PRESENTED TO

____

BY

____

DATE

____

The New Oxford American Dictionary

SECOND EDITION

The New Oxford American Dictionary

SECOND EDITION

FIRST EDITION

Elizabeth J. Jewell
Frank Abate

SECOND EDITION

Erin McKean

2005

OXFORD
UNIVERSITY PRESS

Oxford University Press, Inc., publishes works that further
Oxford University's objective of excellence
in research, scholarship, and education.

Oxford New York
Auckland Cape Town Dar es Salaam Hong Kong Karachi
Kuala Lumpur Madrid Melbourne Mexico City Nairobi
New Delhi Shanghai Taipei Toronto

With offices in
Argentina Austria Brazil Chile Czech Republic France Greece
Guatemala Hungary Italy Japan Poland Portugal Singapore
South Korea Switzerland Thailand Turkey Ukraine Vietnam

The first edition of the *New Oxford American Dictionary* was based on *The New Oxford Dictionary of English*, published in the United Kingdom in 1998.

Published by Oxford University Press, Inc.
198 Madison Avenue, New York, New York, 10016
www.oup.com/us
www.askoxford.com

Library of Congress Cataloging-in-Publication Data

The new Oxford American dictionary.-- 2nd ed.
p. cm.
ISBN 0-19-517077-6
1. English language--United States--Dictionaries. 2. Americanisms--Dictionaries.
PE1628.N429 2005
423'.1--dc22
2005000941

10 9 8 7 6 5 4 3 2 1

Printed in the United States of America on acid-free paper

Contents

Staff

FOR THE FIRST EDITION

Principal Editors:
Elizabeth J. Jewell
Frank R. Abate

Senior Project Editor:
Christine A. Lindberg

Senior Staff Editors:
Suzanne Stone Burke
Erin McKean
Joseph Patwell

Staff Editors:
Martin Coleman
Andrea Nagy
Laurie Ongley

Consulting Editors:
Donna Farina
Mark LaFlaur
Maurice Lee
Julie Marsh
Lois Principe
Susan Sigalis
Dawn Thornton
Wendy Vidou

Pronunciations Editor:
Linda Costa

Consulting Pronunciations Editors:
John Bollard
Sharon Goldstein
Anne Marie Hamilton
Katherine Isaacs
Ellen Johnson
William Kretzschmar
Rima McKinzey
Lisa Cohen Minnick
Katherine Sietsema
Susan Tamasi
Matthew Zimmerman

Editorial Assistants:
Karen Fisher
Kimberly Roberts

Etymologies Editor:
Martha Mayou

Keyboarder:
Tina Wholean

Illustrations Editor:
Debra Argosy

Assistant Illustrations Editors:
Katherine Adzima
Lisa Barnett
Benjamin Keene
James Marra
David Roberts

Illustrators:
Marta Cone
Elizabeth Gaus
Matthew Hansen
Mike Malkovas
Susan Van Winkle

Contributors, New Entries:
Jeri Famighetti
Archie Hobson
Christine Grove
Orin Hargraves
Nancy LaRoche
Sidney Landau
Paul Lagassé
Eric Sinkins
Sue Ellen Thompson

Proofreaders:
Linda Ciacchi
Alan Hartley
William Herzog
Linda Legassie
Douglas Jacobs-Moore
Adrienne Makowski
Susan Norton
Daniel Partner
Joseph Sigalis

Computer Programmer:
Thomas L. Jewell

Reference Computing Programmers:
Stephen Perkins, *dataformat.com, LLC*
Paul Hayslett, *Cow Bay Software*
Dan Barker, Ewen Fletcher, and
Laura Elliott,
OED *Technology Group*

Type Compositor:
dataformat.com, LLC

FOR THE SECOND EDITION

Principal Editor:
Erin McKean

Managing Editor:
Constance Baboukis

Senior Project Editor:
Christine A. Lindberg

Consulting Editor:
Alan Hartley

Review Editors:
Cynthia Barnhart
Carol Braham
Nancy LaRoche
Joseph Patwell
Julia Penelope
Deborah Posner

Pronunciations Editor:
Enid Pearsons

Data Conversions/Analyses:
Helen Langone, *Neologica*

Biographical and Geographical Entries Editor, Photo Permissions:
Georgia Maas

Revised Maps:
Michael Kelly

New Entries Editor:
Orin Hargraves

Etymologies Editor:
Martha Mayou

Keyboarding and Proofreading:
Johanna Baboukis
John Baboukis
Marina Padakis
Katherine Sietsema

Editorial Assistant:
David Bowers

Advisory Board

Ronald Butters, Professor of English and Cultural Anthropology; Chair, Linguistics Program, Duke University

William J. Frawley, Dean of the Columbian College of Arts and Sciences and Professor of Anthropology and Psychology, The George Washington University

Joan Houston Hall, Chief Editor, *Dictionary of American Regional English*

William A. Kretzschmar, Jr., CHA Willson Professor in Humanities, University of Georgia

(for the first edition) Mark Liberman, Director, Linguistic Data Consortium, University of Pennsylvania

(for the second edition) Nancy Ide, Professor and Chair, Department of Computer Science, Vassar College, Technical Director, American National Corpus

Specialist Subject Consultants

AGRICULTURE

Farming ..... **Robert C. Hughes**, farmer

ARTS

Architecture ..... **Benjamin E. Northrup**, Lecturer, Yale University

Art ..... **Michael Harvey**

Ballet/Dance ..... **Dominique Bourassa**

Bell-Ringing ..... **Richard Parsons**, Tower Captain, St. James Church, Hendersonville, NC

Film ..... **Peter DeCherney**, Postdoctoral Fellow, Center for Research on Culture and Literature, Johns Hopkins University

Handwriting ..... **David R. Evans**, Professor of English and Chair, Department of English, Speech, and Journalism, Georgia College and State University

Musical Direction ..... **Marguerite L. Brooks**, Associate Professor, Choral Director, Yale University

Musical Instruments ..... **Nicholas Renouf**, Associate Curator, Yale University Collection of Musical Instruments

Music, Classical and General ..... **James Haar**, Professor, Department of Music, College of Arts & Sciences, The University of North Carolina–Chapel Hill

Music, General ..... **Frederick T. Gerhardt**, musician and educator

Music, Popular ..... **Elysia M. Stobbe**, Director, Market Development, Marketing One, Baltimore, MD

Photography ..... **Peter Craig**, photographer and instructor

Theater ..... **Joseph V. Melillo**, Executive Producer, Brooklyn Academy of Music, Brooklyn, NY

ASTRONOMY

Astronomy/Space ..... **Jennifer Wiseman**, Hubble Fellow, Department of Physics and Astronomy, Johns Hopkins University

BIOLOGY

Biology ..... **Pamela Mulligan**, Ph.D. in Biology

Birds ..... **Jacqueline Weicker**, Scientific Assistant, Department of Ornithology, American Museum of Natural History

Breeds ..... **Carole A. Zerbe**, Assistant Professor of Internal Medicine, School of Veterinary Medicine, University of Pennsylvania

Ecology ..... **Daniel B. Botkin**, Research Professor, University of California–Santa Barbara

Falconry ..... **Frederick W. Holderman**, Master Falconer

Insects ..... **Phillip J. Pellitteri**, Distinguished Outreach Specialist, Lecturer, and Insect Diagnostician, Department of Entomology, University of Wisconsin–Madison

Invertebrates ..... **Alan J. Kohn**, Professor Emeritus, Zoology, University of Wisconsin

Lower Plants ..... **Carol Brittnacher**, undergraduate researcher, University of Washington–St. Louis

Mammals ..... **Link Olsen**, Professor, Department of Cell and Molecular Biology, Northwestern University Medical School

Paleontology ..... **Carl Mendelson**, Professor, Department of Geology, Benoit College

Reptiles ..... **Robert B. Stuebing**, Associate Professor of Biology, National University of Malaysia (Sabah Campus) and Research Associate, Field Museum of Natural History, Chicago

CHEMISTRY

Biochemistry .... **Pamela Mulligan**, Ph.D. in Biology
Chemistry, Inorganic .... **Thomas Schweiger**, Research Associate, E.I du Pont de Nemours & Co., Inc.
Chemistry, Organic .... **Robert C. Everich**, Senior Scientist, Makhteshim-Agan of North America, Inc.

COMMERCE

Commerce .... **Ellen M. Whitener**, Professor of Commerce, McIntire School of Commerce, University of Virginia
Currency/Finance .... **Mark A. White**, Associate Professor of Commerce, McIntire School of Commerce, University of Virginia
Economics .... **Donna M. Bombino**, credit analyst
Stock Market .... **Richard F. DeMong**, Chaired Professor, Investments and Corporate Finance, McIntire School of Commerce, University of Virginia

COMPUTING

Computing .... **Gareth Branwyn**, Editor of "Jargon Watch," *Wired*

CRAFTS

Carpentry .... **Kevin Ireton**, Chief Editor, *Fine Homebuilding*
Printing/Bookbinding .... **David R. Evans**, Professor of English and Chair, Department of English, Speech, and Journalism, Georgia College and State University

EARTH SCIENCES

Epochs .... **Dale A. Springer**, Professor, Geosciences, Department of Geography and Geosciences, Bloomsburg University
Geology/Rocks .... **Michael J. Soreghan**, Lecturer/Researcher, School of Geology and Geophysics, University of Oklahoma
Minerals .... **Lois K. Ongley**, Professor, Geology Department, Bates College
Mining .... **Helen Mango**, Professor, Department of Natural Science, Castleton State College

EDUCATION

Education .... **Ronald D. Anderson**, Professor of Education, University of Colorado

FASHION

Clothing/Dyeing/Needlework/Textiles/Hairdressing .... **Ursula McCarty**
Jewelry .... **Gary A. Melillo**, jewelry designer and sculptor
Knitting .... **Suzanne Stone Burke**, Editor, Oxford University Press

FISHING

Fishing/Commercial Fishing ... **Edward J. Everich**, independent marine consultant

FOOD

Food and Beverages .... **Mary Deirdre Donovan**, Senior Editor, The Culinary Institute of America

FORESTRY

Forestry .... **Daniel B. Botkin**, Research Professor, University of California–Santa Barbara
Timber .... **R. Bruce Hoadley**, Professor, Wood Science and Technology, University of Massachusetts–Amherst

HERALDRY

Heraldry .... **David Robert Wooten**, Fellow, Board of Governors; Secretary-Treasurer, Editor, *The Armiger's News*, American College of Heraldry

HISTORY

Archaeology/Greek Antiquities .... **Joseph Patwell**, Editor, Oxford University Press

HORTICULTURE

Flowers, Trees, and Shrubs ..... **Christine A. Lindberg**, Senior Project Editor, Oxford University Press

HUMAN BODY

Anatomy .... **William E. Burkel**, Director of Medical Anatomy, University of Michigan Medical School
Physiology .... **Tomuo Hoshiko**, Professor Emeritus of Physiology and Biophysics, Case Western Reserve University School of Medicine

HUNTING

Hunting .... **Ronald D. Anderson**, Professor of Education, University of Colorado
Stephen E. Lindberg, hunter

LANGUAGE

Black Slang/Black English ..... **Elysia M. Stobbe**, Director, Market Development, Marketing One, Baltimore, MD
Grammar/Greek Letters .... **Joseph Patwell**, Editor, Oxford University Press
Linguistics .... **William J. Frawley**, The George Washington University
Phonetics .... **John Bollard**, lexicographer and phonetician
Vulgar Slang/Homosexual Terms .... **Ronald R. Butters**, Professor of English and Cultural Anthropology; Chair, Linguistics Program, Duke University

LAW

Law .... **Bryan A. Garner**, attorney and lexicographer; President, LawProse, Inc.
Archie Hobson, lexicographer

LITERATURE

Literature .... **David R. Evans**, Professor of English; Chair, Department of English, Speech, and Journalism, Georgia College and State University
Prosody .... **Sue Ellen Thompson**, lexicographer and poet
Rhetoric .... **Joseph Patwell**, Editor, Oxford University Press

MATHEMATICS

Mathematics/Geometry .... **Michelle LeMasurier**, Assistant Professor, Mathematics, Franklin and Marshall College
Statistics .... **Ingram Olkin**, Professor, Statistics and Education, Stanford University

MECHANICAL ENGINEERING

Aeronautics/Engineering .... **Ralph Costa**, mechanical engineer
Building .... **Faith Gavin Kuhn**, Connecticut Builders & Industry Association (CBIA)
Mechanical Engineering .... **Benson H. Tongue**, Professor of Mechanical Engineering, University of California–Berkeley
Railroads .... National Railway Historical Society

MEDICINE

Medicine .... **John M. Last**, Professor Emeritus, Epidemiology, University of Ottawa
Microbiology .... **Robert C. Everich**, Senior Scientist, Makhteshim-Agan of North America, Inc.
Surgery .... **William Silen**, Johnson & Johnson Distinguished Professor of Surgery; Dean, Faculty Development and Diversity, Harvard Medical School

MILITARY

Weapons/Medals/Rank .... **William L. Faistenhammer**, Colonel, US Army
Military History .... **Mary R. Habeck**, Assistant Professor, Department of History, Yale University

MYTHOLOGY

Mythology .... **Joseph Patwell**, Editor, Oxford University Press

NAUTICAL TERMS

Nautical/Knots .... **Alan H. Hartley**, lexicographer

NUMISMATICS

Numismatics .... **Robert W. Hoge**, Curator, Museum of the American Numismatic Association

PHARMACOLOGY

Drugs .... **Gail Winger**, Senior Research Scientist, Department of Pharmacology, University of Michigan–Ann Arbor

PHILATELY
Philately .... **American Philatelic Society**, State College, PA

PHILOSOPHY
Philosophy/Logic .... **Barry Stroud**, Mills Professor of Metaphysics and Epistemology, University of California–Berkeley

PHYSICS
Elements .... **Robert C. Everich**, Senior Scientist, Makhteshim-Agan of North America, Inc.
Optics................................. **Steve E. Watkins**, Associate Professor of Electrical and Computer Engineering, University of Missouri–Rolla
Physics .... **Harry Lustig**, Professor of Physics Emeritus, City College, City University of New York; Treasurer Emeritus, American Physical Society

PSYCHIATRY
Psychiatry........................... **Samuel B. Guze**, Spencer T. Olin Professor of Psychiatry, Department of Psychiatry, Washington University School of Medicine

PSYCHOLOGY
Psychology .... **Alan E. Kazdin**, Professor and Chair, Department of Psychology, Yale University

RELIGION
Bible .... **Timothy E. Haut**, minister, Congregational Church, Deep River, CT
Buddhism/Hinduism .... **Leonard Zwilling**, University of Wisconsin; *Dictionary of American Regional English*, Madison, WI
Christianity/Ecclesiology......... **Peter Rodgers**, Rector, St. John's Episcopal Church, New Haven, CT
Islam.................................. **Abdulaziz A. Sachedina**, Professor, Islamic Studies, Department of Religious Studies, University of Virginia
Roman Catholic Church .... **Joseph Patwell**, Editor, Oxford University Press
Theology............................. **Maurice Lee**, Researcher, Systematic Theology, Yale University

SOCIOLOGY
American Indians .... **Richard B. Buckley**
Ethnic Groups .... **Alan Hartley**, lexicographer
Sociology .... **Ned Polsky**, Professor of Sociology, SUNY

SPORTS and GAMES
Billiards.............................. **Ned Polsky,** Professor of Sociology, SUNY, international billiard tournament referee
Bridge/Cards .... **Carrie Estill**, former editor, *Dictionary of American Regional English*
Chess.................................. **Peter J. Kurzdorfer**, U.S. Chess Federation titles
Golf .... **Anthony F. Salvati**
Horse Racing........................ **The Jockey Club**
Lawn Bowling...................... **Jack Phillips**, President, American Lawn Bowls Association
Riding .... **Jennifer Bryant**, Editor-at-Large, *USDF Connection*, (U.S. Dressage Federation magazine)
Sports................................. **Frank R. Abate**, lexicogapher
Archie Hobson, lexicographer

TELEVISION
Video .... **Michael Harvey**

Preface to the Second Edition

The first edition of the innovative *New Oxford American Dictionary* was published in 2001. For this second edition, the text has been completely updated, including the addition of nearly 3,000 new words, senses, and phrases to ensure that the dictionary continues to be the most accurate and up-to-date description of American English available. In compiling this new edition, we have continued to draw upon Oxford's extensive worldwide language resources, especially the database of the Oxford North American Reading Program, consisting of nearly 87 million words.

This second edition also includes two new features of especial utility for writers: *The Right Word* synonym studies, which help distinguish among closely related synonyms, and the *Language Guide* appendix, which is a complete yet concise guide to questions of grammar, punctuation, and spelling.

Included with this new edition (a first for an American dictionary of this size and scope) is a complete CD version for installation and use on PDA's and smartphones, enabling quick and easy reference to the *New Oxford American Dictionary* at any time, from anywhere.

Apart from the editors and contributors listed on the staff page, the U.S. Dictionaries program would like to thank Judy Pearsall and James McCracken of the UK Current English Dictionaries Program, Timothy DeWerff of Scholarly Reference in the U.S., and Jesse Sheidlower of the North American Unit of the *OED* for their help during the preparation of this edition.

Preface to the First Edition

The *New Oxford American Dictionary* is a completely new American dictionary, written on new principles. It builds on the excellence of the lexicographical traditions of scholarship and analysis of evidence as set down by the *Oxford English Dictionary* over a century ago, but it is also a new departure. The *New Oxford American Dictionary* is a dictionary of current American English, based on currently available evidence and current thinking about language and cognition. It is an inventory of the words and meanings of present-day English, both those in actual use and those found in the literature of the past. The compilers have gone to the heart of the traditional practices of dictionary making and reappraised the principles on which lexicography is based. In particular, the focus has been on a different approach to an understanding of "meaning" and how this relates to the structure, organization, and selection of material for the dictionary.

Linguists, cognitive scientists, and others have been developing new techniques for analyzing usage and meaning, and the *New Oxford American Dictionary* has taken full advantage of these developments. Foremost among them is an emphasis on identifying what is "central and typical," as distinct from the time-honored search for "necessary conditions" of meaning (that is, a statement of the conditions that would enable someone to pick out all and only the cases of the term being defined). Past attempts to cover the meaning of all possible uses of a word have tended to lead to a blurred, unfocused result, in which the core of the meaning is obscured by many minor uses. In the *New Oxford American Dictionary*, meanings are linked to central norms of usage as observed in the language. The result is fewer meanings, with sharper, crisper definitions.

The style of definition adopted for the *New Oxford American Dictionary* aims in part to account for the dynamism, imaginativeness, and flexibility of ordinary American usage. The *New Oxford American Dictionary* records and explains all normal meanings and uses of well-attested words, but also illustrates transferred, figurative, and derivative meanings, insofar as these are conventional within the language.

The layout and organization of each entry in the dictionary reflect this new approach to meaning. Each entry has at least one core meaning, to which a number of subsenses, logically connected to it, may be attached. The text design is open and accessible, making it easy to find the core meanings and so to navigate the entry as a whole.

At the heart of this dictionary lies the evidence. This evidence forms the basis for everything that we, as lexicographers, are able to say about the language and the words within it. In particular, the large databank of searchable electronic texts collected by Oxford gives, with its 100 million words, a selection of real, modern, and everyday language, equivalent to an ordinary person's reading over ten years or more. Using computational tools to analyze this databank and other corpora, the editors have been able to look at the behavior of each word in detail in its natural contexts, and so to build up a picture for every word in the dictionary.

Databank analysis has been complemented by analysis of other types of evidence: the *New Oxford American Dictionary* makes extensive use of the citation database of the Oxford North American Reading Program, a collection of citations (currently standing at over 64 million words and growing at a rate of about 4.5 million words a year) taken from a variety of sources from all the English-speaking countries of the world. In addition, a specially commissioned reading program has targeted previously neglected specialist fields as diverse as computing, alternative medicine, antique collecting, and sports.

The general approach to defining in the *New Oxford American Dictionary* has particular application for specialist vocabulary. Here, in the context of dealing with highly technical information that may be unfamiliar to the nonspecialist reader, the focus on clarity of expression is of great importance. Avoidance of overtechnical terminology and an emphasis on explaining and describing as well as defining are balanced by the need to maintain a high level of technical information and accuracy. In many cases, additional technical information is presented separately in an easily recognizable alternative format.

The *New Oxford American Dictionary* views the language from the perspective that English, although a world language, is now centered in the United States, and that American vocabulary and usage deserve special attention. Although the focus is on American English, a network of consultants throughout the English-speaking world has enabled us to ensure excellent coverage of world English, from the United Kingdom and Canada to the Caribbean, India, South Africa, Australia, and New Zealand. We have been indebted to the opportunities provided for communication by the Internet; lively discussions by e-mail across the oceans have formed an everyday part of the dictionary-making process.

Many people have been involved in the preparation of this dictionary, and thanks are due to them all. The U.S. Dictionaries Program would like to give special thanks to Judy Pearsall, Patrick Hanks, and the lexicographers of the Current English Dictionaries department in the United Kingdom for creating the foundation on which we have built. We would also like to express our gratitude to Stephen Perkins of dataformat.com, without whose patience and intelligence this dictionary would not have been possible.

Introduction

The *New Oxford American Dictionary* has been compiled according to principles that are quite different from those of traditional American dictionaries. New types of evidence are now available in sufficient quantity to allow lexicographers to construct a picture of the language that is more accurate than has been possible before. The approach to structuring and organizing within individual dictionary entries has been rethought, as has the approach to the selection and presentation of information in every aspect of the dictionary: definitions, choice of examples, grammar, word histories, and every other category. New approaches have been adopted in response to a reappraisal of the workings of language in general and its relationship to the presentation of information in a dictionary in particular. The aim of this introduction is to give the reader background information for using this dictionary and to explain some of the thinking behind these new approaches.

Structure: Core Sense and Subsense

The first part of speech is the primary one for that word: thus, for **bag** and **balloon** the senses of the noun are given before those for the verb, while for **babble** and **bake** the senses of the verb are given before those of the noun.

cocoon

CORE SENSE

a silky case spun by the larvae of many insects for protection as pupae.

subsense	subsense	subsense
a similar structure made by other animals.	a covering that prevents the corrosion of metal equipment.	something that envelops or surrounds, esp. in a protective or comforting way: *the* ***cocoon of*** *her kimono* | figurative ***a*** *warm* ***cocoon of*** *love.*

Within each part of speech, the first definition given is the **core sense.** The general principle on which the senses in the *New Oxford American Dictionary* are organized is that each word has at least one core meaning, to which a number of subsenses may be attached. If there is more than one core sense (see following page), this is introduced by a bold sense number. Core meanings represent typical, central uses of the word in question in modern standard English, as established by research on and analysis of American and World English through corpora (language databanks) and citation databases. The core meaning is the one that represents the most literal sense that the word has in ordinary modern American usage. This is not necessarily the same as the oldest meaning, because word meanings change over time. Nor is it necessarily the most frequent meaning, because figurative senses are sometimes the most frequent. It is the meaning accepted by native speakers as the one that is most established as literal and central.

The core sense also acts as a gateway to other, related subsenses. These subsenses are grouped under the core sense, each one being introduced by a solid square symbol.

	co·coon
CORE SENSE	a silky case spun by the larvae of many insects for protection as pupae.
subsense	■ a similar structure made by other animals. ■ a covering that prevents the corrosion of metal equipment. ■ something that envelops or surrounds, esp. in a protective or comforting way: *the* ***cocoon of*** *her kimono* | *figurative* ***a*** *warm* ***cocoon of*** *love.*

There is a logical relationship between each subsense and the core sense under which it appears. The organization of senses according to this logical relationship is designed to help the user, not only in being able to navigate the entry more easily and find relevant senses more readily, but also in building up an understanding of how senses in the language relate to one another and how the language is constructed on this model. The main types of relationship of core sense to subsense are as follows:

(a) figurative extension of the core sense, e.g.,

	back·bone
CORE SENSE	the series of vertebrae extending from the skull to the pelvis; the spine.
subsense	■ *figurative* the chief support of a system or organization; the mainstay: *these firms are the backbone of our industrial sector.*

	bank·rupt
CORE SENSE	(of a person or organization) declared in law unable to pay outstanding debts: *the company was declared bankrupt*
subsense	■ *figurative* completely lacking in a particular quality or value: *their cause is morally bankrupt.*

(b) specialized case of the core sense, e.g.,

	zone
CORE SENSE	[usu. with *adj.*] an area or stretch of land having a particular characteristic, purpose, or use, or subject to particular restrictions: *a pedestrian zone*
subsense	■ *Geography* a well-defined region extending around the earth between definite limits, esp. between two parallels of latitude: *a zone of easterly winds.*
subsense	■ *Sports* In basketball, football, and hockey, a specific area of the court, field, or rink, esp. one to be defended by a particular player, or the mode of defensive play using this system.

	de·mand
CORE SENSE	an insistent and peremptory request, made as if by right: *a series of* ***demands for*** *far-reaching reforms.*
subsense	■ *Economics* the desire of purchasers, consumers, clients, employers, etc., for a particular commodity, service, or other item: *a recent slump in demand* | *a demand for specialists.*

(c) other extension or shift in meaning, retaining one or more elements of the core sense, e.g.,

	bam·boo
CORE SENSE	a giant woody grass that grows chiefly in the tropics, where it is widely cultivated.
subsense	■ the hollow jointed stem of this plant, used as a cane or to make furniture and implements: [as *adj.*] *a bamboo serving tray.*

	man·age·ment
CORE SENSE	the process of dealing with or controlling things or people: *the management of elk herds.*
subsense	■ *Medicine & Psychiatry* the treatment or control of diseases, injuries, or disorders, or the care of patients who suffer from them: *the use of combination chemotherapy in the management of breast cancer.*

	man·da·rin
CORE SENSE	an official in any of the nine top grades of the former imperial Chinese civil service.
subsense	■ a powerful official or senior bureaucrat, esp. one perceived as reactionary and secretive: *a civil service mandarin.*

Many entries have just one core sense. However some entries are more complex and have different strands of meaning, each constituting a core sense. In this case, each core sense is introduced by a bold sense number, and each potentially has its own block of sub-senses relating to it.

	belt
CORE SENSE	**1** a strip of leather or other material worn around the waist or across the chest, esp. in order to support clothes or carry weapons: *a sword belt* | [as *adj.*] *a belt buckle.*
subsenses	■ short for SEAT BELT. ■ a belt worn as a sign of rank or achievement: *he was awarded the victor's belt.* ■ a belt of a specified color, marking the attainment of a particular level in judo, karate, or similar sports: [as *adj.*] *brown-belt level.* ■ a person who has reached such a level: *I am a karate black belt.* ■ (**the belt**) the punishment of being struck with a belt.
CORE SENSE	**2** a strip of material used in various technical applications, in particular:
subsenses	■ a continuous band of material used in machinery for transferring motion from one wheel to another. ■ a conveyor belt. ■ a flexible strip carrying machine-gun cartridges.
CORE SENSE	**3** a strip or encircling band of something having a specified nature or composition that is different from its surroundings: *the asteroid belt* | *a belt of trees.*
CORE SENSE	**4** a heavy blow: *she ran in to administer a good belt with her stick.*
CORE SENSE	**5** *informal* a gulp or shot of liquor: *they could probably use a few belts.*

Specialist Vocabulary

One of the most important uses of a dictionary is to provide explanations of terms in specialized fields that are unfamiliar to a general reader. Yet in many traditional dictionaries, the definitions have been written by specialists as if for other specialists, and as a result the definitions are often opaque and difficult for the general reader to understand.

One of the primary aims of the *New Oxford American Dictionary* has been to break down the barriers to understanding specialist vocabulary. The challenge has been, on the one hand, to give information that is comprehensible, relevant, and readable, suitable for the general reader, while on the other hand maintaining the high level of technical information and accuracy suitable for the more specialist reader.

This has been achieved in some cases, notably entries for plants and animals and chemical substances, by separating technical information from the rest of the definition:

	A·mer·i·can croc·o·dile
DEFINITION	a crocodile with a long tapering head, occurring from southernmost Florida to Ecuador.
technical information	• *Crocodylus acutus,* family Crocodylidae.

	ben·zo·py·rene
DEFINITION	*Chemistry* a compound that is the major carcinogen present in cigarette smoke. It also occurs in coal tar.
technical information	• A polycyclic aromatic hydrocarbon; chem. formula: $C_{20}H_{12}$.

In other cases, it is achieved by giving additional explanatory information within the definition itself:

	curl·ing
DEFINITION	a game played on ice, esp. in Scotland and Canada, in which large, round, flat stones are slid across the surface toward a mark.
additional information	Members of a team use brooms to sweep the surface of the ice in the path of the stone to control its speed and direction.

	al·che·my
DEFINITION	the medieval forerunner of chemistry, based on the supposed transformation of matter.
additional information	It was concerned particularly with attempts to convert base metals into gold or to find a universal elixir.
	■ *figurative* a process by which paradoxical results are achieved or incompatible elements combined with no obvious rational explanation: *his conducting managed by some alchemy to give a sense of fire and ice.*

As elsewhere, the purpose is to give information that is relevant and interesting, aiming not just to define the word but also to describe and explain its context in the real world. Additional information of this type, where it is substantial, is given in the form of separate boxed features:

	earth
CORE SENSE	(also **Earth**) the planet on which we live; the world: *the diversity of life **on earth**.*
additional boxed information	The earth is the third planet from the sun in the solar system, orbiting between Venus and Mars at an average distance of 90 million miles (149.6 million km) from the sun, and has one natural satellite, the moon. It has an equatorial diameter of 7,654 miles (12,756 km), an average density 5.5 times that of water, and is believed to have formed about 4,600 million years ago. The earth, which is three-quarters covered by oceans and has a dense atmosphere of nitrogen and oxygen, is the only planet known to support life.

	E·o·cene
CORE SENSE	*Geology* of, relating to, or denoting the second epoch of the Tertiary period, between the Paleocene and Oligocene epochs.
subsense	■ [as *n.*] (**the Eocene**) the Eocene epoch or the system of rocks deposited during it.
additional boxed information	The Eocene epoch lasted from 56.5 million to 35.4 million years ago. It was a time of rising temperatures, and there was an abundance of mammals, including the first horses, bats, and whales.

An especially important feature of the *New Oxford American Dictionary* is the coverage of American animals and plants. In-depth research and a thorough review have been carried out for animals and plants in the Americas and throughout the world and, as a result, a large number of entries have been included that have never before been included in general American dictionaries. The style and presentation of these entries follow the general principles for specialist vocabulary in the *New Oxford American Dictionary*: the entries not only give the technical information, but also describe, in everyday English, the appearance and other characteristics (of behavior, medicinal or culinary use, mythological significance, reason for the name, etc.) and the typical habitat and distribution:

CORE SENSE	**black·tail deer**
technical information	a type of mule deer with black markings on the upper side of its tail, found west of the crest of the Cascade Mountains.
	• *Odocoileus hemionus* subsp. *columbianus*, family Cervidae.

CORE SENSE	**chi·a**
technical information	a plant of the mint family with clusters of small two-lipped purple flowers. Chia is common throughout California and the Great Basin.
	• *Salvia columbariae*, family Labiatae.

Encyclopedic Material

Some dictionaries do not include entries for the names of people and places and other proper names, or include them only in separate sections. The argument for this is based on a distinction between "words" and "facts," by which dictionaries are about "words" while encyclopedias and other reference works are about "facts." The distinction is an interesting theoretical one, but in practice there is a considerable overlap: names such as *Shakespeare* and *Mississippi* are as much part of the language as words such as *drama* or *river*, and they belong in a large dictionary.

The *New Oxford American Dictionary* includes all those terms forming part of the enduring common knowledge of English speakers, regardless of whether they are classified as "words" or "names." The information given is the kind of information that people are likely to need from a dictionary, however that information may traditionally be classified. Both the style of definitions in the *New Oxford American Dictionary* and the inclusion of additional material in separate blocks reflect this approach. The *New Oxford American Dictionary* includes more than 5,000 place-name entries, 4,000 biographical entries, and just under 3,000 other proper names. The biographical entries are designed to provide not just the basic facts (such as birth and death dates, full name, and nationality), but also a brief context giving information about, for example, a person's life and why he or she is important.

For a few particularly important encyclopedic entries—for example, countries—a fuller treatment is given and additional information appears in a separate boxed note.

Grammar

In recent years, grammar has begun to enjoy greater prominence than in the past few decades. It is once again being taught explicitly in schools throughout the United States. In addition, there is a recognition that different meanings of a word are closely associated with different lexical and syntactic patterns. The *New Oxford American Dictionary* records and exemplifies the most important of these patterns at the relevant senses of each word, thus giving guidance on language use as well as word meaning.

For example, with the word **bomb,** it is possible to distinguish the main senses of the verb simply on the basis of the grammar: whether the verb is transitive (takes a direct object) or intransitive (no direct object):

CORE SENSE	attack *(a place or vehicle)* with a bomb or bombs: **London* was bombed, night after night*
grammar	[*trans.*]

(the asterisks shown here match the direct object in the example with the parenthetical item in the definition)

CORE SENSE	*informal* (of a movie, play, or other event) fail miserably: *a big-budget movie that bombed at the box office*
grammar	[*intrans.*]

This has particular relevance for a dictionary such as the *New Oxford American Dictionary*, where the aim is to present information in such a way that it helps to explain the structure of the language itself, not just the meanings of individual senses. For this reason, special attention has been paid to the grammar of each word, and grammatical structures are given explicitly.

Where possible, the syntactic behavior of a word is presented directly: for example, if a verb is normally found in a particular sense followed by a certain preposition, this is indicated before the definition, in bold:

> **build**
>
> (**build on**) use as a basis for further progress or development: *the nation should build on the talents of its workforce.*

In other cases, collocations that are typical of the term in use, though not obligatory, are shown highlighted within the example sentence:

> **ball game**
>
> a particular situation, esp. one that is completely different from the previous situation: *making the film was **a whole new ball game** for her.*
>
> **bet**
>
> a candidate or course of action to choose; an option: ***your best bet** is to call a professional exterminator.*

Great efforts have been made to use a minimum of specialist terminology. Nevertheless, a small number of terms are essential in explaining the grammar of a word. The less familiar terms are explained below. All terms are, of course, defined and explained under their own entries in the dictionary.

Terms relating to nouns

[as adj.]: used to mark a noun that can be placed before another noun in order to modify its meaning, e.g.,

> **boom**
>
> [often as *adj.*] a movable arm over a television or movie set, carrying a microphone or camera: *a boom mike.*
>
> **beside**
>
> the space beside a bed, typically that of someone who is ill: *he was summoned to the bedside of a dying man* | [as *adj.*] *a bedside lamp.*

[treated as sing.]: used to mark a noun that is plural in form but is used with a singular verb, e.g., **mumps** in *mumps is one of the major childhood diseases* or **genetics** in *genetics has played a major role in this work.*

[treated as sing. or pl.]: used to mark a noun that can be used with either a singular or a plural verb without any change in meaning or in the form of the headword (often called *collective nouns*, because they typically denote groups of people considered collectively), e.g., *the staff are committed to this policy* or *the staff is trying to gag its critics.*

[in sing.]: used to mark a noun that is used as a count noun but is never or rarely found in the plural, e.g., **ear** in *an ear for rhythm.*

Terms relating to verbs

[trans.]: used to mark a verb that is transitive, i.e., takes a direct object (the type of direct object often being shown in parentheses in the definition), e.g.,

> **escort**
>
> accompany (someone or something) somewhere, esp. for protection or security, or as a mark of rank: *Shiona escorted Janice to the door* | *the shipment was escorted by armed patrol boats.*

[intrans.]: used to mark a verb that is intransive, i.e., takes no direct object, e.g.,

> **quibble**
> [*intrans.*] argue or raise objections about a trivial matter: *they are always quibbling about the amount they are prepared to pay.*

[with adverbial]: used to mark a verb that takes an obligatory adverbial, typically a prepositional phrase, without which the sentence in which the verb occurs would sound unnatural or weird, e.g.,

> **dance**
> [with *adverbial of direction*] (of a person) move in a quick and lively way: *Sheila danced in gaily.*

Terms relating to adjectives

[attrib.]: used to mark an adjective that is normally used attributively, i.e., comes before the noun that it modifies, e.g., **certain** in *a certain man* (not *the man is certain,* which has a very different meaning). Note that attributive use is standard for many adjectives, especially in specialist fields: the [attrib.] label is used only to mark those cases in which predicative use would be less usual.

[as predic. adj.]: used to mark an adjective that is normally used predicatively, i.e., comes after the verb, e.g., **ajar** in *the door was ajar* (not *the ajar door*).

[postpositive]: used to mark an adjective that is used postpositively, i.e., typically comes immediately after the noun that it modifies (such uses are unusual in English and generally arise because the adjective has been adopted from a language where postpositive use is standard), e.g., **galore** in *there were prizes galore.*

Terms relating to adverbs

[sentence adverb]: used to mark an adverb that stands outside a sentence or clause, providing commentary on it as a whole or showing the speaker's or writer's attitude to what is being said, rather than the manner in which something was done. Sentence adverbs most frequently express the speaker's or writer's point of view, although they may also be used to set a context by stating a field of reference, e.g.,

> **certainly**
> [*sentence adverb*] undoubtedly; definitely; surely: *the prestigious address certainly adds to the firm's appeal | it certainly isn't worth risking your life.*

[as submodifier]: used to mark an adverb that is used to modify an adjective or another adverb, e.g.,

> **com·par·a·tive·ly**
> [as *submodifier*] to a moderate degree as compared to something else; relatively: *inflation was comparatively low.*

Evidence and Illustrative Examples

The information presented in the dictionary about individual words is based on close analysis of how words behave in real, natural language. Behind every dictionary entry are examples of the word in use—often hundreds and thousands of them—that have been analyzed to give information about typical usage, about distribution (whether typically American or typically British, for example), about register (whether informal or derogatory, for example), about currency (whether archaic or dated, for example), and about subject field (whether used only in medicine or finance, for example).

Databank and Citation Evidence

Extensive use has been made of Oxford's text databank resources, which include a carefully balanced selection of 100 million words of written and spoken English text (equivalent to one person's reading over ten years) in machine-readable form, available for computational analysis, and nearly 87 million words of citations from Oxford's own North American Reading Program, an ongoing research project in which readers select citations from a huge variety of specialist and nonspecialist sources in all varieties of English. These resources mean that Oxford lexicographers are in a position to see how words normally behave. By using concordancing techniques, each word can be viewed almost instantaneously in the immediate contexts in which it is used. (See Figure 1.) Since the Oxford Reading Program is ongoing, and growing at a rate of 4.5 million words a year, Oxford lexicographers have the most up-to-date language resource of an American dictionary, with the majority of the citations coming from sources of the past two decades.

The Oxford databank shows at a glance that some combinations of words (called "collocations") occur together much more often than others. For example, in the concordance on page xvii, "end in," "end the," and "end up" all occur quite often. But are any of these combinations important enough to be given special treatment in the dictionary?

Recent research has focused on identifying combinations that are not merely frequent but also statistically significant. In the Oxford databank, the two words "end the" occur frequently together but they do not form a statistically significant unit, since the word "the" is the commonest in the language. The combinations **end up** and **end in**, on the other hand, are shown to be more significant and tell the lexicographer something about the way the verb **end** behaves in normal use. Of course, a dictionary for general use cannot go into detailed statistical analysis of word combinations, but it can present examples that are typical of normal usage. In the *New Oxford American Dictionary* particularly significant or important patterns are highlighted, in bold or in bold italics, e.g.,

> **end**
> [*intrans.*] (**end in**) have as its final part, point, or result: *one in three marriages is now likely to end in divorce.* ■ [*intrans.*] (**end up**) eventually reach or come to a specified place, state, or course of action: *I **ended up in** Connecticut | you could **end up with** a higher income.*

For further details, see the previous section on *Grammar.*

Specialist Reading

A general dictionary databank does not, by definition, contain large quantities of specialized terminology. For this reason, additional research and collection of citations in a number of neglected fields (for example, antique collecting, food and cooking, boats and sailing, photography, video and audio, martial arts, and alternative medicine) was done to ensure the thorough coverage of these fields. Additionally, specialists in nearly 100 different areas reviewed entries for accuracy.

Examples

The *New Oxford American Dictionary* contains many more examples of words in use than any other comparable dictionary. Generally, they are there to show typical uses of the word or sense. All examples are authentic, in that they represent actual usage. In the past, dictionaries typically have used made-up examples, partly because not enough authentic text was available and partly

hectic moment here will not **end** in the disappearance of the birds but in the stillness
that more and more marriages **end** in divorce, it can do much to alleviate children's
movies and life did not have to **end** in physical and moral victory.
still do, that the jump could **end** in serious injury and somehow disrupt the carefully
stump, which grow at the cut **end** into nodules called neuromas, continue to generate
of short films stitched end-to- **end**, incorporating whatever zingy image or experiment he
fine tubules of which many **end** in what is termed a flame cell. This misleading name
surface, being at the posterior **end** in the male and in the female about one-third of the body
is a means to an end, not an **end**, not an end in itself. Buy the book, it's a great resource.
Great Leveller has a bizarre **end** in store for the most famous Axumite ruler of Yemen,
of Massachusetts and could **end** my days there in some small fishing village, sailing a
my failed expedition did not **end** my romance with pastures, words, and streams, with what
1940. When the war came to an **end** my mother was really up the creek. A bitter little
will not allow another woman to **end** my life while it is still morning!
of recent years, the **end** objective remains the same as it ever was: to create
-platform applets and client- **end** objects being distributed from a server has been around
by continued firing. At this **end** occur the greatest temperatures and pressures, and here
be for weeks. You see, it's the **end** of <i>al-kaws</i>, the season of storms, and everyone's
One is through the closed- **end**, single country funds that trade on the New York Stock
of the routers goes down, the **end** systems automatically switch their load to the other.
by selecting Miami defensive **end** Shane Curry, who was projected as a middle-rounder.
for a coil of rope. Tying one **end** snuggly around his waist, he coiled the rest and stuff
But almost to the **end** she could laugh till the tears ran down and till our
Dennis Ransom, a Redskins tight **end**, showed some midseason intensity
and in the **end**, the man who helped empower a generation is leaving a
He was able to **end** the conversation and rescue his underwear from the dryer.
and more deeply ironic; in the **end**, the lawyer gives up his reputation for savoir faire and
natural resources. To this **end**, the administration has developed a plan to expedite the
a deputation to Napoleon III to **end** the use of horses in vivisection. Christina was a fierce
and we were pushing hard to **end** the 1980&en;81 year with 50,000 members in our state.
some 5,100 feet. At the lower **end**, the bend reverses direction. Power-conduit water tunnels
government could then seek to **end** the contest before it became necessary to attack Soviet
I spent in New York so I could **end** up acting in Hollywood. But in every script they've sent
The characters almost never **end** up acting out of alighment after this, and it can be seen
the real enthusiasts **end** up adding a hack bike for winter use, a pannier-equipped
the toss, which may even **end** up adding to the overall cost of administering civil
something about the places we **end** up after the diets and health kicks have failed.
stupid or unlucky enough to **end** up alone in a room with them.
can eat decently and won't **end** up among the homeless when they move to Geriatrica.
men so frightened they might **end** up another jousting trophy in our showcase that they have
is where you'll want to **end** up anyway: the gift shop often possesses more gawk value
so if Continental does **end** up arm-in-arm with Pirelli
Africa as a tourist, only to **end** up arrested during a riot and charged with couriering a
the computer scientists will **end** up as "road kills" when the digital highways are
and a lot of men end **end** up as "throwaways," says Pratto, resulting in even
superhighway of science and **end** up in a blind alley.
Buyers will probably **end** up with deals that average 50% less than the original
these students may **end** up having relatively little contact with their more
drawn to the very thing that I **end** up critiquing in my book&em;the apparent stillness of
simply combing your hair can **end** up making it look worse!
soil sample on a regular basis **end** up overspreading commercial fertilizers and those
accounts of various charities **end** up in the pockets of the head honchos, and perhaps
then back from Boston, but **end** up overhearing the conversation at the next desk.
contradictions simply **end** up reasserting that the classical ways to assert truth
get blown away, and we all **end** up in jail or juvenile court at least.

Figure 1: Extract from a concordance from the Oxford North American Reading Program, showing the word 'end.'

through an assumption that made-up examples were somehow better in that they could be tailored to the precise needs of the dictionary entry. Such a view finds little favor today, and it is now generally recognized that the "naturalness" provided by authentic examples is of the utmost importance in giving an accurate picture of language in use.

Word Histories

The etymologies in standard dictionaries explain the language from which a word was brought into English, the period at which it is first recorded in English, and the development of modern word forms. While the *New Oxford American Dictionary* does this, it also goes further. It explains sense development as well as morphological (or form) development. Information is presented clearly and with a minimum of technical terminology, and the perspective taken is that of the general reader who would like to know about word origins but who is not a philological specialist. In this context, the history of how and why a particular meaning developed from an apparently quite different older meaning is likely to be at least as interesting as, for example, what the original form was in Latin or Greek.

For example, the word history for the word **oaf** shows how the present meaning developed from the meaning 'elf,' while the entry for **compass** shows how the sense 'magnetic compass' may have been influenced by Italian:

oaf

DEFINITION a stupid, uncultured, or clumsy person.

ORIGIN ▷early 17th cent.: variant of obsolete *auf,* from Old Norse *álfr* 'elf.' The original meaning was 'elf's child, changeling,' later 'idiot child' and 'halfwit,' generalized in the current sense.

com·pass

DEFINITION an instrument containing a magnetized pointer that shows the direction of magnetic north and bearings from it.

ORIGIN ▷Middle English: from Old French *compas* (noun), *compasser* (verb), based on Latin *com-* 'together' + *passus* 'a step or pace.' Several senses ('measure,' 'artifice,' 'circumscribed area,' and 'pair of compasses') that appeared in Middle English are also found in Old French, but their development and origin are uncertain. The transference of sense to the magnetic compass is held to have occurred in the related Italian word *compasso*, from the circular shape of the compass box.

Additional special features of the *New Oxford American Dictionary* include "internal etymologies" and "folk etymologies." Internal etymologies are given within entries to explain the origin of particular senses, phrases, or idioms. For example, how did the figurative use of **red herring** come about? Why do we call something a **flash in the pan**?

red herring

DEFINITION **1** a dried smoked herring, which is turned red by the smoke.
2 something, esp. a clue, that is or is intended to be misleading or distracting: *the book is fast-paced, exciting, and full of red herrings.*
ORIGIN [so named from the practice of using the scent of red herring in training hounds.]

flash

DEFINITION ▸*PHRASES* □ **flash in the pan** a thing or person whose sudden but brief success is not repeated or repeatable: *our start to the season was just a flash in the pan.*
ORIGIN [with allusion to the firing of a flintlock weapon, the ineffective flash that results from the ignition of the priming powder in the gunlock's pan without the desired ignition of the main charge in the gun's chamber.]

The *New Oxford American Dictionary* presents the information in a straightforward, user-friendly fashion immediately following the relevant definition.

In a similar vein, folk etymologies—those explanations that are unfounded but nevertheless well known to many people—have traditionally simply been ignored in dictionaries. The *New Oxford American Dictionary* gives an account of widely held but often erroneous folk etymologies for the benefit of the general reader, explaining competing theories and assessing their relative merits where applicable.

posh

ORIGIN ▷early 20th cent.: perhaps from slang *posh*, denoting a dandy. There is no evidence to support the folk etymology that *posh* is formed from the initials of *port out starboard home* (referring to the practice of using the more comfortable accommodations, out of the heat of the sun, on ships between England and India).

cherub

ORIGIN ▷Old English *cherubin*, ultimately (via Latin and Greek) from Hebrew *kĕrūḇ*, plural *kĕrūḇîm*. A rabbinic folk etymology, which explains the Hebrew singular form as representing Aramaic *kĕ-raḇyā* 'like a child,' led to the representation of the cherub as a child.

Researching word histories is similar in some respects to archaeology: the evidence is often partial or not there at all, and etymologists must make informed decisions using the evidence available, however inadequate it may be. From time to time, new evidence becomes available, and the known history of a word may need to be reconsidered. In this, the *New Oxford American Dictionary* has been able to draw on the extensive expertise and ongoing research of the *Oxford English Dictionary*.

For more on reading etymologies in the *New Oxford American Dictionary*, please see the essay on page xxxviii.

Usage Notes

Interest in questions of good usage is widespread among English speakers everywhere, and many issues are hotly debated. In the *New Oxford American Dictionary*, traditional issues have been reappraised, and guidance is given on various points, old and new. The aim is to help people to use the language more accurately, more clearly, and more elegantly, and to give information and offer reassurance in the face of some of the more baffling assertions about "correctness" that are sometimes made.

This reappraisal has involved looking carefully at evidence of actual usage (in the Oxford databank, the British National Corpus, the citations collected by the Oxford North American Reading Program, and other sources) in order to find out where mistakes are actually being made, and where confusion and ambiguity actually arise. The issues on which journalists and others tend to comment have been reassessed and a judgment made about whether their comments are justified.

From the 15th century onward, traditionalists have been objecting to particular senses of certain English words and phrases, for example, "due to" and "hopefully." Certain grammatical structures, too, have been singled out for adverse comment, notably the split infinitive and the use of a preposition at the end of a clause. Some of these objections are founded on very dubious arguments, for example, the notion that English grammatical structures should precisely parallel those of Latin or that meaning change of any kind is inherently suspect.

preposition

USAGE NOTE **USAGE:** There is a traditional view, as set forth by the 17th-century poet and dramatist John Dryden, that it is incorrect to put a preposition at the end of a sentence, as in *where do you come* ***from?*** or *she's not a writer I've ever come* ***across***. The rule was formulated on the basis that, since in Latin a preposition cannot come after the word it governs or is linked with, the same should be true of English. What this rule fails to take into account is that English is not like Latin in this respect, and in many cases (particularly in questions and with phrasal verbs) the attempt to move the preposition produces awkward, unnatural-sounding results. Winston Churchill famously objected to the rule, saying *"This is the sort of English* ***up with*** *which I will not* ***put****."* In standard English, the placing of a preposition at the end of a sentence is widely accepted, provided the use sounds natural and the meaning is clear.

due

USAGE NOTE ***USAGE*** The use of **due to** as a prepositional phrase meaning 'because of,' as in *he had to retire* ***due to*** *an injury* first appeared in print in 1897, and traditional grammarians have opposed this prepositional usage for more than a century on the grounds that it is a misuse of the adjectival phrase **due to** in the sense of 'attributable to, likely or expected to' (*the train is due to arrive at 11:15*), or 'payable or owed to' (*render unto Caesar what is due to Caesar*). Nevertheless, this prepositional usage is now widespread and common in all types of literature and must be regarded as standard English. The phrase **due to the fact that** is very common in speech, but it is wordy, and, especially in writing, one should use the simple word 'because.'

hopefully

USAGE NOTE ***USAGE*** The traditional sense of **hopefully**, 'in a hopeful manner' (*he stared hopefully at the trophy*), has been used since 1593. The first recorded use of **hopefully** as a sentence adverb, meaning 'it is to be hoped that' (*hopefully, we'll see you tomorrow*), appears in 1702 in the *Magnalia Christi Americana*, written by Massachusetts theologian and writer Cotton Mather. This use of **hopefully** is now the most common one. Sentence adverbs in general (*frankly, honestly, regrettably, seriously*) are found in English since at least the 1600s, and their use has become common in recent decades. However, most traditionalists take the view that all sentence adverbs are inherently suspect. Although they concede that the battle over **hopefully** is lost on the popular front, they continue to withhold approval of its use as a sentence adverb. Attentive ears are particularly bothered when the sentence that follows does not match the promise of the introductory adverb, as when *frankly* is followed not by an expression of honesty but by a self-serving proclamation (*frankly, I don't care if you go or not*). See also **usage** at SENTENCE ADVERB and THANKFULLY.

The usage notes in the *New Oxford American Dictionary* take the view that English is English, not Latin, and that English is, like all living languages, subject to change. Good usage is usage that gets the speaker's or writer's message across, not usage that conforms to some arbitrary rules that fly in the face of historical fact or current evidence. The editors of the *New Oxford American Dictionary* are well aware that the prescriptions of pundits in the past have had remarkably little practical effect on the way the language is actually used. A good dictionary reports the language as it is, not as the editors (or anyone else) would wish it to be, and the usage notes must give guidance that accords with observed facts about present-day usage.

This is not to imply that the issues are straightforward or that there are simple solutions, however. Much of the debate about use of language is highly political, and controversy is, occasionally, inevitable. Changing social attitudes have stigmatized long-established uses, such as the word "man" to denote the human race in general, for example, and have highlighted the absence of a gender-neutral singular pronoun meaning both "he" and "she" (for which purpose "they" is now often used). Similarly, words such as "race" and "native" are now associated with particular problems of sensitivity in use. The usage notes in the *New Oxford American Dictionary* offer information and practical advice on such issues.

USAGE NOTE

man

USAGE Traditionally, the word **man** has been used to refer not only to adult males but also to human beings in general, regardless of sex. There is a historical explanation for this: in Old English, the principal sense of **man** was 'a human being,' and the words **wer** and **wif** were used to refer specifically to 'a male person' and 'a female person,' respectively. Subsequently, **man** replaced **wer** as the normal term for 'a male person,' but at the same time the older sense 'a human being' remained in use.

In the second half of the 20th century, the generic use of **man** to refer to 'human beings in general' (*reptiles were here long before man appeared on the earth*) became problematic; the use is now often regarded as sexist or old-fashioned. In some contexts, terms such as **the human race** or **humankind** may be used instead of **man** or **mankind**. However, in other cases, particularly in compound forms, alternatives have not yet become established: there are no standard accepted alternatives for **manpower** or the verb **man**, for example.

USAGE NOTE

native

USAGE: In contexts such as *a **native** of Boston*, the use of the noun **native** is quite acceptable. But when used as a noun without qualification, as in *this dance is a favorite with the **natives***, it is more problematic. In modern use, it is used humorously to refer to the local inhabitants of a particular place: *New York in the summer was too hot even for the **natives***. In other contexts, it has an old-fashioned feel and, because of being closely associated with a colonial European outlook on nonwhite peoples living in remote places, it may cause offense.

The Right Word

These notes show fine distinctions in meaning among closely related synonyms, with extra information about the connotations of each word and additional examples to help pinpoint the exact shad of meaning desired.

THE RIGHT WORD **economical, frugal, miserly, parsimonious, provident, prudent, sparing, thrifty**

If you don't like to spend money unnecessarily, you may simply be **economical**, which means that you manage your finances wisely and avoid any unnecessary expenses.

If you're **thrifty**, you're both industrious and clever in managing your resources (*a thrifty shopper who never leaves home without her coupons*).

Frugal, on the other hand, means that you tend to be sparing with money—sometimes getting a little carried away in your efforts—by avoiding any form of luxury or lavishness (*too frugal to take a taxi, even at night*).

If you're **sparing**, you exercise such restraint in your spending that you sometimes deprive yourself (*sparing to the point where she allowed herself only one new item of clothing a season*).

If you're **provident**, however, you're focused on providing for the future (*never one to be provident, she spent her allowance the day she received it*).

Miserly and **parsimonious** are both used to describe frugality in its most extreme form. But while being *frugal* might be considered a virtue, being *parsimonious* is usually considered to be a fault or even a vice (*they could have been generous with their wealth, but they chose to lead a parsimonious life*).

And no one wants to be called *miserly*, which implies being stingy out of greed rather than need (*so miserly that he reveled in his riches while those around him were starving*).

Standard English

Unless otherwise stated, the words and senses recorded in this dictionary are all part of standard English; that is, they are in normal use in both speech and writing everywhere in the world, at many different levels of formality, ranging from official documents to casual conversation. Some words, however, are appropriate only in particular contexts, and these are labeled accordingly. The technical term for a particular level of use in language is **register**.

The *New Oxford American Dictionary* uses the following register labels:

formal: normally used only in writing, in contexts such as official documents.

informal: normally used only in contexts such as conversations or letters between friends.

dated: no longer used by the majority of English speakers, but still encountered occasionally, especially among the older generation.

archaic: very old-fashioned language, not in ordinary use at all today, but sometimes used to give a deliberately old-fashioned effect, or found in works of the past that are still widely read.

historical: still used today, but only to refer to some practice or artifact that is no longer part of the modern world.

literary: found only or mainly in literature written in an "elevated" style.

poetic: found only or mainly in poetry.

technical: normally used only in technical and specialist language, though not necessarily restricted to any specific subject field.

rare: not in normal use.

humorous: used with the intention of sounding funny or playful.

dialect: not used in standard American English, but still widely used in certain local regions of the United States.

offensive: language that is likely to cause offense, particularly racial offense, whether the speaker intends it or not.

derogatory: language intended to convey a low opinion or cause personal offense.

vulgar slang: informal language that may cause offense, often because it refers to the bodily functions of sexual activity or excretion, which are still widely regarded as taboo.

World English

English is spoken as a first language by more than 300 million people throughout the world, and used as a second language by many millions more. It is the language of international communication in business, diplomacy, sports, science, technology, and countless other fields.

The main regional standards are American, British, Canadian, Australian and New Zealand, South African, Indian, and West Indian. Within each of these regional varieties, a number of highly differentiated local dialects may be found. For example, within American English, Southern and Appalachian English have a long history and a number of distinctive features, which have in turn influenced other varieties.

The scope of a dictionary such as the *New Oxford American Dictionary*, given the breadth of material it aims to cover, must be limited for the most part to the vocabulary of the standard language of the United States rather than world English variation. Nevertheless, the *New Oxford American Dictionary* includes thousands of regionalisms encountered in standard contexts in the different English-speaking areas of the world, e.g.,

bun·yip

Austral. **1** a fabulous amphibious monster inhabiting inland waterways.
2 [often as *adj.*] an impostor or pretender: *Australia's bunyip aristocracy.*
▷from Wemba-Wemba *banib.*

ka·ross

S. African a rug or blanket of sewn animal skins, formerly worn as a garment by African people, now used as a bed or floor covering.
▷South African Dutch, from Khoikhoi *karos.*

par·kade

Canadian a multistory parking garage.
▷1950s: from PARK, on the pattern of *arcade.*

ser·vi·ette

Brit. & Canadian a table napkin.
▷late 15th cent.: from Old French, from *servir* 'to serve.'

snog

Brit., informal ▶*v.* (**snogged**, **snog·ging**) [*trans.*] kiss and caress amorously.
▶*n.* an act or spell of amorous kissing and caressing.

tyke

1 [usu. with *adj.*] *informal* a small child: *is the little tyke up to his tricks again?*
■ [usu. as *adj.*] *Canadian* an initiation level of sports competition for young children: *tyke hockey.*
2 *dated, chiefly Brit.* an unpleasant or coarse man.
3 a dog, esp. a mongrel.
▷late Middle English (in senses 2 and 3): from Old Norse *tík* 'bitch.'

The underlying approach has been to get away from the traditional, parochial notion that "correct" English belongs to a chosen few in any one geographical area or social class. A network of consultants in all parts of the English-speaking world has assisted in this by giving information and answering queries—by e-mail, on a regular, often daily basis—on all aspects of the language in a particular region. Often, the aim has been to find out whether a particular word, sense, or expression, well known and standard in American English, is used anywhere else. The picture that emerges is one of complex interactions among an overlapping set of regional standards.

The vast majority of words and senses in the *New Oxford American Dictionary* are common to all the major regional standard varieties of English, but where important local differences exist, the *New Oxford American Dictionary* records them. There are over 6,000 geographical labels on words and senses in this dictionary, but this contrasts with more than ten times that number that are not labeled at all.

The complexity of the overall picture has necessarily been simplified, principally for reasons of space and clarity of presentation. For example, a label such as "chiefly Brit." implies, but does not state, that a term is not standard in American English, though it may nevertheless be found in some local varieties in the United States. The label "Brit.," on the other hand, implies that the use is found typically in standard British English but is not found in standard American English, though it may be found elsewhere.

Spelling

It is often said that English spelling is both irregular and illogical, and it is certainly true that it is only indirectly related to contemporary pronunciation. English spelling reflects not modern pronunciation but the pronunciation of the 16th and 17th centuries, in particular through the influence of the works of Shakespeare and the Authorized Version of the Bible. However, in the two centuries between Chaucer and Shakespeare, English pronunciation had undergone huge changes, but spelling had failed to follow.

In the 18th century, standard spelling became almost completely fixed. The dictionaries written in this period, particularly Samuel Johnson's *Dictionary of the English Language* (1755), helped establish this standard, which, with only minor change and variation, is the standard accepted in British English today. Just over fifty years after the American colonies became independent, in 1828, Noah Webster published a dictionary with many of the spellings that we recognize today as being distinctly American rather than British. The complex history of the English language, together with the absence of any ruling body imposing "spelling reform," has ensured that many idiosyncrasies and anomalies in standard spelling have not only arisen but have also been preserved.

The *New Oxford American Dictionary* gives advice and information on spelling, particularly those cases that are irregular or that otherwise cause difficulty for native speakers. The main categories are summarized below.

Variant spellings

The main form of each word given in the *New Oxford American Dictionary* is always the standard American spelling. If there is a standard variant, e.g., a standard British spelling variant, this is indicated at the top of the entry and is cross-referred if its alphabetical position is more than five entries distant from the main entry.

esophagus (Brit. **oesophagus**)

oesophagus British spelling of ESOPHAGUS.

phyllo (also **filo**)

filo variant spelling of PHYLLO.

Other variants, such as archaic, old-fashioned, or informal spellings, are cross-referred to the main entry, but are not themselves listed at the parent entry.

cyder archaic spelling of CIDER.

Hyphenation

Although standard spelling in English is fixed, the use of hyphenation is not. In standard American English, a few general rules are followed, and these are outlined below.

Hyphenation of noun compounds: There is no hard-and-fast rule to determine whether, for example, **airstream, air stream,** or **air-stream** is correct. All forms are found in use: all are recorded in the Oxford databank and other standard texts. However, there is a broad tendency to avoid hyphenation for noun compounds in modern English (except when used to show grammatical function: see below). Thus there is, for example, a preference for **airstream** rather than **air-stream,** and for **air raid** rather than **air-raid**. Although this is a tendency in both American and British English, there is an additional preference in American English for the form to be one word and in British English for the form to be two words, e.g., **airfare** tends to be the most common form in American English, while **air fare** tends to be the most common form in British English. To save space and avoid confusion, only one of the three potential forms of each noun compound (the standard American one) is generally used as the headword form in the *New Oxford American Dictionary*. This does not, however, imply that other forms are incorrect or not used.

Grammatical function: Hyphens are also used to perform certain grammatical functions. When a noun compound made up of two separate words (e.g., **credit card**) is placed before another noun and used to modify it, the general rule is that the noun compound becomes hyphenated, e.g., *I have overused my credit card and am now in credit-card debt.* This sort of regular alternation is seen in example sentences in the *New Oxford American Dictionary* but is not otherwise explicitly mentioned in the dictionary entries.

A similar alternation is found in compound adjectives such as **well intentioned**. When used predicatively (i.e., after the verb), such adjectives are unhyphenated, but when used attributively (i.e., before the noun), they are hyphenated: *his remarks were well intentioned*; *a well-intentioned remark*.

A general rule governing verb compounds means that, where a noun compound is two words (e.g., **beta test**), any verb derived from it is normally hyphenated (**to beta-test**: *the system was beta-tested*). Similarly, verbal nouns and adjectives are more often hyphenated than ordinary noun or adjective compounds (e.g., **epoch-making**, **nation-building**).

Inflection

Compared with other languages, English has comparatively few inflections, and those that exist are remarkably regular. We add an *-s* to most nouns to make a plural; we add *-ed* to most verbs to make a past tense or a past participle, and *-ing* to make a present participle.

Occasionally, a difficulty arises: for example, a single consonant after a short stressed vowel is doubled before adding *-ed* or *-ing* (**hum**, **hums**, **humming**, **hummed**). In addition, words borrowed from other languages generally bring their foreign inflections with them, causing problems for English speakers who are not proficient in those languages.

In all such cases, guidance is given in the *New Oxford American Dictionary*. The main areas covered are outlined below.

Verbs

The following forms are regarded as regular and are therefore not shown in the dictionary:

- third person singular present forms adding *-s* to the stem (or *-es* to stems ending in *-s, -x, -z, -sh,* or soft *-ch*), e.g., **find** → **finds**; **crush** → **crushes**
- past tenses and past participles dropping a final silent *e* and adding *-ed* to the stem, e.g., **change** → **changed**; **dance** → **danced**
- present participles dropping a final silent *e* and adding *-ing* to the stem, e.g., **change** → **changing**; **dance** → **dancing**

Other forms are given in the dictionary, notably for:

- verbs that inflect by doubling a consonant, e.g., **bat** → **batted**, **batting**
- verbs ending in *-y* that inflect by changing *-y* to *-i*, e.g., **try** → **tries**, **tried**
- verbs in which past tense and past participle do not follow the regular *-ed* pattern, e.g., **feel** → *past* **felt**; **awake** → *past* **awoke**; → *past part.* **awoken**
- present participles that add *-ing* but retain a final *e* (in order to make clear that the pronunciation of *g* remains soft), e.g., **singe** → **singeing**

Nouns

Plurals formed by adding *-s* (or *-es* when they end in *-s, -x, -z, -sh,* or soft *-ch*) are regarded as regular and are not shown, e.g., **dog** → **dogs**; **lunch** → **lunches**

Other plural forms are given in the dictionary, notably for:

- nouns ending in *-i* or *-o*, e.g., **agouti** → **agoutis**; **albino** → **albinos**
- nouns ending in *-a*, *-um*, or *-us* that are or appear to be Latinate forms, e.g., **alumna** → **alumnae**; **spectrum** → **spectra**; **alveolus** → **alveoli**
- nouns ending in *-y*, e.g., **fly** → **flies**; **party** → **parties**
- nouns with more than one plural form, e.g., **crux** → **cruxes** or **cruces**; **money** → **moneys** or **monies**
- nouns with plurals showing a change in the stem, e.g., **foot** → **feet**; **louse** → **lice**
- nouns with plurals unchanged from the singular form are indicated by (*pl.* same).
- for polysyllabic words, only the changed syllables are shown.

Adjectives

The following forms for comparative and superlative are regarded as regular and are not shown in the dictionary:

- words of one syllable adding *-er* and *-est*, e.g., **great** → **greater**, **greatest**
- words of one syllable ending in silent e, which drop the *-e* and add *-er* and *-est*, e.g., **brave** → **braver**, **bravest**
- words that form the comparative and superlative by adding "more" and "most"; e.g., **beautiful** → **more beautiful, most beautiful**

Other forms are given in the dictionary, notably for:

- adjectives that form the comparative and superlative by doubling a final consonant, e.g., **hot** → **hotter**, **hottest**
- two-syllable adjectives that form the comparative and superlative with *-er* and *-est* (typically adjectives ending in *-y* and their negative forms), e.g., **happy** → **happier**, **happiest**; **unhappy** → **unhappier**, **unhappiest**
- only the changed final syllables are shown.

Syllabification

In the *New Oxford American Dictionary*, syllable breaks are shown for main entries and derivatives. Although all possible breaks are shown, there are some conventions that govern how writers break words at the ends of lines. Guidelines include:

- Avoid a break that will leave one letter and a hyphen at the end of the line or one letter (or one letter and a punctuation mark such as a period) at the beginning of a line.
- Avoid breaking a word that is already hyphenated except at that hyphen (e.g., *self-affirmation*; *leather-bound*).
- Never break proper names.
- Avoid breaking abbreviations.

How to use this dictionary

Each new part of speech (introduced by ▶)

Part of speech

ear[1] /i(ə)r/ ▶*n.* the organ of hearing and balance in humans and other vertebrates, esp. the external part of this. ■ an organ sensitive to sound in other animals. ■ [in *sing.*] an ability to recognize, appreciate, and reproduce sounds, esp. music or language: ***an ear for** melody.* ■ used to refer to a person's willingness to listen and pay attention to something: *she offers a sympathetic ear to worried pet owners.* ■ an ear-shaped thing, esp. the handle of a jug.

Core sense

Subsenses (introduced by ■)

The ear of a mammal is composed of three parts. The outer or external ear consists of a fleshy external flap and a tube leading to the eardrum or tympanum. The middle ear is an air-filled cavity connected to the throat, containing three small linked bones that transmit vibrations from the eardrum to the inner ear. The inner ear is a complex fluid-filled labyrinth including the spiral cochlea (where vibrations are converted to nerve impulses) and the three semicircular canals (forming the organ of balance). The ears of other vertebrates are broadly similar.

Encyclopedic information (in separate block)

▷Old English *ēare*, of Germanic origin; related to Dutch *oor* and German *Ohr*, from an Indo-European root shared by Latin *auris* and Greek *ous*. **—eared** *adj.* [in *combination*] *long-eared.* **—ear·less** *adj.*
▶***PHRASES*** □ **be all ears** *informal* be listening eagerly and attentively. □ **bring something (down) about one's ears** bring something, esp. misfortune, on oneself: *she brought her world crashing about her ears.* □ **one's ears are burning** one is subconsciously aware of being talked about or criticized. □ **grin** (or **smile**) **from ear to ear** smile broadly. □ **have something coming out of one's ears** *informal* have a substantial or excessive amount of something: *that man's got money coming out of his ears.* □ **have someone's ear** have access to and influence with someone: *he claimed to have the prime minister's ear.* □ **have** (or **keep**) **an ear to the ground** be well informed about events and trends. □ **in one ear and out the other** heard but disregarded or quickly forgotten: *whatever he tells me seems to go in one ear and out the other.* □ **listen with half an ear** not give one's full attention. □ **be out on one's ear** *informal* be dismissed or ejected ignominiously. □ **up to one's ears in** *informal* very busy with or deeply involved in: *I'm up to my ears in work here.*

Label (showing level of formality)

Phrases (introduced by □)

Example (showing typical use)

Homonym number (indicates different word with the same spelling)

ear[2] ▶*n.* the seed-bearing head or spike of a cereal plant. ■ a head of corn. ▷Old English *ēar*, of Germanic origin; related to Dutch *aar* and German *Ähre*.

Pronunciation

Ear·hart /ˈe(ə)rˌhärt/, Amelia (Mary) (1898–1937), U.S. aviator. In 1932, she became the first woman to fly an airplane across the Atlantic Ocean by herself. In 1937, her plane disappeared somewhere over the Pacific Ocean during an around-the-world flight.

Encyclopedic entry (biography)

Common collocation (highlighted within the example)

earn /ərn/ ▸*v.* [*trans.*] (of a person) obtain (money) in return for labor or services: *they earn $35 per hour | he now* ***earns his living*** *as a truck driver.* ■ [with *two objs.*] (of an activity or action) cause (someone) to obtain (money): *this latest win earned them $50,000 in prize money.* ■ (of capital invested) gain (money) as interest or profit. ■ gain or incur deservedly in return for one's behavior or achievements: *through the years she has earned affection and esteem.* ▷Old English *earnian*, from a base shared by Old English *esne* 'laborer.'
▸*PHRASE* □ **earn one's keep** work in return for food and accommodations. ■ be worth the time, money, or effort spent on one.

ear·wig /ˈi(ə)rˌwig/ ▸*n.* a small elongated insect with a pair of terminal appendages that resemble pincers. The females typically care for their eggs and young until they are grown. • Order Dermaptera: several families.
▸*v.* (**-wigged**, **-wig·ging**) [*intrans.*] *informal, chiefly Brit.* eavesdrop on a conversation: *he looked behind him to see if anyone was earwigging.* ■ [*trans.*] *archaic* influence (someone) by secret means. ▷Old English *ēarwicga*, from *ēare* 'ear' + *wicga* 'earwig' (probably related to *wiggle*). The insect is so named because it was once thought to crawl into the human ear.

Label (showing regional distribution)

Label (showing currency)

Word origin (showing morphological and sense development; introduced by ▷)

e·bul·lient /iˈbo͝olyənt; iˈbəlyənt/ ▸*adj.* **1** cheerful and full of energy: *she sounded ebullient and happy.* **2** *archaic or poetic/literary* (of liquid or matter) boiling or agitated as if boiling: *misted and ebullient seas.* ▷late 16th cent. (in the sense 'boiling'): from Latin *ebullient-* 'boiling up,' from the verb *ebullire*, from *e-* (variant of *ex-*) 'out' + *bullire* 'to boil.' —**e·bul·lience** *n.* —**e·bul·lient·ly** *adv.*

ec·dy·sis /ˈekdəsis/ ▸*n.* *Zoology* the process of shedding the old skin (in reptiles) or casting off the outer cuticle (in insects and other arthropods). ▷mid 19th cent.: from Greek *ekdusis*, from *ekduein* 'put off,' from *ek-* 'out, off' + *duein* 'put.' —**ec·dys·i·al** /ekˈdizēəl/ *adj.*

Subject label

Alternative name

e·chid·na /əˈkidnə/ ▸*n.* a spiny insectivorous egg-laying mammal with a long snout and claws, native to Australia and New Guinea. Also called SPINY ANTEATER. • Family Tachyglossidae, order Monotremata: two genera and species, in particular *Tachyglossus aculeatus*. ▷mid 19th cent.: modern Latin, from Greek *ekhidna* 'viper,' also the name of a mythical creature that gave birth to the many-headed Hydra; compare with *ekhinos* 'sea urchin, hedgehog.'

Technical information (chiefly for animals and plants)

Ec·ua·dor /ˈekwəˌdôr/ a republic in northwestern South America, on the Pacific coast; pop. 13,212,700; capital, Quito; languages, Spanish (official), Quechua. —**Ec·ua·dor·e·an** /ˌekwəˈdôrēən/ *adj.* & *n.*

Encyclopedic entry (place name)

Additional information (in separate block)

Formerly part of the Inca empire, Ecuador was conquered by the Spanish in 1534. It remained part of Spain's American empire until 1822, when independence was gained.

Verb inflections

ed·it /ˈedit/ ▸*v.* (**ed·it·ed**, **ed·it·ing**) [*trans.*] (often **be edited**) prepare (written material) for publication by correcting, condensing, or otherwise modifying it: *Volume I was edited by J. Johnson.* ■ choose material for (a movie or a radio or television program) and arrange it to form a coherent whole: *the footage wasn't good enough to be edited into broadcast form* | [as *adj.*] (**edited**) *an edited version drawn from several prerecorded performances.* ■ be editor of (a newspaper or magazine). ■ (**edit something out**) remove unnecessary or inappropriate words, sounds, or scenes from a text, movie, or radio or television program.
▸*n.* a change or correction made as a result of editing. ▷late 18th cent. (as a verb): partly a back-formation from **EDITOR**, reinforced by French *éditer* 'to edit' (from *édition* 'edition').

Typical form (in bold)

Typical pattern (in bold)

Plural form

elf /elf/ ▸*n.* (*pl.* **elves** /elvz/) a supernatural creature of folk tales, typically represented as a small, elusive figure in human form with pointed ears, magical powers, and a capricious nature. ▷Old English, of Germanic origin; related to German *Alp* 'nightmare.' **—elf·ish** *adj.* **—elv·en** /ˈelvən/ *adj.* (*poetic/literary*) **—elv·ish** /ˈelvish/ *adj.*

Derivatives (in alphabetical order; introduced by —)

Grammatical information (in square brackets)

en·large /enˈlärj/ ▸*v.* make or become bigger or more extensive: [*trans.*] *recently my son enlarged our garden pond* | [*intrans.*] *lymph nodes enlarge and become hard* | [as *adj.*] (**enlarged**) *an enlarged spleen.* ■ [*trans.*] (often **be enlarged**) develop a bigger print of (a photograph).
▸*phrasal v.* □ **enlarge on/upon** speak or write about (something) in greater detail: *I would like to enlarge on this theme.* ▷Middle English (formerly also as *inlarge*): from Old French *enlarger*, from *en-* (expressing a change of state) + *large* 'large.'

Phrasal verbs (introduced by □)

e·o·hip·pus /ˌēōˈhipəs/ ▸*n.* (*pl.* **-pus·es**) another term for **HYRACOTHERIUM**. ▷late 19th cent.: from Greek *ēōs* 'dawn' + *hippos* 'horse.'

Cross reference entry

Variant spelling

ep·i·cen·ter /ˈepiˌsentər/ (*Brit.* **ep·i·cen·tre**) ▸*n.* the point on the earth's surface vertically above the focus of an earthquake. ■ *figurative* the central point of something, typically a difficult or unpleasant situation: *the patient was at the epicenter of concern.* ▷late 19th cent.: from Greek *epikentros* 'situated on a center,' from *epi* 'upon' + *kentron* 'center.'

American Voices

Children hear and come to recognize the voices of their mothers as perhaps their first cognitive act. Some evidence suggests that this process of recognition may begin even before children are born. As we grow and live, we all come to recognize many voices, those of family members, of friends, and of many people whose paths we cross on a regular basis—even the voices of politicians or actors whom we do not know but just hear with some regularity on television or through other media. Individual voices are unique. No two of us have exactly the same pitch or timbre. And no two of us have exactly the same habits in expression, whether habits in pronunciation, in word choice, or in ways of putting words together to say what we want to say. We all have the same kind of teeth and bones and muscles that allow us to talk, but subtle differences in our individual bodies, and in the speech habits we each develop, create in each of us the special qualities of voice that our family and friends can recognize. Voice recognition helps give children the comfort of knowing that they live with those who love them. For adults, the recognition of voices becomes something we use everyday, whether to tell who is on the other end of the telephone or to find one another in a crowd. Moreover, our recognition of voices goes beyond our ability to identify people we know personally; we can often tell when people that we have never met happen to come from the same community that we do, or from some community that we do not belong to. This kind of recognition does not depend on the pitch and timbre of the individual voice, but rather upon habits in pronunciation, in word choice, or in ways of putting words together that have come to be shared by many members of a community. If we hear somebody with a "drawl," we can guess that we are in the presence of a Southerner. If we hear somebody use technical medical or legal terms, we can guess that we are listening to a doctor or a lawyer. If we hear somebody use "whom," or carefully mark the differences between "shall" and "will" or between "lie" and "lay" in their speech, we can guess that our speaker has done well in English classes in school. Of course our guesses might be wrong, because these speech habits only tend to be used by members of a group. They do not have to be used all of the time or by all of the members. Not all Southerners have a "drawl," and some doctors and lawyers will talk to us without using technical terms, and not all highly-educated people distinguish "who/whom," "shall/will," and "lie/lay" in their speech (and there are people with little formal education who do distinguish them). Yet we all do routinely use habits of speech like these to try to identify the people we talk to as coming from different regions or from different social conditions, quite often with good success. Just as the recognition of individual voices is something that we can use to help us every day, we can also use the recognition that particular speakers come from a community of speakers, from some place or from some occupational or social group, to tell us how we should act towards them or what we should expect from them. Our judgments sometimes depend on stereotypes and are the worse for it. To think that all Southerners are slow, or that all New Yorkers are rude, is certainly a mistake. Our better judgments come from our varied experience with people from different walks of life, and they can help us to cooperate and to communicate better in our conversations with different people.

When we speak of American English, we refer to habits in pronunciation, in word choice, or in ways of putting words together that tend to be shared by many Americans. There are now nearly three-hundred-million individual American voices. Every American belongs to many communities—local, regional, occupational, social—and the speech habits of every individual American both contribute to and reflect the speech habits of those communities. The speech habits of a region are composed of the speech habits of its people; the speech habits associated with an occupation like law or medicine, or like mining or telemarketing or automobile assembly, are composed of the speech habits of its practitioners; and the speech habits of any and every social group are composed of the speech habits of its members. Therefore, when we speak of American English, we are not talking about a uniform system of language that must be used by every American, but instead we are talking about a more or less consistent collection of speech habits that arises from all of those individual American voices. When we speak of American English, we are not talking about an exclusive language code, but rather something that includes the recognizable voices of all of the various communities in which Americans participate. When we speak of American English, we are not talking about a form of language that experts say that Americans must or should use, but on the contrary we are talking about the common speech by means of which Americans voluntarily talk to each other. American English is not what makes someone an American, but instead it is that kind of English that Americans together create for themselves.

The term "American English" is chiefly useful for comparisons with other national varieties of English, such as British English or Canadian English. The other national varieties result from the same circumstances that make

American English. British English, for instance, is a more or less consistent collection of speech habits that arises from nearly sixty million individual British voices, and from the speech habits of British regional and social communities. While Canada shares a continent with the United States, and Canadian speech habits are generally closer to those of Americans than they are to British speech, Canadian English is not the same as American English; Canadian English is composed of millions of individual Canadian voices, and of the speech habits of Canadian regional and social communities. Every country that has speakers of English as a native language has its own variety: Australia, India, Jamaica, New Zealand, Nigeria, Singapore, South Africa, and others. In every case, a national variety of a language is composed of a more or less consistent collection of speech habits contributed and reflected by the speakers of the country. Of course there are many elements of language that all English speakers share. We have a common core vocabulary, and we are not all that different in the way that we put words together. The elements of English that we hold in common allow English speakers all over the world to communicate with each other. Even so, there is plenty of room in the language left over for every individual and every community and every country to develop particular and characteristic speech habits. While the common elements of English contribute to the function of communication, all of these characteristic speech habits identify the speakers, whether as themselves, or as members of communities, or as citizens of a country. The special characteristic features also have a function, because they help us to identify the people we talk to. They help us to communicate better in our conversations with people from different regional, social, or national circumstances. They also help us to recognize members of our own communities and thus grant us the comfort of fellow feeling. And every time we speak, our own characteristic speech habits announce who we are to the people we talk to.

Telling Voices Apart

Pronunciation can vary in two different ways to help create different voices. For any given word, different speakers can employ different speech sounds. For instance, many Americans can pronounce the word *room* as either /ro͞om/ or /ro͝om/. This difference is called "phonetic" because it consists of an actual difference in how a speaker produces the sounds. Phonetic differences in American English are widespread. Sometimes phonetic differences occur without apparent cause, as in the pronunciations of *room*. Sometimes phonetic differences occur in patterns, as in the noun *mania* /ˈmānēə/ and the adjective *manic* /ˈmanik/. Here the noun form and the adjective form of what is really the same word have a different vowel in the stressed syllable, just as many other similar noun-adjective pairs do. Another kind of pronunciation difference is called "phonemic," and refers to the set of speech sounds that can be used to tell words apart. In the words *father* and *feather*, the difference in pronunciation between /ä/ and /e/ in the stressed vowel is how we know that these are two different words. Thus we can call /ä/ and /e/ different phonemes of American English. British English shares the American distinction between /ä/ and /e/ for telling words apart, but it does have a somewhat different set of phonemes, especially the vowels, from American English. For instance, British speakers typically pronounce the words *pot* and *hot* with a vowel sound halfway between American /ä/ and /ô/, and this sound can be used in British English to tell words apart. British English has a phoneme that is not available in most American voices. Within American English different communities can also have different sets of phonemes. For example, the words *cot* and *caught* have different sounds for many Americans, /ä/ and /ô/, which serve as phonemes, but for other Americans and most Canadians *cot* and *caught* rhyme; the latter group has lost a phonemic distinction still made by the former group.

Besides phonetic and phonemic differences in speech sounds, different speakers can also use different patterns of stress and intonation. While some Americans pronounce the word *Thanksgiving* /THaNGksˈgiviNG/, with the accent on the second syllable, others pronounce it with the accent on the first syllable, /ˈTHaNGksˌgiviNG/. As a general rule, Americans have a heavier pattern of stresses than British speakers, so that Americans often have two stressed syllables in words where British speakers have only a single stressed syllable, as in American *baseball* /ˈbāsˌbôl/ and British /ˈbāsbôl/. "Intonation" refers to an overall change in pitch across several words, for instance the way that English speakers tend to raise their pitch at the end of a question. Intonation and some other aspects of how we utter sentences, such as one's rate of speech, may well be important factors in how we tell different voices apart, but they have not yet received as much study as phonetic, phonemic, and stress differences.

While we often think of different voices solely in terms of pronunciation, individual and community voices also have differences in word choices (our vocabulary, or lexicon), and in the way that we put words together to say what we need to say (our grammar, or syntax). Different voices sometimes have different words. What an Australian English speaker calls a *billabong*, an American English speaker might call a *stream*, or a *stream bed* in the dry season. And within the United States different regional voices have other different words that correspond to *billabong*: *bayou*, *branch*, *brook*, *creek*, *run*, and other words; and in the dry season *arroyo*, *wash*, and other similar words. The same word can also have different meanings for different voices. While *July 4th* is just a summer day for many English speakers around the world, it has the special meaning of 'Independence Day' for Americans. More subtle differences also occur frequently. *Regular coffee*, besides caffeine, has both cream and sugar in New England, just milk in New York City, and neither cream nor sugar in most of the rest of the country. *Tea* is sweet and cold in the American South, but hot and unsweetened elsewhere. The meanings of words are strongly affected by such local customs, and it is not wrong to say that all words take on local flavor as a result of their historical and cultural associations in particular communities. Grammar works the same way. While all English speakers share a core grammar, plenty of room remains for different grammatical habits within different communities. Within some communities it would be very odd never to say *ain't* or never to say *seen* and *come* as the past-tense forms of *to see* and *to come*. In other communities just the reverse is true: it would be very odd ever to say them. When different Americans are not feeling well, they might say that they feel *sick to*, *sick at*, or *sick in* their stomachs, depending on where they live and what social group they belong to. When the big hand of the clock is on the nine, now a rarer occurrence in the digital age, Americans from different communities might say that it was *quarter to*, *quarter till*, or *quarter of* the hour. People choose their verbs and prepositions not according to how the grammar book tells them, but out of the habits ingrained in them by talking with people in their communities.

We usually tell community voices apart not on the basis of pronunciations of words that are dead giveaways, but instead on the basis of many clues. If we had to wait until we heard somebody pronounce the word *very* as /ˈvärē/, it might be a long time before we could guess that our speaker was from the Appalachian region. We do not want to wait to hear a *milkshake* called a *frappe* or a *cabinet* to decide whether someone is from eastern Massachusetts or Rhode Island, respectively. Words and pronunciations strictly limited to just one place or social group are quite rare. Instead, we form an overall impression of both the subtle and the blatant clues in the speech of the people we talk to, based on our lifelong experience with a great many speakers—and if we are often right, we are also often wrong, especially in these days of geographic and social mobility.

The *New Oxford American Dictionary* is a witness to all of these kinds of differences. A dictionary by its nature takes the lexicon for its organizing principle, and yet it also includes a great deal of information about pronunciation and grammar in addition to its coverage of the meanings of words. This dictionary highlights the American voice among English speakers. It does not exclude some coverage of other national voices, for one of the best ways to recognize the American voice in English is to know what it is not. The dictionary does include those many aspects of English that are shared by English speakers around the world, for the American voice participates in these elements of the language. This dictionary does not include every subtlety of English to be found in the United States. How could it, given the enormous variety of local, regional, and social voices to be found in the country? Readers will find coverage appropriate to the dictionary's scope of both subtle and more obvious American features of pronunciation and grammar, besides special words and meanings of words used by Americans, all within the greater context of English worldwide.

Finding an American Voice

Note: Square brackets [ ] are used in the following discussion below to indicate that the sounds being referred to are not the broad phones of the dictionary pronunciation system, which are always shown between slashes / /.

American English began as soon as English speakers settled on the continent. The language of the first English-speaking settlers, therefore, comes from about the time of Shakespeare, which is also the time of first publication of the King James Version of the Bible. Most people today think of the English of the King James Version as "Biblical language," when in fact the KJV illustrates an artful use of the common idiom of that time period, called Early Modern English by historians of the language. A familiar passage can illustrate some differences, when God asks Adam about eating the apple (Gen. 3.11): "Hast thou eaten of the tree, whereof I commanded thee that thou shouldest not eat?" We see the different pronouns in use at the time, *thee* and *thou*, and the *-st* verb ending that went with them. We would no longer say *eaten of the tree*, but rather "eaten from the tree," or better yet "eaten something from the tree," because we now prefer a different preposition, and we prefer that the verb *eat* take an object in a phrase like this. The word *whereof* sounds like legal language to us, because the language of law is very conservative and has retained the word in its modern usage, just as the KJV has preserved it in a sacred text. But all of these usages were part of the common speech in the early seventeenth century; they would not have sounded "biblical" or "legal" to the people of the time.

The pronunciation of Early Modern English was also quite different from modern pronunciation. Here are some famous lines of Shakespeare from *Sonnet 30*, rendered into Early Modern English pronunciation with the dictionary's pronunciation system:

When to the sessions of sweet silent thought
I summon up remembrance of things past
I see the lack of many a thing I sought
And with old woes new wail my dear time's waste. . . .

[hwen to͞o T͟Hə sesyənz ôv swēt səilənt THôo͝oKHt]
[əi so͝omən o͝op rəmembrəns ôv THiNGZ päst]
[əi sē T͟Hə läk ôv mänē ə THiNG əi sôo͝oKHt]
[änd wiTH ôld wôz nyo͞o weil məi dēr təimz wäst]

In the first line we can find several differences from Modern English in America. Most Americans today would not pronounce an /h/ sound in *when*, though many do; we no longer pronounce the word *session* so that the second syllable is like the one in *onion*; our modern /ī/ sound in *silent* is not the same as the Early Modern English [əi] sound, which many Americans today might hear as being closer to the modern /oi/ sound, or to the [əi~o͝oi] sound for the phoneme /ī/ as used in Britain today (although the modern British pronunciation is also not the same as Shakespeare's); both the vowel and the final consonant cluster of *thought* are also quite different from the modern sounds, in that they still have sounds preserved in the spelling, [ôo͝o] for *ou* and [KHt] for *ght*, that we no longer use in modern pronunciation. Some words are quite similar in pronunciation *(to, the, remembrance, things, a, with*), while others have undergone phonetic changes, as with the sounds [əi, ô] which have become /ī, ō/ across the whole range of words pronounced with those phonemes, or like Modern *new* /no͞o/ from Early Modern [nyo͞o], a phonetic change in the word, though some Americans and many Britons still say [nyo͞o]. The pronunciation of *summon up* from Early Modern English may still be heard today in the more northerly voices of British English, while the pronunciation has changed for American English and southern British English. Spelling and rhymes help historians of the language to reconstruct the pronunciation of earlier forms of English, as does a knowledge of the pronunciation of different varieties of English spoken today.

Even though American English began about the same time as Shakespeare lived, nobody today still speaks Shakespeare's English, not anywhere. To go looking for Shakespeare's English, or to think that people in remote Appalachian valleys still speak it, becomes the height of folly as soon as we realize that nothing we do can prevent a language from changing. Just as all speakers of a language develop their own speech habits within their regional and social communities, those habits change over time. New communities arise and old ones fade away. Within any continuing community the individual speakers, out of whose individual habits the community's speech habits take shape, change with the generations. As all parents realize, children never perfectly reproduce the behavior of their elders, in speech or in anything else—and neither do their children's children. Linguistic change is as inevitable as death or taxes, so long as there are living native speakers of the language. The language does not become worse as time marches on, only different. Even if community elders do not approve of the younger generation's new linguistic behavior, as seems always to be the case, the living speakers of a language will not fail to bring change. As for the English language, American English began to diverge from the English spoken in Britain as soon as communities began to form in North America. The speakers in each place changed the language in their own ways. As we have seen, some parts of Shakespeare's English have become very different in Modern English while others have remained unchanged until the present day. The parts that have changed have changed differently in Britain and America. This being so, British English cannot be said to be more "original" or more "correct" than American English, because both are, so to speak, merely different branches off the same tree trunk. American English is not a corruption of British English, any more than British English itself is a corruption of Shakespeare's English. The best way to think about British English and American English is that they are both records of the varied speech habits of the people in their various regional and social communities.

One of the first to comment on the changes in colonial American English from British English was John Witherspoon. Born near Edinburgh, Scotland, he became the president of the College of New Jersey (the forerunner of Princeton University) in 1768. Witherspoon wrote of a great many "Americanisms" (usages "peculiar to this country") and also of "vulgarisms," slang, and other aspects of language of which he disapproved that were common in both America and Britain. Witherspoon believed, as did many men of the age, in the development of purity and perfection in modern languages, on the model of Classical Latin and Greek. He also believed that the standard for English was still to be found in Britain. Thus Americanisms were just one class among many sorts of errors and imperfections. He mentioned use in America, among other usages, of the word *notify*, of the phrase *fellow countrymen,* of the sentence "I do not consider myself equal to the task" without the word *as* before "equal," of the phrase "a certain Thomas Benson" when in Britain people would say "a certain man called Thomas Benson," of the use of the word *mad* to mean 'angry,' and of the phrase "a clever man" to indicate only a favorable judgment when in Britain the use of *clever* might entail either a favorable or a critical judgment. Each of these usages is thoroughly acceptable in modern American English, and many of them have now become acceptable in Britain as well. Before the late seventeenth and eighteenth centuries, there was little notion of "correctness" with regard to the living modern languages. The things that Witherspoon complained about in American English were nothing more than the normal adjustments, whether in lexicon or grammar, that might be expected of a living language, especially when it had been carried to communities in a new and remote place. The mistake of the men of his age was to think that such living languages could be judged according to standards such as those that could be compiled for Classical Latin and Greek, which had no more living native speakers. While we may see the error of Witherspoon's interpretation of emerging changes in American English, we can be glad that he was motivated to document some of those changes.

Another early commentator was Anne Royall. She was not a college president but a journalist. She traveled the country in the early nineteenth century, and she published comments from her travels that included frequent observations on the local language. From West Virginia, for instance, she reported hearing the expression *lettinon*, as in "she is only lettinon," to mean 'adopt a pretence,' something still current in the area today. In actuality, she was recording the regional American pronunciation of *letting on*, with its new, particularly American meaning. She herself often engaged in dialect writing intended to give an indication of local pronunciation and the everyday grammar of country people, for example the lack of pronunciation of *r* after vowels ("postvocalic /r/") in Virginia country speech. She also commented on the speech of those in high society, for example the common use of "my dear" in the speech of Washington, DC, or what she called the "whining tone" of Philadelphians. In these passages we can glimpse a number of aspects of modern American English that were already present in everyday speech, although we also see Mrs. Royall's prejudice in the comment about Philadelphia speech. Mrs. Royall, like Witherspoon, was interested in the social dynamics of local speech, and particularly interested in portraying speech that did not rise to her own standards. American English grew up in a prescriptive age in which social differences in language were a common topic for comment.

Noah Webster turned this notion of standards in a new direction with his publication of *The American Spelling Book* (1783) and his *American Dictionary of the English Language* (1828). Webster believed that spelling should be practical, not merely traditional, and he defended the idea that grammar should come from the usage of the people, not just from self-appointed experts. As the titles above indicate, Webster also championed the American voice as against a British standard. The spelling reforms that he advocated in *The American Spelling Book* form the basis of present-day differences between American and British spelling. While most other attempts at spelling reform for English have failed, Webster succeeded because his "blue-backed speller" became a standard textbook in American elementary schools and one of the best-selling textbooks in history—with sales of up to 100 million copies. His *American Dictionary* was also highly influential though not a commercial success; his name has become synonymous with American dictionaries, and many companies now attach the name "Webster" to their products. In the modern era the idea that American English could serve as a standard appears obvious to many, because of American commercial and political influence in the world. In the early nineteenth century, however, the United States was still a provincial place in the view of British and even much of American high society, even though the former colonies were no longer under British control. Webster's advocacy of an American standard was therefore highly controversial, and all the more amazing for its success in that it turned upside down the conventional view of what should constitute a linguistic standard.

One explanation for Webster's success comes from the social dynamic of early settlement in America. During the colonial period some settlers did not come by choice: large numbers of petty criminals were transported as a punishment to America by London courts during the seventeenth century, and large numbers of Africans were shipped to America as slaves. However, much larger numbers of settlers did come to America voluntarily, as part of a great social movement to acquire land and to obtain economic and religious control of their own lives. In his famous essay "What is an American?" (1784), J. Hector St. John de Crèvecoeur enthusiastically described the process of becoming an American. He emphasized the collective nature of the experience, how new settlers occupied and improved the land with the help of their neighbors. Just as new immigrants needed to acquire new skills and capital for successful settlement, in Crèvecoeur's description they also became integrated with their new communities and thereby began to acquire linguistic habits. Whereas society in the Old World was fractured by inherited divisions, New World society was characterized by common purpose that could encourage the development of shared linguistic habits.

Several early commentators, including Witherspoon, mention the relative uniformity of colonial American English compared to the dialects of English in the long-settled regions of Britain. This so-called "colonial leveling" is the expected result of early settlement, because the mixture of settlers from different parts of Great Britain, or from language backgrounds other than English, would be expected to dilute the influence of any old-world variety of English. While the speech of the original founding population in an area would exert a larger influence on its eventual speech habits than would the speech of later settlers, the speech of the founding population in an area could not be maintained without change. The only exceptions to this generalization were those communities that moved to an area and kept to themselves without admitting outsiders, such as the "Pennsylvania Dutch" and other strict religious communities. Most communities with originally uniform settlement but without a close-knit, closed-community ideology tended to lose their distinctive language habits over time, some by only the second or third generation after original settlement. Those areas of colonial America with mixed and open communities were influenced by old-world habits, and would not immediately possess their own distinctive voices.

Research on communities with more recent original settlement, such as New Zealand, suggests that settlers in the first and second generation have not yet established stable community speech habits, but that community habits will emerge soon thereafter. Early records from the seventeenth century, such as depositions from the Salem witch trials, use Early Modern English features but show no strong evidence of a new American voice, however important such records are for the development of American culture. Even the earliest records, however, do illustrate place names and words drawn from the Native Americans who already lived here, for instance in John Smith's *Generall Historie of Virginia* (1624) which includes a short glossary of Indian words. Regional American voices began to emerge by the eighteenth century. Witherspoon lists "localisms" from New England (*improve* a horse 'to ride,' *have occasion* 'opportunity'), the middle colonies (*chunks* 'partly burned pieces of wood,' *once in a while* 'sometimes'), and the South (*raw salad* 'salad,' *tote* 'carry'). Diaries and letters by relatively uneducated people show evidence of regional pronunciation habits through their idiosyncratic spelling, and dialect writers like Mrs. Royall also provide pronunciation clues.

The primary cultural centers through which immigration occurred in the eighteenth century became influential "focal" areas for the development of speech habits. Boston, Philadelphia, Eastern Virginia, and Charleston were the original centers, followed by New York City as English settlers overwhelmed the founding Dutch population, and later Pittsburgh at the head of the Ohio River. According to Crèvecoeur's description, many new immigrants would work for some time to provide labor near the cultural centers in order to build capital and learn skills necessary to stay alive when they acquired their own land. The immigrants then carried the speech habits that they had learned in the cultural centers into the interior of the country, and thus spread the speech of the cultural centers into the hinterlands. In the later eighteenth century and into the nineteenth century, the second wave of American settlement carried Atlantic coastal speech habits west in three broad bands. The Northern path of settlement carried Northern speech habits west along the Erie Canal and Great Lakes in the Northern tier of states as far as Minnesota. The Midland band of settlement began in Philadelphia, the largest colonial city, and proceeded west in two different pathways. The North Midland path followed the National Road to Pittsburgh and the head waters of the Ohio River, and from there west across Ohio and Indiana to Illinois. The South Midland path extended southwest down the Shenandoah Valley to the Cumberland Gap in Tennessee, which was the gateway to settlement west of the Appalachians. The Southern band of settlement had its roots in Virginia and the Carolinas, and proceeded west across the Old South into those areas best suited for large-scale plantation agriculture. The parts of the Old South that permitted only subsistence agriculture (especially the mountains and the Piney Woods) were settled by South Midland speakers. African Americans were carried west by the planters. The greatest growth of the African American population occurred during the eighteenth-century expansion of the plantation system. Crèvecoeur's account of his visit to Charleston, South Carolina, included a brief piece of dialogue from an African American slave, just enough to show that the development of African American English was then already well underway. By the Civil War, the Northern, Midland, and Southern settlement areas were well established as far west as the Mississippi—with cultural (and linguistic) differences between the regions that were great enough to fight over.

During the nineteenth-century westward expansion of America, the American ideal of land ownership continued, and, if anything, became even more intense. A great many immigrants from Europe arrived, often in large numbers at times of trouble in the Old Country. The great wave of settlement by the Scots-Irish occurred at the end of the eighteenth century, as the resettlement of Scots in Northern Ireland turned out to be less successful than the British had hoped and the new Scots-Irish emigrated to the colonies. The great wave of Southern Irish settlement occurred in the early nineteenth century, in consequence of the potato famine. Germans and Scandinavians emigrated in large numbers later in the century. All of these groups, and more besides (such as the French and Dutch), had settled alongside the English founding population in the coastal colonies, but mass settlement in waves in the nineteenth century often left more pronounced cultural effects. We can still see prominent German cultural practices such as beer brewing and sausage making in Milwaukee and St. Louis, and Scandinavian cultural practices in Minnesota. The nineteenth century also saw the growth of industry in the cities, and many immigrants ended up not on homesteads but in sweatshops. Settlement in the later nineteenth century from Eastern Europe made New York a center of Ashkenazic Jewish culture and Chicago a center of Polish culture, for instance, and many cities came to have Italian, Greek, and Chinese districts. Settlement west of the Mississippi in the later nineteenth century and early twentieth century did not occur in broad pathways through cultural centers, so the West is not divided into the same broad bands that are found in the East. The more recent settlement in the West suggests that more time will be needed before a Western voice develops, if its low population density and great expanse ever allow for a common Western voice to emerge beyond the local voices of its different communities. Ranching and cowboy culture in the West, including their contribution to the language, have been popular and influential, and not only in America, but these are not the same thing as the development of a Western voice.

More recent changes in the American population have also had their effects on the American voice. During the twentieth century, especially after World War II, homesteading was only possible in Alaska, and the American ideal changed from land ownership (although that has remained a mark of success) to economic independence apart from working the land. Millions of immigrants, many from parts of the world that were not well represented in nineteenth-century immigration, have joined the labor force, most in cities though some still on the land. During the last decade of the twentieth century, for instance, the United States received a massive new influx of Hispanic and Asian immigrants, many of them not from traditional Mexican and Chinese sources. Millions more Americans have left their ancestral homes and changed regions in search of better opportunities. During the Great Depression millions of Southerners, both Black and white, moved away from failing small farms to look for new opportunities in Northern and Western cities. During the energy crisis of the 1970s a great many Northerners moved away from the old industrial Rust Belt to look for new opportunities in new industries in the South. These movements reduced the rural population and increased it in the cities. This mobility and population mixture has not led to a more uniform American voice, as many have thought. Contemporary investigation by William Labov has confirmed that the voices of American cities are more different today than they have ever been. The population density of working people in urban areas has promoted the growth of shared speech habits that are different in every city. We have largely lost the rural Southern voice of the plantation areas which have been widely depopulated by internal American migrations, especially among younger speakers, except as it survives in the speech of African Americans in urban enclaves across the country. Yet many American speakers have voices that continue to correspond to the broad Northern, North Midland, and South Midland cultural regions in the eastern states. We can expect that the voices of such broad rural areas will continue as long as there is a rural population to support them.

As a product of the history of settlement and resettlement by many ethnic and regional groups, Americans now have many choices for communities with which to associate themselves, in speech habits and other kinds of behavior. The colonial American ideal encouraged conformity to community norms, as the royalist Crèvecoeur found out when his Revolutionary neighbors burned his house. The American ideal has grown along with the country, and for a great many Americans the ideal has gradually come to embody cultural pluralism, the idea that we can all still be Americans even if we also place value on our own different ethnic and cultural roots. The contemporary American voice therefore includes a multitude of regional, social, urban, ethnic, and cultural communities, each of which (even the non-English-speaking ones) contributes words and other speech habits to American English. To be an American today means acceptance of, and for most people pride in, the fact that a great many communities come together to form the national culture and voice. If we are what we eat, then Americans are made up of *okra* and *gumbo* (African); *squash*, *pecan*s, and *succotash* (Native American); *pumpkins*, *brioche*, *chowder*, *filet mignon*, and *jambalaya* (French); *chili*, *tacos*, *burritos*, and *tequila* (Spanish); *cookies*, *cole slaw*, and *waffles* (Dutch); *bock beer*, *bratwurst*, *pretzels*, and *hamburgers* (German); *chow mein* and *chop suey* (Chinese); *spaghetti*, *pizza*, and *ravioli* (Italian); and many others too numerous to name. To these ethnic choices, we may add the sum total of American inventiveness in industry and culture, in terms like *quality control* and *(production) line*; *jazz*, *movie*, *baseball*, and *(American) football*; *space shuttle*, *PC*, and *atom bomb*; *crack baby* and *quality time*. American companies have contributed their trade names, not always willingly, to the American voice as the common names of their products and their functions: *Coke*, *Kleenex*, *Linoleum*, *Xerox*. Americans are more free today to choose their own forms of cultural expression than at any time in American history, and these choices are reflected in the American voice.

Increased mobility in the late twentieth century has had a special effect on the most highly educated Americans. Transportation systems have grown enormously after World War II, including the construction of the Interstate highway system, construction of elaborate freeway systems in and around urban areas, and the great expansion of air travel. Improved transportation offers new opportunities to those people who are willing to leave their local communities in search of better jobs. Since World War II, about 20% of the American population moves to a new residence each year. Most people move within the same locality; over 60% of the American people still live in the state of their birth. Only 3% of the population moves out of state each year, and people with a college or higher degree are about twice as likely to move to a different region as those with less education. These statistics indicate that blue-collar Americans can and do move long distances, but because of economically-stratified housing patterns they are likely to find new neighbors who are long-time residents of their new state and locality. White-collar Americans are far more likely to move as part of a national job marketplace in the professions, and they are likely to live in neighborhoods with a smaller proportion of people who were born in the same state. These circumstances have led to maintenance and growth of regional and local urban speech habits among blue-collar Americans, while white-collar Americans are more and more likely not to participate as fully in the regional and urban voices of their communities.

New population patterns have created new social differences in the American voice. Before World War II, professionals and the cultural elite were not so likely to move out of region, and they participated in regional speech patterns.

Their education and cultural experience merely shaped what they learned in their communities, made them less likely, for instance, to use words like *ain't*, or to say *seen* and *come* as the past-tense forms of *to see* and *to come*. They still knew and used the special pronunciation and vocabulary of the region. But now, especially among younger speakers, the avoidance of speech habits that belong to any regional or local urban voice has come to be a mark of education. Highly-educated American speakers commonly limit their use of regional or urban features when they talk in formal situations. A great many educated speakers still know and use regional and local features when they talk in informal settings, as when they are among family or local friends, but many educated speakers grow up in communities where they have little opportunity to acquire regional or local speech habits. The new patterns of population movement among highly-educated Americans have thus created a new social division between the speech habits of blue-collar and white-collar Americans.

Individual speakers, whether educated or not, now have the choice of associating themselves through their speech habits with speakers of increasingly rural regional voices, with speakers of growing local urban voices, or with speakers who limit their use of regional or urban habits. People will choose to talk like the people they want to be like, and their choices may change from one conversation to another. And the success of their choice of voices will be measured through their acceptance by the people they talk to, one conversation at a time. Blue-collar speakers may attempt to limit their use of regional and local urban speech habits, especially when they find themselves in formal situations with highly-educated speakers. So, too, many young educated speakers take an interest in hip-hop culture, with its urban roots, and try to talk the part. People who are able to enact more than one voice with perfect fluency are very rare, just as there are few people who master another language so well that they have perfect ease of expression and no accent. Yet most individual Americans are to some degree able to enact the speech habits from a range of voices from different American communities, according to their experience, opportunity, and ability, as they try to cooperate in conversation with the diverse speakers they encounter in their daily lives.

The American Voice in The New Oxford American Dictionary

Even though this dictionary cannot describe every aspect of every American voice, it can and does present a very large number of words that come from particular American voices. It covers food terms from *bagels* to *cornpone* to *grits* to *wienies* that come from many different American communities. It covers the flora and fauna of America, from *buckeyes* to *trillium*, and from *armadillos* to *wolverines*. It covers terms from baseball and American football. For users with medical interests, it defines the word at *estrogen* and *esophagus* rather than at *oestrogen* and *oesophagus*. All of these American words come from American voices as they have been described in this essay. All are included here because they are not known only to the participants in separate communities, but have achieved more general currency among Americans.

No dictionary could present even a small portion of all of the speech habits of all of the voices that come together to create the American voice. Some words and meanings of words that are not widely used can be labeled as having special regional or social use or currency. Not even this much can be done for all of the pronunciation variation in the voices of American regional and urban and social communities. This dictionary, therefore, must focus on the common habits of American English, and allow other, more specialized references to cover the particular qualities of all of the different regional and social voices. Individual words and meanings of words have been assessed individually by the editors for their use and meanings for Americans. For pronunciation, the editors have adopted a pronunciation model as described below which excludes pronunciations that Americans would recognize as coming from any particular region or city or social group ("marked" pronunciations), and which presents those pronunciations that are common to many American voices. This model follows the trend among younger educated speakers of exclusion of regional features. It is also quite similar to the speech of most national broadcasters, since the national broadcast media has long embraced the more general trend of younger educated speakers. The editorial necessity of offering a common pronunciation model should in no way suggest that any of the American pronunciations that are not represented here are less real or less valid because they have been omitted. We hope that the users of the dictionary will have a chance to hear and enjoy as much as they can of the variety in American pronunciation, and will appreciate each voice for its special contribution to American English. If the American users of the dictionary sometimes do not find a word they know or a pronunciation they use, they can suppose that their usage still belongs to an American voice, as this essay outlines them, even if the dictionary has not been able to include it among the headwords.

The set of symbols in the pronunciation key yields transcriptions that are broadly phonetic. That is, the transcriptions represent actual pronunciations, often with variant forms per headword, not abstract sound units which include and hide potential variation. For instance, both /ro͞om/ and /ro͝om/ are possible pronunciations of *room*, both /eks-/ and /egz-/ are presented for some words beginning with *ex-* plus a vowel. A limited symbol set results in broad transcriptions, but the intention is always to indicate actual sounds to be produced.

While it is possible to hear a variety of voices in every American city or town, even the speech habits that come to be characteristic of each place are generally not mutually exclusive. Particular features like absence of postvocalic /r/ (pronunciation of an /r/ sound after a vowel, before a consonant or pause) are often shared by different regions. Postvocalic /r/ is not pronounced by many speakers in Eastern New England, New York City, and the Coastal South. The special combination and distribution of speech habits, not just one or another particular habit, creates the broad range of American regional, urban, and social voices. Canadian English preserves some different speech habits from the speech of the United States, particularly in Ontario and the Maritime Provinces. The pronunciation of Canadians in the West, however, is often much the same as that of Americans in the western states. Pronunciations which are distinctively Canadian are not included here.

The following comments on particular features of American English pronunciation should make clear the major decisions in the creation of the pronunciation model for the dictionary, and thus explain why some pronunciations are included and why others have been left out.

Postvocalic /r/ is often not pronounced in Eastern New England, New York City, and the Coastal South. Various speakers from these areas, for example, might pronounce the word *poor* as [pō], as [pōə], or as [pŏŏə], among a range of possible pronunciations. Younger and more educated speakers in these regions increasingly do pronounce /r/ after vowels. The pronunciation respellings in this dictionary always include postvocalic /r/ because the various pronunciations without it are regionally marked.

A number of phonemes have variant pronunciations depending on their position in a word or phrase, or on the geographical and social background of the speaker. For example, Americans pronounce the phonemes /t/ and /r/ in a wide variety of different ways. The [t] between vowels, as in *latter*, or before an *r*, as in *forty*, is pronounced differently from other [t] sounds, and may be heard by many as a /d/ sound. Final [t] sounds are often pronounced by many Americans as glottal stops (the "Cockney" sound of [t]) or are not fully articulated; all [t] sounds are transcribed here as /t/. On the other hand, the /r/ phoneme may be realized as a trill (a "Scottish" *r*), or with other sorts and degrees of articulation, but all [r] sounds are here transcribed /r/.

The sound represented in the pronunciation key by /ī/ is actually a combination of two vowel sounds which, to use other symbols from the pronunciation key, can be represented as [äi]. Such combinations of vowel sounds in a single stressed position in a word, called "diphthongs," occur frequently in American pronunciation. The pronunciation of a particular stressed vowel in American English words with one vowel sound or with two sounds, or with different combinations of vowel sounds, is what we hear as a difference in many different American voices, including what many people call a "drawl" or "nasal" pronunciation. Pronunciations in which the second vowel sound in [äi] is weak or absent, so that the word *right* may sound like *rot*, or the word *ride* may sound like *rod*, are characteristic of the regional voices of the Coastal South, the South Midland, and large parts of the Great Plains and Southwest. They are also possible for many other speakers in rapid speech. These variants are not included in the pronunciation respellings in this dictionary because most Americans would recognize them as regional. Many vowels in American English are pronounced as diphthongs depending on where the vowel occurs in the word. It is common in all regions to pronounce /o͞o/ as [o͝oo͞o] or /ē/ as [iē] when the vowel occurs at the end of a word, or when the speaker puts extra stress on the word. These variants are also not offered in the transcriptions, as a matter of keeping things simple for users. A widespread habit of many Americans is to add an /ə/ sound between a stressed vowel and a following /r/, so that *fire* could be pronounced as either /fīr/ or /fīər/, and *hour* as either /our/ or /ouər/. Pronunciations of such words have been presented with the variant thought most common by the editors. Finally, some additions of vowel sounds to make diphthongs are possible in many regions but are characteristic of a particular place. The pronunciations of *bed* as [beəd] and pit as [piət], for example, are commonly associated with the Coastal South and South Midland. These variants, too, have not been shown.

Many American voices sound different because they use different vowels in particular words and sets of words. Some of these vowel alternations are shown in the pronunciation respellings, some not.

/e/~/a/~/ā/—In words spelled with *a* or *e* before r, whether or not followed by another vowel, as in *care, carry, marry, merry, Mary*, the transcriptions generally present /e(ə)/, /e/, or /a/. A range of pronunciations is possible in different areas, such as *Mary* pronounced with /ā/ (in the South) or *very* pronounced with /ä/ (in Appalachia); words like *carry, marry* are pronounced with /a/ mostly along the Atlantic Coast. In Eastern New England /a/ is realized as a sound halfway between /ä/ and /a/ before consonant sounds like *s, th, f, n*, as in *ask, path, half*, and *aunt*. Outside of New England, some cultivated speakers who may view it as a prestige pronunciation, and many African American speakers, realize this vowel as /ä/ in particular words such as *aunt* or *ask*, though not systematically. The /a/ sound may also be pronounced more like /e/ in different regions, particularly before /NG/ or /NGk/ as in the pronunciation [beNGk] for *bank*, but these variations are not shown here.

/ä/~/ô/—The complicated history of the contrast between these sounds deserves a long discussion, not possible here. American voices are highly variable in the pronunciation of these vowels, and a change is now taking place for many speakers in which words pronounced with these historically different vowels now have the same vowel sound. For all words that historically had the /ô/ pronunciation, the transcriptions also provide an /ä/ pronunciation. Rather than present both pronunciations for all words with historical /ä/, which would offer some pronunciations that many Americans would recognize as regional or Canadian, the following practices have been followed: 1) words spelled with *o* like *cot, lot* are transcribed with /ä/; 2) words with *or* spellings are transcribed with /ôr/; 3) words spelled with *o* before g, *ng, nk* are transcribed with /ô/; 4) words spelled with *wa* like *water, wash, watch*, are transcribed with both /ä/ and /ô/.

/ō/~/ô/—When an *o* sound occurs before /r/, this sound is indicated consistently as /ô/ in the respellings, as /fôr/, /bôr/ for *four, bore*. These respellings will not keep separate such potentially differing pairs as *horse/hoarse* or *morning/mourning*; most Americans would no longer recognize any pronunciation difference between these pairs. In some words, like *forest, tomorrow*, the stressed vowel can sometimes be realized as /ä/, as represented in the respellings.

American speakers very often simplify consonant clusters in particular environments. For example, when *-nt-* occurs between vowels and the *t* does not begin a new stressed syllable, a great many Americans would drop or weaken the /t/ sound much of the time, as in ['twen(t)ē], ['man(t)l] for *twenty, mantle*, but /kən'tān/ for *contain*. Groups of consonants are most often reduced at the ends of words, especially with addition of suffixes: *asked* is normally pronounced /ast/, not /askt/, although *ask* is pronounced /ask/.

/iNG/ is very often replaced by [in] in the ending *-ing* in informal speech throughout America. It is not represented in the respellings.

Americans love spelling, even if many of them love to hate it, as shown in our tradition of school spelling bees. Perhaps as a legacy of long use of Webster's "blue-backed speller," our pronunciation is often influenced by spelling, even if such a pronunciation has no historical justification. Words like *calm, palm*, and *salmon* are often pronounced with an /l/ sound in this manner, and even *sword* can sometimes be heard with a /w/ sound. Common spelling pronunciations are represented in the dictionary as optional, as in *palm* /pä(l)m/. Americans are no worse than anybody else at pronouncing unfamiliar words and foreign words and names. Those speakers who have the experience or education to try to pronounce such words as the dictionary would advise, or according to foreign pronunciation patterns, will do so. Everybody else will attempt to pronounce the word or name as it is spelled.

British dictionaries usually mark vowel length, but the duration of vowels is not marked in the transcriptions here. The duration of pronunciation of a vowel only rarely makes the only difference between two American English words (one of the few examples is *have* vs *halve*). Some lengthening of vowels typically occurs before some consonants (the vowel of *grade* lasts longer than the same /ā/ in *grate*), and vowels at the ends of words are usually of longer duration than the same vowel in the middle of a word (the vowel of *go* lasts longer than the same /ō/ in *goat*). American dictionaries, including this one, make use of what is traditionally known as a "length" mark over some vowels, as in /ā, ē, ī, ō, o͞o/. This "length" mark has nothing to do with the duration of pronunciation of the vowel, but instead is merely a conventional name for a difference in the quality of the vowel sound, something that many American users of dictionaries will find to be familiar.

American English is characterized by a heavier pattern of stresses than that found in British English. Americans most often use secondary stress on syllables with unreduced vowels or diphthongs, where British English has an unstressed reduced vowel or an elided syllable. Thus /ˈdikSHəˌnerē/ is the characteristic American pronunciation of *dictionary*, as opposed to British English [ˈdikSHənrē]. Americans also use a variable stress pattern in polysyllabic words. Where British speakers would use only one strong stress in a word, Americans frequently employ more than one, sometimes even with variation in the location of the stresses. Thus in a word like *everlasting*, it is possible for Americans to put a strong stress on both *ever* and on *last*, or just put strong stress on *last*. The tendency toward level stress also applies to compound words, like *downstairs*, which can take strong stress just on *down*, just on *stairs*, or on both *down* and *stairs*. Variable stress of this kind is not represented in the dictionary; the editors have selected the most common stress pattern for the word.

Stress patterns also influence the quality of vowels. In unstressed syllables, /i/ or /ə/ will generally be pronounced no matter what vowel is used in the spelling. In the dictionary, /i/ is shown in those syllables where it precedes word-final /k/, /SH/, and /j/; where it precedes /v/ in derivational suffixes, and where it occurs in the /-iNG/ suffix. The /ə/ sound is used in the *-er* suffix /ər/ as in *leader*, and in *-ion* endings, like /SHən/ and /ZHən/ in *relation*, *equation*. For other words, neighboring sounds determine which unstressed vowel appears in the respelling. If the preceding syllable contains a high-front vowel /i, ē/ or a diphthong ending in a high-front vowel /ā, ī/, the unstressed vowel will usually be /i/; otherwise the /ə/ sound will usually appear. The same factor determines the choice of unstressed vowel in the derivational suffixes *-ness* and *-less*. These decisions about unstressed vowels represent the best judgment of the editors, but it is also true that many American English speakers alternate between the variants /i/ and /ə/ in each of the situations considered here.

The American English pronunciation model that results from these decisions gives the editors a systematic means to decide what transcriptions should be presented among the many possibilities to be found in all the different American voices. However, the editors have reviewed every headword independently, and have occasionally included pronunciations that do not fit the model when they are warranted by widespread use.

Differences between American English and British English

The differences between British English and American English did not wait for the Revolution but began to develop as soon as there were American communities speaking English in the seventeenth century. While the American branch of the English family tree may have begun small, it is now nearly five times larger than the British branch, at least in terms of relative population of the United States and the United Kingdom. In the world today, however, there are many more speakers of voices that sound like British English than of American voices. We can count more recent branches of the tree like Australia, India, New Zealand, and South Africa as sounding more like British English than American English, and we can also count as British voices the habits of all of the learners of English as a second language who have acquired British English from British sources. The British had a strong interest in exporting their language during the years of Empire, and have kept a strong commercial interest in teaching English to the world during the last century as well. American English has become an important commodity to most of the world only since World War II.

Differences in pronunciation between contemporary British and American English can be attributed to divergence in speech habits over nearly four hundred years of separation. There have always been many voices in Britain, just as there have always been many voices in America. When we compare the two national voices today, we cannot account for all of the different habits of all of the contemporary voices in the two countries. Instead, we will do best to compare the American English of white-collar Americans in the national job marketplace with the form of British English called Received Pronunciation (RP). Historically, RP has been the English of only the most elite British speakers, although it is related most closely to the variety of English spoken widely in the southeastern part of the country around London. Today, the best definition of RP speakers includes a wider group of educated Englishmen, and this "advanced" RP, with some recognizable variations in accent from Northern England, Scotland, and Northern Ireland, can now be heard on the world broadcasts of the BBC.

RP and educated American English pronunciation differ mainly in the vowels and in the pronunciation of postvocalic /r/. Many of the vowels in the two systems are very similar: /ā, ô, e, ē, i, o͝o, o͞o/. The vowel of *half* is different; in British English it may sound like /ä/ or like a vowel halfway between /ä/ and /a/. The vowel of modern RP *but* or *love* is closer to the vowel /o͝o/ than in American English and is noticeably different from American /bət, ləv/. British English has one vowel phoneme that most American voices do not have, the vowel in British *pot*. Americans hear this British vowel as something between the /ä/ sound and the /ô/

sound. The RP version of American /ī/, which is actually a diphthong [äi], is a diphthong with a different first vowel, the vowel of RP *but*, *love*. Similarly, the RP version of American /ō/, which is actually another diphthong [ōŏŏ], also is a diphthong with a different first sound [əŏŏ]. None of these differences between RP and American English vowels are very large in terms of articulation, but the set of differences makes a strikingly different impression on the listener.

Postvocalic /r/ is either not pronounced or is articulated as [ə] in RP, much as in the Eastern New England, New York City, and Coastal Southern American voices. Historically, the loss of pronunciation of postvocalic /r/ began about Shakespeare's time, but some areas of England still pronounce postvocalic /r/, just as many American voices have it. The most common explanation for the lack of pronunciation of postvocalic /r/ in some American English areas is that the coastal regions maintained close contact with England for a longer period during settlement, and thus were influenced by the growing loss of postvocalic /r/ in the Old Country. This explanation is too simple an account, since loss of postvocalic /r/ is highly variable on both sides of the Atlantic. It is not just a matter of pronouncing it or not; different regions of both England and America pronounce postvocalic /r/ in different environments in words, and many voices on either side replace postvocalic /r/ with a vowel, usually [ə], or lengthen the preceding vowel, or use another articulation instead of the /r/. Moreover, some areas in both England (including RP) and America (such as Eastern New England) have "linking /r/," which puts back the postvocalic /r/ sound that these speakers would otherwise omit in situations, like *fear o*f, where the postvocalic /r/ occurs just before a word beginning with a vowel. Speakers from both sides of the Atlantic who normally do not pronounce postvocalic /r/ may also use an "intrusive /r/," which inserts an /r/ sound between a word that ends with a vowel and a word that begins with a vowel, as in *law(r) and order*. Both sides of the Atlantic also see "intrusive /r/" in some other situations, such as in RP as an unhistorical /r/ on a word ending in an unstressed vowel, like *idea(r)*, and such as in some regional American voices as a word-internal *r* as sometimes heard in *warsh*, *Warshington*. Under such complicated circumstances it would be better to describe the workings of /r/ for the voices of each national variety, separately and in detail, before attempting any comprehensive explanation.

British and American English have a different rhythm. Differences in stress patterns between the varieties, as mentioned earlier, play a role in rhythm. There are also characteristic differences in intonation, but these have not been well studied even though familiar to many listeners. The rhythm of British and American English sentences may be affected by the use of "tag questions" like "don't you think?" attached to otherwise declarative statements, a habit more common in Britain than America. Other differences in the way RP and American English speakers put words together are more subtle. The British "Mind your Head" is somehow appropriate to the national voice, as is the American "Caution: Low Clearance." As with small differences in vowels, these factors work together to create a characteristic impression in the minds of listeners.

Finally, there are differences between British and American English in what dictionaries do best, the lexicon. According to one way of thinking, every word of English must have a different meaning in Britain and America, because each word is embedded in a different culture and must have different associations. The word *park*, for instance, even if we limit its meanings just to those referring to natural land areas, is different for Americans and Britons. London, for the British, has Hyde Park and St. James Park among city parks, each with its own character and history. Americans think of Central Park in New York, or Grant Park in Chicago, each of which contributes its own special character and history to the meaning of *park* in the national voice. In England one of the principle meanings of *park* is the land maintained around a country house, while in America the word is more often used for the place where baseball is played, or where a children's playground may be found. The same word takes on the meanings of the different cultures. There are also different words for the same thing. Americans play *soccer* on a *field*, while the English play *football* on a *pitch*. The dictionary contains a great many examples of such words, some marked with usage labels but many others, in a dictionary that highlights American English, presented with the meanings that are current in America.

Future Voices

Most commentators without training in the history and development of languages seem to take it for granted that there is one best English (the one taught in the schools), and that eventually everybody will be speaking it. Commentators on each side of the Atlantic think the same thing—of course about different varieties. Their opinions reflect their own experience and values. If their families and friends talk as they do, with the voices that the commentators recognize and trust, then why should voices like those not be best for all English speakers? If our societies in both countries have such an investment in education, why should those values not be transmitted to all the members of the society and be duly accepted by the citizens?

The facts of language behavior in England, America, and elsewhere argue against such an idea. The historical division between the voices of the highly educated and the voices of working people, now in America as well as Britain, is a symptom of the natural human capacity and need to form communities, and for those communities to possess voices that both identify and are recognized by community members. The commentators, whether they are highly educated themselves or they just want people to enjoy the social benefits that come with educational advancement, propose an agenda that is well suited to people who believe strongly in what the schools have to offer. But in Britain, America, and elsewhere the group of people with college or higher degrees is a relatively small fraction of the population. Most of the people outside of that highly-educated community continue to speak with each other according to the regional, ethnic, urban, social, and cultural community ties that are most important to them in their lives, and not with the school English that takes on the value of familiarity or represents social advancement for the commentators. Truth to tell, the commentators themselves actually enact different voices when they talk to members of the different communities to which they belong, just as everybody else does, although some might not realize it.

In just the same way that the commentators prefer the educated voice, so too do the rest of the people recognize and trust the voices of their friends and family. The distance between communities has not disappeared with the rise of public education, and it shows little sign of doing so. And while the voices of every community continue to change over time, the fact that communities are defined in part by their different voices ensures that linguistic changes will not all occur in the direction of linguistic uniformity, whether school English or some other voice. Unless some as yet unanticipated social change can keep people from forming communities of family and friends—and why anyone should desire such a thing is difficult to understand—the outlook remains excellent for the continuing existence and development of a multitude of regional, ethnic, urban, social, and cultural voices. As we extend our view beyond Britain and America, we can see that the globalization of English will only create more English voices worldwide, not fewer. And that is not such a bad thing, if we appreciate the cultural richness that it reflects and represents. The continuation and development of different English voices is also not such a bad thing for dictionaries. There will be a continuing need for a witness that highlights the American national voice, a need that the *New Oxford American Dictionary*, and its successors, can satisfy.

William A. Kretzschmar, Jr.
University of Georgia

How to Read an Etymology

While reading the word histories given in this dictionary, several things should be taken into consideration, though most of what is written here is self-explanatory.

A Few Obvious Cases

Some words easily reveal their origin to the uninitiated. Such are *moo* and *bow-wow*, for example. They are sound imitative (or echoic), and little else can be said about them, except that in different languages people choose different combinations of vowels and consonants to render the dog's bark but seldom disagree about *moo*. Relatively few surprises await the user of the dictionary in this part of the vocabulary. Yet an attentive browser will notice verbs like *crunch* (echoic, but less obviously so than *moo*), *gargoyle*, from French, but a close relative of *gargle* (another echoic verb), and *chatter*, called sound imitative, though it is not immediately clear what sound group *chat* imitates.

As a general rule, only simple words need an etymology, but in many compounds whose form seems to be transparent, the origin of the meaning needs further research. Sometimes the dictionary offers only a guess (the case in point is *butterfly*, for all intents and purposes, *butter* + *fly*, but why *butter*?); in other cases it knows the answer. Thus it explains that *peacock* has nothing to do with peas: the first element here is a reshaping of an old word that itself meant 'peacock.' Nor does pea in *pea jacket* go back to the name of a vegetable. Shorter derivatives may also pose problems. *Doggo* in *lie doggo*, as the dictionary says, is of obscure origin, "apparently from DOG + -O." This circumspect statement implies that although the form of the word suggests an easy solution, appearances may be deceptive. One of the joys of reading word histories consists in discovering how cleverly language disguises its origins.

The Limits of Our Knowledge. Words of Unknown Origin

For many centuries people have been trying to understand "why we say so." Linguists have developed an efficient method of answering the age-old question, but as always in history, the course of some events remains obscure. Therefore, the dictionary often says "of unknown origin." This statement does not mean that no conjectures on the word's etymology exist, for usually the contrary is true: the more impenetrable the past, the more attempts have been made to dispel the obscurity. Rather it implies that none of the existing hypotheses is convincing enough. No etymology is always preferable to a wrong one. Some words of unknown origin were recorded more than a thousand years ago (for example, *adze*), others made their way into manuscripts and books a few centuries later (one of them is *boy*), still others are relatively recent (the fish name *shark* is such), or are 19th century acquisitions (see *skedaddle*), or were coined in recent memory (*nerd*). It will be seen that even the most common words may turn out to be of unascertained origin. Finally, it may happen that we know only the immediate source of a word. Both *basket* and *coat* have come to English from French; the unresolved matter is how they arose there. Hence the formulation in the dictionary: ". . . of unknown ultimate origin."

The Periodization of the History of English. The Importance of a Word's Oldest Attested Form and Meaning

To penetrate the origin of a word, unless its history has been preserved in documents (as happened, for example, to *nylon*, *jeep*, and *quark*), it is desirable to know its oldest form, because both the sounds and the senses of most words change over time. For instance, *marshal* must once have sounded approximately like *mearhscealc* in England (from *mearh* 'mare' and *scealc* 'servant') and meant 'a person in charge of horses'; *girl* usually occurred in the plural and denoted children of both sexes, and *nice* goes back to 'stupid' and, still earlier, 'ignorant.' If we had not known those facts and attempted to reconstruct the origin of *marshal*, *girl*, and *nice* from their present-day form and meaning, we would be looking in a wrong direction. All three cases are typical. Our success in finding the oldest form depends on the preservation of manuscripts and books. In the history of English, we have about 12 centuries of written evidence.

Literacy in its modern form was brought to England with the Anglo-Saxons' conversion to Christianity, but there is little to read in English before the 9th century. It is customary to divide the history of English into three periods: Old English (from the appearance of the first written documents to the Norman Conquest, 1066), Middle English (from 1066 to the beginning of book printing, 1474), and Modern English. These dates are conventional (for people did not adopt a new language in 1067 or 1475), but they reflect the truth in a general way. The terms *late Old English*, *late Middle English*, and the like are also common and turn up in the dictionary in appropriate places. Modern English is divided into early Modern English (which includes the epoch of Shakespeare), 17th century English, and so on.

Not too many words recorded in Old English have survived. Thousands of them have been lost and are therefore of no interest to modern speakers. Conversely, some existed in the ancient period but surfaced in texts later, which means that we have no access to their Old English form. However, even if we had known that form, it would not have been the original one. Obviously, most words were not coined on the day when, by pure chance, they were used by some writer. The Middle English word stock has kept much better, but a great part of it did not continue into the present either. The dates given are those of words' first known attestation, not of their "birth."

The alphabet of Old English was partly different from the one in use today. In this dictionary, the system of transliteration (from Old to Modern English) has been simplified to a maximum. Only a few signs may look unfamiliar. A horizontal line over a vowel (called macron) designates length. For example, ū in ***hus*** 'house' should be pronounced as *o* in Modern English *who*, a in ***stan*** 'stone' as *a* in *father*, i in *risan* 'to rise' as *ee* in *feet*, e in *eage* 'eye' as *e* in *pen* but longer, and o in *boc* 'book' as the vowel in *pour*. (Note that the correspondence is not the same as the one in modern dictionaries, in which "long i" is the vowel of *mine*, etc.) The vowel *y*, short and long (see the Old English forms of *fill* and *hide*), was pronounced like *u* in Modern French or ü in Modern German. The ligature æ in words like *baec* 'back' had the phonetic value of a in Modern English *back*. (In Icelandic words, the accent mark has the function of the macron in Old English. It does not designate stress.)

Related Forms

Languages form families. Members of such families, which share a number of features in their sound systems, grammar, and vocabulary, are traceable to the same parent. As a general rule, that parent is not given in direct observation but is a product of reconstruction. The languages of the huge Eurasian belt from Norway to Ceylon form the so-called Indo-European family, divided into several groups, Germanic, Romance, and Celtic among them. The Germanic group includes English, German, Dutch, Frisian, Yiddish, and five Scandinavian languages (Norwegian, Swedish, Danish, Icelandic, and Faroese); *Germanic* is thus not a synonym of *German*. Among the Germanic languages, the affinity between English and Dutch/German is especially strong, which explains why the dictionary cites the forms of those two languages so regularly. All three are part of the West Germanic group. The noun *beacon* is said to be "of West Germanic origin." It has cognates in Dutch, German, and Frisian, but not in Gothic, the now extinct East Germanic language, while a similar form in Scandinavian is believed to be a borrowing from Old English.

To obtain an etymology, linguists look for both a word's oldest attested form and its cognates (related, or allied, forms in other languages). For example, the cognates of *house* are Dutch *huis* and German *Haus*. This short list tells us only that the English word is not isolated. But quite often, cognates show differences in form and meaning, and important conclusions can be drawn from this circumstance. For example, the Icelandic cognate of *friend* means 'kinsman', and it follows that the meaning recorded in English, German, and Dutch is secondary. In the Middle Ages and earlier, the people we now call "friends" were members of one's family and could rely on its support. Consequently, the Indo-European root 'to love,' mentioned in the word history **friend**, must also be understood in a meaning different from ours: one "loved", that is, was loyal to one's relatives. The more cognates we know, the clearer the picture of the word's history and prehistory will be. If a word has broad connections in the entire Indo-European family, this fact is noted in the word history; the references are usually to Greek, Latin (see **father**), and more rarely Sanskrit (see **red**). Occasionally references to Celtic are necessary (see **iron**).

Some words across language borders seem to be related, but there is no certainty. They are usually said to be obscurely or distantly related. In such cases, the dictionary uses the verb "compare." In the section "origin" concluding the entry *nudge*, we read that the word, which first turned up in texts in the 17th century, is of unknown origin; "compare with Norwegian dialect[al] *nugga*, *nyggja* 'to push, rub'." This is no more than a hint: the Scandinavian verbs may not be related to *nudge*, but the similarity is worthy of notice, even if its nature remains unclear.

Borrowed Words

In the course of its history, English has absorbed thousands of foreign words. The main sources of borrowings in English have been French, Latin, Scandinavian, Dutch, and Northern German. Since speakers of Old Germanic and Old Romance languages (Old Franconian and Old French, to be exact) lived side by side for many centuries, it happened more than once that a Germanic word would be borrowed into Old French and much later return to English, strongly or slightly "Frenchifed." English *garden* sounds almost like German *Garten*, but its Franconian cognate first went to Old French and was reborrowed from the northern dialect of Old French into Middle English. If it had stayed at home, it would have sounded more like *yard*, which, from the historical point of view, is the same word (see the word history at **garden**).

As pointed out above, some words that English has taken over are of unknown origin in their languages. Even when the origin is known, a dictionary of English cannot trace their history in detail. However, more than once, this dictionary says enough for the browser to learn the most basic facts. For example, it is stated that *parallel* is from French, via Latin from Greek, where it is a compound consisting of two elements meaning 'alongside' and 'one another' respectively. On the same page, we find *parakeet*, and read that the word came to English from Old French and has cognates in Italian and Spanish: "origin uncertain, perhaps (via Italian) based on a diminutive meaning 'little wig,' referring to head plumage, or (via Spanish) based on a diminutive of the given name *Pedro*. In their entirety, the word histories give a broad picture of the origin of words in languages from Native American to Chinese.

Connection Among Words

Sometimes it is enough to cite one word to explain another. This is typical of opaque derivatives. For instance, *wrestle* is explained as a frequentative form of an Old English verb meaning 'to wrest' (frequentative verbs denote repetition or intensity of action). A *ladle* is a utensil with which "to lade" food. But more often an elucidating reference is needed to a more remote word with the same root. Following the lead, we can detect the connections that would otherwise have been lost. *Wheat*, we learn, is related not only to similar words in Dutch and German but also to *white*. Probably *white* got its name from the color of *wheat*. Likewise, *green*, as it turns out, is related to *grass* and *grow*. Apparently, the underlying meaning of *green* was "the color of vegetation." *Gold* is "of Germanic origin, from an Indo-European root shared by YELLOW." To the ancestors of Germanic speakers gold was "a yellow metal." *Beacon*, mentioned above, is related to *beckon*, which makes excellent sense, because beacons send signals. Many words that stand apart in our linguistic intuition were closely related in the past. Word histories, in addition to summarizing individual etymologies, restore the ties no longer obvious to modern speakers.

Anatoly Liberman
University of Minnesota

Key to the Pronunciations

This dictionary uses a simple respelling system to show how entries are pronounced, using the symbols listed below. Generally, only the first of two or more identical headwords will have a pronunciation respelling. Where a derivative simply adds a common suffix such as **-less**, **-ness**, or **-ly** to the headword, the derivative may not have a pronunciation respelling unless some other element of the pronunciation also changes.

a *as in* **hat** /hat/, **fashion** /ˈfasHən/, **carry** /ˈkarē/
ā *as in* **day** /dā/, **rate** /rāt/, **maid** /mād/, **prey** /prā/
ä *as in* **lot** /lät/, **father** /ˈfäT͟Hər/, **barnyard** /ˈbärnˌyärd/
b *as in* **big** /big/
CH *as in* **church** /CHərCH/, **picture** /ˈpikCHər/
d *as in* **dog** /dôg/, **bed** /bed/
e *as in* **men** /men/, **bet** /bet/, **ferry** /ˈferē/
ē *as in* **feet** /fēt/, **receive** /riˈsēv/
e(ə)r *as in* **air** /e(ə)r/, **care** /ke(ə)r/
ə *as in* **about** /əˈbout/, **soda** /ˈsōdə/, **mother** /ˈməT͟Hər/, **person** /ˈpərsən/
f *as in* **free** /frē/, **graph** /graf/, **tough** /təf/
g *as in* **get** /get/, **exist** /igˈzist/, **egg** /eg/
h *as in* **her** /hər/, **behave** /biˈhāv/
i *as in* **fit** /fit/, **guild** /gild/, **women** /ˈwimin/
ī *as in* **time** /tīm/, **guide** /gīd/, **hire** /hī(ə)r/, **sky** /skī/
i(ə)r *as in* **ear** /i(ə)r/, **beer** /bi(ə)r/, **pierce** /pi(ə)rs/
j *as in* **judge** /jəj/, **carriage** /ˈkarij/
k *as in* **kettle** /ˈketl/, **cut** /kət/, **quick** /kwik/
l *as in* **lap** /lap/, **cellar** /ˈselər/, **cradle** /ˈkrādl/
m *as in* **main** /mān/, **dam** /dam/
n *as in* **need** /nēd/, **honor** /ˈänər/, **maiden** /ˈmādn/
NG *as in* **sing** /siNG/, **anger** /ˈaNGgər/
ō *as in* **go** /gō/, **promote** /prəˈmōt/
ô *as in* **law** /lô/, **thought** /THôt/, **lore** /lôr/
oi *as in* **boy** /boi/, **noisy** /ˈnoizē/
o͝o *as in* **wood** /wo͝od/, **football** /ˈfo͝otˌbôl/, **sure** /SHo͝or/
o͞o *as in* **food** /fo͞od/, **music** /ˈmyo͞ozik/
ou *as in* **mouse** /mous/, **coward** /ˈkou(ə)rd/
p *as in* **put** /po͝ot/, **cap** /kap/
r *as in* **run** /rən/, **fur** /fər/, **spirit** /ˈspirit/
s *as in* **sit** /sit/, **lesson** /ˈlesən/, **face** /fās/
SH *as in* **shut** /SHət/, **social** /ˈsōSHəl/, **action** /ˈaksHən/
t *as in* **top** /täp/, **seat** /sēt/, **forty** /ˈfôrte/
TH *as in* **thin** /THin/, **truth** /tro͞oTH/
T͟H *as in* **then** /T͟Hen/, **father** /ˈfäT͟Hər/
v *as in* **never** /ˈnevər/, **very** /ˈverē/
w *as in* **wait** /wāt/, **quit** /kwit/
(h)w *as in* **when** /(h)wen/, **which** /(h)wiCH/
y *as in* **yet** /yet/, **accuse** /əˈkyo͞oz/
z *as in* **zipper** /ˈzipər/, **musician** /myo͞oˈziSHən/
ZH *as in* **measure** /ˈmeZHər/, **vision** /ˈviZHən/

Foreign Sounds

KH *as in* **Bach** /bäKH/
A fricative consonant pronounced with the tongue in the same position as for /k/, as in German *Buch* and *ich*, or Scottish *loch*.

N *as in* **en route** /äN ˈro͞ot/, **Rodin** /rōˈdaN/
The /N/ does not represent a separate sound; it indicates that the preceding vowel is nasalized, as in French *bon* (bon voyage) and *en* (en route).

œ *as in* **hors d'oeuvre** /ôr ˈdœvrə/, **Goethe** /ˈgœtə/
A vowel made by rounding the lips as with /ô/ while saying /e/ or /ā/, as in French *boeuf* and *feu*, or German *Hölle* and *Höhle*.

Y *as in* **Lully** /lYˈlē/, **Utrecht** /ˈYˌtreKHt/
A vowel made by rounding the lips as with /o͝o/ or /o͞o/ while saying /i/ or /ē/, as in French *rue* or German *fühlen*.

Stress Marks

Stress (or accent) is represented by marks placed before the affected syllable. The primary stress mark is a short, raised vertical line /ˈ/ which signifies that the heaviest emphasis should be placed on the syllable that follows. The secondary stress mark is a short, lowered vertical line /ˌ/ which signifies a somewhat weaker emphasis than on the syllable with primary stress.

Variant Pronunciations

There are several ways in which variant pronunciations are indicated in the respellings.

Some respellings show a pronunciation symbol within parentheses to indicate a possible variation in pronunciation; for example, in **sandwich** /ˈsan(d)wiCH/ sometimes the /d/ is pronounced, while at other times it is not.

Variant pronunciations may be respelled in full, separated by semicolons. The more common pronunciation is listed first, if this can be determined, but many variants are so common and widespread as to be of equal status.

Variant pronunciations may be indicated by respelling only the part of the word that changes. A hyphen will replace the part of the pronunciation that has remained the same. These 'cutback' respellings will occur primarily in three areas:

a) where the headword has a variant pronunciation:
quasiparticle /ˌkwāzīˈpärtikəl; ˌkwāzē-/

b) in derivative forms:
dangle /ˈdaNGgəl/
dangler /-glər/
dangly /-glē/

Note: Cutbacks in derivatives always refer back to the headword respelling, not the preceding derivative.

c) at irregular plurals:
parenthesis /pəˈrenTHəsis/
parentheses /-ˌsēz/

Note: A hyphen sometimes serves to separate syllables where the respelling might otherwise look confusing, as at reinforce /ˌrē-inˈfôrs/.

Key to the Abbreviations

abbr.	abbreviation
adj.	adjective
adv.	adverb
attrib.	attributive
Austral.	Australian
Brit.	British
C	Celsius
c.	circa ('about, around')
cent.	century
chem.	chemical
cm	centimeter, centimeters
comb.	combining
conj.	conjunction
cu.	cubic
e.g.	exempli gratia ('for example')
esp.	especially
etc.	et cetera ('and the rest')
exclam.	exclamation
F	Fahrenheit
fem.	feminine
fl.	flourished
fl. oz.	fluid ounce, fluid ounces
ft.	foot, feet
I.	Island
i.e.	id est ('that is')
in.	inch, inches
intrans.	intransitive
kg	kilogram, kilograms
km	kilometer, kilometers
L.	Lake
l	liter, liters
lb.	pound, pounds
m	meter, meters
masc.	masculine
mi.	mile, miles
ml	milliliter, milliliters
mm	millimeter, millimeters
mph	miles per hour
n.	noun
N. Amer.	North American
N. English	Northern English
N. Irish	Northern Irish
NZ	New Zealand
obj.	object
oz.	ounce, ounces
part.	participle
pl.	plural
pop.	population
prep.	preposition
pron.	pronoun
R.	River
rpm	revolutions per minute
S. African	South African
sing.	singular
sq.	square
Str.	Strait
trans.	transitive
UK	United Kingdom
U.S.	United States
usu.	usually
v.	verb
var.	variety
vs.	versus
W. Indian	West Indian
yd.	yard, yards

The New Oxford American Dictionary

Aa

A[1] /ā/ (also **a**) ▸*n.* (*pl.* **As** or **A's**) **1** the first letter of the alphabet. ■ denoting the first in a set of items, categories, sizes, etc. ■ denoting the first of two or more hypothetical people or things: *suppose A had killed B.* ■ the highest class of academic mark. ■ (**a**) *Chess* denoting the first file from the left, as viewed from white's side of the board. ■ (usu. ***a***) the first fixed quantity in an algebraic expression. ■ (**A**) the human blood type (in the ABO system) containing the A agglutinogen and lacking the B. **2** a shape like that of a capital A: [in *combination*] *an A-shape.* See also **A-FRAME**, **A-LINE**. **3** *Music* the sixth note of the diatonic scale of C major. ■ a key based on a scale with A as its keynote.
▸***PHRASES*** □ **from A to B** from one's starting point to one's destination: *most road atlases will get you from A to B.* □ **from A to Z** over the entire range; completely: *make sure you understand the subject from A to Z.*

A[2] ▸*abbr.* ■ ace (used in describing play in bridge and other card games): *you cash AK of hearts.* ■ ampere(s). ■ (**Å**) ångstrom(s). ■ answer: *Q: What's the senator's zodiac sign? A: He's a Leo.* ■ (in personal ads) Asian. ■ a dry cell battery size. ■ *Brit., informal* A level.

a /ā; ə/ (**an** before a vowel sound) [called the *indefinite article*] ▸*adj.* **1** used when referring to someone or something for the first time in a text or conversation: *a man came out of the room | it has been an honor to have you | we need people with a knowledge of languages.* Compare with **THE**. ■ used with units of measurement to mean one such unit: *a hundred | a quarter of an hour.* ■ [with *negative*] one single; any: *I simply haven't a thing to wear.* ■ used when mentioning the name of someone not known to the speaker: *a Mr. Smith telephoned.* ■ someone like (the name specified): *you're no better than a Hitler.* **2** used to indicate membership of a class of people or things: *he is a lawyer | this car is a BMW.* **3** used when expressing rates or ratios; in, to, or for each; per: *typing 60 words a minute | cost as much as eight dollars a dozen.* ▷Middle English: weak form of Old English *ān* 'one.'

> ***USAGE*** **1** The article **a** can be pronounced either /ā/, when stressed ("He gave you *a* flower?"—that is, only one flower), or /ə/, when unstressed ("He gave you a *flower*?"—that is, the emphasis is on *flower*, not on the number of flowers). The form **an** is used before words beginning with a vowel sound.
> 2 On the question of using **a** or **an** before words beginning with **h**, see also **usage** at **AN**.

a-[1] ▸*prefix* not; without: *atheistic | atypical.* ▷from Greek.

a-[2] ▸*prefix* to; toward: *aside | ashore.* ■ in a specified state or manner: *asleep | aloud.* ■ in the process of (an activity) *a-hunting.* ■ on: *afoot.* ■ in: *nowadays.* ▷Old English, unstressed form of **ON**.

a-[3] ▸*prefix* variant spelling of **AD-** assimilated before *sc, sp,* and *st* (as in *ascend, aspire,* and *astringent*).

a-[4] ▸*prefix* **1** of: *anew.* [unstressed form of **OF**] **2** utterly: *abash.* [from Anglo-Norman French (corresponding to Old French *e-, es-*), from Latin *ex.*]

-a[1] ▸*suffix* forming: **1** ancient or Latinized modern names of animals and plants: *primula.* **2** names of oxides: *baryta.* **3** geographical names: *Africa.* **4** ancient or Latinized modern feminine forenames: *Lydia.* **5** nouns from Italian, Portuguese, and Spanish: *duenna | stanza.* ▷representing a Greek, Latin, or Romance feminine singular.

-a[2] ▸*suffix* forming plural nouns: **1** from Greek or Latin neuter plurals corresponding to a singular in *-um* or *-on* (such as *addenda, phenomena.*) **2** in names (often from modern Latin) of zoological groups: *Protista | Insectivora.*

-a[3] ▸*suffix informal* **1** of: *coupla.* **2** have: *mighta.* **3** to: *oughta.* ▷representing a casual pronunciation.

A1 ▸*adj. informal* very good or well; excellent: *guitar in A1 condition.* ■ *Nautical* (of a vessel) equipped to the highest standard, esp. as certified by a classification society; first-class.

A3 ▸*n.* [*mass noun*] a standard European size of paper, 420 × 297 mm: [as *modifier*] *A3 posters.* ■ paper of this size: *a prospectus printed on A3.*

A4 ▸*n.* [*mass noun*] a standard European size of paper, 210 × 297 mm: [as *modifier*] *an A4 page.* ■ paper of this size: *several sheets of A4.*

A5 ▸*n.* [*mass noun*] a standard European size of paper, 210 × 148 mm: [as *modifier*] *a little A5 booklet.* ■ paper of this size: *printed on A5.*

AA ▸*abbr.* ■ Alcoholics Anonymous. ■ antiaircraft. ■ administrative assistant. ■ Associate of Arts. ■ a dry cell battery size.

aa /'ä,ä/ ▸*n. Geology* basaltic lava forming very rough jagged masses with a light frothy texture. Often contrasted with **PAHOEHOE**. ▷mid 19th cent.: from Hawaiian *'a-'a.*

AAA /,tripəl 'ā/ ▸*abbr.* American Automobile Association. ■ *Baseball* see **TRIPLE A**. ■ a 1.5 volt dry cell battery size.

AAAS ▸*abbr.* American Association for the Advancement of Science.

Aa·chen /'äkʜən/ an industrial city and spa in western Germany, in North Rhine-Westphalia; pop. 244,440. French name **AIX-LA-CHAPELLE**.

AAD ▸*abbr.* analog analog digital, indicating that a musical recording was made and mastered in analog form before being stored digitally.

Aal·borg /'ôl,bôr(g)/ (also **Ål·borg**) an industrial city and port in northern Jutland, Denmark; pop. 155,000.

Aal·to /'ältō/, (Hugo) Alvar (Henrik) (1898–1976), Finnish architect and designer. He is known as the inventor of bent plywood furniture.

AAM ▸*abbr.* air-to-air missile.

A&M ▸*abbr.* Agricultural and Mechanical (college): *Texas A&M.*

A&R ▸*abbr.* artist(s) and repertory, used to denote employees of a record company who select and sign new artists.

aard·vark /'ärd,värk/ ▸*n.* a nocturnal burrowing mammal with long ears, a tubular snout, and a long extensible tongue, feeding on ants and termites. Aardvarks are native to Africa and have no close relatives. Also called **ANT BEAR**. • *Orycteropus afer*, the only living member of the family Orycteropidae and order Tubulidentata. ▷late 18th cent.: from South African Dutch, from *aarde* 'earth' + *vark* 'pig.'

aard·wolf /'ärd,wo͝olf/ ▸*n.* (*pl.* **-wolves**) a nocturnal black-striped African mammal of the hyena family, feeding mainly on termites. • *Proteles cristatus*, family Hyaenidae. ▷mid 19th cent.: from South African Dutch, from *aarde* 'earth' + *wolf* 'wolf.'

aargh /är; ärg/ ▸*exclam.* used as an expression of anguish, horror, rage, or other strong emotion, often with humorous intent. ▷late 18th cent.: imitative, lengthened form of **AH**, to express a prolonged cry.

Aar·hus /'ôr,ho͞os/ (also **År·hus**) a city on the coast of eastern Jutland, Denmark; pop. 261,440.

Aar·on[1] /'e(ə)rən; 'ar-/ (in the Bible) brother of Moses and traditional founder of the Jewish priesthood (see Exod. 28:1).

Aar·on[2] /'e(ə)rən; 'ar-/, Hank (1934–), U.S. baseball player; full name *Henry Louis Aaron.* He set the all-time career record for home runs (755) and runs batted in (2,297). Baseball Hall of Fame (1982).

Aar·on's beard ▸*n.* a name given to various plants, esp. the **ROSE OF SHARON** (sense 2). ▷early 19th cent.: alluding to **AARON**, whose beard "went down to the skirts of his garments" (Psalms 133:2), because of the prominent hairy stamens or the long runners that some of these plants put out.

Aar·on's rod ▸*n.* another term for the great or common mullein. ▷mid 18th cent.: alluding to **AARON**, whose staff was said to have flowered (Numbers 17:8).

AARP /ärp; 'ā 'ā 'ār 'pē/ ▸*abbr.* American Association of Retired Persons.

AAU ▸*abbr.* Amateur Athletic Union.

AAUP ▸*abbr.* ■ American Association of University Presses. ■ American Association of University Professors.

AAVE ▸*abbr. Linguistics* African-American Vernacular English.

AB[1] ▸*n.* a human blood type (in the ABO system) containing both the A and B agglutinogens. In blood transfusion, a person with blood of this group is a potential universal recipient.

AB[2] ▸*abbr.* ■ able seaman; able-bodied seaman. [from *able-bodied.*] ■ Bachelor of Arts. [from Latin *Artium Baccalaureus.*] ■ airman basic. ■ *Baseball* at bat. ■ Alberta (in official postal use).

Ab[1] /äb; äv/ (also **Av**) ▸*n.* (in the Jewish calendar) the eleventh month of the civil year and the fifth month of the religious year, usually coinciding with parts of July and August. ▷from Hebrew *'āḇ.*

Ab[2] *Biology* ▸*abbr.* antibody.

ab- (also **abs-**) ▸*prefix* away; from: *abaxial | abominate.* ▷from Latin.

ABA ▸*abbr.* ■ American Bar Association. ■ American Basketball Association. ■ American Bankers Association. ■ American Booksellers Association.

a·ba·ca /,abə'kä/ ▸*n.* a large herbaceous Philippine plant of the banana family that yields Manila hemp. • *Musa textilis*, family Musaceae. ■ Manila hemp. ▷mid 18th cent.: via Spanish from Tagalog *abaká.*

a·back /ə'bak/ ▸*adv.* **1** *archaic* toward or situated to the rear: *the little strip of pasture aback of the house.* **2** *Sailing* with the sail pressed backward against the mast by a headwind. ▷Old English *on bæc.* Long written as two words, the term came to be treated as a single word in nautical use.
▸***PHRASE*** □ **take someone aback** shock or surprise someone: *he was taken aback by the sharpness in her voice.*

ab·a·cus /'abəkəs/ ▸*n.* (*pl.* **-cus·es**) **1** an oblong frame with rows of wires or grooves along which beads are slid, used for calculating. **2** *Architecture* the flat slab on top of a capital, supporting the architrave. ▷late Middle English (denoting a board strewn with sand on which to draw figures): from Latin, from Greek *abax, abak-* 'slab, drawing board,' of Semitic origin; probably related to Hebrew *'āḇāq* 'dust.'

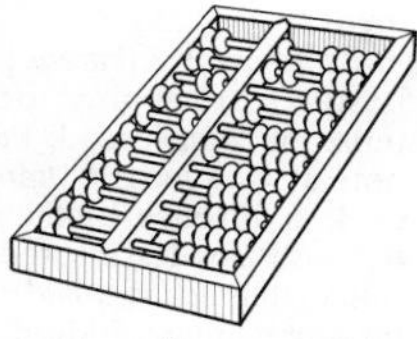

Abacus

A·ba·dan /,äbə'dän; ,abə'dan/ a major port and oil-refining center on an island of the same name on the Shatt al-Arab waterway in western Iran; pop. 308,000.

A·bad·don /ə'badn/ a name for the Devil (Rev. 9:11) or for hell. ▷late Middle English : via Greek from

Pronunciation Key ə *ago*; ər *over*; 'ə *or* ,ə *up*; 'ər *or* ,ər *fur*; a *hat*; ā *rate*; ä *car*; ᴄʜ *chew*; e *let*; ē *see*; e(ə)r *air*; i *fit*; ī *by*; i(ə)r *ear*; ɴɢ *sing*; ō *go*; ô *for*; oi *boy*; o͝o *good*; o͞o *goo*; ou *out*; ѕʜ *she*; ᴛʜ *thin*; T͟H *then*; (h)w *why*; ᴢʜ *vision*

Hebrew *'ăḇaddōn* 'destruction.' Its use for 'hell' arose in the late 17th cent.

a·baft /ə'baft/ *Nautical* ▸*adv.* in or behind the stern of a ship.

▸*prep.* nearer the stern than; behind: *the yacht has a shower just abaft the galley.* ▷Middle English (in the sense 'backward'): from **A-**[2] (expressing motion) + archaic *baft* 'in the rear.'

A·ba·kan /ˌäbə'kän; ˌəbə-/ an industrial city in south central Russia, capital of the republic of Khakassia; pop. 154,000. Former name (until 1931) **UST-ABAKANSKOE.**

ab·a·lo·ne /ˌabə'lōnē; 'abəˌlōnē/ ▸*n.* an edible mollusk of warm seas that has a shallow ear-shaped shell lined with mother-of-pearl and pierced with respiratory holes. Also called **EAR SHELL.** • Genus *Haliotis*, family Haliotidae, class Gastropoda. ▷mid 19th cent.: via Latin American Spanish from *aulun*, from an American Indian language of Monterey Bay, California.

a·ban·don /ə'bandən/ ▸*v.* [*trans.*] **1** give up completely (a course of action, a practice, or a way of thinking): *he had clearly abandoned all pretense of trying to succeed.* See note at **RELINQUISH.** ■ discontinue (a scheduled event) before completion: *against the background of perceived threats, the tour was abandoned.* **2** cease to support or look after (someone); desert: *her natural mother had abandoned her at an early age.* ■ leave (a place, typically a building) empty or uninhabited, without intending to return: *derelict houses were abandoned.* ■ leave (something, typically a vehicle or a vessel) decisively, esp. as an act of survival: *he abandoned his vehicle and tried to flee on foot.* ■ (**abandon someone/something to**) condemn someone or something to (a specified fate) by ceasing to take an interest in or look after them: *it was an attempt to persuade businesses not to abandon the area to inner-city deprivation.* **3** (**abandon oneself to**) allow oneself to indulge in (a desire or impulse): *abandoning herself to moony fantasies.*

▸*n.* complete lack of inhibition or restraint: *she sings and sways with total abandon.* ▷late Middle English: from Old French *abandoner*, from *a-* (from Latin *ad* 'to, at') + *bandon* 'control,' based on late Latin *bannus*, *bannum* (see **BAN**[1]). The original sense was 'bring under control,' later 'give in to the control of, surrender to' (sense 3). **—a·ban·don·ment** *n.*

▸*PHRASE* □ **abandon ship** leave a ship because it is sinking.

a·ban·doned /ə'bandənd/ ▸*adj.* **1** (of a person) having been deserted or cast off: *a home for orphan and abandoned boys.* **2** (of a building or vehicle) remaining empty or unused; having been left for good: *an abandoned jeep stood in the street.* **3** unrestrained; uninhibited: *a wild, abandoned dance.*

a·base /ə'bās/ ▸*v.* [*trans.*] behave in a way so as to belittle or degrade (someone): *I watched my colleagues* ***abasing themselves*** *before the board of trustees.* See note at **HUMBLE.** ▷late Middle English: from Old French *abaissier*, from *a-* (from Latin *ad* 'to, at') + *baissier* 'to lower,' based on late Latin *bassus* 'short of stature.' The spelling has been influenced by **BASE**[2]. **—a·base·ment** *n.*

a·bash /ə'basн/ ▸*v.* [*trans.*] [usu. as *adj.*] (**abashed**) cause to feel embarrassed, disconcerted, or ashamed: *she was not abashed at being caught.* ▷Middle English: from Anglo-Norman French *abaïss-*; compare with Old French *esbaïss-*, lengthened stem of *esbair*, from *es-* 'utterly' + *bair* 'astound.' **—a·bash·ment** *n.*

a·bate /ə'bāt/ ▸*v.* [*intrans.*] (of something perceived as hostile, threatening, or negative) become less intense or widespread: *the storm suddenly abated.* See note at **ALLEVIATE.** ■ [*trans.*] cause to become smaller or less intense: *nothing abated his crusading zeal.* ■ [*trans.*] *Law* lessen, reduce, or remove (esp. a nuisance): *this action would not have been sufficient to abate the odor nuisance.* ▷Middle English (in the legal sense 'put a stop to (a nuisance)'): from Old French *abatre* 'to fell,' from *a-* (from Latin *ad* 'to, at') + *batre* 'to beat' (from Latin *battere*, *battuere* 'to beat').

a·bate·ment /ə'bātmənt/ ▸*n.* (often in legal use) the ending, reduction, or lessening of something: *noise abatement | an abatement in the purchase price.* ▷Middle English: from Anglo-Norman French, from Old French *abatre* 'fell, put an end to' (see **ABATE**).

ab·at·toir /'abəˌtwär/ ▸*n.* a slaughterhouse. ▷early 19th cent.: from French, from *abattre* 'to fell.'

a bat·tu·ta /ˌä bä'tōōtä/ ▸*adv. Music* (typically as a direction) returning to strict tempo. ▷Italian, literally 'to the beating.'

ab·ax·i·al /ab'aksēəl/ ▸*adj. Botany* facing away from the stem of a plant (esp. denoting the lower surface of a leaf). The opposite of **ADAXIAL.**

abaya /ə'bīə/ ▸*n.* a full-length, sleeveless outer garment worn by Arabs. ▷mid 19th cent.: from Arabic *'abāya.*

Ab·ba /'äbä; 'abä/ ▸*n.* (in the New Testament) an intimate term for God as father. ■ (in the Syrian Orthodox and Coptic churches) a title given to bishops and patriarchs. ▷via Greek from Aramaic *'abbā* 'daddy.'

ab·ba·cy /'abəsē/ ▸*n.* (*pl.* **-cies**) the office or period of office of an abbot or abbess. ▷late Middle English: from ecclesiastical Latin *abbacia*, from *abbas*, *abbat-* (see **ABBOT**).

Ab·bas /ä'bäs/, Ferhat (1899–1989), Algerian nationalist leader. He was president of the Algerian provisional government from 1958 and then president of the constituent assembly of independent Algeria 1962–63.

Ab·bas·id /'abəsid; ə'basid/ ▸*adj.* of or relating to a dynasty of caliphs who ruled in Baghdad from 750 to 1258.

▸*n.* a member of this dynasty.

ab·ba·tial /ə'bāsнəl/ ▸*adj.* of or relating to an abbey, abbot, or abbess. ▷late 17th cent.: from medieval Latin *abbatialis*, from *abbas*, *abbat-* (see **ABBOT**).

ab·bé /a'bā/ ▸*n.* (in France) an abbot or other cleric: *the abbé was his confessor* | [as *title*] *Abbé Pierre.* ▷mid 16th cent.: French, from ecclesiastical Latin *abbas*, *abbat-* (see **ABBOT**).

ab·bess /'abis/ ▸*n.* a woman who is the head of an abbey of nuns. ▷Middle English: from Old French *abbesse* 'female abbot,' from ecclesiastical Latin *abbatissa*, from *abbas*, *abbat-* (see **ABBOT**).

Abbe·vill·i·an /ab'vilēən; ˌabə-/ (also **Abbe·vil·l·ean**) ▸*adj. dated Archaeology* of, relating to, or denoting the first Paleolithic culture in Europe. It is now usually referred to as the Lower Acheulean. ■ [as *n.*] (**the Abbevillian**) the Abbevillian culture or period. ▷1930s: from French *Abbevillien* 'from *Abbeville*,' a town in northern France where tools from this culture were discovered.

ab·bey /'abē/ ▸*n.* (*pl.* **-beys**) the building or buildings occupied by a community of monks or nuns. ■ a church or house that was formerly an abbey. ▷Middle English: from Old French *abbeïe*, from medieval Latin *abbatia* 'abbacy,' from *abbas*, *abbat-* (see **ABBOT**).

Ab·bey Road /'abē/ a road in northwestern London in England, west of Regents Park, the site of recording studios that are associated with the Beatles and other pop music figures.

ab·bot /'abət/ ▸*n.* a man who is the head of an abbey of monks. ▷Old English *abbod*, from ecclesiastical Latin *abbas*, *abbat-*, from Greek *abbas* 'father,' from Aramaic *'abbā* (see **ABBA**).

Ab·bott /'abət/ Berenice, (1898–1991), U.S. photographer and teacher of photography. She is noted for her documentation of New York City in the 1930s, published in *Changing New York* (1939). She edited *The World of Atgel* (1964).

abbr. ▸*abbr.* abbreviation.

ab·bre·vi·ate /ə'brēvēˌāt/ ▸*v.* [*trans.*] (usu. **be abbreviated**) shorten (a word, phrase, or text): *the business of artists and repertory, commonly abbreviated to A&R* | [as *adj.*] (**abbreviated**) *this book is an abbreviated version of the earlier work.* ▷late Middle English: from late Latin *abbreviat-* 'shortened,' from the verb *abbreviare*, from Latin *brevis* 'short.'

ab·bre·vi·a·tion /əˌbrēvē'āsнən/ (abbr.: **abbr.**) ▸*n.* a shortened form of a word or phrase. ■ the process or result of abbreviating.

ABC[1] ▸*n.* the alphabet. ■ (also **ABCs**) the rudiments of a subject: *the ABCs of emergency heart-lung resuscitation.* ■ an alphabetical guide: *an ABC of Civil War battlefields.*

▸*PHRASE* □ **easy** (or **simple**) **as ABC** extremely easy or straightforward.

ABC[2] ▸*abbr.* American Broadcasting Company.

ABC Is·lands an acronym for the Caribbean islands of Aruba, Bonaire, and Curaçao.

ABD ▸*abbr.* all but dissertation, used to denote a student who has completed all other parts of a doctorate: *ABDs will be considered, but receipt of the doctorate will be a condition of tenure.*

ab·di·cate /'abdiˌkāt/ ▸*v.* [*intrans.*] (of a monarch) renounce one's throne: *in 1918 Kaiser Wilhelm abdicated as German emperor* | [*trans.*] *Ferdinand abdicated the throne in favor of the emperor's brother.* ■ [*trans.*] fail to fulfill or undertake (a responsibility or duty): *the government was accused of abdicating its responsibility* | [*intrans.*] *the secretary of state should not* ***abdicate from*** *leadership on educational issues.* ▷mid 16th cent.: from Latin *abdicat-* 'renounced,' from the verb *abdicare*, from *ab-* 'away, from' + *dicare* 'declare.' **—ab·di·ca·tion** /-'kāsнən/ *n.*

ab·do·men /'abdəmən; ab'dōmən/ ▸*n.* the part of the body of a vertebrate containing the digestive organs; the belly. In humans and other mammals, it is contained bounded by the diaphragm and the pelvis. ■ *Zoology* the posterior part of the body of an arthropod, esp. the segments of an insect's body behind the thorax. ▷mid 16th cent.: from Latin. **—ab·dom·i·nal** /ab'dämənl/ *adj.*

ab·du·cens nerve /ab'd(y)ōōsənz/ ▸*n. Anatomy* each of the sixth pair of cranial nerves, supplying the muscles concerned with the lateral movement of the eyeballs. ▷early 19th cent.: *abducens* (modern Latin, 'leading away'), from the Latin verb *abducere.*

ab·duct /ab'dəkt/ ▸*v.* [*trans.*] **1** take (someone) away illegally by force or deception; kidnap: *the millionaire who disappeared may have been abducted.* **2** *Physiology* (of a muscle) move (a limb or part) away from the midline of the body or from another part. The opposite of **ADDUCT**[1]. ▷early 17th cent.: from Latin *abduct-* 'led away,' from *abducere*, from *ab-* 'away, from'+ *ducere* 'to lead.'

ab·duct·ee /ˌabdək'tē/ ▸*n.* a person who has been abducted.

ab·duc·tion /ab'dəksнən/ ▸*n.* **1** the action or an instance of forcibly taking a person or persons away against their will: *they organized the abduction of Mr. Cordes on his way to the airport | abductions by armed men in plain clothes.* ■ (in legal use) the illegal removal of a child from parents or guardians. **2** *Physiology* the movement of a limb or other part away from the midline of the body, or from another part. The opposite of **adduction** (see **ADDUCT**[1]).

ab·duc·tor /ab'dəktər/ ▸*n.* **1** a person who abducts another person. **2** (also **abductor muscle**) *Anatomy* a muscle whose contraction moves a limb or part away from the midline of the body, or from another part. Compare with **ADDUCTOR.** ■ any of a number of specific muscles in the hand, forearm, or foot: [followed by Latin genitive] *abductor pollicis.* ▷early 17th cent. (as a term in anatomy): modern Latin (see **ABDUCT**).

Ab·dul Ha·mid II /ˌäbdōōl hä'mēd/ (1842–1918), the last sultan of Turkey 1876–1909. An autocratic ruler, he was deposed after the revolt of the Young Turks.

Ab·dul-Jab·bar /ab'dōōl jə'bär/, Kareem, (1947–), U.S. basketball player; former name *Lewis Ferdinand Alcindor.* He played professionally for the Milwaukee Bucks 1969–75 and the Los Angeles Lakers 1975–89 and holds several records.

Ab·dul·lah ibn Hus·sein /ˌäbdōōl'ä ˌibən hōō'sān/ (1882–1951), king of Jordan 1946–51. After serving as emir of Transjordan from 1921, he became king of Jordan at the time of independence. He was assassinated in 1951.

Ab·dul·lah II /ˌäbdōōl'ä/ ▸(1962–), king of Jordan since 1999; full name *Abdullah ibn al-Hussein.*The son of King Hussein, he maintained a moderate political stance and initiated economic reforms.

King Abdullah

Ab·dul Rah·man /äb'dōōl 'rämən; 'räkнmän; räkн 'män/, Tunku (1903–90), Malayan statesman; prime minister of Malaya 1957–63 and of Malaysia 1963–70.

a·beam /ə'bēm/ ▸*adv.* on a line at right angles to a ship's or an aircraft's length. ■ (**abeam of**) opposite the middle of (a ship or aircraft): *she was lying almost abeam of us.* ▷mid 19th cent.: from **A-**[2] (expressing general direction) + **BEAM.**

a·be·ce·dar·i·an /ˌābēsē'de(ə)rēən/ ▸*adj.* **1** arranged alphabetically: *in abecedarian sequence.* **2** rudimentary; elementary: *abecedarian technology.*

▸*n.* a person who is just learning; a novice. ▷mid 17th cent.: from late Latin *abecedarius* 'alphabetical' (from the names of the letters *a, b, c, d*) + **-AN**.

a·bed /ə'bed/ ▸*adv. archaic* in bed. ▷Middle English: from **A-**2 'in, on' + **BED**.

A·bel1 /'ābəl/ (in the Bible) the second son of Adam and Eve, murdered by his brother Cain.

A·bel2 /'ābəl/, Niels Henrik (1802–29), Norwegian mathematician. He developed the concept of elliptic functions, independently of Jacobi, and did work on integral equations and power series.

Ab·e·lard /'abə,lärd/, Peter (1079–1142), French scholar, theologian, and philosopher. He is famous for his tragic love affair with his student Héloïse. See also **HÉLOÏSE**.

a·bele /ə'bēl/ ▸*n.* the white poplar. ▷Middle English: via Old French from medieval Latin *albellus*, diminutive of *albus* 'white.' The term was reintroduced in the late 16th cent. from Dutch *abeel* (from Old French *abel*), when specimens were imported from the Netherlands.

A·be·li·an /ə'bēlēən; -yən/ ▸*adj. Mathematics* (of a group) having members related by a commutative operation (i.e., $a \times b = b \times a$). ▷mid 19th cent.: named after N. H. *Abel* (see **ABEL**2).

A·be·na·ki /,abə'nakē; ,äbə'nä-/ ▸*n.* variant spelling of **ABNAKI**.

A·be·o·ku·ta /ä'bā-ōko͞o,tä/ a city in southwestern Nigeria, capital of the state of Ogun; pop. 308,800.

Ab·er·deen /,abər'dēn; 'abər,dēn/ **1** a city and seaport in northeastern Scotland, a center of the offshore North Sea oil industry; pop. 201,100. **2** a town in northeastern Maryland, on Chesapeake Bay; pop. 13,087. A major military test range is nearby. **3** a city in northeastern South Dakota, a dairy center; pop. 24,658.

Ab·er·deen An·gus ▸*n.* an animal of a Scottish breed of hornless black beef cattle. Also called **BLACK ANGUS**. ▷mid 19th cent.

Ab·er·nath·y /'abər,naTHē/, Ralph David (1926–90), U.S. minister and civil rights activist. He served as president of the Southern Christian Leadership Conference (SCLC) from 1968 until 1977. His autobiography, *And the Walls Came Tumbling Down*, was published in 1989.

ab·er·rant /'abərənt; ə'ber-/ ▸*adj.* departing from an accepted standard. ■ *chiefly Biology* diverging from the normal type: *aberrant chromosomes*. ▷mid 16th cent.: from Latin *aberrant-* 'wandering away,' from the verb *aberrare*, from *ab-* 'away, from' + *errare* 'to stray.' **—ab·er·rance** *n.* **—ab·er·ran·cy** *n.* **—ab·er·rant·ly** *adv.*

ab·er·ra·tion /,abə'rāSHən/ ▸*n.* a departure from what is normal, usual, or expected, typically one that is unwelcome: *they described the outbreak of violence in the area as an aberration.* ■ a person whose beliefs or behavior are unusual or unacceptable: *evil men are an aberration.* ■ a departure from someone's usual moral character or mental ability, typically for the worse: *I see these activities as some kind of mental aberration.* ■ *Biology* a characteristic that deviates from the normal type: *color aberrations.* ■ *Optics* the failure of rays to converge at one focus because of limitations or defects in a lens or mirror. ■ *Astronomy* the apparent displacement of a celestial object from its true position, caused by the relative motion of the observer and the object. ▷late 16th cent.: from Latin *aberratio(n-)*, from *aberrare* 'to stray' (see **ABERRANT**). **—ab·er·ra·tion·al** /-SHənl/ *adj.*

Ab·er·ta·we /,abər'tou-ē/ see **SWANSEA**.

a·bet /ə'bet/ ▸*v.* (**a·bet·ted, a·bet·ting**) [*trans.*] encourage or assist (someone) to do something wrong, in particular, to commit a crime or other offense: *he was not guilty of murder but was guilty of* ***aiding and abetting*** *others.* ■ encourage or assist someone to commit (a crime): *we are* ***aiding and abetting*** *this illegal traffic.* ▷late Middle English (in the sense 'urge to do something good or bad'): from Old French *abeter*, from *a-* (from Latin *ad* 'to, at') + *beter* 'hound, urge on.' **—a·bet·ment** *n.* **—a·bet·tor** /ə'betər/ (also **a·bet·ter**) *n.*

a·bey·ance /ə'bāəns/ ▸*n.* a state of temporary disuse or suspension: *matters were* ***held in abeyance*** *pending further inquiries.* ■ *Law* the position of being without, or waiting for, an owner or claimant. ▷late 16th cent. (in the legal sense): from Old French *abeance* 'aspiration to a title,' from *abeer* 'aspire after,' from *a-* 'toward' + *beer* 'to gape.' **—a·bey·ant** /ə'bāənt/ *adj.*

ab·hor /ab'hôr/ ▸*v.* (**-horred, -hor·ring**) [*trans.*] *formal* regard with disgust and hatred: *professional tax preparers abhor a flat tax because it would dry up their business.* See note at **DESPISE**. ▷late Middle English: from Latin *abhorrere*, from *ab-* 'away from' + *horrere* 'to shudder.' **—ab·hor·rer** *n.*

ab·hor·rence /ab'hôrəns; -'här-/ ▸*n.* a feeling of repulsion; disgusted loathing: *the thought of marrying him filled her with abhorrence | society's* ***abhorrence of*** *crime.*

ab·hor·rent /ab'hôrənt; -'här-/ ▸*adj.* inspiring disgust and loathing; repugnant: *racial discrimination was* ***abhorrent to*** *us all.* See note at **OFFENSIVE**. ▷late 16th cent.: from Latin *abhorrent-* 'shuddering away from in horror,' from the verb *abhorrere* (see **ABHOR**).

a·bide /ə'bīd/ ▸*v.* **1** [*intrans.*] (**abide by**) accept or act in accordance with (a rule, decision, or recommendation): *I said I would abide by their decision.* **2** [*trans.*] (**can/could not abide**) *informal* be unable to tolerate (someone or something): *if there is one thing I cannot abide it is a lack of discipline.* **3** [*intrans.*] (of a feeling or a memory) continue without fading or being lost. ■ *archaic* live; dwell. ▷Old English *ābīdan* 'wait,' from *ā-* 'onward' + *bīdan* (see **BIDE**).

a·bid·ing /ə'bīdiNG/ ▸*adj.* [*attrib.*] (of a feeling or a memory) lasting a long time; enduring: *he had an abiding respect for her.* **—a·bid·ing·ly** *adv.*

Ab·i·djan /,abi'jän/ the chief port of the Ivory Coast, the capital 1935–83; pop. 1,850,000.

Abi·lene /'abə,lēn/ **1** a commercial city in east central Kansas; pop. 6,242. It was the first terminus of the Chisholm Trail. **2** a city in north central Texas, an agricultural and oil industry center; pop. 106,654.

a·bil·i·ty /ə'bilitē/ ▸*n.* (*pl.* **-ties**) **1** [in *sing.*, with *infinitive*] the capacity to do something: *the manager had lost his ability to motivate the players | the tax bears no relationship to people's ability to pay.* **2** talent that enables someone to achieve a great deal: *a man of exceptional ability.* ■ (in the context of education) a level of mental power: *a student of below average ability | students of all abilities.* ■ a special talent or skill: *much depends on the person's abilities and aptitudes.* ▷late Middle English: from Old French *ablete*, from Latin *habilitas*, from *habilis* 'able.'

-ability ▸*suffix* forming nouns of quality corresponding to adjectives ending in *-able* (such as *suitability* corresponding to *suitable*). ▷from French *-abilité* or Latin *-abilitas*, noun endings.

Ab·ing·ton /'abiNGtən/ a township in southeastern Pennsylvania, north of Philadelphia; pop. 56,103.

ab in·i·ti·o /,ab ə'niSHē,ō/ ▸*adv.* from the beginning (used chiefly in formal or legal contexts): *the agreement should be declared void ab initio.*

▸*adj.* [*attrib.*] starting from the beginning: *he was instructing ab initio pilots.* ▷early 17th cent.: Latin.

a·bi·o·gen·e·sis /,ābī-ō'jenəsis/ ▸*n.* technical term for **SPONTANEOUS GENERATION**. ▷late 19th cent.: from **A-**1 'not' + Greek *bios* 'life' + **GENESIS**.

a·bi·ot·ic /,ābī'ätik/ ▸*adj.* physical rather than biological; not derived from living organisms. ■ devoid of life; sterile.

Ab·i·qui·u /,abə'kē-o͞o/ a ranching community in northern New Mexico, the longtime home of artist Georgia O'Keeffe.

ab·ject /'ab,jekt; ab'jekt/ ▸*adj.* **1** [*attrib.*] (of a situation or condition) extremely bad, unpleasant, and degrading: *abject poverty.* ■ (of an unhappy state of mind) experienced to the maximum degree: *his letter plunged her into abject misery.* ■ (of a failure) absolute and humiliating. **2** (of a person or their behavior) completely without pride or dignity; self-abasing: *an abject apology.* ▷late Middle English (in the sense 'rejected'): from Latin *abjectus*, past participle of *abjicere* 'reject,' from *ab-* 'away' + *jacere* 'to throw.' **—ab·jec·tion** /ab'jekSHən/ *n.* **—ab·ject·ly** *adv.* **—ab·ject·ness** *n.*

ab·jure /ab'jo͝or/ ▸*v.* [*trans.*] *formal* solemnly renounce (a belief, cause, or claim): *his refusal to abjure the Catholic faith.* ▷late Middle English: from Latin *abjurare*, from *ab-* 'away' + *jurare* 'swear.' **—ab·ju·ra·tion** /,abjə'rāSHən/ *n.*

▸*PHRASE* □ **abjure the realm** *historical* swear an oath to leave a country or realm forever.

Ab·khaz /äb'käz; ab'kaz; əb'KHäz/ (also **Ab·kha·zi·an** /ab'kazHən; -zēən; äb'kä-/) ▸*adj.* of or relating to Abkhazia, its people, or their language.

▸*n.* **1** a member of a Caucasian people living in Abkhazia. **2** a Northwest Caucasian language.

Ab·kha·zi·a /äb'käzēə; ab'kāzH(ē)ə/ an autonomous territory in northwestern Georgia, south of the Caucasus mountains on the Black Sea; pop. 537,500; capital, Sokhumi. In 1992, Abkhazia unilaterally declared itself independent, sparking ongoing armed conflict with Georgia.

ab·la·tion /ə'blāSHən/ ▸*n.* **1** the surgical removal of body tissue. **2** the removal of snow and ice by melting or evaporation, typically from a glacier or iceberg. ■ the erosion of rock, typically by wind action. ■ the loss of surface material from a spacecraft or meteorite through evaporation or melting caused by friction with the atmosphere. ▷late Middle English (in the general sense 'taking away, removal'): from late Latin *ablatio(n-)*, from Latin *ablat-* 'taken away,' from *ab-* 'away' + *lat-* 'carried' (from the verb *ferre*). **—ab·late** /ə'blāt/ *v.*

ab·la·tive /'ablətiv/ ▸*adj.* [*attrib.*] **1** *Grammar* relating to or denoting a case (esp. in Latin) of nouns and pronouns (and words in grammatical agreement with them) indicating separation or an agent, instrument, or location. **2** (of surgical treatment) involving ablation. **3** of, relating to, or subject to ablation through melting or evaporation: *the spacecraft's ablative heat shield.*

▸*n. Grammar* a word in the ablative case. ■ (**the ablative**) the ablative case. ▷late Middle English: from Old French *ablative* (feminine of *ablatif*), Latin *ablativus*, from *ablat-* 'taken away' (see **ABLATION**).

ab·la·tive ab·so·lute ▸*n.* a construction in Latin that consists of a noun and participle or adjective in the ablative case and that is syntactically independent of the rest of the sentence.

ab·laut /'ab,lout/ ▸*n.* a change of vowel in related words or forms, e.g., in Germanic strong verbs (e.g., in *sing, sang, sung*). ▷mid 19th cent.: from German, from *ab* 'off' + *Laut* 'sound.'

a·blaze /ə'blāz/ ▸*adj.* [*predic.*] burning fiercely: *his clothes were ablaze |* [as *complement*] *farm buildings were* ***set ablaze.*** ■ very brightly colored or lighted: *New England is* ***ablaze with*** *color in autumn.* ■ made bright by a strong emotion: *his eyes were* ***ablaze with*** *anger.*

a·ble /'ābəl/ ▸*adj.* (**a·bler, a·blest**) **1** [with *infinitive*] having the power, skill, means, or opportunity to do something: *he was able to read Greek at the age of eight | he would never be able to afford such a big house.* **2** having considerable skill, proficiency, or intelligence: *the dancers were technically very able.* ▷late Middle English (also in the sense 'easy to use, suitable'): from Old French *hable*, from Latin *habilis* 'handy,' from *habere* 'to hold.'

-able /əbəl/ ▸*suffix* forming adjectives meaning: **1** able to be: *calculable.* **2** due to be: *payable.* **3** subject to: *taxable.* **4** relevant to or in accordance with: *fashionable.* **5** having the quality to: *suitable | comfortable.* ▷from French *-able* or Latin *-abilis*, adjectival endings; originally found in words only from these forms but later used to form adjectives directly from English verbs ending in *-ate*, e.g., *educable* from *educate*. The unrelated **ABLE** has probably influenced terms such as *bearable, salable.*

a·ble-bod·ied ▸*adj.* fit, strong, and healthy; not physically disabled: *he was the only able-bodied man on the farm.*

a·ble-bod·ied sea·man ▸*n.* (also **a·ble sea·man**) a merchant seaman qualified to perform all routine duties.

a·bled /'ābəld/ ▸*adj.* having a full range of physical or mental abilities; not disabled. See also **DIFFERENTLY ABLED**. ▷1980s: back-formation from **DISABLED**.

a·ble·ism /'ābə,lizəm/ (also **a·blism**) ▸*n.* discrimination in favor of able-bodied people. **—a·ble·ist** *n.* & *adj.*

a·ble sea·man ▸*n.* an able-bodied seaman.

a·bloom /ə'blo͞om/ ▸*adj.* [*predic.*] covered in flowers.

ab·lu·tion /ə'blo͞oSHən/ ▸*n.* (usu. **ablutions**) the act of washing oneself (often used for humorously formal effect): *the women performed their ablutions.* ■ a ceremonial act of washing parts of the body or sacred containers. ▷late Middle English: from Latin *ablutio(n-)*, from *abluere*, from *ab-* 'away' + *luere* 'wash.' The original use was as a term in chemistry and alchemy meaning 'purification by using liquids,' hence 'purification of the body by washing' (mid 16th cent.). **—ab·lu·tion·ar·y** *adj.*

a·bly /'āblē/ ▸*adv.* skillfully; competently: *Steven has summed up our concerns very ably.*

-ably ▸*suffix* forming adverbs corresponding to adjectives ending in *-able* (such as *suitably* corresponding to *suitable*).

ABM ▸*abbr.* antiballistic missile.

Pronunciation Key ə *ago;* ər *over;* 'ə *or* ,ə *up;* 'ər *or* ,ər *fur;* a *hat;* ā *rate;* ä *car;* CH *chew;* e *let;* ē *see;* e(ə)r *air;* i *fit;* ī *by;* i(ə)r *ear;* NG *sing;* ō *go;* ô *for;* oi *boy;* o͝o *good;* o͞o *goo;* ou *out;* SH *she;* TH *thin;* TH *then;* (h)w *why;* ZH *vision*

Ab·na·ki /ab'nakē; äb'nä-/ (also **Ab·e·na·ki** /ˌabə'nakē; ˌäbə'nä-/) ▸*n.* (*pl.* same or **-kis**) **1** a member of a North American Indian people of Maine on the Atlantic coast to southern Quebec. **2** either or both of two Algonquian languages, **Eastern Abnaki** and **Western Abnaki**, now nearly extinct.
▸*adj.* of or relating to this people or their language. ▷from French *Abénaqui*, from Eastern Abnaki.

ab·ne·gate /'abniˌgāt/ ▸*v.* [*trans.*] renounce or reject (something desired or valuable): *he attempts to abnegate personal responsibility.* ▷early 17th cent.: from Latin *abnegat-* 'renounced,' from the verb *abnegare*, from *ab-* 'away, off' + *negare* 'deny.' —**ab·ne·ga·tor** /-ˌgātər/ *n.*

ab·ne·ga·tion /ˌabni'gāshən/ ▸*n.* the act of renouncing or rejecting something: *abnegation of political lawmaking power.* ■ self-denial. ▷Middle English: from Latin *abnegatio(n-)*, from the verb *abnegare* (see ABNEGATE).

ab·nor·mal /ab'nôrməl/ ▸*adj.* deviating from what is normal or usual, typically in a way that is undesirable or worrying: *the illness is recognizable from the patient's abnormal behavior.* ▷mid 19th cent.: alteration (by association with Latin *abnormis* 'monstrosity') of 16th-cent. *anormal*, from French, variant of *anomal*, via Latin from Greek *anōmalos* (see ANOMALOUS). —**ab·nor·mal·ly** *adv.*

ab·nor·mal·i·ty /ˌabnôr'malitē/ ▸*n.* (*pl.* **-ties**) an abnormal feature, characteristic, or occurrence, typically in a medical context: *a chromosome abnormality.* ■ the quality or state of being abnormal.

A·bo /'abō/ (also **a·bo**) *Austral., informal, offensive* ▸*n.* (*pl.* **A·bos**) an Aborigine.
▸*adj.* Aboriginal. ▷early 20th cent.: abbreviation.

Å·bo /'ôbo͞o/ Swedish name for **TURKU**.

a·board /ə'bôrd/ ▸*adv.* & *prep.* on or into (a ship, aircraft, train, or other vehicle): [as *adv.*] *welcome aboard, sir | the plane crashed, killing all 158 people aboard* | [as *prep.*] *climbing aboard the yacht.* ■ on or onto (a horse): [as *adv.*] *with Migliore aboard, he won the cup at a gallop.* ■ *figurative* into an organization or team as a new member: [as *adv.*] *coming aboard as IBM's new chairman.* ■ *Baseball* on base as a runner: *putting their first batter aboard.* ▷late Middle English: from A-2 (expressing motion) + BOARD, reinforced by Old French *à bord*.
▸*PHRASE* □ **all aboard!** a call warning passengers to get on a ship, train, or bus that is about to depart.

a·bode1 /ə'bōd/ ▸*n. formal* or *poetic/literary* a place of residence; a house or home: *her current abode* | (*humorous*) *my humble abode.* ■ residence: *a place of abode.* ■ *archaic* a stay; a sojourn. ▷Middle English (in the sense 'act of waiting'): verbal noun from ABIDE.

a·bode2 ▸*v.* archaic past of ABIDE.

a·bol·ish /ə'bälish/ ▸*v.* [*trans.*] formally put an end to (a system, practice, or institution): *the tax was abolished in 1977.* ▷late Middle English: from Old French *aboliss-*, lengthened stem of *abolir*, from Latin *abolere* 'destroy.' —**a·bol·ish·er** *n.* —**a·bol·ish·ment** *n.*

ab·o·li·tion /ˌabə'lishən/ ▸*n.* the action or an act of abolishing a system, practice, or institution: *the abolition of child labor.* ▷early 16th cent.: from Latin *abolitio(n-)*, from *abolere* 'destroy.'

ab·o·li·tion·ist /ˌabə'lishənist/ ▸*n.* a person who favors the abolition of a practice or institution, esp. capital punishment or (formerly) slavery. —**ab·o·li·tion·ism** *n.*

ab·o·ma·sum /ˌabə'māsəm/ ▸*n.* (*pl.* **-sa** /-sə/) *Zoology* the fourth stomach of a ruminant, which receives food from the omasum and passes it to the small intestine. ▷late 17th cent.: modern Latin, from *ab-* 'away, from' + *omasum* (see OMASUM).

A-bomb ▸*n.* short for ATOM BOMB.

Ab·o·mey /ˌabə'mā; ə'bōmē/ a town in southern Benin, capital of the former kingdom of Dahomey; pop. 54,400.

a·bom·i·na·ble /ə'bäm(ə)nəbəl/ ▸*adj.* causing moral revulsion: *the uprising was suppressed with abominable cruelty.* See note at OFFENSIVE. ■ *informal* very unpleasant: *a cup of abominable tea.* ▷Middle English: via Old French from Latin *abominabilis*, from *abominari* (see ABOMINATE). The term was once widely believed to be from AB- 'away from' + Latin *homine* (from *homo* 'human being'), thus 'inhuman, beastly,' and frequently spelled *abhominable* until the 17th cent. —**a·bom·i·na·bly** /-blē/ *adv.*

A·bom·i·na·ble Snow·man ▸*n.* (*pl.* **-men**) another term for YETI.

a·bom·i·nate /ə'bäməˌnāt/ ▸*v.* [*trans.*] *formal* detest; loathe: *they abominated the very idea of monarchy.* ▷mid 17th cent.: from Latin *abominat-* 'deprecated,' from the verb *abominari*, from *ab-* 'away, from' + *omen, omin-* 'omen.' —**a·bom·i·na·tor** /-ˌnātər/ *n.*

a·bom·i·na·tion /əˌbämə'nāshən/ ▸*n.* a thing that causes disgust or hatred: *the Pharisees regarded Gentiles as an abomination to God* | (*informal*) *concrete abominations masquerading as hotels.* ■ a feeling of hatred: *their abomination of indulgence.* ▷Middle English: from Latin *abominatio(n-)*, from the verb *abominari* (see ABOMINATE).

ab·o·ral /ab'ôrəl/ ▸*adj.* *Zoology* relating to or denoting the side or end that is furthest from the mouth, esp. in animals that lack clear upper and lower sides, such as echinoderms. ■ moving or leading away from the mouth: *propagated in an aboral direction.* —**ab·o·ral·ly** *adv.*

ab·o·rig·i·nal /ˌabə'rijənl/ ▸*adj.* (of human races, animals, and plants) inhabiting or existing in a land from the earliest times or from before the arrival of colonists; indigenous. See note at NATIVE. ■ (**Aboriginal**) of or relating to the Australian Aboriginals or their languages.
▸*n.* an aboriginal inhabitant of a place. ■ (**Aboriginal**) a person belonging to one of the indigenous peoples of Australia. ▷mid 17th cent.: from Latin *aborigines* 'original inhabitants' (see ABORIGINE) + -AL.

USAGE Both **Aboriginals** and **Aborigines**) are standard plural forms when referring to Australian Aboriginal peoples.

Ab·o·rig·i·nal·i·ty /ˌabəˌrijə'nalitē/ ▸*n.* the distinctive culture of aboriginal peoples, esp. those in Australia: *their music reflects their Aboriginality.*

ab·o·rig·i·ne /ˌabə'rijənē/ ▸*n.* a person, animal, or plant that has been in a country or region from earliest times. ■ (**Aborigine**) an aboriginal inhabitant of Australia. ▷mid 19th cent.: back-formation from the 16th-cent. plural *aborigines* 'original inhabitants' (in classical times referring to those of Italy and Greece), from the Latin phrase *ab origine* 'from the beginning.'

USAGE See usage at ABORIGINAL.

a·born·ing /ə'bôrniNG/ ▸*adv.* while being born or produced: *the idea died aborning.*
▸*adj.* [*predic.*] being born or produced: *in the early 1960s, hippiedom was aborning.* ▷1930s: from *a-* 'in the process of' + *borning*, verbal noun from *born* (North American dialect usage) 'to be born.'

a·bort /ə'bôrt/ ▸*v.* [*trans.*] **1** carry out or undergo the abortion of (a fetus). ■ [*intrans.*] (of a pregnant woman or female animal) have a miscarriage, with loss of the fetus. ■ [*intrans.*] *Biology* (of an embryonic organ or organism) remain undeveloped; fail to mature. **2** bring to a premature end because of a problem or fault: *the pilot aborted his landing.*
▸*n. informal* or *technical* an act of aborting a flight, space mission, or other enterprise: *there was an abort because of bad weather.* ▷mid 16th cent.: from Latin *aboriri* 'miscarry,' from *ab-* 'away, from' + *oriri* 'be born.'

a·bor·ti·fa·cient /əˌbôrtə'fāshənt/ *Medicine* ▸*adj.* (chiefly of a drug) causing abortion.
▸*n.* an abortifacient drug.

a·bor·tion /ə'bôrshən/ ▸*n.* **1** the deliberate termination of a human pregnancy, most often performed during the first 28 weeks of pregnancy. ■ the expulsion of a fetus from the uterus by natural causes before it is able to survive independently. ■ *Biology* the arrest of the development of an organ, typically a seed or fruit. **2** an object or undertaking regarded by the speaker as unpleasant or badly made or carried out. ▷mid 16th cent.: from Latin *abortio(n-)*, from *aboriri* 'miscarry' (see ABORT).

a·bor·tion·ist /ə'bôrshənist/ ▸*n.* a person who carries out abortions (typically applied to someone not working in a hospital, or used to convey disapproval of abortion.

a·bor·tion pill ▸*n. informal* a drug that can induce abortion, esp. mifepristone.

a·bor·tive /ə'bôrtiv/ ▸*adj.* **1** failing to produce the intended result: *she made two abortive attempts at suicide.* **2** *Biology, dated* (of an organ or organism) rudimentary; arrested in development: *abortive medusae.* ■ *Medicine* (of a virus infection) failing to produce symptoms. **3** [*attrib.*] *rare* causing or resulting in abortion: *abortive techniques.* ▷Middle English (as a noun denoting a stillborn child or animal): via Old French from Latin *abortivus*, from *aboriri* 'miscarry' (see ABORT). —**a·bor·tive·ly** *adv.*

a·bor·tus fe·ver /ə'bôrtəs/ ▸*n.* the commonest form of undulant fever in humans. • This disease is caused by the bacterium *Brucella abortus*, which is also the chief cause of brucellosis in cattle. ▷1920s: from Latin *abortus* 'miscarriage.'

ABO system ▸*n.* a system of four basic types (A, AB, B, and O) into which human blood may be classified, based on the presence or absence of certain inherited antigens.

a·bou·li·a /ə'bo͞olēə/ ▸*n.* variant spelling of ABULIA.

a·bound /ə'bound/ ▸*v.* [*intrans.*] exist in large numbers or amounts: *rumors of a further scandal abound.* ■ (**abound in/with**) have in large numbers or amounts: *this land abounds with wildlife.* ▷Middle English (in the sense 'overflow, be abundant'): from Old French *abunder*, from Latin *abundare* 'overflow,' from *ab-* 'from' + *undare* 'surge' (from *unda* 'a wave').

a·bout /ə'bout/ ▸*prep.* **1** on the subject of; concerning: *I was thinking about you | I asked him about his beliefs.* ■ so as to affect: *there's nothing we can do about it.* ■ (**be about**) be involved or to do with; have the intention of: *it's **all about** having fun.* **2** used to indicate movement within a particular area: *she looked about the room.* **3** used to express location in a particular place: *rugs strewn about the hall | he produced a knife from somewhere about his person.* ■ used to describe a quality apparent in a person: *there was a look about her that said everything.*
▸*adv.* **1** used to indicate movement in an area: *men were floundering about | finding my way about.* **2** used to express location in a particular place: *there was a lot of flu about | a thief about in the hotel.* **3** (used with a number or quantity) approximately: *reduced by about 5 percent | he's about 35.* ▷Old English *onbūtan*, from *on* + *būtan* 'outside of.'
▸*PHRASES* □ **about to do something** intending to do something or close to doing something very soon: *the ceremony was about to begin.* □ **be not about to do something** be unwilling to do something: *he is not about to step down after so long.* □ **how about** see HOW1. □ **just about** see JUST. □ **know what one is about** *informal* be aware of the implications of one's actions or of a situation, and of how best to deal with them. □ **up and about** see UP. □ **what about** see WHAT.

a·bout-face ▸*n.* (chiefly in military contexts) a turn made so as to face the opposite direction: *he did an about-face and marched out of the tent.* ■ *informal* a complete change of opinion or policy: *he threatened to stop helping us, but did a complete about-face.*
▸*v.* [*intrans.*] turn so as to face the opposite direction.
▸*exclam.* (**about face!**) (in military contexts) a command to make an about-face. ▷mid 19th cent.: shortening of *right-about face*.

a·bove /ə'bəv/ ▸*prep.* **1** in extended space over and not touching: *a display of fireworks above the town* | [with *v.*] *a cable runs above the duct.* ■ extending upward over: *her arms above her head.* ■ higher than and to one side of; overlooking: *in the hills above the capital | on the wall above the altar.* **2** at a higher level or layer than: *bruises above both eyes | small windows above the aisles.* ■ higher in grade or rank than: *at a level above the common people.* ■ considered of higher status or worth than; too good for: *she **married above her** | above reproach.* ■ in preference to: *they cynically chose profit above car safety.* ■ at a higher volume or pitch than: *above a whisper | it went unheard above the din.* **3** higher than (a specified amount, rate, or norm): *above average | above freezing | above sea level | the unemployment rate will **soar above** its present level.*
▸*adv.* at a higher level or layer: *place a quantity of mud in a jar with water above.* ■ higher in grade or rank: *an officer of the rank of superintendent or above.* ■ higher than a specified amount, rate, or norm: *boats of 31 ft. or above.* ■ (in printed text) mentioned earlier or further up on the same page: *the two cases described above | see above left* | [as *adj.*] *at the above address* | [as *n.*] *since writing **the above**, I have reconsidered.* ▷Old English *abufan* (as an adverb), from *a-* 'on' + *bufan* (from *bi* 'by' + *ufan* 'above').
▸*PHRASES* □ **above all** (**else**) more so than anything else: *he was concerned above all to speak the truth.* □ **above oneself** conceited; arrogant. □ **from above** from overhead: *branches rained from above.* ■ from a position of higher rank or authority: *mass culture is imposed from above.* □ **not be above** be capable of stooping to (an unworthy act): *he was not above practical jokes.* □ **over and above** see OVER.

a·bove·board /ə'bəvˌbôrd/ ▸*adj.* legitimate, honest, and open: *certain transactions were not totally aboveboard.*
▸*adv.* legitimately, honestly, and openly: *the accountants acted completely aboveboard.*

ab o·vo /ab 'ōˌvō; äb/ ▸*adv.* from the very beginning. ▷early 18th cent.: Latin, literally 'from the egg.'

Abp. ▸*abbr.* Archbishop.

ab·ra·ca·dab·ra /ˌabrəkəˈdabrə/ ▸*exclam.* a word said by magicians when performing a magic trick.
▸*n. informal* the implausibly easy achievement of difficult feats: *where a computer and a little abracadabra turn a freeze-dried steak into a romantic dinner.* ■ language, typically in the form of gibberish, used to give the impression of arcane knowledge or power: *I get so fed up with all the mumbo jumbo and abracadabra.* ▷late 17th cent. (as a mystical word engraved and used as a charm to ward off illness): from Latin, first recorded in a 2nd-cent. poem by Q. Serenus Sammonicus, from a Greek base.

a·brade /əˈbrād/ ▸*v.* [*trans.*] scrape or wear away by friction or erosion: *a landscape slowly abraded by a fine, stinging dust.* ▷late 17th cent.: from Latin *abradere,* from *ab-* 'away, from' + *radere* 'to scrape.' —**a·brad·er** *n.*

A·bra·ham /ˈābrəˌham/ (in the Bible) the Hebrew patriarch from whom all Jews trace their descent (Gen. 11:27–25:10).

A·bra·ham, Plains of see **PLAINS OF ABRAHAM.**

A·bra·ham·ic /ˌābrəˈhamik/ (also **a·bra·ham·ic**) ▸*adj.* **1** denoting any or all of the religions (Judaism, Christianity, and Islam) that revere Abraham, the Biblical patriarch: *the monotheistic faiths that grew out of the Abrahamic heritage.* **2** relating specifically to the Biblical patriarch Abraham.

A·bra·hams /ˈābrəˌhamz/, Harold (Maurice) (1899–1978), English athlete. In 1924 he became the first Englishman to win the 100 meters in the Olympic Games. His story was retold in the movie *Chariots of Fire* (1981).

a·bra·sion /əˈbrāzʜən/ ▸*n.* the process of scraping or wearing away: *the metal is resistant to abrasion.* ■ an area damaged by scraping or wearing away: *there were cuts and abrasions to the lips and jaw.* ▷mid 17th cent.: from Latin *abrasio(n-),* from the verb *abradere* (see **ABRADE**).

a·bra·sive /əˈbrāsiv; -ziv/ ▸*adj.* (of a substance or material) capable of polishing or cleaning a hard surface by rubbing or grinding. ■ tending to rub or graze the skin: *the trees were abrasive to the touch.* ■ *figurative* (of sounds or music) rough to the ear; harsh: *fast abrasive rhythms.* ■ *figurative* (of a person or manner) showing little concern for the feelings of others; harsh: *her abrasive and arrogant personal style won her few friends.*
▸*n.* a substance used for grinding, polishing, or cleaning a hard surface. ▷mid 19th cent. (as a noun): from Latin *abras-* 'abraded,' from the verb *abradere* (see **ABRADE**), + **-IVE**.

a·bra·zo /əˈbräsō/ ▸*n.* (*pl.* **-zos**) an embrace. ▷Spanish.

ab·re·act /ˌabrēˈakt/ ▸*v.* [*trans.*] *Psychology* release (an emotion) by abreaction. ■ cause (someone) to undergo abreaction. ▷early 20th cent.: back-formation from **ABREACTION**.

ab·re·ac·tion /ˌabrēˈaksʜən/ ▸*n. Psychology* the expression and consequent release of a previously repressed emotion, achieved through reliving the experience that caused it (typically through hypnosis or suggestion). ▷early 20th cent.: from **AB-** 'away from' + **REACTION**, translating German *Abreagierung.* —**ab·re·ac·tive** /-tiv/ *adj.*

a·breast /əˈbrest/ ▸*adv.* **1** side by side and facing the same way: *the path was wide enough for two people to walk abreast | they were riding three abreast.* **2** alongside or even with something: *the cart came* **abreast of** *the Americans in their ricksha.* ■ *figurative* up to date with the latest news, ideas, or information: ***keeping abreast of*** *developments.* ▷late Middle English: from **A-**[2] 'in' + **BREAST**.

a·bridge /əˈbrij/ ▸*v.* [*trans.*] (usu. **be abridged**) **1** shorten (a book, movie, speech, or other text) without losing the sense: *the cassettes have been abridged from the original stories* | [as *adj.*] (**abridged**) *an abridged text of his speech.* **2** *Law* curtail (rights or privileges): *even the right to free speech can be abridged.* ▷Middle English (in the sense 'deprive of'): from Old French *abregier,* from late Latin *abbreviare* 'cut short' (see **ABBREVIATE**). —**a·bridg·er** *n.*

a·bridg·ment /əˈbrijmənt/ (also **a·bridge·ment**) ▸*n.* **1** a shortened version of a larger work: *an abridgment of Shakespeare's Henry VI.* **2** *Law* a curtailment of rights: *the abridgment of the rights of ownership.* ▷late Middle English: from Old French *abregement,* from the verb *abreg(i)er* (see **ABRIDGE**).

a·broad /əˈbrôd/ ▸*adv.* **1** in or to a foreign country or countries: *we usually* **go abroad** *for a week in May | competition from companies* **at home and abroad.** ■ *dated* or *humorous* out of doors: *few people ventured abroad from their warm houses.* **2** in different directions; over a wide area: *millions of seeds are annually scattered abroad.* ■ (of a feeling or rumor) widely current: *there is a new buccaneering spirit abroad.* ■ freely moving about: *con artists abroad on the streets of the town.* **3** *archaic* wide of the mark; in error.
▸*n.* foreign countries considered collectively: *servicemen returning* **from abroad.** ▷Middle English: from **A-**[2] 'on' + **BROAD**.

ab·ro·gate /ˈabrəˌgāt/ ▸*v.* [*trans.*] *formal* repeal or do away with (a law, right, or formal agreement): *a proposal to abrogate temporarily the right to strike.* See note at **VOID**. ▷early 16th cent.: from Latin *abrogat-* 'repealed,' from the verb *abrogare,* from *ab-* 'away, from' + *rogare* 'propose a law.' —**ab·ro·ga·tion** /ˌabrəˈgāsʜən/ *n.*

> *USAGE* The verbs **abrogate** and **arrogate** are quite different in meaning. While **abrogate** means 'repeal (a law),' **arrogate** means 'take or claim (something) for oneself without justification,' often in the structure *arrogate something to oneself,* as in *the emergency committee arrogated to itself whatever powers it chose.*

ab·rupt /əˈbrəpt/ ▸*adj.* **1** sudden and unexpected: *I was surprised by the abrupt change of subject | our round of golf came to an abrupt end on the 13th hole.* **2** brief to the point of rudeness; curt: *you were rather abrupt with that young man.* ■ (of a style of speech or writing) not flowing smoothly; disjointed. **3** steep; precipitous: *the abrupt double peak of the mountain.* ▷late 16th cent.: from Latin *abruptus* 'broken off, steep,' past participle of *abrumpere,* from *ab-* 'away, from' + *rumpere* 'break.' —**ab·rupt·ly** *adv.* —**ab·rupt·ness** *n.*

ab·rup·tion /əˈbrəpsʜən/ ▸*n. technical* the sudden breaking away of a portion from a mass. ■ (also **placental abruption**) *Medicine* separation of the placenta from the wall of the uterus, esp. when it occurs prematurely during pregnancy. ▷early 17th cent.: from Latin *abruptio(n)-,* from *abrumpere* 'break off' (see **ABRUPT**).

ABS ▸*abbr.* ■ acrylonitrile-butadiene-styrene, a composite plastic used to make car bodies and cases for computers and other appliances. ■ anti-lock braking system (for motor vehicles).

abs /abz/ *informal* ▸*n.* the abdominal muscles.

abs- ▸*prefix* variant spelling of **AB-** before *c, q,* and *t* (as in *abscond, abstain*).

Ab·sa·ro·ka Range /abˈsärəkə/ a range of the Rocky Mountains in Montana and Wyoming.

ab·scess /ˈabˌses/ ▸*n.* a swollen area within body tissue, containing an accumulation of pus. ▷mid 16th cent.: from Latin *abscessus* 'a going away,' from the verb *abscedere,* from *ab-* 'away from' + *cedere* 'go,' referring to the elimination of infected matter via the pus.

ab·scise /abˈsīz/ ▸*v.* [*trans.*] cut off or away. ■ [*intrans.*] *Botany* separate by abscission; fall off.

ab·scis·ic ac·id /abˈsisik/ ▸*n. Biochemistry* a plant hormone that promotes leaf detachment, induces seed and bud dormancy, and inhibits germination. ▷1960s: *abscisic* from the earlier name for the hormone *abscisin,* from **ABSCISSION**.

ab·scis·sa /abˈsisə/ ▸*n.* (*pl.* **-scis·sae** /-ˈsisē/ or **-scis·sas**) *Mathematics* (in a system of coordinates) the *x*-coordinate, the distance from a point to the vertical or *y*-axis measured parallel to the horizontal or *x*-axis. Compare with **ORDINATE**. ▷early 17th cent. (denoting the part of a line between a point on it and the point of intersection with an ordinate): from modern Latin *abscissa (linea)* 'cutoff (line),' feminine past participle of *abscindere* (see **ABSCISSION**).

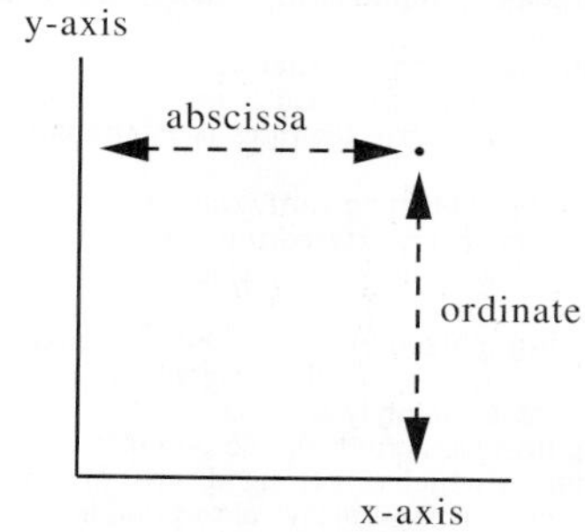

y-axis
abscissa
ordinate
x-axis

abscissa and ordinate

ab·scis·sion /abˈsizʜən/ ▸*n. Botany* the natural detachment of parts of a plant, typically dead leaves and ripe fruit. ■ any act of cutting off. ▷early 17th cent.: from Latin *abscissio(n-),* from *abscindere,* from *ab-* 'off, away' + *scindere* 'to cut.'

ab·scond /abˈskänd/ ▸*v.* [*intrans.*] leave hurriedly and secretly, typically to avoid detection of or arrest for an unlawful action such as theft: *she absconded with the remaining thousand dollars.* ■ (of someone on bail) fail to surrender oneself for custody at the appointed time. ■ (of a person kept in detention or under supervision) escape: *176 detainees absconded.* ■ (of a colony of honeybees, esp. Africanized ones) entirely abandon a hive or nest. ▷mid 16th cent. (in the sense 'hide, conceal (oneself)'): from Latin *abscondere* 'hide,' from *ab-* 'away, from' + *condere* 'stow.' —**ab·scond·er** *n.*

ab·seil /ˈäpˌzīl; ˈabˌsāl/ ▸*n.* & *v.* another term for **RAPPEL**. ▷1930s: from German *abseilen,* from *ab* 'down' + *Seil* 'rope.' —**ab·seil·er** *n.*

ab·sence /ˈabsəns/ ▸*n.* the state of being away from a place or person: *the letter had arrived during his absence | I supervised the rehearsal* **in the absence of** *the director.* ■ an occasion or period of being away from a place or person: *repeated absences from school.* ■ (**absence of**) the nonexistence or lack of: *she found his total absence of facial expression disconcerting.* See note at **LACK**. ▷late Middle English: from Old French, from Latin *absentia,* from *absens, absent-* (see **ABSENT**).
▸*PHRASES* □ **absence makes the heart grow fonder** *proverb* you feel more affection for those you love when parted from them. □ **absence of mind** failure to concentrate on or remember what one is doing.

ab·sent ▸*adj.* /ˈabsənt/ **1** not present in a place or at an occasion: *most students were* **absent from** *school at least once | absent colleagues.* ■ (of a part or feature of the body) not forming part of a creature in which it might be expected: *wings are absent in several species of crane flies.* **2** (of an expression or manner) showing that someone is not paying attention to what is being said or done: *she looked up with an absent smile.*
▸*v.* /abˈsent/ (**absent oneself**) stay or go away: *various people absented themselves because of his presence | halfway through the meal, he* **absented himself from** *the table.*
▸*prep.* /abˈsent/ *formal* without: *employees could not be fired absent other evidence.* ▷Middle English: via Old French from Latin *absens, absent-* 'being absent,' present participle of *abesse,* from *ab-* 'from, away' + *esse* 'to be.' —**ab·sent·ly** *adv.* (in sense 2).

ab·sen·tee /ˌabsənˈtē/ ▸*n.* a person who is expected or required to be present at a place or event but is not.

ab·sen·tee bal·lot ▸*n.* a ballot completed and typically mailed in advance of an election by a voter who is unable to be present at the polls.

ab·sen·tee·ism /ˌabsənˈtēˌizəm/ ▸*n.* the practice of regularly staying away from work or school without good reason.

ab·sen·tee land·lord ▸*n.* a landlord who does not live at and rarely visits the property that they rent out.

ab·sent·mind·ed /ˈabsəntˌmīndid/ ▸*adj.* (of a person or a person's behavior or manner) having or showing a habitually forgetful or inattentive disposition: *an absentminded smile.* —**ab·sent·mind·ed·ly** *adv.* —**ab·sent·mind·ed·ness** *n.*

ab·sinthe /ˈabˌsinтʜ/ (also **ab·sinth**) ▸*n.* **1** the shrub wormwood. ■ an essence made from this. **2** a potent green aniseed-flavored liqueur that turns milky when water is added. Prepared from wormwood, it is now largely banned because of its toxicity. ▷late Middle English: from French *absinthe,* from Latin *absinthium,* from Greek *apsinthion* 'wormwood.'

ab·sit o·men /ˈabsit/ ▸*exclam.* used to express the hope that a reference to something undesirable should not foreshadow its arrival or occurrence. ▷late 16th cent.: Latin, literally 'may this (evil) omen be absent.'

ab·so·lute /ˈabsəˌlo͞ot; ˌabsəˈlo͞ot/ ▸*adj.* **1** not qualified or diminished in any way; total: *absolute secrecy | absolute silence | the attention he gave you was absolute.* ■ used for general emphasis when expressing an opinion: *the policy is absolute folly.* ■ (of powers or rights) not subject to any limitation; unconditional: *no one dared challenge her absolute authority | human right to life is absolute.* ■ (of a ruler) having unrestricted power: *he proclaimed himself absolute monarch.* ■ *Law* (of a decree) final: *the decree of nullity was made absolute.* ■ *Law* see **ABSOLUTE TITLE**. **2** viewed or existing independently and not in relation to other

Pronunciation Key ə *ago;* ər *over;* ˈə or ˌə *up;* ˈər or ˌər *fur;* a *hat;* ā *rate;* ä *car;* cʜ *chew;* e *let;* ē *see;* e(ə)r *air;* i *fit;* ī *by;* i(ə)r *ear;* ɴɢ *sing;* ō *go;* ô *for;* oi *boy;* o͝o *good;* o͞o *goo;* ou *out;* sʜ *she;* тʜ *thin;* T͟H *then;* (h)w *why;* zʜ *vision*

things; not relative or comparative: *absolute moral standards.* ■ *Grammar* (of a construction) syntactically independent of the rest of the sentence, as in *dinner being over, we left the table.* ■ *Grammar* (of a transitive verb) used without an expressed object (e.g., *guns kill*). ■ *Grammar* (of an adjective) used without an expressed noun (e.g., *the brave*).

▸*n. Philosophy* a value or principle that is regarded as universally valid or that may be viewed without relation to other things: *good and evil are presented as absolutes.* ■ (**the absolute**) *Philosophy* that which exists without being dependent on anything else. ■ (**the absolute**) *Theology* ultimate reality; God. ▷late Middle English: from Latin *absolutus* 'freed, unrestricted,' past participle of *absolvere* (see ABSOLVE). **—ab·so·lute·ness** *n.*

ab·so·lute ad·van·tage ▸*n. Economics* the ability of an individual or group to carry out a particular economic activity more efficiently than another individual or group.

ab·so·lute al·co·hol ▸*n.* ethanol containing less than one percent of water by weight.

ab·so·lute·ly /ˌabsəˈlo͞otlē/ ▸*adv.* **1** with no qualification, restriction, or limitation; totally: *she trusted him absolutely* | [as *submodifier*] *you're absolutely right.* ■ used to emphasize the truth or appropriateness of a very strong or exaggerated statement: *he absolutely adores that car* [as *submodifier*] *Dad was absolutely furious.* ■ [with *negative*] none whatsoever: *she had absolutely no idea what he was talking about.* ■ [*sentence adverb*] used to emphasize a statement or opinion: *it's absolutely pouring out there* | *it's absolutely ages since I went to a party.* ■ [as *exclam.*] *informal* used to express and emphasize one's assent or agreement: *"Did they give you a free hand when you joined the band?" "Absolutely!"* **2** independently; not viewed in relation to other things or factors: *white-collar crime increased both absolutely and in comparison with other categories.* ■ *Grammar* (of a verb) without a stated object.

ab·so·lute mag·ni·tude ▸*n. Astronomy* the magnitude (brightness) of a celestial object as it would be seen at a standard distance of 10 parsecs. Compare with APPARENT MAGNITUDE.

ab·so·lute ma·jor·i·ty ▸*n.* a majority over all rivals combined; more than half.

ab·so·lute mu·sic ▸*n.* instrumental music composed purely as music, and not intended to represent or illustrate something else. Compare with PROGRAM MUSIC.

ab·so·lute pitch ▸*n. Music* the ability to recognize the pitch of a note or produce any given note; perfect pitch. ■ pitch according to a fixed standard defined by the frequency of the sound vibration.

ab·so·lute tem·per·a·ture ▸*n.* a temperature measured from absolute zero in kelvins. (Symbol: **T**)

ab·so·lute ti·tle ▸*n. Law* guaranteed title to the ownership of a property or lease.

ab·so·lute u·nit ▸*n.* a unit of measurement that is defined in terms of the fundamental units of a system (mass, length, and time) and is not based on arbitrary definitions.

ab·so·lute val·ue ▸*n.* **1** *Mathematics* the magnitude of a real number without regard to its sign. Also called MODULUS. • The absolute value of a complex number $a + ib$ is the positive square root of $a^2 + b^2$. **2** *technical* the actual magnitude of a numerical value or measurement, irrespective of its relation to other values.

ab·so·lute ze·ro ▸*n.* the lowest temperature that is theoretically possible, at which the motion of particles that constitutes heat would be minimal. It is zero on the Kelvin scale, equivalent to –273.15°C or –459.67°F.

ab·so·lu·tion /ˌabsəˈlo͞osHən/ ▸*n.* formal release from guilt, obligation, or punishment. ■ an ecclesiastical declaration of forgiveness of sins: *the priest administered absolution.* ▷Middle English: via Old French from Latin *absolutio(n-)*, from the verb *absolvere* (see ABSOLVE).

ab·so·lut·ism /ˈabsəlo͞oˌtizəm/ ▸*n.* the acceptance of or belief in absolute principles in political, philosophical, ethical, or theological matters. **—ab·so·lut·ist** *n.* & *adj.*

ab·so·lut·ize /ˈabsəlo͞oˌtīz/ ▸*v.* [*trans.*] *chiefly Philosophy & Theology* make (or treat as) absolute. **—ab·so·lut·i·za·tion** /ˌabsəˌlo͞otiˈzāsHən/ *n.*

ab·solve /əbˈzälv; -ˈsälv/ ▸*v.* [*trans.*] set or declare (someone) free from blame, guilt, or responsibility: *the pardon* ***absolved*** *them* ***of*** *any crimes.* ■ *Christian Theology* give absolution for (a sin). ▷late Middle English: from Latin *absolvere* 'set free, acquit,' from *ab-* 'from' + *solvere* 'loosen.'

THE RIGHT WORD **absolve, acquit, exempt, exonerate, forgive, pardon, vindicate**

To varying degrees, all of these words mean to free from guilt or blame, and some are most frequently heard in a legal or political context.

Absolve is the most general term, meaning to set free or release—not only from guilt or blame, but from a duty or obligation (*absolved from her promise to serve on the committee*) or from the penalties for their violation.

Pardon is usually associated with the actions of a government or military official (*President Gerald Ford pardoned Richard Nixon following his resignation in the wake of the Watergate scandal*) and specifically refers to a release from prosecution or punishment.

It is usually a legal official who decides to **acquit** someone—that is, release someone from a specific and formal accusation of wrongdoing (*the court acquitted the accused due to lack of evidence*).

Exonerate suggests relief (its origin suggests the lifting of a burden), often in a moral sense, from a definite charge so that not even the suspicion of wrongdoing remains (*completely exonerated from the accusation of cheating*).

A person who is **vindicated** is also off the hook, usually due to the examination of evidence (*she vindicated herself by producing the missing documents*).

Exempt has less to do with guilt and punishment and more to do with duty and obligation (*exempt from paying taxes*).

To **forgive**, however, is the most magnanimous act of all: It implies not only giving up on the idea that an offense should be punished, but also relinquishing any feelings of resentment or vengefulness (*"To err is human; to forgive divine"*).

ab·so·nant /ˈabsənənt/ ▸*adj. archaic* discordant or unreasonable. ▷mid 16th cent.: from Latin *ab-* 'away, from' + *sonant-* 'sounding,' from *sonare*, on the pattern of words such as *dissonant*.

ab·sorb /əbˈzôrb; -ˈsôrb/ ▸*v.* [*trans.*] **1** take in or soak up (energy, or a liquid or other substance) by chemical or physical action, typically gradually: *buildings can be designed to absorb and retain heat* | *steroids are* ***absorbed into*** *the bloodstream.* ■ take in and assimilate (information, ideas, or experience): *she absorbed the information in silence.* ■ take control of (a smaller or less powerful entity), making it a part of oneself by assimilation: *the family firm was* ***absorbed into*** *a larger group.* ■ use or take up (time or resources): *arms spending absorbs roughly 2 percent of the national income.* ■ take up and reduce the effect or intensity of (sound or an impact): *deep-pile carpets absorbed all sound of the outside world.* **2** engross the attention of (someone): *the work absorbed him and continued to make him happy.* ▷late Middle English: from Latin *absorbere*, from *ab-* 'from' + *sorbere* 'suck in.' **—ab·sorb·er** *n.*

ab·sorb·a·ble /əbˈzôrbəbəl; -ˈsôr-/ ▸*adj.* able to be absorbed, esp. into the body. **—ab·sorb·a·bil·i·ty** /əbˌzôrbəˈbilitē; -ˌsôr-/ *n.*

ab·sorb·ance /əbˈzôrbəns; -ˈsôr-/ ▸*n. Physics* a measure of the capacity of a substance to absorb light of a specified wavelength. It is equal to the logarithm of the reciprocal of the transmittance.

ab·sorbed /əbˈzôrbd; -ˈsôrbd/ ▸*adj.* [*predic.*] intensely engaged; engrossed: *she sat in an armchair,* ***absorbed in*** *a book.* **—ab·sorb·ed·ly** /-bidlē/ *adv.*

ab·sorbed dose ▸*n. Physics* the energy of ionizing radiation absorbed per unit mass by a body, often measured in rads.

ab·sorb·ent /əbˈzôrbənt; -ˈsôr-/ ▸*adj.* (of a material) able to soak up liquid easily: *drain on absorbent paper towels.*

▸*n.* a substance or item that soaks up liquid easily. ▷early 18th cent.: from Latin *absorbent-* 'swallowing up,' from the verb *absorbere* (see ABSORB). **—ab·sorb·en·cy** *n.*

ab·sorb·ent cot·ton ▸*n.* fluffy wadding of a kind originally made from raw cotton, used for cleansing wounds, removing cosmetics, and padding delicate objects.

ab·sorb·ing /əbˈzôrbiNG; -ˈsôr-/ ▸*adj.* intensely interesting; engrossing: *an absorbing account of their marriage.* **—ab·sorb·ing·ly** *adv.*

ab·sorp·tion /əbˈzôrpsHən; -ˈsôrp-/ ▸*n.* **1** the process or action by which one thing absorbs or is absorbed by another: | *East Germany's* ***absorption into*** *West Germany* | *shock absorption.* ■ *Physics* the process or action by which neutrons are absorbed by the nucleus. **2** the fact or state of being engrossed in something: *her* ***absorption in*** *the problems of the Third World.* ▷late 16th cent. (in the sense 'the swallowing up of something'): from Latin *absorptio(n-)*, from *absorbere* 'swallow up' (see ABSORB). **—ab·sorp·tive** /-tiv/ *adj.*

ab·sorp·tion neb·u·la ▸*n. Astronomy* another term for DARK NEBULA.

ab·sorp·tion spec·trum ▸*n. Physics* a spectrum of electromagnetic radiation transmitted through a substance, showing dark lines or bands due to absorption of specific wavelengths. Compare with EMISSION SPECTRUM.

ab·squat·u·late /abˈskwäcHəˌlāt/ ▸*v.* [*intrans.*] *humorous* leave abruptly: *some overthrown dictator who had absquatulated to the U.S.A.* ▷mid 19th cent.: blend, simulating a Latin form, of *abscond*, *squattle* 'depart,' and *perambulate*. **—ab·squat·u·la·tion** /abˌskwäcHəˈlāsHən/ *n.*

ab·stain /abˈstān/ ▸*v.* [*intrans.*] **1** restrain oneself from doing or enjoying something: ***abstaining from*** *chocolate.* ■ refrain from drinking alcohol: *most pregnant women abstain or drink very little.* **2** formally decline to vote either for or against a proposal or motion: *forty-one voted with the opposition, and some sixty more abstained.* ▷late Middle English: from Old French *abstenir*, from Latin *abstinere*, from *ab-* 'from' + *tenere* 'hold.' **—ab·stain·er** *n.*

ab·ste·mi·ous /abˈstēmēəs/ ▸*adj.* not self-indulgent, esp. when eating and drinking: *"We only had a bottle." "Very abstemious of you."* ▷early 17th cent.: from Latin *abstemius* (from *ab-* 'from' + a word related to *temetum* 'strong drink') + **-ous**. **—ab·ste·mi·ous·ly** *adv.* **—ab·ste·mi·ous·ness** *n.*

ab·sten·tion /abˈstensHən/ ▸*n.* **1** an instance of declining to vote for or against a proposal or motion: *a resolution passed by 126 votes to none, with six abstentions.* **2** the fact or practice of restraining oneself from indulging in something; abstinence: *alcohol consumption versus abstention.* ▷early 16th cent. (denoting the act of keeping back or restraining): from late Latin *abstentio(n-)*, from the verb *abstinere* (see ABSTAIN). **—ab·sten·tion·ism** /-ˌnizəm/ *n.*

ab·sti·nence /ˈabstənəns/ ▸*n.* the fact or practice of restraining oneself from indulging in something, typically alcohol: *I started drinking again after six years of abstinence.* ▷Middle English: from Old French, from Latin *abstinentia*, from the verb *abstinere* (see ABSTAIN). **—ab·sti·nent** *adj.* **—ab·sti·nent·ly** *adv.*

THE RIGHT WORD **abstinence, abnegation, abstemiousness, continence, forbearance, moderation, temperance**

Abstinence implies voluntary self-denial and is usually associated with the non-indulgence of an appetite (*total abstinence from cigarettes and alcohol*).

Abstemiousness is the quality or habit of being abstinent; an abstemious person would be one who is moderate when it comes to eating and drinking.

Continence, **temperance**, and **moderation** all imply various forms of self-restraint or self-denial: *moderation* is the avoidance of extremes or excesses (*he drank in moderation*); *temperance* is habitual moderation, or even total abstinence, particularly with regard to alcohol (*the nineteenth-century temperance movement*); and *continence* (in this regard) refers to self-restraint with regard to sexual activity.

Forbearance is self-control, the patient endurance that characterizes deliberately holding back from action or response.

Abnegation is the rejection or renunciation of something that is generally held in high esteem (*abnegation of the Christian Church*), although it can also mean to refuse or deny oneself a particular right, claim, or convenience (*abnegation of worldly goods*).

ab·stract ▸*adj.* /abˈstrakt; ˈabˌstrakt/ existing in thought or as an idea but not having a physical or concrete existence: *abstract concepts such as love or beauty.* ■ dealing with ideas rather than events: *the novel was too abstract and esoteric to sustain much attention.* ■ not based on a particular instance; theoretical: *we have been discussing the problem in a very abstract manner.* ■ (of a word, esp. a noun) denoting an idea, quality, or state rather than a concrete object: *abstract words like truth or equality.* ■ of or relating to abstract art: *abstract pictures that look like commercial color charts.*

▸*v.* /abˈstrakt/ [*trans.*] **1** consider (something) theoretically or separately from something else: *to* ***abstract*** *science and religion* ***from*** *their historical context can lead to anachronism.* ■ [*intrans.*] form a general idea in this way: *he cannot form a general notion by* ***abstracting from*** *particulars.* **2** extract or remove (something): *applications to* ***abstract*** *more water* ***from*** *streams.* ■ used euphemistically to say that someone has stolen something: *his pockets contained all he had been able to* ***abstract from*** *the apartment.* ■ (**abstract oneself**) withdraw: *as our relationship deepened you seemed to abstract yourself.* **3** make a written summary of (an article or book): *staff who index and abstract material for an online database.*

▸*n.* /ˈabˌstrakt/ **1** a summary or statement of the contents of a book, article, or formal speech: *the abstracts must be as concise as possible.* **2** an abstract work of art: *a big unframed abstract.* **3** (**the abstract**) that which is abstract; the theoretical consideration of something: *the abstract must be made concrete by examples.* ▷Middle English: from Latin *abstractus*, literally 'drawn away,' past participle of *abstrahere*, from *ab-* 'from' + *trahere* 'draw off.' —**ab·stract·ly** *adv.* —**ab·strac·tor** /-tər/ *n.* (in sense 3 of the *v.*).

▸*PHRASE* □ **in the abstract** in a general way; without reference to specific instances: *there's a fine line between promoting U.S. business interests in the abstract and promoting specific companies.*

ab·stract art ▸*n.* art that does not attempt to represent external, recognizable reality but seeks to achieve its effect using shapes, forms, colors, and textures.

ab·stract·ed /abˈstraktid/ ▸*adj.* showing a lack of concentration on what is happening around one: *she seemed abstracted and unaware of her surroundings | an abstracted smile.* —**ab·stract·ed·ly** *adv.*

ab·stract ex·pres·sion·ism ▸*n.* a development of abstract art that originated in New York in the 1940s and 1950s and aimed at subjective emotional expression with particular emphasis on the creative spontaneous act (e.g., action painting). Leading figures were Jackson Pollock and Willem de Kooning. —**ab·stract ex·pres·sion·ist** *n.*

ab·strac·tion /abˈstrakSHən/ ▸*n.* **1** the quality of dealing with ideas rather than events: *topics will vary in degrees of abstraction.* ■ something that exists only as an idea: *the question can no longer be treated as an academic abstraction.* **2** freedom from representational qualities in art: *geometric abstraction has been a mainstay in her work.* ■ an abstract work of art. **3** a state of preoccupation: *she sensed his momentary abstraction.* **4** the process of considering something independently of its associations, attributes, or concrete accompaniments: *they tend to interpret Jesus's words* ***in abstraction from*** *any historical context.* **5** the process of removing something, esp. water from a river or other source: *the abstraction of water from springs and wells.* ▷late Middle English: from Latin *abstractio(n-)*, from the verb *abstrahere* 'draw away' (see **ABSTRACT**).

ab·strac·tion·ism /abˈstrakSHəˌnizəm/ ▸*n.* the principles and practice of abstract art. ■ the presentation of ideas in abstract terms. —**ab·strac·tion·ist** *n.*

ab·stract of ti·tle /ˈabˌstrakt/ ▸*n. Law* a summary giving details of the title deeds and documents that prove an owner's right to dispose of land, together with any encumbrances that relate to the property.

ab·struse /abˈstro͞os/ ▸*adj.* difficult to understand; obscure: *an abstruse philosophical inquiry.* See note at **OBSCURE.** ▷late 16th cent.: from Latin *abstrusus* 'put away, hidden,' from *abstrudere* 'conceal,' from *ab-* 'from' + *trudere* 'to push.' —**ab·struse·ly** *adv.* —**ab·struse·ness** *n.*

ab·surd /əbˈsərd; -ˈzərd/ ▸*adj.* (of an idea or suggestion) wildly unreasonable, illogical, or inappropriate: *it would be absurd to blame contemporary Germans for Nazi crimes | so you think I'm a spy? How absurd!* | [as *n.*] (**the absurd**) *he had a keen eye for the incongruous and the absurd.* ■ (of a person or a person's behavior or actions) foolish; unreasonable: *she was being absurd—and imagining things.* ■ (of an object or situation) arousing amusement or derision; ridiculous: *gym shorts and knee socks looked absurd on such a tall girl.* ▷mid 16th cent.: from Latin *absurdus* 'out of tune,' hence 'irrational'; related to *surdus* 'deaf, dull.' —**ab·surd·ly** *adv.*

THE RIGHT WORD **absurd, foolish, ludicrous, preposterous, ridiculous, unreasonable**

We call something **absurd** when it is utterly inconsistent with what common sense or experience tells us (*she found herself in the absurd position of having to defend the intelligence of a cockroach*).

Ludicrous applies to whatever is so incongruous that it provokes laughter or scorn (*a ludicrous suggestion that he might escape unnoticed if he dressed up as a woman*), and **ridiculous** implies that ridicule or mockery is the only appropriate response (*she tried to look younger, but succeeded only in making herself look ridiculous*).

Foolish behavior shows a lack of intelligence or good judgment (*it was foolish to keep that much money under a mattress*), while **unreasonable** behavior implies that the person has intentionally acted contrary to good sense (*his response was totally unreasonable in view of the fact that he'd asked for their honest opinion*).

Preposterous should be reserved for those acts or situations that are glaringly absurd or ludicrous. For example, it might be *unreasonable* to judge an entire nation on the basis of one tourist's experience and *foolish* to turn down an opportunity to visit that country on those grounds alone, but it would be *preposterous* to suggest that everyone who comes to the U.S. will be robbed at gunpoint.

ab·surd·ism /əbˈsərdˌizəm; -ˈzərd-/ ▸*n.* the belief that human beings exist in a purposeless, chaotic universe. —**ab·surd·ist** *adj.* & *n.*

ab·surd·i·ty /əbˈsərditē; -ˈzərd-/ ▸*n.* (*pl.* **-ties**) the quality or state of being ridiculous or wildly unreasonable: *Duncan laughed at the absurdity of the situation | the absurdities of haute cuisine.* ▷late Middle English (in the sense 'dissonance'): from Latin *absurditas*, from *absurdus* (see **ABSURD**).

a·bub·ble /əˈbəbəl/ ▸*adj.* [*predic.*] full of excitement and enthusiasm: *he was* ***abubble with*** *the news.* ▷1930s: from **A-**[2] 'in the process of' + **BUBBLE**.

A·bu Dha·bi /ˌäbo͞o ˈT͟Häbē; ˈdäbē/ the largest of the seven member states of the United Arab Emirates, lying between Oman and the Gulf coast; pop. 670,125. The former sheikhdom joined the federation of the United Arab Emirates in 1971. ■ the capital of this state; pop. 242,975. It is also the federal capital of the United Arab Emirates.

A·bu·ja /äˈbo͞oyä/ a newly built city in central Nigeria, designated in 1982 to replace Lagos as the national capital; pop. 378,670.

a·bu·li·a /əˈbo͞olēə/ (also **a·bou·li·a**) ▸*n.* an absence of willpower or an inability to act decisively, as a symptom of mental illness. ▷mid 19th cent.: coined from **A-**[1] 'without' + Greek *boulē* 'the will.'

Abu Mu·sa /ˌäbo͞o ˈmo͞osə/ a small island in the Persian Gulf. Formerly held by the emirate of Sharjah, it was occupied by Iran by agreement from 1971 until it was taken over by them in 1992.

A·bu·na /əˈbo͞onə/ ▸*n.* a title given to the Patriarch of the Ethiopian Orthodox Church. ▷Amharic, from Arabic *ʼabūnā* 'our father.'

a·bun·dance /əˈbəndəns/ ▸*n.* a very large quantity of something: *the tropical island boasts an* ***abundance of*** *wildlife.* ■ the quantity or amount of something, e.g., a chemical element or an animal or plant species, present in a particular area, volume, sample, etc.: *estimates of abundance of harp seals | the* ***relative abundances*** *of carbon and nitrogen.* ■ (in solo whist) a bid by which a player undertakes to make nine or more tricks. ■ the state or condition of having a copious quantity of something; plentifulness: *vines and figs grew* ***in abundance.*** ■ plentifulness of the good things of life; prosperity: *the growth of industry promised wealth and abundance.* ▷Middle English: from Latin *abundantia*, from *abundant-* 'overflowing,' from the verb *abundare* (see **ABOUND**).

a·bun·dant /əˈbəndənt/ ▸*adj.* existing or available in large quantities; plentiful: *there was abundant evidence to support the theory.* See note at **PREVALENT.** ■ [*predic.*] (**abundant in**) having plenty of something: *the riverbanks were abundant in wild plants.* ▷late Middle English: from Latin *abundant-* 'abounding,' from the verb *abundare* (see **ABOUND**).

a·bun·dant·ly /əˈbəndəntlē/ ▸*adv.* in large quantities; plentifully: *the plant grows abundantly in the wild.* ■ [as *submodifier*] extremely: *my boss* ***made it abundantly clear*** *that if I didn't like it, I should look for another job.*

a·buse ▸*v.* /əˈbyo͞oz/ [*trans.*] **1** use (something) to bad effect or for a bad purpose; misuse: *the judge abused his power by imposing the fines.* ■ make excessive and habitual use of (alcohol or drugs, esp. illegal ones). **2** treat (a person or an animal) with cruelty or violence, esp. regularly or repeatedly: *riders who abuse their horses should be prosecuted.* ■ assault (someone, esp. a woman or child) sexually: *he was a depraved man who had abused his two young daughters* | [as *adj.*] (**abused**) *abused children.* ■ use or treat in such a way as to cause damage or harm: *he had been abusing his body for years.* ■ speak in an insulting and offensive way to or about (someone): *the referee was abused by players from both teams.*

▸*n.* /əˈbyo͞os/ **1** the improper use of something: *alcohol abuse | an* ***abuse of*** *public funds.* ■ unjust or corrupt practice: *protection against fraud and abuse | human rights abuses.* **2** cruel and violent treatment of a person or animal: *a black eye and other signs of physical abuse.* ■ violent treatment involving sexual assault, esp. on a repeated basis: *young people who have suffered sexual abuse.* ■ insulting and offensive language: *waving his fists and* ***hurling abuse at*** *the driver.* ▷late Middle English: via Old French from Latin *abus-* 'misused,' from the verb *abuti*, from *ab-* 'away' (i.e., 'wrongly') + *uti* 'to use.'

a·bus·er /əˈbyo͞ozər/ ▸*n.* [usu. with *adj.*] someone who regularly or habitually abuses someone or something, in particular: ■ someone who makes excessive use of alcohol or illegal drugs: *intravenous drug abusers.* ■ someone who sexually assaults another person, esp. a woman or child: *an alleged child abuser.*

A·bu Sim·bel /ˌäbo͞o ˈsimbəl/ the site of two huge rock-cut temples in southern Egypt, built during the reign of Ramses II in the 13th century BC, and commemorating him and his first wife Nefertari. Following the building of the High Dam at Aswan, the monument was rebuilt higher on the hillside.

a·bu·sive /əˈbyo͞osiv; -ziv/ ▸*adj.* **1** extremely offensive and insulting: *abusive language | he became quite abusive and swore at her.* **2** engaging in or characterized by habitual violence and cruelty: *abusive parents | an abusive relationship.* **3** involving injustice or illegality: *the abusive and predatory practices of businesses.* —**a·bu·sive·ly** *adv.* —**a·bu·sive·ness** *n.*

a·bus·tle /əˈbəsəl/ ▸*adj.* [*predic.*] bustling; busy: *the main drag is always* ***abustle with*** *inventive sidewalk artists.* ▷1930s: from **A-**[2] 'in the process of' + **BUSTLE**[1].

a·but /əˈbət/ ▸*v.* (**a·but·ted, a·but·ting**) [*trans.*] (of an area of land or a building) be next to or have a common boundary with: *gardens abutting Great Prescott Street* | [*intrans.*] *a park* ***abutting on*** *an area of wasteland.* ■ touch or lean upon: *masonry may crumble where a roof abuts it.* ▷late Middle English: the sense 'have a common boundary' from Anglo-Latin *abuttare*, from *a-* (from Latin *ad* 'to, at') + Old French *but* 'end'; the sense 'lean upon' (late 16th cent.) from Old French *abouter*, from *a-* (from Latin *ad* 'to, at') + *bouter* 'strike, butt,' of Germanic origin.

a·bu·ti·lon /əˈbyo͞otlˌän/ ▸*n.* a herbaceous plant or shrub of the mallow family, native to warm climates and typically bearing showy yellow, red, or mauve flowers. • Genus *Abutilon*, family Malvaceae. ▷modern Latin, from Arabic *ūbūṭīlūn* 'Indian mallow.'

a·but·ment /əˈbətmənt/ ▸*n.* a structure built to support the lateral pressure of an arch or span, e.g., at the ends of a bridge. ■ the process of supporting something with such a structure. ■ a point at which something abuts against something else.

a·but·ter /əˈbətər/ ▸*n.* the owner of property that abuts (touches on) another.

a·buzz /əˈbəz/ ▸*adj.* [*predic.*] filled with a continuous humming sound: *the room was* ***abuzz with*** *mosquitoes* | (*figurative*) *the city was* ***abuzz with*** *rumors.*

ABV ▸*abbr.* alcohol by volume.

a·bysm /əˈbizəm/ ▸*n.* a literary or poetic term for **ABYSS**: *the abysm from which nightmares crawl.* ▷Middle English: from Old French *abisme*, medieval Latin *abysmus*, alteration of late Latin *abyssus* 'bottomless pit,' the ending being assimilated to the Greek ending *-ismos*.

a·bys·mal /əˈbizməl/ ▸*adj.* **1** *informal* extremely bad; appalling: *the quality of her work is abysmal.* **2** *poetic/literary* very deep. ▷mid 17th cent. (used literally as in sense 2): from **ABYSM**. Sense 1 dates from the early 19th cent. —**a·bys·mal·ly** *adv.*

a·byss /əˈbis/ ▸*n.* a deep or seemingly bottomless chasm: *a rope led down into the dark abyss* | (*figurative*) *I was stagnating in an abyss of boredom.* ■ *figurative* a wide or profound difference between people; a gulf: *the* ***abyss between*** *the two nations.* ■ *figurative* the regions of hell conceived of as a bottomless pit: *Satan's dark abyss.* ■ (**the abyss**) *figurative* a catastrophic situation seen as likely to occur: *teetering on* ***the edge of the abyss*** *of a total political wipeout.* ▷late Middle English (in the sense 'infernal pit'): via late Latin from Greek *abussos* 'bottomless,' from *a-* 'without' + *bussos* 'depth.'

a·byss·al /əˈbisəl/ ▸*adj. chiefly technical* relating to or denoting the depths or bed of the ocean, esp. between about 10,000 and 20,000 feet (3,000 and 6,000 m) down: *the genera found in the abyssal North Atlantic.* ■ *Geology* another term for **PLUTONIC** (sense 1). ▷mid 17th cent.: from late Latin *abyssalis* 'belonging to an abyss' (see **ABYSS**).

Pronunciation Key ə *ago*; ər *over*; ˈə or ˌə *up*; ˈər or ˌər *fur*; a *hat*; ā *rate*; ä *car*; CH *chew*; e *let*; ē *see*; e(ə)r *air*; i *fit*; ī *by*; i(ə)r *ear*; NG *sing*; ō *go*; ô *for*; oi *boy*; o͝o *good*; o͞o *goo*; ou *out*; SH *she*; TH *thin*; T͟H *then*; (h)w *why*; ZH *vision*

Ab·ys·sin·i·a /ˌabəˈsinēə/ former name for **ETHIOPIA.**

Ab·ys·sin·i·an /ˌabəˈsinēən/ ▸*adj. historical* of or relating to Abyssinia or its people.
▸*n.* **1** *historical* a native of Abyssinia. **2** (also **Abyssinian cat**) a domestic cat of a breed having long ears and short brown hair flecked with gray.

Ab·zug /ˈabˌzo͝og/, Bella (Savitsky) (1920–98), U.S. politician, lawyer, and women's rights activist. She helped to found Women Strike for Peace in 1961. Serving in Congress as a Democrat from New York, she fought for the rights of women and of the poor.

AC ▸*abbr.* ■ (also **ac**) alternating current: ■ (also **ac**) air conditioning: *a sedan with power steering and AC.* ■ before Christ. [from Latin *ante Christum.*] ■ appellation contrôlée: *AC Sauvignon and Chardonnay.* ■ athletic club. ■ (**ac.**) acre: *a 22-ac. site.*

Ac ▸*symbol* the chemical element actinium.

a/c ▸*abbr.* ■ account. [from the obsolete phrase *account current* denoting a continuous account detailing sums paid and received.] ■ (also **A/C**) air conditioning.

ac- ▸*prefix* variant spelling of **AD-** assimilated before *c* and *q* (as in *accept, acquit,* and *acquiesce*).

-ac ▸*suffix* forming adjectives that are also often (or only) used as nouns, such as *maniac.* Compare with **-ACAL.** ▷from Greek *-akos* via Latin *-acus* or French *-aque.*

a·ca·cia /əˈkāsʜə/ (also **a·ca·cia tree**) ▸*n.* a tree or shrub of warm climates that bears spikes or clusters of yellow or white flowers and is frequently thorny. • Genus *Acacia,* family Leguminosae: numerous species, including *A. senegal,* which yields gum arabic. ■ see **FALSE ACACIA.** ▷late Middle English: via Latin from Greek *akakia.*

ac·a·deme /ˌakəˈdēm; ˈakəˌdēm/ ▸*n.* the academic environment or community; academia: *bridging the gap between industry and academe* | **the groves of academe.** ▷late 16th cent. (in the sense 'academy'): from Latin *academia,* reinforced by Greek *Akadēmos* (see **ACADEMY**).

ac·a·de·mi·a /ˌakəˈdēmēə/ ▸*n.* the environment or community concerned with the pursuit of research, education, and scholarship: *he spent his working life in academia.* ▷1950s: from Latin (see **ACADEMY**).

ac·a·dem·ic /ˌakəˈdemik/ ▸*adj.* **1** of or relating to education and scholarship: *academic achievement* | *he had no academic qualifications.* ■ of or relating to an educational or scholarly institution or environment: *students resplendent in academic dress.* ■ (of an institution or a course of study) placing a greater emphasis on reading and study than on technical or practical work: *an academic high school that prepares students for the best colleges and universities.* ■ (of a person) interested in or excelling at scholarly pursuits and activities: *Ben is not an academic child but he tries hard.* ■ (of an art form) conventional, esp. in an idealized or excessively formal way: *academic painting.* **2** not of practical relevance; of only theoretical interest: *the debate has been largely academic.*
▸*n.* a teacher or scholar in a college or institute of higher education. ▷mid 16th cent.: from French *académique* or medieval Latin *academicus,* from *academia* (see **ACADEMY**). —**ac·a·dem·i·cal·ly** *adv.* [*sentence adverb*] .

ac·a·de·mi·cian /ˌakədəˈmisʜən; əˌkadə-/ ▸*n.* **1** an academic; an intellectual. **2** a member of an academy, esp. of the Royal Academy of Arts, the Académie Française, or the Russian Academy of Sciences. ▷mid 18th cent.: from French *académicien,* from medieval Latin *academicus* (see **ACADEMIC**).

ac·a·dem·i·cism /ˌakəˈdeməˌsizəm/ (also **a·cad·e·mism** /əˈkadəˌmizəm/) ▸*n.* adherence to formal or conventional rules and traditions in art or literature: *the opposition between academicism and creative authenticity.*

ac·a·dem·ic year ▸*n.* the period of the year during which students attend an educational institution, usually from September to June. Also called **SCHOOL YEAR.**

a·cad·e·my /əˈkadəmē/ ▸*n.* (*pl.* **-mies**) **1** a place of study or training in a special field: *a police academy.* ■ *historical* a place of study. ■ a secondary school, typically a private one: *he had passed all his finals at Ephebus Academy.* ■ (**the Academy**) the teaching school founded by Plato. **2** a society or institution of distinguished scholars, artists, or scientists, that aims to promote and maintain standards in its particular field: *the National Academy of Sciences.* ■ the community of scholars; academe: *a writing and publishing world outside the academy.* ▷late Middle English (denoting the garden where Plato taught): from French *académie* or Latin *academia,* from Greek *akadēmeia,* from *Akadēmos,* the hero after whom Plato's garden was named.

A·cad·e·my A·ward ▸*n. trademark* any of a series of awards of the Academy of Motion Picture Arts and Sciences in Hollywood given annually since 1928 for achievement in the movie industry in various categories; an Oscar.

A·ca·di·a /əˈkādēə/ a former French colony established in 1604 in the territory that now forms Nova Scotia in Canada. Contested by France and Britain, it was ceded to Britain in 1763, and French Acadians were deported to other parts of North America, esp. Louisiana. ▷from *Acadie,* the French name for Nova Scotia.

A·ca·di·an /əˈkādēən/ *chiefly historical* ▸*adj.* of or relating to Acadia or its people.
▸*n.* a native or inhabitant of Acadia. ■ *chiefly Canadian* a French-speaking descendant of the early French settlers in Acadia. ■ a descendant of the Acadians deported to Louisiana in the 18th century; a Cajun.

ac·a·jou /ˈakəˌzʜo͞o; -ˌjo͞o/ ▸*n.* **1** the wood of certain tropical timber-yielding trees, esp. mahogany. **2** another term for **CASHEW.** ▷late 16th cent.: from French, via Portuguese from Tupi *acajú.*

-acal ▸*suffix* forming adjectives from nouns and adjectives usually ending in *-ac,* such as *maniacal,* often making a distinction from nouns ending in *-ac* (as in *maniacal* compared with *maniac*).

a·cal·cu·li·a /ˌākalˈkyo͞olēə/ ▸*n. Medicine* loss of the ability to perform simple arithmetic calculations, typically resulting from disease or injury of the parietal lobe of the brain. ▷early 20th cent.: from **A-**[1] 'not' + Latin *calculare* 'calculate' + **-IA**[1].

acantho- (also **acanth-** before a vowel) ▸*comb. form* having thornlike characteristics. ▷from Greek *akantha* 'thorn.'

A·can·tho·ceph·a·la /əˌkanтʜōˈsefələ/ *Zoology* a small phylum of parasitic invertebrates that comprises the thorny-headed worms. ▷modern Latin, from **ACANTHO-** 'thorn' + Greek *kephalē* 'head.' —**a·can·tho·ceph·a·lan** *adj.* & *n.* —**a·can·tho·ceph·a·lid** /-lid/ *adj.* & *n.*

ac·an·tho·di·an /ˌakənˈтʜōdēən/ ▸*n.* a small spiny-finned, jawed fossil fish of a group found chiefly in the Devonian period. • Class (or subclass) Acanthodii. ▷mid 19th cent.: from modern Latin *Acanthodii* (from **ACANTHO-**) + **-AN.**

a·can·thus /əˈkanтʜəs/ ▸*n.* **1** a herbaceous plant or shrub with bold flower spikes and spiny decorative leaves, native to Mediterranean regions. • Genus *Acanthus,* family Acanthaceae: many species. [via Latin from Greek *akanthos,* from *akantha* 'thorn,' from *akē* 'sharp point.'] **2** *Architecture* a conventionalized representation of an acanthus leaf, used esp. as a decoration for Corinthian column capitals.

acanthus 2

a cap·pel·la /ˌä kəˈpelə/ ▸*adj.* & *adv.* (with reference to choral music) without instrumental accompaniment: [as *adj.*] *an a cappella Mass* | [as *adv.*] *the trio usually performs a cappella.* ■ [as *adj.*] relating to or concerned with such music: *the English a cappella tradition.* ▷Italian, literally 'in chapel style.'

A·ca·pul·co /ˌäkəˈpo͞olkō; ˌak-; -ˈpo͞olkō/ a port and resort in southern Mexico, on the Pacific coast; pop. 592,290. Full name **ACAPULCO DE JUÁREZ** .

Ac·a·ri /ˈakəˌrī/ (also **Ac·a·ri·na** /akəˈrīnə/) *Zoology* a large order (or subclass) of small arachnids that comprises the mites and ticks. They are distinguished by an apparent lack of body divisions. ▷modern Latin (plural), from *acarus,* from Greek *akari* 'mite.' —**ac·a·rid** /-rid/ *n.* & *adj.* —**ac·a·rine** /-ˌrīn; -ˌrēn/ *n.* & *adj.*

a·car·i·cide /əˈkarəˌsīd; ˈakərə-/ ▸*n.* a substance poisonous to mites or ticks. ▷late 19th cent.: from Greek *akari* 'mite, tick' + **-CIDE.**

ac·a·rol·o·gy /ˌakəˈräləjē/ ▸*n.* the study of mites and ticks. ▷early 20th cent.: from Greek *akari* 'mite, tick' + **-LOGY.** —**ac·a·rol·o·gist** /-jist/ *n.*

a·cat·a·lec·tic /āˌkatlˈektik/ *Prosody* ▸*adj.* (of a line of verse) having the full number of syllables.
▸*n.* a line of verse of such a type.

Ac·ca·di·an /əˈkādēən/ ▸*n.* variant spelling of **AKKADIAN.**

ac·cede /akˈsēd/ ▸*v.* [*intrans.*] *formal* **1** assent or agree to a demand, request, or treaty: *the authorities did not* **accede to** *the strikers' demands.* **2** assume an office or position: *he* **acceded to** *the post of director in September.* ■ become a member of a community or organization: *Albania acceded to the IMF in 1990.* ▷late Middle English (in the general sense 'come forward, approach'): from Latin *accedere,* from *ad-* 'to' + *cedere* 'give way, yield.'

ac·cel·er·an·do /äkˌseləˈrändō; ak-; äˌcʜelə-/ *Music* ▸*adj.* & *adv.* with a gradual increase of speed (used chiefly as a direction).
▸*n.* (*pl.* **-dos** or **-di** /-dē/) a passage to be performed with such an acceleration. ▷Italian.

ac·cel·er·ant /akˈselərənt/ ▸*n.* a substance used to aid the spread of fire: *stolen accelerants could be used as firebombs.*
▸*adj.* accelerating or causing acceleration: *accelerant factors for carcinoma.*

ac·cel·er·ate /akˈseləˌrāt/ ▸*v.* [*intrans.*] (of a vehicle or other physical object) begin to move more quickly: *the car accelerated toward her.* ■ increase in amount or extent: *inflation started to accelerate* | [as *adj.*] (**accelerating**) *accelerating industrial activity.* ■ *Physics* undergo a change in velocity. ■ [*trans.*] cause to go faster: *the key question is whether stress accelerates aging.* ▷early 16th cent. (in the sense 'hasten the occurrence of'): from Latin *accelerat-* 'hastened,' from the verb *accelerare,* from *ad-* 'toward' + *celer* 'swift.' —**ac·cel·er·a·tive** /-ərətiv; -ˌrātiv/ *adj.*

ac·cel·er·at·ed learn·ing ▸*n.* **1** an intensive method of study employing techniques that enable material to be learned in a relatively short time. **2** a program of learning that allows certain students, esp. those more academically able, to progress through school more rapidly than others.

ac·cel·er·a·tion /akˌseləˈrāsʜən/ ▸*n.* increase in the rate or speed of something: *the acceleration of the industrialization process* | **an acceleration in** *the divorce rate.* ■ *Physics* the rate of change of velocity per unit of time. ■ a vehicle's capacity to gain speed within a short time: *a Formula One car is superior to an Indy car in its acceleration.*

ac·cel·er·a·tor /akˈseləˌrātər/ ▸*n.* something that brings about acceleration, in particular: ■ the device, typically a pedal, that controls the speed of a vehicle's engine. ■ *Physics* an apparatus for accelerating charged particles to high velocities. ■ a substance that speeds up a chemical process, typically the vulcanization of rubber or the curing of a plastic. ■ *Computing* short for **ACCELERATOR BOARD.**

ac·cel·er·a·tor board (also **accelerator card**) ▸*n.* an accessory circuit board that can be plugged into a small computer to increase the speed of its processor or input/output operations.

ac·cel·er·om·e·ter /akˌseləˈrämitər/ ▸*n.* an instrument for measuring acceleration, typically that of an automobile, ship, aircraft, or spacecraft, or that involved in the vibration of a machine, building, or other structure. ▷early 20th cent.: from **ACCELERATE** + **-METER.**

ac·cent ▸*n.* /ˈakˌsent/ **1** a distinctive mode of pronunciation of a language, esp. one associated with a particular nation, locality, or social class: *a strong German accent.* ■ the mode of pronunciation used by native speakers of a language: *she never mastered the French accent.* **2** a distinct emphasis given to a syllable or word in speech by stress or pitch. ■ a mark on a letter or word to indicate pitch, stress, or vowel quality. ■ *Music* an emphasis on a particular note or chord. **3** [in *sing.*] a special or particular emphasis: **the accent is on** *participation.* ■ a feature that gives a distinctive visual emphasis to something: *blue woodwork and accents of red.*
▸*v.* /ˈakˌsent; akˈsent/ [*trans.*] emphasize (a particular feature): *fabrics that accent the background colors in the room.* ■ *Music* play (a note, a beat of the bar, etc.) with an accent. ▷late Middle English (in the sense 'intonation'): from Latin *accentus* 'tone, signal, or intensity' (from *ad-* 'to' + *cantus* 'song'), translating Greek *prosōidia* 'a song sung to music, intonation.' —**ac·cen·tu·al** /akˈsencʜo͞oəl/ *adj.*

ac·cent·ed /ˈakˌsentid; akˈsen-/ ▸*adj.* **1** spoken with or characterized by a particular accent: *he spoke in slightly accented English.* **2** (of a word or syllable) marked with a stress or other accent.

ac·cen·tor /ˈaksentər/ ▸*n.* a small Eurasian songbird with generally drab-colored plumage. • Family Prunellidae and genus *Prunella*: several species. ▷early 19th cent.: from late Latin, from *ad-* 'to' + *cantor* 'singer.'

ac·cen·tu·ate /akˈsencʜo͞oˌāt/ ▸*v.* [*trans.*] make more noticeable or prominent: *his jacket unfortunately* *accentuated his paunch.* ▷mid 18th cent.: from medieval Latin *accentuat-* 'accented,' from the verb *accentuare*, from *accentus* 'tone' (see ACCENT).

ac·cen·tu·a·tion /ak,senCHo͞o'āsHən/ ▶*n.* the action of emphasizing something: *the accentuation of the Treasury's currency policy.* ■ the prominence of a thing relative to the normal: *a condition where there is an accentuation of female characteristics.* ■ the manner in which accents are apparent in pronunciation, or indicated in writing.

ac·cept /ak'sept/ ▶*v.* [*trans.*] **1** consent to receive (a thing offered): *he accepted a pen as a present.* ■ agree to undertake (an offered position or responsibility). ■ give an affirmative answer to (an offer or proposal); say yes to: *he would accept their offer and see what happened* | [*intrans.*] *Tim offered Brian a lift home and he accepted.* ■ *dated* say yes to a proposal of marriage from (a man): *Ronald is a good match and she ought to accept him.* ■ receive as adequate, valid, or suitable: *the college accepted her as a student* | *credit cards are widely accepted.* ■ regard favorably or with approval; welcome: *the Harvard literati never accepted him as one of them.* ■ agree to meet (a draft or bill of exchange) by signing it. ■ (of a thing) be designed to allow (something) to be inserted or applied: *vending machines that accepted 100-yen coins for cans of beer.* **2** believe or come to recognize (an opinion, explanation, etc.) as valid or correct: *this tentative explanation came to be accepted by the group* | [with *clause*] *it is accepted that aging is a continuous process* | [as *adj.*] (**accepted**) *he wasn't handsome in the accepted sense.* ■ be prepared to subscribe to (a belief or philosophy): *accept the tenets of the Episcopalian faith.* ■ take upon oneself (a responsibility or liability); acknowledge: *Jenkins is willing to accept his responsibility* | [with *clause*] *he accepts that he made a mistake.* ■ tolerate or submit to (something unpleasant or undesired): *they accepted the need to cut expenses.* ▷late Middle English: from Latin *acceptare*, frequentative of *accipere* 'take something to oneself,' from *ad-* 'to' + *capere* 'take.' —**ac·cept·er** *n.*

USAGE **Accept**, which means 'take (that which is offered),' may be confused with the verb **except**, which means 'exclude.' Thus: *I* **accept** *the terms of your offer, but I wish to* **except** *the clause calling for repayment of the deposit.*

ac·cept·a·ble /ak'septəbəl/ ▶*adj.* **1** able to be agreed on; suitable: *has tried to find a solution* **acceptable to** *everyone.* ■ adequate; satisfactory: *an acceptable substitute for champagne.* ■ pleasing; welcome: *some coffee would be most acceptable.* **2** able to be tolerated or allowed: *pollution in the city had reached four times the acceptable level.* ▷late Middle English: from Old French, from late Latin *acceptabilis*, from *acceptare* (see ACCEPT). —**ac·cept·a·bil·i·ty** /-,septə'bilitē/ *n.* —**ac·cept·a·ble·ness** *n.* —**ac·cept·a·bly** /-blē/ *adv.*

▶*PHRASE* □ **the acceptable face of** the tolerable or attractive manifestation or aspect of: *he presents himself as the acceptable face of gambling.*

ac·cept·ance /ak'septəns/ ▶*n.* **1** the action of consenting to receive or undertake something offered: *charges involving the acceptance of bribes* | [as *adj.*] *an acceptance speech* | *he had an acceptance from the magazine.* ■ agreement to meet a draft or bill of exchange, effected by signing it. ■ a draft or bill so accepted. **2** the action or process of being received as adequate or suitable, typically to be admitted into a group: *you must wait for acceptance into the club.* **3** agreement with or belief in an idea, opinion, or explanation: *acceptance of the teaching of the church.* ■ approval or favorable regard: *the options proposed by the report gained acceptance.* ■ willingness to tolerate a difficult or unpleasant situation: *a mood of resigned acceptance.* ▷mid 16th cent.: from Old French, from *accepter* (see ACCEPT).

ac·cept·ant /ak'septənt/ ▶*adj.* (**acceptant of**) *rare* willingly accepting. ▷late 16th cent.: from French, 'accepting,' present participle of *accepter* 'to accept.'

ac·cep·ta·tion /,aksep'tāsHən/ ▶*n.* a particular sense or the generally recognized meaning (**common acceptation**) of a word or phrase. ▷late Middle English (originally in the sense 'favorable reception, approval'): from late Latin *acceptatio(n-)*, from the verb *acceptare* (see ACCEPT). The current sense dates from the early 17th cent.

ac·cep·tor /ak'septər/ ▶*n.* a person or thing that accepts something, in particular: ■ a person or bank that accepts a draft or bill of exchange. ■ *Chemistry* an atom or molecule that is able to bind to or accept an electron or other species. ■ *Physics* such an atom forming a positive hole in a semiconductor.

ac·cess /'ak,ses/ ▶*n.* **1** a means of approaching or entering a place: *the staircase gives* **access to** *the top floor* | *wheelchair access* | *the building has a side access.* ■ the right or opportunity to use or benefit from something: *do you* **have access to** *a computer?* | *awards to help people* **gain access to** *training.* ■ the right or opportunity to approach or see someone: *we were* **denied access to** *our grandson.* ■ the action or process of obtaining or retrieving information stored in a computer's memory: *this prevents unauthorized access or inadvertent deletion of the file.* ■ the condition of being able to be reached or obtained: *a campaign to improve road access for the disabled.* ■ [as *adj.*] denoting noncommercial broadcasting produced by local independent groups, rather than by professionals: ***public-access television.*** **2** [in *sing.*] an attack or outburst of an emotion: *I was suddenly overcome with* **an access of** *rage.*

▶*v.* [*trans.*] (usu. **be accessed**) **1** *Computing* obtain, examine, or retrieve (data or a file). **2** approach or enter (a place): *single rooms have private baths accessed via the balcony.* **3** gain the right or opportunity to use or benefit from (something). ▷Middle English (in the sense 'sudden attack of illness'): from Latin *accessus*, from the verb *accedere* 'to approach' (see ACCEDE). Sense 1 is first recorded in the early 17th cent.

USAGE The verb **access** is standard and common in computing and related terminology. But its use outside computing contexts, although well established in the language, is sometimes criticized as being 'jargon' (*you must use a password to* **access** *the account*). Other words or phrases such as 'enter' or 'gain access to' are suggested as ready substitutes. For another example of a controversial formation of a verb from a noun, see **usage** at IMPACT.

ac·cess charge (also **access fee**) ▶*n.* a charge made for the use of computer or local telephone-network facilities.

ac·cess course ▶*n.* an educational course enabling those without traditional qualifications to become eligible for higher education.

ac·ces·si·ble /ak'sesəbəl/ ▶*adj.* **1** (of a place) able to be reached or entered: *the town is* **accessible by** *bus* | *the building has been made* **accessible to** *disabled people.* ■ (of an object, service, or facility) able to be easily obtained or used: *making learning opportunities more* **accessible to** *adults.* ■ easily understood: *his Latin grammar is lucid and accessible.* ■ able to be reached or entered by people in wheelchairs: *it provides specialized features such as nonslip floors and accessible entrances.* **2** (of a person, typically one in a position of authority or importance) friendly and easy to talk to; approachable: *he is more accessible than most tycoons.* ▷late Middle English: from late Latin *accessibilis*, from Latin *access-* 'approached,' from the verb *accedere* (see ACCEDE). —**ac·ces·si·bil·i·ty** /-,sesə'bilitē/ *n.* —**ac·ces·si·bly** /-blē/ *adv.*

ac·ces·sion /ak'sesHən/ ▶*n.* **1** the attainment or acquisition of a position of rank or power, typically that of monarch or president: *the queen's* **accession to the throne** | *lost the vote on the Fortas accession to the chief justiceship.* ■ the action or process of formally joining or being accepted by an association, institution, or group: *the accession of Spain and Portugal into the European Community.* **2** a new item added to an existing collection of books, paintings, or artifacts. ■ an amount added to an existing quantity of something: *did not anticipate any further accession of wealth from the man's estate.* **3** the formal acceptance of a treaty or agreement: *accession to the Treaty of Paris.*

▶*v.* [*trans.*] (usu. **be accessioned**) record the addition of (a new item) to a library, museum, or other collection. ▷late 16th cent. (in the general sense 'something added'): from Latin *accession-*, from the verb *accedere* 'approach, come to' (see ACCEDE).

ac·ces·so·rize /ak'sesə,rīz/ ▶*v.* [*trans.*] provide or complement (a garment) with fashion accessories: *the leisure suits were accessorized with white vinyl loafers and matching belts.* ■ serve as a fashion accessory to (a garment): *leggings accessorize the shortest skirts.*

ac·ces·so·ry /ak'ses(ə)rē/ (also **ac·ces·sa·ry**) ▶*n.* (*pl.* **-ries**) **1** a thing that can be added to something else in order to make it more useful, versatile, or attractive: *a range of bathroom accessories.* ■ a small article or item of clothing carried or worn to complement a garment or outfit: *among the hottest items are hair accessories such as rhinestone-studded barrettes.* **2** *Law* someone who gives assistance to the perpetrator of a crime, without directly committing it, sometimes without being present: *she was charged as an* **accessory to** *murder.*

▶*adj.* [*attrib.*] *chiefly technical* contributing to or aiding an activity or process in a minor way; subsidiary or supplementary: *functionally the maxillae are a pair of accessory jaws.* ▷late Middle English: from medieval Latin *accessorius* 'additional thing,' from Latin *access-* 'increased,' from the verb *accedere* (see ACCEDE).

▶*PHRASE* □ **accessory before** (or **after**) **the fact** *Law, dated* a person who incites or assists someone to commit a crime (or knowingly aids someone who has committed a crime).

ac·ces·so·ry cell ▶*n.* *Physiology* any of various cells of the immune system that interact with T cells in the initiation of the immune response.

ac·ces·so·ry min·er·al ▶*n.* *Geology* a constituent mineral present in small quantity and not taken into account in identifying a rock.

ac·ces·so·ry nerve ▶*n.* *Anatomy* each of the eleventh pair of cranial nerves, supplying certain muscles in the neck and shoulder.

ac·cess pro·vid·er ▶*n.* another term for SERVICE PROVIDER.

ac·cess road ▶*n.* a road giving access to a place or to another road.

ac·cess time ▶*n.* *Computing* the time taken to retrieve data from storage.

ac·ciac·ca·tu·ra /ä,cHäkə'to͝orə/ ▶*n.* (*pl.* **-tu·ras** or **-tu·re** /-'to͝orā; -'to͝orē/) *Music* a grace note performed as quickly as possible before an essential note of a melody. ▷Italian, from *acciaccare* 'to crush.'

ac·ci·dence /'aksidəns/ ▶*n.* the part of grammar that deals with the inflections of words. ▷early 16th cent.: from late Latin *accidentia* (translation of Greek *parepomena* 'things happening alongside'), neuter plural of the present participle of *accidere* 'happen' (see ACCIDENT).

ac·ci·dent /'aksidənt/ ▶*n.* **1** an unfortunate incident that happens unexpectedly and unintentionally, typically resulting in damage or injury: *he had an accident at the factory* | *if you are unable to work owing to accident or sickness* | [as *adj.*] *an accident investigator.* ■ a crash involving road or other vehicles, typically one that causes serious damage or injury: *four people were killed in a car accident.* ■ *informal* used euphemistically to refer to an incidence of incontinence, typically by a child or an animal. **2** an event that happens by chance or that is without apparent or deliberate cause: *the pregnancy was an accident* | ***it is no accident that*** *my tale features a tragic romance.* ■ the working of fortune; chance: *my faith is an* ***accident of birth,*** *not a matter of principled commitment* | *he came to Harvard largely through accident.* **3** *Philosophy* (in Aristotelian thought) a property of a thing that is not essential to its nature. ▷late Middle English (in the general sense 'an event'): via Old French from Latin *accident-* 'happening,' from the verb *accidere*, from *ad-* 'toward, to' + *cadere* 'to fall.'

▶*PHRASES* □ **an accident waiting to happen** **1** a potentially disastrous situation, typically caused by negligent or faulty procedures. **2** a person certain to cause trouble. □ **accidents will happen** however careful you try to be, it is inevitable that some unfortunate or unforeseen events will occur: *problems like these should not occur, but accidents will happen.* □ **by accident** unintentionally; by chance.

ac·ci·den·tal /,aksi'dentl/ ▶*adj.* **1** happening by chance, unintentionally, or unexpectedly: *a verdict of accidental death* | *the damage might have been accidental.* **2** incidental; subsidiary: *the location is accidental and contributes nothing to the tension between the characters in the poem.* **3** *Philosophy* (in Aristotelian thought) relating to or denoting properties that are not essential to a thing's nature.

▶*n.* **1** *Music* a sign indicating a momentary departure from the key signature by raising or lowering a note. **2** *Ornithology* another term for VAGRANT. ▷late Middle English (in senses 2 and 3 of the adjective): from late Latin *accidentalis*, from Latin *accident-* 'happening' (see ACCIDENT). —**ac·ci·den·tal·ly** *adv.*

THE RIGHT WORD **accidental, adventitious, casual, contingent, fortuitous, incidental**

Things don't always go as planned, but there are many ways to describe the role that chance plays.

Accidental applies to events that occur entirely by chance (*an accidental encounter with the candidate outside the men's room*); but it is so strongly influenced by the noun "accident" that it carries connotations of undesirable or possibly disastrous results (*an dental miscalculation of the distance he had to jump*).

A **casual** act or event is one that is random or unpremeditated (*a casual conversation with her son's teacher in the grocery store*), in which the role that chance plays is not always clear.

Something that is **incidental** may or may not involve chance; it typically refers to what is secondary or nonessential (*incidental expenses in the budget*) or what occurs without design or regularity (*incidental lighting throughout the garden*).

Adventitious also implies the lack of an essential relationship, referring to something that is a mere random occurrence (*adventitious circumstances that led to victory*).

In contrast, **contingent** points to something that is entirely dependent on an uncertain event for its existence or occurrence (*travel plans that are contingent upon the weather*).

Fortuitous refers to chance events of a fortunate nature; it is about as far as one can get from *accidental* (*a fortuitous meeting with the candidate outside the men's room just before the press conference*).

ac·ci·dent-prone ▶*adj.* tending to be involved in a greater than average number of accidents.

ac·ci·die /'aksidē/ ▶*n.* acedia. ▷Middle English: via Old French from medieval Latin *accidia*, alteration of **ACEDIA**. Obsolete after the 16th cent., the term was revived in the late 19th cent.

ac·cip·i·ter /ak'sipitər/ ▶*n. Ornithology* a hawk of a group distinguished by short, broad wings and relatively long legs, adapted for fast flight in wooded country. • *Accipiter* and related genera, family Accipitridae: numerous species, including the goshawk. ▷late 19th cent.: Latin, literally 'hawk, bird of prey.'

ac·cip·i·trine /ak'sipitrin; -ˌtrīn/ ▶*adj.* [*attrib.*] *Ornithology* of or relating to birds of a family that includes most diurnal birds of prey other than falcons, New World vultures, and the osprey. • Family Accipitridae; treated as a subfamily (Accipitrinae) in this sense when the osprey is included in this family. ▷mid 19th cent.: from French, from Latin *accipiter* 'bird of prey.'

ac·claim /ə'klām/ ▶*v.* [*trans.*] (usu. **be acclaimed**) praise enthusiastically and publicly: *the conference was* **acclaimed as** *a considerable success* | [*trans.*] *he was acclaimed a great painter.* See note at **PRAISE**.
▶*n.* enthusiastic and public praise: *she has won acclaim for her commitment to democracy.* ▷early 17th cent. (in the sense 'express approval,': from Latin *acclamare*, from *ad-* 'to' + *clamare* 'to shout.' The spelling has been influenced by association with **CLAIM**. Current senses date from the 17th cent.

ac·cla·ma·tion /ˌaklə'māsнən/ ▶*n.* loud and enthusiastic approval, typically to welcome or honor someone or something: *the tackle brought the fans to their feet in acclamation* | *the president was again greeted by the acclamations of all present.* ▷mid 16th cent.: from Latin *acclamatio(n-)*, from *acclamare* 'shout at,' later 'shout in approval' (see **ACCLAIM**).
▶*PHRASE* □ **by acclamation** **1** (of election, agreement, etc.) by overwhelming vocal approval and without ballot. **2** *Canadian* (of election) by virtue of being the sole candidate.

ac·cli·mate /'akləˌmāt; ə'klīmit/ ▶*v.* [*intrans.*] (usu. **be acclimated**) become accustomed to a new climate or to new conditions: *it will take a few days to get* **acclimated to** *the altitude.* ■ *Biology* respond physiologically or behaviorally to a change in a single environmental factor: *trees may* **acclimate to** *high CO_2 levels by reducing the number of stomata.* Compare with **ACCLIMATIZE**. ■ [*trans.*] *Botany & Horticulture* harden off (a plant). ▷late 18th cent.: from French *acclimater*, from *a-* (from Latin *ad* 'to, at') + *climat* 'climate.' **—ac·cli·ma·tion** /ˌaklə'māsнən/ *n.*

ac·cli·ma·tize /ə'klīməˌtīz/ ▶*v.* [*intrans.*] acclimate: *they* **acclimatized themselves** *before ascending Everest.* ■ *Biology* respond physiologically or behaviorally to changes in a complex of environmental factors. Compare with **ACCLIMATE**. ■ [*trans.*] *Botany & Horticulture* harden off (a plant). ▷mid 19th cent.: from French *acclimater* 'acclimatize' + **-IZE**. **—ac·cli·ma·ti·za·tion** /əˌklīmətə'zāsнən/ *n.*

ac·cliv·i·ty /ə'klivitē/ ▶*n.* (*pl.* **-ties**) an upward slope. ▷early 17th cent.: from Latin *acclivitas*, from *acclivis*, from *ad-* 'toward' + *clivus* 'a slope.' **—ac·cliv·i·tous** /-itəs/ *adj.*

ac·co·lade /'akəˌlād; -ˌläd/ ▶*n.* **1** an award or privilege granted as a special honor or as an acknowledgment of merit: *the ultimate official accolade of a visit by the president.* ■ an expression of praise or admiration. **2** a touch on a person's shoulders with a sword at the bestowing of a knighthood. ▷early 17th cent.: from French, from Provençal *acolada*, literally 'embrace around the neck (when bestowing knighthood),' from Latin *ad-* 'at, to' + *collum* 'neck.'

ac·com·mo·date /ə'käməˌdāt/ ▶*v.* [*trans.*] **1** (of physical space, esp. a building) provide lodging or sufficient space for: *the cabins accommodate up to 6 people.* **2** fit in with the wishes or needs of: *any language must accommodate new concepts.* ■ [*intrans.*] (**accommodate to**) adapt to: *making consumers accommodate to the realities of today's marketplace.* ▷mid 16th cent.: from Latin *accommodat-* 'made fitting,' from the verb *accommodare*, from *ad-* 'to' + *commodus* 'fitting.' **—ac·com·mo·da·tive** /-ˌdātiv/ *adj.*

ac·com·mo·dat·ing /ə'käməˌdātiNG/ ▶*adj.* fitting in with someone's wishes or demands in a helpful way. **—ac·com·mo·dat·ing·ly** *adv.*

ac·com·mo·da·tion /əˌkämə'dāsнən/ ▶*n.* **1** an action of accommodating or the process of being accommodated. ■ (usu. **accommodations**) a room, group of rooms, or building in which someone may live or stay: *the cost includes airfare and hotel accommodations.* ■ (**accommodations**) lodging; room and board: *the company offers a number of guesthouse accommodations in Cape Cod.* ■ the available space for occupants in a building, vehicle, or vessel: *there was lifeboat accommodation for 1,178 people.* ■ the provision of a room or lodging: *the building is used exclusively for the accommodation of guests.* **2** a convenient arrangement; a settlement or compromise: *management was seeking an accommodation with labor.* ■ the process of adapting or adjusting to someone or something: *accommodation to a separate political entity was not possible.* ■ the automatic adjustment of the focus of the eye by flattening or thickening of the lens. ▷early 17th cent.: from Latin *accommodatio(n-)*, from *accommodare* 'fit one thing to another' (see **ACCOMMODATE**).

ac·com·mo·da·tion·ist /əˌkämə'dāsнənist/ ▶*n.* a person who seeks compromise with an opposing point of view, typically a political one.

ac·com·mo·da·tion lad·der ▶*n.* a ladder or stairway up the side of a ship allowing access, esp. to and from a small boat, or from a dock.

ac·com·pa·ni·ment /ə'kəmp(ə)nimənt/ ▶*n.* **1** a musical part that supports or partners a solo instrument, voice, or group: *she sang to a guitar accompaniment* | *sonatas for piano with violin accompaniment.* ■ music played to complement or as background to an activity: *lush string accompaniments to romantic scenes in movies.* **2** something that is supplementary to or complements something else, typically food: *sugar snap peas make a delicious accompaniment for salmon.* ▷early 18th cent.: from French *accompagnement*, from *accompagner* 'accompany.'
▶*PHRASE* □ **to the accompaniment of** **1** with accompanying or background music or sound from: *we filed out to the accompaniment of the organ.* **2** with another event happening at the same time as: *the dam was completed to the accompaniment of numerous scandals.*

ac·com·pa·nist /ə'kəmpənist/ ▶*n.* a person who provides a musical accompaniment to another musician or to a singer.

ac·com·pa·ny /ə'kəmp(ə)nē/ ▶*v.* (**-nies, -nied**) [*trans.*] **1** go somewhere with (someone) as a companion or escort: *the two sisters were to accompany us to New York* | *he was at the banquet accompanied by his daughter.* **2** (usu. **be accompanied**) be present or occur at the same time as (something else): *the illness is often accompanied by nausea.* ■ provide (something) as a complement or addition to something else: *home-cooked ham accompanied by brown bread.* **3** play a musical accompaniment for. ▷late Middle English: from Old French *accompagner*, from *a-* (from Latin *ad* 'to, at') + *compagne*, from Old French *compaignon* 'companion.' The spelling change was due to association with **COMPANY**.

ac·com·plice /ə'kämplis/ ▶*n.* a person who helps another commit a crime. ▷mid 16th cent.: alteration (probably by association with **ACCOMPANY**) of Middle English *complice* 'an associate,' via Old French from late Latin *complex, complic-* 'allied,' from *com-* 'together' + the root of *plicare* 'to fold.'

ac·com·plish /ə'kämplisн/ ▶*v.* [*trans.*] achieve or complete successfully: *the planes accomplished their mission.* ▷late Middle English: from Old French *acompliss-*, lengthened stem of *acomplir*, based on Latin *ad-* 'to' + *complere* 'to complete.'

ac·com·plished /ə'kämplisнt/ ▶*adj.* highly trained or skilled: *an accomplished pianist.* ■ *dated* having a higher level of education than average and good social skills.

ac·com·plish·ment /ə'kämplisнmənt/ ▶*n.* something that has been achieved successfully: *the reduction of inflation was a remarkable accomplishment.* ■ the successful achievement of a task: *the accomplishment of planned objectives.* ■ an activity that a person can do well, typically as a result of study or practice: *long-distance running was another of her accomplishments.* ■ skill or ability in an activity: *a poet of considerable accomplishment.*

ac·cord /ə'kôrd/ ▶*v.* **1** [*trans.*] give or grant someone (power, status, or recognition): *the powers* **accorded to** *the head of state* | [with *two objs.*] *the young man had accorded her little notice.* **2** [*intrans.*] (**accord with**) (of a concept or fact) be harmonious or consistent with.
▶*n.* an official agreement or treaty. ■ agreement or harmony: *the government and the rebels are in accord on one point* | *function and form in harmonious accord.* ▷Old English, from Old French *acorder* 'reconcile, be of one mind,' from Latin *ad-* 'to' + *cor, cord-* 'heart'; influenced by **CONCORD**.
▶*PHRASES* □ **in accord with** according to. □ **of its own accord** without outside intervention: *the rash may go away of its own accord.* □ **of one's own accord** voluntarily: *he would not seek treatment of his own accord.* □ **with one accord** in a united way.

ac·cord·ance /ə'kôrdns/ ▶*n.* (in phrase **in accordance with**) in a manner conforming with: *the product is disposed of in accordance with federal regulations.* ▷Middle English: from Old French *acordance*, from *acorder* 'bring to an agreement' (see **ACCORD**).

ac·cord·ant /ə'kôrdnt/ ▶*adj.* [*predic.*] *archaic* agreeing or compatible: *I found the music* **accordant with** *the words of the service.* ▷Middle English: from Old French *acordant*, from *acorder* 'bring to an agreement' (see **ACCORD**).

ac·cord·ing /ə'kôrdiNG/ ▶*adv.* **1** (**according to**) as stated by or in: *the outlook for investors is not bright, according to financial experts.* ■ in a manner corresponding or conforming to: *cook the rice according to the instructions.* ■ in proportion or relation to: *salary will be fixed according to experience.* **2** (**according as**) depending on whether.

ac·cord·ing·ly /ə'kôrdiNGlē/ ▶*adv.* **1** in a way that is appropriate to the particular circumstances: *we have to discover what his plans are and act accordingly.* **2** [*sentence adverb*] consequently; therefore: *There was no breach of the rules. Accordingly, there will be no disciplinary inquiry.*

ac·cor·di·on /ə'kôrdēən/ ▶*n.* a portable musical instrument with metal reeds blown by bellows, played by means of keys and buttons: [as *adj.*] *an accordion player.* ■ [as *adj.*] folding like the bellows of an accordion: *an accordion pleat.* ▷mid 19th cent.: from German *Akkordion*, from Italian *accordare* 'to tune.' **—ac·cor·di·on·ist** /-nist/ *n.*

accordion

ac·cor·di·on sched·ul·ing ▶*n.* the practice of continually adjusting the work schedule of part-time or temporary workers to accommodate a company's changing labor requirements.

ac·cost /ə'kôst; ə'käst/ ▶*v.* [*trans.*] approach and address (someone) boldly or aggressively: *reporters accosted him in the street.* ■ approach (someone) with hostility or harmful intent: *he was accosted by a thief, demanding his money or his life.* ■ approach and address (someone) with sexual intent: *a man tried to accost the girl on her way to school.* ▷late 16th cent. (originally in the sense 'lie or go alongside'): from French *accoster*, from Italian *accostare*, from Latin *ad-* 'to' + *costa* 'rib, side.'

ac·couche·ment /ˌäko͞osн'mäN; ə'ko͞osнmənt/ ▶*n. archaic* the action of giving birth to a baby. ▷late 18th cent.: French, from *accoucher* 'act as midwife,' from *a-* (from Latin *ad* 'to, at') + *coucher* 'put to bed' (see **COUCH**).

ac·cou·cheur /ˌäko͞o'sнər/ ▶*n.* a male midwife. ▷mid 18th cent.: French, from *accoucher* (see **ACCOUCHEMENT**).

ac·count /ə'kount/ ▶*n.* **1** a report or description of an event or experience: *a detailed account of what has been achieved.* ■ an interpretation or rendering of a piece of music: *a lively account of Offenbach's score.* **2** (abbr.: **acct.**) a record or statement of financial expenditure or receipts relating to a particular period or purpose: *the ledger contains all the income and expense accounts* | *he submitted a quarterly account.* ■ the department of a company that deals with such records. **3** (abbr.: **acct.**) an arrangement by which a body holds funds on behalf of a client or supplies goods

or services to the client on credit: *a bank account | charge it to my account | I began buying things* ***on account.*** ■ the balance of funds held under such an arrangement: *I wanted to get some money from the ATM and check my account.* ■ a client having such an arrangement with a supplier: *selling bibles to established accounts in the North.* ■ a contract to do work periodically for a client: *another agency was awarded the account.* **4** importance: *money was* ***of no account*** *to her.*
▶*v.* [*trans.*] consider or regard in a specified way: *her visit could not be accounted a success | he* ***accounted himself*** *the unluckiest man alive.*
▶*phrasal v.* □ **account for 1** give a satisfactory record of (something, typically money, that one is responsible for). ■ provide or serve as a satisfactory explanation or reason for: *he was brought before the Board to account for his behavior.* ■ (usu. **be accounted for**) know the fate or whereabouts of (someone or something), esp. after an accident: *everyone was accounted for after the floods.* ■ succeed in killing, destroying, or defeating: *a mishit drive accounted for Jones, who had scored 32.* **2** supply or make up a specified amount or proportion of: *social security accounts for about a third of total public spending.* ▷Middle English (in the sense 'counting,' 'to count'): from Old French *acont* (noun), *aconter* (verb), based on *conter* 'to count.'
▶*PHRASES* □ **by** (or **from**) **all accounts** according to what one has heard or read: *by all accounts he is a pretty nice guy.* □ **call** (or **bring**) **someone to account** require someone to explain a mistake or poor performance. □ **give a good** (or **bad**) **account of oneself** make a favorable (or unfavorable) impression through one's performance. □ **keep an account of** keep a record of. □ **leave something out of account** fail or decline to consider a factor. □ **on someone's account** for a specified person's benefit: *don't bother on my account.* □ **on account of** because of. □ **on no account** under no circumstances: *on no account let anyone know we're interested.* □ **on one's own account** with one's own money or assets, rather than for an employer or client: *he began trading on his own account.* □ **settle** (or **square**) **accounts with** pay money owed to (someone). ■ have revenge on: *the dirty business of settling accounts with former Communists.* □ **take something into account** (or **take account of**) consider a specified thing along with other factors before reaching a decision or taking action. □ **there's no accounting for tastes** (or **taste**) *proverb* it is impossible to explain why different people like different things, esp. those things that the speaker considers unappealing. □ **turn something to** (**good**) **account** turn something to one's advantage.

USAGE Use with *as* (*we* ***accounted*** *him* ***as*** *wise*) is considered incorrect.

ac·count·a·ble /ə'kountəbəl/ ▶*adj.* **1** (of a person, organization, or institution) required or expected to justify actions or decisions; responsible: *government must be* ***accountable to*** *its citizens | parents could be* ***held accountable for*** *their children's actions.* See note at **RESPONSIBLE. 2** explicable; understandable: *the delayed introduction of characters' names is accountable, if we consider that names have a low priority.* —**ac·count·a·bil·i·ty** /ə,kountə'bilitē/ *n.* —**ac·count·a·bly** /-blē/ *adv.*

ac·count·an·cy /ə'kount(ə)nsē/ ▶*n.* the profession or duties of an accountant.

ac·count·ant /ə'kount(ə)nt/ (abbr.: **acct.**) ▶*n.* a person whose job is to keep or inspect financial accounts. ▷Middle English: from legal French, present participle of Old French *aconter* (see **ACCOUNT**). The original use was as an adjective meaning 'liable to give an account,' hence denoting a person who must do so.

ac·count ex·ec·u·tive ▶*n.* a business executive who manages the interests of a particular client, typically in advertising.

ac·count·ing /ə'kountiNG/ ▶*n.* the action or process of keeping financial accounts.

ac·counts pay·a·ble ▶*plural n.* money owed by a company to its creditors.

ac·counts re·ceiv·a·ble ▶*plural n.* money owed to a company by its debtors.

ac·cou·tre /ə'kōōtər/ (also **ac·cou·ter**) ▶*v.* (**-tred, -tring; -tered, -ter·ing**) [*trans.*] (usu. **be accoutred**) clothe or equip, typically in something noticeable or impressive. ▷mid 16th cent.: from French *accoutrer,* from Old French *acoustrer,* from *a-* (from Latin *ad* 'to, at') + *cousture* 'sewing' (see **COUTURE**).

ac·cou·tre·ment /ə'kōōtərmənt; -trə-/ (also **ac·cou·ter·ment**) ▶*n.* (usu. **accoutrements**) additional items of dress or equipment, or other items carried or worn by a person or used for a particular activity: *the accoutrements of religious ritual.* ■ a soldier's outfit other than weapons and garments. ▷mid 16th cent.: from French, from *accoutrer* 'clothe, equip' (see **ACCOUTRE**).

Ac·cra /'äkrə; 'akrə; ə'krä/ the capital of Ghana, a port on the Gulf of Guinea; pop. 867,460.

ac·cred·it /ə'kredit/ ▶*v.* (**-it·ed, -it·ing**) [*trans.*] (usu. **be accredited**) **1** give credit (to someone) for: *he was* ***accredited with*** *being one of the world's fastest sprinters.* ■ attribute (an action, saying, or quality) to: *the discovery of distillation is usually* ***accredited to*** *the Arabs.* **2** (of an official body) give authority or sanction to (someone or something) when recognized standards have been met: *institutions that do not meet the standards will not be accredited for teacher training.* **3** give official authorization for (someone, typically a diplomat or journalist) to be in a particular place or to hold a particular post: *Arab ambassadors* ***accredited to*** *Baghdad.* ▷early 17th cent. (sense 2): from French *accréditer,* from *a-* (from Latin *ad* 'to, at') + *crédit* 'credit.' —**ac·cred·i·ta·tion** /ə,kredi'tāSHən/ *n.*

ac·cred·it·ed /ə'kreditid/ ▶*adj.* (of a person, organization, or course of study) officially recognized or authorized: *an accredited chiropractic school.*

ac·crete /ə'krēt/ ▶*v.* [*intrans.*] grow by accumulation or coalescence: *ice that had accreted grotesquely into stalactites.* ■ [*trans.*] form (a composite whole or a collection of things) by gradual accumulation: *the collection of art he had accreted was to be sold.* ■ *Astronomy* (of matter) come together under the influence of gravitation; (of a body) be formed from such matter: *the gas will cool and then* ***accrete to*** *the galaxy's core.* ■ [*trans.*] *Astronomy* cause (matter) to come together in this way. ▷late 18th cent.: from Latin *accret-* 'grown,' from the verb *accrescere,* from *ad-* 'to' + *crescere* 'grow.'

ac·cre·tion /ə'krēSHən/ ▶*n.* the process of growth or increase, typically by the gradual accumulation of additional layers or matter: *the accretion of sediments in coastal mangroves |* (*figurative*) *the growing accretion of central government authority.* ■ a thing formed or added by such growth or increase: *about one-third of California was built up by accretions | the city has a historic core surrounded by recent accretions.* ■ *Astronomy* the coming together and cohesion of matter under the influence of gravitation to form larger bodies. ▷early 17th cent.: from Latin *accretion-,* from *accrescere* 'become larger' (see **ACCRETE**). —**ac·cre·tive** /ə'krētiv/ *adj.*

ac·cre·tion·ar·y prism /ə'kreSHə,nerē/ (also **accretionary wedge**) ▶*n. Geology* a mass of sedimentary material scraped off a region of oceanic crust during subduction and piled up at the edge of the overriding plate.

ac·cre·tion disk ▶*n. Astronomy* a rotating disk of matter formed by accretion around a massive body (such as a black hole) under the influence of gravitation.

ac·crue /ə'krōō/ ▶*v.* (**-crues, -crued, -cru·ing**) [*intrans.*] (of sums of money or benefits) be received by someone in regular or increasing amounts over time: *financial benefits will* ***accrue from*** *restructuring |* [as *adj.*] (**accrued**) *the accrued interest.* ■ [*trans.*] accumulate or receive (such payments or benefits). ■ [*trans.*] make provision for (a charge) at the end of a financial period for work that has been done but not yet invoiced. ▷late Middle English: from Old French *acreue,* past participle of *acreistre* 'increase,' from Latin *accrescere* 'become larger' (see **ACCRETE**). —**ac·cru·al** /ə'krōōəl/ *n.*

acct. ▶*abbr.* ■ account. ■ accountant.

ac·cul·tur·ate /ə'kəlCHə,rāt/ ▶*v.* assimilate or cause to assimilate a different culture, typically the dominant one: [*intrans.*] *those who have* ***acculturated to*** *the U.S.* [*trans.*] *the next weeks were spent acculturating the field staff* | [as *adj.*] (**acculturated**) *an acculturated Cherokee.* ▷mid 20th cent.: from **AC-** + **CULTURE** + **-ATE**[1]. The noun *acculturation* dates from the late 19th cent. —**ac·cul·tur·a·tion** /ə,kəlCHə'rāSHən/ *n.* —**ac·cul·tur·a·tive** /-ərətiv; -ə,rātiv/ *adj.*

ac·cum·bent ▶*adj. Botany* (of a cotyledon) lying edgewise against the folded radicle in the seed. ▷early 19th cent.: from Latin *accumbent-* 'reclining,' from *accumbere,* from *ad-* 'to' + a verb related to *cubare* 'to lie.'

ac·cu·mu·late /ə'kyōōmyə,lāt/ ▶*v.* [*trans.*] gather together or acquire an increasing number or quantity of: *investigators have yet to accumulate enough evidence.* ■ gradually gather or acquire (a resulting whole): *her goal was to accumulate a huge fortune.* ■ [*intrans.*] gather or build up: *the toxin accumulated in their bodies.* ▷late 15th cent.: from Latin *accumulat-* 'heaped up,' from the verb *accumulare,* from *ad-* 'to' + *cumulus* 'a heap.'

ac·cu·mu·la·tion /ə,kyōōmyə'lāSHən/ ▶*n.* the acquisition or gradual gathering of something: *the accumulation of wealth.* ■ a mass or quantity of something that has gradually gathered or been acquired: *the accumulation of paperwork on her desk.* ■ the growth of a sum of money by the regular addition of interest.

ac·cu·mu·la·tive /ə'kyōōmyələtiv; -,lātiv/ ▶*adj.* [*attrib.*] gathering or growing by gradual increases: *the accumulative effects of pollution.*

ac·cu·mu·la·tor /ə'kyōōmyə,lātər/ ▶*n.* a person or thing that accumulates things: ***accumulator of*** *capital.* ■ *Computing* a register used to contain the results of an arithmetical or logical operation.

ac·cu·ra·cy /'akyərəsē/ ▶*n.* (*pl.* **-cies**) the quality or state of being correct or precise: *we have confidence in the accuracy of the statistics.* ■ the ability to perform a task with precision: *she hit the ball with great accuracy.* ■ *technical* the degree to which the result of a measurement, calculation, or specification conforms to the correct value or a standard: *the accuracy of radiocarbon dating | accuracies of 50–70%.* Compare with **PRECISION**.

ac·cu·rate /'akyərit/ ▶*adj.* **1** (of information, measurements, statistics, etc.) correct in all details; exact: *accurate information about the illness is essential.* ■ (of an instrument or method) capable of giving such information: *an accurate thermometer.* ■ (of a piece of work) meticulously careful and free from errors. ■ faithfully or fairly representing the truth about someone or something: *the portrait is an accurate likeness of Mozart | we were fairly accurate in our predictions.* **2** (of a weapon or the person using it) capable of reaching the intended target. ■ (of a shot or throw, or the person making it) successful in reaching a target. ▷late 16th cent.: from Latin *accuratus* 'done with care,' past participle of *accurare,* from *ad-* 'toward' + *cura* 'care.' —**ac·cu·rate·ly** *adv.*

ac·curs·ed /ə'kərst; ə'kərsid/ ▶*adj.* **1** *poetic/literary* under a curse: *the Angel of Death walks this accursed house.* **2** [*attrib.*] *informal, dated* used to express strong dislike of or anger toward someone or something: *those accursed books!* ▷Middle English: past participle of obsolete *accurse,* from *a-* (expressing intensity) + **CURSE**.

ac·cu·sal /ə'kyōōzəl/ ▶*n.* another term for **ACCUSATION**.

ac·cu·sa·tion /,akyə'zāSHən; ,akyōō-/ ▶*n.* a charge or claim that someone has done something illegal or wrong: *accusations of bribery.* ■ the action or process of making such a charge or claim: *there was accusation in Brian's voice.* ▷late Middle English: from Old French, from Latin *accusatio(n-),* from *accusare* 'call to account' (see **ACCUSE**).

ac·cu·sa·tive /ə'kyōōzətiv/ *Grammar* ▶*adj.* relating to or denoting a case of nouns, pronouns, and adjectives that expresses the object of an action or the goal of motion.
▶*n.* a word in the accusative case. ■ (**the accusative**) the accusative case. ▷late Middle English: from Latin *(casus) accusativus,* literally 'relating to an accusation or (legal) case,' translating Greek *(ptōsis) aitiatikē* '(the case) showing cause.'

ac·cu·sa·to·ri·al /ə,kyōōzə'tôrēəl/ ▶*adj.* [*attrib.*] *Law* (esp. of a trial or legal procedure) involving accusation by a prosecutor and a verdict reached by an impartial judge or jury. Often contrasted with **INQUISITORIAL**.

ac·cu·sa·to·ry /ə'kyōōzə,tôrē/ ▶*adj.* indicating or suggesting that one believes a person has done something wrong: *he pointed an accusatory finger in her direction.*

ac·cuse /ə'kyōōz/ ▶*v.* [*trans.*] (often **be accused**) charge (someone) with an offense or crime: *he was* ***accused of*** *murdering his wife's lover.* ■ claim that (someone) has done something wrong: *he was* ***accused of*** *favoritism.* ▷Middle English: from Old French *acuser,* from Latin *accusare* 'call to account,' from *ad-* 'toward' + *causa* 'reason, motive, lawsuit.' —**ac·cus·er** *n.*

ac·cused /ə'kyōōzd/ ▶*n.* [treated as *sing.* or *pl.*] (**the accused**) a person or group of people who are charged with or on trial for a crime: *the accused was ordered to stand trial on a number of charges.*

ac·cus·ing /ə'kyōōziNG/ ▶*adj.* (of an expression, gesture, or tone of voice) indicating a belief in someone's guilt or culpability: *she stared at him with accusing eyes.* —**ac·cus·ing·ly** *adv.*

ac·cus·tom /ə'kəstəm/ ▶*v.* [*trans.*] make (someone or

A

something) accept something as normal or usual: *I accustomed my eyes to the lenses* | [*trans.*] *tried to accustom him to their lighthearted ways.* ■ (**be accustomed to**) be used to: *my eyes gradually became accustomed to the darkness.* ▷late Middle English: from Old French *acostumer*, from *a-* (from Latin *ad* 'to, at') + *costume* 'custom.'

ac·cus·tomed /əˈkəstəmd/ ▸*adj.* [*attrib.*] customary or usual: *his accustomed route.*

AC/DC ▸*adj.* alternating current/direct current. ■ *informal* bisexual.

ACE ▸*abbr.* Army Corps of Engineers.

ace /ās/ ▸*n.* **1** a playing card with a single spot on it, ranked as the highest card in its suit in most card games: *the ace of diamonds* | (*figurative*) *life had started dealing him aces again.* ■ *informal Golf* a hole in one. **2** [often with *adj.*] *informal* a person who excels at a particular sport or other activity: *a motorcycle ace.* ■ a pilot who has shot down many enemy aircraft, esp. in World War I or World War II. **3** (in tennis and similar games) a service that an opponent is unable to return and thus wins a point.
▸*adj. informal* very good: *an ace swimmer.*
▸*v.* [*trans.*] *informal* (in tennis and similar games) serve an ace against (an opponent). ■ *Golf* score an ace on (a hole) or with (a shot). ■ get an A or its equivalent in (a test or exam): *I aced my grammar test.* ■ (**ace someone out**) outdo someone in a competitive situation: *the magazine won an award, acing out its rivals* | *it wasn't our intention to* **ace** *Phil* **out of** *a job.* ▷Middle English (denoting the "one" on dice): via Old French from Latin *as* 'unity, a unit.'
▸*PHRASES* □ **an ace up one's sleeve** (or **in the hole**) a plan or piece of information kept secret until it becomes necessary to use it. □ **hold all the aces** have all the advantages. □ **play one's ace** use one's best resource: *deciding to play her ace, Emily showed the letter to Vic.* □ **within an ace of** very close to: *they* **came within an ace of** *death.*

-acea ▸*suffix Zoology* forming the names of zoological groups: *Crustacea.* Compare with **-ACEAN**. ▷from Latin, 'of the nature of,' neuter plural adjectival ending.

-aceae ▸*suffix Botany* forming the names of families of plants: *Liliaceae.* ▷from Latin, 'of the nature of,' feminine plural adjectival ending.

-acean ▸*suffix Zoology* forming adjectives and nouns from taxonomic names ending in *-acea* (such as *crustacean* from *Crustacea*). ▷from Latin *-aceus*, adjectival ending meaning 'of the nature of.'

Ace band·age ▸*n. trademark* an elastic bandage, used to wrap sprained or strained ankles, wrists, or other joints.

a·ce·di·a /əˈsēdēə/ ▸*n.* spiritual or mental sloth; apathy. ▷early 17th cent.: late Latin, from Greek *akēdia* 'listlessness,' from *a-* 'without' + *kēdos* 'care.'

a·cel·lu·lar /āˈselyələr/ ▸*adj. Biology* not consisting of, divided into, or containing cells. ■ (esp. of protozoa) consisting of one cell only.

-aceous ▸*suffix* **1** *Botany* forming adjectives from nouns ending in *-aceae* (such as *ericaceous* from *Ericaceae*). **2** *chiefly Biology & Geology* forming adjectives describing similarity, esp. in shape, texture, or color: *arenaceous* | *foliaceous* | *olivaceous.* ▷from Latin *-aceus*, adjectival ending meaning 'of the nature of.'

a·ceph·a·lous /āˈsefələs/ ▸*adj.* **1** no longer having a head: *an acephalous skeleton.* ■ *Zoology* not having a head. ■ having no leader or chief: *an acephalous society.* **2** *Prosody* lacking a syllable or syllables in the first foot. ▷mid 18th cent.: via medieval Latin from Greek *akephalos* 'headless' (from *a-* 'without' + *kephalē* 'head') + **-OUS**.

a·cerb /əˈsərb/ ▸*adj.* another term for **ACERBIC**. ▷early 17th cent.: from Latin *acerbus* 'sour-tasting.'

a·cer·bic /əˈsərbik/ ▸*adj.* **1** (esp. of a comment or style of speaking) sharp and forthright: *his acerbic wit.* **2** *archaic* or *technical* tasting sour or bitter. ▷mid 19th cent.: from Latin *acerbus* 'sour-tasting' + **-IC**. —**a·cer·bi·cal·ly** *adv.* —**a·cer·bi·ty** /-bitē/ *n.*

acet- ▸*prefix* variant spelling of **ACETO-** shortened before a vowel (as in *acetaldehyde*).

ac·e·tab·u·lum /ˌasiˈtabyələm/ ▸*n.* (*pl.* **-la** /-lə/) *Anatomy* the socket of the hipbone, into which the head of the femur fits. ■ *Zoology* any cup-shaped structure, esp. a sucker. ▷late Middle English (denoting a vinegar cup, hence a cup-shaped cavity): from Latin, from *acetum* 'vinegar' + *-abulum*, denoting a container.

ac·e·tal /ˈasiˌtal/ ▸*n. Chemistry* an organic compound formed by the condensation of two alcohol molecules with an aldehyde molecule. • Acetals have the general formula $R^1CH(OR^2)_2$, where R^1 and R^2 are alkyl groups. ▷mid 19th cent.: from **ACETIC** + *-al* from *alcohol, aldehyde.*

ac·et·al·de·hyde /ˌasiˈtaldəˌhīd/ ▸*n. Chemistry* a colorless volatile liquid aldehyde obtained by oxidizing ethanol. • Alternative name: ethanal; chem. formula: CH_3CHO.

a·cet·am·ide /əˈsetəˌmīd/ ▸*n. Chemistry* the crystalline amide of acetic acid. • Chem. formula: CH_3CONH_2. ▷mid 19th cent.: from **ACETYL** + **AMIDE**.

a·ce·ta·min·o·phen /əˌsētəˈminəfən/ ▸*n.* an analgesic drug used to treat headaches, arthritis, etc., and also to reduce fever, often as an alternative to aspirin. Proprietary names include *Tylenol.* • Chem. formula: $C_8H_9NO_2$. ■ a tablet of this drug.

ac·et·an·i·lide /ˌasiˈtanəˌlīd/ ▸*n. Chemistry* a crystalline solid prepared by acetylation of aniline, used in dye manufacture. • Chem. formula: $C_6H_5NHCOCH_3$. ▷mid 19th cent.: from *acet(yl)* + *anil(ine)* + **-IDE**.

ac·e·tate /ˈasiˌtāt/ ▸*n.* **1** *Chemistry* a salt or ester of acetic acid, containing the anion CH_3COO^- or the group $-OOCCH_3$. **2** cellulose acetate, esp. as used to make textile fibers or plastic: [as *adj.*] *acetate silk.* ■ a transparency made of cellulose acetate film. ■ a recording disk coated with cellulose acetate. ▷late 18th cent.: from **ACETIC** + **-ATE**[1].

a·ce·tic /əˈsētik/ ▸*adj.* of or like vinegar or acetic acid. ▷late 18th cent.: from French *acétique*, from Latin *acetum* 'vinegar.'

a·ce·tic ac·id /əˈsētik/ ▸*n. Chemistry* the acid that gives vinegar its characteristic taste. The pure acid is a colorless viscous liquid or glassy solid. • Chem. formula: CH_3COOH. ▷late 18th cent.: *acetic* from French *acétique*, from Latin *acetum* 'vinegar.'

a·ce·tic an·hy·dride ▸*n. Chemistry* the anhydride of acetic acid. It is a colorless pungent liquid, used in making synthetic fibers. • Chem. formula: $(CH_3CO)_2O$.

aceto- (also **acet-** before a vowel) ▸*comb. form Chemistry* representing **ACETIC** or **ACETYL**.

a·ce·to·bac·ter /əˌsētəˈbaktər; ˌasitə-/ ▸*n.* bacteria that oxidize organic compounds to acetic acid, as in vinegar formation. • Genus *Acetobacter*; Gram-negative oval or rod-shaped bacteria. ▷modern Latin (genus name), from **ACETO-** + **BACTERIUM**.

a·ce·to·gen·ic /əˌsētəˈjenik; ˌasitə-/ ▸*adj.* (of bacteria) forming acetate or acetic acid as a product of metabolism.

ac·e·tone /ˈasiˌtōn/ ▸*n. Chemistry* a colorless volatile liquid ketone made by oxidizing isopropanol, used as an organic solvent and synthetic reagent. • Chem. formula: CH_3COCH_3. ▷mid 19th cent.: from **ACETIC** + **-ONE**.

a·ce·to·ne·mi·a /əˌsētəˈnēmēə; ˌasitə-/ ▸*n.* another term for **KETONEMIA**.

ac·e·to·ni·trile /ˌasitōˈnitril; -trēl; əˌsētō-/ ▸*n. Chemistry* a toxic odoriferous liquid, used as a solvent in high-performance liquid chromatography. • Alternative name: methyl cyanide; chem. formula: $CH_3C{\equiv}N$.

ac·e·tous /əˈsētəs; ˈasitəs/ ▸*adj.* producing or resembling vinegar: *acetous fermentation.* ▷late Middle English (rare before the late 18th cent.): from late Latin *acetosus* 'sour,' from Latin *acetum* 'vinegar.'

a·ce·tyl /əˈsētl; ˈasitl/ ▸*n.* [as *adj.*] *Chemistry* the acyl radical $-C(O)CH_3$, derived from acetic acid: *acetyl chloride* | *an acetyl group.* ▷mid 19th cent.: from **ACETIC** + **-YL**.

a·cet·y·late /əˈsetlˌāt/ ▸*v.* [*trans.*] *Chemistry* introduce an acetyl group into (a molecule or compound): [as *adj.*] (**acetylated**) *the acetylated forms of chloramphenicol.* —**a·cet·y·la·tion** /əˌsetlˈāsʜən/ *n.*

a·ce·tyl·cho·line /əˌsētlˈkōˌlēn; ˌasitl-/ ▸*n. Biochemistry* a compound that occurs throughout the nervous system, in which it functions as a neurotransmitter.

a·ce·tyl·cho·lin·es·ter·ase /əˈsētlˌkōləˈnestəˌrās; -ˌrāz; ˈasitl-/ ▸*n. Biochemistry* an enzyme that causes rapid hydrolysis of acetylcholine. Its action serves to stop excitation of a nerve after transmission of an impulse.

a·ce·tyl·co·en·zyme A ▸*n. Biochemistry* the acetyl ester of coenzyme A, involved as an acetylating agent in many biochemical processes.

a·cet·y·lene /əˈsetlən; -ˌēn/ ▸*n. Chemistry* a colorless pungent-smelling hydrocarbon gas, which burns with a bright flame, used in welding and formerly in lighting. • Alternative name: ethyne; chem. formula: C_2H_2. ▷mid 19th cent.: from **ACETIC** + **-YL** + **-ENE**.

a·cet·y·lide /əˈsetlˌīd/ ▸*n. Chemistry* a saltlike compound formed from acetylene and a metal, containing the anion $(C{\equiv}C)^{2-}$ or $HC{\equiv}C^-$. Acetylides are typically unstable or explosive.

a·ce·tyl·sal·i·cyl·ic ac·id /əˌsētlˌsaliˈsilik/ ▸*n.* systematic chemical name for **ASPIRIN**.

ACH ▸*abbr.* Automated Clearinghouse.

A·chae·a /əˈkēə; əˈkāə/ a region of ancient Greece on the north coast of the Peloponnesus.

A·chae·an /əˈkēən/ ▸*adj.* of or relating to Achaea in ancient Greece. ■ *poetic/literary* (esp. in Homeric contexts) Greek.
▸*n.* an inhabitant of Achaea. ■ *poetic/literary* (esp. in Homeric contexts) a Greek.

The Achaeans were among the earliest Greek-speaking inhabitants of Greece, being established there well before the 12th century BC. Some scholars identify them with the Mycenaeans of the 14th–13th centuries BC. The Greek protagonists in the Trojan War are regularly called Achaeans in the *Iliad*, though this may have referred only to the leaders.

A·chae·me·nid /əˈkēmənid/ (also **A·chae·me·ni·an** /ˌakəˈmēnēən/) ▸*adj.* of or relating to the dynasty ruling in Persia from Cyrus I to Darius III (553–330 BC).
▸*n.* a member of this dynasty. ▷from Greek *Akhaimenēs* 'Achaemenes' (the reputed ancestor of the dynasty) + **-ID**[1].

ach·a·la·sia /ˌakəˈlāzʜ(ē)ə/ ▸*n. Medicine* a condition in which the muscles of the lower part of the esophagus fail to relax, preventing food from passing into the stomach. ▷early 20th cent.: from **A-**[1] 'without, not' + Greek *khalasis* 'loosening' (from *khalan* 'relax') + **-IA**[1].

a·cha·ry·a /əˈcʜə-rēə/ ▸*n.* (in India) a Hindu or Buddhist spiritual teacher or leader. ■ an influential mentor. ▷early 19th cent.: from Sanskrit *ācārya* 'master, teacher.'

A·cha·tes /əˈkātēz/ *Greek Roman Mythology* a companion of Aeneas. His loyalty to his friend was so exemplary as to become proverbial, hence the term *fidus Achates* ('faithful Achates').

ache /āk/ ▸*n.* a continuous or prolonged dull pain in a part of one's body: *the ache in her head worsened.* ■ [in *sing.*] *figurative* an emotion experienced with painful or bittersweet intensity: *an ache in her heart.*
▸*v.* [*intrans.*] **1** (of a person) suffer from a continuous dull pain: *I'm aching all over.* ■ (of a part of one's body) be the source of such a pain: *my legs ached from the previous day's exercise* | [as *adj.*] (**aching**) *aching feet.* ■ *figurative* feel intense sadness or compassion: *she sat still and silent, her heart aching she looked so tired that my heart* **ached for** *her.* **2** feel an intense desire for: *she* **ached for** *his touch* | [with *infinitive*] *he was aching to get his hands on the ball.* ▷Old English *æce* (noun), *acan* (verb). In Middle and early modern English the noun was spelled *atche* and pronounced so as to rhyme with 'batch,' the verb was spelled and pronounced as it is today. The noun began to be pronounced like the verb around 1700. The modern spelling is largely due to Dr. Johnson, who mistakenly assumed its derivation to be from Greek *akhos* 'pain,' —**ach·ing·ly** *adv.* [as *submodifier*] *a sound that was achingly familiar to me.*
▸*PHRASE* □ **aches and pains** minor pains and discomforts, typically in the muscles.

A·che·be /äˈcʜābā/, Chinua (1930–), Nigerian novelist, poet, short-story writer, and essayist; born *Albert Chinualumgu.* Notable works: *Things Fall Apart* (1958), *A Man of the People* (1966), and *Anthills of the Savannah* (1988). Nobel Prize for Literature (1989).

a·chene /āˈkēn/ ▸*n. Botany* a small, dry, one-seeded fruit that does not open to release the seed. ▷mid 19th cent.: from modern Latin *achaenium*, derived irregularly from *a-* 'not' + Greek *khainein* 'to gape.'

A·cher·nar /ˈakərˌnär; ˈäk-/ *Astronomy* the ninth brightest star in the sky, and the brightest in the constellation Eridanus. It marks the southern limit of Eridanus, and is only visible to observers in the southern hemisphere. ▷from Arabic, 'end of the river (i.e., Eridanus).'

Ach·er·on /ˈakəˌrän; -rən/ *Greek Mythology* one of the rivers of Hades. ■ *poetic/literary* hell. ▷early 16th cent.: Latin from Greek *Akherōn.*

Ach·e·son /ˈacʜəsən/, Dean Gooderham (1893–1971), U.S. statesman; secretary of state 1949–53. He urged international control of nuclear power, was instrumental in the formation of NATO, and implemented the Marshall Plan and the Truman Doctrine.

A·cheu·le·an /əˈsʜōōlēən/ (also **A·cheu·li·an**) ▸*adj. Archaeology* of, relating to, or denoting the main Lower Paleolithic culture in Europe, represented by hand-ax industries, and dated to about 1,500,000–150,000 years ago. See also **ABBEVILLIAN**. ■ [as *n.*] (**the**

Acheulean) the Acheulean culture or period. ▷early 20th cent.: from French *Acheuléen*, from *St-Acheul* near Amiens in northern France, where objects from this culture were found.

a·chieve /ə'CHēv/ ▸*v.* [*trans.*] reach or attain (a desired objective, level, or result) by effort, skill, or courage: *he achieved his ambition to become a journalist* | [*intrans.*] *people striving to achieve.* ■ accomplish or bring about: *the communist system achieved a basic economic modernization.* ▷Middle English (in the sense 'complete successfully'): from Old French *achever* 'come or bring to a head,' from *a chief* 'to a head.' —**a·chiev·a·ble** *adj.* —**a·chiev·er** *n.*

a·chieve·ment /ə'CHēvmənt/ ▸*n.* **1** a thing done successfully, typically by effort, courage, or skill: *to reach this stage is a great achievement.* **2** the process or fact of achieving something: *the achievement of professional recognition* | *sense of achievement.* ■ a child's or student's progress in a course of learning, typically as measured by standardized tests or objectives: *assessing ability in terms of academic achievement* | [as *adj.*] *an achievement test.* **3** *Heraldry* a representation of a coat of arms with all the adjuncts to which a bearer of arms is entitled.

ach·il·le·a /ə'kilēə/ ▸*n.* a plant of the daisy family, which typically has heads of small white or yellow flowers and fernlike leaves. • Genus *Achillea*, family Compositae: numerous species, including the common yarrow. ▷via Latin from Greek *Akhilleios*, denoting a plant supposed to have been used medicinally by Achilles.

A·chil·les /ə'kilēz/ *Greek Mythology* a hero of the Trojan War, son of Peleus and Thetis. During his infancy his mother plunged him in the Styx, thus making his body invulnerable except for the heel by which she held him. During the Trojan War, Achilles killed Hector but was later wounded in the heel by an arrow shot by Paris and died.

Achil·les heel ▸*n.* a weakness or vulnerable point. ▷early 19th cent.: alluding to the vulnerability of ACHILLES.

Achil·les ten·don ▸*n.* the tendon connecting calf muscles to the heel.

a·chim·e·nes /ə'kimə,nēz/ ▸*n.* (*pl.* same) a tropical American plant with tubular or trumpet-shaped flowers. • Genus *Achimenes*, family Gesneriaceae. ▷modern Latin, either from Greek *akhaimenis*, denoting a different plant (euphorbia), or from *a-* 'not' + *kheimanein* 'expose to the cold.'

a·chi·o·te /,äCHē'ōtē; ,äkē-/ ▸*n.* annatto. ▷mid 17th cent.: from Spanish, from Nahuatl *achiotl*.

a·chlor·hy·dri·a /,āklôr'hīdrēə/ ▸*n. Medicine* absence of hydrochloric acid in the gastric secretions.

Acholi /ə'kōlē; ə'CHō-/ ▸*n.* **1** (*pl.* same) a member of a farming and pastoral people of northern Uganda and southern Sudan. **2** the Nilotic language of this people.
▸*adj.* of or relating to this people or their language. ▷the name in Acholi.

a·chon·dro·pla·sia /ā,kändrə'plāZH(ē)ə/ ▸*n.* a hereditary condition in which the growth of long bones by ossification of cartilage is retarded, resulting in very short limbs and sometimes a face that is small in relation to the (normal-sized) skull. ▷late 19th cent.: from A-[1] 'without' + Greek *khondros* 'cartilage' + *plasis* 'molding' + -IA[1]. —**a·chon·dro·plas·tic** /-'plastik/ *adj.*

ach·ro·mat /'akrə,mat/ ▸*n.* another term for ACHROMATIC LENS.

ach·ro·mat·ic /,akrə'matik; ,ākrə-/ ▸*adj.* [*attrib.*] **1** relating to, employing, or denoting lenses that transmit light without separating it into constituent colors. **2** *poetic/literary* without color: *achromatic gloom.* ▷late 18th cent.: via French from Greek *a-* 'without' + *khrōmatikos* (from *khrōma* 'color').

ach·ro·mat·ic lens ▸*n.* a lens that transmits light without separating it into constituent colors.

ach·y /'ākē/ ▸*adj.* [*predic.*] suffering from continuous dull pain: *she felt tired and achy.*

a·cic·u·lar /ə'sikyələr/ ▸*adj. technical* (chiefly of crystals) needle-shaped. ▷early 18th cent.: from late Latin *acicula* 'small needle,' diminutive of *acus.*

ac·id /'asid/ ▸*n.* a chemical substance that neutralizes alkalis, dissolves some metals, and turns litmus red; typically, a corrosive or sour-tasting liquid of this kind: *rainwater is a very weak acid* | *traces of acid.* Often contrasted with ALKALI or BASE[1]. ■ *figurative* bitter or cutting remarks or tone of voice: *she was unable to quell the acid in her voice.* ■ *informal* the drug LSD. ■ *Chemistry* a molecule or other entity that can donate a proton or accept an electron pair in reactions.

Acids are compounds that release hydrogen ions (H^+) when dissolved in water. Any solution with a pH of less than 7 is acidic, strong acids such as sulfuric or hydrochloric acid having a pH as low as 1 or 2. Most organic acids (**carboxylic** or **fatty acids**) contain the carboxyl group —COOH.

▸*adj.* **1** containing acid or having the properties of an acid; in particular, having a pH of less than 7: *poor, acid soils.* Often contrasted with ALKALINE or BASIC. ■ *Geology* (of rock, esp. lava) containing a relatively high proportion of silica. ■ *Metallurgy* relating to or denoting steelmaking processes involving silica-rich refractories and slags. **2** sharp-tasting or sour: *acid fruit.* ■ (of a person's remarks or tone) bitter or cutting. ■ (of a color) intense or bright: *an acid green.* ▷early 17th cent. (in the sense 'sour-tasting'): from Latin *acidus*, from *acere* 'be sour.' —**ac·id·y** *adj.*

ac·id·head /'asid,hed/ ▸*n. informal* a habitual user of the drug LSD.

ac·id house ▸*n.* a kind of popular synthesized dance music with a fast repetitive beat, popular in the 1980s and associated with the taking of drugs such as Ecstasy.

a·cid·ic /ə'sidik/ ▸*adj.* **1** having the properties of an acid, or containing acid; having a pH below 7. Often contrasted with ALKALINE or BASIC. ■ *Geology* (of rock, esp. lava) relatively rich in silica. ■ *Metallurgy* relating to or denoting steelmaking processes involving silica-rich refractories and slags. **2** sharp-tasting or sour: *acidic wine.* ■ (of a person's remarks or tone) bitter or cutting: *the occasional acidic comment.* ■ (of a color) intense or bright: *an acidic yellow.* **3** of or relating to acid rock or acid house music.

a·cid·i·fy /ə'sidə,fī/ ▸*v.* (**-fies, -fied**) make or become acid: [*trans.*] *pollutants can acidify surface water* | [*intrans.*] *the paper was acidifying.* —**a·cid·i·fi·ca·tion** /ə,sidəfi'kāSHən/ *n.*

ac·i·dim·e·try /,asi'dimitrē/ ▸*n.* measurement of the strengths of acids.

a·cid·i·ty /ə'siditē/ ▸*n.* **1** the level of acid in substances such as water, soil, or wine. ■ such a level in the gastric juices, typically when excessive and causing discomfort. **2** the bitterness or sharpness of a person's remarks or tone: *the cutting acidity in his voice.*

ac·id jazz ▸*n.* a kind of popular dance music incorporating elements of jazz, funk, soul, and hip-hop. ▷apparently coined from ACID HOUSE and popularized by the *Acid Jazz* record label founded in 1988.

ac·id·ly /'asidlē/ ▸*adv.* with bitterness or sarcasm: *"Is it up to you to make that decision?" she asked acidly.*

a·cid·o·phil /ə'sidə,fil; 'asidə-/ ▸*n. Biology* an acidophilic white blood cell.

a·cid·o·phil·ic /ə,sidə'filik; ,asidə-/ ▸*adj. Biology* **1** (of a cell or its contents) readily stained with acid dyes. **2** (of a microorganism or plant) growing best in acidic conditions. ▷early 20th cent.: from ACID + *-philic* (see -PHILIA).

ac·i·doph·i·lus /,asi'däfələs/ ▸*n.* a bacterium that is used to make yogurt and to supplement the intestinal flora. • *Lactobacillus acidophilus*, a Gram-positive rod-shaped bacterium. ▷1920s: modern Latin, literally 'acid-loving.'

ac·i·do·sis /,asi'dōsis/ ▸*n. Medicine* an excessively acid condition of the body fluids or tissues. —**ac·i·dot·ic** /-'dätik/ *adj.*

ac·id rad·i·cal ▸*n. Chemistry* a radical formed by the removal of hydrogen ions from an acid.

ac·id rain ▸*n.* rainfall made sufficiently acidic by atmospheric pollution that it causes environmental harm, typically to forests and lakes. The main cause is the industrial burning of coal and other fossil fuels, the waste gases from which contain sulfur and nitrogen oxides, which combine with atmospheric water to form acids.

ac·id re·flux ▸*n.* a condition in which gastric acid is regurgitated.

ac·id rock ▸*n.* a type of rock music, mainly of the late 1960s, associated with or inspired by the use of hallucinogenic drugs.

ac·id salt ▸*n. Chemistry* a salt formed by incomplete replacement of the hydrogen of an acid, e.g., potassium hydrogen sulfate ($KHSO_4$).

ac·id test ▸*n.* [in *sing*] a conclusive test of the success or value of something: *the pact with the rebels is an acid test of the government's sincerity.* ▷figuratively, from the original use denoting a test for gold using nitric acid.

a·cid·u·late /ə'sijə,lāt/ ▸*v.* [*trans.*] [usu. as *adj.*] (**acidulated**) make slightly acidic: *acidulated water.* ▷mid 18th cent.: from Latin *acidulus* (from *acidus* 'sour') + -ATE[3]. —**a·cid·u·la·tion** /ə,sijə'lāSHən/ *n.*

a·cid·u·lous /ə'sijələs/ ▸*adj.* sharp-tasting or sour. ■ (of a person's remarks or tone) bitter or cutting. ▷mid 18th cent.: from Latin *acidulus* (from *acidus* 'sour') + -OUS.

ac·i·nus /'asənəs/ ▸*n.* (*pl.* **-ni** /-,nī/) *Anatomy* **1** a small saclike cavity in a gland, surrounded by secretory cells. **2** a region of the lung supplied with air from one of the terminal bronchioles. ▷mid 18th cent.: Latin, literally 'a kernel.'

-acious ▸*suffix* (forming adjectives) inclined to; having as a capacity: *audacious* | *capacious.* ▷from the Latin ending *-ax, -acis* (especially forming adjectives from verbal stems) + -OUS.

-acity ▸*suffix* forming nouns of quality or state corresponding to adjectives ending in *-acious* (such as *audacity* corresponding to *audacious*). ▷from French *-acité* or Latin *-acitas*, noun endings.

ack-ack /'ak ,ak/ *informal Military* ▸*n.* an antiaircraft gun or regiment. ■ antiaircraft gunfire: [as *adj.*] *a quick burst of ack-ack fire.* ▷World War II: signalers' name for the letters *AA.*

ac·kee ▸*n.* variant spelling of AKEE.

ac·knowl·edge /ak'nälij/ ▸*v.* **1** [*reporting verb*] accept or admit the existence or truth of: [*trans.*] *the plight of the refugees was acknowledged by the authorities* | [with *clause*] *the government* **acknowledged that** *the tax was unfair* | [with *direct speech*] *"That's true," she acknowledged.* **2** [*trans.*] (of a body of opinion) recognize the fact or importance or quality of: *the art world has begun to acknowledge his genius* | *he's generally acknowledged to be the game's finest coach.* ■ express or display gratitude for or appreciation of: *he received a letter acknowledging his services.* ■ accept the validity or legitimacy of: *Henry acknowledged Richard as his heir.* **3** [*trans.*] show that one has noticed or recognized (someone) by making a gesture or greeting: *she refused to acknowledge my presence.* ■ confirm (receipt of something). ▷late 15th cent.: from the obsolete Middle English verb *knowledge*, influenced by obsolete *acknow* 'acknowledge, confess.'

ac·knowl·edg·ment /ak'nälijmənt/ (also **ac·knowl·edge·ment**) ▸*n.* **1** acceptance of the truth or existence of something: *there was no acknowledgment of the family's trauma.* **2** the action of expressing or displaying gratitude or appreciation for something: *he received an award* **in acknowledgment of** *his work.* ■ the action of showing that one has noticed someone or something: *he touched his hat* **in acknowledgment of** *the salute.* ■ a letter confirming receipt of something: *I received an acknowledgment of my application.* **3** (usu. **acknowledgments**) an author's or publisher's statement of indebtedness to others, typically one printed at the beginning of a book.

ACL ▸*abbr.* anterior cruciate ligament.

a·clin·ic line /ā'klinik/ ▸*n.* another term for MAGNETIC EQUATOR. ▷mid 19th cent.: *aclinic* from Greek *aklinēs*, from *a-* 'not' + *klinein* 'to bend.'

ACLU ▸*abbr.* American Civil Liberties Union.

ac·me /'akmē/ ▸*n.* [in *sing.*] the point at which someone or something is best, perfect, or most successful: *physics is the acme of scientific knowledge.* ▷late 16th cent.: from Greek *akmē* 'highest point.' Until the 18th cent. it was often consciously used as a Greek word and often written in Greek letters.

Ac·me·ist /'akmē-ist/ ▸*adj.* denoting or relating to an early 20th century movement in Russian poetry that rejected the values of symbolism in favor of formal technique and clarity of exposition. Notable members were Anna Akhmatova and Osip Mandelstam.
▸*n.* a member of this movement. —**Ac·me·ism** /-,izəm/ *n.*

ac·ne /'aknē/ ▸*n.* the occurrence of inflamed or infected sebaceous glands in the skin; in particular, a condition characterized by red pimples on the face, prevalent chiefly among teenagers. ▷mid 19th cent.: via modern Latin from Greek *aknas*, a misreading of *akmas*, accusative plural of *akmē* 'highest point, peak, or facial eruption'; compare with ACME. —**ac·ned** *adj.*

ac·o·lyte /'akə,līt/ ▸*n.* a person assisting the celebrant in a religious service or procession. ■ an assistant or follower. ▷Middle English: from Old French *acolyt* or ecclesiastical Latin *acolytus*, from Greek *akolouthos* 'follower.'

A·con·ca·gua /,akən'kägwə; ,äk-/ an extinct volcano

Pronunciation Key ə *ago*; ər *over*; 'ə *or* ,ə *up*; 'ər *or* ,ər *fur*; a *hat*; ā *rate*; ä *car*; CH *chew*; e *let*; ē *see*; e(ə)r *air*; i *fit*; ī *by*; i(ə)r *ear*; NG *sing*; ō *go*; ô *for*; oi *boy*; o͝o *good*; o͞o *goo*; ou *out*; SH *she*; TH *thin*; TH *then*; (h)w *why*; ZH *vision*

in the Andes, on the border between Chile and Argentina, rising to 22,834 feet (6,960 m). It is the highest mountain in the western hemisphere.

ac·o·nite /ˈakəˌnīt/ ▸*n.* a poisonous plant of the buttercup family, which bears hooded pink or purple flowers. It is native to temperate regions of the northern hemisphere. • Genus *Aconitum*, family Ranunculaceae: many species, including monkshood and wolfsbane. ■ an extract of such a plant, used as a poison or in medicinal preparations. ▷mid 16th cent.: via French and Latin from Greek *akoniton*.

a·con·i·tine /əˈkäniˌtēn/ ▸*n. Chemistry* a poisonous alkaloid obtained from monkshood and related plants.

a·corn /ˈāˌkôrn/ ▸*n.* the fruit of the oak, a smooth oval nut in a rough cuplike base. ▷Old English *æcern*, of Germanic origin; related to Dutch *aker*, also to ACRE, later associated with OAK and CORN[1].

a·corn bar·na·cle ▸*n.* a stalkless barnacle that attaches itself to a variety of surfaces including rocks, ships, and marine animals. Large numbers of individuals may form a heavy encrustation that can affect the progress of a ship. • Genus *Balanus*, family Balanidae.

a·corn squash ▸*n.* a winter squash, typically of a dark green variety, with a longitudinally ridged rind.

a·corn worm ▸*n.* a burrowing wormlike marine animal of shallow waters. Its body consists of a proboscis, a collar, and a long trunk with gill slits, and contains a notochordlike structure. • Class Enteropneusta, phylum Hemichordata.

a·cot·y·le·don /ˌākätlˈēdn/ ▸*n.* a plant with no distinct seed-leaves, esp. a fern or moss. ▷mid 18th cent.: from modern Latin plural *acotyledones* (see A-[1], COTYLEDON). **—a·cot·y·le·don·ous** *adj.*

a·cous·tic /əˈko͞ostik/ ▸*adj.* [*attrib.*] **1** relating to sound or the sense of hearing: *dogs have a much greater acoustic range than humans.* ■ (of building materials) used for soundproofing or modifying sound: *acoustic tiles.* ■ (of an explosive mine or other weapon) able to be set off by sound waves. **2** (of music or musical instruments) not having electrical amplification: *acoustic guitar.* ■ (of a person or group) playing such instruments.

▸*n.* **1** (usu. **acoustics**) the properties or qualities of a room or building that determine how sound is transmitted in it: *Symphony Hall has perfect acoustics.* ■ (**acoustic**) the acoustic properties or ambience of a sound recording or of a recording studio. **2** (**acoustics**) [treated as *sing.*] the branch of physics concerned with the properties of sound. **3** a musical instrument without electrical amplification, typically a guitar. ▷mid 17th cent.: from Greek *akoustikos*, from *akouein* 'hear.' **—a·cous·ti·cal** *adj.* **—a·cous·ti·cal·ly** /-ik(ə)lē/ *adv.*

a·cous·tic cou·pler ▸*n. Electronics* see COUPLER.

ac·ous·ti·cian /ˌako͞oˈstisHən/ ▸*n.* an expert in the branch of physics concerned with the properties of sound.

a·cous·tic im·ped·ance ▸*n. Physics* the ratio of the pressure over an imaginary surface in a sound wave to the rate of particle flow across the surface.

a·cous·tic shock ▸*n.* damaged hearing suffered by the user of a listening device as a result of sudden excessive noise.

ac·quaint /əˈkwānt/ ▸*v.* [*trans.*] (**acquaint someone with**) make someone aware of or familiar with: *new staff should be acquainted with fire exit routes | you need to* ***acquaint yourself with*** *the house style.* ■ (**be acquainted**) be an acquaintance: *I am not* ***acquainted with*** *any young lady of that name | I'll leave you two to* ***get acquainted.*** ▷Middle English: from Old French *acointier* 'make known,' from late Latin *accognitare*, from Latin *accognoscere*, from *ad-* 'to' + *cognoscere* 'come to know.'

ac·quaint·ance /əˈkwāntns/ ▸*n.* **1** a person's knowledge or experience of something: *the students had little* ***acquaintance with*** *the language.* ■ one's slight knowledge of or friendship with someone: *I renewed my* ***acquaintance with*** *Herbert | most men* ***of her acquaintance*** *were in uniform now.* **2** a person one knows slightly, but who is not a close friend: *a wide circle of friends and acquaintances.* ■ such people considered collectively: *his extensive acquaintance included Oscar Wilde and Yeats.* ▷Middle English (in the sense 'mutual knowledge, being acquainted'): from Old French *acointance*, from *acointier* 'make known' (see ACQUAINT). **—ac·quaint·ance·ship** /-ˌSHip/ *n.*

▸*PHRASE* □ **make the acquaintance of** (or **make someone's acquaintance**) meet someone for the first time and become only slightly familiar: *they are anxious to make your acquaintance.*

ac·quaint·ance rape ▸*n.* rape by a person who is known to the victim.

ac·qui·esce /ˌakwēˈes/ ▸*v.* [*intrans.*] accept something reluctantly but without protest: *Sara* ***acquiesced in*** *his decision.* ▷early 17th cent.: from Latin *acquiescere*, from *ad-* 'to, at' + *quiescere* 'to rest.' **—ac·qui·es·cence** /-ˈesəns/ *n.*

ac·qui·es·cent /ˌakwēˈesənt/ ▸*adj.* (of a person) ready to accept something without protest, or to do what someone else wants: *the unions were acquiescent and there was no overt conflict.* ▷early 17th cent.: from Latin *acquiescent-* 'remaining at rest,' from the verb *acquiescere* (see ACQUIESCE).

ac·quire /əˈkwī(ə)r/ ▸*v.* [*trans.*] buy or obtain (an object or asset) for oneself. See note at GET. ■ learn or develop (a skill, habit, or quality): *you must acquire the rudiments of Greek | I've never acquired a taste for whiskey.* ■ achieve (a particular reputation) as a result of one's behavior or activities. ▷late Middle English *acquere*, from Old French *aquerre*, based on Latin *acquirere* 'get in addition,' from *ad-* 'to' + *quaerere* 'seek.' The English spelling was modified (*c.*1600) by association with the Latin word. **—ac·quir·a·ble** *adj.* **—ac·quir·er** *n.*

▸*PHRASE* □ **acquired taste** **1** a thing that one has come to like only through experience: *pumpkin pie is an acquired taste.* **2** a liking of this kind: *an acquired taste for tobacco.*

ac·quired char·ac·ter·is·tic (also **ac·quired char·ac·ter**) ▸*n. Biology* a modification or change in an organ or tissue during the lifetime of an organism due to use, disuse, or environmental effects, and not inherited.

ac·quired im·mune de·fi·cien·cy syn·drome ▸ see **AIDS**.

ac·quire·ment /əˈkwī(ə)rmənt/ ▸*n.* the action of acquiring: *the acquirement of self control.* ■ something acquired, typically a skill.

ac·qui·si·tion /ˌakwəˈzisHən/ ▸*n.* **1** an asset or object bought or obtained, typically by a library or museum. ■ an act of purchase of one company by another: *there were many acquisitions among travel agents | expanding by growth or acquisition.* ■ buying or obtaining an asset or object: *Western culture places a high value on material acquisition.* **2** the learning or developing of a skill, habit, or quality: *the acquisition of management skills.* ▷late Middle English (in the sense 'act of acquiring something'): from Latin *acquisitio(n-)*, from the verb *acquirere* (see ACQUIRE).

ac·quis·i·tive /əˈkwizitiv/ ▸*adj.* excessively interested in acquiring money or material things. See note at GREEDY. ▷mid 19th cent.: from French *acquisitif*, *-tive*, from late Latin *acquisitivus*, from Latin *acquisit-* 'acquired,' from the verb *acquirere* (see ACQUIRE). **—ac·quis·i·tive·ly** *adv.* **—ac·quis·i·tive·ness** *n.*

ac·quit /əˈkwit/ ▸*v.* (**-quit·ted**, **-quit·ting**) **1** [*trans.*] (usu. **be acquitted**) free (someone) from a criminal charge by a verdict of not guilty: *she was acquitted on all counts | the jury* ***acquitted*** *him* ***of*** *murder.* See note at ABSOLVE. **2** (**acquit oneself**) conduct oneself or perform in a specified way: *the Israeli windsurfers acquitted themselves well at the 1994 championship.* ■ (**acquit oneself of**) *archaic* discharge (a duty or responsibility): *they acquitted themselves of their charge with vigilance.* ▷Middle English (originally in the sense 'pay a debt, discharge a liability'): from Old French *acquiter*, from medieval Latin *acquitare* 'pay a debt,' from *ad-* 'to' + *quitare* 'set free.'

ac·quit·tal /əˈkwitl/ ▸*n.* a judgment that a person is not guilty of the crime with which the person has been charged: *the trial resulted in an acquittal | the women felt their chances of acquittal were poor.*

ac·quit·tance /əˈkwitns/ ▸*n. dated Law* a written receipt attesting the settlement of a fine or debt. ▷Middle English: from Old French, from *aquiter* 'discharge (a debt)' (see ACQUIT).

a·cra·sia /əˈkrāzH(ē)ə/ ▸*n.* variant spelling of AKRASIA.

A·cre /ˈäkrə; ˈäkər; ˈākər/ **1** an industrial seaport of Israel; pop. 39,100. Also called **AKKO**. **2** /ˈäkrə; ˈäkrā/ a state in western Brazil, on the border with Peru; capital, Rio Branco.

a·cre /ˈākər/ ▸*n.* a unit of land area equal to 4,840 square yards (0.405 hectare): [as *adj.*] *a 15-acre estate.* ■ (**acres of**) *informal* a large extent or amount of something: *acres of space.* ▷Old English *æcer* (denoting the amount of land a yoke of oxen could plow in a day), of Germanic origin; related to Dutch *akker* and German *Acker* 'field,' from an Indo-European root shared by Sanskrit *ajra* 'field,' Latin *ager*, and Greek *agros*. **—a·cred** /ˈākərd/ *adj.* [in *combination*] : *a many-acred park.*

a·cre·age /ˈāk(ə)rij/ ▸*n.* an area of land, typicially when used for agricultural purposes, but not necessarily measured in acres: *a 35% increase in net acreage.*

a·cre-foot ▸*n.* (*pl.* **a·cre-feet**) a unit of volume equal to the volume of a sheet of water one acre (0.405 hectare) in area and one foot (30.48 cm) in depth; 43,560 cubic feet (1233.5 cu m).

ac·rid /ˈakrid/ ▸*adj.* having an irritatingly strong and unpleasant taste or smell: *acrid fumes.* ■ angry and bitter: *an acrid farewell.* ▷early 18th cent.: formed irregularly from Latin *acer*, *acri-* 'sharp, pungent' + -ID[1], probably influenced by *acid*. **—a·crid·i·ty** /əˈkriditē/ *n.* **—ac·rid·ly** *adv.*

ac·ri·dine /ˈakriˌdēn/ ▸*n. Chemistry* a colorless solid compound obtained from coal tar, used in the manufacture of dyes and drugs. • Chem. formula: $C_{13}H_9N$. ▷late 19th cent.: coined in German from ACRID + -INE[4].

ac·ri·fla·vine /ˌakrəˈflāvēn/ ▸*n.* a bright orange-red dye derived from acridine, used as an antiseptic. ▷early 20th cent.: formed irregularly from ACRIDINE and FLAVINE.

Ac·ri·lan /ˈakrəˌlan/ ▸*n. trademark* a synthetic acrylic textile fiber. ▷1950s: from ACRYLIC + Latin *lana* 'wool.'

ac·ri·mo·ni·ous /ˌakrəˈmōnēəs/ ▸*adj.* (typically of speech or a debate) angry and bitter: *an acrimonious dispute about wages.* ▷early 17th cent. (in the sense 'bitter, pungent'): from ACRIMONY + -OUS. **—ac·ri·mo·ni·ous·ly** *adv.*

ac·ri·mo·ny /ˈakrəˌmōnē/ ▸*n.* bitterness or ill feeling: *a quagmire of lawsuits, acrimony, and finger-pointing.* ▷mid 16th cent. (in the sense 'bitter taste or smell'): from French *acrimonie* or Latin *acrimonia*, from *acer*, *acri-* 'pungent, acrid.'

ac·ro·bat /ˈakrəˌbat/ ▸*n.* **1** an entertainer who performs gymnastic feats. **2** a person noted for constant change of mind, allegiance, etc. ▷early 19th cent.: from French *acrobate*, from Greek *akrobatēs*, from *akrobatos* 'walking on tiptoe,' from *akron* 'tip' + *bainein* 'to walk.'

ac·ro·bat·ic /ˌakrəˈbatik/ ▸*adj.* performing, involving, or adept at spectacular gymnastic feats: *an acrobatic dive.* **—ac·ro·bat·i·cal·ly** /-ik(ə)lē/ *adv.*

ac·ro·bat·ics /ˌakrəˈbatiks/ ▸*plural n.* [usu. treated as *sing.*] gymnastic feats: *figurative goes through all sorts of financial acrobatics to make the monthly payments.*

ac·ro·cy·a·no·sis /ˌakrōˌsīəˈnōsis/ ▸*n. Medicine* bluish or purple coloring of the hands and feet caused by slow circulation. ▷late 19th cent.: from Greek *akron* 'tip' + CYANOSIS.

ac·ro·lect /ˈakrəˌlekt/ ▸*n. Linguistics* the most prestigious dialect or variety of a particular language (used esp. in the study of Creoles). Compare with BASILECT, MESOLECT. ▷1960s: from Greek *akron* 'summit' + *-lect* as in *dialect*. **—ac·ro·lec·tal** /akrəˈlektl/ *adj.*

ac·ro·meg·a·ly /ˌakrōˈmegəlē/ ▸*n. Medicine* abnormal growth of the hands, feet, and face, caused by overproduction of growth hormone by the pituitary gland. ▷late 19th cent.: coined in French from Greek *akron* 'tip, extremity' + *megas*, *megal-* 'great.' **—ac·ro·me·gal·ic** /-məˈgalik/ *adj.*

ac·ro·nym /ˈakrəˌnim/ ▸*n.* a word formed from the initial letters of other words (e.g., *radar*, *laser*). ▷1940s: from Greek *akron* 'end, tip' + *onuma* 'name,' on the pattern of *homonym*.

a·crop·e·tal /əˈkräpitl/ ▸*adj. Botany* (of growth or development) upward from the base or point of attachment. The opposite of BASIPETAL. ■ (of the movement of dissolved substances) outward toward the shoot and root apexes. ▷late 19th cent.: from Greek *akron* 'tip' + Latin *petere* 'seek.' **—a·crop·e·tal·ly** *adv.*

ac·ro·pho·bi·a /ˌakrəˈfōbēə/ ▸*n.* extreme or irrational fear of heights. ▷late 19th cent.: from Greek *akron* 'summit' + -PHOBIA. **—ac·ro·pho·bic** /-ˈfōbik/ *adj.* & *n.*

a·crop·o·lis /əˈkräpəlis/ ▸*n.* a citadel or fortified part of an ancient Greek city, typically built on a hill. ■ (**the Acropolis**) the ancient citadel at Athens, containing the Parthenon and other notable buildings, mostly dating from the 5th century BC. ▷Greek, from *akron* 'summit' + *polis* 'city.'

a·cross /əˈkrôs; əˈkräs/ ▸*prep.* & *adv.* from one side to the other of (something): ■ expressing movement over a place or region: *I ran across the street | traveling across Europe |* [as *adv.*] *he had swum across.* ■ expressing position or orientation: *they lived across the street from one another | the bridge across the river |* [as *adv.*] *he* *looked across at me | halfway across, Jenny jumped.* ■ [as *adv.*] used with an expression of measurement: *can grow to 4 feet across.* ■ [as *adv.*] with reference to a crossword puzzle answer that reads horizontally: *19 across.* ▷Middle English (as an adverb meaning 'in the form of a cross'): from Old French *a croix, en croix* 'in or on a cross,' later regarded as being from A-[2] + CROSS.

▸*PHRASES* □ **across from** opposite: *she sat across from me.* □ **across the board** applying to all: *the cutbacks might be across the board.* ■ (in horse racing) denoting a bet in which equal amounts are staked on the same horse to win, place, or show in a race.

a·cros·tic /ə'krôstik; ə'kräs-/ ▸*n.* a poem, word puzzle, or other composition in which certain letters in each line form a word or words. ▷late 16th cent.: from French *acrostiche,* from Greek *akrostikhis,* from *akron* 'end' + *stikhos* 'row, line of verse.' The spelling change was due to association with -IC.

A·crux /'ā,krəks/ the star Alpha Crucis, the brightest star in the Southern Cross (Crux). It is the twelfth brightest star in the sky. ▷from *A* for alpha + CRUX.

a·cryl·a·mide /ə'krilə,mīd; ,akrə'lamīd/ ▸*n. Chemistry* a colorless crystalline solid that readily forms water-soluble polymers. • The amide of acrylic acid; chem. formula: $CH_2=CHCONH_2$. ▷late 19th cent.: from ACRYLIC + AMIDE.

a·cryl·ic /ə'krilik/ ▸*adj.* (of synthetic resins and textile fibers) made from polymers of acrylic acid or acrylates: *a red acrylic sweater.* ■ of, relating to, or denoting paints based on acrylic resin as a medium: *acrylic colors | an acrylic painting.*

▸*n.* **1** an acrylic textile fiber: *a sweater in four-ply acrylic.* **2** (often **acrylics**) an acrylic paint: *washes of white acrylic.* ▷mid 19th cent.: from the liquid aldehyde *acrolein* (from Latin *acer, acri-* 'pungent' + *ol(eum)* 'oil' + -IN[1]) + -YL + -IC.

a·cryl·ic ac·id ▸*n. Chemistry* a pungent liquid organic acid that can be polymerized to make synthetic resins. • Chem. formula: $CH_2CH=COOH$. —**ac·ry·late** /'akrə,lāt/ *n.*

ac·ry·lo·ni·trile /,akrəlō'nītril; -trēl; -trīl/ ▸*n. Chemistry* a pungent, toxic liquid, used in making artificial fibers and other polymers. • The nitrile of acrylic acid: chem. formula: $CH_2=CHCN$.

ACT ▸*abbr.* ■ American College Test. ■ Australian Capital Territory.

act /akt/ ▸*v.* [*intrans.*] **1** take action; do something: *they urged Washington to act* | [with *infinitive*] *governments must act to reduce pollution.* ■ (**act on**) take action according to or in the light of: *I shall certainly act on his suggestion.* ■ (**act for**) take action in order to bring about: *one's ability to act for community change.* ■ (**act for/on behalf of**) represent (someone) on a contractual, legal, or paid basis: *he chose an attorney to act for him.* ■ (**act from/out of**) be motivated by: *you acted from greed.* **2** [with *adverbial*] behave in the way specified: *they followed the man who was seen acting suspiciously | he acts as if he owned the place.* ■ (**act as/like**) behave in the manner of: *try to act like civilized adults.* **3** (**act as**) fulfill the function or serve the purpose of: *they need volunteers to act as foster parents.* ■ have the effect of: *a five-year sentence will act as a deterrent.* **4** take effect; have a particular effect: *bacteria* **act on** *proteins and sugar.* **5** perform a fictional role in a play, movie, or television production: *she acted in her first professional role at the age of six.* ■ [*trans.*] perform (a part or role): *he acted the role of the dragon | he got the chance to* **act out** *other people's jobs.* ■ [with *complement*] behave so as to appear to be; pretend to be: *I acted dumb at first.* ■ [*trans.*] (**act something out**) perform a narrative as if it were a play: *encouraging students to act out the stories.* ■ [*trans.*] (**act something out**) *Psychoanalysis* express repressed or unconscious feelings in overt behavior: *the impulses of hatred and killing which some human beings act out.*

▸*phrasal v.* □ **act out** misbehave, esp. when unhappy or stressed: *many children who act out while awaiting placement in a health care facility end up in juvenile detention.* □ **act up** (of a thing) fail to function properly: *the plane's engine was acting up.* ■ (of a person) misbehave.

▸*n.* **1** a thing done; a deed: *a criminal act* | **the act of** *writing down one's thoughts | an act of heroism.* **2** [in *sing.*] a pretense: *she was* **putting on an act** *and laughing a lot.* ■ [with *adj.*] a particular type of behavior or routine: *he did his Sir Galahad act.* **3** *Law* a written ordinance of Congress, or another legislative body; a statute: *the act to abolish slavery.* ■ a document attesting a legal transaction. ■ (often **acts**) *dated* the recorded decisions or proceedings of a committee or an academic body. **4** a main division of a play, ballet, or opera. ■ a set performance: *her one-woman poetry act.* ■ a performing group: *an act called the Apple Blossom Sisters.* ▷late Middle English: from Latin *actus* 'event, thing done,' *act-* 'done,' from the verb *agere,* reinforced by the French noun *acte.* —**act·a·bil·i·ty** /,aktə'bilitē/ *n.* (in sense 5 of the *verb*). —**act·a·ble** *adj.* (in sense 5 of the *verb*).

▸*PHRASES* □ **act of God** an instance of uncontrollable natural forces in operation (often used in insurance claims). □ **act of grace** a privilege or concession that cannot be claimed as a right. □ **catch someone in the act** (usu. **be caught in the act**) surprise someone in the process of doing something wrong: *the thieves were caught in the act.* □ **clean up one's act** behave in a more acceptable manner. □ **get one's act together** *informal* organize oneself in the manner required in order to achieve something. □ **get** (or **be**) **in on the act** *informal* become or be involved in a particular activity, in order to gain profit or advantage. □ **in the act of** in the process of: *they photographed him in the act of reading other people's mail.* □ **read the Riot Act** see RIOT ACT. □ **a tough** (or **hard**) **act to follow** an achievement or performance that sets a standard regarded as being difficult for others to measure up to.

Ac·tae·on /ak'tēən/ *Greek Mythology* a hunter who, because he accidentally saw Artemis bathing, was changed into a stag and killed by his own hounds.

ac·tant /'aktənt/ ▸*n.* (in literary theory) a person, creature, or object playing any of a set of active roles in a narrative: *the room has become an actant, a surrogate for the heroine herself.*

ACTH ▸*Biochemistry abbr.* adrenocorticotropic (or adrenocorticotrophic) hormone.

ac·tin /'aktən/ ▸*n. Biochemistry* a protein that forms (together with myosin) the contractile filaments of muscle cells, and is also involved in motion in other types of cells. ▷1940: from Greek *aktis, aktin-* 'ray' + -IN[1].

act·ing /'aktiNG/ ▸*n.* the art or occupation of performing in plays, movies, or television productions: *she studied acting in New York.*

▸*adj.* [*attrib.*] temporarily doing the duties of another person: *acting director.*

ac·tin·i·an /ak'tinēən/ ▸*n. Zoology* a sea anemone. ▷mid 18th cent.: from the modern Latin genus name *Actinia* (from Greek *aktis, aktin-* 'ray') + -AN.

ac·tin·ic /ak'tinik/ ▸*adj.* [*attrib.*] (of light or lighting) able to cause photochemical reactions, as in photography, through having a significant short wavelength or ultraviolet component. ■ relating to or caused by such light: *actinic degradation.* ▷mid 19th cent.: from Greek *aktis, aktin-* 'ray' + -IC. —**ac·tin·ism** /'aktə,nizəm/ *n.*

ac·ti·nide /'aktə,nīd/ ▸*n. Chemistry* any of the series of fifteen metallic elements from actinium (atomic number 89) to lawrencium (atomic number 103) in the periodic table. They are all radioactive, the heavier members being extremely unstable and not of natural occurrence. ▷1940s: from ACTINIUM + -IDE, on the pattern of *lanthanide.*

ac·tin·i·um /ak'tinēəm/ ▸*n.* the chemical element of atomic number 89, a radioactive metallic element of the actinide series. It is rare in nature, occurring as an impurity in uranium ores. (Symbol: **Ac**) ▷early 20th cent.: from Greek *aktis, aktin-* 'ray' + -IUM.

ac·ti·nom·e·ter /,aktə'nämitər/ ▸*n. Physics* an instrument for measuring the intensity of radiation, typically ultraviolet radiation. ▷mid 19th cent.: from Greek *aktis, aktin-* 'ray' + -METER.

ac·ti·no·mor·phic /,aktənō'môrfik/ ▸*adj. Biology* characterized by radial symmetry, such as a starfish or the flower of a daisy. Compare with ZYGOMORPHIC. ▷late 19th cent.: from Greek *aktis, aktin-* 'ray' + *morphē* 'form' + -IC. —**ac·tin·o·mor·phy** /ak'tinə,môrfē/ *n.*

ac·ti·no·my·cete /,aktənō'mī,sēt; -mī'sēt/ ▸*n.* a bacterium of an order of typically nonmotile filamentous form. They include the economically important streptomycetes, and were formerly regarded as fungi. • Order Actinomycetales; Gram-positive. ▷1920s (originally only in the plural): modern Latin, from Greek *aktis, aktin-* 'ray' + *mukētes,* plural of *mukēs* 'fungus.'

ac·tion /'akSHən/ ▸*n.* **1** the fact or process of doing something, typically to achieve an aim: *demanding tougher action against terrorism | if there is a breach of regulations, we will* **take action.** ■ the way in which something such as a chemical has an effect or influence: *the seeds require the catalytic action of water to release hotness.* ■ armed conflict: *servicemen listed as* **missing in action** *during the war.* ■ a military engagement: *a rearguard action.* ■ the events represented in a story or play: *the action is set in the country.* ■ *informal* exciting or notable activity: *the nonstop action of mountain biking | people in the media want to be* **where the action is.** ■ *informal* betting. ■ [as *exclam.*] used by a movie director as a command to begin: *lights, camera, action!* **2** a thing done; an act: *she frequently questioned his actions | I would not be responsible for my actions if I saw him.* ■ a legal process; a lawsuit: *an action for damages.* ■ a gesture or movement: *his actions emphasized his words.* **3** [usu. with *adj.*] a manner or style of doing something, typically the way in which a mechanism works or a person moves: *a high paddle action in canoeing | the weapon has speed and smooth action.* ■ the mechanism that makes a machine or instrument work: *a piano with an escapement action.* ▷late Middle English: via Old French from Latin *actio(n-),* from *agere* 'do, act.'

▸*PHRASES* □ **go into action** start work or activity. □ **in action** engaged in a certain activity; in operation. □ **out of action** temporarily unable to engage in a certain activity; not working: *a heart attack put him out of action | the ship was out of action for 16 days.* □ **put into action** put into effect; carry out.

ac·tion·a·ble /'akSHənəbəl/ ▸*adj. Law* **1** giving sufficient reason to take legal action: *slanderous remarks are actionable.* **2** able to be done or acted on; having practical value: *insightful and actionable information on the effect advertising is having on your brand.*

ac·tion com·mit·tee (also **action group**) ▸*n.* a body formed to campaign politically, typically on a particular issue.

ac·tion fig·ure ▸*n.* a doll representing a person or fictional character known for vigorous action, such as a soldier or superhero. The figure typically is posable, with jointed limbs.

ac·tion paint·ing ▸*n.* a technique and style of abstract painting in which paint is randomly splashed, thrown, or poured on the canvas. It was made famous by Jackson Pollock, and formed part of the more general movement of abstract expressionism.

ac·tion po·ten·tial ▸*n. Physiology* the change in electrical potential associated with the passage of an impulse along the membrane of a muscle cell or nerve cell.

Ac·ti·um, Bat·tle of /'akSHēəm; -tē-/ a naval battle which took place in 31 BC off the promontory of Actium in western Greece, in the course of which Octavian defeated Mark Antony.

ac·ti·vate /'aktə,vāt/ ▸*v.* [*trans.*] make (something) active or operative: *fumes from cooking are enough to activate the alarm.* ■ convert (a substance, molecule, etc.) into a reactive form: [as *adj.*] (**activated**) *activated chlorine* . —**ac·ti·va·tion** /,aktə'vāSHən/ *n.* —**ac·ti·va·tor** /-,vātər/ *n.*

ac·ti·vat·ed car·bon (also **activated charcoal**) ▸*n.* charcoal that has been heated or otherwise treated to increase its adsorptive power.

ac·ti·vat·ed sludge ▸*n.* aerated sewage containing aerobic microorganisms that help to break it down.

ac·ti·va·tion a·nal·y·sis /,aktə'vāSHən/ ▸*n. Chemistry* a technique of analysis in which atoms of a particular element in a sample are made radioactive, typically by irradiation with neutrons, and their concentration is then determined radiologically.

ac·ti·va·tion en·er·gy ▸*n. Chemistry* the minimum quantity of energy that the reacting species must possess in order to undergo a specified reaction.

ac·tive /'aktiv/ ▸*adj.* **1** (of a person) engaging or ready to engage in physically energetic pursuits: *I needed to change my lifestyle and become more active.* ■ moving or tending to move about vigorously or frequently: *active fish need a larger tank.* ■ characterized by energetic activity: *they enjoyed an active social life.* ■ (of a person's mind or imagination) alert and lively. **2** doing things for an organization, cause, or campaign, rather than simply giving it one's support: *she was an active member of the church | he had never been very* **active in** *the affairs of the institute | he enjoyed the active support of the government.* ■ (of a person) participating or engaged in a particular sphere or activity: *a politically active student body.* ■ [*predic.*] (of a person or animal) pursuing their usual occupation or activity, typically at a particular place or time: *tigers are active mainly at night.* **3** working; operative: *the old mill was active until 1960.* ■ (of a bank account) in continuous use. ■ (of an electrical circuit) capable of modifying its state or characteristics automatically

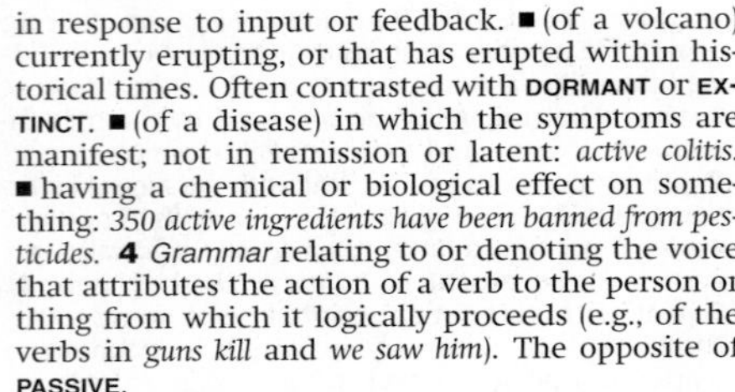

in response to input or feedback. ■ (of a volcano) currently erupting, or that has erupted within historical times. Often contrasted with DORMANT or EXTINCT. ■ (of a disease) in which the symptoms are manifest; not in remission or latent: *active colitis.* ■ having a chemical or biological effect on something: *350 active ingredients have been banned from pesticides.* **4** *Grammar* relating to or denoting the voice that attributes the action of a verb to the person or thing from which it logically proceeds (e.g., of the verbs in *guns kill* and *we saw him*). The opposite of PASSIVE.

▸*n. Grammar* an active form of a verb. ■ (**the active**) the active voice. ▷Middle English (in the sense 'preferring action to contemplation'): from Latin *activus*, from *act-* 'done,' from the verb *agere.* —**ac·tive·ly** *adv.*

ac·tive bar·ri·er ▸*n.* a barrier that allows passage of defined agents while preventing or impeding others, in particular: ■ a security barrier that responds to attempted entries with sensors or personnel. ■ a physical or chemical barrier that intercepts contaminants, debris, or other unwanted substances.

ac·tive du·ty ▸*n.* full-time service in the police or armed forces. ■ the playing of a direct role in the operational work of the police or armed forces as opposed to doing administrative work.

ac·tive im·mu·ni·ty ▸*n. Physiology* the immunity that results from the production of antibodies by the immune system in response to the presence of an antigen. Compare with PASSIVE IMMUNITY.

ac·tive lay·er ▸*n. Geography* the seasonally thawed surface layer above permafrost.

ac·tive list ▸*n.* a list of the officers in an armed service who are liable to be called on for duty.

ac·tive ma·trix ▸*n. Electronics* a display system in which each pixel is individually controlled.

ac·tive serv·ice ▸*n.* direct participation in warfare as a member of the armed forces.

ac·tive site ▸*n. Biochemistry* a region on an enzyme that binds to a protein or other substance during a reaction.

ac·tive trans·port ▸*n. Biology* the movement of ions or molecules across a cell membrane into a region of higher concentration, assisted by enzymes and requiring energy.

ac·tive·wear /ˈaktivˌwe(ə)r/ ▸*n.* clothing designed to be worn for sports, exercise, and outdoor activities.

ac·tiv·ism /ˈaktəˌvizəm/ ▸*n.* the policy or action of using vigorous campaigning to bring about political or social change. —**ac·tiv·ist** *n.*

ac·tiv·i·ty /akˈtivitē/ ▸*n.* (*pl.* **-ties**) **1** the condition in which things are happening or being done: *there has been a sustained level of activity in the economy* | *16 is the general age of consent for sexual activity.* ■ busy or vigorous action or movement: *the room was a* ***hive of activity.*** **2** (usu. **activities**) a thing that a person or group does or has done: *the firm's marketing activities.* ■ a recreational pursuit or pastime: *a range of sports activities.* ■ (**activities**) actions taken by a group in order to achieve their aims: *the police were investigating anarchist activities.* **3** the degree to which something displays its characteristic property or behavior: *abnormal liver enzyme activities.* ■ *Chemistry* a thermodynamic quantity representing the effective concentration of a particular component in a solution or other system, equal to its concentration multiplied by an **activity coefficient**. ▷late Middle English: from French *activité* or late Latin *activitas*, from Latin *act-* 'done,' from the verb *agere.*

act of con·tri·tion ▸*n.* (in the Roman Catholic Church) a penitential prayer.

ac·to·my·o·sin /ˌaktəˈmīəsin/ ▸*n. Biochemistry* a complex of actin and myosin of which the contractile protein filaments of muscle tissue are composed. ▷1940s: from ACTIN + MYOSIN.

ac·tor /ˈaktər/ ▸*n.* a person whose profession is acting on the stage, in movies, or on television. ■ a person who behaves in a way that is not genuine: *in war one must be a good actor.* ■ a participant in an action or process: *employers are key actors within industrial relations.* ▷late Middle English (originally denoting an agent or administrator): from Latin, 'doer, actor,' from *agere* 'do, act.' The theater sense dates from the 16th cent.

Ac·tors' Stu·di·o an acting workshop in New York City, founded in 1947 by Elia Kazan and others, and a leading center of method acting.

ac·tress /ˈaktris/ ▸*n.* a female actor.

ac·tress·y /ˈaktrisē/ ▸*adj.* characteristic of an actress; stereotypically being self-consciously theatrical or emotionally volatile: *her actressy manner was an irritant to the others.*

Acts /akts/ (also **Acts of the Apostles**) ▸a New Testament book immediately following the Gospels and relating the history of the early Church.

ac·tu·al /ˈakCHo͞oəl/ ▸*adj.* **1** existing in fact; typically as contrasted with what was intended, expected, or believed: *the estimate was much less than the actual cost* | *those were his actual words.* See note at GENUINE. ■ used to emphasize the important aspect of something: *the book could be condensed into half the space, but what of the actual content?* **2** existing now; current: *using actual income to measure expected income.* ▷Middle English: from Old French *actuel* 'active, practical,' from late Latin *actualis*, from *actus* (see ACT).

▸PHRASE □ **in actual fact** used to emphasize a comment, typically one that modifies or contradicts a previous statement: *people talk as if he were a monster—in actual fact he was a very kind guy.*

ac·tu·al·i·ty /ˌakCHo͞oˈalitē/ ▸*n.* (*pl.* **-ties**) actual existence, typically as contrasted with what was intended, expected, or believed: *the building looked as impressive* ***in actuality*** *as it did in magazines* | *a mission was sent to investigate the actuality of the situation.* ■ (**actualities**) existing conditions or facts: *the grim actualities of prison life.* ▷late Middle English (in the sense 'activeness'): from Old French *actualite* or medieval Latin *actualitas*, from *actualis* 'active, practical,' from *actus* (see ACT).

ac·tu·al·ize /ˈakCHo͞oəˌlīz/ ▸*v.* [*trans.*] make a reality of: *he had actualized his dream and achieved the world record.* —**ac·tu·al·i·za·tion** /ˌakCHo͞oələˈzāSHən/ *n.*

ac·tu·al·ly /ˈakCHo͞oəlē/ ▸*adv.* **1** as the truth or facts of a situation; really: *we must pay attention to what young people are actually doing* | *the time actually worked on a job.* **2** [as *sentence adverb*] used to emphasize that something someone has said or done is surprising: *he actually expected me to be pleased about it!* ■ used when expressing an opinion, typically one that is not expected: *"Actually," she said icily, "I don't care who you go out with."* ■ used when expressing a contradictory opinion or correcting someone: *"Tom seems to be happy." "He isn't, actually, not any more."* ■ used to introduce a new topic or to add information to a previous statement: *he had a thick Brooklyn accent—he sounded like my grandfather actually.*

ac·tu·ar·y /ˈakCHo͞oˌerē/ ▸*n.* (*pl.* **-ar·ies**) a person who compiles and analyzes statistics and uses them to calculate insurance risks and premiums. ▷mid 16th cent. (originally denoting a clerk or registrar of a court): from Latin *actuarius* 'bookkeeper,' from *actus* (see ACT). The current sense dates from the mid 19th cent. —**ac·tu·ar·i·al** /ˌakCHo͞oˈe(ə)rēəl/ *adj.* —**ac·tu·ar·i·al·ly** *adv.*

ac·tu·ate /ˈakCHo͞oˌāt/ ▸*v.* **1** [*trans.*] cause (a machine or device) to operate: *the pendulum actuates an electrical switch.* **2** (usu. **be actuated**) cause (someone) to act in a particular way; motivate: *the defendants were actuated by malice.* ▷late 16th cent.: from medieval Latin *actuat-* 'carried out, caused to operate,' from the verb *actuare*, from Latin *actus* (see ACT). The original sense was 'carry out in practice,' later 'stir into activity, enliven'; sense 1 dates from the mid 17th cent. —**ac·tu·a·tion** /ˌakCHo͞oˈāSHən/ *n.* —**ac·tu·a·tor** /-ˈātər/ *n.*

ac·tus re·us /ˌaktəs ˈrēəs; ˈrāəs/ ▸*n. Law* action or conduct that is a constituent element of a crime, as opposed to the mental state of the accused. Compare with MENS REA. ▷early 20th cent.: Latin, literally 'guilty act.'

a·cu·i·ty /əˈkyo͞oitē/ ▸*n.* sharpness or keenness of thought, vision, or hearing: *intellectual acuity* | *visual acuity.* ▷late Middle English: from Old French *acuite* or medieval Latin *acuitas*, from Latin *acuere* 'sharpen' (see ACUTE).

a·cu·le·ate /əˈkyo͞olēət; -ˌāt/ ▸*adj.* **1** *Entomology* (of an insect) having a sting. **2** *Botany* sharply pointed; prickly.

▸*n. Entomology* a stinging insect of a group that includes the bees, wasps, and ants. • Section Aculeata, suborder Apocrita, order Hymenoptera. ▷mid 17th cent.: from Latin *aculeatus*, from *aculeus* 'a sting,' diminutive of *acus* 'needle.'

a·cu·men /əˈkyo͞omən; ˈakyə-/ ▸*n.* the ability to make good judgments and quick decisions, typically in a particular domain: *business acumen.* ▷late 16th cent.: from Latin, 'sharpness, point,' from *acuere* 'sharpen' (see ACUTE).

a·cu·mi·nate /əˈkyo͞omənit; -ˌnāt/ ▸*adj. Biology* (of a plant or animal structure, e.g., a leaf) tapering to a point. ▷late 16th cent.: from late Latin *acuminatus* 'pointed,' from *acuminare* 'sharpen to a point,' from *acuere* 'sharpen' (see ACUTE).

ac·u·pres·sure /ˈakyəˌpresHər/ ▸*n.* another term for SHIATSU. ▷1950s: blend of ACUPUNCTURE and PRESSURE.

ac·u·punc·ture /ˈakyəˌpəNGkCHər/ ▸*n.* a system of complementary medicine that involves pricking the skin or tissues with needles, used to alleviate pain and to treat various physical, mental, and emotional conditions. Originating in ancient China, acupuncture is now widely practiced in the West. ▷late 17th cent.: from Latin *acu* 'with a needle' + PUNCTURE. —**ac·u·punc·tur·ist** /-ist/ *n.*

a·cut·ance /əˈkyo͞otns/ ▸*n.* the sharpness of a photographic or printed image. ■ a measure of this. ▷1950s: from ACUTE + -ANCE.

a·cute /əˈkyo͞ot/ ▸*adj.* **1** (of a bad, difficult, or unwelcome situation or phenomenon) present or experienced to a severe or intense degree: *an acute housing shortage* | *the problem is acute and getting worse.* See note at CRUCIAL. ■ (of a disease or its symptoms) of short duration but typically severe: *acute appendicitis.* Often contrasted with CHRONIC. ■ denoting or designed for patients with such conditions: *acute hospital services* | *acute patients.* **2** having or showing a perceptive understanding or insight: shrewd: *an acute awareness of changing fashions.* ■ (of a physical sense or faculty) highly developed; keen: *an acute sense of smell.* See note at KEEN. **3** (of an angle) less than 90°. ■ having a sharp end; pointed. ■ (of a sound) high; shrill.

▸*n.* short for ACUTE ACCENT. ▷late Middle English (sense 2): from Latin *acutus*, past participle of *acuere* 'sharpen,' from *acus* 'needle.' —**a·cute·ly** *adv.* —**a·cute·ness** *n.*

a·cute ac·cent ▸*n.* a mark (´) placed over certain letters in some languages to indicate an alteration of a sound, as of quality, quantity, or pitch, e.g., in *risqué*).

-acy ▸*suffix* forming nouns of state or quality: *celibacy* | *lunacy.* ▷a branch of the suffix **-CY**, from Latin *-atia* (medieval Latin *-acia*), or from Greek *-ateia*, noun suffixes.

a·cy·clic /āˈsīklik; āˈsik-/ ▸*adj.* not displaying or forming part of a cycle. ■ (of a woman) not having a menstrual cycle. ■ *Chemistry* (of a compound or molecule) containing no rings of atoms.

a·cy·clo·vir /āˈsīkləˌvi(ə)r/ ▸*n. Medicine* an antiviral drug used esp. in the treatment of herpes and AIDS. Also called ZOVIRAX (*trademark*).

ac·yl /ˈasəl/ ▸*n.* [as *adj.*] *Chemistry* a radical of general formula −C(O)R, where R is an alkyl group, derived from a carboxylic acid: *acyl groups.* ▷late 19th cent.: formed in German, from Latin *acidus* (see ACID) + **-YL**.

ac·yl·ate /ˈasəˌlāt/ ▸*v.* [*trans.*] *Chemistry* introduce an acyl group into (a molecule or compound): [as *adj.*] (**acylated**) *an acylated glycine derivative.* —**ac·yl·a·tion** /ˌasəˈlāSHən/ *n.*

AD ▸*abbr.* ■ *Military* active duty. ■ armored division. ■ (usu. AD) Anno Domini (used to indicate that a date comes the specified number of years after the accepted date of Christ's birth). ■ athletic director.

USAGE The abbreviation for Anno Domini, AD, typically is written in small capitals and should be placed before the numerals, as in *AD 375* (not *375 AD*). However, when the date is spelled out, it is normal to write, for example, *the third century AD* (not *AD the third century*). The abbreviation BC (before Christ) appears after the date: *Plato was born in 427 BC*—that is to say, in the fifth century BC. In recent years, some writers have begun using the abbreviations CE (of the Common Era) in place of AD, and BCE (before the Common Era) in place of BC, in consideration of a more secular and international readership.

ad[1] /ad/ ▸*n. informal* an advertisement. ▷mid 19th cent.: abbreviation.

ad[2] ▸*n. informal Tennis* short for ADVANTAGE.

A/D *Electronics* ▸*abbr.* analog to digital.

ad- ▸*prefix* denoting motion or direction to: *advance* | *adduce.* ■ reduction or change into: *adapt* | *adulterate.* ■ addition, increase, or intensification: *adjunct* | *adhere* | *admixture.* ▷from Latin *ad* 'to'; in the 16th cent. the use of *ad-* and its variants was extended to replace *a-* from a different origin such as Latin *ab-* (e.g., *advance*, from French *avancer*, based on late Latin *abante* 'in front').

USAGE The prefix **ad-** is also found assimilated in the following forms: **a-** before *sc, sp, st*; **ac-** before *c, q*; **af-** before *f*; **ag-** before *g*; **al-** before *l*; **an-** before *n*; **ap-** before *p*; **ar-** before *r*; **as-** before *s*; **at-** before *t*.

-ad[1] ▸*suffix* forming nouns: **1** in collective numerals:

pentad | *triad.* ■ in groups, periods, or aggregates: *Olympiad.* **2** in names of females in classical mythology, such as *Dryad* and *Naiad.* ■ in names of districts such as *Troad.* **3** in names of poems and similar compositions: *Iliad* | *jeremiad.* **4** forming names of members of some taxonomic groupings: *bromeliad.* ▷from Greek *-ad-* (from nouns ending in *-as*).

-ad[2] ▸*suffix* forming nouns such as *ballad, salad.* Compare with **-ADE**[1]. ▷representing the French noun ending *-ade.*

A·da /'ādə/ ▸*n.* a high-level computer programming language used esp. in real-time computerized control systems, e.g., for aircraft navigation. ▷1980s: from the name of *Ada* Lovelace (see **LOVELACE**[1]).

ad·age /'adij/ ▸*n.* a proverb or short statement expressing a general truth: *the old adage "out of sight out of mind."* See note at **SAYING.** ▷mid 16th cent.: from French, from Latin *adagium* 'saying,' based on an early form of *aio* 'I say.'

a·da·gio /ə'däjō; ə'däzhē,ō/ *Music* ▸*adj.* & *adv.* (esp. as a direction) in slow tempo.
▸*n.* (also **A·da·gio**) (*pl.* **-gios**) a movement or composition marked to be played adagio. ▷Italian, from *ad agio* 'at ease.'

Ad·am[1] /'adəm/ (in the biblical and Koranic traditions) the first man. According to the Book of Genesis, Adam was created by God as the progenitor of the human race and lived with Eve in the Garden of Eden. ▷from Hebrew *'ādām* 'man,' later taken to be a name.
▸*PHRASE* □ **not know someone from Adam** not know or be completely unable to recognize the person in question.

Ad·am[2], Robert (1728–92), Scottish architect. and furniture designer. With his brother James (1730–94), he was influential in the change from the prevailing Palladian fashion to a neoclassical style.

ad·a·mant /'adəmənt/ ▸*adj.* refusing to be persuaded or to change one's mind: *he is **adamant that** he is not going to resign.*
▸*n. archaic* a legendary rock or mineral to which many, often contradictory, properties were attributed, formerly associated with diamond or lodestone. ▷Old English (as a noun), from Old French *adamaunt-*, via Latin from Greek *adamas, adamant,* 'untamable, invincible' (later used to denote the hardest metal or stone, hence diamond), from *a-* 'not' + *daman* 'to tame.' The phrase *to be adamant* dates from the 1930s, although adjectival use had been implied in such collocations as "an adamant heart" since the 16th cent. **—ad·a·mance** *n.* **—ad·a·man·cy** /-mənsē/ *n.* **—ad·a·mant·ly** *adv.*

ad·a·man·tine /,adə'man,tīn; -tin-; -,tēn/ ▸*adj. poetic/literary* unbreakable: *adamantine chains* | *figurative her adamantine will.*

Ad·ams[1] /'adəmz/, Abigail (Smith) (1744–1818), U.S. first lady 1797–1801, the wife of President John Adams and mother of President John Quincy Adams. She is noted for her letters that gave an insider's view of the times.

Abigail Adams

Ad·ams[2], Alice (1926–99), U.S. writer and editor. She wrote about women's lives in her novels *Families and Survivors* (1975), *Superior Women* (1984), and *Southern Exposure* (1995), among others, and in short stories that are collected in such works as *To See You Again* (1982).

Ad·ams[3], Ansel (Easton) (1902–84), U.S. photographer, noted for his black-and-white photographs of American landscapes. Many of his collections, such as *My Camera in the National Parks* (1950) and *This is the American Earth* (1960), reflect his interest in conservation.

Ad·ams[4], John (1735–1826), 2nd president of the U.S. 1797–1801. A Massachusetts Federalist, he was a delegate to the Continental Congress 1774–78 and helped draft the Declaration of Independence in 1776. With John Jay and Benjamin Franklin, he negotiated the Treaty of Paris, which ended the American Revolution in 1783. Adams was minister to Great Britain 1785–88 before becoming the first vice president of the U.S. 1789–97.

John Adams

Ad·ams[5], John Couch (1819–92), English astronomer. He postulated the existence of an eighth planet in 1843, three years before Le Verrier discovered Neptune.

Ad·ams[6], John Quincy (1767–1848), 6th president of the U.S. 1825–29; eldest son of President John Adams. A Massachusetts Democratic-Republican, he served as minister to the Netherlands 1794–96, Germany 1796–1801, St. Petersburg 1809–11, and Great Britain 1815–17. He held a seat in the U.S. Senate 1803–08 and helped negotiate the Treaty of Ghent 1814, which ended the War of 1812. As President Monroe's secretary of state 1817–24, he was the chief architect of the Monroe doctrine. Two of Adams's most impassioned personal causes were the abolition of slavery and the safeguarding of freedom of speech.

John Quincy Adams

Ad·ams[7], Samuel (1722–1803), U.S. patriot. One of the leaders of the Boston Tea Party in 1773, he was active in the pre-Revolution anti-British activities that took place in that city. He served in the First and Second Continental Congresses 1774–75 and was a signer of the Declaration of Independence 1776.

Ad·am's ale ▸*n. dated, humorous* water.

Ad·am's ap·ple ▸*n.* the projection at the front of the neck formed by the thyroid cartilage of the larynx, often prominent in men.

Ad·am's Bridge a line of shoals lying between northwestern Sri Lanka and the southeastern coast of Tamil Nadu in India. It separates the Palk Strait from the Gulf of Mannar.

Ad·am's nee·dle (also **Ad·am's nee·dle-and-thread**) ▸*n.* a frost-hardy yucca native to the eastern U.S., with long leaves that are edged with white threads. • *Yucca filamentosa,* family Agavaceae.

Adam's needle

Ad·am's Peak a mountain in south central Sri Lanka, rising to 7,360 feet (2,243 m). It is regarded as sacred by Buddhists, Hindus, and Muslims.

A·da·na /,ädə'nä/ a town in southern Turkey, capital of a province of the same name; pop. 916,150.

a·dapt /ə'dapt/ ▸*v.* [*trans.*] make (something) suitable for a new use or purpose; modify: [*trans.*] *hospitals have had to be **adapted for** modern medical practice* | *the policies can be adapted to suit individual needs and requirements* | [as *adj.*] (**adapted**) *mink are well adapted to hunting prey.* ■ [*intrans.*] become adjusted to new conditions: *a large organization can be slow to **adapt to** change* ■ alter (a text) to make it suitable for filming, broadcasting, or the stage: *the miniseries was **adapted from** Wouk's novel.* ▷late Middle English: from French *adapter,* from Latin *adaptare,* from *ad-* 'to' + *aptare* (from *aptus* 'fit'). **—a·dap·tive** /-tiv/ *adj.*

USAGE Avoid confusing **adapt** with **adopt.** Trouble sometimes arises because in *adapting* to new conditions, an animal or plant can be said to *adopt* something, e.g., a new color or behavior pattern.

a·dapt·a·ble /ə'daptəbəl/ ▸*adj.* able to adjust to new conditions: *rats are highly **adaptable to** change.* ■ able to be modified for a new use or purpose: *a workforce with adaptable skills.* **—a·dapt·a·bil·i·ty** /ə,daptə'bilitē/ *n.* **—a·dapt·a·bly** /-blē/ *adv.*

ad·ap·ta·tion /,adap'tāshən; ,adəp-/ ▸*n.* the action or process of adapting or being adapted: *the adaptation of teaching strategy to meet students' needs* | *adaptations to the school curriculum.* ■ a movie, television drama, or stage play that has been adapted from a written work, typically a novel: *filming her adaptation of a beloved children's book.* ■ *Biology* a change by which an organism or species becomes better suited to its environment: *living in groups is an adaptation that increases the efficiency of hunting.* ■ the process of making such changes: *biochemical adaptation in parasites.* ▷early 17th cent.: from French, from late Latin *adaptatio(n-),* from Latin *adaptare* (see **ADAPT**).

ad·ap·ta·tion·ism /,adap'tāshə,nizəm; ,adəp-/ ▸*n. Biology* the belief or assumption, now generally held, that each feature of an organism is the result of evolutionary adaptation for a particular function. **—ad·ap·ta·tion·ist** *n.* & *adj.*

a·dapt·er /ə'daptər/ (also **a·dap·tor**) ▸*n.* **1** a device for connecting pieces of equipment that cannot be connected directly. **2** a person who adapts a text to make it suitable for filming, broadcasting, or the stage.

a·dap·tion /ə'dapshən/ ▸*n.* another term for **ADAPTATION.**

a·dap·tive ex·pec·ta·tions hy·poth·e·sis *Economics* a hypothesis that supposes that expectations of future values of a variable can be based primarily on its values in the recent past. Compare with **RATIONAL EXPECTATIONS HYPOTHESIS.**

a·dap·tive ra·di·a·tion ▸*n. Biology* the diversification of a group of organisms into forms filling different ecological niches.

a·dapt·o·gen /ə'daptəjən/ ▸*n.* (in herbal medicine) a natural substance considered to help the body adapt to stress and to exert a normalizing effect upon bodily processes. A well-known example is ginseng. ▷1960s: a term used by N. V. Lazarev, Russian scientist, from **ADAPT + -GEN.** **—a·dapt·o·gen·ic** /ə,daptə'jenik/ *adj.*

A·dar /ä'där; 'ä,där/ ▸*n.* (in the Jewish calendar) the sixth month of the civil and twelfth of the religious year, usually coinciding with parts of February and March. It is known in leap years as **Second Adar.** ■ an intercalary month preceding this in leap years, also called **First Adar.** ▷from Hebrew *'ădār.*

ad·ax·i·al /ad'aksēəl/ ▸*adj. Botany* facing toward the stem of a plant (esp. denoting the upper surface of a leaf). The opposite of **ABAXIAL.**

ad·bot /'ad,bät/ ▸*n.* a computer program that caches advertising on personal computers from an Internet-connected server and then displays the advertising when certain linked programs are being used. ▷blend of *ad(vertising)* and *(ro)bot.*

ADC ▸*abbr.* ■ aide-de-camp. ■ Aid to Dependent Children. ■ Air Defense Command. ■ analog-to-digital converter.

ADD ▸*abbr.* ■ analog digital digital, indicating that a music recording was made in analog format before being mastered and stored digitally. ■ attention deficit disorder.

A

add /ad/ ▸*v.* [*trans.*] **1** join (something) to something else so as to increase the size, number, or amount: *a new wing was* **added to** *the building* | *some box offices now* **add on** *a handling charge* | [as *adj.*] (**added**) *one vitamin tablet daily will give added protection* | [*intrans.*] *this development* **added to** *the problems facing the staff.* ■ [*intrans.*] (**add up**) increase in amount, number, or degree: *watch those air miles add up!* ■ put or mix (an ingredient) together with another as one of the stages in the preparation of a dish: **add** *the flour* **to** *the eggs, stirring continuously.* ■ put (something) in or on something else so as to improve or alter its quality or nature: *chlorine is* **added to** *the water to kill bacteria* | [as *adj.*] (**added**) *the fruit juice contains no added sugar.* ■ contribute (an enhancing quality) to something: *the canopy will* **add** *a touch of class* **to** *your bedroom.* **2** put together (two or more numbers or amounts) to calculate their total value: *they* **added** *all the figures* **up** | **add** *the two numbers* **together** | [*intrans.*] *children learned to add and subtract quickly and accurately.* ■ [*intrans.*] (**add up to**) amount to: *this adds up to a total of 400 calories* | *figurative these isolated incidents don't add up to a true picture of the situation.* ■ [*intrans.*] [usu. with *negative*] (**add up**) *informal* seem reasonable or consistent; make sense: *many things in her story didn't add up.* **3** [*reporting verb*] say as a further remark: [with *direct speech*] *"I hope we haven't been too much trouble," she added politely* | [*trans.*] *we would like to add our congratulations* | [with *clause*] *he* **added that** *few of America's allies would support military action.* ▷late Middle English: from Latin *addere*, from *ad-* 'to' + the base of *dare* 'put.'

Ad·dams[1] /ˈadəmz/, Charles (Samuel) (1912–88), U.S. cartoonist, noted for his macabre characters, which were brought to life in the television series "The Addams Family" (1964–66) and later in the movies in the 1970s and 1990s. His cartoons appeared in the *New Yorker* magazine from 1935.

Ad·dams[2], Jane (1860–1935), U.S. social reformer, feminist, and pacifist. In 1889 she founded Hull House, a center for the care and education of Chicago's poor and a national model for combating urban poverty and treating youthful offenders. She was a leader of the suffrage movement and an active pacifist. Nobel Peace Prize (1931).

Jane Addams

ad·dax /ˈadˌaks/ ▸*n.* a large antelope with a mainly grayish and white coat, native to the deserts of North Africa. • *Addax nasomaculatus*, family Bovidae. ▷late 17th cent.: from Latin, from an African word recorded by Pliny.

ad·den·dum /əˈdendəm/ ▸*n.* (*pl.* **-da** /-də/, **-dums**) **1** an item of additional material, typically omissions, added at the end of a book or other publication. **2** *Engineering* the radial distance from the pitch circle of a cogwheel, worm wheel, etc., to the crests of the teeth or ridges. Compare with **DEDENDUM**. ▷late 17th cent.: Latin, 'that which is to be added,' gerundive of *addere* (see **ADD**).

ad·der /ˈadər/ ▸*n.* a small venomous Eurasian snake that has a dark zigzag pattern on its back and bears live young. Also called **VIPER**. • *Vipera berus*, family Viperidae. ■ used in names of similar or related snakes, e.g., **death adder**, **puff adder**. ▷Old English *nædre* 'serpent, adder,' of Germanic origin; related to Dutch *adder* and German *Natter*. The initial *n* was lost in Middle English by wrong division of *a naddre*; compare with **APRON**, **AUGER**, and **UMPIRE**.

ad·der's tongue (also **ad·der's-tongue**) ▸*n.* **1** a widely distributed atypical fern that has a single pointed oval leaf and a straight unbranched spore-bearing stem. • Genus *Ophioglossum*, family Ophioglossaceae, in particular *O. vulgatum*. **2** another term for **DOG-TOOTH VIOLET**, esp. a trout lily.

ad·dict /ˈadikt/ ▸*n.* a person who is addicted to a particular substance, typically an illegal drug: *a former heroin addict.* ■ [with *adj.*] *informal* an enthusiastic devotee of a specified thing or activity: *a must book for the crossword-puzzle addict* | *a self-confessed chocolate addict.* ▷early 20th cent.: from the obsolete verb *addict*, which was a back-formation from **ADDICTED**.

ad·dict·ed /əˈdiktid/ ▸*adj.* physically and mentally dependent on a particular substance, and unable to stop taking it without incurring adverse effects: *she became* **addicted to** *alcohol and diet pills.* ■ enthusiastically devoted to a particular thing or activity: *he's* **addicted to** *computers.* ▷mid 16th cent.: from the obsolete adjective *addict* 'bound or devoted (to someone),' from Latin *addict-* 'assigned,' from the verb *addicere*, from *ad-* 'to' + *dicere* 'say.'

ad·dic·tion /əˈdikSHən/ ▸*n.* the fact or condition of being addicted to a particular substance, thing, or activity: *he committed the theft to finance his drug addiction* | *an addiction to gambling.* ▷late 16th cent. (denoting a person's inclination or proclivity): from Latin *addictio(n-)*, from *addicere* 'assign' (see **ADDICT**).

ad·dic·tive /əˈdiktiv/ ▸*adj.* (of a substance, thing, or activity) causing or likely to cause someone to become addicted to it: *a highly addictive drug* | *gambling can become addictive.* ■ of, relating to, or susceptible to the fact of being or becoming addicted to something: *addictive behavior* | *I have a very addictive personality.*

add-in ▸*n.* a printed circuit board capable of being fitted internally to a computer or accommodated in an externally accessible slot.

Ad·dis A·ba·ba /ˌadəs ˈabəbə; ˌädəs ˈäbəbə/ (also **A·dis A·be·ba**) the capital of Ethiopia, in the central part of the country, at an altitude of about 8,000 feet (2,440 m); pop. 2,113,000.

Ad·di·son[1] /ˈadəsən/ a village in northeastern Illinois, northwest of Chicago; pop. 32,058.

Ad·di·son[2], Joseph (1672–1719), English essayist, poet, dramatist, and Whig politician. He is noted for his simple unornamented prose style. In 1711 he founded the *Spectator* with Sir Richard Steele.

Ad·di·so·ni·an /ˌadəˈsōnēən/ ▸*adj.* **1** of, relating to, or characteristic of the works or style of Joseph Addison. **2** *Medicine* of, relating to, or characterized by Addison's disease.

Ad·di·son's dis·ease ▸*n.* a disease characterized by progressive anemia, low blood pressure, great weakness, and bronze discoloration of the skin. It is caused by inadequate secretion of hormones by the adrenal cortex. ▷mid 19th cent.: named after Thomas *Addison* (1793–1860), the English physician who described the disease.

ad·di·tion /əˈdiSHən/ (abbr.: **addn.**) ▸*n.* **1** the action or process of adding something to something else: *the hotel has been extended* **with the addition of** *more rooms.* ■ a person or thing added or joined, typically in order to improve something: *you will find the coat a useful* **addition** *to your wardrobe.* **2** (abbr.: **addn.**) the process or skill of calculating the total of two or more numbers or amounts: *she began with simple arithmetic, addition and then subtraction.* ■ *Mathematics* the process of combining matrices, vectors, or other quantities under specific rules to obtain their sum. ▷late Middle English: from Latin *additio(n-)*, from the verb *addere* (see **ADD**).

▸*PHRASE* □ **in addition** as an extra person, thing, or circumstance: *members of the board were paid a small allowance* **in addition to** *their normal salary.*

ad·di·tion·al /əˈdiSHənl/ ▸*adj.* added, extra, or supplementary to what is already present or available: *we require additional information.*

ad·di·tion·al·ly /əˈdiSHənl-ē/ ▸*adv.* as an extra factor or circumstance: *brokers finance themselves additionally by short-term borrowing.* ■ [as *sentence adverb*] used to introduce a new fact or argument: *Additionally, the regulations require escape hatches.*

ad·di·tion re·ac·tion ▸*n.* *Chemistry* a reaction in which one molecule combines with another to form a larger molecule with no other products.

ad·di·tive /ˈaditiv/ ▸*n.* a substance added to something in small quantities, typically to improve or preserve it: *many foods contain chemical additives.*

▸*adj.* characterized by, relating to, or produced by addition: *an additive process* | *the combination of these factors has an additive effect.* ■ *technical* of or relating to the reproduction of colors by the superimposition of primary colors: *the video monitor uses the* **additive colors** *red, green, and blue.* ▷late 17th cent. (as an adjective): from late Latin *additivus*, from Latin *addit-* 'added,' from the verb *addere* (see **ADD**). The noun dates from the 1940s.

ad·dle /ˈadl/ ▸*v.* [*trans.*] *chiefly humorous* make unable to think clearly; confuse: *being in love must have addled your brain.*

▸*adj.* *archaic* (of an egg) rotten. ▷Middle English: from Old English *adela* 'liquid filth,' of Germanic origin; related to Dutch *aal* and German *Adel* 'mire, puddle.'

ad·dle·brained /ˈadlˌbrānd/ (also **ad·dle·head·ed** /-ˌhedid/, **ad·dle·pat·ed** /-ˌpātid/) ▸*adj.* lacking in common sense; having a muddled mind: *made the addlebrained decision to install an uncertain rookie at point guard.*

addn. ▸*abbr.* addition.

add-on ▸*n.* something that has been or can be added to an existing object or arrangement: *we offer skiing lessons as add-ons to our chalet vacations* | [as *adj.*] *cars with add-on extras.* ■ an accessory device designed to increase the capability of a computer or hi-fi system. ■ a unit of construction added to an existing construction: *the new kitchen replaces an add-on that was torn down in 1980.*

ad·dress /əˈdres; ˈaˌdres/ ▸*n.* **1** the particulars of the place where someone lives or an organization is situated: *they exchanged addresses and agreed to keep in touch.* ■ the place itself: *our officers went to the address.* ■ *Computing* a binary number that identifies a particular location in a data storage system or computer memory. **2** a formal speech delivered to an audience: *delivered an address to the National Council of Teachers.* ■ *archaic* a person's manner of speaking to someone else: *his address was abrupt and unceremonious.* ■ (**addresses**) *archaic* courteous or amorous approaches to someone: *he persecuted her with his addresses.* **3** *dated* skill, dexterity, or readiness: *he rescued me with the most consummate address.*

▸*v.* [*trans.*] **1** write the name and address of the intended recipient on (an envelope, letter, or package): *I* **addressed** *my letter* **to** *him personally* | [as *adj.*] (**addressed**) *an addressed envelope.* **2** speak to (a person or an assembly), typically in a formal way: *she addressed an audience of the most important Shawnee chiefs* | *they* **addressed themselves to** *my father.* ■ (**address someone as**) name someone in a specified way when talking or writing: *she addressed my father as "Mr. Stevens."* ■ (**address something to**) say or write remarks or a protest to (someone): *address your complaints to the Board of Review.* **3** think about and begin to deal with (an issue or problem): *a fundamental problem has still to be addressed.* **4** *Golf* take up one's stance and prepare to hit (the ball). ▷Middle English (as a verb in the senses 'set upright' and 'guide, direct,' hence 'write directions for delivery on' and 'direct spoken words to'): from Old French, based on Latin *ad-* 'toward' + *directus* (see **DIRECT**). The noun is of mid 16th-cent. origin in the sense 'act of approaching or speaking to someone.' —**ad·dress·er** *n.*

▸*PHRASE* □ **form of address** a name or title used in speaking or writing to a person of a specified rank or function: *"Venerable" was the usual form of address for a priest at that time.*

ad·dress·a·ble /əˈdresəbəl/ ▸*adj.* *Computing* relating to or denoting a memory unit in which all locations can be separately accessed by a particular program.

ad·dress·ee /ˌadreˈsē; əˌdreˈsē/ ▸*n.* the person to whom something, typically a letter, is addressed.

Ad·dres·so·graph /əˈdresəˌgraf/ ▸*n.* *trademark* a machine for printing addresses on envelopes.

ad·duce /əˈd(y)o͞os/ ▸*v.* [*trans.*] cite as evidence: *a number of factors are adduced to explain the situation.* ▷late Middle English: from Latin *adducere*, from *ad-* 'toward' + *ducere* 'to lead.' —**ad·duc·i·ble** *adj.*

ad·duct[1] /əˈdəkt/ ▸*v.* [*trans.*] (of a muscle) move (a limb or other part of the body) toward the midline of the body or toward another part. The opposite of **ABDUCT**. ▷mid 19th cent.: back-formation from late Middle English *adduction*, from late Latin *adductio(n-)* 'bringing forward,' from the verb *adducere* 'bring in' (see **ADDUCE**). —**ad·duc·tion** /əˈdəkSHən/ *n.*

ad·duct[2] ▸*n.* *Chemistry* the product of an addition reaction between two compounds. ▷1940s: from German *Addukt* (blend of *Addition* and *Produkt*).

ad·duc·tor /əˈdəktər/ (also **adductor muscle**) ▸*n.* *Anatomy* a muscle whose contraction moves a limb or other part of the body toward the midline of the body or toward another part. Compare with **ABDUCTOR**. ■ any of a number of specific muscles in the hand, foot, or thigh: [followed by Latin genitive] *adductor hallucis.* ▷early 17th cent.: modern Latin, from Latin *adduct-* 'brought in,' from the verb *adducere* (see **ADDUCE**).

ad·dy /ˈadē/ ▸*n.* (*pl.* **-dies**) *informal* an address, especially an e-mail address: *I just sent you a note from my other addy.* ▷by shortening and alteration.

-ade[1] ▸*suffix* forming nouns: **1** denoting an action that is completed: *barricade* | *blockade*. **2** denoting the body concerned in an action or process: *brigade* | *cavalcade*. **3** denoting the product or result of an action or process: *arcade* | *lemonade* | *marmalade*. ▷from French via Portuguese, Provençal, and Spanish *-ada* or via Italian *-ata*, from Latin *-atus* (past participial suffix of verbs ending in *-are*).

-ade[2] ▶*suffix* forming nouns such as *decade*. Compare with **-AD**[1]. ▷representing the French noun ending *-ade*, from Greek.

-ade[3] ▶*suffix* forming nouns: **1** equivalent to **-ADE**[1]: *brocade*. **2** denoting a person : *renegade*. ▷from Spanish or Portuguese *-ado*, masculine form of *-ada* (see **-ADE**[1]).

Ad·e·laide /ˈadl,ād/ a city in southern Australia, the capital and chief port of the state of South Australia; pop. 1,050,000.

A·dé·lie Land /əˈdālē; ˈadl-ē/ (also **Adélie Coast**) a section of the Antarctic continent south of the 60th parallel, between Wilkes Land and King George V Land.

A·dé·lie pen·guin /əˈdālē/ ▶*n.* a gregarious and territorial penguin of Antarctica, perhaps the most familiar of all the penguins. The adults have a distinctive white ring around the eye. • *Pygoscelis adeliae*, family Spheniscidae.

Adélie penguin

A·den /ˈädn; ˈādn/ a port in Yemen at the mouth of the Red Sea; pop. 417,370. Formerly under British rule, first as part of British India from 1839 and then from 1935 as a Crown Colony, it was capital of former South Yemen 1967–90.

A·den, Gulf of a part of the eastern Arabian Sea that lies between the southern coast of Yemen and the Horn of Africa.

A·de·nau·er /ˈadn,ou(ə)r/, Konrad (1876–1967), German statesman, first chancellor of the Federal Republic of Germany 1949–63.

ad·e·nine /ˈadn,ēn; -,īn/ ▶*n.* *Biochemistry* a compound that is one of the four constituent bases of nucleic acids. A purine derivative, it is paired with thymine in double-stranded DNA. • Alternative name: 6-aminopurine; chem. formula: $C_5H_5N_5$. ▷late 19th cent.: coined in German from Greek *adēn* 'gland' + **-INE**[4].

adeno- ▶*comb. form* relating to a gland or glands: *adenocarcinoma*. ▷from Greek *adēn* 'gland.'

ad·e·no·car·ci·no·ma /,adn-ō,kärsəˈnōmə/ ▶*n.* (*pl.* **-mas** or **-ma·ta** /-ˈnōmətə/) *Medicine* a malignant tumor formed from glandular structures in epithelial tissue.

ad·e·noids /ˈadn,oidz/ ▶*plural n.* a mass of enlarged lymphatic tissue between the back of the nose and the throat, often hindering speaking and breathing in young children. ▷late 19th cent.: from Greek *adēn* 'gland' + **-OID**. —**ad·e·noi·dal** /,adnˈoidl/ *adj.*

ad·e·no·ma /,adnˈōmə/ ▶*n.* (*pl.* **-mas** or **-ma·ta** /-mətə/) *Medicine* a benign tumor formed from glandular structures in epithelial tissue. ▷late 19th cent.: from Latin, from Greek *adēn* 'gland' + **-OMA**.

a·den·o·sine /əˈdenə,sēn; -sin/ ▶*n.* *Biochemistry* a compound consisting of adenine combined with ribose, one of four nucleoside units in RNA. ▷early 20th cent.: blend of **ADENINE** and **RIBOSE**.

a·den·o·sine de·am·i·nase /dēˈamə,nās; -,nāz/ ▶*n.* *Biochemistry* an enzyme that catalyzes the deamination of adenosine to inosine.

a·den·o·sine mon·o·phos·phate /,mänōˈfäs,fāt/ (abbr.: **AMP**) ▶*n.* *Biochemistry* a compound consisting of an adenosine molecule bonded to one acidic phosphate group, present in most DNA and RNA. It often exists in a cyclic form with the phosphate bonded to the nucleoside at two points.

a·den·o·sine tri·phos·phate /trīˈfäs,fāt/ (abbr.: **ATP**) ▶*n.* *Biochemistry* a compound consisting of an adenosine molecule bonded to three phosphate groups, present in all living tissue. The breakage of one phosphate linkage (to form **adenosine diphosphate, ADP**) provides energy for physiological processes such as muscular contraction.

ad·e·no·vi·rus /,adn-ōˈvīrəs/ ▶*n.* *Medicine* any of a group of DNA viruses first discovered in adenoid tissue, most of which cause respiratory diseases.

a·den·yl·ate cy·clase /əˈdenl,āt ˈsī,klās; -,klāz; əˈdenl-it/ (also **ad·en·yl cy·clase** /ˈadn-il/) ▶*n.* *Biochemistry* an enzyme that catalyzes the formation of cyclic adenylic acid from adenosine triphosphate.

ad·e·nyl·ic ac·id /,adnˈilik/ ▶*n.* another term for **ADENOSINE MONOPHOSPHATE**. ▷late 19th cent.: *adenylic* from **ADENINE** + **-YL** + **-IC**.

a·dept ▶*adj.* /əˈdept/ very skilled or proficient at something: *he is **adept at** cutting through red tape* | *an adept negotiator*.
▶*n.* /ˈadept; əˈdept/ a person who is skilled or proficient at something: ***they are adepts at** kung fu and karate*. ▷mid 17th cent.: from Latin *adeptus* 'achieved,' past participle of *adipisci* 'obtain, attain.' —**a·dept·ly** *adv.* —**a·dept·ness** *n.*

ad·e·quate /ˈadikwit/ ▶*adj.* satisfactory or acceptable in quality or quantity: *this office is perfectly **adequate for** my needs* | *the law is **adequate to** deal with the problem* | *adequate resources and funding*. ▷early 17th cent.: from Latin *adaequatus* 'made equal to,' past participle of the verb *adaequare*, from *ad-* 'to' + *aequus* 'equal.' —**ad·e·qua·cy** /-kwəsē/ *n.* —**ad·e·quate·ly** *adv.*

à deux /ä ˈdœ/ ▶*adv.* for or involving two people: *dinner à deux*. ▷late 19th cent.: French.

ADF ▶*abbr.* automatic direction finder, a device used by pilots to aid navigation.

ad fin. ▶*adv.* at or near the end of a piece of writing. ▷mid 17th cent.: from Latin *ad finem* 'at the end.'

ADH *Biochemistry* ▶*abbr.* antidiuretic hormone.

ADHD ▶*abbr.* attention deficit hyperactivity disorder.

ad·here /adˈhi(ə)r/ ▶*v.* [*intrans.*] (**adhere to**) stick fast to (a surface or substance): *paint won't adhere well to a greasy surface*. ■ believe in and follow the practices of: *the people adhere to the Muslim religion*. ■ represent truthfully and in detail: *the account adhered firmly to fact*. ▷late 15th cent.: from Latin *adhaerere*, from *ad-* 'to' + *haerere* 'to stick.'

ad·her·ent /adˈhi(ə)rənt; -ˈher-/ ▶*n.* someone who supports a particular party, person, or set of ideas: *he was a strong **adherent of** monetarism*.
▶*adj.* sticking fast to an object or surface: *the eggs have thick sticky shells to which debris is often adherent*. ▷late Middle English: from Old French *adherent*, from Latin *adhaerent-* 'sticking to,' from the verb *adhaerere* (see **ADHERE**). —**ad·her·ence** *n.*

ad·he·sion /adˈhēZHən/ ▶*n.* **1** the action or process of adhering to a surface or object: *the adhesion of the Scotch tape to the paper*. ■ the frictional grip of wheels, shoes, etc., on a road, track, or other surface: *the front tires were struggling for adhesion* ■ *Physics* the sticking together of particles of different substances. ■ allegiance or faithfulness to a particular person, party, or set of ideas: *he was harshly criticized for his adhesion to the old bureaucracy*. **2** *Medicine* an abnormal union of membranous surfaces due to inflammation or injury: *endoscopic surgery for pelvic adhesions*. ▷late 15th cent.: from French *adhésion*, from Latin *adhaesio(n-)*, from the verb *adhaerere* (see **ADHERE**).

ad·he·sive /adˈhēsiv; -ziv/ ▶*adj.* able to stick fast to a surface or object; sticky: *an adhesive label*.
▶*n.* a substance used for sticking objects or materials together; glue. ▷late 17th cent. (in the sense 'tending to adhere or cling to'): from French *adhésif*, *-ive*, from the verb *adhérer*, from Latin *adhaerere* 'stick to' (see **ADHERE**). —**ad·he·sive·ly** *adv.* —**ad·he·sive·ness** *n.*

ad·he·sive cap·sul·i·tis /,kapsəˈlītis/ ▶*n.* extreme stiffness or immobility in the shoulder joint, usu. following injury and caused by the adhesions in the joint and inflammation of the capsule of the humerus. Also called **frozen shoulder**.

ad·hib·it /adˈhibit/ ▶*v.* (**-it·ed**, **-it·ing**) [*trans.*] *formal* apply or affix (something) to something else: *signed by a partner who would either adhibit the firm's signature or his own*. ▷early 16th cent. (in the sense 'take in, include'): from Latin *adhibit-* 'brought in,' from the verb *adhibere*, from *ad-* 'to' + *habere* 'hold, have.' —**ad·hi·bi·tion** /,ad(h)əˈbisHən/ *n.*

ad hoc /ˈad ˈhäk; ˈhōk/ ▶*adj.* & *adv.* formed, arranged, or done for a particular purpose only: [as *adj.*] *an ad hoc committee* | *the discussions were on an ad hoc basis* | [as *adv.*] *the group was constituted ad hoc*. ▷mid 16th cent.: Latin, literally 'for this.'

ad·hoc·ra·cy /adˈhäkrəsē/ ▶*n.* a flexible, adaptable, and informal organizational structure without bureaucratic policies or procedures. ▷1970s: blend of **AD HOC** and **-CRACY**.

ad ho·mi·nem /ˈad ˈhämənəm/ ▶*adv.* & *adj.* **1** (of an argument or reaction) arising from or appealing to the emotions and not reason or logic. ■ attacking an opponent's motives or character rather than the policy or position they maintain: *vicious ad hominem attacks*. **2** relating to or associated with a particular person: [as *adv.*] *the office was created ad hominem for Fenton*. | [as *adj.*] *an ad hominem response*. ▷late 16th cent.: Latin, literally 'to the person.'

ad·i·a·bat·ic /,ādīəˈbatik; ,adēə-/ *Physics* ▶*adj.* relating to or denoting a process or condition in which heat does not enter or leave the system concerned. ■ impassable to heat.
▶*n.* a curve or formula representing adiabatic phenomena. ▷late 19th cent.: from Greek *adiabatos* 'impassable,' from *a-* 'not' + *dia* 'through' + *batos* 'passable' (from *bainein* 'go'), + **-IC**. —**ad·i·a·bat·i·cal·ly** /-ik(ə)lē/ *adv.*

ad·i·a·bat·ic lapse rate ▶*n.* *Meteorology* the rate at which atmospheric temperature decreases with increasing altitude in conditions of thermal equilibrium.

ad·i·an·tum /,adēˈantəm/ ▶*n.* technical term for **MAIDENHAIR**.

a·dieu /əˈd(y)o͞o; äˈdyœ/ *chiefly poetic/literary* ▶*exclam.* another term for **GOODBYE**.
▶*n.* (*pl.* **a·dieus** or **a·dieux**) a goodbye: *he whispered a fond adieu* | *they **bade** us all **adieu***. ▷late Middle English: from Old French, from *à* 'to' + *Dieu* 'God'; compare with **ADIOS**.

A·di Granth /,ädē ˈgrənt/ the principal sacred scripture of Sikhism. Original compiled under the direction of Arjan Dev (1563–1606), the fifth Sikh guru, it contains hymns and religious poetry as well as the teachings of the first five gurus. Also called **GRANTH**, **GRANTH SAHIB** ('Revered Book'). ▷from Sanskrit *ādigrantha*, literally 'first book,' based on *grantha* 'literary composition,' from *granth* 'to tie.'

ad in·fi·ni·tum /,ad infəˈnītəm/ ▶*adv.* again and again in the same way; forever: *registration is for seven years and may be renewed ad infinitum*. ▷early 17th cent.: Latin, literally 'to infinity.'

ad·i·os /,ädēˈōs; ,adē-/ ▶*exclam.* & *n.* Spanish term for **GOODBYE**. ▷Spanish *adiós*, from *a* 'to' + *Dios* 'God'; compare with **ADIEU**.

a·dip·ic ac·id /əˈdipik/ ▶*n.* *Chemistry* a crystalline fatty acid obtained from natural fats and used esp. in the manufacture of nylon. • Alternative name: hexanedioic acid; chem. formula: $HOOC(CH_2)_4COOH$. ▷mid 19th cent.: from Latin *adeps*, *adip-* 'fat' (because the acid was first prepared by oxidizing fats) + **-IC**. —**ad·i·pate** /ˈadə,pāt/ *n.*

ad·i·po·cere /ˈadəpō,si(ə)r/ ▶*n.* a grayish waxy substance formed by the decomposition of soft tissue in dead bodies subjected to moisture. ▷early 19th cent.: from French *adipocire*, from Latin *adeps*, *adip-* 'fat' + French *cire* 'wax' (from Latin *cera*).

ad·i·po·cyte /ˈadəpə,sīt/ ▶*n.* *Biology* a cell specialized for the storage of fat, found in connective tissue. ▷1930s: from **ADIPOSE** + **-CYTE**.

ad·i·pose /ˈadə,pōs/ ▶*adj.* *technical* (esp. of body tissue) used for the storage of fat. ▷mid 18th cent.: from modern Latin *adiposus*, from *adeps*, *adip-* 'fat.' —**ad·i·pos·i·ty** /,adəˈpäsitē/ *n.*

ad·i·pose fin ▶*n.* *Zoology* a small, rayless, fleshy, dorsal fin present in certain fishes, notably in the salmon family.

Ad·i·ron·dack chair /,adəˈrän,dak/ ▶*n.* an outdoor wooden armchair constructed of wide slats. The seat typically slants downward toward the sloping back.

Adirondack chair

Ad·i·ron·dack Moun·tains (also **the Ad·i·ron·dacks**) a range of mountains in New York, source of the Hudson and Mohawk rivers.

Adi·ron·dack Park a state preserve in north central New York, the largest park in the contiguous U.S.

A·dis A·be·ba variant spelling of **ADDIS ABABA**.

ad·it /ˈadit/ ▶*n.* a horizontal passage leading into a mine for the purposes of access or drainage. ▷early 17th cent.: from Latin *aditus* 'approach, entrance,' from *adit-* 'approached,' from the verb *adire*, from *ad-* 'toward' + *ire* 'go.'

adj. ▶*abbr.* ■ adjective. ■ adjustment. ■ adjunct. ■ (**Adj.**) adjutant.

ad·ja·cent /ə'jāsənt/ ▸*adj.* **1** next to or adjoining something else: *adjacent rooms* | *the area* ***adjacent to*** *the fire station.* **2** *Geometry* (of angles) having a common vertex and a common side. ▷late Middle English: from Latin *adjacent-* 'lying near to,' from *adjacere*, from *ad-* 'to' + *jacere* 'lie down.' **—ad·ja·cen·cy** *n.*

ad·jec·tive /'ajiktiv/ ▸*n.* *Grammar* a word or phrase naming an attribute, added to or grammatically related to a noun to modify or describe it. ▷late Middle English: from Old French *adjectif, -ive*, from Latin *adject-* 'added,' from the verb *adjicere*, from *ad-* 'toward' + *jacere* 'throw.' The term was originally used in the phrase *noun adjective*, translating Latin *nomen adjectivum*, the latter being a translation of Greek *onoma epitheton* 'attributive name.' **—ad·jec·ti·val** /,ajik'tīvəl/ *adj.* **—ad·jec·ti·val·ly** /,ajik'tīvəlē/ *adv.*

ad·join /ə'join/ ▸*v.* [*trans.*] be next to and joined with (a building, room, or piece of land): *the dining room adjoins a small library* | [as *adj.*] (**adjoining**) *adjoining room.* ▷Middle English: from Old French *ajoindre*, from Latin *adjungere*, from *ad-* 'to' + *jungere* 'to join.'

ad·joint /'ajoint/ *Mathematics* ▸*adj.* relating to or denoting a function or quantity related to a given function or quantity by a particular process of transposition. ■ denoting a matrix that is the transpose of the cofactors of a given square matrix.
▸*n.* an adjoint matrix, function, or quantity. ▷late 19th cent.: from French, literally 'joined to,' from *adjoindre* (see **ADJOIN**).

ad·journ /ə'jərn/ ▸*v.* [*trans.*] (usu. **be adjourned**) break off (a meeting, legal case, or game) with the intention of resuming it later: *the meeting was adjourned until December 4* [*intrans.*] *let's adjourn and reconvene at 2 o'clock.* See note at **POSTPONE**. ■ [*intrans.*] (of people who are together) go somewhere else, typically for refreshment: *they* ***adjourned to*** *a local bar.* ■ put off or postpone (a resolution or sentence): *the sentence was adjourned.* ▷Middle English (in the sense 'summon someone to appear on a particular day'): from Old French *ajorner*, from the phrase *a jorn (nome)* 'to an (appointed) day.' **—ad·journ·ment** *n.*

ad·judge /ə'jəj/ ▸*v.* [*trans.*] (usu. **be adjudged**) consider or declare to be true or the case: *she was adjudged guilty* | [*trans.*] *he was adjudged to be offensive.* ■ (**adjudge something to**) (in legal use) award something judicially to (someone): *the court adjudged legal damages to her.* ■ [*trans.*] (in legal use) condemn (someone) to pay a penalty: *the defaulter was adjudged to pay the whole amount.* ▷late Middle English: from Old French *ajuger*, from Latin *adjudicare*, from *ad-* 'to' + *judicare*, from *judex, judic-* 'a judge.' **—ad·judg·ment** (also **ad·judge·ment**) *n.*

ad·ju·di·cate /ə'jo͞odi,kāt/ ▸*v.* [*intrans.*] make a formal judgment or decision about a problem or disputed matter: *the committee* ***adjudicates on*** *all betting disputes* | [*trans.*] *the case was adjudicated in the Supreme Court.* ■ act as a judge in a competition: *we asked him to adjudicate at the local flower show.* ■ [*trans.*] pronounce or declare judicially: *he was adjudicated bankrupt.* ▷early 18th cent. (in the sense 'award judicially'): from Latin *adjudicat-* 'awarded judicially,' from the verb *adjudicare* (see **ADJUDGE**). The noun *adjudication* dates from the early 17th cent. **—ad·ju·di·ca·tion** /ə,jo͞odi'kāsʜən/ *n.* **—ad·ju·di·ca·tive** /-,kātiv/ *adj.* **—ad·ju·di·ca·tor** /-,kātər/ *n.*

ad·junct /'ajəɴɢkt/ ▸*n.* **1** a thing added to something else as a supplementary rather than an essential part: *computer technology is an* ***adjunct to*** *learning.* ■ a person who is another's assistant or subordinate. **2** *Grammar* a word or phrase used to amplify or modify the meaning of another word or words in a sentence.
▸*adj.* [*attrib.*] connected or added to something, typically in an auxiliary way: *other alternative or adjunct therapies include immunotherapy.* ■ (of an academic post) attached to the staff of a university in a temporary or assistant capacity: *an adjunct professor of entomology.* [as *n.*] *both adjuncts and tenured professors tend to inflate grades.* ▷early 16th cent. (as an adjective meaning 'joined on, subordinate'): from Latin *adjunctus*, past participle of *adjungere* (see **ADJOIN**). **—ad·junc·tive** /ə'jəɴɢ(k)tiv/ *adj.*

ad·junc·tion /ə'jəɴɢ(k)sʜən/ ▸*n.* **1** *Mathematics* the joining of two sets that without overlapping jointly constitute a larger set, or the relation between two such sets. **2** *Logic* the asserting in a single formula of two previously asserted formulae. ▷late 16th cent.: from Latin *adjunctio(n-)*, from the verb *adjungere* (see **ADJOIN**).

ad·jure /ə'jo͝or/ ▸*v.* [*trans.*] *formal* urge or request (someone) solemnly or earnestly to do something: *I adjure you to tell me the truth.* ▷late Middle English (in the sense 'put a person on oath'): from Latin *adjurare*, from *ad-* 'to' + *jurare* 'swear' (from *jus, jur-* 'oath'). **—ad·ju·ra·tion** /,ajə'rāsʜən/ *n.* **—ad·jur·a·to·ry** /-ə,tôrē/ *adj.*

ad·just /ə'jəst/ ▸*v.* **1** [*trans.*] alter or move (something) slightly in order to achieve the desired fit, appearance, or result: *he smoothed his hair and adjusted his tie* | *the interest rate should be* ***adjusted for*** *inflation.* ■ [*intrans.*] permit small alterations or movements so as to allow a desired fit, appearance, or result to be achieved: *a harness that* ***adjusts to*** *the correct fit.* ■ [*intrans.*] adapt or become used to a new situation: *she must be allowed to grieve and to adjust in her own way* | *his eyes had* ***adjusted to*** *semidarkness.* **2** [*trans.*] assess (loss or damages) when settling an insurance claim. ▷early 17th cent. (in the senses 'harmonize discrepancies' and 'assess (loss or damages)'): from obsolete French *adjuster*, from Old French *ajoster* 'to approximate,' based on Latin *ad-* 'to' + *juxta* 'near.' **—ad·just·a·bil·i·ty** /ə,jəstə'bilitē/ *n.* **—ad·just·a·ble** *adj.* **—ad·just·er** *n.* **—ad·just·ment** *n.*

adjustable rate mortgage (abbr.: **ARM**) ▸*n.* a mortgage whose rate of interest is adjusted periodically to reflect market conditions. Also called **VARIABLE RATE MORTGAGE**.

ad·ju·tant /'ajətənt/ ▸*n.* **1** a military officer who acts as an administrative assistant to a senior officer. ■ a person's assistant or deputy. **2** (also **adjutant stork** or **adjutant bird**) a large black-and-white stork with a massive bill and a bare head and neck, found in India and Southeast Asia. • Genus *Leptoptilos*, family Ciconiidae: two species. ▷early 17th cent. (in the sense 'assistant, helper'): from Latin *adjutant-* 'being of service to,' from *adjutare*, frequentative of *adjuvare* 'assist' (see **ADJUVANT**). **—ad·ju·tan·cy** *n.*

ad·ju·tant gen·er·al ▸*n.* (*pl.* **ad·ju·tants gen·er·al**) the adjutant of a unit having a general staff. ■ (**the Adjutant General**) (in the U.S. Army) the chief administrative officer. ■ the senior officer in the National Guard of a U.S. state.

ad·ju·vant /'ajəvənt/ ▸*adj.* *Medicine* (of therapy) applied after initial treatment for cancer, esp. to suppress secondary tumor formation.
▸*n.* *Medicine* a substance that enhances the body's immune response to an antigen. ▷late 16th cent.: from Latin *adjuvant-* 'helping toward,' from the verb *adjuvare*, from *ad-* 'toward' + *juvare* 'to help.'

Ad·ler /'adlər; 'äd-/, Alfred (1870–1937), Austrian psychologist and psychiatrist. Adler disagreed with Freud's idea that mental illness was caused by sexual conflicts in infancy, arguing that society and culture were significant factors. He introduced the concept of the inferiority complex. **—Ad·le·ri·an** /ad'li(ə)rēən; äd-; -'ler-/ *adj.* & *n.*

ad lib /'ad 'lib/ ▸*v.* (**ad libbed, ad lib·bing**) [*intrans.*] speak or perform in public without previously preparing one's words: *Charles had to ad lib because he'd forgotten his script* | [*trans.*] *she ad libbed half the speech.*
▸*n.* something spoken or performed in such a way: *he came up with an apt ad lib.*
▸*adv.* & *adj.* **1** spoken or performed without previous preparation: *an ad lib commentary* | [as *adv.*] *speaking ad lib.* **2** as much and as often as desired: [as *adv.*] *the price includes meals and drinks ad lib* | [as *adj.*] *the pigs are fed on an ad lib system.* **3** *Music* (in directions) in an improvised manner with freedom to vary tempo and instrumentation. ▷early 19th cent. (as an adverb): abbreviation of **AD LIBITUM**.

ad lib·i·tum /ad 'libitəm/ ▸*adv.* & *adj.* more formal term for **AD LIB** (sense 2). ▷early 17th cent.: Latin, literally 'according to pleasure.'

ad li·tem /ad 'lītem/ ▸*adj.* *Law* (esp. of a guardian) appointed to act in a lawsuit on behalf of a child or other person who is not considered capable of representing themselves. ▷mid 18th cent.: Latin, literally 'for the lawsuit.'

ad loc. ▸*abbr.* to or at that place.

Adm. ▸*abbr.* Admiral.

ad·man /'ad,man/ ▸*n.* (*pl.* **-men**) *informal* a person who works in advertising.

ad·min /'ad,min/ ▸*n.* *informal* the administration of a business, organization, etc.: [as *adj.*] *admin staff.* ▷1940s: abbreviation.

ad·min·is·ter /əd'minəstər/ ▸*v.* [*trans.*] **1** manage and be responsible for the running of (a business, organization, etc.): *each school was administered separately.* ■ be responsible for the implementation or use of (law or resources): *a federal agency would administer new regulations.* **2** dispense or apply (a remedy or drug): *paramedic crews are capable of administering drugs.* ■ deal out or inflict (punishment): *retribution was administered to those found guilty.* ■ (of a priest) perform the rites of (a sacrament, typically the Eucharist). ■ *archaic* or *Law* direct the taking of (an oath): *the chief justice will administer the oath of office.* **3** [*intrans.*] give help or service: *we must selflessly* ***administer to*** *his needs.* ▷late Middle English: via Old French from Latin *administrare*, from *ad-* 'to' + *ministrare* (see **MINISTER**). **—ad·min·is·tra·ble** /-strəbəl/ *adj.*

ad·min·is·trate /əd'minə,strāt/ ▸*v.* [*trans.*] less common term for **ADMINISTER** (sense 1). ▷mid 16th cent.: from Latin *administrat-* 'managed,' from the verb *administrare* (see **ADMINISTER**).

ad·min·is·tra·tion /əd,minə'strāsʜən/ (abbr.: **admin.**) ▸*n.* **1** the process or activity of running a business, organization, etc.: *the day-to-day administration of the company* | *a career in arts administration* | [as *adj.*] *administration costs.* ■ (**the administration**) the people responsible for this, regarded collectively: *the university administration took their demands seriously.* ■ the management of public affairs; government: *the inhabitants of the island voted to remain under French administration.* ■ *Law* the management and disposal of the property of an intestate, deceased person, debtor, or other individual, or of an insolvent company, by a legally appointed administrator: *the company* ***went into administration*** | [as *adj.*] *an administration order.* **2** the officials in the executive branch of government under a particular chief executive: *the Bush Administration's demand that the missiles be removed.* ■ the term of office of a political leader or government: *the early years of the Reagan Administration.* ■ a government agency: *the U.S. Food and Drug Administration.* **3** the action of dispensing, giving, or applying something: *the oral administration of the antibiotic* | *the administration of justice.* ▷Middle English: from Latin *administratio(n-)*, from the verb *administrare* (see **ADMINISTER**).

ad·min·is·tra·tive /əd'mini,strātiv; -strətiv/ ▸*adj.* of or relating to the running of a business, organization, etc.: *administrative problems* | *administrative staff.* ▷mid 18th cent.: from Latin *administrativus*, from *administrat-* 'managed,' from the verb *administrare* (see **ADMINISTRATE**). **—ad·min·is·tra·tive·ly** *adv.*

ad·min·is·tra·tive law ▸*n.* *Law* legislative requirements, typically for businesses, issued by government agencies in published regulations.

ad·min·is·tra·tor /əd'minə,strātər/ ▸*n.* a person responsible for running a business, organization, etc. ■ *Law* a person legally appointed to manage and dispose of the estate of an intestate, deceased person, debtor, or other individual, or of an insolvent company. ■ a person who performs official duties in some sphere, esp. dealing out punishment or giving a religious sacrament: *administrators of justice.*

ad·min·is·tra·trix /əd,minə'strātriks/ ▸*n.* *Law* a female administrator of an estate.

ad·mi·ra·ble /'admərəbəl/ ▸*adj.* arousing or deserving respect and approval: *he has one admirable quality—he is totally honest* | *what is admirable in one sex is disdained in the other.* ▷late Middle English: via Old French from Latin *admirabilis* 'to be wondered at,' from *admirari* (see **ADMIRE**). **—ad·mi·ra·bly** /-blē/ *adv.*

ad·mi·ral /'admərəl/ ▸*n.* **1** a commander of a fleet or naval squadron, or a naval officer of very high rank. ■ a commissioned officer of very high rank in the U.S. Navy or Coast Guard, ranking above a vice admiral. ■ short for **VICE ADMIRAL** or **REAR ADMIRAL**. **2** [with *adj.*] a butterfly that has dark wings with bold colorful markings. • Several species in the subfamilies Limenitidinae and Nymphalinae, family Nymphalidae. See **RED ADMIRAL**, **WHITE ADMIRAL**. ▷Middle English (denoting an emir or Saracen commander): from Old French *amiral, admirail*, via medieval Latin from Arabic *'amīr* 'commander' (from *'amara* 'to command'). The ending *-al* was from Arabic *-al-* in the sense 'of the' used in forming titles (e.g., *'amīr-al-'umarā* 'ruler of rulers'), later assimilated to the familiar Latinate suffix **-AL**. **—ad·mi·ral·ship** /-,sʜip/ *n.*

Ad·mi·ral of the Fleet ▸*n.* the highest rank of admiral in the Royal Navy. Compare with **FLEET ADMIRAL**.

ad·mi·ral·ty /'admərəltē/ ▸*n.* (*pl.* **-ties**) **1** the rank or office of an admiral. **2** *Law* the jurisdiction of courts of law over cases concerning ships or the sea and other navigable waters (maritime law). **3** (**Admiralty**) the department of the British government that once administered the Royal Navy. ▷late Middle English: from Old French *admiralte*, from *admirail* 'emir, leader' (see **ADMIRAL**).

Ad·mi·ral·ty Is·lands /'admərəltē/ a group of about 40 islands in the western Pacific, part of Papua New

Guinea. In 1884 the islands became a German protectorate, but after 1920 they were administered as an Australian mandate.

ad·mi·ra·tion /ˌadməˈrāshən/ ▸*n.* respect and warm approval: *their* **admiration for** *each other was genuine.* ■ **(the admiration of)** the object of such feelings: *her house was the admiration of everyone.* ■ pleasurable contemplation: *they were lost in admiration of the scenery.* ▷late Middle English (in the sense 'marveling, wonder'): from Latin *admiratio(n-)*, from the verb *admirari* (see **ADMIRE**).

ad·mire /ədˈmī(ə)r/ ▸*v.* [*trans.*] regard (an object, quality, or person) with respect or warm approval: *I admire your courage* | [as *adj.*] **(admiring)** *she couldn't help but notice his admiring glance.* See notes at **ESTEEM, REVERE.** ■ look at with pleasure: *we were just admiring your garden.* ▷late 16th cent.: from Latin *admirari*, from *ad-* 'at' + *mirari* 'wonder.' **—ad·mir·ing·ly** *adv.*

ad·mir·er /ədˈmī(ə)rər/ ▸*n.* someone who has a particular regard for someone or something: *he was a great admirer of Mark Twain.* ■ a man who is attracted to a particular woman or a woman who is attracted to a particular man: *she's got a secret admirer.*

ad·mis·si·ble /ədˈmisəbəl/ ▸*adj.* **1** acceptable or valid, esp. as evidence in a court of law: *the Court unanimously held that the hearsay was admissible* | *legally admissible evidence.* **2** having the right to be admitted to a place: *foreigners were admissible only as temporary workers.* ▷early 17th cent.: from medieval Latin *admissibilis*, from Latin *admittere* (see **ADMIT**). **—ad·mis·si·bil·i·ty** /-ˌmisəˈbilitē/ *n.*

ad·mis·sion /ədˈmishən/ ▸*n.* **1** a statement acknowledging the truth of something: *an admission of guilt* | *a tacit* **admission that** *things had gone wrong* | *a man who,* **by his own admission,** *fell in love easily.* **2** the process or fact of entering or being allowed to enter a place, organization, or institution: *I had some difficulty securing admission to the embassy* | *the country's admission to the UN* | *her condition required frequent hospital admissions* | [as *adj.*] **(admissions)** *the university admissions office.* ■ the money charged for allowing someone to enter a public place: *admission is $1 for adults and 50 cents for children.* ■ **(admissions)** the number of people entering a place: *hospital admissions decreased nearly 65 percent.* ▷late Middle English: from Latin *admission-*, from the verb *admittere* (see **ADMIT**).

USAGE **Admission** traditionally referred to the price paid for entry or the right to enter: ***admission*** *was $5.* **Admittance** more often referred to physical entry: *we were denied* **admittance** *by a large man with a forbidding scowl.* In the sense of 'permission or right to enter,' these words have become almost interchangeable, although *admittance* is more formal and technical.

ad·mit /ədˈmit/ ▸*v.* **(-mit·ted, -mit·ting) 1** [*reporting verb*] confess to be true or to be the case, typically with reluctance: [with *clause*] *the office finally* **admitted that** *several prisoners had been injured* | ***I have to admit*** *I was relieved when he left* | [with *direct speech*] *"I am feeling pretty tired," Jan admitted* | [*trans.*] *she admitted her terror of physical contact.* ■ [*trans.*] confess to (a crime or fault, or one's responsibility for it): *he was sentenced to prison after admitting 47 charges of burglary* | [*intrans.*] *he had* **admitted to** *a long history of sexual misconduct.* ■ acknowledge (a failure or fault): *after searching for an hour, she finally had to* **admit defeat** | [*intrans.*] *he* **admits to** *having lied.* **2** [*trans.*] allow (someone) to enter a place: *senior citizens are* **admitted** *free to the museum.* ■ (of a ticket) give (someone) the right to enter a place: *the voucher* **admits** *up to four people* **to** *the theme park.* ■ carry out the procedures necessary for (someone) to be received into a hospital for treatment: *she was* **admitted to** *the hospital suffering from a chest infection.* ■ allow (a person, country, or organization) to join an organization or group: *Canada was* **admitted to** *the League of Nations.* ■ allow (someone) to share in a privilege: *the doctrine held that only a chosen few were* **admitted to** *the covenant.* ■ [*trans.*] accept as valid: *the courts can refuse to admit police evidence which has been illegally obtained.* **3** [*intrans.*] **(admit of)** allow the possibility of: *the need to inform him was too urgent to admit of further delay.* ▷late Middle English: from Latin *admittere*, from *ad-* 'to' + *mittere* 'send.'

ad·mit·tance /ədˈmitns/ ▸*n.* **1** the process or fact of entering or being allowed to enter a place or institution: *people were unable to* **gain admittance to** *the hall.* **2** *Physics* a measure of electrical conduction, numerically equal to the reciprocal of the impedance.

USAGE See usage at **ADMISSION**.

ad·mit·ted·ly /ədˈmitidlē/ ▸*adv.* [*sentence adverb*] used to introduce a concession or recognition that something is true or is the case: *admittedly, the salary was not wonderful, but the duties were light* | *this is admittedly an extreme case.*

ad·mix /adˈmiks/ ▸*v.* [*trans.*] *chiefly technical* mix (something) with something else. ▷late Middle English: back-formation from the obsolete adjective *admixt*, from Latin *admixtus* 'mixed together,' past participle of *admiscere*, from *ad-* 'to' + *miscere* 'to mix.'

ad·mix·ture /adˈmikschər/ ▸*n.* a mixture: *he felt that his work was an admixture of aggression and creativity.* ■ something mixed with something else, typically as a minor ingredient: *green with an admixture of black.* ■ the action of adding such an ingredient. ▷early 17th cent. (in the sense 'act of admixing'): from **AD-** (expressing addition) + **MIXTURE**.

ad·mon·ish /ədˈmänish/ ▸*v.* [*trans.*] warn or reprimand someone firmly: *she admonished me for appearing at breakfast unshaven* | [*trans.*] *"You mustn't say that, Shiona," Ruth admonished her.* See note at **REBUKE**. ■ [*trans.*] advise or urge (someone) earnestly: *she admonished him to drink no more than one glass of wine.* ■ *archaic* warn (someone) of something to be avoided: *he* **admonished** *the people* **against** *the evil of such practices.* ▷Middle English *amonest* 'urge, exhort,' from Old French *amonester*, based on Latin *admonere* 'urge by warning.' In late Middle English, the final *t* of *amonest* was taken to indicate the past tense, and its present tense *admonesse* changed on the pattern of verbs such as *abolish*; the prefix *a-* became *ad-* in the 16th cent. by association with the Latin form. **—ad·mon·ish·ment** *n.*

ad·mo·ni·tion /ˌadməˈnishən/ ▸*n.* an act or action of admonishing; authoritative counsel or warning: *the old judge's admonition to the jury on this point was particularly weighty.* ▷late Middle English: from Old French *amonition*, from Latin *admonitio(n-)* '(cautionary) reminder' (see **ADMONISH**).

ad·mon·i·to·ry /ədˈmänəˌtôrē/ ▸*adj.* giving or conveying a warning or reprimand: *the sergeant lifted an admonitory finger.* ▷late 16th cent.: from medieval Latin *admonitorius*, from *admonit-* 'urged,' from Latin *admonere* (see **ADMONISH**).

ad·nate /ˈadˌnāt/ ▸*adj.* *Botany* joined by having grown together. ▷mid 17th cent.: from Latin *adnatus*, variant of *agnatus* (see **AGNATE**), by association with **AD-**.

ad nau·se·am /ad ˈnôzēəm/ ▸*adv.* referring to something that has been done or repeated so often that it has become annoying or tiresome: *the inherent risks of nuclear power have been debated ad nauseam.* ▷mid 18th cent.: Latin, literally 'to sickness.'

ad·nex·a /adˈneksə/ ▸*plural n.* *Anatomy* the parts adjoining an organ. ▷late 19th cent.: Latin, neuter plural of *adnexus* 'joined,' from *adnectere* 'fasten to.' **—ad·nex·al** *adj.*

ad·nom·i·nal /adˈnämənl/ ▸*adj.* *Grammar* attached to or modifying a noun. ▷mid 19th cent.: from Latin *adnomen* 'added name' + **-AL**.

a·do /əˈdo͞o/ ▸*n.* trouble or difficulty: *she had* **much ado** *to keep up with him.* ■ fuss, esp. about something that is unimportant: *on the face of it, this is* **much ado** *about almost nothing.* ▷late Middle English (originally in the sense 'action, business'): from northern Middle English *at do* 'to do,' from Old Norse *at* (used to mark an infinitive) and **DO**[1].

▸*PHRASE* □ **without further** (or **more**) **ado** without any fuss or delay; immediately.

-ado ▸*suffix* forming nouns such as *bravado, desperado* Compare with **-ADE**[3]. ▷representing Spanish and Portuguese noun ending *-ado* or refashioning of Italian *-ata*, Spanish *-ada*, based on Latin *-atus* (past participial suffix of verbs ending in *-are*).

a·do·be /əˈdōbē/ ▸*n.* a kind of clay used as a building material, typically in the form of sun-dried bricks: [as *adj.*] *adobe houses.* ■ a brick of such a type. ■ a building constructed from such material. ▷mid 18th cent.: from Spanish, from *adobar* 'to plaster,' from Arabic *aṭ-ṭūb*, from *al* 'the' + *ṭūb* 'bricks.'

a·do·bo /əˈdōbō/ ▸*n.* (*pl.* **-bos**) a spicy dish or sauce, in particular: ■ a Filipino dish of chicken or pork stewed in vinegar, garlic, soy sauce, bay leaves, and peppercorns. ■ a paste or marinade made from chili peppers, vinegar, herbs, and spices, used in Mexican cooking. ▷Spanish, literally 'marinade.'

ad·o·les·cence /ˌadlˈesəns/ ▸*n.* the period following the onset of puberty during which a young person develops from a child into an adult. ▷late Middle English: from French, from Latin *adolescentia*, from *adolescere* 'grow to maturity' (see **ADOLESCENT**).

ad·o·les·cent /ˌadlˈesənt/ ▸*adj.* (of a young person) in the process of developing from a child into an adult. See note at **YOUTHFUL**. ■ relating to or characteristic of this process: *his adolescent years* | *adolescent problems.*
▸*n.* an adolescent boy or girl. ▷late Middle English (as a noun): via French from Latin *adolescent-* 'coming to maturity,' from *adolescere*, from *ad-* 'to' + *alescere* 'grow, grow up,' from *alere* 'nourish.' The adjective dates from the late 18th cent.

A·do·nai /ˌädōˈnī; -ˈnoi/ ▸*n.* a Hebrew name for God. ▷from Hebrew *'ăḏōnāy*; see also **JEHOVAH**.

A·don·is /əˈdänis/ *Greek Mythology* a beautiful youth loved by both Aphrodite and Persephone. He was killed by a boar, but Zeus decreed that he should spend the winter of each year in the underworld with Persephone and the summer months with Aphrodite. ■ [as *n.*] **(an Adonis)** an extremely handsome young man.

A·don·is blue ▸*n.* a small Eurasian butterfly, the male of which has vivid sky-blue wings. • *Lysandra bellargus*, family Lycaenidae.

a·dopt /əˈdäpt/ ▸*v.* [*trans.*] legally take another's child and bring it up as one's own: *there are many people eager to adopt a baby.* ■ take up or start to use or follow (an idea, method, or course of action): *this approach has been adopted by many big banks.* ■ take on or assume (an attitude or position): *he adopted a patronizing tone* | *adopt a slightly knees-bent position.* ■ **(adopt someone as)** choose someone to receive special recognition: *at least 23 people adopted as "prisoners of conscience" remain in jail.* ■ formally approve or accept (a report or suggestion): *the committee voted 5–1 to adopt the proposal.* ■ choose (a textbook) as standard or required for a course of study. ■ choose (an animal) to become a house pet: *the best way to know a dog's traits is to adopt a mature dog.* ■ (of a local authority) accept responsibility for the maintenance of (a road). ▷late 15th cent.: via French from Latin *adoptare*, from *ad-* 'to' + *optare* 'choose.' **—a·dopt·a·ble** *adj.* **—a·dopt·ee** /-ˈtē/ *n.* **—a·dopt·er** *n.*

USAGE See usage at **ADAPT**.

a·dop·tion /əˈdäpshən/ ▸*n.* the action or fact of adopting or being adopted: *she gave up her children for adoption* | *the widespread adoption of agricultural technology* | [as *adj.*] *an adoption agency* ▷Middle English: from Latin *adoptio(n-)*, from *ad-* 'to' + *optio(n-)* 'choosing' (see **OPTION**).

A·dop·tion·ist /əˈdäpshənist/ ▸*n.* *chiefly historical, Christian Theology* a person holding the view that Jesus is the Son of God by adoption only. **—A·dop·tion·ism** /-ˌnizəm/ *n.*

a·dop·tive /əˈdäptiv/ ▸*adj.* [*attrib.*] as a result of the adoption of another's child: *adoptive parents.* ■ denoting a country or city to which a person has moved and in which they have chosen to make their permanent place of residence. ▷late Middle English: via Old French from Latin *adoptivus*, from *adoptare* 'select for oneself' (see **ADOPT**). **—a·dop·tive·ly** *adv.*

a·dor·a·ble /əˈdôrəbəl/ ▸*adj.* inspiring great affection; delightful; charming: *she looked just adorable* | *I have four adorable Siamese cats.* ▷early 17th cent. (in the sense 'worthy of divine worship'): from French, from Latin *adorabilis*, from the verb *adorare* (see **ADORE**). **—a·dor·a·bil·i·ty** /əˌdôrəˈbilitē/ *n.* **—a·dor·a·ble·ness** *n.* **—a·dor·a·bly** /-blē/ *adv.*

ad·o·ral /aˈdôrəl/ ▸*adj.* *Zoology* relating to or denoting the side or end where the mouth is situated, esp. in animals, such as echinoderms, that lack clear upper and lower sides. ▷late 19th cent.: from **AD-** 'at' + **ORAL**. **—ad·o·ral·ly** *adv.*

a·dore /əˈdôr/ ▸*v.* [*trans.*] love and respect (someone) deeply: *he adored his mother.* See note at **REVERE**. ■ worship; venerate: *he adored the Sacred Host.* ■ *informal* like (something or someone) very much: *she adores Mexican cuisine* | [as *adj.*] **(adoring)** *blowing a farewell kiss to an adoring crowd.* ▷late Middle English: via Old French from Latin *adorare* 'to worship,' from *ad-* 'to' + *orare* 'speak, pray.' **—ad·o·ra·tion** /ˌadəˈrāshən/ *n.* **—a·dor·er** *n.* **—a·dor·ing·ly** *adv.*

a·dorn /əˈdôrn/ ▸*v.* [*trans.*] make more beautiful or attractive: *pictures and prints adorned his walls.* ▷late Middle English: via Old French from Latin *adornare*, from *ad-* 'to' + *ornare* 'deck, add luster.' **—a·dorn·er** *n.* **—a·dorn·ment** *n.*

A·dor·no /äˈdôrnō/, Theodor Wiesengrund (1903–69), German philosopher, sociologist, and musicologist; born *Theodor Wiesengrund.*

Pronunciation Key ə *ago;* ər *over;* ˈə or ˌə *up;* ˈər or ˌər *fur;* a *hat;* ā *rate;* ä *car;* CH *chew;* e *let;* ē *see;* e(ə)r *air;* i *fit;* ī *by;* i(ə)r *ear;* NG *sing;* ō *go;* ô *for;* oi *boy;* o͝o *good;* o͞o *goo;* ou *out;* SH *she;* TH *thin;* T͟H *then;* (h)w *why;* ZH *vision*

A

ADP ▸*abbr.* ■ *Biochemistry* adenosine diphosphate. ■ automatic data processing.

ad·pressed /ad'prest/ ▸*adj.* *Botany* lying closely against the adjacent part, or against the ground. ▷early 19th cent.: from Latin *adpress-* 'pressed near,' from *adprimere*, from *ad* 'to, at' + *premere* 'to press,' + -ED[2].

ADR ▸*abbr.* ■ alternative dispute resolution. ■ American depositary receipt.

Adrar des Ifo·ras /ä'drär dāz ˌēfôr'ä/ a massif region in the central Sahara, on the border between Mali and Algeria.

ad rem /'ad 'rem/ ▸*adv.* & *adj.* *formal* relevant to what is being done or discussed at the time. ▷late 16th cent.: Latin, literally 'to the matter.'

ad·re·nal /ə'drēnl/ ▸*adj.* of, relating to, or denoting a pair of ductless glands situated above the kidneys. Each consists of a core region (**adrenal medulla**) secreting epinephrine and norepinephrine, and an outer region (**adrenal cortex**) secreting corticosteroids.
▸*n.* (usu. **adrenals**) an adrenal gland. ▷late 19th cent.: from AD- + RENAL.

a·dren·al·ine /ə'drenl-in/ (also **a·dren·al·in**) ▸*n.* another term for EPINEPHRINE: *performing live really gets your adrenaline going.* ■ (**Adrenalin**) *trademark* the hormone epinephrine extracted from animals or prepared synthetically for medicinal purposes. ▷early 20th cent.: from ADRENAL + -IN[1].

a·dre·nal·ized /ə'drēnlˌīzd/ ▸*adj.* affected with adrenaline. ■ *informal* excited, charged, or tense: *they possess an adrenalized vigor that distinguishes them from other bands.*

ad·ren·er·gic /ˌadrə'nərjik/ ▸*adj.* *Physiology* relating to or denoting nerve cells in which epinephrine (adrenaline), norepinephrine (noradrenaline), or a similar substance acts as a neurotransmitter. Contrasted with CHOLINERGIC. ▷1930s: from ADRENALINE + Greek *ergon* 'work' + -IC.

a·dre·no·cor·ti·co·trop·ic hor·mone /ə'drēnōˌkôrtikō 'träpik; -'trōpik/ (also **a·dre·no·cor·ti·co·troph·ic hor·mone** /-'träfik; -'trōfik/) (abbr.: **ACTH**) ▸*n.* *Biochemistry* a hormone secreted by the pituitary gland and stimulating the adrenal cortex. ▷1930s: from *adreno-* and *cortico-* (combining forms of ADRENAL and CORTEX) + -TROPHIC or -TROPIC.

a·dre·no·cor·ti·co·tro·pin /ə'drēnōˌkôrtikō'trōpin/ (also **a·dre·no·cor·ti·co·tro·phin** /-'trōfin/) ▸*n.* another term for ADRENOCORTICOTROPIC HORMONE.

A·dri·an /'ādrēən/ a city in southeastern Michigan; pop. 22,097.

A·dri·an IV /'ādrēən/ (*c.*1100–59), pope 1154–59; born *Nicholas Breakspear*. He is the only person from England to have held the office of pope.

A·dri·at·ic /ˌādrē'atik/ ▸*adj.* of or relating to the region comprising the Adriatic Sea and its coasts and islands.
▸*n.* (**the Adriatic**) the Adriatic Sea or its coasts and islands.

A·dri·at·ic Sea an arm of the Mediterranean Sea between the Balkans and the Italian peninsula.

a·drift /ə'drift/ ▸*adj.* [*predic.*] & *adv.* (of a boat or its passengers) floating without being either moored or steered: [as *adv.*] *a cargo ship* ***went adrift*** | [as *adj.*] *the seamen are adrift in lifeboats.* ■ *figurative* (of a person) without purpose or guidance; lost and confused: [as *predic. adj.*] *he was adrift in a strange country* | [as *adv.*] *they were* ***cast adrift*** *in a sea of events.* ▷late 16th cent.: from A-[2] 'on, in' + DRIFT.

a·droit /ə'droit/ ▸*adj.* clever or skillful in using the hands or mind: *he was* ***adroit at*** *tax avoidance.* ▷mid 17th cent.: from French, from *à droit* 'according to right, properly.' —**a·droit·ly** *adv.* —**a·droit·ness** *n.*

ad·sci·ti·tious /ˌadsi'tisʜəs/ ▸*adj.* *rare* forming an addition or supplement; not integral or intrinsic. ▷early 17th cent.: from Latin *adscit-* 'admitted, adopted,' from *adsciscere*, + -ITIOUS[1], on the pattern of *adventitious*.

ADSL ▸*abbr.* *Telecommunications* asynchronous (or asymmetric) digital subscriber line, a method of routing digital data on copper telephone wires, allowing high-speed Internet access and simultaneous use of the line for voice transmission.

ad·sorb /ad'zôrb; -'sôrb/ ▸*v.* [*trans.*] (of a solid) hold (molecules of a gas or liquid or solute) as a thin film on the outside surface or on internal surfaces within the material: *charcoal will not adsorb nitrates* | *the dye is* ***adsorbed onto*** *the fiber.* ▷late 19th cent.: blend of AD- (expressing adherence) + ABSORB. —**ad·sorb·a·ble** *adj.* —**ad·sorp·tion** *n.* —**ad·sorp·tive** *adj.*

ad·sorb·ate /ad'zôrbit; -'sôr-; -ˌbāt/ ▸*n.* a substance adsorbed.

ad·sorb·ent /ad'zôrbənt; -'sôr-/ ▸*n.* a substance that adsorbs another.
▸*adj.* able to adsorb substances.

ad·stra·tum /ad'strātəm; -'stratəm/ ▸*n.* (*pl.* **-stra·ta** /-'strātə; -'stratə/) *Linguistics* a language or group of elements within it that is responsible for changes in a neighboring language. ▷1930s: modern Latin, from Latin *ad* 'to' + *stratum* 'something laid down.' —**ad·strate** /'adˌstrāt/ *adj.*

ad·su·ki /ad'so͝okē; -'zo͞o-/ ▸*n.* variant spelling of ADZUKI.

ad·u·late /'ajəˌlāt/ ▸*v.* [*trans.*] praise (someone) excessively or obsequiously. ▷mid 18th cent.: from Latin *adulat-* 'fawned on,' from the verb *adulari*. —**ad·u·la·tor** /-ˌlātər/ *n.* —**ad·u·la·to·ry** /-ləˌtôrē/ *adj.*

ad·u·la·tion /ˌajə'lāsʜən/ ▸*n.* obsequious flattery; excessive admiration or praise: *he found it difficult to cope with the adulation of the fans.* ▷late Middle English: from Latin *adulatio(n-)*, from *adulari* 'fawn on.'

a·dult /ə'dəlt; 'adˌəlt/ ▸*n.* a person who is fully grown or developed: *children should be accompanied by an adult.* ■ a fully developed animal. ■ *Law* a person who has reached the age of majority. See MAJORITY (sense 2).
▸*adj.* (of a person or animal) fully grown or developed: *the adult inhabitants of the U.S.* ■ of or for adult people: *adult education* | *the responsibilities of adult life.* ■ emotionally and mentally mature: *an effort to be adult and civilized.* ■ sexually explicit or pornographic (used euphemistically to refer to a movie, book, or magazine). ▷mid 16th cent.: from Latin *adultus*, past participle of *adolescere* 'grow to maturity' (see ADOLESCENT). —**a·dult·hood** /-ˌho͝od/ *n.*

a·dult chil·dren ▸*n.* [pl.] adults considered in relation to childhood trauma associated with parents: *adult children of divorce.*

a·dult ed·u·ca·tion ▸*n.* educational programs or courses for adults who are out of school or college.

a·dul·ter·ant /ə'dəltərənt/ ▸*n.* a substance used to adulterate another.
▸*adj.* used in adulterating something. ▷mid 18th cent.: from Latin *adulterant-* 'corrupting,' from the verb *adulterare* (see ADULTERATE).

a·dul·ter·ate /ə'dəltəˌrāt/ ▸*v.* [*trans.*] render (something) poorer in quality by adding another substance, typically an inferior one: *the meat was ground fine and adulterated with potato flour.* See note at POLLUTE. ▷early 16th cent. (as an adjective meaning 'spurious'): from Latin *adulterat-* 'corrupted,' from the verb *adulterare*. —**a·dul·ter·a·tion** /əˌdəltə'rāsʜən/ *n.* —**a·dul·ter·a·tor** /-ˌrātər/ *n.*

a·dul·ter·er /ə'dəltərər/ ▸*n.* a person who commits adultery. ▷early 16th cent.: from the obsolete verb *adulter* 'commit adultery,' from Latin *adulterare* 'debauch, corrupt,' replacing an earlier Middle English noun *avouterer*, from Old French *avoutrer* 'commit adultery,' likewise from Latin *adulterare*.

a·dul·ter·ess /ə'dəlt(ə)ris/ ▸*n.* a female adulterer.

a·dul·ter·ine /ə'dəltəˌrēn; -ˌrīn/ ▸*adj.* (of a child) born as the result of an adulterous relationship. ■ *archaic* & *historical* illegal, unlicensed, or spurious: *an adulterine castle.* ▷mid 18th cent. (in the sense 'due to adulteration'): from Latin *adulterinus*, from *adulterare* 'debauch, corrupt.'

a·dul·ter·ous /ə'dəlt(ə)rəs/ ▸*adj.* of or involving adultery: *an adulterous affair.* ▷mid 16th cent.: from the obsolete noun *adulter* 'adulterer' (see ADULTERY) + -OUS. —**a·dul·ter·ous·ly** *adv.*

a·dul·ter·y /ə'dəlt(ə)rē/ ▸*n.* voluntary sexual intercourse between a married person and a person who is not his or her spouse: *she was* ***committing adultery with*** *a much younger man.* ▷late 15th cent.: from the obsolete noun *adulter*, from Latin *adulter* 'adulterer,' replacing an earlier form *avoutrie*, from Old French *avouterie*, likewise based on Latin *adulter*.

ad·ult·es·cent /ˌadl'tesənt; əˌdəl-/ ▸*n.* *informal* a middle-aged person whose clothes, interests, and activities are typically associated with youth culture. ▷1990s: blend of *adult* and *adolescent*.

ad·um·brate /'adəmˌbrāt; ə'dəm-/ ▸*v.* [*trans.*] *formal* report or represent in outline: *James Madison adumbrated the necessity that the Senate be somewhat insulated from public passions.* ■ indicate faintly: *the walls were not more than adumbrated by the meager light.* ■ foreshadow or symbolize: *what qualities in Christ are adumbrated by the vine?* ■ overshadow: *her happy reminiscences were adumbrated by consciousness of something else.* ▷late 16th cent.: from Latin *adumbrat-* 'shaded,' from the verb *adumbrare*, from *ad-* 'to' (as an intensifier) + *umbrare* 'cast a shadow' (from *umbra* 'shade'). —**ad·um·bra·tion** /ˌadəm'brāsʜən/ *n.* —**ad·um·bra·tive** /ə'dəmbrətiv; 'adəmˌbrā-/ *adj.*

Ad·vai·ta /əd'vītə/ ▸*n.* *Hinduism* a Vedantic doctrine that identifies the individual self (atman) with the ground of reality (brahman). It is associated esp. with the Indian philosopher Shankara (*c* 788–820). ▷Sanskrit, literally 'nonduality.'

ad va·lo·rem /ˌad və'lôrəm/ ▸*adv.* & *adj.* (of the levying of tax or customs duties) in proportion to the estimated value of the goods or transaction concerned. ▷late 17th cent.: Latin, literally 'according to the value.'

ad·vance /əd'vans/ ▸*v.* **1** [*intrans.*] move forward, typically in a purposeful way: *the troops* ***advanced on*** *the capital* | *she stood up and advanced toward him.* ■ make progress: *our knowledge is advancing all the time.* ■ [*trans.*] cause (an event) to occur at an earlier date than planned: *I advanced the date of the meeting by several weeks.* ■ [*trans.*] promote or help the progress of (a person, cause, or plan): *it was a chance to advance his own interests.* ■ [*trans.*] put forward (a theory or suggestion): *the hypothesis I wish to advance in this article.* ■ (esp. of shares of stock) increase in price: *two stocks advanced for every one that fell.* **2** [with *two objs.*] lend (money) to (someone): *the bank advanced them a loan.* ■ pay (money) to (someone) before it is due: *he advanced me a month's salary.*
▸*n.* **1** a forward movement: *the rebels' advance on Madrid was well under way* | *figurative the advance of civilization.* ■ a development or improvement: *genuine* ***advances in*** *engineering techniques* | *decades of great scientific advance.* ■ an increase or rise in amount, value, or price: *bond prices posted vigorous advances.* **2** an amount of money paid before it is due or for work only partly completed: *the author was paid a $250,000 advance* | *I asked for an* ***advance on*** *next month's salary.* ■ a loan: *an advance from the bank.* **3** (usu. **advances**) an approach made to someone, typically with the aim of initiating a sexual encounter: *women accused him of* ***making*** *improper* ***advances.***
▸*adj.* done, sent, or supplied beforehand: *advance notice* | *advance payment.* ▷Middle English: from Old French *avance* (noun), *avancer* (verb), from late Latin *abante* 'in front,' from *ab* 'from' + *ante* 'before.' The initial *a-* was erroneously assimilated to AD- in the 16th cent. —**ad·vanc·er** *n.*
▸*PHRASES* □ **in advance** ahead in time: *you need to book weeks in advance.* □ **in advance of** ahead of in time or space; before: *we went on ahead in advance of the main group.*

ad·vanced /əd'vanst/ ▸*adj.* far on or ahead in development or progress: *negotiations are at an advanced stage* | *the cancer is hopelessly advanced* | *people of advanced years.* ■ new and not yet generally accepted: *his advanced views made him unpopular.*

ad·vanced de·gree ▸*n.* a postgraduate degree, esp. a master's degree or a doctorate.

ad·vanced gas-cooled re·ac·tor (abbr.: **AGR**) ▸*n.* a nuclear reactor in which the coolant is carbon dioxide, with uranium oxide fuel clad in steel and using graphite as a moderator.

ad·vance di·rec·tive ▸*n.* a written statement of a person's wishes regarding medical treatment, often including a living will, made to ensure those wishes are carried out should the person be unable to communicate them to a doctor.

ad·vanced place·ment (abbr.: **AP**) ▸*n.* the placement of a student in a high school course that offers college credit if successfully completed: [as *adj.*] *advanced placement English and chemistry courses.*

ad·vance guard ▸*n.* a body of soldiers preceding and making preparations for the main body of an army.

ad·vance man ▸*n.* a person who visits a location before the arrival of an important visitor to make the appropriate arrangements.

ad·vance·ment /əd'vansmənt/ ▸*n.* the process of promoting a cause or plan: *their lives were devoted to the advancement of science.* ■ the promotion of a person in rank or status: *opportunities for career advancement.* ■ development or improvement: *technological advancements.* ▷Middle English: from Old French *avancement*, from *avancer* 'to advance.'

ad·van·tage /əd'vantij/ ▸*n.* a condition or circumstance that puts one in a favorable or superior position: *companies with a computerized database are* ***at an advantage*** | *she had an* ***advantage over*** *her mother's generation.* ■ the opportunity to gain something; benefit or profit: *you could learn something* ***to your advantage*** | *he saw some advantage in the proposal.* ■ a favorable or desirable circumstance or feature; a benefit: *the village's proximity to the town is an advantage.* ■ *Tennis* a

player's score in a game when they have won the first point after deuce (and will win the game if they win the next point).
▸v. [trans.] put in a favorable or more favorable position. ▷Middle English: from Old French avantage, from avant 'in front,' from late Latin abante (see ADVANCE). —ad·van·ta·geous /ˌadvənˈtājəs; -van-/ adj. —ad·van·ta·geous·ly /ˌadvənˈtājəslē; -van-/ adv.
▸PHRASES □ **have the advantage of** dated be in a stronger position than. □ **take advantage of 1** make unfair demands on (someone) who cannot or will not resist; exploit or make unfair use of for one's own benefit: *people tend to take advantage of a placid nature.* ■ dated (used euphemistically) seduce. **2** make good use of the opportunities offered by (something): *take full advantage of the facilities available.* □ **to advantage** in a way which displays or makes good use of the best aspects of something: *her shoes showed off her legs to advantage | plan your space **to its best advantage**.* □ **turn something to advantage** (or **to one's advantage**) handle or respond to something in such a way as to benefit from it.

ad·van·taged /ədˈvantijd/ ▸adj. having a comparatively favorable position, typically in terms of economic or social circumstances: *children from less advantaged homes.*

ad·vec·tion /adˈvekSHən/ ▸n. the transfer of heat or matter by the flow of a fluid, esp. horizontally in the atmosphere or the sea. ▷early 20th cent.: from Latin advectio(n-), from advehere 'bring,' from ad- 'to' + vehere 'carry.' —**ad·vect** /-ˈvekt/ v. —**ad·vec·tive** /-tiv/ adj.

ad·vent /ˈadˌvent/ ▸n. [in sing.] the arrival of a notable person, thing, or event: *the advent of television.* ■ (**Advent**) the first season of the church year, leading up to Christmas and including the four preceding Sundays. ■ (**Advent**) Christian Theology the coming or second coming of Christ. ▷Old English, from Latin adventus 'arrival,' from advenire, from ad- 'to' + venire 'come.'

Ad·vent cal·en·dar ▸n. a calendar containing small numbered flaps, one of which is opened on each day of Advent to reveal a picture appropriate to the season.

Ad·vent·ist /ˈadˌventist/ ▸n. a member of any of various Christian sects emphasizing belief in the imminent second coming of Christ. See also SEVENTH-DAY ADVENTIST. —**Ad·vent·ism** /-ˌtizəm/ n.

ad·ven·ti·tia /ˌadvenˈtiSH(ē)ə/ ▸n. the outermost layer of the wall of a blood vessel. ▷late 19th cent.: from modern Latin (tunica) adventitia 'additional (sheath).' —**ad·ven·ti·tial** adj.

ad·ven·ti·tious /ˌadvenˈtiSHəs/ ▸adj. happening or carried on according to chance rather than design or inherent nature: *my adventures were always adventitious, always thrust on me.* See note at ACCIDENTAL. ■ coming from outside; not native: *the adventitious population.* ■ Biology formed accidentally or in an unusual anatomical position: *propagation of sour cherries by adventitious shoots.* ■ Botany (of a root) growing directly from the stem or other upper part of a plant. ▷early 17th cent.: from Latin adventicius 'coming to us from abroad' (from advenire 'arrive') + -OUS (see also -ITIOUS²). —**ad·ven·ti·tious·ly** adv.

Ad·vent Sun·day ▸n. the first Sunday in Advent, falling on or near November 30.

ad·ven·ture /adˈvenCHər; əd-/ ▸n. an unusual and exciting, typically hazardous, experience or activity: *her recent adventures in Italy.* ■ daring and exciting activity calling for enterprise and enthusiasm: *she traveled the world in search of adventure | a sense of adventure.* ■ archaic a commercial speculation.
▸v. [intrans.] dated engage in hazardous and exciting activity, esp. the exploration of unknown territory: *they had **adventured into** the forest.* ■ [trans.] dated put (something, esp. money or one's life) at risk: *he adventured $3,000 in the purchase of land.* ▷Middle English: from Old French aventure (noun), aventurer (verb), based on Latin adventurus 'about to happen,' from advenire 'arrive.'

ad·ven·ture game ▸n. a type of computer game in which the participant plays a fantasy role in an episodic adventure story.

ad·ven·tur·er /adˈvenCHərər; əd-/ ▸n. a person who enjoys or seeks adventure. ■ a person willing to take risks or use dishonest methods for personal gain: *a political adventurer.* ■ archaic a financial speculator. ■ archaic a mercenary soldier. ▷late 15th cent. (denoting a gambler): from French aventurier, from aventurer 'venture upon' (see ADVENTURE).

ad·ven·ture·some /adˈvenCHərsəm; əd-/ ▸adj. given to adventures or to running risks; adventurous: *three adventuresome, energetic boys.* ▷early 17th cent. —**ad·ven·ture·some·ness** n.

ad·ven·tur·ess /adˈvenCHəris; əd-/ ▸n. a woman who enjoys or seeks adventure. ■ a woman who seeks social or financial advancement by dishonest or unscrupulous methods: *a sexual adventuress scheming to make a profitable marriage.*

ad·ven·tur·ism /adˈvenCHəˌrizəm; əd-/ ▸n. the willingness to take risks in business or politics (esp. in the context of foreign policy); actions, tactics, or attitudes regarded as daring or reckless. —**ad·ven·tur·ist** n. & adj.

ad·ven·tur·ous /adˈvenCHərəs; əd-/ ▸adj. willing to take risks or to try out new methods, ideas, or experiences: *let's be adventurous | an adventurous traveler.* ■ involving new ideas or methods: *they wanted more adventurous meals.* ■ full of excitement: *my life couldn't be more adventurous.* ▷Middle English: from Old French aventureus, from aventure (see ADVENTURE). —**ad·ven·tur·ous·ly** adv. —**ad·ven·tur·ous·ness** n.

Ad·vent wreath ▸n. a wreath of evergreen foliage in which four candles are set, one to be lit on each Sunday of Advent.

ad·verb /ˈadˌvərb/ ▸n. Grammar a word or phrase that modifies or qualifies an adjective, verb, or other adverb or a word-group, expressing a relation of place, time, circumstance, manner, cause, degree, etc. (e.g., *gently, quite, then, there*). ▷late Middle English: from Latin adverbium, from ad- 'to' (expressing addition) + verbum 'word, verb.'

ad·ver·bi·al /adˈvərbēəl/ Grammar ▸adj. like or relating to an adverb.
▸n. a word or phrase functioning like an adverb. —**ad·ver·bi·al·ly** adv.

ad·ver·game /ˈadvərˌgām/ ▸n. a downloadable or Internet-based computer game that advertises a brand-name product by featuring it as part of the game. ▷blend of advertisement and game. —**ad·ver·gam·ing** n.

ad·ver·sar·i·al /ˌadvərˈse(ə)rēəl/ ▸adj. involving or characterized by conflict or opposition: *industry and government had an adversarial relationship.* ■ opposed; hostile: *Williams had an uncertain relationship to Marxism, sometimes adversarial, sometimes allied.* ■ Law (of a trial or legal procedure) in which the parties in a dispute have the responsibility for finding and presenting evidence: *equality between prosecution and defense is essential in an adversarial system of justice.* Compare with INQUISITORIAL. —**ad·ver·sar·i·al·ly** adv.

ad·ver·sar·y /ˈadvərˌserē/ ▸n. (pl. **-sar·ies**) one's opponent in a contest, conflict, or dispute: *Davis beat his old adversary in the quarterfinals.* ■ (**the Adversary**) the Devil.
▸adj. another term for ADVERSARIAL: *the confrontations of adversary politics.* ▷Middle English: from Old French adversarie, from Latin adversarius 'opposed, opponent,' from adversus (see ADVERSE).

ad·ver·sa·tive /ədˈvərsətiv/ ▸adj. Grammar (of a word or phrase) expressing opposition or antithesis. ▷late Middle English: from French adversatif, -ive or late Latin adversativus, from Latin adversari 'oppose,' from adversus (see ADVERSE).

ad·verse /adˈvərs; ˈadvərs/ ▸adj. preventing success or development; harmful; unfavorable: *taxes are having an **adverse effect** on production | **adverse** weather **conditions**.* See note at HOSTILE. ▷late Middle English: from Old French advers, from Latin adversus 'against, opposite,' past participle of advertere, from ad- 'to' + vertere 'to turn.' Compare with AVERSE. —**ad·verse·ly** adv.

> USAGE **Adverse** means 'hostile, unfavorable, opposed,' and is usually applied to situations, conditions, or events—not to people: *the dry weather has had an **adverse** effect on the garden.* **Averse** is related in origin and also has the sense of 'opposed,' but is usually employed to describe a person's attitude: *I would not be **averse** to making the repairs myself.* See also **usage** at AVERSE.

ad·ver·si·ty /adˈvərsitē/ ▸n. (pl. **-ties**) difficulties; misfortune: *resilience in the face of adversity | she overcame many adversities.* ▷Middle English: from Old French adversite, from Latin adversitas, from advertere 'turn toward.'

ad·vert¹ /ˈadˌvərt/ ▸n. Brit., informal an advertisement. ▷mid 19th cent.: abbreviation.

ad·vert² /adˈvərt; ədˈvərt/ ▸v. [intrans.] (**advert to**) formal refer to in speaking or writing: *he had failed to advert to the consequences that his conduct was having.* ▷late Middle English: from Old French avertire, from Latin advertere 'turn toward' (see ADVERSE). The original sense was 'turn one's attention to,' later 'bring to someone's attention.'

ad·ver·tise /ˈadvərˌtīz/ ▸v. [trans.] describe or draw attention to (a product, service, or event) in a public medium in order to promote sales or attendance: *a billboard advertising beer | many rugs are **advertised as** machine washable | [intrans.] we had a chance to advertise on television.* ■ seek to fill (a vacancy) by putting a notice in a newspaper or other medium: *for every job we advertise we get a hundred applicants | [intrans.] he **advertised for** dancers in the trade papers.* ■ make (a quality or fact) known: *Meryl coughed briefly to advertise her presence.* ■ archaic notify (someone) of something: *some prisoners **advertised** the French **of** this terrible danger.* ▷late Middle English: from Old French advertiss-, lengthened stem of advertir, from Latin advertere 'turn toward' (see ADVERT²). —**ad·ver·tis·er** n.

ad·ver·tise·ment /ˈadvərˌtīzmənt; ədˈvərtiz-/ ▸n. a notice or announcement in a public medium promoting a product, service, or event or publicizing a job vacancy: ***advertisements for** alcoholic drinks | we received only two replies to our advertisement.* ■ (**advertisement for**) informal a person or thing regarded as a means of recommending something: *unhappy clients are not a good advertisement for the company.* ■ archaic a notice to readers in a book. ▷late Middle English (denoting a statement calling attention to something): from Old French advertissement, from the verb advertir (see ADVERTISE).

ad·ver·tis·ing /ˈadvərˌtīziNG/ ▸n. the activity or profession of producing advertisements for commercial products or services: *movie audiences are receptive to advertising | [as adj.] an advertising agency.*

ad·ver·to·ri·al /ˌadvərˈtôrēəl/ ▸n. a newspaper or magazine advertisement giving information about a product in the style of an editorial or objective journalistic article. ▷1960s (originally U.S.): blend of ADVERTISEMENT and EDITORIAL.

ad·vice /ədˈvīs/ ▸n. guidance or recommendations concerning prudent future action, typically given by someone regarded as knowledgeable or authoritative: *she visited the island **on** her doctor's **advice** | even successful businessmen **asked** his **advice**.* ■ a formal notice of a financial transaction: *remittance advices.* ■ archaic information; news: *fresh advices from Europe* ▷Middle English: from Old French avis, based on Latin ad 'to' + visum, past participle of videre 'to see.' The original sense was 'way of looking at something, judgment,' hence later 'an opinion given.'
▸PHRASE □ **take advice** obtain information and guidance, typically from an expert: *he should take advice from his accountant.* ■ (usu. **take someone's advice**) act according to recommendations given: *he took my advice and put his house up for sale.*

ad·vis·a·ble /ədˈvīzəbəl/ ▸adj. [often with infinitive] (of a course of action) to be recommended; sensible: *it is advisable to carry one of the major credit cards | early booking is advisable.* —**ad·vis·a·bil·i·ty** /-ˌvīzəˈbilitē/ n. —**ad·vis·a·bly** /-blē/ adv.

ad·vise /ədˈvīz/ ▸v. [reporting verb] offer suggestions about the best course of action to someone: [trans.] *I advised him to go home | [trans.] he advised caution | [intrans.] we **advise against** sending cash by mail | [with direct speech] "Go to Paris," he advised.* ■ [trans.] recommend (something): *sleeping pills are not advised.* ■ [trans.] inform (someone) about a fact or situation, typically in a formal or official way: *you will be advised of the requirements | [trans.] the lawyer advised the court that his client wished to give evidence.* ▷Middle English: from Old French aviser, based on Latin ad- 'to' + visere, frequentative of videre 'to see.' The original senses included 'look at' and 'consider,' hence 'consider jointly, consult with others.'

ad·vised /ədˈvīzd/ ▸adj. behaving as someone, esp. the speaker, would recommend; sensible; wise: *the department **would be advised to** do some research.*

ad·vis·ed·ly /ədˈvīzidlē/ ▸adv. deliberately and after consideration (used esp. of what might appear a mistake or oversight): *I've used the term "old" advisedly.*

ad·vi·see /adˌvīˈzē; ˌadvī-/ ▸n. a person who meets with an adviser.

ad·vise·ment /ədˈvīzmənt/ ▸n. careful consideration. ■ advice or counsel. ▷Middle English: from Old French avisement, from aviser 'look at' (see ADVISE).
▸PHRASE □ **take something under advisement** reserve judgment while considering something.

ad·vis·er /ədˈvīzər/ (also **ad·vi·sor**) ▸n. a person who

Pronunciation Key ə ago; ər over; ˈə or ˌə up; ˈər or ˌər fur; a hat; ā rate; ä car; CH chew; e let; ē see; e(ə)r air; i fit; ī by; i(ə)r ear; NG sing; ō go; ô for; oi boy; o͝o good; o͞o goo; ou out; SH she; TH thin; T͟H then; (h)w why; ZH vision

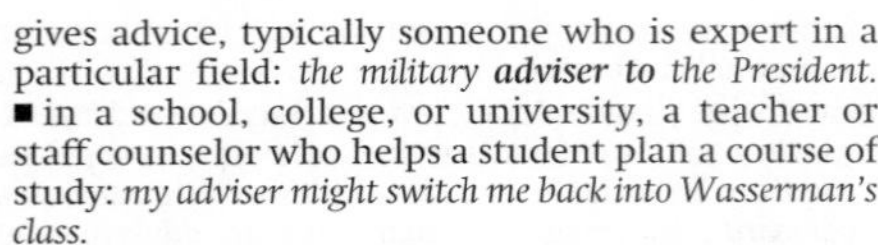

gives advice, typically someone who is expert in a particular field: *the military* ***adviser to*** *the President.* ■ in a school, college, or university, a teacher or staff counselor who helps a student plan a course of study: *my adviser might switch me back into Wasserman's class.*

USAGE The spellings **adviser** and **advisor** are both correct. **Adviser** is the more common spelling in North America; **advisor** is more common in Britain. In both places, however, the adjectival form is **advisory**. In the U.S., **adviser** may be seen as less formal, while **advisor** often suggests an official position.

ad·vi·so·ry /əd'vīzərē/ ▸*adj.* having or consisting in the power to make recommendations but not to take action enforcing them: *an independent advisory committee | the Commission acts in an advisory capacity to the government.* ■ recommended but not compulsory: *universities may treat the recommendations as advisory.*
▸*n.* (*pl.* **-ries**) an official announcement, typically a warning about bad weather conditions: *a frost advisory.*

ad·vo·ca·cy /'advəkəsē/ ▸*n.* public support for or recommendation of a particular cause or policy: *their* ***advocacy of*** *traditional family values.* ■ the profession or work of a legal advocate. ▷late Middle English: via Old French from medieval Latin *advocatia*, from *advocare* 'summon, call to one's aid' (see ADVOCATE).

ad·vo·cate ▸*n.* /'advəkit/ a person who publicly supports or recommends a particular cause or policy: *he was an untiring* ***advocate of*** *economic reform.* ■ a person who pleads on someone else's behalf: *care managers can become advocates for their clients.* ■ a pleader in a court of law; a lawyer: *Marshall was a skilled advocate but a mediocre judge.*
▸*v.* /-ˌkāt/ [*trans.*] publicly recommend or support: *they advocated strict adherence to Islam.* ▷Middle English: from Old French *avocat*, from Latin *advocatus*, past participle (used as a noun) of *advocare* 'call (to one's aid),' from *ad-* 'to' + *vocare* 'to call.' —**ad·vo·ca·tion** /ˌadvə'kāsHən/ *n.* —**ad·vo·ca·tor** /-ˌkātər/ *n.*

ad·vow·son /əd'vouzən/ ▸*n.* (in English ecclesiastical law) the right to recommend a member of the Anglican clergy for a vacant benefice, or to make such an appointment. ▷Middle English (in the sense 'guardianship or patronage of a religious house or benefice,' with the obligation to defend it and speak for it): from Old French *avoeson*, from Latin *advocatio(n-)*, from *advocare* 'summon' (see ADVOCATE).

advt. ▸*abbr.* advertisement.

ad·ware /'adˌwe(ə)r/ ▸*n.* adjunct software that displays advertising while the program it is attached to is running.

A·dy·gea /ˌädə'gāə/ an autonomous republic in the northwestern Caucasus in southwestern Russia; pop. 432,000; capital, Maikop. Its population is largely Muslim. Full name ADYGEI AUTONOMOUS REPUBLIC.

ad·y·tum /'aditəm/ ▸*n.* (*pl.* **-ta** /-tə/) the innermost sanctuary of an ancient Greek temple. ▷Latin, from Greek *aduton*, neuter singular of *adutos* 'impenetrable,' from *a-* 'not' + *duein* 'enter.'

adze /adz/ (**adz**) ▸*n.* a tool similar to an ax with an arched blade at right angles to the handle, used for cutting or shaping large pieces of wood. ▷Old English *adesa*, of unknown origin.

ad·zu·ki /ad'zōōkē/ (also **adzuki bean**) ▸*n.* **1** a small, round, dark-red edible bean. **2** the bushy leguminous Asian plant that produces this bean. • *Vigna angularis*, family Leguminosae. ▷early 18th cent.: from Japanese *azuki*.

AE ▸*abbr.* autoexposure.

Æ (also **æ**) *n.* a ligatured letter used in Old English to represent either a long sound like that in modern American English *hair* or the short vowel of *hat;* currently used in some phonetic alphabets to represent the vowel of *hat,* which is symbolized in this dictionary by /a/ (see ASH[2]).

-ae ▸*suffix* forming plural nouns: **1** used in names of animal and plant families and other groups: *Felidae | Gymnospermae.* **2** used instead of *-as* in the plural of many nonnaturalized or unfamiliar nouns ending in *-a* derived from Latin or Greek: *alumnae | larvae.* ▷representing Latin plural, or the Greek plural ending *-ai* of some nouns.

AEC *historical* ▸*abbr.* Atomic Energy Commission.

ae·dile /'ēˌdīl/ ▸*n. Roman history* either of two (later four) Roman magistrates responsible for public buildings and originally also for the public games and the supply of grain to the city. ▷mid 16th cent.: from Latin *aedilis* 'concerned with buildings,' from *aedes* 'building.' —**ae·dile·ship** /-ˌsHip/ *n.*

AEF ▸*abbr.* American Expeditionary Force.

Ae·ge·an /i'jēən/ ▸*adj.* of or relating to the region comprising the Aegean Sea and its coasts and islands.
▸*n.* (**the Aegean**) the Aegean Sea or its region. ▷early 17th cent.: via Latin from Greek *Aigaios* + -EAN.

Ae·ge·an Is·lands a group of islands in the Aegean Sea that form a region of Greece. The principal islands in the group are Chios, Samos, Lesbos, the Cyclades, and the Dodecanese.

Ae·ge·an Sea a part of the Mediterranean Sea that lies between Greece and Turkey, bounded on the south by Crete and Rhodes and linked to the Black Sea by the Dardanelles, the Sea of Marmara, and the Bosporus.

ae·gis /'ējis/ ▸*n.* [in *sing.*] the protection, backing, or support of a particular person or organization: *negotiations were conducted* ***under the aegis of*** *the UN.* ■ (in classical art and mythology) an attribute of Zeus and Athena (or their Roman counterparts Jupiter and Minerva) usually represented as a goatskin shield. ▷early 17th cent. (denoting armor or a shield, esp. that of a god): via Latin from Greek *aigis* 'shield of Zeus.'

Ae·gis·thus /ē'jisTHəs/ *Greek Mythology* the son of Thyestes and lover of Agamemnon's wife Clytemnestra.

Ael·fric /'alfrik/ (*c.*955–*c.*1020) Anglo-Saxon monk, writer, and grammarian; called **Grammaticus**. He wrote *Lives of the Saints* (993–996).

-aemia ▸*comb. form* British spelling of -EMIA.

Ae·ne·as /i'nēəs/ *Greek Roman Mythology* a Trojan leader, son of Anchises and Aphrodite, and legendary ancestor of the Romans. When Troy fell to the Greeks he escaped and after wandering for many years eventually reached Italy. The story of his voyage is recounted in Virgil's *Aeneid*.

Ae·ne·id /i'nēid/ a Latin epic poem in twelve books by Virgil, that relates the travels and experiences of Aeneas after the fall of Troy.

ae·o·li·an /ē'ōlēən; ā'ō-/ (also **e·o·li·an**) ▸*adj.* **1** *Greek Mythology* of or relating to Aeolus. ■ *poetic/literary* characterized by a sighing or moaning sound as if produced by the wind: *there is a pure aeolian quality, a music as of storms telling their secret.* **2** *chiefly Geology* see EOLIAN. ▷early 17th cent.: from the name AEOLUS + -IAN.

ae·o·li·an harp ▸*n.* a stringed instrument that produces musical sounds when a current of air passes through it.

Ae·o·li·an Is·lands /ē'ōlēən; ā'ōlēən/ ancient name for LIPARI ISLANDS.

Ae·o·li·an mode ▸*n. Music* the mode represented by the natural diatonic scale A–A (containing a minor 3rd, 6th, and 7th). ▷late 18th cent.: from Latin *Aeolius* 'from Aeolis' (an ancient coastal district of Asia Minor) + -AN.

Ae·o·lus /'ēələs/ *Greek Mythology* the god of the winds. ▷from Greek *Aiolos*, from *aiolos* 'swift, changeable.'

ae·on ▸*n. Brit.* variant spelling of EON.

ae·py·or·nis /ˌēpē'ôrnis/ ▸*n.* another term for ELEPHANT BIRD. ▷mid 19th cent.: modern Latin, from Greek *aipus* 'high' + *ornis* 'bird.'

aer·ate /'e(ə)rāt/ ▸*v.* [*trans.*] introduce air into (a material): *she would aerate the lawn with high heels.* ▷late 18th cent.: from Latin *aer* 'air' + -ATE[3], influenced by French *aérer*. —**aer·a·tion** /e(ə)r'āsHən/ *n.* —**aer·a·tor** /-ātər/ *n.*

aer·en·chy·ma /e(ə)'reNGkəmə/ ▸*n. Botany* a soft plant tissue containing air spaces, found esp. in many aquatic plants. ▷late 19th cent.: from Greek *aēr* 'air' + *enkhuma* 'infusion.' —**aer·en·chy·ma·tous** /-mətəs/ *adj.*

aer·i·al /'e(ə)rēəl/ ▸*adj.* [*attrib.*] existing, happening, or operating in the air: *an aerial battle | an intrepid aerial adventurer.* ■ coming or carried out from the air, esp. using aircraft: *aerial bombardment of civilian targets | aerial photography.* ■ (of part of a plant) growing above ground: *knobby sections of aerial roots.* ■ (of a bird) spending much of its time in flight. ■ of or in the atmosphere; atmospheric. ■ insubstantial and hard to grasp or define: *the church may draw fine and aerial distinctions.*
▸*n.* **1** another term for ANTENNA (sense 2): *jiggle the aerial on the radio.* **2** (**aerials**) a type of maneuver in gymnastics, skiing, or surfing involving freestyle jumps or somersaults. ▷late 16th cent. (in the sense 'thin as air, imaginary'): via Latin *aerius* from Greek *aerios* (from *aēr* 'air') + -AL. —**aer·i·al·ly** *adv.*

aer·i·al·ist /'e(ə)rēəlist/ ▸*n.* a person who performs acrobatics high above the ground on a tightrope or trapezes.

aer·i·al lad·der ▸*n.* a long extension ladder, esp. on a fire engine, used to reach high places.

aer·i·al per·spec·tive ▸*n. Art* the technique of representing more distant objects as fainter and more blue.

aer·ie /'e(ə)rē; 'i(ə)rē/ (also **eyr·ie**) ▸*n.* a large nest of a bird of prey, esp. an eagle, typically built high in a tree or on a cliff. ▷late 15th cent.: from medieval Latin *aeria, aerea, eyria*, probably from Old French *aire*, from Latin *area* 'level piece of ground,' in late Latin 'nest of a bird of prey.'

aer·o /'e(ə)rō/ ▸*adj.* **1** short for AERODYNAMIC: *the cars have a lower, more aero front end.* **2** *archaic* short for **aeronautical** (see **aeronautics**): *an aero club | an aero engine.*

aero- ▸*comb. form* **1** of or relating to air: *aerobe | aerobics.* **2** of or relating to aviation: *aerodynamics | aeronautics.* ▷from Greek *aēr* 'air.'

aer·o·bat·ics /ˌe(ə)rə'batiks/ ▸*plural n.* [usu. treated as *sing.*] feats of spectacular flying performed in one or more aircraft to entertain an audience on the ground. ▷World War I: from AERO- + a shortened form of ACROBATICS. —**aer·o·bat·ic** *adj.*

aer·obe /'e(ə)rˌōb/ ▸*n.* a microorganism that grows in the presence of air or requires oxygen for growth. ▷late 19th cent.: coined in French from Greek *aēr* 'air' + *bios* 'life.'

aer·o·bic /ə'rōbik; e(ə)'rō-/ ▸*adj. Biology* relating to, involving, or requiring free oxygen: *simple aerobic bacteria.* ■ relating to or denoting exercise that improves or is intended to improve the efficiency of the body's cardiovascular system in absorbing and transporting oxygen. ▷late 19th cent.: from AERO- + Greek *bios* 'life' + -IC. —**aer·o·bi·cal·ly** *adv.*

aer·o·bics /ə'rōbiks; e(ə)'rō-/ ▸*plural n.* [often treated as *sing.*] vigorous exercises, such as swimming or walking, designed to strengthen the heart and lungs.

aer·o·bi·ol·o·gy /ˌe(ə)rōbī'äləjē/ ▸*n.* the study of airborne microorganisms, pollen, spores, and seeds, esp. as agents of infection.

aer·o·brake /'e(ə)rōˌbrāk/ ▸*v.* [*intrans.*] *technical* cause a spacecraft to slow down by flying through a planet's rarefied atmosphere to produce aerodynamic drag.
▸*n.* a mechanism for aerobraking.

aer·o·drome /'e(ə)rəˌdrōm/ ▸*n.* British term for AIRDROME.

aer·o·dy·nam·ic /ˌe(ə)rōdī'namik/ ▸*adj.* of or relating to aerodynamics: *aerodynamic forces.* ■ of or having a shape that reduces the drag from air moving past: *the plane has a more aerodynamic shape.* —**aer·o·dy·nam·i·cal·ly** *adv.*

aer·o·dy·nam·ics /ˌe(ə)rōdī'namiks/ ▸*plural n.* [treated as *sing.*] the study of the properties of moving air, and esp. of the interaction between the air and solid bodies moving through it. ■ the properties of a solid object regarding the manner in which air flows around it. ■ [treated as *pl.*] these properties insofar as they result in maximum efficiency of motion. —**aer·o·dy·nam·i·cist** /-'naməsist/ *n.*

aer·o·dyne /'e(ə)rəˌdīn/ ▸*n.* any heavier-than-air aircraft that derives its lift principally from aerodynamic forces.

aer·o·e·las·tic·i·ty /ˌe(ə)rō-iˌla'stisitē; -ˌēla-/ ▸*n.* the science of the interaction between aerodynamic forces and nonrigid structures. —**aer·o·e·las·tic** /-i'lastik/ *adj.*

aer·o·foil /'e(ə)rəˌfoil/ ▸*n.* British term for AIRFOIL.

aer·o·gel /'e(ə)rəˌjel/ ▸*n.* a solid material of extremely low density, produced by removing the liquid component from a conventional gel. Also called FROZEN SMOKE.

aer·o·gramme /'e(ə)rəˌgram/ (also **aer·o·gram**) ▸*n.* a sheet of light paper folded and sealed to form a letter for sending by airmail.

aer·o·lite /'e(ə)rəˌlīt/ ▸*n.* a stony meteorite, composed mainly of silicates.

aer·ol·o·gy /e(ə)'räləjē/ ▸*n. dated* the study of the atmosphere, esp. away from ground level. —**aer·o·log·i·cal** /ˌe(ə)rə'läjikəl/ *adj.*

aer·o·mag·net·ic /ˌe(ə)rōmag'netik/ ▸*adj.* relating to or denoting the measurement of the earth's magnetic field using airborne instruments.

aer·o·med·i·cal /ˌe(ə)rō'medikəl/ ▸*adj.* **1** of or relating to the use of aircraft for medical purposes such as transporting patients to a hospital. **2** relating to medical issues associated with air travel.

aer·o·med·i·cine /ˌe(ə)rōˈmedəsən/ ▸*n.* a branch of medicine relating to conditions specific to flight.

aer·o·naut /ˈe(ə)rəˌnôt/ ▸*n. chiefly historical* a traveler in a hot-air balloon, airship, or other flying craft. ▷late 18th cent.: from French *aéronaute*, from Greek *aēr* 'air' + *nautēs* 'sailor.'

aer·o·nau·tics /ˌe(ə)rəˈnôtiks/ ▸*plural n.* [treated as *sing.*] the science or practice of travel through the air. ▷early 19th cent.: from modern Latin *aeronautica* 'matters relating to aeronautics' (see AERONAUT). **—aer·o·nau·tic** *adj.* (*rare*) **—aer·o·nau·ti·cal** *adj.*

ae·ron·o·my /eˈränəmē/ ▸*n.* the science of the upper atmosphere, esp. those regions where there is significant ionization of gases.

aer·o·pha·gia /ˌe(ə)rəˈfājə; -jēə/ ▸*n. Medicine* the swallowing of air, whether deliberately to stimulate belching, accidentally, or as an involuntary habit.

aer·o·phone /ˈe(ə)rəˌfōn/ ▸*n. technical Music* a wind instrument.

aer·o·plane /ˈe(ə)rəˌplān/ ▸*n.* British term for AIRPLANE. ▷late 19th cent.: from French *aéroplane*, from *aéro-* 'air' + Greek *-planos* 'wandering.'

aer·o·shell /ˈe(ə)rōˌshel/ ▸*n.* a casing that protects a spacecraft during reentry.

aer·o·sol /ˈerəˌsôl; -ˌsäl/ ▸*n.* a substance enclosed under pressure and able to be released as a fine spray, typically by means of a propellant gas. ■ a container holding such a substance. ■ *Chemistry* a colloidal suspension of particles dispersed in air or gas. ▷1920s: from AERO- + SOL[2].

aer·o·sol·ize /ˈe(ə)rəsôˌlīz; -sä-/ ▸*v.* [*trans.*] *technical* convert into a fine spray or colloidal suspension in air: [as *adj.*] (**aerosolized**) *the drug is being tested in an aerosolized form.*

aer·o·space /ˈe(ə)rōˌspās/ ▸*n.* the branch of technology and industry concerned with both aviation and space flight.

aer·o·stat /ˈe(ə)rəˌstat/ ▸*n.* an airship or hot-air balloon, esp. one that is tethered. ▷late 18th cent.: from French *aérostat*, from Greek *aēr* 'air' + *statos* 'standing.'

Aes·chi·nes /ˈeskəˌnēz/ (*c.*390–*c.*314 BC), Athenian orator and statesman. He opposed Demosthenes' efforts to unite the Greek city-states against Macedon.

Aes·chy·lus /ˈeskələs/ (*c.*525–*c.*456 BC), Greek dramatist. He is best known for his trilogy, the *Oresteia* (458 BC), consisting of the tragedies *Agamemnon*, *Choephoroe*, and *Eumenides*.

Aes·cu·la·pi·an /ˌesk(y)əˈlāpēən/ ▸*adj. archaic* of or relating to medicine or physicians. ▷late 16th cent.: from Latin *Aesculapius*, the name of the Roman god of medicine, + -IAN.

Aes·cu·la·pi·an snake ▸*n.* a long, slender olive-brown to grayish snake found in Europe and southwestern Asia. In ancient times it was protected because of its mythical link with the god of healing, Aesculapius. • *Elaphe longissima*, family Colubridae.

Ae·sir /ˈāzir; ˈāsir/ *Scandinavian Mythology* the Norse gods and goddesses collectively, including Odin, Thor, and Balder.

Ae·sop /ˈēˌsäp; ˈēsəp/ (6th century BC), Greek storyteller. The moral animal fables associated with Aesop were probably collected from many sources and initially communicated orally.

aes·thete /ˈesˌthēt/ (also **es·thete**) ▸*n.* a person who has or affects to have a special appreciation of art and beauty. ▷late 19th cent.: from Greek *aisthētēs* 'a person who perceives,' or from AESTHETIC, on the pattern of the pair *athlete*, *athletic*.

aes·thet·ic /esˈthetik/ (also **es·thet·ic**) ▸*adj.* concerned with beauty or the appreciation of beauty: *the pictures give great aesthetic pleasure.* ■ giving or designed to give pleasure through beauty; of pleasing appearance.
▸*n.* [in *sing.*] a set of principles underlying and guiding the work of a particular artist or artistic movement: *the Cubist aesthetic.* ▷late 18th cent. (in the sense 'relating to perception by the senses'): from Greek *aisthētikos*, from *aisthēta* 'perceptible things,' from *aisthesthai* 'perceive.' The sense 'concerned with beauty' was coined in German in the mid 18th cent. and adopted into English in the early 19th cent., but its use was controversial until late in the century. **—aes·thet·i·cal·ly** /-ik(ə)lē/ *adv.* [as *submodifier*] *an aesthetically pleasing color combination.*

aes·the·ti·cian /ˌesthəˈtishən/ (also **es·the·ti·cian**) ▸*n.* **1** a person who is knowledgeable about the nature and appreciation of beauty, esp. in art. **2** a beautician.

aes·thet·i·cism /esˈthetəˌsizəm/ ▸*n.* the approach to art exemplified by (but not restricted to) the Aesthetic Movement.

aes·thet·i·cize /esˈthetəˌsīz/ ▸*v.* [*trans.*] represent (something) as being beautiful or artistically pleasing.

Aes·thet·ic Move·ment a literary and artistic movement that flourished in England in the 1880s, devoted to "art for art's sake" and rejecting the notion that art should have a social or moral purpose. Its chief exponents included Oscar Wilde, Max Beerbohm, and Aubrey Beardsley.

aes·thet·ics /esˈthetiks/ (also **es·thet·ics**) ▸*plural n.* [usu. treated as *sing.*] a set of principles concerned with the nature and appreciation of beauty, esp. in art. ■ the branch of philosophy that deals with the principles of beauty and artistic taste.

aes·ti·val ▸*adj.* variant spelling of ESTIVAL.

aes·ti·vate ▸*v.* variant spelling of ESTIVATE.

aes·ti·va·tion ▸*n.* variant spelling of ESTIVATION.

aet. (also **aetat.**) ▸*abbr.* aetatis.

ae·ta·tis /īˈtātis; ēˈtātis/ ▸*adj.* of or at the age of: *his son, aetatis 13, learned in nothing.* ▷early 19th cent.: Latin.

ae·ther ▸*n.* variant spelling of ETHER (senses 2 and 3).

AF ▸*abbr.* ■ air force. ■ audio frequency. ■ autofocus.

af- ▸*prefix* **1** variant spelling of AD- **2** assimilated before *f* (as in *affiliate*, *affirm*).

A·far /ˈäˌfär/ ▸*n.* **1** (*pl.* same or **A·fars**) a member of a people living in Djibouti, Eritrea, and Ethiopia. **2** the Cushitic language of this people.
▸*adj.* of or relating to this people or their language. ▷from Afar *qafar*.

a·far /əˈfär/ ▸*adv. chiefly poetic/literary* at or to a distance: *our hero traveled afar | for months he had loved her* ***from afar.*** ▷Middle English *of feor* 'from far.'

A·fars and Is·sas, French Territory of the /ˈäˌfärz ənd ēˈsäz/ former name (1946–77) of DJIBOUTI.

AFB ▸*abbr.* Air Force Base.

AFC ▸*abbr.* ■ American Football Conference. ■ automatic frequency control, a system in radios and television that keeps them tuned to an incoming signal.

AFDC ▸*abbr.* Aid to Families with Dependent Children, a welfare benefit program of the federal government.

a·feard /əˈfi(ə)rd/ (also **a·feared**) ▸*adj. archaic* or *dialect* afraid. ▷Old English, from *āfǣran* 'frighten,' from *ā-* (expressing intensity) + *fǣran* (see FEAR); used commonly by Shakespeare, but rarely after 1700 in written form.

a·fe·brile /āˈfebrəl; -ˈfē-/ ▸*adj. Medicine* not feverish. ▷late 19th cent.: from A-[1] 'not' + FEBRILE.

af·fa·ble /ˈafəbəl/ ▸*adj.* friendly, good-natured, or easy to talk to: *an affable and agreeable companion.* ▷late Middle English: via Old French from Latin *affabilis*, from the verb *affari*, from *ad-* 'to' + *fari* 'speak.' **—af·fa·bil·i·ty** /ˌafəˈbilitē/ *n.* **—af·fa·bly** /-blē/ *adv.*

af·fair /əˈfe(ə)r/ ▸*n.* **1** an event or sequence of events of a specified kind or that has previously been referred to: *the board admitted responsibility for the affair | I wanted the funeral to be a family affair.* ■ a matter that is a particular person's concern or responsibility: *what you do in your spare time is your affair.* ■ (**affairs**) matters of public interest and importance: *commissions were created to advise on foreign affairs.* ■ (**affairs**) business and financial dealings: *his time was spent in winding up his affairs.* ■ [with *adj.*] *informal* an object of a particular type: *her dress was a black low-cut affair.* **2** a love affair: *his wife is having an affair.* ▷Middle English: from Old French *afaire*, from *à faire* 'to do'; compare with ADO.

af·faire /äˈfe(ə)r; äˈfer/ (also **af·faire de** or **du cœur** /də ˈkœr/) ▸*n.* a love affair. ▷early 19th cent.: French, literally 'affair (of the heart).'

af·fect[1] /əˈfekt/ ▸*v.* [*trans.*] have an effect on; make a difference to: *the dampness began to affect my health |* [with *clause*] *your attitude will* ***affect how*** *successful you are.* ■ touch the feelings of (someone); move emotionally: [as *adj.*] (**affecting**) *a highly affecting account of her experiences in prison.* See note at MOVING. ■ (of an illness) attack or infect: *people who are affected by AIDS.* ▷late Middle English (in the sense 'attack as a disease'): from French *affecter* or Latin *affect-* 'influenced, affected,' from the verb *afficere* (see AFFECT[2]). **—af·fect·ing·ly** *adv.*

USAGE **Affect** and **effect** are both verbs and nouns, but only **effect** is common as a noun, usually meaning 'a result, consequence, impression, etc.': *my father's warnings had no* ***effect*** *on my adventurousness.* The noun **affect** is restricted almost entirely to psychology (see AFFECT[2]). As verbs, they are used differently. **Affect** most commonly means 'produce an effect on, influence': *smoking during pregnancy can* ***affect*** *the baby's development.* **Affect** also means 'pretend to have or feel (something)' (see AFFECT[3]): *she affected a concern for those who had lost their jobs.* **Effect** means 'bring about': *the negotiators* ***effected*** *an agreement despite many difficulties.*

af·fect[2] /əˈfekt/ ▸*v.* [*trans.*] pretend to have or feel (something): *as usual I affected a supreme unconcern* [with *infinitive*] *a book that affects to loathe the modern world.* ■ use, wear, or assume (something) pretentiously or so as to make an impression on others: *an American who had affected a British accent.* ▷late Middle English: from French *affecter* or Latin *affectare* 'aim at,' frequentative of *afficere* 'work on, influence,' from *ad-* 'at, to' + *facere* 'do.' The original sense was 'like, love,' hence '(like to) use, assume, etc.'

USAGE See **usage** at AFFECT[1].

af·fect[3] /ˈafekt; əˈfekt/ ▸*n. Psychology* emotion or desire, esp. as influencing behavior or action. See note at EMOTION. ▷late 19th cent.: coined in German from Latin *affectus* 'disposition,' from *afficere* 'to influence' (see AFFECT[2]). **—af·fect·less** *adj.* **—af·fect·less·ness** *n.*

USAGE See **usage** at AFFECT[1].

af·fec·ta·tion /ˌafekˈtāshən/ ▸*n.* behavior, speech, or writing that is artificial and designed to impress: *the affectation of a man who measures every word for effect | she called the room her boudoir, which he thought an affectation.* ■ a studied display of real or pretended feeling: *an affectation of calm.* ▷mid 16th cent.: from Latin *affectatio(n-)*, from the verb *affectare* (see AFFECT[2]).

af·fect·ed /əˈfektid/ ▸*adj.* **1** influenced or touched by an external factor: *apply moist heat to the affected area.* **2** artificial, pretentious, and designed to impress: *the gesture appeared both affected and stagy.* **3** [*predic.*] *archaic* disposed or inclined in a specified way: *you might become differently affected toward him.* **—af·fect·ed·ly** *adv.* (in sense 2).

af·fect·ed class ▸*n.* a group adversely affected from a common cause, as defined by legislation, litigation, or prevailing practice: *any employee in an affected class may volunteer to be laid off.*

af·fec·tion /əˈfekshən/ ▸*n.* **1** a gentle feeling of fondness or liking: *she felt* ***affection for*** *the wise old lady | he won a place in her affections.* ■ physical expressions of these feelings: *the prisoners crave affection and hence participate in sexual relationships.* **2** *archaic* the act or process of affecting or being affected. ■ a condition of disease: *an affection of the skin.* ■ a mental state; an emotion. ▷Middle English: via Old French from Latin *affectio(n-)*, from *afficere* 'to influence' (see AFFECT[2]). **—af·fec·tion·al** /-shənl/ *adj.*

af·fec·tion·ate /əˈfekshənit/ ▸*adj.* readily feeling or showing fondness or tenderness: *a happy and affectionate family.* ■ expressing fondness: *an affectionate kiss.* ▷late 15th cent. (in the sense 'disposed, inclined toward'): from French *affectionné* 'beloved' or medieval Latin *affectionatus* 'devoted,' from *affectio(n-)*, from *afficere* 'to influence' (see AFFECT[2]). **—af·fec·tion·ate·ly** *adv.*

af·fec·tive /əˈfektiv/ ▸*adj. chiefly Psychology* relating to moods, feelings, and attitudes: *affective disorders.* ▷late Middle English: via French from late Latin *affectivus*, from *afficere* (see AFFECT[2]). **—af·fec·tive·ly** *adv.* **—af·fec·tiv·i·ty** /ˌafekˈtivitē/ *n.*

af·fen·pin·scher /ˈäfənˌpinchər/ ▸*n.* a dog of a small breed resembling a griffin. ▷early 20th cent.: from German, from *Affe* 'monkey' + *Pinscher* 'terrier.'

af·fer·ent /ˈaf(ə)rənt/ ▸*adj. Physiology* conducting or conducted inward or toward something (for nerves, the central nervous system; for blood vessels, the organ supplied). The opposite of EFFERENT.
▸*n.* an afferent nerve fiber or vessel. ▷mid 19th cent.: from Latin *afferent-* 'bringing toward', from the verb *afferre*, from *ad-* 'to' + *ferre* 'bring.'

af·fi·ance /əˈfīəns/ ▸*v.* (**be affianced**) *poetic/literary* be engaged to marry: *Ann Elliott was* ***affianced to*** *Col. Lewis Morris.* ▷late 15th cent.: from Old French *afiancer*, from *afier* 'promise, entrust,' from medieval Latin *affidare* 'declare on oath,' from *ad-* 'toward' + *fides* 'trust.'

af·fi·ant /əˈfīənt/ ▸*n. Law* a person who swears to an

affidavit. ▷early 19th cent.: from French, present participle of *afier,* from medieval Latin *affidare* 'declare on oath' (see AFFIANCE).

af·fi·da·vit /ˌafiˈdāvit/ ▸*n. Law* a written statement confirmed by oath or affirmation, for use as evidence in court. ▷mid 16th cent.: from medieval Latin, literally 'he has stated on oath,' from *affidare.*

af·fil·i·ate ▸*v.* /əˈfilēˌāt/ [*trans.*] (usu. **be affiliated with**) officially attach or connect (a subsidiary group or a person) to an organization: *the college is* ***affiliated with*** *the University of Wisconsin* | [as *adj.*] (**affiliated**) *affiliated union members.* ■ [*intrans.*] officially join or become attached to an organization: *the membership of the National Writers Union voted to* ***affiliate with*** *the United Auto Workers.*
▸*n.* /-it/ a person or organization officially attached to a larger body: *the company established links with British affiliates.* ▷mid 18th cent.: from medieval Latin *affiliat-* 'adopted as a son,' from the verb *affiliare,* from *ad-* 'toward' + *filius* 'son.' **—af·fil·i·a·tive** /-ətiv; -ˌātiv/ *adj.*

af·fil·i·a·tion /əˌfilēˈāsʜən/ ▸*n.* the state or process of affiliating or being affiliated: *he had no particular affiliation, no close associates* | *his political affiliations.* ▷late 18th cent.: from French, from medieval Latin *affiliatio(n-),* from the verb *affiliare* (see AFFILIATE).

af·fine /əˈfīn; ˈafīn/ ▸*adj. Mathematics* allowing for or preserving parallel relationships.
▸*n. Anthropology* a relative by marriage. ▷early 16th cent. (as a noun): from Old French *afin* or Latin *affinis* 'related' (see AFFINITY). The mathematical sense dates from the early 20th cent.

af·fined /əˈfīnd/ ▸*adj. archaic* related or connected. ▷late 16th cent.: from Latin *affinis* 'related' (see AFFINITY) + -ED[1].

af·fin·i·ty /əˈfinitē/ ▸*n.* (*pl.* **-ties**) (often **affinity between/for/with**) a spontaneous or natural liking or sympathy for someone or something: *he has an affinity for the music of Berlioz.* ■ a similarity of characteristics suggesting a relationship, esp. a resemblance in structure between animals, plants, or languages: *a building with no* ***affinity to*** *contemporary architectural styles.* See note at LIKENESS. ■ relationship, esp. by marriage as opposed to blood ties. ■ *chiefly Biochemistry* the degree to which a substance tends to combine with another: *the affinity of hemoglobin for oxygen.* ▷Middle English (in the sense 'relationship by marriage'): via Old French from Latin *affinitas,* from *affinis* 'related' (literally 'bordering on'), from *ad-* 'to' + *finis* 'border.'

af·fin·i·ty card ▸*n.* a credit card carrying the name of an organization to which a portion of the money spent using the card is paid.

af·fin·i·ty group ▸*n.* a group of people linked by a common interest or purpose.

af·firm /əˈfərm/ ▸*v.* [*reporting verb*] state as a fact; assert strongly and publicly: [*trans.*] *he affirmed the country's commitment to peace* | [with *clause*] *we affirm that God's grace is available to all.* | [with *direct speech*] *"Pessimism," she affirmed, "is the most rational view."* ■ [*trans.*] declare one's support for; uphold or defend: *the referendum affirmed the republic's right to secede.* ■ [*trans.*] *Law* accept or confirm the validity of (a judgment or agreement); ratify. ■ [*intrans.*] *Law* make a formal declaration rather than taking an oath (e.g., to testify truthfully). ■ *Law* [*trans.*] (of a court) uphold (a decision) on appeal. ▷Middle English (in the sense 'make firm'): via Old French from Latin *affirmare,* from *ad-* 'to' + *firmus* 'strong.' **—af·firm·er** *n.*

af·firm·a·tion /ˌafərˈmāsʜən/ ▸*n.* the action or process of affirming or being affirmed: *an affirmation of basic human values* | *he nodded in affirmation.* ■ *Law* a formal declaration by a person who declines to take an oath for reasons of conscience. ▷late Middle English: from Latin *affirmation-,* from the verb *affirmare* (see AFFIRM).

af·firm·a·tive /əˈfərmətiv/ ▸*adj.* agreeing with a statement or to a request: *an affirmative answer.* ■ (of a vote) expressing approval or agreement. ■ supportive, hopeful, or encouraging: *the music's natural buoyancy and affirmative character.* ■ active or obligatory: *they have an affirmative duty to stop crime in their buildings* | *using affirmative measures to influence human rights policies.* ■ *Grammar & Logic* stating that a fact is so; making an assertion. Contrasted with INTERROGATIVE and NEGATIVE.
▸*n.* a statement of agreement with an assertion or request: *he accepted her reply as an affirmative.* ■ (**the affirmative**) a position of agreement or confirmation: *his answer veered toward the affirmative.* ■ *Grammar* a word or particle used in making assertions. ■ *Logic* a statement asserting that something is true of the subject of a proposition.
▸*exclam.* expressing agreement with a statement or request; yes. ▷late Middle English (in the sense 'assertive, positive'): via Old French from late Latin *affirmativus,* from *affirmare* 'assert' (see AFFIRM). **—af·firm·a·tive·ly** *adv.*
▸*PHRASE* □ **in the affirmative** so as to accept or agree to a statement or request: *he answered the question in the affirmative.*

af·firm·a·tive ac·tion ▸*n.* an action or policy favoring those who tend to suffer from discrimination, esp. in relation to employment or education; positive discrimination.

af·fix ▸*v.* /əˈfiks/ [*trans.*] stick, attach, or fasten (something) to something else: *he licked the stamp and* ***affixed it to*** *the envelope.*
▸*n.* /ˈaˌfiks/ *Grammar* an additional element placed at the beginning or end of a root, stem, or word, or in the body of a word, to modify its meaning. See also INFIX, PREFIX, SUFFIX. ▷late Middle English: from Old French *affixer* or medieval Latin *affixare,* frequentative of Latin *affigere,* from *ad-* 'to' + *figere* 'to fix.' **—af·fix·a·tion** /ˌafikˈsāsʜən/ *n.*

af·fla·tus /əˈflātəs/ ▸*n. formal* a divine creative impulse or inspiration. ▷mid 17th cent.: from Latin, from the verb *afflare,* from *ad-* 'to' + *flare* 'to blow.'

af·flict /əˈflikt/ ▸*v.* [*trans.*] (of a problem or illness) cause pain or suffering to; affect or trouble: *serious ills afflict the industry* | *his younger child was afflicted with a skin disease* | [as *plural n.*] (**the afflicted**) *he comforted the afflicted.* ■ *Astrology* (of a celestial body) be in a stressful aspect with (another celestial body or a point on the ecliptic): *Jupiter is afflicted by Mars in opposition.* ▷late Middle English (in the sense 'deject, humiliate'): from Latin *afflictare* 'injure, harass,' or from *afflict-* 'knocked down, weakened': both from the verb *affligere,* from *ad-* 'to' + *fligere* 'to strike, dash.' **—af·flic·tive** /-tiv/ *adj.* (*archaic*).

af·flic·tion /əˈfliksʜən/ ▸*n.* something that causes pain or suffering: *a crippling affliction of the nervous system.* ■ pain or suffering: *poor people in great affliction.* ■ *Astrology* an instance of one celestial body afflicting another. ▷Middle English (originally in the sense 'infliction of pain or humiliation,' specifically 'religious self-mortification'): via Old French from Latin *afflictio(n-),* from the verb *affligere* (see AFFLICT).

af·flu·ent /ˈaflo͞oənt; əˈflo͞o-/ ▸*adj.* **1** (esp. of a group or area) having a great deal of money; wealthy: *the affluent societies of the western world* | [as *plural n.*] (**the affluent**) *only the affluent could afford to travel abroad.* See note at WEALTHY. **2** *archaic* (of water) flowing freely or in great quantity.
▸*n. archaic* a tributary stream. ▷late Middle English (sense 2): via Old French from Latin *affluent-* 'flowing toward, flowing freely,' from the verb *affluere,* from *ad-* 'to' + *fluere* 'to flow.' **—af·flu·ence** *n.* **—af·flu·ent·ly** *adv.*

af·flu·en·tial /ˌaflo͞oˈencʜəl/ *informal* ▸*adj.* rich and socially influential: *the daughter of an affluential businessman.*
▸*n.* a rich and socially influential person: *the local affluentials have driven up property values.* ▷1970s: blend of *affluent* and *influential.*

af·flu·en·za /ˌaflo͞oˈenzə/ ▸*n.* a psychological malaise supposedly affecting wealthy young people, symptoms of which include a lack of motivation, feelings of guilt, and a sense of isolation. ▷1970s: blend of *affluent* and *influenza.*

af·flux /ˈaˌfləks/ ▸*n. archaic* a flow of something, esp. water or air. ▷early 17th cent.: from medieval Latin *affluxus,* from *affluere* 'flow freely' (see AFFLUENT).

af·ford /əˈfôrd/ ▸*v.* [*trans.*] **1** (**can/could afford**) have enough money to pay for: *the best that I could afford was a first-floor room* | [with *infinitive*] *we could never have afforded to heat the place.* ■ have (a certain amount of something, esp. money or time) available or to spare: *it was taking up more time than he could afford.* ■ [with *infinitive*] be able to do something without risk of adverse consequences: *kings could afford to be wrathful.* **2** provide or supply (an opportunity or facility): *the rooftop terrace affords beautiful views* | [with *two objs.*] *they were afforded the luxury of bed and breakfast.* See note at GIVE. ▷late Old English *geforthian,* from *ge-* + *forthian* 'to further,' from FORTH. The original sense was 'promote, perform, accomplish,' later 'manage, be in a position to do.'

af·ford·a·ble /əˈfôrdəbəl/ ▸*adj.* inexpensive; reasonably priced: *affordable housing.* **—af·ford·a·bil·i·ty** /əˌfôrdəˈbilitē/ *n.*

af·for·est·a·tion /əˌfôrəˈstāsʜən; əˌfär-/ ▸*v.* [*trans.*] the conversion (of land) into forest, esp. for commercial use. ▷early 16th cent.: from medieval Latin *afforestare,* from *ad-* 'to' (expressing change) + *foresta* 'forest.' **—af·for·est** /əˈfôrist; əˈfär-/ *v.*

af·fran·chise /əˈfranˌcʜīz/ ▸*v.* [*trans.*] *archaic* release from servitude. ▷late 15th cent.: from Old French *afranchiss-,* lengthened stem of *afranchir,* from *a-* (from Latin *ad* 'to, at') + *franc* 'free.'

af·fray /əˈfrā/ ▸*n. Law, dated* an instance of group fighting in a public place that disturbs the peace: *Lowe was charged with* ***causing an affray*** | *a person guilty of affray.* ▷Middle English (in the general sense 'disturbance, fray'): from Anglo-Norman French *afrayer* 'disturb, startle,' based on an element of Germanic origin related to Old English *frithu* 'peace, safety' (compare with German *Friede* 'peace').

af·fri·cate /ˈafrikit/ ▸*n. Phonetics* a phoneme that combines a plosive with an immediately following fricative or spirant sharing the same place of articulation, e.g., *ch* as in *chair* and *j* as in *jar.* ▷late 19th cent.: from Latin *affricatus,* past participle of *affricare,* from *ad-* 'to' + *fricare* 'to rub.'

af·fright /əˈfrīt/ *archaic* ▸*v.* [*trans.*] frighten (someone): *ghosts could never affright her.*
▸*n.* fright: *the deer gazed at us in affright.* ▷late Middle English: in early use from *āfyrhted* 'frightened' in Old English; later by vague form association with FRIGHT.

Af·fri·la·chi·an /ˌafriˈlācʜ(ē)ən/ ▸*n.* an African American who is native to or resides in Appalachia: [as *modifier*] *Affrilachian poets.* ▷blend of *African (American)* and *Appalachian.*

af·front /əˈfrənt/ ▸*n.* an action or remark that causes outrage or offense: *he took his son's desertion as a personal affront* | *privilege publicly worn is* ***an affront to*** *democracy.*
▸*v.* [*trans.*] (usu. **be affronted**) offend the modesty or values of: *she was affronted by his familiarity.* ▷Middle English (as a verb): from Old French *afronter* 'to slap in the face, insult,' based on Latin *ad frontem* 'to the face.'

af·fron·té /ˌafrənˈtā; əˈfrəntē/ (also **af·fron·ty** /əˈfrəntē/) ▸*adj.* [*predic.* or *postpositive*] *Heraldry* (esp. of an animal's head) facing the observer. ▷mid 16th cent. (as *affronty*): French, past participle of *affronter* 'to face.'

Af·ghan /ˈafˌgan/ ▸*n.* **1** a native or national of Afghanistan, or a person of Afghan descent. **2** another term for PASHTO. **3** (**afghan**) a woolen blanket or shawl, typically one knitted or crocheted in strips or squares. **4** short for AFGHAN HOUND.
▸*adj.* of or relating to Afghanistan, its people, or their language. ▷from Pashto *afghānī.*

Af·ghan hound ▸*n.* a tall hunting dog of a breed with long silky hair.

Afghan hound

af·ghan·i /afˈganē; -ˈgä-/ ▸*n.* (*pl.* **-ghan·is**) the basic monetary unit of Afghanistan, equal to 100 puls. ▷from Pashto *afghānī.*

Af·ghan·i·stan /afˈganəˌstan/ a mountainous landlocked republic in central Asia; pop. 16,600,000; capital, Kabul; official languages, Pashto and Dari (the local form of Persian).

Part of the Indian Mogul empire, Afghanistan became independent in the mid 18th century. It was occupied by Soviet forces 1979–89; after they withdrew, the country was thrown into turmoil with various Islamic groups struggling for power. The Taliban seized power in 1996; following the attacks of September 11, 2001, U.S.-led forces invaded Afghanistan and toppled the Taliban. A new government was formed, and a constitution was signed January 16, 2004, but instability continued in many areas of the country.

a·fi·ci·o·na·do /əˌfisн(ē)əˈnädō; əˌfisyə-/ ▸*n.* (*pl.* **-dos**) a person who is very knowledgeable and enthusiastic about an activity, subject, or pastime: *aficionados of the finest wines.* ▷mid 19th cent. (denoting a devotee of bullfighting): from Spanish, 'amateur,' past participle of *aficioner* 'become fond of' used as a noun, based on Latin *affectio(n-)* '(favorable) disposition toward' (see AFFECTION).

a·field /əˈfēld/ ▸*adv.* **1** to or at a distance: *competitors from* ***as far afield*** *as Hong Kong.* **2** in the field (usually in reference to hunting): *the satisfaction of a day afield.* ▷Middle English (sense 2): from A-[2] 'on, in' + FIELD.

a·fire /əˈfī(ə)r/ ▸*adv.* & *adj. chiefly poetic/literary* on fire; burning: [as *predic. adj.*] *the whole mill was afire.*

a·flame /əˈflām/ ▸*adv.* & *adj.* in flames; burning: [as *adv.*] *pour brandy over the steaks and then set aflame.*

af·la·tox·in /ˌafləˈtäksən/ ▸*n. Chemistry* any of a class of toxic compounds that are produced by certain molds found in food, and can cause liver damage and cancer. • These are produced by fungi of the *Aspergillus flavus* group, subdivision Deuteromycotina. ▷1960s: from elements of the modern Latin taxonomic name (see above) + TOXIN.

AFL-CIO ▸*abbr.* American Federation of Labor and Congress of Industrial Organizations.

a·float /əˈflōt/ ▸*adj.* & *adv.* floating in water; not sinking: [as *adv.*] *they trod water to keep afloat* | [as *predic. adj.*] *the canoes were still afloat.* ■ on board a ship or boat: [as *adv.*] *flotilla sailing is a sociable way to explore while living afloat.* ■ *figurative* out of debt or difficulty: [as *adv.*] *I contrived to stay afloat in honest self-employment.* ■ in general circulation; current: [as *predic. adj.*] *the rumor has been afloat that I am far advanced in years.* ▷Old English *on flote* (see A-[2], FLOAT), influenced in Middle English by Old Norse *á flot(i)* and Old French *en flot.*

a·foot /əˈfo͝ot/ ▸*adv.* **1** in preparation or progress; happening or beginning to happen: [as *predic. adj.*] *plans are afoot for a festival.* **2** on foot: [as *adv.*] *they were forced to go afoot.*

a·fore /əˈfôr/ ▸*prep. archaic* or *dialect* before. ▷Old English *onforan* (see A-[2], FORE).

afore- ▸*prefix* before; previously.

a·fore·men·tioned /əˈfôrˌmensнənd/ ▸*adj.* denoting a thing or person previously mentioned: *songs from the aforementioned album.*

a·fore·said /əˈfôrˌsed/ ▸*adj.* another term for AFOREMENTIONED.

a·fore·thought /əˈfôrˌтнôt/ ▸*adj.* see MALICE AFORETHOUGHT.

a for·ti·o·ri /ˈä ˌfôrtēˈôrē; ˈā ˌfôrtēˈôrī/ ▸*adv.* & *adj.* used to express a conclusion for which there is stronger evidence than for a previously accepted one: [as *adv.*] *they reject all absolute ideas of justice, and a fortiori the natural-law position.* ▷early 17th cent.: Latin, from *a fortiori argumento* 'from stronger argument.'

a·foul /əˈfoul/ ▸*adv.* into conflict or difficulty with.
▸*PHRASES* □ **fall afoul of** see FALL. □ **run afoul of** see RUN.

a·fraid /əˈfrād/ ▸*adj.* [*predic.*] feeling fear or anxiety; frightened: *I'm* ***afraid of*** *dogs* | *she tried to think about the future without feeling afraid.* ■ worried that something undesirable will occur or be done: *he was* ***afraid that*** *the farmer would send the dog after them* | *she was* ***afraid of*** *antagonizing him.* ■ [with *infinitive*] unwilling or reluctant to do something for fear of the consequences: *I'm often afraid to go out on the streets.* ■ (**afraid for**) anxious about the well-being or safety of someone or something: *William was suddenly afraid for her.* ▷Middle English: past participle of the obsolete verb *affray,* from Anglo-Norman French *afrayer* (see AFFRAY).
▸*PHRASE* □ **I'm afraid** [with *clause*] used to express polite or formal apology or regret: *I'm afraid I don't understand.*

A-frame ▸*n.* a frame shaped like a capital letter A. ■ a house built around such a timber frame.

af·reet /ˈafrēt; əˈfrēt/ (also **af·rit**) ▸*n.* (in Arabian and Muslim mythology) a powerful jinn or demon. ▷late 18th cent.: from Arabic *ʿifrīt.*

a·fresh /əˈfresн/ ▸*adv.* in a new or different way: *she left the job to start afresh.*

Af·ri·ca /ˈafrikə/ the second largest continent (11.62 million square miles; 30.1 million sq km), a southward projection of the Old World landmass divided roughly in half by the equator and surrounded by sea except where the Isthmus of Suez joins it to Asia. *See map on following page.*

Af·ri·can /ˈafrikən/ ▸*n.* a person from Africa, esp. a black person. ■ a person of black African descent.
▸*adj.* of or relating to Africa or people of African descent. ▷from Latin *Africanus,* from *Africa (terra)* '(land) of the *Afri,*' an ancient people of North Africa.

Af·ri·ca·na /ˌafriˈkanə; -ˈkänə/ ▸*plural n.* books, artifacts, and other collectors' items connected with Africa, in particular southern Africa.

Af·ri·can A·mer·i·can ▸*n.* a black American.
▸*adj.* (**African-American**) of or relating to black Americans.

USAGE See usage at BLACK.

Af·ri·can buf·fa·lo ▸*n.* a buffalo with large horns, native to Africa south of the Sahara. • *Syncerus caffer,* family Bovidae; sometimes considered to be two species, the **Cape buffalo** and the **forest** (or **dwarf**) **buffalo**.

Af·ri·can dai·sy ▸*n.* a plant of the daisy family, sometimes cultivated for its bright flowers. • Family Compositae: several genera, in particular *Dimorphotheca, Arctotis,* and *Gerbera.*

Af·ri·can·der ▸*n.* variant spelling of AFRIKANDER.

Af·ri·can el·e·phant ▸*n.* the elephant native to Africa, which is larger than the Indian elephant and has larger ears and a two-lipped trunk. • *Loxodonta africana,* family Elephantidae.

Af·ri·can Eve hy·poth·e·sis ▸*n.* another term for EVE HYPOTHESIS.

Af·ri·can horse sick·ness ▸*n.* a notifiable viral disease of horses, which is usually fatal. It is transmitted by biting insects and occurs chiefly in Africa, the Middle East, and the Mediterranean.

Af·ri·can·ism /ˈafrikəˌnizəm/ ▸*n.* **1** a feature of language or culture regarded as characteristically African. **2** the belief that black Africans and their culture should predominate in Africa. —**Af·ri·can·ist** *n.* & *adj.*

Af·ri·can·ist /ˈafrikənist/ ▸*n.* **1** someone who studies the culture, history, and languages of Africa. **2** someone who espouses a belief in Africanism.

Af·ri·can·ize /ˈafrikəˌnīz/ ▸*v.* [*trans.*] **1** make African in character: [as *adj.*] (**Africanized**) *an Africanized form of Cajun music.* ■ (in Africa) restructure (an organization) by replacing white employees with black Africans. **2** [usu. as *adj.*] (**Africanized**) hybridize (honeybees of European stock) with bees of African stock, producing an aggressive strain. In recent years hybrids have spread from Brazil to the U.S., where they have become known colloquially as "killer bees." —**Af·ri·can·i·za·tion** /ˌafrikənəˈzāsнən/ *n.*

Af·ri·can lynx ▸*n.* another term for CARACAL.

Af·ri·can Na·tion·al Con·gress (abbr.: **ANC**) a South African political party and black nationalist organization. Having been banned by the South African government 1960–90, the ANC was victorious in the country's first democratic elections in 1994 and its leader, Nelson Mandela, became the country's president.

Af·ri·can vi·o·let ▸*n.* a small East African plant with heart-shaped velvety leaves and violet, pink, or white flowers. • Genus *Saintpaulia,* family Gesneriaceae: several species, in particular *S. ionantha,* a popular houseplant.

Af·ri·kaans /ˌafriˈkänz/ ▸*n.* a language of southern Africa, derived from the form of Dutch brought to the Cape by Protestant settlers in the 17th century, and an official language of South Africa.
▸*adj.* relating to the Afrikaner people, their way of life, or their language. ▷the name in Afrikaans, from Dutch, literally 'African.'

A-frame

Af·ri·ka Korps /ˈafrikə ˌkôr; ˈäfrēkä/ a German army force sent to North Africa in 1941 under General Rommel.

Af·ri·kan·der /ˌafriˈkandər/ ▸*n.* an animal of a South African breed of sheep or longhorn cattle. ▷early 19th cent. (an early form of AFRIKANER, having the same senses): via Afrikaans from South African Dutch.

Af·ri·ka·ner /ˌafriˈkänər/ ▸*n.* an Afrikaans-speaking person in South Africa, esp. one descended from the Dutch and Huguenot settlers of the 17th century. ▷Afrikaans, from South African Dutch *Africander,* from Dutch *Afrikaan* 'an African' + the personal suffix *-der,* on the pattern of *Hollander* 'Dutchman.' —**Af·ri·ka·ner·dom** /-dəm/ *n.*

af·rit ▸*n.* variant spelling of AFREET.

Af·ro /ˈafrō/ ▸*n.* a thick hairstyle with very tight curls that sticks out all around the head, like the natural hair of some black people. ▷1930s: independent usage of AFRO-, or an abbreviation of AFRICAN.

Afro- ▸*comb. form* African; African and ... : *Afro-Asiatic* | *Afro-Belizean.* ■ relating to Africa: *Afrocentric.* ▷from Latin *Afer, Afr-* 'African.'

Af·ro-A·mer·i·can ▸*adj.* & *n.* another term for AFRICAN AMERICAN.

USAGE See usage at BLACK.

Af·ro-A·si·at·ic ▸*adj.* relating to or denoting a family of languages spoken in the Middle East and North Africa. The family is commonly divided into five groups: Semitic, Omotic, Berber, Cushitic, and Chadic. Ancient Egyptian was also a member of this family. Also called HAMITO-SEMITIC.

Af·ro-Car·ib·be·an ▸*n.* a person of African descent living in or coming from the Caribbean.
▸*adj.* of or relating to Afro-Caribbeans.

Af·ro·cen·tric /ˌafrōˈsentrik/ ▸*adj.* regarding African or black culture as preeminent. —**Af·ro·cen·trism** /-trizəm/ *n.* —**Af·ro·cen·trist** /-trist/ *n.*

aft /aft/ ▸*adv.* & *adj.* at, near, or toward the stern of a ship or tail of an aircraft: [as *adv.*] *Travis made his way aft* | [as *adj.*] *the aft cargo compartment.* ▷early 17th cent.: probably from obsolete *baft* (see ABAFT), influenced by Low German and Dutch *achter* 'abaft, after.'

af·ter /ˈaftər/ ▸*prep.* **1** during the period of time following (an event): *shortly after Christmas* | *there's only one thing to do after an experience like that* | [as *conj.*] *bathtime ended in a flood after the faucets were left running* | [as *adv.*] *Duke Frederick died soon after.* ■ with a period of time rather than an event: *after a while he returned.* ■ in phrases indicating something happening continuously or repeatedly: ***day after day*** *we kept studying.* ■ (used in specifying a time) past: *I strolled in about ten minutes after two.* ■ during the time following the departure of (someone): *she cooks for him and cleans up after him.* **2** behind: *she went out, shutting the door after her.* ■ (with reference to looking or speaking) in the direction of someone who is moving further away: *she stared after him.* **3** in pursuit or quest of: *chasing after something you can't have* | *most of them are after money* | *Jenny still yearned after him.* **4** next to and following in order or importance: *in their order of priorities health* ***comes after*** *housing* | *x comes after y in the series.* **5** in allusion to (someone or something with the same or a related name): *they named her Pauline, after Barbara's mother.* ■ in imitation of: *a drawing after Millet's* The Reapers. **6** concerning or about: *she has asked after Iris's mother.*
▸*adj.* [*attrib.*] **1** *archaic* later: *he was sorry in after years.* **2** *Nautical* nearer the stern: *the after cabin.* ▷Old English *æfter,* of Germanic origin; related to Dutch *achter.*
▸*PHRASES* □ **after all** in spite of any indications or expectations to the contrary: *I called and told her I couldn't come after all* | *you are my counselor, after all.* □ **after hours** after normal working or opening hours, typically those of licensed premises: [as *adv.*] *she was going in to work after hours* [as *adj.*] *an after-hours jazz club.* □ **after you** a polite formula used to suggest that someone goes in front of or takes a turn before oneself: *after you, Mr. Pritchard.*

af·ter·birth /ˈaftərˌbərтн/ ▸*n.* the placenta and fetal

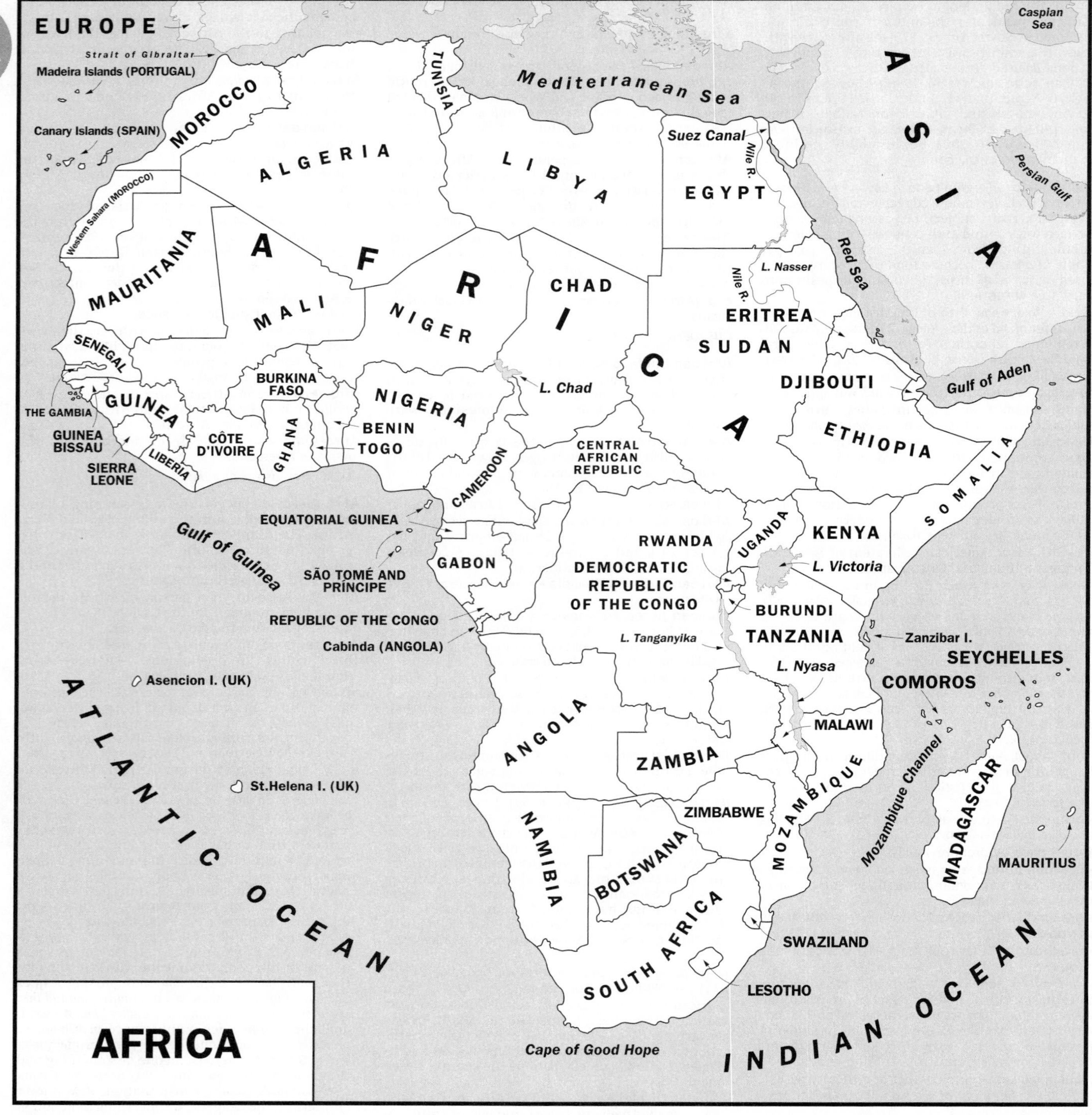

membranes discharged from the uterus after the birth of offspring.

af·ter·burn·er /ˈaftər,bərnər/ ▸*n.* an auxiliary burner fitted to the exhaust system of a turbojet engine to increase thrust.

af·ter·care /ˈaftər,ke(ə)r/ ▸*n.* **1** subsequent care or maintenance, in particular: ■ care of a patient after a stay in the hospital or of a person on release from prison. **2** childcare for the period between the end of the school day and the end of a parent's working day: [as *modifier*] *an aftercare facility at the local YMCA.*

af·ter·damp /ˈaftər,damp/ ▸*n.* choking gas, rich in carbon monoxide, left after an explosion of firedamp in a mine.

af·ter·deck /ˈaftər,dek/ ▸*n.* an open deck toward the stern of a ship.

af·ter·ef·fect /ˈaftəri,fekt/ ▸*n.* an effect that follows after the primary action of something: *he was suffering the aftereffects of the drug.*

af·ter·glow /ˈaftər,glō/ ▸*n.* [in *sing.*] light or radiance remaining in the sky after the sun has set. ■ good feelings remaining after a pleasurable or successful experience: *basking in the afterglow of victory.*

af·ter·im·age /ˈaftər,imij/ ▸*n.* an impression of a vivid sensation (esp. a visual image) retained after the stimulus has ceased.

af·ter·life /ˈaftər,līf/ ▸*n.* [usu. in *sing.*] **1** (in some religions) life after death: *most Christians believe in an afterlife.* **2** later life: *they spent much of their afterlife trying to forget the fire.*

af·ter·mar·ket /ˈaftər,märkit/ ▸*n.* the market for spare parts, accessories, and components, esp. for motor vehicles. ■ *Stock Market* the market for shares and bonds after their original issue.

af·ter·math /ˈaftər,maTH/ ▸*n.* **1** the consequences or aftereffects of an event, esp. when unpleasant: *food prices soared* ***in the aftermath of*** *the drought.* **2** *Farming* new grass growing after mowing or harvest. ▷late 15th cent. (sense 2): from AFTER (as an adjective) + dialect *math* 'mowing,' of Germanic origin; related to German *Mahd.*

af·ter·most /ˈaftər,mōst/ ▸*adj.* [*attrib.*] nearest the stern of a ship or tail of an aircraft. ▷late 18th cent.: from AFTER (as an adjective) + -MOST.

af·ter·noon /,aftərˈnoon/ ▸*n.* the time from noon or lunchtime to evening: *I telephoned* ***this afternoon*** | *I'll be back at three in the afternoon* | *she worked on Tuesday afternoons* | [as *adj.*] *the afternoon sunshine.* ■ this time on a particular day, characterized by a specified type of activity or particular weather conditions: *it was an afternoon of drama and tension.*
▸*adv.* (**afternoons**) *informal* in the afternoon; every afternoon.
▸*exclam. informal* short for GOOD AFTERNOON.

af·ter·pains /ˈaftər,pānz/ ▸*plural n.* pains after childbirth caused by contraction of the uterus.

af·ters /ˈaftərz/ ▸*plural n. Brit., informal* dessert: *there was apple pie for afters.*

af·ter·shave /ˈaftər,SHāv/ ▸*n.* an astringent, typically scented lotion for applying to the skin after shaving.

af·ter·shock /ˈaftər,SHäk/ ▸*n.* a smaller earthquake following the main shock of a large earthquake.

af·ter·sun /ˈaftər,sən/ ▸*adj.* denoting a product intended for application to the skin after exposure to the sun: *aftersun lotion.*

af·ter·taste /ˈaftər,tāst/ ▸*n.* a taste, typically an unpleasant one, remaining in the mouth after eating or drinking something.

af·ter-tax ▸*adj.* relating to income that remains after the deduction of taxes due.

af·ter·thought /ˈaftər,THôt/ ▸*n.* an item or thing that is thought of or added later: *as an afterthought she said "Thank you."*

af·ter·touch /ˈaftər,təCH/ ▸*n.* a facility on an electronic music keyboard by which an effect is produced by the player depressing a key after striking it.

af·ter·ward /ˈaftərwərd/ (also **af·ter·wards** /-wərdz/) ▸*adv.* at a later or future time; subsequently: *the offender was arrested shortly afterward.* ▷Old English *æftewearde,* from *æftan* (see AFT) + -WARD, influenced by AFTER. *Afterwards* from *afterward* + adverbial genitive *-es, -s.*

af·ter·word /ˈaftər,wərd/ ▸*n.* a concluding section in a book, typically by a person other than the author.

af·ter·world /ˈaftər,wərld/ ▸*n.* a world entered after death.

AG ▸*abbr.* ■ adjutant general. ■ Aktiengesellschaft, used in the names of German joint-stock companies. ■ attorney general.

Ag[1] ▸*symbol* the chemical element silver. ▷from Latin *argentum.*

Ag[2] *Biochemistry* ▸*abbr.* antigen.

ag *informal* ▸*adj.* short for AGRICULTURAL.
▸*n.* short for AGRICULTURE.

ag- ▸*prefix* variant spelling of AD- assimilated before *g* (as in *aggravate, aggress*).

a·ga /ˈägə/ ▸*n. chiefly historical* (in Muslim countries, esp. under the Ottoman Empire) a military commander or official. ▷mid 16th cent.: from Turkish *ağa* 'master, lord,' from Mongolian *aqa.*

A·ga·dir /,ägəˈdi(ə)r/ a seaport and resort on the Atlantic coast of Morocco; pop. 110,500.

a·gain /əˈgen; əˈgān/ ▸*adv.* another time; once more: *it was great to meet old friends again* | *they were disappointed* **yet again.** ■ returning to a previous position or condition: *he rose, tidied the bed, and sat down again.* ■ in addition to what has already been mentioned: *the wages were low, but they made half as much again in tips.* ■ [*sentence adverb*] used to introduce a further point for consideration, supporting or contrasting with what has just been said: *I never saw any signs, but* **then again,** *maybe I wasn't looking.* ■ used to ask someone to repeat something: *what was your name again?* ▷Old English *ongēan, ongægn,* etc., of Germanic origin; related to German *entgegen* 'opposite.'
▸*PHRASE* □ **again and again** repeatedly: *I read this author again and again.*

a·gainst /əˈgenst; əˈgānst/ ▸*prep.* **1** in opposition to: *the fight against crime* | *he decided against immediate publication* | *swimming against the tide.* ■ in opposition to, with reference to legal action: *allegations against police officers* | *the first victim gave evidence against him.* ■ in opposition to, with reference to an athletic contest: *the championship game against Virginia.* ■ (in betting) in anticipation of the failure of: *the odds were 5–1 against Pittsburgh.* **2** in anticipation of and preparation for (a problem or difficulty): *insurance against sickness and unemployment.* ■ in resistance to; as protection from: *he turned up his collar against the wind.* ■ in relation to (an amount of money owed or due) so as to reduce or cancel it: *money was advanced against the value of the property.* **3** in conceptual contrast to: *the benefits must be weighed against the costs* | *the instilling of habits* **as against** *the development of understanding.* ■ in visual contrast to: *he was silhouetted against the light of the window.* **4** in or into physical contact with (something), typically so as to be supported by or collide with it: *she stood with her back against the door* | *his lips brushed against her hair.* ▷Middle English: from AGAIN + *-s* (adverbial genitive) + *-t* probably by association with superlatives (as in *amongst*).
▸*PHRASE* □ **have something against someone** dislike or bear a grudge against someone: *I have nothing against you personally.*

A·ga Khan /,ägə ˈkän/ ▸*n.* the title of the spiritual leader of the Nizari sect of Ismaili Muslims. The first Aga Khan was given his title in 1818 by the shah of Persia. The present (fourth) Aga Khan (**Karim Al-Hussain Shah,** b.1937) inherited the title in 1957.

a·gal /äˈgäl/ ▸*n.* a headband worn by Bedouin Arab men to keep the keffiyeh in place. ▷mid 19th cent.: representing a Bedouin pronunciation of Arabic *ʿiḳāl* 'bond, hobble.'

ag·a·ma /əˈgämə; ˈagəmə/ ▸*n.* an Old World lizard with a large head and a long tail, typically showing a marked difference in color and form between the sexes. • Genus *Agama,* family Agamidae: many species. ■ any lizard of the agama family. ▷late 18th cent.: perhaps from Carib.

Ag·a·mem·non /,agəˈmem,nän/ *Greek Mythology* king of Mycenae and brother of Menelaus, commander in chief of the Greek expedition against Troy. On his return home from Troy, he was murdered by his wife Clytemnestra and her lover Aegisthus; his murder was avenged by his son Orestes and daughter Electra.

a·gam·ic /āˈgamik; əˈgam-/ ▸*adj. Biology* asexual; reproducing asexually: *winged agamic females.* ▷mid 19th cent.: from Greek *agamos* 'unmarried' + -IC.

ag·a·mid /ˈagə,mid/ ▸*n. Zoology* a lizard of the agama family (Agamidae). ▷late 19th cent.: from modern Latin *Agamidae,* from AGAMA.

a·gam·ma·glob·u·li·ne·mi·a /,āgamə,gläbyələˈnēmēə/ ▸*n. Medicine* lack of gamma globulin in the blood plasma, causing immune deficiency.

ag·a·mo·sper·my /āˈgamə,spərmē; ˈagəmō-/ ▸*n. Botany* asexual reproduction in which seeds are produced from unfertilized ovules. ▷1930s: from Greek *agamos* 'unmarried' + *sperma* 'seed.' **—ag·a·mo·sper·mous** /ā,gaməˈspərməs; ,agəmō-/ *adj.*

ag·a·pan·thus /,agəˈpanTHəs/ ▸*n.* a South African plant of the lily family, with funnel-shaped bluish flowers that grow in rounded clusters. Also called LILY-OF-THE-NILE. • Genus *Agapanthus,* family Liliaceae (or Alliaceae). ▷modern Latin, from Greek *agapē* 'love' + *anthos* 'flower.'

a·gape[1] /əˈgāp/ ▸*adj.* [*predic.*] (of the mouth) wide open, esp. with surprise or wonder: *Downes listened, mouth agape with incredulity.* ▷mid 17th cent.: from A-[2] 'on' + GAPE.

a·ga·pe[2] /äˈgä,pā; ˈägə-/ ▸*n. Christian Theology* Christian love, esp. as distinct from erotic love or emotional affection. ■ a communal meal in token of Christian fellowship, as held by early Christians in commemoration of the Last Supper. ▷early 17th cent.: from Greek *agapē* 'selfless love.'

a·gar /ˈä,gär; ˈā,gär/ (also **a·gar-a·gar** /ˈägär ˈä,gär; ˈāgär ˈā,gär/) ▸*n.* a gelatinous substance obtained from various kinds of red seaweed and used in biological culture media and as a thickener in foods. ▷early 19th cent.: from Malay.

ag·a·ric /ˈagərik; əˈgar-/ ▸*n.* a fungus with a fruiting body that resembles the ordinary mushroom, having a convex or flattened cap with gills on the underside. • Order Agaricales, class Basidiomycetes, in particular the mushroom family Agaricaceae. ▷late Middle English (originally denoting various bracket fungi with medicinal or other uses): from Latin *agaricum,* from Greek *agarikon* 'tree fungus.'

a·gar·ose /ˈagə,rōs; -,rōz/ ▸*n. Biochemistry* a substance that is the main constituent of agar and is used esp. in gels for electrophoresis. It is a polysaccharide mainly containing galactose residues.

A·gar·ta·la /,əgərtəˈlä/ a city in northeastern India, capital of the state of Tripura, situated near the border with Bangladesh; pop. 157,640.

Ag·as·si /ˈagəsē/, André (1970–), U.S. tennis player. Ranked third in the world by the age of 18, he won the men's singles title at Wimbledon in 1992, at the U.S. Open in 1994 and 1999, at the Australian Open in 1995, 2000, 2001, and 2002, and at the French Open in 1999.

Ag·as·siz /ˈagəsē/, Jean Louis Rodolphe (1807–73), U.S. zoologist, geologist, and paleontologist; born in Switzerland. In 1837, he was the first to propose that much of Europe had once been in the grip of an ice age.

Ag·as·siz, Lake /ˈagə,sē/ a prehistoric glacial lake of the Pleistocene epoch that covered parts of present-day Minnesota and North Dakota in the U.S. and Manitoba and Ontario in Canada.

ag·ate /ˈagit/ ▸*n.* an ornamental stone consisting of a hard variety of chalcedony, typically banded in appearance. ■ a colored toy marble resembling a banded gemstone. ▷late 15th cent.: from French, via Latin from Greek *akhatēs.*

a·ga·ve /əˈgävē/ ▸*n.* a succulent plant with rosettes of narrow spiny leaves and tall flower spikes, native to the southern U.S. and tropical America. • Genus *Agave,* family Agavaceae: numerous species, including the century plant. ▷Latin, from Greek *Agauē,* the name of one of the daughters of Cadmus in Greek mythology, from *agauos* 'illustrious.'

AGC *Electronics* ▸*abbr.* automatic gain control.

age /āj/ ▸*n.* **1** the length of time that a person has lived or a thing has existed: *he died from a heart attack at the age of 51* | *his wife is the same age as Carla* | *he must be nearly 40 years* **of age** | *young people between the ages of 11 and 18.* ■ a particular stage in someone's life: *children of primary school age.* ■ the latter part of life or existence; old age: *with age this gland can become sluggish.* **2** a distinct period of history: *an age of technological growth* | *a child of the television age.* ■ *Geology* a division of time that is a subdivision of an epoch, corresponding to a stage in chronostratigraphy. ■ *archaic* a lifetime taken as a measure of time; a generation: *Nestor is said to have lived three ages when he was ninety years old.* ■ **(ages/an age)** *informal* a very long time: *I haven't seen her for ages* | *it would take an age to tell her everything.*
▸*v.* **(ag·ing)** [*intrans.*] grow old or older, esp. visibly and obviously so: *you haven't aged a lot* | *the tiredness we feel as we age.* See note at MATURE. ■ [*trans.*] cause to grow, feel, or appear older: *he even tried aging the painting with a spoonful of coffee.* ■ (esp. with reference to an alcoholic drink) mature or allow to mature: [*intrans.*] *the wine ages in open vats or casks.* ■ [*trans.*] determine how old (something) is: *we didn't have a clue how to age these animals.* ▷Middle English: from Old French, based on Latin *aetas, aetat-,* from *aevum* 'age, era.'
▸*PHRASES* □ **act** (or **be**) **one's age** [usu. in *imperative*] behave in a manner appropriate to someone of one's age and not to someone much younger: *"Act your age" is not advice to behave like an adolescent.* □ **come of age** (of a person) reach adult status. ■ (of a movement or activity) become fully established: *space travel will then finally come of age.* □ **of an age 1** old enough to be able or expected to do something: *the sons are of an age to marry.* **2** (of two or more people or things) of a similar age: *the children all seemed of an age.* □ **through the ages** throughout history.

-age ▸*suffix* forming nouns: **1** denoting an action: *leverage* | *voyage.* ■ the product of an action: *spillage* | *wreckage.* ■ a function; a sphere of action: *homage* | *peerage.* **2** denoting an aggregate or number of: *mileage* | *percentage* | *signage.* ■ fees payable for; the cost of using: *postage* | *tonnage.* **3** denoting a place or abode: *vicarage* | *village.* ▷from Old French, based on Latin *-aticum,* neuter form of the adjectival ending *-aticus.*

aged ▸*adj.* **1** /ājd/ [*predic.* or *postpositive*] having lived for a specified length of time; of a specified age: *young people aged 14 to 18* | *he died aged 60.* ■ (of a horse or farm animal) over a certain defined age of maturity, typically 6 to 12 years for horses, 3 or 4 years for cattle. **2** /ˈājid/ having lived or existed for a long time; old: *aged men with white hair* | [as *plural n.*] **(the aged)** *Methodist homes for the aged.* See note at OLD. **3** /ājd/ that has been subjected to aging: *jeans in hardrock wash give a unique aged appearance.*

A·gee /ˈājē/, James (Rufus) (1909–55), U.S. writer. He wrote *Let Us Now Praise Famous Men* (1941) after touring the South with photographer Walker Evans and *A Death in the Family* (1955), for which he was posthumously awarded a Pulitzer Prize. He also wrote the screenplays for *The African Queen* (1951) and *The Night of the Hunter* (1955).

age gap ▸*n.* a difference in age between people, esp. as a potential source of misunderstanding.

age group ▸*n.* a number of people or things classed together as being of similar age.

age hard·en·ing ▸*n.* spontaneous hardening of a metal that occurs if it is quenched and then stored at ambient temperature or treated with mild heat. **—age-hard·ened** *adj.*

age·ing /ˈājiNG/ ▸*adj.* & *n.* variant spelling of AGING.

age·ism /ˈāj,izəm/ (also **ag·ism**) ▸*n.* prejudice or discrimination on the basis of a person's age. **—age·ist** (also **ag·ist**) *adj.* & *n.*

age·less /ˈājlis/ ▸*adj.* never growing or appearing to

grow old: *the town retains an ageless charm.* **—age•less•ness** *n.*

age-long ▸*adj.* [*attrib.*] having existed for a very long time: *the will to change age-long habits.*

age-mate ▸*n.* a person or animal that is the same age as another.

a•gen•cy /ˈājənsē/ ▸*n.* **1** [often with *adj.*] a business or organization established to provide a particular service, typically one that involves organizing transactions between two other parties: *an advertising agency | aid agencies.* ■ a department or body providing a specific service for a government or similar organization: *the Environmental Protection Agency.* **2** action or intervention, esp. such as to produce a particular effect: *canals carved* ***by the agency of*** *running water | a belief in various forms of supernatural agency.* ■ a thing or person that acts to produce a particular result: *the movies could be an agency molding the values of the public.* ▷mid 17th cent.: from medieval Latin *agentia*, from *agent-* 'doing' (see **AGENT**).

a•gen•da /əˈjendə/ ▸*n.* a list of items of business to be considered and discussed at a meeting: *the question of nuclear weapons had been removed from the agenda.* ■ a list or program of things to be done or problems to be addressed: *he vowed to put jobs at the top of his agenda | the government had its own agenda.* ▷early 17th cent. (in the sense 'things to be done'): from Latin, neuter plural of *agendum*, gerund of *agere* 'do.'

▸*PHRASES* □ **on the agenda** scheduled for discussion at a meeting: *the rights of minorities would be high on the agenda at the conference.* ■ likely or needing to be dealt with or done: *his release was not on the agenda | national problems loomed large on the domestic agenda.* □ **set the agenda** draw up a list of items to be discussed at a meeting. ■ influence or determine a program of action: *the activists set the agenda, and timorous administrators usually go along.*

USAGE Although **agenda** ('things to be done') is the plural of *agendum* in Latin, in standard modern English it is a normal singular noun with a normal plural form (**agendas**). See also **usage** at **DATA** and **MEDIA**[1].

a•gent /ˈājənt/ ▸*n.* **1** a person who acts on behalf of another, in particular: ■ a person who manages business, financial, or contractual matters for an actor, performer, or writer. ■ a person or company that provides a particular service, typically one that involves organizing transactions between two other parties: *a travel agent | shipping agents | a real-estate agent.* ■ a person who obtains information for a government or other official body, typically in secret: *a trained intelligence agent | KGB agents | an FBI agent.* **2** a person or thing that takes an active role or produces a specified effect: *agents of change | bleaching agents.* ■ *Grammar* the doer of an action, typically expressed as the subject of an active verb or in a *by* phrase with a passive verb. ▷late Middle English (in the sense 'someone or something that produces an effect'): from Latin *agent-* 'doing,' from *agere.*

a•gent-gen•er•al ▸*n.* (*pl.* **a•gents-gen•er•al**) the representative of an Australian state or Canadian province in a major foreign city.

a•gent noun ▸*n.* a noun denoting someone or something that performs the action of a verb, typically ending in *-er* or *-or*, e.g., *worker, accelerator.*

A•gent Or•ange ▸*n.* a defoliant chemical used by the U.S. in the Vietnam War.

a•gent pro•vo•ca•teur /äˌzʜän(t) prəˌväkəˈtər/ ▸*n.* (*pl.* **a•gents pro•vo•ca•teurs** *pronunc.* same or /-ˈtərz/) a person who induces others to break the law so that they can be convicted. ▷late 19th cent.: French, literally 'provocative agent.'

age of con•sent ▸*n.* the age at which a person's, typically a girl's, consent to sexual intercourse is valid in law.

age of dis•cre•tion ▸*n.* the age at which someone is considered able to manage their own affairs or take responsibility for their actions.

age-old ▸*adj.* having existed for a very long time: *the haunting, age-old love call of the prairie chicken.*

ag•glom•er•ate ▸*v.* /əˈglämәˌrāt/ collect or form into a mass or group: [*trans.*] *companies agglomerate multiple sites such as chains of stores* [*intrans.*] *these small particles soon agglomerate together.*

▸*n.* /-rit/ a mass or collection of things: *a multimedia agglomerate.* ■ *Geology* a volcanic rock consisting of large fragments bonded together.

▸*adj.* /-rit/ collected or formed into a mass. ▷late 17th cent.: from Latin *agglomerat-* 'added to,' from the verb *agglomerare*, from *ad-* 'to' + *glomerare* (from *glomus* 'ball'). **—ag•glom•er•a•tion** /əˌgläməˈrāsʜən/ *n.* **—ag•glom•er•a•tive** /-ˌrātiv; -rətiv/ *adj.*

ag•glu•ti•nate /əˈglo͞otnˌāt/ ▸*v.* firmly stick or be stuck together to form a mass: [as *adj.*] (**agglutinated**) *rhinoceros horns are agglutinated masses of hair.* ■ *Biology* (with reference to bacteria or red blood cells) clump together: [*trans.*] *these strains agglutinate human red cells* [*intrans.*] *cell fragments agglutinate and form intricate meshes.* ■ [*trans.*] *Linguistics* combine (simple words or parts of words) without change of form to express compound ideas. ▷mid 16th cent.: from Latin *agglutinat-* 'caused to adhere,' from the verb *agglutinare*, from *ad-* 'to' + *glutinare* (from *gluten* 'glue'). **—ag•glu•ti•na•tion** /əˌglo͞otnˈāsʜən/ *n.*

ag•glu•ti•na•tive /əˈglo͞otn-ətiv/ ▸*adj.* *Linguistics* (of a language) forming words predominantly by agglutination, rather than by inflection or by using isolated elements. Examples include Hungarian, Turkish, Korean, and Swahili.

ag•glu•ti•nin /əˈglo͞otn-in/ ▸*n.* *Biology* an antibody, lectin, or other substance that causes agglutination. ▷late 19th cent.: from **AGGLUTINATE** + **-IN**[1].

ag•glu•tin•o•gen /əˈglo͞otn-əjən/ ▸*n.* *Biology* an antigen that stimulates the production of an agglutinin.

ag•gra•da•tion /ˌagrəˈdāsʜən/ ▸*n.* the deposition of material by a river, stream, or current. ▷late 19th cent.: from **AG-** (expressing increase) + *(de)gradation.*

ag•gran•dize /əˈgranˌdīz/ ▸*v.* [*trans.*] increase the power, status, or wealth of: *an action intended to aggrandize the Frankish dynasty.* ■ enhance the reputation of (someone) beyond what is justified by the facts: *he hoped to aggrandize himself by dying a hero's death.* ▷mid 17th cent. (in the general sense 'increase, magnify'): from French *agrandiss-*, lengthened stem of *agrandir*, probably from Italian *aggrandire*, from Latin *grandis* 'large.' The ending was changed by association with verbs ending in **-IZE**. **—ag•gran•dize•ment** /-ˌdīzmənt; -diz-/ *n.* **—ag•gran•diz•er** *n.*

ag•gra•vate /ˈagrəˌvāt/ ▸*v.* [*trans.*] **1** make (a problem, injury, or offense) worse or more serious: *military action would only aggravate the situation.* **2** *informal* annoy or exasperate (someone), esp. persistently: [as *adj.*] (**aggravating**) *she found him thoroughly aggravating and unprofessional.* ▷mid 16th cent.: from Latin *aggravat-* 'made heavy,' from the verb *aggravare*, from *ad-* (expressing increase) + *gravis* 'heavy.' **—ag•gra•vat•ing•ly** *adv.*

USAGE **Aggravate** in the sense 'annoy or exasperate' dates back to the 17th century and has been so used by respected writers ever since. This use is still regarded as incorrect by some traditionalists on the grounds that it is too radical a departure from the etymological meaning of 'make heavy.' It is, however, comparable to meaning changes in hundreds of other words which have long been accepted without comment. See also **usage** at **EXASPERATE**.

ag•gra•vat•ed /ˈagrəˌvātid/ ▸*adj.* [*attrib.*] (of an offense) made more serious by attendant circumstances (such as frame of mind): *aggravated burglary.* ■ (of a penalty) made more severe in recognition of the seriousness of an offense: *aggravated damages.*

ag•gra•va•tion /ˌagrəˈvāsʜən/ ▸*n.* **1** an intensification of a negative quality or aspect: *Negotiators were optimistic despite the aggravation of the standoff caused by the press release.* ■ (in homeopathy) the temporary appearance or worsening of symptoms that a remedy is intended to eliminated, taken to be caused by too strong a dose. **2** the state of being aggravated: *Internet users' aggravation with the deluge of pop-up ads.* **3** a cause of annoyance or irritation: *the aggravations of living with a self-confessed sports junkie.*

ag•gre•gate ▸*n.* /ˈagrigit/ **1** a whole formed by combining several (typically disparate) elements: *the council was an aggregate of three regional assemblies.* ■ the total number of points scored by a player or team in a series of sporting contests: *the result put the sides even* ***on aggregate.*** **2** a material or structure formed from a loosely compacted mass of fragments or particles. ■ pieces of broken or crushed stone or gravel used to make concrete, or more generally in building and construction work.

▸*adj.* [*attrib.*] /ˈagrigit/ formed or calculated by the combination of many separate units or items; total: *the aggregate amount of grants made.* ■ *Botany* (of a group of species) comprising several very similar species formerly regarded as a single species. ■ *Economics* denoting the total supply or demand for goods and services in an economy at a particular time: *aggregate demand | aggregate supply.*

▸*v.* /-ˌgāt/ form or group into a class or cluster: [*intrans.*] *the butterflies aggregate in dense groups.* ▷late Middle English: from Latin *aggregat-* 'herded together,' from the verb *aggregare*, from *ad-* 'toward' + *grex, greg-* 'a flock.' **—ag•gre•ga•tion** /ˌagriˈgāsʜən/ *n.* **—ag•gre•ga•tive** /-ˌgātiv/ *adj.*

▸*PHRASE* □ **in (the) aggregate** in total; as a whole.

ag•gre•gate fruit ▸*n.* *Botany* a fruit formed from several carpels derived from the same flower, e.g., a raspberry.

ag•gre•ga•tor /ˈagriˌgātər/ ▸*n.* *Computing* an Internet company that collects information about competing products and services and distributes it through a single Web site: *a travel insurance aggregator.*

ag•gres•sion /əˈgresʜən/ ▸*n.* hostile or violent behavior or attitudes toward another; readiness to attack or confront: *his chin was jutting with aggression | territorial aggression between individuals of the same species.* ■ the action of attacking without provocation, esp. in beginning a quarrel or war: *the dictator resorted to armed aggression | he called for an end to foreign aggression against his country.* ■ forceful and sometimes overly assertive pursuit of one's aims and interests. ▷early 17th cent. (in the sense 'an attack'): from Latin *aggressio(n-)*, from *aggredi* 'to attack,' from *ad-* 'toward'+ *gradi* 'proceed, walk.'

ag•gres•sive /əˈgresiv/ ▸*adj.* ready or likely to attack or confront; characterized by or resulting from aggression: *he's very uncooperative and aggressive | aggressive behavior.* ■ pursuing one's aims and interests forcefully, sometimes unduly so: *an aggressive businessman.* See note at **BOLD**. ▷early 19th cent.: from Latin *aggress-* 'attacked' (from the verb *aggredi*) + **-IVE**; compare with French *agressif, -ive.* **—ag•gres•sive•ly** *adv.* **—ag•gres•sive•ness** *n.*

ag•gres•sor /əˈgresər/ ▸*n.* a person or country that attacks another first. ▷mid 17th cent.: from late Latin, from *aggredi* 'to attack' (see **AGGRESSION**).

ag•grieved /əˈgrēvd/ ▸*adj.* feeling resentment at having been unfairly treated: *they were aggrieved at the outcome | she did not see herself as the aggrieved party.* ▷Middle English (in the sense 'distressed'): past participle of *aggrieve*, from Old French *agrever* 'make heavier,' based on Latin *aggravare* (see **AGGRAVATE**). **—ag•griev•ed•ly** /-vidlē/ *adv.*

ag•gro /ˈagrō/ ▸*n.* *Brit., informal* aggressive, violent behavior. ■ problems and difficulties. ▷1960s: abbreviation of *aggravation* (see **AGGRAVATE**), or of **AGGRESSION**.

a•ghast /əˈgast/ ▸*adj.* [*predic.*] filled with horror or shock: *when the news came out they were aghast.* ▷late Middle English: past participle of the obsolete verb *agast, gast* 'frighten,' from Old English *gǣsten.* The spelling with *gh* (originally Scots) became general by about 1700, probably influenced by **GHOST**; compare with **GHASTLY**.

ag•ile /ˈajəl/ ▸*adj.* able to move quickly and easily: *Ruth was as agile as a monkey | figurative his vague manner concealed an agile mind.* ▷late Middle English: via French from Latin *agilis*, from *agere* 'do.' **—ag•ile•ly** /ˈajə(l)lē/ *adv.* **—a•gil•i•ty** /əˈjilitē/ *n.*

ag•ile gib•bon ▸*n.* a gibbon with color varying from light buff to black, found in Southeast Asia. • *Hylobates agilis*, family Hylobatidae.

a•gin /əˈgin/ ▸*prep.* dialect form of **AGAINST**. ▷early 19th cent.: variant of the obsolete preposition *again*, with the same meaning.

Ag•in•court, Bat•tle of /ˈajinˌkôrt; äzʜanˈko͞or/ a battle in northern France in 1415 during the Hundred Years War, in which the English under Henry V defeated a large French army. The victory, achieved largely by use of the longbow, allowed Henry to occupy Normandy.

ag•ing /ˈājiɴɢ/ (also **age•ing**) ▸*n.* the process of growing old: *the external signs of aging* | [as *adj.*] *the aging process.* ■ the process of change in the properties of a material occurring over a period, either spontaneously or through deliberate action.

▸*adj.* (of a person) growing old; elderly: *looking after aging relatives | an aging population.* ■ (of a thing) reaching the end of useful life; obsolescent: *the world's aging fleet of oil tankers.*

ag•ism ▸*n.* variant spelling of **ageism**. **—ag•ist** *adj.* & *n.*

ag•i•tate /ˈajiˌtāt/ ▸*v.* [*trans.*] make (someone) troubled or nervous: *the thought of questioning Toby agitated him extremely* | [as *adj.*] (**agitated**) *she was red and agitated with the effort of arguing.* ■ [*intrans.*] campaign to arouse public concern about an issue in the hope of prompting action: ***they agitated for*** *a reversal of the decision.* ■ stir or disturb (something, esp. a liquid) briskly: *agitate the water to disperse the oil.* ▷late

Middle English (in the sense 'drive away'): from Latin *agitat-* 'agitated, driven,' from *agitare*, frequentative of *agere* 'do, drive.' —**ag·i·tat·ed·ly** *adv.*

ag·i·ta·tion /ˌajiˈtāsʜən/ ▸*n.* **1** a state of anxiety or nervous excitement: *she was wringing her hands in agitation.* ■ the action of arousing public concern about an issue and pressing for action on it: *widespread agitation for social reform.* **2** the action of briskly stirring or disturbing something, esp. a liquid. ▷mid 16th cent. (in the sense 'action, being active'): from Latin *agitatio(n-)*, from the verb *agitare* (see AGITATE).

a·gi·ta·to /ˌajiˈtätō/ ▸*adv.* & *adj. Music* (esp. as a direction after a tempo marking) in an agitated manner: *allegro agitato.* ▷Italian, literally 'agitated.'

ag·i·ta·tor /ˈajiˌtātər/ ▸*n.* **1** a person who urges others to protest or rebel: *a communist agitator.* **2** an apparatus for stirring liquid, as in a washing machine or a photographic developing tank. ▷mid 17th cent. (denoting a delegate of private soldiers in the Parliamentary Army during the English Civil War (1642–49)) from Latin, from *agitare* (see AGITATE). Sense 1 dates from the mid 18th cent.

ag·it·prop /ˈajitˌpräp/ ▸*n.* political (originally communist) propaganda, esp. in art or literature: [as *adj.*] *agitprop painters.* ▷1930s: Russian, blend of *agitatsiya* 'agitation' and *propaganda* 'propaganda.'

a·gleam /əˈglēm/ ▸*adj.* [*predic.*] gleaming: *yellow fur agleam in the sun.*

ag·let /ˈaglit/ ▸*n.* a metal or plastic tube fixed tightly around each end of a shoelace. ▷late Middle English: from French *aiguillette* 'small needle,' diminutive of *aiguille* (see AIGUILLE).

a·gley /əˈglā; əˈglē/ ▸*adv. Scottish* askew; awry. ▷late 18th cent.: from A-[2] 'on' + Scots *gley* 'squint,' of unknown origin.

a·glow /əˈglō/ ▸*adj.* [*predic.*] glowing: *his bald head aglow under the lights.*

ag·ma /ˈagmə/ ▸*n.* the speech sound represented by *ng* as in *thing*, a velar nasal consonant. ■ represented by ŋ in the International Phonetic Alphabet. ▷1950s: from late Greek, from Greek, literally 'fragment.'

ag·nail /ˈagˌnāl/ ▸*n.* another term for HANGNAIL.

ag·nate /ˈagˌnāt/ *chiefly Law* ▸*n.* a person descended from the same male ancestor as another specified or implied person, esp. through the male line.

▸*adj.* descended from the same male ancestor as a specified or implied subject, esp. through the male line. Compare with COGNATE (sense 2). ■ of the same clan or nation. ▷late 15th cent. (as a noun): from Latin *agnatus*, from *ad-* 'to' + *gnatus*, *natus* 'born.' —**ag·nat·ic** /agˈnatik/ *adj.* —**ag·na·tion** /agˈnāsʜən/ *n.*

Ag·na·tha /ˈagnəᴛʜə/ *Zoology* a group of primitive jawless vertebrates that includes the lampreys, hagfishes, and many fossil fishlike forms. Compare with CYCLOSTOME. • Superclass Agnatha: the living forms are in the classes Myxini (hagfishes) and Cephalaspidomorphi (lampreys). ▷from modern Latin *Agnatha* (superclass name), from A-[1] 'without' + Greek *gnathos* 'jaw.' —**ag·na·than** *n.* & *adj.*

Ag·nes, St.[1] /ˈagnəs/ (died *c.*304), Roman martyr. The patron saint of virgins, her emblem is a lamb (Latin *agnus*). Feast day, January 21.

Ag·nes, St.[2] (*c.*1211–82), patron saint of Bohemia. She was canonized in 1989. Feast day, March 2.

Agne·si /änˈyāzē/, Maria Gaetana (1718–99), Italian mathematician and philosopher. She wrote a mathematics textbook and was the first woman appointed to a university chair in mathematics.

Ag·new /ˈagn(y)o͞o/, Spiro T(heodore) (1918–96), U.S. politician. He served as Richard Nixon's vice president 1969–73 but was forced to resign because of corruption charges against him that stemmed from his time as governor of Maryland 1967–69.

Ag·ni /ˈagnē; ˈəg-/ the Vedic god of fire, the priest of the gods and the god of the priests.

a·gno·lot·ti /ˌanyəˈlätē/ ▸ *n.* pasta squares stuffed with a variety of fillings, like small ravioli. ▷Italian.

ag·no·sia /agˈnōzʜ(ē)ə/ ▸*n. Medicine* inability to interpret sensations and hence to recognize things, typically as a result of brain damage. ▷early 20th cent.: coined in German from Greek *agnōsia* 'ignorance.'

ag·nos·tic /agˈnästik/ ▸*n.* a person who believes that nothing is known or can be known of the existence or nature of God or of anything beyond material phenomena; a person who claims neither faith nor disbelief in God.

▸*adj.* of or relating to agnostics or agnosticism. ▷mid 19th cent.: from A-[1] 'not' + GNOSTIC. —**ag·nos·ti·cism** /-təˌsizəm/ *n.*

Ag·nus De·i /ˈagnəs ˈdāˌē; ˈdēˌī; ˈänyo͞os/ ▸*n.* **1** a figure of a lamb bearing a cross or flag, as an emblem of Christ. **2** *Christian Church* an invocation beginning with the words "Lamb of God" forming a set part of the liturgy. ■ a musical setting of this. ▷late Middle English: from Latin, literally 'Lamb of God.'

a·go /əˈgō/ ▸*adv.* (used after a measurement of time) before the present; earlier: *he went five minutes ago* | *as long ago as 1942* | *not long ago.* ▷Middle English *ago*, *agone*, past participle of the obsolete verb *ago* 'pass,' used to express passage of time.

USAGE When **ago** is followed by a clause, the clause is normally introduced by *that* rather than *since*: *it was sixty years ago* **that** *I left this place* (not *it was sixty years ago* **since** *I left this place*). The use of *since* is redundant and is not correct in standard English.

a·gog /əˈgäg/ ▸*adj.* [*predic.*] very eager or curious to hear or see something: *I'm* **all agog** *to see London* | *New York is agog at the gossip.* ▷mid 16th cent.: from Old French *en gogues*, from *en* 'in' + the plural of *gogue* 'fun.'

a·gog·ic /əˈgäjik; əˈgō-/ *Music* ▸*adj.* relating to or denoting an accent produced by lengthening the time value of a note.

▸*plural n.* (**agogics**) [usu. treated as *sing.*] the use of agogic accents. ▷late 19th cent.: coined in German from Greek *agōgos* 'leading,' from *agein* 'to lead,' + -IC.

a·go·go /əˈgōgō/ ▸*n.* a small bell made of two metal cones, used as a percussion instrument in African and Latin music. ▷from Yoruba.

a go·go /ə ˈgōˌgō/ ▸*adj.* [*postpositive*] *informal* in abundance; galore: *Gershwin a gogo—all the hits.* ▷1960s: from French *à gogo*, from Old French *gogue* 'fun.'

a·gon·ic line /əˈgänik/ ▸*n.* an imaginary line around the earth passing through both the north pole and the north magnetic pole, at any point on which a compass needle points to true north. ▷mid 19th cent.: from Greek *agōnios*, *agōnos* (from *a-* 'without' + *gonia* 'angle') + -IC.

ag·o·nist /ˈagənist/ ▸*n.* **1** *Biochemistry* a substance that initiates a physiological response when combined with a receptor. Compare with ANTAGONIST. **2** *Anatomy* a muscle whose contraction moves a part of the body directly. Often contrasted with ANTAGONIST. **3** another term for PROTAGONIST. ▷early 20th cent.: from Greek *agōnistēs* 'contestant' (a sense reflected in English in the early 17th cent.), from *agōn* 'contest.' —**ag·o·nism** /-ˌnizəm/ *n.*

ag·o·nis·tic /ˌagəˈnistik/ ▸*adj.* combative; polemical. ■ *Zoology* (of animal behavior) associated with conflict. ■ *Biochemistry* of, relating to, or acting as an agonist. ▷mid 17th cent.: via late Latin from Greek *agōnistikos*, from *agōnistēs* 'contestant,' from *agōn* 'contest.' —**ag·o·nis·ti·cal·ly** /-ik(ə)lē/ *adv.*

ag·o·nize /ˈagəˌnīz/ ▸*v.* [*intrans.*] undergo great mental anguish through worrying about something: *I didn't agonize over the problem.* ■ [*trans.*] cause mental anguish to (someone). ▷late 16th cent.: from French *agoniser* or late Latin *agonizare*, from Greek *agōnizesthai* 'contend,' from *agōn* 'contest.'

ag·o·nized /ˈagəˌnīzd/ ▸*adj.* manifesting, suffering, or characterized by great physical or mental pain: *she gave an agonized cry* | *months of agonized discussion.*

ag·o·niz·ing /ˈagəˌnīzɪɴɢ/ (also **ag·o·nis·ing**) ▸*adj.* causing great physical or mental pain: *there is an agonizing choice to make* | *an agonizing death.* —**ag·o·niz·ing·ly** *adv.* [as *submodifier*] *agonizingly slow steps.*

ag·o·ny /ˈagənē/ ▸*n.* (*pl.* **-nies**) extreme physical or mental suffering: *he crashed to the ground in agony.* ■ [with *adj.*] the final stages of a difficult or painful death: *his last agony* | *the death agony.* ▷late Middle English (originally denoting mental anguish alone): via Old French and late Latin from Greek *agōnia*, from *agōn* 'contest.' The sense of physical suffering dates from the early 17th cent.

ag·o·ny col·umn ▸*n. Brit., informal* a column in a newspaper or magazine offering advice on personal problems to readers who write in. ■ *dated* a personal column.

ag·o·ra[1] /ˈagərə/ ▸*n.* (*pl.* **-rae** /-rē/ or **-ras**) (in ancient Greece) a public open space used for assemblies and markets. ▷from Greek.

a·go·ra[2] /əˈgôrə; ˌägôˈrä/ ▸*n.* (*pl.* **a·go·rot** /əˈgôrōt; ˌägôˈrōt/ or **a·go·roth** /əˈgôrōt; ˌägôˈrōt/) a monetary unit of Israel, equal to one hundredth of a shekel. ▷from Hebrew *ʾăgōrāh* 'small coin.'

ag·o·ra·pho·bi·a /ˌagərəˈfōbēə/ ▸*n.* extreme or irrational fear of crowded spaces or enclosed public places. ▷late 19th cent.: from Greek *agora* 'place of assembly, marketplace' + -PHOBIA. —**ag·o·ra·pho·bic** /-ˈfōbik/ *adj.* & *n.* —**ag·o·ra·phobe** /ˈagərəˌfōb/ *n.*

Agou·ra Hills /əˈgo͝orə/ a city in southwestern California, northwest of Los Angeles; pop. 20,390.

a·gou·ti /əˈgo͞otē/ ▸*n.* (*pl.* same or **-tis**) a large, long-legged burrowing rodent related to the guinea pig, native to Central and South America. • Genera *Agouti* and *Dasyprocta*, family Dasyproctidae: several species. ■ fur in which each hair has alternate dark and light bands, producing a grizzled appearance. ■ a rodent, esp. a mouse, having fur of this type. ▷mid 16th cent.: via French or from Spanish *aguti*, from Tupi *akutí*.

A·gra /ˈägrə/ a city on the Jumna River in Uttar Pradesh state, northern India; pop. 899,000. Once the capital of the Mogul empire 1566–1658, it is the site of the Taj Mahal.

a·gran·u·lo·cy·to·sis /āˌgranyələsīˈtōsis/ ▸*n. Medicine* a deficiency of granulocytes in the blood, causing increased vulnerability to infection.

a·grar·i·an /əˈgre(ə)rēən/ ▸*adj.* of or relating to cultivated land or the cultivation of land. ■ relating to landed property.

▸*n.* a person who advocates a redistribution of landed property. ▷early 17th cent. (originally designating a Roman law for the division of conquered lands): from Latin *agrarius*, from *ager*, *agr-* 'field.'

A·grar·i·an Rev·o·lu·tion the transformation of British agriculture during the 18th century, characterized by the enclosure of common land and the introduction of technological innovations such as the seed drill and the rotation of crops.

a·gree /əˈgrē/ ▸*v.* (**a·grees**, **a·greed**, **a·gree·ing**) [*intrans.*] **1** have the same opinion about something; concur: *I completely* **agree with** *your recent editorial* | *we both agreed on issues such as tougher penalties for criminals* | [with *clause*] *the authors agree that Jerusalem must remain united* | [with *direct speech*] *"Yes, it's dreadful, isn't it," she agreed.* ■ (**agree with**) approve of (something) with regard to its moral correctness: *I'm not sure I agree with abortion.* **2** (**agree to** or **to do something**) consent to do something that has been suggested by another person: *she had agreed to go and see a movie with him.* ■ [*intrans.*] reach agreement about (something), typically after a period of negotiation: *the commission* **agreed on** *a proposal to limit imports* | [*trans.*] *chiefly Brit. if they had agreed a price, the deal would have gone through.* **3** (**agree with**) be consistent with: *your body language does not agree with what you are saying.* ■ *Grammar* have the same number, gender, case, or person as: *the writer made the verb agree with the subject.* ■ [usu. with *negative*] be healthy or appropriate for someone: *she's eaten something that did not agree with her.* ▷late Middle English: from Old French *agreer*, based on Latin *ad-* 'to' + *gratus* 'pleasing.'

▸*PHRASE* □ **agree to differ** see DIFFER.

USAGE Note the distinction between **agreeing to** something like a plan, scheme, or project and **agreeing with** somebody: *I* **agree to** *the repayment schedule suggested; Danielle* **agrees with** *Eric that we should all go hiking on Saturday; humid weather does not* **agree with** *me.* The construction **agree with** is also used regarding two things that go together: *that story does not* **agree with** *the facts; the verb must* **agree with** *the noun in person and number.*

a·gree·a·ble /əˈgrēəbəl/ ▸*adj.* **1** enjoyable and pleasurable; pleasant: *a cheerful and agreeable companion.* See note at PLEASANT. **2** [*predic.*] willing to agree to something: *they were agreeable to its publication.* ■ (of a course of action) acceptable: *a compromise that might be agreeable to both management and unions.* ▷late Middle English: from Old French *agreable*, from *agreer* 'make agreeable to' (see AGREE). —**a·gree·a·ble·ness** *n.* —**a·gree·a·bly** /-blē/ *adv.* [as *submodifier*] *an agreeably warm day.*

a·greed /əˈgrēd/ ▸*adj.* [*attrib.*] discussed or negotiated and then accepted by all parties: *the agreed time* | *the* **agreed upon** *percentage.* ■ [*predic.*] (of two or more parties) holding the same view or opinion on something: *all the republics are agreed on the necessity of a common defense policy* | [with *clause*] *we are* **agreed that** *what is needed is a catchy title.*

a·gree·ment /əˈgrēmənt/ ▸*n.* harmony or accordance in opinion or feeling; a position or result of agreeing: *the governments failed to* **reach agreement** | *the two officers nodded* **in agreement** | *there is wide agreement*

A

A

that investment is necessary. ■ a negotiated and typically legally binding arrangement between parties as to a course of action: *a trade agreement* | *a verbal agreement to sell.* ■ the absence of incompatibility between two things; consistency: *agreement between experimental observations and theory.* ■ *Grammar* the condition of having the same number, gender, case, or person. ▷late Middle English: from Old French, from *agreer* 'make agreeable to' (see **AGREE**).

a·gres·tal /ə'grestl/ ▶*adj. Botany* growing wild in cultivated fields. ▷mid 19th cent.: from Latin *agrestis* 'relating to the country' (see **AGRESTIC**) + **-AL**.

a·gres·tic /ə'grestik/ ▶*adj. chiefly poetic/literary* of or relating to the country; rural; rustic. ▷early 17th cent.: from Latin *agrestis*, from *ager*, *agr-* 'field' + **-IC**.

agri- ▶*comb. form* variant spelling of **AGRO-**: *agriculture* | *agribusiness.*

ag·ri·busi·ness /'agrə,biznis/ ▶*n.* **1** agriculture conducted on commercial principles, esp. using advanced technology. ■ an organization engaged in this. **2** the group of industries dealing with agricultural produce and services required in farming. ▷1950s (originally U.S.): blend of **AGRICULTURE** and **BUSINESS**. **—ag·ri·busi·ness·man** *n.* (*pl.* **-men**).

A·gric·o·la /ə'grikələ/, Gnaeus Julius (AD 40–93), Roman general and governor of Britain 78–84. As governor he completed the subjugation of Wales and defeated the Scottish Highland tribes.

ag·ri·cul·tur·al /,agri'kəlCHərəl/ ▶*adj.* of or relating to agriculture: *agricultural land* | *an agricultural worker.* **—ag·ri·cul·tur·al·ist** /-ist/ *n.* **—ag·ri·cul·tur·al·ly** *adv. agriculturally fertile plains.*

ag·ri·cul·tur·al fair ▶*n.* see **FAIR**[2].

ag·ri·cul·ture /'agri,kəlCHər/ ▶*n.* the science or practice of farming, including cultivation of the soil for the growing of crops and the rearing of animals to provide food, wool, and other products. ▷late Middle English: from Latin *agricultura*, from *ager*, *agr-* 'field' + *cultura* 'growing, cultivation.' **—ag·ri·cul·tur·ist** /-rist/ *n.*

ag·ri·mo·ny /'agrə,mōnē/ ▶*n.* (*pl.* **-nies**) a plant of the rose family bearing slender flower spikes and spiny fruits. Native to north temperate regions, it has been used traditionally in herbal medicine and dyeing. • Genus *Agrimonia*, family Rosaceae: several species, in particular *A. eupatoria*, which has small yellow flowers. ▷late Middle English: directly or (in early use) via Old French from Latin *agrimonia*, alteration of *argemonia*, from Greek *argemōnē* 'poppy.'

A·grip·pa /ə'gripə/, Marcus Vipsanius (63–12 BC), Roman general. Augustus's adviser and son-in-law, he played an important part in the naval victories over Mark Antony.

ag·ri·sci·ence /'agri,sīəns/ ▶*n.* the application of science to agriculture. **—ag·ri·sci·en·tist** /-tist/ *n.*

ag·ri·tain·ment /,agri'tānmənt/ ▶*n.* farm-based entertainment, typically developed as a revenue source for small-scale farmers and including a wide range of activities, such as hayrides, pony rides, wine tasting, cornfield-maze contests, and harvest festivals.

agro- (also **agri-**) ▶*comb. form* agricultural: *agro-industry* | *agrobiology* | *agribusiness.* ■ agriculture and . . . : *agroforestry.* ▷from Greek *agros* 'field.'

ag·ro·bi·ol·o·gy /,agrōbī'äləjē/ ▶*n.* the branch of biology that deals with soil science and plant nutrition and its application to crop production. **—ag·ro·bi·o·log·i·cal** /-bīə'läjikəl/ *adj.* **—ag·ro·bi·ol·o·gist** /-jist/ *n.*

ag·ro·chem·i·cal /,agrō'kemikəl/ ▶*n.* a chemical used in agriculture, such as a pesticide or a fertilizer.

ag·ro·for·est·ry /,agrō'fôrəstrē; -'fär-/ ▶*n.* agriculture incorporating the cultivation and conservation of trees.

ag·ro·in·dus·try ▶*n.* industry connected with agriculture. ■ agriculture developed along industrial lines. **—ag·ro·in·dus·tri·al** *adj.*

a·grol·o·gy /ə'gräləjē/ ▶*n. Canadian* the application of science to agriculture. **—a·grol·o·gist** /-jist/ *n.*

a·gron·o·my /ə'gränəmē/ ▶*n.* the science of soil management and crop production. ▷early 19th cent.: from French *agronomie*, from *agronome* 'agriculturist,' from Greek *agros* 'field' + *-nomos* 'arranging' (from *nemein* 'arrange'). **—ag·ro·nom·ic** /,agrə'nämik/ *adj.* **—ag·ro·nom·i·cal** /,agrə'nämikəl/ *adj.* **—ag·ro·nom·i·cal·ly** /,agrə'nämik(ə)lē/ *adv.* **—a·gron·o·mist** /-mist/ *n.*

Agro Pontino Italian name for **PONTINE MARSHES**.

ag·ros·tol·o·gy /,agrə'stäləjē/ ▶*n.* the branch of botany concerned with grasses. ▷mid 19th cent.: from Greek *agrōstis* (denoting a kind of grass) + **-LOGY**.

a·ground /ə'ground/ ▶*adj.* & *adv.* (with reference to a ship) on or onto the bottom in shallow water: [as *adv.*] *the ships must slow to avoid* ***running aground*** | [as *predic. adj.*] *a cargo ship aground in the Mediterranean.* ▷Middle English (in the sense 'on the ground'): from **A-**[2] 'on' + **GROUND**[1].

Ag·ua Pri·e·ta /'ägwə prē'ātə/ a city in Sonora, in northwestern Mexico, near the Arizona border; pop. 38,000.

a·guar·dien·te /,ägwär'dyentā/ ▶*n.* (in Spanish-speaking regions) a distilled liquor resembling brandy, esp. as made in South America from sugar cane. ▷from Spanish, from *agua* 'water' + *ardiente* 'fiery.'

A·guas·ca·lien·tes /,ägwä,skäl'yen,tās; ,äwä-/ a state in central Mexico. ■ its capital, a health resort noted for its hot springs; pop. 506,000. ▷Spanish, literally 'hot waters.'

a·gue /'ā,gyōō/ ▶*n. archaic* malaria or some other illness involving fever and shivering. ■ a fever or shivering fit. ▷Middle English: via Old French from medieval Latin *acuta (febris)* 'acute (fever).' **—a·gued** *adj.* **—a·gu·ish** *adj.*

A·gul·has, Cape /ə'gələs/ the most southern point of the continent of Africa, in Western Cape province, South Africa.

A·gul·has Cur·rent an ocean current in the Indian Ocean that flows southward along the east coast of Africa.

AH ▶*abbr.* in the year of the Hegira (used in the Muslim calendar for reckoning years from Muhammad's departure from Mecca in AD 622); of the Muslim era: *a Koran dated 556* AH. ▷from Latin *anno Hegirae*.

ah /ä/ ▶*exclam.* used to express a range of emotions including surprise, pleasure, sympathy, and realization: *ah, there you are!* | *ah, this is the life.* ▷Middle English: from Old French.

AHA ▶*abbr.* ■ alpha-hydroxy acid. ■ American Heart Association.

a·ha /ä'hä/ ▶*exclam.* used to express satisfaction, triumph, or surprise: *aha! So that's your secret plan!* ▷Middle English: from **AH** + **HA**[1].

A·hag·gar Moun·tains /ə'hägər; ,ähə'gär/ another name for **HOGGAR MOUNTAINS**.

a·head /ə'hed/ ▶*adv.* further forward in space; in the line of one's forward motion: *he had to give his attention to the road ahead* | *he was striding ahead toward the stream.* ■ further forward in time; in advance; in the near future: *he contemplated the day ahead* | *we have to plan ahead.* ■ onward so as to make progress. ■ in the lead: *the Bucks were ahead by four* | *he was slightly ahead on points.* ■ higher in number, amount, or value than previously: *profits were slightly ahead.* ▷mid 16th cent. (originally in nautical use): from **A-**[2] 'in, at' + **HEAD**.

▶*PHRASES* □ **ahead of** in front of or before: *she walked ahead of him along the corridor* ■ in store for; awaiting: *we have a long drive ahead of us.* ■ earlier than planned or expected: *elimination of trade barriers came five years ahead of schedule.* □ **ahead of one's** (or **its**) **time** innovative and radical by the standards of the time; more characteristic of a later age.

a·hem /ə'hem; ə'hm/ ▶*exclam.* used to represent the noise made when clearing the throat, typically to attract attention or express disapproval or embarrassment. ▷mid 18th cent.: lengthened form of **HEM**[2].

a·hi /'ähē/ ▶noun Japanese name for **YELLOWFIN**.

a·him·sa /ə'him,sä/ ▶*n.* (in the Hindu, Buddhist, and Jain tradition) the principle of nonviolence toward all living things. ▷Sanskrit, from *a* 'non-, without' + *hiṃsā* 'violence.'

a·his·tor·i·cal /,āhi'stôrikəl; -'stär-/ ▶*adj.* lacking historical perspective or context: *ahistorical nostalgia that misunderstands cultural history.*

Ah·mad·a·bad /'ämədə,bäd/ (also **Ah·med·a·bad**) an industrial city in the state of Gujarat in western India; pop. 2,873,000.

a·ho·le·ho·le /ə'hōlē'hōlē/ ▶*n.* a small silvery fish occurring only in the shallow waters around the Hawaiian islands, where it is a food fish. • *Kuhlia sandvicensis*, family Kuhliidae. ▷from Hawaiian.

-aholic (also **-oholic**) ▶*suffix* denoting a person addicted to something: *shopaholic* | *workaholic.* ▷on the pattern of *(alc)oholic*.

a·hoy /ə'hoi/ ▶*exclam. Nautical* a call used in hailing: *ahoy there!* | *ship ahoy!* ▷mid 18th cent.: from **AH** + **HOY**[1].

▶*PHRASE* □ **land ahoy!** an exclamation announcing the sighting of land from a ship.

Ah·ri·man /'ärimən/ the evil spirit in the doctrine of Zoroastrianism, the opponent of Ahura Mazda.

A·hu·ra Maz·da /ə,hōōrə 'mäzdə/ the creator god of Zoroastrianism, the force for good and the opponent of Ahriman. Also called **ORMAZD**. ▷Avestan, literally 'wise deity.'

Ah·vaz /ä'väz/ (also **Ah·waz** /ä'wäz/) a town in western Iran; pop. 725,000.

Ah·ve·nan·maa /'ävə,nän,mä/ Finnish name for **ÅLAND ISLANDS**.

AI ▶*abbr.* ■ Amnesty International. ■ artificial insemination. ■ artificial intelligence.

AID ▶*abbr.* ■ Agency for International Development. ■ artificial insemination by donor.

aid /ād/ ▶*n.* help, typically of a practical nature: *he saw the pilot slumped in his cockpit and* ***went to his aid*** | *within six weeks he was walking* ***with the aid*** *of a walker.* ■ financial or material help given to a country or area in need: *700,000 tons of food aid* | [as *adj.*] *aid convoys.* ■ a person or thing that is a source of help or assistance: *exercise is an important* ***aid to*** *recovery after heart attacks* | *a teaching aid.* ■ *historical* a grant of subsidy or tax to a king.

▶*v.* [*trans.*] help, assist, or support (someone or something) in the achievement of something: *women were aided in childbirth by midwives* | [*intrans.*] *the heel was slanted to aid in climbing hilly terrain.* ■ promote or encourage (something): *diet and exercise aid healthy skin.* ▷late Middle English: from Old French *aïde* (noun), *aïdier* (verb), based on Latin *adjuvare*, from *ad-* 'toward' + *juvare* 'to help.'

▶*PHRASES* □ **aid and abet** see **ABET**. □ **in aid of** *chiefly Brit.* in support of; for the purpose of raising money for: *a concert in aid of Armenia.*

Ai·dan, St. /'ādn/ (d. AD 651), Irish missionary. While a monk in the monastery at Iona he set out to Christianize Northumbria, founding a church and monastery on the island of Lindisfarne in 635 and becoming its first bishop.

aid climb·ing ▶*n.* rock climbing using the assistance of objects such as pitons placed in the rock. Compare with **FREE CLIMBING**. **—aid climb** *n.* **—aid-climb** *v.*

aide /ād/ ▶*n.* an assistant to an important person, esp. to a political leader: *a presidential aide.* ■ short for **AIDE-DE-CAMP**.

aide-de-camp /'ād də 'kamp/ ▶*n.* (*pl.* **aides-de-camp** /'ādz/ *pronunc.* same) a military officer acting as a confidential assistant to a senior officer. ▷late 17th cent.: from French, 'camp adjutant.'

aide-me·moire /'ād mem'wär/ ▶*n.* (*pl.* **aides-me·moires** or **aides-me·moire** *pronunc.* same) an aid to the memory, esp. a book or document. ■ an informal diplomatic message. ▷mid 19th cent.: from French *aide-mémoire*, from *aider* 'to help' and *mémoire* 'memory.'

AIDS /ādz/ ▶*n.* acquired immune deficiency syndrome, a disease in which there is a severe loss of the body's cellular immunity, greatly lowering the resistance to infection and malignancy.

The cause is a virus (called the human immunodeficiency virus or HIV) transmitted in blood and in sexual fluids, and though the incubation period may be long, the fully developed disease is invariably fatal. AIDS was first identified in the early 1980s and now affects millions of people. In the developed world the disease first spread among homosexuals, intravenous drug users, and recipients of infected blood transfusions, before reaching the wider population. This has tended to overshadow a greater epidemic in parts of Africa, where transmission is mainly through heterosexual contact.

▷1980s: acronym.

AIDS-re·lat·ed com·plex ▶*n.* the symptoms of a person who is infected with HIV but does not necessarily develop the disease.

ai·grette /ā'gret/ ▶*n.* a headdress consisting of a white egret's feather or other decoration such as a spray of gems. ▷mid 18th cent.: French, literally 'egret.'

ai·guille /ā'gwēl/ ▶*n.* a sharp pinnacle of rock in a mountain range. ▷mid 18th cent.: French, literally 'needle'.

ai·guil·lette /,āgwə'let/ ▶*n.* an ornament on some military and naval uniforms, consisting of braided loops hanging from the shoulder and on dress uniforms ending in points. ▷mid 16th cent.: from French, literally 'small needle,' diminutive of *aiguille*.

aiguillette

Ai·ken /ˈākən/ a resort city in west central South Carolina; pop. 25,337.

ai·ki·do /ˌīkēˈdō; īˈkēdō/ ▸*n.* a Japanese form of self-defense and martial art that uses locks, holds, throws, and the opponent's own movements. ▷1950s: from Japanese *aikidō*, literally 'way of adapting the spirit,' from *ai* 'together, unify' + *ki* 'spirit' + *dō* 'way.'

ail /āl/ ▸*v.* [*trans.*] trouble or afflict (someone) in mind or body: *exercise is good for whatever ails you.* ▷Old English *eglian, eglan*, from *egle* 'troublesome,' of Germanic origin; related to Gothic *agls* 'disgraceful.'

ai·lan·thus /āˈlanTHəs/ ▸*n.* a tall large-leaved deciduous tree that is widely grown as an ornamental or shade tree. Native to Asia and Australasia, it has been naturalized in North America and central and southern Europe. • Genus *Ailanthus*, family Simaroubaceae: several species, in particular the tree of heaven. ▷modern Latin, from French *ailante*, from Amboinese *ailanto*, literally 'tree of heaven' (the ending being influenced by names ending with *-anthus*, from Greek *anthos* 'flower').

ai·ler·on /ˈāləˌrän/ ▸*n.* a hinged surface in the trailing edge of an airplane wing, used to control lateral balance. ▷early 20th cent.: French, literally 'small wing'

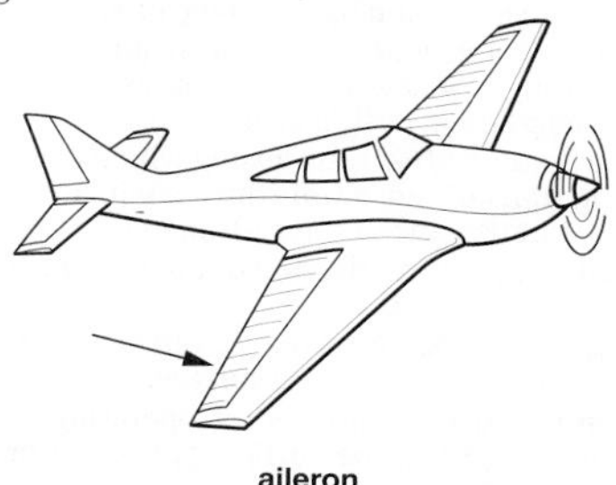

aileron

Ai·ley /ˈālē/, Alvin (1931–89), U.S. dancer and choreographer. He founded the Alvin Ailey Dance Theater in 1958 and helped to establish modern dance as an American art form; he incorporated ballet, jazz, and Afro-Caribbean idioms in his choreography.

ail·ing /ˈāliNG/ ▸*adj.* in poor health: *I went to see my ailing mother* | *figurative the ailing economy.*

ail·ment /ˈālmənt/ ▸*n.* an illness, typically a minor one.

ai·lur·o·phile /īˈlo͝orəˌfīl; āˈlo͝or-/ ▸*n.* a cat lover.

ai·lu·ro·pho·bi·a /īˌlo͝orəˈfōbēə; āˌlo͝or-/ ▸*n.* extreme or irrational fear of cats. ▷early 20th cent.: from Greek *ailuros* 'cat' + **-PHOBIA**. —**ai·lu·ro·phobe** /īˈlo͝orəˌfōb; āˈlo͝or-/ *n.*

AIM /ām/ ▸*abbr.* American Indian Movement.

aim /ām/ ▸*v.* **1** [*trans.*] point or direct (a weapon or camera) at a target: ***aim*** *the camcorder* ***at*** *some suitable object* | [*intrans.*] ***aim for*** *the middle of the target.* ■ direct (an object or blow) at someone or something: *she had* ***aimed*** *the bottle* ***at*** *his head.* ■ **(aim something at)** direct information or an action toward (a particular group): *the TV campaign is aimed at the 16-24 age group.* **2** [*intrans.*] have the intention of achieving: *new French cooking* ***aims at*** *producing clear, fresh flavors and light textures* | [with *infinitive*] *we aim to give you the best possible service.* See note at **INTEND**.

▸*n.* **1** a purpose or intention; a desired outcome: *our primary aim is to achieve financial discipline.* **2** [in *sing.*] the directing of a weapon or object at a target: *his aim was perfect, and the guard's body collapsed backward.* ▷Middle English: from Old French *amer*, variant of *esmer* (from Latin *aestimare* 'assess, estimate'), reinforced by *aemer, aesmer* (from late Latin *adaestimare*, intensified form of *aestimare*).

▸*PHRASES* □ **aim high** be ambitious. □ **take aim** point a weapon or camera at a target.

aim·less /ˈāmlis/ ▸*adj.* without purpose or direction: *an aimless, ungratifying life.* —**aim·less·ly** *adv.* —**aim·less·ness** *n.*

ai·nhum /ˈīnəm/ ▸*n.* *Medicine* a condition in which a band of fibrous tissue grows around the base of a toe, esp. the fifth, eventually resulting in loss of the digit. It occurs mainly in the tropics and is associated with going barefoot, though its cause is unknown. ▷late 19th cent.: from Portuguese, based on Yoruba *eyun* 'saw.'

ain't /ānt/ *informal* ▸*contraction of* ■ am not; are not; is not: *if it ain't broke, don't fix it.* [originally representing London dialect.] ■ has not; have not: *they ain't got nothing to say.* [from dialect *hain't*.]

USAGE The use of **ain't** was widespread in the 18th century and is still perfectly normal in many dialects and informal contexts in both North America and Britain. Today, however, it does not form part of standard English and should not be used in formal contexts.

Ain·tab /īnˈtäb/ former name (until 1921) of **GAZIANTEP**.

Ai·nu /ˈīˌno͞o/ ▸*n.* **1** (*pl.* same or **-nus**) a member of an aboriginal people of Japan, physically distinct (with light skin color and round eyes) from the majority population. **2** the language of this people, of unknown affinity.

▸*adj.* of or relating to this people or their language. ▷early 19th cent.: the name in Ainu, literally 'man, person.'

ai·o·li /īˈōlē; āˈō-/ (also **aï·o·li**) ▸*n.* mayonnaise seasoned with garlic. ▷French, from Provençal *ai* 'garlic' + *oli* 'oil.'

air /e(ə)r/ ▸*n.* **1** the invisible gaseous substance surrounding the earth, a mixture mainly of oxygen and nitrogen. ■ this substance regarded as necessary for breathing: *the air was stale* | *the doctor told me to get some fresh air.* ■ the free or unconfined space above the surface of the earth: *he celebrated by tossing his hat high in the air.* ■ [as *adj.*] used to indicate that something involves the use of aircraft: *air travel.* ■ the earth's atmosphere as a medium for transmitting radio waves: *radio stations have successfully sold products* ***over the air.*** ■ air considered as one of the four elements in ancient philosophy and in astrology (associated with the signs of Gemini, Aquarius, and Libra). ■ a breeze or light wind. See also **LIGHT AIR**. ■ air conditioning. ■ a jump off the ground on a snowboard. [Middle English: from Old French *air*, from Latin *aer*, from Greek *aēr*, denoting the gas.] **2** (**air of**) an impression of a quality or manner given by someone or something: *she answered with a faint air of boredom.* ■ (**airs**) an annoyingly affected and condescending manner: *he began to* ***put on airs*** *and think he could boss us around.* [late 16th cent.: from French *air*, probably from Old French *aire* 'site, disposition,' from Latin *ager, agr-* 'field' (influenced by sense 1).] **3** *Music* a tune or short melodious composition, typically a song. [late 16th cent.: from Italian *aria* (see **ARIA**).]

▸*v.* **1** [*trans.*] (often **be aired**) express (an opinion or grievance) publicly: *a meeting in which long-standing grievances were aired.* ■ broadcast (a program) on radio or television: *the programs were aired on India's state TV network.* ■ *archaic* parade or show (something) ostentatiously: *airing a snowy hand and signet ring.* **2** [*trans.*] expose (a room) to the open air in order to ventilate it: *the window sashes were lifted regularly to air the room.* ■ **(air oneself)** *archaic* go out in the fresh air.

▸*PHRASES* □ **airs and graces** *derogatory* an affectation of superiority. □ **by air** in an aircraft: *all goods must come in by air.* □ **in the air** noticeable all around; becoming prevalent: *I smell violence in the air.* □ **on** (or **off**) **the air** being (or not being) broadcast on radio or television. □ **take the air** go out of doors. □ **up in the air** (of a plan or issue) still to be settled; unresolved: *the fate of the power station is up in the air.* □ **walk on air** feel elated.

air bag ▸*n.* a safety device fitted inside a road vehicle, consisting of a cushion designed to inflate rapidly in the event of a collision and positioned so as to prevent passengers from being flung against the vehicle's structure.

air ball ▸*n.* *informal Basketball* a shot that misses the backboard, rim, and net entirely.

air·base /ˈe(ə)rˌbās/ ▸*n.* a base for the operation of military aircraft.

air bear·ing ▸*n.* a bearing in which moving surfaces are kept apart by a layer of air provided by jets.

air bed ▸*n.* an inflatable mattress.

air blad·der ▸*n.* an air-filled bladder or sac found in certain animals and plants. ■ another term for **SWIM BLADDER**.

air·boat /ˈe(ə)rˌbōt/ ▸*n.* a shallow-draft boat powered by an aircraft engine, for use in swamps.

air·borne /ˈe(ə)rˌbôrn/ ▸*adj.* transported by air: *airborne pollutants.* ■ (of an aircraft) in the air after taking off.

air brake ▸*n.* a brake worked by air pressure. ■ a movable flap or other device on an aircraft to reduce its speed.

air bridge ▸*n.* British term for **JETWAY**.

air·brush /ˈe(ə)rˌbrəSH/ ▸*n.* an artist's device for spraying paint by means of compressed air.

▸*v.* [*trans.*] paint with an airbrush: *a cab airbrushed with a mural of a sunset.* ■ alter or conceal (a photograph or a detail in one) using an airbrush: *a picture of a man with wings airbrushed onto his shoulders.* ■ [usu. as *adj.*] (**airbrushed**) *figurative* represent or describe (someone or something) as better or more beautiful than they in fact are: *an airbrushed vision of the decade.*

airbrush

air·burst /ˈe(ə)rˌbərst/ ▸*n.* an explosion in the air, typically of a nuclear bomb or large meteor.

▸*v.* [*intrans.*] explode in the air.

air·bus /ˈe(ə)rˌbəs/ ▸*n.* *trademark* an aircraft designed to carry a large number of passengers economically, esp. over relatively short routes.

air clean·er ▸ another term for **AIR FILTER**.

air com·mand ▸*n.* a high-level organizational unit in the U.S. Air Force.

air con·di·tion·ing ▸*n.* a system for controlling the humidity, ventilation, and temperature in a building or vehicle, typically to maintain a cool atmosphere in warm conditions. —**air con·di·tioned** *adj.* —**air con·di·tion·er** *n.*

air-cooled ▸*adj.* cooled by means of a flow of air.

air cor·ri·dor ▸*n.* a route to which aircraft are restricted, esp. over a foreign country.

air cov·er ▸*n.* protection from aircraft for land-based or naval operations in war situations.

air·craft /ˈe(ə)rˌkraft/ ▸*n.* (*pl.* same) an airplane, helicopter, or other machine capable of flight.

air·craft car·ri·er ▸*n.* a large warship equipped to serve as a base for aircraft that can take off from and land on its deck.

air·crew /ˈe(ə)rˌkro͞o/ ▸*n.* (*pl.* **-crews**) [treated as *sing.* or *pl.*] the crew manning an aircraft. ■ (*pl.* same) a member of such a crew: *each aircraft carried three aircrew.*

air cush·ion ▸*n.* **1** an inflatable cushion. **2** the layer of air supporting a hovercraft or similar vehicle.

air dam ▸*n.* a streamlining device below the front bumper of a vehicle; a front spoiler.

air date ▸*n.* the date on which a recorded program is to be broadcast.

air·drome /ˈe(ə)rˌdrōm/ ▸*n.* an airport. ■ a military air base.

air·drop /ˈe(ə)rˌdräp/ ▸*n.* an act of dropping supplies, troops, or equipment by parachute from an aircraft.

▸*v.* (**-dropped**, **-drop·ping**) [*trans.*] drop (such things) by parachute.

air-dry ▸*v.* make or become dry through contact with unheated air.

▸*adj.* not giving off any moisture on exposure to air.

Aire·dale /ˈe(ə)rˌdāl/ ▸*n.* a large terrier of a rough-coated black and tan breed. ▷late 19th cent.: from *Airedale*, a district in Yorkshire, England, where the dog was bred.

Airedale

air·fare /ˈe(ə)rˌfe(ə)r/ ▸*n.* the price of a passenger ticket for travel by aircraft: *save a bundle in airfare by flying standby.*

Pronunciation Key ə *ago*; ər *over*; ˈə *or* ˌə *up*; ˈər *or* ˌər *fur*; a *hat*; ā *rate*; ä *car*; CH *chew*; e *let*; ē *see*; e(ə)r *air*; i *fit*; ī *by*; i(ə)r *ear*; NG *sing*; ō *go*; ô *for*; oi *boy*; o͝o *good*; o͞o *goo*; ou *out*; SH *she*; TH *thin*; TH *then*; (h)w *why*; ZH *vision*

air·field /ˈe(ə)rˌfēld/ ▸*n.* an area of land set aside for the takeoff, landing, and maintenance of aircraft.

air fil·ter ▸*n.* a device for filtering particles of dust, soot, etc., from the air passing through it, esp. one protecting the air inlet of an internal combustion engine.

air·flow /ˈe(ə)rˌflō/ ▸*n.* the flow of air, esp. that encountered by a moving aircraft or vehicle.

air·foil /ˈe(ə)rˌfoil/ ▸*n.* a structure with curved surfaces designed to give the most favorable ratio of lift to drag in flight, used as the basic form of the wings, fins, and tailplanes of most aircraft.

air force ▸*n.* (often **the air force** or **the Air Force**) the branch of a nation's armed services that conducts military operations in the air.

Air Force One the designation (when the president of the U.S. is aboard) of any of several specially equipped jetliners maintained by the U.S. Air Force.

air·frame /ˈe(ə)rˌfrām/ ▸*n.* the body of an aircraft as distinct from its engine.

air·freight /ˈe(ə)rˌfrāt/ ▸*n.* the transportation of goods by aircraft. ■ goods in transit, or to be carried, by aircraft.
▸*v.* [*trans.*] carry or send (goods) by aircraft.
▸*adv.* by airfreight: *the exhibit was flown airfreight.*

air fresh·en·er ▸*n.* a substance or device for making the air in a room smell fresh or clean.

air·glow /ˈe(ə)rˌglō/ ▸*n.* a glow in the night sky caused by radiation from the upper atmosphere.

air gui·tar ▸*n. informal* used to describe the actions of someone playing an imaginary guitar: *we like our audiences to sing along and play air guitar.*

air gun ▸*n.* a gun that fires pellets using compressed air.

air·head[1] /ˈe(ə)rˌhed/ ▸*n. Military* a base secured in enemy territory where supplies and troops can be received and evacuated by air. ▹World War II: on the pattern of *bridgehead*.

air·head[2] ▸*n. informal* a silly or foolish person.

air·ing /ˈe(ə)riNG/ ▸*n.* [in *sing.*] **1** an exposure to warm or fresh air, for the purpose of ventilating or removing dampness from something: *somebody had given the place a thorough airing.* ■ a walk or outing to take air or exercise: *taking the baby out for an airing.* **2** a public expression of an opinion or subject: *these are ideas I feel might be worth an airing.* ■ a transmission of a television or radio program.

air-kiss ▸*v.* [*trans.*] purse the lips as if kissing (someone), without making contact: *the media crowd who lunch, gossip, and air-kiss one another.*
▸*n.* (**air kiss**) a simulated kiss, without physical contact.

air lane ▸*n.* a path or course regularly used by aircraft.

air lay·er·ing ▸*n. Horticulture* a form of layering in which the branch is potted or wrapped in a moist growing medium to promote root growth.

air·less /ˈe(ə)rlis/ ▸*adj.* stuffy; not ventilated: *a dusty, airless basement.* ■ without wind or breeze; still: *a hot, airless night.* **—air·less·ness** *n.*

air let·ter ▸*n.* another term for **AEROGRAMME**.

air·lift /ˈe(ə)rˌlift/ ▸*n.* an act of transporting supplies by aircraft, typically in a blockade or other emergency: *a massive airlift of food, blankets, and medical supplies.*
▸*v.* [*trans.*] transport (troops or supplies) by aircraft, typically when transportation by land is difficult: *helicopters were employed to airlift the troops out of danger.*

air·line /ˈe(ə)rˌlīn/ ▸*n.* **1** an organization providing a regular public service of air transportation on one or more routes. ■ (usu. **air line**) a route that forms part of a system regularly used by aircraft. **2** (usu. **air line**) a pipe supplying air: *use an air line to inflate those tires.*

air·lin·er /ˈe(ə)rˌlīnər/ ▸*n.* a large passenger aircraft.

air·lock /ˈe(ə)rˌläk/ (also **air lock**) ▸*n.* **1** a blockage of the flow in a pump or pipe, caused by an air bubble. **2** a compartment with controlled pressure and parallel sets of doors, to permit movement between areas at different pressures.

air·mail /ˈe(ə)rˌmāl/ ▸*n.* a system of transporting mail by aircraft, typically overseas. ■ a letter carried by aircraft.
▸*v.* [*trans.*] send (mail) by aircraft: *a recent letter that I airmailed to Miss Sifton.*

air·man /ˈe(ə)rmən/ ▸*n.* (*pl.* **-men**) a pilot or member of the crew of an aircraft, esp. in an air force. ■ a member of the U.S. Air Force of the lowest rank, below sergeant. ■ a member of the U.S. Navy whose general duties are concerned with aircraft.

air·man·ship /ˈe(ə)rmənˌSHip/ ▸*n.* skill in flying an aircraft.

air mass ▸*n. Meterology* a body of air with horizontally uniform temperature, humidity, and pressure.

air mat·tress ▸*n.* an inflatable mattress.

air mile ▸*n.* a nautical mile used as a measure of distance flown by aircraft. ■ (**Air Miles**) *trademark* points (equivalent to miles of free air travel) accumulated by buyers of airline tickets and other products and redeemable against the cost of air travel with a particular airline.

air·mo·bile /ˈe(ə)rˌmōbəl/ ▸*adj.* (of troops) moved about by helicopters.

air pis·tol ▸*n.* a pistol that fires pellets using compressed air.

air·plane /ˈe(ə)rˌplān/ ▸*n.* a powered flying vehicle with fixed wings and a weight greater than that of the air it displaces.

air plant ▸*n.* a typically epiphytic, sometimes rootless, tropical American plant with grasslike or fingerlike leaves through which water and airborne or waterborne nutrients are absorbed. • Genus *Tillandsia*, family Bromeliaceae: several species, including Spanish moss.

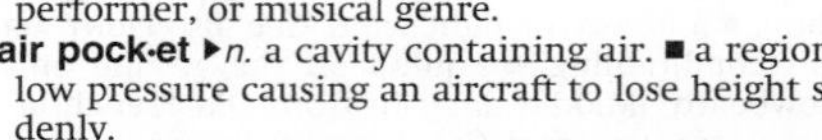
air plant

air·play /ˈe(ə)rˌplā/ ▸*n.* broadcasting time devoted to a particular record, performer, or musical genre.

air pock·et ▸*n.* a cavity containing air. ■ a region of low pressure causing an aircraft to lose height suddenly.

air·port /ˈe(ə)rˌpôrt/ ▸*n.* a complex of runways and buildings for the takeoff, landing, and maintenance of civil aircraft, with facilities for passengers. ■ [as *modifier*] relating to or denoting light popular fiction such as is offered for sale to travelers in airports: *another airport thriller.*

air·pot /ˈe(ə)rˌpät/ ▸*n.* a container for storing and dispensing coffee or other beverages that maintains a constant temperature by use of glass insulation.

air pow·er ▸*n.* airborne military forces.

air pump ▸*n.* a device for pumping air into or out of an enclosed space.

air qual·i·ty ▸*n.* the degree to which the ambient air is pollution-free, assessed by measuring a number of indicators of pollution.

air rage ▸*n.* violent anger directed mainly at inflight airline personnel and arising from the frustrations and stresses of air travel.

air raid ▸*n.* an attack in which bombs are dropped from aircraft onto a ground target.

air ri·fle ▸*n.* a rifle that fires pellets using compressed air.

air sac ▸*n.* a lung compartment containing air; an alveolus. ■ an extension of a bird's lung cavity into a bone or other part of the body.

air·screw /ˈe(ə)rˌskro͞o/ ▸*n. Brit.* an aircraft propeller.

air-sea res·cue ▸*n.* a rescue from the sea using aircraft.

air shaft ▸*n.* a straight, typically vertical passage admitting air into a mine, tunnel, or building.

air·ship /ˈe(ə)rˌSHip/ ▸*n.* a power-driven aircraft that is kept buoyant by a body of gas (typically helium, formerly hydrogen) that is lighter than air.

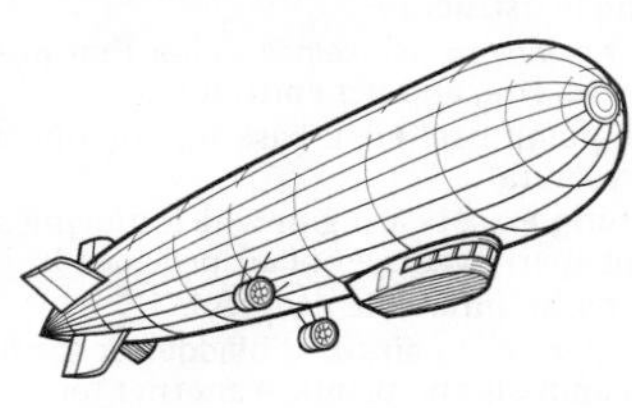
airship

air show ▸*n.* a show at which aircraft perform aerial displays.

air·sick /ˈe(ə)rˌsik/ ▸*adj.* affected with nausea due to travel in an aircraft. **—air·sick·ness** *n.*

air·sick·ness bag ▸*n.* a paper bag provided in an aircraft or ship as a receptacle for vomit.

air·side /ˈe(ə)rˌsīd/ ▸*n.* the side of an airport terminal from which aircraft can be observed; the area beyond security checks and passport and customs control.
▸*adv.* on or to this side of an airport terminal: *a new executive lounge has opened airside.*

air·space /ˈe(ə)rˌspās/ ▸*n.* space available in the atmosphere immediately above the earth: *temples and mosques fight for airspace with skyscrapers.* ■ the air available to aircraft to fly in, esp. the part subject to the jurisdiction of a particular country: *the airliner was refused permission to enter Maltese airspace.* ■ *Law* the right of a private landowner to the space above his land and any structures on it, which he can use for ordinary purposes such as the erection of signposts or fences. ■ space left to be occupied by air for purposes of insulation.

air·speed /ˈe(ə)rˌspēd/ ▸*n.* the speed of an aircraft relative to the air through which it is moving. Compare with **GROUNDSPEED**.

air sta·tion ▸*n.* an airfield operated by a navy or marine corps.

air·stream /ˈe(ə)rˌstrēm/ ▸*n.* a current of air.

air strike ▸*n.* an attack made by aircraft.

air·strip /ˈe(ə)rˌstrip/ ▸*n.* a strip of ground set aside for the takeoff and landing of aircraft.

air sup·port ▸*n.* assistance given to ground or naval forces in an operation by their own or allied aircraft.

air·tight /ˈe(ə)rˌtīt/ ▸*adj.* not allowing air to escape or pass through. ■ having no weaknesses; unassailable: *Scamp had an airtight alibi.*

air·time /ˈe(ə)rˌtīm/ ▸*n.* time during which a broadcast is being transmitted. ■ time during which a cellular phone is in use, including calls made and received.

air-to-air ▸*adj.* [*attrib.*] directed or operating from one aircraft to another in flight.

air-to-ground ▸*adj.* directed or operating from an aircraft in flight to the land surface.

air-to-sur·face ▸*adj.* directed or operating from an aircraft in flight to the surface of the sea or other body of water.

air traf·fic con·trol ▸*n.* the ground-based personnel and equipment concerned with monitoring and controlling air traffic within a particular area. **—air traf·fic con·trol·ler** *n.*

air·waves /ˈe(ə)rˌwāvz/ ▸*plural n.* the radio frequencies used for broadcasting: *football pervades the airwaves.*

air·way /ˈeərˌwā/ ▸*n.* **1** the passage by which air reaches a person's lungs. ■ a tube for supplying air to a person's lungs in an emergency. ■ a ventilating passage in a mine. **2** a recognized route followed by aircraft. ■ (**Airways**) in names of airlines: *British Airways.*

air·wor·thy /ˈe(ə)rˌwərT͟Hē/ ▸*adj.* (of an aircraft) safe to fly. **—air·wor·thi·ness** *n.*

air·y /ˈe(ə)rē/ ▸*adj.* (**airier, airiest**) **1** (of a room or building) spacious, well lit, and well ventilated. ■ delicate, as though filled with or made of air: *airy clouds.* ■ *figurative* giving an impression of light gracefulness and elegance: *her airy presence filled the house.* **2** giving an impression of being unconcerned or not serious, typically about something taken seriously by others: *her airy unconcern for economy.* **—air·i·ly** /-əlē/ *adv.* (in sense 2) **—air·i·ness** *n.*

air·y-fair·y ▸*adj. informal, derogatory, chiefly Brit.* impractical and foolishly idealistic: *love might seem an airy-fairy, romantic concept.*

aisle /īl/ ▸*n.* a passage between rows of seats in a building such as a church or theater, an airplane, or a train: *the musical had the audience dancing in the aisles.* ■ a passage between shelves of goods in a supermarket or other building. ■ *Architecture* (in a church) a lower part parallel to and at the side of a nave, choir, or transept, from which it is divided by pillars. ▹late Middle English *ele, ile,* from Old French *ele,* from Latin *ala* 'wing.' The spelling change in the 17th cent. was due to confusion with *isle* and influenced by French *aile* 'wing.' **—aisled** /īld/ *adj.*
▸*PHRASE* □ **lead someone up the aisle** get married to someone.

aitch /āCH/ ▸*n.* the name of the letter H. ▹mid 16th cent.: from Old French *ache.*
▸*PHRASE* □ **drop one's aitches** fail to pronounce the letter *h* at the beginning of words, a common feature of dialect speech.

aitch·bone /ˈāCHˌbōn/ ▸*n.* the buttock or rump bone of cattle. ■ a cut of beef lying over this. ▹late 15th cent.: from dialect *nache* 'rump,' from Old French, based on Latin *natis* 'buttock(s),' + **BONE**. The initial *n* in *a nache-bone* was lost by wrong division; compare with **ADDER**.

Aix-en-Pro·vence /ˌeks äN prōˈväNs; ˌäks/ a city in Provence in southern France; pop. 126,850.

Aix-la-Cha·pelle /ˌeks lä SHäˈpel; ˌäks/ French name for **Aachen**.

Ai·zawl /īˈzoul/ a city in northeastern India, capital of the state of Mizoram; pop. 154,000.

A·jac·cio /ˌäˌZHäkˈsyō/ a port on the west coast of Corsica; pop. 59,320.

A·jan·ta Caves /əˈjəntə/ a series of caves in the state of Maharashtra, south central India, that contain Buddhist frescos and sculptures dating from the 1st century BC to the 7th century AD.

a·jar[1] /əˈjär/ ▸*adv.* & *adj.* (of a door or other opening) slightly open: [as *adv.*] *she had **left** the window **ajar** that morning* | [as *predic. adj.*] *the door to the sitting room was ajar.* ▷late 17th cent.: from **a-**[2] 'on' + obsolete *char* (Old English *cerr*) 'a turn, return.'

a·jar[2] ▸*adv. archaic* out of harmony. ▷mid 19th cent.: from **a-**[2] 'in, at' + **jar**[2].

A·jax /ˈāˌjaks/ *Greek Mythology* **1** a Greek hero of the Trojan War, son of Telamon, king of Salamis. He was proverbial for his size and strength. **2** a Greek hero, son of Oileus, king of Locris.

a·ji·no·mo·to /ˌäjēnōˈmōtō/ ▸*n.* the Japanese name for **monosodium glutamate**.

Aj·man /ajˈmän; -ˈman/ the smallest of the seven emirates of the United Arab Emirates; pop. 64,320. ■ its capital city.

Aj·mer /ˌəjˈmi(ə)r/ a city in northwestern India, in the state of Rajasthan; pop. 402,000.

aj·o·wan /ˈajəˌwän/ ▸*n.* an annual plant (*Trachyspermum ammi*) of the parsley family, with feathery leaves and white flowers, native to India. ■ the aromatic seeds of the ajowan plant, used as a culinary spice. ■ the essential oil of the ajowan plant. ▷from Hindi *ajvāyn*.

a·ju·ga /ˈajəgə/ ▸*n.* a plant of a genus that includes bugle. • Genus *Ajuga*, family Labiatae: numerous species. ▷modern Latin, from medieval Latin *ajuga*.

AK ▸*abbr.* Alaska (in official postal use).

AK-47 ▸*n.* a type of assault rifle, originally manufactured in the Soviet Union. ▷acronym for Russian *Avtomat Kalashnikova 1947*, the designation of the original model, designed in 1947 by Mikhail T. Kalashnikov (b. 1919).

aka ▸*abbr.* also known as: *John Merrick, aka the Elephant Man.*

A·kan /ˈäˌkän/ ▸*n.* **1** (*pl.* same) a member of a people inhabiting southern Ghana and adjacent parts of Ivory Coast. **2** the Kwa language spoken by this people. There are two main dialects, Ashanti and Fante. Also called **Twi**.
▸*adj.* of or relating to this people or their language. ▷the name in Akan.

a·ka·sha /əˈkäSHə/ ▸*n. chiefly Hinduism* a supposed universal etheric field in which a record of past events is imprinted. ▷from Sanskrit *ākāśa*. **—a·ka·shic** /-SHik/ *adj.*

A·ka·shi /äˈkäSHē/ an industrial port city in west central Japan, on southwestern Honshu Island; pop. 271,000. Standard time for Japan is set here.

ak·a·this·ia /ˌakəˈTHiZHə; -ˈTHiZēə/ ▸*n.* a state of agitation, distress, and restlessness that is an occasional side-effect of antipsychotic and antidepressant drugs.

Ak·bar /ˈäkˌbär; ˈakbər/, Jalaludin Muhammad (1542–1605), Mogul emperor of India 1556–1605; known as **Akbar the Great**. Akbar expanded the Mogul empire to incorporate northern India.

AKC ▸*abbr.* American Kennel Club.

a·ke·bi·a /əˈkēbēə/ ▸*n.* a climbing shrub with purplish flowers, deeply divided leaves, and purple berries. Native to eastern Asia, it is grown as an ornamental in North America. • *Akebia quinata*, family Lardizabalaceae. ▷1837: modern Latin, coined by J. Decaisne, French botanist, from Japanese *akebi*.

a·kee /aˈkē; ˈakē/ (also **ac·kee**) ▸*n.* a tropical tree that is cultivated for its fruit. Native to West Africa, it has been introduced into the West Indies and elsewhere. • *Blighia sapida*, family Sapindaceae. ■ the fruit of this tree, widely eaten as a vegetable, but which can be poisonous unless cooked. ▷late 18th cent.: from Kru *ākee*.

A·khe·na·ten /ˌäk(ə)ˈnätn/ (also **A·khe·na·ton** or **Ikh·na·ton** /ikˈnätn/) (14th century BC), Egyptian pharaoh of the 18th dynasty; reigned 1379–1362 BC; came to the throne as *Amenhotep IV*. He renounced polytheism, introducing a monotheistic cult based on worship of the sun-disk, Aten, in whose honor he changed his name. The husband of Nefertiti, he moved the capital from Thebes to the newly built city of Akhetaten. The empire began to disintegrate during his reign.

Akh·ma·to·va /äKHˈmätəvə/, Anna (1889–1966), Russian poet; pseudonym of *Anna Andreevna Gorenko*. Akhmatova was a member of the Acmeist group of poets.

A·ki·hi·to /ˌäkēˈhētō/, (1933–), emperor of Japan 1989–; full name *Tsugu Akihito*. He is the son of Emperor Hirohito.

a·kim·bo /əˈkimbō/ ▸*adv.* with hands on the hips and elbows turned outward: *she stood with **arms akimbo**, frowning at the small boy.* ■ (of other limbs) flung out widely or haphazardly. ▷late Middle English: from *in kenebowe* in Middle English, probably from Old Norse.

a·kin /əˈkin/ ▸*adj.* of similar character: *something **akin to** gratitude overwhelmed her* | *genius and madness are akin.* ■ related by blood. ▷mid 16th cent.: contracted form of *of kin*.

a·ki·ne·sia /ˌākiˈnēZHə; ˌäkī-/ ▸*n. Medicine* loss or impairment of the power of voluntary movement. ▷mid 19th cent.: from Greek *akinēsia* 'quiescence,' from *a-* 'without' + *kinēsis* 'motion.' **—a·ki·net·ic** /-ˈnetik/ *adj.*

A·ki·ta[1] /äˈkētə/ an industrial port city in northeastern Japan, on northern Honshu Island; pop. 302,000.

A·ki·ta[2] ▸*n.* a spitz (dog) of a Japanese breed. ▷early 20th cent.: from *Akita*, the name of a district in northern Japan.

Akita[2]

Ak·kad /ˈakˌad; ˈäkˌäd/ the capital city that gave its name to an ancient kingdom, traditionally founded by Sargon in north central Mesopotamia. Its location is unknown.

Ak·ka·di·an /əˈkādēən; əˈkäd-/ ▸*adj.* of or relating to Akkad in ancient Babylonia or its people or their language.
▸*n.* **1** an inhabitant of Akkad. **2** the Semitic language of Akkad.

Akkadian, known from cuneiform inscriptions, is the oldest Semitic language for which records exist. It was used in Mesopotamia from about 3500 BC; two dialects, Assyrian and Babylonian, were widely spoken in the Middle East for the next 2,000 years, and the Babylonian form functioned as a lingua franca until replaced by Aramaic around the 6th century BC.

Ak·ko /äˈkō/ another name for **Acre** 1.

Ak-Me·chet /ˌäk miˈCHet/ former name for **Simferopol**.

a·kra·sia /əˈkrāZH(ē)ə/ (also **a·cra·sia**) ▸*n. chiefly Philosophy* the state of mind in which someone acts against their better judgment through weakness of will. ▷early 19th cent.: from Greek, from *a-* 'without' + *kratos* 'power, strength.' The term is used esp. with reference to Aristotle's *Nicomachean Ethics*. **—a·krat·ic** /əˈkratik/ (also **a·crat·ic**) *adj.*

Ak·ron /ˈakrən/ a city in northeastern Ohio; pop. 217,074. Noted as a center for the rubber industry, the first rubber factory was established in 1870 by B. F. Goodrich.

Ak·sai Chin /ˈakˌsī ˈCHin/ a region of the Himalayas occupied by China since 1950, but claimed by India as part of Kashmir.

Ak·sum /ˈäkˌsŏŏm/ (also **Ax·um**) a town in the province of Tigray in northern Ethiopia. A religious center, it was the capital of the powerful Axumite kingdom between the 1st and 6th centuries AD. **—Ak·sum·ite** /ˈäksŏŏˌmīt/ *adj.* & *n.*

ak·va·vit /ˈäkvəˌvēt/ ▸*n.* variant spelling of **aquavit**.

AL ▸*abbr.* ■ Alabama (in official postal use). ■ *Baseball* American League. ■ American Legion.

Al ▸*symbol* the chemical element aluminum.

al- ▸*prefix* variant spelling of **ad-** assimilated before *-l* (as in *alleviate, allocate*).

-al ▸*suffix* **1** (forming adjectives) relating to; of the kind of: ■ from Latin words: *annual* | *infernal* ■ from Greek words: *historical* | *comical.* ■ from English nouns: *tidal*. **2** forming nouns chiefly denoting verbal action: *arrival* | *transmittal.* ▷sense 1 from French *-el* or Latin *-alis*; sense 2 from French *-aille* or from Latin *-alis* functioning as a noun ending.

Ala. ▸*abbr.* Alabama.

à la /ˈä ˌlä; ˈä lə/ ▸*prep.* (of a dish) cooked or prepared in a specified style or manner: *fish cooked à la meunière.* ■ *informal* in the style or manner of: *afternoon talk shows à la Oprah.* ▷French, from **à la mode**.

Al·a·bam·a /ˌaləˈbamə/ a state in the southeastern U.S., on the Gulf of Mexico; pop. 4,447,100; capital, Montgomery; statehood, Dec. 14, 1819 (22). Visited by Spanish explorers in the mid 16th century and later settled by the French, it passed to Britain in 1763 and to the U.S. in 1783. **—Al·a·bam·an** *adj.* & *n.*

Al·a·bam·a Riv·er a river in southern Alabama that flows for 315 miles (507 km) to meet the Mobile River.

al·a·bas·ter /ˈaləˌbastər/ ▸*n.* a fine-grained, translucent form of gypsum, typically white, often carved into ornaments.
▸*adj.* made of alabaster. ■ *poetic/literary* like alabaster in whiteness and smoothness: *her alabaster cheeks flushed with warmth.* ▷late Middle English: via Old French from Latin *alabaster, alabastrum*, from Greek *alabastos, alabastros*.

à la carte /ˌä lä ˈkärt; lə/ ▸*adj.* (of a menu or restaurant) listing or serving food that can be ordered as separate items, rather than part of a set meal. ■ (of food) available on such a menu.
▸*adv.* as separately priced items from a menu, not as part of a set meal: *wine and good food served à la carte.* ▷early 19th cent.: French, literally 'according to the (menu) card.'

a·lack /əˈlak/ (also **a·lack-a-day**) ▸*exclam. archaic* an expression of regret or dismay. ▷late Middle English: probably from **ah** + **lack**.

a·lac·ri·ty /əˈlakritē/ ▸*n.* brisk and cheerful readiness: *she accepted the invitation with alacrity.* ▷late Middle English: from Latin *alacritas*, from *alacer* 'brisk.'

A·lad·din /əˈladn/ the hero of a story in the *Arabian Nights*, who finds an old lamp that, when rubbed, summons a genie who obeys the will of the owner. ▷from Arabic *ʿAlā' al-dīn*.

A·lad·din's lamp ▸*n.* a talisman enabling its holder to gratify any wish. ▷from **Aladdin**.

Alain-Four·nier /äˈlaN fŏŏrnˈyā/ (1886–1914), French novelist; pseudonym of *Henri-Alban Fournier*.

à la king /ˌä lä l(ə) ˈkiNG; ˌal (ə)/ ▸*adj.* (of a dish) with diced meat in a cream sauce, usually with green peppers and pimientos.

Al·a·me·da /ˌaləˈmēdə; -ˈmādə/ a port city in north central California, on San Francisco Bay, just southwest of Oakland; pop. 76,459.

al·a·me·da /ˌaləˈmādə/ ▸*n.* (in Spain and Spanish-speaking regions) a public walkway or promenade shaded with trees. ▷late 18th cent.: Spanish, from *álamo* 'cottonwood' + *-eda* 'grove' from Latin *-etum* (see **-etum**.).

A·la·mein /ˌaləˈmān/ see **El Alamein, Battle of.**

Al·a·mo /ˈaləˌmō/ (**the Alamo**) a mission in San Antonio, Texas, site of a siege in 1836 by Mexican forces, in which all 180 defenders were killed.

The Alamo

à la mode /ˌä lä ˈmōd/ ▸*adv.* & *adj.* **1** in fashion; up to date. **2** served with ice cream. **3** (of beef) braised in wine, typically with vegetables. ▷late 16th cent.: French, literally 'in the fashion.'

Al·a·mo·gor·do /ˌaləməˈgôrdō/ a city in southern New Mexico; pop. 35,582. White Sands and other military and aerospace facilities are nearby.

Pronunciation Key ə *ago*; ər *over*; ˈə *or* ˌə *up*; ˈər *or* ˌər *fur*; a *hat*; ā *rate*; ä *car*; CH *chew*; e *let*; ē *see*; e(ə)r *air*; i *fit*; ī *by*; i(ə)r *ear*; NG *sing*; ō *go*; ô *for*; oi *boy*; ŏŏ *good*; o͞o *goo*; ou *out*; SH *she*; TH *thin*; T͟H *then*; (h)w *why*; ZH *vision*

Å·land Is·lands /ˈōlənd/ a group of islands in the Gulf of Bothnia that forms an autonomous region in Finland; capital, Mariehamn (known in Finnish as Maarianhamina). Finnish name **AHVENANMAA**.

al·a·nine /ˈaləˌnēn/ ▶*n. Biochemistry* an amino acid that is a constituent of most proteins. • Alternative name: 2-aminopropanoic acid; chem. formula: $CH_3CH(NH_2)COOH$. **β-alanine**, an isomer of this, is 3-aminopropanoic acid, $(NH_2)CH_2CH_2COOH$. ▷mid 19th cent.: coined in German as *Alanin*, from **ALDEHYDE** + *-an* (for ease of pronunciation) + **-INE**[4].

Al-A·non /ˈal əˌnän/ a mutual support organization for the families and friends of alcoholics, esp. those of members of Alcoholics Anonymous.

a·lap /ˈälˌäp/ ▶*n.* (in Indian music) the improvised section of a raga, forming a prologue to the formal expression. ▷from Hindi *ālāp*.

a la plan·cha /ˌä lə ˈplänchə/ ▶*adv. adj.* (of meat or fish) pan-fried or cooked on a griddle. ▷Spanish.

A·lar /ˈāˌlär/ ▶*n.* trademark for **DAMINOZIDE**.

a·lar /ˈālər/ ▶*adj. chiefly Zoology* of or relating to a wing or wings. ■ *Anatomy* winglike or wing-shaped. ■ *Botany* another term for **AXILLARY**. ▷mid 19th cent.: from Latin *alaris*, from *ala* 'wing.'

A·lar·cón /ˌälärˈkôn/, Pedro Antonio de (1833–91), Spanish novelist and short-story writer. His notable works include *The Three-Cornered Hat* (1874).

A·lar·cón y Men·do·za see **RUIZ DE ALARCÓN Y MENDOZA**.

Al·a·ric /ˈalərik/ (*c.*370–410), king of the Visigoths 395–410. He captured Rome in 410.

a·larm /əˈlärm/ ▶*n.* an anxious awareness of danger: *the boat tilted and the boatmen cried out* ***in alarm*** | *he views the right-wing upsurge in Europe* ***with alarm***. ■ [in *sing.*] a warning of danger: *I hammered on several doors to* ***raise the alarm*** | *Oliver smelled smoke and* ***gave the alarm***. ■ a warning sound or device: *a burglar alarm.* ■ an alarm clock.
▶*v.* **1** [*trans.*] cause (someone) to feel frightened, disturbed, or in danger: *the government was alarmed by an outbreak of unrest* | [as *adj.*] (**alarming**) *children were dying at an alarming rate.* **2** (**be alarmed**) be fitted or protected with an alarm: *this door is locked and alarmed between 11 p.m. and 6 a.m.* ▷late Middle English (as an exclamation meaning 'to arms!'): from Old French *alarme*, from Italian *allarme*, from *all' arme!* 'to arms!' **—a·larm·ing·ly** *adv.*

a·larm bell ▶*n.* a bell rung as a warning of danger. ■ *figurative* a thing that alerts people to possible problems or danger and causes anxiety: *Scientology's expansion has* ***set alarm bells ringing***.

a·larm call ▶*n.* a warning cry made by a bird or other animal when startled.

a·larm clock ▶*n.* a clock with a device that can be made to sound at the time set in advance, used to wake someone up.

a·larm·ist /əˈlärmist/ ▶*n.* someone who is considered to be exaggerating a danger and so causing needless worry or panic.
▶*adj.* creating needless worry or panic: *alarmist rumors.* **—a·larm·ism** /-ˌmizəm/ *n.*

a·lar·um /əˈlärəm; əˈlar-/ ▶*n.* archaic term for **ALARM**.
▶*PHRASE* □ **alarums and excursions** *humorous* confused activity and uproar.

a·las /əˈlas/ ▶*exclam. chiefly poetic/literary* or *humorous* an expression of grief, pity, or concern: *alas, my funds have some limitations.* ▷Middle English: from Old French *a las, a lasse*, from *a* 'ah' + *las(se)* (from Latin *lassus* 'weary').

Alas. ▶*abbr.* Alaska.

A·las·ka /əˈlaskə/ the largest state in the U.S., in northwestern North America, with coasts on the Arctic and North Pacific oceans and on the Bering Sea, separated from the contiguous 48 U.S. states by Canada; pop. 626,932; capital, Juneau; statehood: Jan. 3, 1959 (49). The territory was purchased from Russia in 1867. After oil was discovered in 1968, a pipeline was completed in 1977 to carry the oil from the North Slope to Valdez. **—A·las·kan** *adj.* & *n.*

A·las·ka, Gulf of a part of the northeastern Pacific Ocean between the Alaska Peninsula and the Alexander Archipelago.

A·las·ka ce·dar ▶*n.* another term for **NOOTKA CYPRESS**.

A·las·ka High·way see **ALCAN HIGHWAY**.

A·las·kan mal·a·mute /əˈlaskən/ (also **A·las·kan mal·e·mute**) ▶*n.* a powerful dog of a breed with a thick, gray coat, bred by the Inuit and typically used to pull sleds. ▷late 19th cent.: from Inuit *malimiut*, the name of a people of Kotzebue Sound, Alaska, who developed the breed.

A·las·ka Pen·in·su·la a peninsula on the south coast of Alaska. It extends south-westward into the northeastern Pacific Ocean and is continued in the Aleutian Islands.

A·las·ka Range a mountain chain that lies across southern Alaska. Mt. McKinley, rising to 20,320 feet (6,194 m), is its high point.

a·late /ˈāˌlāt/ ▶*adj. Botany* & *Entomology* (chiefly of insects or seeds) having wings or winglike appendages. ▷mid 17th cent.: from Latin *alatus*, from *ala* 'wing.'

alb /alb/ ▶*n.* a white vestment worn by clergy and servers in some Christian Churches. ▷Old English *albe*, from ecclesiastical Latin *tunica* (or *vestis*) *alba* 'white garment,' from Latin *albus* 'white.'

alb

al·ba /ˈalbə/ ▶*n.* a shrub rose of a variety with gray-green leaves and pinkish-white, sweet-scented flowers. ▷mid 19th cent.: from Latin *alba*, feminine of *albus* 'white,' from the name *rosa alba*, an old white garden rose.

Al·ba·ce·te /ˌälväˈsātā/ a city in Albacete Province in southeastern Spain; pop. 134,600.

al·ba·core /ˈalbəˌkôr/ (also **albacore tuna**) ▶*n.* a tuna that travels in large schools and is of commercial importance as a food fish. • Two species in the family Scombridae: *Thunnus alalunga* and the **false albacore** (*Euthynus alletteratus*). ▷late 16th cent.: from Portuguese *albacora*, from Arabic *al-bakūra*, perhaps from *al* 'the' + *bakūr* 'premature, precocious.'

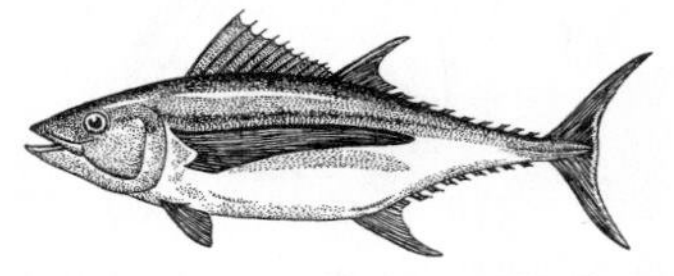

albacore

Al·ba Iu·lia /ˌälbə ˈyoolyə/ a city in west central Romania, north of the Transylvanian Alps; pop. 72,330. Founded by the Romans in the 2nd century AD, it was the capital of Transylvania.

Al·ban, St. /ˈôlbən; ˈal-/ (3rd century), the first English Christian martyr, a native of Verulamium (now St. Albans). He was put to death for sheltering a fugitive priest. Feast day, June 22.

Al·ba·ni·a /alˈbānēə; ôl-/ a republic in southeastern Europe that borders on the Adriatic Sea; pop. 3,500,000; capital, Tirana; official language, Albanian.

Previously part of the Byzantine and later the Ottoman empires, Albania gained independence in 1912. It became a Stalinist regime under Enver Hoxha after World War II and remained extremely isolationist in policy and outlook until the Communists lost power in 1992.

Al·ba·ni·an /alˈbānēən; ôl-/ ▶*adj.* of or relating to Albania or its people or their language.
▶*n.* **1** a native or national of Albania, or a person of Albanian descent. **2** the language of Albania.

Albanian constitutes a separate branch of the Indo-European language group, spoken in Albania, Serbia (Kosovo), and elsewhere.

Al·ba·ny /ˈôlbənē/ **1** a city in southwestern Georgia; pop. 76,939. **2** the capital of New York, in the eastern part of the state, on the western bank of the Hudson River; pop. 95,658. **3** a city in northwestern Oregon; pop. 40,852.

al·ba·tross /ˈalbəˌtrôs; -ˌträs/ ▶*n.* (*pl.* **-tross·es**) a very large oceanic bird related to the shearwaters, with long narrow wings. Albatrosses, some species of which have wingspans greater than 10 feet (3.3 m), are found mainly in the southern oceans, with three kinds in the North Pacific. • Genera *Diomedea* and *Phoebetria*, family Diomedeidae: several species, including the **sooty albatross** (*P. fusca*), **Laysan albatross** (*D. immutablis*), and **wandering albatross** (*D. exulans*). ■ a source of frustration or guilt; an encumbrance (in allusion to Coleridge's *The Rime of the Ancient Mariner*): *an albatross of a marriage.* ■ *Golf* another term for **DOUBLE EAGLE**. ▷late 17th cent.: alteration (influenced by Latin *albus* 'white') of 16th-cent. *alcatras*, applied to various seabirds including the frigate bird and pelican, from Spanish and Portuguese *alcatraz*, from Arabic *al-ġaṭṭās* 'the diver.'

albatross

al·be·do /alˈbēdō/ ▶*n.* (*pl.* **-dos**) *chiefly Astronomy* the proportion of the incident light or radiation that is reflected by a surface, typically that of a planet or moon. ▷mid 19th cent.: ecclesiastical Latin, 'whiteness,' from Latin *albus* 'white.'

Al·bee /ˈôlbē; ˈalbē/, Edward Franklin (1928–), U.S. playwright. Notable works: *Who's Afraid of Virginia Woolf* (1962), *A Delicate Balance* (1966), *Seascape* (1975), and the prize-winning *The Goat, or Who Is Sylvia?* (2001).

al·be·it /ôlˈbē-it; al-/ ▶*conj.* although: *he was making progress, albeit rather slowly.* ▷late Middle English: from the phrase *all be it* 'although it be (that).'

Al·be·marle Sound /ˈalbəˌmärl/ an inlet of the Atlantic Ocean in northeastern North Carolina, inside the Outer Banks.

Al·bers /ˈalbərz; ˈôl-/, Josef (1888–1976), U.S. artist, designer, and teacher; born in Germany. He is associated with the Bauhaus and constructivism and is best known for his series of abstract canvases *Homage to the Square*, which he began in 1950.

Al·bert /ˈalbərt/, Carl (1908–2000), U.S. politician. A Democrat from Oklahoma, he served in the U.S. House of Representatives 1947–76 and became Speaker of the House in 1971.

Al·bert, Lake /ˈalbərt/ a lake in the Rift Valley of east-ern central Africa, on the border between the Democratic Republic of the Congo (formerly Zaire) and Uganda. It is linked to Lake Edward by the Semliki River and to the White Nile by the Albert Nile. Also called **LAKE MOBUTU SESE SEKO**.

Al·bert, Prince /ˈalbərt/ (1819–61), consort to Queen Victoria and prince of Saxe-Coburg-Gotha; full name *Albert Francis Charles Augustus Emmanuel*.

al·bert /ˈalbərt/ (also **albert chain**) ▶*n. Brit.* a watch-chain with a bar at one end for attaching to a buttonhole. ▷mid 19th cent.: named after *Prince Albert* (see **ALBERT, PRINCE**).

Al·ber·ta /alˈbərtə/ a prairie province in western Canada, bounded on the south by the U.S. and on the west by the Rocky Mountains; capital, Edmonton; pop. 2,545,553.

Al·ber·ta Clip·per ▶*Meteorology n.* a fast-moving winter weather system originating in the lee of the Canadian Rockies that typically brings snow, high winds, and cold temperatures across the northern U.S.

Al·ber·ti /älˈbertē/, Leon Battista (1404–72), Italian architect, humanist, painter, and art critic. He wrote *On Painting* (1435), which was the first account of the theory of perspective in the Renaissance.

Al·bert Nile the upper part of the Nile River that flows through northwestern Uganda between Lake Albert and the Ugandan–Sudanese border.

Al·ber·tus Mag·nus, St. /alˈbərtəs ˈmagnəs/ (*c.*1200–80), Dominican theologian, philosopher, and scientist; known as **Doctor Universalis**. A teacher of St. Thomas Aquinas, he was a pioneer in the study of Aristotle. Feast day, November 15.

al·bes·cent /alˈbesənt/ ▶*adj. chiefly poetic/literary* growing or shading into white: *the albescent waves on the* *horizon.* ▷early 18th cent.: from Latin *albescere* 'become white,' from *albus* 'white.'

Al·bi·gen·ses /ˌalbiˈjensēz/ ▶*plural n.* the members of a heretical sect in southern France in the 12th–13th centuries, identified with the Cathars. Their teaching was a form of Manichaean dualism, with an extremely strict moral and social code. ▷medieval Latin, from *Albiga*, the Latin name of *Albi* in southern France. **—Al·bi·gen·si·an** /-ˈjentsēən; -SHən/ *adj.*

al·bi·no /alˈbīnō/ ▶*n.* (*pl.* **-nos**) a person or animal having a congenital absence of pigment in the skin and hair (which are white) and the eyes (which are typically pink). ■ *informal* an abnormally white animal or plant: [as *modifier*] *an albino tiger.* ▷early 18th cent.: from Portuguese (originally denoting albinos among African blacks) and Spanish, from *albo* (from Latin *albus* 'white') + the suffix *-ino* (see **-INE**[1]). **—al·bi·nism** /ˈalbəˌnizəm/ *n.*

Al·bi·nus /ˈalbīnəs/ see **ALCUIN**.

Al·bi·on /ˈalbēən/ ▶*n.* a poetic or literary term for Britain or England (often used in referring to ancient or historical times). ▷Old English, from Latin, probably of Celtic origin and related to Latin *albus* 'white' (in allusion to the white cliffs of Dover). The phrase *perfidious Albion* (mid 19th cent.) translates the French *la perfide Albion*, alluding to alleged treachery to other nations.

al·bite /ˈalˌbīt/ ▶*n.* a sodium-rich mineral of the plagioclase feldspar group, typically white, occurring widely in igneous rocks. ▷early 19th cent.: from Latin *albus* 'white' + **-ITE**[1].

al·biz·zi·a /alˈbizēə; -ˈbitsēə/ (also **al·biz·i·a**) ▶*n.* a leguminous tree or shrub with feathery leaves and densely clustered plumelike flowers. Native to warm climates, it is sometimes grown as a shade tree or ornamental. • Genus *Albizia*, family Leguminosae: several species. ▷modern Latin, named after Filippo degli *Albizzi*, a Tuscan nobleman who introduced the silk tree *A. julibrizzen* into Italy in the mid 18th cent.

al·bon·di·gas /älbônˈdēgäs/ ▶*plural n.* small meatballs, prepared in the Mexican, Spanish, or South American way. ▷Spanish, from Arabic *al-bunduq*, 'hazel nut'

Ål·borg /ˈôlˌbôrg/ variant spelling of **AALBORG**.

Al·bright /ˈôlˌbrīt/, Madeleine Korbel (1937–), U.S. secretary of state 1997–2001; born in Czechoslovakia. After serving as U.S. ambassador to the United Nations 1993–1997, she became the first woman to head the U.S. Department of State. She emigrated to the U.S. with her family in 1948 during the Communist takeover in Czechoslovakia and earned a Ph.D. in government from Columbia University in 1976.

Madeleine Korbel Albright

al·bum /ˈalbəm/ ▶*n.* **1** a blank book for the insertion of photographs, stamps, or pictures: *the wedding pictures had pride of place in the family album.* **2** a collection of recordings, on long-playing record, cassette, or compact disc, that are issued as a single item. ▷early 17th cent.: from Latin, neuter of *albus* 'white' used as a noun meaning 'a blank tablet.' Taken into English from the German use of the Latin phrase *album amicorum* 'album of friends,' it was originally used consciously as a Latin word with Latin inflections.

al·bu·men /alˈbyo͞omən/ ▶*n.* egg white, or the protein contained in it. ▷late 16th cent.: from Latin, 'egg white,' from *albus* 'white.'

USAGE The words **albumen** and **albumin** have the same origin but are not identical in meaning. **Albumen** refers specifically to egg white or the protein found in egg white. **Albumin**, on the other hand, refers to the more general category of protein that is soluble in water and that is coagulated on heating, of which **albumen** is just one type.

al·bu·min /alˈbyo͞omən/ ▶*n. Biochemistry* a simple form of protein that is soluble in water and coagulable by heat, such as that found in egg white, milk, and (in particular) blood serum. ▷mid 19th cent.: from French *albumine*, based on Latin *albumen, albumin-* (see **ALBUMEN**).

USAGE See **usage** at **ALBUMEN**.

al·bu·mi·noid /alˈbyo͞oməˌnoid/ ▶*n.* another term for **SCLEROPROTEIN**.

al·bu·mi·nous /alˈbyo͞omənəs/ ▶*adj.* consisting of, resembling, or containing albumen.

al·bu·mi·nu·ri·a /alˌbyo͞oməˈn(y)o͝orēə/ ▶*n. Medicine* the presence of albumin in the urine, typically as a symptom of kidney disease.

Al·bu·quer·que[1] /ˈalb(y)əˌkərkē/ city in central New Mexico, on the Rio Grande; pop. 448,607. It is the largest city in the state.

Al·bu·quer·que[2], Alfonso de (1453–1515), Portuguese colonial statesman. He conquered Goa (1510) and made it the capital of the Portuguese empire in the east.

Al·cae·us /alˈsēəs/ (*c.*620–*c.*580 BC), Greek lyric poet. He invented a new form of lyric meter called the alcaic. His works were a model for the Roman poet Horace and the verse of the Renaissance.

al·ca·hest /ˈalkəˌhest/ ▶*n.* variant spelling of **ALKAHEST**.

al·ca·ic /alˈkā-ik/ *Prosody* ▶*adj.* a four-line verse stanza in the meter invented by the Greek poet Alcaeus, and later used in a slightly altered form by the Roman poet Horace.
▶*n.* (usu. **alcaics**) alcaic verse. ▷mid 17th cent.: via late Latin from Greek *alkaikos*, from *Alkaios* (see **ALCAEUS**).

Al·ca·lá de He·na·res /ˌälkəˈlä dā āˈnäräs/ a city in central Spain, on the Henares River, 15 miles (25 km) northeast of Madrid; pop. 162,780.

al·cal·de /älˈkäldē; al-/ ▶*n.* a magistrate or mayor in a Spanish, Portuguese, or Latin American town. ▷mid 16th cent.: Spanish, from Arabic *al-ḳāḍī* 'the judge' (see **CADI**).

Al·can High·way /ˈalˌkan/ (also **Alaska Highway**) a military road, built during World War II to link Dawson Creek in the Yukon Territory with Fairbanks in Alaska, as part of a supply route to the Soviet Union and the Pacific Ocean.

Al·ca·traz /ˈalkəˌtraz/ a rocky island in San Francisco Bay, California. It was the site of a top-security federal prison between 1934 and 1963 and since 1972 has been administered by the National Park Service.

al·ca·zar /ˌalkəˈzär; alˈkazər/ (often **Al·ca·zar**) ▶*n.* a Spanish palace or fortress of Moorish origin. ▷early 17th cent.: from Spanish *alcázar*, from Arabic *al-ḳaṣr* 'the castle.'

Al·ces·tis /alˈsestis/ *Greek Mythology* wife of Admetus, king of Pherae in Thessaly, whose life she saved by consenting to die on his behalf.

al·che·my /ˈalkəmē/ ▶*n.* the medieval forerunner of chemistry, based on the supposed transformation of matter. It was concerned particularly with attempts to convert base metals into gold or to find a universal elixir. ■ *figurative* a process by which paradoxical results are achieved or incompatible elements combined with no obvious rational explanation: *his conducting managed by some alchemy to give a sense of fire and ice.* ▷late Middle English: via Old French and medieval Latin from Arabic *alkīmiyā'*, from *al* 'the' + *kīmiyā'* (from Greek *khēmia, khēmeia* 'art of transmuting metals'). **—al·chem·ic** /alˈkemik/ *adj.* **—al·chem·i·cal** /alˈkemikəl/ *adj.* **—al·che·mist** /-mist/ *n.* **—al·che·mize** /-ˌmīz/ *v.*

Al·ci·an blue /ˈalsēən/ ▶*n. trademark* a water-soluble copper-containing blue dye used as a histological stain for glycosaminoglycans. ▷1940s: *Alcian* perhaps from *(phth)al(o)cyan(ine)* with a phonetic respelling.

Al·ci·bi·a·des /ˌalsəˈbīəˌdēz/ (*c.*450–404 BC), Athenian general and statesman who held commands during the Peloponnesian Wars against Sparta (431–404).

al·cid /ˈalsid/ ▶*n. Ornithology* a bird of the auk family (Alcidae); an auk or puffin. ▷late 19th cent.: modern Latin *Alcidae*, from *Alca* (genus name), based on Old Norse *álka* 'razorbill'; compare with **AUK**.

Al·cin·dor /alˈsindər/, Lewis Ferdinand, see **ABDUL-JABBAR**.

Al·clad /ˈalˌklad/ ▶*n. trademark* a composite material consisting of sheets of aluminum alloy coated with pure aluminum or a different alloy to increase corrosion resistance. ▷1920s: from *al(uminium)* + **CLAD**[1].

Al·cock /ˈôlˌkäk/, Sir John William (1892–1919), English aviator. With Sir Arthur Whitten Brown, he made the first nonstop transatlantic flight in June 1919.

al·co·hol /ˈalkəˌhôl; -ˌhäl/ ▶*n.* a colorless volatile flammable liquid that is the intoxicating constituent of wine, beer, spirits, and other drinks, and is also used as an industrial solvent and as fuel. • Alternative names: ethanol, ethyl alcohol; chem. formula: C_2H_5OH. ■ drink containing this: *he has not taken alcohol in twenty-five years.* ■ *Chemistry* any organic compound whose molecule contains one or more hydroxyl groups attached to a carbon atom. ▷mid 16th cent.: French (earlier form of *alcool*), or from medieval Latin, from Arabic *al-kuḥl* 'the kohl.' In early use the term denoted powders, specifically kohl, and esp. those obtained by sublimation; later 'a distilled or rectified spirit' (mid 17th cent.).

al·co·hol-free ▶*adj.* **1** (of a drink) not containing alcohol (denoting varieties of normally alcoholic drinks from which the alcohol has been removed): *alcohol-free wines.* **2** where, or during which, alcoholic drinks are not consumed: *the hotel has an alcohol-free bar.*

al·co·hol·ic /ˌalkəˈhôlik; -ˈhäl-/ ▶*adj.* containing or relating to alcoholic liquor: *beer is the favorite alcoholic drink.* ■ caused by the excessive consumption of alcohol: *alcoholic liver disease.* ■ suffering from alcoholism: *his alcoholic daughter was the cause of his anxiety.*
▶*n.* a person suffering from alcoholism.

Al·co·hol·ics A·non·y·mous (abbr.: **AA**) a self-help organization for people fighting alcoholism, founded in the U.S. in 1935 and now having branches worldwide.

al·co·hol·ism /ˈalkəhôˌlizəm; -hä-/ ▶*n.* an addiction to the consumption of alcoholic liquor or the mental illness and compulsive behavior resulting from alcohol dependency: *he had a long history of depression, drug abuse and alcoholism.*

al·co·hol·om·e·ter /ˌalkəhôˈlämitər; -hä-/ ▶*n.* an instrument for measuring the concentration of alcohol in a liquid. **—al·co·hol·om·e·try** /-trē/ *n.*

Al·cott[1] /ˈôlkət; ˈal-; -ˌkät/, (Amos) Bronson (1799–1888), U.S. educator; father of Louisa May Alcott. He advocated radical reforms in education, including racial integration in the classroom. Appointed superintendent of schools in Concord, Massachusetts, in 1859, he created the first parent-teacher association.

Al·cott[2], Louisa May (1832–88), U.S. novelist. Her novel *Little Women* (1868–69) was based on her New England childhood and was written for adolescent girls. She wrote a number of sequels to this, as well as novels for adults. Alcott was involved in the women's suffrage movement and served as a nurse during the Civil War.

al·cove /ˈalˌkōv/ ▶*n.* a recess, typically in the wall of a room or of a garden. ▷late 16th cent.: from French *alcôve*, from Spanish *alcoba*, from Arabic *al-ḳubba* 'the vault.'

Al·cuin /ˈalkwən/ (*c.*735–804) English scholar, theologian, and adviser to Charlemagne; also known as **Albinus**. He is credited with the transformation of Charlemagne's court into a cultural center during the Carolingian Renaissance.

Al·da /ˈôldə/, Alan (1936–), U.S. actor, director, and writer; born *Alphonso D'Abruzzo*. He won five Emmys for his role as Hawkeye Pierce on the television series "M*A*S*H" 1972–83. His movies include *Same Time, Next Year (1978), California Suite* (1978), *The Seduction of Joe Tynan* (1979), and *Everyone Says I Love You* (1996).

Al·dab·ra /alˈdabrə/ a coral island group in the Indian Ocean, northwest of Madagascar. Formerly part of the British Indian Ocean Territory, it became an outlying dependency of the Seychelles in 1976.

Al·dan Riv·er /ˌəlˈdän/ a river in the eastern Siberian area of Russia that rises in the Stanovoy Khrebet

Mountains and flows for 1,400 miles (2,240 km) into the Lena River east of Yakutsk.

Al·deb·a·ran /al'debərən/ the brightest star in the constellation Taurus. It is a binary system of which the main star is a red giant. ▷Arabic, 'the follower (of the Pleiades).'

al·de·hyde /'aldə,hīd/ ▸*n. Chemistry* an organic compound containing the group –CHO, formed by the oxidation of alcohols. Typical aldehydes include methanal (formaldehyde) and ethanal (acetaldehyde). ▷mid 19th cent.: shortened from Latin *alcohol dehydrogenatum* 'alcohol deprived of hydrogen.' **—al·de·hy·dic** /,aldə'hīdik/ *adj.*

al den·te /äl 'dentā; al/ ▸*adj. & adv.* (of food, typically pasta) cooked so as to be still firm when bitten. ▷Italian, literally 'to the tooth.'

al·der /'ôldər/ (also **alder tree**) ▸*n.* a widely distributed tree of the birch family that has toothed leaves and bears male catkins and woody female cones.
• Genus *Alnus*, family Betulaceae: many species, including the **European** (or **black**) **alder** (*A. glutinosa*), common in damp ground and on riverbanks. ▷Old English *alor, aler*, of Germanic origin; related to German *Erle*; forms spelled with *d* are recorded from the 14th cent.

al·der·fly /'ôldər,flī/ (also **al·der fly**) ▸*n.* (*pl.* **-flies**) a brownish flylike insect that lives near water and has predatory aquatic larvae. • Family Sialidae, order Neuroptera: several genera.

al·der·man /'ôldərmən/ ▸*n.* (*pl.* **-men**) an elected member of a municipal council. ■ (in England before 1974) a member of a county or borough council, next in status to the Mayor. ■ (in Anglo-Saxon England) a noble serving the king as a chief officer in a district or shire. ▷Old English *aldormann* (originally in the general sense 'a man of high rank'), from *aldor, ealdor* 'chief, patriarch,' from *ald* 'old' + MAN. Later the sense 'warden of a guild' arose; then, as the guilds became identified with the ruling municipal body, 'local magistrate, municipal officer,' the status and method of appointment varying in different times and places. **—al·der·man·ic** /,ôldər'manik/ *adj.* **—al·der·man·ship** /-,SHip/ *n.*

Al·der·ney /'ôldərnē/ an island in the English Channel, to the northeast of Guernsey; pop. 2,130. It is the third largest of the Channel Islands.

al·der·per·son /'ôldər,pərsən/ ▸*n.* an alderman or alderwoman (used as a neutral alternative).

al·der·wom·an /'ôldər,wŏŏmən/ ▸*n.* (*pl.* **-wom·en**) an elected female member of a municipal council.

al·di·carb /'aldi,kärb/ ▸*n.* a systemic agricultural pesticide used particularly against some mites, insects, and nematode worms. ▷1970s: blend of ALDEHYDE and *carbamide* (from CARBO- + AMIDE).

Al·dine /'ôl,dīn; -,dēn/ ▸*adj.* of or relating to the Venetian printer Aldus Manutius, or to the books printed by him, or to certain styles of display types. ▷early 19th cent.: from Latin *Aldinus*, from *Aldus*, the printer's given name.

Al·dis lamp /'ôldis/ ▸*n. trademark* a hand-held lamp for signaling in Morse code. ▷World War I: named after A. C. W. *Aldis* (1878–1953), its British inventor.

Al·diss /'ôldəs/, Brian (Wilson) (1925–), English novelist and critic, best known for his science fiction. He wrote *Frankenstein Unbound* (1973).

al·dol /'al,dôl; -,däl/ ▸*n. Chemistry* a viscous liquid obtained when acetaldehyde dimerizes in dilute alkali or acid. • Alternative name: 3-hydroxybutanal; chem. formula: $CH_3CH(OH)CH_2CHO$. ▷late 19th cent.: from *ald(ehyde)* + -OL.

al·dos·te·rone /al'dästə,rōn/ ▸*n. Biochemistry* a corticosteroid hormone that stimulates absorption of sodium by the kidneys and so regulates water and salt balance. ▷1950s: blend of ALDEHYDE and STEROID, + -ONE.

al·do·ster·on·ism /,aldō'stərə,nizəm; al'dästərə-/ ▸*n. Medicine* a condition in which there is excessive secretion of aldosterone. This disturbs the balance of sodium, potassium, and water in the blood and so leads to high blood pressure.

Al·drin /'ôldrin/, Buzz (1930–), U.S. astronaut; full name *Edwin Eugene Aldrin*. He became an astronaut in 1963, and walked in space for 5 hours and 37 minutes during the 1966 Gemini 12 mission. In 1969 he took part in the first moon landing, the Apollo 11 mission, becoming the second person, after Neil Armstrong, to set foot on the moon.

al·drin /'ôldrin/ ▸*n.* a toxic synthetic insecticide, now generally banned. • A chlorinated polycyclic hydrocarbon; chem. formula: $C_{12}H_8Cl_6$. ▷1940s: from the name of K. *Alder* (see DIELS–ALDER REACTION) + -IN[1].

Al·dus Ma·nu·ti·us /'ôldəs mə'n(y)ōōsH(ē)əs/ (1450–1515), Italian scholar, printer, and publisher; Latinized name of *Teobaldo Manucci*; also known as **Aldo Manuzio**.

ale /āl/ ▸*n.* a type of beer with a bitter flavor and higher alcoholic content: *amber-colored beers, ales, and stouts.* ■ *chiefly Brit.* beer. ▷Old English *alu, ealu*, of Germanic origin; related to Old Norse *ǫl*. Formerly the word referred esp. to unhopped or paler-colored varieties of beer.

a·le·a·tor·ic /,ālēə'tôrik; ,al-/ ▸*adj.* another term for ALEATORY. ▷1960s: from Latin *aleatorius*, from *aleator* 'dice player,' from *alea* 'die,' + -IC.

a·le·a·to·ry /'ālēə,tôrē; 'al-/ ▸*adj.* depending on the throw of a die or on chance; random. ■ relating to or denoting music or other forms of art involving elements of random choice (sometimes using statistical or computer techniques) during their composition, production, or performance. ▷late 17th cent.: from Latin *aleatorius* (see ALEATORIC).

al·ec /'alik/ (also **al·eck** or **al·ick**) ▸*n. Austral., informal* a stupid person: *what sort of alec do you take me for?* ▷late 20th cent.: shortening of SMART ALECK.

ale·cost /'āl,kôst; -,käst/ ▸*n.* **1** a wild plant with small daisylike flowers that has culinary and folk-medicinal uses. • *Chrysanthemum balsamita*, family Compositae. **2** another name for COSTMARY.

A·lec·to /ə'lektō/ (also **Al·lec·to**) *Greek Mythology* one of the Furies.

a·lee /ə'lē/ ▸*adv. & adj.* [*predic.*] on the side of a ship that is sheltered from the wind. ■ (of the helm) moved around to leeward in order to tack a vessel or to bring its bows up into the wind. ▷late Middle English: from A-[2] 'on' + LEE.

ale·house /'āl,hous/ ▸*n. dated* a tavern.

A·lei·chem /ə'läKHəm; -kəm/ see SHOLOM ALEICHEM.

Ale·khine /,əl'yôKH(y)in/, Alexander (1892–1946), French chess player; born in Russia; world champion 1927–35 and 1937-46.

A·lek·san·dro·pol /,alik'sändrə,pōl; ,əlyiksən'drôpəl/ (also **A·lex·an·dro·pol**) former name (1840–1924) for GYUMRI.

A·lek·san·drovsk /,əlyik'sändrəfsk/ former name (until 1921) of ZAPORIZHZHYA.

a·lem·bic /ə'lembik/ ▸*n.* a distilling apparatus, now obsolete, consisting of a rounded, necked flask and a cap with a long beak for condensing and conveying the products to a receiver. ▷Middle English: via Old French from medieval Latin *alembicus*, from Arabic *al-'anbīķ*, from *al-* 'the' + *'anbīķ* 'still' (from Greek *ambix, ambik-* 'cup, cap of a still').

albembic

a·leph /'älif; 'älef/ ▸*n.* the first letter of the Hebrew alphabet. ▷Middle English: from Hebrew *'ālep*, literally 'ox' (the character in Phoenician and ancient Hebrew possibly being derived from a hieroglyph of an ox's head).

A·lep·po /ə'lepō/ a city in northern Syria; pop. 1,355,000.

A·lep·po gall ▸*n.* a hard nutlike gall that forms on the Valonia oak (formerly known as the Aleppo oak) in response to the developing larva of a gall wasp. It is used as a source of gallic acid and tannin. • The wasp is *Cynips tinctoria*, family Cynipidae.

a·ler·ce /ə'lərsə/ ▸*n.* a cypress tree that is valued for its timber. • Several species in the family Cupressaceae, in particular the **sandarac tree** (*Tetraclinis articulata*) of southern Spain and northwestern Africa, from which the resin sandarac is obtained. ■ the wood of such a tree, esp. the sandarac tree. ▷mid 19th cent.: from Spanish, 'larch.'

a·lert /ə'lərt/ ▸*adj.* quick to notice any unusual and potentially dangerous or difficult circumstances; vigilant: *an alert police officer discovered a truck full of explosives | schools need to be constantly* **alert to** *this problem.* See note at VIGILANT. ■ able to think clearly; intellectually active: *she remained active and alert until well into her eighties.*
▸*n.* the state of being watchful for possible danger: *security forces were placed* **on alert**. ■ an announcement or signal warning of danger: *a bomb alert | an alert sounded and all the fighters took off.* ■ a period of vigilance in response to such a warning: *traffic was halted during the alert.*
▸*v.* [*trans.*] warn (someone) of a danger, threat, or problem, typically with the intention of having it avoided or dealt with: *he* **alerted** *people* **to** *the dangers of smoking | police were alerted after three men drove away without paying.* ▷late 16th cent. (originally in military use): from French *alerte*, from Italian *all' erta* 'to the watchtower.' **—a·lert·ly** *adv.* **—a·lert·ness** *n.*
▸*PHRASE* □ **on the alert** vigilant and prepared: *the security forces must be on the alert for an upsurge in violence.*

-ales ▸*suffix Botany* forming the names of orders of plants: *Rosales.* ▷from the plural of the Latin adjectival suffix *-alis* (see -AL).

a·leth·ic /ə'leTHik; ə'lē-/ ▸*adj. Philosophy* denoting modalities of truth, such as necessity, contingency, or impossibility. ▷1950s: from Greek *alētheia* 'truth' + -IC.

A·letsch·horn /'äliCH,hôrn/ a mountain in Switzerland, in the Bernese Alps, that rises to 13,763 feet (4,195 m). Its glaciers are among the largest in Europe.

al·eu·rone /'alyə,rōn; ə'lŏŏrōn/ ▸*n. Botany* protein stored as granules in the cells of plant seeds. ▷mid 19th cent.: from Greek *aleuron* 'flour.'

Al·eut /ə'lŏŏt; 'alē,ōōt/ ▸*n.* **1** a member of a people inhabiting the Aleutian Islands, other islands in the Bering Sea, and parts of western Alaska. **2** the language of this people, related to Eskimo.
▸*adj.* of or relating to this people or their language. ▷from Russian, from an unknown source.

A·leu·tian Is·lands /ə'lōōSHən/ (also **the A·leu·tians**) a chain of U.S. volcanic islands that extend southwest from the Alaska Peninsula.

A·leu·tian Range /ə'lōōSHən/ an extension of the Coast Ranges in southwestern Alaska. It contains many volcanoes.

A lev·el ▸*n.* (in the UK except Scotland) the higher of the two main levels of standardized examinations in secondary schools. Compare with O LEVEL. ▷short for *advanced level.*

al·e·vin /'aləvən/ ▸*n.* a newly spawned salmon or trout still carrying the yolk. ▷mid 19th cent.: from Old French, based on Latin *allevare* 'raise up.'

ale·wife /'āl,wīf/ ▸*n.* (*pl.* **-wives** /-,wīvz/) a northwestern Atlantic fish of the herring family that swims up rivers to spawn and is found also in the Great Lakes. • *Alosa pseudoharengus*, family Clupeidae. ▷mid 17th cent.: possibly from earlier *alewife* 'woman who keeps an alehouse,' with reference to the fish's large belly.

Al·ex·an·der[1] /,alig'zandər/ (356–323 BC), king of Macedon 336–323; son of Philip II; known as **Alexander the Great**. He conquered Persia, Egypt, Syria, Mesopotamia, Bactria, and the Punjab; he founded the city of Alexandria in Egypt.

Al·ex·an·der[2] three kings of Scotland: ■ **Alexander I** (*c.*1077–1124), son of Malcolm III; reigned 1107–24. ■ **Alexander II** (1198–1249), son of William I of Scotland; reigned 1214–49. ■ **Alexander III** (1241–86), son of Alexander II; reigned 1249–86. He annexed the Hebrides and the Isle of Man in 1266.

Al·ex·an·der[3] three tsars of Russia: ■ **Alexander I** (1777–1825), reigned 1801–25. During his reign, Napoleon unsuccessfully invaded Russia 1812. ■ **Alexander II** (1818–81), son of Nicholas I; reigned 1855–81; known as **Alexander the Liberator**. His reforms included limited emancipation of the serfs. ■ **Alexander III** (1845–94), son of Alexander II; reigned 1881–94.

Al·ex·an·der[4], Grover Cleveland (1887–1950), U.S. baseball player; known as **Pete**. A 20-season pitcher for the Philadelphia Phillies 1911–17, the Chicago Cubs 1917–26, and the St. Louis Cardinals 1926–30, he retired with 373 career wins and 90 shutouts. Baseball Hall of Fame (1938).

Al·ex·an·der[5], Harold (Rupert Leofric George), 1st Earl Alexander of Tunis (1891–1969), British field marshal and statesman.

Al·ex·an·der Ar·chi·pel·a·go a group of more than 1,000 U.S. islands off the coast of southeastern Alaska.

Al·ex·an·der Nev·sky, St. /'nefskē/ (also **Nev·ski**) (*c.*1220–63), prince of Novgorod 1236-63; born *Aleksandr Yaroslavich*. He defeated the Swedes on the banks of the Neva River in 1240. Feast day, August 30 or November 23.

Al·ex·an·der tech·nique a system of body awareness designed to promote well-being by ensuring minimum effort in maintaining postures and carrying out movements. ▷1930s: named after Frederick

Matthias *Alexander* (1869–1955), Australian-born actor and physical therapist who developed it.

Al·ex·an·dret·ta /ˌaligzan'dretə/ former name for **ISKENDERUN.**

Al·ex·an·dri·a /ˌalig'zandrēə/ **1** the chief port of Egypt; pop. 2,893,000. Founded in 332 BC by Alexander the Great, it was a major center of Hellenistic culture, renowned for its library and for the Pharos lighthouse. **2** an industrial city in central Louisiana, on the Red River; pop. 46,342. **3** a city in northern Virginia, on the Potomac River, across from Washington, DC; pop. 128,283.

Al·ex·an·dri·an /ˌalig'zandrēən/ ▸*adj.* of or relating to Alexandria in Egypt. ■ belonging to or akin to the schools of literature and philosophy of ancient Alexandria. ■ (of a writer) derivative or imitative rather than creative; fond of recondite learning.

al·ex·an·drine /ˌalig'zandrin; -ˌdrēn/ *Prosody* ▸*adj.* (of a line of verse) having six iambic feet.
▸*n.* (usu. **alexandrines**) an alexandrine line. ▷late 16th cent.: from French *alexandrin*, from *Alexandre* (see **ALEXANDER**[1]), the subject of an Old French poem in this meter.

al·ex·an·drite /ˌalig'zanˌdrīt/ ▸*n.* a gem variety of chrysoberyl that appears green in daylight and red in artificial light. ▷mid 19th cent.: from the name of Tsar *Alexander* II of Russia (see **ALEXANDER**[3]) + **-ITE**[1].

Al·ex·an·dro·pol variant spelling of **ALEKSANDROPOL.**

a·lex·i·a /ə'leksēə/ ▸*n.* the inability to see words or to read, caused by a defect of the brain. Also called **WORD BLINDNESS.** Compare with **DYSLEXIA.** ▷late 19th cent.: from **A-**[1] 'without' + Greek *lexis* 'speech,' from *legein* 'speak,' which was confused with Latin *legere* 'read.'

al·fal·fa /al'falfə/ ▸*n.* a leguminous plant with cloverlike leaves and bluish flowers. Native to southwestern Asia, it is widely grown for fodder. Also called **LUCERNE.** • *Medicago sativa*, family Leguminosae. ▷mid 19th cent.: from Spanish, from Arabic *al-fasfaṣa*, a green fodder.

Al Fa·tah /ˌäl fə'tä/ see **FATAH, AL.**

al·fi·sol /'alfiˌsôl; -ˌsäl/ ▸*n. Soil Science* a soil of an order comprising leached basic or slightly acid soils with a clay-enriched B horizon (subsoil). ▷1960s: from the arbitrary element *Alfi-* + **-SOL.**

Al·fon·so XIII /al'fänsō; äl'fônsō/ (1886–1941), king of Spain 1886–1931. He was forced into exile after elections indicating a preference for a republic.

Al·fred /'alfrəd/ (849–99), king of Wessex 871–899; known as **Alfred the Great.** His military resistance saved southwestern England from Viking occupation.

Al·fre·do /al'frādō/ ▸*n.* a sauce for pasta incorporating butter, cream, garlic, and Parmesan cheese. ▷named after *Alfredo* di Lelio, the Italian chef and restaurateur who invented the sauce.

al·fres·co /al'freskō; äl/ ▸*adv.* & *adj.* in the open air: [as *adj.*] *an alfresco luncheon.* ▷mid 18th cent.: from Italian *al fresco* 'in the fresh (air).'

Al Fu·jay·rah /ˌäl fə'jīrə; ˌal/ another name for **FUJAIRAH.**

Alf·vén /äl'vān/, Hannes Olof Gösta (1908–95), Swedish theoretical physicist. His work was important for controlled thermonuclear fusion. Nobel Prize for Physics (1970, shared with Louis Néel 1904–2000).

Alf·vén wave ▸*n. Physics* a hydromagnetic shear wave in a plasma that moves along magnetic field lines. The velocity of such waves (the **Alfvén velocity** or **speed**) is characteristic for a plasma of given properties.

al·ga /'algə/ ▸*n.* (usu. in *pl.* **-gae** /-jē/) a simple nonflowering plant of a large group that includes the seaweeds and many single-celled forms. Algae contain chlorophyll but lack true stems, roots, leaves, and vascular tissue. • Divisions Chlorophyta (**green algae**), Heterokontophyta (**brown algae**), and Rhodophyta (**red algae**); some (or all) are frequently placed in the kingdom Protista. See also **BLUE-GREEN ALGAE.** ▷mid 16th cent.: from Latin, 'seaweed.' **—al·gal** /-gəl/ *adj.*

al·ge·bra /'aljəbrə/ ▸*n.* the part of mathematics in which letters and other general symbols are used to represent numbers and quantities in formulae and equations. ■ a system of this based on given axioms. ▷late Middle English: from Italian, Spanish, and medieval Latin, from Arabic *al-jabr* 'the reunion of broken parts,' 'bone setting,' from *jabara* 'reunite, restore.' The original sense, 'the surgical treatment of fractures,' probably came via Spanish, in which it survives; the mathematical sense comes from the title of a book, *'ilm al-jabr wa'l-mukābala* 'the science of restoring what is missing and equating like with like,' by the mathematician al-Kwārizmī (see **ALGORITHM**). **—al·ge·bra·ist** /-ˌbrā-ist/ *n.*

al·ge·bra·ic /ˌaljə'brā-ik/ ▸*adj.* relating to or involving algebra. ■ (of a mathematical expression or equation) in which a finite number of symbols is combined using only the operations of addition, subtraction, multiplication, division, and exponentiation with constant rational exponents. Compare with **TRANSCENDENTAL.** **—al·ge·bra·i·cal** *adv.* **—al·ge·bra·i·cal·ly** *adv.*

Al·ge·ci·ras /ˌälkhä'thēˌräs; -'sēˌräs/ a ferry port and resort in southern Spain, on the Strait of Gibraltar; pop. 101,365.

Al·ger /'aljər/, Horatio, Jr. (1832–99), U.S. author. His novels, most notably *Ragged Dick* (1867), were infused with the message that honest hard work can overcome poverty.

Al·ge·ri·a /al'ji(ə)rēə/ a republic in northwestern Africa, on the Mediterranean coast; pop. 32,100,000; capital, Algiers; official language, Arabic. **—Al·ge·ri·an** *adj.* & *n.*

Algeria was colonized by France in the mid 19th century and was for a time closely integrated with metropolitan France. Following civil war in the 1950s, it achieved independence in 1962. A brief period of multiparty democracy was ended by a military takeover in 1992 after the fundamentalist Islamic Salvation Front had won the first round of the national elections. This prompted a low-level civil war until 2000 when the Islamic Salvation Army, the armed segment of the Islamic Salvation Front, was dissolved in an effort to achieve national reconciliation.

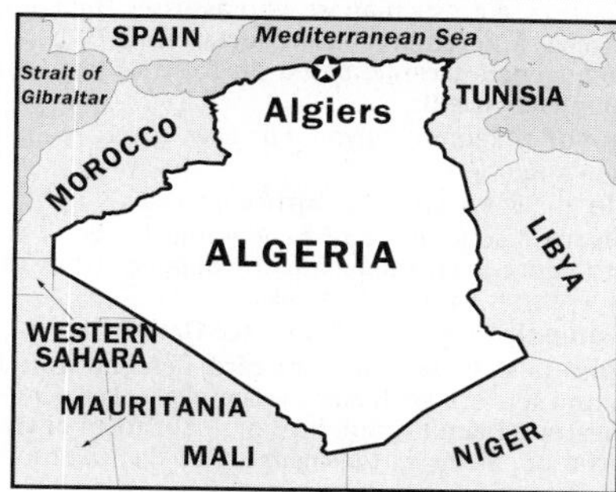

-algia ▸*comb. form* denoting pain in a specified part of the body: *neuralgia* | *myalgia.* ▷from Greek *algos* 'pain.' **—algic** *comb. form* in corresponding adjectives.

-algic ▸*comb. form* in adjectives corresponding to nouns ending in *-algia* (such as *neuralgic* corresponding to *neuralgia*).

al·gi·cide /'aljəˌsīd/ ▸*n.* a substance that is poisonous to algae.

Al·giers /al'ji(ə)rz/ the capital of Algeria and one of the leading Mediterranean ports of North Africa; pop. 1,722,000.

al·gin·ic ac·id /al'jinik/ ▸*n. Chemistry* an insoluble gelatinous carbohydrate found (chiefly as salts) in many brown seaweeds. The sodium salt is used as a thickener in foods and many other materials. ▷late 19th cent.: *alginic* from **ALGA** + **-IN**[1] + **-IC.** **—al·gi·nate** /'aljəˌnāt/ *n.*

algo- ▸*comb. form* pain: *algolagnia.*

Al·gol[1] /'alˌgôl; -ˌgäl/ *Astronomy* a variable star or star system in the constellation Perseus, regarded as the prototype of eclipsing binary stars. ▷from Arabic *al ġūl* 'the ghoul.'

Al·gol[2] ▸*n.* one of the early high-level computer programming languages that was devised to carry out scientific calculations. ▷1950s: from *algo(rithmic)* + the initial letter of **LANGUAGE.**

al·go·lag·ni·a /ˌalgō'lagnēə/ ▸*n. Psychiatry* desire for sexual gratification through inflicting pain on oneself or others; sadomasochism. ▷early 20th cent.: coined in German from Greek *algos* 'pain' + *lagneia* 'lust.'

al·gol·o·gy /al'gäləjē/ ▸*n.* the study of algae. **—al·go·log·i·cal** /ˌalgə'läjikəl/ *adj.* **—al·gol·o·gist** /-jist/ *n.*

Al·gon·qui·an /al'gängk(w)ēən/ (also **Al·gon·ki·an** /-kēən/) ▸*adj.* denoting, belonging to, or relating to a family of North American Indian languages formerly spoken across a vast area from the Atlantic seaboard to the Great Lakes and the Great Plains.
▸*n.* **1** this family of languages. **2** a speaker of any of these languages.

Algonquian is one of the largest groups of American Indian languages, including Ojibwa, Cree, Blackfoot, Cheyenne, Fox, Menominí, and Delaware, which are or were spoken mainly in the northern Midwest, Montana, and southern Canada. Many English words have been adopted from these languages, e.g., *moccasin, moose,* and *toboggan.*

▷from **ALGONQUIN** + **-IAN.**

Al·gon·quin /al'gängk(w)ən/ (also **Al·gon·kin**) ▸*n.* **1** a member of a North American Indian people living in Canada along the Ottawa River and its tributaries and westward to the north of Lake Superior. **2** the dialect of Ojibwa spoken by this people.
▸*adj.* of or relating to this people or their language. ▷French, contraction of obsolete *Algoumequin*, probably from Malecite *elægómogwik* meaning 'they are our relatives or allies.'

USAGE The use of **Algonquin** to refer generically to the Algonquian peoples or their languages is incorrect.

al·go·rithm /'algəˌriT͟Həm/ ▸*n.* a process or set of rules to be followed in calculations or other problem-solving operations, esp. by a computer: *a basic* **algorithm** *for division.* ▷late 17th cent.: variant (influenced by Greek *arithmos* 'number') of Middle English *algorism*, via Old French from medieval Latin *algorismus*. The Arabic source, *al-Kwārizmī* 'the man of Kwārizm' (now Khiva), was the cognomen of the 9th-cent. mathematician Abū Ja'far Muhammad ibn Mūsa. **—al·go·rith·mic** /ˌalgə'riT͟Hmik/ *adj.* **—al·go·rith·mi·cal·ly** /ˌalgə'riT͟Hmik(ə)lē/ *adv.*

Al·gren /'ôlgrən/, Nelson (Abraham) (1909–81), U.S. novelist. He drew on his childhood experiences in the slums of Chicago for his vivid, realistic novels of social protest, such as *Somebody in Boots* (1935). Other notable works: *The Man with the Golden Arm* (1949) and *Walk on the Wild Side* (1956).

al·ha·ji /äl'häjē; al'hajē/ ▸*n.* (*pl.* **-ha·jis**) (*fem.* **-ha·ja**) (in West Africa) a Muslim who has been to Mecca as a pilgrim (often used as a title). ▷Hausa, from Turkish, from *al* 'the' + *hājī* 'pilgrim.'

Al·ham·bra /al'hambrə/ a city in southwestern California, northeast of Los Angeles; pop. 82,106.

Al·ham·bra (**the Alhambra**) a fortified Moorish palace, the last stronghold of the Muslim kings of Granada, built between 1248 and 1354 near Granada in Spain.

The Alhambra

Al-Hu·day·da Arabic name for **HODEIDA.**

A·li[1] /ä'lē/, Muhammad, see **MUHAMMAD ALI**[1].

A·li[2] /ä'lē; 'älē/, Muhammad (1942–), U.S. boxer; born *Cassius Marcellus Clay.* He won the world heavyweight title in 1964, 1974, and 1978, becoming the only boxer to be world heavyweight champion three times. After converting to Islam and changing his name, he was stripped of his title for refusing army service on conscientious objector grounds. This decision was overturned by the U.S. Supreme Court in 1976, and his title was reinstated.

a·li·as /'ālēəs/ ▸*adv.* used to indicate that a named person is also known or more familiar under another specified name: *Eric Blair, alias George Orwell.* ■ *informal* indicating another term or synonym: *the catfish—alias bullhead—is a mighty tasty fry-up.*
▸*n.* a false or assumed identity: *a spy operating* **under the alias** *Barsad.* ■ *Computing* an alternative name or

label that refers to a file, command, address, or other item, and can be used to locate or access it. ■ *Telecommunications* each of a set of signal frequencies that, when sampled at a given uniform rate, would give the same set of sampled values, and thus might be incorrectly substituted for one another when reconstructing the original signal.
▸*v.* [*trans.*] (usu. **be aliased**) *Physics & Telecommunications* misidentify (a signal frequency), introducing distortion or error. ▷late Middle English: from Latin, 'at another time, otherwise.'

a·li·as·ing /ˈālēəsiNG/ ▸*n.* **1** *Physics & Telecommunications* the misidentification of a signal frequency, introducing distortion or error. **2** *Computing* in computer graphics, the jagged, or saw-toothed appearance of curved or diagonal lines on a low-resolution monitor.

A·li Ba·ba /ˌälē ˈbäbə/ the hero of a story supposed to be from the *Arabian Nights*, who discovered the magic formula ("Open Sesame!") that opened a cave where forty robbers kept their treasure.

al·i·bi /ˈaləˌbī/ ▸*n.* (*pl.* **-bis**) a claim or piece of evidence that one was elsewhere when an act, typically a criminal one, is alleged to have taken place: *she **has an alibi** for the whole of yesterday evening | a defense of alibi.* ■ *informal* an excuse or pretext: *a catch-all alibi for failure and inadequacy.*
▸*v.* (**-bis, -bied, -bi·ing**) [*trans.*] *informal* offer an excuse or defense for (someone), esp. by providing an account of their whereabouts at the time of an alleged act: *her friend agreed to alibi her.* ■ [*intrans.*] make excuses: *not once do I recall him whining or alibiing.* ▷late 17th cent. (as an adverb in the sense 'elsewhere'): from Latin, 'in another place; elsewhere.' The noun use dates from the late 18th cent.

USAGE The weakened nonlegal use of **alibi** to mean simply 'an excuse' is a fairly common and natural extension of the core meaning. It is acceptable in standard English, although regarded as incorrect by some traditionalists.

Al·i·can·te /ˌaliˈkantē; ˌäləˈkäntā/ a seaport on the Mediterranean coast of southeastern Spain, the capital of Alicante Province; pop. 270,950.

Al·ice-in-Won·der·land /ˈalis in ˈwəndərˌland/ ▸*adj.* [*attrib.*] not logically explicable or predictable: *this Alice-in-Wonderland economic system.*

Al·ice Springs /ˈalis/ a railroad terminus and supply center serving the outback of Northern Territory, Australia; pop. 20,450.

al·i·cy·clic /ˌaləˈsīklik; -ˈsik-/ *Chemistry* ▸*adj.* relating to or denoting organic compounds that combine cyclic structure with aliphatic properties, e.g., cyclohexane and other saturated cyclic hydrocarbons. Compare with **AROMATIC**.
▸*n.* (usu. **alicyclics**) an alicyclic compound. ▷late 19th cent.: blend of **ALIPHATIC** and **CYCLIC**.

al·i·dade /ˈaliˌdād/ ▸*n.* a sighting device or pointer for determining directions or measuring angles, used in surveying and (formerly) astronomy. ▷late Middle English: directly or (in modern use) via French and Spanish from Arabic *al-ʿiḍāda* 'the revolving radius,' probably based on *ʿaḍud* 'upper arm.'

a·li·en /ˈālyən; ˈālēən/ ▸*adj.* belonging to a foreign country or nation. ■ unfamiliar and disturbing or distasteful: *bossing anyone around was **alien to** him | they found the world of adult education a little alien.* ■ [*attrib.*] relating to or denoting beings supposedly from other worlds; extraterrestrial: *an alien spacecraft.* ■ (of a plant or animal species) introduced from another country and later naturalized.
▸*n.* a foreigner, esp. one who is not a naturalized citizen of the country where they are living: *an illegal alien.* ■ a hypothetical or fictional being from another world. ■ a plant or animal species originally introduced from another country and later naturalized. ▷Middle English: via Old French from Latin *alienus* 'belonging to another,' from *alius* 'other.' **—al·ien·ness** *n.*

al·ien·a·ble /ˈālēənəbəl; ˈālyənə-/ ▸*adj.* *Law* able to be transferred to new ownership. **—a·lien·a·bil·i·ty** /ˌālēənəˈbilitē; ˌālyən-/ *n.*

al·ien·age /ˈālēənij; ˈālyə-/ ▸*n.* the state or condition of being an alien.

al·ien·ate /ˈālēəˌnāt; ˈālyə-/ ▸*v.* [*trans.*] **1** cause (someone) to feel isolated or estranged: *an urban environment that would alienate its inhabitants* | [as *adj.*] (**alienated**) *an alienated angst-ridden 22-year-old.* ■ cause (someone) to become unsympathetic or hostile: *the association does not wish to alienate its members.* **2** *Law* transfer ownership of (property rights) to another person or group. ▷early 16th cent.: from Latin *alienat-* 'estranged,' from the verb *alienare*, from *alienus* 'of another' (see **ALIEN**).
▸*PHRASE* □ **alienate someone's affections** *Law* induce someone to transfer their affection from a person (such as a spouse) with legal rights or claims on them.

al·ien·a·tion /ˌālēəˈnāsHən; ˌālyə-/ ▸*n.* the state or experience of being isolated from a group or an activity to which one should belong or in which one should be involved: *unemployment may generate a sense of political alienation.* See note at **SOLITUDE**. ■ loss or lack of sympathy; estrangement: *public **alienation from** bureaucracy.* ■ (in Marxist theory) a condition of workers in a capitalist economy, resulting from a lack of identity with the products of their labor and a sense of being controlled or exploited. ■ *Psychiatry* a state of depersonalization or loss of identity in which the self seems unreal, thought to be caused by difficulties in relating to society and the resulting prolonged inhibition of emotion. ■ a type of faulty recognition in which familiar situations or persons appear unfamiliar. Compare with **DÉJÀ VU**. ■ (also **alienation effect**) *Theater* an effect, sought by some dramatists, whereby the audience remains objective and does not identify with the actors. ■ *Law* the transfer of the ownership of property rights. ▷late Middle English: from Latin *alienatio(n-)*, from the verb *alienare* 'estrange,' from *alienus* (see **ALIEN**). The term *alienation effect* (1940s) is a translation of German *Verfremdungseffekt*.

al·ien·ee /ˌālēəˈnē; ˌālyə-/ ▸*n.* *Law* dated term for **GRANTEE**.

al·ien·ist /ˈālēənist; ˈālyə-/ ▸*n.* former term for **PSYCHIATRIST**. ■ a psychiatrist who assesses the competence of a defendant in a court. ▷mid 19th cent.: from French *aliéniste*, based on Latin *alienus* 'of another' (see **ALIEN**).

al·ien·or /ˈālēənər; ˈālyə-/ ▸*n.* *Law* dated term for **GRANTOR**.

a-life /ˈā ˌlīf/ ▸*n.* short for **ARTIFICIAL LIFE**.

al·i·form /ˈaləˌfôrm; ˈālə-/ ▸*adj.* wing-shaped. ▷early 18th cent.: from modern Latin *aliformis*, from Latin *ala* 'wing' + *-formis* (see **-FORM**).

A·li·ghie·ri /ˌäləgˈyerē/, Dante, see **DANTE**.

a·light[1] /əˈlīt/ ▸*v.* [*intrans.*] (of a bird) descend from the air and settle: *a lovely blue swallow alighted on a branch.* ■ descend from a train, bus, or other form of transportation: *the conductor alights to push the cable car completely around.*
▸*phrasal v.* □ **alight on** find by chance; notice: *her eyes alighted on the item in question.* ▷Old English *ālīhtan*, from *ā-* (as an intensifier) + *līhtan* 'descend' (see **LIGHT**[3]).

a·light[2] ▸*adv. & adj.* on fire; burning: [as *adj.*] *the house was well alight when the firemen arrived* | [as *adv.*] *flammable liquid was **set alight**.* ■ shining brightly: [as *adj.*] *a single lamp was alight* | *figurative the boy's face was **alight with** excitement.* ▷late Middle English: probably from the phrase *on a light* (= lighted) *fire*.

a·lign /əˈlīn/ ▸*v.* **1** [*trans.*] place or arrange (things) in a straight line: *gently brush the surface to align the fibers.* ■ put (things) into correct or appropriate relative positions: *the fan blades are carefully aligned* | *figurative aligning domestic prices with prices in world markets.* ■ [*intrans.*] lie in a straight line, or in correct relative positions: *the pattern of the border at the seam should align perfectly.* **2** (**align oneself with**) give support to (a person, organization, or cause): *newspapers usually align themselves with certain political parties.* ■ [*intrans.*] come together in agreement or alliance: *all of them must now align against the foe* | [as *adj.*] (**aligned**) *forces aligned with Russia.* ▷late 17th cent.: from French *aligner*, from *à ligne* 'into line.'

a·lign·ment /əˈlīnmənt/ ▸*n.* **1** arrangement in a straight line, or in correct or appropriate relative positions: *the tiles had slipped out of alignment.* ■ the act of aligning parts of a machine: *oil changes, lube jobs, and wheel alignments.* ■ the route or course of a road or railroad: *four railroads, all on different alignments.* **2** a position of agreement or alliance: *a firm famous for its liberal alignment.* ▷late 18th cent.: from French *alignement*, from *aligner* (see **ALIGN**).

a·like /əˈlīk/ ▸*adj.* [*predic.*] (of two or more subjects) similar to each other: *the brothers were very much alike | the houses all looked alike.*
▸*adv.* in the same or a similar way: *the girls dressed alike in black pants and jackets.* ■ used to show that something applies equally to a number of specified subjects: *he talked in a friendly manner to staff and patients alike.* ▷Old English *gelīc*, of Germanic origin; related to Dutch *gelijk* and German *gleich*, reinforced in Middle English by Old Norse *álíkr* (adjective) and *álíka* (adverb).

al·i·ment /ˈaləmənt/ ▸*n.* *archaic* food; nourishment. ■ support; sustenance.
▸*v.* provide with nourishment or sustenance. ▷late 15th cent.: from Latin *alimentum*, from *alere* 'nourish.'

al·i·men·ta·ry /ˌaləˈment(ə)rē/ ▸*adj.* of or relating to nourishment or sustenance. ▷late 16th cent.: from Latin *alimentarius*, from *alimentum* 'nourishment' (see **ALIMENT**).

al·i·men·ta·ry ca·nal ▸*n.* the whole passage along which food passes through the body from mouth to anus. It includes the esophagus, stomach, and intestines.

al·i·men·ta·tion /ˌaləmenˈtāsHən/ ▸*n.* *formal* the provision of nourishment or other necessities of life. ▷late 16th cent. (in the sense 'maintenance, support'): from medieval Latin *alimentatio(n-)*, from late Latin *alimentare* 'to feed,' from *alimentum* 'nourishment' (see **ALIMENT**).

al·i·mo·ny /ˈaləˌmōnē/ ▸*n.* a husband's or wife's court-ordered provision for a spouse after separation or divorce. ▷early 17th cent. (in the sense 'nourishment, means of subsistence'): from Latin *alimonia* 'nutriment,' from *alere* 'nourish.'

A-line /ˈā ˌlīn/ ▸*adj.* (of a garment) slightly flared from a narrow waist or shoulders: *A-line skirts.*

al·i·phat·ic /ˌaləˈfatik/ *Chemistry* ▸*adj.* relating to or denoting organic compounds in which carbon atoms form open chains (as in the alkanes), not aromatic rings. Compare with **ALICYCLIC**.
▸*n.* (usu. **aliphatics**) an aliphatic compound. ▷late 19th cent. (originally used of the fatty acids): from Greek *aleiphar, aleiphat-* 'fat' + **-IC**.

al·i·quot /ˈalikwət/ ▸*n.* a portion of a larger whole, esp. a sample taken for chemical analysis or other treatment. ■ (also **aliquot part** or **portion**) *Mathematics* a quantity that can be divided into another an integral number of times.
▸*v.* [*trans.*] (usu. **be aliquoted**) divide (a whole) into aliquots; take aliquots from (a whole). ▷late 16th cent.: from French *aliquote*, from Latin *aliquot* 'some, so many,' from *alius* 'one of two' + *quot* 'how many.'

al·i·sphe·noid /ˌaləˈsfēˌnoid/ ▸*n.* (also **alisphenoid bone**) *Anatomy & Zoology* a winglike cartilaginous bone within the mammalian skull, forming part of the socket of the eye. ▷mid 19th cent.: from Latin *ala* 'wing' + **SPHENOID**.

A-list /ˈā ˌlist/ (or **B-list** /ˈbē ˌlist /) ▸*n.* a real or imaginary list of the most (or, for B-list, second-most) celebrated or sought-after individuals, especially in show business: [as *modifier*] *an A-list celebrity.*

a·lit·er·ate /āˈlitərit/ ▸*adj.* unwilling to read, although able to do so.
▸*n.* an aliterate person. **—a·lit·er·a·cy** /-əsē/ *n.*

a·live /əˈlīv/ ▸*adj.* [*predic.*] **1** (of a person, animal, or plant) living, not dead: *hopes of finding anyone still alive were fading | he was kept alive by a feeding-tube.* ■ (of a feeling or quality) continuing in existence: *keeping hope alive.* ■ continuing to be supported or in use: *militarism was kept alive by pure superstition.* **2** (of a person or animal) alert and active; animated: *Ken **comes alive** when he hears his music played.* ■ *figurative* having interest and meaning: *we hope we will make history **come alive** for the children.* **3** (**alive to**) aware of and interested in; responsive to: *always alive to new ideas.* **4** (**alive with**) swarming or teeming with: *in spring those cliffs are alive with auks and gulls.* ▷Old English *on life*, literally 'in life.' **—a·live·ness** *n.*
▸*PHRASES* □ **alive and kicking** *informal* prevalent and very active: *bigotry is still alive and kicking.* □ **alive and well** still existing or active (often used to deny rumors or beliefs that something has disappeared or declined): *Jefferson's ideas are alive and well today in Washington.* □ **look alive** another term for **look lively** (see **LIVELY**).

THE RIGHT WORD **alive, animate, animated, living, vital**

Dead is dead, but one can be **alive** to varying degrees. The broadest of these terms describing what has life or shows signs of having it, *alive* can refer to what barely exists (*he was unconscious but still alive when they found him*) as well as to what is bursting with (literal or figurative) life (*her face was alive with excitement and anticipation*).

Living, on the other hand, is more limited in scope and implies the condition of not being dead (*at 92, she was the oldest living member of the family*) or a state of continued existence or activity (*America's greatest living historian*).

Animate has fewer connotations than *living* or *alive*; though rare, it is used to distinguish living organisms as opposed to dead ones (*one of the few animate creatures after the devastating explosion*).
Animated, on the other hand, is used to describe inanimate things to which life or the appearance of life has been given (*an animated cartoon*), or things that are vigorous and lively (*an animated debate on the death penalty*).
Anything that is essential to life is **vital** (*vital functions; vital organs*), but *vital* can also be used to describe the energy, activity, and alertness of living things (*an aging but vital member of the historical society*).

a·li·yah /ˌälēˈä/ ▸*n.* (*pl.* **a·li·yoth** /ˌälēˈōt/) *Judaism* **1** immigration to Israel: *students **making aliyah**.* **2** the honor of being called upon to read from the Torah: *I was called up for an aliyah.* ▷from Hebrew *ʿălīyāh* 'ascent.'

a·liz·a·rin /əˈlizərin/ ▸*n. Chemistry* a red pigment present in madder root, used in dyeing. • Alternative name: 1,2-dihydroxyanthraquinone; chem. formula: $C_{14}H_8O_4$. ■ [as *adj.*] denoting dyes derived from or similar to this pigment: *alizarin crimson.* ▷mid 19th cent.: from French *alizarine*, from *alizari* 'madder,' from Arabic *al-ʿiṣāra* 'pressed juice,' from *ʿaṣara* 'to press fruit.'

Al Ji·zah /äl ˈjēzə/ variant form of **GIZA**.

al·ka·hest /ˈalkəˌhest/ (also **al·ca·hest**) ▸*n. historical* the hypothetical universal solvent sought by alchemists. ▷mid 17th cent.: sham Arabic, probably invented by Paracelsus.

al·ka·li /ˈalkəˌlī/ ▸*n.* (*pl.* **-lis**) a chemical compound that neutralizes or effervesces with acids and turns litmus blue; typically, a caustic or corrosive substance of this kind such as lime or soda. Often contrasted with **ACID**; compare with **BASE**[1].

Alkalis release hydroxide ions (OH^-) when dissolved in water. An alkaline solution has a pH greater than 7.

▷late Middle English (denoting a saline substance derived from the ashes of various plants, including glasswort): from medieval Latin, from Arabic *al-ḳalī* 'calcined ashes (of the glasswort, etc.),' from *ḳalā* 'fry, roast.'

al·kal·ic ▸*adj. Geology* (of a rock or mineral) richer in sodium and/or potassium than is usual for its type.

al·ka·li feld·spar ▸*n. Geology* any of the group of feldspars rich in sodium and/or potassium.

al·ka·li met·al ▸*n. Chemistry* any of the elements lithium, sodium, potassium, rubidium, cesium, and francium, occupying Group IA (1) of the periodic table. They are very reactive, electropositive, monovalent metals forming strongly alkaline hydroxides.

al·ka·line /ˈalkəlin; -ˌlīn/ ▸*adj.* having the properties of an alkali, or containing alkali; having a pH greater than 7. Often contrasted with **ACID** or **ACIDIC**; compare with **BASIC**. **—al·ka·lin·i·ty** /ˌalkəˈlinitē/ *n.*

al·ka·line bat·ter·y ▸*n.* a long-lived dry cell with an alkaline electrolyte of potassium hydroxide, which deters corrosion.

al·ka·line earth (also **alkaline earth metal**) ▸*n.* any of the elements beryllium, magnesium, calcium, strontium, barium, and radium, occupying Group IIA (2) of the periodic table. They are reactive, electropositive, divalent metals, and form basic oxides that react with water to form comparatively insoluble hydroxides.

al·ka·lize /ˈalkəˌlīz/ (also **al·ka·lin·ize** /ˈalkəliˌnīz/) ▸*v.* [*trans.*] [usu. as *adj.*] (**alkalized** or **alkalizing**) treat with alkali. **—al·ka·li·za·tion** /ˌalkəliˈzāsHən/ *n.* **—al·ka·liz·er** *n.*

al·ka·loid /ˈalkəˌloid/ ▸*n. Chemistry* any of a class of nitrogenous organic compounds of plant origin that have pronounced physiological actions on humans. They include many drugs (morphine, quinine) and poisons (atropine, strychnine). ▷early 19th cent.: coined in German from **ALKALI**.

al·ka·lo·sis /ˌalkəˈlōsis/ ▸*n. Medicine* an excessively alkaline condition of the body fluids or tissues that may cause weakness or cramps.

al·kane /ˈalˌkān/ ▸*n. Chemistry* any of the series of saturated hydrocarbons including methane, ethane, propane, and higher members. • Alkanes have the general formula: C_nH_{2n+2}. ▷late 19th cent.: from **ALKYL** + **-ANE**[2].

al·kene /ˈalˌkēn/ ▸*n. Chemistry* any of the series of unsaturated hydrocarbons containing a double bond, including ethylene and propylene. • Alkenes have the general formula: C_nH_{2n}. ▷late 19th cent.: from **ALKYL** + **-ENE**.

al·ky /ˈalkē/ (also **al·kie**) ▸*n.* (*pl.* **-kies**) *informal* an alcoholic.

al·kyd /ˈalkid/ ▸*n. Chemistry* any of a group of synthetic polyester resins derived from various alcohols and acids, used in varnishes, paints, and adhesives. ▷1920s: blend of **ALKYL** and **ACID**.

al·kyl /ˈalkəl/ ▸*n.* [as *adj.*] *Chemistry* of or denoting a hydrocarbon radical derived from an alkane by removal of a hydrogen atom. ▷late 19th cent.: German, from *Alkohol* 'alcohol' + **-YL**.

al·kyl·ate /ˈalkəˌlāt/ ▸*v.* [*trans.*] [usu. as *adj.*] (**alkylating** or **alkylated**) *Chemistry* introduce an alkyl radical into (a compound): *alkylating agents.* **—al·kyl·a·tion** /ˌalkəˈlāsHən/ *n.*

al·kyne /ˈalˌkīn/ ▸*n. Chemistry* any of the series of unsaturated hydrocarbons containing a triple bond, including acetylene. • Alkynes have the general formula: C_nH_{2n-2}. ▷early 20th cent.: from **ALKYL** + **-YNE**.

all /ôl/ ▸*predeterminer, adj., & pron.* used to refer to the whole quantity or extent of a particular group or thing: [as *predeterminer*] *all the people I met | she left all her money to him* | [as *adj.*] *10% of all cars sold | he slept all day* | [as *pron.*] *four bedrooms, all with balconies | carry **all** of the blame | the men are all bearded.* ■ [*adj.*] any whatever: *assured beyond all doubt | he denied all knowledge.* ■ [*adj.*] used to emphasize the greatest possible amount of a quality: *they were **in all** probability completely unaware | **with all** due respect.* ■ *informal* dominated by a particular feature or characteristic: *an eleven-year-old string bean, all elbows and knees.* ■ [*pron.*] [with *clause*] the only thing (used for emphasis): *all I want is to be left alone.* ■ [*pron.*] (used to refer to surroundings or a situation in general) everything: *all was well | it was all very strange.* ■ *informal* used to indicate more than one person or thing: *a team of specialists who all know the patient.* ■ *dialect* consumed; finished; gone: *the cake is all.*
▸*adv.* **1** used for emphasis: ■ completely: *dressed all in black | she's been all around the world | all by himself.* ■ consisting entirely of: *all leather varsity jacket.* **2** (in games) used after a number to indicate an equal score: *after extra time it was still two all.*
▸*n.* the whole of one's possessions, energy, or interest: ***giving** their **all** for what they believed.* ▷Old English *all, eall*, of Germanic origin; related to Dutch *al* and German *all*.
▸*PHRASES* □ **all along** all the time; from the beginning: *she'd known all along.* □ **all and sundry** everyone: *insolent drivers crying to all and sundry to get out of the way.* □ **all around** (*Brit.* also **all round**) **1** in all respects: *it was a bad day all around.* **2** for or by each person: *drinks all around | good acting all around.* □ **all but 1** very nearly: *the subject was all but forgotten.* **2** all except: *we have support from all but one of the networks.* □ **all comers** *chiefly informal* anyone who chooses to take part in an activity, typically a competition: *the champion took on all comers.* □ **all for** *informal* strongly in favor of: *I was all for tolerance.* □ **all in** *informal* exhausted: *he was all in by halftime.* □ **all in all** everything considered; on the whole: *all in all it's been a good year.* □ **all kinds** (or **sorts**) **of** many different kinds of: *how to install paneling on all kinds of walls.* □ **all manner of** see **MANNER**. □ **all of** as much as (typically used ironically of a quantity considered small by the speaker): *the show lasted all of six weeks.* □ **all of a sudden** see **SUDDEN**. □ **all one to someone** making no difference to someone: *simple cases or hard cases, it's all one to me.* □ **all out** using all one's strength or resources: *going all out to win* | [as *adj.*] *an all-out effort.* □ **all over 1** completely finished: *it's all over between us.* **2** *informal* everywhere: *there were bodies all over.* ■ with reference to all parts of the body: *I was shaking all over.* **3** *informal* typical of the person mentioned: *that's our management all over!* **4** *informal* effusively attentive to (someone): *James was all over her.* □ **all over the place** (or **map**) *informal* everywhere: *we've been all over the place looking for you.* ■ in a state of disorder: *my hair was all over the place.* □ **all sorts of** see **all kinds of** above. □ **all's well that ends well** *proverb* if the outcome of a situation is happy, this compensates for any previous difficulty or unpleasantness. □ **all that ——** see **THAT**. □ **all the same** see **SAME**. □ **all the ——** see **THE** (sense 6). □ **all there** [usu. with *negative*] *informal* in full possession of one's mental faculties: *he's not quite all there.* □ **all the time** see **TIME**. □ **all together** all in one place or in a group; all at once: *5,000 people all together | they arrived all together.* Compare with **ALTOGETHER**. □ **all told** in total: *they tried a dozen times all told.* □ **all very well** *informal* used to express criticism or rejection of a favorable or consoling remark: *your proposal is all very well in theory, but in practice it will not pay.* □ **all the way** *informal* without limit or reservation: *I'm with you all the way.* See also **go all the way** at **WAY**. □ **—— and all** used to emphasize something additional that is being referred to: *she threw her coffee over him, mug and all.* ■ *informal* as well: *it must hit him hard, being so young and all.* □ **at all** [with *negative* or in *questions*] (used for emphasis) in any way; to any extent: *I don't like him at all | did he suffer at all?* □ **be all up with** see **UP**. □ **for all ——** in spite of ——: *for all its clarity and style, the book is not easy reading.* □ **in all** in total number; altogether: *there were about 5,000 people in all.* □ **of all** see **OF**. □ **on all fours** see **FOUR**. □ **one and all** see **ONE**.

al·la bre·ve /ˌälə ˈbrev(ā)/ ▸*n. Music* a time signature indicating 2 or 4 half-note beats in a bar. ▷Italian, literally 'according to the breve.'

Al·la·gash Riv·er /ˈaləˌgasH/ a river in northern Maine, noted as a canoeing route.

Al·lah /ˈälə; ˈalə/ the name of God among Muslims (and Arab Christians). ▷from Arabic *ʾallāh*, contraction of *al-ʾilāh* 'the god.'

Al·lah·a·bad /ˈäləhəˌbäd; ˈaləhəˌbad/ a city in Uttar Pradesh state, in north central India; pop. 806,000. Situated at the confluence of the sacred Jumna and Ganges rivers, it is a place of Hindu pilgrimage.

al·la·man·da /ˌaləˈmandə/ ▸*n.* any of a number of tropical shrubs or climbers that bear showy flowers, typically of yellow or purple. • Species in several families, in particular members of the genus *Allamanda*, family Apocynaceae, including the South American **yellow allamanda** (*A. cathartica*), which is cultivated as an ornamental. ▷modern Latin, from the name of Jean-Nicholas-Sébastien *Allamand* (1713–87), Swiss naturalist.

all-A·mer·i·can ▸*adj.* **1** possessing qualities characteristic of American ideals, such as honesty, industriousness, and health: *his all-American wholesomeness.* **2** having members or contents drawn only from America or the U.S.: *an all-American anthology.* ■ involving or representing the whole of America or the U.S.: *an all-American final.* ■ (also **all-America**) (of a sports player) honored as one of the best amateur competitors in the U.S.: *an all-American wrestler.*
▸*n.* (also **all-America**) a sports player honored as one of the best amateurs in the U.S.

al·lan·to·in /əˈlantō-in/ ▸*n. Biochemistry* a crystalline compound formed in the nitrogen metabolism of many mammals (excluding primates). • A cyclic compound related to hydantoin; chem. formula: $C_4H_6N_4O_3$. ▷mid 19th cent.: from **ALLANTOIS** (because it was discovered in the allantoic fluid of cows) + **-IN**[1].

al·lan·to·is /əˈlantō-is/ ▸*n.* (*pl.* **al·lan·to·i·des** /ˌalənˈtō-idēz/) the fetal membrane lying below the chorion in many vertebrates, formed as an outgrowth of the embryo's gut. In birds and reptiles it grows to surround the embryo; in eutherian mammals it forms part of the placenta. ▷mid 17th cent.: modern Latin, based on Greek *allantoeidēs* 'sausage-shaped.' **—al·lan·to·ic** /ˌalənˈtō-ik/ *adj.* **—al·lan·toid** /-toid/ *adj.*

al·lar·gan·do /ˌälärˈgändō/ ▸*adv.* & *adj. Music* (esp. as a direction) getting slower and slower, and often also fuller in tone. ▷Italian, 'broadening.'

all-a·round (*Brit.* **all-round**) ▸*adj.* having many uses or abilities; versatile: *an all-around artist.* ■ in many or all respects: *his all-around excellence.* ■ comprehensive; extensive: *the need of college students for an all-around education.*
▸*n. Gymnastics* an event in which the scores of each individual exercise are totaled to determine the winner.

al·lay /əˈlā/ ▸*v.* [*trans.*] diminish or put at rest (fear, suspicion, or worry): *the report attempted to educate the public and allay fears.* ■ relieve or alleviate (pain or hunger): *some stale figs partly allayed our hunger.* See note at **ALLEVIATE**. ▷Old English *ālecgan* 'lay down or aside.'

all clear ▸*n.* a signal that danger or difficulty is over: *she was given **the all-clear** to travel home.*

all-day ▸*adj.* lasting or available throughout the day: *an all-day barn-raising event.*

al·lée /äˈlā/ ▸*n.* an alley in a formal garden or park, bordered by trees or bushes. ▷mid 18th cent.: French.

al·le·ga·tion /ˌaliˈgāsHən/ ▸*n.* a claim or assertion that someone has done something illegal or wrong, typically one made without proof: *he made allegations of corruption against the administration | **allegations that***

the army was operating a shoot-to-kill policy. ▷late Middle English: from Latin *allegatio(n-)*, from *allegare* 'allege.'

al·lege /ə'lej/ ▶*v.* [*reporting verb*] claim or assert that someone has done something illegal or wrong, typically without proof that this is the case: [with *clause*] *he* **alleged that** *he had been assaulted* | [*trans.*] *the offenses are alleged to have been committed outside the woman's home* | *he is* **alleged to have** *assaulted five men.* ■ (usu. **be alleged**) suppose or affirm to be the case: *the first artifact ever alleged to be from Earhart's aircraft.* ▷Middle English (in the sense 'declare on oath'): from Old French *esligier*, based on Latin *lis, lit-* 'lawsuit'; confused in sense with Latin *allegare* 'allege.'

al·leged /ə'lejd/ ▶*adj.* [*attrib.*] (of an incident or a person) said, without proof, to have taken place or to have a specified illegal or undesirable quality: *the alleged conspirators.* **—al·leg·ed·ly** /-idlē/ *adv.* [*sentence adverb*] *he was allegedly a leading participant in the coup attempt.*

Al·le·ghe·ny Moun·tains /ˌalə'gānē; -'genē/ (also **the Al·le·ghe·nies**) a mountain range, part of the Appalachian system in the eastern U.S., that extends from West Virginia through Pennsylvania.

Al·le·ghe·ny Riv·er a river that flows for 325 miles (523 km) through New York and Pennsylvania to Pittsburgh where it joins the Monongahela River to form the Ohio River.

al·le·giance /ə'lējəns/ ▶*n.* loyalty or commitment of a subordinate to a superior or of an individual to a group or cause: *those wishing to receive citizenship must* **swear allegiance to** *the republic* | *a complex pattern of cross-party allegiances.* ▷late Middle English: from Anglo-Norman French, variant of Old French *ligeance*, from *lige, liege* (see **LIEGE**), perhaps by association with Anglo-Latin *alligantia* 'alliance.'

al·le·gor·i·cal /ˌali'gôrikəl; -'gär-/ ▶*adj.* constituting or containing allegory: *an allegorical painting.* **—al·le·gor·ic** *adj.* **—al·le·gor·i·cal·ly** *adv.*

al·le·go·rize /'aligəˌrīz/ ▶*v.* [*trans.*] interpret or represent symbolically: *the picture is interpreted as allegorizing an alienated society.* **—al·le·go·ri·za·tion** /ˌaliˌgôri'zāshən/ *n.*

al·le·go·ry /'aləˌgôrē/ ▶*n.* (*pl.* **-ries**) a story, poem, or picture that can be interpreted to reveal a hidden meaning, typically a moral or political one: *Pilgrim's Progress is an allegory of the spiritual journey.* ■ the genre to which such works belong. ■ a symbol. ▷late Middle English: from Old French *allegorie*, via Latin from Greek *allēgoria*, from *allos* 'other' + *-agoria* 'speaking.' **—al·le·go·rist** /-ist/ *n.*

al·le·gret·to /ˌali'gretō/ *Music* ▶*adj.* & *adv.* (esp. as a direction) at a fairly brisk tempo.
▶*n.* (*pl.* **-tos**) a movement or piece to be played fairly briskly. ▷Italian, diminutive of **ALLEGRO**.

al·le·gro /ə'legrō/ *Music* ▶*adj.* & *adv.* (esp. as a direction) at a brisk tempo.
▶*n.* (*pl.* **-gros**) a passage or movement in an allegro tempo. ▷Italian, literally 'lively, gay.'

al·lele /ə'lēl/ ▶*n.* *Genetics* one of two or more alternative forms of a gene that arise by mutation and are found at the same place on a chromosome. Also called **ALLELOMORPH**. ▷1930s: from German *Allel*, abbreviation of **ALLELOMORPH**. **—al·lel·ic** /ə'lēlik; ə'lel-/ *adj.*

al·le·lo·chem·i·cal /əˌlēlō'kemikəl; ə'lel-/ ▶*n.* a chemical produced by a living organism, exerting a detrimental physiological effect on the individuals of another species when released into the environment. ▷1970s: from Greek *allēl-* 'one another' + **CHEMICAL**.

al·le·lo·morph /əˌlēlə'môrf; əˌlel-/ ▶*n.* another term for **ALLELE**. ▷early 20th cent.: from Greek *allēl-* 'one another' + *morphē* 'form.' **—al·le·lo·mor·phic** /-'môrfik/ *adj.*

al·le·lop·a·thy /əlē'läpəthē; ˌalə-/ ▶*n.* the chemical inhibition of one plant (or other organism) by another, due to the release into the environment of substances acting as germination or growth inhibitors. ▷1950s: from Greek *allēl-* 'one another' + **-PATHY**.

al·le·lu·ia /ˌalə'lo͞oyə/ ▶*exclam.* variant spelling of **HALLELUJAH**. ▷Old English, via ecclesiastical Latin from Greek *allēlouia* (in the Septuagint), from Hebrew *hallĕlūyāh* 'praise ye the Lord.'

al·le·mande /'aləˌmand; -ˌmänd/ ▶*n.* any of a number of German dances. ■ the music for any of these, esp. as a movement of a suite. ■ a figure in country dancing in which adjacent dancers link arms or join or touch hands and make a full or partial turn. ▷late 16th cent.: from French, 'German (dance).'

all-em·brac·ing ▶*adj.* including or covering everything or everyone; comprehensive: *the goal is not one all-embracing religion.*

Al·len[1] /'alən/, Ethan (1738–89), American soldier. He fought the British in the American Revolution and led the Green Mountain Boys in their campaign to gain independence for the state of Vermont. He died two years before Vermont achieved statehood.

Al·len[2], Gracie (*c.*1902–64), U.S. comedian and television actress. She was the wife and comedy partner of George Burns.

Al·len[3], Steve (1921–2000), U.S. television pioneer, humorist, and songwriter; full name *Stephen Valentine Patrick William Allen.*. He was host and creator of "The Tonight Show" (1954–57) and host of "The Steve Allen Show" (1956–64). He also appeared in the movie *The Benny Goodman Story* (1963).

Al·len[4], Woody (1935–), U.S. movie director, writer, and actor; born *Allen Stewart Konigsberg.* Allen stars in most of his movies, many of which have won Academy Awards and which humorously explore themes of neuroses and sexual inadequacy. Notable works: *Bananas* (1971), *Play it Again, Sam* (1972), *Sleeper* (1973), *Annie Hall* (1977), *Hannah and Her Sisters* (1986), *Crimes and Misdemeanors* (1989), and *Small Time Crooks* (2000).

Al·len·by /'alənbē/, Edmund Henry Hynman, 1st Viscount (1861–1936), British soldier. Commander of the Egyptian Expeditionary Force against the Turks, he captured Jerusalem in 1917 and defeated the Turkish forces at Megiddo in 1918.

Al·len·de /ä'yenˌdā/, Salvador (1908–73), Chilean statesman; president 1970–73. The first avowed Marxist to win a presidency in a free election, he was overthrown and killed in a military coup.

Al·len·stein /'älənˌshtīn/ German name for **OLSZTYN**.

Al·len·town /'alənˌtoun/ a commercial and industrial city in eastern Pennsylvania, on the Lehigh River; pop. 106,632.

Al·len wrench (also **al·len wrench**) ▶*n.* an L-shaped metal bar with a hexagonal head at each end, used to turn bolts and screws having hexagonal sockets. ▷1960s: from the name of the manufacturer, the *Allen* Manufacturing Company, of Hartford, Connecticut.

al·ler·gen /'alərjən/ ▶*n.* a substance that causes an allergic reaction. ▷early 20th cent.: blend of **ALLERGY** and **-GEN**. **—al·ler·gen·ic** /ˌalər'jenik/ *adj.* **—al·ler·ge·nic·i·ty** /ˌalərjə'nisitē/ *n.*

al·ler·gic /ə'lərjik/ ▶*adj.* caused by or relating to an allergy: *an allergic reaction to penicillin.* ■ having an allergy to (a substance): *Heather was* **allergic to** *the sting of bees.* ■ (**allergic to**) *informal* having a strong dislike for: *it's just that I'm allergic to the hype.*

al·ler·gist /'alərjist/ ▶*n.* a medical practitioner specializing in the diagnosis and treatment of allergies.

al·ler·gy /'alərjē/ ▶*n.* (*pl.* **-gies**) a damaging immune response by the body to a substance, esp. pollen, fur, a particular food, or dust, to which it has become hypersensitive. ■ *informal* an antipathy: *their* **allergy to** *free enterprise.* ▷early 20th cent.: from German *Allergie*, from Greek *allos* 'other,' on the pattern of *Energie* 'energy.'

Al·le·rød /'aləˌro͝od; -ˌrœd/ ▶*n.* (**the Allerød**) *Geology* the second climatic stage of the late-glacial period in northern Europe, between the two Dryas stages (about 12,000 to 10,800 years ago). It was an interlude of warmer weather marked by the spread of birch, pine, and willow. ▷1920s: place name near Copenhagen in Denmark.

al·le·vi·ate /ə'lēvēˌāt/ ▶*v.* [*trans.*] make (suffering, deficiency, or a problem) less severe: *he couldn't prevent her pain, only alleviate it* | *measures to alleviate unemployment.* ▷late Middle English: from late Latin *alleviat-* 'lightened,' from the verb *alleviare*, from Latin *allevare*, from *ad-* 'to' + *levare* 'raise,' influenced by *levis* 'light.' **—al·le·vi·a·tion** /əˌlēvē'āshən/ *n.* **—al·le·vi·a·tor** /-ˌātər/ *n.*

THE RIGHT WORD **abate, allay, alleviate, assuage, mitigate, relieve, temper**

To **alleviate** is to make something easier to endure (*alleviate the pain following surgery*); **allay** is often used interchangeably, but it also means to put to rest, to quiet or calm (*to allay their suspicions*).

Assuage and *allay* both suggest the calming or satisfying of a desire or appetite, but *assuage* implies a more complete or permanent satisfaction (*we allay our hunger by nibbling hors d'oeuvres, but a huge dinner assuages our appetite*).

To **relieve** implies reducing the misery or discomfort to the point where something is bearable (*relieve the monotony of the cross-country bus trip*), and **mitigate**, which comes from a Latin word meaning to soften, usually means to lessen in force or intensity (*mitigate the storm's impact*).

Abate suggests a progressive lessening in degree or intensity (*her fever was abating*).

To **temper** is to soften or moderate (*to temper justice with mercy*), but it can also mean the exact opposite: to harden or toughen something (*tempering steel; a body tempered by lifting weights*).

al·ley[1] /'alē/ ▶*n.* (*pl.* **-leys**) a narrow passageway between or behind buildings. ■ a path lined with trees, bushes, or stones. Compare with **ALLÉE**. ■ [with *modifier*] a long, narrow area in which games such as bowling are played. ■ *Tennis* either of the two areas of the court between the doubles sideline and the singles or service sideline. ■ *Baseball* the area between the outfielders in left center or right center field. ▷late Middle English: from Old French *alee* 'walking or passage,' from *aler* 'go,' from Latin *ambulare* 'to walk.'
▶***PHRASE*** □ **up one's alley** (or **right up one's alley**) *informal* well suited to one's tastes, interests, or abilities: *this job would be right up your alley.*

al·ley[2] (also **al·ly**) ▶*n.* (*pl.* **-leys**) a toy marble made of marble, alabaster, or glass. ▷early 18th cent.: perhaps a diminutive of **ALABASTER**.

al·ley cat ▶*n.* a cat that lives wild in a town.

al·ley-oop /ˌalē 'o͞op/ ▶*exclam.* used to encourage or draw attention to the performance of some physical, esp. acrobatic, feat.
▶*n.* (also **alley-oop pass**) *Basketball* a high pass caught by a leaping teammate who tries to dunk the ball before landing. ▷early 20th cent.: perhaps from French *allez!* 'go on!' (expressing encouragement) + a supposedly French pronunciation of **UP**.

al·ley·way /'alēˌwā/ ▶*n.* another term for **ALLEY**[1].

all-fired *informal* ▶*adv.* *informal* extremely: *if I was so all-fired bright . . . why did I have to keep learning this same thing over and over?*
▶*adj.* extreme.

All Fools' Day *n.* another term for **APRIL FOOL'S DAY**.

all fours ▶*n.* a card game, now rarely played, in which points are scored for being dealt the highest or lowest trump, capturing the jack of trump, and taking the highest value of cards in tricks.
▶***PHRASE*** □ **on all fours** on hands and knees or (of an animal) on all four legs rather than just the hind ones: *Frankie scuttled away on all fours.*

all hail ▶*excl.* *dated* a cry of greeting.

All Hal·lows *n.* another term for **ALL SAINTS' DAY**.

all·heal /'ôlˌhēl/ ▶*n.* any of a number of plants, in particular valerian, used in herbal medicine and traditionally considered to be effective in treating a variety of conditions.

al·li·a·ceous /ˌalē'āshəs/ ▶*adj.* *Botany* of, relating to, or denoting plants of a group that comprises the onions and other alliums. ▷late 18th cent.: from Latin *allium* 'garlic' + **-ACEOUS**; compare with the modern Latin taxonomic family name *Alliaceae.*

al·li·ance /ə'līəns/ ▶*n.* a union or association formed for mutual benefit, esp. between countries or organizations: *a defensive alliance between Australia and New Zealand* | *divisions within the alliance.* ■ a relationship based on an affinity in interests, nature, or qualities: *an alliance between medicine and morality.* ■ a state of being joined or associated: *his party is* **in alliance with** *the Greens.* ▷Middle English: from Old French *aliance*, from *aliere* 'to ally' (see **ALLY**[1]).

al·li·cin /'alisin/ ▶*n.* *Chemistry* a pungent oily liquid with antibacterial properties, present in garlic. • Chem. formula: $(C_3H_5S)_2O$. ▷from Latin *allium* 'garlic' + **-IN**[1].

al·lied /ə'līd; 'alˌīd/ ▶*adj.* joined by or relating to members of an alliance: *allied territories* | *the allied fleet.* ■ (usu. **Allied**) of or relating to the U.S. and its allies in World War I and World War II and after: *the liberation of Paris by Allied troops.* ■ (**allied to/with**) in combination or working together with: *skilled craftsmanship allied to advanced technology.* ■ connected or related: *members of the medical and allied professions.*

Al·lier /äl'yā/ a river in central France that rises in the Cévennes Mountains and flows northwest for 258 miles (410 km) to meet the Loire River.

al·li·ga·tor /'aliˌgātər/ ▶*n.* a large semiaquatic reptile similar to a crocodile but with a broader and shorter head, native to the Americas and China. • Genus *Alligator*, family Alligatoridae, order Crocodylia: the **American alligator** (*A. mississippiensis*) and the

Chinese alligator (*A. sinensis*). ■ the skin of the alligator or material resembling it. ▷late 16th cent.: from Spanish *el lagarto* 'the lizard,' probably based on Latin *lacerta*.

alligator

al·li·ga·tor clip ▸*n.* a sprung metal clip with long, serrated jaws, used attached to an electric cable for making a temporary connection to a battery or other component.

alligator clip

al·li·ga·tor fish ▸*n.* a slender bottom-dwelling fish of the northwestern Atlantic, with an armor of bony plates and two curved spines on the snout. • *Aspidophoroides monopterygius*, family Agonidae.

al·li·ga·tor liz·ard ▸*n.* a short-limbed, long-tailed, slim lizard native to North America and Mexico. • Genus *Gerrhonotus*, family Anguidae: several species, including the **northern alligator lizard** (*G. coerulus*) and the **panamint alligator lizard** (*G. panamintinus*).

al·li·ga·tor pear ▸*n.* another term for AVOCADO.

al·li·ga·tor snap·ping tur·tle (also **al·li·ga·tor snap·per**) ▸*n.* a large-headed, long-tailed snapping turtle of the southeastern U.S., found esp. in the Gulf States. Weighing up to 150 pounds (67.5 kg), it is the largest freshwater turtle in North America. • *Macroclemys temminckii*, family Chelydridae.

all-im·por·tant ▸*adj.* vitally important; crucial: *the town's all-important tourist industry.*

all-in·clu·sive ▸*adj.* including everything or everyone: *the tab for the all-inclusive dinner is $38.*

all-in-one ▸*adj.* [*attrib.*] combining two or more items or functions in a single unit: *an all-in-one shampoo/conditioner.*

al·lit·er·ate /əˈlitəˌrāt/ ▸*v.* [*intrans.*] (of a phrase or line of verse) contain words that begin with the same sound or letter: *his first and last names alliterated.* ■ use words that begin with the same sound or letter. ▷late 18th cent.: back-formation from ALLITERATION.

al·lit·er·a·tion /əˌlitəˈrāSHən/ ▸*n.* the occurrence of the same letter or sound at the beginning of adjacent or closely connected words. ▷early 17th cent.: from medieval Latin *alliteratio(n-)*, from Latin *ad-* (expressing addition) + *littera* 'letter.'

al·lit·er·a·tive /əˈlitərətiv; -ˌrātiv/ ▸*adj.* relating to or marked by alliteration. **—al·lit·er·a·tive·ly** *adv.*

al·li·um /ˈalēəm/ ▸*n.* (*pl.* **-ums**) a bulbous plant of a genus that includes the onion and its relatives (e.g., garlic, leek, and chives). • Genus *Allium*, family Liliaceae (or Alliaceae). ▷early 19th cent.: Latin, literally 'garlic.'

all-night ▸*adj.* [*attrib.*] lasting, open, or operating throughout the night: *an all-night party.*

all-night·er /ˌôl ˈnītər/ ▸*n. informal* an event or task that continues throughout the night, esp. a study session before an examination: *he would do an all-nighter, the way he used to in school.*

allo- ▸*comb. form* other; different: *allopatric* | *allotrope.* ▷from Greek *allos* 'other.'

al·lo·cate /ˈaləˌkāt/ ▸*v.* [*trans.*] distribute (resources or duties) for a particular purpose: *the authorities allocated 50,000 places to refugees* | [with *two objs.*] *he has been allocated a generous slice of the annual budget.* ▷mid 17th cent.: from medieval Latin *allocat-* 'allotted,' from the verb *allocare*, from *ad-* 'to' + *locare* (see LOCATE). **—al·lo·ca·ble** /-kəbəl/ *adj.* **—al·lo·ca·tor** /-ˌkātər/ *n.*

al·lo·ca·tion /ˌaləˈkāSHən/ ▸*n.* the action or process of allocating or distributing something: *more efficient allocation of resources* | *ticket allocation.* ■ an amount or portion of a resource assigned to a particular recipient. ▷late Middle English: from medieval Latin *allocatio(n-)*, from the verb *allocare* (see ALLOCATE). **—al·lo·ca·tive** /ˈaləˌkātiv/ *adj. chiefly Economics* .

al·loch·tho·nous /əˈläkTHənəs/ ▸*adj. Geology* denoting sediment or rock that originated at a distance from its present position. Often contrasted with AUTOCHTHONOUS. ▷early 20th cent.: from ALLO- 'other' + Greek *khthōn* 'earth' + -OUS.

al·lo·cu·tion /ˌaləˈkyo͞oSHən/ ▸*n.* a formal speech giving advice or a warning. ▷early 17th cent.: from Latin *allocutio(n-)*, from *alloqui* 'speak to,' from *ad-* 'to' + *loqui* 'speak.'

al·log·a·my /əˈlägəmē/ ▸*n. Botany* the fertilization of a flower by pollen from another flower, esp. one on a different plant. Compare with AUTOGAMY. ▷late 19th cent.: from ALLO- 'other, different' + Greek *-gamia* (from *gamos* 'marriage'). **—al·log·a·mous** /-məs/ *adj.*

al·lo·ge·ne·ic /ˌaləjəˈnē-ik/ ▸*adj. Immunology* denoting, relating to, or involving tissues or cells that are genetically dissimilar and hence immunologically incompatible, although from individuals of the same species. Compare with XENOGENEIC. ▷1960s: from ALLO- 'different' + Greek *genea* 'race, stock' + -IC.

al·lo·gen·ic /ˌaləˈjenik/ ▸*adj.* **1** *Geology* (of a mineral or sediment) transported to its present position from elsewhere. Often contrasted with AUTHIGENIC. **2** *Ecology* (of a successional change) caused by nonliving factors in the environment.

al·lo·graft /ˈaləˌgraft/ ▸*n.* a tissue graft from a donor of the same species as the recipient but not genetically identical. Compare with HOMOGRAFT.

al·lo·graph /ˈaləˌgraf/ ▸*n. Linguistics* each of two or more alternative forms of a letter of an alphabet or other grapheme. The capital, lowercase, italic, and various handwritten forms of the letter A are allographs. ■ *Phonetics* each of two or more letters or letter-combinations representing a single phoneme in different words. Allographs of the phoneme include the (f) of "fake" and the (ph) of "phase." ▷1950s: from ALLO- 'other, different' + GRAPHEME.

al·lom·e·try /əˈlämitrē/ ▸*n. Biology* the growth of body parts at different rates, resulting in a change of body proportions. ■ the study of such growth. **—al·lo·met·ric** /ˌaləˈmetrik/ *adj.*

al·lo·morph /ˈaləˌmôrf/ ▸*n. Linguistics* any of the versions of a morpheme, such as the plural endings /s/ (as in *bats*), /z/ (as in *bugs*), and /iz/ (as in *buses*) for the plural morpheme. ▷1940s: from ALLO- 'other, different' + MORPHEME. **—al·lo·mor·phic** /ˌaləˈmôrfik/ *adj.*

al·lo·path /ˈaləˌpaTH/ ▸*n.* a person who practices allopathy.

al·lop·a·thy /əˈläpəTHē/ ▸*n.* the treatment of disease by conventional means, i.e., with drugs having opposite effects to the symptoms. Often contrasted with HOMEOPATHY. **—al·lo·path·ic** /ˌaləˈpaTHik/ *adj.* **—al·lop·a·thist** /-THist/ *n.*

al·lo·pat·ric /ˌaləˈpatrik/ ▸*adj. Biology* (of animals or plants, esp. of related species or populations) occurring in separate nonoverlapping geographical areas. Compare with SYMPATRIC. ■ (of speciation) taking place as a result of such separation. ▷1940s: from ALLO- 'other' + Greek *patra* 'fatherland' + -IC. **—al·lop·a·try** /ˈaləˌpatrē/ *n.*

al·lo·phone /ˈaləˌfōn/ ▸*n. Linguistics* any of the speech sounds that represent a single phoneme, such as the aspirated *k* in *kit* and the unaspirated *k* in *skit*, which are allophones of the phoneme *k*. ▷1930s: from ALLO- 'other, different' + PHONEME. **—al·lo·phon·ic** /ˌaləˈfänik/ *adj.*

al·lo·pu·ri·nol /aləˈpyo͝oriˌnôl; -ˌnäl/ ▸*n. Medicine* a synthetic drug that inhibits uric acid formation in the body and is used to treat gout and related conditions. ▷1960s: from ALLO- 'other' + PURINE + -OL.

all-or-none ▸*adj.* another way of saying ALL-OR-NOTHING. ■ *Physiology* (of a response) having a strength independent of the strength of the stimulus that caused it.

all-or-noth·ing ▸*adj.* having no middle position or compromise available: *an all-or-nothing decision.*

al·lo·saur /ˈaləˌsôr/ (also **al·lo·sau·rus** /ˌaləˈsôrəs/) ▸*n.* a large bipedal carnivorous dinosaur of the late Jurassic period. • Genus *Allosaurus*, suborder Theropoda, order Saurischia. ▷modern Latin, from Greek *allos* 'other' + *sauros* 'lizard.' **—al·lo·sau·ri·an** *adj.*

al·lo·sta·sis /ˌaləˈstāsis/ ▸*n.* the process by which the body responds to stressors in order to regain homeostasis. **—al·lo·sta·tic** /-ˈstatik/ *adj.*

al·lo·ster·ic /ˌaləˈsterik; -ˈsti(ə)r-/ ▸*adj. Biochemistry* relating to or denoting the alteration of the activity of a protein through the binding of an effector molecule at a specific site. **—al·lo·ster·i·cal·ly** *adv.*

al·lot /əˈlät/ ▸*v.* (**-lot·ted, -lot·ting**) [*trans.*] give or apportion (something) to someone as a share or task: *equal time was allotted to each* | [with *two objs.*] *I was allotted a little room in the servants' block.* ▷late 15th cent.: from Old French *aloter*, from *a-* (from Latin *ad* 'to') + *loter* 'divide into lots.'

al·lot·ment /əˈlätmənt/ ▸*n.* the amount of something allocated to a particular person: *the gadget shuts off the television set when a kid has used up his allotment.* ■ *chiefly historical* a piece of land deeded by the government to an American Indian. ■ the action of allotting: *the allotment of equity securities.*

al·lo·trope /ˈaləˌtrōp/ ▸*n. Chemistry* each of two or more different physical forms in which an element can exist. Graphite, charcoal, and diamond are all allotropes of carbon. ▷late 19th cent.: back-formation from ALLOTROPY.

al·lot·ro·py /əˈlätrəpē/ ▸*n. Chemistry* the existence of two or more different physical forms of a chemical element. ▷mid 19th cent.: from Greek *allotropos* 'of another form,' from *allo-* 'other' + *tropos* 'manner' (from *trepein* 'to turn'). **—al·lo·trop·ic** /ˌaləˈträpik; -ˈtrō-/ *adj.*

al·lot·tee /ˌaləˈtē; əˌläˈtē/ ▸*n.* a person to whom something is allotted, esp. land or shares.

all-ov·er ▸*adj.* [*attrib.*] covering the whole of something: *a carpet with an all-over pattern.*

al·low /əˈlou/ ▸*v.* [*trans.*] **1** admit (an event or activity) as legal or acceptable: *a plan to allow Sunday shopping* | *a reservoir with no hunting or overnight camping allowed.* ■ [*trans.*] give (someone) permission to do something: *the dissident was allowed to leave the country.* ■ [*trans.*, with *two objs.*] permit (someone) to have (something): *he was allowed his first sip of Scotch and soda.* ■ [*trans.*] permit (someone) to enter a place or go in a particular direction: *the river was patrolled and few people were allowed across.* ■ [*trans.*] fail to prevent (something) from happening: *I could not believe that we would allow the opportunity to slip away.* **2** give the necessary time or opportunity for: *they agreed to a cease-fire to allow talks with the government* | [*trans.*] *he stopped for a moment to allow his eyes to adjust* | [*intrans.*] *dated my household duties were too many to* **allow of** *a visit to the hospital.* ■ [*intrans.*] (**allow for**) make provision or provide scope for (something): *the house was demolished to allow for road widening.* ■ [*intrans.*] (**allow for**) take (something) into consideration when making plans or calculations: *income rose by 11 percent allowing for inflation.* ■ [*trans.*] provide or set aside (a specified amount of something) for a specific purpose: *allow an hour or so for driving.* **3** [*reporting verb*] admit the truth of; concede: [with *clause*] *he* **allowed that** *the penalty appeared too harsh for the crime* | [with *direct speech*] *"Could happen," she allowed indifferently.* ■ [with *clause*] *informal or dialect* assert; be of the opinion: *Lincoln* **allowed that** *he himself could never support the man.* ▷Middle English (originally in the senses 'commend, sanction' and 'assign as a right'): from Old French *alouer*, from Latin *allaudare* 'to praise,' reinforced by medieval Latin *allocare* 'to place' (see ALLOCATE). **—al·low·a·ble** *adj.* **—al·low·a·bly** /-əblē/ *adv.*

al·low·ance /əˈlou-əns/ ▸*n.* the amount of something that is permitted, esp. within a set of regulations or for a specified purpose: *a seventy-five-pound baggage allowance.* ■ a sum of money paid regularly to a person, typically to meet specified needs or expenses. ■ a small amount of money that a parent regularly gives a child. ■ an amount of money that can be earned or received free of tax: *a personal allowance.* ■ a reduction in price, typically for the exchange of used goods: *he made the down payment with the trade-in allowance.* ■ *Horse Racing* a deduction in the weight that a horse is required to carry in a race. ■ *archaic* tolerance; sufferance: *the allowance of slavery in the South.*

▸*v.* [*trans.*] *archaic* give (someone) a sum of money regularly as an allowance. ▷late Middle English: from Old French *alouance*, from *alouer* (see ALLOW).

▸*PHRASE* □ **make allowance(s) for 1** take into consideration when planning or making calculations: *a special circuit makes allowances for changes in the ambient temperature.* **2** regard or treat leniently on account of mitigating circumstances: *she liked them and made allowances for their faults.*

al·low·ed·ly /əˈlou-idlē/ ▸*adv.* [*sentence adverb*] as is generally admitted to be true.

al·lox·an /əˈläksən/ ▸*n. Chemistry* an acidic compound obtained by the oxidation of uric acid and isolated as an efflorescent crystalline hydrate. • Chem. formula: $C_4H_2N_2O_4$. ▷mid 19th cent.: from *all(antoin)* + *ox(alic)* + **-AN.**

al·loy ▸*n.* /ˈaˌloi/ a metal made by combining two or more metallic elements, esp. to give greater strength or resistance to corrosion: *an alloy of nickel, bronze, and zinc* | *flat pieces of alloy* | [as *adj.*] *alloy wheels.* ■ an inferior metal mixed with a precious one.
▸*v.* /ˈaˌloi; əˈloi/ [*trans.*] mix (metals) to make an alloy: *alloying tin with copper to make bronze.* ■ *figurative* debase (something) by adding something inferior. ▷late 16th cent.: from Old French *aloi* (noun) and French *aloyer* (verb), both from Old French *aloier, aleier* 'combine,' from Latin *alligare* 'bind.'

all-par·ty ▸*adj.* [*attrib.*] involving all political parties: *the measure received all-party support.*

all-per·vad·ing (also **all-per·va·sive**) ▸*adj.* having an effect on everything or throughout something: *the all-pervading excitement.*

all-points bul·le·tin (abbr.: **APB**) ▸*n.* a radio message sent to every officer in a police force giving details of a suspected criminal or stolen vehicle.

all-pow·er·ful ▸*adj.* having complete power; almighty: *an all-powerful dictator.*

all-pur·pose ▸*adj.* having many uses, esp. all that might be expected from something of its type: *an all-purpose kitchen knife.*

all right ▸*adj.* satisfactory but not especially good; acceptable: *the tea was all right.* ■ (of a person) in a satisfactory mental or physical state: *"Are you all right? You were screaming."* ■ permissible; allowable: *it's all right for you to go now.*
▸*adv.* **1** in a satisfactory manner or to a satisfactory extent; fairly well: *everything will turn out all right.* **2** used to emphasize how certain one is about something: *"Are you sure it's him?" "It's him all right."*
▸*exclam.* expressing or asking for assent, agreement, or acceptance: *all right, I'll tell you.*

USAGE See usage at **ALRIGHT.**

all-round ▸*adj.* British term for **ALL-AROUND.**

All Saints' Day ▸*n.* a Christian festival in honor of all the saints, held (in the Western Church) on November 1.

all·seed /ˈôlˌsēd/ ▸*n.* any of a number of plants producing a great deal of seed for their size, such as knotgrass and goosefoot.

All Souls' Day ▸*n.* a festival in some Christian churches with prayers for the souls of the dead, held on November 2.

all·spice /ˈôlˌspīs/ ▸*n.* **1** the dried aromatic fruit of a West Indian tree, used whole or ground as a culinary spice. **2** a tree of the myrtle family from which this spice is obtained. Also called **PIMENTO.** • *Pimenta dioica*, family Myrtaceae. **3** an aromatic North American tree or shrub. • Genus *Calycanthus*, family Calycanthaceae: several species, in particular **Carolina allspice** (*C. floridus*) and **smooth allspice** (*C. fertilis*).

all-star ▸*adj.* [*attrib.*] composed wholly of outstanding performers or players: *an all-star cast.*
▸*n.* a member of such a group or team.

All·ston /ˈôlstən/, Washington (1779–1843), U.S. landscape painter. The first major artist of the American romantic movement, his paintings exhibit a taste for the monumental, apocalyptic, and melodramatic. Notable works: *The Deluge* (1804), *Belshazzar's Feast* (1817–43), and *Moonlit Landscape* (1819).

all-ter·rain ve·hi·cle (abbr.: **ATV**) ▸*n.* a small open motor vehicle with one or two seats and three or more wheels fitted with large tires, designed for use on rough ground.

all-time ▸*adj.* [*attrib.*] unsurpassed: *all-time favorite* | *interest rates hit an all-time high.*

al·lude /əˈlo͞od/ ▸*v.* [*intrans.*] (**allude to**) suggest or call attention to indirectly; hint at: *she had a way of alluding to Jean but never saying her name.* ■ mention without discussing at length: *we will allude briefly to the main points.* ■ (of an artist or a work of art) recall (an earlier work or style) in such a way as to suggest a relationship with it: *the photographs allude to Italian Baroque painting.* ▷late 15th cent. (in the sense 'hint at, suggest'): from Latin *alludere*, from *ad-* 'toward' + *ludere* 'to play.'

al·lure /əˈlo͝or/ ▸*n.* the quality of being powerfully and mysteriously attractive or fascinating: *people for whom gold holds no allure.*
▸*v.* [*trans.*] powerfully attract or charm; tempt: [as *adj.*] (**alluring**) *the town offers alluring shops and restaurants.* See note at **TEMPT.** ▷late Middle English (in the sense 'tempt, entice'): from Old French *aleurier* 'attract,' from *a-* (from Latin *ad* 'to') + *luere* 'a lure' (originally a falconry term). **—al·lure·ment** *n.* **—al·lur·ing·ly** *adv.*

al·lu·sion /əˈlo͞ozhən/ ▸*n.* an expression designed to call something to mind without mentioning it explicitly; an indirect or passing reference: ***an allusion** to Shakespeare* | *a classical allusion.* ■ the practice of making such references, esp. as an artistic device. ▷mid 16th cent. (denoting a pun, metaphor, or parable): from French, or from late Latin *allusio(n-)*, from the verb *alludere* (see **ALLUDE**).

al·lu·sive /əˈlo͞osiv/ ▸*adj.* (of a remark or reference) working by suggestion rather than explicit mention: *allusive references to the body.* **—al·lu·sive·ly** *adv.* **—al·lu·sive·ness** *n.*

al·lu·vi·al /əˈlo͞ovēəl/ ▸*adj.* of, relating to or derived from alluvium: *rich alluvial soils.*

al·lu·vi·al fan ▸*n.* a fan-shaped mass of alluvium deposited as the flow of a river decreases in velocity.

al·lu·vi·on /əˈlo͞ovēən/ ▸*n.* *Law* the action of the sea or a river in forming new land by deposition. Compare with **AVULSION.** ▷mid 16th cent. (originally denoting a flood, esp. one in which the water carries suspended material that is then deposited): from French, from Latin *alluvion-*, from *ad-* 'toward' + *luere* 'to wash.'

al·lu·vi·um /əˈlo͞ovēəm/ ▸*n.* a deposit of clay, silt, sand, and gravel left by flowing streams in a river valley or delta, typically producing fertile soil. ▷mid 17th cent.: Latin, neuter of *alluvius* 'washed against,' from *ad-* 'toward' + *luere* 'to wash.'

all-weath·er ▸*adj.* including or suitable for all types of weather: *all-weather tennis courts.*

all-wheel drive ▸*n.* a transmission system that always operates in four-wheel drive and does not alternate with two-wheel drive.

al·ly[1] ▸*n.* /ˈalī/ (*pl.* **-lies**) a state formally cooperating with another for a military or other purpose, typically by treaty. ■ a person or organization that cooperates with or helps another in a particular activity: *he was forced to dismiss his closest political ally.* ■ (**the Allies**) a group of nations taking military action together, in particular the countries that fought with the U.S. in World War I and World War II.
▸*v.* /əˈlī/ (**-lies, -lied**) [*trans.*] (**ally something to/with**) combine or unite a resource or commodity with (another) for mutual benefit: *he allied his racing experience with his father's business acumen.* ■ (**ally oneself with**) side with or support (someone or something): *he allied himself with the forces of change.* ▷Middle English (as a verb): from Old French *alier*, from Latin *alligare* 'bind together,' from *ad-* 'to' + *ligare* 'to bind'; the noun is partly via Old French *alie* 'allied.' Compare with **ALLOY.**

al·ly[2] ▸*n.* (*pl.* **-lies**) variant spelling of **ALLEY**[2].

-ally ▸*suffix* forming adverbs from adjectives ending in *-al* (such as *radically* from *radical*). Compare with **-AL, -LY**[2]**, -ICALLY.**

al·lyl /ˈalil/ ▸*n.* [as *modifier*] *Chemistry* the unsaturated hydrocarbon radical $-CH{=}CHCH_2$: *allyl alcohol.* ▷mid 19th cent.: from Latin *allium* 'garlic' + **-YL. —al·lyl·ic** /əˈlilik/ *adj.*

Al·ma-A·ta variant spelling of **ALMATY.**

Al Ma·di·nah /ˌäl mäˈdēnə/ Arabic name for **MEDINA.**

Al·ma·gest /ˈalməˌjest/ ▸*n.* (**the Almagest**) an Arabic version of Ptolemy's astronomical treatise. ■ (also **almagest**) (in the Middle Ages) any celebrated textbook on astrology and alchemy. ▷late Middle English: from Old French *almageste*, based on Arabic, from *al* 'the' + Greek *megistē* 'greatest (composition).'

al·ma ma·ter /ˈälmə ˈmätər; ˈalmə/ ▸*n.* (**one's Alma Mater**) the school, college, or university that one once attended. ■ the anthem of a school, college, or university. ▷mid 17th cent. (in the general sense 'someone or something providing nourishment'): Latin, literally 'bounteous mother.'

al·ma·nac /ˈôlməˌnak; ˈal-/ (also, esp. in titles, **al·ma·nack**) ▸*n.* an annual calendar containing important dates and statistical information such as astronomical data and tide tables. ■ a handbook, typically published annually, containing information of general interest or on a sport or pastime. ▷late Middle English: via medieval Latin from Greek *almenikhiaka*, of unknown origin.

al·man·dine /ˈalmənˌdēn/ ▸*n.* a kind of garnet with a violet tint. ▷late Middle English: from obsolete French, alteration of *alabandine*, from medieval Latin *alabandina (gemma)* 'jewel from *Alabanda*,' an ancient city in Asia Minor where these stones were cut.

Al·ma·ty /ˌalməˈtē/ (also **Al·ma-A·ta** /ˌalmə əˈtä/) the capital of Kazakhstan, in the southeastern part of the republic; pop. 1,515,300. Former name (until 1921) **VERNY.**

Al·me·ría /ˌälmāˈrēə/ a town in Almeria Province in southern Spain; pop. 157,760.

al·might·y /ôlˈmītē/ ▸*adj.* having complete power; omnipotent: *God almighty.* ■ (**the Almighty**) a name or title for God: *I wanted to beg the Almighty for mercy.* ■ *informal* very great; enormous: *the silence was broken by an almighty roar.* ▷Old English *ælmihtig* (see **ALL, MIGHTY**).

Al·mo·had /ˈalməˌhad/ (also **Al·mo·hade** /-ˌhād; -ˌhad/) ▸*n.* (*pl.* **-hads**) a member of a Berber Muslim movement and dynasty that conquered the Spanish and North African empire of the Almoravids in the 12th century.

al·mond /ˈä(l)mənd; ˈa(l)-/ ▸*n.* **1** the oval nutlike seed (kernel) of the almond tree, used as food. **2** (also **almond tree**) the tree that produces this nut, belonging to the rose family and related to the peach and plum. Native to western Asia, it is widely cultivated in warm climates. • Genus *Prunus*, family Rosaceae: one species, *P. dulcis* (**sweet almond**), and a variety, *P. dulcis amara* (**bitter almond**).
▸*adj.* made of or flavored with almonds: *almond cookies.* ■ of an oval shape, pointed at one or both ends: *her almond eyes.* ■ a pale tan color, as of an almond shell: *the kitchen was done in almond.* ▷Middle English: from Old French *alemande*, from medieval Latin *amandula*, from Greek *amugdalē.*

al·mond oil ▸*n.* oil expressed from bitter almonds, used for cosmetic preparations, flavoring, and medicinal purposes.

al·mond paste ▸*n.* another term for **MARZIPAN.**

al·mon·er /ˈalmənər; ˈäm-/ ▸*n.* *historical* an official distributor of alms. ▷Middle English: from Old French *aumonier*, based on medieval Latin *eleemosynarius*, from *eleemosyna* 'alms' (see **ALMS**).

al·mon·ry /ˈalmənrē; ˈäm-/ ▸*n.* (*pl.* **-ries**) a building or place where alms were formerly distributed. ▷late Middle English: from Old French *au(l)mosnerie*, from medieval Latin *eleemosynarius* (see **ALMONER**).

Al·mo·ra·vid /ˌalməˈrävid; älˈmôrə-/ (also **Al·mo·ra·vide** /-ˌvīd/) ▸*n.* (*pl.* **-vids**) a member of a federation of Muslim Berber peoples that established an empire in Morocco, Algeria, and Spain in the 11th century. They were in turn driven out by the Almohads.

al·most /ôlˈmōst; ˈôlˌmōst/ ▸*adv.* not quite; very nearly: *he almost knocked Georgina over* | *Rachel laughed, almost apologetically* | *the place was almost empty* | *it will eat almost anything* | *the storm was almost upon them.* ▷Old English *æl mæst* 'for the most part' (see **ALL, MOST**).

alms /ä(l)mz/ ▸*plural n.* (in historical contexts) money or food given to poor people. ▷Old English *ælmysse, ælmesse*, from Christian Latin *eleemosyna*, from Greek *eleēmosunē* 'compassion,' from *eleēmōn* 'compassionate,' from *eleos* 'mercy.'

alms·house /ˈä(l)mzˌhous/ ▸*n.* a house built originally by a charitable person or organization for poor people to live in.

al-Nak·ba /al ˈnakbä/ ▸*n.* the Arabic term for the events of 1948, when many Palestinians were displaced from their homeland by the creation of the new state of Israel. ▷from Arabic, literally 'the disaster.'

al·oe /ˈalō/ ▸*n.* **1** a succulent plant, typically having a rosette of toothed fleshy leaves and bell-shaped or tubular flowers on long stems. Native to the Old World tropics, several species are cultivated commercially or as ornamentals. • Genus *Aloe*, family Liliaceae (or Aloaceae). ■ (**aloes** or **bitter aloes**) a strong laxative obtained from the bitter juice of various kinds of aloe. ■ (also **American aloe**) another term for **CENTURY PLANT.** **2** (**aloes**) (also **aloeswood**) the fragrant heartwood of a tropical Asian tree. • The wood is obtained from two trees of the genus *Aquilaria*, family Thymelaeaceae, esp. *A. agallocha.* ■ the resin obtained from this wood, used in perfume, incense, and medicine. ▷Old English *alewe, alwe* (denoting the fragrant resin or heartwood of certain Oriental trees), via Latin from Greek *aloē*; reinforced in late Middle English by Old French *aloes* 'aloe,' hence frequently used in the plural.

al·oe ver·a /ˈalō ˈverə; ˈvi(ə)rə/ ▸*n.* **1** a gelatinous substance obtained from a kind of aloe, used esp. in cosmetics as an emollient and for the treatment of burns. **2** the plant that yields this substance, grown chiefly in the Caribbean area and the southern U.S. • *Aloe vera*, family Liliaceae (or Aloaceae). ▷early 20th cent.: modern Latin, literally 'true aloe,' probably in contrast to the American agave, which closely resembles aloe vera: both plants were formerly classified together in the lily family.

a·loft /ə'lôft/ ▸*adj.* [*predic.*] & *adv.* up in or into the air; overhead: *the congregation sways, hands aloft* | [as *adv.*] *she held her glass aloft.* ■ up the mast or into the rigging of a sailing vessel. ▷Middle English: from Old Norse *á lopt, á lopti,* from *á* 'in, on, to' + *lopt* 'air.'

a·log·i·cal /ā'läjikəl/ ▸*adj.* opposed to or lacking in logic.

A·lo·ha /ə'lō,hä/ a community in northwestern Oregon, west of Portland; pop. 34,284.

a·lo·ha /ə'lō,hä/ ▸*exclam.* & *n.* Hawaiian word used when greeting or parting from someone.

a·lo·ha shirt ▸*n.* a loose, brightly patterned Hawaiian shirt.

A·lo·ha State a nickname for the state of HAWAII.

a·lone /ə'lōn/ ▸*adj.* & *adv.* **1** having no one else present; on one's own: [as *predic. adj.*] *she was alone that evening* | [as *adv.*] *he lives alone.* ■ without others' help or participation; single-handed: *team members are more effective than individuals working alone.* ■ [as *adj.*] isolated and lonely: *she was terribly alone and exposed.* ■ having no companions in a particular position or course of action: *they were* **not alone** *in dissenting from the advice.* **2** [as *adv.*] indicating that something is confined to the specified subject or recipient: *we agreed to set up such a test for him alone* | *it is Congress alone that can declare war.* ■ used to emphasize that only one factor out of several is being considered and that the whole is greater or more extreme: *there were fifteen churches in the town center alone.* ▷Middle English: from ALL + ONE. **—a·lone·ness** /ə'lōn(n)əs/ *n.*

▸*PHRASES* □ **go it alone** *informal* act by oneself without assistance. □ **leave** (or **let**) **someone/something alone 1** abandon or desert someone or something. **2** stop disturbing or interfering with someone or something. □ **let alone** see LET[1].

a·long /ə'lông; ə'läng/ ▸*prep.* **1** moving in a constant direction on (a path or any more or less horizontal surface): *soon we were driving along a narrow road* | *he saw Gary run along the top of the wall* | [as *adv.*] *she sailed along* | *we continued to plod along.* ■ used metaphorically to refer to the passage of time or the making of progress: *they can be helped along the road to modernity* | *we passed along snatches of information* | *you'll pick up some valuable tips along the way* [as *adv.*] *they asked how the construction was coming along.* **2** extending in a more or less horizontal line on: *cars were parked along the grass border* | *the path along the cliff* | *hotels are springing up all along the coast.*

▸*adv.* in or into company with others: *he had brought along a friend of his* | *I went along to see Ray.* ■ at hand; with one: *take along a camcorder when you visit.* ▷Old English *andlang*; related to LONG[1].

▸*PHRASES* □ **along about** *informal* or *dialect* around about (a specified time or date): *he generally leaves there along about daylight.* □ **along of** *archaic* or *dialect* **1** on account of: *the trouble I've had along of that lady's crankiness.* **2** with: *you'll have to make a break for it along of me.* □ **along the lines (of)** in conformity with: *a highway patrol organized along the lines of the New Jersey State Police.* □ **along with** in company with or at the same time as: *I was chosen, along with twelve other artists.* □ **be** (or **come**) **along** arrive: *she'll be along soon* | *a chance like this doesn't come along every day.*

a·long·shore /ə'lông'shôr; ə'läng-/ ▸*adv.* along or by the shore: *currents flowing alongshore.*

a·long·side /ə'lông'sīd; ə'läng-/ ▸*prep.* (also **alongside of**) close to the side of; next to: *she was sitting alongside him* | *the road passes alongside the viaduct* | [as *adv.*] *the boat came alongside.* ■ together and in cooperation with: *a care assistant was working alongside him.* ■ at the same time as or in coexistence with: *alongside the development of full-time courses there had to be provision for the part-time student.*

a·loof /ə'lo͞of/ ▸*adj.* not friendly or forthcoming; cool and distant: *they were courteous but faintly aloof* | *an aloof and somewhat austere figure.* ■ conspicuously uninvolved and uninterested, typically through distaste: *he stayed* **aloof from** *the bickering.* ▷mid 16th cent.: from A-[2] (expressing direction) + LUFF. The term was originally an adverb in nautical use, meaning 'away and to windward!,' i.e., with the ship's head kept close to the wind away from a lee shore, etc., toward which it might otherwise drift. From this arose the sense 'at a distance' literally or figuratively. **—a·loof·ly** *adv.* **—a·loof·ness** *n.*

al·o·pe·ci·a /,alə'pēsh(ē)ə/ ▸*n. Medicine* the partial or complete absence of hair from areas of the body where it normally grows; baldness. ▷late Middle English: via Latin from Greek *alōpekia,* literally 'fox mange,' from *alōpēx* 'fox.'

A·lor Se·tar /,al,ôr sē'tär; ,äl,ôr/ a city near the west coast of the central Malay Peninsula in Malaysia; pop. 71,682.

a·loud /ə'loud/ ▸*adv.* **1** audibly; not silently or in a whisper: *he read the letter aloud.* **2** *archaic* loudly: *he wept aloud.* ▷Middle English: from A-[2] (expressing manner) + LOUD.

a·low /ə'lō/ ▸*adv. archaic* or *dialect* below; downward. ■ *Nautical* in or into the lower part of a ship, e.g., down from the rigging, or below deck. ▷late Middle English (in nautical use since the early 16th cent.): from A-[2] 'on' + LOW[1].

alp /alp/ ▸*n.* a high mountain, esp. a snowcapped one. ■ (in Switzerland) an area of green pasture on a mountainside. ▷late Middle English: singular of ALPS.

alpaca

al·pac·a /al'pakə/ ▸*n.* (*pl.* same or **-pac·as**) a long-haired domesticated South American mammal related to the llama, valued for its wool. • *Lama pacos,* family Camelidae, probably descended from the wild guanaco. ■ the wool of the alpaca. ■ fabric made from this wool, with or without other fibers: [as *adj.*] *an alpaca jersey.* ▷late 18th cent.: from Spanish, from Aymara *allpaca.*

al·par·ga·ta /,alpər'gätə/ ▸*n.* a light canvas shoe with a plaited fiber sole; an espadrille. ▷early 19th cent.: from Spanish.

al·pen·glow /'alpən,glō/ ▸*n.* the rosy light of the setting or rising sun seen on high mountains. ▷late 19th cent.: a partial translation of German *Alpenglühen,* literally 'Alp glow.'

al·pen·horn /'alpən,hôrn/ (also **alp·horn** /'alp,hôrn/) ▸*n.* a valveless wooden horn up to 12 feet (4 m) long, used for signaling in the Alps. ▷late 19th cent.: from German, literally 'Alp horn.'

al·pen·stock /'alpən,stäk/ ▸*n.* a long iron-tipped staff used by hikers and mountain climbers. ▷early 19th cent.: from German, literally 'Alp stick.'

Al·pert /'alpərt/, Herb (1935–), U.S. musician and producer. A jazz trumpeter, he co-founded A & M Records with Jerry Moss in 1962 and went on to record many successful albums with the Tijuana Brass.

al·pha /'alfə/ ▸*n.* **1** the first letter of the Greek alphabet (A, α), transliterated as "a." ■ [as *adj.*] denoting the first of a series of items or categories, e.g., forms of a chemical compound: *alpha interferon* | *the α and β chains of hemoglobin.* ■ short for ALPHA TEST. ■ (**Alpha**) [followed by Latin genitive] the first (typically the brightest) star in a constellation: *Alpha Centauri.* ■ [as *adj.*] relating to alpha decay or alpha particles: *an alpha emitter.* ■ (of animals in a group) the socially dominant individual: *he rose to be alpha male of his troop at the very early age of 16.* **2** a code word representing the letter A, used in radio communication.

▸*symbol* ■ (α) a plane angle. ■ (α) angular acceleration. ■ (α) *Astronomy* right ascension. ▷from Semitic; cf. Phoenician *'alp,* lit. 'ox,' and Hebrew *'aleph* 'aleph'.

▸*PHRASE* □ **alpha and omega** the beginning and the end (esp. used by Christians as a title for Jesus). ■ the essence or most important features: *collective bargaining is seen as the alpha and omega of trade unionism.*

al·pha·bet /'alfə,bet; -bit/ ▸*n.* a set of letters or symbols in a fixed order, used to represent the basic sounds of a language; in particular, the set of letters from A to Z. ■ the basic elements in a system which combine to form complex entities: *DNA's 4-letter alphabet.*

> The alphabet has its roots in Phoenician writing of the 2nd millennium BC, from which the modern Hebrew and Arabic systems are ultimately derived. The Greek alphabet, which emerged in 1000–900 BC, developed two branches, Cyrillic (which became the script of Russian) and Etruscan (from which derives the Roman alphabet used in the West).

▷early 16th cent.: from late Latin *alphabetum,* from Greek *alpha, bēta,* the first two letters of the Greek alphabet.

al·pha·bet·i·cal /,alfə'betikəl/ ▸*adj.* of or relating to an alphabet: *alphabetical characters.* ■ in the order of the letters of the alphabet: *an alphabetical index* | *in alphabetical order.* **—al·pha·bet·ic** *adj.* **—al·pha·bet·i·cal·ly** /-ik(ə)lē/ *adv.*

al·pha·bet·ize /'alfəbi,tīz/ ▸*v.* [*trans.*] arrange (words or phrases) in alphabetical order: *the listings are arranged by state and alphabetized by city.* **—al·pha·bet·i·za·tion** /,alfə,betə'zāshən/ *n.*

al·pha·bet soup ▸*n. informal* incomprehensible or confusing language, typically containing many abbreviations or symbols. ▷early 20th cent.: alluding to a kind of clear soup containing pasta in the shapes of letters.

al·pha block·er ▸*n. Medicine* any of a class of drugs that prevent the stimulation of the adrenergic receptors responsible for increased blood pressure.

Al·pha Cen·tau·ri /sen'tôrē/ *Astronomy* the third brightest star in the sky, in the constellation Centaurus, visible only to observers in the southern hemisphere. It is the nearest bright star to the solar system (distance 4.34 light years), and is a visual binary. Also called RIGIL KENTAURUS.

al·pha-fe·to·pro·tein /,fētō'prōtē(ə)n/ ▸*n. Medicine* a protein produced by a fetus that is present in amniotic fluid and the bloodstream of the mother. Levels of the protein can be measured to detect certain congenital defects such as spina bifida and Down syndrome.

alpha globulin ▸*n.* see GLOBULIN.

al·pha-hy·drox·y ac·id / hī'dräksē/ ▸*n. Chemistry* an organic acid containing a hydroxyl group bonded to the carbon atom adjacent to the carboxylic acid group. A number of such compounds are used in skin-care preparations for their exfoliating properties. Also called FRUIT ACID.

al·pha·nu·mer·ic /,alfən(y)o͞o'merik/ ▸*adj.* consisting of or using both letters and numerals: *alphanumeric data* | *an alphanumeric keyboard.*

▸*n.* a character that is either a letter or a number. ▷1950s: blend of ALPHABETICAL and NUMERICAL. **—al·pha·nu·mer·i·cal** *adj.*

al·pha par·ti·cle ▸*n. Physics* a helium nucleus emitted by some radioactive substances, originally regarded as a ray.

al·pha ra·di·a·tion ▸*n.* ionizing radiation consisting of alpha particles, emitted by some substances undergoing radioactive decay.

Al·pha·ret·ta /,alfə'retə/ a city in northwestern Georgia, a suburb of Atlanta; pop. 34,854.

al·pha rhythm ▸*n. Physiology* the normal electrical activity of the brain when conscious and relaxed, consisting of oscillations (**alpha waves**) with a frequency of 8 to 13 hertz.

al·pha test ▸*n.* a trial of machinery, software, or other products carried out by a developer before a product is made available for beta testing.

▸*v.* (**al·pha-test**) [*trans.*] subject (a product) to a test of this kind.

alp·horn /'alp,hôrn/ ▸*n.* another term for ALPENHORN.

al·pine /'al,pīn/ ▸*adj.* [usu. *attrib*] of or relating to high mountains: *alpine and subalpine habitats.* ■ (in the names of plants and animals) growing or found on high mountains: *the alpine forget-me-not.* ■ (**Alpine**) of or relating to the Alps: *the major Alpine ski venues.* ■ (also **Alpine**) (of skiing) involving downhill racing: *an alpine ski team.*

▸*n.* **1** a plant native to mountain districts, often suitable for growing in rock gardens. **2** a North American butterfly that typically has brownish-black wings with orange-red markings. • Genus *Erebia,* subfamily Satyrinae, family Nymphalidae: several species. ▷late Middle English: from Latin *Alpinus,* from *Alpes* 'Alps' (see ALPS).

al·pine house ▸*n.* an unheated greenhouse used to grow alpine plants.

al·pin·ist /'alpənist/ ▸*n.* a climber of high mountains, esp. in the Alps. ▷late 19th cent.: from French *alpiniste,* from *alpin* (see ALPINE).

al·pra·zo·lam /al'prazə,lam/ ▸*n. Medicine* a drug of the benzodiazepine group, used in the treatment of anxiety. ▷1970s: from *al-* of unknown origin + *p(henyl)* + *(t)r(i)azol(e)* + *(-azep)am.*

Alps /alps/ a mountain system in Europe that extends in a curve from the coast of southeastern France through northwestern Italy, Switzerland, Liechtenstein, and southern Germany into Austria. The highest peak, Mont Blanc, rises to a height of 15,771 feet (4,807 m). ▷late Middle English: via

Pronunciation Key ə *ago;* ər *over;* 'ə or ,ə *up;* 'ər or ,ər *fur;* a *hat;* ā *rate;* ä *car;* CH *chew;* e *let;* ē *see;* e(ə)r *air;* i *fit;* ī *by;* i(ə)r *ear;* NG *sing;* ō *go;* ô *for;* oi *boy;* o͝o *good;* o͞o *goo;* ou *out;* SH *she;* TH *thin;* TH *then;* (h)w *why;* ZH *vision*

French from Latin *Alpes*, from Greek *Alpeis*, of unknown origin.

al Qae·da /al 'kīdə; 'kādə; kä'ēdə/, (also **al-Qa'i·dah**, **al-Qae·da**) a militant Islamic fundamentalist group. Founded in the late 1980s to combat the Soviets in Afghanistan, its goal is to establish a pan-Islamic caliphate by collaborating with Islamic extremists to overthrow non-Islamic regimes and to expel Westerners and non-Muslims from Muslim countries. ▷Arabic, literally 'the base.'

Al Qa·hi·ra /äl 'kähērə/ Arabic name for CAIRO.

al-Qods /al 'kôdz/ ▶the Arabic name for Jerusalem.

al·read·y /ôl'redē/ ▶*adv.* **1** before or by now or the time in question: *Anna has suffered a great deal already.* ■ as surprisingly soon or early as this: *at 31, he already suffers from arthritis | already it was past four o' clock.* **2** *informal* used as an intensive after a word or phrase to express impatience: *enough already with these crazy kids and their wacky dances!* ▷Middle English: from ALL (as an adverb) + READY; sense 2 is influenced by Yiddish use.

al·right /ôl'rīt/ ▶ variant spelling of ALL RIGHT.

USAGE The merging of *all* and *right* to form the one-word spelling **alright** is first recorded toward the end of the 19th century (unlike other similar merged spellings such as **altogether** and **already**, which date from much earlier). There is no logical reason for insisting that **all right** be two words when other single-word forms such as **altogether** have long been accepted. Nevertheless, although found widely, **alright** remains nonstandard.

ALS ▶*abbr.* amyotrophic lateral sclerosis.

Al·sace /al'sas; -'säs/ a region of northeastern France, on the borders with Germany and Switzerland. It was annexed by Prussia, along with part of Lorraine, to form **Alsace-Lorraine** after the Franco-Prussian War of 1870–71. It was restored to France after World War I.

Al·sa·tian /al'sāshən/ ▶*n.* **1** *chiefly Brit.* another term for GERMAN SHEPHERD. **2** a native or inhabitant of Alsace.
▶*adj.* of or relating to Alsace or its inhabitants. ▷from medieval Latin *Alsatia* 'Alsace' + -AN.

al·sike /'al,sik; -,sīk/ (also **alsike clover**) ▶*n.* a tall clover that is widely grown for fodder. Native to Europe, it has become naturalized in North America. • *Trifolium hybridum*, family Leguminosae. ▷mid 19th cent.: named after *Alsike* in Sweden; Linnaeus mentions the plant growing there.

al·so /'ôlsō/ ▶*adv.* in addition; too: *a brilliant linguist, he was also interested in botany | dyslexia, also known as word-blindness | [sentence adverb] also, a car is very expensive to run.* ▷Old English *alswā* 'quite so, in that manner, similarly' (see ALL, SO[1]).

al·so-ran ▶*n.* a loser in a race or contest, esp. by a large margin. ■ an undistinguished or unsuccessful person or thing. ▷late 19th cent.: originally applied to horses in a race that do not get a "place."

al·stroe·me·ri·a /,alstrə'mi(ə)rēə/ ▶*n.* a South American plant with showy lilylike flowers, often cultivated as an ornamental. • Genus *Alstroemeria*, family Liliaceae: several species, in particular the Peruvian lily. ▷late 18th cent.: modern Latin, named after Klas von *Alstroemer* (1736–96), Swedish naturalist.

Alt /ôlt/ ▶*n.* short for ALT KEY.

alt. ▶*abbr.* ■ alternate. ■ altimeter. ■ altitude.

alt. (also **alt-**) ▶*combining form* denoting a version of something that is intended as a challenge to the traditional version: *an alt.classical quartet.* ▷1990s: abbr. of *alternative*, influenced by the *alt.* prefix of some Usenet newsgroups.

Alta. ▶*abbr.* Alberta.

Al·ta·de·na /,altə'dēnə/ a residential suburb in southwestern California, just north of Pasadena; pop. 42,658.

Al·tai /'al,tī; 'äl-/ (also **Al·tay**) a krai (administrative territory) of Russia in southwestern Siberia, on the border with Kazakhstan; capital, Barnaul.

Al·ta·ic /al'tāik/ ▶*adj.* **1** of or relating to the Altai Mountains. **2** denoting or belonging to a phylum of languages that includes the Turkic, Mongolian, Tungusic, and Manchu languages. They are characterized by agglutination and vowel harmony.
▶*n.* the Altaic family of languages.

Al·tai Moun·tains a mountain system in central Asia that extends east for about 1,000 miles (1,600 km) from Kazakhstan into western Mongolia and northern China.

Al·tair /'al,te(ə)r; -,tī(ə)r; al'tī(ə)r; -'te(ə)r/ *Astronomy* the brightest star in the constellation Aquila. ▷Arabic, literally 'flying eagle.'

Al·ta·mi·ra /,altə'mi(ə)rə/ the site of a cave with Paleolithic rock paintings, south of Santander in northern Spain, discovered in 1879.

al·tar /'ôltər/ ▶*n.* the table in a Christian church at which the bread and wine are consecrated in communion services. ■ a table or flat-topped block used as the focus for a religious ritual, esp. for making sacrifices or offerings to a deity. ▷Old English *altar*, *alter*, based on late Latin *altar*, *altarium*, from Latin *altus* 'high.'
▶*PHRASES* □ **lead someone to the altar** marry. □ **sacrifice someone/something on/at the altar of someone/something** cause someone or something to suffer in the interests of someone or something else: *no businessman is going to sacrifice his company on the altar of such altruism.*

al·tar boy ▶*n.* a boy who acts as a priest's assistant, esp. in the Roman Catholic Church.

al·tar call ▶*n.* a summons to the altar at a Christian worship service to those wishing to show their commitment: *I never responded to an altar call, or if my pastor gave an altar call, I didn't think it applied to me.*

al·tar girl ▶*n.* a girl who acts as a priest's assistant during a service, esp. in the Roman Catholic Church.

al·tar·piece /'ôltər,pēs/ ▶*n.* a work of art, esp. a painting on wood, set above and behind an altar.

al·tar rail ▶*n.* a railing in front of the altar, separating the chancel from the nave.

Al·tay variant spelling of ALTAI.

alt·az·i·muth /al'tazəməth/ ▶*n.* **1** (also **altazimuth mount** or **mounting**) *Astronomy* a telescope mounting that moves in azimuth (about a vertical axis) and in altitude (about a horizontal axis). Compare with EQUATORIAL MOUNT. ■ (also **altazimuth telescope**) a telescope on such a mounting. **2** a surveying instrument for measuring vertical and horizontal angles, resembling a theodolite but larger and more precise. ▷mid 19th cent.: blend of ALTITUDE and AZIMUTH.

alt.coun·try /'ôlt 'kəntrē/ (also **alt-coun·try**) ▶*n.* a style of country music that is influenced by alternative rock.

Alt·dor·fer /'ält,dôrfər/, Albrecht (*c.*1485–1538), German painter and engraver. He was the principal artist of the Danube School.

al·ter /'ôltər/ ▶*v.* change or cause to change in character or composition, typically in a comparatively small but significant way: *[trans.] Eliot was persuaded to alter the passage | nothing alters the fact that children are our responsibility | [intrans.] our outward appearance alters as we get older | [as adj.] (***altered***) an altered state.* ■ *[trans.]* make structural changes to (a building): *plans to alter the dining hall.* ■ *[trans.]* tailor (clothing) for a better fit or to conform to fashion: *skirts with the hemlines altered a dozen different times.* ■ *[trans.]* castrate or spay (a domestic animal). ▷late Middle English: from Old French *alterer*, from late Latin *alterare*, from Latin *alter* 'other.' **—al·ter·a·ble** *adj.*

al·ter·a·tion /,ôltə'rāshən/ ▶*n.* the action or process of altering or being altered: *timetables are subject to alteration without notice | alterations had to be made.* ▷late Middle English: from Old French, or from late Latin *alteratio(n-)*, from the verb *alterare* (see ALTER).

al·ter·cate /'ôltər,kāt/ ▶*v.* [*intrans.*] *archaic* dispute or argue noisily and publicly. ▷mid 16th cent.: from Latin *altercat-* 'wrangled,' from *altercari*.

al·ter·ca·tion /,ôltər'kāshən/ ▶*n.* a noisy argument or disagreement, esp. in public: *I had an altercation with the conductor.* See note at QUARREL. ▷late Middle English: from Latin *altercatio(n-)*, from the verb *altercari* (see ALTERCATE).

al·ter e·go ▶*n.* a person's secondary or alternative personality. ■ an intimate and trusted friend. ▷mid 16th cent.: Latin, 'other self.'

al·ter·i·ty /ôl'teritē/ ▶*n.* *formal* the state of being other or different; otherness. ▷mid 17th cent.: from late Latin *alteritas*, from *alter* 'other.'

al·ter·nant /'ôltərnənt/ ▶*n.* an alternative form of a word or other linguistic unit; a variant.
▶*adj.* alternating; changing from one to the other. ▷mid 17th cent.: from Latin *alternant-* 'doing things by turns,' from the verb *alternare* (see ALTERNATE).

al·ter·nate ▶*v.* /'ôltər,nāt/ [*intrans.*] occur in turn repeatedly: *the governorship* ***alternated between*** *the Republican and Democratic parties | bouts of depression* ***alternate with*** *periods of elation | [as adj.] (***alternating***) a season of alternating hot days and cool nights.* ■ [*trans.*] do or perform in turn repeatedly: *some adults who wish to* ***alternate*** *work* ***with*** *education.*
▶*adj.* /'ôltərnit/ (abbr.: **alt.**) [*attrib.*] **1** every other; every second: *she was asked to attend on alternate days.* ■ (of two things) each following and succeeded by the other in a regular pattern: *alternate bouts of intense labor and of idleness.* ■ (of a sequence) consisting of alternate items. ■ *Botany* (of leaves or shoots) placed alternately on the two sides of the stem. **2** taking the place of; alternative: *the rerouted traffic takes a variety of alternate routes.*
▶*n.* /-nit/ (abbr.: **alt.**) a person who acts as a deputy or substitute. ▷early 16th cent.: from Latin *alternat-* 'done by turns,' from *alternare*, from *alternus* 'every other,' from *alter* 'other, the other.' **—al·ter·nate·ly** /-nitlē/ *adv.* **—al·ter·na·tion** /,ôltər'nāshən/ *n.*

USAGE See **usage** at ALTERNATIVE.

al·ter·nate an·gles ▶*plural n.* two angles, not adjoining one another, that are formed on opposite sides of a line that intersects two other lines. If the original two lines are parallel, the alternate angles are equal.

al·ter·nat·ing cur·rent (abbr.: **AC** or **ac**) ▶*n.* an electric current that reverses its direction many times a second at regular intervals, typically used in power supplies. Compare with DIRECT CURRENT.

al·ter·na·tion of gen·er·a·tions ▶*n.* *Biology* a pattern of reproduction occurring in the life cycles of many lower plants and some invertebrates, involving a regular alternation between two distinct forms. The generations are alternately sexual and asexual (as in ferns) or dioecious and parthenogenetic (as in some jellyfish).

al·ter·na·tive /ôl'tərnətiv/ ▶*adj.* [*attrib.*] (of one or more things) available as another possibility: *the various alternative methods for resolving disputes | the alternative definition of democracy as popular power.* ■ (of two things) mutually exclusive: *the facts fit two alternative scenarios.* ■ of or relating to behavior that is considered unconventional and is often seen as a challenge to traditional norms: *an alternative lifestyle | they have one foot in alternative music and the other in rock.*
▶*n.* one of two or more available possibilities: *audiocassettes are an interesting* ***alternative to*** *reading | she had no alternative but to break the law.* ▷mid 16th cent. (in the sense 'alternating, alternate'): from French *alternatif, -ive* or medieval Latin *alternativus*, from Latin *alternare* 'interchange' (see ALTERNATE). **—al·ter·na·tive·ly** *adv.* [*sentence adverb*] *alternatively, you may telephone us direct.*

USAGE 1 **Alternate** can be a verb, noun, or adjective, while **alternative** can be a noun or adjective. In both American and British English, the adjective **alternate** means 'every other' (*there will be a dance on* ***alternate*** *Saturdays*) and the adjective **alternative** means 'available as another choice' (*an* ***alternative*** *route;* ***alternative*** *medicine;* ***alternative*** *energy sources*). In American usage, however, **alternate** can also be used to mean 'available as another choice': *an* ***alternate*** *plan called for construction to begin immediately rather than waiting for spring.* Likewise, a book club may offer an 'alternate selection' as an alternative to the main selection.
2 Some traditionalists maintain, from an etymological standpoint, that you can have only two alternatives (from the Latin *alter* 'other (of two); the other') and that uses of more than two alternatives are erroneous. Such uses are, however, normal in modern standard English.

al·ter·na·tive dis·pute res·o·lu·tion (abbr.: **ADR**) ▶*n.* the use of methods such as mediation and arbitration to resolve a dispute instead of litigation.

al·ter·na·tive en·er·gy ▶*n.* energy generated in ways that do not deplete natural resources or harm the environment, esp. by avoiding the use of fossil fuels and nuclear power.

al·ter·na·tive fu·el ▶*n.* a fuel other than gasoline for powering motor vehicles, such as natural gas, methanol, or electricity.

al·ter·na·tive med·i·cine ▶*n.* any of a range of medical therapies that are not regarded as orthodox by the medical profession, such as herbalism, homeopathy, and acupuncture. See also COMPLEMENTARY MEDICINE.

al·ter·na·tor /'ôltər,nātər/ ▶*n.* a generator that produces an alternating current.

Al·thing /'ôl,thing; 'äl-/ the bicameral legislative assembly of Iceland. ▷Icelandic, from Old Norse.

alt·horn /'alt,hôrn/ ▶*n.* a musical instrument of the saxhorn family, esp. the alto or tenor saxhorn in

E flat. ▷mid 19th cent.: from German, from *alt* 'high' (from Latin *altus*) + *Horn* 'horn.'

al·though /ôl'THō/ ▸*conj.* in spite of the fact that; even though: *although the sun was shining it wasn't that warm* | *although small, the room has a spacious feel.* ■ however; but: *he says he has the team jersey, although I've never seen him wear it.* ▷Middle English: from ALL (as an adverb) + THOUGH.

USAGE **Although** and **though** are interchangeable in the senses listed above, the only difference being that use of **though** tends to be less formal than that of **although**. In formal writing, **although** tends to sound better than **though** as the opening word of a sentence. Some uses of **though**, however, are not interchangeable with **although**—e.g., adverbial uses (*it was nice of him to phone, though*) and uses in conjunction with 'as' or 'even' (*she doesn't look as though she's listening*).

Alt·hus·ser /'ält,hōōsər; ,ält(h)ōō'sā/, Louis (1918–90), French philosopher. He reinterpreted traditional Marxism in the light of structuralist theories. Notable works: *For Marx* (1965) and *Reading Capital* (1970).

al·tim·e·ter /al'timitər/ (abbr.: **alt.**) ▸*n.* an instrument for determining altitude attained, esp. a barometric or radar device used in an aircraft. ▷early 20th cent.: from Latin *altus* 'high' + -METER.

al·tim·e·try /al'timitrē/ ▸*n.* the measurement of height or altitude. ▷late Middle English: from medieval Latin *altimetria*. —**al·ti·met·ric** /,altə'metrik/ *adj.* —**al·ti·met·ri·cal·ly** /,altə'metrik(ə)lē/ *adv.*

al·ti·pla·no /alti'plänō/ ▸*n.* (*pl.* **-nos**) the high tableland of central South America. ▷early 20th cent.: from Spanish.

al·tis·si·mo /al'tisə,mō; äl-/ ▸*adj. Music* very high in pitch: *the extreme altissimo range of his horn.* ▷Italian, superlative of *alto* 'high.'

al·ti·tude /'alti,t(y)ōōd/ (abbr.: **alt.**) ▸*n.* the height of an object or point in relation to sea level or ground level: *flight data including airspeed and altitude* | *flying at altitudes over 15,000 feet.* ■ great height: *the mechanism can freeze at altitude.* ■ *Astronomy* the apparent height of a celestial object above the horizon, measured as an angle. ■ *Geometry* the length of the perpendicular line from a vertex to the opposite side of a figure. ▷late Middle English: from Latin *altitudo*, from *altus* 'high.' —**al·ti·tu·di·nal** /,alti't(y)ōōdn-əl/ *adj.*

al·ti·tude sick·ness ▸*n.* illness caused by ascent to a high altitude and the resulting shortage of oxygen, characterized chiefly by hyperventilation, nausea, exhaustion, and cerebral edema.

Alt key /'ôlt/ ▸*n. Computing* a key on a keyboard that when pressed at the same time as another key gives the second key an alternative function. ▷late 20th cent.: abbreviation of *alt(ernative) key*.

Alt·man /'ôltmən/, Robert (1925–), U.S. movie director. He made his name with *M*A*S*H* (1970), a black comedy about an army surgical hospital at the front in the Korean War. Other notable movies: *Nashville* (1975), *The Player* (1992), and *Gosford Park* (2001).

al·to /'altō/ ▸*n.* (*pl.* **-tos**) *Music* a voice, instrument, or part below the highest range and above tenor, in particular: ■ the highest adult male singing voice; countertenor. ■ the lowest female singing voice; contralto. ■ [as *adj.*] denoting the member of a family of instruments pitched second or third highest: *alto flute.* ■ an alto instrument, esp. an alto saxophone. ▷late 16th cent.: from Italian *alto* (*canto*) 'high (song).'

al·to clef ▸*n.* a clef placing middle C on the middle line of the staff, now used chiefly for viola music.

al·to·cu·mu·lus /,altō'kyōōmyələs/ ▸*n.* (*pl.* **-li** /-,lī/) cloud forming a layer of rounded masses with a level base, occurring at medium altitude, usually 6,500–23,000 feet (2–7 km). ▷late 19th cent.: from modern Latin *alto-* (from Latin *altus* 'high') + CUMULUS.

al·to·geth·er /,ôltə'geTHər/ ▸*adv.* completely; totally: *I stopped seeing her altogether* | [as *submodifier*] *I'm not altogether sure that I'd trust him.* ■ including everything or everyone; in total: *he had married several times and had forty-six children altogether.* ■ [*sentence adverb*] taking everything into consideration; on the whole: *altogether it was a great evening.* ▷Old English (see ALL, TOGETHER).

▸*PHRASE* □ **in the altogether** *informal* without any clothes on; naked: *she's agreed to pose in the altogether.*

USAGE Note that **altogether** and **all together** do not mean the same thing. **Altogether** means 'in total, totally' as in *there are six bedrooms altogether*, or *that is a different matter altogether*, whereas **all together** means 'all in one place' or 'all at once,' as in *it was good to have a group of friends all together*, or *they came in all together*.

Al·ton /'ôlt(ə)n/ an industrial city in southwestern Illinois, on the Mississippi River, north of St. Louis in Missouri; pop. 32,905.

Al·too·na /al'tōōnə/ a city in south central Pennsylvania, in the Allegheny Mountains; pop. 49,523. A noted railroad center, it is near Horseshoe Curve, where rails first crossed the Alleghenies.

al·to-re·lie·vo /'altō rə'lēvō/ ▸*n.* (*pl.* **-vos**) *Sculpture* another term for **high relief** at **relief** (sense 4). ■ a sculpture or carving in high relief. ▷mid 17th cent.: from Italian *alto-rilievo*.

al·to·stra·tus /,altō'strātəs; -'stratəs/ ▸*n.* cloud forming a continuous uniform layer that resembles stratus but occurs at medium altitude, usually 6,500–23,000 feet (2–7 km). ▷late 19th cent.: from modern Latin *alto-* (from Latin *altus* 'high') + STRATUS.

al·tri·cial /al'trisHəl/ *Zoology* ▸*adj.* (of a young bird or other animal) hatched or born in an undeveloped state and requiring care and feeding by the parents. Also called NIDICOLOUS. Often contrasted with PRECOCIAL. ■ (of a particular species) having such young.

▸*n.* an altricial bird. ▷late 19th cent.: from Latin *altrix, altric-*, feminine of *altor* 'nourisher,' from *alere* 'nourish.'

al·tru·ism /'altrōō,izəm/ ▸*n.* the belief in or practice of disinterested and selfless concern for the well-being of others: *some may choose to work with vulnerable elderly people out of altruism.* ■ *Zoology* behavior of an animal that benefits another at its own expense. ▷mid 19th cent.: from French *altruisme*, from Italian *altrui* 'somebody else,' from Latin *alteri huic* 'to this other.' —**al·tru·ist** *n.* —**al·tru·is·tic** /,altrōō'istik/ *adj.* —**al·tru·is·ti·cal·ly** *adv.*

Al·tus /'altəs/ a city in southwestern Oklahoma; pop. 21,910.

ALU *Computing* ▸*abbr.* arithmetic logic unit.

al·u·del /'alyə,del/ ▸*n.* a pear-shaped earthenware or glass pot, open at both ends to enable a series to be fitted one above another, formerly used in sublimation and other chemical processes. ▷late Middle English: from Old French *alutel*, via Spanish from Arabic *al-'uṯāl* 'the sublimation vessel.'

al·u·la /'alyələ/ ▸*n.* (*pl.* **-u·lae** /-yə,lē/) technical term for BASTARD WING. ▷late 18th cent.: modern Latin, literally 'small wing,' diminutive of *ala*.

a·lum /'aləm/ ▸*n. Chemistry* a colorless astringent compound that is a hydrated double sulfate of aluminum and potassium, used in solution medicinally and in dyeing and tanning. Also called POTASH ALUM. • Chem. formula: $AlK(SO_4)_2.12H_2O$. ■ any of a number of analogous crystalline double sulfates of a monovalent metal (or group) and a trivalent metal. ▷late Middle English: via Old French from Latin *alumen, alumin-*; related to *aluta* 'tawed leather.'

a·lu·mi·na /ə'lōōmənə/ ▸*n.* a white solid, aluminum oxide, that occurs in bauxite and is found in crystalline form as the main constituent of corundum, sapphire, and other minerals. • Aluminum oxide; chem. formula: Al_2O_3. ▷late 18th cent.: from Latin *alumen* (see ALUM), on the pattern of words such as *magnesia*.

a·lu·mi·nize /ə'lōōmə,nīz/ ▸*v.* [*trans.*] [usu. as *adj.*] (**aluminized**) coat with aluminum: *an aluminized reflector.*

a·lu·mi·no·sil·i·cate /ə,lōōmənə'silikit/ ▸*n. Chemistry* a silicate in which aluminum replaces some of the silicon, esp. a rock-forming mineral such as a feldspar or a clay mineral. ▷early 20th cent.: from *alumino-* (combining form of ALUMINUM) + SILICATE.

a·lu·mi·nous /ə'lōōmənəs/ ▸*adj.* (chiefly of minerals and rocks) containing alumina or aluminum. ▷late Middle English: from Latin *aluminosus*, from *alumen, alumin-* (see ALUM).

a·lu·mi·num /ə'lōōmənəm/ (*Brit.* **al·u·min·i·um** /,alyə'minēəm/) ▸*n.* the chemical element of atomic number 13, a light silvery-gray metal. (Symbol: **Al**)

Aluminum is the most abundant metal in the earth's crust and is obtained mainly from bauxite. Its lightness, resistance to corrosion, and strength (esp. in alloys) have led to widespread use in domestic utensils, engineering parts, and aircraft construction.

▷early 19th cent.: from *alumin(a)* + *(i)um*.

a·lu·mi·num bronze ▸*n.* an alloy of copper and aluminum.

a·lum·na /ə'ləmnə/ ▸*n.* (*pl.* **-nae** /-nē; -nī/) a female graduate or former student of a particular school, college, or university. ▷late 19th cent.: from Latin, feminine of *alumnus* (see ALUMNUS).

USAGE See **usage** at ALUMNUS.

a·lum·nus /ə'ləmnəs/ ▸*n.* (*pl.* **-ni** /-nī; -nē/) a graduate or former student, esp. male, of a particular school, college, or university: *a Harvard alumnus.* ▷mid 17th cent.: from Latin, 'nursling, pupil,' from *alere* 'nourish.'

USAGE In the singular, **alumnus** nearly always means a male, but the plural **alumni** usually refers to graduates or former students of either sex. See also ALUMNA.

al·um·root /'aləm,rōōt; -,rōōt/ (also **al·um root**) ▸*n.* a heuchera, esp. the green-flowered *H. americana* and the white-flowered *H. parvifolia*.

Al Uq·sur /äl 'ōōk,sōōr/ Arabic name for LUXOR.

Al·va·rez /'alvə,rez/, Luis Walter (1911–88), U.S. physicist. In particle physics, he made the first measurement of the neutron's magnetic moment. He also developed the bubble chamber. In 1980 Alvarez and his son identified iridium in sediment from the Cretaceous–Tertiary boundary and proposed that this resulted from a catastrophic meteorite impact. Nobel Prize for Physics (1968).

al·ve·o·lar /al'vēələr/ ▸*adj.* of or relating to an alveolus, in particular: ■ *Anatomy* relating to or denoting the bony ridge that contains the sockets of the upper teeth. ■ *Phonetics* (of a consonant) pronounced with the tip of the tongue on or near this ridge (e.g., *n, s, t*). ■ *Anatomy* of or relating to an alveolus or the alveoli of the lung.

▸*n. Phonetics* an alveolar consonant.

al·ve·o·lus /al'vēələs/ ▸*n.* (*pl.* **-li** /-,lī/) *chiefly Anatomy* a small cavity, pit, or hollow, in particular: ■ any of the many tiny air sacs in the lungs where the exchange of oxygen and carbon dioxide takes place. ■ the bony socket for the root of a tooth. ■ an acinus in a gland. ▷late 17th cent.: from Latin, 'small cavity,' diminutive of *alveus*. —**al·ve·o·late** /-lit; -,lāt/ *adj.*

al·ways /'ôl,wāz; -wēz/ (*archaic* **al·way**) ▸*adv.* **1** at all times; on all occasions: *the sun always rises in the east.* ■ throughout a long period of the past: *she had always been an obstinate sort.* ■ for all future time; forever: *she will always be missed.* ■ repeatedly and annoyingly: *she is always making derogatory remarks.* **2** as a last resort; failing all else: *if the marriage doesn't work out, we can always get divorced.* ▷Middle English: genitive case of *all way*, the inflection probably giving the sense 'at every time' as opposed to 'at one uninterrupted time'; the difference between the two is no longer distinct.

a·lys·sum /ə'lisəm/ ▸*n.* (*pl.* **-sums**) a herbaceous Eurasian plant that bears small flowers in a range of colors, typically white or yellow. Several kinds are widely cultivated in gardens. • Genera *Alyssum* and *Lobularia*, family brassicaceae: many species, including **sweet alyssum** (*L. maritima*), with fragrant white flowers. ▷mid 16th cent. (used loosely to denote various medicinal herbs): modern Latin, from Latin *alysson*, from Greek *alusson*, from *a-* 'without' + *lussa* 'rabies' (referring to early herbalist use).

Alz·hei·mer's dis·ease /'älts,hīmərz; 'ôlts-; 'älz-; 'ôlz-/ ▸*n.* progressive mental deterioration that can occur in middle or old age, due to generalized degeneration of the brain. It is the most common cause of premature senility. ▷early 20th cent.: named after Alois *Alzheimer* (1864–1915), German neurologist who first identified it.

AM ▸*abbr.* ■ amplitude modulation. ■ Master of Arts. [Latin *artium magister*.]

Am ▸*symbol* the chemical element americium.

am /am/ ▸ 1st person singular present of BE.

a.m. ▸*abbr.* before noon, used with times of day between midnight and noon: *we can deliver your most time-sensitive shipments by 10:30 a.m.* ▷from Latin *ante meridiem*.

AMA ▸*abbr.* ■ American Management Association. ■ American Medical Association. ■ American Motorcycle Association.

a·mah /'ämə/ ▸*n.* a nursemaid or maid in the Far East or India. ▷from Portuguese *ama* 'nurse.'

A·mal /ä'mäl/ a Lebanese Shiite Muslim organization founded in 1975 and having political and paramilitary wings. ▷from Arabic *'amal* 'hope.'

a·mal·gam /ə'malgəm/ ▶*n.* a mixture or blend: *a curious amalgam of the traditional and the modern.* ■ *Chemistry* an alloy of mercury with another metal, esp. one used for dental fillings. ▷late 15th cent.: from French *amalgame* or medieval Latin *amalgama*, from Greek *malagma* 'an emollient.'

a·mal·ga·mate /ə'malgə,māt/ ▶*v.* combine or unite to form one organization or structure: [*trans.*] *he* ***amalgamated*** *his company* ***with*** *another.* | [*intrans.*] *numerous small railroad companies amalgamated* | [as *adj.*] (**amalgamated**) *his true genius lies in synthesis, in an amalgamated vision.* ■ *Chemistry* [*trans.*] alloy (a metal) with mercury: [as *adj.*] (**amalgamated**) *amalgamated zinc.* ▷early 17th cent.: from medieval Latin *amalgamat-* 'formed into a soft mass,' from the verb *amalgamare*, from *amalgama* (see **AMALGAM**).

a·mal·ga·ma·tion /ə,malgə'māsʜən/ ▶*n.* the action, process, or result of combining or uniting: *the threat of* ***amalgamation with*** *a competitor* | *an amalgamation of two separate companies.* ■ *Chemistry* the action or process of alloying a metal with mercury. ▷early 17th cent.: from medieval Latin *amalgamare* (see **AMALGAMATE**).

Am·al·the·a /,aməl'ᴛʜēə; əmal-/ *Astronomy* satellite V of Jupiter, the third closest to the planet. It is reddish in color and heavily cratered, with a diameter of 106 miles (170 km). ▷from the name of a goat in Greek Mythology, which suckled the infant Zeus.

A·man·a Col·o·nies /ə'manə/ a group of seven villages in east central Iowa. Settled by a German religious group, they are famous for manufacturing appliances.

a·man·dine /,ämən'dēn; ,amən-/ ▶*adj.* (of a dish) prepared or garnished with sliced almonds.

a·man·u·en·sis /ə,manyo͞o'ensis/ ▶*n.* (*pl.* **-ses** /-,sēz/) a literary or artistic assistant, in particular one who takes dictation or copies manuscripts. ▷early 17th cent.: Latin, from *(servus) a manu* '(slave) at hand(writing), secretary' + *-ensis* 'belonging to.'

am·a·ranth /'amə,ranᴛʜ/ ▶*n.* **1** any plant of the genus *Amaranthus*, typically having small green, red, or purple tinted flowers. Certain varieties are grown for food. • Family Amaranthaceae: several genera, esp. *Amaranthus*. **2** an imaginary flower that never fades. **3** a purple color. ▷mid 16th cent.: from French *amarante* or modern Latin *amaranthus*, alteration (on the pattern of plant names ending in *-anthus*, from Greek *anthos* 'flower') of Latin *amarantus*, from Greek *amarantos* 'everlasting,' from *a-* 'not' + *marainein* 'wither.' **—am·a·ran·thine** /,amə'ranᴛʜin; -,ᴛʜīn/ *adj.*

am·a·ret·ti /,amə'retē/ ▶*plural n.* Italian almond-flavored cookies. ▷Italian, based on *amaro* 'bitter'; compare with **AMARETTO**.

am·a·ret·to /,amə'retō; ,äm-/ ▶*n.* a sweet, almond-flavored liqueur. ▷Italian, diminutive of *amaro* 'bitter' (with reference to bitter almonds).

Am·a·ril·lo /,amə'rilō/ an industrial and commercial city in northwestern Texas, in the Panhandle; pop. 173,627.

am·a·ryl·lis /,amə'rilis/ ▶*n.* a bulbous plant with white, pink, or red flowers and straplike leaves, of the type genus of the amaryllis family, Amaryllidaceae. • A South African plant (*Amaryllis belladonna*, also called **BELLADONNA LILY**), and (popularly) a tropical South American plant that is frequently grown as a houseplant (hybrids of the genus *Hippeastrum*, formerly *Amaryllis*). ▷modern Latin, from Latin *Amaryllis* (from Greek *Amarullis*), a name for a country girl in pastoral poetry.

amaryllis
genus *Hippeastrum*

a·mass /ə'mas/ ▶*v.* [*trans.*] gather together or accumulate (a large amount or number of valuable material or things) over a period of time: *starting from nothing he had amassed a huge fortune.* ■ [*intrans.*] *archaic* (of people) gather together in a crowd or group: *the soldiers were amassing from all parts of Spain.* ▷late 15th cent.: from French *amasser* or medieval Latin *amassare*, based on Latin *massa* 'lump' (see **MASS**). **—a·mass·er** *n.*

A·ma·te·ra·su /,ämäte'räso͞o/ the principal deity of the Japanese Shinto religion, the sun goddess and ancestor of Jimmu, founder of the imperial dynasty.

am·a·teur /'amətər; -,tər; -,cʜo͝or; -cʜər/ ▶*n.* a person who engages in a pursuit, esp. a sport, on an unpaid basis. ■ a person considered contemptibly inept at a particular activity: *that bunch of stumbling amateurs.*
▶*adj.* engaging or engaged in without payment; nonprofessional: *an amateur archaeologist* | *amateur athletics.* ■ inept or unskillful: *it's all so amateur!* ▷late 18th cent.: from French, from Italian *amatore*, from Latin *amator* 'lover,' from *amare* 'to love.' **—am·a·teur·ism** /-,rizəm/ *n.*

am·a·teur·ish /,amə'tərisʜ; -'t(y)o͝or-; -'cʜo͝or-/ ▶*adj.* unskillful; inept: *the editing is choppy and amateurish* | *amateurish actors.* **—am·a·teur·ish·ly** *adv.* **—am·a·teur·ish·ness** *n.*

A·ma·ti /ä'mätē/ a family of Italian violin-makers from Cremona. In the 16th and 17th centuries three generations, including **Andrea** (*c.*1520–80), his sons **Antonio** (1550–1638) and **Girolamo** (1551–1635), and the latter's son **Nicolò** (1596–1684), developed the basic proportions of the violin, viola, and cello.

am·a·tol /'amə,tôl; -,täl/ ▶*n.* a high explosive consisting of a mixture of TNT and ammonium nitrate. ▷early 20th cent.: formed irregularly from *am(monium)* + *tol(uene)*.

am·a·to·ry /'amə,tôrē/ ▶*adj.* [*attrib.*] relating to or induced by sexual love or desire: *his amatory exploits.* ▷late 16th cent.: from Latin *amatorius*, from *amator* (see **AMATEUR**).

am·au·ro·sis /,amô'rōsis/ ▶*n. Medicine* partial or total blindness without visible change in the eye, typically due to disease of the optic nerve, spinal cord, or brain. ▷mid 17th cent.: from Greek *amaurōsis*, from *amauroun* 'darken,' from *amauros* 'dim.' **—am·au·rot·ic** /-'rätik/ *adj.*

a·maze /ə'māz/ ▶*v.* [*trans.*] (often **be amazed**) surprise (someone) greatly; fill with astonishment: *he was* ***amazed at*** *how modern everything was* | [*trans.*] *she was* ***amazed that*** *Paul should notice her* | [as *adj.*] (**amazed**) *she shook her head in amazed disbelief.* ▷Old English *āmasian*, of unknown origin.

a·maze·ment /ə'māzmənt/ ▶*n.* a feeling of great surprise or wonder: *she shook her head* ***in amazement*** | *he found* ***to his amazement*** *that it was a passageway.*

a·maz·ing /ə'māziɴɢ/ ▶*adj.* causing great surprise or wonder; astonishing: *an amazing number of people registered* | *it is amazing how short your memory is.* ■ *informal* startlingly impressive: *she makes the most amazing cakes.* **—a·maz·ing·ly** *adv.* [*sentence adverb*] amazingly, *Alan escaped with a few cuts and bruises* | [as *submodifier*] *an amazingly good idea.*

Am·a·zon[1] /'amə,zän; -zən/ a river in South America that flows more than 4,150 miles (6,683 km) through Peru, Colombia, and Brazil into the Atlantic Ocean. It drains two-fifths of the continent and, in terms of water-flow, is the largest river in the world. ▷the river bore various names after its discovery in 1500 and was finally called *Amazon* after a legendary tribe of female warriors believed to live on its banks. **—Am·a·zo·ni·an** /,amə'zōnēən/ *adj.*

Am·a·zon[2] ▶*n.* **1** a member of a legendary race of female warriors believed by the ancient Greeks to exist in Scythia (near the Black Sea in modern Russia) or elsewhere on the edge of the known world. ■ (also **amazon**) a tall and strong or athletic woman. **2** (**amazon**) a parrot, typically green and with a broad rounded tail, found in Central and South America. • Genus *Amazona*, family Psittacidae: numerous species. ▷late Middle English: via Latin from Greek *Amazōn*, explained by the Greeks as 'breastless' (as if from *a-* 'without' + *mazos* 'breast'), referring to the fable that the Amazons cut off the right breast so as not to interfere with the use of a bow, but probably a popular etymology of an unknown foreign word. **—Am·a·zo·ni·an** *adj.*

am·a·zon ant ▶*n.* a small reddish ant that captures the pupae of other ant colonies to raise as slaves. • Genus *Polyergus*, family Formicidae.

Am·a·zo·ni·a /,amə'zōnēə/ the area around the Amazon River in South America, principally in Brazil, but also extending into Peru, Colombia, and Bolivia. This region comprises approximately one-third of the world's remaining tropical rain forest.

am·bas·sa·dor /am'basədər; -,dôr/ ▶*n.* an accredited diplomat sent by a country as its official representative to a foreign country: *the French* ***ambassador to*** *Portugal.* ■ a person who acts as a representative or promoter of a specified activity: *he is a good ambassador for the industry.* ▷late Middle English: from French *ambassadeur*, from Italian *ambasciator*, based on Latin *ambactus* 'servant.' **—am·bas·sa·do·ri·al** /am-,basə'dôrēəl/ *adj.* **—am·bas·sa·dor·ship** /-,sʜip/ *n.*

am·bas·sa·dor-at-large ▶*n.* an ambassador with special duties, not appointed to a particular country.

am·bas·sa·dress /am'basədris/ ▶*n.* a female ambassador. ■ *archaic* an ambassador's wife.

Am·ba·to /äm'bätō/ a market town in the Andes of central Ecuador; pop. 229,190.

am·ber /'ambər/ ▶*n.* hard translucent fossilized resin produced by extinct coniferous trees of the Tertiary period, typically yellowish in color.

> Amber has been used in jewelry since antiquity. It is found chiefly along the southern shores of the Baltic Sea; pieces often contain the bodies of trapped insects. When rubbed, amber becomes charged with static electricity: the word *electric* is derived from the Greek word for amber.

■ a honey-yellow color typical of this substance. ■ a yellow light used as a cautionary signal between green for "go" and red for "stop": *the lights were at amber.*
▶*adj.* made of amber: *amber beads.* ■ having the yellow color of amber: *her amber eyes.* ▷late Middle English (also in the sense 'ambergris'): from Old French *ambre*, from Arabic *'anbar* 'ambergris,' later 'amber.'

AMBER A·lert /'ambər ə,lərt/ (also **Am·ber A·lert**) ▶*n.* an emergency response system that disseminates information about a missing person (usually a child), by media broadcasting or electronic roadway signs: *our state's AMBER Alert became operational last September.* ■ a public announcement or alert that uses this system: *the AMBER alert gave a description of the suspected abductor.* ▷acronym from America's Missing: Broadcast Emergency Response, named after Amber Hagerman, a child kidnapped in Texas in 1996.

am·ber·gris /'ambər,gris; -,grē(s)/ ▶*n.* a waxlike substance that originates as a secretion in the intestines of the sperm whale, found floating in tropical seas and used in perfume manufacture. ▷late Middle English: from Old French *ambre gris* 'gray amber,' as distinct from *amber jaune* 'yellow amber' (the resin).

am·ber·jack /'ambər,jak/ ▶*n.* a large marine game fish found in inshore tropical and subtropical waters of the Atlantic and South Pacific. • Genus *Seriola*, family Carangidae: several species. ▷late 19th cent.: from **AMBER** (because of its yellowish tail) + **JACK**[1].

am·bi·ance ▶*n.* variant spelling of **AMBIENCE**.

am·bi·dex·trous /,ambi'dekst(ə)rəs/ ▶*adj.* (of a person) able to use the right and left hands equally well: *few of us are naturally ambidextrous.* ■ (of an implement) designed to be used by left-handed and right-handed people with equal ease. ▷mid 17th cent.: from late Latin *ambidexter* (from Latin *ambi-* 'on both sides' + *dexter* 'right-handed') + **-OUS**. **—am·bi·dex·ter·i·ty** /-dek'steritē/ *n.* **—am·bi·dex·trous·ly** *adv.*

am·bi·ence /'ambēəns/ (also **am·bi·ance**) ▶*n.* [usu. in *sing.*] the character and atmosphere of a place: *the relaxed ambience of the cocktail lounge is popular with guests.* ■ background noise added to a musical recording to give the impression that it was recorded live. ▷late 19th cent.: from **AMBIENT** + **-ENCE**, or from French *ambiance*, from *ambiant* 'surrounding.'

am·bi·ent /'ambēənt/ ▶*adj.* [*attrib.*] of or relating to the immediate surroundings of something: *the liquid is stored at below ambient temperature.*
▶*n.* (also **ambient music**) a style of instrumental music with electronic textures and no persistent beat, used to create or enhance a mood or atmosphere. ▷late 16th cent.: from French *ambiant* or Latin *ambient-* 'going around,' from *ambire*.

am·bi·gu·i·ty /,ambi'gyo͞o-itē/ ▶*n.* (*pl.* **-ties**) uncertainty or inexactness of meaning in language: *we can detect no ambiguity in this section of the Act* | *ambiguities in such questions are potentially very dangerous.* ■ a lack of decisiveness or commitment resulting from a failure to make a choice between alternatives: *the film is fraught with moral ambiguity.* ▷late Middle English: from Old French *ambiguite* or Latin *ambiguitas*, from *ambiguus* 'doubtful' (see **AMBIGUOUS**).

am·big·u·ous /am'bigyo͞oəs/ ▶*adj.* (of language) open to more than one interpretation; having a double meaning: *the question is rather ambiguous* | *ambiguous phrases.* See note at **DOUBTFUL**. ■ unclear or inexact because a choice between alternatives has not been made: *this whole society is morally ambiguous* | *the election result was ambiguous.* ▷early 16th cent. (in the sense 'indistinct, obscure'): from Latin *ambiguus* 'doubtful' (from *ambigere* 'waver, go around,' from *ambi-* 'both ways' + *agere* 'to drive') + **-OUS**. **—am·big·u·ous·ly** *adv.*

am·bi·sex·u·al /,ambi'seksʜo͞oəl/ ▶*adj.* bisexual or androgynous.
▶*n.* an ambisexual person: *ambisexuals, who get equal*

sexual pleasure from women and men. ▷1930s: from Latin *ambi-* 'on both sides' + **SEXUAL.** —**am·bi·sex·u·al·ly** *adv.*

am·bi·son·ic /ˌambiˈsänik/ ▶*adj.* denoting or relating to a high-fidelity audio system that reproduces the directional and acoustic properties of recorded sound using two or more channels.
▶*n.* (**ambisonics**) [treated as *sing.*] ambisonic reproduction or systems. ▷1970s: from Latin *ambi-* 'on both sides' + **SONIC.**

am·bit /ˈambit/ ▶*n.* [in *sing.*] the scope, extent, or bounds of something: *within the ambit of federal law.* ▷late Middle English (in the sense 'precincts, environs'): from Latin *ambitus* 'circuit,' from *ambire* 'go around.'

am·bi·tion /amˈbisʜən/ ▶*n.* a strong desire to do or to achieve something, typically requiring determination and hard work: *her ambition was to become a model | he achieved his ambition of making a fortune.* ■ desire and determination to achieve success: *life offered few opportunities for young people with ambition.* ▷Middle English: via Old French from Latin *ambitio(n-)*, from *ambire* 'go around (canvassing for votes).'

am·bi·tious /amˈbisʜəs/ ▶*adj.* having or showing a strong desire and determination to succeed: *his mother was hard-working and ambitious for her four children.* ■ (of a plan or piece of work) intended to satisfy high aspirations and therefore difficult to achieve: *the scope of the book is very ambitious | an ambitious enterprise.* ▷late Middle English: from Old French *ambitieux* or Latin *ambitiosus*, from *ambitio* (see **AMBITION**). —**am·bi·tious·ly** *adv.* —**am·bi·tious·ness** *n.*

am·biv·a·lent /amˈbivələnt/ ▶*adj.* having mixed feelings or contradictory ideas about something or someone: *some loved her, some hated her, few were ambivalent about her | an ambivalent attitude to terrorism.* ▷early 20th cent.: from *ambivalence* (from German *Ambivalenz*), on the pattern of *equivalent.* —**am·biv·a·lence** *n.* —**am·biv·a·lent·ly** *adv.*

am·bi·vert /ˈambəˌvərt/ ▶*n. Psychology* a person whose personality has a balance of extrovert and introvert features. ▷1920s: from Latin *ambi-* 'on both sides,' on the pattern of *extrovert* and *introvert.* —**am·bi·ver·sion** /ˌambiˈvərzʜən/ *n.*

am·ble /ˈambəl/ ▶*v.* [*intrans.*] walk or move at a slow, relaxed pace: *they ambled along the riverbank | he ambled into the foyer.*
▶*n.* a walk at a slow, relaxed pace, esp. for pleasure: *a peaceful riverside amble.* ▷Middle English (originally denoting a horse's gait): from Old French *ambler*, from Latin *ambulare* 'to walk.' —**am·bler** /-blər/ *n.*

am·bly·o·pi·a /ˌambléˈōpēə/ ▶*n. Medicine* impaired or dim vision without obvious defect or change in the eye. ▷early 18th cent.: from Greek *ambluōpia* 'dimsightedness,' from *ambluōpos* (adjective), from *amblus* 'dull' + *ōps, ōp-* 'eye.' —**am·bly·op·ic** /-ˈäpik/ *adj.*

am·bo /ˈamˌbō/ ▶*n.* (*pl.* **am·bos** or **am·bo·nes** /amˈbōnēz/) (in an early Christian church) an oblong pulpit with steps at each end. ▷mid 17th cent.: via medieval Latin from Greek *ambōn* 'rim' (in medieval Greek 'pulpit').

Am·boi·na wood /amˈboinə/ (also **Am·boy·na wood**) ▶*n.* the decorative wood of a rapidly growing Southeast Asian tree, often used for furniture making. • The tree is *Pterocarpus indicus*, family Leguminosae. ▷mid 19th cent.: named after *Amboina* Island (see **AMBON**).

Am·boi·nese /ˌamboiˈnēz; -ˈnēs; ˌäm-/ ▶*adj.* of or relating to the island of Ambon, its people, or their language.
▶*n.* **1** a native or inhabitant of Ambon. **2** the Indonesian language of this people. ▷from *Amboina* (see **AMBON**) + **-ESE.**

Am·bon /ˈämˈbôn; ˈamˌbän/ (also **Am·boi·na** /amˈboinə/) a mountainous island in eastern Indonesia, one of the Molucca Islands. ■ a port on this island, the capital of the Molucca Islands; pop. 80,000.

Am·brose, St. /ˈamˌbrōz; -ˌbrōs/ (*c.*339–397), doctor of the Church. As bishop of Milan from 374, he introduced much Eastern theology and liturgical practice into the West. Feast day, December 7.

am·bro·sia /amˈbrōzʜ(ē)ə/ ▶*n. Greek & Roman Mythology* the food of the gods. ■ something very pleasing to taste or smell: *the tea was ambrosia after the slop I'd been drinking.* ■ a fungal product used as food by ambrosia beetles. ■ another term for **BEEBREAD.** ■ a dessert made with oranges and shredded coconut. ▷mid 16th cent.: via Latin from Greek, 'elixir of life,' from *ambrotos* 'immortal.' —**am·bro·sial** *adj.*

am·bro·sia bee·tle ▶*n.* a small dark wood-boring beetle, the adults and larvae of which feed on a fungus that they cultivate, called ambrosia. • Genus *Platypus* (family Platypodidae), and *Xyleborus* and other genera (family Scolytidae).

am·bry /ˈômbrē/ (also **aum·bry**) ▶*n.* (*pl.* **-bries**) a small recess or cupboard in the wall of a church. ▷Middle English: from Old French *armarie*, from Latin *armarium* 'closet, chest,' from *arma* 'utensils.'

am·bu·lac·rum /ˌambyəˈlakrəm; -ˈlākrəm/ ▶*n.* (*pl.* **-lac·ra** /-ˈlakrə; -ˈlākrə/) *Zoology* (in a starfish or other echinoderm) each of the radially arranged bands, together with their underlying structures, through which the double rows of tube feet protrude. ▷early 19th cent.: Latin, 'avenue,' from *ambulare* 'to walk.' —**am·bu·lac·ral** /-rəl/ *adj.*

am·bu·lance /ˈambyələns/ ▶*n.* a vehicle specially equipped for taking sick or injured people to and from the hospital, esp. in emergencies. ▷early 19th cent.: French, from *hôpital ambulant* 'mobile (horse-drawn) field hospital,' from Latin *ambulant-* 'walking' (see **AMBULANT**).

am·bu·lance chas·er ▶*n. derogatory* a lawyer who specializes in bringing cases seeking damages for personal injury. ▷late 19th cent.: from the reputation gained by certain lawyers for attending accidents and encouraging victims to sue.

am·bu·lant /ˈambyələnt/ ▶*adj. Medicine* (of a patient) able to walk around; not confined to bed. ■ (of treatment) not confining a patient to bed. ▷early 17th cent.: from Latin *ambulant-* 'walking,' from *ambulare.*

am·bu·late /ˈambyəˌlāt/ ▶*v.* [*intrans.*] *formal* or *technical* walk; move about: *making use of crutches to ambulate | tortoises are diurnally active, ambulating mainly over the course of the day.* ▷early 17th cent.: from Latin *ambulat-* 'walked,' from the verb *ambulare.* —**am·bu·la·tion** /ˌambyəˈlāsʜən/ *n.*

am·bu·la·to·ry /ˈambyələˌtôrē/ ▶*adj.* relating to or adapted for walking. ■ *Medicine* able to walk; not bedridden: *ambulatory patients.* ■ *Medicine* relating to patients who are able to walk: *an ambulatory care facility.* ■ movable; mobile: *an ambulatory ophthalmic service.*
▶*n.* (*pl.* **-ries**) a place for walking, esp. an aisle around the apse or a cloister in a church or monastery. ▷mid 16th cent. (as a noun): from Latin *ambulatorius*, from *ambulare* 'to walk.'

am·bu·lo·ce·tus /ˌambyəlōˈsētəs/ ▶*n.* a large carnivorous amphibian (*Ambulocetus natans*, order Cetacea) of the Eocene epoch, an early ancestor of today's whales. ▷1990s (following the discovery of bones in Pakistan): modern Latin, from Latin *ambulare* 'to walk' + *cetus* 'whale.'

am·bus·cade /ˈambəˌskād; ˌambəˈskād/ ▶*n. dated* an ambush.
▶*v.* [*trans.*] *archaic* attack from an ambush. ■ [*intrans.*] *archaic* lie in ambush: [as *adj.*] (**ambuscaded**) *ambuscaded thousands might swarm up over the embankment.* ▷late 16th cent.: from French *embuscade*, from Italian *imboscata*, Spanish *emboscada*, or Portuguese *embuscada*, based on a late Latin word meaning 'to place in a wood'; related to **BUSH**[1].

am·bush /ˈamˌbŏŏsʜ/ ▶*n.* a surprise attack by people lying in wait in a concealed position: *seven members of a patrol were killed in an ambush | terrorists waiting **in ambush**.*
▶*v.* [*trans.*] (often **be ambushed**) make a surprise attack on (someone) from a concealed position: *they were ambushed and taken prisoner by the enemy | figurative representatives were ambushed by camera crews.* ▷Middle English (in the sense 'place troops in hiding in order to surprise an enemy'): from Old French *embusche* (noun), *embuschier* (verb), based on a late Latin word meaning 'to place in a wood'; related to **BUSH**[1]. The noun use dates from the late 15th cent.

am-dram /ˈam ˌdram/ ▶*n. chiefly Brit. informal* [treated as *sing.* or *pl.*] amateur dramatics: *a performance poised somewhere between slapstick and below-average am-dram.* ▷blend.

AME ▶*abbr.* African Methodist Episcopal.

a·me·ba /əˈmēbə/ (also **a·moe·ba**) ▶*n.* (*pl.* **-bas** or **-bae** /-bē/) a single-celled animal that catches food and moves about by extending fingerlike projections of protoplasm. Amebas are either free-living in damp environments or parasitic. • Many families and genera in the phylum Rhizopoda, kingdom Protista, including the aquatic *Amoeba proteus.* ▷mid 19th cent.: modern Latin, from Greek *amoibē* 'change, alternation.' —**a·me·bic** /-bik/ *adj.* —**a·me·boid** /-boid/ *adj.*

am·e·bi·a·sis /ˌaməˈbīəsis/ (also **am·oe·bi·a·sis**) ▶*n. Medicine* infection with amebas, esp. as causing dysentery. ▷early 20th cent.: from **AMEBA** + **-ASIS.**

a·me·bic dys·en·ter·y /əˈmēbik/ ▶*n.* dysentery caused by infection of the intestines by the protozoan *Entamoeba histolytica*, mostly in warm climates, and spread by contaminated food and water.

A·me·che /əˈmēcʜē/, Don (1908–93), U.S. actor; born *Dominic Felix Amici.* A leading man in movies of the 1930s and 1940s, he made a comeback in the 1980s in such movies as *Trading Places* (1983), *Cocoon* (Academy Award; 1985), and *Cocoon: The Return* (1989).

am·e·lan·chi·er /ˌaməˈlaɴɢkēər/ ▶*n.* a shrub of a genus that includes the juneberries. • Genus *Amelanchier*, family Rosaceae. ▷from French dialect *amelancier* 'medlar.'

a·me·lio·rate /əˈmēlyəˌrāt; əˈmēlēə-/ ▶*v.* [*trans.*] make (something bad or unsatisfactory) better: *the reform did much to ameliorate living standards.* ▷mid 18th cent.: alteration of **MELIORATE**, influenced by French *améliorer*, from *meilleur* 'better.' —**a·me·lio·ra·tion** /əˌmēlyəˈrāsʜən/ *n.* —**a·me·lio·ra·tive** /-rətiv; -ˌrātiv/ *adj.* —**a·me·lio·ra·tor** /-ˌrātər/ *n.*

a·men /āˈmen; āˈmen/ ▶*exclam.* uttered at the end of a prayer or hymn, meaning 'so be it.' ■ used to express agreement or assent: *amen to that!*
▶*n.* an utterance of "amen." ▷Old English, from ecclesiastical Latin, from Greek *amēn*, from Hebrew *ʼāmēn* 'truth, certainty,' used adverbially as expression of agreement or consent, and adopted in the Septuagint as a solemn expression of belief or affirmation.

a·me·na·ble /əˈmēnəbəl; əˈmen-/ ▶*adj.* (of a person) open and responsive to suggestion; easily persuaded or controlled: *parents who have had easy babies and amenable children.* ■ [*predic.*] (**amenable to**) (of a thing) capable of being acted upon in a particular way; susceptible to: *the patients had cardiac failure not amenable to medical treatment.* ▷late 16th cent. (in the sense 'liable to answer (to a law or tribunal)'): an Anglo-Norman French legal term, from Old French *amener* 'bring to,' from *a-* (from Latin *ad*) 'to' + *mener* 'bring' (from late Latin *minare* 'drive (animals),' from Latin *minari* 'threaten'). —**a·me·na·bil·i·ty** /əˌmēnəˈbilitē; əˌmen-/ *n.* —**a·me·na·bly** /-blē/ *adv.*

a·men cor·ner ▶*n.* (in some Protestant churches) seats, usually near the preacher, occupied by those who lead responses from the congregation.

a·mend /əˈmend/ ▶*v.* [*trans.*] make minor changes in (a text) in order to make it fairer, more accurate, or more up-to-date: *the rule was amended to apply only to nonmembers.* ■ modify formally, as a legal document or legislative bill: *did she amend her original will later on? | pressuring Panama to amend its banking laws.* ■ make better; improve: *if you can amend or alter people's mind-set.* ■ *archaic* put right: *a few things had gone wrong, but these had been amended.* ▷Middle English: from Old French *amender*, based on Latin *emendare* (see **EMEND**). —**a·mend·a·ble** *adj.* —**a·mend·er** *n.*

a·mend·ment /əˈmen(d)mənt/ ▶*n.* a minor change in a document. ■ a change or addition to a legal or statutory document: *an **amendment to** existing bail laws.* ■ (**Amendment**) an article added to the U.S. Constitution: *the First Amendment.* ■ something that is added to soil in order to improve its texture or fertility. ▷Middle English (in the sense 'improvement, correction'): from Old French *amendement*, from *amender* (see **AMEND**).

a·mends /əˈmendz/ ▶*plural n.* [treated as *sing.*] reparation or compensation. ▷Middle English: from Old French *amendes* 'penalties, fine,' plural of *amende* 'reparation,' from *amender* (see **AMEND**).
▶*PHRASES* □ **make amends** do something in order to make up for a wrong inflicted on someone: *try to **make amends for** the rude way you spoke to Lucy.* □ **an offer of amends** *Law* an offer to publish a correction and an apology for an act of libel.

a·men·i·ty /əˈmenitē; əˈmē-/ ▶*n.* (*pl.* **-ties**) (usu. **amenities**) a desirable or useful feature or facility of a building or place: *heating is regarded as a basic amenity.* ■ the pleasantness of a place or a person: *the exertion of amenity toward the boss.* ▷late Middle English: from Old French *amenite* or Latin *amoenitas*, from *amoenus* 'pleasant.'

a·men·or·rhe·a /āˌmenəˈrēə/ (*Brit.* **a·men·or·rhoe·a**) ▶*n.* an abnormal absence of menstruation. ▷early 19th cent.: from **A-**[1] 'without' + **MENO-** + **-RRHEA.**

am·ent /ˈāment; ˈam-/ ▶*n. Botany* a catkin. ▷mid 18th cent.: from Latin *amentum* 'thong.'

a·men·tia /āˈmencʜēə/ ▶*n.* severe congenital mental handicap. ▷late Middle English: from Latin, literally 'madness,' from *amens, ament-* 'mad,' from *a-* 'without' + *mens* 'the mind.'

A

Am·er·a·sian /ˌamərˈāZHən/ ▸*adj.* having one American and one Asian parent.
▸*n.* a person with one American and one Asian parent. ▹1960s: blend of AMERICAN and ASIAN.

a·merce·ment /əˈmərsmənt/ ▸*n. historical English Law* a fine. ▹late Middle English: from Anglo-Norman French *amerciment*, based on *estre amercie* 'be at the mercy of another' (with respect to the amount of a fine), from *a merci* 'at (the) mercy.' —**a·merce** *v.*

A·mer·i·ca /əˈmerikə/ (also **the A·mer·i·cas**) a landmass in the western hemisphere that consists of the continents of North and South America joined by the Isthmus of Panama. The continent was originally inhabited by American Indians and Inuits. The northeast coastline of North America was visited by Norse seamen in the 8th or 9th century, but for the modern world the continent was first reached by Christopher Columbus in 1492. ■ used as a name for the United States. ▹the name *America* dates from the early 16th cent. and is believed to derive from the Latin form (*Americus*) of the name of Amerigo Vespucci, who sailed along the west coast of South America in 1501.

A·mer·i·can /əˈmerikən/ ▸*adj.* of, relating to, or characteristic of the United States or its inhabitants: *the election of a new American president.* ■ relating to or denoting the continents of America: *the American continent south of the tropic of Cancer.*
▸*n.* **1** a native or citizen of the United States. ■ [usu. with *adj.*] a native or inhabitant of any of the countries of North, South, or Central America. **2** the English language as it is used in the United States; American English. ▹from modern Latin *Americanus*, from AMERICA. —**A·mer·i·can·ness** *n.*

A·mer·i·ca·na /əˌmeriˈkänə; -ˈkanə/ ▸*plural n.* things associated with the culture and history of America, esp. the United States.

A·mer·i·can al·oe ▸ another term for CENTURY PLANT.

A·mer·i·can bald ea·gle ▸*n.* another term for BALD EAGLE.

A·mer·i·can cheese ▸*n.* a type of mild-flavored semisoft processed cheese.

A·mer·i·can Civ·il War the war between the northern U.S. states (usually known as the Union) and the Confederate states of the South, 1861–65.

The war was fought over the issues of slavery and states' rights. The pro-slavery southern states seceded from the Federal Union following the election of Abraham Lincoln on an anti-slavery platform, but were defeated by the North.

A·mer·i·can croc·o·dile ▸*n.* a crocodile with a long tapering head, occurring from southernmost Florida to Ecuador. • *Crocodylus acutus,* family Crocodylidae.

American crocodile

A·mer·i·can de·pos·i·tar·y re·ceipt (abbr.: **ADR**) (also **American depositary share**) ▸*n.* (in the U.S.) a negotiable certificate of title to a number of shares in a non-U.S. company that are deposited in an overseas bank.

A·mer·i·can dream ▸*n.* the traditional social ideals of the U.S., such as equality, democracy, and material prosperity.

A·mer·i·can ea·gle ▸*n.* another term for BALD EAGLE.

A·mer·i·can e·gret ▸*n.* another term for GREAT EGRET.

A·mer·i·can Eng·lish ▸*n.* the English language as spoken and written in the U.S.

A·mer·i·can Falls ▸ see NIAGARA FALLS.

A·mer·i·can Fed·er·a·tion of La·bor a federation of North American trade unions, merged in 1955 with the Congress of Industrial Organizations to form the American Federation of Labor and Congress of Industrial Organizations (AFL–CIO).

A·mer·i·can foot·ball ▸*n.* British term for FOOTBALL.

A·mer·i·can Goth·ic ▸*n.* a noted 1930 painting by Grant Wood (1891–1942), depicting a dour-faced farmer and his daughter in front of their house, with a Gothic-style window in the background. It is representative of traditional American rural values, and is widely copied and parodied. ■ [as *adj.*] conservative in moral and social views.

A·mer·i·can In·de·pend·ence, War of British term for AMERICAN REVOLUTION.

A·mer·i·can In·di·an ▸*n.* a member of any of the indigenous peoples of North, Central, and South America, esp. those of North America.
▸*adj.* of or relating to any of these groups.

USAGE The term **American Indian** has been steadily replaced, esp. in official contexts, by the more recent term **Native American** (first recorded in the 1950s and becoming prominent in the 1970s). The latter is preferred by some as being a more accurate description (the word *Indian* recalling Columbus's assumption that, on reaching America, he had reached the east coast of India). **American Indian** is still widespread in general use, however, partly because it is not normally regarded as offensive by American Indians themselves.
See also NATIVE AMERICAN, AMERINDIAN, and INDIAN.

A·mer·i·can·ism /əˈmerikəˌnizəm/ ▸*n.* a word or phrase peculiar to or originating from the U.S. ■ the qualities regarded as definitive of America or Americans: *the same Americanism that Whitman sees in the farmer.*

A·mer·i·can·ize /əˈmerikəˌnīz/ ▸*v.* [*trans.*] make American in character or nationality: *trying to Americanize the immigrant children* | [as *adj.*] (**Americanized**) *an Americanized accent.* —**A·mer·i·can·i·za·tion** /əˌmerikəniˈzāSHən/ *n.*

A·mer·i·can League ▸*n.* one of the two major leagues in American professional baseball.

A·mer·i·can Le·gion an association of former U.S. servicemen formed in 1919.

A·mer·i·can lo·tus ▸*n.* see LOTUS.

A·mer·i·can or·gan ▸*n.* a type of reed organ resembling the harmonium but in which air is sucked (not blown) through reeds.

A·mer·i·can plan ▸*n.* (in hotels) a system of paying a single daily rate that covers the room and all meals. Often contrasted with EUROPEAN PLAN.

A·mer·i·can Rev·o·lu·tion the war of 1775–83 in which the American colonists won independence from British rule. Called in Britain the WAR OF AMERICAN INDEPENDENCE.

The war was triggered by resentment at the economic policies of Britain, particularly the right of Parliament to tax the colonies, and by the exclusion of the colonists from participation in political decisions affecting their interests. Following disturbances such as the Boston Tea Party of 1773, fighting broke out in 1775; a year later the Declaration of Independence was signed. The Americans gained the support of France and Spain, and French sea power eventually played a crucial role in the decisive surrender of a British army at Yorktown in 1781.

Amer·i·can Riv·er a river in north central California that joins the Sacramento River at Sacramento. Gold was discovered here in 1848, setting off the California gold rush.

A·mer·i·can sad·dle horse ▸*n.* a light, strong horse of a breed developed in Kentucky to be comfortable to ride over long distances.

A·mer·i·can Sa·mo·a /səˈmōə/ an unincorporated overseas territory of the U.S. that is composed of a group of islands in the southern Pacific Ocean, east of Western Samoa and south of Kiribati; pop. 57,900; capital, Fagatogo. The U.S. acquired rights to the islands by agreement with Germany and Britain in 1899, and the two main islands were ceded to the U.S. by their chiefs in April 1900.

A·mer·i·can Sign Lan·guage (abbr.: **ASL**) ▸*n.* a form of sign language developed in the U.S. for the use of the deaf, consisting of over 4,000 signs.

A·mer·i·can Stand·ard Ver·sion (abbr.: **ASV**) ▸*n.* an English translation of the Bible published in the U.S. in 1901, based on the Revised Version of 1881–95 with the incorporation of material produced by American scholars.

A·mer·i·cas /əˈmerikəz/ (**the Americas**) another name for AMERICA.

A·mer·i·ca's Cup an international yachting race held every three to four years.

A·mer·i·ca's Dair·y·land a nickname for the state of WISCONSIN[1].

am·er·i·ci·um /aməˈrisHēəm/ ▸*n.* the chemical element of atomic number 95, a radioactive metal of the actinide series. (Symbol: **Am**)

Americium does not occur naturally and was first made by bombarding plutonium with neutrons. It has been used in industrial measuring equipment as a source of gamma rays.

▹1940s: from AMERICA (where it was first made) + -IUM.

Am·er·in·di·an /ˌaməˈrindēən/ (also **Am·er·ind** /ˈamərind/) ▸*adj.* & *n.* another term for AMERICAN INDIAN, used chiefly in anthropological and linguistic contexts. ▹late 19th cent.: blend of AMERICAN and INDIAN.

USAGE See usage at INDIAN.

Ames /āmz/ a city in central Iowa, home to Iowa State University; pop. 50,731.

Am·e·slan /ˈam(i)ˌslan/ ▸ another term for AMERICAN SIGN LANGUAGE. ▹1970s: acronym.

Ames test /ˈāmz/ ▸*n. Medicine* a test to determine the mutagenic activity of chemicals by observing whether they cause mutations in sample bacteria. ▹1970s: named after Bruce N. *Ames* (born 1928), the American biochemist who devised it.

am·e·thyst /ˈaməTHəst/ ▸*n.* a precious stone consisting of a violet or purple variety of quartz. ■ a violet or purple color. ▹Middle English: via Old French from Latin *amethystus*, from Greek *amethustos* 'not drunken' (because the stone was believed to prevent intoxication). —**am·e·thys·tine** /ˌaməˈTHistin; -ˌtīn/ *adj.*

Amex /ˈameks/ ▸*abbr.* ■ *trademark* American Express. ■ American Stock Exchange.

Am·ha·ra /ämˈhärə/ ▸*n.* (*pl.* same or **-ras**) a member of an Amharic-speaking Semitic people of central Ethiopia.

Am·har·ic /amˈharik/ ▸*n.* the Semitic language descended from Ge'ez that is the official language of Ethiopia.
▸*adj.* of or relating to this language. ▹mid 18th cent.: from AMHARA + -IC.

Am·herst[1] /ˈam(h)ərst/ **1** a town in west central Massachusetts, home to several colleges and universities; pop. 35,228. **2** a town in western New York, northeast of Buffalo; pop. 111,711.

Am·herst[2] /ˈamərst/, Lord Jeffrey (1717–97), English soldier and military commander in North America. He was appointed governor general of British North America 1760–63 and served as commander in chief of the British army 1772–95.

a·mi·a·ble /ˈāmēəbəl/ ▸*adj.* having or displaying a friendly and pleasant manner: *an amiable, unassuming fellow.* ▹late Middle English (originally in the senses 'kind' and 'lovely, lovable'): via Old French from late Latin *amicabilis* 'amicable.' The current sense, influenced by modern French *aimable* 'trying to please,' dates from the mid 18th cent. —**a·mi·a·bil·i·ty** /ˌāmēəˈbilitē/ *n.* —**a·mi·a·bly** /-blē/ *adv.* —**a·mi·a·ble·ness** *n.*

am·i·ca·ble /ˈamikəbəl/ ▸*adj.* (of relations between people) having a spirit of friendliness; without serious disagreement or rancor: *there will be an amicable settlement of the dispute.* ▹late Middle English (in the sense 'pleasant, benign,' applied to things): from late Latin *amicabilis*, from Latin *amicus* 'friend.' —**am·i·ca·bil·i·ty** /ˌamikəˈbilitē/ *n.* —**am·i·ca·bly** /-blē/ *adv.*

am·ice[1] /ˈamis/ ▸*n.* a white linen cloth worn on the neck and shoulders, under the alb, by a priest celebrating the Eucharist. ▹late Middle English: from medieval Latin *amicia*, *amisia*, of unknown origin.

am·ice[2] ▸*n.* a cap, hood, or cape worn by members of

certain religious orders. ▷late Middle English: from Old French *aumusse*, from medieval Latin *almucia*, of unknown origin.

A·mi·ci /ə'mēCHē/, Dominic Felix, see **AMECHE**.

a·mi·cus /ə'mēkəs; ə'mī-/ (in full **a·mi·cus cu·ri·ae** /'kyŏŏrē,ī; -ē,ē/) ▶*n.* (*pl.* **a·mi·ci** /ə'mēkē; ə'mīkī/, **a·mi·ci cu·ri·ae**) an impartial adviser, often voluntary, to a court of law in a particular case: [as *adj.*] *he was planning to advance this position in an* ***amicus brief.*** ▷early 17th cent.: from modern Latin *amicus curiae*, literally 'friend of the court.'

a·mid /ə'mid/ ▶*prep.* surrounded by; in the middle of: *our dream home, set amid magnificent rolling countryside.* ■ in an atmosphere or against a background of: *talks broke down amid accusations of a hostile takeover bid.* ▷Middle English *amidde(s)*.

A·mi·dah /ə'mēdä/ ▶*n. Judaism* a prayer, part of the Jewish liturgy, consisting of a varying number of blessings recited while the worshipers stand. ▷late 19th cent.: Hebrew, literally 'standing.'

am·ide /'amīd; -id/ ▶*n. Chemistry* an organic compound containing the group $-C(O)NH_2$, related to ammonia by replacing a hydrogen atom by an acyl group. ■ a compound derived from ammonia by replacement of a hydrogen atom by a metal, containing the anion NH_2^-. ▷mid 19th cent.: from **AMMONIA + -IDE**.

a·mid·ships /ə'mid,SHips/ (also **a·mid·ship**) ▶*adv.* & *adj.* in the middle of a ship: [as *adv.*] *the destroyer rammed her amidships* | [as *adj.*] *an amidships engine.* ▷late 17th cent.: from **A-**[2] (expressing position or direction) + **MIDSHIPS** (as a noun meaning 'midship,' influenced by **AMID**.

a·midst /ə'midst/ ▶*prep.* variant of **AMID**.

Am·i·ens /'ameənz; äm'yeN/ a town in northern France; pop. 136,230.

a·mi·go /ə'mēgō/ ▶*n.* (*pl.* **-gos**) *informal* used to address or refer to a friend, chiefly in Spanish-speaking areas: *I will think about it, amigo.* ▷mid 19th cent.: Spanish.

A·min /ä'mēn/, Idi (1925–2003), Ugandan soldier and head of state 1971–79; full name *Idi Amin Dada*. He was deposed after a rule that was characterized by the murder of political opponents.

A·min·di·vi Is·lands /,əmən'dēvē/ the northernmost group of islands in Lakshadweep, India's Union Territory in the Indian Ocean.

a·mine /ə'mēn; 'amēn/ ▶*n. Chemistry* an organic compound derived from ammonia by replacement of one or more hydrogen atoms by organic radicals. ▷mid 19th cent.: from **AMMONIA + -INE**[4].

a·mi·no /ə'mēnō/ ▶*n.* [as *adj.*] *Chemistry* the group $-NH_2$, present in amino acids, amides, and many amines. ▷late 19th cent.: from **AMINE**.

amino- ▶*comb. form* designating or containing the group $-NH_2$: *aminobutyric.*

a·mi·no ac·id ▶*n. Biochemistry* a simple organic compound containing both a carboxyl ($-COOH$) and an amino ($-NH_2$) group.

Amino acids occur naturally in plant and animal tissues and are the basic constituents of proteins.

a·mir /ə'mi(ə)r/ ▶*n.* an Arab ruler. ▷late 16th cent.: from Persian and Urdu, from Arabic *'amīr* 'commander,' from *'amara* 'to command'; compare with **ADMIRAL, EMIR**.

Am·i·rante Is·lands /'amə,rant/ a group of coral islands in the Indian Ocean that form part of the Seychelles.

A·mis[1] /'āməs/, Sir Kingsley (1922–95), English novelist and poet, who achieved popular success with his first novel, *Lucky Jim* (1954). Other notable works: *The Old Devils* (1986), *The Folks that Live on the Hill* (1990), and *You Can't Do Both* (1994).

A·mis[2], Martin (Louis) (1949–), English novelist, son of Kingsley Amis. Notable works: *The Rachel Papers* (1973), *Money* (1984), and *Night Train* (1997).

A·mish /'ämisH/ ▶*plural n.* the members of a strict Mennonite sect that established major settlements in Pennsylvania, Ohio, and elsewhere in North America from 1720 onward.
▶*adj.* of or relating to this sect. ▷mid 19th cent.: apparently from German *amisch*.

Am·ish Coun·try name for areas, chiefly in southeastern Pennsylvania and northeastern Ohio, that are inhabited by the Amish, an agricultural religious sect.

a·miss /ə'mis/ ▶*adj.* [*predic.*] not quite right; inappropriate or out of place: *there was* ***something amiss*** *about his calculations.*
▶*adv. dated* wrongly or inappropriately: *how terrible was the danger of her loving amiss.* ▷Middle English: probably from Old Norse *á mis* 'so as to miss,' from *á* 'on' + *mis* (related to **MISS**[1]).
▶*PHRASE* □ **take something amiss** be offended by something that is said, typically through misinterpreting the intentions behind it: *don't take this amiss, it's all good-humored teasing.*

am·i·tot·ic /,āmī'tätik; ,amī-/ ▶*adj. Biology* relating to or denoting the division of a cell nucleus into two parts by constriction without the involvement of a mitotic apparatus. —**am·i·to·sis** /-'tōsis/ *n.* —**am·i·tot·i·cal·ly** /-ik(ə)lē/ *adv.*

am·i·trip·ty·line /,ami'triptə,lēn; -lin/ ▶*n. Medicine* an antidepressant drug of the tricyclic group, with a mild tranquilizing action. ▷1960s: from *ami(ne)* + **TRI-** + *(he)ptyl* + **-INE**[4].

am·i·ty /'amitē/ ▶*n.* a friendly relationship: *international amity and goodwill.* ▷late Middle English: from Old French *amitie*, based on Latin *amicus* 'friend.'

Am·man /ä'män; ə'män; ə'man/ the capital of Jordan, located in the northwestern part of the country; pop. 1,160,000.

am·me·ter /'a(m),mētər/ ▶*n.* an instrument for measuring electric current in amperes. ▷late 19th cent.: from **AMPERE + -METER**.

am·mo /'amō/ ▶*n.* informal term for **AMMUNITION**.

Am·mon /'amən/ Greek and Roman form of **AMUN**.

am·mo·nia /ə'mōnyə; -nēə/ ▶*n.* a colorless gas with a characteristic pungent smell. It dissolves in water to give a strongly alkaline solution. • Chem. formula: NH_3. ■ a solution of this gas, used as a cleaning fluid. ▷late 18th cent.: modern Latin, from *sal ammoniacus* (see **SAL AMMONIAC**).

am·mo·ni·a·cal /,amə'nīikəl/ ▶*adj.* of or containing ammonia. ▷mid 18th cent.: from Middle English *ammoniac*, via Old French from Latin *ammoniacus*. This represented the Greek word *ammōniakos* 'of Ammon,' used as a name for the salt and gum obtained near the temple of *Jupiter Ammon* (the Greek name for the Egyptian deity *Amen*) at Siwa in Egypt. Compare with **SAL AMMONIAC**.

am·mo·ni·at·ed /ə'mōnē,ātid/ ▶*adj.* combined or treated with ammonia. —**am·mo·ni·a·tion** /ə,mōnē'āsHən/ *n.*

am·mo·nite /'amə,nīt/ ▶*n.* an ammonoid that belongs to the order *Ammonitida*, typically having elaborately frilled suture lines. • Typified by ammonoids of the order Ammonitida. ▷mid 18th cent.: from modern Latin *ammonites*, from medieval Latin *cornu Ammonis* 'horn of Ammon,' from the fossil's resemblance to the ram's horn associated with Jupiter Ammon (see **AMMONIACAL**).

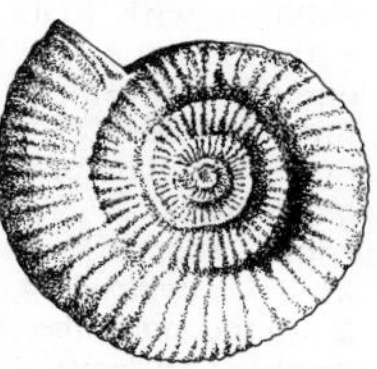
ammonite

am·mo·ni·um /ə'mōnēəm/ ▶*n.* [as *adj.*] *Chemistry* the cation NH_4^+, present in solutions of ammonia and in salts derived from ammonia. ▷early 19th cent.: from **AMMONIA + -IUM**.

am·mo·ni·um car·bon·ate ▶*n. Chemistry* a white crystalline solid that slowly decomposes giving off ammonia and is an ingredient of sal volatile. • Chem. formula: $(NH_4)_2CO_3$. Commercial forms often contain other, related, salts.

am·mo·ni·um chlo·ride ▶*n. Chemistry* a white crystalline salt used chiefly in dry cells, as a mordant, and as soldering flux. Also called **SAL AMMONIAC**. • Chem. formula: NH_4Cl.

am·mo·ni·um ni·trate ▶*n. Chemistry* a white crystalline solid used as a fertilizer and as a component of some explosives. • Chem. formula: NH_4NO_3.

am·mo·noid /'amə,noid/ *Paleontology* ▶*n.* an extinct cephalopod mollusk with a flat-coiled spiral shell, found commonly as a fossil in marine deposits from the Devonian to the Cretaceous periods. • Subclass Ammonoidea, class Cephalopoda: numerous families. See **AMMONITE, CERATITE**, and **GONIATITE**.
▶*adj.* of or relating to the ammonoids. ▷mid 19th cent.: from modern Latin *Ammonoidea*, based on **AMMON** (see **AMMONITE**).

am·mu·ni·tion /,amyə'nisHən/ ▶*n.* a supply or quantity of bullets and shells. ■ *figurative* considerations that can be used to support one's case in debate: *these figures provide ammunition to the argument for more resources.* ▷late 16th cent.: from obsolete French *amunition*, alteration (by wrong division) of *la munition* 'the munition' (see **MUNITION**).

am·ne·sia /am'nēZHə/ ▶*n.* a partial or total loss of memory. ▷late 18th cent.: from Greek *amnēsia* 'forgetfulness.' —**am·ne·si·ac** /am'nēzē,ak; -ZHē,ak/ *n.* & *adj.* —**am·ne·sic** /-zik; -sik/ *adj.* & *n.* —**am·nes·tic** /am'nestik/ *adj.*

am·nes·ty /'amnistē/ ▶*n.* (*pl.* **-ties**) an official pardon for people who have been convicted of political offenses: *an amnesty for political prisoners* | *the new law granted amnesty to those who illegally left the country.* ■ an undertaking by the authorities to take no action against specified offenses or offenders during a fixed period: *a month-long weapons amnesty.*
▶*v.* (**-ties, -tied**) [*trans.*] grant an official pardon to: *the guerrillas would be amnestied and allowed to return to civilian life.* ▷late 16th cent.: via Latin from Greek *amnēstia* 'forgetfulness.'

Am·nes·ty In·ter·na·tion·al an independent international organization in support of human rights, esp. for prisoners of conscience. It was awarded the Nobel Peace Prize in 1977.

am·ni·o /'amnē-ō/ ▶*n.* (*pl.* **-os**) informal term for **AMNIOCENTESIS**.

am·ni·o·cen·te·sis /,amnē-ōsen'tēsis/ ▶*n.* (*pl.* **-ses** /-sēz/) *Medicine* the sampling of amniotic fluid using a hollow needle inserted into the uterus, to screen for developmental abnormalities in a fetus. ▷1950s: from **AMNION** + Greek *kentēsis* 'pricking' (from *kentein* 'to prick').

am·ni·on /'amnē,än; -ən/ ▶*n.* (*pl.* - or **-ni·a** /-nēə/) the innermost membrane that encloses the embryo of a mammal, bird, or reptile. ▷mid 17th cent.: from Greek, 'caul,' diminutive of *amnos* 'lamb.' —**am·ni·ot·ic** /,amnē'ätik/ *adj.*

am·ni·ote /'amnē,ōt/ ▶*n. Zoology* an animal whose embryo develops in an amnion and chorion and has an allantois; a mammal, bird, or reptile. ▷late 19th cent.: from modern Latin *Amniota*, back-formation from *amniotic* (see **AMNION**).

am·ni·ot·ic flu·id /,amnē'ätik/ ▶*n.* the fluid surrounding a fetus within the amnion.

amn't /ant; 'amənt/ *chiefly Scottish Irish* ▶*contraction of* am not.

a·moe·ba ▶*n.* (*pl.* **-bas** or **-bae** /-bē/) variant spelling of **AMEBA**. —**a·moe·bic** *adj.* —**a·moe·boid** *adj.*

a·mok /ə'mək; ə'mäk/ (also **a·muck**) ▶*adv.* (in phrase **run amok**) behave uncontrollably and disruptively: *stone-throwing anarchists running amok* | *figurative her feelings seemed to be running amok.* ▷mid 17th cent.: via Portuguese *amouco*, from Malay *amok* 'rushing in a frenzy.' Early use was as a noun denoting a Malay in a homicidal frenzy; the adverb use dates from the late 17th cent.

a·mo·le /ə'mōlā; -lē/ ▶*n.* a plant of a group native to Mexico and the southern U.S. whose roots are used as detergent, esp. the soap plant or the lechuguilla. ▷mid 19th cent.: Mexican Spanish.

A·mon ▶ variant spelling of **AMUN**.

a·mong /ə'məNG/ (*chiefly Brit.* also **a·mongst** /ə'məNGst/) ▶*prep.* **1** surrounded by; in the company of: *wild strawberries hidden among the roots of the trees* | *you're among friends.* **2** being a member or members of (a larger set): *he was among the first 29 students enrolled* | *snakes are among the animals most feared by humans.* **3** occurring in or practiced by (some members of a community): *a drop in tooth decay among children* | *this pronunciation is not popular among the general public* | *rooting out abuses among the clergy.* ■ involving most or all members of a group reciprocally: *members of the government bickered* ***among themselves.*** **4** indicating a division, choice, or differentiation involving three or more participants: *the king called the three princesses to divide his kingdom among them* | *choosing a privatization scheme from among five models.* ▷Old English *ongemang* (from *on* 'in' + *gemang* 'assemblage, mingling'). The *-st* of *amongst* represents *-s* (adverbial genitive) + *-t* probably by association with superlatives (as in *against*).

USAGE See usage at **BETWEEN**.

a·mon·til·la·do /ə,mäntl'ädō; -tē'yädō/ ▶*n.* (*pl.* **-dos**) a medium dry sherry. ▷Spanish, from *Montilla*, the name of a town in southern Spain where the original wine was produced.

a·mor·al /ā'môrəl/ ▶*adj.* lacking a moral sense; unconcerned with the rightness or wrongness of something: *an amoral attitude to sex.* —**a·mo·ral·i·ty** /,āmə'ralitē/ *n.* —**a·mor·al·ism** /-,lizəm/ *n.* —**a·mor·al·ist** /-list/ *n.*

USAGE See usage at **IMMORAL**.

am·o·ret·to /ˌaməˈretō/ ▶*n.* (*pl.* **-ret·ti** /-ˈretē/) a representation of Cupid in a work of art. ▷late 17th cent. (denoting a lover or a love song): Italian, diminutive of *amore* 'love,' from Latin *amor.*

am·o·rist /ˈamərist/ ▶*n.* a person who is in love or who writes about love. ▷late 16th cent.: from Latin *amor* or French *amour* 'love' + **-IST**.

Am·o·rite /ˈaməˌrīt/ ▶*n.* a member of seminomadic people living in Mesopotamia, Palestine, and Syria in the 3rd millennium BC, founders of Mari on the Euphrates and the first dynasty of Babylon.
▶*adj.* of or relating to this people. ▷from Hebrew *'ĕmōrī*, from Akkadian *'amurrū* + **-ITE**[1].

a·mo·ro·so[1] /ˌäməˈrōsō/ ▶*adv.* & *adj. Music* (esp. as a direction) in a loving or tender manner. ▷Italian, from medieval Latin *amorosus* (see **AMOROUS**).

a·mo·ro·so[2] ▶*n.* a sweetened oloroso sherry. ▷late 19th cent.: Spanish, literally 'amorous,' from medieval Latin *amorosus* (see **AMOROUS**).

am·o·rous /ˈamərəs/ ▶*adj.* showing, feeling, or relating to sexual desire: *she rejected his amorous advances.* ▷Middle English: via Old French from medieval Latin *amorosus*, from Latin *amor* 'love.' **—am·o·rous·ly** *adv.* **—am·o·rous·ness** *n.*

a·mor·phous /əˈmôrfəs/ ▶*adj.* without a clearly defined shape or form: *amorphous blue forms and straight black lines.* ■ vague; ill-organized; unclassifiable: *make explicit the amorphous statements.* ■ (of a group of people or an organization) lacking a clear structure or focus: *an amorphous and leaderless legislature.* ■ *Mineralogy* & *Chemistry* (of a solid) noncrystalline; having neither definite form nor apparent structure. ▷mid 18th cent.: from modern Latin *amorphus*, from Greek *amorphos* 'shapeless' (from *a-* 'without' + *morphē* 'form') + **-OUS**. **—a·mor·phous·ly** *adv.* **—a·mor·phous·ness** *n.*

am·or·tize /ˈamərˌtīz/ ▶*v.* [*trans.*] reduce or extinguish (a debt) by money regularly put aside: *loan fees can be amortized over the life of the mortgage.* ■ gradually write off the initial cost of (an asset): *they want to amortize the tooling costs quickly.* ▷late Middle English (in the senses 'deaden' and 'transfer (land) to a corporation in mortmain'): from Old French *amortiss-*, lengthened stem of *amortir*, based on Latin *ad* 'to, at' + *mors, mort-* 'death.' **—am·or·ti·za·tion** /ˌamərtiˈzāsʜən; əˌmôrti-/ *n.*

A·mos /ˈāməs/ a Hebrew minor prophet (*c.*760 BC), a shepherd of Tekoa, near Jerusalem. ■ a book of the Bible containing his prophecies.

am·o·site /ˈaməˌsīt/ ▶*n.* an iron-rich amphibole asbestos, mined in South Africa. ▷early 20th cent.: from the initial letters of Asbestos Mines of South Africa + **-ITE**[1].

a·mount /əˈmount/ ▶*n.* a quantity of something, typically the total of a thing or things in number, size, value, or extent: *the sport gives an enormous* **amount of** *pleasure to many people | the substance is harmless if taken in small amounts.* ■ a sum of money: *they have spent a colossal amount rebuilding the stadium.*
▶*v.* [*intrans.*] (**amount to**) come to be (the total) when added together: *losses amounted to over 10 million dollars.* ■ be the equivalent of: *their actions amounted to a conspiracy.* ■ develop into; become: *you'll never amount to anything.* ▷Middle English (as a verb): from Old French *amunter*, from *amont* 'upward,' literally 'uphill,' from Latin *ad montem*. The noun use dates from the early 18th cent.
▶*PHRASES* □ **any amount of** a great deal or number of: *a good marriage can withstand any amount of external pressure.* □ **no amount of** not even the greatest possible amount of: *no amount of talk is going to change anything.*

a·mour /əˈmo͝or; äˈmo͝or/ ▶*n.* a secret or illicit love affair or lover. ▷Middle English (originally in the sense 'love, affection'): via Old French from Latin *amor* 'love.' The current sense dates from the late 16th cent.

a·mour fou /äˈmo͝or ˈfo͞o/ ▶*n.* uncontrollable or obsessive passion. ▷1970s: French, literally 'insane love.'

a·mour pro·pre /äˌmo͝or ˈprôpr(ə)/ ▶*n.* a sense of one's own worth; self-respect: *few indications in him of ordinary* amour propre *or common vanity.* ▷late 18th cent.: French, literally 'self-esteem, vanity.'

a·mox·i·cil·lin /əˌmäksəˈsilin/ (also **a·mox·y·cil·lin**) ▶*n.* a broad-spectrum semisynthetic penicillin, closely related to ampicillin but better absorbed when taken orally, used esp. for ear and upper respiratory infections. ▷late 20th cent.: blend of **AMINO** + contractions of **HYDROXY** + **PENICILLIN**.

A·moy /äˈmoi/ another name for **XIAMEN**.

AMP ▶*Biochemistry abbr.* adenosine monophosphate.

amp[1] /amp/ ▶*n.* short for **AMPERE**.

amp[2] ▶*n. informal* short for **AMPLIFIER**.
▶*v.* (often **amp something up**) **1** play (music) through electric amplification: *their willingness to amp up traditional songs virtually began the folk-rock genre.* **2** [as *adj.*] (**amped** or **amped up**) *informal* full of nervous energy: *third-ranked Ohio State (5-0) visits an amped-up Madison for a date with 4-1 Wisconsin.*

Am·pa·kine /ˈampəˌkīn/ ▶*n. trademark* any of a class of synthetic compounds that facilitate transmission of nerve impulses in the brain and appear to improve memory and learning capacity. ▷1990s: from *AMPA* (an acronym denoting certain receptors in the brain) + Greek *kinein* 'to move.'

am·pe·lop·sis /ˌampəˈläpsis/ ▶*n.* (*pl.* same) any of several woody vines of the grape family. • Genus *Ampelopsis*, family Vitaceae: several species, including **American ampelopsis** (*A. cordata*), the **PEPPER VINE** (*ampelopsis arborea*) and the **PORCELAINBERRY** (*A. brevipedunculata*). ▷modern Latin, from Greek *ampelos* 'vine' + *opsis* 'appearance.'

am·per·age /ˈamp(ə)rij/ ▶*n.* the strength of an electric current in amperes.

Am·père /äɴˈper/, André-Marie (1775–1836), French physicist, mathematician, and philosopher, who analyzed the relationship between magnetic force and electric current.

am·pere /ˈamˌpi(ə)r/ (abbr.: **A**) ▶*n.* a unit of electric current equal to a flow of one coulomb per second. • The SI base unit of electric current, 1 ampere is precisely defined as that constant current which, if maintained in two straight parallel conductors of infinite length, of negligible circular cross-section, and placed 1 meter apart in a vacuum, would produce between these conductors a force of 2×10^{-7} newton per meter. ▷late 19th cent.: named after A. M. **AMPÈRE**.

am·per·sand /ˈampərˌsand/ ▶*n.* the sign & (standing for *and*, as in *Smith & Co.*, or the Latin *et*, as in *&c.*). ▷mid 19th cent.: alteration of *and per se and* '& by itself is *and*,' chanted as an aid to learning the sign.

am·phet·a·mine /amˈfetəˌmēn; -min/ ▶*n.* a synthetic, addictive, mood-altering drug, used illegally as a stimulant and legally as a prescription drug to treat children with ADD and adults with narcolepsy. • Alternative name: **1-phenyl-2-aminopropane** (or one of its salts, esp. **amphetamine sulfate**); chem. formula: $C_6H_5CH_2CH(CH_3)NH_2$. ▷1930s: abbreviation of its chemical name, *a(lpha-)m(ethyl) phe(ne)t(hyl)amine.*

amphi- ▶*comb. form* **1** both: *amphibian.* ■ of both kinds: *amphipod.* ■ on both sides: *amphiprostyle.* **2** around: *amphitheater.* ▷from Greek.

am·phib·i·an /amˈfibēən/ ▶*n. Zoology* a cold-blooded vertebrate animal of a class that comprises the frogs, toads, newts, and salamanders. They are distinguished by having an aquatic gill-breathing larval stage followed (typically) by a terrestrial lung-breathing adult stage. • Class Amphibia: orders Urodela (newts and salamanders), Anura (frogs and toads), and Gymnophiona (caecilians). ■ a seaplane, tank, or other vehicle that can operate on land and on water.
▶*adj. Zoology* of or relating to this class of animals: *reptile and amphibian biology.* ▷mid 17th cent. (in the sense 'having two modes of existence or of doubtful nature'): from modern Latin *amphibium* 'an amphibian,' from Greek *amphibion* (noun use of *amphibios* 'living both in water and on land,' from *amphi* 'both' + *bios* 'life').

am·phib·i·ous /amˈfibēəs/ ▶*adj.* relating to, living in, or suited for both land and water: *amphibious habitats | an amphibious vehicle.* ■ (of a military operation) involving forces landed from the sea: *an amphibious assault.* ■ (of forces) trained for such operations. ▷mid 17th cent.: from modern Latin *amphibium*, from Greek *amphibion* (see **AMPHIBIAN**) + **-OUS**.

am·phi·bole /ˈamfəˌbōl/ ▶*n.* any of a class of rock-forming silicate or aluminosilicate minerals typically occurring as fibrous or columnar crystals. ▷early 19th cent.: from French, from Latin *amphibolus* 'ambiguous' (so called because of the varied structure of these minerals), from Greek *amphibolos*, from *amphi-* 'both, on both sides' + *ballein* 'to throw.'

am·phib·o·lite /amˈfibəˌlīt/ ▶*n. Geology* a granular metamorphic rock consisting mainly of hornblende and plagioclase. ▷early 19th cent.: from **AMPHIBOLE** + **-ITE**[1].

am·phi·bol·o·gy /ˌamfəˈbäləjē/ ▶*n.* (*pl.* **-gies**) a phrase or sentence that is grammatically ambiguous, such as *she sees more of her children than her husband.* ▷late Middle English: from Old French *amphibologie*, from late Latin *amphibologia*, from Latin *amphibolia*, from Greek *amphibolos* 'ambiguous' (see **AMPHIBOLE**). **—am·phib·o·lous** /amˈfibələs/ *adj.*

am·phib·o·ly /amˈfibəlē/ ▶*n.* (*pl.* **-lies**) another term for **AMPHIBOLOGY**.

am·phi·brach /ˈamfəˌbrak/ ▶*n. Prosody* a metrical foot consisting of a stressed syllable between two unstressed syllables or (in Greek and Latin) a long syllable between two short syllables. ▷late 16th cent. (originally in the Latin forms *amphibrachus, amphibrachys*): via Latin from Greek *amphibrakhus* 'short at both ends.'

am·phi·mix·is /ˌamfəˈmiksis/ ▶*n. Botany* sexual reproduction involving the fusion of two different gametes to form a zygote. Often contrasted with **APOMIXIS**. ▷late 19th cent.: from **AMPHI-** + Greek *mixis* 'mingling.' **—am·phi·mic·tic** /-ˈmiktik/ *adj.*

am·phi·ox·us /ˌamfēˈäksəs/ ▶*n.* a lancelet that is caught for food in parts of Asia. • Genus *Branchiostoma* (formerly *Amphioxus*), family Branchiostomidae. ▷mid 19th cent.: modern Latin, from **AMPHI-** + Greek *oxus* 'sharp.'

am·phi·path·ic /ˌamfəˈpaᴛʜik/ ▶*adj. Biochemistry* (of a molecule, esp. a protein) having both hydrophilic and hydrophobic parts. ▷1930s: from **AMPHI-** + Greek *pathikos* (from *pathos* 'experience').

am·phi·phil·ic /ˌamfəˈfilik/ ▶*adj. Biochemistry* another term for **AMPHIPATHIC**.

Am·phip·o·da /amˈfipədə/ *Zoology* an order of crustaceans with a laterally compressed body and a large number of leglike appendages. ▷modern Latin (plural), from **AMPHI-** 'of both kinds' (because some legs are specialized for swimming and some for feeding) + Greek *pous, pod-* 'foot.' **—am·phi·pod** /ˈamfəˌpäd/ *n.*

am·phip·ro·style /amˈfiprəˌstīl; ˌamfəˈprō-/ ▶*adj.* (of a classical building) having a portico at each end and no columns along the sides. ▷early 18th cent.: via Latin from Greek *amphiprostulos*, from *amphi-* 'both, on both sides'+ *prostulos* 'having pillars in front' (see **PROSTYLE**).

am·phis·bae·na /ˌamfəsˈbēnə/ ▶*n. Mythology* & *poetic/literary* a legendary serpent with a head at each end. ▷late Middle English: via Latin from Greek *amphisbaina*, from *amphis* 'both ways' + *bainein* 'go.'

Am·phis·bae·ni·a /ˌamfisˈbēnēə/ *Zoology* a group of reptiles that comprises the worm lizards. • Suborder Amphisbaenia, order Squamata. ▷modern Latin, from Greek *amphisbaina*, from *amphis* 'both' + *bainein* 'go, walk.' **—am·phis·bae·ni·an** *n.* & *adj.*

am·phi·the·a·ter /ˈamfəˌᴛʜēətər/ ▶*n.* (esp. in Greek and Roman architecture) a round building, typically unroofed, with a central space for the presentation of dramatic or sporting events. Tiers of seats for spectators surround the central space. ■ a sloping, semicircular seating gallery: *I was permitted to attend a lecture in the amphitheater of the hospital.* ■ a large circular hollow in rocks or hills: *that vast amphitheater chiseled out of the mountain.* ▷late Middle English: via Latin from Greek *amphitheatron*, from *amphi* 'on both sides' + *theatron* (see **THEATER**).

amphitheater

Am·phi·tri·te /ˌamfiˈtrītē/ *Greek Mythology* a sea goddess, wife of Poseidon and mother of Triton.

am·phi·u·ma /ˌamfēˈyo͞omə/ ▶*n.* a fully aquatic eellike amphibian with very small limbs, found in stagnant water and swamps in the southeastern U.S. • Family Amphiumidae and genus *Amphiuma*: three species (identified by the number of toes on each limb), the one-toed *A. pholeter*, the two-toed *A. means*, and the three-toed *A. tridactylum*.

am·pho·ra /ˈamfərə/ ▶*n.* (*pl.* **-rae** /-ˌrē/ or **-ras**) a tall ancient Greek or Roman jar with two handles and a narrow neck. ▷Latin, from Greek *amphoreus*, or from French *amphore*.

am·pho·ter·ic /ˌamfəˈterik/ ▶*adj. Chemistry* (of a compound, esp. a metal oxide or hydroxide) able to react both as a base and as an acid. ▷mid 19th cent.: from Greek *amphoteros*, comparative of *amphō* 'both,' + **-IC**.

am·pi·cil·lin /ˌampiˈsilin/ ▸*n. Medicine* a semisynthetic form of penicillin used chiefly to treat infections of the urinary and respiratory tracts. ▷1960s: blend of **AMINO** and a contraction of **PENICILLIN**.

am·ple /ˈampəl/ ▸*adj.* (**-pler, -plest**) enough or more than enough; plentiful: *there is ample time for discussion | an ample supply of consumer goods.* ■ large and accommodating: *he leaned back in his ample chair.* ■ used euphemistically to convey that someone is fat: *she stood with her hands on her ample hips.* ▷late Middle English: via French from Latin *amplus* 'large, capacious, abundant.' **—am·ple·ness** *n.* **—am·ply** /-p(ə)lē/ *adv.*

am·plex·i·caul /amˈpleksiˌkôl/ ▸*adj. Botany* (of a leaf) embracing and surrounding the stem.

am·plex·us /amˈpleksəs/ ▸*n. Zoology* the mating position of frogs and toads, in which the male clasps the female about the back. ▷1930s: from Latin, literally 'an embrace.'

am·pli·fi·er /ˈampləˌfīər/ ▸*n.* an electronic device for increasing the amplitude of electrical signals, used chiefly in sound reproduction. ■ a device of this kind combined with a loudspeaker, used to amplify electric guitars and other musical instruments.

am·pli·fy /ˈampləˌfī/ ▸*v.* (**-fies, -fied**) [*trans.*] (often **be amplified**) increase the volume of (sound), esp. using an amplifier: *the accompanying chords have been amplified in our arrangement.* ■ increase the amplitude of (an electrical signal or other oscillation). ■ cause to become more marked or intense: *urban policy initiatives amplified social polarization.* ■ *Genetics* make multiple copies of (a gene or DNA sequence). ■ enlarge upon or add detail to (a story or statement): *the notes amplify information contained in the statement.* ▷late Middle English (in the general sense 'increase, augment'): from Old French *amplifier*, from Latin *amplificare*, from *amplus* 'large, abundant.' **—am·pli·fi·ca·tion** /ˌampləfiˈkāsʜən/ *n.*

am·pli·tude /ˈampliˌt(y)o͞od/ ▸*n.* **1** *Physics* the maximum extent of a vibration or oscillation, measured from the position of equilibrium. ■ the maximum difference of an alternating electrical current or potential from the average value. **2** *Astronomy* the angular distance of a celestial object from the true east or west point of the horizon at rising or setting. **3** breadth, range, or magnitude: *the amplitude of the crime of manslaughter lies beneath murder.* **4** *Mathematics* the angle between the real axis of an Argand diagram and a vector representing a complex number. ▷mid 16th cent. (in the senses 'physical extent' and 'grandeur'): from Latin *amplitudo*, from *amplus* 'large, abundant.'

am·pli·tude mod·u·la·tion (abbr.: **AM**) ▸*n.* the modulation of a wave by varying its amplitude, used chiefly as a means of radio broadcasting, in which an audio signal is combined with a carrier wave. Often contrasted with **FREQUENCY MODULATION**. ■ the system of radio transmission using such modulation.

am·poule /ˈamˌp(y)o͞ol/ (also **am·pul** or **am·pule**) ▸*n.* a sealed glass capsule containing a liquid, esp. a measured quantity ready for injecting: *an ampoule of epinephrine.* ▷early 20th cent.: from French, from Latin *ampulla* (see **AMPULLA**).

am·pul·la /amˈpo͝olə; -ˈpələ/ ▸*n.* (*pl.* **-lae** /-lē/) a roughly spherical flask with two handles, used in ancient Rome. ■ a flask for sacred uses such as holding holy oil. ■ *Anatomy & Zoology* a cavity, or the dilated end of a duct, shaped like a Roman ampulla. ▷late Middle English: from Latin, diminutive of *ampora*, variant of *amphora* (see **AMPHORA**).

am·pu·tate /ˈampyəˌtāt/ ▸*v.* [*trans.*] cut off (a limb), typically by surgical operation: *surgeons had to amputate her left hand | the wounded had to* **have** *legs or arms* **amputated**. ▷mid 16th cent.: from Latin *amputat-* 'lopped off,' from *amputare*, from *am-* (for *amb-* 'around') + *putare* 'to prune.' **—am·pu·ta·tion** /ˌampyəˈtāsʜən/ *n.*

am·pu·tee /ˌampyəˈtē/ ▸*n.* a person who has had a limb amputated.

AMRAAM /ˈamˌram/ ▸*abbr.* advanced medium range air-to-air missile.

am·rit /ˈəmrit/ (also **am·ri·ta** /əmˈrētə/) ▸*n.* a syrup considered divine by Sikhs and taken by them in religious observances. ▷from Sanskrit *amṛta* 'immortal.'

Am·rit·sar /ˌəmˈritsər; äm-/ a city in the state of Punjab in northwestern India; pop. 709,000. The center of the Sikh faith, it is the site of its Golden Temple.

am·scray /ˈamˌskrā/ ▸*v.* [*intrans.*] leave quickly; scram: *just amscray and be done with it.* ▷Pig Latin.

Am·ster·dam /ˈamstərˌdam/ the capital and largest city of the Netherlands; pop. 702,440 . It is an important port and financial center, esp. known for its diamond industry.

AMT ▸*abbr.* alternative minimum tax, introduced to prevent companies and individuals using deductions and credits to pay no tax.

am·trac /ˈamˌtrak/ (also **am·track, am·trak**) ▸*n.* an amphibious tracked vehicle used for landing assault troops on a shore. ▷World War II: blend of **AMPHIBIOUS** and **TRACTOR**.

Am·trak /ˈamˌtrak/ *trademark* a federal passenger railroad service in the U.S., operated by the National Railroad Passenger Corporation.

amu ▸*abbr.* atomic mass unit.

a·muck /əˈmək/ ▸*adv.* variant spelling of **AMOK**.

A·mu Dar·ya /ˌämo͞o ˈdäryə/ a river in central Asia that rises in the Pamirs and flows 1,500 miles (2,400 km) into the Aral Sea. In classical times, it was known as the Oxus.

am·u·let /ˈamyəlit/ ▸*n.* an ornament or small piece of jewelry thought to give protection against evil, danger, or disease. ▷late 16th cent.: from Latin *amuletum*, of unknown origin.

A·mun /ˈämən/ (also **A·mon**) *Egyptian Mythology* a supreme god of the ancient Egyptians, identified with the sun god Ra and in Greek and Roman times with Zeus and Jupiter (under the name **Ammon**).

A·mund·sen /ˈämənsən/, Roald (1872–1928), Norwegian explorer. Amundsen was the first to navigate the Northwest Passage (1903–06), during which expedition he located the site of the magnetic North Pole. In 1911, he became the first person to reach the South Pole.

A·mur /äˈmo͝or/ a river of northeastern Asia that forms, for much of its length, the boundary between Russia and China. Its length is about 2,737 miles (4,350 km). Chinese name **HEILONG**.

a·muse /əˈmyo͞oz/ ▸*v.* [*trans.*] **1** cause (someone) to find something funny; entertain: *he made faces to amuse her |* [as *adj.*] (**amused**) *people looked on with amused curiosity.* **2** provide interesting and enjoyable occupation for (someone): *the hotel has planned many activities to amuse its guests | they* **amused themselves** *digging through an old encyclopedia |* [as *adj.*] (**amused**) *elegant shops that will keep any browser amused for hours.* ▷late 15th cent. (in the sense 'delude, deceive'): from Old French *amuser* 'entertain, deceive,' from *a-* (expressing causal effect) + *muser* 'stare stupidly.' The current senses date from the mid 17th cent. **—a·mus·ed·ly** /-zidlē/ *adv.* (in sense 1).

a·muse-gueule /ˌämo͞oz ˈgəl/ ▸*n.* (*pl.* **a·muse-gueules** *pronunc.* same) a small, savory item of food served as an appetizer before a meal. ▷late 20th cent.: French, literally 'amuse mouth.'

a·muse·ment /əˈmyo͞ozmənt/ ▸*n.* the state or experience of finding something funny: *we looked with amusement at our horoscopes.* ■ the provision or enjoyment of entertainment: *an evening's amusement.* ■ something that causes laughter or provides entertainment: *his daughter was an amusement to him.* ▷early 17th cent. (in the sense 'musing, diversion of the attention'): from French, from the verb *amuser* (see **AMUSE**).

a·muse·ment park ▸*n.* a large outdoor area with fairground rides, shows, refreshments, games of chance or skill, and other entertainments.

a·mus·ing /əˈmyo͞oziɴɢ/ ▸*adj.* causing laughter or providing entertainment: *such a likable, amusing man!* **—a·mus·ing·ly** *adv.*

a·myg·da·la /əˈmigdələ/ ▸*n.* (*pl.* **-lae** /-lē/) *Anatomy* a roughly almond-shaped mass of gray matter deep inside each cerebral hemisphere, associated with the sense of smell. ▷late Middle English: via Latin from Greek *amugdalē* 'almond.'

a·myg·da·lin /əˈmigdəlin/ ▸*n. Chemistry* a bitter crystalline compound, found in bitter almonds and the stones of peaches, apricots, and other fruit. ▷mid 19th cent.: from Latin *amygdala* 'almond' + **-IN**[1].

a·myg·da·loid /əˈmigdəˌloid/ ▸*adj. technical* shaped like an almond.

▸*n.* **1** (also **amygdaloid nucleus**) *Anatomy* another term for **AMYGDALA**. **2** *Geology* volcanic rock with amygdules. ▷mid 18th cent.: from Latin *amygdala* 'almond' + **-OID**.

a·myg·da·loi·dal /əˌmigdəˈloidl/ ▸*adj. Geology* relating to or containing amygdules.

a·myg·dule /əˈmigˌd(y)o͞ol/ (also **a·myg·dale** /-ˌdāl/) ▸*n.* *Geology* a vesicle in an igneous rock, containing secondary minerals. ▷late 19th cent.: from French, from Latin *amygdala* (see **AMYGDALA**).

am·yl /ˈaməl/ ▸*n.* [as *adj.*] *Chemistry* the straight-chain pentyl radical $-C_5H_{11}$. ■ *informal* short for **AMYL NITRITE**. ▷mid 19th cent.: from Latin *amylum* 'starch' + **-YL**.

am·yl·ase /ˈaməˌlās; -ˌlāz/ ▸*n. Biochemistry* an enzyme, found chiefly in saliva and pancreatic fluid, that converts starch and glycogen into simple sugars.

am·yl ni·trate ▸*n. Chemistry* a colorless synthetic liquid used as an additive in diesel fuel to improve its ignition properties. • Chem. formula: $C_5H_{11}NO_3$.

USAGE **Amyl nitrate** and **amyl nitrite** are quite distinct substances, but **amyl nitrate** is often mistakenly used to refer to the street drug (inhaled and used as a stimulant and vasodilator), which is correctly called **amyl nitrite**.

am·yl ni·trite ▸*n.* a yellowish volatile synthetic liquid used medicinally as a vasodilator. It is rapidly absorbed by the body on inhalation, and is sometimes used for its stimulatory effects. • Chem. formula: $C_5H_{11}NO_2$.

USAGE See **usage** at **AMYL NITRATE**.

am·y·loid /ˈaməˌloid/ *Medicine* ▸*n.* a starchlike protein that is deposited in the liver, kidneys, spleen, or other tissues in certain diseases. ■ another term for **AMYLOIDOSIS**.

am·y·loi·do·sis /ˌaməloiˈdōsis/ ▸*n. Medicine* a disorder marked by deposition of amyloid in the body.

am·y·lo·pec·tin /ˌaməlōˈpektin/ ▸*n. Biochemistry* the noncrystallizable form of starch, consisting of branched polysaccharide chains.

am·yl·ose /ˈaməˌlōs; -ˌlōz/ ▸*n. Biochemistry* the crystallizable form of starch, consisting of long unbranched polysaccharide chains.

a·my·o·troph·ic lat·er·al scle·ro·sis /ˌāmīəˈtrāfik/ (abbr.: **ALS**) ▸*n.* a progressive degeneration of the motor neurons of the central nervous system, leading to wasting of the muscles and paralysis. Also called **LOU GEHRIG'S DISEASE**.

am·y·ot·ro·phy /ˌāmīˈätrəfē/ ▸*n. Medicine* muscular atrophy. ▷late 19th cent.: from **A-**[1] 'not' + Greek *mus, muo-* 'muscle' + **-TROPHY** (see **-TROPHIC**). **—a·my·o·troph·ic** /ˌāmīəˈtrāfik; -əˈtrō-/ *adj.*

Am·y·tal /ˈaməˌtôl; -ˌtal/ ▸*n. trademark* a barbiturate drug used as a sedative and a hypnotic. • Alternative name: 5-ethyl-5-isopropylbarbituric acid, or its sodium salt (**sodium amytal**); chem. formula: $C_{11}H_{18}N_2O_3$. ▷1920s: from **AMYL** + *-t-* (for ease of pronunciation) + **-AL**.

an /an/ ▸*adj.* the form of the indefinite article (see **A**) used before words beginning with a vowel sound.

USAGE The traditional rule about whether to use **a** or **an** before a word beginning with *h* is that if the *h* is sounded, **a** is the correct form (*a hospital; a hotel*). But if the accent is on the second syllable (*historic; habitual*), there is greater likelihood that, at least in speaking, 'an habitual' will sound more natural. One form is not more correct than the other, although some constructions may strike readers as pretentious or old-fashioned (*an heroic act; an humanitarian*). See also **usage** at **A**.

an-[1] ▸*prefix* variant spelling of **A-**[1] before a vowel (as in *anemia, anechoic*). ▷from Greek.

an-[2] ▸*prefix* variant spelling of **AD-** assimilated before *n* (as in *annihilate, annotate*).

an-[3] ▸*prefix* variant spelling of **ANA-** shortened before a vowel (as in *aneurysm*).

-an (also **-ean** or **-ian**) ▸*suffix* **1** forming adjectives and nouns esp. from: ■ names of places: *Ohioan | Russian.* ■ names of systems: *Anglican | Presbyterian.* ■ names of zoological classes or orders: *crustacean.* ■ names of founders or leaders when referring to them as sources: *Chomskyan | Lutheran.* **2** *Chemistry* forming names of organic compounds, chiefly polysaccharides: *dextran.* ▷based on Latin *-(i)anus, -aeus*, adjectival endings.

ana- (usu. **an-** before a vowel) ▸*prefix* **1** up: *anabasis.* **2** back: *anamnesis.* **3** again: *anabiosis.* ▷from Greek *ana* 'up.'

-ana ▸*suffix* (forming plural nouns) denoting things associated with a person, place, or field of interest:

A

Americana | Victoriana. ▷from the neuter plural of the Latin adjectival ending *-anus.*

An·a·bap·tism /ˌanəˈbapˌtizəm/ ▶*n.* the doctrine that baptism should only be administered to believing adults, held by a radical Protestant sect that emerged during the 1520s and 1530s. ▷mid 16th cent.: via ecclesiastical Latin from Greek *anabaptismos,* from *ana-* 'over again' + *baptismos* 'baptism.' **—An·a·bap·tist** *n.* & *adj.*

an·a·bas /ˈanəˌbas/ ▶*n.* any of the freshwater fish of the climbing perch family native to Asia and Africa, esp. the genus *Anabas,* able to breathe air and move on land.

a·nab·a·sis /əˈnabəsis/ ▶*n.* (*pl.* **-ses** /-ˌsēz/) *rare* a march from a coast into the interior, as that of the younger Cyrus into Asia in 401 BC, as narrated by Xenophon in his work *Anabasis.* ■ a military advance. ▷early 18th cent.: Greek, literally 'ascent.'

an·a·bat·ic /ˌanəˈbatik/ ▶*adj. Meteorology* (of a wind) caused by local upward motion of warm air; compare with**KATABATIC**.. ▷early 20th cent.: from Greek *anabatikos,* from *anabatēs* 'a person who ascends,' from *anabainein* 'walk up.'

an·a·bi·o·sis /ˌanəbīˈōsis/ ▶*n. Zoology* a temporary state of suspended animation or greatly reduced metabolism. ▷late 19th cent.: from Greek *anabiōsis,* from *anabioein* 'return to life.' **—an·a·bi·ot·ic** /-ˈätik/ *adj.*

an·a·bol·ic /ˌanəˈbälik/ ▶*adj. Biochemistry* relating to or promoting anabolism.

an·a·bol·ic ste·roid ▶*n.* a synthetic steroid hormone that resembles testosterone in promoting the growth of muscle. Such hormones are used medicinally to treat some forms of weight loss and (illegally) by some athletes and others to enhance physical performance.

a·nab·o·lism /əˈnabəˌlizəm/ ▶*n. Biochemistry* the synthesis of complex molecules in living organisms from simpler ones together with the storage of energy; constructive metabolism. ▷late 19th cent.: from Greek *anabolē* 'ascent,' from *ana-* 'up' + *ballein* 'to throw.'

a·nach·ro·nism /əˈnakrəˌnizəm/ ▶*n.* a thing belonging or appropriate to a period other than that in which it exists, esp. a thing that is conspicuously old-fashioned: *everything was as it would have appeared in centuries past apart from one anachronism, a bright yellow construction crane.* ■ an act of attributing a custom, event, or object to a period to which it does not belong. ▷mid 17th cent.: from Greek *anakhronismos,* from *ana-* 'backward' + *khronos* 'time.' **—a·nach·ro·nis·tic** /əˌnakrəˈnistik/ *adj.* **—a·nach·ro·nis·ti·cal·ly** /-ˈnistik(ə)lē/ *adv.*

an·a·clit·ic /ˌanəˈklitik/ ▶*adj. Psychoanalysis* relating to or characterized by a strong emotional dependence on another or others: *anaclitic depression.* ▷1920s: from Greek *anaklitos* 'for reclining,' from *anaklinein* 'recline.'

an·a·co·lu·thon /ˌanəkəˈlo͞oTHän/ ▶*n.* (*pl.* **-tha** /-THə/) a sentence or construction that lacks grammatical sequence, such as *while in the garden, the door banged shut.* ▷early 18th cent.: via late Latin from Greek *anakolouthon,* from *an-* 'not' + *akolouthos* 'following.' **—an·a·co·lu·thic** /-THik/ *adj.*

an·a·con·da /ˌanəˈkändə/ ▶*n.* a semiaquatic snake of the boa family that may grow to a great size, native to tropical South America. • Genus *Eunectes,* family Boidae: several species, in particular the **green anaconda** (*E. murinus*). ▷mid 18th cent. (originally denoting a kind of Sri Lankan snake): unexplained alteration of Latin *anacandaia* 'python,' from Sinhalese *henakaňdayā* 'whipsnake,' from *hena* 'lightning' + *kaňda* 'stem.'

A·nac·re·on /əˈnakrēən; -ˌän/ (*c.*570–478 BC), Greek lyric poet, best known for his celebrations of love and wine.

a·nac·re·on·tic /əˌnakrēˈäntik/ (also **A·nac·re·on·tic**) *Prosody* ▶*adj.* (of a poem) composed in the manner of the Greek poet Anacreon, known for his lyrics praising wine, women, and song.
▶*n.* (usu. **anacreontics**) an anacreontic poem. ▷early 17th cent. (as an adjective): from late Latin *anacreonticus,* from Greek *Anakreōn* (see **ANACREON**).

an·a·cru·sis /ˌanəˈkro͞osis/ ▶*n.* (*pl.* **-ses** /-sēz/) **1** *Prosody* one or more unstressed syllables at the beginning of a verse. **2** *Music* one or more unstressed notes before the first bar line of a piece or passage. ▷mid 19th cent.: modern Latin, from Greek *anakrousis* 'prelude,' from *ana-* 'up' + *krousis,* from *krouein* 'to strike.'

an·a·dam·a bread /ˌanəˈdamə ˌbred/ ▶*n.* a type of yeast bread typically made with cornmeal and dark molasses.

a·nad·ro·mous /əˈnadrəməs/ ▶*adj. Zoology* (of a fish, such as the salmon) migrating up rivers from the sea to spawn. The opposite of **CATADROMOUS**. ▷mid 18th cent.: from Greek *anadromos* (from *ana-* 'up' + *dromos* 'running') + **-OUS**.

a·nae·mi·a ▶*n.* British spelling of **ANEMIA**.

a·nae·mic ▶*adj.* British spelling of **ANEMIC**.

an·aer·obe /ˈanəˌrōb/ ▶*n. Biology* an organism that grows without air, or requires oxygen-free conditions to live. ▷late 19th cent.: from **AN-**[1] + **AEROBE**.

an·aer·o·bic /ˌane(ə)ˈrōbik; ˌanə-/ ▶*adj. Biology* relating to, involving, or requiring an absence of free oxygen: *anerobic bacteria.* ■ relating to or denoting exercise that does not improve or is not intended to improve the efficiency of the body's cardiovascular system in absorbing and transporting oxygen. **—an·aer·o·bi·cal·ly** /-bik(ə)lē/ *adv.*

an·aes·the·sia, etc. ▶*n.* British spelling of **ANESTHESIA**, etc.

an·a·gen·e·sis /ˌanəˈjenəsis/ ▶*n. Biology* species formation without branching of the evolutionary line of descent. Compare with **CLADOGENESIS**. **—an·a·ge·net·ic** /-jəˈnetik/ *adj.*

an·a·glyph /ˈanəˌglif/ ▶*n.* **1** *Photography* a stereoscopic photograph with the two images superimposed and printed in different colors, producing a stereo effect when the photograph is viewed through correspondingly colored filters. **2** an object, such as a cameo, embossed or carved in low relief. ▷late 16th cent. (sense 2): from Greek *anagluphē,* from *ana-* 'up' + *gluphē* (from *gluphein* 'carve'). Sense 1 dates from the late 19th cent. **—an·a·glyph·ic** /ˌanəˈglifik/ *adj.*

an·a·gram /ˈanəˌgram/ ▶*n.* a word, phrase, or name formed by rearranging the letters of another, such as *cinema,* formed from *iceman.*
▶*v.* (**-grammed**, **-gram·ming**) another term for **ANAGRAMMATIZE**. ▷late 16th cent.: from French *anagramme* or modern Latin *anagramma,* from Greek *ana-* 'back, anew' + *gramma* 'letter.' **—an·a·gram·mat·ic** /ˌanəgrəˈmatik/ *adj.* **—an·a·gram·mat·i·cal** /ˌanəgrəˈmatikəl/ *adj.*

an·a·gram·ma·tize /ˌanəˈgraməˌtīz/ ▶*v.* [*trans.*] make an anagram of (a word, phrase, or name). **—an·a·gram·ma·ti·za·tion** /-ˌgramətəˈzāSHən/ *n.*

An·a·heim /ˈanəˌhīm/ a city in California, southeast of Los Angeles; pop. 328,014. It is home to Disneyland.

a·nal /ˈānl/ ▶*adj.* involving, relating to, or situated near the anus. ■ (in Freudian psychoanalysis) relating to or denoting a stage of infantile psychosexual development supposedly preoccupied with the anus and defecation. ■ *informal* anal-retentive: *he's anal about things like that.* ▷mid 18th cent.: from modern Latin *analis,* from Latin *anus* (see **ANUS**). **—a·nal·ly** *adv.*

an·a·lects /ˈanlˌek(t)s/ (also **an·a·lec·ta** /ˌanlˈektə/) ▶*plural n.* a collection of short literary or philosophical extracts. ▷late Middle English: via Latin from Greek *analekta* 'things gathered up,' from *analegein* 'pick up,' from *ana-* 'up' + *legein* 'gather.'

an·a·lep·tic /ˌanəˈleptik/ *Medicine* ▶*adj.* (chiefly of a drug) tending to restore a person's health or strength; restorative.
▶*n.* a restorative drug. ■ a drug that stimulates the central nervous system. ▷late 16th cent.: via late Latin from Greek *analēptikos* 'restorative.'

a·nal fin ▶*n. Zoology* an unpaired fin located on the underside of a fish posterior to the anus.

an·al·ge·si·a /ˌanlˈjēzēə; -ZHə/ ▶*n. Medicine* the inability to feel pain. ▷early 18th cent.: from Greek *analgēsia* 'painlessness,' from *an-* 'not' + *algeein* 'feel pain.'

an·al·ge·sic /ˌanlˈjēzik; -sik/ *Medicine* ▶*adj.* (chiefly of a drug) acting to relieve pain.
▶*n.* an analgesic drug.

an·a·log /ˈanlˌôg; -ˌäg/ (also **an·a·logue**) ▶*n.* a person or thing seen as comparable to another: *the idea that the fertilized egg contains a miniature analog of every adult structure.* ■ *Chemistry* a compound with a molecular structure closely similar to that of another.
▶*adj.* relating to or using signals or information represented by a continuously variable physical quantity such as spatial position or voltage. Often contrasted with **DIGITAL** (sense 1). ■ (of a clock or watch) showing the time by means of hands rather than displayed digits. ▷early 19th cent.: from French, from Greek *analogon,* neuter of *analogos* 'proportionate.'

a·nal·o·gize /əˈnaləˌjīz/ ▶*v.* [*trans.*] make a comparison of (something) with something else to assist understanding: *he could* **analogize** *birth* **to** *the coming into being of a poem.*

a·nal·o·gous /əˈnaləgəs/ ▶*adj.* (often **analogous to**) comparable in certain respects, typically in a way that makes clearer the nature of the things compared: *they saw the relationship between a ruler and his subjects as analogous to that of father and children.* ■ *Biology* (of structures) performing a similar function but having a different evolutionary origin, such as the wings of insects and birds. Often contrasted with **HOMOLOGOUS**. ▷mid 17th cent.: via Latin from Greek *analogos* 'proportionate' + **-OUS**. **—a·nal·o·gous·ly** *adv.*

an·a·log-to-dig·it·al con·vert·er (abbr.: **ADC**) ▶*n.* a device for converting analog signals to digital form.

an·a·logue ▶*n.* & *adj.* variant spelling of **ANALOG**.

a·nal·o·gy /əˈnaləjē/ ▶*n.* (*pl.* **-gies**) a comparison between two things, typically on the basis of their structure and for the purpose of explanation or clarification: *an* **analogy between** *the workings of nature and those of human societies | he interprets logical functions* **by analogy with** *machines.* ■ a correspondence or partial similarity: *the syndrome is called deep dysgraphia because of its* **analogy to** *deep dyslexia.* See note at **LIKENESS**. ■ a thing that is comparable to something else in significant respects: *works of art were seen as an analogy for works of nature.* ■ *Logic* a process of arguing from similarity in known respects to similarity in other respects. ■ *Linguistics* a process by which new words and inflections are created on the basis of regularities in the form of existing ones. ■ *Biology* the resemblance of function between organs that have a different evolutionary origin. ▷late Middle English (in the sense 'appropriateness, correspondence'): from French *analogie,* Latin *analogia* 'proportion,' from Greek, from *analogos* 'proportionate.' **—an·a·log·i·cal** /ˌanəˈläjikəl/ *adj.* **—an·a·log·i·cal·ly** *adv.*

an·al·pha·bet·ic /ˌanalfəˈbetik/ ▶*adj.* **1** representing sounds by composite signs rather than by single letters or symbols: *Chinese has an analphabetic writing system.* **2** completely illiterate.

a·nal-re·ten·tive *Psychoanalysis* ▶*adj.* (of a person) excessively orderly and fussy (supposedly owing to conflict over toilet-training in infancy).
▶*n.* (also **anal retentive**) a person who is excessively orderly and fussy. **—a·nal re·ten·tion** *n.* **—a·nal re·ten·tive·ness** *n.*

an·al·y·sand /əˈnaləˌsand; -ˌzand/ ▶*n.* a person undergoing psychoanalysis.

an·a·lyse ▶*v.* British spelling of **ANALYZE**.

a·nal·y·sis /əˈnaləsis/ ▶*n.* (*pl.* **-ses** /-ˌsēz/) detailed examination of the elements or structure of something, typically as a basis for discussion or interpretation: *statistical analysis | an analysis of popular culture.* ■ the process of separating something into its constituent elements. Often contrasted with **SYNTHESIS**. ■ the identification and measurement of the chemical constituents of a substance or specimen. ■ short for **PSYCHOANALYSIS**. ■ *Linguistics* the use of separate, short words and word order rather than inflection or agglutination to express grammatical structure. ■ *Mathematics* the part of mathematics concerned with the theory of functions and the use of limits, continuity, and the operations of calculus. ▷late 16th cent.: via medieval Latin from Greek *analusis,* from *analuein* 'unloose,' from *ana-* 'up' + *luein* 'loosen.'
▶*PHRASE* □ **in the final** (or **last**) **analysis** when everything has been considered (used to suggest that a statement expresses the basic truth about a complex situation): *in the final analysis it is a question of political history.*

an·a·lyst /ˈanl-ist/ ▶*n.* a person who conducts analysis, in particular: ■ an investment expert, typically in a specified field: *rising consumer confidence and falling oil prices are the keys to any upturn, many analysts believe.* ■ short for **PSYCHOANALYST**. ■ a chemist who analyzes substances. ■ short for **SYSTEMS ANALYST**. ▷mid 17th cent.: from French *analyste,* from the verb *analyser* (see **ANALYZE**).

an·a·lyt·ic /ˌanlˈitik/ ▶*adj.* another term for **ANALYTICAL**. ■ *Logic* true by virtue of the meaning of the words or concepts used to express it, so that its denial would be a self-contradiction. Compare with **SYNTHETIC**. ■ *Linguistics* (of a language) tending not to alter the form of its words and to use word order rather than inflection or agglutination to express grammatical structure. Often contrasted with **SYNTHETIC**. ▷early 17th cent.: via Latin from Greek *analutikos,* from *analuein* 'unloose.' The term was adopted in the late 16th cent. as a noun denoting the branch of logic dealing with analysis, with specific reference to Aristotle's treatises on logic, the Analytics (Greek *analutika*).

an·a·lyt·i·cal /ˌanlˈitikəl/ ▸*adj.* relating to or using analysis or logical reasoning: *analytical methods* | *a suave, analytical type who missed his calling as a lawyer.* —**an·a·lyt·i·cal·ly** /-ik(ə)lē/ *adv.*

an·a·lyt·i·cal ge·om·e·try ▸*n.* geometry using coordinates.

an·a·lyt·i·cal phi·los·o·phy (also **an·a·lyt·ic phi·los·o·phy**) ▸*n.* a method of approaching philosophical problems through analysis of the terms in which they are expressed, associated with Anglo-American philosophy of the early 20th century.

an·a·lyt·i·cal psy·chol·o·gy ▸*n.* the psychoanalytic system of psychology developed and practiced by Carl Jung.

an·a·lyze /ˈanlˌīz/ (*Brit.* **an·a·lyse**) ▸*v.* [*trans.*] examine methodically and in detail the constitution or structure of (something, esp. information), typically for purposes of explanation and interpretation: *we need to analyze our results more clearly.* ■ discover or reveal (something) through such examination: *I intend to analyze the sexism in such texts* | [with *clause*] *he tried to analyze exactly what was going on.* ■ psychoanalyze (someone). ■ identify and measure the chemical constituents of (a substance or specimen). ■ *Grammar* resolve (a sentence) into its grammatical elements; parse. ▷late 16th cent.: influenced by French *analyser,* from medieval Latin *analysis* (see **ANALYSIS**). —**an·a·lyz·a·ble** /ˌanəˈlīzəbəl/ *adj.* —**an·a·lyz·er** *n.*

an·am·ne·sis /ˌanəmˈnēsis/ ▸*n.* (*pl.* **-ses** /-sēz/) recollection, in particular: ■ the remembering of things from a supposed previous existence (often used with reference to Platonic philosophy). ■ *Medicine* a patient's account of a medical history. ■ *Christian Church* the part of the Eucharist in which the Passion, Resurrection, and Ascension of Christ are recalled. ▷late 16th cent.: from Greek *anamnēsis* 'remembrance.'

an·am·nes·tic /ˌanamˈnestik/ ▸*adj. Medicine* denoting an enhanced reaction of the body's immune system to an antigen that is related to an antigen previously encountered.

an·a·mor·pho·sis /ˌanəˈmôrfəsis/ ▸*n.* **1** a distorted projection or drawing that appears normal when viewed from a particular point or with a suitable mirror or lens. ■ the process by which such images are produced. **2** *Biology* a gradual, ascending progression or change of form to a higher type. ■ development of the adult form through a series of small changes, esp. in some arthropods, the acquisition of additional body segments after hatching. ▷early 18th cent.: from Greek *anamorphōsis* 'transformation,' from *ana-* 'back, again' + *morphosis* 'a shaping' (from *morphoun* 'to shape,' from *morphē* 'shape, form'). —**an·a·mor·phic** /-fik/ *adj.*

a·nan·da /ˈänəndə/ ▸*n.* (in Hinduism, Buddhism, and Jainism) extreme happiness, one of the highest states of being. ▷from Sanskrit *ānanda* 'blessedness, bliss.'

an·an·da·mide /əˈnandəˌmīd/ ▸*n.* a naturally-occurring arachidonic acid derivative, present in some foods and in mammalian brains, where it acts as a messenger molecule and plays a role in pain, depression, appetite, memory, and fertility.

An·a·ni·as /ˌanəˈnīəs/ two figures in the New Testament: ■ the husband of Sapphira, struck dead because he lied (Acts 5). ■ the Jewish high priest before whom St. Paul was brought (Acts 23).

an·a·pest /ˈanəˌpest/ (*Brit.* **an·a·paest**) ▸*n. Prosody* a metrical foot consisting of two short or unstressed syllables followed by one long or stressed syllable. ▷late 16th cent.: via Latin from Greek *anapaistos* 'reversed,' from *ana-* 'back' + *paiein* 'strike' (so called because it is the reverse of a dactyl). —**an·a·pes·tic** /ˌanəˈpestik/ *adj.*

an·a·phase /ˈanəˌfāz/ ▸*n. Genetics* the stage of meiotic or mitotic cell division in which the chromosomes move away from one another to opposite poles of the spindle.

an·a·phor /ˈanəˌfôr/ ▸*n.* a word or phrase that refers to an earlier word or phrase (e.g., in *my cousin said she was coming, she* is used as an anaphor for *my cousin*). ▷1970s: back-formation from **ANAPHORA**.

a·naph·o·ra /əˈnafərə/ ▸*n.* **1** *Grammar* the use of a word referring to or replacing a word used earlier in a sentence, to avoid repetition, such as *do* in *I like it and so do they.* **2** *Rhetoric* the repetition of a word or phrase at the beginning of successive clauses. ▷late 16th cent.: senses 1 and 2 via Latin from Greek, 'repetition,' from *ana-* 'back' + *pherein* 'to bear.' —**an·a·phor·ic** /ˌanəˈfôrik/ *adj.*

an·aph·ro·dis·i·ac /anˌafrəˈdizēˌak; -ˈdēzē-; -ˈdēzhē-/ *Medicine* ▸*adj.* (chiefly of a drug) tending to reduce sexual desire.
▸*n.* an anaphrodisiac drug.

an·a·phy·lax·is /ˌanəfəˈlaksis/ ▸*n.* (also **an·a·phy·lac·tic shock** /-ˈlaktik/) *Medicine* an extreme, often life-threatening, allergic reaction to an antigen (e.g., a bee sting) to which the body has become hypersensitive following an earlier exposure. ▷early 20th cent.: modern Latin, from Greek *ana-* 'again' + *phulaxis* 'guarding.' —**an·a·phy·lac·tic** /-ˈlaktik/ *adj.*

a·nap·sid /əˈnapsid/ ▸*n. Zoology* a reptile of a group characterized by the lack of temporal openings in the skull, including the turtles and their relatives. • Sometimes placed in a subclass Anapsida, though this taxon is now often not recognized. ▷1930s: from modern Latin *Anapsida,* from Greek *an-* 'without' + *apsis, apsid-* 'arch.'

an·ap·tyx·is /ˌanapˈtiksis/ ▸*n. Phonetics* the insertion of a vowel between two consonants in pronunciation, as in *filim* for *film.* ▷late 19th cent.: modern Latin, from Greek *anaptuxis* 'unfolding,' from *ana-* 'back, again' + *ptuxis* 'folding.' —**anaptyctic** /-ˈtiktik/ *adj.*

an·arch /ˈanˌärk/ ▸*n. poetic/literary* an anarchist.
▸*adj.* anarchic. ▷mid 17th cent.: from Greek *anarkhos* 'without a chief' (see **ANARCHY**).

an·ar·chic /aˈnärkik/ ▸*adj.* with no controlling rules or principles to give order: *an anarchic and bitter civil war.* ■ (of comedy or a person's sense of humor) uncontrolled by convention: *his anarchic wit.* —**an·ar·chi·cal** /-kikəl/ *adj.* —**an·ar·chi·cal·ly** *adv.*

an·ar·chism /ˈanərˌkizəm/ ▸*n.* belief in the abolition of all government and the organization of society on a voluntary, cooperative basis without recourse to force or compulsion. ■ anarchists as a political force or movement: *socialism and anarchism emerged to offer organized protest against the injustices of Spanish society.* ▷mid 17th cent.: from Greek *anarkhos* 'without a chief' (see **ANARCHY**) + **-ISM**; later influenced by French *anarchisme.*

an·ar·chist /ˈanərkist/ ▸*n.* a person who believes in or tries to bring about anarchy.
▸*adj.* relating to or supporting anarchy or anarchists: *an anarchist newspaper.* ▷mid 17th cent.: from Greek *anarkhos* 'without a chief' (see **ANARCHY**) + **-IST**; later influenced by French *anarchiste.* —**an·ar·chis·tic** /ˌanərˈkistik/ *adj.*

an·ar·chy /ˈanərkē/ ▸*n.* a state of disorder due to absence or nonrecognition of authority: *he must ensure public order in a country threatened with anarchy.* ■ absence of government and absolute freedom of the individual, regarded as a political ideal. ▷mid 16th cent.: via medieval Latin from Greek *anarkhia,* from *anarkhos,* from *an-* 'without' + *arkhos* 'chief, ruler.'

A·na·sa·zi /ˌanəˈsäzē/ ▸*n.* (*pl.* same or **-zis**) a member of an ancient American Indian people of the southwestern U.S., who flourished between *c.*200 BC and AD 1500. The earliest phase of their culture, typified by pit dwellings, is known as the Basket Maker period; the present day Pueblo culture developed from a later stage. ▷1930s: from Navajo, literally 'ancestors of our enemies (the Pueblo peoples).'

an·as·tig·mat /ˌanəˈstigˌmat/ ▸*n.* an anastigmatic lens system.

an·as·tig·mat·ic /ˌanəstigˈmatik/ ▸*adj.* (of a lens system) constructed so that the astigmatism of each element is canceled out. ▷late 19th cent.: from **AN-**[1] 'not' + *astigmatic* (see **ASTIGMATISM**).

a·nas·to·mose /əˈnastəˌmōz; -ˌmōs/ ▸*v.* [*intrans.*] *Medicine* be linked by anastomosis: *adjacent veins may anastomose.* ■ [*trans.*] (usu. **be anastomosed**) link by anastomosis: *the graft is anastomosed to the vein of the recipient.* ▷late 17th cent.: coined in French from Greek *anastomōsis* (see **ANASTOMOSIS**).

a·nas·to·mo·sis /əˌnastəˈmōsis/ ▸*n.* (*pl.* **-ses** /-sēz/) *technical* a cross-connection between adjacent channels, tubes, fibers, or other parts of a network. ■ *Medicine* a connection made surgically between adjacent blood vessels, parts of the intestine, or other channels of the body, or the operation in which this is constructed. ▷late 16th cent.: modern Latin, from Greek *anastomōsis,* from *anastomoun* 'provide with a mouth.' —**a·nas·to·mot·ic** /-ˈmätik/ *adj.* & *n.*

a·nas·tro·phe /əˈnastrəfē/ ▸*n. Rhetoric* the inversion of the usual order of words or clauses. ▷mid 16th cent.: from Greek *anastrophē* 'turning back,' from *ana-* 'back' + *strephein* 'to turn.'

an·as·tro·zole /anˈastrəˌzōl/ ▸*n.* a nonsteroidal aromatase inhibitor used in the treatment and prevention of breast cancer. It has been observed to have fewer adverse side effects than tamoxifen.

anat. ▸*abbr.* ■ anatomical. ■ anatomy.

an·a·tase /ˈanəˌtās; -ˌtāz/ ▸*n.* one of the tetragonal forms of titanium dioxide, usually found as brown crystals, used as a pigment in paints and inks. ▷early 19th cent.: from French, from Greek *anatasis* 'extension', with allusion to the length of the crystals.

a·nath·e·ma /əˈnaᴛʜəmə/ ▸*n.* **1** something or someone that one vehemently dislikes: *racial hatred was* ***anathema to her.*** **2** a formal curse by a pope or a council of the Church, excommunicating a person or denouncing a doctrine. ■ *poetic/literary* a strong curse: *the sergeant clutched the ruined communicator, muttering anathemas.* ▷early 16th cent.: from ecclesiastical Latin, 'excommunicated person, excommunication,' from Greek *anathema* 'thing dedicated,' (later) 'thing devoted to evil, accursed thing,' from *anatithenai* 'to set up.'

a·nath·e·ma·tize /əˈnaᴛʜəməˌtīz/ ▸*v.* [*trans.*] curse; condemn: *she anathematized Tom as the despoiler of a helpless widow.* ▷mid 16th cent.: from French *anathématiser,* from Latin *anathematizare,* from Greek *anathematizein,* from *anathema* (see **ANATHEMA**).

An·a·to·li·a /ˌanəˈtōlēə/ the western peninsula of Asia, bounded by the Black, Aegean, and Mediterranean seas, that forms the greater part of Turkey.

An·a·to·li·an /ˌanəˈtōlēən/ ▸*adj.* of or relating to Anatolia, its inhabitants, or their ancient languages.
▸*n.* **1** a native or inhabitant of Anatolia. **2** an extinct group of ancient languages constituting a branch of the Indo-European language family and including Hittite, Luwian, Lydian, and Lycian.

an·a·tom·i·cal /ˌanəˈtämikəl/ (abbr.: **anat.**) ▸*adj.* of or relating to bodily structure: *anatomical abnormalities.* ■ of or relating to anatomy: *anatomical lectures.* ▷late 16th cent.: from late Latin *anatomicus,* from *anatomia* (see **ANATOMY**), + **-AL**. —**an·a·tom·i·cal·ly** /-ik(ə)lē/ *adv.*

an·a·tom·i·cal·ly cor·rect /ˌanəˈtämik(ə)lē/ ▸*adj.* (of a doll) having the sexual organs plainly represented.

a·nat·o·mist /əˈnatəmist/ ▸*n.* an expert in anatomy; a dissector. ▷mid 16th cent.: from French *anatomiste,* from a medieval Latin derivative of *anatomizare* (see **ANATOMIZE**).

a·nat·o·mize /əˈnatəˌmīz/ ▸*v.* [*trans.*] dissect (a body). ■ examine and analyze in detail: *successful comedy is notoriously difficult to anatomize.* ▷late Middle English: from medieval Latin *anatomizare,* from *anatomia* (see **ANATOMY**).

a·nat·o·my /əˈnatəmē/ (abbr.: **anat.**) ▸*n.* (*pl.* **-mies**) the branch of science concerned with the bodily structure of humans, animals, and other living organisms, esp. as revealed by dissection and the separation of parts. ■ the bodily structure of an organism: *descriptions of the cat's anatomy and behavior.* ■ *informal, humorous* a person's body: *he left dusty handprints on his lady customers' anatomies.* ■ *figurative* a study of the structure or internal workings of something: *Machiavelli's anatomy of the art of war.* ▷late Middle English: from Old French *anatomie* or late Latin *anatomia,* from Greek, from *ana-* 'up' + *tomia* 'cutting' (from *temnein* 'to cut').

a·nat·to /əˈnätō/ ▸*n.* (**-tos**) variant spelling of **ANNATTO**.

An·ax·ag·o·ras /ˌanəkˈsagərəs; ˌanak-/ (*c.*500–*c.*428 BC), Greek philosopher. He believed that all matter was infinitely divisible and motionless until animated by mind (*nous*).

A·nax·i·man·der /əˌnaksəˈmandər; əˈnaksəˌmandər/ (*c.*610–*c.*545 BC), Greek scientist from Miletus. He believed the earth to be cylindrical and poised in space and is reputed to have taught that life began in water and that humans originated from fish.

An·ax·im·e·nes /ˌanakˈsiməˌnēz/ (*c.*546 BC), Greek philosopher and scientist from Miletus. He believed the earth to be flat and shallow, a view of astronomy that was a retrograde step from that of Anaximander.

ANC ▸*abbr.* African National Congress.

-ance /əns; ns/ ▸*suffix* forming nouns: **1** denoting a quality or state or an instance of one: *allegiance* | *extravagance* | *perseverance.* **2** denoting an action: *appearance* | *utterance.* ▷representing French suffix *-ance,* from Latin nouns ending in *-antia, -entia* (from present participial stems *-ant-, -ent-*).

an·ces·tor /ˈanˌsestər/ ▸*n.* a person, typically one more remote than a grandparent, from whom one is descended: *my ancestor Admiral Anson circumnavigated the globe 250 years ago.* ■ an early type of animal or plant from which others have evolved. ■ an early

Pronunciation Key ə *ago;* ər *over;* ˈə *or* ˌə *up;* ˈər *or* ˌər *fur;* a *hat;* ā *rate;* ä *car;* CH *chew;* e *let;* ē *see;* e(ə)r *air;* i *fit;* ī *by;* i(ə)r *ear;* NG *sing;* ō *go;* ô *for;* oi *boy;* o͝o *good;* o͞o *goo;* ou *out;* SH *she;* TH *thin;* T͟H *then;* (h)w *why;* ZH *vision*

version of a machine, artifact, system, etc., that later became more developed. ▷Middle English: from Old French *ancestre*, from Latin *antecessor*, from *antecedere*, from *ante* 'before' + *cedere* 'go.'

an·ces·tral /an'sestrəl/ ▸*adj.* [*attrib.*] of, belonging to, inherited from, or denoting an ancestor or ancestors: *the family's ancestral home | the only records of the ancestral forms are their fossils.* ▷late Middle English: from Old French *ancestrel*, from *ancestre* (see **ANCESTOR**).

an·ces·tress /'an,sestris/ ▸*n.* a female ancestor.

an·ces·try /'an,sestrē/ ▸*n.* (*pl.* **-tries**) [usu. in *sing.*] one's family or ethnic descent: *his dark eyes came from his Jewish ancestry.* ■ the evolutionary or genetic line of descent of an animal or plant: *the ancestry of the rose is extremely complicated.* ■ *figurative* the origin or background of something: *the book traces the ancestry of women's poetry.* ▷Middle English: alteration of Old French *ancesserie*, from *ancestre* (see **ANCESTOR**).

An·chi·ses /ang'kīsēz/ *Greek Roman Mythology* the father of the Trojan hero Aeneas.

an·cho /'ancHō; 'än-/ (also **ancho chili**) ▸*n.* a large aromatic variety of chili, used (usually dried) in dishes of Mexican origin or style. ▷from Mexican Spanish *(chile) ancho* 'wide (chili).'

an·choï·ade (also **an·choi·ade**) /,ansHwī'äd; -cHoi'äd/ ▸*n.* a purée of anchovies, crushed garlic, and olive oil that is served with vegetables as a dip or spread on bread. ▷Provençal, from French *anchois* 'anchovy.'

an·chor /'angkər/ ▸*n.* **1** a heavy object attached to a rope or chain and used to moor a vessel to the sea bottom, typically one having a metal shank with a ring at one end for the rope and a pair of curved and/or barbed flukes at the other. ■ *figurative* a person or thing that provides stability or confidence in an otherwise uncertain situation: *the European Community is the economic anchor of the New Europe.* ■ (in full **anchor store**) a store, e.g., a department store, that is the principal tenant of a mall or a shopping center. **2** an anchorman or anchorwoman, esp. in broadcasting or athletics: *he signed off after nineteen years as CBS news anchor.*
▸*v.* [*trans.*] **1** moor (a ship) to the sea bottom with an anchor: *the ship was anchored in the lee of the island |* [*intrans.*] *we anchored in the harbor.* ■ secure firmly in position: *with cords and pitons they* **anchored** *him* **to** *the rock | the tail is used as a hook with which the fish* **anchors itself to** *coral | figurative the first baseman is anchored to the bag.* ■ provide with a firm basis or foundation: *it is important that policy be anchored to some acceptable theoretical basis.* **2** to act or serve as an anchor for (a news program or sporting event): *she anchored a television documentary series in the early 1980s.* ▷Old English *ancor, ancra*, via Latin from Greek *ankura*; reinforced in Middle English by Old French *ancre*. The current form is from *anchora*, an erroneous Latin spelling. The verb (from Old French *ancrer*) dates from Middle English.
▸*PHRASES* □ **at anchor** (of a ship) moored by means of an anchor. □ **drop anchor** (of a ship) let down the anchor and moor. □ **weigh** (or **raise** or **heave**) **anchor** (of a ship) take up the anchor when ready to depart.

anchor 1
types of anchors

An·chor·age /'angk(ə)rij/ a seaport in southern Alaska, on an inlet of the Pacific Ocean, the state's largest city; pop. 260,283 .

an·chor·age /'angk(ə)rij/ ▸*n.* **1** an area that is suitable for a ship to anchor. ■ the action of securing something to a base or the state of being secured: *the plant needs firm anchorage | figurative the mother provides emotional anchorage.* **2** *historical* an anchorite's dwelling place.

an·cho·ress /'angkəris/ ▸*n.* *historical* a female anchorite.

an·cho·rite /'angkə,rīt/ ▸*n.* *historical* a religious recluse. ▷late Middle English: from medieval Latin *anchorita* (ecclesiastical Latin *anchoreta*), from ecclesiastical Greek *anakhōrētēs*, from *anakhōrein* 'retire,' from *ana-* 'back' + *khōra, khōr-* 'a place.' —**an·cho·rit·ic** /,angkə'ritik/ *adj.*

an·chor·man /'angkər,man/ ▸*n.* (*pl.* **-men**) a man who presents and coordinates a live television or radio program involving other contributors. ■ a man who plays the most crucial part or is the most dependable contributor. ■ the member of a relay team who runs the last leg.

an·chor·per·son /'angkər,pərsən/ ▸*n.* (*pl.* **-per·sons** or **-peo·ple**) an anchorman or anchorwoman (used as a neutral alternative).

an·chor text ▸*n.* the text that appears highlighted in a hypertext link and that can be clicked to open the target Web page.

an·chor·wom·an /'angkər,wŏŏmən/ ▸*n.* (*pl.* **-wom·en**) a woman who presents and coordinates a live television or radio program involving other contributors.

an·cho·vy /'an,cHōvē; an'cHōvē/ ▸*n.* (*pl.* **-ies**) a small shoaling fish of commercial importance as a food fish and as bait. It is strongly flavored and is usually preserved in salt and oil. • Genus *Engraulis*, family Engraulidae: several species, including *E. encrasicolus* of European waters. ▷late 16th cent.: from Spanish and Portuguese *anchova*, of unknown origin.

an·chu·sa /ang'kyōōzə/ ▸*n.* an Old World plant of the borage family, often cultivated for its bright, typically blue, flowers. • Genus *Anchusa*, family Boraginaceae. ▷via Latin from Greek *ankhousa*.

an·cien ré·gime /än'syan rā'zHēm/ ▸*n.* (*pl.* **an·ciens ré·gimes** *pronunc.* same) a political or social system that has been displaced, typically by one more modern. ■ (**Ancien Régime**) the political and social system in France before the Revolution of 1789. ▷late 18th cent.: French, literally 'old rule.'

an·cient[1] /'āncHənt/ ▸*adj.* belonging to the very distant past and no longer in existence: *the ancient civilizations of the Mediterranean.* See note at **OLD**. ■ having been in existence for a very long time: *an ancient gateway | ancient forests.* ■ *chiefly humorous* showing or feeling signs of age or wear: *an ancient pair of jeans | you make me feel ancient.*
▸*n.* *archaic* or *humorous* an old person: *a solitary ancient in a tweed jacket.* ▷late Middle English: from Old French *ancien*, based on Latin *ante* 'before.' —**an·cient·ness** *n.*
▸*PHRASES* □ **the Ancient of Days** a biblical title for God. □ **the ancients** the people of ancient times, esp. the Greeks and Romans of classical antiquity. ■ the classical Greek and Roman authors: *a thorough knowledge of the ancients is a prerequisite of criticism.*

an·cient[2] ▸*n.* *archaic* a standard, flag, or ensign. ▷mid 16th cent.: alteration of **ENSIGN** by association with *ancien*, an early form of **ANCIENT**[1].

an·cient his·to·ry ▸*n.* the history of the ancient civilizations of the Mediterranean area and the Near East up to the fall of the Western Roman Empire in AD 476. ■ *informal* something that is already long familiar and no longer new, interesting, or relevant: *the New Wave is ancient history now.* —**an·cient his·to·ri·an** *n.*

an·cient·ly /'āncHəntlē/ ▸*adv.* long ago: *the area was anciently called Dalriada.*

an·cient world ▸*n.* the region around the Mediterranean and the Near East before the fall of the Western Roman Empire in AD 476.

an·cil·lar·y /'ansə,lerē/ ▸*adj.* providing necessary support to the primary activities or operation of an organization, institution, industry, or system: *the development of ancillary services to support its products.* ■ additional; subsidiary: *paragraph 19 was merely* **ancillary to** *paragraph 16.*
▸*n.* (*pl.* **-laries**) a person whose work provides necessary support to the primary activities of an organization, institution, or industry: *the employment of specialist teachers and ancillaries.* ■ something that functions in a supplementary or supporting role: *undergraduate courses of three main subjects with related ancillaries.* ▷mid 17th cent.: from Latin *ancillaris*, from *ancilla* 'maidservant.'

an·con /'ang,kän/ ▸*n.* (*pl.* **an·co·nes** /,ang'kōnēz/) *Architecture* **1** a console or bracket, typically with two volutes, that supports or appears to support a cornice. **2** each of a pair of projections on either side of a block of stone or other material, used for lifting it. ▷early 18th cent. (denoting the corner or quoin of a wall or rafter): via Latin from Greek *ankōn* 'bend, elbow.'

ancon 1

An·co·na[1] /än'kōnə; äng-/ a port on the Adriatic coast of central Italy, capital of Marche region; pop. 103,270.

An·co·na[2] ▸*n.* a chicken of a breed with mottled black and white plumage. ▷mid 19th cent.: from the place name *Ancona* (see **ANCONA**[1]).

-ancy ▸*suffix* (forming nouns) denoting a quality or state: *buoyancy | expectancy.* Compare with **-ANCE**. ▷representing Latin suffix *-antia* (see also **-ENCY**).

an·cy·lo·sto·mi·a·sis /,angkəlōstə'mīəsis; ,ansə-/ (also **an·ky·lo·sto·mi·a·sis**) ▸*n.* *Medicine* hookworm infection of the small intestine, often leading to anemia. • The infecting organism is typically *Ancylostoma duodenale*, class Phasmida (or Secernentea). ▷late 19th cent.: from modern Latin *Ancylostoma* (from Greek *ankulos* 'crooked' + *stoma* 'mouth') + **-IASIS**.

An·cy·ra /an'sīrə/ ancient Roman name for **ANKARA**.

and /and/ ▸*conj.* **1** used to connect words of the same part of speech, clauses, or sentences that are to be taken jointly: *bread and butter | red and black tiles | they can read and write | a hundred and fifty.* ■ used to connect two clauses when the second happens after the first: *he turned around and walked out | she washed and dried her hair.* ■ used to connect two clauses, the second of which results from the first: *do that once more, and I'll skin you alive.* ■ connecting two identical comparatives, to emphasize a progressive change: *getting better and better | he felt more and more like an outsider.* ■ connecting two identical words, implying great duration or great extent: *I cried and cried | it takes hours and hours.* ■ used to connect two identical words to indicate that things of the same name or class have different qualities: *all human conduct is determined or caused—but there are causes and causes.* ■ used to connect two numbers to indicate that they are being added together: *six and four make ten.* ■ *archaic* used to connect two numbers, implying succession: *a line of men marching two and two.* **2** used to introduce an additional comment or interjection: *if it came to a choice—and this was the worst thing—she would turn her back on her parents | they believe they are descended from him, and quite right, too.* ■ used to introduce a question in connection with what someone else has just said: *"I found the letter in her bag." "And did you steam it open?"* ■ (esp. in broadcasting) used to introduce a statement about a new topic: *and now to the dessert.* **3** *informal* used after some verbs and before another verb to indicate intention, instead of "to": *I would* **try and** *do what he said |* **come and** *see me.* See **usage** below.
▸*n.* (usu. **AND**) *Logic Electronics* a Boolean operator that gives the value one if and only if all the operands are one and otherwise has a value of zero. ■ (also **AND gate**) a circuit that produces an output signal only when signals are received simultaneously through all input connections. ▷Old English *and, ond*, of Germanic origin; related to Dutch *en* and German *und*.
▸*PHRASE* □ **and/or** either or both of two stated possibilities: *audio and/or video components.*

USAGE **1** It is still widely taught and believed that conjunctions such as **and** (and also **but** and **because**) should not be used to start a sentence, the argument being that a sentence starting with **and** expresses an incomplete thought and is therefore incorrect. Writers down the centuries have readily ignored this advice, however, using **and** to start a sentence, typically for rhetorical effect: *What are the government's chances of winning in court? And what are the consequences?*

2 A small number of verbs—notably **try**, **come**, and **go**—can be followed by 'and' with another verb, as in sentences like *we're going to* **try and** *explain it to them* or *why don't you* **come and** *see the film?* Such structures in these verbs correspond to the use of the infinitive 'to,' as in *we're going to* **try to** *explain it to them* or *why don't you* **come to** *see the film?* Since these structures are grammatically odd and, though extremely common, are mainly restricted to informal English, they are regarded as wrong by some and should be avoided in formal standard English. Notice that the use is normally only possible with the infinitive of the verb—that is, it is not possible to say *I tried and explained it to them.*

3 On whether it is more correct to say *both the*

boys and the girls or both the boys and girls, see usage at BOTH.

4 Where a number of items are separated by and, the following verb needs to be in the plural: see usage at OR1.

-and ▶suffix (forming nouns) denoting a person or thing to be treated in a specified way: *analysand.* ▷from Latin gerundive ending *-andus.*

An·da·lu·sia /ˌandəˈlo͞ozн(ē)ə/ the southernmost region of Spain, bordering on the Atlantic Ocean and the Mediterranean Sea; capital, Seville. The region was under Moorish rule from 711 to 1492.

An·da·lu·sian /ˌandəˈlo͞ozн(ē)ən; -sн(ē)ən/ ▶adj. of or relating to Andalusia or its people or their dialect. ▶n. **1** a native or inhabitant of Andalusia. **2** the dialect of Spanish spoken in Andalusia. **3** a light horse of a strong breed from Andalusia.

an·da·lu·site /ˌandlˈo͞oˌsīt/ ▶n. a gray, green, brown, or pink aluminosilicate mineral occurring mainly in metamorphic rocks as elongated rhombic prisms, sometimes of gem quality. ▷early 19th cent.: from the name of the Spanish region of ANDALUSIA + -ITE1.

An·da·man and Nic·o·bar Is·lands /ˈandəmən and ˈnikəˌbär; ˈandəˌman/ two groups of islands in the Bay of Bengal that constitute a Union Territory in India; pop. 279,110; capital, Port Blair.

an·dan·te /änˈdänˌtā/ *Music* ▶adj. & adv. (esp. as a direction) in a moderately slow tempo.
▶n. a movement or composition marked to be played andante. ▷Italian, literally 'going,' present participle of *andare.*

an·dan·ti·no /ˌändänˈtēnō/ *Music* ▶adj. & adv. (esp. as a direction) more lighthearted than andante, and in most cases quicker.
▶n. (pl. **-nos**) a movement or composition marked to be played andantino. ▷Italian, diminutive of ANDANTE.

An·de·an /ˈandēən; anˈdē-/ ▶adj. of or relating to the Andes.
▶n. a native or inhabitant of the Andes.

An·de·an con·dor ▶ see CONDOR.

An·der·sen /ˈandərsən; ˈänərsən/, Hans Christian (1805–75), Danish author. He is noted for his fairy tales, published from 1835, such as "The Snow Queen," "The Ugly Duckling," and "The Little Match Girl."

An·der·son1 /ˈandərsən/ **1** an industrial city in east central Indiana; pop. 59,734. **2** a city in northwestern South Carolina; pop. 25,514. **3** a city in north central California; pop. 62,195.

An·der·son2, Carl David (1905–91), U.S. physicist. In 1932 he discovered the positron—the first antiparticle known. Nobel Prize for Physics (1936, shared with Victor F. Hess).

An·der·son3, Elizabeth Garrett (1836–1917), English physician. In 1866 she established a dispensary for women and children in London.

An·der·son4, Marian (1902–93), U.S. opera singer. Initially barred from giving concerts in the U.S. because of racial discrimination, she gained international success during several European tours 1925–35. Her U.S. career flourished from 1936; in 1955, she became the first black singer to perform at the Metropolitan Opera House in New York.

An·der·son5, Maxwell (1888–1959), U.S. playwright. His plays, many of which are written in verse, deal with social and moral problems. He also wrote many historical dramas. Notable works: *Elizabeth the Queen* (1930), *Key Largo* (1939), *Anne of the Thousand Days* (1948), and *The Bad Seed* (1954).

An·der·son6, Philip Warren (1923–), American physicist. He made significant contributions to the study of solid-state physics, investigating magnetism and superconductivity. Nobel Prize for Physics (1977).

An·der·son7, Sherwood (1876–1941), U.S. author. He is noted for *Winesburg, Ohio* (1919), a collection of interrelated short stories that explore the loneliness and frustration of small-town life.

An·der·son·ville /ˈandərsənˌvil/ a village in southwestern Georgia, near Americus, that was the site of a large and infamous Confederate prison camp during the Civil War.

An·des /ˈandēz/ a major mountain system that runs the length of the Pacific coast of South America. It extends more than 5,000 miles (8,000 km), with a continuous height of more than 10,000 feet (3,000 m). Its highest peak is Aconcagua.

an·des·ite /ˈandiˌzīt/ ▶n. *Geology* a dark, fine-grained, brown or grayish volcanic rock that is intermediate in composition between rhyolite and basalt. ▷mid 19th cent.: named after the ANDES mountains, where it is found + -ITE1. —**an·de·sit·ic** /ˌandiˈzitik/ adj.

An·dhra Pra·desh /ˌəndrə prəˈdäsн; ˈändrə; prəˈdesн/ a state in southeastern India, on the Bay of Bengal; capital, Hyderabad.

and·i·ron /ˈanˌdīərn/ ▶n. a metal support, typically one of a pair, that holds wood burning in a fireplace. ▷Middle English: from Old French *andier,* of unknown origin. The ending was altered by association with IRON.

andirons

An·dor·ra /anˈdôrə/ a small autonomous principality in southwestern Europe, in the southern Pyrenees, between France and Spain; pop. 69,800; capital, Andorra la Vella; Catalan (official) and French. —**An·dor·ran** adj. & n.

Andorra's independence dates from the late 8th century, when Charlemagne is said to have granted the Andorrans self-government for their help in defeating the Moors. Since World War II, tourism has driven the economy.

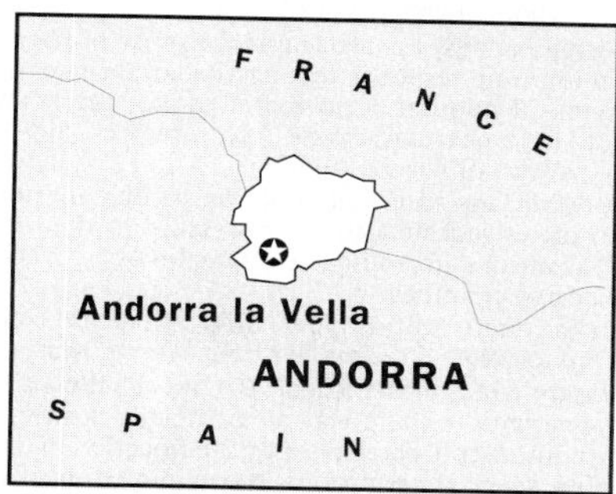

an·dou·ille /anˈdo͞o-ē/ ▶n. a spicy pork sausage seasoned with garlic, used esp. in Cajun cooking. ▷early 17th cent.: French.

an·douil·lette /ˌandwēˈyet/ ▶n. a very small French sausage similar to andouille. ▷French.

An·do·ver /ˈanˌdōvər; ˈandəvər/ a town in northeastern Massachusetts, home to Phillips Academy, a noted prep school; pop. 29,151.

andr- ▶comb. form variant spelling of ANDRO- shortened before a vowel (as in *androecium*).

an·dra·dite /ˈandrəˌdīt/ ▶n. a mineral of the garnet group, containing calcium and iron. It occurs as yellow, green, brown, or black crystals, sometimes of gem quality. ▷mid 19th cent.: named after J. B. de *Andrada* e Silva (c.1763–1838), Brazilian geologist, + -ITE1.

An·dre /ˈänˌdrā/, Carl (1935–), U.S. sculptor. Many of his works are ready-made units, such as bricks, stacked according to a mathematical system and without adhesives or joints.

An·dré /ˈandrē/, John (1750–80), British soldier. He successfully negotiated with Benedict Arnold for the betrayal of West Point to the British 1779–80. Captured while returning from West Point, he was tried and hanged as a spy.

An·dre·an·of Is·lands /ˌandrēˈanôf; -əf; ˌändrēˈänəf/ an island group in southwestern Alaska, part of the Aleutian Islands.

An·dret·ti /anˈdretē/, Mario (Gabriele) (1940–), U.S. race car driver, born in Italy. He won the Daytona 500 in 1967, the Indianapolis 500 in 1969, and the Grand Prix world driving championship in 1978.

An·drew, Prince /ˈandro͞o/, (1960–), British prince; second son of Elizabeth II; full name *Andrew Albert Christian Edward, Duke of York.* He married Sarah Ferguson in 1986, but the couple divorced in 1996; they have two children, Princess Beatrice (1988–) and Princess Eugenie (1990–).

An·drew, St., an Apostle; the brother of St. Peter. The X-shaped cross is associated with him because he is said to have been crucified on such a cross. He is the patron saint of Scotland and Russia. Feast day, November 30.

An·drews1 /ˈanˌdro͞oz/, Julie (1935–), English actress and singer; born *Julia Elizabeth Wells.* She is best known for the movies *Mary Poppins* (1964), for which she won an Academy Award, and *The Sound of Music* (1965).

An·drews2, Thomas (1813–85), Irish physical chemist. He discovered the critical temperature of carbon dioxide and showed that ozone is an allotrope of oxygen.

An·drew·sar·chus /ˌandro͞oˈsärkəs/ ▶n. a very large carnivorous mammal (*Andrewsarchus mongoliensis,* order Creodonta) of the Eocene epoch. ▷modern Latin: from the name of U.S. paleontologist Roy Chapman *Andrews* (1884-1960), who led the expedition on which the animal's fossils were found, + Greek *arkhos* 'ruler.'

andro- (usu. **andr-** before a vowel) ▶comb. form man (as opposed to woman): *androcentric | androgenize.*

an·dro·cen·tric /ˌandrōˈsentrik/ ▶adj. focused or centered on men: *in the radical feminist view science is sexist and androcentric.* ▷early 20th cent.: from Greek *anēr, andr-* 'man' + -CENTRIC.

An·dro·cles /ˈandrəˌklēz/ a runaway slave in a story by Aulus Gellius (2nd century AD) who extracted a thorn from the paw of a lion, which later recognized him and refrained from attacking him when he faced it in the arena.

an·droc·ra·cy /anˈdräkrəsē/ ▶n. (pl. **-cies**) a social system ruled or dominated by men. —**an·dro·crat·ic** /ˌandrəˈkratik/ adj.

an·droe·ci·um /anˈdrēsн(ē)əm/ ▶n. (pl. **-ci·a** /-sн(ē)ə/) *Botany* the stamens of a flower collectively. ▷mid 19th cent.: modern Latin, from Greek *anēr, andr-* 'man' + *oikion* 'house.'

an·dro·gen /ˈandrəjən/ ▶n. *Biochemistry* a male sex hormone, such as testosterone. ▷1930s: from Greek *anēr, andr-* 'man' + -GEN. —**an·dro·gen·ic** /ˌandrəˈjenik/ adj.

an·dro·gen·ize /anˈdräjəˌnīz/ ▶v. [trans.] [usu. as adj.] (**androgenized**) treat with or expose to male hormones, typically resulting in the production of male sexual characteristics. —**an·drog·e·ni·za·tion** /anˌdräjənəˈzāsнən/ n.

an·dro·gyne /ˈandrəˌjīn/ ▶n. an androgynous individual. ■ a hermaphrodite. ▷mid 16th cent. (as a noun): via Latin from Greek *androgunos,* from *anēr, andr-* 'man' + *gunē* 'woman.'

an·drog·y·nous /anˈdräjənəs/ ▶adj. partly male and partly female in appearance; of indeterminate sex. ■ having the physical characteristics of both sexes; hermaphrodite. ▷early 17th cent.: from Latin *androgynus* (see ANDROGYNE) + -OUS. —**an·drog·y·ny** /-nē/ n.

an·droid /ˈanˌdroid/ ▶n. (in science fiction) a robot with a human appearance. ▷early 18th cent. (in the modern Latin form): from modern Latin *androides,* from Greek *anēr, andr-* 'man' + -OID.

An·drom·a·che /anˈdräməkē/ *Greek Mythology* the wife of Hector. She became the slave of Neoptolemus (son of Achilles) after the fall of Troy.

An·drom·e·da /anˈdrämidə/ **1** *Greek Mythology* an Ethiopian princess whose mother Cassiopeia boasted that she herself (or, in some stories, her daughter) was more beautiful than the Nereids. In revenge, Poseidon sent a sea monster to ravage the country; to placate him, Andromeda was fastened to a rock and exposed to the monster, from which she was rescued by Perseus. **2** *Astronomy* a large northern constellation between Perseus and Pegasus, with few bright stars. It is chiefly notable for the **Andromeda Galaxy** (or **Great Nebula of Andromeda**), a conspicuous spiral galaxy probably twice as massive as our own and located 2 million light years away. ■ [as genitive] (**Andromedae** /-ˌdē/) used with a preceding letter or numeral to designate stars in this constellation: *the star Gamma Andromedae.*

an·drom·e·da /anˈdrämidə/ ▶n. an evergreen shrub of the heath family, typically with clusters of small bell-like flowers. • Two genera in the family Ericaceae: several species, including the **bog rosemary** (*Andromeda glaucophylla* and *A. polifolia*) of north temperate regions, and the widely cultivated **Japanese andromeda** (*Pieris japonica*).

an·dro·pause /ˈandrəˌpôz/ ▶n. a collection of symptoms, including fatigue and a decrease in libido, experienced by some middle-aged men and attributed to a gradual decline in testosterone levels. ▷1960s: from **andro-**, on the pattern of *menopause.* **—an·dro·pau·sal**,andrə'pôzəl *adj.*

An·dro·pov1 /an'dräpôf; än'drôpəf/ former name (1984–89) for **RYBINSK**.

An·dro·pov2 /än'drôpəf/, Yuri (Vladimirovich) (1914–84), Soviet statesman; general secretary of the Communist Party of the USSR 1982–84 and president 1983–84. As president he initiated the reform process that was carried out by Mikhail Gorbachev, his successor.

An·dro·scog·gin Riv·er /ˌandrə'skägən/ a river that flows for 175 miles (280 km) from northern New Hampshire through southwestern Maine to the Atlantic Ocean.

an·dro·stene·di·one /ˌandrəˌstēn'dīōn/ ▶*n.* a naturally occurring steroid hormone, also available as a dietary supplement, believed to increase levels of serum testosterone. Also called **ANDRO**.

an·dros·ter·one /an'drästəˌrōn/ ▶*n. Biochemistry* a relatively inactive male sex hormone produced by metabolism of testosterone. ▷1930s: from Greek *anēr, andr-* 'man' + **STEROL** + **-ONE**.

-androus ▶*comb. form Botany & Zoology* having male organs or stamens of a specified number: *monandrous* | *protandrous.* ▷based on modern Latin *-andrus,* from Greek *-andros,* from *andros,* genitive of *anēr* 'man.'

-ane1 ▶*suffix* variant spelling of **-AN**, usually with a distinction of sense (such as *humane* compared with *human*) but sometimes with no corresponding form in *-an* (such as *mundane*).

-ane2 ▶*suffix Chemistry* forming names of saturated hydrocarbons: *methane* | *propane.* ▷on the pattern of words such as *-ene, -ine.*

an·ec·dot·age /'anikˌdōtij/ ▶*n.* **1** anecdotes collectively: *a number of reports cannot be dismissed as anecdotage.* [early 19th cent.: from **ANECDOTE** + **-AGE**.] **2** *humorous* old age, esp. in someone who is inclined to be garrulous. [late 18th cent.: from a blend of **ANECDOTE** and **DOTAGE**.]

an·ec·do·tal /ˌanik'dōtl/ ▶*adj.* (of an account) not necessarily true or reliable, because based on personal accounts rather than facts or research: *while there was much anecdotal evidence there was little hard fact* | *these claims were purely anecdotal.* ■ characterized by or fond of telling anecdotes: *her book is anecdotal and chatty.* ■ [*attrib.*] (of a painting) depicting small narrative incidents: *nineteenth-century French anecdotal paintings.* **—an·ec·do·tal·ist** /-tl-ist/ *n.* **—an·ec·do·tal·ly** *adv.*

an·ec·dote /'anikˌdōt/ ▶*n.* a short and amusing or interesting story about a real incident or person: *told anecdotes about his job* | *he had a rich store of anecdotes.* ■ an account regarded as unreliable or hearsay: *his wife's death has long been the subject of rumor and anecdote.* ■ the depiction of a minor narrative incident in a painting. ▷late 17th cent.: from French, or via modern Latin from Greek *anekdota* 'things unpublished,' from *an-* 'not' + *ekdotos,* from *ekdidōnai* 'publish.'

an·e·cho·ic /ane'kō-ik/ ▶*adj. technical* free from echo: *an anechoic chamber.* ■ (of a coating or material) tending to deaden sound.

a·nele /ə'nēl/ ▶*v.* [*trans.*] *archaic* anoint (someone), esp. as part of the Christian rite of giving extreme unction to the dying. ▷Middle English: from *an-* 'on' + archaic *elien* 'to oil' (from Old English *ele,* from Latin *oleum* 'oil').

a·ne·mi·a /ə'nēmēə/ (*Brit.* **a·nae·mi·a**) ▶*n.* a condition marked by a deficiency of red blood cells or of hemoglobin in the blood, resulting in pallor and weariness. ▷early 19th cent.: via modern Latin from Greek *anaimia,* from *an-* 'without' + *haima* 'blood.'

a·ne·mic /ə'nēmik/ (*Brit.* **a·nae·mic**) ▶*adj.* suffering from anemia. ■ *figurative* lacking in color, spirit, or vitality.

anemo- ▶*comb. form* wind: *anemometer.*

a·nem·o·graph /ə'neməˌgraf/ ▶*n.* an anemometer that records on paper the speed, duration, and sometimes also the direction of the wind. ▷mid 19th cent.: from Greek *anemos* 'wind' + **-GRAPH**.

an·e·mom·e·ter /ˌanə'mämitər/ ▶*n.* an instrument for measuring the speed of the wind, or of any current of gas. ▷early 18th cent.: from Greek *anemos* 'wind' + **-METER**. **—an·e·mom·e·try** /-trē/ *n.* **—an·e·mo·met·ric** /-mə'metrik/ *adj.*

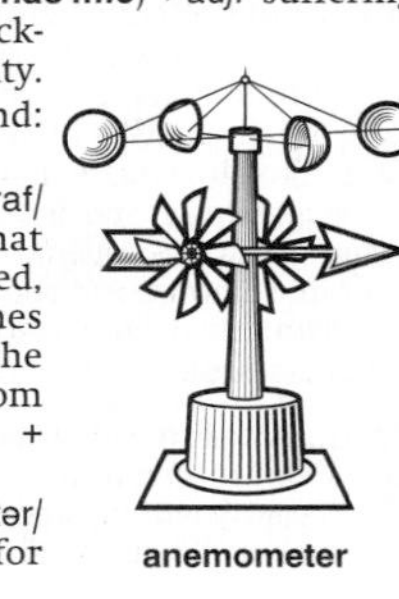
anemometer

a·nem·o·ne /ə'nemənē/ ▶*n.* **1** a plant of the buttercup family, typically bearing brightly colored flowers. Anemones are widely distributed in the wild, and several kinds are popular garden plants. • Genus *Anemone,* family Ranunculaceae: numerous species, including the North American **wood anemone** (*A. quinquefolia*). **2** short for **SEA ANEMONE**. ▷mid 16th cent.: from Latin, said to be from Greek *anemōnē* 'windflower,' literally 'daughter of the wind,' from *anemos* 'wind,' thought to be so named because the flowers open only when the wind blows.

a·nem·o·ne fish ▶*n.* another term for **CLOWNFISH**.

an·e·moph·i·lous /ˌanə'mäfələs/ ▶*adj. Botany* (of a plant) wind-pollinated. ▷late 19th cent.: from Greek *anemos* 'wind' + *-philous* (see **-PHILIA**). **—an·e·moph·i·ly** /-lē/ *n.*

an·en·ce·phal·ic /ˌanensə'falik/ *Medicine* ▶*adj.* having part or all of the cerebral hemispheres and the rear of the skull congenitally absent.
▶*n.* an anencephalic fetus or infant. ▷mid 19th cent.: from Greek *anenkephalos* 'without brain' + **-IC**. **—an·en·ceph·a·ly** /-'sefəlē/ *n.*

a·nent /ə'nent/ ▶*prep. chiefly archaic* concerning; about: *I'll say a few words anent the letter.* ▷Old English *on efen* 'in line with, in company with.'

-aneous ▶*suffix* forming adjectives from Latin words: *cutaneous* | *spontaneous.* ▷from the Latin suffix *-aneus* + **-OUS**.

an·er·gi·a /a'nərj(ē)ə/ ▶*n. Psychiatry* abnormal lack of energy. ▷late 19th cent.: modern Latin, from Greek *an-* 'without' + *ergon* 'work.'

an·er·gy /'anərjē/ ▶*n.* **1** *Medicine* absence of the normal immune response to a particular antigen or allergen. **2** another term for **ANERGIA**. ▷early 20th cent.: from German *Anergie,* from Greek *an-* 'not,' on the pattern of *Allergie* 'allergy.'

an·er·oid /'anəˌroid/ ▶*adj.* relating to or denoting a barometer that measures air pressure by the action of the air in deforming the elastic lid of an evacuated box or chamber.
▶*n.* a barometer of this type. ▷mid 19th cent.: coined in French from Greek *a-* 'without' + *nēros* 'water.'

an·es·the·sia /ˌanəs'THēZHə/ (*Brit.* **an·aes·the·sia**) ▶*n.* insensitivity to pain, esp. as artificially induced by the administration of gases or the injection of drugs before surgical operations. ■ the induction of this state, or the branch of medicine concerned with it. ▷early 18th cent.: from modern Latin *anaesthesia,* from Greek *anaisthēsia,* from *an-* 'without' + *aisthēsis* 'sensation.'

an·es·the·si·ol·o·gy /ˌanəsˌTHēzē'äləjē/ (*Brit.* **an·aes·the·si·ol·o·gy**) ▶*n.* the branch of medicine concerned with anesthesia and anesthetics. **—an·es·the·si·ol·o·gist** /-jist/ *n.*

an·es·thet·ic /ˌanəs'THetik/ (*Brit.* **an·aes·thet·ic**) ▶*n.* **1** a substance that induces insensitivity to pain. **2** (**anesthetics**) [treated as *sing.*] the study or practice of anesthesia.
▶*adj.* inducing or relating to insensitivity to pain. ▷mid 19th cent.: from Greek *anaisthētos* 'insensible,' related to *anaisthēsia* (see **ANESTHESIA**), + **-IC**.

an·es·the·tist /ə'nesTHitist/ (*Brit.* **an·aes·the·tist**) ▶*n.* a medical specialist who administers anesthetics.

an·es·the·tize /ə'nesTHiˌtīz/ (*Brit.* **an·aes·the·tize**) ▶*v.* [*trans.*] administer an anesthetic to: *in fetal surgery, doctors anesthetize both the mother and the fetus.* ■ *figurative* deprive of feeling or awareness: *tragedy of a magnitude that anesthetizes the mind.* **—an·es·the·ti·za·tion** /-THitə'zāSHən/ *n.*

an·eu·ploid /'anyo͝oˌploid/ ▶*adj. Genetics* having particular genes or chromosomal regions present in extra or fewer copies than in the normal type: *aneuploid colon cancer cells missegregate their chromosomes.* **—an·eu·ploi·dy** *n.*

an·eu·rysm /'anyəˌrizəm/ (also **an·eu·rism**) ▶*n. Medicine* an excessive localized enlargement of an artery caused by a weakening of the artery wall. ▷late Middle English: from Greek *aneurusma* 'dilatation,' from *aneurunein* 'widen out.' **—an·eu·rys·mal** /-ˌrizməl/ *adj.*

a·new /ə'n(y)o͞o/ ▶*adv. chiefly poetic/literary* in a new or different, typically more positive, way: *her career had* ***begun anew,*** *with a lucrative Japanese modeling contract.* ■ once more; again: *tears filled her eyes anew.*

an·frac·tu·ous /an'frakCHo͞oəs/ ▶*adj. rare* sinuous or circuitous. ▷late 16th cent.: from late Latin *anfractuosus,* from Latin *anfractus* 'a bending.' **—an·frac·tu·os·i·ty** /-ˌfrakCHo͞o'äsitē/ *n.*

An·ga·ra Riv·er /ˌäNGgə'rä; ˌəNG-/ a river in the southeastern part of Siberia in Russia that flows northwest and west for 1,039 miles (1,779 km) from Lake Baikal to meet the Yenisei River south of Yeniseysk.

an·gel /'ānjəl/ ▶*n.* **1** a spiritual being believed to act as an attendant, agent, or messenger of God, conventionally represented in human form with wings and a long robe: *God sent an angel to talk to Gideon* | *the* ***Angel of Death*** | (*figurative*) *Ella, ever the* ***angel of mercy,*** *organized the girls into baking cookies.* ■ an attendant spirit, esp. a benevolent one: *there was an angel watching over me.* See also **GUARDIAN ANGEL**. ■ *informal* a financial backer of an enterprise, typically in the theater. ■ in traditional Christian angelology, a being of the lowest order of the celestial hierarchy. ■ *informal Aviation* an unexplained radar echo. **2** a person of exemplary conduct or virtue: *women were then seen as angels or whores* | *I know I'm* ***no angel.*** ■ used in similes or comparisons to refer to a person's outstanding beauty, qualities, or abilities: *you sang* ***like an angel.*** ■ used in approval when a person has been or is expected to be kind or willing to oblige: ***be an angel*** *and let us come in.* ■ used as a term of endearment: *I miss you too, angel.* **3** *historical* an English coin minted between 1470 and 1634 and bearing the figure of the archangel Michael killing a dragon. **4** (**angels**) *informal, Aviation* an aircraft's altitude (often used with a numeral indicating thousands of feet): *we rendezvous at angels nine.* ▷Old English *engel,* ultimately via ecclesiastical Latin from Greek *angelos* 'messenger'; superseded in Middle English by forms from Old French *angele.*
▶***PHRASES*** □ **the angel in the house** *chiefly ironic* a woman who is completely devoted to her husband and family. [phrase from a poem by Coventry Patmore.] □ **on the side of the angels** on the side of what is right and just.

an·gel dust ▶*n. informal* **1** the hallucinogenic drug phencyclidine hydrochloride. **2** another term for **CLENBUTEROL**.

An·ge·le·no /ˌanjə'lēnō/ (also **Los An·ge·le·no**, **An·ge·li·no**) ▶*n.* (*pl.* **-nos**) a native or inhabitant of Los Angeles: [as *adj.*] *Angeleno sports fans.* ▷late 19th cent.: from American Spanish.

An·gel Falls /'ānjəl/ a waterfall in the Guiana Highlands of southeastern Venezuela. The highest waterfall in the world, it has an uninterrupted descent of 3,210 feet (978 m). The falls were discovered in 1935 by U.S. aviator and prospector **James Angel** (*c.*1899–1956).

an·gel·fish /'ānjəlˌfisH/ ▶*n.* (*pl.* same or **-fish·es**) any of a number of laterally compressed deep-bodied fish with extended dorsal and anal fins, typically brightly colored or boldly striped, including: • a freshwater fish native to the Amazon basin (genus *Pterophyllum,* family Cichlidae), in particular *P. scalare,* popular in tropical aquariums. • a coastal marine fish (several genera in the family Pomacanthidae), including the blue and yellow **queen angelfish** (*Holacanthus ciliaris*) and the more drably colored **gray angelfish** (*Pomacanthus arcuatus*). • another term for **BATFISH** (sense 2).

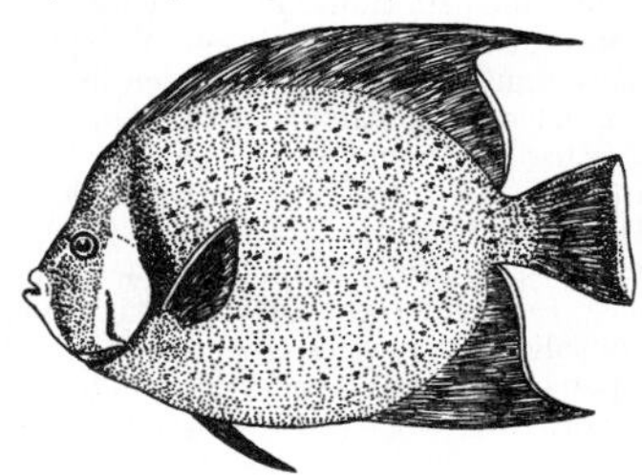
gray angelfish

an·gel food cake (*Brit.* **angel cake**) ▶*n.* a light, pale sponge cake made of flour, egg whites, and no fat, typically baked in a ring shape and covered with soft icing.

an·gel hair (also **an·gel's hair**) ▶*n.* a type of pasta consisting of very fine long strands.

an·gel·ic /an'jelik/ ▶*adj.* of or relating to angels: *the angelic hosts.* ■ (of a person) exceptionally beautiful, innocent, or kind: *she looks remarkably young and angelic.* ▷late Middle English: from French *angélique,* via late Latin from Greek *angelikos,* from *angelos* (see **ANGEL**). **—an·gel·i·cal** *adj.* **—an·gel·i·cal·ly** /-ik(ə)lē/ *adv.*

an·gel·i·ca /an'jelikə/ ▸*n.* a tall aromatic plant of the parsley family, with large leaves and yellowish-green flowers. Native to both Eurasia and North America, it is used in cooking and herbal medicine. • Genus *Angelica*, family Umbelliferae: many species, esp. the cultivated *A. archangelica*. ■ the candied stalk of this plant. ▷early 16th cent.: from medieval Latin *(herba) angelica* 'angelic (herb),' so named because it was believed to be efficacious against poisoning and disease.

an·gel·i·ca tree ▸*n.* another term for **devil's walking stick** (see **HERCULES-CLUB**).

An·gel·ic Doc·tor the nickname of St. Thomas Aquinas.

An·ge·li·co /än'jelikō/, Fra (*c.*1400–55), Italian painter and Dominican friar; born *Guido di Pietro*; monastic name *Fra Giovanni da Fiesole*. Notable works: the frescos in the convent of San Marco, Florence (*c.*1438–47).

An·ge·li·no ▸*n.* variant spelling of **ANGELENO**.

An·gel Is·land an island in San Francisco Bay, in north central California, that was the chief immigration station on the U.S. western coast. It is now a state park.

An·gel·man syn·drome /'ānɢ(g)əlmən/ (also **An·gel·man's syn·drome**) ▸*n.* a rare congenital disorder characterized by mental retardation and a tendency toward jerky movement, caused by the absence of certain genes normally present on the copy of chromosome 15 inherited from the mother. ▷1970s: named after Harold *Angelman*, British doctor who described the condition.

an·gel·ol·o·gy /,ānjə'läləjē/ ▸*n.* theological dogma or speculation concerning angels: *Gnostic angelology influenced Pseudo-Dionysius.* ▷mid 19th cent. **—an·gel·ol·o·gist** /-jist/ *n.*

An·ge·lou /'anjə,lō; -,lo͞o/, Maya (1928–), U.S. novelist and poet; born *Marguerite Johnson*. The first volume of her autobiography, *I Know Why the Caged Bird Sings* (1970), which recounts her harrowing experiences as a black child in the U.S. South, was followed by four more: *Gather Together in My Name* (1974), *Singin' and Swingin' and Gettin' Merry Like Christmas* (1976), *The Heart of a Woman* (1981), and *All God's Children Need Traveling Shoes* (1986).

an·gel shark ▸*n.* an active bottom-dwelling cartilaginous fish with broad winglike pectoral fins. • Family Squatinidae and genus *Squatina*: several species, in particular the **Atlantic angel shark** (*S. dumerili*).

an·gel's trum·pet ▸*n.* a South American shrub or small tree of the nightshade family, with distinctive trumpet-shaped flowers, cultivated as an ornamental and in some regions consumed for its narcotic properties. • Genus *Brugmansia*, family Solanaceae.

An·ge·lus /'anjələs/ (also **an·ge·lus**) ▸*n.* [in *sing.*] a Roman Catholic devotion commemorating the Incarnation of Jesus and including the Hail Mary, said at morning, noon, and sunset. ■ a ringing of church bells announcing this. ▷mid 17th cent.: from the Latin phrase *Angelus domini* 'the angel of the Lord,' the opening words of the devotion.

an·gel wings ▸*plural n.* [treated as *sing.*] a white edible piddock found on the east coast of North America and in the West Indies. • *Barnea costata*, family Pholadidae.

an·ger /'anɢgər/ ▸*n.* a strong feeling of annoyance, displeasure, or hostility: *the colonel's anger at his daughter's disobedience.*
▸*v.* [*trans.*] (often **be angered**) fill (someone) with such a feeling; provoke anger in: *she was angered by his terse answer* | [*trans.*] *I was angered to receive a further letter from them* | [*trans.*] *he was angered that he had not been told.* ▷Middle English: from Old Norse *angr* 'grief,' *angra* 'vex.' The original use was in the Old Norse senses; current senses date from late Middle English.

An·gers /'anjərz; än'ZHā/ a town in western France, capital of the former province of Anjou; pop. 146,160 .

An·ge·vin /'anjəvən/ ▸*n.* a native, inhabitant, or ruler of Anjou. ■ any of the Plantagenet kings of England, esp. those who were also counts of Anjou (Henry II, Richard I, and John).
▸*adj.* of or relating to Anjou. ■ of, relating to, or denoting the Plantaganets. ▷from French, from medieval Latin *Andegavinus*, from *Andegavum* 'Angers' (see **ANGERS**).

an·gi·na /an'jīnə/ ▸*n.* **1** (also **an·gi·na pec·to·ris** /'pektəris/) a condition marked by severe pain in the chest, often also spreading to the shoulders, arms, and neck, caused by an inadequate blood supply to the heart. **2** [with *adj.*] any of a number of disorders in which there is an intense localized pain: *Ludwig's angina.* ▷mid 16th cent. (in the Latin sense): from Latin, 'quinsy,' from Greek *ankhonē* 'strangling'; *pectoris* (sense 1): Latin, 'of the chest.'

angio- ▸*comb. form* relating to blood vessels: *angiography.* ■ relating to seed vessels: *angiosperm.* ▷from Greek *angeion* 'vessel.'

an·gi·o·gen·e·sis /,anjē-ō'jenəsis/ ▸*n. Medicine* the development of new blood vessels. **—an·gi·o·gen·ic** /-'jenik/ *adj.*

an·gi·o·gram /'anj(ē)ə,gram/ ▸*n.* an X-ray photograph of blood or lymph vessels, made by angiography.

an·gi·og·ra·phy /,anjē'ägrəfē/ ▸*n.* examination by X-ray of blood or lymph vessels, carried out after introduction of a radiopaque substance. **—an·gi·o·graph·ic** /-ə'grafik/ *adj.* **—an·gi·o·graph·i·cal·ly** /-ə'grafik(ə)lē/ *adv.*

an·gi·o·ma /,anjē'ōmə/ ▸*n.* (*pl.* **-mas** or **-ma·ta** /-mətə/) *Medicine* an abnormal growth produced by the dilatation or new formation of blood vessels. ▷late 19th cent.: from Greek *angeion* 'vessel' + **-OMA**.

an·gi·o·plas·ty /'anjēə,plastē/ ▸*n.* (*pl.* **-ties**) surgical repair or unblocking of a blood vessel, esp. a coronary artery. See also **BALLOON ANGIOPLASTY**.

an·gi·o·sperm /'anjēə,spərm/ ▸*n. Botany* a plant that has flowers and produces seeds enclosed within a carpel. The angiosperms are a large group and include herbaceous plants, shrubs, grasses, and most trees. Compare with **GYMNOSPERM**. • Subdivision Angiospermae, division Spermatophyta.

an·gi·o·sta·tin /,anjēō'statn/ ▸*n. Medicine* a drug used to inhibit the growth of new blood vessels in malignant tumors.

an·gi·o·ten·sin /,anjē-ō'tensin/ ▸*n. Biochemistry* a protein whose presence in the blood promotes aldosterone secretion and tends to raise blood pressure. ▷1950s: from **ANGIO-** + *(hyper)tens(ion)* + **-IN**[1].

Ang·kor /'anɢkər; 'anɢ,kôr/ the capital of the ancient kingdom of Khmer in northwestern Cambodia; noted for its temples, esp. the **Angkor Wat** (mid 12th century), the site was rediscovered in 1860.

Angkor Wat

An·gle /'anɢgəl/ ▸*n.* a member of a Germanic people, originally inhabitants of what is now Schleswig-Holstein, who migrated to England in the 5th century AD. The Angles founded kingdoms in Mercia, Northumbria, and East Anglia and gave their name to England and the English. ▷from Latin *Anglus*, (plural) *Angli* 'the people of *Angul*,' a district of Schleswig (now in northern Germany), so called because of its shape; of Germanic origin, related to Old English *angul* (see **ANGLE**[2]). Compare with **ENGLISH**.

an·gle[1] /'anɢgəl/ ▸*n.* **1** the space (usually measured in degrees) between two intersecting lines or surfaces at or close to the point where they meet. ■ a corner, esp. an external projection or an internal recess of a part of a building or other structure: *a skylight in the angle of the roof.* ■ slope; a measure of the inclination of two lines or surfaces with respect to each other, equal to the amount that one would have to be turned in order to point in the same direction as the other: *sloping at an angle of 33° to the horizontal* | *he trudged back, the angle of his shoulders spelling dejection.* ■ a position from which something is viewed or along which it travels or acts, often as measured by its inclination from an implicit horizontal or vertical baseline: *from this angle, Maggie could not see Naomi's face* | *camera angles.* **2** a particular way of approaching or considering an issue or problem: *discussing the problems from every conceivable angle* | *he always had a fresh* ***angle on*** *life.* ■ one part of a larger subject, event, or problem: *a black prosecutor who downplayed the racial angle* | *his chosen angle was the language of the Old Testament.* ■ a bias or point of view: *Zimmer saw the world from an angle that few could understand.* **3** [often with *adj.*] *Astrology* each of the four mundane houses (the first, fourth, seventh, and tenth of the twelve divisions of the heavens) that extend counterclockwise from the cardinal points of the compass. **4** angle iron or a similar construction material made of another metal.

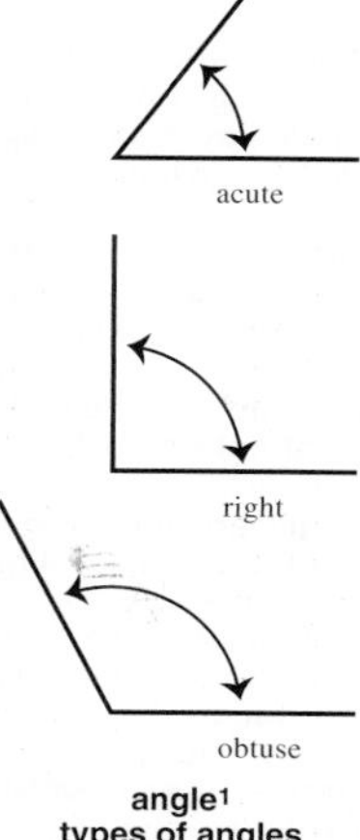

angle[1]
types of angles

▸*v.* [*trans.*] direct or incline at an angle: *Anna angled her camera toward the tree* | *he angled his chair so that he could watch her.* ■ [*intrans.*] move or be inclined at an angle: *the cab angled across two lanes and skidded to a stop* | *the sun angled into the dining room.* ■ [*trans.*] present (information) to reflect a particular view or have a particular focus. ▷late Middle English: from Old French, from Latin *angulus* 'corner.'
▸*PHRASES* □ **at an angle** in a direction or at an inclination markedly different from parallel, vertical, or horizontal with respect to an implicit baseline: *she wore her beret at an angle* | *an armchair was drawn up* ***at an angle to*** *his desk.* □ **from all angles** from every direction or point of view: *they come shooting at us from all angles* | *looking at the problem from all angles.*

an·gle[2] ▸*v.* [*intrans.*] fish with rod and line: *there are no big fish left to* ***angle for.*** ■ seek something desired by indirectly prompting someone to offer it: *Ralph had begun to* ***angle for*** *an invitation* | [with *infinitive*] *her husband was angling to get into the Cabinet.*
▸*n. archaic* a fishhook. ▷Old English *angul* (noun); the verb dates from late Middle English.

an·gle brack·et ▸*n.* **1** either of a pair of marks in the form < >, used to enclose words or figures so as to separate them from their context. **2** another term for **BRACKET** (sense 3).

an·gled /'anɢgəld/ ▸*adj.* **1** placed or inclined at an angle to something else: *he sent an angled shot into the net* | *a sharply angled flight of stairs.* **2** [in *combination*] (of an object or shape) having an angle or angles of a specified type or number: *a right-angled bend* | *an obtuse-angled triangle.* ■ (of information) presented so as to reflect a particular view or to have a particular focus.

an·gle i·ron ▸*n.* a construction material consisting of pieces of steel with an L-shaped cross-section, able to be bolted together. ■ a piece of metal of this kind.

an·gle of at·tack ▸*n.* the angle between the chord of an airfoil and the direction of the surrounding undisturbed flow of gas or liquid.

an·gle of in·ci·dence ▸*n. Physics* the angle that an incident line or ray makes with a perpendicular to the surface at the point of incidence.

an·gle of re·flec·tion ▸*n. Physics* the angle made by a reflected ray with a perpendicular to the reflecting surface.

an·gle of re·frac·tion ▸*n. Physics* the angle made by a refracted ray with a perpendicular to the refracting surface.

an·gle of re·pose ▸*n.* the steepest angle at which a sloping surface formed of of a particular loose material is stable.

an·gler /'anɢglər/ ▸*n.* a person who fishes with a rod and line: [with *adj.*] *a carp angler.* ■ short for **ANGLERFISH**.

an·gler·fish /'anɢglər,fiSH/ ▸*n.* (*pl.* same or **-fish·es**) a fish that lures prey with a fleshy lobe attached to a filament that arises from the snout and hangs in front of the mouth. Most anglerfishes have a very

A

large head and wide mouth, with a small body and tail. • Order Lophiiformes: several families. Some rest motionless on the seabed, in particular those of the family Lophiidae); many others are deep-sea fish.

An·gle·sey /ˈaNGgəlsē/ an island in northwestern Wales, separated from the mainland by the Menai Strait.

an·gle shades ▸*plural n.* [treated as *sing.*] a moth with wings patterned in muted green, red, and pink. • *Phlogophora meticulosa*, family Noctuidae and other species.

An·gli·an /ˈaNGglēən/ ▸*adj.* of or relating to the ancient Angles. ▷1960s: from Latin *Angli* (see **Angle**) + **-ian**.

An·gli·can /ˈaNGglikən/ ▸*adj.* of, relating to, or denoting the Church of England or any Church in communion with it.
▸*n.* a member of any of these Churches. ▷early 17th cent.: from medieval Latin *Anglicanus* (its adoption suggested by *Anglicana ecclesia* 'the English church' in the Magna Carta), from *Anglicus*, from *Angli* (see **Angle**). **—An·gli·can·ism** /-ˌnizəm/ *n.*

An·gli·can chant ▸*n.* a method of singing unmetrical psalms and canticles to short harmonized melodies, the first note being extended to accommodate as many syllables as necessary.

An·gli·can com·mun·ion the group of Christian Churches derived from or related to the Church of England, including the Episcopal Church in the U.S. and other national, provincial, and independent Churches. The body's primate is the Archbishop of Canterbury.

An·gli·cism /ˈaNGgləˌsizəm/ ▸*n.* **1** a word or phrase that is peculiar to British English: *this new autobiography is studded with Anglicisms like lorries, plimsolls, and doing a bunk.* ■ the quality of being typically English or of favoring English things. **2** a word or phrase borrowed from English into a foreign language: *"purists" condemn the use of "fin de semaine" because it is an anglicism.* ▷mid 17th cent.: from Latin *Anglicus*, from *Angli* (see **Angle**) + **-ism**.

an·gli·cize /ˈaNGgləˌsīz/ ▸*v.* [*trans.*] make English in form or character: *he anglicized his name to Goodman* | [as *adj.*] (**anglicized**) *an anglicized form of a Navajo word.* **—an·gli·ci·za·tion** /ˌaNGgləsəˈzāSHən/ *n.*

an·gling /ˈaNG(g)(ə)liNG/ ▸*n.* the sport or pastime of fishing with a rod and line: [as *adj.*] *an angling club* | *an angling license.*

An·glo /ˈaNGglō/ ▸*n.* (*pl.* **-glos**) a white, English-speaking American as distinct from a Hispanic American: [as *adj.*] *Anglo neighborhoods.* ▷early 19th cent.: independent usage of **Anglo-**.

Anglo- ▸*comb. form* English: *anglophone.* ■ of English origin: *Anglo-Saxon.* ■ English and ... : *Anglo-Latin.* ■ British and ... : *Anglo-Indian.* ▷modern Latin, from Latin *Anglus* 'English.'

An·glo-A·mer·i·can ▸*adj.* of or relating to both Britain and the U.S.: *the older Anglo-American conception of the American as an offshoot of the Anglo-Saxons.* ■ of English descent, but born or living in the U.S.
▸*n.* an American born in England or of English ancestry. ■ an American whose native tongue is English.

An·glo-Cath·o·lic ▸*adj.* of or relating to Anglo-Catholicism.
▸*n.* a member of an Anglo-Catholic Church.

An·glo-Ca·thol·i·cism ▸*n.* a tradition within the Anglican Church that is close to Catholicism in its doctrine and worship and is broadly identified with High Church Anglicanism. Anglo-Catholicism grew out of the Oxford Movement of the 1830s and 1840s.

An·glo-Celt ▸*n.* a person of British or Irish descent (typically used outside Britain and Ireland). **—An·glo-Celt·ic** *adj.*

An·glo·cen·tric /ˌaNGglōˈsentrik/ ▸*adj.* centered on or considered in terms of England or Britain: *an Anglocentric, white view of Australian history.*

An·glo-In·di·an ▸*adj.* of, relating to, or involving both Britain and India: *Anglo-Indian business cooperation.* ■ (esp. of a person living in the Indian subcontinent) of mixed British and Indian parentage. ■ *chiefly historical* of British descent or birth but living or having lived long in India. ■ (of a word) adopted into English from an Indian language.
▸*n.* an Anglo-Indian person.

An·glo-I·rish ▸*adj.* of or relating to both Britain and Ireland (or specifically the Republic of Ireland). ■ of English descent but born or resident in Ireland. ■ [as *plural n.*] (**the Anglo-Irish**) people of English descent but born or resident in Ireland. ■ of mixed English and Irish parentage.
▸*n.* the English language as used in Ireland.

An·glo-I·rish Trea·ty an agreement signed in 1921 by representatives of the British government and the provisional Irish Republican government, by which Ireland was partitioned and the Irish Free State created.

An·glo-Lat·in ▸*adj.* of, in, or relating to Latin as used in medieval England.
▸*n.* this form of Latin.

An·glo·ma·ni·a /ˌaNGglōˈmānēə/ ▸*n.* excessive admiration of English customs.

An·glo-Nor·man French (also **An·glo-Nor·man**) ▸*n.* the variety of Norman French used in England after the Norman Conquest. It remained the language of the English nobility for several centuries and has had a strong influence on legal phraseology in English.
▸*adj.* of or relating to this language.

An·glo·phile /ˈaNGgləˌfīl/ ▸*n.* a person who is fond of or greatly admires England or Britain.
▸*adj.* fond or admiring of England or Britain. **—An·glo·phil·ia** /ˌaNGgləˈfilēə/ *n.*

An·glo·phobe /ˈaNGgləˌfōb/ ▸*n.* a person who greatly hates or fears England or Britain.
▸*adj.* greatly hating or fearing England or Britain. **—An·glo·pho·bi·a** /ˌaNGgləˈfōbēə/ *n.*

an·glo·phone /ˈaNGgləˌfōn/ ▸*adj.* English-speaking: *anglophone students* | *the population is largely anglophone.*
▸*n.* an English-speaking person. ▷early 20th cent. (as a noun; rare before the 1960s): from **Anglo-** + **-phone**, on the pattern of *francophone.*

An·glo-Sax·on ▸*adj.* relating to or denoting the Germanic inhabitants of England from their arrival in the 5th century up to the Norman Conquest. ■ of English descent. ■ of, in, or relating to the Old English language. ■ *informal* (of an English word or expression) plain, in particular vulgar: *using a lot of good old Anglo-Saxon expletives.*
▸*n.* **1** a Germanic inhabitant of England between the 5th century and the Norman Conquest. ■ a person of English descent. ■ any white, English-speaking person. **2** another term for **Old English**. ■ *informal* plain English, in particular vulgar slang. ▷from modern Latin *Anglo-Saxones* (plural), medieval Latin *Angli Saxones.*

An·go·la /aNGˈgōlə; anˈgōlə/ a republic on the west-ern coast of southern Africa; pop. 10,978,000; capital, Luanda; languages, Portuguese (official), Bantu languages. **—An·go·lan** *adj.* & *n.*

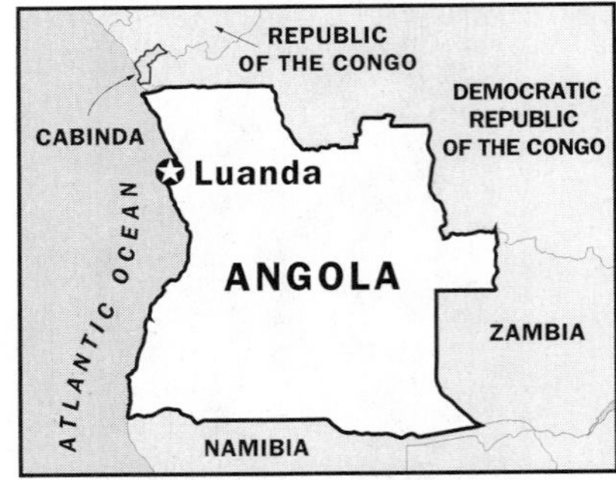

Angola was a Portuguese possession from the end of the 16th century until it achieved independence in 1975. Independence was followed by years of civil war, chiefly between the ruling Marxist MPLA and the UNITA movement.

An·go·ra /aNGˈgôrə/ former name (until 1930) of **Ankara**.

an·go·ra /aNGˈgôrə/ ▸*n.* [often as *adj.*] a cat, goat, or rabbit of a long-haired breed: *angora rabbits.* ■ a fabric made from the hair of the angora goat or rabbit: [as *adj.*] *an angora cardigan.* ▷early 19th cent. (denoting a long-haired breed): from the place name **Angora**.

an·go·ra wool ▸*n.* a mixture of sheep's wool and angora rabbit hair.

An·gos·tu·ra /ˌaNGgəˈst(y)o͝orə/ former name (until 1846) for **Ciudad Bolívar**.

an·gos·tu·ra /ˌaNGgəˈst(y)o͝orə/ (also **angostura bark**) ▸*n.* an aromatic bitter bark from some South American trees, used as a flavoring, and formerly as a tonic and to reduce fever. • This bark is taken from the trees *Angostura febrifuga* and *Galipea officinalis*, family Rutaceae. ■ short for **Angostura bitters**. ▷late 18th cent.: from the place name **Angostura**.

An·gos·tu·ra bit·ters ▸ *n. trademark* a kind of tonic first made in Angostura.

an·gry /ˈaNGgrē/ ▸*adj.* (**-gri·er**, **-gri·est**) having a strong feeling of or showing annoyance, displeasure, or hostility; full of anger: *why are you* **angry with** *me?* | *an angry customer* | *Christine had* **made him angry** | *I'm* **angry that** *she didn't call me.* ■ *figurative* (of the sea or sky) stormy, turbulent, or threatening: *the wild, angry sea.* ■ (of a wound or sore) red and inflamed: *her skin was splotched with angry red burns.* **—an·gri·ly** /-grəlē/ *adv.*

an·gry white male ▸*n. derogatory* a politically conservative or anti-liberal white man.

an·gry young man ▸*n.* a young man dissatisfied with and outspoken against existing social and political structures. ■ (**Angry Young Men**) a number of British playwrights and novelists of the early 1950s whose work was marked by irreverence toward the Establishment and disgust at the survival of class distinctions and privilege. Notable members of the group were John Osborne and Kingsley Amis.

angst /aNG(k)st; äNG(k)st/ ▸*n.* a feeling of deep anxiety or dread, typically an unfocused one about the human condition or the state of the world in general: *adolescent angst.* ■ *informal* a feeling of persistent worry about something trivial: *my hair causes me angst.* ▷1920s: from German, 'fear, anxiety.'

Ång·ström /ˈôNGstrəm; ˈaNG-/, Anders Jonas (1814–1874), Swedish physicist. He proposed a relationship between the emission and absorption spectra of chemical elements and measured optical wavelengths in the unit later named in his honor.

ang·strom /ˈaNGstrəm/ (also **ång·ström**, **angstrom unit**) (abbr.: **Å**) ▸*n.* a unit of length equal to one hundred-millionth of a centimeter, 10^{-10} meter, used mainly to express wavelengths and interatomic distances. ▷late 19th cent.: named after A. J. **Ångström**.

An·guil·la /aNGˈgwilə; an-/ the northernmost island of the Leeward Islands in the West Indies; pop. 7,020; capital, The Valley. Formerly a British colony and briefly united with St. Kitts and Nevis in 1967, it is now a self-governing dependency of the UK. **—An·guil·lan** *adj.* & *n.*

an·guish /ˈaNGgwiSH/ ▸*n.* severe mental or physical pain or suffering: *she shut her eyes* **in anguish** | *Philip gave a cry of anguish.*
▸*v.* suffer or cause someone to suffer anguish: *he anguished over how to reply.* ▷Middle English: via Old French from Latin *angustia* 'tightness,' (plural) 'straits, distress,' from *angustus* 'narrow.'

an·guished /ˈaNGgwiSHt/ ▸*adj.* experiencing or expressing severe mental or physical pain or suffering: *he gave an anguished cry* | *when she turned, her face was anguished.* ▷early 17th cent.: past participle of the rare verb *anguish*, from Old French *anguissier*, from ecclesiastical Latin *angustiare* 'to distress,' from Latin *angustia* (see **anguish**).

an·gu·lar /ˈaNGgyələr/ ▸*adj.* **1** (of an object, outline, or shape) having angles or sharp corners: *angular chairs* | *Adam's angular black handwriting.* ■ (of a person or part of their body) lean and having a prominent bone structure: *her angular face.* ■ (of a person's way of moving) not flowing smoothly; awkward or jerky: *his movements were stiff and angular* | *figurative the music is angular and sardonic.* ■ placed or directed at an angle: *the large angular writing was typical of the officers and the noncoms.* **2** *chiefly Physics* denoting physical properties or quantities measured with reference to or by means of an angle, esp. those associated with rotation: *angular acceleration.* **3** *Astrology* located in or relating to one of the houses that begin at the four cardinal points. ▷late Middle English (as an astrological term): from Latin *angularis*, from *angulus* (see **angle**[1]). **—an·gu·lar·i·ty** /ˌaNGgyəˈlaritē/ *n.* **—an·gu·lar·ly** *adv.*

an·gu·lar di·am·e·ter ▸*n. Astronomy* the apparent diameter of a planet or other celestial object measured by the angle that it subtends at the point of observation.

an·gu·lar mo·men·tum ▸*n. Physics* the quantity of rotation of a body, which is the product of its moment of inertia and its angular velocity.

an·gu·lar ve·loc·i·ty ▸*n. Physics* the rate of change of angular position of a rotating body.

an·gu·late /ˈaNGgyəˌlāt/ ▸*v.* [*trans.*] (often **be angulated**) *technical* hold, bend, or distort (a part of the body, esp. of an animal) so as to form an angle or angles: [as *adj.*] (**angulated**) *the hindquarters are more strongly angulated than the forequarters.* ■ *Skiing* incline (the upper body) sideways and outward during a turn: [*intrans.*] *angulate slightly with the knees.* ▷late

15th cent. (as *angulated*, used chiefly as a botanical or zoological term): from Latin *angulatus*, past participle of *angulare*, from *angulus* 'angle.' —**an·gu·la·tion** /ˌaNGgyəˈlāSHən/ *n.*

ang·wan·ti·bo /aNGˈ(g)wäntəˌbō/ ▸*n.* (*pl.* **-bos**) a small rare nocturnal primate of west central Africa, related to the potto. • *Arctocebus calabarensis*, family Lorisidae. ▷mid 19th cent.: from Efik.

an·har·mon·ic /ˌanhärˈmänik/ ▸*adj. Physics* relating to or denoting motion that is not simple harmonic. —**an·har·mo·nic·i·ty** /anˌhärməˈnisitē/ *n.*

an·he·do·ni·a /ˌanhēˈdōnēə; -hi-/ ▸*n. Psychiatry* inability to feel pleasure. ▷late 19th cent.: from French *anhédonie*, from Greek *an-* 'without' + *hēdonē* 'pleasure.' —**an·he·don·ic** /-ˈdänik/ *adj.*

an·he·dral /anˈhēdrəl/ ▸*adj. Crystallography* (of a crystal) having no plane faces.
▸*n. Aeronautics* downward inclination of an aircraft's wing, or the angle of this. Compare with **DIHEDRAL**. ▷late 19th cent. (as an adjective): from **AN-**[1] 'not' + *-hedral* (see **-HEDRON**).

an·hin·ga /anˈhiNGgə/ ▸*n.* a long-necked fish-eating bird related to the cormorants, typically found in fresh water. Anhingas spear fish with their long pointed bills and frequently swim submerged to the neck. Also called **DARTER, SNAKEBIRD**. • Family Anhingidae and genus *Anhinga*: four species. ▷mid 18th cent.: from Portuguese, from Tupi *áyinga*.

An·hui /ˈänˈhwā/ (also **An·hwei**) a province in eastern China; capital, Hefei.

an·hy·dride /anˈhīˌdrīd/ ▸*n. Chemistry* the compound obtained by removing the elements of water from a particular acid. ■ [usu. with *adj.*] an organic compound containing the group −C(O)OC(O)−, derived from a carboxylic acid. ▷mid 19th cent.: from Greek *anudros* (see **ANHYDROUS**) + **-IDE**.

an·hy·drite /anˈhīˌdrīt/ ▸*n.* a white mineral consisting of anhydrous calcium sulfate. It typically occurs in evaporite deposits. ▷early 19th cent.: from Greek *anudros* (see **ANHYDROUS**) + **-ITE**[1].

an·hy·drous /anˈhīdrəs/ ▸*adj. Chemistry* (of a substance, esp. a crystalline compound) containing no water. ▷early 19th cent.: from Greek *anudros* (from *an-* 'without' + *hudōr* 'water') + **-OUS**.

a·ni /äˈnē/ ▸*n.* (*pl.* **a·nis**) a glossy black long-tailed bird of the cuckoo family, with a large deep bill, found in Central and South America. • Genus *Crotophaga*, family Cuculidae: three species. ▷early 19th cent.: from Spanish *ani*, Portuguese *anum*, from Tupi *anū*.

an·i·line /ˈanl-in/ ▸*n. Chemistry* a colorless oily liquid present in coal tar. It is used in the manufacture of dyes, drugs, and plastics, and was the basis of the earliest synthetic dyes. • Chem. formula: $C_6H_5NH_2$. ▷mid 19th cent.: from *anil* 'indigo' (from which it was originally obtained), via French and Portuguese from Arabic *an-nīl* (from Sanskrit *nīlī*, from *nīla* 'dark blue').

an·i·line dye ▸*n. chiefly historical* a synthetic dye, esp. one made from aniline.

a·ni·lin·gus /ˌānəˈliNGgəs/ ▸*n.* sexual stimulation of the anus by the tongue or mouth. ▷1960s: from Latin *anus* 'anus' on the pattern of *cunnilingus*.

an·i·ma /ˈanəmə/ ▸*n. Psychology* Jung's term for the feminine part of a man's personality: Often contrasted with **ANIMUS** (sense 3). ■ the part of the psyche that is directed inward, and is in touch with the subconscious. Often contrasted with **PERSONA**. ▷1920s: from Latin, literally 'mind, soul.'

an·i·mad·ver·sion /ˌanəmadˈvərZHən/ ▸*n. formal* criticism or censure: *her animadversion against science.* ■ a comment or remark, esp. a critical one: *animadversions that the poet receives quite humbly.* ▷mid 16th cent.: from French, or from Latin *animadversio(n-)*, from the verb *animadvertere* (see **ANIMADVERT**).

an·i·mad·vert /ˌanəmadˈvərt/ ▸*v.* [*intrans.*] (**animadvert on/upon/against**) *formal* pass criticism or censure on; speak out against: *we shall be obliged to animadvert most severely upon you in our report | many travelers animadvert against their own towns and cities.* ▷late Middle English (in the sense 'pay attention to'): from Latin *animadvertere*, from *animus* 'mind' + *advertere* (from *ad-* 'toward' + *vertere* 'to turn').

an·i·mal /ˈanəməl/ ▸*n.* a living organism that feeds on organic matter, typically having specialized sense organs and nervous system and able to respond rapidly to stimuli: *animals such as spiders | wild animals adapt badly to a caged life | humans are the only animals who weep.* ■ any such living organism other than a human being: *are humans superior to animals, or just different?* ■ a mammal, as opposed to a bird, reptile, fish, or insect: *the snowfall seemed to have chased all birds, animals, and men indoors.* ■ a person whose behavior is regarded as devoid of human attributes or civilizing influences, esp. someone who is very cruel, violent, or repulsive: *those men have to be animals—what they did to that boy was savage.* ■ [with *adj.*] a particular type of person or thing: *a regular party animal | the government that followed the election was a very* ***different animal***.

Animals are generally distinguished from plants by being unable to synthesize organic molecules from inorganic ones, so that they have to feed on plants or on other animals. They are typically able to move about, although this ability is sometimes restricted to a particular stage in the life cycle. The great majority of animals are invertebrates, of which there are some thirty phyla; the vertebrates constitute but a single subphylum.
See also **HIGHER ANIMALS, LOWER ANIMALS**.

▸*adj.* [*attrib.*] of, relating to, or characteristic of animals: *the evolution of animal life | animal welfare.* ■ of animals as distinct from plants: *tissues of animal and vegetable protein.* ■ characteristic of the physical and instinctive needs of animals; of the flesh rather than the spirit or intellect: *a crude surrender to animal lust.* ▷Middle English: as a noun from Latin *animal*, based on Latin *animalis* 'having breath,' from *anima* 'breath'; as an adjective via Old French, from Latin *animalis*.

an·i·mal crack·er ▸*n.* a type of sweet cracker made in various animal shapes.

an·i·mal·cule /ˌanəˈmalˌkyo͞ol/ ▸*n. archaic* a microscopic animal. ▷late 16th cent.: from modern Latin *animalculum*, from *animal* 'an animal' + **-CULE**.

an·i·mal hus·band·ry ▸*n.* the science of breeding and caring for farm animals.

an·i·mal·ism /ˈanəməˌlizəm/ ▸*n.* behavior that is characteristic of or appropriate to animals, particularly in being physical and instinctive. ■ religious worship of or concerning animals. —**an·i·mal·is·tic** /ˌanəməˈlistik/ *adj.*

an·i·mal·i·ty /ˌanəˈmalitē/ ▸*n.* animal nature or character: *a prehuman condition of animality.* ■ physical, instinctive behavior or qualities: *what attracted me to her was her animality.* ▷early 17th cent.: from French *animalité*, from *animal* (adjective), from Latin *animalis* 'animate, living' (see **ANIMAL**).

an·i·mal·ize /ˈanəməˌlīz/ ▸*v.* [*trans.*] make into or like an animal. —**an·i·mal·i·za·tion** /ˌanəməliˈzāSHən/ *n.*

an·i·mal mag·net·ism ▸*n.* **1** a quality of sexual attractiveness: *he had an animal magnetism that women found irresistible.* **2** *historical* a supposed emanation to which the action of hypnotism was ascribed.

an·i·mal pole ▸*n. Biology* the portion of an egg that contains the nucleus and less yolk, opposite the vegetal pole.

an·i·mal rights ▸*plural n.* rights believed to belong to animals to live free from use in medical research, hunting, and other services to humans.

an·i·mal spir·its ▸*plural n.* natural exuberance.

an·i·mate ▸*v.* /ˈanəˌmāt/ [*trans.*] **1** *chiefly figurative* bring to life: *the desert is like a line drawing waiting to be animated with color.* ■ give inspiration, encouragement, or renewed vigor to: *she has animated the nation with a sense of political direction.* See note at **QUICKEN**. **2** (usu. **be animated**) give (a movie or character) the appearance of movement using animation techniques.
▸*adj.* /-mit/ alive or having life (often as a contrast with **INANIMATE**): *all of creation, animate and inanimate.* ■ lively and active: *party photos of animate socialites.* See note at **ALIVE**. ▷late Middle English: from Latin *animat-* 'instilled with life,' from the verb *animare*, from *anima* 'life, soul.'

an·i·mat·ed /ˈanəˌmātid/ ▸*adj.* **1** full of life or excitement; lively: *an animated conversation.* See note at **ALIVE**. **2** (of a movie) made using animation techniques: *an animated version of the classic fairytale.* ■ moving or appearing to move as if alive: *animated life-size figures.* —**an·i·mat·ed·ly** *adv.*

an·i·mat·ic /ˌanəˈmatik/ ▸*n.* a preliminary version of a movie, produced by shooting successive sections of a storyboard and adding a soundtrack. ▷1970s: from *animat(ed)* + **-IC**, or a blend of **ANIMATED** and **SCHEMATIC**.

an·i·ma·tion /ˌanəˈmāSHən/ ▸*n.* **1** the state of being full of life or vigor; liveliness: *they started talking with animation.* ■ *chiefly archaic* the state of being alive. **2** the technique of filming successive drawings or positions of puppets or models to create an illusion of movement when the movie is shown as a sequence: [as *adj.*] *animation techniques | animations as backdrops for live action.* ■ (also **computer animation**) the manipulation of electronic images by means of a computer in order to create moving images. ▷mid 16th cent. (in the sense 'encouragement'): from Latin *animatio(n-)*, from *animare* 'instill with life' (see **ANIMATE**). Sense 1 dates from the early 19th cent.

a·ni·ma·to /ˌänəˈmätō/ *Music* ▸*adj.* & *adv.* (esp. as a direction) in an animated manner.
▸*n.* (*pl.* **-ma·tos** or **-ma·ti** /-ˈmätē/) a passage marked animato. ▷Italian.

an·i·ma·tor /ˈanəˌmātər/ ▸*n.* a person who animates something, esp. a person who prepares animated movies: *some animators in Europe are looking at much cheaper ways of making computer graphics.*

an·i·ma·tron·ics /ˌanəməˈträniks/ ▸*plural n.* [treated as *sing.*] the technique of making and operating lifelike robots, typically for use in film or other entertainment. ▷1970s: blend of **ANIMATED** and **ELECTRONICS**. —**an·i·ma·tron·ic** *adj.*

an·i·me /ˈanəˌmā/ ▸*n.* Japanese movie and television animation, often having a science fiction theme and sometimes including violent or explicitly sexual material. Compare with **MANGA**. ▷1980s: Japanese.

an·i·mism /ˈanəˌmizəm/ ▸*n.* **1** the attribution of a soul to plants, inanimate objects, and natural phenomena. **2** the belief in a supernatural power that organizes and animates the material universe. ▷mid 19th cent.: from Latin *anima* 'life, soul' + **-ISM**. —**an·i·mist** *n.* —**an·i·mis·tic** /ˌanəˈmistik/ *adj.*

an·i·mos·i·ty /ˌanəˈmäsitē/ ▸*n.* (*pl.* **-ties**) strong hostility: *he no longer felt any* ***animosity toward*** *her | the* ***animosity between*** *the King and his brother | the five decided to put aside their animosities.* ▷late Middle English (originally in the sense 'spirit, courage'): from Old French *animosité* or late Latin *animositas*, from *animosus* 'spirited,' from Latin *animus* 'spirit, mind.' The current sense dates from the early 17th cent.

an·i·mus /ˈanəməs/ ▸*n.* **1** hostility or ill feeling: *the author's animus toward her.* **2** motivation to do something: *the reformist animus came from within the Party.* **3** *Psychology* Jung's term for the masculine part of a woman's personality. Often contrasted with **ANIMA**. ▷early 19th cent.: from Latin, 'spirit, mind.'

an·i·on /ˈanˌīən/ ▸*n. Chemistry* a negatively charged ion, i.e., one that would be attracted to the anode in electrolysis. The opposite of **CATION**. ▷mid 19th cent.: from **ANODE** or **ANA-**, + **ION**. —**an·i·on·ic** /ˌanīˈänik/ *adj.*

an·ise /ˈanis/ ▸*n.* **1** a Mediterranean plant of the parsley family, cultivated for its aromatic seeds, which are used in cooking and herbal medicine. • *Pimpinella anisum*, family Umbelliferae. See also **ANISEED**. **2** an Asian or American tree or shrub that bears fruit with an aniseedlike odor. • Genus *Illicium*, family Illiciaceae: many species, esp. **star anise** (*I. verum*), used in Chinese cooking. ▷Middle English: via Old French from Latin *anisum*, from Greek *anison* 'anise, dill.'

an·i·seed /ˈanə(s)ˌsēd/ ▸*n.* the seed of the anise, used in cooking and herbal medicine. ▷late Middle English: from **ANISE** + **SEED**.

an·i·sette /ˌaniˈset; -ˈzet/ ▸*n.* a liqueur flavored with aniseed. ▷mid 19th cent.: from French, diminutive of *anis* (see **ANISE**).

an·i·sog·a·my /ˌaniˈsägəmē/ ▸*n. Biology* sexual reproduction by the fusion of dissimilar gametes. Often contrasted with **ISOGAMY**. ▷late 19th cent.: from Greek *anisos* 'unequal' + *-gamy* (from *gamos* 'marriage'). —**an·i·sog·a·mous** /-məs/ *adj.*

an·i·so·trop·ic /anˌīsəˈtrōpik; -ˈträpik/ ▸*adj. Physics* (of an object or substance) having a physical property that has a different value when measured in different directions. A simple example is wood, which is stronger along the grain than across it. ■ (of a property or phenomenon) varying in magnitude according to the direction of measurement. ▷late 19th cent.: from Greek *anisos* 'unequal' + *tropos* 'turn' + **-IC**. —**an·i·sot·ro·py** /ˌaniˈsätrəpē/ *n.*

An·jou /ˈanjo͞o; äNˈZHo͞o/ a former province of western France, on the Loire River. It was an English possession 1154–1204.

An·ka·ra /ˈäNGkərə; ˈaNG-/ the capital of Turkey since 1923; pop. 2,559,470. Prominent in Roman times as Ancyra, it later declined in importance until chosen by Kemal Atatürk in 1923 as his seat of government. Former name (until 1930) **ANGORA**.

ankh /ängk/ ▸*n.* an object or design resembling a cross but having a loop instead of the top arm, used in ancient Egypt as a symbol of life. ▷late 19th cent.: from Egyptian, literally 'life, soul.'

ankh

an·kle /'angkəl/ ▸*n.* the joint connecting the foot with the leg: [as *adj.*] *an ankle injury.* ■ the narrow part of the leg between the foot and the calf: *her slim ankles | I stood* **up to my ankles in** *snow | the men are ankle-deep in mud |* [as *adj.*] *ankle socks.*
▸*v.* **1** *informal* [*trans.*] leave: *he ankled the series to do a movie.* ■ [*intrans.*] walk. **2** [*intrans.*] [usu. as *n.*] (**ankling**) flex the ankles while cycling in order to increase pedaling efficiency. ▷Old English *ancleow*, of Germanic origin; superseded in Middle English by forms from Old Norse; related to Dutch *enkel* and German *Enkel*, from an Indo-European root shared by **ANGLE**[1].

an·kle-bit·er ▸*n. humorous* a child: *traveling overseas with an ankle-biter has its advantages.*

an·kle bone ▸*n.* the chief bone of the ankle joint; the talus.

an·klet /'angklit/ ▸*n.* **1** a sock that reaches just above the ankle. **2** an ornament worn around an ankle. ▷early 19th cent.: from **ANKLE** + **-LET**, on the pattern of *bracelet.*

an·ky·lo·saur /'angkəlō,sôr/ (also **an·ky·lo·sau·rus** /,angkəlō'sôrəs/) ▸*n.* a heavily built quadrupedal herbivorous dinosaur primarily of the Cretaceous period, armored with bony plates. • Infraorder Ankylosauria, order Ornithischia: several genera, in particular *Ankylosaurus.* ▷early 20th cent.: from modern Latin *Ankylosaurus*, from Greek *ankulos* (see **ANKYLOSIS**) + *sauros* 'lizard.' —**an·ky·lo·sau·ri·an** *adj.*

an·ky·lose /'angkə,lōs; -,lōz/ ▸*v. Medicine* (**be/become ankylosed**) (of bones or a joint) be or become stiffened or united by ankylosis. ▷late 18th cent.: back-formation from **ANKYLOSIS**, on the pattern of words such as *anastomose.*

an·ky·los·ing spon·dy·li·tis /'angkə,lōsing ,spändl-'ītis; -,lōzing/ ▸*n. Medicine* a form of spinal arthritis, chiefly affecting young males, that eventually causes ankylosis of vertebral and sacro-iliac joints.

an·ky·lo·sis /,angkə'lōsis/ ▸*n. Medicine* abnormal stiffening and immobility of a joint due to fusion of the bones. ▷early 18th cent.: from Greek *ankulōsis*, from *ankuloun* 'to crook,' from *ankulos* 'crooked.' —**an·ky·lot·ic** /-'lätik/ *adj.*

an·la·ge /'än,lägə/ ▸*n.* (*pl.* **-lag·en** /-,lägən/) *Biology* the rudimentary basis of a particular organ or other part, esp. in an embryo. ▷late 19th cent.: from German, 'foundation, basis.'

An·na·ba /an'äbə/ a port of northeastern Algeria; pop. 348,000. The modern town is adjacent to the site of Hippo Regius, a prominent city in Roman Africa and the home and bishopric of St. Augustine of Hippo from 396 to 430. Former name **BÔNE**.

An Na·jaf /,an 'najaf/ another name for **NAJAF**.

an·nal·ist /'anl-ist/ ▸*n.* a person who writes annals. —**an·nal·is·tic** /,anl'istik/ *adj.*

an·nals /'anlz/ ▸*plural n.* a record of events year by year: *eighth-century Northumberland annals.* ■ historical records: *the annals of the famous European discoverers | figurative the deed will live forever in the annals of infamy.* ■ (**Annals**) used in the titles of learned journals: *Annals of Internal Medicine.* ▷mid 16th cent.: from Latin *annales (libri)* 'yearly (books),' from *annus* 'year.'

An·nan /ə'nän/, Kofi (Atta) (1938–), Ghanaian diplomat; secretary general of the UN 1997–.

Kofi Annan

An·nan·dale /'anən,dāl/ a residential suburb in northern Virginia, southwest of Washington, DC; pop. 50,975.

An·nap·o·lis /ə'nap(ə)ləs/ the state capital of Maryland, on the western coast of Chesapeake Bay; pop. 35,838. It is the home of the U.S. Naval Academy.

An·na·pur·na /,anə'pərnə/ a ridge of the Himalayas, in north central Nepal. Its highest peak rises to 26,503 ft. (8,078 m.).

Ann Ar·bor /,an 'ärbər/ a city in southeastern Michigan, home to the University of Michigan; pop. 114,024.

An·na's hum·ming·bird /'anəz/ ▸*n.* a North American hummingbird that lives chiefly in California. The male has an iridescent rose-red head and throat. • *Calypte anna*, family Trochilidae. ▷mid 19th cent.: named after *Anna*, the wife of Prince François Massena (*c.*1795–1863), Duc de Ravoli, who obtained the original specimen.

an·nat·to /ə'nätō/ (also **a·nat·to**) ▸*n.* (*pl.* **-tos**) **1** an orange-red dye obtained from the pulp of a tropical fruit, used for coloring foods and fabric. **2** the tropical American tree from which this fruit is obtained. • *Bixa orellana*, family Bixaceae. ▷early 17th cent.: from Carib.

Ann, Cape /an/ a peninsula in northeastern Massachusetts, noted for its resorts and scenery.

Anne /an/ (1665–1714), queen of England and Scotland (known as Great Britain from 1707) and Ireland 1702–14. The last of the Stuart monarchs and daughter of the Catholic James II (but herself a Protestant), she succeeded her brother-in-law William III to the throne.

Anne, Princess, (1950–), daughter of Queen Elizabeth II; full name *Anne Elizabeth Alice Louise, the Princess Royal.* Her two children are Peter (1977–) and Zara (1981–), by her former husband, Captain Mark Philips.

Anne, St., traditionally the mother of the Virgin Mary; first mentioned by name in the apocryphal gospel of James (2nd century). Feast day, July 26.

an·neal /ə'nēl/ ▸*v.* [*trans.*] heat (metal or glass) and allow it to cool slowly, in order to remove internal stresses and toughen it. ■ *Biochemistry* recombine (DNA) in the double-stranded form following separation by heat. ■ [*intrans.*] *Biochemistry* (of DNA) undergo this process. ▷Old English *onǣlan*, from *on* + *ǣlan* 'burn, bake,' from *āl* 'fire, burning.' The original sense was 'set on fire,' hence (in late Middle English) 'subject to fire, alter by heating'; sense 1 dates from the mid 17th cent. —**an·neal·er** *n.*

Anne Bol·eyn see **BOLEYN**.

An·nel·i·da /ə'nelidə/ *Zoology* a large phylum that comprises the segmented worms, which include earthworms, lugworms, and leeches. ▷modern Latin (plural), from French *(animaux) annelés* 'ringed (animals),' from Old French *anel* 'a ring,' from Latin *anellus*, diminutive of *anulus* 'a ring.' —**an·ne·lid** /'anl-,id/ *n.* & *adj.* —**an·nel·i·dan** /ə'nelidn/ *n.* & *adj.*

Anne of Cleves /klēvz/ (1515–57), fourth wife of Henry VIII. The politically arranged marriage was dissolved after only six months.

an·nex ▸*v.* /ə'neks; 'aneks/ [*trans.*] (often **be annexed**) append or add as an extra or subordinate part, esp. to a document: *the first ten amendments were* **annexed to** *the Constitution in 1791 |* [as *adj.*] (**annexed**) *the annexed diagram.* ■ add (territory) to one's own territory by appropriation: *Moldova was annexed by the Soviet Union in 1940.* ■ *informal* take for oneself; appropriate: *it was bad enough that Richard should have annexed his girlfriend.* ■ *archaic* add or attach as a condition or consequence.
▸*n.* /'aneks; -iks/ (*chiefly Brit.* also **an·nexe**) (*pl.* **-nex·es**) **1** a building joined to or associated with a main building, providing additional space or accommodations. **2** an addition to a document: *an annex to the report.* ▷late Middle English: from Old French *annexer*, from Latin *annectere* 'connect,' from *ad-* 'to' + *nectere* 'tie, fasten.' —**an·nex·a·tion** /,anek'sāshən; ,anik-/ *n.* —**an·nex·a·tion·ist** *n.* & *adj.*

An·ni·go·ni /,änə'gōnē/, Pietro (1910–88), Italian painter. One of the few 20th-century artists to practice the techniques of the Old Masters, he is noted for his portraits of Queen Elizabeth II (1955, 1970) and of President John F. Kennedy (1961).

an·ni·hi·late /ə'nī-ə,lāt/ ▸*v.* [*trans.*] destroy utterly; obliterate: *a simple bomb of this type could annihilate them all | a crusade to annihilate evil.* See note at **DESTROY**. ■ defeat utterly: *the stronger force annihilated its opponent virtually without loss.* ■ *Physics* convert (a subatomic particle) into radiant energy. ▷late Middle English (originally as an adjective meaning 'destroyed, annulled'): from late Latin *annihilatus* 'reduced to nothing,' from the verb *annihilare*, from *ad-* 'to' + *nihil* 'nothing.' The verb sense 'destroy utterly' dates from the mid 16th cent. —**an·ni·hi·la·tor** /-,lātər/ *n.* —**an·ni·hi·la·tion** /ə,nīə'lāshən/ *n.*

An·nis·ton /'anəstən/ an industrial and military city in northeastern Alabama; pop. 26,623.

an·ni·ver·sa·ry /,anə'vərsərē/ ▸*n.* (*pl.* **-ries**) the date on which an event took place in a previous year: *the 50th anniversary of the start of World War II |* [as *adj.*] *anniversary celebrations.* ■ the date on which a country or other institution was founded in a previous year: *Canada's 125th anniversary.* ■ the date on which a couple was married in a previous year: *he even forgot our tenth anniversary!* ■ *informal* the date on which a romance began in a previous month or week. ▷Middle English: from Latin *anniversarius* 'returning yearly,' from *annus* 'year' + *versus* 'turning.'

An·no Dom·i·ni /'anō 'dämənē; -nī; 'änō/ ▸*adv.* full form of **AD**. ▷mid 16th cent.: Latin, literally 'in the year of the Lord.'

an·no·tate /'anə,tāt/ ▸*v.* [*trans.*] add notes to (a text or diagram) giving explanation or comment: *documentation should be* **annotated with** *explanatory notes |* [as *adj.*] (**annotated**) *an annotated bibliography.* ▷late 16th cent.: from Latin *annotat-* 'marked,' from the verb *annotare*, from *ad-* 'to' + *nota* 'a mark.' —**an·no·tat·a·ble** *adj.* —**an·no·ta·tor** /-,tātər/ *n.*

an·no·ta·tion /,anə'tāshən/ ▸*n.* a note of explanation or comment added to a text or diagram: *marginal annotations.* ■ the action of annotating a text or diagram: *annotation of prescribed texts.* ▷late Middle English: from French, or from Latin *annotatio(n-)*, from the verb *annotare* (see **ANNOTATE**).

an·nounce /ə'nouns/ ▸*v.* [*reporting verb*] make a public and typically formal declaration about a fact, occurrence, or intention: [with *clause*] *the president's office announced that the state of siege would be lifted |* [*trans.*] *he announced his retirement from football |* [with *direct speech*] *"I have a confession to make," she announced.* ■ [*trans.*] make known: *we announce our failures by warring against ourselves and others | these glossy and expensive volumes announce anxiety.* ■ [*trans.*] give information about (transportation) in a station or airport via a public address system: *they were announcing her train.* ■ [*trans.*] (of a notice, letter, sound, etc.) give information to (someone) via the senses of sight or hearing: *storms came announced by long wisps that lashed out from a snow cloud's body | she heard the traditional strains of music announcing her arrival in the church.* ■ [*trans.*] make known the arrival or imminence of (a guest or a meal) at a formal social occasion: *dinner was announced.* ▷late 15th cent.: from French *annoncer*, from Latin *annuntiare*, from *ad-* 'to' + *nuntiare* 'declare, announce' (from *nuntius* 'messenger').

THE RIGHT WORD **announce, blazon, declare, proclaim, promulgate, publish**

When you **announce** something, you communicate it in a formal and public manner, often for the first time (*to announce the arrival of the guest of honor*). But just how you go about announcing something depends on what you're trying to convey.

If you want to make sure no one misses your message, use **blazon** (*signs along the highway blazoned the local farmers' complaints*).

If you plan to make your views known to the general public through the medium of writing, use **publish** (*to publish a story on drunk driving in the local newspaper*).

Use **proclaim** if you have something of great importance that you want to announce formally and officially (*proclaim a national day of mourning*).

Although **declare** also implies a very formal announcement (*declare war*), it can refer to any clear and explicit statement (*declare one's love*).

Promulgate is usually associated with the communication of a creed, doctrine, or law (*promulgate the views of the Democratic Party*).

an·nounce·ment /ə'nounsmənt/ ▸*n.* a public and typically formal statement about a fact, occurrence, or intention: *the spokesperson was about to* **make an announcement** *| a policy announcement | he was shaken by her announcement.* ■ the action of making such a statement: *the announcement of the decision of the president.* ■ a notice appearing in a newspaper or public place and announcing something such as a birth, death, or marriage: *an announcement is appearing in the* Morning Post *tomorrow.* ■ a statement of information given over a public address system: *a loudspeaker announcement echoed across the field.*

an·nounc·er /ə'nounsər/ ▸*n.* a person who announces

something, in particular someone who introduces or gives information about programs on radio or television.

an·noy /əˈnoi/ ▸*v.* [*trans.*] (often **be annoyed**) irritate (someone); make (someone) a little angry: *he was* ***annoyed at*** *being woken up so early* | *Kelly was* ***annoyed with*** *herself for feeling a pang of jealousy* | *your damned cheerfulness has always annoyed me* | [*intrans.*] *rock music loud enough to annoy.* ■ *archaic* harm or attack repeatedly: *a gallant Saxon, who annoyed this Coast.* ▷Middle English (in the sense 'be hateful to'): from Old French *anoier* (verb), *anoi* (noun), based on Latin *in odio* in the phrase *mihi in odio est* 'it is hateful to me.'

an·noy·ance /əˈnoi-əns/ ▸*n.* the feeling or state of being annoyed; irritation: *a look of annoyance on his face* | ***annoyance at*** *government interference* | *he turned his charm on Tara,* ***much to*** *Herbert's* ***annoyance.*** ■ a thing that annoys someone; a nuisance: *the Council found him an annoyance.* ▷late Middle English: from Old French *anoiance*, from *anoier* (see ANNOY).

an·noy·ing /əˈnoi-ɪɴɢ/ ▸*adj.* causing irritation or annoyance: *annoying habits* | *unsolicited calls are annoying.* —**an·noy·ing·ly** *adv.*

an·nu·al /ˈanyo͞oəl/ ▸*adj.* occurring once every year: *the union's annual conference* | *the sponsored walk became an annual event* | *an annual report.* ■ calculated over or covering a period of a year: *annual accounts* | *an annual rate of increase* | *his basic annual income.* ■ (of a plant) living for a year or less, perpetuating itself by seed: *annual flowers.*
▸*n.* a book or magazine that is published once a year under the same title but with different contents: *a Christmas annual* | *trade journals, annuals, and directories.* ■ an annual plant: *sow annuals in spring.* ▷late Middle English: from Old French *annuel*, from late Latin *annualis*, based on Latin *annus* 'year.' —**an·nu·al·ly** *adv.*

an·nu·al·ized /ˈanyo͞oəˌlīzd/ ▸*adj.* (of a rate of interest, inflation, or return on an investment) recalculated as an annual rate: *an annualized yield of about 11.5%.*

an·nual ring ▸*n.* another term for TREE RING.

an·nu·i·tant /əˈn(y)o͞oitənt/ ▸*n.* *formal* a person who receives an annuity. ▷early 18th cent.: from ANNUITY, on the pattern of *accountant.*

an·nu·i·ty /əˈn(y)o͞oitē/ ▸*n.* (*pl.* **-ties**) a fixed sum of money paid to someone each year, typically for the rest of their life: *he left her an annuity of $1,000 in his will.* ■ a form of insurance or investment entitling the investor to a series of annual sums: [as *adj.*] *an annuity plan.* ▷late Middle English: from French *annuité*, from medieval Latin *annuitas*, from Latin *annus* 'yearly,' from *annus* 'year.'

an·nul /əˈnəl/ ▸*v.* (**-nulled**, **-nul·ling**) [*trans.*] (usu. **be annulled**) declare invalid (an official agreement, decision, or result): *the elections were annulled by the general amid renewed protests.* See note at VOID. ■ declare (a marriage) to have had no legal existence: *her first marriage was finally annulled by His Holiness.* ▷late Middle English: from Old French *anuller*, from late Latin *annullare*, from *ad-* 'to' + *nullum* 'nothing.' —**an·nul·ment** *n.*

an·nu·lar /ˈanyələr/ ▸*adj.* *technical* ring-shaped. ▷late 16th cent.: from French *annulaire* or Latin *annularis*, from *anulus*, *annulus* 'a ring.' —**an·nu·lar·ly** *adv.*

an·nu·lar e·clipse ▸*n.* an eclipse of the sun in which the edge of the sun remains visible as a bright ring around the moon.

an·nu·late /ˈanyəlit; -ˌlāt/ ▸*adj.* *chiefly Zoology* having rings; marked with or formed of rings: *an annulate worm.* ▷early 19th cent.: from Latin *annulatus*, from *anulus*, *annulus* 'a ring.' —**an·nu·lat·ed** *adj.* —**an·nu·la·tion** /ˌanyəˈlāsʜən/ *n.*

an·nu·let /ˈanyəlit/ ▸*n.* **1** *Architecture* a small fillet or band encircling a column. **2** *Heraldry* a charge in the form of a small ring. ▷late Middle English (sense 2): from Old French *anelet*, from Latin *anulus*, *annulus* 'ring' + -ET[1]. The spelling change in the 16th cent. was due to association with the Latin.

an·nu·lus /ˈanyələs/ ▸*n.* (*pl.* **-li** /-ˌlī/) *technical* a ring-shaped object, structure, or region. ▷mid 16th cent.: from Latin *anulus*, *annulus.*

an·nun·ci·ate /əˈnənsēˌāt/ ▸*v.* [*trans.*] *archaic* announce (something). ▷late Middle English (originally as a past participle): from medieval Latin *annunciat-*, variant spelling of Latin *annuntiat-* 'announced,' from the verb *annuntiare.*

an·nun·ci·a·tion /əˌnənsēˈāsʜən/ ▸*n.* (usu. **the Annunciation**) the announcement of the Incarnation by the angel Gabriel to Mary (Luke 1:26–38). ■ the church festival commemorating this, held on March 25 (Lady Day). ■ a painting or sculpture depicting this. ■ *formal* or *archaic* the announcement of something: *the annunciation of a set of rules applying to the relationships between states.* ▷Middle English: from Old French *annonciation*, from late Latin *annuntiatio(n-)*, from the verb *annuntiare* (see ANNUNCIATE).

an·nun·ci·a·tor /əˈnənsēˌātər/ ▸*n.* a bell, light, or other device that provides information on the state or condition of something by indicating which of several electrical circuits has been activated: [as *adj.*] *the annunciator panel and warning lights.*

an·nus hor·ri·bi·lis /ˈanəs həˈribəlis/ ▸*n.* a year of disaster or misfortune. ▷late 20th cent.: modern Latin on the pattern of ANNUS MIRABILIS.

an·nus mi·ra·bi·lis /ˈanəs məˈräbəlis/ ▸*n.* a remarkable or auspicious year. ▷mid 17th cent.: modern Latin, literally 'wonderful year.'

a·no·a /əˈnōə/ ▸*n.* (*pl.* same or **-as**) a small deerlike water buffalo, native to Sulawesi. • Genus *Bubalus*, family Bovidae: two species. ▷mid 19th cent.: a local name.

an·ode /ˈanōd/ ▸*n.* the positively charged electrode by which the electrons leave a device. The opposite of CATHODE. ■ the negatively charged electrode of a device supplying current such as a primary cell. ▷mid 19th cent.: from Greek *anodos* 'way up,' from *ana* 'up' + *hodos* 'way.' —**an·od·al** /anˈōdl; āˈnōdl/ *adj.* —**an·od·ic** /anˈädik/ *adj.*

an·o·dize /ˈanəˌdīz/ ▸*v.* [*trans.*] [usu. as *adj.*] (**anodized**) coat (a metal, esp. aluminum) with a protective oxide layer by an electrolytic process in which the metal forms the anode. —**an·o·diz·er** *n.*

an·o·dyne /ˈanəˌdīn/ ▸*adj.* not likely to provoke dissent or offense; uncontentious or inoffensive, often deliberately so: *anodyne new age music* | *I attempted to keep the conversation as anodyne as possible.*
▸*n.* a pain-killing drug or medicine. ■ *figurative* something that alleviates a person's mental distress: *an anodyne to the misery she had put him through.* ▷mid 16th cent.: via Latin from Greek *anōdunos* 'painless,' from *an-* 'without' + *odunē* 'pain.'

a·no·gen·i·tal /ˌānōˈjenitl/ ▸*adj.* *Medicine & Anatomy* of or relating to the anus and genitals. ▷early 20th cent.: from Latin *ano-* (combining form of ANUS) + GENITAL.

a·noint /əˈnoint/ ▸*v.* [*trans.*] smear or rub with oil, typically as part of a religious ceremony: *bodies were anointed after death for burial.* ■ (**anoint something with**) smear or rub something with (any other substance): *Cuna Indians anoint the tips of their arrows with poison.* ■ ceremonially confer divine or holy office upon (a priest or monarch) by smearing or rubbing with oil: [*trans.*] *the Lord has anointed me to preach to the poor* | [*trans.*] *Samuel anointed him king.* ■ *figurative* nominate or choose (someone) as successor to or leading candidate for a position: *he was anointed as the organizational candidate of the party* | [as *adj.*] (**anointed**) *his officially anointed heir.* ▷Middle English: from Old French *enoint* 'anointed,' past participle of *enoindre*, from Latin *inungere*, from *in-* 'upon' + *ungere* 'anoint, smear with oil.'
▸***PHRASES*** □ **Anointing of the Sick** (in the Roman Catholic Church) the sacramental anointing of the ill or infirm with blessed oil; unction. □ **God's** (or **the Lord's**) **anointed** a monarch ruling by divine right.

a·no·le /əˈnōlē/ ▸*n.* a small, mainly arboreal American lizard with a throat fan that (in the male) is typically brightly colored. Anoles have some ability to change color. Also called CHAMELEON. • Genus *Anolis*, family Iguanidae: numerous species, in particular the **green anole** (*A. carolinensis*), which is popular as a pet. ▷early 18th cent.: from Carib.

a·nom·a·lis·tic month /əˌnäməˈlistik/ ▸*n.* a month measured between successive perigees of the moon (approximately 27½ days).

a·nom·a·lis·tic year ▸*n.* a year measured between successive perihelia of the earth (approximately 365 ¼ days).

a·nom·a·lous /əˈnäməlәs/ ▸*adj.* deviating from what is standard, normal, or expected: *an anomalous situation* | *sentences that are grammatically anomalous.* ▷mid 17th cent.: via late Latin from Greek *anōmalos* (from *an-* 'not' + *homalos* 'even') + -OUS. —**a·nom·a·lous·ly** *adv.* —**a·nom·a·lous·ness** *n.*

a·nom·a·ly /əˈnäməlē/ ▸*n.* (*pl.* **-lies**) **1** something that deviates from what is standard, normal, or expected: *there are a number of anomalies in the present system* | *a legal anomaly* | [with *clause*] *the apparent* ***anomaly that*** *those who produced the wealth were the poorest* | *the position abounds in anomaly.* **2** *Astronomy* the angular distance of a planet or satellite from its last perihelion or perigee. ▷late 16th cent.: via Latin from Greek *anōmalia*, from *anōmalos* (see ANOMALOUS).

a·no·mi·a /əˈnōmēə/ ▸*n.* *Medicine* a form of aphasia in which the patient is unable to recall the names of everyday objects. ▷early 20th cent.: formed irregularly from A-[1] 'without, not' + Latin *nomen* 'name' + -IA[1]. —**a·nom·ic** /əˈnämik; əˈnō-/ *adj.*

an·o·mie /ˈanəˌmē/ (also **anomy**) ▸*n.* lack of the usual social or ethical standards in an individual or group: *the theory that high-rise architecture leads to anomie in the residents.* ▷1930s: from French, from Greek *anomia*, from *anomos* 'lawless.' —**a·nom·ic** /əˈnämik; əˈnō-/ *adj.*

a·non /əˈnän/ ▸*adv.* *archaic* soon; shortly: *I'll see you anon.* ▷Old English *on ān* 'into one,' *on āne* 'in one.' The original sense was 'in or into one state, course, etc.,' which developed into the temporal sense 'at once.'

anon. ▸*abbr.* anonymous.

a·non·y·mize /əˈnänəˌmīz/ ▸*v.* [*trans.*] make anonymous: *manuscripts will be anonymized by the editorial assistant.* ■ [usu. as *adj.*] (**anonymized**) *Medicine* remove identifying particulars from (test results) for statistical or other purposes: *anonymized testing of routine blood samples.* ▷1970s: from ANONYMOUS + -IZE.

a·non·y·mous /əˈnänəməs/ ▸*adj.* (of a person) not identified by name; of unknown name: *the anonymous author of* Beowulf | *the donor's wish to remain anonymous* | *an anonymous phone call.* ■ having no outstanding, individual, or unusual features; unremarkable or impersonal: *the anonymous black car waiting to take him to the airport* | *a faceless, anonymous group.* ■ [*postpositive*] used in names of support groups for addicts of a substance or behavior to indicate the confidentiality maintained among members of the group: *Alcoholics Anonymous* | *Debtors Anonymous.* ▷late 16th cent.: via late Latin from Greek *anōnumos* 'nameless' (from *an-* 'without' + *onoma* 'name') + -OUS. —**an·o·nym·i·ty** /ˌanəˈnimitē/ *n.* —**a·non·y·mous·ly** *adv.*

a·non·y·mous FTP ▸*n.* *Computing* part of the File Transfer Protocol (FTP) on the Internet that lets anyone log on to an FTP server, using a general username and without a password.

a·noph·e·les /əˈnäfəˌlēz/ (also **anopheles mosquito**) ▸*n.* a mosquito of a genus that is particularly common in warmer countries and includes the mosquitoes that transmit the malarial parasite to humans. Compare with CULEX. • Genus *Anopheles*, subfamily Anophelinae, family Culicidae. ▷late 19th cent.: modern Latin, from Greek *anōphelēs* 'unprofitable, useless.' —**a·noph·e·line** /-ˌlīn; -lin/ *adj.* & *n.*

An·o·plu·ra /ˌanəˈplo͝orə/ *Entomology* an order of insects that comprises the sucking lice. Also called SIPHUNCULATA. See also PHTHIRAPTERA. ▷modern Latin (plural), from *anoplos* 'unarmed' + *oura* 'tail.' —**an·o·plu·ran** *n.* & *adj.*

an·o·rak /ˈanəˌrak/ ▸*n.* a waterproof jacket, typically with a hood, of a kind originally used in polar regions. ▷1920s: from Greenland Eskimo *anoraq.*

an·o·rec·tal /ˈanəˈrektəl/ ▸*adj.* *Medicine & Anatomy* of or relating to the anus and rectum. ▷late 19th cent.: from French *ano-rectal*, from Latin *ano-* (combining form of ANUS) + *rectal* (see RECTAL).

an·o·rex·i·a /ˌanəˈreksēə/ ▸*n.* a lack or loss of appetite for food (as a medical condition). ■ (also **an·o·rex·i·a ner·vo·sa** /nərˈvōsə/) an emotional disorder characterized by an obsessive desire to lose weight by refusing to eat; compare with BULIMIA. ▷late 16th cent.: via late Latin from Greek, from *an-* 'without' + *orexis* 'appetite.'

an·o·rex·ic /ˌanəˈreksik/ (also **an·o·rec·tic** /ˌanəˈrektik/) ▸*adj.* relating to, characterized by, or suffering from anorexia. ■ *informal* extremely thin.
▸*n.* **1** a person suffering from anorexia. **2** (**anorectic**) a medicine that produces a loss of appetite.

an·or·gas·mi·a /ˌanôrˈgazmēə/ ▸*n.* *Medicine* persistent inability to achieve orgasm despite responding to sexual stimulation. ▷1970s: from AN-[1] + ORGASM + -IA[1]. —**an·or·gas·mic** /-mik/ *adj.*

an·or·thite /anˈôrˌᴛʜīt/ ▸*n.* a calcium-rich mineral of the plagioclase feldspar group, typically white, occurring esp. in limestones metamorphosed by contact with an igneous intrusion. ▷mid 19th cent.: from AN-[1] + Greek *orthos* 'straight' + -ITE[1].

an·or·tho·site /əˈnôrᴛʜəˌsit/ ▸*n.* *Geology* a plutonic rock composed largely of calcic plagioclase. ▷mid 19th cent.: from French *anorthose* 'plagioclase' + -ITE[1].

Pronunciation Key ə *ago*; ər *over*; ˈə *or* ˌə *up*; ˈər *or* ˌər *fur*; a *hat*; ā *rate*; ä *car*; ᴄʜ *chew*; e *let*; ē *see*; e(ə)r *air*; i *fit*; ī *by*; i(ə)r *ear*; ɴɢ *sing*; ō *go*; ô *for*; oi *boy*; o͝o *good*; o͞o *goo*; ou *out*; sʜ *she*; ᴛʜ *thin*; T̲H̲ *then*; (h)w *why*; ᴢʜ *vision*

an·os·mi·a /a'näzmēə; a'näs-/ ▶*n.* *Medicine* the loss of the sense of smell, either total or partial. It may be caused by head injury, infection, or blockage of the nose. ▷early 19th cent.: from **AN-**2 + Greek *osmē* 'smell.' —**an·os·mic** /-mik/ *adj.*

an·oth·er /ə'nə*TH*ər/ ▶*adj.* & *pron.* **1** used to refer to an additional person or thing of the same type as one already mentioned or known about; one more; a further: [as *adj.*] *have another drink | I didn't say another word* | [as *pron.*] *they have two practices, one in the morning and another in the afternoon | she was to become* ***another of*** *his stars.* ■ [usu. as *adj.*] used with a proper name to indicate someone or something's similarity to the person or event specified: *they said I was another Ryan Giggs! | this will not be another Vietnam.* **2** used to refer to a different person or thing from one already mentioned or known about: [as *adj.*] *come back another day | his wife left him for another man* | [as *pron.*] *moving from one place to another |* ***it is one thing*** *to formulate policies and* ***quite another*** *to implement them.* ■ [*adj.*] used to refer to someone sharing an attribute in common with the person already mentioned: *his kiss with another man caused a tabloid rumpus.* ▷Middle English: as *an other* until the 16th cent.

A·nouilh /ä'noo͞ē; än'wē/, Jean (1910–87), French playwright. Notable works: *Ring Around the Moon* (1947), *Thieves' Carnival* (1932), and *Antigone* (1944).

ANOVA /'anōvə/ ▶*n.* analysis of variance, a statistical method in which the variation in a set of observations is divided into distinct components. ▷1960s: acronym.

an·ov·u·lant /an'ävyələnt/ *Medicine* ▶*adj.* (chiefly of a drug) preventing ovulation.
▶*n.* an anovulant drug. ▷1960s: from **AN-**1 + *ovul(ation)* + **-ANT**.

an·ov·u·la·to·ry /an'ävyələ,tôrē/ ▶*adj.* *Medicine* (of a menstrual cycle) in which ovulation does not occur.

an·ox·i·a /a'näksēə/ ▶*n.* *technical* an absence of oxygen. ■ *Medicine* an absence or deficiency of oxygen reaching the tissues; severe hypoxia. ▷1930s: from **AN-**1 + *ox(ygen)* + **-IA**1. —**an·ox·ic** /-sik/ *adj.*

ANS ▶*abbr.* autonomic nervous system.

An·schluss /'än,shloo͞s/ the annexation of Austria by Germany in 1938. Hitler had forced the resignation of the Austrian chancellor by demanding that he admit Nazis into his Cabinet. The new chancellor, a pro-Nazi, invited German troops to enter the country on the pretext of restoring law and order. ▷German, from *anschliessen* 'to join.'

An·selm, St. /'an,selm/ (*c.*1033–1109), English philosopher and theologian; born in Italy; archbishop of Canterbury 1093–1109. Feast day, April 21.

An·shan /'än'shän/ a city in Liaoning, China; pop. 1,370,000. It is situated close to major iron-ore deposits, and China's largest iron and steel complex is nearby.

ANSI /'ansē/ ▶*abbr.* American National Standards Institute.

an·swer /'ansər/ ▶*n.* a thing said, written, or done to deal with or as a reaction to a question, statement, or situation: *he knocked and entered without waiting for an answer.* ■ a thing written or said in reaction to a question in a test or quiz: *write your answers on a postcard.* ■ the correct solution to such a question: *the answer is 280°.* ■ a solution to a problem or dilemma: *the* ***answer to*** *poverty and unemployment is a properly funded range of services.* ■ [in *sing.*] (**answer to**) a thing or person that imitates or fulfills the same role as something or someone else: *the press called her Britain's answer to Marilyn Monroe.* ■ *Law* the defendant's reply to the plaintiff's charges.
▶*v.* **1** [*reporting verb*] say or write something to deal with or as a reaction to someone or something: [with *direct speech*] *"Of course I can," she answered* | [with *clause*] *she answered that she would take nothing but the ring* | [*trans.*] *she tried to answer his questions truthfully | I didn't answer him* | [*intrans.*] *Steve was about to answer, but Hazel spoke first.* ■ [*trans.*] provide the required responses to (a test or quiz): *answer the questions below for a chance to win a vacation.* ■ [*intrans.*] (**answer back**) respond impudently or disrespectfully to someone, esp. when being criticized or told to do something: *one couldn't argue with a parent; one couldn't answer back* | [*trans.*] *Mary resisted the temptation to answer her mother back.* ■ [*trans.*] act in reaction to (a sound such as a telephone ringing or a knock or ring on a door): *David answered the door* | [*intrans.*] *she called Edward's house, hoping he would answer.* ■ [*trans.*] act in response to (a stimulus): *answering the call of nature.* ■ [*trans.*] discharge (a responsibility or claim): *they answered the call of duty in World War II.* ■ [*trans.*] defend oneself against (a charge, accusation, or criticism): *he said he would return to Spain to answer all charges.* ■ [*intrans.*] (**answer for**) be responsible or to blame for: *the dust mite* ***has a lot to answer for****, especially if you are asthmatic.* ■ [*intrans.*] (**answer to**) be responsible or report to (someone): *I answer to the assistant commissioner.* ■ [*intrans.*] (**answer to**) be required to explain or justify oneself to (someone): *you will have the police to answer to.* **2** be suitable for fulfilling (a need); satisfy: [*trans.*] *entrepreneurship is necessary to answer the needs of national and international markets* [*intrans.*] *nothing short of that would answer.* ▷Old English *andswaru* (noun), *andswarian* (verb), of Germanic origin; from a base shared by **SWEAR**. —**an·swer·er** *n.* **an·swer·less** *adj.*
▶*PHRASES* □ **answer the description of** correspond to a description, esp. one of a suspect issued by the police: *he answers the description of being slightly taller than his two supposed companions.* □ **answer to (the name of)** *often humorous* be called: *an attractive woman answering to the name of Suzanne.* □ **have** (or **know**) **all the answers** *informal* be confident in one's knowledge of something, typically unjustifiably so: *it was his air of knowing all the answers that riled Mrs. Farrar.* □ **in answer to** as a response to or as a result of: *in answer to the stresses on modern woman, we have developed a range of beauty treatments.*

an·swer·a·ble /'ansərəbəl/ ▶*adj.* **1** [*predic.*] (**answerable to**) required to explain or justify one's actions to; responsible or having to report to: *I'm not answerable to you for my every movement.* See note at **RESPONSIBLE**. ■ (**answerable for**) responsible for: *an employer is answerable for the negligence of his employees.* **2** (of a question) able to be answered: *straightforward and answerable questions.*

an·swer·ing ma·chine ▶*n.* a tape recorder or digital device that supplies a recorded answer to a telephone call and can record a message from the caller.

an·swer·ing serv·ice ▶*n.* a business that receives and answers telephone calls for its clients.

ant /ant/ ▶*n.* a small insect, often with a sting, that usually lives in a complex social colony with one or more breeding queens. It is wingless except for fertile adults, which often form large mating swarms, and is proverbial for industriousness. • Family Formicidae, order Hymenoptera: several subfamilies. ▷Old English *ǣmete*; related to German *Ameise*. Compare with **EMMET**.
▶*PHRASE* □ **have ants in one's pants** *informal* be fidgety or restless.

ant- ▶*prefix* variant spelling of **ANTI-** before a vowel or *h* (as in *Antarctic*).

-ant ▶*suffix* **1** (forming adjectives) denoting attribution of an action or state: *arrogant | expectant.* **2** (forming nouns) denoting an agent: *deodorant | propellant.* ▷from Latin or French present participial verb stems (see also **-ENT**).

Ant·a·buse /'antə,byoo͞s/ ▶*n.* trademark for **DISULFIRAM**. ▷1940s: from **ANTI-** + **ABUSE**.

ant·ac·id /ant'asid/ ▶*adj.* (chiefly of a medicine) preventing or correcting acidity, esp. in the stomach.
▶*n.* an antacid medicine.

An·tae·us /an'tēəs; -'tā-/ *Greek Mythology* a giant, the son of Poseidon and Earth, who compelled all comers to wrestle with him, overcoming and killing them all them until he was defeated by Hercules.

an·tag·o·nism /an'tagə,nizəm/ ▶*n.* active hostility or opposition: *the* ***antagonism between*** *them | his* ***antagonism toward*** *the local people | petty antagonisms and jealousies.* ■ *Biochemistry* inhibition of or interference with the action of one substance or organism by another. ▷early 19th cent.: from French *antagonisme*, from Greek *antagōnizesthai* 'struggle against' (see **ANTAGONIST**).

an·tag·o·nist /an'tagənist/ ▶*n.* a person who actively opposes or is hostile to someone or something; an adversary: *he turned to confront his antagonist.* ■ *Biochemistry* a substance that interferes with or inhibits the physiological action of another. Compare with **AGONIST**. ■ *Anatomy* a muscle whose action counteracts that of another specified muscle. Compare with **AGONIST**. ▷late 16th cent.: from French *antagoniste* or late Latin *antagonista*, from Greek *antagōnistēs*, from *antagōnizesthai* 'struggle against' (see **ANTAGONIZE**).

an·tag·o·nis·tic /an,tagə'nistik/ ▶*adj.* showing or feeling active opposition or hostility toward someone or something: *he was* ***antagonistic to*** *the government's reforms | an antagonistic group of bystanders.* ■ *Biochemistry* & *Physiology* of or relating to an antagonist or its action. —**an·tag·o·nis·ti·cal·ly** /-ik(ə)lē/ *adv.*

an·tag·o·nize /an'tagə,nīz/ ▶*v.* [*trans.*] cause (someone) to become hostile: *he antagonized many colleagues during the budget wars.* ■ *Biochemistry* (of a substance) act as an antagonist of (a substance or its action): *two other drugs antagonized the antidepressantlike effect.* ▷mid 18th cent. (in the sense 'struggle against'): from Greek *antagōnizesthai*, from *ant-* 'against' + *agōnizesthai* 'struggle' (from *agōn* 'contest').

An·ta·kya /,äntäk'yä/ Turkish name for **ANTIOCH**.

An·tal·ya /,än,täl'yä; ,äntl'yä/ a port in southern Turkey; pop. 378,200.

An·ta·na·na·ri·vo /,äntə,nänə'rēvō; ,antə,nanə-/ the capital of Madagascar, located in the central plateau; pop. 802,390. Former name (until 1975) **TANANARIVE**.

Ant·arc·tic /ant'ärktik; -'ärtik/ ▶*adj.* of or relating to the south polar region or Antarctica. ■ *Botany* of, relating to, or denoting a phytogeographical kingdom comprising New Zealand, southern parts of Chile and Argentina, and islands in the South Atlantic and southern Indian Ocean.
▶*n.* (**the Antarctic**) the Antarctic region. ▷late Middle English: from Old French *antartique* or Latin *antarcticus*, from Greek *antarktikos* 'opposite to the north,' from *ant-* 'against' + *arktikos* (see **ARCTIC**).

Ant·arc·ti·ca /ant'ärktikə; -'ärtikə/ a continent around the South Pole, situated mainly within the Antarctic Circle and almost entirely covered by ice sheets. Its exploitation is governed by an international treaty of 1959, which was renewed in 1991.

Ant·arc·tic Cir·cle the parallel of latitude 66° 33′ south of the equator. It marks the southernmost point at which the sun is visible on the southern winter solstice and the northernmost point at which the midnight sun can be seen on the southern summer solstice.

Ant·arc·tic Con·ver·gence the zone of the Antarctic Ocean where the cold, nutrient-laden Antarctic surface water sinks beneath the warmer waters to the north.

Ant·arc·tic O·cean the sea surrounding Antarctica. It consists of parts of the southern Atlantic, Pacific, and Indian oceans. Also called **SOUTHERN OCEAN**.

Ant·arc·tic Pen·in·su·la a mountainous peninsula of Antarctica between the Bellingshausen and Weddell seas that extends northward toward Cape Horn and the Falkland Islands.

An·tar·es /an'te(ə)rēz; -'tar-/ the brightest star in the constellation Scorpius. It is a binary star of which the main component is a red supergiant. ▷Greek, literally 'simulating Mars (in color).'

ant bear ▶*n.* **1** another term for **AARDVARK**. **2** the giant anteater. (See **ANTEATER**.

ant·bird /'ant,bərd/ ▶*n.* an insectivorous, long-legged, short-tailed bird that typically has dark gray plumage in the male and brown in the female. Antbirds, found mainly in the tropical forests of South America, often feed on insects that have been disturbed by swarms of army ants. • Family Formicariidae: several genera, in particular *Myrmeciza*, *Cercomacra*, and *Drymophila*.

an·te /'antē/ ▶*n.* a stake put up by a player in poker and similar games before receiving cards.
▶*v.* (**-tes, -ted, -te·ing**) [*trans.*] (**ante something up**) put up an amount as an ante in poker and similar games. ■ *informal* pay an amount of money in advance: *he anted up $925,000 of his own money.* ■ [*intrans.*] (**ante up**) *informal* put up one's money; pay up: *the owners have to ante up if they want to attract the best talent.* ▷early 19th cent.: from Latin, literally 'before.'
▶*PHRASE* □ **up** (or **raise**) **the ante** increase what is at stake or under discussion, esp. in a conflict or dispute: *he decided to up the ante in the trade war.*

ante- ▶*prefix* before; preceding: *antechapel | antecedent.* ▷from Latin *ante* 'before.'

ant·eat·er /'ant,ētər/ ▶*n.* a mammal that feeds on ants and termites. It has a long snout and sticky tongue. • Most anteaters are edentates of the Central and South American family Myrmecophagidae, which includes the **giant anteater** and the tamanduas. The echidna, numbat, and pangolin are also known as **spiny anteater**, **banded anteater**, and **scaly anteater**, respectively.

an·te·bel·lum /,antē'beləm/ ▶*adj.* [*attrib.*] occurring or existing before a particular war, esp. the American Civil War: *the conventions of the antebellum South.* ▷mid 19th cent.: from Latin, from *ante* 'before' and *bellum* 'war.'

an·te·ced·ent /,antə'sēdnt/ ▶*n.* a thing or event that existed before or logically precedes another: *some antecedents to the African novel might exist in Africa's oral traditions.* ■ (**antecedents**) a person's ancestors or family and social background: *her early life and antecedents have been traced.* ■ *Grammar* a word, phrase, clause, or sentence to which another word (esp. a

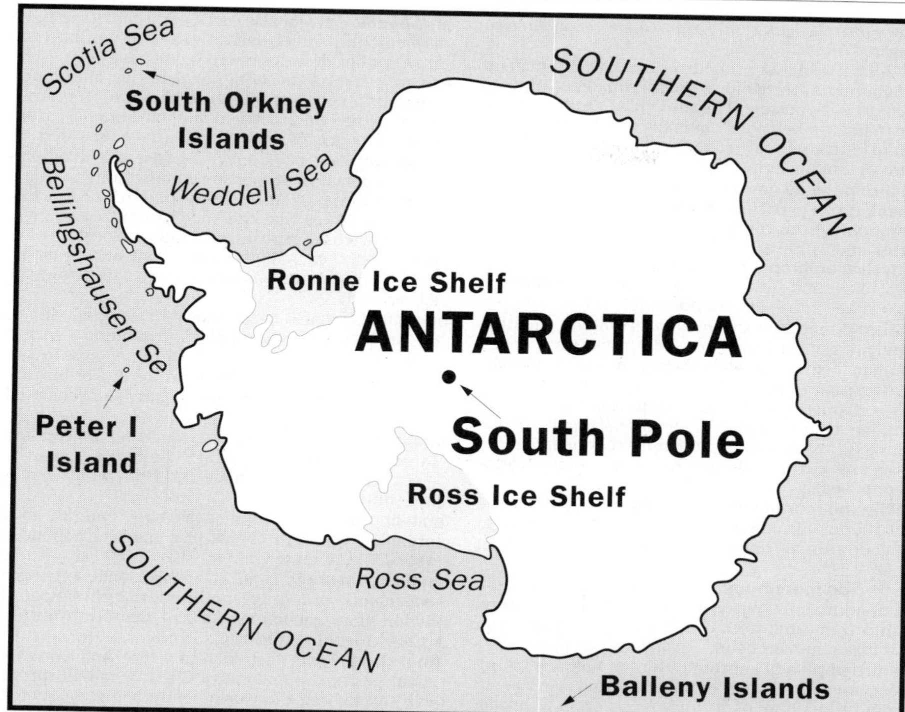

following relative pronoun) refers. ■ *Logic* the statement contained in the "if" clause of a conditional proposition. ■ *Mathematics* the first term in a ratio.
▶*adj.* preceding in time or order; previous or preexisting: *the antecedent events that prompt you to break a diet.* ■ denoting a grammatical antecedent. ▷late Middle English: from Old French or from Latin *antecedent-* 'going before,' from *antecedere*, from *ante* 'before' + *cedere* 'go.' **—an·te·ced·ence** *n.*

an·te·cham·ber /ˈantē,CHāmbər/ ▶*n.* a small room leading to a main one. ▷mid 17th cent. (as *antichamber*): from French *antichambre*, from Italian *anticamera*, from *anti-* 'preceding' + *camera* (see **CHAMBER**).

an·te·chap·el /ˈantē,CHapəl/ ▶*n.* a vestibule for a college chapel, lying beyond the west end of the nave.

ant·e·chi·nus /,antēˈkīnəs/ ▶*n.* a marsupial mouse of shrewlike habits and appearance, found in Australia, New Guinea, and Tasmania. • Genera *Antechinus* and *Parantechinus*, family Dasyuridae: several species. ▷modern Latin, from Greek *anti-* 'simulating' + *ekhinos* 'sea urchin, hedgehog' (from its bristly fur).

an·te·date /ˈanti,dāt/ ▶*v.* [*trans.*] precede in time; come before (something) in date: *a civilization that antedated the Roman Empire.* ■ indicate that (a document or event) should be assigned to an earlier date: *there are no references to him that would antedate his birth.*

an·te·dat·ing /ˈanti,dātiNG/ ▶*n.* an example or instance of (a sense of) a word, phrase, etc., at a date earlier than previously known or recorded; a citation of this: *antedatings of some prize-fighting terms.*

an·te·di·lu·vi·an /,antēdəˈlo͞ovēən/ ▶*adj.* [*attrib.*] of or belonging to the time before the biblical Flood: *gigantic bones of antediluvian animals.* ■ *chiefly humorous* ridiculously old-fashioned: *they maintain antediluvian sex-role stereotypes.* See note at **OLD**. ▷mid 17th cent.: from **ANTE-** + Latin *diluvium* 'deluge' + **-AN**.

an·te·lope /ˈantl,ōp/ ▶*n.* (*pl.* same or **-lopes**) a swift-running deerlike ruminant with smooth hair and upward-pointing horns, native to Africa and Asia. • Many genera and species, in the family Bovidae. ■ another term for **PRONGHORN**. ▷late Middle English (originally the name of a fierce mythical creature with long serrated horns, said to live on the banks of the Euphrates): via Old French and medieval Latin from late Greek *antholops*, of unknown origin and meaning.

an·te·mor·tem /,antēˈmôrtəm/ ▶*adj.* & *adv.* before death: [as *adj.*] *the antemortem instructions of the dead leader* | [as *adv.*] *abnormalities of the sinus are difficult to demonstrate antemortem.* ▷late 19th cent.: Latin, literally 'before death.'

an·te·na·tal /,antēˈnātl/ ▶*adj.* [*attrib.*] before birth; during or relating to pregnancy; prenatal: *antenatal care.*
▶*n. informal* a medical examination during pregnancy. **—an·te·na·tal·ly** *adv.*

an·ten·na /anˈtenə/ ▶*n.* **1** *Zoology* (*pl.* **-ten·nae** /-ˈtenē/) either of a pair of long, thin sensory appendages on the heads of insects, crustaceans, and some other arthropods. ■ (**antennae**) *figurative* the faculty of instinctively detecting and interpreting subtle signs: *he has the political antennae of a party whip.* **2** (*pl.* **-ten·nas**) a rod, wire, or other device used to transmit or receive radio or television signals. ▷mid 17th cent.: from Latin, alteration of *antemna* 'yard' (of a ship), used in the plural to translate Greek *keraioi* 'horns (of insects),' used by Aristotle. **—an·ten·nal** /-ˈtenl/ *adj.* (in sense 1). **—an·ten·na·ry** /-ˈtenərē/ *adj.* (in sense 1).

an·ten·nule /anˈten,yo͞ol/ ▶*n. Zoology* a small antenna, esp. either of the first pair of antennae in a crustacean. ▷mid 19th cent.: diminutive of **ANTENNA**.

an·te·par·tum /,antēˈpärtəm/ ▶*adj.* [*attrib.*] *Medicine* occurring not long before childbirth. ▷late 19th cent.: from Latin, 'before birth.'

an·te·pe·nul·ti·mate /,antēpəˈnəltəmit/ ▶*adj.* [*attrib.*] last but two in a series; third last: *the antepenultimate item on the agenda.* | *the antepenultimate syllable.*

an·te·ri·or /anˈti(ə)rēər/ ▶*adj.* **1** *technical, chiefly Anatomy* & *Biology* nearer the front, esp. situated in the front of the body, or nearer to the head or forepart: *the veins* ***anterior to*** *the heart.* The opposite of **POSTERIOR**. ■ *Botany* (of a part of a flower or leaf) situated further away from the main stem. **2** *formal* coming before in time; earlier: *there are few examples of gold and silver work* ***anterior to*** *the dynasty of the Romanoffs.* ▷mid 16th cent.: from French *antérieur* or Latin *anterior*, comparative of *ante* 'before.' **—an·te·ri·or·i·ty** /an,ti(ə)rēˈôritē; -ˈär-/ *n.* **—an·te·ri·or·ly** *adv.*

antero- ▶*comb. form chiefly Anatomy* representing **ANTERIOR**: *anteroposterior.*

an·ter·o·grade /ˈantərō,grād/ ▶*adj.* directed forward in time. The opposite of **RETROGRADE**. ■ of or denoting a type of amnesia involving inability to remember any new information. ▷late 19th cent.: from **ANTERIOR**, on the pattern of *retrograde.*

an·ter·o·lat·er·al /,antərōˈlatərəl/ ▶*adj. chiefly Anatomy* both anterior and lateral.

an·te·room /ˈantē,ro͞om; -,ro͝om/ ▶*n.* an antechamber, typically serving as a waiting room. ■ *Military* a sitting room in an officers' mess.

an·ter·o·pos·te·ri·or /,antərōpäˈstirēər; -pō-/ ▶*adj. chiefly Anatomy* relating to or directed toward both front and back: *an anteroposterior axis.*

an·te·vert·ed /ˈantē,vərtid/ ▶*adj. Anatomy* & *Medicine* (of an organ of the body, typically the uterus) inclined forward. ▷mid 19th cent.: from Latin *antevertere*, from *ante* 'before' + *vertere* 'to turn' + **-ED**[2].

ant·he·li·on /antˈhēlēən; anˈTHē-/ ▶*n.* (*pl.* **-li·a** /-lēə/) a luminous halo around a shadow projected by the sun on to a cloud or fog bank. ■ a parhelion seen opposite the sun in the sky. ▷late 17th cent.: from Greek *anthēlion*, neuter of *anthēlios* 'opposite to the sun,' from *anth-* (variant of *anti-* 'against') + *hēlios* 'sun.'

ant·hel·min·tic /,ant-helˈmintik; ,anTHel-/ *Medicine* ▶*adj.* [*attrib.*] (chiefly of medicines) used to destroy parasitic worms.
▶*n.* an anthelmintic medicine. ▷late 17th cent. (as an adjective): from *anth-* (variant of *anti* 'against') + Greek *helmins*, *helminth-* 'worm' + **-IC**.

an·them /ˈanTHəm/ ▶*n.* **1** a rousing or uplifting song identified with a particular group, body, or cause: *the song became the anthem for hippie activists.* ■ (also **national anthem**) a solemn patriotic song officially adopted by a country as an expression of national identity. **2** a choral composition based on a biblical passage, for singing by a choir in a church service. ▷Old English *antefn*, *antifne* (denoting a composition sung antiphonally), from late Latin *antiphona* (see **ANTIPHON**). The spelling with *th*, which began in the 16th cent., was on the pattern of similar words, such as *Antony*, *Anthony* or *amarant*, *amaranth*.

an·the·mic /anˈTHēmik; -ˈTHemik/ ▶*adj.* (of a song) like an anthem in being rousing or uplifting.

an·the·mi·on /anˈTHēmēən/ ▶*n.* (*pl.* **-mi·a** /-mēə/) a flowerlike ornament used in the decorative arts. ▷mid 19th cent.: from Greek, literally 'flower.'

an·ther /ˈanTHər/ ▶*n. Botany* the part of a stamen that contains the pollen. ▷early 18th cent.: from French *anthère* or modern Latin *anthera*, from Greek *anthēra* 'flowery,' from *anthos* 'flower.'

an·ther·id·i·um /,anTHəˈridēəm/ ▶*n.* (*pl.* **-ther·id·i·a** /-THəˈridēə/) *Botany* the male sex organ of algae, mosses, ferns, fungi, and other nonflowering plants. ▷mid 19th cent.: modern Latin, from *anthera* (see **ANTHER**) + *-idium* (from the Greek diminutive suffix *-idion*). **—an·ther·id·i·al** /-T͟Həˈridēəl/ *adj.*

an·ther·o·zo·id /,anTHərəˈzō-id; ˈanTHərə,zoid/ ▶*n. Botany* another term for **SPERMATOZOID**. ▷mid 19th cent.: from **ANTHER** + **ZOOID**.

an·the·sis /anˈTHēsis/ ▶*n. Botany* the flowering period of a plant, from the opening of the flower bud. ▷mid 19th cent.: from Greek *anthēsis* 'flowering,' from *anthein* 'to blossom.'

ant·hill /ˈant,hil/ ▶*n.* a moundlike nest built by ants or termites.

antho- ▶*comb. form* of or relating to flowers: *anthophilous.* ▷from Greek *anthos* 'flower.'

an·tho·cy·a·nin /,anTHəˈsīənin/ ▶*n. Chemistry* a blue, violet, or red flavonoid pigment found in plants. ▷mid 19th cent.: from German *Anthocyan*, from Greek *anthos* 'flower' + *kuanos* 'blue' + **-IN**[1].

an·thol·o·gize /anˈTHälə,jīz/ ▶*v.* [*trans.*] [usu. as *adj.*] (**anthologized**) include (an author or work) in an anthology: *the most anthologized of today's poets.*

an·thol·o·gy /anˈTHäləjē/ ▶*n.* (*pl.* **-gies**) a published collection of poems or other pieces of writing: *an anthology of European poetry.* ■ a similar collection of songs or musical compositions issued in one album. ▷mid 17th cent.: via French or medieval Latin from Greek *anthologia*, from *anthos* 'flower' + *-logia* 'collection' (from *legein* 'gather'). In Greek, the word originally denoted a collection of the "flowers" of verse, i.e., small choice poems or epigrams, by various authors. **—an·thol·o·gist** /-jist/ *n.*

An·tho·ny /ˈanTHənē/, Susan B(rownell) (1820–1906), U.S. social reformer and leader of the woman suffrage movement. She traveled, lectured, and cam-

Susan B. Anthony

Pronunciation Key ə *ago*; ər *over*; ˈə *or* ,ə *up*; ˈər *or* ,ər *fur*; a *hat*; ā *rate*; ä *car*; CH *chew*; e *let*; ē *see*; e(ə)r *air*; i *fit*; ī *by*; i(ə)r *ear*; NG *sing*; ō *go*; ô *for*; oi *boy*; o͝o *good*; o͞o *goo*; ou *out*; SH *she*; TH *thin*; T͟H *then*; (h)w *why*; ZH *vision*

paigned throughout her life for women's rights. With Elizabeth Cady Stanton, she organized the National Woman Suffrage Association in 1869. With Stanton and Matilda Joslyn Gage, she compiled the *History of Woman Suffrage* (1881–1902).

An·tho·ny, St. /'anTHənē/ (also **An·to·ny** /'antənē/) (*c.*251–356), Egyptian hermit; the founder of monasticism. Feast day, January 17.

An·tho·ny of Pad·u·a, St. (also **An·to·ny** /'antənē/) (1195–1231), Portuguese Franciscan friar. His devotion to the poor is commemorated by alms known as St. Anthony's bread; he is invoked to find lost articles. Feast day, June 13.

an·thoph·i·lous /an'THäfələs/ ▸*adj. Zoology* (of insects or other animals) frequenting flowers.

An·tho·zo·a /,anTHə'zōə/ *Zoology* a large class of sedentary marine coelenterates that includes the sea anemones and corals. They are either solitary or colonial, and have a central mouth surrounded by tentacles. ▷modern Latin (plural), from Greek *anthos* 'flower' + *zōia* 'animals.' **—an·tho·zo·an** *n.* & *adj.*

an·thra·cene /'anTHrə,sēn/ ▸*n. Chemistry* a colorless crystalline aromatic hydrocarbon obtained by the distillation of crude oils and used in chemical manufacture. • A tricyclic compound; chem. formula: $C_{14}H_{10}$. ▷mid 19th cent.: from Greek *anthrax, anthrak-* 'coal' + **-ENE**.

an·thra·cite /'anTHrə,sīt/ ▸*n.* coal of a hard variety that contains relatively pure carbon and burns with little flame and smoke. Also called **HARD COAL**. ▷late 16th cent. (denoting a gem described by Pliny and said to resemble coals, supposedly hydrophane): from Greek *anthrakitēs*, from *anthrax, anthrak-* 'coal.' **—an·thra·cit·ic** /,anTHrə'sitik/ *adj.*

an·thrac·nose /an'THrak,nōs/ ▸*n.* a mainly fungal disease of plants, causing dark lesions. • This is usually caused by fungi of the subdivision Deuteromycotina. ▷late 19th cent.: coined in French from Greek *anthrax, anthrak-* 'coal' + *nosos* 'disease.'

an·thra·qui·none /,anTHrəkwi'nōn; -'kwēnōn/ ▸*n. Chemistry* a yellow crystalline compound obtained by oxidation of anthracene. It is the basis of many natural and synthetic dyes. • Chem. formula: $C_{14}H_8O_2$. ▷late 19th cent.: from *anthra(cene)* + **QUINONE**.

an·thrax /'an,THraks/ ▸*n.* a notifiable bacterial disease of sheep and cattle, typically affecting the skin and lungs. It can be transmitted to humans, causing severe skin ulceration or a form of pneumonia (also called **WOOL-SORTERS' DISEASE**). ▷late Middle English: Latin, 'carbuncle' (the earliest sense in English), from Greek *anthrax, anthrak-* 'coal, carbuncle,' with reference to the skin ulceration in humans.

an·throp·ic prin·ci·ple /an'THräpik/ *n.* the cosmological principle that theories of the universe are constrained by the necessity to allow human existence.

In its 'weak' form the principle affirms that a universe in which living observers cannot exist is inherently unobservable. 'Strong' forms take this line of reasoning further, seeking to explain features of the universe as being so because they are necessary for human existence.

▷1970s: *anthropic* from Greek *anthrōpikos*, from *anthrōpos* 'human being.'

anthropo- ▸*comb. form* human; of a human being: *anthropometry.* ■ relating to humankind: *anthropology.* ▷from Greek *anthrōpos* 'human being.'

An·thro·po·cene /'anTHrəpə,sēn/ ▸*n.* the current geological age, viewed as having begun about 200 years ago with the significant impact of human activity on the ecosphere. ▷2000: based on Greek *anthrōpos* 'human being' + *kainos* 'recent'; reportedly coined by chemist Paul Crutzen (1933–).

an·thro·po·cen·tric /,anTHrəpō'sentrik/ ▸*adj.* regarding humankind as the central or most important element of existence, esp. as opposed to God or animals. **—an·thro·po·cen·tri·cal·ly** /-trik(ə)lē/ *adv.* **—an·thro·po·cen·trism** /-,trizəm/ *n.*

an·thro·po·gen·ic /,anTHrəpō'jenik/ ▸*adj.* (chiefly of environmental pollution and pollutants) originating in human activity: *anthropogenic emissions of sulfur dioxide.* **—an·thro·po·gen·i·cal·ly** /-ik(ə)lē/ *adv.*

an·thro·pog·e·ny /,anTHrə'päjənē/ ▸*n.* the study of the origin of humankind.

an·thro·poid /'anTHrə,poid/ ▸*adj.* resembling a human being in form: *cartoons of anthropoid frogs.* ■ *Zoology* of or relating to the group of higher primates, which includes monkeys, apes, and humans. ■ *Zoology* (of an ape) belonging to one of the families of great apes. ■ *informal, derogatory* (of a person) apelike in appearance or behavior: *his crewcut sloped down from the back of his head to a low-cut, anthropoid forehead.*
▸*n. Zoology* a higher primate, esp. an ape or apeman. • Suborder Anthropoidea, order Primates. ■ *informal, derogatory* a person that resembles an ape in appearance or behavior: *anthropoids ruled the streets.* ▷mid 19th cent.: from Greek *anthrōpoeidēs*, from *anthrōpos* 'human being' + **-OID**.

an·thro·pol·o·gy /,anTHrə'päləjē/ ▸*n.* the study of humankind, in particular: ■ (also **cultural** or **social anthropology**) the comparative study of human societies and cultures and their development. ■ (also **physical anthropology**) the science of human zoology, evolution, and ecology. **—an·thro·po·log·i·cal** /-pə'läjikəl/ *adj.* **—an·thro·pol·o·gist** /-jist/ *n.*

an·thro·pom·e·try /,anTHrə'pämitrē/ ▸*n.* the scientific study of the measurements and proportions of the human body. **—an·thro·po·met·ric** /-pō'metrik/ *adj.*

an·thro·po·mor·phic /,anTHrəpə'môrfik/ ▸*adj.* relating to or characterized by anthropomorphism. ■ having human characteristics: *anthropomorphic bears and monkeys.* ▷early 19th cent.: from Greek *anthrōpomorphos* (see **ANTHROPOMORPHOUS**) + **-IC**. **—an·thro·po·mor·phi·cal·ly** /-ik(ə)lē/ *adv.*

an·thro·po·mor·phism /,anTHrəpə'môr,fizəm/ ▸*n.* the attribution of human characteristics or behavior to a god, animal, or object. **—an·thro·po·mor·phize** /-,fīz/ *v.*

an·thro·po·mor·phous /,anTHrəpə'môrfəs/ ▸*adj.* (of a god, animal, or object) human in form or nature. ▷mid 18th cent.: from Greek *anthrōpomorphos* (from *anthrōpos* 'human being' + *morphē* 'form') + **-OUS**.

an·thro·poph·a·gi /,anTHrə'päfəjī; -gī/ ▸*plural n.* cannibals, esp. in legends or fables. ▷mid 16th cent.: from Latin, plural of *anthropophagus*, from Greek *anthrōpophagos* 'man-eating,' from *anthrōpos* 'human being' + *-phagos* (see **-PHAGOUS**).

an·thro·poph·a·gy /,anTHrə'päfəjē/ ▸*n.* the eating of human flesh by human beings. ▷mid 17th cent.: from Greek *anthrōpophagia*, from *anthrōpophagos* (see **ANTHROPOPHAGI**). **—an·thro·poph·a·gous** /-gəs/ *adj.*

an·thro·pos·o·phy /,anTHrə'päsəfē/ ▸*n.* a formal educational, therapeutic, and creative system established by Rudolf Steiner, seeking to use mainly natural means to optimize physical and mental health and well-being. ▷early 20th cent.: from **ANTHROPO-** + Greek *sophia* 'wisdom.' **—an·thro·po·soph·i·cal** /-pə'säfikəl/ *adj.*

an·thu·ri·um /an'THōōrēəm/ ▸*n.* (*pl.* **-ums**) a tropical American plant often grown elsewhere for its ornamental foliage or brightly colored flowering spathes. • Genus *Anthurium*, family Araceae. ▷modern Latin, from Greek *anthos* 'flower' + *oura* 'tail.'

an·ti /'an,tī; 'antē/ ▸*prep.* opposed to; against: *I'm anti the abuse of drink and the hassle that it causes.*
▸*adj.* [*predic.*] *informal* opposed: *one big soul fight in the GOP concerns immigration—illegal and legal, anti or pro.*
▸*n.* (*pl.* **an·tis**) *informal* a person opposed to a particular policy, activity, or idea: *a shadow army of antis who endanger your sport.* ▷late 18th cent. (as a noun): independent usage of **ANTI-**.

anti- (also **ant-**) ▸*prefix* opposed to; against: *antiaircraft.* ■ preventing: *antibacterial.* ■ reversing or undoing: *anticoagulant | antigravity | antipruritic.* ■ the opposite of: *anticlimax.* ■ *Physics* the opposite state of matter or of a specified particle: *antimatter | antiproton.* ■ acting as a rival: *antipope.* ■ unlike the conventional form: *anti-hero.* ▷representing Greek *anti* 'against.'

an·ti·a·bor·tion /,antēə'bôrSHən; ,antī-/ ▸*adj.* [*attrib.*] opposing or legislating against medically induced abortion. **—an·ti·a·bor·tion·ist** *n.*

an·ti·air·craft /,antē'er,kraft; ,antī-/ (also **an·ti-air·craft**) (abbr.:**AA**) ▸*adj.* [*attrib.*] (esp. of a gun or missile) used to attack enemy aircraft.

an·ti·a·li·as·ing /,antē'ālēəsiNG; ,antī-/ ▸*n.* (in computer graphics) a technique used to add greater realism to a digital image by smoothing jagged edges on curved lines and diagonals.

an·ti·bac·te·ri·al /,antēbak'ti(ə)rēəl; ,antī-/ ▸*adj.* [*attrib.*] active against bacteria.

an·ti·bal·lis·tic mis·sile /,antēbə'listik; ,antī-/ (abbr.: **ABM**) ▸*n.* a missile designed for intercepting and destroying a ballistic missile while in flight.

An·tibes /än'tēb/ a fishing port and resort in southeastern France; pop. 70,690.

an·ti·bi·o·sis /,antēbī'ōsis; ,antī-/ ▸*n. Biology* an antagonistic association between two organisms (esp. microorganisms), in which one is adversely affected. See also **SYMBIOSIS**. ▷late 19th cent.: from **ANTI-** + a shortened form of **SYMBIOSIS**.

an·ti·bi·ot·ic /,antēbī'ätik; ,antī-/ ▸*n.* a medicine (such as penicillin or its derivatives) that inhibits the growth of or destroys microorganisms.
▸*adj.* relating to, involving, or denoting antibiotics. ▷mid 19th cent. (in the sense 'doubting the possibility of life in a particular environment'): from **ANTI-** + Greek *biōtikos* 'fit for life' (from *bios* 'life').

an·ti·bod·y /'anti,bädē/ ▸*n.* (*pl.* **-bod·ies**) a blood protein produced in response to and counteracting a specific antigen. Antibodies combine chemically with substances that the body recognizes as alien, such as bacteria, viruses, and foreign substances in the blood. ▷early 20th cent.: from **ANTI-** + **BODY**, translating German *Antikörper*, from *anti-* 'against' + *Körper* 'body.'

an·ti·bub·ble /'antē,bəbəl; 'antī-/ ▸*n.* a membrane of air, submerged in liquid and surrounding a sphere of liquid.

an·tic /'antik/ ▸*adj. poetic/literary* grotesque or bizarre. ▷early 16th cent.: from Italian *antico* 'antique,' used to mean 'grotesque.'

an·ti·cath·ode /,antē'ka,THōd; ,antī-/ ▸*n. Physics* the target (or anode) of an X-ray tube that is struck by electrons from the cathode and from which X-rays are emitted.

an·ti·choice /,antē'CHois; ,antī-/ ▸*adj.* opposed to a pregnant woman's choice of a medically induced abortion. Compare with **PRO-LIFE**.

an·ti·cho·lin·er·gic /,antē,kōlə'nərjik; ,antī-/ ▸*Medicine adj.* (chiefly of a drug) inhibiting the physiological action of acetylcholine, esp. as a neurotransmitter.
▸*n.* an anticholinergic drug.

An·ti·christ /'antē,krīst; 'antī-/ ▸*n.* (**the An·ti·christ**) a great personal opponent of Christ who will spread evil throughout the world before being conquered at Christ's second coming. ■ a person or force seen as opposing Christ or the Christian Church. ▷Old English, via Old French or ecclesiastical Latin from Greek *antikhristos*, from *anti* 'against' + *Khristos* (see **CHRIST**).

an·ti-Chris·tian /,antē'krisCHən; ,antī-/ ▸*adj.* opposed to Christianity or Christian values. ■ of or relating to the Antichrist.
▸*n.* a person who opposes Christianity.

an·tic·i·pate /an'tisə,pāt/ ▸*v.* [*trans.*] **1** regard as probable; expect or predict: *she anticipated scorn on her return to the theater* | [with *clause*] *it was anticipated that the rains would slow the military campaign.* ■ guess or be aware of (what will happen) and take action in order to be prepared: *they failed to anticipate a full scale invasion.* ■ look forward to: *Stephen was eagerly anticipating the break from the routine of business.* ■ use or spend in advance. **2** act as a forerunner or precursor of: *he anticipated Bates's theories on mimicry and protective coloration.* ■ come or take place before (an event or process expected or scheduled for a later time). ■ react or respond to (someone) too quickly, without giving them a chance to do or say something. ■ pay (a debt) before it is due. ▷mid 16th cent. (in the senses 'to take something into consideration,' 'mention something before the proper time'): from Latin *anticipat-* 'acted in advance,' from *anticipare*, based on *ante-* 'before' + *capere* 'take.' **—an·tic·i·pa·tor** /-,pātər/ *n.*

USAGE Anticipate in the sense 'expect, foresee' (as in sense 1 above) is well established in informal use (*he anticipated a restless night*), but is regarded as a weakening of the meaning by many traditionalists. The formal sense is more specific in its meaning, 'be aware of and deal with beforehand' (*the doctor anticipated the possibility of a relapse by prescribing new medications*).

an·tic·i·pa·tion /an,tisə'pāSHən/ ▸*n.* the action of anticipating something; expectation or prediction: *her eyes sparkled* ***with anticipation***. ■ *Music* the introduction in a composition of part of a chord that is about to follow in full. ▷late Middle English: from Latin *anticipatio(n-)*, from the verb *anticipare* (see **ANTICIPATE**).
▸***PHRASE*** □ **in anticipation** with the probability or expectation of something happening: *they manned the telephones* ***in anticipation of*** *a flood of calls.*

an·tic·i·pa·to·ry /an'tisəpə,tôrē/ ▸*adj.* happening, performed, or felt in anticipation of something: *an anticipatory flash of excitement.* ■ *Law* (of a breach of contract) taking the form of an announcement or indication that a contract will not be honored.

an·ti·cler·i·cal /,antē'klerikəl; ,antī-/ *chiefly historical* ▸*adj.* opposed to the power or influence of the clergy, esp. in politics.
▸*n.* a person holding such views. **—an·ti·cler·i·cal·ism** /-,lizəm/ *n.*

an·ti·cli·max /ˌantēˈklīˌmaks; ˌantī-/ ▸*n.* a disappointing end to an exciting or impressive series of events: *the rest of the journey was an anticlimax by comparison | a sense of anticlimax and incipient boredom.* —**an·ti·cli·mac·tic** /-klīˈmaktik/ *adj.* —**an·ti·cli·mac·ti·cal·ly** /-klīˈmaktik(ə)lē/ *adv.*

an·ti·cline /ˈantēˌklīn; ˈantī-/ ▸*n. Geology* a ridge-shaped fold of stratified rock in which the strata slope downward from the crest. Compare with SYNCLINE. ▷mid 19th cent.: from ANTI- + Greek *klinein* 'lean,' on the pattern of *incline.* —**an·ti·cli·nal** /ˌantēˈklīnl; ˌantī-/ *adj.*

an·ti·clock·wise /ˌantēˈkläkˌwīz; ˌantī-/ ▸*adv. & adj.* British term for COUNTERCLOCKWISE.

an·ti·co·ag·u·lant /ˌantēkōˈagyələnt; ˌantī-/ ▸*adj.* having the effect of retarding or inhibiting the coagulation of the blood.
▸*n.* an anticoagulant substance.

an·ti·co·don /ˌantēˈkōdän; ˌantī-/ ▸*n. Biochemistry* a sequence of three nucleotides forming a unit of genetic code in a transfer RNA molecule, corresponding to a complementary codon in messenger RNA.

an·ti·com·pet·i·tive /ˌantēkəmˈpetitiv; ˌantī-/ ▸*adj.* tending to stifle or suppress competition, esp. when this violates antitrust laws: *an anticompetitive advantage in the software industry.* —**an·ti·com·pet·i·tive·ly** *adv.* —**an·ti·com·pet·i·tive·ness** *n.*

an·ti·con·vul·sant /ˌantēkənˈvəlsənt; ˌantī-/ ▸*adj.* (chiefly of a drug) used to prevent or reduce the severity of epileptic fits or other convulsions.
▸*n.* an anticonvulsant drug.

an·tics /ˈantiks/ ▸*plural n.* foolish, outrageous, or amusing behavior: *the antics of our political parties.* ▷early 16th cent.: from ANTIC.

an·ti·cy·clone /ˌantēˈsīklōn; ˌantī-/ ▸*n.* a weather system with high atmospheric pressure at its center, around which air slowly circulates in a clockwise (northern hemisphere) or counterclockwise (southern hemisphere) direction. Anticyclones are associated with calm, fine weather. —**an·ti·cy·clon·ic** /-sīˈklänik/ *adj.*

an·ti·de·pres·sant /ˌantēdəˈpresnt; ˌantī-/ ▸*adj.* (chiefly of a drug) used to alleviate depression.
▸*n.* an antidepressant drug.

an·ti·di·ar·rhe·al /ˌantēˌdīəˈrēəl; ˌantī-/ ▸*adj.* (of a drug) used to alleviate diarrhea.
▸*n.* an antidiarrheal drug.

an·ti·di·u·ret·ic hor·mone /ˌantēˌdīəˈretik; ˌantī-/ (abbr.: **ADH**) ▸*n.* another term for VASOPRESSIN.

an·ti·dote /ˈantiˌdōt/ ▸*n.* a medicine taken or given to counteract a particular poison. ■ something that counteracts or neutralizes an unpleasant feeling or situation: *laughter is a good antidote to stress.* ■ (in homeopathy) a substance that cancels or opposes the effect of a remedy.
▸*v.* [*trans.*] (**-dotes, -dot·ed, -dot·ing**) counteract or cancel with an antidote: *What remedy will antidote Bryonia?* ▷late Middle English: via Latin, from Greek *antidoton,* neuter of *antidotos* 'given against,' from *anti-* 'against' + *didonai* 'give.' —**an·ti·dot·al** /ˌantiˈdōtl/ *adj.*

an·ti·drom·ic /ˌantiˈdrämik/ ▸*adj. Physiology* (of an impulse) traveling in the opposite direction to that normal in a nerve fiber. The opposite of ORTHODROMIC. ▷early 20th cent.: from ANTI- + Greek *dromos* 'running' + -IC.

an·ti·e·met·ic /ˌantēəˈmetik; ˌantī-/ ▸*adj.* (chiefly of a drug) preventing vomiting.
▸*n.* an antiemetic drug.

an·ti·es·tab·lish·ment /ˌantē-iˈstablishmənt; ˌantī-/ ▸*adj.* against the establishment or established authority.

An·tie·tam /anˈtētəm/ historic site in northwestern Maryland, on Antietam Creek, southeast of Sharpsburg, scene of a major Civil War battle in September 1862.

an·ti·feed·ant /ˌantēˈfēdnt; ˌantī-/ ▸*n.* a naturally occurring substance in certain plants that adversely affects insects or other animals that eat them. ▷1960s: from ANTI- + FEED + -ANT.

an·ti·fer·ro·mag·net·ic /ˌantēˌferōməgˈnetik; ˌantī-/ ▸*adj. Physics* designating or exhibiting a form of magnetism characterized by an antiparallel alignment of adjacent electron spins in a crystal lattice. Compare with FERRIMAGNETIC.

an·ti·foul·ing /ˌantēˈfouliNG; ˌantī-/ ▸*n.* treatment of a boat's hull with a paint or similar substance designed to prevent fouling. ■ an antifouling substance.

an·ti·freeze /ˈantiˌfrēz/ ▸*n.* a liquid, typically one based on ethylene glycol, which can be added to water to lower the freezing point, chiefly used in the radiator of a motor vehicle.

an·ti-g /ˌantēˈjē; ˌantī-/ ▸*adj.* short for ANTIGRAVITY. ▷1940s: from ANTI- + *g,* the symbol for acceleration due to gravity.

an·ti·gen /ˈantijən/ ▸*n.* a toxin or other foreign substance that induces an immune response in the body, esp. the production of antibodies. ▷early 20th cent.: via German from French *antigène* (see ANTI-, -GEN). —**an·ti·gen·ic** /ˌantiˈjenik/ *adj.*

an·ti·gen·ic de·ter·mi·nant ▸*n. Biochemistry* another term for EPITOPE.

an·ti·glob·al·i·za·tion /ˌantēˌglōbələˈzāshən; ˌantī-/ ▸*n.* opposition to the agendas and actions of groups perceived to favor globalization, such as the IMF, the World Trade Organization, and the G8 countries: [as *modifier*] *antiglobalization protesters.*

An·tig·o·ne /anˈtigənē/ *Greek Mythology* daughter of Oedipus and Jocasta, the subject of a tragedy by Sophocles. She was sentenced to death for defying her uncle Creon, king of Thebes, but she took her own life before the sentence could be carried out, and Creon's son Haemon, who was engaged to her, killed himself over her body.

an·tig·o·rite /anˈtigəˌrīt/ ▸*n.* a mineral of the serpentine group, occurring typically as thin green plates.

an·ti·gov·ern·ment /ˌantēˈgəvər(n)mənt; ˌantī-/ ▸*adj.* against a government or the administration in office.

an·ti·grav·i·ty /ˌantēˈgravitē; ˌantī-/ ▸*n. Physics* a hypothetical force opposing gravity.
▸*adj.* [*attrib.*] (chiefly of clothing for a pilot or astronaut) designed to counteract the effects of high acceleration.

An·ti·gua /anˈtēgwə; -ˈtigwə/ (also **An·ti·gua Gua·te·ma·la** /ˌgwätəˈmälə/) a town in the central highlands of Guatemala; pop. 26,630.

An·ti·gua and Bar·bu·da /bärˈbo͞odə/ a country in the western West Indies, in the Leeward Islands, that consists of two main islands (Antigua and Barbuda) and Redonda, a smaller island to the southwest of Antigua; pop. 68,320; capital, St. John's (on Antigua); languages, English (official), Creole. —**An·ti·guan** *adj. & n.*

Discovered in 1493 by Columbus and settled by the English in 1632, Antigua became a British colony with Barbuda as its dependency; the islands gained independence within the Commonwealth of Nations in 1981.

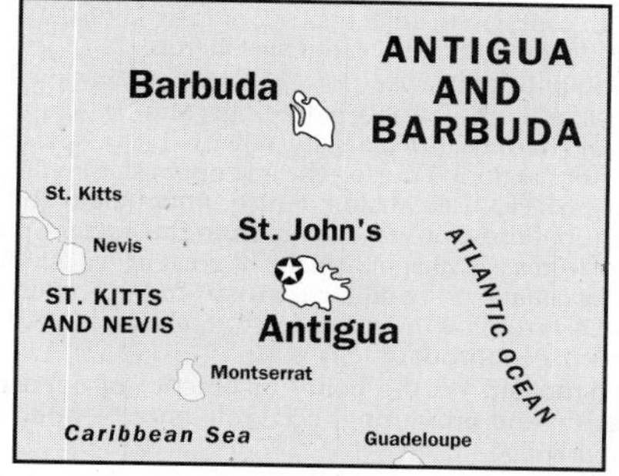

an·ti·he·ro /ˈantēˌhi(ə)rō; ˈantī-/ ▸*n.* a central character in a story, movie, or drama who lacks conventional heroic attributes.

an·ti·her·o·ine /ˈantēˌherōin; ˈantī-/ ▸*n.* a female antihero.

an·ti·his·ta·mine /ˌantēˈhistəmin; -mēn/ ▸*n.* [usu. as *adj.*] a drug or other compound that inhibits the physiological effects of histamine, used esp. in the treatment of allergies: *an antihistamine injection.*

an·ti·in·fec·tive /ˌantēinˈfektiv; ˌantī-/ ▸*adj.* (of a drug) used to prevent infection.
▸*n.* an anti-infective drug.

an·ti·in·flam·ma·to·ry /ˌantēinˈflaməˌtôrē; ˌantī-/ ▸*adj.* (chiefly of a drug) used to reduce inflammation.
▸*n.* (*pl.* **-ries**) an anti-inflammatory drug.

an·ti·in·tel·lec·tu·al /ˌantēˌintlˈekcho͞oəl; ˌantī-/ ▸*n.* a person who scorns intellectuals and their views and methods.
▸*adj.* characteristic of a such a person. —**an·ti·in·tel·lec·tu·al·ism** *n.*

an·ti·knock /ˌantēˈnäk; ˌantī-/ ▸*n.* a substance (such as tetraethyl lead) added to gasoline to inhibit preignition.

An·ti-Leb·a·non Moun·tains /ˌantēˈlebənən; -əˌnän/ a range of mountains that run north to south along the border between Lebanon and Syria, east of the Lebanon range.

an·ti-life /ˌantēˈlīf; ˌantī-/ ▸*adj.* opposed to or restricting the full development of life: *the new industrial age was anti-life.* ■ opposing the development of life by advocating abortion.

An·til·les /anˈtilēz/ a group of islands that form the greater part of the West Indies. The **Greater Antilles** extend roughly east to west and are comprised of Cuba, Jamaica, Hispaniola (Haiti and the Dominican Republic), and Puerto Rico; the **Lesser Antilles,** to the southeast, include the Virgin, Leeward, and Windward islands, as well as various small islands to the north of Venezuela. See also NETHERLANDS ANTILLES.

an·ti·lock /ˌantēˈläk; ˌantī-/ (also **an·ti-lock**) ▸*adj.* [*attrib.*] (of brakes) designed so as to prevent the wheels from locking and the vehicle from skidding if applied suddenly.

an·ti·log /ˈantēˌlôg; ˈantī-; -ˌläg/ ▸*n.* short for ANTILOGARITHM.

an·ti·log·a·rithm /ˌantēˈlôgəˌri*TH*əm; -ˈläg-; ˌantī-/ ▸*n.* the number to which a logarithm belongs.

an·ti·ma·cas·sar /ˌantēməˈkasər/ ▸*n. chiefly historical* a piece of cloth put over the back of a chair to protect it from grease and dirt or as an ornament. ▷mid 19th cent.: from ANTI- + MACASSAR.

an·ti·mag·net·ic /ˌantēmagˈnetik; ˌantī-/ ▸*adj.* (esp. of watches) resistant to magnetization.

an·ti·mat·ter /ˈantēˌmatər; ˈantī-/ ▸*n. Physics* molecules formed by atoms consisting of antiprotons, antineutrons, and positrons. Stable antimatter does not appear to exist in our universe.

an·ti·me·tab·o·lite /ˌantēmiˈtabəˌlīt; ˌantī-/ ▸*n. Physiology* a substance that interferes with the normal metabolic processes within cells, typically by combining with enzymes.

an·ti·mon·ar·chist /ˌantēˈmänərkist; ˌantī-/ ▸*n.* an opponent of monarchy.

an·ti·mo·ny /ˈantəˌmōnē/ ▸*n.* the chemical element of atomic number 51, a brittle silvery-white metalloid. (Symbol: **Sb**)

Antimony was known from ancient times; the naturally occurring black sulfide was used as the cosmetic kohl. The element is used in alloys, usually with lead, such as pewter, type-metal, and Britannia metal.

▷late Middle English (denoting stibnite, the most common ore of the metal): from medieval Latin *antimonium,* of unknown origin. The current sense dates from the early 19th cent. —**an·ti·mo·ni·al** /ˌantəˈmōnēəl/ *adj.* —**an·ti·mo·nic** /ˌantəˈmänik/ *adj.* —**an·ti·mo·ni·ous** /ˌantəˈmōnēəs/ *adj.*

an·ti·na·tion·al /ˌantēˈnashənl; ˌantī-/ ▸*adj.* opposed to national interests or nationalism: *the Communists were seen as antinational party.*

an·ti·neu·tron /ˌantēˈn(y)o͞oträn; ˌantī-/ ▸*n. Physics* the antiparticle of a neutron.

an·ti·node /ˈantiˌnōd/ ▸*n. Physics* the position of maximum displacement in a standing wave system.

an·ti·noise /ˌantēˈnoiz; ˌantī-/ ▸*adj.* [*attrib.*] promoting the suppression or reduction of noise: *stringent antinoise regulations.*
▸*n.* sound generated for the purpose of reducing noise by interference.

an·ti·no·mi·an /ˌantiˈnōmēən/ ▸*adj.* of or relating to the view that Christians are released by grace from the obligation of observing the moral law.
▸*n.* a person holding this view. ▷mid 17th cent.: from medieval Latin *Antinomi,* the name of a 16th-cent. sect in Germany alleged to hold this view, from Greek *anti-* 'opposite, against' + *nomos* 'law.' —**an·ti·no·mi·an·ism** /-ˌnizəm/ *n.*

an·tin·o·my /anˈtinəmē/ ▸*n.* (*pl.* **-mies**) a contradiction between two beliefs or conclusions that are in themselves reasonable; a paradox. ▷late 16th cent. (in the sense 'a conflict between two laws'): from Latin *antinomia,* from Greek, from *anti* 'against' + *nomos* 'law.'

an·ti·nu·cle·ar ▸*adj.* [*attrib.*] opposed to the development of nuclear weapons or nuclear power.

An·ti·och /ˈäntēˌäk/ **1** a city in southern Turkey, near the Syrian border; pop. 123,871. Antioch was the ancient capital of Syria under the Seleucid kings, who founded it *c.*300 BC. Turkish name **ANTAKYA. 2** a city in ancient Phrygia. **3** a city in north central California; pop. 62,195.

An·ti·o·chus /an'tīəkəs/ the name of eight Seleucid kings, notably: ■ **Antiochus III** (*c.*242–187 BC), reigned 223–187 BC; known as **Antiochus the Great**. He restored and expanded the Seleucid empire. ■ **Antiochus IV** (*c.*215–163 BC), son of Antiochus III; reigned 175–163 BC; known as **Antiochus Epiphanes**. His attempt to Hellenize the Jews resulted in the revival of Jewish nationalism and the Maccabean revolt.

an·ti·ox·i·dant /ˌantē'äksidənt; ˌantī-/ ▸*n.* a substance that inhibits oxidation, esp. one used to counteract the deterioration of stored food products. ■ a substance such as vitamin C or E that removes potentially damaging oxidizing agents in a living organism.

an·ti·par·al·lel /ˌantē'parəˌlel; ˌantī-/ ▸*adj. Physics* parallel but moving or oriented in opposite directions.

an·ti·par·ti·cle /'antēˌpärtikəl; 'antī-/ ▸*n. Physics* a subatomic particle having the same mass as a given particle but opposite electric or magnetic properties. Every kind of subatomic particle has a corresponding antiparticle, e.g., the positron has the same mass as the electron but an equal and opposite charge.

an·ti·pas·to /ˌantē'pästō; ˌän-/ ▸*n.* (*pl.* **-pas·ti** /-'pästē/) (in Italian cooking) an appetizer typically consisting of olives, anchovies, cheeses, and meats. ▷Italian, from *anti-* 'before' + *pasto* (from Latin *pastus* 'food').

an·ti·pa·thet·ic /anˌtipə'THetik/ ▸*adj.* showing or feeling a strong aversion: *it is human nature to be* ***antipathetic to*** *change.* ▷mid 19th cent.: from ANTIPATHY, on the pattern of *pathetic.*

an·tip·a·thy /an'tipəTHē/ ▸*n.* (*pl.* **-thies**) a deep-seated feeling of dislike; aversion: *his fundamental* ***antipathy to*** *capitalism* | *a thinly disguised mutual antipathy.* ▷late 16th cent. (in the sense 'opposition of feeling, nature, or disposition'): from French *antipathie* or Latin *antipathia*, from Greek *antipatheia*, from *antipathēs* 'opposed in feeling,' from *anti* 'against' + *pathos* 'feeling.'

an·ti·per·son·nel /ˌantēˌpərsə'nel; ˌantī-/ ▸*adj.* [*attrib.*] (of weapons, esp. bombs) designed to kill or injure people rather than to damage buildings or equipment.

an·ti·per·spi·rant /ˌanti'pərspərənt/ ▸*n.* a substance that is applied to the skin, esp. under the arms, to prevent or reduce perspiration.

an·ti·phon /'antəˌfän/ ▸*n.* (in traditional western Christian liturgy) a short sentence sung or recited before or after a psalm or canticle. ■ a musical setting of such a sentence or sentences. ▷late Middle English: via ecclesiastical Latin from Greek *antiphōna* 'harmonies,' neuter plural of *antiphōnos* 'responsive,' from *anti* 'in return' + *phōnē* 'sound.'

an·tiph·o·nal /an'tifənl/ ▸*adj.* (in traditional western Christian liturgy) (of a short sentence or its musical setting) sung, recited, or played alternately by two groups.
▸*n.* another term for ANTIPHONARY. —**an·tiph·o·nal·ly** *adv.*

an·tiph·o·nar·y /an'tifəˌnerē/ ▸*n.* (*pl.* **-nar·ies**) a collection of antiphons. ▷early 17th cent.: from ecclesiastical Latin *antiphonarium*, from *antiphona* (see ANTIPHON).

an·tiph·o·ny /an'tifənē/ ▸*n.* antiphonal singing, playing, or chanting.

an·tip·o·dal /an'tipədl/ ▸*adj.* relating to or situated on the opposite side of the earth. ■ (**antipodal to**) diametrically opposed to something. ■ *Botany* relating to or denoting cells formed at the chalazal end of the embryo sac.

an·ti·pode /'antiˌpōd/ ▸*n.* the direct opposite of something else: *the pole and its antipode.* ▷early 17th cent. (denoting an inhabitant of the opposite side of the earth): back-formation from ANTIPODES.

an·tip·o·des /an'tipədēz/ ▸*plural n.* (**the An·tip·o·des**) Australia and New Zealand (used by inhabitants of the northern hemisphere). ■ the direct opposite of something: *we are the very* ***antipodes of*** *labor unions.* ▷late Middle English: via French or late Latin from Greek *antipodes* 'having the feet opposite,' from *anti* 'against, opposite' + *pous, pod-* 'foot.' The term originally denoted the inhabitants of opposite sides of the earth, or of the side opposite to oneself, and was later transferred to the places where they live (mid 16th cent.). —**an·tip·o·de·an** /anˌtipə'dēən/ *adj., n.*

an·ti·pope /'antiˌpōp/ ▸*n.* a person established as pope in opposition to one held by others to be canonically chosen. ▷late Middle English *antipape*, via French from medieval Latin *antipapa* (on the pattern of *Antichrist*). The spelling change in the 17th cent. was due to association with POPE[1].

an·ti·pro·ton /'antēˌprōtän; 'antī-/ ▸*n. Physics* the negatively charged antiparticle of a proton.

an·ti·pru·rit·ic /ˌantēprə'ritik; ˌantī-/ ▸*adj.* [*attrib.*] (chiefly of a drug) used to relieve itching.
▸*n.* an antipruritic drug. ▷late 19th cent.: from ANTI- + *pruritic* (see PRURITUS).

an·ti·psy·chot·ic /ˌantēsī'kätik; ˌantī-/ ▸*adj.* [*attrib.*] (chiefly of a drug) used to treat psychotic disorders.
▸*n.* an antipsychotic drug.

an·ti·py·ret·ic /ˌantēˌpī'retik; ˌantī-/ ▸*adj.* (chiefly of a drug) used to prevent or reduce fever.
▸*n.* an antipyretic drug.

an·ti·quar·i·an /ˌanti'kwe(ə)rēən/ ▸*adj.* relating to or dealing in antiques or rare books. ■ valuable because rare or old: *out-of-print and antiquarian books.*
▸*n.* a person who studies or collects antiques or antiquities. ▷early 17th cent.: from Latin *antiquarius* (see ANTIQUARY). —**an·ti·quar·i·an·ism** /-ˌnizəm/ *n.*

an·ti·quark /'antēˌkwôrk; 'antī-/ ▸*n. Physics* the antiparticle of a quark.

an·ti·quar·y /'antiˌkwerē/ ▸*n.* (*pl.* **-quar·ies**) another term for ANTIQUARIAN. ▷mid 16th cent.: from Latin *antiquarius*, from *antiquus* (see ANTIQUE).

an·ti·quat·ed /'antiˌkwātid/ ▸*adj.* old-fashioned or outdated: *this antiquated central heating system.* See note at OLD. ▷late 16th cent. (in the sense 'old, of long standing'): from ecclesiastical Latin *antiquare* 'make old,' from *antiquus* (see ANTIQUE).

an·tique /an'tēk/ ▸*n.* a collectible object such as a piece of furniture or work of art that has a high value because of its considerable age: *Pauline loves collecting antiques* | [as *adj.*] *an antique dealer.*
▸*adj.* **1** (of a collectible object) having a high value because of considerable age: *an antique clock.* ■ (of a method of finishing a wooden surface) intended to resemble the appearance of antique furniture: *bookshelves with an antique finish.* **2** belonging to ancient times: *statues of antique gods.* ■ old-fashioned or outdated: *trade unions defending antique work practices.* ■ *often humorous* showing signs of great age or wear: *an antique divorcee in reduced circumstances.*
▸*v.* **1** (**-tiques, -tiqued, -ti·quing**) [*trans.*] [usu. as *adj.*] (**antiqued**) make (something) resemble an antique by artificial means: *an antiqued door.* **2** (**go antiquing**) shop in stores where antiques are sold: *we would often go antiquing in search of furnishings.* ▷late 15th cent. (as an adjective): from Latin *antiquus, anticus* 'former, ancient,' from *ante* 'before.'

an·tiq·ui·ty /an'tikwitē/ ▸*n.* (*pl.* **-ties**) **1** the ancient past, esp. the period before the Middle Ages: *the great civilizations of antiquity.* ■ [with *adj.*] a specified historical period during the ancient past: *cameos dating from classical antiquity.* ■ (usu. **antiquities**) an object, building, or work of art from the ancient past: *a collection of Islamic antiquities.* **2** great age: *a church of great antiquity.* ▷Middle English: from Old French *antiquite*, from Latin *antiquitas*, from *antiquus* 'old, former' (see ANTIQUE).

an·ti·rac·ism ▸*n.* the policy or practice of opposing racism and promoting racial tolerance. —**an·ti·rac·ist** *n.* & *adj.*

an·ti·re·tro·vi·ral /ˌantēˌretrō'vīrəl; ˌantī-/ ▸*adj.* working against or targeted against retroviruses, especially HIV: *antiretroviral therapy.*
▸*n.* an antiretroviral drug.

an·ti·roll bar ▸*n.* a rubber-mounted bar fitted in the suspension of a vehicle to increase its stability, esp. when cornering.

an·tir·rhi·num /ˌanti'rīnəm/ ▸*n.* (*pl.* **-nums**) a plant of the figwort family, with showy two-lipped flowers. • Genus *Antirrhinum*, family Scrophulariaceae: several species, in particular the snapdragon. ▷from Latin, from Greek *antirrhinon*, from *anti-* 'counterfeiting' + *rhis, rhin-* 'nose,' from the resemblance of the flower to an animal's snout.

an·ti·scor·bu·tic /ˌantēskôr'byōōtik; ˌantī-/ *Medicine* ▸*adj.* (chiefly of a drug) having the effect of preventing or curing scurvy.
▸*n.* an antiscorbutic food or drug.

an·ti-Sem·i·tism ▸*n.* hostility to or prejudice against Jews. —**an·ti-Sem·ite** *n.* —**an·ti-Se·mit·ic** *adj.*

an·ti·sense /'antēˌsens; 'antī-/ ▸*adj. Genetics* having a sequence of nucleotides complementary to (and hence capable of binding to) a coding sequence, which may be either that of the strand of a DNA double helix that undergoes transcription, or that of a messenger RNA molecule.

an·ti·sep·sis /'antiˌsepsis/ ▸*n.* the practice of using antiseptics to eliminate the microorganisms that cause disease. Compare with ASEPSIS.

an·ti·sep·tic /ˌanti'septik/ ▸*adj.* of, relating to, or denoting substances that prevent the growth of disease-causing microorganisms. ■ (of medical techniques) based on the use of such substances. See note at SANITARY. ■ *figurative* scrupulously clean or pure, esp. so as to be bland or characterless: *the antiseptic modernity of a conference center.*
▸*n.* an antiseptic compound or preparation. —**an·ti·sep·ti·cal·ly** /-ik(ə)lē/ *adv.*

an·ti·se·rum /'antiˌsi(ə)rəm/ ▸*n.* (*pl.* **-se·ra** /-ˌsi(ə)rə/) a blood serum containing antibodies against specific antigens, injected to treat or protect against specific diseases.

an·ti·so·cial /ˌantē'sōsHəl; ˌantī-/ ▸*adj.* **1** contrary to the laws and customs of society; devoid of or antagonistic to sociable instincts or practices: *a dangerous, unprincipled, antisocial type of man.* **2** not sociable; not wanting the company of others.

USAGE See usage at UNSOCIABLE.

an·ti·spas·mod·ic /ˌantēspaz'mätik; ˌantī-/ ▸*adj.* (chiefly of a drug) used to relieve spasm of involuntary muscle.
▸*n.* an antispasmodic drug.

an·ti·stat·ic ▸*adj.* [*attrib*] preventing the buildup of static electricity or reducing its effects.

an·tis·tro·phe /an'tistrəfē/ ▸*n.* the second section of an ancient Greek choral ode or of one division of it. Compare with STROPHE and EPODE (sense 2). ▷mid 16th cent. (as a term in rhetoric denoting the repetition of words in reverse order): via late Latin from Greek *antistrophē*, from *antistrephein* 'turn against,' from *anti* 'against' + *strephein* 'to turn.'

an·ti·sym·met·ric /ˌantēsə'metrik; ˌantī-/ ▸*adj. Mathematics & Physics* unaltered in magnitude but changed in sign by exchange of two variables or by a particular symmetry operation.

an·ti·tank ▸*adj.* [*attrib.*] for use against enemy tanks: *new antitank missiles.*

an·ti·ter·ror·ism /ˌantē'terəˌrizəm; ˌantī-/ ▸*n.* the prevention or abatement of terrorism: *a meeting of experts on antiterrorism* [as *modifier*] *antiterrorism measures.* —**an·ti·ter·ror·ist** *n.* & *adj.*

an·ti·tet·a·nus ▸*adj. Medicine* preventing or effective against tetanus: *an antitetanus injection.*

an·tith·e·sis /an'tiTHəsis/ ▸*n.* (*pl.* **-ses** /-ˌsēz/) a person or thing that is the direct opposite of someone or something else: *love is the antithesis of selfishness.* ■ a contrast or opposition between two things: *the* ***antithesis between*** *occult and rational mentalities.* ■ a figure of speech in which an opposition or contrast of ideas is expressed by parallelism of words that are the opposites of, or strongly contrasted with, each other, such as "hatred stirs up strife, but love covers all sins": *his sermons were full of startling antitheses.* ■ (in Hegelian philosophy) the negation of the thesis as the second stage in the process of dialectical reasoning. Compare with SYNTHESIS. ▷late Middle English (originally denoting the substitution of one grammatical case for another): from late Latin, from Greek *antitithenai* 'set against,' from *anti* 'against' + *tithenai* 'to place.' The earliest current sense, denoting a rhetorical or literary device, dates from the early 16th cent.

an·ti·thet·i·cal /ˌantə'THetikəl/ ▸*adj.* **1** directly opposed or contrasted; mutually incompatible: *people whose religious beliefs are* ***antithetical to*** *mine* | *two antithetical emotions pulled at her.* See note at OPPOSITE. **2** [*attrib.*] connected with, containing, or using the rhetorical device of antithesis. ▷late 16th cent. (sense 2): from Greek *antithetikos*, from *antithetos* 'placed in opposition,' from *antitithenai* 'set against.' —**an·ti·thet·ic** *adj.* —**an·ti·thet·i·cal·ly** *adv.*

an·ti·tox·in /ˌantē'täksin/ ▸*n. Physiology* an antibody that counteracts a toxin. —**an·ti·tox·ic** /-sik/ *adj.*

an·ti·trades /'antiˌtrādz/ ▸(also **an·ti·trade winds**) *plural n.* steady winds that blow in the opposite direction to and overlie the trade winds.

an·ti·trust /ˌantē'trəst; ˌantī-/ ▸*adj.* [*attrib.*] of or relating to legislation preventing or controlling trusts or other monopolies, with the intention of promoting competition in business.

an·ti·type /'antiˌtīp/ ▸*n.* **1** a person or thing that represents the opposite of someone or something else. **2** something that is represented by a symbol: *the ship in danger is easily understood to be its old antitype, the Commonwealth.* ▷early 17th cent.: from late Latin *antitypus*, from Greek *antitupos* 'corresponding as an impression to the die,' from *anti* 'against, opposite' + *tupos* 'type, a stamp.' **—an·ti·typ·i·cal** /ˌantiˈtipikəl/ *adj.*

an·ti·ven·in /ˌantēˈvenin; ˌantī-/ ▸*n.* an antiserum containing antibodies against specific poisons, esp. those in the venom of snakes, spiders, and scorpions. Also called **antivenom**. ▷late 19th cent.: from ANTI- + *ven(om)* + -IN[1].

an·ti·vi·ral /ˌantēˈvīrəl; ˌantī-/ ▸*adj. Medicine* (chiefly of a drug or treatment) effective against viruses.

an·ti·vi·rus /ˌantēˈvīrəs; ˌantī-/ ▸*adj.* [*attrib.*] *Computing* (of software) designed to detect and destroy computer viruses.

an·ti·viv·i·sec·tion /ˌantēˌviviˈsekshən; ˌantī-/ ▸*adj.* [*attrib.*] opposed to operations on live animals for scientific research. **—an·ti·viv·i·sec·tion·ism** /-ˌnizəm/ *n.* **—an·ti·viv·i·sec·tion·ist** /-nist/ *n. & adj.*

ant·ler /ˈantlər/ ▸*n.* one of the branched horns on the head of an adult (usually male) deer, which are made of bone and are grown and cast off annually. ■ one of the branches on such a horn. ▷late Middle English (originally denoting the lowest (forward-directed) branch of the antler): from Anglo-Norman French, variant of Old French *antoillier*, of unknown origin. The current sense dates from the early 19th cent. **—ant·lered** *adj.*

Ant·li·a /ˈantlēə/ *Astronomy* a small and faint southern constellation (the Air Pump), between Hydra and Vela. ■ [as *genitive*] (**Antliae** /-lēˌē/) used with a preceding letter or numeral to designate stars in the constellation: *the star Alpha Antliae.* ▷Latin, from Greek.

ant li·on ▸*n.* an insect that resembles a dragonfly, with predatory larvae that construct conical pits into which insect prey, esp. ants, fall. • Family Myrmeleontidae, order Neuroptera.

An·to·fa·gas·ta /ˌäntōfəˈgästə/ a port in northern Chile, capital of Antofagasta region; pop. 218,750.

An·to·nine /ˈantəˌnīn/ ▸*adj.* [*attrib*] of or relating to the Roman emperors Antoninus Pius and Marcus Aurelius or their rules (AD 137–80).
▸*plural n.* (**the Antonines**) the Antonine emperors.

An·to·ni·nus Pi·us /ˌantəˈnīnəs ˈpīəs/ (86–161), Roman emperor 138–161. The adopted son and successor of Hadrian, his reign was generally peaceful.

An·to·nio·ni /ˌantōnēˈōnē; -təˈnyō-/, Michelangelo (1912–), Italian movie director. Notable movies: *L'avventura* (1960), *Blow-Up* (1966), *Zabriskie Point* (1970), and *Beyond the Clouds* (1995).

an·to·no·ma·sia /anˌtänəˈmāzh(ē)ə/ ▸*n. Rhetoric* the substitution of an epithet or title for a proper name (e.g., *the Bard* for Shakespeare). ■ the use of a proper name to express a general idea (e.g., *a Scrooge* for a miser). ▷mid 16th cent.: via Latin from Greek, from *antonomazein* 'name instead,' from *anti-* 'against, instead' + *onoma* 'a name.'

An·to·ny /ˈantənē; ˈanthənē/, Mark (*c.*83–30 BC), Roman general and triumvir; Latin name *Marcus Antonius.* Following Julius Caesar's assassination in 44 BC, he took charge of the Eastern Empire, where he established his association with Cleopatra. Quarrels with Octavian led finally to his defeat at the battle of Actium and to his suicide.

An·to·ny, St. see ANTHONY, ST.

An·to·ny of Pad·u·a, St. see ANTHONY OF PADUA, ST.

an·to·nym /ˈantəˌnim/ ▸*n. Linguistics* a word opposite in meaning to another (e.g., *bad* and *good*). ▷mid 19th cent.: from French *antonyme*, from *ant-* (from Greek *anti-* 'against') + Greek *onuma* 'a name.' **—an·ton·y·mous** /anˈtänəməs/ *adj.*

an·trec·to·my /anˈtrektəmē/ ▸*n.* surgical removal of an antrum, esp. the antrum of the stomach.

An·trim /ˈantrəm/ one of the six counties of Northern Ireland, formerly an administrative area. ■ a town in this county, on the northeastern shore of Lough Neagh; pop. 21,000.

An·tron /ˈanˈträn/ ▸*n. trademark* a type of strong, light nylon fiber used chiefly in making carpets and upholstery. ▷1960s: invented name.

an·trum /ˈantrəm/ ▸*n.* (*pl.* **-tra** /-trə/) *Anatomy* a natural chamber or cavity in a bone or other anatomical structure. ■ the part of the stomach just inside the pylorus. ▷early 19th cent.: from Latin, from Greek *antron* 'cave.' **—an·tral** /-trəl/ *adj.*

ant·sy /ˈantsē/ ▸*adj.* agitated, impatient, or restless: *he was too antsy to stay in one place for long.* ▷mid 19th cent.: probably from the phrase *have ants in one's pants* (see ANT).

ant·thrush ▸*n.* any of a number of thrush-sized ant-eating birds: • a large antbird (three genera in the family Formicariidae). • an African thrush (genus *Neocossyphus*, subfamily Turdinae, family Muscicapidae: four species). • another term for PITTA[2].

antlers

An·tung /ˈänˈdoong/ former name for **DANDONG**.

Ant·werp /ˈanˌtwərp/ a port in northern Belgium, on the Scheldt River; pop. 467,520. By the 16th century, it was a leading European commercial and financial center. French name **ANVERS**, Flemish name **ANTWERPEN**. ■ a province of Belgium of which Antwerp is the capital.

A·nu·bis /əˈnoobis/ *Egyptian Mythology* the god of mummification, protector of tombs, typically represented as having the head of a jackal.

Anubis

An·u·ra /əˈn(y)oorə/ *Zoology* an order of tailless amphibians that comprises the frogs and toads. Also called **SALIENTIA** or **BATRACHIA**. ■ [as *plural n.*] (**anura**) amphibians of this order; frogs and toads. ▷modern Latin, from AN-[1] + Greek *oura* 'tail.' **—an·u·ran** *n. & adj.*

A·nu·ra·dha·pu·ra /ˌənəˌrädəˈpoorə/ a city in north central Sri Lanka; pop. 36,000. The ancient capital of Sri Lanka, it is a center of Buddhist pilgrimage.

an·u·ri·a /əˈn(y)oorēə/ ▸*n. Medicine* failure of the kidneys to produce urine. ▷mid 19th cent.: from AN-[1] + -URIA. **—an·u·ric** /-ik/ *adj.*

a·nus /ˈānəs/ ▸*n. Anatomy & Zoology* the opening at the end of the alimentary canal through which solid waste matter leaves the body. ▷late Middle English: from Latin, originally 'a ring.'

An·vers /änˈver(s)/ French name of **ANTWERP**.

an·vil /ˈanvil/ ▸*n.* a heavy steel or iron block with a flat top, concave sides, and typically a pointed end, on which metal can be hammered and shaped. ■ the horizontally extended upper part of a cumulonimbus cloud: [as *adj.*] *anvil clouds.* ■ *Anatomy* another term for INCUS. ▷Old English *anfilte*, from the Germanic base of ON + a verbal stem meaning 'beat.'

anvil

ANWR ▸*n.* the Arctic National Wildlife Refuge, a wilderness area in Alaska. ■ a Congressional bill that would open up this area to oil exploration and drilling: [as *modifier*] *to date, ANWR language has not gained enough bipartisan backing.*

anx·i·e·ty /angˈzī-itē/ ▸*n.* (*pl.* **-ties**) a feeling of worry, nervousness, or unease, typically about an imminent event or something with an uncertain outcome: *he felt a surge of anxiety* | ***anxieties about** the moral decline of today's youth.* ■ [*with infinitive*] desire to do something, typically accompanied by unease: *the housekeeper's eager anxiety to please.* ■ *Psychiatry* a nervous disorder characterized by a state of excessive uneasiness and apprehension, typically with compulsive behavior or panic attacks. ▷early 16th cent.: from French *anxiété* or Latin *anxietas*, from *anxius* (see ANXIOUS).

anx·i·o·lyt·ic /ˌangzēəˈlitik/ *Medicine* ▸*adj.* (chiefly of a drug) used to reduce anxiety.
▸*n.* an anxiolytic drug. ▷1960s: from ANXIETY + -LYTIC.

anx·ious /ˈang(k)shəs/ ▸*adj.* **1** experiencing worry, unease, or nervousness, typically about an imminent event or something with an uncertain outcome: *she was extremely anxious about her exams.* ■ [*attrib.*] (of a period of time or situation) causing or characterized by worry or nervousness: *there were some anxious moments.* **2** [usu with *infinitive*] wanting something very much, typically with a feeling of unease: *the company was anxious to avoid any trouble* | [with *clause*] *my parents were anxious that I get an education.* ▷early 17th cent.: from Latin *anxius* (from *angere* 'to choke') + -OUS. **—anx·ious·ly** *adv.* **—anx·ious·ness** *n.*

USAGE **Anxious** and **eager** both mean 'looking forward to something,' but they have different connotations. **Eager** suggests enthusiasm about something, a positive outlook: *I'm **eager** to get started on my vacation.* **Anxious** implies worry about something: *I'm **anxious** to get started before it rains.*

A

an·y /ˈenē/ ▸*adj.* & *pron.* **1** [usu. with *negative* or in *questions*] used to refer to one or some of a thing or number of things, no matter how much or many: [as *adj.*] *I don't have any choice* | *do you have any tips to pass on?* | [as *pron.*] *someone asked him for a match, but Joe didn't have any* | *you don't know* **any of** *my friends* | *if there is any left, throw it away.* ■ [as *pron.*] anyone: *it ceased payments to any but the elderly or disabled.* **2** whichever of a specified class might be chosen: [as *adj.*] *these constellations are visible at any hour of the night* | *any fool knows that* | [as *pron.*] *the illness may be due to* **any of** *several causes.*
▸*adv.* [usu. with *negative* or in *questions*] [as *submodifier*] (used for emphasis) at all; in some degree: *he wasn't any good at basketball* | *no one would be* **any the wiser.** ■ *informal* used alone, not qualifying another word: *I didn't hurt you any.* ▷Old English *ǣnig* (see **ONE**, **-Y**[1]), of Germanic origin; related to Dutch *eenig* and German *einig*.
▸*PHRASES* □ **any amount of** see **AMOUNT**. □ **any old** see **OLD**. □ **any time** (also **anytime**) **1** at whatever time: *she can come any time.* **2** without exception or doubt: *I can handle a shrimp like him anytime.* □ **any time** (or **day** or **minute**, etc.) **now** *informal* very soon: *we'll get them back any day now.* □ **be not having any** (**of it**) *informal* be unwilling to cooperate: *I tried to make polite conversation, but he wasn't having any.* □ **hardly any** see **HARDLY**. □ **not just any** — a particular or special thing of its type rather than an ordinary one of that type: *he had an acting job at last, and not just any part, but the lead in a new film.*

USAGE When used as a pronoun, **any** can be used with either a singular or a plural verb, depending on the context: *we needed more sugar but there wasn't any left* (singular verb) or *are any of the new videos available?* (plural verb).

an·y·bod·y /ˈenēˌbädē; -ˌbədē/ ▸*pron.* **1** anyone: *there wasn't anybody around.* **2** a person of any importance: *everybody who was anybody in state government turned out to be involved.*
▸*PHRASE* □ **anybody's guess** see **GUESS**.

an·y·how /ˈenēˌhou/ ▸*adv.* **1** another term for **ANYWAY**. **2** in a careless or haphazard way: *two suitcases flung anyhow.*

an·y·more /ˌenēˈmôr/ (also **any more**) ▸*adv.* [usu. with *negative* or in *questions*] to any further extent; any longer: *she refused to listen anymore* | *you don't get men like him anymore.*

an·y·one /ˈenēˌwən/ ▸*pron.* **1** [usu. with *negative* or in *questions*] any person or people: *there wasn't anyone there* | *does anyone remember him?* | *I was afraid to tell anyone.* ■ [without *negative*] used for emphasis: *anyone could do it.* **2** a person of importance or authority: *they are read by* **anyone who's anyone.**
▸*PHRASES* □ **be anyone's** *informal* (of a person) be open to sexual advances from anyone: *three drinks and he's anyone's.* □ **anyone's game** an evenly balanced contest: *it was still anyone's game at halftime.* □ **anyone's guess** see **GUESS**.

USAGE **Any one** is not the same as **anyone**, and the two forms should not be used interchangeably. **Any one**, meaning 'any single (person or thing),' is written as two words to emphasize singularity: *any one of us could do the job*; *not more than ten new members are chosen in any one year.* Otherwise it is written as one word: *anyone who wants to come is welcome.* (Note that this distinction is structurally similar to, although not identical with, the difference between *every day* and *everyday.* See **usage** at **EVERYDAY**.)

an·y·place /ˈenēˌplās/ ▸*adv.* informal term for **ANYWHERE**: *Miami is hotter than anyplace else.*

an·y·thing /ˈenēˌTHiNG/ ▸*pron.* [usu. with *negative* or in *questions*] used to refer to a thing, no matter what: *nobody was saying anything* | *have you found anything?* | *he inquired whether there was anything he could do.* ■ [without *negative*] used for emphasis: *I was ready for anything.* ■ used to indicate a range: *he trains anything from seven to eight hours a day.*
▸*PHRASES* □ **anything but** not at all (used for emphasis): *he is anything but racist.* □ **anything like** — [with *negative*] at all like— (used for emphasis): *it doesn't taste anything like wine.* □ (**as**) — **as anything** *informal* extremely—: *she said it out loud, clear as anything.* □ **if anything** see **IF**. □ **like anything** see **LIKE**[1]. □ **or anything** [usu. with *negative* or in *questions*] *informal* added as a general reference to other things similar to the thing mentioned: *no strings attached, you don't have to join up or anything.*

an·y·time /ˈenēˌtīm/ ▸*adv.* variant of **any time** at **ANY**.

An·y·town /ˈenēˌtoun/ ▸*n.* (also **Anytown U.S.A.**) any real or fictional place regarded as being typical of American small-town appearance or values: *the party was looking for that elusive candidate from Anytown.*

an·y·way /ˈenēˌwā/ ▸*adv.* **1** used to confirm or support a point or idea just mentioned: *I told you, it's all right, and anyway, it was my fault* | *it's too late now anyway.* ■ used in questions to emphasize the speaker's wish to obtain the truth: *"What are you doing here, anyway?"* **2** used in conversations: ■ to change the subject or to resume a subject after interruption: *How she lives with him is beyond me. Anyway, I really like her.* ■ to indicate that the speaker wants to end the conversation: *"Anyway, Dot, I must go."* ■ to indicate that the speaker is passing over less significant aspects of an account in order to focus on the most important points: *"Poor John always enjoyed a drink. Anyway, he died last year."* **3** used to indicate that something happened or will happen in spite of something else: *nobody invited Miss Honey to sit down so she sat down anyway.*

an·y·ways /ˈenēˌwāz/ ▸*adv.* informal or dialect form of **ANYWAY**: *you wouldn't understand all them long words anyways.*

an·y·where /ˈenēˌ(h)we(ə)r/ ▸*adv.* [usu. with *negative* or in *questions*] in or to any place: *he couldn't be found anywhere.* ■ [without *negative*] used for emphasis: *I could go anywhere in the world.* ■ used to indicate a range: *this iron garden seat dates anywhere from 1890 to 1920* | *she could have been* **anywhere between** *twenty-five and forty.*
▸*pron.* any place: *he doesn't have anywhere to live.*
▸*PHRASE* □ **anywhere near** [with *negative* or in *questions*] (used for emphasis) at all near: *I wouldn't dream of letting a surgeon anywhere near my eyes.* ■ remotely close to in extent, level, or scope: *imitations rarely look anywhere near as good as the real thing.*

an·y·wheres /ˈenēˌ(h)we(ə)rz/ ▸*adv.* & *pron.* informal or dialect form of **ANYWHERE**: [as *adv.*] *I'll see if I can find your clothes anywheres.*

an·y·wise /ˈenēˌwīz/ ▸*adv.* *archaic* in any manner or way. ▷Old English *on ǣnige wīsan* 'in any wise.'

An·zac /ˈanˌzak/ ▸*n.* a soldier in the Australian and New Zealand Army Corps (1914–18). ■ *dated* a person, esp. a member of the armed services, from Australia or New Zealand. ▷acronym.

An·zio /ˈäntsēˌō; ˈanzēō/ a seaport in western Italy, south of Rome; pop. 36,000. It was a popular resort for citizens of ancient Rome. Allied troops landed here in January 1944, amid fierce fighting, to begin their drive to capture Rome.

AOC ▸*abbr.* *appellation d'origine contrôlée* (see **APPELLATION CONTRÔLÉE**).

ao dai /ˈou ˌdī; ˈō/ ▸*n.* (*pl.* **ao dais**) a Vietnamese woman's long-sleeved tunic with ankle-length panels at front and back, worn over trousers. ▷1960s: Vietnamese.

A-OK (also **A-o·kay**) *informal* ▸*adj.* in good order or condition; all right: *everything will be A-OK.*
▸*adv.* in a good manner or way; all right: *we hit it off A-OK.* ▷1960s (originally an astronauts' term): from *all systems OK.*

AOR ▸*n.* [usu. as *adj.*] a type of popular music in which a hard rock background is combined with softer or more melodic elements. ▷1970s: from *album-oriented rock* or *adult-oriented rock.*

Ao·ra·ki/Mount Cook /ouˈrakē ˌmount ˈko͝ok/ *n.* official name (since 1999) for Mount Cook, the highest peak in New Zealand: 12,349 feet (3,764 m).

A·o·ran·gi /ouˈräNGē/ Maori name for **COOK, MOUNT**.

a·o·rist /ˈāərist/ *Grammar* ▸*n.* (esp. in Greek) an unqualified past tense of a verb without reference to duration or completion of the action.
▸*adj.* relating to or denoting this tense. ▷late 16th cent.: from Greek *aoristos* 'indefinite,' from *a-* 'not' + *horizein* 'define, limit.' **—a·o·ris·tic** /ˌāəˈristik/ *adj.*

a·or·ta /āˈôrtə/ ▸*n.* the main artery of the body, supplying oxygenated blood to the circulatory system. In humans it passes over the heart from the left ventricle and runs down in front of the backbone. ▷mid 16th cent.: from Greek *aortē* (used in the plural by Hippocrates for the branches of the windpipe, and by Aristotle for the great artery), from *aeirein* 'raise.' **—a·or·tic** /-tik/ *adj.*

Ao·te·a·ro·a /ˌouˌtāəˈrōə/ the Maori name for **NEW ZEALAND**. ▷Maori, literally "land of the long white cloud."

a·ou·dad /ˈä-o͞oˌdad/ ▸*n.* another term for **BARBARY SHEEP**. ▷early 19th cent.: from French, from Berber *udād.*

à ou·trance /ˌä o͞oˈträns/ ▸*adv.* *poetic/literary* to the death or the very end: *a duel à outrance.* ▷early 17th cent.: French, literally 'to the utmost.'

Aou·zou Strip /ouˈzo͞o/ a narrow corridor of disputed desert land in northern Chad. It forms the border between Chad and Libya. In 1994, Libya agreed to withdraw its troops from the area.

AP ▸*abbr.* ■ advanced placement. ■ American plan. ■ Associated Press.

ap-[1] ▸*prefix* variant spelling of **AD-** assimilated before *p* (as in *apposite, apprehend*).

ap-[2] ▸*prefix* variant spelling of **APO-** before *h* (as in *aphelion*).

a·pace /əˈpās/ ▸*adv.* *poetic/literary* swiftly; quickly: *work continues apace.* ▷late Middle English: from Old French *a pas* 'at (a considerable) pace.'

A·pach·e ▸/əˈpacHē/ *n.* **1** (*pl.* same or **A·pach·es**) a member of a North American Indian people living chiefly in New Mexico and Arizona. The Apache put up fierce resistance to the European settlers and were, under the leadership of Geronimo, the last American Indian people to be conquered. **2** the Athabaskan language of this people.
▸*adj.* of or relating to the Apache or their language. ▷from Mexican Spanish, probably from Zuni *Apachu*, literally 'enemy.'

a·pache /əˈpasH; äˈpäsH/ ▸*n.* (*pl.* **a·paches** *pronunc.* same) a violent street ruffian, originally in Paris. ▷early 20th cent.: French, from **APACHE**, by association with the reputed ferocity of the American Indian people.

Apa·la·chi·co·la Riv·er /ˌapəˌlacHiˈkōlə/ see **CHATTAHOOCHEE RIVER**.

a·part /əˈpärt/ ▸*adv.* **1** (of two or more people or things) separated by a distance; at a specified distance from each other in time or space: *his parents are now living apart* | *two stone gateposts some thirty feet apart* | *countries* **as far apart as** *New Zealand and the U.S.* | *figurative the two sides remained far apart on the issue.* **2** to or on one side; at a distance from the main body: *Isabel stepped away from Joanna and stood apart* *figurative their religious commitment sets them apart.* ■ used after a noun to indicate that someone or something has distinctive qualities that mark them out from other people or things: *wrestlers were a breed apart.* ■ used after a noun to indicate that someone or something has been dealt with sufficiently or is being excluded from what follows: *Alaska apart, much of America's energy business concentrates on producing gas.* **3** so as to be shattered; into pieces: *he leapt out of the car just before it was blown apart.* ▷late Middle English: from Old French, from Latin *a parte* 'at the side.' **—a·part·ness** *n.*
▸*PHRASES* □ **apart from 1** except for: *the whole world seemed to be sleeping, apart from Barbara.* **2** in addition to; as well as: *quite apart from all the work, he had such financial problems.* □ **tell apart** distinguish or separate one from another: *the twins were so identical that it was impossible to tell them apart.*

a·part·heid /əˈpärtˌ(h)āt; -ˌ(h)īt/ ▸*n.* *historical* (in South Africa) a policy or system of segregation or discrimination on grounds of race. ■ segregation in other contexts: *sexual apartheid.*

Adopted by the successful Afrikaner National Party as a slogan in the 1948 election, apartheid extended and institutionalized existing racial segregation. Despite rioting and terrorism at home and isolation abroad from the 1960s onward, the white regime maintained the apartheid system with only minor relaxation until February 1991.

▷1940s: Afrikaans, literally 'separateness,' from Dutch *apart* 'separate' + *-heid* (equivalent of **-HOOD**).

a·part·ment /əˈpärtmənt/ (abbr.: **apt.**) ▸*n.* a suite of rooms forming one residence, typically in a building containing a number of these. ■ a large building containing such suites; an apartment building. ■ (**apartments**) a suite of rooms in a very large or grand house set aside for the private use of a monarch or noble: *the Imperial apartments.* ▷mid 17th cent. (denoting a suite of rooms for the use of a particular person or group): from French *appartement*, from Italian *appartamento*, from *appartare* 'to separate,' from *a parte* 'apart.'

a·part·ment build·ing (also **apartment block** or **apartment house**) ▸*n.* a large building divided into separate apartments.

ap·a·thet·ic /ˌapəˈTHetik/ ▸*adj.* showing or feeling no interest, enthusiasm, or concern: *apathetic slackers who don't vote.* ▷mid 18th cent.: from **APATHY**, on the pattern of *pathetic.* **—ap·a·thet·i·cal·ly** /-ik(ə)lē/ *adv.*

ap·a·thy /ˈapəTHē/ ▸*n.* lack of interest, enthusiasm, or concern: *widespread apathy among students.* ▷early

17th cent.: from French *apathie*, via Latin from Greek *apatheia*, from *apathēs* 'without feeling,' from *a-* 'without' + *pathos* 'suffering.'

ap·a·tite /ˈapəˌtīt/ ▸*n.* a widely occurring pale green to purple mineral, consisting of calcium phosphate with some fluorine, chlorine, and other elements. It is used in the manufacture of fertilizers. ▷early 19th cent.: coined in German from Greek *apatē* 'deceit' (from the mineral's diverse forms and colors).

a·pa·to·saur /əˈpatōˌsôr/ (also **a·pa·to·sau·rus** /əˌpatōˈsôrəs/) ▸*n.* a huge herbivorous dinosaur of the late Jurassic period, with a long neck and tail. Also called **BRONTOSAURUS**. • Genus *Apatosaurus* (popularly *Brontosaurus*), infraorder Sauropoda, order Saurischia. ▷modern Latin, from Greek *apatē* 'deceit' + *sauros* 'lizard.' —**a·pa·to·sau·ri·an** *adj.*

APB ▸*abbr.* all-points bulletin.

APC ▸*abbr.* ■ armored personnel carrier. ■ aspirin, phenacetin, and caffeine, a compound used in some analgesics.

ape /āp/ ▸*n.* a large primate that lacks a tail, including the gorilla, chimpanzees, orangutan, and gibbons. See also **GREAT APE, GIBBON**. • Families Pongidae and Hylobatidae. ■ used in names of macaque monkeys with short tails, e.g., **Barbary ape**. ■ (in general use) any monkey. ■ an unintelligent or clumsy person. ■ *archaic* an inferior imitator or mimic: *cunning is but the ape of wisdom.*
▸*v.* [*trans.*] imitate the behavior or manner of (someone or something), esp. in an absurd or unthinking way: *new architecture can respect the old without aping its style.* See note at **IMITATE**. ▷Old English *apa*, of Germanic origin; related to Dutch *aap* and German *Affe*.
▸*PHRASE* □ **go ape** *informal* express wild excitement or anger: *your kids will go ape over these Popsicles!* | *a washerwoman gone ape with a butcher knife.*

APEC /ˈāˌpek/ ▸*abbr.* Asia Pacific Economic Cooperation, a regional economic forum established in 1989, including the U.S., Japan, China, Australia, Indonesia, Hong Kong, and Thailand.

A·pel·doorn /ˈapəlˌdôrn/ a town in the east central Netherlands; pop. 148,200. It is the site of the summer residence of the Dutch royal family.

ape·man /ˈāpˌman/ ▸*n.* (*pl.* **-men**) an extinct apelike primate believed to be related or ancestral to present-day humans.

Ap·en·nines /ˈapəˌnīnz/ a mountain range in Italy that extends for 880 miles (1,400 km) from the northwest to the southern tip of the country.

a·per·çu /äperˈso͞o/ ▸*n.* (*pl.* **-çus** *pronunc.* same) a comment or brief reference that makes an illuminating or entertaining point. ▷early 19th cent.: from French, past participle of *apercevoir* 'perceive.'

a·per·i·ent /əˈpi(ə)rēənt/ *Medicine* ▸*adj.* (chiefly of a drug) used to relieve constipation.
▸*n.* an aperient drug. ▷early 17th cent.: from Latin *aperient-* 'opening,' from *aperire*.

a·pe·ri·od·ic /ˌāpi(ə)rēˈädik/ ▸*adj. technical* not periodic; irregular: *aperiodic fluctuations.* ■ *Physics* denoting a potentially oscillating or vibrating system (such as an instrument with a pointer) that is damped to prevent oscillation or vibration. —**a·pe·ri·o·dic·i·ty** /āˌpi(ə)rēəˈdisitē/ *n.*

a·pe·ri·tif /äˌperiˈtēf; -əˌper-/ ▸*n.* an alcoholic drink taken before a meal to stimulate the appetite. ▷late 19th cent.: from French *apéritif*, from medieval Latin *aperitivus*, based on Latin *aperire* 'to open.'

ap·er·ture /ˈapərˌcнər/ ▸*n. chiefly technical* an opening, hole, or gap: *the bell ropes passed through apertures in the ceiling.* ■ a space through which light passes in an optical or photographic instrument, esp. the variable opening by which light enters a camera. ▷late Middle English: from Latin *apertura*, from *apert-* 'opened,' from *aperire* 'to open.'

ap·er·ture pri·or·i·ty ▸*n. Photography* an exposure system used in some automatic cameras in which the aperture is selected by the user and the appropriate shutter speed is controlled automatically. Compare with **SHUTTER PRIORITY**.

ap·er·y /ˈāpərē/ ▸*n. archaic* the act of imitating the behavior or manner of someone, esp. in an absurd or unthinking way.

ape·shit /ˈāpˌsнit/ ▸*n.*
▸*PHRASE* □ **go apeshit** *vulgar slang* another way of saying **go ape** (see **APE**).

a·pet·al·ous /āˈpetl-əs/ ▸*adj. Botany* (of a flower) having no petals. ▷early 18th cent.: from modern Latin *apetalus*, from Greek *apetalos* 'leafless' (from *a-* 'without' + *petalon* 'leaf') + **-OUS**.

A·pex /ˈāpeks/ ▸*n.* [usu. as *adj.*] a system of reduced fares for scheduled airline flights and railroad journeys that must be booked and paid for before a certain period in advance of departure: *Apex fares.* ▷1970s: from Advance Purchase Excursion.

a·pex /ˈāpeks/ ▸*n.* (*pl.* **a·pex·es** or **a·pi·ces** /ˈāpəˌsēz; ˈapə-/) the top or highest part of something, esp. one forming a point: *the living-room extends right up into the apex of the roof* | *figurative the apex of his career was when he hoisted aloft the World Cup.* ■ *Geometry* the highest point in a plane or solid figure, relative to a base line or plane. ■ *Botany* the growing point of a shoot. ■ the highest level of a hierarchy, organization, or other power structure regarded as a triangle or pyramid: *the central bank is at the apex of the financial system.*
▸*v.* [*intrans.*] reach a high point or climax: *melodic lines build up to the chorus and it apexes at the solo.* ▷early 17th cent.: from Latin, 'peak, tip.'

Ap·gar score /ˈapˌgär/ ▸*n. Medicine* a measure of the physical condition of a newborn infant. It is obtained by adding points (2, 1, or 0) for heart rate, respiratory effort, muscle tone, response to stimulation, and skin coloration; a score of ten represents the best possible condition. ▷1960s: named after Virginia *Apgar* (1909–74), American anesthesiologist who devised this method of assessment in 1953.

a·phaer·e·sis /əˈferəsis/ ▸*n. Linguistics* the loss of a sound or sounds at the beginning of a word, e.g., in the derivation of *adder* from *nadder*.
▸(usu. **a·pher·e·sis**) *Medicine* /ˌafəˈrēsis/ the removal of blood plasma from the body by the withdrawal of blood, its separation into plasma and cells, and the reintroduction of the cells, used esp. to remove antibodies in treating autoimmune diseases. ▷mid 16th cent.: via late Latin from Greek *aphairesis*, from *aphairein* 'take away,' from *apo* 'from' + *hairein* 'take.'

a·pha·sia /əˈfāzнə/ ▸*n. Medicine* loss of ability to understand or express speech, caused by brain damage. Compare with **APHONIA**. ▷mid 19th cent.: from Greek, from *aphatos* 'speechless,' from *a-* 'not' + *phanai* 'speak.' —**a·pha·sic** /-zik/ *adj.* & *n.*

a·phe·li·on /əˈfēlyən; əˈfēlēən/ ▸*n.* (*pl.* **a·phe·li·a** /əfēlyə; əˈfēlēə/ or **a·phe·li·ons**) *Astronomy* the point in the orbit of a planet, asteroid, or comet at which it is furthest from the sun: *Mars is* ***at aphelion***. The opposite of **PERIHELION**. ▷mid 17th cent.: alteration of modern Latin *aphelium* (by substitution of the Greek inflection *-on*), from Greek *aph' hēlion* 'from the sun.'

aph·e·sis /ˈafisis/ ▸*n. Linguistics* the loss of an unstressed vowel at the beginning of a word (e.g., of *a* from *around* to form *round*). ▷late 19th cent.: from Greek, literally 'letting go,' from *apo* 'from' + *hienai* 'let go, send.' —**a·phet·ic** /əˈfetik/ *adj.* —**a·phet·i·cal·ly** /əˈfetik(ə)lē/ *adv.*

a·phi·cide /ˈāfiˌsīd; ˈaf-/ ▸*n.* an insecticide used against aphids.

a·phid /ˈāfid; ˈaf-/ ▸*n.* a minute bug that feeds by sucking sap from plants. It reproduces rapidly, often producing live young without mating, and may live in large colonies that cause extensive damage to crops. • Superfamily Aphidoidea, suborder Homoptera. ▷late 19th cent.: back-formation from *aphides*, plural of **APHIS**.

aphid

a·phis /ˈāfis; ˈaf-/ ▸*n.* (*pl.* **a·phi·des** /ˈāfiˌdēz; ˈafi-/) an aphid, esp. one of the genus *Aphis*. ▷late 18th cent.: modern Latin, from Greek, perhaps a misreading of *koris* 'bug' (misinterpreting the Greek characters κορ 'kor' as αφ 'aph').

a·pho·ni·a /āˈfōnēə/ (also **aph·o·ny** /ˈafəˌnē/) ▸*n. Medicine* loss of ability to speak through disease of or damage to the larynx or mouth. Compare with **APHASIA**. ▷late 17th cent.: modern Latin, from Greek *aphōnia*, from *aphōnos* 'voiceless,' from *a-* 'without' + *phōnē* 'voice.'

aph·o·rism /ˈafəˌrizəm/ ▸*n.* a pithy observation that contains a general truth, such as, "if it ain't broke, don't fix it." See note at **SAYING**. ■ a concise statement of a scientific principle, typically by an ancient classical author. ▷early 16th cent.: from French *aphorisme* or late Latin *aphorismus*, from Greek *aphorismos* 'definition,' from *aphorizein* 'define.' —**aph·o·rist** *n.* —**aph·o·ris·tic** /ˌafəˈristik/ *adj.* —**aph·o·ris·ti·cal·ly** /ˌafəˈristik(ə)lē/ *adv.* —**aph·o·rize** /-ˌrīz/ *v.*

aph·ro·dis·i·ac /ˌafrəˈdizēˌak; -ˈdēzē-; -ˈdēzнē-/ ▸*n.* a food, drink, or drug that stimulates sexual desire: *the Romans worshiped the apple as an aphrodisiac* | [*as adj.*] *aphrodisiac powers.* ■ a thing that causes excitement: *for a few seconds she'd fallen for the powerful aphrodisiac of music* | *power is an aphrodisiac.* ▷early 18th cent.: from Greek *aphrodisiakos*, from *aphrodisios*, from *Aphroditē* (see **APHRODITE**.

Aph·ro·di·te /ˌafrəˈdītē/ *Greek Mythology* the goddess of beauty, fertility, and sexual love. She is variously described as the daughter of Zeus and Dione, or as being born from the sea. Roman equivalent **VENUS**. ▷Greek, literally 'foam-born,' from *aphros* 'foam.'

aph·tha /ˈafтнə/ ▸*n.* (*pl.* **-thae** /-тнē/) *Medicine* a small ulcer occurring in groups in the mouth or on the tongue. ■ a condition in which such ulcers occur. ▷mid 17th cent.: via Latin from Greek, connected with *haptein* 'set on fire.' —**aph·thous** /-тнəs/ *adj.*

API ▸*abbr.* ■ American Petroleum Institute. ■ *Computing* application programming interface.

A·pi·a /əˈpēə; äˈpēə/ the capital of Samoa; pop. 32,200.

a·pi·an /ˈāpēən/ ▸*adj.* [*attrib.*] of or relating to bees. ▷early 19th cent.: from Latin *apianus*, from *apis* 'bee.'

a·pi·ar·y /ˈāpēˌerē/ ▸*n.* (*pl.* **-ar·ies**) a place where bees are kept; a collection of beehives. ▷mid 17th cent.: from Latin *apiarium*, from *apis* 'bee.' —**a·pi·ar·i·an** /ˌāpēˈe(ə)rēən/ *adj.* —**a·pi·a·rist** /-əˌrist/ *n.*

a·pi·cal /ˈāpikəl; ˈap-/ ▸*adj. technical* of, relating to, or denoting an apex. ■ *Phonetics* (of a consonant) formed with the tip of the tongue. ▷early 19th cent.: from Latin *apex, apic-* (see **APEX**) + **-AL**.

a·pi·ces /ˈāpəˌsēz; ˈapə-/ ▸ plural form of **APEX**.

A·pi·com·plex·a /ˌāpikəmˈpleksə/ ▸ another term for **SPOROZOA**.

a·pi·cul·ture /ˈāpiˌkəlcнər/ ▸*n.* technical term for **BEEKEEPING**. ▷mid 19th cent.: from Latin *apis* 'bee' + **CULTURE**, on the pattern of words such as *agriculture*. —**a·pi·cul·tur·al** /ˌāpiˈkəlcнərəl/ *adj.* —**a·pi·cul·tur·ist** /ˌāpiˈkəlcнərist/ *n.*

a·piece /əˈpēs/ ▸*adv.* (used after a noun or an amount) to, for, or by each one of a group: *we sold 385 prints at $10 apiece.* ▷late Middle English: from **A** + **PIECE**.

A·pis /ˈäpis/ *Egyptian Mythology* a god depicted as a bull, symbolizing fertility and strength in war.

ap·ish /ˈāpisн/ ▸*adj.* of or resembling an ape in appearance: *Australopithecus had an apish cranium and a humanlike jaw.* ■ resembling or likened to an ape in being foolish or silly. —**ap·ish·ly** *adv.* —**ap·ish·ness** *n.*

a·pi·ther·a·py /ˌāpiˈтнerəpē/ ▸*n.* the use of products derived from bees as medicine, including venom, honey, pollen, and royal jelly.

ap·la·nat /ˈapləˌnat/ ▸*n. Physics* a reflecting or refracting surface that is free from spherical aberration. ▷late 19th cent.: coined in German from Greek *aplanētos* 'free from error,' from *a-* 'not' + *planan* 'wander.' —**ap·la·nat·ic** /ˌapləˈnatik/ *adj.*

a·pla·sia /əˈplāzнə/ ▸*n. Medicine* the failure of an organ or tissue to develop or to function normally. ▷late 19th cent.: from **A-**[1] 'without' + Greek *plasis* 'formation.' —**a·plas·tic** /āˈplastik/ *adj.*

a·plas·tic a·ne·mi·a /āˈplastik əˈnēmēə/ ▸*n. Medicine* deficiency of all types of blood cells caused by failure of bone marrow development.

a·plen·ty /əˈplentē/ ▸*adj.* [*postpositive*] in abundance: *there are going to be disasters aplenty in the garden.*

a·plomb /əˈpläm; əˈpləm/ ▸*n.* self-confidence or assurance, esp. when in a demanding situation: *Diana passed the test* ***with aplomb***. ▷late 18th cent. (in the sense 'perpendicularity, steadiness'): from French, from *à plomb* 'according to a plummet.'

ap·ne·a /ˈapnēə; apˈnēə/ (*Brit.* **ap·noe·a**) ▸*n. Medicine* temporary cessation of breathing, esp. during sleep: *thousands suffer from* ***sleep apnea***. ▷early 18th cent.: modern Latin, from Greek *apnoia*, from *apnous* 'breathless.'

APO ▸*abbr.* ■ (U.S.) Air Force Post Office. ■ (U.S.) Army Post Office.

apo- ▸*prefix* **1** away from: *apocrypha* | *apostrophe*. ■ separate: *apocarpous.* **2** *Astronomy* denoting the furthest point in the orbit of a body in relation to the primary: *apolune*. Compare with **PERI-**. ▷from Greek *apo* 'from, away, quite, un-.'

Apoc. ▸*abbr.* ■ Apocalypse. ■ Apocrypha. ■ Apocryphal.

a·poc·a·lypse /əˈpäkəˌlips/ ▸*n.* (often **the Apocalypse**) the complete final destruction of the world, as described in the biblical book of Revelation. ■ an event involving destruction or damage on an

Pronunciation Key ə *ago*; ər *over*; ˈə or ˌə *up*; ˈər or ˌər *fur*; a *hat*; ā *rate*; ä *car*; cн *chew*; e *let*; ē *see*; e(ə)r *air*; i *fit*; ī *by*; i(ə)r *ear*; nɢ *sing*; ō *go*; ô *for*; oi *boy*; o͝o *good*; o͞o *goo*; ou *out*; sн *she*; тн *thin*; <u>TH</u> *then*; (h)w *why*; zн *vision*

A

awesome or catastrophic scale: *a stock market apocalypse | an era of ecological apocalypse.* ■ (**the Apocalypse**) (esp. in the Vulgate Bible) the book of Revelation. ▷Old English, via Old French and ecclesiastical Latin from Greek *apokalupsis*, from *apokaluptein* 'uncover, reveal,' from *apo-* 'un-' + *kaluptein* 'to cover.'

a·poc·a·lyp·tic /ə,päkə'liptik/ ▶*adj.* describing or prophesying the complete destruction of the world: *the apocalyptic visions of ecologists.* ■ resembling the end of the world; momentous or catastrophic: *the struggle between the two countries is assuming apocalyptic proportions.* ■ of or resembling the biblical Apocalypse: *apocalyptic imagery.* ▷early 17th cent. (as a noun denoting the writer of the Apocalypse, St. John): from Greek *apokaluptikos*, from *apokaluptein* 'uncover' (see **APOCALYPSE**). **—a·poc·a·lyp·ti·cal·ly** /-ik(ə)lē/ *adv.*

ap·o·car·pous /,apə'kärpəs/ ▶*adj. Botany* (of a flower, fruit, or ovary) having distinct carpels that are not joined together. The opposite of **SYNCARPOUS**. ▷mid 19th cent.: from **APO-** + Greek *karpos* 'fruit' + **-OUS**.

ap·o·chro·mat /,apə'krōmat/ ▶*n. Physics* a lens or lens system that reduces spherical and chromatic aberration. ▷early 20th cent.: from **APO-** + **CHROMATIC**. **—ap·o·chro·mat·ic** /-krō'matik/ *adj.*

a·poc·o·pe /ə'päkəpē/ ▶*n. Linguistics* the loss of a sound or sounds at the end of a word, e.g., in the derivation of *curio* from *curiosity*. ▷mid 16th cent.: from late Latin, from Greek *apokoptein* 'cut off,' from *apo-* 'from' + *koptein* 'to cut.'

Apocr. ▶*abbr.* Apocrypha.

ap·o·crine /'apəkrin; -,krin; -,krēn/ ▶*adj. Physiology* relating to or denoting multicellular glands that release some of their cytoplasm in their secretions, esp. the sweat glands associated with hair follicles in the armpits and pubic regions. Compare with **ECCRINE**. ▷early 20th cent.: from **APO-** + Greek *krinein* 'to separate.'

A·poc·ry·pha /ə'päkrəfə/ ▶*plural n.* [treated as *sing.* or *pl.*] biblical or related writings not forming part of the accepted canon of Scripture. ■ (**apocrypha**) writings or reports not considered genuine. ▷late Middle English: from ecclesiastical Latin *apocrypha (scripta)* 'hidden (writings),' from Greek *apokruphos*, from *apokruptein* 'hide away.'

a·poc·ry·phal /ə'päkrəfəl/ ▶*adj.* (of a story or statement) of doubtful authenticity, although widely circulated as being true: *an apocryphal story about a former president.* See note at **SPURIOUS**. ■ (also **Apocryphal**) of or belonging to the Apocrypha: *the Apocryphal Gospel of Thomas.*

ap·o·dal /ā'pōdl/ ▶*adj. Zoology* without feet or having undeveloped feet. ■ (of fish) without ventral fins. ▷early 19th cent.: from Greek *apous, apod-* 'footless' (from *a-* 'without' + *pous, pod-* 'foot') + **-OUS**.

ap·o·dic·tic /,apə'diktik/ (also **ap·o·deic·tic** /-'dīktik/) ▶*adj. formal* clearly established or beyond dispute. ▷mid 17th cent.: via Latin from Greek *apodeiktikos*, from *apodeiknunai* 'show off, demonstrate.'

a·pod·o·sis /ə'pädəsis/ ▶*n.* (*pl.* **-ses** /-,sēz/) *Grammar* the main (consequent) clause of a conditional sentence (e.g., *I would agree* in *if you asked me I would agree*). Often contrasted with **PROTASIS**. ▷early 17th cent.: via late Latin from Greek, from *apodidonai* 'give back.'

ap·o·dous /'apədəs/ ▶*adj. Zoology* without feet or having only rudimentary feet.

ap·o·gee /'apəjē/ ▶*n. Astronomy* the point in the orbit of the moon or a satellite at which it is furthest from the earth. The opposite of **PERIGEE**. ■ *figurative* the highest point in the development of something; the climax or culmination of something: *the White House is considered **the apogee of** American achievement.* ▷late 16th cent.: from French *apogée* or modern Latin *apogaeum*, from Greek *apogaion (diastēma)* '(distance) away from earth,' from *apo* 'from' + *gaia, gē* 'earth.'

a·po·lar /ā'pōlər/ ▶*adj. chiefly Biochemistry* having no electrical polarity.

a·po·lit·i·cal /,āpə'litikəl/ ▶*adj.* not interested or involved in politics: *a former apolitical housewife.*

A·pol·li·naire /ə,pälə'ne(ə)r/, Guillaume (1880–1918), French poet; pseudonym of *Wilhelm Apollinaris de Kostrowitzki*. He coined the term *surrealist* and was acknowledged by the surrealist poets as their precursor. Notable works: *Les Alcools* (1913) and *Calligrammes* (1918).

A·pol·li·nar·is /ə,pälə'ne(ə)ris/ ■ (*c.*310–*c.*390), bishop of Laodicea in Asia Minor. He upheld the heretical doctrine that Jesus Christ had a human body and soul but no human spirit, this being replaced by the divine Logos. **—A·pol·li·nar·i·an** *adj.* & *n.*■

A·pol·lo /ə'pälō/ **1** *Greek Mythology* a god, son of Zeus and Leto and brother of Artemis. He is associated with music, poetic inspiration, archery, prophecy, medicine, pastoral life, and in later poetry with the sun; the sanctuary at Delphi was dedicated to him. **2** the American space program for landing astronauts on the moon. *Apollo 8* was the first mission to orbit the moon (1968), *Apollo 11* was the first to land astronauts (July 20, 1969), and five further landings took place up to 1972.

Ap·ol·lo·ni·an /,apə'lōnēən/ ▶*adj.* **1** *Greek Mythology* of or relating to the god Apollo. **2** of or relating to the rational, ordered, and self-disciplined aspects of human nature: *the struggle between cold Apollonian categorization and Dionysiac lust and chaos.* Compare with **DIONYSIAN**.

Ap·ol·lo·ni·us[1] /,apə'lōnēəs/ (*c.*260–190 BC), Greek mathematician; known as **Apollonius of Perga**. He examined and redefined the various conic sections and was the first to use the terms *ellipse, parabola,* and *hyperbola* for these classes of curve.

Ap·ol·lo·ni·us[2] (3rd century BC), Greek poet and grammarian; known as **Apollonius of Rhodes**. He wrote *Argonautica*, an epic poem in Homeric style.

A·pol·lyon /ə'pälyən/ a name for the Devil (Rev. 9:11). ▷from late Latin (Vulgate), from Greek *Apolluōn* 'destroyer' (translating **ABADDON**), from *apollunai*, from *apo-* 'quite' + *ollunai* 'destroy.'

a·pol·o·get·ic /ə,pälə'jetik/ ▶*adj.* regretfully acknowledging or excusing an offense or failure: *she was very apologetic about the whole incident.* ■ of the nature of a formal defense or justification of something such as a theory or religious doctrine: *the apologetic proposition that production for profit is the same thing as production for need.*
▶*n.* a reasoned argument or writing in justification of something, typically a theory or religious doctrine: *the unconvincing apologetic of modern Muslim writers.* ▷late Middle English (as a noun denoting a formal defense or justification): from French *apologétique* or late Latin *apologeticus*, from Greek *apologētikos*, from *apologeisthai* 'speak in one's own defense,' from *apologia* (see **APOLOGY**). The current sense dates from the mid 19th cent. **—a·pol·o·get·i·cal·ly** /-ik(ə)lē/ *adv.*

a·pol·o·get·ics /ə,pälə'jetiks/ ▶*plural n.* [treated as *sing.* or *pl.*] reasoned arguments or writings in justification of something, typically a theory or religious doctrine. ▷mid 18th cent.: from **APOLOGETIC**.

ap·o·lo·gi·a /,apə'lōj(ē)ə/ ▶*n.* a formal written defense of one's opinions or conduct: *an apologia for book banning.* ▷late 18th cent.: from Latin (see **APOLOGY**).

a·pol·o·gist /ə'päləjist/ ▶*n.* a person who offers an argument in defense of something controversial: *an enthusiastic **apologist for** fascism in the 1920s.* ▷mid 17th cent.: from French *apologiste*, from Greek *apologizesthai* 'give an account' (see **APOLOGIZE**).

a·pol·o·gize /ə'pälə,jīz/ ▶*v.* [*intrans.*] express regret for something that one has done wrong: *I must **apologize for** disturbing you like this | we **apologize to** him for our error.* ▷late 16th cent. (in the sense 'make a defensive argument, offer a justification'): from Greek *apologizesthai* 'give an account,' from *apologos* (see **APOLOGUE**). In English the verb has always been used as if it were a direct derivative of *apology*.

ap·o·logue /'apə,lôg; -,läg/ ▶*n.* a moral fable, esp. one with animals as characters. ▷mid 16th cent.: from French, via Latin from Greek *apologos* 'story.'

a·pol·o·gy /ə'päləjē/ ▶*n.* (*pl.* **-gies**) **1** a regretful acknowledgment of an offense or failure: *we owe you an apology | my apologies for the delay | I make no apologies for supporting that policy.* ■ a formal, public statement of regret, such as one issued by a newspaper, government, or other organization: *the Prime Minister demanded an apology from the ambassador.* ■ (**apologies**) used to express formally one's regret at being unable to attend a meeting or social function: ***apologies for absence** were received from Miss Brown.* **2** (**an apology for**) a very poor or inadequate example of: *we were shown into an apology for a bedroom.* **3** a reasoned argument or writing in justification of something, typically a theory or religious doctrine: *a specious apology for capitalism.* ▷mid 16th cent. (denoting a formal defense against an accusation): from French *apologie*, or via late Latin from Greek *apologia* 'a speech in one's own defense,' from *apo* 'away'+ *-logia* (see **-LOGY**).
▶*PHRASE* □ **with apologies to** used before the name of an author or artist to indicate that something is a parody or adaptation of their work: *here, with apologies to Rudyard Kipling, is a more apt version of "If."*

ap·o·lune /'apə,loon/ ▶*n.* the point at which a spacecraft in lunar orbit is furthest from the moon. The opposite of **PERILUNE**. ▷1960s: from **APO-** + Latin *luna* 'moon,' on the pattern of *apogee*.

ap·o·mict /'apə,mikt/ ▶*n. Botany* a plant that reproduces by apomixis.

ap·o·mix·is /,apə'miksis/ ▶*n. Botany* asexual reproduction in plants, in particular agamospermy. Often contrasted with **AMPHIMIXIS**. ▷early 20th cent.: from **APO-** + Greek *mixis* 'mingling.' **—ap·o·mic·tic** /-'miktik/ *adj.*

ap·o·mor·phine /,apə'môrfēn; -fin/ ▶*n. Medicine* a white crystalline compound used as an emetic and in the treatment of Parkinson's disease. • A morphine derivative; chem. formula: $C_{17}H_{17}NO_2$.

ap·o·neu·ro·sis /,apən(y)oo'rōsis/ ▶*n.* (*pl.* **-ses** /-,sēz/) *Anatomy* a sheet of pearly-white fibrous tissue that takes the place of a tendon in sheetlike muscles having a wide area of attachment. ▷late 17th cent.: modern Latin, from Greek *aponeurōsis*, from *apo* 'off, away' + *neuron* 'sinew' + **-OSIS**. **—ap·o·neu·rot·ic** /-'rätik/ *adj.*

ap·o·phat·ic /,apə'fatik/ ▶*adj. Theology* (of knowledge of God) obtained through negation. The opposite of **CATAPHATIC**. ▷mid 19th cent.: from Greek *apophatikos* 'negative,' from *apophasis* 'denial,' from *apo-* 'other than' + *phanai* 'speak.' **—ap·o·pha·ti·cal·ly** /-ik(ə)lē/ *adv.* **—ap·o·pha·ti·cism** /-,sizəm/ *n.*

ap·o·phthegm ▶*n.* British spelling of **APOTHEGM**.

a·poph·yl·lite /ə'päfə,līt; ,apə'filīt/ ▶*n.* a mineral occurring typically as white glassy prisms, usually as a secondary mineral in volcanic rocks. It is a hydrated silicate and fluoride of calcium and potassium. ▷early 19th cent.: from **APO-** + Greek *phullon* 'leaf' + **-ITE**[1].

a·poph·y·sis /ə'päfəsis/ ▶*n.* (*pl.* **-ses** /-,sēz/) *Zoology & Anatomy* a natural protuberance from a bone, or inside the shell or exoskeleton of a sea urchin or insect, for the attachment of muscles. ■ *Botany* a swelling at the base of the sporangium in some mosses. ■ *Geology* a small offshoot extending from an igneous intrusion into the surrounding rock. ▷late 16th cent.: modern Latin, from Greek *apophusis* 'offshoot,' from *apo-* 'from, away' + *phusis* 'growth.' **—a·po·phys·e·al** /ə,päfə'sēəl/ *adj.*

ap·o·plec·tic /,apə'plektik/ ▶*adj. informal* overcome with anger; extremely indignant: *Mark was **apoplectic with** rage at the decision.* ■ *dated* relating to or denoting apoplexy (stroke): *an apoplectic attack.* ▷early 17th cent.: from French *apoplectique* or late Latin *apoplecticus*, from Greek *apoplēktikos*, from *apoplēssein* 'disable by a stroke' (see **APOPLEXY**). **—ap·o·plec·ti·cal·ly** /-ik(ə)lē/ *adv.*

ap·o·plex·y /'apə,pleksē/ ▶*n.* (*pl.* **-plex·ies**) *dated* unconsciousness or incapacity resulting from a cerebral hemorrhage or stroke. ■ *informal* incapacity or speechlessness caused by extreme anger: *this drives the social engineers of government into apoplexy.* ▷late Middle English: from Old French *apoplexie*, from late Latin *apoplexia*, from Greek *apoplēxia*, from *apoplēssein* 'disable by a stroke.'

ap·o·pro·tein /,apə'prō,tēn; -'prōtēən/ ▶*n. Biochemistry* a protein that together with a prosthetic group forms a particular biochemical molecule such as a hormone or enzyme.

ap·op·to·sis /,apə(p)'tōsis/ ▶*n. Physiology* the death of cells that occurs as a normal and controlled part of an organism's growth or development. Also called **PROGRAMMED CELL DEATH**. ▷1970s: from Greek *apoptōsis* 'falling off,' from *apo* 'from' + *ptōsis* 'falling, a fall.' **—ap·op·tot·ic** /-'tätik/ *adj.*

a·po·ri·a /ə'pôrēə/ ▶*n.* an irresolvable internal contradiction or logical disjunction in a text, argument, or theory: *the celebrated aporia whereby a Cretan declares all Cretans to be liars.* ■ *Rhetoric* the expression of doubt. ▷mid 16th cent.: via late Latin from Greek, from *aporos* 'impassable,' from *a-* 'without' + *poros* 'passage.'

ap·o·se·mat·ic /,apəsi'matik/ ▶*adj. Zoology* (of coloration or markings) serving to warn or repel predators. ■ (of an animal) having such coloration or markings. **—ap·o·se·ma·tism** /,apə'sēmə,tizəm/ *n.*

ap·o·si·o·pe·sis /,apə,sīə'pēsis/ ▶*n.* (*pl.* **-ses** /-sēz/) *Rhetoric* the device of suddenly breaking off in speech. ▷late 16th cent.: via Latin from Greek *aposiōpēsis*, from *aposiōpan* 'be silent.' **—ap·o·si·o·pet·ic** /-'petik/ *adj.*

a·pos·ta·sy /ə'pästəsē/ ▶*n.* the abandonment or renunciation of a religious or political belief. ▷Middle English: from ecclesiastical Latin *apostasia*, from a late Greek alteration of Greek *apostasis* 'defection.'

a·pos·tate /ə'päs,tāt; -tit/ ▶*n.* a person who renounces a religious or political belief or principle.

▸*adj.* abandoning a religious or political belief or principle. ▷Middle English: from ecclesiastical Latin *apostata*, from Greek *apostatēs* 'apostate, runaway slave.' —**ap·o·stat·i·cal** /ˌapəˈstatikəl/ *adj.*

a·pos·ta·tize /əˈpästəˌtīz/ ▸*v.* [*intrans.*] renounce a religious or political belief or principle. ▷mid 16th cent.: from medieval Latin *apostatizare*, from *apostata* (see APOSTATE).

a pos·te·ri·o·ri /ˈä päˌsti(ə)rēˈôrˌē; -ˈôrˌī/ ▸*adj.* relating to or denoting reasoning or knowledge that proceeds from observations or experiences to the deduction of probable causes. Compare with A PRIORI. ■ [*sentence adverb*] (loosely) of the nature of an afterthought or subsequent rationalization.
▸*adv.* in a way based on reasoning from known facts or past events rather than by making assumptions or predictions. ■ (loosely) with hindsight; as an afterthought. ▷early 17th cent.: Latin, 'from what comes after.'

a·pos·tle /əˈpäsəl/ ▸*n.* (often **Apostle**) each of the twelve chief disciples of Jesus Christ. ■ any important early Christian teacher, esp. St. Paul. ■ (**Apostle of**) the first successful Christian missionary in a country or to a people: *Kiril and Metodije, the Apostles of the Slavs.* ■ a vigorous and pioneering advocate or supporter of a particular policy, idea, or cause: *Leo Buscaglia, leading apostle of love and okayness.* ■ a messenger or representative: *apostles of doom and defeat.* ■ one of the twelve administrative officers of the Mormon church.

The twelve Apostles were Peter, Andrew, James, John, Philip, Bartholomew, Thomas, Matthew, James (the Less), Judas (or Thaddaeus), Simon, and Judas Iscariot. After the suicide of Judas Iscariot his place was taken by Matthias.

▷Old English *apostol*, via ecclesiastical Latin from Greek *apostolos* 'messenger,' from *apostellein* 'send forth.' —**a·pos·tle·ship** /-ˌSHip/ *n.*

A·pos·tle Is·lands an island group in northern Wisconsin, in Lake Superior.

A·pos·tles' Creed a statement of Christian belief used in the Western Church, dating from the 4th century and traditionally ascribed to the twelve Apostles.

A·pos·tle spoon (also **Apostle teaspoon**) ▸*n.* a teaspoon with the figure of an Apostle or saint on the handle.

a·pos·to·late /əˈpästəˌlāt; -lit/ ▸*n.* (chiefly in Roman Catholic contexts) the position or authority of an Apostle or a religious leader. ■ a group of Apostles or religious leaders. ■ religious or evangelistic activity or works: *our apostolate of hospitality to the elderly.* ▷late Middle English: from ecclesiastical Latin *apostolatus*, from *apostulus* (see APOSTLE).

ap·os·tol·ic /ˌapəˈstälik/ ▸*adj.* *Christian Church* of or relating to the Apostles: *apostolic writings | a simple apostolic life.* ■ of or relating to the pope, esp. when he is regarded as the successor to St. Peter: *an apostolic nuncio.* ▷Middle English: from French *apostolique* or ecclesiastical Latin *apostolicus*, from Greek *apostolikos*, from *apostolos* (see APOSTLE).

Ap·os·tol·ic Fa·thers ▸*plural n.* the Christian leaders immediately succeeding the Apostles.

ap·os·tol·ic suc·ces·sion ▸*n.* (in Christian thought) the uninterrupted transmission of spiritual authority from the Apostles through successive popes and bishops, taught by the Roman Catholic Church but denied by most Protestants.

a·pos·tro·phe[1] /əˈpästrəfē/ ▸*n.* a punctuation mark (') used to indicate either possession e.g., *Harry's book; boys's coats*) or the omission of letters or numbers (e.g., *can't; he's; class of '99*). ▷mid 16th cent. (denoting the omission of one or more letters): via late Latin, from Greek *apostrophos* 'accent of elision,' from *apostrephein* 'turn away,' from *apo* 'from' + *strephein* 'to turn.'

USAGE The apostrophe is used to indicate missing letters or numbers (*bo'sun; the summer of '63*), to form some possessives (see **usage** at POSSESSIVE), and to form some plurals (see **usage** at PLURAL.)

a·pos·tro·phe[2] ▸*n.* *Rhetoric* an exclamatory passage in a speech or poem addressed to a person (typically one who is dead or absent) or thing (typically one that is personified). ▷mid 16th cent.: via Latin from Greek *apostrophē* 'turning away,' from *apostrephein* 'turn away' (see APOSTROPHE[1]).

a·pos·tro·phize /əˈpästrəˌfīz/ ▸*v.* [*trans.*] **1** *Rhetoric* address an exclamatory passage in a speech or poem to (someone or something). **2** punctuate (a word) with an apostrophe.

a·poth·e·car·ies' meas·ure /əˈpäTHiˌkerēz/ (also **apothecaries' weight**) ▸*n.* *historical* systems of units formerly used in pharmacy for liquid volume (or weight). They were based respectively on the fluid ounce (= 8 drachms or 480 minims) and the ounce troy (= 8 drams or 24 scruples or 480 grains).

a·poth·e·car·y /əˈpäTHiˌkerē/ ▸*n.* (*pl.* **-car·ies**) *archaic* a person who prepared and sold medicines and drugs. ▷late Middle English: via Old French from late Latin *apothecarius*, from Latin *apotheca*, from Greek *apothēkē* 'storehouse.'

ap·o·thegm /ˈapəˌTHem/ (*Brit.* **ap·oph·thegm** /ˈapəˌTHem/) ▸*n.* a concise saying or maxim; an aphorism. ▷mid 16th cent.: from French *apophthegme* or modern Latin *apothegma*, from Greek, from *apophthengesthai* 'speak out.' —**ap·o·theg·mat·ic** /ˌapəTHegˈmatik/ *adj.*

ap·o·them /ˈapəˌTHem/ ▸*n.* *Geometry* a line from the center of a regular polygon at right angles to any of its sides. ▷late 19th cent.: from Greek *apotithenai* 'put aside, deposit,' from *apo* 'away' + *tithenai* 'to place.'

a·poth·e·o·sis /əˌpäTHēˈōsis; ˌapəˈTHēəsis/ ▸*n.* (*pl.* **-ses** /-ˌsēz/) [usu. in *sing.*] the highest point in the development of something; culmination or climax: *his appearance as Hamlet was the apotheosis of his career.* ■ the elevation of someone to divine status; deification. ▷late 16th cent.: via ecclesiastical Latin from Greek *apotheōsis*, from *apotheoun* 'make a god of,' from *apo* 'from' + *theos* 'god.'

a·poth·e·o·size /əˈpäTHēəˌsīz; ˌapəˈTHēə-/ ▸*v.* [*trans.*] elevate to, or as if to, the rank of a god; idolize.

ap·o·tro·pa·ic /ˌapətrəˈpā-ik/ ▸*adj.* supposedly having the power to avert evil influences or bad luck: *apotropaic statues.* ▷late 19th cent.: from Greek *apotropaios* 'averting evil,' from *apotrepein* 'turn away or from' + -IC. —**ap·o·tro·pa·i·cal·ly** /-ik(ə)lē/ *adv.*

app /ap/ ▸*n.* *Computing* short for APPLICATION (sense 5).

Ap·pa·la·chi·a /ˌapəˈlāCH(ē)ə; -lāCH-; -ˈlāSH-/ a term for areas in the Appalachian Mountains of the eastern U.S. that exhibit longterm poverty and distinctive folkways. —**Ap·pa·la·chi·an** *adj.*

Ap·pa·la·chi·an dul·ci·mer ▸*n.* see DULCIMER.

Ap·pa·la·chi·an Moun·tains /ˌapəˈlāCH(ē)ən; -ˈlaCH-; -ˈlāSH-/ (also **the Ap·pa·la·chi·ans**) a mountain system in eastern North America that stretches from Quebec and Maine in the north to Georgia and Alabama in the south. Its highest peak, Mount Mitchell in North Carolina, rises to 6,684 feet (2,037 m).

Ap·pa·la·chi·an Trail an approximately 2,000-mi. (3,200-km.) footpath through the Appalachian Mountains from Mount Katahdin in Maine to Springer Mountain in Georgia.

ap·pall /əˈpôl/ ▸*v.* (**-palled**, **-pall·ing**) [*trans.*] (usu. **be appalled**) greatly dismay or horrify: *bankers are **appalled at** the economic incompetence of some officials* | [as *adj.*] (**appalled**) *Alison looked at me, appalled.* ▷Middle English: from Old French *apalir* 'grow pale,' from *a-* (from Latin *ad* 'to, at') + *palir* 'to pale.' The original sense was 'grow pale,' later 'make pale,' hence 'dismay, horrify' (late Middle English).

ap·pall·ing /əˈpôliNG/ ▸*adj.* *informal* awful; terrible: *his conduct was appalling.* —**ap·pall·ing·ly** *adv.*

Ap·pa·loo·sa /ˌapəˈlo͞osə/ ▸*n.* a horse of a North American breed having dark spots on a light background. ▷1920s: from *Opelousas* in Louisiana, or *Palouse*, a river in Idaho.

ap·pa·nage /ˈapənij/ (also **ap·a·nage**) ▸*n.* *archaic* a gift of land, an official position, or money given to the younger children of kings and princes to provide for their maintenance. ■ a necessary accompaniment: *there is a tendency to make microbiology an **apanage of** organic chemistry.* ▷early 17th cent.: from French, based on medieval Latin *appanare* 'provide with the means of subsistence,' from *ad-* 'to' + *panis* 'bread.'

ap·pa·rat /ˈäpəˌrät; ˌapə-/ ▸*n.* *chiefly historical* the administrative system of a communist party, typically in a communist country. ▷1940s: Russian, from German, literally 'apparatus.'

ap·pa·rat·chik /ˌäpəˈräCHik/ ▸*n.* (*pl.* **-chiks** or **-chi·ki** /-CHiˌkē/) *derogatory* or *humorous* an official in a large organization, typically a political one: *Tory apparatchiks.* ■ *chiefly historical* a member of a communist party apparat. ▷1940s: from Russian, from *apparat* (see APPARAT).

ap·pa·rat·us /ˌapəˈratəs; -ˈrātəs/ ▸*n.* (*pl.* **-us·es**) **1** the equipment needed for a particular activity or purpose: *laboratory apparatus.* See note at TOOL. ■ the organs used to perform a particular bodily function: *the specialized male and female sexual apparatus.* **2** a complex structure within an organization or system: *the apparatus of government.* **3** (also **critical apparatus** or **apparatus criticus**) a collection of notes, variant readings, and other matter accompanying a printed text. ▷early 17th cent.: from Latin, from *apparare* 'make ready for,' from *ad-* 'toward' + *parare* 'make ready.'

ap·par·el /əˈparəl/ ▸*n.* *formal* clothing. ■ (**apparels**) embroidered ornamentation on ecclesiastical vestments.
▸*v.* (**-eled**, **-el·ing**; *Brit.* **-elled**, **-el·ling**) [*trans.*] *archaic* clothe (someone): *all the vestments in which they used to apparel their Deities.* ▷Middle English (as a verb in the sense 'make ready or fit'; as a noun 'furnishings, equipment'): from Old French *apareillier*, based on Latin *ad-* 'to' (expressing change) + *par* 'equal.'

ap·par·ent /əˈparənt; əˈpe(ə)r-/ ▸*adj.* clearly visible or understood; obvious: [with *clause*] *it became apparent that he was talented | for no apparent reason she laughed.* ■ seeming real or true, but not necessarily so: *his apparent lack of concern.* See note at OSTENSIBLE. ▷late Middle English: from Old French *aparant*, from Latin *apparent-* 'appearing,' from the verb *apparere* (see APPEAR).

ap·par·ent ho·ri·zon ▸*n.* see HORIZON (sense 1).

ap·par·ent·ly /əˈparəntlē; əˈpe(ə)r-/ ▸*adv.* [*sentence adverb*] as far as one knows or can see: *the child nodded, apparently content with the promise.* ■ used by speakers or writers to avoid committing themselves to the truth of what they are saying: *foreign ministers met but apparently failed to make progress.*

ap·par·ent mag·ni·tude ▸*n.* *Astronomy* the magnitude of a celestial object as it is actually measured from the earth. Compare with ABSOLUTE MAGNITUDE.

ap·par·ent so·lar time ▸*n.* *Astronomy* time as calculated by the motion of the apparent (true) sun. The time indicated by a sundial corresponds to apparent solar time. Compare with MEAN SOLAR TIME.

ap·par·ent time ▸*n.* another term for MEAN SOLAR TIME.

ap·pa·ri·tion /ˌapəˈriSHən/ ▸*n.* a ghost or ghostlike image of a person. ■ the appearance of something remarkable or unexpected, typically an image of this type: *twentieth-century apparitions of the Virgin.* ▷late Middle English (in the sense 'the action of appearing'): from Latin *apparitio(n-)* 'attendance,' from the verb *apparere* (see APPEAR). —**ap·pa·ri·tion·al** /-SHənl/ *adj.*

ap·peal /əˈpēl/ ▸*v.* [*intrans.*] **1** make a serious or urgent request, typically to the public: *police are **appealing for** information about the incident | she **appealed to** Germany for political asylum.* **2** *Law* apply to a higher court for a reversal of the decision of a lower court: *he said he would **appeal against** the conviction* | [*trans.*] *they have 48 hours to appeal the decision.* ■ *Baseball* (of the defensive team) call on the umpire to rule a strike or out on a completed play. ■ (**appeal to**) address oneself to (a principle or quality in someone) in anticipation of a favorable response: *I appealed to his sense of justice.* **3** be attractive or interesting: *the range of topics will **appeal to** youngsters.*
▸*n.* **1** a serious or urgent request, typically one made to the public: *his mother made an appeal for for the return of the ring.* ■ an attempt to obtain financial support: *a public appeal to raise $120,000.* ■ entreaty: *a look of appeal on his face.* **2** *Law* an application to a higher court for a decision to be reversed: *he has 28 days in which to **lodge an appeal** | the right of appeal.* ■ an address to a principle or quality in anticipation of a favorable response: *an appeal to black pride.* **3** the quality of being attractive or interesting: *the popular appeal of football.* ▷Middle English (in legal contexts): from Old French *apel* (noun), *apeler* (verb), from Latin *appellare* 'to address,' based on *ad-* 'to' + *pellere* 'to drive.' —**ap·peal·er** *n.*

ap·peal·ing /əˈpēliNG/ ▸*adj.* **1** attractive or interesting: *the rural life is somehow more appealing | an appealing young woman.* **2** (of an expression or tone of voice) showing that one wants help or sympathy: *an appealing look.* —**ap·peal·ing·ly** *adv.*

ap·peals court ▸*n.* a court that hears appeals from a lower court.

ap·pear /əˈpi(ə)r/ ▸*v.* [*intrans.*] **1** come into sight; become visible or noticeable, typically without visible agent or apparent cause: *smoke appeared on the horizon.* ■ come into existence or use: *the major life forms appeared on earth.* ■ (of a book) be published: *the paperback edition didn't appear for another two years.*

Pronunciation Key ə *ago*; ər *over*; ˈə or ˌə *up*; ˈər or ˌər *fur*; a *hat*; ā *rate*; ä *car*; CH *chew*; e *let*; ē *see*; e(ə)r *air*; i *fit*; ī *by*; i(ə)r *ear*; NG *sing*; ō *go*; ô *for*; oi *boy*; o͝o *good*; o͞o *goo*; ou *out*; SH *she*; TH *thin*; T͟H *then*; (h)w *why*; ZH *vision*

■ feature or be shown: *the symbol **appears in** many paintings of the period.* ■ perform publicly in a movie, play, etc.: *he **appeared on** Broadway.* ■ (of an accused person, witness, or lawyer) make an official appearance in a court of law: *he **appeared on** six charges of theft.* ■ *informal* arrive at a place: *by ten o'clock Bill still hadn't appeared.* **2** seem; give the impression of being: [with *infinitive*] *she appeared not to know what was happening* | [with *clause*] ***it appears** unlikely that interest rates will fall* | [with *complement*] *he appeared unaware of the rebuke.* ▷Middle English: from Old French *apareir*, from Latin *apparere*, from *ad-* 'toward' + *parere* 'come into view.'

ap·pear·ance /ə'pi(ə)rəns/ ▶*n.* **1** the way that someone or something looks: *I like the appearance of stripped antique pine* | *they are similar **in appearance**.* ■ an impression given by someone or something, although this may be misleading: *she read it with every appearance of interest.* **2** an act of performing or participating in a public event: *he is well-known for his television appearances.* **3** [usu. in *sing.*] an act of becoming visible or noticeable; an arrival: *the sudden appearance of her daughter startled her.* ■ a process of coming into existence or use: *the appearance of the railroad.* ▷late Middle English: from Old French *aparance, aparence*, from late Latin *apparentia*, from Latin *apparere* (see APPEAR).
▶*PHRASES* □ **keep up appearances** maintain an impression of wealth or well-being, typically to hide the true situation. □ **make** (or **put in**) **an appearance** attend an event briefly, typically out of courtesy. □ **to** (or **by**) **all appearances** as far as can be seen: *to all appearances, it had been a normal day.*

ap·pear·ance mon·ey ▶*n.* money paid to secure the appearance of a celebrity, typically a sports figure, at a particular event.

ap·pease /ə'pēz/ ▶*v.* [*trans.*] **1** pacify or placate (someone) by acceding to their demands: *amendments have been added to appease local pressure groups.* See note at PACIFY. **2** relieve or satisfy (a demand or a feeling): *we give to charity because it appeases our guilt.* ▷Middle English: from Old French *apaisier*, from *a-* (from Latin *ad* 'to, at') + *pais* 'peace.' **—ap·pease·ment** *n.* **—ap·peas·er** *n.*

Ap·pel /'äpəl/, Karel (1921–), Dutch painter, sculptor, and graphic artist.

ap·pel·lant /ə'pelənt/ ▶*n.* *Law* a person who applies to a higher court for a reversal of the decision of a lower court. ▷late Middle English: from French *apelant*, literally 'appealing,' from the verb *apeler* (see APPEAL).

ap·pel·late /ə'pelit/ ▶*adj.* [*attrib.*] *Law* (typically of a court) concerned with or dealing with applications for decisions to be reversed. ▷late Middle English (originally in the sense 'appealed against, accused'): from Latin *appellatus* 'appealed against,' from the verb *appellare* (see APPEAL). The current sense dates from the mid 18th cent.

ap·pel·la·tion[1] /,apə'lāsʜən/ ▶*n.* *formal* a name or title: *the city fully justifies its appellation "the Pearl of the Orient."* ■ the action of giving a name to a person or thing. ▷late Middle English: via Old French from Latin *appellatio(n-)*, from the verb *appellare* (see APPEAL).

ap·pel·la·tion[2] /äpelä'syôɴ/ ▶*n.* an appellation contrôlée. ■ a wine bearing such a guarantee. ■ the district in which such wine is produced. ▷late 20th cent.: abbreviation of *appellation (d'origine) contrôlée.*

ap·pel·la·tion con·trô·lée /äpelä'syôɴ ,kôntrô'lā/ (also **ap·pel·la·tion d'ori·gi·ne con·trô·lée** /dôrē'zʜēn/) ▶*n.* a description awarded to French wine guaranteeing that it was produced in the region specified, using vines and production methods that satisfy the regulating body. ▷mid 20th cent.: French, literally 'controlled appellation.'

ap·pel·la·tive /ə'pelətiv/ ▶*adj.* *formal* relating to or denoting the giving of a name.
▶*n.* *Grammar* a common noun, such as "doctor," "mother," or "sir," used as a vocative. ▷late Middle English: from late Latin *appellativus*, from *appellat-* 'addressed,' from the verb *appellare* (see APPEAL).

ap·pel·lee /,apə'lē/ ▶*n.* *Law* the respondent in a case appealed to a higher court. ▷mid 16th cent.: from French *appelé*, past participle of *appeler* 'call,' from Latin *appellare* 'to address' (see APPEAL).

ap·pend /ə'pend/ ▶*v.* [*trans.*] add (something) as an attachment or supplement: *the results of the survey are **appended to** this chapter.* ▷late Middle English: from Latin *appendere* 'hang on,' from *ad-* 'to' + *pendere* 'hang.'

ap·pend·age /ə'pendij/ ▶*n.* (often with negative or pejorative connations) a thing that is added or attached to something larger or more important: *they treat Scotland as a mere appendage of England.* ■ *Biology* a projecting part of an invertebrate or other living organism, with a distinct appearance or function: *many species have specialized clutching appendages.*

ap·pend·ant /ə'pendənt/ *formal archaic* ▶*adj.* attached or added, typically in a subordinate capacity.
▶*n.* a subordinate person or thing. ▷late Middle English (in legal contexts): from Old French *apendant*, from *apendre* 'depend on, belong to,' from Latin *appendere* (see APPEND).

ap·pen·dec·to·my /,apən'dektəmē/ (*Brit.* also **ap·pen·di·cec·to·my** /ə,pendə'sektəmē/) ▶*n.* (*pl.* **-mies**) a surgical operation to remove the appendix.

ap·pen·di·ci·tis /ə,pendə'sītis/ ▶*n.* a serious medical condition in which the appendix becomes inflamed and painful.

ap·pen·dic·u·lar /apən'dikyələr/ ▶*adj.* *technical* relating to or denoting an appendage or appendages. ■ *Anatomy* of or relating to a limb or limbs: *the appendicular skeleton.* ▷mid 17th cent.: from Latin *appendicula* 'small appendage,' diminutive of *appendix*, + -AR[1].

ap·pen·dix /ə'pendiks/ ▶*n.* (*pl.* **-di·ces** /-di,sēz/; **-dix·es**) **1** *Anatomy* a tube-shaped sac attached to and opening into the lower end of the large intestine in humans and some other mammals. Also called VERMIFORM APPENDIX.

> In humans the appendix is small and has no known function, but in rabbits, hares, and some other herbivores it is involved in the digestion of cellulose.

2 a section or table of additional matter at the end of a book or document. ▷mid 16th cent. (sense 2): from Latin, from *appendere* 'hang upon' (see APPEND). Sense 1 dates from the early 17th cent.

ap·per·cep·tion /,apər'sepsʜən/ ▶*n.* *dated Psychology* the mental process by which a person makes sense of an idea by assimilating it to the body of ideas he or she already possesses. ■ fully conscious perception: *an immediate apperception of a unity lying beyond.* ▷mid 18th cent.: from French *aperception* or modern Latin *apperceptio(n-)*, from Latin *ad-* 'to' + *percipere* 'perceive.' **—ap·per·cep·tive** /-tiv/ *adj.*

ap·per·tain /,apər'tān/ ▶*v.* [*intrans.*] **1** (**appertain to**) relate to; concern: *the answers generally appertain to improvements in standards of service.* **2** be appropriate or applicable: *the institutional arrangements that appertain under the system.* ▷late Middle English: from Old French *apertenir*, from late Latin *appertinere*, from *ad-* 'to' + Latin *pertinere* 'to pertain.'

ap·pe·stat /'apə,stat/ ▶*n.* *Physiology* the region of the hypothalamus of the brain that is believed to control a person's appetite for food. ▷1950s: from APPETITE, probably on the pattern of *thermostat.*

ap·pe·ten·cy /'apitənsē/ ▶*n.* (*pl.* **-cies**) *archaic* a longing or desire. ■ a natural tendency or affinity. ▷early 17th cent.: from Latin *appetentia*, from *appetere* 'seek after' (see APPETITE).

ap·pe·tite /'api,tīt/ ▶*n.* [usu. in *sing.*] a natural desire to satisfy a bodily need, esp. for food: *he has a healthy appetite* | *they suffered from loss of appetite.* ■ a strong desire or liking for something: *an unquenchable appetite for life.* ▷Middle English: from Old French *apetit* (modern *appétit*), from Latin *appetitus* 'desire for,' from *appetere* 'seek after,' from *ad-* 'to' + *petere* 'seek.'

ap·pe·ti·tive /'api,tītiv/ ▶*adj.* characterized by a natural desire to satisfy bodily needs: *the appetitive behavior of animals.* ▷mid 16th cent.: from French *appétitif* or medieval Latin *appetitivus*, from *appetire* 'seek after' (see APPETITE). **—ap·pe·ti·tive·ness** *n.* **ap·pe·ti·tive·ly** *adv.*

ap·pe·tiz·er /'api,tīzər/ ▶*n.* a small dish of food or a drink taken before a meal or the main course of a meal to stimulate one's appetite.

ap·pe·tiz·ing /'api,tīzɪɴɢ/ (also **ap·pe·tis·ing**) ▶*adj.* stimulating one's appetite: *the appetizing aroma of sizzling bacon.* ▷mid 17th cent.: from French *appétissant*, irregular formation from *appétit* (see APPETITE). **—ap·pe·tiz·ing·ly** *adv.*

Ap·pi·an Way /'apēən/ in classical times, the principal road south from Rome, named after the censor Appius Claudius Caecus, who built the section to Capua in 312 BC; it was later extended to Brindisi. Latin name VIA APPIA.

ap·plaud /ə'plôd/ ▶*v.* [*intrans.*] show approval or praise by clapping: *the crowd whistled and applauded* | [*trans.*] *his speech was loudly applauded.* ■ [*trans.*] show strong approval of (a person or action); praise: *Jill applauded the decision.* ▷late 15th cent.: from Latin *applaudere*, from *ad-* 'to' + *plaudere* 'to clap,' reinforced by French *applaudir*.

ap·plause /ə'plôz/ ▶*n.* approval or praise expressed by clapping: *they **gave him a round of applause**.* ▷late Middle English: from medieval Latin *applausus*, from the verb *applaudere* (see APPLAUD).

ap·ple /'apəl/ ▶*n.* **1** the round fruit of a tree of the rose family, which typically has thin red or green skin and crisp flesh. Many varieties have been developed as dessert or cooking fruit or for making cider. ■ [with *adj.*] an unrelated fruit that resembles this in some way. See also CUSTARD APPLE, THORN APPLE. **2** (also **apple tree**) the tree bearing such fruit. • Genus *Malus*, family Rosaceae: numerous hybrids and cultivars. **3** (**the Apple**) short for the BIG APPLE. ▷Old English *æppel*, of Germanic origin; related to Dutch *appel* and German *Apfel*.
▶*PHRASES* □ **the apple never falls far from the tree** *proverb* family characteristics are usually inherited. □ **the apple of one's eye** a person of whom one is extremely fond and proud. [originally denoting the pupil of the eye, considered to be a globular solid body, extended as a symbol of something cherished.] □ **apples and oranges** (of two people or things) irreconcilably or fundamentally different. □ **a rotten** (or **bad**) **apple** *informal* a bad or corrupt person in a group, typically one whose behavior is likely to have a detrimental influence on his or her associates. [with reference to the effect that a rotten apple has on fruit with which it is in contact.] □ **upset the applecart** spoil a plan or disturb the status quo.

ap·ple but·ter ▶*n.* a paste of spiced stewed apple used as a spread or condiment, typically made with cider.

ap·ple-cheeked ▶*adj.* (of a person) having round rosy cheeks.

ap·ple green ▶*n.* a bright yellowish green.

Ap·ple Isle (also **Ap·ple Is·land**) *Austral.* a nickname for Tasmania.

ap·ple·jack /'apəl,jak/ ▶*n.* an alcoholic drink distilled from fermented cider. ▷early 19th cent.: from APPLE + JACK[1].

ap·ple pie ▶*n.* [in *sing.*] used to represent a cherished ideal of comfort and familiarity: *to say I'm fed up with the Olympics is like being against **motherhood and apple pie**.*
▶*PHRASE* □ **as American as apple pie** typically American in character.

ap·ple-pie or·der ▶*n.* perfect order or neatness: *everything was **in apple-pie order**.*

ap·ple pol·ish·er ▶*n.* *informal* a person who behaves obsequiously to someone important. **—ap·ple-pol·ish·ing** *n.*

ap·ple·sauce /'apəl,sôs/ ▶*n.* **1** a purée of stewed apples, typically sweetened. **2** *informal* nonsense: *Equal Opportunity for All—Elmer says that's all applesauce.*

Ap·ple·seed /'apəl,sēd/, Johnny (1774–1845), U.S. folk hero; born *John Chapman*. A missionary, he traveled throughout Ohio and Indiana planting and caring for apple orchards.

ap·plet /'aplit/ ▶*n.* *Computing* a very small application, esp. a utility program performing one or a few simple functions. ▷1990s: blend of APPLICATION and -LET.

Ap·ple·ton[1] /'apəltən/ an industrial and academic city in east central Wisconsin; pop. 70,087.

Ap·ple·ton[2], Sir Edward Victor (1892–1965), English physicist. He discovered a region of ionized gases (the Appleton layer) in the atmosphere above the Heaviside or E layer. Nobel Prize for Physics (1947).

Ap·ple Val·ley **1** a town in southwestern California, northeast of Los Angeles; pop. 46,079. **2** a city in southeastern Minnesota, south of Minneapolis; pop. 34,598.

ap·ple·wood /'apəl,wo͝od/ ▶*n.* the timber of the apple tree, used in carpentry and to smoke food.

ap·pli·ance /ə'plīəns/ ▶*n.* **1** a device or piece of equipment designed to perform a specific task, typically a domestic one. See note at TOOL. ■ an apparatus fitted by a surgeon or a dentist for corrective or therapeutic purpose: *electrical and gas appliances.* **2** *Brit.* the action or process of bringing something into operation: *the appliance of science could increase crop yields.*

ap·pli·anced /ə'plīənst/ ▶*adj.* (of a kitchen) having or fitted with appliances.

ap·pli·ca·ble /'aplikəbəl; ə'plik-/ ▶*adj.* relevant or appropriate: *the same considerations are equally applicable to accident claims.* ▷mid 16th cent. (in the sense 'compliant'): from Old French, or from medieval Latin *applicabilis*, from the verb *applicare* (see APPLY).

—**ap·pli·ca·bil·i·ty** /ˌaplikəˈbilitē/ *n.* —**ap·pli·ca·bly** /-blē/ *adv.*

ap·pli·cant /ˈaplikənt/ ▸*n.* a person who makes a formal application for something, typically a job. ▷early 19th cent.: from APPLICATION + -ANT.

ap·pli·ca·tion /ˌapliˈkāshən/ ▸*n.* **1** a formal request to an authority for something: *an* **application for** *leave* | [with *infinitive*] *an application to join the forum* | [as *adj.*] *application form.* ■ the action or process of making such a request: *licenses are available* **on application**. **2** the action of putting something into operation: *the application of general rules to particular cases* | *massage has far-reaching medical applications.* ■ [often with *negative*] practical use or relevance: *this principle has no application to the present case.* **3** the action of putting something on a surface: *a fresh application of makeup* | *paints suitable for application on fabric.* ■ a medicinal substance put on the skin. **4** sustained effort; hard work: *the job takes a great deal of patience and application.* **5** *Computing* a program or piece of software designed and written to fulfill a particular purpose of the user: *a database application.* ▷Middle English: via Old French from Latin *applicatio(n-)*, from the verb *applicare* (see APPLY). —**ap·pli·ca·tion·al** /-shənl/ *adj.*

ap·pli·ca·tion pro·gram ▸*n.* another term for APPLICATION (sense 5).

ap·pli·ca·tion pro·gram·ming in·ter·face (abbr.: **API**) ▸*n.* *Computing* a system of tools and resources in an operating system, enabling developers to create software applications.

ap·pli·ca·tive /ˈapliˌkātiv; əˈplikə-/ ▸*adj.* relating to or involving the application of a subject or idea; practical or applied: *applicative algebra.* ▷mid 17th cent.: from Latin *applicat-* 'set close or in contact, fastened to,' from the verb *applicare* (see APPLY).

ap·pli·ca·tor /ˈapliˌkātər/ ▸*n.* a device used for inserting something or for applying a substance to a surface. ■ a person who applies a substance or installs something, such as house siding. ▷mid 17th cent.: from Latin *applicat-* 'fastened to' (from the verb *applicare*) + -OR[1].

ap·plied /əˈplīd/ ▸*adj.* [*attrib.*] (of a subject or type of study) put to practical use as opposed to being theoretical: *applied chemistry.* Compare with PURE.

ap·plied math·e·mat·ics ▸ see MATHEMATICS.

ap·pli·qué /ˌapliˈkā/ ▸*n.* ornamental needlework in which pieces of fabric are sewn or stuck onto a large piece of fabric to form pictures or patterns.
▸*v.* (**-qués, -quéd, -qué·ing**) [*trans.*] (usu. **be appliquéd**) decorate (a piece of fabric) in such a way: *the coat is* **appliquéd with** *exotic-looking cloth* | [as *adj.*] (**appliquéd**) *19th-century appliquéd silks.* ■ sew or stick (pieces of fabric) onto a large piece of fabric to form pictures or patterns: *the floral motifs are* **appliquéd to** *christening robes.* ▷mid 18th cent.: from French, past participle of *appliquer* 'apply,' from Latin *applicare* (see APPLY).

ap·ply /əˈplī/ ▸*v.* (**-plies, -plied**) **1** [*intrans.*] make a formal application or request: *you need to* **apply to** *the local authorities for a grant* | [with *infinitive*] *a number of people have applied to vote by proxy.* ■ put oneself forward formally as a candidate for a job: *she had* **applied for** *a number of positions.* **2** [*intrans.*] be applicable or relevant: *the offer does not* **apply to** *unionized workers* | *normal rules apply.* **3** [*trans.*] put or spread (something) on a surface: *the sealer can be* **applied to** *new wood.* ■ administer: *smooth over with a cloth, applying even pressure.* **4** (**apply oneself**) give one's full attention to a task; work hard. **5** [*trans.*] bring or put into operation or practical use: *the oil industry has failed to apply appropriate standards of care.* ▷late Middle English: from Old French *aplier*, from Latin *applicare* 'fold, fasten to,' from *ad-* 'to' + *plicare* 'to fold.'

ap·pog·gia·tu·ra /əˌpäjəˈto͝orə/ ▸*n.* (*pl.* **-tu·ras** or **-tu·re** /-ˈto͝orā/) *Music* a grace note performed before a note of the melody and typically having half its time value. ▷Italian, from *appoggiare* 'lean upon, rest.'

ap·point /əˈpoint/ ▸*v.* [*trans.*] **1** assign a job or role to (someone): *she has been* **appointed to** *the board* | [*trans.*] *a delegated engineer will be appointed to oversee each graduate they* **appointed** *her* **as** *personnel manager.* **2** determine or decide on (a time or a place): *they appointed a day in May for the meeting.* ■ *archaic* decree: *such laws are appointed by God.* **3** *Law* decide the disposal of (property of which one is not the owner) under powers granted by the owner: *trustees appoint the capital to the beneficiaries.* ▷late Middle English: from Old French *apointer*, from *a point* 'to a point.' —**ap·point·ee** /əˌpoinˈtē/ *n.* —**ap·point·er** *n.*

ap·point·ed /əˈpointid/ ▸*adj.* **1** (of a time or place) decided on beforehand; designated: *she arrived at the appointed time.* **2** (of a building or room) equipped or furnished in a specified way or to a specified standard: *a luxuriously appointed lobby.*

ap·poin·tive /əˈpointiv/ ▸*adj.* (of a job) relating to or filled by appointment rather than election.

ap·point·ment /əˈpointmənt/ ▸*n.* **1** an arrangement to meet someone at a particular time and place: *she* **made an appointment** *with my receptionist.* **2** an act of appointing; assigning a job or position to someone: *his appointment as president.* ■ a job or position: *she took up an appointment as head of communications.* ■ a person appointed to a job or position. **3** (**appointments**) furniture or fittings: *the room was spartan in its appointments.* ▷Middle English: from Old French *apointement*, from *apointer* (see APPOINT).
▸*PHRASES* □ **by appointment** having previously made an arrangement to do something: *visits are by appointment only.* □ **power of appointment 1** power to select the holder of a particular job or position. **2** *Law* power to decide the disposal of property, in exercise of a right conferred by the owner.

Ap·po·mat·tox /ˌapəˈmatəks/ a historic site in central Virginia, at the head of the Appomattox River, where Robert E. Lee's surrender of his Confederate forces in April 1865 ended the Civil War.

ap·por·tion /əˈpôrshən/ ▸*v.* [*trans.*] divide and allocate: *voting power will be apportioned according to contribution.* ■ assign: *they did not* **apportion** *blame or liability* **to** *any one individual.* ▷late 16th cent.: from Old French *apportionner* or medieval Latin *apportionare*, from *ad-* 'to' + *portionare* 'divide into portions.'

ap·por·tion·ment /əˈpôrshənmənt/ ▸*n.* the action or result of apportioning something: *an exercise in apportionment of blame.* ■ the determination of the proportional number of members each U.S. state sends to the House of Representatives, based on population figures.

ap·pose /əˈpōz/ ▸*v.* [*trans.*] *technical* place (something) in proximity to or juxtaposition with something else: *the specimen was* **apposed to** *X-ray film.* ▷late 16th cent.: from Latin *apponere*, on the pattern of words such as *compose*, *expose*.

ap·po·site /ˈapəzit/ ▸*adj.* apt in the circumstances or in relation to something: *an apposite quotation* | *the observations are* **apposite to** *the discussion.* ▷late 16th cent.: from Latin *appositus*, past participle of *apponere* 'apply,' from *ad-* 'toward' + *ponere* 'put.' —**ap·po·site·ly** *adv.* —**ap·po·site·ness** *n.*

ap·po·si·tion /ˌapəˈzishən/ ▸*n.* **1** *chiefly technical* the positioning of things or the condition of being side by side or close together. **2** *Grammar* a relationship between two or more words or phrases in which the two units are grammatically parallel and have the same referent (e.g., *my friend Sue; the first U.S. President, George Washington*). ▷late Middle English: from late Latin *appositio(n-)*, from *apponere* 'to apply' (see APPOSITE).

ap·po·si·tion·al /ˌapəˈzishənl/ *Grammar* ▸*adj.* of or relating to apposition.
▸*n.* a term standing in apposition.

ap·pos·i·tive /əˈpäzitiv/ ▸*adj.* & *n.* *Grammar* another term for APPOSITIONAL. ▷late 17th cent.: from late Latin *appositivus* 'subsidiary.'

ap·prais·al /əˈprāzəl/ ▸*n.* an act of assessing something or someone: *treatment begins with a thorough appraisal of the patient's condition* | *the report has been subject to appraisal.* ■ an expert estimate of the value of something: *the final figure is just a little more than triple the appraisal.*

ap·prais·al drill·ing ▸*n.* drilling undertaken to establish the quality, quantity, and other characteristics of oil or gas in a newly discovered field.

ap·praise /əˈprāz/ ▸*v.* [*trans.*] assess the value or quality of: *she stealthily appraised him in a pocket mirror* | [*intrans.*] *the interviewer's job is to appraise and evaluate.* ■ (of an official or expert) set a price on; value: *they appraised the painting at $200,000.* ▷late Middle English (in the sense 'set a price on'): alteration of APPRIZE, by association with PRAISE. The current sense dates from the mid 19th cent. —**ap·prais·er** *n.* —**ap·prais·ing·ly** *adv.*

USAGE **Appraise**, meaning 'evaluate,' should not be confused with **apprise**, which means 'inform': *the painting was appraised at $3,000,000; they gasped when apprised of this valuation.*

ap·pre·ci·a·ble /əˈprēsh(ē)əbəl/ ▸*adj.* large or important enough to be noticed: *tea and coffee both contain appreciable amounts of caffeine.* See note at TANGIBLE. ▷early 19th cent.: from French *appréciable*, from *apprécier* (see APPRECIATE). —**ap·pre·ci·a·bly** /-blē/ *adv.*

ap·pre·ci·ate /əˈprēshēˌāt/ ▸*v.* [*trans.*] **1** recognize the full worth of: *she feels that he does not appreciate her.* See note at ESTEEM. ■ be grateful for (something): *I'd appreciate any information you could give me.* **2** understand (a situation) fully; recognize the full implications of: *they failed to appreciate the pressure he was under* | [with *clause*] *I appreciate that you cannot be held totally responsible.* **3** [*intrans.*] rise in value or price: *they expected the house to* **appreciate in value.** ▷mid 16th cent.: from late Latin *appretiat-* 'set at a price, appraised,' from the verb *appretiare*, from *ad-* 'to' + *pretium* 'price.' —**ap·pre·cia·tive** /-sh(ē)ətiv/ *adj.* (in sense 1). —**ap·pre·cia·tive·ly** *adv.* (in sense 1). —**ap·pre·ci·a·tor** /-ˌātər/ *n.*

ap·pre·ci·a·tion /əˌprēshēˈāshən/ ▸*n.* **1** the recognition and enjoyment of the good qualities of someone or something: *I smiled in appreciation* | *she shows a fine appreciation of obscure thinkers.* ■ gratitude for something: *they would be the first to* **show their appreciation.** ■ a piece of writing in which the qualities of a person or the person's work are discussed and assessed. ■ sensitive understanding of the aesthetic value of something: *courses in music appreciation.* **2** a full understanding of a situation: *they have an appreciation of the needs of users* | *the bank's lack of appreciation of their problems.* **3** increase in monetary value: *the appreciation of the franc against the dollar.* ▷early 17th cent.: from French *appréciation*, from late Latin *appretiatio(n-)*, from the verb *appretiare* 'set at a price, appraise' (see APPRECIATE).

ap·pre·hend /ˌapriˈhend/ ▸*v.* [*trans.*] **1** arrest (someone) for a crime: *a warrant was issued but he has not been apprehended.* **2** understand or perceive: *great art invites us to apprehend beauty.* ■ *archaic* anticipate (something) with uneasiness or fear. ▷late Middle English (originally in the sense 'grasp, get hold of (physically or mentally)'): from French *appréhender* or Latin *apprehendere*, from *ad-* 'toward' + *prehendere* 'lay hold of.'

ap·pre·hen·si·ble /ˌapriˈhensəbəl/ ▸*adj.* *archaic* or *poetic/literary* capable of being understood or perceived: *a bat whirred, apprehensible only from the displacement of air.* ▷early 17th cent.: from late Latin *apprehensibilis*, from Latin *apprehendere* (see APPREHEND).

ap·pre·hen·sion /ˌapriˈhenshən/ ▸*n.* **1** anxiety or fear that something bad or unpleasant will happen: *he felt sick with apprehension* | *she had some apprehensions about the filming.* **2** understanding; grasp: *the pure apprehension of the work of art.* **3** the action of arresting someone: *they acted with intent to prevent lawful apprehension.* ▷late Middle English (in the sense 'learning, acquisition of knowledge'): from late Latin *apprehensio(n-)*, from *apprehendere* 'seize, grasp' (see APPREHEND).

ap·pre·hen·sive /ˌapriˈhensiv/ ▸*adj.* **1** anxious or fearful that something bad or unpleasant will happen: *he felt apprehensive about going home* | [with *clause*] *they were apprehensive that something might go wrong.* **2** *archaic* or *poetic/literary* of or relating to perception or understanding. ▷late Middle English (sense 2): from French *appréhensif* or medieval Latin *apprehensivus*, from Latin *apprehendere* 'seize, grasp' (see APPREHENSION). —**ap·pre·hen·sive·ly** *adv.* —**ap·pre·hen·sive·ness** *n.*

ap·pren·tice /əˈprentis/ ▸*n.* a person who is learning a trade from a skilled employer, having agreed to work for a fixed period at low wages: [as *adj.*] *an apprentice electrician.* ■ [usu. as *adj.*] a beginner at something: *an apprentice confidence trickster.* See note at NOVICE.
▸*v.* [*trans.*] (usu. **be apprenticed**) employ (someone) as an apprentice: *Edward was* **apprenticed to** *a printer.* ■ [*intrans.*] serve as an apprentice: *she apprenticed with midwives in San Francisco.* ▷Middle English: from Old French *aprentis* (from *apprendre* 'learn,' from Latin *apprehendere* 'apprehend'), on the pattern of words ending in *-tis, -tif*, from Latin *-tivus* (see -IVE). —**ap·pren·tice·ship** /-ˌship/ *n.*

ap·press /əˈpres/ ▸*v.* [*trans.*] (usu. **be appressed**) *technical* press (something) close to something else: *the two cords can be closely* **appressed to** *one another.* ▷early 17th cent.: from Latin *appress-* 'pressed close,' from the verb *apprimere*, from *ad-* 'to' + *premere* 'to press.'

ap·prise /əˈprīz/ ▸*v.* [*trans.*] inform or tell (someone): *I thought it right to* **apprise** *Chris* **of** *what had happened.* ▷late 17th cent.: from French *appris, apprise*, past participle of *apprendre* 'learn, teach,' from Latin *apprehendere* (see APPREHEND).

USAGE See usage at APPRAISE.

ap·prize /ə'prīz/ ▸*v.* [*trans.*] *archaic* put a price upon; appraise: *the sheriff was to apprize the value of the lands.* ■ value highly; esteem: *how highly your Highness apprizeth peace.* ▷late Middle English: from Old French *aprisier*, from *a-* (from Latin *ad* 'to, at') + *prisier* 'to price, prize,' from *pris* (see **PRICE**). The spelling change in the 17th cent. was due to association with **PRIZE**[1].

ap·proach /ə'prōCH/ ▸*v.* [*trans.*] **1** come near or nearer to (someone or something) in distance: *the train approached the main line* | [*intrans.*] *she hadn't heard him approach* | [as *adj.*] (**approaching**) *an approaching car.* ■ come near or nearer to (a future time or event): *he was approaching retirement.* ■ [*intrans.*] (of a future time) come nearer: *the time is approaching when you will be destroyed.* ■ come close to (a number, level, or standard) in quality or quantity: *the population will approach 12 million by the end of the decade.* ■ (of an aircraft) descend toward and prepare to land on (an airfield, runway, etc.): *the single-seater plane hit a post as it was approaching the runway.* ■ *archaic* bring nearer: *all those changes shall serve to approach him the faster to the blest mansion.* **2** speak to (someone) for the first time about something, typically with a proposal or request: *the department had been approached about funding.* **3** start to deal with (something) in a certain way: *one must approach the matter with caution.*
▸*n.* **1** a way of dealing with something: *we need a whole new* ***approach to*** *the job.* **2** an act of speaking to someone for the first time about something, typically a proposal or request: *the landowner made an approach to the developer.* ■ (**approaches**) *dated* behavior intended to propose personal or sexual relations with someone: *feminine resistance to his approaches.* **3** [in *sing.*] the action of coming near or nearer to someone or something in distance or time: *the approach of winter.* ■ (**approach to**) an approximation to something: *the past is impossible to recall with any approach to accuracy.* ■ the part of an aircraft's flight in which it descends gradually toward an airfield or runway for landing. **4** (usu. **approaches**) a road, sea passage, or other way leading to a place: *the eastern* ***approach to*** *the town.* ▷Middle English: from Old French *aprochier*, *aprocher*, from ecclesiastical Latin *appropiare* 'draw near,' from *ad-* 'to' + *propius* (comparative of *prope* 'near').

ap·proach·a·ble /ə'prōCHəbəl/ ▸*adj.* **1** friendly and easy to talk to: *managers should be approachable.* **2** (of a place) able to be reached from a particular direction or by a particular means: *at night parrotfish are approachable as they sleep in nooks and crannies on the reef.* **—ap·proach·a·bil·i·ty** /ə,prōCHə'bilitē/ *n.*

ap·proach shot ▸*n.* *Golf* a stroke that sends the ball from the fairway onto or nearer the green.

ap·pro·bate /'aprə,bāt/ ▸*v.* [*trans.*] *rare* approve formally; sanction: *a letter approbating the affair.* ▷late Middle English: from Latin *approbat-* 'approved,' from the verb *approbare*, from *ad-* 'to' + *probare* 'try, test' (from *probus* 'good').

ap·pro·ba·tion /,aprə'bāSHən/ ▸*n.* *formal* approval or praise: *the opera met with high approbation.* ▷late Middle English: via Old French from Latin *approbatio(n-)*, from the verb *approbare* (see **APPROBATE**). **—ap·pro·ba·tive** /'aprə,bātiv; ə'prōbətiv/ *adj.* **—ap·pro·ba·to·ry** /ə'prōbə,tôrē/ *adj.*

ap·pro·pri·ate ▸*adj.* /ə'prōprē-it/ suitable or proper in the circumstances: *a measure appropriate to a wartime economy.*
▸*v.* /-,āt/ [*trans.*] **1** take (something) for one's own use, typically without the owner's permission: *his images have been appropriated by advertisers.* **2** devote (money or assets) to a special purpose: *there can be problems in* ***appropriating*** *funds* ***for*** *legal expenses.* ▷late Middle English: from late Latin *appropriatus*, past participle of *appropriare* 'make one's own,' from *ad-* 'to' + *proprius* 'own, proper.' **—ap·pro·pri·ate·ly** /-itlē/ *adv.* [*sentence adverb*] *appropriately, the first recital will be given at the festival.* **—ap·pro·pri·ate·ness** /-itnis/ *n.* **—ap·pro·pri·a·tor** /-,ātər/ *n.*

ap·pro·pri·a·tion /ə,prōprē'āSHən/ ▸*n.* **1** the action of taking something for one's own use, typically without the owner's permission: *the appropriation of parish funds.* ■ *often derogatory* the artistic practice or technique of reworking images from well-known paintings, photographs, etc., in one's own work. **2** a sum of money or total of assets devoted to a special purpose. ▷late Middle English: from late Latin *appropriatio(n-)*, from *appropriare* 'make one's own' (see **APPROPRIATE**).

ap·pro·pri·a·tion·ist /ə,prōprē'āSHənist/ ▸*n.* *often derogatory* an artist whose work contains reworkings of well-known images by other artists: [as *adj.*] *appropriationist art.*

ap·prov·al /ə'prōōvəl/ ▸*n.* **1** the action of officially agreeing to something or accepting something as satisfactory: *the road plans have been given approval* | *they have delayed the launch to await project approvals.* ■ the belief that someone or something is good or acceptable: *step-parents need to win a child's approval.* **2** (usu. **approvals**) *Philately* stamps sent by request to a collector or potential customer.
▸*PHRASES* □ **on approval** (of goods) supplied on condition that they may be returned if not satisfactory. □ **seal** (or **stamp**) **of approval** an official statement or indication that something is accepted or regarded favorably.

ap·prove /ə'prōōv/ ▸*v.* [*trans.*] **1** officially agree to or accept as satisfactory: *the budget was approved by Congress* | [as *adj.*] (**approved**) *an approved profit-sharing plan.* ■ [*intrans.*] believe that someone or something is good or acceptable: *I don't* ***approve of*** *the way she pampers my father and brothers.* **2** *archaic* prove; show: *he* ***approved himself*** *ripe for military command.* ▷Middle English: from Old French *aprover*, from Latin *approbare* (see **APPROBATE**). The original sense was 'prove, demonstrate,' later 'corroborate, confirm,' hence 'pronounce to be satisfactory' (late Middle English). **—ap·prov·ing·ly** *adv.*

THE RIGHT WORD **approve, certify, commend, endorse, ratify, sanction**

There are a number of ways to show your support for something. The most general way is to **approve** it, a term that covers everything from simple, technical agreement (*to approve the plan*) to enthusiastic support (*she was quick to approve her son's decision to marry*).

Endorse implies a more public and official expression of support and is used primarily in reference to things that require promotion or publicity (*endorse a political candidate*), while **commend** is to make a formal and usually public statement of approval or congratulation (*he was commended for his heroism*).

Sanction, **certify**, and **ratify** imply that approval is not only official but that it makes something legal. To *sanction* is not only to *approve* but to authorize (*school authorities would not sanction the wearing of hats in class*), while *certify* implies conformity with certain standards (*certified to teach in the State of New York*).

Ratify is usually confined to only the most official and authoritative settings. For example, an employer might *sanction* the idea of hiring a woman to perform a job that only men have performed in the past, and the woman in question might have to *certify* that she possesses the necessary training and qualifications. But to *ratify* a constitutional amendment granting equal rights to women requires a lengthy set of legislative procedures.

approx. ▸*abbr.* approximate(ly).

ap·prox·i·mate ▸*adj.* /ə'präksəmit/ close to the actual, but not completely accurate or exact: *the calculations are very approximate.*
▸*v.* /-,māt/ [*intrans.*] come close or be similar to something in quality, nature, or quantity: *a leasing agreement approximating to ownership* | [*trans.*] *reality can be approximated by computational techniques.* ■ [*trans.*] estimate or calculate (a quantity) fairly accurately: *I had to approximate the weight of my horse.* ▷late Middle English (in the adjectival sense 'close, similar'): from late Latin *approximatus*, past participle of *approximare*, from *ad-* 'to' + *proximus* 'very near.' The verb (originally meaning 'bring close') arose in the mid 17th cent.; the current adjectival sense dates from the early 19th cent. **—ap·prox·i·mate·ly** *adv.* **—ap·prox·i·ma·tion** /ə,präksə'māSHən/ *n.*

ap·prox·i·ma·tive /ə'präksə,mātiv/ ▸*adj.* (of a method, description, etc.) giving only an approximation to something: *a crudely approximative outline.*

ap·pur·te·nance /ə'pərtn-əns/ ▸*n.* (usu. **appurtenances**) an accessory or other item associated with a particular activity or style of living: *all the appurtenances of luxurious travel.* ▷Middle English: from Old French *apertenance*, based on late Latin *appertinere* 'belong to' (see **APPERTAIN**).

ap·pur·te·nant /ə'pərtn-ənt/ ▸*adj.* belonging; pertinent: *secondary buildings that are* ***appurtenant to*** *the main building.* ▷late Middle English: from Old French *apartenant* 'appertaining,' from the verb *apartenir* (see **APPERTAIN**).

APR ▸*abbr.* annual or annualized percentage rate, typically of interest on loans or credit.

Apr. ▸*abbr.* April.

a·prax·i·a /ā'praksēə/ ▸*n.* *Medicine* inability to perform particular purposive actions, as a result of brain damage. ▷late 19th cent.: from German *Apraxie*, from Greek *apraxia* 'inaction.' **—a·prax·ic** /-sik/ *adj.*

après- ▸*prefix informal, humorous* coming after in time, typically specifying a period following an activity: *a low-fat, après-workout snack.* ▷mid 20th cent.: French, literally 'after,' used in combinations on the pattern of *après-ski*.

a·près-ski /,äprā 'skē/ ▸*n.* the social activities and entertainment following a day's skiing: [as *adj.*] *the après-ski disco.* ▷1950s: French, literally 'after skiing.' **—a·près-ski·ing** *n.*

ap·ri·cot /'apri,kät; 'āpri-/ ▸*n.* **1** a juicy, soft fruit, resembling a small peach, of an orange-yellow color. ■ an orange-yellow color like the skin of a ripe apricot. **2** (also **apricot tree**) the tree bearing this fruit. • *Prunus armeniaca*, family Rosaceae. ▷mid 16th cent.: from Portuguese *albricoque* or Spanish *albaricoque*, from Spanish Arabic *al* 'the' + *barḳūḳ* (from late Greek *praikokion*, from Latin *praecoquum*, variant of *praecox* 'early ripe'); influenced by Latin *apricus* 'ripe' and by French *abricot*.

A·pril /'āprəl/ ▸*n.* the fourth month of the year, in the northern hemisphere usually considered the second month of spring: *the prison was to close in April* | [as *adj.*] *April showers.* ▷Old English, from Latin *Aprilis*.

A·pril fool ▸*n.* a person who is the victim of a trick or hoax on April 1: [as *exclam.*] *Lucy was waiting right outside. "April fool!" she said.* ■ a trick or hoax on April 1: [as *adj.*] *an April fool joke.*

A·pril Fool's Day (also **A·pril Fools' Day**) ▸*n.* April 1, in many Western countries traditionally an occasion for playing tricks. This custom has been observed for hundreds of years, but its origin is unknown. Also called **ALL FOOLS' DAY**.

a pri·o·ri /'ä prē'ôrē; prī'ôrī; 'ā/ ▸*adj.* relating to or denoting reasoning or knowledge that proceeds from theoretical deduction rather than from observation or experience: *a priori assumptions about human nature.*
▸*adv.* in a way based on theoretical deduction rather than empirical observation: *sexuality may be a factor, but it cannot be assumed a priori.* | [*sentence adverb*] *a priori, it would seem that his government was an extension of Soviet power.* ▷late 16th cent.: Latin, 'from what is before.' **—a·pri·o·rism** /,āprī'ôrizəm; -prē-; ,äprē-/ *n.*

a·pron /'āprən/ ▸*n.* **1** a protective or decorative garment worn over the front of one's clothes, either from chest or waist level, and tied at the back. ■ a similar garment worn as part of official dress, as by an Anglican bishop or a Freemason. ■ a sheet of lead worn to shield the body during an X-ray examination. **2** a small area adjacent to another larger area or structure: *a tiny* ***apron of*** *garden.* ■ a hard-surfaced area on an airfield used for maneuvering or parking aircraft. ■ (also **apron stage**) a projecting strip of stage for playing scenes in front of the curtain. ■ a broadened area of pavement at the end of a driveway. ■ the narrow strip of the floor of a boxing ring lying outside the ropes. ■ the outer edge or border of a golf green. ■ *Geology* an extensive outspread deposit of sediment, typically at the foot of a glacier or mountain. **3** an object resembling an apron in shape or function, in particular: ■ a covering protecting an area or structure, for example, from water erosion. ■ [often as *adj.*] an endless conveyor made of overlapping plates: *apron feeders bring coarse ore to a grinding mill.* ■ *Medicine* a pendulous fold of abdominal fat that obscures the genital region. ▷Middle English *naperon*, from Old French, diminutive of *nape*, *nappe* 'tablecloth,' from Latin *mappa* 'napkin.' The *n* was lost by wrong division of *a napron*; compare with **ADDER**.
▸*PHRASE* □ (**tied to**) **someone's apron strings** (too much under) the influence and control of someone: *we have all met sturdy adults who are tied to mother's apron strings.*

ap·ro·pos /,aprə'pō/ ▸*prep.* with reference to; concerning: *she remarked* ***apropos of*** *the initiative, "It's not going to stop the abuse."*
▸*adv.* [*sentence adverb*] (**apropos of nothing**) used to state a speaker's belief that someone's comments or acts are unrelated to any previous discussion or situation: *Isabel kept smiling apropos of nothing.*
▸*adj.* [*predic.*] very appropriate to a particular situation: *the composer's reference to child's play is apropos.* ▷mid 17th cent.: from French *à propos* '(with regard) to (this) purpose.'

ap·sa·ra /'əpsərə/ (also **ap·sa·ras** /-sərəs/) ▸*n.* (*pl.* **-ras** or **-ra·ses** /-rəsiz/) *Hindu Mythology* a celestial nymph, typically the consort of a gandharva or heavenly musician. ▷from Hindi *apsarā*, from Sanskrit *apsarās*.

apse /aps/ ▸*n.* **1** a large semicircular or polygonal recess in a church, arched or with a domed roof, typically at the eastern end, and usually containing the altar. **2** another term for APSIS. ▷early 19th cent. (sense 2): from Latin *apsis* (see APSIS). —**ap·si·dal** /'apsidl/ *adj.*

ap·sis /'apsis/ ▸*n.* (*pl.* **-si·des** /-si,dēz/) either of two points on the orbit of a planet or satellite that are nearest to or furthest from the body around which it moves. ▷early 17th cent. (denoting the orbit of a planet): via Latin from Greek *apsis, hapsis* 'arch, vault,' perhaps from *haptein* 'fasten, join.' —**ap·si·dal** /'apsidl/ *adj.*

apt /apt/ ▸*adj.* **1** appropriate or suitable in the circumstances: *an apt description of her nature.* **2** [*predic.*] (**apt to do something**) having a tendency to do something: *she was apt to confuse the past with the present.* **3** quick to learn: *he proved an apt scholar.* ▷late Middle English (in the sense 'suited, appropriate'): from Latin *aptus* 'fitted,' past participle of *apere* 'fasten.' —**apt·ly** *adv.* —**apt·ness** *n.*

apt. ▸*abbr.* ■ apartment. ■ aptitude.

ap·ter·ous /'aptərəs/ ▸*adj. Entomology* (of an insects) having no wings. ▷late 18th cent.: from Greek *apteros* (from *a-* 'without' + *pteron* 'wing') + -OUS.

Ap·ter·y·go·ta /ap,teri'gōtə/ *Entomology* a group of insects that includes the bristletails and springtails. They have a primitive body form that lacks wings and typically have no distinct larval stage. Compare with PTERYGOTA. • Subclass Apterygota, class Insecta (or Hexapoda): several orders, some of which are sometimes not included with the Insecta. ▷modern Latin *Apterygota*, from Greek *a-* 'not' + *pterugōtos* 'winged.' —**ap·ter·y·gote** /ap'teri,gōt/ *n.*

ap·ti·tude /'apti,t(y)o͞od/ ▸ **1** *n.* (abbr.: **apt.**) (often **aptitude for**) a natural ability to do something: *he had a remarkable* ***aptitude for*** *learning words.* ■ a natural tendency: *his natural* ***aptitude for*** *failure.* **2** *archaic* suitability or fitness: *aptitude of expression.* ▷late Middle English: via Old French from late Latin *aptitudo*, from *aptus* (see APT).

ap·ti·tude test ▸*n.* a test designed to determine a person's ability in a particular skill or field of knowledge.

APU ▸*abbr.* auxiliary power unit, a device used on aircraft to provide power while on the ground and to start the main engines.

Ap·u·le·ius /,apyə'lēəs/ (born *c.*AD 123), Roman writer; born in Africa. He wrote *Metamorphoses* (*The Golden Ass*).

A·pus /'āpəs/ *Astronomy* a faint southern constellation, the Bird of Paradise, close to the south celestial pole. ■ [as *genitive*] (**Apodis** /'apədis/) used with a preceding letter or numeral to designate stars: *the star Beta Apodis.* ▷Latin, denoting a kind of bird, from Greek *apous.*

A·qa·ba /'äkəbə; 'ak-/ Jordan's only port, at the head of the Gulf of Aqaba; pop. 40,000.

A·qa·ba, Gulf of part of the Red Sea that extends northward between the Sinai and Arabian peninsulas.

aq·ua /'äkwə; 'ak-/ ▸*n.* a light bluish-green color; aquamarine: *houses of yellow and aqua* | [as *adj.*] *aqua blue.* ▷1930s: abbreviation of AQUAMARINE.

aqua- ▸*comb. form* relating to water: *aquaculture.* ■ relating to water sports or aquatic entertainment: *aquacade.* ▷from Latin *aqua* 'water.'

aq·ua·cade /'äkwə,kād; 'ak-/ ▸*n.* a spectacle involving swimming and diving, usually with musical accompaniment.

aq·ua·cul·ture /'äkwə,kəlCHər; 'ak-/ ▸*n. Botany* the rearing of aquatic animals or the cultivation of aquatic plants for food. ▷mid 19th cent.: from Latin *aqua* 'water' + CULTURE, on the pattern of words such as *agriculture.*

aq·ua for·tis /'äkwə 'fôrtis; 'ak-/ ▸*n.* archaic term for NITRIC ACID. ▷late 15th cent.: from Latin, literally 'strong water.'

aq·ua·lung /'äkwə,ləNG; 'ak-/ ▸*n.* a portable breathing apparatus for divers, consisting of cylinders of compressed air strapped on the diver's back, feeding air automatically through a mask or mouthpiece.
▸*v.* [*intrans.*] *dated* swim underwater using such an apparatus. ▷1950s (originally a proprietary name in the U.S.): from Latin *aqua* 'water' + LUNG.

aq·ua·ma·rine /,äkwəmə'rēn; ,ak-/ ▸*n.* a precious stone consisting of a light bluish-green variety of beryl. ■ a light bluish-green color: *the aquamarine of the Atlantic Ocean* | [as *adj.*] *the aquamarine water.* ▷early 18th cent.: from Latin *aqua marina* 'seawater.'

aq·ua·naut /'äkwə,nôt; 'ak-/ ▸*n.* a person who swims underwater using an aqualung. ▷late 19th cent.: from Latin *aqua* 'water' + Greek *nautēs* 'sailor.'

aq·ua·plane /'äkwə,plān; 'ak-/ ▸*n.* a board for riding on water, pulled by a speedboat.
▸*v.* [*intrans.*] [often as *n.*] (**aquaplaning**) ride standing on an aquaplane. ■ (of a vehicle) slide uncontrollably on a wet surface: *the plane is believed to have aquaplaned on the runway.* ▷early 20th cent. (originally U.S.): from Latin *aqua* 'water' + PLANE[1].

aq·ua re·gi·a /'äkwə 'rejēə; 'ak-/ ▸*n. Chemistry* a mixture of concentrated nitric and hydrochloric acids. It is a highly corrosive liquid that will dissolve gold and other resistant substances. ▷early 17th cent.: Latin, literally 'royal water.'

aq·ua·relle /,äkwə'rel; ,ak-/ ▸*n.* a style of painting using thin, typically transparent, watercolors. ■ a painting in such a style. ▷mid 19th cent.: from French, from Italian *acquarella* 'watercolor,' diminutive of *acqua*, from Latin *aqua* 'water.'

A·quar·i·an /ə'kwe(ə)rēən/ *Astrology* ▸*n.* a person born under the sign of Aquarius.
▸*adj.* of or relating to people born under the sign of Aquarius. ■ of or relating to the Age of Aquarius or the New Age.

a·quar·ist /ə'kwe(ə)rist/ ▸*n.* a person who keeps an aquarium.

a·quar·i·um /ə'kwe(ə)rēəm/ ▸*n.* (*pl.* **-i·ums** or **-i·a** /-ēə/) a transparent tank of water in which fish and other water creatures and plants are kept. ■ a building containing such tanks, esp. one that is open to the public. ▷mid 19th cent.: from Latin, neuter of *aquarius* 'of water,' on the pattern of *vivarium.*

A·quar·i·us /ə'kwe(ə)rēəs/ **1** *Astronomy* a large constellation, the Water-carrier or Water-bearer, said to represent a man pouring water from a jar. It contains no bright stars but has several planetary nebulae. ■ [as *genitive*] (**Aquarii** /-ē,ī/) used with a preceding letter or numeral to designate stars: *the star Alpha Aquarii.* **2** *Astrology* the eleventh sign of the zodiac, which the sun enters about January 21. ■ (**an Aquarius**) a person born when the sun is in this sign. ▷Latin *aquarius* 'of water,' used as a noun to mean 'water carrier.'
▸*PHRASE* □ **Age of Aquarius** an age that the world has just entered or is about to enter, believed by some to signal a period of peace and harmony.

a·quat·ic /ə'kwätik; ə'kwat-/ ▸*adj.* of or relating to water. ■ (of a plant or animal) growing or living in or near water: *the bay could support aquatic life.* ■ (of a sport) played in or on water. ■ (of a shop or dealer) specializing in products for ponds or aquariums.
▸*n.* **1** an aquatic plant or animal, typically one suitable for a pond or aquarium. **2** (**aquatics**) sports played in or on water. ▷late 15th cent. (in the sense 'watery, rainy'): from Old French *aquatique* or Latin *aquaticus*, from *aqua* 'water.'

aq·ua·tint /'äkwə,tint; 'ak-/ ▸*n.* a print resembling a watercolor, produced from a copper plate etched with nitric acid. ■ the technique or process of making pictures in such a way.
▸*v.* [*trans.*] create (a scene or picture) in such a way. ▷late 18th cent.: from French *aquatinte*, from Italian *acqua tinta* 'colored water.'

aq·ua·vit /'äkwə,vēt; 'ak-/ (also **ak·va·vit** /'äkvä,vēt/) ▸*n.* an alcoholic spirit made from potatoes or other starchy plants. ▷late 19th cent.: from Norwegian, Swedish, and Danish *akvavit* (see AQUA VITAE).

aq·ua vi·tae /'äkwə 'vītē; 'vē,tī; 'akwə/ ▸*n.* strong alcoholic spirit, esp. brandy. ▷late Middle English: from Latin, literally 'water of life'; compare with AQUAVIT, EAU-DE-VIE, USQUEBAUGH, and WHISKEY.

aq·ue·duct /'äkwə,dəkt; 'ak-/ ▸*n.* an artificial channel for conveying water, typically in the form of a bridge supported by tall columns across a valley. ■ *Anatomy* a small canal containing fluid. ▷mid 16th cent.: from obsolete French (now *aqueduc*), from Latin *aquae ductus* 'conduit,' from *aqua* 'water' + *ducere* 'to lead.'

Roman aquaduct
Segovia, Spain

a·que·ous /'äkwēəs; 'ak-/ ▸*adj.* of or containing water, typically as a solvent or medium: *an aqueous solution of potassium permanganate.* ■ *figurative* like water; watery: *a great hall of aqueous marble.* ▷mid 17th cent.: from medieval Latin *aqueus*, from Latin *aqua* 'water.'

a·que·ous hu·mor ▸*n.* the clear fluid filling the space in the front of the eyeball between the lens and the cornea. Compare with VITREOUS HUMOR.

A·quid·neck /ə'kwid,nek/ the former name of Rhode Island, the largest island in Narragansett Bay, part of the state of Rhode Island.

aq·ui·fer /'äkwəfər; 'ak-/ ▸*n.* a body of permeable rock that can contain or transmit groundwater. ▷early 20th cent.: from Latin *aqui-* (from *aqua* 'water') + *-fer* 'bearing' (from *ferre* 'to bear').

A·quil·a /ə'kwilə; 'akwələ/ *Astronomy* a small northern constellation, the Eagle, said to represent the eagle that carried Ganymede to Olympus. It contains the bright star Altair, and some rich star fields of the Milky Way. ■ [as *genitive*] (**Aquilae** /-lē/) used with a preceding letter or numeral to designate stars: *the star Beta Aquilae.* ▷Latin.

aq·ui·le·gi·a /,akwə'lēj(ē)ə/ ▸*n.* a plant of the buttercup family, bearing showy flowers with backward-pointing spurs. Native to temperate regions of the northern hemisphere, it is widely grown in gardens. • Genus *Aquilegia*, family Ranunculaceae. See also COLUMBINE. ▷from medieval Latin, probably from Latin *aquilegus* 'water collecting.'

aq·ui·line /'akwə,līn; -lin/ ▸*adj.* like an eagle. ■ (of a person's nose) hooked or curved like an eagle's beak. ▷mid 17th cent.: from Latin *aquilinus*, from *aquila* 'eagle.'

A·qui·nas, St. Thom·as /ə'kwīnəs/ (1225–74), Italian philosopher, theologian, and Dominican friar; known as *the Angelic Doctor*. He is regarded as the greatest figure of scholasticism. One of his most important achievements was the introduction of the work of Aristotle to Christian western Europe. His works include commentaries on Aristotle as well as the *Summa Contra Gentiles* and *Summa Theologiae*. Feast day, January 28.

A·qui·no /ä'kēnō; ə'kē-/ (Maria) Corazón (1933–), Filipino stateswoman and president 1986–92.

Aq·ui·taine[1] /'akwə,tān/ a region and former province in southwestern France, on the Bay of Biscay. It became an English possession as a result of the marriage of Eleanor of Aquitaine to Henry II in 1152 and remained so until 1453.

Aq·ui·taine[2], Eleanor of, see ELEANOR OF AQUITAINE.

a·quiv·er /ə'kwivər/ ▸*adj.* [*predic.*] quivering; trembling: *her face aquiver with pleasure.*

AR ▸*abbr.* ■ (also **A/R**) accounts receivable. ■ Arkansas (in official postal use). ■ Army Regulation. ■ Autonomous Republic.

Ar ▸*symbol* the chemical element argon.

ar- ▸*prefix* variant spelling of AD- assimilated before *r* (as in *arrive, arrogate*).

-ar[1] ▸*suffix* **1** (forming adjectives) of the kind specified; relating to: *lunar* | *molecular.* **2** forming nouns such as *scholar.* ▷from Old French *-aire, -ier*, or from Latin *-aris.*

-ar[2] ▸*suffix* forming nouns such as *pillar.* ▷from French *-er* or representing Latin *-ar, -are* (neuter of *-aris*).

-ar[3] ▸*suffix* forming nouns such as *bursar, vicar.* ▷from Old French *-aire, -ier*, or from Latin *-arius, -arium.*

-ar[4] ▸*suffix* alteration of -ER[1], -OR[1] (as in *beggar, liar*).

A·ra /'arə; 'e(ə)rə/ *Astronomy* a small and faint southern constellation, the Altar, in the Milky Way near Scorpius. ■ [as *genitive*] (**Arae** /-rē/) used with a preceding letter or numeral to designate stars: *the star Delta Arae.* ▷Latin.

Ar·ab /'arəb/ ▸*n.* **1** a member of a Semitic people, originally from the Arabian peninsula and neighboring territories, inhabiting much of the Middle East and North Africa. **2** an Arabian horse.
▸*adj.* of or relating to Arabia and the people of Arabia: *Arab countries.* ▷from French *Arabe*, via Latin and Greek from Arabic *'arab.*

USAGE See **usage** at ARABIAN.

arabesque

ar·a·besque /ˌarəˈbesk/ ▸*n.* **1** an ornamental design consisting of intertwined flowing lines, originally found in Arabic or Moorish decoration: [as *adj.*] *arabesque scrolls.* ■ *Music* a passage or composition with fanciful ornamentation of the melody. **2** *Ballet* a posture in which the body is supported on one leg, with the other leg extended horizontally backward. ▷mid 17th cent.: from French, from Italian *arabesco* 'in the Arabic style,' from *arabo* 'Arab.'

A·ra·bi·a /əˈrābēə/ (also **Arabian peninsula**) a peninsula in southwestern Asia, largely desert, that lies between the Red Sea and the Persian Gulf and is bounded on the north by Jordan and Iraq. The original homeland of the Arabs and the historic center of Islam, it comprises the states of Saudi Arabia, Yemen, Oman, Bahrain, Kuwait, Qatar, and the United Arab Emirates.

A·ra·bi·an /əˈrābēən/ ▸*adj. historical* of or relating to Arabia or Arabs.

▸*n. historical* **1** a native or inhabitant of Arabia. **2** (also **Arabian horse**) a horse of a breed originating in Arabia, with a distinctive dished face and high-set tail.

USAGE Arab is now generally used in reference to people; the use of **Arabian** in this sense is historical.

A·ra·bi·an cam·el ▸*n.* the domesticated one-humped camel, probably native to the deserts of North Africa and southwestern Asia. See also **DROMEDARY**. • *Camelus dromedarius*, family Camelidae.

A·ra·bi·an Des·ert /əˈrābēən/ a desert in eastern Egypt, between the Nile River and the Red Sea. Also called the **EASTERN DESERT**.

A·ra·bi·an Gulf another name for **PERSIAN GULF**.

A·ra·bi·an Nights a collection of stories and romances written in Arabic. The stories include the tales of Aladdin and Sinbad the Sailor. Also called the **THOUSAND AND ONE NIGHTS**.

A·ra·bi·an pen·in·su·la another name for **ARABIA**.

A·ra·bi·an Sea the northwestern part of the Indian Ocean, between Arabia and India.

Ar·a·bic /ˈarəbik/ ▸*n.* the Semitic language of the Arabs, spoken by some 150 million people throughout the Middle East and North Africa.

▸*adj.* of or relating to the literature or language of Arab people.

Arabic is written from right to left in a characteristic cursive script of twenty-eight consonants, the vowels being indicated by additional signs. The script has been adapted for various languages, including Persian, Urdu, Malay, and (formerly) Turkish.

▷Middle English: via Latin from Greek *arabikos*, from *Araps, Arab-* 'Arab.'

a·rab·i·ca /əˈrabikə/ ▸*n.* **1** coffee from the most widely grown kind of coffee plant. **2** the bush of the bedstraw family that produces these beans, native to the Old World tropics. • *Coffea arabica*, family Rubiaceae. ▷1920s: from Latin, feminine of *arabicus* (see **ARABIC**).

Ar·a·bic nu·mer·al ▸*n.* any of the numerals 0, 1, 2, 3, 4, 5, 6, 7, 8, and 9. Arabic numerals reached western Europe through Arabia, replacing Roman numerals, by about AD 1200, but probably originated in India.

a·rab·i·nose /əˈrabəˌnōs; ˈarəbə-/ ▸*n. Chemistry* a sugar of the pentose class that is a constituent of many plant gums. ▷late 19th cent.: from *arabin*, a carbohydrate derived from gum arabic, (based on **GUM ARABIC** + **-IN**[1]) + **-OSE**[2].

ar·a·bis /ˈarəbəs/ ▸*n.* a low-growing herbaceous plant that typically bears white or pink flowers and is frequently grown in rock gardens. Also called **ROCK CRESS**. • Genus *Arabis*, family Brassicaceae. ▷via medieval Latin from Greek, feminine of *Araps, Arab-* (see **ARAB**).

Ar·ab·ism /ˈarəˌbizəm/ ▸*n.* **1** Arab culture or identity. ■ support for Arab nationalism or political interests. **2** an Arabic linguistic usage, word, or phrase.

Ar·ab·ist /ˈarəbist/ ▸*n.* a person who studies Arabic civilization or language. ■ a person who supports Arab nationalism or political interests.

Ar·ab·ize /ˈarəˌbīz/ ▸*v.* [*trans.*] [usu. as *adj.*] (**Arabized**) give (someone or something) an Arab or Arabic character: *an Arabized script.* —**Ar·ab·i·za·tion** /ˌarəbəˈzāsHən/ *n.*

ar·a·ble /ˈarəbəl/ ▸*adj.* (of land) used or suitable for growing crops. ■ (of crops) able to be grown on such land. ■ concerned with growing such crops: *arable farming.*

▸*n.* land or crops of this type. ▷late Middle English: from Old French, or from Latin *arabilis*, from *arare* 'to plow.'

A·ra·ca·jú /ˌärəkəˈzHo͞o/ a port in eastern Brazil, on the Atlantic coast; pop. 404,828.

a·ra·ca·ri /ˌärəˈsärē/ ▸*n.* (*pl.* **-ris**) a small toucan with a serrated bill, and typically with a green back and wings, yellow underside, and red rump. • Genus *Pteroglossus*, family Ramphastidae: several species. ▷early 19th cent.: via Portuguese from Tupi *arasa'ri*.

ar·a·chi·don·ic ac·id /ˌarəkiˈdänik/ ▸*n. Biochemistry* a polyunsaturated fatty acid present in animal fats. It is important in metabolism, esp. in the synthesis of prostaglandins and leukotrienes, and is an essential constituent of the diet. • Alternative name: eicosa-5,8,11,14-enoic acid; chem. formula: $C_{19}H_{31}COOH$. ▷early 20th cent.: *arachidonic* formed irregularly from *arachidic* (a saturated fatty acid) + **-ONE** + **-IC**.

A·rach·ne /əˈraknē/ *Greek Mythology* a woman of Colophon in Lydia, a skillful weaver who challenged Athena to a contest. Athena destroyed Arachne's work and Arachne tried to hang herself, but Athena changed her into a spider. ▷from Greek *arakhnē* 'spider.'

A·rach·ni·da /əˈraknidə/ *Zoology* a class of chelicerate arthropods that includes spiders, scorpions, mites, and ticks. They have become adapted for a terrestrial life and possess book lungs and tracheae, and many have silk or poison glands. ▷modern Latin (plural), from Greek *arakhnē* 'spider.' —**a·rach·nid** *n.* & *adj.*

a·rach·noid /əˈrakˌnoid/ ▸*adj.* like a spider or arachnid.

▸*n.* (also **arachnoid membrane** or **arachnoid mater**) *Anatomy* a fine, delicate membrane, the middle one of the three membranes or meninges that surround the brain and spinal cord, situated between the dura mater and the pia mater. ▷mid 18th cent.: from modern Latin *arachnoides*, from Greek *arakhnoeidēs* 'like a cobweb,' from *arakhnē* 'spider.'

a·rach·no·pho·bi·a /əˌraknəˈfōbēə/ ▸*n.* extreme or irrational fear of spiders. ▷1920s: modern Latin, from Greek *arakhnē* 'spider' + **-PHOBIA**. —**a·rach·no·phobe** /əˈraknəˌfōb/ *n.* —**a·rach·no·pho·bic** /-bik/ *adj.*

Ar·a·fat /ˈarəˌfat/, Yasser (1929–2004), Palestinian statesman, chairman of the Palestine Liberation Organization from 1968 and Palestinian president 1996–2004. Nobel Peace Prize (1994, shared with Israel's Yitzhak Rabin and Shimon Peres).

A·ra·fu·ra Sea /ˌarəˈfo͝orə/ a sea that lies between northern Australia and eastern Indonesia and New Guinea.

A·ra·gon[1] /ˈarəˌgän; -gən/ an autonomous region in northeastern Spain, bounded on the north by the Pyrenees and on the east by Catalonia and Valencia; capital, Saragossa. Formerly an independent kingdom, it was united with Catalonia in 1137 and with Castile in 1479.

A·ra·gon[2], Catherine of, see **CATHERINE OF ARAGON**.

a·rag·o·nite /əˈragəˌnīt; ˈarəgə-/ ▸*n.* a mineral consisting of calcium carbonate, typically occurring in white seashells and as colorless prisms in deposits in hot springs. ▷early 19th cent.: from the place name **ARAGON**[1] + **-ITE**[1].

ar·ak ▸*n.* variant spelling of **ARRACK**.

a·ra·li·a /əˈrālēə; -yə/ ▸*n.* a plant of a diverse group of trees and shrubs of the ginseng family, native to America and Asia. Several kinds are cultivated for their foliage and profusion of tiny flowers, and some are used in herbal medicine. • Genus *Aralia*, family Araliaceae: several species, including the **bristly sarsaparilla** (*A. hispida*). ▷modern Latin, of unknown origin.

Ar·al Sea /ˈarəl/ an inland sea in central Asia, on the border between Kazakhstan and Uzbekistan. Its area was reduced by one-third and serious environmental consequences resulted between 1960 and 1990 after water was diverted for irrigation.

Ar·a·mae·an /ˌarəˈmāən; -ˈmēən/ ▸*n.* a member of an ancient Aramaic-speaking people inhabiting Aram (modern Syria) and part of Babylonia in the 11th–8th centuries BC.

▸*adj.* of or relating to Aram or the Aramaeans. ▷from Latin *Aramaeus* (from Greek *Aramaios*: see **ARAMAIC**) + **-AN**.

Ar·a·ma·ic /ˌarəˈmāik/ ▸*n.* a Semitic language, a Syrian dialect of which was used as a lingua franca in the Near East from the 6th century BC. It gradually replaced Hebrew as the language of the Jews in those areas and was itself supplanted by Arabic in the 7th century AD.

▸*adj.* of or in this language. ▷mid 19th cent.: from Greek *Aramaios* 'of Aram' (the biblical name of Syria) + **-IC**.

ar·a·me /ˈarəˌmā; əˈrä-/ ▸*n.* an edible Pacific seaweed with broad brown leaves, used in Japanese cooking. • *Ecklonia bicyclis*, class Phaeophyceae.

ar·a·mid /ˈarəmid/ ▸*n.* any of a class of synthetic polymers, related to nylon, that yield fibers of exceptional strength and thermal stability. ▷1970s: from *ar(omatic)* + *(poly)amid(e)*.

Ar·an /ˈarən/ ▸*adj.* denoting a type of knitwear with traditional patterns, typically involving a raised cable stitch and large diamond designs. ▷1960s: from the **ARAN ISLANDS**.

a·ra·ne·id /əˈrānēid/ ▸*n. Zoology* an invertebrate of an order that comprises the spiders. • Order Araneae, in particular the family Araneidae. ▷late 19th cent.: from modern Latin *Araneida* (former order name), from *aranea* 'spider.'

Ar·an Is·lands three islands, Inishmore, Inishmaan, and Inisheer, located off the west coast of the Republic of Ireland.

A·ran·ya·ka /äˈrənyəkə/ ▸*n.* each of a set of Hindu sacred treatises based on the Brahmanas, composed in Sanskrit *c.*700 BC. Intended only for initiates, the Aranyakas contain mystical and philosophical material and explications of esoteric rites.

A·rap·a·ho /əˈrapəˌhō/ ▸*n.* **1** (*pl.* same or **-hos**) a member of a North American Indian people living chiefly on the Great Plains, esp. in Wyoming. **2** the Algonquian language of this people.

▸*adj.* of or relating to this people or their language. ▷from Crow *aaraxpéahu*, probably literally 'those having many tattoo marks.'

ar·a·pai·ma /ˌarəˈpīmə/ ▸*n.* a large, long edible freshwater fish native to tropical South America. • *Arapaima gigas*, family Osteoglossidae. ▷mid 19th cent.: from Tupi.

Ar·a·rat, Mount /ˈarəˌrat/ two volcanic peaks in eastern Turkey, near the borders with Armenia and Iran. The higher peak, which rises to 16,946 feet (5,165 m), is the traditional site of the resting place of Noah's ark after the Flood (Gen. 8:4).

a·ra·tion·al /āˈrasHənl/ ▸*adj.* not based on or governed by reason.

Ar·au·ca·ni·an /ˌarôˈkānēən/ ▸*n.* **1** a member of a group of South American Indian peoples of Chile and adjacent parts of Argentina, of which the only people that has a surviving cultural identity is the Mapuche. **2** the family of languages spoken by this people.

▸*adj.* relating to or denoting this people or their language. See also **MAPUCHE**. ▷from Spanish *Araucania*, a region in Chile, + **-AN**.

ar·au·car·i·a /ˌarôˈke(ə)rēə/ ▸*n.* an evergreen conifer of a genus that includes the monkey puzzle and the Norfolk Island pine, having stiff sharp leaves. • Genus *Araucaria*, family Araucariaceae. ▷modern Latin, from Spanish *Arauco*, the name of a province of Araucania, Chile.

Ar·a·wak /ˈarəˌwäk/ ▸*n.* (*pl.* same or **-waks**) **1** a member of a native people originally of the Greater Antilles and adjacent South America, now living mainly in Guiana. They were forced out of the Antilles by the more warlike Caribs shortly before Spanish expansion in the Caribbean. **2** any of the Arawakan languages of these peoples.

▸*adj.* designating or relating to this people or their languages.

Ar·a·wak·an /ˌarəˈwäkən/ ▸*adj.* **1** of or relating to the Arawak people. **2** denoting or belonging to a widely scattered family of South American Indian languages, most of which are now extinct or nearly so.

▸*n.* this family of languages.

arb /ärb/ ▸*n. informal* short for **ARBITRAGEUR**.

ar·ba·lest /ˈärbəlist/ ▸*n. historical* a crossbow with a special mechanism for drawing back and releasing the string. ▷Old English *arblast*, from Old French *arbaleste*, from late Latin *arcubalista*, from Latin *arcus* 'bow' + *ballista* (see **BALLISTA**).

ar·bi·ter /ˈärbitər/ ▸*n.* a person who settles a dispute or has ultimate authority in a matter: *the military acted as arbiter of conflicts between political groups.* ■ (usu. **arbiter of**) a person whose views or actions have great influence over trends in social behavior: *an arbiter of* *taste.* ▷late Middle English: from Latin, 'judge, supreme ruler.'

ar·bi·ter e·le·gan·ti·a·rum /ˌeliˌganshēˈe(ə)rəm/ (also **ar·bi·ter e·le·gan·ti·ae** /ˌeliˈganshēˌē/) ▶*n.* a judge of artistic taste and etiquette. ▷early 19th cent.: Latin, 'judge of elegance,' used by Tacitus to describe PETRONIUS, arbiter of taste at Nero's court.

ar·bi·trage /ˈärbiˌträzh/ ▶*n.* the simultaneous buying and selling of securities, currency, or commodities in different markets or in derivative forms in order to take advantage of differing prices for the same asset.
▶*v.* [*intrans.*] buy and sell assets in such a way. ▷late Middle English (originally denoting the exercise of individual judgment): from French, from *arbitrer* 'give judgment,' from Latin *arbitrari* (see ARBITRATE). The current sense dates from the late 19th cent.

ar·bi·tra·geur /ˌärbiträˈzhər; ˈärbiˌträzhər/ (also **ar·bi·tra·ger** /ˈärbiˌträzhər/) ▶*n.* a person who engages in arbitrage. ▷late 19th cent.: from French, from *arbitrer* 'give judgment,' from Latin *arbitrari* (see ARBITRATE).

ar·bi·tral /ˈärbitrəl/ ▶*adj.* [*attrib.*] relating to or resulting from the use of an arbitrator to settle a dispute. ▷late 15th cent.: from late Latin *arbitralis*, from *arbiter* 'judge, supreme ruler.'

ar·bit·ra·ment /ärˈbitrəmənt/ ▶*n.* the settling of a dispute by an arbitrator. ■ an authoritative decision made by an arbitrator. ▷late Middle English: from Old French *arbitrement*, from medieval Latin *arbitramentum*, from *arbitrari* (see ARBITRATE).

ar·bi·trar·y /ˈärbiˌtrerē/ ▶*adj.* based on random choice or personal whim, rather than any reason or system: *his mealtimes were entirely arbitrary.* ■ (of power or a ruling body) unrestrained and autocratic in the use of authority: *arbitrary rule by King and bishops has been made impossible.* ■ *Mathematics* (of a constant or other quantity) of unspecified value. ▷late Middle English (in the sense 'dependent on one's will or pleasure, discretionary'): from Latin *arbitrarius*, from *arbiter* 'judge, supreme ruler,' perhaps influenced by French *arbitraire*. **—ar·bi·trar·i·ly** /ˌärbiˈtre(ə)rəlē/ *adv.* **—ar·bi·trar·i·ness** *n.*

ar·bi·trate /ˈärbiˌtrāt/ ▶*v.* [*intrans.*] (of an independent person or body) reach an authoritative judgment or settlement: *the board has the power to arbitrate in disputes* | [*trans.*] *it set up a commission to arbitrate border tensions.* ▷mid 16th cent.: from Latin *arbitrat-* 'judged,' from *arbitrari*, from *arbiter* 'judge, supreme ruler.'

ar·bi·tra·tion /ˌärbiˈtrāshən/ ▶*n.* the use of an arbitrator to settle a dispute.
▶*PHRASE* □ **go to arbitration** submit a dispute to an arbitrator.

ar·bi·tra·tor /ˈärbiˌtrātər/ ▶*n.* an independent person or body officially appointed to settle a dispute.

ar·bor[1] /ˈärbər/ ▶*n.* an axle or spindle on which something revolves. ■ a device holding a tool in a lathe. ▷mid 17th cent.: from French *arbre* 'tree, axis.' The spelling change was due to association with Latin *arbor* 'tree.'

ar·bor[2] (*Brit.* **ar·bour**) ▶*n.* a shady garden alcove with sides and a roof formed by trees or climbing plants trained over a wooden framework. ▷Middle English (also denoting a lawn or flower bed): from Old French *erbier*, from *erbe* 'grass, herb,' from Latin *herba*. The phonetic change to *ar-* (common in words having *er-* before a consonant) was assisted by association with Latin *arbor* 'tree.'

Ar·bor Day ▶*n.* a day dedicated annually to public tree-planting in the U.S., Australia, and other countries. It is usually observed in late April or early May. ▷from Latin *arbor* 'tree.'

ar·bo·re·al /ärˈbôrēəl/ ▶*adj.* (chiefly of animals) living in trees: *arboreal rodents.* ■ of or relating to trees. ▷mid 17th cent.: from Latin *arboreus*, from *arbor* 'tree,' + -AL. **—ar·bo·re·al·i·ty** /ärˌbôrēˈalitē/ *n.*

ar·bo·res·cent /ˌärbəˈresənt/ ▶*adj.* *chiefly Botany* treelike in growth or appearance: *arborescent ferns.* ▷late 17th cent.: from Latin *arborescent-* 'growing into a tree,' from *arborescere*, from *arbor* 'tree.' **—ar·bo·res·cence** *n.*

ar·bo·re·tum /ˌärbəˈrētəm/ ▶*n.* (*pl.* **-re·tums** or **-re·ta** /-ˈrētə/) a botanical garden devoted to trees. ▷early 19th cent.: from Latin, 'a place with trees,' from *arbor* 'tree' + -ETUM.

ar·bor·i·cul·ture /ˈärbəriˌkəlchər; ärˈbôri-/ ▶*n.* the cultivation of trees and shrubs. ▷early 19th cent.: from Latin *arbor* 'tree' + CULTURE, on the pattern of words such as *agriculture.* **—ar·bor·i·cul·tur·al** /ˌärbəriˈkəlchərəl; ärˈbôriˌkəl-/ *adj.* **—ar·bor·i·cul·tur·ist** /ˌärbəriˈkəlchərist; ärˈbôrəˌkəl-/ *n.*

Ar·bo·ri·o /ärˈbôrēˌō/ (also **ar·bo·ri·o**) ▶*n.* a variety of round-grained rice produced in Italy and used in making risotto. ▷Italian.

ar·bor·i·za·tion /ˌärbərəˈzāshən/ ▶*n.* *Anatomy* a fine branching structure at the end of a nerve fiber.

ar·bor vi·tae /ˈärbər ˈvītē/ (also **ar·bor·vi·tae**) ▶*n.* **1** a North American and eastern Asian evergreen coniferous tree of the cypress family. • Genus *Thuja*, family Cupressaceae: several species, in particular the northern white cedar (see WHITE CEDAR). **2** the arborescent appearance of the white matter in a vertical section of the cerebellum. ▷mid 16th cent.: from Latin, literally 'tree of life,' probably with reference to its medicinal use.

ar·bour ▶*n.* British spelling of ARBOR[2].

ar·bo·vi·rus /ˈärbəˌvīrəs/ ▶*n.* *Medicine* any of a group of viruses that are transmitted by mosquitoes, ticks, or other arthropods. They include encephalitis, dengue, and yellow fever. ▷1950s: from *ar(thropod)-bo(rne)* + VIRUS.

Ar·bus /ˈärbəs/, Diane (1923–71), U.S. photographer. She is best known for her disturbing images of people, esp. the poor or unusual, on city streets.

Ar·buth·not /ärˈbəthnət; ˈärbəthˌnät/, John (1667–1735), Scottish physician and writer. His satirical *History of John Bull* (1712) was the origin of John Bull as the personification of the typical Englishman.

ar·bu·tus /ärˈbyo͞otəs/ ▶*n.* either of two evergreen plants of the family Ericaceae (heath family): • a tree or shrub of the genus *Arbutus*, which includes the strawberry tree. • (also **trailing arbutus**) a North American trailing plant that bears pink or white flowers (Epigaea repens). Also called MAYFLOWER. ▷from Latin.

ARC /ärk/ ▶*abbr.* ■ *Medicine* AIDS-related complex. ■ American Red Cross.

arc /ärk/ ▶*n.* **1** a part of the circumference of a circle or other curve. ■ a curved shape, or something shaped like a curve: *the huge* **arc** *of the sky.* ■ a curving trajectory: *he swung his flashlight in a wide arc.* ■ [as *adj.*] *Mathematics* indicating the inverse of a trigonometrical function. [from the former method of defining trigonometrical functions by arcs.] **2** (also **electric arc**) a luminous electrical discharge between two electrodes or other points.
▶*v.* (**arced**; **arc·ing**) [*intrans.*] **1** [with *adverbial of direction*] move with a curving trajectory: *the ball arced across the room.* **2** [usu. as *n.*] (**arcing**) form an electric arc: *check that switches operate properly with no sign of arcing.* ▷late Middle English (denoting the path of a celestial object, esp. the sun, from horizon to horizon): via Old French from Latin *arcus* 'bow, curve.'
▶*PHRASES* □ **minute of arc** see MINUTE[1] (sense 2). □ **second of arc** see SECOND[2] (sense 2).

ar·cade /ärˈkād/ ▶*n.* **1** a covered passageway with arches along one or both sides. ■ a covered walk with stores along one or both sides. ■ *Architecture* a series of arches supporting a wall, or set along it. **2** short for VIDEO ARCADE. ▷late 17th cent.: from French, from Provençal *arcada* or Italian *arcata*, based on Latin *arcus* 'bow' (see ARC). **—ar·cad·ed** *adj.* **—ar·cad·ing** *n.*

Ar·ca·di·a /ärˈkādēə/ **1** a mountainous district in the Peloponnese of southern Greece. In poetic fantasy it represents a pastoral paradise, and in Greek mythology it is the home of Pan. **2** a city in southwestern California, northeast of Los Angeles; pop. 48,290. The Santa Anita racetrack is here.

Ar·ca·di·an /ärˈkādēən/ ▶*n.* a native of Arcadia. ■ *poetic/literary* an idealized country dweller.
▶*adj.* of or relating to Arcadia. ■ *poetic/literary* of or relating to an ideal rustic paradise. ▷late 16th cent.: from Latin *Arcadius*, from Greek *Arkadia* (see ARCADIA).

Ar·ca·dy /ˈärkədē/ ▶*n.* *poetic/literary* an ideal rustic paradise. ▷late 16th cent.: from Greek *Arkadia* (see ARCADIA).

ar·ca·na /ärˈkānə/ ▶*plural n.* [treated as *sing.* or *pl.*] (*sing.* **-num** /-nəm/) secrets or mysteries: *his knowledge of federal budget arcana is legendary.* ■ [treated as *sing.*] either of the two groups of cards in a tarot pack: the twenty-two trump cards (the **major arcana**) and the fifty-six suit cards (the **minor arcana**). ▷mid 16th cent.: from Latin, neuter plural of *arcanus* (see ARCANE).

ar·cane /ärˈkān/ ▶*adj.* understood by few; mysterious or secret: *modern math and its arcane notation.* ▷mid 16th cent.: from Latin *arcanus*, from *arcere* 'to shut up,' from *arca* 'chest.' **—ar·cane·ly** *adv.*

Ar·ca·ro /ärˈkarō; -ˈke(ə)rō/, Eddie (1916–), U.S. jockey; full name *George Edward Arcaro*. He was the first two-time Triple Crown winner, riding Whirlaway in 1941 and Citation in 1948.

Arc de Tri·omphe /ˈärk də trēˈônf/ a ceremonial arch standing at the top of the Champs Élysées in Paris, commissioned by Napoleon to commemorate his victories in 1805–06. Inspired by the Arch of Constantine in Rome, it was completed in 1836.

Arc de Triomphe

arc fur·nace ▶*n.* a furnace that uses an electric arc as a heat source, esp. for steelmaking.

arch[1] /ärch/ ▶*n.* a curved symmetrical structure spanning an opening and typically supporting the weight of a bridge, roof, or wall above it. ■ a structure of this type forming a passageway or a ceremonial monument: *a triumphal arch.* ■ a shape resembling such a structure or a thing with such a shape: *the delicate* **arch of** *his eyebrows.* ■ the inner side of the foot.
▶*v.* **1** [*intrans.*] have the curved shape of an arch: *a beautiful bridge that* **arched over** *a canal.* ■ form or cause to form the curved shape of an arch: [*intrans.*] *her eyebrows arched in surprise* | [*trans.*] *she arched her back.* **2** [*trans.*] [usu. as *adj.*] (**arched**) provide (a bridge, building, or part of a building) with an arch: *high arched windows.* ■ *archaic* or *poetic/literary* span (something) by or as if by an arch: *the vine arched his evening seat.* ▷Middle English: from Old French *arche*, based on Latin *arcus* 'bow' (see ARC).

arch[2] ▶*adj.* deliberately or affectedly playful and teasing: *arch observations about even the most mundane matters.* ▷mid 16th cent. (in the sense 'chief, principal'): from ARCH-, because of its association with words such as *rogue*. **—arch·ly** *adv.* **—arch·ness** *n.*

arch- ▶*comb. form* chief; principal: *archbishop.* ■ preeminent of its kind: *archenemy.* ■ (in unfavorable senses) out-and-out: *arch-scoundrel.* ▷via Latin from Greek *arkhi-*, from *arkhos* 'chief.'

ar·chae·a /ärˈkēə/ ▶*plural n.* another term for ARCHAEBACTERIA. **—ar·chae·an** *adj.* & *n.*

Ar·chae·an ▶*adj.* British spelling of ARCHEAN.

ar·chae·bac·te·ri·a /ˌärkēˌbakˈti(ə)rēə/ ▶*plural n.* (*sing.* **-te·ri·um** /-ˈti(ə)rēəm/) *Biology* microorganisms that are similar to bacteria in size and simplicity of structure but radically different in molecular organization. They are now believed to constitute an ancient intermediate group between the bacteria and eukaryotes. Also called ARCHAEA. ▷modern Latin (plural), from Greek *arkhaios* 'primitive.' **—ar·chae·bac·te·ri·al** *adj.*

archaeo- (also **archeo-**) ▶*comb. form* relating to archaeology or prehistoric times: *archaeoastronomy* | *archaeomagnetism.* ▷from Greek *arkhaios* 'ancient,' from *arkhē* 'beginning.'

ar·chae·o·as·tron·o·my /ˌärkēō-əˈstränəmē/ ▶*n.* the investigation of the astronomical knowledge of prehistoric cultures. Also called ASTROARCHAEOLOGY.

ar·chae·ol·o·gy /ˌärkēˈäləjē/ (also **ar·che·ol·o·gy**) ▶*n.* the study of human history and prehistory through the excavation of sites and the analysis of artifacts and other physical remains. ▷early 17th cent. (in the sense 'ancient history'): from modern Latin *archaeologia*, from Greek *arkhaiologia* 'ancient history,' from *arkhaios* 'ancient' (see ARCHAEO-). The current sense dates from the mid 19th cent. **—ar·chae·o·log·ic** /-əˈläjik/ *adj.* **—ar·chae·o·log·i·cal** /-əˈläjikəl/ *adj.* **—ar·chae·o·log·i·cal·ly** *adv.* **—ar·chae·ol·o·gist** /-jist/ *n.*

ar·chae·op·ter·yx /ˌärkēˈäptəriks/ ▶*n.* the oldest known fossil bird, of the late Jurassic period. It had feathers, wings, and hollow bones like a bird, but teeth, a bony tail, and legs like a small coelurosaur

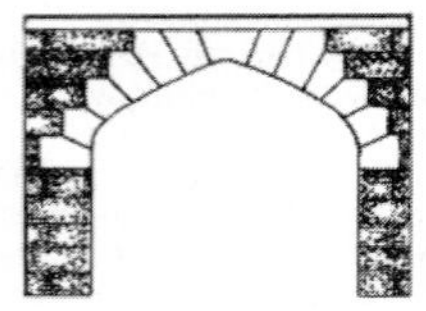

Tudor

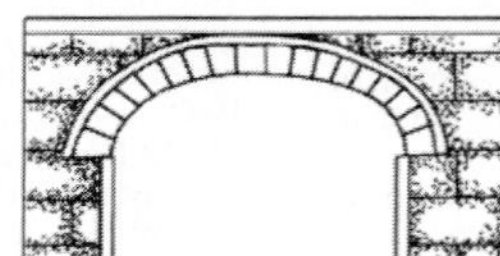

basket handle

rampant

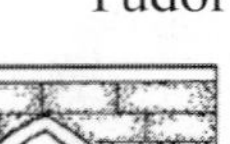

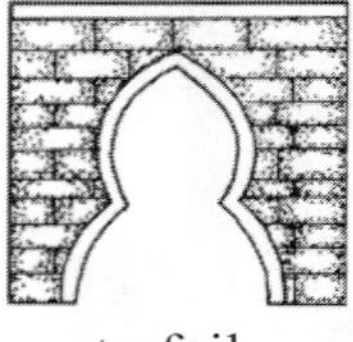

trefoil

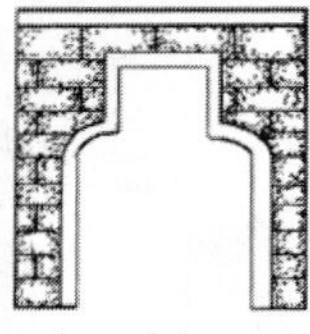

shouldered

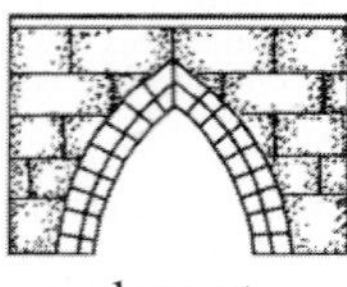

lancet

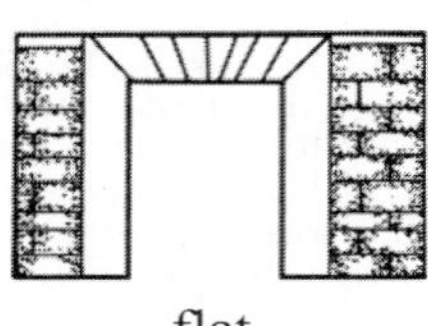

flat

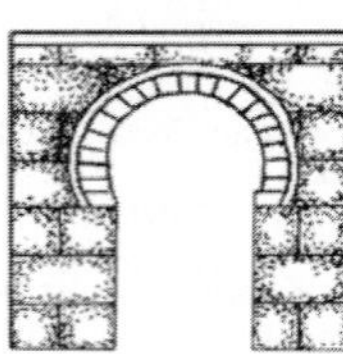

horseshoe

equilateral

round

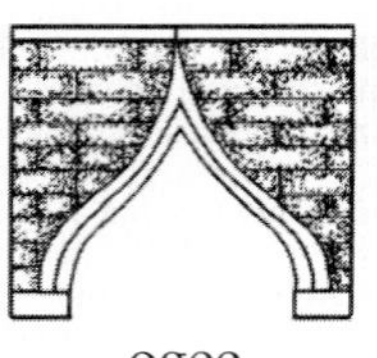

ogee

arch[1]
types of arches

dinosaur. • *Archaeopteryx lithographica*, subclass Archaeornithes. ▷from Greek *arkhaios* 'ancient' (see **ARCHAEO-**) + *pterux* 'wing.'

ar·cha·ic /är'kāik/ ▸*adj.* very old or old-fashioned: *prisons are run on archaic methods.* See note at **OLD**. ■ (of a word or a style of language) no longer in everyday use but sometimes used to impart an old-fashioned flavor. ■ of an early period of art or culture, esp. the 7th–6th centuries BC in Greece: *the archaic temple at Corinth.* ▷mid 19th cent.: from French *archaïque*, from Greek *arkhaikos*, from *arkhaios*, from *arkhē* 'beginning.' **—ar·cha·i·cal·ly** *adv.*

ar·cha·ism /'ärkē,izəm; 'ärkā-/ ▸*n.* a thing that is very old or old-fashioned. ■ an archaic word or style of language or art. ■ the use or conscious imitation of very old or old-fashioned styles or features in language or art. ▷mid 17th cent.: from modern Latin *archaismus*, from Greek *arkhaismos*, from *arkhaizein* 'imitate archaic styles,' from *arkhaios* 'ancient,' from *arkhē* 'beginning.' **—ar·cha·is·tic** /,ärkē'istik; ,ärkā-/ *adj.*

ar·cha·iz·ing /'ärkē,īziNG; 'ärkā-/ ▸*adj.* consciously imitating a word or a style of language or art that is very old or old-fashioned: *some archaizing poetry.*

Arch·an·gel /'ärk,ānjəl/ a port in northwestern Russia, on the White Sea; pop. 419,000. It is named after the monastery of the Archangel Michael that is situated here. Russian name **ARKHANGELSK**.

arch·an·gel /'ärk,ānjəl/ ▸*n.* an angel of high rank. ■ in traditional Christian angelology, a being of the eighth order of the ninefold celestial hierarchy. ▷Middle English, from Anglo-Norman French *archangele*, via ecclesiastical Latin from ecclesiastical Greek *arkhangelos*, from *arkhi-* 'chief' + *angelos* 'messenger, angel.' **—arch·an·gel·ic** /,ärkan'jelik/ *adj.*

arch·bish·op /'ärCH'bisHəp/ ▸*n.* the chief bishop responsible for an archdiocese. ▷Old English, from **ARCH-** 'chief' + *biscop* (see **BISHOP**), replacing earlier *heah-biscop* 'high bishop.'

arch·bish·op·ric /,ärCH'bisHəprik/ ▸*n.* the office of an archbishop. ■ an archdiocese. ▷Old English *arcebiscoprice* (see **ARCH-**, **BISHOPRIC**).

arch·dea·con /'ärCH'dēkən/ ▸*n.* a senior Christian cleric (in the early Church a deacon, in the modern Anglican church a priest) to whom a bishop delegates certain responsibilities. ▷Old English *arcediacon*, *ercediacon*, from ecclesiastical Latin *archidiaconus*, from ecclesiastical Greek *arkhidiakonos*, from *arkhi-* 'chief' + *diakonos* (see **DEACON**).

arch·dea·con·ry /,ärCH'dēkənrē/ ▸*n.* (*pl.* **-ries**) the office of an archdeacon. ■ the district for which an archdeacon is responsible. ■ the residence of an archdeacon.

arch·di·o·cese /,ärCH'dīəsis; -,sēz/ ▸*n.* the district for which an archbishop is responsible. **—arch·di·oc·e·san** /,ärCHdī'äsəsən/ *adj.*

arch·duch·ess /'ärCH'dəCHis/ ▸*n. historical* the wife or widow of an archduke. ■ a daughter of the emperor of Austria.

arch·duke /'ärCH'd(y)o͞ok/ ▸*n. historical* a son of the emperor of Austria. ▷early 16th cent.: from Old French *archeduc*, from Merovingian Latin *archidux*, *archiduc-*, from *archi-* 'chief' + *dux*, *duc-* (see **DUKE**). **—arch·du·cal** /,ärCH'd(y)o͞okəl/ *adj.*

Ar·che·an /är'kēən/ (*Brit.* **Ar·chae·an**) ▸*adj. Geology* of, relating to, or denoting the eon that constitutes the earlier (or middle) part of the Precambrian, in which there was no life on earth. It precedes the Proterozoic eon. Also called **AZOIC**. ■ [as *n.*] (**the Archean**) the Archean eon or the system of rocks deposited during it.

The Archean extended from the origin of the earth (see **PRECAMBRIAN**) to about 2,500 million years ago. In models that include the Priscoan eon, the Archean began about 4,000 million years ago.

▷late 19th cent.: from Greek *arkhaios* 'ancient' + **-AN**.

ar·che·go·ni·um /,ärki'gōnēəm/ ▸*n.* (*pl.* **-ni·a** /-nēə/) *Botany* the female sex organ in mosses, liverworts, ferns, and most conifers. ▷mid 19th cent.: modern Latin, from Greek *arkhegonos*, from *arkhe-* 'first' + *gonos* 'race.'

arch·en·e·my /'ärCH'enəmē/ ▸*n.* a person who is extremely hostile or opposed to someone or something: *the twins were archenemies.* ■ (**the Archenemy**) the Devil.

arch·en·ter·on /ärk'entə,rän/ ▸*n. Embryology* the rudimentary alimentary cavity of an embryo at the gastrula stage. ▷late 19th cent.: from Greek *arkhē* 'beginning' + *enteron* 'intestine.'

archeo- ▸*comb. form* variant spelling of **ARCHAEO-**.

ar·che·ol·o·gy ▸*n.* variant of **ARCHAEOLOGY**.

arch·er /'ärCHər/ ▸*n.* a person who shoots with a bow and arrows, esp. at a target for sport. ■ (**the Archer**) the zodiacal sign or constellation Sagittarius. ▷Middle English: from Old French *archier*, based on Latin *arcus* 'bow.'

ar·cher·fish /'ärCHər,fisH/ ▸*n.* (*pl.* same or **-fish·es**) a freshwater fish that knocks insect prey off overhanging vegetation by spitting water at it. It is native to Asia, Australia, and the Philippines. • Genus *Toxotes*, family Toxotidae: several species, in particular *T. jaculator*.

ar·cher·y /'ärCHərē/ ▸*n.* the sport or skill of shooting with a bow and arrows, esp. at a target. ▷late Middle English: from Old French *archerie*, from *archier* (see **ARCHER**).

arch·es /'ärCHiz/ ▸*plural n.* [treated as *sing.*] used in names of moths with curving archlike patterns on the wings, such as **dark arches**. • Several genera in the families Noctuidae and Notodontidae.

ar·che·typ·al /,ärk(i)'tīpəl/ ▸*adj.* very typical of a certain kind of person or thing: *the archetypal country doctor.* ■ recurrent as a symbol or motif in literature, art, or mythology: *an archetypal journey representing the quest for identity.* ■ of, relating to, or denoting an original that has been imitated: *the archetypal believer, Abraham.* ■ relating to or denoting Jungian archetypes.

ar·che·type /'ärk(i),tīp/ ▸*n.* a very typical example of a certain person or thing: *the book is a perfect archetype of the genre.* See note at **MODEL**. ■ an original that has been imitated: *the archetype of faith is Abraham.* ■ a recurrent symbol or motif in literature, art, or mythology: *mythological archetypes of good and evil.* ■ *Psychoanalysis* (in Jungian psychology) a primitive mental image inherited from the earliest human ancestors, and supposed to be present in the collective unconscious. ▷mid 16th cent.: via Latin from Greek *arkhetupon* 'something molded first as a model,' from *arkhe-* 'primitive' + *tupos* 'a model.' **—ar·che·typ·i·cal** /,ärk(i)'tipikəl/ *adj.*

arch·fiend /'ärCH'fēnd/ ▸*n. poetic/literary* a chief fiend, esp. the Devil.

ar·chi·di·ac·o·nal /,ärkidī'akənl/ ▸*adj.* of or relating to an archdeacon. ▷late Middle English: from medieval Latin *archidiaconalis*, from *archi-* 'chief' + *diaconalis* (see **DIACONAL**). **—ar·chi·di·ac·o·nate** /-nit/ *n.*

ar·chi·e·pis·co·pal /,ärkēə'piskəpəl/ ▸*adj.* of or relating to an archbishop. ▷early 17th cent.: via ecclesiastical Latin from Greek *arkhiepiskopos* 'archbishop' (from *arkhi-* 'chief' + *episkopos* 'bishop') + **-AL**. **—ar·chi·e·pis·co·pa·cy** /-ə'piskəpəsē/ *n.* (*pl.* **-cies**) **—ar·chi·e·pis·co·pate** /-pit; -,pāt/ *n.*

ar·chil /'ärkəl; -CHəl/ ▸*n.* archaic spelling of **ORCHIL**.

Ar·chil·o·chus /är'kiləkəs/ (8th or 7th century BC), Greek poet. He is credited with the invention of iambic meter.

ar·chi·man·drite /,ärkə'man,drīt/ ▸*n.* the head of a large monastery or group of monasteries in the Orthodox Church. ■ an honorary title given to a monastic priest. ▷mid 17th cent.: via ecclesiastical Latin, from ecclesiastical Greek *arkhimandritēs*, from *arkhi-* 'chief' + *mandra* 'monastery.'

Ar·chi·me·de·an screw /,ärkə'mēdēən/ ▸*n.* a device invented by Archimedes for raising water by means of a spiral within a tube.

Ar·chi·me·des /,ärkə'mēdēz/ (*c.*287–212 BC), Greek mathematician and inventor from Syracuse. He is noted for his discovery of Archimedes' principle (legend has it that he made this discovery while taking a bath and ran through the streets shouting "Eureka!"). Among his mathematical discoveries are the ratio of the radius of a circle to its circumference and formulas for the surface area and volume of a sphere and of a cylinder. **—Ar·chi·me·de·an** /-'mēdēən/ *adj.*

Ar·chi·me·des' prin·ci·ple *Physics* a result stating that a body totally or partially immersed in a fluid is subject to an upward force equal in magnitude to the weight of fluid it displaces.

ar·chi·pel·a·go /,ärkə'pelə,gō/ ▸*n.* (*pl.* **-gos** or **-goes**) a group of islands. ■ a sea or stretch of water containing many islands. ▷early 16th cent.: from Italian *arcipelago*, from Greek *arkhi-* 'chief' + *pelagos* 'sea.' The word was originally used as a proper name (*the Archipelago* 'the Aegean Sea'): the generalization of meaning occurred because the Aegean Sea is remarkable for its large numbers of islands.

Ar·chi·pen·ko /,ärkə'p(y)eNGkō/, Aleksandr (Porfirevich) (1887–1964), U.S. sculptor; born in Russia. He adapted cubist techniques to sculpture.

Ar·chi·pié·la·go de Co·lón /,ärCHē'pyālä,gō dā kō'lōn/ official Spanish name for **GALÁPAGOS ISLANDS**.

ar·chi·tect /'ärki,tekt/ ▸*n.* a person who designs buildings and in many cases also supervises their construction. ■ a person who is responsible for inventing or realizing a particular idea or project: *a chief architect of the plan to slash income taxes.*
▸*v.* [*trans.*] (usu. **be architected**) *Computing* design and make: *few software packages were architected with Ethernet access in mind.* ▷mid 16th cent.: from French *architecte*, from Italian *architetto*, via Latin from Greek *arkhitektōn*, from *arkhi-* 'chief' + *tektōn* 'builder.'

ar·chi·tec·ton·ic /,ärkitek'tänik/ ▸*adj.* of or relating to architecture or architects. ■ (of an artistic composition or physical appearance) having a clearly defined structure, esp. one that is artistically pleasing: *the painting's architectonic harmony.*
▸*n.* (**architectonics**) [usu. treated as *sing.*] the

scientific study of architecture. ■ musical, literary, or artistic structure: *the architectonics of Latin prose.* ▷mid 17th cent.: via Latin from Greek *arkhitektonikos,* from *arkhitektōn* (see ARCHITECT). —**ar·chi·tec·ton·i·cal·ly** /-ik(ə)lē/ *adv.*

ar·chi·tec·ture /ˈärkiˌtekCHər/ ▸*n.* **1** the art or practice of designing and constructing buildings. ■ the style in which a building is designed or constructed, esp. with regard to a specific period, place, or culture: *Victorian architecture.* **2** the complex or carefully designed structure of something: *the chemical* ***architecture of*** *the human brain.* ■ the conceptual structure and logical organization of a computer or computer-based system: *a client/server architecture.* ▷mid 16th cent.: from Latin *architectura,* from *architectus* (see ARCHITECT). —**ar·chi·tec·tur·al** /ˌärkiˈtekCHərəl/ *adj.* —**ar·chi·tec·tur·al·ly** /ˌärkiˈtekCHərəlē/ *adv.*

ar·chi·trave /ˈärkiˌtrāv/ ▸*n.* **1** (in classical architecture) a main beam resting across the tops of columns, specifically the lower third entablature. **2** the molded frame around a doorway or window. ■ a molding around the exterior of an arch. ▷mid 16th cent.: from French, from Italian, from *archi-* 'chief' + *-trave* from Latin *trabs, trab-* 'a beam.'

ar·chive /ˈärˌkīv/ (usu. **archives**) ▸*n.* a collection of historical documents or records providing information about a place, institution, or group of people: *source materials in local archives* | [as *adj.*] *a section of archive film.* ■ the place where such documents or records are kept: *to get into the archives I had to fill in a request form.*
▸*v.* [*trans.*] place or store (something) in such a collection or place. ■ *Computing* transfer (data) to a less frequently used storage medium such as magnetic tape, typically external to the computer system and having a greater storage capacity. ▷early 17th cent. (in the sense 'place where records are kept'): from French *archives* (plural), from Latin *archiva, archia,* from Greek *arkheia* 'public records,' from *arkhē* 'government.' The verb dates from the late 19th cent. —**ar·chi·val** /ärˈkīvəl/ *adj.*

ar·chi·vist /ˈärkəvist; -ˌkī-/ ▸*n.* a person who maintains and is in charge of archives.

ar·chi·volt /ˈärkəˌvōlt/ ▸*n.* a band of molding, resembling an architrave, around the lower curve of an arch. ■ the lower curve itself from impost to impost of the columns. ▷mid 17th cent.: from French *archivolte* or Italian *archivolto,* based on Latin *arcus* 'bow, arch' + *volvere* 'to roll.'

arch·lute /ˈärCHˌlo͞ot/ ▸*n.* a bass lute with an extended neck and unstopped bass strings. ▷mid 17th cent.: from French *archiluth,* from *archi-* 'chief' + *luth* (see LUTE[1]).

ar·chon /ˈärˌkän/ ▸*n.* each of the nine chief magistrates in ancient Athens. ■ any ruler: *rock's archons are disc jockeys and concert promoters.* ▷late 16th cent.: from Greek *arkhōn* 'ruler,' noun use of the present participle of *arkhein* 'to rule.' —**ar·chon·ship** /-ˌSHip/ *n.*

ar·cho·saur /ˈärkəˌsôr/ (also **ar·cho·sau·rus** /ˌärkəˈsôrəs/) ▸*n. Zoology & Paleontology* a reptile of a large group that includes the dinosaurs and pterosaurs, represented today only by the crocodilians. • Subdivision Archosauria, subclass Diapsida. ▷1930s: from modern Latin *Archosauria,* from Greek *arkhos* 'chief' or *arkhōn* 'ruler' + -SAUR. —**ar·cho·sau·ri·an** /ˌärkəˈsôrēən/ *adj.*

arch·priest /ˈärCHˈprēst/ ▸*n.* a chief priest.

arch·way /ˈärCHˌwā/ ▸*n.* a curved structure forming a passage or entrance.

arc light (also **arc lamp**) ▸*n.* a light source using an electric arc.

arc min·ute /ˈminit/ ▸*n.* see MINUTE[1] (sense 2).

arc sec·ond (also **second of arc**) ▸*n.* see SECOND[2] (sense 2).

arc sine (abbr.: **arc·sin**) ▸*n.* a mathematical function that is the inverse of the sine function.

arc tan·gent (abbr.: **arctan**) ▸*n.* a mathematical function that is the inverse of the tangent function.

Arc·tic /ˈärktik; ˈärtik/ ▸*adj.* **1** of or relating to the regions around the North Pole: *an Arctic explorer.* ■ (of animals or plants) living or growing in such regions. ■ designed for use in such regions: *Arctic clothing.* **2** (**arctic**) *informal* (of weather conditions) very cold.
▸*n.* **1** (**the Arctic**) the regions around the North Pole. **2** (**arc·tics** /ˈärtiks/) thick waterproof overshoes extending to the ankle or above. **3** (**arctic**) a drab-colored hairy butterfly of the arctic and subarctic regions of the New World. • Genus *Oenis,* subfamily Satyrinae, family Nymphalidae. ▷late Middle English: via Old French from Latin *arcticus, articus,* from Greek *arktikos,* from *arktos* 'bear, Ursa Major, North Star.'

Arc·tic Ar·chi·pel·a·go the name for all of the islands that lie north of mainland Canada and the Arctic Circle. Sparsely populated, they have varied mineral resources and wildlife. Baffin Island is the largest of the group.

Arc·tic char ▸*n.* see CHAR[4].

Arc·tic Cir·cle the parallel of latitude 66° 33′ north of the equator. It marks the northernmost point at which the sun is visible on the northern winter solstice and the southernmost point at which the midnight sun can be seen on the northern summer solstice.

Arc·tic fox ▸*n.* a fox with a thick coat that turns white in winter, found on the tundra of North America and Eurasia. • *Alopex lagopus,* family Canidae.

Arc·tic hare ▸*n.* a hare whose coat turns white in winter, found in the arctic areas of North America. • *Lepus arcticus,* family Leporidae.

Arc·tic O·cean a sea that surrounds the North Pole and lies within the Arctic Circle. Much of the sea is covered with pack ice throughout the year.

Arc·tic tern ▸*n.* a red-billed tern that breeds in the Arctic and adjacent areas, migrating to Antarctic regions for the winter. • *Sterna paradisaea,* family Sternidae.

Arc·tic wil·low (also **arc·tic wil·low**) ▸*n.* a shrub, *Salix arctica,* found in the Canadian tundra.

Arc·to·gae·a /ˌärktəˈjēə/ (also **Arc·to·ge·a**) *Zoology* a major zoogeographical area comprising the Palaearctic, Nearctic, Ethiopian, and Oriental regions. ▷modern Latin, from Greek *arktos* 'northern' + *gaia* 'earth.' —**Arc·to·gae·an** *adj.*

arc·to·phile /ˈärktəˌfīl/ ▸*n.* a person who collects or is very fond of teddy bears. ▷1970s: from Greek *arktos* 'bear' + *philos* 'loving.' —**arc·to·phil·i·a** /ˌärktəˈfilēə/ *n.* —**arc·toph·il·ist** /ärkˈtäfilist/ *n.* — **arc·toph·il·y** /-ˈtäfilē/ *n.*

Arc·tu·rus /ärkˈt(y)o͝orəs/ *Astronomy* the fourth brightest star in the sky, and the brightest in the constellation Boötes. It is an orange giant. ▷from Greek *arktos* 'bear' + *ouros* 'guardian' (because of its position in line with the tail of Ursa Major).

ar·cu·ate /ˈärkyo͞oit; -ˌāt/ ▸*adj. technical* shaped like a bow; curved: *the arcuate sweep of the chain of islands.* ▷late Middle English: from Latin *arcuatus,* past participle of *arcuare* 'to curve,' from *arcus* 'bow, curve.'

ar·cus se·ni·lis /ˈärkəs səˈnīlis/ ▸*n. Medicine* a narrow opaque band encircling the cornea, common in old age. ▷late 18th cent.: Latin, literally 'senile bow.'

arc weld·ing ▸*n.* a technique in which metals are welded using heat generated by an electric arc.

-ard ▸*suffix* forming nouns such as *bollard, wizard.* ■ forming nouns having a depreciatory sense: *drunkard* | *dullard.* ▷Middle English and Old French, from German *-hard* 'hard, hardy.'

Ar·den /ˈärdn/, Elizabeth (*c.*1880–1966), U.S. executive in the cosmetics industry; born in Canada; born *Florence Nightingale Graham.*

Ar·dennes /ärˈden/ a forested upland region extending over parts of southeastern Belgium, northeastern France, and Luxembourg. It was the scene of fierce fighting in both world wars.

ar·dent /ˈärdnt/ ▸*adj.* enthusiastic or passionate: *an ardent baseball fan* | *an ardent suitor.* See note at EAGER. ■ *archaic* or *poetic/literary* burning; glowing: *the ardent flames.* ▷Middle English: from Old French *ardant,* from Latin *ardens, ardent-,* from *ardere* 'to burn.' —**ar·dent·ly** *adv.*

Ard·more /ˈärdˌmôr/ a city in southern Oklahoma, in an oil-producing and agricultural area; pop. 23,711.

ar·dor /ˈärdər/ (*Brit.* **ar·dour**) ▸*n.* enthusiasm or passion: *they felt the stirrings of revolutionary ardor.* ▷late Middle English: via Old French from Latin *ardor,* from *ardere* 'to burn.'

ar·du·ous /ˈärjo͞oəs/ ▸*adj.* involving or requiring strenuous effort; difficult and tiring: *an arduous journey.* See note at HARD. ▷mid 16th cent.: from Latin *arduus* 'steep, difficult' + -OUS. —**ar·du·ous·ly** *adv.* —**ar·du·ous·ness** *n.*

are[1] /är/ ▸ 2nd person singular present and 1st, 2nd, 3rd person plural present of BE.

are[2] /är; e(ə)r/ ▸*n. historical* a metric unit of measure, equal to 100 square meters (about 119.6 square yards). ▷late 18th cent.: from French, from Latin *area* (see AREA).

ar·e·a /ˈe(ə)rēə/ ▸*n.* **1** a region or part of a town, a country, or the world: *rural areas of New Jersey* | *people living in the area are at risk.* ■ [with *adj.*] a space allocated for a specific purpose: *the dining area.* ■ a part of an object or surface: *areas of the body.* ■ a subject or range of activity or interest: *the key areas of science.* ■ [usu. as *adj.*] *Brit.* a sunken enclosure giving access to the basement of a building: *a bicycle padlocked to the area railing.* **2** the extent or measurement of a surface or piece of land: *the area of a triangle* | *the room is twelve square feet* ***in area.*** ▷mid 16th cent. (in the sense 'space allocated for a specific purpose'): from Latin, literally 'vacant piece of level ground.' —**ar·e·al** *adj.*

ar·e·a code ▸*n.* a three-digit number that identifies one of the telephone service regions into which the U.S., Canada, and certain other countries are divided and that is dialed when calling from one area to another.

ar·e·a rug ▸*n.* a rug that covers only a part of a floor in a room.

ar·e·a·way /ˈe(ə)rēəˌwā/ ▸*n.* a sunken enclosure giving access to the basement of a building. ■ a passageway between buildings.

a·re·ca /əˈrēkə; ˈarikə; ˈe(ə)r-/ (also **areca palm**) ▸*n.* a tropical Asian palm. • Genus *Areca,* family Palmae: several species, in particular *A. catechu.* ▷via Portuguese from Malayalam *aḍekka.*

a·re·ca nut ▸*n.* the astringent seed of an areca palm (*Areca catechu*), which is often chewed with betel leaves. Also called BETEL NUT.

A·re·ci·bo /ˌärəˈsēbō/ a community in northwestern Puerto Rico, west of San Juan; pop. 49,545. It is an academic center noted for its huge radio telescope facility.

a·re·li·gious /ˌāriˈlijəs/ ▸*adj.* not influenced by or practicing religion: *the sexual mores of today's secular and areligious culture.*

a·re·na /əˈrēnə/ ▸*n.* a level area surrounded by seats for spectators, in which sports, entertainments, and other public events are held. ■ a place or scene of activity, debate, or conflict: *he has reentered the political arena.* ▷early 17th cent.: from Latin *harena, arena* 'sand, sand-strewn place of combat.'

ar·e·na·ceous /ˌarəˈnāSHəs/ ▸*adj. Geology* consisting of sand or sandlike particles. ■ *Biology* (of animals or plants) living or growing in sand. ▷mid 17th cent.: from Latin *arenaceus,* from *arena, harena* 'sand.'

Ar·endt /ˈärənt/, Hannah (1906–75), U.S. philosopher and political theorist; born in Germany. A student of Martin Heidegger, she established her reputation as a political thinker with one of the first works to propose that Nazism and Stalinism had common roots. Notable works: *The Origins of Totalitarianism* (1951), *Eichmann in Jerusalem* (1963), and *On Violence* (1970).

a·re·no·sol /əˈrēnəˌsôl; -ˌsäl/ ▸*n.* a soil type consisting mainly of sand with very little organic matter and supporting limited amounts of specialized vegetation.

aren't /är(ə)nt/ ▸*contraction of* ■ are not: *they aren't here.* ■ am not (only used in questions): *I'm right, aren't I?* | *why aren't I being given a pay raise?*

a·re·o·la /əˈrēələ/ ▸*n.* (*pl.* **-lae** /-ˌlē/) *Anatomy* a small circular area, in particular the ring of pigmented skin surrounding a nipple. ■ *Biology* any of the small spaces between the veins on a leaf or the nervures on an insect's wing. ■ *Medicine* a reddened patch around a spot or papule. ▷mid 17th cent. (in the sense 'small space or interstice'): from Latin, literally 'small open space,' diminutive of *area* (see AREA). —**a·re·o·lar** *adj.* —**a·re·o·late** /-lit; -ˌlāt/ *adj.*

ar·e·ole /ˈe(ə)rēˌōl/ ▸*n. Biology* an areola, esp. a small area bearing spines or hairs on a cactus. ▷mid 19th cent.: from French *aréole,* from Latin (see AREOLA).

ar·e·ol·o·gy /ˌe(ə)rēˈäləjē/ ▸*n.* the study of the planet Mars. ▷late 19th cent.: from *Ares* (Greek equivalent of the Roman war god Mars) + *-ology.* —**ar·e·o·log·i·cal** /ˌe(ə)rēəˈläjikəl/ *adj.* —**ar·e·ol·o·gist** *n.* & *adj.*

Ar·e·op·a·gus /ˌarēˈäpəgəs/ (in ancient Athens) a hill on which met the highest governmental council and later a judicial court. ▷from Greek *Areios pagos* 'hill of *Ares*'; the name for the site came to denote the court itself.

a·re·pa /äˈrāpə/ ▸*n.* a corn pancake, sweetened or unsweetened, eaten in Venezuela and Colombia. ▷Cariban.

A·re·qui·pa /ˌärəˈkēpə/ a city in southern Peru, in the Andes; pop. 634,500.

Ar·es /ˈe(ə)rēz/ *Greek Mythology* the Greek war god, son of Zeus and Hera. Roman equivalent **MARS**.

a·rête /əˈrāt/ ▸*n.* a sharp mountain ridge. ▷early 19th cent.: from French, from Latin *arista* 'ear of wheat, fish bone, spine.'

ar·e·thu·sa /ˌarəˈTHo͞ozə/ ▸*n.* a pinkish-red North American wild orchid that grows in boggy ground. Also called **DRAGON'S MOUTH**. • *Arethusa bulbosa*, family Orchidaceae.

arf /ärf/ ▸*exclam.* (usu. **arf arf**) used to imitate or represent a dog's bark.

ar·ga·li /ˈärgəlē/ ▸*n.* (*pl.* same) the largest wild sheep, which has massive horns and is found in mountainous areas of Asia. • *Ovis ammon*, family Bovidae. ▷late 18th cent.: from Mongolian.

Ar·gand di·a·gram /ˈärgənd; -gand/ ▸*n.* *Mathematics* a diagram on which complex numbers are represented geometrically using Cartesian axes, the horizontal coordinate representing the real part of the number and the vertical coordinate the complex part. ▷early 20th cent.: named after J. R. *Argand* (1768–1822), French mathematician.

Ar·gand lamp ▸*n.* *historical* an oil or gas lamp equipped with a tubular wick that allowed air to pass both inner and outer surfaces of the flame, securing more perfect combustion and brighter light. ▷late 18th cent.: named after A. *Argand* (1755–1803), French physicist.

ar·gan oil /ˈärgən/ ▸*n.* an aromatic culinary oil expressed from the seeds of the argan tree, native to an area of southwestern Morocco. • *Argania spinosa*, family Sapotaceae.

ar·gent /ˈärjənt/ ▸*adj.* *poetic/literary* & *Heraldry* silver; silvery white: *the argent moon.*
▸*n.* *Heraldry* silver as a heraldic tincture. ▷late Middle English (denoting silver coins): via Old French from Latin *argentum* 'silver.'

ar·gen·tif·er·ous /ˌärjənˈtifərəs/ ▸*adj.* (of rocks or minerals) containing silver. ▷late 18th cent.: from Latin *argentum* 'silver' + **-FEROUS**.

Ar·gen·ti·na /ˌärjənˈtēnə/ a republic that occupies much of the southern part of South America; pop. 39,144,000; capital, Buenos Aires; official language, Spanish. **—Ar·gen·tine** /ˈärjənˌtēn; -ˌtīn/ *adj.* & *n.* **—Ar·gen·tin·i·an** /-ˈtinēən/ *adj.* & *n.*

Colonized by the Spanish in the 16th century, Argentina declared its independence in 1816. It emerged as a democratic republic in the mid 19th century, but has periodically fallen under military rule. In 1982, Argentina's claim to the Falkland Islands led to an unsuccessful war with Britain.

ar·gen·tine /ˈärjənˌtīn; -ˌtēn/ ▸*adj.* *archaic* of or resembling silver.
▸*n.* a small marine fish with a silvery sheen. • Family Argentinidae: two genera and several species, in particular *Argentina silus* of the North Atlantic. ▷late Middle English: from Old French *argentin*, *argentine*, from *argent* 'silver,' from Latin *argentum*.

Ar·gen·tine ant ▸*n.* a small South American ant that has become established in parts of the U.S. • *Iridomyrmex humilis*, family Formicidae.

ar·gil·la·ceous /ˌärjəˈlāSHəs/ ▸*adj.* *Geology* (of rocks or sediment) consisting of or containing clay. ▷late 17th cent.: from Latin *argillaceus* (from *argilla* 'clay') + **-OUS**.

ar·gil·lite /ˈärjəˌlīt/ ▸*n.* *Geology* a sedimentary rock that does not split easily, formed from consolidated clay. ▷late 18th cent.: from Latin *argilla* 'clay' + **-ITE**[1].

ar·gi·nine /ˈärjəˌnēn; -ˌnīn/ ▸*n.* *Biochemistry* a basic amino acid that is a constituent of most proteins. It is an essential nutrient in the diet of vertebrates. • Chem. formula: $HN{=}C(NH_2)NH(CH_2)_3CH(NH_2)COOH$. ▷late 19th cent.: from German *Arginin*, perhaps from Greek *arginoeis* 'bright-shining, white.'

Ar·give /ˈärˌjīv; -ˌgīv/ ▸*adj.* of or relating to the ancient city of Argos. ■ (esp. in Homer) Greek.
▸*n.* a citizen of Argos. ■ (esp. in Homer) a Greek person. ▷from Latin *Argivus*, from Greek *Argeios* 'relating to Argos.'

ar·gle-bar·gle /ˈärgəl ˈbärgəl/ ▸*n.* **1** copious but meaningless talk or writing; nonsense: *bureaucratic argle-bargle.* **2** another term for **ARGY-BARGY**. ▷early 19th cent.: reduplication of dialect *argle*, a late 16th-cent. alteration of **ARGUE**.

Ar·go /ˈärgō/ (in full **Argo Navis**) *historical Astronomy* a large southern constellation (the ship *Argo*), which is now divided into the constellations Carina, Puppis, and Vela. ▷Latin.

ar·gol /ˈärgəl/ ▸*n.* tartar obtained from wine fermentation. ▷Middle English: from Anglo-Norman French *argoile*, of unknown origin.

ar·gon /ˈärˌgän/ ▸*n.* the chemical element of atomic number 18, an inert gaseous element of the noble gas group. Argon is the most common noble gas, making up nearly one percent of the earth's atmosphere. (Symbol: **Ar**) ▷late 19th cent.: from Greek, neuter of *argos* 'idle,' from *a-* 'without' + *ergon* 'work.'

ar·go·naut /ˈärgəˌnôt/ ▸*n.* a small floating octopus, the female of which has webbed arms like sails and secretes a thin, coiled, papery shell in which the eggs are laid. Also called **PAPER NAUTILUS**. • Genus *Argonauta*, order Octopoda.

Ar·go·nauts /ˈärgəˌnôts/ *Greek Mythology* a group of heroes who accompanied Jason on board the ship *Argo* in the quest for the Golden Fleece. ▷*argonaut* from Greek *argonautēs* 'sailor in the ship *Argo*.'

Ar·gonne /ärˈgän; ˈärˌgän/ a wooded plateau in northeastern France, near the Belgian border. The region is thinly populated. A major Allied offensive was staged here during World War I; during World War II the region was occupied by Germany from 1940 until 1944.

Ar·gos /ˈärgəs; -gôs/ a city in southern Greece, in the northeastern Peloponnese; pop. 20,702. One of the oldest cities of ancient Greece, it dominated the Peloponnese and the western Aegean in the 7th century BC.

ar·go·sy /ˈärgəsē/ ▸*n.* (*pl.* **-sies**) *poetic/literary* a large merchant ship, originally one from Ragusa (now Dubrovnik) or Venice. ▷late 16th cent.: apparently from Italian *Ragusea (nave)* '(vessel) of *Ragusa*' (see **RAGUSA**).

ar·got /ˈärgō; -gət/ ▸*n.* the jargon or slang of a particular group or class: *teenage argot.* See note at **DIALECT**. ▷mid 19th cent. (originally denoting the jargon or slang of criminals): from French, of unknown origin.

ar·gu·a·ble /ˈärgyo͞oəbəl/ ▸*adj.* able to be argued or asserted: *an arguable case for judicial review* | [with *clause*] *it is* **arguable that** *egg donation raises a series of moral and practical problems.* ■ open to disagreement; not obviously correct: *a highly arguable assumption.*

ar·gu·a·bly /ˈärgyo͞oəblē/ ▸*adv.* [*sentence adverb*] it may be argued (used to qualify the statement of an opinion or belief): *she is arguably the greatest woman tennis player of all time.*

ar·gue /ˈärgyo͞o/ ▸*v.* (**-gues**, **-gued**, **-gu·ing**) **1** [*reporting verb*] give reasons or cite evidence in support of an idea, action, or theory, typically with the aim of persuading others to share one's view: [with *clause*] *defense attorneys* **argue that** *the police lacked "probable cause" to arrest the driver* | [with *direct speech*] *"It stands to reason," she argued.* ■ [*trans.*] (**argue someone into/out of**) persuade someone to do or not to do (something) by giving reasons: *I tried to argue him out of it.* **2** [*intrans.*] exchange or express diverging or opposite views, typically in a heated or angry way: *don't* **argue with** *me* | *figurative I wasn't going to* **argue** *with a gun* | [*trans.*] *she was too tired to* **argue the point.** ▷Middle English: from Old French *arguer*, from Latin *argutari* 'prattle,' frequentative of *arguere* 'make clear, prove, accuse.' **—ar·gu·er** *n.*

ar·gu·fy /ˈärgyəˌfī/ ▸*v.* (**-fies**, **-fied**) [*intrans.*] *humorous* or *dialect* argue or quarrel, typically about something trivial: *it won't do to argufy, I tell you.* ▷late 17th cent.: fanciful formation from **ARGUE**; compare with *speechify.*

ar·gu·ment /ˈärgyəmənt/ ▸*n.* **1** an exchange of diverging or opposite views, typically a heated or angry one: *I've had an* **argument with** *my father* | *heated arguments over public spending* | *there was some argument about the decision.* **2** a reason or set of reasons given with the aim of persuading others that an action or idea is right or wrong: *there is a strong argument for submitting a formal appeal* | [with *clause*] *he rejected the* **argument that** *keeping the facility would be costly.* **3** *Mathematics* an independent variable associated with a function and determining the value of the function. For example, in the expression $y = F(x_1, x_2)$, the arguments of the function F are x_1 and x_2, and the value is *y*. ■ another term for **AMPLITUDE** (sense 4). ■ *Computing* a value or address passed to a procedure or function at the time of call. ■ *Linguistics* any of the noun phrases in a clause that are related directly to the verb, typically the subject, direct object, and indirect object. ■ *Logic* the middle term in a syllogism. **4** *archaic* a summary of the subject matter of a book. ▷Middle English (in the sense 'process of reasoning'): via Old French from Latin *argumentum*, from *arguere* 'make clear, prove, accuse.'
▸*PHRASE* □ **for the sake of argument** as a basis for discussion or reasoning.

ar·gu·men·ta·tion /ˌärgyəmənˈtāSHən/ ▸*n.* the action or process of reasoning systematically in support of an idea, action, or theory: *lines of argumentation used to support his thesis.* ▷late Middle English: via Old French from Latin *argumentatio(n-)*, from *argumentat-* 'conducted as an argument,' from *argumentari.*

ar·gu·men·ta·tive /ˌärgyəˈmentətiv/ ▸*adj.* **1** given to expressing divergent or opposite views: *an argumentative child.* **2** using or characterized by systematic reasoning: *the highest standards of argumentative rigor.* ▷late Middle English: from Old French *argumentatif, -ive* or late Latin *argumentativus*, from *argumentari* 'conduct an argument.' **—ar·gu·men·ta·tive·ly** *adv.* **—ar·gu·men·ta·tive·ness** *n.*

ar·gu·ment from de·sign ▸*n.* *Christian Theology* the argument that God's existence is demonstrable from the evidence of design in the universe.

ar·gus /ˈärgəs/ ▸*n.* **1** (**Argus**) *Greek Mythology* a monster with a hundred eyes, used by Hera to watch over Io. He was killed by Hermes, and Hera then used his eyes to deck the peacock's tail. ■ an alert, watchful guardian. **2** (also **argus pheasant**) a long-tailed pheasant with generally brown plumage, found in Southeast Asia and Indonesia. • Two species in the family Phasianidae: the male **great argus** (*Argusianus argus*) has lengthened secondary wing feathers bearing eyespots, spread during display; the **crested argus** (*Rheinartia ocellata*) has the longest tail feathers of any bird. **3** a small brown or bluish Eurasian butterfly that typically has eyelike markings near the wing margins. • *Aricia* and other genera, family Lycaenidae. **4** (also **argus fish**) a silvery deep-bodied fish with round spots, widely distributed throughout the tropical Indo-Pacific region in both fresh and salt water. • *Scatophagus argus*, family Scatophagidae. ▷late Middle English: from Latin, from Greek *Argos*, the name of a mythical watchman with a hundred eyes.

Ar·gus-eyed /ˈärgəs/ ▸*adj.* *poetic/literary* vigilant.

ar·gy-bar·gy /ˈärjē ˈbärjē/ ▸*n.* (*pl.* **-gies**) *informal, chiefly Brit.* noisy quarreling or wrangling. ▷late 19th cent. (originally Scots): rhyming jingle based on **ARGUE**.

ar·gyle /ˈärˌgīl/ ▸*n.* [usu. as *adj.*] a pattern composed of diamonds of various colors on a plain background, used in knitted garments such as sweaters and socks. ■ a sock with such a pattern. ▷1940s: from *Argyll*, a family name and a former county of Scotland. The pattern is based on the tartan of the *Argyll* branch of the Campbell clan.

argyle

ar·hat /ˈärhət/ ▸*n.* (in Buddhism and Jainism) someone who has attained the goal of the religious life. ▷late 19th cent.: from Sanskrit, literally 'meritorious.'

År·hus variant spelling of AARHUS.

a·rhyth·mic ▶*adj.* variant spelling of ARRHYTHMIC.

a·ri·a /ˈärēə/ ▶*n. Music* a long, accompanied song for a solo voice, typically one in an opera or oratorio. ▷early 18th cent.: from Italian, from Latin *aer* 'air.'

Ar·i·ad·ne /ˌarēˈadnē/ *Greek Mythology* the daughter of King Minos of Crete and Pasiphaë. She helped Theseus to escape from the Minotaur's labyrinth by giving him a ball of thread, which he unraveled as he went in and used to trace his way out again after killing the Minotaur.

Ar·i·an /ˈe(ə)rēən/ ▶*n.* **1** an adherent of the doctrine of Arianism. **2** a person born under the sign of Aries.
▶*adj.* **1** of or concerning Arianism. **2** of or relating to a person born under the sign of Aries.

-arian ▶*suffix* (forming adjectives and corresponding nouns) having a concern or belief in a specified thing: *antiquarian | humanitarian | vegetarian.* ▷from the Latin suffix *-arius.*

Ar·i·an·ism /ˈe(ə)rēəˌnizəm/ ▶*n. Christian Theology* an influential heresy denying the divinity of Christ, originating with the Alexandrian priest Arius (*c.*250–*c.*336). Arianism maintained that the Son of God was created by the Father and was therefore neither coeternal with the Father, nor consubstantial.

A·ri·as Sanchez /ˈärē-äs ˈsänchəs/, Oscar (1941–), Costa Rican president 1986–90. He worked to achieve peace in Central America, particularly in Nicaragua. Nobel Peace Prize (1987).

ar·id /ˈarid/ ▶*adj.* (of land or a climate) having little or no rain; too dry or barren to support vegetation: *hot and arid conditions.* See note at DRY. ■ *figurative* lacking in interest, excitement, or meaning: *his arid years in suburbia.* ▷mid 17th cent.: from French *aride* or Latin *aridus,* from *arere* 'be dry or parched.' **—a·rid·i·ty** /əˈriditē/ *n.* **—ar·id·ly** *adv.* **—ar·id·ness** *n.*

a·rid·i·sol /əˈridiˌsôl; -ˌsäl/ ▶*n. Soil Science* a soil of an order comprising typically saline or alkaline soils with very little organic matter, characteristic of arid regions.

Ar·i·el /ˈe(ə)rēəl/ **1** *Astronomy* a satellite of Uranus discovered in 1851, the twelfth closest to the planet and the fourth largest, with a diameter of 721 miles (1,160 km). **2** a series of six American and British satellites devoted to studies of the ionosphere and X-ray astronomy (1962-79). ▷named after a fairy or spirit in Shakespeare's *The Tempest.*

ar·i·el /ˈe(ə)rēəl/ ▶*n.* a gazelle found in the Middle East and North Africa. • Genus *Gazella,* family Bovidae: the mountain gazelle (*G. gazella*) or the dorcas gazelle (*G. dorcas*). ▷mid 19th cent.: from Arabic *ʼaryal.*

Ar·ies /ˈe(ə)rēz/ **1** *Astronomy* a small constellation (the Ram), said to represent the ram whose Golden Fleece was sought by Jason and the Argonauts. ■ [as *genitive*] (**Arietis** /əˈri-itis/) used with a preceding letter or numeral to designate stars: *the star Beta Arietis.* **2** *Astrology* the first sign of the zodiac, which the sun enters at the vernal equinox (about March 20). ■ (**an Aries**) (*pl.* same) a person born when the sun is in this sign. ▷Latin.
▶*PHRASE* □ **First Point of Aries** *Astronomy* the point on the celestial sphere where the path of the sun crosses the celestial equator from south to north in March, marking the zero point of right ascension. Owing to precession of the equinoxes, it has moved from Aries into Pisces, and is now approaching Aquarius. Also called VERNAL EQUINOX.

a·right /əˈrīt/ ▶*adv. dialect* correctly; properly: *I wondered if I'd heard aright.* ▷Old English *on riht, ariht* (see A-[2] 'in,' RIGHT).

ar·il /ˈarəl/ ▶*n. Botany* an extra seed-covering, typically colored and hairy or fleshy, e.g., the red fleshy cup around a yew seed. ▷mid 18th cent.: from modern Latin *arillus,* of unknown origin; perhaps related to medieval Latin *arilli* 'dried grapestones.' **—ar·il·late** /-lit; -ˌlāt/ *adj.*

a·rio·so /ˌärēˈōsō; -zō/ *Music* ▶*adj. & adv.* in a melodious, expressive, songlike style.
▶*n.* (*pl.* **-sos**) a piece of music to be performed in this way. ▷Italian, from ARIA.

A·ri·os·to /ˌärēˈästō; -ˈôstō/, Ludovico (1474–1533), Italian poet; noted for his romantic epic *Orlando Furioso* (final version 1532).

-arious ▶*suffix* forming adjectives such as *gregarious, vicarious.* ▷from the Latin suffix *-arius* + **-OUS**.

a·rise /əˈrīz/ ▶*v.* (*past* **a·rose** /əˈrōz/; *past part.* **a·ris·en** /əˈrizən/) [*intrans.*] **1** (of a problem, opportunity, or situation) emerge; become apparent: *new difficulties had arisen.* ■ come into being; originate: *the practice arose in the nineteenth century.* ■ (**arise from/out of**) occur as a result of: *most conflicts arise from ignorance or uncertainty.* **2** *formal* or *poetic/literary* get or stand up: *he arose at 9:30 and went out for a walk.* ▷Old English *ārīsan,* from *ā-* 'away' (as an intensifier) + the verb RISE.

Ar·is·tar·chus[1] /ˌarəˈstärkəs/ (3rd century BC), Greek astronomer; known as **Aristarchus of Samos**. Founder of an important school of Hellenic astronomy, he was aware of the rotation of the earth around the sun and so was able to account for the seasons.

Ar·is·tar·chus[2] (*c.*217–145 BC), Greek scholar; known as **Aristarchus of Samothrace**. He is noted for his editions of the writings of Homer and other Greek authors.

A·ri·stide /ärēˈstēd/, Jean-Bertrand (1953–), Haitian president 1990–96 and ex-Roman Catholic priest. He led a movement against the dictatorship of Duvalier in the 1980s and was elected president of Haiti in 1990, but was forced into exile 1991–94 by a military coup. U.S. troops faciliated his return, and he served as president 1994–96 and 2001–04, when he was again forced into exile.

Ar·is·ti·des /ˌarəˈstīˌdēz/ (5th century BC), Athenian statesman and general; known as **Aristides the Just**. He commanded the Athenian army at the battle of Plataea (479 BC).

Ar·is·tip·pus /ˌarəˈstipəs/ (late 5th century BC), Greek philosopher; known as **Aristippus the Elder (of Cyrene)**. He is considered the founder of the Cyrenaic school.

a·ris·to /əˈristō/ ▶ informal term for ARISTOCRAT.

ar·is·toc·ra·cy /ˌariˈstäkrəsē/ ▶*n.* (*pl.* **-cies**) [treated as *sing.* or *pl.*] (usu. **the aristocracy**) the highest class in certain societies, esp. those holding hereditary titles or offices: *the ancient Polish aristocracy had hereditary right to elect the king.* ■ a form of government in which power is held by the nobility. ■ a state governed in this way. ■ *figurative* a group regarded as privileged or superior in a particular sphere: *high-level technocrats make up a large part of this "technical aristocracy."* ▷late 15th cent.: from Old French *aristocratie,* from Greek *aristokratia,* from *aristos* 'best' + *-kratia* 'power.' The term originally denoted the government of a state by its best citizens, later by the rich and wellborn, hence the sense 'nobility,' regardless of the form of government (mid 17th cent.).

> *USAGE* **Aristocracy, oligarchy,** and **plutocracy** are sometimes confused. All mean some form of rule by a small elite. **Aristocracy** is rule by a traditional elite, held to be made up of 'the best' people, and is usually hereditary. **Oligarchy** is literally rule by a few. **Plutocracy** is rule by the (necessarily few) very rich.

a·ris·to·crat /əˈristəˌkrat/ ▶*n.* a member of the aristocracy: *an aristocrat by birth.* ■ something believed to be the best of its kind: *the trout is the aristocrat of freshwater fish.* ▷late 18th cent.: from French *aristocrate* (a word of the French Revolution), from *aristocratie* (see ARISTOCRACY).

a·ris·to·crat·ic /əˌristəˈkratik/ ▶*adj.* of or relating to the aristocracy: *an aristocratic family.* ■ distinguished in manners or bearing: *a stately, aristocratic manner.* ■ grand; stylish: *aristocratic-sounding names | a snob with aristocratic aspirations.* ▷early 17th cent.: from French *aristocratique,* from Greek *aristokratikos,* from *aristokratia* (see ARISTOCRACY). **—a·ris·to·crat·i·cal·ly** /-ik(ə)lē/ *adv.*

Ar·is·toph·a·nes /ˌarəˈstäfəˌnēz/ (*c.*450–*c.*385 BC), Greek comic playwright. Notable works: *Lysistrata, The Birds,* and *The Frogs.*

Ar·is·to·te·lian /əˌristəˈtēlyən; ˌaristə-; -lēən/ ▶*adj.* of or relating to Aristotle or his philosophy.
▶*n.* a student of Aristotle or an adherent of his philosophy.

Ar·is·to·te·lian log·ic ▶*n.* the traditional system of logic expounded by Aristotle and developed in the Middle Ages, concerned chiefly with deductive reasoning as expressed in syllogisms. Compare with SYMBOLIC LOGIC.

Ar·is·tot·le /ˈarəˌstätl; ˌarəˈstätl/ (384–322 BC), Greek philosopher and scientist. A student of Plato and tutor to Alexander the Great, he founded a school (the Lyceum) outside Athens. He is one of the most influential thinkers in the history of Western thought. His surviving works cover a vast range of subjects, including logic, ethics, metaphysics, politics, natural science, and physics.

Ar·is·tot·le's lan·tern ▶*n. Zoology* a conical structure of calcareous plates and muscles supporting the rasping teeth of a sea urchin.

A·ri·ta /əˈrētə/ ▶*n.* a type of Japanese porcelain characterized by asymmetric decoration. ▷late 19th cent.: named after *Arita,* a town in Japan, where it is made.

a·rith·me·tic ▶*n.* /əˈriTHməˌtik/ the branch of mathematics dealing with the properties and manipulation of numbers: *the laws of arithmetic.* ■ the use of numbers in counting and calculation: *he could do arithmetic in his head.* ■ *figurative* those aspects of a particular situation that can be expressed in numerical terms: *some unsettling parliamentary arithmetic.*
▶*adj.* (**ar·ith·met·ic**) /ˌariTHˈmetik/ (also **ar·ith·met·i·cal**) of or relating to arithmetic: *perform arithmetic functions.* ▷Middle English: from Old French *arismetique,* based on Latin *arithmetica,* from Greek *arithmētikē (tekhnē)* '(art) of counting,' from *arithmos* 'number.' **—a·rith·me·ti·cian** /əˌriTHməˈtiSHən/ *n.*

ar·ith·met·ic log·ic u·nit /ˌariTHˈmetik/ ▶*n.* a unit in a computer that carries out arithmetic and logical operations.

ar·ith·met·ic mean /ˌariTHˈmetik/ ▶*n.* the average of a set of numerical values, calculated by adding them together and dividing by the number of terms in the set.

ar·ith·met·ic pro·gres·sion /ˌariTHˈmetik/ (also **arithmetic series**) ▶*n.* a sequence of numbers in which each differs from the preceding by a constant quantity (e.g., 3, 6, 9, 12, etc.; 9, 7, 5, 3, etc.). ■ the relationship between numbers in such a sequence: *the numbers are in arithmetic progression.*

ar·ith·met·ic u·nit ▶*n.* another term for ARITHMETIC LOGIC UNIT.

a·rith·me·tize /əˈriTHməˌtīz/ ▶*v.* [*trans.*] express arithmetically; reduce to arithmetic form.

-arium ▶*suffix* forming nouns usually denoting a place: *planetarium | vivarium.* ▷from Latin, neuter ending of adjectives in *-arius.*

Ariz. ▶*abbr.* Arizona.

Ar·i·zo·na /ˌarəˈzōnə/ a state in the southwestern U.S., on the border with Mexico; pop. 5,130,632; capital, Phoenix; statehood, Feb. 14, 1912 (48). Part of New Spain until 1821, it was organized as a U.S. territory in 1863 from lands ceded by the Treaty of Guadalupe Hidalgo in 1848 and the Gadsden Purchase in 1853. **—Ar·i·zo·nan** *n. & adj.*

Ar·ju·na /ˈärjənə; ˈər-/ *Hinduism* a hero prince in the Mahabharata, one of the two main characters in the Bhagavadgita.

ark /ärk/ ▶*n.* **1** (**the ark**) (in the Bible) the ship built by Noah to save his family and two of every kind of animal from the Flood; Noah's ark. ■ *figurative* a vessel or sanctuary that serves as protection against extinction: *a starship ark built by their android protectors.* ■ *archaic* a chest or box: *the ark was of Italian walnut.* ■ a large, flat-bottomed boat. **2** short for ARK OF THE COVENANT. ■ (also **Holy Ark**) a chest or cupboard housing the Torah scrolls in a synagogue. **3** (also **ark shell**) a widely distributed bivalve mollusk that typically attaches itself to rocks with byssus threads. • Order Arcoidea: *Arca* and other genera. ▷Old English *ærc,* from Latin *arca* 'chest.'

Ark. ▶*abbr.* Arkansas.

Ar·kan·sas /ˈärkənˌsô/ a state in the southern central U.S., on the western banks of the Mississippi River; pop. 2,673,400; capital, Little Rock; statehood, June 15, 1836 (25). Arkansas seceded from the Union in 1861 to fight for the Confederacy during the Civil War and rejoined the Union in 1868. In 1957, federal troops were needed to enforce school desegregation in Little Rock.

Ar·kan·sas Riv·er /ˈärkənˌsô; ärˈkanzəs/ a river in the southwestern U.S., that flows for 1,450 miles (2,320 km) from the Rockies in Colorado to join the Mississippi River in Arkansas. It has been made navigable for oceangoing vessels as far west as Tulsa, Oklahoma.

Ar·khan·gelsk /ärˈKHängilsk; ärˈkaNGˌgelsk/ Russian name for ARCHANGEL.

Ark of the Cov·e·nant (also **Ark of the Testimony**) the wooden chest that contained the tablets of the laws of the ancient Israelites. Carried by the Israelites on their wanderings in the wilderness, it was later placed by Solomon in the Temple at Jerusalem.

ar·kose /ˈärˌkōs/ ▸*n. Geology* a coarse-grained sandstone that is at least 25 percent feldspar. ▹mid 19th cent.: from French, probably from Greek *arkhaios* 'ancient.' —**ar·ko·sic** /ärˈkōsik/ *adj.*

Ark·wright /ˈärkˌrīt/, Sir Richard (1732–92), English inventor and industrialist. In 1767 he patented a water-powered spinning machine known as the spinning jenny.

Arles /ärl/ a city in southeastern France; pop. 52,590. It was the capital of the medieval kingdom of Arles, formed in the 10th century by the union of the kingdoms of Provence and Burgundy.

Ar·ling·ton /ˈärliNGtən/ **1** a county in northern Virginia, forming a suburb of Washington. It is the site of the Pentagon and Arlington National Cemetery. **2** a town in eastern Massachusetts, northwest of Boston; pop. 44,630. **3** an industrial city in northern Texas, between Dallas and Fort Worth; pop. 332,969.

Arlington National Cemetery

Ar·ling·ton Heights a village in northeastern Illinois, northwest of Chicago; pop. 76,031.

ARM ▸*abbr.* ADJUSTABLE RATE MORTGAGE.

arm[1] /ärm/ ▸*n.* **1** each of the two upper limbs of the human body from the shoulder to the hand: *she held the baby in her arms.* ■ (in technical use) each of these upper limbs from the shoulder to the elbow. ■ each of the forelimbs of an animal. ■ a flexible limb of an invertebrate animal, e.g., an octopus. ■ a sleeve of a garment. ■ an ability to throw a ball skillfully: *he has a good arm.* ■ an athlete with such an ability: *he wasn't the best arm in the outfield, but his performance at the plate more than compensated.* ■ used to refer to the holding of a person's arm in support or companionship: *as they walked he offered her his arm | he arrived with a pretty girl on his arm.* ■ used to refer to something perceived as powerful or protective: *the comforting arms of the church.* **2** a thing resembling an arm in form or function, in particular: ■ a side part of a chair or other seat on which a sitter's arm can rest. ■ a narrow strip of water or land projecting from a larger body. ■ a large branch of a tree. ■ *figurative* a long, narrow shape or object: *a long arm of sunshine.* **3** a branch or division of a company or organization: *the political arm of the separatist group.* ■ one of the types of troops of which an army is composed, such as infantry or artillery. [also understood as a figurative use of ARM[2].] **4** *Mathematics* each of the lines enclosing an angle. ▹Old English *arm, earm*, of Germanic origin; related to Dutch *arm* and German *Arm.* —**arm·ful** /-ˌfo͝ol/ *n.* (*pl.* **-fuls**) —**arm·less** *adj.*

▸*PHRASES* □ **arm in arm** (of two or more people) with arms linked. □ **the long arm of the law** used to refer to the criminal justice system as far-reaching: *act now before the long arm of the law catches up with you.* □ **as long as one's** (or **someone's**) **arm** *informal* very long: *I have a list of vices as long as your arm.* □ **at arm's length** away from the body, with the arm fully extended: *I held the telephone at arm's length.* □ **cost an arm and a leg** *informal* be extremely expensive. □ **give one's right arm** *informal* used to convey a strong desire to have or do something: *I'd give my right arm to go with them.* □ **in arms** (of a baby) too young to walk: *a babe in arms.* □ **into the arms of** into the possession or control of: *the violin passed into the arms of a wealthy dilettante.* □ **keep someone/something at arm's length** avoid intimacy or close contact with someone or something. □ **put the arm on** *informal* attempt to force or coerce (someone) to do something: *she started putting the arm on them for donations.* □ **under one's arm** between one's arm and one's body: *Barbara tucked the papers under her arm.* □ **with open arms** with great affection or enthusiasm: *schools have welcomed such arrangements with open arms.* □ **within arm's reach** near enough to reach by extending one's arm.

arm[2] ▸*v.* [*trans.*] supply or provide with weapons: *both sides **armed themselves with** grenades and machine guns.* ■ supply or provide with equipment, tools, or other items in preparation or readiness for something: *she **armed** them **with** brushes and mops.* ■ activate the fuse of (a bomb or other device) so that it is ready to explode.

▸*n.* see ARMS. ▹Middle English: from Old French *armer* (verb), from Latin *armare*, from *arma* 'armor, arms.'

ar·ma·da /ärˈmädə/ ▸*n.* a fleet of warships: *an armada of destroyers, minesweepers, and gunboats.* ■ (**the Spanish Armada**) a Spanish naval invasion force sent against England by Philip II of Spain. It was defeated by the English fleet and almost completely destroyed by storms off the Hebrides. ▹mid 16th cent.: from Spanish, from *armata*, feminine past participle of Latin *armare* 'to arm.' Compare with ARMY.

ar·ma·dil·lo /ˌärməˈdilō/ ▸*n.* (*pl.* **-los**) a nocturnal omnivorous mammal that has large claws for digging and a body covered in bony plates. Armadillos are native to the south central U.S. and Central and South America. • Family Dasypodidae, order Xenarthra (or Edentata): several genera and species, including the **nine-banded armadillo** (*Dasypus novemcinctus*), which has spread into the southern U.S. ▹late 16th cent.: from Spanish, diminutive of *armado* 'armed man,' from Latin *armatus*, past participle of *armare* 'to arm.'

armadillo

Ar·ma·ged·don /ˌärməˈgedn/ ▸*n.* (in the New Testament) the last battle between good and evil before the Day of Judgment. ■ a biblical hill of Megiddo, an archaeological site on the plain of Esdraelon, south of present-day Haifa in Israel. See also MEGIDDO. ■ the place where the last battle between good and evil will be fought. ■ a dramatic and catastrophic conflict, typically seen as likely to destroy the world or the human race: *nuclear Armageddon.* ▹Greek, from Hebrew *har məgiddōn* 'hill of Megiddo' (Rev. 16:16.)

Ar·magh /ärˈmä; ˈärˌmä/ one of the six counties of Northern Ireland, formerly an administrative area. ■ the chief town of this county; pop. 12,700.

Ar·mag·nac /ˌärmənˈyak; -ˈyäk/ *n.* a type of brandy, traditionally made in Aquitaine in southwestern France.

Ar·ma·lite /ˈärməˌlīt/ ▸*n. trademark* a type of light automatic rifle.

ar·ma·ment /ˈärməmənt/ ▸*n.* (also **armaments**) military weapons and equipment: *chemical weapons and other unconventional armaments.* ■ the process of equipping military forces for war. ■ *archaic* a military force equipped for war. ▹late 17th cent. (in the sense 'force equipped for war'): from Latin *armamentum*, from *armare* 'to arm' (see ARM[2]).

ar·ma·men·tar·i·um /ˌärməmənˈte(ə)rēəm/ ▸*n.* (*pl.* **-tar·i·a** /-ˈte(ə)rēə/) the medicines, equipment, and techniques available to a medical practitioner. ■ a collection of resources available for a certain purpose: *the entire armamentarium of electronic surveillance.* ▹late 19th cent.: from Latin, 'arsenal, armory.'

Ar·ma·ni /ärˈmänē/, Giorgio (1935–), Italian fashion designer.

ar·ma·ture /ˈärməCHər; -ˌCHo͝or/ ▸*n.* **1** the rotating coil or coils of a dynamo or electric motor. ■ any moving part of an electrical machine in which a voltage is induced by a magnetic field. ■ a piece of iron or other object acting as a keeper for a magnet. **2** a metal framework on which a sculpture is molded with clay or similar material. **3** *Biology* the protective covering of an animal or plant. ■ *archaic* armor. ▹late Middle English: from French, from Latin *armatura* 'armor,' from *armare* 'to arm' (see ARM[2]). The original sense was 'armor,' hence 'protective covering' (sense 3, early 18th cent.), later 'keeper of a magnet,' source of sense 1 (mid 19th cent.).

arm·band /ˈärmˌband/ ▸*n.* a band worn around a person's upper arm to hold up a shirtsleeve or as a symbol.

arm can·dy ▸*n. informal* a sexually attractive companion accompanying a person, esp. a celebrity, at social events: *the athletes and their arm candy clustered around the bar.*

arm·chair ▸*n.* /ˈärmˌCHe(ə)r/ a comfortable chair, typically upholstered, with side supports for a person's arms.

▸*adj.* [*attrib.*] lacking or not involving practical or direct experience of a particular subject or activity: *armchair adventurers.*

Arm·co /ˈärmkō/ ▸*n. trademark* a very pure soft iron, used in particular for roadside guardrails. ▹early 20th cent.: acronym from *American Rolling Mill Company.*

armed /ärmd/ ▸*adj.* **1** equipped with or carrying a weapon or weapons: *the security forces are **armed with** automatic rifles | heavily armed troops.* ■ involving the use of firearms: *armed robbery.* ■ (of a bomb, alarm, or other device) prepared to activate or explode. ■ *figurative* supplied with equipment, tools, or other items in preparation or readiness for something: *he is armed with a list of questions.* **2** *Heraldry* having claws, a beak, etc., of a specified tincture.

▸*PHRASE* □ **armed to the teeth** see TEETH.

armed camp ▸*n.* a town, territory, or group of people fully armed for war.

armed forc·es (also **armed services**) ▸*plural n.* a country's military forces, esp. its army, navy, and air force.

Ar·me·ni·a /ärˈmēnēə/ a landlocked country in southwestern Asia, in the Caucasus; pop. 2,991,000; capital, Yerevan; official languages, Armenian and Russian.

The Armenian homeland fell under Turkish rule from the 16th century and with the decline of the Ottomans was divided among Turkey, Iran, and Russia. In 1915 the Turks forcibly deported 1,750,000 Armenians to the deserts of Syria and Mesopotamia; more than 600,000 were killed or died on forced marches. Russian Armenia was absorbed into the Soviet Union in 1922 and gained independence as a member of the Commonwealth of Independent States in 1991. Since 1988 there has been conflict with neighboring Azerbaijan over the ethnically Armenian enclave of Nagorno-Karabakh and the predominantly Azerbaijani territory of Naxçivan.

Ar·me·ni·an /ärˈmēnēən; -yən/ ▸*adj.* of or relating to Armenia, its language, or the Christian Church established there.

▸*n.* **1** a native of Armenia or a person of Armenian descent. **2** the Indo-European language of Armenia, spoken by around 4 million people and written in a distinctive alphabet of thirty-eight letters.

Ar·me·ni·an Church (also **Armenian Apostolic Orthodox Church**) an independent Christian Church established in Armenia since *c.*300 and influenced by Roman and Byzantine as well as Syrian traditions. A small Armenian Catholic Church also exists (see UNIATE).

Arm·gard /ˈärmˌgärd/, Beatrix Wilhelmina, see BEATRIX.

arm·guard /ˈärmˌgärd/ ▸*n.* another term for BRACER[2].

arm·hole /ˈärmˌhōl/ ▸*n.* each of two openings in a garment through which the wearer puts their arms.

ar·mi·ger /ˈärmijər/ ▸*n.* a person entitled to heraldic arms. ▹mid 16th cent.: Latin, literally 'bearing arms,' from *arma* 'arms' + *gerere* 'to bear.' —**ar·mig·er·ous** /ärˈmijərəs/ *adj.*

ar·mil·lar·y sphere /ˈärməˌlerē/ ▸*n.* a model of the celestial globe constructed from rings and hoops representing the equator, the tropics, and other celestial circles, and able to revolve on its axis. ▷mid 17th cent.: from modern Latin *armillaris* 'relating to an *armilla*,' an astronomical instrument consisting of a hoop fixed in the plane of the equator (sometimes crossed by one in the plane of the meridian), used by the ancient astronomers to show the recurrence of equinoxes and solstices; from Latin *armilla* 'bracelet.'

Ar·min·i·an /är'minēən/ ▸*adj.* relating to the doctrines of Jacobus Arminius (Latinized name of Jakob Hermandszoon, 1560–1609), a Dutch Protestant theologian, who rejected the Calvinist doctrine of predestination. His teachings had a considerable influence on Methodism.
▸*n.* an adherent of these doctrines. **—Ar·min·i·an·ism** /-,nizəm/ *n.*

ar·mi·stice /'ärməstis/ ▸*n.* an agreement made by opposing sides in a war to stop fighting for a certain time; a truce. ▷early 18th cent.: from French, or from modern Latin *armistitium*, from *arma* 'arms' (see **ARM**2) + *-stitium* 'stoppage.'

Ar·mi·stice Day ▸*n.* the anniversary of the armistice of November 11, 1918, now replaced by Veterans Day in the U.S.

arm·let /'ärmlit/ ▸*n.* **1** a band or bracelet worn around the upper part of a person's arm. **2** a small inlet of a sea or branch of a river.

arm·load /'ärm,lōd/ ▸*n.* the amount that can be carried with one arm or in both arms.

arm·lock /'ärm,läk/ ▸*n.* a method of restraining someone by holding an arm tightly behind their back.

ar·moire /ärm'wär; 'ärm ,wär/ ▸*n.* a wardrobe or movable cabinet, typically one that is ornate or antique. ▷late 16th cent.: from French, from Old French *armarie* (see **AUMBRY**).

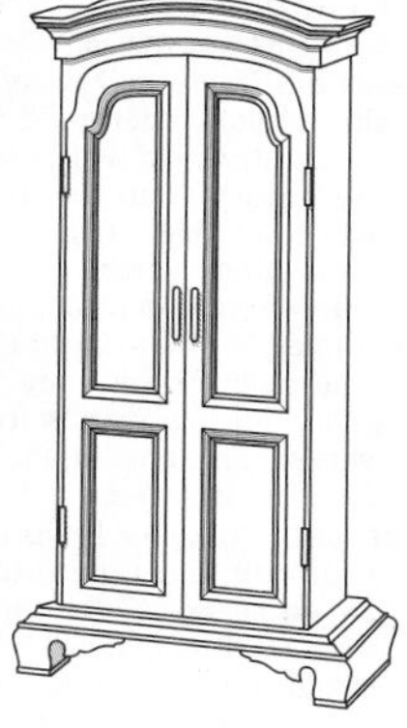
armoire

ar·mor /'ärmər/ (*Brit.* **ar·mour**) ▸*n.* the metal coverings formerly worn by soldiers or warriors to protect the body in battle: *knights in armor | a suit of armor.* ■ (also **armor plate**) the tough metal layer covering a military vehicle or ship to defend it from attack. ■ military vehicles collectively: *the contingent includes infantry, armor, and logistic units.* ■ the protective layer or shell of some animals and plants. ■ a person's emotional, social, or other defenses: *his armor of self-confidence.*
▸*v.* [*trans.*] provide (someone) with emotional, social, or other defenses: *the knowledge* ***armored*** *him* ***against*** *her.* ▷Middle English: from Old French *armure*, from Latin *armatura*, from *armare* 'to arm' (see **ARM**2). **—ar·mor-plat·ed** *adj.*

ar·mored /'ärmərd/ (*Brit.* **ar·moured**) ▸*adj.* (of a military vehicle or ship) covered with a tough metal layer as a defense against attack: *armored vehicles.* ■ (of troops) equipped with such vehicles: *the 2nd Armored Division.* ■ (of some animals and plants) having a protective layer or shell: *armored fish.* ■ *historical* (of a soldier) wearing armor: *armored and mounted knights.*

ar·mored per·son·nel car·ri·er ▸*n.* an armored military vehicle used to transport troops.

ar·mor·er /'ärmərər/ (*Brit.* **ar·mour·er**) ▸*n.* **1** a maker, supplier, or repairer of weapons or armor. **2** an official in charge of the arms of a military unit. ▷Middle English: from Old French *armurier*, from *armure* (see **ARMOR**).

ar·mo·ri·al /är'môrēəl/ ▸*adj.* of or relating to heraldry or heraldic devices: *armorial shields.*
▸*n.* a book of heraldic devices. ▷late Middle English: from Old French *armoierie* (see **ARMORY**1).

ar·mor·y1 /'ärmərē/ (*Brit.* **ar·mour·y**) ▸*n.* (*pl.* **-mor·ies**) **1** a place where arms are kept. ■ a supply of arms: *the most powerful weapon in our armory.* ■ a place where arms are manufactured. ■ [in *sing.*] *figurative* an array of resources available for a particular purpose: *his armory of comic routines.* **2** a place where military reservists are trained or headquartered. ▷Middle English (in the sense 'armor'): from Old French *armoirie, armoierie*, from *armoier* 'to blazon,' from *arme* 'weapon' (see **ARMS**). The spelling change in the 17th cent. was due to association with **ARMOR**.

ar·mor·y2 ▸*n.* [*mass noun*] heraldry. ▷late Middle English: from Old French *armoierie* (see **ARMOURY**).

Ar·mour /'ärmər/, Philip Danforth (1832–1901), U.S. industrialist. He reorganized his brother Herman's grain commission house into the Armour & Co. meat-packing plant in 1870.

ar·mour /'ärmər/ ▸*n.* British spelling of **ARMOR**.

ar·mour·er ▸*n.* British spelling of **ARMORER**.

ar·mour·y ▸*n.* British spelling of **ARMORY**1.

arm·pit /'ärm,pit/ ▸*n.* a hollow under the arm at the shoulder; also called **AXILLA**. ■ *informal* a place regarded as extremely unpleasant: *they call the region the armpit of America.*
▸*PHRASE* □ **up to one's armpits** deeply involved in a particular unpleasant situation or enterprise: *the country is* ***up to its armpits*** *in drug trafficking.*

arm·rest /'ärm,rest/ ▸*n.* a padded or upholstered arm of a chair or other seat on which a sitter's arm can comfortably rest.

arms /ärmz/ ▸*plural n.* **1** weapons and ammunition; armaments: *they were subjugated by force of arms* | [as *adj.*] *arms exports.* **2** distinctive emblems or devices, originally borne on shields in battle and now forming the heraldic insignia of families, corporations, or countries. See also **COAT OF ARMS**. ▷Middle English: from Old French *armes*, from Latin *arma*.
▸*PHRASES* □ **a call to arms** a call to prepare for confrontation: *a call to arms to defend against a takeover.* □ **lay down (one's) arms** cease fighting. □ **take up arms** begin fighting. □ **under arms** equipped and ready for war or battle: *Iraq had up to one million men under arms.* □ **up in arms (about/over)** protesting vigorously about something: *teachers are up in arms about new school tests.*

arms con·trol ▸*n.* international disarmament or arms limitation, esp. by mutual consent.

arm's-length ▸*adj.* [*attrib.*] avoiding intimacy or close contact: *an arm's-length relationship.*

arms race ▸*n.* a competition between nations for superiority in the development and accumulation of weapons, esp. between the U.S. and the former USSR during the Cold War.

Arm·strong1 /'ärm,strôNG/, Edwin Howard (1890–1954), U.S. electrical engineer, inventor of the superheterodyne radio receiver and the frequency modulation (FM) system.

Arm·strong2, Lance (1971–) U.S. cyclist. He won the Tour de France in 1999 after successfully battling advanced testicular cancer. He repeated the win in 2000, 2001, 2002, 2003, and 2004.

Arm·strong3, (Daniel) Louis (1900–71), U.S. jazz musician; known as **Satchmo**. A major influence on Dixieland jazz, he was a trumpet and cornet player, as well as a bandleader and a distinctive singer. He also appeared in many movies, including *The Birth of the Blues* (1941).

Arm·strong4, Neil (Alden) (1930–), U.S. astronaut. He commanded the Apollo 11 mission, during which he became the first man to set foot on the Moon (July 20, 1969).

Neil Armstrong

arm-twist·ing ▸*n.* *informal* persuasion by the use of physical force or moral pressure: *eight years of arguing and diplomatic arm-twisting.* **—arm-twist** *v.*

arm-wres·tling ▸*n.* a trial of strength in which two people sit opposite each other with one elbow resting on a table, clasp each other's hands, and try to force each other's arm down onto the table. **—arm-wres·tle** *v.*

ar·my /'ärmē/ ▸*n.* (*pl.* **-mies**) an organized military force equipped for fighting on land: *the two armies were in position.* ■ (**the army** or **the Army**) the branch of a nation's armed services that conducts military operations on land: *an enlisted man in the army* | [as *adj.*] *army officers.* ■ (**an army of** or **armies of**) a large number of people or things, typically formed or organized for a particular purpose: *an army of photographers | armies of cockroaches.* ▷late Middle English: from Old French *armee*, from *armata*, feminine past participle of Latin *armare* 'to arm.'
▸*PHRASES* □ **an army marches on its stomach** see **STOMACH**. □ **you and whose army?** *informal* used as an expression of disbelief in someone's ability to carry out a threat: *"One word to him and I'll nail you." "You and whose army?"*

ar·my ant ▸*n.* a blind nomadic tropical ant that forages in large columns, preying chiefly on insects and spiders. Also called **DRIVER ANT**. • Subfamily Dorylinae, family Formicidae.

ar·my brat ▸*n.* *informal* a child of a career soldier, esp. one who has lived in various places as a result of military transfers.

ar·my is·sue ▸*n.* [usu. as *adj.*] equipment or clothing supplied by the army.

ar·my-na·vy ▸*adj.* denoting the type of store that specializes in military surplus equipment, or the goods sold there.

ar·my sur·plus ▸*n.* goods and equipment that are in excess of the army's requirements: [as *adj.*] *an army surplus store.*

ar·my worm ▸*n.* any of a number of insect larvae that occur in large numbers, in particular: • the caterpillars of some moths, which feed on cereals and other crops, moving *en masse* when the food is exhausted (*Spodoptera* and other genera, family Noctuidae). • the small maggots of certain fungus gnats, which move in very large numbers within secreted slime (genus *Sciara*, family Mycetophilidae).

Arne /ärn/, Thomas (1710–78), English composer of the music for "Rule, Brittania."

Ar·nel /är'nel/ ▸*n.* *trademark* a synthetic fiber made from cellulose triacetate. ■ fabric made from fibers of this type.

Arn·hem /'ärnəm; 'ärn,hem/ a town in the eastern Netherlands, situated on the Rhine River; pop. 131,700.

Arn·hem Land a peninsula in Northern Territory, Australia.

ar·ni·ca /'ärnikə/ ▸*n.* a plant of the daisy family that bears yellow daisylike flowers. Native to cooler regions of the northern hemisphere, it is sometimes cultivated as an ornamental. • Genus *Arnica*, family Compositae: many species, esp. mountain tobacco (*A. montana*) of central Europe. ■ a preparation of this plant used medicinally, esp. for the treatment of bruises. ▷mid 18th cent.: modern Latin, of unknown origin.

Ar·no /'ärnō/ a river that rises in the Apennines in northern Italy and flows west for 150 miles (240 km) through Florence and Pisa to the Ligurian Sea.

Ar·nold1 /'ärnld/, Benedict (1741–1801), American general and traitor. During the American Revolution, with Ethan Allan, he was instrumental in the capture of Fort Ticonderoga but later planned to betray West Point to the British. He fled behind British lines and lived the rest of his life in Britain. His name became synonymous with "traitor."

Ar·nold2, Matthew (1822–88), English poet, essayist, and social critic. He is known for such poems as "The Scholar-Gipsy" and "Dover Beach" and was professor of poetry at Oxford 1857–67.

ar·oid /'aroid/ (also **aroid lily**) ▸*n.* *Botany* a plant of the arum family (Araceae). ▷late 19th cent.: from **ARUM** + **-OID**.

a·rol·la /ə'rälə; ə'rō-/ (also **arolla pine**) ▸*n.* a tall pine tree native to the Alps and Carpathian mountains, often planted in dense clumps as an avalanche break. • *Pinus cembra*, family Pinaceae. ▷late 19th cent.: from Swiss French *arol(l)e*.

a·ro·ma /ə'rōmə/ ▸*n.* a distinctive, typically pleasant smell: *the tantalizing aroma of fresh coffee.* See note at **SMELL**. ■ a subtle, pervasive quality or atmosphere of a particular type: *the aroma of officialdom.* ▷Middle English (usually in the plural denoting fragrant plants or spices): via Latin from Greek *arōma* 'spice.'

a·ro·ma·tase /ə'rōmə,tās/ ▸*n.* an adrenal enzyme that converts androstenedione and estrone to estrogen. Inhibiting its action is one approach to breast cancer prevention and treatment.

A

a·ro·ma·ther·a·py /əˌrōməˈTHerəpē/ ▸*n.* the use of aromatic plant extracts and essential oils in massage or baths. **—a·ro·ma·ther·a·peu·tic** /-ˌTHerəˈpyōōtik/ *adj.* **—a·ro·ma·ther·a·pist** /-pist/ *n.*

ar·o·mat·ic /ˌarəˈmatik/ ▸*adj.* **1** having a pleasant and distinctive smell: *a massage with aromatic oils.* **2** *Chemistry* (of an organic compound) containing a planar unsaturated ring of atoms that is stabilized by an interaction of the bonds forming the ring. Such compounds are typified by benzene and its derivatives. Compare with **ALICYCLIC**.
▸*n.* **1** a substance or plant emitting a pleasant and distinctive smell. **2** (usu. **aromatics**) *Chemistry* an aromatic compound. ▷late Middle English: via Old French from late Latin *aromaticus*, from Greek *arōmatikos*, from *arōma* (see **AROMA**). **—ar·o·mat·i·cal·ly** *adv.* **—ar·o·ma·tic·i·ty** /-məˈtisitē/ *n.* (*Chemistry*).

a·ro·ma·tize /əˈrōməˌtīz/ ▸*v.* [*trans.*] **1** *Chemistry* convert (a compound) into an aromatic structure. **2** cause to have a pleasant and distinctive smell: *vinegar aromatized with plant juices and honey.* ▷late Middle English: from Old French *aromatiser*, from late Latin *aromatizare*, from Greek *arōmatizein* 'to spice.' **—a·ro·ma·ti·za·tion** /əˌrōmətiˈzāSHən/ *n.*

a·rose /əˈrōz/ ▸ past of **ARISE**.

a·round /əˈround/ ▸*adv.* **1** (*Brit.* also **round**) located or situated on every side: *the mountains towering all around | a building visible for miles around.* ■ so as to surround someone or something: *everyone crowded around | a pool with banks all the way around.* ■ *figurative* so as to give support and companionship: *if one girl is distraught, the others will rally around.* ■ with circular motion: *the boats were spun around by waterspouts.* ■ so as to cover or take in the whole area surrounding a particular center: *she paused to glance around admiringly at the décor.* ■ so as to reach everyone in a particular group or area: *he passed a newspaper clipping around.* **2** (*Brit.* also **round**) so as to rotate and face in the opposite direction: *Jack seized her by the shoulders and turned her around | figurative having him in my corner has turned my career around.* ■ so as to lead in another direction: *it was the last house before the road curved around.* ■ used in describing the position of something, typically with regard to the direction in which it is facing or its relation to other items: *the picture shows the pieces the wrong way around.* ■ used to describe a situation in terms of the relation between people, actions, or events: *it was he who was attacking her, not the other way around.* **3** (*Brit.* also **round**) so as to reach a new place or position, typically by moving from one side of something to the other: *he made his way around to the back of the building | they went* **the long way around** *by the main road.* ■ in or to many places throughout a locality: *his only ambition is to drive around in a sports car | word got around that he was on the verge of retirement.* ■ used to convey an ability to navigate or orient oneself: *I like pupils to* **find** *their own* **way around**. ■ *informal* used to convey the idea of visiting someone else: *why don't you come around to my office?* ■ randomly or unsystematically; here and there: *John tried to focus on her but she kept moving around | one of them was glancing nervously around.* **4** (*Brit.* also **round**) in existence, in the vicinity, or in active use: *there was no one around | by being around I threaten her happiness | barley has been around for a long time.* ■ near at hand: *he would want to have her around as much as possible.* **5** approximately; about: *software costs would be around $1,500 |* [as *prep.*] *I returned to my hotel around 3 a.m.*
▸*prep.* (*Brit.* also **round**) **1** on every side of: *the palazzo is built around a courtyard | the hills around the city.* ■ (of something abstract) having (the thing mentioned) as a focal point: *our entire culture is built around those loyalties | you can organize your essay around an existing critical controversy.* **2** in or to many places throughout (a community or locality): *cycling around the village | a number of large depots around the country.* ■ on the other side of (a corner or obstacle): *Steven parked the car around the corner.* ■ so as to hit (something) in passing: *if he didn't shut up, he might get a slap around the ear.* **3** so as to encircle or embrace (someone or something): *he put his arm around her | warming her hands around a cup of coffee | the polar vortex around Antarctica.* ■ (of a person's arm or arms) partially encircling (another person) as part of a gesture of affection: *Mike put an arm around Mary and kissed her.* ■ following an approximately circular route: *he walked around the airfield | it can drill around corners | the contour followed around a curve to the north.* ■ so as to cover or take in the whole area of (a place): *she went around the house and saw that all the windows were barred.* ▷Middle English: from **A-**[2] 'in, on' + **ROUND**.
▸*PHRASES* □ **around the bend** see **BEND**[1]. □ **have been around** *informal* have a lot of varied experience and understanding of the world.

USAGE Are **around** and **round** (as preposition and adverbial particle) interchangeable? In U.S. English, the normal form in most contexts is **around**; **round** is generally regarded as informal or nonstandard and is standard only in certain fixed expressions, as in *the park is open* ***year round*** and *they went* ***round and round*** *in circles.*

a·rouse /əˈrouz/ ▸*v.* [*trans.*] **1** evoke or awaken (a feeling, emotion, or response): *something about the man aroused the guard's suspicions | the letter* **aroused in** *him a sense of urgency.* ■ excite or provoke (someone) to anger or strong emotions: *an ability to influence the audience and to arouse the masses.* See note at **INCITE**. ■ excite (someone) sexually. **2** awaken (someone) from sleep: *she had been aroused by the telephone.* ▷late 16th cent.: from **ROUSE**, on the pattern of the pair of *rise, arise.* **—a·rous·al** /-zəl/ *n.*

ARP ▸*abbr.* adjustable-rate preferred.

Arp /ärp/, Jean (1887–1966), French painter, sculptor, and poet; also known as **Hans Arp**. He was a cofounder of the Dada movement.

ar·peg·gi·ate /ärˈpejēˌāt/ ▸*v.* [*trans.*] *Music* play (a chord) as a series of ascending or descending notes. **—ar·peg·gi·a·tion** /ärˌpejēˈāSHən/ *n.* **—ar·peg·gi·a·tor** /-ˌātər/ *n.*

ar·peg·gi·o /ärˈpejēˌō/ ▸*n.* (*pl.* **-os**) *Music* the notes of a chord played in succession, either ascending or descending. ▷Italian, from *arpeggiare* 'play the harp,' from *arpa* 'harp.'

ar·peg·gio·ne /ärˌpejēˈōnē; ˌärpeˈjyōnē/ ▸*n.* an early 19th-century stringed instrument resembling a guitar in shape and having six strings and frets, but played with a bow like a cello. ▷late 19th cent.: from German, from **ARPEGGIO**.

ar·que·bus /ˈärk(w)əbəs/ ▸*n.* variant spelling of **HARQUEBUS**.

arr. ▸*abbr.* ■ (of a piece of music) arranged by: *Variations on a theme of Corelli (arr. Wild).* ■ (with reference to the arrival time of a bus, train, or airplane) arrives.

ar·rack /ˈarək; əˈrak/ (also **ar·ak**) ▸*n.* an alcoholic liquor typically distilled from the sap of the coconut palm or from rice. ▷early 17th cent.: from Arabic *'arak* 'sweat,' from the phrase *'arak al-tamr*, denoting an alcoholic spirit made from dates.

ar·raign /əˈrān/ ▸*v.* (often **be arraigned**) [*trans.*] call or bring (someone) before a court to answer a criminal charge: *her sister was* **arraigned on** *attempted murder charges.* ■ find fault with (someone or something); censure: *the soldiers bitterly arraigned the government for failing to keep its word.* ▷late Middle English: from Old French *araisnier*, based on Latin *ad-* 'to' + *ration-* 'reason, account.' **—ar·raign·ment** *n.*

Ar·ran /ˈarən/ an island in the Firth of Clyde, in the west of Scotland.

ar·range /əˈrānj/ ▸*v.* [*trans.*] **1** put (things) in a neat, attractive, or required order: *she had just finished arranging the flowers | the columns are* **arranged in** *12 rows.* **2** organize or make plans for (a future event): *they hoped to arrange a meeting | we've* **arranged** *the funeral* **for** *Saturday |* [*intrans.*] *my aunt* **arranged for** *the furniture to be stored.* ■ [*intrans.*] reach agreement about an action or event in advance: *I* **arranged with** *my boss to have the time off |* [with *infinitive*] *they* **arranged to** *meet at eleven o'clock.* ■ ensure that (something) is done or provided by organizing it in advance: *accommodations can be arranged if required.* **3** *Music* adapt (a composition) for performance with instruments or voices other than those originally specified: *songs* **arranged for** *viola and piano.* **4** *archaic* settle (a dispute or claim): *the quarrel, partly by the interference of the Crown Prince, was arranged.* ▷late Middle English: from Old French *arangier*, from *a-* (from Latin *ad* 'to, at') + *rangier* 'to range' (see **RANGE**). **—ar·range·a·ble** *adj.* **—ar·rang·er** *n.*

ar·ranged mar·riage ▸*n.* a marriage planned and agreed to by the families or guardians of the bride and groom, who have little or no say in the matter themselves.

ar·range·ment /əˈrānjmənt/ ▸*n.* **1** the action, process, or result of arranging or being arranged: *the arrangement of the furniture in the room.* ■ a thing that has been arranged in a neat or attractive way: *flower arrangements | an intricate arrangement of gravel paths.* **2** (usu. **arrangements**) plans or preparations for a future event: *all the* **arrangements for** *the wedding were made.* ■ an agreement with someone: *the travel agents have an* **arrangement with** *the hotel |* **by special arrangement**, *students can take a course in other degree programs.* **3** *Music* a composition adapted for performance with different instruments or voices than those originally specified: *Mozart's symphonies in* **arrangements for** *cello and piano.* **4** *archaic* a settlement of a dispute or claim.

ar·rant /ˈarənt/ ▸*adj.* [*attrib.*] *dated* complete, utter: *what arrant nonsense!* ▷Middle English: variant of **ERRANT**, originally in phrases such as *arrant thief* ('outlawed, roving thief').

Ar·ras /äˈräs; ˈarəs/ a town in northeastern France; pop. 42,700. In medieval times, it was a center for the manufacture of tapestries.

ar·ras /ˈarəs/ ▸*n.* a rich tapestry, typically hung on the walls of a room or used to conceal an alcove. ▷late Middle English (originally denoting the fabric itself): named after the French town of **ARRAS**.

ar·ray /əˈrā/ ▸*n.* **1** an impressive display or range of a particular type of thing: *there is a vast array of literature on the topic | a bewildering array of choices.* **2** an ordered arrangement, in particular: ■ an arrangement of troops. ■ *Mathematics* an arrangement of quantities or symbols in rows and columns; a matrix. ■ *Computing* an ordered set of related elements. ■ *Law* a list of jurors empaneled. **3** *poetic/literary* elaborate or beautiful clothing: *he was clothed in fine array.*
▸*v.* **1** [*trans.*] (usu. **be arrayed**) display or arrange (things) in a particular way: *arrayed across the table was a buffet | the forces arrayed against him.* **2** [*trans.*] (usu. **be arrayed in**) dress someone in (the clothes specified): *they were arrayed in Hungarian national dress.* **3** [*trans.*] *Law* empanel (a jury). ▷Middle English (in the senses 'preparedness' and 'place in readiness'): from Old French *arei* (noun), *areer* (verb), based on Latin *ad-* 'toward' + a Germanic base meaning 'prepare.'

ar·rears /əˈri(ə)rz/ ▸*plural n.* money that is owed and should have been paid earlier: *he was suing the lessee for the arrears of rent.* ▷Middle English (first used in the phrase *in arrear*): from *arrear* (adverb) 'behind, overdue,' from Old French *arere*, from medieval Latin *adretro*, from *ad-* 'toward' + *retro* 'backward.' **—ar·rear·age** /əˈri(ə)rij/ *n.*
▸*PHRASE* □ **in arrears** (also *chiefly Law* **in arrear**) behind in paying money that is owed: *two out of three tenants are in arrears.* ■ (of payments made or due for wages, rent, etc.) at the end of each period of work or occupancy: *you will be paid monthly in arrears.*

ar·rest /əˈrest/ ▸*v.* [*trans.*] **1** seize (someone) by legal authority and take into custody: *the police* **arrested** *him* **for** *possession of marijuana | two youths aged 16 were arrested.* **2** stop or check (progress or a process): *the spread of the disease can be arrested |* [as *adj.*] (**arrested**) *arrested development may occur.* **3** attract the attention of (someone): *his attention was arrested by a strange sound.*
▸*n.* **1** the action of seizing someone to take into custody: *I have a warrant for your arrest | they* **placed** *her* **under arrest** *| at least 69 arrests were made.* **2** a stoppage or sudden cessation of motion: [with *adj.*] *a cardiac arrest.* ▷late Middle English: from Old French *arester*, based on Latin *ad-* 'at, to' + *restare* 'remain, stop.'

ar·rest·ee /əˌresˈtē/ ▸*n.* a person who has been arrested.

ar·rest·er /əˈrestər/ (also **ar·res·tor**) ▸*n.* [usu. with *adj.*] a device that prevents or stops a specified thing: *a spark arrester | a lightning arrester.* ■ a device on an aircraft carrier that slows aircraft after landing by means of a hook and cable.

ar·rest·ing /əˈrestiNG/ ▸*adj.* **1** striking; eye-catching: *at 6 feet 6 inches he was an arresting figure.* **2** a person or agency that seizes and detains (someone or something) by legal authority: *the arresting officer.* **—ar·rest·ing·ly** *adv.*

Ar·re·tine /ˈariˌtīn; -ˌtēn/ ▸*adj.* denoting fine red pottery made at Arretium, an ancient city in central Italy, and elsewhere from *c.*100 BC until the late 1st century AD. ▷late 18th cent.: from the name of the city *Arretium* (modern *Arezzo*) + **-INE**[1].

Ar·rhe·ni·us /əˈrēnēəs; -ˈrā-/, Svante August (1859–1927), Swedish chemist, noted for his work on electrolytes. Nobel Prize for Chemistry (1903).

ar·rhyth·mi·a /āˈriTHmēə; əˈriTH-/ ▸*n.* *Medicine* a condition in which the heart beats with an irregular or abnormal rhythm. ▷late 19th cent.: from Greek *arruthmia* 'lack of rhythm,' from *a-* 'without' + *rhuthmos* (see **RHYTHM**).

ar·rhyth·mic /əˈriTHmik/ (also **a·rhyth·mic**) ▸*adj.* not rhythmic; without rhythm or regularity: *the arrhythmic clip-clop of pony steps.* ■ *Medicine* of, relating to, or suffering from cardiac arrhythmia. **—ar·rhyth·mi·cal** *adj.* **—ar·rhyth·mi·cal·ly** /-mik(ə)lē/ *adv.*

ar·rière-pen·sée /ä,ryer pän'sä/ ▸*n.* a concealed thought or intention; an ulterior motive. ▷early 19th cent.: French, literally 'behind thought.'

ar·ris /'aris/ ▸*n. Architecture* a sharp edge formed by the meeting of two flat or curved surfaces. ▷late 17th cent.: alteration of early modern French *areste* 'sharp ridge,' earlier form of ARÊTE.

ar·ri·val /ə'rīvəl/ ▸*n.* the action or process of arriving: *Ruth's arrival in New York | he was dead* **on arrival** *at the hospital.* ■ a person who has arrived somewhere: *hotel staff greeted the late arrivals.* ■ the emergence or appearance of a new development, phenomenon, or product: *the arrival of democracy.* ■ such a new development, phenomenon, or product: *sociology is a relatively new arrival on the academic scene.* ▷late Middle English: from Anglo-Norman French *arrivaille*, from Old French *arriver* (see ARRIVE).

ar·rive /ə'rīv/ ▸*v.* [*intrans.*] reach a place at the end of a journey or a stage in a journey: *we* **arrived at** *his house and knocked at the door | the team* **arrived in** *New Delhi on July 30 | they had recently* **arrived from** *Turkey.* ■ (of a thing) be brought or delivered: *the invitation arrived a few days later.* ■ (**arrive at**) reach (a conclusion or decision): *they arrived at the same conclusion.* ■ (of an event or a particular moment) happen or come: *we will be in touch with them when the time arrives.* ■ (of a new development or product) come into existence or use: *microcomputers arrived at the start of the 1970s.* ■ (of a baby) be born: *he will feel jealous when a new baby arrives.* ■ *informal* achieve success or recognition. ▷Middle English (in the sense 'reach the shore after a voyage'): from Old French *ariver*, based on Latin *ad-* 'to' + *ripa* 'shore.'

ar·ri·viste /,ärē'vēst/ ▸*n.* an ambitious or ruthlessly self-seeking person, esp. one who has recently acquired wealth or social status. ▷early 20th cent.: from French, from *arriver* (see ARRIVE).

ar·ro·gant /'arəgənt/ ▸*adj.* having or revealing an exaggerated sense of one's own importance or abilities: *he's arrogant and opinionated | a typically arrogant assumption.* ▷late Middle English: via Old French from Latin *arrogant-* 'claiming for oneself,' from the verb *arrogare* (see ARROGATE). **—ar·ro·gance** *n.* **—ar·ro·gant·ly** *adv.*

ar·ro·gate /'arə,gāt/ ▸*v.* [*trans.*] take or claim (something) for oneself without justification: *they* **arrogate to themselves** *the ability to divine the nation's true interests.* ▷mid 16th cent.: from Latin *arrogat-* 'claimed for oneself,' from the verb *arrogare*, from *ad-* 'to' + *rogare* 'ask.' **—ar·ro·ga·tion** /,arə'gāshən/ *n.*

USAGE See usage at ABROGATE.

ar·ron·disse·ment /ə'rändismənt; ä'rändēs,män/ ▸*n.* a subdivision of a department in France, for purposes of local government administration. ■ an administrative district of certain large French cities, in particular Paris. ▷French, from *arrondir* 'make round.'

Ar·row /'arō/, Kenneth Joseph (1921–), U.S. economist, noted chiefly for his work on general economic equilibrium and social choice. His *Social Choices and Individual Values* (1951) argued the impossibility of aggregating the preferences of individuals into a single combined order of priorities for society as a whole. Nobel Prize for Economics (1972).

ar·row /'arō/ ▸*n.* a shaft sharpened at the front and with feathers or vanes at the back, shot from a bow as a weapon or for sport: *his ability to launch an arrow accurately.* ■ a mark or sign resembling an arrow, used to show direction or position; a pointer: *we drove in the main gate and followed a series of arrows | [as adj.] you can use the up and down arrow keys.* ▷Old English *arewe, arwe*, from Old Norse. **—ar·row·y** *adj.*

▸*PHRASES* □ **arrow of time** (or **time's arrow**) the direction of travel from past to future in time considered as a physical dimension. □ **straight as an arrow** perfectly straight, with no deviation.

ar·row·head /'arō,hed/ ▸*n.* **1** the pointed end of an arrow, typically wedge-shaped. ■ a decorative device resembling an arrowhead. **2** an aquatic or semiaquatic plant with arrow-shaped leaves and three-petaled white flowers. • Genus *Sagittaria*, family Alismataceae: several species, in particular the common **broad-leaved arrowhead** *S. latifolia*.

broad-leaved arrowhead

ar·row·root /'arō,ro͞ot; -,ro͝ot/ ▸*n.* a West Indian herbaceous plant from which a starch is prepared. • *Maranta arundinacea*, family Marantaceae. ■ the fine-grained starch obtained from this plant, used in cooking and medicine. ▷late 17th cent.: alteration of Arawak *aru-aru* (literally 'meal of meals') by association with ARROW and ROOT[1], the tubers being used to absorb poison from arrow wounds.

ar·row-slit ▸*n.* (esp. in a medieval fortified building) a narrow vertical slit in a wall for shooting or looking through, or to admit light and air.

ar·row-straight ▸*adj.* & *adv.* completely straight: [as *adj.*] *the roads are empty and arrow-straight* | [as *adv.*] *an index leads the reader arrow-straight to documents of interest.*

ar·row worm ▸*n.* a slender transparent wormlike animal with fins, having spines on the head for grasping prey. It is common in marine plankton. Also called **chaetognath.** • Phylum Chaetognatha.

ar·roy·o /ə'roi,ō/ ▸*n.* (*pl.* **-os**) a steep-sided gully cut by running water in an arid or semiarid region. ▷mid 19th cent.: from Spanish.

ar·roz /ä'rōs/ ▸*n.* Spanish word for RICE, used in the names of various dishes.

ar·roz con pol·lo /kōn 'pô(l)yō/ ▸*n.* a Spanish and Latin American dish of chicken and rice simmered with tomatoes, stock, and herbs. ▷Spanish, 'chicken with rice.'

arse /ärs/ ▸ British spelling of ASS[2]. ▷Old English *ærs*, of Germanic origin; related to Dutch *aars* and German *Arsch*.

ar·se·nal /'ärs(ə)-nl/ ▸*n.* a collection of weapons and military equipment stored by a country, person, or group: *Britain's nuclear arsenal.* ■ a place where weapons and military equipment are stored or made. ■ [in *sing.*] *figurative* an array of resources available for a certain purpose: *an arsenal of computers at our disposal.* ▷early 16th cent. (denoting a dock for the construction and repair of ships): from French, or from obsolete Italian *arzanale*, based on Arabic *dār-aṣ-ṣinā'a*, from *dār* 'house' + *al-* '(of) the' + *sinā'a* 'art, industry' (from *ṣana'a* 'make, fabricate').

ar·se·nate /'ärs(ə)nit; -,nāt/ ▸*n. Chemistry* a salt or ester of arsenic acid.

ar·se·nic ▸*n.* /'ärs(ə)nik/ the chemical element of atomic number 33, a brittle steel-gray metalloid. (Symbol: **As**)

Arsenic compounds (and their poisonous properties) have been known since ancient times, and the metallic form was isolated in the Middle Ages. Arsenic occurs naturally in orpiment, realgar, and other minerals, and rarely as the free element. Arsenic is used in semiconductors and some specialized alloys; its toxic compounds are widely used in wood preservation.

▸*adj.* (**ar·sen·ic**) /är'senik/ of or relating to arsenic. ■ *Chemistry* of arsenic with a valence of five; of arsenic(V). ▷late Middle English (denoting yellow orpiment, arsenic sulfide): via Old French from Latin *arsenicum*, from Greek *arsenikon* 'yellow orpiment,' identified with *arsenikos* 'male,' but in fact from Arabic *al-zarnīk* 'the orpiment,' based on Persian *zar* 'gold.'

ar·sen·ic ac·id /är'senik/ ▸*n. Chemistry* a weakly acidic crystalline solid with oxidizing properties, formed when arsenic reacts with nitric acid. • Chem. formula: H_3AsO_4.

ar·sen·i·cal /är'senikəl/ ▸*adj.* of or containing arsenic. ▸*n.* (usu. **arsenicals**) an arsenical drug or other compound.

ar·se·nide /'ärs(ə),nīd/ ▸*n. Chemistry* a binary compound of arsenic with a metallic element.

ar·se·no·py·rite /,ärsənō'pī,rīt; är,senō-/ ▸*n.* a silvery-gray mineral consisting of an arsenide and sulfide of iron. • Chem. formula FeAsS.

ar·sine /'ärsēn; är'sēn/ ▸*n. Chemistry* a poisonous gas smelling slightly of garlic, made by the reaction of some arsenides with acids. • Arsenic trihydride; chem. formula: AsH_3. ▷late 19th cent.: from ARSENIC, on the pattern of *amine*.

ar·sis /'ärsis/ ▸*n.* (*pl.* **-ses** /-,sēz/) *Prosody* the unstressed syllable of a metrical foot. The opposite of THESIS (sense 3). To the Greeks, the two terms designated the raising and lowering of the foot in walking, but their meanings became reversed in the Latin tradition, where grammarians identified them with the lowering and raising of the voice. ▷late Middle English: via late Latin from Greek, literally 'lifting,' from *airein* 'raise.'

ar·son /'ärsən/ ▸*n.* the criminal act of deliberately setting fire to property: *police are treating the fire as arson* | [as *adj.*] *an arson attack.* ▷late 17th cent.: an Anglo-Norman French legal term, from medieval Latin *arsio(n-)*, from Latin *ardere* 'to burn.' **—ar·son·ist** /-nist/ *n.*

ars·phen·a·mine /ärs'fenəmən; -,mēn/ ▸*n. Medicine* a synthetic organic arsenic compound formerly used to treat syphilis and other diseases. ▷early 20th cent.: blend of ARSENIC, PHENYL, and AMINE.

ar·sy-ver·sy /'ärsē 'vərsē/ *informal, chiefly Brit.* ▸*adj.* in a confused, disordered, or perversely contrary state or condition: *the whole place was arsy-versy | they got things all arsy-versy.* ▷mid 16th cent.: from ARSE + Latin *versus* 'turned,' the addition of -Y[1] to both elements forming a jingle.

art[1] /ärt/ ▸*n.* **1** the expression or application of human creative skill and imagination, typically in a visual form such as painting or sculpture, producing works to be appreciated primarily for their beauty or emotional power: *the art of the Renaissance | great art is concerned with moral imperfections | she studied art in Paris.* ■ works produced by such skill and imagination: *his collection of modern art | an exhibition of Tibetan art* | [as *adj.*] *an art critic.* ■ creative activity resulting in the production of paintings, drawings, or sculpture: *she's good at art.* **2** (**the arts**) the various branches of creative activity, such as painting, music, literature, and dance: *the visual arts* | [in *sing.*] *the art of photography.* **3** (**arts**) subjects of study primarily concerned with the processes and products of human creativity and social life, such as languages, literature, and history (as contrasted with scientific or technical subjects): *the belief that the arts and sciences were incompatible | the Faculty of Arts.* **4** a skill at doing a specified thing, typically one acquired through practice: *the art of conversation.* ▷Middle English: via Old French from Latin *ars, art-*.

▸*PHRASES* □ **art for art's sake** used to convey the idea that the chief or only aim of a work of art is the self-expression of the individual artist who creates it. □ **art is long, life is short** *proverb* there is so much knowledge to acquire that a lifetime is not sufficient. □ **art of war** the strategy, tactics, and techniques of combat.

art[2] ▸ archaic or dialect 2nd person singular present of BE.

art. ▸*abbr.* ■ article. ■ artificial. ■ artillery.

Ar·taud /är'tō/, Antonin (1896–1948), French actor, director, and poet. He developed the concept of the nonverbal Theater of Cruelty.

art car ▸*n.* a car or other four-wheel motor vehicle decorated as a work of art.

art dec·o ▸*n.* the predominant decorative art style of the 1920s and 1930s, characterized by precise and boldly delineated geometric shapes and strong colors, and used most notably in household objects and in architecture. ▷1960s: shortened from French *art décoratif* 'decorative art,' from the 1925 *Exposition des Arts décoratifs* in Paris.

ar·te·fact ▸*n.* British spelling of ARTIFACT.

ar·tel /är'tel/ ▸*n. historical* (in prerevolutionary Russia) a cooperative association of craftsmen living and working together. ▷from Russian *artel'*.

Ar·te·mis /'ärtəməs/ *Greek Mythology* a goddess, daughter of Zeus and sister of Apollo. She was a huntress and is typically depicted with a bow and arrows. Roman equivalent DIANA.

ar·te·mis·i·a /,ärtə'mēzh(ē)ə/ ▸*n.* an aromatic or bitter-tasting plant of a genus that includes wormwood, mugwort, and sagebrush. Several kinds of artemisia are used in herbal medicine and many are cultivated for their feathery gray foliage. • Genus *Artemisia*, family Compositae. ▷Middle English: via Latin from Greek, 'wormwood,' named after the goddess ARTEMIS, to whom it was sacred.

ar·te·mis·in·in /,ärtə'mēsənin; -'mis-/ ▸*n.* another term for QINGHAOSU. ▷1970s: blend of ARTEMISIA and QUININE.

Ar·te Po·ver·a /'ärtä 'pōvərə; 'pô-/ ▸*n.* a style and movement in art originating in Italy in the 1960s combining aspects of conceptual, minimalist, and performance art, and making use of worthless or common materials such as stones or newspapers, in

A

the hope of subverting the commercialization of art. ▷1960s: Italian, literally 'impoverished art,' from *arte* 'art' + *povera* (feminine of *povero* 'needy').

ar·te·ri·al /är'ti(ə)rēəl/ ▶*n.* a through road: *sabotaged arterials needed for evacuation of civilians.*

▶*adj.* [*attrib.*] of or relating to an artery or arteries. ■ denoting an important route in a system of roads, railroad lines, or rivers: *one of the main arterial routes from New York.* ▷late Middle English: from medieval Latin *arterialis*, from Latin *arteria* (see ARTERY).

ar·te·ri·al·ize /är'ti(ə)rēə,līz/ ▶*v.* [*trans.*] [usu. as *adj.*] (**arterialized**) convert venous into arterial (blood) by reoxygenation, esp. in the lungs. —**ar·te·ri·al·i·za·tion** /är,ti(ə)rēələ'zāsHən/ *n.*

arterio- ▶*comb. form* of or relating to the arteries: *arteriosclerosis.* ▷from Greek *artēria* (see ARTERY).

ar·te·ri·og·ra·phy /är,ti(ə)rē'ägrəfē/ ▶*n. Medicine* radiography of an artery, carried out after injection of a radio-opaque substance.

ar·te·ri·ole /är'ti(ə)rē,ōl/ ▶*n. Anatomy* a small branch of an artery leading into capillaries. ▷mid 19th cent.: from French *artériole*, diminutive of *artère* (see ARTERY). —**ar·te·ri·o·lar** /är,ti(ə)rē'ōlər/ *adj.*

ar·te·ri·o·scle·ro·sis /är,ti(ə)rēōsklə'rōsis/ ▶*n. Medicine* the thickening and hardening of the walls of the arteries, occurring typically in old age. —**ar·te·ri·o·scle·rot·ic** /-'rätik/ *adj.*

ar·te·ri·o·ve·nous /är,ti(ə)rēō'vēnəs/ ▶*adj. Anatomy* of, relating to, or affecting an artery and a vein.

ar·te·ri·tis /,ärtə'rītis/ ▶*n. Medicine* inflammation of the walls of an artery.

ar·ter·y /'ärtərē/ ▶*n.* (*pl.* **-ter·ies**) any of the muscular-walled tubes forming part of the circulation system by which blood (mainly that which has been oxygenated) is conveyed from the heart to all parts of the body. Compare with VEIN (sense 1). ■ an important route in a system of roads, rivers, or railroad lines: *the east-west artery between San Francisco and Sacramento.* ▷late Middle English: from Latin *arteria*, from Greek *artēria*, probably from *airein* 'raise.'

ar·te·sian /är'tēzHən/ ▶*adj.* relating to or denoting a well bored perpendicularly into water-bearing strata lying at an angle, so that natural pressure produces a constant supply of water with little or no pumping: *the water from* **artesian wells** *makes agriculture possible.* ▷mid 19th cent.: from French *artésien* 'from *Artois*' (see ARTOIS), where such wells were first made.

art film ▶*n.* a film that is artistic or experimental in its primary intent.

art form ▶*n.* a conventionally established form of artistic composition, such as the novel, sonata, or sonnet. ■ any activity regarded as a medium of imaginative or creative self-expression: *he elevates stage managing to an art form.*

art·ful /'ärtfəl/ ▶*adj.* **1** (of a person or action) clever or skillful, typically in a crafty or cunning way: *her artful wiles.* **2** showing creative skill or taste: *an artful photograph of a striking woman.* —**art·ful·ly** *adv.* —**art·ful·ness** *n.*

art his·to·ry ▶*n.* the academic study of the history and development of painting, sculpture, and the other visual arts. —**art his·to·ri·an** *n.* —**art his·tor·i·cal** *adj.*

art house ▶*n.* a movie theater that specializes in films that are artistic or experimental rather than merely entertaining.

ar·thral·gia /är'THralj(ē)ə/ ▶*n. Medicine* pain in a joint. ▷mid 19th cent.: from Greek *arthron* 'joint' + -ALGIA.

ar·thri·tis /är'THrītis/ ▶*n.* painful inflammation and stiffness of the joints. ▷mid 16th cent.: via Latin from Greek, from *arthron* 'joint.' *Arthritic* was already used in late Middle English. —**ar·thrit·ic** /-'THritik/ *adj.* & *n.*

arthro- ▶*comb. form* of a joint; relating to joints: *arthroscope.* ▷from Greek *arthron* 'joint.'

ar·throd·e·sis /är'THrädəsis/ ▶*n.* surgical immobilization of a joint by fusion of the adjacent bones. ▷early 20th cent.: from ARTHRO- + Greek *desis* 'binding together.'

Ar·throp·o·da /är'THräpədə/ *Zoology* a large phylum of invertebrate animals that includes insects, spiders, crustaceans, and their relatives. They have a segmented body, an external skeleton, and jointed limbs, and are sometimes divided among several phyla. ▷late 19th cent.: modern Latin (plural), from Greek *arthron* 'joint' + *pous, pod-* 'foot.' —**ar·thro·pod** /'ärTHrə,päd/ *n.*

ar·thro·scope /'ärTHrə,skōp/ ▶*n. Medicine* an instrument through which the interior of a joint may be inspected or operated on. —**ar·thro·scop·ic** /,ärTHrə'skäpik/ *adj.* —**ar·thros·co·py** /är'THräskəpē/ *n.*

Ar·thur[1] /'ärTHər/ a legendary king of Britain, historically perhaps a 5th- or 6th-century Romano-British chieftain or general. Stories of his life, the exploits of his knights, and the Round Table of the court at Camelot were developed by Malory, Chrétien de Troyes, and other medieval writers and became the subject of many legends. —**Ar·thu·ri·an** /är'THŏŏrēən/ *adj.*

Ar·thur[2], Chester Alan (1830–86), 21st president of the U.S. 1881–85. A New York Republican, he became James Garfield's vice president in March 1881, succeeding to the presidency upon the assassination of Garfield six months later. During his term of office, he was responsible for the enactment of Civil Service reforms and for improving the strength of the U.S. Navy.

Chester Alan Arthur

ar·ti·choke /'ärti,CHōk/ ▶*n.* **1** (also **globe artichoke**) a European plant cultivated for its large thistlelike flowerheads. • *Cynara scolymus*, family Compositae. ■ the unopened flowerhead of this, of which the heart and the fleshy bases of the bracts are edible. **2** see JERUSALEM ARTICHOKE. ▷mid 16th cent.: from northern Italian *articiocco*, from Spanish *alcarchofa*, from Arabic *al-karšūfa.*

artichoke

ar·ti·choke gall ▶*n.* a hard egg-shaped gall which forms inside an artichoke bud in response to the developing larva of a gall wasp. • The wasp is *Andricus fecundator*, family Cynipidae.

ar·ti·cle /'ärtikəl/ ▶*n.* **1** a particular item or object, typically one of a specified type: *small household articles | articles of clothing.* **2** a piece of writing included with others in a newspaper, magazine, or other publication: *an article about middle-aged executives.* **3** a separate clause or paragraph of a legal document or agreement, typically one outlining a single rule or regulation: [as *adj.*] *it is an offense under Article 7 of the treaty.* **4** *Grammar* see DEFINITE ARTICLE, INDEFINITE ARTICLE.

▶*v.* [*trans.*] (usu. **be articled**) bind by the terms of a contract, as one of apprenticeship. ▷Middle English (denoting a separate clause of the Apostles' Creed): from Old French, from Latin *articulus* 'small connecting part,' diminutive of *artus* 'joint.'

▶*PHRASES* □ **an article of faith** a firmly held belief: *it was an article of faith with this circle that women must free themselves.* □ **the genuine article** a person or thing considered to be an authentic and excellent example of their kind.

Ar·ti·cle 15 ▶*n.* a section of the Uniform Code of Military Justice allowing commanders to carry out discretionary punishments without judicial proceedings ■ a judgment or punishment issued under this provision: *if I agree to accept the Article 15, am I admitting guilt?*

Ar·ti·cles of Con·fed·er·a·tion ▶*n.* the original constitution of the U.S., ratified in 1781, which was replaced by the U.S. Constitution in 1789.

ar·tic·u·lar /är'tikyələr/ ▶*adj.* [*attrib.*] of or relating to a joint or the joints: *articular cartilage.* ▷late Middle English: from Latin *articularis*, from *articulus* 'small connecting part' (see ARTICLE).

ar·tic·u·late ▶*adj.* /är'tikyəlit/ **1** (of a person or a person's words) having or showing the ability to speak fluently and coherently: *an articulate account of their experiences.* **2** having joints or jointed segments. ■ *Zoology* denoting a brachiopod that has projections and sockets that form a hinge joining the two halves of the shell.

▶*v.* /-,lāt/ **1** [*trans.*] express (an idea or feeling) fluently and coherently: *they were unable to articulate their emotions.* ■ pronounce (something) clearly and distinctly: *he articulated each word with precision* | [*intrans.*] *people who do not articulate well are more difficult to lip-read.* **2** [*intrans.*] form a joint: *the mandible is a solid piece* **articulating with** *the head.* ■ (**be articulated**) be connected by joints: *the wing is articulated to the thorax.* ▷mid 16th cent.: from Latin *articulatus*, past participle of *articulare* 'divide into joints, utter distinctly,' from *articulus* 'small connecting part' (see ARTICLE). —**ar·tic·u·la·ble** *adj.* —**ar·tic·u·la·cy** /-ləsē/ *n.* —**ar·tic·u·late·ly** *adv.* —**ar·tic·u·late·ness** *n.* —**ar·tic·u·la·tor** /-,lātər/ *n.*

ar·tic·u·lat·ed /är'tikyə,lātid/ ▶*adj.* **1** having two or more sections connected by a flexible joint: *eight articulated trailer coaches | the trilobite's thorax has a variable number of articulated segments.* **2** (of an idea or feeling) expressed; put into words: *the lack of a clearly articulated policy.*

ar·tic·u·la·tion /är,tikyə'lāsHən/ ▶*n.* **1** the action of putting into words an idea or feeling of a specified type: *it would involve the articulation of a theory of the just war.* ■ the formation of clear and distinct sounds in speech: *the articulation of vowels and consonants.* ■ *Music* clarity in the production of successive notes: *beautifully polished articulation from the violins.* ■ *Phonetics* the act or manner of uttering a speech sound, esp. a consonant. **2** the state of being jointed: *the area of articulation of the lower jaw.* ■ [with *adj.*] a specified joint: *the leg articulation.* ▷late Middle English (in the senses 'joint,' 'joining'): from Latin *articulatio(n-)*, from the verb *articulare* (see ARTICULATE).

ar·tic·u·la·to·ry /är'tikyələ,tôrē/ ▶*adj.* [*attrib.*] of or relating to the formation of speech sounds.

ar·ti·fact /'ärtə,fakt/ (*Brit.* **ar·te·fact**) ▶*n.* **1** an object made by a human being, typically an item of cultural or historical interest: *gold and silver artifacts.* ■ *Archaeology* such an object as distinguished from a similar object naturally produced. **2** something observed in a scientific investigation or experiment that is not naturally present but occurs as a result of the preparative or investigative procedure: *widespread tissue infection may be a technical artifact.* ▷early 19th cent.: from Latin *arte* 'by or using art' + *factum* 'something made' (neuter past participle of *facere* 'make'). —**ar·ti·fac·tu·al** /,ärtə'fakCHŏŏəl/ *adj.*

ar·ti·fice /'ärtəfis/ ▶*n.* clever or cunning devices or expedients, esp. as used to trick or deceive others: *artifice and outright fakery | the style is not free from the artifices of the period.* ▷late Middle English (in the sense 'workmanship'): from Old French, from Latin *artificium*, based on *ars, art-* 'art' + *facere* 'make.'

ar·tif·i·cer /är'tifəsər/ ▶*n. archaic* a skilled craftsman or inventor. ■ *Brit., Military* a skilled mechanic in the armed forces. ▷late Middle English: from Anglo-Norman French, probably an alteration of Old French *artificien*, from *artifice* (see ARTIFICE).

ar·ti·fi·cial /,ärtə'fisHəl/ ▶*adj.* **1** made or produced by human beings rather than occuring naturally, typically as a copy of something natural: *her skin glowed in the artificial light | an artificial limb | artificial flowers.* ■ (of a situation or concept) not existing naturally; contrived or false: *the artificial division of people into age groups.* See note at SPURIOUS. ■ *Bridge* (of a bid) conventional as opposed to natural. **2** (of a person or a person's behavior) insincere or affected: *an artificial smile.* ▷late Middle English: from Old French *artificiel* or Latin *artificialis*, from *artificium* 'handicraft' (see ARTIFICE). —**ar·ti·fi·ci·al·i·ty** /-,fisHē'alitē/ *n.* —**ar·ti·fi·cial·ly** *adv.*

ar·ti·fi·cial climb·ing ▶*n.* the sport of climbing on an indoor or outdoor wall whose surface simulates a mountain.

ar·ti·fi·cial ho·ri·zon ▶*n.* a gyroscopic instrument or a fluid surface, typically one of mercury, used to provide a horizontal reference plane for navigational measurement.

ar·ti·fi·cial in·sem·i·na·tion (abbr.: **AI**) ▶*n.* the injection of semen into the vagina or uterus other than by sexual intercourse.

ar·ti·fi·cial in·tel·li·gence (abbr.: **AI**) ▶*n.* the theory and development of computer systems able to perform tasks that normally require human intelligence, such as visual perception, speech recognition, decision-making, and translation between languages.

ar·ti·fi·cial life ▶*n.* the production or action of computer programs or computerized systems that simulate the behavior, population dynamics, or other characteristics of living organisms.

ar·ti·fi·cial res·pi·ra·tion ▸*n.* the restoration or substitution of someone's breathing by manual, mechanical, or mouth-to-mouth methods.

ar·ti·fi·cial sat·el·lite ▸*n.* another term for SATELLITE (sense 1).

ar·ti·fi·cial sur·face ▸*n. Sports* (also **artificial turf**) a carpetlike playing surface used in stadiums instead of natural grass.

ar·til·ler·y /är'tilərē/ ▸*n.* (*pl.* **-ler·ies**) large-caliber guns used in warfare on land: *tanks and heavy artillery.* ■ a military detachment or branch of the armed forces that uses such guns. ▷late Middle English: from Old French *artillerie*, from *artiller*, alteration of *atillier* 'equip, arm,' probably a variant of *atirier*, from *a-* (from Latin *ad* 'to, at') + *tire* 'rank, order.' **—ar·til·ler·ist** /-rist/ *n.* **—ar·til·ler·y·man** /-mən/ *n.*

Ar·ti·o·dac·ty·la /ˌärtē-ō'daktl-ə/ *Zoology* an order of mammals that comprises the even-toed ungulates. Compare with PERISSODACTYLA. ▷modern Latin (plural), from Greek *artios* 'even' + *daktulos* 'finger, toe.' **—ar·ti·o·dac·tyl** /-'daktl/ *n.* & *adj.*

ar·ti·san /'ärtizən/ ▸*n.* a worker in a skilled trade, esp. one that involves making things by hand. ▷mid 16th cent.: from French, from Italian *artigiano*, based on Latin *artitus*, past participle of *artire* 'instruct in the arts,' from *ars, art-* 'art.' **—ar·ti·san·al** /-zənl/ *adj.*

art·ist /'ärtist/ ▸*n.* a person who produces paintings or drawings as a profession or hobby. ■ a person who practices any of the various creative arts, such as a sculptor, novelist, poet, or filmmaker. ■ a person skilled at a particular task or occupation: *a surgeon who is an artist with the scalpel.* ■ a performer, such as a singer, actor, or dancer. ■ *informal* [with *adj.*] a habitual practitioner of a specified reprehensible activity: *a con artist | rip-off artists.* ▷early 16th cent. (denoting a master of the liberal arts): from French *artiste*, from Italian *artista*, from *arte* art, from Latin *ars, art-*.

ar·tiste /är'tēst/ ▸*n.* a professional entertainer, esp. a singer or dancer: *cabaret artistes.* ▷early 19th cent.: from French (see ARTIST).

ar·tis·tic /är'tistik/ ▸*adj.* having or revealing natural creative skill: *my lack of artistic ability.* ■ of, relating to, or characteristic of art or artistry: *a denial of artistic freedom | her artistic temperament.* ■ aesthetically pleasing: *computer programs that produce artistic designs.* **—ar·tis·ti·cal·ly** /-ik(ə)lē/ *adv.*

ar·tis·tic di·rec·tor ▸*n.* the person with overall responsibility for the selection and interpretation of the works performed by a theater, ballet, or opera company.

art·ist·ry /'ärtistrē/ ▸*n.* creative skill or ability: *the artistry of the pianist.*

art·ist's fun·gus ▸*n.* a bracket fungus that has the shape of an artist's palette, with a reddish-brown upper surface, found in both Eurasia and North America. • *Ganoderma applanatum*, family Ganodermataceae, class Hymenomycetes.

art·less /'ärtlis/ ▸*adj.* without guile or deception: *an artless, naive girl | artless sincerity.* ■ without effort or pretentiousness; natural and simple: *an artless literary masterpiece.* ■ without skill or finesse: *her awkward, artless prose.* **—art·less·ly** *adv.*

art nou·veau /är(t) nōō'vō/ ▸*n.* a style of decorative art, architecture, and design prominent in western Europe and the U.S. from about 1890 until World War I and characterized by intricate linear designs and flowing curves based on natural forms. ▷early 20th cent.: from French, literally 'new art.'

Ar·tois /är'twä/ a region and former province of northwestern France.

art pa·per ▸*n.* [*mass noun*] high-quality paper coated with china clay or a similar substance to give it a smooth surface.

arts and crafts ▸*plural n.* decorative design and handicraft.

Arts and Crafts Move·ment an English decorative arts movement of the second half of the 19th century that sought to revive the ideal of craftsmanship in an age of increasing mechanization and mass production. William Morris was its most prominent member.

art song ▸*n. Music* a song written to be sung in recital, typically with piano accompaniment and often set to a poem.

art·sy /'ärtsē/ (also **art·y** /'ärtē/) ▸*adj.* (**-si·er, -si·est**) *informal* making a strong, affected, or pretentious display of being artistic or interested in the arts: *the artsy town of Taos | artsy French flicks.* **—art·si·ness** *n.*

art·sy-craft·sy /'kraftsē/ *informal* ▸*adj.* interested or involved in making decorative, artistic objects, typically ones perceived as quaint or homespun: *artsy-craftsy gift shops.*

art·sy-fart·sy /'färtsē/ ▸*adj. informal, derogatory* associated with or showing a pretentious interest in the arts: *you can wear a turtleneck to join your artsy-fartsy friends.*

art ther·a·py ▸*n.* a form of psychotherapy involving the encouragement of free self-expression through painting, drawing, or modeling, used as a remedial activity or an aid to diagnosis.

art·work /'ärtˌwərk/ ▸*n.* illustrations, photographs, or other nontextual material prepared for inclusion in a publication. ■ paintings, drawings, or other artistic works: *a collection of artwork from tribal cultures | each artwork is reproduced in color on a full page.*

A·ru·ba /ə'rōōbə/ an island in the Caribbean Sea, close to the Venezuelan coast; pop. 60,000; capital, Oranjestad. Formerly part of the Netherlands Antilles, it separated in 1986 to become a self-governing territory of the Netherlands.

a·ru·gu·la /ə'rōōgələ/ (also **ru·co·la, ru·go·la**) ▸*n.* the rocket plant, used in cooking. ▷1970s: from Italian dialect, ultimately a diminutive of Latin *eruca*, 'downy-stemmed plant.'

ar·um /'arəm/ ▸*n.* a North American and European plant that has arrow-shaped leaves and a broad leafy spathe enclosing a club-shaped spadix, and that bears bright red berries in late summer. • *Arum, Arisaema*, and other genera, family Araceae (the **arum family**): several species, including jack-in-the-pulpit, cuckoopint, and skunk cabbage. The arum family also contains a number of popular houseplants, such as philodendrons and calla lilies. ▷late Middle English: from Latin, from Greek *aron*.

ar·um lil·y ▸*n.* chiefly British term for **calla lily** (see CALLA).

Aru·na·chal Pra·desh /ˌärə'nächəl prə'dāsh; prə'desh/ a mountainous state in far northeastern India that lies on the border of Tibet to the north and Myanmar (Burma) to the east; capital, Itanagar. It became a state of India in 1986.

Ar·va·da /är'vadə; -'vädə/ a city in north central Colorado, northwest of Denver; pop. 102,153.

-ary[1] ▸*suffix* **1** forming adjectives such as *budgetary, primary.* **2** forming nouns such as *dictionary, granary.* ▷from French *-aire* or Latin *-arius* 'connected with.'

-ary[2] ▸*suffix* forming adjectives such as *capillary, military.* ▷from French *-aire* or Latin *-aris* 'belonging to.'

Ar·ya·bha·ta I /ˌäryə'bətə/, (476–*c.*550), Indian astronomer and mathematician. His surviving work, *Aryabhatiya* (499), deals with mathematics, the measurement of time, planetary models, the sphere, and eclipses.

Ar·y·an /'e(ə)rēən; 'ar-; -yən/ ▸*n.* a member of a people speaking an Indo-European language who invaded northern India in the 2nd millennium BC, displacing the Dravidian and other aboriginal peoples. ■ dated term for PROTO-INDO-EUROPEAN or for INDO-IRANIAN. ■ (in Nazi ideology) a person of Caucasian race not of Jewish descent.

The idea that there was an "Aryan" race corresponding to the parent Indo-European language was proposed by certain 19th century writers and was taken up by Hitler and other proponents of racist ideology, but it has been generally rejected by scholars.

▸*adj.* of or relating to this people or their language. ▷from Sanskrit *ārya* 'noble' + **-AN**.

ar·yl /'arəl/ ▸*n.* [as *adj.*] *Chemistry* of or denoting a radical derived from an aromatic hydrocarbon by removal of a hydrogen atom: *aryl groups.* ▷early 20th cent.: from **AROMATIC + -YL**.

ar·y·te·noid /ə'ritnˌoid; ˌarə'tēˌnoid; ˌer-/ *Anatomy* ▸*adj.* [*attrib.*] of, relating to, or denoting a pair of cartilages at the back of the larynx.

▸*n.* either of these cartilages. ▷early 18th cent.: from modern Latin *arytaenoides*, from Greek *arutainoeidēs*, from *arutaina* 'funnel.'

AS ▸*abbr.* ■ American Samoa. ■ Anglo-Saxon. ■ Associate in Science.

As ▸*symbol* the chemical element arsenic.

as[1] /az/ ▸*adv.* (usu. **as —— as**) used in comparisons to refer to the extent or degree of something: *hailstones as big as tennis balls | go as fast as you can | it tasted like grape juice but not as sweet.* ■ used to emphasize an amount: ***as many as*** *twenty-two rare species may be at risk.*

▸*conj.* **1** used to indicate that something happens during the time when something is taking place: *Frank watched him as he ambled through the crowd | as she grew older, she kept more to herself.* **2** used to indicate by comparison the way that something happens or is done: *dress as you would if you were having guests | they can do as they wish |* [as *adv.*] *she kissed him goodbye,* ***as usual*** *| as in the past, a collection is to be taken.* ■ used to add or interject a comment relating to the statement of a fact: *as you can see, I didn't go after all | he has, as you know, called for a referendum.* **3** because; since: *I must stop now as I have to go out.* **4** even though: *sweet as he is, he doesn't pay his bills | try as he might, he failed to pull it off.*

▸*prep.* **1** used to refer to the function or character that someone or something has: *he got a job as a cook | they were treated as foreigners | it came as a shock | as a U.S. adviser, he is a target for terrorism.* **2** during the time of being (the thing specified): *he had often been sick as a child | as a student, my nickname was Space.* ▷Middle English: reduced form of Old English *alswā* 'similarly' (see ALSO).

▸*PHRASES* □ **as and when** at the time when (used to refer to an uncertain future event): *they deal with an issue as and when it rears its head.* □ **as for** with regard to: *as for you, you'd better be quick.* □ **as if** (or **as though**) as would be the case if: *she behaved as if he weren't there.* □ **as if!** *informal* I very much doubt it: *You know how lottery winners always say it won't change their lives? Yeah, as if!* □ **as (it) is** in the existing circumstances: *I've got enough on my plate as it is.* □ **as it were** in a way (used to be less precise): *areas that have been, as it were, pushed aside.* □ **as long as** see LONG[1]. □ **as much** see MUCH. □ **as of** used to indicate the time or date from which something starts: *as of January 1, a free market will be created | I'm on unemployment as of today.* □ **as per** see PER. □ **as such** see SUCH. □ **as though** see **as if** above. □ **as to** with respect to; concerning: *decisions as to which patients receive treatment.* □ **as well** see WELL[1]. □ **as yet** [usu. with *negative*] until now or a particular time in the past: *the damage is as yet undetermined.*

USAGE 1 A small, seemingly innocent word, **as** is so frequently misused (or not used where needed) that interested writers are advised to consult a full-length usage guide for counsel on its proper use. **As** is often used in causal senses in place of *because* or *since* (*As Julie wasn't hungry, she ordered only a cup of coffee*); in such constructions, where **as** may cause confusion, it is generally advisable to use the unambiguous *because*, or *since*.

2 On whether it is more correct to say *he's not as shy* **as I** rather than *he's not as shy* **as me** or *I live in the same street* **as she** rather than *I live in the same street* **as her**, see **usage** at PERSONAL PRONOUN.

3 For a discussion of when to use **as** rather than **like**, see **usage** at LIKE.

as[2] /as/ ▸*n.* (*pl.* **as·ses**) an ancient Roman copper coin. ▷early 17th cent.: Latin, literally 'a unit.'

as- ▸*prefix* variant spelling of **AD-** assimilated before *s* (as in *assemble, assess*).

ASA ▸*abbr.* American Standards Association (esp. in film-speed specification): *color film from 50 to 400 ASA.*

a·sa·fet·i·da /ˌasə'fetidə/ (*Brit.* **a·sa·foet·i·da**) ▸*n.* **1** a fetid resinous gum obtained from the roots of a herbaceous plant, used in herbal medicine and Indian cooking. **2** a Eurasian plant of the parsley family, from which this gum is obtained. • *Ferula*, family Apiaceae. ▷late Middle English: from medieval Latin *asafoetida*, from *asa* (from Persian *azā* 'mastic') + *foetida* (see FETID).

a·sa·na /'äsənə/ ▸*n.* a posture adopted in performing hatha yoga. ▷from Sanskrit *āsana*.

A·san·sol /ˌəsən'sōl/ an industrial city in northeastern India, in West Bengal, northwest of Calcutta; pop. 262,000 .

A·san·te /ə'sänˌtē/ variant spelling of **ASHANTI**[1].

ASAP (also **asap**) ▸*abbr.* as soon as possible.

as·bes·tos /as'bestəs; az-/ ▸*n.* a heat-resistant fibrous silicate mineral that can be woven into fabrics, and is used in fire-resistant and insulating materials such as brake linings: *asbestos was used for pipe insulation |* [as *adj.*] *asbestos shingles.* ■ fabric containing such a mineral.

The asbestos minerals include chrysotile (**white asbestos**) and several kinds of amphibole, notably amosite (**brown asbestos**) and crocidolite (**blue asbestos**). The danger to health caused by breathing in highly carcinogenic asbestos particles has led to stringent control of its use.

▷early 17th cent.: via Latin from Greek *asbestos* 'unquenchable' (applied by Dioscurides to quicklime), from *a-* 'not' + *sbestos* (from *sbennumi* 'quench').

as·bes·to·sis /ˌasbesˈtōsis; ˌaz-/ ▸*n.* a lung disease resulting from the inhalation of asbestos particles, marked by severe fibrosis and a high risk of mesothelioma (cancer of the pleura).

As·bury Park /ˈazˌberē; -b(ə)rē/ a city in east central New Jersey, on the Atlantic Ocean, long a noted resort; pop. 16,799.

ASCAP ▸*abbr.* American Society of Composers, Authors, and Publishers.

as·ca·ri·a·sis /ˌaskəˈrīəsis/ ▸*n.* *Medicine* infection of the intestine with ascarids.

as·ca·rid /ˈaskərid/ (also **as·ca·ris** /-ris/) ▸*n.* *Zoology* a parasitic nematode worm of a family (Ascaridae) whose members typically live in the intestines of vertebrates. ▷late 17th cent.: back-formation from Greek *askarides*, plural of *askaris* 'intestinal worm.'

as·cend /əˈsend/ ▸*v.* **1** [*trans.*] go up or climb: *she ascended the stairs* | [*intrans.*] *new magmas were created and ascended to the surface.* ■ climb to the summit of (a mountain or hill): *the first traveler to ascend the mountain.* ■ (of a fish or boat) move upstream along (a river). **2** [*intrans.*] rise through the air: *we had ascended 3,000 ft.* ■ (of a road or flight of steps) slope or lead up: *the road* ***ascends to*** *the lake.* ■ move up the social or professional scale: *he took exams to* ***ascend through*** *the ranks.* ■ (**ascend to**) rise to (an important position or a higher level): *some executives ascend to top-level positions.* ■ (of a spiritual being or soul) rise into heaven: *the Prophet* ***ascended to heaven*** | [as *adj.*] (**ascended**) *the risen and ascended Christ.* ■ (of a voice or sound) rise in pitch: *Carolyn's voice had ascended into high-pitched giggles.* ▷late Middle English: from Latin *ascendere*, from *ad-* 'to' + *scandere* 'to climb.'

▸*PHRASE* □ **ascend the throne** become king or queen.

as·cend·an·cy /əˈsendənsē/ (also **as·cend·en·cy**) ▸*n.* occupation of a position of dominant power or influence: *the ascendancy of good over evil* | *they have a moral ascendancy over the rich.*

as·cend·ant /əˈsendənt/ (also **as·cend·ent**) ▸*adj.* **1** rising in power or influence: *ascendant moderate factions in the party.* **2** *Astrology* (of a planet, zodiacal degree, or sign) just above the eastern horizon.

▸*n.* *Astrology* the point on the ecliptic at which it intersects the eastern horizon at a particular time, typically that of a person's birth. ■ the point on an astrological chart representing this. ▷late Middle English: via Old French from Latin *ascendent-* 'climbing up,' from the verb *ascendere* (see **ASCEND**).

▸*PHRASE* □ **in the ascendant** rising in power or influence: *the reformers are in the ascendant.*

as·cend·er /əˈsendər/ ▸*n.* a person or thing that ascends, in particular: ■ a part of a letter that extends above the main part (as in *b* and *h*). ■ a letter having such a part. ■ a device used in climbing that can be clipped to a rope to act as a foothold or handhold, or to keep something in position.

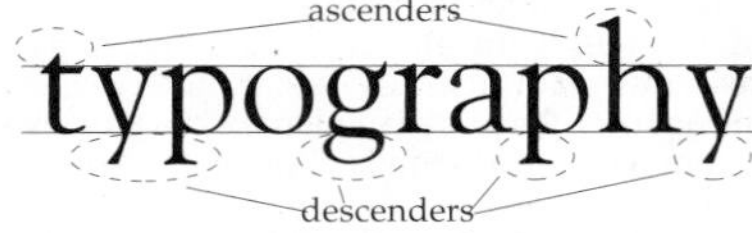

ascenders and descenders

as·cend·ing /əˈsendiNG/ ▸*adj.* [*attrib.*] **1** increasing in size or importance: *incomes ranked* ***in ascending order*** *of size.* **2** sloping or leading upward: *a gently ascending forest path* | *blood pressure in the ascending aorta.*

as·cend·ing co·lon ▸*n.* *Anatomy* the first main part of the large intestine, which passes upward from the cecum on the right side of the abdomen.

as·cen·sion /əˈsenSHən/ ▸*n.* [in *sing.*] the act of rising to an important position or a higher level: *his* ***ascension*** *to the ranks of pop star.* ■ (**Ascension**) the ascent of Christ into heaven on the fortieth day after the Resurrection. ▷Middle English (referring to the ascent of Christ): via Old French from Latin *ascensio(n-)*, from the verb *ascendere* (see **ASCEND**).

As·cen·sion Day the fortieth day after Easter, on which Christ's Ascension is celebrated in the Christian Church; also called Holy Thursday.

As·cen·sion Is·land /əˈsenSHən/ a small island in the South Atlantic Ocean, with St. Helena it is a dependency of the UK; pop. 1,007.

as·cent /əˈsent/ ▸*n.* **1** a climb or walk to the summit of a mountain or hill: *the first ascent of the Matterhorn* | *the routes of ascent can be retraced.* ■ an upward slope or path: *the ascent grew steeper.* **2** [in *sing.*] an instance of rising through the air: *the first balloon ascent was in 1783.* ■ [in *sing.*] a rise to an important position or a higher level: *his* ***ascent to*** *power.* ▷late 16th cent.: from **ASCEND**, on the pattern of the pair of *descend, descent.*

as·cer·tain /ˌasərˈtān/ ▸*v.* [*trans.*] find (something) out for certain; make sure of: *an attempt to ascertain the cause of the accident* | [with *clause*] *management should* ***ascertain whether*** *adequate funding can be provided.* ▷late Middle English (in the sense 'assure, convince'): from Old French *acertener*, based on Latin *certus* 'settled, sure.' —**as·cer·tain·a·ble** *adj.* —**as·cer·tain·ment** *n.*

as·cet·ic /əˈsetik/ ▸*adj.* characterized by or suggesting the practice of severe self-discipline and abstention from all forms of indulgence, typically for religious reasons: *an ascetic life of prayer, fasting, and manual labor* | *a narrow, humorless, ascetic face.* See note at **SEVERE**.

▸*n.* a person who practices such self-discipline and abstention. ▷mid 17th cent.: from medieval Latin *asceticus* or Greek *askētikos*, from *askētēs* 'monk,' from *askein* 'to exercise.' —**as·cet·i·cal·ly** /-ik(ə)lē/ *adv.* —**as·cet·i·cism** /-ˌsizəm/ *n.*

As·cham /ˈaskəm/, Roger (*c.*1515–68), English humanist scholar and writer. He was noted for his treatise on archery, *Toxophilus* (1545), and for *The Scholemaster* (1570), a practical and influential tract on education.

asc·hel·minth /ˈaskhelˌminTH/ ▸*n.* (*pl.* **asc·hel·minths** or **asc·hel·min·thes** /ˌaskhelˈminTHēz/) *Zoology* an invertebrate animal belonging to a group of phyla that are distinguished by the lack of a well-developed coelom and blood vessels. Most aschelminths are minute wormlike animals, including the nematode worms, rotifers, and water bears. • Phylum Nematoda and about seven minor phyla, formerly placed in a phylum Aschelminthes. ▷from modern Latin *Aschelminthes* (former phylum name), from Greek *askos* 'sac' + *helminth* 'worm' (from the former belief that animals of this group had a fluid-filled internal sac).

as·ci /ˈasī; -kī; -kē/ ▸ plural form of **ASCUS**.

as·cid·i·an /əˈsidēən/ ▸*n.* *Zoology* a sea squirt. • Phylum Chordata, Subphylum Urochordata, class Ascidiacea. ▷mid 19th cent.: from modern Latin plural *Ascidia* (genus name), from Greek *askidion*, diminutive of *askos* 'wineskin.'

ASCII /ˈaskē/ *Computing* ▸*abbr.* American Standard Code for Information Interchange, a set of digital codes representing letters, numerals, and other symbols, widely used as a standard format in the transfer of text between computers.

as·ci·tes /əˈsītēz/ ▸*n.* *Medicine* the accumulation of fluid in the peritoneal cavity, causing abdominal swelling. ▷late Middle English: via late Latin from Greek *askitēs*, from *askos* 'wineskin.' —**as·cit·ic** /əˈsitik/ *adj.*

As·cle·pi·us /əˈsklēpēəs/ *Greek Mythology* a hero and god of healing, son of Apollo.

as·co·my·cete /ˌaskəˈmīsēt; -mīˈsēt/ ▸*n.* *Botany* a fungus whose spores develop within asci. The ascomycetes include most molds, mildews, and yeasts, the fungal component of most lichens, and a few large forms such as morels and truffles. Compare with **BASIDIOMYCETE**. • Phylum Ascomycota (formerly subdivision Ascomycotina), class Ascomycetes. ▷mid 19th cent.: from modern Latin *Ascomycetes* (former class name), from Greek *askos* 'sac' + *muketēs* 'fungi.'

as·con /ˈaskän/ ▸*n.* *Zoology* a sponge of the simplest structure, with a tubelike or baglike form lined with choanocytes. Compare with **LEUCON** and **SYCON**. • Phylum Porifera. ▷late 19th cent.: modern Latin (genus name), from Greek *askos* 'bag.' —**as·co·noid** /-kəˌnoid/ *adj.*

a·scor·bic ac·id /əˈskôrbik/ ▸*n.* a vitamin found particularly in citrus fruits and green vegetables. It is essential in maintaining healthy connective tissue, and is also thought to act as an antioxidant. Severe deficiency causes scurvy. Also called **VITAMIN C**. • A lactone; chem. formula: $C_6H_8O_6$. ▷1930s: from **A-**[1] 'without' + medieval Latin *scorbutus* 'scurvy' + **-IC**. —**a·scor·bate** /-bāt; -bit/ *n.*

As·cot /ˈasˌkät; -kət/ a town in southern England, southwest of London. It is the site of an annual horse race.

ascot

as·cot /ˈasˌkät; -kət/ ▸*n.* (also **ascot tie**) a man's broad silk necktie. ▷early 20th cent.: from the place name **ASCOT**, by association with formal dress at race meetings held there.

as·cribe /əˈskrīb/ ▸*v.* [*trans.*] (**ascribe something to**) attribute something to (a cause): *he ascribed Jane's short temper to her upset stomach.* ■ (usu. **be ascribed to**) attribute (a text, quotation, or work of art) to a particular person or period: *a quotation ascribed to Thomas Cooper.* ■ (usu. **be ascribed to**) regard (a quality) as belonging to: *tough-mindedness is a quality commonly ascribed to top bosses.* ▷Middle English: from Latin *ascribere*, from *ad-* 'to' + *scribere* 'write.' —**a·scrib·a·ble** *adj.*

as·crip·tion /əˈskripSHən/ ▸*n.* the attribution of something to a cause: *an* ***ascription*** *of effect* ***to*** *cause.* ■ the attribution of a text, quotation, or work of art to a particular person or period: *her* ***ascription*** *of the text* ***to*** *Boccaccio* | *questions of authorial ascription.* ■ the action of regarding a quality as belonging to someone or something: *the author's* ***ascription*** *of human attributes* ***to*** *his hero or villain.* ■ a preacher's words ascribing praise to God at the end of a sermon. ▷late 16th cent.: from Latin *ascriptio(n-)*, from the verb *ascribere* (see **ASCRIBE**).

as·cus /ˈaskəs/ ▸*n.* (*pl.* **as·ci** /ˈasī; ˈaskī; -kē/) *Botany* a sac, typically cylindrical in shape, in which the spores of ascomycete fungi develop. ▷mid 19th cent.: modern Latin, from Greek *askos* 'bag.'

asdic /ˈazˌdik/ (also **ASDIC**) ▸*n.* *chiefly Brit.* an early form of sonar used to detect submarines. ▷World War II: acronym from *Allied Submarine Detection Investigation Committee.*

-ase ▸*suffix* *Biochemistry* forming names of enzymes: *amylase.* ▷from *(diast)ase.*

ASEAN /ˈäsēˌän; ˈas-/ ▸*abbr.* Association of Southeast Asian Nations.

a·seis·mic /āˈsīzmik/ ▸*adj.* *Geology* not characterized by earthquake activity.

a·sep·sis /āˈsepsis/ ▸*n.* the absence of bacteria, viruses, and other microorganisms. ■ the exclusion of bacteria and other microorganisms, typically during surgery. Compare with **ANTISEPSIS**.

a·sep·tic /āˈseptik/ ▸*adj.* free from contamination caused by harmful bacteria, viruses, or other microorganisms. ■ [*attrib.*] (of surgical practice) aiming at the complete exclusion of harmful microorganisms. ■ [*attrib.*] (of a wound, instrument, or dressing) surgically sterile or sterilized.

a·sex·u·al /āˈsekSHōōəl/ ▸*adj.* without sex or sexuality, in particular: ■ *Biology* (of reproduction) not involving the fusion of gametes. ■ *Biology* without sex or sexual organs: *asexual parasites.* ■ without sexual feelings or associations: *she rested her hand on the back of his head, in a maternal, wholly asexual, gesture.* —**a·sex·u·al·i·ty** /āsekSHōōˈalitē/ *n.* —**a·sex·u·al·ly** *adv.*

As·gard /ˈasˌgärd; ˈaz-/ *Scandinavian Mythology* a region in the center of the universe, inhabited by the gods.

ash[1] /aSH/ ▸*n.* the powdery residue left after the burning of a substance: *cigarette ash* | *a day's worth of paper* ***burned to ashes.*** ■ (**ashes**) the remains of something destroyed; ruins: *democracies taking root in the ashes of the Soviet empire.* ■ (**ashes**) the remains of the human body after cremation or burning: *his ashes were scattered on a Welsh mountainside.* ■ powdery material thrown out by a volcano: *the plains have been showered by volcanic ash.* ■ the mineral component of an organic substance, as assessed from the residue left after burning: *coal contains higher levels of ash than premium fuels.* ▷Old English *æsce, aexe*, of Germanic origin; related to Dutch *as* and German *Asche.*

▸*PHRASES* □ (**turn to**) **ashes in one's mouth** (become) something that is bitterly disappointing or worthless: *they found words such as "heroic" turn to ashes in their mouths during the scandal.* □ **rise** (or **emerge**) **from the ashes** be renewed after destruction: *Atlanta has risen from the ashes.* [compare with *rise like a phoenix from the ashes* (see **PHOENIX**).]

ash[2] ▸*n.* **1** (also **ash tree**) a tree with silver-gray bark and compound leaves. The ash is widely distributed throughout north temperate regions where it can form forests. • Genus *Fraxinus*, family Oleaceae: many species, including the North American **white**

ash (*F. americana*) and the **European ash** (*F. excelsior*). ■ the hard pale wood of this tree. ■ [with *adj.*] any of a number of unrelated trees with similar leaves. See also MOUNTAIN ASH. **2** an Old English runic letter (so named from the word of which it was the first letter). ■ the symbol æ or Æ, used in the Roman alphabet in place of the runic letter, and as a phonetic symbol. See also **Æ**. ▷Old English *æsc*, of Germanic origin; related to Dutch *es* and German *Esche*.

a·shamed /əˈsʜāmd/ ▸*adj.* [*predic.*] embarrassed or feeling guilt because of something one has done or a characteristic one has: *you should be ashamed of yourself* | [with *clause*] *she felt ashamed that she had hit him.* ■ (**ashamed to do something**) reluctant to do something through fear of embarrassment or humiliation: *I'm ashamed to say I followed him home* | *I am not ashamed to be seen with them.* ■ embarrassed or humiliated to be associated with a person: *his clothes and manners made me* ***ashamed of*** *him.* ▷Old English *āscamod*, past participle of *āscamian* 'feel shame,' from *ā-* (as an intensifier) + the verb SHAME. **—a·sham·ed·ly** /əˈsʜāmidlē/ *adv.*

A·shan·ti[1] /əˈsʜäntē; əˈsʜantē/ (also **A·san·te** /əˈsäntē; əˈsantē/) a region of central Ghana. Annexed by Britain in 1902, it became part of the former British colony of the Gold Coast.

A·shan·ti[2] (also **A·san·te**) ▸*n.* (*pl.* same) **1** a member of a people of south central Ghana. **2** the dialect of Akan spoken by this people.
▸*adj.* relating to or denoting this people or their language. ▷the name in Akan.

ash blond (also **ash blonde**) ▸*adj.* (of a person or their hair) very pale blond.
▸*n.* a very pale blond color. ■ a person with hair of such a color.

ash·can /ˈasʜˌkan/ ▸*n.* a metal receptacle for trash or ashes. ■ *military slang* a depth charge.

Ash·can School /ˈasʜˌkan/ a group of American realist painters active from *c.*1908 until World War I, who painted scenes from the slums of New York. The school grew out of the group called "the Eight."

Ash·croft[1] /ˈasʜˌkrôft/, John (1942–), U.S. attorney general 2001–05. Under him, the Justice Department was reorganized to focus on antiterrorism, a national concern that had heightened following the terrorist attacks of September 11, 2001.

Ash·croft[2], Dame Peggy (1907–91), English actress; born *Edith Margaret Emily Ashcroft*. She won an Academy Award for best supporting actress in the movie *A Passage to India* (1984).

Ashe /asʜ/, Arthur (Robert) (1943–93), U.S. tennis player. He won the U.S. Open championship in 1968 and Wimbledon in 1975, becoming the first black male player to achieve world rankings. He died of AIDS, having contracted HIV from a blood transfusion.

ash·en[1] /ˈasʜən/ ▸*adj.* of the pale gray color of ash: *the ashen morning sky.* See note at PALE. ■ (of a person's face) very pale with shock, fear, or illness. ■ of or resembling ashes: *the volcano's ashen breath.*

ash·en[2] ▸*adj. archaic* or *poetic/literary* made of timber from the ash tree.

Ash·er /ˈasʜər/ (in the Bible) a Hebrew patriarch, son of Jacob and Zilpah (Gen. 30:12, 13). ■ the tribe of Israel traditionally descended from him.

Ashe·ville /ˈasʜvəl; -ˌvil/ a city in western North Carolina, a resort in the Blue Ridge Mountains; pop. 68,889. The Biltmore estate is here.

Ash·ga·bat /ˈäsʜgəˌbät; ˈasʜgəˌbat/ (also **Ash·kha·bad** /ˈäsʜkəˌbäd; ˈasʜkəˌbad/) the capital of the central Asian republic of Turkmenistan; pop. 407,200. Former name (1919–27) POLTORATSK.

a·shine /əˈsʜīn/ ▸*adj.* [*predic.*] *poetic/literary* shining: *eyes ashine in the darkness.*

Ash·ke·naz·i /ˌasʜkəˈnazē; ˌäsʜkəˈnäzē/ ▸*n.* (*pl.* **-naz·im** /-ˈnazim; -ˈnäzim/) a Jew of central or eastern European descent. More than 80 percent of Jews today are Ashkenazim; they preserve Palestinian rather than Babylonian Jewish traditions, and some still use Yiddish. Compare with SEPHARDI. ▷from modern Hebrew, from *Ashkenaz*, son of Japheth, one of the sons of Noah (Gen. 10:3). **—Ash·ke·naz·ic** /-ˈnazik; -ˈnä-/ *adj.*

Ash·ke·na·zy /ˌasʜkəˈnäzē; ˌäsʜ-/, Vladimir (Davidovich) (1937–), Russian pianist. A child prodigy, he left the Soviet Union in 1963, finally settling in Iceland in 1973.

Ash·kha·bad /ˈäsʜkəˌbäd/ variant spelling of ASHGABAT.

Ash·land /ˈasʜlənd/ **1** a city in northeastern Kentucky, on the Ohio River; pop. 21,981. It is a center of the area's coal industry. **2** a city in north central Ohio; pop. 20,079.

ash·lar /ˈasʜlər/ ▸*n.* masonry made of large square-cut stones, typically used as a facing on walls of brick or stone. ■ a stone used in such masonry. ▷Middle English: from Old French *aisselier*, from Latin *axilla*, diminutive of *axis* 'plank.'

ash·lar·ing /ˈasʜləriNG/ ▸*n.* **1** ashlar masonry. **2** upright boarding fixed from the joists to the rafters of an attic to cut off the acute angle between the roof and the floor.

Ash·ley /ˈasʜlē/, Laura (1925–85), Welsh fashion and textile designer; known for her use of floral patterns and romantic Victorian and Edwardian styles.

Ash·mo·le·an Mu·se·um /asʜˈmōlēən/ a museum of art and antiquities in Oxford, England. It opened in 1683 and was the first public institution of its kind in England.

Ash·more and Car·ti·er Is·lands /ˈasʜˌmôr; ˈkärtēˌā; ˌkärtēˈā/ uninhabited islands in the Indian Ocean, an external territory of Australia.

A·sho·ka variant spelling of ASOKA.

a·shore /əˈsʜôr/ ▸*adv.* to or on the shore from the direction of the sea: *the seals come ashore to breed.* ■ on land as opposed to at sea: *we spent the day ashore.*

ash pan ▸*n.* a tray fitted beneath a grate in which ashes can be collected and removed.

ash·ram /ˈäsʜrəm/ ▸*n.* (in the Indian subcontinent) a hermitage, monastic community, or other place of religious retreat for Hindus. ■ a place of religious retreat or community life modeled on the Indian ashram. ▷from Sanskrit *āśrama* 'hermitage.'

Ash Sha·ri·qah /ˌäsʜ ˈsʜärēkə/ variant form of SHARJAH.

Ash·ta·bu·la /ˌasʜtəˈbyo͞olə/ a port city in northeastern Ohio, on Lake Erie; pop. 21,633.

ash·tang·a /asʜˈtäNGə/ (also **as·tang·a** /as-/) ▸*n.* a type of yoga based on eight principles and consisting of a series of poses executed in swift succession, combined with deep, controlled breathing. ▷from Hindi *aṣṭaṅ* or its source, Sanskrit *ashṭaṅga* 'having eight parts,' from *ashtán* 'eight.'

Ash·ton /ˈasʜtən/, Sir Frederick (William Mallandaine) (1904–88), British ballet dancer, choreographer, and director.

ash·tray /ˈasʜˌtrā/ ▸*n.* a receptacle for tobacco ash and cigarette butts.

A·shur·ba·ni·pal /ˌäsʜo͝orˈbäniˌpäl/, king of Assyria *c.*668–627 BC; grandson of Sennacherib. A patron of the arts, he established a library of more than 20,000 clay tablets at Nineveh.

Ash Wednes·day ▸*n.* the first day of Lent in the Western Christian Church, marked by services of penitence. ▷from the custom of marking the foreheads of penitents with ashes on that day.

ash·y /ˈasʜē/ ▸*adj.* **1** of a pale grayish color; ashen: *the ashy shadows of the mountains.* **2** covered with, consisting of, or resembling ashes: *an ashy sediment.*

ASI ▸*abbr.* airspeed indicator.

A·sia /ˈāzʜə/ the largest of the world's continents, constituting nearly one-third of the landmass, lying entirely north of the equator except for some Southeast Asian islands. It is connected to Africa by the Isthmus of Suez and borders Europe (part of the same landmass) along the Ural Mountains and across the Caspian Sea.

as·i·a·go /ˌäsēˈägō; äˈsyä-/ ▸*n.* a strong-flavored cow's milk cheese originally made in northern Italy. ▷named after *Asiago*, the plateau and town in northern Italy where the cheese was first made.

A·sia Mi·nor /ˈmīnər/ western peninsula of Asia that now constitutes most of modern Turkey.

A·sian /ˈāzʜən/ ▸*adj.* of or relating to Asia or its people, customs, or languages.
▸*n.* a native of Asia or a person of Asian descent. ▷late Middle English: from Latin *Asianus*, from Greek *Asianos*, from *Asia* (see ASIA).

USAGE See usage at ORIENTAL.

A·sian A·mer·i·can ▸*n.* an American who is of Asian (chiefly Far Eastern) descent.
▸*adj.* of or relating to such people.

A·sian co·bra ▸*n.* another term for SPECTACLED COBRA.

A·sian De·vel·op·ment Bank a bank with forty-seven member countries (thirty-two are from the Asia-Pacific region) located in Manila. Its aim is to promote the economic and social progress of its developing member countries.

A·sian el·e·phant ▸*n.* another term for INDIAN ELEPHANT.

A·sian long-horned bee·tle ▸*n.* a large black beetle with white spots whose larvae feed on hardwoods. Infestations in the U.S. have led to large-scale destruction of trees in order to eradicate the pest. • *Anoplophora glabripennis*, family Cerambycidae.

A·sian pear ▸*n.* the crisp apple-shaped fruit of a tree that is native to Japan and China and cultivated in Australia and New Zealand. Also called NASHI. • This fruit is obtained from varieties of *Pyrus pyrifolia*, family Rosaceae.

A·sian swamp eel ▸*n.* a freshwater eel that can breathe air and traverse land. Its introduction in the southeastern U.S. threatens some native aquatic fauna. • *Monopterus albus*, family Synbranchidae.

A·sia-Pa·cif·ic ▸*n.* (also **Asia-Pacific region**) a business region consisting of the whole of Asia as well as the countries of the Pacific Rim.

A·si·at·ic /ˌāzʜēˈatik; ˌāzē-/ ▸*adj.* relating to or deriving from Asia: *Asiatic cholera* | *Asiatic coastal regions.*
▸*n. often offensive* an Asian person. ▷via Latin *Asiaticus* from Greek *Asiatikos*, from *Asia* (see ASIA).

USAGE The standard and accepted term when referring to individual people is **Asian** rather than **Asiatic**, which can be offensive. However, **Asiatic** is standard in scientific and technical use, for example in biological and anthropological classifications.
See also **usage** at ORIENTAL.

ASIC /ˈāsik/ *Electronics* ▸*abbr.* application specific integrated circuit.

a·side /əˈsīd/ ▸*adv.* to one side; out of the way: *he pushed his plate aside* | *they stood aside to let a car pass* | *she must put aside all her antagonistic feelings.* ■ in reserve; for future use: *she set aside some money for rent.* ■ used to indicate that one is dismissing something from consideration, or that one is shifting from one topic or tone of discussion to another: ***joking aside****, I've certainly had my fill.*
▸*n.* **1** a remark or passage by a character in a play that is intended to be heard by the audience but unheard by the other characters in the play. ■ a remark not intended to be heard by everyone present: *"Does that make him a murderer?" whispered Alice in an aside to Fred.* **2** a remark that is not directly related to the main topic of discussion: *the recipe book has little asides about the importance of home and family.* ▷Middle English (originally *on side*): see A-[2], SIDE.
▸*PHRASES* □ **aside from** apart from. □ **set something aside 1** remove land from agricultural production for fallow or other use: *with 15% of land set aside, cereal production will fall* | [as *adj.*] *using his set-aside acreage to work clover into his rotation.* **2** annul a legal decision or process. **3** put in reserve: *he was setting aside a few dollars a week.* □ **take** (or **draw**) **someone aside** move someone away from a group of people in order to talk privately.

A-side ▸*n.* the side of a pop single or album regarded as the main release.

As·i·mov /ˈazəˌmôv; -ˌmôf/, Isaac (1920–92), U.S. writer and scientist; born in Russia; particularly known for his works of science fiction, his books on science for nonscientists, and his essays on a wide variety of subjects. Building on Karel Čapek's concept of the robot, in 1941, Asimov coined the term *robotics*. Notable science-fiction works: *I, Robot* (1950) and *Foundation* (trilogy, 1951–53).

as·i·nine /ˈasəˌnīn/ ▸*adj.* extremely stupid or foolish: *Lydia ignored his asinine remark.* See note at STUPID. ▷late 15th cent.: from Latin *asininus*, from *asinus* 'ass.' **—as·i·nin·i·ty** /ˌasəˈninitē/ *n.*

A·sir Moun·tains /äˈsi(ə)r/ a range of mountains in southwestern Saudi Arabia that run parallel to the Red Sea.

-asis (often **-iasis**) ▸*suffix* forming the names of diseases: *onchocerciasis* | *psoriasis.* ▷via Latin from Greek in nouns denoting a state or condition.

as·i·ty /ˈasitē/ ▸*n.* (*pl.* **-ties**) a stocky perching bird related to the pittas, found only in Madagascar. • Family Philepittidae: two genera, in particular *Philepitta* (two species). See also FALSE SUNBIRD. ▷probably a local name.

ask /ask/ ▸*v.* **1** [*reporting verb*] say something in order to obtain an answer or some information: [with *clause*] *he* ***asked if*** *she wanted coffee* | *he* ***asked whether*** *his electric wheelchair would fit through their doors* | [*trans.*] *people are always asking questions* | [with *direct speech*] *"How much further?" I asked* | [*intrans.*] *the old man* ***asked about*** *her job.* ■ [*intrans.*] (**ask around**) talk to various people in order to find something out: *there are fine meals to be had if you ask around.* ■ [*intrans.*] (**ask after**) inquire about the health or well-being of:

Mrs. Savage asked after Iris's mother. **2** [*trans.*] request (someone) to do or give something: *Mary* ***asked*** *her father* ***for*** *money* | [*trans.*] *I asked him to call the manager* | [*intrans.*] *don't be afraid to* ***ask for*** *advice.* ■ [with *clause*] request permission to do something: *she* ***asked if*** *she could move in* | [with *infinitive*] *he asked to see the officer involved.* ■ [*intrans.*] (**ask for**) request to speak to: *when I arrived, I asked for Catherine.* ■ request (a specified amount) as a price for selling something: *he was* ***asking*** *$250* ***for*** *the guitar.* ■ expect or demand (something) of someone: *it's asking a lot, but could you look through Billy's things?* **3** [*trans.*] invite (someone) to one's home or a function: *it's about time we* ***asked*** *Pam* ***to*** *dinner.* ■ (**ask someone along**) invite someone to join one on an outing: *do you want to ask him along?* ■ (**ask someone out**) invite someone out socially, typically on a date.

▸*n.* [in *sing.*] **1** a request, especially for a donation: *Somebody inside the university will want to make the ask, because it's prestigious, it will make him look good.* **2** the price at which an item, esp. a financial security, is offered for sale: [as *adj.*] *ask prices for bonds.* ▷Old English *āscian, āhsian, āxian.* —**ask·er** *n.*

▸*PHRASES* □ **be asking for it** (or **trouble**) *informal* behave in a way that is likely to result in difficulty for oneself: *they accused me of asking for it* | *you're asking for trouble.* □ **don't ask me!** *informal* used to indicate that one does not know the answer to a question and that one is surprised or irritated to be questioned: *"Is he her boyfriend then?" "Don't ask me!"* □ **for the asking** used to indicate that something can be easily obtained: *the job was his for the asking.* □ **I ask you!** *informal* an exclamation of shock or disapproval intended to elicit agreement from one's listener: *a soap opera based on Congress, I ask you.* □ **if you ask me** *informal* used to emphasize that a statement is one's personal opinion: *if you ask me, it's just an excuse for laziness.*

USAGE See usage at **REQUEST**.

a·skance /ə'skans/ (also **a·skant** /ə'skant/) ▸*adv.* with an attitude or look of suspicion or disapproval: *the reformers* ***looked askance at*** *the mystical tradition* | *a waiter* ***looked askance at*** *Charlie's jeans.* ▷late 15th cent.: of unknown origin.

as·ka·ri /'askərē/ ▸*n.* (*pl.* same or **-ris**) (in East Africa) a soldier or police officer. ▷late 19th cent.: from Arabic *'askarī* 'soldier.'

as·ke·sis /ə'skēsis/ (also **as·ce·sis** /ə'sēsis/) ▸*n.* the practice of severe self-discipline, typically for religious reasons. ▷late 19th cent.: from Greek *askēsis* 'training,' from *askein* 'to exercise.'

a·skew /ə'skyōō/ ▸*adv.* & *adj.* not in a straight or level position: [as *adv.*] *the door was hanging askew on one twisted hinge* | [as *predic. adj.*] *her hat was slightly askew.* ■ *figurative* wrong; awry: [as *adv.*] *the plan went sadly askew* | [as *adj.*] *outrageous humor with a decidedly askew point of view.* ▷mid 16th cent.: from **A-**[2] 'on' + **SKEW**.

ask·ing price ▸*n.* the price at which something is offered for sale.

ASL ▸*abbr.* American Sign Language.

a·slant /ə'slant/ ▸*adv.* at an angle or in a sloping direction: *some of the paintings hung aslant.*

▸*prep.* across at an angle or in a sloping direction: *rays of light fell aslant a door.*

a·sleep /ə'slēp/ ▸*adj.* & *adv.* in or into a state of sleep: [as *adj.*] *she had been asleep for over three hours* | [as *adv.*] *Bob regularly* ***fell asleep*** *in his recliner.* ■ not attentive or alert; inactive: [as *adj.*] *the competition was not asleep.* ■ (of a limb) having no feeling; numb: [as *adj.*] *his legs were asleep.* ■ *poetic/literary* used euphemistically to say that someone is dead.

▸*PHRASE* □ **asleep at the switch** (or **wheel**) *informal* not attentive or alert; inactive: *someone must have been asleep at the switch to allow this.*

a·slope /ə'slōp/ ▸*adv.* & *adj. archaic* or *poetic/literary* in a sloping position: [as *adj.*] *the steps are aslope and broken* | [as *adv.*] *against the mast he leans aslope.* ▷late Middle English: origin uncertain; this form appears earlier than **SLOPE**.

ASM ▸*abbr.* ■ air-to-surface missile. ■ assistant stage manager.

As·ma·ra /äz'märə/ (also **As·me·ra** /az'merə/) the capital of Eritrea; pop. 358,000.

a·so·cial /ā'sōSHəl/ ▸*adj.* avoiding social interaction; inconsiderate of or hostile to others: *the cat's independence has encouraged a view that it is asocial.*

A·so·ka /ə'sōkə/ (also **A·sho·ka** /ə'SHōkə/) (died *c.*232 BC), emperor of India *c.*269–232 BC. He converted to Buddhism and established it as the state religion.

A·so·ka pil·lar (also **A·sho·ka pil·lar**) the pillar of the Emperor Asoka with four lions on the capital, built at Sarnath in Uttar Pradesh to mark the spot where the Buddha publicly preached his doctrine, and adopted as a symbol by the government of India. ▷*Asoka* from Sanskrit *aśoka*.

asp /asp/ ▸*n.* (also **asp viper**) a small southern European viper with an upturned snout. • *Vipera aspis*, family Viperidae. ■ another term for **EGYPTIAN COBRA**. ▷Middle English: from Latin *aspis*, from Greek.

ASP ▸*abbr.* application service provider, a company providing Internet access to software applications that would otherwise have to be installed on individual computers.

as·par·a·gine /ə'sparə,jēn; -jin/ ▸*n.* *Biochemistry* a hydrophilic amino acid that is a constituent of most proteins. • An amide of aspartic acid; chem. formula: $CONH_2CH_2CH(NH_2)COOH$. ▷early 19th cent.: from **ASPARAGUS** (which contains it) + **-INE**[4].

as·par·a·gus /ə'sparəgəs/ ▸*n.* a tall plant of the lily family with fine feathery foliage, cultivated for its edible shoots. • *Asparagus officinalis*, family Liliaceae. ■ the tender young shoots of this plant, eaten as a vegetable and considered a delicacy. ▷mid 16th cent.: via Latin from Greek *asparagos*.

as·par·a·gus bee·tle ▸*n.* a small, boldly marked leaf beetle whose adults and larvae feed on the leaves of asparagus. • *Crioceris asparagi*, family Chrysomelidae.

as·par·a·gus fern ▸*n.* a decorative indoor or greenhouse plant with feathery foliage, related to the edible asparagus. • Genus *Asparagus*, family Liliaceae: several species, in particular *A. plumosus*.

as·par·tame /'aspär,tām/ ▸*n.* a very sweet substance used as an artificial sweetener, chiefly in low-calorie products. It is a derivative of aspartic acid and phenylalanine.

as·par·tic ac·id /ə'spärtik/ ▸*n.* *Biochemistry* an acidic amino acid that is a constituent of most proteins and also occurs in sugar cane. It is important in the metabolism of nitrogen in animals and also acts as a neurotransmitter. • Chem. formula: $COOHCH_2CH(NH_2)COOH$. ▷mid 19th cent.: *aspartic* from French *aspartique*, formed arbitrarily from Latin *asparagus* (see **ASPARAGUS**). —**as·par·tate** /-tāt/ *n.*

ASPCA ▸*abbr.* American Society for the Prevention of Cruelty to Animals.

as·pect /'aspekt/ ▸*n.* **1** a particular part or feature of something: *the financial aspect can be overstressed.* ■ a specific way in which something can be considered: *from every aspect, theirs was a changing world.* ■ [in *sing.* with *adj.*] a particular appearance or quality: *the air of desertion lent the place a sinister aspect | a man of decidedly foreign aspect.* **2** [usu. in *sing.*] the positioning of a building or thing in a specified direction: *a greenhouse with a southern aspect.* ■ the side of a building facing a particular direction: *the front aspect of the hotel was unremarkable.* ■ *Astrology* a particular position of a planet or other celestial body relative to another, as measured by angular distance: *the sun in Aries formed an adverse aspect with Uranus in Capricorn.* **3** *Grammar* a grammatical category or form that expresses the way in which time is denoted by the verb: *the semantics of tense and aspect | four verbal aspects.*

There are two aspects in English, the progressive or continuing aspect (expressing duration, typically using the auxiliary verb *be* with a form in *-ing*, as in *I was reading a book*) and the perfect or perfective (expressing completed action, typically using the auxiliary verb *have* with a past participle, as in *I have read the book*).

▸*v.* [*trans.*] (usu. **be aspected**) *Astrology* (of a planet) form an aspect with (another celestial body): *the sun is superbly aspected by your ruler Mars on the 19th.* ▷late Middle English (denoting the action or a way of looking at something): from Latin *aspectus*, from *aspicere* 'look at,' from *ad-* 'to, at' + *specere* 'to look.' —**as·pec·tu·al** /a'spekCHōōəl/ *adj.*

as·pect ra·tio ▸*n.* the ratio of two dimensions of something as considered from a specific direction, in particular: ■ the ratio of the width to the height of the image on a television screen. ■ *Aeronautics* the ratio of the span to the mean chord of an airfoil.

As·pen /'aspən/ a resort in south central Colorado; pop. 6,850. A thriving recreational center, it is noted particularly for its skiing facilities.

as·pen /'aspən/ ▸*n.* a poplar tree with rounded, long-stalked, and typically coarsely-toothed leaves that tremble in even a slight breeze. • Genus *Populus*, family Salicaceae: several species, in particular the North American **quaking aspen** (*P. tremuloides*) and **bigtooth aspen** (*P. grandidentata*) and the European *P. tremula*. ▷late Middle English: from dialect *asp* (in the same sense) + **-EN**[2], forming an adjective later used as a noun (late 16th cent.).

as·per·ges /ə'spərjəz/ ▸*n.* *Christian Church* the rite of sprinkling holy water at the beginning of the Mass, still used occasionally in Catholic churches. ■ another term for **ASPERGILLUM**. ▷late 16th cent.: the first word of the Latin text of Psalms 50(51):9 (literally 'thou shalt purge'), recited before Mass during the sprinkling of holy water.

as·per·gil·lo·sis /,asperjə'lōsis/ ▸*n.* a condition in which certain fungi infect the tissues. It most commonly affects the lungs, owing to inhalation of spores from moldy hay, and is then informally called **farmer's lung**. • The fungi that cause this condition are blackish molds of the genus *Aspergillus*, phylum Ascomycota. ▷late 19th cent.: from modern Latin *Aspergillus*, from **ASPERGILLUM**, + **-OSIS**.

as·per·gil·lum /,aspər'jiləm/ ▸*n.* (*pl.* **-gil·la** /-'jilə/ or **-gil·lums**) an implement for sprinkling holy water. ▷mid 17th cent.: from Latin.

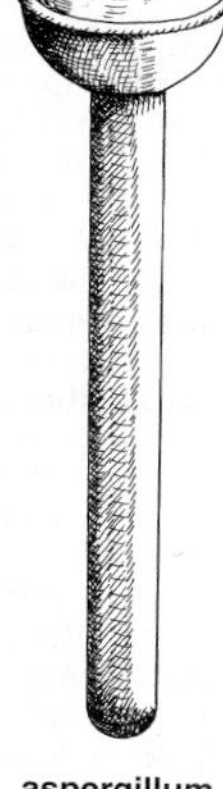
aspergillum

as·per·i·ty /ə'speritē/ ▸*n.* (*pl.* **-ties**) harshness of tone or manner: *he pointed this out with some asperity.* ■ (**asperities**) harsh qualities or conditions: *the asperities of a harsh and divided society.* ■ (usu. **asperities**) a rough edge on a surface: *the asperities of the metal surfaces.* ▷Middle English (in the sense 'hardship, rigor'): from Old French *asperite*, or Latin *asperitas*, from *asper* 'rough.'

a·sper·mi·a /ā'spərmēə/ ▸*n.* *Medicine* failure to produce semen, or absence of sperm in the semen.

as·perse /ə'spərs/ ▸*v.* [*trans.*] *rare* attack or criticize the reputation or integrity of: *he aspersed the place and its inhabitants.* ▷late 15th cent. (in the sense 'sprinkle or spatter with liquid'): from Latin *aspers-* 'sprinkled,' from the verb *aspergere*, from *ad-* 'to' + *spargere* 'sprinkle.'

as·per·sion /ə'spərZHən/ ▸*n.* (usu. **aspersions**) an attack on the reputation or integrity of someone or something: *I don't think anyone is **casting aspersions on** you.* ▷late Middle English (denoting the sprinkling of water, esp. at baptism): from Latin *aspersio(n-)*, from *aspergere* (see **ASPERSE**).

as·phalt /'asfôlt/ ▸*n.* a mixture of dark bituminous pitch with sand or gravel, used for surfacing roads, flooring, roofing, etc. ■ the pitch used in this mixture, sometimes found in natural deposits but usually made by the distillation of crude oil.
▸*v.* [*trans.*] cover with asphalt. ▷late Middle English: from French *asphalte*, based on late Latin *asphalton*, *asphaltum*, from Greek *asphalton*. —**as·phal·tic** /as'fôltik/ *adj.*

as·phalt jun·gle ▸*n.* the modern city, esp. when considered as a place of poverty and crime.

a·spher·i·cal /ā'sferikəl/ ▸*adj.* (esp. of the surface of an optical lens) not spherical. —**a·spher·ic** *adj.*

as·pho·del /'asfə,del/ ▸*n.* **1** a Eurasian plant of the lily family, typically having long slender leaves and flowers borne on a spike. • Genera *Asphodelus* and *Asphodeline*, family Liliaceae. See also **BOG ASPHODEL**. **2** *poetic/literary* an immortal flower said to grow in the Elysian fields. ▷late Middle English: via Latin from Greek *asphodelos*; compare with **DAFFODIL**.

as·phyx·i·a /as'fiksēə/ ▸*n.* a condition arising when the body is deprived of oxygen, causing unconsciousness or death; suffocation. ▷early 18th cent. (in the sense 'stopping of the pulse'): modern Latin, from Greek *asphuxia*, from *a-* 'without' + *sphuxis* 'pulse.' —**as·phyx·i·al** *adj.* —**as·phyx·i·ant** /-sēənt/ *adj.* & *n.*

as·phyx·i·ate /as'fiksē,āt/ ▸*v.* [*trans.*] (usu. **be asphyxiated**) kill (someone) by depriving them of air: *they were asphyxiated by the carbon monoxide fumes* | [as *adj.*] (**asphyxiating**) *figurative avoiding asphyxiating government control.* ■ [*intrans.*] die in this way: *they slowly asphyxiated.* —**as·phyx·i·a·tion** /as,fiksē'āSHən/ *n.*

as·pic /'aspik/ ▸*n.* a savory jelly, often made with meat stock, used as a garnish, or to contain pieces of food such as meat, seafood, or eggs, set in a mold. ▷late 18th cent.: from French, literally 'asp,' from the colors of the jelly as compared with those of the snake.

as·pi·dis·tra /,aspi'distrə/ ▸*n.* a bulbous plant with broad tapering leaves, native to eastern Asia and often grown as a houseplant. • Genus *Aspidistra*, family Liliaceae. ▷early 19th cent.: modern Latin, from Greek *aspis*, *aspid-* 'shield' (because of the shape of the stigma), on the pattern of *Tupistra*, a related genus.

as·pir·ant /'aspərənt; ə'spī-/ ▸*adj.* [*attrib.*] (of a person) having ambitions to achieve something, typically to follow a particular career: *an aspirant politician.*
▸*n.* a person who has ambitions to achieve something: *an **aspirant to** the throne.* ▷mid 18th cent. (as a noun): from Latin *aspirant-* 'aspiring,' from the verb *aspirare* (see **ASPIRE**).

as·pi·rate ▸*v.* /'aspə,rāt/ [*trans.*] **1** *Phonetics* pronounce (a sound) with an exhalation of breath: [as *adj.*] (**aspirated**) *the aspirated allophone of p occurs in "pie."* ■ [*intrans.*] pronounce the sound *h* at the beginning of a word. **2** (usu. **be aspirated**) *Medicine* draw (fluid) by suction from a vessel or cavity. ■ draw fluid in such a way from (a vessel or cavity). ■ breathe (something) in; inhale: *some drowning victims don't aspirate any water.* **3** [usu. as *adj.*] (**aspirated**) provide (an internal combustion engine) with air: *the superchargers produce twice the power of standard aspirated engines.* See also **NORMALLY ASPIRATED**.
▸*n.* /'asp(ə)rit/ **1** *Phonetics* an aspirated consonant. ■ the sound *h* or a character used to represent this sound. **2** *Medicine* matter that has been drawn from the body by aspiration: *gastric aspirate | esophageal aspirates.*
▸*adj.* /'asp(ə)rit/ *rare Phonetics* (of a sound) pronounced with an exhalation of breath; aspirated. ▷mid 16th cent. (as an adjective): from Latin *aspiratus* 'breathed,' past participle of *aspirare* (see **ASPIRE**).

as·pi·ra·tion /,aspə'rāSHən/ ▸*n.* **1** (usu. **aspirations**) a hope or ambition of achieving something: *he had nothing tangible to back up his literary aspirations | the yawning gulf between aspiration and reality.* ■ the object of such an ambition; a goal: *fabrics and oriental rugs were my aspirations.* **2** the action of pronouncing a sound with an exhalation of breath. **3** *Medicine* the action of drawing fluid by suction from a vessel or cavity. ▷late Middle English (sense 2): from Latin *aspiratio(n-)*, from the verb *aspirare* (see **ASPIRE**). —**as·pi·ra·tion·al** /-SHənl/ *adj.* (in sense 1).

as·pi·ra·tor /'aspə,rātər/ ▸*n.* *Medicine* an instrument or apparatus for aspirating fluid from a vessel or cavity.

as·pire /ə'spī(ə)r/ ▸*v.* [*intrans.*] direct one's hopes or ambitions toward achieving something: *we never thought that we might **aspire to** those heights* | [with *infinitive*] *other people will aspire to be like you* | [as *adj.*] (**aspiring**) *an aspiring artist.* ■ *poetic/literary* rise high; tower: *above the domes of loftiest mosques, these pinnacles of death aspire.* ▷late Middle English: from French *aspirer* or Latin *aspirare*, from *ad-* 'to' + *spirare* 'breathe.'

as·pi·rin /'asp(ə)rin/ ▸*n.* a synthetic compound used medicinally to relieve mild or chronic pain and to reduce fever and inflammation. • Alternative name: acetylsalicylic acid; chem. formula: $C_6H_4(OCOCH_3)COOH$. ■ (*pl.* same or **-rins**) a tablet containing this. ▷late 19th cent.: from German, from *acetylierte Spirsäure* 'acetylated salicylic acid' (the element *Spir-* being from the plant genus name *Spiraea*).

as·por·ta·tion /,aspər'tāSHən/ ▸*n.* *Law, rare* the detachment, movement, or carrying away of property, considered an essential component of the crime of larceny. ▷late 15th cent.: from Latin *asportation-*, from *asportare* 'carry away.'

a·sprawl /ə'sprôl/ ▸*adv.* & *adj.* sprawling: [as *adv.*] *he slipped on the greasy tiles and fell asprawl* | [as *predic. adj.*] *she lay, legs and arms asprawl.*

a·squint /ə'skwint/ ▸*adv.* & *adj.* with a glance to one side or from the corner of the eyes: [as *adv.*] *a woman **looked asquint at** me.* ▷Middle English: perhaps from **A-**[2] 'on' + a Low German or Dutch word related to modern Dutch *schuinte* 'slant.'

As·quith /'askwəTH/, Herbert Henry, 1st Earl of

Pronunciation Key ə *ago*; ər *over*; 'ə or ,ə *up*; 'ər or ,ər *fur*; a *hat*; ā *rate*; ä *car*; CH *chew*; e *let*; ē *see*; e(ə)r *air*; i *fit*; ī *by*; i(ə)r *ear*; NG *sing*; ō *go*; ô *for*; oi *boy*; ŏŏ *good*; ōō *goo*; ou *out*; SH *she*; TH *thin*; TH *then*; (h)w *why*; ZH *vision*

Oxford and Asquith (1852–1928), British statesman; prime minister 1908–16.

ass[1] /as/ ▸*n.* **1** a hoofed mammal of the horse family with a braying call, typically smaller than a horse and with longer ears. • Genus *Equus*, family Equidae: *E. africanus* of Africa, which is the ancestor of the domestic ass or donkey, and *E. hemionus* of Asia. ■ (in general use) a donkey. **2** *informal* a foolish or stupid person: *that ass of a young man.* ▷Old English *assa*, from a Celtic word related to Welsh *asyn*, Breton *azen*, based on Latin *asinus*.

▸*PHRASE* □ **make an ass of oneself** *informal* behave in a way that makes one look foolish or stupid: *he is stewed and about to make an ass of himself.*

ass[2] (*Brit.* **arse**) ▸*n. vulgar slang* a person's buttocks or anus. ■ a stupid, irritating, or contemptible person. ■ women regarded as a source of sexual gratification. ■ oneself (used in phrases for emphasis): *get your ass in here fast | the bureaucrat who wants everything in writing so as to cover his ass.* **—assed** /ast/ *adj.* [in *combination*] *fat-assed guys.*

▸*PHRASES* □ **bust one's ass** try very hard to do something. □ **bust someone's ass** use physical force to injure someone in a fight. □ **chew** (**someone's**) **ass** reprimand severely. □ **get your ass in** (or **into**) **gear** [in *imperative*] hurry: *if you get your ass in gear, you can make it out of here tonight.* □ **get off one's ass** stop being lazy. □ **haul** (or **drag** or **tear**) **ass** hurry or move fast: *I just turn around and haul ass right out of there.* □ **kick** (**some**) **ass** (or **kick someone's ass**) see KICK[1]. □ **kiss ass** see KISS. □ **my ass** used to convey that one does not believe something that has just been said: *sold out, my ass!* □ **not give a rat's ass** not care at all about something. □ **not know one's ass from a hole in the ground** (or **from one's elbow**) be totally ignorant or incompetent. □ **a pain in the ass** see PAIN. □ **a piece of ass** see PIECE. □ **put** (or **have**) **someone's ass in a sling** get someone in trouble: *you managed to put his ass in a sling along with your own.* □ **up your ass** used to express contempt for someone or something. □ **you bet your ass** you can be very sure: [*with clause*] *you can bet your ass I'll go for it every time.*

-ass ▸*comb. form* used in slang terms as an intensifier, often with depreciatory reference: *smart-ass | lame-ass.* ▷see ASS[2].

As·sad /ä'säd; 'ä,säd/, Hafiz al- (1928–2000), Syrian statesman; president 1971–2000. While in office, he ensured the strengthening of Syria's oil-based economy and suppressed political opposition such as the uprising of Muslim extremists (1979–82). He supported the coalition forces during the 1991 Gulf War. His son Bashar Assad (1965–) succeeded him in 2000.

as·sa·gai ▸*n.* & *v.* variant spelling of ASSEGAI.

as·sa·i /ä'sī/ ▸*adv. Music* (esp. as a direction after a tempo marking) very: *allegro assai.* ▷Italian, 'very much.'

as·sail /ə'sāl/ ▸*v.* [*trans.*] make a concerted or violent attack on: *the Scots army assailed Edward's army from the rear.* See note at ATTACK. ■ (usu. **be assailed**) (of an unpleasant feeling or physical sensation) come upon (someone) suddenly and strongly: *she was assailed by doubts and regrets.* ■ criticize (someone) strongly. ▷Middle English: from Old French *asaill-*, stressed stem of *asalir*, from medieval Latin *assalire*, from Latin *assilire*, from *ad-* 'to' + *salire* 'to leap'; compare with ASSAULT. **—as·sail·a·ble** *adj.*

as·sail·ant /ə'sālənt/ ▸*n.* a person who physically attacks another.

As·sam /ä'säm; ə'sam; 'as,am/ a state in northeastern India, much of which lies in the valley of the Brahmaputra River, noted for its production of tea; capital, Dispur.

As·sa·mese /,äsə'mēz/ ▸*n.* (*pl.* same) **1** a native or inhabitant of Assam. **2** the Indic language, related to Bengali, that is the offical language of Assam.

▸*adj.* of or relating to Assam, its people, or its language.

as·sas·sin /ə'sasin/ ▸*n.* a murderer of an important person in a surprise attack for political or religious reasons. ■ (**Assassin**) *historical* a member of the Nizari branch of Ismaili Muslims at the time of the Crusades, when the newly established sect ruled part of northern Persia (1094–1256). They were renowned as militant fanatics, and were popularly reputed to use hashish before going on murder missions. ▷mid 16th cent.: from French, or from medieval Latin *assassinus*, from Arabic *ḥašīšī* 'hashish eater.'

as·sas·si·nate /ə'sasə,nāt/ ▸*v.* (often **be assassinated**) murder (an important person) in a surprise attack for political or religious reasons. See note at KILL. ▷early 17th cent.: from medieval Latin *assassinat-* 'killed,' from the verb *assassinare*, from *assassinus* (see ASSASSIN). **—as·sas·si·na·tion** /ə,sasə'nāsHən/ *n.*

as·sas·sin bug ▸*n.* a long-legged predatory or bloodsucking bug that occurs chiefly in the tropics and feeds mainly on other arthropods. Some of those that bite humans can transmit microorganisms such as the one causing Chagas' disease. • Family Reduviidae, suborder Heteroptera: numerous species.

As·sa·teague Is·land /'asə,tēg/ a barrier island in southeastern Maryland and northeastern Virginia, on the Atlantic Ocean, noted for its wild ponies.

as·sault /ə'sôlt/ ▸*v.* [*trans.*] make a physical attack on: *he pleaded guilty to assaulting a police officer | she was sexually assaulted as a child.* See note at ATTACK. ■ *figurative* attack or bombard (someone or the senses) with something undesirable or unpleasant: *her right ear was assaulted with a tide of music.* ■ carry out a military attack or raid on (an enemy position): *they left their strong position to assault the hill.* ■ rape.

▸*n.* **1** a physical attack: *his imprisonment for an* ***assault on*** *the film director | sexual assaults.* ■ *Law* an act, criminal or tortious, that threatens physical harm to a person, whether or not actual harm is done: *he appeared in court charged with assault.* ■ a military attack or raid on an enemy position: *troops began an* ***assault on*** *the city* | [as *adj.*] *an assault boat.* ■ a strong verbal attack: *the* ***assault on*** *the party's tax policies.* **2** a concerted attempt to do something demanding: *a winter* ***assault on*** *Mt. Everest.* ▷Middle English: from Old French *asaut* (noun), *assauter* (verb), based on Latin *ad-* 'to' + *saltare*, frequentative of *salire* 'to leap.' Compare with ASSAIL. **—as·sault·er** *n.*

as·sault and bat·ter·y ▸*n. Law* the crime of threatening a person together with the act of making physical contact with them.

as·saul·tive /ə'sôltiv/ ▸*adj.* tending or likely to commit an assault: *they found that assaultive men had abusive parents.* ■ extremely aggressive or forcefully assertive: *his loud, assaultive playing style can leave you cowering.*

as·sault ri·fle ▸*n.* a rapid-fire, magazine-fed automatic rifle designed for infantry use.

as·say /'a,sā; a'sā/ ▸*n.* the testing of a metal or ore to determine its ingredients and quality: *submission of plate for assay.* ■ a procedure for measuring the biochemical or immunological activity of a sample: *each assay was performed in duplicate | the results of sequential assay of serum were analyzed immunofluorescence assay.*

▸*v.* [*trans.*] **1** determine the content or quality of (a metal or ore). ■ determine the biochemical or immunological activity of (a sample): *cell contents were* ***assayed for*** *enzyme activity.* ■ examine (something) in order to assess its nature: *stepping inside, I quickly assayed the clientele.* **2** *archaic* attempt: *I assayed a little joke of mine on him.* ▷Middle English (in the general sense 'testing, or a test of, the merit of someone or something'): from Old French *assai* (noun), *assaier* (verb), variant of *essai* 'trial,' *essayer* 'to try' (see ESSAY). **—as·say·er** *n.*

ass-back·wards *informal* ▸*adv.* & *adj.* (used disparagingly) backwards or in a contrary way.

ass ban·dit ▸*n. vulgar slang* (also **ass burglar**) **1** a male homosexual sodomite or pederast. **2** an eager seducer of young women.

as·se·gai /'asə,gī/ (also **as·sa·gai**) ▸*n.* (*pl.* **-gais**) **1** a slender, iron-tipped, hardwood spear used chiefly by southern African peoples. **2** (also **assegai wood**) a South African tree of the dogwood family that yields hard timber. • *Curtisia dentata*, family Cornaceae.

▸*v.* (**-gaied**, **-gai·ing**) [*trans.*] (often **be assegaied**) wound or kill with an assegai. ▷early 17th cent.: from obsolete French *azagaie* or Portuguese *azagaia*, from Arabic *az-zaġ ēğāyah*, from *az*, *al* 'the' + Berber *zaġ ēğāyah* 'spear.'

as·sem·blage /ə'semblij/ ▸*n.* a collection or gathering of things or people: *a wondrous assemblage of noble knights, cruel temptresses, and impossible loves.* ■ a machine or object made of pieces fitted together: *some vast assemblage of gears and cogs.* ■ a work of art made by grouping found or unrelated objects. ■ the action of gathering or fitting things together.

as·sem·ble /ə'sembəl/ ▸*v.* **1** [*intrans.*] (of people) gather together in one place for a common purpose: *a crowd had assembled outside the gates.* See note at GATHER. ■ [*trans.*] bring (people or things) together for a common purpose: *he assembled the surviving members of the group for a tour.* ■ [usu. as *n.*] (**assembling**) *Entomology* (of male moths) gather for mating in response to a pheromone released by a female. **2** [*trans.*] fit together the separate component parts of (a machine or other object): *a factory that assembled parts for trucks.* ■ *Computing* translate (a program) from assembly language into machine code. ▷Middle English: from Old French *asembler*, based on Latin *ad-* 'to' + *simul* 'together.'

as·sem·bler /ə'semblər/ ▸*n.* **1** a person who assembles a machine or its parts. **2** *Computing* a program for converting instructions written in low-level symbolic code into machine code. ■ another term for ASSEMBLY LANGUAGE.

as·sem·bly /ə'semblē/ ▸*n.* (*pl.* **-blies**) **1** a group of people gathered together in one place for a common purpose: *an assembly of scholars and poets.* ■ a group of people elected to make laws or decisions for a particular country or region, esp. the lower legislative house in some U.S. states: *the Connecticut General Assembly.* **2** the action of gathering together as a group for a common purpose: *a decree guaranteeing freedom of assembly.* ■ a regular gathering of the teachers and students of a school: *catcalling occurred during the assembly.* ■ (usu. **the assembly**) *chiefly historical* a signal for troops to assemble, given by drum or bugle. **3** [often as *adj.*] the action of fitting together the component parts of a machine or other object: *a car assembly plant.* ■ a unit consisting of components that have been fitted together: *the tail assembly of the aircraft.* ■ [usu. as *adj.*] *Computing* the conversion of instructions in low-level code to machine code by an assembler. ▷Middle English: from Old French *asemblé*, feminine past participle of *asembler* (see ASSEMBLE).

as·sem·bly lan·guage ▸*n. Computing* a low-level symbolic code converted by an assembler.

as·sem·bly line ▸*n.* a series of workers and machines in a factory by which a succession of identical items is progressively assembled: *their latest economy car rolled off the assembly line last August figurative new teenage idols were pouring off the assembly line.* Compare with PRODUCTION LINE.

as·sem·bly·man /ə'semblēmən/ ▸*n.* a person who is a member of a legislative assembly.

as·sem·bly·wo·man /ə'semblē,wŏŏmən/ ▸*n.* a woman who is a member of a legislative assembly.

as·sent /ə'sent/ ▸*n.* the expression of approval or agreement: *a loud murmur of assent | he* ***nodded assent.*** ■ official agreement or sanction: *the governor has power to withhold his assent from a bill.*

▸*v.* [*intrans.*] express approval or agreement, typically officially: *Roosevelt assented to the agreement* | [with *direct speech*] *"Guest house, then," Frank assented cheerfully.* ▷Middle English: from Old French *as(s)enter* (verb), *as(s)ente* (noun), based on Latin *assentiri*, from *ad-* 'toward' + *sentire* 'feel, think.' **—as·sent·er** *n.*

as·sert /ə'sərt/ ▸*v.* [*reporting verb*] state a fact or belief confidently and forcefully: [with *clause*] *the company asserts that the cuts will not affect development* | [*trans.*] *he asserted his innocence* | [with *direct speech*] *"I don't know why she came," he asserted.* ■ [*trans.*] cause others to recognize (one's authority or a right) by confident and forceful behavior: *the good librarian is able to assert authority when required.* ■ (**assert oneself**) behave or speak in a confident and forceful manner: *it was time to assert himself.* ▷early 17th cent.: from Latin *asserere* 'claim, affirm,' from *ad-* 'to' + *serere* 'to join.' **—as·sert·er** *n.*

as·ser·tion /ə'sərsHən/ ▸*n.* a confident and forceful statement of fact or belief: [with *clause*] *his* ***assertion that*** *his father had deserted the family.* ■ the action of stating something or exercising authority confidently and forcefully: *the assertion of his legal rights.*

as·ser·tive /ə'sərtiv/ ▸*adj.* having or showing a confident and forceful personality: *patients should be more assertive with their doctors.* **—as·ser·tive·ly** *adv.* **—as·ser·tive·ness** *n.*

as·ses /'asiz/ ▸ plural form of AS[2], ASS[1], ASS[2].

as·sess /ə'ses/ ▸*v.* [*trans.*] evaluate or estimate the nature, ability, or quality of: *the committee must assess the relative importance of the issues* | [with *clause*] *it is difficult to assess whether this is a new trend.* ■ (usu. **be assessed**) calculate or estimate the price or value of: *the damage was assessed at $5 billion.* ■ (often **be assessed**) set the value of a tax, fine, etc., for (a person or property) at a specified level: *all empty properties will be* ***assessed at*** *50 percent.* ▷late Middle English: from Old French *assesser*, based on Latin *assidere* 'sit by' (in medieval Latin 'levy tax'), from *ad-* 'to, at' + *sedere* 'sit.' Compare with ASSIZE. **—as·sess·a·ble** *adj.*

A

as·sess·ment /ə'sesmənt/ ▸*n.* the evaluation or estimation of the nature, quality, or ability of someone or something: *the assessment of educational needs | he made a rapid assessment of the situation assessments of market value.*

as·ses·sor /ə'sesər/ ▸*n.* a person who assesses someone or something, in particular: ■ a person who calculates or estimates the value of something or an amount to be paid, chiefly for tax or insurance purposes. ■ a person who is knowledgeable in a particular field and is called upon for advice, typically by a judge or committee of inquiry. ▷late Middle English: from Old French *assessour,* from Latin *assessor* 'assistant judge' (in medieval Latin 'assessor of taxes'), from Latin *assidere* (see ASSESS).

as·set /'aset/ ▸*n.* a useful or valuable thing, person, or quality: *quick reflexes were his chief asset | the school is an* ***asset to*** *the community.* ■ (usu. **assets**) property owned by a person or company, regarded as having value and available to meet debts, commitments, or legacies: *growth in net assets | [as adj.] debiting the asset account.* ■ (**assets**) military equipment, such as planes, ships, communications and radar installations, employed or targeted in military operations. ▷mid 16th cent. (in the plural in the sense 'sufficient estate to allow discharge of a will'): from an Anglo-Norman French legal term, from Old French *asez* 'enough,' based on Latin *ad* 'to' + *satis* 'enough.'

as·set-backed ▸*adj.* [*attrib.*] denoting securities having as collateral the return on a series of mortgages, credit agreements, or other forms of lending.

as·set-strip·ping ▸*n.* the practice of taking over a company in financial difficulties and selling each of its assets separately at a profit without regard for the company's future. —**as·set-strip·per** *n.*

as·sev·er·a·tion /ə,sevə'rāsʜən/ ▸*n.* the solemn or emphatic declaration or statement of something: *I fear that you offer only unsupported asseveration | the dogmatic outlook marks many of his asseverations.* ▷mid 16th cent.: from Latin *asseveratio(n-),* from the verb *asseverare,* from *ad-* 'to' + *severus* 'serious.' —**as·sev·er·ate** /ə'sevə,rāt/ *v.*

ass·hole /'as,hōl/ ▸*n. vulgar slang* the anus. ■ an irritating or contemptible person.

as·sib·i·late /ə'sibə,lāt/ ▸*v.* [*trans.*] *Phonetics* pronounce (a sound) as a sibilant or affricate ending in a sibilant (e.g., sound *t* as *ts*). ▷mid 19th cent.: from Latin *assibilat-* 'hissed at,' from the verb *assibilare,* from *ad-* 'to' + *sibilare* 'to hiss.' —**as·sib·i·la·tion** /ə,sibə'lāsʜən/ *n.*

as·si·du·i·ty /,asi'd(y)o͞oitē/ ▸*n.* (*pl.* **-ties**) constant or close attention to what one is doing: *the assiduity with which he could wear down his opponents.* ■ (**assiduities**) *archaic* or *poetic/literary* constant attentions to someone. ▷late Middle English: from Latin *assiduitas,* from *assiduus* 'occupied with' (see ASSIDUOUS).

as·sid·u·ous /ə'sijəwəs/ ▸*adj.* showing great care and perseverance: *she was* ***assiduous in*** *pointing out every feature.* See note at BUSY. ▷mid 16th cent.: from Latin *assiduus,* from *assidere* 'be engaged in doing' (see ASSESS), + -OUS. —**as·sid·u·ous·ly** *adv.* —**as·sid·u·ous·ness** *n.*

as·sign /ə'sīn/ ▸*v.* [*trans.*] **1** allocate (a job or duty): *Congress* ***assigned*** *the task* ***to*** *the agency | [trans., with two objs.] his leader assigned him this mission.* ■ (often **be assigned**) appoint (someone) to a particular job, task, or organization: *she has been* ***assigned to*** *a new job | [trans.] he was assigned to prosecute the case.* **2** designate or set (something) aside for a specific purpose: *managers happily* ***assign*** *large sums of money* ***to*** *travel budgets.* ■ (**assign something to**) attribute something as belonging to: *it is difficult to decide whether to assign the victory to Goodwin.* **3** transfer (legal rights or liabilities): *they will ask you to assign your rights against the airline.*

▸*n. Law* another term for ASSIGNEE (sense 1). ▷Middle English: from Old French *asigner, assiner,* from Latin *assignare,* from *ad-* 'to' + *signare* 'to sign.' —**as·sign·a·ble** *adj.* (in sense 3 of the *verb*). —**as·sign·er** *n.* —**as·sign·or** /ə'sīnər/ *n.* (in sense 3 of the *verb*).

as·sig·na·tion /,asig'nāsʜən/ ▸*n.* **1** an appointment to meet someone in secret, typically one made by lovers: *his* ***assignation with*** *an older woman.* **2** the allocation or attribution of someone or something as belonging to something. ▷late Middle English (in the senses 'command, appointment to office, or allotment of revenue'): via Old French from Latin *assignatio(n-),* from the verb *assignare* (see ASSIGN).

as·sign·ee /ə,sī'nē/ ▸*n.* *chiefly Law* **1** a person to whom a right or liability is legally transferred. **2** a person appointed to act for another. ▷Middle English: from Old French *assigne,* past participle of *assigner* 'allot' (see ASSIGN).

as·sign·ment /ə'sīnmənt/ ▸*n.* **1** a task or piece of work assigned to someone as part of a job or course of study: *a homework assignment.* ■ the allocation of a job or task to someone: *the effective assignment of tasks.* ■ the task or post to which one has been appointed: *his assignment was to the County Court | I was* ***on assignment*** *for a German magazine.* **2** the attribution of someone or something as belonging: *the* ***assignment*** *of individuals* ***to*** *particular social positions.* **3** an act of making a legal transfer of a right, property, or liability: *an assignment of leasehold property.* ■ a document effecting such a transfer. ▷late Middle English: from Old French *assignement,* from medieval Latin *assignamentum,* from Latin *assignare* 'allot' (see ASSIGN).

as·sim·i·late /ə'simə,lāt/ ▸*v.* [*trans.*] **1** take in (information, ideas, or culture) and understand fully: *Marie tried to assimilate the week's events.* ■ (usu. **be assimilated**) absorb and integrate (people, ideas, or culture) into a wider society or culture: *pop trends are* ***assimilated into*** *the mainstream with alarming speed | [intrans.] the converts were assimilated into the society of their conquerors.* ■ absorb and integrate and use for one's own benefit: *the music business assimilated whatever aspects of punk it could turn into profit.* ■ (usu. **be assimilated**) (of the body or any biological system) absorb and digest (food or nutrients): *the sugars in the fruit are readily assimilated by the body.* **2** cause (something) to resemble; liken: *philosophers had* ***assimilated*** *thought* ***to*** *perception.* ■ [*intrans.*] come to resemble: *the churches* ***assimilated to*** *a certain cultural norm.* ■ *Phonetics* make (a sound) more like another in the same or next word. ▷late Middle English: from Latin *assimilat-* 'absorbed, incorporated,' from the verb *assimilare,* from *ad-* 'to' + *similis* 'like.' —**as·sim·i·la·ble** /-ləbəl/ *adj.* —**as·sim·i·la·tion** /ə,simə'lāsʜən/ *n.* —**as·sim·i·la·tive** /-,lātiv; -lətiv/ *adj.* —**as·sim·i·la·tor** /-,lātər/ *n.* —**as·sim·i·la·to·ry** /-lə,tôrē/ *adj.*

as·sim·i·la·tion·ist /ə,simə'lāsʜə,nist/ ▸*n.* a person who advocates or participates in racial or cultural integration: [*as adj.*] *the assimilationist policies of the right.*

As·sin·i·boin /ə'sinə,boin/ (also **As·sin·i·boine**) ▸*n.* (*pl.* same or **-boins**) **1** a member of an American Indian people formerly living in southern Manitoba, but now living in Montana, Alberta, and Saskatchewan. **2** the Siouan language of this people.

▸*adj.* of or relating to the Assiniboin or their language. ▷late 17th cent.: from Canadian French, from Ojibwa *assini:pwa:n* 'stone Sioux,' from *assin* 'stone' + *pwa:n* 'Sioux.'

As·si·ni·boine Riv·er /ə'sinə,boin/ a river in south central Canada that flows for 590 miles (950 km) from eastern Saskatchewan into Manitoba to join the Red River at Winnipeg.

As·si·si[1] /ə'sēsē; -zē/ a town in the province of Umbria in central Italy; pop. 24,790. It is the birthplace of St. Francis, whose tomb is located there.

As·si·si[2] see CLARE OF ASSISI, ST.

As·si·si[3] see FRANCIS OF ASSISI, ST.

as·sist /ə'sist/ ▸*v.* [*trans.*] help (someone), typically by doing a share of the work: *a senior academic would assist him in his work | [trans.] he assisted her to find employment | [intrans.] their presence would* ***assist in*** *keeping the peace.* ■ help by providing money or information: *they were assisting police with their inquiries | [intrans.] funds to* ***assist with*** *capital investment.* ■ [*intrans.*] be present as a helper or spectator: *two midwives who* ***assisted at*** *a water birth.*

▸*n.* an act of help, typically by providing money: *the budget must have an assist from tax policies.* ■ (chiefly in ice hockey, basketball, or baseball) the act of touching the puck or ball in a play in which a teammate scores or an opposing batter is put out: *he led the league with 14 outfield assists.* ■ [*in combination*] a mechanical device that provides help: *the implant is a ventricular-assist device.* ▷late Middle English: from Old French *assister,* from Latin *assistere* 'take one's stand by,' from *ad-* 'to, at' + *sistere* 'take one's stand.' —**as·sist·er** *n.*

as·sis·tance /ə'sistəns/ ▸*n.* the provision of money, resources, or information to help someone: *plans offering financial* ***assistance to*** *employers | she will be glad to give advice and assistance.* ■ the action of helping someone with a job or task: *the work was completed* ***with the assistance of*** *carpenters.* ▷late Middle English: from Old French, or from medieval Latin *assistentia,* from Latin *assistere* (see ASSIST).

▸*PHRASES* □ **be of assistance** be of practical use or help: *the guide will* ***be of assistance to*** *development groups.* □ **come to someone's assistance** act to help someone.

as·sis·tant /ə'sistənt/ ▸*n.* a person who ranks below a senior person: *the managing director and his assistant | [as adj.] an assistant manager.* ■ [with *adj.* or *modifier*] a person who helps in particular work: *a laboratory assistant.* ▷late Middle English: from Old French, or from medieval Latin *assistent-* 'taking one's stand beside,' from the verb *assistere* (see ASSIST).

as·sis·tant pro·fes·sor ▸*n.* a college teacher ranking immediately below an associate professor.

as·sis·tant·ship /ə'sistənt,sʜip/ ▸*n.* a paid academic appointment made to a graduate student that involves part-time teaching or research.

as·sist·ed liv·ing ▸*n.* housing for the elderly or disabled that provides nursing care, housekeeping, and prepared meals as needed.

as·sist·ed su·i·cide ▸*n.* the suicide of a patient suffering from an incurable disease, effected by the taking of lethal drugs provided by a doctor for this purpose.

as·size /ə'sīz/ ▸*n.* (usu. **assizes**) *historical* a court that formerly sat at intervals in each county of England and Wales to administer the civil and criminal law. In 1972 the civil jurisdiction of assizes was transferred to the High Court, and the criminal jurisdiction to the Crown Court. ▷Middle English: from Old French *assise,* feminine past participle of *asseeir* 'sit, settle, assess,' from Latin *assidere* (see ASSESS).

ass-kiss·ing ▸*n. vulgar slang* the use of compliments, flattery, or other obsequious behavior in order to gain favor. —**ass-kiss·er** *n.*

ass-lick·ing *vulgar slang* ▸ another term for ASS-KISSING.

assn. ▸*abbr.* association.

Assoc. ▸*abbr.* ■ Associate. ■ (as part of a title) Association.

as·so·ci·ate ▸*v.* /ə'sōsē,āt; -sʜē-/ [*trans.*] connect (someone or something) with something else in one's mind: *I* ***associated*** *wealth* ***with*** *freedom.* ■ (usu. **be associated**) connect (something) with something else because they occur together or one produces another: *the environmental problems* ***associated with*** *nuclear waste.* ■ (**associate oneself with**) allow oneself to be connected with or seen to be supportive of: *I cannot associate myself with some of the language used.* ■ (**be associated with**) be involved with: *she has been associated with the project from the first.* ■ [*intrans.*] meet or have dealings with someone commonly regarded with disapproval: *she began* ***associating with*** *socialists.*

▸*n.* /-it/ **1** a partner or colleague in business or at work: *he arranged for a close associate to take control of the institute.* ■ a companion or friend: *his old friend and hearty associate.* **2** a person with limited or subordinate membership in an organization. ■ a person who holds an academic degree conferred by a junior college (only in titles or set expressions): *an associate's degree in science | an Associate of Arts.* **3** *chiefly Psychology* a concept connected with another.

▸*adj.* /-it/ [*attrib.*] joined or connected with an organization or business: *an associate company.* ■ denoting shared function or membership but with a lesser status: *the associate director of the academy.* ▷late Middle English (as a verb in the sense 'join with in a common purpose'; as an adjective in the sense 'allied'): from Latin *associat-* 'joined,' from the verb *associare,* from *ad-* 'to' + *socius* 'sharing, allied.' —**as·so·ci·a·bil·i·ty** /ə,sōsʜ(ē)ə'bilitē; -sʜē-/ *n.* —**as·so·ci·a·ble** /ə'sōsʜ(ē)əbəl; -sʜē-/ *adj.* —**as·so·ci·ate·ship** /-,sʜip/ *n.*

as·so·ci·at·ed /ə'sōsē,ātid; -sʜē-/ ▸*adj.* (of a person or thing) connected with something else: *two associated events.* ■ (of a company) connected or amalgated with another company or companies. ■ *Chemistry* (of liquids) in which the molecules are held together by hydrogen bonding or other weak interaction.

As·so·ci·at·ed Press (abbr.: **AP**) an international news agency based in New York City.

As·so·ci·ate of Arts (abbr.: **AA**) (also **Associate's degree**) ▸*n.* a degree granted after a two-year course of study, esp. by a community or junior college.

as·so·ci·ate pro·fes·sor ▸*n.* an academic ranking immediately below full professor.

as·so·ci·a·tion /ə,sōsē'āsʜən; -sʜē-/ ▸*n.* **1** (abbr.: **assn.**) (often in names) a group of people organized for a joint purpose: *the National Association of*

Broadcasters. ■ *Ecology* a plant community defined by a characteristic group of dominant plant species. **2** a connection or cooperative link between people or organizations: *he developed a close* **association with** *the university* | *the program was promoted* **in association with** *the Department of Music.* ■ the action or state of becoming a member of an organization with subordinate status: [as *adj.*] *Slovenia signed association agreements with the European Union.* ■ *Chemistry* the linking of molecules through hydrogen bonding or other interaction short of full bond formation. **3** (usu. **associations**) a mental connection between ideas or things: *the word bureaucracy has unpleasant associations.* ■ the action of making such a connection: *the association of alchemy with "hieroglyphics" and "cabala."* ■ the fact of occurring with something else; co-occurrence: *cases of cancer found* **in association with** *colitis.* ▷mid 16th cent. (in the sense 'uniting in a common purpose'): from medieval Latin *associatio(n-)*, from Latin *associare* 'to unite, ally' (see ASSOCIATE). **—as·so·ci·a·tion·al** /-SHənl/ *adj.*

as·so·ci·a·tion ar·e·a ▶*n. Anatomy* a region of the cortex of the brain that connects sensory and motor areas, and that is thought to be concerned with higher mental activities.

As·so·ci·a·tion Foot·ball ▶*n.* more formal term for SOCCER. ▷so called because it is played according the rules of the Football *Association.*

as·so·ci·a·tion·ism /ə,sōsē'āSHə,nizəm; -,sōSHē-/ ▶*n.* a theory in philosophy or psychology that regards the simple association or co-occurrence of ideas or sensations as the primary basis of meaning, thought, or learning. **—as·so·ci·a·tion·ist** *n.* & *adj.*

As·so·ci·a·tion of South·east A·sian Na·tions (abbr.: **ASEAN**) a regional organization intended to promote economic cooperation and now comprising the countries of Indonesia, Malaysia, the Philippines, Singapore, Thailand, Brunei, Vietnam, Laos, Myanmar, and Cambodia.

as·so·ci·a·tive /ə'sōsē,ātiv; -SHē-; -sēətiv; -SHətiv/ ▶*adj.* **1** of or involving the action of associating ideas or things: *an associative, nonlinear mode of thought.* ■ [*attrib.*] *Computing* of or denoting computer storage in which items are identified by content rather than by address. **2** *Mathematics* involving the condition that a group of quantities connected by operators gives the same result whatever their grouping, as long as their order remains the same, e.g., $(a \times b) \times c = a \times (b \times c)$.

as·so·ci·a·tive mem·o·ry ▶*n. Computing* a memory capable of determining whether a given datum (the search word) is contained in one of its addresses or locations.

as·so·nance /'asənəns/ ▶*n.* in poetry, the repetition of the sound of a vowel or diphthong in nonrhyming stressed syllables near enough to each other for the echo to be discernible (e.g., *penitence, reticence*). Compare with ALLITERATION. ▷early 18th cent.: from French, from Latin *assonare* 'respond to,' from *ad-* 'to' + *sonare* (from *sonus* 'sound'). **—as·so·nant** *adj.* **—as·so·nate** /-,nāt/ *v.*

as·sort /ə'sôrt/ ▶*v.* **1** [*intrans.*] *Genetics* (of genes or characters) become distributed among cells or progeny. **2** [*trans.*] *archaic* place in a group; classify: *he would* **assort** *it* **with** *the fabulous dogs as a monstrous invention.* ▷late 15th cent.: from Old French *assorter*, from *a-* (from Latin *ad* 'to, at') + *sorte* 'sort, kind.'

as·sort·a·tive /ə'sôrtətiv/ ▶*adj.* [*attrib.*] denoting or involving the preferential mating of animals or marrying of people with similar characteristics.

as·sort·ed /ə'sôrtid/ ▶*adj.* [*attrib.*] of various sorts put together; miscellaneous: *bowls in assorted colors.*

as·sort·ment /ə'sôrtmənt/ ▶*n.* a miscellaneous collection of things or people: *the room was filled with* **an assortment of** *clothes.*

ASSR *historical* ▶*abbr.* Autonomous Soviet Socialist Republic.

Asst. ▶*abbr.* Assistant.

as·suage /ə'swāj/ ▶*v.* [*trans.*] make (an unpleasant feeling) less intense: *the letter assuaged the fears of most members.* See note at ALLEVIATE. ■ satisfy (an appetite or desire): *an opportunity occurred to assuage her desire for knowledge.* ▷Middle English: from Old French *assouagier, asouagier*, based on Latin *ad-* 'to' (expressing change) + *suavis* 'sweet.' **—as·suage·ment** *n.*

As Su·lay·ma·ni·yah /äs ,sōōli,mä'nē(y)ə/ variant form of SULAYMANIYAH.

as·sume /ə'sōōm/ ▶*v.* [*trans.*] **1** suppose to be the case, without proof: *you're afraid of what people are going to assume about me* | [with *clause*] *it is reasonable to assume that such changes have significant social effects* | [*trans.*] *they were assumed to be foreign.* **2** take or begin to have (power or responsibility): *he assumed full responsibility for all organizational work.* ■ seize (power or control): *the rebels assumed control of the capital.* **3** take on (a specified quality, appearance, or extent): *militant activity had assumed epidemic proportions.* ■ adopt falsely: *Oliver assumed an expression of penitence* | [as *adj.*] (**assumed**) *a man living under an assumed name.* ▷late Middle English: from Latin *assumere*, from *ad-* 'toward' + *sumere* 'take.' **—as·sum·ed·ly** /-midlē/ *adv.*

as·sum·ing /ə'sōōmiNG/ ▶*conj.* used for the purpose of argument to indicate a premise on which a statement can be based: **assuming that** *the treaty is ratified, what is its relevance?*
▶*adj. archaic* arrogant or presumptuous.

as·sump·tion /ə'səm(p)SHən/ ▶*n.* **1** a thing that is accepted as true or as certain to happen, without proof: *they made certain assumptions about the market* | [with *clause*] *we're working on the assumption that the time of death was after midnight.* **2** the action of taking or beginning to take power or responsibility: *the assumption of an active role in regional settlements.* **3** (**Assumption**) the reception of the Virgin Mary bodily into heaven. This was formally declared a doctrine of the Roman Catholic Church in 1950. See also DORMITION. ■ the feast in honor of this, celebrated on August 15. **4** *archaic* arrogance or presumption. ▷Middle English (sense 3): from Old French *asompsion* or Latin *assumptio(n-)*, from the verb *assumere* (see ASSUME).

as·sump·tive /ə'səm(p)tiv/ ▶*adj.* **1** *rare* of the nature of an assumption. **2** *archaic* apt to seize something for oneself. ▷mid 16th cent. (in the sense 'taken, adopted'): from Latin *assumptivus*, from the verb *assumere* (see ASSUME).

as·sur·ance /ə'SHŏŏrəns/ ▶*n.* **1** a positive declaration intended to give confidence; a promise: [with *clause*] *he* **gave an assurance that** *work would not recommence until Wednesday.* **2** confidence or certainty in one's own abilities: *she drove with assurance.* ■ certainty about something: *assurance of faith depends on our trust in God.* **3** *chiefly Brit.* insurance, specifically life insurance. ▷late Middle English (sense 2): from Old French, from *assurer* 'assure.'

as·sure /ə'SHŏŏr/ ▶*v.* **1** [*reporting verb*] tell someone something positively or confidently to dispel any doubts they may have: [*trans.*] *Tony assured me that there was a supermarket in the village* | [*trans.*] *"I quite understand," Mrs. Lewis assured her* | [*trans.*] *they* **assured** *him* **of** *their full confidence.* ■ make (someone) sure of something: *you would be assured of a fine welcome* | *she* **assured herself** *that he was asleep.* **2** [*trans.*] (often **be assured**) make (something) certain to happen: *victory was now assured* | [with *clause*] *their influence assured that the report would be tough.* ■ *chiefly Brit.* cover (a person) with life insurance. ■ secure the future payment of (an amount) with insurance. ▷late Middle English: from Old French *assurer*, based on Latin *ad-* 'to' (expressing change) + *securus* (see SECURE). **—as·sur·er** *n.*

as·sured /ə'SHŏŏrd/ ▶*adj.* **1** confident: *"Certainly not," was her assured reply.* **2** [*attrib.*] protected against discontinuance or change: *an assured tenancy.* **—as·sur·ed·ly** /ə'SHŏŏridlē/ *adv.* [*sentence adverb*] *if they lose their hold, they will assuredly drown.*

As·syr·i·a /ə'si(ə)rēə/ an ancient country in what is now northern Iraq. From the early part of the 2nd millennium BC, Assyria was the center of a succession of empires .

As·syr·i·an /ə'si(ə)rēən/ ▶*n.* **1** an inhabitant of ancient Assyria. **2** the language of ancient Assyria, a dialect of Akkadian. **3** a dialect of Aramaic still spoken by a group of people of mainly Christian faith living in the mountains of Syria, northern Iraq, and surrounding regions.
▶*adj.* **1** of or relating to ancient Assyria or its language. **2** relating to or denoting modern Assyrian or its speakers.

As·syr·i·ol·o·gy /ə,si(ə)rē'äləjē/ ▶*n.* the study of the language, history, and antiquities of ancient Assyria. **—As·syr·i·o·log·i·cal** /ə,si(ə)rēə'läjikəl/ *adj.* **—As·syr·i·ol·o·gist** /-jist/ *n.*

AST ▶*abbr.* Atlantic Standard Time (see ATLANTIC TIME).

a·sta·ble /ā'stābəl/ ▶*adj. chiefly Electronics* of or relating to a system or electric circuit that oscillates spontaneously between unstable states.

A·staire /ə'ste(ə)r/, Fred (1899–1987), U.S. dancer, singer, and actor; born *Frederick Austerlitz.* He starred in a number of movie musicals, including *Top Hat* (1935) and *Shall We Dance?* (1937), with Ginger Rogers and in *Easter Parade* (1948) with Judy Garland.

As·ta·na /äs'tänə/ the capital of Kazakhstan (since 1998); pop. 287,000. Formerly called **Aqmola** and, earlier, **Tselinograd.**

as·tang·a /as'täNGə/ ▶*n.* variant spelling of ASHTANGA.

As·tar·te /ə'stärtē/ *Mythology* a Phoenician goddess of fertility and sexual love who corresponds to the Babylonian and Assyrian goddess Ishtar and who became identified with the Egyptian Isis, the Greek Aphrodite, and others.

a·stat·ic /ā'statik/ ▶*adj.* not keeping a steady position or direction, in particular: ■ *Physics* (of a system or instrument) consisting of or employing a combination of magnets suspended in a uniform magnetic field on a single wire or thread in such a way that no torque is present (e.g., to minimize the effect of the earth's magnetic field). ▷early 19th cent.: from Greek *astatos* 'unstable' + -IC.

as·ta·tine /'astə,tēn; -tin/ ▶*n.* the chemical element of atomic number 85, a radioactive member of the halogen group. Astatine was first produced by bombarding bismuth with alpha particles, and it occurs in traces in nature as a decay product. (Symbol: **At**) ▷1940s: from Greek *astatos* 'unstable' + -INE[4].

New England aster

as·ter /'astər/ ▶*n.* **1** a plant of the daisy family that has bright rayed flowers, typically of purple or pink. • Genus *Aster*, family Compositae: numerous species, many of which bloom in autumn, including the wild purple **New England aster** (*A. novae-angliae*). See also CHINA ASTER. **2** *Biology* a star-shaped structure formed during division of the nucleus of an animal cell. ▷early 17th cent. (in the Greek sense): via Latin from Greek *astēr* 'star.'

-aster ▶*suffix* forming nouns: **1** denoting poor quality: *criticaster* | *poetaster.* **2** *Botany* denoting incomplete resemblance: *oleaster.* ▷from Latin.

as·ter·isk /'astə,risk/ ▶*n.* a symbol (*) used to mark printed or written text, typically as a reference to an annotation or to stand for omitted matter. ■ a thing resembling a star in shape: *soft asterisks of pollen.*
▶*v.* [*trans.*] [usu. as *adj.*] (**asterisked**) mark (printed or written text) with an asterisk: *asterisked entries.* ▷late Middle English: via late Latin from Greek *asteriskos* 'small star,' diminutive of *astēr.*

USAGE Avoid pronouncing this word /'astə,riks/ or /'astə,rik/, as many regard such pronunciations as uneducated.

as·ter·ism /'astə,rizəm/ ▶*n.* **1** *Astronomy* a prominent pattern or group of stars, typically having a popular name but smaller than a constellation. **2** a group of three asterisks (⁂) drawing attention to following text. ▷late 16th cent.: from Greek *asterismos*, from *astēr* 'star.'

a·stern /ə'stərn/ ▶*adv.* **1** behind or toward the rear of a ship or aircraft: *the engine rooms lay astern.* **2** (of a ship) backward: *the lifeboat was carried astern by the tide.* ▷late Middle English: from A-[2] (expressing position or direction) + STERN[2].

as·ter·oid /'astə,roid/ ▶*n.* a small rocky body orbiting the sun. Large numbers of these, ranging in size from nearly 600 miles (1,000 km) across (Ceres) to dust particles, are found (as the **asteroid belt**) esp. between the orbits of Mars and Jupiter, though some have more eccentric orbits, and a few pass close to the earth or enter the atmosphere as meteors. ▷early 19th cent.: from Greek *asteroeidēs* 'starlike,' from *astēr* 'star.' **—as·ter·oi·dal** /,astə'roidl/ *adj.*

As·ter·oi·de·a /,astə'roidēə/ *Zoology* a class of echinoderms that comprises the starfishes. ▷modern Latin (plural), from Greek *asteroeidēs* 'starlike,' from *astēr* 'star.' **—as·ter·oid** /'astə,roid/ *n.* & *adj.*

as·the·ni·a /as'THēnēə/ ▶*n. Medicine* abnormal physical weakness or lack of energy. ▷late 18th cent.: modern Latin, from Greek *astheneia*, from *asthenēs* 'weak.'

as·then·ic /as'THenik/ ▶*adj. Medicine* relating to, involving, or suffering from asthenia. ▷late 18th cent.: from Greek *asthenikos*, from *asthenēs* 'weak.'

as·then·o·sphere /as'THenə,sfi(ə)r/ ▶*n. Geology* the upper layer of the earth's mantle, below the lithosphere, in which there is relatively low resistance to plastic flow and convection is thought to occur.

▷early 20th cent.: from Greek *asthenēs* 'weak' + SPHERE. —**as·then·o·spher·ic** /as,THenə'sfi(ə)rik; -'sferik/ *adj.*

asth·ma /'azmə/ ▶*n.* a respiratory condition marked by spasms in the bronchi of the lungs, causing difficulty in breathing. It usually results from an allergic reaction or other forms of hypersensitivity. ▷late Middle English: from medieval Latin *asma*, from Greek *asthma*, from *azein* 'breathe hard.'

asth·mat·ic /az'matik/ ▶*adj.* relating to or suffering from asthma.
▶*n.* a person who suffers from asthma. ▷early 16th cent.: via Latin from Greek *asthmatikos*, from *asthma* (see ASTHMA). —**asth·mat·i·cal·ly** /-ik(ə)lē/ *adv.*

As·ti /'ästē/ ▶*n.* **1** a white wine from the province of Asti and neighboring parts of Piedmont. **2** a light sparkling wine from this region.

a·stig·ma·tism /ə'stigmə,tizəm/ ▶*n.* a defect in the eye or in a lens caused by a deviation from spherical curvature, which results in distorted images, as light rays are prevented from meeting at a common focus. ▷mid 19th cent.: from A-[1] 'without' + Greek *stigma* 'point' + -ISM. —**as·tig·mat·ic** /,astig'matik/ *adj.*

a·stil·be /ə'stilbē/ ▶*n.* an Old World plant of the saxifrage family, with plumes of tiny white, pink, or red flowers. • Genus *Astilbe*, family Saxifragaceae. ▷modern Latin, from Greek *a-* 'not' + *stilbē*, feminine of *stilbos* 'glittering' (because the individual flowers are small and inconspicuous).

a·stir /ə'stər/ ▶*adj.* [*predic.*] in a state of excited movement: *the streets are all astir.* ■ awake and out of bed: *he woke before anyone else was astir.* ▷late 18th cent.: from A-[2] 'on' + the noun STIR[1].

As·ti Spu·man·te /'ästē sp(y)ōō'mäntē/ ▶ former term for ASTI (sense 2).

As·ton /'astən/, Francis William (1877–1945), English physicist. He invented the mass spectrograph (with J. J. Thomson) and eventually discovered many of the 287 naturally occurring isotopes of nonradioactive elements. Nobel Prize for Chemistry (1922).

as·ton·ish /ə'stäniSH/ ▶*v.* [*trans.*] surprise or impress (someone) greatly: *you never fail to astonish me* | [*trans.*] *it astonished her that Mrs. Browing could seem so anxious* | [as *adj.*] (**astonishing**) *an astonishing achievement.* ▷early 16th cent. (as *astonished*, in the sense 'stunned, bewildered, dismayed'): from obsolete *astone* 'stun, stupefy,' from Old French *estoner*, based on Latin *ex-* 'out' + *tonare* 'to thunder.' —**as·ton·ish·ing·ly** *adv.* [as *submodifier*] *an astonishingly successful program.*

as·ton·ish·ment /ə'stäniSHmənt/ ▶*n.* great surprise: *she looked at him* ***in astonishment.***

As·tor[1] /'astər/, John Jacob (1763–1848), U.S. merchant; born in Germany. He emigrated to the U.S. in 1784 and made a fortune in the fur trade.

As·tor[2], Nancy Witcher Langhorne, Viscountess (1879–1964), British politician; born in the U.S. She became the first woman to sit in the House of Commons when she succeeded her husband as a member of Parliament.

As·to·ri·a /ə'stôrēə/ **1** a city in northwestern Oregon, near the mouth of the Columbia River on the Pacific coast; pop. 10,069. In the 19th century it was a noted fur-trading center. **2** a section of northwestern Queens in New York City, noted for its large Greek-American population.

as·tound /ə'stound/ ▶*v.* [*trans.*] shock or greatly surprise: *her bluntness astounded him.* ▷Middle English (as an adjective in the sense 'stunned'): from *astoned*, past participle of obsolete *astone* (see ASTONISH).

as·tound·ing /ə'stoundiNG/ ▶*adj.* surprisingly impressive or notable: *the summit offers astounding views.* —**as·tound·ing·ly** *adv.* [as *submodifier*] *an astoundingly good performance.*

a·strad·dle /ə'stradl/ ▶*prep.* with the legs stretched widely on each side of: *policemen sitting astraddle motorcycles.*
▶*adj.* & *adv.* with the legs stretched widely on each side.

As·trae·a /a'strēə/ *Astronomy* asteroid 5, discovered in 1845 (diameter 125 km). ▷from the name of a Roman goddess associated with justice.

as·tra·gal /'astrəgəl/ ▶*n.* a convex molding or wooden strip across a surface or separating panels, typically semicircular in cross-section. ■ *Architecture* a small semicircular molding around the top or bottom of a column. ■ a wooden molding that covers the gap between a pair of doors or casement windows. ■ a glazing bar, typically one used in cabinet-making. ▷mid 17th cent.: from ASTRAGALUS, partly via French *astragale.*

as·trag·a·lus /ə'stragələs/ ▶*n.* (*pl.* **-li** /-,lī/) *chiefly Zoology* another term for TALUS[1] (ankle bone). ▷mid 16th cent.: via Latin from Greek *astragalos* 'ankle bone, molding,' also the name of a vetch.

As·tra·khan /'astrə,kan; -kən/ a city in southern Russia, on the delta of the Volga River; pop. 509,000.

as·tra·khan /'astrəkən; -,kan/ ▶*n.* the dark curly fleece of young karakul lambs from central Asia: [as *adj.*] *an astrakhan collar.* ■ a cloth imitating this. ▷mid 18th cent.: named after the city of ASTRAKHAN in Russia, from which the fleeces were exported.

as·tral /'astrəl/ ▶*adj.* [*attrib.*] of, connected with, or resembling the stars: *astral navigation.* ■ of or relating to a supposed nonphysical realm of existence to which various psychic and paranormal phenomena are ascribed, and in which the physical human body is said to have a counterpart. ▷early 17th cent.: from late Latin *astralis*, from *astrum* 'star.'

a·stray /ə'strā/ ▶*adv.* **1** away from the correct path or direction: *we went astray but a man redirected us.* **2** into error or morally questionable behavior: *he was led astray by boozy colleagues.* ▷Middle English (in the sense 'distant from the correct path'): from an Anglo-Norman French variant of Old French *estraie*, past participle of *estraier*, based on Latin *extra* 'out of bounds' + *vagari* 'wander.'
▶*PHRASE* □ **go astray** (of an object) become lost or mislaid: *the money had gone astray.*

a·stride /ə'strīd/ ▶*prep.* with a leg on each side of: *he was* ***sitting astride*** *the bike* | *a figure astride a horse* | [as *adv.*] *he sat on the chair astride.* ■ extending across: *the port* ***stands astride*** *an international route* | *why do people build their dream homes astride some seismic fault?* ■ [as *adv.*] with legs apart: *he stood, legs astride.*

as·trin·gent /ə'strinjənt/ ▶*adj.* **1** causing the contraction of body tissues, typically of the skin: *an astringent skin lotion.* **2** sharp or severe in manner or style: *her astringent words had their effect.* ■ (of taste or smell) sharp or bitter: *an astringent smell of rotting apples.*
▶*n.* a substance that causes the contraction of body tissues, typically used to protect the skin and to reduce bleeding from minor abrasions. ▷mid 16th cent.: from French, from Latin *astringent-* 'pulling tight,' from the verb *astringere*, from *ad-* 'toward' + *stringere* 'bind, pull tight.' —**as·trin·gen·cy** *n.* —**as·trin·gent·ly** *adv.* (in sense 2 of the *adjective*).

astro- ▶*comb. form* relating to the stars, celestial objects, or outer space: *astrocompass* | *astrophysics* | *astrochemistry* | *astrophotography.* ▷from Greek *astron* 'star.'

as·tro·ar·chae·ol·o·gy /'astrō,ärkē'äləjē/ (also **as·tro·ar·chae·ol·o·gy**) ▶*n.* another term for ARCHAEOASTRONOMY.

as·tro·bi·o·lo·gy /,astrōbī'äləjē/ ▶*n.* the science concerned with life in space.

as·tro·bleme /'astrə,blēm/ ▶*n.* *Geology* an eroded remnant of a large crater made by the impact of a meteorite or comet. ▷mid 20th cent.: from Greek *astron* 'star' + *blēma* 'wound.'

as·tro·chem·is·try /,astrō'keməstrē/ ▶*n.* the study of the chemical substances and species occurring in stars and interstellar space. —**as·tro·chem·i·cal** /-kəl/ *adj.* —**as·tro·chem·ist** /'astrō,kemist/ *n.*

as·tro·com·pass /'astrō,kəmpəs; -,käm-/ ▶*n.* an instrument designed to indicate direction with respect to the stars.

as·tro·cyte /'astrə,sīt/ ▶*n.* *Anatomy* a star-shaped glial cell of the central nervous system. —**as·tro·cyt·ic** /,astrə'sitik/ *adj.*

as·tro·dome /'astrə,dōm/ ▶*n.* **1** a domed window in an aircraft for astronomical observations. **2** (**the Astrodome**) an enclosed stadium in Houston with a domed roof.

as·tro·ga·tion /,astrə'gāSHən/ ▶*n.* (in science fiction) navigation in outer space. ▷1930s: blend of ASTRO- and NAVIGATION. —**as·tro·ga·tor** /'astrə,gātər/ *n.*

as·troid /'astroid/ ▶*n.* *Mathematics* a hypocycloid with four cusps (like a square with concave sides).

as·tro·labe /'astrə,lāb/ ▶*n.* *chiefly historical* an instrument formerly used to make astronomical measurements, typically of the altitudes of celestial bodies, and in navigation for calculating latitude, before the development of the sextant. In its basic form (known from classical times), it consists of a disk with the edge marked in degrees and a pivoted pointer. ▷late Middle English: from Old French *astrelabe*, from medieval Latin *astrolabium*, from Greek *astrolabon*, neuter of *astrolabos* 'star-taking.'

as·trol·o·gy /ə'stráləjē/ ▶*n.* the study of the movements and relative positions of celestial bodies interpreted as having an influence on human affairs and the natural world.

Ancient observers of the heavens developed elaborate systems of explanation based on the movements of the sun, moon, and planets through the constellations of the zodiac, for predicting events and for casting horoscopes. By 1700 astrology had lost intellectual credibility in the West, but continued to have popular appeal. Modern astrology is based on that of the Greeks, but other systems are extant, notably those of China and India.

▷late Middle English: from Old French *astrologie*, from Latin *astrologia*, from Greek, from *astron* 'star.' The term (in full *natural astrology*) originally denoted the practical uses of astronomy, applied in the measurement of time and the prediction of natural phenomena. The current sense (in full *judicial astrology*, relating to human affairs) dates from the mid 16th cent. —**as·trol·o·ger** /-jər/ *n.* —**as·tro·log·i·cal** /,astrə'läjikəl/ *adj.* —**as·trol·o·gist** /-jist/ *n.*

as·tro·met·ric bi·na·ry /,astrō'metrik 'bīnərē/ ▶*n.* *Astronomy* a binary star system in which one companion is invisible, but is known to be present from its effect on measurements relating to the other.

as·trom·e·try /ə'strämitrē/ ▶*n.* the measurement of the positions, motions, and magnitudes of stars. —**as·tro·met·ric** /,astrō'metrik/ *adj.*

as·tro·naut /'astrə,nôt/ ▶*n.* a person who is trained to travel in a spacecraft. ▷1920s: from ASTRO-, on the pattern of *aeronaut* and *aquanaut.* —**as·tro·nau·ti·cal** /,astrə'nôtikəl/ *adj.*

as·tro·nau·tics /,astrə'nôtiks/ ▶*n.* the science and technology of human space travel and exploration.

as·tro·nav·i·ga·tion /,astrō,navi'gāSHən/ ▶*n.* determination of the position and course of an aircraft or a spacecraft by means of observation of the stars. ▷mid 20th cent.: from ASTRO- + NAVIGATION. —**as·tro·nav·i·ga·tor** /-'navi,gātər/ *n.*

as·tron·o·mer /ə'stränəmər/ ▶*n.* an expert in or student of astronomy.

as·tro·nom·i·cal /,astrə'nämikəl/ ▶*adj.* **1** of or relating to astronomy. **2** *informal* (of an amount) extremely large: *he wanted an astronomical fee.* ▷mid 16th cent.: via Latin from Greek *astronomikos*, from *astronomia* (see ASTRONOMY). —**as·tro·nom·ic** *adj.* (in sense 2). —**as·tro·nom·i·cal·ly** /-ik(ə)lē/ *adv.*

as·tro·nom·i·cal u·nit (abbr.: **AU**) ▶*n.* *Astronomy* a unit of measurement equal to 149.6 million kilometers, the mean distance from the center of the earth to the center of the sun.

as·tro·nom·i·cal year ▶ See YEAR (sense 1).

as·tron·o·my /ə'stränəmē/ ▶*n.* the branch of science that deals with celestial objects, space, and the physical universe as a whole.

In ancient times, observation of the sun, moon, stars, and planets formed the basis of timekeeping and navigation. Astronomy was greatly furthered by the invention of the optical telescope, but modern observations are made in all parts of the spectrum, including X-ray and radio frequencies, using terrestrial and orbiting instruments and space probes.

▷Middle English (also denoting astrology): from Old French *astronomie*, from Latin *astronomia*, from Greek, from *astronomos* (adjective) 'star-arranging.'

as·tro·pho·tog·ra·phy /,astrōfə'tägrəfē/ ▶*n.* the use of photography in astronomy; the photographing of celestial objects and phenomena. —**as·tro·pho·tog·ra·pher** /-fər/ *n.* —**as·tro·pho·to·graph·ic** /-,fōtə'grafik/ *adj.*

as·tro·phys·ics /,astrō'fiziks/ ▶*n.* the branch of astronomy concerned with the physical nature of stars and other celestial bodies, and the application of the laws and theories of physics to the interpretation of astronomical observations. —**as·tro·phys·i·cal** /-ikəl/ *adj.* —**as·tro·phys·i·cist** /-isist/ *n.*

As·tro·Turf /'astrō,tərf/ ▶*n.* *trademark* an artificial grass surface, used for athletic fields. ▷1960s: from ASTRODOME (sense 1), where it was first used, + TURF. —**As·tro·Turfed** *adj.*

As·tu·ri·as[1] /ə'st(y)ŏŏrēəs/ an autonomous region and former principality in northwestern Spain; capital, Oviedo.

As·tu·ri·as[2], Miguel Ángel (1899–1974), Guatemalan novelist and poet, best known for his experimental novel *The President* (1946). Nobel Prize for Literature (1967).

as·tute /ə'st(y)o͞ot/ ▸*adj.* having or showing an ability to accurately assess situations or people and turn this to one's advantage: *an astute businessman.* See note at **KEEN**. ▷early 17th cent.: from obsolete French *astut* or Latin *astutus*, from *astus* 'craft.' —**as·tute·ly** *adv.* —**as·tute·ness** *n.*

a·sty·lar /ā'stīlər/ ▸*adj. Architecture* (of a classical building) lacking columns or pilasters. ▷mid 19th cent.: from **A-**[1] 'without' + Greek *stulos* 'column' + **-AR**[1].

A·sun·ción /ä,so͞onsē'ōn; -'syōn/ the capital and chief port of Paraguay, on the Paraguay River; pop. 729,300.

a·sun·der /ə'səndər/ ▸*adv. archaic* or *poetic/literary* apart; divided: *those whom God hath joined together let no man put asunder.* ■ into pieces: *the desk burst asunder.* ▷Old English *on sundran* 'in or into a separate place'; compare with **SUNDER**.

a·su·ra /'əsərə/ ▸*n.* a member of a class of divine beings in the Vedic period, which in Indian mythology tend to be evil and in Zoroastrianism are benevolent. Compare with **DEVA**, **AHURA MAZDA**.

As·wan /as'wän; äs-/ a city on the Nile River in southern Egypt, 10 miles (16 km), north of Lake Nasser; pop. 195,700. Two dams across the Nile have been built nearby. The controlled release of water from Lake Nasser behind the High Dam produces the greater part of Egypt's electricity.

a·swarm /ə'swôrm/ ▸*adj.* [*predic.*] crowded; full of moving beings or objects: *the streets were* ***aswarm with*** *vendors.*

as well as ▸*conj.* and also; and in addition: *genuine sentiment as well as a fair degree of realism.*

a·swim /ə'swim/ ▸*adj.* [*predic.*] swimming: *sardines aswim in oil.*

a·swirl /ə'swərl/ ▸*adj. & adv.* swirling; covered or surrounded with something swirling: [*predic. adj.*] *flowers aswirl with bees* | [*adv.*] *she shook her head, sending the streamers aswirl.*

a·sy·lum /ə'sīləm/ ▸*n.* **1** (also **political asylum**) the protection granted by a nation to someone who has left their native country as a political refugee: *granting asylum to foreigners persecuted for political reasons.* ■ shelter or protection from danger: *asylum for those too ill to care for themselves.* **2** *dated* an institution offering shelter and support to the mentally ill: *he'd been committed to an asylum.* ▷late Middle English (in the sense 'place of refuge,' esp. for criminals): via Latin from Greek *asulon* 'refuge,' from *asulos* 'inviolable,' from *a-* 'without' + *sulon* 'right of seizure.' The current senses date from the 18th cent.

a·sym·met·ri·cal /,āsə'metrikəl/ ▸*adj.* having parts that fail to correspond to one another in shape, size, or arrangement; lacking symmetry: *the church has an asymmetrical plan with an aisle only on one side.* ■ having parts or aspects that are not equal or equivalent; unequal in some respect: *the asymmetrical relationship between a landlord and a tenant.* —**a·sym·met·ric** *adj.* —**a·sym·met·ri·cal·ly** /-ik(ə)lē/ *adv.*

a·sym·met·ri·cal war·fare ▸*n.* warfare involving surprise attacks by small, simply armed groups on a nation armed with modern high-tech weaponry.

a·sym·met·ric bars /,āsə'metrik/ ▸*plural n.* British term for **UNEVEN BARS**.

a·sym·me·try /ā'simitrē/ ▸*n.* (*pl.* **-tries**) lack of equality or equivalence between parts or aspects of something; lack of symmetry. ▷mid 17th cent.: from Greek *asummetria*, from *a-* 'without' + *summetria* (see **SYMMETRY**).

a·symp·to·mat·ic /,āsim(p)tə'matik/ ▸*adj. Medicine* (of a condition or a person) producing or showing no symptoms.

as·ymp·tote /'asəm(p),tōt/ ▸*n.* a line that continually approaches a given curve but does not meet it at any finite distance. ▷mid 17th cent.: from modern Latin *asymptota (linea)* '(line) not meeting,' from Greek *asumptōtos* 'not falling together,' from *a-* 'not' + *sun* 'together' + *ptōtos* 'apt to fall' (from *piptein* 'to fall'). —**as·ymp·tot·ic** /,asəm(p)'tätik/ *adj.* —**as·ymp·tot·i·cal·ly** /-ik(ə)lē/ *adv.*

a·syn·chro·nous /ā'siNGkrənəs/ ▸*adj.* **1** *Computing & Telecommunications* of or requiring a form of computer control timing protocol in which a specific operation begins upon receipt of an indication (signal) that the preceding operation has been completed. **2** not going at the same rate and exactly together with something else, in particular: ■ (of a machine or motor) not working in time with the alternations of current. ■ *Astronomy* (of a satellite) revolving around the parent planet at a different rate from that at which the planet rotates. ■ *Astronomy* (of an orbit) such that a satellite in it is asynchronous. **3** (of two or more objects or events) not existing or happening at the same time. —**a·syn·chro·nous·ly** *adv.*

a·syn·de·ton /ə'sində,tän/ ▸*n.* (*pl.* **-de·ta** /-dətə/) the omission or absence of a conjunction between parts of a sentence. ▷mid 16th cent.: modern Latin, from Greek *asundeton*, neuter of *asundetos* 'unconnected,' from *a-* 'not' + *sundetos* 'bound together.' —**as·yn·det·ic** /,asən'detik/ *adj.*

At ▸*symbol* the chemical element astatine.

at[1] /at/ ▸*prep.* **1** expressing location or arrival in a particular place or position: *they live at Conway House* | *she was constantly at the telex machine* | *they stopped at a small trattoria.* ■ used in speech to indicate the sign @: *the children go to bed at nine o'clock* | *his death came at a time when the movement was split.* ■ [without *adj.*] denoting a particular period of time: *the sea is cooler at night.* ■ [without *adj.*] denoting the time spent by someone attending an educational institution, a workplace, or their home: *we all need to get involved in fighting crime whether it's at work, at home, or at school.* **3** denoting a particular point or segment on a scale: *prices start at $18,500* | *driving at 50 mph.* ■ referring to someone's age: *at fourteen he began to work as a mailman.* **4** expressing a particular state or condition: *placed them at a serious disadvantage* | *the coroner accepted that the machines were at fault.* ■ expressing a relationship between an individual and a skill: *boxing was the only sport I was any good at* | *he is poor at giving instructions.* **5** expressing the object of a look, gesture, thought, action, or plan: *I looked at my watch* | *Leslie pointed at him.* ■ expressing the target of a shot from a weapon: *they tore down the main street, firing at anyone in sight.* ■ emphasizing the directing of an action toward a specified object: *she clutched at the thin gown* | *he hit at her face with the gun.* **6** expressing the means by which something is done: *holding a corrections officer at knifepoint* | *figurative her pride had taken a beating at his hands.* ▷Old English *æt*, of Germanic origin; related to Old Frisian *et* and Old Norse *at*, from an Indo-European root shared by Latin *ad* 'to.'

▸*PHRASES* □ **at all** see **ALL**. □ **at first** see **FIRST**. □ **at it** engaged in some activity, typically a reprehensible one: *the guy who faked the Hitler diaries is at it again.* □ **at last** see **LAST**[1]. □ **at least** see **LEAST**. □ **at most** see **MOST**. □ **at once** see **ONCE**. □ **at that** in addition; furthermore: *it was not fog but smoke, and very thick at that.* □ **not at all** see **NOT**. □ **where it's at** *informal* the fashionable place, possession, or activity: *New York is where it's at, stylewise.*

at[2] /ät/ ▸*n.* a monetary unit of Laos, equal to one hundredth of a kip.

at- ▸*prefix* variant spelling of **AD-** assimilated before *t* (as in *attend, attenuate*).

At·a·brine /'atəbrin; -,brēn/ ▸ trade name for **QUINACRINE**.

A·ta·ca·ma Des·ert /,ätə'kämə; ,atə-/ an arid region in western Chile that extends roughly 600 miles (965 km) south from the Peruvian border.

a·tac·tic /ā'taktik/ ▸*adj. Chemistry* (of a polymer or polymer structure) in which the repeating units have no regular stereochemical configuration. ▷mid 19th cent.: from Greek *ataktos*, from *a-* 'not' + *taktos* 'arranged' + **-IC**.

At·a·lan·ta /,atə'läntə/ *Greek Mythology* a huntress who would marry only someone who could beat her in a foot race. She was beaten when a suitor threw down three golden apples which she stopped to pick up.

at·a·man /'atəmən/ ▸*n.* (*pl.* **-mans**) a Cossack leader. See also **HETMAN**. ▷mid 19th cent.: from Russian.

at·a·rax·y /'atə,raksē/ (also **at·a·rax·i·a** /,atə'raksēə/) ▸*n.* a state of serene calmness. ▷early 17th cent.: from French *ataraxie*, from Greek *ataraxia* 'impassiveness,' from *a-* 'not' + *tarassein* 'disturb.' —**at·a·rac·tic** /,atə'raktik/ *adj.* —**at·a·rax·ic** /,atə'raksik/ *adj.*

A·tas·ca·de·ro /ə,taskə'de(ə)rō/ a city in southwestern California; pop. 23,138.

A·ta·türk /,atə'tərk/, Kemal (1881–1938), Turkish general and statesman; president 1923–38; born *Mustafa Kemal*; also called **Kemal Pasha**. As the first president of the Turkish republic, he abolished the caliphate and introduced other policies designed to make Turkey a modern secular state.

at·a·vis·tic /,atə'vistik/ ▸*adj.* relating to or characterized by reversion to something ancient or ancestral: *atavistic fears and instincts.* ▷late 19th cent.: based on Latin *atavus* 'forefather,' via French *atavisme*, + **-IC**. —**at·a·vism** /'atə,vizəm/ *n.* —**at·a·vis·ti·cal·ly** /-tik(ə)lē/ *adv.*

a·tax·i·a /ə'taksēə/ (also **a·tax·y** /ə'taksē/) ▸*n. Medicine* the loss of full control of bodily movements. ▷late 19th cent.: modern Latin, from Greek, from *a-* 'without' + *taxis* 'order.' The original sense was 'irregularity, disorder,' later (in medical use) denoting irregularity of function or symptoms. —**a·tax·ic** /-sik/ *adj.*

ATB ▸*abbr.* all-terrain bike.

at bat *Baseball* ▸*n.* a player's turn at batting, as officially recorded: *O'Neill had three singles in four at bats.* Compare with **PLATE APPEARANCE**.

▸*adv.* batting.

ATC ▸*abbr.* ■ air traffic control. ■ air traffic controller.

A·tchaf·a·lay·a Riv·er /(ə),CHafə'līə/ a river in south central Louisiana that flows south for 170 miles (275 km) to the Gulf of Mexico. It is used to control flooding on the Red and Mississippi rivers.

ATE ▸*abbr.* automated test equipment.

ate /āt/ ▸ past of **EAT**.

-ate[1] ▸*suffix* forming nouns: **1** denoting status or office: *doctorate* | *episcopate.* ■ a state or function: *curate* | *mandate.* **2** denoting a group: *electorate.* **3** *Chemistry* denoting a salt or ester, esp. of an acid with a corresponding name ending in *-ic*: *chlorate* | *nitrate.* **4** denoting a product (of a chemical process): *condensate* | *filtrate.* ▷representing Old French *-at* or *-é(e)*, or from Latin *-atus* (as a noun or past participial form).

-ate[2] ▸*suffix* **1** forming adjectives and nouns such as *associate, duplicate, separate.* **2** forming adjectives from Latin: *caudate.* ▷representing French *-é* or its Latin source *-atus* (past participial suffix).

-ate[3] ▸*suffix* forming verbs such as *fascinate, hyphenate.* ▷representing French *-er* or its Latin source *-are.* Originally forms were based on existing past participial adjectives ending in *-atus*, later extended to any verb ending in *-are.*

A-team ▸*n.* a group of elite soldiers or the top advisers or workers in an organization. ▷1970s: from sports terminology in which an organization's A-team is its best team.

at·e·lec·ta·sis /,atl'ektəsis/ ▸*n. Medicine* partial or complete collapse of the lung. ▷mid 19th cent.: from Greek *atelēs* 'imperfect' + *ektasis* 'extension.'

at·el·ier /,atl'yā/ ▸*n.* a workshop or studio, esp. one used by an artist or designer. ▷late 17th cent.: from French, from Old French *astelle* 'splinter of wood,' from Latin *astula.*

a tem·po /ä 'tempō/ ▸*adv. Music* (esp. as a direction) in the previous or original tempo. ▷Italian, literally 'in time.'

a·tem·po·ral /ā'temp(ə)rəl/ ▸*adj.* existing or considered without relation to time. —**a·tem·po·ral·i·ty** /,ātempə'ralitē/ *n.*

A·ten /'ätn/ (also **A·ton**) *Egyptian Mythology* the sun or solar disk, the deity of a strong monotheistic cult, particularly during the reign of Akhenaten.

a·ten·o·lol /ə'tenə,lôl; -,läl/ ▸*n. Medicine* a beta blocker used mainly to treat angina and high blood pressure. ▷1970s: perhaps from *a(ngina)* + *ten(sion)* + *(propran)olol*, a related compound.

ATF ▸*abbr.* (Federal Bureau of) Alcohol, Tobacco, and Firearms.

Ath·a·bas·ca Riv·er /,aTHə'baskə/ a river in Canada that flows northeast for 765 miles (1,230 km) from the Rocky Mountains across Alberta to Lake Athabasca, Canada's fourth-largest lake. The river valley has large oil tar deposits.

Ath·a·bas·kan /,aTHə'baskən/ (also **Ath·a·pas·kan** /-'pas-/) ▸*adj.* denoting, belonging to, or relating to a family of North American Indian languages including esp. Navajo and various Apache languages of the southwest U.S., several languages of coastal California and Oregon, and many languages of Alaska and northwestern Canada, including Chipewyan.

▸*n.* **1** this family of languages. **2** a speaker of any of these languages. ▷from *Athabasca*, the name of a lake in western Canada, from Cree *athapaskaw* 'grass and reeds here and there,' + **-AN**.

Ath·a·na·sian Creed /,aTHə'nāZHən/ a summary of Christian doctrine formerly attributed to St. Athanasius, but probably dating from the 5th century.

Ath·a·na·sius, St. /,aTHə'nāSHəs/ (*c.*296–373), Greek theologian and upholder of Christian orthodoxy against the Arian heresy. Feast day, May 2.

ath·a·nor /'athə,nôr/ ▸*n.* a type of furnace used by alchemists, able to maintain a steady heat for long periods. ▷late 15th cent.: from Arabic *at-tannūr*, from *al-* 'the' + *tannūr* 'baker's oven.' Compare with TANDOOR.

A·thar·va Ve·da /əˈtärvə ˈvādə; ˈvēdə/ *Hinduism* a collection of hymns and ritual utterances, written in early Sanskrit and added at a later stage to the existing Vedic material. ▷from Sanskrit *Atharvan* (the name of Brahma's eldest son, said to be the author of the collection) + *vēda* '(sacred) knowledge.'

a·the·ism /ˈāTHēˌizəm/ ▸*n.* the theory or belief that God does not exist. ▷late 16th cent.: from French *athéisme*, from Greek *atheos*, from *a-* 'without' + *theos* 'god.' **—a·the·ist** *n.* **—a·the·is·tic** /ˌāTHēˈistik/ *adj.* **—a·the·is·ti·cal** /-ˈistikəl/ *adj.*

ath·el·ing /ˈaTHəliNG; ˈaTH-/ ▸*n. historical* a prince or lord in Anglo-Saxon England. ▷Old English *ætheling*, from a base meaning 'race, family.'

Ath·el·stan /ˈaTHəlˌstan/ (895–939), king of England 925–939.

a·the·mat·ic /ˌāTHiˈmatik/ ▸*adj.* **1** *Music* (of a composition) not based on the use of themes. **2** *Grammar* (of a verb form) having a suffix attached to the stem without a connecting (thematic) vowel.

A·the·na /əˈTHēnə/ (also **A·the·ne** /-nē/) *Greek Mythology* the patron goddess of Athens, worshiped as the goddess of wisdom, handicrafts, and warfare. She is often allegorized into a personification of wisdom. Also called PALLAS. Identified with the Roman goddess MINERVA.

ath·e·nae·um /ˌaTHəˈnēəm/ (also **ath·e·ne·um**) ▸*n.* used in the names of libraries or institutions for literary or scientific study: *the Boston Athenaeum.* ■ used in the titles of periodicals concerned with literature, science, and art. ▷mid 18th cent.: via Latin from Greek *Athēnaion*, denoting the temple of Athena.

A·then·i·an em·pire /əˈTHēnēən/ see DELIAN LEAGUE.

Ath·ens /ˈaTHənz/ **1** the capital of Greece, in the southern part of the country; pop. 3,096,775. A flourishing city-state in ancient Greece, it was an important cultural center in the 5th century BC. It came under Roman rule in 146 BC and fell to the Goths in AD 267. After its capture by the Turks in 1456, Athens declined to the status of a village until chosen as the capital of a newly independent Greece in 1834. Greek name ATHÍNAI. **2** a city in northeastern Georgia, the seat of the University of Georgia; pop. 45,734. **3** a city in southeastern Ohio, the seat of Ohio University; pop. 21,265. **—A·the·ni·an** /əˈTHēnēən/ *adj.* & *n.*

ath·er·o·gen·ic /ˌaTH(ə)rōˈjenik/ ▸*adj. Physiology* tending to promote the formation of fatty plaques in the arteries. ▷1950s: from ATHEROMA + -GENIC. **—ath·er·o·gen·e·sis** /-əsis/ *n.*

ath·er·o·ma /ˌaTHəˈrōmə/ ▸*n. Medicine* degeneration of the walls of the arteries caused by accumulated fatty deposits and scar tissue, and leading to restriction of the circulation and a risk of thrombosis. See also ATHEROSCLEROSIS. ■ the fatty material that forms plaques in the arteries. ▷late 16th cent.: via Latin from Greek *athērōma*, from *athērē*, *atharē* 'groats.' **—ath·er·om·a·tous** /-ˈrämətəs; -ˈrō-/ *adj.*

ath·er·o·scle·ro·sis /ˌaTHərōskləˈrōsis/ ▸*n. Medicine* a disease of the arteries characterized by the deposition of plaques of fatty material on their inner walls. See also ATHEROMA and ARTERIOSCLEROSIS. ▷early 20th cent.: coined in German from Greek *athērē* 'groats' + *sklērōsis* 'hardening' (see SCLEROSIS). **—ath·er·o·scle·rot·ic** /-ˈrätik/ *adj.*

ath·e·tize /ˈaTHiˌtīz/ ▸*v.* [*trans.*] *rare* reject (a passage in a text) as spurious. ▷late 19th cent.: from Greek *athetos* 'without position' + -IZE, rendering the Greek verb *athetein*. **—ath·e·te·sis** /ˌaTHiˈtēsis/ *n.*

ath·e·to·sis /ˌaTHiˈtōsis/ ▸*n. Medicine* a condition in which abnormal muscle contractions cause involuntary writhing movements. It affects some people with cerebral palsy, impairing speech and use of the hands. ▷late 19th cent.: from Greek *athetos* 'without position' + -OSIS. **—ath·e·toid** /ˈaTHiˌtoid/ *adj.* **—ath·e·tot·ic** /-ˈtätik/ *adj.*

A·thí·nai /äˈTHēne/ variant spelling of ATHENS.

a·thirst /əˈTHərst/ ▸*adj.* [*predic.*] *archaic* thirsty. ■ very eager to get something: *she was* **athirst** *for news.* ▷Old English *ofthyrst*, shortened from *ofthyrsted*, past participle of *ofthyrstan* 'be thirsty.'

ath·lete /ˈaTHˌlēt/ ▸*n.* a person who is proficient in sports and other forms of physical exercise. ■ *chiefly Brit.* a person who is skilled in competitive track and field events (athletics). ▷late Middle English: from Latin *athleta*, from Greek *athlētēs*, from *athlein* 'compete for a prize,' from *athlon* 'prize.'

ath·lete's foot ▸*n.* a fungal infection affecting the skin between the toes. It is a form of ringworm.

ath·let·ic /aTHˈletik/ ▸*adj.* **1** [*attrib.*] of or relating to athletes or athletics: *athletic events* | *an athletic club.* **2** physically strong, fit, and active: *big, muscular, athletic boys.* ▷mid 17th cent.: from French *athlétique* or Latin *athleticus*, from Greek *athlētikos*, from *athlētēs* (see ATHLETE). **—ath·let·i·cal·ly** /-ik(ə)lē/ *adv.* **—ath·let·i·cism** /-ˌsizəm/ *n.*

ath·let·ics /aTHˈletiks/ ▸*plural n.* [usu. treated as *sing.*] physical sports and games of any kind. ■ *chiefly Brit.* the sport of competing in track and field events, including running races and various competitions in jumping and throwing: [as *adj.*] *athletics championships.*

ath·let·ic sup·port·er ▸*n.* another term for JOCKSTRAP.

at-home ▸*n.* an informal party in a person's home. ■ *dated* a period when a person has announced that they will receive visitors in their home.
▸*adj.* occurring in or suited to one's home: *at-home athletic equipment.*

Ath·os, Mount /ˈaTHˌäs; ˈāˌTHäs/ a narrow, mountainous peninsula in northeastern Greece that projects into the Aegean Sea. It is inhabited by Greek Orthodox monks, who forbid women and even female animals to set foot on the peninsula. **—Ath·o·nite** /ˈaTHəˌnīt/ *adj.* & *n.*

a·thwart /əˈTHwôrt/ ▸*prep.* **1** from side to side of; across: *a long counter thrown athwart the entranceway.* **2** in opposition to; counter to: *these statistics* **run** *sharply* **athwart** *conventional presumptions.*
▸*adv.* **1** across from side to side; transversely: *one table running athwart was all the room would hold.* **2** so as to be perverse or contradictory: *our words* **ran athwart** *and we ended up at cross purposes.* ▷late Middle English: from A-² 'on' + THWART.

-atic ▸*suffix* forming adjectives and nouns such as *aquatic, idiomatic.* ▷from French *-atique* or Latin *-aticus*, often based on Greek *-atikos*.

-ation ▸*suffix* (forming nouns) denoting an action or an instance of it: *exploration* | *hesitation.* ■ denoting a result or product of action: *plantation.* ▷representing French *-ation* or Latin *-ation-*.

At·i·van /ˈatiˌvan/ ▸*n.* trademark for LORAZEPAM.

-ative ▸*suffix* (forming adjectives) denoting a characteristic or propensity: *pejorative* | *talkative.* ▷representing French *-atif, -ative*, or from Latin *-ativus*.

At·kins di·et /ˈatkinz/ ▸*n.* a diet high in protein and fat and low in carbohydrates, prescribed for weight loss. ▷1972: after its originator, cardiologist Dr. Robert C. Atkins (1930–2003) and his book *Dr. Atkins' Diet Revolution* (1972).

At·kin·son /ˈatkinsən/, Sir Harry (Albert) (1831–92), New Zealand statesman; born in Britain; prime minister 1876–77, 1883–84, and 1887–91.

At·lan·ta /ətˈlantə; at-/ the capital of the state of Georgia in the U.S., in northwest central Georgia; pop. 416,474. It was burned by Union forces under Gen. William T. Sherman in 1864 during the Civil War.

at·lan·tes /atˈlantēz/ ▸ plural form of ATLAS (sense 3).

At·lan·tic /ətˈlantik; at-/ ▸*adj.* [*attrib.*] of or adjoining the Atlantic Ocean: *an Atlantic storm* | *the Atlantic coast of Europe.*
▸*n.* short for ATLANTIC OCEAN. ▷late Middle English: via Latin from Greek *Atlantikos*, from *Atlas, Atlant-* (see ATLAS). The term originally referred to the Atlas Mountains in Libya, hence to the sea near the west African coast, later being extended to the whole ocean.

At·lan·tic, Battle of the a succession of sea operations during World War II in which Axis naval and air forces attempted to destroy shipping carrying supplies from North America to the UK.

At·lan·tic Char·ter a declaration of eight common principles in international relations drawn up by Churchill and Roosevelt in August 1941, which provided the ideological basis for the United Nations organization.

At·lan·tic Cit·y a resort city in southeastern New Jersey, on the Atlantic Ocean; pop. 37,986. It is noted for its gambling casinos and its boardwalk.

At·lan·tic In·tra·coast·al Wa·ter·way a water route in the U.S. that allows sheltered boat passage for 1,900 miles (3,100 km) along the Atlantic coast between Boston and Key West.

At·lan·ti·cism /ətˈlantiˌsizəm/ ▸*n.* belief in or support for a close relationship between western Europe and the U.S., or particularly for NATO. **—At·lan·ti·cist** *n.* & *adj.*

At·lan·tic O·cean the ocean that lies between Europe and Africa on the east and North and South America on the west. It is divided by the equator into the North Atlantic and the South Atlantic oceans.

At·lan·tic Prov·in·ces another name for MARITIME PROVINCES.

At·lan·tic seal ▸*n.* another term for GRAY SEAL.

At·lan·tic time the standard time in a zone including the easternmost parts of mainland Canada, Puerto Rico, and the Virgin Islands, specifically: • (**Atlantic Standard Time**, abbrev.: **AST**) standard time based on the mean solar time at the longitude 60° W, four hours behind GMT. • (**Atlantic Daylight Time**, abbrev.: **ADT**) Atlantic time during daylight savings, three hours behind GMT.

At·lan·tis /ətˈlantis; at-/ a legendary island, beautiful and prosperous, which sank into the sea. **—At·lan·te·an** /ˌatlanˈtēən; atˈlantēən/ *adj.*

At·las /ˈatləs/ *Greek Mythology* one of the Titans, who was punished for his part in their revolt against Zeus by being made to support the heavens. He became identified with the Atlas Mountains. **—At·lan·te·an** /ˌatlanˈtēən; atˈlantēən/ *adj.*

at·las /ˈatləs/ ▸*n.* **1** (*pl.* **at·las·es**) a book of maps or charts: *I looked in the atlas to find a map of Italy* | *a road atlas.* ■ a book of illustrations or diagrams on any subject: *Atlas of Surgical Operations.* **2** (*pl.* **at·las·es**) (also **atlas vertebra**) *Anatomy* the topmost vertebra of the backbone, articulating with the occipital bone of the skull. **3** (*pl.* **at·lan·tes** /atˈlantēz/) *Architecture* a stone carving of a male figure, used as a column to support the entablature of a Greek or Greek-style building. ▷late 16th cent. (originally denoting a person who supported a great burden): via Latin from Greek *Atlas* (see ATLAS).

at·las moth ▸*n.* a very large, boldly marked silkworm moth that occurs in both the Old and New World tropics. • Genus *Attacus*, family Saturniidae: several species, in particular *A. atlas* of Asia, which is the largest moth in the world.

At·las Moun·tains a range of mountains in North Africa that extends from Morocco to Tunisia in a series of chains, including the Anti-Atlas, High Atlas, Middle Atlas, Rif Mountains, Tell Atlas, and Sahara Atlas.

ATM ▸*abbr.* ■ *Telecommunications* asynchronous transfer mode. ■ automated (or automatic) teller machine.

atm *Physics* ▸*abbr.* atmosphere(s), as a unit of pressure.

at·man /ˈätmən/ (also **At·man**) ▸*n. Hinduism* the spiritual life principle of the universe, esp. when regarded as inherent in the real self of the individual. ■ a person's soul. ▷from Sanskrit *ātman*, literally 'essence, breath.'

at·mos·phere /ˈatməsˌfi(ə)r/ ▸*n.* [usu. in *sing.*] **1** the envelope of gases surrounding the earth or another planet: *part of the sun's energy is absorbed by the earth's atmosphere.* ■ the air in any particular place: *we couldn't breathe in the dusty atmosphere of his apartment.* ■ (abbr.: **atm**) *Physics* a unit of pressure equal to mean atmospheric pressure at sea level, 101,325 pascals. **2** the pervading tone or mood of a place, situation, or work of art: *the hotel is famous for its friendly, welcoming atmosphere* | *this crisis further compounded the prevailing atmosphere of gloom.* ■ a pleasurable and interesting or exciting mood: *a superb restaurant, full of atmosphere.* ▷mid 17th cent.: from modern Latin *atmosphaera*, from Greek *atmos* 'vapor' + *sphaira* 'ball, globe.'

at·mos·pher·ic /ˌatməsˈfi(ə)rik; -ˈferik/ ▸*adj.* **1** of or relating to the atmosphere of the earth or (occasionally) another planet: *atmospheric conditions such as fog, snow, rain.* **2** creating a distinctive mood, typically of romance, mystery, or nostalgia: *atmospheric lighting.* **—at·mos·pher·i·cal** *adj.* (*archaic*) **—at·mos·pher·i·cal·ly** *adv.*

at·mos·pher·ic pres·sure ▸*n.* the pressure exerted by the weight of the atmosphere, which at sea level has a mean value of 101,325 pascals (roughly 14.6959 pounds per square inch). Also called BAROMETRIC PRESSURE.

at·mos·pher·ics /ˌatməsˈfi(ə)riks; -ˈferiks/ ▸*plural n.* **1** electrical disturbances in the atmosphere due to lightning and other phenomena, esp. as they interfere with telecommunications. **2** effects intended to create a particular atmosphere or mood, esp. in music: *a jazz sound with spooky atmospherics.*

at·oll /ˈatˌôl; ˈatˌäl; ˈāˌtôl; ˈāˌtäl/ ▸*n.* a ring-shaped reef, island, or chain of islands formed of coral. ▷early 17th cent.: from Maldivian *atoḷu*.

at·om /ˈatəm/ ▸*n.* the basic unit of a chemical element. ■ such particles as a source of nuclear energy: *the power of the atom.* ■ [usu. with *negative*] an extremely small amount of a thing or quality: *I shall not have one atom of strength left.*

An atom, roughly 10^{-8} cm in diameter, consists of a tiny, dense, positively charged nucleus made of neutrons and protons, surrounded by a cloud of negatively charged electrons. Each chemical element consists of atoms that possess a characteristic number of protons. Atoms are held together in molecules by sharing electrons.

▷late 15th cent.: from Old French *atome*, via Latin from Greek *atomos* 'indivisible,' based on *a-* 'not' + *temnein* 'to cut.'

at·om bomb (also **a·tom·ic bomb**) ▸*n.* a bomb that derives its destructive power from the rapid release of nuclear energy by fission of heavy atomic nuclei, causing damage through heat, blast, and radioactivity. Compare with HYDROGEN BOMB.

In such a bomb two pieces of a fissile material are brought together by a conventional explosion to form a super critical mass. Neutrons then cause an uncontrolled fission chain reaction that quickly releases large amounts of energy.

a·tom·ic /əˈtämik/ ▸*adj.* of or relating to an atom or atoms: *the atomic nucleus.* ■ *Chemistry* (of a substance) consisting of uncombined atoms rather than molecules: *atomic hydrogen.* ■ of or forming a single irreducible unit or component in a larger system: *a society made up of atomic individuals pursuing private interests.* ■ relating to, denoting, or using the energy released in nuclear fission or fusion: *the atomic age required a new way of political thinking | atomic weapons.* ▷late 17th cent.: from modern Latin *atomicus*, from *atomus* 'indivisible' (see ATOM). —**a·tom·i·cal·ly** /-ik(ə)lē/ *adv.*

a·tom·ic age ▸*n.* another term for NUCLEAR AGE.

a·tom·ic clock ▸*n.* an extremely accurate type of clock that is regulated by the vibrations of an atomic or molecular system such as cesium or ammonia.

at·o·mic·i·ty /ˌatəˈmisitē/ ▸*n.* **1** *Chemistry* the number of atoms in the molecules of an element. **2** the state or fact of being composed of indivisible units.

a·tom·ic mass ▸*n.* the mass of an atom of a chemical element expressed in atomic mass units. It is approximately equivalent to the number of protons and neutrons in the atom (the mass number) or to the average number allowing for the relative abundances of different isotopes.

a·tom·ic mass u·nit (abbr.: **amu**) ▸*n.* a unit of mass used to express atomic and molecular weights, equal to one-twelfth of the mass of an atom of carbon-12. It is equal to approximately 1.66×10^{-27} kg.

a·tom·ic num·ber ▸*n.* *Chemistry & Physics* the number of protons in the nucleus of an atom, which determines the chemical properties of an element and its place in the periodic table. (Symbol: **Z**)

a·tom·ic phys·ics ▸*plural n.* [treated as *sing.*] the branch of physics concerned with the structure of the atom, its energy states, and its interactions with particles and fields.

a·tom·ic pile ▸*n.* dated term for NUCLEAR REACTOR.

a·tom·ic pow·er ▸*n.* another term for NUCLEAR POWER.

a·tom·ic spec·trum ▸*n.* the spectrum of frequencies of electromagnetic radiation emitted or absorbed during transitions of electrons between energy levels within an atom. Each element has a characteristic spectrum by which it can be recognized.

a·tom·ic the·o·ry ▸*n.* the theory that all matter is made up of tiny indivisible particles (atoms). According to the modern version, the atoms of each element are effectively identical, but differ from those of other elements, and unite to form compounds in fixed proportions. ■ in any field, a theory that proposes the existence of distinct, separable, independent components: *an atomic theory of heredity.*

a·tom·ic vol·ume ▸*n.* *Chemistry* the volume occupied by one gram-atom of an element under standard conditions.

a·tom·ic weight ▸*n.* *Chemistry* another term for ATOMIC MASS.

at·om·ism /ˈatəˌmizəm/ ▸*n.* *chiefly Philosophy* a theoretical approach that regards something as interpretable through analysis into distinct, separable, and independent elementary components. The opposite of HOLISM. —**at·om·ist** *n.* —**at·om·is·tic** /ˌatəˈmistik/ *adj.*

at·om·ize /ˈatəˌmīz/ ▸*v.* [*trans.*] convert (a substance) into very fine particles or droplets: *the CO_2 depressurized, atomizing the paint into a mist of even-size particles.* ■ reduce (something) to atoms or other small distinct units: *by disrupting our ties with our neighbors, crime atomizes society.* —**at·om·i·za·tion** /ˌatəməˈzāshən/ *n.*

at·om·iz·er /ˈatəˌmīzər/ (*Brit.* also **at·om·is·er**) ▸*n.* a device for emitting water, perfume, or other liquids as a fine spray.

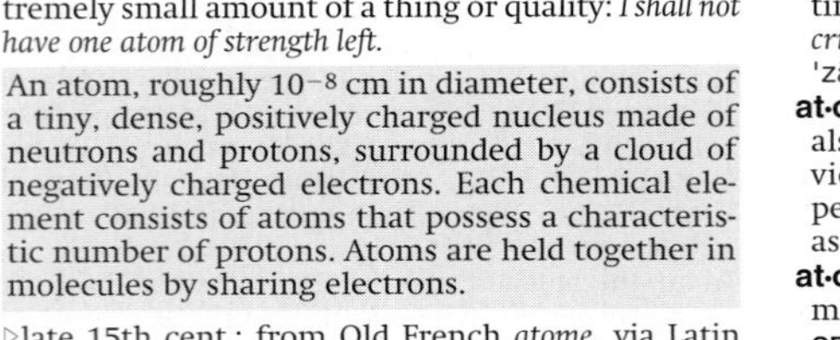

atomizer

at·om smash·er ▸*n.* informal term for PARTICLE ACCELERATOR.

at·o·my /ˈatəmē/ ▸*n.* (*pl.* **-mies**) *archaic* a skeleton or emaciated body. ▷late 16th cent.: from ANATOMY, taken as *an atomy.*

A·ton variant spelling of ATEN.

a·ton·al /āˈtōnl/ ▸*adj.* *Music* not written in any key or mode. —**a·ton·al·ism** /-ˌizəm/ *n.* —**a·ton·al·ist** /-ist/ *n.* —**a·to·nal·i·ty** /ˌātōˈnalitē;/ *n.*

a·tone /əˈtōn/ ▸*v.* [*intrans.*] make amends or reparation: *he was being helpful, to* ***atone for*** *his past mistakes.* ▷Middle English (originally in the sense 'make or become united or reconciled,' rare before the 16th cent.): from *at one* in early use; later by back-formation from ATONEMENT.

a·tone·ment /əˈtōnmənt/ ▸*n.* reparation for a wrong or injury: *she wanted to* ***make atonement for*** *her husband's behavior.* ■ *Religion* reparation or expiation for sin: *the High Priest offered the sacrifice as* ***atonement for*** *all the sins of Israel.* ■ (**the Atonement**) *Christian Theology* the reconciliation of God and humankind through Jesus Christ. ▷early 16th cent. (denoting unity or reconciliation, esp. between God and man): from *at one* + -MENT, influenced by medieval Latin *adunamentum* 'unity,' and earlier *onement* from an obsolete verb *one* 'to unite.'

a·ton·ic /āˈtänik/ ▸*adj.* **1** *Linguistics* (of a syllable) without accent or stress. **2** *Physiology* lacking muscular tone. —**at·o·ny** /ˈatnē/ *n.*

a·top /əˈtäp/ ▸*prep.* on the top of: *the weathervane is perched atop the barn.*
▸*adv.* on the top: *the air raid siren* ***atop of*** *the courthouse.*

a·top·ic /āˈtäpik/ ▸*n.* denoting a form of allergy in which a hypersensitivity reaction such as dermatitis or asthma may occur in a part of the body not in contact with the allergen. ▷early 20th cent.: from Greek *atopia* 'a being out of place,' from *atopos* 'out of place,' from *a-* 'without' + *topos* 'place.' —**at·o·py** /ˈatəpē/ *adj.*

-ator ▸*suffix* forming agent nouns such as *agitator.* ■ used in names of implements, machines, etc.: *escalator.* ▷from Latin, or sometimes representing French *-ateur.*

-atory ▸*suffix* (forming adjectives) relating to or involving an action: *explanatory | predatory.* ▷from Latin *-atorius.*

ATP ▸*abbr.* *Biochemistry* adenosine triphosphate.

at·ra·bil·ious /ˌatrəˈbilēəs; -ˈbilyəs/ ▸*adj.* *poetic/literary* melancholy or ill-tempered. ▷mid 17th cent. (in the sense 'affected by black bile,' one of the four supposed cardinal humors of the body, believed to cause melancholy): from Latin *atra bilis* 'black bile,' translation of Greek *melankholia* 'melancholy,' + -IOUS. —**at·ra·bil·ious·ness** *n.*

a·trau·mat·ic /ˌātrəˈmatik; ˌātrou-; ˌātrô-/ ▸*adj.* (of a medical or surgical procedure) causing minimal tissue injury.

at·ra·zine /ˈatrəˌzēn/ ▸*n.* a synthetic compound used as an agricultural herbicide. • A triazine derivative; chem. formula: $C_8H_{14}N_5Cl$. ▷1960s: blend of AMINO and TRIAZINE

a·trem·ble /əˈtrembəl/ ▸*adj.* [*predic.*] *poetic/literary* trembling: *the breeze failed to set a single leaf atremble.*

a·tre·sia /əˈtrēzh(ē)ə/ ▸*n.* **1** *Medicine* absence or abnormal narrowing of an opening or passage in the body. **2** *Physiology* the degeneration of those ovarian follicles that do not ovulate during the menstrual cycle. ▷early 19th cent.: from A-[1] 'without' + Greek *trēsis* 'perforation' + -IA[1].

A·tre·us /āˈtrēəs; ˈātro͞os/ *Greek Mythology* the son of Pelops and father of Agamemnon and Menelaus. He quarreled with his brother Thyestes and invited him to a banquet at which he served up the flesh of Thyestes' own children.

a·tri·o·ven·tric·u·lar /ˌātrē-ōvenˈtrikyələr/ ▸*adj.* *Anatomy & Physiology* relating to the atrial and ventricular chambers of the heart, or the connection or coordination between them.

at-risk ▸*adj.* vulnerable, especially to abuse or delinquency: *a church-run school for the most at-risk children.*

a·tri·um /ˈātrēəm/ ▸*n.* (*pl.* **a·tri·a** /ˈātrēə/ or **a·tri·ums**) **1** *Architecture* an open-roofed entrance hall or central court in an ancient Roman house. ■ a central hall or court in a modern building, with rooms or galleries opening off it, often glass-covered. **2** *Anatomy* each of the two upper cavities of the heart from which blood is passed to the ventricles. The right atrium receives deoxygenated blood from the veins of the body; the left atrium receives oxygenated blood from the pulmonary vein. Also called AURICLE. ▷late 16th cent.: from Latin. —**a·tri·al** /ˈātrēəl/ *adj.*

a·tro·cious /əˈtrōshəs/ ▸*adj.* horrifyingly wicked: *atrocious cruelties.* ■ of a very poor quality; extremely bad or unpleasant: *he attempted an atrocious imitation of my English accent | atrocious weather.* ▷mid 17th cent.: from Latin *atrox, atroc-* 'cruel' + -IOUS. —**a·tro·cious·ly** *adv.* —**a·tro·cious·ness** *n.*

a·troc·i·ty /əˈträsitē/ ▸*n.* (*pl.* **-ties**) an extremely wicked or cruel act, typically one involving physical violence or injury: *war atrocities | scenes of hardship and atrocity.* ■ *humorous* a highly unpleasant or distasteful object: *the house was a split-level atrocity.* ▷mid 16th cent. (in the sense 'cruelty'): from French *atrocité* or Latin *atrocitas*, from *atrox, atroc-* 'cruel.'

at·ro·phy /ˈatrəfē/ ▸*v.* (**-phies**, **-phied**) [*intrans.*] (of body tissue or an organ) waste away, typically due to the degeneration of cells, or become vestigial during evolution: *without exercise, the muscles will atrophy* | [as *adj.*] (**atrophied**) *in some beetles, the hind wings are atrophied.* ■ *figurative* gradually decline in effectiveness or vigor due to underuse or neglect: *her artistic skills atrophied from lack of use.*
▸*n.* the condition or process of atrophying: *gastric atrophy.* ■ *figurative* the gradual decline of effectiveness or vigor due to underuse or neglect: *extensive TV viewing may lead to atrophy of children's imaginations.* ▷late 16th cent.: from French *atrophier* (verb), *atrophie* (noun), from late Latin *atrophia*, from Greek, 'lack of food,' from *a-* 'without' + *trophē* 'food.' —**a·troph·ic** /āˈtrōfik; āˈträfik/ *adj.*

at·ro·pine /ˈatrəˌpēn/ ▸*n.* *Chemistry* a poisonous compound found in deadly nightshade and related plants. It is used in medicine as a muscle relaxant, e.g., in dilating the pupil of the eye. • An alkaloid; chem. formula: $C_{17}N_{23}NO_3$. ▷mid 19th cent.: modern Latin *Atropa belladonna* 'deadly nightshade,' from ATROPOS + -INE[4].

At·ro·pos /ˈatrəˌpäs/ *Greek Mythology* one of the three Fates. ▷Greek, literally 'inflexible.'

at sign ▸*n.* the symbol @.

At·si·na /atˈsēnə/ ▸*n.* (*pl.* same or **-nas**) a member of a North American Indian people living chiefly in the north central plains region. They speak an Algonquian language. Also called GROS VENTRE.
▸*adj.* of or relating to the Atsina.

at·ta·boy /ˈatəˌboi/ ▸*exclam.* an informal expression of encouragement or admiration, typically to a man or boy.
▸*n.* a piece of encouragement or congratulations, esp. a letter: *our boss will write you guys an attaboy.* ▷early 20th cent.: probably representing a casual pronunciation of *that's the boy.*

at·tach /əˈtach/ ▸*v.* [*trans.*] fasten; join: *he made certain that the trailer was securely* ***attached to*** *the van.* ■ fasten (a related document) to another: *I attach a copy of the memo for your information.* ■ include (a condition) as part of an agreement: *the Commission can attach appropriate conditions to the operation of the agreement.* ■ used to indicate that someone regards something as important or valuable: *he doesn't* ***attach*** *too much importance* ***to*** *radical ideas.* ■ [*intrans.*] (**attach to**) used to indicate someone regards something as important or valuable: *in South Korea enormous importance is attached to respect for the dead.* ■ (**attach oneself to**) join (someone or something) without being invited: *they were all too ready to attach themselves to you for the whole day.* ■ (usu. **be attached**) appoint (someone) for special or temporary duties: *I was* ***attached to*** *another department.* ■ *Law* seize (a person's property) by legal authority: *the court attached his wages for child support.* ▷Middle English (in the sense 'seize by legal authority'): from Old French *atachier* or *estachier* 'fasten, fix,' based on an element of Germanic origin related to STAKE[1]; compare with ATTACK. —**at·tach·a·ble** *adj.*

at·ta·ché /ˌatəˈsʜā ˌata-/ ▸*n.* **1** a person on the staff of an ambassador, typically with a specialized area of responsibility: *military attachés.* **2** short for ATTACHÉ CASE. ▷early 19th cent.: from French, literally 'attached,' past participle of *attacher.*

at·ta·ché case ▸*n.* a small, flat, rectangular case used for carrying documents.

at·tached /əˈtacʜt/ ▸*adj.* **1** joined or fastened to something: *please complete the attached form.* ■ (of a building or room) adjacent to and typically connected with another building or room: *a ground-floor bedroom with a bathroom attached.* **2** full of affection or fondness: *during his visit, Mark became increasingly **attached to** Tara.* **3** (**attached to**) (of a person) appointed to an organization or group for special or temporary duties: *he was attached to military intelligence.* ■ (of an organization or body) affiliated to another larger organization or body: *a public relations agency attached to the university.*

at·tach·ment /əˈtacʜmənt/ ▸*n.* **1** an extra part or extension that is or can be attached to something to perform a particular function: *the food processor comes with a blender attachment.* ■ a computer file appended to an e-mail. **2** the condition of being attached to something or someone, in particular: ■ affection, fondness, or sympathy for someone or something: *she felt a sentimental **attachment to** the place.* ■ an affectionate relationship between two people: *he formed an attachment with a young widow.* **3** the action of attaching something: *the case has a loop for attachment to your belt.* ■ legal seizure of property. ▷late Middle English (in the sense 'arrest for contempt of court'): from Old French *attachement,* from *atachier* 'fasten, fix' (see ATTACH).

at·tack /əˈtak/ ▸*v.* [*trans.*] take aggressive action against (a place or enemy forces) with weapons or armed force, typically in a battle or war: *in December, the Japanese attacked Pearl Harbor* | [*intrans.*] *the terrorists did not attack again until March.* ■ (of a person or animal) act against (someone or something) aggressively in an attempt to injure or kill: *a doctor was attacked by two youths.* ■ (of a disease, chemical substance, or insect) act harmfully on: *HIV is thought to attack certain cells in the brain.* ■ criticize or oppose fiercely and publicly: *he attacked the government's defense policy.* ■ begin to deal with (a problem or task) in a determined and vigorous way: *a plan of action to attack unemployment.* ■ [*intrans.*] make an aggressive or forceful attempt to score a goal or point, or gain or exploit an advantage in a game against an opposing team or player: [as *adj.*] (**attacking**) *the home team showed some good attacking play.* ■ *Chess* move into or be in a position to capture (an opponent's piece).
▸*n.* an aggressive and violent action against a person or place: *he was killed in an **attack on** a checkpoint* | *three classrooms were gutted in the arson attack.* ■ destructive action by a disease, chemical, or insect: *the tissue is open to attack by fungus.* ■ a sudden short bout of an illness or stress: *an attack of nausea* | *an asthma attack.* ■ an instance of fierce public criticism or opposition: *he launched a stinging **attack on** the White House.* ■ a determined attempt to tackle a problem or task: *an **attack on** inflation.* ■ *Music* the manner of beginning to play or sing a passage. ■ forceful and decisive style in performing music or another art: *the sheer attack of Hendrix's playing.* ■ an aggressive attempt to score a goal, win points, or gain or exploit an advantage in a game. ■ *Chess* a threat to capture an opponent's piece. ▷early 17th cent.: from French *attaque* (noun), *attaquer* (verb), from Italian *attacco* 'an attack,' *attaccare* 'join battle,' based on an element of Germanic origin (see ATTACH).
▸*PHRASE* □ **under attack** subject to aggressive, violent, or harmful action: *his paintings have come under attack for their satanic content.*

THE RIGHT WORD **assail, assault, attack, beset, besiege, bombard, charge, molest, storm**

There is no shortage of "fighting words." **Attack** is the most general verb, meaning to set upon someone or something in a violent, forceful, or aggressive way (*the rebels attacked at dawn*); but it can also be used figuratively (*attack the government's policy*).

Assault implies a greater degree of violence or viciousness and the infliction of more damage. As part of the legal term "assault and battery," it suggests an attempt or threat to injure someone physically.

Molest is another word meaning to *attack* and is used today almost exclusively of sexual molestation (*she had been molested as a child*).

Charge and **storm** are primarily military words, both suggesting a forceful assault on a fixed position. To *charge* is to make a violent onslaught (*the infantry charged the enemy camp*) and is often used as a command (| *"Charge!" the general cried*). To *storm* means to take by force, with all the momentum and fury of a storm (*after days of planning, the soldiers stormed the castle*), but there is often the suggestion of a last-ditch, all-out effort to end a long siege or avoid defeat.

To **assail** is to attack with repeated thrusts or blows, implying that victory depends not so much on force as on persistence.

To **bombard** is to assail continuously with bombs or shells (*they bombarded the city without mercy for days*).

Besiege means to surround with an armed force (*to besiege the capital city*). When used figuratively, its meaning comes close to that of *assail,* but with an emphasis on being hemmed in and enclosed rather than punished repeatedly (*besieged with fears*). **Beset** also means to attack on all sides (*beset by enemies*), but it is also used frequently in other contexts to mean set or placed upon (| *a bracelet beset with diamonds*).

at·tack·er /əˈtakər/ ▸*n.* a person or animal that attacks someone or something. ■ (in soccer and other games) a player that makes an assertive or aggressive attempt to score; a forward.

at·ta·girl /ˈatəˌgərl/ ▸*exclam.* an informal expression of encouragement or admiration to a woman or girl. ▷1920s: on the pattern of *attaboy.*

at·tain /əˈtān/ ▸*v.* [*trans.*] succeed in achieving (something that one desires and has worked for): *clarify your objectives and ways of attaining them* | *he attained the rank of admiral* | *human beings can attain happiness.* See note at GET. ■ reach (a specified age, size, or amount): *dolphins can attain remarkable speeds in water.* ▷Middle English (in the senses 'bring to justice' and 'reach (a state)'): from Old French *ateindre,* from Latin *attingere,* from *ad-* 'at, to' + *tangere* 'to touch.' **—at·tain·a·bil·i·ty** /əˌtānəˈbilitē/ *n.* **—at·tain·a·ble** *adj.*

at·tain·der /əˈtāndər/ ▸*n. historical* the forfeiture of land and civil rights suffered as a consequence of a sentence of death for treason or felony. ▷late Middle English: from Anglo-Norman French, variant (used as a noun) of Old French *ateindre* in the sense 'convict, bring to justice' (see ATTAIN).
▸*PHRASE* □ **bill of attainder** an item of legislation inflicting attainder without judicial process.

at·tain·ment /əˈtānmənt/ ▸*n.* the action or fact of achieving a goal toward which one has worked: *the attainment of a mystical state of communion with God.* ■ (often **attainments**) a thing achieved, esp. a skill or educational achievement: *scholarly attainments.*

at·taint /əˈtānt/ ▸*v.* [*trans.*] **1** (usu. **be attainted**) *historical* subject to attainder. **2** *archaic* affect or infect with disease or corruption. ▷Middle English (in the sense 'touch, reach, attain'): from obsolete *attaint* (adjective), from Old French *ataint, ateint,* past participle of *ateindre* 'bring to justice' (see ATTAIN); influenced in meaning by TAINT.

At·ta·lid /ˈatlˌid/ ▸*n.* a member of a Hellenistic dynasty centered on the city of Pergamum in Asia Minor and named after Attalus I (reigned 241–197 BC), which flourished in the 3rd and 2nd centuries BC.
▸*adj.* of or relating to this dynasty.

at·tar /ˈatər/ (also **ot·to** /ˈätō/) ▸*n.* a fragrant essential oil, typically made from rose petals. ▷late 17th cent.: via Persian from Arabic *'aṭir* 'fragrant.'

at·tempt /əˈtem(p)t/ ▸*v.* [*trans.*] make an effort to achieve or complete (something, typically a difficult task or action): *she attempted a comeback in 1989* | [with *infinitive*] *those who attempted to flee were captured at the border.* ■ try to climb to the top of (a mountain): *the group's next plan was to attempt Everest.* ■ *archaic* try to take (a life): *he would not have attempted the life of a friend.*
▸*n.* an act of trying to achieve something, typically one that is unsuccessful or not certain to succeed: [with *infinitive*] *an attempt to halt the bombings any **attempt at** talking politics ended in a fit of laughter* | *an abortive coup attempt.* ■ an effort to surpass a record or conquer a mountain: *we made an **attempt on** the southwest buttress.* ■ a bid to kill someone: *Karakozov made an **attempt on** the tsar's life.* ■ a thing produced as a result of trying to make or achieve something: *her first **attempt at** a letter ended up in the wastebasket.* ▷late Middle English: from Old French *attempter,* from Latin *attemptare,* from *ad-* 'to' + *temptare* 'to tempt.'

At·ten·bor·ough /ˈatnb(ə)rə/, Sir Richard (Samuel), Baron Attenborough of Richmond-upon-Thames (1923–), English movie actor, producer, and director; brother of David Attenborough (1926–). He directed *Oh! What a Lovely War* (1969), *A Bridge Too Far* (1977), *Gandhi* (Academy Award, 1982), and *Shadowlands* (1993).

at·tend /əˈtend/ ▸*v.* **1** [*trans.*] be present at (an event, meeting, or function): *the entire sales force attended the conference* | *she was unable to attend the wedding.* ■ go regularly to (an educational, religious, social, or clinical institution): *all children are required to attend school.* **2** [*intrans.*] (**attend to**) deal with: *he muttered that he had business to attend to.* ■ give practical help and care to; look after: *the severely wounded had two medics to attend to their wounds* | [*trans.*] *each of the beds in the intensive care unit is attended by a nurse.* ■ pay attention to: *Alice hadn't attended to a word of his sermon.* **3** [*trans.*] (usu. **be attended**) occur with or as a result of: *people feared that the switch to a peacetime economy would be attended by a severe slump.* ■ escort or accompany (a member of royalty or other important personage) so as to assist them; wait on: *Her Royal Highness was attended by two capable women.* ▷Middle English (in the sense 'apply one's mind, one's energies to'): from Old French *atendre,* from Latin *attendere,* from *ad-* 'to' + *tendere* 'stretch.' **—at·tend·er** /əˈtendər/ *n.*

at·tend·ance /əˈtendəns/ ▸*n.* the action or state of going regularly to or being present at a place or event: *my **attendance at** church was very irregular.* ■ the number of people present at a particular event, function, or meeting: *reports placed the attendance at 500,000.* ▷late Middle English: from Old French, from *atendre* 'give one's attention to' (see ATTEND).
▸*PHRASE* □ **in attendance** present at a function or a place. ■ accompanying a member of royalty or the aristocracy in the capacity of an assistant or servant.

at·tend·ant /əˈtendənt/ ▸*n.* **1** a person employed to provide a service to the public in a particular place: *a flight attendant* | *a gas station attendant.* ■ an assistant to an important person; a servant or courtier. **2** a person who is present at an event, meeting, or function: *he had become a regular attendant at chapel.*
▸*adj.* occurring with or as a result of; accompanying: *the sea and its attendant attractions* | *he warns against the dangers **attendant on** solitary life.* ■ (of a person or animal) accompanying another as a companion or assistant: *a pair of blind tourists with their attendant dogs.* ▷late Middle English (as an adjective): from Old French, from *atendre* 'give one's attention to' (see ATTEND).

at·tend·ee /əˌtenˈdē; ˌaten-/ ▸*n.* a person who attends a conference or other gathering.

at·ten·tion /əˈtensʜən/ ▸*n.* **1** notice taken of someone or something; the regarding of someone or something as interesting or important: *he **drew attention to** three spelling mistakes* | *you've never **paid** that much **attention** to her opinions.* ■ the mental faculty of considering or taking notice of someone or something: *he **turned his attention to** the educational system.* **2** the action of dealing with or taking special care of someone or something: *the business needed her attention* | *he failed to give the patient adequate medical attention.* ■ (**attentions**) a person's interest in someone, esp. when unwelcome or regarded as excessive: *his primary aim was to avoid the attentions of the newspapers.* ■ (**attentions**) a person's actions intended to express interest of a sexual or romantic nature in someone, sometimes when unwelcome: *she felt flattered by his attentions.* **3** *Military* a position assumed by a soldier, standing very straight with the heels together and the arms straight down the sides of the body: *the squadron **stood to attention** when we arrived* | *midshipmen standing **at attention.*** ■ [as *exclam.*] an order to assume such a position. ▷late Middle English: from Latin *attentio(n-),* from the verb *attendere* (see ATTEND). **—at·ten·tion·al** /-sʜənl/ *adj.*

at·ten·tion def·i·cit dis·or·der (also **attention deficit hyperactivity disorder**) (abbr.: **ADD** or **ADHD**) ▸*n.* any of a range of behavioral disorders occurring primarily in children, including such symptoms as poor concentration, hyperactivity, and impulsivity.

at·ten·tion span ▸*n.* the length of time for which a person is able to concentrate mentally on a particular activity.

at·ten·tive /əˈtentiv/ ▸*adj.* paying close attention to something: *never before had she had such an attentive audience* | *Congress should be more **attentive to** the interests of taxpayers.* ■ assiduously attending to the comfort or wishes of others; very polite or courteous: *the hotel has a pleasant atmosphere and attentive service.*

A

▷late Middle English: from Old French *attentif, -ive*, from *atendre* 'give one's attention to' (see ATTEND). —**at·ten·tive·ly** *adv.* —**at·ten·tive·ness** *n.*

at·ten·u·ate ▶*v.* /ə'tenyo͞o,āt/ [*trans.*] (often **be attenuated**) reduce the force, effect, or value of: *her intolerance was attenuated by a rather unexpected liberalism.* ■ reduce the amplitude of (a signal, electric current, or other oscillation). ■ [*intrans.*] (of a signal, electric current, or other oscillation) be reduced in amplitude. ■ [usu. as *adj.*] (**attenuated**) reduce the virulence of (a pathogenic organism or vaccine): *attenuated strains of rabies virus.* ■ reduce in thickness; make thin: *the trees are attenuated from being grown too close together.*
▶*adj.* /-wit; -,wāt/ *rare* reduced in force, effect, or physical thickness. ▷mid 16th cent.: from Latin *attenuat-* 'made slender,' from the verb *attenuare*, from *ad-* 'to' + *tenuare* 'make thin' (from *tenuis* 'thin'). —**at·ten·u·a·tion** /ə,tenyo͞o'āsʜən/ *n.*

at·ten·u·at·ed /ə'tenyo͞o,ātid/ ▶*adj.* unnaturally thin: *she was a drooping, attenuated figure.* ■ weakened in force or effect: *Roman influence became attenuated.*

at·ten·u·a·tor /ə'tenyo͞o,ātər/ ▶*n.* a device consisting of an arrangement of resistors that reduces the strength of a radio or audio signal.

at·test /ə'test/ ▶*v.* [*trans.*] provide or serve as clear evidence of: *his status is attested by his recent promotion* | [*intrans.*] *his numerous drawings of ships* **attest to** *his fascination with them.* ■ [*intrans.*] declare that something exists or is the case: *I can* **attest to** *his tremendous energy* | [with *clause*] *the deceased's attorney attested that he had been about to institute divorce proceedings.* ■ be a witness to; certify formally: *the witnesses must attest and sign the will in the testator's presence.* ▷early 16th cent.: from French *attester*, from Latin *attestari*, from *ad-* 'to' + *testari* 'to witness' (from *testis* 'a witness'). —**at·tes·ta·tion** /,ate'stāsʜən/ *n.*

At·tic /'atik/ ▶*adj.* of or relating to Athens or Attica, or the dialect of Greek spoken there in ancient times.
▶*n.* the dialect of Greek used by the ancient Athenians, the chief literary form of classical Greek. ▷late 16th cent.: via Latin from Greek *Attikos*.

at·tic /'atik/ ▶*n.* a space or room just below the roof of a building. ▷late 17th cent. (as an architectural term designating a small order (column and entablature) above a taller one): from French *attique*, from Latin *Atticus* 'relating to Athens or Attica.'

At·ti·ca /'atikə/ **1** a triangular promontory in eastern Greece. With the islands in the Saronic Gulf, it forms a department of Greece, of which Athens is the capital. **2** a town in western New York, the scene of a bloody 1971 prison uprising; pop. 7,383.

at·ti·cism /'atə,sizəm/ (often **At·ti·cism**) ▶*n.* a word or form characteristic of Attic Greek. ▷late 16th cent.: from Greek *Attikismos*, from *Attikos* (see ATTIC). From the original sense of 'the Greek language as used by the Athenians,' arose the meaning 'refined, elegant Greek,' later extended to language in general.

At·ti·la /ə'tilə; 'atl-ə/ (406–453), king of the Huns 434–453. He ravaged vast areas between the Rhine and the Caspian Sea before being defeated by the joint forces of the Roman army and the Visigoths at Châlons in 451.

at·tire /ə'tī(ə)r/ ▶*n.* clothes, esp. fine or formal ones: *holiday attire.*
▶*v.* (**be attired**) be dressed in clothes of a specified kind: *Donna was* **attired in** *an elaborate evening gown* | [as *adj.*, with *submodifier*] (**attired**) *the outrageously attired rock star.* ▷Middle English: from Old French *atirier, atirer* 'equip,' from *a tire* 'in order,' of unknown origin.

At·tis /'atis/ *Anatolian Mythology* the youthful consort of Cybele. His death and resurrection were associated with the spring festival.

at·ti·tude /'ati,t(y)o͞od/ ▶*n.* a settled way of thinking or feeling about someone or something, typically one that is reflected in a person's behavior: *she took a tough attitude toward other people's indulgences* | *being competitive is* **an attitude of mind** | *differences in attitude were apparent between ethnic groups.* ■ a position of the body proper to or implying an action or mental state: *the boy was standing in an* **attitude of** *despair, his chin sunk on his chest.* ■ *informal* truculent or uncooperative behavior; a resentful or antagonistic manner: *I asked the waiter for a clean fork, and all I got was attitude.* ■ *informal* individuality and self-confidence as manifested by behavior or appearance; style: *she snapped her fingers* **with attitude.** ■ the orientation of an aircraft or spacecraft, relative to the direction of travel. ■ *Ballet* a position in which one leg is lifted behind with the knee bent at right angles and turned out, and the corresponding arm is raised above the head, the other extended to the side. ▷late 17th cent. (denoting the placing or posture of a figure in art): from French, from Italian *attitudine* 'fitness, posture,' from late Latin *aptitudo*, from *aptus* 'fit.' —**at·ti·tu·di·nal** /,ati't(y)o͞odn-əl/ *adj.*

at·ti·tu·di·nize /,ati't(y)o͞odn,īz/ ▶*v.* [*intrans.*] adopt or express a particular attitude or attitudes, typically just for effect. ▷late 16th cent.: from Italian *attitudine* (see ATTITUDE) + -IZE. —**at·ti·tu·di·niz·er** *n.*

At·tle·boro /'atl,bərō; -,bərə; -,bə-rō; ,bə-rə/ an industrial city in southeastern Massachusetts, northeast of Providence in Rhode Island; pop. 38,383.

Att·lee /'atlē/, Clement Richard, 1st Earl Attlee (1883–1967), British statesman; Labour prime minister 1945–51. His term saw the creation of the modern welfare state and the nationalization of major industries.

attn. ▶*abbr.* (on an envelope, packet, package, or cover letter) attention (i.e., for the attention of): *attn.: Harold Carter.*

atto- ▶*comb. form Mathematics* (used in units of measurement) denoting a factor of 10^{-18} : *attowatt.* ▷from Danish or Norwegian *atten* 'eighteen.'

at·torn /ə'tərn/ ▶*v.* [*intrans.*] *Law* formally make or acknowledge a transfer of something. ■ [*trans.*] *archaic* transfer (something) to someone else. ▷Middle English (in the senses 'turn, change, transform'): from Old French *atorner* 'appoint, assign,' from *a-* (from Latin *ad* 'to, at') + *torner* 'to turn.'
▶PHRASE □ **attorn tenant** *Law* formally make or acknowledge a transfer of tenancy.

at·tor·ney /ə'tərnē/ ▶*n.* (*pl.* **-neys**) **1** a person appointed to act for another in business or legal matters. **2** a lawyer. ▷Middle English: from Old French *atorne*, past participle of *atorner* 'assign,' from *a* 'toward' + *torner* 'turn.' —**at·tor·ney·ship** /-,sʜip/ *n.*

at·tor·ney-at-law ▶*n.* a lawyer who is qualified to represent a client in court.

at·tor·ney gen·er·al (abbr.: **AG** or **Atty. Gen.**) ▶*n.* (*pl.* **at·tor·neys gen·er·al**) the principal legal officer who represents a country or a state in legal proceedings and gives legal advice to the government. ■ the head of the U.S. Department of Justice.

at·tract /ə'trakt/ ▶*v.* [*trans.*] cause to come to a place or participate in a venture by offering something of interest, favorable conditions, or opportunities: *a campaign to attract more visitors to West Virginia* | *he hoped this strategy would attract foreign investment by multinationals.* ■ evoke (a specified reaction): *I did not want to attract attention* | *his criticism of the government attracted widespread support.* ■ cause (someone) to have a liking for or interest in something: *I was* **attracted to** *the idea of working for a ballet company.* ■ cause (someone) to have a sexual or romantic interest in someone: *it was her beauty that attracted him.* ■ exert a force on (an object) that is directed toward the source of the force: *the negatively charged ions attract particles of dust.* ▷late Middle English: from Latin *attract-* 'drawn near,' from the verb *attrahere*, from *ad-* 'to' + *trahere* 'draw.' —**at·trac·tor** /-tər/ *n.*

at·tract·ant /ə'traktənt/ ▶*n.* a substance that attracts something (esp. animals): *a sex attractant given off by female moths to attract a mate.*
▶*adj.* attracting.

at·trac·tion /ə'traksʜən/ ▶*n.* the action or power of evoking interest, pleasure, or liking for someone or something: *she has romantic ideas about sexual attraction* | *the timeless attraction of a good tune.* ■ a quality or feature of something or someone that evokes interest, liking, or desire: *this reform has many* **attractions for** *those on the left* | *the main attraction of Peking duck is the crackling texture of its skin.* ■ a thing or place that draws visitors by providing something of interest or pleasure: *the church is the town's main tourist attraction.* ■ *Physics* a force under the influence of which objects tend to move toward each other: *gravitational attraction.* ■ *Grammar* the influence exerted by one word on another that causes it to change to an incorrect form, e.g., *the wages of sin is* (for *are*) *death.* ▷late Middle English (denoting the action of a poultice in drawing matter from the tissues): from Latin *attractio(n-)*, from the verb *attrahere* (see ATTRACT).

at·trac·tive /ə'traktiv/ ▶*adj.* (of a thing) pleasing or appealing to the senses: *an attractive home* | *foliage can be as attractive as flowers.* See note at PLEASANT. ■ (of a person) appealing to look at; sexually alluring: *an attractive, charismatic man.* ■ (of a thing) having beneficial qualities or features that induce someone to accept what is being offered: *the site is close to the high-rent district, which should make it* **attractive to** *developers.* ■ of or relating to attraction between physical objects. ▷late Middle English (in the sense 'absorbent'): from French *attractif, -ive*, from late Latin *attractivus*, from the verb *attrahere* (see ATTRACT). —**at·trac·tive·ly** *adv.* —**at·trac·tive·ness** *n.*

at·trib·ute ▶*v.* /ə'tri,byo͞ot/ [*trans.*] (**attribute something to**) regard something as being caused by (someone or something): *he attributed the firm's success to the efforts of the managing director* | *the bombing was attributed to the IRA.* ■ ascribe a work or remark to (a particular author, artist, or speaker): *the building was attributed to Frank Lloyd Wright.* ■ regard a quality or feature as characteristic of or possessed by (someone or something): *ancient peoples attributed magic properties to certain stones.*
▶*n.* (**at·tri·bute**) /'atrə,byo͞ot/ a quality or feature regarded as a characteristic or inherent part of someone or something: *flexibility and mobility are the key attributes of our army.* ■ a material object recognized as symbolic of a person, esp. a conventional object used in art to identify a saint or mythical figure. See note at EMBLEM. ■ *Grammar* an attributive adjective or noun. ■ *Statistics* a real property that a statistical analysis is attempting to describe. ▷late 15th cent.: as a noun from Old French *attribut*, and as a verb from Latin *attribut-* 'allotted,' both from the verb *attribuere*, from *ad-* 'to' + *tribuere* 'assign.' —**at·trib·ut·a·ble** /ə'tribyətəbəl/ *adj.* —**at·tri·bu·tion** /,atrə'byo͞osʜən/ *n.*

at·tri·bu·tion the·o·ry /,atrə'byo͞osʜən/ ▶*n. Psychology* a theory that supposes that one attempts to understand the behavior of others by attributing feelings, beliefs, and intentions to them.

at·trib·u·tive /ə'tribyətiv/ ▶*adj. Grammar* (of an adjective or noun) preceding the word it qualifies or modifies and expressing an attribute, as *old* in *the old dog* (but not in *the dog is old*) and *expiration* in *expiration date* (but not in *date of expiration*). Often contrasted with PREDICATIVE. ▷mid 18th cent. (as a noun in the sense 'a word expressing an attribute'): from French *attributif, -ive*, from *attribut* 'an attribute,' from Latin *attribuere* 'add to' (see ATTRIBUTE). —**at·trib·u·tive·ly** *adv.*

at·trit /ə'trit/ ▶*v.* (**-trit·ted, -trit·ting**) [*trans.*] *informal* wear down (an opponent or enemy) by sustained action: *his defense was designed to attrit us.* ▷1950s: back-formation from ATTRITION.

at·tri·tion /ə'trisʜən/ ▶*n.* **1** the action or process of gradually reducing the strength or effectiveness of someone or something through sustained attack or pressure: *the council is trying to wear down the opposition by attrition* | *the squadron suffered severe attrition of its bombers.* ■ the gradual reduction of a workforce by employees' leaving and not being replaced rather than by their being laid off: *with so few retirements since March, the year's attrition was insignificant.* ■ wearing away by friction; abrasion: *the skull shows attrition of the edges of the teeth.* **2** (in scholastic theology) sorrow, but not contrition, for sin. ▷late Middle English (sense 2): from late Latin *attritio(n-)*, from *atterere* 'to rub.' —**at·tri·tion·al** /-sʜənl/ *adj.*

At·tu /'a,to͞o/ an island in southwestern Alaska, the westernmost of the Aleutian Islands. During World War II, it was occupied by Japanese forces.

At·tucks /'atəks/, Crispus (c.1723–70), American revolutionary. Believed to have been either an escaped or freed slave, he was one of five colonists killed by British soldiers in the Boston Massacre on March 5, 1770.

at·tune /ə't(y)o͞on/ ▶*v.* [*trans.*] (usu. **be attuned**) make receptive or aware: *a society more* **attuned to** *consumerism than ideology* | [as *adj.*] (**attuned**) *the department is very attuned politically.* ■ accustom or acclimatize: *students are not* **attuned to** *making decisions.* ■ [*intrans.*] become receptive to or aware of: *a conscious attempt to* **attune to** *the wider audience.* ■ make harmonious: *the interests of East and West are now closely attuned.* ▷late 16th cent.: from AT- + TUNE.

Atty. ▶*abbr.* Attorney.

Atty. Gen. ▶*abbr.* Attorney General.

ATV ▶*abbr.* all-terrain vehicle.

At·wa·ter /'at,wôtər; -,wätər/ a city in central California; pop. 22,282.

At·wood /'at,wo͝od/, Margaret (Eleanor) (1939–), Canadian novelist, poet, critic, and short-story writer. Notable works: *The Edible Woman* (1969), *The Handmaid's Tale* (1985), *Cat's Eye* (1989), and *Alias Grace* (1996).

a·typ·i·cal /ā'tipikəl/ ▶*adj.* not representative of a type, group, or class: *a sample of people who are rather atypical of the target audience* | *there were somewhat atypical results in May and November.* —**a·typ·i·cal·ly** *adv.*

AU ▶*abbr.* ■ ångström unit(s). ■ (also **a.u.**) astronomical unit(s).

Au ▸*symbol* the chemical element gold. ▷from Latin *aurum.*

au·bade /ō'bäd/ ▸*n.* a poem or piece of music appropriate to the dawn or early morning. ▷late 17th cent.: from French, from Spanish *albada,* from *alba* 'dawn.'

au·berge /ō'berzн/ ▸*n.* an inn in French-speaking countries. ▷French, from Provençal *alberga* 'lodging.'

au·ber·gine /'ōbər,zнēn/ ▸*n. chiefly Brit.* another term for EGGPLANT. ■ a dark purple color like that of eggplant.

Au·brey /'ôbrē/, John (1626–97), English antiquarian and author. He is noted for *Brief Lives,* a collection of biographies of eminent people.

au·brie·tia /ô'brēsн(ē)ə/ (also **au·bre·ti·a**) ▸*n.* a dwarf evergreen Eurasian trailing plant with dense masses of foliage and purple, pink, or white flowers. It is widely cultivated in rock gardens and on banks. • *Aubrieta deltoidea,* family Brassicaceae. ▷early 19th cent.: modern Latin, named after Claude *Aubriet* (1668–1743), French botanist. The name of the genus was originally, and remains, *Aubrieta,* but in ordinary speech the form ending in *-tia* has become normal.

Au·burn /'ôbərn/ **1** an academic city in eastern Alabama, home to Auburn University; pop. 42,987. **2** an industrial city in southwestern Maine, on the Androscoggin River, across from Lewiston; pop. 23,203. **3** an industrial and commercial city in west central New York, on Owasco Lake; pop. 31,258. **4** an industrial city in west central Washington; pop. 33,102.

au·burn /'ôbərn/ ▸*adj.* (chiefly of a person's hair) of a reddish-brown color.
▸*n.* a reddish-brown color. ▷late Middle English: from Old French *auborne, alborne,* from Latin *alburnus* 'whitish,' from *albus* 'white.' The original sense was 'yellowish white,' but the word became associated with *brown* because in the 16th and 17th centuries it was often written *abrune* or *abroun.*

Au·bus·son /'ōbə,sôn/ ▸*n.* a kind of French tapestry or carpet, principally from the 18th century. ▷from *Aubusson,* the name of a town in central France where the tapestries were made.

AUC ▸*abbr.* used to indicate a date reckoned from 753 BC, the year of the foundation of Rome: *765* AUC. ▷from Latin *ab urbe condita* 'from the foundation of the city,' also *anno urbis conditae* 'in the year of the founding of the city.'

Au·chin·closs /'ôkən,kläs/, Louis Stanton (1917–), U.S. lawyer and author; early pseudonym *Andrew Lee.* His novels often depict life among the elite of New York City.

Auck·land /'ôklənd/ the largest city and chief seaport of New Zealand, on North Island; pop. 309,400. It was the capital of New Zealand until 1865.

au cou·rant /,ō 'ko͝orän/ ▸*adj.* aware of what is going on; well informed: *they were* ***au courant with*** *the literary scene.* ■ fashionable: *light, low-fat, au courant recipes.* ▷mid 18th cent.: from French, literally 'in the (regular) course.'

auc·tion /'ôksнən/ ▸*n.* a public sale in which goods or property are sold to the highest bidder: *the books are expected to fetch a six-figure sum at tomorrow's auction* | [as *adj.*] *an auction sale.* ■ the action or process of selling something in this way: *the Ferrari sold* ***at auction*** *for $10 million.* ■ *Bridge* the part of the play in which players bid to decide the contract in which the hand shall be played.
▸*v.* [*trans.*] (often **be auctioned**) sell or offer for sale at an auction: *his collection of vintage cars is to be* ***auctioned off*** *tomorrow.* ▷late 16th cent.: from Latin *auction-* 'increase, auction,' from the verb *augere* 'to increase.'
▸PHRASE □ **on the auction block** see **on the block** at BLOCK.

auc·tion bridge ▸*n.* an obsolete form of the card game bridge, in which all tricks won count toward the game whether bid or not.

auc·tion·eer /,ôksнə'ni(ə)r/ ▸*n.* a person who conducts auctions by accepting bids and declaring goods sold. —**auc·tion·eer·ing** *n.*

auc·tion house ▸*n.* a company that runs auctions.

au·da·cious /ô'dāsнəs/ ▸*adj.* **1** showing a willingness to take surprisingly bold risks: *a series of audacious takeovers.* See note at BOLD. **2** showing an impudent lack of respect: *an audacious remark.* ▷mid 16th cent.: from Latin *audax, audac-* 'bold' (from *audere* 'dare') + -IOUS. —**au·da·cious·ly** *adv.* —**au·da·cious·ness** *n.*

au·dac·i·ty /ô'dasitē/ ▸*n.* **1** the willingness to take bold risks: *her audacity came in handy during our most recent emergency.* See note at TEMERITY. **2** rude or disrespectful behavior; impudence: *she* ***had the audacity to*** *pick up the receiver and ask me to hang up.* ▷late Middle English: from medieval Latin *audacitas,* from *audax, audac-* 'bold' (see AUDACIOUS).

Au·den /'ôdn/, W. H. (1907–73), British poet; full name *Wystan Hugh Auden.* He was a leading left-wing poet and was awarded the Pulitzer Prize for *The Age of Anxiety* (1947).

Audh variant spelling of OUDH.

au·di·al /'ôdēəl/ ▸*adj.* relating to or perceived through the sense of hearing. ▷late 20th cent.: formed irregularly from Latin *audire* 'hear' (compare with AUDILE), on the pattern of *visual.*

au·di·ble /'ôdəbəl/ ▸*adj.* able to be heard: *ultrasound is audible to dogs.*
▸*n. Football* a change in the offensive play called by the quarterback at the line of scrimmage. ▷late 15th cent.: from late Latin *audibilis,* from *audire* 'hear.' —**au·di·bil·i·ty** /,ôdə'bilitē/ *n.* —**au·di·bly** /-blē/ *adv.*

au·di·ence /'ôdēəns/ ▸*n.* **1** the assembled spectators or listeners at a public event, such as a play, movie, concert, or meeting: *the orchestra was given an enthusiastic ovation from the audience.* ■ the people who watch or listen to a television or radio program: *the program attracted an audience of almost twenty million.* ■ the readership of a book, magazine, or newspaper: *the newspaper has a sophisticated audience.* ■ the people giving or likely to give attention to something: *there will always be an audience for romantic literature.* **2** a formal interview with a person in authority: *he demanded an audience with the pope.* **3** *archaic* formal hearing. ▷late Middle English: from Old French, from Latin *audientia,* from *audire* 'hear.'

au·dile /'ô,dīl/ ▸*adj.* another term for AUDITORY. ▷late 19th cent.: formed from Latin *audire* 'hear,' on the pattern of *tactile.*

au·di·o /'ôdē,ō/ ▸*n.* [usu. as *adj.*] sound, esp. when recorded, transmitted, or reproduced: *audio equipment* | *the machine can retrieve and play audio from a CD-ROM.* ▷1930s: independent usage of AUDIO-.

audio- ▸*comb. form* relating to hearing or sound: *audiometer* | *audio-visual.* ▷from Latin *audire* 'hear.'

Au·di·o-An·i·ma·tron·ics /,anəmə'träniks/ ▸*plural n.* trademark for ANIMATRONICS. —**Au·di·o-An·i·ma·tron·ic** *adj.*

au·di·o·book /'ôdē-ō,bo͝ok/ (also **au·di·o book**) ▸*n.* an audiocassette recording of a reading of a book, typically a novel.

au·di·o·cas·sette /,ôdē-ōkə'set/ ▸*n.* a cassette of audiotape.

au·di·o fre·quen·cy ▸*n.* a frequency of oscillation capable of being perceived by the human ear, generally between 20 and 20,000 Hz.

au·di·o·gram /'ôdēə,gram/ ▸*n.* a graphic record produced by audiometry.

au·di·ol·o·gy /,ôdē'äləjē/ ▸*n.* the branch of science and medicine concerned with the sense of hearing. —**au·di·o·log·i·cal** /-ə'läjikəl/ *adj.* —**au·di·ol·o·gist** /-jist/ *n.*

au·di·om·e·try /,ôdē'ämitrē/ ▸*n.* measurement of the range and sensitivity of a person's sense of hearing. —**au·di·om·e·ter** /-itər/ *n.* —**au·di·o·met·ric** /-ə'metrik/ *adj.*

au·di·o·phile /'ôdē-ō,fīl/ ▸*n.* a hi-fi enthusiast.

au·di·o·tape /'ôdē-ō,tāp/ ▸*n.* magnetic tape on which sound can be recorded. ■ a length of this, typically in the form of a cassette.
▸*v.* [*trans.*] record (sound) on tape: *each interview was audiotaped and transcribed.*

au·di·o·vis·u·al /,ôdē-ō'vizнo͞oəl/ ▸*adj.* using both sight and sound, typically in the form of slides or video and recorded speech or music: *audiovisual presentations.*

au·dit /'ôdit/ ▸*n.* an official inspection of an individual's or organization's accounts, typically by an independent body. ■ a systematic review or assessment of something: *a complete audit of flora and fauna at the site.*
▸*v.* (**-dit·ed, -dit·ing**) [*trans.*] **1** conduct an official financial examination of (an individual's or organization's accounts): *companies must have their accounts audited.* ■ conduct a systematic review of: *auditing obstetrical and neonatal care.* **2** attend (a class) informally, not for academic credit. ▷late Middle English: from Latin *auditus* 'hearing,' from *audire* 'hear,' in medieval Latin *auditus (compoti)* 'audit (of an account),' an audit originally being presented orally.

au·di·tion /ô'disнən/ ▸*n.* an interview for a particular role or job as a singer, actor, dancer, or musician, consisting of a practical demonstration of the candidate's suitability and skill.
▸*v.* [*intrans.*] perform an audition: *he was* ***auditioning for*** *the lead role in the play.* ■ [*trans.*] assess the suitability of (someone) for a role by means of an audition: *she was* ***auditioning*** *people* ***for*** *her new series.* ▷late 16th cent. (in the sense 'power of hearing or listening'): from Latin *auditio(n-),* from *audire* 'hear.' The current sense of the noun dates from the late 19th cent.

au·di·tive /'ôditiv/ ▸*adj.* another term for AUDITORY.

au·di·tor /'ôditər/ ▸*n.* **1** a person who conducts an audit. **2** a listener: *so low was Jim's voice that his auditors had to give it close attention.* ■ a person who attends a class informally without working for academic credit. ▷Middle English: from Old French *auditeur,* from Latin *auditor,* from *audire* 'to hear.' —**au·di·to·ri·al** /,ôdə'tôrēəl/ *adj.*

au·di·to·ri·um /,ôdi'tôrēəm/ ▸*n.* (*pl.* **-to·ri·ums** or **-to·ri·a** /-'tôrēə/) **1** the part of a theater, concert hall, or other public building in which the audience sits. **2** a large building or hall used for public gatherings, typically concerts or sports events. ■ a large room for such gatherings, esp. in a school. ▷early 17th cent. (originally in the general sense 'a place for hearing'): from Latin, neuter of *auditorius* 'relating to hearing' (see AUDITORY).

au·di·to·ry /'ôdi,tôrē/ ▸*adj.* of or relating to the sense of hearing: *the auditory nerves* | *teaching methods use both visual and auditory stimulation.* ▷late 16th cent.: from Latin *auditorius,* from *audire* 'hear.'

Au·du·bon /'ôdə,bän/, John James (1785–1851), U.S. naturalist and artist. His most notable work is *The Birds of America* (1827–38), in which he portrayed even the largest birds life-size and painted them in action.

Au·er·bach[1] /'ou-ər,bäk; -,bäкн/, Frank (1931–), British painter, born in Germany.

Au·er·bach[2] /'ou-ər,bak; -,bäk/, Red (1917–), U.S. basketball coach; full name *Arnold Jacob Auerbach.* As coach of the Boston Celtics 1950–66, he led the team to nine National Basketball Association (NBA) championships 1957, 1959–66. Basketball Hall of Fame (1968).

au fait /,ō 'fe/ ▸*adj.* (**au fait with**) having a good or detailed knowledge of something: *you should* ***be*** *reasonably* ***au fait with*** *the company and its products.* ▷mid 18th cent.: from French, literally 'to the fact, to the point.'

au fond /,ō 'fôɴ/ ▸*adv.* in essence: *she might be,* au fond, *quite a pleasant woman.* ▷late 18th cent.: French, literally 'at bottom.'

Aug. ▸*abbr.* August.

Au·ge·an /ô'jēən/ ▸*adj.* of or relating to Augeas: *the Augean stables.* ■ (of a task or problem) requiring so much effort to complete or solve as to seem impossible: *Augean amounts of debris to clear.*

Au·ge·as /ô'jēəs/ *Greek Mythology* a legendary king whose vast stables had never been cleaned. Hercules cleaned them in a day by diverting the Alpheus River to flow through them.

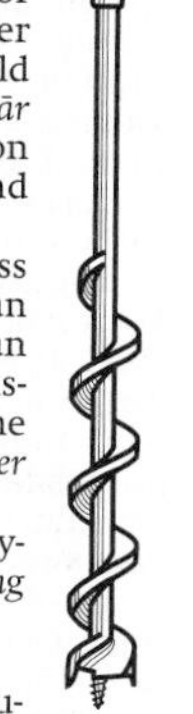
auger

au·ger /'ôgər/ ▸*n.* a tool with a helical bit for boring holes in wood. ■ a similar larger tool for boring holes in the ground. ▷Old English *nafogār,* from *nafu* (see NAVE[2]) + *gār* 'piercer.' The *n* was lost by wrong division of *a nauger;* compare with ADDER and APRON.

Au·ger ef·fect /ō'zнā/ ▸*n. Physics* a process in which an electron in an outer shell of an atom makes a transition to a vacancy in an inner shell. The energy gained is transferred to an electron that escapes from the atom. ▷1930s: named after Pierre V. *Auger* (1899-1944), French physicist.

aught[1] /ôt/ (also **ought**) *archaic* ▸*pron.* anything at all: *know you aught of this fellow, young sir?* ▷Old English *āwiht* (see AYE[2], WIGHT).

aught[2] ▸*n.* the digit 0; zero.

au·gite /'ô,jīt/ ▸*n.* a dark green or black aluminosilicate mineral of the pyroxene group. It occurs in many igneous rocks, including basalt, gabbro, and diabase. ▷early 19th cent.: from Latin *augites,* denoting a precious stone (probably turquoise), from Greek *augitēs,* from *augē* 'luster.'

aug·ment ▸*v.* /ôg'ment/ [*trans.*] make (something)

Pronunciation Key ə ago; ər over; 'ə or ,ə up; 'ər or ,ər fur; a hat; ā rate; ä car; cн chew; e let; ē see; e(ə)r air; i fit; ī by; i(ə)r ear; ɴɢ sing; ō go; ô for; oi boy; o͝o good; o͞o goo; ou out; sн she; тн thin; <u>тн</u> then; (h)w why; zн vision

A

greater by adding to it; increase: *he augmented his summer income by painting houses.*
▶*n.* /ˈôgˌment; -mənt/ *Linguistics* a vowel prefixed to past tenses of verbs in Greek and other Indo-European languages. ▷late Middle English: from Old French *augmenter* (verb), *augment* (noun), or late Latin *augmentare*, from Latin *augere* 'to increase.'

aug·men·ta·tion /ˌôgmenˈtāSHən/ ▶*n.* the action or process of making or becoming greater in size or amount: *the augmentation of the curriculum with new subjects.* ■ *Music* the lengthening of the time values of notes in a melodic part. ■ *Heraldry* an addition to a coat of arms granted as a mark of special honor. ▷late Middle English: from late Latin *augmentatio(n-)*, from the verb *augmentare* (see **AUGMENT**).

aug·ment·a·tive /ôgˈmentətiv/ ▶*adj. Grammar* (of an affix or derived word) reinforcing the idea of the original word, esp. by meaning 'a large —,' as with the Italian suffix *-one* in *borrone* 'ravine,' compared with *borro* 'ditch.' ▷late Middle English (in the sense 'having a tendency to increase'): from Old French *augmentatif, -ive* or medieval Latin *augmentativus*, from the verb *augmentare* (see **AUGMENT**).

aug·ment·ed /ôgˈmentid/ ▶*adj.* **1** having been made greater in size or value: *augmented pensions for those retiring at 65.* **2** *Music* denoting or containing an interval that is one semitone greater than the corresponding major or perfect interval: *augmented fourths.*

au grat·in /ˌō ˈgrätn; ˈgratn; graˈtaN/ ▶*adj.* [*predic.*] sprinkled with breadcrumbs or grated cheese, or both, and browned: *lentils and mushrooms au gratin.* ▷early 19th cent.: French, literally 'by grating.'

Augs·burg /ˈôgzˌbərg; ˈouksˌbŏŏrk/ a city in southern Germany, in Bavaria; pop. 259,880.

Augs·burg Con·fes·sion a statement of the Lutheran position, drawn up mainly by Melanchthon and approved by Luther before being presented to the Emperor Charles V at Augsburg on June 25, 1530.

au·gur /ˈôgər/ ▶*v.* [*intrans.*] (**augur well/badly/ill**) (of an event or circumstance) portend a good or bad outcome: *the end of the Cold War seemed to augur well | the return to the gold standard augured badly for industry.* See note at **PREDICT**. ■ [*trans.*] portend or bode (a specified outcome): *they feared that these happenings augured a neo-Nazi revival.* ■ [*trans.*] (*archaic*) foresee or predict.
▶*n. historical* (in ancient Rome) a religious official who observed natural signs, esp. the behavior of birds, interpreting these as an indication of divine approval or disapproval of a proposed action. ▷late Middle English (as a noun): from Latin, 'diviner.' **—au·gu·ral** /ˈôgyərəl/ *adj.* (*archaic*).

au·gu·ry /ˈôgyərē/ ▶*n.* (*pl.* **-ries**) a sign of what will happen in the future; an omen: *they heard the sound as an augury of death.* See note at **SIGN**. ■ the work of an augur; the interpretation of omens. ▷late Middle English (in the sense 'divination'): from Old French *augurie* or Latin *augurium* 'interpretation of omens,' from *augur* (see **AUGUR**).

Au·gust /ˈôgəst/ ▶*n.* the eighth month of the year, in the northern hemisphere usually considered the last month of summer: *the sultry haze of late August |* [as *adj.*] *an August cold snap.* ▷Old English, from Latin *augustus* 'consecrated, venerable'; named after **AUGUSTUS** Caesar, the first Roman emperor.

au·gust /ôˈgəst/ ▶*adj.* respected and impressive: *she was in august company.* ▷mid 17th cent.: from French *auguste* or Latin *augustus* 'consecrated, venerable.' **—au·gust·ly** *adv.*

Au·gus·ta /əˈgəstə/ **1** a resort in eastern Georgia; pop. 44,640. **2** the capital of Maine, in the southwestern part of the state, on the Kennebec River; pop. 18,560.

Au·gus·tan /ôˈgəstən/ ▶*adj.* connected with or occurring during the reign of the Roman emperor Augustus. ■ relating to or denoting Latin literature of the reign of Augustus, including the works of Virgil, Horace, Ovid, and Livy. ■ relating to or denoting 17th- and 18th-century English literature of a style considered refined and classical, including the works of Pope, Addison, and Swift.
▶*n.* a writer of the (Latin or English) Augustan age. ▷from Latin *Augustanus* 'relating to Augustus' (see **AUGUSTUS**).

Au·gus·tine /ˈôgəˌstēn; ôˈgəstin/ ▶*n.* an Augustinian friar. ▷late Middle English: from Old French *augustin*, from Latin *Augustinus* 'Augustine' (see **AUGUSTINIAN**).

Au·gus·tine, St.[1] /ˈôgəˌstēn; əˈgəstən/ (died *c.*604), Italian churchman; known as **St. Augustine of Canterbury**. Sent from Rome by Pope Gregory the Great, he founded a monastery at Canterbury and became its first archbishop. Feast day, May 26.

Au·gus·tine, St.[2] (354–430), doctor of the Church; known as **St. Augustine of Hippo**. He became bishop of Hippo in North Africa in 396. His writings, such as *Confessions* (400) and *City of God* (412–427), dominated subsequent Western theology. Feast day, August 28.

Au·gus·tin·i·an /ˌôgəˈstinēən/ ▶*adj.* **1** of or relating to St. Augustine of Hippo or his theological doctrines. **2** of or relating to a religious order observing a rule derived from St. Augustine's writings.
▶*n.* **1** a member of an Augustinian order. **2** an adherent of the doctrines of St. Augustine.

Au·gus·tus /əˈgəstəs/ (63 BC–AD 14), the first Roman emperor; born *Gaius Octavianus*; also called **Octavian**. He was adopted in the will of his great-uncle Julius Caesar and gained supreme power by his defeat of Antony in 31 BC. In 27 BC he was given the title Augustus ("venerable") and became in effect emperor.

au jus /ō ˈZHŏŏs; ˈZHY/ ▶*adj.* (of meat) with its own natural juices from cooking. ▷French 'with the juice.'

auk /ôk/ ▶*n.* a short-winged diving seabird found in northern oceans, typically with a black head and back and white underparts. • Family Alcidae (the **auk family**), which comprises the guillemots, murres, razorbills, puffins, and their relatives. See also **GREAT AUK, DOVEKIE**. ▷late 17th cent.: from Old Norse *álka* 'razorbill.'

auk·let /ˈôklit/ ▶*n.* a small stubby auk found in the North Pacific, typically with gray underparts. • *Aethia* and three other genera, family Alcidae: several species.

auld /ôld/ ▶*adj.* Scottish form of **OLD**. ▷Old English *ald*, Anglian form of **OLD**.

auld lang syne /ôld laNG ˈzīn/ ▶*n.* times long past. ▷late 18th cent.: Scots (see **AULD, LANG SYNE**). The phrase was popularized as the title and refrain of a song by Robert Burns (1788).
▶*PHRASE* □ **for auld lang syne** for old times' sake.

aum·bry /ˈambrē/ ▶*n.* variant spelling of **AMBRY**.

au na·tu·rel /ˌō ˌnaCHəˈrel/ ▶*adj.* & *adv.* with no elaborate treatment, dressing, or preparation: [as *adv.*] *I wear my hair au naturel these days |* [as *adj.*] *the cheese is delicious whether au naturel or seasoned.* ■ (humorous) naked. ▷early 19th cent.: French, literally 'in the natural (state).'

Aung San /ˈouNG ˈsän/ (1914–47), Burmese nationalist leader. As leader of the Council of Ministers, he negotiated a promise of self-government from the British shortly before his assassination.

Aung San Suu Kyi /ˈouNG ˈsän ˈsŏŏ ˈCHē/ (1945–), Burmese political leader, daughter of Aung San and leader of the National League for Democracy (NLD) 1988– . She was kept under house arrest 1989–95, and the military government refused to recognize her party's victory in the 1990 elections. Nobel Peace Prize (1991). She was again placed under house arrest in 2003.

San Suu Kyi Aung

aunt /ant; änt/ ▶*n.* the sister of one's father or mother or the wife of one's uncle. ■ *informal* an unrelated older woman friend, esp. of a child. ▷Middle English: from Old French *ante*, from Latin *amita*.

aunt·ie /ˈantē; ˈän-/ (also **aunt·y**) ▶*n.* (*pl.* **-ies**) informal term for **AUNT**.

Aunt Sal·ly /ˌant ˈsalē; ˌänt/ ▶*n.* (*pl.* **Aunt Sal·lies**) a game played in some parts of Britain in which players throw sticks or balls at a wooden dummy. ■ a dummy used in this game. ■ *figurative* a person or thing that is subjected to much criticism, esp. one set up as an easy target for it.

au pair /ˌō ˈpe(ə)r/ ▶*n.* a young foreign person, typically a woman, who helps with housework or child care in exchange for room and board. ▷late 19th cent.: from French, literally 'on equal terms.' The phrase was originally adjectival, describing an arrangement between two parties paid for by the exchange of mutual services; the noun usage dates from the 1960s.

au·ra /ˈôrə/ ▶*n.* (*pl.* **au·ras**) [usu. in *sing.*] the distinctive atmosphere or quality that seems to surround and be generated by a person, thing, or place: *the ceremony retains an aura of mystery.* ■ a supposed emanation surrounding the body of a living creature, viewed by mystics, spiritualists, and some practitioners of complementary medicine as the essence of the individual, and allegedly discernible by people with special sensibilities. ■ any invisible emanation, esp. a scent or odor: *there was a faint aura of disinfectant.* ■ *Medicine* (*pl.* also **au·rae** /ˈôrē/) a warning sensation experienced before an attack of epilepsy or migraine. ▷late Middle English (originally denoting a gentle breeze): via Latin from Greek, 'breeze, breath.' Current senses date from the 18th cent.

au·ral /ˈôrəl/ ▶*adj.* of or relating to the ear or the sense of hearing: *aural anatomy | information held in written, aural, or database form.* ▷mid 19th cent.: from Latin *auris* 'ear' + **-AL**. **—au·ral·ly** *adv.*

USAGE The words **aural** and **oral** have the same pronunciation in standard English, which is sometimes a source of confusion. However, alternative pronunciations for **aural**, such as /ˈourəl/ (the first syllable rhyming with *cow*), have not yet become standard.

Au·rang·zeb /ˌôrəNGˈzeb/ (1618–1707), Mogul emperor of Hindustan 1658–1707, who increased the Mogul empire to its greatest extent.

au·rar /ˈouˌrär; ˈoi-/ ▶*n.* plural form of **EYRIR**.

au·re·ate /ˈôrē-it; -ˌāt/ ▶*adj.* denoting, made of, or having the color of gold. ■ (of language) highly ornamented or elaborate. ▷late Middle English: from late Latin *aureatus*, from Latin *aureus* 'golden,' from *aurum* 'gold.'

Au·re·li·an /ôˈrēlēən/ (*c.*215–275), Roman emperor 270–275; Latin name *Lucius Domitius Aurelianus*.

Au·re·li·us /ôˈrēlēəs/, Marcus (121–80), Roman emperor 161–180; full name *Caesar Marcus Aurelius Antoninus Augustus*. He was occupied for much of his reign with wars against invading Germanic tribes. His *Meditations* are evidence of his philosophical interest.

au·re·ole /ˈôrēˌōl/ (also **au·re·o·la** /ôˈrēələ/) ▶*n.* a circle of light or brightness surrounding something, esp. as depicted in art around the head or body of a person represented as holy. ■ another term for **CORONA**[1] (sense 1, of the sun or moon). ■ another term for **AREOLA**. ■ *Geology* the zone of metamorphosed rock surrounding an igneous intrusion. ▷Middle English: from Old French *aureole*, from Latin *aureola* (*corona*) 'golden (crown),' feminine of *aureolus* (diminutive of *aureus*, from *aurum* 'gold').

au·re·us /ˈôrēəs/ ▶*n.* (*pl.* **au·re·i** /ˈôrēˌī/) a gold coin of ancient Rome, worth 25 silver denarii. ▷Latin, noun use of *aureus* 'golden,' from *aurum* 'gold.'

au re·voir /ˌō rəvˈwär/ ▶*exclam.* good-bye until we meet again. ▷late 17th cent.: from French, literally 'to the seeing again.'

Au·ric /ôˈrēk/, Georges (1899–1983), French composer. He is best known for his scores for movies such as *The Lavender Hill Mob* (1951) and *Moulin Rouge* (1952).

au·ric[1] /ˈôrik/ ▶*adj.* of or relating to the aura supposedly surrounding a living creature.

au·ric[2] ▶*adj. Chemistry* of gold with a valence of three. ▷early 19th cent.: from Latin *aurum* 'gold' + **-IC**.

au·ri·cle /ˈôrikəl/ ▶*n. Anatomy & Biology* a structure resembling an ear or earlobe. ■ another term for **ATRIUM** (of the heart). ■ strictly, a small muscular appendage of each atrium. ■ the external part or pinna of the ear. ▷late Middle English: from Latin *auricula* 'external part of the ear,' diminutive of *auris* 'ear.'

au·ric·u·lar /ôˈrikyələr/ ▶*adj.* **1** of or relating to the ear or hearing. **2** of, relating to, or shaped like an auricle. ▷late Middle English: from late Latin *auricularis*, from *auricula*, diminutive of *auris* 'ear.'

au·ric·u·late /ôˈrikyəlit; -ˌlāt/ ▶*adj. Botany & Zoology* having one or more structures shaped like an ear or earlobe. ▷early 18th cent.: from Latin *auricula* 'external part of the ear' (diminutive of *auris* 'ear') + **-ATE**[2].

au·ric·u·lo·ther·apy /ˌôˌrikyəlōˈTHerəpē/ ▸*n.* a form of acupuncture applied to points on the ear in order to treat other parts of the body. ▷1970s: from Latin *auricula* 'external part of the ear' + *therapy*.

au·rif·er·ous /ôˈrifərəs/ ▸*adj.* (of rocks or minerals) containing gold. ▷mid 17th cent.: from Latin *aurifer* 'gold-bearing' (from *aurum* 'gold') + **-ous**.

Au·ri·ga /ôˈrīgə/ *Astronomy* a large northern constellation (the Charioteer), said to represent a man holding a whip. ■ [as *genitive*] (**Aurigae** /-jē/) used with a preceding letter or numeral to designate stars: *the star Theta Aurigae.* ▷Latin.

Au·ri·gna·cian /ˌôriˈgnāSHən; ˌôrinˈyā-/ ▸*adj. Archaeology* of, relating to, or denoting the early stages of the Upper Paleolithic culture in Europe and the Near East. It is dated in most places to about 34,000–29,000 years ago and is associated with Cro-Magnon Man. ■ [as *n.*] (**the Aurignacian**) the Aurignacian culture or period. ▷early 20th cent.: from French *Aurignacien*, from *Aurignac* in southwestern France, where remains of this culture were found.

au·ri·scope /ˈôriˌskōp/ (also **au·ro·scope** /ˈôrə-/) ▸*n.* another term for **otoscope**. ▷mid 19th cent.: from Latin *auris* 'ear' + **-scope**.

au·rochs /ˈouräks; ˈōˌräks/ ▸*n.* (*pl.* same) a large wild Eurasian ox that was the ancestor of domestic cattle. It was probably exterminated in Britain in the Bronze Age, and the last one was killed in Poland in 1627. Also called **urus**. • *Bos taurus* (formerly **primigenius**) , family Bovidae. ▷late 18th cent.: from German, early variant of *Auerochs*, from Old High German *ūrohso*, from *ūr* (form also found in Old English, of unknown origin) + *ohso* 'ox.'

Au·ro·ra[1] /əˈrôrə/ **1** a city in north central Colorado, east of Denver; pop. 276,393. **2** an industrial city in northeastern Illinois; pop. 142,990.

Au·ro·ra[2] /əˈrôrə; ôˈrôrə/ *Roman Mythology* goddess of the dawn. Greek equivalent **Eos**.

au·ro·ra /əˈrôrə; ôˈrôrə/ ▸*n.* (*pl.* **au·ro·ras** or **au·ro·rae** /ôˈrôrē/) **1** a natural electrical phenomenon characterized by the appearance of streamers of reddish or greenish light in the sky, usually near the northern or southern magnetic pole.

The effect is caused by the interaction of charged particles from the sun with atoms in the upper atmosphere. In northern and southern regions it is respectively called **aurora borealis** or **northern lights** and **aurora australis** or **southern lights**. [*borealis* from Latin, 'northern,' based on Greek *Boreas*, the god of the north wind; *australis* from Latin, 'southern,' from *Auster* 'the south, the south wind.']

2 [in *sing.*] *poetic/literary* the dawn. ▷late Middle English (originally in sense 2): from Latin, 'dawn, goddess of the dawn.' Sense 1 dates from the early 18th cent. —**au·ro·ral** *adj.*

A.U.S. ▸*abbr.* Army of the United States.

Ausch·witz /ˈouSHvits/ a Nazi concentration camp in World War II, near the town of Oświęcim (Auschwitz) in Poland.

Ausch·witz Lie (also **Ausch·witz lie**) ▸*n.* the assertion that the Holocaust did not take place or that the number of deaths is exaggerated. ▷from *Auschwitz*, a concentration camp in Poland.

aus·cul·ta·tion /ˌôskəlˈtāSHən/ ▸*n.* the action of listening to sounds from the heart, lungs, or other organs, typically with a stethoscope, as a part of medical diagnosis. ▷mid 17th cent.: from Latin *auscultatio(n-)*, from *auscultare* 'listen to.' —**aus·cul·tate** /ˈôskəlˌtāt/ *v.* —**aus·cul·ta·to·ry** /ôˈskəltəˌtôrē/ *adj.*

Aus·le·se /ˈouslāzə/ ▸*n.* a white wine of German origin or style made from selected bunches of grapes picked later than the general harvest. ▷from German, from *aus* 'out' + *Lese* 'picking, vintage.'

aus·pice /ˈôspis/ ▸*n. archaic* a divine or prophetic token. ▷mid 16th cent. (originally denoting the observation of bird flight in divination): from French, or from Latin *auspicium*, from *auspex* 'observer of birds,' from *avis* 'bird' + *specere* 'to look.'

▸*PHRASE* □ **under the auspices of** with the help, support, or protection of: *the delegation's visit was arranged under UN auspices.*

aus·pi·cious /ôˈspiSHəs/ ▸*adj.* conducive to success; favorable: *it was not the most auspicious moment to hold an election.* ■ giving or being a sign of future success: *they said it was an auspicious moon—it was rising.* ■ *archaic* characterized by success; prosperous: *he was respectful to his auspicious customers.* ▷late 16th cent.: from **auspice** + **-ous**. —**aus·pi·cious·ly** *adv.* —**aus·pi·cious·ness** *n.*

Aus·sie /ˈôsē/ ▸*n.* (*pl.* **-sies**) & *adj.* informal term for **Australia** or **Australian**.

Aus·ten /ˈôstən/, Jane (1775–1817), English novelist. Her major novels are *Sense and Sensibility* (1811), *Pride and Prejudice* (1813), *Mansfield Park* (1814), *Emma* (1815), *Northanger Abbey* (1818), and *Persuasion* (1818).

aus·ten·ite /ˈôstəˌnīt/ ▸*n. Metallurgy* a solid solution of carbon in a nonmagnetic form of iron, stable at high temperatures. It is a constituent of some forms of steel. ▷early 20th cent.: from the name of Sir William Roberts-*Austen* (1843–1902), English metallurgist, + **-ite**[1]. —**aus·ten·it·ic** /ˌôstəˈnitik/ *adj.*

aus·tere /ôˈsti(ə)r/ ▸*adj.* (**-ter·er**, **-ter·est**) severe or strict in manner, attitude, or appearance: *an austere man, with a rigidly puritanical outlook* | *an austere expression.* See note at **severe**. ■ (of living conditions or a way of life) having no comforts or luxuries; harsh or ascetic: *conditions in the prison could hardly be more austere.* ■ having an extremely plain and simple style or appearance; unadorned: *the cathedral is impressive in its austere simplicity.* ■ (of an economic policy or measure) designed to reduce a budget deficit, esp. by cutting public expenditure. ▷Middle English: via Old French from Latin *austerus*, from Greek *austēros* 'severe.' —**aus·tere·ly** *adv.*

aus·ter·i·ty /ôˈsteritē/ ▸*n.* (*pl.* **-ties**) sternness or severity of manner or attitude: *he was noted for his austerity and his authoritarianism.* ■ extreme plainness and simplicity of style or appearance: *the room was decorated with a restraint bordering on austerity.* ■ (**austerities**) conditions characterized by severity, sternness, or asceticism: *his austerities had undermined his health* | *the simple life of prayer and personal austerity.* ■ difficult economic conditions created by government measures to reduce a budget deficit, esp. by reducing public expenditure: *a period of austerity* | [as *adj.*] *austerity measures.* ▷late Middle English: from French *austérité*, from Latin *austeritas*, from *austerus* 'severe' (see **austere**).

Aus·ter·litz, Battle of /ˈôstərˌlits; ˈoustər-/ a battle in 1805 near the town of Austerlitz (now in the Czech Republic), in which Napoleon defeated the Austrians and Russians.

Aus·tin[1] /ˈôstən/ **1** a city in southeastern Minnesota, noted for its meatpacking industry; pop. 21,907. **2** the capital of Texas; pop. 656,562. First settled by Anglo-Americans in 1835 (a year before Texas gained independence from Mexico), it was named **Waterloo** until 1839, when it was renamed to honor Stephen F. Austin.

Aus·tin[2], J. L. (1911–60), English philosopher; full name *John Langshaw Austin*. Notable works: *Sense and Sensibilia* and *How to Do Things with Words* (both 1962).

Aus·tin[3], John (1790–1859), English jurist. His work is significant for its strict delimitation of the sphere of law and its distinction from that of morality.

Aus·tin[4], Stephen Fuller (1793–1836), colonizer of Texas. He founded the first recognized Anglo-American settlement in Texas 1822 and served briefly as secretary of state of the Republic of Texas 1836. His colonization of Texas was a continuation of the effort begun by his father, Moses Austin (1761–1821), who in 1821 became the first man allowed to bring Anglo-American settlers into Spanish Texas.

Aus·tin[5] ▸*adj.* & *n.* another name for **Augustinian**.

aus·tral /ˈôstrəl/ ▸*adj.* of or relating to the south, in particular: ■ *technical* of the southern hemisphere: *the austral spring.* ■ (**Austral**) of Australia or Australasia. ▷late 15th cent.: from Latin *australis*, from *Auster* 'the south, the south wind.'

Aus·tral·a·sia /ˌôstrəˈlāZHə/ the region that consists of Australia, New Zealand, New Guinea, and the neighboring islands of the Pacific Ocean. —**Aus·tral·a·sian** *adj.* & *n.*

Aus·tral·ia /ôˈstrālyə; əˈstrāl-/ an island country and continent in the southern hemisphere, in the southwestern Pacific Ocean, a member state of the Commonwealth of Nations; pop. 19,900,000; capital, Canberra; official language, English.

Inhabited by Aboriginal peoples since prehistoric times, Australia was explored by the Dutch from 1606; British colonization began in 1788, as did the transportation of convicts from Britain, a practice that was discontinued in 1868. Australia was declared a commonwealth in 1901 when the six colonies (New South Wales, Victoria, Queensland, South Australia, Western Australia, and the offshore island of Tasmania) federated as sovereign states; Northern Territory achieved similar status in 1978.

Aus·tral·ian /ôˈstrālyən/ ▸*n.* a native or national of Australia, or a person of Australian descent.
▸*adj.* of or relating to Australia. ■ *Zoology* of, relating to, or denoting a zoogeographical region comprising Australasia together with Indonesia east of Wallace's line, in which monotremes and marsupials dominate the fauna. Compare with **Notogaea**, **oriental**. ■ *Botany* of, relating to, or denoting a phytogeographical kingdom comprising only Australia and Tasmania. ▷from French *australien*, from Latin *australis* in the phrase *Terra Australis* 'the southern land,' the name of the supposed southern continent. —**Aus·tral·ian·ism** /-ˌnizəm/ *n.*

Aus·tral·ian Ant·arc·tic Ter·ri·to·ry an area of Antarctica that lies between longitudes 142° east and 136° east. It is administered by Australia.

Aus·tral·ian Cap·i·tal Ter·ri·to·ry a federal territory in New South Wales, Australia, that consists of two enclaves ceded by New South Wales—one in 1911 to contain Canberra, the other in 1915 containing Jervis Bay.

Aus·tral·ian crawl ▸*n. chiefly Austral.* another term for **crawl** (sense 2).

Aus·tral·ian La·bor Par·ty (abbr.: **ALP**) Australia's oldest political party, founded in 1891. The party is moderately liberal; it has provided three recent Australian Prime Ministers, Gough Whitlam, Bob Hawke, and Paul Keating.

Aus·tral·ian pine ▸*n.* another name for the **beefwood** tree, especially in its role as an invasive pest in subtropical areas of the U.S.

Aus·tral·ian Rules (also **Australian Rules football**) ▸*n.* a form of football played on an oval ground with an oval ball by teams of eighteen players. Official name **Australian National football**.

The game dates from 1858. Players may run with the ball if they touch it to the ground every fifteen meters, and may pass it in any direction by punching. There are both inner and outer goalposts: a behind (between the outer posts) scores one point and a goal (between the inner posts) scores six.

Aus·tral·ian salm·on ▸*n.* see **salmon** (sense 2).

Aus·tral·ian ter·ri·er ▸*n.* a wire-haired terrier of a breed originating in Australia.

Aus·tral·ian wil·low ▸*n.* another term for **wilga**.

Aus·tral Is·lands /ˈôstrəl/ another name for **Tubuai Islands**.

aus·tra·lite /ˈôstrəˌlīt/ ▸*n. Geology* a tektite from the strewn field in Australia.

Aus·tra·loid /ˈôstrəˌloid/ ▸*adj. often offensive* of or belonging to the division of humankind represented by Australian Aboriginal peoples.
▸*n. often offensive* a person belonging to this division of humankind.

USAGE The term **Australoid**, together with other terms such as **Caucasoid**, **Negroid**, and **Mongoloid**, belong to the systems of human classification developed by 19th-century anthropologists and physiologists and relate to outdated notions of race that have largely been abandoned. Such terms are potentially offensive today and, when referring to native peoples of a particular region, it is preferable, e.g., to refer to 'Australian Aboriginals' or 'Aboriginals.' See also **usage** at **Caucasian** and **Mongoloid**.

Aus·tra·lo·pith·e·cus /ˌôstrəlōˈpiTHikəs; ôˌstrālō-/ ▸*n.* a fossil bipedal primate with both apelike and human characteristics, found in Pliocene and lower Pleistocene deposits (*c.*4 million to 1 million years old) in Africa. • Genus *Australopithecus*, family Hominidae: several species, including the lightly built *A. africanus*, which is thought to be the immediate ancestor of the human genus *Homo*. The more heavily built forms (often placed in the genus *Paranthropus*), such as *A. robustus* and *A.* (or **Zinjanthropus**) *boisei*, were probably evolutionary dead ends. ▷modern Latin, from Latin *australis* 'southern' (see **austral**) + Greek *pithēkos* 'ape.' —**aus·tra·lo·pith·e·cine** /-ˌsēn; -ˌsīn/ *n.* & *adj.*

Aus·tral·orp /ˈôstrəˌlôrp/ ▸*n.* a black Orpington chicken of an Australian breed. ▷early 20th cent.: blend of **Australian** and **Orpington**.

Aus·tri·a /ˈôstrēə/ a republic in central Europe; pop. 8,100,000; capital, Vienna; official language, German. —**Aus·tri·an** *adj.* & *n.*

Austria was dominated from the early Middle Ages by the Habsburg family and became the center of a massive central European empire that lasted

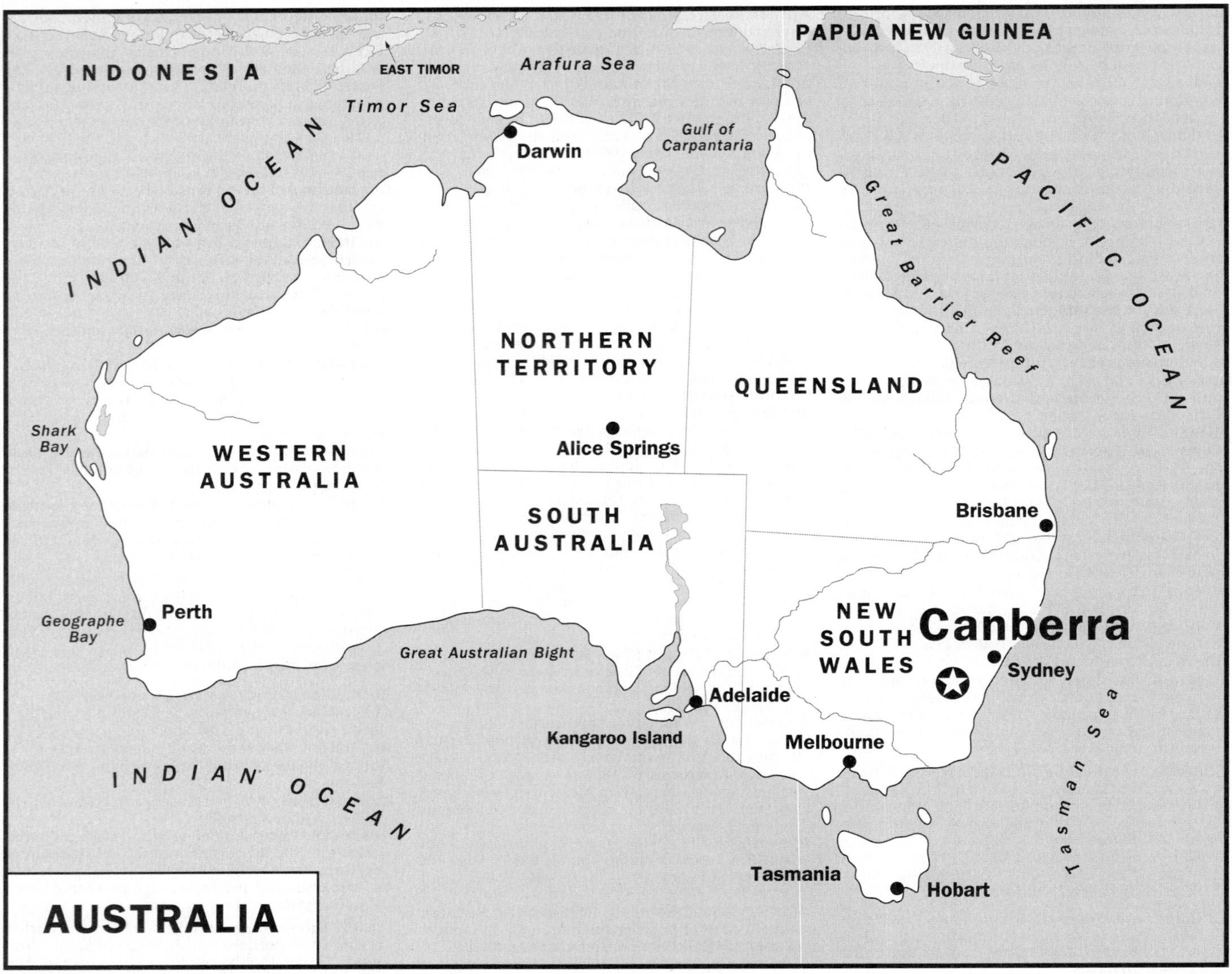

AUSTRALIA

until 1918. The country was incorporated within the Nazi Reich in 1938 and after World War II was occupied by the Allies before regaining its sovereignty in 1955. A referendum in 1994 approved Austria's entry into the European Union.

Aus·tri·a-Hun·ga·ry (also **Aus·tro-Hun·gar·i·an em·pire** /ˈôstrō/) the dual monarchy established in 1867 by the Austrian emperor Franz Josef, according to which Austria and Hungary became autonomous states under a common sovereign.

Aus·tri·an shade /ˈôstrēən/ ▸*n.* a window shade made from fabric shirred in puffy frills or pleats, extending about a third of the way down a window.

Aus·tri·an Suc·ces·sion, War of the a group of several related conflicts (1740–48), involving most of the states of Europe, that were triggered by the death of the Emperor Charles VI and the accession of his daughter Maria Theresa in 1740 to the Austrian throne. See also PRAGMATIC SANCTION.

Austro-[1] ▸*comb. form* Austrian; Austrian and . . . : *Austro-Hungarian.*

Austro-[2] ▸*comb. form* Australian; Australian and . . . : *Austro-Malayan.* ■ southern: *Austro-Asiatic.* ▷from Latin *australis* 'southern.'

Aus·tro-A·si·at·ic /ˈôstrō ˌāzhēˈatik; -shē-; -zē-/ ▸*adj.* of, relating to, or denoting a phylum of languages spoken in Southeast Asia, consisting of the Mon-Khmer family, the Munda family, and one or two other isolated languages.
▸*n.* this phylum of languages. ▷early 20th cent.: from AUSTRO-[2] 'southern' + ASIATIC.

Aus·tro·ne·sian /ˌôstrōˈnēzhən/ ▸*adj.* of, relating to, or denoting a family of languages spoken in an area extending from Madagascar in the west to the Pacific islands in the east. Also called MALAYO-POLYNESIAN.
▸*n.* this family of languages. ▷from German *austronesisch*, based on Latin *australis* 'southern' (see AUSTRAL) + Greek *nēsos* 'island.'

aut- ▸*prefix* variant spelling of AUTO- shortened before a vowel (as in *autarky*).

au·tarch /ˈôtärk/ ▸*n.* a ruler who has absolute power. ▷early 19th cent.: from Greek *autarkhos*, from *autos* 'self' + *arkhos* 'leader.'

au·tar·chy /ˈôˌtärkē/ ▸*n.* (*pl.* **-chies**) **1** another term for AUTOCRACY. **2** variant spelling of AUTARKY. ▷mid 17th cent.: from modern Latin *autarchia*, from Greek *autos* 'self' + *-arkhia* (from *arkhein* 'take the lead'), on the pattern of *monarckhia* 'monarchy.' **—au·tar·chic** /ôˈtärkik/ *adj.*

au·tar·ky /ˈôˌtärkē/ ▸*n.* economic independence or self-sufficiency. ■ a country, state, or society that is economically independent. ▷early 17th cent.: from Greek *autarkeia*, from *autarkēs* 'self-sufficiency,' from *autos* 'self' + *arkein* 'suffice.' **—au·tar·kic** /ôˈtärkik/ *adj.*

aut·e·col·o·gy /ôtiˈkäləjē/ (also **au·to·e·col·o·gy**) ▸*n. Biology* the ecological study of an individual organism, or sometimes a particular species. Contrasted with SYNECOLOGY. **—aut·ec·o·log·i·cal** /ˌôtekəˈläjikəl; -ēkə-/ *adj.*

au·teur /ôˈtər/ ▸*n.* a filmmaker whose movies are characterized by a filmmaker's creative influence. ▷1960s: French, literally 'author.' **—au·teur·ism** /-ˌizəm/ *n.* **—au·teur·ist** /-ist/ *adj.*

auth. ▸*abbr.* ■ authentic. ■ author. ■ authority. ■ authorized.

au·then·tic /ôˈthentik/ (abbr.: **auth.**) ▸*adj.* **1** of undisputed origin; genuine: *the letter is now accepted as an authentic document | authentic 14th-century furniture.* See note at GENUINE. ■ made or done in the traditional or original way, or in a way that faithfully resembles an original: *the restaurant serves authentic Italian meals | every detail of the movie was totally authentic.* ■ based on facts; accurate or reliable: *an authentic depiction of the situation.* ■ (in existentialist philosophy) relating to or denoting an emotionally appropriate, significant, purposive, and responsible mode of human life. **2** *Music* (of a church mode) comprising the notes lying between the principal note or final and the note an octave higher. Compare with PLAGAL. ▷late Middle English: via Old French from late Latin *authenticus*, from Greek *authentikos* 'principal, genuine.' **—au·then·ti·cal·ly** /-ik(ə)lē/ *adv.* [as *submodifier*] *the food is authentically Cajun.* **—au·then·tic·i·ty** /ˌôthenˈtisitē/ *n.*

au·then·ti·cate /ôˈthentiˌkāt/ ▸*v.* [*trans.*] prove or show (something, esp. a claim or an artistic work) to be true or genuine: *they were invited to authenticate* *artifacts from the Italian Renaissance.* ■ validate: *the nationalist statements authenticated their leadership among the local community.* ■ [*intrans.*] *Computing* (of a user or process) have one's identity verified. ▷early 17th cent.: from medieval Latin *authenticat-* 'established as valid,' from the verb *authenticare*, from late Latin *authenticus* 'genuine' (see **AUTHENTIC**). **—au·then·ti·ca·tion** /ô,THenti'kāSHən/ *n.* **—au·then·ti·ca·tor** /-,kātər/ *n.*

au·thi·gen·ic /,ôTHi'jenik/ ▶*adj. Geology* (of minerals and other materials) formed in their present position. Often contrasted with **ALLOGENIC**. ▷late 19th cent.: from Greek *authigenēs* 'born on the spot' + **-IC**.

au·thor /'ôTHər/ (abbr.: **auth.**) ▶*n.* a writer of a book, article, or report: *he is the author of several books on the subject.* ■ someone who writes books as a profession: *my favorite authors are Kurt Vonnegut and Aldous Huxley.* ■ the writings of such a person: *I had to read authors I disliked.* ■ *figurative* an originator or creator of something, esp. a plan or idea: *the authors of the peace plan.*
▶*v.* [*trans.*] be the author of (a book or piece of writing): *she has authored several articles on wildlife.* ■ *figurative* be the originator of; create: *the concept has been authored largely by insurance companies.* ▷Middle English (in the sense 'a person who invents or causes something'): from Old French *autor*, from Latin *auctor*, from *augere* 'increase, originate, promote.' The spelling with *th* arose in the 15th cent., and perhaps became established under the influence of *authentic*. **—au·tho·ri·al** /ô'THôrēəl/ *adj.*

USAGE In the sense 'be the author of,' the verb **author** is objected to by some traditionalists who regard it as an awkward or pretentious substitute for *write* or *compose*. It is widespread and well established though, especially in North America, and has been in use since the end of the 16th century. The verb **coauthor**, for which there is no common synonym, is useful and unobjectionable.

au·thor·ess /'ôTHəris/ ▶*n.* a female author.

USAGE See **usage** at **-ESS**.

au·thor·ing /'ôTHəriNG/ ▶*n. Computing* the creation of programs and databases for computer applications such as computer-assisted learning or multimedia products: [as *adj.*] *an authoring system.*

au·thor·i·tar·i·an /ə,THôri'te(ə)rēən; ô,THär-/ ▶*adj.* favoring or enforcing strict obedience to authority, esp. that of the government, at the expense of personal freedom: *the transition from an authoritarian to a democratic regime.* ■ showing a lack of concern for the wishes or opinions of others; domineering; dictatorial: *he had an authoritarian and at times belligerent manner.*
▶*n.* an authoritarian person. **—au·thor·i·tar·i·an·ism** *n.*

au·thor·i·ta·tive /ə'THôri,tātiv; ə'THär-/ ▶*adj.* **1** able to be trusted as being accurate or true; reliable: *clear, authoritative information and advice | an authoritative source.* ■ (of a text) considered to be the best of its kind and unlikely to be improved upon: *the authoritative study of mollusks.* **2** commanding and self-confident; likely to be respected and obeyed: *she had an authoritative air | his voice was calm and authoritative.* ■ proceeding from an official source and requiring compliance or obedience: *authoritative directives.* **—au·thor·i·ta·tive·ly** *adv.* **—au·thor·i·ta·tive·ness** *n.*

au·thor·i·ty /ə'THôritē; ô'THär-/ (abbr.: **auth.**) ▶*n.* (*pl.* **-ties**) **1** the power or right to give orders, make decisions, and enforce obedience: *he had absolute* ***authority over*** *his subordinates | positions of authority | they acted* ***under the authority*** *of the UN Security Council | a rebellion against those* ***in authority****.* See note at **JURISDICTION**. ■ [often with *infinitive*] the right to act in a specified way, delegated from one person or organization to another: *military forces have the legal authority to arrest drug traffickers.* ■ official permission; sanction: *the money was spent without congressional authority.* **2** (often **authorities**) a person or organization having power or control in a particular, typically political or administrative, sphere: *the health authorities | the Chicago Transit Authority | the authorities ordered all foreign embassies to close | she wasn't used to dealing with authority.* **3** the power to influence others, esp. because of one's commanding manner or one's recognized knowledge about something: *he has the natural authority of one who is used to being obeyed | he spoke* ***with authority*** *on the subject.* ■ the confidence resulting from personal expertise: *he hit the ball with authority.* ■ a person with extensive or specialized knowledge about a subject; an expert: *she was* ***an authority on*** *the stockmarket.* ■ a book or other source able to supply reliable information or evidence, typically to settle a dispute: *the court cited a series of authorities supporting their decision.* ▷Middle English: from Old French *autorite*, from Latin *auctoritas*, from *auctor* 'originator, promoter' (see **AUTHOR**).
▶***PHRASE*** □ **have something on good authority** have ascertained something from a reliable source: *I have it on good authority that there is a waiting list of up to five weeks.*

au·thor·i·za·tion /,ôTHərə'zāSHən/ ▶*n.* the action or fact of authorizing or being authorized: *the raising of revenue and the authorization of spending | power stations will have to obtain authorizations to continue their operations.* ■ a document giving permission or authority.

au·thor·ize /'ôTHə,rīz/ ▶*v.* [*trans.*] give official permission for or approval to (an undertaking or agent): *the government authorized further aircraft production | [as adj.]* (**authorized**) *an authorized dealer | [trans.] the troops were authorized to use force.* ▷late Middle English: from Old French *autoriser*, from medieval Latin *auctorizare*, from *auctor* 'originator, promoter' (see **AUTHOR**).

Au·thor·ized Ver·sion ▶*n. chiefly Brit.* another name for **KING JAMES BIBLE**.

au·thor·ship /'ôTHər,SHip/ ▶*n.* the fact or position of someone's having written a book or other written work: *an investigation into the authorship of the Gospels | joint authorship.* ■ the occupation of writing: *he took to authorship.*

au·tism /'ô,tizəm/ ▶*n. Psychiatry* a mental condition, present from early childhood, characterized by great difficulty in communicating and forming relationships with other people and in using language and abstract concepts. ■ a mental condition in which fantasy dominates over reality, as a symptom of schizophrenia and other disorders. ▷early 20th cent.: from Greek *autos* 'self' + **-ISM**. **—au·tis·tic** /ô'tistik/ *adj.* & *n.*

au·to /'ôtō/ ▶*n.* (*pl.* **-tos**) [usu. as *modifier*] *informal* an automobile: *the auto industry.* ▷late 19th cent.: abbreviation of **AUTOMOBILE**.

auto- (usu. **aut-** before a vowel) ▶*comb. form* **1** self: *autoanalysis.* ■ one's own: *autograph.* ■ by oneself or spontaneous: *autoxidation.* ■ by itself or automatic: *autofocusing.* **2** relating to cars: *autocross.* ▷from Greek *autos* 'self.' Sense 2 is a backformation from *automobile*.

au·to·an·ti·bod·y /,ôtō'anti,bädē/ ▶*n.* (*pl.* **-bod·ies**) *Physiology* an antibody produced by an organism in response to a constituent of its own tissues.

au·to·bahn /'ôtə,bän/ ▶*n.* a German, Austrian, or Swiss expressway. ▷1930s: from German, from *Auto* 'automobile' + *Bahn* 'path, road.'

au·to·bi·o·graph·i·cal /,ôtəbīə'grafikəl/ ▶*adj.* (of a written work) dealing with the writer's own life: *an autobiographical account | the book is partly autobiographical.* **—au·to·bi·o·graph·ic** /-fik/ *adj.*

au·to·bi·og·ra·phy /,ôtəbī'ägrəfē/ ▶*n.* (*pl.* **-phies**) an account of a person's life written by that person: *he gives a vivid description of his childhood in his autobiography.* ■ such writing as a literary genre. **—au·to·bi·og·ra·pher** /-fər/ *n.*

au·to·ca·tal·y·sis /,ôtəkə'taləsis/ ▶*n. Chemistry* catalysis of a reaction by one of its products. **—au·to·cat·a·lyst** /-'katl-ist/ *n.* **—au·to·cat·a·lyt·ic** /-,katl'itik/ *adj.*

au·to·ceph·a·lous /,ôtə'sefələs/ ▶*adj.* (of an Eastern Christian Church) appointing its own head, not subject to the authority of an external patriarch or archbishop. ▷mid 19th cent.: from Greek *autokephalos* (from *autos* 'self' + *kephalē* 'head') + **-OUS**.

au·to·chrome /'ôtə,krōm/ ▶*n.* [usu. as *adj.*] an early form of color photography using plates coated with dyed starch grains, patented by the Lumière brothers in 1904: *the autochrome process.* ■ a color photograph made by this process.

au·toch·thon /ô'täkTHən/ ▶*n.* (*pl.* **-thons** or **-tho·nes** /-THə,nēz/) an original or indigenous inhabitant of a place; an aborigine. ▷late 16th cent.: from Greek, literally 'sprung from the earth,' from *autos* 'self' + *khthōn* 'earth, soil.'

au·toch·tho·nous /ô'täkTHənəs/ ▶*adj.* (of an inhabitant of a place) indigenous rather than descended from migrants or colonists. ■ *Geology* (of a deposit or formation) formed in its present position. Often contrasted with **ALLOCHTHONOUS**.

au·to·clave /'ôtə,klāv/ ▶*n.* a strong, heated container used for chemical reactions and other processes using high pressures and temperatures, e.g., steam sterilization.
▶*v.* [*trans.*] heat (something) in an autoclave. ▷late 19th cent.: from French, from *auto-* 'self' + Latin *clavus* 'nail' or *clavis* 'key' (so called because it is self-fastening).

au·to·com·plete /,ôtōkəm'plēt/ *Computing* ▶*n.* a software function that gives users the option of completing words or forms by a shorthand method on the basis of what has been typed before: *features like autocomplete, spell-checking, and other niceties could be added.*
▶*v.* [*trans* .] complete (a word or form) in this way. **—au·to·com·ple·tion** *n.* /-kəm'plēSHən/

au·to·cor·re·la·tion /,ôtō,kôrə'lāSHən/ ▶*n. Statistics* correlation between the elements of a series and others from the same series separated from them by a given interval. ■ a calculation of such correlation.

au·toc·ra·cy /ô'täkrəsē/ ▶*n.* (*pl.* **-cies**) a system of government by one person with absolute power. ■ a regime based on such a principle of government. ■ a country, state, or society governed in such a way. ■ domineering rule or control: *a boss who shifts between autocracy, persuasion, and consultation.* ▷mid 17th cent. (in the sense 'autonomy'): from Greek *autokrateia*, from *autokratēs* (see **AUTOCRAT**).

au·to·crat /'ôtə,krat/ ▶*n.* a ruler who has absolute power. ■ someone who insists on complete obedience from others; an imperious or domineering person. ▷early 19th cent.: from French *autocrate*, from Greek *autokratēs*, from *autos* 'self' + *kratos* 'power.'

au·to·crat·ic /,ôtə'kratik/ ▶*adj.* of or relating to a ruler who has absolute power: *the constitutional reforms threatened his autocratic power.* ■ taking no account of other people's wishes or opinions; domineering: *an autocratic management style.* **—au·to·crat·i·cal·ly** /-ik(ə)lē/ *adv.*

au·to·cross /'ôtō,krôs; -,kräs/ ▶*n.* a form of competition in which cars are driven around an obstacle course, typically marked out by cones. ▷1960s: blend of **AUTOMOBILE** and **CROSS-COUNTRY**.

au·to-da-fé /'ôtō də 'fā/ ▶*n.* (*pl.* **au·tos-da-fé**) the burning of a heretic by the Spanish Inquisition. ■ a sentence of such a kind. ▷early 18th cent.: from Portuguese, literally 'act of the faith.'

au·to·di·al /'ôtō,dī(ə)l/ ▶*n.* a function of telephonic equipment that allows for automatic dialing of preprogrammed or of randomly selected numbers: *have a telephone with autodial by your bed.*
▶*v.* (**-di·aled**, **-di·al·ing**; *Brit.* **-di·alled**, **-di·al·ling**) automatically dial a telephone number, with or without human prompting: [*intrans.*] *it had autodialed and been online for over 2 hours* | [*trans.*] *if the first number is busy the modem autodials the backup number.*

au·to·dial·er /'ôtō,dī(ə)lər/ ▶*n.* an electronic device that dials telephone numbers randomly or from a list and may also leave messages and request information.

au·to·di·dact /,ôtō'dī,dakt/ ▶*n.* a self-taught person. ▷mid 18th cent.: from Greek *autodidaktos* 'self-taught,' from *autos* 'self' + *didaskein* 'teach.' **—au·to·di·dac·tic** /-,dī'daktik/ *adj.*

au·to·e·col·o·gy /,ôtō-i'käləjē/ ▶*n.* variant spelling of **AUTECOLOGY**.

au·to·e·rot·ic /,ôtō-i'rätik/ ▶*adj.* of or relating to sexual excitement generated by stimulating or fantasizing about one's own body. **—au·to·e·rot·i·ci·sm** /-,sizəm/ *n.*

au·to·e·rot·ic as·phyx·i·a ▶*n.* asphyxia that results from intentionally strangling oneself while masturbating, in an attempt to heighten sexual pleasure by limiting the oxygen supply to the brain.

au·to·ex·po·sure /'ôtō-ik'spōZHər/ ▶*n.* a device that sets the exposure automatically on a camera or other piece of equipment. ■ the facility to set exposure automatically.

au·to·fo·cus /'ôtō,fōkəs/ ▶*n.* a device that focuses a camera or other piece of equipment automatically. ■ automatic focusing. **—au·to·fo·cus·ing** /-siNG/ *n.*

au·tog·a·my /ô'tägəmē/ ▶*n. Biology* self-fertilization, esp. the self-pollination of a flower. ▷late 19th cent.: from **AUTO-** 'self' + Greek *-gamia* (from *gamos* 'marriage'). **—au·tog·a·mous** /-məs/ *adj.*

au·to·ge·net·ic /,ôtōjə'netik/ ▶*adj. technical* self-generated: *autogenetic succession.*

au·to·gen·ic train·ing /ôtə'jenik/ ▶*n.* a form of relaxation therapy involving autosuggestion.

au·tog·e·nous /ô'täjənəs/ ▶*adj.* arising from within or from a thing itself. ■ (of welding) done either without solder or with a filler of the same metal as the pieces being welded.

Pronunciation Key ə *ago*; ər *over*; 'ə or ,ə *up*; 'ər or ,ər *fur*; a *hat*; ā *rate*; ä *car*; CH *chew*; e *let*; ē *see*; e(ə)r *air*; i *fit*; ī *by*; i(ə)r *ear*; NG *sing*; ō *go*; ô *for*; oi *boy*; o͝o *good*; o͞o *goo*; ou *out*; SH *she*; TH *thin*; T͟H *then*; (h)w *why*; ZH *vision*

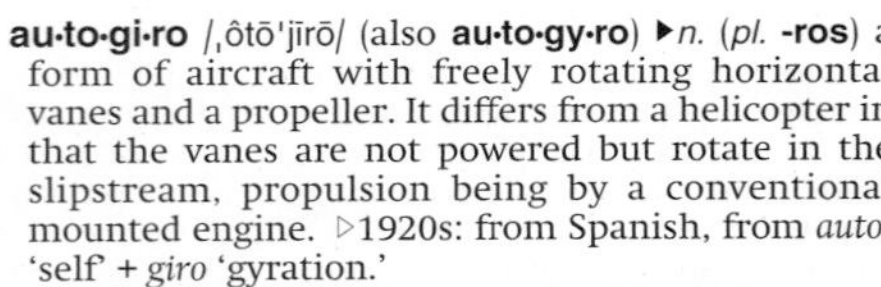

au·to·gi·ro /ˌôtōˈjīrō/ (also **au·to·gy·ro**) ▸*n.* (*pl.* **-ros**) a form of aircraft with freely rotating horizontal vanes and a propeller. It differs from a helicopter in that the vanes are not powered but rotate in the slipstream, propulsion being by a conventional mounted engine. ▷1920s: from Spanish, from *auto-* 'self' + *giro* 'gyration.'

au·to·graft /ˈôtəˌgraft/ ▸*n.* a graft of tissue from one point to another of the same individual's body.

au·to·graph /ˈôtəˌgraf/ ▸*n.* **1** a signature, esp. that of a celebrity written as a memento for an admirer: *fans surged around the car asking for autographs.* **2** a manuscript or musical score in the author's or musician's own handwriting. ■ a person's handwriting: *a songbook in Purcell's autograph.*
▸*v.* [*trans.*] (of a celebrity) write one's signature on (something); sign: *the whole team autographed a shirt for him* | [as *adj.*] (**autographed**) *an autographed photo.*
▸*adj.* written in the author's own handwriting: *an autograph manuscript.* ■ (of a painting or sculpture) done by the artist, not by a copier. ▷early 17th cent.: from French *autographe* or late Latin *autographum*, from Greek *autographon*, neuter of *autographos* 'written with one's own hand,' from *autos* 'self' + *graphos* 'written.'

au·tog·ra·phy /ôˈtägrəfē/ ▸*n.* (*pl.* **-phies**) an autobiography: *Arthur Miller's splendid autography,* Timebends.

Au·to·harp /ˈôtōˌhärp/ ▸*n. trademark* a kind of zither with a mechanical device that allows the playing of a chord by damping all the other strings.

au·to·hyp·no·sis /ˌôtōhipˈnōsis/ ▸*n.* induction of a hypnotic state in oneself; self-hypnosis. **—au·to·hyp·not·ic** /-ˈnätik/ *adj.*

au·to·im·mune /ˌôtōəˈmyo͞on/ ▸*adj. Medicine* of or relating to disease caused by antibodies or lymphocytes produced against substances naturally present in the body: *the infection triggers an autoimmune response.* **—au·to·im·mu·ni·ty** /-nitē/ *n.*

au·to·in·tox·i·ca·tion /ˌôtō-inˌtäksiˈkāsʜən/ ▸*n. Medicine* poisoning by a toxin formed within the body itself.

au·to·load /ˈôtōˌlōd/ ▸*adj.* self-loading; semiautomatic: *24mm film in autoload cartridges.* **—au·to·load·er** *n.* **—au·to·load·ing** *n.*

au·tol·o·gous /ôˈtäləgəs/ ▸*adj.* (of cells or tissues) obtained from the same individual: *autologous bone marrow transplants.*

au·tol·y·sis /ôˈtäləsis/ ▸*n. Biology* the destruction of cells or tissues by their own enzymes, esp. those released by lysosomes. **—au·to·lyt·ic** /ˌôtlˈitik/ *adj.*

au·to·mat /ˈôtəˌmat/ ▸*n. historical* a cafeteria in which food and drink were obtained from vending machines. ▷late 17th cent. (denoting an automaton): from German, from French *automate*, from Latin *automaton* (see **AUTOMATON**). The current sense dates from the early 20th cent.

au·to·mate /ˈôtəˌmāt/ ▸*v.* [*trans.*] convert (a process or facility) to largely automatic operation: *industry is investing in automating production* | [as *adj.*] (**automated**) *a fully automated process.* ▷1950s: back-formation from **AUTOMATION**.

Au·to·mat·ed Clear·ing·house /ˈôtəˌmātid ˈkli(ə)rɪɴɢ ˌhous/ ▸*n.* the clearing and settlement system used by U.S. commercial banks and other institutions.

au·to·mat·ed tell·er ma·chine (also **au·to·mat·ic tell·er ma·chine**) (abbr.: **ATM**) ▸*n.* a machine that automatically provides cash and performs other banking services on insertion of a special card by the account holder.

au·to·mat·ic /ˌôtəˈmatik/ ▸*adj.* **1** (of a device or process) working by itself with little or no direct human control: *an automatic kettle that switches itself off when it boils* | *calibration is fully automatic.* ■ (of a firearm) self-loading and able to fire continuously until the ammunition is exhausted or the pressure on the trigger is released: *automatic weapons.* ■ (of a motor vehicle or its transmission) using gears that shift by themselves according to speed and acceleration: *a four-speed automatic gearbox.* **2** done or occurring spontaneously, without conscious thought or intention: *automatic physical functions such as breathing* | *"Nice to meet you," he said, with automatic politeness.* ■ occurring as a matter of course and without debate: *he is the automatic choice for the senior team.* ■ (esp. of a legal sanction) given or imposed as a necessary and inevitable result of a fixed rule or particular set of circumstances: *for missing the team workout, he received an automatic one-game suspension.*
▸*n.* **1** an automatic machine or device, in particular: ■ a gun that continues firing until the ammunition is exhausted or the pressure on the trigger is released. ■ a vehicle with automatic transmission. **2** *Football* another term for **AUDIBLE**. ▷mid 18th cent.: from Greek *automatos* 'acting of itself' (see **AUTOMATON**) + **-IC**. **—au·to·mat·i·cal·ly** /-ik(ə)lē/ *adv.* **—au·to·ma·tic·i·ty** /-məˈtisitē/ *n.*

au·to·mat·ic gain con·trol (abbr.: **AGC**) ▸*n. Electronics* a feature of certain amplifier circuits that gives a constant output over a wide range of input levels.

au·to·mat·ic pi·lot ▸*n.* a device for keeping an aircraft on a set course without the intervention of the pilot: *figurative cruising through life* ***on automatic pilot.***

au·to·mat·ic writ·ing ▸*n.* writing said to be produced by a spiritual, occult, or subconscious agency rather than by the conscious intention of the writer.

au·to·ma·tion /ˌôtəˈmāsʜən/ ▸*n.* the use of largely automatic equipment in a system of manufacturing or other production process: *unemployment due to the spread of automation* | *the automation of office tasks.* ▷1940s (originally U.S.): irregular formation from **AUTOMATIC** + **-ATION**.

au·tom·a·tism /ôˈtäməˌtizəm/ ▸*n.* the performance of actions without conscious thought or intention. ■ *Art* the avoidance of conscious intention in producing works of art, esp. by using mechanical techniques or subconscious associations. ■ an action performed unconsciously or involuntarily. ▷mid 19th cent.: from French *automatisme*, from *automate* 'automaton,' from Greek *automatos* 'acting of itself' (see **AUTOMATON**).

au·tom·a·tize /ôˈtäməˌtīz/ ▸*v.* [*trans.*] [usu. as *adj.*] (**automatized**) make automatic or habitual: *the need to refresh automatized forms of literature.* **—au·tom·a·ti·za·tion** /ôˌtämətiˈzāsʜən/ *n.*

au·tom·a·ton /ôˈtämətən; -ˌtän/ ▸*n.* (*pl.* **-ta** /-tə/ or **-tons**) a moving mechanical device made in imitation of a human being. ■ a machine that performs a function according to a predetermined set of coded instructions, esp. one capable of a range of programmed responses to different circumstances. ■ used in similes and comparisons to refer to a person who seems to act in a mechanical or unemotional way: *she went about her preparations like an automaton.* ▷early 17th cent.: via Latin from Greek, neuter of *automatos* 'acting of itself,' from *autos* 'self.'

au·to·mim·ic·ry /ˌôtəˈmimikrē/ ▸*n.* the mimicking or accentuation of some characteristic of one's own species as an adaptive response.

au·to·mize /ˈôtəˌmīz/ ▸*v.* **1** another term for **AUTOMATE**. **2** another term for **AUTOMATIZE**.

au·to·mo·bile /ˌôtəmōˈbēl/ ▸*n.* a road vehicle, typically with four wheels, powered by an internal combustion engine or electric motor and able to carry a small number of people. ▷late 19th cent.: from French, from *auto-* 'self' + *mobile* 'mobile.'

au·to·mo·tive /ˌôtəˈmōtiv/ ▸*adj.* [*attrib.*] of, relating to, or concerned with motor vehicles.

au·to·nom·ic /ˌôtəˈnämik/ ▸*adj.* [*attrib.*] *chiefly Physiology* involuntary or unconscious; relating to the autonomic nervous system. ▷mid 19th cent. (in the sense 'self-governing'): from **AUTONOMY** + **-IC**.

au·to·nom·ic nerv·ous sys·tem ▸*n.* the part of the nervous system responsible for control of the bodily functions not consciously directed, such as breathing, the heartbeat, and digestive processes.

au·ton·o·mous /ôˈtänəməs/ ▸*adj.* (of a country or region) having self-government, at least to a significant degree: *the federation included sixteen autonomous republics.* ■ acting independently or having the freedom to do so: *an autonomous committee of the school board* | *autonomous underwater vehicles.* ■ (in Kantian moral philosophy) acting in accordance with one's moral duty rather than one's desires. ▷early 19th cent.: from Greek *autonomos* 'having its own laws' + **-OUS**. **—au·ton·o·mous·ly** *adv.*

au·ton·o·my /ôˈtänəmē/ ▸*n.* (*pl.* **-mies**) (of a country or region) the right or condition of self-government, esp. in a particular sphere: *Tatarstan demanded greater autonomy within the Russian Federation.* ■ a self-governing country or region. ■ freedom from external control or influence; independence: *economic autonomy is still a long way off for many women.* ■ (in Kantian moral philosophy) the capacity of an agent to act in accordance with objective morality rather than under the influence of desires. ▷early 17th cent.: from Greek *autonomia*, from *autonomos* 'having its own laws,' from *autos* 'self' + *nomos* 'law.' **—au·ton·o·mist** /-mist/ *n.* & *adj.*

au·to·pa·thog·ra·phy /ˌôtōpəˈᴛʜägrəfē/ ▸*n.* (*pl.* **-phies**) an autobiography dealing primarily with the influence of a disease, disability, or psychological disorder on the author's life. ▷blend of *autobiography* and *pathography.*

au·to·pi·lot /ˈôtōˌpīlət/ ▸*n.* short for **AUTOMATIC PILOT**.

au·top·sy /ˈôˌtäpsē/ ▸*n.* (*pl.* **-sies**) a postmortem examination to discover the cause of death or the extent of disease: [as *adj.*] *an autopsy report.*
▸*v.* (**-sies, -sied**) [*trans.*] perform a postmortem examination on (a body or organ): [as *adj.*] (**autopsied**) *an autopsied brain.* ▷mid 17th cent. (in the sense 'personal observation'): from French *autopsie* or modern Latin *autopsia*, from Greek, from *autoptēs* 'eyewitness,' from *autos* 'self' + *optos* 'seen.'

au·to·ra·di·o·gram /ˌôtōˈrādēəˌgram/ ▸*n.* another term for **AUTORADIOGRAPH**.

au·to·ra·di·o·graph /ˌôtōˈrādēəˌgraf/ ▸*n.* a photograph of an object produced by radiation from radioactive material in the object and revealing the distribution or location of labeled material in the object.
▸*v.* [*trans.*] make an autoradiograph of. **—au·to·ra·di·o·graph·ic** /-ˌrādēəˈgrafik/ *adj.* **—au·to·ra·di·og·ra·phy** /-ˌrādēˈägrəfē/ *n.*

au·to·ro·ta·tion /ˌôtōrōˈtāsʜən/ ▸*n.* rotation of an object caused by the flow of moving air or water around the shape of the object (e.g., a winged seed). ■ such rotation in the rotor blades of a helicopter that is descending without engine power. **—au·to·ro·tate** /-ˈrōtāt/ *v.*

au·to·route /ˈôtōˌro͞ot/ ▸*n.* a highway in a French-speaking country. ▷1960s: from French, from *auto(mobile)* 'car' + *route* 'route.'

au·to·shap·ing /ˈôtōˌsʜāpɪɴɢ/ ▸*n. Psychology* a method of conditioning in which the conditioned response has not been reinforced by reward or punishment, but is a modified instinctive response to certain stimuli.

au·to·some /ˈôtəˌsōm/ ▸*n. Biology* any chromosome that is not a sex chromosome. **—au·to·so·mal** /ˌôtōˈsōməl/ *adj.*

au·to·stra·da /ˈôtōˌsträdə/ ▸*n.* (*pl.* **-stra·das** or **-stra·de** /-ˌsträdē/) an Italian highway. ▷1920s: from Italian, from *auto* 'automobile' + *strada* 'road.'

au·to·sug·ges·tion /ˌôtōsə(g)ˈjescʜən/ ▸*n.* the hypnotic or subconscious adoption of an idea that one has originated oneself, e.g. through repetition of verbal statements to oneself in order to change behavior.

au·to·tel·ic /ˌôtəˈtelik/ ▸*adj. formal* (of an activity or a creative work) having an end or purpose in itself. ▷early 20th cent.: from **AUTO-** 'self' + Greek *telos* 'end' + **-IC**.

au·tot·o·my /ôˈtätəmē/ ▸*n. Zoology* the casting off of a part of the body (e.g., the tail of a lizard) by an animal under threat.

au·to·tox·in /ˈôtōˌtäksin/ ▸*n.* a substance produced by an organism that is toxic to the organism itself. **—au·to·tox·ic** /ˌôtōˈtäksik/ *adj.*

au·to·trans·form·er /ˌôtōtransˈfôrmər/ ▸*n.* an electrical transformer that has a single coil winding, part of which is common to both primary and secondary circuits.

au·to·trans·plan·ta·tion /ˌôtōˌtransplanˈtāsʜən/ ▸*n.* transplantation of tissue from one site to another in the same individual. **—au·to·trans·plant** /-ˈtrans ˌplant/ *n.* **—au·to·trans·plant·ed** /-transˈplantid/ *adj.*

au·to·troph /ˈôtəˌträf; -ˌtrōf/ ▸*n. Biology* an organism that is able to form nutritional organic substances from simple inorganic substances such as carbon dioxide. Compare with **HETEROTROPH**. **—au·to·troph·ic** *adj.* **—au·tot·ro·phy** *n.*

au·to·wind·er /ˈôtōˌwīndər/ ▸*n.* a device that automatically advances the film in a camera after a picture has been taken. **—au·to·wind** *n.* & *v.*

au·to·work·er /ˈôtōˌwərkər/ ▸*n.* a worker in the automobile industry.

au·tox·i·da·tion /ˌôtäksiˈdāsʜən/ ▸*n. Chemistry* spontaneous oxidation of a substance at ambient temperatures in the presence of oxygen. **—au·tox·i·dize** /ôˈtäksiˌdīz/ *v.*

Au·try /ˈôtrē/, (Orvon) Gene (1907–98), U.S. singer and actor; known as **the Singing Cowboy**. His credits include the first cowboy song recording (1929) and many musical western movies.

au·tumn /ˈôtəm/ ▸*n.* the third season of the year, when crops and fruits are gathered and leaves fall, in the northern hemisphere from September to November and in the southern hemisphere from March to May: *the countryside is ablaze with color in autumn* | [as *adj.*] *autumn leaves* | *figurative he was* ***in the autumn of*** *his life.* ■ *Astronomy* the period from the autumnal equinox to the winter solstice. ▷late Middle

English: from Old French *autompne*, or later directly from Latin *autumnus*.

au·tum·nal /ô'təmnəl/ ▶*adj.* of, characteristic of, or occurring in autumn: *chilly autumnal weather* ▷late 16th cent.: from Latin *autumnalis*, from *autumnus* 'autumn.'

au·tum·nal e·qui·nox ▶*n.* the equinox in autumn, on about September 22 in the northern hemisphere and March 20 in the southern hemisphere.

au·tumn cro·cus ▶*n.* a crocuslike Eurasian plant of the lily family, cultivated for its autumn-blooming flowers. • Genus *Colchicum*, family Liliaceae: several species, in particular meadow saffron.

au·tun·ite /ô'tənīt; 'ôtn,īt/ ▶*n.* a yellow or pale green mineral occurring as square crystals that fluoresce in ultraviolet light. It is a hydrated phosphate of calcium and uranium. ▷mid 19th cent.: from *Autun*, the name of a town in eastern France, + -ITE[1].

Au·vergne /ō'vern(yə); ō'vərn/ a region in south central France that was a province of the Roman Empire. The region is mountainous and contains extinct volcanic cones known as the Puys. ▷from Latin *Arverni*, the name of a Celtic tribe that lived there in Roman times.

aux·il·ia·ry /ôg'zilyərē; -'zil(ə)rē/ ▶*adj.* providing supplementary or additional help and support: *an auxiliary nurse | auxiliary airport staff.* ■ (of equipment) held in reserve: *the ship has an auxiliary power source.* ■ (of troops) engaged in the service of a nation at war but not part of the regular army, and often of foreign origin. ■ (of a sailing vessel) equipped with a supplementary engine.
▶*n.* (*pl.* **-ries**) a person or thing providing supplementary or additional help and support: *a nursing auxiliary | there are two main fuel tanks and two auxiliaries.* ■ a group of volunteers giving supplementary support to an organization or institution: *members of the Volunteer Fire Department's women's auxiliary.* ■ (**auxiliaries**) troops engaged in the service of a nation at war but not part of the regular army, and often of foreign origin. ■ *Grammar* an auxiliary verb. ■ a naval vessel with a supporting role, not armed for combat. ▷late Middle English: from Latin *auxiliarius*, from *auxilium* 'help.'

aux·il·ia·ry verb ▶*n. Grammar* a verb used in forming the tenses, moods, and voices of other verbs. See also MODAL VERB.

The primary auxiliary verbs in English are *be, do,* and *have*; the modal auxiliaries are *can, could, may, might, must, shall, should, will,* and *would.*

aux·in /'ôksin/ ▶*n.* a plant hormone that causes the elongation of cells in shoots and is involved in regulating plant growth. ▷1930s: coined in German from Greek *auxein* 'to increase' + -IN[1].

aux·o·troph /'ôksə,trāf; -,trōf/ ▶*n. Biology* a mutant organism (typically a bacterium or fungus) that requires a particular additional nutrient that the normal strain does not. ▷1950s: from Latin *auxilium* 'help' + Greek *trophos* 'feeder.' **—aux·o·troph·ic** /,ôksə'träfik; -'trō-/ *adj.*

AV ▶*abbr.* ■ audiovisual (teaching aids). ■ Authorized Version.

Av ▶*n.* variant spelling of AB[1].

av·a·da·vat /'avədə,vat/ (also **am·a·da·vat** /'am-/) ▶*n.* a small South Asian waxbill that is often kept as a caged bird. The male has red or green plumage and a red bill. • Genus *Amandava*, family Estrildidae: the **red avadavat** (*A. amandava*) and the **green avadavat** (*A. formosa*). ▷late 17th cent.: named after the city of AHMADABAD in India, where the birds were sold.

a·vail /ə'vāl/ ▶*v.* **1** (**avail oneself of**) use or take advantage of (an opportunity or available resource): *my daughter did not avail herself of my advice.* **2** help or benefit: [*trans.*] *no amount of struggle availed Charles |* [*intrans.*] *the dark and narrow hiding place did not avail to save the fugitives.* ▷Middle English: from obsolete *vail* 'be of use or value' (apparently on the pattern of pairs such as *amount, mount*), from Old French *valoir*, from Latin *valere* 'be strong, be of value.'
▶*PHRASES* □ **avail someone nothing** *archaic* (of an action) be of no help at all to someone: *this protest availed her nothing.* □ **of little** (or **no**) **avail** not very (or not at all) effective or successful: *Latin was of little avail in the practical affairs of life.* □ **to little** (or **no**) **avail** with little (or no) success or benefit: *he tried to get his work recognized, but to little avail.*

a·vail·a·ble /ə'vāləbəl/ ▶*adj.* able to be used or obtained; at someone's disposal: *refreshments will be available all afternoon | a slush fund* **available to** *universities.* ■ (of a person) not otherwise occupied; free to do something: *the nurse is only available at certain times | the minister was not available for comment.* ■ not currently involved in a sexual or romantic relationship: *there's a dearth of available women here.* ▷late Middle English (in the senses 'effectual, serviceable' and 'legally valid'): from AVAIL + -ABLE. Sense 1 dates from the early 19th cent. **—a·vail·a·bil·i·ty** /ə,vālə'bilitē/ *n.*

av·a·lanche /'avə,lanCH/ ▶*n.* a mass of snow, ice, and rocks falling rapidly down a mountainside. ■ a large mass of any material moving rapidly downhill: *an avalanche of mud.* ■ *figurative* a sudden arrival or occurrence of something in overwhelming quantities: *we have had an avalanche of applications.* ■ *Physics* a cumulative process in which a fast-moving ion or electron generates further ions and electrons by collision.
▶*v.* [*intrans.*] (of a mass of snow, ice, and rocks) descend rapidly down a mountainside. ■ [*trans.*] (usu. **be avalanched**) engulf or carry off by such a mass of material: *the climbers were avalanched down the south face of the mountain.* ■ [*intrans.*] *Physics* undergo a rapid increase in conductivity due to an avalanche process. ▷late 18th cent.: from French, alteration of the Alpine dialect word *lavanche* (of unknown origin), influenced by *avaler* 'descend'; compare with Italian *valanga*.

Av·a·lon /'avə,län/ (in Arthurian legend) the place to which Arthur was conveyed after death.

a·vant-garde /'ävänt 'gärd; ,avän/ ▶*n.* (usu. **the avant-garde**) new and unusual or experimental ideas, esp. in the arts, or the people introducing them: *works by artists of the Russian avant-garde.*
▶*adj.* favoring or introducing such new ideas: *a controversial avant-garde composer.* ▷late Middle English (denoting the vanguard of an army): from French, literally 'vanguard.' Current senses date from the early 20th cent. **—a·vant-gard·ism** /-,dizəm/ *n.* **—a·vant-gard·ist** /-dist/ *n.*

av·a·rice /'avəris/ ▶*n.* extreme greed for wealth or material gain. ▷Middle English: from Old French, from Latin *avaritia*, from *avarus* 'greedy.'

av·a·ri·cious /,avə'risHəs/ ▶*adj.* having or showing an extreme greed for wealth or material gain: *a corrupt and avaricious government.* See note at GREEDY. ▷late Middle English: from Old French *avaricieux*, based on Latin *avarus* 'greedy' (see AVARICE). **—av·a·ri·cious·ly** *adv.* **—av·a·ri·cious·ness** *n.*

a·vas·cu·lar /ə'vaskyələr; ā'vas-/ ▶*adj. Medicine* characterized by or associated with a lack of blood vessels.

a·vast /ə'vast/ ▶*exclam. Nautical* stop; cease: *you, young man, avast there!* ▷early 17th cent.: from Dutch *hou'vast, houd vast* 'hold fast!'

av·a·tar /'avə,tär/ ▶*n. chiefly Hinduism* a manifestation of a deity or released soul in bodily form on earth; an incarnate divine teacher. ■ an incarnation, embodiment, or manifestation of a person or idea: *he set himself up as a new avatar of Arab radicalism.* ■ *Computing* a movable icon representing a person in cyberspace or virtual reality graphics. ▷from Sanskrit *avatāra* 'descent,' from *ava* 'down' + *tar-* 'to cross.'

a·vaunt /ə'vônt/ ▶*exclam. archaic* go away: *avaunt, you worm-faced fellows of the night!* ▷late Middle English: from an Anglo-Norman French variant of Old French *avant*, from Latin *ab* 'from' + *ante* 'before.'

a·ve /'ä,vā/ ▶*exclam. poetic/literary* used to express good wishes on meeting or parting.
▶*n.* **1** (**Ave**) short for AVE MARIA. **2** *poetic/literary* a shout of welcome or farewell. ▷Middle English: from Latin, 'fare well!', singular imperative of *avere*.

Ave. ▶*abbr.* Avenue.

Ave·bur·y /'āvb(ə)rē; 'āv,berē/ a village in Wiltshire, site of one of Britain's major henge monuments of the late Neolithic period.

A·ve Ma·ri·a /'ävā mə'rēə/ ▶*n.* a prayer to the Virgin Mary used in Catholic worship. The first line is adapted from Luke 1:28. Also called HAIL MARY. ▷Middle English: the opening words in Latin, literally 'Hail, Mary!'

a·venge /ə'venj/ ▶*v.* [*trans.*] inflict harm in return for (an injury or wrong done to oneself or another): *his determination to avenge the murder of his brother | they are eager to avenge last year's Super Bowl defeat.* ■ inflict such harm on behalf of (oneself or someone else previously wronged or harmed): *we must avenge our dead | she* **avenged herself** *after he broke off their engagement | the warrior swore he would be* **avenged on** *their prince.* ▷late Middle English: from Old French *avengier*, from *a-* (from Latin *ad* 'to') + *vengier*, from Latin *vindicare* 'vindicate.' **—a·veng·er** *n.*

av·ens /'avənz/ ▶*n.* a plant of the rose family, typically having serrated, divided leaves and seeds bearing small hooks. Several kinds are grown in gardens. • Genus *Geum*, family Rosaceae: several species, including the widespread **water avens** (*G. rivale*), with drooping pinkish flowers, and the mat-forming **alpine avens** (*G. montanum*). ▷Middle English: from Old French *avence* (medieval Latin *avencia*), of unknown origin.

a·ven·tu·rine /ə'venCHə,rēn; -,rīn/ ▶*n.* brownish glass containing sparkling particles of copper or gold: [as *adj.*] *aventurine glass.* ■ a translucent mineral containing small reflective particles, typically quartz containing mica or iron compounds, or feldspar containing hematite. ▷early 18th cent.: from French, from Italian *avventurino*, from *avventura* 'chance' (because of its accidental discovery).

av·e·nue /'avə,n(y)ōō/ ▶*n.* **1** a broad road in a town or city, typically having trees at regular intervals along its sides: *tree-lined avenues surround the hotel |* [in *proper names*] *Euclid Avenue.* ■ [in *proper names*] a thoroughfare running at right angles to the streets in a city laid out on a grid pattern: *7th Avenue.* ■ a tree-lined road or path, esp. one that leads to a country house or similar building: *an avenue of limes.* **2** a way of approaching a problem or making progress toward something: *three possible avenues of research suggested themselves.* ▷early 17th cent. (sense 2): from French, feminine past participle of *avenir* 'arrive, approach,' from Latin *advenire*, from *ad-* 'toward' + *venire* 'come.'

a·ver /ə'vər/ ▶*v.* (**a·verred**, **a·ver·ring**) [*reporting verb*] *formal* state or assert to be the case: [with *clause*] *he averred that he was innocent of the allegations |* [with *direct speech*] *"You're the most beautiful girl in the world," he averred.* ■ [*trans.*] *Law* allege as a fact in support of a plea. ▷late Middle English (in the sense 'declare or confirm to be true'): from Old French *averer*, based on Latin *ad* 'to' (implying 'cause to be') + *verus* 'true.'

av·er·age /'av(ə)rij/ (abbr.: **avg.**) ▶*n.* **1** the result obtained by adding several quantities together and then dividing this total by the number of quantities; the mean: *the housing prices there are twice the national average.* Compare with MEAN[3] (sense 1). ■ an amount, standard, level, or rate regarded as usual or ordinary: *the month's snowfall is* **below average** *| they take about thirty minutes* **on average**. See note at NORMAL. **2** the apportionment of financial liability resulting from loss of or damage to a ship or its cargo. ■ reduction in the amount payable under an insurance policy, e.g., in respect of partial loss.
▶*adj.* constituting the result obtained by adding together several quantities and then dividing this total by the number of quantities: *the average temperature in May was 64°F.* ■ of the usual or ordinary standard, level, or quantity: *a woman of average height.* ■ having qualities that are seen as typical of a particular person or thing: *the average teenager prefers comfort to high fashion.* ■ mediocre; not very good: *a very average director who made very average movies.*
▶*v.* [*trans.*] achieve or amount to as an average rate or amount over a period of time: *annual inflation averaged 2.4 percent.* ■ calculate or estimate the average of (figures or measurements): *their earnings,* **averaged out** *over the month, were only $62 a week.* ■ [*intrans.*] (**average out**) result in an even distribution; even out: *it is reasonable to hope that the results will average out.* ■ [*intrans.*] (**average out at/to**) result in an average figure of: *the cost should average out to about $6 per page.* ▷late 15th cent.: from French *avarie* 'damage to ship or cargo,' earlier 'customs duty,' from Italian *avaria*, from Arabic *'awār* 'damage to goods'; the suffix *-age* is on the pattern of *damage*. Originally denoting a charge or customs duty payable by the owner of goods to be shipped, the term later denoted the financial liability from goods lost or damaged at sea, and specifically the equitable apportionment of this between the owners of the vessel and the cargo (late 16th cent.); this gave rise to the general sense of the equalizing out of gains and losses by calculating the mean (mid 18th cent.). **—av·er·age·ly** *adv.*

a·ver·ment /ə'vərmənt/ ▶*n. formal* an affirmation or allegation. ■ *Law* a formal statement by a party in a case of a fact or circumstance that the party offers to prove or substantiate. ▷late Middle English: from Old French *averrement, averement*, from *averer* 'declare true' (see AVER).

A·ver·ro·ës /ə'verō,ēz; ,avə'rō-ēz/ (c.1126–98), Islamic philosopher, judge, and physician, born in Spain; Arabic name *ibn-Rushd*. His highly influential commentaries on Aristotle sought to reconcile the Greek philosophical tradition with the Arabic.

a·verse /ə'vərs/ ▸*adj.* [*predic.*] [usu. with *negative*] (**averse to**) having a strong dislike of or opposition to something: *as a former CIA director, he is not averse to secrecy* | [in *combination*] *the bank's approach has been risk-averse.* ▷late 16th cent.: from Latin *aversus* 'turned away from,' past participle of *avertere* (see AVERT).

USAGE The widespread phrase for expressing dislike, opposition, or hostility (to things, usually not people) is **averse to**. Similarly, one may be said to have an **aversion to** (usually not **aversion from**) certain things or activities (but usually not people): *Katherine was known for her* ***aversion to*** *flying, but she was brave and boarded the plane anyway.* **Averse from** is found more often in British than U.S. English, following the prescription of Samuel Johnson and other traditionalists, who have condemned **averse to** as nonsensical (the Latin origin of **averse** has the meaning 'turn from'). In the U.S., however, **averse to** is by far the more common occurrence. See also **usage** at ADVERSE.

a·ver·sion /ə'vərZHən/ ▸*n.* a strong dislike or disinclination: *he had a deep-seated* ***aversion to*** *most forms of exercise.* ■ someone or something that arouses such feelings. ▷late 16th cent. (originally denoting the action of turning away or averting one's eyes): from Latin *aversio(n-)*, from *avertere* 'turn away from' (see AVERT). **—a·ver·sive** /-siv; -ziv/ *adj.*

a·ver·sion ther·a·py ▸*n.* a type of behavior therapy designed to make a patient give up an undesirable habit by causing them to associate it with an unpleasant effect.

a·vert /ə'vərt/ ▸*v.* [*trans.*] **1** turn away (one's eyes or thoughts): *she averted her eyes during the more violent scenes.* **2** prevent or ward off (an undesirable occurrence): *talks failed to avert a rail strike.* ▷late Middle English (in the sense 'divert or deter someone from a place or a course of action'): from Latin *avertere*, from *ab-* 'from' + *vertere* 'to turn'; reinforced by Old French *avertir*.

A·ves /'āvāz/ *Zoology* a class of vertebrates that comprises the birds. ▷Latin, plural of *avis* 'bird.'

A·ves·ta /ə'vestə/ ▸*n.* the sacred writings of Zoroastrianism, compiled in the 4th century AD. ▷Persian.

A·ves·tan /ə'vestən/ ▸*adj.* of or relating to the Avesta or to the ancient Indo-Iranian language in which it is written, closely related to Vedic Sanskrit.
▸*n.* the Avestan language.

avg. ▸*abbr.* average.

av·gas /'av,gas/ ▸*n.* aircraft fuel. ▷mid 20th cent.: from *av(iation)* + GAS.

a·vi·an /'āvēən/ ▸*adj.* of or relating to birds: *avian tuberculosis.*
▸*n.* a bird. ▷late 19th cent.: from Latin *avis* 'bird' + -AN.

a·vi·an in·flu·en·za ▸the technical name for BIRD FLU.

a·vi·ar·y /'āvē,erē/ ▸*n.* (*pl.* **-ar·ies**) a large cage, building, or enclosure for keeping birds in. ▷late 16th cent.: from Latin *aviarium*, from *avis* 'bird.'

a·vi·ate /'āvē,āt/ ▸*v.* pilot or fly in an airplane: [*trans.*] *an aircraft that can be aviated without effort* | [*intrans.*] *there are fewer opportunities to aviate in winter.* ▷late 19th cent.: back-formation from AVIATION.

a·vi·a·tion /,āvē'āSHən/ ▸*n.* the flying or operating of aircraft: [as *adj.*] *the aviation industry* | *aviation engineering.* ▷mid 19th cent.: from French, formed irregularly from Latin *avis* 'bird.'

a·vi·a·tor /'āvē,ātər/ ▸*n. dated* a pilot.

a·vi·a·tor glass·es ▸*n.* a style of sunglasses with thin wire frames and large lenses.

a·vi·a·trix /,āvē'ātriks/ ▸*n.* (*pl.* **-tri·ces** /-trisēz/) *dated* a female pilot.

Av·i·cen·na /,avə'senə/ (980–1037), Islamic philosopher and physician, born in Persia; Arabic name *ibn-Sina.* His philosophical system was the major influence on the development of scholasticism.

a·vic·u·lar·i·um /ə,vikyə'le(ə)rēəm/ ▸*n.* (*pl.* **-lar·i·a** /-'le(ə)rēə/) *Zoology* (in some bryozoans) any of a number of modified zooids that take the form of a pair of snapping jaws resembling a bird's head, serving to prevent other organisms from settling on the colony. Compare with VIBRACULUM. ▷mid 19th cent.: modern Latin, from *avicula*, diminutive of *avis* 'bird.'

a·vi·cul·ture /'āvi,kəlCHər; 'avi-/ ▸*n.* the breeding and rearing of birds. ▷early 20th cent.: from Latin *avis* 'bird' + CULTURE. **—a·vi·cul·tur·al** /,āvi'kəlCHərəl; ,avi-/ *adj.* **—a·vi·cul·tur·al·ist** /,āvi'kəlCHərəlist; ,avi-/ *n.* **—a·vi·cul·tur·ist** /-rist/ *n.*

av·id /'avid/ ▸*adj.* having or showing a keen interest in or enthusiasm for something: *an avid reader of science fiction* | *she took an avid interest in the project.* See note at EAGER. ■ (**avid for**) having an eager desire for something: *she was avid for information about the murder inquiry.* ▷mid 18th cent.: from French *avide* or Latin *avidus*, from *avere* 'crave.' **—av·id·ly** *adv.*

av·i·din /'avidin/ ▸*n. Biochemistry* a protein found in raw egg white, which combines with biotin and hinders its absorption. ▷1940s: from AVID + -IN[1].

a·vid·i·ty /ə'viditē/ ▸*n.* extreme eagerness or enthusiasm: *he read detective stories with avidity.* ■ *Biochemistry* the overall strength of binding between an antibody and an antigen. ▷late Middle English: from French *avidité* or Latin *aviditas*, from *avidus* 'eager, greedy.'

a·vi·fau·na /,āvə'fônə; ,avə-/ ▸*n.* the birds of a particular region, habitat, or geological period. ▷late 19th cent.: from Latin *avis* 'bird' + FAUNA. **—a·vi·fau·nal** *adj.*

A·vi·gnon /,āvēn'yôN/ a city on the Rhône River in southeastern France; pop. 89,440. From 1309 until 1377, it was the residence of the popes during their exile from Rome and was papal property until the French Revolution.

Á·vi·la, Te·re·sa of see TERESA OF ÁVILA, ST.

a·vi·on·ics /,āvē'äniks/ ▸*plural n.* [usu. treated as *sing.*] electronics as applied to aviation. ■ electronic equipment fitted in an aircraft. ▷1940s: blend of AVIATION and ELECTRONICS.

a·vir·u·lent /ā'vir(y)ələnt/ ▸*adj.* (of a microorganism) not virulent.

a·vi·ta·min·o·sis /ā,vītəmi'nōsis/ ▸*n.* (*pl.* **-ses** /-sēz/) *Medicine* a condition resulting from a deficiency of one or more particular vitamins.

av·o·ca·do /,avə'kädō; ,ävə-/ ▸*n.* (*pl.* **-dos**) **1** a pear-shaped fruit with a rough leathery skin, smooth oily edible flesh, and a large stone: *serve with slices of avocado.* Also called ALLIGATOR PEAR. ■ a light green color like that of the flesh of avocados. **2** the tropical evergreen tree that bears this fruit. It is native to Central America and widely cultivated elsewhere. • *Persea americana*, family Lauraceae. ▷mid 17th cent.: from Spanish, alteration (influenced by *avocado* 'advocate') of *aguacate*, from Nahuatl *ahuacatl*.

av·o·ca·tion /,avə'kāSHən/ ▸*n.* a hobby or minor occupation. ▷mid 17th cent.: from Latin *avocatio(n-)*, from *avocare* 'call away,' from *ab-* 'from' + *vocare* 'to call.' **—av·o·ca·tion·al** /-SHənl/ *adj.*

av·o·cet /'avə,set/ ▸*n.* a long-legged wading bird with a slender upturned bill and strikingly patterned plumage. • Genus *Recurvirostra*, family Recurvirostridae: four species, including the **American avocet** (*R. americana*), which has black and white plumage. ▷late 17th cent.: from French *avocette*, from Italian *avosetta*.

A·vo·ga·dro /,ävə'gäd,rō; ,ävō-/, Amedeo (1776–1856), Italian chemist and physicist. His law, formulated in 1811, was used to derive both molecular weights and a system of atomic weights.

A·vo·ga·dro's law *Chemistry* a law stating that equal volumes of gases at the same temperature and pressure contain equal numbers of molecules.

A·vo·ga·dro's num·ber (also **Avogadro's constant**) *Chemistry* the number of atoms or molecules in one mole of a substance, equal to 6.023×10^{23}.

a·void /ə'void/ ▸*v.* [*trans.*] **1** keep away from or stop oneself from doing (something): *avoid excessive exposure to the sun* | *the kind of place that Robyn would normally have* ***avoided like the plague.*** ■ contrive not to meet (someone): *boys lined up to meet Gloria, but avoided her bossy sister.* ■ (of a person or a route) not go to or through (a place): *this route avoids downtown Boston.* ■ prevent from happening: *make the necessary adjustments to avoid an accident.* **2** *Law* repudiate, nullify, or render void (a decree or contract). ▷late Middle English: from Old French *evuider* 'clear out, get rid of,' from *vuide* 'empty' (see VOID). **—a·void·a·ble** *adj.* **—a·void·a·bly** /-əblē/ *adv.* **—a·void·ance** /ə'voidns/ *n.* **—a·void·er** *n.*

a·void·ance re·la·tion·ship ▸*n.* a familial relationship that is forbidden according to rules operating in some traditional societies. In Australian Aboriginal society, for example, mothers-in-law and sons-in-law may not meet face to face or speak directly with one another.

av·oir·du·pois /,ävərdə'poiz/ ▸*n.* a system of weights based on a pound of 16 ounces or 7,000 grains, widely used in English-speaking countries: [as *adj.*] *avoirdupois weights* | [*postpositive*] *a pound avoirdupois.* Compare with TROY. ■ *humorous* weight; heaviness: *she was putting on the avoirdupois like nobody's business.* ▷Middle English (denoting merchandise sold by weight): from Old French *aveir de peis* 'goods of weight,' from *aveir* 'to have' (infinitive used as a noun, from Latin *habere*) + *peis* 'weight' (see POISE[1]).

A·von /'āvən; 'ā,vän/ **1** a river in central England that rises near the border between the counties of Leicestershire and Northamptonshire and flows 96 miles (154 km) southwest through Stratford to the Severn River. **2** a river in southwestern England that rises near the Gloucestershire–Wiltshire border and flows 75 miles (121 km) through Bath and Bristol to the Severn River. **3** a county in southwestern England; county town, Bristol.

Av·on·dale /'avən,dāl/ a city in south central Arizona, a western suburb of Phoenix; pop. 35,883.

a·vouch /ə'vouCH/ ▸*v.* [*trans.*] *archaic* affirm or assert. ▷late 15th cent.: from Old French *avochier*, from Latin *advocare* 'summon in defense,' from *ad-* 'to' + *vocare* 'to call.' **—a·vouch·ment** *n.*

a·vow /ə'vou/ ▸*v.* [*reporting verb*] assert or confess openly: [with *clause*] *he avowed that he had voted Republican in every election* | [*trans.*] *he avowed his change of faith* | [as *adj.*] (**avowed**) *an avowed Marxist.* ▷Middle English (in the senses 'acknowledge, approve' and 'vouch for'): from Old French *avouer* 'acknowledge,' from Latin *advocare* 'summon in defense' (see AVOUCH). **—a·vow·al** /ə'vouəl/ *n.* **—a·vow·ed·ly** /ə'vou-idlē/ *adv.*

a·vul·sion /ə'vəlSHən/ ▸*n. chiefly Medicine* the action of pulling or tearing away. ■ *Law* the sudden separation of land from one property and its attachment to another, esp. by flooding or a change in the course of a river. Compare with ALLUVION. ▷early 17th cent.: from Latin *avulsion-*, from the verb *avellere*, from *ab-* 'from' + *vallere* 'pluck.' **—a·vulse** /ə'vəls/ *v.*

a·vun·cu·lar /ə'vəNGkyələr/ ▸*adj.* **1** of or relating to an uncle. ■ kind and friendly toward a younger or less experienced person: *an avuncular manner.* **2** *Anthropology* of or relating to the relationship between men and their siblings' children. ▷mid 19th cent.: from Latin *avunculus* 'maternal uncle,' diminutive of *avus* 'grandfather.'

a·vun·cu·late /ə'vəNGkyəlit; -,lāt/ ▸*n.* (**the avunculate**) *Anthropology* the special relationship in some societies between a man and his sister's son. ▷early 20th cent.: from Latin *avunculus* 'maternal uncle' + -ATE[2].

aw /ô/ ▸*exclam.* used to express mild protest, entreaty, commiseration, or disapproval: *aw, Dad, that's not fair.* ▷natural exclamation: first recorded in American English in the mid 19th cent.

AWACS /'ā,waks/ ▸*n.* a long-range airborne radar system for detecting enemy aircraft and missiles and directing attacks on them. ■ an aircraft equipped with this radar system. ▷1960s: acronym from *airborne warning and control system.*

Awadh variant spelling of OUDH.

a·wait /ə'wāt/ ▸*v.* [*trans.*] (of a person) wait for (an event): *we await the proposals with impatience* | *prisoners awaiting trial* | [as *adj.*, with *submodifier*] (**awaited**) *an eagerly awaited debut.* ■ (of an event or circumstance) be in store for (someone): *many dangers await them.* ▷Middle English: from Anglo-Norman French *awaitier*, from *a-* (from Latin *ad* 'to, at') + *waitier* 'to wait.'

a·wake /ə'wāk/ ▸*v.* (*past* **a·woke** /ə'wōk/; *past part.* **a·wok·en** /ə'wōkən/) [*intrans.*] stop sleeping; wake from sleep: *she awoke to find the streets covered in snow.* ■ [*trans.*] cause (someone) to wake from sleep: *my screams awoke my parents.* ■ regain consciousness: *I awoke six hours after the operation.* ■ (**awake to**) *figurative* become aware of; come to a realization of: *the authorities finally awoke to the extent of the problem.* ■ make or become active again: *there were echoes and scents that awoke some memory in me.*
▸*adj.* [*predic.*] not asleep: *the noise might keep you awake at night.* ■ (**awake to**) aware of: *too few are awake to the dangers.* ▷Old English *āwæcnan*, *āwacian*, both used in the sense 'come out of sleep' (see A-[2], WAKE[1]).

a·wak·en /ə'wākən/ ▸*v.* [*trans.*] rouse from sleep; cause to stop sleeping: *Anna was awakened by the telephone.* ■ [*intrans.*] stop sleeping: *he sighed but did not awaken.* ■ rouse (a feeling): *different images can awaken new emotions within us.* ■ (**awaken someone to**) make someone aware of (something) for the first time: *the movie helped to awaken the public to the horrors of apartheid.* ▷Old English *onwæcnan*, from *on* 'on' + WAKEN.

a·wak·en·ing /ə'wāk(ə)niNG/ ▸*n.* [in *sing.*] an act or moment of becoming suddenly aware of something: *the war came as* ***a rude awakening*** *to the hardships of life.*

■ *formal* an act of waking from sleep. ■ the beginning or rousing of something: *the awakening of democracy in Eastern Europe.*
▸*adj.* [*attrib.*] coming into existence or awareness: *his awakening desire | an awakening conscience.*

a·ward /ə'wôrd/ ▸*v.* [with *two objs.*] give or order the giving of (something) as an official payment, compensation, or prize to (someone): *he was awarded the Purple Heart | the 3.5 percent pay raise was awarded to the staff.* See note at **GIVE**. ■ grant or assign (a contract or commission) to (a person or organization).
▸*n.* a prize or other mark of recognition given in honor of an achievement: *the company's annual award for high-quality service* | [as *adj.*] *an award ceremony.* ■ an amount of money paid to someone as an official payment, compensation, or grant: *a generous award given to promising young dancers.* ■ the action of giving a payment, compensation, or prize: *the award of an honorary doctorate | an award of damages.* ▷late Middle English (in the sense 'issue a judicial decision,' also denoting the decision itself): from Anglo-Norman French *awarder*, variant of Old French *esguarder* 'consider, ordain,' from *es-* (from Latin *ex* 'thoroughly') + *guarder* 'watch (over),' based on a word of Germanic origin related to **WARD**; compare with **GUARD**. **—a·ward·ee** /ə,wôr'dē/ *n.* **—a·ward·er** *n.*

a·ware /ə'we(ə)r/ ▸*adj.* [*predic.*] having knowledge or perception of a situation or fact: *most people are* ***aware of*** *the dangers of sunbathing | I am* ***well aware of*** *the problem* | [with *clause*] *he was aware that a problem existed* ***as far as I'm aware****, no one has complained.* ■ [with *adverbial*] concerned and well-informed about a particular situation or development: *unless everyone becomes more* ***environmentally aware****, catastrophe is inevitable | a* ***politically aware*** *electorate.* ▷Old English *gewær*; related to German *gewahr*, also to **WARE**[2]. **—a·ware·ness** *n.*

a·wash /ə'wôsн; ə'wäsн/ ▸*adj.* [*predic.*] covered or flooded with water, esp. seawater or rain: *the boat rolled violently, its decks awash | figurative the city was* ***awash with*** *journalists.* ■ level with the surface of water, esp. the sea, so that it just washes over: *a rock awash outside the reef entrance.*

a·way /ə'wā/ ▸*adv.* **1** to or at a distance from a particular place, person, or thing: *she landed badly, and crawled away | they walked* ***away from*** *the church in silence | Bernice pushed him away | we'll be away for four nights | there's a river* ***not far away****.* ■ at a specified distance: *when he was ten or twelve feet away, he stopped | a loud explosion* ***a short distance away*** *| we have had patients* ***from as far away as*** *Toronto.* ■ at a specified future distance in time: *the wedding is only weeks away.* ■ toward a lower level; downward: *in front of them the land fell away to the river.* ■ conceptually to one side, so as no longer to be the focus of attention: *the museum has shifted its emphasis* ***away from*** *research toward exhibitions.* **2** into an appropriate place for storage or safekeeping: *he put away the lawn furniture | Philip locked away all the cash every night.* ■ toward or into nonexistence: *the sound of hoofbeats died away | Marie felt her distress ebbing away.* **3** constantly, persistently, or continuously: *there was little Edgar crooning away | have your camera ready and click away when you spot something.*
▸*adj.* (of a sports competition) played at the opponents' grounds: *tomorrow night's away game at Yankee Stadium.* ▷Old English *onweg, aweg* 'on one's way' (see **A-**[2], **WAY**).
▸*PHRASE* □ **away with** said as an exhortation to overcome or be rid of something; let us be rid of: *away with poverty!*

a·way mes·sage ▸*n.* a voice or text message directed to callers of a cell phone whose owner cannot answer.

AWB an extreme right-wing white political party in South Africa violently opposed to majority rule. ▷abbreviation from *Afrikaner Weerstandsbeweging* 'Afrikaner Resistance Movement.'

awe /ô/ ▸*n.* a feeling of reverential respect mixed with fear or wonder: *they gazed in awe at the small mountain of diamonds | the sight filled me with awe | his staff members* ***are in awe of*** *him.* ■ *archaic* capacity to inspire awe: *is it any wonder that Christmas Eve has lost its awe?*
▸*v.* [*trans.*] (usu. **be awed**) inspire with awe: *they were both awed by the vastness of the forest* | [as *adj.*] (**awed**) *he spoke in a hushed, awed whisper.* ▷Old English *ege* 'terror, dread, awe,' replaced in Middle English by forms related to Old Norse *agi*.

a·weigh /ə'wā/ ▸*adj. Nautical* (of an anchor) raised just clear of the sea or riverbed. ▷early 17th cent.: from **A-**[2] 'on'+ **WEIGH**[1].

awe-in·spir·ing ▸*adj.* arousing awe through being impressive, formidable, or magnificent: *Michelangelo's awe-inspiring masterpiece.*

awe·some /'ôsəm/ ▸*adj.* extremely impressive or daunting; inspiring great admiration, apprehension, or fear: *the awesome power of the atomic bomb.* ■ *informal* extremely good; excellent: *the band is truly awesome!* ▷late 16th cent. (in the sense 'filled with awe'): from **AWE** + **-SOME**[1]. **—awe·some·ly** *adv.* **—awe·some·ness** *n.*

awe·struck /'ô,strək/ (also **awe·strick·en** /'ô,strikən/) ▸*adj.* filled with or revealing awe: *people were awestruck by the pictures sent back to earth.*

aw·ful /'ôfəl/ ▸*adj.* **1** very bad or unpleasant: *the place smelled awful | I look awful in a swimsuit | an awful speech.* ■ extremely shocking; horrific: *awful, bloody images.* ■ [*attrib.*] used to emphasize the extent of something, esp. something unpleasant or negative: *I've made an awful fool of myself.* ■ (of a person) very unwell, troubled, or unhappy: *I felt awful for being so angry with him | you look awful—you should go and lie down.* **2** *archaic* inspiring reverential wonder or fear.
▸*adv.* [as *submodifier*] *informal* awfully; very: *we're an awful long way from the main road.* ▷Old English (see **AWE**, **-FUL**). **—aw·ful·ness** *n.*
▸*PHRASE* □ **an awful lot** a very large amount; a great deal: *we've had an awful lot of letters | you've still got an awful lot to learn.*

aw·ful·ize /'ôfə,līz/ ▸*v.* to imagine (something) to be as bad as it can possibly be: [*trans.*] *one way to make yourself miserable is awfulizing a situation, or imposing impossible standards upon yourself and others* | [as *gerund*] (**awfulizing**) *I bravely boarded, managed to find a seat, stash my overnight bag, and engage in some steady awfulizing.*

aw·ful·ly /'ôf(ə)lē/ ▸*adv.* **1** [as *submodifier*] (used esp. in spoken English) very: *I'm awfully sorry to bother you so late | an awfully nice man.* **2** very badly or unpleasantly: *we played awfully.*

a·while /ə'(h)wīl/ ▸*adv.* for a short time: *stand here awhile.* ▷Old English *āne hwīle* '(for) a while.'

USAGE The adverb **awhile** (*we paused awhile*) should be written as one word. The noun phrase, meaning 'a period of time,' esp. when preceded by a preposition, should be written as two words (*Margaret rested for* ***a while****; we'll be there in* ***a while***). See also **usage** at **WORTHWHILE**.

a·whirl /ə'(h)wərl/ ▸*adj.* [*predic.*] in a whirl; whirling: *her mind was* ***awhirl with*** *images.*

awk·ward /'ôkwərd/ ▸*adj.* **1** causing difficulty; hard to do or deal with: *one of the most awkward jobs is painting a ceiling | some awkward questions | the wheelbarrow can be awkward to maneuver.* ■ deliberately unreasonable or uncooperative: *you're being damned awkward! | please excuse my daughter—she's at an awkward age.* **2** causing or feeling embarrassment or inconvenience: *he had put her in a very awkward situation.* **3** not smooth or graceful; ungainly: *Luther's awkward movements impeded his progress | she was long-legged and rather awkward.* ■ uncomfortable or abnormal: *make sure the baby isn't sleeping in an awkward position.* ▷late Middle English (in the sense 'the wrong way around, upside down'): from dialect *awk* 'backward, perverse, clumsy' (from Old Norse *afugr* 'turned the wrong way') + **-WARD**. **—awk·ward·ly** *adv.* **—awk·ward·ness** *n.*

awk·ward age ▸*n.* the period of adolescence marked by self-consciousness and moody behavior.

awl /ôl/ ▸*n.* a small pointed tool used for piercing holes, esp. in leather. ▷Old English *æl*, of Germanic origin; related to German *Ahle*.

awl

awn /ôn/ ▸*n. Botany* a stiff bristle, esp. one of those growing from the ear or flower of barley, rye, and many grasses. ▷Old English, from Old Norse *ǫgn*; related to Swedish *agn*, Danish *avn*. **—awned** *adj.*

awn·ing /'ôniNG/ ▸*n.* a sheet of canvas or other material stretched on a frame and used to keep the sun or rain off a storefront, window, doorway, or deck. ▷early 17th cent. (originally in nautical use): of unknown origin.

a·woke /ə'wōk/ ▸ past of **AWAKE**.

a·wo·ken /ə'wōkən/ ▸ past participle of **AWAKE**.

AWOL /'ā,wôl/ ▸*adj.* [*predic.*] *Military* absent from one's post but without intent to desert: *the men have gone AWOL | humorous now the parrot has* ***gone AWOL****.* ▷1920s: acronym from *absent without (official) leave.*

a·wry /ə'rī/ ▸*adv. & adj.* away from the appropriate, planned, or expected course; amiss: [as *adv.*] *many youthful romances* ***go awry*** | [as *predic. adj.*] *I got the impression that something was awry.* ■ out of the normal or correct position; askew: [as *predic. adj.*] *he was hatless, his silver hair awry.* ▷late Middle English: from **A-**[2] 'on' + **WRY**.

aw-shucks ▸*adj.* [*attrib.*] *informal* (of a personal quality or manner) self-deprecating and shy: *his aw-shucks niceness disguised his conniving nature.* ▷late 20th cent.: from **AW** + *shucks* (see **SHUCK**).

ax /aks/ (also **axe**) ▸*n.* **1** a tool typically used for chopping wood, usually a steel blade attached at a right angle to a wooden handle. ■ *figurative* a measure intended to reduce costs drastically, esp. one that involves elimination of staff: *thirty workers are* ***facing the ax*** *in the assembly department.* **2** *informal* a musical instrument, esp. a jazz musician's saxophone or a bass guitar.
▸*v.* [*trans.*] **1** end, cancel, or dismiss suddenly and ruthlessly: *the company is axing 125 jobs | 2,500 staff were axed as part of the realignment.* ■ reduce (costs or services) drastically: *the candidates all promised to ax government spending.* **2** cut or strike with an ax, esp. violently or destructively: *the door had been axed by the firefighters.* ▷Old English *æx*, of Germanic origin; related to Dutch *aaks* and German *Axt*.
▸*PHRASE* □ **have an ax to grind** have a self-serving reason for doing or being involved in something: *she joined the board because she had an ax to grind with the school system.*

ax

ax·el /'aksəl/ (also **Ax·el**) ▸*n. Figure Skating* a jump with a forward takeoff from the forward outside edge of one skate to the backward outside edge of the other, with one and a half turns in the air. ▷1930s: named after *Axel* R. Paulsen (1885–1938), Norwegian skater.

a·xen·ic /ā'zēnik; ā'zen-/ ▸*adj. chiefly Botany* of, relating to, or denoting a culture that is free from living organisms other than the species required. ▷1940s: from *a-* 'not' + Greek *xenikos* 'alien, strange' + **-IC**. **—a·xen·i·cal·ly** /-ik(ə)lē/ *adv.*

ax·es /'ak,sēz/ ▸ plural form of **AXIS**.

ax·i·al /'aksēəl/ ▸*adj.* of, forming, or relating to an axis: *the main axial road.* ■ around an axis: *the axial rotation rate of the earth.* **—ax·i·al·ly** *adv.*

ax·il /'aksəl/ ▸*n. Botany* the upper angle between a leaf stalk or branch and the stem or trunk from which it is growing. ▷late 18th cent.: from Latin *axilla* 'armpit' (see **AXILLA**).

axil

ax·il·la /ak'silə/ ▸*n.* (*pl.* **ax·il·lae** /ak'silē/) *Anatomy* the space below the shoulder through which vessels and nerves enter and leave the upper arm; a person's armpit. ■ *Botany* an axil. ▷early 17th cent.: from Latin, diminutive of *ala* 'wing.'

ax·il·lar·y /'aksə,lerē/ ▸*adj. Anatomy* of or relating to the armpit: *enlargement of the axillary lymph nodes.* ■ *Botany* in or growing from an axil: *axillary shoots.* Often contrasted with **TERMINAL**.

ax·il·lar·y bud ▸*n.* a bud that grows from the axil of a leaf and may develop into a branch or flower cluster. Also called **LATERAL BUD**.

awning

Pronunciation Key ə *ago*; ər *over*; 'ə or ,ə *up*; 'ər or ,ər *fur*; a *hat*; ā *rate*; ä *car*; CH *chew*; e *let*; ē *see*; e(ə)r *air*; i *fit*; ī *by*; i(ə)r *ear*; NG *sing*; ō *go*; ô *for*; oi *boy*; o͝o *good*; o͞o *goo*; ou *out*; SH *she*; TH *thin*; T͟H *then*; (h)w *why*; ZH *vision*

ax·i·om /ˈaksēəm/ ▸*n.* a statement or proposition that is regarded as being established, accepted, or self-evidently true: *the **axiom** that supply equals demand.* ■ *chiefly Mathematics* a statement or proposition on which an abstractly defined structure is based. ▷late 15th cent.: from French *axiome* or Latin *axioma,* from Greek *axiōma* 'what is thought fitting,' from *axios* 'worthy.'

ax·i·o·mat·ic /ˌaksēəˈmatik/ ▸*adj.* self-evident or unquestionable: *it is **axiomatic that** dividends have to be financed.* ■ [*attrib.*] *chiefly Mathematics* relating to or containing axioms. ▷late 18th cent.: from Greek *axiōmatikos,* from *axiōma* 'what is thought fitting' (see AXIOM). **—ax·i·o·mat·i·cal·ly** /-ik(ə)lē/ *adv.*

ax·i·on /ˈaksēˌän/ ▸*n. Physics* a hypothetical subatomic particle postulated to account for the rarity of processes that break charge-parity symmetry. It is very light, electrically neutral, and pseudoscalar. ▷1970s: from AXIAL + -ON.

ax·is /ˈaksis/ ▸*n.* (*pl.* **ax·es** /ˈaksēz/) **1** an imaginary line about which a body rotates: *the earth revolves on its axis once every 24 hours.* ■ *Geometry* an imaginary straight line passing through the center of a symmetrical solid, and about which a plane figure can be conceived as rotating to generate the solid. ■ an imaginary line that divides something into equal or roughly equal halves, esp. in the direction of its greatest length. **2** *Mathematics* a fixed reference line for the measurement of coordinates: *the variable that is thought of as a cause is placed on the horizontal axis, and the variable that is thought of as an effect on the vertical axis.* **3** a straight central part in a structure to which other parts are connected. ■ *Botany* the central column of an inflorescence or other growth. ■ *Zoology* the skull and backbone of a vertebrate animal. **4** *Anatomy* the second cervical vertebra, below the atlas at the top of the backbone. **5** an agreement or alliance between two or more countries that forms a center for an eventual larger grouping of nations: *the Anglo-American axis.* ■ (**the Axis**) the alliance of Germany and Italy formed before and during World War II, later extended to include Japan and other countries: [as *adj.*] *the Axis Powers.* ▷late Middle English: from Latin, 'axle, pivot.'

ax·is deer (also **ax·is**) ▸*n.* a deer that has lyre-shaped antlers and a yellowish-brown coat with white spots, native to India and Sri Lanka. • *Cervus axis,* family Cervidae. ▷early 17th cent.: *axis* from Latin, the name of an Indian animal mentioned by Pliny.

ax·i·sym·met·ric /ˌaksēsəˈmetrik/ ▸*adj. Geometry* symmetrical about an axis.

ax·le /ˈaksəl/ ▸*n.* a rod or spindle (either fixed or rotating) passing through the center of a wheel or group of wheels: [as *adj.*] *axle grease axle loads.* ▷Middle English (originally *axle-tree*): from Old Norse *ǫxultré.*

ax·man /ˈaksˌman/ (also **axe·man**) ▸*n.* (*pl.* **-men**) **1** a person who works with an ax: *he was like an axman at work in a tangled thicket.* **2** *informal* a rock or jazz guitarist.

Ax·min·ster /ˈaksˌminstər/ (also **Axminster carpet**) ▸*n.* a kind of machine-woven patterned carpet with a cut pile. ▷early 19th cent.: named after the town of *Axminster* in southern England, noted since the 18th cent. for the production of carpets.

ax·o·lotl /ˈaksəˌlätl/ ▸*n.* a Mexican salamander which in natural conditions retains its aquatic newtlike larval form throughout life but is able to breed. • *Ambystoma mexicanum,* family Ambystomatidae. ▷late 18th cent.: from Nahuatl, from *atl* 'water' + *xolotl* 'servant.'

ax·on /ˈakˌsän/ ▸*n.* the long threadlike part of a nerve cell along which impulses are conducted from the cell body to other cells. ▷mid 19th cent. (denoting the body axis): from Greek *axōn* 'axis.' **—ax·on·al** /ˈaksənl; akˈsänl/ *adj.*

ax·o·neme /ˈaksəˌnēm/ ▸*n. Biology* the central strand of a cilium or flagellum. It is composed of an array of microtubules, typically in nine pairs around two single central ones. ▷early 20th cent.: from Greek *axōn* 'axis' + *nēma* 'thread.' **—ax·o·ne·mal** /aksəˈnēməl/ *adj.*

ax·o·no·met·ric /ˌaksənōˈmetrik/ ▸*adj.* using or designating an orthographic projection of an object, such as a building, on a plane inclined to each of the three principal axes of the object; three-dimensional but without perspective.

ax·o·plasm /ˈaksəˌplazəm/ ▸*n. Biology* the cytoplasm of a nerve axon. **—ax·o·plas·mic** /ˌaksəˈplazmik/ *adj.*

Ax·um variant spelling of AKSUM.

ay /ī; ā/ ▸*exclam.* & *n.* variant spelling of AYE.

A·ya·cu·cho /ˌäyəˈkōōchō/ a city in the Andes in south central Peru; pop. 101,600.

a·yah /ˈäyə/ ▸*n.* a native maid or nursemaid employed by Europeans in India. ▷Anglo-Indian, from Portuguese *aia* 'nurse,' feminine of *aio* 'tutor.'

a·ya·huas·ca /ˌäyəˈwäskə/ ▸*n.* a tropical vine native to the Amazon region, noted for its hallucinogenic properties. • Genus *Banisteriopsis,* family Malpighiaceae: several species, in particular *B. caapi.* ■ a hallucinogenic drink prepared from the bark of this. ▷1940s: from South American Spanish, from Quechua *ayawáskha,* from *aya* 'corpse' + *waskha* 'rope.'

a·ya·tol·lah /ˌäyəˈtōlə/ ▸*n.* a Shiite religious leader in Iran. ▷1950s: from Persian, from Arabic *āyatu-llāh,* literally 'token of God.'

A·ya·tol·lah Kho·mei·ni see KHOMEINI.

Ayck·bourn /ˈākˌbôrn/, Sir Alan (1939–), English playwright. Notable plays: *Relatively Speaking* (1967), *Absurd Person Singular* (1973), and *A Chorus of Disapproval* (1985).

aye[1] /ī/ (also **ay**) ▸*exclam. archaic* or *dialect* said to express assent; yes: *aye, you're right about that.* ■ (**aye, aye**) *Nautical* a response acknowledging an order: *aye, aye, captain.* ■ (in voting) I assent: *all in favor say, "aye."*

▸*n.* an affirmative answer or assent, esp. in voting: *the House was divided: Ayes 211, Noes 271.* ▷late 16th cent.: probably from *I,* first person personal pronoun, expressing assent.

▸*PHRASE* □ **the ayes have it** the affirmative votes are in the majority.

aye[2] /ā/ ▸*adv. archaic* or *Scottish* always or still. ▷Middle English: from Old Norse *ei, ey;* related to Latin *aevum* 'age' and Greek *aie(i)* 'ever,' *aiōn;* 'aeon.'

▸*PHRASE* □ **for aye** forever: *I shall treasure the memory for aye.*

aye-aye /ˈī ˈī/ ▸*n.* a rare nocturnal Madagascan primate allied to the lemurs. It has rodentlike incisor teeth and an elongated twiglike finger on each hand with which it pries insects from bark. • *Daubentonia madagascariensis,* the only member of the family Daubentoniidae. ▷late 18th cent.: from French, from Malagasy *aiay.*

Ayer /e(ə)r/, Sir A. J. (1910–89), English philosopher; full name *Alfred Jules Ayer.* He was an important proponent of logical positivism. Notable works: *Language, Truth, and Logic* (1936) and *The Problem of Knowledge* (1956).

Ayers Rock /e(ə)rz/ a red rock mass in Northern Territory, Australia, southwest of Alice Springs. The largest monolith in the world, it is 1,143 feet (348 m) high and about 6 miles (9 km) in circumference. Aboriginal name **ULURU**.

A·ye·sha /äˈ(y)ēshə/ the wife of Muhammad.

Ay·ma·ra /ˌīmäˈrä/ ▸*n.* (*pl.* same or **-ras**) **1** a member of a South American Indian people inhabiting the high plateau region of Bolivia and Peru near Lake Titicaca. **2** the language of this people, related to Quechua.

▸*adj.* of or relating to this people or their language. ▷Spanish.

Ayr·shire /ˈe(ə)rshər; -ˌshi(ə)r/ ▸*n.* an animal of a mainly white breed of dairy cattle. ▷mid 19th cent.: named after *Ayrshire,* a former Scottish county where the cattle were bred.

AYT ▸*abbr. informal Computing* (in e-mail) are you there?

A·yub Khan /äˈyōōb ˈkän; ˈkhän/, Muhammad (1907–74), Pakistani soldier and statesman; president 1958–69.

A·yur·ve·da /ˌäyərˈvādə; -ˈvēdə/ ▸*n.* the traditional Hindu system of medicine, which is based on the idea of balance in bodily systems and uses diet, herbal treatment, and yogic breathing. ▷from Sanskrit *āyus* 'life' + *veda* 'science.' **—A·yur·ve·dic** /-ˈvedik/ *adj.*

AZ ▸*abbr.* Arizona (in official postal use).

A·zad Kash·mir /ˈäzäd käshˈmi(ə)r; kash-/ an autonomous state in northeastern Pakistan, formerly part of Kashmir; administrative center, Muzzafarabad. It was established in 1949 after Kashmir was split as a result of the partition of India. ▷from Urdu, literally 'Free Kashmir.'

a·zal·ea /əˈzālyə/ ▸*n.* a deciduous flowering shrub of the heath family with clusters of brightly colored, sometimes fragrant flowers. Technically classified as rhododenrons, azaleas are characteristically smaller than most other rhododendrons. • Genus *Rhododendron,* family Ericaceae: many cultivars. ▷mid 18th cent.: modern Latin, from Greek, feminine of *azaleos* 'dry,' because the shrub flourishes in dry soil.

a·zan /äˈzän/ ▸*n.* the Muslim call to ritual prayer, typically made by a muezzin from the minaret of a mosque. ▷mid 19th cent.: from Arabic *'aḏān* 'announcement.' Compare with MUEZZIN.

a·za·role /ˈazəˌrōl/ ▸*n.* a small tree related to the hawthorn, cultivated in southern Europe for its small, yellow or reddish fruit. • *Crataegus azarolus,* family Rosaceae.

a·ze·o·trope /āˈzēəˌtrōp/ ▸*n. Chemistry* a mixture of two liquids that has a constant boiling point and composition throughout distillation. ▷early 20th cent.: from A-[1] 'without' + Greek *zein* 'to boil' + *tropos* 'turning.' **—a·ze·o·trop·ic** /ˌāzēəˈträpik; -ˈtrōpik/ *adj.*

Az·er·bai·jan /ˌazərˌbīˈjän; ˌäz-; -ˈzhän/ a country in southwestern Asia, in the Caucasus, on the western shore of the Caspian Sea; pop. 7,868,000; capital, Baku; languages, Azerbaijani (official), Russian.

Historically, the name Azerbaijan refers to a larger region that formed part of Persia. The northern part of this was ceded to Russia in the early 19th century; the southern part remained a region in northwestern Iran. Russian Azerbaijan was absorbed into the Soviet Union in 1922 and gained independence on the breakup of the USSR in 1991. Azerbaijan contains the predominantly Armenian region of Nagorno-Karabakh, over which open conflict with Armenia broke out in 1988. The Azeri autonomous republic of Naxçivan forms an enclave within the Republic of Armenia and similarly continues to be the subject of armed conflict.

A·zer·bai·ja·ni /ˌazərbīˈjänē; ˌäzər-/ ▸*adj.* of or relating to Azerbaijan or its people or their language.

▸*n.* (*pl.* **-nis**) **1** a native or national of Azerbaijan or a person of Azerbaijani descent. **2** the Turkic language of Azerbaijan.

A·ze·ri /əˈzerē/ ▸*n.* (*pl.* **-ris**) **1** a member of a Turkic people forming the majority population of Azerbaijan, and also living in Armenia and northern Iran. **2** the Azerbaijani language.

▸*adj.* of, relating to, or denoting this people or their language. ▷from Turkish *azerī.*

az·ide /ˈāˌzīd; ˈazˌīd/ ▸*n. Chemistry* a compound containing the univalent group $-N_3^-$. ▷early 20th cent.: from AZO- + -IDE.

a·zi·do·thy·mi·dine /ˌazidōˈthīməˌdēn; əˌzī-; əˌzē-/ ▸*n.* trademark for the drug ZIDOVUDINE.

A·zi·ki·we /ˌäziˈkēwā/, (Benjamin) Nnamdi (1904–96), Nigerian statesman; the first governor-general of independent Nigeria 1960–63 and its first president 1963-66.

az·i·muth /ˈazəməth/ ▸*n.* the direction of a celestial object from the observer, expressed as the angular distance from the north or south point of the horizon to the point at which a vertical circle passing through the object intersects the horizon. ■ the horizontal angle or direction of a compass bearing. ▷late Middle English (denoting the arc of a celestial circle from the zenith to the horizon): from Old French *azimut,* from Arabic *as-samt,* from *al* 'the' + *samt* 'way, direction.' **—az·i·muth·al** /ˌazəˈməthəl/ *adj.*

az·i·muth·al pro·jec·tion /ˌazəˈməthəl/ ▸*n.* a map projection in which a region of the earth is projected onto a plane tangential to the surface, typically at a pole or the equator.

az·ine /ˈazˌēn; ˈāˌzēn/ ▸*n. Chemistry* a cyclic organic compound having a ring including one or (typically) more nitrogen atoms. ▷late 19th cent.: from AZO- + -INE[4].

azo- ▸*prefix Chemistry* containing two adjacent nitrogen atoms between carbon atoms: *azobenzene.*

▷from obsolete *azote* 'nitrogen,' from French, from Greek *azōos* 'without life.'

az·o·ben·zene /ˌazō'benzēn; -ben'zēn; ˌāzō-/ ▶*n. Chemistry* a synthetic crystalline organic compound used chiefly in dye manufacture. • Chem. formula: $(C_6H_5)N{=}N(C_6H_5)$.

az·o dye /'azō; 'āzō/ ▶*n. Chemistry* any of a large class of synthetic dyes whose molecules contain two adjacent nitrogen atoms between carbon atoms.

a·zo·ic /ā'zō-ik; ə'zō-/ ▶*adj.* having no trace of life or organic remains. ■ (**Azoic**) *Geology* another term for **ARCHEAN.** ▷mid 19th cent.: from Greek *azōos* 'without life' + **-IC**.

a·zon·al /ā'zōnl/ ▶*adj.* (esp. of soils) having no zonal organization or structure.

a·zo·o·sper·mi·a /ˌāzōə'spərmēə/ ▶*n. Medicine* absence of motile (and hence viable) sperm in the semen. **—a·zo·o·sper·mic** /-'spərmik/ *adj.*

A·zores /ə'zôrz; 'āˌzôrz/ a group of volcanic islands in the Atlantic Ocean, west of Portugal, a possession of Portugal but partially autonomous; pop. 241,590; capital, Ponta Delgada.

A·zores High ▶*Meteorology n.* a semipermanent area of high pressure located over the Azores in winter and early spring. Compare with **BERMUDA HIGH**.

az·o·tu·ri·a /ˌazə't(y)ŏŏrēə/ ▶*n. Medicine* abnormal excess of nitrogen compounds in the urine. ■ *Veterinary Medicine* a condition of horses that causes stiffness and pain in the muscles of the hindquarters and back, and the production of dark-colored urine containing myoglobin. ▷mid 19th cent.: from obsolete *azote* 'nitrogen' + **-URIA**.

A·zov, Sea of /'azˌôf; 'āˌzôf/ an inland sea in southern Russia and Ukraine, separated from the Black Sea by the Crimea and linked to it by a narrow strait.

Az·ra·el /'azrēˌel; ˌäzrē'el/ *Jewish & Islamic Mythology* the angel who severs the soul from the body at death.

AZT ▶*abbr. trademark* azidothymidine.

Az·tec /'azˌtek/ ▶*n.* **1** a member of the American Indian people dominant in Mexico before the Spanish conquest of the 16th century. **2** the extinct language of this people, a Uto-Aztecan language from which modern Nahuatl is descended.
▶*adj.* of, relating to, or denoting this people or their language. ▷from French *Aztèque* or Spanish *Azteca*, from Nahuatl *aztecatl* 'person of Aztlan,' their legendary place of origin.

a·zu·le·jo /ˌazhə'lāˌhō; ˌazyə-/ ▶*n.* (*pl.* **-jos**) a kind of glazed colored tile traditionally used in Spanish and Portuguese buildings. ▷from Spanish, from *azul* 'blue.'

az·ure /'azhər/ ▶*adj.* bright blue in color, like a cloudless sky: *white beaches surrounded by azure seas.* ■ *Heraldry* blue: [*postpositive*] *a saltire azure.*
▶*n.* **1** a bright blue color. ■ *poetic/literary* the clear sky. **2** a small butterfly that is typically blue or purplish, with color differences between the sexes. • *Celastrina* and other genera, family Lycaenidae. ▷Middle English (denoting a blue dye): from Old French *asur, azur*, from medieval Latin *azzurum, azolum*, from Arabic *al* 'the' + *lāzaward* (from Persian *lāžward* 'lapis lazuli').

az·ur·ite /'azhəˌrīt/ ▶*n.* a blue mineral consisting of copper hydroxyl carbonate. It occurs as blue prisms or crystal masses, often with malachite. ▷early 19th cent.: from **AZURE** + **-ITE**[1].

Azu·sa /ə'zōōsə/ a city in southwestern California, northeast of Los Angeles; pop. 41,333.

az·y·gos vein /'azəgəs/ ▶*n. Anatomy* a large vein on the right side at the back of the thorax, draining into the superior vena cava. ▷mid 17th cent.: *azygos* from Greek *azugos*, from *a-* 'without' + *zugon* 'yoke,' the vein not being one of a pair.

az·y·gous /ā'zīgəs; 'azə-/ ▶*adj. Anatomy & Biology* (of an organic structure) single; not existing in pairs. ▷mid 19th cent.: from Greek *azugos* 'unyoked' (from *a-* 'without' + *zugon* 'yoke') + **-OUS**.

Az Zar·qa /äz 'zärˌkä/ variant form of **ZARQA**.

Bb

B[1] /bē/ (also **b**) ▸*n.* (*pl.* **Bs** or **B's**) **1** the second letter of the alphabet. ■ the second highest class of academic mark. ■ denoting the second-highest-earning socioeconomic category for marketing purposes, including intermediate management and professional personnel. ■ (**b**) *Chess* denoting the second file from the left, as viewed from White's side of the board. ■ (usu. **b**) the second constant to appear in an algebraic equation. ■ *Geology* denoting a soil horizon of intermediate depth, typically the subsoil. ■ the human blood type (in the ABO system) containing the B antigen and lacking the A. **2** (usu. **B**) *Music* the seventh note of the diatonic scale of C major. ■ a key based on a scale with B as its keynote.
▸*PHRASE* □ **plan B** an alternative strategy: *it's time I put plan B into action.*

B[2] ▸*abbr.* ■ (used in recording moves in chess) bishop: *Be5.* ■ black (used in describing grades of pencil lead): *2HB pencils.* ■ (in personal ads) Black. ■ bomber (in designations of U.S. aircraft types): *a B52.* ■ a dry cell battery size.
▸*symbol* ■ the chemical element boron. ■ *Physics* magnetic flux density.

b ▸*abbr.* ■ *Physics* barn(s). ■ (**b.**) born (used to indicate a date of birth): *George Lloyd (b. 1913).* ■ billion. ■ bass. ■ basso.

BA ▸*abbr.* ■ Bachelor of Arts: *David Brown, BA.* ■ *Baseball* batting average. ■ Buenos Aires.

Ba ▸*symbol* the chemical element barium.

baa /bä/ ▸*v.* (**baas, baaed** /bäd/, **baa·ing**) [*intrans.*] (of a sheep or lamb) bleat.
▸*n.* the cry of a sheep or lamb. ▷early 16th cent.: imitative.

Baa·de /'bädə/ (Wilhelm Heinrich) Walter (1893–1960), U.S. astronomer, born in Germany. He proved that the Andromeda galaxy was much farther away than had been thought, which implied that the universe was much older and more extensive than had been supposed. He also contributed to the understanding of the life cycles of stars.

Baa·der-Mein·hof Group /,bädər 'mīnhäf/ another name for **Red Army Faction**.

Ba·al /'bā(ə)l/ (also **Bel** /bel/) (*pl.* **Ba·a·lim** /'bāə,lim/ or **Ba·als**) a male fertility god whose cult was widespread in ancient Phoenician and Canaanite lands. ▷from Hebrew *ba'al* 'lord.'

Baal·bek /'bäl,bek; 'bāəl-/ a town in eastern Lebanon, site of the ancient city of Heliopolis.

Ba·ath Par·ty /bäTH/ (also **Ba'ath**) a pan-Arab socialist party founded in Syria in 1943. Different factions of the Baath Party hold power in Syria and formerly held power in Iraq. ▷*Baath*, from Arabic *ba'ṯ* 'resurrection, renaissance.' **—Ba·ath·ism** /-izəm/ *n.* **—Ba·ath·ist** /-ist/ *adj.* & *n.*

ba·ba[1] /'bä,bä/ (also **ba·ba au rhum** /ō 'rəm/) ▸*n.* a small rich sponge cake, typically soaked in rum-flavored syrup. ▷early 19th cent.: via French from Polish, literally 'married peasant woman.'

ba·ba[2] ▸*n. Indian, informal* **1** father (often as a proper name or as a familiar form of address). ■ a respectful form of address for an older man: *"Sit down, baba, you like tea?"* ■ (often **Baba**) a holy man (often as a proper name or form of address). **2** a child, esp. a male one (often in names or as an affectionate form of address). ▷from Hindi *bābā*.

ba·ba gha·nouj /,bäbə gə'nōōZH/ (also **ba·ba ga·noush** /gə'nōōSH/) ▸*n.* a thick sauce or spread made from ground eggplant and sesame seeds, olive oil, lemon, and garlic, typical of eastern Mediterranean cuisine. ▷from Egyptian Arabic, from Arabic *bābā*, literally 'father' + *gannuug*, perhaps a personal name.

ba·bas·su /,bäbə'sōō/ (also **ba·ba·çú**) ▸*n.* a Brazilian palm that yields an edible oil sometimes used in cosmetics. • Genus *Orbignya*, family Palmae. ▷1920s: from Brazilian Portuguese *babaçú*, from Tupi *ybá* 'fruit' + *guasu* 'large.'

Bab·bage /'babij/, Charles (1791–1871), English mathematician, inventor, and pioneer of machine computing. With Ada Lovelace, he designed a mechanical computer that would perform calculations and print the results, but he was unable to complete it during his lifetime.

Bab·bitt[1] /'babit/, Bruce Edward (1938–), U.S. politician and lawyer. A noted environmentalist, he served as governor of Arizona 1978–87 and U.S. secretary of the interior 1993–2001.

Bab·bitt[2], Milton (Byron) (1916–), U.S. composer and mathematician. His compositions developed from the twelve-note system of Arnold Schoenberg and Anton von Webern.

Bab·bitt[3] ▸*n. dated* a materialistic, complacent, and conformist businessman. ▷1922: from the name George *Babbitt*, the protagonist of the novel *Babbitt* by Sinclair Lewis. **—Bab·bitt·ry** /-trē/ *n.*

bab·ble /'babəl/ ▸*v.* [*intrans.*] talk rapidly and continuously in a foolish, excited, or incomprehensible way: *he would* **babble on** *in his gringo Spanish.* ■ [*reporting verb*] utter something rapidly and incoherently: [with *direct speech*] *I gasped and stared and babbled, "Look at this!"* | [*trans.*] *he began to babble an apology.* ■ reveal something secret or confidential by talking impulsively or carelessly: *he babbled to another convict while he was in jail* | [*trans.*] *my father* **babbled out** *the truth.* ■ [usu. as *adj.*] (**babbling**) (of a stream) make the continuous murmuring sound of water flowing over stones: *a gently babbling brook.*
▸*n.* [in *sing.*] the sound of people talking quickly and in a way that is difficult or impossible to understand: *a babble of protest.* ■ foolish, excited, or confused talk: *her soft voice stopped his babble.* ■ [usu. in *combination* or with *adj.*] pretentious jargon from a specified field: *to shed light on such transatlantic psychobabble.* ■ the continuous murmuring sound of water flowing over stones in a stream: *the babble of a brook.* ■ background disturbance caused by interference from conversations on other telephone lines. ▷Middle English: from Middle Low German *babbelen*, or an independent English formation, as a frequentative based on the repeated syllable *ba*, typical of a child's early speech.

bab·bler /'bab(ə)lər/ ▸*n.* **1** a person who babbles. **2** a thrushlike Old World songbird with a long tail, short rounded wings, and typically a loud discordant or musical voice. • Family Timaliidae (the **babbler family**): numerous genera.

babe /bāb/ ▸*n.* **1** *chiefly poetic/literary* a baby: ***a babe in arms**, less than twelve months old.* ■ *figurative* an innocent or helpless person: *cable TV is no longer a babe in swaddling clothes.* **2** *informal* an affectionate form of address, typically for someone with whom one has a sexual or romantic relationship: *I'm the golden boy, babe.* ■ a form of address for a young woman or girl (often considered sexist): *oh, babe, waltz with me.* ■ a sexually attractive young woman or girl: *he's been pumping up his pecs to impress the babes.* ▷late Middle English: probably imitative of an infant's first attempts at speech. Compare with **baby**.

ba·bel /'babəl; 'bā-/ ▸*n.* [in *sing.*] a confused noise, typically that made by a number of voices: *the babel of voices on the road.* ■ a scene of noisy confusion. ▷early 16th cent.: from *Babel* (see **Tower of Babel**), where, according to the biblical story in Gen. 11:4–9, God confused the languages of the builders.

Ba·bel, Tower of see **Tower of Babel**.

ba·be·li·cious /,bābə'liSHəs; ,bab-/ ▸*adj. informal* (of a woman) sexually very attractive. ▷1992: coined in the film *Wayne's World*.

ba·be·si·o·sis /bə,bēzē'ōsis/ (also **ba·be·si·a·sis** /,babi'zīəsis; -'sī-/) ▸*n.* a disease of cattle and other livestock, transmitted by the bite of ticks. It affects the red blood cells and causes the passing of red or blackish urine. Also called **piroplasmosis**. • This is caused by protozoans of the genus *Babesia*, phylum Sporozoa. ▷early 20th cent.: from modern Latin *Babesia*, from the name Victor *Babès* (1854–1926), Romanian bacteriologist.

Ba·bi /'bäbē/ ▸*n.* an adherent of Babism.

ba·biche /bə'bēSH/ ▸*n.* rawhide, typically formed into strips, as used by North American Indians for making fastenings, animal snares, snowshoes, etc. ▷early 19th cent.: from Canadian French, from Micmac *a:papi:č*.

Ba·bin·ski re·flex /bə'binskē/ ▸*n.* a reflex action in which the big toe remains extended or extends itself when the sole of the foot is stimulated. ▷named for Joseph François Felix Babinski (1857–1932), French neurologist.

bab·i·ru·sa /,bäbə'rōōsə; ,bab-/ ▸*n.* a forest-dwelling wild pig with several upturned hornlike tusks, native to Malaysia. • *Babyrousa babyrussa*, family Suidae. ▷late 17th cent.: from Malay, from *babi* 'hog' + *rusa* 'deer.'

babirusa

Bab·ism /'bäbizəm/ ▸*n.* a religion founded in 1844 by the Persian Mirza Ali Muhammad of Shiraz (1819–50) (popularly known as "the Bab"), who taught that a new prophet would follow Muhammad. See also **Baha'i**. ▷mid 19th cent.: via Persian from Arabic *bāb* 'intermediary,' literally 'gate' (taken as a name by the founder) + **-ism**.

bab·ka /'bäbkə/ ▸*n.* a loaf-shaped coffee cake made with sweet yeast dough to which raisins, chocolate, or nuts may be added. ▷from Polish, diminutive of *baba* (see **baba**).

ba·boon /ba'bōōn/ ▸*n.* a large Old World ground-dwelling monkey with a long doglike snout, large teeth, and naked callosities on the buttocks. Baboons are social animals and live in troops. • Genera *Papio* and *Mandrillus*, family Cercopithecidae: several species, including the drill and mandrill. ■ an ugly or uncouth person. ▷Middle English (denoting a grotesque figure used in architecture): from Old French *babuin* or medieval Latin *babewynus*, perhaps from Old French *baboue* 'muzzle, grimace.'

Ba·bo·qui·va·ri Moun·tains /,bäbōkə'värē/ a range in southern Arizona that rises to 7,734 feet (2,357 m) at Baboquivari Peak.

ba·bouche /bə'bōōSH/ ▸*n.* a heelless slipper, typically in oriental style. ▷late 17th cent.: from French, from Arabic *bābūj*, Persian *pāpūš*, literally 'foot covering.'

Ba·bruisk /bä'brōō-isk/ (also **Ba·bruysk, Bo·bruisk**, or **Bo·bruysk**) a river port in central Belarus, on the Berezina River, southeast of Minsk; pop. 222,900.

ba·bu /'bäbōō/ ▸*n.* (*pl.* **ba·bus**) *Indian* a respectful title or form of address for a man, esp. an educated one: *I could see Kana-babu's shop.* ■ an office worker; a clerk. ▷from Hindi *bābū*, literally 'father.'

ba·bul /bəˈbo͞ol/ ▶*n.* (in the Indian subcontinent) a tropical acacia introduced from Africa, used as a source of fuel, gum arabic, and (formerly) tannin. • *Acacia nilotica*, family Leguminosae. ▷early 19th cent.: from Hindi *babūl*.

Ba·bur /ˈbäbo͝or/ (1483–1530), first Mogul emperor of India *c.*1525–30; descendant of Tamerlane; born *Zahir ad-Din Muhammad*. He invaded India *c.*1525 and conquered the territory that extended from the Oxus to Patna.

ba·bush·ka /bəˈbo͞oshkə/ ▶*n.* (in Poland and Russia) an old woman or grandmother. ■ a headscarf tied under the chin, typical of those worn by Polish and Russian women. ▷mid 20th cent.: Polish, Russian, 'grandmother.'

Ba·bu·yan Is·lands /ˌbäbo͞oˈyän/ a group of 24 volcanic islands lying to the north of the island of Luzon in the northern Philippines.

ba·by /ˈbābē/ ▶*n.* (*pl.* **-bies**) **1** a very young child, esp. one newly or recently born: *his wife's just had a baby* | [as *adj.*] *a baby girl.* ■ a young or newly born animal. ■ the youngest member of a family or group: *Clara was the baby of the family.* ■ a timid or childish person: *"Don't be such a baby!" she said witheringly.* ■ (**one's baby**) *figurative* one's particular responsibility, achievement, or concern: *"This is your baby, Gerry," she said, handing him the brief.* **2** *informal* a young woman or a person with whom one is having a romantic relationship (often as a form of address): *my baby left me for another guy* | *baby, don't cry!* ■ a thing regarded with affection or familiarity: *this baby can reach speeds of 140 mph.*
▶*adj.* [*attrib.*] comparatively small or immature of its kind: *a baby grand piano.* ■ (of vegetables) picked before reaching their usual size: *baby carrots.*
▶*v.* (**-bies, -bied**) [*trans.*] treat (someone) as a baby; pamper or be overprotective toward: *her aunt babied her and fussed over her clothes.* ▷late Middle English: probably imitative of an infant's first attempts at speech. —**ba·by·hood** /-ˌho͝od/ *n.*
▶*PHRASE* □ **throw the baby out with the bathwater** discard something valuable along with other things that are inessential or undesirable.

Ba·by Bell ▶*n. informal* a nickname for any of the telephone companies created in 1984 from the breakup of American Telephone and Telegraph Corporation, which was nicknamed "Ma Bell."

ba·by blue ▶*n.* a pale shade of blue. ■ (**baby blues**) *informal* blue eyes. ■ (**baby blues**) depression affecting a woman after giving birth; postnatal depression.

ba·by-blue-eyes ▶*n.* a plant of western North America with blue bowl-shaped flowers. • Genus *Nemophila*, family Hydrophyllaceae: several species, in particular *N. menziesii* of California and southern Oregon.

ba·by boom ▶*n. informal* a temporary marked increase in the birth rate, esp. the one following World War II.

ba·by bug·gy ▶*n.* a baby carriage.

ba·by bust ▶*n. informal* a temporary marked decrease in the birth rate. —**ba·by bust·er** *n.*

ba·by car·riage ▶*n.* a four-wheeled carriage for a baby, typically with a retractable hood, pushed by a person on foot.

Baby Doc see DUVALIER.

ba·by doll ▶*n.* a doll designed to look like a baby. ■ a girl or woman with pretty, ingenuous, childlike looks.
▶*adj.* [*attrib.*] denoting a style of women's clothing or sleepwear resembling that traditionally worn by a doll or young child, esp. short, high-waisted, short-sleeved dresses.

ba·by face ▶*n.* a smooth round face like a baby's.

ba·by-faced ▶*adj.* having a youthful or innocent face: *baby-faced tough guys.*

ba·by grand ▶*n.* the smallest size of grand piano, about 4.5 feet (1.5 m) long.

ba·by·ish /ˈbābē-ish/ ▶*adj. derogatory* (of appearance or behavior) characteristic of a baby: *he pursed his mouth into a babyish pout.* ■ (of clothes or toys) suitable for a baby: *he declared that dolls were silly, babyish things.* —**ba·by·ish·ly** *adv.* —**ba·by·ish·ness** *n.*

Bab·y·lon[1] /ˈbabəˌlän; -ˌlən/ **1** an ancient city in Mesopotamia, the capital of Babylonia in the 2nd millennium BC. The city was on the banks of the Euphrates River and was noted for its luxury, its fortifications, and, particularly, for the Hanging Gardens of Babylon. **2** a town on the southern shore of Long Island in New York that includes the villages of Babylon and Amityville; pop. 202,889. ▷Greek *Babulōn* (from Hebrew *bāḇel*), also the name of the mystical city of the Apocalypse. Compare with BABEL.

Bab·y·lon[2] ▶*n. black English* (chiefly among Rastafarians) a contemptuous or dismissive term for aspects of a society seen as degenerate or oppressive, esp. the police: *praise them for bringing a new rectitude to Babylon.* ▷1940s: by association with BABYLON[1].

Bab·y·lo·ni·a /ˌbabəˈlōnēə/ an ancient region of Mesopotamia, formed when the kingdoms of Akkad in the north and Sumer in the south combined in the first half of the 2nd millennium BC.

Bab·y·lo·ni·an /ˌbabəˈlōnēən/ ▶*n.* **1** an inhabitant of Babylon or Babylonia. **2** the dialect of Akkadian spoken in ancient Babylon.
▶*adj.* of or relating to Babylon or Babylonia.

Bab·y·lo·ni·an Cap·tiv·i·ty the captivity of the Israelites in Babylon, lasting from their deportation by Nebuchadnezzar in 586 BC until their release by Cyrus the Great in 539 BC.

ba·by·moth·er /ˈbābēˌmə<u>th</u>ər/ (or **ba·by·fa·ther** /ˈbābēˌfä<u>th</u>ər/) ▶*n. black English* the mother (or father) of one or more of one's children: *I knew his babymother, Miss Richards, as we went to school and grew up together.*

ba·by oil ▶*n.* a mineral oil used to soften the skin.

ba·by's breath ▶*n.* a herbaceous plant of delicate appearance that bears tiny scented pink or white flowers. • *Gypsophila paniculata*, family Caryophyllaceae.

ba·by·sit /ˈbābēˌsit/ ▶*v.* (**-sit·ting**; *past* and *past part.* **-sat**) [*intrans.*] look after a child or children while the parents are out: *I babysit for my neighbor sometimes* | [*trans.*] *she was babysitting Sophie* | [as *n.*] (**babysitting**) *part-time jobs such as babysitting.* —**ba·by·sit·ter** *n.*

ba·by talk ▶*n.* childish talk used by or to young children.

ba·by tooth ▶*n.* another term for MILK TOOTH.

ba·ca·lao /ˌbäkəˈlou/ ▶*n.* codfish, often dried or salted, as used in Spanish and Latin American cooking. ▷Spanish.

Ba·call /bəˈkôl/, Lauren (1924–), U.S. actress; born *Betty Joan Perske*. She co-starred with husband Humphrey Bogart in a number of successful movies, including *The Big Sleep* (1946) and *Key Largo* (1948).

Ba·car·di /bəˈkärdē/ ▶*n.* (*pl.* **-dis**) *trademark* a West Indian rum produced originally in Cuba. ▷named after the Compania Ron *Bacardi* of Cuba (now *Bacardi* & Co. Ltd., Nassau).

bac·ca·la /ˌbakəˈlä; ˈbakəˌlä/ ▶*n.* Italian term for BACALAO.

bac·ca·lau·re·ate /ˌbakəˈlôrēit/ ▶*n.* **1** a college bachelor's degree. **2** *Brit.* an examination intended to qualify successful candidates for higher education. **3** *Brit.* a religious service held at some educational institutions before commencement, containing a farewell sermon to the graduating class. ▷mid 17th cent. (sense 1): from French *baccalauréat* or medieval Latin *baccalaureatus*, from *baccalaureus* 'bachelor.' The earlier form *baccalarius* was altered by wordplay to conform with *bacca lauri* 'laurel berry,' because of the laurels awarded to scholars. Sense 2 dates from 1970.

bac·ca·rat /ˈbäkəˌrä; ˌbakəˈrä/ ▶*n.* a gambling card game in which players hold two- or three-card hands, the winning hand being that giving the highest remainder when its face value is divided by ten. ▷mid 19th cent.: from French *baccara*, of unknown origin.

bac·cate /ˈbakˌāt/ ▶*adj.* bearing berries; berried. ■ of the nature of a berry; berrylike.

Bac·chae /ˈbakē; ˈbäkē/ the priestesses or female devotees of the Greek god Bacchus.

bac·cha·nal /ˌbäkəˈnäl; ˌbak-; ˈbakənl/ *chiefly poetic/literary* ▶*n.* **1** an occasion of wild and drunken revelry. ■ a drunken reveler. **2** a priest, worshiper, or follower of Bacchus.
▶*adj.* another term for BACCHANALIAN. ▷mid 16th cent.: from Latin *bacchanalis*, from the name of the god BACCHUS.

Bac·cha·na·li·a /ˌbakəˈnālyə; ˌbäk-/ ▶*plural n.* [also treated as *sing.*] the Roman festival of Bacchus. ■ (**bacchanalia**) drunken revelry. ▷late 16th cent.: from Latin *bacchanalia*, neuter plural of the adjective *bacchanalis* (see BACCHANAL).

bac·cha·na·li·an /ˌbäkəˈnālyən; -ˈnālēən; ˌbakə-/ ▶*adj.* characterized by or given to drunken revelry; riotously drunken: *a bacchanalian orgy.*

bac·chant /bəˈkänt; -ˈkant/ ▶*n.* (*pl.* **-chants** or **-chantes** /-ˈkäntēz/; *fem.* **-chan·te** /-tē/) a priest, priestess, or follower of Bacchus. ▷late 16th cent.: from French *bacchante*, from Latin *bacchari* 'celebrate the feast of Bacchus.'

Bac·chus /ˈbäkəs; ˈbak-/ *Greek Mythology* another name for DIONYSUS. ▷Latin, from Greek *Bakkhos*. —**Bac·chic** /-kik/ *adj.*

bac·cy /ˈbakē/ ▶*n. chiefly Brit.* informal term for TOBACCO.

Bach /bäkh; bäk/, Johann Sebastian (1685–1750), German composer. An exceptional and prolific baroque composer, his compositions range from violin concertos, suites, and the six *Brandenburg Concertos* (1720–21) to clavier works and sacred cantatas. Large-scale choral works include *The Passion according to St. John* (1723), *The Passion according to St. Matthew* (1729), and the *Mass in B minor* (1733–38). Three of his sons were also well-known composers: **J(ohann) C(hristian) Bach,** (1735–82), known as **the London Bach, J(ohann) C(hristoph) F(riedrich) Bach,** (1732–95), known as **the Bückeburg Bach,** and **W(ilhelm) F(riedemann) Bach,** (1710–84), known as **the Halle Bach.**

Bach·a·rach /ˈbakəˌrak/, Burt (1929–), U.S. writer of popular songs. His songs, many of which were written with lyricist Hal David (1921–), include "Walk On By" (1961), "Alfie" (1966), and "Raindrops Keep Falling on my Head" (1969).

ba·cha·ta /bäˈchätä/ ▶*n.* a style of romantic music originating in the Dominican Republic. ■ a song in this style. ▷Caribbean Spanish, literally 'a party, good time.'

bach·e·lor /ˈbach(ə)lər/ ▶*n.* **1** a man who is not and has never been married: *Mark is a* ***confirmed bachelor*** | *one of the country's most* ***eligible bachelors.*** ■ *Zoology* a male bird or mammal without a mate, esp. one prevented from breeding by a dominant male. **2** a person who holds an undergraduate degree from a university or college (only in titles or set expressions): *he graduated with a bachelor's degree in philosophy* | *a Bachelor of Arts.* **3** *historical* a young knight serving under another's banner. See also KNIGHT BACHELOR. [said to be from French *bas chevalier*, literally 'low knight' (i.e., knight of a low order).] ▷Middle English: from Old French *bacheler*; of uncertain origin. —**bach·e·lor·hood** /-ˌho͝od/ *n.*

bach·e·lor a·part·ment ▶*n.* an apartment occupied by a bachelor. ■ an apartment consisting of a single large room serving as bedroom and living room, with a separate bathroom.

bach·e·lor·ette /ˌbach(ə)ləˈret/ ▶*n.* **1** a young unmarried woman. **2** a small bachelor apartment: *a bachelorette in a high-rise complex.*

bach·e·lor·ette par·ty ▶*n.* a party given for a woman who is about to get married, typically one attended by women only.

bach·e·lor girl ▶*n.* an independent, unmarried young woman.

bach·e·lor par·ty ▶*n.* a party given for a man who is about to get married, typically attended by men only.

bach·e·lor's but·tons ▶*plural n.* [treated as *sing.* or *pl.*] any of a number of ornamental plants that bear small, buttonlike, double flowers, in particular the vivid blue cornflower *Centaurea cyanus*.

Bach·man /ˈbäkmən/, Richard see KING[4].

ba·cil·li·form /bəˈsiləˌfôrm/ ▶*adj. chiefly Biology* rod-shaped.

ba·cil·lus /bəˈsiləs/ ▶*n.* (*pl.* **-cil·li** /-ˈsilī/) a disease-causing bacterium. ■ a rod-shaped bacterium. ▷late 19th cent.: from late Latin, diminutive of Latin *baculus* 'stick.' —**bac·il·lar·y** /ˈbasəˌlerē/ *adj.*

USAGE All bacteria belonging to the genus *Bacillus* are called **bacilli**, but not all bacteria called **bacilli** belong to the genus *Bacillus*.

bac·i·tra·cin /ˌbasiˈtrāsin/ ▶*n.* an antibiotic typically used topically for skin and eye infections. • The drug is obtained from the bacterium *Bacillus subtilis*.

back /bak/ ▶*n.* **1** the rear surface of the human body from the shoulders to the hips: *he lay on his back* | *Forbes slapped me on the back* | [as *adj.*] *back pain.* ■ the corresponding upper surface of an animal's body. ■ the spine of a person or animal. ■ the part of a chair against which the sitter's back rests. ■ the part of a garment that covers a person's back. ■ a person's torso or body regarded in terms of wearing clothes: *all he owned were the clothes on his back.* ■ a person's back regarded as carrying a load or bearing an imposition: *they wanted the government off their backs.* **2** the side or part of something that is away from the spectator or from the direction in which it moves or faces; the rear: *at the back of the hotel is a secluded garden | an empty spot in the back of the plane.* ■ [in *sing.*] the position directly behind someone or something: *she unbuttoned her dress from the back.* ■ the side or part of an object opposed to the one that is normally seen or used; the less active, visible, or important part of something: *write on the back of a postcard | he wiped his mouth with the back of his hand.* ■ the part of a book where the pages are held together by a binding. **3** a player in a field game whose initial position is behind the front line: *their backs showed some impressive running and passing.* ■ the position taken by such a player.

▸*adv.* **1** toward the rear; in the opposite direction from the one that one is facing or traveling: *she moved back a pace | she walked away without looking back.* ■ expressing movement of the body into a reclining position: *he leaned back in his chair | sit back and relax.* ■ at a distance away: *I thought you were miles back | the officer pushed the crowd back.* ■ (**back of**) behind: *he knew that other people were back of him.* **2** expressing a return to an earlier or normal condition: *she put the book back on the shelf | drive to Montreal and back | I went back to sleep | he was given his job back.* ■ fashionable again: *sideburns are back.* **3** in or into the past: *he made his fortune back in 1955.* ■ at a place previously left or mentioned: *the folks back home are counting on him.* **4** in return: *they wrote back to me.*

▸*v.* **1** [*trans.*] give financial, material, or moral support to: *he had a newspaper empire backing him | go up there and tell them—I'll back you up.* ■ bet money on (a person or animal) winning a race or contest: *he backed the horse at 33–1.* ■ be in favor of: *over 97 percent backed the changes.* ■ supplement in order to reinforce or strengthen: *U.S. troops were* **backed up** *by forces from European countries.* **2** [*trans.*] (often **be backed**) cover the back of (an object) in order to support, protect, or decorate it: *a mirror backed with tortoiseshell.* ■ (esp. in popular music) provide musical accompaniment to (a singer or musician): *brisk guitar work backed by drums, bass, fiddle, and accordion.* ■ put a song or piece of music on the less important side of (a recording): *the new single is backed with a track from the LP.* **3** [*intrans.*] walk or drive backward: *she tried to back away | backing down the stairs | figurative the administration* **backed away from** *the plan* | [*trans.*] *he backed the Mercedes into the yard.* ■ [*intrans.*] (of the wind) change direction counterclockwise around the points of the compass: *the wind had backed to the northwest.* The opposite of VEER[1]. ■ [*trans.*] *Sailing* put (a sail) aback in order to slow the vessel down. **4** [*intrans.*] (of a property) have its back adjacent to (a piece of land or body of water): *a row of cottages* **backed on** *the water | his garage wall backs onto the neighboring property.* ■ [*trans.*] (usu. **be backed**) lie behind or at the back of: *the promenade is backed by lots of cafes.*

▸*phrasal v.* □ **back down** withdraw a claim or assertion in the face of opposition: *the contenders* **backed down from** *their original pledge.* □ **back off** draw back from action or confrontation: *they* **backed off from** *fundamental reform of the system.* ■ another way of saying BACK DOWN. □ **back out** withdraw from a commitment: *if he* **backs out of** *the deal they'll sue him.* □ **back up 1** (of vehicles) form a line due to congestion: *the traffic began to back up.* **2** (of running water) accumulate behind an obstruction. □ **back something up** *Computing* make a spare copy of data or a disk. (usu. **be backed up**) cause vehicles to form into a queue due to congestion: *the traffic was backed up a couple of miles in each direction.*

▸*adj.* [*attrib.*] **1** of or at the back of something: *the back garden | the back pocket of his jeans.* ■ situated in a remote or subsidiary position: *back roads.* **2** (esp. of wages or something published or released) from or relating to the past: *she was owed back pay.* **3** directed toward the rear or in a reversed course: *back currents.* **4** *Phonetics* (of a sound) articulated at the back of the mouth. ▷Old English *bæc*, of Germanic origin; related to Middle Dutch and Old Norse *bak*. The adverb use dates from late Middle English and is a shortening of ABACK.

▸*PHRASES* □ **at someone's back** in pursuit or support of someone. □ **back and fill** trim the sails of a vessel so that the wind alternately fills and spills out of them, in order to maneuver in a limited space. ■ zigzag or vacillate. □ **back and forth** to and fro. □ **someone's back is turned** someone's attention is elsewhere: *he kissed her quickly, when the landlady's back was turned.* □ **the back of (the) beyond** a remote or inaccessible place. □ **the back of one's mind** used to express that something is in one's mind but is not consciously thought of or remembered: *she had a little nagging worry at the back of her mind.* □ **back to front** /ˈˌbak tə ˈfrənt/ *Brit.* reversed; backward: *the exhausts had been fitted back to front | a back-to-front baseball cap.* □ **back through the box** see BOX[1]. □ **back water** reverse the action of the oars while rowing, causing a boat to slow down or stop. □ **back the wrong horse** make a wrong or inappropriate choice. □ **behind someone's back** without a person's knowledge and in an unfair or dishonorable way: *Carla made fun of him behind his back.* □ **get** (or **put**) **someone's back up** make someone annoyed or angry. □ **in back** at the back of something, esp. a building: *my dad demolished an old shed* **in back of** *his barn.* □ **know something like the back of one's hand** be entirely familiar with a place or route. □ **on one's back** in bed recovering from an injury or illness. ■ full-length on the ground: *he slipped off the heap and landed* **flat on his back**. □ **put one's back into** approach (a task) with vigor. □ **turn one's back on** ignore (someone) by turning away. ■ reject or abandon: *she turned her back on her career to devote her life to animals.* □ **with one's back to** (or **up against**) **the wall** in a desperate situation; hard-pressed.

back·ache /ˈbakˌāk/ ▸*n.* a prolonged pain in one's back.

back al·ley ▸*n.* a narrow passage behind or between buildings.
▸*adj.* [*attrib.*] secret or illegal, as might be found in a back alley: *a back-alley drug deal.*

back·bar /ˈbakˌbär/ ▸*n.* a structure behind a bar counter, with shelves for holding bottles and other supplies.

Back Bay a historic residential and commercial district in western Boston, Massachusetts, on land along the Charles River that was reclaimed in the 19th century.

back·beat /ˈbakˌbēt/ ▸*n. Music* a strong accent on one of the normally unaccented beats of the bar, used esp. in jazz and popular music.

back·bench /ˈbakˈbenCH/ ▸*n.* (in the UK) the benches behind the front benches on either side of the House of Commons, occupied by members of parliament who do not hold office in the government or opposition: [as *adj.*] *backbench MPs.* ■ (**the backbenches**) these members of parliament: *the support of the Tory backbenches.* —**back·bench·er** *n.*

back·bit·ing /ˈbakˌbītiNG/ ▸*n.* malicious talk about someone who is not present. —**back·bite** /-ˌbīt/ *v.* —**back·bit·er** /-tər/ *n.*

back·board /ˈbakˌbôrd/ ▸*n.* a board placed at or forming the back of something, such as a collage or piece of electronic equipment. ■ *Basketball* an upright board behind the basket, off which the ball may rebound. ■ a board used to support or straighten a person's back, esp. after an accident.

back·bone /ˈbakˌbōn/ ▸*n.* the series of vertebrae extending from the skull to the pelvis; the spine. ■ *figurative* the chief support of a system or organization; the mainstay: *these firms are the backbone of our industrial sector.* ■ *figurative* strength of character; firmness: *he has the backbone to see us through this difficulty.* ■ the spine of a book. ■ *Biochemistry* the main chain of a polymeric molecule.

back-break·ing (also **back·break·ing**) ▸*adj.* [*attrib.*] (esp. of manual labor) physically demanding: *a day's back-breaking work.*

back burn·er ▸*n.* a state of inaction or suspension; a position of relatively little importance: *priorities that have been* **placed on the back burner** *year after year.*
▸*v.* [*trans.*] (usu. **be back-burnered**) postpone consideration of or action on: *a planned test of the new ale has been back-burnered.*

back·cast /ˈbakˌkast/ *Fishing* ▸*n.* a backward swing of a fishing line preparatory to casting.
▸*v.* (*past* and *past part.* **-cast**) [*intrans.*] make such a backward swing.

back cat·a·log (also **back cat·a·logue**) ▸*n.* all the works previously produced by a recording artist or record company. ■ a similar archived collection of movies or television programs.

back·chan·nel /ˈbakˌCHanl/ (also **back chan·nel**) ▸*n.* **1** a secondary or covert route for the passage of information: *the agency offered a reliable backchannel to Washington* | [as *adj.*] *backchannel briefings.* **2** *Psychology* a sound or gesture made to give continuity to a conversation by a person who is listening to another.

back·chat /ˈbakˌCHat/ ▸*n.* another term for BACK TALK.

back·coun·try /ˈbakˌkəntrē/ ▸*n.* (**the backcountry**) sparsely inhabited rural areas; wilderness: *exploring the backcountry on horseback* | [as *adj.*] *backcountry skiing.*

back·court /ˈbakˌkôrt/ ▸*n.* (in tennis, basketball, and similar games) the part of each side of the court nearest the back wall or back boundary line. ■ the defensive players in a basketball team.

back·cross /ˈbakˌkrôs/ *Genetics* ▸*v.* [*trans.*] cross (a hybrid) with one of its parents or an organism with the same genetic characteristics as one of the parents: [as *adj.*] (**backcrossed**) *after five generations the backcrossed dogs were indistinguishable from purebred dalmatians* | [*intrans.*] *they backcrossed with red-flowered parents to reinforce the effect.*
▸*n.* an instance of backcrossing. ■ the product of such a cross.

back·date /ˈbakˌdāt/ ▸*v.* [*trans.*] put an earlier date to (a document or agreement) than the actual one: *they backdated the sale documents to evade a court order.*

back door ▸*n.* the door or entrance at the back of a building.
▸*adj.* (also **back·door**) [*attrib.*] (of an activity) clandestine; underhanded: *backdoor private deals.*

back·door sell·ing /ˈbakˌdôr/ ▸*n.* the selling by wholesalers directly to the public, seen as detrimental to retailers.

back·down /ˈbakˌdoun/ ▸*n.* an act of backing down.

back·draft /ˈbakˌdraft/ (*Brit.* **back·draught**) ▸*n.* **1** a current of air or water that flows backward down a chimney, pipe, etc. **2** a phenomenon in which a fire that has consumed all available oxygen suddenly explodes when more oxygen is made available, typically because a door or window has been opened. —**back·draft·ing** *n.*

back·drop /ˈbakˌdräp/ ▸*n.* a painted cloth hung at the back of a theater stage as part of the scenery. ■ *figurative* the setting or background for a scene, event, or situation: *the conference took place* **against a backdrop of** *increasing diplomatic activity.*
▸*v.* (**-dropped**, **-drop·ping**) provide a background or setting for: *an ornate fountain, and at its center, backdropped with golden spray, a statue of a young girl.*

back end ▸*n.* the end of something that is farthest from the front or the working end: *the back end of the car swung around.* ■ *chiefly Brit.* the latter part of a period of time or process: *the book takes us up to the back end of last year.*
▸*adj.* [*attrib.*] **1** relating to the end or outcome of a project, process, or investment: *many annuities have back-end surrender charges.* **2** *Computing* denoting a subordinate processor or program, not directly accessed by the user, which performs a specialized function on behalf of a main processor or software system: *a back-end database server.*

back·er /ˈbakər/ ▸*n.* a person, institution, or country that supports something, esp. financially: *$3.3 million was provided by the project's backers.* ■ a person who bets on a horse.

back-fanged ▸*adj. Zoology* (of a snake such as a boomslang) having the rear one or two pairs of teeth modified as fangs, with grooves to conduct the venom. Compare with FRONT-FANGED.

back fat ▸*n.* fat on the back of a meat-producing animal.

back·field /ˈbakˌfēld/ ▸*n. Football* the area of play behind either the offensive or defensive line. ■ the players positioned in this area.

back·fill /ˈbakˌfil/ ▸*v.* [*trans.*] refill (an excavated hole) with the material dug out of it: *they backfill the hole to street level.*
▸*n.* material used for backfilling.

back·fire /ˈbakˌfī(ə)r/ ▸*v.* [*intrans.*] **1** (of an engine) undergo a mistimed explosion in the cylinder or exhaust: *a car backfired in the road.* **2** (of a plan or action) rebound adversely on the originator; have the opposite effect to what was intended: *overzealous publicity* **backfired on** *her.*
▸*n.* **1** a mistimed explosion in the cylinder or exhaust of a vehicle or engine. **2** a fire set intentionally to arrest the progress of an approaching fire by creating a burned area in its path, thus depriving the fire of fuel.

back·flip /ˈbakˌflip/ ▸*n.* a backward somersault done in the air with the arms and legs stretched out straight.

back fo·cus ▸*n. Photography* the distance between the back of a lens and the image of an object at infinity.

back-for·ma·tion ▸*n.* a word that is formed from an already existing word from which it appears to be a derivative, often by removal of a suffix (e.g., *laze* from *lazy* and *edit* from *editor*). ■ the process by which such words are formed.

back·gam·mon /ˈbak,gamən/ ▶*n.* a board game in which two players move their pieces around twenty-four triangular points according to the throw of dice, the winner being the first to remove all their pieces from the board. ■ the most complete form of win in this game. ▷mid 17th cent.: from BACK + GAMMON².

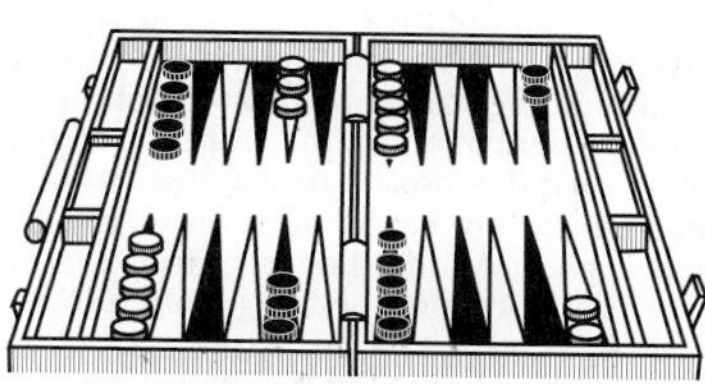

backgammon board and pieces

back·ground /ˈbak,ground/ ▶*n.* **1** [in *sing.*] the area or scenery behind the main object of contemplation, esp. when perceived as a framework for it: *the house stands against a background of sheltering trees.* ■ the part of a picture or design that serves as a setting to the main figures or objects, or that appears furthest from the viewer: *the background shows a landscape of domes and minarets | the word is written in white on a red background.* ■ a position or function that is not prominent or conspicuous: *after that evening, Athens remained* ***in the background.*** **2** the general scene, surroundings, or circumstances: *the black cab blends beautifully into the city background | the events occurred against a background of continuing civil war.* ■ the circumstances, facts, or events that influence, cause, or explain something: *the political and economic background* | [as *adj.*] *background information.* ■ a person's education, experience, and social circumstances: *she has a background in nursing | a mix of students from many different backgrounds.* **3** a persistent level of some phenomenon or process, against which particular events or measurements are distinguished, in particular: ■ *Physics* low-intensity radiation from radioisotopes present in the natural environment. ■ unwanted signals, such as noise in the reception or recording of sound. **4** *Computing* used to describe tasks or processes running on a computer that do not need input from the user: *programs can be left running in the background* | [as *adj.*] *background processing.*

back·ground·er /ˈbak,groundər/ ▶*n.* an official briefing or handout giving background information: *their departure had to explained by aides in a backgrounder the next day.*

back·ground mu·sic ▶*n.* music intended as an unobtrusive accompaniment to some activity, such as dining in a restaurant, or to provide atmosphere in a movie.

back·ground ra·di·a·tion ▶*n.* *Astronomy* the uniform microwave radiation remaining from the big bang. See also BIG BANG.

back·hand /ˈbak,hand/ ▶*n.* **1** (in tennis and other racket sports) a stroke played with the back of the hand facing in the direction of the stroke, typically starting with the arm crossing the body: *he drove a backhand into the net* | [as *adj.*] *a backhand volley.* ■ a blow or stroke of any kind made in this way, or in a direction opposite to the usual: *ground balls hit to my backhand* | [as *adj.*] *he made a backhand stop of the ball.* **2** handwriting that slopes to the left.
▶*v.* [*trans.*] strike with a backhanded blow or stroke: *in a flash, he backhanded Ace across the jaw.*

back·hand·ed /ˈbak,handid/ ▶*adj.* made with the back of the hand facing in the direction of movement: *a backhanded pass.* ■ *figurative* indirect; ambiguous or insincere: *coming from me, teasing is a* ***backhanded compliment.***
▶*adv.* with the back of the hand or with the hand turned backward: *Frank hit him backhanded.*

back·hand·er /ˈbak,handər/ ▶*n.* **1** a backhand stroke or shot in a game. ■ a blow made with the back of the hand. **2** *Brit., informal* a secret payment, typically one made illegally; a bribe.

back·haul /ˈbak,hôl/ ▶*n.* **1** a cargo carried on a return journey. **2** an unedited video transmission via satellite or other means to a network or station. ■ a frequency on which such transmissions occur.
▶*v.* carry (freight) on a return journey.

back·hoe /ˈbak,hō/ (*Brit.* also **backhoe loader**) ▶*n.* a mechanical excavator that draws toward itself a bucket attached to a hinged boom.

back·ing /ˈbakiNG/ ▶*n.* **1** support or help: *he accepted the backing of the police group | they had financial backing from local firms.* ■ a layer of material that forms, protects, or strengthens the back of something: *the fabric has a special backing for durability.* ■ (esp. in popular music) the music or singing that accompanies the main singer or soloist: *the trio provided backing to some of the most popular vocalists of the day* | [as *adj.*] *backing vocals.* **2** *Phonetics* the movement of the place of formation of a sound toward the back of the mouth.

back·ing track ▶*n.* a recorded musical accompaniment, esp. for a soloist to play or sing along with.

back is·sue ▶*n.* a past issue of a journal or magazine.

back·land /ˈbak,land/ ▶*n.* **1** (also **backlands**) another term for BACKCOUNTRY. **2** land behind or beyond an area that is built on or otherwise developed.

back·lash /ˈbak,lasH/ ▶*n.* **1** [in *sing.*] a strong and adverse reaction by a large number of people, esp. to a social or political development: *a public* ***backlash against*** *racism.* **2** recoil arising between parts of a mechanism. ■ degree of play between parts of a mechanism.

back·less /ˈbaklis/ ▶*adj.* (of a woman's garment) cut low at the back: *a backless lycra dress.*

back·light /ˈbak,līt/ ▶*n.* illumination from behind. —**back·light·ing** *n.* .

back·list /ˈbak,list/ ▶*n.* a publisher's list of older books still in print.

back·lit /ˈbak,lit/ ▶*adj.* (esp. in photography or of a graphic display) illuminated from behind: *she was backlit by the morning sun | a backlit LCD screen.*

back·load /ˈbak,lōd/ ▶*v.* [*trans.*] (usu. **be backloaded**) place more charges at the later stages of (a financial agreement) than at the earlier stages.

back·log /ˈbak,lôg; -,läg/ ▶*n.* an accumulation of something, esp. uncompleted work or matters that need to be dealt with: *the company took on extra staff to clear the backlog of work.* ■ a reserve; reserves: *backlogs of experience.*

back·lot /ˈbak,lät/ ▶*n.* an outdoor area in a movie studio where large exterior sets are made and some outside scenes are filmed.

back num·ber ▶*n.* an issue of a periodical earlier than the current one. ■ *informal* a person or thing seen as old-fashioned.

back·pack /ˈbak,pak/ ▶*n.* a bag, often supported by a metal frame, with shoulder straps that allow it to be carried on someone's back. A backpack is typically made of a strong, waterproof material and carried by hikers. ■ a knapsack used by students as a bookbag, or any small bag carried on the back. ■ a load or piece of equipment carried on a person's back: *a two-tank scuba backpack.*
▶*v.* [*intrans.*] [usu. as *n.*] (**backpacking**) travel or hike carrying one's belongings in a backpack: *a week's backpacking in the Pyrenees | he has backpacked around the world.* —**back·pack·er** *n.*

back·pay /ˈbak,pā; ,bakˈpā/ ▶*n.* payment for work done in the past that was withheld at the time, usually because of a dispute: *Hickman should be provided backpay plus any expenses.*

> ***USAGE*** Though still somewhat more frequent as an open compound that most dictionaries have not defined, *backpay* is now gaining considerable ground as a closed compound, with an attendant shift in stress to the first syllable.

back·ped·al /ˈbak,pedl/ ▶*v.* (**-ped·aled, -ped·al·ing;** *Brit.* **-ped·alled, -ped·al·ling**) [*intrans.*] move the pedals of a bicycle backward in order to brake. ■ move hastily backward: *backpedaling furiously, he flipped a perfect pass.* ■ reverse one's previous action or opinion: *you've criticized him for backpedaling on budget reform.*

back·plane /ˈbak,plān/ ▶*n.* a board to which the main circuit boards of a computer may be connected and that provides connections between them.

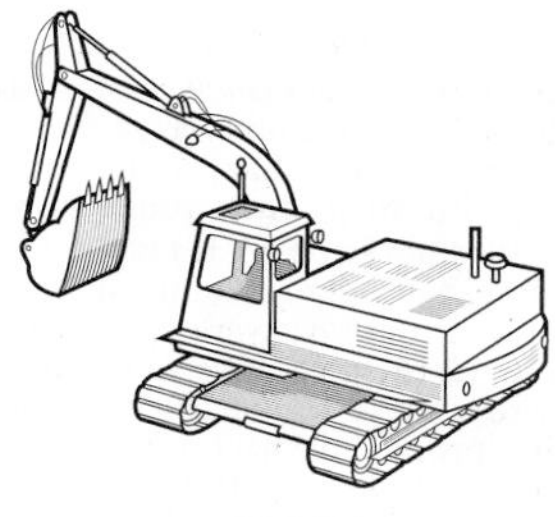

backhoe

back·plate /ˈbak,plāt/ ▶*n.* a plate placed at or forming the back of something.

back-pro·jec·tion ▶*n.* another term for REAR PROJECTION.

back·rest /ˈbak,rest/ ▶*n.* a support for a person's back when the person is seated.

back·ro·nym /ˈbakrə,nim/ ▶*n.* a fanciful expansion of an existing acronym or word, such as "port out, starboard home" for *posh.* ▷blend of *back* and *acronym.*

back room ▶*n.* a place where secret, administrative, or supporting work is done: *this would lead to weak government and deals in back rooms* | [as *adj.*] *back-room strategists.*

back·saw /ˈbak,sô/ ▶*n.* a type of saw with a reinforced back edge that keeps the thin blade from being distorted.

back·scat·ter /ˈbak,skatər/ ▶*n.* *Physics* deflection of radiation or particles through an angle of 180°. ■ radiation or particles that have been deflected in this way. ■ *Photography* light from a flashgun or other light source that is deflected directly into a lens: *backscatter causes an underexposed picture with a blizzard effect.*
▶*v.* [*trans.*] *Physics* deflect (radiation or particles) through an angle of 180°: [as *adj.*] (**backscattered**) *backscattered sound reaches the sonar receiver.*

back·scratch·er /ˈbak,skracHər/ ▶*n.* a rod terminating in a clawed hand for scratching one's own back.

back·scratch·ing /ˈbak,skracHiNG/ ▶*n.* the mutual providing of favors or services, esp. when the legitimacy of such dealings is doubtful: *the friendship thrives on little more than mutual backscratching.*

back seat (also **back·seat**) ▶*n.* a seat at the back of a vehicle.
▶*PHRASE* □ **take a back seat** take or be given a less important position or role: *printed words will take a back seat to TV and video screens.*

back·seat driv·er /ˈbakˈsēt/ ▶*n.* a passenger in a car who gives the driver unwanted advice. ■ a person who is eager to advise without responsibility. —**back·seat driv·ing** *n.*

back·shift /ˈbak,sHift/ ▶*n.* *Grammar* the changing of a present tense in direct speech to a past tense in reported speech (or a past tense to pluperfect).

back·side /ˈbak,sīd/ ▶*n.* *informal* a person's buttocks or rump. ■ the rear side or view of a thing: *the backside of the hill.*
▶*adj.* (of a maneuver in surfing and other board sports) done clockwise for a regular rider and counterclockwise for a goofy rider.

back slang ▶*n.* slang in which words are spoken as though they were spelled backward (e.g., *redraw* for *warder*).

back·slap·ping /ˈbak,slapiNG/ ▶*n.* the action of effusively congratulating or encouraging someone, typically by slapping a person's back: *effusive displays of backslapping and arm-punching.*
▶*adj.* vigorously hearty: *those cheerful, backslapping journalists.* —**back·slap** *v.* & *n.* **back·slap·per** *n.*

back·slash /ˈbak,slasH/ ▶*n.* *Computing* a backward-sloping diagonal line (\), used to separate file and folder names in a path statement.

back·slide /ˈbak,slīd/ ▶*v.* (*past* **-slid**; *past part.* **-slid** or **-slid·den** /-,slidn/) [*intrans.*] relapse into bad ways or error: *converted vegetarians backslide to T-bones* | [as *n.*] (**backsliding**) *there would be no backsliding from the administration's sound policies.* —**back·slid·er** *n.*

back·space /ˈbak,spās/ ▶*n.* **1** a key on a typewriter or computer keyboard that causes the carriage or cursor to move backward. **2** a device on a video recorder or camcorder that produces a slight backward run between shots to eliminate disturbance caused by the interruption of the scanning process.
▶*v.* [*intrans.*] move a typewriter carriage or computer cursor back one or more spaces.

back·spin /ˈbak,spin/ ▶*n.* a backward spin given to a moving ball, causing it to stop more quickly or rebound at a steeper angle on hitting a surface.

back·splash /ˈbak,splasH/ ▶*n.* a panel behind a sink or stove that protects the wall from splashes.

back·stab·bing /ˈbak,stabiNG/ ▶*n.* the action or practice of criticizing someone in a treacherous manner while feigning friendship.
▶*adj.* (of a person) behaving in such a way. —**back·stab** *v.* —**back·stab·ber** *n.*

back·stage /ˈbakˈstāj/ ▶*n.* the area in a theater out of

view of the audience, esp. in the wings or dressing rooms: *backstage was the scene of pleasant pandemonium.*
▸*adj.* of, relating to, or situated in the area behind the stage in a theater: *a backstage tour of the opera house.* ■ *figurative* kept from public scrutiny; secret: *backstage deals.*
▸*adv.* in or to the backstage area in a theater: *I went backstage after the show.* ■ *figurative* not known to the public; in secret: *we planned our strategies backstage.*

B

back·stairs /ˈbakˈste(ə)rz/ ▸*plural n.* stairs at the back or side of a building.
▸*adj.* [*attrib.*] underhanded or clandestine: *I won't make backstairs deals with politicians.*

back·stay /ˈbak,stā/ ▸*n.* a stay on a sailing ship leading downward and aft from the top or upper part of a mast.

back·stitch /ˈbak,sticн/ ▸*n.* sewing with overlapping stitches.
▸*v.* sew using backstitches: [*trans.*] *you can simply backstitch the edges* | [*intrans.*] *this method avoids having to backstitch through open loops.*

back·stop /ˈbak,stäp/ ▸*n.* a person or thing placed at the rear of or behind something as a barrier, support, or reinforcement: *bullets volleyed into the backstop of a flood-control canal.* ■ *Baseball* a high fence or similar structure behind the home plate area. ■ *informal Baseball* a catcher: *he tore the chest protector completely off the big Yankee backstop.* ■ *figurative* an emergency precaution or last resort: *the human operator has to act as the ultimate backstop when things go badly wrong.*
▸*v.* [*trans.*] support or reinforce: *the founding banks were backstopping the loans.* ■ *Hockey* act as goaltender for: *the man who backstopped the Edmonton Oilers.*

back·sto·ry /ˈbak,stôrē/ ▸*n.* (*pl.* **-ries**) a history or background created for a fictional character in a motion picture or television program. ■ similar background information about a real person or thing that promotes fuller understanding of it: *the little-known backstory about the theory of evolution.*

back·street /ˈbak,strēt/ ▸*n.* a minor street remote from a main road: *the fetid backstreets of the shanty town* | [as *adj.*] *a backstreet garage.*
▸*adj.* [*attrib.*] operating or performed secretly, and typically illegally: *a loophole that allowed backstreet chemists to make methamphetamine.*

back·stretch /ˈbakˈstrecн/ ▸*n.* the part of a racecourse that is farthest from the grandstand and parallel to the homestretch. ■ the area adjacent to a racetrack where the horses are stabled and stable employees have temporary living accommodations.

back·stroke /ˈbak,strōk/ ▸*n.* [in *sing.*] a swimming stroke performed on the back with the arms lifted alternately out of the water in a backward circular motion and the legs extended and kicking: *I concentrated on the backstroke most of the time* | [as *adj.*] *I won the backstroke and breaststroke events* | [as *adv.*] *they would swim freestyle and then backstroke.* ■ (**the backstroke**) a race, typically of a specified length or kind, in which such a style of swimming is used: *he was fifth in the 200-meter backstroke.* —**back·strok·er** *n.*

back·swept /ˈbak,swept/ ▸*adj.* swept, slanted, or sloped backward: *his backswept hair.*

back·swim·mer /ˈbak,swimər/ ▸*n.* a predatory aquatic bug that swims on its back using its long back legs as oars. It is able to capture large prey such as tadpoles and fish. See also **WATER BOATMAN**. • Family Notonectidae, suborder Heteroptera: *Notonecta* and other genera.

backswimmer

back·swing /ˈbak,swiɴɢ/ ▸*n.* a backward swing, esp. of an arm or of a golf club when about to hit a ball.

back·sword /ˈbak,sôrd/ ▸*n.* a sword with only one cutting edge.

back talk ▸*n. informal* rude or impertinent remarks made in reply to someone in authority: *no back talk, I'm warning you.*

back-to-back ▸*adj.* consecutive: *back-to-back homers in a major league baseball game.*
▸*adv.* (**back to back**) **1** (of two people) facing in opposite directions with backs touching: *they sat on the ground, leaning back to back.* **2** consecutively; in succession: *the games were played back to back.*

back-to-na·ture ▸*adj.* [*attrib.*] advocating or relating to reversion to a simpler way of life: *a back-to-nature lifestyle.*

back·track /ˈbak,trak/ ▸*v.* **1** [*intrans.*] retrace one's steps: *she had to bypass two closer farms and backtrack to them later* | *figurative to backtrack a little, the case is a complex one.* ■ *figurative* reverse one's previous action or opinion: *the unions have had to* **backtrack on** *their demands.* **2** [*trans.*] pursue, trace, or monitor: *he was able to backtrack the buck to a ridge nearby.*

back·up /ˈbak,əp/ ▸*n.* **1** help or support: *no police backup could be expected.* ■ a person or thing that can be called on if necessary; a reserve: *I've got a security force as backup* | *the filter is an excellent backup to other systems* | [as *adj.*] *a backup generator.* **2** *Computing* the procedure for making extra copies of data in case the original is lost or damaged: *automatic online backup* | [as *adj.*] *a backup system.* ■ a copy of this type. **3** an overflow caused by a stoppage, as in water or automobile traffic: *there are long backups on all routes.*

back·up light ▸*n.* a light at the rear of a vehicle that comes on when the vehicle is in reverse gear.

back·ward /ˈbakwərd/ ▸*adj.* **1** [*attrib.*] directed behind or to the rear: *she left the room without a backward glance* | *a gradual backward movement.* ■ looking toward the past, rather than being progressive; retrograde: *he said the decision was a backward step.* **2** (of a person) having learning difficulties: *a lively child but a bit backward.* ■ having made less than normal progress: *economically backward countries.*
▸*adv.* (also **back·wards**) **1** (of a movement) away from one's front; in the direction of one's back: *he took a step backward* | *Harry suddenly fell backward into a somersault.* ■ in reverse of the usual direction or order: *counting backward* | *baseball caps turned backward.* ■ with the rear facing forward: *the canoe turned around backward.* **2** toward or into the past: *a loving look backward at his early life.* ■ toward or into a worse state: *a giant step backward for child-centered education.* ▷Middle English: from earlier *abackward*, from **ABACK**. —**back·ward·ly** *adv.* —**back·ward·ness** *n.*
▸*PHRASES* □ **backward and forward** in both directions alternately; to and fro. □ **bend** (or **lean**) **over backward to do something** *informal* make every effort, esp. to be fair or helpful: *Jensen bent over backward to be fair.* □ **know something backward** (**and forward**) be entirely familiar with something.

USAGE In U.S. English, the adverb form is sometimes spelled **backwards** (*the ladder fell backwards*), but the adjective is almost always **backward** (*a backward glance*). Directional words using the suffix *-ward* tend to have no *s* ending in U.S. English, although **backwards** is more common than *afterwards, towards,* or *forwards*. The *s* ending often (but not always) appears in the phrases *backwards and forwards* and *bending over backwards*. In British English, the spelling **backwards** is more common than **backward**.

back·ward com·pat·i·ble (also **back·wards com·pat·i·ble**) ▸*adj.* (of computer hardware or software) able to be used with an older piece of hardware or software without special adaptation or modification. —**back·ward com·pat·i·bil·i·ty** *n.*

back·wash /ˈbak,wôsн; -,wäsн/ ▸*n.* the motion of receding waves. ■ a backward current of water or air created by the motion of an object through it: *the backwash of a truck on the highway.* ■ *figurative* repercussions: *the backwash of the Cuban missile crisis.*
▸*v.* [*trans.*] clean (a filter) by reversing the flow of fluid through it.

back·wa·ter /ˈbak,wôtər; -,wätər/ ▸*n.* a part of a river not reached by the current, where the water is stagnant: *the eels inhabit backwaters.* ■ an isolated or peaceful place: *a sleepy Midwest backwater.* ■ a place or condition in which no development or progress is taking place: *the country remained an economic backwater.*

back·wind /ˈbak,wind/ *Sailing* ▸*v.* [*trans.*] (of a sail or vessel) deflect a flow of air into the back of (another sail or vessel).
▸*n.* a flow of air deflected into the back of a sail.

back·woods /ˈbakˈwo͝odz/ ▸*plural n.* [often as *adj.*] remote uncleared forest land: *backwoods homesteads.* ■ a remote or sparsely inhabited region, esp. one considered backward. —**back·woods·man** /-mən/ *n.*

back·yard /ˈbakˈyärd/ ▸*n.* **1** a yard behind a house or other building, typically surrounded by a fence: *a tree-shaded succession of backyards* | [as *adj.*] *a casual backyard party.* **2** the area close to where one lives, or the territory close to a particular country, regarded with proprietorial concern: *anything was preferable to a nuclear dump* **in their own backyard.**

Ba·co·lod /bəˈkō,lôd/ a city in the central Philippines, a port on the northwestern coast of the island of Negros; pop. 364,180.

Ba·con[1] /ˈbākən/, Francis, Baron Verulam and Viscount St. Albans (1561–1626), English statesman and philosopher. As a scientist he advocated the inductive method. Notable works: *The Advancement of Learning* (1605) and *Novum Organum* (1620).

Ba·con[2], Francis (1909–92), Irish painter. His work chiefly depicts human figures in grotesquely distorted postures, their features blurred or erased.

Ba·con[3], Roger (*c.*1214–94), English philosopher, scientist, and Franciscan monk. Most notable for his work in the field of optics, he emphasized the need for an empirical approach to scientific study.

ba·con /ˈbākən/ ▸*n.* cured meat from the back or sides of a pig. ▷Middle English: from Old French, from a Germanic word meaning 'ham, flitch'; related to **BACK**.
▸*PHRASES* □ **bring home the bacon** *informal* **1** supply material provision or support; earn a living. **2** achieve success. □ **save someone's bacon** see **SAVE**[1].

Ba·co·ni·an /bāˈkōnēən/ ▸*adj.* of or relating to Sir Francis Bacon or his inductive method of reasoning and philosophy. ■ relating to or denoting the theory that Bacon wrote the plays attributed to Shakespeare.
▸*n.* an adherent of Bacon's philosophical system. ■ a supporter of the theory that Bacon wrote the plays attributed to Shakespeare.

bac·te·re·mi·a /,baktəˈrēmēə/ (*Brit.* **bac·te·rae·m·i·a**) ▸*n. Medicine* the presence of bacteria in the blood. ▷late 19th cent.: from **BACTERIUM** + **-EMIA**. —**bacteremic** /-mik/ *adj.*

bac·te·ri·a /bakˈti(ə)rēə/ ▸ plural form of **BACTERIUM**.

USAGE See usage at **BACTERIUM**.

bac·te·ri·cide /bakˈti(ə)rə,sīd/ ▸*n.* a substance that kills bacteria. —**bac·te·ri·cid·al** /-,ti(ə)rəˈsīdl/ *adj.*

bacterio- (also **bacteri-**; also **bacter-** before a vowel) ▸*comb. form* representing **BACTERIUM**.

bac·te·ri·o·cin /bakˈti(ə)rēəsin/ ▸*n. Biology* a protein produced by bacteria of one strain and active against those of a closely related strain. ▷1950s: from French *bactériocine*, from Greek *baktērion* 'small cane' + a shortened form of **COLICIN**.

bac·te·ri·o·log·i·cal /bak,ti(ə)rēəˈläjikəl/ ▸*adj.* [*attrib.*] of or relating to bacteriology or bacteria. ■ relating to or denoting germ warfare. —**bac·te·ri·o·log·ic** /-jik/ *adj.* —**bac·te·ri·o·log·i·cal·ly** /-ik(ə)lē/ *adv.*

bac·te·ri·ol·o·gy /bak,ti(ə)rēˈäləjē/ ▸*n.* the study of bacteria. —**bac·te·ri·ol·o·gist** /-jist/ *n.*

bac·te·ri·ol·y·sis /bak,ti(ə)rēˈäləsis/ ▸*n. Biology* the rupture of bacterial cells, esp. by an antibody. —**bac·te·ri·o·lyt·ic** /-,ti(ə)rēəˈlitik/ *adj.*

bac·te·ri·o·phage /bakˈti(ə)rēə,fāj/ ▸*n. Biology* a virus that parasitizes a bacterium by infecting it and reproducing inside it. ▷1920s: from **BACTERIUM** + Greek *phagein* 'eat.'

bac·te·ri·o·rho·dop·sin /bak,ti(ə)rēō-rōˈdäpsin/ ▸*n.* a protein pigment in the bacterium *Halobacterium halobium* that when illuminated transports protons across the cytoplasmic membrane in large numbers.

bac·te·ri·o·stat /bakˈti(ə)rēə,stat/ ▸*n.* a substance that prevents the multiplying of bacteria without destroying them. ▷early 20th cent.: from **BACTERIUM** + Greek *statos* 'standing.' —**bac·te·ri·o·sta·sis** /-,ti(ə)rēəˈstāsis/ *n.* —**bac·te·ri·o·stat·ic** /-,ti(ə)rēəˈstatik/ *adj.* —**bac·te·ri·o·stat·i·cal·ly** *adv.*

bac·te·ri·um /bakˈti(ə)rēəm/ ▸*n.* (*pl.* **-te·ri·a** /-ˈti(ə)rēə/) a member of a large group of unicellular microorganisms that have cell walls but lack organelles and an organized nucleus, including some that can cause disease.

Bacteria are widely distributed in soil, water, and air, and on or in the tissues of plants and animals. Formerly included in the plant kingdom, they are now classified separately (as prokaryotes). They play a vital role in global ecology, as the chemical changes they bring about include those of organic decay and nitrogen fixation. Much modern biochemical knowledge has been gained from the study of bacteria because they grow easily and reproduce rapidly in laboratory cultures.

▷mid 19th cent.: modern Latin, from Greek *baktērion*, diminutive of *baktēria* 'staff, cane' (because the first ones to be discovered were rod-shaped). Compare with **BACILLUS**. —**bac·te·ri·al** /-ˈti(ə)rēəl/ *adj.*

USAGE Bacteria is the plural form (derived from Latin) of **bacterium**. Like any other plural, it should be used with the plural form of the verb: *the **bacteria** causing salmonella **are** killed by thorough cooking*, not *the **bacteria** . . . **is** killed* . . . . However, the unfamiliarity of the form means that **bacteria** is often mistakenly treated as a singular form, as in the example above.

bac·te·ri·u·ri·a /bakˌti(ə)rē'yŏŏrēə/ ▸*n. Medicine* the presence of bacteria in the urine.

bac·te·rize /'baktəˌrīz/ ▸*v.* [*trans.*] (usu. **be bacterized**) treat with bacteria. —**bac·te·ri·za·tion** /ˌbaktərə'zāshən/ *n.*

bac·te·roid /'baktəˌroid/ ▸*adj.* of the nature of or resembling a bacterium.
▸*n.* a bacteroid organism or structure, esp. a modified cell formed by a symbiotic bacterium in a root nodule of a leguminous plant.

Bac·tri·a /'baktrēə/ an ancient country in central Asia, corresponding to the northern part of modern Afghanistan. —**Bac·tri·an** *adj.* & *n.*

Bac·tri·an cam·el /'baktrēən/ ▸*n.* the two-humped camel, which has been domesticated but is still found wild in central Asia. • *Camelus bactrianus* (formerly **ferus**)), family Camelidae.

bac·u·lo·vi·rus /'bakyəlōˌvīrəs/ ▸*n. Biology* a member of a family of DNA viruses infecting only invertebrate animals. Some have a very specific insect host and may be used in biological pest control. ▷1980s: from Latin *baculum* 'rod, stick' + VIRUS.

bac·u·lum /'bakyŏŏləm/ ▸*n.* (*pl.* **-la** /-lə/) another term for OS PENIS. ▷1930s: modern Latin.

bad /bad/ ▸*adj.* (**worse** /wərs/; **worst** /wərst/) **1** of poor quality; inferior or defective: *a bad diet* | *bad eyesight.* ■ (of a person) not able to do something well; incompetent: *I'm so **bad at** names* | *a bad listener.* **2** unpleasant or unwelcome: *bad news* | *bad weather.* ■ unsatisfactory or unfortunate: *bad luck* | [as *n.*] (**the bad**) *taking the good with the bad.* ■ (of an unwelcome thing) serious; severe: *bad headaches* | *a bad crash* | *a bad mistake.* ■ unfavorable; adverse: *bad reviews.* ■ harmful: *soap was **bad for** his face.* ■ not suitable: *morning was a bad time to ask Andy about anything.* **3** (of food) decayed; putrid: *everything in the fridge would go bad.* ■ (of the atmosphere) polluted; unhealthy: *bad air.* **4** (of parts of the body) injured, diseased, or causing pain: *a bad back.* ■ [as *complement*] (of a person) unwell: *I feel bad.* **5** [as *complement*] regretful, guilty, or ashamed about something: *working mothers who feel bad about leaving their children.* **6** morally depraved; wicked: *the bad guys* | *bad language* | *a bad reputation.* ■ naughty; badly behaved: *what a bad girl* | *bad behavior.* **7** worthless; not valid: *he ran up 87 bad checks.* **8** (**bad·der**, **bad·dest**) *informal* good; excellent: *they want the baddest, best-looking Corvette there is.*
▸*adv. informal* badly: *he beat her up real bad.* ▷Middle English: perhaps representing Old English *bǣddel* 'hermaphrodite, womanish man.' —**bad·dish** *adj.* —**bad·ness** *n.*
▸*PHRASES* □ **come to a bad end** see END. □ **from bad to worse** into an even worse state: *the country's going from bad to worse.* □ **in a bad way** ill: *Sammy shivered. He was in a bad way.* ■ in trouble: *the fleet was in a bad way, mainly due to a shortage of spares.* □ **not** (or **not so**) **bad** *informal* fairly good: *she discovered he wasn't so bad after all.* □ **to the bad** to ruin: *I hate to see you going to the bad.* ■ in deficit: *he was $80 to the bad.* □ **too bad** *informal* used to indicate that something is regrettable but now beyond retrieval: *too bad, but that's the way it is.*

USAGE Confusion in the use of **bad** versus **badly** usually has to do with verbs called copulas, such as *feel* or *seem*. Thus, standard usage calls for *I feel bad*, not *I feel badly*. As a precise speaker or writer would explain, *I feel badly* means 'I do not have a good sense of touch.' See also **usage** at GOOD.

bad·ass /'badˌas/ *informal* ▸*n.* a tough, aggressive, or uncooperative person: *one of them is a real badass, the other's pretty friendly.*
▸*adj.* **1** tough or aggressive: *a strange fellow with a badass temper.* ■ particularly bad or severe: *some badass virus I'd caught at sea.* **2** formidable; excellent: *this was one badass camera.* ▷1950s: from the adjective BAD + ASS[2].

bad blood ▸*n.* ill feeling: *there has always been bad blood between these families.*

bad break ▸*n. informal* a piece of bad luck: *a weird coincidence and a bad break.*

bad breath ▸*n.* unpleasant-smelling breath; halitosis.

bad debt ▸*n.* a debt that cannot be recovered.

bad·de·ley·ite /'bad(ə)lēˌīt/ ▸*n.* a mineral consisting largely of zirconium dioxide, ranging from colorless to yellow, brown, or black. ▷late 19th cent.: named after Joseph *Baddeley*, English traveler, + -ITE[1].

bad·der·locks /'badərˌläks/ ▸*plural n. chiefly Scottish* an edible seaweed with a long greenish frond and prominent midrib, occurring in northern Europe. • *Alaria esculenta*, class Phaeophyceae. ▷late 18th cent.: perhaps from *Balderlocks*, based on the name of the god BALDER.

bad·dy /'badē/ (also **bad·die**) *informal* ▸*n.* (*pl.* **-dies**) a villain or criminal in a story, movie, etc.

bade /bad; bād/ ▸ past of BID[2].

bad egg ▸*n.* see EGG[1] (sense 2).

Ba·den /'bädn/ a spa town in eastern Austria, south of Vienna; pop. 24,000. It is noted for its warm mineral springs .

Ba·den-Ba·den /ˌbädn 'bädn/ a spa town in the Black Forest in southwestern Germany; pop. 48,700.

Ba·den-Pow·ell /ˌbädn 'pōəl; 'pou-əl/, Robert (Stephenson Smyth), 1st Baron Baden-Powell of Gilwell (1857–1941), English soldier and founder of the Boy Scout movement.

Ba·den-Würt·tem·berg /'wərtəmˌbərg; 'vyrtəmˌberk/ a state of western Germany; capital, Stuttgart.

bad faith ▸*n.* intent to deceive: *the owners have bargained **in bad faith**.* ■ (in existentialist philosophy) refusal to confront facts or choices.

bad form ▸*n.* an offense against current social conventions: *it was considered bad form to talk about money.*

badge /baj/ ▸*n.* a distinctive emblem worn as a mark of office, membership, achievement, licensed employment, etc.: *name badges* | *a Girl Scout badge.* ■ a distinguishing object or emblem: *a large gold key hung around his neck as his badge of office.* ■ *figurative* a feature or sign that reveals a particular condition or quality: *my jeans had patches on the knees, like badges of courage marking encounters with barbed wire.*
▸*v.* [*trans.*] mark with a badge or other distinguishing emblem. ▷late Middle English: of unknown origin.

badge en·gi·neer·ing ▸*n.* the practice of marketing a motor vehicle under two or more brand names.

badg·er /'bajər/ ▸*n.* **1** a heavily built omnivorous nocturnal mammal of the weasel family, typically having a gray and black coat. • Several genera and species in the family Mustelidae, in particular the Eurasian *Meles meles*, which has a white head with two black stripes, and the North American *Taxidea taxus*, with a white stripe on the head. **2** (**Badger**) *informal* a native of Wisconsin.
▸*v.* [*trans.*] ask (someone) repeatedly and annoyingly for something; pester: *journalists **badgered** him **about** the deals* | *Tom had finally **badgered** her **into** going* | [*trans.*] *his daughter was always badgering him to let her join.* ▷early 16th cent.: perhaps from BADGE, with reference to its distinctive head markings. The verb sense (late 18th cent.) originates from the formerly popular sport of badger baiting.

badger 1

Badg·er State a nickname for the state of WISCONSIN[1].

bad hair day ▸*n. informal* a day on which everything seems to go wrong, characterized as a day on which one's hair is particularly unmanageable.

bad·i·nage /ˌbadn'äzh/ ▸*n.* humorous or witty conversation: *cultured badinage about art and life.* ▷mid 17th cent.: from French, from *badiner* 'to joke,' from *badin* 'fool,' based on Provençal *badar* 'gape.'

bad·lands /'badˌlandz/ ▸*plural n.* extensive tracts of heavily eroded, uncultivable land with little vegetation. ■ (**the Badlands**) a barren plateau region of the western U.S., mainly in southwestern South Dakota and northwestern Nebraska, south of the Black Hills, noted for its harsh terrain. ▷mid 19th cent. (originally U.S.): translation of French *mauvaises terres*.

bad·ly /'badlē/ ▸*adv.* (**worse** /wərs/, **worst** /wərst/) **1** in an unsatisfactory, inadequate, or unsuccessful way: *a badly managed company* | *the war was going badly.* ■ in an unfavorable way: *try not to think badly of me.* ■ in an unacceptable or unpleasant way: *she realized she was behaving rather badly.* **2** to a great or serious degree; severely: *the building was badly damaged by fire* | *I wanted a baby so badly* | *things had begun to go badly wrong.*
▸*adj. informal* [as *complement*] guilty or regretful: *I felt badly about my unfriendliness of the previous evening.*
▸*PHRASE* □ **badly off** in an unfavorable situation: *her belief that children are worse off when their parents divorce.* ■ having little money.

USAGE See **usage** at BAD.

bad·min·ton /'badmintn/ ▸*n.* a game with rackets in which a shuttlecock is played back and forth across a net. ▷named after *Badminton*, a country home in southwestern England.

bad-mouth ▸*v.* [*trans.*] *informal* criticize (someone or something); speak disloyally of: *no one wants to hire an individual who bad-mouths a prior employer.*

bad news ▸*n. informal* an unpleasant or undesirable person or thing: *dry weather is always bad news for gardeners.*

bad-tem·pered ▸*adj.* easily annoyed or made angry: *in a heat wave, many people become increasingly bad-tempered.* ■ characterized by anger or ungraciousness: *Mary was feeling very bad-tempered* | *a bad-tempered exchange.* —**bad-tem·pered·ly** *adv.*

Bae·de·ker /'bādikər; 'bed-/, Karl (1801–59), German publisher of travel guidebooks. He is remembered chiefly for the series of guidebooks to which he gave his name and which are still published.

Bae·ke·land /'bakəˌlänt; 'bāk(ə)lənd/, Leo Hendrik (1863–1944), U.S. chemist and inventor; born in Belgium. He invented and developed the synthetic resin Bakelite in 1907.

Baer /be(ə)r/, Karl Ernest von (1792–1876), German biologist. He discovered that ova are particles within the ovarian follicles, and he formulated the principle that general characters appear before special ones do in the developing embryo. His studies were used by Darwin in the theory of evolution.

Bae·yer /'bāər/, Adolph Johann Friedrich Wilhelm von (1835–1917), German organic chemist. He prepared the first barbiturates, investigated dyes, and synthesized indigo. Nobel Prize for Chemistry (1905).

Ba·ez /'bīˌez; bī'ez/, Joan (1941–), U.S. folk singer and civil rights activist. She is best known for her performances at civil rights demonstrations in the early 1960s. Notable albums: *Any Day Now* (1968) and *Diamonds and Rust* (1975).

Baf·fin /'bafən/, William (*c.*1584–1622), English navigator and explorer, the pilot of several expeditions in search of the Northwest Passage 1612–16. He discovered the largest island of the Canadian Arctic in 1616; this and the strait between it and Greenland are named after him.

Baf·fin Bay an extension of the North Atlantic Ocean between Baffin Island and Greenland, linked to the Arctic Ocean by three passages. It is largely icebound in winter.

Baf·fin Is·land a large island in the Canadian Arctic Ocean, situated at the mouth of Hudson Bay. It is separated from Greenland by Baffin Bay.

baf·fle /'bafəl/ ▸*v.* [*trans.*] **1** totally bewilder or perplex: *an unexplained occurrence that baffled everyone* | [as *adj.*] (**baffling**) *the baffling murder of her sister.* See note at THWART. **2** restrain or regulate (a fluid, a sound, etc.): *to baffle the noise further, I pad the gunwales.*
▸*n.* a device used to restrain the flow of a fluid, gas, or loose material or to prevent the spreading of sound or light in a particular direction. ▷late 16th cent. (in the sense 'cheat, deceive'): perhaps related to French *bafouer* 'ridicule' or obsolete French *beffer* 'mock, deceive.' —**baf·fle·ment** *n.* (in sense 1 of the *verb*). —**baf·fling·ly** *adv.* (in sense 1 of the *verb*).

baf·fle·gab /'bafəlˌgab/ ▸*n. informal* incomprehensible or pretentious language, esp. bureaucratic jargon: *the smooth chairman who had elevated bafflegab to an art form.*

bag /bag/ ▸*n.* **1** a container of flexible material with an opening at the top, used for carrying things: *brown paper bags* | *a shopping bag.* ■ an amount held by such a container: *a **bag of** apples.* ■ a thing resembling a bag in shape: *this year's sweater is a big bag of* *natural Shetland.* ■ a woman's handbag or purse. ■ a piece of luggage: *she began to unpack her bags.* ■ *Baseball* a base. ■ (**bags**) *informal, chiefly Brit.* plenty of something: *I had* ***bags of*** *energy.* **2** the amount of game shot by a hunter. **3** (usu. **bags**) a loose fold of skin under a person's eye: *the bags under his eyes gave him a sad appearance.* **4** a sac in an animal, such as the udder of a cow. **5** *informal, derogatory* a woman, esp. an older one, perceived as unpleasant, bad-tempered, or unattractive: *an interfering* ***old bag.*** **6** (**one's bag**) *informal* one's particular interest or taste: *if religion and politics are your bag, you'll find something to interest you here.*

▶*v.* (**bagged, bag·ging**) [*trans.*] **1** put (something) in a bag: *customers bagged their own groceries | we* ***bagged up*** *the apples.* **2** (of a hunter) succeed in killing or catching an animal: *in 1979, handgun hunters bagged 677 deer.* ■ *figurative* succeed in securing (something): *we've bagged three awards for excellence.* ■ *informal* take, occupy, or reserve (something) before someone else can do so: *get there early to bag a seat in the front row.* **3** [*intrans.*] (of clothes, esp. pants) hang loosely or lose shape: *these trousers never bag at the knee.* ■ swell or bulge. **4** quit; give up on: *it was a drag to be in the ninth grade at 17, so he bagged it.* ▷Middle English: perhaps from Old Norse *baggi.* **—bag·ful** /-ˌfo͝ol/ *n.* (*pl.* **-fuls**) .

▶*PHRASES* □ **bag and baggage** with all one's belongings: *he threw her out bag and baggage.* □ **a bag of bones** an emaciated person or animal: *the pony is just a bag of bones.* □ **a bag** (or **whole bag**) **of tricks** *informal* a set of ingenious plans, techniques, or resources: *hoteliers are using a whole new bag of tricks to keep their guests on the premises.* □ **be left holding the bag** see HOLD. □ **in the bag** *informal* **1** (of something desirable) as good as secured: *the election is in the bag.* **2** drunk: *I don't think my parents even suspected that I was* ***half in the bag.***

Ba·gan·da /bəˈgändə/ (also **Gan·da**) ▶*plural n.* (*sing.* **Mu·gan·da** /mo͞oˈgändə/) a Bantu people of the kingdom of Buganda, now forming part of Uganda. Their language is Luganda.

▶*adj.* of or relating to the Baganda. ▷a local name; compare with Kiswahili *Waganda.*

ba·gasse /bəˈgas/ ▶*n.* the dry pulpy residue left after the extraction of juice from sugar cane, used as fuel for electricity generators, etc. ▷early 19th cent.: from French, from Spanish *bagazo* 'pulp.'

bag·a·telle /ˌbagəˈtel/ ▶*n.* **1** a thing of little importance; a very easy task: *dealing with these boats was* ***a mere bagatelle*** *for the world's oldest yacht club.* **2** a game in which small balls are hit and then allowed to roll down a sloping board on which there are holes, each numbered with the score achieved if a ball goes into it, with pins acting as obstructions. **3** a short, light piece of music, esp. one for the piano. ▷mid 17th cent. (sense 1): from French, from Italian *bagatella*, perhaps from *baga* 'baggage' or from a diminutive of Latin *baca* 'berry.' Sense 2 dates from the early 19th cent.

ba·gel /ˈbāgəl/ ▶*n.* a dense bread roll in the shape of a ring, made by boiling dough and then baking it. ▷early 20th cent. (as *beigel*): from Yiddish *beygel.*

bag·gage /ˈbagij/ ▶*n.* **1** personal belongings packed in suitcases for traveling; luggage. ■ the portable equipment of an army. ■ *figurative* past experiences or long-held ideas regarded as burdens and impediments: *the emotional baggage I'm hauling around | the party jettisoned its traditional ideological baggage.* **2** *dated, derogatory* a cheeky or disagreeable girl or woman. ▷late Middle English: from Old French *bagage* (from *baguer* 'tie up'), or *bagues* 'bundles'; perhaps related to BAG.

bag·gage claim ▶*n.* [in *sing.*] the area in an airport where arriving passengers collect luggage that has been carried in the hold of the aircraft.

Bag·gie /ˈbagē/ ▶*n.* (*pl.* **-gies**) *trademark* a plastic bag typically used for storing food. ■ (**baggie**) *informal* any small plastic bag.

bag·ging /ˈbagiNG/ ▶*n.* material out of which bags are made.

bag·gy /ˈbagē/ ▶*adj.* (**-gi·er, -gi·est**) (of clothing) loose and hanging in folds: *baggy pants.* ■ (of eyes) with folds of puffy skin below them: *his eyes were baggy with the fatigue of overwork.*

▶*n.* (**baggies**) *informal* loose and wide-legged pants, shorts, or swim trunks. **—bag·gi·ly** /ˈbagəlē/ *adv.* **—bag·gi·ness** *n.*

Bagh·dad /ˈbagˌdad; bagˈdad/ the capital of Iraq, on the Tigris River; pop. 4,648,600

bag la·dy ▶*n.* *informal* a homeless woman who carries her possessions in shopping bags.

bag lunch ▶*n.* a cold lunch prepared at home and carried in a bag to work, to school, or on an excursion.

bag·man /ˈbagˌman; -mən/ ▶*n.* (*pl.* **-men**) **1** *informal* an agent who collects or distributes the proceeds of illicit activities: *one million dollars cash paid to the general's bagman.* **2** *Canadian* a political fund-raiser: *a Tory bagman.* **3** *Brit., dated, informal* a traveling salesman.

bagn·io /ˈbanyō; ˈbän-/ ▶*n.* (*pl.* **-ios**) **1** *archaic* a brothel. **2** *historical* an oriental prison. **3** *historical* a bathhouse in Turkey or Italy. ▷late 16th cent. (sense 2): from Italian *bagno*, from Latin *balneum* 'bath.'

bag of wa·ters ▶*n.* the fluid-filled sac that contains and protects the fetus in the womb and that releases its fluids when it breaks during birth.

bag·pipe /ˈbagˌpīp/ ▶*n.* (usu. **bagpipes**) a musical instrument with reed pipes that are sounded by the pressure of wind emitted from a bag squeezed by the player's arm. Bagpipes are associated esp. with Scotland, but are also used in folk music in Ireland, Northumberland, and France. **—bag·pip·er** /ˈbagˌpīpər/ *n.*

bagpipes

ba gua /ˌbä ˈgwä/ (also **pa kua**) ▶*n.* a Chinese religious motif incorporating the eight trigrams of the *I Ching*, typically arranged octagonally around a symbol denoting the balance of yin and yang, or around a mirror. ■ this motif regarded in feng shui as a pattern determining the significance and auspicious qualities of spatial relationships. ■ a Chinese martial art in which movements are focused on a circle and the defense of eight points around it. ▷from Chinese *bā* 'eight' + *guà* 'divinatory symbols.'

ba·guette /baˈget/ ▶*n.* **1** a long, narrow loaf of French bread. **2** a gem, esp. a diamond, cut in a long rectangular shape: [often as *modifier*] *a baguette diamond.* **3** *Architecture* a small molding, semicircular in section. **4** a slim, rectangular handbag. ▷early 18th cent. (sense 3): from French, from Italian *bacchetto*, diminutive of *bacchio*, from Latin *baculum* 'staff.' Senses 1 and 2 date from the 20th cent.

bag·wig /ˈbagˌwig/ ▶*n.* a wig fashionable in the 18th century with the back hair enclosed in an ornamental bag.

bag·worm /ˈbagˌwərm/ ▶*n.* a drab moth, the caterpillar and flightless female of which live in a portable protective case constructed out of plant debris. • Family Psychidae: many genera.

bah /bä/ ▶*exclam.* an expression of contempt or disagreement: *You think it was an accident? Bah!* ▷early 19th cent.: probably from French.

Ba·ha·'i /bəˈhī/ (also **Ba·ha·i**) ▶*n.* (*pl.* **-ha·'is**) a monotheistic religion founded in the 19th century as a development of Babism, emphasizing the essential oneness of humankind and of all religions and seeking world peace. The Baha'i faith was founded by the Persian Baha'ullah (1817–92) and his son Abdul Baha (1844–1921). ■ an adherent of the Baha'i faith. ▷Persian, from Arabic *bahā'* 'splendor.' **—Ba·ha·'ism** /-ˌizəm/ *n.*

Ba·ha·mas /bəˈhäməz/ a country in the northwestern West Indies, an archipelago off the southeastern coast of Florida; pop. 299,600; capital, Nassau; languages, English (official), Creole. **—Ba·ha·mi·an** /bəˈhāmēən; -ˈhäm-/ *adj.* & *n.*

It was here that Columbus first landed in the New World (Oct. 12, 1492). The islands were a British colony from the 18th century until they gained independence within the Commonwealth of Nations in 1973.

Ba·ha·sa In·do·ne·sia /bəˈhäsə ˌindəˈnēZHə/ ▶*n.* the official language of Indonesia. See INDONESIAN. ▷from Malay *bahasa* 'language.'

Ba·ha·sa Ma·lay·sia /bəˈhäsə məˈlāZHə/ ▶*n.* the official language of Malaysia. See MALAY.

Ba·ha·wal·pur /bəˈhä-wəlˌpo͝or/ a city in east central Pakistan, in Punjab province; pop. 250,000.

Ba·hi·a /bäˈēə; bəˈhēə/ **1** a state of eastern Brazil, on the Atlantic coast; capital, Salvador. **2** former name for SALVADOR.

Ba·hí·a Blan·ca /bäˈēə ˈbläNGkə/ a port in Argentina serving the southern part of the country; pop. 271,500.

Bah·rain /bäˈrān/ a country in western Asia that consists of a group of islands in the Persian Gulf; pop. 677,800; capital, Manama; official language, Arabic. **—Bah·rain·i** /-ˈrānē/ *adj.* & *n.*

Ruled by the Portuguese in the 16th century and the Persians in the 17th century, Bahrain became a British protectorate in 1861 and gained independence in 1971. Its economy is dependent on the refining and export of oil.

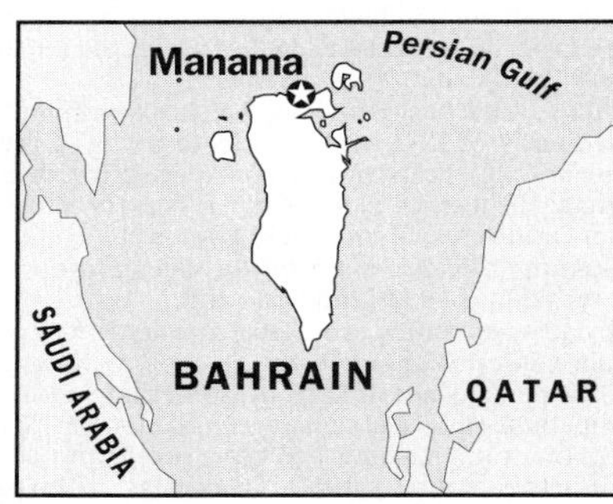

baht /bät/ ▶*n.* (*pl.* same) the basic monetary unit of Thailand, equal to 100 satangs. ▷from Thai *bāt.*

Ba·hu·tu /bäˈho͞oˌto͞o/ ▶ plural form of HUTU.

Bai·kal, Lake /bīˈkäl; -ˈkôl; -ˈkal/ (also **Bay·kal**) a large lake in southern Siberia, in Russia, the largest freshwater lake in Europe and Asia and, with a depth of 5,714 feet (1,743 m), the deepest lake in the world.

bail[1] /bāl/ ▶*n.* the temporary release of an accused person awaiting trial, sometimes on condition that a sum of money be lodged to guarantee their appearance in court: *he has been released* ***on bail.*** ■ money paid by or for such a person as security.

▶*v.* [*trans.*] (usu. **be bailed**) release or secure the release of (a prisoner) on payment of bail: *his son called home to get* ***bailed out*** *of jail.* See also BAIL OUT at BAIL[3]. ▷Middle English: from Old French, literally 'custody, jurisdiction,' from Old French *bailler* 'take charge of,' from Latin *bajulare* 'bear a burden.' **—bail·a·ble** *adj.*

▶*PHRASES* □ **jump bail** *informal* fail to appear for trial after being released on bail: *he jumped bail and was on the run until his arrest.* □ **go bail** (or **stand bail**) act as surety for an accused person. □ **post bail** pay a sum of money as bail: *I posted bail for him.*

bail[2] ▶*n.* **1** a bar that holds something in place, in particular: ■ *Fishing* a bar that guides fishing line on a reel. ■ a bar on a typewriter or computer printer that holds the paper steady. ■ *Mountaineering* a bar on a crampon that fits into a groove in the sole of a boot. ■ a bar separating horses in an open stable. **2** an arched handle, such as on a bucket or a teapot: [as *adj.*] *drawers fitted with brass bail handles.* **3** (usu. **bails**) *Cricket* either of the two crosspieces bridging the stumps, which the bowler and fielders try to dislodge with the ball to get the batsman out. ▷Middle English (denoting the outer wall of a castle): from Old French *baile* 'palisade, enclosure,' *baillier* 'enclose,' perhaps from Latin *baculum* 'rod, stick.' Compare with BAILEY.

bail[3] ▶*v.* **1** [*trans.*] scoop water out of (a ship or boat): *the first priority is to* ***bail out*** *the boat with buckets.* ■ scoop (water) out of a ship or boat: *I started to use my hands to* ***bail out*** *the water.* **2** [*intrans.*] abandon a commitment, obligation, or responsibility: *after 12 years of this, including Sunday Mass with the family, I bailed.* ■ (**bail on**) let (someone) down by failing to fulfill a commitment, obligation, or responsibility: *he looks a little like the guy who bailed on me.*

▶*phrasal v.* □ **bail out** (of a member of an aircrew) make an emergency parachute descent from an aircraft; eject. ■ *figurative* become free of an obligation or commitment; discontinue an activity: *she felt ready to bail out of the corporate rat race.* ▫ **bail someone/something out** release someone or something from a difficulty; rescue: *the state will not bail out loss-making enterprises.* ▷early 17th cent.: from obsolete *bail* 'bucket,' from French *baille,* based on Latin *bajulus* 'carrier.' —**bail·er** *n.*

Bai·le Átha Cli·ath /blä 'klēə/ Irish name for **DUBLIN**.

bail·ee /bā'lē/ ▸*n. Law* a person or party to whom goods are delivered for a purpose, such as custody or repair, without transfer of ownership.

Bai·ley /'bālē/, Frederick Augustus Washington, see **DOUGLASS**.

bai·ley /'bālē/ ▸*n.* (*pl.* **-leys**) the outer wall of a castle. ▪ a court enclosed by this. ▷Middle English: probably from Old French *baile* 'palisade, enclosure' (see **BAIL**[2]).

bail·ie /'bālē/ ▸*n.* (*pl.* **-ies**) *chiefly historical* a municipal officer and magistrate in Scotland. ▷Middle English (originally used interchangeably with **BAILIFF**): from Old French *bailli.*

bail·iff /'bālif/ ▸*n.* a person who performs certain actions under legal authority, in particular: ▪ an official in a court of law who keeps order, looks after prisoners, etc. ▪ *chiefly Brit.* a sheriff's officer who executes writs and processes and carries out distraints and arrests. ▪ *Brit.* the agent or steward of a landlord. ▷Middle English: from Old French *baillif,* inflected form of *bailli,* based on Latin *bajulus* 'carrier, manager.'

bail·i·wick /'bālə,wik/ ▸*n. Law* the district or jurisdiction of a bailie or bailiff. ▪ (**one's bailiwick**) *informal* one's sphere of operations or particular area of interest: *you never give the presentations—that's my bailiwick.* ▷late Middle English: from **BAILIE** + **WICK**[2].

bail·ment /'bālmənt/ ▸*n. Law* an act of delivering goods to a bailee for a particular purpose, without transfer of ownership.

bail·or /'bālər/ ▸*n. Law* a person or party that entrusts goods to a bailee.

bail·out /'bāl,out/ ▸*n. informal* an act of giving financial assistance to a failing business or economy to save it from collapse.

Bain·bridge Island /'bān,brij/ an island in western Washington, in Puget Sound, west of Seattle.

bain-ma·rie /,ban mə'rē/ ▸*n.* (*pl.* **bains-ma·rie** *pronunc.* same) a container holding hot water into which a pan is placed for slow cooking. ▪ *chiefly Brit.* a double boiler. ▷early 18th cent.: French, translation of medieval Latin *balneum Mariae* 'bath of Maria,' translating Greek *kaminos Marias* 'furnace of Maria,' said to be a Jewish alchemist.

Baird /be(ə)rd/, John Logie (1888–1946), Scottish inventor. He made the first transatlantic transmission and demonstration of color television in 1928 using a mechanical system that was soon superseded by an electronic system.

Bai·ri·ki /'bī,rēkē/ the capital of Kiribati, on South Tarawa Island; pop. 2,200.

bairn /be(ə)rn/ ▸*n. chiefly Scottish & N. Engl.* a child. ▷Old English *bearn,* of Germanic origin; related to the verb **BEAR**[1].

Bai·sak·hi /bī'säkē/ ▸*n.* a Sikh festival held annually to commemorate the founding of the khalsa by Gobind Singh in 1699. ▷from Sanskrit *Vaiśākha,* denoting a month of the Hindu lunar year corresponding to April–May, regarded in some areas as the start of the new year.

bait /bāt/ ▸*n.* **1** food used to entice fish or other animals as prey: *herrings make excellent bait for pike | fishing with live baits.* ▪ *figurative* an allurement; a thing intended to tempt or entice: *she used the prospect of freedom as bait to trap him into talking | many potential buyers are reluctant to* ***take the bait.*** **2** variant spelling of **BATE**.
▸*v.* [*trans.*] **1** deliberately annoy or taunt (someone): *the other boys reveled in* ***baiting*** *him* ***about*** *his love of literature.* ▪ torment (a trapped or restrained animal), esp. by allowing dogs to attack it. **2** prepare (a hook, trap, net, or fishing area) with bait to entice fish or animals as prey: *she baited a trap with carrots and corn.* ▪ *figurative* lure; entice: *workers baited by your carrot powers of hiring.* **3** [*intrans.*] *archaic* stop on a journey to take food or a rest: *they stopped to bait at an inn.* ▪ [*trans.*] give food to (horses) on a journey: *while their horses were baited, they entered the public room.* ▷Middle English: from Old Norse *beit* 'pasture, food,' *beita* 'to hunt or chase.'
▸*PHRASES* ▫ **fish or cut bait** *informal* stop vacillating and act on something or disengage from it: *when it comes to flagging brands, companies are being forced to fish or cut bait.* ▫ **rise to the bait** react to a provocation or temptation exactly as intended: *Jenny was being provocatively rude, but he never rose to the bait.* ▫ **with baited breath** misspelling of **WITH BATED BREATH**.

USAGE See usage at **BATED**

bait-and-switch ▸*n.* the action (generally illegal) of advertising goods that are an apparent bargain, with the intention of substituting inferior or more expensive goods: [as *adj.*] *a bait-and-switch scheme.*

bait·fish /'bāt,fisH/ ▸*n.* a fish used as bait to catch a larger fish.

bai·za /'bīzə/ ▸*n.* (*pl.* same or **bai·zas**) a monetary unit of Oman, equal to one thousandth of a rial.

baize /bāz/ ▸*n.* a coarse, feltlike, woolen material that is typically green, used for covering billiard and card tables and for aprons. ▷late 16th cent.: from French *baies,* feminine plural of *bai* 'chestnut-colored' (see **BAY**[4]), treated as a singular noun. The name is presumably from the original color of the cloth, although several colors are recorded.

Ba·ja Ca·li·for·nia /'bähä ,kalə'fôrnyə/ a mountainous peninsula in northwestern Mexico that extends southward from the border with California and separates the Gulf of California from the Pacific Ocean. It consists of two states of Mexico: **Baja California** (capital, Mexicali) and **Baja California Sur** (capital, La Paz). Also called **LOWER CALIFORNIA**.

ba·ja·da /bə'hädə/ ▸*n.* a broad slope of alluvial material at the foot of an escarpment or mountain. ▷mid 19th cent.: from Spanish, 'descent, slope.'

Ba·jan /'bājən/ ▸*adj. & n.* informal term for **BARBADIAN** (see **BARBADOS**).

Ba·ka /'bäkə/ ▸*n.* (*pl.* same) **1** a member of a nomadic Pygmy people inhabiting the rain forests of southeastern Cameroon and northern Gabon. **2** the Bantu language of the Baka. ▷the name in Baka.

bake /bāk/ ▸*v.* [*trans.*] **1** cook (food) by dry heat without direct exposure to a flame, typically in an oven or on a hot surface: *they bake their own bread and cakes* | [with *two objs.*] *I baked him a cake for his birthday* | [as *adj.*] (**baked**) *baked apples.* ▪ [*intrans.*] (of food) be cooked in such a way: *the bread was baking on hot stones.* **2** (of the sun or other agency) subject (something) to dry heat, esp. so as to harden it: *the sun has baked the earth a dusty brown.* ▪ [*intrans.*] *informal* (of a person or place) be or become extremely hot in prolonged sun or hot weather: *the city was baking in a heat wave* | [as *adj.*] (**baking**) *the summer's baking heat.*
▸*n.* [with *adj.*] a social gathering at which baked food is eaten: *lobster bakes on deserted islands.* ▷Old English *bacan,* of Germanic origin; related to Dutch *bakken* and German *backen.*

baked A·las·ka ▸*n.* sponge cake and ice cream in a meringue covering, cooked for a very short time. ▷named after the state of **ALASKA**.

baked beans ▸*plural n.* short for **BOSTON BAKED BEANS**.

Baked Bean State a nickname for the state of **MASSACHUSETTS**.

bake·house /'bāk,hous/ ▸*n. dated* a building or area in which bread is made.

Ba·ke·lite /'bāk(ə),līt/ ▸*n. trademark* an early form of brittle plastic, typically dark brown, made from formaldehyde and phenol, used chiefly for electrical equipment. ▷early 20th cent.: named after Leo H. *Baekeland* (1863–1944), the Belgian-born American chemist who invented it, + **-ITE**[1].

Bak·er /'bākər/, Josephine (1906–75), U.S. dancer. She was a star of the Folies-Bergère in Paris in the 1930s, famed for her exotic dancing and risqué clothing.

bak·er /'bākər/ ▸*n.* a person who makes bread and cakes, esp. commercially. ▪ [often with *adj.*] an oven for a particular purpose: *a bread baker.* ▷Old English *bæcere,* from *bacan* (see **BAKE**).

Ba·ker Is·land an uninhabited island in the central Pacific Ocean, near the equator, claimed by the U.S. in 1857. Once a guano source, it is now a wildlife refuge.

bak·er's doz·en ▸*n.* a group or set of thirteen: *a baker's dozen of love songs.* ▷late 16th cent.: from the former bakers' custom of adding an extra loaf to a dozen sold, this constituting the retailer's profit.

Ba·kers·field /'bākərz,fēld/ an industrial city in south central California, an oil industry center in the San Joaquin Valley; pop. 247,057.

bak·er's yeast ▸*n.* a dried preparation of yeast used or suitable for use as leaven.

bak·er·y /'bāk(ə)rē/ ▸*n.* (*pl.* **-er·ies**) a place where bread and cakes are made or sold: *delicious aromas wafting from the bakery* | [as *adj.*] *an assortment of bakery goods.* ▪ baked goods such as bread and cakes: *a table overflowing with homemade bakery and wine.*

bake·shop /'bāk,sHäp/ ▸*n.* a place where bread and cakes are made or sold.

bake·ware /'bāk,we(ə)r/ ▸*n.* tins, trays, and other items placed in the oven during baking.

bak·ing pow·der ▸*n.* a mixture of sodium bicarbonate and cream of tartar, used instead of yeast in baking.

bak·ing so·da ▸*n.* sodium bicarbonate used in cooking, for cleaning, or in toothpaste.

Bak·ker /'bakər/, Robert T. (1945–), U.S. paleontologist. He proposed the controversial idea that dinosaurs were both active and warm-blooded.

ba·kla·va /,bäklə'vä/ ▸*n.* a dessert originating in the Middle East made of phyllo pastry filled with chopped nuts and soaked in honey. ▷Turkish.

bak·sheesh /'baksHēsH; bak'sHēsH/ ▸*n.* (in parts of Asia) a small sum of money given as alms, a tip, or a bribe. ▷based on Persian *bakšīš,* from *bakšīdan* 'give.'

Bakst /bäkst/, Léon (1866–1924), Russian painter and designer; born *Lev Samuilovich Rozenberg.* He was a member of the Ballets Russes, for which he designed exotic, richly colored sets and costumes.

Ba·ku /bä'ko͞o/ the capital of Azerbaijan, on the Caspian Sea; pop. 1,780,000. It is an industrial port and a center of the oil industry.

Ba·ku·nin /bə'ko͞onyin/, Mikhail (Aleksandrovich) (1814–76), Russian anarchist and writer who participated in the revolutionary movements of 1848–49.

Bal·a·cla·va, Battle of /,balə'klävə/ a battle of the Crimean War, fought between Russia and an alliance of British, French, and Turkish forces in and around the port of Balaclava (now Balaklava) in the southern Crimea in 1854. The battle ended inconclusively; and is chiefly remembered as the scene of the Charge of the Light Brigade.

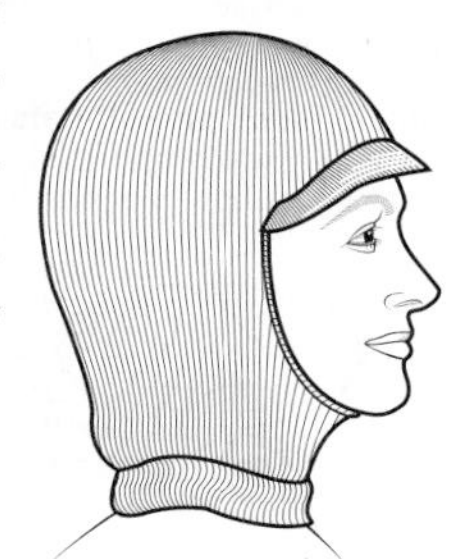
balaclava

bal·a·cla·va /,balə'klävə/ (also **balaclava helmet**) ▸*n.* a close-fitting garment covering the whole head and neck except for parts of the face, typically made of wool. ▷late 19th cent. (denoting a garment worn originally by soldiers serving in the Crimean War): named after the village of *Balaclava* in the Crimea (see **BALACLAVA, BATTLE OF**).

bal·a·fon /'balə,fōn/ ▸*n.* a large xylophone having hollow gourds as resonators, used in West African music. ▷late 18th cent.: via French from Manding *bala* 'xylophone' + *fo* 'to play.'

bal·a·lai·ka /,balə'līkə/ ▸*n.* a guitarlike musical instrument with a triangular body and two, three, or four strings, popular in Russia and other Slavic countries. ▷late 18th cent.: from Russian, of Tartar origin.

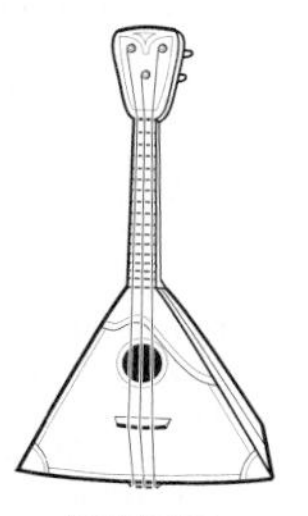
balalaika

bal·ance /'baləns/ ▸*n.* **1** an even distribution of weight enabling someone or something to remain upright and steady: *slipping in the mud but* ***keeping*** *their* ***balance*** | *she* ***lost*** *her* ***balance*** *before falling.* ▪ stability of one's mind or feelings: *the way to some kind of peace and personal balance.* ▪ *Sailing* the ability of a boat to stay on course without adjustment of the rudder. **2** a condition in which different elements are equal or in the correct proportions: *overseas investments can add balance to an investment portfolio* | [in *sing.*] *try to keep a* ***balance between*** *work and relaxation.* ▪ *Art* harmony of design and proportion. ▪ [in *sing.*] the relative volume of various sources of sound: *the balance of the voices is good.* **3** an apparatus for weighing, esp. one with a central pivot, beam, and a pair of scales. ▪ (**the Balance**) the zodiacal sign or constellation Libra. **4** a counteracting weight or force. ▪ (also **bal-**

Pronunciation Key ə *ago;* ər *over;* 'ə *or* ,ə *up;* 'ər *or* ,ər *fur;* a *hat;* ā *rate;* ä *car;* CH *chew;* e *let;* ē *see;* e(ə)r *air;* i *fit;* ī *by;* i(ə)r *ear;* NG *sing;* ō *go;* ô *for;* oi *boy;* o͝o *good;* o͞o *goo;* ou *out;* SH *she;* TH *thin;* TH *then;* (h)w *why;* ZH *vision*

ance wheel) the regulating device in a mechanical clock or watch. **5** a predominating weight or amount; the majority: ***the balance of*** *opinion was that work was more important than leisure.* **6** a figure representing the difference between credits and debits in an account; the amount of money held in an account: *he accumulated a healthy balance with the savings bank.* ■ the difference between an amount due and an amount paid: *unpaid credit-card balances.* ■ [in *sing.*] an amount left over.

▸*v.* [*trans.*] **1** keep or put (something) in a steady position so that it does not fall: *a mug that she* ***balanced on*** *her knee.* ■ [*intrans.*] remain in a steady position without falling: *Richard* ***balanced on*** *the ball of one foot.* **2** offset or compare the value of (one thing) with another: *the cost of obtaining such information needs to be* ***balanced against*** *its benefits.* ■ counteract, equal, or neutralize the weight or importance of: *he* ***balanced*** *his radical remarks* ***with*** *more familiar declarations.* ■ establish equal or appropriate proportions of elements in: *balancing work and family life.* **3** compare debits and credits in (an account), typically to ensure that they are equal: *the law requires the council to* ***balance its books*** *each year.* ■ [*intrans.*] (of an account) have credits and debits equal. ▷Middle English (sense 3): from Old French *balance* (noun), *balancer* (verb), based on late Latin *(libra) bilanx* '(balance) having two scalepans,' from *bi-* 'twice, having two' + *lanx* 'scalepan.' **—bal·anc·er** *n.*

▸*PHRASES* □ **balance of payments** the difference in total value between payments into and out of a country over a period. □ **balance of power 1** a situation in which nations of the world have roughly equal power. **2** the power held by a small group when larger groups are of equal strength. □ **balance of trade** the difference in value between a country's imports and exports. □ **in the balance** uncertain; at a critical stage: *his survival* ***hung in the balance*** *for days.* □ **on balance** with all things considered: *but on balance he was pleased.* □ **strike a balance** choose a moderate course or compromise: *she's decided to strike a balance between fashionable and accessible.* □ **throw** (or **catch**) **someone off balance** cause someone to become unsteady and in danger of falling. ■ *figurative* confuse or bewilder someone.

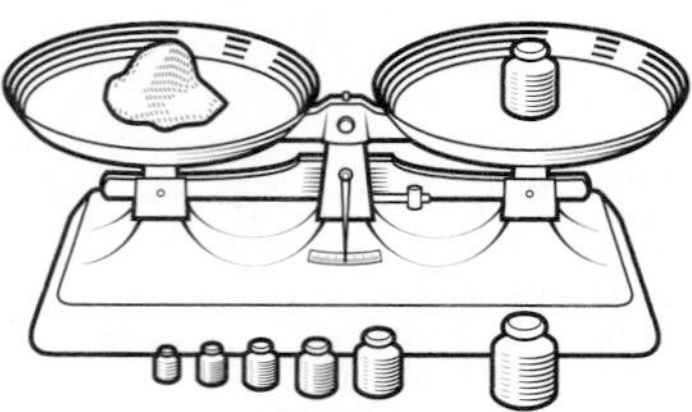

balance 3

bal·ance beam ▸*n.* a narrow horizontal bar raised off the floor, on which a gymnast balances while performing exercises. ■ [in *sing.*] the set of exercises performed on such a piece of equipment.

bal·anced /ˈbalənst/ ▸*adj.* keeping or showing a balance; arranged in good proportions: *she assembled a balanced team.* ■ taking everything into account; fairly judged or presented: *accurate and balanced information.* ■ (esp. of food) having different elements in the correct proportions: *a healthy, balanced diet.* ■ (of a person or state of mind) having no emotion lacking or too strong; stable: *a balanced personality.* ■ (of an account or budget) having debits and credits equal: *a balanced budget.* ■ (of an electrical circuit or signal) being symmetrical with respect to a reference point, typically ground.

bal·ance sheet ▸*n.* a statement of the assets, liabilities, and capital of a business or other organization at a particular point in time, detailing the balance of income and expenditure over the preceding period.

bal·ance tab ▸*n.* a tab on a control surface of an aircraft that reduces the amount of force needed to move the control surface by moving in the opposite direction.

bal·ance wheel ▸*n.* the regulating device in a watch or clock.

Bal·an·chine /ˌbalənˈCHēn; ˈbalənˌCHēn/, George (1904–83), U.S. ballet dancer and choreographer; born in Russia; born *Georgi Melitonovich Balanchivadze.* He was chief choreographer of Diaghilev's Ballets Russes during the 1920s, and in 1934 he cofounded the company that later became the New York City Ballet. Notable ballets: *The Firebird* (1949) and *A Midsummer Night's Dream* (1962).

bal·anc·ing act ▸*n.* an action or activity that requires a delicate balance between different situations or requirements: *our balancing act between working more to buy luxuries and having enough leisure to enjoy them.*

bal·as ru·by /ˈbaləs/ ▸*n.* a spinel of a delicate rose-red variety. ▷late Middle English: from Old French *balais,* from Arabic *balakš,* from Persian *Badakšān,* a district of Afghanistan, where it is found.

ba·la·ta /bəˈlätə/ ▸*n.* a tropical American tree that bears edible fruit and produces latex. • Several species in the family Sapotaceae, in particular, *Manilkara bidentata.* ■ the dried sap of this tree used as a substitute for rubber. ▷early 17th cent.: from Carib *balatá.*

Ba·la·ton, Lake /ˈbôləˌtōn; ˈbäləˌtän/ a large shallow lake in west central Hungary, situated in a wine-producing and resort region south of the Bakony mountains.

Bal·bo·a /balˈbōə/, Vasco Núñez de (1475–1519), Spanish explorer. In 1513 he reached the western coast of the isthmus of Darien (Panama), thereby becoming the first European to see the eastern shores of the Pacific Ocean.

bal·bo·a /balˈbōə/ ▸*n.* the basic monetary unit of Panama, equal to 100 centésimos. ▷named after Vasco Núñez de BALBOA.

bal·brig·gan /balˈbrigən/ ▸*n.* a fine, unbleached knitted cotton fabric, used for stockings and underwear. ▷late 19th cent.: named after the town of *Balbriggan* in Ireland, where it was originally made.

Bal·co·nes Es·carp·ment /balˈkōnəs/ the scarp marking the geologic fault that separates the plains of eastern Texas from highlands to the west. San Antonio, Austin, and Waco lie near or on it.

bal·co·ny /ˈbalkənē/ ▸*n.* (*pl.* **-nies**) **1** a platform enclosed by a wall or balustrade on the outside of a building, with access from an upper-floor window or door. **2** (**the balcony**) the upstairs seats in a theater, concert hall, or auditorium. ▷early 17th cent.: from Italian *balcone,* probably ultimately of Germanic origin. **—bal·co·nied** *adj.*

bald /bôld/ ▸*adj.* **1** having a scalp wholly or partly lacking hair: *he had a shiny bald head | he was starting to* ***go bald.*** See note at NAKED. ■ (of an animal) not covered by the usual fur, hair, or feathers: *hedgehogs are born bald.* ■ (of a plant or an area of land) not covered by the usual leaves, bark, or vegetation: *the bald trunks with their empty branches.* ■ (of a tire) having the tread worn away: *my car had two bald tires.* **2** [*attrib.*] without any extra detail or explanation; plain or blunt: *the bald statement in the preceding paragraph requires amplification.* ▷Middle English: probably from a base meaning 'white patch,' whence the archaic sense 'marked or streaked with white.' **—bald·ish** *adj.* **—bald·ly** *adv.* (in sense 2) *"I want to leave," Stephen said baldly.* **—bald·ness** *n.*

bal·da·chin /ˈbôldəkin/ (also **bal·da·quin**) ▸*n.* a ceremonial canopy of stone, metal, or fabric over an altar, throne, or doorway. ▷late 16th cent. (denoting an embroidered material, woven with silk and gold thread): from Italian *baldacchino,* from *Baldacco* 'Baghdad,' place of origin of the original brocade.

bald cy·press ▸*n.* a deciduous North American conifer with exposed buttress roots and ball-shaped cones, typically growing in swamps and on water margins. • *Taxodium distichum,* family Taxodiaceae.

bald ea·gle ▸*n.* a white-headed North American eagle that includes fish among its prey. Now most common in Alaska, it is the national emblem of the U.S. • *Haliaeetus leucocephalus,* family Accipitridae.

bald eagle

Bal·der /ˈbôldər/ *Scandinavian Mythology* a son of Odin and god of the summer sun. He was invulnerable to all things except mistletoe, with which the god Loki, by a trick, induced the blind god Hödur to kill him.

bal·der·dash /ˈbôldərˌdaSH/ ▸*n.* senseless talk or writing; nonsense: *she dismissed talk of plots as "bunkum and balderdash."* ▷late 16th cent. (denoting a frothy liquid; later, an unappetizing mixture of drinks): of unknown origin.

bald-faced ▸*adj.* **1** (of an animal) having white markings on the face. **2** shameless and undisguised; bare-faced: *a bald-faced lie.*

bald·ing /ˈbôldiNG/ ▸*adj.* going bald: *a man in his late twenties, prematurely balding.*

bald·pate /ˈbôldˌpāt/ ▸*n.* the American wigeon, in allusion to its white-crowned head.

bal·dric /ˈbôldrik/ ▸*n.* *historical* a belt for a sword or other piece of equipment, worn over one shoulder and reaching down to the opposite hip. ▷Middle English *baudry,* from Old French *baudre,* of unknown ultimate origin.

Bald·win[1] /ˈbôldwin/, Henry (1780–1844), U.S. Supreme Court associate justice 1830–44. He also served in Congress as a representative from Pennsylvania 1817–22.

Bald·win[2], James (Arthur) (1924–87), U.S. writer and civil rights activist. Notable works: novels *Go Tell It on the Mountain* (1953), *Giovanni's Room* (1956), and *Another Country* (1962); essay collections *Nobody Knows My Name* (1961) and *The Price of a Ticket* (1985).

Bald·win[3], Stanley, 1st Earl Baldwin of Bewdley (1867–1947), British statesman; prime minister 1923–24, 1924–29, and 1935–37.

Bald·win Park a city in southwestern California, east of Los Angeles; pop. 69,330.

bald·y /ˈbôldē/ (also **bald·ie**) ▸*n.* (*pl.* **bald·ies**) *informal, derogatory* a baldheaded person.

▸*adj.* [*attrib.*] *chiefly Scottish & Irish* bald: *a baldy head.*

Bâle /bäl/ French name for BASLE.

bale[1] /bāl/ ▸*n.* a bundle of paper, hay, cotton, etc., tightly wrapped and bound with cords or hoops: *the fire destroyed 500* ***bales of*** *hay.* ■ the quantity in a bale as a measure, esp. 500 pounds of cotton.

▸*v.* [*trans.*] make (something) into bales: *they baled a lot of good hay* | [as *n.*] (**baling**) *most baling and field work have been finished.* ▷Middle English: probably from Middle Dutch, from Old French; ultimately of Germanic origin and related to BALL[1].

bale[2] ▸*n.* *archaic* or *poetic/literary* evil considered as a destructive force. ■ evil suffered; physical torment or mental suffering. ▷Old English *balu, bealu,* of Germanic origin.

Bal·e·ar·ic Is·lands /ˌbalēˈarik/ (also **the Bal·e·ar·ics**) a group of four large and seven small islands in the Mediterranean off the eastern coast of Spain that form an autonomous region of Spain; capital, Palma (on the island of Majorca).

ba·leen /bəˈlēn/ ▸*n.* whalebone. ▷Middle English (also denoting a whale): from Old French *baleine,* from Latin *balaena* 'whale.'

ba·leen whale ▸*n.* a whale that has plates of whalebone in the mouth for straining plankton from the water. Baleen whales include the rorquals, humpback, right whales, and gray whale. Also called WHALEBONE WHALE. • Suborder Mysticeti, order Cetacea: three families and ten species.

bale·fire /ˈbālˌfīr/ ▸*n.* a large open-air fire; a bonfire. ▷Old English (recorded in poetry), from obsolete *bale* 'great fire' + FIRE.

bale·ful /ˈbālfəl/ ▸*adj.* threatening harm; menacing: *Bill shot a baleful glance in her direction | the baleful light cast trembling shadows.* ■ having a harmful or destructive effect: *drug money has had a baleful impact on the country.* ▷Old English *bealufull* (see BALE[2], -FUL). **—bale·ful·ly** *adv.* **—bale·ful·ness** *n.*

Ba·len·ci·a·ga /ˌbälensēˈägə; ˌbälenˈTHyägə/, Cristóbal (1895–1972), Spanish couturier. In the 1950s he contributed to the move away from the tight-waisted New Look originated by Christian Dior to a looser, semifitted style.

bal·er /ˈbālər/ ▸*n.* a machine for making paper, hay, or cotton into bales.

Bal·four /ˈbalˌfôr/, Arthur James, 1st Earl of Balfour (1848–1930), British statesman; prime minister 1902–05. In 1917, as foreign secretary, he issued the Balfour Declaration that favored a Jewish national home in Palestine.

Ba·li /ˈbälē; ˈbalē/ a mountainous island in Indonesia, east of Java; chief city, Denpasar; pop. 2,856,000. It is noted for its beauty and the richness of its culture.

Ba·li·nese /ˌbäləˈnēz; ˌbal-; -ˈnēs/ ▸*adj.* of or relating to Bali or its people or language.
▸*n.* (*pl.* same) **1** a native of Bali. **2** the Indonesian language of Bali. ▷from BALI, on the pattern of Dutch *Balinees*.

balk /bôk/ (*Brit.* also **baulk**) ▸*v.* [*intrans.*] **1** hesitate or be unwilling to accept an idea or undertaking: *any gardener will at first* **balk at** *enclosing the garden.* ■ [*trans.*] thwart or hinder (a plan or person): *the utmost of his influence will be invoked to balk the law.* See note at THWART. ■ [*trans.*] (**balk someone of**) prevent a person or animal from having (something): *the lions, fearing to be balked of their prey.* ■ (of a horse) refuse to go on. ■ [*trans.*] *archaic* miss or refuse (a chance or invitation). **2** *Baseball* (of a pitcher) make an illegal motion, penalized by an advance of the base runners: *the rookie balked and permitted Robinson to score.*
▸*n.* **1** *Baseball* an illegal motion made by a pitcher that may deceive a base runner. **2** a roughly squared timber beam. **3** any area on a pool or billiard table in which play is restricted in some way. **4** a ridge left unplowed between furrows. ▷late Old English *balc*, from Old Norse *bálkr* 'partition.' The original use was 'unplowed ridge,' in late Middle English 'land left unplowed by mistake,' hence 'blunder, omission' (giving rise to the verb sense 'miss (a chance)'). A late Middle English sense 'obstacle' gave rise to the verb senses 'hesitate' and 'hinder.'

Bal·kan·ize /ˈbôlkəˌnīz/ ▸*v.* [*trans.*] divide (a region or body) into smaller mutually hostile states or groups. ▷1920s: from *Balkan* Peninsula (where this was done in the late 19th and early 20th cent.) + -IZE. —**Bal·kan·i·za·tion** /ˌbôlkənəˈzāshən/ *n.*

Bal·kans /ˈbôlkənz/ **1** (also **Bal·kan Moun·tains**) a range of mountains stretching east across Bulgaria from the Serbian frontier to the Black Sea. The highest point is Botev Peak (7,793 feet; 2,375 m). **2** the countries occupying the part of southeastern Europe that lies south of the Danube and Sava rivers and forms a peninsula bounded by the Adriatic and Ionian seas in the west, the Aegean and Black seas in the east, and the Mediterranean Sea in the south. —**Bal·kan** *adj.*

Bal·kan Wars /ˈbôlkən/ two wars of 1912–13 that were fought over the last European territories of the Ottoman Empire.

In 1912 Bulgaria, Serbia, Greece, and Montenegro forced Turkey to give up Albania and Macedonia, leaving the area around Constantinople (Istanbul) as the only Ottoman territory in Europe. The following year Bulgaria disputed with Serbia, Greece, and Romania for possession of Macedonia, which was partitioned between Greece and Serbia.

balk·line /ˈbôkˌlīn/ (also **balk line**) ▸*n.* a line on a billiard table marking off an area in which play is restricted.

balk·y /ˈbôkē/ (*Brit.* also **baulk·y**) ▸*adj.* (**balk·i·er**, **balk·i·est**) reluctant; uncooperative: *he was trying to get his balky horse to move.*

Ball[1] /bôl/, John (died 1381), English rebel. He was a priest who preached egalitarianism. Following the Peasants' Revolt, he was hanged as a traitor.

Ball[2], Lucille (Désirée) (1911–89), U.S. comedienne known in particular for the popular television series *I Love Lucy* (1951–55). Notable movies: *Stage Door* (1937), *Sorrowful Jones* (1949), and *Yours, Mine, and Ours* (1968).

Lucille Ball

ball[1] /bôl/ ▸*n.* **1** a solid or hollow sphere or ovoid, esp. one that is kicked, thrown, or hit in a game: *a soccer ball.* ■ a ball-shaped object: *a* **ball of** *wool* | *he crushed the card into a ball.* ■ *historical* a solid nonexplosive missile for a firearm. ■ a game played with a ball, esp. baseball: *young men would graduate from college and enter pro ball.* **2** *Baseball* a pitch delivered outside the strike zone that the batter does not attempt to hit: *the umpire called it a ball.* ■ *Sports* a pass of a ball from one player to another: *Whelan sent a long ball to Goddard.* **3** (in full **the ball of the foot**) the rounded protuberant part of the foot at the base of the big toe. ■ (in full **the ball of the thumb**) the rounded protuberant part of the hand at the base of the thumb. **4** (**balls**) *vulgar slang* testicles. ■ (**ball**) an act of sexual intercourse. ■ courage or nerve. ■ nonsense; rubbish (often said to express strong disagreement).
▸*v.* [*trans.*] **1** (usu. **ball up**) squeeze or form (something) into a rounded shape: *Robert* **balled up** *his napkin and threw it on to his plate.* ■ clench or screw up (one's fist) tightly: *she balled her fist so that the nails dug into her palms.* ■ [*intrans.*] form a round shape: *the fishing nets eventually* **ball up** *and sink.* ■ wrap the rootball of (a tree or shrub) in burlap to protect it during transportation. **2** *vulgar slang* have sexual intercourse with.
▸*phrasal v.* □ **ball** (*Brit.* **balls**) **something up** bungle something. ▷Middle English: from Old Norse *bǫllr*, of Germanic origin.
▸*PHRASES* □ **balled up 1** formed into a ball. **2** entangled; confused: *I got slightly balled up in my facts.* **3** used as a euphemism for *constipated.* □ **the ball is in your court** it is up to you to make the next move. □ **a ball of fire** a person full of energy and enthusiasm. □ **keep the ball rolling** maintain the momentum of an activity. □ **keep one's eye on** (or **take one's eye off**) **the ball** keep (or fail to keep) one's attention focused on the matter in hand. □ **on the ball** alert to new ideas, methods, and trends: *maintaining contact with customers keeps me on the ball.* ■ indicating competence, alertness, or intelligence: *a woman like that, with so much on the ball.* □ **play ball** play a ball game such as baseball: *we noticed some youngsters playing ball in a vacant lot.* ■ *informal* work willingly with others; cooperate: *if his lawyers won't play ball, there's nothing we can do.* ■ *Baseball* the umpire's command to begin or resume play. □ **start** (or **get** or **set**) **the ball rolling** set an activity in motion; make a start: *to start the ball rolling, the government was asked to contribute a million dollars to the fund.* □ **the whole ball of wax** *informal* everything.

ball[2] ▸*n.* a formal social gathering for dancing: *the social season was highlighted by debutante balls* | [as *adj.*] *a ball gown.* ▷early 17th cent.: from French *bal* 'a dance,' from late Latin *ballare* 'to dance'; related to Greek *ballizein* 'to dance' (also *ballein* 'to throw').
▸*PHRASE* □ **have a ball** *informal* enjoy oneself greatly; have a lot of fun: *I had a ball on my fortieth birthday.*

bal·lad /ˈbaləd/ ▸*n.* a poem or song narrating a story in short stanzas. Traditional ballads are typically of unknown authorship, having been passed on orally from one generation to the next as part of the folk culture. ■ a slow sentimental or romantic song. ▷late 15th cent. (denoting a light, simple song): from Old French *balade*, from Provençal *balada* 'dance, song to dance to,' from *balar* 'to dance,' from late Latin *ballare* (see BALL[2]). The sense 'narrative poem' dates from the mid 18th cent.

bal·lade /bəˈläd/ ▸*n.* **1** a poem normally composed of three stanzas and an envoy. The last line of the opening stanza is used as a refrain, and the same rhymes, strictly limited in number, recur throughout. **2** a short, lyrical piece of music, esp. one for piano. ▷late Middle English: earlier spelling and pronunciation of BALLAD.

bal·lad·eer /ˌbaləˈdi(ə)r/ ▸*n.* a singer or composer of ballads.

bal·lad op·er·a ▸*n.* a theatrical entertainment popular in early 18th-century England, taking the form of a satirical play interspersed with traditional or operatic songs. The best-known example is John Gay's *The Beggar's Opera* (1728).

bal·lad·ry /ˈbalədrē/ ▸*n.* ballads collectively. ■ the art of writing or performing ballads.

bal·lad stan·za ▸*n.* a four-line stanza in iambic meter in which the first and third unrhymed lines have four metrical feet and the second and fourth rhyming lines have three metrical feet.

ball and chain ▸*n.* a heavy metal ball secured by a chain to the leg of a prisoner to prevent escape. ■ *figurative* a crippling encumbrance: *the ball and chain of debt.*

ball-and-sock·et joint ▸*n.* a natural or manufactured joint or coupling, such as the hip joint, in which a partially spherical end lies in a socket, allowing multidirectional movement and rotation.

ball-and-socket joint

Bal·lard /ˈbalərd/, J. G. (1930–), British novelist and short-story writer; full name *James Graham Ballard*. Notable works: *The Drowned World* (1962), *Crash* (1973), and *Empire of the Sun* (1984).

bal·last /ˈbaləst/ ▸*n.* **1** heavy material, such as gravel, sand, iron, or lead, placed low in a vessel to improve its stability. ■ a substance of this type carried in an airship or on a hot-air balloon to stabilize it, and jettisoned when greater altitude is required. ■ *figurative* something that gives stability or substance: *the film is an entertaining comedy with some serious ideas thrown in for ballast.* **2** gravel or coarse stone used to form the bed of a railroad track or road. ■ a mixture of coarse and fine aggregate for making concrete. **3** a passive component used in an electric circuit to moderate changes in current.
▸*v.* [*trans.*] (usu. **be ballasted**) **1** give stability to (a ship) by putting a heavy substance in its bilge: *the vessel has been ballasted to give the necessary floating stability.* **2** form (the bed of a railroad line or road) with gravel or coarse stone. ▷mid 16th cent.: probably of Low German or Scandinavian origin.
▸*PHRASE* □ **in ballast** (of a ship) laden only with ballast.

ball bear·ing ▸*n.* a bearing between a wheel and a fixed axle, in which the rotating part and the stationary part are separated by a ring of small solid metal balls that reduce friction. ■ a ball used in such a bearing.

ball bearing

ball boy ▸*n.* a boy who retrieves balls that go out of play during a game such as tennis or baseball, and who supplies players or umpires with new balls.

ball-break·er (also **ball-bust·er**) ▸*n.* *informal* a sexually demanding woman who destroys men's self-confidence. ■ a demanding and punishing task or situation: *Vietnam was a ball-breaker.* —**ball-break·ing** *adj.*

ball·car·ri·er /ˈbôlˌkarēər/ ▸*n.* *Football* a player in possession of the ball and attempting to advance it.

ball cock ▸*n.* a valve that automatically fills a tank after liquid has been drawn from it. Used, for example, in a flush toilet, a ball cock has a float on the end of a pivoting arm that opens the valve when the arm drops.

bal·le·ri·na /ˌbaləˈrēnə/ ▸*n.* a female ballet dancer. ▷late 18th cent.: from Italian, feminine of *ballerino* 'dancing master,' from *ballare* 'to dance,' from late Latin.

Bal·le·ste·ros /ˌbīyəˈstārōs; ˌbäləˈste(ə)rōs/, Severiano, known as **Sevvy**, (1957–), Spanish golfer. In 1979, he became the youngest player in the 20th century to win the British Open, and he won it again in 1984 and 1988. In 1980, he was the youngest-ever and the second European to win the U.S. Masters; he won it again in 1983.

bal·let /baˈlā/ ▸*n.* an artistic dance form performed to music using precise and highly formalized set steps and gestures. Classical ballet, which originated in Renaissance Italy and established its present form during the 19th century, is characterized by light, graceful, fluid movements and the use of pointe shoes. ■ a creative work of this form or the music written for it. ■ a group of dancers who regularly perform such works: *the New York City Ballet.* ■ [in *sing.*] *figurative* an elaborate or complicated interaction between people: *that delicate and cautious ballet known as the planning process.* ▷mid 17th cent.: from French, from Italian *balletto*, diminutive of *ballo* 'a dance,' from late Latin *ballare* 'to dance' (see BALL[2]).

bal·let·ic /ba'letik; bə-/ ▶*adj.* of, relating to, or characteristic of ballet: *a graceful, balletic movement.* —**bal·let·i·cal·ly** /-ik(ə)lē/ *adv.*

bal·let mas·ter ▶*n.* a person employed by a ballet company to teach and rehearse dancers.

bal·let·o·mane /bə'letə,mān; ba-/ ▶*n.* a ballet enthusiast. —**bal·let·o·ma·ni·a** /-,letə'mānēə/ *n.*

Bal·lets Russes /,balā 'ro͞os/ a ballet company formed in Paris in 1909 by Sergei Diaghilev.

The company presented a unified whole encompassing music, dance, decor, and costume: music was commissioned from the composers Stravinsky, Satie, and Rimsky-Korsakov, while Picasso and Jean Cocteau designed sets. The company's choreographers and dancers included Michel Fokine, Anna Pavlova, Vaslav Nijinsky, and George Balanchine. It was responsible for reviving ballet as an art form in western Europe.

ball float ▶*n.* the spherical float attached to the pivoting arm of the ball cock in a toilet tank.

ball game ▶*n.* **1** a game played with a ball. ■ a baseball game: *I took the afternoon off and went to a ball game.* **2** [in *sing.*] *informal* a particular situation, esp. one that is completely different from the previous situation: *making the film was* ***a whole new ball game*** *for her.*

ball girl ▶*n.* a girl who retrieves balls that go out of play during a game such as tennis or baseball, and who supplies players or umpires with new balls.

ball·hawk /'bôl,hôk/ ▶*n. informal* a skilled ball player, in particular a football or basketball player adept at stealing or intercepting the ball or an outfielder in baseball skilled at catching fly balls. —**ball·hawk·ing** *n.*

bal·lis·ta /bə'listə/ ▶*n.* (*pl.* **-tae** /-tē/ or **-tas**) a catapult used in ancient warfare for hurling large stones. ■ a large crossbow for firing a spear. ▷early 16th cent.: from Latin, based on Greek *ballein* 'to throw.'

bal·lis·tic /bə'listik/ ▶*adj.* [*attrib.*] **1** of or relating to projectiles or their flight. **2** moving under the force of gravity only. ▷late 18th cent.: from BALLISTA + -IC. —**bal·lis·ti·cal·ly** /-ik(ə)lē/ *adv.*

▶*PHRASE* □ **go ballistic** *informal* fly into a rage.

bal·lis·tic mis·sile ▶*n.* a missile with a high, arching trajectory, that is initially powered and guided but falls under gravity onto its target. Compare with GUIDED.

bal·lis·tics /bə'listiks/ ▶*plural n.* [treated as *sing.*] the science of projectiles and firearms. ■ the study of the effects of being fired on a bullet, cartridge, or gun.

bal·lis·to·car·di·o·gram /bə,listə'kärdēə,gram/ ▶*n.* a record made by a ballistocardiograph.

bal·lis·to·car·di·o·graph /bə,listə'kärdēə,graf/ ▶*n.* an instrument for recording the movements of the body caused by ejection of blood from the heart at each beat.

ball light·ning ▶*n.* a rare and little known kind of lightning having the form of a moving globe of light several centimeters across that persists for periods of up to a minute.

bal·locks ▶*n.* variant spelling of BOLLOCKS.

bal·lon /bə'lôn/ ▶*n.* **1** (in dancing) the ability to appear effortlessly suspended while performing movements during a jump. **2** variant spelling of BALLOON (sense 3). ▷French, from Italian *ballone*, from *balla* 'ball.'

bal·lo·net /,balə'nā/ (also **bal·lon·net**) ▶*n.* the compartment in a balloon or airship into which air or another gas can be forced in order to maintain the craft's shape as buoyant gas is released.

bal·loon /bə'lo͞on/ ▶*n.* **1** a brightly colored rubber sac inflated with air and then sealed at the neck, used as a children's toy or a decoration: *the room was festooned with balloons and streamers* | *figurative his derision pricked the fragile balloon of her vanity.* ■ a round or pear-shaped outline in which the words or thoughts of characters in a comic strip or cartoon are written: *a balloon reading "Ka-Pow!"* **2** a large bag filled with hot air or gas to make it rise in the air, typically carrying a basket for passengers: *a hot-air balloon.* **3** (also **balloon glass**) a large rounded drinking glass, used for brandy and other drinks.

▶*v.* [*intrans.*] **1** swell out in a spherical shape; billow: *the trousers* ***ballooned out*** *below his waist* | [*trans.*] *the wind ballooned her sleeves.* ■ (of an amount of money) increase rapidly: *the company's debt has ballooned in the last five years* | [as *adj.*] (**ballooning**) *ballooning government spending.* ■ swell dramatically in size or number: *the public payroll ballooned from about 27,000 people to about 66,000 people* ■ (of a person) increase rapidly and dramatically in weight: *I had ballooned on the school's starchy diet.* **2** travel by hot-air balloon: *he is famous for ballooning across oceans.*

▶*adj.* resembling a balloon; puffed: *a flouncy balloon curtain.* ▷late 16th cent. (originally denoting a game played with a large inflated leather ball): from French *ballon* or Italian *ballone* 'large ball.'

bal·loon an·gi·o·plas·ty ▶*n. Medicine* surgical widening of a blocked or narrowed blood vessel, esp. a coronary artery, by means of a balloon catheter.

bal·loon cath·e·ter ▶*n. Medicine* a type of catheter incorporating a small balloon that may be introduced into a canal, duct, or blood vessel and then inflated in order to clear an obstruction or dilate a narrowed region.

bal·loon·ing /bə'lo͞oniNG/ ▶*n.* the sport or pastime of flying in a balloon. —**bal·loon·ist** /-nist/ *n.*

bal·loon mort·gage ▶*n.* a mortgage in which a large portion of the borrowed principal is repaid in a single payment at the end of the loan period.

bal·loon pay·ment ▶*n.* a repayment of the outstanding principal sum made at the end of a loan period, interest only having been paid hitherto.

bal·loon tire ▶*n.* a large tire containing air at low pressure. —**bal·loon-tired** *adj.*

bal·loon vine ▶*n.* a tropical American vine with inflated balloonlike pods. • *Cardiospermum halicacabum*, family Sapiondaceae.

bal·lot /'balət/ ▶*n.* a process of voting, in writing and typically in secret: *next year's primary ballot* | *the commissioners were elected* ***by ballot.*** ■ (**the ballot**) the total number of votes cast in such a process: *he won 54 percent of the ballot.* ■ the piece of paper used to record someone's vote in such a process. ■ a list of candidates or issues to be voted on: *he agreed to have his name placed on California's primary ballot.* ■ the right to vote: *they were a contrivance to deny the ballot to Negro voters.*

▶*v.* (**-lot·ed**, **-lot·ing**) [*trans.*] (of an organization) elicit a secret vote from (members) on a particular issue: *the union is preparing to ballot its members on the same issue.* ■ [*intrans.*] cast one's vote on a particular issue: *ambulance crews balloted unanimously to reject the deal.* ■ decide the allocation of (something) to applicants by drawing lots. ▷mid 16th cent. (originally denoting a small colored ball placed in a container to register a vote): from Italian *ballotta*, diminutive of *balla* (see BALL[1]).

bal·lot box ▶*n.* a sealed box into which voters put completed ballots. ■ (**the ballot box**) democratic principles and methods: *the proper remedy was the ballot box and not the court.*

bal·lo·tin /'balətin/ ▶*n.* a decorative cardboard box, slightly larger at the top and with broad flaps, in which chocolates are sold. ▷French, from *ballot* 'a small package of goods.'

bal·lot·tine /'balə,tēn/ ▶*n.* a dish of meat, poultry, or fish that is stuffed and rolled and usually served hot. ▷French.

ball·park /'bôl,pärk/ ▶*n.* a baseball stadium or field. ■ *informal* a particular area or range: *we can make a pretty good guess that this figure's in the ballpark.*

▶*adj.* [*attrib.*] *informal* (of prices or costs) approximate; rough: *the* ***ballpark figure*** *is $400–500.*

ball-peen ham·mer ▶*n.* a hammer with a rounded end opposite the face.

ball·point /'bôl,point/ (also **ballpoint pen**) ▶*n.* a pen with a tiny ball as its writing point. The ball transfers ink from a cartridge to the paper.

ball race ▶*n. Mechanics* either of the components of a ball bearing that have ring-shaped grooves in which the balls run.

ball·room /'bôl,ro͞om; -,ro͝om/ ▶*n.* a large room used for dancing.

ball·room danc·ing ▶*n.* formal social dancing in couples, popular as a recreation and also as a competitive activity. The ballroom dance repertoire includes dances developed from old European folk dances such as the waltz, Latin American dances such as the tango, rumba, and cha-cha, and dances of 20th-century origin such as the foxtrot and quickstep. —**ball·room dance** *n.*

balls-up ▶*n. Brit., vulgar slang* a bungled or badly carried out task or action; a mess.

balls·y /'bôlzē/ ▶*adj.* (**balls·i·er**, **balls·i·est**) *informal* tough and courageous: *a cool, ballsy woman who could not be intimidated.* ▷1950s: from BALL[1] (sense 4 of *noun*). + -Y[1]. —**balls·i·ness** *n.*

ball valve ▶*n.* **1** a one-way valve that is opened and closed by pressure on a ball that fits into a cup-shaped opening. **2** *Brit.* another term for BALL COCK.

bal·ly·hoo /'balē,ho͞o/ *informal* ▶*n.* extravagant publicity or fuss: *after all the ballyhoo, the film was a flop.*

▶*v.* (**-hoos**, **-hooed**) [*trans.*] praise or publicize extravagantly: [as *adj.*] (**ballyhooed**) *a much-ballyhooed musical extravaganza.* ▷late 19th cent.: American coinage of unknown origin.

balm /bä(l)m/ ▶*n.* **1** a fragrant ointment or preparation used to heal or soothe the skin. ■ *figurative* something that has a comforting, soothing, or restorative effect: *the murmur of the water can provide balm for troubled spirits.* **2** a tree that yields a fragrant resinous substance, typically one used in medicine. • Species in several families, in particular those of the genus *Commiphora* (family Burseraceae). ■ such a substance. **3** (also **lemon balm** or **sweet balm**) a bushy herb of the mint family, with leaves smelling and tasting of lemon. • *Melissa officinalis*, family Labiatae. ■ used in names of other aromatic herbs of the mint family, e.g., **bee balm**. ▷Middle English (in the sense 'preparation for embalming, fragrant resinous substance'): from Old French *basme*, from Latin *balsamum* (see BALSAM).

bal·ma·caan /,balmə'kan; -'kän/ ▶*n.* a loose overcoat with raglan sleeves.

Bal·mer se·ries /'bämər/ *Physics* a series of lines in the visible and ultraviolet spectrum of atomic hydrogen, between 656 and 365 nanometers.

balm of Gil·e·ad /'gilēəd/ ▶*n.* **1** a fragrant medicinal resin obtained from certain kinds of tree. **2** a tree that yields such a resin, in particular: • an Arabian tree traditionally of importance in medicine and perfumery (*Commiphora gileadensis*, family Burseraceae). • either of two poplars with sticky aromatic buds (*Populus* × *gileadensis* (or **candicans**)) and the balsam poplar, family Salicaceae). • the balsam fir. ▷early 16th cent.: *balm* from a translation in Coverdale's Bible (Gen. 37:25), rendered 'resin' in the Vulgate; *Gilead* from the assumption that this resin is the substance mentioned in the Bible as coming from Gilead.

bal·mor·al /bal'môrəl/ (also **Bal·mor·al**) ▶*n.* **1** a type of brimless round cocked hat with a cockade or ribbons attached, worn by certain Scottish regiments. **2** a heavy laced leather walking boot. **3** *historical* a stiff woolen or horsehair petticoat worn under a skirt. ▷mid 19th cent.: named after BALMORAL CASTLE in Scotland.

Bal·mor·al Cas·tle a vacation residence of the British royal family, on the Dee River in Scotland.

balm·y /'bä(l)mē/ ▶*adj.* (**balm·i·er**, **balm·i·est**) **1** (of the weather) pleasantly warm: *the balmy days of late summer.* **2** *informal* extremely foolish; eccentric: *this is a balmy decision.* | *I think he's* ***gone balmy*** *again.* —**balm·i·ness** *n.*

bal·ne·ol·o·gy /,balnē'äləjē/ ▶*n.* the study of therapeutic bathing and medicinal springs. ■ another term for BALNEOTHERAPY. ▷mid 19th cent.: from Latin *balneum* 'bath' + -LOGY. —**bal·ne·o·log·i·cal** /-nēə'läjikəl/ *adj.* —**bal·ne·ol·o·gist** /-jist/ *n.*

bal·ne·o·ther·a·py /,balnēə'THerəpē/ ▶*n.* the treatment of disease by bathing in mineral springs. ▷late 19th cent.: from Latin *balneum* 'bath' + THERAPY.

ba·lo·ney /bə'lōnē/ ▶*n. informal* **1** foolish or deceptive talk; nonsense: *typical salesman's baloney.* [corruption of BOLOGNA.] **2** variant of BOLOGNA.

Bal·qash, Lake /bäl'käsH; bal'kasH/ (also **Bal·khash**) a shallow salt lake in Kazakhstan.

bal·sa /'bôlsə/ ▶*n.* **1** (also **balsa wood**) a very lightweight wood used in particular for making models and rafts. **2** the fast-growing tropical American tree from which this wood is obtained. • *Ochroma lagopus* (or **pyramidale**) , family Bombacaceae. ▷early 17th cent. (denoting a kind of South American raft or fishing boat): from Spanish, 'raft.'

bal·sam /'bôlsəm/ ▶*n.* **1** an aromatic resinous substance, such as balm, exuded by various trees and shrubs and used as a base for certain fragrances and medical preparations. ■ an aromatic ointment or other resinous medicinal or cosmetic preparation. ■ a tree or shrub that yields balsam. **2** a herbaceous plant cultivated for its flowers, which are typically pink or purple and carried high on the stem. • Genus *Impatiens*, family Balsaminaceae: several species, including **garden balsam** (*I. balsamina*) and **Himalayan balsam** (*I. glandulifera*), which is naturalized in Europe and North America, sometimes to the detriment of the native flora. ▷Old English, via Latin from Greek *balsamon*. —**bal·sam·ic** /bôl'samik/ *adj.*

bal·sam ap·ple ▶*n.* another name for BITTER MELON.

bal·sam fir ▶*n.* a North American fir tree that yields Canada balsam. • *Abies balsamea*, family Pinaceae.

bal·sam·ic vin·e·gar ▸*n.* dark, sweet Italian vinegar that has been matured in wooden barrels.

bal·sam pop·lar ▸*n.* a North American poplar tree that yields balsam. • *Populus balsamifera,* family Salicaceae.

Bal·sas, Ri·o /ˌrēō ˈbôlsəs/ a river that flows 450 miles (725 km) through central Mexico, through Puebla, Guerrero, and Michoacán states, into the Pacific Ocean.

bal·sa wood ▸*n.* see BALSA (sense 1).

Balt /bôlt/ ▸*n.* **1** a speaker of a Baltic language; a Lithuanian or Latvian. **2** a native or inhabitant of one of the Baltic States of Lithuania, Latvia, and Estonia. ■ *historical* a German-speaking inhabitant of any of these states.
▸*adj.* of or relating to the Balts. ▷late 19th cent.: from late Latin *Balthae* 'dwellers near the Baltic Sea.'

Bal·tha·sar /bôlˈTHazər; bal-; ˈbôlTHəˌzär/ (also **Bal·tha·zar**) one of the three Magi.

Bal·tha·zar /bôlˈTHazər; bal-; ˈbôlTHəˌzär/ ▸*n.* a very large wine bottle, with a capacity of 12 liters, equivalent to that of 16 ordinary wine bottles. ▷1930s: from *Balthazar,* the name of the King of Babylon, who "made a great feast . . . and drank wine before a thousand" (Dan. 5:1).

Bal·tic /ˈbôltik/ ▸*adj.* **1** of or relating to the Baltic Sea or the region surrounding it. **2** denoting, belonging to, or relating to a branch of the Indo-European family of languages consisting of Lithuanian, Latvian, and Old Prussian.
▸*n.* **1** (**the Baltic**) the Baltic Sea or the Baltic States. **2** the Baltic languages collectively. ▷late 16th cent.: from medieval Latin *Balticus,* from late Latin *Balthae* 'dwellers near the Baltic Sea.'

Bal·tic Sea a sea in northern Europe. Almost landlocked, it is linked with the North Sea by Kattegat Strait and the Øresund Channel.

Bal·tic States **1** the independent republics of Estonia, Latvia, and Lithuania. **2** the ten members of the Council of Baltic States established in 1992: Denmark, Estonia, Finland, Germany, Latvia, Lithuania, Norway, Poland, Russia, and Sweden.

Bal·ti·more /ˈbôltəˌmôr; ˈbôlt(ə)mər/ a seaport in northern Maryland, the largest city in Maryland, on Chesapeake Bay; pop. 651,154 . ▷named after George Calvert, the first Baron *Baltimore* (*c.*1580–1632), who in 1632 obtained a grant of land for the colony that later became Maryland.

Bal·ti·more Coun·ty a county in north central Maryland that surrounds but does not include the city of Baltimore; pop. 692,134. Towson is its seat.

Bal·ti·stan /ˌbôltəˈstan; ˌbəl-; -ˈstän/ a region of the Karakoram range of the Himalayas, to the south of K2 peak. Also called LITTLE TIBET.

Bal·to-Slav·ic /ˈbôltō ˈslävik/ ▸*n.* a branch of the Indo-European language family that includes the Baltic and Slavic languages. **—Bal·to-Slav·ic** *adj.*

Ba·lu·chi /bəˈlo͞oCHē/ (also **Ba·luch** /-ˈlo͞oCH/) ▸*n.* (*pl.* same or **-chis**) **1** a native or inhabitant of Baluchistan. **2** the Iranian language of Baluchistan.
▸*adj.* of or relating to this people or their language. ▷from Persian *Balūčī.*

Ba·lu·chi·stan /bəˌlo͞oCHiˈstan; -ˈstän/ **1** a mountainous region of western Asia that includes part of southeastern Iran, southwestern Afghanistan, and western Pakistan. **2** a province of western Pakistan; capital, Quetta.

Ba·lun·da /bəˈlo͝ondə; -ˈlo͞on-/ ▸*n.* plural form of LUNDA.

bal·us·ter /ˈbaləstər/ ▸*n.* a short pillar or column, typically decorative in design, in a series supporting a rail or coping. ■ [as *adj.*] (of a furniture leg or other decorative item) having the form of a baluster. ▷early 17th cent.: from French *balustre,* from Italian *balaustro,* from *balaust(r)a* 'wild pomegranate flower' (via Latin from Greek *balaustion*), so named because part of the pillar resembles the curving calyx tube of the flower.

bal·us·trade /ˈbaləˌstrād/ ▸*n.* a railing supported by balusters, esp. an ornamental parapet on a balcony, bridge, or terrace. ▷mid 17th cent.: from French, from *balustre* (see BALUSTER). **—bal·us·trad·ed** *adj.*

balustrade

Bal·zac /ˈbôlˌzak; ˈbal-/, Honoré de (1799–1850), French novelist; chiefly remembered for his series of ninety-one interconnected novels and stories known collectively as *La Comédie humaine.* **—Bal·zac·i·an** /bôlˈzakēən; bal-/ *adj.*

bam /bam/ ▸*exclam.* used to imitate the sound of a hard blow or to convey the abruptness of an occurrence: *he'll have to make a dash for it, and when he does, bam, he's dead.* ▷1920s: imitative.

Ba·ma·ko /ˈbäməˌkō; ˈbam-/ the capital of Mali, in the south part of the country, on the Niger River; pop. 646,000.

Bam·ba·ra /bämˈbärə/ ▸*n.* (*pl.* same or **-ras**) a member of a native people living chiefly in Mali. ■ the Mande language of this people.
▸*adj.* of or relating to this people or their language.

bam·bi·no /bamˈbēnō/ ▸*n.* (*pl.* **-ni** /-nē/) *often humorous* a baby or young child. ■ an image of the infant Jesus. ▷early 18th cent.: Italian, diminutive of *bambo* 'silly.'

bam·boo /ˌbamˈbo͞o/ ▸*n.* a giant woody grass that grows chiefly in the tropics, where it is widely cultivated. • *Bambusa* and other genera, family Gramineae. ■ the hollow jointed stem of this plant, used as a cane or to make furniture and implements: [as *adj.*] *a bamboo serving tray.* ▷late 16th cent.: from Dutch *bamboes,* based on Malay *mambu.*

bam·boo cur·tain ▸*n.* (often **the Bamboo Curtain**) a political and economic barrier between China and noncommunist countries.

bam·boo shoot ▸*n.* a young shoot of bamboo, eaten as a vegetable.

bam·boo·zle /bamˈbo͞ozəl/ ▸*v.* [*trans.*] *informal* fool or cheat (someone): *Tom Sawyer bamboozled the neighborhood boys into doing it for him.* ■ (often **be bamboozled**) confound or perplex: *bamboozled by the number of savings plans being offered.* ▷early 18th cent.: of unknown origin.

bamboo

bam·my /ˈbamē/ (also **bam·mie**) ▸*n.* (*pl.* **-my** or **-mies**) (in the West Indies) a flat roll or pancake made from cassava flour. ▷probably from a West African language.

ban[1] /ban/ ▸*v.* (**banned, ban·ning**) [*trans.*] (often **be banned**) officially or legally prohibit: *he was* **banned from** *driving for a year | a proposal to ban all trade in ivory.* See note at PROHIBIT. ■ officially exclude (someone) from a place: *he once was banned from a casino in Reno.*
▸*n.* **1** an official or legal prohibition: *a proposed* **ban on** *cigarette advertising | a three-year driving ban.* ■ an official exclusion of a person from an organization, country, or activity: *a* **ban on** *homosexuals in the armed forces.* ■ *archaic* a curse. **2** a tacit prohibition by public opinion: *Barenboim proposed to defy an unwritten ban on Wagner's works.* ▷Old English *bannan* 'summon by a public proclamation,' of Germanic origin, reinforced by Old Norse *banna* 'curse, prohibit'; the noun is partly from Old French *ban* 'proclamation, summons, banishment.'

ban[2] /bän/ ▸*n.* (*pl.* **ba·ni** /ˈbänē/) a monetary unit of Romania, equal to one hundredth of a leu. ▷Romanian.

Ba·na·ba /bəˈnäbə; -ˈnabə/ an island in the western Pacific, just south of the equator to the west of the Gilbert Islands. Formerly within the Gilbert and Ellice Islands, it has been part of Kiribati since 1979. Also called OCEAN ISLAND.

ba·nal /ˈbānl; bəˈnal; -ˈnäl/ ▸*adj.* so lacking in originality as to be obvious and boring: *songs with banal, repeated words.* ▷mid 18th cent. (originally relating to feudal service in the sense 'compulsory,' hence 'common to all'): from French, from *ban* 'a proclamation or call to arms'; ultimately of Germanic origin and related to BAN[1]. **—ba·nal·i·ty** /bəˈnalitē/ *n.* (*pl.* **-ties**) **—ba·nal·ly** *adv.*

ba·nan·a /bəˈnanə/ ▸*n.* **1** a long curved fruit that grows in clusters and has soft pulpy flesh and yellow skin when ripe. **2** (also **banana plant** or **banana tree**) the tropical and subtropical treelike plant that bears this fruit. It has very large leaves and resembles a palm, but lacks a woody trunk. • Genus *Musa,* family Musaceae: several species, in particular *M. sapientum.* **3** *adj.* (**bananas**) *informal* insane or extremely silly: *he's beginning to think I'm bananas.* ▷late 16th cent.: via Portuguese or Spanish from Mande.
▸*PHRASES* □ **go bananas** *informal* go insane: *Roy's customers think the council has gone bananas.* ■ rave; cheer wildly: *I have never had a product that people* **went** *so* **bananas over.** ■ become extremely angry or excited: *she went bananas when I said I was going to leave the job.* □ **second banana** *informal* the second most important person in an organization or activity. □ **top banana** *informal* the most important person in an organization or activity.

ba·nan·a belt ▸*n.* *informal* a region with a comparatively warm climate.

ba·nan·a oil ▸*n.* a colorless liquid with a bananalike odor used in flavorings and as a solvent. • Chem. formula: $CH_3CO_2C_5H_{11}$.

ba·nan·a plug ▸*n.* *Electronics, informal* a single-pole connector with a curved spring along its tip.

ba·nan·a·quit /bəˈnanəˌkwit/ ▸*n.* a small songbird with a curved bill, typically with a white stripe over the eye, a sooty gray back, and yellow underparts. It is common in the West Indies and Central and South America. • *Coereba flaveola,* the only member of the family Coerebidae (sometimes placed in the subfamily Parulinae, family Emberizidae). ▷see QUIT[2].

ba·nan·a re·pub·lic ▸*n.* *chiefly derogatory* a small nation, esp. in Central America, dependent on one crop or the influx of foreign capital.

ba·nan·a seat ▸*n.* a narrow, elongated bicycle seat that curves up toward the rear.

ba·nan·a split ▸*n.* a dessert made with a split banana, ice cream, sauce, whipped cream, nuts, and a cherry.

ba·nau·sic /bəˈnôzik; -sik/ ▸*adj.* *formal* not operating on a refined or elevated level; mundane. ■ relating to technical work. ▷mid 19th cent.: from Greek *banausikos* 'of or for artisans.'

ban·co /ˈbaNGkō/ ▸*exclam.* used in baccarat, chemin de fer, and similar games to express a player's willingness to meet the banker's whole stake single-handed. ▷late 18th cent.: via French from Italian.

Ban·croft /ˈbanˌkrôft; ˈbaNG-; -ˌkräft/, Anne (1931–), U.S. actress; born *Anna Maria Luisa Italiano.* She won a 1959 Tony Award for her performance in the play *The Miracle Worker* and an Academy Award for her performance in the movie version in 1962.

band[1] /band/ ▸*n.* **1** a flat, thin strip or loop of material put around something, typically to hold it together or to decorate it: *wads of banknotes fastened with gummed paper bands.* ■ a strip of material forming part of a garment: *hatband | waistband.* ■ a plain ring for the finger, esp. a gold wedding ring: *a narrow* **band of gold** *was her only jewelry.* ■ *Ornithology* a ring of metal placed around a bird's leg to identify it. ■ (**bands**) a collar with two hanging strips, worn by certain clerics and academics as part of their formal dress. ■ *Mechanics* a belt connecting wheels or pulleys. **2** a stripe or elongated area of a different color, texture, or composition than its surroundings: *a long, narrow band of cloud.* **3** a range of frequencies or wavelengths in a spectrum (esp. of radio frequencies): *channels in the UHF band.* **4** (on a long-playing record) a set of grooves onto which sound has been recorded, separated from other sections of the record by grooves with no sound. **5** *archaic* a thing that restrains, binds, or unites.
▸*v.* [*trans.*] (usu. **be banded**) **1** surround (an object) with something in the form of a strip or ring, typically for reinforcement or decoration: *doors are banded with iron to make them stronger.* ■ *Ornithology* put a band on (a bird) for identification. **2** mark (something) with a stripe or stripes of a different color: *the bird's bill is banded across the middle with black |* [as *adj.*] (**banded**) *banded agate.* ▷late Old English (sense 5), from Old Norse, reinforced in late Middle English by Old French *bande,* of Germanic origin; related to BIND.

band[2] ▸*n.* **1** a group of people who have a common interest or purpose: *guerrilla bands | a determined band of activists.* ■ *Anthropology* a subgroup of a tribe. **2** a group of musicians who play together, in particular: ■ a small group of musicians and vocalists who play pop, jazz, or rock music: *the band's last two albums | a rock band.* ■ a group of musicians who play brass, wind, or percussion instruments: *a military band.* ■ *informal* an orchestra. **3** a herd or flock: *moving bands of caribou.*
▸*v.* [*intrans.*] (of people or organizations) form a group for a mutual purpose: *local people* **banded together** *to fight the company.* ▷late Middle English: from Old French *bande,* of Germanic origin; related to BANNER.

Ban·da /ˈbandə/, Hastings Kamuzu (1906–1997), Malawian statesman; prime minister 1964–94; the first president of the Republic of Malawi 1966–94.

band·age /ˈbandij/ ▸*n.* a strip of material used to bind a wound or to protect an injured part of the body: *her leg was swathed in bandages | a sterile adhesive bandage with nonstick pad.*
▸*v.* [*trans.*] bind (a wound or a part of the body) with a protective strip of material: *bandage the foot so that the ankle is supported | the doctors **bandaged up** his wounds.* ▷late 16th cent.: from French, from *bande* (see BAND²).

band·ag·ing /ˈbandijiNG/ ▸*n.* the action of binding a strip or strips of material around a wound or an injured part of the body. ■ the material used for this.

Band-Aid /ˈband ˌād/ ▸*n. trademark* an adhesive bandage with a gauze pad in the center, used to cover minor wounds. ■ *figurative* (also **band-aid**) a makeshift or temporary solution: [as *adj.*] *a band-aid solution to a much deeper problem.*

ban·dan·na /banˈdanə/ ▸*n.* a large handkerchief or neckerchief, typically of silk or cotton, often having a colorful pattern. ▷mid 18th cent.: probably via Portuguese from Hindi.

Ban·da·ra·nai·ke /ˌbəndərəˈnīkə/, Sirimavo Ratwatte Dias (1916–2000), Sinhalese stateswoman; prime minister of Sri Lanka 1960–65, 1970–77, and 1994–2000. The world's first woman prime minister, she succeeded her husband, S. W. R. D. Bandaranaike, after his assassination. Her daughter Chandrika Kumaratunga became president in 1994.

Ban·dar Lam·pung /ˈbəndər ˈlämˌpoŏNG/ a city at the southern tip of Sumatra, in Indonesia; pop. 284,275. It was created in the 1980s as a result of the amalgamation of the city of Tanjungkarang and the nearby port of Telukbetung.

Ban·dar Se·ri Be·ga·wan /ˈbänˌdär ˈserē beˈgäwən/ the capital of Brunei, in the northern part of the country; pop. 46,000.

Ban·da Sea /ˈbandə; ˈbändə/ a sea in eastern Indonesia, between the central and south Molucca Islands.

b. & b. (also **B&B**) ▸*abbr.* bed and breakfast.

band·box /ˈbandˌbäks/ ▸*n.* a cardboard box, typically circular, for carrying hats. ▷mid 17th cent.: from BAND² + BOX¹, the box being used originally for neckbands.

B&E ▸*abbr.* breaking and entering.

ban·deau /banˈdō/ ▸*n.* (*pl.* **-deaux** /-ˈdōz/) a narrow band worn around the head to hold the hair in position: *their dusty blonde hair smoothly combed in bandeaux.* ■ a woman's strapless top formed from a band of fabric fitting around the bust: *white two-piece bathing suit with quilted sateen bandeau top.* ▷early 18th cent.: from French, from Old French *bandel*, diminutive of *bande* (see BAND²).

ban·de·ril·la /ˌbandəˈrēə/ ▸*n.* a decorated dart thrust into a bull's neck or shoulders during a bullfight. ▷Spanish, diminutive of *bandera* 'banner.'

ban·de·ril·le·ro /ˌbandərēˈyerō/ ▸*n.* (*pl.* **-ros**) a bullfighter who uses banderillas. ▷Spanish.

ban·de·role /ˈbandəˌrōl/ (also **ban·de·rol**) ▸*n.* a narrow flaglike object, in particular: ■ a long, narrow flag with a cleft end, flown at a masthead. ■ an ornamental streamer on a knight's lance. ■ a ribbonlike stone scroll bearing an inscription. ▷mid 16th cent.: from French, from Italian *banderuola*, diminutive of *bandiera* 'banner.'

ban·di·coot /ˈbandiˌko͞ot/ ▸*n.* a mainly insectivorous marsupial native to Australia and New Guinea. • Family Peramelidae: several genera and species, some of which are endangered or extinct, including the **short-nosed** (or **southern brown**) **bandicoot** (*Isodon obesulus*). ▷late 18th cent.: from Telugu *pandikokku*, literally 'pig-rat.'

short-nosed bandicoot

ban·di·coot rat ▸*n.* an Asian rat that is often a destructive pest. • Genera *Bandicota* and *Nesokia*, family Muridae: four species, in particular the large *B. indica*.

band·ing /ˈbandiNG/ ▸*n.* **1** the presence or formation of visible stripes of contrasting color: *the yellow and black banding of bees and wasps.* ■ *Biochemistry* the pattern of regions on a chromosome made visible by staining. ■ *Biochemistry* the separation of molecules into bands of concentration in a gel. **2** the marking of individual birds or other animals with bands or rings: *banding is a useful tool for the study of migration.*

ban·dit /ˈbandit/ ▸*n.* (*pl.* **ban·dits** or **ban·dit·ti** /banˈdītē/) a robber or outlaw belonging to a gang and typically operating in an isolated or lawless area: *the bandit produced a weapon and demanded money.* ■ *figurative* [with *modifier*] a person notably proficient at something, esp. in contrast to or at the expense of a rival or opponent: *he was no base-running bandit, but he got the job done.* ■ *military slang* an enemy aircraft. ▷late 16th cent.: from Italian *bandito*, literally 'banned,' past participle of *bandire*. —**ban·dit·ry** /-trē/ *n.*
▸*PHRASE* □ **make out like a bandit** profit greatly from an activity.

band·lead·er /ˈbandˌlēdər/ (also **band lead·er**) ▸*n.* a player or conductor at the head of a musical band.

band·mas·ter /ˈbandˌmastər/ ▸*n.* the conductor of a musical band, esp. a brass or military one.

ban·dog /ˈbanˌdôg/ ▸*n.* a fighting dog bred for its strength and ferocity by crossing aggressive breeds. ▷Middle English (originally denoting a dog kept on a chain or "band"): from BAND¹ + DOG.

ban·do·lier /ˌbandəˈli(ə)r/ (also **ban·do·leer**) ▸*n.* a shoulder-belt with loops or pockets for cartridges. ▷late 16th cent.: from French *bandoulière*; perhaps from Spanish *bandolera* (from *banda* 'sash'), or from Catalan *bandolera* (from *bandoler* 'bandit').

bandolier

ban·do·ne·on /banˈdōnēən/ ▸*n.* a type of concertina used esp. in South America. ▷via Spanish from German *Bandonion*, named after Heinrich *Band*, the 19th-cent. German musician who invented it, + *-on-* (as in *Harmonika* 'harmonica') + *-ion* (as in *Akkordion* 'accordion').

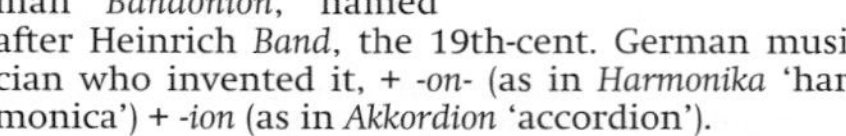

ban·do·ra /banˈdôrə/ ▸*n.* a bass stringed instrument of the cittern family, having a long neck and a scallop-shaped body. ▷mid 16th cent.: origin uncertain; compare with Dutch *bandoor*, Spanish *bandurria*, also with BANJO.

band·pass /ˈbandˌpas/ ▸*adj. Electronics* (of a filter) transmitting only a set range of frequencies: *a 1–40 Hz bandpass filter.*
▸*n.* the range of frequencies transmitted through such a filter.

band·saw /ˈbandˌsô/ (also **band saw**) ▸*n.* an endless saw, consisting of a steel band with a serrated edge running over wheels.

band·shell /ˈbandˌSHel/ (also **band shell**) ▸*n.* a bandstand in the form of a large concave shell with special acoustic properties.

bands·man /ˈbandzmən/ ▸*n.* (*pl.* **-men**) a player in a musical band, esp. a military or brass one.

band·stand /ˈbandˌstand/ ▸*n.* a covered outdoor platform for a band to play on, typically in a park. ■ a raised platform for performing musicians in a restaurant or dance hall.

Ban·dung /ˈbänˌdo͝oNG/ a city in Indonesia; pop. 2,056,900. Founded by the Dutch in 1810, it was the capital of the former Dutch East Indies.

band·wag·on /ˈbandˌwagən/ ▸*n.* **1** a wagon used for carrying a band in a parade or procession. **2** [usu. in *sing.*] a particular activity or cause that has suddenly become fashionable or popular: *the local deejays are on the home-team bandwagon.*
▸*PHRASE* □ **jump** (or **climb**) **on the bandwagon** join others in doing or supporting something fashionable or likely to be successful: *scientists and doctors alike have jumped on the bandwagon.*

band·width /ˈbandˌwidTH/ ▸*n. Electronics* a range of frequencies within a given band, in particular: ■ the range of frequencies used for transmitting a signal. ■ the range of frequencies over which a system or a device can operate effectively. ■ the transmission capacity of a computer network or other telecommunication system. ■ *figurative* the breadth of a person's interests or mental capacity.

ban·dy¹ /ˈbandē/ ▸*adj.* (**-di·er**, **-di·est**) (of a person's legs) curved so as to be wide apart at the knees. ■ (often **bandy-legged**) (of a person) having legs that are curved in such a way; bowlegged. ▷late 17th cent.: perhaps from obsolete *bandy* 'curved stick used in hockey.'

ban·dy² ▸*v.* (**-dies**, **-died**) [*trans.*] (usu. **be bandied about/around**) pass on or discuss an idea or rumor in a casual way: *$40,000 is the figure that has been bandied about.* ■ exchange; pass back and forth: *they bandied words and laughs from one to another.*
▸*n.* a game similar to field hockey. ■ the stick used to play this game. ▷late 16th cent. (in the sense 'pass (a ball) to and fro'): perhaps from French *bander* 'take sides in a tennis match,' from *bande* 'band, crowd' (see BAND²).
▸*PHRASE* □ **bandy words with** argue pointlessly or rudely: *don't **bandy words with** me, Sir!*

bane /bān/ ▸*n.* [usu. in *sing.*] a cause of great distress or annoyance: *the bane of the decorator is the long, narrow hall | the depressions that were the **the bane of** her existence.* ■ *archaic* something, typically poison, that causes death. ▷Old English *bana* 'thing causing death, poison,' of Germanic origin. —**bane·ful** /-fəl/ *adj. archaic*.

bane·ber·ry /ˈbānˌberē/ ▸*n.* (*pl.* **-ries**) a plant of the buttercup family that bears fluffy spikes of creamy-white flowers followed by shiny berries. Native to north temperate regions, it was formerly used in medicine. • Genus *Actaea*, family Ranunculaceae: many species, including the North American **white baneberry** (*A. pachypoda*), with clusters of black-eyed white berries on red stalks. ■ the bitter, typically poisonous berry of this plant. ▷mid 18th cent.: from BANE in the sense 'poison' + BERRY.

bang¹ /baNG/ ▸*n.* **1** a sudden loud noise: *the door slammed with a bang | I heard a series of loud bangs.* ■ a sharp blow causing such a loud noise: *I went to answer a bang on the front door.* ■ a sudden painful blow: *a nasty bang on the head.* **2** (**bangs**) a fringe of hair cut straight across the forehead: *she brushed back her wispy bangs.* [from a use of the adverb *bang* to mean 'abruptly.'] **3** *vulgar slang* an act of sexual intercourse. **4** *Computing* the character "!"
▸*v.* **1** [*trans.*] strike or put down (something) forcefully and noisily, typically in anger or in order to attract attention: *he began to bang the table with his fist | Sarah **banged** the phone **down** |* [*intrans.*] *someone was **banging on** the door.* ■ [*trans.*] come into contact with (something) suddenly and sharply, typically by accident: *I banged my head on the low beams |* [*intrans.*] *she banged into some shelves in the darkness.* ■ [*intrans.*] make a sudden loud noise, typically repeatedly: *the shutter was banging in the wind.* ■ [*trans.*] (of a door) open or close violently and noisily: *he **banged** the kitchen door **shut** behind him |* [*intrans.*] *the door **banged open** and a man staggered out.* ■ [*intrans.*] (of a person) move around or do something noisily, esp. as an indication of anger or irritation: *she was banging around the kitchen.* ■ [*trans.*] (of a sports player) hit (a ball or a shot) forcefully and successfully: *in his second start he banged out two hits.* ■ *vulgar slang* (of a man) have sexual intercourse with (a woman). **2** cut (hair) in a fringe.
▸*phrasal v.* □ **bang away at** *informal* do something in a persistent or dogged way: *he was banging away at his novel.* □ **bang something out** *informal* **1** play music noisily, enthusiastically, and typically unskillfully: *Dad was annihilating a Beethoven sonata, banging out notes.* **2** produce hurriedly or in great quantities: *they weren't banging out ads in my day the way they are now.* □ **bang someone/something up** *informal* damage or injure someone or something: *he banged up his knee.* ■ *Brit., informal* imprison someone: *they've been banged up for something they didn't do.*
▸*adv. informal chiefly Brit.* exactly: *bang in the middle of town.* ■ completely: *bring your wardrobe bang up to date.*
▸*exclam.* **1** used to express or imitate the sound of a sudden loud noise: *firecrackers **went bang** | Bang, Bang! You're dead.* **2** used to convey the suddenness of an action or process: *the minute something becomes obsolete, bang, it's gone.* ▷mid 16th cent.: imitative, perhaps of Scandinavian origin; compare with Old Norse *bang* 'hammering.'
▸*PHRASES* □ **bang for one's** (or **the**) **buck** *informal* value for money; performance for cost: *this cross between a sports car and a family sedan gave a lot of bang for the buck.* □ **bang** (or **knock** or **crack**) **people's heads together** reprimand people severely, esp. in the attempt to make them stop arguing. □ **get a bang out of** *informal* derive excitement or pleasure from: *some*

people get a bang out of reading that stuff. □ **go (off) with a bang** go successfully: *the occasion went with a bang.* □ **with a bang 1** abruptly: *the remark brought me down to earth with a bang.* **2** impressively or spectacularly: *the day starts with a bang—the steep climb to the mountain top.*

bang[2] ▶*n.* variant spelling of BHANG.

Ban·ga·lore /ˌbaNGgəˈlôr/ a city in south central India, capital of the state of Karnataka; pop. 2,651,000.

ban·ga·lore tor·pe·do (also **Ban·ga·lore tor·pe·do**) ▶*n.* a tube containing explosives used by infantry for blowing up barriers.

bang·er /ˈbaNGər/ ▶*n. chiefly Brit.* **1** *informal* a sausage: *bangers and beans.* **2** *informal* a car in poor condition, esp. a noisy one: *they've got an old banger.* **3** a loud explosive firework.

Bang·kok /ˈbaNG,käk; baNGˈkäk/ the capital and chief port of Thailand, on the Chao Phraya waterway, 25 miles (40 km) upstream from its outlet into the Gulf of Thailand; pop. 5,876,000.

Bang·la·desh /ˌbängglәˈdesH; ˌbaNGlә-/ a country in southern Asia, in the Ganges River delta, on the Bay of Bengal; pop. 141,340, 000; capital, Dhaka; official language, Bengali. **—Bang·la·desh·i** /-ˈdesHē/ *adj.* & *n.*

Formerly part of British India, the region, as East Pakistan, became one of the two geographical units of Pakistan. After civil war, the independent republic of Bangladesh was proclaimed in 1971. Cyclones in the Bay of Bengal cause repeated devastation to the country.

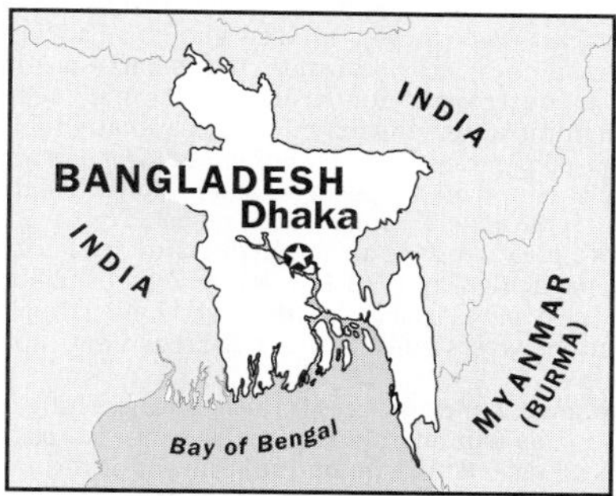

ban·gle /ˈbaNGgəl/ ▶*n.* a rigid bracelet or anklet. ▷late 18th cent.: from Hindi *baṅglī* 'glass bracelet.'

Ban·gor /ˈbaNGgər/ an industrial city in east central Maine, on the Penobscot River, formerly a lumbering center; pop. 31,473.

bang·tail /ˈbaNG,tāl/ ▶*n.* a horse's tail that has been cut straight across just below the level of the hocks.

Ban·gui /bäNGˈgē; ˈbäNG,gē/ the capital of the Central African Republic, in the southwestern part of the country, on the Ugandi River; pop. 596,800.

bang-up ▶*adj. informal* excellent: *for a novice, he has done a* ***bang-up job.***

ba·ni /ˈbänē/ ▶ plural form of BAN[2].

ban·ian ▶*n.* variant spelling of BANYAN.

ban·ish /ˈbanisH/ ▶*v.* [*trans.*] (often **be banished**) send (someone) away from a country or place as an official punishment: *they were* ***banished to*** *Siberia for political crimes.* ■ forbid, abolish, or get rid of (something unwanted): *it's perfectly feasible to banish the smoke without banning smoking | all thoughts of romance were* ***banished from*** *her head.* ▷late Middle English: from Old French *baniss-*, lengthened stem of *banir*; ultimately of Germanic origin and related to BAN[1]. **—ban·ish·ment** *n.*

ban·is·ter /ˈbanəstər/ (also **ban·nis·ter**) ▶*n.* (also **banisters**) the structure formed by uprights and a handrail at the side of a staircase. ■ a single upright at the side of the staircase: *I stuck my head between the banisters.* ▷mid 17th cent.: from earlier *barrister*, alteration of BALUSTER.

Ban·ja Lu·ka /ˌbänyə ˈlo͞okə/ a spa town in northern Bosnia and Herzegovina; pop. 143,000. It served as a base for Bosnian Serbs during their war against Bosnian Muslims in the 1990s.

Ban·jar·ma·sin /ˌbänjərˈmäsən; ˌban-/ a deep-water port in Indonesia, on the southern part of the island of Borneo; pop. 480,700.

ban·jax /ˈban,jaks/ ▶*v.* [*trans.*] *Brit., informal* ruin; incapacitate: *he said the scheme was banjaxing the tourist industry.* ▷1930s: originally Anglo-Irish, of unknown origin.

ban·jo /ˈbanjō/ ▶*n.* (*pl.* **-jos** or **-joes**) a stringed musical instrument with a long neck and a round open-backed body consisting of parchment stretched over a metal hoop like a tambourine, played by plucking or with a plectrum. It is used esp. in American folk music. ■ an object resembling this in shape: [as *adj.*] *a banjo clock.* ▷mid 18th cent.: originally a black American alteration of earlier *bandore*; probably based on Greek *pandoura* 'three-stringed lute.' Compare with BANDORA. **—ban·jo·ist** /-ist/ *n.*

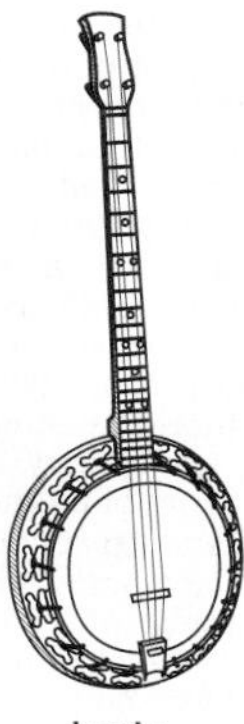
banjo

Ban·jul /ˈbän,jo͞ol/ the capital of the Gambia; pop. 44,540. Until 1973 it was known as Bathurst.

bank[1] /baNGk/ ▶*n.* **1** the land alongside or sloping down to a river or lake: *willows lined the bank.* **2** a slope, mass, or mound of a particular substance: *a bank of clouds | a bank of snow.* ■ an elevation in the seabed or a riverbed; a mudbank or sandbank. ■ a transverse slope given to a road, railroad, or sports track to enable vehicles or runners to maintain speed around a curve. ■ the sideways tilt of an aircraft when turning in flight: *flying with small amounts of bank.* **3** a set or series of similar things, esp. electrical or electronic devices, grouped together in rows: *the DJ had big banks of lights and speakers on either side of his console.* ■ a tier of oars: *the early ships had only twenty-five oars in each bank.* **4** the cushion of a pool table: [as *adj.*] *a bank shot.*
▶*v.* [*trans.*] **1** heap (a substance) into a mass or mound: *the rain* ***banked*** *the soil* ***up*** *behind the gate | snow was banked in humps at the roadside.* ■ [*intrans.*] rise or form into a mass or mound: *purple clouds* ***banked up*** *over the hills.* ■ heap a mass or mound of a substance against (something): *people were banking their houses with earth.* ■ heap (a fire) with tightly packed fuel so that it burns slowly: *she could have made a fire and banked it with dirt.* ■ edge or surround with a ridge or row of something: *steps banked with pots of chrysanthemums.* **2** (of an aircraft or vehicle) tilt or cause to tilt sideways in making a turn: [*intrans.*] *the plane banked as if to return to the airport* | [*trans.*] *I banked the aircraft steeply and turned.* ■ [*intrans.*] build (a road, railroad, or sports track) higher at the outer edge of a bend to facilitate fast cornering. **3** (in pool and other games) play (a ball) so that it rebounds off a surface such as a backboard or cushion. ▷Middle English: from Old Norse *bakki*, of Germanic origin; related to BENCH. The senses 'set of similar things in sloping rows' and 'tier of oars' are from French *banc*, of the same ultimate origin.

bank[2] ▶*n.* a financial establishment that invests money deposited by customers, pays it out when required, makes loans at interest, and exchanges currency: *I paid the money straight into my bank.* ■ a stock of something available for use when required: *a blood bank | building a bank of test items is the responsibility of teachers.* ■ a place where something may be safely kept: *the computer's memory bank.* ■ (**the bank**) the store of money or tokens held by the banker in some gambling or board games. ■ the person holding this store; the banker. ■ *Brit.* a site or receptacle where something may be deposited for recycling: *a paper bank.*
▶*v.* [*trans.*] deposit (money or valuables) in a bank: *I banked the check.* ■ [*intrans.*] have an account at a particular bank: *he did not* ***bank with*** *the old family banks.* ■ *informal* (esp. of a competitor in a game or race) win or earn (a sum of money): *he banked $100,000 for a hole-in-one.* ■ store (something, esp. blood, tissue, or sperm) for future use: *the sperm is banked or held in storage for the following spring.*
▶*phrasal v.* □ **bank on** base one's hopes or confidence on: *they can bank on my winning 25 games next year.* ▷late 15th cent. (originally denoting a money dealer's table): from French *banque* or Italian *banca*, from medieval Latin *banca*, *bancus*, of Germanic origin; related to BANK[1] and BENCH.
▶*PHRASE* □ **break the bank** (in gambling) win more money than is held by the bank. ■ [usu. with *negative*] *informal* cost more than one can afford: *Christmas need not break the bank.*

bank·a·ble /ˈbaNGkəbəl/ ▶*adj.* (esp. in the entertainment industry) certain to bring profit and success: *he needed some bankable names to star in the film.* ■ reliable: *a bankable assurance.* **—bank·a·bil·i·ty** /ˌbaNGkəˈbilitē/ *n.*

bank bal·ance ▶*n.* the amount of money held in a bank account at a given moment.

bank bill ▶*n.* **1** *Brit.* a bill of exchange drawn by one bank on another. **2** another term for BANKNOTE.

bank·book /ˈbaNGk,bo͝ok/ ▶*n.* another term for PASSBOOK.

bank card ▶*n.* a card issued by a bank for the purpose of identifying a customer, as at an automated teller machine. ■ a credit card issued by a bank.

bank dis·count ▶*n.* interest computed on the face value of a loan and deducted in advance from the loan by the lending bank.

bank draft ▶*n.* a check drawn by a bank on its own funds in another bank.

bank·er /ˈbaNGkər/ ▶*n.* an officer or owner of a bank or group of banks. ■ the person running the table, controlling play, or acting as dealer in some gambling or board games. ▷mid 16th cent.: from French *banquier*, from *banque* (see BANK[2]).

bank·er's hours ▶*plural n.* short working hours (in reference to the typical opening hours of a bank in former times).

Bank·head /ˈbaNGk,hed/, Tallulah (1903–68), U.S. actress noted for her uninhibited public persona, rich laugh, and harsh drawl. Her most successful movie appearance was in Alfred Hitchcock's *Lifeboat* (1944).

bank hol·i·day ▶*n. Brit.* a day on which banks are officially closed, observed as a public holiday.

bank·ing /ˈbaNGkiNG/ ▶*n.* the business conducted or services offered by a bank: *with this account, you are entitled to free banking.* ■ the occupation of a banker: [as *adj.*] *to pursue a banking career.*

bank ma·chine ▶*n.* another term for AUTOMATED TELLER MACHINE.

bank·note /ˈbaNGk,nōt/ (also **bank note**) ▶*n.* a piece of paper money, constituting a central bank's promissory note to pay a stated sum to the bearer on demand: *is the $1 bill the only banknote with George Washington's picture on it?*

bank rate ▶*n.* the rate of discount set by a central bank.

bank·roll /ˈbaNGk,rōl/ ▶*n.* a roll of paper money. ■ *figurative* financial resources: *his bankroll allowed him to run campaigns all over the U.S.*
▶*v.* [*trans.*] *informal* support (a person, organization, or project) financially: *the project is bankrolled by wealthy expatriates.*

bank·rupt /ˈbaNGk,rəpt; -rəpt/ ▶*adj.* (of a person or organization) declared in law unable to pay outstanding debts: *the company was declared bankrupt | he committed suicide after* ***going bankrupt.*** ■ impoverished or depleted: *a bankrupt country with no natural resources.* ■ *figurative* completely lacking in a particular quality or value: *their cause is morally bankrupt.*
▶*n.* a person judged by a court to be insolvent, whose property is taken and disposed of for the benefit of creditors.
▶*v.* [*trans.*] reduce (a person or organization) to bankruptcy: *the strike nearly bankrupted the union.* ▷mid 16th cent.: from Italian *banca rotta* 'broken bench,' from *banca* (see BANK[2]) and *rompere* 'to break.' The change in the ending was due to association with Latin *rupt-* 'broken.'

bank·rupt·cy /ˈbaNGk,rəp(t)sē; -rəp(t)sē/ ▶*n.* (*pl.* **-cies**) the state of being bankrupt: *many companies were facing bankruptcy | a series of bankruptcies and scandals* | [as *adj.*] *bankruptcy proceedings.* ■ *figurative* the state of being completely lacking in a particular quality or value: *the moral bankruptcy of terrorism.*

Banks[1] /baNGks/, Ernie (1931–), U.S. baseball player; full name *Ernest Banks*; known as **Mr. Cub**. He played first base or shortstop for the Chicago Cubs from 1953 until 1971. Baseball Hall of Fame (1977).

Banks[2], Sir Joseph (1743–1820), English botanist. He accompanied Captain James Cook on his first voyage to the Pacific.

bank·si·a /ˈbaNGksēə/ ▶*n.* an evergreen Australian shrub that typically has narrow, leathery leaves and spikes of bottlebrushlike flowers. • Genus *Banksia*, family Proteaceae. ▷modern Latin, named after Sir Joseph BANKS[2].

bank state·ment ▶*n.* a printed record of the balance in a bank account and the amounts that have been paid into it and withdrawn from it, issued periodically to the holder of the account.

bank swal·low ▶*n.* another term for SAND MARTIN.

bank vole ▸*n.* a common reddish-brown Eurasian vole that lives in woodland and scrub. • *Clethrionomys glareolus*, family Muridae.

Ban·ne·ker /ˈbanikər/, Benjamin (1731–1806), U.S. inventor, astronomer, and mathematician. Born to a slave father and freed slave mother, he published an almanac 1791–1802 that featured his astronomical and tide calculations. On the recommendation of Thomas Jefferson, he was hired to assist in the surveying of the District of Columbia 1790.

B

ban·ner /ˈbanər/ ▸*n.* **1** a long strip of cloth bearing a slogan or design, hung in a public place or carried in a demonstration or procession: *a banner in the front window announced "Grand Reopening"* | *students waved banners and chanted slogans.* ■ a flag on a pole used as the standard of a monarch, army, or knight. ■ *figurative* an idea or principle used to rally public opinion: *the administration is flying the free trade banner.* **2** (also **banner ad**) an advertisement appearing across the top of a web page: *to get a new banner now, click Step 1.* [as modifier] *advertise and promote your site on thousands of web sites all around the world for free utilizing our award winning banner exchange engine and free web tools!*
▸*adj.* [*attrib.*] excellent; outstanding: *I predict that 1998 will be a banner year.* ▷Middle English: from Old French *baniere*, ultimately of Germanic origin and related to BAND². —**ban·nered** *adj.*
▸*PHRASE* □ **under the banner of** claiming to support a particular cause or set of ideas: *campaigns fought under the banner of multiculturalism.* ■ as part of a particular group or organization: *the party is running under the banner of the Left-Wing Alliance.*

ban·ner·et /ˈbanərit; ˌbanəˈret/ ▸*n. historical* **1** a knight who commanded his own troops in battle under his own banner. **2** a knighthood given on the battlefield for courage. ▷Middle English: from Old French *baneret*, literally 'bannered,' from *baniere* 'banner.'

ban·ner head·line ▸*n.* a newspaper headline running across a whole page, esp. one on the front page.

Ban·nis·ter /ˈbanəstər/, Sir Roger (Gilbert) (1929–), British middle-distance runner and neurologist. In 1954, he became the first man to run a mile in under 4 minutes.

ban·nis·ter ▸*n.* variant spelling of BANISTER.

ban·nock /ˈbanək/ ▸*n.* a round, flat loaf, typically unleavened, associated with Scotland and northern England. ▷Old English *bannuc*, of Celtic origin; related to Welsh *ban*, Breton *bannac'h*, *banne*, and Cornish *banna* 'a drop.'

Ban·nock·burn, Battle of /ˈbanəkˌbərn/ a battle that took place near Stirling in central Scotland in 1314, in which the English army of Edward II, advancing to break the siege of Stirling Castle, was defeated by the Scots under Robert the Bruce.

banns /banz/ ▸*plural n.* a notice read out on three successive Sundays in a parish church, announcing an intended marriage and giving the opportunity for objections. ▷Middle English: plural of BAN¹.

ban·quet /ˈbaNGkwit/ ▸*n.* an elaborate and formal evening meal for many people, often followed by speeches: *the Austrian emperor's lavish banquets* [as *adj.*] *a banquet table.* ■ an elaborate and extensive meal; a feast: *a ten-course Chinese banquet.*
▸*v.* (**-quet·ed, -quet·ing**) [*trans.*] entertain with a banquet: *there are halls for banqueting up to 3,000 people* | [as *adj.*] (**banqueting**) *a banqueting hall.* ▷late 15th cent.: from French, diminutive of *banc* 'bench' (see BANK¹). —**ban·quet·er** *n.*

ban·quette /baNGˈket/ ▸*n.* **1** an upholstered bench along a wall, esp. in a restaurant or bar. **2** a raised step behind a rampart. ▷early 17th cent. (sense 2): from French, from Italian *banchetta*, diminutive of *banca* 'bench' (see BANK²). Sense 1 dates from the mid 19th cent.

ban·shee /ˈbanSHē/ ▸*n.* (in Irish legend) a female spirit whose wailing warns of an impending death in a house: *the little girl dropped her ice cream and began to howl like a banshee* | [as *adj.*] *a horrible banshee wail.* ▷late 17th cent.: from Irish *bean sídhe*, from Old Irish *ben síde* 'woman of the fairies.'

ban·tam /ˈbantəm/ ▸*n.* **1** a chicken of a small breed, of which the cock is noted for its aggressiveness: *figurative what a wiry bantam he is!* **2** short for BANTAMWEIGHT. ▷mid 18th cent.: apparently named after the province of *Bantam* in Java, although the fowl is not native there.

ban·tam·weight /ˈbantəmˌwāt/ ▸*n.* a weight in boxing and other sports intermediate between flyweight and featherweight. In boxing it ranges from 112 to 118 pounds (51 to 54 kg). ■ a boxer or other competitor of this weight.

ban·teng /ˈbanteNG/ ▸*n.* a Southeast Asian forest ox that resembles the domestic cow. It has been domesticated in Bali. • *Bos javanicus*, family Bovidae. ▷early 19th cent.: from Malay.

ban·ter /ˈbantər/ ▸*n.* the playful and friendly exchange of teasing remarks: *there was much singing and good-natured banter.*
▸*v.* [*intrans.*] talk or exchange remarks in a good-humored teasing way: *the men* ***bantered with*** *the waitresses* | [as *adj.*] (**bantering**) *a bantering tone.* ▷late 17th cent.: of unknown origin.

Ban·ting /ˈbantiNG/, Sir Frederick Grant (1891–1941), Canadian physiologist and surgeon. With the assistance of C. H. Best, Banting discovered insulin 1921–22, using it to treat diabetes. Nobel Prize for Physiology or Medicine (1923, shared with J. J. R. Macleod).

bant·ling /ˈbantliNG/ ▸*n. archaic poetic/literary* a young child; a brat.

Ban·tu /ˈbantoo͞/ ▸*n.* (*pl.* same or **-tus**) **1** a member of an extensive group of native peoples of central and southern Africa. **2** the group of languages spoken by these peoples.

Bantu languages belong to the Niger-Congo language family, and there are more than 400 of them (with over 100 million speakers), of which Swahili, Xhosa, and Zulu are the most important.

▸*adj.* of or relating to these peoples or their languages. ▷plural (in certain Bantu languages) of *-ntu* 'person.'

ban·yan /ˈbanyən/ (also **ban·ian**) ▸*n.* (also **banyan tree**) an Indian fig tree whose branches produce aerial roots that later become accessory trunks. A mature tree may cover several acres in this manner. • *Ficus benghalensis*, family Moraceae. ▷late 16th cent.: from Portuguese, from Gujarati *vāṇiyo* 'man of the trading caste,' from Sanskrit. Originally denoting a Hindu trader or merchant, the term was applied by Europeans in the mid 17th cent. to a particular tree under which such traders had built a pagoda.

ban·zai /ˈbanˈzī/ ▸*exclam.* **1** a Japanese battle cry. [early 20th cent.] **2** a form of greeting used to the Japanese emperor. [late 19th cent.]
▸*adj.* (esp. of Japanese troops) attacking fiercely and recklessly: *a banzai charge.* ▷Japanese, literally 'ten thousand years (of life to you).'

ba·o·bab /ˈbāōˌbab; ˈbā-ō-/ ▸*n.* a short tree with an enormously thick trunk and large edible fruit. It can live to a great age. • Genus *Adansonia*, family Bombacaceae: several species, in particular the African *A. digitata* and the Australian *A. gregorii.* ▷mid 17th cent.: probably from an African language; first recorded in Latin (1592), in a treatise on the plants of Egypt by Prosper Alpinus, Italian botanist.

Bao·tou /ˈbouˈtō/ an industrial city in Inner Mongolia, northern China, on the Yellow River; pop. 1,180,000.

bap·tism /ˈbapˌtizəm/ ▸*n.* (in the Christian Church) the religious rite of sprinkling water onto a person's forehead or of immersion in water, symbolizing purification or regeneration and admission to the Christian Church. In many denominations, baptism is performed on young children and is accompanied by name-giving. ■ a ceremony or occasion at which this takes place. ■ a religious experience likened to this: *baptism in the Holy Spirit.* ■ *figurative* a person's initiation into a particular activity or role, typically one perceived as difficult: *this event constituted his baptism as a politician.* ▷Middle English: from Old French *baptesme*, via ecclesiastical Latin from ecclesiastical Greek *baptismos* 'ceremonial washing,' from *baptizein* 'immerse, baptize.' —**bap·tis·mal** /bapˈtizməl/ *adj.*
▸*PHRASE* □ **baptism of fire** a difficult or painful new undertaking or experience. [from the original sense of 'a soldier's first battle.']

bap·tis·mal name ▸*n.* a personal name given at baptism.

bap·tist /ˈbaptist/ ▸*n.* **1** (**Baptist**) a member of a Protestant Christian denomination advocating baptism only of adult believers by total immersion. Baptists form one of the largest Protestant bodies and are found throughout the world and esp. in the U.S. **2** a person who baptizes someone. ▷Middle English (sense 2): from Old French *baptiste*, via ecclesiastical Latin from ecclesiastical Greek *baptistēs*, from *baptizein* 'immerse, baptize.'

bap·tis·tery /ˈbaptəstrē/ (also **bap·tis·try**) ▸*n.* (*pl.* **-ter·ies**) the part of a church used for baptism. ■ *historical* a building next to a church, used for baptism. ■ (in a Baptist chapel) a sunken receptacle used for baptism by total immersion. ▷Middle English: from Old French *baptistere*, via ecclesiastical Latin from ecclesiastical Greek *baptistērion*, from *baptizein* 'immerse, baptize.'

bap·tize /ˈbapˌtīz; bapˈtīz/ ▸*v.* [*trans.*] administer baptism to (someone); christen: *he was baptized Joshua.* ■ admit (someone) into a specified church by baptism: *Mark had been baptized a Catholic.* ■ give a name or nickname to: *he baptized the science of narrative "narratology."* ▷Middle English: via Old French from ecclesiastical Latin *baptizare*, from Greek *baptizein* 'immerse, baptize.'

bar¹ /bär/ ▸*n.* **1** a long rod or rigid piece of wood, metal, or similar material, typically used as an obstruction, fastening, or weapon. ■ an amount of food or another substance formed into a regular narrow block: ***a bar of*** *chocolate* | *gold bars.* ■ a band of color or light, esp. on a flat surface: *bars of sunlight shafting through the broken windows.* ■ see CROSSBAR. ■ a sandbank or shoal at the mouth of a harbor, bay, or estuary. ■ *Brit.* a rail marking the end of each chamber in the Houses of Parliament. ■ *Heraldry* a charge in the form of a narrow horizontal stripe across the shield. **2** a counter across which alcoholic drinks or refreshments are served. ■ a room in a restaurant or hotel in which alcohol is served. ■ an establishment where alcohol and sometimes other refreshments are served. ■ [usu. with *adj.*] a small store or booth serving refreshments or providing a service: *a dairy bar.* **3** a barrier or restriction to an action or advance: *political differences are not necessarily* ***a bar to*** *a good relationship.* **4** *Music* any of the sections, typically of equal time value, into which a musical composition is divided, shown on a score by vertical lines across the staff. **5** (**the bar**) a partition in a courtroom, now usually notional, beyond which most persons may not pass and at which an accused person stands: *the prisoner* ***at the bar.*** ■ a similar partition in a legislative assembly: *he had to appear at the Bar of the House for a reprimand by the Speaker.* ■ a plea arresting an action or claim in a law case. ■ a particular court of law. ■ any kind of tribunal: *the bar of public opinion.* **6** (**the Bar**) the legal profession. ■ lawyers collectively. ■ *Brit.* barristers collectively.
▸*v.* (**barred, bar·ring**) [*trans.*] **1** fasten (something, esp. a door or window) with a bar or bars: *she bolts and bars the door.* ■ (usu. **be barred**) prevent or forbid the entrance or movement of: *boulders barred her passage* | *she was* ***barred from*** *a men-only dinner.* ■ prohibit (someone) from doing something: *journalists had been* ***barred from*** *covering the elections.* ■ forbid (an activity) to someone: *the job she loved had been* ***barred to*** *her.* ■ exclude (something) from consideration: *nothing is barred in the crime novel.* ■ *Law* prevent or delay (an action) by objection. **2** (usu. **be barred**) mark (something) with bars or stripes: *his face was barred with light.*
▸*prep. chiefly Brit.* except for; apart from: *everyone, bar a few ascetics, thinks it desirable.* ▷Middle English: from Old French *barre* (noun), *barrer* (verb), of unknown origin. —**barred** /bärd/ *adj. barred windows* | *birds with barred breasts* | [in *combination*] *a five-barred gate.*
▸*PHRASES* □ **bar none** with no exceptions: *the greatest living American poet bar none.* □ **behind bars** in prison.

bar² ▸*n.* a unit of pressure equivalent to 100,000 newtons per square meter or approximately one atmosphere. ▷early 20th cent.: from Greek *baros* 'weight.'

Bar. ▸*abbr. Bible* Baruch.

Ba·ra·ta·ria Bay /ˌbärəˈtarēə; -ˈte(ə)rēə/ an inlet of the Gulf of Mexico in southeastern Louisiana, south of New Orleans, associated with Jean Lafitte and other early 19th-century outlaws.

bar·a·the·a /ˌbarəˈTHēə/ ▸*n.* a fine woolen cloth, sometimes mixed with silk or cotton, used chiefly for coats and suits. ▷mid 19th cent.: of unknown origin.

barb¹ /bärb/ ▸*n.* **1** a sharp projection near the end of an arrow, fishhook, or similar item, angled away from the main point so as to make extraction difficult. ■ a cluster of spikes on barbed wire. ■ *figurative* a deliberately hurtful remark: *his barb hurt more than she cared to admit.* ■ a beardlike filament at the mouth of some fish, such as barbel and catfish. ■ one of the fine hairlike filaments growing from the shaft of a feather, forming the vane. **2** a freshwater fish that typically has barbels around the mouth, popular in aquariums. • *Barbus* and other genera, family Cyprinidae: numerous species, including the **tiger barb** (*B. pentazona*) and the **rosy barb** (*B. conchonius*). ▷Middle English: from Old

French *barbe*, from Latin *barba* 'beard.' —**barb·less** *adj.*

barb[2] ▸*n.* a small horse of a hardy breed originally from North Africa. ▷mid 17th cent.: from French *barbe*, from Italian *barbero* 'of Barbary.'

Bar·ba·dos /bär'bādəs; -ˌdōs; -ˌdōz/ a country in the eastern West Indies, one of the Windward Islands; pop. 278,200; capital, Bridgetown; official language, English. —**Bar·ba·di·an** /bär'bādēən/ *adj.* & *n.*

Barbados was a British colony until it gained independence within the Commonwealth of Nations in 1966. Its economy is based on tourism, sugar, and light manufacturing industries.

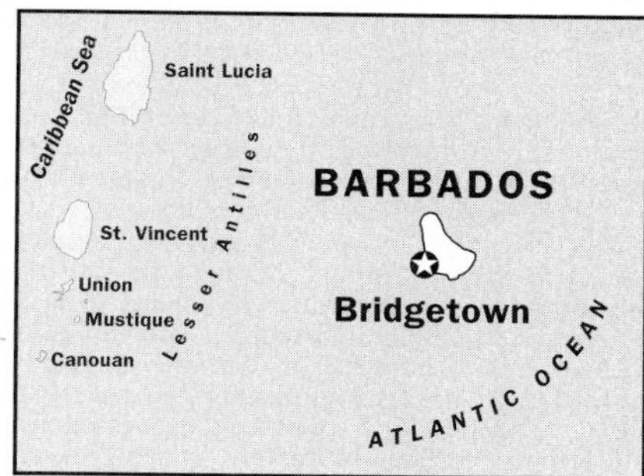

bar·bar·i·an /bär'be(ə)rēən/ ▸*n.* (in ancient times) a member of a community or tribe not belonging to one of the great civilizations (Greek, Roman, Christian). ■ an uncultured or brutish person.
▸*adj.* of or relating to ancient barbarians: *barbarian invasions* | *barbarian peoples.* ■ uncultured; brutish. ▷Middle English (as an adjective used depreciatively to denote a person with different speech and customs): from Old French *barbarien*, from *barbare*, or from Latin *barbarus* (see **BARBAROUS**).

bar·bar·ic /bär'barik/ ▸*adj.* **1** savagely cruel; exceedingly brutal: *he had carried out barbaric acts in the name of war.* **2** primitive; unsophisticated: *the barbaric splendor he found in civilizations since destroyed.* ■ uncivilized and uncultured. ▷late Middle English (as a noun in the sense 'a barbarian'): from Old French *barbarique*, or via Latin from Greek *barbarikos*, from *barbaros* 'foreign' (esp. with reference to speech). —**bar·bar·i·cal·ly** *adv.*

bar·ba·rism /'bärbəˌrizəm/ ▸*n.* **1** absence of culture and civilization: *the collapse of civilization and the return to barbarism.* ■ a word or expression that is badly formed according to traditional philological rules, for example a word formed from elements of different languages, such as *breathalyzer* (English and Greek) or *television* (Greek and Latin). **2** extreme cruelty or brutality: *she called the execution an act of barbarism* | *barbarisms from the country's past.* ▷late Middle English: from Old French *barbarisme*, via Latin from Greek *barbarismos*, from *barbarizein* 'speak like a foreigner,' from *barbaros* 'foreign.'

bar·bar·i·ty /bär'baritē/ ▸*n.* (*pl.* **-ties**) **1** extreme cruelty or brutality: *the barbarity displayed by the terrorists* | *the Nazi barbarities of the last war.* **2** absence of culture and civilization: *beyond the Empire lay barbarity.*

bar·ba·rize /'bärbəˌrīz/ ▸*v.* [*trans.*] [usu. as *adj.*] (**barbarizing**) cause to become savage or uncultured: *the barbarizing effect of four decades of rock 'n' roll.* ▷late Middle English (in the sense 'speak using barbarisms'): from late Latin *barbarizare*, from Greek *barbarizein* 'speak like a foreigner.' —**bar·ba·ri·za·tion** /ˌbärbərə'zāshən/ *n.*

Bar·ba·ros·sa[1] /ˌbärbə'räsə; -'rōsə/ see **FREDERICK I**.

Bar·ba·ros·sa[2], (*c.*1483–1546), Barbary pirate; born *Khair ad-Din.* He was notorious for his successes against Christian vessels in the eastern Mediterranean Sea.

bar·ba·rous /'bärbərəs/ ▸*adj.* **1** savagely cruel; exceedingly brutal: *many early child-rearing practices were barbarous by modern standards.* **2** primitive; uncivilized: *a remote and barbarous country.* ■ (esp. of language) coarse and unrefined. ▷late Middle English (sense 2): via Latin from Greek *barbaros* 'foreign' + **-OUS**. —**bar·ba·rous·ly** *adv.*

Bar·ba·ry /'bärbərē/ (also **Barbary States**) a former name for the Saracen countries of north and northwestern Africa, together with Moorish Spain. The area was noted between the 16th and 18th centuries as a haunt of pirates. Compare with **MAGHRIB**. ▷based on Arabic *barbar* (see **BERBER**).

Bar·ba·ry ape ▸*n.* a tailless macaque monkey that is native to northwestern Africa and also found on the Rock of Gibraltar. • *Macaca sylvana*, family Cercopithecidae.

Bar·ba·ry Coast a former name for the Mediterranean coast of North Africa from Morocco to Egypt.

Bar·ba·ry sheep ▸*n.* a short-coated sheep with a long neck ruff, found in the high deserts of northern Africa. Also called **AOUDAD**. • *Ammotragus lervia*, family Bovidae.

bar·be·cue /'bärbiˌkyoo/ ▸*n.* a meal or gathering at which meat, fish, or other food is cooked out of doors on a rack over an open fire or on a portable grill. ■ a portable grill used for the preparation of food at a barbecue, or a brick fireplace containing a grill. ■ food cooked in such a way.
▸*v.* (**-cued, -cu·ing**) [*trans.*] cook (meat, fish, or other food) on a barbecue: *fish barbecued with herbs* | [as *adj.*] (**barbecued**) *barbecued chicken.* ▷mid 17th cent.: from Spanish *barbacoa*, perhaps from Arawak *barbacoa* 'wooden frame on posts.' The original sense was 'wooden framework for sleeping on, or for storing meat or fish to be dried.'

bar·be·cue sauce ▸*n.* a highly seasoned sauce containing vinegar, spices, and usually chilies.

barbed /bärbd/ ▸*adj.* having a barb or barbs: *barbed arrows.* ■ *figurative* (of a remark or joke) deliberately hurtful: *a fair degree of barbed wit.*

barbed wire ▸*n.* wire with clusters of short, sharp spikes set at intervals along it, used to make fences or in warfare as an obstruction.

barbed wire

bar·bel /'bärbəl/ ▸*n.* **1** a fleshy filament growing from the mouth or snout of a fish. **2** a large European freshwater fish of the minnow family that has such filaments hanging from its mouth. It lives in running water. • *Barbus barbus*, family Cyprinidae. **3** [with *adj.*] a marine or freshwater African fish with barbels around the mouth. • Species in several families, including *Tachysurus feliceps* (family Ariidae), of southern African coasts and estuaries, whose toxin-coated spines can inflict a dangerous wound. ▷late Middle English (sense 2): via Old French from late Latin *barbellus*, diminutive of *barbus* 'barbel,' from *barba* 'beard.'

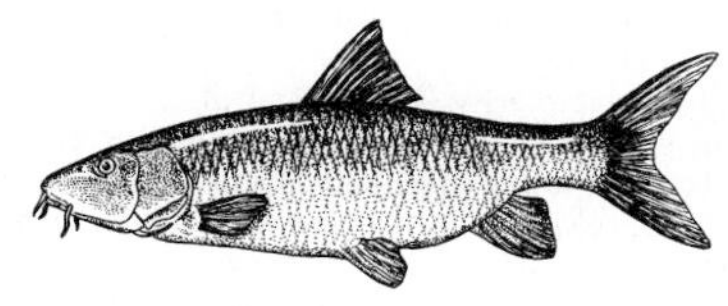

barbel 2

bar·bell /'bärˌbel/ ▸*n.* a long metal bar to which disks of varying weights are attached at each end, used for weightlifting. ▷late 19th cent.: from **BAR**[1] + **BELL**[1].

bar·be·que /'bärbiˌkyoo/ ▸*n.* & *v.* a common misspelling of barbecue.

USAGE This common form arises understandably from a confused conflation of the proper spelling *barbecue*, the abbreviation *Bar-B-Q*, and phonetic spelling. Its frequency does not quite justify it: in no other English word does *que* attain the status of a stand-alone, terminal syllable.

Bar·ber /'bärbər/, Samuel (1910–81), U.S. composer. He developed a style based on romanticism allied to classical forms. Notable works: *Adagio for Strings* (1936) and *Vanessa* (opera, 1958).

bar·ber /'bärbər/ ▸*n.* a person who cuts hair, esp. men's, and shaves or trims beards as an occupation.
▸*v.* [*trans.*] cut or trim (a man's hair): *his hair was neatly barbered.* ▷Middle English: via Anglo-Norman French from Old French *barbe* (see **BARB**[1]).

bar·ber·ry /'bärˌberē; -bərē/ ▸*n.* (*pl.* **-ries**) a thorny shrub that bears yellow flowers and red or blue-black berries. • Genus *Berberis*, family Berberidaceae: many species, including the **American barberry** (*B. canadensis*), with widely toothed leaves, and the **European barberry** (*B. vulgaris*), with more closely toothed leaves. ▷late Middle English: from Old French *berberis*. The change in the ending was due to association with **BERRY**.

bar·ber·shop /'bärbərˌshäp/ ▸*n.* a shop where a barber works. ■ [often as *adj.*] a popular style of close harmony singing, typically for four male voices: *a barbershop quartet.* [from the custom in the 16th and 17th centuries of passing time in a barbershop by harmonizing to a lute or guitar provided to entertain customers waiting their turn.]

bar·ber's itch ▸*n.* ringworm of the face or neck communicated by unsterilized shaving apparatus.

bar·ber's pole (also **bar·ber pole**) ▸*n.* a pole painted with spiraling red and white stripes and hung outside barbershops as a business sign.

Bar·ber·ton /'bärbərtən/ a city in northeastern Ohio, southwest of Akron; pop. 27,623.

bar·bet /'bärbit/ ▸*n.* a large-headed, brightly colored, fruit-eating bird that has a stout bill with tufts of bristles at the base. Barbets are found on all continents, esp. in the tropics. • Family Capitonidae: numerous genera and species. ▷late 16th cent. (denoting a poodle until the early 19th cent.): from French, from *barbe* 'beard' (see **BARB**[1]). The current sense dates from the early 19th cent.

bar·bette /bär'bet/ ▸*n.* a fixed armored housing at the base of a gun turret on a warship or armored vehicle. ■ *historical* a platform on which a gun is placed to fire over a parapet. ▷late 18th cent.: from French, diminutive of *barbe* 'beard' (see **BARB**[1]).

bar·bi·can /'bärbikən/ ▸*n.* the outer defense of a city or castle, esp. a double tower above a gate or drawbridge. ▷Middle English: from Old French *barbacane*; probably based on Arabic.

bar·bi·cel /'bärbəˌsel/ ▸*n.* any of the minute hooked filaments that interlock the barbules of a bird's feathers.

bar·bie /'bärbē/ ▸*n.* (*pl.* **-bies**) *informal, chiefly Austral.* a barbecue. ▷1970s: abbreviation.

Bar·bie doll /'bärbē/ ▸*n. trademark* a doll representing a conventionally attractive young woman. ■ *informal* a woman who is attractive in a glossily artificial way and is typically considered to be stupid and characterless. ▷1950s: *Barbie*, diminutive of the given name *Barbara.*

bar·bi·tal /'bärbiˌtäl; -ˌtôl/ ▸*n.* a long-acting sedative and sleep-inducing drug of the barbiturate type. • Alternative name: **diethylbarbituric acid**; chem. formula: $C_6H_{12}O_3N_2$. ▷early 20th cent.: from **BARBITURIC ACID**, on the pattern of *veronal* (an alternative name).

bar·bi·tone /'bärbiˌtōn/ ▸*n.* British term for **BARBITAL**. ▷early 20th cent.: from **BARBITURIC ACID** + **-ONE**.

bar·bi·tu·rate /bär'bichərit; -əˌrāt/ ▸*n.* any of a class of sedative and sleep-inducing drugs derived from barbituric acid. ■ *Chemistry* a salt or ester of barbituric acid.

bar·bi·tu·ric ac·id /ˌbärbi'choorik/ ▸*n.* *Chemistry* a synthetic organic acid from which the barbiturates are derived. • A cyclic drivative of urea and malonic acid; chem. formula: $C_4H_4O_3N_2$. ▷mid 19th cent.: from French *barbiturique*, from German *Barbitursäure*, from the given name *Barbara* + *Säure* 'acid.'

Bar·bi·zon School /'bärbəˌzän/ a mid-19th-century school of French landscape painters who reacted against classical conventions and based their art on direct study of nature. Led by Théodore Rousseau, the group included Charles Daubigny and Jean-François Millet. ▷named after *Barbizon*, a small village in the forest of Fontainebleau, near Paris, where Rousseau and others worked.

Bar·bour /'bärbər/, Philip Pendleton (1783–1841), U.S. Supreme Court associate justice 1836–41. He also served in Congress as a representative from Virginia 1814–25; 1827–30.

B

Bar·bu·da /bär'bo͞odə/ see **Antigua and Barbuda.** —**Bar·bu·dan** /bär'bo͞odn/ *adj.* & *n.*

bar·bule /'bär,byo͞ol/ ▸*n.* a minute filament projecting from the barb of a feather. ▷mid 19th cent.: from Latin *barbula*, diminutive of *barba* 'beard.'

barb·wire /'bärb'wīr/ ▸*n.* barbed wire.

Bar·ca·Loung·er /'bärkə,lounjər/ ▸*n. trademark* a type of deeply padded reclining chair. ▷1970s: from the name of Edward J. *Barcolo*, who acquired the original license to manufacture the chairs, and *lounger*.

bar·ca·role /'bärkə,rōl/ (also **bar·ca·rolle**) ▸*n.* a song traditionally sung by Venetian gondoliers. ■ a musical composition in the style of such a song. ▷late 18th cent.: from French *barcarolle*, from Venetian Italian *barcarola* 'boatman's song,' from *barca* 'boat.'

Bar·ce·lo·na /,bärsə'lōnə/ a city on the coast of northeastern Spain, capital of Catalonia; pop. 1,653,175.

Bar·ce·lo·na chair ▸*n. trademark* an armless chair with a curved stainless steel frame and padded leather cushions.

bar·chan /bär'kän/ ▸*n.* a crescent-shaped shifting sand dune, concave on the leeward side. ▷late 19th cent.: from Turkic *barkhan*.

bar chart ▸*n.* another term for **bar graph.**

Bar-Coch·ba /'bär 'kôkнbə/ Jewish rebel leader; known as **Simeon** in Jewish sources. He led the rebellion in AD 132 against the Romans and was accepted by some of his Jewish contemporaries as the Messiah.

bar code ▸*n.* a machine-readable code in the form of numbers and a pattern of parallel lines of varying widths, printed on and identifying a product. Also called **Universal Product Code.**

bard[1] /bärd/ ▸*n. archaic* or *poetic/literary* a poet, traditionally one reciting epics and associated with a particular oral tradition. ■ (**the Bard** or **the Bard of Avon**) Shakespeare. ▷Middle English: from Scottish Gaelic *bàrd*, Irish *bard*, Welsh *bardd*, of Celtic origin. In Scotland in the 16th cent. it was a derogatory term for an itinerant musician, but was later romanticized by Sir Walter Scott. —**bard·ic** /-dik/ *adj.*

bard[2] ▸*n.* a slice of bacon placed on meat or game before roasting.
▸*v.* [*trans.*] cover (meat or game) with slices of bacon. ▷early 18th cent.: from French *barde*, a transferred sense of *barde* 'armor for the breast and flanks of a warhorse,' based on Arabic *bard̲a'a* 'saddlecloth, padded saddle.'

Bar·deen /bär'dēn/, John (1908–91), U.S. physicist. With William Shockley and Walter Brattain he developed a point-contact transistor. He also worked on the theory of superconductivity. Nobel Prize for Physics in 1956, shared with Shockley and Brattain, and in 1972, shared with Leon N. Cooper (1930–) and John R. Schreiffer (1931–).

bar·do /'bär,dō/ ▸*n.* (in Tibetan Buddhism) a state of existence between death and rebirth, varying in length according to a person's conduct in life and manner of, or age at, death. ■ an indeterminate, transitional state: *wandering adrift in a bardo of intense negativity, blame, disappointment, criticism, and denial.* ▷Tibetan *bár-do*, from *bar* 'interval' + *do* 'two.'

bard·ol·a·try /bär'dälətrē/ ▸*n. humorous* excessive admiration of Shakespeare. —**bard·ol·a·ter** /-'dälitər/ (or **bard·o·la·tor**) *n.*

Bar·do·li·no /,bärdl'ēnō/ ▸*n.* a red wine from the Veneto region of Italy. ▷Italian.

Bar·dot /bär'dō/, Brigitte (1934–), French actress; born *Camille Javal*. The movie *And God Created Woman* (1956) established her reputation as an international sex symbol.

bare /be(ə)r/ ▸*adj.* **1** (of a person or part of the body) not clothed or covered: *he was bare from the waist up* | *she padded in bare feet toward the door.* See note at **naked.** ■ without the appropriate, usual, or natural covering: *a clump of bare aspen trees* | *bare floorboards.* ■ without the appropriate or usual contents: *a bare cell with just a mattress.* ■ unconcealed; without disguise: *an ordeal that would* **lay bare** *a troubled family background.* **2** without addition; basic and simple: *he outlined the bare essentials of the story* | *a strange, bare production of* Twelfth Night. ■ [*attrib.*] only just sufficient: *a bare majority.* ■ [*attrib.*] surprisingly small in number or amount: *all you need to get started with this program is a bare 10K bytes of memory.*
▸*v.* [*trans.*] uncover (a part of the body or other thing) and expose it to view: *he bared his chest to show his scar.* ▷Old English *bær* (noun), *barian* (verb), of Germanic origin; related to Dutch *baar*. —**bare·ness** *n.*
▸*PHRASES* □ **bare all** take off all of one's clothes and display oneself to others: *Lysette bared all for* Playboy *in 1988.* □ **the bare bones** the basic facts about something, without any detail: *the bare bones of the plot.* □ **bare of** without: *the interior, bare of plaster, leaked a smell of old timbers.* □ **bare one's soul** reveal one's innermost secrets and feelings to someone. □ **bare one's teeth** show one's teeth, typically when angry. □ **with one's bare hands** without using tools or weapons.

bare·back /'be(ə)r,bak/ ▸*adj.* & *adv.* on an unsaddled horse or other animal: [as *adj.*] *a bareback circus rider* | [as *adv.*] *riding bareback.*

bare·back·ing /'be(ə)r,bakiNG/ ▸*n. vulgar slang* anal intercourse without a condom.

bare·boat /'be(ə)r,bōt/ ▸*adj.* [*attrib.*] relating to or denoting a boat or ship hired without a crew: *bareboat charters.* —**bare·boat·ing** *n.*

bare·faced /'be(ə)r,fāst/ ▸*adj.* **1** [*attrib.*] shameless; undisguised: *a barefaced lie.* **2** having an uncovered face, so as to be exposed or vulnerable to something: *his years of working barefaced, breathing down dust.*

bare·foot /'be(ə)r,fo͝ot/ (also **bare·foot·ed** /-,fo͝otid/) ▸*adj.* & *adv.* wearing nothing on the feet: [as *adv.*] *I won't walk barefoot.*

bare·foot doc·tor ▸*n.* a paramedical worker with basic medical training working in a rural district in China.

ba·rège /bə'rezн/ (also **ba·rege**) ▸*n.* a light, silky dress fabric resembling gauze, typically made from wool. ▷French, named after the village of *Barèges* in southwestern France, where it was originally made.

bare·hand /'be(ə)r,hand/ ▸*v.* (in baseball) field with one's bare hand.

bare·hand·ed /'be(ə)r'handid/ ▸*adj.* & *adv.* with nothing in or covering one's hands: *his running, barehanded catch in foul territory.* ■ carrying no weapons.

bare·head·ed /'be(ə)r,hedid/ ▸*adj.* & *adv.* without a covering for one's head: [as *adv.*] *he walked bareheaded in the teeming rain.*

Ba·reil·ly /bə'rālē/ an industrial city in northern India, in Uttar Pradesh; pop. 583,000.

bare-knuck·le (also **bare-knuck·led** or **bare-knuck·les**) ▸*adj.* [*attrib.*] (of a boxer or boxing match) without gloves. ■ *informal* with no scruples or reservations: *an apostle of bare-knuckled capitalism.*

bare·leg·ged /'be(ə)r,legid/ ▸*adj.* & *adv.* without a covering on the legs: *barelegged models strutted down the runway.*

bare·ly /'be(ə)rlē/ ▸*adv.* **1** only just; almost not: *she nodded, barely able to speak* | [as *submodifier*] *a barely perceptible pause.* ■ only a short time before: *they had barely sat down when forty policemen swarmed in.* **2** in a simple and sparse way: *their barely furnished house.* **3** *archaic* openly; explicitly.

Bar·en·boim /'barən,boim/, Daniel (1942–), Israeli pianist and conductor. He was musical director of the Orchestre de Paris 1975–88 and of the Chicago Symphony Orchestra from 1991.

Bar·ents /'barənts; 'bär-/, Willem (died 1597), Dutch explorer. The leader of several expeditions in search of the Northeast Passage to Asia, Barents discovered Spitsbergen and reached Novaya Zemlya.

Bar·ents Sea a part of the Arctic Ocean north of Norway and Russia, bounded on the west by Svalbard, on the north by Franz Josef Land, and on the east by Novaya Zemlya.

barf /bärf/ *informal* ▸*v.* [*intrans.*] vomit.
▸*n.* vomited food. ▷1960s: of unknown origin.

barf bag ▸*n.* a bag provided for airplane passengers for use in case of vomiting associated with motion sickness.

bar·fly /'bär,flī/ ▸*n.* (*pl.* **-flies**) *informal* a person who spends much time drinking in bars.

bar·gain /'bärgən/ ▸*n.* **1** an agreement between two or more parties as to what each party will do for the other: *the extraconstitutional bargain between the northern elite and the southern planters.* **2** a thing bought or offered for sale more cheaply than is usual or expected: *the secondhand table was a real bargain* | [as *adj.*] *household and electrical goods at bargain prices.*
▸*v.* [*intrans.*] negotiate the terms and conditions of a transaction: *he* **bargained with** *the city council to rent the stadium* | [as *n.*] (**bargaining**) *many statutes are passed by political bargaining.* ■ [*trans.*] (**bargain something away**) part with something after negotiation but get little or nothing in return: *his determination not to bargain away any of the province's existing economic powers.* ■ (**bargain for/on**) be prepared for; expect: *I got more information than I'd bargained for* | *he didn't bargain on this storm.* ▷Middle English: from Old French *bargaine* (noun), *bargaignier* (verb); probably of Germanic origin and related to German *borgen* 'borrow.' —**bar·gain·er** *n.*
▸*PHRASES* □ **drive a hard bargain** be uncompromising in making a deal. □ **into (in) the bargain** in addition to what was expected; moreover: *an upstate yokel and a raving paranoiac into the bargain.* □ **keep one's side of the bargain** carry out the promises one has made as part of an agreement. □ **strike a bargain** make a bargain; agree to a deal.

bar·gain base·ment ▸*n.* a part of a store where goods are sold cheaply, typically because they are old or imperfect: [as *adj.*] *bargain-basement prices* | *figurative a mixture of styles from pop culture's bargain basement.*

bar·gain·ing chip ▸*n.* a potential concession or other factor that can be used to advantage in negotiations.

barge /bärj/ ▸*n.* a flat-bottomed boat for carrying freight, typically on canals and rivers, either under its own power or towed by another. ■ a long ornamental boat used for pleasure or ceremony. ■ a boat used by the chief officers of a warship.
▸*v.* **1** [*intrans.*] move forcefully or roughly: *we can't just* **barge into** *a private garden.* ■ (**barge in**) intrude or interrupt rudely or awkwardly: *sorry to* **barge in on** *your cozy evening.* ■ (chiefly in a sporting context) collide with: *displays of dissent, such as deliberately* **barging into** *the umpire.* **2** [*trans.*] convey (freight) by barge. ▷Middle English (denoting a small seagoing vessel): from Old French, perhaps ultimately from Greek *baris* 'Egyptian boat.'

barge·board /'bärj,bôrd/ ▸*n.* a board, typically ornamental, fixed to the gable end of a roof to hide the ends of the roof timbers. ▷mid 19th cent.: from mid 16th-cent. *barge-* (used in architectural terms relating to the gable of a building).

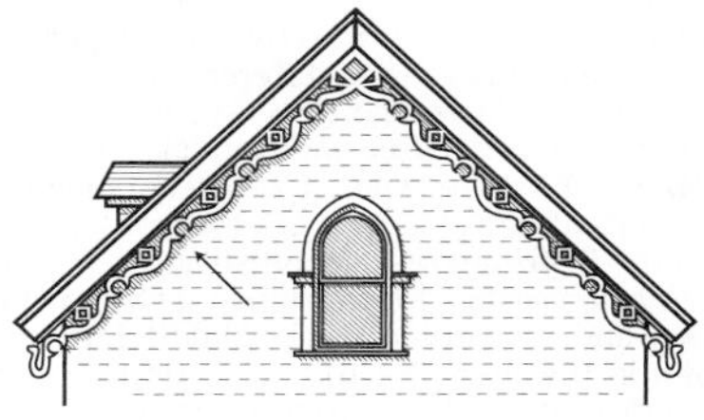

bargeboard

barg·ee /bär'jē/ ▸*n. chiefly Brit.* a bargeman.

Bar·gel·lo /bär'jelō; -'zнelō/ (also **bar·gel·lo**) ▸*n.* a kind of embroidery, typically worked on upholstery fabrics, in stitch patterns suggestive of flames. Also called **flame stitch.** ▷1940s: named after *Bargello* Palace, in Florence, Italy, which contains upholstered chairs with such embroidery.

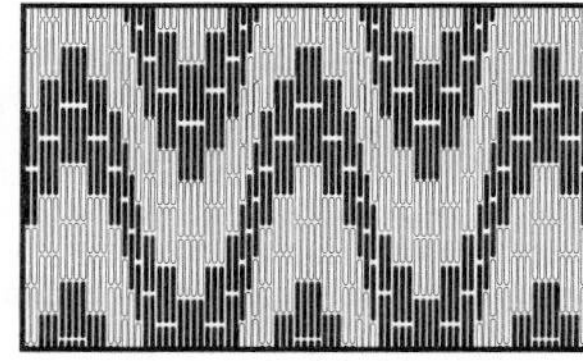

Bargello

barge·man /'bärjmən/ ▸*n.* (*pl.* **-men**) a person who has charge of, or works on, a barge.

bar graph (also **bar chart**) ▸*n.* a diagram in which the numerical values of variables are represented by the height or length of lines or rectangles of equal width.

Bar Har·bor /bär/ a resort town in southern central Maine, on Mount Desert Island; pop. 4,443.

bar·hop /'bär,häp/ ▸*v.* [*intrans.*] drink at a number of bars during a single day or evening.

Ba·ri /'bärē/ an industrial seaport on the Adriatic coast of southeastern Italy; pop. 353,030.

bar·i·at·rics /,barē'atriks/ ▸*n.* the branch of medicine that deals with the study and treatment of obesity. —**bar·i·at·ric** *adj.*

bar·i·at·ric sur·ger·y ▸*n.* surgical removal of parts of the stomach and small intestines to induce weight loss.

ba·ril·la /bə'rilə; -'rēə/ ▸*n.* an impure alkali formerly made from the ashes of burned plants, esp. saltworts. ▷early 17th cent.: from Spanish *barrilla*, diminutive of *barra* 'bar.'

Ba·ri·sal /'barə,sôl/ a river port in southern Bangladesh, on the Ganges delta; pop. 180,010.

ba·ri·sta /bə'rēstə/ ▸n. a person who serves in a coffee bar. ▷1980s: Italian, 'barman.'

bar·ite /'be(ə)rīt; 'bar-/ ▸n. a mineral consisting of barium sulfate, typically occurring as colorless prismatic crystals or thin white flakes.

bar·i·tone /'bari,tōn/ ▸n. **1** an adult male singing voice between tenor and bass: *he sang in a rich baritone.* ■ a singer with such a voice. ■ a part written for such a voice. **2** an instrument that is second lowest in pitch in its family. ■ a large, valved brass instrument in coiled oval form, used esp. in military or street bands.
▸adj. second lowest in musical pitch. ▷early 17th cent.: from Italian *baritono*, from Greek *barutonos*, from *barus* 'heavy' + *tonos* (see TONE).

bar·i·um /'be(ə)rēəm; 'bar-/ ▸n. the chemical element of atomic number 56, a soft white reactive metal of the alkaline earth group. (Symbol: **Ba**) ■ a mixture of barium sulfate and water, opaque to X-rays, that is swallowed to permit radiological examination of the stomach or intestines: [as adj.] *a barium meal.*

Barium compounds are used in water purification, the glass industry, and pigments, and as an ingredient of signal flares and fireworks, giving a bright yellowish-green color. Barium oxide is a component of high-temperature superconductors.

▷early 19th cent.: from BARYTA + -IUM.

bar·i·um sul·fate ▸n. an odorless, insoluble white powder used in the making of pigments, paper, textiles, and plastics, and ingested as a contrasting agent in X-raying the digestive tract. • Chem. formula: $BaSO_4$.

bark[1] /bärk/ ▸n. the sharp explosive cry of certain animals, esp. a dog, fox, or seal. ■ a sound resembling this cry, typically one made by someone laughing or coughing: *a short bark of laughter.*
▸v. **1** [intrans.] (of a dog or other animal) emit a bark: *a dog **barked at** her.* ■ (of a person) make a sound, such as a cough or a laugh, resembling a bark: *she barked with laughter.* **2** [trans.] utter (a command or question) abruptly or aggressively: *he began **barking out** his orders* | [with direct speech] *"Nobody is allowed up here," he barked* | [intrans.] *he was **barking at** me to make myself presentable.* ■ [intrans.] call out in order to sell or advertise something: *doormen bark at passersby, promising hot music and cold beer.* ▷Old English *beorc* (noun), *beorcan* (verb), of Germanic origin; possibly related to BREAK.
▸PHRASES □ **someone's bark is worse than their bite** someone is not as ferocious as they appear or sound. □ **be barking up the wrong tree** informal be pursuing a mistaken or misguided line of thought or course of action.

bark[2] ▸n. the tough, protective outer sheath of the trunk, branches, and twigs of a tree or woody shrub. ■ this material used for tanning leather, making dyestuffs, or as a mulch in gardening.
▸v. [trans.] **1** strip the bark from (a tree or piece of wood). ■ scrape the skin off (one's shin) by accidentally hitting it against something hard. **2** technical tan or dye (leather or other materials) using the tannins found in bark. ▷Middle English: from Old Norse *bǫrkr*; perhaps related to BIRCH. —**barked** adj. [in combination] *the red-barked dogwood.*

bark[3] ▸n. (also **barque**) a sailing ship, typically with three masts, in which the foremast and mainmast are square-rigged and the mizzenmast is rigged fore-and-aft. ■ archaic or poetic/literary a ship or boat. ▷late Middle English: variant of BARQUE.

bark bee·tle ▸n. a small wood-boring beetle that tunnels under the bark of trees, which die if heavily infested. • Family Scolytidae: many genera and species, including the **smaller European elm bark beetle** (*Scolytus multistriatus*), which is responsible for the spread of the fungus that causes Dutch elm disease.

bark·cloth /'bärk,klôTH/ ▸n. cloth made from the inner bark of the paper mulberry or similar tree.

bar·keep·er /'bär,kēpər/ (also **bar·keep**) ▸n. a person who owns or serves drinks in a bar.

bark·en·tine /'bärkən,tēn/ (Brit. **bar·quen·tine**) ▸n. a sailing ship similar to a bark but square-rigged only on the foremast. ▷late 17th cent.: from BARK[3], on the pattern of *brigantine.*

bark·er /'bärkər/ ▸n. informal a person who stands in front of a theater, sideshow, etc., and calls out to passersby to attract customers. ▷late Middle English: from BARK[1] + -ER[1]. The original sense was 'a person or animal that barks; noisy protester,' hence the current sense (late 17th cent.).

bark·ing deer ▸n. another term for MUNTJAC.

Bark·ley[1] /'bärklē/, Alben William (1877–1956), U.S. politician. He served as Harry S Truman's vice president 1949–53. He also served in the U.S. Senate 1927–49; 1955–56.

Bark·ley[2], Charles (Wade) (1963–), U.S. basketball player. A five-time All-NBA player, he played for the Philadelphia 76ers 1984–92, the Phoenix Suns 1992–97, and the Houston Rockets 1997–2000. He was also a member of the U.S. Olympic "Dream" Team in 1992.

bar·ley /'bärlē/ ▸n. a hardy cereal that has coarse bristles extending from the ears. It is widely cultivated, chiefly for use in brewing and stockfeed. • Genus *Hordeum*, family Gramineae. ■ the grain of this plant. See also PEARL BARLEY. ▷Old English *bærlic* (adjective), from *bære*, *bere* 'barley' + *-lic* (see -LY[1]).

bar·ley·corn /'bärlē,kôrn/ ▸n. a grain of barley. ■ a former unit of measurement (about a third of an inch) based on the length of a grain of barley.

bar·ley sug·ar ▸n. an amber-colored candy made of boiled sugar, traditionally shaped as a twisted stick.
▸adj. (**bar·ley-sug·ar**) [attrib.] shaped like twisted barley-sugar sticks.

bar·ley wa·ter ▸n. a drink made from water and a boiled barley mixture, typically flavored with orange or lemon.

bar·ley wine ▸n. a strong English ale.

bar line ▸n. Music a vertical line used in a musical score to mark a division between bars.

Bar·low knife /'bärlō/ ▸n. a large single-bladed pocketknife. ▷named for Russell Barlow, 18th-cent. English inventor.

barm /bärm/ ▸n. the froth on fermenting malt liquor. ■ archaic or dialect yeast or leaven. ▷Old English *beorma.*

bar·maid /'bär,mād/ ▸n. **1** a waitress who serves drinks in a bar. **2** Brit. a woman bartender.

bar·man /'bärmən/ ▸n. (pl. **-men**) chiefly Brit. a male bartender.

Bar·me·cide /'bärmə,sīd/ (also **Bar·me·cid·al** /,bärmə'sīdl/) rare ▸adj. [attrib.] illusory or imaginary and therefore disappointing.
▸n. a person who offers benefits that are illusory or disappointing. ▷early 18th cent. (as a noun): from Arabic *Barmakī*, the name of a prince in the *Arabian Nights' Entertainments*, who gave a beggar a feast consisting of ornate but empty dishes.

bar mitz·vah /,bär 'mitsvə/ ▸n. the religious initiation ceremony of a Jewish boy who has reached the age of 13 and is regarded as ready to observe religious precepts and eligible to take part in public worship. ■ the boy undergoing this ceremony.
▸v. [trans.] (usu. **be bar mitzvahed**) celebrate the bar mitzvah of (a boy). ▷mid 19th cent.: from Hebrew *bar miṣwāh*, literally 'son of the commandment.'

barm·y /'bärmē/ ▸adj. (**barm·i·er**, **barm·i·est**) Brit. another term for BALMY (sense 2). ▷late 15th cent. (in the sense 'frothy'): from BARM + -Y[1]. —**barm·i·ly** /-məlē/ adv. —**barm·i·ness** n.

barn[1] /bärn/ ▸n. a large farm building used for storing grain, hay, or straw or for housing livestock. ■ a large shed used for storing vehicles. ■ a large and unattractive building: *moved into that **barn of a** house.* ▷Old English *bern*, *berern*, from *bere* 'barley' + *ern*, *ærn* 'house.'

barn[2] (abbr.: **b**) ▸n. Physics a unit of area, 10^{-28} square meters, used esp. in particle physics. ▷1940s: apparently from the phrase *as big as a barn door.*

Bar·na·bas, St. /'bärnəbəs/ (died c.61), a Cypriot Levite and apostle. The traditional founder of the Cypriot Church, he is said to have been martyred in Cyprus. Feast day, June 11.

bar·na·cle /'bärnəkəl/ ▸n. a marine crustacean with an external shell, which attaches itself permanently to a variety of surfaces. Barnacles feed by filtering particles from the water using their modified feathery legs. • Class Cirripedia. See ACORN BARNACLE, GOOSE BARNACLE. ■ used figuratively to describe a tenacious person or thing: *buses careered along with men hanging from their doors like barnacles.* ▷late 16th cent.: from medieval Latin *bernaca*, of unknown origin. In Middle English the term denoted the barnacle goose, whose breeding grounds were long unknown and which was believed to hatch from the shell of the crustacean to which it gave its name. —**bar·na·cled** adj.

bar·na·cle goose ▸n. a goose with a white face and black neck, breeding in the arctic tundra of Greenland and northern Europe. • *Branta leucopsis*, family Anatidae. ▷mid 18th cent.: see BARNACLE.

Bar·nard /'bärnərd/, Christiaan Neethling (1922–2001), South African surgeon; a pioneer in human heart transplantation. He performed the first heart transplant in December 1967.

Bar·na·ul /,bərnə'o͞ol/ the capital of Altai territory in southern Russia, on the Ob River; pop. 603,000.

barn burn·er (also **barn·burn·er**) ▸n. informal an event, typically a sports contest, that is very exciting or intense.

barn dance ▸n. an informal social gathering for square dancing, originally held in a barn.

barn door ▸n. the large door of a barn. ■ a target too large to be missed: *on the shooting range he **could not hit a barn door.*** ■ a hinged metal flap fitted to a spotlight to control the direction and intensity of its beam.

Bar·ne·gat Bay /'bärni,gat; -gət/ a tidal body in southeastern New Jersey, shielded from the Atlantic Ocean by barrier islands, the site of numerous resorts.

barn owl ▸n. an owl with a heart-shaped face, dark eyes, and relatively long, slender legs. It typically nests in farm buildings or in holes in trees. • Genus *Tyto*, family Tytonidae: three species, esp. the white-faced *T. alba*, which is found throughout the world.

Barns·ley /'bärnzlē/ a town in northern England; pop. 217,300.

Barn·sta·ble /'bärnstəbəl/ a town in southeastern Massachusetts, on the southwestern part of Cape Cod; pop. 40,949. It is the commercial center for a resort area.

barn·storm /'bärn,stôrm/ ▸v. [intrans.] tour rural districts giving theatrical performances, originally often in barns. ■ [trans.] make a rapid tour of (an area), typically as part of a political campaign. ■ travel around giving exhibitions of flying and performing aeronautical stunts: [as n.] (**barnstorming**) *barnstorming had become a popular occupation among many trained pilots.* —**barn·storm·er** n.

barn swal·low ▸n. see SWALLOW[2].

Bar·num /'bärnəm/, P. T. (1810–91), U.S. showman; full name *Phineas Taylor Barnum*. He was noted for his extravagant advertising and exhibition of freaks at his museum in New York City. When his circus opened in 1871, he billed it as "The Greatest Show on Earth"; ten years later, he founded the Barnum and Bailey circus with former rival Anthony Bailey (1847–1906).

Bar·num ef·fect ▸n. Psychology the tendency to accept certain information as true, such as character assessments or horoscopes, even when the information is so vague as to be worthless. ▷named after P. T. BARNUM; the word *Barnum* was in use from the mid 19th cent. as a noun in the sense 'nonsense, humbug.'

barn·yard /'bärn,yärd/ ▸n. the area of open ground around a barn.
▸adj. (esp. of manners or language) typical of a barnyard; earthy: *a polite way of avoiding barnyard language.*

baro- ▸comb. form relating to pressure: *barotrauma* | *baroreceptor.* ▷from Greek *baros* 'weight.'

bar·o·gram /'barə,gram/ ▸n. a record traced by a barograph.

bar·o·graph /'barə,graf/ ▸n. a barometer that records its readings on a moving chart. ▷mid 19th cent.: from Greek *baros* 'weight' + -GRAPH.

Ba·ro·lo /bə'rōlō/ ▸n. a full-bodied red Italian wine from Barolo, a region of Piedmont.

ba·rom·e·ter /bə'rämitər/ ▸n. an instrument measuring atmospheric pressure, used esp. in forecasting the weather and determining altitude. ■ something that reflects changes in circumstances or opinions: *furniture is **a barometer of** changing tastes.* ▷mid 17th cent.: from Greek *baros* 'weight' + -METER. —**bar·o·met·ric** /,barə'metrik/ adj. —**bar·o·met·ri·cal** adj. —**ba·rom·e·try** /-'rämitrē/ n.

bar·o·met·ric pres·sure ▸n. another term for ATMOSPHERIC PRESSURE.

bar·on /'barən/ ▸n. a member of the lowest order of the British nobility. The term "Baron" is not used as a form of address in Britain, barons usually being referred to as "Lord." ■ a similar member of a foreign nobility. ■ historical a person who held lands or property from the sovereign or a powerful overlord. ■ [with *adj.*] an important or powerful person in a specified business or industry: *a press baron.* ▷Middle English: from Old French, from medieval Latin *baro, baron-* 'man, warrior,' probably of Germanic origin.

bar·on·age /'barənij/ ▸*n.* **1** [treated as *sing.* or *pl.*] barons or nobles collectively. **2** an annotated list of barons or peers. ▷Middle English: from Old French *barnage* (from *baron*), or from medieval Latin *baronagium*, from *baro* (see BARON).

bar·on·ess /'barənis/ ▸*n.* the wife or widow of a baron. The term "Baroness" is not used as a form of address in Britain, baronesses usually being referred to as "Lady." ■ a woman holding the rank of baron either as a life peerage or as a hereditary rank. ▷late Middle English: from Old French *baronesse*, from *baron* (see BARON).

bar·on·et /'barənit; ˌbarə'net/ ▸*n.* a member of the lowest hereditary titled British order, with the status of a commoner but able to use the prefix "Sir." ▷late Middle English: from Anglo-Latin *baronettus*, from Latin *baro, baron-* 'man, warrior.' The term originally denoted a gentleman, not a nobleman, summoned by the king to attend parliament; the current order was instituted in the early 17th cent.

bar·on·et·age /'barənitij; ˌbarə'netij/ ▸*n.* **1** [treated as *sing.* or *pl.*] baronets collectively. **2** an annotated list of baronets.

bar·on·et·cy /'barənitsē/ ▸*n.* (*pl.* **-cies**) the rank of a baronet.

ba·ro·ni·al /bə'rōnēəl/ ▸*adj.* belonging or relating to a baron or barons. ■ suitable for a baron: *vast halls of baronial splendor.*

bar·on of beef ▸*n.* a joint of beef consisting of two sirloins joined at the backbone.

bar·o·ny /'barənē/ ▸*n.* (*pl.* **-nies**) **1** the rank and estates of a baron. **2** *historical* (in Ireland) a division of a county. **3** *historical* (in Scotland) a large manor or estate.

ba·roque /bə'rōk/ ▸*adj.* relating to or denoting a style of European architecture, music, and art of the 17th and 18th centuries that followed mannerism and is characterized by ornate detail. In architecture the period is exemplified by the palace of Versailles and by the work of Bernini in Italy. Major composers include Vivaldi, Bach, and Handel; Caravaggio and Rubens are important baroque artists. ■ highly ornate and extravagant in style: *the candles were positively baroque.*
▸*n.* the baroque style. ■ the baroque period. ▷mid 18th cent.: from French (originally designating a pearl of irregular shape), from Portuguese *barroco*, Spanish *barrueco*, or Italian *barocco*; of unknown ultimate origin.

bar·o·re·cep·tor /ˌbarōri'septər/ ▸*n.* *Zoology* a receptor sensitive to changes in pressure.

bar·o·trau·ma /ˌbarō'troumə; -'trô-/ ▸*n.* *Medicine* injury caused by a change in air pressure, typically affecting the ear or the lung.

ba·rouche /bə'rōōsh/ ▸*n.* *historical* a four-wheeled horse-drawn carriage with a collapsible hood over the rear half, a seat in front for the driver, and seats facing each other for the passengers, used esp. in the 19th century. ▷early 19th cent.: from German dialect *Barutsche*, from Italian *baroccio*, based on Latin *birotus* 'two-wheeled,' from *bi-* 'having two' + *rota* 'wheel.'

barouche

barque /bärk/ ▸*n.* variant spelling of BARK[3]. ▷Middle English: from Old French, probably from Provençal *barca*, from late Latin *barca* 'ship's boat.'

bar·quen·tine /'bärkənˌtēn/ ▸*n.* British spelling of BARKENTINE.

Bar·qui·si·me·to /ˌbärkēsē'mātō/ a city in northwestern Venezuela; pop. 602,620.

bar·rack[1] /'barək/ ▸*v.* [*trans.*] (often **be barracked**) provide (soldiers) with accommodations in a building or set of buildings: *the granary in which the platoons were barracked.* ▷early 18th cent.: from BARRACKS.

bar·rack[2] ▸*v.* [*trans.*] *Brit.* & *Austral./NZ* jeer loudly at (someone performing or speaking in public) in order to express disapproval or to create a distraction: *opponents barracked him when he addressed the opening parliamentary session* | [as *n.*] (**barracking**) *the disgraceful barracking which came from the mob.* ■ [*intrans.*] (**barrack for**) *Austral./NZ* give support and encouragement to: *I take it you'll be barracking for Labour tonight?* ▷late 19th cent.: probably from Northern Irish dialect.

bar·racks /'barəks/ ▸*plural n.* [often treated as *sing.*] a building or group of buildings used to house soldiers: *the troops were ordered back to barracks.* ■ a building or group of buildings used to house large numbers of people. ▷late 17th cent.: *barrack* from French *baraque*, from Italian *baracca* or Spanish *barraca* 'soldier's tent,' of unknown origin.

bar·racks bag ▸*n.* a large cloth bag for carrying clothing, equipment, and personal items; a duffel bag.

bar·ra·coon /ˌbarə'kōōn/ ▸*n.* *historical* an enclosure in which black slaves were confined for a limited period. ▷mid 19th cent.: from Spanish *barracón*, from *barraca* 'soldier's tent' (see BARRACKS).

bar·ra·cu·da /ˌbarə'kōōdə/ ▸*n.* (*pl.* same or **-das**) a large, predatory tropical marine fish with a slender body and large jaws and teeth. • Genus *Sphyraena*, family Sphyraenidae: several species, in particular the inedible and poisonous **great barracuda** (*S. barracuda*) and the edible **Pacific barracuda** (*S. argentea*). ▷late 17th cent.: of unknown origin.

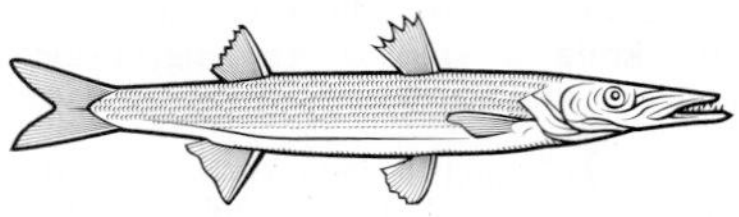

Pacific barracuda

bar·rage /bə'räzh/ ▸*n.* a concentrated artillery bombardment over a wide area. ■ *figurative* a concentrated outpouring, as of questions or blows: *she was not prepared for his* **barrage of** *questions* | *a barrage of 60-second television spots.*
▸*v.* [*trans.*] (usu. **be barraged**) bombard (someone) with something: *his doctor was* **barraged with** *unsolicited advice.* ▷mid 19th cent.: from French, from *barrer* 'to bar,' of unknown origin.

bar·rage bal·loon ▸*n.* a large balloon anchored to the ground by cables and often with netting suspended from it, serving as an obstacle to low-flying enemy aircraft.

bar·ra·mun·di /ˌbarə'məndē/ ▸*n.* (*pl.* same or **-dis**) any of a number of large, chiefly freshwater, fishes of Australia and Southeast Asia: • a fish that migrates between the sea and rivers and is valued as a food fish (*Lates calcarifer*, family Centropomidae). • a mouthbrooder (genus *Scleropages*, family Osteoglossidae), in particular *S. leichardti*, which is popular with fly fishermen. ▷late 19th cent.: probably from an Aboriginal language of Queensland, Australia.

bar·ran·ca /bə'rängkə/ (also **bar·ran·co** /-kō/) ▸*n.* (*pl.* **-cas** also **-cos**) a narrow, winding river gorge. ▷late 17th cent.: from Spanish.

Bar·ran·quil·la /ˌbärən'kē(y)ə/ the chief port of Colombia; pop. 1,018,700. Founded in 1629, it lies at the mouth of the Magdalena River, near the Caribbean Sea.

bar·ra·try /'barətrē/ ▸*n.* **1** *archaic* fraud or gross negligence of a ship's master or crew at the expense of its owners or users. **2** *Law* vexatious litigation or incitement to it. **3** *historical* trade in the sale of church or state appointments. ▷late Middle English (sense 3): from Old French *baraterie*, from *barater* 'deceive,' based on Greek *prattein* 'do, perform, manage' (sometimes dishonestly); perhaps influenced by Old Norse *barátta* 'contest.' **—bar·ra·tor** /'barətər/ *n.* (*historical*) (in sense 2). **—bar·ra·trous** /-trəs/ *adj.*

Barr bod·y /bär/ ▸*n.* *Anatomy & Physiology* a small, densely staining structure in the cell nuclei of female mammals, consisting of a condensed, inactive X chromosome. It is regarded as diagnostic of genetic femaleness.

barre /bär/ ▸*n.* a horizontal bar at waist level on which ballet dancers rest a hand for support during exercises. ▷early 20th cent.: French, literally 'bar.'

bar·ré /bä'rā/ ▸*n.* *Music* a method of playing a chord on the guitar or similar instrument with a finger laid across the strings at a particular fret, raising their pitch. ▷late 19th cent.: French, literally 'barred,' past participle of *barrer*.

barred owl ▸*n.* large gray-brown North American owl with brown eyes and a barred pattern across the chest. • *Strix varia*, family Strigidae.

bar·rel /'barəl/ ▸*n.* **1** a cylindrical container bulging out in the middle, traditionally made of wooden staves with metal hoops around them. ■ such a container together with its contents: ***a barrel of*** *beer.* ■ a measure of capacity used for oil and beer. It is usually equal to 36 imperial gallons for beer and 35 imperial gallons or 42 U.S. gallons (roughly 192 liters) for oil. **2** a tube forming part of an object such as a gun or a pen. **3** the belly and loins of a four-legged animal such as a horse.
▸*v.* (**-reled, -rel·ing**; *Brit.* **-relled, -rel·ling**) **1** [*intrans.*] *informal* drive or move fast, often heedless of surroundings or conditions: *we barreled across the Everglades* | ***barreling along*** *the Ventura freeway.* **2** [*trans.*] put into a barrel or barrels. ▷Middle English: from Old French *baril*, from medieval Latin *barriclus* 'small cask.'
▸***PHRASES*** □ **a barrel of laughs** [often with *negative*] *informal* a source of fun or amusement: *life is not exactly a barrel of laughs at the moment.* □ **on the barrel** (of payment) without delay: *I gotta be paid cash on the barrel.* □ **over a barrel** *informal* in a helpless position; at someone's mercy. □ **with both barrels** *informal* with unrestrained force or emotion.

bar·rel cac·tus ▸*n.* a spiny, ribbed cylindrical cactus. • *Ferocactus, Echinocereus*, and other genera, family Cactaceae: numerous species, including the **Arizona barrel cactus** (*F. wislizenii*), with yellow, orange, or red flower.

bar·rel-chest·ed ▸*adj.* having a large rounded chest.

bar·rel dis·tor·tion ▸*n.* a type of defect in optical or electronic images in which vertical or horizontal straight lines appear as convex curves.

bar·rel·head /'barəlˌhed/ ▸*n.* the flat top of a barrel.
▸***PHRASE*** □ **on the barrelhead** another way of saying ON THE BARREL (see BARREL).

bar·rel·house /'barəlˌhous/ ▸*n.* **1** a cheap or disreputable bar. **2** [usu. as *adj.*] an unrestrained and unsophisticated style of jazz music. ▷late 19th cent.: so named because of the rows of barrels along the walls of such a bar.

bar·rel knot ▸*n.* another term for BLOOD KNOT.

bar·rel or·gan ▸*n.* a mechanical musical instrument from which predetermined music is produced by turning a handle, played, esp. in former times, by street musicians.

bar·rel roll ▸*n.* an aerobatic maneuver in which an aircraft follows a single turn of a spiral while rolling once about its longitudinal axis.

bar·rel vault ▸*n.* *Architecture* a vault forming a half cylinder. **—bar·rel-vault·ed** *adj.*

bar·ren /'barən/ ▸*adj.* **1** (of land) too poor to produce much or any vegetation. See note at NAKED. ■ (of a tree or plant) not producing fruit or seed. ■ *archaic* (of a woman) unable to have children. ■ (of a female animal) not pregnant or unable to become so. ■ showing no results or achievements; unproductive: *much of philosophy has been barren.* **2** (of a place or building) bleak and lifeless: *the sports hall turned out to be a rather barren concrete building.* ■ empty of meaning or value: *those young heads were stuffed with barren facts.* ■ (**barren of**) devoid of: *the room was barren of furniture.*
▸*n.* (usu. **barrens**) a barren tract or tracts of land: *crossing the barrens was no easy feat.* ▷Middle English: from Old French *barhaine*, of unknown origin. **—bar·ren·ness** *n.*

Bar·rett /'barit/, Elizabeth, see BROWNING[1].

bar·rette /bə'ret/ ▸*n.* a typically bar-shaped clip or ornament for the hair. ▷early 20th cent.: from French, diminutive of *barre* 'bar.'

bar·ri·cade /'bariˌkād/ ▸*n.* an improvised barrier erected across a street or other thoroughfare to prevent or delay the movement of opposing forces.
▸*v.* [*trans.*] block or defend with such a barrier: *he barricaded the door with a bureau* | [as *adj.*] (**barricaded**) *the heavily barricaded streets.* ■ shut (oneself or someone) into a place by blocking all the entrances: *detainees who* **barricaded themselves into** *their dormitory.* ▷late 16th cent.: from French, from *barrique* 'cask,' from Spanish *barrica*; related to BARREL (barrels being often used to build barricades).

Bar·rie /'barē/, Sir J. M. (1860–1937), Scottish dramatist and novelist; full name *James Matthew Barrie*. He wrote *Peter Pan* (1904), a fantasy for children about a boy who would not grow up. Other notable plays include *The Admirable Crichton* (1902).

bar·ri·er /'barēər/ ▸*n.* a fence or other obstacle that prevents movement or access. ■ a circumstance or obstacle that prevents communication or that keeps people or things apart: *a language barrier.* ■ something that prevents progress or success: *the cultural* ***barriers to*** *economic growth.* ■ the starting gate of a racecourse. ■ (in full **barrier island**) a long narrow island lying parallel and close to the mainland, protecting the mainland from erosion and storms. ■ *Brit.* a gate at a parking lot that controls access by being raised or lowered. ▷late Middle English (denoting a palisade or fortification defending an entrance): from Old French *barriere*, of unknown origin; related to **BARRE**.

▸*PHRASE* □ **break the barrier** pass or exceed a significant level or amount: *the Tokyo stock exchange reopened to break the 5000-yen barrier.*

bar·ri·er meth·od ▸*n.* a method of contraception using a device or preparation that prevents live sperm from reaching an ovum.

bar·ri·er reef ▸*n.* a coral reef running parallel to the shore but separated from it by a channel of deep water.

bar·ring /ˈbäriNG/ ▸*prep.* except for; if not for: *barring a miracle, he's crippled for life.* ▷late 15th cent.: from the verb **BAR**[1] + **-ING**[2].

bar·ri·o /ˈbärēˌō/ ▸*n.* (*pl.* **-os**) a district of a town in Spain and Spanish-speaking countries. ■ (in the U.S.) the Spanish-speaking quarter of a town or city. ■ a poor neighborhood populated by Spanish-speaking people. ▷Spanish, perhaps from Arabic.

bar·rique /bəˈrēk/ ▸*n.* a wine barrel, especially a small one made of new oak, in which Bordeaux and other wines are aged. ▷late 18th cent.: French.

bar·ris·ter /ˈbarəstər/ (also **bar·ris·ter-at-law**) ▸*n.* *chiefly Brit.* a lawyer entitled to practice as an advocate, particularly in the higher courts. Compare with **ATTORNEY, SOLICITOR**. ▷late Middle English: from the noun **BAR**[1], perhaps on the pattern of *minister*.

bar·room /ˈbärˌro͞om; -ˌro͝om/ ▸*n.* a room where alcoholic drinks are served over a counter. ■ typical of a barroom: *a barroom brawl.*

Bar·row[1] /ˈbarō/ a city in north central Alaska, a commercial center on the Arctic Ocean. It is the northernmost U.S. city; pop. 4,581. Nearby Point Barrow is the northernmost point in the U.S.

Bar·row[2], Clyde (1909–34), U.S. bank robber and murderer. He and his partner, Bonnie Parker, shot and killed at least thirteen people during a notorious two-year crime spree across the Southwest. They were finally stopped and shot to death at a Louisiana roadblock.

bar·row[1] /ˈbarō/ ▸*n.* a metal frame with two wheels used for transporting objects such as luggage. ■ a wheelbarrow. ■ *Brit.* a two-wheeled handcart used esp. by street vendors. ▷Old English *bearwe* 'stretcher, bier,' of Germanic origin; related to **BEAR**[1]. **—bar·row·load** /-ˌlōd/ *n.*

bar·row[2] ▸*n.* *Archaeology* an ancient burial mound. ▷Old English *beorg*, of Germanic origin; related to Dutch *berg*, German *Berg* 'hill, mountain.'

bar·row[3] ▸*n.* a male pig castrated before maturity.

bar·row boy ▸*n.* *Brit.* a boy or man who sells wares from a barrow in the street.

Bar·ry /ˈbarē/, Sir Charles (1795–1860), English architect, designer of the Houses of Parliament.

bar·ry /ˈbarē/ ▸*adj.* *Heraldry* divided into typically four, six, or eight equal horizontal bars of alternating tinctures. ▷late 15th cent.: from French *barré* 'barred, striped,' past participle of *barrer.*

Bar·ry·more /ˈbarəˌmôr/, a U.S. family of film and stage actors, notably **Lionel** (1878–1954), his sister **Ethel** (1879–1959), their brother **John** (1882–1942), and John's granddaughter **Drew** (1975–).

Bar·sac /ˈbärˌsak/ ▸*n.* a sweet white wine from the district of Barsac, a department of the Gironde in France.

bar sin·is·ter ▸*n.* popular and erroneous term for **BEND SINISTER**.

bar·stool /ˈbärˌsto͞ol/ (also **bar stool**) ▸*n.* a tall padded stool for customers at a bar to sit on.

Bar·stow /ˈbärˌstō/ a city in south central California, in the Mojave Desert, northeast of Los Angeles; pop. 21,472.

Bart /bärt/, Lionel (1930–99), English composer and lyricist; born *Lionel Beglieter.* His musicals include *Oliver!* (1960).

Bart. ▸*abbr.* Baronet.

bar tack ▸*n.* a stitch made to strengthen a potential weak spot in a garment or other sewn item. **—bar-tacked** *adj.* **—bar tack·ing** *n.*

bar·tend·er /ˈbärˌtendər/ ▸*n.* a person who mixes and serves drinks at a bar.

bar·ter /ˈbärtər/ ▸*v.* [*trans.*] exchange (goods or services) for other goods or services without using money: *he often* ***bartered*** *a meal* ***for*** *drawings* | [*intrans.*] *the company is prepared to barter for Russian oil.*
▸*n.* the action or system of exchanging goods or services without using money: *it will be paid for by a mixture of barter and cash.* ■ the goods or services used for such an exchange: *I took a supply of coffee and cigarettes to use as barter.* ▷late Middle English: probably from Old French *barater* 'deceive' (see **BARRATRY**). **—bar·ter·er** *n.*

Barth[1] /bärTH/, John (Simmons) (1930–), U.S. novelist and short-story writer noted for complex experimental novels. Notable works: *The Sot-Weed Factor* (1960), *Giles Goat-Boy* (1966), and *Letters* (1979).

Barth[2] /bärt/, Karl (1886–1968), Swiss theologian. His seminal work *Epistle to the Romans* (1919) established a neo-orthodox or theocentric approach to contemporary religious thought that remains influential in Protestant theology.

Barthes /bärt/, Roland (1915–80), French writer and critic. He was a leading exponent of structuralism and semiology in literary criticism. Notable works: *On Racine* (1963), *Mythologies* (1957), and *Elements of Semiology* (1964).

Bar·thol·di /bärˈtôldē/, (Frédéric) Auguste (1834–1904), French sculptor, known primarily as the designer of the *Statue of Liberty* .

Bar·tho·lin's gland /ˈbärtl-inz/ ▸*n.* *Anatomy* one of a pair of glands lying near the entrance of the vagina, which secrete a fluid that lubricates the vulva. ▷early 18th cent.: named by Caspar *Bartholin* (1655–1738), Danish anatomist, as a tribute to his father.

Bar·thol·o·mew, St. /bärˈTHäləˌmyo͞o/, an Apostle; regarded as the patron saint of tanners. Feast day, August 24.

bar·ti·zan /ˈbärtəzən/ ▸*n.* *Architecture* an overhanging corner turret at the top of a castle or church tower. ▷early 19th cent.: from 17th-cent. *bertisene*, Scots variant of *bratticing* 'temporary breastwork or parapet,' from **BRATTICE**; revived and reinterpreted by Sir Walter Scott.

Bar·tles·ville /ˈbärtlzˌvil/ a city in northeastern Oklahoma, noted as an oil industry center; pop. 34,748.

Bart·lett[1] /ˈbärtlit/ a town in southwestern Tennessee, northeast of Memphis; pop. 40,543.

Bart·lett[2] (also **Bartlett pear**) ▸*n.* a dessert pear of a juicy, early-ripening variety.

Bar·tók /ˈbärˌtäk; -ˌtôk/, Béla (1881–1945), Hungarian composer, whose work owes much to Hungarian folk music. Notable works: *Concerto for Orchestra* (1943) and *Duke Bluebeard's Castle* (opera, 1911).

Bar·to·lom·me·o /ˌbärtōləˈmāō/, Fra (*c.*1472–1517), Italian painter; born *Baccio della Porta.* A Dominican friar, he worked chiefly in Florence. Notable works: *The Vision of St. Bernard* (1507) and *The Mystic Marriage of St. Catherine* (1511).

Bar·ton /ˈbärtn/, Clara (1821–1912), U.S. social activist; full name *Clarissa Harlowe Barton.* She founded the American Red Cross and served as its first president 1882–1904.

Clara Barton

bart·si·a /ˈbärtsēə/ ▸*n.* a herbaceous plant of the figwort family. Some kinds obtain additional nourishment by attachment to the roots of other plants, esp. grasses. • *Bartsia* and related genera, family Scrophulariaceae: several species, in particular the pink-flowered **red bartsia** (*Odontites serotina*). ▷modern Latin, from the name of Johann *Bartsch* (1709–38), Prussian botanist.

Ba·ruch[1] /bəˈro͞ok/, Bernard Mannes (1870–1965), U.S. financier and economic adviser. As a sought-after presidential adviser, his many appointments included chairman of the War Industries Board 1918–19 and U.S. representative on the UN Atomic Energy Commission 1946.

Bar·uch[2] a book of the Apocrypha, attributed in the text to Baruch, the scribe of Jeremiah (Jer. 36).

bar·ware /ˈbärˌwe(ə)r/ ▸*n.* glassware of various shapes and sizes used for preparing and serving alcoholic drinks.

bar·y·cen·tric /ˌbarəˈsentrik/ ▸*adj.* [*attrib.*] of or relating to the center of gravity. ▷late 19th cent.: from Greek *barus* 'heavy' + **-CENTRIC**. **—bar·y·cen·ter** /ˈbarəˌsentər/ *n.*

bar·y·on /ˈbarēˌän/ ▸*n.* *Physics* a subatomic particle, such as a nucleon or hyperon, that has a mass equal to or greater than that of a proton. ▷1950s: from Greek *barus* 'heavy' + **-ON**. **—bar·y·on·ic** /ˌbarēˈänik/ *adj.*

bar·y·on·ic mat·ter ▸*n.* matter composed of protons and neutrons; ordinary matter, as distinct from exotic forms.

Ba·rysh·ni·kov /bəˈrisHnəˌkôf; -ˌkôv/, Mikhail (Nikolaevich) (1948–), U.S. ballet dancer, born in Latvia of Russian parents. In 1974 he defected to the West while touring with the Kirov Ballet. He served as the American Ballet Theater's artistic director 1980–89.

Mikhail Baryshnikov

ba·ry·ta /bəˈrītə/ ▸*n.* *Chemistry* barium hydroxide. • Chem. formula: $Ba(OH)_2$. ▷early 19th cent.: from **BARYTE**, on the pattern of words such as *soda.*

bar·yte /ˈbarīt/ (also **ba·ry·tes** /bəˈrītēz/) ▸*n.* *Brit.* variant spelling of **BARITE**. ▷mid 19th cent.: from **BARIUM** + **-ITE**[1].

bar·y·tone[1] ▸*n.* & *adj.* variant spelling of **BARITONE**.

bar·y·tone[2] /ˈbariˌtōn/ ▸*adj.* *Greek Grammar* not having the acute accent on the last syllable. **—bar·y·tone** *n.*

ba·sal /ˈbāsəl; -zəl/ ▸*adj.* [*attrib.*] *chiefly technical* forming or belonging to a bottom layer or base.

ba·sal bod·y (also **ba·sal gran·ule**) ▸*n.* an organelle that forms the base of a flagellum or cilium and that is similar to a centriole in structure and function. Also called **KINETOSOME**.

ba·sal cell ▸*n.* a type of cell in the innermost layer of the epidermis.

ba·sal cell car·ci·no·ma ▸*n.* technical term for **RODENT ULCER**.

ba·sal gan·gli·a ▸*plural n.* *Anatomy* a group of structures linked to the thalamus in the base of the brain and involved in coordination of movement.

ba·sal met·a·bol·ic rate ▸*n.* the rate at which the body uses energy while at rest to keep vital functions going, such as breathing and keeping warm. **—ba·sal me·tab·o·lism** *n.*

ba·salt /bəˈsôlt/ ▸*n.* a dark, fine-grained volcanic rock that sometimes displays a columnar structure. It is typically composed largely of plagioclase with pyroxene and olivine. ■ a kind of black stoneware resembling such rock. ▷early 17th cent. (in the Latin form): from Latin *basaltes* (variant of *basanites*), from Greek *basanitēs*, from *basanos* 'touchstone.' **—ba·sal·tic** /-tik/ *adj.*

bas·cule /ˈbaskyo͞ol/ (also **bascule bridge**) ▸*n.* a type of bridge with a pivoting section that is raised and lowered using counterweights. ■ a moveable section of road forming part of such a bridge. ▷late 19th cent.: earlier denoting a lever apparatus of which one end is raised while the other is lowered, from French (earlier *bacule*), 'seesaw,' from *battre* 'to bump' + *cul* 'buttocks.'

base[1] /bās/ ▸*n.* **1** the lowest part or edge of something, esp. the part on which it rests or is supported: *she sat down at the base of a tree.* ■ *Architecture* the part of a column between the shaft and pedestal or pavement. ■ *Botany & Zoology* the end at which a part or organ is attached to the trunk or main part: *a shoot is produced at the base of the stem.* ■ *Geometry* a line or surface on which a figure is regarded as standing: *the base of the triangle.* ■ *Surveying* a line of known length used in triangulation. ■ *Heraldry* the lowest part of a shield. ■ *Heraldry* the lower third of the field. **2** a conceptual structure or entity on which something draws or depends: *the town's economic base collapsed.* ■ something used as a foundation or starting point for further work; a basis: *uses existing data as the* ***base for*** *the study.* ■ [with *adj.*] a group of people regarded as supporting an organization, for example by buying its products: *a client base.* **3** the main place where a person works or stays: *she makes the studio her base.* ■ *chiefly Military* a place used as a center of operations by the armed forces or others; a headquarters: *an airbase | he headed back to base.* ■ a place from which a particular activity can be carried out: ***a base for*** *shipping operations.* **4** a main or important element or ingredient to which other things are added: *soaps with a vegetable oil base.* ■ a substance used as a foundation for makeup. ■ a substance such as water or oil into which a pigment is mixed to form paint. **5** *Chemistry* a substance capable of reacting with an acid to form a salt and water, or (more broadly) of accepting or neutralizing hydrogen ions. Compare with **ALKALI**. ■ *Biochemistry* a purine or pyrimidine group in a nucleotide or nucleic acid. **6** *Electronics* the middle part of a bipolar transistor, separating the emitter from the collector. **7** *Linguistics* the root or stem of a word or a derivative. ■ the uninflected form of a verb. **8** *Mathematics* a number used as the basis of a numeration scale. ■ a number in terms of which other numbers are expressed as logarithms. **9** *Baseball* one of the four stations that must be reached in turn to score a run.

▸*v.* [*trans.*] **1** (often **be based**) have as the foundation for (something); use as a point from which (something) can develop: *the film is* ***based on*** *a novel by Pat Conroy | inaccurate conclusions based on incomplete facts.* **2** situate as the center of operations: *a research program* ***based at*** *the University of Arizona* | [as *adj.*, in *combination*] (**-based**) *a London-based band.* ▷Middle English: from Old French, from Latin *basis* 'base, pedestal,' from Greek.

▸*PHRASES* □ **get to first base** [usu. with *negative*] *informal* achieve the first step toward one's objective. □ **first base, second base, third base** *informal* used to refer to progressive levels of sexual intimacy. □ **off-base** *informal* mistaken: *the boy is way off-base.* □ **touch base(s)** *informal* briefly make or renew contact with (someone).

base[2] ▸*adj.* (of a person or a person's actions or feelings) without moral principles; ignoble: *the electorate's baser instincts of greed and selfishness | we hope his motives are nothing so base as money.* ■ *archaic* denoting or befitting a person of low social class. ■ (of coins or other articles) not made of precious metal: *the basest coins in the purse were made in the seventh century* AD. ▷late Middle English: from Old French *bas*, from medieval Latin *bassus* 'short' (found in classical Latin as a cognomen). The senses in late Middle English included 'low, short' and 'of inferior quality'; from the latter arose a sense 'low on the social scale, menial,' and hence (mid 16th cent.) 'reprehensibly cowardly, selfish, or mean.' **—base·ly** *adv.* **—base·ness** *n.*

base·ball /ˈbās,bôl/ ▸*n.* a ball game played between two teams of nine on a field with a diamond-shaped circuit of four bases. It is played chiefly in the U.S., Canada, Latin America, and East Asia. ■ the hard ball used in this game.

base·ball cap ▸*n.* a fabric cap of a kind originally worn by baseball players, with a large brim and an adjustable strap at the back.

base·board /ˈbās,bôrd/ ▸*n.* a narrow wooden board running along the base of an interior wall.

base·born /ˈbās,bôrn/ ▸*adj.* [*attrib.*] *archaic* of low birth or origin. ■ illegitimate.

base bur·ner ▸*n.* a coal stove or furnace into which coal is fed automatically from a hopper as the lower layers are burned.

base camp ▸*n.* a camp from which mountaineering expeditions set out.

base dress·ing ▸*n.* the application of manure or fertilizer to the earth, which is then plowed or dug in. Compare with **TOP DRESSING**. ■ manure or fertilizer applied in this way.

base ex·change (abbr.: **BX**) ▸*n.* a nonprofit store for the purchase of personal items, clothing, refreshments, etc., at a naval or air force base.

base·head /ˈbās,hed/ ▸*n. informal* a habitual abuser of freebase or crack cocaine. ▷1980s: from a shortened form of **FREEBASE** + **-HEAD**[2].

base hit ▸*n. Baseball* a fair ball hit such that the batter can advance safely to a base without aid of an error committed by the team in the field.

base hos·pi·tal ▸*n.* a military hospital situated at some distance from the area of active operations during a war.

base jump (also **BASE jump**) ▸*n.* a parachute jump from a fixed point, typically a high building or promontory, rather than an aircraft.

▸*v.* [*intrans.*] [often as *n.*] (**base jumping**) perform such a jump. ▷1980s: *base* from building, *antenna* tower, *span*, *earth* (denoting the types of structure used). **—base jump·er** *n.*

Ba·sel /ˈbäzəl/ German name for **BASLE**.

base·less /ˈbāslis/ ▸*adj.* **1** without foundation in fact: *baseless allegations.* **2** *Architecture* (of a column) not having a base between the shaft and pedestal. **—base·less·ly** *adv.* **—base·less·ness** *n.*

base·line /ˈbās,līn/ ▸*n.* **1** a minimum or starting point used for comparisons. **2** (in tennis, volleyball, etc.) the line marking each end of the court. ■ *Baseball* the line between bases, which a runner must stay close to when running.

base·man /ˈbāsmən/ ▸*n.* (*pl.* **-men**) *Baseball* a fielder designated to cover first, second, or third base.

base·ment /ˈbāsmənt/ ▸*n.* the floor of a building partly or entirely below ground level. ■ *Geology* the oldest formation of rocks underlying a particular area. ▷mid 18th cent.: probably from archaic Dutch *basement* 'foundation,' perhaps from Italian *basamento* 'column base.'

base·ment mem·brane ▸*n. Anatomy* a thin, delicate membrane of protein fibers and glycosaminoglycans separating an epithelium from underlying tissue.

base met·al ▸*n.* a common metal not considered precious, such as copper, tin, or zinc.

ba·sen·ji /bəˈsenjē/ ▸*n.* (*pl.* **-jis**) a small hunting dog of a central African breed, which growls and yelps but does not bark. ▷1930s: a local word.

base on balls (abbr.: **BB**) ▸*n. Baseball* another term for **WALK** *n.* 3.

base pair ▸*n. Biochemistry* a pair of complementary bases in a double-stranded nucleic acid molecule, consisting of a purine in one strand linked by hydrogen bonds to a pyrimidine in the other. Cytosine always pairs with guanine, and adenine with thymine (in DNA) or uracil (in RNA). **—base pair·ing** *n.*

base path ▸*n. Baseball* the straight-line path from one base to the next, defined by the position of the base runner while a play is being made.

base pay ▸*n.* the base rate of pay for a job or activity, not including any additional payments such as overtime or bonuses.

base·plate /ˈbās,plāt/ ▸*n.* a sheet of metal forming the bottom of an object.

base run·ner (also **base·run·ner**) ▸*n. Baseball* a player on the team at bat who is on a base, or running between bases. **—base-run·ning** (or **base·run·ning**) *n.*

ba·ses /ˈbāsēz/ ▸ plural form of **BASIS**.

base u·nit ▸*n.* a fundamental unit that is defined arbitrarily and not by combinations of other units. The base units of the SI system are the meter, kilogram, second, ampere, kelvin, mole, and candela.

bash /basʜ/ ▸*v.* [*trans.*] *informal* strike hard and violently: *bash a mosquito with a newspaper.* ■ (**bash something in**) damage or break something by striking it violently: *the car's rear window had been bashed in.* ■ [*intrans.*] (**bash into**) collide with: *the other vehicle bashed into the back of them.* ■ *figurative* criticize severely: *a remark bashing the Belgian brewing industry.*

▸*phrasal v.* □ **bash something out** produce something rapidly without preparation or attention to detail.

▸*n. informal* **1** a heavy blow: *a* ***bash on*** *the head.* **2** [usu. with *adj.*] *informal* a party or social event: *a birthday bash.* ▷mid 17th cent. (as a verb): imitative, perhaps a blend of **BANG**[1] and **SMASH**, **DASH**, etc. Sense 2 is a 20th-cent. usage.

ba·shaw /bəˈsʜô/ ▸*n.* another term for **PASHA** (sense 1).

-bash·er /-,basʜər/ ▸*comb. form* forming nouns denoting a person who harshly criticizes, debunks, or commits violence against the named party: *theory-basher | world-trade basher.*

ba·shert /bäˈsʜert/ ▸*n.* (in Jewish use) a person's soulmate, especially when considered as an ideal or predestined marriage partner. ▷Yiddish 'fate, destiny.'

bash·ful /ˈbasʜfəl/ ▸*adj.* reluctant to draw attention to oneself; shy: *don't be bashful about telling folks how you feel.* ▷late 15th cent.: from obsolete *bash* 'make or become abashed' (from **ABASH**) + **-FUL**. **—bash·ful·ly** *adv.* **—bash·ful·ness** *n.*

bash·ing /ˈbasʜiɴɢ/ ▸*n.* [usu. with *modifier*] *informal* violent physical assault: *nine incidents of gay bashing were reported to the police.* ■ severe criticism: *press bashing.*

Bash·kir /basʜˈki(ə)r/ ▸*n.* **1** a member of a Muslim people living in the southern Urals. **2** the Turkic language of this people.

▸*adj.* of or relating to this people or their language. ▷via Russian from Turkic *Başkurt*.

Bash·kir·i·a /basʜˈki(ə)rēə/ an autonomous republic in central Russia, west of the Urals; pop. 3,964,000; capital, Ufa. Also called **BASHKIR AUTONOMOUS REPUBLIC, BASHKORTOSTAN**.

BASIC /ˈbāsik/ ▸*n.* a simple high-level computer programming language that uses familiar English words, designed for beginners and formerly widely used on microcomputers. ▷1960s: acronym from *Beginners' All-purpose Symbolic Instruction Code.*

ba·sic /ˈbāsik/ ▸*adj.* **1** forming an essential foundation or starting point; fundamental: *certain basic rules must be obeyed | the laying down of arms is* ***basic to*** *the agreement.* ■ offering or consisting in the minimum required without elaboration or luxury; simplest or lowest in level: *basic and unsophisticated resorts | the food was good, if a bit basic.* ■ common to or required by everyone; primary and ineradicable or inalienable: *basic human rights.* **2** *Chemistry* having the properties of a base, or containing a base; having a pH greater than 7. Often contrasted with **ACID** or **ACIDIC**; compare with **ALKALINE**. ■ *Geology* (of rock, esp. igneous rock) relatively poor in silica. ■ *Metallurgy* relating to or denoting steelmaking processes involving lime-rich refractories and slags.

▸*n.* (**basics**) the essential facts or principles of a subject or skill: *learning the basics of the business | storytelling has reemerged as people have turned* ***back to basics.*** ■ essential food and other supplies: *people are facing a shortage of basics like flour.* ■ *Military* basic training. ▷mid 19th cent.: from **BASE**[1] + **-IC**.

ba·si·cal·ly /ˈbāsik(ə)lē/ ▸*adv.* [often as *submodifier*] in the most essential respects; fundamentally: *we started from a basically simple idea.* ■ [*sentence adverb*] used to indicate that a statement summarizes the most important aspects, or gives a roughly accurate account, of a more complex situation: *I basically played the same tunes every night.*

Ba·sic Eng·lish ▸*n.* a simplified form of English limited to 850 selected words, intended for international communication.

ba·sic·i·ty /bāˈsisitē/ ▸*n. Chemistry* the number of hydrogen atoms replaceable by a base in a particular acid.

ba·sic train·ing ▸*n. Military* the initial period of training for new personnel, involving intense physical activity and behavioral discipline.

ba·sid·i·o·my·cete /bə,sidēōˈmīsēt/ ▸*n. Botany* a fungus whose spores develop in basidia. Basidiomycetes include the majority of familiar mushrooms and toadstools. Compare with **ASCOMYCETE**. • Phylum Basidiomycota: classes Basidiomycetes (mushrooms, toadstools, puffballs, earthstars, stinkhorns, polypores), Teliomycetes (rusts), and Ustomycetes (smuts). ▷late 19th cent.: anglicized singular of modern Latin *Basidiomycetes*, from *basidium* (see **BASIDIUM**) + Greek *mukētes* 'fungi.'

ba·sid·i·o·spore /bəˈsidēō,spôr/ ▸*n.* a spore produced by a basidium.

ba·sid·i·um /bəˈsidēəm/ ▸*n.* (*pl.* **-sid·i·a** /-ˈsidēə/) a microscopic, club-shaped spore-bearing structure produced by certain fungi. ▷mid 19th cent.: modern Latin, from Greek *basidion*, diminutive of *basis* (see **BASIS**).

Ba·sie /ˈbāsē/, Count (1904–84), U.S. jazz pianist, organist, and bandleader; born *William Basie*. In 1935 he formed the Count Basie Orchestra, which became one of the best-known and most successful bands of the swing era.

ba·si·fy /ˈbāsəˌfī/ ▸*v.* [*trans.*] *Chemistry* change into a base; alkalize.

bas·il /ˈbāzəl; ˈbazəl/ ▸*n.* an aromatic annual herb of the mint family, native to tropical Asia. • Genus *Ocimum*, family Labiatae: several species, in particular the common **sweet basil** (*O. basilicum*) and the low-growing, compact **bush basil** *O. minimum*. ■ the leaves of this plant used as a culinary herb, esp. in Mediterranean dishes. ▷late Middle English: from Old French *basile*, via medieval Latin from Greek *basilikon*, neuter of *basilikos* 'royal' (see **BASILICA**).

Bas·il, St. /ˈbazəl; ˈbāzəl/ (*c.*330–379), doctor of the Church; bishop of Caesarea; known as **St. Basil the Great**. Brother of St. Gregory of Nyssa, he staunchly opposed the Arian heresy and established a monastic rule that is still the basis of monasticism in the Eastern Church. Feast day, June 14.

bas·i·lar /ˈbasələr/ ▸*adj.* [*attrib.*] of or situated at the base of something, esp. of the skull, or of the organ of Corti in the ear. ▷mid 16th cent.: from modern Latin *basilaris*, formed irregularly from Latin *basis* (see **BASIS**).

bas·i·lar mem·brane ▸*n.* *Anatomy* a membrane in the cochlea that bears the organ of Corti.

Ba·sil·don /ˈbazəldən/ a town in southeastern England; pop. 157,500.

ba·si·lect /ˈbāzəˌlekt; ˈbaz-/ ▸*n.* *Linguistics* a less prestigious dialect or variety of a particular language (used esp. in the study of Creoles). Compare with **ACROLECT**, **MESOLECT**. —**ba·si·lec·tal** /ˌbāzəˈlektəl; ˌbaz-/ *adj.*

Ba·sil·i·an /bəˈzilyən; -ˈzilēən/ ▸*adj.* of or relating to St. Basil the Great, or the order of monks and nuns following his monastic rule.
▸*n.* a Basilian monk or nun.

ba·sil·i·ca /bəˈsilikə/ ▸*n.* a large oblong hall or building with double colonnades and a semicircular apse, used in ancient Rome as a court or for public assemblies. ■ a similar building used as a Christian church. ■ the name given to certain churches granted special privileges by the pope. ▷mid 16th cent.: from Latin, literally 'royal palace,' from Greek *basilikē*, feminine of *basilikos* 'royal,' from *basileus* 'king.' —**ba·sil·i·can** *adj.*

bas·i·lisk /ˈbasəˌlisk; ˈbaz-/ ▸*n.* **1** a mythical reptile with a lethal gaze or breath, hatched by a serpent from a cock's egg. ■ *Heraldry* another term for **COCKATRICE**. **2** a long, slender, and mainly bright green lizard found in Central America, the male of which has a crest running from the head to the tail. It can swim well and is able to run on its hind legs across the surface of water. • *Basiliscus plumifrons*, family Iguanidae. ▷late Middle English: via Latin from Greek *basiliskos* 'little king, serpent,' from *basileus* 'king.'

basilisk 2

bas·i·lo·sau·rus /ˌbasələˈsôrəs/ ▸*n.* (*pl.* **-sau·rus·es** or **-sau·ri** /-ˈsôrī/) a large marine cetacean (*Basilosaurus isis*) of the Eocene epoch, having a long, slender body and vestigial fore and hind limbs. Fossils were discovered in the early 1990s. ▷modern Latin, from Greek *basileus* 'king' + *sauros* 'lizard.'

ba·sin /ˈbāsən/ ▸*n.* **1** a bowl for washing, typically attached to a wall and having faucets connected to a water supply; a washbasin. **2** a wide, round open container, esp. one used for holding liquid. **3** a natural depression on the earth's surface, typically containing water: *the Indian Ocean basin*. ■ the tract of country that is drained by a river and its tributaries or drains into a lake or sea: *the Amazon basin | a drainage basin*. ■ an enclosed area of water where vessels can be moored: *a yacht basin*. ■ *Geology* a circumscribed area within which the rock strata dip toward the center. ▷Middle English: from Old French *bacin*, from medieval Latin *bacinus*, from *bacca* 'water container,' perhaps of Gaulish origin. —**ba·sin·ful** /-ˌfo͝ol/ *n.*

Ba·sin and Range Province a largely arid intermountain region of the southwestern U.S., chiefly in Nevada, Utah, and California. The Great Basin and Death Valley are parts of the region.

bas·i·net /ˌbasəˈnet/ (also **bas·ci·net**) ▸*n.* a medieval helmet of light steel, fitting close to the wearer's head and typically having a visor. ▷Middle English: from Old French *bacinet* 'little basin.'

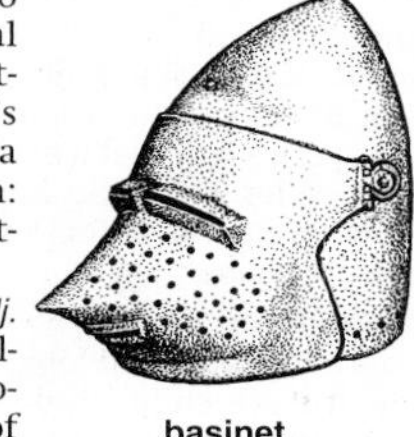

basinet

ba·sip·e·tal /bāˈsipitl/ ▸*adj.* *Botany* (of growth or development) downward toward the base or point of attachment. The opposite of **ACROPETAL**. ■ (of the movement of dissolved substances) inward from the shoot and root apexes. ▷mid 19th cent.: from **BASIS** + Latin *petere* 'seek' + **-AL**. —**ba·sip·e·tal·ly** *adv.*

ba·sis /ˈbāsis/ ▸*n.* (*pl.* **-ses** /-sēz/) the underlying support or foundation for an idea, argument, or process: *trust is the only basis for a good working relationship*. ■ the system or principles according to which an activity or process is carried on: *she needed coaching on a regular basis | flea markets operate on a cash-only basis*. ■ the justification for or reasoning behind something: *on the basis of these statistics, important decisions are made*. ▷late 16th cent. (denoting a base or pedestal): via Latin from Greek, 'stepping.' Compare with **BASE**[1].

ba·sis point ▸*n.* *Finance* one hundredth of one percent, used chiefly in expressing differences of interest rates.

bask /bask/ ▸*v.* [*intrans.*] lie exposed to warmth and light, typically from the sun, for relaxation and pleasure: *sprawled figures **basking in** the afternoon sun*. ■ (**bask in**) *figurative* revel in and make the most of (something pleasing): *he went on **basking in** the **glory** of his first book*. ▷late Middle English (originally in the sense 'bathe'): perhaps related to Old Norse *batha* 'bathe.'

Bas·ker·ville /ˈbaskərˌvil/ ▸*n.* a typeface much used in books. ▷early 19th cent.: named after John *Baskerville* (1706–75), English printer, designer of the typeface.

bas·ket /ˈbaskit/ ▸*n.* **1** a container used to hold or carry things, typically made from interwoven strips of cane or wire: *a laundry basket*. ■ a structure suspended from the envelope of a hot-air balloon for carrying the crew, equipment, and ballast. ■ *Finance* a group or range of currencies or investments: *the European currency unit is made up of **a basket of** ten currencies*. **2** *Basketball* a net fixed on a hoop used as the goal. ■ a goal scored. ▷Middle English: from Old French *basket*, of unknown ultimate origin.

bas·ket·ball /ˈbaskitˌbôl/ ▸*n.* a game played between two teams of five players in which goals are scored by throwing a ball through a netted hoop fixed above each end of the court. ■ the inflated ball used in this game.

bas·ket bin·go ▸*n.* a fund-raising event in which players buy tickets to play bingo for prizes of gift baskets that are made up by donors.

bas·ket case ▸*n.* *informal* a person or thing regarded as useless or unable to cope. ▷early 20th cent.: originally slang denoting a soldier who had lost all four limbs, thus unable to move independently.

bas·ket hilt ▸*n.* a sword hilt with a guard resembling basketwork. —**bas·ket-hilt·ed** *adj.*

Bas·ket Mak·er ▸*n.* a member of a culture of the southwestern U.S., forming the early stages of the Anasazi culture, from the 1st century BC until *c.*AD 700. The name comes from the basketry and other woven fragments found in early cave sites.

bas·ket-of-gold ▸*n.* a cultivated evergreen alyssum, with gray-green leaves and numerous small yellow flowers. • *Alyssum saxatile*, family Brassicaceae.

bas·ket·ry /ˈbaskitrē/ ▸*n.* the craft of basket-making. ■ baskets collectively.

bas·ket star ▸*n.* a brittlestar having branched arms. • Genus *Gorgonocephalus*, family Gorgonocephalidae: several species, including the large *G. eucnemis*.

bas·ket weave ▸*n.* a style of weave or a pattern resembling basketwork.

bas·ket-weav·ing /ˈbaskitˌwēviNG/ ▸*n.* **1** the art or activity of creating woven baskets. **2** *humorous* a college course that is thought to be very easy.

bas·ket·work /ˈbaskitˌwərk/ ▸*n.* material woven in the style of a basket. ■ the craft of making such material.

bask·ing shark ▸*n.* a large shark that feeds exclusively on plankton and often swims slowly close to the surface, found chiefly in the open ocean. • *Cetorhinus maximus*, the only member of the family Cetorhinidae.

Basle /bäl/ a commercial and industrial city on the Rhine River in northwestern Switzerland; pop. 171,000 . French name **BÂLE**, German name **BASEL**.

bas·ma·ti /bäsˈmätē/ (also **basmati rice**) ▸*n.* a kind of long-grain Indian rice of a high quality. ▷from Hindi *bāsmatī*, literally 'fragrant.'

bas mitz·vah /bäs ˈmitsvə/ ▸*n.* a variant of **BAT MITZVAH**.

ba·so·phil /ˈbāsəfil/ ▸*n.* *Physiology* a basophilic white blood cell.

ba·so·phil·i·a /ˌbāsəˈfilēə/ ▸*n.* **1** a tendency to stain readily with a basic dye. **2** a condition of the blood marked by the formation and accumulation of an excess of basophil cells.

ba·so·phil·ic /ˌbāsəˈfilik/ ▸*adj.* *Physiology* (of a cell or its contents) readily stained with basic dyes.

Ba·so·tho /bəˈsōˌtō/ ▸*n.* (*pl.* same or **-thos**) a member of the Sotho people of southern Africa, esp. Lesotho. ▷from Sesotho, from *ba-* (prefix denoting a plural) + **SOTHO**. Compare with **BASUTOLAND**.

Basque /bask/ ▸*n.* **1** a member of a people living in the Basque Country of France and Spain. Culturally one of the most distinct groups in Europe, the Basques were largely independent until the 19th century. **2** the language of this people, which has no known relation to any other language.
▸*adj.* of or relating to the Basques or their language. ▷from French, from Latin *Vasco*; compare with **GASCON**.

basque /bask/ ▸*n.* a close-fitting bodice extending from the shoulders to the waist and often with a short continuation below waist level. ▷mid 19th cent.: from **BASQUE**, referring to Basque dress.

Basque Coun·try /bask/ a region of the western Pyrenees in both France and Spain, the homeland of the Basque people. French name **PAYS BASQUE**.

Basque Prov·in·ces an autonomous region consisting of the provinces of Álava, Guipúzcoa, and Vizcaya in northern Spain, on the Bay of Biscay; capital, Vitoria.

Bas·ra /ˈbäsrə; ˈbäz-/ an oil port in Iraq, on the Shatt al-Arab waterway; pop. 616,700.

bas-re·lief /ˌbä rəˈlēf/ ▸*n.* *Sculpture* see **RELIEF** (sense 4). ■ a sculpture, carving, or molding in bas-relief. ▷early 17th cent. (as *basse relieve*): from Italian *basso-rilievo* 'low relief,' later altered to the French form.

bass[1] /bās/ ▸*n.* a voice, instrument, or sound of the lowest range, in particular: ■ the lowest adult male singing voice. ■ [as *adj.*] denoting the member of a family of instruments that is the lowest in pitch: *a bass clarinet | a bass drum*. ■ *informal* a bass guitar or double bass. ■ the low-frequency output of a radio or audio system, corresponding to the bass in music. ▷late Middle English: alteration of **BASE**[2], influenced by **BASSO**.

bass[2] /bas/ ▸*n.* (*pl.* same or **bass·es**) **1** the common European freshwater perch. **2** any of a number of fish similar to or related to this, in particular: • a mainly marine fish found in temperate waters (family Percichthyidae or Moronidae, including *Dicentrarchus labrax* of European waters and genus *Morone* of North America). • an American freshwater fish of the sunfish family, popular with anglers (genera *Ambloplites* and *Micropterus*, family Centrarchidae). • a sea bass. ▷late Middle English: alteration of dialect *barse*, of Germanic origin; related to Dutch *baars* and German *Barsch*.

bass[3] /bas/ ▸*n.* another term for **BAST**. ▷late 17th cent.: alteration.

bass·ack·wards /ˈbasˈakwərds/ ▸*adv.* & *adj.* *jocular* variant of **ASS-BACKWARDS**.

bass clef /bās klef/ ▸*n.* a clef placing F below middle C on the second-highest line of the staff.

bass drum /bās/ ▸*n.* a large, two-headed drum that has a low booming sound.

Bas·sein /bəˈsān/ a port on the Irrawaddy delta in southwestern Myanmar (Burma); pop. 144,100.

Basse-Nor·man·die /ˈbäs ˌnôrmänˈdē/ a region of

Pronunciation Key ə *ago*; ər *over*; ˈə *or* ˌə *up*; ˈər *or* ˌər *fur*; a *hat*; ā *rate*; ä *car*; CH *chew*; e *let*; ē *see*; e(ə)r *air*; i *fit*; ī *by*; i(ə)r *ear*; NG *sing*; ō *go*; ô *for*; oi *boy*; o͝o *good*; o͞o *goo*; ou *out*; SH *she*; TH *thin*; T͟H *then*; (h)w *why*; ZH *vision*

northwestern France, on the coast of the English Channel, including the Cherbourg peninsula and the city of Caen.

Basse·terre /bäs'ter/ the capital of St. Kitts and Nevis in the Leeward Islands, on the island of St. Kitts; pop. 12,600.

Basse-Terre /bäs 'ter/ the main island of Guadeloupe in the West Indies.

bas·set horn /'basit/ ▸*n.* an alto clarinet in F. ▷mid 19th cent.: from German, translation of French *cor de bassette*, from Italian *corno di bassetto*, from *corno* 'horn' + *di* 'of' + *bassetto* (diminutive of *basso* 'low,' from Latin *bassus* 'short').

bas·set hound /'basit hound/ ▸*n.* a sturdy hunting dog of a breed with a long body, short legs, and big ears. ▷early 17th cent.: from French, diminutive of *bas* 'low,' from medieval Latin *bassus* 'short.'

basset hound

bass fid·dle /bās/ ▸*n.* another term for DOUBLE BASS.

Bas·si /'bäsē/, Laura (1711–78), Bolognese physicist and professor. After receiving her college degree in 1732, she became a professor at the University of Bologna, teaching philosophy, mathematics, and physics. She was the first woman to pursue a scientific career for which she was paid a salary. She also gave private instruction in physics and performed experiments in her home.

bas·si·net /,basə'net/ ▸*n.* a baby's wicker cradle, usually with a hood. ▷mid 19th cent.: from French, diminutive of *bassin* 'basin'; compare with BASINET.

bas·si pro·fun·di /'basē prə'fəndē/ ▸ plural form of BASSO PROFUNDO.

bass·ist /'bāsist/ ▸*n.* a person who plays a double bass or bass guitar.

bass·let /'baslit/ ▸*n.* a small, brightly colored fish related to the sea basses. • Genera *Gramma* and *Lipogramma*, family Grammidae: several species.

bas·so /'basō; bä-/ ▸*n.* (*pl.* **bas·sos** or **bas·si** /'bäsē/) a singer with a bass voice. ▷early 18th cent.: Italian, 'low,' from Latin *bassus* 'short, low.'

bas·soon /bə'so͞on; ba-/ ▸*n.* a bass instrument of the oboe family with a double reed. ▷early 18th cent.: from French *basson*, from Italian *bassone*, from *basso* 'low,' from Latin *bassus* 'short, low.' —**bas·soon·ist** /-nist/ *n.*

bassoon

bas·so pro·fun·do /'basō prō'fəndō; 'bäsō/ ▸*n.* (*pl.* **bas·so pro·fun·dos** or **bas·si pro·fun·di** /'bäsē prō'fəndē/) a bass singer with an exceptionally low range. ▷mid 19th cent.: Italian, from *basso* 'low' + *profondo* 'deep.'

bas·so-re·lie·vo /'basō ri'lēvō/ ▸*n.* (*pl.* **-vos**) *Sculpture* another term for BAS-RELIEF (see RELIEF sense 4). ▷mid 17th cent.: from Italian *basso-rilievo*.

Bass Strait /'bas/ a channel that separates Tasmania from the mainland of Australia.

bass vi·ol /bās 'vīəl/ ▸*n.* a viola da gamba. ■ a double bass.

bass·wood /'bas,wo͝od/ ▸*n.* a North American linden tree, commonly planted along streets. • Genus *Tilia*, family Tiliaceae: several species, in particular the large-leaved *T. americana* (also called **American linden**) of the northern U.S. and Canada. ▷late 17th cent.: from BASS[3] + WOOD.

bast /bast/ ▸*n.* (also **bast fiber**) fibrous material from the phloem of a plant, used as fiber in matting, cord, etc. ■ *Botany* the phloem or vascular tissue of a plant. ▷Old English *bæst*; related to Dutch *bast*, German *Bast*; of unknown origin.

bas·tard /'bastərd/ ▸*n.* **1** *archaic* or *derogatory* a person born of parents not married to each other. **2** *informal* an unpleasant or despicable person: *he lied to me, the bastard!* ■ [with *adj.*] a person (used to suggest an emotion such as pity or envy): *the poor bastard | he was a lucky bastard.* ■ a difficult or awkward thing, undertaking, or situation: *it's been an absolute bastard of a week.*

▸*adj.* [*attrib.*] **1** *archaic* or *derogatory* born of parents not married to each other; illegitimate: *a bastard child.* **2** (of a thing) no longer in its pure or original form; debased: *a bastard Darwinism.* ■ (of a handwriting script or typeface) showing a mixture of different styles. ▷Middle English: via Old French from medieval Latin *bastardus*. —**bas·tar·dy** *n.* (in sense 1 of the *noun*).

USAGE In the past, the word **bastard** was the standard term in both legal and nonlegal use for 'an illegitimate child.' Today, however, it has little importance as a legal term and is retained today in this older sense only as a term of abuse.

bas·tard·ize /'bastər,dīz/ ▸*v.* [*trans.*] **1** [often as *adj.*] (**bastardized**) corrupt or debase (something such as a language or art form), typically by adding new elements: *a strange, bastardized form of French.* **2** *archaic* declare (someone) illegitimate: *to annul the marriage and bastardize the child.* —**bas·tard·i·za·tion** /,bastərdi'zāshən/ *n.*

bas·tard wing ▸*n.* a group of small quill feathers on the first digit of a bird's wing.

baste[1] /bāst/ ▸*v.* [*trans.*] pour juices or melted fat over (meat) during cooking in order to keep it moist. ▷late 15th cent.: of unknown origin.

baste[2] ▸*v.* [*trans.*] *Needlework* tack with long, loose stitches in preparation for sewing. ▷late Middle English: from Old French *bastir* 'sew lightly,' ultimately of Germanic origin and related to BAST.

baste[3] ▸*v.* [*trans.*] *informal, dated* beat (someone) soundly; thrash: *go baste him one!* ▷mid 16th cent.: perhaps a figurative use of BASTE[1].

Bas·tet /'bastet/ *Egyptian Mythology* a goddess usually shown as a woman with the head of a cat, wearing one gold earring. See also SEKHMET.

Ba·sti·a /'bästēə; bäst'yä/ the chief port of the French island of Corsica, on the northeastern coast; pop. 38,730.

Bas·tille /ba'stēl/ a fortress in Paris built in the 14th century and used in the 17th–18th centuries as a state prison. Its storming by the mob on July 14, 1789, marked the start of the French Revolution. ▷via Old French from Provençal *bastida*, from *bastir* 'build.'

Bas·tille Day ▸*n.* July 14, the date of the storming of the Bastille in 1789, celebrated as a national holiday in France.

bas·ti·na·do /,bastə'nādō; -'nädō/ *chiefly historical* ▸*n.* a form of punishment or torture that involves caning the soles of someone's feet.

▸*v.* (**-does, -doed**) [*trans.*] (usu. **be bastinadoed**) punish or torture (someone) in such a way. ▷late 16th cent. (denoting a blow with a stick): from Spanish *bastonada*, from *bastón* 'stick, cudgel,' from late Latin *bastum* 'stick.'

bas·tion /'baschən/ ▸*n.* a projecting part of a fortification built at an angle to the line of a wall, so as to allow defensive fire in several directions. ■ a natural rock formation resembling such a fortification. ■ *figurative* an institution, place, or person strongly defending or upholding particular principles, attitudes, or activities: *the **last bastion of** male privilege.* ▷mid 16th cent.: from French, from Italian *bastione*, from *bastire* 'build.'

bast·naes·ite /'bast-nə,sīt/ ▸*n.* a yellow to brown mineral consisting of a fluoride and carbonate of cerium and other rare earth metals. ▷late 19th cent.: from *Bastnäs*, the name of a district in Västmanland, Sweden, + -ITE[1].

Bas·togne /bä'stōn(yə)/ a town in southeastern Belgium; pop. 11,000. It was the scene of heavy fighting during the Battle of the Bulge in World War II.

ba·su·co /bə'so͞okō/ ▸*n.* impure or low-grade cocaine, esp. when mixed with coca paste and tobacco and marijuana. ▷1980s: from Colombian Spanish; perhaps related to Spanish *bazucar* 'shake violently.'

Ba·su·to·land /bə'so͞otō,land/ former name (until 1966) of LESOTHO. Compare with BASOTHO.

bat[1] /bat/ ▸*n.* an implement with a handle and a solid surface, usually of wood, used for hitting the ball in games such as baseball, cricket, and table tennis. ■ the person batting, esp. in cricket: *the team's opening bat.* ■ each of a pair of objects resembling table tennis bats, used by a person on the ground to guide a taxiing aircraft.

▸*v.* (**bat·ted, bat·ting**) **1** [*intrans.*] (of a team or a player in sports such as baseball) take in turns the role of hitting rather than fielding: *Ruth came to bat in the fifth inning.* **2** [*trans.*] hit at (someone or something) with the palm of one's hand: *he batted the flies away.*

▸*phrasal v.* □ **bat around** (or **about**) *informal* travel widely, frequently, or casually: *I'm always batting around between England and America.* □ **bat something around** (or **about**) *informal* discuss an idea or proposal casually or idly. □ **go to bat for** *informal* defend the interests of; support: *his willingness to go to bat for his employees.* ▷late Old English *batt* 'club, stick, staff,' perhaps partly from Old French *batte*, from *battre* 'to strike.'

▸*PHRASE* □ **right off the bat** at the very beginning.

bat[2] ▸*n.* **1** a mainly nocturnal mammal capable of sustained flight, with membranous wings that extend between the fingers and connecting the forelimbs to the body and the hindlimbs to the tail. • Order Chiroptera: many families and numerous species. The large tropical fruit bats (suborder Megachiroptera) generally have good eyesight and feed mainly on fruit; the numerous smaller bats (suborder Microchiroptera) are mouselike in appearance, mainly insectivorous, and use ultrasonic echolocation. **2** (usu. **old bat**) a woman regarded as unattractive or unpleasant: *some deranged old bat.* ▷late 16th cent.: alteration, perhaps by association with medieval Latin *batta*, *blacta*, of Middle English *bakke*, of Scandinavian origin.

▸*PHRASES* □ **have bats in the** (or **one's**) **belfry** *informal* be eccentric or crazy. □ **like a bat out of hell** *informal* very fast and wildly.

bat[3] ▸*v.* (**bat·ted, bat·ting**) [*trans.*] flutter one's eyelashes, typically in a flirtatious manner: *she batted her long dark eyelashes at him.* ▷late 19th cent.: from dialect *bat* 'to wink, blink,' variant of obsolete *bate* 'to flutter.'

▸*PHRASE* □ **not bat** (or **without batting**) **an eyelid** (or **eye**) *informal* show (or showing) no reaction: *she paid the bill without batting an eyelid.*

Ba·taan /bə'tan; -'tän/ a peninsula and province in the Philippines, on the western part of the island of Luzon, bounded by Manila Bay on the east and the South China Sea on the west; site of World War II battles and the infamous "Death March." Pop. 426,000.

Ba·tak /bə'täk/ ▸*n.* **1** (*pl.* same or **-taks**) a member of a people of northern Sumatra. **2** the Indonesian language of this people.

▸*adj.* of or relating to the Batak or their language. ▷the name in Batak.

Ba·tan Is·lands /bä'tän/ the northernmost islands in the Philippines.

ba·ta·ta /bə'tätə/ ▸*n.* (in the southern West Indies) sweet potato. ▷via Spanish from Taino.

Ba·ta·vi·a /bə'tāvēə/ former name (until 1949) for JAKARTA.

Ba·ta·vi·an /bə'tāvēən/ *historical or archaic* ▸*adj.* of or relating to the ancient Germanic people who inhabited the island of Betuwe between the Rhine and the Waal (now part of the Netherlands). ■ of or relating to the people of the Netherlands. ■ of or relating to Djakarta in Indonesia (formerly the Dutch East Indies).

▸*n.* a Batavian person. ▷from Latin *Batavia* (from *Batavi* 'the people of Betuwe') + -AN.

bat·boy /'bat,boi/ ▸*n.* a boy who is employed to look after and retrieve bats during a baseball game and as a general assistant at other times.

batch /bach/ ▸*n.* a quantity or consignment of goods produced at one time: ***a batch of** cookies | the company undertakes thirty-six separate quality control checks on every batch.* ■ *informal* a number of things or people regarded as a group or set: ***a batch of** hostile letters came.* ■ *Computing* a group of records processed as a single unit, usually without input from a user.

▸*v.* [*trans.*] arrange (things) in sets or groups. ▷late 15th cent. (in the senses 'process of baking,' 'quantity produced at one baking'): based on an Old English word related to *bacan* (see BAKE). Current senses date from the early 18th cent.

batch file ▸*n.* a computer file containing a list of instructions to be carried out in turn.

batch proc·ess·ing ▸*n.* the performing of an industrial process on material in batches of a limited quantity or number. ■ *Computing* the processing of previously collected jobs in a single batch.

bate /bāt/ ▸*v.* [*intrans.*] *Falconry* (of a hawk) beat the wings in an attempt to escape from the perch: *the* *hawks bated when the breeze got in their feathers.* ▷late Middle English: from Old French *batre* 'to beat' (see also **BATTER**[1]).

ba·teau /ba'tō/ ▶*n.* (*pl.* **-teaux** /-'tōz/) a light flat-bottomed riverboat used in eastern and central North America. ▷early 18th cent.: French, literally 'boat.'

bat·ed /'bātid/ ▶*adj.* (in phrase **with bated breath**) in great suspense; very anxiously or excitedly: *he waited for a reply to his offer with bated breath.* ▷late 16th cent.: from the past participle of obsolete *bate* 'restrain,' from **ABATE**.

USAGE The spelling *baited breath* instead of **bated breath** is a common mistake that, in addition to perpetuating a cliché, evokes a distasteful image. Before using the expression **bated breath**, think of the verb *abate*, as in *the winds abated*, not fish bait.

Bates ▶, Alan 1934–2003, English actor. Notable films: *The Caretaker* (1964), *Zorba the Greek* (1964), *The Fixer* (1968), *Women in Love* (1969), and *An Unmarried Woman* (1978). He also played a number of roles on stage and won a Tony Award for his performance in Turgenev's *Fortune's Fool* (2002).

Bates·i·an mim·ic·ry /'bātsēən/ ▶*n. Zoology* mimicry in which an edible animal is protected by its resemblance to a noxious one that is avoided by predators. Compare with **MÜLLERIAN MIMICRY**. ▷late 19th cent.: named after Henry W. *Bates* (1825–92), the English naturalist who first described it.

Bate·son /'bātsən/, William (1861–1926), English geneticist. He coined the term *genetics* in its current sense and publicized the work of Gregor Mendel.

bat·fish /'bat,fisн/ ▶*n.* (*pl.* same or **-fish·es**) **1** a fish of tropical and temperate seas with a flattened body that is round or almost triangular when viewed from above. It typically has a hard or spiny covering. • Family Ogcocephalidae: several genera and species, including the southern African *Halieuta fitzsimonsi*. **2** a deep-bodied, laterally compressed marine fish of the Indo-Pacific region that resembles an angelfish. • Genus *Platax*, family Ephippidae: several species, including the large *P. pinnatus* (also called **ANGELFISH**.)

bat·fowl /'bat,foul/ ▶*v.* [*intrans.*] catch birds at night by dazing them with a light and knocking them down or netting them.

bat·girl /'bat,gərl/ ▶*n.* a girl who is employed to look after and retrieve bats during a baseball game and as a general assistant at other times.

Bath /baтн; bäтн/ a spa town in southwestern England; pop. 79,900.

bath[1] /baтн/ ▶*n.* (*pl.* **baths** /baтнs; baтнz/) an act or process of immersing and washing one's body in a large container of water: *she* **took** *a long, hot* **bath**. ■ such a container and its contents; a bathtub: *he lay thinking* **in the bath**. ■ [with *adj.*] any act of washing or cleansing oneself: *sweat baths | sponge baths.* ■ (usu. **baths**) a public establishment offering bathing facilities. ■ (**baths**) a resort with a mineral spring used for medical treatment. ■ a bathroom. ■ [with *adj.*] a container holding a liquid or other substance in which something is immersed, typically when undergoing a process such as film developing.
▶*v.* [*trans.*] wash (someone) while immersing him or her in a container of water: *how to bath a baby.* ▷Old English *bæth*, of Germanic origin; related to Dutch *bad* and German *Bad*.
▶***PHRASE*** □ **take a bath** *informal* suffer a heavy financial loss.

bath[2] ▶*n.* an ancient Hebrew liquid measure equivalent to about 40 liters or 9 gallons. ▷from Hebrew *baṯ*.

bath chair ▶*n. dated* a kind of wheelchair for invalids, typically with a hood. ▷early 19th cent.: named after the city of **BATH**, which attracted many invalids because of the supposed curative powers of its hot springs.

bathe /bāтн/ ▶*v.* [*intrans.*] wash by immersing one's body in water. ■ spend time in the ocean or a lake, river, or swimming pool for pleasure. ■ [*trans.*] soak or wipe gently with liquid to clean or soothe: *she bathed and bandaged my knee.* ■ [*trans.*] wash (someone) in a bath: *they bathed the baby.* ■ [*trans.*] (usu. **be bathed**) *figurative* suffuse or envelop in something: *the park lay bathed in sunshine | mussels bathed in garlic butter.* ▷Old English *bathian*, of Germanic origin; related to Dutch and German *baden*. **—bath·er** *n.*

bath·house /'baтн,hous/ ▶*n.* **1** a building with baths for communal use. **2** a building where swimmers change clothes.

Bath·i·nette /,baтнə'net/ ▶*n. trademark* a portable folding bathtub for infants. ▷a play on the word **BASSINET**.

bath·ing beau·ty ▶*n.* a contestant in a beauty contest in which bathing suits are worn.

bath·ing cap ▶*n.* a close-fitting elastic cap worn while swimming to keep the hair dry or to reduce friction.

bath·ing ma·chine /'bāтнiNG/ ▶*n. historical* a wheeled hut drawn to the edge of the sea, used for changing in and swimming from.

bath·ing suit ▶*n.* a garment worn for swimming; a swimsuit.

bath mat ▶*n.* a mat for someone to stand on after getting out of a bathtub. ■ a rubber mat placed in the bottom of a bathtub to prevent someone from slipping while getting in or out.

bath·o·lith /'baтнə,liтн/ ▶*n. Geology* a very large igneous intrusion extending deep in the earth's crust. ▷early 20th cent.: coined in German from Greek *bathos* 'depth' + **-LITH**.

ba·thos /'bāтнäs/ ▶*n.* (esp. in a work of literature) an effect of anticlimax created by an unintentional lapse in mood from the sublime to the trivial or ridiculous. ▷mid 17th cent. (first recorded in the Greek sense): from Greek, literally 'depth.' The current sense was introduced by Alexander Pope in the early 18th cent. **—ba·thet·ic** /bə'тнetik/ *adj.*

bath·robe /'baтн,rōb/ ▶*n.* a robe, typically made of terrycloth, worn esp. before and after taking a bath.

bath·room /'baтн,ro͞om; -,ro͝om/ ▶*n.* a room containing a bathtub or a shower and usually also a washbasin and a toilet. ■ a set of matching units to be fitted in such a room, esp. as sold together. ■ a room containing a toilet: *I have to go to the bathroom.*
▶***PHRASE*** □ **go to** (or **use**) **the bathroom** urinate or defecate.

bath salts ▶*plural n.* a crystalline substance that is dissolved in bathwater to soften or perfume the water.

Bath·she·ba /,baтн'sнēbə/ (in the Bible) the mother of Solomon, she was originally the wife of Uriah the Hittite, and later one of the wives of David.

bath sponge ▶*n.* a marine sponge of warm waters, the fibrous skeleton of which is used as a sponge for washing. • Genera *Spongia* and *Hippospongia*, family Spongiidae.

bath·tub /'baтн,təb/ ▶*n.* a tub, usually installed in a bathroom, in which to bathe.

Bath·urst /'baтнərst/ former name (until 1973) of **BANJUL**.

bathy- ▶*comb. form* relating to depth: *bathymetry | bathysphere.* ▷from Greek *bathus* 'deep.'

bath·y·al /'baтнēəl/ ▶*adj.* of or relating to the zone of the sea between the continental shelf and the abyssal zone.

ba·thym·e·ter /bə'тнimitər/ ▶*n.* an instrument used to measure the depth of water in oceans, seas, or lakes. ▷late 19th cent.: from Greek *bathos* 'depth' + **-METER**.

ba·thym·e·try /bə'тнimətrē/ ▶*n.* the measurement of depth of water in oceans, seas, or lakes. ▷mid 19th cent.: from Greek *bathus* 'deep' + **-METRY**. **—bath·y·met·ric** /,baтнə'metrik/ *adj.*

bath·y·pe·lag·ic /,baтнəpə'lajik/ ▶*adj. Biology* (of fish and other organisms) inhabiting the deep sea where the environment is dark and cold, approximately 3,300–9,800 feet (1,000–3,000 m) below the surface.

bath·y·scaphe /'baтнə,skaf/ ▶*n. chiefly historical* a manned submersible vessel of a kind used by the French deep-sea explorer Auguste Piccard (1884–1962). ▷1940s: coined in French by its inventor, Auguste Piccard, from Greek *bathus* 'deep' + *skaphos* 'vessel; hull (of a ship).'

bath·y·sphere /'baтнə,sfir/ ▶*n.* a manned spherical chamber for deep-sea observation, lowered by cable from a ship. ▷1930s: from Greek *bathus* 'deep' + **SPHERE**.

ba·tik /bə'tēk/ ▶*n.* a method (originally used in Java) of producing colored designs on textiles by dyeing them, having first applied wax to the parts to be left undyed. ■ an item or piece of cloth treated in this way. ▷late 19th cent.: from Javanese, literally 'painted.'

Ba·tis·ta /bə'tēstə/, Fulgencio (1901–73), Cuban soldier and statesman; president 1940–44 and 1952–59; full name *Fulgencio Batista y Zaldívar*. Despite support from the U.S., his second government was overthrown by Fidel Castro.

ba·tiste /bə'tēst/ ▶*n.* a fine, light linen or cotton fabric resembling cambric. ▷early 19th cent.: from French (earlier *batiche*); probably related to *battre* 'to beat.'

bat·man /'batmən/ ▶*n.* (*pl.* **-men**) *dated* (in the British armed forces) an officer's personal servant. ▷mid 18th cent. (originally denoting an orderly in charge of the *bat horse* 'packhorse' that carried the officer's baggage): from Old French *bat* (from medieval Latin *bastum* 'packsaddle') + **MAN**.

bat mitz·vah /bät 'mitsvə/ ▶*n.* a religious initiation ceremony for a Jewish girl aged twelve years and one day, regarded as the age of religious maturity. ■ the girl undergoing such a ceremony. ▷from Hebrew *baṯ miṣwāh* 'daughter of the commandment,' on the pattern of **BAR MITZVAH**.

ba·ton /bə'tän/ ▶*n.* a short stick or staff or something resembling one, in particular: ■ a thin stick used by a conductor to direct an orchestra or choir. ■ *Track & Field* a short stick or tube passed from runner to runner in a relay race. ■ a long stick carried and twirled by a drum major. ■ a police officer's club. ■ a staff symbolizing office or authority, esp. one carried by a field marshal. ■ *Heraldry* a narrow bend truncated at each end. ■ a short bar replacing some figures on the dial of a clock or watch. ■ (**batons**) one of the suits in some tarot packs, corresponding to wands in others. ▷early 16th cent. (denoting a staff or cudgel): from French *bâton*, earlier *baston*, from late Latin *bastum* 'stick.'
▶***PHRASES*** □ **pass** (**on**) **the baton** hand over a particular duty or responsibility. □ **take up** (or **pick up**) **the baton** accept a duty or responsibility. □ **under the baton of** (of an orchestra or choir) conducted by: *under the baton of Sir Edward Downes.*

Bat·on Rouge /,batn 'ro͞ozн/ the capital of Louisiana, in the southeastern central part of the state, on the Mississippi River; pop. 227,818. ▷French, literally "red stick," with reference to a post placed as a boundary marker for the settlement.

Ba·tra·chi·a /bə'trākēə/ *Zoology* another term, esp. formerly, for **ANURA**. ▷modern Latin (plural), from Greek *batrakhos* 'frog.' **—ba·tra·chi·an** *n.* & *adj.*

bats /bats/ ▶*adj.* [*predic.*] *informal, dated* (of a person) crazy; insane. ▷early 20th cent.: from the phrase *have bats in the belfry* (see **BAT**[2]).

bats·man /'batsmən/ ▶*n.* (*pl.* **-men**) a player, esp. in baseball and cricket, who is batting or whose chief skill is in batting. **—bats·man·ship** /-,sнip/ *n.*

Bat·swa·na /bät'swänə/ ▶*n.* & *adj.* see **TSWANA**.

batt /bat/ ▶*n.* a piece of felted material used for lining or insulating items such as quilts and sleeping bags. ■ a piece of fiberglass used to insulate buildings. ▷late Middle English (in the general sense 'lump, piece'): of unknown origin.

bat·tal·ion /bə'talyən/ ▶*n.* a large body of troops ready for battle, esp. an infantry unit forming part of a brigade typically commanded by a lieutenant colonel. ■ a large, organized group of people pursuing a common aim or sharing a major undertaking. ▷late 16th cent.: from French *bataillon*, from Italian *battaglione*, from *battaglia* 'battle,' from Latin (see **BATTLE**).

Bat·tam·bang /'batəm,baNG/ (also **Bat·dam·bang**) the capital of a province of the same name in western Cambodia; pop. 551,860.

batte·ment /'batmənt/ ▶*n.* [with *adj.*] *Ballet* a movement in which one leg is moved outward from the body and in again: *performing battements tendus.* ▷mid 19th cent.: French, literally 'beating.'

Bat·ten /'batn/, Jean (1909–82), New Zealand aviator. She was the first woman to fly from England to Australia and back 1934–35.

bat·ten[1] /'batn/ ▶*n.* a long, flat strip of squared wood or metal used to hold something in place or as a fastening against a wall. ■ a strip of wood used for clamping the boards of a door. ■ a strip of wood or metal for securing the edges of a tarpaulin that covers a ship's hatch. ■ a strip of wood or plastic used to stiffen and extend the leech of a sail.
▶*v.* [*trans.*] strengthen or fasten (something) with battens: *Stephen was* **battening down** *the shutters.* ▷late 15th cent.: from Old French *batant*, present participle (used as a noun) of *batre* 'to beat,' from Latin *battuere*.
▶***PHRASE*** □ **batten down the hatches** *Nautical* secure a ship's hatch-tarpaulins, esp. when rough weather is expected. ■ *figurative* prepare for a difficulty or crisis.

bat·ten[2] ▶*v.* [*intrans.*] (**batten on**) thrive or prosper at the expense of (someone): *multinational monopolies batten on the working classes.* ▷late 16th cent. (in the sense 'improve in condition, grow fat'): from Old Norse *batna* 'get better,' related to BETTER[1].

bat·ten·ing /'batn-ING/ ▸*n.* the application or addition of battens. ■ a structure formed with battens.

bat·ter[1] /'batər/ ▸*v.* [*trans.*] strike repeatedly with hard blows; pound heavily and insistently: *a prisoner was* ***battered to death*** *with a table leg* | *figurative their idealism has been battered.* ■ [often as *n.*] (**battering**) subject (one's spouse, partner, or child) to repeated violence and assault. ■ [usu. as *n.*] (**battering**) *figurative* censure, criticize, or defeat severely: *the movie* ***took a battering*** *from critics.* ▹Middle English: from Old French *batre* 'to beat' (from Latin *battuere*) + -ER[3]. —**bat·ter·er** *n.*

bat·ter[2] ▸*n.* **1** a semiliquid mixture of flour, egg, and milk or water used in cooking, esp. for making cakes or for coating food before frying. **2** *Printing, chiefly historical* a damaged area of metal type or a printing block. ▹late Middle English: from Old French *bateure* 'the action of beating,' from *batre* 'to beat.'

bat·ter[3] ▸*n.* (in various sports, esp. baseball) a player who is batting.

bat·ter[4] ▸*n.* a gradual backward slope in a wall or similar structure.
▸*v.* [*intrans.*] (of a wall) have a receding slope. ▹mid 16th cent. (as a verb): of unknown origin.

bat·tered[1] /'batərd/ ▸*adj.* injured by repeated blows or punishment: *he finished the day battered and bruised.* ■ having suffered repeated violence from a spouse, partner, or parent: *a battered wife.* ■ (of a thing) damaged by age and repeated use; shabby: *a pair of battered black boots.*

bat·tered[2] ▸*adj.* (of food) coated in batter and deep-fried until crisp.

bat·tered child syn·drome ▸*n.* the set of symptoms, injuries, and signs of mistreatment seen on a severely or repeatedly abused child.

bat·tered wom·an syn·drome ▸*n.* the set of symptoms, injuries, and signs of mistreatment seen in a woman who has been repeatedly abused by a husband or other male figure.

bat·te·rie /'batərē/ ▸*n. Ballet* the action of beating or crossing the feet or calves together during a leap or jump. ▹early 18th cent.: French, literally 'beating.'

bat·te·rie de cui·sine /ba'trē də kwē'zēn/ ▸*n.* the apparatus or set of utensils for serving or preparing a meal. ▹late 18th cent.: French, literally 'set of equipment for the kitchen.' The sense of 'set' developed from the original meaning of 'collection of artillery equipment (for "beating" the enemy)'; see also BATTERY.

bat·ter·ing par·ent syn·drome ▸*n.* the set of symptoms and signs indicating a psychological disorder in a parent or child-care provider resulting in a tendency toward repeated abuse of a child.

bat·ter·ing ram ▸*n.* a heavy object swung or rammed against a door to break it down: *figurative a battering ram to crush opposing views.* ■ *historical* a heavy beam, originally with an end in the form of a carved ram's head, used in breaching fortifications.

Bat·tery /'batərē/ (**the Battery**) a historic area at the southern end of Manhattan Island in New York City.

bat·ter·y /'batərē/ ▸*n.* (*pl.* **-ter·ies**) **1** a container consisting of one or more cells, in which chemical energy is converted into electricity and used as a source of power: [as *adj.*] *battery power.* **2** a fortified emplacement for heavy guns. ■ an artillery subunit of guns, men, and vehicles. **3** a set of similar units of equipment, typically when connected together: *a battery of equipment to monitor blood pressure.* ■ an extensive series, sequence, or range of things: *children given a battery of tests.* **4** *Law* the crime or tort of unconsented physical contact with another person, even where the contact is not violent but merely menacing or offensive. See also ASSAULT AND BATTERY. **5** (**the battery**) *Baseball* the pitcher and the catcher in a game, considered as a unit. ▹Middle English: from French *batterie,* from *battre* 'to strike,' from Latin *battuere.* The original sense was 'metal articles wrought by hammering,' later 'a number of pieces of artillery used together'; on this was based a sense 'a number of Leyden jars connected up so as to discharge simultaneously' (mid 18th cent.), from which sense 1 developed. The general meaning 'a set or series of similar units' (sense 3) dates from the late 19th cent.

bat·ting ▸*n.* cotton wadding prepared in sheets for use in quilts.

bat·ting av·er·age ▸*n. Baseball* the average performance of a batter, expressed as a ratio of a batter's safe hits per official times at bat.

bat·ting cage ▸*n. Baseball* an area for batting practice that is enclosed by fencing or netting.

bat·ting or·der ▸*n. Baseball* the order in which batters take their turn at bat.

bat·tle /'batl/ ▸*n.* a sustained fight between large, organized armed forces: [in *names*] *the Battle of Shiloh* | *he died* ***in battle.*** ■ a lengthy and difficult conflict or struggle: *the battle over the future shape of Europe* | *the battle against aging.*
▸*v.* [*intrans.*] fight or struggle tenaciously to achieve or resist something: *he has been* ***battling against*** *the illness* | *representatives from eight countries are* ***battling for*** *the title.* ■ [*trans.*] engage in a fight or struggle against: *firefighters battled a 9,800-acre brush fire.* ▹Middle English: from Old French *bataille* (noun), *bataillier* (verb), based on late Latin *battualia* 'military or gladiatorial exercises,' from Latin *battuere* 'to beat.' —**bat·tler** *n.*
▸*PHRASES* □ **battle it out** fight or compete to a definite conclusion. □ **do battle** fight; engage in conflict: *do battle with the forces of evil.* □ **battle royal** (*pl.* **battles royal**) a fiercely contested fight or dispute: *there promises to be a battle royal between the two companies.* □ **battle stations** the positions taken by military personnel in preparation for battle (often used as a command or signal to prepare for battle). □ **half the battle** an important step toward achieving something: *he never gives in, and that's half the battle.*

bat·tle-ax (also **bat·tle-axe**) ▸*n.* **1** a large broad-bladed ax used in ancient warfare. **2** *informal* a formidably aggressive older woman.

Bat·tle-born State /'batl,bôrn/ nickname for NEVADA.

Bat·tle Creek a city in southern Michigan, noted as a center of the cereal industry; pop. 53,540.

bat·tle-cruis·er /'batl,kro͞ozər/ ▸*n. historical* a large warship of a type built in the early 20th century, carrying similar armament to a battleship but faster and more lightly armored.

bat·tle cry ▸*n.* a word or phrase shouted by soldiers going into battle to express solidarity and intimidate the enemy. ■ a slogan expressing the ideals of people promoting a cause.

bat·tle·dore /'batl,dôr/ ▸*n. historical* (also **battledore and shuttlecock**) a game played with a shuttlecock and rackets; a forerunner of badminton. ■ the small racket used in this. ▹late Middle English (in the sense 'a paddle-shaped implement used in washing clothes'): perhaps from Provençal *batedor* 'beater, paddle,' from *batre* 'to beat.'

bat·tle fa·tigue ▸*n.* another term for SHELL SHOCK.

bat·tle·field /'batl,fēld/ (also **bat·tle·ground** /-,ground/) ▸*n.* the piece of ground on which a battle is or was fought: *death on the battlefield* | [as *adj.*] *battlefield conditions.* ■ *figurative* a place or situation of strife or conflict: *an ideological battlefield.*

bat·tle·front /'batl,frənt/ ▸*n.* the region or line along which opposing armies engage in combat. ■ the area in which opponents or opposing ideas meet.

bat·tle group ▸*n.* a military force created to fight together, typically consisting of several different types of troops.

bat·tle jack·et ▸*n.* a style of waist-length jacket worn by army personnel. ■ any jacket of a similar cut.

bat·tle·ment /'batlmənt/ ▸*n.* (usu. **battlements**) a parapet at the top of a wall, usually of a fort or castle, that has regularly spaced, squared openings for shooting through. ■ a section of roof enclosed by this. ▹late Middle English: from Old French *bataillier* 'fortify with movable defense turrets,' possibly related to BATTLE. —**bat·tle·ment·ed** *adj.*

battlement

bat·tler /'batlər; 'batl-ər/ ▸*n.* a person who refuses to admit defeat in the face of difficulty: *a trash talking battler taking swings at opponents and rallying friends.*

> *USAGE* *Battler* is long and firmly established in Antipodean English and summarizes a national character trait for many Australians; it is increasingly common now both in British and American English.

bat·tle·ship /'batl,SHip/ ▸*n.* a heavy warship of a type built chiefly in the late 19th and early 20th centuries, with extensive armor and large-caliber guns. ▹late 18th cent.: shortening of *line-of-battle ship,* originally with reference to the largest wooden warships.

bat·tle·ship gray ▸*n.* a bluish gray color, typically used for warships to reduce their visibility.

bat·tle star ▸*n.* former term for SERVICE STAR.

bat·tle·wag·on /'batl,wagən/ (also **bat·tle wag·on**) ▸*n. informal* a battleship or an armored vehicle.

bat·tue /ba'to͞o/ ▸*n.* the driving of game toward hunters by beaters. ■ a hunting party arranged in such a way. ▹early 19th cent.: from French, feminine past participle of *battre* 'to beat,' from Latin *battuere.*

bat·ty /'batē/ ▸*adj.* (**-ti·er, -ti·est**) *informal* crazy; insane: *you'll drive me batty!* ▹early 20th cent.: from BAT[2] + -Y[1]. Compare with BATS. —**bat·ti·ly** /'batəlē/ *adv.* —**bat·ti·ness** *n.*

bat·wing /'bat,wiNG/ ▸*adj.* [*attrib.*] (of a sleeve) having a deep armhole and a tight cuff. ■ (of a garment) having such sleeves.

bau·ble /'bôbəl/ ▸*n.* **1** a small, showy trinket or decoration. ■ *figurative* something of no importance or worth. **2** *historical* a baton formerly used as an emblem by jesters. ▹Middle English: from Old French *baubel* 'child's toy,' of unknown origin.

Bau·cis /'bôsis/ *Greek Mythology* the wife of Philemon.

baud /bôd/ ▸*n.* (*pl.* same or **bauds**) *chiefly Computing* a unit used to express the speed of transmission of electronic signals, corresponding to one information unit or event per second. ■ a unit of data transmission speed for a modem of one bit per second (in fact there is usually more than one bit per event). ▹1930s: coined in French from the name of J. M. E. *Baudot* (1845–1903), French engineer who invented a telegraph printing system.

Bau·de·laire /,bōdə'le(ə)r; -dl'e(ə)r/, Charles (Pierre) (1821–67), French poet and critic. He is noted for *Les Fleurs du mal* (1857), a series of 101 lyrics that explore his isolation and melancholy and the attraction of evil and the macabre.

Bau·dril·lard /,bōdrē'(y)är/, Jean (1929–), French sociologist and cultural critic, associated with postmodernism.

Baugh /bô/, Sammy (1914–), U.S. football player; full name *Samuel Adrian Baugh*; known as **Slingin' Sammy**. He played for the Washington Redskins 1937–52, where his trademark pinpoint passing revolutionized professional football by making the forward pass a routine play from scrimmage. In 1943, he became the only player to lead the National Football League (NFL) in passing, punting, and interceptions in the same season. Football Hall of Fame (1963).

Bau·haus /'bou,hous/ a school of design established by Walter Gropius in Weimar in 1919, best known for its designs of objects based on functionalism and simplicity. ▹German, 'house of architecture,' from *Bau* 'building' + *Haus* 'house.'

baulk ▸*v.* & *n. Brit.* variant spelling of BALK.

baulk·y ▸*adj.* British spelling of BALKY.

Baum /bôm; bäm/, L(yman) Frank (1856–1919), U.S. journalist and author. His many children's books include *Father Goose: His Book* (1899), *The Wonderful Wizard of Oz* (1900), and other *Oz* books.

Bau·mé scale /bō'mā; 'bōmā/ ▸*n.* a scale with arbitrary markings, used with a hydrometer to measure the relative density of liquids. ▹named for Antoine Baumé (1728–1804), French chemist.

Bausch /bousH/, John Jacob (1830–1926), U.S. businessman, born in Germany. He cofounded (with Henry Lomb) the Bausch & Lomb Optical Company in 1853.

baux·ite /'bôksīt/ ▸*n.* an amorphous clayey rock that is the chief commercial ore of aluminum. It consists largely of hydrated alumina with variable proportions of iron oxides. ▹mid 19th cent.: from French, from *Les Baux* (the name of a village near Arles in southeastern France, near which it was first found) + -ITE[1]. —**baux·it·ic** /,bôk'sitik/ *adj.*

ba·var·dage /,bavər'däzH/ ▸*n.* idle gossip; chitchat. ▹French, from *bavarder* 'to chatter,' from *bavard* 'talkative,' from *bave* 'drivel.'

Ba·var·i·a /bə've(ə)rēə/ a state in southern Germany, formerly an independent kingdom; capital, Munich. German name **BAYERN**.

Ba·var·i·an /bə've(ə)rēən/ ▸*adj.* of or relating to Bavaria, its people, or their language.
▸*n.* **1** a native or inhabitant of Bavaria. **2** the dialect of German used in Bavaria.

ba·va·rois /,bävär'wä/ (also **ba·va·roise** /-'wäz/) ▸*n.* a dessert containing gelatin and whipped cream, served cold. ▷mid 19th cent.: French, literally 'Bavarian.'

baw·bee /'bôbē/ ▸*n. Scottish & N. Irish* a coin of low value. ■ *historical* a former silver coin worth three (later six) Scottish pennies. ▷mid 16th cent.: from the name of the laird of Sille*bawby*, mint master under James V.

bawd /bôd/ ▸*n. archaic* a woman in charge of a brothel. ▷late Middle English: shortened from obsolete *bawdstrot*, from Old French *baudestroyt* 'procuress,' from *baude* 'shameless.'

bawd·ry /'bôdrē/ ▸*n.* obscenity in speech or writing.

bawd·y /'bôdē/ ▸*adj.* (**bawd·i·er**, **bawd·i·est**) dealing with sexual matters in a comical way; humorously indecent.
▸*n.* humorously indecent talk or writing. —**bawd·i·ly** /-dəlē/ *adv.* —**bawd·i·ness** *n.*

bawd·y house ▸*n. archaic* a brothel.

bawl /bôl/ ▸*v.* **1** [*reporting verb*] shout or call out noisily and unrestrainedly: [with *direct speech*] *"Move!" bawled the drill sergeant* | [*trans.*] *lustily* **bawling out** *the hymns* | [*intrans.*] *Joe bawled with laughter.* **2** [*intrans.*] weep or cry noisily: *she began to bawl like a child* | [as *adj.*] (**bawling**) *bawling babies.*
▸*phrasal v.* □ **bawl someone out** reprimand someone angrily: *tales of how she bawled out employees.*
▸*n.* a loud, unrestrained shout. ▷late Middle English (in the sense '(of an animal) howl, bark'): imitative.

Bax·ter /'bakstər/, Anne (1923–85), U.S. actress. She won an Academy Award in 1946 for her supporting role in *The Razor's Edge.*

Bax·ter State Park /'bakstər/ a preserve in northern Maine that incorporates Mount Katahdin and the northern end of the Appalachian Trail.

bay[1] /bā/ ▸*n.* a broad inlet of the sea where the land curves inward: [in *place names*] *San Francisco Bay* | *the Bay of Biscay.* ■ an indentation or recess in a range of hills or mountains. ▷late Middle English: from Old French *baie*, from medieval Latin *baia.*

bay[2] ▸*n.* **1** (also **bay tree**, **bay laurel**, or **sweet bay**) an evergreen Mediterranean shrub of the laurel family, with deep green leaves and purple berries. Its aromatic leaves are used in cooking and were formerly used to make triumphal crowns for victors. • *Laurus nobilis*, family Lauraceae. **2** a similarly aromatic tree or shrub of North America, esp. the bayberry used in the preparation of bay rum. ▷late Middle English (denoting the laurel berry): from Old French *baie*, from Latin *baca* 'berry.'

bay[3] ▸*n.* a recessed or enclosed area, in particular: ■ a space created by a window-line projecting outward from a wall. ■ short for BAY WINDOW. ■ a section of wall between two buttresses or columns, esp. in the nave of a church. ■ [with *adj.*] a compartment with a particular function in a motor vehicle, aircraft, or ship: *an engine bay* | *a bomb bay.* ■ an area allocated or marked off for a specified purpose: *a loading bay.* ■ short for SICKBAY. ■ *Computing* a cabinet, or a space in the cabinet, into which an electronic device is installed: *a drive bay.* ▷late Middle English: from Old French *baie*, from *baer* 'to gape,' from medieval Latin *batare*, of unknown origin.

bay[4] ▸*adj.* (of a horse) brown with black points.
▸*n.* a bay horse. ▷Middle English: from Old French *bai*, from Latin *badius.*

bay[5] ▸*v.* [*intrans.*] (of a dog, esp. a large one) bark or howl loudly: *the dogs bayed* | *a jackal* **baying at the moon.** ■ (of a group of people) shout loudly, typically to demand something: *as a mob bayed below, the king was dead.* ■ [*trans.*] *archaic* bay at: *a pack of wolves baying at the moon.*
▸*n.* the sound of baying, esp. that of hounds in close pursuit of their quarry. ▷Middle English (as a noun): from Old French *(a)bai* (noun), *(a)baiier* (verb) 'to bark,' of imitative origin.
▸*PHRASES* □ **at bay** forced to confront one's attackers or pursuers; cornered. □ **bring someone/something to bay** trap or corner a person or animal being hunted or chased. □ **hold** (or **keep**) **someone/something at bay** prevent someone or something from approaching or having an effect. □ **stand at bay** turn to face one's pursuers.

ba·ya·dère /'bīə,de(ə)r/ ▸*n.* a Hindu dancing girl, in particular one at a southern Indian temple. ▷from French, from Portuguese *bailadeira*, from *bailar* 'to dance' (related to medieval Latin *ballare* 'to dance').

Bay Ar·e·a the region around San Francisco Bay, in north central California. Oakland is the hub of the East Bay, San Jose of the South Bay.

bay·ber·ry /'bā,berē/ ▸*n.* (*pl.* **-ries**) **1** a North American shrub with aromatic leathery leaves and waxy berries. See also WAX MYRTLE. • Genus *Myrica*, family Myricaceae: several species, in particular **northern bayberry** (*M. pensylvanica*) and **black bayberry** (*M. heterophylla*). **2** a tropical American shrub with aromatic leaves that are used in the preparation of bay rum. Also called **bay rum tree.** • *Pimenta racemosa*, family Myrtaceae. ▷late 17th cent.: from BAY[2] + BERRY.

Bay Cit·y industrial city in eastern Michigan, on the Saginaw River, near Lake Huron; pop. 38,936.

Bay·ern /'bīərn/ German name for BAVARIA.

Bayes' the·o·rem /bāz/ *Statistics* a theorem describing how the conditional probability of each of a set of possible causes for a given observed outcome can be computed from knowledge of the probability of each cause and the conditional probability of the outcome of each cause. ▷mid 19th cent.: named after Thomas *Bayes* (1702–61), English mathematician. —**Bayes·i·an** /'bāzēən/ *adj.*

Ba·yeux Tap·es·try /bä'yoo; bā'yoo/ a medieval English embroidery made between 1066 and 1077, telling the story of the Norman Conquest.

Bay·kal, Lake variant spelling of BAIKAL, LAKE.

bay lau·rel ▸*n.* another term for BAY[2].

bay leaf ▸*n.* the aromatic, usually dried, leaf of the bay tree, used in cooking.

Bay·lis /'bālis/, Lilian Mary (1874–1937), English theater manager, noted for her management of the Old Vic and for her initiative in reopening the old Sadler's Wells Theatre in 1931.

Bay·lor /'bālər/, Elgin Gay (1934–), U.S. basketball player. He played for the Minneapolis (from 1960, Los Angeles) Lakers 1958–72. Known for his scoring ability, he reached 71 points in a game against the New York Knicks in December 1960. Basketball Hall of Fame (1976).

Bay of Ben·gal, Bay of Fun·dy, etc. see BENGAL, BAY OF; FUNDY, BAY OF, etc.

Bay of Pigs ▸*n.* an invasion of another nation that results in failure.

The Bay of Pigs is the location of a failed attempt in 1961 by U.S.-trained Cuban exiles to invade Cuba and overthrow the government of Fidel Castro, resulting in considerable embarrassment for the administration of President John F. Kennedy.

bay·o·net /'bāənit; ,bāə'net/ ▸*n.* **1** a swordlike stabbing blade that may be fixed to the muzzle of a rifle for use in hand-to-hand fighting. **2** [as *adj.*] denoting a fitting for a light bulb, camera lens, or other appliance that is engaged by being pushed into a socket and then twisted to lock it in place.
▸*v.* (**-net·ed**, **-net·ing**) [*trans.*] stab (someone) with a bayonet. ▷late 17th cent. (denoting a kind of short dagger): from French *baïonnette*, from *Bayonne*, the name of a town in southwestern France, where they were first made.

bayonet 1

Bay·onne /bā'yōn/ an industrial port city in northeastern New Jersey, on New York Bay; pop. 61,444.

bay·ou /'bīoo; 'bīō/ ▸*n.* (*pl.* **-ous**) (in the southern U.S.) a marshy outlet of a lake or river. ▷mid 18th cent.: from Louisiana French, from Choctaw *bayuk.*

Bay·ou State a nickname for the state of LOUISIANA.

Bay·ou Teche /'bī,oo 'tesh/ a water route in south central Louisiana, at the heart of Cajun Country. Also called **the Teche.**

Bay·reuth /'bī,roit; bī'roit/ a town in Bavaria where Wagner is buried and where festivals of his operas are held regularly.

bay rum ▸*n.* an aromatic liquid, used esp. for the hair or as an aftershave, typically distilled from rum and the leaves of the bayberry.

bay·side /'bā,sīd/ ▸*adj.* on or near the shore of a bay.

Bay State a nickname for the state of MASSACHUSETTS.

Bay·town /'bā,toun/ a city in southeastern Texas, east of Houston, a center of the oil industry; pop. 63,850.

bay tree ▸*n.* see BAY[2].

bay win·dow ▸*n.* a window built to project outward from an outside wall.

ba·zaar /bə'zär/ ▸*n.* a market in a Middle-Eastern country. ■ a fund-raising sale of goods, typically for charity. ■ *dated* a large shop selling miscellaneous goods. ▷late 16th cent.: from Italian *bazarro*, from Turkish, from Persian *bāzār* 'market.'

ba·zil·lion /bə'zilyən/ ▸*cardinal number informal* a very large exaggerated number: *you were going a bazillion miles per hour!* ▷1980s: probably a blend of *billion* and *gazillion* (also a large exaggerated number).

ba·zoo /bə'zoo/ ▸*n. informal* **1** a person's mouth. **2** a person's buttocks or anus. ▷late 19th cent.: of unknown origin; compare with Dutch *bazuin* 'trombone, trumpet.'

ba·zoo·ka /bə'zookə/ ▸*n.* **1** a short-range tubular rocket launcher used against tanks. **2** a trombonelike type of kazoo. ▷1930s (sense 2: apparently from slang BAZOO in the original sense 'kazoo.'

ba·zoom /bə'zoom/ ▸*n.* (usu. **bazooms**) *informal* a woman's breast. ▷1950s: probably an alteration of BOSOM.

bazooka 1

BB ▸*symbol* a standard size of lead pellet used in air rifles.
▸*abbr. Baseball* base on balls.

b-ball ▸*informal* basketball.

BBC ▸*abbr.* British Broadcasting Corporation.

BB gun ▸*n.* an air rifle that fires BBs.

BBIN ▸*abbr.* Bangladesh, Bhutan, India, and Nepal, considered as a group with regard to development, public health, and economic issues.

bbl. ▸*abbr.* barrels (esp. of oil).

b-boy ▸*n. informal* a young man involved with hip-hop culture. ▷1980s.

BBQ ▸*abbr. informal* barbecue.

BBS *Computing* ▸*abbr.* bulletin board system.

BC ▸*abbr.* ■ before Christ (used to indicate that a date is before the Christian Era). ■ British Columbia (in official postal use). ■ Batallion Commander.

USAGE In recent years, some writers have begun using the abbreviations CE (of the Common Era) in place of AD, and BCE (before the Common Era) in place of BC. See also **usage** at **AD.**

bcc ▸*abbr.* blind carbon copy, a copy of an e-mail sent to someone whose name and address isn't visible to other recipients.

BCD ▸*abbr.* ■ *Military* bad conduct discharge. ■ binary coded decimal.

BCE ▸*abbr.* ■ Bachelor of Chemical Engineering. ■ Bachelor of Civil Engineering. ■ before the Common Era (used of dates before the Christian era, esp. by non-Christians).

B cell (also **B-cell**) ▸*n. Physiology* a lymphocyte not processed by the thymus gland, and responsible for producing antibodies. Also called **B** LYMPHOCYTE. Compare with **T** CELL. ▷*B* for BURSA, referring to the organ in birds where it was first identified.

BCF ▸*abbr.* bromochlorodifluoromethane, a substance formerly used in fire extinguishers.

BCG ▸*abbr.* Bacillus Calmette-Guérin, an antituberculosis vaccine.

B com·plex ▸*n.* see VITAMIN **B.**

BD ▸*abbr.* Bachelor of Divinity.

BDD ▸*abbr.* body dysmorphic disorder.

Bde ▸*abbr.* Brigade.

bdel·li·um /'delēəm/ ▸*n.* a fragrant resin produced by a number of trees related to myrrh, used in perfumes. ▷late Middle English: via Latin from Greek *bdellion*, of Semitic origin.

bdrm. ▸*abbr.* bedroom.

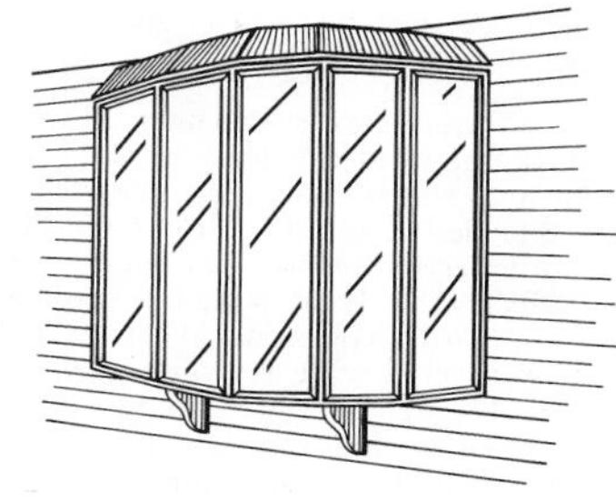

bay window

Pronunciation Key ə *ago*; ər *over*; 'ə *or* ,ə *up*; 'ər *or* ,ər *fur*; a *hat*; ā *rate*; ä *car*; CH *chew*; e *let*; ē *see*; e(ə)r *air*; i *fit*; ī *by*; i(ə)r *ear*; NG *sing*; ō *go*; ô *for*; oi *boy*; oo *good*; oo *goo*; ou *out*; SH *she*; TH *thin*; TH *then*; (h)w *why*; ZH *vision*

BDU ▸*abbr.* battle dress uniform.

BE ▸*abbr.* ■ Bachelor of Education. ■ Bachelor of Engineering. ■ bill of exchange. ■ Black English.

Be ▸*symbol* the chemical element beryllium.

be /bē/ ▸*v.* (*sing. present* **am** /am/; **are** /är/; **is** /iz/; *pl. present* **are**; *1st and 3rd sing. past* **was** /wəz; wäz/; *2nd sing. past and pl. past* **were** /wər/; *present subjunctive* **be**; *past subjunctive* **were**; *present participle* **be·ing** /'bēiNG/; *past part.* **been** /bin/) **1** (usu. **there is/are**) exist: *there are no easy answers | there once was a man | there must be something wrong | I think, therefore I am.* ■ be present: *there is a boy sitting on the step | there were no curtains around the showers | Are there any castles in this area?* **2** [with *adverbial*] occur; take place: *the exhibition will be in November | the opening event is on October 16 | that was before the war.* ■ occupy a position in space: *the Salvation Army store was on his left | she was not at the window.* ■ stay in the same place or condition: *she was here until about ten-thirty | he's a tough customer—**let him be**.* ■ attend: *the days when she was in school.* ■ come; go; visit: *he's from Missouri | I have just been to Thailand | the doctor's been here twice today.* **3** [as *copular verb*] having the state, quality, identity, nature, role, etc., specified: *Amy was 91 | the floor was uneven | I want to be a teacher | father was not well | his hair's brown | it will be Christmas soon | "Be careful," Mr. Carter said.* ■ cost: *the tickets were $25.* ■ amount to: *one and one is two | two sixes are twelve.* ■ represent: *let A be a square matrix of order* n. ■ signify: *we were everything to each other.* ■ consist of; constitute: *the monastery was several three-story buildings.*

▸*phrasal v.* □ **be about** see ABOUT. □ **be off** go away; leave: *he was anxious to be off.*

▸*auxiliary v.* **1** used with a present participle to form continuous tenses: *they are coming | he had been reading | she will be waiting.* **2** used with a past participle to form the passive mood: *it was done | it is said | his book will be published.* **3** [with *infinitive*] used to indicate something due to happen: *construction is to begin next summer | I was to meet him at 6:30.* ■ used to express obligation or necessity: *you are to follow these orders | they said I was to remain on board.* ■ used to express possibility: *these snakes are **to be** found in North America | she was nowhere **to be** seen.* ■ used to hypothesize about something that might happen: *if I **were** to lose | if I was to tell you, you'd think I was crazy | were she to cure me, what could I offer her?* **4** *archaic* used with the past participle of intransitive verbs to form perfect tenses: *I am returned | all humanity is fallen.* ▷Old English *bēon*), an irregular and defective verb, whose full conjugation derives from several originally distinct verbs. The forms *am* and *is* are from an Indo-European root shared by Latin *sum* and *est*. The forms *was* and *were* are from an Indo-European root meaning 'remain.' The forms *be* and *been* are from an Indo-European root shared by Latin *fui* 'I was,' *fio* 'I become' and Greek *phuein* 'bring forth, cause to grow.' The origin of *are* is uncertain.

▸*PHRASES* □ **as/that was** *archaic* as someone or something was previously called: *General Dunstaple had married Miss Hughes that was.* □ **the be-all and end-all** *informal* a feature of an activity or a way of life that is of greater importance than any other. □ **be oneself** act naturally, according to one's character and instincts. □ **be that as it may** see MAY[1]. □ **be there for someone** be available to support or comfort someone while they are experiencing difficulties or adversities. □ **been there, done that** see THERE. □ **not be oneself** not feel well. □ **-to-be** [in *combination*] of the future: *my bride-to-be.*

USAGE For a discussion of whether it is correct to say *that must **be he** at the door* and *it **is I*** rather than *that must **be him** at the door* and *it **is me**,* see **usage** at PERSONAL PRONOUN.

be- ▸*prefix* **1** forming verbs. ■ all over; all around: *bespatter.* ■ thoroughly; excessively: *bewilder.* **2** (added to intransitive verbs) expressing transitive action: *bemoan.* **3** (added to adjectives and nouns) expressing transitive action: *befool | befriend.* **4** (added to nouns) affect with: *befog.* ■ (added to adjectives) cause to be: *befoul.* **5** (forming adjectives ending in *-ed*) having; covered with: *bejeweled.* ▷Old English, weak form of *bī* 'by.'

beach /bēCH/ ▸*n.* a pebbly or sandy shore, esp. by the ocean between high- and low-water marks.

▸*v.* [*trans.*] run or haul up (a boat or ship) onto a beach: *at the water's edge a rowboat was beached | [intrans.] crews would not beach for fear of damaging craft.* ■ [often as *adj.*] (**beached**) cause (a whale or similar animal) to become stranded out of the water. ■ [*intrans.*] (of a whale or similar animal) become stranded out of the water. ■ (of an angler) land (a fish) on a beach. ■ *figurative* cause (someone) to suffer a loss: *competitive procurement seems to have beached several companies.* ▷mid 16th cent. (denoting shingle on the seashore): perhaps related to Old English *bæce, bece* 'brook' (an element that survives in place names such as Wis*bech* and Sand*bach*), assuming an intermediate sense 'pebbly river valley.'

beach ball ▸*n.* a large inflatable ball used for playing games on the beach.

beach bug·gy ▸*n.* another term for DUNE BUGGY.

beach bum ▸*n. informal* a person who loafs on or around a beach.

beach·comb·er /'bēCH,kōmər/ ▸*n.* **1** a vagrant who makes a living by searching beaches for articles of value and selling them. **2** a person who searches beaches for useful or interesting items. **3** a long wave rolling in from the sea; a comber.

beach flea ▸*n.* a small crustacean of the seashore that typically lives among seaweed and leaps when disturbed. Also called SAND FLEA, SAND HOPPER. • *Orchestia* and other genera, order Amphipoda.

beach·front /'bēCH,frənt/ ▸*n.* [usu. in *sing.*] the part of a coastal town next to and directly facing the sea: [as *adj.*] *beachfront property.*

beach grass ▸*n.* marram grass, or any related grass of the genus *Ammophila.*

beach·head /'bēCH,hed/ ▸*n.* a defended position on a beach taken from the enemy by landing forces, from which an attack can be launched. ▷World War II (originally U.S.): formed on the pattern of *bridgehead.*

Beach-la-mar /,bēCH lə 'mär/ ▸*n.* another term for BISLAMA.

beach plum ▸*n.* a maritime shrub related to the plum, native to northeastern North America. • *Prunus maritima*, family Rosaceae. ■ the edible fruit of this tree.

beach·side /'bēCH,sīd/ ▸*adj.* [*attrib.*] next to the beach.

beach·wear /'bēCH,we(ə)r/ ▸*n.* clothing suitable for wearing on the beach, though not necessarily for swimming in.

bea·con /'bēkən/ ▸*n.* a fire or light set up in a high or prominent position as a warning, signal, or celebration: *a chain of beacons carried the news | figurative the prospect of a new government was **a beacon of hope** for millions.* ■ *Brit.* (often in place names) a hill suitable for such a fire or light: *Ivinghoe Beacon | the Brecon Beacons.* ■ a light or other visible object serving as a signal, warning, or guide, esp. at sea or on an airfield. ■ a radio transmitter whose signal helps to fix the position of a ship, aircraft, or spacecraft.

▸*v.* shine like a beacon: *figurative the righteous servant of God who beacons to the nations the Good News.* ▷Old English *bēacn* 'sign, portent, ensign,'; related to BECKON.

Bea·con Hill a historic neighborhood in downtown Boston, Massachusetts, on high ground north of the Boston Common.

bead /bēd/ ▸*n.* **1** a small piece of glass, stone, or similar material, typically rounded and perforated for threading with others as a necklace or rosary or for sewing onto fabric. ■ (**beads**) a necklace made of a string of beads. ■ (**beads**) a rosary. **2** something resembling a bead or a string of beads, in particular: ■ a drop of a liquid on a surface: ***beads of** sweat.* ■ a small knob forming the front sight of a gun. ■ the reinforced inner edge of a pneumatic tire that grips the rim of the wheel. ■ an ornamental molding resembling a string of beads or of a semicircular cross-section.

▸*v.* [*trans.*] **1** [often as *adj.*] (**beaded**) decorate or cover with beads: *a beaded evening bag.* ■ string (beads) together. **2** (often **be beaded**) cover (a surface) with drops of moisture: *his face was **beaded with** perspiration.* ▷Old English *gebed* 'prayer,' of Germanic origin; related to Dutch *bede* and German *Gebet*, also to BID[1]. Current senses derive from the use of a rosary, each bead representing a prayer.

▸*PHRASES* □ **draw** (or **get**) **a bead on** take aim at. □ **tell** (or **say**) **one's beads** use the beads of a rosary in counting prayers.

bead·ing /'bēdiNG/ ▸*n.* decoration or ornamental molding resembling a string of beads or of a semicircular cross section.

bea·dle /'bēdl/ ▸*n. Brit.* a ceremonial officer of a church, college, or similar institution. ■ *Scottish* a church officer assisting the minister. ■ *historical* a minor parish officer dealing with petty offenders. ▷Old English *bydel* 'a person who makes a proclamation,' gradually superseded in Middle English by forms from Old French *bedel*, ultimately of Germanic origin; related to German *Büttel*, also to BID[1].

bead·work /'bēd,wərk/ ▸*n.* decorative work made of beads.

bead·y /'bēdē/ ▸*adj.* (of a person's eyes) small, round, and gleaming. ■ (of a look) bright and penetrating: *she fixed him with a beady stare.* **—bead·i·ly** /'bēdəlē/ *adv.*

bead·y-eyed ▸*adj.* having small, glinting eyes. ■ *informal* keenly observant, typically in a sinister or hostile way.

bea·gle /'bēgəl/ ▸*n.* a small sturdy hound of a breed with a coat of medium length, bred esp. for hunting. ▷late 15th cent.: perhaps from Old French *beegueule* 'open-mouthed,' from *beer* 'open wide' + *gueule* 'throat.' **—bea·gler** /-g(ə)lər/ *n.*

beagle

beak /bēk/ ▸*n.* a bird's horny projecting jaws; a bill. ■ the similar horny projecting jaw of other animals, e.g., a turtle or squid. ■ *informal* a person's nose, esp. a hooked one: *she can't wait to stick her beak in.* ■ a projection at the prow of an ancient warship, typically shaped to resemble the head of a bird or other animal, used to pierce the hulls of enemy ships. ▷Middle English: from Old French *bec*, from Latin *beccus*, of Celtic origin. **—beaked** *adj.* [in *combination*] *a yellow-beaked alpine chough.*

beaked whale ▸*n.* a medium-sized whale with elongated jaws that form a beak, often showing marked differences in size and body form between the sexes. • Family Ziphiidae: four genera and several species.

beak·er /'bēkər/ ▸*n.* a lipped cylindrical glass container for laboratory use. ■ *archaic* or *poetic/literary* a large drinking container with a wide mouth. ■ *Archaeology* a waisted pot characteristic of graves of the Beaker folk. ▷Middle English (in the sense 'large drinking container'): from Old Norse *bikarr*, perhaps based on Greek *bikos* 'drinking bowl.'

Beak·er folk /'bēkər/ ▸*plural n. Archaeology* a late Neolithic and early Bronze Age European people (*c.*2700–1700 BC), named after distinctive waisted pots (**Beaker ware**) that were associated with their burials and appear to have been used for alcoholic drinks.

beak·y /'bēkē/ ▸*adj. informal* (of a person's nose) resembling a bird's beak; hooked. ■ (of a person) having such a nose.

Beale /bēl/, Dorothea (1831–1906), English educator. She campaigned for women's suffrage and for higher education.

Beale Street /bēl/ a historic commercial street in downtown Memphis, Tennessee, that is associated with black music and commerce.

beam /bēm/ ▸*n.* **1** a long, sturdy piece of squared timber or metal spanning an opening or part of a building, usually to support the roof or floor above. ■ another term for BALANCE BEAM. ■ a horizontal piece of squared timber or metal supporting the deck and joining the sides of a ship. ■ *Nautical* the direction of an object visible from the port or starboard side of a ship when it is perpendicular to the center line of the vessel: *there was land in sight **on the port beam**.* ■ a ship's breadth at its widest point: *a cutter with a beam of 16 feet.* ■ [in *sing.*] *informal* the width of a person's hips: *notice how **broad in the beam** she's getting?* ■ the main stem of a stag's antler. ■ the crossbar of a balance. ■ (esp. in a stationary steam engine) an oscillating shaft through which the vertical piston movement is transmitted to the crank or pump. ■ *historical* the main timber of a horse-drawn plow. **2** a ray or shaft of light: *a **beam of light** flashed in front of her | the flashlight beam dimmed perceptibly.* ■ a directional flow of particles or radiation: *beams of electrons.* ■ a series of radio or radar signals emitted to serve as a navigational guide for ships or aircraft. **3** [in *sing.*] a radiant or good-natured look or smile: *a beam of satisfaction.*

▸*v.* **1** [*trans.*] transmit (a radio signal or broadcast) in

cardinal

heavy, triangular beak for cracking seeds

red-tailed hawk

strong, sharp, hooked beak for tearing flesh

great blue heron

long, daggerlike beak for spearing and seizing fish and frogs

ruby-throated hummingbird

needlelike beak for collecting nectar

mallard

wide bill for scooping and sifting vegetation and insects from water's surface

white pelican

long, flat bill with throat pouch for scooping and swallowing fish

roseate spoonbill

spatulate bill that sweeps through the water to scoop up crustaceans and fish

tree swallow

short, wide-opening beak for catching flying insects

red-bellied woodpecker

tapered beak for boring into wood for insects

beaks and bills

a specified direction: *beaming a distress signal into space* | [*intrans.*] *the TV station begins beaming into homes in the new year.* ■ [*trans.*] (**beam someone up/down**) (in science fiction) transport someone instantaneously to another place, esp. to or from a spaceship: *Scotty, beam me up!* [phrase from the television series *Star Trek*.] **2** [*intrans.*] (of a light or light source) shine brightly: *the sun's rays beamed down.* **3** [*intrans.*] smile radiantly: *she beamed with pleasure* | [as *adj.*] (**beaming**) *a beaming smile.* ■ [*trans.*] express (an emotion) with a radiant smile: *the teacher beamed her approval* | [with *direct speech*] *"Isn't that wonderful, Beatrice?" beamed the nun.* **4** (**beamed**) construct a ceiling with exposed beams: *vaulted beamed ceilings in the family room.* ▷Old English *bēam* 'tree, beam,'; related to Dutch *boom* and German *Baum*.

▸***PHRASES*** □ **a beam in one's eye** a fault that is greater in oneself than in the person one is finding fault with. [with biblical allusion to Matt. 7:3.] □ **off** (or **way off**) **beam** *informal* on the wrong track; mistaken: *you're way off beam on this one.* □ **on the beam** *informal* on the right track. □ **on her** (or **its**) **beam-ends** (of a ship) heeled over on its side; almost capsized.

beam com·pass (also **beam com·pass·es**) ▸*n.* a drawing compass consisting of a horizontal rod or beam connected by sliding sockets to two vertical legs, used for drawing large circles.

beam·ish /'bēmisн/ ▸*adj.* beaming with happiness, optimism, or anticipation.

Bea·mon /'bēmən/, Bob (1946–), U.S. long jumper; full name *Robert Beamon*. He set a world record at the 1968 Olympic Games that stood until 1991.

beam sea ▸*n. Nautical* a sea that is running at approximately right angles to a vessel's heading.

beam split·ter ▸*n.* a device for dividing a beam of light or other electromagnetic radiation into two or more separate beams.

beam·y /'bēmē/ ▸*adj.* (of a ship) broad-beamed.

Bean /bēn/, Roy (*c.*1825–1903), U.S. frontiersman; known as **Judge**. In 1882, he named himself justice of the peace in the Texas settlement of Vinegaroon, which he renamed Langtry for his idol Lillie Langtry. He held court in his saloon, the Jersey Lily.

bean /bēn/ ▸*n.* **1** an edible seed, typically kidney-shaped, growing in long pods on certain leguminous plants. ■ the hard seed of coffee, cocoa, and certain other plants. **2** a leguminous plant that bears such seeds in pods. • *Phaseolus* and other genera, family Leguminosae: numerous species, including the **scarlet runner** (*P. coccineus*), **kidney bean** (*P. vulgaris*), and **broad bean** (*Vicia faba*). **3** [with *negative*] (also **beans**) *informal* a very small amount or nothing at all of something (used emphatically): *there is not a single bean of substance in the report* | *I didn't know beans about being a step-parent.* **4** *informal* a person's head, typically when regarded as a source of common sense.

▸*v.* [*trans.*] *informal* hit (someone) on the head: *Boone was nearly beaned by that wild pitch.* ▷Old English *bēan*, of Germanic origin; related to Dutch *boon* and German *Bohne*.

▸***PHRASES*** □ **full of beans** *informal* lively; in high spirits. □ **a hill** (or **row**) **of beans** [with *negative*] anything of any importance or value: *three little people don't amount to a hill of beans in this crazy world.* □ **old bean** *Brit., informal dated* a friendly form of address, usually to a man: *great to see you, old bean!*

bean·bag /'bēn,bag/ ▸*n.* **1** a small bag filled with dried beans and typically used in children's games. ■ *Football* a square of colored plastic with a weighted section, used as a penalty flag. **2** a large cushion, typically filled with polystyrene beads, used as a seat.

▸*v.* [*trans.*] (**-bagged**, **-bag·ging**) *Football* indicate (a penalty) or charge (a player) with a penalty using a beanbag.

bean·ball /'bēn,bôl/ ▸*n. Baseball informal* a ball pitched, esp. intentionally, at the batter's head.

bean count·er ▸*n. informal, derogatory* a person, typically an accountant or bureaucrat, perceived as placing excessive emphasis on controlling expenditure and budgets. —**bean count·ing** *n.*

bean curd ▸*n.* another term for TOFU.

bean·er·y /'bēnərē/ ▸*n.* (*pl.* **-er·ies**) a cheap restaurant.

bean·ie /'bēnē/ ▸*n.* (*pl.* **-ies**) a small, close-fitting hat worn on the back of the head. ▷1940s: perhaps from BEAN (in the sense 'head') + -IE.

bean·pole /'bēn,pōl/ ▸*n.* a stick for supporting bean plants. ■ *informal* a tall, thin person.

bean sprouts ▸*plural n.* the sprouting seeds of certain beans, esp. mung beans, used in oriental cooking.

bean·stalk /'bēn,stôk/ ▸*n.* the stem of a bean plant, proverbially fast growing and tall.

bear[1] /be(ə)r/ ▸*v.* (*past* **bore** /bôr/; *past part.* **borne** /bôrn/) [*trans.*] **1** (of a person) carry: *he was bearing a tray of brimming glasses* | *the warriors bore lances tipped with iron.* ■ (of a vehicle or boat) convey (passengers or cargo): *steamboats bear the traveler out of Kerrerra Sound.* ■ have or display as a visible mark or feature: *a small boat bearing a white flag* | *many of the papers bore his flamboyant signature.* ■ be called by (a name or title): *he bore the surname Tiller.* ■ (**bear oneself**) [with *adverbial*] carry or conduct oneself in a particular manner: *she bore herself with dignity.* **2** support: *walls that cannot bear a stone vault.* ■ take responsibility for: *no one likes to* ***bear the responsibility*** *for such decisions* | *the expert's fee shall be borne by the tenant.* ■ be able to accept or stand up to: *it is doubtful whether either of these distinctions would* ***bear scrutiny.*** **3** endure (an ordeal or difficulty): *she bore the pain stoically.* ■ [with *modal* and *negative*] manage to tolerate (a situation or experience): *she* ***could hardly bear*** *his sarcasm* | [with *infinitive*] *I cannot bear to see you hurt* ■ (**cannot bear someone/something**) strongly dislike: *I can't bear caviar.* **4** give birth to (a child): *she bore six daughters* | [with *two objs.*] *his wife had borne him a son.* ■ (of a tree or plant) produce (fruit or flowers): *a squash that bears fruit shaped like cucumbers.* **5** [*intrans.*] turn and proceed in a specified direction: *bear left and follow the old road.*

▸*phrasal v.* □ **bear away** another way of saying BEAR OFF. □ **bear down** (of a woman in labor) exert downward pressure in order to push the baby out. ■ put pressure on someone or something: *he bore down and allowed the Bears only one more run.* □ **bear down on** move quickly toward someone, in a purposeful or an intimidating manner. ■ take strict measures to deal with: *a commitment to bear down on inflation.* □ **bear off** *Sailing* change course away from the wind. ■ *Nautical* steer away from something, typically the land. □ **bear on** be relevant to (something): *two kinds of theories that bear on literary studies.* ■ [with *adverbial*] be a burden on (someone): *a tax that will* ***bear heavily on*** *poorer households.* □ **bear something out** support or confirm something: *this assumption is not borne out by any evidence.* □ **bear up** remain cheerful in the face of adversity: *she's bearing up remarkably well.* □ **bear with** be patient or tolerant with. ▷Old English *beran*, of Germanic origin; from an Indo-European root shared by Sanskrit *bharati*, Greek *pherein*, and Latin *ferre*.

▸***PHRASES*** □ **be borne in upon** come to be realized by: *the folly of her action was borne in on her with devastating precision.* □ **bear arms 1** carry firearms. **2** wear or display a coat of arms. □ **bear the brunt of** see BRUNT. □ **bear the burden of** suffer the consequences of. □ **bear fruit** *figurative* yield positive results: *plans for power-sharing may be about to bear fruit.* □ **bear someone a grudge** nurture a feeling of resentment against someone. □ **bear a hand** *archaic* help in a task or enterprise. □ **bear someone malice** (or **ill will**) [with *negative*] wish someone harm. □ **bear a resemblance** (or **similarity**) **to** resemble. □ **bear a relation** (or **relationship**) **to** [with *negative*] be logically consistent with: *the map didn't seem to bear any relation to the roads.* □ **bear the stamp of** be clearly identifiable with: *their tactics bear the stamp of Soviet military training.* □ **bear witness** (or **testimony**) **to** testify to: *little is left to bear witness to the past greatness of the city.* □ **bring pressure to bear on** attempt to coerce: *they brought pressure to bear on him to resign.* □ **bring to bear 1** muster and use to effect: *she had reservations about how much influence she could bring to bear.* **2** aim (a weapon): *bringing his rifle to bear on a distant target.* □ **does not bear thinking about** is too terrible to contemplate. □ **grin and bear it** see GRIN. □ **have one's cross to bear** see CROSS.

USAGE In the early 17th century, **borne** and **born** were simply variant forms of the past participle of **bear** used interchangeably with no distinction in meaning. By around 1775, however, the present distinction in use had become established. At that time, **borne** became the standard past participle used in all the senses listed in this dictionary entry, e.g., *she has* ***borne*** *you another son, the findings have been* ***borne*** *out*, and so on. **Born** became restricted to just one very common use (which remains the case today), in the passive, without **by**, as the standard, neutral way to refer to birth: *she was* ***born*** *in 1965, he was* ***born*** *lucky*, or *I was* ***born*** *and bred in Boston.*

bear[2] ▸*n.* **1** a large, heavy, mammal that walks on the soles of its feet, with thick fur and a very short tail. Bears are related to the dog family, but most species are omnivorous. • Family Ursidae: several genera and species. ■ a teddy bear. ■ *informal* a rough, unmannerly, or uncouth person. ■ a large, heavy, cumbersome man: *a lumbering bear of a man.* ■ (**the Bear**) *informal* a nickname for Russia. ■ (**the Bear**) the constellation Ursa Major or Ursa Minor. **2** *Stock Market* a person who forecasts that prices of stocks or commodities will fall, esp. a person who sells shares hoping to buy them back later at a lower price: [as *adj.*] *bear markets.* Often contrasted with BULL[1] (sense 2 of the *noun*). [said to be from a proverb warning against 'selling the bear's skin before one has caught the bear.'] ▷Old English *bera*; related to Dutch *beer* and German *Bär*.

▸*PHRASE* □ **loaded for bear** *informal* fully prepared for any eventuality, typically a confrontation or challenge.

bear·a·ble /ˈbe(ə)rəbəl/ ▸*adj.* able to be endured: *a ceiling fan made the heat bearable.* —**bear·a·bly** *adv.*

bear·bait·ing /ˈbe(ə)rˌbātiNG/ ▸*n.* *historical* a form of entertainment that involved setting dogs to attack a captive bear.

bear·ber·ry /ˈbe(ə)rˌberē/ ▸*n.* (*pl.* **-ries**) a creeping dwarf shrub of the heath family, with pinkish flowers and bright red berries. • Genus *Arctostaphylos*, family Ericaceae: several species, in particular *A. uva-ursi*, found esp. in circumpolar regions.

bear·cat /ˈbe(ə)rˌkat/ ▸*n.* **1** a bearlike climbing mammal, esp. the red panda. **2** a binturong. **3** *Informal* an aggressive or forceful person.

Beard ▸, James (1903–85), U.S. chef and cookbook author. He hosted the first televised cooking show and founded a cooking school in New York.

beard /bi(ə)rd/ ▸*n.* **1** a growth of hair on the chin and lower cheeks of a man's face: *he had a black beard | three days' growth of beard.* ■ a tuft of hair on the chin of certain mammals, for example a lion or goat. ■ an animal's growth or marking that is likened to a beard, e.g., the gills of an oyster, or the beak bristles of certain birds. ■ a tuft of hairs or bristles on certain plants, esp. the awn of a grass. **2** *informal* a person who carries out a transaction, typically a bet, for someone else in order to conceal the other's identity. ■ a person who pretends to have a romantic or sexual relationship with someone else in order to conceal the other's true sexual orientation.

▸*v.* [*trans.*] boldly confront or challenge (someone formidable). ▷Old English; related to Dutch *baard* and German *Bart.* —**beard·ed** *adj.* [in *combination*] *a gray-bearded man.* —**beard·less** *adj.*

▸*PHRASE* □ **beard the lion in his den** (or **lair**) confront or challenge someone on their own ground.

beard·ed col·lie ▸*n.* a dog of a shaggy breed of collie with long hair on the face.

beard·ed vul·ture ▸*n.* another term for LAMMERGEIER.

Beard·more Gla·cier /ˈbi(ə)rdˌmôr/ a glacier in Antarctica that flows from the Queen Maud Mountains to the Ross Ice Shelf, at the southern edge of the Ross Sea, 260 miles (418 km) long.

Beards·ley /ˈbi(ə)rdzlē/, Aubrey (Vincent) (1872–98), English artist and illustrator, associated with art nouveau and the Aesthetic Movement.

beard·tongue /ˈbi(ə)rdˌtəNG/ ▸*n.* a North American plant of the figwort family with showy, five-lobed flowers. Each blossom has a tuft of hair on one of its stamens. • Genus *Penstemon*, family Scrophulariaceae: several species, including **hairy beardtongue** (*P. hirsutus*) and the widespread **foxglove beardtongue** (*P. digitalis*).

bear·er /ˈbe(ə)rər/ ▸*n.* **1** a person or thing that carries or holds something: *I'm sorry to be the bearer of bad tidings* | [in *combination*] *a flag-bearer.* ■ a carrier of equipment on an expedition. ■ a person who carries the coffin at a funeral; pall-bearer. ■ a tree or plant that bears fruit or flowers. **2** a person who presents a check or other order to pay money: *promissory notes payable to the bearer.* ■ [as *adj.*] payable to the possessor: *bearer bonds.*

bear·grass /ˈbe(ə)rˌgras/ (also **bear grass**) ▸*n.* a North American plant with long, coarse, grasslike leaves, in particular: • a wild yucca (genus *Yucca*, family Agavaceae). • a cultivated ornamental plant, the leaves of which were formerly used by American Indians to make watertight baskets (*Xerophyllum tenax*, family Liliaceae). Also called **elk grass**.

bear hug ▸*n.* a rough, tight embrace.

bear·ing /ˈbe(ə)riNG/ ▸*n.* **1** [in *sing.*] a person's way of standing or moving: *a man of precise military bearing.* ■ the way one behaves or conducts oneself: *she has the bearing of a First Lady.* **2** relation or relevance: *the case has no direct* ***bearing on*** *the issues.* **3** the level to which something bad can be tolerated: *school was bad enough, but now it's past bearing.* **4** a part of a machine that bears friction, esp. between a rotating part and its housing. ■ a ball bearing. **5** *Architecture* a structural part that supports weight, such as a wall that supports a beam. ■ the point at which a structural part rests upon a supporting structure, such as the specific area of a beam that rests upon a wall. **6** the direction or position of something, or the direction of movement, relative to a fixed point. It is typically measured in degrees, usually with magnetic north as zero: *the Point is* ***on a bearing*** *of 015°.* ■ (**one's bearings**) awareness of one's position relative to one's surroundings: *he rose unsteadily to his feet and tried to get his bearings.* **7** *Heraldry* a device or charge: *armorial bearings.* **8** the act, capability, or time of producing fruit or offspring: *I gave myself up to the bearing of children.*

bear·ing rein ▸*n.* a fixed rein that causes the horse to raise its head and arch its neck.

bear·ish /ˈbe(ə)riSH/ ▸*adj.* **1** resembling or likened to a bear, typically in being rough, surly, or clumsy: *a bearish figure with muttonchop whiskers.* **2** *Stock Market* characterized by falling share prices. ■ (of a dealer) inclined to sell because of an anticipated fall in prices. —**bear·ish·ly** *adv.* —**bear·ish·ness** *n.*

bear mar·ket ▸*n.* *Stock Market* a market in which prices are falling, encouraging selling.

Bé·ar·naise sauce /ˌberˈnāz/ ▸*n.* a rich sauce thickened with egg yolks and flavored with tarragon. ▷*Béarnaise*, feminine of French *Béarnais* 'of Béarn,' a region of southwestern France.

bear·skin /ˈbe(ə)rˌskin/ ▸*n.* the pelt of a bear, esp. when used as a rug or wrap. ■ a tall cap of black fur worn ceremonially by certain military troops.

Be·as /ˈbēˌäs/ a river in northern India that rises in the Himalayas and flows through Himachal Pradesh to join the Sutlej River in Punjab. It is one of the five rivers that gave Punjab ("five waters") its name.

beast /bēst/ ▸*n.* an animal, esp. a large or dangerous four-footed one: *a wild beast.* ■ (usu. **beasts**) a domestic animal, esp. a bovine farm animal. ■ *archaic* or *humorous* an animal as opposed to a human: *the gift of reason differentiates humanity from the beasts.* ■ an inhumanly cruel, violent, or depraved person: *he is a filthy drunken beast.* ■ *informal* an objectionable or unpleasant person or thing: *a scheming, manipulative little beast.* ■ (**the beast**) a person's brutish or untamed characteristics: ***the beast in*** *you is rearing its ugly head.* ■ [with *adj.*] *informal* a thing or concept possessing a particular quality: *that much-maligned beast, the rave record.* ▷Middle English: from Old French *beste*, based on Latin *bestia*.

beast·ie /ˈbēstē/ ▸*n.* (*pl.* **-ies**) *Scottish* or *humorous* an animal, insect, or germ: *our immune systems are killing millions of wee beasties.* ■ [with *adj.*] a vehicle or device of a particular kind: *these little beasties only have three wheels.*

beast·ings ▸*n.* variant spelling of BEESTINGS.

beast·ly /ˈbēstlē/ ▸*adj.* (**-li·er**, **-li·est**) **1** *informal, chiefly Brit.*, very unpleasant: *this beastly war.* ■ unkind; malicious: *don't be* ***beastly to*** *him.* **2** *archaic* cruel and unrestrained: *beastly immorality.*

▸*adv.* [as *submodifier*] *Brit., informal, dated* possessing a specified characteristic to an intense and unpleasant degree: *a beastly hot summer.* —**beast·li·ness** *n.*

beast of bur·den ▸*n.* an animal such as a mule or donkey that is used for carrying loads.

beast of prey ▸*n.* an animal, esp. a mammal, that kills and eats other animals.

beat /bēt/ ▸*v.* (*past* **beat**; *past part.* **beat·en** /ˈbētn/) [*trans.*] **1** strike (a person or an animal) repeatedly and violently so as to hurt or injure them, usually with an implement such as a club or whip: *she beat me with a stick for the slightest misdemeanor.* ■ strike (an object) repeatedly so as to make a noise: *he beat the table with his hand.* ■ [*intrans.*] (of an instrument) make a rhythmical sound by being struck: *drums were beating in the distance.* ■ strike (a carpet, blanket, etc.) repeatedly in order to remove dust. ■ remove (dust) from something by striking it repeatedly. ■ flatten or shape (metal) by striking it repeatedly with a hammer: *pure gold can be* ***beaten out*** *to form very thin sheets.* ■ (**beat something against/on**) strike something against (something): *she beat her fists against the wood.* ■ [*intrans.*] (**beat on/against**) strike repeatedly on: *Sidney beat on the door with the flat of his hand.* ■ [*intrans.*] (**beat at**) make striking movements toward: *Emmie seized the hearthrug and began to beat at the flames.* ■ move across (an area of land) repeatedly striking at the ground cover in order to raise game birds for shooting. **2** defeat (someone) in a game, competition, election, or commercial venture: *she beat him easily at chess | the Senators* ***beat out*** *the Yankees for the 1933 pennant.* ■ *informal* baffle: ***it beats me how*** *you manage to work in this heat.* ■ overcome (a problem, or disease): *they are investing their savings in hopes of beating inflation | he beat heroin addiction in 1992.* ■ do or be better than (a record or score): *he beat his own world record.* ■ *informal* be better than: ***you can't beat*** *the taste of fresh raspberries.* **3** succeed in getting somewhere ahead of (someone): *I could beat him on my bicycle | the goalie beat him to the ball.* ■ take action to avoid (difficult or inconvenient effects of an event or circumstance): *they set off early to beat the traffic.* **4** [*intrans.*] (of the heart) pulsate: *her heart beat faster with panic.* **5** (of a bird) move (the wings) up and down. ■ (of a bird or its wings) make rhythmic movements through (the air): *black-tipped wings beat the air.* ■ [*intrans.*] (of a bird) fly making rhythmic wing movements: *an owl beat low over the salt marsh.* **6** stir (cooking ingredients) vigorously with a fork, whisk, or beater to make a smooth or frothy mixture. **7** (**beat it**) *informal* leave: [in *imperative*] *now beat it, will you!* **8** [*intrans.*] *Sailing* sail into the wind, following a zigzag course with repeated tacking: *we beat southward all that first day.*

▸*phrasal v.* □ **beat someone back** (usu. **be beaten back**) force (someone attempting to do something) to retreat: *I tried to get in but was beaten back by the flames.* □ **beat down** (of the sun) radiate intense heat and brightness. ■ (of rain) fall hard and continuously. □ **beat something down** quell defense or resistance. □ **beat someone down** force someone to reduce the price of something. □ **beat one's meat** *vulgar slang* (of a man) masturbate. □ **beat off** *vulgar slang* (of a man) masturbate. □ **beat someone/something off** succeed in resisting an attacker or an attack. ■ win against a challenge or rival. □ **beat something out** **1** produce a loud, rhythmic sound by striking something: *he beat out a rhythm on the drums.* **2** extinguish flames by striking at them with a suitable object. □ **beat someone up** **1** assault and severely injure someone by hitting, kicking, or punching them repeatedly. **2** abuse someone verbally. □ **beat up on** another way of saying BEAT SOMEONE UP.

▸*n.* **1** a main accent or rhythmic unit in music or poetry: *the glissando begins on the second beat.* ■ a strong rhythm in popular music: *the music changed to a funky disco beat.* ■ [in *sing*] a regular, rhythmic sound or movement: *the beat of the wipers became almost hypnotic.* ■ the sound made when something, typically a musical instrument, is struck: *he heard a regular drumbeat.* ■ a pulsation of the heart. ■ a periodic variation of sound or amplitude due to the combination of two sounds, electrical signals, or other vibrations having similar but not identical frequencies. ■ the movement of a bird's wings. **2** an area allocated to a police officer to patrol: *a patrolman who strived to make his beat a safe one | public clamor for more police officers* ***on the beat.*** ■ a spell of duty allocated to a police officer: *her beat ended at 6 a.m.* ■ an area regularly frequented by someone, typically a prostitute. ■ *figurative* a person's area of interest: *his beat is construction, property, and hotels.* ■ an area regularly occupied by a shoal of freshwater fish. **3** a brief pause or moment of hesitation, typically one lasting a specified length: *she waited for a beat of three seconds.* [as a stage direction.] **4** *informal* short for BEATNIK.

▸*adj.* **1** [*predic.*] *infomal* completely exhausted: *I'm* ***dead beat.*** **2** [*attrib.*] of or relating to the beat generation or its philosophy: *beat poet Allen Ginsberg.* ▷Old English *bēatan*, of Germanic origin. —**beat·a·ble** *adj.*

▸*PHRASES* □ **beat all** be amazing or impressive: *well, that beats all.* □ **beat around** (or **beat about**) **the bush** discuss a matter without coming to the point. □ **beat someone at their own game** see GAME[1]. □ **beat someone's brains out** see BRAIN. □ **beat one's breast** see BREAST. □ **beat the bushes** *informal* search thoroughly: *I was out* ***beating the bushes for*** *investors to split the risk.* □ **beat the clock** perform a task quickly or within a fixed time limit. □ **beat a dead horse** waste energy on a lost cause or unalterable situation. □ **beat the drum for** see DRUM[1]. □ **beat the hell out of** *informal* **1** beat (someone) very severely. **2** surpass or defeat easily. □ **beat the living daylights out of** see DAYLIGHT (sense 2). □ **beat the pants off** *informal* prove to be vastly superior to. □ **beat a path to someone's door** (of a large number of people) hasten to make contact with someone regarded as interesting or inspiring, or in association with whom one stands to profit. □ **beat a (hasty) retreat** withdraw, typically in order to avoid something unpleasant: *as the bombs started to go off, they beat a hasty retreat across the field.* □ **beat the shit out of** *vulgar slang* beat (someone) very severely. □ **beat the system** succeed in finding a means of getting around rules, regulations, or other means of control. □ **beat time** indicate or follow a musical tempo with a baton or other means. □ **beat someone to it** succeed in doing something or getting somewhere before someone else, to their annoyance. □ **miss a beat** see MISS1. □ **to beat all ——s** that is infinitely better than all the things mentioned: *a PC screen saver to beat all screen savers.* □ **to beat the band** *informal* in such a way as to surpass all competition: *they were talking to beat the band.*

beat·box /ˈbētˌbäks/ ▶*n. informal* a drum machine. ■ a radio or radio cassette player used to play loud music, esp. rap.

beat·en /ˈbētn/ ▶ past participle of BEAT.
▶*adj.* **1** having been defeated: *I knew when I was beaten.* ■ exhausted and dejected: *he sat feeling old and beaten.* **2** having been beaten or struck: *he trudged home like a beaten dog.* ■ (of food) whipped to a uniform consistency: *beaten eggs.* ■ (of metal) shaped by hammering, typically so as to give the surface a dimpled texture. ■ (of precious metal) hammered to form thin foil for ornamental use. **3** (of a path) well trodden; much used.
▶*PHRASE* □ **off the beaten track** (or **path**) in or into an isolated place. ■ unusual: [as *adj.*] *off-the-beaten-track experiences.*

beat·er /ˈbētər/ ▶*n.* **1** a person who hits someone or something, in particular: ■ a person employed to flush out or drive game animals for shooting by striking at the ground cover. ■ a person who beats metal in manufacturing. ■ [in *combination*] a person who habitually hits someone: *a wife-beater.* **2** [often with *adj.*] an implement or machine used for beating something, in particular: ■ (in cooking) a device for whisking or blending ingredients. ■ an implement used to dislodge dirt from rugs and carpets by hitting them. ■ a vacuum-cleaner attachment for rugs and carpets. ■ a stick for beating a drum. **3** [in *combination*] *informal* a means of defeating or preventing something: *a recession-beater.* **4** *informal* a dilapidated but serviceable car: *If you provide the kids with a car, give them an old beater.*

bea·ter bar ▶*n.* the rotating-brush unit within the powerhead of a vacuum cleaner.

beat fre·quen·cy ▶*n. Physics* the number of beats per second, equal to the difference in the frequencies of two interacting tones or oscillations.

beat gen·er·a·tion a movement of young people in the 1950s who rejected conventional society and favored Zen Buddhism, modern jazz, free sexuality, and recreational drugs. Among writers associated with the movement were Jack Kerouac and Allen Ginsberg.

be·a·tif·ic /ˌbēəˈtifik/ ▶*adj.* blissfully happy: *a beatific smile.* ■ *Christian Theology* imparting holy bliss. ▷mid 17th cent.: from French *béatifique* or Latin *beatificus*, from *beatus* 'blessed.' **—be·a·tif·i·cal·ly** /-ik(ə)lē/ *adv.*

be·at·i·fi·ca·tion /bēˌatəfiˈkāSHən/ ▶*n.* (in the Roman Catholic Church) declaration by the pope that a dead person is in a state of bliss, constituting a step toward canonization and permitting public veneration. ▷early 16th cent. (in the sense 'action of making blessed'): from Old French, or from ecclesiastical Latin *beatificatio(n-)*, from *beatificare* 'make blessed,' from Latin *beatus* 'blessed.'

be·at·i·fy /bēˈatəˌfī/ ▶*v.* **(-fies, -fied)** [*trans.*] (in the Roman Catholic Church) announce the beatification of. ■ make (someone) blissfully happy. ▷mid 16th cent. (in the sense 'make blessed or supremely happy'): from Old French *beatifier* or ecclesiastical Latin *beatificare*, from Latin *beatus* 'blessed.'

beat·ing /ˈbētiNG/ ▶*n.* **1** a punishment or assault in which the victim is hit repeatedly: *if he got dirt on his clothes, he'd get a beating | torture methods included beating.* **2** pulsation or throbbing, typically of the heart. **3** a defeat in a competitive situation.
▶*PHRASE* □ **take a beating** *informal* suffer damage or hurt.

be·at·i·tude /bēˈatiˌt(y)o͞od/ ▶*n.* supreme blessedness. ■ **(the Beatitudes)** the blessings listed by Jesus in the Sermon on the Mount (Matt. 5:3–11). ■ **(his/your Beatitude)** a title given to patriarchs in the Orthodox Church. ▷late Middle English: from Old French *beatitude* or Latin *beatitudo*, from *beatus* 'blessed.'

beat·nik /ˈbētnik/ ▶*n.* a young person in the 1950s and early 1960s belonging to a subculture associated with the beat generation. ▷1950s: from BEAT + *-nik* on the pattern of *sputnik*, perhaps influenced by U.S. use of Yiddish *-nik*, denoting someone or something who acts in a particular way.

Bea·ton /ˈbētn/, Sir Cecil (Walter Hardy) (1904–80), English photographer. He is noted for his fashion features and portraits of celebrities.

Be·a·trix /ˈbāəˌtriks; ˈbē-/ (1938–), queen of the Netherlands (1980–); full name *Beatrix Wilhelmina Armgard.*

Beat·tie /ˈbētē/, Ann (1947–), U.S. author. Her works include the novels *Chilly Scenes of Winter* (1976), *Picturing Will* (1989), and *Another You* (1995) and the short-story collection *Park City* (1998).

Beat·ty /ˈbētē; ˈbātē/, Warren (1937–), U.S. actor, director, and screenwriter; born *Henry Warren Beaty*; the brother of actress Shirley MacLaine. He produced *Bonnie and Clyde* (1967), wrote and producted *Shampoo* (1975), codirected *Heaven Can Wait* (1978), and was producer, cowriter, and Academy Award-winning director of *Reds* (1981). He starred in them all. Beatty's later movies include *Dick Tracy* (1990) and *Love Affair* (1994).

beat-up ▶*adj.* [*attrib.*] *informal* (of a thing) worn out by overuse; in a state of disrepair.

Bea·ty1 /ˈbātē; ˈbētē/, Henry Warren, see **BEATTY**.

Bea·ty2 Shirley MacLean, see **MACLAINE**.

beau /bō/ ▶*n.* (*pl.* **beaux** /bōz/ or **beaus**) *dated* **1** a boyfriend or male admirer. **2** a rich, fashionable young man; a dandy. ▷late 17th cent. (sense 2): from French, literally 'handsome,' from Latin *bellus.*

beau·coup /bōˈko͞o; ˈbo͞oˌko͞o/ ▶*n. informal* an abundance; a large quantity.
▶*adj.* many; much: *you can spend beaucoup bucks on software.*
▶*adv.* in abundance. ▷early 20th cent.: from French, literally 'fine stroke'; see BEAU and COUP.

Beau·fort scale /ˈbōfərt/ a scale of wind speed based on a visual estimation of the wind's effects, ranging from force 0 (less than 1 knot or 1 kph, "calm") to force 12 (64 knots or 118 kph and above, "hurricane"). ▷mid 19th cent.: named after Sir Francis *Beaufort* (1774–1857), the English admiral and naval hydrographer who devised it.

Beau·fort Sea a part of the Arctic Ocean that lies to the north of Alaska and Canada. ▷named after Sir Francis *Beaufort* (see **BEAUFORT SCALE**).

beau geste /ˌbō ˈZHest/ ▶*n.* (*pl.* **beaux gestes** *pronunc.* same) a noble and generous act. ▷early 20th cent.: French, literally 'splendid gesture.'

beau i·dé·al /ˌbō ˌēdāˈal; īˈdēəl/ ▶*n.* a person or thing representing the highest possible standard of excellence in a particular respect. ▷early 19th cent.: French, literally 'ideal beauty.'

Beau·jo·lais /ˌbōZHəˈlā/ ▶*n.* a light red or (less commonly) white burgundy wine produced in the Beaujolais district of southeastern France.

Beau·jo·lais Nou·veau /ˌbōZHəˈlā no͞oˈvō/ ▶*n.* a Beaujolais wine sold in the first year of a vintage. ▷from **BEAUJOLAIS** + French *nouveau* 'new.'

Beau·mar·chais /ˌbōmärˈSHā/, Pierre Augustin Caron de (1732–99), French playwright. He is chiefly remembered for his comedies *The Barber of Seville* (1775) and *The Marriage of Figaro* (1784)

beau monde /ˌbō ˈmônd/ ▶*n.* **(the beau monde)** fashionable society. ▷late 17th cent.: French, literally 'fine world.'

Beau·mont1 /ˈbōˌmänt/ an industrial port in southeastern Texas, on the Neches River, a center of the oil industry; pop. 114,323.

Beau·mont2, Francis (1584–1616), English playwright. He collaborated with John Fletcher on *Philaster* (1609), *The Maid's Tragedy* (1610–11), and many other plays. *The Knight of the Burning Pestle* (*c.*1607) is attributed to Beaumont alone.

Beaune /bōn/ ▶*n.* a red burgundy wine from the region around Beaune in eastern France.

Beau·re·gard /ˈbōriˌgärd/, Pierre Gustave Toutant (1818–93), U.S. army officer. He served as superintendent of the U.S. Military Academy at West Point; as the Civil War was about to begin in 1861, he resigned to join the Confederate army with the rank of brigadier general.

beaut /byo͞ot/ *informal*, ▶*n.* a particularly fine example of something: *the idea was a beaut.* ■ a beautiful person. ▷mid 19th cent.: abbreviation of **BEAUTY** or **BEAUTIFUL**.

beau·te·ous /ˈbyo͞otēəs/ ▶*adj. poetic/literary* beautiful: *his beauteous bride.* ▷late Middle English: from **BEAUTY**, on the pattern of *bounteous* and *plenteous.*

beau·ti·cian /byo͞oˈtiSHən/ ▶*n.* a person whose job is to do hair styling, manicures, and other beauty treatments.

beau·ti·ful /ˈbyo͞otəfəl/ ▶*adj.* pleasing the senses or mind aesthetically: *beautiful poetry | a beautiful young woman | the mountains were calm and beautiful.* ■ of a very high standard; excellent: *the house had been left in beautiful order | she spoke in beautiful English.* **—beau·ti·ful·ly** /-f(ə)lē/ *adv.* [as *adj.*] *the rules are beautifully simple.*
▶*PHRASES* □ **the beautiful people** **1** fashionable, glamorous, and privileged people. **2** (in the 1960s) hippies. □ **the body beautiful** an ideal of physical beauty:

B

beau·ti·fy /ˈbyo͞otəˌfī/ ▶*v.* **(-fies, -fied)** [*trans.*] improve the appearance of. **—beau·ti·fi·ca·tion** /ˌbyo͞otəfiˈkāSHən/ *n.* **—beau·ti·fi·er** *n.*

beau·ty /ˈbyo͞otē/ ▶*n.* (*pl.* **-ties**) **1** a combination of qualities, such as shape, color, or form, that pleases the aesthetic senses, esp. the sight: *I was struck by her beauty | an area of outstanding natural beauty.* ■ a combination of qualities that pleases the intellect or moral sense. ■ [as *adj.*] denoting something intended to make a woman more attractive: *beauty products | beauty treatment.* **2** a beautiful or pleasing thing or person, in particular: ■ a beautiful woman. ■ an excellent specimen or example of something: *the fish was a beauty, around 14 pounds.* ■ **(the beauties of)** the pleasing or attractive features of something: *the beauties of the Pennsylvania mountains.* ■ [in *sing.*] the best feature or advantage of something: ***the beauty of** keeping cats is that they don't tie you down.* ▷Middle English: from Old French *beaute*, based on Latin *bellus* 'beautiful, fine.'
▶*PHRASES* □ **beauty is in the eye of the beholder** *proverb* beauty cannot be judged objectively, for what one person finds beautiful or admirable may not appeal to another. □ **beauty is only skin-deep** *proverb* a pleasing appearance is not a guide to character.

beau·ty bush (also **beau·ty·bush**) ▶*n.* a deciduous Chinese shrub of the honeysuckle family, with clusters of yellow-throated pink tubular flowers, widely cultivated as an ornamental. • *Kolkwitzia amabilis*, family Caprifoliaceae.

beau·ty con·test ▶*n.* a competition for a prize given to the woman judged the most beautiful. ■ a contest between rival institutions or political candidates that depends heavily on presentation.

beau·ty mark ▶*n.* another term for BEAUTY SPOT (sense 2).

beau·ty par·lor (also **beauty salon** or **beauty shop**) ▶*n.* an establishment in which hairdressing, makeup, and similar cosmetic treatments are carried out professionally.

beau·ty queen ▶*n.* a woman judged most beautiful in a beauty contest.

beau·ty sleep ▶*n. humorous* sleep considered to be sufficient to keep one looking young and beautiful.

beau·ty spot ▶*n.* **1** a place known for its beautiful scenery. **2** a small natural or artificial mark such as a mole on a woman's face, considered to enhance another feature.

Beau·voir, Simone de, see DE **BEAUVOIR**.

beaux /bōz/ ▶ plural form of **BEAU**.

beaux arts /ˌbō ˈzär/ ▶*plural n.* **1** fine arts. **2** (usu. **Beaux Arts**) [as *adj.*] relating to the classical decorative style maintained by the École des Beaux-Arts in Paris, esp. in the 19th century. ▷from French *beaux-arts.*

bea·ver1 /ˈbēvər/ ▶*n.* (*pl.* same or **-vers**) a large semiaquatic broad-tailed rodent that is native to North America and northern Eurasia. It is noted for its habit of gnawing through tree trunks to fell the trees in order to feed on the bark and build dams.

beaver 1

Pronunciation Key ə *ago*; ər *over*; ˈə or ˌə *up*; ˈər or ˌər *fur*; a *hat*; ā *rate*; ä *car*; CH *chew*; e *let*; ē *see*; e(ə)r *air*; i *fit*; ī *by*; i(ə)r *ear*; NG *sing*; ō *go*; ô *for*; oi *boy*; o͝o *good*; o͞o *goo*; ou *out*; SH *she*; TH *thin*; T͟H *then*; (h)w *why*; ZH *vision*

• Family Castoridae and genus *Castor*: the North American *C. canadensis* and the Eurasian *C. fiber*. ■ the soft light brown fur of the beaver. ■ (also **beaver hat**) *chiefly historical* a hat made of felted beaver fur. ■ (also **beaver cloth**) a heavy woolen cloth resembling felted beaver fur. ■ *figurative* a very hardworking person.
▸*v.* [*intrans.*] *informal* work hard: *Bridget* **beavered away** *to keep things running smoothly.* ▷Old English *beofor, befor*, of Germanic origin; related to Dutch *bever* and German *Biber*, from an Indo-European root meaning 'brown.'

bea·ver[2] ▸*n.* the lower part of the face guard of a helmet in a suit of armor. The term is also used to refer to the upper part or visor, or to a single movable guard. ▷late 15th cent.: from Old French *baviere* 'bib,' from *baver* 'to drool.'

bea·ver[3] ▸*n. vulgar slang* a woman's genitals or pubic area. ■ *offensive* a woman. ▷early 20th cent.: of unknown origin.

bea·ver·board /'bēvər,bôrd/ ▸*n.* a kind of fiberboard used in building. ▷early 20th cent.: from BEAVER[1] + BOARD.

Bea·ver State a nickname for the state of **OREGON**.

Bea·ver·ton /'bēvərtən/ a city in northwestern Oregon, west of Portland, noted for its electronics industry; pop. 76,129.

be·bop /'bē,bäp/ ▸*n.* a type of jazz originating in the 1940s and characterized by complex harmony and rhythms. It is associated particularly with Charlie Parker, Thelonious Monk, and Dizzy Gillespie. ▷1940s (originally U.S.): imitative of the typical rhythm of this music. **—be·bop·per** *n.*

be·calm /bi'kä(l)m/ ▸*v.* [*trans.*] (usu. **be becalmed**) leave (a sailing vessel) unable to move through lack of wind.

be·came /bi'kām/ ▸ past participle of **BECOME**.

be·cause /bi'kôz; -'kəz/ ▸*conj.* for the reason that; since: *we did it because we felt it our duty* | ***just because*** *I'm inexperienced doesn't mean that I lack perception.* ▷Middle English: from the phrase *by cause*, influenced by Old French *par cause de* 'by reason of.'
▸*PHRASE* □ **because of** on account of; by reason of: *they moved here because of the baby.*

USAGE 1 When **because** follows a negative construction, the meaning can be ambiguous. In the sentence *he did not go* ***because*** *he was ill*, for example, it is not clear whether it means either 'the reason he did not go was that he was ill' or 'being ill was *not* the reason for his going—there was another reason.' Some usage guides recommend using a comma when the first interpretation is intended (*he did not go, because he was ill*) and no comma where the second interpretation is intended, but in general it is probably safest to try to avoid such constructions altogether.

2 As with other conjunctions such as **but** and **and**, it is still widely believed and taught that it is incorrect to begin a sentence with **because**. It has, however, long been used in this way in both written and spoken English (typically for rhetorical effect), and it is quite correct—however, the sentence-opening **because** should be used sparingly. See also **usage** at **AND**.

3 On the construction **the reason ... is because**, see **usage** at **REASON**.

4 On the use of **since** in the sense of **because**, see **usage** at **SINCE**.

bec·ca·fi·co /,bekə'fēkō/ ▸*n.* a European songbird, esp. a warbler, eaten as a delicacy. ▷Italian.

bé·cha·mel /,bāshə'mel/ (also **béchamel sauce**) ▸*n.* a rich white sauce made with milk infused with herbs and other flavorings. ▷named after the Marquis Louis de *Béchamel* (died 1703), steward to Louis XIV of France, who is said to have invented a similar sauce.

be·chance /bi'chans/ ▸*v. archaic* happen; befall.

bêche-de-mer /,besh də 'mer/ ▸*n.* (*pl.* same or **bêches-de-mer** *pronunc.* same) **1** a large sea cucumber that is eaten as a delicacy in China and Japan. Also called **TREPANG**. **2** variant spelling of **BEACH-LA-MAR**. ▷late 18th cent.: pseudo-French, alteration of Portuguese *bicho do mar*, literally 'sea worm.'

Bech·stein /'bek,stīn/ ▸*n.* a piano made by the German piano-builder Friedrich Wilhelm Carl Bechstein (1826–1900) or by the firm that he founded in 1856.

beck[1] /bek/ ▸*n. chiefly Brit.* a mountain stream. ▷Middle English: from Old Norse *bekkr*, of Germanic origin; related to Dutch *beek* and German *Bach*. Used as the common term for a brook in the northern areas of England, *beck* often refers, in literature, to a brook with a stony bed or following a rugged course, typical of such areas.

beck[2] ▸*n. poetic/literary* a gesture requesting attention, such as a nod or wave. ▷Middle English: from archaic *beck*, abbreviated form of **BECKON**.
▸*PHRASE* □ **at someone's beck and call** always having to be ready to obey someone's orders immediately.

Beck·er /'bekər/, Boris (1967–), German tennis player. He won the men's singles championship at Wimbledon 1985, 1986, 1989, at the U.S. Open 1989, and at the Australian Open 1991.

beck·et /'bekit/ ▸*n.* a loop of rope or similar device for securing loose items on a ship. ▷early 18th cent.: of unknown origin.

Beck·et, St. Tho·mas à /ə 'bekit/ (*c.*1118–70), English prelate and statesman, archbishop of Canterbury 1162–70. He was assassinated when he opposed Henry II. Feast day, December 29.

Beck·ett /'bekit/, Samuel (Barclay) (1906–89), Irish playwright, novelist, and poet. He is well known for *Waiting for Godot* (1952), a seminal work in the Theater of the Absurd. Nobel Prize for Literature (1969).

Beck·mann[1] /'bekmən/, Ernst Otto (1853–1923), German chemist. He devised a method for determining a compound's molecular weight by measuring the rise in boiling point of a solvent containing the compound.

Beck·mann[2], Max (1884–1950), German painter and graphic artist. His paintings reflect his first-hand experience of human evil during World War I.

beck·on /'bekən/ ▸*v.* [*intrans.*] make a gesture with the hand, arm, or head to encourage someone to come nearer or follow: *Miranda* ***beckoned to*** *Adam.* ■ [*trans.*] attract the attention of and summon (someone) in this way: *he beckoned Christopher over* | [*trans.*] *he beckoned Duncan to follow.* ■ *figurative* seem to be appealing or inviting: *the going is tough, and soft options beckon.* ▷Old English *biecnan, bēcnan*; related to **BEACON**.

be·cloud /bi'kloud/ ▸*v.* [*trans.*] cause to become obscure or muddled: *self-interest beclouds the issue.* ■ (usu. **be beclouded**) cover or surround with clouds.

be·come /bi'kəm/ ▸*v.* (*past* **-came**; *past part.* **-come**) **1** [*intrans.*] begin to be: *they became angry* | *it is becoming clear that we are in a totally new situation.* ■ grow to be; turn into: *the child will become an adult.* ■ (of a person) qualify or be accepted as; acquire the status of: *she wanted to become a doctor.* ■ (**become of**) (in questions) happen to: *what would become of her now?* **2** [*trans.*] (of clothing) look good on or suit (someone): *the dress becomes her.* ■ be appropriate or suitable to (someone): *minor celebrity status did not become him.* ▷Old English *becuman* 'come to a place, come (to be or do something)' (see **BE-**, **COME**), of Germanic origin; related to Dutch *bekomen* and German *bekommen* 'get, receive.'

be·com·ing /bi'kəming/ ▸*adj.* (esp. of clothing) flattering a person's appearance: *what a becoming dress!* | *New beret? It's very becoming.* ■ decorous: *a becoming modesty.*
▸*n. Philosophy* the process of coming to be something or of passing into a state. **—be·com·ing·ly** *adj.*

Bec·que·rel /,bek(ə)'rel/, Antoine-Henri (1852–1908), French physicist. With Marie and Pierre Curie he discovered the natural radioactivity in uranium salts. Nobel Prize for Physics (1903, shared with the Curies).

bec·que·rel /'bekə,rel/ (abbr.: **Bq**) ▸*n. Physics* the SI unit of radioactivity, corresponding to one disintegration per second. ▷late 19th cent.: named after A. H. **BECQUEREL**.

BEd ▸*abbr.* Bachelor of Education.

bed /bed/ ▸*n.* **1** a piece of furniture for sleep or rest, typically a framework with a mattress and coverings: *a large double bed* | *she was* ***in bed*** *by nine* | ***getting out of bed*** *is a real struggle.* ■ a place or article used by a person or animal for sleep or rest: *a bed of straw.* ■ the time for sleeping: *it was time for bed.* ■ a bed and associated facilities making up a place for a patient in a hospital or for a guest at a hotel: *a round of hospital staff layoffs and bed closings* | *few can afford a bed in a hotel.* ■ *informal* used with reference to a bed as the typical place for sexual activity: *some men care very little about pleasing their partners* ***in bed*** | *she'd* ***gone to bed with*** *Tony willingly.* **2** an area of ground, typically in a garden, where flowers and plants are grown: *a bed of tulips* | *vegetable beds.* **3** a flat base or foundation on which something rests or is supported, in particular: ■ the foundation of a road or railroad. ■ the open part of a truck, wagon, or railroad car, where goods are carried. ■ the flat surface beneath the baize of a billiard table. **4** a layer or pile of something, in particular: ■ a layer of food on which other foods are served: *the salad is served on a bed of raw spinach.* ■ a layer of rock or other geological material: *a bed of clay.* ■ any mass or pile resembling a bed: *pots steaming on the fragrant bed of coals* | *a dog knocked the girl into a bed of ants.* **5** the bottom of the sea or a lake or river: *a riverbed.* ■ [with *modifer*] a place on the seabed where shellfish, esp. oysters or mussels, breed or are bred: *mussel beds.*
▸*v.* (**bed·ded, bed·ding**) **1** [*intrans.*] settle down to sleep or rest for the night, typically in an improvised place: *he usually* ***bedded down*** *on newspapers in the church porch.* ■ (**bed someone/something down**) settle a person or animal down to sleep or rest for the night. ■ *informal* have sexual intercourse with: *he should bed a woman his own age.* **2** transfer (a plant) from a pot or seed tray to a garden plot: *I* ***bedded out*** *these houseplants.* **3** (usu. **be bedded in/on**) fix firmly; embed: *the posts should be firmly bedded in concrete.* ■ lay or arrange (something, esp. stone) in a layer. ▷Old English *bed, bedd* (noun), *beddian* (verb), of Germanic origin; related to Dutch *bed* and German *Bett*.
▸*PHRASES* □ **bed of nails** a board with nails pointing out of it, as lain on by fakirs and ascetics. ■ *figurative* a problematic or uncomfortable situation. □ **bed of roses** [often with *negative*] used in reference to a situation or activity that is comfortable or easy: *farming is no bed of roses.* □ **be brought to bed** *archaic* (of a woman) give birth to a child: *she was* ***brought to bed of*** *a daughter.* □ **get up on the wrong side of the bed** start the day in a bad temper. □ **in bed with** *informal* having sexual intercourse with: *he found his wife in bed with one of the neighbors.* ■ *figurative* in undesirably close association with: *these meetings with politicians put the gay movement in bed with the dreaded Establishment.* □ **make a bed** fit a bed with sheets, blankets, and pillows. □ **put someone to bed** take or prepare someone, typically a child, for rest in bed: *Clare put her to bed and gave her a mug of cocoa.* □ **put a newspaper to bed** *informal* prepare a newspaper for press. □ **take to one's bed** stay in bed because of illness.

be·dab·ble /bi'dabəl/ ▸*v.* [*trans.*] (usu. **be bedabbled**) *archaic* stain or splash with dirty liquid or blood: *idols of gold bedabbled all with blood.*

be·dad /bi'dad/ ▸*exclam. Irish* used to express surprise or for emphasis. ▷early 18th cent.: alteration of *by God*; compare with **BEGAD** and **GAD**[2].

bed and break·fast (also **bed-and-break·fast**; abbr.: **b. & b.**) ▸*n.* sleeping accommodations for a night and a morning meal, provided in guest houses and small hotels. ■ a guest house or small hotel offering such accommodations.

be·daub /bi'dôb/ ▸*v.* [*trans.*] (usu. **be bedaubed**) *poetic/literary* smear or daub with a sticky substance: *a dozen maidens, all* ***bedaubed with*** *paint.*

be·daz·zle /bi'dazəl/ ▸*v.* [*trans.*] (often **be bedazzled**) greatly impress (someone) with brilliance or skill: *bedazzled by him, they offered him a job in Paris.* ■ cleverly outwit. **—be·daz·zle·ment** *n.*

bed-block·ing /'bed ,bläking/ ▸*n. Brit.* the long-term occupation of hospital beds, chiefly by the elderly, due to a shortage of suitable care elsewhere.

bed·bug /'bed,bəg/ ▸*n.* a bloodsucking bug that is a parasite of birds and mammals. • Family Cimicidae, suborder Heteroptera: *Cimex* and other genera, and many species, in particular the chiefly nocturnal *C. lectularius*, which feeds mainly on humans, hiding in crevices or among clothing during the day.

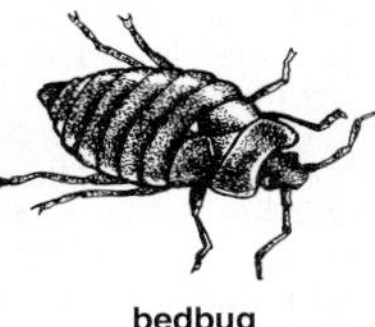

bedbug

bed·cham·ber /'bed,chāmbər/ ▸*n. archaic* a bedroom.

bed·clothes /'bed,klō(th)z/ ▸*plural n.* coverings for a bed, such as sheets and blankets.

bed·cov·er /'bed,kəvər/ ▸*n.* a bedspread.

bed·da·ble /'bedəbəl/ ▸*adj. informal* sexually attractive or available.

bed·ded /'bedid/ ▸*adj. Geology* (of rock) deposited in layers or strata, esp. in a way specified: *thinly bedded carbonate mudstones.*

bed·der /'bedər/ ▸*n.* a plant suitable for use as a bedding plant.

bed·ding /'beding/ ▸*n.* **1** coverings for a bed, such as sheets and blankets. ■ straw or similar material for animals to sleep on. **2** a base or bottom layer: [as *adj.*] *a bedding course of sand.* **3** a display of bedding plants. **4** *Geology* the stratification or layering of rocks or other geological materials: [as *adj.*] *a bedding plane.*

bed·ding plant ▸*n.* a plant set into a garden bed or container when it is about to bloom, usually an annual used for display and discarded at the end of the season.

bed·dy-bye /ˈbedē ˌbī/ ▸*n. informal* a baby-talk word for bed or bedtime: *it was time for beddy-bye* | [as *adj.*] *we got our beddy-bye kisses and trundled up the stairs.* ▷early 20th cent.: from **BED** + **-Y**2 and **BYE-BYE**.

▸*PHRASE* □ **go beddy-bye** go to bed: *for the last ten miles, all I could think about was getting home and going beddy-bye.*

Bede, St. /bēd/ (*c.*673–735), English monk, theologian, and historian; known as **the Venerable Bede**. He wrote *The Ecclesiastical History of the English People* (written in Latin and completed in 731), a primary source for early English history. Feast day, May 27.

be·deck /biˈdek/ ▸*v.* [*trans.*] (often **be bedecked**) decorate: *he led us into a room* ***bedecked with*** *tinsel.*

bed·e·guar /ˈbediˌgär/ (also **bedeguar gall**) ▸ another term for **MOSSY ROSE GALL**. ▷late Middle English: from French *bédégar*, from Persian *bād-āwar*, literally 'wind-brought.'

be·dev·il /biˈdevəl/ ▸*v.* (**-dev·iled**, **-dev·il·ing**; also *chiefly Brit.* **-dev·illed**, **-dev·il·ling**) [*trans.*] (of something bad) cause great and continual trouble to: *inconsistencies that bedevil modern English spelling.* ■ (of a person) torment or harass: *he bedeviled them with petty practical jokes.* —**be·dev·il·ment** *n.*

be·dew /biˈd(y)o͞o/ ▸*v.* [*trans.*] *poetic/literary* cover or sprinkle with drops of water or other liquid.

bed·fel·low /ˈbedˌfelō/ ▸*n.* a person who shares a bed with another. ■ *figurative* a person or thing allied or closely connected with another: *the treaty will make* ***strange bedfellows*** *of a number of enemies.*

Bed·ford /ˈbedfərd/ a city in northeastern Texas, northeast of Fort Worth; pop. 43,762.

Bed·ford cord ▸*n.* a tough woven fabric having prominent ridges, similar to corduroy. ▷late 19th cent.: named after the town of Bedford, England.

Bed·ford-Stuy·ve·sant /ˈstīvəsənt/ a residential and commercial section of northern Brooklyn in New York City, home to one of the largest U.S. black communities.

bed-hop ▸*v.* [*intrans.*] *informal* engage in successive casual sexual affairs: [as *n.*] (**bed-hopping**) *a life of bed-hopping.* —**bed-hop·per** *n.*

be·dight /biˈdīt/ ▸*adj. archaic* adorned: *a Christmas pudding* ***bedight with*** *holly.* ▷late Middle English: past participle of archaic *bedight* 'equip, array' (see **BE-**, **DIGHT**).

be·dim /biˈdim/ ▸*v.* (**-dimmed**, **-dim·ming**) [*trans.*] *poetic/literary* cause to become dim: *a slight cloud would bedim the sky.*

be·di·zened /biˈdīzənd/ ▸*adj. poetic/literary* dressed up or decorated gaudily: *a dress* ***bedizened with*** *resplendent military medals.* ▷mid 17th cent.: from **BE-** (as an intensifier) + obsolete *dizen* 'deck out,' probably of Dutch origin. —**be·di·zen** *v.*

bed·lam /ˈbedləm/ ▸*n.* **1** a scene of uproar and confusion: *there was bedlam in the courtroom.* **2** *historical* (**Bedlam**) a former insane asylum in London. ■ *archaic* used allusively to refer to any insane asylum. ▷late Middle English: early form of **BETHLEHEM**, referring to the hospital of St. Mary of Bethlehem in London, used as an asylum for the insane.

bed lin·en ▸*n.* sheets, pillowcases, and duvet covers.

Bed·ling·ton ter·ri·er /ˈbedliNGtən/ ▸*n.* a terrier of a breed with a narrow head, long legs, and curly hair. ▷mid 19th cent.: named after the village of *Bedlington* in northern England, where the breed originated.

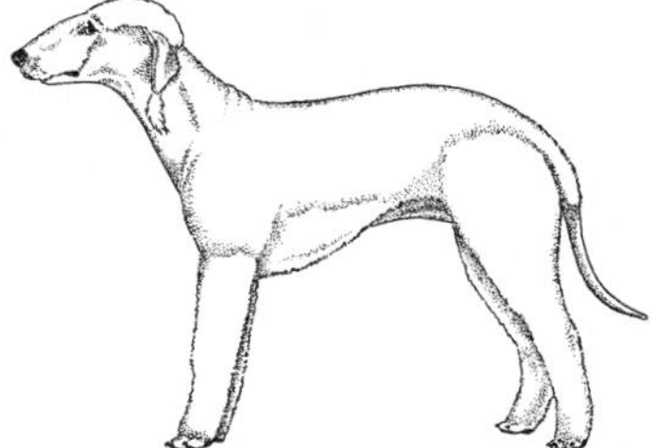

Bedlington terrier

bed·mate /ˈbedˌmāt/ ▸*n.* a person with whom a bed is shared, esp. a sexual partner.

Bed·ou·in /ˈbed(ə)win/ (also **Bed·u·in**) ▸*n.* (*pl.* same) a nomadic Arab of the desert.

▸*adj.* of or relating to the Bedouin. ▷from Old French *beduin*, based on Arabic *badawī*, (plural) *badawīn* 'dwellers in the desert,' from *badw* 'desert.'

bed·pan /ˈbedˌpan/ ▸*n.* a receptacle used by a bedridden patient as a toilet.

bed·plate /ˈbedˌplāt/ ▸*n.* a metal plate forming the base of a machine.

bed·post /ˈbedˌpōst/ ▸*n.* any of the four upright supports of a bedstead.

▸*PHRASE* □ **between you and me and the bedpost** (or **the gatepost** or **the wall**) *informal* in strict confidence.

be·drag·gled /biˈdragəld/ ▸*adj.* dirty and disheveled: *bedraggled refugees* | *we got there, tired and bedraggled.* ▷early 18th cent.: from **BE-** 'thoroughly' + **DRAGGLE** + **-ED**2. —**be·drag·gle** *v.*

bed·rail /ˈbedˌrāl/ ▸*n.* a rail along the side of a bed connecting the headboard to the footboard.

bed rest ▸*n.* confinement of an invalid to bed as part of treatment.

bed·rid·den /ˈbedˌridn/ ▸*adj.* confined to bed by sickness or old age. ▷Middle English: formed irregularly from archaic *bedrid* 'bedridden person,' from the base of the verb **RIDE**.

bed·rock /ˈbedˌräk/ ▸*n.* solid rock underlying loose deposits such as soil or alluvium. ■ *figurative* the fundamental principles on which something is based: *honesty is the bedrock of a good relationship.*

bed·roll /ˈbedˌrōl/ ▸*n.* a sleeping bag or other bedding rolled into a bundle.

bed·room /ˈbedˌro͞om; -ˌro͝om/ (abbr.: **bdrm.**) ▸*n.* a room for sleeping in: [in *combination*] *a three-bedroom house.* ■ [as *adj.*] relating to sexual relations: *bedroom secrets.* ■ [as *adj.*] denoting a small town or suburb whose residents travel to work in a nearby city: *a bedroom community.*

bed·side /ˈbedˌsīd/ ▸*n.* the space beside a bed, typically that of someone who is ill: *he was summoned to the bedside of a dying man* | [as *adj.*] *a bedside lamp.*

▸*PHRASE* □ **bedside manner** a doctor's approach or attitude toward a patient.

bed·sit /ˈbedˌsit/ (also **bed·sit·ter** or **bed-sit·ting room**) ▸*n. Brit., informal* a one-room apartment typically consisting of a combined bedroom and sitting room with cooking facilities.

bed·skirt /ˈbedˌskərt/ ▸*n.* a decorative drapery attached to the frame of a bed; a dust ruffle.

bed·sore /ˈbedˌsôr/ ▸*n.* a sore developed by an invalid because of pressure caused by lying in bed in one position. Also called **DECUBITUS ULCER**.

bed·spread /ˈbedˌspred/ ▸*n.* a decorative cloth used to cover a bed.

bed·stead /ˈbedˌsted/ ▸*n.* the framework of a bed on which the bedsprings and mattress are placed.

bed·straw /ˈbedˌstrô/ ▸*n.* a herbaceous plant with small, lightly perfumed, white or yellow flowers and whorls of slender leaves. It was formerly used for stuffing mattresses. • Genus *Galium*, family Rubiaceae: several species, including **yellow bedstraw** (*G. verum*).

bed·time /ˈbedˌtīm/ ▸*n.* [in *sing.*] the usual time when someone goes to bed: *it was well past her bedtime* | [as *adj.*] *a bedtime story.*

Bed·u·in ▸*n.* & *adj.* variant spelling of **BEDOUIN**.

bed warm·er (also **bed·warm·er**) ▸*n. historical* a device for warming a bed, typically a metal pan filled with warm coals.

bed warmer

bed-wet·ting ▸*n.* involuntary urination during sleep. —**bed-wet·ter** *n.*

bee /bē/ ▸*n.* **1** a honeybee. **2** an insect of a large group to which the honeybee belongs, including many solitary as well as social kinds. • Superfamily Apoidea, order Hymenoptera: several families, often now placed in the single family Apidae. **3** [with *adj.*] a meeting for communal work or amusement: *a quilting bee.* ▷Old English *bēo*, of Germanic origin; related to Dutch *bij* and German dialect *Beie*.

▸*PHRASES* □ **have a bee in one's bonnet** *informal* be preoccupied or obsessed about something, esp. a scheme or plan of action: □ **the bee's knees** *informal* an outstandingly good person or thing. [first used to denote something small and insignificant, transferred to the opposite sense in U.S. slang.]

bee balm ▸*n.* another term for **BERGAMOT** (sense 3).

bee·bread /ˈbēˌbred/ (also **bee bread**) ▸*n.* honey or pollen used as food by bees.

beech /bēCH/ ▸*n.* (also **beech tree**) a large tree with smooth gray bark, glossy leaves, and hard, pale, fine-grained timber. Its fruit, the beechnut, is an important food for numerous wild birds and mammals. • Genera *Fagus* (of the north temperate zone) and *Notofagus* (the **southern beeches**, of Australasia and South America), family Fagaceae: many species, esp. the common **American beech** (*F. grandifolia*) and the **European beech** (*F. sylvatica*). ▷Old English *bēce*, of Germanic origin; related to **BOOK** and to Latin *fagus* 'beech,' Greek *phagos* 'edible oak.'

Bee·cham /ˈbēCHəm/, Sir Thomas (1879–1961), English conductor and impresario. He founded the London Philharmonic 1932 and the Royal Philharmonic 1947.

beech·drops /ˈbēCHˌdräps/ ▸*n.* a broomrape that is parasitic on the roots of beech trees. Unlike most broomrapes, it has branching stems. • *Epifagus virginiana*, family Orobanchaceae.

Bee·cher1 /ˈbēCHər/, Catharine Esther (1800–78), U.S. educator. She promoted educational rights for women and founded the American Women's Education Assocation in 1852. She was the sister of Henry Ward Beecher and Harriet Beecher Stowe.

Bee·cher 2, Henry Ward (1813–87), U.S. clergyman, orator, and writer. Ordained as a Congregationalist in 1837, he became famous as an orator who attacked political corruption and slavery. He was the brother of Catharine Beecher and Harriet Beecher Stowe.

beech fern ▸*n.* a fern with triangular, deeply lobed fronds. Native to eastern North America, it favors moist woodland habitats and streamsides. • Genus *Thelypteris*, family Polypodiaceae: two species, the **broad beech fern** (*T. hexagonptera*) and the **long beech fern** (also **narrow beech fern** or **northern beech fern**) (*T. phegopteris*).

beech mar·ten ▸*n.* another term for **STONE MARTEN**.

beech·mast /ˈbēCHˌmast/ ▸*n.* (collectively, esp. when on the ground) beechnuts. ▷late 16th cent.: from **BEECH** + **MAST**2.

beech·nut /ˈbēCHˌnət/ ▸*n.* the small triangular brown fruit of the beech tree, pairs of which are enclosed in a prickly case; see **BEECHMAST**.

bee dance ▸*n.* a series of movements performed in the hive by worker honeybees to inform the colony of the direction and distance to a food source.

bee·di ▸*n.* (*pl.* **bee·dis**) variant spelling of **BIDI**.

bee-eat·er ▸*n.* a brightly colored insectivorous bird with a large head and a long down-curved bill, and typically with long central tail feathers. • Family Meropidae: three genera, in particular *Merops*, and including the **European bee-eater** (*M. apiaster*).

beef /bēf/ ▸*n.* **1** the flesh of a cow, bull, or ox, used as food. ■ (*pl.* **beeves** /bēvz/) *Farming* a cow, bull, or ox fattened for its meat. ■ *informal* flesh or muscle, typically when well developed: *he needs a little more beef on his bones.* ■ *informal* strength or power: *he's been brought in to give the team more beef.* **2** (*pl.* **beefs**) *informal* a complaint or grievance: *he has a beef with American education: it doesn't teach the basics of investing.* **3** *informal* a criminal charge: *a drunk-driving beef.*

▸*v.* [*intrans.*] *informal* complain: *he was* ***beefing about*** *how the recession was killing the business.*

▸*phrasal v.* □ **beef something up** *informal* give more substance or strength to something: *cost-cutting measures are planned to beef up performance.* ▷Middle English: from Old French *boef*, from Latin *bos*, *bov-* 'ox.' *See page 146.*

beef·a·lo /ˈbēfəˌlō/ ▸*n.* (*pl.* same or **-loes**) a hybrid animal, a cross between cattle and buffalo. ▷1970s: blend of **BEEF** and **BUFFALO**.

beef bour·gui·gnon ▸*n.* variant spelling of **BOEUF BOURGIGNON**.

beef·cake /ˈbēfˌkāk/ ▸*n. informal* an attractive man with well-developed muscles.

beef·eat·er /ˈbēfˌētər/ ▸*n.* a Yeoman Warder or Yeoman of the Guard in the Tower of London. ▷early 17th cent. (originally a derogatory term for a well-fed servant): the current sense dates from the late 17th cent.

bee fly ▸*n.* a squat, hairy, beelike fly that hovers to feed from flowers using its long tongue. Its larvae usually parasitize other insects, esp. bees and wasps. • Family Bombyliidae: many genera.

B

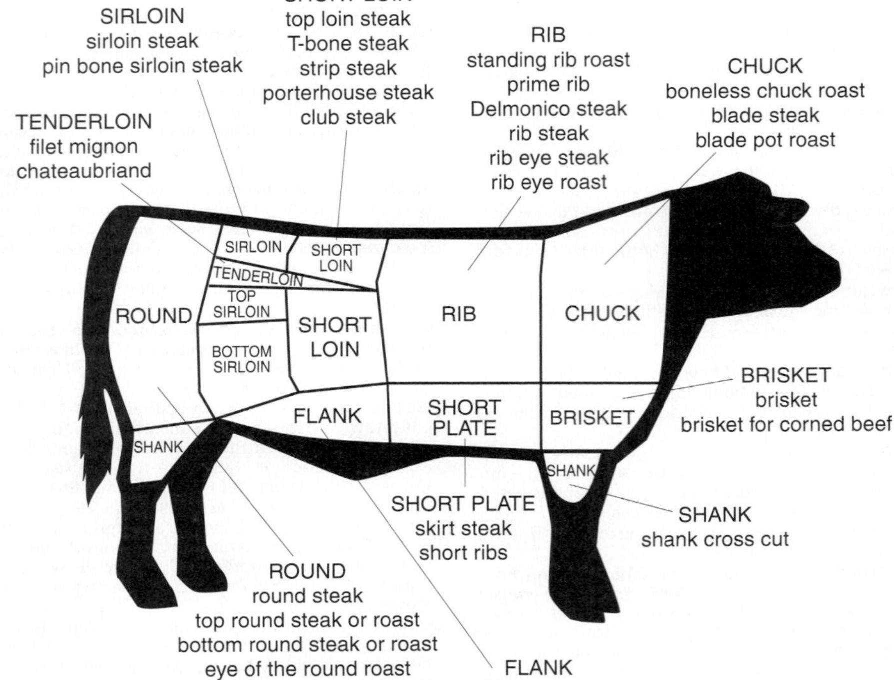

beef 1

beef·steak /ˈbēfˌstāk/ ▸*n.* a thick slice of lean beef, typically from the rump and eaten grilled, broiled, or fried.

beef·steak fun·gus (also **beefsteak mushroom**) ▸*n.* an edible reddish-brown bracket fungus that resembles raw beef. Native to both Eurasia and North America, it usually grows on oak or sweet chestnut trees. • *Fistulina hepatica*, family Fistulinaceae, class Hymenomycetes.

beef·steak to·ma·to ▸*n.* a tomato of an exceptionally large and firm variety.

beef tea ▸*n. chiefly Brit.* a drink made from stewed extract of beef used as nourishment for invalids.

beef Wel·ling·ton ▸*n.* a dish of beef, typically coated in pâté de foie gras, wrapped in puff pastry, and baked.

beef·wood /ˈbēfˌwo͝od/ ▸*n.* a tropical hardwood tree with close-grained red timber. • Species in several families, in particular *Casuarina equisetifolia* (family Casuarinaceae), native to Australia and Southeast Asia.

beef·y /ˈbēfē/ ▸*adj.* (**beef·i·er**, **beef·i·est**) **1** *informal* muscular or robust: *he shrugged his beefy shoulders.* ■ [*attrib.*] large and impressively powerful: *beefy skis.* **2** tasting like beef. —**beef·i·ly** /ˈbēfəlē/ *adv.* —**beef·i·ness** *n.*

bee·hive /ˈbēˌhīv/ ▸*n.* **1** a structure in which bees are kept, typically in the form of a dome or box. ■ [usu. as *adj.*] something having the domed shape of a traditional wicker beehive: *beehive huts* | *beehive ovens.* ■ a busy, crowded place: *the church became* **a beehive of activity**. ■ (**the Beehive** or **the Beehive cluster**) another term for PRAESEPE. **2** a woman's domed and lacquered hairstyle, esp. popular in the 1960s. —**bee·hived** *adj.* (in sense 2).

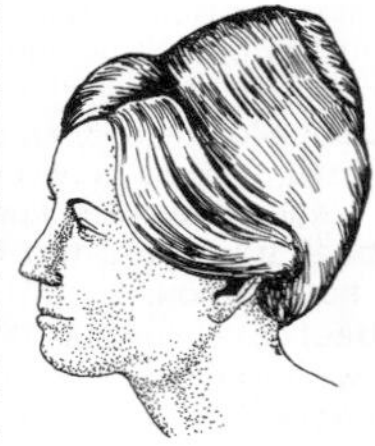
beehive 2

Bee·hive State a nickname for the state of UTAH.

bee·keep·ing /ˈbēˌkēpiNG/ ▸*n.* the occupation of owning and breeding bees for their honey. —**bee·keep·er** /-ˌkēpər/ *n.*

bee·line /ˈbēˌlīn/ ▸*n.* a straight line between two places. ▷early 19th cent.: with reference to the straight line supposedly taken instinctively by a bee when returning to the hive.

▸*PHRASE* □ **make a beeline for** hurry directly to.

Be·el·ze·bub /bēˈelzəˌbəb/ a name for the Devil. ▷from late Latin *Beelzebub*, translating Hebrew *ba'al zəḇūḇ* 'lord of flies,' the name of a Philistine god (2 Kings 1:2), and Greek *Beelzeboul* 'the Devil' (Matt. 12:24).

Bee·mer /ˈbēmər/ (also **Bea·mer**) ▸*n. informal* a car or motorcycle manufactured by the company BMW. ▷1980s (originally U.S.): representing a pronunciation of the first two letters of *BMW* (Bayerische Motoren Werke AG) + *-er*.

been /bin/ ▸ past participle of BE.

Beene /bēn/, Geoffrey (1927–2004), U.S. fashion designer.

beep /bēp/ ▸*n.* a short, high-pitched sound emitted by electronic equipment or a vehicle horn.

▸*v.* [*intrans.*] (of a horn or electronic device) produce such a sound: *radio receivers squawked and beeped.* ■ [*trans.*] summon (someone) by means of a pager: *they have themselves beeped in restaurants.* ▷1920s: imitative.

beep·er /ˈbēpər/ ▸*n.* another term for PAGER.

beer /bi(ə)r/ ▸*n.* an alcoholic drink made from yeast-fermented malt flavored with hops: *a pint of beer* | *I'm dying for a beer.* ■ any of several other fermented drinks: [with *adj.*] *ginger beer.* ▷Old English *bēor*, based on monastic Latin *biber* 'a drink,' from Latin *bibere* 'to drink'; related to Dutch *bier* and German *Bier*.

▸*PHRASE* □ **beer and skittles** [often with *negative*] *Brit.* amusement or enjoyment: *life isn't all beer and skittles.*

beer bel·ly (also *informal* **beer gut**) ▸*n.* a man's fat stomach, caused by excessive consumption of beer. —**beer-bel·lied** *adj.*

Beer·bohm /ˈbi(ə)rˌbōm/, Max (1872–1956), English caricaturist, essayist, and critic; full name *Sir Henry Maximilian Beerbohm*.

Beer·en·aus·le·se /ˌberənˈousˌlāzə/ ▸*n.* a white wine of German origin or style made from selected individual grapes picked later than the general harvest. ▷German, from *Beeren* 'berries' + *aus* 'out' + *lese* 'picking.'

beer gar·den ▸*n.* a garden, typically one attached to a bar or tavern, where beer is served.

beer gut ▸*n.* another term for BEER BELLY.

beer hall ▸*n.* a large room or building where beer is served.

beer mon·ey ▸*n. informal* a small amount of money allowed or earned. ▷early 19th cent.: so named because the allowance of money was made instead of beer.

beer par·lour ▸*n. Canadian* a room in a hotel or tavern where beer is served.

Beer·she·ba /bi(ə)rˈsHēbə/ a town in southern Israel on the northern edge of the Negev Desert; pop. 138,100.

beer-swill·ing ▸*adj.* drinking a lot of beer. ■ disreputable, rowdy.

beer·y /ˈbi(ə)rē/ ▸*adj. informal* relating to or characterized by the drinking of beer, typically in large amounts: *many beery pledges were made* | *stale beery breath.*

beest·ings /ˈbēstiNGz/ (also **beast·ings**) ▸*n.* [treated as *sing.*] the first milk produced by a cow or goat after giving birth. ▷Old English *bȳsting*; related to Dutch *biest* and German *Biest(milch)*.

bee-stung ▸*adj.* [*attrib.*] *informal* (of a woman's lips) full, red, and pouting.

bees·wax /ˈbēzˌwaks/ ▸*n.* **1** the wax secreted by bees to make honeycombs and used to make wood polishes and candles: *turning pollen into beeswax.* **2** *informal* a person's concern or business: *that's none of your beeswax.*

beet /bēt/ ▸*n.* a herbaceous plant widely cultivated as a source of food for humans and livestock, and for processing into sugar. Some varieties are grown for their leaves and some for their large nutritious root. • *Beta vulgaris*, family Chenopodiaceae: several subspecies. ▷Old English *bēte*, from Latin *beta*, perhaps of Celtic origin; related to Dutch *beet* and German *Bete*.

Bee·tho·ven /ˈbāˌtōvən; ˈbātˌō-/, Ludwig van (1770–1827), German composer. Despite increasing deafness, Beethoven wrote prodigiously: nine symphonies, thirty-two piano sonatas, sixteen string quartets, the opera *Fidelio* (1814), and the Mass in D (the *Missa Solemnis*, 1823).

bee·tle[1] /ˈbētl/ ▸*n.* an insect of an order distinguished by forewings typically modified into hard wing cases (elytra) that cover and protect the hind wings and abdomen. • Order Coleoptera: see COLEOPTERA. ■ (loosely) a similar insect, esp. a black one.

▸*v.* [*intrans.*] *informal* make one's way hurriedly or with short, quick steps: *the tourist beetled off.* ▷Old English *bitula*, *bitela* 'biter,' from the base of *bītan* 'to bite.'

bee·tle[2] ▸*n.* a tool with a heavy head and a handle, used for tasks such as ramming, crushing, and driving wedges; a maul. ■ a machine used for heightening the luster of cloth by pressure from rollers.

▸*v.* [*trans.*] ram, crush, or drive with a beetle. ■ finish (cloth) with a beetle. ▷Old English *bētel*, of Germanic origin; related to BEAT.

bee·tle[3] ▸*v.* [*intrans.*] [usu. as *adj.*] (**beetling**) (of a person's eyebrows) project or overhang threateningly: *piercing eyes glittered beneath a great beetling brow.*

▸*adj.* [*attrib.*] (of a person's eyebrows) shaggy and projecting. ▷mid 16th cent. (as an adjective): back-formation from *beetle-browed*. The verb was apparently used as a nonce word by Shakespeare and was later adopted by other writers. —**bee·tle-browed** *adj.*

beet leaf·hop·per ▸*n.* a North American leafhopper found west of the Mississippi River and considered a serious pest to beets and members of the gourd family. It is a principal carrier of the virus that causes curly top. • *Circulifer tenellus*, family Cicadellidae.

bee tree ▸*n.* a hollow tree used by bees for a hive: *in the Appalachians, the tupelo is a prime bee tree.*

beet·root /ˈbētˌro͞ot/ ▸*n. chiefly Brit.* **1** the edible root of a kind of beet that is typically dark red and spherical and eaten as a vegetable. **2** the variety of beet that produces this root. • *Beta vulgaris* subsp. *vulgaris*, family Chenopodiaceae.

beet sug·ar ▸*n.* sugar obtained from sugar beet.

beeves /bēvz/ ▸ plural form of BEEF (sense 1).

BEF ▸*abbr.* British Expeditionary Force.

be·fall /biˈfôl/ ▸*v.* (*past* **-fell**; *past part.* **-fall·en**) [*trans.*] *poetic/literary* (of something bad) happen to someone: *a tragedy befell his daughter* | [*intrans.*] *she was to blame for anything that befell.* See note at HAPPEN. ▷Old English *befeallan* 'to fall' (early use being chiefly figurative); related to German *befallen*.

be·fit /biˈfit/ ▸*v.* (**fit·ted**, **-fit·ting**) [*trans.*] be appropriate for; suit: *the ballet ends nobly, as befits a tragedy* | [as *adj.*] (**befitting**) *I answered in a befitting manner.* —**be·fit·ting·ly** *adv.*

be·fog /biˈfäg/ ▸*v.* (**-fogged**, **-fog·ging**) [*trans.*] cause to become confused: *her brain was befogged with lack of sleep.*

be·fool /biˈfo͞ol/ ▸*v.* [*trans.*] *archaic* make a fool of: *novels that befool almost every intelligence.*

be·fore /biˈfôr/ ▸*prep., conj., & adv.* **1** during the period of time preceding (a particular event, date, or time): [as *prep.*] *she had to rest before dinner* | *the day before yesterday* | *before the war* | [as *conj.*] *they lived rough* *for four days before they were arrested | it wasn't long before I had my first bite* | [as *adv.*] *his playing days had ended six years before | it's never happened to me before.* **2** in front of: [as *prep.*] *Matilda stood before her, panting | the patterns swam before her eyes* | [as *adv.*] *archaic trotting through the city with guards running before and behind.* ■ [*prep.*] in front of and required to answer to (a court of law, tribunal, or other authority): *he could be taken before a magistrate for punishment | a fall in the number of cases brought before the courts.* **3** in preference to; with a higher priority than: [as *prep.*] *a woman who placed duty before all else* | [as *conj.*] *they would die before they would cooperate with each other.* ▷Old English *beforan* (see **BY**, **FORE**), of Germanic origin; related to German *bevor*.

be·fore·hand /bi'fôr,hand/ ▶*adv.* before an action or event; in advance: *rooms must be booked beforehand.* ▷Middle English (originally as two words): from **BEFORE** + **HAND**; probably influenced by Old French *avant main*.

▶*PHRASE* □ **be beforehand with** *archaic* anticipate; forestall.

be·fore·time /bi'fôr,tīm/ ▶*adv. archaic* previously; formerly.

be·foul /bi'foul/ ▶*v.* [*trans.*] make dirty; pollute: *they befoul our water with mining.*

be·friend /bi'frend/ ▶*v.* [*trans.*] act as a friend to (someone) by offering help or support.

be·fud·dle /bi'fədl/ ▶*v.* [*trans.*] [usu. as *adj.*] (**befuddled**) make (someone) unable to think clearly: *he has an air of befuddled unworldliness.* —**be·fud·dle·ment** *n.*

beg /beg/ ▶*v.* (**begged, beg·ging**) **1** [*reporting verb*] ask (someone) earnestly or humbly for something: [*trans.*] *a leper* **begged** *Jesus* **for** *help* | [*trans.*] *she begged me to say nothing to her father* | [*intrans.*] *I must* **beg of** *you not to act impulsively.* ■ ask for (something) earnestly or humbly: *he begged their forgiveness* | [with *direct speech*] *"Don't leave me," she begged.* ■ ask formally for (permission to do something): *I will now* **beg leave** *to make some observations* | [*intrans.*] *we beg to inform you that we are instructed to wait.* **2** [*intrans.*] ask for something, typically food or money, as charity or a gift: *they had to* **beg for** *food.* ■ [*trans.*] acquire (something) from someone in this way: *a piece of bread that I* **begged from** *a farmer.* ■ live by acquiring food or money in this way. ■ (of a dog) sit up with the front paws raised expectantly in the hope of a reward.

▶*phrasal v.* □ **beg off** withdraw from a promise or undertaking. ▷Middle English: probably from Old English *bedecian*, of Germanic origin; related to **BID**[1].

▶*PHRASES* □ **beg, borrow, or steal** *figurative* do whatever may be necessary to acquire something greatly desired: *I'm gonna get the money to buy Casey's ring, even if I have to beg, borrow, or steal.* □ **beg off** request to be excused from a question or obligation: *asked to name her favorites from her films, Hepburn begs off.* □ **beg one's bread** *archaic* live by begging. □ **beg the question 1** (of a fact or action) raise a question or point that has not been dealt with; invite an obvious question. **2** avoid the question; evade the issue. **3** assume the truth of an argument or proposition to be proved, without arguing it. □ **beg to differ** see **DIFFER**. □ **go begging** (of an article) be available for use because unwanted by others: *half the apartments in New York go begging in the summer.* ■ (of an opportunity) not be taken: *we let so many good chances go begging.*

USAGE The original meaning of the phrase **beg the question** belongs to the field of logic. It is a translation of the Latin rhetorical term *petitio principii*, literally meaning 'laying claim to a principle,' that is, assuming something that ought to be proved first, as in the following sentence: *dogs should be locked up, otherwise attacks by wild dogs on children will continue to increase.* This **begs the question** (among other questions) whether, in fact, such attacks are increasing. Usually such a statement will give the impression that the problem of proving the argument has been sidestepped.

From this impression of sidestepping, a new meaning has developed: 'avoid the question, evade the issue,' as in *they said he begged the question by criticizing his opponent's program.* Also, over the last 100 years or so another, more general use has arisen: 'invite an obvious question,' as in *some definitions of mental illness beg the question of what constitutes normal behavior.*

Both of these newer meanings are widely accepted in modern standard English, although they have been criticized as being misunderstandings of the Latin rhetorical term. To some traditionalists, the sense of 'assume the truth of an argument to be proved' is still the only correct meaning of **beg the question**. Both of the newer meanings of **beg** are used not only with *question*, but with other words as well: *beg the point, beg the issue, beg the difficulties.*

THE RIGHT WORD **beg, beseech, entreat, implore, importune, petition, plead, solicit**

How badly do you want something? You can **beg** for it, which implies a humble and earnest approach.

If you **entreat**, you're trying to get what you want by ingratiating yourself (*she entreated her mother to help her prepare for the exam*).

To **plead** involves more urgency (*he pleaded with the judge to spare his life*) and is usually associated with the legal system (| *she was advised to plead guilty*).

Beseech also suggests urgency, as well as an emotional appeal (*he beseeched her to tell the truth*).

Implore is still stronger, suggesting desperation or great distress (*the look in his mother's eyes implored him to have mercy*). If you really want to get your way, you can **importune**, which means to *beg* not only urgently but persistently and to risk making a pest of yourself (*he importuned her daily to accept his invitation*).

Petition suggests an appeal to authority (*to petition the government to repeal an unjust law*), while **solicit** suggests petitioning in a courteous, formal way (*soliciting financial support for the school carnival*).

be·gad /bi'gad/ ▶*exclam. archaic* used to express surprise or for emphasis. ▷late 16th cent.: altered form; compare with **BEDAD** and **GAD**[2].

be·gan /bi'gan/ ▶ past of **BEGIN**.

be·gat /bi'gat/ ▶ archaic past of **BEGET**.

be·gem /bi'jem/ ▶*v.* (**-gemmed, -gem·ming**) [*trans.*] [usu. as *adj.*] (**begemmed**) set or stud with gems: *a begemmed cross.*

be·get /bi'get/ ▶*v.* (**-get·ting**; *past* **-got** /-'gät/; *past part.* **-got·ten**) [*trans.*] *poetic/literary* **1** (typically of a man, sometimes of a man and a woman) bring (a child) into existence by the process of reproduction: *they hoped that the King might beget an heir by his new queen.* **2** give rise to; bring about: *success begets further success.* ▷Old English *begietan* 'get, obtain by effort' (see **BE-**, **GET**). —**be·get·ter** *n.*

beg·gar /'begər/ ▶*n.* **1** a person, typically a homeless one, who lives by asking for money or food. **2** [with *adj.*] *informal* a person of a specified type, often one to be envied or pitied: *poor little beggars.*

▶*v.* [*trans.*] reduce (someone) to poverty: *by being soft to the unfortunate, we beggared ourselves.* ▷Middle English: from **BEG** + **-AR**[3].

▶*PHRASES* □ **beggar belief** (or **description**) be too extraordinary to be believed or described. □ **beggars can't be choosers** *proverb* people with no other options must be content with what is offered. □ **set a beggar on horseback and he'll ride to the Devil** *proverb* someone unaccustomed to power or luxury will abuse or be corrupted by it.

beg·gar·ly /'begərlē/ ▶*adj.* poverty-stricken. ■ pitifully or deplorably bad: *the beggarly physical condition to which I had been reduced.* ■ very small and mean: *the stipend was a beggarly $26.* —**beg·gar·li·ness** *n.*

beg·gar-my-neigh·bor ▶*n.* a card game for two players in which the object is to acquire one's opponent's cards. Players alternately turn cards up and if an honor is revealed, the other player must find an honor within a specified number of turns or else forfeit the cards already played.

▶*adj.* [*attrib.*] (also **beg·gar-thy-neigh·bor**) (esp. of national policy) self-aggrandizing at the expense of competitors: *failure would create a growing risk of trade wars as countries retreated into beggar-thy-neighbor policies.*

beg·gar's purse ▶*n.* an appetizer consisting of a crêpe stuffed with a savory filling, typically caviar and crème fraiche.

beg·gar ticks (also **beg·gar's ticks**) ▶*plural n.* [often treated as *sing.*] a plant of the daisy family with inconspicuous yellow flowers and small barbed fruit that cling to passing animals. Several kinds are widespread weeds. Also called **BUR MARIGOLD**. • Genus *Bidens*, family Compositae: several species, in particular *B. frondosa*. ▷mid 19th cent.: apparently from the resemblance of the seedpods to ticks.

beg·gar·y /'begərē/ ▶*n.* a state of extreme poverty.

Be·gin /'bāgin; bə'gēn/, Menachem (1913–92), Israeli statesman, prime minister 1977–84. His hard line on Arab–Israeli relations softened in a series of meetings with President Anwar al-Sadat of Egypt, which led to a peace treaty between the countries. Nobel Peace Prize (1978, shared with Sadat).

be·gin /bi'gin/ ▶*v.* (**-gin·ning**; *past* **-gan** /-'gan/; *past part.* **-gun** /-'gən/) **1** [*trans.*] start; perform or undergo the first part of (an action or activity): *the Communists have just begun to fight | she began a double life* | (**begin to do/doing something**) *it was beginning to snow* | [*intrans.*] *she* **began by** *rewriting the syllabus.* ■ [*intrans.*] come into being or have its starting point at a certain time or place: *the ground campaign had begun | the story* **begins with** *the death of her senile father | the tour* **begins at** *the active Poas Volcano.* ■ [*intrans.*] (of a person) hold a specific position or role before holding any other: *he* **began as** *a drummer.* ■ [*intrans.*] (of a thing) originate: *Watts Lake* **began as** *a marine inlet.* ■ [*intrans.*] (**begin with**) have as a first element: *words beginning with a vowel.* ■ [*intrans.*] (**begin on/upon**) set to work at: *Picasso began on a great canvas.* ■ [with *direct speech*] start speaking by saying: *"I've got to go to the hotel," she began.* ■ [*intrans.*] (**begin at**) (of an article) cost at least (a specified amount): *rooms begin at $139.* **2** [*intrans.*] [with *negative*] *informal* not have any chance or likelihood of doing a specified thing: *circuitry that Karen could not begin to comprehend.* ▷Old English *beginnan*, of Germanic origin; related to Dutch and German *beginnen*.

▶*PHRASE* □ **to begin with** at first. ■ in the first place: *such a fate is unlikely to befall him: to begin with, his is a genuine talent.*

be·gin·ner /bi'ginər/ ▶*n.* a person just starting to learn a skill or take part in an activity. See note at **NOVICE**.

▶*PHRASE* □ **beginner's luck** good luck supposedly experienced by a beginner at a particular activity.

be·gin·ning /bi'giniNG/ ▶*n.* [usu. in *sing.*] the point in time or space at which something starts: *he left at the beginning of February | they had reached the beginning of the forest.* ■ the process of coming, or being brought into being: *the beginning of active cooperation | the ending of one relationship and the beginning of another.* ■ the first part or earliest stage of something: *the beginning of a letter | she had the beginnings of a headache.* ■ (usu. **beginnings**) the background or origins of anything: *the series explores the beginnings of flight | he had risen from humble beginnings to great wealth.*

▶*adj.* new or inexperienced: *a beginning gardener.* ■ introductory or elementary: *the beginning guitar class.*

▶*PHRASE* □ **the beginning of the end** the event to which ending or failure can be traced.

be·gird /bi'gərd/ ▶*v.* [*trans.*] *chiefly poetic/literary* gird about or around; encompass. ■ besiege.

Be·glie·ter /bi'glītər/, Lionel, see **BART**.

be·gone /bi'gôn; -'gän/ ▶*exclam. poetic/literary* go away (as an expression of annoyance): *begone from my sight!*

be·go·nia /bi'gōnyə; -nēə/ ▶*n.* a herbaceous plant of warm climates, the bright flowers of which have brightly colored sepals but no petals. Numerous cultivated varieties of begonia are grown for their flowers or for their striking foliage. • Genus *Begonia*, family Begoniaceae. ▷modern Latin, named after Michel *Bégon* (1638–1710), French amateur botanist who discovered the plant on the island of Santo Domingo and introduced it to Europe.

be·got /bi'gät/ ▶ past of **BEGET**.

be·got·ten /bi'gätn/ ▶ past participle of **BEGET**.

be·grime /bi'grīm/ ▶*v.* [*trans.*] [often as *adj.*] (**begrimed**) blacken with ingrained dirt: *paint flaking from begrimed walls.*

be·grudge /bi'grəj/ ▶*v.* **1** [with *two objs.*] envy (someone) the possession or enjoyment of (something): *she begrudged Martin his affluence.* **2** [*trans.*] give reluctantly or resentfully: *nobody begrudges a single penny spent on health.* —**be·grudg·ing·ly** *adv.*

be·guile /bi'gīl/ ▶*v.* [*trans.*] **1** charm or enchant (someone), sometimes in a deceptive way: *every prominent American artist has been beguiled by Maine* | [as *adj.*] (**beguiling**) *a beguiling smile.* See note at **TEMPT**. ■ trick (someone) into doing something: *they were beguiled into signing a peace treaty.* **2** *dated* help (time) pass pleasantly: *to beguile some of the time they went to the movie theater.* ▷Middle English (in the sense 'deceive, deprive of by fraud'): from **BE-** 'thoroughly' + obsolete *guile* 'to deceive' (see **GUILE**). —**be·guile·ment** *n.* —**be·guil·er** *n.* —**be·guil·ing·ly** *adv.*

Beg·uine /'begēn; 'bā,gēn; bə'gēn/ ▶*n.* (in the Roman Catholic Church) a member of a Dutch lay sisterhood, formed in the 12th century, and not bound by vows.

be·guine /bi'gēn/ ▶*n.* a popular dance of West Indian

origin, similar to the foxtrot. ▷1930s: from West Indian French, from French *béguin* 'infatuation.'

be·gum /ˈbāgəm; ˈbē-/ ▸*n. Indian* a Muslim lady of high rank. ■ (**Begum**) the title of a married Muslim woman, equivalent to Mrs. ▷from Urdu *begam*, from eastern Turkish *bigim* 'princess,' feminine of *big* 'prince.'

be·gun /biˈgən/ ▸ past participle of BEGIN.

be·half /biˈhaf/ ▸*n.* ▷Middle English: from a mixture of the earlier phrases *on his halve* and *bihalve him*, both meaning 'on his side' (see BY, HALF).

▸*PHRASE* □ **on** (also **in**) **behalf of** (or **on someone's behalf**) **1** in the interests of a person, group, or principle: *votes cast by labor unions on behalf of their members.* **2** as a representative of: *he had to attend the funeral on Mama's behalf.*

be·have /biˈhāv/ ▸*v.* [*intrans.*] **1** [with *adverbial*] act or conduct oneself in a specified way, esp. toward others: *he always behaved like a gentleman | you should* ***behave*** *affectionately* ***toward*** *the patient.* ■ (of a machine or natural phenomenon) work or function in a specified way: *each car behaves differently.* **2** [often in *imperative*] conduct oneself in accordance with the accepted norms of a society or group: *you can go as long as you behave |* (**behave oneself**) *they were expected to behave themselves.* ▷late Middle English: from BE- + HAVE in the sense 'have or bear (oneself) in a particular way' (corresponding to modern German *sich behaben*).

be·haved /biˈhāvd/ ▸*adj.* conducting oneself in a specified way: *some of the boys had been badly behaved |* [in *combination*] *a well-behaved child.*

be·hav·ior /biˈhāvyər/ (*Brit.* **be·hav·iour**) ▸*n.* the way in which one acts or conducts oneself, esp. toward others: *good behavior | his insulting* ***behavior toward*** *me.* ■ the way in which an animal or person acts in response to a particular situation or stimulus: *the feeding behavior of predators.* ■ the way in which a natural phenomenon or a machine works or functions: *the erratic behavior of the old car.* ▷late Middle English: from BEHAVE, on the pattern of *demeanour* (an earlier spelling of DEMEANOR), and influenced by obsolete *haviour* from HAVE.

▸*PHRASE* □ **be on one's best behavior** behave well when being observed: *warn them to be on their best behavior.*

be·hav·ior·al /biˈhāvyərəl/ ▸*adj.* involving, relating to, or emphasizing behavior: *closely related species have similar behavioral patterns | a behavioral approach to children's language.* —**be·hav·ior·al·ly** *adv.*

be·hav·ior·al·ism /biˈhāvyərə,lizəm/ ▸*n.* the methods and principles of the science of animal (and human) behavior. ■ advocacy of or adherence to a behavioral approach to social phenomena. —**be·hav·ior·al·ist** *n.* & *adj.*

be·hav·ior·al sci·ence ▸*n.* the scientific study of human and animal behavior.

be·hav·ior·ism /biˈhāvyə,rizəm/ (*Brit.* **be·hav·iour·ism**) ▸*n. Psychology* the theory that human and animal behavior can be explained in terms of conditioning, without appeal to thoughts or feelings, and that psychological disorders are best treated by altering behavior patterns. ■ such study and treatment in practice. —**be·hav·ior·ist** *n.* & *adj.* —**be·hav·ior·is·tic** /bi,hāvyəˈristik/ *adj.*

be·ha·vior mod·i·fi·ca·tion ▸*n.* **1** the alteration of behavioral patterns through the use of such learning techniques as biofeedback and positive or negative reinforcement. **2** another term for BEHAVIOR THERAPY.

be·hav·ior ther·a·py ▸*n.* the treatment of neurotic symptoms by training the patient's reactions to stimuli.

be·head /biˈhed/ ▸*v.* cut off the head of (someone), typically as a form of execution: [as *n.*] (**beheading**) *Arabs have public beheadings.* ▷Old English *behēafdian*; from BE- 'off' (expressing removal) + *hēafod* (see HEAD).

be·held /biˈheld/ ▸ past and past participle of BEHOLD.

be·he·moth /biˈhēməth; ˈbēəməth/ ▸*n.* a huge or monstrous creature. ■ something enormous, esp. a big and powerful organization: *shoppers are now more loyal to their local stores than to faceless behemoths |* [as *adj.*] *behemoth telephone companies.* ▷late Middle English: from Hebrew *bĕhēmōṯ*, intensive plural of *bĕhēmāh* 'beast.'

be·hest /biˈhest/ ▸*n. poetic/literary* a person's orders or command: *they had assembled* ***at his behest*** *| the slaughter of the male children* ***at the behest of*** *Herod.* ▷Old English *behǣs* 'a vow,' from a Germanic base meaning 'bid'; related to HIGHT.

be·hind /biˈhīnd/ ▸*prep.* **1** at or to the far side of (something), typically so as to be hidden by it: ■ expressing location: *the recording machinery was kept behind screens | sitting behind a luggage cart.* ■ *figurative* hidden from the observer: *the agony behind his decision to retire.* ■ expressing movement: *Jannie instinctively hid her cigarette behind her back.* ■ at the back of (someone), after they have passed through a door: *she ran out of the room, slamming the door behind her.* **2** in a line or procession, following or further back than (another member of the line or procession): *stuck behind a slow-moving tractor.* **3** in support of or giving guidance to (someone else): *whatever you decide to do, I'll be behind you | the power behind the throne.* ■ guiding, controlling, or responsible for (an event or plan): *the chances were that he was behind the death of the girl | the reasoning behind their decisions.* **4** after the departure or death of (the person referred to): *he left behind him a manuscript that was subsequently published.* **5** less advanced than (someone else) in achievement or development: *the government admitted it is ten years behind the West in PC technology.* **6** having a lower score than (another competitor): *Woodnam moved to ten under par, five shots behind Fred Couples.*

▸*adv.* **1** at or to the far side or the back side of something: *as I looked behind, my feet crashed into a basket | Campbell grabbed him from behind.* **2** in a place or time already past: *the adventure lay behind them.* **3** remaining after someone or something is gone: *blocks of ice left behind by a retreating glacier | don't leave me behind.* **4** further back than other members of a group: *Bill led the way, with the others a short distance behind.* **5** (in a game or contest) having a score lower than that of the opposition: *polls showed him as much as 50 points behind.* **6** slow or late in accomplishing a task: *getting* ***behind with*** *my work | things were falling behind.* ■ in arrears: *she was* ***behind with*** *her rent.* **7** underlying or motivating: *behind his winning facade lurks uncertainty.*

▸*adj.* following; lagging: *the team behind could accept a loss.*

▸*n.* **1** *informal* the buttocks: *sitting on her behind.* **2** *Australian Rules Football* a one-point score made by kicking the ball between the outer set of two sets of goalposts (the behind line), or by touching the ball, causing it to pass between the inner posts (goalposts). ▷Old English *behindan*, *bihindan*, from *bi* 'by' + *hindan* 'from behind.'

be·hind·hand /biˈhīnd,hand/ ▸*adj.* late or slow in doing something, esp. paying a debt: *the Yoruba have not been* ***behindhand in*** *economic activity.* ■ *archaic* unaware of recent events: *you are miserably behindhand—Mr. Cole gave me a hint of it six weeks ago.* ▷mid 16th cent.: from BEHIND + HAND, on the pattern of *beforehand*.

be·hold /biˈhōld/ ▸*v.* (*past* and *past part.* **-held** /-ˈheld/) [*trans.*] [often in *imperative*] *archaic* or *poetic/literary* see or observe (a thing or person, esp. a remarkable or impressive one): *behold your king! | the botanical gardens were a wonder* ***to behold.*** ▷Old English *bihaldan*, from *bi-* 'thoroughly' + *haldan* 'to hold.' —**be·hold·er** *n.*

▸*PHRASE* □ **beauty is in the eye of the beholder** see BEAUTY.

be·hold·en /biˈhōldən/ ▸*adj.* [*predic.*] owing thanks or having a duty to someone in return for help or a service: *I don't like to be* ***beholden to*** *anybody.* ▷late Middle English: former past participle of BEHOLD, in the otherwise unrecorded sense 'bound.'

be·hoof /biˈho͞of/ ▸*n. archaic* benefit or advantage: *to make laws* ***for the behoof of*** *the colony.* ▷Old English *behōf*; related to Dutch *behoef* and German *Behuf*, also to HEAVE.

be·hoove /biˈho͞ov/ (*Brit.* **be·hove** /-ˈhōv/) ▸*v.* [*trans.*] (**it behooves someone to do something**) *formal* it is a duty or responsibility for someone to do something; it is incumbent on: *it behooves any coach to study his predecessors.* ■ [with *negative*] it is appropriate or suitable; it befits: ***it ill behooves*** *the opposition constantly to decry the sale of arms to friendly countries.* ▷Old English *behōfian*, from *behōf* (see BEHOOF).

Beh·ring /ˈberiNG/, Emil Adolf von (1854–1917), German bacteriologist; one of the founders of immunology. Nobel Prize for Physiology or Medicine (1901).

Bei·der·becke /ˈbīdər,bek/, Bix (1903–31), U.S. jazz musician and composer; born *Leon Bismarck Beiderbecke*. A self-taught cornettist and pianist, he profoundly influenced the development of jazz.

beige /bāZH/ ▸*adj.* of a pale sandy yellowish-brown color: *the beige tiles of the kitchen floor.*

▸*n.* a pale sandy fawn: *tones of beige, green, and orange | in matching fawns and beiges.* ▷mid 19th cent. (denoting a usually undyed and unbleached woolen fabric of this color): from French, of unknown ultimate origin.

Beige Book ▸*n.* a summary and analysis of economic activity and conditions, prepared with the aid of reports from the district Federal Reserve Banks and issued by the central bank of the Federal Reserve for its policy makers before a Federal Open Market Committee meeting: *Wednesday's Beige Book will be scanned for reports of tightness in labor markets.*

bei·gnet /benˈyā/ ▸*n.* **1** a fritter: *a cheese beignet.* **2** a square of fried dough eaten hot sprinkled with confectioners' sugar. ▷French, from archaic *buyne* 'hump, bump.'

Bei·jing /ˈbāˈjiNG/ the capital of China, in the northeastern part of the country; pop. 6,920,000. It became the country's capital in 1421, at the start of the Ming period, and survived as the capital of the Republic of China after the revolution of 1912. Also called (esp. formerly) PEKING.

be·ing /ˈbēiNG/ ▸ present participle of BE.

▸*n.* **1** existence: *the railway* ***brought*** *many towns* ***into being*** *| the moment when the universe* ***came into being.*** ■ living; being alive: *holism promotes a unified way of being.* **2** [in *sing.*] the nature or essence of a person: *sometimes one aspect of our being has been developed at the expense of the others.* **3** a real or imaginary living creature, esp. an intelligent one: *animals regarded as primitive beings | alien beings.* ■ a human being: *she felt anxiety about so small and vulnerable a being | a rational being.* ■ a supernatural entity: *a being who had made all things.*

Bei·ra /ˈbārə/ a port on the coast of Mozambique; pop. 299,300.

Bei·rut /bāˈro͞ot/ the capital and chief port of Lebanon; pop. 1,500,000. It was badly damaged during the Lebanese civil war of 1975–89.

beit din /ˈbāt ˈdin/ ▸*n.* a rabbinical court that decides questions on the basis of Talmudic law: *would a beit din close Napster down?* ▷Hebrew, literally 'house of judgment.'

Be·ja /ˈbājə/ ▸*n.* (*pl.* same) **1** a member of a nomadic people living between the Nile and the Red Sea. **2** the Cushitic language of this people.

▸*adj.* of or relating to this people or their language.

be·jab·bers /biˈjabərz/ (also **be·ja·bers** /-ˈjā-/) ▸*exclam.* another way of saying BEJESUS. ▷early 19th cent.: alteration of *by Jesus*.

Bé·jart /bāˈyär/, Maurice (1927–), French ballet choreographer; born *Maurice Jean Berger*.

be·je·sus /biˈjēzəs/ (also **be·jee·zus**) ▸*n. informal* an exclamation traditionally attributed to the Irish, used to express surprise or for emphasis: *they were forty minutes late, cocky as bejesus.*

▸*PHRASES* □ **beat the bejesus out of someone** hit someone very hard or for a long time. □ **scare the bejesus out of someone** frighten someone very much.

be·jew·eled /biˈjo͞oəld/ (also **be·jew·elled**) ▸*adj.* adorned with jewels: *a wave of his bejeweled hand.*

Bel /bel/ another name for BAAL.

bel /bel/ ▸*n.* a unit used in the comparison of power levels in electrical communication or of intensities of sound, corresponding to an intensity ratio of 10 to 1. See also DECIBEL. ▷1920s: from the name of Alexander Graham Bell (see BELL[2]).

be·la·bor /biˈlābər/ ▸*v.* [*trans.*] **1** argue or elaborate (a subject) in excessive detail: *critics thought they belabored the obvious.* **2** attack or assault (someone) physically or verbally: *Tyndale seized every opportunity to belabor the Roman Church.* ▷late Middle English: from BE- (expressing transitivity) + the verb LABOR.

Bel Air /bel ˈe(ə)r/ an affluent residential section of Los Angeles, California.

Be·la·rus /,beləˈro͞os; ,bā-/ a country in eastern Europe; pop. 10,328,000; capital, Minsk; official language, Belorussian. Also called WHITE RUSSIA.

Belarus became a republic of the Soviet Union in 1921. It gained independence as a member of the Commonwealth of Independent States in 1991 but in 1996 signed a treaty with Russia that established a Community of Sovereign Republics. In 1999, Belarus signed another agreement with Russia for closer political and economic integration.

be·lat·ed /bi'lātid/ ▸*adj.* coming or happening later than should have been the case: *a belated apology.* ▷early 17th cent. (in the sense 'overtaken by darkness'): past participle of obsolete *belate* 'delay' (see **BE-**, **LATE**). **—be·lat·ed·ly** *adv.* **—be·lat·ed·ness** *n.*

be·lay /bi'lā/ ▸*v.* [*trans.*] **1** fix (a running rope) around a cleat, pin, rock, or other object, to secure it. ■ secure (a mountaineer) in this way: *he belayed his partner across the ice* | [*intrans.*] *it is possible to belay here.* **2** [usu. in *imperative*] *Nautical slang* stop; enough!: *"Belay that, mister. Man your post."*
▸*n.* **1** an act of belaying: *the leader may require belays to tackle more difficult sections.* **2** a spike of rock or other hard material used for belaying. ▷mid 16th cent. (originally in nautical use): from **BE-** + **LAY**[1], on the pattern of Dutch *beleggen.* **—be·lay·er** *n.*

Be·la·ya Riv·er /'byeləyə/ a river in the Bashkir Republic, in eastern Russia, that flows northwest for 700 miles (1,210 km) from the Ural Mountains to the Kama River.

be·lay·ing pin ▸*n.* a pin or rod, typically of metal or wood, used on board ship and in mountaineering to secure a rope fastened around it.

bel can·to /bel 'käntō; 'kan-/ ▸*n.* a lyrical style of operatic singing using a full rich broad tone and smooth phrasing: *a superb piece of bel canto* | [as *adj.*] *the bel canto arias of Bellini.* ▷late 19th cent.: Italian, literally 'fine song.'

belch /belCH/ ▸*v.* **1** [*intrans.*] emit gas noisily from the stomach through the mouth. **2** [*trans.*] (often **belch out/forth/into**) (esp. of a chimney) send (smoke or flames) out or up: *a factory chimney belches out smoke.* ■ [*intrans.*] (often **belch from**) (of smoke or flames) pour out from a chimney or other opening: *flames belch from the wreckage.*
▸*n.* an act of belching: *he gave a loud belch.* ▷Old English *belcettan*, probably imitative.

bel·dam /'beldəm; -,dam/ (also **bel·dame**) ▸*n. archaic* an old woman. ■ a malicious and ugly woman, esp. an old one; a witch. ▷late Middle English (originally in the sense 'grandmother'): from Old French *bel* 'beautiful' + **DAM**[2].

be·lea·guer /bi'lēgər/ ▸*v.* [*trans.*] [usu. as *adj.*] (**beleaguered**) lay siege to: *he is leading a relief force to the aid of the beleaguered city.* ■ beset with difficulties: *the board is supporting the beleaguered director amid calls for his resignation.* ▷late 16th cent.: from Dutch *belegeren* 'camp around,' from *be-* '(all) around' + *leger* 'a camp.'

Be·lém /bā'lem; bə-/ a city and port in northern Brazil, at the mouth of the Amazon River; pop. 1,244,640. It is Brazil's chief commercial center.

bel·em·nite /'beləm,nīt/ ▸*n.* an extinct cephalopod mollusk with a bullet-shaped internal shell that is often found as a fossil in marine deposits of the Jurassic and Cretaceous periods. • Order Belemnoidea, class Cephalopoda: many genera. ▷early 17th cent.: from modern Latin *belemnites*, based on Greek *belemnon* 'dart.'

Bel·fast /'bel,fast; bel'fast/ the capital and chief port of Northern Ireland; pop. 280,970. It suffered damage and population decline from the early 1970s because of sectarian violence by the Irish Republican Army (IRA) and Loyalist paramilitary groups.

Bel·fast sink ▸*n. Brit.* a deep rectangular sink with a drain at one end, traditionally made of glazed white porcelain.

bel·fry /'belfrē/ ▸*n.* (*pl.* **-fries**) a bell tower or steeple housing bells, esp. one that is part of a church. ■ a space for hanging bells in a church tower. ▷Middle English *berfrey*, from Old French *berfrei*, later *belfrei.* The change in the first syllable was due to association with **BELL**[1].
▸*PHRASE* □ **bats in the** (or **one's**) **belfry** see **BAT**[2].

Bel·gae /'beljē; 'bel,gī/ ▸*plural n.* an ancient Celtic people inhabiting Gaul north of the Seine and Marne rivers. ▷from Latin.

Bel·gaum /bel'goum/ an industrial city in western India, in the state of Karnataka; pop. 326,000.

Bel·gian /'beljən/ ▸*adj.* of or relating to Belgium.
▸*n.* a native or national of Belgium or a person of Belgian descent.

Bel·gian en·dive ▸*n.* another term for **ENDIVE** (sense 2).

Bel·gian hare ▸*n.* a rabbit of a dark red long-eared domestic breed.

Bel·gian sheep·dog ▸*n.* a dog of a medium-sized breed, similar in appearance to a German shepherd.

Bel·gian waf·fle ▸*n.* a waffle made with a special tool to have large, deep indentations in it.

Bel·gic /'beljik/ ▸*adj.* of or relating to the Belgae.

Bel·gium /'beljəm/ a low-lying country in western Europe, on the southern shore of the North Sea; pop. 10,340,000; capital, Brussels, official languages, Flemish and French. French name **BELGIQUE**, Flemish name **BELGIË**. ▷Latin, from **BELGAE**.

Belgium became independent from the Netherlands after a nationalist revolt in 1830. Occupied and devastated during both world wars, Belgium formed the Benelux Customs Union with the Netherlands and Luxembourg in 1948 and became a founding member of the EEC. Flemish is spoken mainly in the north, and French and Walloon are spoken in the south.

Bel·go·rod /'byelgərət; 'belgə,räd/ an industrial city in southern Russia, on the Donets River close to the border with Ukraine; pop. 306,000.

Bel·grade /'bel,grād; -,gräd/ the capital of Serbia and Montenegro, on the Danube River; pop. 1,168,450.

Be·li·al /'bēlēəl/ a name for the Devil. ▷from Hebrew *bĕlîyya'al* 'worthlessness.'

be·lie /bi'lī/ ▸*v.* (**-ly·ing**) [*trans.*] **1** (of an appearance) fail to give a true notion or impression of (something); disguise or contradict: *his lively alert manner belied his years.* **2** fail to fulfill or justify (a claim or expectation); betray: *the notebooks belie Darwin's later recollection.* ▷Old English *belēogan* 'deceive by lying,' from **BE-** 'about' + *lēogan* 'to lie.' Current senses date from the 17th cent.

be·lief /bi'lēf/ ▸*n.* **1** an acceptance that a statement is true or that something exists: *his **belief in** God* | *a **belief that** solitude nourishes creativity.* ■ something one accepts as true or real; a firmly held opinion or conviction: *c.ontrary to popular belief, Aramaic is a living language we're prepared to fight for our beliefs.* See note at **OPINION**. ■ a religious conviction: *Christian beliefs* | *I'm afraid to say belief has gone local beliefs and customs.* **2** (**belief in**) trust, faith, or confidence in someone or something: *a belief in democratic politics* | *I've still got belief in myself.* ▷Middle English: alteration of Old English *gelēafa*; compare with **BELIEVE**.
▸*PHRASES* □ **be of the belief that** hold the opinion that; think: *I am firmly of the belief that we need to improve our product.* □ **beyond belief** astonishingly good or bad; incredible: *riches beyond belief* | *the driving we have witnessed was beyond belief.* □ **in the belief that** thinking or believing that: *he took the property in the belief that he had consent.* □ **to the best of my belief** in my genuine opinion; as far as I know: *to the best of my belief, Francis never made a will.*

be·liev·a·ble /bi'lēvəbəl/ ▸*adj.* (of an account or the person relating it) able to be believed; credible. ■ (of a fictional character or situation) convincing or realistic. **—be·liev·a·bil·i·ty** /bi,lēvə'bilitē/ *n.*; **be·liev·a·bly** *adv.*

THE RIGHT WORD believable, cogent, convincing, credible, creditable, plausible, valid

Believable is the most general of these terms, used to describe anything we accept as true, even in the absence of absolute proof (*a believable story about why she was late*).

Credible also means worthy of belief or confidence and is often used interchangeably with *believable*, but it goes one step further: a *credible* excuse is one that is supported by known facts. **Creditable**, often confused with *credible*, at one time meant worthy of belief but nowadays is used to mean respectable or decent, deserving of honor, reputation, or esteem (*leading a creditable life*).

Something that is **convincing** is *believable* because it overcomes doubts or opposition (*a convincing performance*), while something that is **plausible** may appear to be convincing or believable on the surface, but may not be so upon closer examination.

Valid means legally sound, just, or authoritative; a *valid* criticism seldom provokes opposition.

Cogent, on the other hand, means having the power to convince; a *cogent* argument is believable because of its clear, forceful, or incisive presentation.

be·lieve /bi'lēv/ ▸*v.* [*trans.*] **1** accept (something) as true; feel sure of the truth of: *the superintendent believed Lancaster's story* | [with *clause*] *Christians believe that Jesus rose from the dead.* ■ accept the statement of (someone) as true: *he didn't believe her or didn't want to know.* ■ [*intrans.*] have faith, esp. religious faith: *there are those on the fringes of the Church who do not really believe.* ■ (**believe something of someone**) feel sure that (someone) is capable of a particular action: *I wouldn't have believed it of Lois—what an extraordinary woman!* **2** [with *clause*] hold (something) as an opinion; think or suppose: *I believe we've already met* | *things were not as bad as the experts believed* | *humu-humu are, I believe, shrimp fritters* | (**believe someone/something to be**) *four men were believed to be trapped.*
▸*phrasal v.* □ **believe in** **1** have faith in the truth or existence of: *I believe in God.* **2** be of the opinion that (something) is right, proper, or desirable: *I don't believe in censorship of the arts* | *he didn't believe in sex before marriage.* **3** have confidence in (a person or a course of action): *he had finally begun to believe in her.* ▷late Old English *belȳfan, belēfan*, alteration of *gelēfan*, of Germanic origin; related to Dutch *geloven* and German *glauben*, also to **LIEF**.
▸*PHRASES* □ **be unable** (or **hardly able**) **to believe something** be amazed by something: *I couldn't believe what was happening* | *Clarke could hardly believe his luck as he put the ball into the empty net.* □ **be unable** (or **hardly able**) **to believe one's eyes** (or **ears**) be amazed by what one sees or hears: *I couldn't believe my eyes when I opened the box.* □ **believe it or not** used to concede that a proposition or statement is surprising: *believe it or not, the speaker was none other than Horace.* □ **believe me** (or **believe you me**) used to emphasize the truth of a statement or assertion: *believe me, she is a shrewd woman.* □ **don't you believe it!** used to express disbelief in the truth of a statement: *he says he is left of center, but don't you believe it.* □ **would you believe it?** used to express surprise at something one is relating: *they're still arguing, would you believe it?*

be·liev·er /bi'lēvər/ ▸*n.* **1** a person who believes that a specified thing is effective, proper, or desirable: *a **believer in** ghosts* | *a firm **believer that** party politics has no place in local government.* **2** an adherent of a particular religion; someone with religious faith.

be·like /bi'līk/ ▸*adv. archaic* probably; perhaps.

be·lit·tle /bi'litl/ ▸*v.* [*trans.*] make (someone or something) seem unimportant: *this is not to belittle his role* | *she felt belittled.* ▷late 18th cent.: a coinage of Thomas Jefferson originally meaning 'diminish in size, make small'; the current sense dates from the very end of the 18th century. **—be·lit·tle·ment** *n.* **—be·lit·tler** *n.*

Be·li·tung /bā'lē,to͝oNG/ (also **Bil·li·ton** /bi'lē,tōn/) an Indonesian island in the Java Sea, between Borneo and Sumatra.

Be·lize /bə'lēz/ a country in northeastern Central America, on the coast of the Caribbean Sea; pop.

272,000; capital, Belmopan; languages, English (official), Creole, Spanish. Former name (until 1973) **British Honduras.** ▷named after a river with a Mayan name meaning 'muddy water.' **—Be·li·zi·an** /-zēən/ *adj.* & *n.*

Proclaimed as a British Crown Colony in 1862, Belize became independent within the Commonwealth of Nations in 1981. Guatemala, on the west and south, has always claimed the territory on the basis of old Spanish treaties, although in 1992 it agreed to recognize the existence of Belize.

Be·lize Cit·y the principal seaport and former capital (until 1970) of Belize; pop. 46,000.

Bell[1] /bel/ a city in southwestern California, southeast of Los Angeles; pop. 34,365.

Bell[2], Alexander Graham (1847–1922), U.S. scientist, inventor of the telephone and the gramophone; born in Scotland. He invented a method for transmitting speech electrically and gave the first public demonstration of the telephone in 1876; he founded the Bell Telephone Company the following year.

Bell[3], Currier, Ellis, and Acton, the pseudonyms used by Charlotte, Emily, and Anne Brontë respectively.

Bell[4], Vanessa (1879–1961), English painter and designer; born *Vanessa Stephen.* Together with her sister, Virginia Woolf, she was a prominent member of the Bloomsbury Group.

bell[1] /bel/ ▸*n.* **1** a hollow object, typically made of metal and having the shape of a deep inverted cup widening at the lip, that sounds a clear musical note when struck, typically by means of a clapper inside. ■ a device that includes or sounds like a bell, used to give a signal or warning: *a bicycle bell.* ■ the sound of a bell: *at the bell we are both giggling.* ■ (**the bell**) (in boxing and other sports) a bell rung to mark the start or end of a round: *they were dragged off each other at the final bell.* **2** a bell-shaped object or part of one, such as the end of a trumpet. ■ the corolla of a bell-shaped flower: *a flower with small, pale blue bells.* **3** (**bells**) a musical instrument consisting of a set of cylindrical metal tubes of different lengths, suspended in a frame and played by being struck with a hammer. Also called **TUBULAR BELLS. 4** *Nautical* (preceded by a numeral) the time as indicated every half hour of a watch by the striking of the ship's bell one to eight times: *at five bells in the forenoon of June 11.*
▸*v.* **1** [*trans.*] provide with a bell or bells; attach a bell or bells to: *the young men were belling and hobbling the horses before releasing them* | [as *adj.*] (**belled**) *animals in gaudy belled harnesses.* **2** [*intrans.*] make a ringing sound likened to that of a bell: *the organ belling away.* **3** [*intrans.*] spread or flare outward like the lip of a bell: *her shirt* **belled out** *behind.* ▷Old English *belle,* of Germanic origin; related to Dutch *bel,* and perhaps to **BELL**[2].
▸*PHRASES* □ **be saved by the bell** (in boxing and other sports) avoid being counted out by the ringing of the bell at the end of a round. ■ escape from danger narrowly or by an unexpected intervention. □ **bell the cat** take the danger of a shared enterprise upon oneself. [an allusion to a fable in which the mice (or rats) suggest hanging a bell around the cat's neck to have warning of its approach.] □ **bells and whistles** *informal* attractive additional features or trimmings: *an advocate of more bells and whistles on the income tax code.* [an allusion to the various bells and whistles of old fairground organs.] □ **(as) clear** (or **sound**) **as a bell** perfectly clear or sound: *Aunt Nora's words came clear as a bell.* □ **ring a bell** *informal* revive a distant recollection; sound familiar: *the name Woodall rings a bell.* □ **with bells on** *informal* enthusiastically: *everybody's waiting for you with bells on.*

bell[2] ▸*n.* the cry of a stag or buck at rutting time.
▸*v.* [*intrans.*] (of a stag or buck) make this cry. ▷Old English *bellan* 'to bellow,' of Germanic origin; related to German *bellen* 'to bark, bray,' and perhaps also to **BELL**[1].

bel·la·don·na /,belə'dänə/ ▸*n.* deadly nightshade. ■ a drug prepared from the leaves and root of this, containing atropine. ▷mid 18th cent.: from modern Latin, from Italian *bella donna* 'fair lady,' perhaps from the use of its juice to add brilliance to the eyes by dilating the pupils.

bel·la·don·na lil·y ▸*n.* the South African amaryllis.

bell·bird /'bel,bərd/ ▸*n.* **1** a tropical American bird of the cotinga family, with loud explosive calls. There are wattles on the head of the male. • Genus *Procnias,* family Cotingidae: four species. **2** any of a number of Australasian songbirds with ringing bell-like calls, including: • (**New Zealand bellbird**) a New Zealand honeyeater (*Anthornis melanura,* family Meliphagidae). • (**crested bellbird**) an Australian whistler (*Oreoica gutturalis,* family Pachycephalidae). • the bell miner. See **MINER** (sense 2).

bell-bot·toms ▸*plural n.* trousers with a marked flare below the knee: [as *adj.*] (**bell-bottom**) *bell-bottom trousers.* **—bell-bot·tomed** *adj.*

bell·boy /'bel,boi/ ▸*n.* another term for **BELLHOP.**

bell·bu·oy /'bel,bo͞oē; -,boi/ ▸*n.* a buoy equipped with a bell rung by the motion of the sea, warning nearby vessels of shoal waters.

bell cap·tain ▸*n.* the supervisor of a group of bellboys.

bell crank (also **bell crank lever**) ▸*n.* a lever with two arms that have a common fulcrum at their junction.

bell curve ▸*n. Mathematics* a graph of a normal (Gaussian) distribution, with a large rounded peak tapering away at each end.

bell curve

belle /bel/ ▸*n.* a beautiful girl or woman, esp. the most beautiful at a particular event or in a particular group: *the belle of the season.* ▷early 17th cent.: from French, feminine of *beau,* from Latin *bella,* feminine of *bellus* 'beautiful.'
▸*PHRASE* □ **belle of the ball** the most beautiful and popular girl or woman at a dance.

Bel·leau Wood /bel'ō/ (French name **Bois de Belleau**) a forest east of Paris, France, and just east of Château-Thierry, the scene of a June 1918 U.S. victory over the Germans during World War I.

belle é·poque /,bel ā'pək/ ▸*n.* the period of settled and comfortable life preceding World War I: [as *adj.*] *a romantic, belle-époque replica of a Paris bistro.* ▷mid 20th cent.: French, literally 'fine period.'

Bel·ler·o·phon /bə'lerə,fän; -fən/ *Greek Mythology* a hero who slew the monster Chimera with the help of the winged horse Pegasus.

belles-let·tres /,bel 'letrə/ ▸*plural n.* [also treated as *sing.*] **1** essays, particularly of literary and artistic criticism, written and read primarily for their aesthetic effect. **2** literature considered as a fine art. ▷mid 17th cent.: from French, literally 'fine letters.' **—bel·let·rism** /bel'letrizəm/ *n.* **—bel·let·rist** /bel'letrist/ *n.* **—bel·let·ris·tic** /,belə'tristik/ *adj.*

Belle·ville /'bel,vil/ **1** an industrial city in southwestern Illinois; pop. 42,785. **2** an industrial township in northeastern New Jersey; pop. 34,213.

Belle·vue /'bel,vyo͞o/ **1** a city in eastern Nebraska; pop. 44,382. **2** a city in northwestern Washington, across an inlet of Puget Sound to the east of Seattle; pop. 109,569

Bell·flow·er /'bel,flou-ər/ a city in southwestern California, southeast of Los Angeles; pop. 61,815.

bell·flow·er /'bel,flou(-ə)r/ ▸*n.* a plant with bell-shaped flowers that are usually blue, purple, pink, or white. Many kinds are cultivated as ornamentals. • Genus *Campanula,* family Campanulaceae: many species, including the Eurasian **clustered bellflower** (*C. glomerata*) and the harebell.

Bell Gardens an unincorporated suburb east of Los Angeles, California; pop. 42,355.

bell·hop /'bel,häp/ ▸an attendant in a hotel who performs services such as carrying guests' luggage.

bel·li·cose /'beli,kōs/ ▸*adj.* demonstrating aggression and willingness to fight: *a group of bellicose patriots.* See note at **HOSTILE.** ▷late Middle English: from Latin *bellicosus,* from *bellicus* 'warlike,' from *bellum* 'war.' **—bel·li·cos·i·ty** /,belə'käsitē/ *n.*

bel·lig·er·ence /bə'lijərəns/ (also **bel·lig·er·en·cy** /-ənsē/) ▸*n.* aggressive or warlike behavior: *the reaction ranged from wild enthusiasm to outright belligerence.*

bel·lig·er·ent /bə'lijərənt/ ▸*adj.* hostile and aggressive: *a bull-necked, belligerent old man.* See note at **HOSTILE.** ■ engaged in a war or conflict, as recognized by international law.
▸*n.* a nation or person engaged in war or conflict, as recognized by international law. ▷late 16th cent.: from Latin *belligerant-* 'waging war,' from the verb *belligerare,* from *bellum* 'war.' **—bel·lig·er·ent·ly** *adv.*

Bel·ling·ham /'beliNG,ham/ an industrial port city in northwestern Washington, on Bellingham Bay off Puget Sound; pop. 67,171.

Bel·lings·hau·sen Sea /'beliNGz,houzən/ a part of the southeastern Pacific Ocean off the coast of Antarctica, bounded on the east and the south by the Antarctic Peninsula and Ellsworth Land. ▷named after the Russian explorer Fabian Gottlieb von *Bellingshausen* (1778–1852), who in 1819–21 became the first to circumnavigate Antarctica.

Bel·li·ni[1] /bə'lēnē/, **Jacopo** (*c.*1400–70) and his sons **Gentile** (*c.*1429–1507) and **Giovanni** (*c.*1430–1516), Italian painters in Venice.

Bel·li·ni[2], Vincenzo (1801–35), Italian opera composer. Notable works: *La Sonnambula* (1831), *Norma* (1831), and *I Puritani* (1835).

Bel·li·ni /bə'lēnē/ ▸*n.* (*pl.* **-nis**) a cocktail consisting of peach juice mixed with champagne. ▷from the name of Venetian painter Giovanni *Bellini* (*c.* 1430–1516): the cocktail is said to have been invented in Venice during a major exhibition of the artist's work in 1948.

bell jar ▸*n.* a bell-shaped glass cover used for covering delicate objects or used in a laboratory, typically for enclosing samples. ■ *figurative* an environment in which someone is protected or cut off from the outside world: *let him stay in his bell jar of perfectionist concentration.*

bell·man /'belmən/ ▸*n.* (*pl.* **-men**) **1** another term for **BELLHOP. 2** *historical* a town crier.

Bel·loc /bə'lôk/ (Joseph) Hilaire (Pierre René) (1870–1953), British writer, historian, and poet; born in France. He is remembered chiefly for *Cautionary Tales* (1907).

Bel·low /'belō/, Saul (1915–), U.S. novelist; born in Canada. Notable works *The Adventures of Augie March* (1953), *Herzog* (1964), *More Die of Heartbreak* (1987) and *Ravelstein* (2000). Nobel Prize for Literature (1976).

bel·low /'belō/ ▸*v.* [*intrans.*] (of a person or animal) emit a deep loud roar, typically in pain or anger: *he* **bellowed in** *agony* | [as *n.*] (**bellowing**) *the bellowing of a bull.* ■ [*reporting verb*] shout something with a deep loud roar: [*trans.*] *the watchers were bellowing encouragement* | *he* **bellowed out** *the order* | [with *direct speech*] *"God send the right!" he bellowed* | [with *infinitive*] *his desperate parents were* **bellowing at** *her to stop.* ■ [*trans.*] sing (a song) loudly and tunelessly: *he got thrown out of bars for bellowing Portuguese folk songs*
▸*n.* a deep roaring shout or sound: *a bellow of rage* | *he delivers his lines in a bellow.* ▷Middle English: perhaps from late Old English *bylgan.*

bel·lows /'belōz/ ▸*plural n.* [also treated as *sing.*] **1** a device with a bag that emits a stream of air when squeezed: ■ (also **pair of bellows**) a kind with two handles used for blowing air at a fire. ■ a kind used in a harmonium or small organ. **2** an object or device with concertinaed sides to allow it to expand and contract, such as a tube joining a lens to a camera body. ▷Middle English: probably representing Old English *belga,* plural of *belig* (see **BELLY**), used as a shortened form of earlier *blǣstbelig* 'blowing bag.'

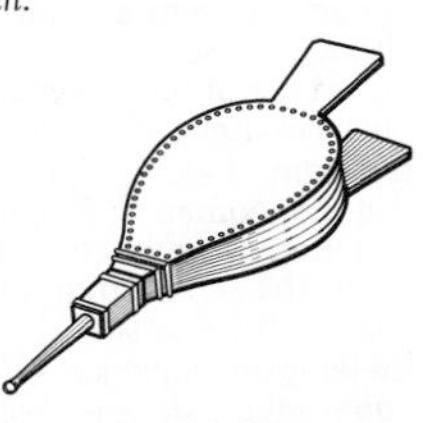
pair of bellows

bell pep·per ▸*n.* another term for **SWEET PEPPER.**

bell pull ▸*n.* a cord or handle that rings a bell when pulled, typically used to summon someone from another room.

bell-ring·ing ▸*n.* the activity or pastime of ringing church bells or handbells. **—bell-ring·er** *n.*

Bell's pal·sy ▸*n.* paralysis of the facial nerve, causing muscular weakness in one side of the face. ▷mid 19th cent.: named after Sir Charles Bell (1774–1842), the Scottish anatomist who first described it.

bell·weth·er /'bel,weT͟Hər/ ▸*n.* the leading sheep of a flock, with a bell on its neck. ■ an indicator or predictor of something: *college campuses are often the bellwether of change* | [as *adj.*] *the market's bellwether stock.*

Bell·wood /'bel,wo͝od/ a village in northeastern Illinois, west of Chicago; pop. 20,421.

bell·wort /'bel,wərt; -,wôrt/ ▸*n.* a plant of the lily family bearing slender yellow bell-like flowers and found chiefly in eastern North America. • Genus *Uvularia,* family Liliaceae: several species, including the **large-flowered bellwort** (*U. grandiflora*) and the **perfoliate bellwort** (*U. perfoliata*).

bel·ly /'belē/ ▸*n.* (*pl.* **-lies**) the human trunk below the ribs, containing the stomach and bowels. ■ the front of this part of the body: *he fell flat on his belly.* ■ the stomach, esp. as representing the body's need for food: *they'll fight all the better on empty bellies.* ■ the underside of a bird or other animal. ■ a cut of pork from the underside between the legs. ■ a pig's belly as food, esp. as a traded commodity. ■ the rounded underside of a ship or aircraft. ■ the top surface of an instrument of the violin family, across which the strings are placed.

▸*v.* (**-lies, -lied**) **1** [*intrans.*] swell; bulge: *as she leaned forward her pullover* ***bellied out.*** ■ [*trans.*] cause to swell or bulge: *the wind* ***bellied*** *the sail* ***out.*** **2** [*intrans.*] (**belly up to**) *informal* move or sit close to (a bar or table): *regulars who first bellied up to the bar years before.* ▷Old English *belig* 'bag,' of Germanic origin, from a base meaning 'swell, be inflated.' —**bel·lied** *adj.* [usu. in *combination*] *fat-bellied men.*

▸*PHRASE* □ **go belly up** *informal* go bankrupt.

bel·ly·ache /ˈbelē,āk/ *informal* ▸*n.* an abdominal pain.
▸*v.* [*intrans.*] complain noisily or persistently: *heads of departments* ***bellyaching about*** *lack of resources* | [as *n.*] (**bellyaching**) *there was plenty of bellyaching.* —**bel·ly·ach·er** *n.*

bel·ly·band /ˈbelē,band/ ▸*n.* **1** a band placed round a horse's belly to harness it to the shafts of a cart. **2** a cloth band placed around the belly of an infant to protect the navel. **3** a band wrapped around a product to prevent it from opening.

bel·ly but·ton ▸*n. informal* a person's navel.

bel·ly dance ▸*n.* a dance originating in the Middle East, typically performed by a woman and involving undulating movements of the belly and rapid gyration of the hips. —**bel·ly danc·er** *n.* —**bel·ly danc·ing** *n.*

bel·ly·flop /ˈbelē,fläp/ *informal* ▸*n.* a dive into water, landing flat on one's front. ■ *figurative* a commercial failure: *the film's bellyflop at the box office is unsurprising.*
▸*v.* (**-flopped, -flop·ping**) [*intrans.*] perform such a dive. ■ (of an aircraft) perform a belly landing.

bel·ly·ful /ˈbelē,fo͝ol/ ▸*n.* (*pl.* **-fuls**) a quantity of food sufficient to fill one's stomach; a sustaining meal.
▸*PHRASE* □ **have a** (or **one's**) **bellyful** *informal* become intolerant of someone or something after lengthy or repeated contact: *he had had his bellyful of hospitals.*

bel·ly land·ing ▸*n.* a crash-landing of an aircraft on the underside of the fuselage, without lowering the undercarriage.

bel·ly laugh ▸*n.* a loud, unrestrained laugh.

Bel·mont /ˈbel,mänt/ **1** a city in north central California, southeast of San Francisco; pop. 24,127. **2** a town in eastern Massachusetts, northwest of Boston; pop. 24,720.

Bel·mo·pan /ˈbelmə,pan/ the capital of Belize since 1970, in the central part of the country. It is one of the smallest capital cities in the world; pop. 3,850.

Be·lo Ho·ri·zon·te /,bālō ,hôrəˈzôntā/ a city in eastern Brazil, the first planned city in Brazil; pop. 2,020,160.

Be·loit /bəˈloit/ an industrial and academic city in southeastern Wisconsin; pop. 35,573.

be·long /biˈlôNG/ ▸*v.* [*intrans.*] **1** [with *adverbial of place*] (of a thing) be rightly placed in a specified position: *learning to place the blame where it belongs.* ■ be rightly classified in or assigned to a specified category: *bony fish: the vast majority of living fish belong here.* **2** [usu. with *adverbial of place*] (of a person) fit in a specified place or environment: *she is a stranger, and doesn't belong here* | *you and me, we belong together* | [as *n.*] (**belonging**) *we feel a real* ***sense of belonging.*** ■ have the right personal or social qualities to be a member of a particular group: *young people are generally very anxious to belong.* ■ (**belong to**) be a member or part of (a particular group, organization, or class): *they belong to garden and bridge clubs.* **3** (**belong to**) be the property of: *the vehicle did not belong to him.* ■ be the rightful possession of; be due to: *most of the credit belongs to Paul.* ■ (of a contest or period of time) be dominated by: *the race belonged completely to Ferguson.* ▷Middle English (in the sense 'be appropriately assigned to'): from **BE-** (as an intensifier) + the archaic verb *long* 'belong,' based on Old English *gelang* 'at hand, together with.' —**be·long·ing·ness** *n.*

be·long·ings /biˈlôNGiNGz/ ▸*plural n.* one's movable possessions.

Be·lo·rus·sian /,belōˈrəSHən/ (also **Bye·lo·rus·sian** /,byelō-/) ▸*adj.* of or relating to Belarus, its people, or its language.
▸*n.* **1** a native or national of Belarus. ■ a person of Belorussian descent. **2** the East Slavic language of Belarus.

Be·lo·stok /,byeləˈstôk/ Russian name for **BIAŁYSTOK**.

be·lov·ed /biˈləv(i)d/ ▸*adj.* dearly loved. ■ (**beloved by/of**) very popular with or much used by a specified set of people: *being so close, the mountain hut is beloved of families on a day's outing.*
▸*n.* a much loved person: *he watched his beloved.* ▷late Middle English: past participle of obsolete *belove* 'be pleasing,' later 'love.'

be·low /biˈlō/ ▸*prep.* **1** extending underneath: *the tunnel below the crags* | *cables running below the floorboards* | *hanging space below a top storage shelf.* **2** at a lower level or layer than: *just below the pocket was a stain* | *blistered skin below his collar.* ■ lower in grade or rank than: *they rated its financial soundness below its competitor's.* **3** lower than (a specified amount, rate, or norm): *below average* | *below freezing* | *a dive to below 60 feet.*
▸*adv.* at a lower level or layer: *he jumped from the window into the moat below.* ■ under the surface of the water: *trout lying more than 20 feet below.* ■ on earth: *deflections of the stars from their proper orbits with fatal results here below.* ■ in hell: *traitors gnash their teeth below.* ■ lower than zero (esp. zero degrees Fahrenheit) in temperature: *there's a north wind blowing, and it's 30 below.* ■ (in printed text) mentioned later or further down on the same page: *our nutritionist is pictured below right* | *the most common methods are shown below.* ■ *Nautical* below deck: *I'll* ***go below*** *and fix us a drink.* ▷late Middle English (as an adverb): from **BE-** 'by' + the adjective **LOW**[1]. Not common until the 16th cent., the word developed a prepositional use and was frequent in Shakespeare.

▸*PHRASE* □ **below** (**the**) **ground** beneath the surface of the ground: *60 feet below ground.*

be·low decks (also **be·low deck**) ▸*adj.* & *adv.* in or into the space below the main deck of a ship: [as *adj.*] *the sleeping quarters were below decks* | [as *adv.*] *nuclear weapons stored below decks.*
▸*plural n.* (**belowdecks**) the space below the main deck of a ship.

Bel Pa·e·se /,bel päˈāzē/ ▸*n. trademark* a rich, white, mild, creamy cheese of a kind originally made in Italy. ▷Italian, literally 'fair country.'

Bel·sen /ˈbelsən/ a Nazi concentration camp in World War II, near the village of Belsen in northwestern Germany.

Bel·shaz·zar /ˈbelSHə,zär; belˈSHazər/ (6th century BC), last king of Babylon, son of Nebuchadnezzar. According to Daniel 5, he was killed in the sack of the city and his doom was foretold by writing that appeared on the palace walls at a great banquet.

belt /belt/ ▸*n.* **1** a strip of leather or other material worn around the waist or across the chest, esp. in order to support clothes or carry weapons: *a sword belt* | [as *adj.*] *a belt buckle.* ■ short for **SEAT BELT**. ■ a belt worn as a sign of rank or achievement: *he was awarded the victor's belt.* ■ a belt of a specified color, marking the attainment of a particular level in judo, karate, or similar sports: [as *adj.*] *brown-belt level.* ■ a person who has reached such a level: *I am a karate black belt.* ■ (**the belt**) the punishment of being struck with a belt. **2** a strip of material used in various technical applications, in particular: ■ a continuous band of material used in machinery for transferring motion from one wheel to another. ■ a conveyor belt. ■ a flexible strip carrying machine-gun cartridges. **3** a strip or encircling band of something having a specified nature or composition that is different from its surroundings: *the asteroid belt* | *a belt of trees.* **4** a heavy blow: *she ran in to administer a good belt with her stick.* **5** *informal* a gulp or shot of liquor: *they could probably use a few belts.*
▸*v.* [*trans.*] **1** [*trans.*] fasten with a belt: *she paused only to belt a robe about her waist* | *she belted her raincoat firmly.* ■ [*intrans.*] be fastened with a belt: *the jacket belts at the waist.* ■ attach or secure with a belt: *he was securely belted into the passenger seat.* **2** beat or strike (someone), esp. with a belt, as a punishment. ■ hit (something) hard: *he belted the ball to the left-field fence.* **3** gulp a drink quickly: *belting down shots of a potent drink called arrack.* **4** [*intrans.*] move quickly in a specified direction: *they belted along the empty road.* ■ (of rain) fall hard: *the rain* ***belted down*** *on the tin roof.*
▸*phrasal v.* □ **belt something out** sing or play a song loudly and forcefully. ▷Old English, of Germanic origin, from Latin *balteus* 'girdle.' —**belt·ed** *adj.* (usu. in sense 1 of the *noun*).
▸*PHRASES* □ **below the belt** unfair or unfairly; disregarding the rules: *there has been yet another below-the-belt blow to the workers of Chicago.* [from the notion of an unfair and illegal blow in boxing.] □ **tighten one's belt** cut one's spending; live more frugally. □ **under one's belt** **1** safely or satisfactorily achieved, experienced, or acquired: *I want to get more experience under my belt* | *he now has almost a year as president under his belt.* **2** (of food or drink) consumed: *Gus already had a large brandy under his belt.*

Bel·tane /ˈbel,tān/ ▸*n.* an ancient Celtic festival celebrated on May Day. ▷late Middle English: from Scottish Gaelic *bealltainn.*

belt drive ▸*n.* a mechanism in which power is transmitted by a continuous flexible belt.

belt·ed gal·lo·way ▸*n.* an animal belonging to a variety of the galloway breed of cattle (see **GALLOWAY**).

belt·er /ˈbeltər/ ▸*n. informal* a loud forceful singer. ■ a loud forceful song.

belt·ing /ˈbeltiNG/ ▸*n.* **1** belts collectively, or material for belts: *a small piece of plastic belting.* **2** a beating, esp. with a belt, as a punishment.

belt sand·er ▸*n.* a sander that uses a moving abrasive belt to smooth surfaces.

belt-tight·en·ing ▸*n.* the introduction of rigorous reductions in spending: [as *adj.*] *belt-tightening measures.*

B

belt·way /ˈbelt,wā/ ▸*n.* a highway encircling an urban area. ■ (**Beltway**) [often as *adj.*] Washington, DC, esp. as representing the perceived insularity of the U.S. government: *conventional beltway wisdom.* [transferred use by association with the beltway encircling Washington.]

Belt·way ban·dit ▸*n. informal* a company that does a large percentage of its business as a federal government contractor. See **BELTWAY**.

be·lu·ga /bəˈlo͞ogə/ ▸*n.* (*pl.* same or **-gas**) **1** a small, white-toothed whale related to the narwhal, living in herds mainly in Arctic coastal waters. Also called **WHITE WHALE**. • *Delphinapterus leucas*, family Monodontidae. **2** a very large sturgeon occurring in the inland seas and associated rivers of central Eurasia. • *Huso huso*, family Acipenseridae. ■ (also **beluga caviar**) caviar obtained from this fish. ▷late 16th cent. (sense 2): from Russian *belukha* (sense 1), *beluga* (sense 2), both from *belyĭ* 'white.'

bel·ve·dere /ˈbelvi,di(ə)r/ ▸*n.* a summerhouse or open-sided gallery, usually at rooftop level, commanding a fine view. ▷late 16th cent.: from Italian, literally 'fair view,' from *bel* 'beautiful' + *vedere* 'to view.'

be·ly·ing /biˈlī-iNG/ ▸ present participle of **BELIE**.

BEM ▸*abbr.* Bachelor of Engineering of Mines.

be·ma /ˈbēmə/ ▸*n.* (*pl.* **-mas** or **-ma·ta** /-mətə/) the altar part or sanctuary in ancient and Orthodox churches. ■ (**bi·ma, bi·mah**) *Judaism* the podium or platform in a synagogue from which the Torah and Prophets are read. ■ *historical* the platform from which orators spoke in ancient Athens. ▷late 17th cent.: from Greek *bēma* 'step, raised place.'

Bem·ba /ˈbembə/ ▸*n.* (*pl.* same) **1** a member of a native people of Zambia. **2** the Bantu language of this people.
▸*adj.* of or relating to this people or their language. ▷of Bemba origin.

be·mire /biˈmī(ə)r/ ▸*v.* [*trans.*] *archaic* cover or stain with mud: *his shoes were bemired, as if he had been traveling on foot.* ■ (**be bemired**) be stuck in mud: *men and horses and wagons all bemired.* ▷mid 16th cent.: from **BE-** (expressing transitivity) + **MIRE**.

be·moan /biˈmōn/ ▸*v.* [*trans.*] *often humorous* express discontent or sorrow over (something): *single women bemoaning the absence of men.* See note at **MOURN**. ▷Old English *bemǣnan* 'complain, lament.' The change in the second syllable (16th cent.) was due to association with **MOAN**, to which it is related.

be·muse /biˈmyo͞oz/ ▸*v.* [*trans.*] [usu. as *adj.*] (**bemused**) puzzle, confuse, or bewilder (someone): *her bemused expression* | *she was accepted with bemused resignation by her parents as a hippie.* ▷mid 18th cent.: from **BE-** (as an intensifier) + **MUSE**. —**be·mus·ed·ly** /-zidlē/ *adv.* —**be·muse·ment** *n.*

ben[1] /ben/ ▸*n. Scottish* a high mountain or mountain peak (esp. in place names): *Ben Nevis.* ▷late 18th cent.: from Scottish Gaelic and Irish *beann.*

ben[2] ▸*n. Scottish* & *N. Irish* an inner room in a two-roomed cottage. ▷late 18th cent.: dialect variant of Middle English *binne* 'within' (adverb), from Old English *binnan* (related to Dutch and German *binnen*).

Be·na·res /bəˈnäris; -ēz/ former name for **VARANASI**.

Ben Bel·la /ben ˈbelə/, (Muhammad) Ahmed (1918–), Algerian statesman; prime minister 1962–63; president 1963–65. The first president of an independent Algeria, he was overthrown in a military coup.

Bench /benCH/, Johnny Lee (1947–), U.S. baseball player. He was a catcher for the Cincinnati Reds from 1967 until 1983. Baseball Hall of Fame (1989).

bench /benCH/ ▸*n.* **1** a long seat for several people, typically made of wood or stone. **2** a long, sturdy work table used by a carpenter, mechanic, scientist, or other worker. **3** (**the bench**) the office of judge or magistrate: *his appointment to the civil bench.*

■ a judge's seat in a court. ■ judges or magistrates collectively: *rulings from the bench.* **4** *Brit.* a seat in Parliament for politicians of a specified party or position: *the Conservative benches* | *the Opposition benches.* ■ the politicians occupying such a seat: *the pledge that was given by the Opposition benches yesterday.* **5** (**the bench**) a seat on which sports coaches and players sit during a game when they are not playing. **6** a flat ledge in masonry or on sloping ground.

▸*v.* [*trans.*] **1** exhibit (a dog) at a show: *Affenpinschers and Afghans were benched side by side.* [from the practice of exhibiting dogs on benches.] **2** withdraw (a sports player) from play; substitute: *the coach benched quarterback Randall Cunningham in favor of Jim McMahon.* **3** short for BENCH PRESS. ▷Old English *benc*, of Germanic origin; related to Dutch *bank* and German *Bank*, also to BANK[1].

▸*PHRASE* □ **on the bench** **1** appointed as or in the capacity of a judge or magistrate: *he retired after twenty-five years on the bench.* **2** acting as one of the possible substitutes in a sports contest.

bench·er /ˈbenCHər/ ▸*n. Law* (in the UK) a senior member of any of the Inns of Court.

Bench·ley /ˈbenCHlē/ a family of U.S. writers, including: **Robert Charles Benchley** (1889–1945), drama critic, actor, and humorist. He was a theater critic for *Life* magazine (1920–29) and the *New Yorker* (1929–40). His son **Nathaniel Benchley** (1915–81) was the author of humorous novels, including *Lassiter's Folly* (1971). **Peter Benchley** (1940–), the son of Nathaniel, wrote *Jaws* (1974), *The Deep* (1976), and *White Shark* (1994).

bench·mark /ˈbenCH,märk/ ▸*n.* **1** a standard or point of reference against which things may be compared or assessed: [as *adj.*] *a benchmark case.* ■ a problem designed to evaluate the performance of a computer system: *Xstones is a graphics benchmark.* **2** a surveyor's mark cut in a wall, pillar, or building and used as a reference point in measuring altitudes.

▸*v.* [*trans.*] evaluate or check (something) by comparison with a standard: *we are* ***benchmarking*** *our performance* ***against*** *external criteria.* ■ [*intrans.*] evaluate or check something in this way: *we continue to benchmark against the competition.* ■ [*intrans.*] show particular results during a benchmark test: *the device should benchmark at between 100 and 150 MHz.*

bench·mark test ▸*n.* a test using a benchmark to evaluate a computer system's performance.

bench press ▸*n.* a bodybuilding and weightlifting exercise in which a lifter lies on a bench with feet on the floor and raises a weight with both arms.

▸*v.* (**bench-press**) [*trans.*] raise (a weight) in a bench press: *Josh can bench-press more than 400 pounds* | [*intrans.*] *my elbow hurts when I bench-press.*

bench run ▸*n.* & *v.* another term for BENCH TEST.

bench seat ▸*n.* a seat across the whole width of a car.

bench test *chiefly Computing* ▸*n.* a test carried out on a machine, a component, or software before it is released for use, to ensure that it works properly.

▸*v.* (**bench-test**) [*trans.*] run a bench test on (something): *they are offering you the chance to bench-test their applications.* ■ [*intrans.*] give particular results during a bench test: *it bench-tests two times faster than the previous version.*

bench·warm·er /ˈbenCH,wôrmər/ ▸*n. informal* a sports player who does not get selected to play; a substitute.

bench war·rant ▸*n.* a written order issued by a judge authorizing the arrest of a person charged with some contempt, crime, or misdemeanor.

bench·work /ˈbenCH,wərk/ ▸*n.* work carried out at a bench in a laboratory or workshop.

Bend /bend/ a city in central Oregon; pop. 52,029.

bend[1] /bend/ ▸*v.* (*past* **bent** /bent/) **1** [*trans.*] shape or force (something straight) into a curve or angle: *the rising wind bent the long grass.* ■ [*intrans.*] (of something straight) be shaped or forced into a curve or angle: *the oar bent as Lance heaved angrily at it.* ■ *figurative* force or be forced to submit: [*trans.*] *they want to* ***bend*** *me* ***to*** *their will* | [*intrans.*] *a refusal to* ***bend to*** *mob rule.* ■ [*intrans.*] (of a road, river, or path) deviate from a straight line in a specified direction; have a sharply curved course: *the road bent left and then right* | *the river slowly bends around Davenport.* **2** [*intrans.*] (of a person) incline the body downward from the vertical: *he* ***bent down*** *and picked her up* | *I* ***bent over*** *my plate* | [with *infinitive*] *he bent to tie his shoelaces.* ■ [*trans.*] move (a jointed part of the body) to an angled position: *extend your left leg and bend your right* | *Irene bent her head over her work.* **3** [*trans.*] interpret or modify (a rule) to suit oneself or somebody else: *we cannot bend the rules, even for Darren.* **4** [*trans.*] direct or devote (one's attention or energies) to a task: *Eric* ***bent*** *all his efforts* ***to*** *persuading them to donate some blankets* | [*intrans.*] *she* ***bent*** *once more* ***to*** *the task of diverting the wedding guests.* **5** [*trans.*] *Nautical* attach (a sail or rope) by means of a knot: *sailors were* ***bending*** *sails* ***to*** *the spars.*

▸*n.* **1** a curve, esp. a sharp one, in a road, river, racecourse, or path. **2** a curved or angled part or form of something: *making a bend in the wire.* **3** a kind of knot used to join two ropes, or to tie a rope to another object, e.g. a carrick bend. **4** (**the bends**) decompression sickness, esp. in divers. ▷Old English *bendan* 'put in bonds, tension a bow by means of a string,' of Germanic origin; related to BAND[1]. —**bend·a·ble** *adj.*

▸*PHRASES* □ **bend someone's ear** *informal* talk to someone, esp. with great eagerness or in order to ask a favor: *she regularly bent Michael's ear with her problems.* □ **bend one's elbow** drink alcohol. □ **bend one's** (or **the**) **knee** *figurative* submit: *a country no longer willing to* ***bend its knee to*** *foreign powers.* □ **bend over backward** see BACKWARD. □ **on bended knee** (or **knees**) kneeling, esp. when pleading or showing great respect. □ **around the bend** *informal* crazy; insane: *I'd tell you if you were* ***going around the bend.***

bend[2] ▸*n. Heraldry* an ordinary in the form of a broad diagonal stripe from top left (dexter chief) to bottom right (sinister base) of a shield or part of one. ▷late Middle English: from Anglo-Norman French *bande*, Old French *bende* 'flat strip.'

bend·er /ˈbendər/ *informal* ▸*n.* **1** [usu. in *combination*] an object or person that bends something else: *a fender bender.* **2** a wild drinking spree. ▷late 15th cent. (denoting instruments such as pliers, for bending things): from BEND[1] + -ER[1].

bend sin·is·ter ▸*n. Heraldry* a broad diagonal stripe from top right to bottom left of a shield (a supposed sign of bastardy).

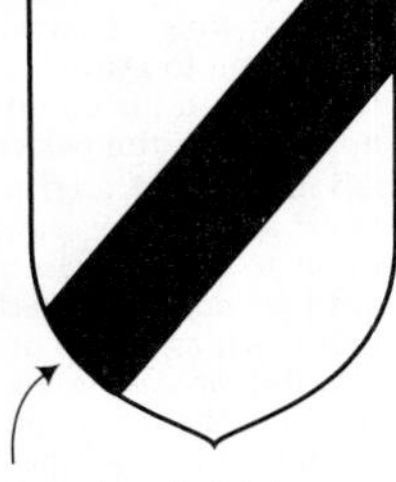
bend sinister

bend·y /ˈbendē/ ▸*adj.* (**bend·i·er, bend·i·est**) *informal* capable of bending; soft and flexible. —**bend·i·ness** *n.*

be·neath /biˈnēTH/ ▸*prep.* **1** extending or directly underneath, typically with close contact: *in the labyrinths beneath central Moscow.* ■ underneath so as to be hidden, covered, or protected: *unaltered even after years beneath the sea.* **2** at a lower level or layer than: *beneath this floor there's a cellar* | *her eyes were dull with dark shadows beneath them.* ■ lower in grade or rank than: *relegated to the rank beneath theirs.* ■ considered of lower status or worth than: *taking jobs beneath my abilities.* ■ behind (a physical surface): *they found another layer beneath the stucco.* ■ behind or hidden behind (an appearance): *beneath the gloss of success.*

▸*adv.* **1** extending or directly underneath something: *a house built on stilts to allow air to circulate beneath.* **2** at a lower level or layer: *the runways had cracked open, exposing the black earth beneath.* ■ behind or hidden behind an appearance: *the smile revealed the evil beneath.* ▷Old English *binithan, bineothan*, from *bi* (see BY) + *nithan, neothan* 'below,' of Germanic origin; related to NETHER.

Ben·e·det·to /,beniˈdetō/, Anthony Dominick, see BENNETT.

ben·e·dic·i·te /,beniˈdisitē/ ▸*n.* a blessing, esp. a grace said at table in religious communities. [Middle English] ■ (**the Benedicite**) the canticle used in the Anglican service of matins beginning "O all ye works of the Lord, bless ye the Lord," the text being taken from the Apocrypha. [mid 17th cent.] ▷Latin, 'bless ye!,' plural imperative from *benedicere* 'wish well'; the first word of the canticle in Latin.

Ben·e·dict, St. /ˈbeni,dikt/ (*c.*480–*c.*550), Italian hermit. He established a monastery at Monte Cassino and his *Regula Monachorum* (known as the Rule of St. Benedict) formed the basis of Western monasticism. Feast day, July 11 (formerly March 21).

Ben·e·dic·tine /,beniˈdik,tēn; -tin/ ▸*n.* **1** a monk or nun of an order following the rule of St. Benedict. **2** *trademark* a liqueur based on brandy, originally made by Benedictine monks in France.

▸*adj.* of St. Benedict or the Benedictines. ▷from French *bénédictine* or modern Latin *benedictinus*, from the name *Benedictus* (see BENEDICT, ST.).

ben·e·dic·tion /,beniˈdikSHən/ ▸*n.* the utterance or bestowing of a blessing, esp. at the end of a religious service. ■ (**Benediction**) a service in which the congregation is blessed with the Blessed Sacrament, held mainly in the Roman Catholic Church. ■ devout or formal invocation of blessedness: *her arms outstretched in benediction.* ■ the state of being blessed: *he eventually wins benediction.* ▷late Middle English: via Old French from Latin *benedictio(n-)*, from *benedicere* 'wish well, bless,' from *bene* 'well' + *dicere* 'say.'

Ben·e·dict's so·lu·tion /ˈbeni,dikts/ (also **Benedict's reagent**) ▸*n.* a chemical solution that changes color in the presence of glucose and other reducing sugars, used in clinical urine tests for diabetes. It is a mixture of sodium or potassium citrate, sodium carbonate, and copper sulfate. ▷named after S. R. *Benedict* (1884–1936), American chemist.

Ben·e·dic·tus /,beniˈdiktəs/ ▸*n. Christian Church* **1** an invocation beginning *Benedictus qui venit in nomine Domini* (Blessed is he who comes in the name of the Lord) forming a set part of the Mass. **2** a canticle beginning *Benedictus Dominus Deus* (Blessed be the Lord God) from Luke 1:68–79. ▷mid 16th cent.: Latin, 'blessed,' past participle of *benedicere* 'wish well.'

ben·e·fac·tion /,benəˈfakSHən/ ▸*n.* a donation or gift. ▷mid 17th cent.: from late Latin *benefactio(n-)*, from *bene facere* 'do good (to),' from *bene* 'well' + *facere* 'do.'

ben·e·fac·tive /,benəˈfaktiv/ *Grammar* ▸*adj.* denoting a semantic case or construction that expresses the person or thing that benefits from the action of the verb, for example *for you* in *I bought this for you.*

▸*n.* the benefactive case, or a word or expression in it. ▷1940s: from Latin *benefactus* 'capable of giving' + -IVE.

ben·e·fac·tor /ˈbenə,faktər; ,benəˈfaktər/ ▸*n.* a person who gives money or other help to a person or cause. ▷late Middle English: from Latin, from *bene facere* 'do good (to)' (see BENEFACTION).

ben·e·fac·tress /ˈbenə,faktris; ,benəˈfaktris/ ▸*n.* a female benefactor.

be·nef·ic /bəˈnefik/ ▸*adj. rare* beneficent or kindly. ■ *Astrology* relating to or denoting the planets Jupiter and Venus, traditionally considered to have a favorable influence. ▷early 17th cent.: from Latin *beneficus*, from *bene facere* 'do good (to).'

ben·e·fice /ˈbenəfis/ ▸*n.* a permanent Church appointment, typically that of a rector or vicar, for which property and income are provided in respect of pastoral duties. ▷Middle English: via Old French from Latin *beneficium* 'favor, support,' from *bene* 'well' + *facere* 'do.' —**ben·e·ficed** *adj.*

be·nef·i·cent /bəˈnefəsənt/ ▸*adj.* (of a person) generous or doing good. ■ resulting in good: *a beneficent democracy.* ▷early 17th cent.: from Latin *beneficent-* (stem of *beneficentior*, comparative of *beneficus* 'favorable, generous'), from *bene facere* 'do good (to).' —**be·nef·i·cence** *n.* —**be·nef·i·cent·ly** *adv.*

ben·e·fi·cial /,benəˈfiSHəl/ ▸*adj.* favorable or advantageous; resulting in good: *the beneficial effect on the economy* | *discoveries* ***beneficial to*** *mankind.* ■ *Law* of or relating to rights, other than legal title: *the beneficiary will be taxed on the value of his beneficial use of the property.* ▷late Middle English: from late Latin *beneficialis*, from *beneficium* (see BENEFICE). —**ben·e·fi·cial·ly** *adv.*

ben·e·fi·cials /,benəˈfiSHəlz/ ▸ *plural n.* insects that are a boon to gardeners: *daisies that are highly attractive to five key kinds of beneficials (ladybugs, lacewings, hover flies, tachinid flies, and miniwasps).*

ben·e·fi·ci·ar·y /,benəˈfiSHē,erē/ ▸*n.* (*pl.* **-ar·ies**) a person who derives advantage from something, esp. a trust, will, or life insurance policy. ▷early 17th cent.: from Latin *beneficiarius*, from *beneficium* (see BENEFICE).

ben·e·fit /ˈbenəfit/ ▸*n.* **1** an advantage or profit gained from something: *tenants bought their houses* ***with the benefit of*** *a discount* | *enjoy the benefits of being a member* | *uninformed criticism is* ***of benefit to*** *no one.* **2** a payment or gift made by an employer, the state, or an insurance company: *welfare benefits* | *wages and benefits.* **3** a public performance or other entertainment of which the proceeds go to a particular charitable cause.

▸*v.* (**-fit·ed, -fit·ing** or **-fit·ted, -fit·ting**) [*intrans.*] receive an advantage; profit; gain: *areas that would* ***benefit from*** *regeneration.* ■ [*trans.*] bring advantage to: *the bill will benefit the nation.* ▷late Middle English (originally denoting a kind deed or something well done): from Old French *bienfet*, from Latin *benefactum* 'good deed,' from *bene facere* 'do good (to).'

▸*PHRASES* □ **benefit of clergy** **1** *historical* exemption of the English clergy and nuns from the jurisdiction of the ordinary civil courts, granted in the

Middle Ages but abolished in 1827. **2** ecclesiastical sanction or approval: *they lived together **without benefit of clergy**.* □ **the benefit of the doubt** a concession that a person or fact must be regarded as correct or justified, if the contrary has not been proven: *I'll **give you the benefit of the doubt** as to whether it was deliberate or not.* □ **for the benefit of 1** in order to help, guide, or be of service to: *a man who has spent his life fighting evil for the benefit of the community.* **2** in order to interest or impress someone: *it was all an act put on for his benefit.* □ **give someone the benefit of** *often ironic* explain or recount to someone at length: *the whole assembly was given the benefit of his opinions.*

Ben·e·lux /ˈbenl,əks/ a collective name for Belgium, the Netherlands, and Luxembourg, esp. with reference to their economic union. ▷1947: acronym from *Be*lgium, *Ne*therlands, and *Lux*embourg.

be·nev·o·lent /bəˈnevələnt/ ▸*adj.* well meaning and kindly: *a benevolent smile.* ■ (of an organization) serving a charitable rather than a profit-making purpose: *a benevolent fund.* ▷late Middle English: from Old French *benivolent,* from Latin *bene volent-* 'well wishing,' from *bene* 'well' + *velle* 'to wish.' **—be·nev·o·lence** *n.* **—be·nev·o·lent·ly** *adv.*

Ben·ford's Law /ˈbenfərdz/ ▸*n. Mathematics* the principle that in any large, randomly produced set of natural numbers, such as tables of logarithms or corporate sales statistics, around 30 percent will begin with the digit 1, 18 percent with 2, and so on, with the smallest percentage beginning with 9. The law is applied in analyzing the validity of statistics and financial records. ▷Named for U.S. physicist Frank Benford, whose 1938 paper demonstrated the statistical validity of the phenomenon.

BEng ▸*abbr.* Bachelor of Engineering.

beng·a /ˈbeNGgə/ ▸*n.* a style of African popular music originating in Kenya, characterized by a fusion of traditional Kenyan music and a lively arrangement of guitars, bass, and vocals. ▷1980s: from Luo (a Kenyan language).

Ben·gal /benˈgôl; beNG-; -ˈgäl/ a region in the northeast of the Indian subcontinent that contains the Ganges and Brahmaputra river deltas. In 1947, the province was divided into West Bengal, which has remained a state of India, and East Bengal, which is now Bangladesh.

Ben·gal, Bay of a part of the Indian Ocean that lies between India on the west and Myanmar (Burma) and Thailand on the east.

Ben·ga·li /,beNGˈgälē/ ▸*n.* (*pl.* **-lis**) **1** a native of Bengal. **2** the Indic language of Bangladesh and West Bengal.
▸*adj.* of or relating to Bengal, its people, or their language. ▷from Hindi *baṅgālī.*

ben·ga·line /ˈbeNGgə,lēn/ ▸*n.* a strong ribbed fabric made of a mixture of silk and either cotton or wool. ▷late 19th cent.: from French, so named because of a similarity with archaic *Bengals* denoting fabrics, usually silks, imported from Bengal.

Ben·gal light /,beNGˈgäl/ ▸*n.* a kind of firework giving off a blue flame and used for lighting or signaling.

Ben·gha·zi /benˈgäzē; beNG-/ a Mediterranean port in northeastern Libya; pop. 485,400. It was the joint capital (with Tripoli) 1951–72.

Ben·guel·a /benˈgwelə; beNG-/ a port and railroad terminal in Angola, on the Atlantic coast; pop. 155,000. Copper is brought here from Zambia and the Democratic Republic of the Congo (formerly Zaire).

Ben·guel·a Cur·rent a cold ocean current that flows north from Antarctica along the west coast of southern Africa as far as Angola.

Ben-Gu·rion /ben ˈgŏŏrēən/, David (1886–1973), Israeli statesman; prime minister 1948–53 and 1955–63. He was Israel's first prime minister and minister of defense.

Be·ni Riv·er /ˈbānē/ a river that flows for 1,000 miles (1,600 km) from central to northern Bolivia, east of the Andes, into the Madeira River.

Be·ni·cia /bəˈnēSHə/ a city in north central California, north of San Francisco Bay; pop. 24,437.

be·night·ed /biˈnītid/ ▸*adj.* **1** in a state of pitiful or contemptible intellectual or moral ignorance, typically owing to a lack of opportunity: *they saw themselves as bringers of culture to poor benighted peoples.* **2** overtaken by darkness: *a storm developed and we were forced to wait benighted near the summit.* ▷late 16th cent. (sense 2): past participle of archaic *benight* 'cover in the darkness of night, obscure' (see **BE-**, **NIGHT**). **—be·night·ed·ness** *n.*

be·nign /biˈnīn/ ▸*adj.* **1** gentle; kindly: *her face was calm and benign | his benign but firm manner.* ■ (of a climate or environment) mild and favorable: ■ not harmful to the environment: [in *combination*] *an ozone-benign refrigerant.* **2** *Medicine* (of a disease) not harmful in effect: in particular, (of a tumor) not malignant. ▷Middle English: from Old French *benigne,* from Latin *benignus,* probably from *bene* 'well' + *-genus* '-born.' Compare with **GENTLE**. **—be·nign·ly** *adv.*

be·nig·nant /biˈnignənt/ ▸*adj.* **1** kindly and benevolent: *an old man, with a face noble and benignant.* **2** *Medicine* less common term for **BENIGN** (sense 2). ■ *archaic* having a good effect; beneficial: *the benignant touch of love and beauty.* ▷late 18th cent.: from **BENIGN**, or Latin *benignus,* on the pattern of *malignant.* **—be·nig·nan·cy** *n.* **—be·nig·nant·ly** *adv.*

be·nig·ni·ty /biˈnignitē/ ▸*n.* (*pl.* **-ties**) kindness or tolerance toward others: *his air of benignity.* ■ *archaic* an act of kindness. ▷late Middle English: from Old French *benignite* or Latin *benignitas,* from *benignus* (see **BENIGN**).

be·nign ne·glect ▸*n.* a noninterference that is intended to benefit someone or something more than continual attention would.

Be·nin /bəˈnēn; -ˈnin/ a country in West Africa, just west of Nigeria; pop. 7,250,000; capital, Porto Novo; languages, French (official), West African languages. Former name (until 1975) **DAHOMEY**. ▷name adopted in 1975, formerly used by an African kingdom, powerful in the 14th–17th cents. **—Be·ni·nese** /,benəˈnēz; -ˈnēs/ *adj.* & *n.*

The country was conquered by the French in 1893 and became part of French West Africa. In 1960, it achieved independence.

Be·nin, Bight of a wide bay on the coast of Africa north of the Gulf of Guinea, bordered by Togo, Benin, and southwestern Nigeria. Lagos is its chief port.

ben·i·son /ˈbenəsən; -zən/ ▸*n. poetic/literary* a blessing: *the rewards and benisons of marriage.* ▷Middle English: from Old French *beneiçun,* from Latin *benedictio* (see **BENEDICTION**).

Ben·ja·min /ˈbenjəmən/ (in the Bible) a Hebrew patriarch, the youngest son of Jacob and Rachel, and Jacob's favorite (Gen. 35:18, 42, etc.). ■ the smallest tribe of Israel, traditionally descended from him.

ben·ne /ˈbenē/ ▸*n.* another term for **SESAME**. ▷mid 18th cent.: from Malay *bene.*

Ben·nett /ˈbenit/, Tony (1926–), U.S. singer; born *Anthony Dominick Benedetto.* A popular jazz singer in the early 1950s with such hits as "Because of You" (1951), he made a successful comeback during the 1990s.

Ben Ne·vis /ben ˈnevəs/ a mountain in western Scotland. Rising to 4,406 feet (1,343 m), it is the highest mountain in the British Isles.

Ben·ning·ton /ˈbeniNGtən/ a historic town in southwestern Vermont; pop. 15,737.

Ben·ny /ˈbenē/, Jack (1894–1974), U.S. comedian and actor; born *Benjamin Kubelsky.* He made his radio debut in 1931 on *The Ed Sullivan Show* and launched his own series in 1932. *The Jack Benny Show* was successfully transferred to television in 1950 and ran until 1965. Benny was renowned for his timing, delivery, and mordant, self-effacing humor.

Jack Benny

ben·ny[1] /ˈbenē/ ▸*n.* (*pl.* **-nies**) *informal* a tablet of Benzedrine.

ben·ny[2] ▸*n.* (*pl.* **-nies**) *informal* a benefit attached to employment.

ben·o·myl /ˈbenə,mil/ ▸*n.* a systemic fungicide used on fruit and vegetable crops, derived from imidazole. ▷1960s: from *ben(z)o-* + *m(eth)yl.*

Be·no·ni /bəˈnōnē/ a city in South Africa, east of Johannesburg; pop. 206,800. It is a gold-mining center.

Ben·sa·lem /benˈsāləm/ a township in southeastern Pennsylvania; pop. 58,434.

Ben·son·hurst /ˈbensən,hərst/ a residential section in southwestern Brooklyn in New York City.

bent[1] /bent/ ▸ past and past participle of **BEND**[1].
▸*adj.* **1** sharply curved or having an angle: *a piece of bent wire | his bent shoulders.* **2** *informal, chiefly Brit.* dishonest; corrupt: *a bent cop.* ■ stolen. ■ homosexual. **3** (**bent on**) determined to do or have something: *a missionary bent on saving souls | a mob bent on violence.*
▸*n.* a natural talent or inclination: *a man of religious bent | she had no natural **bent for** literature.*
▸*PHRASE* □ **bent out of shape** *informal* angry or agitated: *it was just a mistake, nothing to get bent out of shape about.*

bent[2] ▸*n.* **1** (also **bent grass**) a stiff grass that is used for lawns and is a component of pasture and hay grasses. • *Agrostis* and other genera, family Gramineae: several species, including **common bent** (*A. capillaris* (or **tenuis**)). ■ the stiff flowering stalk of a grass. ■ *archaic* any stiff-stemmed or rushlike grass or sedge. **2** *Brit., archaic* or *dialect* a heath or unenclosed pasture. ▷Middle English: representing Old English *beonet* (recorded in place names); related to German *Binse.*

Ben·tham /ˈbenTHəm/, Jeremy (1748–1832), English philosopher and jurist, the first major proponent of utilitarianism. He wrote *Introduction to the Principles of Morals and Legislation* (1789).

ben·thos /ˈben,THäs/ ▸*n. Ecology* the flora and fauna found on the bottom, or in the bottom sediments, of a sea, lake, or other body of water. ▷late 19th cent.: from Greek, 'depth of the sea.' **—ben·thic** /-THik/ *adj.*

ben·to /ˈbentō/ ▸*n.* (*pl.* **-tos**) a lacquered or decorated wooden Japanese lunchbox. ■ a Japanese-style packed lunch, consisting of such items as rice, vegetables, and sashimi (raw fish with condiments). ▷Japanese.

Ben·ton[1] /ˈbentn/, Thomas Hart (1782–1858), U.S. politician. A Democratic member of the U.S. Senate from Missouri (1821–51), he supported frontier explorations and opposed extending slavery to the territories.

Ben·ton[2], Thomas Hart (1889–1975), U.S. painter, a grandnephew of Senator Thomas Hart Benton. His paintings, of the American naturalist school, represent life in the Midwest.

ben·ton·ite /ˈbentn,īt/ ▸*n.* a kind of absorbent clay formed by the breakdown of volcanic ash, used esp.

as a filler. ▷late 19th cent.: from the name of Fort *Benton* in Montana, where it is found, + **-ITE**[1].

Bent·sen /'bentsən/, Lloyd (Millard, Jr.) (1921–), U.S. politician. He was a Demmocratic member of the U.S. Senate from Texas 1971–93, a vice presidential candidate 1988, and secretary of the treasury 1993–94.

Bent's Fort /bents/ a historic site in east central Colorado, northeast of La Junta, on the Arkansas River and the former Santa Fe Trail.

bent·wood /'bent,wo͝od/ ▸*n.* wood that is artificially shaped for use in making furniture: [as *adj.*] *bentwood chairs.*

bentwood chair

Be·nue-Con·go /'bān,wā/ ▸*n.* a major branch of the Niger-Congo family of languages, spoken mainly in Nigeria and including Efik and Fula.
▸*adj.* of, relating to, or denoting this group of languages. ▷from the names of rivers.

Be·nue Riv·er a river that flows for 870 miles (1,400 km) from northern Cameroon into Nigeria, where it joins the Niger River.

be·numb /bi'nəm/ ▸*v.* [*trans.*] [often as *adj.*] (**benumbed**) deprive of physical or emotional feeling: *a hoarse shout cut through his benumbed senses.* ▷late 15th cent.: from obsolete *benome*, past participle of *benim* 'deprive,' from **BE-** (expressing removal) + Old English *niman* 'take.'

Ben·xi /'ben'CHē/ a city in northeastern China, in the province of Liaoning; pop. 920,000.

Benz /benz; bents/, Karl Friedrich (1844–1929), German engineer and automobile manufacturer. In 1885 he built the first vehicle to be powered by an internal combustion engine. His company merged with the Daimler Motor Company to form Daimler-Benz AG in 1926.

benz·al·de·hyde /ben'zaldə,hīd/ ▸*n. Chemistry* a colorless liquid aldehyde with the odor of bitter almonds, used in the manufacture of dyes and perfumes. • Chem. formula: C_6H_5CHO.

Ben·ze·drine /'benzə,drēn/ ▸*n.* trademark for **AMPHETAMINE.** ▷1930s: blend of **BENZOIN** and **EPHEDRINE.**

ben·zene /'ben,zēn; ben'zēn/ ▸*n.* a colorless volatile liquid hydrocarbon present in coal tar and petroleum, used in chemical synthesis. Its use as a solvent has been reduced because of its carcinogenic properties. • Chem. formula: C_6H_6. ▷mid 19th cent.: from **BENZOIN** + **-ENE.**

ben·zene hex·a·chlor·ide /,heksə'klôr,īd/ (abbr.: **BHC**) ▸*n.* **1** a compound of benzene and chlorine used as an insecticide. • Chem. formula: $C_6H_6Cl_6$. **2** used as a general term for **LINDANE.**

ben·zene ring ▸*n. Chemistry* the hexagonal unsaturated ring of six carbon atoms present in benzene and many other aromatic molecules.

ben·ze·noid /'benzə,noid/ ▸*adj. Chemistry* having the six-membered ring structure or aromatic properties of benzene.

ben·zi·dine /'benzi,dēn/ ▸*n.* a crystalline base used in making dyes and in detecting blood stains. • Chem. formula: $NH_2C_6H_4C_6H_4NH_2$.

ben·zine /'ben,zēn; ben'zēn/ (also **ben·zin** /'benzin/) ▸*n.* a mixture of liquid hydrocarbons obtained from petroleum. ▷mid 19th cent. (denoting benzene): from **BENZOIN** + **-INE**[4].

ben·zo·caine /'benzə,kān/ ▸*n.* a white, odorless, crystalline powder used in ointments as a local anesthetic and to protect against sunburn. • Chem. formula: $NH_2C_6H_4C_6H_4NH_2$.

ben·zo·di·az·e·pine /,benzō,dī'azə,pēn/ ▸*n. Medicine* any of a class of heterocyclic organic compounds used as tranquilizers, such as Librium and Valium. ▷1930s: from **BENZENE** + **DI-**[1] + **AZO-** + **EPI-** + **-INE**[4].

ben·zo·ic ac·id /ben'zō-ik/ ▸*n. Chemistry* a white crystalline substance present in benzoin and other plant resins, and used as a food preservative. • Chem. formula: C_6H_5COOH. **—ben·zo·ate** /'benzō,āt/ *n.*

ben·zo·in /'benzō-in; -,zoin/ ▸*n.* **1** (also **gum benzoin**) a fragrant gum resin obtained from a tropical tree of eastern Asia, used in medicines, perfumes, and incense. Also called **GUM BENJAMIN.** • This is obtained from several species of the genus *Styrax*, family Styracaceae, in particular *S. benzoin.* **2** *Chemistry* a white crystalline aromatic ketone present in this resin. • Alternative name: 2-hydroxy-1, 2-diphenylethanone; chem. formula: $C_6H_5CHOHCOC_6H_5$. ▷mid 16th cent.: from French *benjoin*, based on Arabic *lubānjāwī* 'incense of Java.'

ben·zo·phe·none /,benzōfi'nōn; -'fē,nōn/ ▸*n.* a white, crystalline ketone that is used in perfume, sunscreen, and as a flavoring agent. • Chem. formula: $C_6H_5COC_6H_5$.

ben·zo·py·rene /,benzō'pīrēn/ ▸*n. Chemistry* a compound that is the major carcinogen present in cigarette smoke. It also occurs in coal tar. • A polycyclic aromatic hydrocarbon; chem. formula: $C_{20}H_{12}$.

ben·zo·qui·none /,benzōkwi'nōn; -'kwinōn/ ▸*n. Chemistry* a yellow crystalline compound related to benzene but having two hydrogen atoms replaced by oxygen. • Chem. formula: $C_6H_4O_2$; there are two isomers, with the oxygen atoms on opposite (**1,4-benzoquinone**) or adjacent (**1,2-benzoquinone**) carbon atoms.

ben·zo·yl /'benzō-il/ ▸*n.* [as *adj.*] *Chemistry* the acyl radical $-C(O)C_6H_5$, derived from benzoic acid: *benzoyl peroxide.*

ben·zo·yl per·ox·ide ▸*n.* an antibacterial ingredient used in acne medications.

ben·zyl /'benzil/ ▸*n.* [as *adj.*] *Chemistry* the radical $-CH_2C_6H_5$, derived from toluene: *benzyl benzoate.*

Be·o·thuk /'bāə,THo͝ok/ ▸*n.* (*pl.* same or **-thuks**) **1** a member of an extinct North American Indian people of Newfoundland. **2** the language of this people, of unknown affinity.
▸*adj.* of or relating to this people or their language. ▷probably the name in Beothuk.

Be·o·wulf /'bāə,wo͝olf/ an Old English epic poem celebrating the legendary Scandinavian hero Beowulf.

Generally dated to the 8th century, it was the first major poem in a European vernacular language and is the only complete Germanic epic that survives. It describes Beowulf's killing of the water monster Grendel and its mother and his death in combat with a dragon, and includes both pagan and Christian elements.

be·queath /bi'kwēTH; -'kwē<u>TH</u>/ ▸*v.* [*trans.*] leave (a personal estate or one's body) to a person or other beneficiary by a will: *an identical sum was bequeathed by Margaret | he bequeathed his art collection to the town.* ■ pass (something) on or leave (something) to someone else: *he is ditching the unpopular policies bequeathed to him.* ▷Old English *becwethan*, from **BE-** 'about' (expressing transitivity) + *cwethan* 'say' (see **QUOTH**). **—be·queath·er** *n.*

be·quest /bi'kwest/ ▸*n.* a legacy: *her $135,000 was the largest bequest the library ever has received.* ■ the action of bequeathing something: *a painting acquired by bequest.* ▷Middle English: from **BE-** 'about' + Old English *cwis* 'speech,' influenced by **BEQUEATH.**

be·rate /bi'rāt/ ▸*v.* [*trans.*] scold or criticize (someone) angrily: *my son berated me for not giving him a Jewish upbringing.* See note at **SCOLD.** ▷mid 16th cent.: from **BE-** 'thoroughly' + **RATE**[2].

Ber·ber /'bərbər/ ▸*n.* **1** a member of an indigenous people of North Africa. The majority of Berbers are settled farmers or (now) migrant workers. **2** the Afro-Asiatic language of these peoples. There are several different dialects; some of them, e.g., Tamashek, are regarded by some scholars as separate languages.
▸*adj.* of or relating to these peoples or their language. ▷from Arabic *barbar*, from Greek *barbarus* 'foreigner' (see **BARBARIAN**).

ber·be·rine /'bərbə,rēn/ ▸*n. Chemistry* a bitter yellow compound of the alkaloid class obtained from barberry and other plants. ▷early 19th cent.: from **BERBERIS** + **-INE**[4].

ber·ceuse /ber'so͞oz; -'sœz/ ▸*n.* (*pl.* **-ceuses** *pronunc.* same) a lullaby. ■ a piece of instrumental music in the style of a lullaby. ▷French, from *bercer* 'to rock.'

Berch·tes·ga·den /'berKHtəs,gädn/ a town in southern Germany, in the Bavarian Alps close to the border with Austria; pop. 8,186. Adolf Hitler had a fortified retreat there.

be·reave /bi'rēv/ ▸*v.* (**be bereaved**) be deprived of a loved one through a profound absence, esp. due to the loved one's death: *the year after they had been bereaved* | [as *adj.*] (**bereaved**) *bereaved families* | [as *plural n.*] (**the bereaved**) *those who counsel the bereaved.* ▷Old English *berēafian* (see **BE-**, **REAVE**). The original sense was 'deprive of' in general. **—be·reave·ment** *n.*

be·reft /bi'reft/ ▸ archaic past participle of **BEREAVE.**
▸*adj.* deprived of or lacking something, esp. a nonmaterial asset: *her room was stark and* **bereft of** *color.* ■ (of a person) lonely and abandoned, esp. through someone's death or departure: *his death in 1990 left her bereft.*

Ber·e·ni·ce /,berə'nīsē; -'nēs/ (3rd century BC), Egyptian queen; wife of Ptolemy III. She offered her hair for the safe return of her husband from an expedition; the hair was stolen and, according to legend, placed in the heavens. The constellation Coma Berenices (*Berenice's hair*) is named after her.

be·ret /bə'rā/ ▸*n.* a round flattish cap of felt or cloth. ▷early 19th cent.: from French *béret* 'Basque cap,' from Old Provençal *berret*, based on late Latin *birrus* 'hooded cape.' Compare with **BIRETTA.**

be·ret·ta ▸*n.* variant spelling of **BIRETTA.**

Berg /berKH/, Alban (Maria Johannes) (1885–1935), Austrian composer, a leading exponent of twelve-tone composition.

berg /bərg/ ▸*n.* short for **ICEBERG.**

ber·ga·mot /'bərgə,mät/ ▸*n.* **1** an oily substance extracted from the rind of the fruit of a dwarf variety of the Seville orange tree. It is used in cosmetics and as flavoring in tea. **2** (also **bergamot orange**) the tree that bears this fruit. • *Citrus aurantium* subsp. *bergamia*, family Rutaceae. **3** an aromatic North American herb of the mint family, grown for its bright flowers and traditionally used in American Indian medicine. Also called **BEE BALM**; **OSWEGO TEA.** • *Monarda didyma*, family Labiatae. ▷late 17th cent. (sense 2): named after the city and province of *Bergamo* in northern Italy.

Ber·gen /'bərgən; 'ber-/ a seaport in southwestern Norway; pop. 213,344. It is a center of the fishing and North Sea oil industries.

Ber·gen·field /'bərgən,fēld/ a suburban borough in northeastern New Jersey; pop. 24,458.

Ber·ger[1] /'bərgər/, Hans (1873–1941), German psychiatrist. He detected electric currents in the brain's cortex and developed encephalography.

Ber·ger[2], Thomas (1924–), U.S. writer. His works include *Crazy in Berlin* (1958), *Little Big Man* (1964), *The Feud* (1983), and *Meeting Evil* (1992).

Ber·ge·rac see **CYRANO DE BERGERAC.**

ber·gère /ber'ZHer/ ▸*n.* a long-seated upholstered armchair fashionable in the 18th century. ■ a later example of this, in which the upholstery is replaced with canework seat, back, and sides.

Ber·gi·us /'bergēo͞os/, Friedrich Karl Rudolf (1884–1949), German industrial chemist. Nobel Prize for Chemistry (1931, shared with Carl Bosch 1874–1940).

Berg·man[1] /'bərgmən; 'ber(yə),män/, (Ernst) Ingmar (1918–), Swedish movie and theater director. He used haunting imagery and symbolism. Notable films: *Smiles of a Summer Night* (1955), *The Seventh Seal* (1956), and *Fanny and Alexander* (1982).

Berg·man[2] /'bərgmən/, Ingrid (1915–82), Swedish actress. Notable movies: *Casablanca* (1942), *Gaslight* (Academy Award, 1944), *Anastasia* (Academy Award, 1956), and *Murder on the Orient Express* (Academy Award, 1974).

Berg·son /'bergsən; berk'sôN/, Henri (Louis) (1859–1941), French philosopher. He wrote *Creative Evolution* (1907). Nobel Prize for Literature (1927).

Be·ri·a /'byeryə/, Lavrenti (Pavlovich) (1899–1953), Soviet politician and head of the secret police 1938–53. After Joseph Stalin's death, he was arrested and executed.

be·rib·boned /bi'ribənd/ ▸*adj.* decorated with many ribbons.

ber·i·ber·i /'berē'berē/ ▸*n.* a disease causing inflammation of the nerves and heart failure, caused by a deficiency of vitamin B_1. ▷early 18th cent.: from Sinhalese, from *beri* 'weakness.'

Ber·ing /'beriNG/, Vitus (Jonassen) (1681–1741), Danish navigator and explorer. He led several Russian expeditions to determine whether Asia and North America were connected by land. The Bering Sea and Bering Strait are named after him.

Be·rin·gi·a /bə'rinjēə/ the area comprising the Bering Strait and adjacent parts of Siberia and Alaska, esp. in connection with the migration of animals across the former Bering land bridge. See **BERING STRAIT.** **—Beringian** *adj.*

Ber·ing Sea an arm of the North Pacific Ocean that lies between northeastern Siberia in Russia and Alaska, bounded on the south by the Aleutian Islands. It is linked to the Arctic Ocean by the Bering Strait. Both the sea and the strait are named after Vitus Bering.

Ber·ing Strait a narrow sea passage that separates the eastern tip of Siberia in Russia from Alaska and links the Arctic Ocean with the Bering Sea, about 53 miles (85 km) wide at its narrowest point. During the Ice Age, as a result of a drop in sea levels, the **Bering land bridge** formed between the two continents, allowing the migration of animals and dispersal of plants in both directions.

Berke·ley[1] /'bərklē/ a city in western California, on San Francisco Bay, site of a campus of the University of California; pop. 102,724.

Berke·ley[2] /'bərklē/, Busby (1895–1976), U.S. choreographer and movie director; born *William Berkeley Enos*. He is remembered for his spectacular movie sequences in which dancers formed kaleidoscopic patterns on the screen. Notable movies: *Gold Diggers* series (1922–37) and *Babes in Arms* (1939).

Berke·ley[3] /'bärklē; 'bər-/, George (1685–1753), Irish philosopher and bishop. He argued that material objects exist only by being perceived. **—Berke·le·ian·ism** /'bärkləə,nizəm; 'bər-/ *n.*

ber·ke·li·um /bər'kēlēəm/ ▸*n.* the chemical element of atomic number 97, a radioactive metal of the actinide series. Berkelium does not occur naturally and was first made by bombarding americium with helium ions. (Symbol: **Bk**) ▷1949: from BERKELEY[1], California (where it was first made) + -IUM.

Berk·shire /'bərkSHər; -,SHi(ə)r/ (in full **Berkshire Pig**) ▸*n.* a pig of a black breed, now rarely kept commercially.

Berk·shire Hills /'bərkSHər/ an upland in western Massachusetts, noted as a resort area.

Berle /bərl/, Milton (1908–2002), U.S. comedian and actor; real name *Milton Berlinger*. He began as a vaudeville entertainer and went on to star on radio, stage, movies and, in particular, on television with the "Texaco Star Theater" from 1948 until 1956 (renamed "The Milton Berle Show" in 1953).

Ber·lin[1] /bər'lin/ the capital of Germany; pop. 3,102,500. At the end of World War II, the city was occupied by the Allies and divided into two parts: **West Berlin** and **East Berlin.** Between 1961 and 1989, the Berlin Wall separated the two parts, which were reunited in 1990.

Ber·lin[2], Irving (1888–1989), U.S. composer of popular music; born in Russia; born *Israel Baline*. He wrote more than 800 songs, many of which are regarded as popular "standards" or classics. Notable works: "Alexander's Ragtime Band" (1911), "God Bless America" (1939), and "White Christmas" (1942), and the musical *Annie get Your Gun* (1946; film 1950).

Ber·li·ner /bər'linər/ ▸*n.* a native or citizen of Berlin. ▷mid 19th cent.: German.

Berlinger, Milton, see BERLE.

Ber·lin Wall a fortified and heavily guarded wall built on the boundary between East and West Berlin in 1961 by the communist authorities, chiefly to curb the flow of East Germans to the West. It was opened in November 1989 after the collapse of the communist regime in East Germany and subsequently was dismantled.

Ber·lin work ▸*n.* worsted embroidery on canvas.

Ber·li·oz /'berlē,ōz; ber'lyôz/, Hector (1803–69), French composer; full name *Louis-Hector Berlioz*. Notable works: *Les Troyens* (opera, 1856–59), *Symphonie fantastique* (1830), and *La Damnation de Faust* (cantata, 1846).

berm /bərm/ ▸*n.* a flat strip of land, raised bank, or terrace bordering a river or canal. ■ a path or grass strip beside a road. ■ an artificial ridge or embankment, e.g., as a defense against tanks. ■ a narrow space, esp. one between a ditch and the base of a parapet. ▷early 18th cent. (DENOTING A NARROW SPACE): from French *berme*, from Dutch *berm*.

Ber·mu·da /bər'myōōdə/ (also **the Ber·mu·das**) a British crown colony made up of about 150 small islands about 650 miles (1,046 km) east of the coast of North Carolina; pop. 58,000; capital, Hamilton. Inhabited since 1609, it now has internal self-government. ▷named after a Spanish sailor, Juan *Bermúdez*, who sighted the islands early in the 16th cent. **—Ber·mu·dan** /-'myōōdn/ *adj. & n.* **—Ber·mu·di·an** /-'myōōdēən/ *adj. & n.*

Ber·mu·da grass ▸*n.* a creeping grass common in warmer parts of the world, used for lawns and pasture. • *Cynodon dactylon*, family Gramineae.

Ber·mu·da High ▸*Meteorology n.* a semipermanent area of high pressure located over Bermuda in summer and fall that steers many storm systems westward across the Atlantic. Compare with AZORES HIGH.

Ber·mu·da Hun·dred a locality southeast of Richmond in Virginia, the site of an 1864 Civil War battle.

Ber·mu·da on·ion ▸*n.* a variety of cultivated onion with a mild flavor and a flattened shape.

Ber·mu·da rig ▸*n.* a tall yachting rig with a high, tapering fore-and-aft mainsail.

Ber·mu·da shorts (also **Ber·mu·das**) ▸*plural n.* casual knee-length shorts.

Ber·mu·da Tri·an·gle an area of the western Atlantic Ocean between Florida, Bermuda, and Puerto Rico where a large number of ships and aircraft are said to have disappeared mysteriously.

Ber·na·dette, St. /,bərnə'det/ (1844–79), French peasant girl; born *Marie Bernarde Soubirous*. Her visions of the Virgin Mary at Lourdes in 1858 led to the town's establishment as a center of pilgrimage. Feast day, February 18.

Ber·na·dotte[1] /,bernə'dät; -'dôt/, Folke, Count (1895–1948), Swedish statesman. As vice president of the Swedish Red Cross he arranged the exchange of prisoners of war and in 1945 conveyed a German offer of capitulation to the Allies. Appointed as UN mediator in Palestine in 1948, he was assassinated by the Stern Gang.

Ber·na·dotte[2], Jean Baptiste Jules (1763–1844), French soldier who became king of Sweden as Charles XIV 1818–44. One of Napoleon's marshals, he was adopted by Charles XIII of Sweden in 1810 and later became king, thus founding Sweden's present royal house.

Ber·nard /ber'när/, Claude (1813–78), French physiologist. He showed the role of the pancreas in digestion, the method of regulation of body temperature, and the function of nerves that supply the internal organs.

Ber·nard, St. /bər'närd; ber'när/ (*c.*996–*c.*1081), French monk. He founded two hospices for travelers in the Alps. The St. Bernard passes, where the hospices were situated, and St. Bernard dogs, once kept by the monks and trained to aid travelers, are named after him. Feast day, May 28.

Ber·nard of Clair·vaux, St. /bər'närd əv kler'vō; ber'när/ (1090–1153), French theologian and abbot. The first abbot of Clairvaux, his monastery was one of the chief centers of the Cistercian order. Feast day, August 20.

Berne /bern; bərn/ (also **Bern**) the capital of Switzerland, in the west central part of the country; pop. 134,620. ■ a canton of Switzerland. **—Ber·nese** /bər'nēz; -'nēs; bər-/ *adj. & n.*

Ber·nese moun·tain dog /'bərnēz; -nēs; bər'nēz; -'nēs/ ▸*n.* a large muscular dog of a Swiss breed with a silky black coat, having white and russet markings.

Bern·hardt /'bərn,härt/, Sarah (1844–1923), French actress; born *Henriette Rosine Bernard*. She was noted for her portrayal of Marguerite in *La Dame aux camélias* and of Cordelia in *King Lear*.

Ber·ni·ni /bər'nēnē/, Gian Lorenzo (1598–1680), Italian sculptor, painter, and architect. His work includes the great canopy over the altar and the colonnade around the piazza at St. Peter's in Rome.

Ber·noul·li /bər'nōō(l)ē/ a Swiss family that produced many eminent mathematicians and scientists: ■ **Jakob** (1654–1705), a professor of mathematics; also known as *Jacques* or *James Bernoulli*. He made discoveries in calculus and contributed to geometry and the theory of probabilities. ■ **Johann** (1667–1748), the brother of Jakob; also known as *Jean* or *John Bernoulli*. He contributed to differential and integral calculus. ■ **Daniel** (1700–82), son of Johann. His greatest contributions were to hydrodynamics and mathematical physics.

Ber·noul·li's prin·ci·ple ▸*n.* the principle in hydrodynamics that an increase in the velocity of a stream of fluid results in a decrease in pressure. Also called **Ber·noul·li ef·fect** or **Ber·noul·li the·o·rem.** ▷Named for Swiss mathematician Daniel Bernoulli (1700–82).

Bern·stein[1] /'bərn,stēn; -,stīn/, Carl (1944–), U.S. journalist. He was the *Washington Post* reporter who, with Bob Woodward, broke the story of the Watergate burglary and traced the financial payoffs to President Nixon. With Woodward, he wrote *All The President's Men* (1974) and *The Final Days* (1976).

Bern·stein[2], Leonard (1918–90), U.S. composer, conductor, and pianist. He was a conductor with the New York Philharmonic Orchestra 1945–48 and 1957–69. Notable works: *The Age of Anxiety* (symphony, 1947–49), *West Side Story* (musical, 1957), and music for the movie *On the Waterfront* (1954).

Ber·ra /'berə/, Yogi (1925–), U.S. baseball player; born *Lawrence Peter Berra*. He was especially noted as a catcher with the New York Yankees, setting the record for the most home runs (313) by a catcher in the American League. He became known for his pithy sayings, such as "You can't think and hit at the same time." Baseball Hall of Fame (1972).

ber·ried /'berēd/ ▸*adj.* **1** bearing or covered with berries. **2** like a berry or berries, as in flavor or shape. **3** (of crustaceans or fish) bearing eggs.

Ber·ry /'berē/, Chuck (1931–), U.S. rock-and-roll singer, guitarist, and songwriter; born *Charles Edward Berry*. One of the first great rock-and-roll stars, his recording career was interruped by a period of imprisonment 1962–64. Notable songs: Maybelline" (1955), "Johnny B Goode" (1958), and "My Ding A Ling" (1972).

Chuck Berry

ber·ry /'berē/ ▸*n.* (*pl.* **-ries**) a small roundish juicy fruit without a stone: *juniper berries* | [as *adj.*] *berry clusters.* ■ *Botany* any fruit that has its seeds enclosed in a fleshy pulp, for example, a banana or tomato. ■ any of various kernels or seeds, such as the coffee bean. ■ a fish egg or the roe of a lobster or similar creature. ▷Old English *berie*, of Germanic origin; related to Dutch *bes* and German *Beere*.

ber·ry·ing /'berēiNG/ ▸*n.* the activity of gathering berries: *let's go berrying.*

Ber·ry·man /'berēmən/, John (1914–72), U.S. poet and educator. His notable works include the Pulitzer Prize-winning *77 Dream Songs* (1964).

ber·seem clo·ver /bər'sēm/ ▸*n.* a white-flowered clover. Native to Egypt and Syria, it is an established forage plant in the southern U.S. Also called EGYPTIAN CLOVER. • *Trifolium alexandrinum*, family Leguminosae.

ber·serk /bər'zərk; -'sərk/ ▸*adj.* (of a person or animal) out of control with anger or excitement; wild or frenzied: *after she left him, he* **went berserk***, throwing things about the apartment.* ■ (of a mechanical device or system) operating in a wild or erratic way; out of control: *the climate control went berserk and either roasted or froze us.* ■ (of a procedure, program, or activity) fluctuating wildly: *the stock market's gone berserk, with sugar at 15.27 cents a pound.* ▷early 19th cent. (originally as a noun denoting a wild Norse warrior who fought with frenzy): from Old Norse *berserkr* (noun), probably from *birn-*, *bjǫrn* (see BEAR[2]) + *serkr* 'coat,'

Leonard Bernstein

Pronunciation Key ə *ago*; ər *over*; 'ə or ,ə *up*; 'ər or ,ər *fur*; a *hat*; ā *rate*; ä *car*; CH *chew*; e *let*; ē *see*; e(ə)r *air*; i *fit*; ī *by*; i(ə)r *ear*; NG *sing*; ō *go*; ô *for*; oi *boy*; ŏŏ *good*; ōō *goo*; ou *out*; SH *she*; TH *thin*; TH *then*; (h)w *why*; ZH *vision*

but also possibly from *berr* 'bare' (i.e., without armor).

ber·serk·er /bər'zərkər; -'sər-/ ▶*n.* an ancient Norse warrior who fought in a wild frenzy.

berth /bərTH/ ▶*n.* **1** a ship's allotted place at a wharf or dock. **2** a fixed bed or bunk on a ship, train, or other means of transport. **3** *informal* (often in a sports context) a situation or position in an organization or event: *today's victory clinched a berth for the Orioles in the playoffs.*
▶*v.* [*trans.*] **1** moor (a ship) in its allotted place: *these modern ships can almost berth themselves.* ■ [*intrans.*] (of a ship) dock: *the Dutch freighter berthed at the Brooklyn docks.* **2** (of a passenger ship) provide a sleeping place for (someone). ▷early 17th cent. (in the sense 'adequate sea room'): probably from a nautical use of BEAR[1] + -TH[2].
▶*PHRASE* □ **give a wide berth** steer (a ship) well clear of something while passing it: *ships are advised to give a wide berth to the Outer Banks.* ■ *figurative* stay away from someone or something: *I'd sworn to give women a wide berth.*

ber·tha /'bərTHə/ ▶*n. chiefly historical* a deep collar, typically made of lace, attached to the top of a dress that has a low neckline. ▷mid 19th cent.: from the given name *Bertha.*

berth·ing /'bərTHiNG/ ▶*n.* **1** the action of mooring a ship: *as soon as the berthing was complete, they went ashore.* **2** mooring position; accommodation in berths: *there were more than 12 miles of berthing.*

Ber·til·lon /'bərtl,än; ,bertē'yôN/, Alphonse (1853–1914), French criminologist. He devised a system of body measurements (the **Bertillon system**) for the identification of criminals, which was widely used until superseded by the technique of finger printing at the beginning of the 20th century.

Ber·to·luc·ci /,bertl'ōōCHē/, Bernardo (1940–), Italian movie director. Notable works: *The Spider's Stratagem* (1970), *Last Tango in Paris* (1972), *The Last Emperor* (Academy Award, 1988), and *The Dreamers* (2003).

Ber·wyn /'bər,win/ a city in northeastern Illinois, west of Chicago; pop. 45,426.

ber·yl /'berəl/ ▶*n.* a transparent pale green, blue, or yellow mineral consisting of a silicate of beryllium and aluminum, sometimes used as a gemstone. ▷Middle English: from Old French *beril*, via Latin from Greek *bērullos.*

be·ryl·li·o·sis /bə,rilē'ōsis/ ▶*n. Medicine* poisoning by beryllium or beryllium compounds, esp. by inhalation causing fibrosis of the lungs.

be·ryl·li·um /bə'rilēəm/ ▶*n.* the chemical element of atomic number 4, a hard gray metal. (Symbol: **Be**)

Beryllium is the lightest of the alkaline earth metals, and its chief source is the mineral beryl. It is used in the manufacture of light corrosion-resistant alloys and in windows in X-ray equipment.

Ber·ze·li·us /bər'zālēəs; -'zē-/, Jöns Jakob (1779–1848), Swedish analytical chemist. He determined the atomic weights of many elements and discovered cerium, selenium, and thorium.

Bes /bes/ *Egyptian Mythology* a grotesque god depicted as having short legs, an obese body, and an almost bestial face, who dispelled evil spirits.

Be·san·çon /bəzäN'sôN/ a city in northeastern France; pop. 119,200.

Besch·loss /'besHlôs/, Michael (1955–), U.S. historian and writer. Among his books on the twentieth-century presidency are *Mayday: Eisenhower, Khrushchev, and the U-2 Affair* (1986), *The Crisis Years: Kennedy and Khrushchev, 1960–1963* (1991), and *The Conquerors: Roosevelt, Truman, and the Destruction of Hitler's Germany, 1941–1945* (2002). He is a commentator on PBS and ABC.

be·seech /bi'sēCH/ ▶*v.* (*past* **-sought** /-'sôt/ or **-seeched**) [*reporting verb*] *formal* or *literary* ask (someone) urgently and fervently to do something; implore; entreat: [*trans.*] *they beseeched him to stay* | [*trans.*] *"You have got to believe me," Gloria beseeched him* | [*trans.*] *they earnestly beseeched his forgiveness* | [as *adj.*] (**beseeching**) *a beseeching gaze.* See note at BEG. ▷Middle English: from BE- (as an intensifier) + Old English *sēcan* (see SEEK). **—be·seech·ing·ly** *adv.*

be·seem /bi'sēm/ ▶*v.* [*trans.*] *archaic* seem; befit.

be·set /bi'set/ ▶*v.* (**-set·ting**; *past* and *past part.* **-set**) [*trans.*] **1** (of a problem or difficulty) trouble or threaten persistently: *the social problems that beset the inner city* | *she was* **beset with** *self-doubt* | [as *adj.*] *poverty is a besetting problem.* ■ surround and harass; assail on all sides: *I was beset by clouds of flies.* See note at ATTACK. ■ hem in; enclose: *the ship was beset by ice.* **2** (**be beset with**) *archaic* be covered or studded with: *blades of grass beset with glistening drops of dew.* ▷Old English *besettan*, from BE- 'around' + *settan* (see SET[1]).

be·shrew /bi'SHrōō/ ▶*v.* [*trans.*] *archaic* **1** make wicked; deprave. **2** invoke evil upon; curse; blame for a misfortune.

be·side /bi'sīd/ ▶*prep.* **1** at the side of; next to: *he sat beside me in the front seat* | *on the table beside the bed.* ■ compared with: *beside Beth's idealism, my priorities looked shabby.* **2** in addition to; apart from: *he commissioned work from other artists beside Rivera.* ▷Old English *be sīdan* (adverb) 'by the side' (see BY, SIDE).
▶*PHRASES* □ **beside oneself** overcome with worry or anger; distraught: *she was* **beside herself with** *anguish.* □ **beside the point** see POINT.

USAGE It is sometimes said that **beside** should not be used to mean 'apart from' and that **besides** should be used instead (*he commissioned work from other artists* **besides** *Minton* rather than *he commissioned work from other artists* **beside** *Minton*). Although there is little logical basis for such a view, and in standard English both **beside** and **besides** are used for this sense, it is worth being aware of the potential ambiguity in the use of **beside**: ***beside*** *the cold meat, there are platters of trout and salmon* means either 'the cold meat is next to the trout and salmon' or 'apart from the cold meat, there are also trout and salmon'. **Beside** is the word to use in the phrases **beside the point** and **beside oneself.**

be·sides /bi'sīdz/ ▶*prep.* in addition to; apart from: *I have no other family besides my parents* | *besides being a player, he was my friend.*
▶*adv.* in addition; as well: *I'm capable of doing the work, and a lot more besides.* ■ moreover; anyway: *I had no time to warn you. Besides, I wasn't sure.*

USAGE See **usage** at BESIDE.

be·siege /bi'sēj/ ▶*v.* [*trans.*] surround (a place) with armed forces in order to capture it or force its surrender; lay siege to: *the guerrillas continued to besiege other major cities to the north* | [as *adj.*] (**besieged**) *the besieged city.* See note at ATTACK. ■ crowd around oppressively; surround and harass: *she spent the whole day besieged by newsmen.* ■ (**be besieged**) be inundated by large numbers of requests or complaints: *the television station was* **besieged with** *calls.* ▷Middle English: alteration (by change of prefix) of *assiege*, from Old French *asegier.* **—be·sieg·er** *n.*

be·smear /bi'smi(ə)r/ ▶*v.* [*trans.*] *poetic/literary* smear or cover with a greasy or sticky substance. ▷Old English *bismierwan* (see BE-, SMEAR).

be·smirch /bi'smərCH/ ▶*v.* [*trans.*] damage the reputation of (someone or something) in the opinion of others: *he had besmirched the good name of his family.* ■ *poetic/literary* make (something) dirty or discolored: *the ground was besmirched with blood.* ▷from BE- + SMIRCH.

be·som /'bēzəm/ ▶*n.* a broom made of twigs tied around a stick. ▷Old English *besema*; related to Dutch *bezem* and German *Besen.*

besom

be·sot·ted /bi'sätid/ ▶*adj.* **1** strongly infatuated: *he became* **besotted with** *his best friend's sister.* **2** *archaic* intoxicated; drunk. ▷late 16th cent.: past participle of *besot* 'make foolishly affectionate,' from BE- 'cause to be' + SOT.

be·sought /bi'sôt/ ▶ past and past participle of BESEECH.

be·spat·ter /bi'spatər/ ▶*v.* [*trans.*] splash small drops of a liquid substance all over (an object or surface): *his shoes were* **bespattered with** *mud.*

be·speak /bi'spēk/ ▶*v.* (*past* **-spoke**; *past part.* **-spoken**) [*trans.*] **1** (of an appearance or action) suggest; be evidence of: *the attractive tree-lined road bespoke money.* **2** order or reserve (something) in advance: *obtaining the affidavits that it has been necessary to bespeak.* **3** *archaic* speak to: *and in disgrace bespoke him thus.* ▷Old English *bisprecan* 'speak up, speak out' (see BE-, SPEAK), later 'discuss, decide on,' hence 'arrange, order' (sense 2, late 16th cent.).

be·spec·ta·cled /bi'spektəkəld/ ▶*adj.* (of a person) wearing eyeglasses: *a bespectacled, studious youth.*

be·spoke /bi'spōk/ ▶ past of BESPEAK.
▶*adj.* [*attrib.*] *chiefly Brit.* (of goods, esp. clothing) made to order: *a bespoke suit.* ■ (of a trader) making such goods: *bespoke tailors.*

be·spo·ken /bi'spōkən/ ▶ past participle of BESPEAK.

be·sprent /bi'sprent/ ▶*adj.* [*archaic*] sprinkled.

be·sprin·kle /bi'spriNGkəl/ ▶*v.* [*trans.*] *poetic/literary* sprinkle all over with small drops or amounts of a substance: *their lips were* **besprinkled with** *flakes of pastry.*

Bes·sa·ra·bi·a /,besə'rābēə/ a region in eastern Europe between the Dniester and Prut rivers. It was part of Romania 1918–40, but now lies in Moldova and Ukraine. **—Bes·sa·ra·bi·an** *adj.* & *n.*

Bes·sel /'besəl/, Friedrich Wilhelm (1784–1846), German astronomer and mathematician. He determined the positions of about 75,000 stars, obtained accurate measurements of stellar distances, and, following a study of the orbit of Uranus, predicted the existence of an eighth planet.

Bes·se·mer[1] /'besəmər/ a city in north central Alabama, a steel and industrial center southwest of Birmingham; pop. 29,672.

Bes·se·mer[2], Sir Henry (1813–98), English engineer and inventor. By 1860 he had developed the Bessemer process, the first successful method of making steel in quantity at low cost.

Bes·se·mer proc·ess ▶*n.* a steelmaking process, now largely superseded, in which carbon, silicon, and other impurities are removed from molten pig-iron by oxidation in a blast of air in a special tilting retort (a **Bessemer converter**).

Best /best/, Charles Herbert (1899–1978), Canadian physiologist; born in the U.S. He assisted F. G. Banting in research leading to the discovery of insulin in 1922.

best /best/ superlative of GOOD. ▶*adj.* of the most excellent, effective, or desirable type or quality: *the best pitcher in the league* | *how to obtain the best results from your machine* | *her best black suit.* ■ most enjoyable: *some of the best times of my life.* ■ most appropriate, advantageous, or well advised: *do whatever you think best* | *it's best if we both go.*
▶*adv.* superlative of WELL[1]. ■ to the highest degree; most: *the one we liked best* | *you knew him best* | *well-drained soil suits it best.* ■ most excellently or effectively: *the best-dressed man in Hollywood* | *the things we do best.* ■ most suitably, appropriately, or usefully: *this is best done at home* | *jokes are best avoided in essays.*
▶*n.* (usu. **the best**) that which is the most excellent, outstanding, or desirable: *buy the best you can afford* | *Sarah always had to be* **the best at** *everything* | *a theory embodying the best of both socialism and capitalism.* ■ the most meritorious aspect of a thing or person: *he* **brought out the best in** *people.* ■ (**one's best**) the peak of condition; the highest standard or level that a person or thing can reach: *this is jazz* **at its best** | *try to* **look your best.** ■ (**one's best**) one's finest or most formal clothes: *she dressed in her best.* ■ (in sports) a record of a specified kind, esp. a personal one: *achieving a lifetime best of 12.0 seconds* | **a personal best.**
▶*v.* [*trans.*] *informal* outwit or get the better of (someone): *she refused to allow herself to be bested.* ▷Old English *betest* (adjective), *betost, betst* (adverb), of Germanic origin; related to Dutch and German *best*, also to BETTER[1].
▶*PHRASES* □ **all the best** said or written to wish a person well on ending a letter or parting. □ **as best one can** (or **may**) as effectively as possible under the circumstances: *I went about my job as best I could.* □ **at best** taking the most optimistic or favorable view: *signs of recovery are patchy at best.* □ **at** (or **in**) **the best of times** even in the most favorable circumstances: *his memory is poor at the best of times.* □ **be best friends** be mutually closest friends: *he's* **best friends with** *Eddie.* □ **be for** (or **all for**) **the best** be desirable in the end, although not at first seeming so. □ **one's best friend** one's closest or favorite friend. □ **the best of friends** very good friends. □ **the best of three** (or **five**, etc.) victory achieved by winning the majority of a specified (usually odd) number of games. □ **the best part of** most of: *it took them the best part of 10 years.* □ **best wishes** an expression of hope for someone's future happiness or welfare: *we sent our* **best wishes for** *a speedy recovery.* ■ written at the end of a letter: *Best wishes, Celia.* □ **one's best years** the most vigorous and productive period of one's life; one's prime: *he had spent* **the best years of his life** *working at the stables.* □ **do** (or **try**) **one's best** do all one can: *Ruth* **did her best to** *reassure her.* □ **get the best of** overcome (someone): *his drinking got the best of him and he was fired.* □ **had best do something** find it most sensible or well advised to do the thing mentioned: *I'd best be going.* □ **make the best of** derive

what limited advantage one can from (something unsatisfactory or unwelcome): *you'll just have to make the best of the situation.* ■ use (resources) as well as possible: *he tried to make the best of his talents.* □ **to the best of one's ability** (or **knowledge**) as far as one can do or know: *the text is free of factual errors, to the best of my knowledge.* □ **with the best of them** as well or as much as anyone: *he'll be out there dancing with the best of them.*

USAGE On the punctuation of **best** in compound adjectives, see **usage** at WELL[1].

best ball ▸*n. Golf* the better score at a hole of two or more players competing as a team: [as *adj.*] *a best-ball match.*

best boy ▸*n.* the assistant to the chief electrician of a movie crew.

bes·tial /ˈbēsCHəl; ˈbes-/ ▸*adj.* of or like an animal or animals: *Darwin's revelations about our bestial beginnings.* ■ savagely cruel and depraved: *bestial and barbaric acts.* ▷late Middle English: via Old French from late Latin *bestialis*, from Latin *bestia* 'beast.' —**bes·tial·ly** *adv.*

bes·ti·al·i·ty /ˌbēsCHēˈalitē; ˌbes-/ ▸*n.* **1** savagely cruel or depraved behavior: *there seems no end to the bestiality of human beings.* **2** sexual intercourse between a person and an animal. ▷late Middle English: from Old French *bestialite*, from *bestial* (see BESTIAL).

bes·ti·ar·y /ˈbēsCHēˌerē; ˈbes-/ ▸*n.* (*pl.* **-ar·ies**) a descriptive or anecdotal treatise on various real or mythical kinds of animals, esp. a medieval work with a moralizing tone. ▷mid 19th cent.: from medieval Latin *bestiarium*, from Latin *bestia* 'beast.'

be·stir /biˈstər/ ▸*v.* (**-stirred, -stir·ring**) (**bestir oneself**) make a physical or mental effort; exert or rouse oneself: *they rarely bestir themselves except in the most pressing of circumstances.*

best man ▸*n.* [in *sing.*] a male friend or relative chosen by a bridegroom to assist him at his wedding.

best-of /ˈbest ˌəv; əv/ ▸*n.* a list or collection comprising the best examples of something: *foodies have flocked like sheep to this critic's best-ofs.* ▸*adj.* denoting such a collection or list.

be·stow /biˈstō/ ▸*v.* [*trans.*] confer or present (an honor, right, or gift): *the office was **bestowed on** him by the chief of state* | *thank you for this honor that you have **bestowed upon** me* | *figurative she bestowed her nicest smile on Jim.* See note at GIVE. ▷Middle English *bistowen* (in the sense 'use for, devote to'): from BE- (as an intensifier) + *stowen* 'to place', from Old English *stōw* 'place.' —**be·stow·al** /-əl/ *n.*

be·strew /biˈstro͞o/ ▸*v.* (*past part.* **-strewed** or **-strewn**) [*trans.*] *poetic/literary* cover or partly cover (a surface) with scattered objects: *the bride's train was **bestrewn with** rose petals.* ■ (of objects) lie scattered over (a surface): *sweeping away the sand and rubbish that bestrewed it.* ▷Old English *bestrēowian* (see BE-, STREW).

be·stride /biˈstrīd/ ▸*v.* (*past* **-strode**; *past part.* **-strid·den**) [*trans.*] stand astride over; span or straddle: *figurative creatures that bestride the dividing line between amphibians and reptiles.* ■ sit astride on: *he bestrode his horse with the easy grace of a born horseman.* ▷Old English *bestrīdan* (see BE-, STRIDE).

best sell·er ▸*n.* a book or other product that sells in very large numbers: *her autobiography is an international best seller.*

best-sell·ing ▸*adj.* [*attrib.*] (of a book or other product) having very large sales; very popular: *a best-selling novel.*

be·suit·ed /biˈso͞otid/ ▸*adj.* (of a person, esp. a man) wearing a suit: *the personification of Bloated Washington, heaving his besuited bulk from stump to stump.*

bet /bet/ ▸*v.* (**bet·ting**; *past* **bet** or **bet·ted**) **1** [*intrans.*] risk something, usually a sum of money, against someone else's on the basis of the outcome of a future event, such as the result of a race or game: ***betting on** horses* | [with *clause*] *I would be prepared to bet that what he really wanted was to settle down* | [*trans.*] *most people would **bet** their life savings **on** this prospect.* ■ [*trans.*] risk a sum of money against (someone) on the outcome or happening of a future event: [with *two objs.*] *I'll bet you $15 you won't find a single scratch.* **2** [with *clause*] *informal* feel sure: ***I bet** this place is really spooky late at night* | *he'll be surprised to see me, **I'll bet.*** ▸*n.* an act of risking a sum of money in this way: *every Saturday she had **a bet on** the horses.* ■ a sum of money staked in this way: *the bookies are taking bets on his possible successor.* ■ [with *adj.*] *informal* a candidate or course of action to choose; an option: ***your best bet** is to call a professional exterminator.* ■ (**one's bet**) *informal* an opinion, typically one formed quickly or spontaneously: *my bet is that the president will veto the bill.* ▷late 16th cent.: perhaps a shortening of the obsolete noun *abet* 'abetment.' ▸*PHRASES* □ **all bets are off** *informal* the outcome of a situation is unpredictable. □ **don't** (or **I wouldn't**) **bet on it** *informal* used to express doubt about an assertion or situation: *he may be a suitable companion—but don't bet on it.* □ **want to** (or **wanna**) **bet?** *informal* used to express vigorous disagreement with a confident assertion: *"You can't be with me every moment." "Want to bet?"* □ **you bet** *informal* you may be sure; certainly: *"Would you like this piece of pie?" "You bet!"*

bet. ▸*abbr.* between.

be·ta /ˈbātə/ ▸*n.* the second letter of the Greek alphabet (**Β, β**), transliterated as 'b.' ■ [as *adj.*] denoting the second of a series of items, categories, forms of a chemical compound, etc.: *beta carotene* | *beta blocker.* ■ *informal* short for BETA TEST: *their database system is currently **in beta*** | [as *adj.*] *a beta version.* ■ (**Beta**) [followed by Latin genitive] the second (usually second-brightest) star in a constellation: *Beta Virginis.* ■ [as *adj.*] relating to beta decay or beta particles: *beta emitters.*

be·ta-ad·ren·er·gic ▸*adj.* of, relating to, or affecting beta receptors: *sympathetic nerves that stimulate beta-adrenergic receptors.*

be·ta block·er ▸*n.* any of a class of drugs that prevent the stimulation of the adrenergic receptors responsible for increased cardiac action. Beta blockers are used to control heart rhythm, treat angina, and reduce high blood pressure.

Be·ta·cam /ˈbātəˌkam/ ▸*n. trademark* a high quality format for video cameras and recorders. ■ a camera using this format.

be·ta·car·o·tene /ˌbātəˈkarəˌtēn/ (also **be·ta-car·o·tene**) ▸*n.* see CAROTENE.

be·ta cell ▸*n.* any of the insulin-producing cells in the islets of Langerhans.

be·ta de·cay ▸*n.* radioactive decay in which an electron is emitted.

be·ta en·dor·phin ▸*n.* an endorphin produced in the pituitary gland that is a powerful pain suppressor.

be·ta glob·u·lin ▸*n.* see GLOBULIN.

be·ta·ine /ˈbētəˌēn/ ▸*n. Chemistry* a crystalline compound with basic properties found in many plant juices. • Chem. formula: $(CH_3)_3N^+{-}CH_2CO_2^-$. ■ any zwitterionic compound of the same type. ▷mid 19th cent.: formed irregularly from Latin *beta* 'beet' (because originally isolated from sugar beet) + -INE[4].

be·take /biˈtāk/ ▸*v.* (*past* **-took**; *past part.* **-tak·en**) [*trans.*] (**betake oneself to**) *poetic/literary* go to: *I shall betake myself to my room.*

Be·ta·max /ˈbātəˌmaks/ ▸*n. trademark* a format for video recorders, now largely obsolete.

be·ta par·ti·cle (also **beta ray**) ▸*n. Physics* a fast-moving electron emitted by radioactive decay of substances. (The emission of beta particles was originally regarded as a ray.)

be·ta re·cep·tor ▸*n.* an adrenergic receptor in the sympathetic nervous system, stimulation of which results esp. in increased cardiac activity.

be·ta rhythm ▸*n. Physiology* the normal electrical activity of the brain when conscious and alert, consisting of oscillations (**beta waves**) with a frequency of 18 to 25 hertz.

be·ta test ▸*n.* a trial of machinery, software, or other products, in the final stages of its development, carried out by a party unconnected with its development. ▸*v.* (**be·ta-test**) [*trans.*] subject (a product) to such a test.

be·ta·tron /ˈbātəˌträn/ ▸*n. Physics* an apparatus for accelerating electrons in a circular path by magnetic induction. ▷1940s: from BETA + -TRON.

bet·cha /ˈbeCHə/ ▸*v.* a nonstandard contraction of "bet you," used in representing informal speech: *betcha can't find a better apartment.*

be·tel /ˈbētl/ ▸*n.* **1** the leaf of an Asian evergreen climbing plant that is used in the East as a mild stimulant. Parings of areca nut, lime, and cinnamon are wrapped in the leaf, which is then chewed, causing the saliva to go red and, with prolonged use, the teeth to go black. **2** the plant, related to pepper, from which these leaves are taken. • *Piper betle*, family Piperaceae. ▷mid 16th cent.: via Portuguese from Malayalam *verrila*.

Be·tel·geuse /ˈbētlˌjo͞os; ˈbetl-; -ˌjo͞oz/ (also **Be·tel·geux**) *Astronomy* the tenth brightest star in the sky, in the constellation Orion. It is a red supergiant, and variations in its brightness are associated with pulsations in its outer envelope. ▷French, alteration of Arabic *yad al-jauzā* 'hand of the giant' (the giant being Orion).

be·tel nut ▸*n.* another term for ARECA NUT. ▷Portuguese *betel*.

be·tel palm ▸*n.* another term for ARECA.

bête noire /ˌbāt ˈnwär; ˌbet/ ▸*n.* (*pl.* **bêtes noires** *pronunc.* same or /ˈnwärz/) a person or thing that one particularly dislikes: *great-uncle Edward was my father's bête noire.* ▷mid 19th cent.: French, literally 'black beast.'

beth /bās; bāt; bet/ ▸*n.* the second letter of the Hebrew alphabet.

Beth·an·y /ˈbeTHənē/ a city in central Oklahoma, west of Oklahoma City; pop. 20,075.

Beth·el /ˈbeTHəl/ a town in the Catskill Mountains, in southeastern New York; pop. 3,693. It is the actual site of the 1969 Woodstock music festival.

beth·el /ˈbeTHəl/ ▸*n.* **1** a holy place. **2** a chapel for seamen. **3** *Brit.* a Nonconformist chapel.

Beth·el Park a borough in southwestern Pennsylvania, south of Pittsburgh; pop. 33,823.

Be·thes·da /bəˈTHezdə/ an affluent unincorporated suburb in central Maryland, north of Washington, DC. It is home to the National Institutes of Health; pop. 62,936.

be·think /biˈTHiNGk/ ▸*v.* (*past* and *past part.* **-thought**) (**bethink oneself**) *formal* or *archaic* think on reflection; come to think: *he **bethought himself of** the verse from the Book of Proverbs* | [with *clause*] *the council bethought itself that this plan would leave room for future expansion.* ▷Old English *bithencan* (see BE-, THINK).

Beth·le·hem /ˈbeTHliˌhem; -lēəm/ **1** a small town 5 miles (8 km) south of Jerusalem, in the West Bank; pop. 14,000. It was the native city of King David and is the reputed birthplace of Jesus. **2** an industrial city in eastern Pennsylvania, on the Lehigh River; pop. 71,329. It is noted for the manufacturing of steel.

Be·thune /bəˈTH(y)o͞on/, Mary McLeod (1875–1955), U.S. educator. In 1904, she founded the Daytona Normal and Industrial Institute for Negro Girls, which, with the Cookman Institute, became Bethune-Cookman College in 1923. Bethune was founder and first president 1935–49 of the National Council of Negro Women.

be·tide /biˈtīd/ ▸*v.* [*intrans.*] *poetic/literary* happen: *I waited with beating heart, as yet not knowing what would betide.* ■ [*trans.*] happen to (someone): *she was trembling with fear lest worse might betide her.* ▷Middle English: from BE- (as an intensifier) + obsolete *tide* 'befall,' from Old English *tīdan* 'happen,' from *tīd* (see TIDE). ▸*PHRASE* □ **woe betide** see WOE.

be·times /biˈtīmz/ ▸*adv. poetic/literary* before the usual or expected time; early: *next morning I was up betimes.* ▷Middle English: from obsolete *betime* (see BY, TIME).

bê·tise /beˈtēz/ ▸*n.* a foolish or ill-timed remark or action. ▷early 19th cent.: French, literally 'stupidity.'

be·to·ken /biˈtōkən/ ▸*v.* [*trans.*] *poetic/literary* be a sign of; indicate: *she wondered if his cold, level gaze betokened indifference or anger.* ■ be a warning or indication of (a future event): *the falling comet betokened the true end of Merlin's powers.* ▷Old English *betācnian*, from BE- (as an intensifier) + *tācnian* 'signify,' of Germanic origin; related to TOKEN.

bet·o·ny /ˈbetn-ē/ ▸*n.* (*pl.* **-nies**) a Eurasian plant of the mint family that bears spikes of showy purple flowers. • *Stachys officinalis*, family Labiatae. ■ used in names of plants that resemble the betony, e.g., **wood betony**. ▷Middle English: from Old French *betoine*, based on Latin *betonica*, perhaps from the name of an Iberian tribe.

be·took /biˈto͝ok/ ▸ past of BETAKE.

be·tray /biˈtrā/ ▸*v.* [*trans.*] be disloyal to: *his friends were shocked when he betrayed them.* ■ be disloyal to (one's country, organization, or ideology) by acting in the interests of an enemy: *he could betray his country for the sake of communism.* ■ treacherously inform an enemy of the existence or location of (a person or organization): *this group was betrayed by an informer.* ■ treacherously reveal (secrets or information): *many of those employed by diplomats betrayed secrets and sold classified documents.* ■ *figurative* reveal the presence of; be evidence of: *she drew a deep breath that betrayed her indignation.* ▷Middle English: from BE- 'thoroughly' + obsolete *tray* 'betray,' from Old French *trair*, based on Latin *tradere* 'hand over.'

Pronunciation Key ə *ago*; ər *over*; ˈə or ˌə *up*; ˈər or ˌər *fur*; a *hat*; ā *rate*; ä *car*; CH *chew*; e *let*; ē *see*; e(ə)r *air*; i *fit*; ī *by*; i(ə)r *ear*; NG *sing*; ō *go*; ô *for*; oi *boy*; o͝o *good*; o͞o *goo*; ou *out*; SH *she*; TH *thin*; TH *then*; (h)w *why*; ZH *vision*

B

Compare with TRAITOR. —**be·tray·al** /-əl/ *n.* —**be·tray·er** *n.*

be·troth /bə'trōT͟H; -'trôTH/ ▸*v.* [*trans.*] (usu. **be betrothed**) *dated* enter into a formal agreement to marry: *soon I shall be* **betrothed to** *Isabel* | [as *n.*] (**betrothed**) *how long have you known your betrothed?* ▷Middle English *betreuthe*: from BE- (expressing transitivity) + TRUTH. The change in the second syllable was due to association with TROTH. —**be·troth·al** /-əl/ *n.*

Bet·tel·heim /'betl,hīm/, Bruno (1903–90), U.S. psychologist; born in Austria. His experiences in Nazi Germany helped him to develop revolutionary theories and therapies for autistic children.

Bet·ten·dorf /'betn,dôrf/ an industrial city in southeastern Iowa, on the Mississippi River; pop. 31,275. It is one of the Quad Cities.

bet·ter[1] /'betər/ ▸*adj.* **1** comparative of GOOD and WELL. ■ of a more excellent or effective type or quality: *hoping for better weather* | *the new facilities were far better* | *I'm* **better at** *algebra than Alice.* ■ more appropriate, advantageous, or well advised: *there couldn't be a better time to start this job* | *it might be better to borrow the money.* **2** [*predic.*] partly or fully recovered from illness or injury: *she's much better today* | *his leg was getting better.* ■ fitter and healthier; less unwell: *we'll feel a lot better after a decent night's sleep.*

▸*adv.* comparative of WELL[1]. ■ more excellently or effectively: *Johnny could do better if he tried* | *instruments are generally better made these days.* ■ to a greater degree; more: *I liked it better when we lived in the country* | *you may find alternatives that suit you better.* ■ more suitably, appropriately, or usefully: *the money could be better spent on more urgent cases.*

▸*n.* **1** the better one; that which is better: *the Natural History Museum book is by far the better of the two* | *a change* **for the better**. **2** (**one's betters**) *chiefly dated* or *humorous* one's superiors in social class or ability: *amusing themselves by imitating their betters.*

▸*v.* [*trans.*] improve on or surpass (an existing or previous level or achievement): *bettering his previous time by ten minutes.* ■ make (something) better; improve: *his ideas for bettering the working conditions.* ■ (**better oneself**) achieve a better social position or status: *the residents are mostly welfare mothers who have bettered themselves.* ■ overcome or defeat (someone): *she bettered him at archery.* ▷Old English *betera* (adjective), of Germanic origin; related to Dutch *beter* and German *besser*, also to BEST.

▸*PHRASES* □ **be better off** be in a better position, esp. in financial terms: *the promotion would make her about $750 a year better off* | [as *plural n.*] (**the better off**) *a paper read mainly by the better off.* □ **the —— the better** used to emphasize the importance or desirability of the quality or thing specified: *the sooner we're off, the better* | *the more people there the better.* □ **the better part of** almost all of; most of: *it is the better part of a mile.* □ **better safe than sorry** *proverb* it's wiser to be cautious than to be hasty or rash and so do something you may later regret. □ **better than** more than: *he'd lived there for better than twenty years.* □ **the better to ——** so as to —— better: *he leaned closer the better to hear her.* □ **for better or (for) worse** whether the outcome is good or bad: *ours, for better or for worse, is the century of youth.* □ **get the better of** (often of something immaterial) win an advantage over (someone); defeat or outwit: *curiosity got the better of her.* □ **go one better** narrowly surpass a previous effort or achievement: *I want to go one better this time and score.* ■ narrowly outdo (another person): *he went one better than Jack by reaching the finals.* □ **had better do something** would find it wiser to do something; ought to do something: *you had better be careful.* □ **have the better of** be more successful in a contest: *she usually had the better of these debates.* □ **no** (or **little**) **better than** just (or almost) the same as; merely: *government officials who were often no better than bandits.*

USAGE 1 In the verb phrase **had** *better do something*, the word **had** acts like an auxiliary verb; in informal spoken contexts, it is often dropped, as in *you* **better** *not come tonight.* In writing, the **had** may be contracted to **'d** (*you'd better call*), but it should not be dropped altogether (not *you better call*).

2 On the punctuation of **better** in compound adjectives, see **usage** at WELL[1].

bet·ter[2] ▸*n.* variant spelling of BETTOR.

bet·ter half ▸*n. informal* a person's wife, husband, or partner.

bet·ter·ment /'betərmənt/ ▸*n.* the act or process of improving something: *they believed that what they were doing was vital for the betterment of society* | [as *adj.*] *working at betterment projects throughout the city.* ■ the enhanced value of real property arising from local improvements: [as *adj.*] *a betterment charge.*

bet·ting /'betiNG/ ▸*n.* the act of gambling money on the outcome of a race, game, or other unpredictable event: *there was a good deal of* **betting on** *the races going on.*

bet·tong /be'tôNG; -'täNG/ ▸*n.* a short-nosed rat kangaroo found in Australia. • Family Potoroidae: two genera, in particular *Bettongia*, and several species. ▷early 19th cent.: from Dharuk.

bet·tor /'betər/ (also **bet·ter**) ▸*n.* a person who bets, typically regularly or habitually.

be·tween /bi'twēn/ (abbr.: **bet.**) ▸*prep.* **1** at, into, or across the space separating (two objects or regions): ■ expressing location: *traffic was at a standstill between exits 12 and 14* | *a rope bridge strung between two cliff ledges* | *the border between Mexico and the U.S.* ■ expressing movement to a point: *the dog crawled between us and lay down at our feet.* ■ expressing movement from one side or point to the other and back again: *traveling by train between London and Paris.* **2** in the period separating (two points in time): *they snack between meals* | *the long, cold nights between autumn and spring.* **3** in the interval separating (two points on a scale): *a man aged between 18 and 30* | *between 25 and 40 percent off children's clothes* | *the difference between income and expenditure.* **4** indicating a connection or relationship involving two or more parties: *the relationship between Pauline and Chris* | *negotiations between Russia, Ukraine, and Romania* | *links between science and industry.* ■ with reference to a collision or conflict: *a collision in midair between two light aircraft above Geneva* | *the wars between Russia and Poland.* ■ with reference to a choice or differentiation involving two or more things being considered together: *if you have to choose between two or three different options.* **5** by combining the resources or actions of (two or more people or other entities): *we have created something between us* | *China and India between them account for a third of the global population.* ■ shared by (two or more people or things): *they had drunk between them a bottle of Chianti.*

▸*adv.* **1** in or along the space separating two objects or regions: *layers of paper with tar* **in between** | *from Leipzig to Dresden, with the gentle Elbe flowing between.* **2** in the period separating two points in time: *sets of exercises with no rest* **in between**. ▷Old English *betwēonum*, from *be* 'by' + a Germanic word related to TWO.

▸*PHRASES* □ **between ourselves** (or **you and me**) in confidence: *just between you and me, I don't think it is going to happen.* □ (**in**) **between times** in the intervals between other actions: *I have seen to the needs of my child, and in between times I have cooked the meals.*

USAGE 1 **Between** is used in speaking of only two things, people, etc.: *we must choose between two equally unattractive alternatives.* **Among** is used for collective and undefined relations of usually three or more: *agreement on landscaping was reached among all the neighbors.* But where there are more than two parties involved, **between** may be used to express one-to-one relationships of pairs within the group or the sense 'shared by': *there is close friendship between the members of the club; diplomatic relations between the U.S., Canada, and Mexico.*

2 *Between you and I, between you and he*, etc., are incorrect; **between** should be followed only by the objective case: *between you and me, between you and him*, etc. See also **usage** at PERSONAL PRONOUN.

be·twixt /bi'twikst/ ▸*prep.* & *adv.* archaic term for BETWEEN. ▷Old English *betwēox*, from *be* 'by' + a Germanic word related to TWO.

▸*PHRASE* □ **betwixt and between** *informal* neither one thing nor the other.

beurre blanc /'bər 'bläNGk/ ▸*n.* a creamy sauce made with butter, onions or shallots, and vinegar or lemon juice, usually served with seafood dishes. ▷mid 20th cent.: French, literally 'white butter.'

beurre noir /'bər 'nwär/ ▸*n.* French term for BLACK BUTTER.

beurre noi·sette /'bər nwä'zet/ ▸*n.* a sauce of butter cooked until golden or brown, usually flavored with capers, herbs, vinegar, etc. ▷French, literally 'hazelnut butter.'

Beu·then /'boitn/ German name for BYTOM.

BEV ▸*abbr. Linguistics* Black English Vernacular.

BeV ▸ another term for GEV. ▷1940s: from *b*illion (10⁹) *e*lectron*v*olts.

bev·a·tron /'bevə,trän/ ▸*n.* a synchrotron used to accelerate protons to energies in the billion electronvolt range. ▷1940s: from BEV + -TRON.

bev·el /'bevəl/ ▸*n.* a slope from the horizontal or vertical in carpentry and stonework; a sloping surface or edge. ■ (in full **bev·el square**) a tool for marking angles in carpentry and stonework.

▸*v.* (**bev·eled, bev·el·ing** or **bev·elled, bev·el·ling**) [*trans.*] [often as *adj.*] (**beveled**) reduce (a square edge on an object) to a sloping edge: *a beveled mirror.* ▷late 16th cent. (as an adjective in the sense 'oblique'): from an Old French diminutive of *baif* 'open-mouthed,' from *baer* 'to gape' (see BAY[5]).

bev·el gear ▸*n.* a gear working another gear at an angle to it by means of bevel wheels.

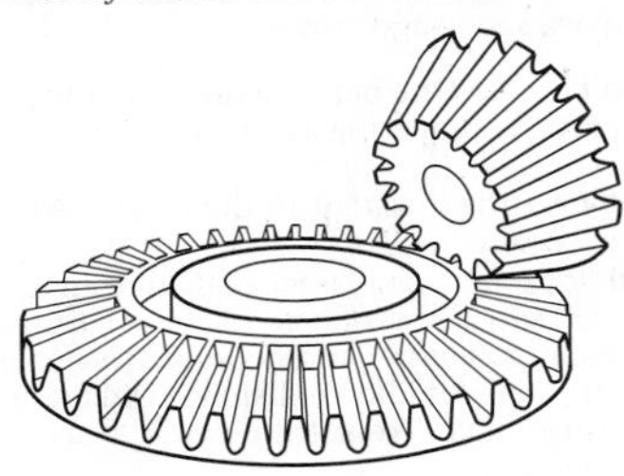

bevel gear

bev·el wheel ▸*n.* a toothed wheel whose working face is oblique to the axis.

bev·er·age /'bev(ə)rij/ ▸*n.* a drink, esp. one other than water. ▷Middle English: from Old French *bevrage*, based on Latin *bibere* 'to drink.'

Bev·er·ly /'bevərlē/ an industrial and resort city in northeastern Massachusetts; pop. 38,195.

Bev·er·ly Hills a largely residential city in California, on the northwestern side of the Los Angeles conurbation; pop. 31,970. It is known as the home of many movie stars.

Bev·in /'bevən/, Ernest (1881–1951), British statesman and trade unionist. As foreign secretary 1945–51, he helped to establish NATO 1949.

bev·y /'bevē/ ▸*n.* (*pl.* **bev·ies**) a large group of people or things of a particular kind: *he was surrounded by* **a bevy of** *beautiful girls.* ■ a group of birds, particularly when closely gathered on the ground: *a bevy of quail stayed through winter, feeding on our locust beans.* ▷late Middle English: of unknown origin.

be·wail /bi'wāl/ ▸*v.* [*trans.*] express great regret, disappointment, or bitterness over (something) by complaining about it to others: *he bewailed the fact that heart trouble had slowed him down.* ■ cry or wail loudly about (something).

be·ware /bi'we(ə)r/ ▸*v.* [*intrans.*] [in *imperative* or *infinitive*] be cautious and alert to the dangers of: *consumers were warned to* **beware of** *faulty packaging* | *Beware! Dangerous submerged rocks ahead* | [*trans.*] *we should beware the incompetence of legislators.* ▷Middle English: from the phrase *be ware* (see BE-, WARE[2]).

be·whisk·ered /bi'(h)wiskərd/ ▸*adj.* having hair or whiskers growing on the face.

be·wigged /bi'wigd/ ▸*adj.* (of a person) wearing a wig.

be·wil·der /bi'wildər/ ▸*v.* [*trans.*] [often as *adj.*] (**bewildered**) cause (someone) to become perplexed and confused: *she seemed frightened and bewildered* | *his reaction had bewildered her* | [as *adj.*] (**bewildering**) *there is a bewildering array of desserts to choose from.* ▷late 17th cent.: from BE- 'thoroughly' + obsolete *wilder* 'lead or go astray,' of unknown origin. —**be·wil·dered·ly** *adv.* —**be·wil·der·ing·ly** *adv.* —**be·wil·der·ment** *n.*

be·witch /bi'wiCH/ ▸*v.* [*trans.*] (often **be bewitched**) cast a spell on and gain control over (someone) by magic: *his relatives were firmly convinced that he was bewitched.* ■ enchant and delight (someone): *they both were bewitched by the country and its culture* | [as *adj.*] (**bewitching**) *she was certainly a bewitching woman.* ▷Middle English: from BE- 'thoroughly' + WITCH. —**be·witch·ing·ly** *adv.* —**be·witch·ment** *n.*

bey /bā/ ▸*n.* (*pl.* **beys**) *historical* the governor of a district or province in the Ottoman Empire. ■ formerly used in Turkey and Egypt as a courtesy title. ▷Turkish, modern form of *beg* 'prince, governor.'

be·yond /bē'änd; bi'yänd/ ▸*prep.* & *adv.* **1** at or to the further side of: [as *prep.*] *he pointed to a spot beyond the trees* | *passengers traveling to destinations beyond Boston* | [as *adv.*] *there was the terminal and, beyond, an endless line of warehouses.* ■ [*prep.*] outside the physical limits or range of: *the land sloped away until far beyond sight it reached the Great Plains.* ■ *figurative* more extensive or extreme than; further-reaching than: [as *prep.*] *what these children go through is* **far beyond** *what most adults endure in a lifetime.* | [as *adv.*] *pushing the laws to their* **limits and beyond**. **2** happening or continuing after (a specified time or event): [as *prep.*] *we can manage another two years, but beyond that the system is not viable*

| [as *adv.*] *music going on into the night* ***and beyond.*** **3** having progressed or achieved more than (a specified stage or level): [as *prep.*] *we need to get beyond square one.* ■ above or greater than (a specified amount): [as *prep.*] *the absenteeism had gone beyond 15%* | [as *adv.*] *he could count up to a billion now,* ***and beyond.*** **4** [*prep.*] to a degree or condition where a specified action is impossible: *the landscape has changed beyond recognition.* ■ too much for (someone) to achieve or understand: *I did something that I thought was beyond me.* **5** [*prep.*] [with *negative*] apart from; except: *beyond telling us that she was well educated, he has nothing to say about her* | *there was little vegetation beyond scrub and brush.*

▸*n.* (**the beyond**) the unknown after death: *messages from the beyond.* ▷Old English *begeondan,* from *be* 'by' + *geondan* of Germanic origin (related to YON and YONDER).

▸*PHRASE* □ **the back of beyond** see BACK.

bez·ant /ˈbezənt/ ▸*n.* **1** *historical* a gold or silver coin originally minted at Byzantium. **2** *Heraldry* a roundel or (i.e., a solid gold circle). ▷Middle English: from Old French *besant,* from Latin *Byzantius* 'Byzantine.' Sense 2 dates from the late 15th cent.

bez·el /ˈbezəl/ ▸*n.* a grooved ring holding the glass or plastic cover of a watch face or other instrument in position. ■ a groove holding the crystal of a watch or the stone of a gem in its setting. ▷late 16th cent.: from Old French, of unknown origin.

be·zique /bəˈzēk/ ▸*n.* a trick-taking card game for two, played with a double pack of 64 cards, including the seven to ace only in each suit. ■ the holding of the queen of spades and the jack of diamonds in this game. ▷mid 19th cent.: from French *bésigue,* perhaps from Persian *bāzīgar* 'juggler' or *bāzī* 'game.'

be·zoar /ˈbēzôr/ ▸*n.* a small stony concretion that may form in the stomachs of certain animals, esp. ruminants, and which was once used as an antidote for various ailments. ▷late 15th cent. (in the general sense 'stone or concretion'): from French *bezoard,* based on Arabic *bāzahr, bādizahr,* from Persian *pādzahr* 'antidote.'

b.f. ▸*abbr.* ■ *Printing* boldface. ■ board foot. ■ (also **b/f** or **B/F**) (in bookkeeping) brought forward.

BG (also **B Gen**) ▸*abbr.* brigadier general.

BGH ▸*abbr.* bovine growth hormone.

B-girl (also **bar girl**) ▸*n.* an attractive woman employed to encourage customers to buy drinks at a bar. ▷mid 20th cent.: alteration of *bar girl.*

Bh ▸*symbol* the chemical element bohrium.

BHA ▸*abbr.* butylated hydroxyanisole.

Bha·ga·vad·gi·ta /ˌbəgəvədˈgētə; ˌbägəväd-/ (also **Gi·ta**) *Hinduism* a poem composed between the 2nd century BC and the 2nd century AD and incorporated into the Mahabharata. Presented as a dialogue between the warrior prince Arjuna and his divine charioteer Krishna, it stresses the importance of doing one's duty and of faith in God.

Bhag·wan /ˌbəgˈwän/ ▸*n. Indian* God. ■ a guru or revered person (often as a proper name or form of address). ▷from Hindi *bhagwān,* from Sanskrit *bhagavān,* from the root *bhaj* 'adore'.

bha·jan /ˈbəjən; ˈbäˌjän/ ▸*n. Hinduism* a devotional song. ▷from Sanskrit *bhajana.*

bhak·ti /ˈbəktē; ˈbäk-/ ▸*n. Hinduism* devotional worship directed to one supreme deity, usually Vishnu (esp. in his incarnations as Rama and Krishna) or Shiva, by whose grace salvation may be attained by all regardless of sex, caste, or class. It is practiced by the majority of Hindus today. ▷Sanskrit.

bhang /bang/ (also **bang**) ▸*n.* the leaves and flower-heads of cannabis, used as a narcotic. ▷from Hindi *bhāṅg.*

bhan·gra /ˈbängGrə/ ▸*n.* a type of popular music combining Punjabi folk traditions with Western pop music. ▷1960s (denoting a traditional folk dance): from Punjabi *bhāṅgrā.*

Bha·rat /ˈbə-rət/ Hindi name for INDIA.

Bhav·na·gar /bouˈnəgər/ an industrial port in northwestern India, in Gujarat, on the Gulf of Cambay; pop. 401,000.

bhik·khu /ˈbikoo/ ▸*n.* a Theravada Buddhist monk. ▷Pali.

bhik·khu·ni /biˈkoonē/ ▸*n. historical* formerly, a member of an order of Theravada Buddhist nuns. ▷Pali.

Bhn (also **BHN**) ▸*abbr.* Brinell hardness number.

Bhoj·pu·ri /ˌbōjˈpoorē/ ▸*n.* a Bihari language spoken in western Bihar and eastern Uttar Pradesh.

Bho·pal /bōˈpäl/ a city in central India, the capital of the state of Madhya Pradesh; pop. 1,604,000. In December 1984, leakage of poisonous gas from a U.S.-owned pesticide factory in the city caused the death of about 2,500 people.

b.h.p. ▸*abbr.* brake horsepower.

BHT ▸*abbr.* butylated hydroxytoluene.

Bhu·ba·nes·war /ˌboovəˈnäsHwər/ a city in eastern India, capital of the state of Orissa; pop. 412,000.

bhu·na /ˈboonə/ (also **bhoo·na**) ▸*n.* a medium-hot, dry curry originating in Bengal, prepared typically by frying meat with spices at a high temperature: *lamb bhuna.* ▷1950s: from Bengali, Urdu *bhunnā* 'to be fried,' ultimately from Sanskrit *bhrajj* 'to fry, parch, roast.'

Bhu·tan /booˈtän; -ˈtan/ a small independent kingdom in southern Asia, on the southeastern slopes of the Himalayas, north of India; pop. 810,000; capital, Thimphu; languages, Dzongkha (official), Nepali. —**Bhu·tan·ese** /ˌbootnˈēz; -ˈēs/ *adj.* & *n.*

A British protectorate from 1910, it became independent in 1949, with continuing help from India regarding its foreign policy and aid.

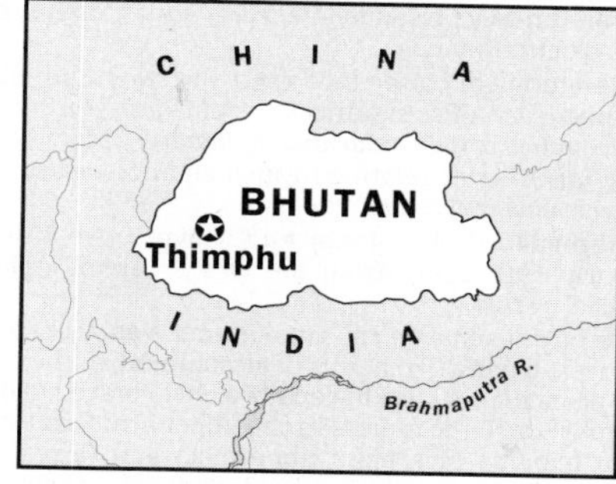

Bhut·to[1] /ˈbootō/, Benazir (1953–), Pakistani stateswoman; prime minister 1988–90 and 1993–96; daughter of Zulfikar Ali Bhutto. She was the first woman prime minister of a Muslim country and brought Pakistan back into the Commonwealth of Nations.

Bhut·to[2], Zulfikar Ali (1928–79), Pakistani statesman; president 1971–73; prime minister 1973–77. He was ousted by a military coup and executed for conspiring to murder a political rival.

BI ▸*abbr.* Block Island.

Bi ▸*symbol* the chemical element bismuth.

bi /bī/ ▸*abbr. informal* bisexual.

bi- (often **bin-** before a vowel) ▸*comb. form* two; having two: *bicolored* | *biathlon* | *binocular.* ■ occurring twice in every one: *biannual* | *bimonthly.* ■ occurring once in every two: *bicentennial* | *biennial.* ■ lasting for two: *biennial* | *biennium.* ■ doubly; in two ways: *biconcave.* ■ *Chemistry* a substance having a double proportion of the radical, group, etc., indicated by the simple word: *bicarbonate* | *binoxalate.* ■ *Botany & Zoology* (of division and subdivision) twice over: *bipinnate.* ▷from Latin, earlier *dui-,* related to Greek *di-* 'two' and Sanskrit *dvi-* 'doubly, having two.'

USAGE On the ambiguity of words like **bimonthly, biweekly,** see **usage** at BIENNIAL, BIMONTHLY.

Bi·a·fra /bēˈafrə; bī-/ a state proclaimed in 1967, when part of eastern Nigeria, inhabited chiefly by the Ibo people, sought independence from the rest of the country. In the ensuing civil war the new state's troops were overwhelmed by numerically superior forces, and by 1970 it had ceased to exist. —**Bi·a·fran** *adj.* & *n.*

bi·a·ly /bēˈälē/ ▸*n.* (*pl.* **-lys**) a flat bread roll topped with chopped onions. ▷mid 20th cent.: from *Białystok,* where the bread originated.

Bia·ły·stok /byäˈwiˌstôk/ an industrial city in northeastern Poland, close to the border with Belarus; pop. 270,568. Russian name BELOSTOK.

bi·an·nu·al /bīˈanyooəl/ ▸*adj.* occurring twice a year: *the biannual meeting of the planning committee.* —**bi·an·nu·al·ly** *adv.*

USAGE See **usage** at BIENNIAL.

Biar·ritz /ˌbēəˈrits; ˈbēəˌrits/ a seaside resort in southwestern France, on the Bay of Biscay; pop. 28,890.

bi·as /ˈbīəs/ ▸*n.* **1** prejudice in favor of or against one thing, person, or group compared with another, usually in a way considered to be unfair: *there was evidence of* ***bias against*** *foreign applicants* | *the* ***bias toward*** *younger people in recruitment* | [in *sing.*] *a systematic* ***bias in favor of*** *the powerful.* ■ [in *sing.*] a concentration on or interest in one particular area or subject: *he worked on a variety of Greek topics, with a discernible bias toward philosophy.* ■ *Statistics* a systematic distortion of a statistical result due to a factor not allowed for in its derivation. **2** an edge cut obliquely across the grain of a fabric. **3** in some sports, such as lawn bowling, the irregular shape given to a ball. ■ the oblique course that such a shape causes a ball to run. **4** *Electronics* a steady voltage, magnetic field, or other factor applied to an electronic system or device to cause it to operate over a predetermined range.

▸*v.* (**bi·ased, bi·as·ing** or **bi·assed, bi·as·sing**) **1** [*trans.*] (usu. **be biased**) show prejudice for or against (someone or something) unfairly: *readers said the paper was* ***biased toward*** *the conservatives* | *the tests were* ***biased against*** *women and minorities* | [as *adj.*] (**biased**) *a biased view of the world.* ■ influence unfairly to invoke favoritism: *her well-rehearsed sob story failed to bias the jury.* **2** give a bias to: *bias the ball.* ▷mid 16th cent. (in the sense 'oblique line'; also as an adjective meaning 'oblique'): from French *biais,* from Provençal, perhaps based on Greek *epikarsios* 'oblique.'

▸*PHRASE* □ **cut on the bias** (of a fabric or garment) cut obliquely or diagonally across the grain.

THE RIGHT WORD **bias, bigotry, intolerance, narrow-mindedness, parochialism, partiality, prejudice, provincialism**

Bias is a predisposition either for or against something; one can have a *bias* against police officers or a *bias* for French food and wines.

Partiality, on the other hand, is a favorable bias (*the partiality of parents for their own children; the partiality of Americans for fast food*), while **prejudice** implies a preconceived and usually negative judgment or opinion (*a decision motivated by racial prejudice*).

Bigotry is an even stronger term, referring to an intense dislike and often violent hatred for the members of a particular race, religion, or ethnic group.

Narrow-mindedness also points to rigidly preconceived ideas, but implies that they are the result of lack of education or understanding, rather than outright hostility (*her parents' narrow-mindedness prevented her from meeting any boys her age*).

Parochialism is another term meaning excessive narrowness of mind (from "parochial," pertaining to a parish or parishes; that is, concerned mainly about local issues), while **provincialism** is narrow-mindedness that results from lack of exposure to cultural or intellectual activity, characteristic of a province or non-urban area.

Intolerance is a broad term used to describe the inability to put up with almost anything (*parents' intolerance of their children's misbehavior*).

bi·as-cut ▸*adj.* (of a garment or fabric) cut obliquely or diagonally across the grain.

bi·as-ply ▸*adj.* (of a tire) having fabric layers with their threads running diagonally, crosswise to each other. Compare with RADIAL (sense 1).

bi·as tape (also **bias binding**) ▸*n.* a narrow strip of fabric cut obliquely and used to bind edges or for decoration.

bi·ath·lon /bīˈaTHlän/ ▸*n.* an athletic contest combining two events, esp. cross-country skiing and rifle shooting. ▷1950s: from BI- 'two' + Greek *athlon* 'contest,' on the pattern of *pentathlon.* —**bi·ath·lete** /-ˌlēt/ *n.*

bi·ax·i·al /bīˈaksēəl/ ▸*adj.* having or relating to two axes. ■ (of crystals) having two optic axes, as in the orthorhombic, monoclinic, and triclinic systems.

bib[1] /bib/ ▸*n.* a piece of cloth or plastic fastened around a person's neck to keep their clothes clean while eating. ■ the part above the waist of the front of an apron or pair of overalls. ■ a loose-fitting, sleeveless garment worn for identification, esp. by competitors and officials at sporting events. ■ a patch of color on the throat of a bird or other animal: *a black bird with a white bib.* ▷late 16th cent.: probably from BIB[2].

▸*PHRASE* □ **one's best bib and tucker** *informal* one's finest clothes.

bib[2] ▸*v.* (**bibbed, bib·bing**) [*trans.*] *archaic* drink (something alcoholic). ▷late Middle English: probably from Latin *bibere* 'to drink.'

Pronunciation Key ə ago; ər over; ˈə or ˌə up; ˈər or ˌər fur; a hat; ā rate; ä car; CH chew; e let; ē see; e(ə)r air; i fit; ī by; i(ə)r ear; NG sing; ō go; ô for; oi boy; oo good; oo goo; ou out; SH she; TH thin; TH then; (h)w why; ZH vision

B

bib·ber /ˈbibər/ ▸*n.* [usu. in *combination*] a person who regularly drinks a particular drink: *a wine-bibber.*

bibb let·tuce /bib/ (also **Bibb**) ▸*n.* a variety of butterhead lettuce that has crisp dark-green leaves. ▷late 19th cent.: named after Jack *Bibb* (1789–1884), the American horticulturalist who developed it.

bib·cock /ˈbib,käk/ ▸*n.* a faucet with a bent nozzle fixed at the end of a pipe. ▷late 18th cent.: perhaps from BIB[1] and COCK[1].

bibcock

bi·be·lot /ˈbib(ə),lō/ ▸*n.* a small, decorative ornament or trinket. ▷late 19th cent.: from French, fanciful formation based on *bel* 'beautiful.'

bibl. (also **Bibl.**) ▸*abbr.* biblical.

Bi·ble /ˈbībəl/ ▸*n.* (**the Bible**) the Christian scriptures, consisting of the 66 books of the Old and New Testaments. ■ (**the Bible**) the Jewish scriptures, consisting of the Torah or Law, the Prophets, and the Hagiographa or Writings. ■ (also **bible**) a copy of the Christian or Jewish scriptures: *clutching a large black Bible under his arm.* ■ a particular edition or translation of the Bible: *the New English Bible.* ■ (**bible**) *informal* any authoritative book: *"Larousse Gastronomique," the bible of French cooking.* ■ the scriptures of any religion. ▷Middle English: via Old French from ecclesiastical Latin *biblia*, from Greek *biblia* 'books,' from *biblion* 'book,' originally a diminutive of *biblos* 'papyrus, scroll,' of Semitic origin.

Bi·ble Belt ▸*n.* (**the Bible Belt**) *informal* those areas of the southern and midwestern U.S. and western Canada where Protestant fundamentalism is widely practiced.

Bi·ble-thump·ing ▸*adj.* [*attrib.*] denoting a person who expounds or follows the teachings of the Bible in an aggressively evangelical way: *a Bible-thumping evangelical Protestant.* —**Bi·ble-thump·er** *n.*

bib·li·cal /ˈbiblikəl/ (also **Bib·li·cal**) (abbr.: **bibl.** or **Bibl.**) ▸*adj.* of, relating to, or contained in the Bible: *the biblical account of creation | biblical times.* ■ resembling the language or style of the Bible: *there is a biblical cadence in the last words he utters.* ■ very great; on a large scale: *they see themselves as victims of almost biblical dimensions.* —**bib·li·cal·ly** /-ik(ə)lē/ *adv.*

bib·li·cist /ˈbibləsist/ ▸*n.* **1** one who is an expert in the Bible. **2** one who interprets the Bible literally. —**bib·li·cism** /-,sizəm/ *n.*

biblio- ▸*comb. form* relating to a book or books: *bibliomania | bibliophile.* ▷from Greek *biblion* 'book.'

bibliog. ▸*abbr.* bibliography.

bib·li·og·ra·phy /,biblēˈägrəfē/ (abbr.: **bibliog.**) ▸*n.* (*pl.* **-phies**) a list of the books referred to in a scholarly work, usually printed as an appendix. ■ a list of the books of a specific author or publisher, or on a specific subject: *a bibliography of his publications.* ■ the history or systematic description of books, their authorship, printing, publication, editions, etc.: *he regarded bibliography as a science.* ■ any book containing such information. ▷early 19th cent.: from French *bibliographie* or modern Latin *bibliographia*, from Greek *biblion* 'book' + *-graphia* 'writing.' —**bib·li·og·ra·pher** /-fər/ *n.* —**bib·li·o·graph·ic** /-lēəˈgrafik/ *adj.* —**bib·li·o·graph·i·cal** /-ˈgrafikəl/ *adj.* —**bib·li·o·graph·i·cal·ly** *adv.*

bib·li·ol·a·try /,biblēˈälətrē/ ▸*n.* **1** an excessive adherence to the literal interpretation of the Bible. **2** an excessive love of books. —**bib·li·ol·at·er** /-ˈälətər/ *n.* —**bib·li·ol·a·trous** /-ˈälətrəs/ *adj.*

bib·li·o·man·cy /ˈbiblēə,mansē/ ▸*n. rare* foretelling the future by interpreting a randomly chosen passage from a book, esp. the Bible.

bib·li·o·ma·ni·a /,biblēəˈmānēə/ ▸*n.* passionate enthusiasm for collecting and possessing books. —**bibli·o·ma·ni·ac** /-nē,ak/ *n.* & *adj.*

bib·li·o·phile /ˈbiblēə,fīl/ ▸*n.* a person who collects or has a great love of books. ▷early 19th cent.: from French, from Greek *biblion* 'book' + *philos* 'loving.' —**bib·li·o·phil·ic** /,biblēəˈfilik/ *adj.* —**bib·li·oph·i·ly** /,biblēˈäfəlē/ *n.*

bib·li·o·pole /ˈbiblēə,pōl/ ▸*n. archaic* a person who buys and sells books, esp. rare ones. ▷late 18th cent.: via Latin from Greek *bibliopōlēs*, from *biblion* 'book' + *pōlēs* 'seller.'

bib·li·o·the·ca /,biblēəˈTHēkə/ ▸*n.* (*pl.* **-cae** /-kē/ or **-cas**) a library. ■ a list of books in a catalog, esp. for use by a bookseller.

bib·li·ot·ics /,biblēˈätiks/ ▸*plural n.* [treated as *sing.*] the study of documents, handwriting, and writing materials to determine authenticity. —**bib·li·ot·ic** *n.* —**bib·li·o·tist** /ˈbiblēətist/ *n.*

bib o·ver·alls ▸*n.* see OVERALLS.

bib·u·lous /ˈbibyələs/ ▸*adj. formal* excessively fond of drinking alcohol. ▷late 17th cent. (in the sense 'absorbent'): from Latin *bibulus* 'freely or readily drinking' (from *bibere* 'to drink') + **-OUS**.

bi·cam·er·al /bīˈkamərəl/ ▸*adj.* (of a legislative body) having two branches or chambers. ▷mid 19th cent.: from **BI-** 'two' + Latin *camera* 'chamber' + **-AL**. —**bi·cam·er·al·ism** /-,lizəm/ *n.*

bi·carb /bīˈkärb/ ▸*n. informal* sodium bicarbonate.

bi·car·bo·nate /bīˈkärbə,nāt; -nit/ ▸*n. Chemistry* a salt containing the anion HCO_3^-. ■ (also **bicarbonate of soda**) sodium bicarbonate.

bice /bīs/ (also **blue bice** or **bice blue**) ▸*n.* a medium blue pigment made from basic copper carbonate. ■ the color of this. ▷Middle English (originally in the sense 'dark or brownish gray'): from Old French *bis* 'dark gray.'

bi·cen·ten·ar·y /,bīsenˈtenərē/ ▸*n.* & *adj.* another term for **BICENTENNIAL**.

bi·cen·ten·ni·al /,bīsenˈtenēəl/ ▸*n.* the two-hundredth anniversary of a significant event: *last year's commemoration of* **the bicentennial of** *Mozart's birth.*
▸*adj.* [*attrib.*] of or relating to such an anniversary: *the bicentennial celebrations.*

bi·ceph·a·lous /bīˈsefələs/ ▸*adj.* having two heads. ▷early 19th cent.: from **BI-** 'two' + Greek *kephalē* 'head' + **-OUS**.

bi·ceps /ˈbī,seps/ ▸*n.* (*pl.* same or **-ceps·es** /-sepsiz/) a muscle having two points of attachment at one end, in particular: ■ (also **bi·ceps bra·chi·i** /ˈbrākē,ī; -kē,ē; ˈbrak-/) the large muscle in the upper arm that turns the hand to face palm uppermost and flexes the arm and forearm: *he clenched his fist and exhibited his bulging biceps.* ■ (also **bi·ceps fem·o·ris** /ˈfemərIs/) *Anatomy* the muscle in the back of the thigh that helps to flex the leg. ▷mid 17th cent.: from Latin, literally 'two-headed,' from *bi-* 'two' + *-ceps* (from *caput* 'head').

bich·ir /ˈbiCHər/ ▸*n.* an elongated African freshwater fish with an armor of hard shiny scales and a series of separate fins along its back. • Genus *Polypterus*, family *Polypteridae*: several species, including *P. senegalus*. ▷1960s: via French from dialect Arabic *abu shīr*.

Bi·chon Fri·sé /ˈbēSHän friˈzā; ˈfrēz; ˈbēSHôN frēˈzā/ (also **Bi·chon Fri·se**) ▸*n.* (*pl.* **Bi·chons Fri·sés** *pronunc.* same) a small sturdy dog of a breed with a curly white coat and a tail that curves over its back.

Bichon Frise

bi·chro·mate /bīˈkrōmāt/ ▸*adj.* another term for **DICHROMATE**.

bi·cip·i·tal /bīˈsipitl/ ▸*adj.* **1** two-headed. **2** of or relating to biceps.

Bick·el /ˈbikəl/, Ernest Frederick McIntyre see **MARCH**[2].

bick·er /ˈbikər/ ▸*v.* [*intrans.*] **1** argue about petty and trivial matters: *whenever the phone rings, they* **bicker over** *who must answer it* | [as *n.*] (**bickering**) *the constant* **bickering between** *Edgar and his mother.* **2** *poetic/literary* (of water) flow or fall with a gentle repetitive noise; patter: *against the glass the rain did beat and bicker.* ■ (of a flame or light) flash, gleam, or flicker: *the restless wheels whose flashing spokes bicker and burn.* ▷Middle English: of unknown origin.

bi·coast·al /bīˈkōstəl/ ▸*adj.* of or relating to two coasts, esp. the east and west coast regions of the U.S.: *a bicoastal custody settlement.* ■ traveling frequently from one coast to the other: *a bicoastal businessman.* ■ located along both the east and west coasts.

bi·col·or /ˈbī,kələr/ ▸*adj.* having two colors: *a male bicolor damselfish.*
▸*n.* a bicolor blossom or animal. —**bi·col·ored** *adj.* & *n.*

bi·con·cave /bīˈkän,kāv; ,bīkänˈkāv/ ▸*adj.* concave on both sides.

bi·con·vex /bīˈkän,veks; ,bīkänˈveks/ ▸*adj.* convex on both sides.

bi·cul·tur·al /bīˈkəlCHərəl/ ▸*adj.* having or combining the cultural attitudes and customs of two nations, peoples, or ethnic groups: *there is too little recognition of the children's bilingual and bicultural status.* —**bi·cul·tur·al·ism** /-,lizəm/ *n.*

bi·cus·pid /bīˈkəspid/ ▸*adj.* having two cusps or points.
▸*n.* a tooth with two cusps, esp. a human premolar tooth. ▷mid 19th cent.: from **BI-** 'two' + Latin *cuspis, cuspid-* 'sharp point.'

bi·cus·pid valve ▸*n. Anatomy* another term for **MITRAL VALVE**.

bi·cy·cle /ˈbīsikəl/ ▸*n.* a vehicle composed of two wheels held in a frame one behind the other, propelled by pedals and steered with handlebars attached to the front wheel.
▸*v.* [*intrans.*] ride a bicycle in a particular direction: *they had spent the day bicycling around the island.* ▷mid 19th cent.: from **BI-** 'two' + Greek *kuklos* 'wheel.' —**bi·cy·clist** /-siklist/ *n.*

bi·cy·cle chain ▸*n.* a chain that transmits the driving power from the pedals of a bicycle to its rear wheel.

bi·cy·cle clip ▸*n.* either of a pair of metal clips worn by cyclists around their ankles to prevent their pants legs from becoming entangled in the bicycle chain.

bi·cy·cle pump ▸*n.* a portable pump for inflating bicycle tires.

bi·cy·cle rick·sha ▸*n.* a three-wheeled bicycle for public hire, with a covered seat for passengers behind the driver.

bi·cy·clic /bīˈsīklik; -ˈsik-/ ▸*adj. Chemistry* having two rings of atoms in its molecule.

bid[1] /bid/ ▸*v.* (**bid·ding**; *past* and *past part.* **bid**) [*trans.*] offer (a certain price) for something, esp. at an auction: *a consortium of dealers bid a world record price for a snuff box | what am I bid?* | [*intrans.*] *guests will* **bid for** *pieces of fine jewelry.* ■ [*intrans.*] (**bid for**) (of a contractor) offer to do (work) for a stated price; tender for: *nineteen companies have indicated their intention to bid for the contract.* ■ [*intrans.*] (**bid for**) make an effort or attempt to achieve: *the two freshmen are bidding for places in the varsity swim team.* ■ *Bridge* make a statement during the auction undertaking to make (a certain number of tricks with a stated suit as trumps) if the bid is successful and one becomes the declarer: *North bids four hearts* | [*intrans.*] *with this hand, South should not bid.*
▸*n.* an offer of a price, esp. at an auction: *several buyers* **made bids for** *the Van Gogh sketches.* ■ an offer to buy the shares of a company in order to gain control of it: *a takeover bid.* ■ an offer to do work or supply goods at a stated price; a tender. ■ an attempt or effort to achieve something: [with *infinitive*] *an investigation would be carried out* **in a bid** *to establish what had happened | she did not hesitate to help him* **make a bid for** *the presidency.* ■ *Bridge* an undertaking by a player in the auction to make a stated number of tricks with a stated suit as trumps. ▷Old English *bēodan* 'to offer, command,' of Germanic origin; related to Dutch *bieden* and German *bieten*. —**bid·der** *n.*

bid[2] ▸*v.* (**bid·ding**; *past* **bid** or **bade** /bad; bād/; *past part.* **bid**) [*trans.*] **1** utter (a greeting or farewell) to: *a chance to bid farewell to their president.* **2** *archaic* or *poetic/literary* command or order (someone) to do something: *I did as he bade me.* ■ invite (someone) to do something: *he bade his companions enter.* ▷Old English *biddan* 'ask,' of Germanic origin; related to German *bitten*.
▸*PHRASE* □ **bid fair to** *archaic* or *poetic/literary* seem likely to: *the girl bade fair to be pretty.*

bi·dar·ka /bīˈdärkə/ ▸*n.* a canoe covered with animal skins, used by the Inuit of Alaska and adjacent regions. ▷early 19th cent.: from Russian *baĭdarka*, diminutive of *baĭdara* 'an umiak.'

bid cal·ler ▸*n.* one who announces the bids and recognizes bidders at an auction.

bid·da·ble /ˈbidəbəl/ ▸*adj.* **1** meekly ready to accept and follow instructions; docile and obedient. See note at **OBEDIENT**. **2** *Bridge* strong enough to justify a bid. —**bid·da·bil·i·ty** /,bidəˈbilitē/ *n.*

Bid·de·ford /ˈbidəfərd/ an industrial city in southwestern Maine; pop. 20,942.

bid·den /ˈbidn/ ▸*archaic* or *poetic.literary* past participle of **BID**[2].

ordinary (or penny-farthing) (1880s)

ladies' safety bicycle (1890s)

mountain bike

racing bike

tandem

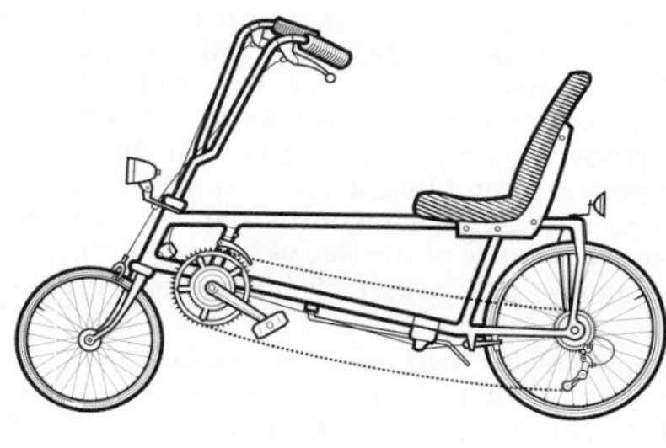
recumbent

bicycles

bid·ding /ˈbidiNG/ ▸*n.* **1** the offering of particular prices for something, esp. at an auction: *their first sale produced a wide range of lots and some energetic bidding | other companies* ***in the bidding*** *include General Electric.* ■ the offers made in such a situation: *from a cautious opener of $30, the bidding soared to $450.* ■ (in bridge and whist) the action of stating before play how many tricks one intends to make. **2** the ordering or requesting of someone to do something: *the clandestine associations that would act* ***at their bidding*** | [in *sing.*] *I never needed a second bidding.*
▸*PHRASE* □ **do someone's bidding** do what someone orders or requests, typically in a way considered overly slavish.

bid·ding pad·dle ▸*n.* a paddle-shaped baton, usually marked with an identifying number, used to signal bids at auctions.

bid·ding prayer ▸*n.* a prayer inviting the congregation to join in, now usually used to describe a group of intercessionary prayers.

bid·dy /ˈbidē/ ▸*n.* (*pl.* **-dies**) *informal* a woman, usually an elderly one regarded as annoying or interfering: *the* ***old biddies*** *were muttering in his direction.* ▷early 17th cent. (originally denoting a chicken): of unknown origin; probably influenced by the use of *biddy* denoting an Irish maidservant, from *Biddy*, nickname for the given name *Bridget.*

bide /bīd/ ▸*v.* [*intrans.*] *archaic* or *dialect* remain or stay somewhere: *how long must I bide here to wait for the answer?* ▷Old English *bīdan*, of Germanic origin.
▸*PHRASE* □ **bide one's time** wait quietly for a good opportunity to do something: *she bided her time, patiently reading a magazine and planning her escape.*

bi·det /biˈdā/ ▸*n.* a low oval basin used for washing one's genital and anal area. ▷mid 17th cent. (in the sense 'horse'): from French, literally 'pony,' from *bider* 'to trot,' of unknown origin.

bi·di /ˈbēdē/ (also **bee·di** or **bi·ri** /ˈbērē/) ▸*n.* (*pl.* **bi·dis**) (in the Indian subcontinent) a type of cheap cigarette made of unprocessed tobacco wrapped in leaves. ▷from Hindi *bīḍī* 'betel plug, cigar,' from Sanskrit *viṭikā.*

bi·di·rec·tion·al /ˌbīdiˈreksHənl/ ▸*adj.* functioning in two directions.

bi·don·ville /ˌbēdôNˈvēl; biˈdôN,vēl/ ▸*n.* a shanty town built of oil drums or other metal containers, esp. on the outskirts of a North African city. ▷1950s: from French, from *bidon* 'container for liquids' + *ville* 'town.'

bid price ▸*n.* the price that a dealer or other prospective buyer is prepared to pay for securities or other assets. Often contrasted with **OFFERING PRICE.**

Bie·der·mei·er /ˈbēdər,mīər/ ▸*adj.* denoting or relating to a style of furniture and interior decoration current in Germany in the period 1815–48, characterized by restraint, conventionality, and utilitarianism. ▷from the name of Gottlieb *Biedermeier*, a fictitious German provincial schoolmaster and poet created by German satirist Ludwig Eichrodt (1827–92) in 1854.

Bie·le·feld /ˈbēlə,feld/ an industrial city in western Germany, in North Rhine-Westphalia; pop. 322,130.

Bien Hoa /ˈbyen ˈhwä/ an industrial city in southern Vietnam, north of Ho Chi Minh City; pop. 314,000. A major U.S. airbase was here during the Vietnam War.

biennale /ˌbē-enˈälā/ ▸*n.* a large art exhibition or music festival, usually one held biennially. ▷1930s (used originally as the name of an international art exhibition held in Venice): from Italian, literally 'biennial.'

bi·en·ni·al /bīˈenēəl/ ▸*adj.* **1** taking place every other year: *summit meetings are normally biennial.* **2** (esp. of a plant) living or lasting for two years.
▸*n.* **1** a plant that takes two years to grow from seed to fruition and die. Compare with **ANNUAL, PERENNIAL. 2** an event celebrated or taking place every two years. ▷early 17th cent.: from Latin *biennis* (from *bi-* 'twice' + *annus* 'year') + **-AL.** **—bi·en·ni·al·ly** *adv.*

USAGE **Biennial** means 'lasting or occurring every two years': *congressional elections are a biennial phenomenon. A biennial plant* is one that lives a two-year cycle, flowering and producing seed in the second year. **Biannual** means 'twice a year': *the solstice is a biannual event.*

bi·en·ni·um /bīˈenēəm/ ▸*n.* (*pl.* **-en·ni·ums** or **-en·ni·a** /-ˈenēə/) (usu. **the biennium**) a specified period of two years: *the budget for the next biennium.* ▷early 20th cent.: from Latin, from *bi-* 'twice' + *annus* 'year.'

bien pensant /ˌbyeN pänˈsäN/ ▸*adj.* right-thinking; orthodox.
▸*n.* (**bien-pensant**) a right-thinking or orthodox person. ▷French, from *bien* 'well' + *pensant*, present participle of *penser* 'think.'

bier /bi(ə)r/ ▸*n.* a movable frame on which a coffin or a corpse is placed before burial or cremation or on which it is carried to the grave. ▷Old English *bēr*, of Germanic origin; related to German *Bahre*, also to **BEAR**[1].

Bierce /bi(ə)rs/, Ambrose (Gwinnett) (1842–*c.*1914), U.S. writer, best known for his sardonic short stories that include *Cobwebs from an Empty Skull* (1874), *In the Midst of Life* (1898), and *The Devil's Dictionary* (1911). In 1913, he traveled to Mexico and mysteriously disappeared.

bi·face /ˈbī,fās/ ▸*n. Archaeology* a type of prehistoric stone implement flaked on both faces.

bi·fa·cial /bīˈfāsHəl/ ▸*adj.* having two faces, in particular: ■ *Botany* (of a leaf) having upper and lower surfaces that are structurally different. ■ *Archaeology* (of a flint or other artifact) worked on both faces.

biff /bif/ *informal* ▸*v.* [*trans.*] strike (someone) roughly or sharply, usually with the fist: *he biffed me on the nose.*
▸*n.* a sharp blow with the fist. ▷mid 19th cent.: symbolic of a short sharp movement.

bi·fid /ˈbīfid/ ▸*adj. Botany & Zoology* (of a part of a plant or animal) divided by a deep cleft or notch into two parts: *a bifid leaf | the gut is bifid.* ▷mid 17th cent.: from Latin *bifidus*, from *bi-* 'doubly' + *fidus* (from *findere* 'to split').

bi·fi·lar /bīˈfīlər/ ▸*adj.* consisting of or involving two threads or wires. ▷mid 19th cent.: from **BI-** 'two' + *filum* 'thread' + **-AR**[1].

bi·fla·gel·late /bīˈflajəlit; -,lāt/ ▸*adj.* having two flagella: *various types of biflagellate spermatozoa.*

bi·fo·cal /ˈbī,fōkəl/ ▸*adj.* (usually of a pair of eyeglasses) having lenses each with two parts with different focal lengths, one for distant vision and one for near vision.
▸*n.* (**bifocals**) a pair of eyeglasses having two such parts.

bi·fold /ˈbī,fōld/ ▸*adj.* double or twofold.

bi·func·tion·al /bīˈfəNGksHənl/ ▸*adj.* **1** having two functions. **2** *Chemistry* having two highly reactive binding sites in each molecule: *bifunctional enzymes retain stable levels of activity.*

bi·fur·cate ▸*v.* /ˈbīfər,kāt/ divide into two branches or forks: [*intrans.*] *just below Cairo the river bifurcates* | [*trans.*] *the trail was bifurcated by a mountain stream.*
▸*adj.* /bīˈfərkāt; ˈbīfərkit/ forked; branched: *a bifurcate tree.* ▷early 17th cent.: from medieval Latin

bifurcat- 'divided into two forks,' from the verb *bifurcare*, from Latin *bifurcus* 'two-forked,' from *bi-* 'having two' + *furca* 'a fork.'

bi·fur·ca·tion /ˌbīfərˈkāSHən/ ▸*n.* the division of something into two branches or parts: *the bifurcation of the profession into social do-gooders and self-serving iconoclasts.* ■ a thing divided in this way or either of the branches: *the bifurcation of the aorta is a site commonly affected first.*

B

big /big/ ▸*adj.* (**big·ger, big·gest**) **1** of considerable size, extent, or intensity: *big hazel eyes | big buildings | big cuts in staff.* ■ [*attrib.*] of a large or the largest size: *my big toe.* ■ grown up: *I'm a big girl now.* ■ elder: *my big sister.* ■ [*attrib.*] *informal* doing a specified action very often or on a very large scale: *a big eater | a big gambler.* ■ *informal* on an ambitiously large scale: *a small company with big plans.* ■ *informal* popular or exciting interest among the public: *Latino bands that are big in Los Angeles.* ■ showing great enthusiasm: *a big tennis fan | he tells me the Inuits of the Arctic are very* **big on** *Jim Reeves.* ■ (**big with**) *archaic* advanced in pregnancy: *my wife was big with child | figurative a word big with fate.* **2** of considerable importance or seriousness: *it's a big decision | Mark's biggest problem is money | he made a big mistake.* ■ *informal* holding an important position or playing an influential role: *as a senior in college, he was a big man on campus.* **3** [*predic.*] *informal often ironic* generous: *"I'm inclined to take pity on you." "That's* **big of you***!"*
▸*n.* (**the bigs**) *informal* the major league in a professional sport: *the day he made it to the bigs, he forgot every minor league ballpark he ever played in.* ▷Middle English (in the sense 'strong, mighty'): of unknown origin. **—big·gish** *adj.* **—big·ness** *n.*
▸*PHRASES* □ **big bucks** *informal* large amounts of money, esp. as pay or profit: *Emily earns big bucks on Wall Street.* □ **big idea** *chiefly ironic* a clever or important intention or scheme: *okay, what's the big idea?* □ **the big lie** a gross distortion or misrepresentation of the facts, esp. when used as a propaganda device by a politician or official body. □ **big screen** *informal* the movies: *the play was adapted for the big screen.* □ **big shot** (also **big noise**) *informal* an important or influential person. □ **big stick** *informal* the use or threat of force or power: *the authorities used quiet persuasion instead of a big stick.* □ **the Big Three, Four,** etc. *informal* the dominant group of three, four, etc.: *increased competition between the Big Three networks.* □ **go over big** *informal* have a great effect; be a success: *the story went over big with the children.* □ **in a big way** *informal* on a large scale; with great enthusiasm: *he contributed to the project in a big way | they went for it in a big way.* □ **make it big** *informal* become very successful or famous: *Simon had made it big in the financial world.* □ **talk big** *informal* talk confidently or boastfully: *he talked big, blinding her with legal jargon.* □ **think big** *informal* be ambitious: *to trade in a heavyweight world market we must think big.* □ **too big for one's britches** (or **breeches**) *informal* conceited.

big air ▸*n. informal* a high jump in sports such as skateboarding, snowboarding, and BMX.

big·a·my /ˈbigəmē/ ▸*n.* the act of going through a marriage ceremony while already married to another person. ▷Middle English: from Old French *bigamie*, from *bigame* 'bigamous,' from late Latin *bigamus*, from *bi-* 'twice' + Greek *-gamos* 'married.' **—big·a·mist** /-mist/ *n.* **—big·a·mous** /-məs/ *adj.*

Big Ap·ple nickname for New York City.

big band ▸*n.* a large group of musicians playing jazz or dance music: [as *adj.*] *the big band sound.*

big bang (also **Big Bang**) ▸*n. Astronomy* the explosion of dense matter that, according to current cosmological theories, marked the origin of the universe.

In the beginning, a fireball of radiation at extremely high temperature and density, but occupying a tiny volume, is believed to have formed. This expanded and cooled, extremely fast at first, but more slowly as subatomic particles condensed into matter that later accumulated to form galaxies and stars. The galaxies are currently still retreating from one another. What was left of the original radiation continued to cool and has been detected as a uniform background of weak microwave radiation.

Big Bear Lake a reservoir and recreational center in southern California, in the San Bernardino Mountains, east northeast of Los Angeles.

big beat ▸*n.* popular music with a steady, prominent beat: [as *adj.*] *had my big beat box and I was jammin'.*

Big Ben the great clock tower of the Houses of Parliament in London and its bell.

Big Bend Na·tion·al Park a U.S. national park in a bend of the Rio Grande, in the desert lands of southern Texas on the border with Mexico. In 1975, fossil remains of the pterosaur were discovered here.

Big Bend State a nickname for the state of TENNESSEE.

Big Black Riv·er a river in Mississippi that flows 330 miles (530 km) into the Mississippi River near Vicksburg.

Big Board informal term for the New York Stock Exchange.

Big Broth·er ▸*n. informal* a person or organization exercising total control over people's lives. ▷1950s: from the name of the head of state in Orwell's *Nineteen Eighty-four* (1949). **—Big Broth·er·ism** /ˈbrəT͟Hərˌizəm/ *n.*

big busi·ness ▸*n.* large-scale or important financial or commercial activity: *the children's toy market is big business now.*

big cat ▸*n.* any of the large members of the cat family, including the lion, tiger, leopard, jaguar, snow leopard, clouded leopard, cheetah, and cougar. • *Panthera* and other genera, family Felidae.

big crunch ▸*n. Astronomy* a contraction of the universe to a state of extremely high density and temperature, hypothesized as a possible scenario for its demise.

Big Dad·dy (also **Big Chief**) ▸*n. informal* a person in authority; the head of an organization or enterprise.

Big Dip·per ▸*n.* **1** a prominent group of seven stars in the constellation Ursa Major (the Great Bear), containing the Pointers that indicate the direction to Polaris. **2** *Brit.* (also **big dipper**) a roller coaster.

bi·gem·i·ny /bīˈjemənē/ ▸*n.* a cardiac rhythm in which each normal beat is followed by an abnormal one. **—bi·gem·i·nal** /-ˈjemənl/ *adj.*

big end ▸*n.* (in an engine) the end of the connecting rod that encircles the crankpin.

bi·ge·ner·ic /ˌbījəˈnerik/ ▸*adj. Botany* relating to or denoting a hybrid between two genera.

big·eye /ˈbigˌī/ ▸*n.* **1** (also **bigeye tuna**) a large migratory tuna that is very important to the commercial fishing industry. • *Thunnus obesus*, family Scombridae. **2** a reddish, large-eyed fish that lives in moderately deep waters of the tropical Atlantic and the western Indian Ocean. Also called CATALUFA. • *Priacanthus arenatus*, family Priacanthidae.

Big·foot /ˈbigˌfo͝ot/ ▸*n.* (*pl.* **-feet**) a large, hairy, apelike creature resembling a yeti, supposedly found in northwestern America. Also called SASQUATCH. ▷so named because of the size of its footprints.

big game ▸*n.* large animals hunted for sport: [as *adj.*] *a big-game hunter.*

big·gie /ˈbigē/ ▸*n.* (*pl.* **-gies**) *informal* a big, important, or successful person or thing: *composers including most of the biggies like Brahms, Wagner, Mendelssohn.*

big·git·y /ˈbigitē/ (also **big·get·y**) ▸*adj. informal* conceited, self-important, or boastful: *we had no truck with biggety Yankees.*
▸*adv.* rudely; impudently: *so that's why you talked to him so biggity.*

big gov·ern·ment ▸*n.* government perceived as excessively interventionist and intruding into all aspects of the lives of its citizens.

big gun ▸*n. informal* a powerful or influential person: *the first baseman and the center fielder were the big guns of that team.* ■ a significant or influential thing, esp. when presented as an ultimate means of persuasion: *the blackmailer's big gun was the threat of photographs.*

big hair ▸*n. informal* a bouffant hairstyle, typically one that has been teased, permed, or sprayed to create volume.

big·head /ˈbigˌhed/ ▸*n. informal* a conceited or arrogant person. **—big·head·ed** *adj.* **—big·head·ed·ness** *n.*

big·heart·ed /ˈbigˌhärtid/ ▸*adj.* (of a person or action) kind and generous.

big hit·ter ▸ another term for HEAVY HITTER.

big·horn /ˈbigˌhôrn/ (in full **American bighorn sheep**) ▸*n.* a stocky brown North American wild sheep, found esp. in the Rocky Mountains. Also called MOUNTAIN SHEEP. • *Ovis canadensis*, family Bovidae.

Big·horn Moun·tains /ˈbigˌhôrn/ a range of the Rocky Mountains in Montana and Wyoming. The Bighorn River flows along its west side.

big house ▸*n. informal* a prison: *he's doing a stint in the big house.*

bight /bīt/ ▸*n.* a curve or recess in a coastline, river, or other geographical feature. ■ a loop of rope, as distinct from the rope's ends. ▷Old English *byht* 'a bend or angle,' of Germanic origin; related to BOW[2].

Big Is·land a popular name for the island of HAWAII.

big league ▸*n.* a group of teams in a professional sport, esp. baseball, competing for a championship at the highest level: [as *adj.*] *big league teams.* ■ (**the big league**) *informal* a very successful or important group: *the film brought him into the movie world's big league.* **—big lea·guer** *n.*

big·mouth /ˈbigˌmouTH/ ▸*n.* **1** *informal* an indiscreet or boastful person. **2** Another term for LARGEMOUTH BASS; see BLACK BASS. **—big·mouthed** *adj.*

Big Mud·dy a popular name for the Missouri River, whose waters are muddier than those of the Mississippi River.

big name ▸*n. informal* a person who is famous in a certain sphere: *he's a big name in gymnastics.*

big noise ▸*n. informal* another term for BIG SHOT.

big·o·rex·i·a /ˌbigəˈreksēə/ ▸*n.* informal term for MUSCLE DYSMORPHIA. ▷ *big* + Greek *orexis* 'appetite,' on the pattern of *anorexia.* **—big·o·rex·ic** *adj.* & *n.*

big·ot /ˈbigət/ ▸*n.* a person who is bigoted: *religious bigots.* See note at ZEALOT. ▷late 16th cent. (denoting a superstitious religious hypocrite): from French, of unknown origin.

big·ot·ed /ˈbigətid/ ▸*adj.* obstinately convinced of the superiority or correctness of one's own opinions and prejudiced against those who hold different opinions: *a bigoted group of reactionaries.* ■ expressing or characterized by prejudice and intolerance: *a thoughtless and bigoted article.*

big·ot·ry /ˈbigətrē/ ▸*n.* bigoted attitudes; intolerance toward those who hold different opinions from oneself: *the report reveals racism and right-wing bigotry.* See note at BIAS. ▷late 17th cent.: from BIGOT, reinforced by French *bigoterie.*

big rig ▸*n. informal* another term for TRACTOR-TRAILER.

Big Rip ▸*n.* a theory about the end of the universe holding that the accelerating forces driving its expansion will eventually rend all currently organized matter. ▷early 21st cent.: on the pattern of *Big Bang.*

big sci·ence ▸*n. informal* scientific research that is expensive and involves large teams of scientists.

Big Sioux Riv·er a river in South Dakota and Iowa that flows for 420 miles (680 km) to the Missouri River.

Big Sky Coun·try a nickname for the state of MONTANA[1].

Big Spring a city in west Texas, an oil industry center northeast of Midland; pop. 23,093.

Big Sur /ˈsər/ a scenic locality in west central California, south of Monterey on the Pacific coast.

big tent ▸*n.* used in reference to a political party's policy of permitting or encouraging a broad spectrum of views among its members: *the struggle to change Wyoming takes place inside the Republican Party and its "big tent."*

Big Thick·et a forested area in eastern Texas, north of Beaumont, noted for its biological diversity.

big-tick·et ▸*adj.* [*attrib.*] *informal* constituting a major expense: *big-ticket items such as cars, houses, and expensive vacations.*

big time *informal* ▸*n.* (**the big time**) the highest or most successful level in a career, esp. in entertainment: *a bit-part actor who finally made the big time in Hollywood.*
▸*adv.* on a large scale; to a great extent: *this time they've messed up big time.* **—big-tim·er** *n.*

big top ▸*n.* the main tent in a circus.

big tree ▸*n.* another term for giant redwood (see REDWOOD).

big·wig /ˈbigˌwig/ ▸*n. informal* an important person, usually in a particular sphere. Also called **big wheel.**

bighorn (male)

Bi·har /bi'här/ a state in northeastern India; capital, Patna.

Bi·ha·ri /bi'härē/ ▸*n.* **1** a native or inhabitant of Bihar. **2** a group of three closely related Indic languages, Bhojpuri, Maithili, and Magahi, spoken principally in Bihar.
▸*adj.* of or relating to this people, their languages, or Bihar. ▷from Hindi *Bihārī*.

bi·jou /'bēzHōō/ ▸*adj.* (esp. of a residence or business establishment) small and elegant: *the greasy spoons have given way to bijou restaurants.*
▸*n.* (*pl.* **-joux** /-zHōō(z)/) *archaic* a jewel or trinket. ▷French, from Breton *bizou* 'finger ring,' from *biz* 'finger.'

bi·jou·te·rie /bē'zHōōtərē/ ▸*n.* jewelry or trinkets: *strewn about were bric-a-brac and bijouterie.* ▷French, from BIJOU.

bike /bīk/ *informal* ▸*n.* a bicycle or motorcycle: *I'm going* **by bike** | [as *adj.*] *a bike ride.*
▸*v.* [*intrans.*] ride a bicycle or motorcycle: *we hope to encourage as many people as possible to bike to work* | [as *n.*] (**biking**) *the terrain is perfect for biking.* ▷late 19th cent.: abbreviation.

bike lane ▸*n.* a division of a road marked off with painted lines, for use by cyclists.

bike path ▸*n.* a path or road for bicycles and not motor vehicles.

bik·er /'bīkər/ ▸*n.* *informal* a motorcyclist: [as *adj.*] *her biker boyfriend.* ■ a member of a motorcycle gang or club. ■ a cyclist: *a mountain biker.*

bike·way /'bīk,wā/ ▸*n.* a path or lane for the use of bicycles.

Bi·ki·ni /bi'kēnē/ an atoll in the Marshall Islands, in the western Pacific Ocean, used by the U.S. 1946–58 as a site for testing nuclear weapons.

bi·ki·ni /bi'kēnē/ ▸*n.* (*pl.* **-nis**) a very brief two-piece swimsuit for women. ■ (also **bi·ki·nis**) scanty underpants. ▷1940s: named after BIKINI, where an atomic bomb was exploded in 1946 (because of the supposed 'explosive' effect created by the garment).

bi·ki·ni line ▸*n.* the area of skin around the edge of the bottom half of a bikini, used esp. with reference to the cosmetic removal of the pubic hair in this area.

Bi·ko /'bēkō/, Steve (1946–77), South African radical leader; full name *Stephen Biko*. He was banned from political activity in 1973. After his death in police custody, he became a symbol of heroic resistance to apartheid.

Bi·kol /bi'kōl/ (also **Bi·col**) ▸*n.* (*pl.* same or **-kols**) a member of an indigenous people of southeastern Luzon in the Philippines. ■ the Austronesian language of this people.
▸*adj.* of or relating to this people or their language.

bi·la·bi·al /bī'lābēəl/ ▸*adj.* *Phonetics* (of a speech sound) formed by closure or near closure of the lips, as in *p, b, m, w*.
▸*n.* a consonant sound made in such a way.

bi·lat·er·al /bī'latərəl/ ▸*adj.* having or relating to two sides; affecting both sides: *bilateral hearing is essential for sound location.* ■ involving two parties, usually countries: *the recently concluded bilateral agreements with Japan.* —**bi·lat·er·al·ly** *adv.*

bi·lat·er·al sym·me·try ▸*n.* the property of being divisible into symmetrical halves on either side of a unique plane.

bi·lay·er /'bī,lāər/ ▸*n.* *Biochemistry* a film two molecules thick (formed, e.g., by lipids), in which each molecule is arranged with its hydrophobic end directed inward toward the opposite side of the film and its hydrophilic end directed outward.

Bil·ba·o /bil'bou/ a seaport and industrial city in northern Spain; pop. 372,200.

bil·ber·ry /'bil,berē/ ▸*n.* (*pl.* **-ries**) a hardy dwarf shrub closely related to the blueberry, with red drooping flowers and dark blue edible berries. • Genus *Vaccinium*, family Ericaceae: several species, including the **tundra bilberry** (*V. uliginosum*). ■ the small blue edible berry of this plant. ▷late 16th cent.: probably of Scandinavian origin; compare with Danish *bøllebær*.

bil·bo /'bilbō/ ▸*n.* (*pl.* **-bos** or **-boes**) a sword used in former times, noted for the temper and elasticity of its blade. ▷mid 16th cent.: from *Bilboa*, an earlier English form of the name BILBAO, noted for the manufacture of fine blades.

bil·boes /'bilbōz/ ▸*plural n.* an iron bar with sliding shackles formerly used for confining a prisoner's ankles. ▷mid 16th cent.: of unknown origin.

Bil·dungs·ro·man /'bildōōNGzrō,män; 'bēldōōNGks-/ ▸*n.* a novel dealing with one person's formative years or spiritual education. ▷German, from *Bildung* 'education' + *Roman* 'a novel.'

bile /bīl/ ▸*n.* a bitter greenish-brown alkaline fluid that aids digestion and is secreted by the liver and stored in the gallbladder. ■ *figurative* anger; irritability: *that topic is sure to stir up plenty of bile.* ▷mid 16th cent.: from French, from Latin *bilis*.

bile duct ▸*n.* the duct that conveys bile from the liver and the gallbladder to the duodenum.

bi-lev·el /'bī,levəl/ (also **bi·lev·el**) ▸*adj.* [*attrib.*] having or functioning on two levels; arranged on two planes: *the unit's bi-level design keeps water in the sink.* ■ denoting a style of two-story house in which the lower story is partially sunk below ground level, and the main entrance is between the two stories; split-level. ■ denoting a railroad passenger coach or a bus with seats on two levels.
▸*n.* a bi-level house: *a three-bedroom bi-level.*

bilge /bilj/ ▸*n.* the area on the outer surface of a ship's hull where the bottom curves to meet the vertical sides. ■ (**bilges**) the lowest internal portion of the hull. ■ bilgewater. ■ *figurative, informal* nonsense; rubbish: *romantic bilge dreamed up by journalists.*
▸*v.* [*trans.*] *archaic* break a hole in the bilge of (a ship): *she was hopelessly bilged, her back broken.* ▷late 15th cent.: probably a variant of BULGE.

bilge keel ▸*n.* each of a pair of plates or timbers fastened under the sides of the hull of a ship to provide lateral resistance to the water, prevent rolling, and support its weight in dry dock.

bil·har·zi·a /bil'härzēə/ ▸*n.* a chronic disease, endemic in parts of Africa and South America, caused by infestation with blood flukes (schistosomes). Also called BILHARZIASIS or SCHISTOSOMIASIS. ■ the fluke (schistosome) itself. ▷mid 19th cent.: modern Latin, former name of the genus *Schistosoma*, named after T. *Bilharz* (1825–62), the German physician who discovered the parasite.

bil·har·zi·a·sis /,bilhär'zīəsis/ ▸*n.* *Medicine* another term for BILHARZIA (the disease).

bil·i·ar·y /'bilē,erē; 'bilyərē/ ▸*adj.* *Medicine* of or relating to bile or the bile duct. ▷mid 18th cent.: from French *biliaire*, from *bile* 'bile.'

bi·lin·e·ar /bī'linēər/ ▸*adj.* *Mathematics* **1** *rare* of, relating to, or contained by two straight lines. **2** of, relating to, or denoting a function of two variables that is linear and homogeneous in both independently.

bi·lin·gual /bī'liNGgwəl/ ▸*adj.* (of a person) speaking two languages fluently: *a bilingual secretary.* ■ (of a text or an activity) written or conducted in two languages: *bilingual dictionaries* | *bilingual education.* ■ (of a country, city, or other community) using two languages, esp. officially: *the town is virtually bilingual in Dutch and German.*
▸*n.* a person fluent in two languages. ▷mid 19th cent.: from Latin *bilinguis*, from *bi-* 'having two' + *lingua* 'tongue' + -AL. —**bi·lin·gual·ism** /-,lizəm/ *n.*

bil·ious /'bilyəs/ ▸*adj.* affected by or associated with nausea or vomiting: *I had eaten something that didn't agree with me and I was a little bilious.* ■ (of a color) lurid or sickly: *a bilious olive hue.* ■ *figurative* spiteful; bad-tempered: *outbursts of bilious misogyny.* ■ *Physiology* of or relating to bile. ▷mid 16th cent. (in the sense 'biliary'): from Latin *biliosus*, from *bilis* 'bile.' —**bil·ious·ly** *adv.* —**bil·ious·ness** *n.*

bil·i·ru·bin /'bili,rōōbin/ ▸*n.* *Biochemistry* an orange-yellow pigment formed in the liver by the breakdown of hemoglobin and excreted in bile. ▷late 19th cent.: coined in German from Latin *bilis* 'bile' + *ruber* 'red' + -IN[1].

bil·i·ver·din /,bilə'vərdn; 'bili,vərdn/ ▸*n.* *Biochemistry* a green pigment excreted in bile. It is an oxidized derivative of bilirubin.

bilk /bilk/ *informal* ▸*v.* [*trans.*] **1** obtain or withhold money from (someone) by deceit or without justification; cheat or defraud: *government waste has* **bilked** *the taxpayer* **of** *billions of dollars.* ■ obtain (money) fraudulently: *some businesses bilk thousands of dollars from unsuspecting elderly consumers.* **2** *archaic* evade; elude: *I ducked into the pantry, bilking Edward for the third time this week.* ▷mid 17th cent. (originally used in cribbage meaning 'spoil one's opponent's score'): perhaps a variant of BALK. —**bilk·er** *n.*

bill[1] /bil/ ▸*n.* **1** an amount of money owed for goods supplied or services rendered, set out in a printed or written statement of charges: *he was* **running up a bill** *of hundreds of dollars* | *the bill for their meal came to $17.* **2** a draft of a proposed law presented to parliament for discussion: *a debate over the civil rights bill.* **3** a program of entertainment, esp. at a theater: *she was* **top of the bill** *at America's leading vaudeville house.* **4** a banknote; a piece of paper money: *a ten-dollar bill.* **5** a poster or handbill: *the circus promoters were* **posting bills** *all over town.*
▸*v.* [*trans.*] **1** (usu. **be billed**) list (a person or event) in a program: *they were billed to appear but didn't show up.* ■ (**bill someone/something as**) describe someone or something in a particular, usually promotional, way, esp. as a means of advertisement: *he was billed as "the new Sean Connery."* **2** send a note of charges to (someone): *we shall be billing them for the damage caused* | [with *two objs.*] *he had been billed $3,000 for his license.* ■ charge (a sum of money): *we billed her $400,000.* ▷Middle English (denoting a written list or catalog): from Anglo-Norman French *bille*, probably based on medieval Latin *bulla* 'seal, sealed document' (see also BULL[2]). —**bill·a·ble** *adj.*
▸*PHRASES* □ **fit** (or **fill**) **the bill** be suitable for a particular purpose: *a partner is an ally or a companion, and you don't seem to fit the bill.* □ **foot** (or **pick up**) **the bill** see FOOT (sense 1 of the *verb*).

bill[2] ▸*n.* the beak of a bird, esp. when it is slender, flattened, or weak, or belongs to a web-footed bird or a bird of the pigeon family. ■ the muzzle of a platypus. ■ the point of an anchor fluke. ■ *Brit.* a stiff brim at the front of a cap.
▸*v.* [*intrans.*] (of birds, esp. doves) stroke bill with bill during courtship. ▷Old English *bile*, of unknown origin. —**billed** *adj.* [usu. in *combination*] *the red-billed weaverbird.*
▸*PHRASE* □ **bill and coo** *informal* exchange caresses or affectionate words; behave or talk in a very loving or sentimental way.

bill[3] ▸*n.* a medieval weapon like a halberd with a hook instead of a blade. ▷Old English *bil*; related to German *Bille* 'ax.'

bil·la·bong /'bilə,bôNG/ ▸*n.* *Austral.* a branch of a river forming a backwater or stagnant pool, made by water flowing from the main stream during a flood. ▷mid 19th cent.: from Wiradhuri *bilabang* (originally as the name of the Bell River, New South Wales), from *billa* 'water' + *bang* 'channel that is dry except after rain.'

bill·board /'bil,bôrd/ ▸*n.* a large outdoor board for displaying advertisements.

bill·bug /'bil,bəg/ ▸*n.* a typically large weevil that feeds on various grasses and grains. • Genus *Sphenophorus*, subfamily Rhynchophorinae, family Curculionidae: numerous species, including the **maize billbug** (*S. maidis*), which can cause serious damage to corn plants and can harm or kill poultry by clamping on to the bird's throat or tongue.

Bille·rica /bil'rikə; ,belə-/ a town in northeastern Massachusetts, south of Lowell; pop. 37,609.

bil·let[1] /'bilit/ ▸*n.* a place, usually a civilian's house or other nonmilitary facility, where soldiers are lodged temporarily.
▸*v.* (**-let·ed, -let·ing**) [*trans.*] (often **be billeted**) lodge (soldiers) in a particular place, esp. a civilian's house or other nonmilitary facility: *he didn't belong to the regiment billeted at the hotel.* ▷late Middle English (originally denoting a short written document): from Anglo-Norman French *billette*, diminutive of *bille* (see BILL[1]). The verb is recorded in the late 16th cent., and the noun sense 'a written order requiring a householder to lodge the bearer, usually a soldier,' from the mid 17th cent.; hence the current meaning.

bil·let[2] ▸*n.* a thick piece of wood. ■ a small bar of metal for further processing. ■ *Architecture* each of a series of short cylindrical pieces inserted at intervals in decorative hollow moldings. ■ *Heraldry* a rectangle placed vertically as a charge. ▷late Middle English: from Old French *billette* and *billot*, diminutives of *bille* 'tree trunk,' from medieval Latin *billa*, *billus* 'branch, trunk,' probably of Celtic origin.

bil·let-doux /'bilā 'dōō; 'bēyā-/ ▸*n.* (*pl.* **bil·lets-doux** *pronunc.* same or /-'dōōz/) *dated* or *humorous* a love letter. ▷late 17th cent.: French, literally 'sweet note.'

bill·fish /'bil,fisH/ ▸*n.* (*pl.* same or **-fish·es**) a large, fast-swimming fish of open seas, with a streamlined body and a long, pointed, spearlike snout. It occurs on the surface in warmer waters and is a popular sporting fish. • Family Istiophoridae: three genera and several species, including the marlins, sailfish, and spearfishes.

bill·fold /'bil,fōld/ ▸*n.* a thin wallet with few compartments, typically made of leather. ■ any wallet.

bill·hook /ˈbil,ho͝ok/ ▸*n.* a tool with a sickle-shaped blade with a sharp inner edge, used for pruning or lopping branches or other vegetation.

bil·liard /ˈbilyərd/ ▸*n.* **1** (**billiards**) [usu. treated as *sing.*] a game usually for two people, played on a billiard table, in which three balls are struck with cues into pockets around the edge of the table: *play billiards at home* | [as *adj.*] (**billiard**) *billiard ball* | *billiard room.* ■ (in full **English billiards**) a game played on a billiard table with pockets, in which points are made by caroms, pocketing an object ball, or caroming the cue ball into a pocket: **2** a stroke in which the cue ball strikes two balls successively. ▷late 16th cent.: from French *billard*, denoting both the game and the cue, diminutive of *bille* (see BILLET2).

bil·liard ta·ble ▸*n.* a smooth rectangular cloth-covered table used for billiards and some forms of pool, with six pockets at the corners and sides into which the balls can be struck. ■ a similar table but without pockets used for playing carom billiards.

bill·ing /ˈbiliNG/ ▸*n.* **1** the action or fact of publicizing or being publicized in a particular way: *they can justify their billing as the American League favorites.* ■ prominence in publicity, esp. as an indication of importance: *he shared **top billing** with his wife.* **2** the process of making out or sending invoices: *faster, more accurate order fulfillment and billing.* ■ the total amount of business conducted in a given time, esp. that of an advertising agency: *the account was worth about $2 million a year in billings.*

Bil·lings /ˈbiliNGz/ a commercial city in south central Montana, the state's largest city; pop. 89,847.

Bil·lings meth·od ▸*n.* a system for finding the time of ovulation by examining cervical mucus. It can be used as a form of birth control by avoiding sexual intercourse at that time. ▷1960s: named after Drs. John and Evelyn *Billings*, who devised the method.

bil·lion /ˈbilyən/ ▸*cardinal number* (*pl.* **-lions** or (with numeral or quantifying word) same) the number equivalent to the product of a thousand and a million; 1,000,000,000 or 10^9: *a world population of over 6 billion* | *half a billion dollars.* ■ (**billions**) *informal* a very large number or amount of something: *our immune systems are killing billions of germs right now.* ■ a billion dollars (or pounds, etc.): *the problem persists despite the billions spent on it.* ■ *dated, chiefly Brit.* a million million (1,000,000,000,000 or 10^{12}). ▷late 17th cent.: from French, from *million*, by substitution of the prefix *bi-* 'two' for the initial letters. —**bil·lionth** /-yənTH/ *ordinal number* .

bil·lion·aire /ˈbilyə,ne(ə)r/ ▸*n.* a person possessing assets worth at least a billion dollars (or pounds, etc.). ▷mid 19th cent.: from BILLION, on the pattern of *millionaire.*

bill of at·tain·der ▸*n. Law* an item of legislation (prohibited by the U.S. Constitution) that inflicts attainder without judicial process: *during the Revolutionary War, bills of attainder were passed to a wide extent.*

bill of ex·change ▸*n.* a written order to a person requiring the person to make a specified payment to the signatory or to a named payee; a promissory note.

bill of fare ▸*n. dated* a menu. ■ *informal* the selection of food available to or consumed by (a person or animal): *our bill of fare in Alaska included clams, mussels, and herring.* ■ a program for a theatrical event.

bill of goods ▸*n.* a consignment of merchandise.

▸*PHRASE* □ **sell someone a bill of goods** deceive someone, usually by persuading them to accept something untrue or undesirable: *she was sold a bill of goods about that dog's pedigree.*

bill of health ▸*n.* a certificate relating to the incidence of infectious disease on a ship or in the port from which it has sailed.

▸*PHRASE* □ **a clean bill of health** a declaration or confirmation that someone is healthy or that something is in good condition: *a survey gave the property a clean bill of health.*

bill of in·dict·ment ▸*n.* a written accusation as presented to a grand jury.

bill of lad·ing ▸*n.* a detailed list of a shipment of goods in the form of a receipt given by the carrier to the person consigning the goods.

Bill of Rights ▸*n. Law* a statement of the rights of a class of people, in particular: ■ the first ten amendments to the U.S. Constitution, ratified in 1791 and guaranteeing such rights as the freedoms of speech, assembly, and worship. ■ the English constitutional settlement of 1689, confirming the deposition of James II and the accession of William and Mary, guaranteeing the Protestant succession, and laying down the principles of parliamentary supremacy.

bill of sale ▸*n.* a certificate of transfer of personal property.

bil·lon /ˈbilən/ ▸*n.* an alloy formerly used for coinage, containing gold or silver with a predominating amount of copper or other base metal. ▷early 18th cent.: from French, literally 'bronze or copper money,' in Old French 'ingot,' from *bille* (see BILLET2).

bil·low /ˈbilō/ ▸*n.* a large undulating mass of something, typically cloud, smoke, or steam. ■ *archaic* a large sea wave.

▸*v.* [*intrans.*] (of fabric) fill with air and swell outward: *her dress **billowed out** around her.* ■ (of smoke, cloud, or steam) move or flow outward with an undulating motion: *smoke was billowing from the chimney.* ▷mid 16th cent.: from Old Norse *bylgja.* —**bil·low·y** /ˈbilō-ē/ *adj.*

bill·post·er /ˈbil,pōstər/ ▸*n.* a person who posts advertisements, notices, or posters. —**bill·post·ing** /-,pōstiNG/ *n.*

bil·ly /ˈbilē/ ▸*n.* (*pl.* **-lies**) **1** short for BILLY GOAT. **2** (also **billy club**) a truncheon; a cudgel. ▷mid 19th cent.: from *Billy*, nickname for the given name *William.*

bil·ly goat ▸*n.* a male goat.

Bil·ly the Kid see BONNEY.

bi·lobed /bīˈlōbd/ (also **bi·lo·bate** /-ˈlōbāt/) ▸*adj.* having or consisting of two lobes.

bi·lo·ca·tion /,bīlōˈkāSHən/ ▸*n.* the supposed phenomenon of being in two places simultaneously.

Bi·loxi /biˈləksē; -ˈläksē/ a city in southeastern Mississippi, on the Gulf of Mexico; pop. 50,644. It is a noted fishing and tourist center.

bil·tong /ˈbil,tôNG/ ▸*n. chiefly S. African* lean meat that is salted and dried in strips. ▷Afrikaans, from Dutch *bil* 'buttock' + *tong* 'tongue.'

bi·man·u·al /bīˈmanyo͞oəl/ ▸*adj.* performed with both hands. —**bi·man·u·al·ly** *adv.*

bim·bo /ˈbimbō/ (also **bim·bette** /bimˈbet/) ▸*n.* (*pl.* **-bos**) *informal* an attractive but empty-headed young woman, esp. one perceived as a willing sex object. ▷early 20th cent. (originally in the sense 'fellow, man'): from Italian, literally 'little child.'

bi·me·tal·lic /,bīməˈtalik/ ▸*adj.* made or consisting of two metals. ■ *historical* of or relating to bimetallism. ▷late 19th cent.: from French *bimétallique*, from *bi-* 'two' + *métallique* 'metallic.'

bi·me·tal·lic strip ▸*n.* a temperature-sensitive electrical contact used in some thermostats, consisting of two bands of different metals joined face to face along their lengths. When heated, the metals expand at different rates, causing the strip to bend.

bi·met·al·lism /bīˈmetl,izəm/ ▸*n. historical* a system allowing the unrestricted currency of two metals (e.g., gold and silver) as legal tender at a fixed ratio to each other. —**bi·met·al·list** *n.*

bi·mil·le·nar·y /bīˈmilə,nerē/; ▸*adj.* [*attrib.*] of or relating to a period of two thousand years or a two-thousandth anniversary.

▸*n.* (*pl.* **-nar·ies**) a period of two thousand years or a two-thousandth anniversary.

Bim·i·ni /ˈbimənē/ (also **Biminis**) resort islands in the northwestern Bahamas. The legendary Fountain of Youth sought by Ponce de León was thought to be here.

bi·mod·al /bīˈmōdl/ ▸*adj.* having or involving two modes, in particular (of a statistical distribution) having two maxima.

bi·mo·lec·u·lar /,bīməˈlekyələr/ ▸*adj. Chemistry* consisting of or involving two molecules.

bi·month·ly /bīˈmənTHlē/ ▸*adj.* occurring or produced twice a month or every two months: *a bimonthly newsletter.*

▸*adv.* twice a month or every two months: *the magazine appears bimonthly.*

▸*n.* (*pl.* **-lies**) a periodical produced twice a month or every two months.

> *USAGE* The meaning of **bimonthly** (and other similar words such as **biweekly** and **biyearly**) is ambiguous. The only way to avoid this ambiguity is to use alternative expressions like *every two months* and *twice a month.* In the publishing world, the meaning of **bimonthly** is more fixed and is invariably used to mean 'every two months.' See also **usage** at BIENNIAL.

bin /bin/ ▸*n.* [with *adj.*] a receptacle for storing a specified substance: *a vegetable bin.* ■ a receptacle in which to deposit trash or recyclables: *we tossed the soda cans in the bin marked "aluminum only."* ■ *Statistics* each of a series of ranges of numerical value into which data are sorted in statistical analysis. ■ short for LOONY BIN: *back in the bin, she suffers from dreadful nightmares.*

▸*v.* (**binned, bin·ning**) [*trans.*] place (something) in a bin. ■ *Statistics* group together (data) in bins. ▷Old English *bin(n)*, *binne*, of Celtic origin; related to Welsh *ben* 'cart.' The original meaning was 'receptacle' in a general sense; also specifically 'a receptacle for provender in a stable' and 'a receptacle for storing grain, bread, or other foodstuffs.' The sense 'receptacle for trash' dates from the mid 19th cent.

bin- ▸*prefix* variant spelling of BI- before a vowel (as in *binaural*).

bi·na·ry /ˈbī,nerē; -nərē/ ▸*adj.* **1** relating to, using, or expressed in a system of numerical notation that has 2 rather than 10 as a base. ■ in binary format: *it is stored as a binary file.* **2** relating to, composed of, or involving two things: *testing the so-called binary, or dual-chemical, weapons.*

▸*n.* (*pl.* **-ries**) **1** the binary system: binary notation: *the device is counting in binary.* **2** something having two parts. ■ a binary star. ▷late Middle English (in the sense 'duality, a pair'): from late Latin *binarius*, from *bini* 'two together.'

bi·na·ry code ▸*n. Electronics* a coding system using the binary digits 0 and 1 to represent a letter, digit, or other character in a computer or other electronic device.

bi·na·ry cod·ed dec·i·mal (abbr.: **BCD**) ▸*n. Electronics* a system for coding a number in which each digit of a decimal number is represented individually by its binary equivalent. ■ a number represented in this way.

bi·na·ry dig·it ▸*n.* one of two digits (0 or 1) in a binary system of notation.

bi·na·ry op·er·a·tion ▸*n.* a mathematical operation, such as addition or multiplication, performed on two elements of a set to derive a third element.

bi·na·ry star ▸*n.* a system of two stars in which one star revolves around the other or both revolve around a common center.

bi·na·ry sys·tem ▸*n.* **1** a system in which information can be expressed by combinations of the digits 0 and 1. **2** a system consisting of two parts: *the binary system of state and public schools.* ■ *Astronomy* a star system containing two stars orbiting around each other.

bi·na·ry tree ▸*n. Computing* a data structure in which a record is linked to two successor records, usually referred to as the left branch when greater and the right when less than the previous record.

bi·nate /ˈbīnāt/ ▸*adj. Botany* growing in pairs. ■ composed of two equal parts. ▷early 19th cent.: from modern Latin *binatus*, from Latin *bini* 'two together.'

bi·na·tion·al /bīˈnaSHənl/ ▸*adj.* concerning or consisting of two nations.

bin·au·ral /bīˈnôrəl; bin-/ ▸*adj.* of, relating to, or used with both ears: *human hearing is binaural.* ■ of or relating to sound recorded using two microphones and usually transmitted separately to the two ears of the listener.

bind /bīnd/ ▸*v.* (*past* and *past part.* **bound** /bound/) [*trans.*] **1** tie or fasten (something) tightly: *floating bundles of logs **bound together** with ropes* | *the magician bound her wrists with a silk scarf.* ■ restrain (someone) by the tying up of hands and feet: *the raider then bound and gagged Mr. Glenn.* ■ wrap (something) tightly: *her hair was **bound up** in a towel.* ■ bandage (a wound): *he cleaned the wound and **bound** it **up** with a clean dressing* | *she had bound his wounds with a poultice of herbs.* ■ (**be bound with**) (of an object) be encircled by something, typically metal bands, in order to strengthen it: *an ancient oak chest, bound with brass braces.* ■ *Linguistics* (of a rule or set of grammatical conditions) determine the relationship between (coreferential noun phrases). **2** cause (people) to feel that they belong together or form a cohesive group: *the comradeship that had **bound** such a disparate bunch of young men **together**.* ■ (**bind someone to**) cause someone to feel strongly attached to (a person or place): *loosened the ties that had bound him to the university.* ■ cohere or cause to cohere in a single mass: [*trans.*] *with the protection of trees to bind soil and act as a windbreak* | [*intrans.*] *clay is made up chiefly of tiny soil particles that **bind together** tightly.* ■ cause (ingredients) to cohere by adding another ingredient: *mix the flour with the coconut and enough egg white to bind them.* ■ cause (painting pigments) to form a smooth medium by mixing them with oil: *use a white that is bound in linseed oil.* ■ hold by chemical bonding: *a protein in* *a form that can bind DNA.* ■ [*intrans.*] (**bind to**) combine with (a substance) through chemical bonding: *these proteins have been reported to* **bind to** *calmodulin.* **3** *formal* impose a legal or contractual obligation on: *a party who signs a document will normally be bound by its terms.* ■ indenture (someone) as an apprentice: *he was* **bound apprentice** *at the age of sixteen.* ■ (**bind oneself**) *formal* make a contractual or enforceable undertaking: *the government cannot bind itself as to the form of subsequent legislation.* ■ secure (a contract), typically with a sum of money. ■ (**be bound by**) be hampered or constrained by: *Sarah did not want to be bound by a rigid timetable.* **4** fix together and enclose (the pages of a book) in a cover: *a small, fat volume, bound in red morocco.* **5** trim (the edge of a piece of material) with a decorative strip: *a ruffle with the edges* **bound in** *a contrasting color.* **6** *Logic* (of a quantifier) be applied to (a given variable) so that the variable falls within its scope. • For example, in an expression of the form 'For every *x*, if *x* is a dog, *x* is an animal,' the universal quantifier is binding the variable *x*.

▶*phrasal v.* □ **bind off** cast off in knitting. □ **bind someone over** (usu. **be bound over**) (of a court of law) require someone to fulfill an obligation, typically by paying a sum of money as surety: *he was bound over for trial on a felony charge.*

▶*n.* **1** a problematical situation: *he is in a political bind over the welfare issue.* **2** *formal* a statutory constraint: *the moral bind of the law.* **3** *Music* another term for **TIE**. **4** another term for **BINE**. ▷Old English *bindan*, of Germanic origin; related to Dutch and German *binden*, from an Indo-European root shared by Sanskrit *bandh*.

▶**PHRASE** □ **bind someone hand and foot** see **HAND**.

bind·er /ˈbīndər/ ▶*n.* a thing or person that binds something, in particular: ■ a cover for holding loose sheets of paper, magazines, etc., together. ■ a substance that acts cohesively. ■ a reaping machine that binds grain into sheaves. ■ a bookbinder.

bind·er twine ▶*n.* (in farming) strong cord made from plastic or natural fiber, used in a baling machine or binder to tie hay and straw bales.

bind·er·y /ˈbīndərē/ ▶*n.* (*pl.* **-er·ies**) a workshop or factory in which books are bound.

bin·di /ˈbindē/ ▶*n.* a decorative mark worn in the middle of the forehead by Indian women. ▷from Hindi *bindī*.

bin·di-eye ▶*n.* a small perennial Australian plant of the daisy family that has a burlike fruit. • *Calotis cuneifolia*, family Compositae. ▷early 20th cent.: perhaps from an Aboriginal language.

bind·ing /ˈbīndiNG/ ▶*n.* **1** a strong covering holding the pages of a book together. ■ fabric such as braid used for binding the edges of a piece of material. **2** (also **ski binding**) a mechanical device fixed to a ski to grip a ski boot, esp. either of a pair used for downhill skiing that hold the toe and heel of the boot and release it automatically in a fall. **3** the action of fastening, holding together, or being linked by chemical bonds: *the binding of antibodies to cell surfaces.* ■ (in Chomskyan linguistics) the relationship between a referentially dependent form (such as a reflexive) and the independent noun phrase that determines its reference.

▶*adj.* (of an agreement or promise) involving an obligation that cannot be broken: *business agreements are intended to be legally binding.*

bind·ing en·er·gy ▶*n. Physics* the energy that holds a nucleus together, equal to the mass defect of the nucleus.

bind·ing post ▶*n. Electronics* a connector consisting of a threaded screw to which bare wires are attached and held in place by a nut.

bin·dle·stiff /ˈbindlˌstif/ ▶*n. informal* a tramp or a hobo, esp. one carrying a bundle containing a bedroll and other gear. ▷early 20th cent.: probably from an alteration of **BUNDLE** + **STIFF** (in the sense 'useless person').

bind·weed /ˈbīndˌwēd/ ▶*n.* a twining plant with trumpet-shaped flowers. Several kinds are invasive weeds. • Genera *Convolvulus* and *Calystegia*, family Convolvulaceae: several species, including the widespread **hedge bindweed** (or **wild morning glory**) (*Calystegia* (or **Convolvulus**) *sepium*). ■ used in names of similar twining plants, e.g., **black bindweed**.

bine /bīn/ ▶*n.* a long flexible stem of a climbing plant, esp. the hop. ▷early 19th cent.: originally a dialect form of **BIND**.

Bi·net /bəˈnā/, Alfred (1857–1911), French psychologist. He devised a mental age scale that described performance in relation to the average performance of students of the same physical age. With psychiatrist **Théodore Simon** (1873–1961), he was responsible for a pioneering system of intelligence tests.

Bi·net–Si·mon scale /biˈnā ˈsīmən/ ▶*n.* the measurement of intelligence by the application of a test (see **BINET-SIMON TEST**) consisting of tasks and problems graded in terms of mental age.

Bi·net–Si·mon test /biˈnā ˈsīmən/ (also **Bi·net test**) ▶*adj. Psychology* a test used to measure intelligence, esp. that of children.

Bing /biNG/, Sir Rudolf (1902–97), British opera conductor and manager; born in Austria. He was conductor and director of the Metropolitan Opera in New York City 1950–72. In 1955, he hired Marian Anderson, ending the Met's unwritten ban against African Americans. He was knighted in 1971.

bing /biNG/ ▶*exclam.* indicating a sudden action or event: *Bing! They've hit you with something.* ▷late 19th cent. (originally dialect in the sense 'sudden bang'): imitative.

Bing cher·ry /biNG/ ▶*n.* a large heart-shaped cherry, juicy, sweet and dark blackish-red.

binge /binj/ *informal* ▶*n.* a short period devoted to indulging in an activity, esp. drinking alcohol, to excess: *he* **went on a binge** *and was in no shape to drive* | [as *adj.*] *binge eating* | [with *adj.*] *a spending binge.*

▶*v.* (**bing·ing** or **binge·ing**) [*intrans.*] indulge in an activity, esp. eating, to excess: *some dieters say they cannot help* **binging on** *chocolate* | [as *n.*] (**binging**) *her secret binging and vomiting.* ▷early 19th cent.: of unknown origin. —**bing·er** *n.*

binge-eat·ing syn·drome ▶*n.* see **BULIMIA**.

binge-purge syn·drome ▶*n.* see **BULIMIA**.

Bing·ham /ˈbiNGəm/, George Caleb (1811–79), U.S. artist. His paintings of the U.S. frontier include *The Fur Traders Descending the Missouri* (1845), *The Trappers Return* (1851), and *The Country Election* (1851–52).

Bing·ham·ton /ˈbiNGəmtən/ an industrial city in south central New York, on the Susquehanna River, near the Pennsylvania border; pop. 47,380.

bin·go /ˈbiNGgō/ ▶*n.* a game in which players mark off numbers on cards as the numbers are drawn randomly by a caller, the winner being the first person to mark off five numbers in a row or another required pattern.

▶*exclam.* used to express satisfaction or surprise at a sudden positive event or outcome: *bingo, she leapfrogged into a sales trainee position.* ■ a call by someone who wins a game of bingo. ▷1920s (as an interjection): of unknown origin.

bin·na·cle /ˈbinəkəl/ ▶*n.* a built-in housing for a ship's compass. ▷late 15th cent. (as *bittacle*): from Spanish *bitácula*, *bitácora* or Portuguese *bitacola*, from Latin *habitaculum* 'dwelling place,' from *habitare* 'inhabit.' The change to *binnacle* occurred in the mid 18th cent.

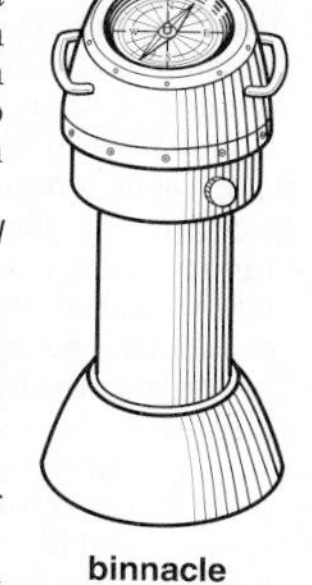
binnacle

bin·ocs /biˈnäks/ ▶*plural n. informal* short for **BINOCULARS**.

bin·oc·u·lar /biˈnäkyələr/ ▶*adj.* adapted for or using both eyes: *a binocular microscope.* ▷early 18th cent. (in the sense 'having two eyes'): from Latin *bini* 'two together' + *oculus* 'eye,' on the pattern of *ocular*.

bin·oc·u·lars /biˈnäkyələrz/ ▶*plural n.* an optical instrument with a lens for each eye, used for viewing distant objects. ▷late 19th cent.: plural of **BINOCULAR**.

bin·oc·u·lar vi·sion ▶*n.* vision using two eyes with overlapping fields of view, allowing good perception of depth.

bi·no·mi·al /bīˈnōmēəl/ ▶*n.* **1** *Mathematics* an algebraic expression of the sum or the difference of two terms. **2** a two-part name, esp. the Latin name of a species of living organism (consisting of the genus followed by the specific epithet). **3** *Grammar* a noun phrase with two heads joined by a conjunction, in which the order is relatively fixed (as in *knife and fork*).

▶*adj.* **1** *Mathematics* consisting of two terms. ■ of or relating to a binomial or to the binomial theorem. **2** having or using two names, used esp. of the Latin name of a species of living organism. ▷mid 16th cent.: from French *binôme* or modern Latin *binomium* (from *bi-* 'having two' + Greek *nomos* 'part, portion') + **-AL**.

bi·no·mi·al dis·tri·bu·tion ▶*n. Statistics* a frequency distribution of the possible number of successful outcomes in a given number of trials in each of which there is the same probability of success.

bi·no·mi·al no·men·cla·ture ▶*n. Biology* the system of nomenclature in which two terms are used to denote a species of living organism, the first one indicating the genus and the second the specific epithet. Compare with **SYSTEMATIC NAME**.

bi·no·mi·al the·o·rem ▶*n.* a formula for finding any power of a binomial without multiplying at length.

bin·tu·rong /binˈto͝orôNG/ ▶*n.* a tree-dwelling Asian civet with a coarse blackish coat and a muscular prehensile tail. • *Arctictis binturong*, family Viverridae. ▷early 19th cent.: from Malay.

bi·nu·cle·ate /bīˈn(y)o͞oklēit; -ˌāt/ ▶*adj.* having two nuclei.

bi·o /ˈbīō/ ▶*n.* (*pl.* **-os**) *informal* **1** biology: [as *modifier*] *he dated a bio major in college.* **2** a biography: *the latest in a series of unauthorized bios.*

▶*adj. informal* **1** biological: *studying the effects of bio treatment.* **2** biographical: *it was excluded from her official bio material.* ▷mid 20th cent.: abbreviation.

bio- ▶*comb. form* **1** of or relating to life: *biosynthesis.* ■ biological; relating to biology: *biohazard.* ■ of living beings: *biogenesis.* **2** relating to or involving the use of toxic biological or biochemical substances as weapons of war: *bioterrorism.* ▷from Greek *bios* '(course of) human life.' The sense is extended in modern scientific usage to mean 'organic life.'

bi·o·ac·cu·mu·late /ˌbīōəˈkyo͞omyəˌlāt/ ▶*v.* [*intrans.*] (of a substance) become concentrated inside the bodies of living things. —**bi·o·ac·cu·mu·la·tion** /-ˌkyo͞omyəˈlāSHən/ *n.*

bi·o·a·cous·tics /ˌbīōəˈko͞ostiks/ ▶*plural n.* [treated as *sing.*] the branch of acoustics concerned with sounds produced by or affecting living organisms, esp. as relating to communication.

bi·o·ac·tive /ˌbīōˈaktiv/ ▶*adj.* (of a substance) having a biological effect. —**bi·o·ac·tiv·i·ty** /-akˈtivitē/ *n.*

bi·o·as·say /ˌbīōəˈsā; -ˈasā/ ▶*n.* measurement of the concentration or potency of a substance by its effect on living cells or tissues. ▷early 20th cent.: from **BIO-** 'life' + **ASSAY**.

bi·o·as·tro·nau·tics /ˌbīōˌastrəˈnôtiks/ ▶*n.* the study of the effects of space flight on living organisms.

bi·o·a·vail·a·bil·i·ty /ˌbīōˌəvāləˈbilitē/ ▶*n. Physiology* the proportion of a drug or other substance that enters the circulation when introduced into the body and so is able to have an active effect. —**bi·o·a·vail·a·ble** /-əˈvāləbəl/ *adj.*

bi·o·bib·li·og·ra·phy /ˌbīōˌbiblēˈägrəfē/ ▶*n.* a bibliography containing biographical information about the author(s).

bi·o·cat·a·lyst /ˌbīōˈkatl-ist/ ▶*n.* a substance, such as an enzyme or hormone, that initiates or increases the rate of a chemical reaction. —**bi·o·cat·a·lyt·ic** /ˌbīōˌkatlˈitik/ *adj.*

bi·o·ce·no·sis /ˌbīōsiˈnōsis/ (also **bi·o·coe·no·sis**) ▶*n.* (*pl.* **-no·ses** /-ˈnōsēz/) *Ecology* an association of different organisms forming a closely integrated community. ▷late 19th cent.: modern Latin, from **BIO-** 'life' + Greek *koinōsis* 'sharing' (from *koinos* 'common').

bi·o·cen·trism /ˌbīōˈsentrizəm/ ▶*n.* the view or belief that the rights and needs of humans are not more important than those of other living things. —**bi·o·cen·tric** /-trik/ *adj.* —**bi·o·cen·trist** *n.*

bi·o·chem·i·cal ox·y·gen de·mand /ˌbīōˈkemikəl/ (abbr.: **BOD**) ▶*n.* the amount of dissolved oxygen that must be present in water in order for microorganisms to decompose the organic matter in the water, used as a measure of the degree of pollution. Also called **BIOLOGICAL OXYGEN DEMAND**.

bi·o·chem·is·try /ˌbīōˈkeməstrē/ ▶*n.* the branch of science concerned with the chemical and physicochemical processes that occur within living organisms. ■ processes of this kind: *abnormal brain biochemistry.* —**bi·o·chem·i·cal** /-ˈkemikəl/ *adj.* —**bi·o·chem·i·cal·ly** *adv.* —**bi·o·chem·ist** /-ˈkemist/ *n.*

bi·o·chip /ˈbīōˌCHip/ ▶*n.* a microchip intended to function in a biological environment, esp. inside a living organism. ■ a logical device analogous to the silicon chip, whose components are formed from biological molecules or structures.

bi·o·cide /ˈbīəˌsīd/ ▶*n.* **1** a poisonous substance, esp. a pesticide. **2** the destruction of life: *our whims have brought us to the brink of biocide.* ▷1940s: from **BIO-** 'life' + **-CIDE**. —**bi·o·cid·al** /ˌbīəˈsīdl/ *adj.*

bi·o·cir·cuit /ˈbīō,sərkit/ ▸*n.* an integrated circuit incorporating biological molecules or structures. —**bi·o·cir·cuit·ry** /,bīōˈsərkitrē/ *n.*

bi·o·cli·mat·ic /,bīōklīˈmatik/ ▸*adj.* *Ecology* of or relating to the interrelation of climate and the activities and distribution of living organisms.

bi·o·cli·ma·tol·o·gy /,bīō,klīməˈtäləjē/ ▸*n.* the study of climate in relation to living organisms and esp. to human health. —**bi·o·cli·mat·o·log·i·cal** /-,klīmətl-ˈäjikəl/ *adj.*

bi·o·com·pat·i·ble /,bīōkəmˈpatəbəl/ ▸*adj.* (esp. of materials used in surgical implants) not harmful to living tissue. —**bi·o·com·pat·i·bil·i·ty** /-,patəˈbilitē/ *n.*

bi·o·com·pu·ter /ˈbīōkəm,pyo͞otər/ ▸*n.* a hypothetical computer based on circuits and components formed from biological molecules or structures that would be smaller and faster than an equivalent computer built from semiconductor components. ■ a human being, or the human mind, regarded as a computer.

bi·o·com·put·ing /,bīōkəmˈpyo͞otiNG/ ▸*n.* the design and construction of computers using biochemical components. ■ an approach to programming that seeks to emulate or model biological processes. ■ computing in a biological context or environment.

bi·o·con·trol /,bīōkənˈtrōl/ ▸*n.* short for BIOLOGICAL CONTROL.

bi·o·con·ver·sion /,bīōkənˈvərZHən/ ▸*n.* the conversion of organic matter, such as animal or plant waste, into a source of energy through the action of microorganisms.

bi·o·de·grad·a·ble /,bīōdiˈgrādəbəl/ ▸*adj.* (of a substance or object) capable of being decomposed by bacteria or other living organisms. —**bi·o·de·grad·a·bil·i·ty** /-,grādəˈbilitē/ *n.*

bi·o·de·grade /,bīōdiˈgrād/ ▸*v.* [*intrans.*] (of a substance or object) be decomposed by bacteria or other living organisms: *most plastics will not biodegrade at all.* —**bi·o·deg·ra·da·tion** /-,degrəˈdāSHən/ *n.*

bi·o·die·sel /ˈbīō,dēzəl; -səl/ ▸*n.* [*mass noun*] a biofuel intended as a substitute for diesel.

bi·o·di·ver·si·ty /,bīōdiˈvərsitē/ ▸*n.* the variety of life in the world or in a particular habitat or ecosystem.

bi·o·dy·nam·ics /,bīōdīˈnamiks/ ▸*plural n.* [treated as *sing.*] **1** the study of physical motion or dynamics in living systems. **2** a method of organic farming involving such factors as the observation of lunar phases and planetary cycles and the use of incantations and ritual substances. —**bi·o·dy·nam·ic** *adj.*

bi·o·e·lec·tric /,bīōiˈlektrik/ ▸*adj.* of or relating to electricity or electrical phenomena produced within living organisms. —**bi·o·e·lec·tri·cal** *adj.*

bi·o·e·lec·tron·ics /,bīōilekˈträniks; -,ēlek-/ ▸*plural n.* [usu. treated as *sing.*] **1** the study and application of electronics in medicine and biological processes. **2** the integration of biological principles in electronic technology: *the impact of bioelectronics on computer hardware.* —**bi·o·e·lec·tron·ic** *adj.* —**bi·o·e·lec·tron·i·cal·ly** /-ik(ə)lē/ *adv.*

bi·o·en·er·get·ics /,bīō,enərˈjetiks/ ▸*plural n.* [treated as *sing.*] **1** the study of the transformation of energy in living organisms. **2** a system of alternative psychotherapy based on the belief that emotional healing can be aided through resolution of bodily tension. —**bi·o·en·er·get·ic** *adj.*

bi·o·en·gi·neer·ing /,bīō,enjəˈni(ə)riNG/ ▸*n.* **1** another term for GENETIC ENGINEERING. **2** the use of artificial tissues, organs, or organ components to replace damaged or absent parts of the body, such as artificial limbs and heart pacemakers. **3** the use in engineering or industry of biological organisms or processes. —**bi·o·en·gi·neer** *n.* & *v.*

bi·o·eth·ics /,bīōˈeTHiks/ ▸*plural n.* [treated as *sing.*] the ethics of medical and biological research. —**bi·o·eth·i·cal** /-ˈeTHikəl/ *adj.* —**bi·o·eth·i·cist** /-ˈeTHəsist/ *n.*

bi·o·feed·back /,bīōˈfēd,bak/ ▸*n.* the use of electronic monitoring of a normally automatic bodily function in order to train someone to acquire voluntary control of that function.

bi·o·film /ˈbīō,film/ ▸*n.* a thin, slimy film of bacteria that adheres to a surface.

bi·o·fla·vo·noid /,bīōˈflāvə,noid/ ▸*n.* any of a group of compounds occurring mainly in citrus fruits and black currants, formerly regarded as vitamins. Also called CITRIN. See also VITAMIN P.

bi·o·foul·ing /ˈbīō,fouliNG/ ▸*n.* the fouling of pipes and underwater surfaces by organisms such as barnacles and algae.

bi·o·fu·el /ˈbīō,fyo͞oəl/ ▸*n.* a fuel derived directly from living matter.

bi·o·gas /ˈbīō,gas/ ▸*n.* gaseous fuel, esp. methane, produced by the fermentation of organic matter.

bi·o·gen·e·sis /,bīōˈjenəsis/ ▸*n.* the synthesis of substances by living organisms. ■ *historical* the hypothesis that living matter arises only from other living matter. —**bi·o·ge·net·ic** /-jəˈnetik/ *adj.*

bi·o·ge·net·ic law /,bīōjəˈnetik/ ▸*n.* the theory that evolutionary stages are repeated in the growth of a young animal. Also called RECAPITULATION THEORY.

bi·o·gen·ic /,bīōˈjenik/ ▸*adj.* [*attrib.*] produced or brought about by living organisms: *biogenic sediments.*

bi·o·ge·o·chem·i·cal /,bīō,jēōˈkemikəl/ ▸*adj.* relating to or denoting the cycle in which chemical elements and simple substances are transferred between living systems and the environment. —**bi·o·ge·o·chem·ist** /-ˈkemist/ *n.* —**bi·o·ge·o·chem·is·try** /-ˈkeməstrē/ *n.*

bi·o·ge·og·ra·phy /,bīōjēˈägrəfē/ ▸*n.* the branch of biology that deals with the geographical distribution of plants and animals. —**bi·o·ge·og·ra·pher** /-fər/ *n.* —**bi·o·ge·o·graph·ic** /-,jēəˈgrafik/ *adj.* —**bi·o·ge·o·graph·i·cal** /-,jēəˈgrafikəl/ *adj.* —**bi·o·ge·o·graph·i·cal·ly** *adv.*

bi·og·ra·phee /bī,ägrəˈfē/ ▸*n.* one who is the subject of a biography.

bi·og·ra·phy /bīˈägrəfē/ ▸*n.* (*pl.* **-phies**) an account of someone's life written by someone else. ■ writing of such a type as a branch of literature. ■ a human life in its course: *although their individual biographies are different, both are motivated by a similar ambition.* ▷late 17th cent.: from French *biographie* or modern Latin *biographia*, from medieval Greek, from *bios* 'life' + *-graphia* 'writing.' —**bi·og·ra·pher** /-fər/ *n.* —**bi·o·graph·ic** /,bīəˈgrafik/ *adj.* —**bi·o·graph·i·cal** /,bīəˈgrafikəl/ *adj.*

bi·o·hack·ing /,bīōˈhakiNG/ ▸*n.* the activity of exploiting genetic material experimentally without regard to accepted ethical standards, or for criminal purposes. —**bi·o·hack·er** *n.*

bi·o·haz·ard /ˈbīō,hazərd/ ▸*n.* a risk to human health or the environment arising from biological work, esp. with microorganisms.

bi·o·in·di·ca·tor /,bīōˈindi,kātər/ ▸*n.* an organism whose status in an ecosystem is analyzed as an indication of the ecosystem's heath: *spruce, which is the main tree species in Austria, was used as bioindicator.* —**bi·o·in·di·ca·tion** /-,indiˈkāSHən/ *n.*

bi·o·in·for·mat·ics /,bīō,infərˈmatiks/ ▸*plural n.* [treated as *sing.*] the science of collecting and analyzing complex biological data such as genetic codes. —**bi·o·in·for·mat·ic** *adj.*

Bi·o·ko /bēˈōkō/ an island in Equatorial Guinea, in the eastern part of the Gulf of Guinea. Its chief town is Malabo, which is also the capital of Equatorial Guinea. Known as Fernando Póo until 1973, it was called Macias Nguema 1973–79.

biol. ▸*abbr.* ■ biological. ■ biologist. ■ biology.

bi·o·log·i·cal /,bīəˈläjikəl/ (abbr.: **biol.**) ▸*adj.* of or relating to biology or living organisms. ■ genetically related; related by blood: *the alleged rights of the biological father.* ■ (of a detergent or other cleaning product) containing enzymes to assist the process of cleaning.

▸*n.* a therapeutic substance, such as a vaccine or drug, derived from biological sources: [usu. *plural*] *an international biotechnology company with interests in biologicals, agriculture, and pharmaceutical products.* —**bi·o·log·i·cal·ly** /-ik(ə)lē/ *adv.*

bi·o·log·i·cal clock ▸*n.* an innate mechanism that controls the physiological activities of an organism that change on a daily, seasonal, yearly, or other regular cycle.

bi·o·log·i·cal con·trol ▸*n.* the control of a pest by the introduction of a natural enemy or predator.

bi·o·log·i·cal ox·y·gen de·mand (abbr.: **BOD**) ▸*n.* another term for BIOCHEMICAL OXYGEN DEMAND.

bi·o·log·i·cal war·fare ▸*n.* the use of toxins of biological origin or microorganisms as weapons of war: *opposed to chemical and biological warfare.*

bi·ol·o·gism /bīˈälə,jizəm/ ▸*n.* the interpretation of human life from a strictly biological point of view. —**bi·ol·o·gis·tic** /-,äləˈjistik/ *adj.*

bi·ol·o·gy /bīˈäləjē/ (abbr.: **biol.**) ▸*n.* the study of living organisms, divided into many specialized fields that cover their morphology, physiology, anatomy, behavior, origin, and distribution. ■ the plants and animals of a particular area: *the biology of Chesapeake Bay.* ■ the physiology, behavior, and other qualities of a particular organism or class of organisms: *human biology.* ▷early 19th cent.: coined in German, via French from Greek *bios* 'life' + -LOGY. —**bi·ol·o·gist** /-jist/ *n.*

bi·o·lu·mi·nes·cence /,bīō,lo͞oməˈnesəns/ ▸*n.* the biochemical emission of light by living organisms such as fireflies and deep-sea fishes. ■ the light emitted in such a way. —**bi·o·lu·mi·nes·cent** /-ˈnesənt/ *adj.*

bi·o·mag·net·ism /,bīōˈmagni,tizəm/ ▸*n.* the interaction of living organisms with magnetic fields.

bi·o·mass /ˈbīō,mas/ ▸*n.* the total mass of organisms in a given area or volume. ■ organic matter used as a fuel, esp. in a power station for the generation of electricity.

bi·o·ma·ter·i·al /,bīōməˈti(ə)rēəl/ ▸*n.* synthetic or natural material suitable for use in constructing artificial organs and prostheses or to replace bone or tissue.

bi·o·math·e·mat·ics /,bīō,maTHəˈmatiks/ ▸*plural n.* [treated as *sing.*] the science of the application of mathematics to biology.

bi·ome /ˈbī,ōm/ ▸*n.* *Ecology* a large naturally occurring community of flora and fauna occupying a major habitat, e.g., forest or tundra. ▷early 20th cent.: from BIO- 'life' + -OME.

bi·o·me·chan·ics /,bīōməˈkaniks/ ▸*plural n.* [treated as *sing.*] the study of the mechanical laws relating to the movement or structure of living organisms.

bi·o·med·i·cal /,bīōˈmedikəl/ ▸*adj.* of or relating to both biology and medicine. —**bi·o·med·i·cine** /-ˈmedəsən/ *n.*

bi·o·me·te·or·ol·o·gy /,bīō,mētēəˈräləjē/ ▸*n.* the study of the relationship between living organisms and weather. —**bi·o·me·te·or·o·log·i·cal** /-ərəˈläjikəl/ *adj.*

bi·o·met·ric read·er /,bīōˈmetrik/ ▸*n.* an electronic device that determines identity by detecting and matching physical characteristics.

bi·o·met·rics /,bīōˈmetriks/ ▸*n.* **1** another term for BIOMETRY. **2** another term for BIOSTATISTICS.

bi·o·met·ric sig·na·ture ▸*n.* the unique pattern of a bodily feature such as the retina, iris, or voice, encoded on an identity card and used for recognition and identification purposes.

bi·om·e·try /bīˈämitrē/ ▸*n.* the application of statistical analysis to biological data. Also called BIOMETRICS. —**bi·o·met·ric** /,bīōˈmetrik/ *adj.* —**bi·o·met·ri·cal** /,bīōˈmetrikəl/ *adj.* —**bi·o·me·tri·cian** /,bīōməˈtriSHən/ *n.*

bi·o·mi·met·ic /,bīōmiˈmetik/ ▸*adj.* *Biochemistry* relating to or denoting synthetic methods that mimic biochemical processes. —**bi·o·mi·met·ics** *n.*

bi·o·morph /ˈbīō,môrf/ ▸*n.* a decorative form or object based on or resembling a living organism. ■ a graphical representation of an organism generated on a computer, used to model evolution. —**bi·o·mor·phic** /,bīōˈmôrfik/ *adj.*

bi·on·ic /bīˈänik/ ▸*adj.* having artificial body parts, esp. electromechanical ones. ■ *informal* having ordinary human powers increased by or as if by the aid of such devices (real or fictional): *working out in gymnasiums to become bionic men.* ■ of or relating to bionics. ▷1960s: from BIO- 'human,' on the pattern of *electronic.* —**bi·on·i·cal·ly** /-ik(ə)lē/ *adv.*

bi·on·ics /bīˈäniks/ ▸*plural n.* [treated as *sing.*] the study of mechanical systems that function like living organisms or parts of living organisms.

bi·o·nom·ics /bīəˈnämiks/ ▸*plural n.* [treated as *sing.*] the study of the mode of life of organisms in their natural habitat and their adaptations to their surroundings; ecology. ▷late 19th cent.: from BIO- 'life,' on the pattern of *economics.* —**bi·o·nom·ic** *adj.*

bi·o·phys·ics /,bīōˈfiziks/ ▸*plural n.* [treated as *sing.*] the science of the application of the laws of physics to biological phenomena. —**bi·o·phys·i·cal** /-ˈfizikəl/ *adj.* —**bi·o·phys·i·cist** /-ˈfizəsist/ *n.*

bi·o·pic /ˈbīō,pik/ ▸*n.* *informal* a biographical movie. ▷1950s: blend of *biographical* (see BIOGRAPHY) and PIC.

bi·o·pi·ra·cy /,bīōˈpīrəsē/ ▸*n.* bioprospecting that exploits plant and animal species by claiming patents to restrict their general use.

bi·o·pol·y·mer /,bīōˈpäləmər/ ▸*n.* a polymeric substance occurring in living organisms, e.g., a protein, cellulose, or DNA.

bi·o·pros·pect·ing /,bīōˈpräspektiNG/ ▸*n.* the search for plant and animal species from which medicinal drugs and other commercially valuable compounds can be obtained. ▷1990s: from *bio(diversity) prospecting.* —**bi·o·pros·pec·tor** /-ˈpräspektər/ *n.*

bi·op·sy /ˈbī,äpsē/ ▸*n.* (*pl.* **-sies**) an examination of tissue removed from a living body to discover the presence, cause, or extent of a disease. ▷late 19th cent.: coined in French from Greek *bios* 'life' + *opsis* 'sight,' on the pattern of *necropsy.*

bi·o·psy·chol·o·gy /ˌbīōsīˈkäləjē/ ▸*n.* the branch of psychology concerned with its biological and physiological aspects.

bi·o·re·ac·tor /ˌbīōrēˈaktər/ ▸*n.* an apparatus in which a biological reaction or process is carried out, esp. on an industrial scale.

bi·o·re·gion /ˈbīōˌrējən/ ▸*n.* a region defined by characteristics of the natural environment rather than by man-made divisions. —**bi·o·re·gion·al** /ˌbīōˈrējənl/ *adj.*

bi·o·re·gion·al·ism /ˌbīōˈrējənlˌizəm/ ▸*n.* advocacy of the belief that human activity should be largely restricted to distinct ecological and geographical regions. —**bi·o·re·gion·al·ist** *n.*

bi·o·re·me·di·a·tion /ˌbīōriˌmēdēˈāsʜən/ ▸*n.* the use of either naturally occurring or deliberately introduced microorganisms or other forms of life to consume and break down environmental pollutants, in order to clean up a polluted site.

bi·o·rhythm /ˈbīōˌriT͟Həm/ ▸*n.* a recurring cycle in the physiology or functioning of an organism, such as the daily cycle of sleeping and waking. ■ a cyclic pattern of physical, emotional, or mental activity said to occur in the life of a person. —**bi·o·rhyth·mic** /ˌbīōˈriT͟Hmik/ *adj.*

BIOS /ˈbīōs/ ▸*n.* *Computing* a set of computer instructions in firmware that control input and output operations. ▷acronym from *Basic Input-Output System.*

bi·o·sat·el·lite /ˌbīōˈsatlˌīt/ ▸*n.* an artificial satellite that serves as an automated laboratory, conducting biological experiments on living organisms.

bi·o·sci·ence /ˈbīōˌsīəns/ ▸*n.* any of the life sciences. —**bi·o·sci·en·tist** /ˌbīōˈsīəntist/ *n.*

bi·o·sen·sor /ˈbīōˌsensər/ ▸*n.* a device that uses a living organism or biological molecules, esp. enzymes or antibodies, to detect the presence of chemicals.

bi·o·so·cial /ˌbīōˈsōsʜəl/ ▸*adj.* of or relating to the interaction of biological and social factors.

bi·o·sol·ids /ˈbīōˌsälidz/ ▸*plural n.* organic matter recycled from sewage, esp. for use in agriculture.

bi·o·sphere /ˈbīəˌsfi(ə)r/ ▸*n.* the regions of the surface, atmosphere, and hydrosphere of the earth (or analogous parts of other planets) occupied by living organisms. ▷late 19th cent.: coined in German from Greek *bios* 'life' + *sphaira* (see SPHERE). —**bi·o·spher·ic** /ˌbīəˈsfi(ə)rik; -ˈsfer-/ *adj.*

bi·o·sta·tis·tics /ˌbīōstəˈtistiks/ ▸*plural n.* [treated as *sing.*] the branch of statistics that deals with data relating to living organisms. Also called BIOMETRICS. —**bi·o·sta·tis·ti·cal** /-tikəl/ *adj.* —**bi·o·stat·is·ti·cian** /-ˌstatəˈstisʜən/ *n.*

bi·o·stra·tig·ra·phy /ˌbīōstrəˈtigrəfē/ ▸*n.* the branch of stratigraphy concerned with fossils and their use in dating rock formations. —**bi·o·stra·tig·ra·pher** /-fər/ *n.* —**bi·o·strat·i·graph·ic** /-ˌstratiˈgrafik/ *adj.* —**bi·o·strat·i·graph·i·cal** /-ˌstratiˈgrafikəl/ *adj.* —**bi·o·strat·i·graph·i·cal·ly** *adv.*

bi·o·sur·ge·ry /ˌbīōˈsərjərē/ ▸*n.* the medical use of maggots to clean infected wounds, especially in cases where a patient is resistant to conventional antibiotic treatment.

bi·o·syn·the·sis /ˌbīōˈsinTHəsis/ ▸*n.* the production of complex molecules within living organisms or cells. —**bi·o·syn·thet·ic** /-ˌsinˈTHetik/ *adj.*

bi·o·sys·tem·at·ics /ˌbīōˌsistəˈmatiks/ ▸*plural n.* [treated as *sing.*] taxonomy based on the study of the genetic evolution of plant and animal populations. —**bi·o·sys·tem·a·tist** /-ˈsistəməˌtist/ *n.*

bi·o·ta /bīˈōtə/ ▸*n.* *Ecology* the animal and plant life of a particular region, habitat, or geological period: *the biota of the river.* ▷early 20th cent.: modern Latin, from Greek *biotē* 'life.'

bi·o·tech /ˌbīōˈtek; ˈbīōˌtek/ ▸*n.* *informal* short for BIOTECHNOLOGY.
▸*adj.* *informal* genetically modified: *biotech corn.*

bi·o·tech·nol·o·gy /ˌbīōtekˈnäləjē/ ▸*n.* the exploitation of biological processes for industrial and other purposes, esp. the genetic manipulation of microorganisms for the production of antibiotics, hormones, etc.

bi·o·te·lem·e·try /ˌbīōtəˈlemitrē/ ▸*n.* the detection or measurement of human or animal physiological functions from a distance using a telemeter: *a review of underwater biotelemetry, with emphasis on ultrasonic techniques.* —**bi·o·tel·e·me·tric** /-ˌteləˈmetrik/ *adj.*

bi·o·ter·ror·ism /ˌbīōˈterəˌrizəm/ ▸*n.* terrorism involving the release of toxic biological agents.

bi·o·ther·a·py /ˌbīōˈTHerəpē/ ▸*n.* (*pl.* **-pies**) the treatment of disease using substances obtained or derived from living organisms.

bi·ot·ic /bīˈätik/ ▸*adj.* [*attrib.*] of, relating to, or resulting from living things, esp. in their ecological relations: *the preservation of biotic diversity.* ▷mid 19th cent.: from French *biotique*, or via late Latin from Greek *biōtikos*, from *bios* 'life.'

bi·o·tin /ˈbīətin/ ▸*n.* *Biochemistry* a vitamin of the B complex, found in egg yolk, liver, and yeast. It is involved in the synthesis of fatty acids and glucose. Also called VITAMIN H. ▷1930s: coined in German from Greek *bios* 'life' + -IN[1].

bi·o·tite /ˈbīəˌtīt/ ▸*n.* a black, dark brown, or greenish black variety of mica, occurring in many igneous and metamorphic rocks. ▷mid 19th cent.: named after J.-B. *Biot* (1774–1862), French mineralogist.

bi·o·tope /ˈbīəˌtōp/ ▸*n.* *Ecology* the region of a habitat associated with a particular ecological community. ▷1920s: from German *Biotop*, based on Greek *topos* 'place.'

bi·o·trans·for·ma·tion /ˌbīōˌtransfərˈmāsʜən/ ▸*n.* the alteration of a substance, such as a drug, within the body.

bi·o·tur·ba·tion /ˌbīōtərˈbāsʜən/ ▸*n.* *Geology* the disturbance of sedimentary deposits by living organisms. —**bi·o·tur·ba·ted** /-ˈtərbātid/ *adj.*

bi·o·type /ˈbīəˌtīp/ ▸*n.* a group of organisms having an identical genetic constitution.

bi·o·war·fare /ˌbīōˈwôrˌfe(ə)r/ ▸*n.* biological warfare, including the use of toxins of biological origin or microorganisms as weapons of war.

bi·o·weap·on /ˈbīōˌwepən/ ▸*n.* a biological weapon: *fears mount about smallpox as a bioweapon.*

bi·par·ti·san /bīˈpärtəzən/ ▸*adj.* of or involving the agreement or cooperation of two political parties that usually oppose each other's policies: *educational reform received considerable bipartisan approval.* —**bi·par·ti·san·ship** /-ˌsʜip/ *n.*

USAGE See usage at CROSS-PARTY.

bi·par·tite /bīˈpärˌtīt/ ▸*adj.* involving or made by two separate parties: *the bipartite system of elementary and secondary schools.* ■ *technical* consisting of two parts: *a bipartite uterus.* ▷late Middle English (in the sense 'divided into two parts'): from Latin *bipartitus*, past participle of *bipartire*, from *bi-* 'two' + *partire* 'to part.'

bi·ped·al /bīˈpedl/ ▸*adj.* *Zoology* (of an animal) using only two legs for walking. ▷early 17th cent.: from Latin *bipes, biped-* (from *bi-* 'having two' + *pes, ped-* 'foot') + -AL. —**bi·ped** /ˈbīped/ *n.* & *adj.* —**bi·ped·al·ism** /bīˈpedlˌizəm/ *n.* —**bi·pe·dal·i·ty** /ˌbīpiˈdalitē/ *n.*

bi·pha·sic /bīˈfāzik/ ▸*adj.* having two phases: the patient's biphasic recovery curve.

bi·phen·yl /bīˈfenl/ ▸*n.* *Chemistry* an organic compound containing two phenyl groups bonded together, e.g., the PCBs.

bi·pin·nate /bīˈpinˌāt/ ▸*adj.* *Botany* (of a pinnate leaf) having leaflets that are further subdivided in a pinnate arrangement.

bi·plane /ˈbīˌplān/ ▸*n.* an early type of aircraft with two pairs of wings, one above the other.

biplane

bi·pod /ˈbīˌpäd/ ▸*n.* a two-legged stand or support.

bi·po·lar /bīˈpōlər/ ▸*adj.* having or relating to two poles or extremities: *a sharply bipolar division of affluent and underclasses.* ■ (of a plant or animal species) of or occurring in both polar regions. ■ (of a nerve cell) having two axons, one on either side of the cell body. ■ *Electronics* (of a transistor or other device) using both positive and negative charge carriers. —**bi·po·lar·i·ty** /ˌbīpōˈlaritē; -pə-/ *n.*

bi·po·lar dis·or·der ▸*n.* a mental disorder marked by alternating periods of elation and depression. Also called **bipolar illness**. Also called, esp. formerly, MANIC DEPRESSION. Compare with UNIPOLAR.

bi·ra·cial /bīˈrāsʜəl/ ▸*adj.* concerning or containing members of two racial groups.

bi·ra·mous /bīˈrāməs/ ▸*adj.* *Zoology* (esp. of crustacean limbs and antennae) dividing to form two branches. ▷late 19th cent.: from BI- 'two' + RAMUS + -OUS.

birch /bərcʜ/ ▸*n.* **1** (also **birch tree**) a slender, fast-growing tree that has thin bark (often peeling) and bears catkins. Birch trees grow chiefly in north temperate regions, some reaching the northern limit of tree growth. • Genus *Betula*, family Betulaceae: many species, including the **yellow birch** (*B. alleghaniensis*) of North America. ■ (also **birch·wood**) the hard fine-grained pale wood of any of these trees. **2** (**the birch**) *chiefly historical* a formal punishment in which a person is flogged with a bundle of birch twigs.
▸*v.* [*trans.*] *chiefly historical* beat (someone) with a bundle of birch twigs as a formal punishment. ▷Old English *bierce, birce*, of Germanic origin; related to German *Birke*. —**birch·en** /-cʜən/ *adj.* (*archaic*).

birch·bark /ˈbərcʜˌbärk/ (also **birch bark**) ▸*n.* the impervious bark of the North American paper birch, *Betula papyrifera*, used, esp. formerly by American Indians, to make canoes and containers: *stretched the birchbark over a cedar frame* | [as *adj.*] *birchbark baskets.* ■ a canoe of this material.

Birch·er /ˈbərcʜər/ ▸*n.* a member or supporter of the John Birch Society, a conservative anticommunist American organization founded in 1958. ▷from the name of John *Birch*, a Baptist missionary and U.S. Army Air Force officer and called the "first casualty of the Cold War," killed by Chinese communists in 1945.

Bird /bərd/, Larry (1956–), U.S. basketball player and coach. He played for the Boston Celtics 1979–92 and coached the Indiana Pacers 1997–2000. Basketball Hall of Fame (1998).

bird /bərd/ ▸*n.* **1** a warm-blooded egg-laying vertebrate distinguished by the possession of feathers, wings, and a beak and (typically) by being able to fly. • Class Aves; birds probably evolved in the Jurassic period from small dinosaurs that may already have been warm-blooded. ■ an animal of this type that is hunted for sport or used for food: *carve the bird at the dinner table.* ■ a clay pigeon. ■ *informal* an aircraft, spacecraft, satellite, or guided missile: *the crews worked frantically to ready their birds for flight.* **2** [usu. with *adj.*] *informal* a person of a specified kind or character: *I'm a pretty tough* **old bird.** ■ *Brit., informal* a young woman; a girlfriend. ▷Old English *brid* 'chick, fledgling,' of unknown origin.
▸***PHRASES*** □ **a bird in the hand is worth two in the bush** *proverb* it's better to be content with what you have than to risk losing everything by seeking more. □ **the birds and the bees** basic facts about sex and reproduction, as told to a child. □ **birds of a feather flock together** *proverb* people of the same sort or with the same tastes and interests will be found together: *these health professionals were birds of a feather.* □ **eat like a bird** see EAT. □ **flip someone the bird** stick one's middle finger up at someone as a sign of contempt or anger, meaning 'fuck you'. Compare with *give someone the finger* in FINGER. □ (**strictly**) **for the birds** *informal* not worth consideration; unimportant: *this piece of legislation is for the birds.* □ **give someone the bird** see FLIP SOMEONE THE BIRD. □ **have a bird** *informal* be very shocked or agitated: *the press corps would have a bird if the president-to-be appointed his wife to a real job.* □ **kill two birds with one stone** see KILL[1]. □ **a little bird told me** *humorous* used to say that the speaker knows something but prefers to keep the identity of the informant a secret: *a little bird told me it was your birthday.*

bird band·ing ▸*n.* the practice of catching birds, marking them with an identifying band around the leg, and then releasing them. —**bird band·er** *n.*

bird·bath /ˈbərdˌbaTH/ ▸*n.* a small basin filled with water for birds to bathe in, typically found in a garden.

bird·brain /ˈbərdˌbrān/ ▸*n.* *informal* an annoyingly stupid and shallow person. —**bird·brained** *adj.*

bird·cage /ˈbərdˌkāj/ ▸*n.* a cage for pet birds, typically made of wire or cane. ■ an object resembling such a cage: *the elevator was an elegant and gilded birdcage.*

bird call ▸*n.* a note uttered by a bird for the purpose of contact, alarm, or marking its territory. ■ an instrument imitating such a sound, used esp. by hunters.

bird cher·ry ▸*n.* a small wild cherry tree or shrub, with bitter black fruit that is eaten by birds. • Genus *Prunus*, family Rosaceae: many species, including the **pin cherry** (*P. pensylvanica*) of North America.

bird colo·nel ▸*n.* *informal* a full colonel. ▷mid 20th cent.; from the silver eagle indicating the rank of full colonel.

bird dog ▸*n.* a gun dog trained to retrieve birds. ■ *informal* a person whose job involves searching, esp. a talent scout for a sports team.
▸*v.* (**bird-dog**) [*trans.*] search out or pursue with dogged determination: *he ordered the vice president to bird-dog Congress for funds.*

bird·er /ˈbərdər/ ▸*n. informal* a bird-watcher.

bird flu ▸*n.* an often fatal flu virus of birds, esp. poultry, that is transmissible from them to humans, in whom it may also prove fatal. • the virus is an *Influenza A* virus, family Orthomyxoviridae.

B

bird·house /ˈbərd,hous/ ▸*n.* a box, typically made to resemble a house, provided for a bird to make its nest in.

bird·ie /ˈbərdē/ ▸*n.* (*pl.* **bird·ies**) **1** *informal* a little bird. **2** *Golf* a score of one stroke under par at a hole.
▸*v.* (**bird·ie·ing**) *Golf* [*trans.*] play (a hole) with a score of one stroke under par: *she wound up birdieing the hole from 20 feet.* ▷late 18th cent.: diminutive of BIRD; the golf term from slang *bird*, denoting any first-rate thing.

bird·ing /ˈbərdiNG/ ▸*n.* the observation of birds in their natural habitats as a hobby.

bird·lime /ˈbərd,līm/ ▸*n.* a sticky substance spread on twigs to trap small birds.
▸*v.* spread with birdlime: *he birdlimed the branch.* ■ catch or trap with birdlime. ■ *figurative* entrap by clever deception; inveigle: *they were birdlimed by his slick line of flattery.*

bird of par·a·dise ▸*n.* **1** (*pl.* **birds of par·a·dise**) a tropical Australasian bird, the male of which is noted for the beauty and brilliance of its plumage and its spectacular courtship display. Most kinds are found in New Guinea, where their feathers are used in ornamental dress. • Family Paradisaeidae: numerous genera. [early 17th cent.: *paradise* suggested by the modern Latin family name *Paradisaeidae* (plural).] **2** (also **bird of paradise flower**) a southern African plant related to the banana. It bears a showy irregular flower with a long projecting tongue. • Genus *Strelitzia*, family Strelitziaceae: several species, in particular *S. regina*, whose orange and dark blue flowers are pollinated by a sunbird. [late 19th cent.: named from the protrusion of flowers from a green spathe, resembling a bird of paradise in flight.]

bird of pas·sage ▸*n. dated* a migratory bird. ■ a person who passes through or visits a place without staying for long.

bird of prey ▸*n.* a predatory bird, distinguished by a hooked bill and sharp talons; a raptor. • Orders Falconiformes (the diurnal birds of prey) and Strigiformes (the owls).

bird pep·per ▸*n.* a tropical American pepper thought to be the ancestor of both sweet and chili peppers. • *Capsicum annuum* var. *glabriusculum* (or *C. frutescens* var. *typicum*), family Solanaceae. ■ the small, red, very hot fruit of this plant. ■ a variety of small hot pepper grown in Asia or Africa.

bird·seed /ˈbərd,sēd/ ▸*n.* any seed or blend of seed for feeding birds.

Birds·eye /ˈbərd,zī/, Clarence (1886–1956), U.S. businessman and inventor. A former fur trader, he had observed food preservation techniques practiced by the people of Labrador. He developed a process of rapidly freezing foods in small packages that were suitable for retail sale and created a revolution in eating habits.

bird's-eye ▸*n.* **1** [usu. as *adj.*] any of a number of plants with small flowers that have contrasting petals and centers, in particular: • (also **bird's-eye primrose**) a primrose with yellow-centered purple flowers (*Primula farinosa*, family Primulaceae). • (also **bird's-eye speedwell**) a speedwell with bright blue flowers, also known as GERMANDER SPEEDWELL. **2** (also **bird's-eye chili** or **bird's-eye pepper**) a small, very hot chili pepper. **3** a small geometric pattern woven with a dot in the center, typically used in suiting and lining fabrics.

bird's-eye ma·ple ▸*n.* the lumber from an American maple, typically the sugar maple, that contains eyelike markings, used in decorative woodwork.

bird's-eye view ▸*n.* a general view from above: *we had a bird's-eye view from the attic window.* ■ a general view as if from above: *the map gives a bird's-eye view of the route.* ■ a broad, general, or superficial consideration (of something): *this introductory bird's-eye view will survey the animal kingdom.*

bird's-foot tre·foil (also **birds·foot tre·foil**) ▸*n.* a small plant of the pea family with leaves that consist of three leaflets, yellow flowers streaked with red, and triple pods that resemble the feet of a bird. • *Lotus corniculatus*, family Leguminosae.

bird·shot /ˈbərd,SHät/ ▸*n.* the smallest size of shot for shotguns.

bird's-nest ▸*n.* **1** a North American brownish or yellowish flowering plant of the wintergreen family, with scalelike leaves. The bird's-nest is a saprophyte that lacks chlorophyll. Also called **giant bird's-nest** • *Pterospora andromeda*, family Monotropaceae. **2** (also **bird's-nest fungus**) a fungus of worldwide distribution that grows on dead wood and other plant debris. It produces a small bowl-shaped fruiting body that opens to reveal egg-shaped organs containing the spores. • Family Nidulariaceae, class Basidiomycetes: several genera and species, including the common *Crucibulum levis*.

bird's-nest or·chid ▸*n.* a European woodland orchid that lacks chlorophyll, the whole plant being yellowish-brown. It obtains nourishment by linking its nestlike mass of thick roots to a soil-dwelling fungus from which it absorbs nutrients. • *Neottia nidus-avis*, family Orchidaceae.

bird's nest soup ▸*n.* a Chinese soup made from the dried gelatinous coating of the nests of swifts and other birds.

bird·song /ˈbərd,sôNG/ ▸*n.* the musical vocalizations of a bird or birds, typically uttered by a male songbird in characteristic bursts or phrases for territorial purposes.

bird strike (also **bird-strike**) ▸*n.* a collision between a bird or flock of birds and an aircraft.

bird-watch·er (also **bird·watch·er**) ▸*n.* a person who observes birds in their natural surroundings as a hobby. —**bird-watch·ing** *n.*

Bird Wom·an see SACAJAWEA.

bi·re·frin·gent /,bīriˈfrinjənt/ ▸*adj. Physics* having two different refractive indices. ■ *Optics* of or relating to optically anisotropic material: *double refraction will occur in a birefringent material such as quartz.* —**bi·re·frin·gence** *n.*

bi·reme /ˈbī,rēm/ ▸*n.* an ancient warship with two files of oarsmen on each side. ▷late 16th cent.: from Latin *biremis*, from *bi-* 'having two' + *remus* 'oar.'

bi·ret·ta /bəˈretə/ (also **be·ret·ta**) ▸*n.* a square cap with three flat projections on top, worn by Roman Catholic clergymen. ▷late 16th cent.: from Italian *berretta* or Spanish *birreta*, based on late Latin *birrus* 'hooded cape.' Compare with BERET.

Bir·git·ta, St. /birˈgitə/ see BRIDGET, ST.[2]

bi·ri /ˈbi(ə)rē/ ▸*n.* (*pl.* **-ris**) variant spelling of BIDI.

bi·ri·a·ni /,birēˈänē/ ▸*n.* variant spelling of BIRYANI.

Bir·ken·head /ˈbərkən,hed/ a town in northwestern England on the Wirral Peninsula on the Mersey River, opposite Liverpool; pop. 116,000.

Bir·ken·stock /ˈbərkən,stäk/ ▸*n. trademark* a type of shoe or sandal with a contoured cork-filled sole and a thick leather upper. ■ [as *modifier*] denoting people concerned with political correctness or conservationist issues: *home builders are no longer content to leave environmentalism to the Birkenstock crowd.* ▷1970s: from the name of the manufacturer.

Bir·man /ˈbərmən/ ▸*n.* a cat of a long-haired breed, typically with a cream body, a dark head, tail, and legs, and white paws.

Bir·ming·ham **1** /ˈbərmiNG,ham/ an industrial city in north central Alabama; pop. 242,820. **2** /ˈbərmiNG-,ham/ a city in southeastern Michigan, north of Detroit; pop. 19,997. **3** /ˈbərmiNGəm/ an industrial city in west central England; pop. 934,900.

birr /bər/ ▸*n.* the basic monetary unit of Ethiopia, equal to 100 cents. ▷from Amharic.

birth /bərTH/ ▸*n.* the emergence of a baby or other young from the body of its mother; the start of life as a physically separate being: *he was blind* ***from birth*** | *despite a difficult birth he's fit and healthy.* ■ [with *adj.*] a baby born: *the overall rate of incidence of Down syndrome is one in every 800 live births.* ■ the beginning or coming into existence of something: *the birth of democracy.* ■ origin, descent, or ancestry: *the mother is American* ***by birth***. ■ high or noble descent: *she was proud of her beauty and her birth.*
▸*v.* [*trans.*] *informal* give birth to (a baby or other young): *she had carried him and birthed him* | [*intrans.*] *in spring the cows birthed.* ▷Middle English: from Old Norse *byrth*; related to BEAR[1].
▸*PHRASE* □ **give birth** bear a child or young: *she's due to give birth in March* | *she* ***gave birth to*** *a son.*

birth ca·nal ▸*n.* the passageway from the womb through the cervix, the vagina, and the vulva through which a fetus passes during birth.

birth cer·tif·i·cate ▸*n.* an official document issued to record a person's birth, including such identifying data as name, gender, date of birth, place of birth, and parentage.

birth con·trol ▸*n.* the practice of preventing unwanted pregnancies, typically by use of contraception.

birth con·trol pill ▸*n.* a contraceptive pill.

birth·date /ˈbərTH,dāt/ ▸*n.* **1** date of birth: *her baptismal record puts her birthdate as April 26, 1741.* **2** the anniversary of a date of birth, especially for someone dead: *the communists' symbolic vote to clear the name of Stalin came six days after Stalin's birthdate.*

birth·day /ˈbərTH,dā/ ▸*n.* the annual anniversary of the day on which a person was born, typically treated as an occasion for celebration and present-giving: *I'm getting a dollhouse for my birthday* | [as *adj.*] *a birthday cake* | *the birthday boy.* ■ the day of one's birth: *she shares a birthday with Paul McCartney.* ■ the anniversary of something starting or being founded: *the staff celebrated the twenty-fifth birthday of the paper.*
▸*PHRASE* □ **in one's birthday suit** *humorous* naked.

birth de·fect ▸*n.* a physical or biochemical abnormality that is present at birth and that may be inherited or the result of environmental influence.

birth fam·i·ly ▸*n.* one's biological parents and siblings, as opposed to adoptive relatives.

birth·ing /ˈbərTHiNG/ ▸*n.* the action or process of giving birth: [as *adj.*] *a birthing pool.*

birth·ing cen·ter ▸*n.* a medical facility, specializing in childbirth, that is less restrictive and more homelike than a hospital.

birth·ing room ▸*n.* a room in a hospital or other medical facility that is equipped for labor and childbirth and is designed to be comfortable and homelike.

birth·mark /ˈbərTH,märk/ ▸*n.* an unusual and typically permanent brown or red mark on someone's body from birth.

birth moth·er ▸*n.* a woman who has given birth to a child, as opposed to an adoptive mother; a biological mother.

birth pang ▸*n.* [usu. in *pl.*] another term for LABOR PAIN.

birth par·ent ▸*n.* a biological as opposed to an adoptive parent.

birth·place /ˈbərTH,plās/ ▸*n.* the place where a person was born. ■ the place where something started or originated: *Florence was the birthplace of the Renaissance.*

birth rate ▸*n.* the number of live births per thousand of population per year.

birth·right /ˈbərTH,rīt/ ▸*n.* a particular right of possession or privilege one has from birth, esp. as an eldest child. ■ the possession or privilege itself: *your daddy's gold watch is your birthright.* ■ a natural or moral right, possessed by everyone: *she saw a liberal education as the birthright of every child.*

birth·stone /ˈbərTH,stōn/ ▸*n.* a gemstone popularly associated with the month or astrological sign of one's birth.

birth·weight /ˈbərTH,wāt/ ▸*n.* the weight of a baby at birth.

birth·wort /ˈbərTH,wərt; -,wôrt/ ▸*n.* a climbing or herbaceous plant that typically has heart-shaped leaves and deep-throated, often pipe-shaped, flowers. It was formerly used as an aid to childbirth and to induce abortion. • Genus *Aristolochia*, family Aristolochiaceae.

bi·ry·a·ni /,birēˈänē/ (also **bi·ri·a·ni**) ▸*n.* an Indian dish made with highly seasoned rice and meat, fish, or vegetables. ▷Urdu, from Persian *biryānī*, from *biriyān* 'fried, grilled.'

bis /bis/ ▸*adv.* again, as a direction in a musical score indicating that a passage is to be repeated. ▷via French and Italian from Latin, literally 'twice.'

bis- ▸*comb. form Chemistry* used to form the names of compounds containing two groups identically substituted or coordinated: *bis(2-aminoethyl) ether.*

Bis·cay, Bay of /ˈbis,kā/ a part of the North Atlantic Ocean between the northern coast of Spain and the western coast of France, noted for its strong currents and storms.

Bis·cayne Bay /bisˈkān/ an inlet of the Atlantic Ocean in southeastern Florida, south of Miami, noted for its islands and resorts.

bis·cot·ti /biˈskätē/ ▸*plural n.* small, crisp rectangular twice-baked cookies typically containing nuts, made originally in Italy. ▷Italian.

bis·cuit /ˈbiskit/ ▸*n.* **1** a small, typically round cake of bread leavened with baking powder, baking soda, or sometimes yeast. ■ *Brit.* a cookie or cracker. **2** another term for BISQUE[3]: [as *adj.*] *biscuit ware.* **3** a light

brown color. **4** a small flat piece of wood used to join two mortised planks together.
▸*adj.* light brown in color. ▷Middle English: from Old French *bescuit*, based on Latin *bis* 'twice' + *coctus*, past participle of *coquere* 'to cook' (so named because originally biscuits were cooked in a twofold process: first baked and then dried out in a slow oven so that they would keep). **—bis·cuit·y** *adj.*

bi·sect /bī'sekt; 'bī,sekt/ ▸*v.* [*trans.*] divide into two parts: *a landscape of farmland bisected by long straight roads.* ■ *Geometry* divide (a line, angle, shape, etc.) into two equal parts. ▷mid 17th cent.: from **BI-** 'two' + Latin *sect-* (from *secare* 'to cut'). **—bi·sec·tion** /bī'sekSHən/ *n.* **—bi·sec·tor** /bī'sektər; 'bī,sek-/ *n.*

bi·se·ri·al /bī'si(ə)rēəl/ ▸*adj.* *Statistics* referring to the correlation between two sets measurements, one of which is dichotomous. ■ *Botany & Zoology* arranged in or consisting of two series or rows.

bi·sex·u·al /bī'sekSHo͞oəl/ ▸*adj.* sexually attracted to both men and women. ■ *Biology* having characteristics of both sexes.
▸*n.* a person who is sexually attracted to both men and women. **—bi·sex·u·al·i·ty** /,bīsekSHo͞o'alitē/ *n.*

Bish·kek /bisH'kek/ the capital of Kyrgyzstan; pop. 625,000. From 1926 to 1991, the city was named Frunze. Former name (until 1926) **PISHPEK**.

Bi·sho /'bēsHō/ a town in southern South Africa, situated near the coast to the northeast of Port Elizabeth; pop. (with East London) 270,130.

Bish·op /'bisHəp/, Elizabeth (1911–79), U.S. poet. Her poetry contrasts her experiences in South America 1952–67 with her New England origins. She was awarded the Pulitzer Prize for her first two collections, *North and South* (1946) and *A Cold Spring* (1955). Other notable works include *Geography III* (1976).

bish·op /'bisHəp/ ▸*n.* **1** a senior member of the Christian clergy, typically in charge of a diocese and empowered to confer holy orders. **2** (also **bishop bird**) an African weaverbird, the male of which has red, orange, yellow, or black plumage. • Genus *Euplectes*, family Ploceidae: several species, including the **red bishop** (*E. orix*), which has scarlet plumage with a black face and underparts. **3** a chess piece, typically with its top shaped like a miter, that can move in any direction along a diagonal on which it stands. Each player starts the game with two bishops, one moving on white squares and the other on black. **4** mulled and spiced wine. ▷Old English *biscop*, *bisceop*, based on Greek *episkopos* 'overseer,' from *epi* 'above' + *-skopos* '-looking.'

bish·op·ric /'bisHəprik/ ▸*n.* the office or rank of a bishop. ■ a district under a bishop's control; a diocese. ▷Old English *bisceoprīce*, from *bisceop* (see **BISHOP**) + *rīce* 'realm.'

Bis·la·ma /bis'lämə/ ▸*n.* an English-based pidgin language used as a lingua franca in Fiji and the Solomon Islands and as an official language in Vanuatu. Also called **BEACH-LA-MAR**. ▷alteration of Portuguese *bicho do mar* 'sea cucumber'(traded as a commodity, the word later being applied to the language of trade). Compare with **BÊCHE-DE-MER**.

Bis·marck[1] /'biz,märk/ the capital of North Dakota, in the south central part of the state, on the Missouri River; pop. 55,532. It took the name of German Chancellor Bismarck in order to attract German capital for railroad building.

Bis·marck[2], Otto Eduard Leopold von, Prince of Bismarck, Duke of Lauenburg (1815–98), Prussian minister and German statesman; chancellor of the German Empire 1871–90; also known as the **Iron Chancellor**. He was the driving force behind the unification of Germany and orchestrated wars with Denmark 1864, Austria 1866, and France 1870–71 in order to achieve this end.

Bis·marck Ar·chi·pel·a·go an island group in the western Pacific Ocean, part of Papua New Guinea. Held by Germany from 1884 to World War I, it includes New Britain, New Ireland, and several hundred other islands.

Bis·marck Sea an arm of the Pacific Ocean, northeast of New Guinea and north of New Britain. In March 1943, the U.S. destroyed a large Japanese naval force in these waters.

bis·mil·lah /bis'milə/ ▸*exclam.* in the name of Allah (an invocation used by Muslims at the beginning of any undertaking). ▷from Arabic *bi-smi-llāh(i)*, the first phrase of the Koran.

bis·muth /'bizməTH/ ▸*n.* the chemical element of atomic number 83, a brittle reddish-gray metal. (Symbol: **Bi**) ■ a compound of this element used medicinally. ▷mid 17th cent.: from modern Latin *bisemutum*, Latinization of German *Wismut*, of unknown origin.

bi·son /'bīsən; -zən/ ▸*n.* (*pl.* same) a humpbacked shaggy-haired wild ox native to North America and Europe. • Genus *Bison*, family Bovidae: *B. bison* of North American prairies (also called **BUFFALO**), and *B. bonasus* of European forests (also called **WISENT**), now found only in Poland. These are sometimes regarded as a single species. ▷late Middle English: from Latin, ultimately of Germanic origin and related to **WISENT**.

bis·phe·nol A /bis'fēnôl/ ▸*n.* *Chemistry* a synthetic organic compound used in the manufacture of epoxy resins and other polymers. • A bicyclic phenol; chem. formula: $C(CH_3)_2(C_6H_4OH)_2$.

bisque[1] /bisk/ ▸*n.* a rich, creamy soup typically made with shellfish, esp. lobster. ▷mid 17th cent.: French, literally 'crayfish soup.'

bisque[2] ▸*n.* an extra turn, point, or stroke allowed to a weaker player in croquet or court tennis. ▷mid 17th cent. (originally a term in court tennis): from French, of unknown ultimate origin.

bisque[3] ▸*n.* **1** fired unglazed pottery: *using bisque for doll heads* | [as *adj.*] *bisque figurines.* **2** a light brown color: *shades of bisque, taupe, and chocolate brown.*
▸*adj.* light brown in color.

Bis·sau /bi'sou/ the capital of Guinea-Bissau, in the western part of the country; pop. 125,000.

bi·sta·ble /bī'stābəl/ ▸*n.* an electronic circuit that has two stable states.
▸*adj.* (of a system) having two stable states.

bis·ter /'bistər/ (also **bis·tre**) ▸*n.* a brownish-yellowish pigment made from the soot of burned wood. ■ the color of this pigment. ▷early 18th cent.: from French *bistre*, of unknown origin.

bis·tort /'bistôrt/ ▸*n.* a Eurasian herbaceous plant with a spike of flesh-colored flowers and twisted root that is sometimes used medicinally. • Genus *Polygonum*, family Polygonaceae: several species, in particular *P. bistorta*. ▷early 16th cent.: from French *bistorte* or medieval Latin *bistorta*, from *bis* 'twice' + *torta* (feminine past participle of *torquere* 'to twist').

bis·tou·ry /'bistərē/ ▸*n.* (*pl.* **-ries**) a surgical knife with a long, narrow, straight or curved blade. ▷mid 18th cent.: from French *bistouri*, originally *bistorie* 'dagger,' of unknown origin.

bis·tro /'bistrō; 'bē-/ ▸*n.* (*pl.* **-tros**) a small restaurant. ▷1920s: French.

bi·sul·fate /bī'səl,fāt/ (*chiefly Brit.* also **bi·sul·phate**) ▸*n.* *Chemistry* a salt of the anion HSO_4^-.

bi·sul·fide /bī'səl,fīd/ (*chiefly Brit.* **bi·sul·phide**) ▸*n.* another term for **DISULFIDE**.

bi·sul·fite /bī'səl,fīt/ (*chiefly Brit.* also **bi·sul·phite**) ▸*n.* an acid sulfite containing the radical HSO_3.

bit[1] /bit/ ▸*n.* **1** a small piece, part, or quantity of something: *give the duck **a bit of** bread* | *he read **bits of** his work to me.* ■ **(a bit)** a fair amount: *there's a bit to talk about there.* ■ **(a bit)** a short time or distance: *I fell asleep for a bit.* ■ [with *adj.*] *informal* a set of actions or ideas associated with a specific group or activity: *she's gone off to do her theatrical bit.* **2** *informal, dated* a unit of $12^1/_2$ cents (used only in even multiples): *the sideshow admission was twenty-five cents, two bits, the fourth of a dollar.* ▷Old English *bita* 'bite, mouthful,' of Germanic origin; related to German *Bissen*, also to **BITE**.
▸*PHRASES* □ **a bit** somewhat; to some extent: *he came back looking a bit annoyed.* □ **bit by bit** gradually: *the school was built bit by bit over the years.* □ **a bit of a —** used to suggest that something is not severe or extreme, or is true only to a limited extent: *he's a bit of a womanizer.* ■ only a little —; a mere —: *we went on a bit of a walk.* □ **bits and pieces** an assortment of small items: *weird bits and pieces of paraphernalia.* □ **do one's bit** *informal* make a useful contribution to an effort or cause: *she was keen to do her bit to help others.* □ **every bit as** see **EVERY**. □ **not a bit** not at all: *I'm not a bit tired.* □ **to bits 1** into pieces: *he smashed it to bits with a hammer.* **2** *informal* very much; to a great degree: *we've got two great kids whom I love to bits.*

bit[2] ▸ past of **BITE**.

bit[3] ▸*n.* **1** a mouthpiece, typically made of metal, that is attached to a bridle and used to control a horse. **2** a tool or piece for boring or drilling, typically of metal: *a drill bit.* ■ the cutting or gripping part of a plane, pliers, or other tool. ■ the part of a key that engages with the lock lever. ■ the copper head of a soldering iron.
▸*v.* [*trans.*] put a bit into the mouth of (a horse). ■ *figurative* restrain: *my own hysteria was bitted by upbringing and respect.* ▷Old English *bite* 'biting, a bite,' of Germanic origin; related to Dutch *beet* and German *Biss*, also to **BITE**. **—bit·ted** *adj.* [in *combination*] *a double-bitted ax.*
▸*PHRASES* □ **above the bit** (of a horse) carrying its head too high so that it evades correct contact with the bit. □ **behind the bit** (of a horse) carrying its head with the chin tucked in so that it evades contact with the bit. □ **off the bit** (or **bridle**) (of a horse) ridden on a loose rein to allow it to gallop freely, esp. at the end of a race. □ **on the bit** (or **bridle**) (of a horse) ridden with a light but firm contact on the mouth, and accepting the bit in a calm and relaxed manner. □ **take** (or **get** or **have**) **the bit in** (or **between**) **one's teeth** begin to tackle a problem or task in a determined or independent way.

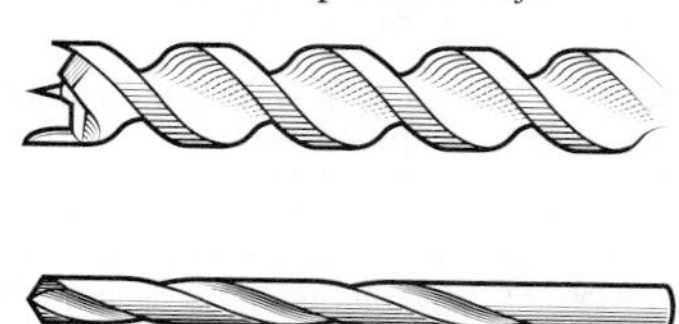

bit[3] **2**

bit[4] ▸*n.* *Computing* a unit of information expressed as either a 0 or 1 in binary notation. ▷1940s: blend of **BINARY** and **DIGIT**.

bi·tar·trate /bī'tär,trāt/ ▸*n.* an acid tartrate containing the radical $C_4H_5O_6$.

bitch /bicH/ ▸*n.* **1** a female dog, wolf, fox, or otter. **2** *informal, derogatory* a woman whom one dislikes or considers to be malicious or unpleasant. ■ [in *sing.*] *informal* a thing or situation that is unpleasant or difficult to deal with: *the stove is a bitch to fix.*
▸*v.* [*intrans.*] *informal* express displeasure; grumble: *they **bitch about** everything* | [as *n.*] (**bitching**) *we're tired of your bitching.* ▷Old English *bicce*, of Germanic origin.

bitch·er·y /'bicHərē/ ▸*n.* bitchy behavior.

bitch·ing /'bicHiNG/ (also **bitch·en** or **bitch·in'** /'bicHən/) ▸*adj.* *informal* excellent: *a bitching new album.*
▸*adv.* [as *submodifier*] extremely: *it's bitchin' hot, ain't it?*

bitch-slap ▸*v.* (**-slapped, -slap·ping**) *vulgar slang* [*trans.*] deliver a stinging blow to (someone), typically in order to humiliate them: *I'd bitch-slap her too if she mouthed off to me like that.* ▷1990s: originally black English, referring to a woman hitting or haranguing her male partner.

bitch·y /'bicHē/ *informal* ▸*adj.* (**bitchier, bitchiest**) (of a person's comments or behavior) malicious or unpleasant: *bitchy remarks.* **—bitch·i·ly** /'bicHəlē/ *adv.* **—bitch·i·ness** *n.*

bite /bīt/ ▸*v.* (*past* **bit** /bit/; *past part.* **bit·ten** /'bitn/) [*intrans.*] **1** (of a person or animal) use the teeth to cut into something in order to eat it: *Rosa **bit into** a cupcake* | [*trans.*] *he bit a mouthful from the sandwich.* ■ [*trans.*] (of an animal or a person) use the teeth in order to inflict injury on: *she had bitten, scratched, and kicked her assailant.* ■ [*trans.*] (of a snake, insect, or arachnid) wound with a sting, pincers, or fangs: *getting bitten by mosquitoes.* ■ (**bite at**) (of an animal) snap at; attempt to bite: *it is not unusual for this dog to bite at its owner's hand.* ■ (of an acid) corrode a surface: *chemicals have **bitten** deep **into** the stone.* ■ (of a fish) take the bait or lure on the end of a fishing line into the mouth. ■ *figurative* (of a person) be persuaded to accept a deal or offer: *a hundred or so retailers should bite.* **2** (of a tool, tire, boot, etc.) grip a surface: *once on the wet grass, my boots failed to bite.* ■ (of an object) press into a part of the body, causing pain: *the handcuffs **bit into** his wrists.* ■ *figurative* cause emotional pain: *Cheryl's betrayal had bitten deep.* ■ (of a policy or situation) take effect, with unpleasant consequences: *when the cuts in art education start to bite.* ■ *informal* be very bad, unpleasant, or unfortunate: *it bites that your mom won't let you go.*
▸*phrasal v.* □ **bite something back** refrain with difficulty from saying something, making a sound, or expressing an emotion: *Melissa bit back a scathing comment.*
▸*n.* **1** an act of biting into something in order to eat it: *Stephen ate a hot dog in three big bites.* ■ a piece cut off by biting: *Robyn took a large bite out of her sandwich.* ■ *informal* a quick snack: *I plan to stop off in the village and have **a bite to eat.*** ■ a small morsel of prepared

food, intended to constitute one mouthful: *minced bacon bites with cheese.* ■ *figurative* a short piece of information: *snack-sized bites of information.* See also SOUND BITE. ■ a wound inflicted by an animal's or a person's teeth: *Perry's dog had given her a nasty bite.* ■ a wound inflicted by a snake, insect, or arachnid: *suspected it to be a tick bite.* ■ an act of bait being taken by a fish: *by four o'clock he still hadn't had a single bite.* ■ *Dentistry* the bringing together of the teeth in occlusion. ■ *Dentistry* the imprint of this in a plastic material. **2** a sharp or pungent flavor: *a fresh, lemony bite.* ■ incisiveness or cogency of style: *his colorful characterizations brought added bite to the story.* ■ a feeling of cold in the air or wind: *by early October there's a bite in the air.* ▷Old English *bītan*, of Germanic origin; related to Dutch *bijten* and German *beissen.* —**bit·er** *n.*

▸*PHRASES* □ **one's bark is worse than one's bite** *proverb* said of someone whose fierce and intimidating manner is not felt by the speaker to reflect the person's nature. □ **be bitten by the —— bug** develop a passionate interest in a specified activity: *Joe was bitten by the showbiz bug at the age of four.* □ **bite the big one** *informal* die. □ **bite the bullet** decide to do something difficult or unpleasant that one has been putting off or hesitating over. [from the old custom of giving wounded soldiers a bullet to bite on when undergoing surgery without anesthetic.] □ **bite the dust** *informal* be killed: *and the bad guys bite the dust with lead in their bellies.* ■ *figurative* fail; come to an end: *she hoped the new program would not bite the dust for lack of funding.* □ **bite the hand that feeds one** deliberately hurt or offend a benefactor. □ **bite someone's head off** see HEAD. □ **bite one's lip** dig one's front teeth into one's lip in embarrassment, grief, or annoyance, or to prevent oneself from saying something or to control oneself when experiencing physical pain. ■ *figurative* forcing oneself to remain silent even though annoyed, provoked, or in possession of information: *he could have mocked Carol's obnoxious behavior, but he bit his lip.* □ **bite off more than one can chew** take on a commitment one cannot fulfill. □ **bite one's tongue** make a desperate effort to avoid saying something: *I had to bite my tongue and accept his explanation.* □ **one could have bitten one's tongue off** used to show that someone profoundly and immediately regrets having said something. □ **once bitten, twice shy** *proverb* an unpleasant experience induces caution. □ **put the bite on** *informal* borrow or extort money from. [1930s: *bite* in the slang sense 'cadging.'] □ **take a bite out of** *informal* reduce by a significant amount: *insurance costs that can take a bite out of your retirement funds.*

bite-sized (also **bite-size**) ▸*adj.* (of a piece of food) small enough to be eaten in one mouthful: *cut the potatoes into bite-sized pieces.* ■ *informal* very small or short: *a series of bite-sized essays.*

bite·wing /ˈbīt,wiNG/ ▸*n.* a dental film for X-raying the crowns of upper and lower teeth simultaneously and that is held in place by a tab between the teeth.

bit·ing /ˈbītiNG/ ▸*adj.* (of insects and certain other animals) able to wound the skin with a sting or fangs: *ridding the premises of biting red ants.* ■ (of wind or cold) so cold as to be painful: *he leaned forward to protect himself against the biting wind.* ■ (of wit or criticism) harsh or cruel: *his biting satire on corruption and power.* —**bit·ing·ly** *adv.*

bit·ing midge ▸*n.* a very small fly that typically occurs in large swarms. The female has piercing mouthparts and feeds on the blood of a variety of animals including humans. • Family Ceratopogonidae: numerous genera and species, including the punkie (*Culicoides* and related genera).

bit·map /ˈbit,map/ *Computing* ▸*n.* a representation in which each item corresponds to one or more bits of information, esp. the information used to control the display of a computer screen.

▸*v.* **(-mapped, -map·ping)** [*trans.*] represent (an item) as a bitmap.

BITNET /ˈbit,net/ (also **Bitnet**) *trademark* a data transmission network founded in 1981 to link North American academic institutions and to interconnect with other information networks.

bi·ton·al /bīˈtōnl/ ▸*adj* (of music) having parts in two different keys sounding together. —**bi·ton·al·i·ty** *n.*

bit part ▸*n.* a small acting role in a play or a movie.

bit rate ▸*n.* *Electronics* the number of bits per second that can be transmitted along a digital network.

bit·stream /ˈbit,strēm/ ▸*n.* *Electronics* a stream of data in binary form. ■ **(Bitstream)** *trademark* a system of digital-to-analog signal conversion used in some audio CD players, in which the signal from the CD is digitally processed to give a signal at a higher frequency before being converted to an analog signal.

bitt /bit/ ▸*n.* [usu. in *pl.*] any of the posts fixed in pairs on the deck of a ship, for fastening cables, belaying ropes, etc.

▸*v.* [*trans.*] coil or fasten around the bitts.

bit·ten /ˈbitn/ ▸ past participle of BITE.

bit·ter /ˈbitər/ ▸*adj.* **1** having a sharp, pungent taste or smell; not sweet: *the raw berries have an intensely bitter flavor.* ■ (of chocolate) dark and unsweetened. **2** (of people or their feelings or behavior) angry, hurt, or resentful because of one's bad experiences or a sense of unjust treatment: *I don't feel jealous or bitter.* **3** harsh or unpleasant, in particular: ■ (often used for emphasis) painful or unpleasant to accept or contemplate: *today's decision has come as **a bitter blow**.* ■ (of a conflict, argument, or opponent) full of anger and acrimony: *a bitter, five-year legal battle.* ■ (of wind, cold, or weather) intensely cold: *a bitter wind blowing from the east.*

▸*n.* **1** [*mass noun*] *Brit.* beer that is strongly flavored with hops and has a bitter taste. **2** (**bitters**) [treated as *sing*] liquor that is flavored with the sharp pungent taste of plant extracts and is used as an additive in cocktails or as a medicinal substance to promote appetite or digestion. ▷Old English *biter*, of Germanic origin; related to Dutch and German *bitter*, and probably to BITE. —**bit·ter·ly** *adv.* —**bit·ter·ness** *n.*

▸*PHRASE* □ **to the bitter end** used to say that one will continue doing something until it is finished, no matter what: *the workers would **fight to the bitter end** for safer conditions.* [perhaps associated with a nautical word *bitter* denoting the last part of a cable inboard of the BITTS, perhaps influenced by the biblical phrase 'her end is bitter as wormwood' (Prov. 5:4).]

bit·ter al·mond ▸*n.* see ALMOND (sense 2).

bit·ter al·oes ▸*n.* see ALOE.

bit·ter ap·ple ▸*n.* another term for COLOCYNTH.

bit·ter·cress /ˈbitər,kres/ ▸*n.* a plant with small white flowers that grows widely as a weed of temperate areas, esp. in damp soils. • Genus *Cardamine*, family Brassicaceae: several species, in particular the **Pennsylvania bittercress** (*C. pensylvanica*) of North America.

bit·ter-end·er ▸*n.* a person who holds out until the end no matter what.

bit·ter gourd ▸*n.* another term for BITTER MELON.

bit·ter greens ▸*plural n.* mixed green leaves of a variety of salad vegetables with a bitter taste, such as kale, mustard, collard, endive, chicory, or spinach.

bit·ter mel·on ▸*n.* a warty, green-colored, unripe fruit of an annual tropical vine, used in Asian cooking and for its medicinal properties. Also called BITTER GOURD. ■ the widespread plant of the gourd family that produces this fruit. • *Momordica charantia*, family Cucurbitaceae.

bit·tern[1] /ˈbitərn/ ▸*n.* a large marsh bird of the heron family, typically smaller than a heron, with brown streaked plumage. The larger kinds are noted for the deep booming call of the male in the breeding season. • Genera *Botaurus* and *Ixobrychus*, family Ardeidae: several species, esp. the **American bittern** (*B. lentiginosus*) and the **least bittern** (*I. exilis*). ▷late Middle English *bitore*, from Old French *butor*, based on Latin *butio* 'bittern' + *taurus* 'bull' (because of its call). The *-n* was added in the 16th cent., perhaps by association with *hern*, obsolete variant of HERON.

bit·tern[2] (also **bitterns**) ▸*n.* a concentrated solution of various salts remaining after the crystallization of salt from seawater. ▷late 17th cent.: probably from the adjective BITTER.

bit·ter or·ange ▸*n.* another term for SEVILLE ORANGE.

bit·ter·root /ˈbitər,ro͞ot; -,ro͝ot/ ▸*n.* a plant of the purslane family with showy pinkish-white flowers on short stems. Found throughout the rocky areas of western North America, it is particularly abundant in Montana, of which it is the state flower. • *Lewisia rediviva*, family Portulacaceae.

Bit·ter·root Range part of the Rocky Mountains in western Montana and eastern Idaho.

bit·ter rot ▸*n.* a disease of apples, characterized by sunken brown spots, caused by the fungus *Glomerella cingulata*.

bit·ter·sweet /ˈbitər,swēt/ ▸*adj.* (of food, drink, or flavor) sweet with a bitter aftertaste. ■ arousing pleasure tinged with sadness or pain: *the room, with all its bittersweet memories.*

▸*n.* **1** another term for woody nightshade (see NIGHTSHADE). **2** (also **climbing bittersweet**) a vinelike climbing plant that bears clusters of bright orange pods. • Genus *Celastrus*, family Celastraceae: several species, in particular *C. scandens*.

bitts /bits/ ▸*plural n.* a pair of posts on the deck of a ship for fastening mooring lines or cables. ▷Middle English: probably of Low German origin.

bit·ty /ˈbitē/ *informal* ▸*adj.* **(-tier, -tiest)** tiny: *a **little bitty** house.* —**bit·ti·ly** /ˈbitəlē/ *adv.* —**bit·ti·ness** *n.*

bi·tu·men /biˈt(y)o͞omən; bī-/ ▸*n.* a black viscous mixture of hydrocarbons obtained naturally or as a residue from petroleum distillation. It is used for road surfacing and roofing. ▷late Middle English (denoting naturally occurring asphalt used as mortar): from Latin.

bi·tu·mi·nize /biˈt(y)o͞omən,īz; bī-/ ▸*v.* [*trans.*] convert into, impregnate with, or cover with bitumen. —**bi·tu·mi·ni·za·tion** /-,t(y)o͞oməniˈzāSHən/ *n.*

bi·tu·mi·nous /biˈt(y)o͞omənəs; bī-/ ▸*adj.* [*attrib.*] of, containing, or of the nature of bitumen. ▷mid 16th cent.: from French *bitumineux*, from Latin *bituminosus*.

bi·tu·mi·nous coal ▸*n.* black coal having a relatively high volatile content. It burns with a characteristically bright smoky flame.

bit·wise /ˈbit,wīz/ ▸*adj.* *Computing* designating an operator in a programming language that manipulates the individual bits in a byte or word.

bi·va·lence /bīˈvāləns/ ▸*n.* *Logic* the existence of only two states or truth values (e.g., true and false).

bi·va·lent /bīˈvālənt/ ▸*adj.* **1** *Biology* (of homologous chromosomes) associated in pairs. **2** *Chemistry* another term for DIVALENT.

▸*n.* *Biology* a pair of homologous chromosomes. ▷mid 19th cent.: from BI- 'two' + Latin *valent-* 'being strong' (from the verb *valere*).

bi·valve /ˈbī,valv/ ▸*n.* an aquatic mollusk that has a compressed body enclosed within two hinged shells, such as oysters, clams, mussels, and scallops. Also called PELECYPOD or LAMELLIBRANCH. • Class Bivalvia (formerly Pelecypoda or Lamellibranchia).

▸*adj.* (also **bi·valved**) *Zoology* (of a mollusk or other aquatic invertebrate) with a hinged double shell. ■ *Botany* having two valves.

bi·var·i·ate /bīˈve(ə)rēit; -ˈve(ə)rē,āt/ ▸*adj.* *Statistics* involving or depending on two variables.

biv·ou·ac /ˈbivo͞o,ak; ˈbivwak/ ▸*n.* a temporary camp without tents or cover, used esp. by soldiers or mountaineers.

▸*v.* [*intrans.*] (**bivouacked, bivouacking**) stay in such a camp: *he'd bivouacked on the north side of the town | the battalion was now bivouacked in a field.* ▷early 18th cent. (denoting a night watch by the whole army): from French, probably from Swiss German *Bîwacht* 'additional guard at night,' apparently denoting a citizens' patrol supporting the ordinary town watch.

bi·week·ly /bīˈwēklē/ ▸*adj.* & *adv.* appearing or taking place every two weeks or twice a week: [as *adj.*] *a biweekly bulletin* | [as *adv.*] *she followed her doctor's instructions to undergo health checks biweekly.*

▸*n.* (*pl.* **-lies**) a periodical that appears every two weeks or twice a week.

USAGE See usage at BIENNIAL and BIMONTHLY.

bi·year·ly /bīˈyi(ə)rlē/ ▸*adj.* & *adv.* appearing or taking place every two years or twice a year.

USAGE See usage at BIENNIAL and BIMONTHLY.

biz /biz/ ▸*n.* [usu. in *sing.*] [usu. with *adj.*] *informal* a business, typically one connected with entertainment: *in the music biz.* ▷mid 19th cent. (originally U.S.): abbreviation.

bi·zarre /biˈzär/ ▸*adj.* very strange or unusual, esp. so as to cause interest or amusement: *her bizarre dresses and outrageous hairdos.* ▷mid 17th cent.: from French, from Italian *bizzarro* 'angry,'. —**bi·zarre·ness** *n.*

bi·zarre·ly ▸*adv.* in a very strange or unusual manner: *bizarrely attired musicians.* ■ [*sentence adverb*] used to express the opinion that something is very strange or unusual: ***bizarrely enough**, he began to trust his abductors.*

bi·zar·re·rie /biˈzärərē/ ▸*n.* (*pl.* **-ries**) a thing considered extremely strange and unusual, typically in an amusing way: *the bizarreries of small talk.* ▷mid 18th cent.: from French, from BIZARRE.

bi·zar·ro /biˈzärō/ ▸*adj.* *informal* bizarre: *a whacked-out frontman for a bizarro fringe rock n' roll band.* ▷perhaps from *Bizarro*, the name of a character in DC Comics' *Superman* comic books, or from *Bizarro*, the name of a comic strip created by Dan Piraro.

Bi·zet /bi'zä/, Georges (1838–75), French composer; born *Alexandre César Léopold Bizet*. He is best known for the opera *Carmen* (1875).

BJ ▶*abbr.* BLOW JOB.

Bjerk·nes /'byerknəs/, Vilhelm Frimann Koren (1862–1951), Norwegian geophysicist and meteorologist. He developed a theory of physical hydrodynamics for atmosphere and oceanic circulation and mathematical models for weather prediction.

Bk ▶*symbol* the chemical element berkelium.

bk ▶*abbr.* ■ bank. ■ book. ■ brick.

BL ▶*abbr.* ■ Bachelor of Law. ■ Bachelor of Letters. ■ bill of lading.

bl ▶*abbr.* ■ bale. ■ barrel. ■ black. ■ blue.

blab /blab/ *informal* ▶*v.* (**blabbed, blab·bing**) [*intrans.*] reveal secrets by indiscreet talk: *she blabbed to the press* | [*trans.*] *there's no need to blab the whole story.*
▶*n.* a person who blabs. ▷Middle English (as a noun): probably of Germanic origin; ultimately imitative.

blab·ber /'blabər/ *informal* ▶*v.* [*intrans.*] talk foolishly, mindlessly, or excessively: *she* ***blabbered on and on***.
▶*n.* a person who talks foolishly or indiscreetly. ■ foolish or mindless talk: *annoyed by their endless blabber.*

blab·ber·mouth /'blabər,mouth/ ▶*n. informal* a person who talks excessively or indiscreetly.

Black[1] /blak/, Hugo Lafayette (1886–1971), U.S. Supreme Court associate justice 1937–71, noted as an advocate of First Amendment rights. He was also a U.S. senator from Alabama 1927–37.

Black[2], Joseph (1728–99), Scottish chemist. He developed accurate techniques for following chemical reactions by weighing reactants and products.

black /blak/ ▶*adj.* **1** of the very darkest color; the opposite of white; colored like coal, due to the absence of or complete absorption of light: *black smoke* | *her hair was black.* ■ (of the sky or night) completely dark due to nonvisibility of the sun, moon, or stars, normally because of dense cloud cover: *the sky was moonless and black.* ■ deeply stained with dirt: *his clothes were absolutely black.* ■ (of a plant or animal) dark in color as distinguished from a lighter variety: *Japanese black pine.* ■ (of coffee or tea) served without milk or cream. ■ of or denoting the suits spades and clubs in a deck of cards. ■ (of a ski run) of the highest level of difficulty, as indicated by black markers positioned along it. **2** (also **Black**) of any human group having dark-colored skin, esp. of African or Australian Aboriginal ancestry: *black adolescents of Jamaican descent.* ■ of or relating to black people: *black culture.* **3** *figurative* (of a period of time or situation) characterized by tragic or disastrous events; causing despair or pessimism: *five thousand men were killed on the blackest day of the war* | *the future looks black for those of us interested in freedom.* ■ (of a person's state of mind) full of gloom or misery; very depressed: *Jean had disappeared and Mary was in a black mood.* ■ (of humor) presenting tragic or harrowing situations in comic terms: *"Good place to bury the bodies," she joked with black humor.* ■ full of anger or hatred: *Roger shot her a black look.* ■ *archaic* very evil or wicked: *my soul is steeped in the blackest sin.*
▶*n.* **1** black color or pigment: *a tray decorated in black and green* | *a series of paintings done only in grays and blacks.* ■ black clothes or material, often worn as a sign of mourning: *dressed in the black of widowhood.* ■ darkness, esp. of night or an overcast sky: *the only thing visible in the black was the light of the lantern.* **2** (also **Black**) a member of a dark-skinned people, esp. one of African or Australian Aboriginal ancestry: *a coalition of blacks and whites against violence.* **3** (in a game or sport) a black piece or ball, in particular: ■ (often **Black**) the player of the black pieces in chess or checkers. ■ the black pieces in chess.
▶*v.* [*trans.*] make black, esp. by the application of black polish: *blacking the prize bull's hooves.* ■ make (one's face, hands, and other visible parts of one's body) black with polish or makeup, so as not to be seen at night or, esp. formerly, to play the role of a black person in a musical show, play, or movie: *white extras* ***blacking up*** *their faces to play Ethiopians.*
▶*phrasal v.* □ **black out** (of a person) undergo a sudden and temporary loss of consciousness: *they knocked me around and I blacked out.* □ **black something out** **1** (usu. **be blacked out**) extinguish all lights or completely cover windows, esp. for protection against an air attack or in order to provide darkness in which to show a movie: *the bombers began to come nightly and the city was blacked out.* ■ subject a place to an electricity failure: *Chicago was blacked out yesterday after a freak flood.* **2** obscure something completely so that it cannot be read or seen: *the license plate had been blacked out with masking tape.* ■ (of a television company) suppress the broadcast of a program: *they blacked out the women's finals on local television.* ▷Old English *blæc*, of Germanic origin. —**black·ish** *adj.* —**black·ly** *adv.* —**black·ness** *n.*
▶*PHRASES* □ **black someone's eye** hit someone in the eye so as to cause bruising. □ **in the black** (of a person or organization) not owing any money; solvent. □ **look on the black side** *informal* view a situation pessimistically. □ **not as black as one is painted** *informal* not as bad as one is said to be.

USAGE Black, designating Americans of African heritage, became the most widely used and accepted term in the 1960s and 1970s, replacing **Negro**. It is not usually capitalized: *black Americans.*
Through the 1980s, the more formal **African American** replaced **black** in much usage, but both are now generally acceptable.
Afro-American, first recorded in the 19th century and popular in the 1960s and 1970s, is now heard mostly in anthropological and cultural contexts.
Colored people, common in the early part of the 20th century, is now usually regarded as offensive, although the phrase survives in the full name of the NAACP, the National Association for the Advancement of Colored People.
An inversion, **people of color**, has gained some favor, but is also used in reference to other nonwhite ethnic groups: *a gathering spot for African Americans and other people of color interested in reading about their cultures.*
See also **usage** at COLORED and PERSON OF COLOR.

black Af·ri·ca the area of Africa, generally south of the Sahara, where black people predominate.

black·a·moor /'blakə,mŏŏr/ ▶*n. dated, offensive* a black African; a very dark-skinned person. ▷early 16th cent.: from BLACK + MOOR.

black and blue ▶*adj.* discolored by bruising: *a black-and-blue mark on his arm.* ■ (of a person) covered in bruises: *they were both black and blue the day after the accident.*

black and tan ▶*n.* **1** a terrier of a breed with a black back and tan markings on face, flanks, and legs. **2** a drink composed of stout (or porter) and ale. **3** *informal* an event or establishment that is attended or frequented by both blacks and whites: *takes this guy out to the black and tan every night* [as *adj.*] *a black and tan nightclub.*

Black and Tans an armed force recruited by the British government to fight Sinn Fein in Ireland in 1921. Their harsh methods caused an outcry in Britain and the U.S. ▷so named because of the mixture of military khaki and black constabulary colors of their uniform.

black and white ▶*adj.* **1** (of a photograph, movie, television program, or illustration) in black, white, shades of gray, and no other color: *old black-and-white movies.* ■ (of a television) displaying images only in black, white, and shades of gray. **2** (of a situation or debate) involving clearly defined opposing principles or issues: *there is nothing black and white about these matters.*
▶*n. informal* a police car.
▶*PHRASE* □ **in black and white** **1** in writing or in print, and regarded as more reliable, credible, or formal than by word of mouth: *getting her contract down in black and white.* **2** in terms of clearly defined opposing principles or issues: *children think in black and white, good and bad.*

Black An·gus ▶*n.* another term for ABERDEEN ANGUS.

black ant ▶*n.* an ant that is black and is often found in and around houses. • Several species in the family Formicidae.

black art ▶*n.* (usu. **the black art**) another term for BLACK MAGIC. ■ *often humorous* a technique or practice considered mysterious and sinister: *the black art of political news management.*

black·ball /'blak,bôl/ ▶*v.* [*trans.*] reject (someone, usually a candidate applying to become a member of a private club), typically by means of a secret ballot: *her husband was blackballed when he tried to join the country club.* ▷late 18th cent.: from the practice of registering an adverse vote by placing a black ball in a ballot box.

black bass /bas/ ▶*n.* a North American freshwater fish of the sunfish family. It is a popular sporting and food fish. • Genus *Micropterus*, family Centrarchidae: several species, in particular the **largemouth bass** (*M. salmoides*) and the **smallmouth bass** (*M. dolomieui*).

black bean ▶*n.* **1** either of two cultivated varieties of bean plant having small black seeds: • a variety of soybean, used fermented in Asian cooking. • a Mexican variety of string bean. ■ the dried seed of such a plant used as a vegetable. **2** either of two Australian plants of the pea family: • a large tree with red or yellow flowers, dark beanlike seeds, and a hard and decorative wood (*Castanospermum australe*, family Leguminosae). • a liana with blackish flowers (*Kennedia nigricans*, family Leguminosae).

black bear ▶*n.* a medium-sized forest-dwelling bear with blackish fur and a paler face, found in North America and eastern Asia. • Two species, family Ursidae: the **American black bear** (*Ursus americanus*), with a wide range of coat color, and the smaller **Asian black bear** (*Selenarctos thibetanus*).

American black bear

Black·beard /'blak,bi(ə)rd/ (died 1718), English pirate; real name *Edward Teach*. Originally a privateer during the War of the Spanish Succession 1701–14, he turned to piracy and concentrated on the West Indies and the Virginia–North Carolina coast of America.

Black Belt an agricultural district in central Alabama and Mississippi, named for its rich soils.

black belt ▶*n.* a black belt worn by an expert in judo, karate, and other martial arts. ■ a person qualified to wear this.

black·ber·ry /'blak,berē/ ▶*n.* (*pl.* **-ries**) **1** an edible soft fruit, consisting of a cluster of soft purple-black drupelets. **2** the prickly climbing shrub of the rose family that bears this fruit and that grows extensively in the wild. • *Rubus fruticosus*, family Rosaceae (sometimes treated as an aggregate of many species).
▶*v.* (**-ries, -ried**) [*intrans.*] [usu. as *n.*] (**blackberrying**) gather blackberries in the wild.

black bile ▶*n.* (in medieval science and medicine) one of the four bodily humors, believed to be associated with a melancholy temperament. Also called MELANCHOLY. ▷late 18th cent.: translation of Greek *melankholia* (see MELANCHOLY). Compare with ATRABILIOUS.

black bind·weed ▶*n.* a twining weed of the dock family, with arrowhead-shaped leaves and small greenish flowers. • *Polygonum convolvulus*, family Polygonaceae.

black birch ▶*n.* another term for SWEET BIRCH.

black·bird /'blak,bərd/ ▶*n.* **1** a European thrush with mainly black plumage. • Genus *Turdus*, subfamily Turdinae, family Muscicapidae: four species, in particular *T. merula*, the male of which has all-black plumage and a yellow bill. **2** an American bird with a strong pointed bill. The male has black plumage that is iridescent or has patches of red or yellow. • Family Icteridae: several genera and species, including the abundant **red-winged blackbird** (*Agelaius phoeniceus*).

black·board /'blak,bôrd/ ▶*n.* a large board with a smooth, typically dark, surface attached to a wall or supported on an easel and used for writing on with chalk, esp. by teachers in schools.

black book ▶*n.* (a book containing) a list of the names of people liable to be censured or punished.

black bot·tom ▶*n.* a popular U.S. dance of the 1920s.

black bot·tom pie ▶*n.* pie with a bottom layer of chocolate cream or custard and a contrasting top layer, usually of whipped cream.

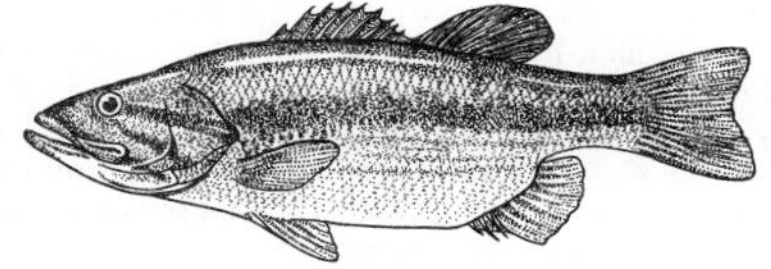
black bass

black box ▸*n.* a flight recorder in an aircraft. ■ any complex piece of equipment, typically a unit in an electronic system, with contents that are mysterious to the user.

black bread ▸*n.* a coarse, dark-colored type of rye bread.

black bry·o·ny ▸*n.* see BRYONY (sense 2).

black·buck /ˈblakˌbək/ ▸*n.* a small Indian gazelle, the horned male of which has a black back and white underbelly, the female being hornless. • *Antilope cervicapra*, family Bovidae.

Black·burn /ˈblakbərn/ an industrial town in northwestern England; pop. 132,800.

black but·ter ▸*n.* a sauce made by heating butter until it is dark brown. It is often flavored with vinegar and herbs.

black·cap /ˈblakˌkap/ ▸*n.* **1** a mainly European warbler with a black cap in the male and a reddish-brown one in the female. • *Sylvia atricapilla*, family Sylviidae. **2** the black-capped chickadee. See CHICKADEE.

black cau·cus ▸*n.* a political caucus composed of black people interested in advancing the concerns of blacks. ■ (**Black Caucus**) a caucus of this kind composed of black members of the U.S. Congress.

black cher·ry ▸*n.* a large North American cherry tree that yields valuable close-grained hard wood. • *Prunus serotina*, family Rosaceae. ■ the bitter blackish fruit of this tree, sometimes used for jellies and regularly eaten by wild birds and animals.

black·cock /ˈblakˌkäk/ ▸*n.* (*pl.* same) the male of the black grouse.

black co·hosh /ˈkōhäsн/ ▸*n.* see COHOSH.

black con·scious·ness ▸*n.* awareness of one's identity as a black person. ■ a political movement or ideology (particularly in the U.S. and South Africa) seeking to unite black people in affirming their common identity.

black cur·rant ▸*n.* (*Brit.* **blackcurrant**) **1** a small round edible black berry that grows in loose hanging clusters. **2** the shrub that produces this fruit. • Genus *Ribes*, family Grossulariaceae: several species, in particular the widely cultivated *Ribes nigrum*.

black·damp /ˈblakˌdamp/ ▸*n.* choking or suffocating gas, typically carbon dioxide, that is found in mines and other underground spaces.

Black Death the great epidemic of bubonic plague that killed a large part of the population of Europe in the mid 14th century. It originated in central Asia and China and spread rapidly through Europe, carried by the fleas of black rats, reaching England in 1348 and killing between one third and one half of the population in a matter of months. ▷a modern term (compare with earlier *the (great) pestilence*, *great death*, *the plague*), said to have been introduced into English history by Mrs. Markham (pseudonym of Mrs. Penrose) in 1823, and into medical literature by a translation of German *der Schwarze Tod* (1833). The epithet *Black* is of uncertain origin; its equivalent was first found in Swedish and Danish chroniclers.

black dia·mond ▸*n.* **1** *informal* a lump of coal. **2** [usu. as *adj.*] a difficult ski slope: *a steep, black diamond run.* **3** another term for CARBONADO.

black dog ▸*n. informal* used as a metaphor for melancholy or depression: *I'm very happy, but the black dog is there, lurking around the corner.* ▷late 18th cent.: figuratively from a cant name used during Queen Anne's reign (1702–14) for a base silver coin (usually a bad shilling).

black duck ▸*n.* a duck with black plumage, esp. the **American black duck** (*Anas rubripes*) of northeastern North America.

black·en /ˈblakən/ ▸*v.* become or make black or dark, esp. as a result of burning, decay, or bruising: [*intrans.*] *he set fire to the paper, watching the end blacken as it burned* | [*trans.*] *she blackened George's eye before he knew what had happened* | [as *adj.*] (**blackened**) *her smile revealed blackened teeth.* ■ [*trans.*] dye or color (the face or hair) black for camouflage or cosmetic effect: *in full combat gear with blackened faces.* ■ [*intrans.*] (of the sky) become dark as night or a storm approaches. ■ [*trans.*] *figurative* damage or destroy (someone's good reputation); defame: *she won't thank you for blackening her husband's name.*

black Eng·lish ▸*n.* any of various nonstandard forms of English spoken by black people, esp. as an urban dialect in the U.S.

Black·ett /ˈblakit/, Patrick Maynard Stuart, Baron (1897–1974), English physicist. He was a member of the Maud Committee, which dealt with the development of the atom bomb. He also modified the cloud chamber for the study of cosmic rays. Nobel Prize for Physics (1948).

black eye ▸*n.* a bruised and discolored area around the eye resulting from a blow: *it's gonna be a doozy of a black eye.* ■ *figurative* a mark or source of dishonor or shame: *legislators have caused the state to suffer yet another black eye.*

black-eyed pea ▸*n.* another term for COWPEA.

black-eyed Su·san ▸*n.* any of a number of flowers that have yellowish petals and a dark center, in particular: • a daisylike North American flower with bristly leaves and stems (*Rudbeckia hirta* and its hybrids, family Compositae). • a slender tropical climber, grown as a popular indoor or greenhouse plant (*Thunbergia alata*, family Acanthaceae).

black·face /ˈblakˌfās/ ▸*n.* the makeup used by a nonblack performer playing a black role. The role played is typically comedic or musical and usually is considered offensive: *he appeared* **in blackface** | [as *adj.*] *the blackface components of the minstrel era.* ■ *figurative* used to imply patronization of blacks by whites or by institutions perceived to be insincerely or ineffectively nonracist.

black·fish /ˈblakˌfisн/ ▸*n.* (*pl.* same or **-fish·es**) **1** any of a number of dark-colored fish, in particular: • an open-ocean fish related to the perches (genera *Centrolophus* and *Schedophilus*, family Centrolophidae), in particular the large and widespread *C. niger*. • (**Alaska blackfish**) a small fish occurring along the Arctic coasts of Alaska and Siberia, noted for its ability to withstand freezing (*Dallia pectoralis*, family Umbridae). • (**river blackfish**) a large fish of Australian rivers (*Gadopsis marmoratus*, family Gadopsidae). • a salmon just after spawning. **2** another term for PILOT WHALE.

black flag ▸*n.* **1** *historical* a pirate's ensign, typically thought to feature a white skull and crossbones on a black background; Jolly Roger. **2** *Auto Racing* a black flag used to signal a driver to make an immediate pit stop as punishment for violating a rule or driving dangerously, or to force inspection of a hazardous condition such as an oil leak.

black fly ▸*n.* (*pl.* **-flies**) **1** a small black fly, the female of which sucks blood and can transmit a number of serious human and animal diseases. Large swarms sometimes cause distress to livestock and humans. • Family Simuliidae: *Simulium* and other genera. **2** a black or dark green aphid that is a common pest of crops and gardens. • Several species in the family Aphididae, in particular *Aphis fabae*.

Black·foot /ˈblakˌfo͝ot/ ▸*n.* (*pl.* same or **-feet**) **1** a member of a confederacy of North American Indian peoples of the northwestern plains. The Blackfoot confederacy comprised three closely related tribes: the Blackfeet proper, the Bloods, and the Piegan. **2** the Algonquian language of this people. **3** a subdivision of the Teton Sioux.

▸*adj.* of or relating to these peoples or the language of the Blackfeet proper.

Black For·est a hilly wooded region of southwestern Germany that lies to the east of the Rhine River valley. German name **SCHWARZWALD**.

Black For·est cake ▸*n.* a chocolate sponge cake with layers of morello cherries or cherry jam and whipped cream and topped with chocolate icing. ▷*Black Forest*, a translation of German *Schwarzwald*, the name of a forested area in southwestern Germany.

Black Fri·ar ▸*n.* a Dominican friar. ▷early 16th cent.: so named because of the color of the order's habit.

black frost ▸*n.* a dry, nonvisible killing frost that turns vegetation black.

black gold ▸*n. informal* petroleum.

black grouse ▸*n.* (*pl.* same) a large Eurasian grouse, the male of which has glossy blue-black plumage and a lyre-shaped tail. The males display in communal leks. • *Tetrao tetrix*, family Tetraonidae (or Phasianidae); the male is called a **blackcock** and the female a **greyhen**.

black·guard /ˈblagərd; ˈblakˌgärd/ ▸*n. dated* a person, particularly a man, who behaves in a dishonorable or contemptible way.

▸*v.* [*trans.*] *dated* abuse or disparage (someone) scurrilously. ▷early 16th cent. (originally as two words): from BLACK + GUARD. The term originally denoted a body of attendants or servants, esp. the menials who had charge of kitchen utensils, but the exact significance of the epithet 'black' is uncertain. The sense 'scoundrel, villain' dates from the mid 18th cent., and was formerly considered highly offensive. —**black·guard·ly** *adj.*

black guil·le·mot ▸*n.* a seabird of the auk family with black summer plumage and large white wing patches, breeding on the coasts of the Arctic and North Atlantic. • *Cepphus grylle*, family Alcidae.

black gum ▸*n.* another term for SOURGUM.

Black Hand ▸*n.* a secret criminal and terrorist society in New York during the early 20th century. ■ any similar society.

Black Hawk (1767–1838), American Indian leader, chief of the Sauk and Fox Indians; native name *Makataimeshekiakiak*. He fought to repossess Indian lands in the Black Hawk War 1832.

black·head /ˈblakˌhed/ ▸*n.* **1** a plug of sebum in a hair follicle, darkened by oxidation. **2** an infectious disease of turkeys producing discoloration of the head, caused by a protozoan.

Black Hills a mountain range in eastern Wyoming and western South Dakota. The highest point is Harney Peak (7,242 feet; 2,207 m); Mount Rushmore is also part of this range.

black hole ▸*n.* *Astronomy* a region of space having a gravitational field so intense that no matter or radiation can escape.

> Black holes are probably formed when a massive star exhausts its nuclear fuel and collapses under its own gravity. If the star is massive enough, no known force can counteract the increasing gravity, and it will collapse to a point of infinite density. Before this stage is reached, within a certain radius (the event horizon), light itself becomes trapped and the object becomes invisible.

■ *informal* a figurative place of emptiness or aloneness: *they think he's sitting in a black hole with no interaction with his people.* ■ *informal, chiefly humorous* a place where money, lost items, etc., are supposed to go, never to be seen again: *the moribund economy has been a black hole for federal funds* | *I wouldn't dare go in that black hole he calls a "garage."* ■ *informal* (of a system, practice, or institution) a state of inadequacy or excessive bureaucracy in which hopes, progress, etc., become futile: *juveniles lost for good in the black hole of the criminal justice system.*

Black Hole of Cal·cut·ta a dungeon 20 feet (6 m) square in Fort William, Calcutta, where perhaps as many as 146 English prisoners were confined overnight following the capture of Calcutta by the nawab of Bengal, in 1756. Only twenty-three of them were still alive the next morning.

black ice ▸*n.* a transparent coating of ice, found esp. on a road or other paved surface.

Black Jack see PERSHING[1].

black·jack /ˈblakˌjak/ ▸*n.* **1** a gambling card game in which players try to acquire cards with a face value as close as possible to 21 without going over. Also called TWENTY-ONE, VINGT-ET-UN. **2** a short, leather-covered, typically lead-filled club with a flexible handle, used as a weapon. **3** *historical* a pirate's black ensign. **4** *historical* a tarred-leather container used for alcoholic drinks.

Black Jew ▸*n.* another term for **FALASHA**.

black·lead /ˈblakˌled/ ▸*n.* another term for GRAPHITE.

black·leg /ˈblakˌleg/ ▸*n.* **1** any of a number of plant diseases in which part of the stem blackens and decays, in particular: • a fungal disease of cabbages and related plants (caused by *Leptosphaeria*, *Pleospora*, and other genera). • a bacterial disease of potatoes (caused by *Erwinia carotovora* subsp. *atroseptica*). **2** an acute infectious bacterial disease of cattle and sheep, causing necrosis in one or more legs. • This disease is caused by *Clostridium chauvoei*. **3** *Brit., derogatory* a strikebreaker. [the reason for the name remains unknown.]

black let·ter ▸*n.* an early, ornate, bold style of type, typically resembling Gothic.

black light ▸*n.* ultraviolet or infrared radiation, invisible to the eye.

black·list /ˈblakˌlist/ ▸*n.* a list of people or products viewed with suspicion or disapproval.

▸*v.* [*trans.*] (often **be blacklisted**) put (a person or product) on such a list: *workers were blacklisted after being quoted in the newspaper.*

black lo·cust ▸*n.* a North American tree with compound leaves and dense, hanging clusters of fragrant white flowers, widely grown as an ornamental. • *Robinia pseudoacacia*, family Leguminosae.

black lung ▸*n.* pneumoconiosis caused by inhalation of coal dust.

black mag·ic ▸*n.* magic involving the supposed invocation of evil spirits for evil purposes.

black·mail /ˈblakˌmāl/ ▸*n.* the action, treated as a

criminal offense, of demanding money from a person in return for not revealing compromising or injurious information about that person: *they were acquitted of charges of blackmail.* ■ money demanded in this way: *we do not pay blackmail.* ■ the use of threats or the manipulation of someone's feelings to force them to do something: *out of fear, she submitted to Jim's* ***emotional blackmail*** | *they are trying to blackmail us with hunger.*
▸*v.* [*trans.*] demand money from (a person) in return for not revealing compromising or injurious information about that person: *trying to blackmail him for $400,000.* ■ force (someone) to do something by using threats or manipulating their feelings: *he had* ***blackmailed*** *her* ***into*** *sailing with him.* ▷mid 16th cent. (denoting protection money levied by Scottish chiefs): from BLACK + obsolete *mail* 'tribute, rent,' from Old Norse *mál* 'speech, agreement.' —**black·mail·er** *n.*

black mam·ba ▸*n.* a highly venomous, slender, olive-brown to dark gray snake that moves with great speed and agility. Native to eastern and southern Africa, it is the largest poisonous snake on the continent. • *Dendroaspis polylepis*, family Elapidae.

Black Ma·ri·a /mə'rīə/ ▸*n. informal* a police vehicle for transporting prisoners. ▷mid 19th cent.: said to be named after a black woman, *Maria Lee*, who kept a boardinghouse in Boston and helped police in escorting drunk and disorderly customers to jail.

black mark ▸*n. informal* used to indicate that someone is remembered and regarded with disfavor: *an arrest will be a black mark on your record* | ***a black mark*** *went down* ***against*** *him for turning down the job.*

black mar·ket ▸*n.* (**the black market**) an illegal traffic or trade in officially controlled or scarce commodities: *they planned to sell the meat* ***on the black market.*** —**black mar·ke·teer** (also **black-mar·ke·teer**) *n.* —**black-mar·ke·teer** *v.* —**black mar·ket·er** *n.*

black mass (often **Black Mass**) ▸*n.* a travesty of the Roman Catholic Mass in worship of Satan.

Black Me·sa an upland in northeastern Arizona, home to many of the Navajo. The Hopi live on extensions to the south.

black met·al ▸*n.* a type of heavy metal music having lyrics that deal with Satan and the supernatural.

Black Mon·day ▸*n.* Monday, October 19, 1987, when the collapse of stock prices on Wall Street triggered similar declines in markets around the world.

black mon·ey ▸*n.* income illegally obtained or not declared for tax purposes.

Black Monk ▸*n.* a Benedictine monk. ▷Middle English: so named because of the color of the order's habit.

Black·more /'blak,môr/, R. D. (1825–1900), English novelist and poet; full name *Richard Doddridge Blackmore*. He is noted for his romantic novel *Lorna Doone* (1869).

Black Moun·tains a range of the Appalachian Mountains in western North Carolina. Mount Mitchell at 6,684 feet (2,039 m) is the high point.

Black·mun /'blakmən/, Harry Andrew (1908–99), U.S. Supreme Court associate justice 1970–94. He is noted as the author of *Roe v. Wade*, which ruled on the right to legal abortion in 1973.

Black Mus·lim ▸*n.* a member of the NATION OF ISLAM.

black na·tion·al·ism ▸*n.* the advocacy of separate national status for black people, esp. in the U.S. —**black na·tion·al·ist** *n.*

black-on-black ▸*adj.* designating harmful actions in which both the perpetrator and the victim are black: *black-on-black violence.*

black·out /'blak,out/ ▸*n.* **1** a period when all lights must be turned out or covered to prevent them being seen by the enemy during an air raid: *people found it difficult to travel in the blackout* | [as *adj.*] *she peered out through the blackout curtains.* ■ (usu. **blackouts**) dark curtains put up in windows to cover lights during an air raid. ■ [often with *adj.*] a failure of electrical power supply: *due to a power blackout, their hotel was in total darkness.* ■ a moment in the theater when the lights on stage are suddenly turned off. **2** a suppression of information, esp. one imposed on the media by government: *there is a total information* ***blackout on*** *minority interests.* ■ a period during which a particular activity is prohibited: *there are no blackout days during the travel period.* **3** a temporary loss of consciousness: *she was suffering from blackouts.*

black oys·ter plant ▸*n.* another term for SCORZONERA.

Black Pan·ther ▸*n.* a member of a militant political organization set up in the U.S. in 1966 to fight for black rights.

black pan·ther ▸*n.* a leopard that has black fur rather than the typical spotted coat.

black pep·per ▸*n.* the dried black berries of the pepper (see PEPPER sense 2), which are harvested while still green and unripe. Black pepper is widely used as a spice and a condiment and may be used whole (peppercorns) or ground.

black·poll /'blak,pōl/ (also **blackpoll warbler**) ▸*n.* a North American warbler, the male of which has a black cap, white cheeks, and white underparts streaked with black. • *Dendroica striata*, subfamily Parulinae, family Emberizidae.

Black·pool /'blak,po͞ol/ a seaside resort in northwestern England; pop. 144,500.

black pow·der ▸*n.* the original gunpowder, composed of charcoal, saltpeter, and sulfur, now used chiefly in antique firearms and in fireworks.

Black Pow·er ▸*n.* a movement in support of rights and political power for black people, esp. prominent in the U.S. in the 1960s and 1970s.

Black Prince (1330–76), eldest son of Edward III of England; name given to *Edward, Prince of Wales and Duke of Cornwall*, most likely because of the black armor he wore when fighting. He was responsible for the British victory at Poitiers in 1356. He predeceased his father, and his son became King Richard II.

black pud·ding ▸*n.* blood sausage.

black rasp·ber·ry ▸*n.* **1** an edible soft fruit related to the blackberry, consisting of a cluster of black drupelets. **2** the prickly arching shrub of the rose family that bears this fruit. • *Rubus occidentalis*, family Rosaceae.

black rat ▸*n.* a rat with dark fur, large ears, and a long tail. It is found throughout the world, being particularly common in the tropics, and is the chief host of the plague-transmitting flea. Also called ROOF RAT. • *Rattus rattus*, family Muridae.

black rhi·noc·er·os ▸*n.* a two-horned rhinoceros with a prehensile upper lip, found in Africa south of the Sahara. • *Diceros bicornis*, family Rhinocerotidae.

Black Riv·er a river that flows southeast for 300 miles (480 km) through Missouri and Arkansas, along the eastern edge of the Ozark Plateau.

Black Rod (in full **Gentleman Usher of the Black Rod**) ▸*n.* (in the UK) the chief usher of the Lord Chamberlain's department of the royal household, who is also usher to the House of Lords. ▷mid 17th cent.: so named because of the black wand carried as a symbol of office.

black rot ▸*n.* a disease of fruits and vegetables caused by bacteria or fungi, producing blackening, rotting, and shriveling.

black sal·si·fy ▸*n.* another term for SCORZONERA.

Blacks·burg /'blaks,bərg/ a town in southwestern Virginia, in the Appalachian Mountains, home to Virginia Polytechnic Institute; pop. 39,573.

Black Sea a tideless almost landlocked sea bounded by Ukraine, Russia, Georgia, Turkey, Bulgaria, and Romania. It is connected to the Mediterranean Sea through the Bosporus and the Sea of Marmara.

black sheep ▸*n. informal* a member of a family or group who is regarded as a disgrace to them: ***the black sheep of the family.*** ▷late 18th cent.: from the proverb *there is a black sheep in every flock.*

black·shirt /'blak,SHərt/ ▸*n.* a member of a fascist organization, in particular: ■ (in Italy) a member of a paramilitary group founded by Mussolini. ■ (in Nazi Germany) a member of the SS. ▷1920s: so named because of the color of the Italian Fascist uniform.

black·smith /'blak,smiTH/ ▸*n.* a person who makes and repairs things in iron by hand. ■ a farrier.

black smok·er ▸*n. Geology* a geothermal vent on the seabed that ejects superheated water containing much suspended matter, typically black sulfide minerals.

black·snake /'blak,snāk/ ▸*n.* a long black American racer, esp. the common **Northern blacksnake** (*Coluber constrictor constrictor*), the adult of which is a patternless black, above and below.

black spot ▸*n.* a disease of plants, esp. of roses, producing black blotches on leaves.

Black·stone Riv·er /'blak,stōn/ a river that flows south for 50 miles (80 km) through Worcester, Massachusetts, to Pawtucket, Rhode Island, below which it is called the Seekonk River. The Blackstone Valley was a site of early U.S. industrial development.

black·strap /'blak,strap/ ▸*n.* a dark, viscous molasses, the byproduct of the final extraction phase of sugar refining, used chiefly in cattle feed and in the industrial production of citric acid and vinegar.

black swan ▸*n.* a mainly black swan with white flight feathers, which is common in Australia and Tasmania and has been introduced widely elsewhere. • *Cygnus atratus*, family Anatidae.

black·tail deer /'blak,tāl/ (also **black-tailed deer**) ▸*n.* a type of mule deer with black markings on the upper side of its tail, found west of the crest of the Cascade Mountains. • *Odocoileus hemionus* subsp. *columbianus*, family Cervidae.

black tea ▸*n.* **1** tea of the most usual type, that is fully fermented before drying. Compare with GREEN TEA. **2** tea served without milk or cream.

black·thorn /'blak,THôrn/ ▸*n.* a thorny Eurasian shrub that bears white flowers before the leaves appear and astringent blue-black fruits. Also called SLOE. • *Prunus spinosa*, family Rosaceae. ■ a walking stick or cudgel made from the wood of this shrub.

black tie ▸*n.* a black bow tie worn with a dinner jacket. ■ formal evening dress: *the audience wears black tie.*
▸*adj.* (**black-tie**) (of an event) requiring formal evening dress: *evening meals were black-tie affairs.*

black·top /'blak,täp/ ▸*n.* asphalt, or other black material used for surfacing roads: [as *adj.*] *blacktop roads.* ■ a road or area surfaced with such material: *playing hopscotch on the blacktop behind the school.*
▸*v.* [*trans.*] surface (a road or area) with such material: *41 miles had been blacktopped to date.*

black tu·pe·lo ▸*n.* another term for SOURGUM.

black vel·vet ▸*n.* a drink consisting of a mixture of stout and champagne.

black vul·ture ▸*n.* **1** a large, aggressive American vulture with black plumage and a short square tail. Also called CARRION CROW. • *Coragyps atratus*, family Cathartidae. **2** a very large Old World vulture with blackish-brown plumage, now rare in Europe. Also called CINEREOUS VULTURE. • *Aygypius monachus*, family Accipitridae.

black wal·nut ▸*n.* see WALNUT.

Black War·ri·or Riv·er a river that flows 178 miles (287 km) across northern Alabama to join the Tombigbee River. Tuscaloosa and the Birmingham area lie along its course.

black wa·ter ▸*n. technical* waste water from toilets. Compare with GRAY WATER.

black·wa·ter fe·ver /'blak,wôtər; -,wätər/ ▸*n.* a severe form of malaria in which blood cells are rapidly destroyed, resulting in dark urine.

Black·well /'blakwəl; -,wel/, Elizabeth (1821–1910), U.S. physician, born in England. She was the first woman to receive a medical degree in the U.S. (1849) and the first woman listed in the Medical Register of the United Kingdom (1859).

black wid·ow ▸*n.* a highly venomous American spider that has a black body with red markings. • *Latrodectus mactans*, family Theridiidae; races also occur on other continents.

black widow

black·work /'blak,wərk/ ▸*n.* a type of embroidery done in black thread on white cloth, esp. popular in England during the Tudor period.

blad·der /'bladər/ ▸*n.* **1** a membranous sac in humans and other animals, in which urine is collected for excretion. **2** anything inflated and hollow: *an air bladder in the arch and collar of the shoe.* ■ *Botany* an inflated fruit or vesicle in various plants: *a dried bladder of seaweed.* ▷Old English *blǣdre*, of Germanic origin; related to Dutch *blaar* and German *Blatter*, also to BLOW[1].

blad·dered /'bladərd/ ▸*adj. Brit. informal* extremely drunk.

blad·der fern ▸*n.* a small delicate fern with rounded spore cases, growing on rocks and walls. Bladder ferns are native to both Eurasia and North America. Also called BRITTLE FERN. • Genus *Cystopteris*, family Dryopteridaceae: several species.

blad·der·nut /'bladər,nət/ ▸*n.* (also **bladder nut**) a shrub or small tree of north temperate regions that bears white flowers and inflated seed capsules.

• Genus *Staphylea*, family Staphyleaceae: several species, in particular the **American bladdernut** (*S. trifolia*) of the eastern U.S. ■ the fruit of this shrub or tree.

blad·der sen·na ▸*n.* a Mediterranean shrub of the pea family that bears yellow flowers followed by inflated reddish pods. • *Colutea arborescens*, family Leguminosae.

blad·der worm ▸*n.* an immature form of a tapeworm, which lives in the flesh of the secondary host. Further development is suspended until it is eaten by the primary host.

blad·der·wort /ˈbladər,wərt; -,wôrt/ ▸*n.* an aquatic plant of north temperate regions with small air-filled bladders that keep the plant afloat and trap tiny animals that provide additional nutrients. • Genus *Utricularia*, family Lentibulariaceae.

blad·der·wrack /ˈbladər,rak/ (also **blad·der wrack**) ▸*n.* a common brown shoreline seaweed that has tough straplike fronds containing air bladders that give buoyancy. • *Fucus vesiculosus*, class Phaeophyceae.

blade /blād/ ▸*n.* **1** the flat cutting edge of a knife, saw, or other tool or weapon. ■ short for RAZOR BLADE. ■ *poetic/literary* a sword. ■ *Archaeology* a long, narrow flake. **2** the flat, wide section of an implement or device such as an oar or a propeller. ■ a thin, flat metal runner on an ice skate. ■ a shoulder bone in a cut of meat, or the cut of meat itself. ■ the flat part of the tongue behind the tip. **3** a long, narrow leaf of grass or another similar plant: ***a blade of*** *grass.* ■ *Botany* the broad thin part of a leaf apart from the stalk. **4** *informal, dated* a dashing or energetic young man.
▸*v.* [*intrans .*] *informal* skate using in-line skates: *we bladed into the parking lot behind Mensky's.* ▷Old English *blæd* 'leaf of a plant' (also in sense 2), of Germanic origin; related to Dutch *blad* and German *Blatt.* —**blad·ed** *adj.* [in *combination*] *double-bladed paddles.*

blague /bläg/ ▸*n.* a joke or piece of nonsense. ▷mid 19th cent.: French, literally 'claptrap, nonsense.'

bla·gueur /bläˈgər/ ▸*n.* a person who talks nonsense. ▷French, from BLAGUE.

blah /blä/ *informal* ▸used to substitute for actual words in contexts where they are felt to be too tedious or lengthy to give in full: *the typical kid, going out every night, blah, blah, blah.*
▸*n.* **1** (also **blah-blah**) used to refer to something that is boring or without meaningful content: *talking all kinds of blah to him* | [as *adj.*] *his blah feeling.* **2** (**the blahs**) depression: *he battled a case of the blahs* | [with *adj.*] *the winter blahs.* ▷early 20th cent. (originally U.S.): imitative.

blain /blān/ ▸*n. rare* an inflamed swelling or sore on the skin. See CHILBLAIN. ▷Old English *blegen*; related to Dutch *blein.*

Blaine /blān/ a city in southeastern Minnesota, north of Minneapolis; pop. 38,975.

Blair[1] /ble(ə)r/, Bonnie (1964–), U.S. speed skater. She is the only U.S. woman to win five Olympic gold medals-in the 500—meter race in 1988, 1992, and 1994 and in the 1,000-meter race in 1992 and 1994.

Blair[2], John (1732–1800), U.S. Supreme Court associate justice 1789–96. He was a member of the Constitutional Convention 1787 and signed the U.S. Constitution. He favored a strong federal government.

Blair[3], Tony (1953–), British statesman; prime minister (1997–); full name *Anthony Charles Lynton Blair.* He was elected leader of the Labour Party in 1994.

Blake[1] /blāk/, Eubie (1883–1983), U.S. jazz pianist and composer. One of the foremost ragtime pianists, he wrote over 300 songs, many in collaboration with lyricist Noble Sissle (1889–1975).

Blake[2], Peter (1932–), English painter. He was prominent in the pop art movement in the late 1950s and early 1960s.

Blake[3], William (1757–1827), English artist and poet. His poems mark the beginning of romanticism and a rejection of the Age of Enlightenment. His watercolors and engravings, like his writings, were not fully appreciated until after his death. Notable collections of poems: *Songs of Innocence* (1789) and *Songs of Experience* (1794).

Bla·key /ˈblākē/, Art (1919–90), U.S. jazz drummer; full name *Arthur Blakey.* A pioneer of the bebop movement, he was known for his group, the Jazz Messengers.

blame /blām/ ▸*v.* [*trans.*] assign responsibility for a fault or wrong: *the inquiry* ***blamed*** *the engineer* ***for*** *the accident.* ■ (**blame something on**) assign the responsibility for something bad to (someone or something): *they blame youth crime on unemployment.*
▸*n.* responsibility for a fault or wrong: *his players had to* ***take the blame*** | *they are trying to* ***put the blame on*** *us.* ■ the action of assigning responsibility for a fault: *he singled out food additives for blame.* ▷Middle English: from Old French *blamer, blasmer* (verb), from a popular Latin variant of ecclesiastical Latin *blasphemare* 'reproach, revile, blaspheme,' from Greek *blasphēmein* (see BLASPHEME). —**blam·a·ble** (also **blame·a·ble**) *adj.* —**blame·ful** /-fəl/ *adj.*
▸*PHRASES* □ **be to blame** be responsible for a fault or wrong: *he* ***was to blame for*** *their deaths.* □ **I don't** (or **can't**) **blame you** (or **her**, etc.) used to indicate that one agrees that the action or attitude taken was reasonable: *he was becoming impatient, and I couldn't blame him.* □ **have only oneself to blame** be solely responsible for something bad that has happened.

blamed /blāmd/ ▸*adj.* & *adv. informal* used for emphasis, esp. to express disapprobation or annoyance: *a blamed old sodden-headed conservative.*

blame·less /ˈblāmlis/ ▸*adj.* innocent of wrongdoing: *he led a blameless life.* —**blame·less·ly** *adv.* —**blame·less·ness** *n.*

blame·wor·thy /ˈblām,wərt͟hē/ ▸*adj.* responsible for wrongdoing and deserving of censure or blame. —**blame·wor·thi·ness** *n.*

blanc fixe /ˈblaNGk ˈfiks; bläN ˈfēks/ ▸*n.* barium sulfate in the form of a white powder used in making pigments and paper.

blanch /blanCH/ ▸*v.* **1** [*trans.*] make white or pale by extracting color; bleach: *the cold light blanched her face.* ■ [*trans.*] whiten (a plant) by depriving it of light: *blanch endive by covering plants with large flowerpots.* ■ [*intrans.*] *figurative* (of a person) grow pale from shock, fear, or a similar emotion: *many* ***people blanch at*** *the suggestion* | *their faces blanched with fear.* **2** [*trans.*] prepare (vegetables) for freezing or further cooking by immersing briefly in boiling water. ■ peel (almonds) by scalding them: [as *adj.*] (**blanched**) *blanched almonds.* ▷Middle English: from Old French *blanchir*, from *blanc* 'white,' ultimately of Germanic origin.

Blan·chard /ˈblanCHərd; bläNˈSHär/, Jean Pierre François (1753–1809), French balloonist. Together with an American, **John Jeffries** (1744–1819), he made the first air crossing of the English Channel, in a balloon, on January 7, 1785.

blanc·mange /bləˈmänj; -ˈmänZH/ ▸*n.* a sweet opaque gelatinous dessert made with cornstarch and milk. ▷late Middle English *blancmanger*, from Old French *blanc mangier*, from *blanc* 'white' + *mangier* 'eat' (used as a noun to mean 'food'). The shortened form without *-er* arose in the 18th cent.

bland /bland/ ▸*adj.* lacking strong features or characteristics and therefore uninteresting: *rebelling against the bland uniformity.* ■ (of food or drink) mild or insipid: *bland and unadventurous vegetarian dish* | *bland beers of mediocre quality.* ■ (of a person or behavior) showing no strong emotion; dull and unremarkable: *offering bland reassurance* | *his expression was bland and unreadable.* ▷late Middle English (in the sense 'gentle in manner'): from Latin *blandus* 'soft, smooth.' —**bland·ly** *adv.* —**bland·ness** *n.*

Blan·da /ˈblandə/, George Frederick (1927–), U.S. football player. The all-time leading scorer (2,002 points) in professional football, he played the most games (340) for the most seasons (26). Football Hall of Fame (1981).

bland·ish /ˈblandisH/ ▸*v.* [*trans.*] *archaic* coax (someone) with kind words or flattery: *I was blandishing her with imprudences to get her off the subject.* ▷Middle English: from Old French *blandiss-*, lengthened stem of *blandir*, from Latin *blandiri*, from *blandus* 'soft, smooth.'

bland·ish·ment /ˈblandisHmənt/ ▸*n.* a flattering or pleasing statement or action used to persuade someone gently to do something: *the blandishments of the travel brochure.*

blank /blaNGk/ ▸*adj.* **1** (of a surface or background) unrelieved by decorative or other features; bare, empty, or plain: *the blank skyline* | *a blank wall.* ■ not written or printed on: *a blank sheet of paper.* ■ (of a document) with spaces left for a signature or details: *blank tax-return forms.* ■ (of a tape) with nothing recorded on it: *blank cassettes.* **2** showing incomprehension or no reaction: *we were met by blank looks.* ■ having temporarily no knowledge or understanding: *her mind went blank.* ■ lacking incident or result: *those blank moments aboard airplanes.* **3** [*attrib.*] complete; absolute (used emphatically with negative force): *he was met with a blank refusal to discuss the issue.*
▸*n.* **1** a space left to be filled in a document: *leave blanks to type in the appropriate names* | *this measure required subjects to* ***fill in the blanks*** *in a story.* ■ a document with blank spaces to be filled. **2** (also **blank cartridge**) a cartridge containing gunpowder but no bullet, used for training or as a signal. **3** an empty space or period of time, esp. in terms of a lack of knowledge or understanding: *my mind was a total blank.* **4** an object that has no mark or design on it, in particular: ■ a roughly cut metal or wooden block intended for further shaping or finishing. ■ a domino with one or both halves blank. ■ a plain metal disk from which a coin is made by stamping a design on it. **5** a dash written instead of a word or letter, esp. instead of an obscenity or profanity. ■ used euphemistically in place of a noun regarded as obscene, profane, or abusive.
▸*v.* [*trans.*] **1** cover up, obscure, or cause to appear blank or empty: *electronic countermeasures* ***blanked out*** *the radar signals.* ■ [*intrans.*] become blank or empty: *the picture* ***blanked out.*** ■ cut (a metal blank): *the complete core disk can be* ***blanked out*** *in one piece.* **2** *informal* defeat (a sports opponent) without allowing the opposition to score: *Baltimore blanked Toronto in a 7–0 victory.* ▷Middle English (in the sense 'white, colorless'): from Old French *blanc* 'white,' ultimately of Germanic origin. —**blank·ly** *adv.* —**blank·ness** *n.*
▸*PHRASES* □ **draw a blank** elicit no successful response; fail: *the search drew a blank.* □ **firing blanks** *informal* (of a man) infertile.

blank check ▸*n.* a bank check with the amount left for the payee to fill in. ■ [in *sing.*] *figurative* an unlimited freedom of action: *he was effectively granted a blank check to conduct a war without congressional authorization.*

blan·ket /ˈblaNGkit/ ▸*n.* **1** a large piece of woolen or similar material used as a bed covering or other covering for warmth. ■ *figurative* a thick mass or layer of a specified material that covers something completely: *a dense gray blanket of cloud.* **2** *Printing* a rubber surface used for transferring the image in ink from the plate to the paper in offset printing.
▸*adj.* covering all cases or instances; total and inclusive: *a blanket ban on tobacco advertising.*
▸*v.* (**-ket·ed, -ket·ing**) [*trans.*] cover completely with a thick layer of something: *the countryside* ***was blanketed in*** *snow.* ■ stifle or keep quiet (sound): *the double glazing blankets the noise a bit.* ■ *Sailing* take wind from the sails of (another craft) by passing to windward. ▷Middle English (denoting undyed woolen cloth): via Old Northern French from Old French *blanc* 'white,' ultimately of Germanic origin.
▸*PHRASE* □ **born on the wrong side of the blanket** *dated* born of parents not lawfully married to each other.

blan·ket·flow·er /ˈblaNGkit,flou(ə)r/ ▸*n.* another term for GAILLARDIA.

blan·ket·ing /ˈblaNGkitiNG/ ▸*n.* **1** material used for making blankets. **2** the action of covering something with or as if with a blanket: *the blanketing of large areas with trees.*

blan·ket roll ▸*n.* a blanket or sleeping bag made into a cylindrical roll for ease of carrying, often with utensils and other personal supplies inside; a bedroll.

blan·ket stitch ▸*n.* a buttonhole stitch used on the edges of a blanket or other material too thick to be hemmed.

blan·ket·weed /ˈblaNGkit,wēd/ ▸*n.* a common green freshwater alga that forms long unbranched filaments. It can be a problem in overenriched water and garden ponds. • Genus *Spirogyra*, phylum Chlorophyta, kingdom Plantae (or Protista).

blank·e·ty /ˈblaNGkitē/ (also **blank·e·ty-blank**) ▸*adj.* & *n. informal* used euphemistically to replace a word considered coarse or vulgar: *it's time to ditch the blankety-blank tax code.*

blank verse ▸*n.* verse without rhyme, esp. that which uses iambic pentameter.

blan·quette /bläNGˈket/ ▸*n.* a dish consisting of white meat in a white sauce. ▷French, based on *blanc* 'white.'

Blan·tyre /ˈblan,tī(ə)r/ the chief commercial and industrial city in Malawi; pop. 331,600 (with Limbe, a town to the southeast). It is named after explorer David Livingstone's birthplace in Scotland.

blare /ble(ə)r/ ▸*v.* [*intrans.*] sound loudly and harshly: *the ambulance arrived outside, siren blaring.* ■ [*trans.*] cause (something) to sound loudly and harshly: *the radio was* ***blaring out*** *organ music.*
▸*n.* a loud harsh sound: *a blare of trumpets.* ▷late Middle English (in the sense 'roar, bellow'): from Middle

Dutch *blaren, bleren,* or Low German *blaren,* of imitative origin. Current senses date from the late 18th cent.

blar·ney /ˈblärnē/ ▸*n.* talk that aims to charm, pleasantly flatter, or persuade: *he had the "street charm" of an Irish politician, but this blarney concealed his inner self.* ■ amusing and harmless nonsense: *this story is perhaps just a bit of blarney.*
▸*v.* (**-neys, -neyed**) [*trans.*] influence or persuade (someone) using charm and pleasant flattery. ▷late 18th cent.: named after *Blarney,* a castle near Cork in Ireland, where there is a stone said to give the gift of persuasive speech to anyone who kisses it.

bla·sé /bläˈzā/ ▸*adj.* unimpressed or indifferent to something because one has experienced or seen it so often before: *she was becoming quite blasé about the dangers.* ▷early 19th cent.: French, past participle of *blaser* 'cloy,' probably ultimately of Germanic origin.

blas·pheme /blasˈfēm; ˈblasˌfēm/ ▸*v.* [*intrans.*] speak irreverently about God or sacred things: *allegations that he had* ***blasphemed against*** *Islam.* ▷Middle English: via Old French from ecclesiastical Latin *blasphemare* 'reproach, revile, blaspheme,' from Greek *blasphēmein,* from *blasphēmos* 'evil-speaking.' Compare with BLAME. **—blas·phem·er** /blasˈfēmər; ˈblasfəmər/ *n.*

blas·phe·mous /ˈblasfəməs/ ▸*adj.* sacrilegious against God or sacred things; profane: *blasphemous and heretical talk.* ▷late Middle English: via ecclesiastical Latin from Greek *blasphēmos* 'evil-speaking' + -OUS. **—blas·phe·mous·ly** *adv.*

blas·phe·my /ˈblasfəmē/ ▸*n.* (*pl.* **-mies**) the act or offense of speaking sacrilegiously about God or sacred things; profane talk: *he was detained on charges of blasphemy | screaming incomprehensible blasphemies.* ▷Middle English: from Old French, via ecclesiastical Latin from Greek *blasphēmia* 'slander, blasphemy.'

blast /blast/ ▸*n.* **1** a destructive wave of highly compressed air spreading outward from an explosion: *they were thrown backward by the blast.* ■ an explosion or explosive firing, esp. of a bomb: *a bomb blast | a shotgun blast.* ■ *figurative* a forceful attack or assault: *he defeated his weakest opponent in such a blast that the fans left unimpressed.* **2** a strong gust of wind or air: *the icy blast hit them.* ■ a strong current of air used in smelting. **3** a single loud note of a horn, whistle, or other noisemaking device: *a blast of the ship's siren.* **4** *informal* a severe reprimand: *I braced myself for the inevitable blast.* **5** *informal* an enjoyable experience or lively party: *it could turn out to be a real blast.*
▸*v.* [*trans.*] **1** blow up or break apart (something solid) with explosives: *quantities of solid rock had to be* ***blasted away*** *| the explosion* ***blasted out*** *hundreds of windows.* ■ produce (damage or a hole) by means of an explosion: *the force of the collision* ***blasted out*** *a tremendous crater.* ■ [*trans.*] force or throw (something) in a specified direction by impact or explosion: *the car was blasted thirty feet into the sky.* ■ shoot with a gun: *Fowler was blasted with an air rifle.* ■ [*intrans.*] move very quickly and loudly in a specified direction: *driving rain blasted through the smashed window.* ■ *informal* criticize fiercely: *the school was blasted by government inspectors.* **2** make or cause to make a loud continuous musical or other noise: [*intrans.*] *music blasted out at full volume |* [*trans.*] *an impatient motorist blasted his horn.* **3** kick, strike, or throw (a ball) hard: *Ripken blasted the ball into the gap in right field.* **4** *poetic/literary* (of a wind or other natural force) wither, shrivel, or blight (a plant): *crops blasted on the eve of harvest.* ■ strike with divine anger: *damn and blast this awful place!* ■ destroy or ruin: *a candidate whose only strategy is to blast the opposition.*
▸*phrasal v.* □ **blast off** (of a rocket or spacecraft) take off from a launching site.
▸*exclam. chiefly Brit., informal* expressing annoyance: *"Blast! The car won't start!"* ▷Old English *blǣst,* of Germanic origin; related to BLAZE³.
▸*PHRASES* □ **a blast from the past** *informal* something forcefully nostalgic: *a request for a real old blast from the past.* □ **(at) full blast** at maximum power or intensity: *the heat is on full blast.*

-blast ▸*comb. form Biology* denoting an embryonic cell: *erythroblast.* Compare with -CYTE. ■ denoting a germ layer of an embryo: *epiblast.* ▷from Greek *blastos* 'sprout.'

blast cell ▸*n.* a primitive, undifferentiated blood cell, often found in the blood of those with acute leukemia.

blast·ed /ˈblastid/ ▸*adj.* **1** [*attrib.*] *informal* used to express annoyance: *make your own blasted coffee!* **2** [*attrib.*] *poetic/literary* withered or blighted; laid waste: *an area of blasted trees.* **3** [*predic.*] *informal* drunk: *the waiter kept bringing us free cocktails; so I got really blasted.*

blas·te·ma /blaˈstēmə/ ▸*n.* (*pl.* **-mas** or **-ma·ta** /-mətə/) the primary formative material of plants and animals, from which cells are developed. **—blas·te·mal** *adj.* **—blas·te·mat·ic** /ˌblastəˈmatik/ *adj.*

blast·er /ˈblastər/ ▸*n.* a person or thing that blasts: *Jake was an explosives specialist, a blaster.* ■ (in science fiction) a weapon that emits a destructive blast. ■ a computer game in which the objective is to shoot as many enemies as possible: *the game is a blaster requiring a gun-happy trigger finger.* ■ short for GHETTO BLASTER.

blast fur·nace ▸*n.* a smelting furnace in the form of a tower into which a blast of hot compressed air can be introduced from below. Such furnaces are used chiefly to make iron from a mixture of iron ore, coke, and limestone.

blast·ing gel·a·tin ▸*n.* another term for GELATIN.

blasto- ▸*comb. form* relating to germination: *blastoderm.* ▷from Greek *blastos* 'germ, sprout.'

blas·to·coel /ˈblastəˌsēl/ (also **blas·to·coele**) ▸*n.* the fluid-filled cavity of a blastula. Also called SEGMENTATION CAVITY. **—blas·to·coel·ic** /ˌblastəˈsēlik/ *adj.*

blas·to·cyst /ˈblastəˌsist/ ▸*n. Embryology* a mammalian blastula in which some differentiation of cells has occurred. Also called **blastodermic vesicle**.

blas·to·derm /ˈblastəˌdərm/ ▸*n. Embryology* the layer of embryonic tissue that forms prior to the development of the embryonic axis. ■ the outer layer of cells that forms the wall of a blastula.

blas·to·disk /ˈblastəˌdisk/ (also **blas·to·disc**) ▸*n. Embryology* a blastula having the form of a disk of cells on top of the yolk in the eggs of reptiles and birds.

blast·off /ˈblastˌôf; -ˌäf/ ▸*n.* the launching of a rocket or spacecraft.

blas·to·gen·e·sis /ˌblastəˈjenəsis/ ▸*n.* **1** the theory of the transmission of inherited characteristics by germ plasm. **2** asexual reproduction of an organism by budding. **3** the development of lymphocytes into larger undifferentiated cells that can undergo mitosis. **—blas·to·gen·ic** /-ˈjenik/ *adj.*

blas·to·ma /blaˈstōmə/ ▸*n.* (*pl.* **-mas** or **-ma·ta** /-mətə/) a neoplasm consisting of immature undifferentiated cells.

blas·to·mere /ˈblastəˌmi(ə)r/ ▸*n. Embryology* a cell formed by cleavage of a fertilized ovum.

blas·to·my·co·sis /ˌblastəmīˈkōsis/ ▸*n. Medicine* a disease caused by infection with parasitic fungi affecting the skin or the internal organs. • The fungi (**blastomycetes**) belong to the genus *Blastomyces,* subdivision Deuteromycotina.

blas·to·pore /ˈblastəˌpôr/ ▸*n.* the opening of the central cavity of an embryo in the early stage of development.

blas·tu·la /ˈblasCHələ/ ▸*n.* (*pl.* **-las** or **-lae** /-ˌlē/) *Embryology* an animal embryo at the early stage of development when it is a hollow ball of cells. Also called **blastosphere**. ▷late 19th cent.: modern Latin, from Greek *blastos* 'sprout.'

blat /blat/ ▸*v.* (**blat·ted, blat·ting**) [*intrans.*] make a bleating sound.
▸*n.* a bleat or similar noise: *the blat of Jack's horn.* ▷mid 19th cent.: imitative.

bla·tant /ˈblātnt/ ▸*adj.* (of bad behavior) done openly and unashamedly: *blatant lies.* ■ completely lacking in subtlety; very obvious: *forcing herself to resist his blatant charm.* ▷late 16th cent.: perhaps an alteration of Scots *blatand* 'bleating.' It was first used by Spenser as an epithet for a thousand-tongued monster produced by Cerberus and Chimera, a symbol of calumny, which he called the *blatant beast.* It was subsequently used to mean 'clamorous, offensive to the ear,' first of people (mid 17th cent.), later of things (late 18th cent.); the sense 'obtrusive to the eye, unashamedly conspicuous' arose in the late 19th cent. **—bla·tan·cy** /ˈblātnsē/ *n.*

bla·tant·ly /ˈblātntlē/ ▸*adv.* in an unsubtle and unashamed manner: *the general staff blatantly manipulated press coverage of the war.* ■ [usu. as *submodifier*] used to emphasize the speaker's opinion that something disapproved of is clearly the case: *he found her remarks blatantly racist.*

Blatch·ford /ˈblaCHfərd/, Samuel (1820–93), U.S. Supreme Court associate justice 1882–93. He was a circuit judge before being appointed to the Court by President Arthur. His specialty was patent law.

blath·er /ˈblaT͟Hər/ (also **bleth·er** /ˈbleT͟Hər/ or **blith·er** /ˈbliT͟Hər/) ▸*v.* [*intrans.*] talk long-windedly without making very much sense: *she began* ***blathering on*** *about spirituality and life after death |* [as *n.*] (**blathering**) *now stop your blathering and get back to work.*
▸*n.* long-winded talk with no real substance. ▷late Middle English (as a verb; originally Scots and northern English dialect): from Old Norse *blathra* 'talk nonsense,' from *blathr* 'nonsense.'

blath·er·skite /ˈblaT͟Hərˌskīt/ ▸*n.* **1** a person who talks at great length without making much sense. ■ foolish talk; nonsense: *politicians get away all the time with their blatherskite.* **2** *informal* a scoundrel: *you lousy, thieving blatherskite!* ▷mid 17th cent.: from BLATHER + *skite,* a Scottish derogatory term adopted into American colloquial speech during the American Revolution, from the Scottish song *Maggie Lauder,* by F. Semphill, which was popular with American troops.

Blau /blou/ see ORMANDY.

Blau·e Rei·ter /ˈblouə ˈrītər/ a group of German expressionist painters formed in 1911, based in Munich. The group included Wassily Kandinsky, Jean Arp, and Paul Klee. ▷German, literally 'blue rider,' the title of a painting by Kandinsky.

Bla·vat·sky /bləˈvatskē; -ˈvätskē/, Helena (Petrovna) (1831–91), Russian spiritualist; born in Ukraine; born *Helena Petrovna Hahn;* known as **Madame Blavatsky**. In 1875, she cofounded the Theosophical Society in New York.

blax·ploi·ta·tion /ˌblaksploiˈtāSHən/ ▸*n.* the exploitation of black people, esp. with regard to stereotyped roles in movies. ▷1970s: blend of *blacks* (plural of noun BLACK) and *exploitation* (see EXPLOIT).

blaze¹ /blāz/ ▸*n.* **1** a very large or fiercely burning fire: *twenty fireman fought the blaze.* ■ a harsh bright light: *a lightning flash changed the gentle illumination of the office into a sudden white blaze.* ■ [in *sing.*] a very bright display of light or color: *the gardens in summer are* ***a blaze of*** *color.* ■ [in *sing.*] *figurative* a conspicuous display or outburst of something: *their relationship broke up in* ***a blaze of publicity.*** **2** (**blazes**) *informal* used in various expressions of anger, bewilderment, or surprise as a euphemism for "hell": *"Go to blazes!" he shouted | what* ***in blue blazes*** *are you all talking about?* [with reference to the flames associated with hell.]
▸*v.* [*intrans.*] **1** burn fiercely or brightly: *the fire blazed merrily.* ■ shine brightly or powerfully: *the sun* ***blazed down*** *| figurative Barbara's eyes were* ***blazing with*** *anger.* **2** (of a gun or a person firing a gun) fire repeatedly or indiscriminately: *two terrorists burst into the house with guns blazing.* **3** *informal* achieve something in an impressive manner: *she blazed to a gold medal in the 200-meter sprint.* ■ [*trans.*] hit (a ball) with impressive strength: *he blazed a drive into the rough.*
▸*phrasal v.* □ **blaze up** burst into flame: *he attacked the fire with poker and tongs until it blazed up.* ■ *figurative* suddenly become angry: *he blazed up without warning.* ▷Old English *blæse* 'torch, bright fire,' of Germanic origin; related ultimately to BLAZE².
▸*PHRASES* □ **like blazes** *informal* very fast or forcefully: *I ran like blazes toward home.* [see sense 2 of the noun.] □ **with all guns blazing** *informal* with great determination and energy, typically without thought for the consequences.

blaze² ▸*n.* **1** a white spot or stripe on the face of a mammal or bird. ■ a broad white stripe running the length of a horse's face. **2** a mark made on a tree by cutting the bark so as to mark a route.
▸*v.* (**blaze a trail**) mark out a path or route. ■ *figurative* set an example by being the first to do something; pioneer: *small firms would set the pace, blazing a trail for others to follow.* ▷mid 17th cent. (sense 1): ultimately of Germanic origin; related to German *Blässe* 'blaze' and *blass* 'pale,' also to BLAZE¹, and probably to BLEMISH.

blaze³ ▸*v.* [*trans.*] (of a newspaper) present or proclaim (news) in a prominent, typically sensational, manner. ▷late Middle English (in the sense 'blow out on a trumpet'): from Middle Low German or Middle Dutch *blāzen* 'to blow'; related to BLOW¹.

blaz·er /ˈblāzər/ ▸*n.* a lightweight jacket, typically solid-colored, often worn as part of a uniform by members of a club, sports team, or school. ■ a plain jacket, typically dark blue, not forming part of a suit but considered appropriate for formal or semiformal wear. ▷late 19th cent.: from BLAZE¹ + -ER¹. The original general sense was 'a thing that blazes or shines' (mid 17th cent.), giving rise to the term for a brightly colored sport coat.

blaz·ing star ▶*n.* any of a number of North American plants, some of which are cultivated for their flowers, in particular: • a plant of the daisy family with tall spikes of purple or white flowers (genus *Liatris*, family Compositae). • a plant of the western U.S. with toothed leaves and yellow flowers (genus *Mentzelia*, family Loasaceae), esp. the gray-leaved, large-flowered **giant blazing star** (*M. laevicaulis*). • devil's bit.

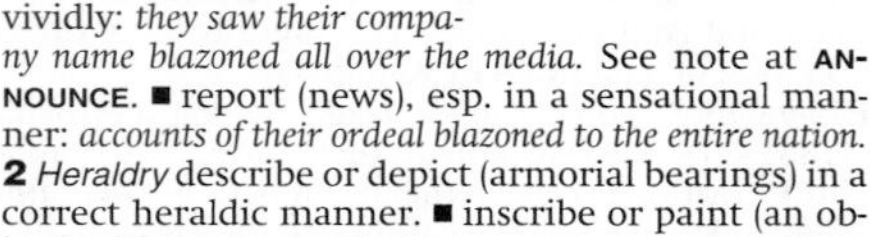
blazing star

bla·zon /ˈblāzən/ ▶*v.* [*trans.*] **1** [with *adverbial of place*] display prominently or vividly: *they saw their company name blazoned all over the media.* See note at ANNOUNCE. ■ report (news), esp. in a sensational manner: *accounts of their ordeal blazoned to the entire nation.* **2** *Heraldry* describe or depict (armorial bearings) in a correct heraldic manner. ■ inscribe or paint (an object) with arms or a name.
▶*n.* *Heraldry* a correct description of armorial bearings. ■ *archaic* a coat of arms. ▷Middle English (denoting a shield, later one bearing a heraldic device): from Old French *blason* 'shield,' of unknown origin. The sense of the verb has been influenced by BLAZE[3].

bla·zon·ry /ˈblāzənrē/ ▶*n.* *Heraldry* the art of describing or painting heraldic devices or armorial bearings. ■ [*plural n.*] devices or bearings of this type.

bldg. ▶*abbr.* building.

bleach /blēCH/ ▶*v.* [*trans.*] whiten by exposure to sunlight or by a chemical process: *paper products are bleached with chlorine* | [as *adj.*] (**bleached**) *permed and bleached hair.* ■ clean and sterilize: *a new formula to bleach and brighten clothing* ■ *figurative* deprive of vitality or substance: *his contributions to the album are bleached of personality.*
▶*n.* a chemical (typically a solution of sodium hypochlorite or hydrogen peroxide) used to whiten or sterilize materials. ▷Old English *blǣcan* (verb), *blǣce* (noun), from *blǣc* 'pale,' of Germanic origin; related to BLEAK[1].

bleach·er /ˈblēCHər/ ▶*n.* **1** a person who bleaches textiles or other material. ■ a container or chemical used in bleaching. **2** (usu. **bleachers**) a cheap bench seat at a sports arena, typically in an outdoor uncovered stand. ■ (also **bleacherite** /ˈblēCHəˌrīt/) a person occupying such a seat: *the bleachers cheered.*

bleach·ing pow·der ▶*n.* a powder containing calcium hypochlorite, used chiefly to remove color from materials.

bleak[1] /blēk/ ▶*adj.* (of an area of land) lacking vegetation and exposed to the elements: *a bleak and barren moor.* ■ (of a building or room) charmless and inhospitable; dreary: *he looked around the bleak little room in despair.* ■ (of the weather) cold and miserable: *a bleak midwinter's day.* ■ (of a situation or future prospect) not hopeful or encouraging; unlikely to have a favorable outcome: *he paints a bleak picture of a company that has lost its way.* ■ (of a person or a person's expression) cold and forbidding: *his bleak, near vacant eyes grew remote.* ▷Old English *blāc* 'shining, white,' or in later use from synonymous Old Norse *bleikr*; ultimately of Germanic origin and related to BLEACH.
—bleak·ly *adv.* **—bleak·ness** *n.*

bleak[2] ▶*n.* a small silvery shoaling fish of the minnow family, found in Eurasian rivers. • Genera *Alburnus* and *Chalcalburnus*, family Cyprinidae: several species, in particular *A. alburnus.* ▷late 15th cent.: from Old Norse *bleikja.*

blear /bli(ə)r/ *archaic* ▶*v.* [*trans.*] make dim; blur: *you would blear your eyes with books.*
▶*adj.* dim, dull, or filmy: *a medicine to lay to sore and blear eyes.*
▶*n.* a film over the eyes; a blur: *he forced his eyes open and shut to rid them of blear.* ▷Middle English (as a verb): probably related to Middle High German *blerre* 'blurred vision' and Low German *blarroged* 'bleary-eyed.'

blear·y /ˈbli(ə)rē/ ▶*adj.* (**blear·i·er**, **blear·i·est**) (of the eyes) unfocused or filmy from sleep or tiredness: *you hate to face the world with bleary, tear-soaked, itching eyes.*
—blear·i·ly /ˈbli(ə)rəlē/ *adv.* **—blear·i·ness** *n.*

blear·y-eyed (also **blear-eyed**) ▶*adj.* (of a person) having bleary eyes.

bleat /blēt/ ▶*v.* [*intrans.*] (of a sheep, goat, or calf) make a characteristic wavering cry: *the lamb was bleating weakly figurative handing the mike to some woman who starts bleating out rap rhymes* | [as *n.*] (**bleating**) *the silence was broken by the plaintive bleating of sheep.* ■ [*reporting verb*] speak or complain in a weak, querulous, or foolish way: *he bleated incoherently about the report.*
▶*n.* [in *sing.*] the wavering cry made by a sheep, goat, or calf: *the distant bleat of sheep in the field.* ■ a person's plaintive cry: *his despairing bleat touched her heart.* ■ *informal* a complaint: *they're hoping that I'll bow to their idiotic arrangements without a bleat.* ▷Old English *blǣtan*, of imitative origin.

bleb /bleb/ ▶*n.* a small blister on the skin. ■ a small bubble in glass or in a fluid. ■ *Biology* a rounded outgrowth on the surface of a cell. ▷early 17th cent.: variant of BLOB.

bleed /blēd/ ▶*v.* (*past* and *past part.* **bled** /bled/) **1** [*intrans.*] lose blood from the body as a result of injury or illness: *the cut was bleeding steadily* | *some casualties were left to* **bleed to death** | [as *n.*] (**bleeding**) *the bleeding has stopped now.* ■ (of a dye or color) seep into an adjacent color or area: *I worked loosely with the oils, allowing colors to bleed into one another.* ■ [*intrans.*] *Printing* (of an illustration or a design) be printed so as to run to the edge of the page: *the picture bleeds on three sides.* ■ [*trans.*] print and trim (an illustration or a design) in such a way. **2** [*trans.*] draw blood from (someone), esp. as a once-common method of treatment in medicine. ■ remove blood from (an animal carcass): *the first steer rolled out on the floor to be bled, skinned, and dressed.* ■ [*trans.*] *informal* drain (someone) of money or resources: *his policy of attempting to bleed unions of funds.* ■ [*trans.*] allow (fluid or gas) to escape from a closed system through a valve: *open the valves and bleed air from the pump chamber.* ■ [*trans.*] treat (a system) in this way: *bleeding the radiator at the air vent.*
▶*n.* an instance of bleeding: *a lot of blood was lost from the placental bleed.* ■ *Printing* an instance of printing an illustration, design, or text to the edge of the page: *it allows printing of a tabloid page with full bleed.* ■ the escape of fluid or gas from a closed system through a valve: *the amount of air bleed from the compressor.* ■ the action or process of a dye, ink, or color seeping into an adjacent color or area: *color bleed is apparent on brighter hues.* ▷Old English *blēdan*, of Germanic origin; related to BLOOD.
▶*PHRASES* □ **bleed someone dry** (or **white**) drain someone of all money or resources: *the railroads claimed that personnel costs were bleeding them dry.* □ **my heart bleeds** (**for you**) used ironically to express the speaker's belief that the person spoken about does not deserve the sympathetic response sought: *"I flew out here feeling tired and overworked." "My heart bleeds for you!" she replied.*

bleed·er /ˈblēdər/ ▶*n.* **1** *informal* a person who bleeds easily, esp. a hemophiliac. ■ a blood vessel that bleeds freely during surgery. **2** *Baseball* a ground ball that barely passes between two infielders.

bleed·ing /ˈblēdiNG/ ▶*adj.* [*attrib.*] *Brit., informal* used for emphasis or to express annoyance.

bleed·ing edge ▶*n.* the very forefront of technological development: [as *modifier*] *an architecture that many people believe is still too bleeding edge for large mission-critical systems.* ▷1980s: on the pattern of *leading edge, cutting edge.*

bleed·ing heart ▶*n.* **1** *informal, derogatory* a person considered to be dangerously softhearted, typically someone considered too liberal in political beliefs: [as *adj.*] *a tirade against bleeding-heart environmentalists.* **2** any of a number of plants that have heart-shaped flowers, typically pink or red, in particular: • a popular herbaceous garden plant (genus *Dicentra*, family Fumariaceae, in particular *D. spectabilus*). • a tropical twining shrub with cream and red flowers, often cultivated under glass (*Clerodendrum thomsoniae*, family Verbenaceae).

bleeding heart 2

bleep /blēp/ ▶*n.* a short high-pitched sound made by an electronic device as a signal or to attract attention: *the autopilot sent back an acknowledgment bleep.* ■ a sound of this type used in broadcasting as a substitute for a censored word or phrase.
▶*v.* [*intrans.*] (of an electronic device) make a short high-pitched sound or repeated sequence of sounds: *the screen flickered for a few moments and bleeped.* ■ [*trans.*] substitute a bleep or bleeps for (a censored word or phrase): *cable operators have* **bleeped out** *the accuser's name.* ■ used in place of an expletive: *"what the bleep are we going to do?" he asked.* ▷1950s: imitative.

bleep·er /ˈblēpər/ ▶*n.* British term for PAGER.

bleep·ing /ˈblēpiNG/ ▶*adj.* (of an electronic device) making a short high-pitched sound or sounds: *a bleeping red display on the exercise machine.* ■ *informal, often humorous* used to express exasperation or annoyance, in place of an expletive: *we didn't do a bleeping thing, and we're still getting hung.* ▷1950s: euphemistically for BLEEDING, by association with the "bleeps" used to dub expletives in broadcast texts.

blem·ish /ˈblemiSH/ ▶*n.* a small mark or flaw that spoils the appearance of something: *the merest blemish on a Rolls Royce might render it unsalable.* ■ *figurative* a moral defect or fault: *the offenses were an uncharacteristic blemish on an otherwise clean record* | *local government is not without blemish.*
▶*v.* [*trans.*] [often as *adj.*] (**blemished**) spoil the appearance of (something) that is otherwise aesthetically perfect: *thousands of Web pages are blemished with embarrassing typos* | *figurative his reign as world champion has been blemished by controversy.* ▷late Middle English (as a verb): from Old French *ble(s)miss-*, lengthened stem of *ble(s)mir* 'make pale, injure'; probably of Germanic origin.

blench[1] /blenCH/ ▶*v.* [*intrans.*] make a sudden flinching movement out of fear or pain: *he blenched and struggled to regain his composure.* ▷Old English *blencan* 'deceive,' of Germanic origin; later influenced by BLINK.

blench[2] ▶*v.* *chiefly dialect* variant spelling of BLANCH.

blend /blend/ ▶*v.* [*trans.*] mix (a substance) with another substance so that they combine together as a mass: **blend** *the cornstarch* **with** *a tablespoon of water* | [*intrans.*] *add the grated cheese and blend well.* ■ [often as *adj.*] (**blended**) mix (different types of the same substance, such as tea, coffee, liquor, etc.) together so as to make a product of the desired quality: *a blended whiskey.* ■ put or combine (abstract things) together: *blend basic information for the novice with some scientific gardening for the more experienced* | [as *n.*] (**blending**) *a blending of romanticism with a more detached modernism.* ■ merge (a color) with another so that one is not clearly distinguishable from the other. ■ [*intrans.*] form a harmonious combination: *costumes, music, and lighting all* **blend together** *beautifully.* ■ (**blend in/into**) be unobtrusive or harmonious by being similar in appearance or behavior: *she would have to employ a permanent bodyguard in the house, someone who would blend in.*
▶*n.* a mixture of different things or people: *knitting yarns in mohair blends.* ■ a mixture of different types or grades of a substance, such as tea, coffee, whiskey, etc. ■ a combination of different abstract things or qualities: *a blend of Marxist and anarchist ideas* | *Ontario offers a cultural blend you'll find nowhere else on earth.* ■ a word made up of the parts of others and combining their meanings, for example *motel* from *motor* and *hotel.* ▷Middle English: probably of Scandinavian origin and related to Old Norse *blanda* 'to mix.'

blende /blend/ ▶*n.* another term for SPHALERITE. ▷late 17th cent.: from German, from *blenden* 'deceive' (so named because it often resembles galena, but is deceptive in that it yields no lead).

blend·ed fam·i·ly ▶*n.* a family consisting of a couple and their children from this and all previous relationships.

blend·er /ˈblendər/ ▶*n.* a person or thing that mixes things together, in particular: ■ an electric mixing machine used in food preparation for liquefying, chopping, or puréeing.

Blen·heim[1] /ˈblenəm/ a battle in 1704 in Bavaria, near the village of Blindheim, in which the English, under the Duke of Marlborough, defeated the French and the Bavarians. See MARLBOROUGH.

Blen·heim[2] ▶*n.* a dog of a small red and white breed of spaniel. ▷mid 19th cent.: from the name of *Blenheim* palace, the Duke of Marlborough's seat in central England, given to the Duke in honor of his victory at Blenheim.

blen·ny /ˈblenē/ ▸*n.* (*pl.* **-nies**) a small, spiny-finned marine fish with scaleless skin and a blunt head, typically living in shallow inshore or intertidal waters. • Family Blennidae: several genera, in particular *Blennius.* ■ [with *adj.*] any of a number of other small fishes that resemble or are related to the true blennies, including the **hairy blenny** (*Labrisomus nuchipinnis*, family Clinidae), found esp. along the Atlantic coast from the Bahamas to Brazil. ▷mid 18th cent.: from Latin *blennius*, from Greek *blennos* 'mucus' (because of its mucous coating).

hairy blenny

blent /blent/ *poetic/literary* ▸ past and past participle of BLEND.

ble·o·my·cin /ˌblēəˈmīsin/ ▸*n. Medicine* an antibiotic used to treat Hodgkin's disease and other cancers. • The drug is obtained from the bacterium *Streptomyces verticillus.* ▷1960s: an arbitrary alteration of earlier *phleomycin*, the name of a related antibiotic.

bleph·a·ri·tis /ˌblefəˈrītis/ ▸*n. Medicine* inflammation of the eyelid. ▷mid 19th cent.: from Greek *blepharon* 'eyelid' + -ITIS.

bleph·a·ro·plas·ty /ˈblefərəˌplastē/ ▸*n. Medicine* surgical repair or reconstruction of an eyelid. ▷mid 19th cent.: from Greek *blepharon* 'eyelid' + -PLASTY.

bleph·a·ro·spasm /ˈblefərəˌspazəm/ ▸*n.* involuntary tight closure of the eyelids. ▷late 19th cent.: from Greek *blepharon* 'eyelid' + SPASM.

Blé·riot /ˈblärēˌō; ble(ə)rˈyō/, Louis (1872–1936), French aviation pioneer. On July 25, 1909, he became the first person to cross the English Channel (Calais to Dover) in a monoplane.

bles·bok /ˈblesˌbäk/ ▸*n.* an antelope with a mainly reddish-brown coat and white face, found in southwestern South Africa. It belongs to the same species as the bontebok. • *Damaliscus dorcas phillipsi*, family Bovidae. ▷early 19th cent.: from Afrikaans, from Dutch *bles* 'blaze' (because of the white mark on its forehead) + *bok* 'buck.'

bless /bles/ ▸*v.* [*trans.*] (of a priest) pronounce words in a religious rite, to confer or invoke divine favor upon; ask God to look favorably on: *he blessed the dying man and anointed him.* ■ consecrate (something) by a religious rite, action, or spoken formula. ■ (esp. in Christian Church services) call (God) holy; praise (God). ■ (**bless someone with**) (of God or some notional higher power) endow (someone) with a particular cherished thing or attribute: *God has blessed us with free will.* ■ express or feel gratitude to; thank: *she silently blessed the premonition which had made her pack her best dress.* ■ (**bless oneself**) *archaic* make the Christian gesture of the sign of the cross: *the poor parson, blessing himself, brought up the rear.* ■ used in expressions of surprise, endearment, gratitude, etc.: *bless my soul, Alan, what are you doing?* | *Lenore,* ***bless her heart,*** *had done just that.* ▷Old English *blēdsian, blētsian*, based on *blōd* 'blood' (i.e., originally perhaps 'mark or consecrate with blood'). The meaning was influenced by its being used to translate Latin *benedicere* 'to praise, worship,' and later by association with BLISS.

▸*PHRASE* □ **bless you!** said to a person who has just sneezed. [from the phrase *(may) God bless you.*]

bless·ed /blest; ˈblesid/ ▸*adj.* **1** made holy; consecrated. ■ a title preceding the name of a dead person considered to have led a holy life, esp. a person formally beatified by the Roman Catholic Church: *the Convent of the Blessed Agnes.* ■ used respectfully in reference to a dead person: *a gracious lady* ***of blessed memory.*** ■ endowed with divine favor and protection: *blessed are the meek.* ■ bringing pleasure or relief as a welcome contrast to what one has previously experienced: *he half stumbled out of the room up to his bed and blessed, blessed sleep.* ■ (**blessed with**) endowed with (a particular quality or attribute): *a beautiful city, steeped in history and blessed with huge sandy beaches.* **2** *informal* used in mild expressions of annoyance or exasperation: *there wasn't a blessed thing anybody could have done.*

▸*plural n.* (**the Blessed** /ˈblesid/) those who live with God in heaven. **—blessedly** /ˈblesidlē/ *adv.*

bless·ed·ness /ˈblesidnis/ ▸*n.* the state of being blessed with divine favor.

Bless·ed Vir·gin Mar·y /ˈblesid/ (also **Bles·sed Vir·gin**) (abbr.: **BVM**) a title given to Mary, the mother of Jesus. See MARY[1].

bless·ing /ˈblesiNG/ ▸*n.* [in *sing.*] God's favor and protection: *may God continue to give us his blessing.* ■ a prayer asking for such favor and protection: *a priest gave a blessing as the ship was launched.* ■ grace said before or after a meal. ■ a beneficial thing for which one is grateful; something that brings well-being: *great intelligence can be a curse as well as a blessing* | *it's a blessing we're alive.* ■ a person's sanction or support: *he gave the plan his blessing even before it was announced.*

▸*PHRASES* □ **a blessing in disguise** an apparent misfortune that eventually has good results. □ **count one's blessings** see COUNT[1].

blest /blest/ ▸*adj.* archaic or literary term for BLESSED.

bleth·er /ˈbleT͟Hər/ ▸*n.* another term for BLATHER.

bleu cheese /bloo͞/ ▸*n.* variant spelling of BLUE CHEESE.

blew /bloo͞/ ▸ past of BLOW[1] and BLOW[3].

blew·it /ˈbloo͞it/ (also **blew·its**) ▸*n.* an edible wild mushroom of Europe and North America, with a pale buff or lilac cap and a lilac stem. • Genus *Lepista*, family Tricholomataceae, class Basidiomycetes: several species, including **common blewit** (*L. saeva*) and **wood blewit** (*L. nuda*). ▷early 19th cent.: probably from BLUE.

Bligh /blī/, William (1754–1817), British naval officer; captain of HMS *Bounty*. In 1789, part of his crew, led by the first mate Fletcher Christian, mutinied and set Bligh adrift in an open boat. Bligh landed safely at Timor, nearly 4,000 miles (6,400 km) away, a few weeks later.

blight /blīt/ ▸*n.* a plant disease, esp. one caused by fungi such as mildews, rusts, and smuts: *the vines suffered blight and disease* | [with *adj.*] *potato blight.* ■ *informal* anything that causes a plant disease or interferes with the healthy growth of a plant. ■ [in *sing.*] a thing that spoils or damages something: *her remorse could be* ***a blight on*** *that happiness.* ■ an ugly, neglected, or rundown condition of an urban area: *the depressing urban blight that lies to the south of the city.*

▸*v.* [*trans.*] (usu. **be blighted**) infect (plants or a planted area) with blight: *a peach tree blighted by leaf curl.* ■ spoil, harm, or destroy: *the scandal blighted the careers of several leading politicians* | [as *adj.*] (**blighted**) *his father's blighted ambitions.* ■ [usu. as *adj.*] (**blighted**) subject (an urban area) to neglect: *plans to establish enterprise zones in blighted areas.* ▷mid 16th cent. (denoting inflammation of the skin): of unknown origin.

blight·er /ˈblītər/ ▸*n.* [with *adj.*] *Brit., informal* a person who is regarded with contempt, irritation, or pity: *you little blighter!* ▷early 19th cent.: from BLIGHT + -ER[1].

Blight·y /ˈblītē/ ▸*n. Brit.* an informal and typically affectionate term for Britain or England, chiefly as used by soldiers of World War I and World War II. ■ *military slang* a wound suffered by a soldier in World War I that was sufficiently serious to merit being shipped home to Britain: *he had copped a Blighty and was on his way home.* ▷first used by soldiers in the Indian army; Anglo-Indian alteration of Urdu *bilāyatī, wilāyatī* 'foreign, European,' from Arabic *wilāyat, wilāya* 'dominion, district.'

bli·mey /ˈblīmē/ ▸*exclam. Brit., informal* used to express one's surprise, excitement, or alarm. ▷late 19th cent.: altered form of *(God) blind (or blame) me!*

blimp /blimp/ ▸*n.* **1** *informal* a small nonrigid airship. ■ an obese person: *I could work out four hours a day and still end up a blimp.* **2** (also **Colonel Blimp**) *Brit.* a pompous, reactionary type of person: *no Colonel Blimp could have been more nationalistic.* **3** a soundproof cover for a movie camera. ▷World War I (sense 1): of uncertain origin. Sense 2 derives from the character invented by cartoonist David Low (1891–1963), used in anti-German or antigovernment drawings before and during World War II. **—blimp·ish** *adj.*

blin /blin/ ▸ singular form of BLINI.

blind /blīnd/ ▸*adj.* **1** unable to see; sightless: *she suffered from glaucoma, which has left her completely blind* | *he was blind in one eye.* ■ [*attrib.*] (of an action, esp. a test or experiment) done without being able to see or without being in possession of certain information; compare with DOUBLE BLIND: *a blind tasting of eight wines.* ■ *Aeronautics* (of flying) using instruments only: *blind landings during foggy conditions.* **2** [*predic.*] lacking perception or discernment: *he's absolutely blind where you're concerned, isn't he?* ■ (**blind to**) unwilling or unable to appreciate or notice something apparent to others: *she was blind to the realities of her position.* ■ [*attrib.*] (of an action or state of mind) not controlled by reason or judgment: *they left in blind panic.* ■ [*attrib.*] not governed by purpose: *moving purposelessly in a world of blind chance.* **3** [*attrib.*] concealed or closed, in particular: ■ (of a corner or bend in a road) impossible to see around: *two trucks collided on a blind curve in the road.* ■ (of a door or window) walled up. ■ closed at one end: *a blind pipe.* ■ (of a plant) without buds, eyes, or terminal flowers: *planting too shallowly is the most common cause of bulbs coming up blind.* **4** [*attrib.*] [with *negative*] *Brit., informal* (used in emphatic expressions) not the slightest: *you don't know a blind thing!* **5** *informal* drunk.

▸*v.* [*trans.*] **1** cause (someone) to be unable to see, permanently or temporarily: *the injury temporarily blinded him* | *eyes blinded with tears.* **2** (**be blinded**) deprive (someone) of understanding, judgment, or perception: *a clever tactician blinded by passion* | *somehow Clare and I were* ***blinded to*** *the truth.* ■ (**blind someone with**) confuse or overawe someone with something difficult to understand: *they try to* ***blind*** *you* ***with science.***

▸*n.* **1** [as *plural n.*] (**the blind**) people who are unable to see: *guide dogs for the blind.* **2** an obstruction to sight or light, in particular: ■ a screen for a window, esp. one on a roller or made of slats: *she pulled down the blinds.* ■ *Brit.* an awning over a shop window. **3** [in *sing.*] something designed to conceal one's real intentions: *he phoned again from his own home: that was just a blind for his wife.* ■ a hiding place: *you can sometimes use your car as a blind.* ■ a camouflaged shelter used by hunters to get close to wildlife: *a duck blind.* **4** *Brit., informal, dated* a heavy drinking bout: *he's off on a blind again.* **5** *Brit.* a legitimate business concealing a criminal enterprise.

▸*adv.* without being able to see clearly: *he was the first pilot in history to fly blind.* ■ without having all the relevant information; unprepared: *he was going into the interview blind.* ■ (of a stake in poker and other games) put up by a player before the cards dealt are seen. ▷Old English, of Germanic origin; related to Dutch and German *blind.* **—blind·ness** *n.*

▸*PHRASES* □ **(as) blind as a bat** *informal* having very bad eyesight. □ **blind drunk** *informal* extremely drunk. □ **effing and blinding** *Brit.* see EFF. □ **rob** (or **steal**) **someone blind** *informal* rob or cheat someone in a comprehensive or merciless way. □ **turn a blind eye** pretend not to notice. [said to be in allusion to Nelson, who lifted a telescope to his blind eye at the Battle of Copenhagen (1801), in order to avoid seeing the signal to 'discontinue the action.']

blind al·ley ▸*n.* an alley or road that is closed at one end. ■ *figurative* a course of action leading nowhere: *many technologies that show early promise lead up blind alleys.*

blind date ▸*n.* a social engagement or date with a person one has not previously met: *a blind date arranged by well-meaning friends.* ■ either person of the couple on a blind date: *where do you take a blind date, anyway?*

blind·er /ˈblīndər/ ▸*n.* (**blinders**) a pair of small leather screens attached to a horse's bridle to prevent it seeing sideways and behind. Also called BLINKERS (see BLINKER). ■ *figurative* something that prevents someone from gaining a full understanding of a situation: *they will wear their cultural blinders to the grave.*

blind·fish /ˈblīndˌfiSH/ ▸*n.* another term for CAVEFISH.

blind·fold /ˈblīndˌfōld/ ▸*v.* [*trans.*] (often **be blindfolded**) deprive (someone) of sight by tying a piece of cloth around the head so as to cover the eyes.

▸*n.* a piece of cloth tied around the head to cover someone's eyes.

▸*adj. poetic/literary* wearing a blindfold. ■ (of a game of chess) conducted without sight of board and pieces.

▸*adv.* with a blindfold covering the eyes: *the reporter was driven blindfold to meet the gangster.* ■ done with great ease and confidence, as if it could have been done wearing a blindfold: *missing putts that he would normally hole blindfold.* ▷mid 16th cent.: alteration, by association with FOLD1, of *blindfeld*, past participle of obsolete *blindfell* 'strike blind, blindfold,' from Old English *geblindfellan* (see BLIND, FELL2).

blind gut ▶*n.* the cecum.

blind·ing /ˈblīndiNG/ ▶*n. Brit.* the process of covering a newly made road with grit to fill cracks. ■ the grit used in such a process.
▶*adj.* [*attrib.*] (of light) very bright and likely to dazzle or temporarily blind someone: *a massive explosion with a blinding flash of light.* ■ (of a thing) temporarily obstructing a person's vision: *he saw the school bus approaching through almost blinding rain.* ■ *figurative* suddenly and overwhelmingly obvious: ***in a blinding flash****, everything fell into place.* ■ *figurative* (of pain or an emotion) so intense as to block out everything else: *I've got a blinding headache.* ■ *figurative* (of a process or action) remarkably fast or skillful; dazzling: *a blinding fastball.* **—blind·ing·ly** *adv.* [as *submodifier*] *the reason was blindingly obvious.*

blind·ly /ˈblīndlē/ ▶*adv.* as if blind; without seeing or noticing: *I continued to stare blindly into my coffee.* ■ without reasoning or questioning: *solutions must be assessed, not blindly accepted.*

blind·man's bluff /ˈblīndmənz/ (also **blind·man's buff**) ▶*n.* a children's game in which a blindfolded player tries to catch others while being pushed about by them. ▷early 17th cent.: *bluff*, alteration of *buff* 'a blow,' from Old French *bufe* (see BUFFET2).

blind pig ▶*n.* another term for BLIND TIGER. ▷late 19th cent.: see BLIND TIGER.

blind pool ▶*n.* a company that sells stock without specifying how invested money will be spent.

blind side ▶*n.* [in *sing.*] a direction in which a person has a poor view, typically of approaching danger: *a minivan nearly clipped him on his blind side.* ■ the side opposite the one toward which a person is looking: *they came at me from my blind side* | [as *adj.*] *the crushing blind-side sack of the quarterback.*
▶*v.* (**blind·side**) [*trans.*] hit or attack (someone) on the blind side: *Jenkins blindsided Adams, knocking him to the sidewalk.* ■ (often **be blindsided**) catch (someone) unprepared; attack from an unexpected position: *protection against being technologically blindsided.*

blind·sight /ˈblīndˌsīt/ ▶*n. Medicine* the ability to respond to visual stimuli without consciously perceiving them. This condition can occur after certain types of brain damage.

blind snake ▶*n.* a small burrowing insectivorous snake that lacks a distinct head and has very small inefficient eyes. Also called WORM SNAKE. • Infraorder Scolecophidia: three families, in particular Typhlopidae, and several genera.

blind spot ▶*n.* **1** *Anatomy* the point of entry of the optic nerve on the retina, insensitive to light. **2** an area where a person's view is obstructed: *the angle rearview mirror eliminates blind spots on both sides of the car.* ■ an area in which a person lacks understanding or impartiality: *Ed had a blind spot where these ethical issues were concerned.* **3** *Telecommunications* a point within the normal range of a transmitter where there is unusually weak reception.

blind stamp·ing (also **blind tooling**) ▶*n.* the impressing of text or a design on a book cover without the use of color or gold leaf.

blind stitch ▶*n.* a sewing stitch producing stitches visible on one side only.
▶*v.* (**blind-stitch**) [*trans.*] sew (something) using such a stitch.

blind ti·ger ▶*n. informal* an illegal bar. ▷mid 19th cent.: probably so named because in order to evade prohibition laws, the bars were disguised as exhibition halls for natural curiosities.

blind trust ▶*n.* a financial arrangement in which a person in public office gives the administration of private business interests to an independent trust in order to prevent conflict of interest. Under the trust, the owner does not know how the assets are managed.

blind·worm /ˈblīndˌwərm/ ▶*n.* another term for SLOWWORM.

bling-bling /ˈbliNG ˌbliNG/ ▶*n. informal* expensive, ostentatious clothing and jewelry, or the wearing of them: *behind the bling-bling: are diamonds worth it?* ▷1990s: perhaps imitative of light reflecting off jewelry, or of jewelry clashing together.

blin·i /ˈblinē; ˈblē-/ (also **blin·y** or **blin·is**) ▶*plural n.* (*sing.* **blin** /blin/) pancakes made from buckwheat flour and served with sour cream. ▷Russian (plural); compare with BLINTZ.

blink /bliNGk/ ▶*v.* [*intrans.*] **1** shut and open the eyes quickly: *she blinked, momentarily blinded* | [*trans.*] *he blinked his eyes nervously.* ■ [*trans.*] clear (dust or tears) from the eyes by this action: *she* ***blinked away*** *her tears.* ■ [*trans.*] (**blink back**) try to control or prevent (tears) by such an action: *Elizabeth blinked back tears.* ■ (**blink at**) look at (someone or something) with one's eyes opening and shutting, typically to register surprise or bewilderment: *Lucy blinked at him, scarcely able to believe her ears.* ■ (**blink at**) [usu. with *negative*] *figurative* react to (something) with surprise or disapproval: *he doesn't blink at the unsavory aspects of his subject.* ■ *figurative* back down from a confrontation: *it seemed that the Iraqis had blinked and that the likelihood of an immediate invasion had decreased.* **2** (of a light or light source) shine intermittently or unsteadily: *the icon for his e-mail was blinking.*
▶*n.* [in *sing.*] **1** an act of shutting and opening the eyes quickly: *he was observing her every blink.* ■ *figurative* a moment's hesitation: *Thompson would have given her all this* ***without a blink.*** **2** a momentary gleam of light. ▷Middle English: from *blenk*, Scots variant of BLENCH1, reinforced by Middle Dutch *blinken* 'to shine.' Early senses included 'deceive,' 'flinch' (compare with BLENCH1), also 'open the eyes after sleep': hence sense 1 (mid 16th cent.).
▶*PHRASES* □ **not blink an eye** show no reaction. □ **in the blink of an eye** (or **in a blink**) *informal* very quickly. □ **on the blink** *informal* (of a machine) not working properly; out of order: *the computer's on the blink.*

blink·er /ˈbliNGkər/ ▶*n.* **1** a device that blinks, esp. a vehicle's turn signal. **2** (**blinkers**) another term for BLINDERS (see BLINDER).
▶*v.* [*trans.*] (often **be blinkered**) put blinders on (a horse). ■ *figurative* cause (someone) to have a narrow or limited outlook on a situation: *college education blinkers researchers so that they see poverty in terms of their own specialization.*

blink·ered /ˈbliNGkərd/ ▶*adj.* (of a horse) wearing blinders. ■ *figurative* having or showing a limited outlook: *a small-minded, blinkered approach.*

blink·ing /ˈbliNGkiNG/ ▶*adj.* [*attrib.*] *Brit., informal* used to express annoyance: *computers can be a blinking nuisance to operators.*

blintz /blints/ (also **blint·ze** /ˈblintsə/) ▶*n.* a thin rolled pancake filled with cheese or fruit and then fried or baked. ▷from Yiddish *blintse*, from Russian *blinets* 'little pancakes'; compare with BLINI.

blin·y ▶*plural n.* variant spelling of BLINI.

blip /blip/ ▶*n.* **1** a short high-pitched sound made by an electronic device. **2** a flashing point of light on a radar screen representing an object, typically accompanied by a high-pitched sound. **3** an unexpected, minor, and typically temporary deviation from a general trend: *an upward blip in house prices.* **4** a brief segment, esp. of a telecast: *the media fire unrelated blips of information at us* | *the blips on the evening news.*
▶*v.* (**blipped, blip·ping**) **1** [*intrans.*] (of an electronic device) make a short high-pitched sound or succession of sounds. **2** [*trans.*] open (the throttle of a motor vehicle) momentarily. ▷late 19th cent. (denoting a sudden rap or tap): imitative; the noun sense 'unexpected deviation' dates from the 1970s.

Bliss /blis/, Sir Arthur (Edward Drummond) (1891–1975), English composer.

bliss /blis/ ▶*n.* perfect happiness; great joy: *she gave a sigh of bliss.* See note at RAPTURE. ■ something providing such happiness: *the steam room was bliss.* ■ a state of spiritual blessedness, typically that reached after death. ▷Old English *blīths*, *bliss*, of Germanic origin; related to BLITHE.
▶*phrasal v.* □ **bliss out** [often as *adj.*] (**blissed out**) *informal* reach a state of perfect happiness, typically so as to be oblivious of everything else: *blissed-out hippies.*

bliss·ful /ˈblisfəl/ ▶*adj.* extremely happy; full of joy: *a blissful couple holding a baby.* ■ providing perfect happiness or great joy: *the blissful caress of cool cotton sheets.* **—bliss·ful·ly** *adv.* **—bliss·ful·ness** *n.*
▶*PHRASE* □ **blissful ignorance** fortunate unawareness of something unpleasant.

B-list /ˈbē ˌlist/ ▶*n.* see A-LIST.

blis·ter /ˈblistər/ ▶*n.* **1** a small bubble on the skin filled with serum and caused by friction, burning, or other damage. ■ a similar swelling, filled with air or fluid, on the surface of a plant, heated metal, painted wood, or other object. ■ *Medicine, chiefly historical* a preparation applied to the skin to cause a blister. **2** *Brit., informal or dated* an annoying person: *the child is a disgusting little blister.*
▶*v.* **1** [*intrans.*] form swellings filled with air or fluid on the surface of something: *the surface of the door began to blister* | [as *adj.*] (**blistered**) *he had blistered feet.* ■ [*trans.*] cause blisters to form on the surface of: *a caustic liquid that blisters the skin.* **2** criticize sharply: *they came out and blistered the girls for pulling leaves off a chestnut tree.* ▷Middle English: perhaps from Old French *blestre* 'swelling, pimple.'

blis·ter a·gent ▶*n.* a chemical weapon that burns and blisters the skin or other tissues.

blis·ter bee·tle ▶*n.* a beetle that, when alarmed or crushed, gives off a substance that causes blisters. The larvae are typically parasites of other insects. • *Lytta* and other genera, family Meloidae: several species. See also SPANISH FLY.

blis·ter cop·per ▶*n.* partly purified copper with a blistered surface formed during smelting.

blis·ter·ing /ˈblistəriNG/ ▶*adj.* (of heat) intense: *the blistering heat of the desert.* ■ *figurative* (of criticism) expressed with great vehemence: *blistering diatribes.* ■ extremely fast, forceful, or impressive: *Burke set a blistering pace.*

blis·ter pack ▶*n.* a type of packaging in which a product is sealed in plastic, often with a cardboard backing.

blis·ter rust ▶*n.* any of several destructive diseases of pine trees caused by fungi of the genus *Conartium*, resulting in orange blisters on the bark and tips of branches.

blithe /blī*TH*; blīTH/ ▶*adj.* showing a casual and cheerful indifference considered to be callous or improper: *a blithe disregard for the rules of the road.* ■ happy or joyous: *a blithe seaside comedy.* ▷Old English *blīthe*, of Germanic origin; related to Dutch *blijde*, also to BLISS. **—blithe·ly** *adv.* **—blithe·ness** *n.* **—blithe·some** /-səm/ *adj.* (*poetic/literary*).

blith·er /ˈbli*TH*ər/ ▶*v.* & *n.* another term for BLATHER.

blith·er·ing /ˈbli*TH*əriNG/ ▶*adj.* [*attrib.*] *informal* senselessly talkative, babbling; used chiefly as an intensive to express annoyance or contempt: *a blithering idiot.* ▷late 19th cent.: from BLITHER (see also BLATHER) + -ING2.

BLitt (also **BLit**) ▶*abbr.* ■ Bachelor of Letters. ■ Bachelor of Literature. ▷from Latin *Baccalaureus Litterarum*.

blitz /blits/ ▶*n.* an intensive or sudden military attack. ■ *informal* a sudden, energetic, and concerted effort, typically on a specific task: *a major press blitz.* ■ *Football* a charge of the passer by the defensive linebackers just after the ball is snapped. ■ (**the Blitz**) the German air raids on Britain in 1940. ■ a form of chess in which moves must be made at very short intervals.
▶*v.* [*trans.*] (often **be blitzed**) attack or damage (a place or building) in a blitz: *news came that Rotterdam had been blitzed* | *figurative organizations blitzed Capitol Hill with mailgrams and postcards.* ■ *Football* attack (the passer) in a blitz. ▷abbreviation of BLITZKRIEG.

blitz·krieg /ˈblitsˌkrēg/ ▶*n.* an intense military campaign intended to bring about a swift victory. ▷World War II: from German, literally 'lightning war.'

Blix·en /ˈbliksən/, Karen (Christentze), Baroness Blixen-Finecke (1885–1962), Danish novelist and short-story writer; born *Karen Dinesen*; also known by the pseudonym of **Isak Dinesen**. She is best known for *Seven Gothic Tales* (1934) and her autobiography *Out of Africa* (1937), which was made into a movie in 1985.

bliz·zard /ˈblizərd/ ▶*n.* a severe snowstorm with high winds and low visibility. ■ *figurative* an overabundance; a deluge: *a* ***blizzard of*** *legal forms.* ▷early 19th cent. (originally U.S., denoting a violent blow): of unknown origin.

bloat1 /blōt/ ▶*v.* [*trans.*] cause to swell with fluid or gas: *the fungus has bloated their abdomens.* ■ [*intrans.*] become swollen with fluid or gas: [as *n.*] (**bloating**) *she suffered from abdominal bloating.*
▶*n.* a disease of livestock characterized by an accumulation of gas in the stomach. ▷late 17th cent. (in the sense 'cause to swell'): from obsolete *bloat* 'swollen, soft,' perhaps from Old Norse *blautr* 'soft, flabby.' The noun sense dates from the late 19th cent.

bloat2 ▶*v.* [*trans.*] cure (a herring) by salting and smoking it lightly. ▷late 16th cent.: related to the adjective *bloat* used in the compound *bloat herring* 'bloater' from the late 16th to mid 17th cent.; of obscure origin.

bloat·ed /ˈblōtid/ ▶*adj.* (of part of the body) swollen with fluid or gas: *he had a bloated, unshaven face.* ■ *figurative* excessive in size or amount: *the company trimmed its bloated labor force.* ■ *figurative* (of a person) excessively wealthy and pampered: *the bloated captains of industry.*

bloat·er[1] /ˈblōtər/ ▸*n.* a herring cured by salting and light smoking.

bloat·er[2] ▸*n.* another term for CISCO.

bloat·ware /ˈblōtˌwe(ə)r/ ▸*n. Computing, informal* software whose usefulness is reduced because of the excessive disk-space and memory it requires.

BLOB /bläb/ ▸*n Computing* binary large objects.

blob /bläb/ ▸*n.* a drop of a thick liquid or other viscous substance: *blobs of paint.* ■ a spot of color: *a badly printed blob on shopping bags.* ■ an indeterminate mass or shape: *a leathery blob commonly known as a sea squirt.*
▸*v.* [*trans.*] (often **be blobbed**) put small drops of thick liquid or spots of color on: *her nose was blobbed with paint.* ▷late Middle English (denoting a bubble): perhaps symbolic of a drop of liquid; compare with BLOTCH, BLUBBER[1], and PLOP. **—blob·by** *adj.*

bloc /bläk/ ▸*n.* a combination of countries, parties, or groups sharing a common purpose: *a center-left voting bloc.* ▷early 20th cent.: from French, literally 'block.'

Bloch /bläk/, Ernest (1880–1959), U.S. composer; born in Switzerland. His work reflects the influence of the late 19th-century romanticism of Franz Liszt and Richard Strauss and of Jewish musical forms. Notable works: *Israel Symphony* (1912–16) and *Solomon* (1916).

block /bläk/ ▸*n.* **1** a large solid piece of hard material, esp. rock, stone, or wood, typically with flat surfaces on each side: *a block of marble.* ■ a sturdy, flat-topped block used as a work surface, typically for chopping food. ■ (usu. **blocks**) any of a set of solid cubes used as a child's toy. ■ a block of stone or low wooden steps from which a rider mounts a horse. ■ (usu. **blocks**) a starting block: *the thrust a sprinter gets when coming* ***out of the blocks.*** ■ *Printing* a piece of wood or metal engraved for printing on paper or fabric. ■ (also **cylinder block** or **engine block**) the main body of an internal combustion engine, containing the pistons. ■ a head-shaped mold used for shaping hats or wigs. **2** the area bounded by four streets in a town or suburb: *she went for a run around the block | ours was the ugliest house* ***on the block.*** ■ the length of one side of such an area, typically as a measure of distance: *he lives a few blocks away from the museum.* **3** [with *adj.*] a building, esp. part of a complex, used for a particular purpose: *a cell block.* ■ *chiefly Brit.* a large single building subdivided into separate rooms, apartments, or offices: *an apartment block.* **4** a large quantity or allocation of things regarded as a unit: *a block of shares* | [as *adj.*] *block grants.* ■ *Computing* a large piece of text processed as a unit. ■ *chiefly Brit.* a set of sheets of paper glued along one edge, used for drawing or writing on: *a sketching block.* ■ an unseparated unit of at least four postage stamps in at least two rows, generally a group of four. **5** an obstacle to the normal progress or functioning of something: *substantial demands for time off may constitute* ***a block to*** *career advancement | an emotional block.* ■ *Sports* a hindering or stopping of an opponent's movement or action. ■ *Tennis* a shot in which the racket is held stationary rather than being swung back, esp. a stop volley. ■ short for MENTAL BLOCK. ■ short for NERVE BLOCK. ■ a chock for stopping the motion of a wheel. **6** a flat area of something, typically a solid area of color: *cover the eyelid with a neutral block of color.* **7** a pulley or system of pulleys mounted in a case. **8** *informal* a person's head: *"I'll knock your block off," he said.*
▸*v.* [*trans.*] **1** make the movement or flow in (a passage, pipe, road, etc.) difficult or impossible: ***block up*** *the holes with sticky tape | a police cordon* ***blocked off*** *roads* | [as *adj.*] (**blocked**) *a blocked nose.* ■ put an obstacle in the way of (something proposed or attempted): *he stood up, blocking her escape | the administration tried to block an agreement on farm subsidies.* ■ restrict the use or conversion of (currency or any other asset). ■ *Sports* hinder or stop the movement or action of (an opponent). ■ *Sports* stop (a blow or ball) from finding its mark: *when driving for a lay-up or leaping to block a shot.* ■ *Medicine* produce insensibility in (a part of the body) by injecting an anesthetic close to the nerves that supply it. ■ *Bridge* play in such a way that an opponent cannot establish (a long suit). **2** impress text or a design on (a book cover). **3** *Theater* design or plan the movements of actors on a stage or movie set. **4** shape or reshape (a hat) using a wooden mold.
▸*phrasal v.* □ **block something in 1** mark something out roughly. ■ add something in a unit: *it's a good idea to block in regular periods of exercise.* ■ paint something with solid areas of color. **2** park one's car in such a way as to prevent another car from moving away: *he blocked in Vera's minivan.* □ **block something out 1** stop something, typically light or noise, from reaching somewhere: *you're blocking out my sun.* ■ *figurative* exclude something unpleasant from one's thoughts or memory. **2** mark or sketch something out roughly. ▷Middle English (denoting a log or tree stump): from Old French *bloc* (noun), *bloquer* (verb), from Middle Dutch *blok,* of unknown ultimate origin.
▸*PHRASES* □ **have been around the block** (**a few times**) *informal* (of a person) have a lot of experience. □ **the new kid on the block** *informal* a newcomer to a particular place or sphere of activity, typically someone who has yet to prove themselves. □ **on the** (**auction**) **block** for sale at auction: *the original first manuscript for Ravel's Bolero goes on the block today | figurative the company put its subsidiary on the block because it did not fit its core business interests.* □ **put** (or **lay**) **one's head** (or **neck**) **on the block** *informal* put one's standing or reputation at risk by proceeding with a particular course of action. [with reference to the executioner's block.]

block·ade /bläˈkād/ ▸*n.* an act of sealing off a place to prevent goods or people from entering or leaving: *the army has imposed an economic blockade.* ■ anything that prevents access or progress: *the police pulled down blockades on the highway.* ■ an obstruction of a physiological or mental function, esp. of a biochemical receptor.
▸*v.* [*trans.*] seal off (a place) to prevent goods or people from entering or leaving. ▷late 17th cent.: from BLOCK + -ADE[1], probably influenced by *ambuscade.* **—blockader** *n.*
▸*PHRASE* □ **run a blockade** (of a ship) manage to enter or leave a blockaded port.

block·ade-run·ner ▸*n.* **1** a vessel that runs or attempts to run into or out of a blockaded port. **2** the owner, master, or one of the crew of such a vessel.

block·age /ˈbläkij/ ▸*n.* an obstruction that makes movement or flow difficult or impossible: *a blockage in the pipes | the pumps are prone to blockage.*

block and tack·le ▸*n.* a mechanism consisting of ropes and one or more pulley-blocks, used for lifting or pulling heavy objects.

block and tackle

block·bust·er /ˈbläkˌbəstər/ ▸*n. informal* a thing of great power or size, in particular: ■ a movie, book, or other product that is a great commercial success: [as *adj.*] *a blockbuster pay-per-view special event.* ■ a huge aerial bomb capable of destroying targets within a wide area.

block·bust·ing /ˈbläkˌbəstiNG/ ▸*adj.* [*attrib.*] very successful commercially: *his blockbusting novel.*
▸*n.* the practice of persuading owners to sell property cheaply because of the fear of people of another race or class moving into the neighborhood, and thus profiting by reselling at a higher price.

block cap·i·tals ▸*plural n.* another term for BLOCK LETTERS.

block di·a·gram ▸*n.* a diagram showing in schematic form the general arrangement of parts or components of a complex system or process, such as an industrial apparatus or an electronic circuit.

block·er /ˈbläkər/ ▸*n.* a person or thing that blocks, in particular: ■ *Football* a player whose task it is to block for the ballcarrier or kicker. ■ a substance that prevents or inhibits a given physiological function.

block grant ▸*n.* a grant from a central government that a local authority can allocate to a wide range of services.

block·head /ˈbläkˌhed/ ▸*n. informal* a stupid person. **—block·head·ed** *adj.*

block heat·er ▸*n.* a device for heating the engine block of a vehicle.

block·house /ˈbläkˌhous/ ▸*n.* a reinforced concrete shelter used as an observation point. ■ *historical* a one-storied timber building with loopholes, used as a fort. ■ a house made of squared logs.

block·ing /ˈbläkiNG/ ▸*n.* **1** the action or process of obstructing movement, progress, or activity, in particular: ■ obstructing or impeding the actions of an opponent in a game, esp. (in ball sports) one who does not have control of the ball. ■ *Psychiatry* the sudden halting of the flow of thought or speech, as a symptom of schizophrenia or other mental disorder. ■ failure to recall or consider an unpleasant memory or train of thought. **2** the grouping or treatment of things (e.g., items of data or shades of color) in blocks. ■ the physical arrangement of actors on a stage or movie set.

block·ish /ˈbläkisH/ ▸*adj.* **1** resembling a block. ■ big, bulky, or crude in form or appearance: *his blockish architecture is ugly if functional.* **2** unintelligent and stupid.

Block Is·land (abbr.: **BI**) a resort island in southern Rhode Island, in the Atlantic Ocean at the eastern end of Long Island Sound.

block let·ters ▸*plural n.* plain capital letters.

block moun·tain ▸*n. Geology* a mountain consisting of a block or blocks bounded by normal faults in the earth's crust. See NORMAL.

block par·ty ▸*n.* a party for all the residents of a block or neighborhood, typically held on a closed-off city street.

block plane ▸*n.* a carpenter's plane with a blade set at an acute angle, used esp. for planing across the end grain of wood.

block sys·tem ▸*n.* a system of railroad signaling that divides the track into sections and allows no train to enter a section that is not completely clear.

block vote ▸*n.* a vote proportional in power to the number of people a delegate represents.

block·y /ˈbläkē/ ▸*adj.* of the nature of or resembling a block or blocks: *blocky granite.*

Bloem·fon·tein /ˈblo͞omfänˌtān/ a city in central South Africa, judicial capital of the country, capital of Orange Free State; pop. 300,150.

blog /bläg/ ▸*n.* a weblog: *blogs run by twenty-something Americans with at least an unhealthy interest in computers.*
▸*v.* (**blogged, blog·ging**) [*intrans.*] add new material to or regularly update a weblog. ▷shortening. **—blog·ger** *n.*

blog·o·sphere /ˈblägəˌsfi(ə)r/ ▸*n.* the world of weblogs.

bloke /blōk/ ▸*n. Brit., informal* a man; a fellow. ▷mid 19th cent.: from Shelta.

blond /bländ/ ▸*adj.* (of hair) fair or pale yellow: *short-cropped blond hair | her hair was dyed blond.* ■ (of a person) having hair of a fair or pale yellow color: *a slim blond woman.* ■ (of a person) having fair hair and a light complexion, typically regarded as a racial characteristic. ■ (of wood and other substances) light in color or tone: *a New York office full of blond wood.*
▸*n.* a person with fair hair and skin. **—blond·ish** *adj.* **—blond·ness** *n.*

USAGE The spellings **blonde** and **blond** correspond to the feminine and masculine forms in French. Although the distinction is usually retained in Britain, American usage since the 1970s has generally preferred the gender-neutral **blond**. The adjective **blonde** may still refer to a woman's (but not a man's) hair color, though use of the noun risks offense (*See that blonde over there?*): the offense arises from the fact that the color of hair is not the person. The adjective applied to inanimate objects (wood, beer) is typically spelled **blond**.

blonde /bländ/ ▸*adj.* (of a woman or a woman's hair) blond.
▸*n.* a blond-haired woman. ▷late 17th cent. (earlier as *blond*): from French, feminine of *blond.*

USAGE See **usage** at BLOND.

blonde mo·ment ▸*n. humorous* an instance of being silly or scatterbrained. ▷late 20th cent.: from the stereotypical perception of blonde-haired women as unintelligent.

Blood /bləd/ ▸*n.* (*pl.* same or **Bloods**) a member of a North American Indian people belonging to the Blackfoot Confederacy.

blood /bləd/ ▸*n.* **1** the red liquid that circulates in the arteries and veins of humans and other vertebrate animals, carrying oxygen to and carbon dioxide from the tissues of the body: *drops of blood.* ■ an internal bodily fluid, not necessarily red, that performs a similar function in invertebrates. ■ *figurative* violence involving bloodshed: *a commando operation full of blood and danger.* ■ *figurative* a person's downfall or punishment, typically as retribution: *the press is baying for blood.*

Pronunciation Key ə *ago;* ər *over;* ˈə *or* ˌə *up;* ˈər *or* ˌər *fur;* a *hat;* ā *rate;* ä *car;* CH *chew;* e *let;* ē *see;* e(ə)r *air;* i *fit;* ī *by;* i(ə)r *ear;* NG *sing;* ō *go;* ô *for;* oi *boy;* o͝o *good;* o͞o *goo;* ou *out;* SH *she;* TH *thin;* TH *then;* (h)w *why;* ZH *vision*

Blood consists of a mildly alkaline aqueous fluid (plasma) containing red cells (erythrocytes), white cells (leukocytes), and platelets; it is red when oxygenated and purple when deoxygenated. Red blood cells carry the protein hemoglobin, which gives blood its color and can combine with oxygen, thus enabling the blood to carry oxygen from the lungs to the tissues. White blood cells protect the body against the invasion of foreign agents (e.g., bacteria). Platelets and other factors present in plasma are concerned in the clotting of blood, preventing hemorrhage. In medieval science and medicine, blood was regarded as one of the four bodily humors, believed to be associated with a confident and optimistic temperament.

B

2 *figurative* temperament or disposition, esp. when passionate: *a ritual that fires up his blood.* **3** [with *adj.*] family background; descent or lineage: *she must have Irish blood in her.* ■ [in *combination*] a person of specified descent: *a mixed-blood.* ■ *informal* a fellow black person. **4** (usu. **Blood**) a member of a Los Angeles street gang. **5** *dated, chiefly Brit.* a fashionable and dashing young man: *a group of* ***young bloods.***
▶*v.* [*trans.*] initiate (someone) in a particular activity: *clubs are too slow in blooding young players.* ■ (in hunting) smear the face of (a novice) with the blood of the kill. ■ (in hunting) give (a hound) a first taste of blood. ▷Old English *blōd*, of Germanic origin; related to German *Blut* and Dutch *bloed*.
▶*PHRASES* □ **be like getting blood out of** (or **from**) **a stone** (or **turnip**) be extremely difficult (said in reference to obtaining something from someone): *getting a story out of her is like getting blood out of a stone!* □ **blood and guts** *informal* violence and bloodshed, typically in fiction. □ **blood and thunder** *informal, chiefly Brit.* unrestrained and violent action or behavior, typically in sports or fiction. □ **blood is thicker than water** *proverb* relationships and loyalties within a family are the strongest and most important ones. □ **blood, sweat, and tears** extremely hard work; unstinting effort. □ **blood will tell** *proverb* family characteristics cannot be concealed. □ **first blood 1** the first shedding of blood, esp. in a boxing match or formerly in dueling with swords. **2** the first point or advantage gained in a contest: *King* ***drew first blood*** *when he took the opening set.* □ **give blood** allow blood to be removed medically from one's body in order to be stored for use in transfusions. □ **have blood on one's hands** be responsible for someone's death. □ **have** (or **get**) **one's blood up** be in a fighting mood. □ **in one's blood** ingrained in or fundamental to one's character: *racing is in his blood.* □ **in cold blood** ruthlessly; without feeling: *proving that he can kill in cold blood.* □ **make someone's blood boil** *informal* infuriate someone. □ **make someone's blood run cold** horrify someone. □ **new** (or **fresh**) **blood** new members admitted to a group, typically as an invigorating force. □ **out for** (**someone's**) **blood** set on getting revenge. □ **taste blood** achieve an early success that stimulates further efforts: *the speculators have tasted blood and could force a devaluation of the franc.* □ **young blood** a younger member or members of a group, typically as an invigorating force.
blood bank ▶*n.* a place where supplies of blood or plasma for transfusion are stored.
blood·bath /ˈbləd,baᴛʜ/ ▶*n.* an event or situation in which many people are killed in a violent manner: *he allowed the protest to go ahead despite warnings that it would spark a bloodbath figurative the bad publicity would be a media bloodbath.*
blood boost·ing ▶*n.* another term for **BLOOD DOPING**.
blood-borne ▶*adj.* (typically of a disease or pathogen) carried by the blood.
blood-brain bar·ri·er ▶*n. Physiology* a filtering mechanism of the capillaries that carry blood to the brain and spinal cord tissue, blocking the passage of certain substances.
blood broth·er ▶*n.* a brother by birth. ■ a man who has sworn to treat another man as a brother, sometimes with a ceremonial mingling of blood.
blood cell ▶*n.* any of the kinds of cell normally found circulating in the blood.
blood clot ▶*n.* a gelatinous or semisolid mass of coagulated blood.
blood count ▶*n.* a determination of the number of corpuscles in a specific volume of blood. ■ the number found in such a procedure: *a low blood count.*
blood·cur·dling /ˈbləd,kərd(ə)liɴɢ/ ▶*adj.* causing terror or horror: *the warrior's bloodcurdling cry.*
blood cur·rant ▶*n.* another term for **RED-FLOWERING CURRANT** (see **FLOWERING CURRANT**).
blood do·nor ▶*n.* a person who gives blood for transfusion.
blood dop·ing (also **blood boosting**) ▶*n.* the injection of oxygenated blood into an athlete before an event in an attempt to enhance athletic performance.
blood·ed /ˈblədid/ ▶*adj.* [usu. in *combination*] having blood or a temperament of a specified kind: *warm-blooded animals.* ■ (of horses or cattle) of good pedigree: *a blooded stallion.*
blood feud ▶*n.* a lengthy conflict between families involving a cycle of retaliatory killings or injury.
blood film ▶*n.* a specimen of blood on a glass slide, used for microscopic investigation of possible abnormalities or pathogens.
blood·fin /ˈbləd,fin/ ▶*n.* a small South American freshwater fish that is silvery-yellow with bright red fins. It is popular in aquariums. • *Aphyocharax rubripinnis*, family Characidae.
blood fluke ▶*n.* another term for **SCHISTOSOME**.
blood group ▶*n.* any of the various types of human blood whose antigen characteristics determine compatibility in transfusion. The best known blood groups are those of the ABO system.
blood·guilt /ˈbləd,gilt/ ▶*n.* guilt resulting from murder or bloodshed. Also called **bloodguiltiness**. **—blood·guilt·y** *adj.*
blood·hound /ˈbləd,hound/ ▶*n.* a large hound of a breed with a very keen sense of smell, used in tracking.

bloodhound

blood knot ▶*n.* a type of knot used by anglers to join two fishing lines. Also called **BARREL KNOT**.
blood·less /ˈblədlis/ ▶*adj.* **1** without blood: *the meat is clean and relatively bloodless.* ■ (of a revolution or conflict) without violence or killing: *a bloodless coup.* ■ (of surgery or other medical procedures) spilling little or no blood: *it is usually the drug of choice for bloodless medicine.* **2** (of the skin or a part of the body) drained of color: *his bloodless lips.* ■ (of a person) cold or unemotional: *a shrewd and bloodless Hollywood mogul.* ■ lacking in vitality; feeble: *their occasionally bloodless chamber jazz.* **—blood·less·ly** *adv.* **—blood·less·ness** *n.*
blood·let·ting /ˈbləd,letiɴɢ/ ▶*n. chiefly historical* the surgical removal of some of a patient's blood for therapeutic purposes. ■ the violent killing and wounding of people during a war or conflict: *gang members have halted their internecine bloodletting.* ■ bitter division and quarreling within an organization.
blood·line /ˈbləd,līn/ ▶*n.* an animal's set of ancestors or pedigree, typically considered with regard to the desirable characteristics bred into it. ■ a set of ancestors or line of descent of a person.
blood·lust /ˈbləd,ləst/ ▶*n.* uncontrollable desire to kill or maim others.
blood meal ▶*n.* dried blood used for feeding animals and as a fertilizer.
blood·mo·bile /ˈblədmə,bēl/ ▶*n.* a motor vehicle equipped for collecting blood from volunteer donors.
blood mon·ey ▶*n.* money paid in compensation to the family of someone who has been killed. ■ money paid to a hired killer. ■ money paid by the police or the media for information about a killer or killing.
blood or·ange ▶*n.* an orange of a variety with red or red-streaked flesh.
blood plate·let ▶*n.* see **PLATELET**.
blood poi·soning ▶*n.* the presence of microorganisms or their toxins in the blood, causing disease; septicemia.
blood pres·sure ▶*n.* the pressure of the blood in the circulatory system, often measured for diagnosis since it is closely related to the force and rate of the heartbeat and the diameter and elasticity of the arterial walls.
blood pud·ding ▶*n.* another term for **BLOOD SAUSAGE**.
blood-red ▶*adj.* of the deep red color of blood: *a blood-red lipstick.*
▶*n.* a deep red.
blood re·la·tion (also **blood rel·a·tive**) ▶*n.* a person related to another by birth rather than by marriage.
blood·root /ˈbləd,ro͞ot; -,ro͝ot/ ▶*n.* **1** a North American plant of the poppy family that has white flowers and fleshy underground rhizomes that exude red sap when cut. • *Sanguinaria canadensis*, family Papaveraceae. **2** a lily-like Australian plant with a red rhizome that is roasted and eaten by some Aboriginals. • *Haemodorum coccineum*, family Haemodoraceae.

North American bloodroot

blood sau·sage (also **blood pudding**) ▶*n.* a dark sausage containing pork, dried pig's blood, and suet.
blood·shed /ˈbləd,sʜed/ ▶*n.* the killing or wounding of people, typically on a large scale during a conflict.
blood·shot /ˈbləd,sʜät/ ▶*adj.* (of the eyes) inflamed or tinged with blood, typically as a result of tiredness.
blood sport ▶*n.* (usu. **blood sports**) a sport involving the shedding of blood, esp. the hunting or killing of animals: *cock-fighting, bullfighting, fox hunting, and other blood sports figurative politics is a blood sport.*
blood·stain /ˈbləd,stān/ ▶*n.* a stain or a spot caused by blood. **—blood·stained** *adj.*
blood·stock /ˈbləd,stäk/ ▶*n.* [treated as *sing.* or *pl.*] thoroughbred horses considered collectively.
blood·stone /ˈbləd,stōn/ ▶*n.* a type of green chalcedony spotted or streaked with red, used as a gemstone.
blood·stream /ˈbləd,strēm/ ▶*n.* [in *sing.*] the blood circulating through the body of a person or animal.
blood·suck·er /ˈbləd,səkər/ ▶*n.* **1** an animal or insect that sucks blood, esp. a leech or a mosquito. **2** a long-tailed arboreal Asian lizard that carries its head in a raised position. Its ability to change color is most marked in the male, whose head and shoulders become bright red when excited. • *Calotes versicolor*, family Agamidae. **3** a person who extorts money. ■ a person who lives off others; a parasite. **—blood·suck·ing** /-,səkiɴɢ/ *adj.*
blood sug·ar ▶*n.* the concentration of glucose in the blood.
blood test ▶*n.* a scientific examination of a sample of blood, typically for the diagnosis of illness or for the detection and measurement of drugs or other substances.
blood·thirst·y /ˈbləd,ᴛʜərstē/ ▶*adj.* (**-thirst·i·er**, **-thirst·i·est**) eager to shed blood: *a bloodthirsty dictator.* ■ (of a story or movie) containing or depicting much violence: *a bloodthirsty novel.* **—blood·thirst·i·ly** /-stəlē/ *adv.* **—blood·thirst·i·ness** *n.*
blood trans·fu·sion ▶*n.* an injection into a patient of blood, previously taken from a healthy person.
blood type ▶*n.* another term for **BLOOD GROUP**.
blood typ·ing ▶*n.* the testing of a sample of blood to determine an individual's blood group.
blood ves·sel ▶*n.* a tubular structure carrying blood through the tissues and organs; a vein, artery, or capillary.
blood·wood /ˈbləd,wo͝od/ ▶*n.* any of a number of hardwood trees with deep red timber, in particular: • an Australian gum tree (genus *Eucalyptus*, family Myrtaceae, in particular *E. gummifera*). • a tree of the Old World tropics (genus *Pterocarpus*, family Leguminosae).
blood·worm /ˈbləd,wərm/ ▶*n.* **1** the bright red aquatic larva of a nonbiting midge, the blood of which contains hemoglobin that allows it to live in poorly oxygenated water. • Genus *Chironomus*, family Chironomidae. **2** another term for **TUBIFEX**.
blood·wort /ˈbləd,wərt; -,wôrt/ ▶*n.* any of various plants having red roots or leaves, esp. the red-veined dock.
blood·y[1] /ˈblədē/ ▶*adj.* (**bloodier**, **bloodiest**) **1** covered, smeared, or running with blood: *a bloody body.* ■ composed of or resembling blood: *a bloody*

discharge. **2** involving or characterized by bloodshed or cruelty: *a bloody coup | the bloody tyrannies of Europe.*
▸*v.* (**blood·ies**, **blood·ied**) [*trans.*] (often **be bloodied**) cover or stain with blood: *he ended the fight with his face bloodied and battered | figurative she has been bloodied in her three years on the commission.* ▷Old English *blōdig* (see BLOOD, -Y1). —**blood·i·ly** /ˈblədəlē/ *adv.* —**blood·i·ness** *n.*
▸*PHRASE* □ **bloody** (or **bloodied**) **but unbowed** proud of what one has achieved despite having suffered great difficulties or losses.

blood·y2 ▸*adj.* **1** [*attrib.*] *informal, chiefly Brit.* used to express anger, annoyance, or shock, or simply for emphasis: *took your bloody time* | [as *exclam.*] *bloody Hell!—what was that?* | [as *submodifier*] *it's bloody cold outside.* **2** *Brit., dated* unpleasant or perverse: *don't be too bloody to poor Jack.* ▷mid 17th cent.: from BLOODY1. The use of *bloody* to add emphasis to an expression is of uncertain origin, but is thought to have a connection with the "bloods" (aristocratic rowdies) of the late 17th and early 18th centuries; hence the phrase *bloody drunk* (= as drunk as a blood) meant 'very drunk indeed.' After the mid 18th cent. until quite recently, *bloody* used as a swearword was regarded as unprintable, probably from the mistaken belief that it implied a blasphemous reference to the blood of Christ, or that the word was an alteration of "by Our Lady"; hence a widespread caution in using the term even in phrases such as *bloody battle* merely referring to bloodshed.

Blood·y Mar·y1 the nickname of Mary I of England (see MARY2).

Blood·y Mar·y2 ▸*n.* a drink consisting of vodka and seasoned tomato juice.

blood·y-mind·ed ▸*adj. Brit., informal* deliberately uncooperative. —**blood·y-mind·ed·ly** *adv.* —**blood·y-mind·ed·ness** *n.*

bloo·ey /ˈblo͞oē/ (also **bloo·ie**) *informal* ▸*adv.* & *adj.* awry; amiss: [as *adv.*] *the ignition switch* **went blooey** | *my head for figures has gone blooey.*
▸*exclam.* used to convey that something has happened in an abrupt way: *and, blooey! He shot himself dead.* ▷1920s: of unknown origin.

bloom1 /blo͞om/ ▸*n.* **1** a flower, esp. one cultivated for its beauty: *an exotic bloom | the hydrangea has a wealth of bloom.* ■ the state or period of flowering: *the apple trees were* **in bloom**. ■ the state or period of greatest beauty, freshness, or vigor: *a young girl, still* **in the bloom of youth**. **2** [in *sing.*] a youthful or healthy glow in a person's complexion: *her face had lost its usual bloom.* **3** a delicate powdery surface deposit on certain fresh fruits, leaves, or stems. ■ (also **algal bloom**) a rapid growth of microscopic algae or cyanobacteria in water, often resulting in a colored scum on the surface. ■ a grayish-white appearance on chocolate caused by cocoa butter rising to the surface. **4** a full bright sound, esp. in a musical recording: *the remastering has lost some of the bloom of the strings.*
▸*v.* [*intrans.*] produce flowers; be in flower: *a rose tree bloomed on a ruined wall.* ■ come into or be in full beauty or health; flourish: *she bloomed as an actress under his tutelage.* ■ (of fire, color, or light) become radiant and glowing: *color bloomed in her cheeks.* ▷Middle English: from Old Norse *blóm* 'flower, blossom,' *blómi* 'prosperity,' *blómar* 'flowers.'
▸*PHRASE* □ **the bloom is off the rose** something is no longer new, fresh, or exciting.

bloom2 ▸*n.* a mass of iron, steel, or other metal hammered or rolled into a thick bar for further working. ■ *historical* an unworked mass of puddled iron.
▸*v.* [*trans.*] [usu. as *n.*] (**blooming**) make (metal) into such a mass. ▷Old English *blōma*, of unknown origin.

Bloom·er /ˈblo͞omər/, Amelia Jenks (1818–94), U.S. suffragette and social reformer. She founded and edited 1849–55 the feminist paper *Lily*, and she wore full pants that came to be known as "bloomers."

bloom·er1 /ˈblo͞omər/ ▸*n.* [usu. in *combination*] a plant that produces flowers at a specified time: *fragrant night-bloomers such as nicotiana.* ■ [with *adj.*] a person who matures or flourishes at a specified time: *he was* **a late bloomer**.

bloom·er2 ▸*n. Brit., informal, dated* a serious or stupid mistake. ▷late 19th cent.: equivalent to *blooming error.*

bloo·mers /ˈblo͞omərz/ ▸*plural n.* women's loose-fitting knee-length underpants, considered old-fashioned. ■ *historical* women's and girls' loose-fitting trousers, gathered at the knee or, originally, the ankle. ▷mid 19th cent.: named after Mrs. Amelia J. *Bloomer* (1818–94), an American social reformer who advocated a similar garment.

Bloom·field1 /ˈblo͞om,fēld/ a township in northeastern New Jersey, north of Newark; pop. 45,061.

Bloom·field2, Leonard (1887–1949), U.S. linguist. One of the founders of American structural linguistics, his primary aim was to establish linguistics as an autonomous and scientific discipline. He wrote *Language* (1933).

bloom·ing /ˈblo͞omiNG/ ▸*adj.* & *adv. Brit., informal* used for emphasis or to express annoyance: [as *adj.*] *I didn't learn a blooming thing* | [as *submodifier*] *a blooming good read.*

Bloom·ing·ton /ˈblo͞omiNGtən/ **1** a commercial city in central Illinois; pop. 51,972. **2** a city in south central Indiana, noted for its limestone industry and home to Indiana University; pop. 69,291. **3** a city in southeastern Minnesota, south of Minneapolis. It is home to the huge Mall of America; pop. 85,172.

Blooms·bur·y /ˈblo͞omzbərē; -,berē/ an area of central London noted for its large squares and gardens and for its associations with the Bloomsbury Group. The British Museum is located here. ■ [as *adj.*] associated with or similar to the Bloomsbury Group.

Blooms·bur·y Group a group of writers, artists, and philosophers living in or associated with Bloomsbury in the early 20th century. Members of the group, which included Virginia Woolf, Lytton Strachey, Vanessa Bell, Duncan Grant, and Roger Fry, were known for their unconventional lifestyles and attitudes and were a powerful force in the growth of modernism.

bloop /blo͞op/ ▸*v.* **1** [*intrans.*] *informal* make a mistake: *the company admitted it had blooped.* ■ [*trans.*] *Baseball* hit a ball weakly or make (a hit) from a poorly hit fly ball landing just beyond the reach of the infielders. **2** [*intrans.*] *chiefly Brit.* (of an electronic device) emit a short low-pitched noise.
▸*n.* **1** *informal* a mistake: *a typical beginner's bloop.* ■ *Baseball* another term for BLOOPER (sense 2): [as *adj.*] *a bloop single.* **2** *chiefly Brit.* a short low-pitched noise emitted by an electronic device. ▷1920s: imitative. —**bloop·y** *adj.*

bloop·er /ˈblo͞opər/ ▸*n. informal* **1** an embarrassing error: *he poked fun at his own tendency to utter bloopers.* ■ a brief television or radio segment containing a humorous error, collected with others for broadcast as a group: *a selection of bloopers and outtakes from the evening.* **2** *Baseball* a weakly hit fly ball landing just beyond the reach of the infielders: *a blooper over the shortstop's head.* ▷1926 (originally denoting a radio that caused others to *bloop*, i.e., emit a loud howling noise): from imitative BLOOP + -ER1.

blos·som /ˈbläsəm/ ▸*n.* a flower or a mass of flowers on a tree or bush: *tiny white blossoms | the slopes were ablaze with almond blossom.* ■ the state or period of flowering: *fruit trees* **in blossom**.
▸*v.* [*intrans.*] (of a tree or bush) produce flowers or masses of flowers: *the mango trees have shed their fruit and blossomed again.* ■ mature or develop in a promising or healthy way: *their friendship* **blossomed into** *romance* | [as *n.*] (**blossoming**) *the blossoming of experimental theater.* ■ seem to grow or open like a flower: *the smile blossomed on his lips.* ▷Old English *blōstm, blōstma* (noun), *blōstmian* (verb), of Germanic origin; related to Dutch *bloesem*, also to BLOOM1. —**blos·som·y** *adj.*

blot /blät/ ▸*n.* a dark mark or stain, typically one made by ink, paint, or dirt: *an ink blot.* ■ a shameful act or quality that tarnishes an otherwise good character or reputation: *the only blot on an otherwise clean campaign.* ■ *Biochemistry* a procedure in which proteins or nucleic acids separated on a gel are transferred directly to an immobilizing medium for identification.
▸*v.* (**blot·ted**, **blot·ting**) [*trans.*] **1** dry (a wet surface or substance) using an absorbent material: *Guy blotted his face with a dust rag.* ■ *Biochemistry* transfer by means of a blot. **2** mark or stain (something): [as *adj.*] (**blotted**) *the writing was messy and blotted.* ■ tarnish the good character or reputation of: *the turmoil blotted his memory of the school.* **3** (**blot something out**) cover writing or pictures with ink or paint so that they cannot be seen. ■ obscure a view: *a dust shield blotting out the sun.* ■ obliterate or disregard something painful in one's memory or existence: *the concentration necessary to her job blotted out all the feelings.* ▷late Middle English: probably of Scandinavian origin and related to Old Norse *blettr.*

blotch /bläCH/ ▸*n.* an irregular patch or unsightly mark on a surface, typically the skin: *red blotches on her face.*
▸*v.* (usu. **be blotched**) cover with blotches: *her face was blotched and swollen with crying.* ▷early 17th cent. (as a verb): partly an alteration of obsolete *plotch* in the same sense (of unknown origin), influenced by BLOT; partly a blend of BLOT and BOTCH. —**blotch·y** *adj.*

blot·ter /ˈblätər/ ▸*n.* **1** a sheet or pad of blotting paper inserted into a frame and kept on a desk. **2** a temporary recording book, esp. a police charge sheet: *the boys ended up on* **police blotters** *for property crimes.*

blot·ting pa·per ▸*n.* absorbent paper used for soaking up excess ink when writing.

blot·to /ˈblätō/ ▸*adj. informal* extremely drunk: *we got blotto.* ▷early 20th cent.: from BLOT + -O.

blouse /blous; blouz/ ▸*n.* a woman's loose upper garment resembling a shirt, typically with a collar, buttons, and sleeves. ■ a loose linen or cotton garment of a type worn by peasants and manual workers, typically belted at the waist. ■ a type of jacket worn as part of military uniform.
▸*v.* [*trans.*] make (a garment) hang in loose folds: *I bloused my trousers over my boots* | [*intrans.*] *my dress bloused out above my waist.* ▷early 19th cent. (denoting a belted loose garment worn by peasants): from French, of unknown origin.

blous·on /ˈblou,sän; -,zän/ ▸*n.* a short loose-fitting jacket, typically bloused and finishing at the waist. ▷early 20th cent.: from French, diminutive of BLOUSE.

blow1 /blō/ ▸*v.* (*past* **blew** /blo͞o/; *past part.* **blown** /blōn/) **1** [*intrans.*] (of wind) move creating an air current: *a cold wind began to blow.* ■ [*trans.*] (of wind) cause to move; propel: *a gust of wind blew a cloud of smoke into his face | the spire was blown down during a gale.* ■ [*intrans.*] be carried, driven, or moved by the wind or an air current: *it was so windy that the tent nearly blew away | cotton curtains blowing in the breeze.* ■ [*trans.*] *informal* leave (a place): *I'm ready to blow town* | [*intrans.*] *I'd better blow.* **2** [*intrans.*] (of a person) expel air through pursed lips: *Willie took a deep breath, and blew | he* **blew on** *his coffee to cool it.* ■ [*trans.*] use one's breath to propel: *he blew cigar smoke in her face.* ■ breathe hard; pant: *Uncle Albert was soon puffing and blowing.* ■ [*trans.*] cause to breathe hard; exhaust of breath: [as *adj.*] (**blown**) *an exhausted, blown horse.* ■ [*trans.*] (of a person) force air through the mouth into (an instrument) in order to make a sound: *the umpire blew his whistle.* ■ (of such an instrument) make a noise through being blown into in such a way: *police whistles blew.* ■ [*trans.*] sound (the horn of a vehicle). ■ *informal* play jazz or rock music in an unrestrained style: *it took him maybe five choruses to warm up, but then he could really blow.* ■ [*trans.*] force air through a tube into (molten glass) in order to create an artifact. ■ [*trans.*] remove the contents of (an egg) by forcing air through it. ■ [with *adverbial of place*] (of flies) lay eggs in or on something: *to repel the hordes of flies that would otherwise blow on the buffalo hide.* ■ (of a whale) eject air and vapor through the blowhole. **3** [*trans.*] (of an explosion or explosive device) displace violently or send flying: *the blast had blown the windows out of the van | the back of his head had been blown away.* ■ [*intrans.*] (of a vehicle tire) burst suddenly while the vehicle is in motion. ■ burst or cause to burst due to pressure or overheating: [*intrans.*] *the engines sounded as if their exhausts had blown* | [*trans.*] *frost will have blown a compression joint.* ■ (of an electrical circuit) burn out or cause to burn out through overloading: [*intrans.*] *the fuse in the plug had blown* | [*trans.*] *the floodlights blew a fuse.* **4** [*trans.*] *informal* spend recklessly: *they blew $100,000 in just eighteen months.* **5** *informal* completely bungle (an opportunity): *the wider issues were to show that politicians had* **blown it**. ■ (usu. **be blown**) expose (a stratagem): *a man whose cover was blown.* **6** (*past part.* **blowed**) [*trans.*] [usu. as *imperative*] *Brit., informal* damn: *"Well,* **blow me,***" he said, "I never knew that"* | [with *clause*] **I'm blowed if** *I want to see him again.* **7** [*trans.*] *vulgar slang* perform fellatio.
▸*phrasal v.* □ **blow someone away** *informal* **1** kill someone using a firearm. **2** (**be blown away**) be extremely impressed: *I'm blown away by his new poem.* □ **blow in** *informal* (of a person) arrive casually and unannounced. □ **blow off** lose one's temper and shout. □ **blow someone off** *informal* fail to keep an appointment with someone. ■ end a romantic or sexual relationship with someone. □ **blow something off** *informal* ignore or make light of something.

Pronunciation Key ə *ago*; ər *over*; ˈə or ,ə *up*; ˈər or ,ər *fur*; a *hat*; ā *rate*; ä *car*; CH *chew*; e *let*; ē *see*; e(ə)r *air*; i *fit*; ī *by*; i(ə)r *ear*; NG *sing*; ō *go*; ô *for*; oi *boy*; o͝o *good*; o͞o *goo*; ou *out*; SH *she*; TH *thin*; T̲H̲ *then*; (h)w *why*; ZH *vision*

B

■ fail to attend something: *Ivy blew off class.* □ **blow out 1** be extinguished by an air current: *the candles blew out.* **2** (of a tire) puncture while the vehicle is in motion. **3** (of an oil or gas well) emit gas suddenly and forcefully. **4** (**blow itself out**) (of a storm) finally lose its force: *figurative the recession may finally have blown itself out.* □ **blow someone out** *informal* defeat someone convincingly. □ **blow something out 1** use one's breath to extinguish a flame: *he blew out the candle.* **2** *informal* render a part of the body useless: *he blew out his arm trying to snap a curveball.* □ **blow over** (of trouble) fade away without serious consequences. □ **blow up 1** explode. ■ (of a person) lose one's temper: *Meg* **blows up at** *Patrick for always throwing his tea bags in the sink.* **2** (of a wind or storm) begin to develop. ■ (of a scandal or dispute) emerge or become public. **3** inflate: *my stomach had started to blow up.* □ **blow something up 1** cause something to explode. **2** inflate something: *a small pump for blowing up balloons.* ■ enlarge a photograph or text.

▸*n.* **1** [in *sing.*] a strong wind: *we're in for a blow.* **2** an act of blowing on an instrument: *a number of blows on the whistle.* ■ [in *sing.*] an act of blowing one's nose: *give your nose a good blow.* ■ [in *sing.*] *informal* a spell of playing jazz or rock music. ■ (in steelmaking) an act of sending an air or oxygen blast through molten metal in a converter. **3** *informal* cocaine. ▷Old English *blāwan*, of Germanic origin; related to German *blähen* 'blow up, swell,' from an Indo-European root shared by Latin *flare* 'blow.'

▸*PHRASES* □ **be blown off course** *figurative* (of a project) be disrupted by some circumstance. □ **be blown out of the water** *figurative* (of a person, idea, or project) be shown to lack all credibility. □ **blow away the cobwebs** refresh oneself when feeling weary, typically by having some fresh air. □ **blow someone's brains out** *informal* kill someone with a shot in the head with a firearm. □ **blow the doors off** *informal* be considerably better or more successful than: *a package that blows the doors off anything on the market.* □ **blow a fuse** see FUSE1. □ **blow a gasket** *informal* lose one's temper. □ **blow one's own horn** see HORN. □ **blow hot and cold** vacillate. □ **blow someone a kiss** kiss the tips of one's fingers then blow across them toward someone as a gesture of affection. □ **blow one's lid** (or **top** or **stack** or **cool**) *informal* lose one's temper. □ **blow the lid off** see LID. □ **blow me down** *Brit.* an exclamation of surprise. □ **blow someone's mind** *informal* affect someone very strongly. □ **blow one's nose** clear one's nose of mucus by blowing through it into a handkerchief. □ **blow off steam** see LET OFF STEAM at STEAM. □ **blow a raspberry** see RASPBERRY. □ **blow someone's socks off** see SOCK. □ **blow something to bits** (or **pieces** or **smithereens**) use bombs or other explosives to destroy something, typically a building, completely. □ **blow something out of proportion** exaggerate the importance of something. □ **blow up in one's face** (of an action, project, or situation) go drastically wrong with damaging effects to oneself. □ **blow the whistle on** see WHISTLE. □ **blow with the wind** be incapable of maintaining a consistent course of action.

blow2 ▸*n.* a powerful stroke with a hand, weapon, or hard object: *he received a blow to the skull.* ■ a sudden shock or disappointment: *the news came as a crushing blow.* ▷late Middle English: of unknown origin.

▸*PHRASES* □ **at one blow** by a single stroke; in one operation: *the letter had destroyed his certainty at one blow.* □ **come to blows** start fighting after a disagreement. □ **soften** (or **cushion**) **the blow** make it easier to cope with a difficult change or upsetting news: *monetary compensation was offered to soften the blow.* □ **strike a blow for** (or **against**) act in support of (or opposition to): *a chance to strike a blow for freedom.*

blow3 *archaic or poetic/literary* ▸*v.* (*past* **blew** /blo͞o/; *past part.* **blown** /blōn/) [*intrans.*] produce flowers or be in flower: *I know a bank where the wild thyme blows.*

▸*n.* the state or period of flowering: *stocks in fragrant blow.* ▷Old English *blōwan*, of Germanic origin; related to Dutch *bloeien* and German *blühen*, also to BLOOM1 and BLOSSOM.

blow·back /ˈblō,bak/ ▸*n.* a process in which gases expand or travel in a direction opposite the usual one, esp. through escape of pressure or delayed combustion.

blow-by-blow ▸*adj.* [*attrib.*] (of a description of an event) giving all the details in the order in which they occurred: *he gave them a* **blow-by-blow account** *of your rescue.*

blow·dart /ˈblō,därt/ ▸*n.* a dart shot from a blowpipe.

blow·down /ˈblō,doun/ ▸*n.* **1** a tree that has been blown down by the wind. ■ such trees collectively: *work to remove blowdown.* ■ the blowing down of a tree or trees: *the measures did not prevent mass blowdown.* **2** the removal of solids or liquids from a container or pipe using pressure.

blow-dry ▸*v.* [*trans.*] arrange (the hair) into a particular style while drying it with a hand-held dryer. ■ [as *adj.*] (**blow-dried**) *figurative* (of a person) well groomed, polished, and assured.

▸*n.* [in *sing.*] an act of arranging the hair in such a way. —**blow-dry·er** (also **blow-dri·er**) *n.*

blow·er /ˈblōər/ ▸*n.* **1** a person or thing that blows, typically a mechanical device for creating a current of air used to dry or heat something. **2** *informal, chiefly Brit.* a telephone.

blow·fish /ˈblō,fish/ ▸*n.* (*pl.* same or **-fish·es**) any of a number of fishes that are able to inflate their bodies when alarmed, such as a globefish.

blow·fly /ˈblō,flī/ ▸*n.* (*pl.* **-flies**) a large and typically metallic-colored fly that lays its eggs on meat and carcasses. • Family Calliphoridae: numerous species, including the bluebottle.

blow·gun /ˈblō,gən/ ▸*n.* a primitive weapon consisting of a long tube through which an arrow or dart is propelled by force of the breath.

blow·hard /ˈblō,härd/ *informal* ▸*n.* a person who blusters and boasts in an unpleasant way: *a bunch of pompous blowhards trying to get on the news* | [as *adj.*] *local blowhard politicians.*

blow·hole /ˈblō,hōl/ ▸*n.* a hole for blowing or breathing through, in particular: ■ the nostril of a whale on the top of its head. ■ a hole in ice to which seals, whales, and other aquatic animals come to breathe. ■ a vent for air or smoke in a tunnel or other structure. ■ a cavity in a metal casting, produced by the escape of air through the liquid metal.

blow job (**BJ**) ▸*n. vulgar slang* an act of fellatio.

blown /blōn/ ▸ past participle of BLOW1.

▸*adj.* destroyed; spoiled: *a blown fuse* | *your cover is blown.* ■ *informal* (of a vehicle or its engine) provided with a turbocharger.

▸*PHRASES* □ **blown away** extremely surprised; flabbergasted: *Sharon was blown away by the place.* □ **blown to bits** (or **smithereens**) completely destroyed.

blow·off /ˈblō,ôf/ ▸*n.* the action of emitting a gas, typically to reduce pressure to a safe level.

blow·out /ˈblō,out/ ▸*n.* **1** a sudden rupture or malfunction of a part or apparatus due to pressure, in particular: ■ a bursting of an automobile tire. ■ *figurative* an outburst of anger; an argument: *that exchange led to a big blowout five years ago.* ■ an uprush of oil or gas from a well. ■ *informal* a melting of an electric fuse. **2** *informal* an easy victory in a sporting contest or an election: *they had lost seven games—four by blowouts and three by slim margins.* **3** *informal* a large or lavish meal or social gathering. **4** a hollow eroded by the wind.

▸*adj.* huge; all-consuming: *year-end blowout sale* | *an all-night blowout bachelor bash.*

blow·pipe /ˈblō,pīp/ ▸*n.* **1** another term for BLOWGUN. **2** a long tube by means of which molten glass is blown into the required shape. ■ a tube used to intensify the heat of a flame by blowing air or other gas through it at high pressure.

blows·y /ˈblouzē/ (also **blowz·y**) ▸*adj.* (of a woman) coarse, untidy, and red-faced: *a blowsy woman wearing Bermuda shorts and a Bally's sweatshirt* | *figurative blowsy, old-fashioned roses.* ▷early 17th cent.: from obsolete *blowze* 'beggar's female companion,' of unknown origin. —**blows·i·ly** /-zəlē/ *adv.* —**blows·i·ness** *n.*

blow·torch /ˈblō,tôrch/ ▸*n.* a portable device producing a hot flame that is directed onto a surface, typically to solder metal.

blow·up /ˈblō,əp/ (also **blow-up**) ▸*n.* **1** an enlargement of a photograph. **2** *informal* an outburst of anger.

▸*adj.* [*attrib.*] inflatable: *a blowup neck pillow.*

blow·y /ˈblō-ē/ ▸*adj.* (**blow·i·er**, **blow·i·est**) having or affected by strong winds; windy or windswept: *a blowy day.*

BLT ▸*n. informal* a sandwich filled with bacon, lettuce, and tomato.

blub·ber1 /ˈbləbər/ ▸*n.* the fat of sea mammals, esp. whales and seals. ■ *informal, derogatory* excessive human fat.

▸*adj.* [*attrib.*] *archaic* (of a person's lips) swollen or protruding. [alteration of obsolete *blabber* 'swollen.'] ▷late Middle English (denoting the foaming of the sea, also a bubble on water): perhaps symbolic; compare with BLOB and BLOTCH. —**blub·ber·y** *adj.*

blub·ber2 ▸*v.* [*intrans.*] *informal* sob noisily and uncontrollably: *he was blubbering like a child* | [with *direct speech*] *"I don't like him," blubbered Jonathan.* ▷late Middle English: probably symbolic; compare with BLOB and BLUBBER1.

blu·chers /ˈblo͞okərz; -chərz/ ▸*plural n. historical* strong leather half-boots or high shoes. ▷mid 19th cent.: named after G. L. von *Blücher* (1742–1819), Prussian general.

bludg·eon /ˈbləjən/ ▸*n.* a thick stick with a heavy end, used as a weapon: *figurative a rhetorical bludgeon in the war against liberalism.*

▸*v.* [*trans.*] beat (someone) repeatedly with a bludgeon or other heavy object. ■ force or bully (someone) to do something: *she was determined not to be* **bludgeoned into** *submission.* ■ (**bludgeon one's way**) make one's way by brute force. ▷mid 18th cent.: of unknown origin.

blue /blo͞o/ ▸*adj.* (**blu·er**, **blu·est**) **1** of a color intermediate between green and violet, as of the sky or sea on a sunny day: *the clear blue sky* | *blue jeans* | *deep blue eyes.* ■ (of a person's skin) having or turning such a color, esp. with cold or breathing difficulties: *Annie went blue, and I panicked.* ■ (of a bird or other animal) having blue markings: *a blue jay.* ■ (of cats, foxes, or rabbits) having fur of a smoky gray color: *the blue fox.* ■ (of a ski run) of the second lowest level of difficulty, as indicated by colored markers positioned along it. ■ *Physics* denoting one of three colors of quark. **2** *informal* (of a person or mood) melancholy, sad, or depressed: *he's feeling blue.* **3** *informal* (of a movie, joke, or story) with sexual or pornographic content: *the blue movies are hugely profitable.* ■ (of language) marked by cursing, swearing, and blasphemy. **4** *informal* rigidly religious or moralistic; puritanical.

▸*n.* **1** blue color or pigment: *she was dressed* **in blue** | *the dark blue of his eyes* | *armchairs in pastel blues and greens.* ■ blue clothes or material: *Susan wore blue.* ■ a blue uniform, or a person wearing a blue uniform, such as a police officer or a baseball umpire. ■ (usu. **Blue**) the Union army in the Civil War, or a member of that army. **2** a blue thing, in particular: ■ a blue ball, piece, etc., in a game or sport. ■ (**the blue**) *poetic/literary* the sky or sea; the unknown: *a lark went trilling up, up* **into the blue**. **3** [usu. with *adj.*] a small butterfly, the male of which is predominantly blue while the female is typically brown. • Numerous genera in the family Lycaenidae. **4** another term for BLUING.

▸*v.* (**blues**, **blued**, **blu·ing** or **blue·ing**) **1** make or become blue: [*trans.*] *the light dims, bluing the retina* | [as *adj.*] (**blued**) *blued paper* | [*intrans.*] *the day would haze, the air bluing with afternoon.* ■ [*trans.*] heat (metal) so as to give it a grayish-blue finish: [as *adj.*] (**blued**) *nickel-plated or blued hooks.* **2** [*trans.*] wash (white clothes) with bluing. ▷Middle English: from Old French *bleu*, ultimately of Germanic origin and related to Old English *blǣwen* 'blue' and Old Norse *blár* 'dark blue'. —**blue·ness** *n.*

▸*PHRASES* □ **do something until** (or **till**) **one is blue in the face** *informal* put all one's efforts into doing something to no avail: *she could talk to him until she was blue in the face, but he was just not hearing.* □ **once in a blue moon** *informal* very rarely. [because a "blue moon" is a phenomenon that never occurs.] □ **out of the blue** (or **out of a clear blue sky**) *informal* without warning; unexpectedly: *she phoned me out of the blue.* [with reference to a "blue" (i.e., clear) sky, from which nothing unusual is expected.] □ **talk a blue streak** *informal* speak continuously and at great length.

blue ba·by ▸*n.* a baby with a blue complexion from lack of oxygen in the blood due to a congenital defect of the heart or major blood vessels.

blue·back /ˈblo͞o,bak/ ▸*n.* a bird or fish, esp. a trout or a sockeye salmon, having a bluish back.

Blue·beard /ˈblo͞o,bi(ə)rd/ a character in a tale by Charles Perrault, who killed several wives in turn for disobeying his order to avoid a locked room, which contained the bodies of his previous wives. Local tradition in Brittany identifies him with Gilles de Rais (*c.*1400–40), a perpetrator of atrocities, although he had only one wife (who left him). ■ [as *n.*] (**a Bluebeard**) a man who murders his wives.

blue beat ▸*n.* another term for SKA.

blue·bell /ˈblo͞o,bel/ ▸*n.* **1** (also **English bluebell**) a widely cultivated European woodland plant of the lily family that produces clusters of bell-shaped blue flowers in spring. • *Hyacinthoides* (or **Endymion**) *nonscripta*, family Liliaceae. **2** any of a number of other plants with blue bell-shaped flowers, in particular: • another term for BELLFLOWER. • chiefly

Scottish term for HAREBELL. • another term for SQUILL and other scillas. • short for VIRGINIA BLUEBELL. • a plant of the bellflower family (genus *Wahlenbergia*, family Campanulaceae), distributed mostly in the southern hemisphere, e.g., the **Australian bluebell** (*W. gloriosa*).

blue·ber·ry /ˈblo͞oˌberē/ ▸*n.* (*pl.* **-ries**) **1** a hardy dwarf shrub of the heath family, with small, whitish drooping flowers and dark blue edible berries. • Genus *Vaccinium*, family Ericaceae: several North American species, including the **common highbush blueberry** (*V. corymbosum*), from which many cultivated varieties originate. **2** the small, sweet edible berry of this plant.

blue bice ▸*n.* see BICE.

blue·bill /ˈblo͞oˌbil/ ▸*n.* any of a number of ducks with blue bills, esp. the scaup.

blue·bird /ˈblo͞oˌbərd/ ▸*n.* an American songbird of the thrush family, the male of which has a blue head, back, and wings. See also FAIRY BLUEBIRD. • Genus *Sialia*, subfamily Turdinae, family Muscicapidae: three species, including the **eastern bluebird** (*S. sialis*).

blue-black ▸*adj.* black with a tinge of blue.

blue blood ▸*n.* noble birth: *blue blood is no guarantee of any particular merit, competence, or expertise.* ■ (also **blueblood**) a person of noble birth: *a comforting figure among that crowd of blue bloods.* —**blue-blood·ed** *adj.*

blue·bon·net /ˈblo͞oˌbänit/ ▸*n.* a blue-flowered lupine, esp. common in Texas. • Genus *Lupinus*, family Leguminosae: several species, in particular the **Texas bluebonnet** (*L. texensis*) and the **shy bluebonnet** (*L. subcarnosus*).

blue book ▸*n.* **1** a listing of socially prominent people. ■ (in full **Kelley Blue Book**) *trademark* a reference book listing the prices of used cars. ■ (**Blue Book**) a report issued by the government. ■ *Brit.* a report issued by Parliament or the Privy Council. **2** a blank book used for written examinations in high school and college.

blue·bot·tle /ˈblo͞oˌbätl/ ▸*n.* **1** a common blowfly with a metallic-blue body, the female of which often comes into houses searching for a suitable food source on which to lay her eggs. • *Calliphora vomitoria*, family Calliphoridae. **2** the wild cornflower.

blue box ▸*n.* an electronic device used to access long-distance telephone lines illegally.

blue cheese ▸*n.* cheese containing veins of blue mold, such as Gorgonzola and Danish Blue.

blue-chip ▸*adj.* [*attrib.*] denoting companies or their shares considered to be a reliable investment, though less secure than gilt-edged stock. ■ of the highest quality: *blue-chip art.* ▹early 20th cent. (originally U.S.): from the *blue chip* used in gambling games, which usually has a high value.

blue chip·per ▸*n.* a highly valued person, esp. an athlete.

blue coat ▸*n.* a person who wears a blue coat, in particular: ■ a soldier in a blue uniform, esp. a Union soldier during the Civil War. ■ a police officer.

blue co·hosh ▸*n.* see COHOSH.

blue-col·lar ▸*adj.* [*attrib.*] of or relating to workers who wear work clothes or specialized protective clothing, as miners, mechanics, etc.: *unskilled blue-collar operators | their speech and attitudes mark them as blue-collar guys.* Compare with WHITE-COLLAR.

blue corn ▸*n.* a variety of corn with bluish grains.

blue crab ▸*n.* a large edible swimming crab of the Atlantic coast of North America. • *Callinectes sapidus*, family Portunidae.

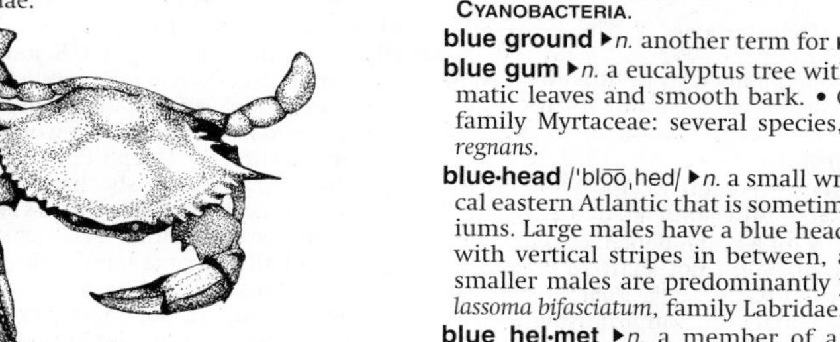

blue crab

blue crane ▸*n.* a large South African crane with blue-gray plumage. Also called STANLEY CRANE. • *Anthropoides paradisea*, family Gruidae. ■ this bird as the national bird of South Africa.

blue·curls /ˈblo͞oˌkərlz/ ▸*n.* a North American plant of the mint family, with small blue flowers and blue-stalked, deeply curled stamens. • Genus *Trichostema*, family Labiatae: several species, in particular *T. dichotomum*, found esp. in the northeastern U.S., and the typically more southern *T. setaceum*.

blue dev·il ▸*n. informal* **1** a blue capsule containing a barbiturate. **2** (**blue devils**) a feeling of despondency or low spirits. **3** (**blue devils**) another term for DELIRIUM TREMENS.

blue dog Dem·o·crat (also **Blue Dog Dem·o·crat**) ▸*n. informal* in the U.S., a Democrat from a Southern state who has a conservative voting record. ▹From the name of a coalition of Southern Democrats in the U.S. Congress formed in 1995. Their name alludes to an older term, "yellow dog Democrat," for a party loyalist who allegedly "would vote for a yellow dog if it were on the ballot as a Democrat." The blue dog Democrats claim that their conservative views have been choked off by their own party to the point that these yellow dogs have turned blue.

blue-eyed boy ▸*n. informal* a person highly regarded by someone and treated with special favor.

blue-eyed grass ▸*n.* a North American plant of the iris family, cultivated for its blue flowers. • Genus *Sisyrinchium*, family Iridaceae: several species, including the flat-stemmed *S. montanum*.

blue-eyed Mar·y ▸*n.* a low-growing plant of the borage family that bears bright blue flowers and spreads by means of runners. • *Omphalodes verna*, family Boraginaceae.

blue·fin /ˈblo͞oˌfin/ (also **bluefin tuna**) ▸*n.* the most common large tuna, which occurs worldwide in warm seas. It is probably the largest bony fish, and is very important as a food and game fish. • *Thunnus thynnus*, family Scombridae.

blue·fish /ˈblo͞oˌfisн/ ▸*n.* (*pl.* same or **-fish·es**) a predatory blue-colored marine fish that inhabits tropical and temperate waters and is popular as a game fish. • *Pomatomus saltatrix*, the only member of the family Pomatomidae.

blue flag ▸*n.* **1** a violet-flowered iris that grows in marshy places and wet meadows. • Genus *Iris*, family Iridaceae: several species, in particular the **larger blue flag** (*I. versicolor*) and the **slender blue flag** (*I. prismatica*). **2** a European award for beaches based on cleanliness and safety.

larger blue flag

blue flu ▸*n.* a sick-out, esp. among police officers.

blue·gill /ˈblo͞oˌgil/ ▸*n.* an edible North American freshwater fish of the sunfish family, with a deep body and bluish cheeks and gill covers. It is popular with anglers. • *Lepomis macrochirus*, family Centrarchidae.

blue·grass /ˈblo͞oˌgras/ ▸*n.* **1** (also **Kentucky bluegrass**) a bluish-green grass that was introduced into North America from northern Europe. It is widely grown for fodder, esp. in Kentucky and Virginia. See also MEADOW GRASS. **2** a kind of country music influenced by jazz and blues and characterized by virtuosic playing of banjos and guitars and high-pitched, close-harmony vocals.

Blue·grass State a nickname for the state of KENTUCKY.

blue-green al·gae ▸*plural n.* another term for CYANOBACTERIA.

blue ground ▸*n.* another term for KIMBERLITE.

blue gum ▸*n.* a eucalyptus tree with blue-green aromatic leaves and smooth bark. • Genus *Eucalyptus*, family Myrtaceae: several species, in particular *E. regnans*.

blue·head /ˈblo͞oˌhed/ ▸*n.* a small wrasse of the tropical eastern Atlantic that is sometimes kept in aquariums. Large males have a blue head and green body with vertical stripes in between, and females and smaller males are predominantly yellowish. • *Thalassoma bifasciatum*, family Labridae.

blue hel·met ▸*n.* a member of a United Nations peacekeeping force.

Blue Hen State a nickname for the state of DELAWARE[1].

blue ice ▸*n.* clean, dense ice of a vivid blue color, formed in glaciers by the recrystallization of snow.

blue·ish /ˈblo͞oisн/ ▸*adj.* variant spelling of BLUISH.

blue·jack·et /ˈblo͞oˌjakit/ ▸*n. informal* a sailor in the navy.

blue jay ▸*n.* a common North American jay with a blue crest, back, wings, and tail. • *Cyanocitta cristata*, family Corvidae.

blue jeans ▸*n.* jeans made of blue denim.

blue law ▸*n.* a law prohibiting certain activities, such as shopping, on a Sunday. ■ (in colonial New England) a strict religious law, particularly one preventing entertainment or leisure activities on a Sunday.

Blue Law State a nickname for the state of CONNECTICUT.

blue line ▸*n. Ice Hockey* either of the two lines midway between the center of the rink and each goal.

blue mold ▸*n.* a bluish fungus that grows on food. Blue molds are deliberately introduced into some cheeses, and some kinds are used to produce antibiotics such as penicillin. • *Penicillium* and other genera, phylum Ascomycota.

Blue Nile one of the two principal headwaters of the Nile River. It rises from Lake Tana in northwestern Ethiopia and flows about 1,000 miles (1,600 km) south and then northwest into Sudan, where it meets the White Nile at Khartoum.

blue·nose /ˈblo͞oˌnōz/ ▸*n. informal* **1** a priggish or puritanical person: [as *adj.*] *the most restrictive, bluenose standards.* **2** (**Bluenose**) a person from Nova Scotia. —**bluenosed** *adj.* (in sense 1).

blue note ▸*n. Music* a minor interval where a major would be expected, used esp. in jazz.

blue-pen·cil ▸*v.* [*trans.*] edit or make cuts in (a manuscript, movie, or other work).

Blue Pe·ter ▸*n.* a blue flag with a white square in the center, raised by a ship about to leave port.

blue plate (also **blue-plate**) ▸*adj.* [*attrib.*] (of a restaurant meal) consisting of a full main course ordered as a single menu item: *the blue plate special.* ▹mid 20th cent.: with reference to the original blue plates divided into compartments, on which fixed-price restaurant meals were served.

blue·point /ˈblo͞oˌpoint/ ▸*n.* a small oyster, in particular one harvested from the oyster beds in Great South Bay, at Blue Point, Long Island. Bluepoints are typically served raw, on the half shell.

blue·print /ˈblo͞oˌprint/ ▸*n.* a design plan or other technical drawing. ■ *figurative* something that acts as a plan, model, or template: *a vague **blueprint for** fundamental land redistribution.*
▸*v.* [*trans.*] draw up (a plan or model): [as *adj.*] (**blueprinted**) *a neatly blueprinted scheme.* ▹late 19th cent.: from the original process in which prints were composed of white lines on a blue ground or of blue lines on a white ground.

blue-rib·bon ▸*adj.* [*attrib.*] of the highest quality; first-class: *blue-ribbon service.* ■ (of a jury or committee) carefully or specially selected.

blue rib·bon ▸*n.* (*Brit.* also **blue rib·and**) a badge made of blue ribbon and given as first prize to the winner of a competition. ■ (in the UK) a badge worn by members of the Order of the Garter.

Blue Ridge Moun·tains a range in the Appalachian Mountains in the eastern U.S. that stretches from southern Pennsylvania to northern Georgia. Mount Mitchell is the highest peak, rising to a height of 6,684 feet (2,037 m).

blue rinse ▸*n.* a preparation used as a rinse on gray or white hair intended to make it look more silver.
▸*adj.* (**blue-rinse** or **blue-rinsed**) [*attrib.*] *informal, derogatory* of or relating to elderly and conservative women: *the blue-rinse brigade.*

blue roan ▸*adj.* denoting an animal's coat consisting of black-and-white hairs evenly mixed, giving it a blue-gray hue.
▸*n.* an animal with such a coat.

blues /blo͞oz/ ▸*plural n.* **1** [treated as *sing.* or *pl.*] (often **the blues**) melancholic music of black American folk origin, typically in a twelve-bar sequence. It developed in the rural southern U.S. toward the end of the 19th century, finding a wider audience in the 1940s as blacks migrated to the cities. This urban blues gave rise to rhythm and blues and rock and roll. ■ [treated as *sing.*] a piece of such music: *we'll do a blues in C.* **2** (**the blues**) *informal* feelings of melancholy, sadness, or depression: *she's **got the blues**.* ▹mid 18th cent. (sense 2): elliptically from *blue devils* 'depression or delirium tremens.' —**blues·y** *adj.* (in sense 1).

blue-screen ▸*adj.* [*attrib.*] *Cinematography* denoting a special-effects technique in which scenes shot

Pronunciation Key ə *ago;* ər *over;* ˈə *or* ˌə *up;* ˈər *or* ˌər *fur;* a *hat;* ā *rate;* ä *car;* CH *chew;* e *let;* ē *see;* e(ə)r *air;* i *fit;* ī *by;* i(ə)r *ear;* NG *sing;* ō *go;* ô *for;* oi *boy;* o͝o *good;* o͞o *goo;* ou *out;* SH *she;* TH *thin;* T͟H *then;* (h)w *why;* ZH *vision*

against a blue background are superimposed on other scenes.

blue shark ▸*n.* a long slender shark with an indigo-blue back and white underparts, typically occurring in the open sea. • *Prionace glauca*, family Carcharhinidae.

blue·shift /ˈblo͞oˌsʜift/ (also **blue shift**) ▸*n. Astronomy* the displacement of the spectrum to shorter wavelengths in the light coming from distant celestial objects moving toward the observer. Compare with **REDSHIFT**.

blue-sky (also **blue-skies**) ▸*adj.* [*attrib.*] *informal* not yet practical or profitable: *blue-sky research.*

blue-sky law ▸*n.* a law regulating the sale of securities, intended to protect the public from fraud.

Blue Springs a city in west central Missouri, east of Kansas City; pop. 48,080.

blue spruce ▸*n.* a North American spruce with sharp, stiff blue-green needles, growing wild in the central Rocky Mountains. Its many cultivated varieties tend to be bluer in color than the wild ones. Also called **COLORADO BLUE SPRUCE**, **COLORADO SPRUCE**. • *Picea pungens*, family Pinaceae.

blue·stem /ˈblo͞oˌstem/ ▸*n.* a coarse North American prairie grass with bluish leaf sheaths, often cultivated as forage. • Genus *Andropogon*, family Gramineae.

blue·stock·ing /ˈblo͞oˌstäkiɴɢ/ ▸*n. often derogatory* an intellectual or literary woman. ▷late 17th cent.: originally used to describe a man wearing blue worsted (instead of formal black silk) stockings; extended to mean 'in informal dress.' Later the term denoted a person who attended the literary assemblies held (*c.*1750) by three London society ladies, where some of the men favored less formal dress. The women who attended became known as *blue-stocking ladies* or *blue-stockingers*.

blue·stone /ˈblo͞oˌstōn/ ▸*n.* any of various bluish or gray building stones. ■ any of the smaller stones made of dolerite found in the inner part of Stonehenge.

blu·et /ˈblo͞oit/ ▸*n.* a low-growing North American plant of the bedstraw family, with small four-petaled flowers and paired leaves. Bluets often grow in large groups. • Genus *Houstonia (or* **Hedyotis**)*, family Rubiaceae: several species, esp.* H. caerulea*, with milky-blue or white flowers, and* **long-leaved bluets** (*H. longifolia*), with white or lavender flowers. ▷early 18th cent.: from French, diminutive of *bleu* 'blue.'

blue·throat /ˈblo͞oˌᴛʜrōt/ ▸*n.* a small, lively thrush found in northern Eurasia and Alaska. The male has a blue throat with a reddish spot in the center. • *Luscinia svecica*, subfamily Turdinae, family Muscicapidae.

blue tit ▸*n.* a small titmouse with a blue cap, greenish-blue back, and yellow underparts, widespread in Eurasia and northwestern Africa. • *Parus caeruleus*, family Paridae.

blue-tongued skink (also **blue-tongued lizard**) ▸*n.* a heavily built Australian skink with a large head, short limbs, and a blue tongue, which is displayed in defense. • Genus *Tiliqua*, family Scincidae: several species, in particular *T. scincoides*, which is commonly kept as a pet.

Blue·tooth /ˈblo͞oˌto͞oᴛʜ/ ▸*n. trademark* a standard for the short-range wireless interconnection of cellular phones, computers, and other electronic devices. ▷1990s: said to be named after King Harald *Bluetooth* (910–985), credited with uniting Denmark and Norway, as Bluetooth technology unifies the telecommunications and computing industries.

blue vit·ri·ol ▸*n. archaic* crystalline copper sulfate.

blue-wa·ter ▸*adj.* relating to or associated with the open sea; oceangoing: *a blue-water navy.*

blue·weed /ˈblo͞oˌwēd/ ▸*n.* another term for **VIPER'S BUGLOSS**.

blue whale ▸*n.* a migratory, mottled bluish-gray rorqual, found in all oceans of the world. Known to grow as long as 110 feet (33 m) and weigh as much as 150 tons (136,000 kg), it is the largest animal ever to inhabit the earth. • *Balaenoptera musculus*, family Balaenopteridae.

bluff[1] /bləf/ ▸*n.* an attempt to deceive someone into believing that one can or will do something: *the offer was denounced as a bluff* | *his game of bluff.*

▸*v.* [*intrans.*] try to deceive someone as to one's abilities or intentions: *he's been bluffing all along* | [with *direct speech*] *"I am an accredited envoy," he bluffed.* ■ [*trans.*] mislead (someone) in this way: *the object is to* **bluff** *your opponent* **into** *submission.* ■ (in a card game) bet heavily on a weak hand in order to deceive opponents. ■ (**bluff one's way**) contrive a difficult escape or other achievement by maintaining a pretense: *he* **bluffed his way** *onto an Antarctic supply vessel.* ▷late 17th cent. (originally in the sense 'blindfold, hoodwink'): from Dutch *bluffen* 'brag,' or *bluf* 'bragging.' The current sense (originally U.S., mid 19th cent.) originally referred to bluffing in the game of poker. —**bluff·er** *n.*

▸*PHRASE* □ **call someone's bluff** challenge someone thought to be bluffing: *she was tempted to call his bluff, hardly believing he'd carry out his threat.*

bluff[2] ▸*adj.* direct in speech or behavior but in a good-natured way: *a big, bluff, hearty man.* See note at **BRUSQUE**. ▷early 18th cent. (in the sense 'surly, abrupt in manner'): figurative use of **BLUFF**[3]. The current positive connotation dates from the early 19th cent. —**bluff·ly** *adv.* —**bluff·ness** *n.*

bluff[3] ▸*n.* **1** a steep cliff, bank, or promontory. **2** *Canadian* a grove or clump of trees.

▸*adj.* (of a cliff or a ship's bow) having a vertical or steep broad front. ▷early 17th cent. (as an adjective, originally in nautical use): of unknown origin. The Canadian sense dates from the mid 18th cent.

blu·ing /ˈblo͞oiɴɢ/ (also **blue·ing**) ▸*n.* **1** *chiefly historical* blue powder used to preserve the whiteness of laundry. **2** a grayish-blue finish on metal produced by heating.

blu·ish /ˈblo͞oisʜ/ (also **blue·ish**) ▸*adj.* having a blue tinge; somewhat blue.

Blum /ˈblo͞om/, Léon (1872–1950), French statesman; prime minister 1936–37, 1938, and 1946–47. As France's first socialist and Jewish prime minister, Blum introduced significant labor reforms.

Blume /blo͞om/, Judy Sussman (1938–), U.S. author, mostly of young adult's fiction. Her works include *Are You There, God? It's Me, Margaret* (1970), *Tales of a Fourth Grade Nothing* (1972), *Forever . . .* (1975), and, for adults, *Wifey* (1977) and *Summer Sisters* (1998).

Blu·men·bach /ˈblo͞omənˌbäkʜ/, Johann Friedrich (1752–1840), German physiologist and anatomist. He is regarded as the founder of physical anthropology, although his approach has since been much modified. He classified modern human beings into five broad categories (Caucasian, Mongoloid, Malayan, Ethiopian, and American), based mainly on cranial measurements.

blun·der /ˈbləndər/ ▸*n.* a stupid or careless mistake. See note at **MISTAKE**.

▸*v.* [*intrans.*] make such a mistake; act or speak clumsily: *the mayor and the City Council have blundered in an ill-advised campaign* | *I* **blundered on** *in my explanation* | [as *adj.*] (**blundering**) *blundering actors.* ■ [*intrans.*] move clumsily or as if unable to see: *we were blundering around in the darkness.* ▷Middle English: probably of Scandinavian origin and related to **BLIND**. —**blun·der·er** *n.* —**blun·der·ing·ly** *adv.*

blun·der·buss /ˈbləndərˌbəs/ ▸*n. historical* a short-barreled large-bored gun with a flared muzzle, used at short range. ■ *figurative* an action or way of doing something regarded as lacking in subtlety and precision: *economists resort too quickly to the blunderbuss of regulation.* ▷mid 17th cent.: alteration (by association with **BLUNDER**) of Dutch *donderbus*, literally 'thunder gun.'

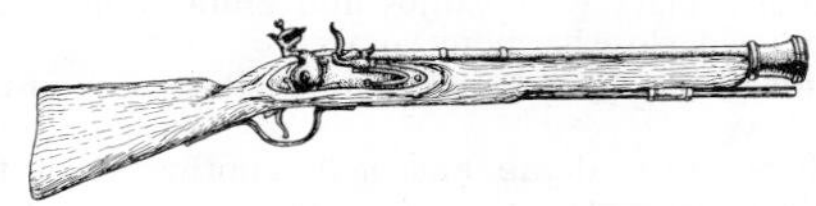

blunderbuss

blunge /blənj/ ▸*v.* [*trans.*] mix (clay or other materials) with water in a revolving apparatus for use in ceramics. ▷early 19th cent.: blend of **BLEND** and **PLUNGE**. —**blung·er** *n.* .

Blunt /blənt/, Anthony (Frederick) (1907–83), British art historian, foreign office official, and Soviet spy.

blunt /blənt/ ▸*adj.* **1** (of a knife, pencil, etc.) having a worn-down edge or point; not sharp: *a blunt knife.* ■ having a flat or rounded end: *the blunt tip of the leaf.* **2** (of a person or remark) uncompromisingly forthright: *he is as blunt as a kick in the shins* | *a blunt statement of fact.* See note at **BRUSQUE**.

▸*n. informal* a hollowed-out cigar filled with marijuana.

▸*v.* make or become less sharp: [*trans.*] *wood can blunt your ax* | [*intrans.*] *the edge may blunt very rapidly.* ■ [*trans.*] *figurative* weaken or reduce (something): *their determination had been blunted.* ▷Middle English (in the sense 'dull, insensitive'): perhaps of Scandinavian origin and related to Old Norse *blunda* 'shut the eyes.' —**blunt·ly** *adv.* —**blunt·ness** *n.*

blunt in·stru·ment ▸*n.* a heavy object without a sharp edge or point, used as a weapon. ■ *figurative* an imprecise or heavy-handed way of doing something: *as a promotional method, direct mail has been a blunt instrument.*

blur /blər/ ▸*v.* (**blurred**, **blur·ring**) make or become unclear or less distinct: [*trans.*] *tears blurred her vision* | *his novels blur the boundaries between criticism and fiction* | [*intrans.*] *as daylight waned, the pages blurred.*

▸*n.* a thing that cannot be seen or heard clearly: *the pale blur of her face* | *the words were a blur.* ■ an indistinct memory or impression of events, typically because they happened very fast: *the day before was a blur.* ▷mid 16th cent. (in the sense 'smear that partially obscures something)': perhaps related to **BLEAR**. —**blur·ry** *adj.* (**blurr·i·er**, **blurr·i·est**).

blurb /blərb/ ▸*n.* a short description of a book, movie, or other product written for promotional purposes and appearing on the cover of a book or in an advertisement.

▸*v.* [*trans.*] *informal* write or contribute such a passage for (a book, movie, or other product). ▷early 20th cent.: coined by Gelett Burgess (died 1951), American humorist.

blurt /blərt/ ▸*v.* [*trans.*] say (something) suddenly and without careful consideration: *she wouldn't* **blurt out** *words she did not mean* | [with *direct speech*] *"It wasn't my idea," Gordon blurted.* ▷late 16th cent.: probably imitative.

blush /bləsʜ/ ▸*v.* [*intrans.*] develop a pink tinge in the face from embarrassment or shame: *she blushed at the unexpected compliment* | [with *complement*] *Kate felt herself blushing scarlet.* ■ feel embarrassed or ashamed: [with *infinitive*] *he blushed to think of how he'd paraded himself.* ■ [often as *adj.*] (**blushing**) (of a flower or other thing) be or become pink or pale red: *the trees are loaded with blushing blossoms.*

▸*n.* **1** a reddening of the face as a sign of embarrassment or shame: *he had brought a faint blush to her cheeks.* ■ a pink or pale red tinge: *the roses were white with a lovely pink blush.* ■ another term for **BLUSHER** (sense 1). **2** (also **blush wine**) a wine with a slight pink tint made in the manner of white wine but from red grape varieties. ▷Old English *blyscan*; related to modern Dutch *blozen*.

▸*PHRASE* □ **at first blush** at the first glimpse or impression.

blush·er /ˈbləsʜər/ ▸*n.* **1** a cosmetic of a powder or cream consistency used to give a warm color to the cheeks. Also called **BLUSH**. **2** (**the blusher**) a woodland toadstool that has a buff cap bearing fluffy white spots and white flesh that turns pink when bruised or cut. It is native to both Eurasia and North America. • *Amanita rubescens*, family Amanitaceae, class Basidiomycetes.

blus·ter /ˈbləstər/ ▸*v.* [*intrans.*] talk in a loud, aggressive, or indignant way with little effect: *you threaten and bluster, but won't carry it through* | [with *direct speech*] *"I don't care what he says," I blustered* | [as *adj.*] (**blustering**) *a blustering bully.* ■ (of a storm, wind, or rain) blow or beat fiercely and noisily: *a winter gale blustered against the sides of the house* | [as *adj.*] (**blustering**) *the blustering wind.*

▸*n.* loud, aggressive, or indignant talk with little effect: *their threats contained a measure of bluster.* ▷late Middle English: ultimately imitative. —**blus·ter·er** *n.*

blus·ter·y /ˈbləstərē/ ▸*adj.* (of weather or a period of time) characterized by strong winds: *a gusty, blustery day.* ■ (of a wind) blowing in strong gusts.

blvd. ▸*abbr.* boulevard.

Bly /blī/, Nellie (1867–1922), U.S. journalist and social reformer; pseudonym of *Elizabeth Jane Cochrane*. As a reporter for the Pittsburgh Dispatch, she wrote about child labor and unsafe working conditions in factories. Hired by Joseph Pulitzer as a reporter for his New York World, she had herself admitted to the insane asylum on Blackwell's Island and wrote a scathing exposé, called Ten Days in a Madhouse (1887), of the terrible conditions she found there. She also wrote *Nellie Bly's Book: Around the World in Seventy-two Days* (1890) about her trip breaking the fictional record set in Jules Vernes's *Around the World in Eighty Days.*

B lym·pho·cyte (also **B-lymphocyte**) ▸*n. Physiology* another term for **B CELL**.

Blythe /blīᴛʜ; blīᴛʜ/, Vernon, see **CASTLE**.

Blythe·ville /ˈblīᴛʜvəl/ a city in northeastern Arkansas; pop. 22,906.

Bly·ton /ˈblītn/, Enid (1897–1968), British writer of children's fiction. Her best-known creation was the character Noddy, who first appeared in 1949. Her books for older children included the series of the *Famous Five* and *Secret Seven* adventure stories.

BM ▸*abbr.* ■ Bachelor of Medicine. ■ Bachelor of Music. ■ bowel movement. ■ basal metabolism. ■ board measure. ■ black male. ■ British Museum.

BMI ▸*abbr.* body mass index.

BMOC ▸*abbr.* big man on campus.

B-mov·ie ▸*n.* a low-budget movie, esp. one made for use as a companion to the main attraction in a double feature: [as *adj.*] *a B-movie actress.*

BMR ▸*abbr.* basal metabolic rate.

BMus ▸*abbr.* Bachelor of Music.

BMX ▸*n.* organized bicycle racing on a dirt track, esp. for youngsters: [as *adj.*] *a BMX track.* ■ a kind of bicycle designed to be used for such racing. ▷1970s: from the initial letters of *bicycle motocross*, with *X* standing for *cross*.

Bn. ▸*abbr.* ■ Baron. ■ Battalion.

bn ▸*abbr.* billion.

B'nai B'rith /bəˈnā ˈbriTH/ a Jewish organization founded in New York in 1843. It pursues educational, humanitarian, and cultural activities and attempts to safeguard the rights and interests of Jews around the world. ▷Hebrew, literally 'sons of the covenant.'

BO ▸*abbr.* ■ *informal* body odor. ■ best offer. ■ box office. ■ back order. ■ (also **B/O** or **b/o**) (in bookkeeping) brought over.

bo ▸*abbr.* best offer.

bo·a /ˈbōə/ ▸*n.* **1** a constrictor snake that bears live young and may reach great size, native to America, Africa, Asia, and some Pacific islands. • Family Boidae, several genera and numerous species. See also BOA CONSTRICTOR. ■ any snake that is a constrictor. **2** a long thin stole of feathers or fur worn around a woman's neck, typically as part of evening dress. ▷late Middle English: from Latin (mentioned in the writings of Pliny), of unknown ultimate origin.

bo·a con·stric·tor ▸*n.* a large and typically boldly marked snake that kills by coiling around its prey and asphyxiating it, native to tropical America. • *Boa constrictor*, family Boidae.

boar /bôr/ ▸*n.* (*pl.* same or **boars**) **1** (also **wild boar**) a tusked Eurasian wild pig from which domestic pigs are descended. • *Sus scrofa*, family Suidae. ■ the flesh of the wild boar as food. **2** an uncastrated domestic male pig. ■ the full-grown male of certain other animals, esp. a badger, guinea pig, or hedgehog. ▷Old English *bār*; related to Dutch *beer* and German *Bär*.

board /bôrd/ ▸*n.* **1** a long, thin, flat piece of wood or other hard material, used for floors or other building purposes: *loose boards creaked as I walked on them* | *sections of board.* ■ (**the boards**) *informal* the stage of a theater. **2** a thin, flat, rectangular piece of wood or other stiff material used for various purposes, in particular: ■ a vertical surface on which to write or pin notices. ■ a horizontal surface on which to cut things, play games, or perform other activities. ■ a flat insulating sheet used as a mounting for an electronic circuit: [with *adj.*] *a graphics board.* ■ the piece of equipment on which a person stands in surfing, skateboarding, snowboarding, and certain other sports. ■ (**boards**) the wooden structure surrounding an ice-hockey rink. ■ (usu. **boards**) *Basketball* informal term for BACKBOARD, referring specifically to rebounding: *the absence of center David Robinson to dominate* **on the boards**. ■ (**boards**) pieces of thick stiff cardboard or, originally, wood used for book covers. **3** [treated as *sing.* or *pl.*] a group of people constituted as the decision-making body of an organization: *he sits on the board of directors* | [in *names*] *the Federal Reserve Board* | [as *adj.*] *a board meeting.* **4** the provision of regular meals when one stays somewhere, in return for payment or services: *your* **room and board** *will be free.* ■ *archaic* a table set for a meal. **5** *Sailing* a distance covered by a vessel in a single tack.
▸*v.* **1** [*trans.*] get on or into (a ship, aircraft, or other vehicle): *we boarded the plane for Oslo* | [*intrans.*] *they would not be able to board without a ticket.* ■ (**be boarding**) (of an aircraft) be ready for passengers to embark: *flight 172 to Istanbul is now boarding at gate 37.* **2** [*intrans.*] live and receive regular meals in a house in return for payment or services: *the cousins boarded for a while with Ruby.* ■ (of a student) live at school during the semester in return for payment. ■ [*trans.*] (often **be boarded**) provide (a person or animal) with regular meals and somewhere to live in return for payment: *dogs may have to be* **boarded at** *kennels.* **3** [*trans.*] (**board something up**) cover or seal a window, storefront, or other structure with pieces of wood: *the shop was still boarded up.* **4** [*intrans.*] ride on a snowboard. ▷Old English *bord*, of Germanic origin; related to Dutch *boord* and German *Bort*; reinforced in Middle English by Old French *bort* 'edge, ship's side' and Old Norse *borth* 'board, table.'
▸*PHRASES* □ **go by the board** (of something planned or previously upheld) be abandoned, rejected, or ignored: *my education just went by the board.* [earlier in nautical use meaning 'fall overboard,' used of a mast falling past the *board*, i.e., the side of the ship.] □ **on board** on or in a ship, aircraft, or other vehicle. ■ *informal* onto a team or group as a member: *the need to bring on board a young manager.* ■ *informal* (of a jockey) riding. ■ *Baseball* on base. □ **take something on board** *informal* fully consider or assimilate a new idea or situation: *we've got to take accusations of sexism on board.* □ **tread the boards** *informal* appear on stage as an actor.

board cer·ti·fi·ca·tion ▸*n.* the process of examining and certifying the qualifications of a physician or other professional by a board of specialists in the field.

board-cer·ti·fied ▸*adj.* having satisfied the requirements for board certification.

board·ed /ˈbôrdid/ ▸*adj.* (of a floor, roof, or other structure) built with pieces of wood. ■ (of a window, storefront, or other structure) covered or sealed with pieces of wood.

board·er /ˈbôrdər/ ▸*n.* **1** a person who receives regular meals when staying somewhere, in return for payment or services. ■ a student who lives at school during the semester in return for payment. **2** a person who boards a ship during or after an attack. **3** a person who takes part in a sport using a board, such as surfing or snowboarding.

board foot ▸*n.* (*pl.* **board feet**) a unit of volume for timber equal to 144 cubic inches, notionally twelve inches by twelve inches by one inch.

board game ▸*n.* any game played on a board, esp. one that involves the movement of pieces on the board, such as chess or checkers.

board·ing /ˈbôrdiNG/ ▸*n.* **1** long, flat, thin pieces of wood used to build or cover something. **2** the procedure according to which students live at school during the semester in return for payment. **3** the action of getting on or into a ship, aircraft, or other vehicle.

board·ing·house /ˈbôrdiNG,hous/ (also **board·ing-house** or **board·ing house**) ▸*n.* a house providing food and lodging for paying guests.

board·ing ken·nel ▸*n.* a place in which dogs are kept and fed, typically while their owners are on vacation.

board·ing pass (also **boarding card**) ▸*n.* a pass for boarding an aircraft, given to a passenger when the ticket is issued or upon check-in at the airport.

board·ing school ▸*n.* a school where students reside during the semester.

board of ed·u·ca·tion ▸*n.* a body of officials elected or appointed to oversee a local or statewide school system or systems. Compare with SCHOOL BOARD.

Board of Trade ▸*n.* **1** another term for CHAMBER OF COMMERCE. ■ (also **Chicago Board of Trade**) the Chicago futures exchange. **2** (**Board of Trade**) a now nominal British government department within the Department of Trade and Industry concerned with commerce and industry.

board·room /ˈbôrd,ro͞om/ ▸*n.* a room in which the members of a board meet regularly. ■ the directors of a company or organization considered collectively.

board·sail·ing /ˈbôrd,sāliNG/ ▸*n.* another term for WINDSURFING. —**board·sail·or** /-,sālər/ *n.*

board·walk /ˈbôrd,wôk/ ▸*n.* a wooden walkway across sand or marshy ground. ■ a promenade along a beach or waterfront, typically made of wood.

Bo·as /ˈbō,az/, Franz (1858–1942), U.S. anthropologist; born in Germany. A pioneer of modern anthropology, he developed the linguistic and cultural components of ethnology. His most notable work was *Race, Language, and Culture* (1940).

boast[1] /bōst/ ▸*v.* **1** [*reporting verb*] talk with excessive pride and self-satisfaction about one's achievements, possessions, or abilities: [with *direct speech*] *Ted used to boast, "I manage ten people"* | [with *clause*] *he boasted that he had taken part in the crime* | [*intrans.*] *she* **boasted about** *her many conquests.* **2** [*trans.*] (of a person, place, or thing) possess (a feature that is a source of pride): *the hotel boasts high standards of comfort.*
▸*n.* an act of talking with excessive pride and self-satisfaction: *I said I would score, and it wasn't an idle boast.* ▷Middle English (as a noun): of unknown origin. —**boast·er** *n.* —**boast·ing·ly** *adv.*

boast[2] ▸*n.* (in squash) a stroke in which the ball is made to hit one of the sidewalls before hitting the front wall. ▷late 19th cent.: perhaps from French *bosse* denoting a rounded projection in the wall of a court for court tennis.

boast·ful /ˈbōstfəl/ ▸*adj.* showing excessive pride and self-satisfaction in one's achievements, possessions, or abilities. —**boast·ful·ly** *adv.* —**boast·ful·ness** *n.*

boat /bōt/ ▸*n.* **1** a small vessel propelled on water by oars, sails, or an engine: *a fishing boat* | [as *adj.*] *a boat trip.* ■ (in general use) a ship of any size. **2** a serving dish in the shape of a boat: *a gravy boat.*
▸*v.* [*intrans.*] travel or go in a boat for pleasure: *they boated through fjords* [as *n.*] (**boating**) *she likes to* **go boating.** ■ [*trans.*] transport (someone or something) in a boat in a specified direction: *they boated the timber down the lake.* ■ [*trans.*] to bring a caught fish into a boat. ▷Old English *bāt*, of Germanic origin. —**boat·ful** /-,fo͝ol/ *n.* (*pl.* **-fuls**).
▸*PHRASES* □ **be in the same boat** *informal* be in the same unfortunate circumstances as others. □ **miss the boat** see MISS[1]. □ **off the boat** *informal* or *often offensive* recently arrived from a foreign country, and by implication naive or an outsider: *what are you, fresh off the boat?* □ **rock the boat** *informal* say or do something to disturb an existing situation.

boat·bill /ˈbōt,bil/ ▸*n.* (also **boat-billed her·on**) a small Central and South American heron with a broad, flattened bill and a prominent black crest. • *Cochlearius cochlearius*, family Ardeidae.

boat·build·ing /ˈbōt,bildiNG/ ▸*n.* the occupation or industry of building boats. —**boat·build·er** /-,bildər/ *n.*

boat deck ▸*n.* the deck from which a ship's lifeboats are launched.

boat·el /,bōˈtel/ ▸*n.* **1** a waterside hotel with facilities for mooring boats. **2** a ship moored at a wharf and used as a hotel. ▷1950s: blend of BOAT and HOTEL.

boat·er /ˈbōtər/ ▸*n.* **1** a flat-topped hardened straw hat with a brim. [so named because originally worn while boating.] **2** a person who uses or travels in a boat for pleasure.

boat·hook /ˈbōt,ho͝ok/ ▸*n.* a long pole with a hook and a spike at one end, used for fending off or pulling a boat.

boat·house /ˈbōt,hous/ ▸*n.* a shed at the edge of a river or lake used for housing boats.

boat·ing /ˈbōtiNG/ ▸*n.* rowing or sailing in boats as a sport or form of recreation.

boat·load /ˈbōt,lōd/ ▸*n.* a number of passengers or amount of cargo that will fill a ship or boat: *a* **boatload of** *coal.* ■ *informal* a large number of people: *the company has signed a* **boatload of** *European distributors for the new product.*

boat·man /ˈbōtmən/ ▸*n.* (*pl.* **-men**) a person who rents out or works on boats.

boat neck (also **boatneck**) ▸*n.* a type of wide neckline on a garment that passes just below the collarbone. ▷from its shape.

boat peo·ple ▸*plural n.* refugees who have left a country by sea, in particular the Vietnamese who fled in small boats to Hong Kong, Australia, and elsewhere after the conquest of South Vietnam by North Vietnam in 1975.

boat shoe (also **deck shoe**) ▸*n.* a type of loafer with a flexible rubber heel and sole to provide good traction on boat decks.

boat·swain /ˈbōsən/ (also **bo'sun** or **bo·sun**) ▸*n.* a ship's officer in charge of equipment and the crew. ▷late Old English *bātswegen* (see BOAT, SWAIN).

boat·swain's chair ▸*n.* a seat suspended from ropes, used in rescues and for work on the body or masts of a ship or the face of a building.

boat train ▸*n.* a train scheduled to connect with the arrival or departure of a boat.

boat·yard /ˈbōt,yärd/ ▸*n.* a place where boats are built, repaired, or stored.

Bo·a Vis·ta /ˈbōə ˈvistə/ a town in northern Brazil; pop. 130,426 (1990).

bob[1] /bäb/ ▸*v.* (**bobbed**, **bob·bing**) [*intrans.*] (of a thing) make a quick short movement up and down: *I could see his red head bobbing around* | *the boat bobbed up and down.* ■ [*trans.*] cause (something) to make such a

movement: *she bobbed her head.* ■ [*intrans.*] make a sudden move in a particular direction so as to appear or disappear: *a lady* **bobbed up** *from beneath the counter.* ■ [*intrans.*] move up and down briefly in a curtsy. ▸*n.* a movement up and down: *she could only manage a slight bob of her head.* ■ another term for BOBBER. ■ a curtsy. ▷late Middle English: of unknown origin.
▸*PHRASES* □ **bob and weave** make rapid bodily movements up and down and from side to side, for example as an evasive tactic by a boxer. □ **bob for apples** try to catch floating or hanging apples with one's mouth alone, as a game.

bob[2] ▸*n.* **1** a style in which the hair is cut short and evenly all around so that it hangs above the shoulders. **2** a weight on a pendulum, plumb line, or kite-tail. **3** a bobsled. **4** a short line at or near the end of a stanza. **5** a horse's tail docked short. ▸*v.* (**bobbed, bob·bing**) **1** [*trans.*] [usu. as *adj.*] (**bobbed**) cut (someone's hair) in a bob: *she tied a headscarf over her bobbed brown hair.* **2** [*intrans.*] ride on a bobsled. ▷late Middle English (denoting a bunch or cluster): of unknown origin.

bob[3] *Brit., informal* ▸*n.* (*pl.* same) a shilling. ■ used with reference to a moderately large but unspecified amount of money: *those vases are worth a few bob.* ▷late 18th cent.: of unknown origin.

bob[4] ▸*n.* a change of order in bell-ringing. ■ used in names of change-ringing methods: *plain bob | bob minor.* ▷late 17th cent.: perhaps connected with BOB[1] in the noun sense 'sudden movement up and down.'

bo·ba tea ▸*n.* another term for BUBBLE TEA.

bob·ber /ˈbäbər/ ▸*n.* a small float placed on a fishing line to hold the hook at the desired depth.

bob·bin /ˈbäbin/ ▸*n.* a cylinder or cone holding thread, yarn, or wire, used esp. in weaving, machine sewing, and lacemaking. ■ a spool or reel. ▷mid 16th cent.: from French *bobine*, of unknown origin.

bob·bi·net /ˌbäbəˈnet/ ▸*n.* machine-made cotton net (imitating lace made with bobbins on a pillow). ▷mid 19th cent.: from BOBBIN + NET[1].

bob·bin lace ▸*n.* lace made by hand with thread wound on bobbins.

bob·ble[1] /ˈbäbəl/ ▸*n.* a small ball made of strands of wool used as a decoration on a hat or on furnishings. ▷1920s: diminutive of BOB[2]. —**bob·bly** /ˈbäb(ə)lē/ *adj.*

bob·ble[2] *informal* ▸*v.* **1** [*trans.*] mishandle (a ball): *Andy bobbled the ball, so his throw home was too late.* **2** [*intrans.*] move with an irregular bouncing motion: *the glare of the snow made the landscape bobble.* ▸*n.* **1** a mishandling of a ball: *a once-a-season bobble by Jordan en route to a breakaway jam.* **2** an irregular bouncing motion. ▷early 19th cent.: frequentative of BOB[1].

Bobb·sey twins /ˈbäbzē/ ▸*n. trademark, humorous* name for two people who are often seen together or who look and act alike. ▷From the characters in a long-running series of children's books (1904–1992), written under the pen name Laura Lee Hope.

bob·by /ˈbäbē/ ▸*n.* (*pl.* **-bies**) *Brit., informal, dated* a police officer. ▷mid 19th cent.: nickname for *Robert*, given name of Sir Robert PEEL.

bob·by pin ▸*n.* a kind of sprung hairpin or small clip. ▸*v.* (**bob·by-pin**) [*trans.*] fix (hair) in place with such a pin or clip. ▷1930s: from BOB[2] (because bobby pins were originally used with bobbed hair) + -Y[2].

bob·by socks (also **bob·by sox**) ▸*plural n. dated* short socks reaching just above the ankle (used chiefly in the 1940s and 1950s to refer to the socks worn by teenage girls). ▷1940s: compare with BOB[2] in the sense 'cut short.'

bob·by-sox·er /ˈbäbē ˌsäksər/ ▸*n. dated, chiefly derogatory* an adolescent girl.

bob·cat /ˈbäbˌkat/ ▸*n.* a small North American cat species with a barred and spotted coat and a short tail. • *Lynx rufus*, family Felidae. Compare with LYNX. ▷late 19th cent.: from BOB[2] (with reference to its short tail) + CAT[1].

Bo·bo-Diou·las·so /ˈbōbō dyōōˈlasō/ a commercial and industrial city in southwestern Burkina Faso; pop. 269,000. It is an agricultural market and rail center.

bob·o·link /ˈbäbəˌliNGk/ ▸*n.* a North American songbird of the American blackbird family, with a finchlike bill. The male has black, buff, and white plumage. • *Dolichonyx oryzivorus*, family Icteridae. ▷late 18th cent. (originally *Bob o'Lincoln, Bob Lincoln*): imitative of its call.

bobolink

bob·sled /ˈbäbˌsled/ ▸*n.* a mechanically steered and braked sled, typically manned by crews of two or four, used for racing down a steep ice-covered run with banked curves. ▸*v.* ride on a bobsled. ▷mid 19th cent. (originally denoting a sled made of two short sleds coupled together and used for hauling logs): from BOB[2] in the sense 'short' + SLED.

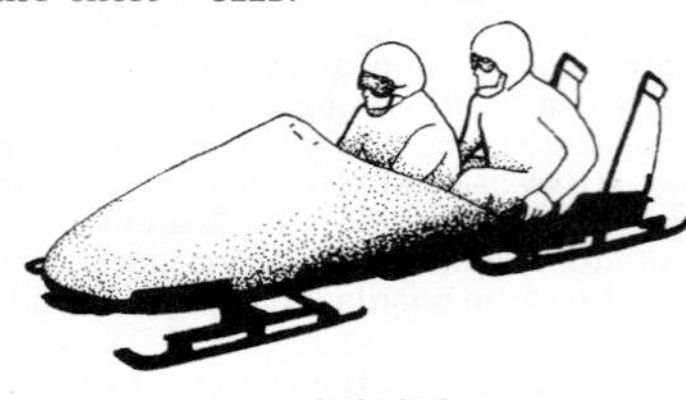
bobsled

bob·sled·ding /ˈbäbˌslediNG/ ▸*n.* riding in a bobsled, esp. as a winter sport.

bob·sleigh /ˈbäbˌslā/ ▸*n.* another term for BOBSLED.

bob·stay /ˈbäbˌstā/ ▸*n.* a rope used to hold down the bowsprit of a ship against the upward pull of the forestay. ▷mid 18th cent.: probably from BOB[1] + STAY[2].

bob·tail /ˈbäbˌtāl/ ▸*n.* a docked tail of a horse or dog. ▸*adj.* (also **bob·tailed**) *figurative* cut short; abbreviated: *the bobtailed 1995 baseball season.* ▷mid 16th cent.: probably from BOB[2] + TAIL[1]. It was originally recorded as a humorous term for a kind of broad-headed arrow, probably because it looked as though it had been cut short.

bob-weight ▸*n.* a component used as a counterweight to a moving part in a machine.

bob·white /ˈbäb(h)wīt/ (also **bobwhite quail**) ▸*n.* a New World quail with mottled reddish-brown plumage, and typically a pale throat and eyestripe. • Genus *Colinus*, family Phasianidae: two species, in particular the **northern** (or **common**) **bobwhite** (*C. virginianus*). ▷early 19th cent.: imitative of its call.

northern bobwhite

bo·cac·cio /bəˈkäCHō; -CHē-ō; bō-/ ▸*n.* an edible rockfish, of particular commercial importance in California. • *Sebastes paucispinis*, family Scorpaenidae. ▷ultimately from American Spanish *bocacho* 'big-mouth(ed)'.

bo·cage /bōˈkäZH/ ▸*n.* (in France) pastureland divided into small hedged fields interspersed with groves of trees. ▷late 16th cent.: from French, from Old French *boscage* (see BOSCAGE).

Bo·ca Ra·ton /ˌbōkə rəˈtōn/ a city and resort in southeastern Florida, on the Atlantic Ocean, north of Fort Lauderdale; pop. 61,492.

Boc·cac·ci·o /bəˈkäCHēˌō/, Giovanni (1313–75), Italian writer, poet, and humanist. He is most noted for the *Decameron* (1348–58), a collection of 100 tales told by ten young people living in the country in order to escape the Black Death.

boc·ce /ˈbäCHē/ (also **boc·cie** or **boc·ci**) ▸*n.* an Italian game similar to lawn bowling but played on a shorter, narrower green. ▷Italian, 'bowls,' plural of *boccia* 'ball.'

Boc·che·ri·ni /ˌbäkəˈrēnē; ˌbōkə-/, Luigi (1743–1805), Italian composer and cellist.

boc·con·ci·ni /ˌbäkənˈCHēnē/ ▸*plural n.* small balls of mozzarella cheese. ▷Italian.

Boche /bôSH; bäSH/ *dated, offensive* ▸*n.* a German, esp. a soldier. ■ (**the Boche**) Germans, esp. German soldiers, considered collectively. ▸*adj.* German. ▷late 19th cent.: French soldiers' slang, originally in the sense 'rascal,' later used in World War I meaning 'German.'

Bo·chum /ˈbōKHŏŏm; ˈbōkəm/ an industrial city in the Ruhr valley, in North Rhine-Westphalia, Germany; pop. 398,580.

bock /bäk/ (also **bock beer**) ▸*n.* a strong dark beer brewed in the fall and drunk in the spring. ▷mid 19th cent.: via French from an abbreviation of German *Eimbockbier* 'beer from *Einbeck*,' a town in Hanover.

BOD ▸*abbr.* biochemical oxygen demand.

bod /bäd/ ▸*n. informal* a body: *shake your bod.* ■ a physique: *Roger was proud of his bod.* ■ *chiefly Brit.* a person: *some clever bod wrote a song about them.* ▷late 18th cent. (originally Scots): abbreviation of BODY.

bo·da·cious /bōˈdāSHəs/ ▸*adj. informal* excellent, admirable, or attractive: *the restaurant serves bodacious grilled lobster.* ■ audacious in a way considered admirable: *those bodacious dudes have an excellent time playing games with death.* ▷mid 19th cent.: perhaps a variant of southwestern English dialect *boldacious*, blend of BOLD and AUDACIOUS.

bode /bōd/ ▸*v.* [*intrans.*] (**bode well/ill**) be an omen of a particular outcome: *their argument did not* **bode well** *for the future* | [*trans.*] *the 12 percent interest rate bodes dark days ahead for retailers.* ▷Old English *bodian* 'proclaim, foretell,' from *boda* 'messenger,' of Germanic origin; related to German *Bote*, also to BID[1].

bo·de·ga /bōˈdāgə/ ▸*n.* a grocery store in a Spanish-speaking neighborhood. ■ a wineshop or wine cellar. ▷mid 19th cent.: from Spanish, via Latin from Greek *apothēkē* 'storehouse.' Compare with APOTHECARY, BOUTIQUE.

Bo·den·see /ˈbōdnˌzā/ German name for Lake Constance (see CONSTANCE, LAKE).

Bodh·ga·ya /ˈbōdˈgīə/ (also **Buddh Ga·ya** /ˈbŏŏdˈgīə/) a village in the state of Bihar in northeastern India, where Buddha attained enlightenment.

bo·dhi·satt·va /ˌbōdiˈsätvə; -ˈsət-/ (also **Bo·dhi·satt·va**) ▸*n.* (in Mahayana Buddhism) a person who is able to reach nirvana but delays doing so out of compassion in order to save suffering beings. ▷early 19th cent.: Sanskrit, 'a person whose essence is perfect knowledge,' from *bodhi-* 'perfect knowledge' (from *budh-* 'awaken'[see BUDDHA]) + *sattva* 'being, essence.'

bo·dhi tree /ˈbōdē/ ▸*n.* another term for BO TREE.

bod·hrán /ˈbôˌrän; -rən/ ▸*n.* a shallow one-sided Irish drum typically played with a short two-headed drumstick. ▷Irish.

bod·ice /ˈbädis/ ▸*n.* the part of a woman's dress (excluding sleeves) that is above the waist. ■ a woman's vest, esp. a laced vest worn as an outer garment. ■ a woman's vest-like undergarment. ▷mid 16th cent. (originally *bodies*): plural of BODY, retaining the original pronunciation. The term probably first denoted an undergarment, then known as a *pair of bodice*, although this sense is not recorded until the early 17th cent.

bodice

bod·ice-rip·per ▸*n. informal, derogatory* or *humorous* a sexually explicit romantic novel or movie with a historical setting. —**bod·ice-rip·ping** *adj.*

bod·i·less /ˈbädēlis/ ▸*adj.* lacking a body: *a bodiless head.* ■ having no material existence; insubstantial: *a sinister, bodiless voice.*

bod·i·ly /ˈbädl-ē/ ▸*adj.* [*attrib.*] of or concerning the body: *children learn to control their bodily functions.* ■ material or actual as opposed to spiritual or incorporeal: *God is not present in bodily form.* ▸*adv.* by taking hold of a person's body, esp. with force: *he hauled her bodily from the van.* ■ with one's whole body; with great force: *he launched himself bodily at the door.*

bod·kin /ˈbädkin/ ▸*n.* a blunt thick needle with a large eye used esp. for drawing tape or cord through a hem. ■ a small pointed instrument used to pierce cloth or leather. ■ *historical* a long pin used for fastening hair. ■ *Printing, chiefly historical* a pointed tool used for removing pieces of metal type for correction. ▷Middle English: perhaps of Celtic origin and related to Irish *bod*, Welsh *bidog*, Scottish Gaelic *biodag* 'dagger.'

Bod·lei·an Li·brar·y /ˈbädlēən/ the main research library of Oxford University, and one of six copyright libraries in the UK.

Bod·ley /ˈbädlē/, Sir Thomas (1545–1613), English scholar and diplomat. He enlarged the Oxford University library, which was renamed the Bodleian in 1604.

Bo·do·ni /bōˈdōnē/, Giambattista (1740–1813), Italian printer. He designed a typeface that is named after him.

bod·y /ˈbädē/ ▸*n.* (*pl.* **bod·ies**) **1** the physical structure of a person or an animal, including the bones, flesh, and organs: *it's important to keep your body in good condition* | [as *adj.*] *body temperature.* ■ a corpse: *they found his body washed up on the beach.* ■ the physical and mortal aspect of a person as opposed to the soul or spirit: *a duality of body and soul.* ■ *informal* a person's body regarded as an object of sexual desire: *he was just after her body.* ■ *informal, dated* a person, often one of a specified type or character: *a motherly body.* **2** the trunk apart from the head and the limbs: *the blow almost severed his head from his body.* ■ [in *sing.*] (**the body of**) the main or central part of something, esp. a building or text: *information that changes regularly is kept apart from the main body of the text.* ■ the main section of a car or aircraft: *the body of the aircraft was filled with smoke.* ■ a large or substantial amount of something; a mass or collection of something: *a rich* **body** *of Canadian folklore* | *large* **bodies** *of seawater.* ■ (in pottery) a clay used for making the main part of ceramic ware, as distinct from a glaze. **3** a group of people with a common purpose or function acting as an organized unit: *a regulatory body* | *international bodies of experts.* **4** [often with *adj.*] *technical* a distinct material object: *the path taken by the falling body.* **5** a full or substantial quality of flavor in wine. ■ fullness or thickness of a person's hair: *designed to add body to limp and straight hair.*

▸*v.* (**bod·ies, bod·ied**) [*trans.*] **1** (**body something forth**) give material form to something abstract: *he bodied forth the traditional Prussian remedy for all ills.* **2** build the bodywork of (a motor vehicle): *an era when automobiles were bodied over wooden frames.* ▷Old English *bodig*, of unknown origin. **—bod·ied** *adj.* [in *combination*] *a wide-bodied jet.*

▸*PHRASES* □ **body and soul** involving every aspect of a person; completely: *the company owned them body and soul.* □ **in a body** all together; as a group: *they departed in a body.* □ **keep body and soul** (or **soul and body**) **together** stay alive, esp. in difficult circumstances: *do you think a man can keep body and soul together by selling coconuts?* □ **over my dead body** *informal* used to emphasize that one opposes something and would do anything to prevent it from happening: *she moves into our home over my dead body.*

THE RIGHT WORD **body, cadaver, carcass, corpse, cremains, remains**

The problem of what to call the human **body** after it has departed this life is a delicate one.

Although a *body* can be either dead or alive, human or animal, a **corpse** is most definitely a dead human body and a **carcass** is the body of a dead animal. The issue has been confused, of course, by the figurative use of *carcass* as a term of contempt (*"Get your carcass out of bed and come down here!"*). While *carcass* is often used humorously, there's nothing funny about *corpse*, a no-nonsense term for a lifeless physical body (*the battlefield was littered with corpses*).

A funeral director is likely to prefer the term **remains**, which is a euphemism for the body of the deceased (*he had his wife's remains shipped home for burial*), or **cremains**, if the body has been cremated.

A medical student, on the other hand, is much more likely to use the term **cadaver**, which is a corpse that is dissected in a laboratory for scientific study.

bod·y ar·mor ▸*n.* clothing worn by military and police personnel to protect against gunfire.

bod·y art ▸*n.* **1** items of jewelry or clothing worn on the body and regarded as art. ■ the practice of decorating the body by means of tattooing, piercing, plastic surgery, etc. **2** an artistic movement originating in the 1970s in which the physical presence of the artist (or of a model) is regarded as an integral part of the work.

bod·y bag ▸*n.* a bag used for carrying a corpse from a battlefield or the scene of an accident or crime.

bod·y blow ▸*n.* a heavy punch to the body. ■ a severe disappointment or crushing setback: *a tax on books would be a body blow for education.*

bod·y·board /ˈbädēˌbôrd/ ▸*n.* a short light type of surfboard ridden in a prone position. **—bod·y·board·er** *n.* **—bod·y·board·ing** *n.*

bod·y·build·ing /ˈbädēˌbildiNG/ ▸*n.* the practice of strengthening and enlarging the muscles of the body through exercise. | **—bod·y·build·er** /-ˌbildər/ *n.*

bod·y-cen·tered ▸*adj.* denoting a crystal structure in which there is an atom at each vertex and at the center of the unit cell. Compare with **FACE-CENTERED.**

bod·y check ▸*n.* a deliberate obstruction of a player (esp. in ice hockey) by placing one's body in the way. ▸*v.* (**bod·y-check**) [*trans.*] obstruct (a player) in such a way.

bod·y clock ▸*n.* a person's or animal's biological clock.

bod·y col·or ▸*n.* an opaque pigment.

bod·y cor·po·rate ▸*n.* formal term for **CORPORATION.**

bod·y count ▸*n.* a list or total of casualties.

bod·y dou·ble ▸*n.* a stand-in for a movie actor used during stunt or nude scenes.

bod·y dys·mor·phic dis·or·der (abbr.: **BDD**) ▸*n.* a psychological disorder in which a person becomes obsessed with imaginary defects in their appearance.

bod·y Eng·lish ▸*n.* a bodily action after throwing, hitting, or kicking a ball, intended as an attempt to influence the ball's trajectory: *see him waving and using body English to try to keep the ball from going foul.*

bod·y·guard /ˈbädēˌgärd/ ▸*n.* a person or group of persons hired to escort and protect another person, esp. a dignitary.

bod·y im·age ▸*n.* the subjective picture or mental image of one's own body.

bod·y·kit /ˈbädˌ ˌkit/ (also **bod·y kit**) ▸*n.* a packaged set of decorations and fittings for customizing a car or motorcycle body.

bod·y lan·guage ▸*n.* the process of communicating nonverbally through conscious or unconscious gestures and movements: *his intent was clearly expressed in his body language.*

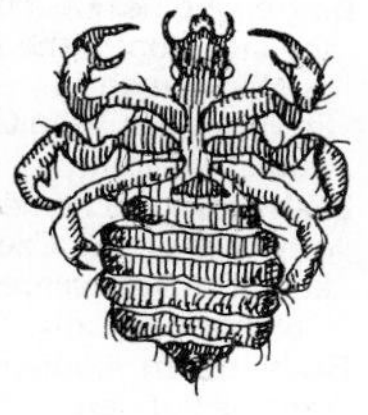

body louse

bod·y louse ▸*n.* a louse of a variety that infests the human body and is especially prevalent where hygiene is poor. It can transmit several diseases through its bite, including typhus. • *Pediculus humanus humanus*, family Pediculidae, order Anoplura. See also **HEAD LOUSE.**

bod·y mass in·dex (abbr.: **BMI**) ▸*n.* (*pl.* **-di·ces** /-dəsēz/ or **-dex·es**) a weight-to-height ratio, calculated by dividing one's weight in kilograms by the square of one's height in meters and used as an indicator of obesity and underweight.

bod·y me·chan·ics ▸*plural n.* [treated as *sing.* or *pl.*] exercises designed to improve posture, coordination, and stamina.

bod·y o·dor ▸*n.* the smell of the human body, esp. when unpleasant.

bod·y pierc·ing ▸*n.* the piercing of holes in parts of the body other than the earlobes in order to insert rings or other decorative objects.

bod·y pol·i·tic ▸*n.* (usu. **the body politic**) the people of a nation, state, or society considered collectively as an organized group of citizens.

bod·y press ▸*n.* *Wrestling* a move in which a wrestler uses their body weight to pin an opponent to the floor.

bod·y scrub ▸*n.* an exfoliating cosmetic preparation, applied to the body to cleanse the skin. ■ a type of beauty treatment in which the skin is cleaned and exfoliated.

bod·y search ▸*n.* a search, typically conducted by customs officials or the police, of a person's body and clothing for illicit weapons, drugs, or other articles.

bod·y shirt ▸*n.* a close-fitting woman's garment for the upper body that is closed at the crotch. ■ a close-fitting blouse or shirt.

bod·y shop ▸*n.* a garage where repairs to the bodies of vehicles are carried out.

bod·y·side /ˈbädeˌsīd/ ▸*n.* the side of the body of a vehicle: [as *adj.*] *bodyside panels.*

bod·y slam ▸*n.* *Wrestling* a move (illegal in some codes) in which the opponent's body is lifted and then thrown hard onto the floor.

bod·y·snatch·er /ˈbädēˌsnaCHər/ ▸*n.* *historical* a person who stole corpses from a graveyard for dissection, for which there was no legal provision until 1832. **—bod·y·snatch·ing** /-ˌsnaCHiNG/ *n.*

bod·y stock·ing ▸*n.* a woman's one-piece undergarment that covers the torso and legs.

bod·y·suit /ˈbädēˌsōōt/ ▸*n.* a close-fitting one-piece stretch garment for women, typically worn for sports.

bod·y·surf /ˈbädēˌsərf/ ▸*v.* [*intrans.*] [often as *n.*] (**body-surfing**) float on the crest of incoming waves without using a board.

bod·y text ▸*n.* (usu. **the body text**) the main part of a printed text, excluding items such as headings and footnotes.

bod·y wall ▸*n.* the external surface of an animal body that encloses the body cavity and consists of ectoderm and mesoderm.

bod·y wave ▸*n.* a soft, light permanent wave designed to give hair fullness.

bod·y·work /ˈbädēˌwərk/ ▸*n.* **1** the metal outer shell of a vehicle. **2** therapies and techniques in complementary medicine that involve touching or manipulating the body. **—bod·y·work·er** *n.* (in sense 2).

bod·y wrap ▸*n.* a type of beauty treatment involving the application of skin-cleansing ingredients to the body, which is then wrapped in hot towels.

boehm·ite /ˈbāmīt; ˈbō-/ ▸*n.* a crystalline mineral compound composed of aluminum oxide and hydroxide and found in bauxite. • Chem. formula: $AlO(OH)$.

Boe·ing /ˈbō-iNG/, William Edward (1881–1956), U.S. industrialist. In 1927, he founded United Aircraft and Transport, which, in 1934, was divided into Boeing Aircraft, United Aircraft, and United Airlines.

Boe·o·tia /bēˈōSHə/ a department in central Greece, north of the Gulf of Corinth, and a region of ancient Greece of which the chief city was Thebes. **—Boe·o·tian** *adj.* & *n.*

Boer /bôr; bŏŏr/ *chiefly historical* ▸*n.* a member of the Dutch and Huguenot population that settled in southern Africa in the late 17th century.

The Boers were Calvinist in religion and fiercely self-sufficient. Conflict with the British administration of Cape Colony after 1806 led to the Great Trek of 1835–37 and the Boer Wars, after which the Boer republics of Transvaal and Orange Free State became part of the Republic of South Africa. The Boers' present-day descendants are the Afrikaners.

▸*adj.* of or relating to the Boers. ▷from Dutch *boer* 'farmer.' Compare with **BOOR.**

boer·bull /ˈbôrˌbŏŏl; ˈbŏŏr-/ (also **boer·bul**) ▸*n.* *S. African* a large dog crossbred from the mastiff and indigenous African dogs. ▷1960s: from Afrikaans *boerboel*, from *boer* (commonly applied to indigenous plants and animals) + *boel*, from Dutch *bul* (as in *bulhond* 'mastiff').

boer goat /bôr; bŏŏr/ ▸*n.* a goat of a hardy breed, originally from South Africa. ▷from Afrikaans *boer* 'farmer' + **GOAT.**

Boer Wars two wars fought by Great Britain in southern Africa.

The first war (1880–81) began with the revolt of the Boer settlers in Transvaal against British rule and ended with the establishment of an independent Boer Republic under British suzerainty. The second (1899–1902) was caused by the Boer refusal to grant equal rights to recent British immigrants and by the imperialist ambitions of Cecil Rhodes. The British eventually won through superior numbers and the employment of concentration camps to control the countryside.

boeuf /bœf/ ▸*n.* *Cooking* French word for **BEEF**, used in the names of various beef dishes.

boeuf bour·gui·gnon /ˈbœf ˌbŏŏrgēˈnyôN/ ▸*n.* a dish consisting of beef stewed in red wine. ▷early 20th cent.: French, literally 'Burgundy beef.'

boff /bäf/ *informal* ▸*v.* [*trans.*] have sexual intercourse with (someone).

▸*n.* an act of sexual intercourse. ▷1920s (in the sense 'blow, punch'): imitative. The current sense dates from the 1950s.

bof·fin /ˈbäfin/ ▸*n.* *informal, chiefly Brit.* a person engaged in scientific or technical research: *a computer boffin.* ■ a person with knowledge or a skill considered to be complex, arcane, and difficult: *he had a reputation as a tax boffin, a learned lawyer.* ▷World War II: of unknown origin. **—bof·fin·y** *adj.*

bof·fo /ˈbäfō/ *informal* ▸*adj.* **1** (of a review of a theatrical production, movie, etc.) wholeheartedly positive; commendatory. ■ resoundingly successful or popular: *a boffo box-office certainty.* **2** (of a laugh) deep and unrestrained. ■ boisterously funny.

▸*n.* (*pl.* **-fos**) a success: *the finale is a genuine boffo.* ▷1940s: from *boff* 'roaring success' + **-o.**

bof·fo·la /bäˈfōlə/ *informal* ▸*n.* a joke or a line in a script meant to get a laugh.

B

▸*adj.* (of a laugh) hearty and unrestrained. ▷1940s: extension of BOFF.

Bo·fors gun /ˈbōfôrz/ ▸*n.* a type of light antiaircraft gun. ▷1930s: named after *Bofors* in Sweden, where it was first manufactured.

bog /bäg; bôg/ ▸*n.* **1** wet muddy ground too soft to support a heavy body: *the island is a wilderness of bog* | *a peat bog figurative a bog of legal complications.* ■ *Ecology* wetland with acid, peaty soil, typically dominated by peat moss. Compare with FEN[1]. **2** (usu. **the bog**) *Brit., informal* a bathroom.

▸*v.* (**bogged, bog·ging**) [*trans.*] (usu. **be bogged down**) cause (a vehicle, person, or animal) to become stuck in mud or wet ground: *the car* ***became bogged down*** *on the beach road.* ■ (**be bogged down**) *figurative* (of a person or process) be unable to make progress: *you must not* ***get bogged down in*** *detail.* ▷Middle English: from Irish or Scottish Gaelic *bogach*, from *bog* 'soft.' **—bog·gy** *adj.* **—bog·gi·ness** *n.*

Bo·garde /ˈbō,gärd/, Sir Dirk (1921–99), British actor and writer; born *Derek Niven van den Bogaerde.* Notable movies: *The Servant* (1963), *Death in Venice* (1971), and *A Bridge Too Far* (1977).

Bo·gart /ˈbō,gärt/, Humphrey (DeForest) (1899–1957), U.S. actor. His success as a ruthless gangster in *The Petrified Forest*, a play, was repeated in the movie of 1936. His many movies include *Casablanca* (1942), *The Big Sleep* (1946, in which he played opposite his fourth wife, Lauren Bacall), and *The African Queen* (1951, for which he won an Academy Award).

bo·gart /ˈbōgärt/ ▸*v.* [*trans.*] *informal* selfishly appropriate or keep (something, esp. a lit marijuana cigarette). ▷1960s: from U.S. actor Humphrey *Bogart* (1899–1957), who often smoked in films.

bog as·pho·del ▸*n.* a yellow-flowered marsh plant of the lily family. • Genus *Narthecium*, family Liliaceae: several species, including *N. ossifragum* of Europe and *N. americanum* of the eastern U.S., esp. New Jersey.

bog·bean /ˈbäg,bēn/ ▸*n.* another term for BUCKBEAN.

bo·gey[1] /ˈbōgē/ *Golf* ▸*n.* (*pl.* **-geys**) a score of one stroke over par at a hole. ■ archaic term for PAR[1] sense 1.

▸*v.* (**-geys, -geyed**) [*trans.*] play (a hole) in one stroke over par. ▷late 19th cent.: perhaps from *Bogey*, denoting the Devil (see BOGEY[2]), regarded as an imaginary player.

bo·gey[2] /ˈbŏŏgē/ (also **bo·gy**) ▸*n.* (*pl.* **-geys**) a person or thing that causes fear or alarm: *the bogey of recession.* ■ an evil or mischievous spirit. ■ *military slang* an enemy aircraft. ▷mid 19th cent. (as a proper name applied to the Devil): of unknown origin; probably related to BOGLE.

bo·gey·man /ˈbŏŏgē,man; ˈbō-/ (also **boo·gey·man, bo·gy·man**) ▸*n.* (*pl.* **-men**) (usu. **the bogeyman**) an imaginary evil spirit, referred to typically to frighten children: *with the blankets pulled over our heads to keep out the bogeyman.* ■ a person or thing that is widely regarded as an object of fear: *the violent criminal has replaced the communist as the bogeyman.*

bog·gle /ˈbägəl/ ▸*v.* [*intrans.*] *informal* (of a person or a person's mind) be astonished or overwhelmed when trying to imagine something: *the mind boggles at the spectacle.* ■ [*trans.*] cause (a person or a person's mind) to be astonished in such a way: *the inflated salary of a CEO* ***boggles the mind*** | [as *adj.*] (**boggling**) *the total was a boggling 1.5 trillion miles.* ■ (**boggle at**) (of a person) hesitate or be anxious at: *you never boggle at plain speaking.* ▷late 16th cent.: probably of dialect origin and related to BOGLE and BOGEY[2].

bo·gie /ˈbōgē/ ▸*n.* (*pl.* **-gies**) *chiefly Brit.* an undercarriage with four or six wheels pivoted beneath the end of a railroad car. ▷early 19th cent. (originally in northern English dialect use): of unknown origin.

bog i·ron ▸*n.* soft, spongy goethite deposited in bogs.

bog·land /ˈbäg,land/ ▸*n.* *chiefly Brit.* marshy land.

bo·gle /ˈbōgəl/ ▸*n.* a phantom or goblin. ■ *Scottish & N. Engl.* a scarecrow. ▷early 16th cent.: of unknown origin; probably related to BOGEY[2].

bog moss ▸*n.* another term for PEAT MOSS (sense 1).

bog myr·tle ▸*n.* another term for SWEET GALE.

bog oak ▸*n.* an ancient oak tree that has been preserved in a black state in peat.

BOGOF /ˈbägôf/ ▸*abbr.* buy one, get one free.

Bog·o·mil /ˈbägəmil/ ▸*n.* *historical* a member of a heretical medieval Balkan sect professing a modified form of Manichaeism. ▷mid 19th cent.: from medieval Greek *Bogomilos*, from *Bogomil*, literally 'beloved of God,' the name of the person who first disseminated the heresy, from Old Church Slavic. **—Bog·o·mil·ism** /-,lizəm/ *n.*

bo·gong /ˈbōgôNG; -gäNG/ (also **bogong moth**) ▸*n.* *Austral.* a large brown moth native to southern Australia, formerly used as food by Aboriginals. • *Agrotis infusa*, family Noctuidae. ▷mid 19th cent.: from Ngayawuh.

Bo·go·tá /ˈbōgə,tä; ,bōgəˈtô/ the capital of Colombia, in the eastern Andes at about 8,560 feet (2,610 m); pop. 4,921,200. It was founded by the Spanish in 1538 on the site of a pre-Columbian center of the Chibcha culture. Official name SANTA FÉ DE BOGOTÁ.

bog rose·mar·y ▸*n.* See ANDROMEDA.

bog spav·in ▸*n.* a soft swelling of the joint capsule of the hock of horses that most commonly occurs in young, fast-growing horses.

bog·trot·ter /ˈbäg,trätər/ ▸*n.* a person who lives or works among bogs. ■ *informal, offensive* an Irish person.

bo·gus /ˈbōgəs/ ▸*adj.* not genuine or true; fake: *a bogus insurance claim.* ▷late 18th cent. (originally U.S., denoting a machine for making counterfeit money): of unknown origin. **—bo·gus·ly** *adv.* **—bo·gus·ness** *n.*

bo·gy /ˈbōgē; ˈbŏŏgē/ ▸*n.* (*pl.* **-gies**) variant spelling of BOGEY[2].

bo·gy·man ▸*n.* variant spelling of BOGEYMAN.

Bo Hai /ˈbō ˈhī/ (also **Po Hai**) a large inlet of the Yellow Sea, on the coast of eastern China. Also called CHIHLI, GULF OF.

bo·hea /bōˈhē/ ▸*n.* a black China tea that comes from the last crop of the season and is typically regarded as of low quality. ▷early 18th cent.: named after the *Bu-yi* (*Wuyi*) hills in China, from where black tea first came to Britain.

Bo·he·mi·a /bōˈhēmēə/ a region that forms the western part of the Czech Republic. Formerly a Slavic kingdom, it became a province in the newly formed Czechoslovakia by the Treaty of Versailles in 1919.

Bo·he·mi·an /bōˈhēmēən/ ▸*n.* **1** a native or inhabitant of Bohemia. **2** (also **bohemian**) a person who has informal and unconventional social habits, esp. an artist or writer: *the young bohemians with their art galleries and sushi bars.* [mid 19th cent.: from French *bohémien* 'gypsy' (because gypsies were thought to come from Bohemia, or because they perhaps entered the West through Bohemia).]

▸*adj.* **1** of or relating to Bohemia or its people. **2** (also **bohemian**) having informal and unconventional social habits: *the bohemian writer's drafty-garret existence.* **—Bo·he·mi·an·ism** /-,nizəm/ *n.* (in sense 2 of the *adjective*).

bo·ho /ˈbō,hō/ ▸*n.* (*pl.* **-hos**) informal term for BOHEMIAN (sense 2).

▸*adj.* informal term for BOHEMIAN (sense 2).

Bo·hol /bōˈhôl/ an island in the central Philippines, north of Mindanao; chief town, Tagbilaran.

Bohr /bôr/, Niels Hendrik David (1885–1962), Danish physicist and pioneer in quantum physics. His theory of the structure of the atom incorporated quantum theory for the first time and is the basis for present-day quantum-mechanical models. Bohr helped to develop the atom bomb in Britain and then in the U.S. Nobel Prize for Physics (1922).

Bohr ef·fect ▸*n.* a decrease in the amount of oxygen associated with hemoglobin and other respiratory compounds in response to a lowered blood pH resulting from an increased concentration of carbon dioxide in the blood. ▷named for Danish physiologist Christian Bohr (1855–1911).

bohr·i·um /ˈbôrēəm/ ▸*n.* the chemical element of atomic number 107, a very unstable element made by high-energy atomic collisions. (Symbol: **Bh**)

Bohr the·o·ry ▸*n.* *Physics* a theory of the structure of atoms stating that electrons revolve in discrete orbits around a positively charged nucleus and that radiation is given off or absorbed only when an electron moves from one orbit to another. ▷named for Danish physicist Niels Henrik David Bohr (1885–1962).

bo·hunk /ˈbō,həNGk/ ▸*n.* *informal, offensive* an immigrant from central or southeastern Europe, esp. a laborer. ■ *informal* a rough or uncivilized person. ▷early 20th cent.: apparently from BOHEMIAN + *-hunk*, alteration of HUNGARIAN.

boil[1] /boil/ ▸*v.* **1** [*trans.*] heat (a liquid) to the temperature at which it bubbles and turns to vapor: *we tried to get people to boil their drinking water* | *I'll* ***boil up*** *the stock.* ■ (of a liquid) be at or reach this temperature: *he waited for the water to boil.* ■ heat (a container) until the liquid in it reaches such a temperature: [*trans.*] *she boiled the kettle and took down a couple of mugs.* ■ [*intrans.*] (of a container) be heated until the liquid in it reaches such a temperature: *the kettle boiled and he filled the teapot.* **2** [*trans.*] subject (something) to the heat of boiling liquid, in particular: ■ cook (food) by immersing in boiling water: *boil the potatoes until well done* | [as *adj.*] (**boiled**) *two boiled eggs.* ■ [*intrans.*] (of food) be cooked in boiling water: *make the sauce while the lobsters are boiling.* ■ wash or sterilize (clothes) in very hot water. ■ *historical* execute (someone) by subjecting them to the heat of boiling liquid. **3** [*intrans.*] (of the sea or clouds) be turbulent and stormy: *a huge cliff with the black sea boiling below.* ■ (of a person or strong emotion) be stirred up or inflamed: *he was* ***boiling with*** *rage.*

▸*phrasal v.* □ **boil away** (of a liquid in a container) boil until the container is empty: *check that the water has not boiled away.* □ **boil down to** be in essence a matter of: *everything boiled down to cash in the end.* □ **boil something down** reduce the volume of a liquid by boiling: *they boil down the syrup until it is very thick.* □ **boil over** (of a liquid) flow over the sides of the container in boiling. ■ *figurative* (of a situation or strong emotion) become so excited or tense as to get out of control: *one woman's anger boiled over.*

▸*n.* **1** [in *sing.*] the temperature at which a liquid bubbles and turns to vapor: *stir in cream and* ***bring to a boil.*** ■ an act or process of heating a liquid to such a temperature. ■ *figurative* a state of vigorous activity or excitement. ■ an area of churning water: *massive current differentials, boils, and braided channels.* ■ *Fishing* a sudden rise of a fish at a fly. **2** an outdoor meal at which seafood is boiled: *everything for a traditional Louisiana seafood boil can be carried down to the beach.* ■ a blend of seasonings added to water to enhance the flavor of boiled seafood: *Chef Eric has blended a salt-free seafood boil by combing mustard and other ingredients.* ▷Middle English: from Old French *boillir*, from Latin *bullire* 'to bubble,' from *bulla* 'bubble.'

▸*PHRASES* □ **keep the pot boiling** maintain the momentum or interest value of something. □ **make one's blood boil** see BLOOD.

boil[2] ▸*n.* an inflamed pus-filled swelling on the skin, typically caused by the infection of a hair follicle. ▷Old English *bȳle, bȳl*; related to Dutch *buil* and German *Beule*.

Boi·leau /bwäˈlō/, Nicholas (1636–1711), French critic and poet; full name *Nicholas Boileau-Despréaux.* One of the founders of French literary criticism, his didactic poem *Art poétique* (1674) defined principles of composition and criticism.

boiled shirt ▸*n.* *dated* a dress shirt with a starched front.

boil·er /ˈboilər/ ▸*n.* a fuel-burning apparatus or container for heating water, in particular: ■ a household device providing a hot-water supply or serving a central heating system. ■ a tank for generating steam under pressure in a steam engine. See also STEAM BOILER. ■ *dated* a metal tub for washing or sterilizing clothes at a very high temperature.

boil·er·mak·er /ˈboilər,mākər/ ▸*n.* **1** a person who makes boilers. ■ a metalworker in heavy industry. **2** a shot of whiskey followed by a glass of beer as a chaser.

boil·er·plate /ˈboilər,plāt/ ▸*n.* **1** rolled steel for making boilers. **2** (**boilerplates**) *mountaineering* smooth, overlapping, and undercut slabs of rock: *the ice-worn boilerplates.* **3** *figurative* writing that is clichéd or expresses a generally accepted opinion or belief: *he accepted Soviet boilerplate at face value.* ■ standardized pieces of text for use as clauses in contracts or as part of a computer program: *some sections have been written as boilerplate for use in all proposals.*

boil·er room ▸*n.* a room in a building (typically in the basement) or a compartment in a ship containing a boiler and related heating or steam-generating equipment. ■ a room used for intensive telephone selling: [as *adj.*] *boiler-room stock salesmen.*

boil·er suit ▸*n.* British term for COVERALLS (see COVERALLS).

boil·ing /ˈboiliNG/ ▸*adj.* (for fresh water at sea level) at 212°F (100°C). ■ (also **boiling hot**) *informal* (used hyperbolically) extremely hot: *Saturday is forecast to be boiling and sunny.* ■ (of an emotion) intensely and powerfully felt: *his boiling hatred of oppression.*

▸*n.* the action of bringing a liquid to the temperature at which it bubbles and turns to vapor. ■ the temperature at which such an event occurs: *reheat gently to just below boiling.*

boil·ing point ▸*n.* the temperature at which a liquid boils and turns to vapor. ■ *figurative* the point at which anger or excitement breaks out into violent expression: *racial tension surges to boiling point.*

boil·ing-wa·ter re·ac·tor (abbr.: **BWR**) ▸*n.* a nuclear reactor in which the fuel is uranium oxide clad in zircaloy and the coolant and moderator is water, which is boiled to produce steam for driving turbines.

boing /boiNG/ ▸*exclam.* representing the noise of a compressed spring suddenly released.
▸*n.* such a noise.
▸*v.* [*intrans.*] make such a noise. ▷1950s: imitative.

Boi·se /ˈboisē; -zē/ a city in southwestern Idaho, the capital of the state; pop. 185,787.

boi·se·rie /bwäzəˈrē/ ▸*n.* wooden paneling. ▷mid 19th cent.: French.

bois·ter·ous /ˈboist(ə)rəs/ ▸*adj.* (of a person, event, or behavior) noisy, energetic, and cheerful; rowdy: *the boisterous conviviality associated with taverns of that period.* See note at **VOCIFEROUS**. ■ (of wind, weather, or water) wild or stormy: *the boisterous wind was lulled.* ▷late Middle English (in the sense 'rough, stiff'): variant of earlier *boistuous* 'rustic, coarse, boisterous,' of unknown origin. —**bois·ter·ous·ly** *adv.* —**bois·ter·ous·ness** *n.*

boîte /bwät/ ▸*n.* (*pl.* same or **boîtes**) a small restaurant or nightclub. ▷French, literally 'box'.

Bo·kas·sa /bəˈkäsə/, Jean Bédel (1921–96), Central African Republic statesman and military leader; president 1972–76; self-styled emperor 1976–79.

bok choy /ˈbäk ˈCHoi/ ▸*n.* Chinese cabbage of a variety with smooth-edged tapering leaves.

bok choy

bo·keh /bōˈkā/ ▸*n.* *Photography* the visual quality of the out-of-focus areas of a photographic image, especially as rendered by a particular lens: *a quick, visual survey of the foreground and background bokeh of a variety of lenses.* ▷from Japanese.

bok·ken /ˈbäkən/ ▸*n.* a wooden sword used as a practice weapon in kendo.

Bok·mål /ˈbo͝ok,môl/ ▸*n.* one of two standard forms of the Norwegian language, a modified form of Danish. See **NORWEGIAN**. ▷from Norwegian *bok* 'book' + *mål* 'language.'

bo·la /ˈbōlə/ (also **bo·las**) ▸*n.* (esp. in South America) a weapon consisting of a number of balls connected by strong cord, which when thrown entangles the limbs of the quarry. ▷early 19th cent.: from Spanish and Portuguese *bolas*, plural of *bola* 'ball.'

bo·la tie /ˈbōlə/ ▸*n.* variant spelling of **BOLO TIE**.

bold /bōld/ ▸*adj.* **1** (of a person, action, or idea) showing an ability to take risks; confident and courageous: *a bold attempt to solve the crisis | he was the only one bold enough to air his dislike.* ■ *dated* (of a person or manner) so confident as to suggest a lack of shame or modesty: *she tossed him a bold look.* **2** (of a color or design) having a strong or vivid appearance: *a coat with bold polka dots.* ■ (of a typeface) having thick strokes. **3** (of a cliff or coastline) steep or projecting: *bold, craggy edges on the lip of the plateau.*
▸*n.* a typeface with thick strokes: *difficult words and phrases are highlighted* **in bold**. ▷Old English *bald*, of Germanic origin; related to Dutch *boud* and to German *bald* 'soon.' —**bold·ly** *adv.* —**bold·ness** *n.*
▸*PHRASES* □ **be** (or **make**) **so bold** (**as to do something**) *formal* dare to do something (often used when politely asking a question or making a suggestion): *what would he be calling for,* ***if I might make so bold*** *as to ask?* □ (**as**) **bold as brass** confident to the point of impudence: *she marched into the library as bold as brass.* □ **a bold stroke** a daring action or initiative. □ **put a bold face on something** see **FACE**.

THE RIGHT WORD **aggressive, audacious, bold, brazen, bumptious, intrepid, presumptuous**

Is walking up to an attractive stranger and asking him or her to have dinner with you tonight a **bold** move or merely an **aggressive** one?

Both words suggest assertive, confident behavior that is a little on the shameless side, but *bold* has a wider range of application. It can suggest self-confidence that borders on impudence (*to be so bold as to call the president by his first name*), but it can also be used to describe a daring temperament that is either courageous or defiant (| *a bold investigator who would not give up*).

Aggressive behavior, on the other hand, usually falls within a narrower range, somewhere between menacing (*aggressive attacks on innocent villagers*) and just plain pushy (| *an aggressive salesperson*).

Brazen implies a defiant lack of modesty (*a brazen stare*), and **presumptuous** goes even further, suggesting over-confidence to the point of causing offense (*a presumptuous request for money*).

Bumptious behavior can also be offensive, but it is usually associated with the kind of cockiness that can't be helped (*a bumptious young upstart*).

An **audacious** person is bold to the point of recklessness (*an audacious explorer*), which brings it very close in meaning to **intrepid**, suggesting fearlessness in the face of the unknown (*the intrepid settlers of the Great Plains*).

bold·face /ˈbōld,fās/ ▸*n.* a typeface with thick strokes.
▸*adj.* printed or displayed in such a typeface. —**bold·faced** *adj.*

bole1 /bōl/ ▸*n.* the trunk of a tree. ▷Middle English: from Old Norse *bolr*; perhaps related to **BALK**.

bole2 ▸*n.* fine, compact, earthy clay, typically of a reddish color, used as a pigment. ▷Middle English: from late Latin *bolus* 'rounded mass' (see **BOLUS**).

bo·lec·tion /bōˈlekSHən/ ▸*n.* [usu. as *adj.*] *Architecture* a decorative molding that separates two planes (or surfaces), esp. around a wooden panel, usually convex. ▷mid 17th cent.: of unknown origin.

bo·le·ro /bəˈle(ə)rō/ ▸*n.* (*pl.* **-ros**) **1** a Spanish dance in simple triple time. ■ a piece of music for this dance. **2** a woman's short open jacket. ▷late 18th cent.: from Spanish.

bolero 2

bo·lete /bōˈlēt/ (also **bo·le·tus** /bōˈlētəs/) ▸*n.* (*pl.* **-letes** or **-le·tus·es** /-ˈlētəsəz/) a mushroom or toadstool with pores rather than gills on the underside of the cap. Boletes often have a thick stem, and several kinds are edible. See also **CEP**. • Genus *Boletus*, family Boletaceae, class Basidiomycetes. ▷from Latin, from Greek *bōlitēs*, perhaps from *bōlos* 'lump.'

Bol·eyn /bo͝oˈlin; ˈbo͝olən/, Anne (1507–36), second wife of Henry VIII; mother of Elizabeth I. Henry divorced Catherine of Aragon in order to marry Anne in 1533, but she fell from favor when she failed to provide him with a male heir. She was eventually executed because of alleged infidelities.

Bol·ger /ˈbōljər/, Ray (1904–87), U.S. dancer and actor; full name *Raymond Wallace Bolger*. He is best known for his role as the scarecrow in *The Wizard of Oz* (1939).

bo·lide /ˈbōlīd; ˈbōlid/ ▸*n.* a large meteor that explodes in the atmosphere. ▷early 19th cent.: from French, from Latin *bolis, bolid-*, from Greek *bolis* 'missile.'

Bol·ing·broke /ˈbōliNG,bro͝ok; ˈbäl-; -,brōk/, the surname of Henry IV of England. (see **HENRY1**).

Bo·ling·brook /ˈbōliNG,bro͝ok/ a village in northeastern Illinois, southwest of Chicago; pop. 40,843.

Bol·i·var /bəˈlē,vär; ˈbäləvər/, Simón (1783–1830), Venezuelan patriot and statesman; known as **the Liberator**. He succeeded in driving the Spanish from Venezuela, Colombia, Peru, and Ecuador. Upper Peru was named Bolivia in his honor.

bol·i·var /bəˈlē,vär; ˈbäləvər/ ▸*n.* the basic monetary unit of Venezuela, equal to 100 centimos. ▷named after S. **BOLÍVAR**.

Bo·liv·i·a /bəˈlivēə/ a landlocked country in western South America; pop. 8,724,000; capital, La Paz; legal capital and seat of the judiciary, Sucre; languages, Spanish (official), Aymara, and Quechua. ▷named after Simón *Bolívar*, who liberated the country from Spanish rule. —**Bo·liv·i·an** *adj.* & *n.*

After the defeat of the Incas, Bolivia became part of Spain's empire in the Americas. Freed from Spanish rule in 1825, it has suffered continually from political instability.

bo·liv·i·a·no /bə,livēˈänō/ ▸*n.* (*pl.* **-nos**) the basic monetary unit of Bolivia (1863–1962 and since 1987), equal to 100 centavos or cents. ▷late 19th cent.: Spanish, literally 'Bolivian,' from **BOLIVIA**.

Böll /bœl/, Heinrich (Theodor) (1917–85), German novelist and short-story writer. Notable works: *Billiards at Half Past Nine* (1959) and *The Lost Honor of Katharina Blum* (1974). Nobel Prize for Literature (1972).

boll /bōl/ ▸*n.* the rounded seed capsule of plants such as cotton or flax. ▷Middle English (originally denoting a bubble): from Middle Dutch *bolle* 'rounded object'; related to **BOWL1**.

bol·lard /ˈbälərd/ ▸*n.* **1** a short, thick post on the deck of a ship or on a wharf, to which a ship's rope may be secured. **2** *Brit.* a short post used to divert traffic from an area or road. ▷Middle English (sense 1): perhaps from Old Norse *bolr* (see **BOLE1**) + **-ARD**.

bol·li·to mis·to /bōˈlētō ˈmistō/ ▸*n.* (*pl.* **bol·li·ti mis·ti** /bōˈlētē ˈmistē/) a dish of mixed kinds of meat, such as chicken, veal, and sausage, boiled with vegetables in broth. ▷Italian, 'boiled mixed meat,' from *bollito* past participle of *bollire* 'to boil' and *misto* 'mixed.'

bol·lix /ˈbäliks/ *vulgar slang* ▸*v.* [*trans.*] (usu. **bollix something up**) bungle (a task).
▸*plural n.* variant spelling of **BOLLOCKS**.

bol·locks /ˈbäləks/ (also **bal·locks** or **bol·lix**) *vulgar slang, chiefly Brit.* ▸*n.* **1** [in *pl.*] the testicles. **2** used to express contempt, annoyance, or defiance. ▷mid 18th cent.: plural of *bollock*, variant of earlier *ballock*, of Germanic origin; related to **BALL1**.

boll wee·vil ▸*n.* a small weevil that feeds on the fibers of the cotton boll. It is a major pest of the American cotton crop. • *Anthonomus grandis*, family Curculionidae. ■ *informal* in the U.S., a conservative Southern Democrat, esp. a member of Congress.

boll·worm /ˈbōl,wərm/ ▸*n.* a moth caterpillar that attacks the cotton boll, in particular: • (**pink bollworm**) a small moth that is a serious pest of the North American cotton crop (*Pectinophora gossypiella*, family Gelechiidae). • (also **cotton bollworm**) another term for **CORN EARWORM**.

boll weevil

Bol·ly·wood /ˈbälē,wo͝od/ ▸*n.* the Indian movie industry, based in Bombay. ▷1970s: blend of **BOMBAY** and **HOLLYWOOD**.

bo·lo /ˈbōlō/ ▸*n.* **1** (*pl.* **-los**) a large single-edged knife used in the Philippines. **2** variant of **BOLA**. **3** short for **BOLO TIE**. ▷Spanish.

Bo·lo·gna /bəˈlōnyə/ a city in northern Italy, northeast of Florence; pop. 411,800. Its university, which dates from the 11th century, is the oldest in Europe.

bo·lo·gna /bəˈlōnē/ (also **bologna sausage**) ▸*n.* a large smoked, seasoned sausage made of various meats, esp. beef and pork. ▷from **BOLOGNA**.

bo·lom·e·ter /bōˈlämitər/ ▸*n.* a sensitive electrical instrument for measuring radiant energy. ▷late 19th cent.: from Greek *bolē* 'ray of light' + **-METER**. —**bo·lo·met·ric** /,bōləˈmetrik/ *adj.*

bo·lo·ney ▸*n.* variant spelling of **BALONEY**.

bo·lo tie (also **bo·la tie** /ˈbōlə/) ▸*n.* a type of tie consisting of a cord worn around the neck with a large, sliding, ornamental fastening at the throat.

bolo tie

Bol·she·vik /ˈbōlsʜəˌvik/ ▸*n. historical* a member of the majority faction of the Russian Social Democratic Party, which was renamed the Communist Party after seizing power in the October Revolution of 1917. ■ *chiefly derogatory* (in general use) a person with politically subversive or radical views; a revolutionary.
▸*adj.* of, relating to, or characteristic of Bolsheviks or their views or policies. ▷Russian, from *bol'she* 'greater' (with reference to the greater faction). **—Bol·she·vism** /-ˌvizəm/ *n.* **—Bol·she·vist** /-vist/ *n.*

Bol·shie /ˈbōlsʜē/ (also **Bol·shy**) ▸*n.* (*pl.* **-shies**) *Brit., informal* a Bolshevik or socialist.
▸*adj.* (**bolshie**) *Brit., informal* or *dated* (of a person or attitude) deliberately combative or uncooperative: *policemen with bolshie attitudes.* ▷early 20th cent.: abbreviation of **BOLSHEVIK**. **—bol·shi·ness** *n.*

bol·ster /ˈbōlstər/ ▸*n.* (also **bolster pillow**) a long, thick pillow that is placed under other pillows for support. ■ a part of a vehicle or tool providing structural support. ■ *Building* a short timber cap over a post designed to increase the bearing of the beams it supports.
▸*v.* [*trans.*] support or strengthen; prop up: *the fall in interest rates is starting to bolster confidence | he wished to bolster up his theories with hard data.* ■ provide (a seat) with padded support: [as *adj.*] (**bolstered**) *I snuggled down into the heavily bolstered seat.* ▷Old English (in the sense 'long, thick pillow'), of Germanic origin; related to Dutch *bolster* and German *Polster*.

Bolt /bōlt/, Robert (Oxton) (1924–95), English writer. His play *A Man for All Seasons* (1960) was made into a movie in 1967, the screenplay for which won an Academy Award. He also wrote the screenplays for *Lawrence of Arabia* (1962), for *Dr. Zhivago* (1965), and for *The Mission* (1986).

bolt[1] /bōlt/ ▸*n.* **1** a metal pin or bar, in particular: ■ a bar that slides into a socket to fasten a door or window. ■ a threaded pin that screws into a nut and is used to fasten things together. ■ the sliding piece of the breech mechanism of a rifle. ■ (in rock climbing) a long pin that is driven into a rock face so that a rope can be attached to it. **2** a short heavy arrow shot from a crossbow. **3** a flash of lightning leaving a jagged line across the sky.
▸*v.* [*trans.*] fasten (something) with a metal pin or bar, in particular: ■ fasten (a door or window) with a bar that slides into a socket: *all the doors were locked and bolted.* ■ [*trans.*] fasten (an object) to something else with a bolt: *the lid was put into position and bolted down | a camera was bolted to the aircraft.* ▷Old English, 'arrow,' of unknown origin; related to Dutch *bout* and German *Bolzen* 'arrow, bolt for a door.'
▸*PHRASES* □ **a bolt from** (or **out of**) **the blue** a sudden and unexpected event or piece of news: *the job came like a bolt from the blue.* □ **bolt upright** upright, with the back rigid and straight: *she sat bolt upright in bed.* □ **have shot one's bolt** *informal* have done all that one is able.

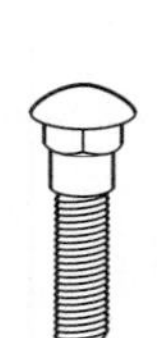

carriage bolt

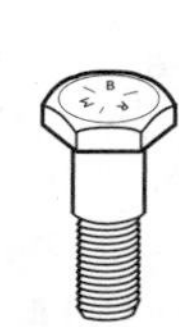

hex-head bolt

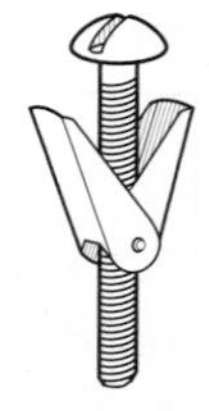

toggle bolt

bolt[1] **1**

bolt[2] ▸*v.* **1** [*intrans.*] (of a horse or other animal) run away suddenly out of control: *the horses shied and bolted.* ■ [*intrans.*] (of a person) move or run away suddenly: *they bolted down the stairs.* ■ [*trans.*] (in hunting) cause (a rabbit or fox) to run out of its burrow or hole. ■ (of a plant) grow tall quickly and stop flowering as seeds develop: *the lettuces have bolted.* **2** [*trans.*] (often **bolt something down**) eat or swallow (food) quickly: *it is normal for puppies to bolt down their food.* ▷Middle English: from **BOLT**[1], expressing the sense 'fly like an arrow.'
▸*PHRASES* □ **make a bolt for** try to escape by moving suddenly toward (something): *Ellie made a bolt for the door.* □ **shut the stable door after the horse has bolted** try to avert something bad or unwelcome when it is already too late to do so.

bolt[3] ▸*n.* a roll of fabric, originally as a measure: *the room is stacked with bolts of cloth.* ▷Middle English: transferred use of **BOLT**[1].

bolt[4] (also **boult**) ▸*v.* [*trans.*] *archaic* pass (flour, powder, or other material) through a sieve. ▷Middle English: from Old French *bulter*, of unknown ultimate origin. The change in the first syllable was due to association with **BOLT**[1].

bolt-ac·tion ▸*adj.* (of a gun) having a breech that is opened by turning a bolt and sliding it back.

bolt-hole ▸*n. figurative* a place where a person can escape and hide: *he thought of Antwerp as a possible bolt-hole.* ■ *chiefly Brit.* a hole or burrow by which a rabbit or other wild animal can escape.

bolt·ing /ˈbōltiɴɢ/ ▸*n.* (in rock climbing) the action of driving metal pins into rock faces so that ropes can be attached to them.

Bol·ton /ˈbōltn/ a town in northwestern England, northwest of Manchester; pop. 253,300 (1991).

bolt-on ▸*adj.* [*attrib.*] (of an extra part of a machine) able to be fastened on with a bolt or catch.
▸*n.* an extra part that can be fastened onto a machine with a bolt or catch.

bolt rope ▸*n.* a rope sewn around the edge of a vessel's sail to prevent tearing.

Boltz·mann /ˈbôltsmən/, Ludwig (1844–1906), Austrian physicist. He made contributions to the kinetic theory of gases, statistical mechanics, and thermodynamics. He also derived the Maxwell–Boltzmann equation for the distribution of energy among colliding atoms.

Boltz·mann dis·tri·bu·tion another term for **MAXWELL–BOLTZMANN DISTRIBUTION**.

Boltz·mann's con·stant *Chemistry* the ratio of the gas constant to Avogadro's number, equal to 1.381 × 10^{-23} joule per kelvin. (Symbol: **k**)

bo·lus /ˈbōləs/ ▸*n.* (*pl.* **bo·luses**) a small rounded mass of a substance, esp. of chewed food at the moment of swallowing. ■ a type of large pill used in veterinary medicine. ■ *Medicine* a single dose of a drug or other medicinal preparation given all at once. ▷mid 16th cent. denoting a large pill of medicine: via late Latin from Greek *bōlos* 'clod.'

Bol·za·no /bōltˈsänō; bōldˈzänō/ a city in northeastern Italy; pop. 100,000.

bomb /bäm/ ▸*n.* **1** a container filled with explosive, incendiary material, smoke, gas, or other destructive substance, designed to explode on impact or when detonated by a time mechanism, remote-control device, or lit fuse. ■ [with *adj.*] an explosive device fitted into a specified object: *a package bomb.* See also **CAR BOMB**, **LETTER BOMB**. ■ (**the bomb**) nuclear weapons considered collectively as agents of mass destruction: *she joined the fight against the bomb.* ■ a small pressurized container that sprays liquid, foam, or gas: *an aerosol bomb.* **2** a thing resembling a bomb in impact, in particular: ■ (also **volcanic bomb**) a lump of lava thrown out by a volcano. ■ *informal* a movie, play, or other event that fails badly: *that bomb of an old movie.* ■ a long forward pass or hit in a ball game: *a big 40-yard bomb down the middle to tight end Howard Cross.* ■ an old car. ■ (**a bomb**) *Brit., informal* a large sum of money: *it will* **cost a bomb** *in call charges.* **3** *informal* (**da** (or **the**) **bomb**) an outstandingly good person or thing: *the site would really be da bomb if its content were updated more frequently.* **4** *informal* a marijuana cigarette.
▸*v.* **1** [*trans.*] attack (a place or vehicle) with a bomb or bombs: *London was bombed, night after night* | [as *n.*] (**bombing**) *a series of bombings.* **2** [*intrans.*] *informal* (of a movie, play, or other event) fail miserably: *a big-budget movie that bombed at the box office | he* **bombed out** *at several tournaments.* **3** [*intrans.*, with *adverbial of direction*] *Brit. informal* move very quickly: *the bus came bombing along.* ▷late 17th cent.: from French *bombe*, from Italian *bomba*, probably from Latin *bombus* 'booming, humming,' from Greek *bombos*, of imitative origin.
▸*PHRASES* □ **go down a bomb** *Brit. informal* be very well received: *those gigs we did went down a bomb.* □ **it looks like a bomb's hit it** *informal* used to describe a place that is extremely messy or untidy in appearance.

bom·bard ▸*v.* /bämˈbärd/ [*trans.*] attack (a place or person) continuously with bombs, shells, or other missiles: *the city was bombarded by federal forces | supporters* **bombarded** *police* **with** *bottles.* See note at **ATTACK**. ■ assail (someone) persistently, as with questions, criticisms, or information: *they will be* **bombarded with** *complaints.* ■ *Physics* direct a high-speed stream of particles at (a substance).
▸*n.* /ˈbämˌbärd/ *historical* a cannon of the earliest type, which originally fired a stone ball. ▷late Middle English (as a noun denoting an early form of cannon, also a shawm): from Old French *bombarde*, probably based on Latin *bombus* 'booming, humming' (see **BOMB**). The verb (late 16th cent.) is from French *bombarder*. **—bom·bard·ment** /bämˈbärdmənt/ *n.*

bom·barde /ˈbämˌbärd/ ▸*n. Music* a medieval alto-pitched shawm. ▷late Middle English: from Old French, denoting a shawm (see **BOMBARD**).

bom·bar·dier /ˌbämbə(r)ˈdi(ə)r/ ▸*n.* **1** a member of a bomber crew in the U.S. Air Force responsible for sighting and releasing bombs. **2** a rank of noncommissioned officer in certain Canadian and British artillery regiments, equivalent to corporal. ▷mid 16th cent. (denoting a soldier in charge of a *bombard*, an early form of cannon): from French, from Old French *bombarde* 'cannon' (see **BOMBARD**).

bom·bar·dier bee·tle ▸*n.* a ground beetle that when alarmed discharges a puff of hot irritant vapor from its anus with an audible pop. • Genus *Brachinus*, family Carabidae: several species .

bom·bar·don /ˈbämbərdən; bämˈbärdn/ ▸*n. Music* a type of valved bass tuba. ■ an organ stop imitating this. ▷mid 19th cent.: from Italian *bombardone*, from *bombardo* 'cannon.'Compare with **BOMBARDE**.

bom·bast /ˈbämbast/ ▸*n.* high-sounding language with little meaning, used to impress people. ▷mid 16th cent. (denoting raw cotton or absorbent cotton used as padding, later used figuratively): from Old French *bombace*, from medieval Latin *bombax*, *bombac-*, alteration of *bombyx* 'silkworm' (see **BOMBAZINE**). **—bom·bas·tic** /bämˈbastik/ *adj.* **—bom·bas·ti·cal·ly** /bämˈbastik(ə)lē/ *adv.*

Bom·bay /bämˈbā/ a city and port on the western coast of India, capital of the state of Maharashtra; pop. 9,990,000. Official name (from 1995) **MUMBAI**.

Bom·bay duck ▸*n.* the bummalo (fish), esp. when dried and eaten as an accompaniment with curry. ▷mid 19th cent.: alteration of **BUMMALO** by association with **BOMBAY** in India, from which bummalo were exported.

bom·ba·zine /ˌbämbəˈzēn; ˈbämbəˌzēn/ ▸*n.* a twilled dress fabric of worsted and silk or cotton. ▷mid 16th cent. (denoting raw cotton): from French *bombasin*, from medieval Latin *bombacinum*, from *bombycinum*, neuter of *bombycinus* 'silken,' based on Greek *bombux* 'silkworm.'

bomb bay ▸*n.* a compartment in the fuselage of an aircraft in which bombs are held and from which they may be dropped.

bomb dis·pos·al ▸*n.* the defusing or removal and detonation of unexploded and delayed-action bombs.

bombe /bäm(b)/ ▸*n.* a frozen dome-shaped dessert. ■ a dome-shaped mold in which this dessert is made. ▷late 19th cent.: French, literally 'bomb.'

bom·bé /bämˈbā/ ▸*adj.* (of furniture) rounded. ▷early 20th cent.: French, literally 'swollen out.'

bombed /bämd/ ▸*adj.* **1** (of an area or building) subjected to bombing: *the rubble of a bombed house.* **2** *informal* intoxicated by drink or drugs: *"we might as well get* **bombed out of our minds,**" *he said, downing another bottle.*

bombed-out ▸*adj.* **1** [*attrib.*] (of a building or city) destroyed by bombing. **2** *informal* another term for **BOMBED** (sense 2).

bomb·er /ˈbämər/ ▸*n.* **1** an aircraft designed to carry and drop bombs. **2** a person who plants, detonates, or throws bombs in a public place, esp. as a terrorist. **3** *informal* a cigarette containing marijuana. **4** short for **BOMBER JACKET**.

bomb·er jack·et ▸*n.* a short jacket, usually leather, tightly gathered at the waist and cuffs by elasticized bands and typically having a zipper front.

bom·bi·nate /ˈbämbəˌnāt/ ▸*v.* [*intrans.*] *poetic/literary* buzz; hum: [as *adj.*] (**bombinating**) *her head had become a bombinating vacuum.* ▷late 19th cent.: from medieval Latin *bombinat-* 'buzzed,' from the verb *bombinare*, from Latin *bombus* 'humming' (see **BOMBARD**).

bomb·ing run ▸*n.* the part of the flight path of a bomber that brings it into position to release its weapons.

bomb·let /ˈbämlit/ ▸*n.* a small bomb.

bom·bor·a /bämˈbôrə/ ▸*n. Austral.* a wave that forms over a submerged offshore reef or rock, sometimes breaking heavily and producing a dangerous stretch of broken water. ▷1930s: from an Aboriginal word, perhaps Dharuk *bumbora*.

bomb·proof /ˈbäm,pro͞of/ ▸*adj.* strong enough to resist the effects of blast from a bomb.

bomb·shell /ˈbäm,sʜel/ ▸*n.* **1** an overwhelming surprise or disappointment: *the news came as a bombshell.* **2** *informal* a very attractive woman: *a twenty-year-old* ***blonde bombshell.*** **3** *dated* an artillery shell.

bomb·sight /ˈbäm,sīt/ ▸*n.* a mechanical or electronic device used in an aircraft for aiming bombs.

bomb squad ▸*n.* a division of a police force assigned to defuse explosive devices.

Bon /bôn/ (also **O-Bon** /ō ˈbôn/) ▸*n.* a Japanese Buddhist festival held annually in August to honor the dead. Also called **Festival of the Dead** and **Lantern Festival.**

Bon, Cape /bôɴ/ a peninsula in northeastern Tunisia.

bo·na fide /ˈbōnə ,fīd; ˈbänə/ ▸*adj.* genuine; real: *only bona fide members of the company are allowed to use the logo.*
▸*adv. chiefly Law* sincerely; without intention to deceive: *the court will assume that they have acted bona fide.* ▷mid 16th cent.: Latin, literally 'with good faith,' ablative singular of **bona fides.**

bo·na fi·des /ˈbōnə ,fīdz; ˈfīdēz; ˈbänə/ ▸*n.* a person's honesty and sincerity of intention: *he went to great lengths to establish his liberal bona fides.* ■ [treated as *pl.*] *informal* documentary evidence showing a person's legitimacy; credentials: *are you satisfied with my bona fides?* [mid 20th cent.] ▷late 18th cent.: Latin, literally 'good faith.'

Bon·aire /bəˈne(ə)r/ one of the two principal islands of the Netherlands Antilles (the other is Curaçao); chief town, Kralendijk; pop. 10,190.

bo·nan·za /bəˈnanzə/ ▸*n.* [often with *adj.*] a situation or event that creates a sudden increase in wealth, good fortune, or profits: *a bonanza in military sales* | [as *adj.*] *a bonanza year for the computer industry.* ■ a large amount of something desirable: *the festive feature film bonanza.* ▷early 19th cent. (originally U.S., esp. with reference to success when mining): from Spanish, literally 'fair weather, prosperity,' from Latin *bonus* 'good.'

Bo·na·parte /ˈbōnə,pärt/ (Italian **Buo·na·parte** /,bwōnäˈpärtä/) a Corsican family, including the three French rulers named Napoleon.

bon ap·pé·tit /ˈbôn ,apəˈtē/ ▸*exclam.* used as a salutation to a person about to eat. ▷mid 19th cent.: French, literally 'good appetite.'

Bon·a·ven·tu·ra, St. /,bônə,venˈto͝orə/ (1221–74), Franciscan theologian; born *Giovanni di Fidanza*; known as **the Seraphic Doctor**. He wrote the official biography of St. Francis. Feast day, July 15 (formerly 14).

bon·bon /ˈbän,bän/ ▸*n.* a piece of candy, esp. one covered with chocolate. ▷late 18th cent.: from French, reduplication of *bon* 'good,' from Latin *bonus*.

bond /bänd/ ▸*n.* **1** (**bonds**) physical restraints used to hold someone or something prisoner, esp. ropes or chains. ■ a thing used to tie something or to fasten things together: *she brushed back a curl that had strayed from its bonds* | *figurative chaos could result if the bonds of obedience and loyalty were broken.* ■ adhesiveness; ability of two objects to stick to each other: *a total lack of effective bond between the concrete and the steel.* ■ *figurative* a force or feeling that unites people; a common emotion or interest: *there was a bond of understanding between them.* ■ (**bonds**) *figurative* restricting forces or circumstances; obligations: *bonds of loyalty.* **2** an agreement or promise with legal force, in particular: ■ *Law* a deed by which a person is committed to make payment to another. ■ a certificate issued by a government or a public company promising to repay borrowed money at a fixed rate of interest at a specified time. ■ (of dutiable goods) a state of storage in a bonded warehouse until the importer pays the duty owing. ■ an insurance policy held by a company, which protects against losses resulting from circumstances such as bankruptcy or misconduct by employees. **3** (also **chemical bond**) a strong force of attraction holding atoms together in a molecule or crystal, resulting from the sharing or transfer of electrons. **4** [with *adj.*] *Building* any of the various patterns in which bricks are conventionally laid in order to ensure the strength of the resulting structure. See **English bond, Flemish bond.** **5** short for **bond paper.**
▸*v.* **1** join or be joined securely to something else, typically by means of an adhesive substance, heat, or pressure: [*trans.*] *press the material to* ***bond*** *the layers* ***together*** | [*intrans.*] *this material will* ***bond*** *well* ***to*** *stainless steel rods* | [as *adj.*] (**bonding**) *a bonding agent.* ■ [*intrans.*] *figurative* establish a relationship with someone based on shared feelings, interests, or experiences: *the failure to properly* ***bond with*** *their children* | *the team has* ***bonded together*** *well* | [as *n.*] (**bonding**) *the film has some great male bonding scenes.* **2** join or be joined by a chemical bond. **3** [*trans.*] [usu. as *adj.*] (**bonding**) lay (bricks) in an overlapping pattern so as to form a strong structure: *a bonding course.* **4** [usu. as *n.*] (**bonding**) place (dutiable goods) in bond. ▷Middle English: variant of **band**[1].

bond·age /ˈbändij/ ▸*n.* **1** the state of being a slave: *the deliverance of the Israelites from Egypt's bondage.* ■ *figurative* a state of being greatly constrained by circumstances or obligations: *young women lost to the bondage of early motherhood.* **2** sexual practice that involves the tying up or restraining of one partner. ▷Middle English: from Anglo-Latin *bondagium*, from Middle English *bond* 'serf' (earlier 'peasant, householder'), from Old Norse *bóndi* 'tiller of the soil,' based on *búa* 'dwell'; influenced in sense by **bond.**

bond·ed /ˈbändid/ ▸*adj.* [*attrib.*] **1** (of a thing) joined securely to another thing, esp. by an adhesive, a heat process, or pressure: *bonded metal plates.* ■ *figurative* emotionally or psychologically linked: *a strongly bonded group of females.* ■ held by a chemical bond: *bonded atoms.* **2** (of a person or company) bound by a legal agreement, in particular: ■ (of a debt) secured by bonds. ■ (of a worker or workforce) obliged to work for a particular employer, often in a condition close to slavery. **3** (of dutiable goods) placed in bond.

bond·ed ware·house ▸*n.* a customs-controlled warehouse for the retention of imported goods until the duty owed is paid.

bond·maid /ˈbänd,mād/ ▸*n. archaic* a slave girl.

bond·man /ˈbänd,mən/ ▸*n. archaic* a serf; a slave.

bond pa·per ▸*n.* high-quality writing paper.

Bonds /bändz/, Barry (1964–), U.S. baseball player; full name *Barry Lamar Bonds.* The winner of six National League Most Valuable Player awards (1990, 1992, 1993, 2001, 2002, 2003), he played for the San Francisco Giants from 1993 and hit his 700th home run in September 2004, a record matched only by Babe Ruth (1934) and Hank Aaron (1973).

bond·serv·ant /ˈbänd,sərvənt/ ▸*n.* a person bound in service without wages. ■ a slave or serf.

bonds·man /ˈbändzmən/ ▸*n.* (*pl.* **-men**) **1** a person who stands surety for a bond. [early 18th cent.: from **bond** + **man.**] **2** *archaic* a slave. [mid 18th cent.: variant of Middle English *bondman*, from obsolete *bond* 'serf' (see also **bondage**).]

bond·wom·an /ˈbänd,wo͝omən/ ▸*n.* (*pl.* **-wom·en**) a female bondservant or slave.

Bône /bōn/ former name for **Annaba.**

bone /bōn/ ▸*n.* **1** any of the pieces of hard, whitish tissue making up the skeleton in humans and other vertebrates: *his injuries included many broken bones* | *a shoulder bone.*

> The substance of bones is formed by specialized cells (osteoblasts) that secrete around themselves a material containing calcium salts (which provide hardness and strength in compression) and collagen fibers (which provide tensile strength). Many bones have a central cavity containing marrow.

■ (**bones**) a person's body: *he hauled his tired bones upright.* ■ (**bones**) a corpse or skeleton: *the diggers turned up the bones of a fifteen-year-old girl* | *bones of prehistoric mammals.* ■ (**bones**) *figurative* the basic or essential framework of something: *you need to put some flesh on the bones of your idea.* ■ a bone of an animal with meat on it, used as food for people or dogs: *stewed in stock made with a ham bone* | *dogs yelping over a bone.* **2** the calcified material of which bones consist: *an earring of bone.* ■ a substance similar to this such as ivory, dentin, or whalebone. ■ (often **bones**) a thing made of, or once made of, such a substance, for example a pair of dice. **3** the whitish color of bone: *the sandals she had dyed bone to match the small purse.* **4** *vulgar slang* a penis.
▸*v.* **1** [*trans.*] remove the bones from (meat or fish): *while the gumbo is simmering, bone the cooked chicken.* **2** [*intrans.*] (**bone up on**) *informal* study (a subject) intensively, often in preparation for something: *she boned up on languages she had learned long ago and went back to New Guinea.* **3** [*trans.*] *vulgar slang* (of a man) have sexual intercourse with (someone). ▷Old English *bān*, of Germanic origin; related to Dutch *been* and German *Bein.*
▸*PHRASES* □ **a bag of bones** see **bag.** □ **the bare bones** see **bare.** □ **be skin and bones** see **skin.** □ **a bone of contention** a subject or issue over which there is continuing disagreement: *the examination system has long been a serious bone of contention.* □ **close to** (or **near**) **the bone** **1** (of a remark) penetrating and accurate to the point of causing hurt or discomfort. **2** destitute; hard up. □ **cut** (or **pare**) **something to the bone** reduce something to the bare minimum: *costs will have to be cut to the bone.* □ (**as**) **dry as a bone** see **dry.** □ **have a bone to pick with someone** *informal* have reason to disagree or be annoyed with someone. □ **have not a —— bone in one's body** (of a person) have not the slightest trace of the specified quality: *there's not a conservative bone in his body.* □ **in one's bones** felt, believed, or known deeply or instinctively: *he has rhythm in his bones* | *something good was bound to happen; he could* ***feel it in his bones.*** □ **make no bones about something** have no hesitation in stating or dealing with something, however awkward or distasteful it is: *the film is an op-ed piece, and the director makes no bones about its biases.* □ **to the bone** **1** (of a wound) so deep as to expose a person's bone: *his thigh had been axed open to the bone* | (*figurative*) *his contempt cut her to the bone.* ■ (esp. of cold) affecting a person in a penetrating way: *chilled to the bone.* **2** (or **to one's bones**) used to emphasize that a person has a specified quality in an overwhelming or fundamental way: *she's a New Englander to her bones* | *he's a cop to the bone.* □ **throw a bone to** give someone only a token concession: *was the true purpose of the minimum wage hike to throw a bone to the unions?* □ **what's bred in the bone will come out in the flesh** (or **blood**) *proverb* a person's behavior or characteristics are determined by heredity. □ **work one's fingers to the bone** work very hard: *Tracy can work her fingers to the bone, but it's Ms. Green who gets the thanks.*

bone ash ▸*n.* the mineral residue of calcined bones, used chiefly in the production of bone china and fertilizers.

bone black ▸*n.* fine charcoal made by burning animal bones in a closed container, used as a pigment and in the refining of sugar.

bone chi·na ▸*n.* fine china made of clay mixed with bone ash.

boned /bōnd/ ▸*adj.* [*attrib.*] **1** (of meat or fish) having had the bones removed before cooking or serving: *boned turkey with cranberry stuffing.* **2** [in *combination*] (of a person) having bones of the specified type: *she was fine-boned and boyishly slim.* **3** (of a garment) stiffened with strips of plastic or whalebone to give shape to the figure or the garment.

bone-dry ▸*adj.* extremely or completely dry.

bone·fish /ˈbōn,fisʜ/ ▸*n.* (*pl.* same or **-fish·es**) a silvery game fish of warm coastal waters. Also called **ladyfish.** • Family Albulidae and genus *Albula*: several species, in particular *A. vulpes.*

bone·head /ˈbōn,hed/ ▸*n. informal* a stupid person. **—bone·head·ed** *adj.*

bone·less /ˈbōnlis/ ▸*adj.* (of a piece of meat or fish) having had the bones removed. ■ *figurative* (of a person) limp; with loose limbs. ■ *figurative* lacking physical or mental strength: *the slack and boneless character of his writing.* **—bone·less·ly** *adv. he collapsed bonelessly into an easy chair.*

bone mar·row ▸*n.* see **marrow** (sense 1).

bone·meal /ˈbōn,mēl/ ▸*n.* crushed or ground bones used as a fertilizer.

bon·er /ˈbōnər/ ▸*n.* **1** *informal* a stupid mistake. **2** *vulgar slang* an erection of the penis. ▷early 20th cent. (originally U.S.): from **bone** + **-er**[1].

bone·set /ˈbōn,set/ ▸*n.* a North American plant of the daisy family that bears clusters of small flowers and is used in herbal medicine. • Genus *Eupatorium*, family Compositae, several species, in particular the white-flowered *E. perfoliatum* and its purple-flowered form, **purple boneset.** ■ another term for **comfrey.** [its ground-up root was formerly used as a 'plaster' to set broken bones.]

bone·set·ter /ˈbōn,setər/ ▸*n. historical* a person, typically not formally qualified, who sets broken or dislocated bones.

bone spav·in ▸*n.* osteoarthritis of the hock in horses, which may cause swelling and lameness.

bone-wea·ry (also **bone-tired**) ▸*adj.* utterly weary; extremely tired.

bone·yard /ˈbōn,yärd/ ▸*n. informal* a cemetery. ■ a place where discarded cars are kept.

bon·fire /ˈbän,fīr/ ▸*n.* a large open-air fire used as part of a celebration, for burning trash, or as a signal. ▷late Middle English: from BONE + FIRE. The term originally denoted a large open-air fire on which bones were burned (sometimes as part of a celebration), also one for burning heretics or proscribed literature. Dr. Johnson accepted the mistaken idea that the word came from French *bon* 'good.'

B

bong[1] /bäNG/ ▸*n.* a low-pitched sound as of a bell: *the clock had struck the hour, and it was only three bongs.*
▸*v.* [*intrans.*] emit such a sound. ▷1920s (originally U.S.): imitative.

bong[2] ▸*n.* a water pipe used for smoking marijuana or other drugs. ▷1970s: from Thai *baung*, literally 'wooden tube.'

bong[3] ▸*n. Mountaineering* a large piton. ▷1960s: probably imitative of the sound of its being hammered into rock.

bon·go[1] /ˈbäNGgō; ˈbôNG-/ (also **bongo drum**) ▸*n.* (*pl.* **-gos** or **-goes**) either of a pair of small, long-bodied drums typically held between the knees and played with the fingers. ▷1920s: from Latin American Spanish *bongó*.

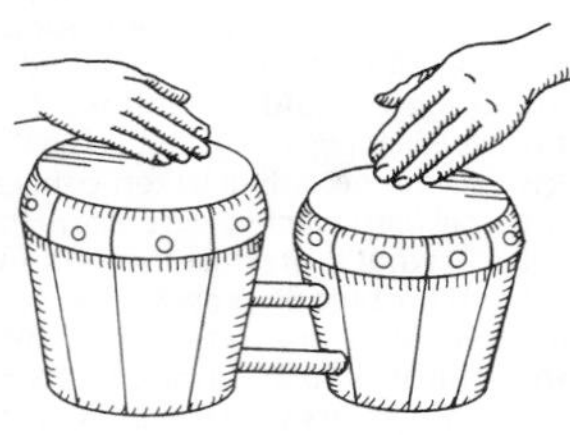

bongo[1]

bon·go[2] ▸*n.* (*pl.* same or **-gos**) a forest antelope that has a chestnut coat with narrow white vertical stripes, native to central Africa. • *Tragelaphus euryceros*, family Bovidae. ▷mid 19th cent.: from Kikongo.

Bon·hoef·fer /ˈbän,hôfər/, Dietrich (1906–45), German Lutheran theologian and pastor. He was an active opponent of Nazism and was involved in the German resistance movement. Arrested in 1943, he was sent to Buchenwald concentration camp and later executed.

bon·ho·mie /ˈbänə,mē; ,bänəˈmē/ ▸*n.* cheerful friendliness; geniality: *he exuded good humor and bonhomie.* ▷late 18th cent.: from French, from *bonhomme* 'good fellow.'

bon·ho·mous /ˈbänəməs/ ▸*adj.* full of cheerful friendliness: *her relaxed, bonhomous nature.* ▷early 20th cent.: from BONHOMIE + -OUS.

bo·ni·a·to /,bānēˈätō/ ▸*n.* a variety of sweet potato with white flesh. ▷American Spanish.

Bon·i·face, St. /ˈbänəfəs/ (680–754), Anglo-Saxon missionary; born *Wynfrith*; known as **the Apostle of Germany**. He was sent to Frisia and Germany to spread the Christian faith and was appointed primate of Germany in 732. He was martyred in Frisia. Feast day, June 5.

bo·ni·to /bəˈnētō/ ▸*n.* (*pl.* **-tos**) a smaller relative of the tunas, with dark oblique stripes on the back and important as a food and game fish. • *Sarda* and related genera, family Scombridae: several species. ■ (also **ocean bonito**) another term for SKIPJACK (sense 1). ▷late 16th cent.: from Spanish.

bonk /bäNGk/ *informal* ▸*v.* **1** [*trans.*] knock or hit (something) so as to cause a reverberating sound: *he bonked his head on the plane's low bulkhead.* **2** [*trans.*] have sexual intercourse with (someone). **3** [*intrans.*] (of a cyclist or runner) reach a point of exhaustion that makes one unable to go further: *I bonked and couldn't pedal another stroke.*
▸*n.* **1** an act of knocking or hitting something that causes a reverberating sound: *give it a bonk with a hammer.* ■ a reverberating sound caused in such a way. **2** an act of sexual intercourse. **3** (**the bonk**) a level of exhaustion that makes a cyclist or runner unable to go further: *we had the bonk when we were saddle sore.* ▷1930s: imitative.

bon·kers /ˈbäNGkərz/ ▸*adj.* [*predic.*] *informal* mad; crazy: *and the fans **go bonkers** | he's driving me bonkers.* ▷1940s: of unknown origin.

bon mot /ˈbän ˈmō; ,bôN ˈmō/ ▸*n.* (*pl.* **bons mots** *pronunc.* same or /ˈmōz/) a witty remark. ▷mid 18th cent.: French, literally 'good word.'

Bonn /bän/ a city in the state of North Rhine-Westphalia in Germany; pop. 296,240. From 1949 until the reunification of Germany in 1990, it was the capital of the Federal Republic of Germany (West Germany).

Bon·nard /bôˈnär/, Pierre (1867–1947), French painter and graphic artist; member of the Nabi Group.

bonne femme /,bän ˈfam/ ▸*adj.* [*postpositive*] (of fish dishes, stews, and soups) cooked in a simple way. ▷French, from the phrase *à la bonne femme* 'in the manner of a good housewife.'

bon·net /ˈbänit/ ▸*n.* **1** a woman's or child's hat tied under the chin, typically with a brim framing the face. ■ (also **war bonnet**) the ceremonial feathered headdress of an American Indian. ■ a soft round brimless hat like a beret, esp. as worn by men and boys in Scotland. ■ *Heraldry* the velvet cap within a coronet. **2** a protective cover or cap over a machine or object, in particular: ■ a cowl on a chimney. ■ *Brit.* the hood of an automobile. **3** *historical, Sailing,* an additional canvas laced to the foot of a sail to catch more wind. ▷late Middle English (denoting a soft brimless hat for men): from Old French *bonet*, from medieval Latin *abonnis* 'headgear.' Sense 1 dates from the late 15th cent. —**bon·net·ed** *adj.* (in sense 1).

Bon·ne·ville Dam /ˈbänə,vil/ hydroelectric dam built in the 1930s on the Columbia River, east of Portland in Oregon.

Bon·ne·ville Salt Flats a desert in northwestern Utah, west of the Great Salt Lake, noted as the site of automotive speed trials.

Bon·ney /ˈbänē/, William H. (1859–81), U.S. outlaw; born *Henry McCarty*; known as **Billy the Kid**. A notorious robber and murderer, he was captured by Sheriff Pat Garrett in 1880 and was shot by Garrett after he had escaped from jail.

Bon·nie Prince Char·lie /ˈbänē ,prins ˈCHärlē/ see STUART[1].

bon·ny /ˈbänē/ (also **bon·nie**) *chiefly Scottish & N. Engl.* ▸*adj.* (**-ni·er**, **-ni·est**) attractive; beautiful: *a bonny lass.* ■ (of a baby) plump and healthy-looking. ■ sizable; considerable (usually expressing approval): *it's worth a thousand pounds, a bonny sum.*
▸*n.* (**my bonny**) *poetic/literary* used as a form of address for one's beloved or baby. ▷late 15th cent.: perhaps related to Old French *bon* 'good.' —**bon·ni·ly** /ˈbänəlē/ *adv.* —**bon·ni·ness** *n.*

bon·ny clab·ber ▸*n.* another term for CLABBER. ▷early 17th cent.: from Irish *bainne clabair*, denoting thick milk for churning.

Bo·no /ˈbōnō/, Sonny (1935–98), U.S. entertainer and politician; born Salvatore Bono. Famed as half of the singing duo Sonny and Cher 1964–74, he became a Republican politician. He was elected mayor of Palm Springs, California, in 1988 and served in the U.S. House of Representatives 1995–98. He died in a skiing accident.

bo·no·bo /bəˈnōbō/ ▸*n.* (*pl.* **-bos**) a chimpanzee with a black face and black hair, found in the rain forests of the Democratic Republic of the Congo (formerly Zaire). Also called PYGMY CHIMPANZEE. • *Pan paniscus*, family Pongidae. ▷1950s: a local word.

bon·sai /bänˈsī; ˈbänsī/ ▸*n.* (*pl.* same) (also **bonsai tree**) an ornamental tree or shrub grown in a pot and artificially prevented from reaching its normal size. ■ the art of growing trees or shrubs in such a way. ▷1950s: from Japanese, from *bon* 'tray' + *sai* 'planting.'

bons mots /ˈmōz/ ▸*n.* plural form of BON MOT.

bon·spiel /ˈbän,spēl/ ▸*n. chiefly Scottish & Canadian* a curling match. ▷mid 16th cent.: probably of Low German origin.

bon·te·bok /ˈbäntē,bäk/ ▸*n.* (*pl.* same or **-boks**) an antelope with a mainly reddish-brown coat and white face, found in eastern South Africa. It belongs to the same species as the blesbok. • *Damaliscus dorcas dorcas*, family Bovidae. ▷late 18th cent.: from Afrikaans, from Dutch *bont* 'pied' + *bok* 'buck.'

bon ton /bän ˈtän; bôN ˈtôN/ ▸*n.* the fashionable world. ▷French, literally 'good taste'.

bo·nus /ˈbōnəs/ ▸*n.* a payment or gift added to what is usual or expected, in particular: See note at PRESENT. ■ an amount of money added to wages on a seasonal basis, esp. as a reward for good performance: *big Christmas bonuses.* ■ something welcome and often unexpected that accompanies and enhances something that is itself good: *good weather is **an added bonus** but the real appeal is the landscape.* ■ *Basketball* an extra free throw awarded to a fouled player when the opposing team has exceeded the number of team fouls allowed during a period. ■ *Brit.* an extra dividend or issue paid to the shareholders of a company. ■ *Brit.* a distribution of profits to holders of an insurance policy. ▷late 18th cent. (probably originally London stock-exchange slang): from Latin *bonus* (masculine) 'good,' used in place of *bonum* (neuter) 'good, good thing.' Compare with BOON[2].

bon vi·vant /ˈbän vēˈvänt; ,bôN vēˈväN/ ▸*n.* (*pl.* **bon vi·vants** or **bons vi·vants** *pronunc.* same or /-ˈvänts/) a person who enjoys a sociable and luxurious lifestyle. ▷late 17th cent.: from French, literally 'person living well,' from *bon* 'good' and *vivre* 'to live.'

bon vi·veur /ˈbän vēˈvər; ,bôN vēˈvœr/ ▸*n.* (*pl.* **bon vi·veurs** or **bons vi·veurs** *pronunc.* same or /-ˈvərz/) another term for BON VIVANT. ▷mid 19th cent.: pseudo-French, from French *bon* 'good' and *viveur* 'a living person,' on the pattern of *bon vivant*.

bon vo·yage /ˈbän voiˈäZH; ˈbōn; bôē/ ▸*exclam.* used to express good wishes to someone about to go on a journey: *good luck and bon voyage! | they had come to **wish** her **bon voyage**.* ▷late 17th cent.: French, literally 'good journey.'

bon·y /ˈbōnē/ ▸*adj.* (**bon·i·er**, **bon·i·est**) of or like bone: *the bony plates that protect turtles and tortoises.* ■ (of a person or part of the body) so thin that the bones are prominent: *he held up his bony fingers.* ■ (of a fish eaten as food) having many bones. —**bon·i·ness** *n.*

bon·y fish ▸*n.* a fish of a large class distinguished by a skeleton of bone, and comprising the majority of modern fishes. Compare with CARTILAGINOUS FISH. • Class Osteichthyes: two or three subclasses.

bon·y lab·y·rinth ▸*n.* see LABYRINTH.

bonze /bänz/ ▸*n.* a Japanese or Chinese Buddhist monk. ▷late 16th cent.: probably from Japanese *bonzō, bonsō* 'priest.'

bon·zer /ˈbänzər/ ▸*adj. Austral./NZ, informal* excellent, first-rate. ▷early 20th cent.: perhaps an alteration of BONANZA.

boo /bo͞o/ ▸*exclam.* **1** said suddenly to surprise someone: *"Boo!" she cried, jumping up to frighten him.* [probably an alteration of earlier *bo*, used in the same way since late Middle English.] **2** said to show disapproval or contempt, esp. at a performance or athletic contest.
▸*n.* an utterance of "boo" to show disapproval or contempt: *the audience greeted this comment with boos and hisses.*
▸*v.* (**boos**, **booed**) say "boo" to show disapproval or contempt: [*intrans.*] *they booed and hissed when he stepped on stage* | [*trans.*] *I was practically **booed off the stage** for talking about cyberpunk.* ▷early 19th cent. (sense 2): imitative of the lowing of oxen. The sound was considered to be derisive; compare with HISS and HOOT.
▸*PHRASES* □ **say boo** [with *negative*] say anything at all; utter a sound: *Walter looked at us, but he didn't say boo.* □ **wouldn't say boo to a goose** *Brit.* used to emphasize that someone is very shy or reticent.

boob[1] /bo͞ob/ *informal* ▸*n.* **1** a foolish or stupid person: *why was that boob given a key investigation?* **2** *Brit.* an embarrassing mistake. ▷early 20th cent.: abbreviation of BOOBY[1].

boob[2] ▸*n.* (usu. **boobs**) *informal* a woman's breast. ▷1950s (originally U.S.): abbreviation of BOOBY[2], from dialect *bubby*, of uncertain origin; perhaps related to German dialect *Bübbi* 'teat.'

boob·oi·sie /,bo͞obwäˈzē/ ▸*n. informal* stupid people as a class. ▷1920s: from BOOB[1], humorous formation on the pattern of *bourgeoisie*.

boo-boo ▸*n. informal* a mistake: *you could make a big boo-boo if you leap to any drastic conclusions.* ■ *informal* a minor injury, such as a scratch: *there is no one to kiss the boo-boo!* ▷1950s (originally U.S.): reduplication of BOOB[1].

boob tube *informal* ▸*n.* (usu. **the boob tube**) television or a television set: *librarians are scrambling for ways to compete with the boob tube.*

boo·by[1] /ˈbo͞obē/ ▸*n.* (*pl.* **-bies**) **1** a stupid or childish person. **2** a large tropical seabird of the gannet family, with brown, black, or white plumage and often brightly colored feet. • Genus *Sula*, family Sulidae: several species, including the common **red-footed booby** (*S. sula*). ▷early 17th cent.: probably from Spanish *bobo* (in both senses), from Latin *balbus* 'stammering.'

boo·by[2] ▸*n.* (*pl.* **-bies**) (usu. **boobies**) *informal* a woman's breast. ▷1930s: alteration of dialect *bubby* (see BOOB[2]).

boo·by hatch ▸*n. informal, offensive* a psychiatric hospital.

boo·by prize ▸*n.* a prize given as a joke to the last-place finisher in a race or competition.

boo·by trap ▸*n.* a thing designed to catch the unwary, in particular: ■ an apparently harmless object containing a concealed explosive device designed to kill or injure anyone who touches it: *miles of mines, booby traps, and underground fortifications.* ■ a trap intended as a practical joke, such as an object placed on top of a door ajar ready to fall on the next person to pass through.
▸*v.* (**boob·y-trap**) [*trans.*] place a booby trap in or on (an object or area): [as *adj.*] (**booby-trapped**) *the area was heavily mined and booby-trapped.*

boo·dle /ˈbo͞odl/ ▸*n.* **1** *informal* money, esp. that gained or spent illegally or improperly: *he spent $30 million of his own boodle trying to buy a Senate seat.* **2** (**boodles**) a great quantity, esp. of money: *Scandinavian Air has boodles of seats for America | the men expected to make boodles.* ▷early 17th cent. (denoting a pack or crowd): from Dutch *boedel, boel* 'possessions, disorderly mass.' Compare with **CABOODLE.**

boo·ga·loo /ˈbo͞ogəˌlo͞o/ ▸*n.* a modern dance to rock-and-roll music performed with swiveling and shuffling movements of the body, originally popular in the 1960s.
▸*v.* (**-loos, -looed**) [*intrans.*] perform this dance. ▷1960s: perhaps an alteration of **BOOGIE-WOOGIE** (see **BOOGIE**).

boog·er /ˈbo͞ogər/ ▸*n.* **1** another term for **BOGEYMAN.** **2** *informal* a piece of dried nasal mucus.

boog·ey·man ▸*n.* variant spelling of **BOGEYMAN.**

boog·ie /ˈbo͝ogē/ ▸*n.* (also **boog·ie-woog·ie** /ˈwo͝ogē/) (*pl.* **boog·ies**) a style of blues played on the piano with a strong, fast beat. ■ *informal* a dance to fast pop or rock music.
▸*v.* (**boog·ie·ing**) [*intrans.*] *informal* dance to fast pop or rock music: *ready to* **boogie down** *to the music of the house band | he can* **boogie the night away.** ■ [*intrans.*] move or leave somewhere fast: *I think we'd better* **boogie on out of here.** ▷early 20th cent. (originally U.S. in the sense 'party'): of unknown origin.

boog·ie board ▸*n.* a short light type of surfboard ridden in a prone position. —**boog·ie board·er** *n.*

boo·hoo /ˈbo͞oˈho͞o/ ▸*exclam.* used to represent the sound of someone crying noisily.
▸*v.* (**-hoos, -hooed**) [*intrans.*] cry noisily: *she broke down and boohooed.* ▷mid 19th cent.: imitative.

boo·jum /ˈbo͞ojəm/ ▸*n.* an imaginary dangerous animal. ▷late 19th cent.: nonsense word coined by Lewis Carroll.

book /bo͝ok/ ▸*n.* **1** a written or printed work consisting of pages glued or sewn together along one side and bound in covers: *a book of selected poems | a* **book on** *cats |* [as *adj.*] *a book report.* ■ a literary composition that is published or intended for publication as such a work: *the book is set in the 1940s | I'm writing a book.* ■ (**the books**) used to refer to studying: *he is so deep in his books he would forget to eat.* ■ a main division of a classic literary work, an epic, or the Bible: *the Book of Genesis.* ■ the libretto of an opera or musical, or the script of a play. ■ (**the book**) the local telephone directory: *is your name in the book?* ■ (**the Book**) the Bible. ■ *informal* a magazine. ■ *figurative* an imaginary record or list (often used to emphasize the thoroughness or comprehensiveness of someone's actions or experiences): *she felt every emotion in the book of love.* **2** [with *adj.*] a bound set of blank sheets for writing or keeping records in: *an accounts book.* ■ (**books**) a set of records or accounts: *he can do more than* **balance the books.** ■ a bookmaker's record of bets accepted and money paid out. **3** a set of tickets, stamps, matches, checks, samples of cloth, etc., bound together: *a pattern book | a book of matches.* ■ (**the book**) the first six tricks taken by the declarer in a hand of bridge.
▸*v.* [*trans.*] **1** reserve (accommodations, a place, etc.); buy (a ticket) in advance: *I have booked a table at the Swan |* [*intrans.*] *book early to avoid disappointment.* ■ reserve accommodations for (someone): *his secretary had* **booked** *him* **into** *the Howard Hotel* [with *two objs.*] *book me a single room at my usual hotel.* ■ engage (a performer or guest) for an occasion or event. ■ (**be booked** (**up**)) have all appointments or places reserved; be full: *I'm booked till, like, 2008.* **2** make an official record of the name and other personal details of (a criminal suspect or offender): *the cop booked me and took me down to the station.* ▷Old English *bōc* (originally also 'a document or charter'), *bōcian* 'to grant by charter,' of Germanic origin; related to Dutch *boek* and German *Buch,* and probably to **BEECH** (on which runes were carved). —**book·a·ble** *adj.*
▸*PHRASES* □ **bring someone to book** bring someone to justice; punish. □ **by the book** strictly according to the rules: *a cop who doesn't exactly* **play it by the book.** □ **close the book on** lay aside; expend no further energy on: *Congress closed the book on wool subsidies.* □ **in someone's bad** (or **good**) **books** *chiefly Brit.* in disfavor (or favor) with a person. □ **in my book** in my opinion: *that counts as a lie in my book.* □ **make book** take bets on the outcome of an event: *figurative I wouldn't make book on it.* □ **one for the books** an extraordinary feat or event. □ **on the books** contained in a book of laws or records: *discriminatory laws still on the books | the longest pitching career on the books.* □ **People of the Book** Jews and Christians as regarded by Muslims. □ **suit one's book** *Brit.* be convenient to one: *it didn't suit her book at all to be moved.* □ **take a leaf from** (or **out of**) **someone's book** imitate or emulate someone in a particular way: *Gorbachev must take a leaf from Deng's book and offer tangible benefits.* □ **throw the book at** *informal* charge or punish (someone) as severely as possible. □ **wrote the book** be the leader in the field: *John wrote the book on goatpacking.* □ **you can't judge a book by its cover** *proverb* outward appearances are not a reliable indication of true character.

book·bind·er /ˈbo͝okˌbīndər/ ▸*n.* a person who binds books as a profession. —**book·bind·ing** /-ˌbīndiNG/ *n.*

book·case /ˈbo͝okˌkās/ ▸*n.* a set of shelves for books set in a surrounding frame or cabinet.

book club ▸*n.* an organization that sells selected books to members or subscribers, often from a mail-order catalog.

book·end /ˈbo͝okˌend/ ▸*n.* a support for the end of a row of books to keep them upright, often one of a pair.
▸*v.* [*trans.*] (usu. **be bookended**) *informal* occur or be positioned at the end or on either side of (something): *the narrative is bookended by a pair of incisive essays.*

book·er /ˈbo͝okər/ ▸*n.* short for **BOOKING AGENT.**

Book·er Prize /ˈbo͝okər/ a literary prize awarded annually for a novel published by a British or Commonwealth citizen during the previous year, financed by the multinational company Booker McConnell.

book hand ▸*n.* a formal style of handwriting as used by professional copiers of books before the invention of printing.

book·ie /ˈbo͝okē/ ▸*n.* (*pl.* **-ies**) informal term for **BOOKMAKER.**

book·ing /ˈbo͝okiNG/ ▸*n.* an act of reserving accommodations, travel, etc., or of buying a ticket in advance: *the hotel does not handle group bookings | early booking is essential.* ■ an engagement for a performance by an entertainer: *TV show bookings were mysteriously canceled.*

book·ing a·gent ▸*n.* a person who makes engagements or reservations for others, in particular: ■ a person who arranges concert or club engagements for performers. ■ a person who makes travel arrangements for clients.

book·ing clerk ▸*n. Brit.* an official selling tickets, esp. at a railroad station.

book·ing hall (also **booking office**) ▸*n. Brit.* a room or area at a railroad station in which tickets are sold.

book·ish /ˈbo͝okiSH/ ▸*adj.* (of a person or way of life) devoted to reading and studying rather than worldly interests: *by comparison I was very bookish, intellectual, and worldy in a wrong way.* ■ (of language or writing) literary in style or allusion: *long bookish scholarship | a bookish but eloquent erotic memoir.* —**book·ish·ly** *adv.* —**book·ish·ness** *n.*

book·keep·ing /ˈbo͝okˌkēpiNG/ ▸*n.* the activity or occupation of keeping records of the financial affairs of a business. —**book·keep·er** /-ˌkēpər/ *n.*

book learn·ing ▸*n.* knowledge gained from books or study; mere theory: *knowledge based on experience rather than book learning.*

book·let /ˈbo͝oklit/ ▸*n.* a small book consisting of a few sheets, typically with paper covers.

book·louse /ˈbo͝okˌlous/ ▸*n.* (*pl.* **-lice**) a minute insect that typically has reduced or absent wings and often lives in books or papers, where it feeds on mold. • Liposcelidae and related families in the order Psocoptera: many species.

book lung ▸*n. Zoology* (in a spider or other arachnid) each of a pair of respiratory organs composed of many fine leaves. They are situated in the abdomen and have openings on the underside.

book·mak·er /ˈbo͝okˌmākər/ ▸*n.* a person who takes bets (esp. on horse races) calculates odds, and pays out winnings. —**book·mak·ing** /-ˌmākiNG/ *n.*

book·man /ˈbo͝okmən/ ▸*n.* (*pl.* **-men**) a literary person, esp. one involved in the business of books.

book·mark /ˈbo͝okˌmärk/ ▸*n.* a strip of leather, cardboard, or other material, used to mark one's place in a book. ■ *Computing* a record of the address of a file, web page, or other data used to enable quick access by a user.
▸*v. Computing* record the address of (a file, web page, or other data) for quick access by a user: *if you think politics is the ultimate game, be sure to bookmark eVote.*

book·mo·bile /ˈbo͝okməˌbēl/ ▸*n.* a truck, van, or trailer serving as a mobile library. ▷1930s: from **BOOK,** on the pattern of *automobile.*

Book of Chang·es ▸*n.* another name for **I CHING.**

Book of Com·mon Prayer ▸*n.* the official service book of the Church of England and, with some variation, of other churches of the Anglican Communion. It was compiled by Thomas Cranmer and others and first issued in 1549.

book of hours ▸*n.* (in the Christian Church) a book containing the prayers or offices to be said at the canonical hours of the day, particularly popular in the Middle Ages.

book page ▸*n.* **1** a page of a book. **2** a page of a newspaper or magazine devoted to book reviews.

book·plate /ˈbo͝okˌplāt/ ▸*n.* a decorative label stuck in the front of a book, bearing the name of the book's owner.

book·rack /ˈbo͝okˌrak/ ▸*n.* a rack or shelf for books. ■ a stand or rack for holding an open book. Also called **BOOKSTAND.**

book·sell·er /ˈbo͝okˌselər/ ▸*n.* a person who sells books, esp. as the owner or manager of a bookstore.

book·shelf /ˈbo͝okˌSHelf/ ▸*n.* (*pl.* **-shelves**) a shelf on which books can be stored.

book·stall /ˈbo͝okˌstôl/ ▸*n.* a stand where books are sold, typically secondhand. ■ *chiefly Brit.* a newsstand.

book·stand /ˈbo͝okˌstand/ ▸*n.* **1** another term for **BOOKSTALL.** **2** another term for **BOOKRACK.**

book·store /ˈbo͝okˌstôr/ (also *chiefly Brit.* **book·shop** /-ˌSHäp/) ▸*n.* a store where books are sold.

book val·ue ▸*n.* the value of a security or asset as entered in a company's books. Often contrasted with **MARKET VALUE.**

book·work /ˈbo͝okˌwərk/ ▸*n.* **1** the activity of keeping records of accounts: *the bookwork has a tendency to pile up if I don't keep on top of it.* **2** the studying of textbooks, as opposed to practical work: *he concentrates mainly on the flying, but the heavy bookwork is in there too.*

book·worm /ˈbo͝okˌwərm/ ▸*n.* **1** *informal* a person devoted to reading. **2** the larva of a wood-boring beetle that feeds on the paper and glue in books.

Boole /bo͞ol/, George (1815–64), English mathematician; responsible for Boolean algebra. The study of mathematical or symbolic logic developed mainly from his ideas.

Bool·e·an /ˈbo͞olēən/ ▸*adj.* denoting a system of algebraic notation used to represent logical propositions, esp. in computing and electronics.
▸*n. Computing* a binary variable, having two possible values called "true" and "false." ▷mid 19th cent.: from the name of G. **BOOLE** + **-AN.**

boom[1] /bo͞om/ ▸*n.* a loud, deep, resonant sound: *the deep boom of the bass drum.* ■ the characteristic resonant call of the bittern.
▸*v.* [*intrans.*] make a loud, deep, resonant sound: *thunder boomed in the sky | her voice* **boomed out.** ■ [with *direct speech*] say in a loud, deep, resonant voice: *the imperative "Silence!" boomed out by Ray himself.* ■ (of a bittern) utter its characteristic resonant call. ▷late Middle English (as a verb): ultimately imitative; perhaps from Dutch *bommen* 'to hum, buzz.' —**boom·y** *adj.*

boom[2] ▸*n.* a period of great prosperity or rapid economic growth: *a boom in precious metal mining |* [as *adj.*] *a boom economy.*
▸*v.* [*intrans.*] enjoy a period of great prosperity or rapid economic growth: *business is booming | the popularity of soy-based foods has boomed in the last two decades.* ▷late 19th cent. (originally U.S.): probably from **BOOM**[1]. —**boom·let** /ˈbo͞omlit/ *n.* —**boom·y** *adj.*

boom[3] ▸*n.* a long pole or rod, in particular: ■ a spar

B

pivoting on the after side of the mast and to which the foot of a vessel's sail is attached, allowing the angle of the sail to be changed. ■ [often as *adj.*] a movable arm over a television or movie set, carrying a microphone or camera: *a boom mike.* ■ a long beam extending upward at an angle from the mast of a derrick, for guiding or supporting objects being moved or suspended. ■ a floating beam used to contain oil spills or to form a barrier across the mouth of a harbor or river. ■ a retractable tube for inflight transferral of fuel from a tanker airplane to another airplane. ▷mid 16th cent. (in the general sense 'beam, pole'): from Dutch, 'beam, tree, pole'; related to BEAM.

boom box ▸*n. informal* a portable sound system, typically including radio and cassette or CD player, capable of powerful sound: *teenagers dance to boom boxes on warm April nights.*

boom·er /ˈbo͞omər/ ▸*n. informal* **1** short for BABY BOOMER (see BABY BOOM). **2** something large or notable of its kind, in particular: ■ *Austral.* a large male kangaroo. ■ a large wave. **3** *informal* a nuclear submarine with ballistic missiles. **4** a transient construction worker, esp. a bridge builder. **5** another name for MOUNTAIN BEAVER. ▷early 19th cent.: probably from the verb BOOM[1] + -ER[1].

boo·mer·ang /ˈbo͞oməˌraNG/ ▸*n.* a curved flat piece of wood that can be thrown so as to return to the thrower, traditionally used by Australian Aboriginals as a hunting weapon.

▸*v.* [*intrans.*] (of a plan or action) return to the originator, often with negative consequences: *misleading consumers about quality will eventually* **boomerang on** *a carmaker.* ▷early 19th cent.: from Dharuk.

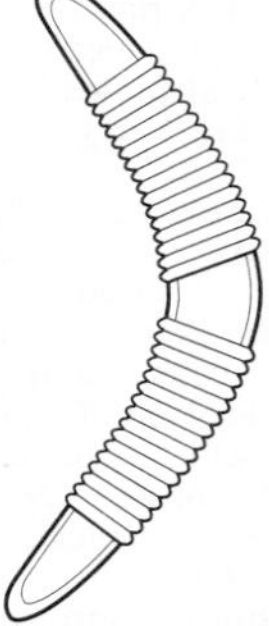
boomerang

boo·mer·ang kid (also **boo·mer·ang·er** /ˈbo͞oməˌraNGər/) ▸*n. informal* a young adult who goes back to live with a parent after a period of independence. ▷allusion to a *boomerang*, which is thrown so as to return to the thrower.

Boom·er State a nickname for the state of OKLAHOMA.

boom·ing /ˈbo͞omiNG/ ▸*adj.* **1** having a period of great prosperity or rapid economic growth: *the booming economy of southern China.* **2** (of a sound or voice) loud, deep, and resonant: *his booming voice | a booming laugh.*

boom·slang /ˈbo͞omˌslaNG/ ▸*n.* a large, highly venomous southern African tree snake, the male of which is bright green and the female dull olive brown. • *Dispholidus typus*, family Colubridae. ▷late 18th cent.: from Afrikaans, from Dutch *boom* 'tree' + *slang* 'snake.'

boom town (also **boom·town**) ▸*n.* a town undergoing rapid growth due to sudden prosperity: *the automobile was in its heady adolescence, and Detroit was America's newest boom town.*

boon[1] /bo͞on/ ▸*n.* **1** [usu. in *sing.*] a thing that is helpful or beneficial: *the navigation system will be a* **boon to** *both civilian and military users.* **2** *archaic* a favor or request: *may I have the inestimable boon of a few minutes' conversation?* ▷Middle English (originally in the sense 'request for a favor'): from Old Norse *bón.*

boon[2] ▸*adj.* (of a companion or friend) close; intimate; favorite: *he debated the question with a few* **boon companions** *in the barroom.* ▷mid 16th cent.: *boon* from Old French *bon*, from Latin *bonus* 'good.' The early literal sense was 'good fellow,' originally denoting a drinking companion.

boon·docks /ˈbo͞onˌdäks/ ▸*plural n. informal* rough, remote, or isolated country: *we're out here in the boondocks, miles from a telephone.* ▷1940s: *boondock* from Tagalog *bundok* 'mountain.'

boon·dog·gle /ˈbo͞onˌdägəl; -ˌdôgəl/ *informal* ▸*n.* work or activity that is wasteful or pointless but gives the appearance of having value: *writing off the cold fusion phenomenon as a boondoggle best buried in literature.* ■ a public project of questionable merit that typically involves political patronage and graft: *they each drew $600,000 in the final months of the great boondoggle.*

▸*v.* [*intrans.*] waste money or time on such projects. ▷1930s: of unknown origin.

Boone /bo͞on/, Daniel (*c.*1734–1820), American pioneer. He made trips west from North Carolina into the unexplored area that is now Kentucky, organizing settlements and successfully defending them against hostile Indians. He later moved further west to what is now Missouri, having been granted land there in 1799.

boon·ies /ˈbo͞onēz/ ▸*plural n.* short for BOONDOCKS.

boor /bo͝or/ ▸*n.* a rude, unmannerly person: *at last the big obnoxious boor had been dealt a stunning blow for his uncouth and belligerent manner.* ■ a clumsy person. ■ a peasant; a yokel. ▷mid 16th cent. (in the sense 'peasant'): from Low German *būr* or Dutch *boer* 'farmer.' Compare with BOER. **—boor·ish** *adj.* **—boor·ish·ly** *adv.* **—boor·ish·ness** *n.*

boost /bo͞ost/ ▸*v.* [*trans.*] help or encourage (something) to increase or improve: *a range of measures to boost tourism.* ■ push from below; assist: *people they were trying to boost over a wall.* ■ amplify (an electrical signal). ■ *informal* steal, esp. by shoplifting or pickpocketing.

▸*n.* a source of help or encouragement leading to increase or improvement: *the cut in interest rates will give a further boost to the economy.* ■ an increase or improvement: *a boost in exports.* ■ a push from below. ▷early 19th cent. (originally in the sense 'push from below'): of unknown origin.

boost·er /ˈbo͞ostər/ ▸*n.* **1** a person or thing that helps increase or promote something, in particular: ■ a keen promoter of a person, organization, or cause: [as *adj.*] *athletic booster clubs.* ■ [in *combination*] a source of help or encouragement: *job fairs are a great morale booster.* ■ *Medicine* a dose of an immunizing agent increasing or renewing the effect of an earlier one. ■ the first stage of a rocket or spacecraft, used to give initial acceleration. ■ a device for increasing electrical voltage or signal strength. **2** *informal* a shoplifter.

boost·er ca·ble ▸*n.* another term for JUMPER CABLE.

boost·er·ish /ˈbo͞ostəriSH/ ▸*adj.* supporting or promoting something enthusiastically, and often uncritically: *the city's boosterish slogan "La Porte's on the Move."*

boost·er·ism /ˈbo͞ostəˌrizəm/ ▸*n.* the enthusiastic promotion of a person, organization, or cause: *a barrage of boosterism about the wonderful recreation facilities.*

boost·er seat ▸*n.* an extra seat or cushion placed on an existing seat for a small child to sit on.

boot[1] /bo͞ot/ ▸*n.* **1** a sturdy item of footwear covering the foot, the ankle, and sometimes the leg below the knee: *walking boots.* ■ a covering or sheath to protect a mechanical connection, as on a gearshift. ■ (also **Denver boot**) a clamp placed by the police on the wheel of an illegally parked vehicle to make it immobile. ■ a covering to protect the lower part of a horse's leg. ■ *historical* an instrument of torture encasing and crushing the foot. **2** *informal* a hard kick: *I* **got a boot in** *the stomach.* **3** *Brit.* the trunk of a car. **4** (also **boot up**) [usu. as *adj.*] the process of starting a computer and putting it into a state of readiness for operation: *a boot disk.* **5** *Military* a navy or marine recruit.

▸*v.* [*trans.*] **1** [usu. as *adj.*] (**booted**) place boots on (oneself, another person, or an animal): *thin, booted legs.* **2** [*trans.*] kick (something) hard in a specified direction: *he ended up booting the ball into the stands.* ■ (in an athletic contest) misplay (a ball); mishandle (a play): *the usually dependable infielder booted the ball.* ■ (**boot someone off**) force someone to leave a vehicle unceremoniously: *the driver booted two teenagers off the bus.* ■ (**boot someone out**) *informal* force someone to leave a place, institution, or job unceremoniously: *she had* **been booted out of** *school.* **3** start (a computer) and put it into a state of readiness for operation: *the menu will be ready as soon as you* **boot up** *your computer | [intrans.] the system won't* **boot from** *the original drive.* [from sense 2 of BOOTSTRAP.] **4** place a Denver boot on (an illegally parked car). ▷Middle English: from Old Norse *bóti* or its source, Old French *bote*, of unknown ultimate origin.

▸*PHRASES* □ **die with one's boots on** die in battle or while otherwise actively occupied. □ **get the boot** *informal* be dismissed from one's job. □ **give someone the boot** *informal* dismiss someone from their job. □ **one's heart sank** (or **fell**) **into one's boots** used to refer to a sudden onset of depression or dismay: *the way your heart drops to your boots if your foal has terribly crooked legs.* □ **you** (**can**) **bet your boots** *informal* used to express certainty about a situation or statement: *you can bet your boots that patrol has raised the alarm.*

boot[2] ▸*n.* (in phrase **to boot**) as well; in addition: *images that are precise, revealing, and often beautiful to boot.* ▷originally 'something extra thrown into a bargain', fromOld English *bōt* 'advantage, remedy,' of Germanic origin; related to Dutch *boete* and German *Busse* 'penance, fine,' also to BETTER[1] and BEST.

boot·a·ble /ˈbo͞otəbəl/ ▸*adj.* (of a disk) containing the software required to boot a computer.

boot·black /ˈbo͞otˌblak/ ▸*n. chiefly historical* a person employed to polish boots and shoes.

boot camp ▸*n.* a military training camp for new recruits, with strict discipline. ■ a prison for youthful offenders, run on military lines.

boot-cut (also **bootcut**) ▸*adj.* (of jeans or other trousers) flared very slightly below the knee, so as to be worn comfortably over boots.

boot·ee /ˈbo͞otē; bo͞oˈtē/ ▸*n.* (*pl.* **-ees**) variant spelling of BOOTIE.

Bo·ö·tes /bōˈōtēz/ *Astronomy* a northern constellation (the Herdsman), said to represent a man holding the leash of two dogs (Canes Venatici) while driving a bear (Ursa Major). It contains the bright star Arcturus. ■ [as *genitive*] (**Boötis** /-ˈōtis/) used with a preceding letter or numeral to designate stars: *the star Gamma Boötis.* ▷Greek.

Booth[1] /bo͞oTH/, John Wilkes (1838–65), U.S. actor. He is better known as the assassin of President Abraham Lincoln at Ford's Theater in Washington, DC.

Booth[2], William (1829–1912), English religious leader; founder and first general of the Salvation Army.

booth /bo͞oTH/ ▸*n.* **1** a small temporary tent or structure, used esp. for the sale or display of goods at a market or fair: *there are booths offering everything from accessories to food to health care.* ■ a small room where a vendor sits separated from customers by a window: *a ticket booth.* **2** an enclosure or compartment for various purposes, such as telephoning, broadcasting, or voting: *the phone booth alongside the highway | ex-athletes in the broadcast booth.* **3** a set of a table and benches in a restaurant or bar: *I sat in a booth with coffee and a roll.* ▷Middle English (in the general sense 'temporary dwelling or shelter'): from Old Norse *buth*, based on *búa* 'dwell.'

Boo·thi·a, Gulf of /ˈbo͞oTHēə/ a gulf in the Canadian Arctic Ocean, in Northwest Territories, between Boothia Peninsula and Baffin Island. ▷named in honor of Sir Felix *Booth* (1775–1850), patron of the expedition to the Arctic (1829–33) led by Sir John Ross.

Boo·thi·a Pen·in·su·la a peninsula in northern Canada, in the Northwest Territories, located between Victoria and Baffin islands.

boot·ie /ˈbo͞otē/ (also **boot·ee**) ▸*n.* (*pl.* **-ies**) **1** a soft shoe, typically knitted, worn by a baby. ■ any soft, socklike shoe. **2** a protective shoe or lining for a shoe. **3** a woman's short boot.

boot·jack /ˈbo͞otˌjak/ ▸*n.* a device for holding a boot by the heel to ease withdrawal of one's foot.

boot·lace /ˈbo͞otˌlās/ ▸*n.* a cord or leather strip for lacing boots.

boot·leg /ˈbo͞otˌleg/ ▸*adj.* [*attrib.*] (esp. of liquor, computer software, or recordings) made, distributed, or sold illegally: *bootleg cassettes | bootleg whiskey.*

▸*v.* (**-legged, -leg·ging**) [*trans.*] make, distribute, or sell (illicit goods, esp. liquor, computer software, or recordings) illegally: [as *n.*] (**bootlegging**) *domestic bootlegging was almost impossible to control* | [as *adj.*] (**bootlegged**) *bootlegged videos.*

▸*n.* **1** an illegal musical recording, esp. one made at a concert. **2** *Football* a play in which the quarterback fakes a handoff and runs with the ball hidden next to his hip: *he scored on a 29-yard bootleg on fourth down.* ▷late 19th cent.: from the smugglers' practice of concealing bottles in their boots. **—boot·leg·ger** *n.*

boot·less /ˈbo͞otlis/ ▸*adj. archaic* (of a task or undertaking) ineffectual; useless: *words at this pass were vain and bootless.* ▷Old English *bōtlēas* 'not able to be compensated for by payment' (see BOOT[2], -LESS).

boot·lick·er /ˈbo͞otˌlikər/ ▸*n. informal* an obsequious or overly deferential person; a toady: *bootlickers telling him what a big star he's going to be.* **—boot·lick·ing** /-ˌlikiNG/ *n.*

boots /bo͞ots/ ▸*n. Brit., dated* a hotel employee who cleans boots and shoes, carries luggage, and performs other menial tasks. ▷late 18th cent.: plural of BOOT[1], used as a singular.

boot-scoot·ing ▸*n.* another term for LINE DANCING.

boot·strap /ˈbo͞otˌstrap/ ▸*n.* **1** a loop at the back of a boot, used to pull it on. ■ [usu. as *adj.*] the technique of starting with existing resources to create something more complex and effective: *her willingness to work night and day in a tiny basement office was evidence of her trademark bootstrap.* **2** *Computing* a technique of loading a program into a computer by means of a

few initial instructions that enable the introduction of the rest of the program from an input device.
▸*v.* (**-strapped, -strap·ping**) **1** [*trans.* with *adverbial of direction*] get (oneself or something) into or out of a situation using existing resources: *the company is bootstrapping itself out of a marred financial past.* **2** [*trans.*] start up (an enterprise), especially one based on the Internet, with minimal resources: *they are bootstrapping their stations themselves, not with lots of dot-com venture capital.*
▸*adj.* (of a person or project) using one's own resources rather than external help: *a bootstrap capitalist's trip up the entrepreneurial ladder.*
▸*PHRASE* □ **pull oneself up by one's (own) bootstraps** improve one's position by one's own efforts.

boot top ▸*n.* the part of a ship's hull just above the waterline, typically marked by a line of contrasting color.

boot-up ▸*n.* see BOOT[1] (sense 4).

boo·ty[1] /'bo͞otē/ ▸*n.* valuable stolen goods, esp. those seized in war: *the militias supply themselves with booty from the raided civilian populations.* ■ *colloq.* something gained or won: *now the booty: four winners will receive prizes.* ▷late Middle English (denoting plunder acquired in common and destined to be divided among the plunderers): from Middle Low German *būte, buite* 'exchange, distribution,' of uncertain ultimate origin.

boo·ty[2] ▸*n.* (*pl.* **-ties**) *informal* a person's buttocks.
▸*PHRASE* □ **shake one's booty** dance energetically.

boo·ty call ▸*n. informal* a sexual invitation or rendezvous. ■ a person regarded for this: *to him, I was just a booty call.* ▷1990s: from *booty* (slang for 'buttocks') and *call.*

boo·ty·li·cious /,bo͞otl'isHəs/ ▸*adj. informal* sexually attractive. ▷early 21st cent.: from *booty* (slang for 'buttocks'), on the pattern of *delicious.*

booze /bo͞oz/ *informal* ▸*n.* alcohol, esp. hard liquor: *they turn to booze to beat work pressure.*
▸*v.* [*intrans.*] drink alcohol, esp. in large quantities: *you used to booze a lot on expensive hard liquor* | [as *n.*] (**boozing**) *Michael is trying to quit boozing.* ▷Middle English *bouse,* from Middle Dutch *būsen* 'drink to excess.' The spelling *booze* dates from the 18th cent.

booze·hound /'bo͞oz,hound/ ▸*n. informal* a person who drinks alcohol often and heavily.

booz·er /'bo͞ozər/ ▸*n. informal* a person who drinks large quantities of alcohol. ■ *Brit.* a pub or bar.

booze-up ▸*n. informal, chiefly Brit.* a drinking spree.

booz·y /'bo͞ozē/ ▸*adj.* (**booz·i·er, booz·i·est**) *informal* intoxicated; addicted to drink: *the boozy and drugged-out wreckage of his later years.* —**booz·i·ly** /-zəlē/ *adv.* —**booz·i·ness** *n.*

bop[1] /bäp/ *informal* ▸*n.* short for BEBOP.
▸*v.* (**bopped, bop·ping**) [*intrans.*] dance to pop music: *bopping to the radio while they made breakfast.* ■ move or travel energetically: *we had been bopping around the county all morning.* ▷1940s: shortening of BEBOP. —**bop·per** *n.*

bop[2] *informal* ▸*v.* (**bopped, bop·ping**) [*trans.*] hit; punch lightly: *I warned him I'd bop him on the nose if he tried it.*
▸*n.* a blow or light punch. ▷1930s: imitative.

Bo·phu·that·swa·na /,bōpo͞o,tät'swänə/ a former homeland established in South Africa for the Tswana people.

bor. ▸*abbr.* borough.

bo·ra /'bôrə/ ▸*n.* a strong, cold, dry northeast wind blowing in the upper Adriatic. ▷mid 19th cent.: dialect variant of Italian *borea,* from Latin *boreas* 'north wind' (see BOREAL).

Bo·ra-Bo·ra /,bôrə 'bôrə/ an island in the Society Islands group in French Polynesia.

bo·rac·ic /bə'rasik/ ▸*adj.* another term for BORIC. ▷late 18th cent.: from medieval Latin *borax, borac-* (see BORAX) + -IC.

bor·age /'bôrij; 'bär-/ ▸*n.* a herbaceous plant with bright blue flowers and hairy leaves, used medicinally and as a salad green. • *Borago officinalis,* family Boraginaceae (the **borage family**). This family includes many plants that typically have blue or purple flowers, including forget-me-not, comfrey, and bugloss. ▷Middle English: from Old French *bourrache,* from medieval Latin *borrago,* probably from Arabic.

bo·rane /'bôrān/ ▸*n. Chemistry* any of a series of unstable binary compounds of boron and hydrogen, analogous to the alkanes. The simplest example is diborane, B_2H_6. ▷early 20th cent.: from BORON + -ANE[2].

Bo·rås /bo͞o'rôs/ an industrial city in southwestern Sweden; pop. 101,770.

bo·rate /'bôrāt/ ▸*n. Chemistry* a salt in which the anion contains both boron and oxygen, as in borax.

bo·rax /'bôraks/ ▸*n.* a white mineral in some alkaline salt deposits, used in making glass and ceramics, as a metallurgical flux, and as an antiseptic. • A hydrated sodium borate; chem. formula: $Na_2B_4O_7(OH)_4.8H_2O$. ▷late Middle English: from medieval Latin, from Arabic *būraḳ,* from Pahlavi *būrak.*

Bo·ra·zon /'bôrə,zän/ ▸*n. trademark* an industrial abrasive consisting of boron nitride. ▷1950s: from BORON, with the insertion of AZO-.

bor·bo·ryg·mus /,bôrbə'rigməs/ ▸*n.* (*pl.* **-mi** /-mī/) *technical* a rumbling or gurgling noise made by the movement of fluid and gas in the intestines. ▷early 18th cent.: modern Latin, from Greek *borborugmos.* —**bor·bo·ryg·mic** /-mik/ *adj.*

Bor·deaux[1] /bôr'dō/ a port in southwestern France, on the Garonne River; pop. 213,270.

Bor·deaux[2] ▸*n.* (*pl.* same) a red, white, or rosé wine from the district of Bordeaux.

Bor·deaux mix·ture ▸*n.* a fungicide for vines, fruit trees, and other plants composed of equal quantities of copper sulfate and calcium oxide in water. ▷late 19th cent.: first used in the vineyards of the Bordeaux region.

bor·de·laise /,bôrdl'āz/ ▸*adj.* served with a sauce of red wine and onions: [*postpositive*] *lobster bordelaise.* ▷French, from *(à la) bordelaise* 'Bordeaux-style.'

bor·del·lo /bôr'delō/ ▸*n.* (*pl.* **-los**) a brothel. ▷late 16th cent. (gradually replacing Middle English *bordel*): from Italian, probably from Old French *bordel,* diminutive of *borde* 'small farm, cottage,' ultimately of Germanic origin.

Bor·den /'bôrdn/, Lizzie Andrew (1860–1927), U.S. accused murderess. Accused of the murder of her father and stepmother in Fall River, Massachusetts, in 1892, she was acquitted in a trial that became a national sensation.

bor·der /'bôrdər/ ▸*n.* **1** a line separating two political or geographical areas, esp. countries: *Iraq's northern* ***border with*** *Turkey* | [as *adj.*] *border patrols.* ■ a district near such a line: *a refugee camp* ***on the border.*** **2** the edge or boundary of something, or the part near it: *the northern border of their distribution area* | *figurative the unknown regions at the borders of physics and electronics.* **3** a band or strip, esp. a decorative one, around the edge of something: *put a white border around the picture.* ■ a strip of ground along the edge of a lawn or path for planting flowers or shrubs: *the garden borders are planted with perennials.*
▸*v.* [*trans.*] form an edge along or beside (something): *a pool* ***bordered by*** *palm trees.* ■ (of a country or area) be adjacent to (another country or area): *regions bordering Azerbaijan* | [*intrans.*] *the mountains* ***bordering on*** *Afghanistan.* ■ [*intrans.*] (**border on**) *figurative* be close to an extreme condition: *Sam arrived in a state of excitement bordering on hysteria.* ■ (usu. **be bordered with**) provide (something) with a decorative edge: *a curving driveway bordered with chrysanthemums.* ▷late Middle English: from Old French *bordeure;* ultimately of Germanic origin and related to BOARD.

THE RIGHT WORD **border, brim, brink, edge, margin, rim, verge**

A **border** is the part of a surface that is nearest to its boundary (*a rug with a flowered border*)—although it may also refer to the boundary line itself (*the border between Vermont and New Hampshire*).

A **margin** is a *border* of a definite width that is usually distinct in appearance from what it encloses; but unlike *border,* it usually refers to the blankness or emptiness that surrounds something (*the margin on a printed page*).

While *border* and *margin* usually refer to something that is circumscribed, **edge** may refer to only a part of the perimeter (*the edge of the lawn*) or the line where two planes or surfaces converge (*the edge of the table*). *Edge* can also connote sharpness (*the edge of a knife*) and can be used metaphorically to suggest tension, harshness, or keenness (*there was an edge in her voice; take the edge off their nervousness*).

Verge may also be used metaphorically to describe the extreme limit of something (*on the verge of a nervous breakdown*), but in a more literal sense, it sometimes is used of the line or narrow space that marks the limit or termination of something (*the verge of a desert or forest*).

Brink denotes the edge of something very steep or an abrupt division between land and water (*the brink of the river*), or metaphorically the very final limit before an abrupt change (*on the brink of disaster*).

Rim and **brim** apply only to things that are circular or curving. But while *rim* describes the edge or lip of a rounded or cylindrical shape (*the rim of a glass*), *brim* refers to the inner side of the rim when the container is completely full (*a cup filled to the brim with steaming coffee*). However, when one speaks of the *brim* of a hat, it comes closer to the meaning of *margin* or *border.*

B

Bor·der col·lie ▸*n.* (also **border collie**) a common working sheepdog, typically with a black and white coat, of a medium-sized breed originating near the border between England and Scotland.

bord·er·er /'bôrdərər/ ▸*n.* a person living near a border.

bord·er·land /'bôrdər,land/ ▸*n.* (usu. **borderlands**) the district near a border. ■ *figurative* an area of overlap between two things: *the murky borderland between history and myth.*

bord·er·line /'bôrdər,līn/ ▸*n.* a line marking a border. ■ *figurative* a division between two distinct (often extreme) conditions: *the borderline between ritual and custom.*
▸*adj.* barely acceptable in quality or as belonging to a category; on the borderline: *references may be requested in borderline cases.*

bor·der state ▸*n.* any of the slave states that bordered the northern free states during the U.S. Civil War. See also BORDER STATES. ■ a U.S. state that borders Canada or Mexico. ■ a small country that borders a larger, more powerful country or that lies between two larger countries.

Bor·der States those U.S. states, including Delaware, Maryland, Kentucky, Virginia, and Missouri, that were slave states but did not secede from the Union during the Civil War.

Bord·er ter·ri·er ▸*n.* a small terrier of a breed with rough hair, originating in the Cheviot Hills.

Bor·det /bôr'dā/, Jules (1870–1961), Belgian bacteriologist and immunologist. He discovered the complement system of blood serum, and developed a vaccine for whooping cough.

bor·dure /'bôrjər/ ▸*n. Heraldry* a broad border used as a charge in a coat of arms, often as a mark of difference. ▷late Middle English: variant of BORDER.

bore[1] /bôr/ ▸*v.* **1** [*trans.*] make (a hole) in something, esp. with a revolving tool: *they bored holes in the sides* | [*intrans.*] *the drill can bore through rock.* ■ [*trans.*] hollow out (a tube or tunnel): *try to bore the tunnel at the correct angle.* ■ [*intrans.*] (**bore into**) *figurative* (of a person's eyes) stare harshly at: *your terrible blue eyes bore into me.* ■ [*trans.*] hollow out (a gun barrel or other tube). **2** [*intrans.*] make one's way through (a crowd).
▸*n.* **1** the hollow part inside a gun barrel or other tube. ■ [often in *combination*] the diameter of this; the caliber: *a small-bore rifle.* ■ [in *combination*] a gun of a specified bore: *he shot a guard in the leg with a twelve-bore.* **2** short for BOREHOLE. ▷Old English *borian* (verb), of Germanic origin; related to German *bohren.*

bore[2] ▸*n.* a person whose talk or behavior is dull and uninteresting: *a* ***crashing bore*** *who tells the same old jokes over and over.* ■ [in *sing.*] a tedious situation or thing: *it's such a bore cooking when one's alone.*
▸*v.* [*trans.*] make (someone) feel weary and uninterested by tedious talk or dullness: *rather than bore you with all the details, I'll hit some of the bright spots.* ▷mid 18th cent. (as a verb): of unknown origin.
▸*PHRASE* □ **bore someone to death** (or **to tears**) weary (a person) in the extreme.

bore[3] ▸*n.* a steep-fronted wave caused by the meeting of two tides or by the constriction of a tide rushing up a narrow estuary. ▷early 17th cent.: perhaps from Old Norse *bára* 'wave'; the term was used in the general sense 'billow, wave' in Middle English.

bore[4] ▸ past of BEAR[1].

bo·re·al /'bôrēəl/ ▸*adj.* of the North or northern regions. ■ *Ecology* relating to or characteristic of the climatic zone south of the Arctic, esp. the cold temperate region dominated by taiga and forests of birch, poplar, and conifers: *northern boreal forest.* ■ (**Boreal**) *Botany* relating to or denoting a phytogeographical kingdom comprising the arctic and temperate regions of Eurasia and North America. ▷late Middle English: from late Latin *borealis,* from

Latin *Boreas*, denoting the god of the north wind, from Greek.

bored[1] /bôrd/ ▸*adj.* feeling weary because one is unoccupied or lacks interest in one's current activity: *she* ***got bored with*** *staring out of the window | they would hang around all day,* ***bored stiff.***

bored[2] ▸*adj.* [in *combination*] (of a gun) having a specified bore: *large-bored guns.*

bore·dom /'bôrdəm/ ▸*n.* the state of feeling bored: *the boredom of afternoon duty could be relieved by friendly conversation.*

bo·reen /bô'rēn/ ▸*n. Irish* a narrow country road. ▷mid 19th cent.: from Irish *bóithrín*, diminutive of *bóthar* 'road.'

bore·hole /'bôr,hōl/ ▸*n.* a deep, narrow hole made in the ground, esp. to locate water or oil.

bo·rek /bô'rek/ ▸*n.* an envelope of thin pastry filled with cheese, spinach, or ground meat and baked or fried. ▷from Turkish, 'pie.'

bor·er /'bôrər/ ▸*n.* **1** a worm, mollusk, insect, or insect larva that bores into wood, other plant material, or rock. **2** a tool for boring.

bore·scope /'bôr,skōp/ ▸*n.* an instrument used to inspect the inside of a structure through a small hole.

Borg /bôrg/, Björn (Rune) (1956–), Swedish tennis player. He won five consecutive men's singles titles at Wimbledon 1976–80 and six French Opens 1974–75 and 1978–81.

bor·ga·ta /bôr'gätə/ ▸*n.* (*pl.* **-tas** or **-te** /-tē/) an organized branch of the Mafia. ▷1960s: from Italian *borgatà* 'district, village.'

Bor·ge /'bôrgə/, Victor (1909–2000), U.S. pianist; born in Denmark. He was noted for his clowning while playing classical music. His one-man show, *Comedy in Music*, began an 849-performance run on Broadway in 1953, with a brief revival in 1977.

Bor·ges /'bôr,hās/, Jorge Luis (1899–1986), Argentine poet, short-story writer, and essayist. His volume of short stories *A Universal History of Infamy* (1935, revised 1954) is regarded as one of the first works of magic realism.

Bor·gia[1] /'bôrzhə/, Cesare (*c.*1476–1507), Italian statesman, cardinal, and general. He was the illegitimate son of Cardinal Rodrigo Borgia (later Pope Alexander VI) and the brother of Lucrezia Borgia.

Bor·gia[2], Lucrezia (1480–1519), Italian noblewoman; sister of Cesare Borgia. She was the illegitimate daughter of Cardinal Rodrigo Borgia (later Pope Alexander VI).

Bor·glum /'bôrgləm/, Gutzon (1867–1941) U.S. sculptor; full name *John Gutzon de la Mothe Borglum*. His most famous work is the Mount Rushmore National Memorial in South Dakota that features the monumental heads of U.S. Presidents Washington, Jefferson, Lincoln, and T. Roosevelt. The work, begun in 1927, was completed in 1941 with the help of his son Lincoln Borglum (1912–86).

Borg·nine /'bôrg,nīn/, Ernest (1917–), U.S. actor; born *Ermes Effron Borgnine*. His movies included *From Here to Eternity* (1953) and *Marty* (Academy Award, 1955). He turned to television during the 1960s, starring in "McHale's Navy" (1962–66). Later, he played in the series "Airwolf" (1984) and "The Single Guy" (1995).

bo·ric /'bôrik/ ▸*adj. Chemistry* of boron: *boric oxide.*

bo·ric ac·id ▸*n. Chemistry* a weakly acid crystalline compound derived from borax, used as a mild antiseptic and in the manufacture of heat-resistant glass and enamels. • Chem. formula: $B(OH)_3$.

bor·ing /'bôriNG/ ▸*adj.* not interesting; tedious: *I've got a boring job in an office.* **—bor·ing·ly** *adv.* [as *submodifier*] *the list is excoriated as boringly predictable.* **—bor·ing·ness** *n.*

Bo·ris Go·du·nov /'bôrəs/ see **GODUNOV**.

bork /bôrk/ (also **Bork**) ▸*v.* [*trans.*] *informal* obstruct (someone, esp. a candidate for public office) through systematic defamation or vilification: [as *n.*] (**borking**) *is fear of borking scaring people from public office?* ▷1980s: from the name of Robert *Bork* (born 1927), an American judge whose nomination to the U.S. Supreme Court (1987) was rejected following unfavorable publicity for his allegedly extreme views.

Bor·laug /'bôr,lôg/, Norman Ernest (1914–), U.S. agronomist. He developed high-yielding cereals for cultivation in less developed countries. He wrote *The Green Revolution, Peace and Humanity* (1971) and *Food Production in a Fertile, Unstable World* (1978). Nobel Peace Prize (1970).

Bor·mann /'bôrmən/, Martin (1900–*c.*1945), German Nazi politician. Considered to be Hitler's closest collaborator, he disappeared at the end of World War II; his skeleton, exhumed in Berlin, was identified in 1973.

Born /bôrn/, Max (1882–1970), German theoretical physicist, a founder of quantum mechanics. Nobel Prize for Physics (1954, shared with Walther Bothe 1891–1957).

born /bôrn/ ▸ past participle of **BEAR**[1] (sense 4).
▸*adj.* existing as a result of birth: *he was born in Seattle | babies* ***born to*** *women aged 25–29 | he was* ***born into*** *a family of wine merchants | she was born Margaret Roberts |* [in *combination*] *a German-born philosopher.* ■ [*attrib.*] having a natural ability to do a particular job or task: *he's a born engineer.* ■ [with *infinitive*] perfectly suited or trained to do a particular job or task: *they believe that they are born to rule.* ■ (of a thing) brought into existence: *her own business was born.* ■ (**born of**) existing as a result of a particular situation or feeling: *a power born of obsession.* ▷Old English *boren*, past participle of *beran* 'to bear' (see **BEAR**[1]).
▸*PHRASES* □ **born and bred** by birth and upbringing, esp. when considered a typical product of a place: *he was a born and bred product of the Bronx.* □ **born on the wrong side of the blanket** see **BLANKET**. □ **born with a silver spoon in one's mouth** see **SILVER**. □ **I** (**she**, etc.) **wasn't born yesterday** used to remind someone that one isn't naive. □ **in all one's born days** used to express surprise or shock at something one has not encountered before: *in all my born days I've never seen the like of it.* □ **there's one** (or **a sucker**) **born every minute** there are many gullible people.

USAGE On the difference between **born** and **borne**, see **usage** at **BEAR**[1].

born-a·gain ▸*adj.* converted to a personal faith in Christ (with reference to John 3:3): *a born-again Christian.* ■ *figurative* having the extreme enthusiasm of the newly converted or reconverted: *born-again environmentalists.*
▸*n.* a born-again Christian.

borne /bôrn/ ▸ past participle of **BEAR**[1] (senses 1, 2, 3, and 5).
▸*adj.* [in *combination*] carried or transported by: *waterborne bacteria | insect-borne pollen.*

Bor·ne·o /'bôrnēō/ a large island in the Malay Archipelago that is comprised of Kalimantan (a region of Indonesia), Sabah and Sarawak (states of Malaysia), and Brunei. **—Bor·ne·an** /-nēən/ *adj.*

Born·holm /'bôrn,hō(l)m/ a Danish island in the Baltic Sea, southeast of Sweden.

Born·holm dis·ease ▸*n.* a viral infection with fever and pain in the muscles of the ribs. ▷1930s: named after the island of **BORNHOLM**, where it was first described.

born·ite /'bôrnīt/ ▸*n.* a brittle reddish-brown crystalline mineral with an iridescent purple tarnish, consisting of a sulfide of copper and iron. ▷early 19th cent.: from the name of Ignatius von *Born* (1742–91), Austrian mineralogist, + **-ITE**[1].

boro- ▸*comb. form Chemistry* representing **BORON**.

Bo·ro·bu·dur /,bôrəbə'do͝or/ a Buddhist monument in central Java, built *c.*800.

Bo·ro·din /,bôrə'dēn/, Aleksandr (Porfirevich) (1833–87), Russian composer. He is noted for the opera *Prince Igor*, which was completed after his death by Nikolai Rimsky-Korsakov and Aleksandr Glazunov (1865–1936).

Bo·ro·di·no, Battle of /,bôrə'dēnō/ a battle in 1812 at Borodino, a village about 110 km (70 miles) west of Moscow, at which Napoleon's forces defeated the Russian army.

bo·ron /'bôrän/ ▸*n.* the chemical element of atomic number 5, a nonmetallic solid. (Symbol: **B**)

Boron is usually prepared as an amorphous brown powder, but when very pure it forms hard, shiny, black crystals with semiconducting properties. The element has some specialized uses, such as in alloy steels and nuclear control rods.

▷early 19th cent.: from **BORAX**, on the pattern of *carbon* (which it resembles in some respects). **—bo·ride** /-rīd/ *n.* .

bo·ro·ni·a /bə'rōnēə/ ▸*n.* a sweet-scented Australian shrub cultivated for its perfume and for use as a cut flower. • Genus *Boronia*, family Rutaceae. ▷modern Latin, named after Francesco *Borone* (1769–94), Italian botanist.

bo·ro·sil·i·cate /,bôrə'silikit; -,kāt/ ▸*n.* [usu. as *adj.*] a low-melting-point glass made from a mixture of silica and boric oxide (B_2O_3).

bor·ough /'bərō/ (abbr.: **bor.**) ▸*n.* a town or district that is an administrative unit, in particular: ■ an incorporated municipality in certain U.S. states. ■ each of five divisions of New York City. ■ in Alaska, a district corresponding to a county elsewhere in the U.S. ■ *Brit.* a town (as distinct from a city) with a corporation and privileges granted by a royal charter. ■ *Brit., historical* a town sending representatives to Parliament. ▷Old English *burg, burh* 'fortress, citadel,' later 'fortified town,' of Germanic origin; related to Dutch *burg* and German *Burg*. Compare with **BURGH**.

Bor·ro·mi·ni /,bôrə'mēnē/, Francesco (1599–1667), Italian architect, a leading figure of the Italian baroque style.

bor·row /'bärō; 'bôrō/ ▸*v.* [*trans.*] take and use (something that belongs to someone else) with the intention of returning it: *he had* ***borrowed*** *a car* ***from*** *one of his colleagues |* [as *adj.*] (**borrowed**) *she was wearing a borrowed jacket.* ■ take and use (money) from a person or bank under an agreement to pay it back later: *I borrowed the money for a return plane ticket |* [*intrans.*] *lower interest rates will make it cheaper for individuals to borrow.* ■ take (a word, idea, or method) from another source and use it in one's own language or work: *the term is* ***borrowed from*** *Greek |* [*intrans.*] *designers consistently* ***borrow from*** *the styles of preceding generations.* ■ take and use (a book) from a library for a fixed period of time. ■ in subtraction, take a unit from the next larger denomination. ■ *Golf* allow (a certain distance) when playing a shot to compensate for sideways motion of the ball due to a slope or other irregularity.
▸*n. Golf* a slope or other irregularity on a golf course that must be compensated for when playing a shot. ▷Old English *borgian* 'borrow against security,' of Germanic origin; related to Dutch and German *borgen*. **—bor·row·er** *n.*
▸*PHRASES* □ **be** (**living**) **on borrowed time** used to say that someone has continued to survive against expectations, with the implication that this will not be for much longer. □ **borrow trouble** take needless action that may have detrimental effects.

bor·row·ing /'bärō-iNG; 'bôr-/ ▸*n.* the action of borrowing something: *the borrowing of clothes.* ■ the action of taking and using money from a bank under an agreement to pay it back later: *a curb on government borrowing | the group had total borrowings of $570 million.* ■ a word, idea, or method taken from another source and used in one's own language or work: *a hard-bop musician with some borrowings from free jazz.*

Bor·sa·li·no /,bôrsə'lēnō/ ▸*n.* (*pl.* **-nos**) *trademark* a man's wide-brimmed felt hat. ▷early 20th cent.: from the name of the manufacturer.

borscht /bôrsHt/ (also **borsch**) ▸*n.* a Russian or Polish soup made with beets and usually served with sour cream. ▷from Russian *borshch*.

Borscht Belt /bôrsHt/ ▸*n.* (**the Borscht Belt**) *humorous* a resort area in the Catskill Mountains frequented chiefly by Jewish guests: [as *adj.*] *Borscht Belt entertainers.*

bor·stal /'bôrstəl/ (also **Bor·stal**) ▸*n. Brit., historical* a custodial institution for youthful offenders. ▷early 20th cent.: named after the village of *Borstal* in southern England, where the first of these was established.

bort /bôrt/ ▸*n.* small, granular, opaque diamonds, used as an abrasive in cutting tools. Compare with **CARBONADO**. ▷early 17th cent.: from Dutch *boort*.

bor·zoi /'bôrzoi/ ▸*n.* (*pl.* **-zois**) a large Russian wolfhound of a breed with a narrow head and silky, often white, coat. ▷late 19th cent.: from Russian *borzoĭ* (adjective) 'swift.'

borzoi

Bosc /bäsk/ (also **Bosc pear**) ▸*n.* a medium- to large-sized variety of pear, golden brown in color and often russeted. The Bosc's dense flesh makes it a common choice for baking and cooking. ▷named after L. *Bosc* d'Antic (1759–1828), French naturalist.

bos·cage /'bäskij/ (also **bos·kage**) ▸*n.* massed trees or shrubs: *the lush subtropical boscage.* ▷late Middle

English: from Old French; ultimately of Germanic origin and related to **BUSH**[1]. Compare with **BOCAGE**.

Bosch /bäsh; bôsh/, Hieronymus (*c.*1450–1516), Dutch painter. His highly detailed works are typically crowded with half-human, half-animal creatures and grotesque demons in settings symbolic of sin and folly.

Bose /bōz/, Satyendra Nath (1894–1974), Indian physicist. With Albert Einstein, he described fundamental particles that later came to be known as *bosons*.

bosh /bäsh/ ▶*n. informal* something regarded as absurd; nonsense: *I think it's a load of bosh* | [as *exclam.*] *bosh! You don't want to go with us.* ▷mid 19th cent.: from Turkish *boş* 'empty, worthless,' which became widely known in English through James Morier's novel *Ayesha* (1834).

bosk /bäsk/ ▶*n.* a thicket of bushes; a small wood.

bosk·y /ˈbäskē/ ▶*adj.* wooded; covered by trees or bushes: *a river meandering between bosky banks.* ▷late 16th cent.: from Middle English *bosk*, variant of **BUSH**[1].

Bos·man rul·ing /ˈbäzmən/ ▶*n.* a European Court ruling that obliges professional soccer or other sports clubs to allow players over the age of 25 to move freely between clubs once their contracts have expired. ▷1990s: named after Jean-Marc *Bosman* (1964–), a Belgian soccer player who brought a legal case that resulted in the ruling.

bo's'n ▶*n.* variant spelling of **BOATSWAIN**.

Bos·ni·a /ˈbäznēə/ a region in the Balkans that forms the larger, northern part of Bosnia and Herzegovina. —**Bos·ni·an** *adj.* & *n.*

Bos·ni·a and Her·ze·go·vi·na /ˌhertsəgōˈvēnə ˌhertsəˈgōvənə/ a country in southeastern Europe, in the Balkans, formerly a constituent republic of Yugoslavia; pop. 4,007,000; capital, Sarajevo; languages, Bosnian, Croatian, Serbian.

Bosnia and Herzegovina were conquered by the Turks in 1463. The province of Bosnia–Herzegovina was annexed by Austria in 1908, an event that contributed to the outbreak of World War I. In 1918, it became part of the Kingdom of Serbs, Croats, and Slovenes, which changed its name to Yugoslavia in 1929. In 1992, Bosnia and Herzegovina followed Slovenia and Croatia in declaring independence, but ethnic conflict among Muslims, Serbs, and Croats quickly reduced the republic to a state of civil war. An accord signed in December 1995 formally brought the conflict to an end.

bos·om /ˈbo͝ozəm/ ▶*n.* a woman's chest: *her ample bosom* | *the dress offered a fair display of bosom.* ■ (usu. **bosoms**) a woman's breast. ■ a part of a woman's dress covering the chest. ■ the space between a person's clothing and chest used for carrying things: *he carried a letter* ***in his bosom.*** ■ (**the bosom of**) *poetic/literary* the loving care and protection of: *Bruno went home each night* ***to the bosom of*** *his family* | *the town has* ***taken*** *the gay community* ***to its bosom.*** ■ used to refer to the chest as the seat of emotions: *quivering dread was settling in her bosom.*
▶*adj.* [*attrib.*] (of a friend) close or intimate: *the two girls had become bosom friends.* ▷Old English *bōsm*; related to Dutch *boezem* and German *Busen*. —**bos·omed** *adj.* [in *combination*] *her small-bosomed physique.*

bos·om·y /ˈbo͝ozəmē/ ▶*adj.* (of a woman) having large breasts.

bo·son /ˈbōsän/ ▶*n. Physics* a subatomic particle, such as a photon, that has zero or integral spin and follows the statistical description given by S. N. Bose and Einstein. ▷1940s: named after S. N. **BOSE** + **-ON**.

Bos·po·rus /ˈbäsp(ə)rəs/ (also **Bos·pho·rus** /ˈbäsf(ə)rəs/) a strait that connects the Black Sea with the Sea of Marmara and separates Europe from the Anatolian peninsula of western Asia. Istanbul is located at its south end.

boss[1] /bôs; bäs/ *informal* ▶*n.* a person in charge of a worker or organization: *I asked my boss for a promotion* | *union bosses.* ■ a person in control of a group or situation: *the boss of the largest crime family in the country.*
▶*v.* [*trans.*] give (someone) orders in a domineering manner: *plump old battle-axes* ***bossing*** *everyone* ***around.***
▶*adj.* [*attrib.*] excellent; outstanding: *she's a real boss chick.* ▷early 19th cent. (originally U.S.): from Dutch *baas* 'master.'
▶*PHRASES* □ **be one's own boss** be self-employed. □ **show someone who's boss** make it clear that one is in charge.

boss[2] ▶*n.* a round knob, stud, or other protuberance, in particular: ■ a stud on the center of a shield. ■ *Architecture* a piece of ornamental carving covering the point where the ribs in a vault or ceiling cross. ■ *Geology* a large mass of igneous rock protruding through other strata. ■ *Mechanics* an enlarged part of a shaft. ▷Middle English: from Old French *boce*, of unknown origin.

boss[3] ▶*n. informal* a cow. Compare with **BOSSY**[2]. ▷early 19th cent.: of unknown origin.

bos·sa no·va /ˈbäsə ˈnōvə; ˈbô-/ ▶*n.* a dance like the samba, originating in Brazil. ■ a piece of music for this dance or in its rhythm. ▷1960s: from Portuguese, from *bossa* 'tendency' and *nova* (feminine of *novo*) 'new.'

Bos·sier Cit·y /ˈbōzhər/ a city in northwestern Louisiana, on the Red River, just northeast of Shreveport; pop. 56,461. It is a center for the oil and gas industry.

boss·ism /ˈbôsizəm; ˈbäs-/ ▶*n.* a situation in which a political party is controlled by party managers.

boss·y[1] /ˈbôsē; ˈbäs-/ ▶*adj.* (**boss·i·er, boss·i·est**) *informal* fond of giving people orders; domineering: *she was headlong, bossy, scared of nobody, and full of vinegar.* —**boss·i·ly** /-səlē/ *adv.* —**boss·i·ness** *n.*

boss·y[2] ▶*n.* (*pl.* **boss·ies**) *informal* a cow or calf. Compare with **BOSS**[3]. ▷mid 19th cent.: of unknown origin.

Bos·ton[1] /ˈbôstən/ a city in eastern Massachusetts, the capital of the state, on Massachusetts Bay; pop. 589,141. It was founded *c.*1630 by the Massachusetts Bay Company under its governor, John Winthrop (1588–1649). Boston was the scene of many disturbances that led to the American Revolution at the end of the 18th century. —**Bos·to·ni·an** /bôˈstōnēən/ *n.* & *adj.*

Bos·ton[2] ▶*n.* **1** a card game resembling solo whist. **2** a variation of the waltz or of the two-step.

Bos·ton baked beans ▶*plural n.* a dish of baked beans with salt pork and molasses.

Bos·ton cream pie ▶*n.* a round, two-layer cake that is filled with custard or cream and frosted, usually with chocolate.

Bos·ton fern ▶*n.* a variety of sword fern, with long, arching bright green fronds, widely cultivated esp. as a hanging houseplant. • *Nephrolepis exaltata bostoniensis*, family Dryopteridaceae.

Bos·ton i·vy ▶*n.* a Virginia creeper with three-lobed leaves, cultivated for its foliage. • *Parthenocissus tricuspidata*, family Vitaceae.

Bos·ton let·tuce ▶*n.* a butterhead lettuce of a variety that has medium or light green leaves.

Bos·ton rock·er ▶*n.* a rocking chair with a decorative panel on a high spindled back and with arms and a seat that curves downward at the front.

Bos·ton Tea Par·ty a violent demonstration in 1773 by American colonists before the American Revolution. Colonists boarded vessels in Boston harbor and threw the cargoes of tea into the water in protest at the imposition of a tax on tea by the British Parliament, in which the colonists had no representation.

Bos·ton ter·ri·er ▶*n.* a small smooth-coated terrier of a breed originating in Massachusetts from a crossing of the bulldog and terrier.

bo·sun (also **bo'sun**) ▶*n.* variant spelling of **BOATSWAIN**.

Bos·well /ˈbäzwəl; -ˌwel/, James (1740–95), Scottish author, companion and biographer of Samuel Johnson. Notable works: *Journal of a Tour to the Hebrides* (1785) and *The Life of Samuel Johnson* (1791).

Bos·worth Field /ˈbäzwərth/ (also **Battle of Bosworth**) a battle of the Wars of the Roses fought in 1485 near Market Bosworth in Leicestershire. Henry Tudor defeated and killed the Yorkist king Richard III, which enabled him to take the throne as Henry VII.

bot[1] /bät/ ▶*n.* the larva of the botfly, which is an internal parasite of animals. It lives typically in the stomach, finally passing through the host's dung and pupating on the ground. ▷early 16th cent.: probably of Low German origin.

bot[2] ▶*n.* (chiefly in science fiction) a robot. ■ *Computing* an autonomous program on a network (esp. the Internet) that can interact with computer systems or users, esp. one designed to respond or behave like a player in an adventure game. ▷1980s: shortening of **ROBOT**.

-bot ▶*comb. form* used to form nouns denoting a computer program or robot with a very specific function: *fembot* | *adbot.* ▷from *robot*.

bot. ▶*abbr.* ■ (with reference to journal titles) botanic; botanical; botany. ■ bottle. ■ bought.

bo·tan·i·cal /bəˈtanikəl/ ▶*adj.* of or relating to plants: *botanical specimens* | *a botanical illustrator.*
▶*n.* (usu. **botanicals**) a substance obtained from a plant and used as an additive, esp. in gin or cosmetics. —**bo·tan·i·cal·ly** /-ik(ə)lē/ *adv.*

bo·tan·i·cal gar·den (also **bo·tan·ic gar·den**) ▶*n.* an establishment where plants are grown for display to the public and often for scientific study.

bot·a·nize /ˈbätnˌīz/ ▶*v.* [*intrans.*] study plants, esp. in their natural habitat: *I'd always be scheming to go off birdwatching or botanizing.* ▷mid 18th cent.: from modern Latin *botanizare*, from Greek *botanizein* 'gather plants,' from *botanē* 'plant.'

Bot·a·ny /ˈbätn-ē/ (also **Botany wool**) ▶*n.* [*mass noun*] merino wool, esp. from Australia. ▷late 19th cent.: named after **BOTANY BAY**, from where the wool originally came.

bot·a·ny /ˈbätn-ē/ ▶*n.* the scientific study of plants, including their physiology, structure, genetics, ecology, distribution, classification, and economic importance. ■ the plant life of a particular region, habitat, or geological period: *the botany of North America.* ▷late 17th cent.: from earlier *botanic* (from French *botanique*, based on Greek *botanikos*, from *botanē* 'plant') + **-Y**[3]. —**bo·tan·ic** /bəˈtanik/ *adj.* —**bot·a·nist** /-ist/ *n.*

Bot·a·ny Bay an inlet of the Tasman Sea just south of Sydney, Australia. It was the site of Captain James Cook's landing in 1770 and of an early British penal settlement. ▷named by Cook after the large variety of plants collected there by his companion, Sir Joseph Banks.

botch /bäch/ ▶*v.* [*trans.*] *informal* carry out (a task) badly or carelessly: *the ability to take on any task without botching it* | *he was in a position to hire people, and he* ***botched*** *that* ***up*** | [as *adj.*] (**botched**) *a botched attempt to kill them.* ■ patch or repair (an object or damage) clumsily.
▶*n.* (also **botch-up**) *informal* a bungled or badly carried out task or action: *I've probably* ***made a botch of*** *things.* ▷late Middle English (in the sense 'repair' but originally not implying clumsiness): of unknown origin. —**botch·er** *n.*

bot·fly /ˈbätˌflī/ ▶*n.* (*pl.* **-flies**) a stout hairy-bodied fly with larvae that are internal parasites of mammals, in particular: • a fly with larvae (bots) that develop within the guts of horses (*Gasterophilus* and other genera, family Gasterophilidae). • a fly of the warble fly family (Oestridae).

both /bōth/ ▶*adj.* & *pron.* used to refer to two people or things, regarded and identified together: [as *adj.*] *both his parents indulged him* | *I urge you to read both these books* | *she held on with both hands he was blind in both eyes* | [as *pron.*] *a picture of both of us together* | *Jackie and I are both self-employed* | *he looked at them both.*
▶*adv.* used before the first of two alternatives to emphasize that the statement being made applies to each (the other alternative being introduced by "and"): *they all loved to play, both the boys and the girls* | *it has won favor with both young and old* | *studies of zebra finches, both in the wild and in captivity.* ▷Middle English: from Old Norse *báthir*.
▶*PHRASE* □ **have it both ways** benefit from two incompatible ways of thinking or behaving: *countries cannot have it both ways: the cost of a cleaner environment may sometimes be fewer jobs.*

USAGE When **both** is used in constructions with **and**, the structures following 'both' and 'and' should be symmetrical in well-formed English. Thus, *studies of zebra finches,* **both** *in the wild* **and** *in captivity* is stronger and clearer than *studies of zebra* *finches, both in the wild and captivity.* In the second example, the symmetry or parallelism of 'in the wild' and 'in captivity' has been lost.

Bo·tha[1] /'bōtə/, Louis (1862–1919), South African soldier and statesman; first prime minister of the Union of South Africa 1910–19.

Bo·tha[2], P. W. (1916–), South African statesman; prime minister 1978–84; state president 1984–89; full name *Pieter Willem Botha.* An authoritarian leader, he continued to enforce apartheid but in response to pressure, he introduced limited reforms.

B

both·er /'bäT͟Hər/ ▸*v.* **1** [with *negative*] take the trouble to do something: *nobody bothered locking the doors | scientists rarely* ***bother with*** *such niceties |* [with *infinitive*] *the driver didn't bother to ask why.* **2** (of a circumstance or event) worry, disturb, or upset (someone): *secrecy is an issue that bothers journalists | it* ***bothered*** *me* ***that*** *I hadn't done anything.* ■ trouble or annoy (someone) by interrupting or causing inconvenience: *she didn't feel she could* ***bother*** *Mike* ***with*** *the problem.* ■ [*intrans.*] [usu. with *negative*] feel concern about or interest in: *don't* ***bother about*** *me—I'll find my own way home |* [as *adj.*] (**bothered**) *I'm not particularly* ***bothered about*** *how I look.* ■ [with *negative*] (**bother oneself**) concern oneself: *he wasn't to* ***bother himself with*** *day-to-day things.*
▸*n.* effort, worry, or difficulty: *he* ***saved me the bother*** *of having to come up with a speech | it may seem like too much bother to cook just for yourself.* ■ (**a bother**) a person or thing that causes worry or difficulty: *I hope she hasn't been a bother.* ■ [with *negative*] a nuisance or inconvenience: ***it's no bother,*** *it's on my way home.* ▷late 17th cent. (as a noun in the dialect sense 'noise, chatter'): of Anglo-Irish origin; probably related to Irish *bodhaire* 'noise,' *bodhraim* 'deafen, annoy.' The verb (originally dialect) meant 'confuse with noise' in the early 18th cent.
▸*PHRASES* □ **can't be bothered** (**to do something**) be unwilling to make the effort to do something: *they couldn't be bothered to look it up.* □ **hot and bothered** in a state of anxiety or physical discomfort.

both·er·a·tion /ˌbäT͟Hə'rāSHən/ *informal* ▸*n.* effort, worry, or difficulty; bother: *he has caused us a deal of unnecessary botheration.*
▸*exclam. dated* used to express mild irritation or annoyance.

both·er·some /'bäT͟Hərsəm/ ▸*adj.* causing bother; troublesome: *most childhood stomachaches, though bothersome, aren't serious.*

Both·ni·a, Gulf of /'bäTHnēə/ a northern arm of the Baltic Sea, between Sweden and Finland.

both·y /'bäTHē/ (also **both·ie**) ▸*n.* (*pl.* **both·ies**) (in Scotland) a small hut or cottage. ▷late 18th cent.: obscurely related to Irish and Scottish Gaelic *both, bothan,* and perhaps to **BOOTH**.

Bo·tox /'bōˌtäks/ ▸*n. trademark* a drug prepared from the bacterial toxin botulin, used medically to treat certain muscular conditions and cosmetically to remove wrinkles by temporarily paralyzing facial muscles. ▷1990s: from *bo(tulinum) tox(in).* **—Bo·toxed** *adj.*

Bo·tox par·ty ▸*n.* a social event at which guests receive Botox injections from a doctor and mingle with each other for mutual support. ▷on the pattern of *Tupperware party.*

bo tree /bō/ (also **bo·dhi tree** /'bōdē/) ▸*n.* a fig tree native to India and Southeast Asia, regarded as sacred by Buddhists. Also called **PEEPUL** or **PIPAL**. • *Ficus religiosa,* family Moraceae. ▷mid 19th cent.: representing Sinhalese *bōgaha* 'tree of knowledge' (Buddha's enlightenment having occurred beneath such a tree), from *bō* (from Sanskrit *budh* 'understand thoroughly') + *gaha* 'tree.'

bot·ry·oi·dal /ˌbätrē'oidl/ ▸*adj.* (chiefly of minerals) having a shape reminiscent of a cluster of grapes. ▷late 18th cent.: from Greek *botruoeidēs* (from *botrus* 'bunch of grapes') + **-AL**.

bo·try·tis /bō'trītis/ ▸*n.* a fungus that forms a grayish powdery mold on a variety of organic matter. It causes a number of fungal plant diseases, including chocolate spot, and is deliberately cultivated (as noble rot) on the grapes used for certain wines. • Genus *Botrytis,* phylum Ascomycota: numerous species, in particular the gray mold *B. cinerea.* ▷modern Latin, from Greek *botrus* 'cluster of grapes.'

Bot·swa·na /bät'swänə/ a landlocked country in southern Africa, the western half of which is the Kalahari Desert; pop. 1,560,000; capital, Gaborone; languages, English (official) and Setswana. **—Bot·swa·nan** *adj.* & *n.*

Inhabited by Sotho people and, in the Kalahari Desert, San (Bushmen), the area was made the British Protectorate of Bechuanaland in 1885. It became an independent republic within the Commonwealth of Nations in 1966 and adopted the name Botswana.

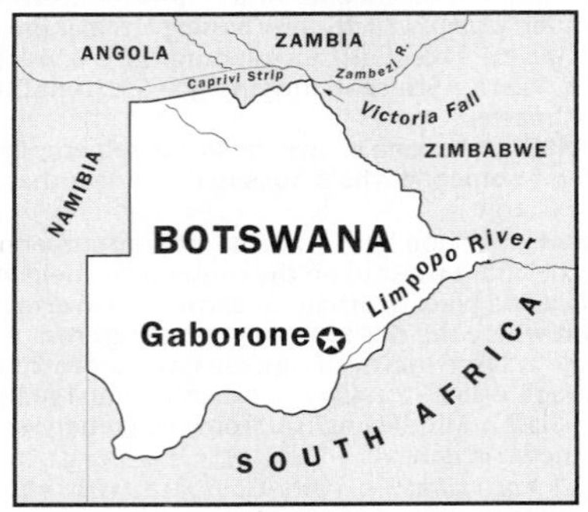

bot·tar·ga /bō'tärgə/ ▸*n.* the dried, pressed roe of the mullet, which is sold in blocks and shaved over Italian dishes. ▷from Italian, from Arabic *butarkhah.*

Bot·ti·cel·li /ˌbätə'CHelē/, Sandro (1445–1510), Italian painter; born *Alessandro di Mariano Filipepi.* He is noted for his mythological works, such as *Primavera* (*c.*1478) and *The Birth of Venus* (*c.*1480).

bot·tle /'bätl/ ▸*n.* a container, typically made of glass or plastic and with a narrow neck, used for storing drinks or other liquids: *a bottle of soda pop.* ■ the contents of such a container: *he managed to put away* ***a bottle of*** *wine.* ■ (**the bottle**) *informal* used in reference to heavy drinking: *more women are* ***taking to the bottle.*** ■ a bottle fitted with a nipple for giving milk or other drinks to babies and very young children: *a bottle of formula.* ■ (**the bottle**) the milk given to a baby from such a bottle: *the age at which parents want a baby to give up the bottle varies.* ■ a large metal cylinder holding liquefied gas.
▸*v.* [*trans.*] (usu. **be bottled**) place (drinks or other liquid) in bottles or jars: *the wine is then bottled |* [as *adj.*] (**bottled**) *bottled beer.* ■ [usu. as *adj.*] (**bottled**) store (gas) in a container in liquefied form: *connecting the bottled gas to the stove.*
▸*phrasal v.* □ **bottle someone up** (usu. **be bottled up**) keep (someone) trapped or contained: *he had to stay bottled up in New York.* □ **bottle something up** repress or conceal feelings over a period of time: *learning how to express anger instead of bottling it up |* [as *adj.*] (**bottled up**) *Lily's bottled-up fury.* ▷late Middle English (denoting a leather bottle): from Old French *boteille,* from medieval Latin *butticula,* diminutive of late Latin *buttis* 'cask, wineskin' (see **BUTT**[4]). **—bot·tler** *n.*
▸*PHRASE* □ **hit the bottle** *informal* drink heavily.

bottle

bot·tle age ▸*n.* time spent by a wine maturing in its bottle.

bot·tle bill ▸*n.* any of several U.S. state laws that require deposits to be paid on beverages sold in recyclable bottles and cans.

bot·tle blond (also **bot·tle blonde**) *derogatory* ▸*adj.* (of a woman's hair) of a light blond shade, as though artificially lightened or bleached.
▸*n.* a woman with such hair.

bot·tle·brush /'bätlˌbrəSH/ ▸*n.* an Australian shrub or small tree with spikes of scarlet or yellow flowers that resemble a cylindrical brush in shape. • Genus *Callistemon,* family Myrtaceae. ■ any of a number of plants bearing similar flowers.

bot·tled gas ▸*n.* butane or propane gas stored under pressure in portable tanks.

bot·tle-feed ▸*v.* [*trans.*] feed (a baby) with milk from a bottle instead of from the mother's breast: [as *adj.*] (**bottle-fed**) *a bottle-fed baby.*

bot·tle green ▸*n.* a dark shade of green.

bot·tle jack ▸*n.* a bottle-shaped hydraulic jack used for lifting heavy objects.

bot·tle·neck /'bätlˌnek/ ▸*n.* **1** the neck or mouth of a bottle. **2** a point of congestion or blockage, in particular: ■ a narrow section of road or a junction that impedes traffic flow: *narrow streets and a lack of parking space combine to make the town a bottleneck.* ■ a situation that causes delay in a process or system: *lack of imports is making the bottlenecks in domestic output worse than usual.* **3** a device shaped like the neck of a bottle, worn on a guitarist's finger to produce special sound effects. ■ (also **bottleneck guitar**) the style of guitar playing that uses such a device.

bot·tle·nose dol·phin /'bätlˌnōz/ (also **bot·tle-nosed dol·phin**) ▸*n.* a stout-bodied dolphin with a distinct short beak, found in tropical and temperate coastal waters. • *Tursiops truncatus,* family Delphinidae.

bot·tle tree ▸*n.* either of two Australian trees with swollen water-containing trunks: • the Australian baobab of the Kimberley region (*Adansonia gregorii,* family Bombacaceae). • a relative of the flame tree occurring in Queensland (*Brachychiton rupestre,* family Sterculiaceae).

bot·tom /'bätəm/ ▸*n.* (usu. **the bottom**) **1** the lowest point or part: *the bottom of the page | she paused at the bottom of the stairs.* ■ the lower surface of something: *place the fruit on the bottom of the dish.* ■ the part on which a thing rests; the underside: *he sat on the bottom of an upturned bucket.* ■ the ground under a sea, river, or lake: *the liner plunged to the bottom of the sea.* ■ (also **bottoms**) another term for **BOTTOMLAND**. ■ the seat of a chair. ■ the lowest position in a competition or ranking: *he started at the bottom and now has his own business.* ■ the basis or origin: *there's a mad scientist* ***at the bottom of it*** *all.* ■ (also **bottoms**) the lower half of a two-piece garment: *pajama bottoms | a skimpy bikini bottom.* ■ the lowest part of the hull of a ship, esp. the relatively flat portion on either side of the keel. ■ *archaic* a ship, esp. considered as a unit of transport capacity. ■ *archaic* stamina or strength of character, esp. of a horse. **2** *informal* the buttocks: *he climbs the side of the gorge, scratching his bottom unselfconsciously.* **3** *Baseball* the second half of an inning: *the bottom of the ninth.* **4** *Physics* one of six flavors of quark. **5** *informal* a male who takes the passive role in homosexual intercourse, esp. anal intercourse.
▸*adj.* in the lowest position: *the books on the bottom shelf.* ■ in the lowest or last position in a competition or ranking: *households in the bottom income bracket.*
▸*v.* [*intrans.*] (of a performance or situation) reach the lowest point before stabilizing or improving: *interest rates have* ***bottomed out.*** ▷Old English *botm,* of Germanic origin; related to Dutch *bodem* 'bottom, ground' and German *Boden* 'ground, earth.' **—bot·tomed** *adj.* [in *combination*] *a glass-bottomed boat | bare-bottomed toddlers.* **—bot·tom·most** /-ˌmōst/ *adj.*
▸*PHRASES* □ **at bottom** basically; fundamentally: *at bottom, science is exploration.* □ **bet your bottom dollar** *informal* stake everything: *you can bet your bottom dollar it'll end in tears.* □ **the bottom falls** (or **drops**) **out** collapse or failure occurs: ***the bottom fell out of*** *the market for classic cars.* □ **bottoms up!** *informal* a call to finish one's drink. □ **from the bottom of one's heart** see **HEART**. □ **from the bottom up 1** completely and thoroughly: *Paul understands me from the bottom up.* **2** by progressing from a lower or more fundamental starting point: *we began to study history from the bottom up.* □ **get to the bottom of** find an explanation for (a mystery): *he hopes to get to the bottom of the scam.*

bot·tom-dwell·ing ▸*adj.* (of an aquatic organism) dwelling on or near the bed of the sea, a lake, or other body of water. ■ (of a person or organization) performing consistently poorly. ■ (of a person or organization) acting or performing questionably or unethically. **—bot·tom-dwell·er** *n.*

bot·tom feed·er ▸*n.* an aquatic creature that feeds at the bottom of a body of water. ■ *figurative* someone who profits from things cast off or left over by others.

bot·tom fer·men·ta·tion ▸*n.* a process in the brewing of certain beers in which the yeast falls to the bottom during fermentation.

bot·tom fish ▸*n.* a species of fish, such as flounder, that is a bottom feeder.
▸*v.* fish for species that are bottom fish. ■ make profits from investments that are of low value or out of favor.

bot·tom·land /ˈbätəm,land/ ▸*n.* low-lying land, typically by a river and subject to overflow during floods.

bot·tom·less /ˈbätəmlis/ ▸*adj.* **1** without a bottom. ■ very deep: *the cold dark sea in whose bottomless depths monsters swam.* ■ *figurative* inexhaustible: *I don't have a* **bottomless pit** *of money | his appetite becomes bottomless.* **2** naked, esp. below the waist.

bot·tom line ▸*n. informal* the final total of an account, balance sheet, or other financial document: *figurative the determination of Japanese companies to ignore the bottom line.* ■ the ultimate criterion: *the bottom line is, does it work?* ■ the underlying or ultimate outcome: *the bottom line is I'm still married to Denny.*

bot·tom round ▸*n.* a steak or other cut from the outer part of a round of beef.

bot·tom·ry /ˈbätəmrē/ ▸*n. dated* a system of merchant insurance in which a ship is used as security against a loan to finance a voyage, the lender losing the investment if the ship sinks. ▹late 16th cent.: from BOTTOM (in the sense 'ship') + -RY, influenced by Dutch *bodemerij.*

bot·tom-up ▸*adj.* proceeding from the bottom of a hierarchy upward or from the beginning of a process forward.

bot·u·lin /ˈbächəlin/ ▸*n.* the bacterial toxin involved in botulism.

bot·u·li·num /,bächəˈlīnəm/ ▸*n.* a rod-shaped bacterium that produces botulin. • *Clostridium botulinum.*

bot·u·li·num tox·in /,bächəˈlīnəm/ (also **bot·u·li·nus tox·in** /-ˈlīnəs/) ▸*n.* another term for BOTULIN.

bot·u·lism /ˈbächə,lizəm/ ▸*n.* food poisoning caused by a bacterium (botulinum) growing on improperly sterilized canned meats and other preserved foods. ▹late 19th cent.: from German *Botulismus*, originally 'sausage poisoning,' from Latin *botulus* 'sausage.'

bou·bou /ˈbo͞o,bo͞o/ ▸*n.* **1** (also **boubou shrike**) an African bush shrike with the upper parts mainly blackish in color. It is noted for the duet of bell-like calls produced by the male and female together. • Genus *Laniarius*, family Laniidae: several species, in particular the **tropical boubou** (*L. aethiopicus*) and the **southern boubou** (*L. ferrugineus*). **2** a long, colorful, loose-fitting garment worn by both sexes in parts of Africa. ▹French, from Malinke *bubu.*

bou·chée /bo͞oˈshā/ ▸*n.* a small pastry with a sweet or savory filling.

Bou·cher /bo͞oˈshā/, François (1703–70), French painter and decorative artist. One of the foremost artists of the rococo style in France, his works include *The Rising of the Sun* (1753) and *Summer Pastoral* (1749).

bou·clé /,bo͞oˈklā/ ▸*n.* [often as *adj.*] yarn with a looped or curled ply, or fabric woven from this yarn: *a bouclé sweater.* ▹late 19th cent.: French, literally 'buckled, curled.'

Bou·dic·ca /bo͞oˈdikə/ (died AD 62), a queen of the Britons; ruler of the Iceni tribe in eastern England; also known as **Boadicea**. She led her forces in revolt against the Romans and sacked Colchester, St. Albans, and London before being defeated by the Roman governor, Suetonius Paulinus.

bou·din /bo͞oˈdan; -ˈdän/ ▸*n.* a French type of blood sausage. ■ a spicy sausage used esp. in Louisiana cuisine. ▹early 19th cent.: French, literally 'blood sausage.'

bou·doir /ˈbo͞o,dwär/ ▸*n. chiefly historical* or *humorous* a woman's bedroom or private room. ▹late 18th cent.: French, literally 'sulking place'.

bouf·fant /bo͞oˈfänt/ ▸*adj.* [*attrib.*] (of a person's hair) styled so as to puff out in a rounded shape: *a blonde lady with bouffant hair.*
▸*n.* a bouffant hairstyle. ▹early 19th cent.: from French, literally 'swelling,' present participle of *bouffer.*

Bou·gain·ville[1] /ˈbo͞ogən,vil; ˈbō-/ a volcanic island in the South Pacific Ocean, the largest of the Solomon Islands. ▹named after Louis de *Bougainville* (see BOUGAINVILLE[2]), who visited it in 1768.

Bou·gain·ville[2] /,bo͞ogänˈvēl/, Louis Antoine de (1729–1811), French explorer. He led the first French circumnavigation of the globe 1766–69, visiting many of the islands of the South Pacific and compiling an invaluable scientific record of his findings.

bou·gain·vil·le·a /,bo͞ogənˈvilyə; -ˈvēə; ,bō-/ (also **bou·gain·vil·lae·a**) ▸*n.* an ornamental climbing plant that is widely cultivated in the tropics. The insignificant flowers are surrounded by brightly colored papery bracts that persist on the plant for a long time. • Genus *Bougainvillea*, family Nyctaginaceae. ▹named after Louis Antoine de *Bougainville* (see BOUGAINVILLE[2]).

bough /bou/ ▸*n.* a main branch of a tree: *apple boughs laden with blossom.* ▹Old English *bōg, bōh* 'bough or shoulder,' of Germanic origin; related to Dutch *boeg* 'shoulders or ship's bow,' German *Bug* 'ship's bow' and 'horse's hock or shoulder,' also to BOW[3].

bought /bôt/ ▸ past and past participle of BUY.

bought·en /ˈbôtn/ ▸*adj. dialect* bought rather than homemade: *wooden boxes full of boughten cookies | her first store-boughten doll.* ▹late 18th cent.: dialect variant of BOUGHT.

bou·gie /ˈbo͞ojē; -zhē/ ▸*n.* (*pl.* **-gies**) *Medicine* a thin, flexible surgical instrument for exploring or dilating a passage of the body. ▹mid 18th cent.: from French, literally 'wax candle,' from Arabic *Bijāya*, the name of an Algerian town that traded in wax.

bouil·la·baisse /,bo͞o(l)yəˈbās; ˈbo͞o(l)yə,bās/ ▸*n.* a rich, spicy stew or soup made with various kinds of fish, originally from Provence. ▹French, from modern Provençal *bouiabaisso* 'boil down.'

bouil·lon /ˈbo͞olyən; -yän/ ▸*n.* a broth made by stewing meat, fish, or vegetables in water. ▹mid 17th cent.: French, literally 'liquid in which something has boiled'.

bouil·lon cube ▸*n.* a cube of concentrated stock, used for making bouillon.

Boul·der /ˈbōldər/ a city in north central Colorado, northwest of Denver, home to the University of Colorado; pop. 94,673.

boul·der /ˈbōldər/ (also **bowl·der**) ▸*n.* a large rock, typically one that has been worn smooth by erosion. ▹late Middle English: shortened from earlier *boulderstone*, of Scandinavian origin. **—boul·der·y** *adj.*

boul·der clay ▸*Brit. n.* another term for TILL[4].

boul·der·ing /ˈbōldəriNG/ ▸*n. Mountaineering* climbing on large boulders, either for practice or as a sport in its own right.

boule[1] /bo͞ol/ (also **boules** pronunc. same) ▸*n.* **1** a French lawn game, played on rough ground with metal balls. **2** a crystal, as of sapphire, synthetically manufactured by fusion and used as a gemstone. **3** a rounded loaf of bread. ▹early 20th cent. (originally denoting a form of roulette): French, literally 'bowl.'

bou·le[2] /bo͞oˈlā; ˈbo͞olē/ ▸*n.* a legislative body of ancient or modern Greece. ▹from Greek *boulē* 'senate.'

boul·e·vard /ˈbo͞olə,värd/ (abbr.: **blvd.**) ▸*n.* a wide street in a town or city, typically one lined with trees: [in *names*] *Sunset Boulevard.* ■ another term for BOULEVARD STRIP. ▹mid 18th cent.: French, literally 'a rampart' (later 'a promenade on the site of one'), from German *Bollwerk* (see BULWARK).

bou·le·var·dier /,bo͞oləvärˈdi(ə)r/ ▸*n.* a wealthy, fashionable socialite. ▹late 19th cent.: from French, originally in the sense 'person who frequents boulevards.'

boul·e·vard strip ▸*n.* a grassy strip between a road and a sidewalk.

bou·le·ver·se·ment /,bo͞oləversəˈmän/ ▸*n.* an inversion, esp. a violent one; an upset or upheaval. ▹from French *bouleverser* 'overturn'.

Bou·lez /bo͞oˈlez/, Pierre (1925–), French composer and conductor. He was principal conductor with the New York Philharmonic Orchestra 1971–78.

boulle /bo͞ol/ ▸*n. Brit.* variant spelling of BUHL.

bounce /bouns/ ▸*v.* [*intrans.*] (of an object, esp. a ball) move quickly away from a surface after hitting it; rebound: *the ball* **bounced off** *the rim |* [*trans.*] *he was bouncing the ball against the wall.* ■ [often with *adv.* or *prep. phrase* showing direction] rebound repeatedly: *the ball bounced away, and he chased it | the puck bounced into the middle of the ice.* ■ (of light, sound, or an electronic signal) come into contact with an object or surface and be reflected: *short sound waves* **bounce off** *even small objects.* ■ (of a thing) move up and down while remaining essentially in the same position: *the gangplank bounced under his confident step.* ■ (of a person) jump repeatedly up and down, typically on something springy: *bouncing up and down on the mattress.* ■ [*trans.*] cause (a child) to move lightly up and down on one's knee as a game: *I remember how you used to bounce me on your knee.* ■ [often with *adv.* or *prep. phrase* showing direction] move in an energetic or happy manner: *Linda bounced in through the open front door.* ■ [often with *adv.* or *prep. phrase* showing direction] (of a vehicle) move jerkily along a bumpy surface: *the car bounced down the narrow track.* ■ (**bounce back**) *figurative* recover well after a setback: *admired for his ability to bounce back from injury.* ■ *Baseball* hit a ball that bounces before reaching a fielder: *bouncing out with the bases loaded |* [*trans.*] *bounced a grounder to third.* ■ *informal* (of a check) be returned by a bank when there are insufficient funds to meet it: *my rent check bounced.* ■ [*trans.*] *informal* write (a check) on insufficient funds: *I've never bounced a check.* ■ [*trans.*] *informal* dismiss (someone) from a job: *those who put in a dismal performance will be* **bounced from** *the tour.* ■ [*trans.*] *informal* eject (a troublemaker) forcibly from a nightclub or similar establishment.
▸*n.* a rebound of a ball or other object: *a bad bounce caused the ball to get away from the second baseman.* ■ an act of jumping or an instance of being moved up and down: *every bounce of the truck brought them into fresh contact | a bounce on your knee or a cuddle and pat on the back.* ■ the power of rebounding: *a large flange with lots of bounce.* ■ a sudden rise in the level of something: *economists agree that there could be a bounce in prices next year.* ■ exuberant self-confidence: *the bounce was now back in Jenny's step.* ■ health and body in the hair: *use conditioner to help hair regain its bounce.* ▹Middle English *bunsen* 'beat, thump.'
▸*PHRASES* □ **bounce an idea off someone** *informal* share an idea with another person in order to get feedback on it. □ **be bouncing off the walls** *informal* be full of nervous excitement or agitation.

bounce flash ▸*n.* a device for giving reflected photographic flashlight. ■ flashlight reflected in this way.

bounc·er /ˈbounsər/ ▸*n.* **1** a person employed by a nightclub or similar establishment to prevent troublemakers from entering or to eject them from the premises. **2** *Baseball* a batted ball that bounces before being fielded.

bounc·ing /ˈbounsiNG/ ▸*adj.* (of a ball) rebounding up and down: *an awkwardly bouncing ball.* ■ (of a baby) vigorous and healthy: *Lisa gave birth to a bouncing baby boy.* ■ lively and confident: *by the next day she was her usual bouncing, energetic self.* ■ *informal* (of a check) returned by a bank because there are insufficient funds in an account to meet it: *attempts to tighten up the law on bouncing checks.*

bounc·ing Bet ▸*n.* another term for SOAPWORT.

bounc·y /ˈbounsē/ ▸*adj.* (**bounc·i·er**, **bounc·i·est**) bouncing well: *a bouncy ball.* ■ resilient; springy: *that bouncy artificial grass.* ■ (of a person) confident and lively: *she was still the girl he remembered, bouncy and full of life.* ■ (of music) having a jaunty rhythm: *the bouncy cheerfulness of polka.* ■ (of the hair) in good condition; having bounce: *hair with shiny, bouncy curls.* **—bounc·i·ly** /-səlē/ *adv.* **—bounc·i·ness** *n.*

bound[1] /bound/ ▸*v.* [*intrans.*] walk or run with leaping strides: *Louis came* **bounding down** *the stairs | the dog* **bounded up to** *him.* ■ (of an object, typically a round one) rebound from a surface: *bullets* **bounded off** *the veranda.*
▸*n.* a leaping movement upward: *I went up the steps in two effortless bounds.* ▹early 16th cent. (as a noun): from French *bond* (noun), *bondir* (verb) 'resound,' later 'rebound,' from late Latin *bombitare*, from Latin *bombus* 'humming.'

bound[2] ▸*n.* (often **bounds**) a territorial limit; a boundary: *the ancient bounds of the forest.* ■ a limitation or restriction on feeling or action: *it is not* **beyond the bounds of possibility** *that the issue could arise again | enthusiasm to join the union* **knew no bounds**. ■ *technical* a limiting value.
▸*v.* [*trans.*] (usu. **be bounded**) form the boundary of; enclose: *the ground was bounded by a main road on one side and a meadow on the other.* ■ place within certain limits; restrict: *freedom of action is bounded by law.* ▹Middle English (in the senses 'landmark' and 'borderland'): from Old French *bodne*, from medieval Latin *bodina*, earlier *butina*, of unknown ultimate origin.
▸*PHRASES* □ **in bounds** *Sports* inside the regular

Pronunciation Key ə *ago*; ər *over*; ˈə *or* ,ə *up*; ˈər *or* ,ər *fur*; a *hat*; ā *rate*; ä *car*; CH *chew*; e *let*; ē *see*; e(ə)r *air*; i *fit*; ī *by*; i(ə)r *ear*; NG *sing*; ō *go*; ô *for*; oi *boy*; o͝o *good*; o͞o *goo*; ou *out*; SH *she*; TH *thin*; TH *then*; (h)w *why*; ZH *vision*

playing area. □ **out of bounds** (of a place) outside the limits of where one is permitted to be: *his kitchen was **out of bounds to** me at mealtimes.* ■ *Sports* outside the regular playing area: *he hit his third shot out of bounds at the 17th.* ■ *figurative* beyond what is acceptable: *Paul felt that this conversation was getting out of bounds.*

bound3 ▸*adj.* heading toward somewhere: *trains **bound for** Chicago* | [in *combination*] *the three moon-bound astronauts.* ■ *figurative* destined or likely to have a specified experience: *they were **bound for** disaster.* ▷Middle English *boun* (in the sense 'ready, dressed'), from Old Norse *búinn*, past participle of *búa* 'get ready'; the final *-d* is euphonic, or influenced by **BOUND**4.

bound4 ▸ past and past participle of **BIND**.
▸*adj.* **1** [in *combination*] restricted or confined to a specified place: *his job kept him city-bound.* ■ prevented from operating normally by the specified conditions: *blizzard-bound Boston.* **2** [with *infinitive*] certain to do or have something: *there is bound to be a change of plan.* ■ obliged by law, circumstances, or duty to do something: *I'm bound to do what I can to help Sam* | *I'm **bound to say** that I'm not sure.* **3** [in *combination*] (of a book) having a specified binding: *fine leather-bound books.* **4** *Linguistics* (of a morpheme) unable to occur alone, e.g., *dis-* in *dismount.* **5** constipated.
▸*PHRASES* □ **bound up in** focusing on, to the exclusion of all else: *she was too bound up in her own misery to care that other people were hurt.* □ **bound up with** (or **in**) closely connected with or related to: *democracy is bound up with a measure of economic and social equality.*

bound·a·ry /'bound(ə)rē/ ▸*n.* (*pl.* **-ries**) a line that marks the limits of an area; a dividing line: *the eastern boundary of the wilderness* | *the boundary between the U.S. and Canada* | [as *adj.*] *a boundary wall.* ■ (often **boundaries**) *figurative* a limit of a subject or sphere of activity: *a community without class or political boundaries.* ▷early 17th cent.: variant of dialect *bounder*, from **BOUND**2 + **-ER**1, perhaps on the pattern of *limitary*.

bound·a·ry con·di·tion ▸*n.* *Mathematics* a condition that is required to be satisfied at all or part of the boundary of a region in which a set of differential equations is to be solved.

bound·a·ry lay·er ▸*n.* a layer of more or less stationary fluid (such as water or air) immediately surrounding an immersed object in relative motion with the fluid.

Bound·a·ry Waters a region in northeast Minnesota, along the Ontario border, known as a canoeing wilderness.

bound·en /'boundən/ ▸ archaic past participle of **BIND**.
▸*PHRASE* □ **one's bounden duty** a responsibility regarded as obligatory: *the Pastor believed that it was his bounden duty to keep them on the right path.*

bound·er /'boundər/ ▸*n.* *informal, dated, chiefly Brit.* a dishonorable man: *he is nothing but a fortune-seeking bounder.*

bound form ▸*n.* a morpheme that occurs only as an element of a compound word and cannot stand on its own, such as *-ing* or *-er*.

bound·less /'boundlis/ ▸*adj.* unlimited; immense: *enthusiasts who devote boundless energy to their hobby.* **—bound·less·ly** *adv.* [as *submodifier*] *the land was boundlessly fertile.* **—bound·less·ness** *n.*

boun·te·ous /'bountēəs/ ▸*adj.* *archaic* generously given or giving; bountiful: *the earth yields a bounteous harvest.* ▷late Middle English: from Old French *bontif, -ive* 'benevolent' (from *bonte* 'bounty'), on the pattern of *plenteous.* **—boun·te·ous·ly** *adv.* **—boun·te·ous·ness** *n.*

Boun·ti·ful /'bountəfəl/ a city in northern Utah, north of Salt Lake City; pop. 41,301.

boun·ti·ful /'bountəfəl/ ▸*adj.* large in quantity; abundant: *the ocean provided a bountiful supply of fresh food.* ■ giving generously: *he was exceedingly bountiful to persons in distress.* ▷early 16th cent.: from **BOUNTY** + **-FUL**. **—boun·ti·ful·ly** *adv.*

Boun·ty /'bountē/ a ship of the British navy on which in 1789 part of the crew, led by Fletcher Christian, mutinied against their commander, William Bligh, and set him adrift in an open boat with eighteen crewmen.

boun·ty /'bountē/ ▸*n.* (*pl.* **-ties**) **1** generosity; liberality: *figurative for millennia the people along the Nile have depended entirely on its bounty.* ■ abundance; plenty: *we ask that growers share their bounty with others.* **2** a monetary gift or reward, typically given by a government, in particular: ■ a sum paid for killing or capturing a person or animal: *there was an increased **bounty on his head.*** ■ *historical* a sum paid to encourage trade: *bounties were paid to colonial producers of indigo dye.* ■ a sum paid to army or navy recruits upon enlistment. ■ *poetic/literary* something given or occurring in generous amounts: *the bounties of nature.* ▷Middle English (denoting goodness or generosity): from Old French *bonte* 'goodness,' from Latin *bonitas*, from *bonus* 'good.' The sense 'monetary reward' dates from the early 18th cent.

boun·ty hunt·er ▸*n.* one who pursues a criminal or seeks an achievement for the sake of the reward.

bou·quet /bō'kā; bo͞o-/ ▸*n.* **1** an attractively arranged bunch of flowers, esp. one presented as a gift or carried at a ceremony. ■ *figurative* an expression of approval; a compliment: *we will happily publish the bouquets.* **2** a characteristic scent, esp. that of a wine or perfume: *the aperitif has a faint bouquet of almonds* | *champagnes have a delicacy of bouquet.* See note at **SMELL**. ▷early 18th cent.: from French (earlier 'clump of trees'), from a dialect variant of Old French *bos* 'wood.' Sense 2 dates from the mid 19th cent.

bou·quet gar·ni /bō'kā gär'nē; bo͞o-/ ▸*n.* (*pl.* **bou·quets gar·nis** *pronunc.* same) a bunch of herbs, typically encased in a cheesecloth bag, used for flavoring a stew or soup. ▷mid 19th cent.: French, literally 'garnished bouquet.'

Bour·bon1 /'bo͝orbən/ the surname of a branch of the royal family of France. The Bourbons ruled France from 1589, when Henry IV succeeded to the throne, until the monarchy was overthrown in 1848, and reached the peak of their power under Louis XIV in the late 17th century. Members of this family have also been kings of Spain (1700–1931 and since 1975).

Bour·bon2 ▸*n.* **1** a reactionary. **2** (also **Bourbon rose**) a rose of a variety that flowers over a long period and has a rich scent. It arose as a natural hybrid on the island of Réunion (formerly Île de Bourbon) and was introduced into Europe in the early 19th century. • *Rosa × borboniana*, a hybrid of *Rosa chinensis* and *R. damascena*, family Rosaceae. ▷mid 19th cent. (sense 1, originally U.S.): from the name of the **BOURBON**1 family. Sense 2 dates from the 1930s.

bour·bon /'bərbən/ ▸*n.* a straight whiskey distilled from a mash having at least 51 percent corn in addition to malt and rye. ▷mid 19th cent.: named after *Bourbon* County, Kentucky, where it was first made.

Bour·bon Coun·ty a county in north central Kentucky, in the Bluegrass region, birthplace of the American whiskey type.

Bour·bon·nais /ˌbo͝orbə'nā/ a former duchy and province in central France; chief town, Moulins.

bour·don /'bo͝ordn/ ▸*n.* **1** *Music* a low-pitched stop in an organ or harmonium, typically a sixteen-foot stopped diapason. **2** the drone pipe of a bagpipe. ▷Middle English (in the sense 'drone of a bagpipe'): from Old French, 'drone,' of imitative origin.

bourg /bo͝org/ ▸*n.* *historical* a town or village under the shadow of a castle. ■ a French market town. ▷French, from late Latin *burgus* 'castle' (in medieval Latin 'fortified town'), ultimately of Germanic origin and related to **BOROUGH**.

bour·geois /bo͝or'zhwä; 'bo͝orzhwä/ ▸*adj.* of or characteristic of the middle class, typically with reference to its perceived materialistic values or conventional attitudes: *a rich, bored, bourgeois family* | *these views will shock the bourgeois critics.* ■ (in Marxist contexts) upholding the interests of capitalism; not communist: *bourgeois society took for granted the sanctity of property.*
▸*n.* (*pl.* same) a bourgeois person: *a self-confessed and proud bourgeois.* ▷mid 16th cent.: from French **BOURG**. Compare with **BURGESS**.

bour·geoise /bo͝or'zhwäz; 'bo͝orzhwäz/ ▸*adj.* of or characteristic of female members of the bourgeoisie.
▸*n.* a female member of the bourgeoisie. ▷late 18th cent.: French, feminine of *bourgeois* 'citizen' (see **BOURGEOIS**).

bour·geoi·sie /ˌbo͝orzhwä'zē/ ▸*n.* (usu. **the bourgeoisie**) the middle class, typically with reference to its perceived materialistic values or conventional attitudes. ■ (in Marxist contexts) the capitalist class who own most of society's wealth and means of production. ▷early 18th cent.: French, from **BOURGEOIS**.

Bour·gogne /bo͝or'gôn(yə)/ French name for **BURGUNDY**.

Bour·gui·ba /bo͝or'gēbə/, Habib ibn Ali (1903–2000), Tunisian nationalist and statesman. He was the first president of independent Tunisia 1957–87.

Bourke-White /'bərk ˌ(h)wīt/, Margaret (1906–71), U.S. photojournalist. During World War II, she was the first female photographer with the U.S. armed forces. At the end of the war, she accompanied the Allied forces when they entered the Nazi concentration camps. Later assignments included the Korean War (1950–53) and work in India and South Africa.

bourn1 /bôrn; bo͝orn/ (also **bourne**) ▸*n.* *dialect* a small stream, esp. one that flows intermittently or seasonally. ▷Middle English: southern English variant of **BURN**2.

bourn2 (also **bourne**) ▸*n.* *poetic/literary* **1** a goal; a destination. **2** a limit; a boundary. ▷early 16th cent. (denoting a boundary of a field): from French *borne*, from Old French *bodne* (see **BOUND**2).

Bourne·mouth /'bôrnməth; 'bo͝orn-/ a resort on the southern coast of England; pop. 154,400.

bour·rée /bo͝o'rā/ ▸*n.* a lively French dance like a gavotte. ■ *Ballet* a series of very fast little steps, with the feet close together, typically performed on pointe and giving the impression that the dancer is gliding over the floor.
▸*v.* [*intrans.*] perform a bourrée. ▷late 17th cent.: French, literally 'faggot of twigs' (the dance being performed around a fire made with such twigs).

bourse /bo͝ors/ ▸*n.* a stock market in a non-English-speaking country, esp. France. ■ (**Bourse**) the Paris stock exchange. ▷mid 16th cent. (as *burse*, the usual form until the mid 19th cent.): from French, literally 'purse,' via medieval Latin from Greek *bursa* 'leather.'

Bour·sin /bo͝or'san/ ▸*n.* *trademark* a kind of soft cheese from France. ▷French.

bou·stro·phe·don /ˌbo͞ostrə'fēdn/ ▸*adj.* & *adv.* (of written words) from right to left and from left to right in alternate lines. ▷early 17th cent.: from Greek, literally 'as an ox turns in plowing,' from *bous* 'ox' + *-strophos* 'turning.'

bout /bout/ ▸*n.* **1** a short period of intense activity of a specified kind: *occasional bouts of strenuous exercise* | *a drinking bout.* ■ an attack of illness or strong emotion of a specified kind: *a severe bout of flu.* ■ a wrestling or boxing match. **2** a curve in the side of a violin, guitar, or other musical instrument. ▷mid 16th cent. (denoting a curve or circuit, hence later a "turn" of activity): from dialect *bought* 'bend, loop'; probably of Low German origin.

bou·tade /bo͞o'täd/ ▸*n.* *formal* a sudden outburst or outbreak. ▷early 17th cent.: French, from *bouter* 'to thrust.'

bou·tique /bo͞o'tēk/ ▸*n.* **1** a small store selling fashionable clothes or accessories. **2** a business that serves a sophisticated or specialized clientele: *a small investment boutique* | [as *adj.*] *a boutique film.* ▷mid 18th cent.: French, literally 'small shop,' via Latin from Greek *apothēkē* 'storehouse.' Compare with **BODEGA**. **—bou·tique·y** *adj.*

bou·tique brew·er·y ▸*n.* another term for **MICROBREWERY**.

bou·tique ho·tel ▸*n.* a small stylish hotel, typically one situated in a fashionable urban location.

bou·ton /bo͞o'tôn/ ▸*n.* *Anatomy* an enlarged part of a nerve fiber or cell, esp. an axon, where it forms a synapse with another nerve. ▷mid 20th cent.: from French, literally 'button.'

bou·ton·nière /ˌbo͞otn'i(ə)r/ ▸*n.* a spray of flowers worn in a buttonhole. ▷late 19th cent.: French, 'buttonhole,' from *bouton* 'button.'

Bou·tros-Gha·li, Boutros (1922–), Egyptian diplomat and politician; secretary-general of the UN 1992–97.

bou·vier /bo͞o'vyā/ ▸*n.* a large, powerful dog of a rough-coated breed originating in Belgium. ▷French 'cowherd'.

bou·zou·ki /bo͞o'zo͞okē/ ▸*n.* (*pl.* **-kis** or **-kia** /-kyä/) a long-necked Greek instrument similar to the mandolin. ▷1950s: from modern Greek *mpouzouki*, possibly related to Turkish *bozuk* 'spoiled' (with reference to roughly made instruments).

bo·vid /'bōvid/ ▸*n.* *Zoology* a mammal of the cattle family (Bovidae). ▷late 19th cent.: from modern Latin *Bovidae*, from *bos, bov-* 'ox.'

bo·vine /'bōvīn; -vēn/ ▸*adj.* of, relating to, or affecting cattle: *bovine tuberculosis* | *bovine tissue.* ■ (of a person) slow-moving and dull-witted: *amiable bovine faces.*
▸*n.* an animal of the cattle group, which also includes buffaloes and bisons. ▷early 19th cent.: from late Latin *bovinus*, from Latin *bos, bov-* 'ox.' **—bo·vine·ly** *adv.*

bo·vine growth hor·mone (abbr.: **BGH**) ▸*n.* a natural hormone in cattle that helps regulate growth and milk production and that may be produced artificially and given to dairy cattle to increase the yield of milk. Also called **BOVINE SOMATROPIN**.

bo·vine so·mat·o·tro·pin /səˌmatə'trōpin/ (abbr.: **BST**) ▸*n.* another term for **BOVINE GROWTH HORMONE**.

bo·vine spon·gi·form en·ceph·a·lop·a·thy ▸*n.* see **BSE**.

Bow /bō/, Clara (1905–65), U.S. actress. One of the most popular stars and sex symbols of the 1920s, she was known as the "It Girl." Her best-known roles were in the silent movies *It* (1927) and *The Wild Party* (1929).

bow[1] /bō/ ▸*n.* **1** a knot tied with two loops and two loose ends, used esp. for tying shoelaces and decorative ribbons: *a girl with long hair tied back* ***in a bow***. ■ a decorative ribbon tied in such a knot. **2** a weapon for shooting arrows, typically made of a curved piece of wood whose ends are joined by a taut string. ■ a bowman. **3** a long, partially curved rod with horsehair stretched along its length, used for playing the violin and other stringed instruments. ■ a single passage of such a rod over the strings. **4** a thing that is bent or curved in shape, in particular: ■ a curved stroke forming part of a letter (e.g., *b*, *p*). ■ a metal ring forming the handle of a key or pair of scissors. ■ a side piece or lens frame of a pair of glasses.
▸*v.* **1** [*trans.*] play (a stringed instrument or music) using a bow: *the techniques by which the pieces were bowed.* **2** bend into the shape of a bow: *the sides of the image are squeezed in or bowed out.* ▷Old English *boga* 'bend, bow, arch,' of Germanic origin; related to Dutch *boog* and German *Bogen*, also to **BOW**[2].

bow[2] /bou/ ▸*v.* [*intrans.*] bend the head or upper part of the body as a sign of respect, greeting, or shame: *he turned and* ***bowed to*** *his father | they refused to* ***bow down before*** *the king* | [as *adj.*] (**bowed**) *councilors stood* ***with heads bowed*** | [*trans.*] *she knelt and bowed her head.* ■ [*trans.*] express (thanks, agreement, or other sentiments) by bending one's head respectfully: *he looked at Hector before bowing grave thanks.* ■ [*intrans.*] bend the body in order to see or concentrate: [as *adj.*] *my mother sat bowed over a library book.* ■ [*trans.*] cause (something) to bend with age or under a heavy weight: *the vines* ***were bowed down with*** *flowers* | [*intrans.*] *the grass bowed down before the wind.* ■ submit to pressure or to someone's demands: *the mayor* ***bowed to*** *public opinion.* ■ [*trans.*] usher (someone) in a specified direction while bowing respectfully: *a gorgeously dressed footman bowed her into the hallway.*
▸*phrasal v.* □ **bow out** withdraw or retire from an activity, role, or commitment: *many artists are forced to* ***bow out of*** *the profession at a relatively early age.*
▸*n.* an act of bending the head or upper body as a sign of respect or greeting: *the man* ***gave a little bow***. ▷Old English *būgan* 'bend, stoop,' of Germanic origin; related to German *biegen*, also to **BOW**[1].
▸**PHRASES** □ **bow and scrape** behave in an obsequious way to someone in authority. □ **make one's bow** make one's first formal appearance in a particular role: *he made his bow as a science fiction writer.* □ **take a bow** (of an actor or entertainer) acknowledge applause after a performance by bowing: *figurative the aides do the grind work while the boss takes the bows.*

bow[3] /bou/ (also **bows**) ▸*n.* the front end of a ship: *water sprayed high over her bows | the two went to stand in the bow.* ▷late Middle English: from Low German *boog*, Dutch *boeg* 'shoulder or ship's bow'; related to **BOUGH**.
▸**PHRASES** □ **on the bow** *Nautical* within 45° of the point directly ahead. □ **a (warning) shot across the bows** a statement or gesture intended to frighten someone into changing their course of action: *supporters are firing a warning shot across the President's bows.*

bow com·pass /bō/ (also **bow com·pass·es**) ▸*n.* a compass with jointed legs.

bowd·ler·ize /ˈbōdlə,rīz; ˈboud-/ ▸*v.* [*trans.*] remove material that is considered improper or offensive from (a text or account), esp. with the result that it becomes weaker or less effective: [as *adj.*] (**bowdlerized**) *a bowdlerized version of the story.* ▷mid 19th cent.: from the name of Dr. Thomas *Bowdler* (1754–1825), who published an expurgated edition of Shakespeare in 1818, + **-IZE**. —**bowd·ler·ism** /-,rizəm/ *n.* —**bowd·ler·i·za·tion** /,bōdləriˈzāsʜən; ,boud-/ *n.*

bow ech·o /bō/ ▸*Meteorology n.* a bow-shaped radar signature associated with fast-moving storm systems accompanied by damaging winds

bow·el /ˈbou(ə)l/ (also **bow·els**) ▸*n.* the part of the alimentary canal below the stomach; the intestine. ■ (**the bowels of ——**) the parts deep inside something large: *the train picks up speed for its final plunge into the subterranean bowels of Manhattan.* ▷Middle English: from Old French *bouel*, from Latin *botellus*, diminutive of *botulus* 'sausage.'

bow·el move·ment ▸*n.* an act of defecation. ■ the feces discharged in an act of defecation.

Bow·en /ˈbōən/, Elizabeth (Dorothea Cole) (1899–1973), British novelist and short-story writer, born in Ireland. Notable works: *The Death of the Heart* (1938) and *The Heat of the Day* (1949).

bow·er[1] /ˈbou(-ə)r/ ▸*n.* a pleasant shady place under trees or climbing plants in a garden or wood. ■ *poetic/literary* a summerhouse or country cottage. ■ *poetic/literary* a lady's private room or bedroom.
▸*v.* [*trans.*] *poetic/literary* shade or enclose (a place or person): [as *adj.*] (**bowered**) *the bowered pathways into the tangle of vines.* ▷Old English *būr* 'dwelling, inner room,' of Germanic origin; related to German *Bauer* 'birdcage.'

bow·er[2] (also **bower anchor**) ▸*n.* each of two anchors carried at a ship's bow. ▷late 15th cent.: from **BOW**[3] + **-ER**[1].

bow·er·bird /ˈbou(-ə)r,bərd/ ▸*n.* a strong-billed Australasian bird, noted for the male's habit of constructing an elaborate run or bower adorned with feathers, shells, and other objects to attract the female for courtship. • Family Ptilonorhynchidae: several genera and species, esp. the **satin bowerbird** (*Ptilonorhynchus violaceus*), which decorates the bower with blue-colored articles.

Bow·er·y /ˈbou(-ə)rē/ a street and district of lower Manhattan in New York City that is associated with drunks and vagrants. ▷mid 17th cent.: built on the site of governor Peter Stuyvesant's *bowery* 'farm,' from Dutch *bouwerij*; the district became noted for its cheap rooming houses and saloons.

bow·fin /ˈbō,fin/ ▸*n.* a predatory American freshwater fish with a large blunt head and a long dorsal fin. It is able to survive for long periods out of water. • *Amia calva*, the only living member of the family Amiidae. ▷late 19th cent.: from **BOW**[1] + **FIN**.

bow-front·ed /bō/ ▸*adj.* (of furniture) having a convexly curved front. —**bow front** *n.* & *adj.*

bow·head /ˈbō,hed/ (also **bowhead whale**) ▸*n.* an Arctic right whale with black skin, feeding by skimming the surface for plankton. Also called **GREENLAND RIGHT WHALE**. • *Balaena mysticetus*, family Balaenidae. ▷late 19th cent.: from **BOW**[1] + **HEAD**.

bow·hunt·ing /ˈbō,həntiɴɢ/ ▸*n.* the practice of hunting animals with a bow rather than a gun. —**bow·hunt·er** /-,həntər/ *n.*

Bow·ie[1] /ˈbōē/ a town in west central Maryland, northeast of Washington, DC; pop. 50,269.

Bow·ie[2] /ˈbo͞o-ē/, David (1947–), English rock singer, songwriter, and actor; born *David Robert Jones*. He is known for his theatrical performances and unconventional stage personae. Notable albums: *Ziggy Stardust* (1972) and *Let's Dance* (1983).

Bow·ie[3] /ˈbōē; ˈbo͞oē/, Jim (1799–1836), U.S. frontiersman; full name *James Bowie*. The Bowie knife was designed either by him or by his brother Rezin. One of the leaders among the U.S. settlers who opposed Mexican rule in Texas, he shared command of the garrison that resisted the Mexican attack on the Alamo. He died during this battle.

bow·ie knife /ˈbo͞oē; ˈbōē/ ▸*n.* a long knife with a blade double-edged at the point. ▷mid 19th cent.: named after Jim *Bowie* or his brother (see **BOWIE**[3]).

bow·knot /ˈbō,nät/ ▸*n.* a double-looped knot in a ribbon, tie, or other fastening.

bowl[1] /bōl/ ▸*n.* **1** a round, deep dish or basin used for food or liquid: *a mixing bowl | a sugar bowl.* ■ the contents of such a container: *huge* ***bowls of*** *steaming spaghetti.* ■ [usu. in *names*] a decorative round dish awarded as a prize in a competition: *the McGeorge Rose Bowl.* ■ a rounded, concave part of an object: *a toilet bowl | the bowl of a spoon.* ■ *Geography* a natural basin. **2** [in *names*] a stadium for sporting or musical events: *the Hollywood Bowl.* ■ a football game played after the regular season between leading or all-star teams: [as *adj.*] *their last four bowl games.* ▷Old English *bolle*, *bolla*, of Germanic origin; related to Dutch *bol* 'round object,' also to **BOLL**. —**bowl·ful** /-,fo͝ol/ *n.*

bowl[2] ▸*n.* a ball made slightly asymmetrical so that it runs on a curved course, used in the game of lawn bowling. ■ a large ball with holes for gripping, used in tenpin bowling.
▸*v.* **1** [*trans.*] roll (a ball or hoop) along the ground: *she snatched her hat off and bowled it ahead of her like a hoop.* **2** [*trans.*] *Cricket* deliver (a ball to a batsman): *Lillee bowled another bouncer* | [*intrans.*] *Sobers bowled to Willis.* ■ (also **bowl out**) dismiss (a batsman) by knocking down the wicket with the ball that one has bowled: *Stewart* ***was bowled for*** *33 in the one-day international.* **3** [*intrans.*] move rapidly and smoothly in a specified direction: *they bowled along the country roads.*
▸*phrasal v.* □ **bowl someone over** knock someone down: *he was almost bowling people over in his haste.* ■ (usu. **be bowled over**) *informal* completely overwhelm or astonish someone, for example by one's good qualities or looks: *when he met Angela, he was just bowled over by her.* ▷late Middle English (in the general sense 'ball'): from Old French *boule*, from Latin *bulla* 'bubble.'

bowl·der ▸*n.* variant spelling of **BOULDER**.

bow legs /bō/ ▸*plural n.* legs that curve outward at the knee; bandy legs. —**bow-leg·ged** /ˈbō ,legid/ *adj.*

bowl·er[1] /ˈbōlər/ ▸*n.* **1** a player at tenpin bowling, lawn bowling, or skittles. **2** *Cricket* a member of the fielding side who bowls or is bowling.

bowl·er[2] (also **bowler hat**) ▸*n.* a man's hard felt hat with a round dome-shaped crown. ▷mid 19th cent.: named after William *Bowler*, the English hatter who designed it in 1850.

Bowles /bōlz/, Paul (Frederick) (1910–99), U.S. writer and composer. In the 1930s, he studied music in Paris and worked as a music critic and composer. His novels, which include *The Sheltering Sky* (1949), *Let It Come Down* (1952), and *The Spider's House* (1966), typically concern Westerners in the Arab world.

bowl hair·cut ▸*n.* a haircut done by or as if by inverting a bowl on a person's head and cutting off the hair left exposed.

bow·line /ˈbōlin; ˈbō,lin/ ▸*n.* **1** a rope attached to the weather leech of a square sail and leading forward, thus helping the ship sail nearer the wind. **2** a nonbinding knot for forming a nonslipping nonjamming loop at the end of a rope. ▷Middle English: from Middle Low German *bōlīne*, Middle Dutch *boechlijne*, from *boeg* 'ship's bow' + *lijne* 'line.'

bowl·ing /ˈbōliɴɢ/ ▸*n.* **1** the game of tenpin bowling as a sport or recreation. ■ the game of candlepin or duckpin bowling. ■ the game of lawn bowling. ■ the game of skittles. **2** *Cricket* the delivery of the ball.

bowl·ing al·ley ▸*n.* a long narrow track along which balls are rolled in the games of tenpin bowling or skittles. ■ a building containing such tracks.

bowl·ing ball ▸*n.* a large, heavy ball with holes for the thumb and two fingers, used in tenpin bowling.

Bowl·ing Green a city in west central Kentucky; pop. 49,296.

bowl·ing green ▸*n.* an area of closely mown grass on which the game of lawn bowling is played.

bowls /bōlz/ ▸*plural n.* [treated as *sing.*] British term for **LAWN BOWLING**. ■ *Brit.* tenpin bowling or skittles.

bow·man[1] /ˈbōmən/ ▸*n.* (*pl.* **-men**) an archer.

bow·man[2] /ˈboumən/ ▸*n.* (*pl.* **-men**) the rower who sits nearest the bow of a boat, esp. a racing boat.

Bow·man's cap·sule /ˈbōmənz/ ▸*n.* a capsule-shaped membranous structure surrounding the glomerulus of each nephron in the kidneys of mammals that extracts wastes, excess salts, and water from the blood.

bow saw /bō/ ▸*n.* a narrow saw stretched like a bowstring on a light frame.

bow·ser /ˈbouzər/ ▸*n.* *trademark* a tanker used for fueling aircraft and other vehicles or for supplying water. ▷1920s: from the name of a company of oil storage engineers.

bow·shot /ˈbō,sʜät/ ▸*n.* [in *sing.*] the distance to which a bow can send an arrow: *the two armies camped almost* ***within bowshot*** *of each other.*

bow·sprit /ˈbou,sprit; ˈbō-/ ▸*n.* a spar extending forward from a ship's bow, to which the forestays are fastened. ▷Middle English: from Middle Low German *bōgsprēt*, Middle Dutch *boechspriet*, from *boech* 'bow' + *spriet* 'sprit.'

bowsprit

Pronunciation Key ə *ago*; ər *over*; ˈə or ,ə *up*; ˈər or ,ər *fur*; a *hat*; ā *rate*; ä *car*; ᴄʜ *chew*; e *let*; ē *see*; e(ə)r *air*; i *fit*; ī *by*; i(ə)r *ear*; ɴɢ *sing*; ō *go*; ô *for*; oi *boy*; o͝o *good*; o͞o *goo*; ou *out*; sʜ *she*; ᴛʜ *thin*; T͟H *then*; (h)w *why*; ᴢʜ *vision*

bow·string /ˈbōˌstriNG/ ▸*n.* the string of an archer's bow, traditionally made of three strands of hemp.
▸*v.* (*past* and *past part.* **-strung**) [*trans.*] *historical* strangle with a bowstring (a former Turkish method of execution).

bow·string hemp ▸*n.* another term for SANSEVIERA.

bow tie /bō/ ▸*n.* a necktie in the form of a bow or a knot with two loops. ■ a pattern used for patchwork quilts, resembling such a necktie: [as *adj.*] *a bow-tie quilt.*

bow wave /bou/ ▸*n.* a wave or system of waves set up at the bows of a moving ship.

bow win·dow /bō/ ▸*n.* a curved bay window.

bow·wood /ˈbōˌwo͝od/ ▸*n.* another name for OSAGE ORANGE.

bow-wow /ˈbou ˈwou/ ▸*exclam.* an imitation of a dog's bark.
▸*n. informal* a child's word for a dog.

bow·yer /ˈbōyər/ ▸*n.* a person who makes or sells archers' bows.

box[1] /bäks/ ▸*n.* **1** a container with a flat base and sides, typically square or rectangular and having a lid: *a cereal box | a hat box.* ■ the contents of such a container: *she ate a whole **box of** chocolates that night.* ■ short for BOOM BOX. ■ *informal* a casing containing a computer. ■ (**the box**) *informal chiefly Brit.* television or a television set: *light entertainment shows on the box.* ■ *informal* a coffin: *I always thought I'd be in a box when I finally left here.* ■ *historical* a coachman's seat. ■ *vulgar slang* a woman's vagina. **2** an area or space enclosed within straight lines, in particular: ■ an area on a printed page that is to be filled in or that is set off by a border: *a picture of Sandy was in the upper right-hand box.* ■ an area on a computer screen for user input or displaying information. ■ (**the box**) (also **the batter's box**) *Baseball* the rectangular area occupied by the batter. ■ *Baseball* the rectangular area behind home plate for the catcher (**catcher's box**), or those near first and third bases, in foul territory, for each base coach (**coach's box**). ■ (**the box**) *Soccer* the penalty area: *he curled in a shot from the edge of the box.* **3** a small structure or building for a specific purpose, in particular: ■ a separate section or enclosed area within a larger building, esp. one reserved for a group of people in a theater or sports ground or for witnesses or the jury in a law court: *a box at the opera | the jury was now in the box.* ■ *Brit.* a small country house for use when hunting or fishing. **4** a protective casing for a piece of a mechanism. ■ *informal* short for GEARBOX. **5** a mailbox at a post office, newspaper office, or other facility where a person may arrange to receive correspondence: *write to me care of PO Box 112.*
▸*v.* [*trans.*] [often as *adj.*] (**boxed**) put in or provide with a box: *the books are sold as a boxed set | Muriel **boxed up** all of Christopher's clothes.* ■ enclose (a piece of text) within printed lines: *boxed sections in magazines.* ■ (**box someone in**) restrict the ability of (someone) to move freely: *a van had double-parked alongside her car and totally boxed her in.*
▸*phrasal v.* □ **box out** *Basketball* block an opponent from an area by the position of one's body: *Miller neglected to box out his man in the final seconds.* ▷late Old English, probably from late Latin *buxis*, from Latin *pyxis* 'boxwood box,' from Greek *puxos* (see BOX[3]). —**box·ful** /-ˌfo͝ol/ *n.* —**box·like** /-ˌlīk/ *adj.*
▸PHRASES □ **back through the box** *Baseball* (of a batted ball) hit in the direction of the pitcher past second base. □ **in a box** restricted or limited: *he will find himself in a box on US policy toward the Soviet Union.* □ **in-a-box** (or **in-the-box**) packaged simply, cheaply, and conveniently: *the Butler-in-a-Box is the gadget of your dreams.* □ (**right**) **out of the box** describing a newly purchased product that works immediately, without any special assembly or training: *a completely preconfigured system you can quickly install right out of the box.* □ **think outside** (**of**) **the box** think in an original or creative way: *you have to give him credit for thinking outside the box.*

box[2] ▸*v.* [*intrans.*] fight an opponent using one's fists; compete in the sport of boxing: *he boxed for England | [trans.] he had to box Bennett for the title.*
▸*n.* [in *sing.*] a slap with the hand on the side of a person's head given as a punishment or in anger: *she gave him **a box on the ear**.* ▷late Middle English (in the general sense 'a blow'): of unknown origin.
▸PHRASE □ **box someone's ears** slap someone on the side of the head as a punishment or in anger.

box[3] ▸*n.* **1** (also **box tree**) a slow-growing European evergreen shrub or small tree with glossy dark green leaves. It is often grown as a hedge and for topiary. • *Buxus sempervirens*, family Buxaceae. ■ (also **box·wood**) the hard, heavy wood of this tree, formerly widely used for engraving and for musical instruments. **2** any of a number of trees that have similar wood or foliage, in particular: • several Australian eucalyptus trees (genus *Eucalyptus*, family Myrtaceae). • the tropical American **Venezuelan** (or **West Indian**) **box** (*Casearia praecox*, family Flacourtiaceae), the wood of which has now largely replaced that of the European box. ▷Old English, via Latin from Greek *puxos*.

box[4] ▸*v.* (in phrase **box the compass**) *chiefly Nautical* **1** recite the compass points in correct order. **2** make a complete change of direction: *by now the breeze had boxed the compass.* ▷mid 18th cent.: perhaps from Spanish *bojar* 'sail around,' from Middle Low German *bōgen* 'bend,' from the base of BOW[1].

box beam ▸*n.* another term for BOX GIRDER.

box·board /ˈbäksˌbôrd/ ▸*n.* a type of stiff cardboard used to make boxes.

box cam·er·a ▸*n.* a simple box-shaped hand camera, typically lacking an adjustment for shutter speed.

box can·yon ▸*n.* a narrow canyon with a flat bottom and vertical walls. ▷mid 19th cent.: probably a calque from Spanish *cajón* 'large box, canyon.'

box·car /ˈbäksˌkär/ ▸*n.* an enclosed railroad freight car, typically with sliding doors on the sides.

box-cut·ter ▸*n.* a thin, inexpensive razor-blade knife designed to open cardboard boxes.

box el·der ▸*n.* an American maple of damp soils that has leaves resembling the ash and green or purplish twigs. • *Acer negundo*, family Aceraceae.

Box·er /ˈbäksər/ ▸*n.* a member of a fiercely nationalistic Chinese secret society that flourished in the 19th century. In 1899 the society led a Chinese uprising (**the Boxer Rebellion**) against Western domination that was eventually crushed by a combined European force, aided by Japan and the U.S. ▷from BOXER, translating Chinese *yì hé quán*, literally 'righteous harmony fists.'

box·er /ˈbäksər/ ▸*n.* **1** a person who takes part in boxing, esp. as a sport. **2** a medium-sized dog of a breed with a smooth brown coat and puglike face.

boxer 2

box·er shorts (also **boxers**) ▸*plural n.* men's loose underpants similar in shape to the shorts worn by boxers.

box·fish /ˈbäksˌfiSH/ ▸*n.* (*pl.* same or **-fish·es**) a tropical marine fish that has a shell of bony plates enclosing the body, from which spines project. Also called TRUNKFISH. • Family Ostraciontidae: numerous genera and species, including the widely distributed *Tetrosomus gibbosus*.

box gird·er ▸*n.* a hollow girder square in cross section.

box·ing /ˈbäksiNG/ ▸*n.* the sport or practice of fighting with the fists, esp. with padded gloves in a roped square ring according to prescribed rules.

Box·ing Day ▸*n.* (in parts of the British Commonwealth) a public holiday celebrated on the first day (strictly, the first weekday) after Christmas Day. ▷mid 19th cent.: from the custom of giving tradespeople a Christmas box on this day.

box·ing glove ▸*n.* a heavily padded mitten worn in boxing.

box jel·ly·fish ▸*n.* a jellyfish with a box-shaped swimming bell, living in warm seas. See also SEA WASP. • Class Cubozoa (formerly order Cubomedusae).

box kite ▸*n.* a tailless kite in the form of a long box open at each end.

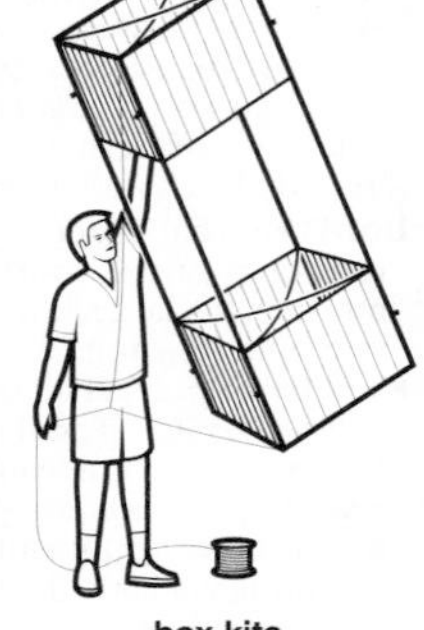
box kite

box lunch ▸*n.* an individual lunch carried in a box rather than a bag.

box of·fice ▸*n.* a place at a theater or other arts establishment where tickets are bought or reserved. ■ [in *sing.*] used to refer to the commercial success of a movie, play, or actor in terms of the audience size or takings they command: [as *adj.*] *the movie was a huge box-office hit.*

box·out /ˈbäksˌout/ ▸*n.* a piece of text written to accompany a larger text and printed in a separate area of the page.

box pew ▸*n.* an old-fashioned church pew enclosed by wooden partitions.

box pleat ▸*n.* a pleat consisting of two parallel creases facing opposite directions and forming a raised section in between.

box score ▸*n.* the tabulated results of a baseball game or other sporting event, with statistics given for each player's performance.

box seat ▸*n.* **1** a seat in a box in a theater or sports stadium. **2** *historical* a coachman's seat.

box so·cial ▸*n.* a fund-raising event in which box lunches are auctioned off.

box spring ▸*n.* each of a set of vertical springs housed in a frame in a mattress or upholstered chair base.

box stall ▸*n.* an enclosed area in a barn in which a single animal can move around freely.

box step ▸*n.* a dance step in which the feet describe the form of a square or rectangle.

box tur·tle ▸*n.* a land-living turtle that has a lower shell with hinged lobes that can be drawn up tightly to enclose the animal. It is native to North America and Mexico and is sometimes kept as a pet. • Genus *Terrapene*, family Emydidae: several species, including the **eastern box turtle** (*T. carolina*) and the **western box turtle** (*T. ornata*).

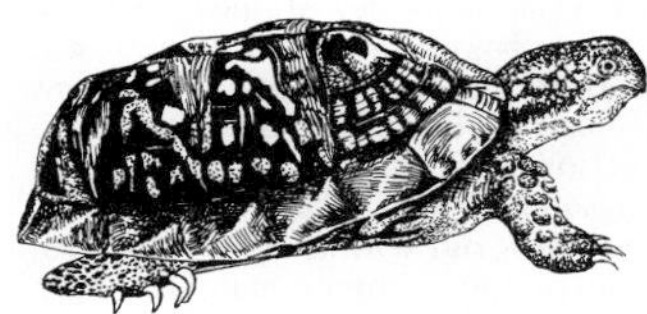
eastern box turtle

box·wood /ˈbäksˌwo͝od/ ▸*n.* see BOX[3] (sense 1).

box wrench ▸*n.* a cylindrical wrench with a hexagonal end fitting over the head of a nut, used esp. when the nut is difficult to reach.

box·y /ˈbäksē/ ▸*adj.* (**box·i·er**, **box·i·est**) squarish in shape: *a boxy jacket | nondescript highrises, boxy and uniform.* ■ (of a room or space) cramped: *the children are too old to share this boxy bedroom.* ■ (of recorded sound) restricted in tone.

boy /boi/ ▸*n.* **1** a male child or young man: *a group of six boys.* ■ a son: *she put **her** little boy to bed.* ■ [with *adj.*] a male child or young man who does a specified job: *a delivery boy.* **2** [usu. with *adj.*] used informally or lightheartedly to refer to a man: *the inspector was a **local boy**.* ■ *dated* used as a friendly form of address from one man to another, often from an older man to a young man: ***my dear boy**, don't say another word!* ■ *dated, offensive* (often used as a form of address) a black male servant or worker. ■ used as a form of address to a male dog: ***down boy**, down!*
▸*exclam. informal* used to express strong feelings, esp. of excitement or admiration: *oh boy, that's wonderful!* ▷Middle English (denoting a male servant): of unknown origin. —**boy·hood** /-ˌho͝od/ *n.*
▸PHRASES □ **the big boys** men or organizations considered to be the most powerful and successful. □ **boys will be boys** used to express the view that mischievous or childish behavior is typical of boys or young men and should not cause surprise when it occurs. □ **one of the boys** an accepted member of a group, esp. a group of men: *he expected to be treated just like one of the boys | Ms. Patton is one of the boys.*

bo·yar /bōˈyär/ ▸*n. historical* a member of the old aristocracy in Russia, next in rank to a prince. ▷late 16th cent.: from Russian *boyarin* 'grandee.'

boy band (or **girl band**) ▸*n.* a pop group composed of attractive young men (or young women) whose music and image are designed to appeal primarily to a young teenage audience.

boy·cott /ˈboiˌkät/ ▸*v.* [*trans.*] withdraw from commercial or social relations with (a country, organization, or person) as a punishment or protest. ■ refuse to buy or handle (goods) as a punishment or protest. ■ refuse to cooperate with or participate in (a policy or event).

▸*n.* a punitive ban that forbids relations with other bodies, cooperation with a policy, or the handling of goods. ▷from the name of Captain C. C. *Boycott* (1832–97), an English land agent in Ireland, so treated in 1880, in an attempt instigated by the Irish to get rents reduced.

Boyd /boid/, Nancy, see **MILLAY**.

Boy·er /boi'(y)ā/, Charles (1897–1978), U.S. actor; born in France. Before going to Hollywood in the 1930s, he enjoyed a successful stage career in France. Notable movies: *Mayerling* (1936), *All This, and Heaven Too* (1940), *Tales of Manhattan* (1942), *Gaslight* (1944), and *Barefoot in the Park* (1968).

boy·friend /'boi,frend/ ▸*n.* a regular male companion with whom one has a romantic or sexual relationship.

boy·ish /'boi-ISH/ ▸*adj.* of, like, or characteristic of a male child or young man: *his boyish charm | she looked boyish and defiant.* —**boy·ish·ly** *adv.* —**boy·ish·ness** *n.*

Boyle /boil/, Robert (1627–91), Irish scientist. He advanced a corpuscular view of matter and is known for his experiments with the air pump that led to the law named after him.

Boyle's law *Chemistry* a law stating that the pressure of a given mass of an ideal gas is inversely proportional to its volume at a constant temperature.

Boyne, Battle of the /boin/ a battle fought near the Boyne River in Ireland in 1690, in which the Protestant army of William of Orange, the newly crowned William III, defeated the Catholic army (including troops from both France and Ireland) led by the recently deposed James II. The battle is celebrated annually (on July 12) in Northern Ireland as a victory for the Protestant cause.

Boyn·ton Beach /'bointən/ a resort city in southeastern Florida; pop. 46,194.

boy·o /'boiō/ ▸*n.* (*pl.* **-os**) *informal, chiefly Welsh & Irish* a boy or man (usually used as a form of address).

Boy Scout ▸*n.* A member of an organization of boys, esp. the **Boy Scouts of America**, that promotes character, outdoor activities, good citizenship, and service to others. ■ an honest, friendly, and typically naive man: [as *adj.*] *his trademark Boy Scout smile.*

boy·sen·ber·ry /'boizən,berē/ ▸*n.* (*pl.* **-ries**) **1** a large red edible blackberrylike fruit. **2** the shrubby plant that bears this fruit, which is a hybrid of several kinds of bramble. • *Rubus loganobaccus*, family Rosaceae. ▷1930s: named after Robert *Boysen* (died 1950), the American horticulturalist who developed it.

Boys Town a village in east central Nebraska, just west of Omaha, noted as a home for troubled youth; pop. 794.

boy toy ▸*n. informal, derogatory* a young woman who offers herself as a sex object for young men. ■ a young man who offers himself as a sex object for women.

boy won·der ▸*n.* an exceptionally talented young man or boy.

Boz /bäz/ the pseudonym used by Charles Dickens in his *Pickwick Papers* and contributions to the *Morning Chronicle*.

Boze·man /'bōzmən/ a city in southwestern Montana; pop. 27,509.

bo·zo /'bōzō/ ▸*n.* (*pl.* **-zos**) *informal* a stupid, rude, or insignificant person, esp. a man. ▷1920s: of unknown origin.

BP ▸*abbr.* ■ before the present (era): *18,000 years BP.* ■ blood pressure. ■ *Baseball* batting practice. ■ boiling point.

Bp. ▸*abbr.* Bishop.

bp ▸*abbr.* ■ baptized. ■ *Biochemistry* base pair(s), as a unit of length in nucleic acid chains. ■ *Finance* basis point(s). ■ (**b.p.**) boiling point.

BPH *Medicine* ▸*abbr.* benign prostatic hyperplasia (or hypertrophy), an enlargement of the prostate gland common in elderly men.

BPh ▸*abbr.* (also **BPhil**) Bachelor of Philosophy.

bpi *Computing* ▸*abbr.* bits per inch, used to indicate the density of data that can be stored on magnetic tape or similar media.

B-pic·ture ▸*n.* another term for **B-MOVIE**.

BPR ▸*abbr.* business process reengineering.

bps *Computing* ▸*abbr.* bits per second.

Bq ▸*abbr.* becquerel.

BR ▸*abbr.* ■ bedroom(s). ■ bills receivable. ■ (in the UK) British Rail or (formerly) British Railways.

Br ▸*symbol* the chemical element bromine.

Br. ▸*abbr.* ■ British. ■ (with reference to religious orders) Brother.

bra /brä/ ▸*n.* an undergarment worn by women to support the breasts. ■ (also **auto bra** or **car bra**) a carbon-based cover that fits over the front bumper of a car, absorbing the microwaves used in police radar equipment to minimize the risk of detection for the speeding motorist. ▷1930s: abbreviation of **BRASSIERE**. —**bra·less** *adj.*

Bra·bant /brə'bant/ a former duchy in western Europe, the capital of which was Brussels. It is now divided into two provinces: North Brabant in the Netherlands, of which the capital is 's-Hertogenbosch; and Brabant in Belgium, of which the capital remains Brussels.

bra burn·er ▸*n. informal* a feminist perceived as militant in the struggle for women's rights. ▷from the mid 20th-cent. urban legend of women of burning bras to symbolize freedom from societal restraints.

brace /brās/ ▸*n.* **1** a device that clamps things tightly together or that gives support, in particular: ■ a device fitted to a weak or injured neck, leg, or other part of the body for support: *a neck brace.* ■ a wire device fitted in the mouth to straighten the teeth. ■ a strengthening piece of iron or timber used in building and carpentry. ■ a tool in carpentry having a crank handle and a socket to hold a bit for boring. ■ a rope leading aft from each yardarm, used for trimming the sail. ■ (**braces**) British term for **SUSPENDERS**. **2** (*pl.* same) a pair of something, typically of birds or mammals killed in hunting: *thirty brace of grouse.* **3** either of the two marks { and }, used either to indicate that two or more items on one side have the same relationship as each other to the single item to which the other side points, or in pairs to show that words between them are connected. ■ *Music* a similar mark connecting staves to be performed at the same time.

▸*v.* [*trans.*] make (a structure) stronger or firmer with wood, iron, or other forms of support: *the posts were braced by lengths of timber.* ■ press (one's body or part of one's body) firmly against something in order to stay balanced: *she* **braced** *her feet* **against** *a projecting shelf* | [as *adj.*] (**braced**) *he stood with legs braced.* ■ prepare (someone or oneself) for something difficult or unpleasant: *both stations* **are bracing themselves for** *job losses | police* **are braced for** *a traffic nightmare.*

▸*phrasal v.* □ **brace up** be strong or courageous. ▷Middle English (as a verb meaning 'clasp, fasten tightly'): from Old French *bracier* 'embrace,' from *brace* 'two arms,' from Latin *bracchia*, plural of *bracchium* 'arm,' from Greek *brakhiōn*.

brace and bit ▸*n.* a revolving tool with a D-shaped crank handle for boring.

brace and bit

brace·let /'brāslit/ ▸*n.* an ornamental band, hoop, or chain worn on the wrist or arm. ■ (**bracelets**) *informal* handcuffs. ▷late Middle English: from Old French, from *bras* 'arm,' from Latin *bracchium.*

brac·er[1] /'brāsər/ ▸*n. informal* an alcoholic drink intended to prepare one for something difficult or unpleasant.

brac·er[2] ▸*n.* a wristguard used in archery, fencing, and other sports. Also called **ARMGUARD**. ■ *historical* a portion of a suit of armor covering the arm. ▷late Middle English: from Old French *braciere*, from *bras* 'arm' (see **BRACELET**).

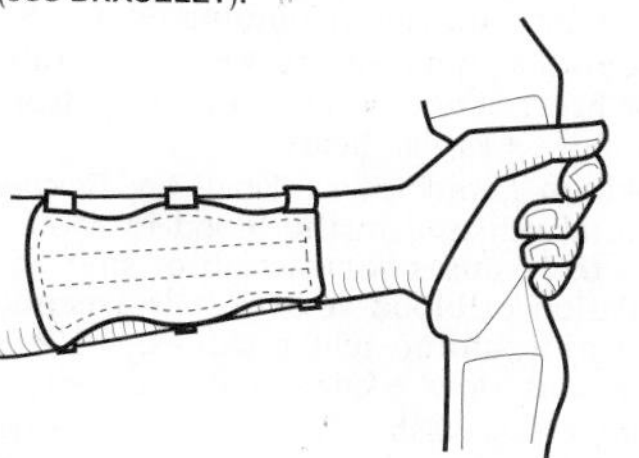

bracer[2]

bra·cer·o /brə'se(ə)rō/ ▸*n.* a Mexican laborer allowed into the U.S. for a limited time as a seasonal agricultural worker. ▷Spanish 'farm worker', from *brazo* 'arm'.

bra·chi·al /'brākēəl; 'brak-/ ▸*adj. Anatomy* of or relating to the arm, specifically the upper arm, or an armlike structure: *the brachial artery.* ■ like an arm. ■ *Zoology* denoting the upper valve of a brachiopod's shell. ▷late Middle English: from Latin *brachialis*, from *brac(c)hium* 'arm.'

bra·chi·ate ▸*v.* /'brākē,āt; 'brak-/ [*intrans.*] (of certain apes) move by using the arms to swing from branch to branch: *the gibbons brachiate energetically across their enclosure.*

▸*adj.* /'brākē,āt; 'brak-; -it/ *Biology* branched, esp. having widely spread paired branches on alternate sides. ■ having arms. ▷mid 18th cent. (originally in the sense 'having paired branches'): from Latin *brachium* 'arm' + **-ATE**[2]. —**bra·chi·a·tion** /,brākē'āSHən; ,brak-/ *n.* —**bra·chi·a·tor** /-,ātər/ *n.*

bra·chi·o·ce·phal·ic /'brākēōsə'falik; 'brak-/ ▸*adj.* of or relating to both arm and head.

Brach·i·op·o·da /,brākē'äpōdə; ,brak-/ *Zoology* a phylum of marine invertebrates that comprises the lamp shells. ▷modern Latin (plural), from Greek *brakhiōn* 'arm' + *pous, pod-* 'foot.' —**bra·chi·o·pod** /'brākēə,päd; 'brak-/ *n.*

bra·chi·o·saur /'brākēə,sôr; 'brak-/ (also **bra·chi·o·sau·rus** /,brākēə'sôrəs; ,brak-/) ▸*n.* a huge herbivorous dinosaur of the late Jurassic to mid Cretaceous periods, with forelegs much longer than the hind legs. • Genus *Brachiosaurus*, infraorder Sauropoda, order Saurischia. ▷modern Latin, from Greek *brakhiōn* 'arm' + *sauros* 'lizard.' —**bra·chi·o·sau·ri·an** *adj.*

bra·chis·to·chrone /brə'kistə,krōn/ ▸*n.* a curve between two points along which a body can move under gravity in a shorter time than for any other curve. ▷late 18th cent.: from Greek *brakhistos* 'shortest' + *khronos* 'time.'

bra·chi·um /'brākēəm; 'brak-/ ▸*n.* the arm, specifically the upper arm from shoulder to elbow.

brachy- ▸*comb. form* short: *brachycephalic.* ▷from Greek *brakhus* 'short.'

brach·y·ce·phal·ic /,brakēsə'falik/ ▸*adj.* having a relatively broad, short skull (usually with the breadth at least 80 percent of the length). Often contrasted with **DOLICHOCEPHALIC**. —**brach·y·ceph·a·ly** /-'sefəlē/ *n.*

brach·y·ther·a·py /,brakē'THerəpē/ ▸*n.* the treatment of cancer, especially prostate cancer, by the insertion of radioactive implants directly into the tissue.

brach·y·u·ra /,brakē'yŏŏrə/ ▸a tribe or suborder of crustaceans that have short abdomens folded toward the ventral surface. It includes the true crabs. ▷from **BRACHY-** + Greek *oura* 'tail'. —**brach·y·u·ral** /-'yŏŏrəl/ *adj.* —**brach·y·u·rous** /-'yŏŏrəs/ *adj.*

brach·y·u·ran /,brakē'yŏŏrən/ ▸*n.* a crab belonging to the brachyura suborder of crustaceans.

brac·ing /'brāsiNG/ ▸*adj.* **1** fresh and invigorating: *the bracing sea air.* **2** [*attrib.*] (of a support) serving to brace a structure: *bracing struts.* —**brac·ing·ly** *adv.* (in sense 1).

bra·ci·o·la /,brächē'ōlə; brä'CHō-/ ▸*n.* a thin slice of beef or other meat wrapped around a filling and cooked in wine. ▷Italian.

brack·en /'brakən/ ▸*n.* a tall fern with coarse lobed fronds that occurs worldwide and can cover large areas. • *Pteridium aquilinum*, family Dennstaedtiaceae (or Hypolepidaceae). ■ (loosely) any large coarse fern resembling this. ▷Middle English: of Scandinavian origin; related to Danish *bregne*, Swedish *bräken*.

brack·et /'brakit/ ▸*n.* **1** each of a pair of marks [ ] used to enclose words or figures so as to separate them from the context: *symbols are* **given in brackets.** **2** [with *adj.*] a category of people or things that are similar or fall between specified limits: *those in a high income bracket.* **3** a right-angled support attached to and projecting from a wall for holding a shelf, lamp, or other object. ■ a shelf fixed with such a support to a wall. **4** *Military* the distance between two artillery shots fired either side of the target to establish range.

▸*v.* (**-et·ed, -et·ing**) [*trans.*] **1** (usu. **be bracketed**) place (one or more people or things) in the same category or group: *he is sometimes bracketed with the "new wave" of film directors.* **2** enclose (words or figures) in brackets: [as *adj.*] (**bracketed**) *the relevant data are included as bracketed points.* ■ *Mathematics* enclose (a complex expression) in brackets to denote that the whole of the expression rather than just a part of it has a particular relation, such as multiplication or division, to another expression. ■ *figurative* surround or enclose (someone or something) physically: *the lines of exhaustion bracketing his mouth.* ■ put (a belief or matter) aside temporarily: *he* ***bracketed off*** *the question of God.* **3** hold or attach (something) by means of a right-angled support: *pipes should be bracketed.* **4** *Military* establish the range of (a target) by firing two preliminary shots, one short of the target and the other beyond it. ■ *Photography* establish (the correct exposure) by taking several pictures with slightly more or less exposure. ▷late 16th cent.: from French *braguette* or Spanish *bragueta* 'codpiece, bracket, corbel,' from Provençal *braga*, from Latin *braca*, (plural) *bracae* 'breeches.'

brack·et creep ▸*n.* movement into a higher tax bracket as taxable income increases.

brack·et fun·gus ▸*n.* a fungus that grows on living trees or dead wood, forming one or more shelflike projections that are the spore-producing bodies. Hyphae spread through the wood absorbing nutrients and can cause the death of the tree. • Several families (formerly in the order Aphyllophorales), class Basidiomycetes.

brack·ish /ˈbrakisн/ ▸*adj.* (of water) slightly salty, as is the mixture of river water and seawater in estuaries. ■ (of fish or other organisms) living in or requiring such water. ■ unpleasant or distasteful: *the lighting in the movie is brackish.* ▷mid 16th cent.: from obsolete *brack* 'salty,' from Middle Low German, Middle Dutch *brac.* **—brack·ish·ness** *n.*

brac·o·nid /ˈbrakənid/ ▸*n. Entomology* a small parasitic wasp of a family (Braconidae) that is related to that of the ichneumons. Unlike the latter, braconids lay numerous eggs in a single host. ▷late 19th cent.: from modern Latin *Braconidae*, formed irregularly from Greek *brakhus* 'short.'

bract /brakt/ ▸*n. Botany* a modified leaf or scale, typically small, with a flower or flower cluster in its axil. Bracts are sometimes larger and more brightly colored than the true flower, as in a poinsettia. ▷late 18th cent.: from Latin *bractea* 'thin plate of metal.' **—brac·te·ate** /-tēit; -tē,āt/ *adj.*

bract of a composite flower

brac·te·o·late /ˈbraktēəlit; -,lāt/ ▸*adj.* having bracteoles.

brac·te·ole /ˈbraktē,ōl/ ▸*n.* a small bract, esp. one on a floral stem.

brad /brad/ ▸*n.* a small wire nail with a small, often asymmetrical head. ▷late Middle English: from Old Norse *broddr* 'spike.'

brad·awl /ˈbrad,ôl/ ▸*n.* a hand boring tool similar to a small, sharpened screwdriver. ▷early 19th cent.: from BRAD + AWL.

Brad·bur·y /ˈbrad,berē; -bərē/, Ray (1920–), U.S. writer of science fiction; full name *Raymond Douglas Bradbury.* Notable works: *The Martian Chronicles* (1950), *Fahrenheit 451* (1951), and *A Graveyard for Lunatics* (1990).

Brad·dock /ˈbradək/, Edward (1695–1755) British soldier. He was commander in chief of the British forces in America in 1754.

Bra·den·ton /ˈbrādntən/ a city in southwestern Florida, noted as a resort and for citrus processing; pop. 43,779.

Brad·ford[1] /ˈbradfərd/ an industrial city in northern England; pop. 449,100.

Brad·ford[2], William (1590–1657), American religious and colonial leader. He was a signer of the Mayflower Compact in 1620 and governor of Plymouth Colony sporadically from 1621 until 1656 (1621–32, 1635, 1637, 1639–43, 1645–56).

Brad·ley[1] /ˈbradlē/, Bill (1943–), U.S. basketball player and politician; full name *William Warren Bradley.* He played professionally for the New York Knicks 1967–77 before entering politics. A New Jersey Democrat, he served as a U.S. senator 1979–97. In 2000, he unsuccessfully campaigned to be the Democratic presidential nominee. Basketball Hall of Fame (1983).

Brad·ley[2] /ˈbradlē/, Joseph (1813–92), U.S. Supreme Court associate justice 1870–92. In 1877, he was part of the Electoral College commission that was formed to resolve the indecisiveness of the Hayes-Tilden presidential election and cast the deciding vote in favor of Rutherford B. Hayes.

Brad·ley[3], Milton (1836–1911), U.S. publisher and manufacturer. His board game "The Checkered Game of Life" (1860) led to the formation of Milton Bradley and Company in 1864. Through the company, he also published books on kindergarten and manufactured materials for kindergartens.

Brad·ley[4], Omar Nelson (1893–1981), U.S. army officer. As a general, he commanded the land contingent during the Normandy campaign of 1944–45. After World War II, he served as chief of staff of the U.S. Army 1948–49, chairman of the U.S. Joint Chiefs of Staff 1949–53, and General of the Army 1950.

Omar Bradley

Brad·ley[5], Thomas (1917–98), U.S. politician and lawyer. Elected mayor of Los Angeles 1973–93, he became the first African-American mayor of a largely white city. He was with the Los Angeles police department 1940–62 and on the city council 1963–73 before becoming mayor.

Brad·ley (in full **Bradley Fighting Vehicle**) ▸*n.* a medium-sized tank equipped for use in combat. ▷named for General Omar *Bradley.*

Brad·man /ˈbradmən/, Don (1908–2001), Australian cricketer; full name *Sir Donald George Bradman.* His test match batting average of 99.94 is well above that of any other cricketer of any era.

Brad·shaw /ˈbradsнô/, Terry Paxton (1948–), U.S. football player. He quarterbacked for the Pittsburgh Steelers 1970–83. Football Hall of Fame (1989).

Brad·street /ˈbrad,strēt/, Anne Dudley (1612–72), American poet. She came from England with her husband Simon Bradstreet to the Massachusetts Bay Colony in 1630. Her poetry is collected in *The Tenth Muse Lately Sprung Up in America* (1650).

Bra·dy /ˈbrādē/, Mathew W. (*c.*1823–96) U.S. photographer. His photographs of the Union armies taken during the Civil War became the basis for his National Photographic Collection, and the publication of his *Gallery of Illustrious Americans* (1850) established him as a leading U.S. photographer.

Bra·dy Bill /ˈbrādē/ (also **Brady Law**) ▸*n.* a provision of U.S. federal law that requires a waiting period for handgun purchases and background checks on those who wish to purchase handguns. ▷For James S. Brady (1940–), who campaigned for the bill, which was signed into law in 1993. Brady was shot and seriously wounded in the 1981 assassination attempt on President Ronald Reagan.

Bra·dy bond ▸*n.* a restructured commercial bank loan to poor countries, denominated in U.S. dollars.

brad·y·car·di·a /,bradiˈkärdēə/ ▸*n. Medicine* abnormally slow heart action. ▷late 19th cent.: from Greek *bradus* 'slow' + *kardia* 'heart.'

brad·y·kin·in /,bradiˈkīnin; -ˈkinin/ ▸*n. Biochemistry* a compound released in the blood in some circumstances that causes contraction of smooth muscle and dilation of blood vessels. It is a peptide comprising nine amino-acid residues. ▷1940s: from Greek *bradus* 'slow' + *kinēsis* 'motion' + -IN[1].

brae /brā/ ▸*n. Scottish & N. Irish* a steep bank or hillside. ▷Middle English: from Old Norse *brá* 'eyelash.' Compare with BROW[1], in which a similar sense development occurred.

Brae·burn /ˈbrābərn/ ▸*n.* a dessert apple of a variety with crisp flesh, first grown in New Zealand.

brag /brag/ ▸*v.* (**bragged, brag·ging**) [*reporting verb*] say in a boastful manner: [with *direct speech*] *"I found them," she bragged* | [with *clause*] *he brags that he wrote 300 pages in 10 days* | [*intrans.*] *they were* ***bragging about*** *how easy it had been.*
▸*n.* **1** a gambling card game that is a simplified form of poker. **2** [in *sing.*] a boastful statement; an act of talking boastfully.
▸*adj.* [*attrib.*] *informal*, excellent; first-rate: *that was my brag heifer.* ▷Middle English (as an adjective in the sense 'boastful'): of unknown origin (French *braguer* is recorded only later). **—brag·ger** *n.* **—brag·ging·ly** *adv.*
▸*PHRASE* □ **bragging rights** used to express pride in bettering a rival: *it took the team seven games to wrest bragging rights from their interstate rivals.*

Bra·gan·za /brəˈgänzə/ the dynasty that ruled Portugal from 1640 until the end of the monarchy in 1910 and Brazil (on its independence from Portugal) from 1822 until the formation of a republic in 1889.

Bragg /brag/, Sir William Henry (1862–1942), English physicist, a founder of solid-state physics. He collaborated with his son, **Sir (William) Lawrence Bragg** (1890–1971), in developing the technique of X-ray diffraction for determining the atomic structure of crystals. Nobel Prize for Physics (1915, shared with his son).

brag·ga·do·ci·o /,bragəˈdōsнē,ō/ ▸*n.* boastful or arrogant behavior. ▷late 16th cent. (denoting a boaster): from *Braggadocchio*, the name of a braggart in Spenser's Faerie Queene, from BRAG or BRAGGART + the Italian suffix *-occio*, denoting something large of its kind.

brag·gart /ˈbragərt/ ▸*n.* a person who boasts about achievements or possessions: [as *adj.*] *braggart men.* ▷late 16th cent.: from French *bragard*, from *braguer* 'to brag.'

brag·ging rights ▸*n.* (esp. of sports teams) the supposed right of a winning team and its fans to brag over the defeat of a close rival. ■ the supposed right to brag about an accomplishment: *the megacompanies compete for bragging rights over which entertainment combine is bigger.*

Brahe /ˈbrä,hē/, Tycho (1546–1601), Danish astronomer. He built an observatory equipped with precision instruments, but despite demonstrating that comets follow sun-centered paths, he adhered to a geocentric system of planetary motions.

Brah·ma /ˈbrämə/ **1** the creator god in later Hinduism, who forms a triad with Vishnu the preserver and Shiva the destroyer. **2** another term for BRAHMAN (sense 2). ▷from Sanskrit *brahman.*

brah·ma /ˈbrämə/ ▸*n.* short for BRAHMAPUTRA.

Brah·man /ˈbrämən/ (also **Brah·min** /-min/) ▸*n.* (*pl.* **-mans** also **-mins**) **1** a member of the highest Hindu caste, that of the priesthood. [from Sanskrit *brāhmaṇa.*] **2** (in Hinduism) the ultimate reality underlying all phenomena. [from Sanskrit *brahman.*] **3** an ox of a humped breed originally domesticated in India that is tolerant of heat and drought and is now kept widely in tropical and warm-temperate countries. Also called ZEBU. • *Bos indicus*, family Bovidae; now usually included under the name *B. taurus* with other domestic cattle. **—Brah·man·ic** /bräˈmanik/ *adj.* **—Brah·man·i·cal** /bräˈmanikəl/ *adj.*

Brah·ma·na /ˈbrämənə/ ▸*n.* (in Hinduism) any of the lengthy commentaries on the Vedas, composed in Sanskrit *c.*900–700 BC and containing expository material relating to Vedic sacrificial ritual.

Brah·man·ism /ˈbrämə,nizəm/ (also **Brah·min·ism**) ▸*n.* the complex sacrificial religion that emerged in post-Vedic India (*c.*900 BC) under the influence of the dominant priesthood (Brahmans), an early stage in the development of Hinduism.

Brah·ma·pu·tra /,brämэˈpo͞otrə/ a river in southern Asia that rises in the Himalayas and flows for 1,800 miles (2,900 km) through Tibet, northeastern India, and Bangladesh to join the Ganges River at its delta on the Bay of Bengal.

Brah·min /ˈbrämin/ ▸*n.* **1** variant spelling of BRAHMAN. **2** a socially or culturally superior person, esp. a member of the upper classes from New England. **—Brah·min·i·cal** /bräˈminikəl/ *adj.* (in sense 1).

Brahms /brämz/, Johannes (1833–97), German composer and pianist. He eschewed program music and opera and concentrated on traditional forms. He wrote four symphonies, four concertos, chamber and piano music, choral works including the *German Requiem* (1857–68), and nearly 200 songs.

braid /brād/ ▸*n.* **1** threads of silk, cotton, or other material woven into a decorative band for edging or trimming garments: *a coat trimmed with gold braid* | *fancy braids.* **2** a length of hair made up of three or more interlaced strands: *women with long black braids.* ■ a length made up of three or more interlaced

strands of any flexible material: *a flexible copper braid | braids of garlic.*
▸*v.* [*trans.*] **1** interlace three or more strands of (hair or other flexible material) to form a length: *their long hair was tightly braided* | [as *adj.*] (**braided**) *horses with braided manes.* **2** [often as *adj.*] (**braided**) edge or trim (a garment) with braid: *braided red trousers.* **3** [usu. as *adj.*] (**braided**) (of a river or stream) flow into shallow interwoven channels divided by deposits of sediment. ▷Old English *bregdan* 'make a sudden movement,' also 'interweave,' of Germanic origin; related to Dutch *breien* (verb).

braid·ing /ˈbrādiNG/ ▸*n.* decorative braid or braided work: *curtains heavy with gold braiding.*

brail /brāl/ *Sailing* ▸*n.* (**brails**) small ropes that are led from the leech of a fore-and-aft sail to pulleys on the mast for temporarily furling it.
▸*v.* [*trans.*] (**brail a sail up**) furl (a sail) by hauling on such ropes. ▷late Middle English: from Old French *braiel,* from medieval Latin *bracale* 'girdle,' from *braca* 'breeches.'

Bră·i·la /brəˈēlä/ an industrial city and port in eastern Romania, on the Danube River; pop. 236,300.

Braille[1] /brāl/, Louis (1809–52), French educator. Blind from the age of 3, he had developed his own system of raised-point reading and writing by the age of 15. His system was officially adopted two years after his death.

Braille[2] ▸*n.* a form of written language for the blind, in which characters are represented by patterns of raised dots that are felt with the fingertips.
▸*v.* [*trans.*] print or transcribe in Braille.

braille·writ·er /ˈbrāl,rītər/ ▸*n.* a machine for writing braille.

brain /brān/ ▸*n.* **1** an organ of soft nervous tissue contained in the skull of vertebrates, functioning as the coordinating center of sensation and intellectual and nervous activity. ■ (**brains**) the substance of such an organ, typically that of an animal, used as food. ■ *informal* an electronic device with functions comparable to those of the human brain.

The human brain consists of three main parts. (i) The forebrain, greatly developed into the cerebrum, consists of two hemispheres joined by a bridge of nerve fibers, and is responsible for thought and control of speech. (ii) The midbrain, the upper part of the tapering brainstem, contains cells involved in eye movements. (iii) The hindbrain, the lower part of the brainstem, contains cells responsible for breathing and for regulating heart action, the flow of digestive juices, and other unconscious actions and processes. The cerebellum, which lies behind the brain stem, plays an important role in the execution of highly skilled movements.

2 intellectual capacity: *I didn't have enough brains for the sciences* | *success requires brain as well as brawn.* ■ (**the brains**) *informal* a clever person who supplies the ideas and plans for a group of people: *Tom was the brains of the outfit.* ■ a person's mind: *a tiny alarm bell began to ring in her brain.* ■ an exceptionally intelligent person: *he was known more as a snappy dresser than a brain.*
▸*v.* [*trans.*] *informal* hit (someone) hard on the head with an object: *she brained me with a rolling pin.* ▷Old English *brægen*; related to Dutch *brein.*
▸*PHRASES* □ **beat** (or **blow**) **someone's brains out** *informal* injure or kill someone with a hard hit on the head. □ **have something on the brain** *informal* be obsessed with something: *John has cars on the brain.*

brain cell ▸*n.* a cell in the tissue of the brain. ■ *informal* regarded as a unit of intellectual power: *it does help if the student has more than one brain cell.*

brain·child /ˈbrān,CHīld/ ▸*n.* (*pl.* **-child·ren**) *informal* an idea or invention considered to be a particular person's creation: *the statue is the brainchild of a local landscape artist.*

brain cor·al ▸*n.* a compact coral with a convoluted surface resembling that of the brain. • *Diploria* and other genera, order Scleractinia.

brain dam·age ▸*n.* injury to the brain that impairs its functions, esp. permanently. **—brain-dam·aged** *adj.*

brain-dead ▸*adj.* having suffered brain death: *brain-dead patients.* ■ *informal* extremely stupid: *the brain-dead politics of the past.*

brain death ▸*n.* irreversible brain damage causing the end of independent respiration, regarded as indicative of death.

brain drain ▸*n.* [in *sing.*] *informal* the emigration of highly trained or intelligent people from a particular country.

Braine /brān/, John (Gerard) (1922–86), English novelist, noted for his novel, *Room at the Top* (1957), whose opportunistic hero is hailed as a representative example of an "angry young man."

brained /brānd/ ▸*adj.* [in *combination*] (of vertebrates) having an organ in the skull of a certain size or kind: *large-brained mammals.* ■ *derogatory* (of a person) having an intellectual capacity of a certain quality or kind: *pea-brained Americans.*

brain fe·ver ▸*n. dated* inflammation of the brain.

brain fin·ger·print·ing ▸*n.* the recording and analysis of an individual's neurological responses to images and words flashed on a screen, esp. to determine if the person is telling the truth.

brain food ▸*n.* food believed to be beneficial to the brain, esp. in increasing intellectual power.

brain·i·ac /ˈbrānē,ak/ ▸*n. informal* an exceptionally intelligent person. ▷1950s: from the name of a super-intelligent alien character of the Superman comic strip, from a blend of **BRAIN** and **MANIAC.**

brain·less /ˈbrānlis/ ▸*adj.* stupid; foolish: *a brainless bimbo.* **—brain·less·ly** *adv.* **—brain·less·ness** *n.*

brain·pan /ˈbrān,pan/ ▸*n. informal* a person's skull.

brain·pow·er /ˈbrān,pouər/ ▸*n.* mental ability; intelligence.

brain·sick /ˈbrān,sik/ ▸*adj.* diseased in the mind; mad or insane.

brain·stem /ˈbrān,stem/ (also **brain stem**) ▸*n. Anatomy* the central trunk of the mammalian brain, consisting of the medulla oblongata, pons, and midbrain, and continuing downward to form the spinal cord.

brain·storm /ˈbrān,stôrm/ ▸*n.* **1** a spontaneous group discussion to produce ideas and ways of solving problems. ■ *informal* a sudden clever idea. **2** *informal* a moment in which one is suddenly unable to think clearly or act sensibly.
▸*v.* [*intrans.*] produce an idea or way of solving a problem by holding a spontaneous group discussion: [as *n.*] (**brainstorming**) *a brainstorming session.*

brain-teas·er (also **brain-twist·er**) ▸*n. informal* a problem or puzzle, typically one designed to be solved for amusement. **—brain-teas·ing** *adj.*

Brain·tree /ˈbrān,trē/ a town in eastern Massachusetts, south of Boston; pop. 32,836.

brain trust ▸*n.* a group of experts appointed to advise a government or politician.

brain·wash /ˈbrān,wôsH; -,wäsH/ ▸*v.* [*trans.*] make (someone) adopt radically different beliefs by using systematic and often forcible pressure: *the organization could brainwash young people* | *they have been* **brainwashed into** *conformity and subservience.*

brain·wave /ˈbrān,wāv/ ▸*n.* (usu. **brainwaves**) an electrical impulse in the brain. ■ [usu. in *sing.*] *informal* a sudden clever idea.

brain·work /ˈbrān,wərk/ ▸*n.* mental activity or effort, esp. as opposed to physical labor.

brain·y /ˈbrānē/ ▸*adj.* (**brain·i·er, brain·i·est**) having or showing intelligence: *a brainy, high-powered lawyer.* **—brain·i·ly** /-nəlē/ *adv.* **—brain·i·ness** *n.*

braise /brāz/ ▸*v.* [*trans.*] fry (food) lightly and then stew it slowly in a closed container: [as *adj.*] (**braised**) *braised veal.* ▷mid 18th cent.: from French *braiser,* from *braise* 'live coals' (in which the container was formerly placed).

brake[1] /brāk/ ▸*n.* a device for slowing or stopping a moving vehicle, typically by applying pressure to the wheels: *he slammed on his brakes* | [as *adj.*] *a brake pedal.* ■ a thing that slows or hinders a process: *China's decision to* **put the brakes on** *economic reform.*
▸*v.* [*intrans.*] make a moving vehicle slow down or stop by using a brake: *drivers who brake abruptly* | [as *adj.*] (**braking**) *an anti-lock braking system.* ▷late 18th cent.: of unknown origin.

brake[2] ▸*n. historical* an open, horse-drawn, four-wheeled carriage. ▷mid 19th cent.

brake[3] ▸*n.* a toothed instrument used for crushing flax and hemp. ■ (also **brake harrow**) a heavy machine formerly used in agriculture for breaking up large lumps of earth. ▷late Middle English: possibly related to Middle Low German *brake* and Dutch *braak,* and perhaps also to **BREAK.**

brake[4] ▸*n. archaic* or *poetic/literary* a thicket. See also **CANEBRAKE, FERNBRAKE.** ▷Old English *bracu* (first recorded in the plural in *fearnbraca* 'thickets of fern'), related to Middle Low German *brake* 'branch, stump.'

brake[5] (also **brake fern**) ▸*n.* a coarse fern of warm and tropical countries, frequently having the fronds divided into long linear segments. • Genus *Pteris,* family Pteridaceae. ■ archaic term for **BRACKEN.** ▷Middle English: perhaps an abbreviation of **BRACKEN** (interpreted as plural).

brake[6] ▸ archaic past of **BREAK.**

brake block ▸*n.* a block of hard material pressed against the rim of a wheel to slow it down by friction, typically one of a pair made of hardened rubber used on a bicycle.

brake disc ▸*n.* the disc attached to the wheel in a disc brake.

brake drum ▸*n.* a broad, very short cylinder attached to a wheel, against which the brake shoes press in a drum brake.

brake flu·id ▸*n.* fluid used in a hydraulic brake system.

brake har·row ▸*n.* see **BRAKE**[3].

brake horse·pow·er ▸*n.* (*pl.* same) the available power of an engine, assessed by measuring the force needed to brake it: *the net brake horsepower is only up by six.*

brake light ▸*n.* a red light at the back of a vehicle that is automatically illuminated when the brakes are applied.

brake lin·ing ▸*n.* a layer of asbestos or a similar material attached to a brake shoe to increase friction against the brake drum.

brake·man /ˈbrākmən/ ▸*n.* (*pl.* **-men**) **1** a railroad worker responsible for a train's brakes and other aspects of its operation. **2** a person in charge of brakes, for instance in a bobsled.

brake pad ▸*n.* either of the thin blocks that grip the disc in a disc brake.

brake shoe ▸*n.* either of the long curved blocks that press on the inside of the brake drum.

brak·ing dis·tance ▸*n.* the approximate distance traveled before coming to a complete stop when the brakes are applied in a vehicle moving at a specified speed.

Bra·man·te /brāˈmäntā/, Donato (di Angelo) (1444–1514), Italian architect. He drew up the first plan for St. Peter's Cathedral, which was begun in 1506, and established the concept of a huge central dome.

bram·ble /ˈbrambəl/ ▸*n.* a prickly scrambling wild shrub of the rose family, esp. a blackberry or (loosely) a dog rose. ■ any rough, prickly vine or shrub. ▷Old English *bræmbel, bræmel,* of Germanic origin; related to **BROOM.** **—bram·bly** /-b(ə)lē/ *adj.*

Bramp·ton /ˈbramtən/ a city in south Ontario, an industrial and residential suburb west of Toronto; pop. 234,445.

bran /bran/ ▸*n.* pieces of grain husk separated from flour after milling. ▷Middle English: from Old French, of unknown origin.

Bran·agh /ˈbranə; ˈbran,ô/, Kenneth (Charles) (1960–), English actor, producer, and director. He is known especially for his Shakespearean films: *Much Ado about Nothing* (1993), *Hamlet* (1996), and *Love's Labour's Lost* (2000).

branch /branCH/ ▸*n.* a part of a tree that grows out from the trunk or from a bough. ■ a lateral extension or subdivision extending from the main part of something, typically one extending from a river, road, or railway: *a branch of the Susquehanna River.* ■ a division or office of a large business or organization, operating locally or having a particular function: *he went to work at our Boston branch.* ■ a conceptual subdivision of something, esp. a family, group of languages, or a subject: *a branch of mathematics called graph theory.* ■ *Computing* a control structure in which one of several alternative sets of program statements is selected for execution.
▸*v.* [*intrans.*] (of a road or path) divide into one or more subdivisions. ■ (of a tree or plant) bear or send out branches: [as *adj.*] (**branched**) *the common sea lavender can be identified by its branched stem.* ■ (**branch off**) diverge from the main route or part: *the road branched off at the town* | *figurative Ellington was constantly branching off with new musical styles.* ■ (**branch out**) extend or expand one's activities or interests in a new direction: *the company is* **branching out into** *Europe.* ▷Middle English: from Old French *branche,* from late Latin *branca* 'paw.' **—branch·let** /-lit/ *n.* **—branch·like** /-,līk/ *adj.* **—branch·y** *adj.*

bran·chi·a /ˈbrangkēə/ ▸*n.* (*pl.* **-chi·ae** /-kē,ē/) the gills of fish and some invertebrate animals. ▷late 17th cent.: from Latin *branchia,* (plural) *branchiae,* from Greek *brankhia* (plural). **—bran·chi·al** /-kēəl/ *adj.*

Bran·chi·op·o·da /ˌbrangkēˈäpədə/ *Zoology* a class of small aquatic crustaceans that includes water fleas and fairy shrimps, which are distinguished by having gills on their feet. ▷modern Latin (plural), from Greek *brankhia* 'gills' + *pous, pod-* 'foot.' **—bran·chi·o·pod** /ˈbrangkēəˌpäd/ *n.*

branch·let /ˈbranchlit/ ▸*n.* a subdivision of a branch; a twig.

branch line ▸*n.* a secondary railroad line branching off from a main line.

branch wa·ter (also **branch**) ▸*n.* ordinary water, esp. when added to alcoholic drinks. ■ water from a stream or brook.

Bran·cu·si /branˈkōōsē; ˈbränˌkōōsh/, Constantin (1876–1957), Romanian sculptor, who spent much of his working life in France. His sculpture represents an attempt to move away from representational art and to capture the essence of forms by reducing them to their ultimate, almost abstract, simplicity.

brand /brand/ ▸*n.* **1** a type of product manufactured by a particular company under a particular name: *a new brand of detergent.* ■ a brand name: *the company will market computer software under its own brand.* ■ a particular type or kind of something: *the Finnish brand of democratic socialism.* **2** an identifying mark burned on livestock or (esp. formerly) criminals or slaves with a branding iron. ■ *archaic* a branding iron. ■ *figurative* a habit, trait, or quality that causes someone public shame or disgrace: *the brand of Paula's alcoholism.* **3** a piece of burning or smoldering wood: *he took two burning brands from the fire.* ■ *poetic/literary* a torch. **4** *poetic/literary* a sword.
▸*v.* [*trans.*] **1** mark (an animal, formerly a criminal or slave) with a branding iron. ■ mark indelibly: *an ointment that branded her with unsightly violet-colored splotches.* ■ describe (someone or something) as something bad or shameful: *the media was intent on* ***branding us as*** *communists* | [*trans.*] *she was branded a liar.* **2** assign a brand name to: [as *adj.*] (**branded**) *branded goods at low prices.* ■ [as *n.*] (**branding**) the promotion of a particular product or company by means of advertising and distinctive design. ▷Old English, of Germanic origin; related to German *Brand,* also to **BURN**[1]. The word originally meant 'burning' or 'a piece of burning or smoldering wood' (sense 3); the verb sense 'mark permanently with a hot iron' dates from late Middle English. The noun sense 'mark of ownership made by branding,' based on the latter, arose in the mid 17th cent., and from it is derived sense 1 (early 19th cent.). **—brand·er** *n.*

bran·dade /bränˈdäd/ ▸*n.* a Provençal dish consisting of salt cod mixed into a purée with olive oil and milk. ▷French, from modern Provençal *brandado,* literally 'something that has been shaken.'

brand a·ware·ness ▸*n.* the extent to which consumers are familiar with the distinctive qualities or image of a particular brand of goods or services.

Bran·deis /ˈbrandīs/, Louis Dembitz (1856–1941), U.S. Supreme Court associate justice 1916–39. He gained an early reputation as the "people's attorney" by defending without a fee Boston residents seeking regulation of local public utilities. His "Brandeis brief" made use of social facts, rather than relying solely on precedent and general arguments.

Bran·den·burg /ˈbrandənˌbərg/ a state in northeastern Germany that surrounds but is independent of the city of Berlin; capital, Potsdam.

Bran·den·burg Gate one of the city gates of Berlin. Built 1788–91, it is the only one that survives. After the construction of the Berlin Wall in 1961, it stood in East Berlin, a conspicuous symbol of a divided city. It was reopened in December 1989.

Brandenburg Gate

brand ex·ten·sion ▸*n.* an instance of using an established brand name or trademark on new products, so as to increase sales.

brand im·age ▸*n.* the impression of a product held by real or potential consumers.

brand·ing i·ron ▸*n.* a metal implement that is heated and used to brand livestock or (esp. formerly) criminals or slaves.

bran·dish /ˈbrandish/ ▸*v.* [*trans.*] wave or flourish (something, esp. a weapon) as a threat or in anger or excitement. ▷Middle English: from Old French *brandiss-,* lengthened stem of *brandir;* ultimately of Germanic origin and related to **BRAND**. **—bran·dish·er** *n.*

brand lead·er ▸*n.* the best-selling or most highly regarded product or brand of its type.

brand·ling /ˈbrandling/ ▸*n.* a red earthworm that has rings of a brighter color, often found in manure, and used as bait by anglers and in composting kitchen waste. • *Eisenia fetida,* family Lumbricidae. ▷mid 17th cent.: from **BRAND** + **-LING**.

brand loy·al·ty ▸*n.* the tendency of some consumers to continue buying the same brand of goods rather than competing brands.

brand name ▸*n.* a name given by the maker to a product or range of products, esp. a trademark. ■ a familiar or widely known name: [as *adj.*] *younger writers who clamber toward brand-name status.*

brand new ▸*adj.* completely new.

Bran·do /ˈbrandō/, Marlon (1924–2004), U.S. actor. An exponent of method acting, he first attracted critical acclaim in the stage production of *A Streetcar Named Desire* (1947) and starred in the movie version four years later. Other notable movies: *On the Waterfront* (1954, for which he won an Academy Award), *The Godfather* (1972), and *Apocalypse Now* (1979).

Brandt /bränt/, Willy (1913–92), German statesman; chancellor of West Germany 1969–74; born *Karl Herbert Frahm.* He achieved international recognition for his policy of détente and the opening of relations with the countries of the Eastern bloc (Ostpolitik). Nobel Peace Prize (1971).

Brand X ▸*n.* a name used for an unidentified brand contrasted unfavorably with a product of the same type being promoted.

bran·dy /ˈbrandē/ ▸*n.* (*pl.* **-dies**) a strong alcoholic spirit distilled from wine or fermented fruit juice. ▷mid 17th cent.: from earlier *brandwine, brandewine,* from Dutch *brandewijn,* from *branden* 'burn, distill' + *wijn* 'wine.'

Bran·dy·wine Creek /ˈbrandēˌwīn/ a historic stream in southeastern Pennsylvania and northern Delaware, the birthplace of the U.S. gunpowder industry.

brane /brān/ ▸*n.* *Physics* an extended object with any given number of dimensions, of which strings in string theory are examples with one dimension. Our universe is a 3-brane. ▷abbr. of *membrane.*

brane world (also **brane-world**) ▸*n.* *Physics* a world model in which our space-time is the result of a 3-brane moving through a space-time of higher dimension, with all interactions except gravity being confined to the 3-brane.

Bran·ford /ˈbranfərd/ a town in south central Connecticut, east of New Haven; pop. 27,603.

branks /brangks/ ▸*plural n.* *historical* an instrument of punishment for a scolding woman, consisting of an iron framework for the head and a sharp metal gag for restraining the tongue. ▷mid 16th cent.: origin uncertain; compare with German *Pranger* 'a pillory or bit for a horse' and Dutch *prang* 'a fetter'; also with late Middle English *barnacle(s),* denoting a powerful bit for restraining a horse.

bran·ni·gan /ˈbranigən/ ▸*n.* *informal* a brawl or violent argument. ▷late 19th cent.: of unknown origin; perhaps from the surname *Brannigan.*

Bran·son[1] /ˈbransən/ a city in southwestern Missouri, on the Ozark Plateau, noted as a resort based on country music; pop. 3,706.

Bran·son[2], Richard (1950–), English businessman and adventurer. He established Virgin Records in 1969 and Virgin Atlantic Airways in 1984. He also made the fastest transatlantic crossing by boat in 1986 and the first by hot-air balloon in 1987.

brant /brant/ ▸*n.* (*pl.* same or **brants**) a small goose with a mainly black head and neck, breeding in the arctic tundra of Eurasia and Canada. • *Branta bernicla,* family Anatidae.

Braque /bräk/, Georges (1882–1963), French painter. His collages, which introduced commercial lettering and fragmented objects into pictures to contrast the real with the "illusory" painted image, were the first stage in the development of synthetic cubism.

brash[1] /brash/ ▸*adj.* self-assertive in a rude, noisy, or overbearing way: *he could be brash, cocky, and arrogant.* ■ strong, energetic, or irreverent: *I like brash, vibrant flavors.* ■ (of a place or thing) having an ostentatious or tasteless appearance: *the cafe was a brash new building.* ▷early 19th cent. (originally dialect); perhaps a form of **RASH**[1]. **—brash·ly** *adv.* **—brash·ness** *n.*

brash[2] ▸*n.* a mass of fragments, in particular: ■ loose broken rock or ice. ▷late 18th cent.: of unknown origin.

Bra·sil /brəˈzil/ Portuguese name for **BRAZIL**[1].

Bra·síl·ia /brəˈzilyə/ the capital, since 1960, of Brazil; pop. 1,601,100. Designed by Lúcio Costa in 1956, the city was built in the center of the country with the intention of drawing people away from the crowded coastal areas.

Bra·şov /bräˈshōv/ a city in Romania; pop. 352,640. It belonged to Hungary until after World War I and was ceded to Romania in 1920. Hungarian name **BRASSÓ**. German name **KRONSTADT**.

brass /bras/ ▸*n.* a yellow alloy of copper and zinc: [as *adj.*] *a brass plate on the door.* ■ a decorative object made of such an alloy: *shining brasses stood on the mantelpiece.* ■ a memorial, typically medieval, consisting of a flat piece of inscribed brass, laid in the floor or set into the wall of a church. ■ a brass block or die used for stamping a design on a book binding. ■ *Brit., informal* money: *they wanted to spend their newly acquired brass.* ■ *Music* brass wind instruments (including trumpet, horn, trombone) forming a band or a section of an orchestra: *the brass and percussion were consistently too loud.* ■ (also **top brass**) *informal* people in authority or of high military rank. ■ *informal* in extended or metaphorical use referring to a person's hardness or effrontery: *he was the only one who* ***had the brass to*** *show his face.* ▷Old English *bræs,* of unknown origin.
▸*PHRASE* □ **the brass ring** *informal* a prize or goal that someone strives for: *Willa* ***went for the brass ring,*** *joining the firm at a whopping salary.* [with reference to the reward of a free ride given on a merry-go-round to the person hooking a brass ring suspended over the horses.]

bras·sard /brəˈsärd; ˈbrasˌärd/ ▸*n.* a band worn on the sleeve, typically having an identifying mark and worn with a uniform. ■ *historical* a piece of armor for the upper arm. ▷late 16th cent. (denoting a piece of armor for the upper arm): from French, from *bras* 'arm.'

brass band ▸*n.* a group of musicians playing brass instruments and sometimes also percussion.

brass-bound ▸*adj.* trimmed or banded with brass fittings. ■ (of a person) adhering inflexibly to tradition or belief. ■ (of a person) brazen or impudent.

bras·se·rie /ˌbrasəˈrē/ ▸*n.* (*pl.* **-ries**) an informal restaurant, esp. one in France or modeled on a French one and with a large selection of drinks. ▷mid 19th cent.: French, originally 'brewery,' from *brasser* 'to brew.'

Bras·sey /ˈbrasē/, Thomas (1805–70), English engineer and railroad contractor. He built more than 6,500 miles (10,000 km) of railroads in Europe, India, South America, and Australia.

brass hat ▸*n.* *informal* a high-ranking officer in the armed forces. ▷late 19th cent.: so named because of the gilt insignia on the caps of such officers.

bras·si·ca /ˈbrasikə/ ▸*n.* a plant of a genus that includes cabbage, turnip, Brussels sprout, and mustard. • Genus *Brassica,* family Brassicaceae. ▷early 19th cent.: Latin, literally 'cabbage.'

brass·ie /ˈbrasē/ (also **brass·y**) ▸*n.* (*pl.* **-ies**) *Golf, informal* a number two wood. ▷late 19th cent.: so named because the wood was originally shod with brass.

bras·siere /brəˈzi(ə)r/ ▸*n.* full form of **BRA**. ▷early 20th cent.: from French, literally 'bodice, child's vest.'

brass in·stru·ment ▸*n.* a wind instrument, such as a trumpet or trombone, typically made of brass.

brass knuck·les ▸*n.* a metal guard worn over the knuckles in fighting, esp. to increase the effect of the blows.

brass knuckles

brass mon·key ▸*n.* *informal* used in phrases to refer to extremely cold weather: *it's brass monkey weather tonight.* ▷late 19th cent.: perhaps from a type of brass rack or 'monkey' in which cannon balls were stored and which contracted in very cold weather, ejecting the balls.

Bras·só /ˈbräsн-sнô/ Hungarian name for **Braşov**.

brass rub·bing ▸*n.* the action of rubbing crayon or chalk over paper laid on an engraved brass to reproduce its design. ■ an image created by doing this.

brass·ware /ˈbras,we(ə)r/ ▸*n.* utensils or other objects made of brass.

brass·y[1] /ˈbrasē/ ▸*adj.* (**brass·i·er**, **brass·i·est**) resembling brass, in particular: ■ bright or harsh yellow. ■ sounding like a brass musical instrument; harsh and loud. ■ (of a person, typically a woman) tastelessly showy or loud in appearance or manner: *her brassy, audacious exterior.* —**brass·i·ly** /ˈbrasəlē/ *adv.* —**brass·i·ness** *n.*

brass·y[2] ▸*n.* variant spelling of **brassie**.

brat /brat/ ▸*n. informal, derogatory* or *humorous* a child, typically a badly behaved one. ▷mid 16th cent. —**brat·tish** *adj.* —**brat·tish·ness** *n.* —**brat·ty** *adj.*

Bra·ti·sla·va /,brätəˈslävə/ the capital of Slovakia, in the western part of the country, a port on the Danube River; pop. 441,450. From 1526 to 1784 it was the capital of Hungary. German name **Pressburg**; Hungarian name **Pozsony**.

brat pack ▸*n. informal* a rowdy and ostentatious group of young celebrities, typically movie stars. —**brat pack·er** *n.*

Brat·tain /ˈbratn/, Walter Houser (1902–87), U.S. physicist and inventor. He co-invented the point-contact transistor 1947 with John Bardeen and William Shockley. Nobel Prize for Physics (1956, shared with Bardeen and Shockley).

brat·tice /ˈbratis/ ▸*n.* a partition or shaft lining in a coal mine, typically made of wood or heavy cloth. ▷Middle English (denoting a temporary wooden gallery for use in a siege): from Old French *bretesche*, from medieval Latin *britisca*, from Old English *brittisc* 'British.' The current sense dates from the mid 19th cent. —**brat·ticed** *adj.*

brat·tle /ˈbratl/ *dialect* ▸*n.* a sharp rattling sound: *a distant brattle of thunder.*
▸*v.* [*trans.*] rattle (something). ■ [*intrans.*] produce a rattling sound. ▷early 16th cent.: probably imitative, from a blend of **break** and **rattle**.

Brat·tle·bo·ro /ˈbratl,bərə; -,bərō/ a town in southeastern Vermont, on the Connecticut River; pop. 12,005.

brat·wurst /ˈbrät,wərst/ (also **brats**) ▸*n.* a type of fine German pork sausage that is typically fried or grilled. ▷German, from *Brat* 'a spit' + *Wurst* 'sausage.'

Braun[1] /broun/, Eva (1910–45), German mistress of Adolf Hitler. Braun and Hitler are thought to have married during the fall of Berlin, shortly before committing suicide together in the air-raid shelter of his Berlin headquarters.

Braun[2] /broun/, Karl Ferdinand (1850–1918), German physicist. He invented the coupled system of radio transmission and the Braun tube (forerunner of the cathode-ray tube), in which a beam of electrons could be deflected. Nobel Prize for Physics (1909, shared with Guglielmo Marconi).

Braun[3] /brôn; broun/, Wernher Magnus Maximilian von (1912–77), U.S. rocket engineer; born in Germany. He led the development of the V-2 rockets used by Germany during World War II. After the war he moved to the U.S., where he worked in the U.S. space program.

Braun·schweig /ˈbroun,sнwīg/ German name for **Brunswick**.

braun·schwei·ger /ˈbroun,sнwīgər/ ▸*n.* a variety of smoked liver sausage.

bra·va /ˈbrävä; bräˈvä/ ▸*exclam.* feminine of **bravo**[1].

bra·va·do /brəˈvädō/ ▸*n.* a bold manner or a show of boldness intended to impress or intimidate. ▷late 16th cent.: from Spanish *bravada*, from *bravo* 'bold' (see **brave**, **-ado**).

brave /brāv/ ▸*adj.* ready to face and endure danger or pain; showing courage: *a brave soldier* | *he* ***put up a brave fight*** *before losing.* ■ *poetic/literary* fine or splendid in appearance: *his medals made a brave show.*
▸*n.* **1** [as *plural n.*] (**the brave**) people who are ready to face and endure danger or pain. **2** *dated* an American Indian warrior. ■ a young man who shows courage or a fighting spirit.
▸*v.* [*trans.*] endure or face (unpleasant conditions or behavior) without showing fear: *we had to brave the full heat of the sun.* ▷late 15th cent.: from French, from Italian *bravo* 'bold' or Spanish *bravo* 'courageous, untamed, savage,' based on Latin *barbarus* (see **barbarous**). —**brave·ly** *adv.* —**brave·ness** *n.*
▸*PHRASES* □ **brave new world** used to refer, often ironically, to a new and hopeful period in history resulting from major changes in society: ***the brave new world of*** *computing.* □ **put a brave face on something** see **face**.

brav·er·y /ˈbrāv(ə)rē/ ▸*n.* courageous behavior or character. ▷mid 16th cent. (in the sense 'bravado'): from French *braverie* or Italian *braveria*, based on Latin *barbarus* (see **barbarous**).

bra·vis·si·mo /bräˈvisə,mō; -ˈvēsē-/ ▸*exclam.* used to express great approval of a performance or performer.

bra·vo[1] /ˈbrävō/ ▸*exclam.* used to express approval when a performer or other person has done something well: *people kept on clapping and shouting "bravo!"*
▸*n.* (*pl.* **-vos**) **1** a cry of bravo: *bravos rang out.* **2** a code word representing the letter B, used in radio communication. ▷mid 18th cent.: from French, from Italian, literally 'bold' (see **brave**).

bra·vo[2] ▸*n.* (*pl.* **-vos** or **-voes**) a thug or hired assassin. ▷late 16th cent.: from Italian, from *bravo* 'bold (one)' (see **brave**).

bra·vu·ra /brəˈv(y)o͞orə/ ▸*n.* great technical skill and brilliance shown in a performance or activity: *the recital ended with a blazing display of bravura* | [as *adj.*] *a bravura performance.* ■ the display of great daring: *the show of bravura hid a guilty timidity.* ▷mid 18th cent.: from Italian, from *bravo* 'bold.'

braw /brô/ ▸*adj. Scottish* fine: *it was a braw day.* ▷late 16th cent.: variant of **brave**. —**braw·ly** *adv.*

brawl /brôl/ ▸*n.* a rough or noisy fight or quarrel.
▸*v.* [*intrans.*] fight or quarrel in a rough or noisy way. ■ *poetic/literary* (of a stream) flow noisily. ▷late Middle English: perhaps ultimately imitative and related to **bray**[1]. —**brawl·er** *n.*

brawn /brôn/ ▸*n.* **1** physical strength in contrast to intelligence: *commando work required as much brain as brawn.* **2** *Brit.* meat from a pig's or calf's head that is cooked and pressed in a pot with jelly. ▷Middle English: from Old French *braon* 'fleshy part of the leg,' of Germanic origin; related to German *Braten* 'roast meat.'

brawn·y /ˈbrônē/ ▸*adj.* (**brawn·i·er**, **brawn·i·est**) physically strong; muscular. —**brawn·i·ness** *n.*

Brax·ton Hicks con·trac·tions /,brakstən ˈhiks/ ▸*plural n. Medicine* intermittent weak contractions of the uterus occurring during pregnancy. ▷early 20th cent.: named after John *Braxton Hicks* (1823–97), English gynecologist.

brax·y /ˈbraksē/ ▸*n.* a fatal bacterial infection of young sheep, caused by ingestion of frozen grass or contaminated feed. • The bacterium is *Clostridium septicum.* ▷late 18th cent.

bray[1] /brā/ ▸*n.* [usu. in *sing.*] the loud, harsh cry of a donkey or mule. ■ a sound, voice, or laugh resembling such a cry.
▸*v.* [*intrans.*] make a loud, harsh cry or sound: *he* ***brayed with laughter.*** ■ [*trans.*] say (something) in a loud, harsh way: *vendors brayed the merits of spiced sausages* | [with *direct speech*] *"Leave," brayed a hoarse voice behind her.* ▷Middle English: from Old French *brait* 'a shriek,' *braire* 'to cry' (the original senses in English), perhaps ultimately of Celtic origin.

bray[2] ▸*v.* [*trans.*] *archaic* pound or crush (something) to small pieces, typically with a pestle and mortar. ▷late Middle English: from Old French *breier*, of Germanic origin; related to **break**, **brioche**.

braze /brāz/ ▸*v.* [*trans.*] [often as *adj.*] (**brazed**) form, fix, or join by soldering with an alloy of copper and zinc at high temperature.
▸*n.* a brazed joint. ▷late 17th cent.: from French *braser* 'solder,' ultimately of Germanic origin.

bra·zen /ˈbrāzən/ ▸*adj.* **1** bold and without shame: *he went about his illegal business with a brazen assurance* | *a brazen hussy!* See note at **bold**. **2** *chiefly poetic/literary* made of brass. ■ harsh in sound: *the music's brazen chords.* ▷Old English *bræsen* 'made of brass,' from *bræs* 'brass,' of unknown ultimate origin. —**bra·zen·ly** *adv.* —**bra·zen·ness** *n.*
▸*phrasal v.* □ **brazen it** (or **something**) **out** endure an embarrassing or difficult situation by behaving with apparent confidence and lack of shame.

bra·zier /ˈbrāzнər/ ▸*n.* **1** a portable heater consisting of a pan or stand for holding lighted coals. **2** a barbecue. ▷late 17th cent.: from French *brasier*, from *braise* 'hot coals.'

Bra·zil[1] /brəˈzil/ the largest country in South America, in the east-central part of the continent, on the Atlantic Ocean; pop. 184,100,000; capital, Brasilia; official language, Portuguese. Portuguese name **Brasil**. —**Bra·zil·ian** *adj.* & *n.*

Brazil is the fifth largest country in the world. Previously inhabited in large part by Tupi and Guarani peoples, Brazil was colonized by the Portuguese, who imported large numbers of slaves from West Africa to work on sugar plantations. The country was proclaimed an independent empire in 1822 and became a republic after the overthrow of the monarchy in 1889.

Bra·zil[2] (also **bra·zil**) ▸*n.* **1** (also **Brazil nut**) a large three-sided nut with an edible kernel, several of which grow inside a large woody capsule. Brazil nuts grow on a South American forest tree, and most are harvested in the wild. • *Bertholletia excelsa*, family Lecythidaceae. **2** (also **Brazil wood**) a hard red wood obtained from a tropical tree and from which dyes may be obtained. • Genus *Caesalpinia*, family Leguminosae: several species. ▷Middle English (sense 2): from medieval Latin *brasilium*. The South American country *Brazil* (see **BRAZIL**[1]) takes its name from the wood.

Braz·os Riv·er /ˈbrazəs/ a river that flows southeast for 840 miles (1,350 km) across Texas, from the Panhandle to the Gulf of Mexico. The cities at its mouth are called collectively Brazosport.

Braz·za·ville /ˈbrazəˌvil; ˈbräzəˌvēl/ the capital of and a major port in the Republic of the Congo; pop. 2,936,000. It was founded in 1880 by French explorer Savorgnan de Brazza (1852–1905) and was capital of French Equatorial Africa 1910–58.

breach /brēCH/ ▸*n.* **1** an act of breaking or failing to observe a law, agreement, or code of conduct: *a breach of confidence | I sued for breach of contract.* ■ a break in relations: *a sudden* ***breach between*** *father and son.* **2** a gap in a wall, barrier, or defense, esp. one made by an attacking army.
▸*v.* [*trans.*] **1** make a gap in and break through (a wall, barrier, or defense): *the river breached its bank.* ■ break or fail to observe (a law, agreement, or code of conduct). **2** [*intrans.*] (of a whale) rise and break through the surface of the water. ▷Middle English: from Old French *breche*, ultimately of Germanic origin; related to **BREAK**.
▸*PHRASES* □ **breach of the peace** an act of violent or noisy behavior that causes a public disturbance and is considered a criminal offense. □ **breach of promise** the action of breaking a sworn assurance to do something, formerly esp. to marry someone. □ **step into the breach** replace someone who is suddenly unable to do a job or task.

bread /bred/ ▸*n.* food made of flour, water, and yeast or another leavening agent, mixed together and baked: *a loaf of bread* | [as *adj.*] *a bread roll | Italian breads.* ■ the bread or wafer used in the Eucharist: *altar bread.* ■ *informal* the money or food that one needs in order to live: *I hate doing this, but I need the bread | his day job puts bread on the table.* ▷Old English *brēad*, of Germanic origin; related to Dutch *brood* and German *Brot*.
▸*PHRASES* □ **best** (or **greatest**) **thing since sliced bread** *informal* used to emphasize one's enthusiasm about a new idea, person, or thing: *they don't consider you to be the greatest thing since sliced bread.* □ **bread and circuses** a diet of entertainment or political policies on which the masses are fed to keep them happy and docile. [translating Latin *panem et circenses* (Juvenal's *Satires*, x.80).] □ **bread and water** a frugal diet that is eaten in poverty, chosen in abstinence, or given as a punishment. □ **bread and wine** the consecrated elements used in the celebration of the Eucharist; the sacrament of the Eucharist. □ **the bread of life** something regarded as a source of spiritual nourishment: *the Roman Catholic Church and faith were the bread of life to the subordinate classes.* □ **break bread** celebrate the Eucharist. ■ *poetic/literary* share a meal with someone. □ **cast one's bread upon the waters** do good without expecting gratitude or reward. [with biblical allusion to Eccles. 11:1.] □ **daily bread** the money or food that one needs in order to live: *she earned her daily bread by working long hours.* □ **know which side one's bread is buttered** (on) *informal* know where one's advantage lies. □ **one cannot live by bread alone** people have spiritual as well as physical needs. [with biblical allusion to Deut. 8:3, Matt. 4:4.] □ **take the bread out of** (or **from**) **people's mouths** deprive people of their livings by competition or unfair working practices. □ **want one's bread buttered on both sides** *informal* want more than is practicable or than is reasonable to expect.

bread and but·ter ▸*n.* a person's livelihood or main source of income, typically as earned by routine work: *their bread and butter is reporting local events* | [as *adj.*] *bread-and-butter occupations.* ■ an everyday or ordinary person or thing: *the bread and butter of non-League soccer* | [as *adj.*] *a good bread-and-butter player.*

bread-and-but·ter let·ter ▸*n.* a letter expressing thanks for hospitality.

bread-and-but·ter pick·le ▸*n.* a variety of sweet pickle made with thin-sliced cucumbers and various seasonings.

Bread and But·ter State a nickname for the state of **MINNESOTA**.

bread·bas·ket /ˈbredˌbaskit/ ▸*n.* **1** a part of a region that produces cereals for the rest of it. **2** *informal* a person's stomach, considered as the target for a blow.

Bread·bas·ket of A·mer·i·ca a nickname for the state of **KANSAS**.

bread·board /ˈbredˌbôrd/ ▸*n.* a board for making an experimental model of an electric circuit.
▸*v.* [*trans.*] make (an experimental circuit).

bread·box /ˈbredˌbäks/ ▸*n.* a box for storing bread and other baked goods.

bread·crumb /ˈbredˌkrəm/ ▸*n.* (usu. **breadcrumbs**) a small fragment of bread. —**bread·crumbed** *adj.*

bread·ed /ˈbredid/ ▸*adj.* (of food) coated with breadcrumbs and then fried: *lightly breaded chicken strips.*

bread·fruit /ˈbredˌfro͞ot/ ▸*n.* **1** the large, round, starchy fruit of a tropical tree, which is used as a vegetable and sometimes to make a substitute for flour. **2** (also **breadfruit tree**) the large evergreen tree that bears this fruit, which is widely cultivated on the islands of the Pacific and the Caribbean. • *Artocarpus altilis*, family Moraceae.

bread knife ▸*n.* a long knife, typically with a serrated edge, for slicing bread.

bread·line /ˈbredˌlīn/ ▸*n.* a line of people waiting to receive free food.

bread mold ▸*n.* any of various fungi, esp. of the genus *Rhizopus*, that grow on bread and other foods.

bread pud·ding ▸*n.* a dessert consisting of slices of bread baked together with dried fruit, sugar, spices, eggs, and milk.

bread·stick /ˈbredˌstik/ ▸*n.* a long, thin, often crisp piece of bread.

bread·stuff /ˈbredˌstəf/ ▸*n.* any bread product. ■ grain or flour used in the making of bread.

breadth /bredTH/ ▸*n.* the distance or measurement from side to side of something; width: *a black sweater outlined the breadth of his shoulders | the boat measured 27 feet* ***in breadth*** *| we traveled the length and breadth of India.* ■ wide range or extent: *she has the advantage of breadth of experience | there is a greater breadth of sound in the later recordings.* ■ the capacity to accept a wide range of ideas or beliefs: *the minister is not noted for his breadth of vision.* ■ *dated* a piece of cloth of standard or full width. ■ overall unity of artistic effect: *these masterpieces showed a new breadth of handling.* ▷early 16th cent.: from obsolete *brede* in the same sense (related to **BROAD**) + **-TH**[2], on the pattern of *length*.

breadth·wise /ˈbredTHˌwīz/ (also **breadth·ways** /-ˌwāz/) ▸*adv.* in a direction parallel with a thing's width.

bread·win·ner /ˈbredˌwinər/ ▸*n.* a person who earns money to support a family. —**bread·win·ning** /-ˌwiniNG/ *n.*

break /brāk/ ▸*v.* (*past* **broke** /brōk/; *past part.* **brok·en** /ˈbrōkən/) **1** separate or cause to separate into pieces as a result of a blow, shock, or strain: [*intrans.*] *the rope broke with a loud snap | the slate fell from my hand and broke in two on the hard floor* | [*trans.*] *windows in the street were broken by the blast | break the chocolate into pieces.* ■ [*trans.*] (of a person or animal) sustain an injury involving the fracture of a bone or bones in (a part of the body): *she had broken her leg in two places.* ■ [*trans.*] sustain such an injury to (a bone in the body). ■ [*intrans.*] (of a part of the body or a bone) sustain a fracture: *what if his leg had broken?* ■ [*trans.*] cause a cut or graze in (the skin): *the bite had scarcely broken the skin.* ■ make or become inoperative: [*intrans.*] *the machine has broken, and they can't fix it until next week* | [*trans.*] *he's broken the video.* ■ (of the amniotic fluid surrounding a fetus) be or cause to be discharged when the sac is ruptured in the first stages of labor: [*intrans.*] *she realized her water had broken.* ■ [*trans.*] open (a safe) forcibly. ■ [*trans.*] use (a piece of paper currency) to pay for something and receive change out of the transaction: *she had to break a ten.* ■ [*trans.*] exchange (a piece of paper currency of large denomination) for the same amount in smaller denominations. ■ [*intrans.*] (of two boxers or wrestlers) come out of a clinch, typically at the referee's command: *I was acting as referee and telling them to break.* ■ [*trans.*] unfurl (a flag or sail). ■ [*trans.*] succeed in deciphering (a code). ■ [*trans.*] open (a shotgun or rifle) at the breech. ■ [*trans.*] disprove (an alibi). ■ [*trans.*] invalidate (a will) through legal process. **2** [*trans.*] interrupt (a continuity, sequence, or course): *the new government broke the pattern of growth | his concentration was broken by a sound.* ■ put an end to (a silence) by speaking or making contact. ■ make a pause in (a journey): *we will break our journey in Venice.* ■ [*intrans.*] stop proceedings in order to have a pause or vacation: *at mid-morning they* ***broke for*** *coffee.* ■ lessen the impact of (a fall): *she put out an arm to break her fall.* ■ stop oneself from being subject to (a habit). ■ put an end to (a tie in a game) by making a score. ■ [*intrans.*] (chiefly of an attacking player or team, or of a military force) make a rush or dash in a particular direction: *the flight broke to the right and formed a defensive circle.* ■ surpass (a record): *the movie broke box-office records.* ■ disconnect or interrupt (an electrical circuit). ■ [*intrans.*] *Sports* (of a pitched or bowled ball) swerve or dip in direction. ■ [*intrans.*] *Soccer* (of the ball) rebound unpredictably: *the ball broke to Craig but his shot rebounded from the post.* ■ [*intrans.*] (of a bowled cricket ball) change direction on bouncing, due to spin. **3** [*trans.*] fail to observe (a law, regulation, or agreement): *the district attorney says she will prosecute retailers who break the law | a legally binding contract that can only be broken by mutual consent.* ■ fail to continue with (a self-imposed discipline): *diets started without preparation are broken all the time.* **4** [*trans.*] crush the emotional strength, spirit, or resistance of: *the idea was to better the prisoners, not to break them.* ■ [*intrans.*] (of a person's emotional strength) give way: *her self-control finally broke.* ■ destroy the power of (a movement or organization). ■ destroy the effectiveness of (a strike), typically by bringing in other people to replace the striking workers. ■ tame or train (a horse). **5** [*intrans.*] undergo a change or enter a new state, in particular: ■ (of the weather) change suddenly: *the weather broke, and thunder rumbled through a leaden sky.* ■ (of a storm) begin violently. ■ (of dawn or day) begin with the sun rising: *dawn was just breaking.* ■ (of clouds) move apart and begin to disperse. ■ (of waves) curl over and dissolve into foam: *the Caribbean sea breaking gently on the shore.* ■ (of a pitched baseball) curve or drop on its way toward the batter. ■ (of the voice) falter and change tone, due to emotion: *her voice broke as she relived the experience.* ■ (of a boy's voice) change in tone and register at puberty. ■ *Phonology* (of a vowel) develop into a diphthong, under the influence of an adjacent sound: [as *n.*] (**breaking**) *breaking due to a following r or h.* ■ (of prices on the stock exchange) fall sharply. ■ (of news or a scandal) suddenly become public: *since the news broke I've received thousands of wonderful letters.* ■ [*trans.*] (**break something to someone**) make bad news known to someone. ■ make the first stroke at the beginning of a game of billiards, pool, or snooker.
▸*phrasal v.* □ **break away** (of a person) escape from someone's hold. ■ escape from the control of a person, group, or practice: *an attempt to* ***break away from*** *the elitism that has dominated the book trade.* ■ (of a competitor in a race) move into the lead. ■ (of a material or object) become detached from its base, typically through decay or under force. □ **break down 1** (of a machine or motor vehicle) suddenly cease to function: *his van broke down.* ■ (of a person) have the vehicle they are driving cease to function: *she broke down on the highway.* ■ (of a relationship, agreement, or process) cease to continue; collapse: *pay negotiations with management broke down.* ■ lose control of one's emotions when in a state of distress: *if she had tried to utter a word, she would have broken down | the old woman broke down in tears.* ■ (of a person's health or emotional control) fail or collapse: *his health broke down under the strain of overwork.* **2** undergo chemical decomposition: *waste products that* ***break down into*** *low-level toxic materials.* □ **break something down 1** demolish a door or other barrier: *they had to get the police to break the door down | figurative race barriers can be broken down by educational reform.* **2** separate something into parts: *each tutorial is broken down into more manageable units.* ■ analyze information: *bar graphs show how the information can be broken down.* ■ convert a substance into simpler compounds by chemical action: *almost every natural substance can be broken down by bacteria.* □ **break even** reach a point in a business venture when the profits are equal to the costs. □ **break forth** burst out suddenly; emerge. □ **break free** another way of saying **BREAK AWAY**. □ **break in 1** force entry to a building: *it sounded like someone trying to break in.* **2** [with *direct speech*] interject: *"I don't want to interfere," Mrs. Hendry broke in.* □ **break someone in** familiarize someone with a new job or situation: *there was no time to break in a new*

executive assistant. ■ (**break a horse**) accustom a horse to a saddle and bridle, and to being ridden. □ **break something in** wear something, typically a pair of new shoes, until it becomes supple and comfortable. □ **break in on** interrupt: *the doctor's voice **broke in on** her thoughts.* □ **break into 1** enter or open a (place, vehicle, or container) forcibly, typically for the purposes of theft: *four men broke into the house | a friend of mine had his car broken into.* ■ succeed in winning a share of (a market or a position in a profession): *Japanese companies failed to break into the U.S. personal-computer market.* ■ interrupt (a conversation). **2** (of a person) suddenly or unexpectedly burst forth into (laughter or song). ■ (of a person's face or mouth) relax into (a smile). **3** change one's pace to (a faster one): *Greg broke into a sprint.* □ **break off** become severed: *the fuselage had broken off just behind the pilot's seat.* ■ abruptly stop talking: *she broke off, stifling a sob.* □ **break something off** remove something from a larger unit or whole: *Tucker broke off a piece of bread.* ■ discontinue talks or relations: *the U.S. threatened to break off diplomatic relations.* □ **break something open** open something forcibly. □ **break out** (of war, fighting, or similarly undesirable things) start suddenly: *forest fires have broken out across Indonesia.* ■ (of a physical discomfort) suddenly manifest itself: *prickles of sweat had broken out along her backbone.* □ **break out in** (of a person or a part of their body) be suddenly affected by an unpleasant sensation or condition: *something had caused him to break out in a rash.* □ **break out of** escape from: *figurative executives looking to break out of the corporate hierarchy.* □ **break something out** *informal* open and start using something: *it was time to break out the champagne.* □ **break through** make or force a way through (a barrier): *demonstrators attempted to break through the police lines | the sun might break through in a few spots.* ■ *figurative* (of a person) achieve success in a particular area: *so many talented players are struggling to break through.* □ **break up** disintegrate; disperse: *the bones had broken up into minute fragments | the gray clouds had begun to break up.* ■ (of a gathering) disband; end. ■ *Brit.* end the school term: *we broke up for the summer.* ■ (of a couple in a relationship) part company. ■ start laughing uncontrollably: *the whole cast broke up.* ■ become emotionally upset. □ **break someone up** cause someone to become extremely upset. □ **break something up** cause something to separate into pieces, parts, or sections: *break up the chocolate, and place it in a bowl | he intends to break the company up into strategic business units.* ■ bring a social event or meeting to an end by being the first person to leave: *Richard was sorry to break up the party.* ■ disperse or put an end to a gathering: *police broke up a demonstration in the capital.* □ **break with** quarrel or cease relations with (someone): *he had broken with his family long before.* ■ act in a way that is not in accordance with (a custom or tradition).

▸*n.* **1** an interruption of continuity or uniformity: *the magazine has been published without a break since 1950.* ■ an act of separating oneself from a state of affairs: *a **break with** the past.* ■ a change in the weather. ■ [with *adj.*] a change of line, paragraph, or page: *dotted lines on the screen show page breaks.* ■ a curve or drop in the path of a pitched baseball. ■ a change of tone in the voice due to emotion: *there was a break in her voice now.* ■ an interruption in an electrical circuit. ■ a rush or dash in a particular direction, esp. by an attacking player or team: *he made a bounce pass for a basket on the break in the second quarter.* ■ a breakout, esp. from prison. ■ a sudden decrease, typically in prices. ■ *informal* an opportunity or chance, esp. one leading to professional success: *his big break came when a critic gave him a rave review.* ■ (also **break of serve** or **service break**) *Tennis* the winning of a game against an opponent's serve. **2** a pause in work: *I need a **break from** mental activity | they take long coffee breaks.* ■ a short vacation: *the Christmas break.* ■ a period of time taken out of one's professional activity in order to do something else: *those returning to work after a career break.* ■ a short solo or instrumental passage in jazz or popular music. **3** a gap or opening: *the spectacular vistas occasionally offered by a break in the rain forest | he stopped to wait for a break in the traffic.* **4** an instance of breaking; the point where something is broken: *a break in the valve was being repaired.* **5** *Billiards & Snooker* a player's turn to make the opening shot of a game or a rack. ■ a consecutive series of successful shots, scoring a specified number of points: *a break of 83 put him in front for the first time.* ▷Old English *brecan* (verb), of Germanic origin; related to Dutch *breken* and German *brechen*, from an Indo-European root shared by Latin *frangere* 'to break.'

▸*PHRASES* □ **break the back of** do the hardest part of (a task): *we've broken the back of the problem.* ■ overwhelm or defeat: *I thought we really had broken the back of inflation.* □ **break the bank** see BANK². □ **break bread** see BREAD. □ **break camp** see CAMP¹. □ **break cover** (of game being hunted) emerge into the open. □ **break someone's heart** see HEART. □ **break the ice** see ICE. □ **break a leg!** *theatrical slang* good luck! □ **break the mold** see MOLD¹. □ **break of day** dawn. □ **break ranks** see RANK¹. □ **break (someone's) serve** (or **service**) win a game in a tennis match against an opponent's service. □ **break step** see STEP. □ **break wind** release gas from the anus. □ **give someone a break** [usu. in *imperative*] *informal* stop putting pressure on someone about something. ■ (**give me a break**) used to express contemptuous disagreement or disbelief about what has been said: *He's seven times as quick and he's only 20 years old. Give me a break.* □ **make a break for** make a sudden dash in the direction of, typically in a bid to escape: *he made a break for the door.* □ **make a clean break** remove oneself completely and finally from a situation or relationship. □ **those are** (or **them's**) **the breaks** that is the way things turn out.

break·a·ble /ˈbrākəbəl/ ▸*adj.* capable of breaking or being broken easily: *breakable ornaments | an encrypted password isn't easily breakable.*
▸*n.* (**breakables**) things that are fragile and easily broken.

break·age /ˈbrākij/ ▸*n.* the action of breaking something: *some breakage of bone has occurred | there had been three breakages in the overhead wires.* ■ a thing that has been broken: *they left minor breakages behind them.*

break·a·way /ˈbrākəˌwā/ ▸*n.* **1** a divergence or radical change from something established or long standing: *rock was a **breakaway from** pop | as [adj.] the breakaway hit movie.* ■ a secession of a number of people from an organization, typically following conflict or disagreement and resulting in the establishment of a new organization: [as *adj.*] *the breakaway republic.* **2** *Sports* a sudden attack or forward movement, esp. in a bicycle race or in hockey or football: *a winning breakaway.* **3** an object, such as a stage prop, designed to break apart easily: [as *adj.*] *barroom brawls are staged with breakaway furniture.*

break·beat /ˈbrākˌbēt/ ▸*n.* *Popular Music* a repeated sample of a drumbeat, usually forming a fast syncopated rhythm, used as a basis for dance music. ■ dance music featuring breakbeats.

break·bone fe·ver /ˈbrākˌbōn/ ▸*n.* another term for DENGUE.

break-bulk ▸*adj.* [*attrib.*] denoting a system of transporting cargo as separate pieces rather than in containers.

break crop ▸*n.* a crop grown between fields of grain to ensure a varied planting pattern.

break·danc·ing /ˈbrākˌdansiNG/ ▸*n.* an energetic and acrobatic style of street dancing, developed by American blacks. —**break·dance** *v.* & *n.* —**break·danc·er** /-ˌdansər/ *n.*

break·down /ˈbrākˌdoun/ ▸*n.* **1** a failure of a relationship or of communication: *the breakdown of their marriage | some of these women will have experienced marital breakdown.* ■ a collapse of a system of authority due to widespread transgression of the rules: *a breakdown in military discipline.* ■ a sudden collapse in someone's mental health. ■ a mechanical failure. ■ [in *sing.*] the chemical or physical decomposition of something: *the breakdown of ammonia to nitrites.* **2** an explanatory analysis, esp. of statistics: *a detailed cost breakdown.* **3** a lively, energetic American country dance.

break·er /ˈbrākər/ ▸*n.* **1** a heavy sea wave that breaks into white foam on the shore or a shoal. **2** a person or thing that breaks something: [in *combination*] *a rule-breaker a code-breaker.* ■ a person who breaks horses. ■ short for CIRCUIT BREAKER. **3** a person who interrupts the conversation of others on a Citizens' Band radio channel, indicating a wish to transmit a message. ■ any CB radio user. **4** a break dancer.

break-e·ven ▸*n.* the point or state at which a person or company breaks even: [as *adj.*] *the break-even point.*

break-fall ▸*n.* (in martial arts) a controlled fall in which most of the impact is absorbed by the arms or legs.

break·fast /ˈbrekfəst/ ▸*n.* a meal eaten in the morning, the first of the day: *I often have toast for my breakfast | I don't eat breakfast.*
▸*v.* [*intrans.*] have this meal: *she **breakfasted on** French toast and bacon.* ▷late Middle English: from the verb BREAK + FAST². —**break·fast·er** *n.* **break·fast·less** *adj.*
▸*PHRASE* □ **have** (or **eat**) **someone for breakfast** *informal* deal with or defeat someone with contemptuous ease.

break·front /ˈbrākˌfrənt/ ▸*n.* a piece of furniture having the line of its front broken by a curve or angle: [as *adj.*] *a breakfront bookcase.*

break-in ▸*n.* a forced or unconsented entry into a building, car, computer system, etc., typically to steal something.

break·ing and en·ter·ing ▸*n.* the crime of entering a building by force so as to commit burglary.

break·ing point ▸*n.* the moment of greatest strain at which someone or something gives way: *the refugee crisis has **reached the breaking point** | her nerves were stretched **to the breaking point**.*

break·neck /ˈbrākˌnek/ ▸*adj.* [*attrib.*] dangerously or extremely fast: *he drove at breakneck speed.*

break-off ▸*n.* an instance of breaking something off or of discontinuing something.

break·out /ˈbrākˌout/ ▸*n.* **1** a forcible escape, typically from prison: *a prison breakout.* ■ [in *sing.*] (in soccer, hockey, and other sports) a sudden attack by a team that had been defending. **2** [in *sing.*] an outbreak: *a breakout of hostilities.* **3** a categorized list: *an excellent breakout of Web sites by topic.* **4** a sudden advance to a new level: *gold was overdue for a breakout.* **5** the deformation or splintering of wood, stone, or other material being drilled or planed.
▸*adj.* *informal* **1** suddenly and extremely popular or successful: *a breakout movie.* **2** denoting or relating to groups that break away from a conference or other larger gathering for discussion: *we divided into 15 breakout groups.*

break point ▸*n.* **1** a place or time at which an interruption or change is made. ■ (usu. **break·point**) *Computing* a place in a computer program where the sequence of instructions is interrupted, esp. by another program or by the operator. **2** *Tennis* the state of a game when the side receiving service needs only one more point to win the game: *he hit a winner to reach break point.* ■ a point of this nature: *he saved three break points.* **3** another term for BREAKING POINT.

Break·spear /ˈbrākˌspi(ə)r/, Nicholas, see ADRIAN IV.

break·through /ˈbrākˌTHro͞o/ ▸*n.* a sudden, dramatic, and important discovery or development, esp. in science: *a major breakthrough in DNA research.* ■ a significant and dramatic overcoming of a perceived obstacle, allowing the completion of a process: *the union's agreement was the key breakthrough on pay and conditions.*

break·through bleed·ing ▸*n.* bleeding from the uterus occurring between menstrual periods, a side effect of some oral contraceptives.

break·through pain ▸*n.* (usually in connection with cancer) severe pain that erupts while a patient is already medicated with a long-acting painkiller.

break·up /ˈbrākˌəp/ ▸*n.* an end to a relationship, typically a marriage. ■ a division of a country or organization into smaller autonomous units: *the breakup of the Soviet Union.* ■ a physical disintegration of something: *large quantities of oil are released after the breakup of a tanker | the spring breakup of the ice.*

break·wa·ter /ˈbrākˌwôtər; -ˌwätər/ ▸*n.* a barrier built out into a body of water to protect a coast or harbor from the force of waves.

bream¹ /brim; brēm/ ▸*n.* (*pl.* same) a greenish-bronze deep-bodied freshwater fish native to Europe, popular with anglers. • *Abramis brama*, family Cyprinidae. ■ used in names of other fishes resembling or related to this, e.g., **sea bream**. ▷late Middle English: from Old French *bresme*, of Germanic origin; related to German *Brachsen, Brassen*.

bream² /brēm/ ▸*v.* [*trans.*] *Nautical, archaic* clear (a ship or its bottom) of weeds, shells, or other accumulated matter by burning and scraping it. ▷late 15th cent.: probably of Low German origin and related to BROOM.

breast /brest/ ▸*n.* either of the two soft, protruding organs on the upper front of a woman's body that secrete milk after pregnancy. ■ the corresponding less-developed part of a man's body. ■ a person's chest: *her heart was hammering in her breast.* ■ the corresponding part of a bird or mammal: [as *adj.*] *the breast feathers of the doves.* ■ a portion of poultry cut from such a part: *a grilled chicken breast.* ■ the part of a garment that covers the chest: [as *adj.*] *a breast pocket.* ■ a person's chest regarded as the seat of the emotions: *wild feelings of frustration were rising up in his breast.*

▸*v.* [*trans.*] face and move forward against or through (something): *I watched him breast the wave.* ■ reach the top of (a hill). ▷Old English *brēost*, of Germanic origin; related to Dutch *borst* and German *Brust.* —**breast·ed** *adj.* [in *combination*] *a bare-breasted woman* | *a crimson-breasted bird.*

▸*PHRASES* □ **beat one's breast** make an exaggerated show of sorrow, despair, or regret. □ **make a clean breast of something** see CLEAN.

breast-beat·ing /ˈbrest,bētiNG/ ▸*n.* a loud, emotional expression of remorse: *the breast-beating of American media commentators* | [as *adj.*] *the breast-beating advocates of the people.*

breast·bone /ˈbrest,bōn/ ▸*n.* a thin, flat bone running down the center of the chest and connecting the ribs. Also called STERNUM.

breast col·lar ▸*n.* a thick chest strap that forms part of a horse's harness, often used instead of an ordinary collar on horses pulling lightweight or show vehicles.

breast drill ▸*n.* a drill on which pressure is brought to bear by the operator's chest.

breast-feed ▸*v.* (*past* and *past part.* **-fed**) [*trans.*] (of a woman) feed (a baby) with milk from the breast: *she breast-fed her first child* | [*intrans.*] *sometimes it is not possible to breast-feed.* ■ [*intrans.*] (of a baby) feed from the breast: *the child began to breast-feed.*

breast-high ▸*adj.* & *adv.* submerged to or as high as the breast: [as *adj.*] *we pushed through breast-high weeds* | [as *adv.*] *a cement patio fenced breast-high.*

breast·hook /ˈbrest,ho͝ok/ ▸*n.* a large piece of shaped timber fitted horizontally in the bows of a ship, used to connect the sides to the stem.

breast im·plant ▸*n.* *Medicine* a prosthesis consisting of a gellike or fluid material in a flexible sac, implanted behind or in place of a female breast in reconstructive or cosmetic surgery.

breast·plate /ˈbrest,plāt/ ▸*n.* **1** a piece of armor covering the chest. **2** *Judaism* in ancient times, a jeweled vestment covering the chest of the Jewish high priest. **3** a set of straps attached to the front of a saddle, which pass across the horse's chest and prevent the saddle from slipping backward. ■ the strap of a harness covering the chest of a horse.

breast pump ▸*n.* a device for drawing milk from a woman's breasts by suction.

breast·stroke /ˈbrest,strōk/ ▸*n.* [in *sing.*] a style of swimming on one's front, in which the arms are pushed forward and then swept back in a circular movement, while the legs are tucked in toward the body and then kicked out in a corresponding movement. ■ (**the breaststroke**) a race, typically of a specified length or kind, in which such a style of swimming is used: *she won the 200 m breaststroke.*

breast·work /ˈbrest,wərk/ ▸*n.* a low temporary defense or parapet.

breath /breTH/ ▸*n.* an inhalation or exhalation of air from the lungs: *she drew in a quick breath* | *take three deep breaths.* ■ an exhalation of air by a person or animal that can be seen, smelled, or heard: *he sighed, his breath hanging like a cloud in the icy air.* ■ the physiological process of taking air into the lungs and expelling it again, esp. the ability to breathe easily: *she paused for breath.* ■ the air taken into or expelled from the lungs: *I was gasping for breath.* ■ *archaic* the power of breathing; life. ■ a brief moment; the time required for one act of respiration: *in Las Vegas, they marry you in a breath.* ■ [in *sing.*] a slight movement of air: *the weather was balmy, not a breath of wind.* ■ [in *sing.*] a sign, hint, or suggestion: *he avoided the slightest breath of scandal.* ▷Old English *brǣth* 'smell, scent,' of Germanic origin; related to BROOD.

▸*PHRASES* □ **a breath of fresh air** a small amount of or a brief time in the fresh air. ■ a refreshing change: *the company's no-nonsense attitude is a breath of fresh air.* □ **the breath of life** a thing that someone needs or depends on: *politics has been the breath of life to her for 50 years.* □ **catch one's breath 1** cease breathing momentarily in surprise or fear. **2** rest after exercise to restore normal breathing: *she stood for a few moments, catching her breath.* □ **don't hold your breath** *informal* used hyperbolically to indicate that something is likely to take a long time: *don't hold your breath waiting for Congress to clean up political action committees.* □ **draw breath** breathe in. □ **get one's breath** (**back**) begin to breathe normally again after exercise or exertion. □ **hold one's breath** cease breathing temporarily. ■ *figurative* be in a state of suspense or anticipation: *France held its breath while the Senate chose its new president.* □ **in the same** (or **next**) **breath** at the same time: *he congratulated Simon on his victory but in the same breath dismissed it.* □ **last breath** the last moment of one's life (often used hyperbolically); death: *she would fight to the last breath to preserve her good name.* □ **out of breath** gasping for air, typically after exercise: *he arrived on the top floor out of breath.* □ **save one's breath** stop wasting time in futile talk: *save your breath; I know all about it.* □ **take someone's breath away** astonish or inspire someone with awed respect or delight. □ **under** (or **below**) **one's breath** in a very quiet voice; almost inaudibly: *he swore violently under his breath.* Compare with SOTTO VOCE. □ **waste one's breath** talk or give advice without effect: *I have better things to do than waste my breath arguing.*

breath·a·ble /ˈbrēT͟Həbəl/ ▸*adj.* (of the air) fit or pleasant to breathe. ■ (of clothes or material) admitting air to the skin and allowing sweat to evaporate.

breath·a·lyze /ˈbreTHə,līz/ ▸*v.* [*trans.*] (usu. **be breathalyzed**) (of the police) use a breathalyzer.

breath·a·lyz·er /ˈbreTHə,līzər/ (also *trademark* **Breath·a·lyz·er**) ▸*n.* a device used by police for measuring the amount of alcohol in a driver's breath. ▷1960s: blend of BREATH and *(an)alyze* + -ER[1].

breath·ar·i·an /breTHˈe(ə)rēən/ ▸*n.* a person who believes that it is possible, through meditation, to reach a level of consciousness where one can obtain all sustenance from the air or sunlight.

breathe /brēT͟H/ ▸*v.* [*intrans.*] take air into the lungs and then expel it, esp. as a regular physiological process: *she was wheezing as she breathed* | ***breathe in*** *through your nose* | *he* ***breathed out*** *heavily* | [*trans.*] *we are polluting the air we breathe.* ■ be or seem to be alive because of this: *at least I'm still breathing.* ■ *poetic/literary* (of wind) blow softly. ■ [with *direct speech*] say something with quiet intensity: *"We're together at last," she breathed.* ■ (of an animal or plant) respire or exchange gases: *plants breathe through their roots.* ■ [*trans.*] give an impression of (something): *the whole room breathed an air of hygienic efficiency.* ■ (of wine) be exposed to fresh air: *red wine needs untold time to breathe.* ■ (of material or soil) admit or emit air or moisture: *let your lawn breathe by putting air into the soil.* ■ [*trans.*] allow (a horse) to rest after exertion. ■ (**breathe upon**) *archaic* or *poetic/literary* tarnish or taint: *before the queen's fair name was breathed upon.* ▷Middle English (in the sense 'exhale, steam'): from BREATH.

▸*PHRASES* □ **breathe** (**freely**) **again** relax after being frightened or tense about something: *she wouldn't breathe freely again until she was airborne.* □ **breathe down someone's neck** follow closely behind someone. ■ constantly check up on someone. □ **breathe one's last** die. □ **breathe** (**new**) **life into** fill with enthusiasm and energy; reinvigorate: *spring breathes new life into a wintry woods.* □ **breathe a sigh of relief** exhale noisily as a sign of relief (often used hyperbolically): *they breathed a great sigh of relief after the election was won.* □ **live and breathe** see LIVE[1]. □ **not breathe a word** remain silent about something; keep secret.

breathed /breTHt/ ▸*adj.* [usu. in *combination*] having breath of a specified kind: *a foul-breathed poodle.*

▸■ (also /brēT͟Hd/) *Phonetics* unvoiced; voiceless.

breath·er /ˈbrēT͟Hər/ ▸*n.* **1** [in *sing.*] *informal* a brief pause for rest: *the director is* ***taking a breather*** *from his furious schedule.* **2** a vent or valve to release pressure or to allow air to move freely around something: *a cask breather* | [as *adj.*] *a breather pipe.* **3** [with *adj.*] a person or animal that breathes in a particular way, or breathes a particular substance: *a heavy breather* | [in *combination*] *reptiles are lung-breathers.*

breath·ing /ˈbrēT͟HiNG/ ▸*n.* **1** the process of taking air into and expelling it from the lungs: *his breathing was shallow.* **2** a sign in Greek (ʼ or [lenis]) indicating the presence of an aspirate (**rough breathing**) or the absence of an aspirate (**smooth breathing**) at the beginning of a word.

breath·ing room *n.* ▸sufficient room to move and breathe comfortably. ■ breathing space.

breath·ing space ▸*n.* [in *sing.*] an opportunity to pause, relax, or decide what to do next.

breath·less /ˈbreTHlis/ ▸*adj.* gasping for breath, typically due to exertion: *the climb left me breathless.* ■ short of breath or appearing this way because of excitement or other strong feelings: *a breathless story about risking death to steal the truth.* ■ (of the air or weather) unstirred by a wind or breeze; stiflingly still: *the warm, breathless air.* —**breath·less·ly** *adv.* —**breath·less·ness** *n.*

breath·tak·ing /ˈbreTH,tākiNG/ ▸*adj.* astonishing or awe-inspiring in quality, so as to take one's breath away: *the scene was one of breathtaking beauty.* —**breath·tak·ing·ly** *adv.*

breath test ▸*n.* a test in which a driver is made to blow into a breathalyzer to check the amount of alcohol that has been drunk.

▸*v.* (**breath-test**) [*trans.*] give (someone) such a test.

breath·y /ˈbreTHē/ ▸*adj.* (**breath·i·er**, **breath·i·est**) producing or causing an audible sound of breathing, often related to physical exertion or strong feelings: *a breathy laugh.* —**breath·i·ly** /ˈbreTHəlē/ *adv.* —**breath·i·ness** *n.*

brec·ci·a /ˈbreCHēə; ˈbresH-/ ▸*n.* *Geology* rock consisting of angular fragments cemented together. ▷late 18th cent.: from Italian, literally 'gravel,' ultimately of Germanic origin and related to BREAK. —**brec·ci·ate** /-ē,āt/ *v.* —**brec·ci·a·tion** /,breCHēˈāsHən; ,bresH-/ *n.*

Brecht /brekt; breKHt/, (Eugen) Bertolt (Friedrich) (1898–1956), German playwright, producer, and poet. His interest in combining music and drama led to collaboration with Kurt Weill in *The Threepenny Opera* (1928). Brecht's later dramas include *Mother Courage* (1941) and *The Caucasian Chalk Circle* (1948).

Breck·in·ridge /ˈbrekən,rij/, John Cabell (1821–75), U.S. politician and vice president of the U.S. 1857–61. He also served as a major general in the Confederate Army 1861.

bred /bred/ ▸ past and participle of BREED.

▸*adj.* [usu. in *combination*] (of a person or animal) reared in a specified environment or way: *a city-bred man.*

Bre·da /brāˈdä; ˈbrādə/ a manufacturing town in southwestern Netherlands; pop. 124,800. Historically, it is noted for the Compromise of Breda of 1566; the 1660 manifesto of Charles II; and the Treaty of Breda.

bred-in-the-bone ▸*adj.* firmly established; deep-rooted. ■ long established and unlikely to change; inveterate.

breech /brēCH/ ▸*n.* **1** the part of a cannon behind the bore. ■ the back part of a rifle or gun barrel. **2** *archaic* a person's buttocks.

▸*v.* [*trans.*] *archaic* put (a boy) into breeches after being in petticoats since birth. ▷Old English *brēc* (plural of *brōc*, of Germanic origin; related to Dutch *broek*), interpreted as a singular form. The original sense was 'garment covering the loins and thighs' (compare with BREECHES), hence 'the buttocks' (sense 2, mid 16th cent.), later 'the hind part' of anything (late 16th cent.).

breech birth (also **breech delivery**) ▸*n.* a delivery of a baby so positioned in the uterus that the buttocks or feet are delivered first.

breech·block /ˈbrēCH,bläk/ ▸*n.* a metal block that closes the aperture at the back part of a rifle or gun barrel.

breech·clout /ˈbrēCH,klout/ ▸*n.* (also **breech·cloth**) another term for LOINCLOTH.

breech·es /ˈbriCHiz; ˈbrē-/ ▸*plural n.* short trousers fastened just below the knee, now chiefly worn for riding a horse or as part of ceremonial dress. ■ *informal* trousers. ▷Middle English: plural of BREECH.

▸*PHRASE* □ **too big for one's breeches** see BIG.

Breech·es Bi·ble ▸*n.* the Geneva Bible of 1560, so named because the word *breeches* is used in Gen. 3:7 for the garments made by Adam and Eve.

breech·es bu·oy ▸*n.* a lifebuoy with canvas breeches attached that, when suspended from a rope, can be used to transfer a person to safety from a ship.

breech·ing /ˈbrēCHiNG/ ▸*n.* **1** a strong leather strap passing around the hindquarters of a horse harnessed to a vehicle. **2** *historical* a thick rope used to secure the carriage of a cannon on a ship and to absorb the force of the recoil. **3** the hair or wool on the hindquarters of an animal.

breech-load·er ▸*n.* a gun designed to have ammunition inserted at the breech rather than through the muzzle. —**breech-load·ing** *adj.*

breech pre·sen·ta·tion ▸*n.* a position of a fetus in which the feet or buttocks appear first during birth.

breed /brēd/ ▸*v.* (*past* and *past part.* **bred** /bred/) [*trans.*] cause (an animal) to produce offspring, typically in a controlled and organized way: *bitches may not* ***be bred from*** *more than once a year.* ■ [*intrans.*] (of animals) mate and then produce offspring: *toads are said to return to the pond of their birth to breed* | [as *adj.*] (**breeding**) *the breeding season.* ■ develop (a kind of animal or plant) for a particular purpose or quality: *these horses* ***are bred for*** *this sport.* ■ raise (livestock or animals): *they live on an island, where they breed Hanoverian horses.* ■ rear and train (someone) to behave in a particular way or have certain qualities: *Theresa had been beautifully bred.* ■ cause (something) to happen or occur, typically over a period of time: *success breeds confidence.* ■ *Physics* create (fissile material) by nuclear reaction.

▸*n.* a stock of animals or plants within a species having a distinctive appearance and typically having been developed by deliberate selection. ■ a sort or kind of person or thing: *a new breed of entrepreneurs was brought into being.* ▷Old English *brēdan* 'produce (offspring), bear (a child),' of Germanic origin; related to German *brüten,* also to **BROOD.**

▸*PHRASES* □ **a breed apart** a sort or kind of person that is very different from the norm: *Japanese capitalism is a breed apart from that found in the U.S.* □ **a dying breed** a sort or kind of person that is slowly disappearing: *the country's dying breed of elder statesmen.* □ **what's bred in the bone will come out in the flesh** (or **blood**) see **BONE.**

breed·er /'brēdər/ ▸*n.* a person who breeds livestock, racehorses, other animals, or plants: *a plant breeder* | *a breeder of fine cattle.* ■ [with *adj.*] an animal that breeds at a particular time or in a particular way: *emperor penguins are winter breeders.* ■ *informal, derogatory* (among homosexuals) a heterosexual person.

breed·er doc·u·ment ▸*n.* a document, genuine or fraudulent, that can serve as a basis to obtain other identification documents or benefits fraudulently.

breed·er re·ac·tor ▸*n.* a nuclear reactor that creates fissile material (typically plutonium-239 by irradiation of uranium-238) at a faster rate than it uses another fissile material (typically uranium-235) as fuel.

breed·ing /'brēdiNG/ ▸*n.* the mating and production of offspring by animals: *palolo worms use the moon to time their breeding.* ■ the activity of controlling the mating and production of offspring of animals: *the breeding of rats and mice for experiments.* ■ training and education, esp. in proper social behavior: *a girl of good breeding.* ■ the good manners regarded as characteristic of the aristocracy and conferred by heredity: *a lady of breeding.*

breed·ing ground ▸*n.* an area where birds, fish, or other animals habitually breed. ■ [usu. in *sing.*] *figurative* a thing that favors the development or occurrence of something: *Austin is a breeding ground for musical talent.*

Breed·love /'brēd,ləv/, Sarah see **WALKER.**

breeks /brēks/ ▸*plural n.* Scottish term for **BREECHES.**

breeze[1] /brēz/ ▸*n.* **1** a gentle wind. ■ [with *adj.*] a wind of force 2 to 6 on the Beaufort scale (4–27 knots or 4.5-31 mph). **2** *informal* a thing that is easy to do or accomplish: *traveling through London was a breeze.*

▸*v.* [*intrans.*] *informal* come or go in a casual or lighthearted manner: *I breezed in as if nothing were wrong.* ■ [*intrans.*] deal with something with apparently casual ease: *the computer has the power to* ***breeze through*** *huge documents* | *he breezed to victory.* ▷mid 16th cent.: probably from Old Spanish and Portuguese *briza* 'northeastern wind' (the original sense in English).

▸*PHRASE* □ **shoot the breeze** see **SHOOT.**

breeze[2] ▸*n.* small cinders mixed with sand and cement to make cinder blocks. ▷late 16th cent.: from French *braise,* (earlier) *brese* 'live coals.'

breeze block ▸*n.* British term for **CINDER BLOCK.**

breeze·way /'brēz,wā/ ▸*n.* a roofed outdoor passage, as between a house and a garage.

breez·y /'brēzē/ ▸*adj.* (**breez·i·er, breez·i·est**) **1** pleasantly windy: *it was a bright, breezy day.* **2** appearing relaxed, informal, and cheerily brisk: *the text is written in a breezy, matter-of-fact manner.* **—breez·i·ly** /-zəlē/ *adv.* **—breez·i·ness** *n.*

breg·ma /'bregmə/ ▸*n.* the point or area of the skull where the sagittal and coronal sutures joining the parietal and frontal bones come together.

Brel /brel/, Jacques (1929–78), Belgian singer and composer.

Brem·en /'brāmən; 'bremən/ a state in northeastern Germany. Divided into two parts, which center on the city of Bremen and the port of Bremerhaven, it is surrounded by the state of Lower Saxony. ■ its capital, an industrial city linked by the Weser River to the port of Bremerhaven and the North Sea; pop. 537,600.

Brem·er·ha·ven /'bremər,hāvən/ a seaport in northwestern Germany, on the North Sea coast, north of Bremen; pop. 131,000. Bremerhaven is one of the largest seaports and fishing centers in Europe. The first regular shipping service between the U.S. and Europe began here. Former name **WESERMÜNDE.**

Brem·er·ton /'bremərtən/ a city in west central Washington, on Puget Sound, home to large naval shipyards; pop. 38,142.

brems·strah·lung /'brem,SHträləNG/ ▸*n. Physics* electromagnetic radiation produced by the acceleration or esp. the deceleration of a charged particle after passing through the electric and magnetic fields of a nucleus. ▷1940s: from German, from *bremsen* 'to brake' + *Strahlung* 'radiation.'

Bren /bren/ (also **Bren gun**) ▸*n.* a lightweight quick-firing machine gun used by the Allied Forces in World War II. ▷blend of *Brno* (a town in the Czech Republic where it was originally made) and *Enfield* in England (site of the Royal Small Arms Factory where it was later made).

Bren·dan, St. /'brendən/ (*c.*486–*c.*575), Irish abbot. Feast day, May 16.

Bren·nan[1] /'brenən/, Walter (1894–1974), U.S. actor. A character actor, he appeared in many movies and was the first actor to win three Academy Awards, all for best supporting actor. His award-winning movies were *Come and Get It* (1936), *Kentucky* (1938), and *The Westerner* (1940).

Bren·nan[2], William Joseph, Jr. (1906–97), U.S. Supreme Court associate justice 1956–90. He was a New Jersey Supreme Court judge 1952–56 before being appointed to the U.S. Supreme Court by President Eisenhower. He was noted for his defense of First Amendment rights.

Bren·ner Pass /'brenər/ an Alpine pass at the border between Austria and Italy, on the route between Innsbruck and Bolzano, at an altitude of 4,450 feet (1,371 m).

brent goose /brent/ ▸*n.* British term for **BRANT.** ▷late Middle English: of unknown origin.

Brent·wood /'brent,wo͝od/ **1** a village in central Long Island in New York; pop. 45,218. **2** a section of West Los Angeles, California, noted for expensive homes and celebrity inhabitants.

bre·sao·la /bre'sōlə; bri'zō-/ ▸*n.* an Italian dish of raw beef cured by salting and air-drying, served typically in slices with a dressing of olive oil, lemon juice, and black pepper. ▷Italian, from *bresada,* past part. of *brasare* 'braise.'

Bre·scia /'brāSHə; 'breSHə/ an industrial city in northern Italy, in the region of Lombardy; pop. 196,770.

Bres·lau /'bres,lou/ German name for **WROCŁAW.**

Bres·lin /'brezlən/, Jimmy (1930–), U.S. journalist and writer. A syndicated columnist and Pulitzer Prize-winner 1986, he wrote *The Gang That Couldn't Shoot Straight* (1969), *He Got Hungry and Forgot His Manners* (1988), *Damon Runyon: A Life* (1991), and *I'd Like to Thank My Brain for Remembering Me* (1996).

Brest /brest/ **1** a port and naval base in northwestern France, on the Atlantic coast of Brittany; pop. 153,100. **2** a river port and industrial city in Belarus, close to the border with Poland; pop. 268,800. The peace treaty between Germany and Russia was signed here in March 1918. Former name (until 1921) **BREST-LITOVSK.** Polish name **BRZEŚĆ NAD BUGIEM.**

Bre·tagne /brə'tänyə/ French name for **BRITTANY.**

breth·ren /'breTH(ə)rin/ ▸ archaic plural form of **BROTHER.**

▸*plural n.* fellow Christians or members of a male religious order. See also **BROTHER** (sense 2). ■ used for humorous or rhetorical effect to refer to people belonging to a particular group: *our brethren in the popular press.*

Bret·on[1] /'bretn/ ▸*n.* **1** a native of Brittany. **2** the Celtic language of Brittany, related to Cornish.

▸*adj.* of or relating to Brittany or its people or language. ▷early 19th cent.: from Old French, literally 'Briton.'

Bret·on[2] /bre'tôN/, André (1896–1966), French poet, essayist, and critic. He launched the surrealist movement, outlining the movement's philosophy in his manifesto of 1924.

Brett /bret/, George (1953–), U.S. baseball player. Playing for the Kansas City Royals 1971–93, he was the American League batting champion in three different decades 1976, 1980, and 1990. Baseball Hall of Fame (1999).

Bret·ton Woods /'bretn/ a resort in the White Mountains of north central New Hampshire, noted as the site of UN conferences at the end of World War II.

Breu·er /'broiər/, Marcel Lajos (1902–81), U.S. architect; born in Hungary. He designed the UNESCO headquarters in Paris 1953–58 and the Whitney Museum of American Art in New York City 1965–66. He is also known for his chair designs.

Bre·vard Coun·ty /brə'värd/ a county in east central Florida, on the Atlantic Ocean, the site of Cape Canaveral and of large citrus and resort industries; pop. 398,978.

breve /brēv; brev/ ▸*n.* **1** a musical note, rarely used in modern music, having the time value of two semibreves or whole notes. **2** a written or printed mark (˘) indicating a short or unstressed vowel. **3** *historical* an authoritative letter from a pope or monarch. ▷Middle English: variant of **BRIEF.** In the musical sense, the term was originally used in a series where a *long* was of greater time value than a *breve.*

bre·vet /brə'vet; 'brevit/ ▸*n.* [often as *adj.*] a former type of military commission conferred esp. for outstanding service by which an officer was promoted to a higher rank without the corresponding pay: *a brevet lieutenant.*

▸*v.* (**-vet·ed** or **-vet·ted, -vet·ing** or **-vet·ting**) [*trans.*] confer a brevet rank on. ▷late Middle English (denoting an official letter, esp. a papal indulgence): from Old French *brievet* 'little letter,' diminutive of *bref.*

bre·vi·ar·y /'brēvē,erē; 'brev-/ ▸*n.* (*pl.* **-ar·ies**) a book containing the service for each day, to be recited by those in orders in the Roman Catholic Church. ▷late Middle English (also denoting an abridged version of the psalms): from Latin *breviarium* 'summary, abridgment,' from *breviare* 'abridge,' from *brevis* 'short, brief.'

brev·i·ty /'brevitē/ ▸*n.* concise and exact use of words in writing or speech. ■ shortness of time: *the brevity of human life.* ▷late 15th cent.: from Old French *brievete,* from Latin *brevitas,* from *brevis* 'brief.'

▸*PHRASE* □ **brevity is the soul of wit** *proverb* the essence of a witty statement lies in its concise wording and delivery. [from Shakespeare's *Hamlet* II. ii. 90.]

brew /bro͞o/ ▸*v.* [*trans.*] **1** make (beer) by soaking, boiling, and fermentation. **2** make (tea or coffee) by mixing it with hot water: *I've just brewed some coffee* | [*intrans.*] *he did a crossword while the tea brewed.* **3** [*intrans.*] (of an unwelcome event or situation) begin to develop: *there was more trouble brewing as the airline pilots went on strike* | *a storm was brewing.*

▸*phrasal v.* □ **brew up** *Brit.* make tea.

▸*n.* **1** a kind of beer: *nonalcoholic brews.* ■ *informal* a serving of beer. **2** a cup or mug of tea or coffee. **3** a mixture of events, people, or things that interact to form a more potent whole: *a dangerous brew of political turmoil and violent conflict.* ▷Old English *brēowan* (verb), of Germanic origin; related to Dutch *brouwen* and German *brauen.* **—brew·er** *n.*

Brew·er /'bro͞oər/, David Josiah (1837–1910), U.S. Supreme Court associate justice 1889–1910. Appointed to the Court by President Benjamin Harrison, he was considered a moderate conservative and generally opposed a strong central government.

brew·er's yeast ▸*n.* a yeast that is used in breadmaking, winemaking, and the brewing of top-fermenting beer. It is also consumed as a source of vitamin B and is used in laboratories as an important research organism. • *Saccharomyces cerevisiae,* phylum Ascomycota.

brew·er·y /'bro͞oərē/ ▸*n.* (*pl.* **-er·ies**) a place where beer is made commercially. ▷mid 17th cent.: from **BREW,** probably on the pattern of Dutch *brouwerij.*

brew·house /'bro͞o,hous/ ▸*n.* a brewery.

brew·mas·ter /'bro͞o,mastər/ ▸*n.* a person who supervises the brewing process in a brewery.

brew·pub /'bro͞o,pəb/ ▸*n.* an establishment selling beer brewed on the premises and often including a restaurant.

brew·ski /'bro͞oskē/ ▸*n. informal* a bottle, can, or glass of beer.

Brey·er /'brīər/, Stephen Gerald (1938–), U.S. Supreme Court associate justice 1994– . He is known for his pragmatic judgments.

Brezh·nev /'brezH,nef; 'brezHnyif/, Leonid (Ilich) (1906–82), Soviet statesman; general secretary of the Communist Party of the Soviet Union 1966–82; president 1977–82. His administration was marked by intensified persecution of dissidents at home and by attempted détente followed by renewed Cold

War in 1968; he was largely responsible for the invasion of Czechoslovakia 1968.

bri·ar[1] /ˈbrī(ə)r/ ▶*n.* variant spelling of BRIER[1].

bri·ar[2] ▶*n.* variant spelling of BRIER[2].

bri·ar·root ▶*n.* variant spelling of BRIERROOT.

bri·ar·wood ▶*n.* variant spelling of BRIERWOOD.

bribe /brīb/ ▶*v.* [*trans.*] persuade (someone) to act in one's favor, typically illegally or dishonestly, by a gift of money or other inducement: *an undercover agent* **bribed** *the judge* **into** *giving a lenient sentence* | [*trans.*] *you weren't willing to be good to your sister without being bribed with a lollipop.* | [*intrans.*] *he has no money to bribe with.*

▶*n.* a sum of money or other inducement offered or given in this way. ▷late Middle English: from Old French *briber, brimber* 'beg,' of unknown origin. The original sense was 'rob, extort,' hence (as noun) 'theft, stolen goods,' also 'money extorted or demanded for favors, ' later 'offer money as an inducement' (early 16th cent.). **—brib·a·ble** *adj.* **—brib·er** *n.*

brib·er·y /ˈbrīb(ə)rē/ ▶*n.* the giving or offering of a bribe: *he was convicted of racketeering and bribery* | [as *adj.*] *a bribery scandal.*

bric-a-brac /ˈbrik ə ˌbrak/ ▶*n.* miscellaneous objects and ornaments of little value. ▷mid 19th cent.: from French, from obsolete *à bric et à brac* 'at random.'

Brick /brik/ a township in southeastern New Jersey; pop. 76,119.

brick ▶*n.* **1** a small rectangular block typically made of fired or sun-dried clay, used in building. ■ bricks collectively as a building material: *this mill was built of brick* [as *modifier*] *a large brick building.* ■ a small, rectangular object: *a* **brick of** *ice cream.* **2** *Brit., informal dated* a generous, helpful, and reliable person.

▶*v.* [*trans.*] (often **be bricked**) block or enclose with a wall of bricks: *the doors have been* **bricked up**. ▷late Middle English: from Middle Low German, Middle Dutch *bricke, brike*; probably reinforced by Old French *brique*; of unknown ultimate origin.

▶*PHRASES* □ **be built like a brick shithouse** see SHITHOUSE. □ **a brick short of a load** see SHORT. □ **hit** (or **run into**) **a brick wall** face an insuperable problem or obstacle while trying to do something. □ **like a ton of bricks** *informal* with crushing weight, force, or authority: *all her years of marriage suddenly fell on her like a ton of bricks.* □ **shit a brick** (or **bricks**) *vulgar slang* be extremely anxious or nervous. □ **you can't make bricks without straw** *proverb* nothing can be made or accomplished without proper or adequate material or information. [with biblical allusion to Exodus 5; "without straw" meant "without having straw provided" (i.e., the Israelites were required to gather the straw for themselves). A misinterpretation has led to the current sense.]

brick·bat /ˈbrikˌbat/ ▶*n.* a piece of brick, typically when used as a weapon. ■ a remark or comment which is highly critical and typically insulting: *the plaudits were beginning to outnumber the brickbats.*

brick-built ▶*adj.* [*attrib.*] (of a building or structure) made of bricks.

brick·field /ˈbrikˌfēld/ ▶*n. Brit.* an area of ground where bricks are made.

brick·lay·er /ˈbrikˌlāər/ ▶*n.* a person whose job is to build walls, houses, and other structures with bricks. **—brick·lay·ing** /-ˌlāiNG/ *n.*

brick red ▶*n.* a deep brownish red: *various shades from blushing pink to angry brick red* | [as *adj.*] *he had a brick-red face.*

bricks and mor·tar ▶*n.* used to denote a business that operates in the physical world rather than over the Internet: [as *modifier*] *the bricks-and-mortar banks.* Compare with CLICKS AND MORTAR.

brick ve·neer ▶*n.* a covering of brick applied to a timber frame. ■ timber frames covered in brick as a building material.

brick·work /ˈbrikˌwərk/ ▶*n.* the bricks in a wall, house, or other structure, typically in terms of their type or layout: *the patterned brickwork of the gables.* ■ the craft or occupation of building walls, houses, or other structures with bricks.

brick·yard /ˈbrikˌyärd/ ▶*n.* a place where bricks are made.

bri·co·lage /ˌbrēkōˈläZH; ˌbrikə-/ ▶*n.* (*pl.* same or **-lag·es**) (in art or literature) construction or creation from a diverse range of available things: *the chaotic bricolage of the novel is brought together in a unifying gesture.* ■ something constructed or created in this way: *bricolages of painted junk.* ▷mid 20th cent.: French, from *bricoler* 'do odd jobs, repair.'

bri·co·leur /ˌbrēkōˈlər; ˌbrikə-/ ▶*n.* a person who engages in bricolage. ▷mid 20th cent.: French, literally 'handyman.'

brid·al /ˈbrīdl/ ▶*adj.* [*attrib.*] of or concerning a bride or a wedding: *her white bridal gown* | *the* **bridal party** *came out into the church porch.* ▷late Middle English: from Old English *brȳd-ealu* 'wedding feast,' from *brȳd* 'bride' + *ealu* 'ale-drinking.' Since the late 16th cent., the word has been associated with adjectives ending in -AL.

brid·al reg·is·try ▶*n.* a service offered by a store or other organization in which a bridal couple's gift preferences are recorded so as to be available to family and friends when shopping at the store.

brid·al suite ▶*n.* a suite of rooms in a hotel for the use of a newly married couple.

brid·al wreath ▶*n.* a spirea with sprays of white flowers. • *Spirea prunifolia*, family Rosaceae.

Bride, St. /brīd; brēd/ see BRIDGET, ST.[1]

bride /brīd/ ▶*n.* a woman on her wedding day or just before and after the event. ▷Old English *brȳd*, of Germanic origin; related to Dutch *bruid* and German *Braut*.

bride·groom /ˈbrīdˌgro͞om/ ▶*n.* a man on his wedding day or just before and after the event. ▷Old English *brȳdguma*, from *brȳd* 'bride' + *guma* 'man.' The change in the second syllable was due to association with GROOM.

bride price ▶*n.* [in *sing.*] a sum of money or quantity of goods given to a bride's family by that of the groom, esp. in tribal societies: *payments of bride price from the husband's kin.*

brides·maid /ˈbrīdzˌmād/ ▶*n.* a girl or woman who accompanies a bride on her wedding day. ▷late 18th cent.: alteration of earlier *bridemaid*.

bride·well /ˈbrīdˌwel; -wəl/ ▶*n.* a prison for petty offenders such as a reform school. ▷mid 16th cent.: named after *St. Bride's Well* in the City of London, near which such a building stood.

bride·zil·la /brīdˈzilə/ ▶*n. humorous* an overzealous bride-to-be who acts irrationally or causes offense. ▷on the pattern of *Godzilla*.

bridge[1] /brij/ ▶*n.* **1** a structure carrying a road, path, railroad, or canal across a river, ravine, road, railroad, or other obstacle: *a bridge across the river* | *a railroad bridge.* ■ something that makes a physical connection between two other things. ■ something that is intended to reconcile or form a connection between two things: *a committee that was formed to create a* **bridge between** *rival parties.* ■ a partial denture supported by natural teeth on either side. See also BRIDGEWORK. ■ the support formed by the hand for the forward part of a billiard cue. ■ a long stick with a frame at the end that is used to support a cue for a shot that is otherwise hard to reach. ■ *Music* an upright piece of wood on a string instrument over which the strings are stretched. ■ *Music* a bridge passage or middle eight. ■ short for LAND BRIDGE. **2** the elevated, enclosed platform on a ship from which the captain and officers direct operations. **3** the upper bony part of a person's nose: *he pushed his spectacles further up the bridge of his nose.* ■ the central part of a pair of glasses, fitting over this: *these sunglasses have a special nose bridge for comfort.* **4** an electric circuit with two branches across which a detector or load is connected. These circuits are used to measure resistance or other property by equalizing the potential across the two ends of a detector, or to rectify an alternating voltage or current.

▶*v.* [*trans.*] be a bridge over (something): *a covered walkway that bridged the gardens.* ■ build a bridge over (something): *earlier attempts to bridge the channel had failed.* ■ make (a difference between two groups) smaller or less significant: *bridging the gap between avant garde art and popular culture.* ▷Old English *brycg* (noun), of Germanic origin; related to Dutch *brug* and German *Brücke*. **—bridge·a·ble** *adj.*

▶*PHRASES* □ **burn one's bridges** see BURN[1]. □ **cross that bridge when one comes to it** deal with a problem when and if it arises.

bridge[2] ▶*n.* a card game descended from whist, played by two partnerships of two players who at the beginning of each hand bid for the right to name the trump suit, the highest bid also representing a contract to make a specified number of tricks with a specified suit as trumps. ▷late 19th cent.: of unknown origin.

bridge-build·ing ▶*n.* the activity of building bridges. ■ *figurative* the promotion of friendly relations between groups. **—bridge-build·er** *n.*

bridge·head /ˈbrijˌhed/ ▶*n.* a strong position secured by an army inside enemy territory from which to advance or attack: *figurative in the 1970s, academic literary theory established bridgeheads in Britain.*

bridge loan ▶*n.* a sum of money lent by a bank to cover an interval between two transactions, typically the buying of one house and the selling of another.

bridge mix ▶*n.* a mixture of various bite-size snack foods, such as nuts, raisins, and chocolates, typically served in a bowl at card games, parties, etc.

Bridge of Sighs a 16th-century enclosed bridge in Venice between the Doges' Palace and the state prison, originally crossed by prisoners on their way to torture or execution.

bridge pas·sage ▶*n.* a transitional section in a musical composition leading to a new section or theme.

Bridge·port /ˈbrijˌpôrt/ an industrial city in southwestern Connecticut, on Long Island Sound; pop. 139,529.

Bridg·es[1] /ˈbrijiz/, Lloyd (Vernet, Jr.) (1913–98), U.S. actor; father of actors **Jeff Bridges** (1949–) and **Beau Bridges** (1941–). His many movie credits include *High Noon* (1952) and *Airplane* (1980). He also starred in the television series "Sea Hunt" (1958–61).

Bridg·es[2], Robert (Seymour) (1844–1930), English poet and literary critic; poet laureate 1913–30. His long philosophical poem, *The Testament of Beauty* (1929), was written in the Victorian tradition.

Bridg·et, St.[1] /ˈbrijət/ (also **Bride** /brīd; brēd/ or **Brig·id** /ˈbrijəd; brēd/) (6th century), Irish abbess; also known as **St. Bridget of Ireland**. She was venerated in Ireland as a virgin saint and noted in miracle stories for her compassion. Feast day, July 23.

Bridg·et, St.[2] (also **Bir·git·ta** /birˈgētə/) (*c.*1303–73), Swedish nun and visionary; also known as **St. Bridget of Sweden**. She experienced her first vision of the Virgin Mary at the age of seven. Feast day, February 1.

Bridge·town /ˈbrijˌtoun/ the capital of Barbados, a port on the southern coast; pop. 6,720.

bridge·work /ˈbrijˌwərk/ ▶*n.* **1** dental bridges collectively. ■ the construction or insertion of such bridges. **2** *Building* the component parts of a bridge. ■ the construction of bridges.

bridg·ing /ˈbrijiNG/ ▶*n.* the action of putting a bridge over something: *the bridging of a ditch.* ■ *Mountaineering* a method of climbing a wide chimney by using the left hand and foot on one sidewall and the right hand and foot on the other.

Bridg·man /ˈbrijmən/, Percy Williams (1882–1961), U.S. physicist. He worked with liquids and solids under very high pressures; his techniques were later used in making artificial minerals (including diamonds). Nobel Prize for Physics (1946).

bri·dle /ˈbrīdl/ ▶*n.* the headgear used to control a horse, consisting of buckled straps to which a bit and reins are attached. ■ a line, rope, or device that is used to restrain or control the action or movement of something. ■ *Nautical* a length of rope, chain, or cable fastened at both ends to an object that is to be secured or moved or to a vessel that is to do the towing, a pull being exerted at the center of its length.

horse's bridle

▶*v.* **1** [*trans.*] (usu. **be bridled**) put a bridle on (a horse). ■ bring (something) under control; curb: *the fact that he was their servant bridled his tongue.* **2** [*intrans.*] show one's resentment or anger, esp. by throwing up the head and drawing in the chin: *ranchers have* **bridled at** *excessive federal control.* ▷Old English *brīdel* (noun), *brīdlian* (verb), of Germanic origin; related to Dutch *breidel* (noun). Sense 2 of the verb use is from the action of a horse when reined in.

▶*PHRASES* □ **off the bridle** see BIT[3]. □ **on the bridle** see BIT[3].

bri·dle path ▶*n.* a path or track used for horseback riding.

Brie /brē/ ▶*n.* a kind of soft, mild, creamy cheese with a firm, white skin. ▷named after *Brie* in northern France, where it was originally made.

brief /brēf/ ▶*adj.* of short duration: *the president made a brief visit to Moscow.* ■ concise in expression; using few words: *introductions were brief and polite.* ■ (of a piece of clothing) not covering much of the body; scanty: *Alice sported a pair of extremely brief black shorts.*

▶*n.* a concise statement or summary: *their comments*

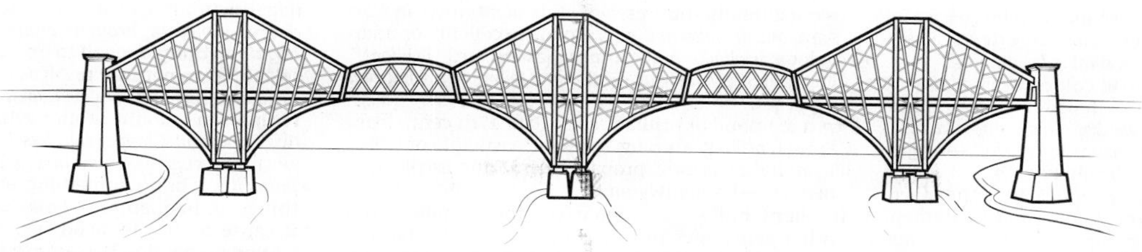
cantilever bridge

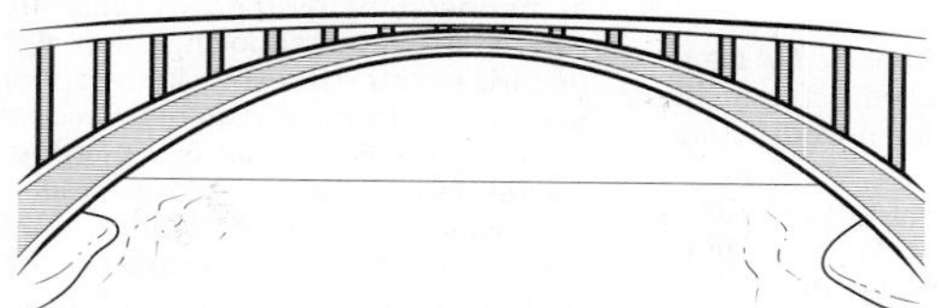
arch bridge

covered bridge

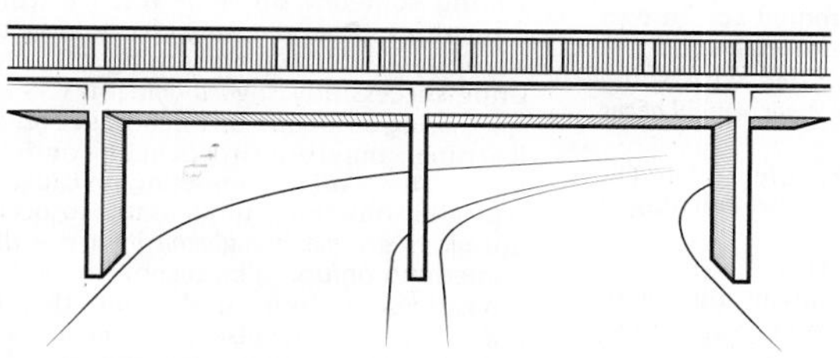
span beam bridge

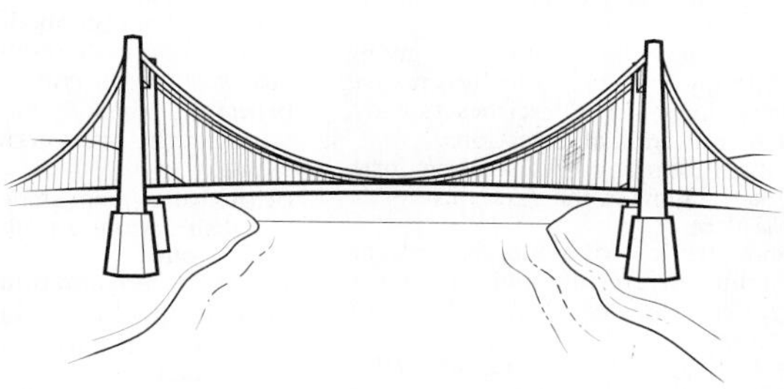
suspension bridge

bridges

were cribbed right from industry briefs. ■ a set of instructions given to a person about a job or task: *his brief is to turn around the country's economy.* ■ a written summary of the facts and legal points supporting one side of a case, for presentation to a court. ■ a letter from the pope to a person or community on a matter of discipline.

▶*v.* [*trans.*] instruct or inform (someone) thoroughly, esp. in preparation for a task: *she briefed him on last week's decisions.* ▷Middle English: from Old French *brief,* from Latin *brevis* 'short.' The noun is via late Latin *breve* 'note, dispatch,' hence 'an official letter.' **—brief·ly** *adv.* [*sentence adverb*] *briefly, the plot is as follows . . .* **—brief·ness** *n.*

▶*PHRASES* □ **hold no brief for** not support or argue in favor of: *I hold no brief for the president.* □ **in brief** in a few words; in short: *he is, in brief, the embodiment of evil | the news in brief.*

brief·case /ˈbrēfˌkās/ ▶*n.* a flat, rectangular container, typically made of leather, for carrying books and papers.

brief·ing /ˈbrēfiNG/ ▶*n.* a meeting for giving information or instructions: *the daily press briefing.* ■ the information or instructions given: *this briefing explains the systems, products and standards.* ■ the action of informing or instructing someone: *today's briefing of NATO allies.*

briefs /brēfs/ ▶*plural n.* close-fitting legless underpants that are cut so as to cover the body to the waist, in contrast to a bikini.

bri·er[1] /ˈbrī(ə)r/ (also **bri·ar**) ▶*n.* any of a number of prickly scrambling shrubs, esp. the sweetbrier and other wild roses. ▷Old English *brǣr, brēr,* of unknown origin. **—bri·er·y** *adj.*

bri·er[2] (also **bri·ar**) ▶*n.* **1** (also **brier pipe**) a tobacco pipe made from nodules borne at ground level by a large woody plant of the heath family. **2** the white-flowered shrub of the heath family that bears these nodules, native chiefly to France and Corsica. • *Erica arborea,* family Ericaceae. ▷mid 19th cent.: from French *bruyère* 'heath, heather,' from medieval Latin *brucus.*

bri·er·root /ˈbrī(ə)rˌro͞ot; -ˌro͝ot/ ▶*n.* wood from the nodules of the brier (*Erica arborea*), used esp. for making tobacco pipes.

bri·er·wood /ˈbrī(ə)rˌwo͝od/ ▶*n.* another term for BRIERROOT.

brig /brig/ ▶*n.* a two-masted, square-rigged ship with an additional gaff sail on the mainmast. ■ *informal* a prison, esp. on a warship. ▷early 18th cent.: abbreviation of BRIGANTINE (the original sense).

Brig. ▶*abbr.* ■ brigade. ■ brigadier.

bri·gade /briˈgād/ ▶*n.* a subdivision of an army, typically consisting of a small number of infantry battalions and/or other units and often forming part of a division: *he commanded a brigade of 3,000 men.* ■ [usu. with *adj.*] an organization with a specific purpose, typically with a military or quasi-military structure: *the local fire brigade.* ■ [in *sing.*] *informal, often derogatory* a group of people with a common characteristic or dedicated to a common cause: *the anti-smoking brigade.*

▶*v.* [*trans.*] (often **be brigaded**) *rare* form into a brigade. ■ associate with (someone or something): *they thought the speech too closely brigaded with illegal action.* ▷mid 17th cent.: from French, from Italian *brigata* 'company,' from *brigare* 'contend,' from *briga* 'strife.'

brig·a·dier /ˌbrigəˈdi(ə)r; ˈbrigəˌdi(ə)bur/ ▶*n.* a rank of officer in the British army, above colonel and below major general. ▷late 17th cent.: from French (see BRIGADE, -IER).

brig·a·dier gen·er·al ▶*n.* (*pl.* **brig·a·dier gen·er·als**) an officer in the U.S. Army, Air Force, or Marine Corps ranking above colonel and below major general.

brig·and /ˈbrigənd/ ▶*n. poetic/literary* a member of a gang that ambushes and robs people in forests and mountains. ▷late Middle English (also denoting an irregular foot soldier): from Old French, from Italian *brigante,* literally '(person) contending,' from *brigare* 'contend' (see BRIGADE). **—brig·and·age** /-dij/ *n.* **—brig·and·ry** /-drē/ *n.*

brig·an·dine /ˈbrigənˌdēn/ ▶*n. historical* a coat of mail, typically one made of iron rings or plates attached to canvas or other fabric. ▷late Middle English: from Old French, from *brigand* (see BRIGAND).

brig·an·tine /ˈbrigənˌtēn/ ▶*n.* a two-masted sailing ship with a square-rigged foremast and a fore-and-aft-rigged mainmast. ▷early 16th cent. (denoting a small vessel used by pirates): from Old French, from Italian *brigantino,* from *brigante* (see BRIGAND).

Briggs /brigz/, Henry (1561–1630), English mathematician. Renowned for his work on logarithms, he introduced the decimal base, made the thousands of calculations necessary for the tables, and popularized their use. He also devised the usual method used for long division.

Bright /brīt/, John (1811–89), English politician and reformer. A noted orator, Bright was the leader, along with Richard Cobden, of the campaign to repeal the Corn Laws and was closely identified with the 1867 Reform Act.

bright /brīt/ ▶*adj.* **1** giving out or reflecting a lot of light; shining: *I have problems seeing when the sun is bright | her bright, dark eyes.* ■ full of light: *the rooms are bright and spacious.* ■ (of a period of time) having sunny, cloudless weather: *the long, bright days of June.* ■ having a vivid color: *the bright flowers | a bright tie.* ■ (of color) vivid and bold: *the bright green leaves.* **2** (of sound) clear, vibrant, and typically high-pitched: *her voice is fresh and bright.* **3** (of a person, idea, or remark) intelligent and quick-witted: *a bright young journalist | a suggestion box for bright ideas.* **4** giving an appearance of cheerful liveliness: *she gave a bright*

smile. ■ (of someone's future) likely to be successful and happy: *the bright prospects for her early retirement.*
▸*adv.* luminously: *a full moon shining bright.*
▸*n.* (**brights**) **1** bold and vivid colors: *webbed gloves in neon brights.* **2** headlights switched to high beam: *he turned the brights on, and we drove along the dirt road.* ▷Old English *beorht,* of Germanic origin. —**bright·ish** *adj.* —**bright·ly** *adv.* —**bright·ness** *n.*
▸*PHRASES* □ **bright and early** very early in the morning. □ **the bright lights** the glamor and excitement of the city: *they hankered for the bright lights of the capital.* □ **look on the bright side** be optimistic or cheerful in spite of difficulties.

THE RIGHT WORD **bright, brilliant, effulgent, luminous, lustrous, radiant, refulgent, resplendent, shining**

Looking for just the right word to capture the quality of the light on a moonlit night or a summer day? All of these adjectives describe an intense, steady light emanating (or appearing to emanate) from a source.

Bright is the most general term, applied to something that gives forth, reflects, or is filled with light (*a bright and sunny day; a bright star*).

Brilliant light is even more intense or dazzling (*the brilliant diamond on her finger*), and **resplendent** is a slightly more formal, even poetic, way of describing a striking brilliance (*the sky was resplendent with stars*).

Poets also prefer adjectives like **effulgent** and **refulgent**, both of which can be applied to an intense, pervading light, sometimes from an unseen source (*her effulgent loveliness*); but *refulgent* specifically refers to reflected light (*a chandelier of refulgent crystal pendants*).

Radiant is used to describe the power of giving off light, either literally or metaphorically (*a radiant June day; the bride's radiant face*); it describes a steady, warm light that is emitted in all directions.

Like *radiant,* **luminous** suggests sending forth light, but light of the glow-in-the-dark variety (*the luminous face of the alarm clock*).

While diamonds are known for being *brilliant,* fabrics like satin and surfaces like polished wood, which reflect light and take on a gloss or sheen, are often called **lustrous**.

If none of these words captures the exact quality of the light you're trying to describe, you can always join the masses and use **shining**, a word that has been overworked to the point of cliché (*my knight in shining armor*).

bright·en /ˈbrītn/ ▸*v.* make or become more light: [*intrans.*] *the day began to brighten in the east* | [*trans.*] *the fire began to blaze fiercely, brightening the room.* ■ [*trans.*] make (something) more attractively and cheerfully colorful: *this colorful hanging ornament will brighten any room* | *daffodils* ***brighten up*** *many gardens and parks.* ■ make or become happier and more cheerful: [*intrans.*] *Sarah* ***brightened up*** *considerably as she thought of Emily's words* | [*trans.*] *she seems to brighten his life.* ▷Old English *(ge)beorhtnian.*

bright-eyed ▸*adj.* **1** having shining eyes. **2** alert and lively: *bright-eyed young lawyers* | *a bright-eyed optimism.*
▸*PHRASE* □ **bright-eyed and bushy-tailed** *informal* alert and lively; eager. [from the conventional description of a squirrel.]

Bright·on /ˈbrītn/ a resort town on the southern coast of England; pop. 133,400.

Brigh·ton Beach /ˈbrītn/ a section of southern Brooklyn in New York City, east of Coney Island, noted for its Jewish community, and now home to a large Russian immigrant population.

Bright's dis·ease ▸*n.* a disease involving chronic inflammation of the kidneys. ▷mid 19th cent.: named after Richard *Bright* (1789–1858), the English physician who established its nature.

bright·work /ˈbrītˌwərk/ ▸*n.* polished metalwork on ships or vehicles.

Brig·id, St. /ˈbrijəd; brēd/ see **BRIDGET, ST.**[1]

brill /bril/ ▸*n.* a European flatfish that resembles a turbot. • *Scophthalmus rhombus,* family Scophthalmidae (or Bothidae). ▷late 15th cent.: of unknown origin.

bril·liance /ˈbrilyəns/ (also **bril·lian·cy** /-sē/) ▸*n.* intense brightness of light: *the nights were dark, lit only by the brilliance of Aegean stars.* ■ vividness of color. ■ exceptional talent or intelligence: *he's played the stock market with great brilliance.*

bril·liant /ˈbrilyənt/ ▸*adj.* **1** (of light) very bright and radiant. See note at **BRIGHT.** ■ (of a color) brightly and intensely vivid. **2** exceptionally clever or talented: *a brilliant young mathematician* | *a brilliant idea.* ■ outstanding; impressive: *his brilliant career at Harvard.* ■ *Brit., informal* very good, excellent, or marvelous: *we had a brilliant time* | [as *exclam.*] *"Brilliant!" he declared excitedly as she finished telling him what had happened.*
▸*n.* a diamond of brilliant cut. ▷late 17th cent.: from French *brillant* 'shining,' present participle of *briller,* from Italian *brillare,* probably from Latin *beryllus* (see **BERYL**). —**bril·liant·ly** *adv.*

bril·liant cut ▸*n.* a circular cut for diamonds and other gemstones in the form of two many-faceted pyramids joined at their bases, the upper one truncated near its apex.

bril·lian·tine /ˈbrilyənˌtēn/ ▸*n.* **1** *dated* scented oil used on men's hair to make it look glossy. **2** shiny dress fabric made from cotton and mohair or cotton and worsted. ▷late 19th cent.: from French *brillantine,* from *brillant* 'shining' (see **BRILLIANT**). —**bril·lian·tined** *adj.* (in sense 1).

Bril·lo /ˈbrilō/ (also **Brillo pad**) ▸*n. informal, often offensive* hair that is wiry or tightly curled. ▷from the trademark *Brillo,* used for soaped, steel-wool scouring pads.

brim /brim/ ▸*n.* the projecting edge around the bottom of a hat: *a soft hat with a turned-up brim.* See note at **BORDER.** ■ the upper edge or lip of a cup, bowl, or other container: *tankards frothing* ***to the brim.***
▸*v.* (**brimmed, brim·ming**) [often as *adj.*] (**brimming**) fill or be full to the point of overflowing: [*intrans.*] *a brimming cup* [*trans.*] *seawater brimmed the riverbanks.* ■ fill something so completely as almost to spill out of it: *large tears brimmed in her eyes.* ■ *figurative* be possessed by or full of feelings or thoughts: *he is* ***brimming with*** *ideas.* ▷Middle English (denoting the edge of the sea or other body of water): perhaps related to German *Bräme* 'trimming.' —**brimmed** *adj.* [in *combination*] : *a wide-brimmed hat.* —**brim·less** *adj.*

brim·ful /ˈbrimˌfo͝ol/ ▸*adj.* [*predic.*] filled with something to the point of overflowing: *a jug brimful of custard.*

brim·stone /ˈbrimˌstōn/ ▸*n. archaic* sulfur. ▷late Old English *brynstān,* probably from *bryne* 'burning' + *stān* 'stone.'
▸*PHRASE* □ **fire and brimstone** see **FIRE.**

brin·dle /ˈbrindl/ ▸*n.* a brownish or tawny color of animal fur, with streaks of other color. ■ an animal with such a coat.
▸*adj.* (also **brin·dled**) (esp. of domestic animals) brownish or tawny with streaks of other color: *a brindle pup.* ▷late 17th cent.: back-formation from *brindled,* alteration of Middle English *brinded* in the same sense, probably of Scandinavian origin.

brine /brīn/ ▸*n.* water saturated or strongly impregnated with salt. ■ seawater: *dolphins and whales can't help taking in the odd gulp of brine as they swallow a fish.* ■ *technical* a strong solution of a salt or salts: *these brines percolated downward.*
▸*v.* [*trans.*] [often as *adj.*] (**brined**) soak in or saturate with salty water: *brined anchovies.* ▷Old English *brine,* of unknown origin.

Bri·nell hard·ness test /briˈnel/ ▸*n.* a test to determine the hardness of metals and alloys by hydraulically pressing a steel ball into the metal and measuring the resulting indentation.

The steel ball used in the test has a diameter of 1.6 millimeters and the applied load has a weight of 12.6 kilograms. The ratio of this load to the area of the resulting indentation is the **Bri·nell hard·ness num·ber**.

▷named for Johan August Brinell (1849–1925), Swedish engineer.

brine shrimp ▸*n.* a small fairy shrimp that lives in brine pools and salt lakes and is used as food for aquarium fish. • *Artemia salina,* class Branchiopoda.

bring /briNG/ ▸*v.* (*past* **brought** /brôt/) [*trans.*] come to a place with (someone or something): *she brought Luke home from the hospital* | [with *two objs.*] *Liz brought her a glass of water.* ■ cause (someone or something) to come to a place: *what brings you here?* | *a felony case brought before a jury* | *figurative his inner confidence has* ***brought*** *him* ***through*** *his ordeal.* ■ make (someone or something) move in a particular direction or way: *he brought his hands out of his pockets* | *heavy rain* ***brought down*** *part of the ceiling.* ■ cause (something): *the bad weather brought famine* | *her letter* ***brought forth*** *a torrent of criticism.* ■ cause (someone or something) to be in or change to a particular state or condition: *I'll give you some aspirin to* ***bring down*** *his temperature* | *his approach* ***brought*** *him* ***into*** *conflict with government.* ■ (**bring someone in**) involve (someone) in a particular activity: *he has brought in a consultant.* ■ initiate (legal action) against someone: *riot and conspiracy charges should* ***be brought against*** *them.* ■ [usu. with *negative*] (**bring oneself to do something**) force oneself to do something unpleasant or distressing: *she could not bring herself to mention it.* ■ cause someone to receive (an amount of money) as income or profit: *two important Chippendale lots brought $10,000 each* | [with *two objs.*] *five more novels brought him $150,000.*
▸*phrasal v.* □ **bring something about 1** cause something to happen: *she brought about a revolution.* **2** cause a ship to head in a different direction. □ **bring something back** cause something to return. ■ reintroduce something: *bringing back capital punishment would solve nothing.* □ **bring someone down** cause someone to fall over, esp. by tackling them during a football game or rugby match. ■ cause someone to lose power: *the vote will not bring down the government.* ■ make someone unhappy. □ **bring someone/something down** cause an animal or person to fall over by shooting them. ■ cause an aircraft or bird to fall from the sky by shooting it. □ **bring something forth** *archaic* or *poetic/literary* give birth to: *why does Elsbeth not bring forth a child?* □ **bring something forward 1** move a meeting or event to an earlier date or time. **2** [often as *adj.*] (**brought forward**) in bookkeeping, transfer a total sum from the bottom of one page to the top of the next: *a profit and loss balance brought forward of $5,000,000.* **3** propose a plan, subject, or idea for consideration. □ **bring something in 1** introduce something, esp. a new law or product: *Congress brought in reforms to prevent abuse of presidential power.* **2** make or earn a particular amount of money: *their fund-raising efforts have brought in more than $1 million.* **3** (of a jury) give a decision in court: *the jury brought in a unanimous verdict.* □ **bring someone off 1** be rescued from a ship in difficulties. **2** *vulgar slang* give someone or oneself an orgasm. □ **bring something off** achieve something successfully: *a good omelet is very hard to bring off.* □ **bring someone on** encourage someone who is learning something to develop or improve at a faster rate. □ **bring something on** cause something, typically something unpleasant, to occur or develop: *ulcers are not brought on by a rich diet.* ■ (**bring something on/upon**) be responsible for something, typically something unpleasant, that happens to oneself or someone else: *the doom that he has* ***brought upon himself.*** □ **bring someone out 1** encourage one to feel more confident or sociable: *she needs friends to* ***bring*** *her* ***out of herself.*** **2** introduce (a young woman) formally into society. **3** introduce (a homosexual) into the homosexual subculture. □ **bring something out** produce and launch a new product or publication: *the band is bringing out a video.* ■ make something more evident; emphasize something: *the shawl brings out the color of your eyes* | *he* ***brought out the best in*** *his team.* □ **bring someone around 1** restore someone to consciousness. **2** persuade someone to do something, esp. to adopt one's own point of view: *my wife has brought me around to eating broiled grouper.* □ **bring someone to** restore someone to consciousness. □ **bring something to** cause a boat to stop, esp. by turning into the wind. □ **bring up** (chiefly of a ship) come to a stop. □ **bring someone up** look after a child until it is an adult. ■ (**be brought up**) be taught as a child to adopt particular behavior or attitudes: *he had been brought up to believe that marriage was forever.* □ **bring something up 1** vomit something. **2** raise a matter for discussion or consideration: *she tried repeatedly to bring up the subject of marriage.* ▷Old English *bringan,* of Germanic origin; related to Dutch *brengen* and German *bringen.* —**bring·er** *n.*
▸*PHRASES* □ **bring home the bacon** see **BACON.** □ **bring something home to someone** see **HOME.** □ **bring the house down** make an audience respond with great enthusiasm, typically as shown by their laughter or applause. □ **bring something into play** cause something to begin operating or to have an effect; activate. □ **bring something to bear** exert influence or pressure so as to cause a particular result: *he was released after pressure had been brought to bear by the aid agencies.* □ **bring someone to book** see **BOOK.** □ **bring something to light** see **LIGHT**[1]. □ **bring someone/something to mind** cause one to remember or think of someone or something: *all that marble brought to mind a mausoleum.* □ **bring something to pass** *chiefly poetic/literary* cause something to happen.

bring·down /ˈbriNGˌdoun/ ▸*n.* a disappointment or letdown; comedown.

Brink /briNGk/, André (1935–), South African novelist, short-story writer, and playwright. His novel,

Looking on Darkness (1973), became the first novel in Afrikaans to be banned by the South African government. Other notable novels: *A Dry White Season* (1979) and *A Chain of Voices* (1982).

brink /briNGk/ ▸*n.* an extreme edge of land before a steep or vertical slope: ***the brink of*** *the cliffs.* ■ a margin or bank of a body of water: ***the brink of*** *the pond.* See note at BORDER. ■ a point at which something, typically an unwelcome or disastrous event, is about to happen: *a hapless dictator teetering on the brink.* ▷Middle English: of Scandinavian origin.

▸*PHRASE* □ **on the brink of** about to experience something, typically a disastrous or unwelcome event: *the country was on the brink of a constitutional crisis.*

Brink·ley /ˈbriNGklē/, David (1920–2003), U.S. news commentator. He reported news for NBC 1951–81, co-anchoring "The Huntley-Brinkley Report" 1956–70 with Chet Huntley. He anchored ABC's "This Week" 1981–97.

brink·man·ship /ˈbriNGkmən,SHip/ (also **brinks·man·ship** /ˈbriNGksmən-/) ▸*n.* the art or practice of pursuing a dangerous policy to the limits of safety before stopping, typically in politics.

brin·y /ˈbrīnē/ ▸*adj.* of salty water or the sea; salty: *the briny tang of the scallops.*

▸*n.* (**the briny**) *Brit., informal* the sea.

bri·o /ˈbrēō/ ▸*n.* vigor or vivacity of style or performance: *she told her story with some brio.* See also CON BRIO. ▷mid 18th cent.: from Italian.

bri·oche /brēˈōSH; -ˈôSH/ ▸*n.* a light, sweet yeast bread typically in the form of a small, round roll. ▷French, from Norman French *brier*, synonym of *broyer*, literally 'split up into very small pieces by pressure;' related to BRAY[2].

bri·quette /briˈket/ (also **bri·quet**) ▸*n.* a block of compressed charcoal or coal dust used as fuel. ▷late 19th cent.: from French, diminutive of *brique* 'brick.'

bris /bris/ ▸*n.* the Jewish ceremony of circumcision. Also called BRITH.

Bris·bane /ˈbrizbən; -,bān/ the capital of Queensland, Australia; pop. 1,273,500. It was founded in 1824 as a penal colony. ▷named after Sir Thomas *Brisbane* (1773–1860), governor of New South Wales 1821–25.

bri·sé /brēˈzā/ ▸*n. Ballet* a jump in which the dancer sweeps one leg into the air to the side while jumping off the other, brings both legs together in the air and beats them before landing. ▷late 18th cent.: French, literally 'broken.'

brisk /brisk/ ▸*adj.* active, fast, and energetic: *a good brisk walk | business appeared to be brisk.* ■ (of the weather or wind) cold but fresh and enlivening. ■ sharp or abrupt: *the brisk, dismissive nod of her head.* ▷late 16th cent.: probably from French *brusque* (see BRUSQUE). —**brisk·ly** *adv.* —**brisk·ness** *n.*

bris·ket /ˈbriskit/ ▸*n.* meat cut from the breast of an animal, typically a cow. ▷Middle English: perhaps from Old Norse *brjósk* 'cartilage, gristle.'

bris·ling /ˈbrizliNG; ˈbris-/ ▸*n.* (*pl.* same or **-lings**) a sprat, typically one seasoned and smoked in Norway and sold in a can. ▷early 20th cent.: from Norwegian and Danish.

bris·tle /ˈbrisəl/ ▸*n.* (usu. **bristles**) a short stiff hair, typically one of those on an animal's skin, a man's face, or a plant. ■ a stiff animal hair, or a man-made substitute, used to make a brush: *a toothbrush with nylon bristles | the heads are made with natural bristle.*

▸*v.* [*intrans.*] **1** (of hair or fur) stand upright away from the skin, esp. in anger or fear: *the hair on the back of his neck bristled.* ■ make one's hair or fur stand on end: *the cat bristled in annoyance.* ■ react angrily or defensively, typically by drawing oneself up: *she* ***bristled at*** *his rudeness.* **2** (**bristle with**) be covered with or abundant in: *the roof bristled with antennas.* ▷Middle English: from Old English *byrst* (of Germanic origin, related to German *Borste*) + -LE[1].

bris·tle·cone pine /ˈbrisəl,kōn/ ▸*n.* a very long-lived shrubby pine of western North America. It has been used in dendrochronology to correct radiocarbon dating. • *Pinus longaeva*, family Pinaceae.

bris·tle fern ▸*n.* a filmy fern with hairlike bristles protruding from the spore-containing bodies. Most bristle ferns have delicate fronds and live in damp shady places, chiefly in tropical areas. • Genus *Trichomanes*, family Hymenophyllaceae.

bris·tle·tail /ˈbrisəl,tāl/ ▸*n.* a small wingless insect that has bristles at the end of the abdomen. • Orders Thysanura (the **true bristletails**, with three bristles, including the silverfish) and Diplura (the **two-pronged bristletails**), subclass Apterygota.

bris·tle worm ▸*n.* a marine annelid worm that has a segmented body with numerous bristles on the fleshy lobes of each segment. Also called **polychaete.** • Class Polychaeta: numerous species, including ragworms, lugworms, fan worms, and their relatives.

bris·tling /ˈbris(ə)liNG/ ▸*adj.* **1** (esp. of hair) close-set, stiff, and spiky: *a bristling beard.* **2** *figurative* aggressively brisk or tense: *he fills the screen with a restless, bristling energy.*

bris·tly /ˈbrislē/ ▸*adj.* (of hair or foliage) having a stiff and prickly texture. ■ covered with short stiff hairs: *he rubbed his bristly chin.*

bris·tly sar·sa·pa·ril·la ▸*n.* see ARALIA.

Bris·tol /ˈbristl/ **1** a city in southwestern England; pop. 370,300. It is located on the Avon River about 6 miles (10 km) from the Bristol Channel. **2** an industrial city and township in west central Connecticut; pop. 60,062. **3** a township in southeastern Pennsylvania, on the Delaware River; pop. 55,521. **4** an industrial city in eastern Tennessee; pop. 23,421.

Bris·tol board ▸*n.* fine, smooth pasteboard used for drawing or cutting. ▷early 19th cent.: named after the city of BRISTOL in southwestern England.

Bris·tol Chan·nel a wide inlet of the Atlantic Ocean between South Wales and the southwestern peninsula of England that narrows into the estuary of the River Severn.

Brit /brit/ *informal* ▸*n.* a British person.

▸*adj.* British. ▷early 20th cent.: abbreviation.

Brit·ain /ˈbritn/ an island that consists of England, Wales, and Scotland and includes the small adjacent islands. The name is broadly synonymous with Great Britain, but the longer form is more usual for the political unit. See also GREAT BRITAIN. ▷Old English *Breoton*, from Latin *Brittones* 'Britons,' superseded in Middle English by forms from Old French *Bretaigne* (from Latin *Brit(t)annia*).

Bri·tan·ni·a /briˈtanyə; -ˈtanēə/ the personification of Britain, usually depicted as a helmeted woman with shield and trident. The figure had appeared on Roman coins and was revived with the name Britannia on the coinage of Charles II. ▷the Latin name for BRITAIN.

Bri·tan·ni·a met·al ▸*n.* a silvery alloy consisting of tin with about 5–15 percent antimony and typically some copper, lead, or zinc.

Bri·tan·nic /briˈtanik/ ▸*adj. dated* (usually in names or titles) of Britain or the British Empire: *he answered His Britannic Majesty's call to arms.* ▷mid 17th cent.: from Latin *Britannicus*, from *Britannia* (see BRITANNIA).

britch·es /ˈbriCHiz/ ▸*n.* variant spelling of BREECHES.

▸*PHRASE* □ **too big for one's britches** see BIG.

brith /bris; brit/ ▸*n.* another term for BRIS. ▷For *brith milah*, from Hebrew *berit mila* 'covenant of circumcision' (Gen 17:9–10).

Brit·i·cism /ˈbriti,sizəm/ (also **Brit·ish·ism** /ˈbritiSH ,izəm/) ▸*n.* an idiom used in Britain but not in other English-speaking countries. ▷mid 19th cent.: from BRITISH, on the pattern of words such as *Gallicism.*

Brit·ish /ˈbritiSH/ ▸*adj.* **1** of or relating to Great Britain or the United Kingdom, or to its people or language. **2** of the British Commonwealth or (formerly) the British Empire.

▸*n.* [*as plural n.*] (**the British**) the British people. ▷Old English *Brettisc* 'relating to the ancient Britons,' from *Bret* 'Briton,' from Latin *Britto*, or its Celtic equivalent. —**Brit·ish·ness** *n.*

Brit·ish Ant·arc·tic Ter·ri·to·ry that part of Antarctica claimed by Britain. It includes about 150,058 square miles (388,500 sq km) of the continent of Antarctica as well as the South Orkney and South Shetland islands in the South Atlantic Ocean.

Brit·ish Broad·cast·ing Cor·po·ra·tion (abbr.: **BBC**) a public corporation for radio and television broadcasting in Britain.

The BBC was established in 1927 by royal charter and held a monopoly until the introduction of the first commercial TV station in 1954. It is financed by the sale of television viewing licenses rather than by revenue from advertising and has an obligation to remain impartial in its reporting.

Brit·ish Co·lum·bi·a a province on the western coast of Canada; pop. 3,282,061; capital, Victoria. Formed in 1866 by the union of Vancouver Island and the mainland area, then called New Caledonia, the province includes the Queen Charlotte Islands.

Brit·ish Com·mon·wealth see COMMONWEALTH (sense 2).

Brit·ish Em·pire a former empire consisting of Great Britain and its possessions, dominions, and dependencies.

Colonization of North America and domination of India began in the 17th century. A series of small colonies, mostly in the West Indies, was gained during the late 17th–early 19th centuries, and Australia, New Zealand, various parts of the Far East, and large areas of Africa were added in the 19th century. Self-government was granted to Canada, Australia, New Zealand, and South Africa in the mid 19th century, and most of the remaining colonies have gained independence since the end of World War II.

Brit·ish Eng·lish ▸*n.* English as used in Great Britain, as distinct from that used elsewhere.

Brit·ish·er /ˈbritiSHər/ ▸*n. informal* (in North America and old-fashioned British English) a native or inhabitant of Britain.

Brit·ish Ex·pe·di·tion·ar·y Force (abbr.: **BEF**) a British force made available by the army reform of 1908 for service overseas against foreign countries. Such forces were sent to France at the outbreak of both world wars.

Brit·ish In·di·a that part of the Indian subcontinent administered by the British from 1765, when the East India Company acquired control over Bengal, until 1947, when India became independent and Pakistan was created. See also INDIA.

Brit·ish In·di·an O·cean Ter·ri·to·ry a British dependency in the Indian Ocean that consists of the islands of the Chagos Archipelago and (until 1976) some other groups that now belong to the Seychelles. Ceded to Britain by France in 1814, the islands became a separate dependency in 1965.

Brit·ish Isles a group of islands lying off the coast of northwestern Europe, from which they are separated by the North Sea and the English Channel. They include Britain, Ireland, the Isle of Man, the Isle of Wight, the Hebrides, the Orkney Islands, the Shetland Islands, the Scilly Isles, and the Channel Islands.

Brit·ish·ism /ˈbritə,SHizəm/ ▸*n.* variant spelling of BRITICISM.

Brit·ish Mu·se·um a national museum of antiquities in Bloomsbury, London. Established with public funds in 1753, it includes among its holdings the Magna Carta, the Elgin Marbles, and the Rosetta Stone.

Brit·ish So·ma·li·land a former British protectorate that was established on the Somali coast of East Africa in 1884. In 1960, it united with a former Italian territory to create the independent republic of Somalia.

Brit·ish ther·mal u·nit (abbr.: **Btu, BTU**) ▸*n.* the amount of heat needed to raise one pound of water at maximum density through one degree Fahrenheit, equivalent to 1.055×10^3 joules.

Brit·ish Vir·gin Is·lands see VIRGIN ISLANDS.

Brit·on /ˈbritn/ ▸*n.* **1** a citizen or native of Great Britain. ■ a person of British descent. **2** one of the people of southern Britain before and during Roman times. ▷from Old French *Breton*, from Latin *Britto, Britton-*, or its Celtic equivalent.

Brit·pop /ˈbrit,päp/ ▸*n.* pop music by a loose affiliation of British groups of the mid 1990s, typically influenced by the Beatles and other British groups of the 1960s and perceived as a reaction against American grunge music.

Brit·ta·ny /ˈbritn-ē/ a region and former duchy of northwestern France that forms a peninsula between the Bay of Biscay and the English Channel. French name BRETAGNE.

Brit·ten /ˈbritn/, (Edward) Benjamin, Lord Britten of Aldeburgh (1913–76), English composer, pianist, and conductor. Notable operas: *Peter Grimes* (1945), *A Midsummer Night's Dream* (1960), and *Death in Venice* (1973).

brit·tle /ˈbritl/ ▸*adj.* hard but liable to break or shatter easily: *her bones became fragile and brittle.* ■ (of a sound, esp. a person's voice) unpleasantly hard and sharp and showing signs of instability or nervousness: *a brittle laugh.* ■ (of a person or behavior) appearing aggressive or hard but unstable or nervous within: *her manner was artificially bright and brittle.*

▸*n.* a candy made from nuts and set melted sugar: *peanut brittle.* ▷late Middle English, ultimately of Germanic origin and related to Old English *brēotan* 'break up.' —**brit·tle·ly** (or **brit·tly**) *adv.* —**brit·tle·ness** *n.*

brit·tle bone dis·ease ▸*n. Medicine* **1** another term for OSTEOGENESIS IMPERFECTA. **2** another term for OSTEOPOROSIS.

brit·tle fern ▸*n.* another term for BLADDER FERN.

brit·tle frac·ture ▸*n.* fracture of a metal or other material occurring without appreciable prior plastic deformation.

brit·tle·star /ˈbritl,stär/ ▸*n.* an echinoderm related to the starfish, with long, thin, flexible arms radiating from a small central disk. • Class Ophiuroidea: *Ophiura* and other genera.

B

Brit·ton·ic /briˈtänik/ ▸*adj.* & *n.* variant of **BRYTHONIC**. ▷from Latin *Britto, Britton-* 'Briton' + -IC.

britz·ka /ˈbrichkə; ˈbrits-/ (also **britz·ska**) ▸*n. historical* an open carriage with calash top and space for reclining. ▷early 19th cent.: from Polish *bryczka*.

Brix scale /briks/ ▸*n.* a hydrometer scale for measuring the amount of sugar in a solution at a given temperature.

Br·no /ˈbərnō/ an industrial city in the Czech Republic; pop. 388,000.

bro /brō/ ▸*n. informal* short for BROTHER: *his baby bro.* ■ [in *sing.*] a friendly greeting or form of address: *"Yo bro!"* ■ (**Bro.**) Brother (used before a first name when referring in writing to a member of a religious order of men): *Bro. Felix.*

broach[1] /brōch/ ▸*v.* [*trans.*] **1** raise (a sensitive or difficult subject) for discussion: *he broached the subject he had been avoiding all evening.* **2** pierce (a cask) to draw liquor. ■ open and start using the contents of (a bottle or other container). **3** [*intrans.*] (of a fish or sea mammal) rise through the water and break the surface: *the salmon broach, then fall to slap the water.* ▷Middle English: from Old French *brochier*, based on Latin *brocchus, broccus* 'projecting.' The earliest recorded sense was 'prick with spurs,' part of the general meaning 'pierce with something sharp,' from which sense 2 arose in late Middle English. Sense 1, a figurative use of this, dates from the late 16th cent.

broach[2] *Nautical* ▸*v.* [*intrans.*] (also **broach to**) (of a ship with the wind on the quarter) veer and pitch forward because of bad steering or a sea hitting the stern, causing it to present a side to the wind and sea, lose steerage, and possibly suffer serious damage: *we had broached badly, side on to the wind and sea | the ship would have broached to if the captain had not sprung to the wheel.*
▸*n.* a sudden and hazardous veering of a ship having such consequences. ▷early 18th cent.: of unknown origin.

broad /brôd/ ▸*adj.* **1** having an ample distance from side to side; wide: *a broad staircase.* ■ (after a measurement) giving the distance from side to side: *the valley is three miles long and half a mile broad.* ■ large in area; spacious: *a broad expanse of prairie.* **2** covering a large number and wide scope of subjects or areas: *a broad range of experience.* ■ having or incorporating a wide range of meanings, applications, or kinds of things; loosely defined: *three broad categories of mutual funds.* ■ including or coming from many people of many kinds: *broad support for the president's foreign policy.* **3** general; without detail: *a broad outline of NATO's position.* ■ (of a hint) clear and unambiguous; not subtle: *a broad hint.* ■ somewhat coarse and indecent: *what we regard as broad or even bawdy is a fact of nature to him.* ■ (of a phonetic transcription) showing only meaningful distinctions in sound and ignoring minor details. **4** (of a regional accent) very noticeable and strong: *his broad Bronx accent.*
▸*n. informal, chiefly derogatory* a woman. ▷Old English *brād*, of Germanic origin; related to Dutch *breed* and German *breit*. —**broad·ness** *n.*
▸*PHRASES* □ **broad in the beam** fat around the hips. □ **in broad daylight** during the day, when it is light, and surprising or unexpected for this reason: *the kidnapping took place in broad daylight.*

broad ar·row ▸*n.* a mark resembling a broad arrowhead, formerly used on British prison clothing, Navy timber, and other government property.

broad·ax /ˈbrôd,aks/ (also **broad·axe**) ▸*n.* an ax with a wide head and a short handle.

broad·band /ˈbrôd,band/ ▸*adj.* of or using signals over a wide range of frequencies in high-capacity telecommunications, esp. as used for access to the Internet: *broadband applications such as video and live audio.*
▸*n.* signals over such a range of frequencies: *our ability to uplink on broadband has been curtailed.*

broad bean ▸*n.* **1** a large edible flat green bean that is typically eaten without the pod. Also called FAVA BEAN, HORSEBEAN. **2** the plant that yields these beans, often cultivated in gardens. • *Vicia faba*, family Leguminosae.

broad·bill /ˈbrôd,bil/ ▸*n.* **1** a small bird of the Old World tropics, with a stocky body, a large head, a flattened bill with a wide gape, and typically very colorful plumage. • Family Eurylaimidae: several genera. **2** a bird with a broad bill, esp. a duck like the shoveler or the scaup. **3** another term for SWORDFISH.

broad-brush ▸*adj.* lacking in detail and subtlety: *a broad-brush measure of inflation.*
▸*n.* (**broad brush**) an approach characterized in this way: *the public painted all evangelists with a broad brush.*

broad·cast /ˈbrôd,kast/ ▸*v.* (*past* **-cast** or **-cast·ed**; *past part.* **-cast** or **-cast·ed**) [*trans.*] **1** (often **be broadcast**) transmit (a program or some information) by radio or television: *the announcement was broadcast live* | [as *n.*] (**broadcasting**) *the 1920s saw the dawn of broadcasting.* ■ [*intrans.*] take part in a radio or television transmission: *the station broadcasts 24 hours a day.* ■ tell (something) to many people; make widely known: *we don't want to broadcast our unhappiness to the world.* **2** scatter (seeds) by hand or machine rather than placing in drills or rows. See note at SCATTER.
▸*n.* a radio or television program or transmission.
▸*adj.* of or relating to such programs: *a broadcast journalist.*
▸*adv.* by scattering: *green manure can be sown broadcast or in rows.* ▷mid 18th cent. (in the sense 'sown by scattering'): from BROAD + the past participle of CAST[1]. Senses relating to radio and television date from the early 20th cent. —**broad·cast·er** *n.*

Broad Church ▸*n.* a tradition or group within the Anglican Church favoring a liberal interpretation of doctrine. ■ a group, organization, or doctrine that allows for and caters to a wide range of opinions and people.

broad·cloth /ˈbrôd,klôth/ ▸*n.* clothing fabric of fine twilled wool or worsted, or plain-woven cotton. ▷late Middle English: originally denoting cloth made 72 inches wide, as opposed to 'strait' cloth, 36 inches wide. The term now implies quality rather than width.

broad·en /ˈbrôdn/ ▸*v.* [*intrans.*] become larger in distance from side to side; widen: *her smile broadened | the river slowed and* ***broadened out*** *slightly.* ■ expand to encompass more people, ideas, or things: *her interests broadened as she grew up* | [*trans.*] *efforts to broaden classical music's appeal.*
▸*PHRASE* □ **broaden one's horizons** expand one's range of interests, activities, and knowledge.

broad gauge ▸*n.* a railroad gauge that is wider than the standard gauge of 56.5 inches (1.435 m).

broad jump ▸*n.* another term for LONG JUMP.

broad·leaf /ˈbrôd,lēf/ ▸*adj.* another term for BROADLEAVED.
▸*n.* (*pl.* **-leaves** or **-leafs**) a tree or plant with wide flat leaves.

broad-leaved /ˈbrôd ,lēvd/ ▸*adj.* [*attrib.*] (of a tree or plant) having relatively wide, flat leaves rather than needles; nonconiferous. ■ (of a wood or woodland) consisting of trees with such leaves: *ancient broadleaved woodlands.*

broad·loom /ˈbrôd,lo͞om/ ▸*n.* carpet woven in wide widths: *wall-to-wall broadloom.* —**broad·loomed** *adj.*

broad·ly /ˈbrôdlē/ ▸*adv.* **1** in general and with the exception of minor details: *the climate is broadly similar in the two regions.* **2** widely and openly: *he was grinning broadly.*

broad-mind·ed ▸*adj.* tolerant or liberal in one's views and reactions; not easily offended: *a broad-minded approach to religion.* —**broad-mind·ed·ness** *n.* —**broad-mind·ed·ly** *adv.*

broad pen·nant (also **broad pen·dant**) ▸*n.* a short swallow-tailed pennant distinguishing the commodore's ship in a squadron.

broad reach *Sailing* ▸*n.* a point of sailing in which the wind blows over a boat's quarter, between the beam and the stern: ***on a broad reach*** *they are magnificent craft.*
▸*v.* (**broad-reach**) [*intrans.*] sail with the wind in this position.

broad·sheet /ˈbrôd,shēt/ ▸*n.* a large piece of paper printed on one side only with information; a broadside. ■ (also **broadsheet newspaper**) a newspaper with a large format regarded as more serious and less sensationalist than tabloids.

broad·side /ˈbrôd,sīd/ ▸*n.* **1** a nearly simultaneous firing of all the guns from one side of a warship. ■ *figurative* a strongly worded critical attack: ***broadsides against*** *the Christian faith.* ■ the set of guns that can fire on each side of a warship. ■ the side of a ship above the water between the bow and quarter. **2** a sheet of paper printed on one side only, forming one large page; also called BROADSHEET: *a broadside of Lee's farewell address.* ■ in 16th- and 17th-century England, a popular ballad. Also called **broadside ballad**.
▸*adv.* with the side turned to a particular thing: *the yacht was drifting* ***broadside to*** *the wind.* ■ on the side: *her car was hit broadside by another vehicle.*
▸*v.* [*trans.*] collide with the side of (a vehicle): *I had to skid my bike sideways to avoid broadsiding her.*

broad-spec·trum ▸*adj.* [*attrib.*] denoting antibiotics, pesticides, etc., effective against a large variety of organisms.

broad·sword /ˈbrôd,sôrd/ ▸*n.* a sword with a wide blade, used for cutting rather than thrusting.

broad·tail /ˈbrôd,tāl/ ▸*n.* a karakul sheep. ■ the fleece or wool from a karakul lamb.

Broad·way /ˈbrôdwā/ a street that runs the length of Manhattan in New York City. It is famous for its theaters, and its name has become synonymous with show business. It is also known as the Great White Way, in reference to its brilliant street illuminations.

broad·way /ˈbrôd,wā/ ▸*n.* (usually in names) a large open or main road.

Broad·way Joe see NAMATH.

broast /brōst/ ▸*v.* prepare food using a cooking process that combines broiling and roasting: [as *adj.*] *broasted chicken.*

Brob·ding·nag·i·an /,bräbdingˈnagēən/ ▸*adj.* gigantic.
▸*n.* a giant. ▷early 18th cent.: from *Brobdingnag*, the name given by Swift (in *Gulliver's Travels*) to a land where everything is of huge size, + -IAN.

bro·cade /brōˈkād/ ▸*n.* a rich fabric, usually silk, woven with a raised pattern, typically with gold or silver thread: [as *adj.*] *a heavy brocade curtain.*
▸*v.* [*trans.*] [usu. as *adj.*] (**brocaded**) weave (something) with this design: *a heavily brocaded blanket.* ▷late 16th cent.: from Spanish and Portuguese *brocado* (influenced by French *brocart*), from Italian *broccato*, from *brocco* 'twisted thread.'

Bro·ca's ar·e·a /ˈbrōkəz/ ▸*n. Anatomy* a region of the brain concerned with the production of speech, located in the cortex of the dominant frontal lobe. Damage in this area causes **Broca's aphasia**, characterized by hesitant and fragmented speech with little grammatical structure. ▷late 19th cent.: named after P. Paul *Broca* (1824–80), French surgeon.

broc·ci·flow·er /ˈbräkə,flou(ə)r/ (also **broc·co·flow·er**) ▸*n.* a light green vegetable that is a cross between broccoli and cauliflower. ▷blend of *broccoli* and *cauliflower*.

broc·co·li /ˈbräk(ə)lē/ ▸*n.* a cabbage of a variety similar to the cauliflower, bearing heads of green or purplish flower buds. It is widely cultivated as a vegetable. • There are several kinds of broccoli, in particular those in the "Italica" group. ■ the flower stalk and head eaten as a vegetable. ▷mid 17th cent.: from Italian, plural of *broccolo* 'cabbage sprout, head,' diminutive of *brocco* 'shoot,' based on Latin *brocchus, broccus* 'projecting.'

broc·co·li·ni /,bräkəˈlēnē/ ▸*n.* a vegetable that is a hybrid of broccoli and kale, with small florets on slender stalks. It has a mild, nutty flavor.

broc·co·li rabe /räb/ (also **broc·co·li raab**) ▸*n.* a leafy green vegetable with broccolilike buds and bitter-flavored greens.

bro·chette /brōˈshet/ ▸*n.* a skewer or spit on which chunks of meat or fish are barbecued, grilled, or roasted: *beef and lamb* ***en brochette.*** ■ a dish of meat or fish chunks cooked in such a way. ▷French, diminutive of *broche* (see BROACH[1]).

bro·chure /brōˈsho͝or/ ▸*n.* a small book or magazine containing pictures and information about a product or service. ▷mid 18th cent.: from French, literally 'something stitched,' from *brocher* 'to stitch' (see BROACH[1]).

bro·chure·ware /brōˈsho͝or,we(ə)r/ ▸*n.* Web sites or Web pages produced by converting a company's printed marketing or advertising material into an Internet format, typically providing little or no opportunity for interactive contact with prospective customers.

Brock /bräk/, Lou (1939–), U.S. baseball player. An outfielder, he played for the Chicago Cubs 1961–64 and the St. Louis Cardinals 1964—79. Baseball Hall of Fame (1985).

Brock·en /ˈbräkən/ a mountain in northern central Germany, in the Harz Mountains, that rises to 3,747 feet (1,143 m). It is noted for the optical phenomenon of the Brocken specter, in which a greatly enlarged image appears projected on clouds, and for witches' revels that reputedly took place here on Walpurgis night.

brock·et /ˈbräkit/ (also **brocket deer**) ▸*n.* a small deer with short, straight antlers, found in Central and South America. • Genus *Mazama*, family Cervidae: four species. ▷late Middle English (denoting any red deer stag in its second year, with straight antlers): from Anglo-Norman French *broquet*, diminutive of *broque*, variant of *broche* (see **BROOCH**). The current sense dates from the mid 19th cent.

Brock·ton /ˈbräktən/ an industrial city in southeastern Massachusetts, south of Boston, noted esp. for shoe manufacture; pop. 94,304.

bro·de·rie an·glaise /ˌbrōdərē äNGˈglez; -ˈgläz/ ▸*n.* open embroidery, typically in white floral patterns, on fine white cotton or linen. ▷mid 19th cent.: French, literally 'English embroidery.'

Brod·sky /ˈbrädskē; ˈbrät-/, Joseph (1940–96), U.S. poet; born in Russia; born *Iosif Aleksandrovich Brodsky*; U.S. poet laureate 1991. Writing both in Russian and in English, he was noted for his collection, *The End of a Beautiful Era* (1977). Nobel Prize for Literature (1987).

Broe·der·bond /ˈbrōdərˌbänd/ a largely secret society in South Africa (founded in 1918) promoting the interests of and restricted in membership to male, Protestant Afrikaners. ▷Afrikaans, from *broeder* 'brother' + *bond* 'league.'

bro·gan /ˈbrogən/ ▸*n.* a coarse, stout leather shoe reaching to the ankle. ▷mid 19th cent.: from Irish *brógán*, Scottish Gaelic *brógan*, literally 'small brogue.'

brogue[1] /brōg/ ▸*n.* a strong outdoor shoe with ornamental perforated patterns in the leather. ■ *historical* a rough shoe of untanned leather, formerly worn in parts of Ireland and the Scottish Highlands. ▷late 16th cent.: from Scottish Gaelic and Irish *bróg*, from Old Norse *brók* (related to **BREECH**).

brogue[2] ▸*n.* [usu. in *sing.*] a marked accent, esp. Irish or Scottish, when speaking English: *a fine Irish brogue* | *a sweet lilt of brogue in her voice.* ▷early 18th cent.: perhaps allusively from **BROGUE**[1], referring to the rough footwear of Irish peasants.

broi·der /ˈbroidər/ ▸*v.* [*trans.*] *archaic* ornament with embroidery.

broil[1] /broil/ ▸*v.* [*trans.*] cook (meat or fish) by exposure to direct, intense radiant heat: *he broiled a wedge of sea bass* | [as *adj.*] (**broiled**) *a broiled sirloin steak.* ■ [*intrans.*] become very hot, esp. from the sun: *the countryside lay broiling in the sun.* ▷late Middle English (also in the sense 'burn, char'): from Old French *bruler* 'to burn,' of unknown origin.

broil[2] ▸*n. archaic* a quarrel or a commotion. ▷early 16th cent.: from obsolete *broil* 'to muddle.' Compare with **EMBROIL**.

broil·er /ˈbroilər/ ▸*n.* **1** (also **broil·er chick·en**) a young chicken suitable for roasting, grilling, or barbecuing. **2** a gridiron, grill, or special part of a stove for broiling meat or fish.

broke /brōk/ ▸ past (and archaic past participle) of **BREAK**.
▸*adj.* [*predic.*] *informal* having completely run out of money: *many farmers went broke.*
▸*PHRASE* □ **go for broke** *informal* risk everything in an all-out effort.

bro·ken /ˈbrōkən/ past participle of **BREAK**. ▸*adj.* **1** having been fractured or damaged and no longer in one piece or in working order: *a broken arm.* ■ rejected, defeated, or despairing: *he went to his grave a broken man* | *a broken heart.* ■ sick or weakened: *broken health.* ■ (of a relationship) ended, typically by betrayal or faithlessness: *a broken marriage.* ■ disrupted or divided: *broken families.* ■ (of an agreement or promise) not observed by one of the parties involved. **2** having gaps or intervals that break a continuity: *a broken white line across the road.* ■ having an uneven and rough surface: *broken ground.* ■ (of speech or a language) spoken falteringly and with many mistakes, as by a foreigner: *a young man talking in broken Italian.* ■ spoken haltingly, as if overcome by emotion: *he whispered in a broken voice.* —**bro·ken·ly** *adv.* —**bro·ken·ness** *n.*
▸*PHRASE* □ **broken record** a scratched record that repeats the same brief passage over and over.

Bro·ken Ar·row a city in northeastern Oklahoma, southeast of Tulsa; pop. 74,859.

bro·ken chord ▸*n.* [usu. as *adj.*] *Music* a chord in which the notes are played successively: *the second entry is a straight broken-chord figure.*

bro·ken-down ▸*adj.* [*attrib.*] worn out and dilapidated by age, use, or ill-treatment: *a broken-down car.* ■ (of a machine or vehicle) not functioning due to a mechanical failure. ■ (of a horse) with serious damage to the legs, in particular the tendons, caused by excessive strain.

bro·ken-field *Football* ▸*adj.* relating to or occurring in the area beyond the line of scrimmage where defenders are relatively scattered: *a broken-field run.* ■ *informal* (of a movement) with starts, stops, and changes of direction, in the manner of a broken-field ballcarrier: *a broken-field chase.*

bro·ken-heart·ed ▸*adj.* overwhelmed by grief or disappointment.

Bro·ken Hill 1 a town in New South Wales in Australia, a center of lead, silver, and zinc mining; pop. 23,260. **2** former name (1904–65) for **KABWE**.

bro·ken home ▸*n.* a family in which the parents are divorced or separated.

bro·ken wind /wind/ ▸*n.* another term for **COPD** in horses. —**bro·ken-wind·ed** *adj.*

bro·ker /ˈbrōkər/ ▸*n.* a person who buys and sells goods or assets for others.
▸*v.* [*trans.*] arrange or negotiate (a settlement, deal, or plan): *fighting continued despite attempts to broker a cease-fire.* ▷Middle English (denoting a retailer or peddler): from Anglo-Norman French *brocour*, of unknown ultimate origin.

bro·ker·age /ˈbrōkərij/ ▸*n.* the business or service of acting as a broker. ■ a fee or commission charged by a broker: *a revenue of $1,400 less a sales brokerage of $12.50.* ■ a company that buys or sells goods or assets for clients.

bro·ker-deal·er ▸*n.* a brokerage firm that buys and sells securities on its own account as a principal before selling the securities to customers.

brol·ga /ˈbrälgə/ ▸*n.* a large gray Australian crane that has an elaborate courtship display that involves much leaping, wing-flapping, and trumpeting. • *Grus rubicundus*, family Gruidae. ▷late 19th cent.: from Kamilaroi *burralga* (also found in other Aboriginal languages).

Brom·berg /ˈbrämbərg/ German name for **BYDGOSZCZ**.

brome /brōm/ ▸*n.* an oatlike grass that is sometimes grown for fodder or ornamental purposes. • Genus *Bromus*, family Gramineae. ▷mid 18th cent.: from modern Latin *Bromus*, from Greek *bromos* 'oat.'

bro·me·li·ad /brōˈmēlēˌad/ ▸*n.* a plant native to tropical and subtropical America, typically having short stems with rosettes of stiff, usually spiny, leaves. Some kinds are epiphytic, and many are cultivated as houseplants. • Family Bromeliaceae: *Bromelia* and other genera, and numerous species, including the pineapple and Spanish moss. ▷mid 19th cent.: from modern Latin *Bromelia* (named by Linnaeus after Olaf *Bromel* (1639–1705), Swedish botanist) + **-AD**[1].

bro·mic ac·id /ˈbrōmik/ ▸*n. Chemistry* a strongly oxidizing acid known only in aqueous solutions. • Chem. formula: $HBrO_3$. —**bro·mate** /ˈbrōˌmāt/ *n.*

bro·mide /ˈbrōmīd/ ▸*n.* **1** *Chemistry* a compound of bromine with another element or group, esp. a salt containing the anion Br^- or an organic compound with bromine bonded to an alkyl radical. ■ a reproduction or piece of typesetting on bromide paper. ■ *dated* a sedative preparation containing potassium bromide. **2** a trite and unoriginal idea or remark, typically intended to soothe or placate: *feel-good bromides create the illusion of problem solving.* —**bro·mid·ic** /brōˈmidik/ *adj.* (in sense 2).

bro·mide pa·per ▸*n.* photographic printing paper coated with silver bromide emulsion.

bro·min·ate /ˈbrōməˌnāt/ ▸*v.* [*trans.*] treat with bromine.
▸■ [usu. as *adj.*] (**brominated**) introduce one or more bromine atoms into a compound or molecule, usually in place of hydrogen: *brominated flame retardants.* —**bro·mi·na·tion** ˌbrōməˈnāSHən *n.*

bro·mine /ˈbrōmēn/ ▸*n.* the chemical element of atomic number 35, a dark red fuming toxic liquid with a choking, irritating smell. It is a member of the halogen group and occurs chiefly as salts in seawater and brines. (Symbol: **Br**) ▷early 19th cent.: from French *brome*, from Greek *brōmos* 'a stink,' + **-INE**[4].

bro·mism /ˈbrōˌmizəm/ ▸*n. dated* a condition of dullness and weakness due to excessive intake of bromide sedatives.

bromo- (usu. **brom-** before a vowel) ▸*comb. form Chemistry* representing **BROMINE**.

Bromp·ton cock·tail /ˈbrämptən/ ▸*n.* a powerful painkiller and sedative consisting of vodka or other liquor laced with morphine and sometimes also cocaine. ▷late 20th cent.: said to be from the name of *Brompton* Hospital, London, where the mixture was invented for cancer patients.

bronc /bräNGk/ ▸*n. informal* short for **BRONCO**.

bron·chi /ˈbräNGkī; -kē/ ▸ plural form of **BRONCHUS**.

bron·chi·a /ˈbräNGkēə/ ▸*n. rare* the ramifications of the two main bronchi in the lungs.

bron·chi·al /ˈbräNGkēəl/ ▸*adj.* of or relating to the bronchi or bronchioles: *bronchial pneumonia.*

bron·chi·al tree ▸*n.* the branching system of bronchi and bronchioles conducting air from the windpipe into the lungs.

bron·chi·al tube ▸*n.* a bronchus or a primary branch off of one.

bron·chi·ec·ta·sis /ˌbräNGkēˈektəsis/ ▸*n. Medicine* abnormal widening of the bronchi or their branches, causing a risk of infection. ▷late 19th cent.: from Greek *bronkhia* (denoting the branches of the main bronchi) + *ektasis* 'dilatation.'

bron·chi·ole /ˈbräNGkēˌōl/ ▸*n. Anatomy* any of the minute branches into which a bronchus divides. ▷mid 19th cent.: from modern Latin *bronchiolus*, *bronchiolum*, diminutives of late Latin *bronchia*, denoting the branches of the main bronchi. —**bron·chi·o·lar** /ˌbräNGkēˈōlər/ *adj.*

bron·chi·o·li·tis /ˌbräNGkēəˈlītis/ ▸*n. Medicine* inflammation of the bronchioles.

bron·chi·tis /bräNGˈkītis/ ▸*n.* inflammation of the mucous membrane in the bronchial tubes. It typically causes bronchospasm and coughing. —**bron·chit·ic** /bräNGˈkitik/ *adj.* & *n.*

bron·chi·um /ˈbräNGkēəm/ ▸*n.* a bronchial tube smaller than a bronchus and larger than a bronchiole.

broncho- ▸*comb. form* of or relating to the bronchi: *bronchopneumonia.* ▷from Greek *bronkho-*, from *bronkhos* (see **BRONCHUS**).

bron·cho·di·la·tor /ˌbräNGkōdīˈlātər; -di-; -ˈdīlātər/ ▸*n. Medicine* a drug that causes widening of the bronchi, e.g., any of those taken by inhalation for the alleviation of asthma.

bron·cho·gen·ic /ˌbräNGkōˈjenik/ ▸*adj.* of bronchial origin.

bron·cho·pneu·mo·nia /ˌbräNGkōn(y)o͞oˈmōnēə; -ˈmōnyə/ ▸*n.* inflammation of the lungs, arising in the bronchi or bronchioles.

bron·cho·scope /ˈbräNGkəˌskōp/ ▸*n.* a fiber-optic cable that is passed into the windpipe in order to view the bronchi. —**bron·chos·co·py** /bräNG ˈkäskəpē/ *n.*

bron·cho·spasm /ˈbräNGkəˌspazəm/ ▸*n. Medicine* spasm of bronchial smooth muscle producing narrowing of the bronchi.

bron·chus /ˈbräNGkəs/ ▸*n.* (*pl.* **-chi** /-kī; -kē/) any of the major air passages of the lungs that diverge from the windpipe. ▷late 17th cent.: from late Latin, from Greek *bronkhos* 'windpipe.'

bron·co /ˈbräNGkō/ ▸*n.* (*pl.* **-cos**) a wild or half-tamed horse, esp. of the western U.S. ▷mid 19th cent.: from Spanish, literally 'rough, rude.'

bron·co·bust·er /ˈbräNGkōˌbəstər/ ▸*n. informal* a cowboy who breaks in wild or half-tamed horses.

Bron·të /ˈbräntē ˈbräntā/ three English novelists: ■ **Charlotte** (1816–55), author of *Jane Eyre* (1847), *Shirley* (1849), and *Villette* (1853). ■ **Emily** (1818–48), author of *Wuthering Heights* (1847); also a poet. ■ **Anne** (1820–49), author of *Agnes Grey* (1845) and *The Tenant of Wildfell Hall* (1847).

bron·to·saur /ˈbräntəˌsôr/ (also **bron·to·sau·rus** /ˌbräntəˈsôrəs/) ▸*n.* another term for **APATOSAUR**. ▷modern Latin from Greek *brontē* 'thunder' + *sauros* 'lizard.' —**bron·to·sau·ri·an** /ˌbräntəˈsôrēən/ *adj.*

bron·to·there /ˈbräntəTHi(ə)r/ ▸*n.* a large ungulate mammal (*Embolotherium andrewsi*) of the Eocene epoch with a hornlike bony growth on the nose. ▷modern Latin, from Greek *brontē* 'thunder' + *thērion* 'wild beast.'

Bronx /bräNGks/ **the Bronx** a borough in northeastern New York City. ▷named after Jonas *Bronck*, a Dutch settler who purchased land here in 1641.

Bronx cheer ▶*n.* a sound of derision or contempt made by blowing through closed lips with the tongue between them; a raspberry. ▷1920s: named after the **BRONX** in New York.

bronze /bränz/ ▶*n.* a yellowish-brown alloy of copper with up to one-third tin. ■ a yellowish-brown color: *rich, gleaming shades of bronze.* ■ a work of sculpture or other object made of bronze. ■ short for **BRONZE MEDAL**.
▶*adj.* made of or colored like bronze: *a bronze statue.*
▶*v.* [*trans.*] (usu. **be bronzed**) make (a person or part of the body) suntanned: *Alison was bronzed by outdoor life* | [as *adj.*] (**bronzed**) *bronzed and powerful arms.* ■ give a surface of bronze or something resembling bronze to: *the doors were bronzed with sculpted reliefs.* ▷mid 17th cent. (as a verb): from French *bronze* (noun), *bronzer* (verb), from Italian *bronzo*, probably from Persian *birinj* 'brass.' —**bronz·y** *adj.*

Bronze Age a prehistoric period that followed the Stone Age and preceded the Iron Age, when certain weapons and tools came to be made of bronze rather than stone.

The Bronze Age began in the Near East and southeastern Europe in the late 4th and early 3rd millennium BC. It is associated with the first European civilizations, the beginnings of urban life in China, and the final stages of some Meso-American civilizations, but did not appear in Africa and Australasia at all.

bronze med·al ▶*n.* a medal made of bronze, customarily awarded for third place in a race or competition.

Bronze Star ▶*n.* a U.S. military decoration awarded for heroic or meritorious achievement not involving participation in aerial flight.

Bron·zi·no /brôn'zēnō/, Agnolo (1503–72), Italian painter; born *Agnolo di Cosimo.*

brooch /brōCH; brōōCH/ ▶*n.* an ornament fastened to clothing with a hinged pin and catch. ▷Middle English: variant of *broach*, a noun originally meaning 'skewer, bodkin,' from Old French *broche* 'spit for roasting,' based on Latin *brocchus, broccus* 'projecting.' Compare with **BROACH**[1].

brood /brōōd/ ▶*n.* a family of young animals, esp. of a bird, produced at one hatching or birth: *a brood of chicks.* ■ bee or wasp larvae. ■ *informal* all of the children in a family: *she was brought up by a loving stepfather as part of a brood of eight.* ■ a group of things or people having a similar character: *a remarkable brood of writers.*
▶*v.* **1** [*intrans.*] think deeply about something that makes one unhappy: *he* **brooded over** *his need to find a wife.* **2** [*trans.*] (of a bird) sit on (eggs) to hatch them. ■ (of a fish, frog, or invertebrate) hold (developing eggs) within the body. **3** [usu. foll. by over] (of silence, a storm, etc.) hang or hover closely: *a winter storm broods over the lake.*
▶*adj.* [*attrib.*] (of an animal) kept to be used for breeding: *a brood mare.* ▷Old English *brōd*, of Germanic origin; related to Dutch *broed* and German *Brut*, also to **BREED**. Sense 1 of the verb was originally used with an object, i.e. 'to nurse (feelings) in the mind' (late 16th cent.), a figurative use of the notion of a hen nursing chicks under her wings.

brood·er /'brōōdər/ ▶*n.* **1** a heated house for chicks or piglets. **2** a person who broods about something.

brood·ing /'brōōdiNG/ ▶*adj.* showing deep unhappiness of thought: *he stared with brooding eyes.* ■ appearing darkly menacing: *a dark, brooding landscape.* —**brood·ing·ly** *adv.*

brood pouch ▶*n.* a pouch in certain fish, frogs, and invertebrates in which the eggs are protected before hatching.

brood·y /'brōōdē/ ▶*adj.* (**brood·i·er**, **brood·i·est**) **1** (of a hen) wishing or inclined to incubate eggs. ■ *informal* (of a woman) having a strong desire to have a baby. **2** thoughtful and unhappy: *his broody concern for the future.* —**brood·i·ly** /-dəlē/ *adv.* —**brood·i·ness** *n.*

brook[1] /brŏŏk/ ▶*n.* a small stream. ▷Old English *brōc*; related to Dutch *broek* and German *Bruch* 'marsh.' —**brook·let** /-lit/ *n.*

brook[2] ▶*v.* [*trans.*] [with *negative*] *formal* tolerate or allow (something, typically dissent or opposition): *Jenny would brook no criticism of Matthew.* ▷Old English *brūcan* 'use, possess,' of Germanic origin; related to Dutch *bruiken* and German *brauchen*. The current sense dates from the mid 16th cent., a figurative use of an earlier sense 'digest, stomach.'

Brooke[1] /brŏŏk/, Edward William (1919–), U.S. lawyer and politician. A Republican senator from Massachusetts 1966–79, he was the first African-American senator popularly elected to the U.S. Senate. He was awarded the Spingarn Medal in 1967.

Brooke[2], Rupert (Chawner) (1887–1915), English poet. He is noted for his wartime poetry, *1914 and Other Poems* (1915).

Brook Farm a historic commune that existed in the 1840s in West Roxbury, now a southwestern section of Boston in Massachusetts, associated with Margaret Fuller and other writers.

Brook·field /'brŏŏk,fēld/ a city in southeastern Wisconsin, west of Milwaukee; pop. 35,184.

Brook·ha·ven /'brŏŏk,hāvən/ a town in eastern Long Island in New York that includes the villages of Brookhaven and Stony Brook, home to a noted nuclear laboratory; pop. 407,779.

brook·lime /'brŏŏk,līm/ ▶*n.* a speedwell with smooth, fleshy leaves and deep blue flowers on long stalks. It grows in wet areas, where the stems take root or float in the water. • Genus *Veronica*, family Scrophulariaceae: several species, in particular *V. beccabunga* of Eurasia and the **American brooklime** (*V. americana*). ▷Middle English *broklemok*, from **BROOK**[1] + *hleomoce*, the name of the plant in Old English.

Brook·line /'brŏŏk,līn/ a town in eastern Massachusetts, on the west side of Boston and almost surrounded by the city; pop. 54,718.

Brook·lyn /'brŏŏklən/ a borough of New York City, at the southwestern corner of Long Island.

Brook·lyn Bridge a suspension bridge between southern Manhattan and northern Brooklyn (on Long Island) in New York City. Constructed 1869–1883, it was one of the period's engineering marvels and is celebrated in art and literature.

Brooklyn Bridge

Brook·lyn·ese /,brŏŏklə'nēz; -'nēs/ ▶*n.* a form of New York speech associated esp. with the borough of Brooklyn.

Brook·lyn Park a city in southeastern Minnesota, north of Minneapolis; pop. 67,388.

Brook·ner /'brŏŏknər/, Anita (1928–), English novelist and art historian. Notable works: *Hotel du Lac* (1984), *Visitors* (1997), *The Bay of Angels* (2001) and *The Rules of Engagement* (2003).

Brooks[1] /brŏŏks/, Cleanth (1906–94), U.S. teacher and critic. A leading proponent of the New Criticism movement, he edited *The Southern Review* 1935–42 and taught at Yale University 1947–75. Notable works: *Modern Poetry and Tradition* (1939) and *The Well-Wrought Urn* (1947).

Brooks[2], Garth (1962–), U.S. country music singer and songwriter; full name *Troyal Garth Brooks*. His albums include *No Fences* (1990), *Ropin' the Wind* (1991), and *Sevens* (1997).

Brooks[3], Gwendolyn (1917– 2000), U.S. poet and writer. She was the first African-American woman named as poetry consultant to the Library of Congress 1985–86 and the first to be awarded a Pulitzer Prize for her poetry collected in *Annie Allen* (1949).

Brooks[4], Mel (1927–), U.S. comedian, movie director and actor; born *Melvin Kaminsky*. He is known esp. for his parodies and farces. His movie debut, *The Producers* (1967), was followed by the spoof *Blazing Saddles* (1974) and *Silent Movie* (1976), which established his characteristic style. Other notable movies: *High Anxiety* (1977), *Spaceballs* (1987), and *Robin Hood: Men in Tights* (1993).

Brooks Range /brŏŏks/ a mountain chain that extends across northern Alaska. It is the northwestern end of the Rocky Mountains; the North Slope lies on its north.

brook trout ▶*n.* see **CHAR**[4].

broom /brōōm; brŏŏm/ ▶*n.* **1** a long-handled brush of bristles or twigs used for sweeping. ■ an implement for sweeping the ice in the game of curling. [formerly made of twigs of broom.] **2** a flowering shrub with long, thin green stems and small or few leaves, that is cultivated for its profusion of flowers. • Genera *Cytisus* and *Genista*, family Leguminosae: many species and cultivated hybrids. See also **SPANISH BROOM**. ▷Old English *brōm* (sense 2), of Germanic origin; related to Dutch *braam*, also to **BRAMBLE**.
▶*PHRASE* □ **a new broom sweeps clean** *proverb* people newly appointed to positions of responsibility tend to be eager to make big or far-reaching changes.

broom·corn /'brōōm,kôrn; 'brŏŏm-/ ▶*n.* a variety of sorghum whose dried inflorescences are used to make brooms.

broom·rape /'brōōm,rāp; 'brŏŏm-/ ▶*n.* a parasitic plant that bears tubular flowers on a leafless brown stem. It is attached by its tubers to the roots of a host plant, which may be any of a number of species. • Genus *Orobanche*, family Orobanchaceae. ▷late 16th cent.: from **BROOM** + Latin *rapum* 'tuber.'

broom·stick /'brōōm,stik; 'brŏŏm-/ ▶*n.* the long handle of a broom. ■ a broom on which, in children's literature, witches are said to fly.

Bros ▶*plural n.* brothers (in names of companies): *Hills Bros. coffee.*

broth /brāTH; brôTH/ ▶*n.* **1** soup consisting of meat or vegetable chunks, and often rice, cooked in stock. ■ meat or fish stock. **2** *Microbiology* liquid medium containing proteins and other nutrients for the culture of bacteria: [as *adj.*] *broth cultures of intestinal tissue.* ■ a liquid mixture for the preservation of tissue: *tissue samples were frozen in a cryoprotective broth.* ▷Old English, of Germanic origin; related to **BREW**.
▶*PHRASE* □ **a broth of a boy** *informal, chiefly Irish* used approvingly to refer to a very lively boy.

broth·el /'brāTHəl; 'brôTHəl/ ▶*n.* a house where men can visit prostitutes. ▷mid 16th cent. (originally *brothel-house*): from late Middle English *brothel* 'worthless man, prostitute,' related to Old English *brēothan* 'degenerate, deteriorate.'

broth·er /'brəT͟Hər/ ▶*n.* **1** a man or boy in relation to other sons and daughters of his parents. ■ a half-brother, stepbrother, or foster brother. ■ a brother-in-law. ■ a male associate or fellow member of an organization: *fraternity brothers.* ■ *informal* a black man (chiefly used as a term of address among black people). ■ a fellow human being. ■ a thing that resembles or is connected to another thing: *the machine is almost identical to its larger brother.* **2** (*pl.* also **breth·ren** /'breT͟Hrin/) *Christian Church* a (male) fellow Christian. ■ a member of a religious order or congregation of men: *a Benedictine brother.*
▶*exclam.* used to express annoyance or surprise. ▷Old English *brōthor*, of Germanic origin; related to Dutch *broeder* and German *Bruder*, from an Indo-European root shared by Latin *frater*. —**broth·er·li·ness** *n.* —**broth·er·ly** *adj.*
▶*PHRASE* □ **brothers in arms** soldiers fighting together, esp. in a war.

broth·er·hood /'brəT͟Hər,hŏŏd/ ▶*n.* **1** the relationship between brothers. ■ the feeling of kinship with and closeness to a group of people or all people: *a gesture of solidarity and brotherhood.* **2** an association, society, or community of people linked by a common interest, religion, or trade: *a religious brotherhood.* ■ a trade union. ▷Middle English: probably from obsolete *brotherred* (based on Old English *-rǣden* 'condition, state'; compare with **KINDRED**). The change of suffix was due to association with words ending in **-HOOD** and **-HEAD**[1].

broth·er-in-law ▶*n.* (*pl.* **broth·ers-in-law**) the brother of one's wife or husband. ■ the husband of one's sister or sister-in-law.

brough·am /'brōōəm; 'brōəm/ ▶*n.* *historical* a horse-drawn carriage with a roof, four wheels, and an open driver's seat in front. ■ an automobile with an open driver's seat. ▷mid 19th cent.: named after Lord *Brougham* (1778–1868), who designed the carriage.

brought /brôt/ ▶ past and past participle of **BRING**.

brou·ha·ha /'brōōhä,hä; brōō'hähä/ ▶*n.* [usu. in *sing.*] a noisy and overexcited critical response, display of interest, or trail of publicity: *24 members resigned over the brouhaha* | *all that election brouhaha.* ▷late 19th cent.: from French, probably imitative.

Brou·wer /'brou-ər/, Adriaen (*c.*1605–38), Flemish painter. Providing an important link between Dutch and Flemish genre painting, his most typical works represent peasant scenes in taverns.

brow[1] /brou/ ▶*n.* **1** a person's forehead: *he wiped his brow.* ■ (usu. **brows**) an eyebrow: *his brows lifted in surprise.* **2** the summit of a hill or pass: *the cottages were built on the brow of a hill.* ▷Old English *brū* 'eyelash, eyebrow,' of Germanic origin. The sense 'forehead' dates from Middle English, and 'top of a hill' from late Middle English; compare with BRAE. **—-browed** *adj.* [in *combination*] *furrow-browed.*

brow[2] ▸*n.* a gangway from a ship to the shore. ■ a hinged part of a ferry or landing craft forming a landing platform or ramp. ▷mid 19th cent.: probably from Norwegian *bru*, from Old Norse *brú* 'bridge.'

Brow·ard Coun·ty /'brou-ərd/ a county in southeastern Florida, on the Atlantic Ocean, north of Miami; pop. 1,255,488. Fort Lauderdale is its seat.

brow·beat /'brou,bēt/ ▸*v.* (*past* **-beat**; *past part.* **-beat·en**) [*trans.*] intimidate (someone), typically into doing something, with stern or abusive words: *a witness is being browbeaten under cross-examination.*

-browed ▸*comb. form* having a specified kind of brow or brows: [in *combination*] *furrow-browed* | *monobrowed.*

Brown[1] /broun/, Sir Arthur Whitten (1886–1948), Scottish aviator. In 1919, he made the first transatlantic flight with Sir John William Alcock.

Brown[2], Ford Madox (1821–93), English painter. His early work was inspired by the Pre-Raphaelites, and in 1861 he became a founder member of William Morris's company, designing stained glass and furniture.

Brown[4], Henry Billings (1836–1913), U.S. Supreme Court associate justice 1890–1906. After serving in several judicial posts in Michigan, he was appointed to the Court by President Benjamin Harrison.

Brown[5], James (1928–), U.S. soul and funk singer and songwriter. In the 1960s he played a leading role in the development of funk with songs such as "Papa's Got a Brand New Bag" (1965) and "Sex Machine" (1970).

Brown[6], Jim (1936–), U.S. football player and actor. He was the National Football League's premier running back, leading the league in rushing in eight of his nine seasons 1957–66 with the Cleveland Browns. He was later featured in several movies, including *The Dirty Dozen* (1967) and *Ice Station Zebra* (1968). Football Hall of Fame (1971).

Brown[7], John (1800–59), U.S. abolitionist. In 1859 he was executed after raiding a government arsenal at Harpers Ferry, Virginia (later part of West Virginia), with the intention of arming slaves and starting a revolt. He became a hero of the abolitionists in the Civil War, and he is commemorated in the song "John Brown's Body."

Brown[8], Lancelot (1716–83), English landscape gardener; known as **Capability Brown**. He evolved an English style of natural-looking landscape parks.

brown /broun/ ▸*adj.* of a color produced by mixing red, yellow, and black, as of dark wood or rich soil: *an old brown coat* | *she had warm brown eyes.* ■ dark-skinned or suntanned: *his face was brown from the sun.* ■ (of bread) made from a dark, unsifted, or unbleached flour.

▸*n.* brown color or pigment: *the brown of his eyes* | *a pair of boots* **in brown** | *the print is rich with velvety browns.* ■ brown clothes or material: *a woman all in brown.*

▸*v.* make or become brown, typically by cooking: [*trans.*] *a skillet in which food has been browned* | [*intrans.*] *bake the pizza until the cheese has browned.*

▸*phrasal v.* □ **brown someone off** [usu. as *adj.*] (**browned off**) make someone feel irritated or depressed: *they are getting browned off with the overtime.* ▷Old English *brūn*, of Germanic origin; related to Dutch *bruin* and German *braun*. **—brown·ish** *adj.* **—brown·ness** *n.* **—brown·y** *adj.*

▸*PHRASES* □ **(as) brown as a berry** (of a person) very suntanned. □ **do something up brown** do something thoroughly or completely: [as *adj.*] *a real picnic, done up brown according to all the rules.* □ **in a brown study** see STUDY.

brown al·gae ▸*plural n.* algae belonging to a large group that includes many seaweeds, typically olive brown or greenish in color. They contain xanthophyll in addition to chlorophyll. • Class Phaeophyceae, phylum Heterokonta, kingdom Protista; formerly division Phaeophyta.

brown bag ▸*n.* a bag made of opaque brown paper. ■ a bag of such a kind in which a lunch is packed and carried to work, school, or informal functions: [as *adj.*] *a brown bag lunch.*

▸*v.* [*trans.*] (**brown bag it**) take a packed lunch to work or school: *no school lunch next week, so I'm brown-bagging it.* **—brown bag·ger** *n.*

brown bag·ging ▸*n.* **1** the practice of bringing one's own packed lunch to work. **2** the practice of bringing one's own liquor to a restaurant or club that may supply setups but can not sell alcoholic beverages.

brown bear ▸*n.* a large bear with a coat color ranging from cream to black, occurring chiefly in forests in Eurasia and North America. See also GRIZZLY BEAR (see GRIZZLY). • *Ursus arctos*, family Ursidae.

brown belt ▸*n.* a brown belt marking a high level of proficiency in judo, karate, or other martial arts, below that of a black belt. ■ a person qualified to wear such a belt.

brown bet·ty ▸*n.* a baked pudding made with apples or other fruit and breadcrumbs.

brown cloud ▸*n.* a visible pall of air pollutants that persists over a city or other area: *the Asian brown cloud* | *throughout the day, air shifts in the valley cause variances in the brown cloud.*

brown coal ▸*n.* another term for LIGNITE.

brown dwarf ▸*n. Astronomy* a celestial object intermediate in size between a giant planet and a small star, believed to emit mainly infrared radiation.

brown earth ▸*n. Soil Science* a type of soil having a brown humus-rich surface layer.

brown fat ▸*n.* a dark-colored adipose tissue with many blood vessels, involved in the rapid production of heat in hibernating animals and human babies.

brown·field /'broun,fēld/ ▸*adj.* [*attrib.*] (of an urban site for potential building development) having had previous development on it. Compare with GREENFIELD.

▸*n.* a former industrial or commercial site where future use is affected by real or perceived environmental contamination.

brown goods ▸*plural n.* television sets, audio equipment, and similar household appliances: *a supply chain that accommodates highly perishable products, as well as white and brown goods.* Compare with WHITE GOODS.

brown hare ▸*n.* a hare found commonly in much of Eurasia. • *Lepus europaeus* (or **capensis**) , family Leporidae.

brown hol·land ▸*n.* unbleached holland linen.

Brown·i·an mo·tion /'brounēən/ ▸*n. Physics* the erratic random movement of microscopic particles in a fluid, as a result of continuous bombardment from molecules of the surrounding medium. ▷late 19th cent.: named after Robert *Brown* (1773–1858), the Scottish botanist who first observed the motion.

Brown·ie /'brounē/ ▸*n.* (*pl.* **-ies**) **1** a member of the junior branch of the Girl Scouts, for girls aged between about 6 and 8. [so named because of the color of the uniform.] **2** (**brownie**) a small square of rich cake, typically chocolate cake with nuts. **3** (**brownie**) a benevolent elf supposed to haunt houses and do housework secretly. [diminutive of BROWN; a "wee brown man" often appears in Scottish ballads and fairy tales; compare with Old Norse *svartálfar*, the dark elves of the Edda.]

▸*PHRASE* □ **brownie point** *informal, humorous* an imaginary award given to someone who does good deeds or tries to please: *his policy will win brownie points with voters.*

Brown·ing[1] /'brouniNG/, Elizabeth Barrett (1806–61), English poet; born *Elizabeth Barrett*. She established her reputation with *Poems* (1844). In 1846, she eloped with Robert Browning. Other notable works: *Sonnets from the Portuguese* (1850), *Aurora Leigh* (novel, 1857), and the posthumous *Last Poems* (1862).

Brown·ing[2], Robert (1812–89), English poet. In 1842, he established his name with *Dramatic Lyrics* that contained "The Pied Piper of Hamelin" and "My Last Duchess." A highly creative period followed his elopement with Elizabeth Barrett. Other notable works: *Dramatic Romances and Lyrics* (1845), *Men and Women* (1855), and *The Ring and the Book* (1868–69).

Brown·ing[3] ▸*n.* (also **Browning machine gun**) a type of water-cooled automatic machine gun. ■ (also **Browning automatic**) a type of automatic pistol. ■ (also **Browning automatic rifle**) a gas-operated automatic rifle, typically fired from a bipod. ▷early 20th cent.: named after J. M. *Browning* (1855–1926), American designer of the weapons.

brown-nose (also **brown·nose**) *informal* ▸*n.* (also **brown-nos·er**) a person who acts in a grossly obsequious way.

▸*v.* [*trans.*] curry favor with (someone) by acting in such a way: *academics were brown-nosing the senior faculty* | [*intrans.*] *I dedicated a book to him—I was not brown-nosing.* ▷the assumed result of ASS-KISSING.

brown·out /'broun,out/ ▸*n.* a partial blackout.

brown owl ▸*n.* another term for TAWNY OWL.

brown rat ▸*n.* a rat found throughout the world, often living in association with man and regarded as a pest. It is commonly kept as a laboratory animal and as a pet, and is also bred in the albino form. Also called COMMON RAT, NORWAY RAT. • *Rattus norvegicus*, family Muridae.

brown rec·luse (also **brown rec·luse spi·der**) ▸*n.* a brown venomous North American spider, identifiable by the dark brown violin-shaped marking on the top of its orange-yellow head. Also called FIDDLEBACK, VIOLIN SPIDER. • *Loxosceles reclusa*, family Loxoscelidae.

brown rice ▸*n.* unpolished rice with only the husk of the grain removed.

brown rot ▸*n.* a fungal disease causing the rotting and browning of parts of plants, in particular: • a disease producing discoloration and shriveling of apples, pears, plums, etc. (caused by fungi of the genus *Monilinia*, phylum Ascomycota). • a disease resulting in the softening and cracking of timber (caused by bracket fungi of the family Polyporaceae, class Basidiomycetes).

brown sauce ▸*n.* a savory sauce made with fat and flour cooked to a brown color.

Brown·shirt /'broun,SHərt/ ▸*n. chiefly historical* a member of an early Nazi militia founded by Hitler in Munich in 1921, with brown uniforms resembling that of Mussolini's Blackshirts.They aided Hitler's rise to power, but were eclipsed by the SS after the "night of the long knives" in June 1934. Also called STORM TROOPS or STURMABTEILUNG.

brown snake ▸*n.* **1** a fast-moving, venomous, and aggressive Australian snake, with a variety of color forms. • *Pseudonaja* and other genera, family Elapidae: several species, in particular *P. textilis*. **2** a small, secretive, harmless North American snake that is typically brownish in color. • *Storeria dekayi*, family Colubridae.

brown·stone /'broun,stōn/ ▸*n.* a kind of reddish-brown sandstone used for building. ■ a building faced with such sandstone.

brown sug·ar ▸*n.* unrefined or partially refined sugar. ■ a consumer product made by adding molasses to white sugar.

Browns·ville **1** a city in southern Texas, on the Rio Grande and the Mexican border; pop. 98,962. **2** a section of eastern Brooklyn in New York City, noted in the early 20th century for its Jewish community, today a struggling inner-city neighborhood. Local name **the 'Ville.**

Brown Swiss ▸*n.* an animal of a brown breed of dairy cattle, originally bred in Switzerland.

brown-tail (also **brown-tail moth**) ▸*n.* a white European moth that has a brown tip to the abdomen and is a pest of tree foliage in several areas, including North America. The caterpillars live communally in web tents and bear irritant hairs that can produce an allergic reaction. • *Euproctis chrysorrhoea*, family Lymantriidae.

brown tree snake ▸*n.* a nocturnal tree snake of Pacific origin that has escaped captivity as a pet to threaten native fauna in many Pacific Rim locations. • *Boiga irregularis*, family Colubridae.

brown trout ▸*n.* (*pl.* same) the common trout of Europe, esp. one of a nonmigratory race with dark spotted skin, that occurs in small rivers and pools. It has been introduced into North America as a game fish. • *Salmo trutta*, family Salmonidae, in particular *S. trutta fario*. Compare with LAKE TROUT, SEA TROUT.

browse /brouz/ ▸*v.* [*intrans.*] **1** survey objects casually, esp. goods for sale: *he stopped to browse around a sporting goods store.* ■ scan through a book or magazine superficially to gain an impression of the contents: *she browsed through the newspaper* [*trans.*] *patrons can browse the shelves of the library.* ■ [*trans.*] *Computing* read or survey (data files), typically via a network. **2** (of an animal) feed on leaves, twigs, or other high-growing vegetation: *they reach upward to* **browse on** *bushes* | [*trans.*] *the animals browse the high foliage of trees.*

▸*n.* **1** [in *sing.*] an act of casual looking or reading: *the brochure is well worth a browse.* **2** vegetation, such as twigs and young shoots, eaten by animals: *a moose needs to eat forty to fifty pounds of browse a day.* ▷late Middle English (sense 2 of the *verb*): from Old French *broster*, from *brost* 'young shoot,' probably of Germanic origin. **—brows·a·ble** *adj.*

brows·er /'brouzər/ ▸*n.* a person who looks casually through books or magazines or at things for sale. ■ an animal that feeds mainly on high-growing vegetation. ■ *Computing* a program with a graphical user interface for displaying HTML files, used to navigate the World Wide Web: *a Web browser.*

brrr /bər/ ▸*exclam.* used to express someone's reaction to feeling cold: *Brrr! It's a freezing cold day.*

Bru·beck /'bro͞o,bek/, Dave (1920–), U.S. jazz pianist, composer, and bandleader; full name *David Warren Brubeck.* He formed the Dave Brubeck Quartet in 1951 and gained a reputation as an experimental musician. He won international recognition with the album *Time Out* (1959), which included "Take Five."

Bruce[1] /bro͞os/, Lenny (1925–66), U.S. comedian; born *Leonard Alfred Schneider.* He gained notoriety for flouting the bounds of respectability with his humor and was imprisoned for obscenity in 1961. In 1963, he was refused entry to Britain and banned in Australia. He died following an accidental drug overdose.

Bruce[2], Robert the, see **Robert** I.

bru·cel·lo·sis /,bro͞osə'lōsis/ ▸*n.* a bacterial disease typically affecting cattle and buffalo and causing undulant fever in humans. • This disease is caused by Gram-negative bacteria of the genus *Brucella*, in particular *B. abortus.* ▷1930s: from modern Latin *Brucella* + **-osis**: named after Sir David *Bruce* (1855–1931), the Scottish physician who identified the bacterium.

bru·cine /'bro͞osēn; -sin/ ▸*n.* a highly toxic alkaloid present in nux vomica. • Chem. formula: $C_{23}H_{26}N_2O_4$.

bru·cite /'bro͞osīt/ ▸*n.* a white, gray, or greenish mineral consisting of magnesium hydroxide. ▷early 19th cent.: named after Archibald *Bruce* (1777–1818), American mineralogist, + **-ite**[1].

Brue·gel /'broigəl/ (also **Breu·ghel** or **Brue·ghel**) a family of Flemish artists: ■ **Pieter** (*c.*1525–69); known as **Pieter Bruegel the Elder.** He produced landscapes, religious allegories, and satires of peasant life. Notable works: *The Procession to Calvary* (1564). ■ **Pieter Bruegel the Younger** (1564–1638), son of Pieter Bruegel the Elder; known as **Hell Bruegel.** A very able copyist of his father's work, he is also noted for his paintings of devils. ■ **Jan** (1568–1623), son of Pieter Bruegel the Elder; known as **Velvet.** He was a celebrated painter of flower, landscape, and mythological pictures.

Bru·ges /bro͞ozн/ a city in northwestern Belgium; pop. 117,000. Flemish name **Brugge.**

Brug·ge /'brʏgə/ Flemish name for **Bruges.**

bru·in /'bro͞oin/ ▸*n.* a bear, esp. in children's fables. ▷late 15th cent.: from Dutch *bruin* (see **brown**); used as a name for the bear in the 13th-cent. fable *Reynard the Fox.*

bruise /bro͞oz/ ▸*n.* an injury appearing as an area of discolored skin on the body, caused by a blow or impact rupturing underlying blood vessels. ■ a similar area of damage on a fruit, vegetable, or plant.
▸*v.* [*trans.*] [often as *adj.*] (**bruised**) inflict such an injury on (someone or something): *a bruised knee.* ■ hurt (someone's feelings): *she tried to bolster her bruised pride.* ■ [*intrans.*] be susceptible to bruising: *potatoes bruise easily, so treat them with care.* ■ crush or pound (something): *bruise the raisins before adding to the mixture.* ▷Old English *brȳsan* 'crush, injure or damage with a blow,' reinforced in Middle English by Old French *bruisier* 'break.'

bruis·er /'bro͞ozər/ ▸*n. informal, chiefly derogatory* a person who is tough and aggressive and enjoys a fight or argument. ■ a professional boxer.

bruis·ing /'bro͞oziNG/ ▸*adj.* causing a bruise or bruises: *his legs took the bruising blows.* ■ *figurative* (of an antagonistic or competitive situation) conducted in an aggressive way and likely to have a stressful effect on those involved: *a bruising congressional battle over public spending.*
▸*n.* bruises on the skin: *her arm showed signs of bruising.*

bruit /bro͞ot/ ▸*v.* [*trans.*] spread (a report or rumor) widely: *I didn't want to have our relationship* ***bruited*** *about the office.*
▸*n.* **1** *archaic* a report or rumor. **2** a sound, typically an abnormal one, heard through a stethoscope; a murmur. ▷late Middle English (as a noun): from Old French *bruit* 'noise,' from *bruire* 'to roar.'

Bru·maire /bro͞o'me(ə)r/ ▸*n.* the second month of the French Republican calendar (1793–1805), originally running from October 22 to November 20. ▷French, from *brume* 'mist.'

bru·mal /'bro͞oməl/ ▸*adj. poetic/literary* of or relating to winter; wintry: *'tis a brumal night.*

brume /bro͞om/ ▸*n. poetic/literary* mist or fog: *the birds rise like brume.* ▷early 18th cent.: from French, from Latin *bruma* 'winter.'

Brum·ma·gem /'brəməjəm/ (also **brum·ma·gem**) ▸*adj.* [*attrib.*] cheap, showy, or counterfeit: *a vile Brummagem substitute for the genuine article.* ▷mid 17th cent.: dialect form of **Birmingham**, England, with reference to counterfeit coins and plated goods once made there.

Brum·mell /'brəməl/, George Bryan (1778–1840), English dandy; known as **Beau Brummell.** He was the arbiter of British fashion for the early 19th century, owing his social position to his friendship with the Prince Regent.

bru·mous /'bro͞oməs/ ▸*adj. poetic/literary* foggy; wintry. ▷mid 19th cent.: from French *brumeux*, from late Latin *brumosus* (from *bruma* 'winter').

brunch /brənCH/ ▸*n.* a late morning meal eaten instead of breakfast and lunch. ▷late 19th cent.: blend of **breakfast** and **lunch.**

Brundt·land /'bro͝ont,länd/, Gro Harlem (1939–), Norwegian stateswoman, prime minister 1981, 1986–89, and 1990–96. As Norway's first female prime minister, she chaired the World Commission on Environment and Development (known as the Brundtland Commission), which produced the *Our Common Future* report in 1987.

Bru·nei /bro͞o'nī; 'bro͞o,nī/ a small oil-rich constitutional sultanate on the northwestern coast of Borneo, divided by parts of Malaysia's state of Sarawak; pop. 365,000; capital, Bandar Seri Begawan; languages, Malay (official), English (official), Chinese. Official name **Brunei Darussalam.** —**Bru·nei·an** /-'nīən/ *adj.* & *n.*

In the 16th century Brunei dominated Borneo and parts of the Philippines, but its power declined as that of the Portuguese and Dutch grew. In 1888, it was placed under British protection; it became a fully independent Commonwealth of Nations state in 1984. Brunei has been ruled by the same family for six centuries.

Bru·nel /bro͞o'nel/, Isambard Kingdom (1806–59), English engineer, son of Sir Marc Isambard Brunel (1769–1849). He designed the *Great Western* (1838), the first transatlantic steamship, and the *Great Eastern* (1858), the world's largest ship until 1899.

Bru·nel·les·chi /,bro͞onl'eskē/, Filippo (1377–1446), Italian architect; born *Filippo di Ser Brunellesco.* He is noted for the dome of Florence Cathedral (1420–61), which he raised without the use of temporary supports.

bru·nette /bro͞o'net/ (also **bru·net**) ▸*adj.* having dark brown hair: *a fresh-faced brunette woman in her thirties.* ■ (of hair) dark brown: *her lustrous brunette tresses.* ▷mid 16th cent.: from French, feminine of *brunet*, diminutive of *brun* 'brown.'

brung /brəNG/ ▸ dialect past and past participle of **bring.**

Brun·hild /'bro͞on,hild; -,hilt/ *Germanic Mythology* in the Nibelungenlied, the wife of Gunther, who instigated the murder of Siegfried. In the Norse versions she is a Valkyrie whom Sigurd (the counterpart of Siegfried) wins by penetrating the wall of fire behind which she lies in an enchanted sleep.

Bru·no /'bro͞onō/, Giordano (1548–1600), Italian philosopher. A supporter of the heliocentric Copernican view of the solar system, envisaging an infinite universe of numerous worlds moving in space, he was tried by the Inquisition for heresy and burned at the stake.

Bru·no, St. /'bro͞onō; brʏ'nō/ (*c.*1032–1101), French churchman, born in Germany. He founded the Carthusian order at La Grande Chartreuse in 1084. Feast day, October 6.

bru·noise /bro͞on'wäz/ ▸*n.* finely diced vegetables that are cooked in butter and used to flavor soups and sauces

Bruns·wick /'brənzwik/ **1** a former duchy and state in central Germany, mostly incorporated into Lower Saxony. German name **Braunschweig.** ■ the capital of this former duchy, an industrial city in Lower Saxony, Germany; pop. 259,130. **2** a town in southwestern Maine, home to Bowdoin College; pop. 21,172.

Bruns·wick stew ▸*n.* a stew originally made with squirrel or rabbit, but now consisting of chicken and vegetables including onion and tomatoes.

brunt /brənt/ ▸*n.* (**the brunt**) the worst part or chief impact of a specified thing: *education will* ***bear the brunt*** *of the cuts.* ▷late Middle English (denoting a blow or an attack, also the force or shock of something): of unknown origin.

bru·schet·ta /bro͞o'sketə/ ▸*n.* toasted Italian bread drenched in olive oil and served typically with garlic or tomatoes. ▷Italian.

brush[1] /brəSH/ ▸*n.* **1** an implement with a handle, consisting of bristles, hair, or wire set into a block, used for cleaning or scrubbing, applying a liquid or powder to a surface, arranging the hair, or other purposes: *a paint brush.* ■ an act of sweeping, applying, or arranging with such an implement or with one's hand: *he gave the seat a brush.* ■ (usu. **brushes**) a thin stick set with long wire bristles, used to make a soft hissing sound on drums or cymbals. ■ the bushy tail of a fox. **2** a slight and fleeting touch: *the lightest brush of his lips against her cheek.* ■ a brief and typically unpleasant or unwelcome encounter with someone or something: *a* ***brush with*** *death.* **3** a piece of carbon or metal serving as an electrical contact with a moving part in a motor or alternator.
▸*v.* **1** [*trans.*] remove (dust or dirt) by sweeping or scrubbing: *we'll be able to* ***brush*** *the mud* ***off*** *easily | he* ***brushed himself down.*** ■ [*trans.*] use a brush or one's hand to remove dust or dirt from (something): *she* ***brushed down*** *her best coat.* ■ [*trans.*] clean (one's teeth) by scrubbing with a brush. ■ [*trans.*] arrange (one's hair) by running a brush through it. ■ [*trans.*] apply a liquid to (a surface) with a brush: *brush the potatoes with oil.* ■ apply (a liquid or substance) to a surface: ***brush on*** *a floor enamel for a long-lasting base coat.* **2** [*intrans.*] touch lightly and gently: *stems of grass* ***brush against*** *her legs.* ■ (**brush past**) touch fleetingly and in passing: *she brushed past him to leave the room.* ■ [*trans.*] push (something) away with a quick movement of the hand: *she* ***brushed*** *a wisp of hair* ***away*** *from her face.* ■ [*trans.*] (**brush something aside**) dismiss (something) curtly and confidently: *people brushed aside the possibility of imminent war.* ■ [*trans.*] (**brush someone/something off**) dismiss in an abrupt, contemptuous way: *the president brushed off a reporter's question about terrorism.*
▸*phrasal v.* □ **brush someone back** *Baseball, informal* (of a pitcher) force a batter to step back to avoid being hit by a ball pitched close to the body. □ **brush up on** improve one's previously good knowledge of or skill at a particular thing: *brush up on your telephone skills.* ▷Middle English: noun from Old French *broisse*; verb partly from Old French *brosser* 'to sweep.' —**brush·less** *adj. chiefly technical*.

brush[2] ▸*n.* undergrowth, small trees, and shrubs. ■ land covered with such growth. ■ cut brushwood. ▷Middle English: from Old French *broce*, perhaps based on Latin *bruscum*, denoting an excrescence on the maple.

brush·back /'brəSH,bak/ (also **brushback pitch**) ▸*n.* *Baseball* a pitch aimed close to the body so that the batter must step back to avoid it.

brushed /brəSHt/ ▸*adj.* having been treated with a brush, in particular: ■ (of fabric) having a soft raised nap: *brushed cotton.* ■ (of metal) finished with a nonreflective surface: *brushed aluminum.*

brush fire (also **brush-fire**) ▸*n.* **1** a fire in brush or scrub. **2** a conflict, esp. an armed conflict, that arises suddenly and is limited in scale or area: [as *adj.*] *fighting brush-fire wars.* ■ a minor crisis.

brush-off ▸*n.* [in *sing.*] *informal* a rejection or dismissal in which someone is treated as unimportant: *he's been* ***giving*** *her* ***the brush-off.***

brush·stroke /'bəsH,strōk/ ▸*n.* **1** the stroke of a brush, especially a hair brush or paintbrush. ■ the mark or effect created by this: *an errant brushstroke doesn't necessarily destroy a painting.* **2** an individual action that contributes to an overall effect or work: *you write in broad, inaccurate brushstrokes, and seem incapable of grasping the meaning of your own words.*

brush tur·key ▸*n.* a large mound-building bird of the megapode family, resembling a turkey and found mainly in New Guinea. • Family Megapodiidae: several genera and species, including *Alectura lathami* of eastern Australia.

brush wolf ▸*n.* another term for **COYOTE**.

brush·wood /ˈbrəsʜˌwo͝od/ ▸*n.* undergrowth, twigs, and small branches, typically used for firewood or kindling.

brush·work /ˈbrəsʜˌwərk/ ▸*n.* the way in which painters use their brush, as evident in their paintings: *canvases characterized by lively, flowing brushwork.*

brush·y /ˈbrəsʜē/ ▸*adj.* **1** covered in or consisting of brushwood: *a brushy hillside.* **2** *Art* relating to or displaying bold use of the brush in painting: *brushy outlining of form.*

brusque /brəsk/ ▸*adj.* abrupt or offhand in speech or manner: *she could be brusque and impatient.* ▷mid 17th cent.: from French, 'lively, fierce,' from Italian *brusco* 'sour.' **—brusque·ly** *adv.* **—brusque·ness** *n.* **—brus·que·rie** /ˌbrəskəˈrē; ˌbro͞o-/ *n.* (*archaic*).

THE RIGHT WORD **bluff, blunt, brusque, curt, gruff, surly**

Brusque, which comes from an Italian word meaning rude, describes an abruptness of speech or manner that is not necessarily meant to be rude (*a brusque handshake; a brusque reply*).

Curt is more deliberately unfriendly, suggesting brevity and coldness of manner (*a curt dismissal*).

There's nothing wrong with being **blunt**, although it implies an honesty and directness that can border on tactlessness (*a blunt reply to his question about where the money went*).

Someone who is **bluff** is usually more likable, possessing a frank, hearty manner that may be a little too outspoken but is seldom offensive (*a bluff man who rarely minced words*).

Exhibiting **gruff** or **surly** behavior will not win friends, since both words suggest bad temper if not rudeness. But *gruff* is used to describe a rough or grouchy disposition and, like *bluff*, is applied more often to a man.

Anyone who has had to deal with an overworked store clerk while shopping during the holidays knows the meaning of *surly*, which is worse than *gruff*. It describes not only a sour disposition but an outright hostility toward people, and it can apply to someone of either sex (*that surly woman at the customer service desk*).

Brus·sels /ˈbrəsəlz/ the capital of Belgium, in the central part of the country; pop. 954,000. The headquarters of the European Commission is located here. French name **BRUXELLES**; Flemish name **BRUSSEL**.

Brus·sels car·pet ▸*n.* a carpet with a heavy woolen pile and a strong linen back. ▷late 18th cent.: named after **BRUSSELS**[1] in Belgium.

Brus·sels lace ▸*n.* an elaborate kind of lace, typically with a raised design, made using a needle or lace pillow.

Brus·sels sprout (also **brus·sels sprout**) ▸*n.* a vegetable consisting of the small compact bud of a variety of cabbage. ■ the plant that yields this vegetable, bearing many such buds along a tall single stem.

Brussels sprouts

brut /bro͞ot/ ▸*adj.* (of sparkling wine) unsweetened; very dry. ▷late 19th cent.: French, literally 'raw, rough.'

bru·tal /ˈbro͞otl/ ▸*adj.* savagely violent: *a brutal murder.* ■ punishingly hard or uncomfortable: *the brutal winter wind.* ■ without any attempt to disguise unpleasantness: *the brutal honesty of his observations.* ▷late 15th cent. (in the sense 'relating to the lower animals'): from Old French, or from medieval Latin *brutalis*, from *brutus* 'dull, stupid' (see **BRUTE**). **—bru·tal·i·ty** /bro͞oˈtalitē/ *n.* **—bru·tal·ly** *adv.*

bru·tal·ism /ˈbro͞otlˌizəm/ ▸*n.* a style of architecture or art characterized by a deliberate plainness, crudity, or violence of imagery. The term was first applied to functionalist buildings of the 1950s and 1960s that made much use of steel and concrete in starkly massive blocks. **—bru·tal·ist** *n.* & *adj.*

bru·tal·ize /ˈbro͞otlˌīz/ ▸*v.* [*trans.*] attack (someone) in a savage and violent way: *they brutalize and torture persons in their custody.* ■ (often **be brutalized**) desensitize (someone) to the pain or suffering of others by exposing them to violent behavior or situations: *he had been brutalized in prison and became cynical* | [as *adj.*] (**brutalizing**) *the brutalizing effects of warfare.* **—bru·tal·i·za·tion** /ˌbro͞otliˈzāsʜən/ *n.*

brute /bro͞ot/ ▸*n.* a savagely violent person or animal: *he was a cold-blooded brute.* ■ *informal* a cruel, unpleasant, or insensitive person: *what an unfeeling little brute you are.* ■ an animal as opposed to a human being. ■ something awkward, difficult, or unpleasant: *a great **brute of a** machine.*

▸*adj.* [*attrib.*] unreasoning and animallike: *a brute struggle for social superiority.* ■ merely physical: *we achieve little by brute force.* ■ harsh, fundamental, or inescapable: *the brute necessities of basic subsistence.* ▷late Middle English (as an adjective): from Old French *brut(e)*, from Latin *brutus* 'dull, stupid.'

brut·ish /ˈbro͞otisʜ/ ▸*adj.* resembling or characteristic of a brute: *brutish behavior.* **—brut·ish·ly** *adv.* **—brut·ish·ness** *n.*

Bru·tus[1] /ˈbro͞otəs/, Lucius Junius, (6th century BC), legendary founder of the Roman Republic. Traditionally, he led a popular uprising, after the rape of Lucretia, against his uncle, the king, and drove him from Rome.

Bru·tus[2], Marcus Junius (85–42 BC), Roman senator. With Cassius he led the conspirators who assassinated Julius Caesar in 44. They were defeated by Caesar's supporters, Antony and Octavian, at the battle of Philippi in 42, after which he committed suicide.

Brux·elles /brʏˈsel/ French name for **BRUSSELS**[1].

brux·ism /ˈbrəksizəm/ ▸*n.* the involuntary or habitual grinding of the teeth, typically during sleep. ▷1930s: from Greek *brukhein* 'gnash the teeth' + **-ISM**.

Bry·an /ˈbrīən/ a city in east central Texas; pop. 55,002.

Bry·ansk /brēˈänsk/ (also **Bri·ansk**) an industrial city in western Russia, southwest of Moscow, on the Desna River; pop. 456,000.

Bry·ant /ˈbrīənt/, William Cullen (1794–1878), U.S. poet and editor. He was co-owner and editor of the New York Evening Post 1829–78; his poems "Thanatopsis" (1811) and "To a Waterfowl" (1821) established him as the leading poet of his time.

Bryce Can·yon /brīs/ a region in south central Utah, site of a national park noted for spectacular rock formations.

Bryl·creem /ˈbrilˌkrēm/ ▸*n. trademark* a cream used on men's hair to give it a smooth, shiny appearance. **—Bryl·creemed** *adj.*

bry·ol·o·gy /brīˈäləjē/ ▸*n.* the study of mosses and liverworts. ▷mid 19th cent.: from Greek *bruon* 'moss' + **-LOGY**. **—bry·o·log·i·cal** /ˌbrīəˈläjikəl/ *adj.* **—bry·ol·o·gist** /-jist/ *n.*

bry·o·ny /ˈbrīənē/ ▸*n.* (*pl.* **-nies**) **1** (also **white bryony**) a climbing plant that has greenish-white flowers, red berries, and springlike tendrils. Native to Eurasia, it is the only British member of the gourd family. • *Bryonia dioica*, family Cucurbitaceae. **2** (**black bryony**) a climbing plant with broad glossy leaves, poisonous red berries, and black tubers. Native to Europe, it is the only British member of the yam family. • *Tamus communis*, family Dioscoreaceae. ▷Old English, via Latin from Greek *bruōnia*.

Bry·oph·y·ta /brīˈäfitə/ *Botany* a division of small, simple plants that comprises the mosses and liverworts. They lack flowers and roots, reproduce by spores released from a stalked capsule, and are anchored to the soil by specialized hairs. • Division Bryophyta: classes Musci (mosses) and Hepaticae (liverworts). ▷modern Latin (plural), from Greek *bruon* 'moss' + *phuta* 'plants.' **—bry·o·phyte** /ˈbrīəˌfīt/ *n.*

Bry·o·zo·a /ˌbrīəˈzōə/ *Zoology* a phylum of sedentary aquatic invertebrates that comprises the moss animals. ▷modern Latin (plural), from Greek *bruon* 'moss' + *zōia* 'animals.' **—bry·o·zo·an** *n.* & *adj.*

Bry·thon·ic /briˈᴛʜänik/ (also **Brit·ton·ic** /briˈtänik/) ▸*adj.* denoting, relating to, or belonging to the southern group of Celtic languages, consisting of Welsh, Cornish, and Breton. Compare with **GOIDELIC**. Also called **P-CELTIC**.

▸*n.* these languages collectively. ▷from Welsh *Brython* 'Britons' + **-IC**.

Brześć nad Bu·giem /bəˈzʜescʜ näd ˈbo͞ogˌyem/ Polish name for **BREST** (sense 2.)

BS ▸*abbr.* ■ Bachelor of Science. ■ balance sheet. ■ Blessed Sacrament. ■ *vulgar slang* used as a euphemism for "bullshit."

BSA ▸*abbr.* Boy Scouts of America.

BSc ▸*abbr.* Bachelor of Science.

B-school /ˈbēˌsko͞ol/ ▸*abbr.* business school.

BSE ▸*abbr.* bovine spongiform encephalopathy, a usually fatal disease of cattle affecting the central nervous system, causing agitation and staggering. It is thought to be caused by an agent such as a prion or a virino, and its possible connection with Creutzfeldt–Jakob disease in humans is still much debated. Also (popularly) called **MAD COW DISEASE**.

B-side ▸*n.* the less important side of a pop single record.

BST ▸*abbr.* ■ bovine somatotropin, esp. as a hormone injected in cattle.

Bt. ▸*abbr.* Baronet.

B-tree ▸*n. Computing* an organizational structure for information storage and retrieval in the form of a tree in which all terminal nodes are the same distance from the base, and all nonterminal nodes have between *n* and 2*n* subtrees or pointers (where *n* is an integer).

Btu (also **BTU**) ▸*abbr.* British thermal unit(s).

btw ▸*abbr.* by the way.

B2B ▸*abbr.* business-to-business, denoting trade conducted via the Internet between businesses.

B2C ▸*abbr.* business-to-consumer, denoting trade conducted via the Internet for businesses and consumers.

bu. ▸*abbr.* ■ bureau. ■ bushel(s).

Bual /bwäl; bo͞oˈäl/ ▸*n.* a variety of wine grape grown chiefly in Madeira. ■ a Madeira wine of a medium sweet type made from such grapes. ▷from Portuguese *boal*.

bub /bəb/ ▸*n. informal* an aggressive or rude way of addressing a boy or man: *hey, bub, I'm looking for someone.* ▷mid 19th cent.

bu·bal /ˈbyo͞obəl/ ▸*n.* a hartebeest, esp. one of an extinct race that was formerly found in North Africa. • *Alcelaphus buselaphus buselaphus*, family Bovidae. ▷late 18th cent.: from French *bubale*, via Latin from Greek *boubalos* 'wild ox, antelope.'

bub·ba /ˈbəbə/ ▸*n. informal* **1** used as an informal or affectionate form of address to a brother: *my sister has always called me bubba.* **2** *derogatory* a working-class white male of the rural South. ▷late 20th cent.: alteration of **BROTHER**.

bub·bie /ˈbo͝obē; ˈbəbē/ ▸*n. informal* (chiefly Jewish) one's grandmother. ▷from Yiddish *bubeleh* 'grandmother.'

bub·ble /ˈbəbəl/ ▸*n.* **1** a thin sphere of liquid enclosing air or another gas. ■ an air- or gas-filled spherical cavity in a liquid or a solidified liquid such as glass or amber. ■ *figurative* a state or feeling that is unstable and unlikely to last: *many companies enjoyed rapid expansion before **the bubble burst** | he said the plan was a bubble.* ■ a brief, sudden, upward change from a general trend: *the slide in soybean prices confirmed that Wednesday's rally was just a bubble.* **2** (also **bubble shell**) a marine mollusk that typically has a thin scroll-like shell. • Bullidae and other families, order Cephalaspidea, class Gastropoda. **3** a transparent domed cover or enclosure: *piglets born into a sterile bubble.* ■ a place or position of isolated safety: *they are not on tour packages seeing foreign ports from a bubble.*

▸*v.* [*intrans.*] (of a liquid) contain bubbles of air or gas rising to the surface: *a pot of soup bubbled away on the stove.* ■ [often as *adj.*] (**bubbling**) make a sound resembling this: *a bubbling fountain.* ■ (**bubble with** or **over with**) *figurative* (of a person) be exuberantly filled with an irrepressible positive feeling: *Ellen was bubbling with such enthusiasm.* ■ (**bubble up**) *figurative* (esp. of a negative feeling) become more intense and approach the point of being vehemently expressed: *the fury bubbling up inside her.* ▷Middle English: partly imitative, partly an alteration of **BURBLE**.

▸*PHRASES* □ **burst someone's bubble** see **BURST**. □ **on the bubble** *informal* (of a sports player or team) last or among the last awaiting news about qualifying for the final place in a competition. [from *sit on the bubble*, with the implication that the bubble may burst.]

bub·ble and squeak ▸*n. Brit.* cooked cabbage fried with cooked potatoes and often meat. ▷late 18th cent.: from the sounds of the mixture cooking.

bub·ble bath ▸*n.* liquid, crystals, or powder added to bathwater to make it foam and have a fragrant smell. ■ a bath of water with such a substance added.

bub·ble can·o·py ▸*n.* a transparent domed canopy on an aircraft or bubble car.

bub·ble car ▸*n.* a small car with a transparent domed canopy and typically three wheels.

B

Pronunciation Key ə *ago*; ər *over*; ˈə or ˌə *up*; ˈər or ˌər *fur*; a *hat*; ā *rate*; ä *car*; cʜ *chew*; e *let*; ē *see*; e(ə)r *air*; i *fit*; ī *by*; i(ə)r *ear*; ɴɢ *sing*; ō *go*; ô *for*; oi *boy*; o͝o *good*; o͞o *goo*; ou *out*; sʜ *she*; ᴛʜ *thin*; T͟H *then*; (h)w *why*; zʜ *vision*

B

bub·ble cham·ber ▸*n. Physics* an apparatus designed to make the tracks of ionizing particles visible as a row of bubbles in a liquid.

bub·ble e·con·o·my ▸*n.* an unstable expanding economy; in particular, a period of heightened prosperity and increased commercial activity in Japan in the late 1980s brought about by artificially adjusted interest rates.

bub·ble·gum /ˈbəbəlˌgəm/ ▸*n.* **1** chewing gum that can be blown into bubbles. ■ (also **bubblegum pink**) the bright pink color of such gum: [as *adj.*] *bubblegum capri pants.* **2** [usu. as *adj.*] a thing considered to be insipid, simplistic, or adolescent in taste or style: *rockers hate bubblegum pop.*

bub·ble·head /ˈbəbəlˌhed/ ▸*n. informal* a foolish or empty-headed person.

bub·ble·jet print·er /ˈbəbəlˌjet/ ▸*n.* a kind of inkjet printer.

bub·ble lift (also **bub·ble**) ▸*n. informal* a ski lift with enclosed cabins.

bub·ble mem·o·ry ▸*n. Computing* a type of memory in which data is stored as a pattern of magnetized regions in a thin layer of magnetic material.

bub·ble pack ▸*n.* another term for **BUBBLE WRAP**.

bub·bler /ˈbəb(ə)lər/ ▸*n.* a drinking fountain.

bub·ble tea ▸*n.* a cold, frothy drink made with iced tea, sweetened milk or other flavorings, and usually with sweet black balls or "pearls" made from tapioca. Also called **BOBA TEA, PEARL TEA.**.

bub·ble wrap (*trademark* **Bub·ble Wrap**) ▸*n.* plastic packaging material in sheets containing numerous small air cushions designed to protect fragile goods.

bub·bly /ˈbəb(ə)lē/ ▸*adj.* (**-bli·er, -bli·est**) containing bubbles: *bake until the top is crisp and bubbly.* ■ *figurative* (of a person) full of cheerful high spirits: *a bright and bubbly personality.*
▸*n. informal* champagne.

Bu·ber /ˈbo͞obər/, Martin (1878–1965), Israeli religious philosopher, born in Austria. In his existentialist work *I and Thou* (1923), he argued that religious experience involves reciprocal relationships with a personal subject, rather than knowledge of some "thing."

bu·bo /ˈb(y)o͞obō/ ▸*n.* (*pl.* **-boes**) a swollen, inflamed lymph node in the armpit or groin. ▷late Middle English: from Latin, from Greek *boubōn* 'groin or swelling in the groin.' **—bu·bon·ic** /b(y)o͞oˈbänik/ *adj.*

bu·bon·ic plague ▸*n.* the commonest form of plague in humans, characterized by fever, delirium, and the formation of buboes.

The plague bacterium, *Yersinia pestis* is transmitted by rat fleas. Epidemics occurred in Europe throughout the Middle Ages (notably as the Black Death and the Great Plague of 1665–66); the disease is still endemic in parts of Asia.

bucatini /ˌbo͞okəˈtēnē/ ▸ *n.* pasta in the shape of small tubes. ▷Italian.

buc·cal /ˈbəkəl/ ▸*adj. technical* of or relating to the mouth: *the buccal cavity.* ■ of or relating to the cheek: *the buccal side of the molars.* ▷early 19th cent.: from Latin *bucca* 'cheek' + **-AL**.

buc·ca·neer /ˌbəkəˈnir/ ▸*n. historical* a pirate, originally off the Spanish-American coasts. ■ a daring, adventurous, and sometimes reckless person, esp. in business: [as *adj.*] *a shrewd and buccaneering businessman.* ▷mid 17th cent. (originally denoting European hunters in the Caribbean): from French *boucanier*, from *boucan* 'a frame on which to cook or cure meat,' from Tupi *mukem*.

buc·ca·neer·ing /ˌbəkəˈniriNG/ ▸*adj.* daring and adventurous (often used in a business context): *the buccaneering nature of the oil-transport industry.*

buc·ci·na·tor /ˈbəksəˌnātər/ ▸*n. Anatomy* a flat, thin muscle in the wall of the cheek. ▷late 17th cent.: from Latin, from *buccinare* 'blow a trumpet,' from *buccina*, denoting a kind of trumpet.

Bu·ceph·a·lus /byo͞oˈsefələs/ the favorite horse of Alexander the Great, who tamed the horse as a boy and took it with him on his campaigns until its death, after a battle, in 326 BC.

Bu·chan·an /byo͞oˈkanən/, James (1791–1868), 15th president of the U.S. 1857–61. A Pennsylvania Democrat, he served as U.S. congressman 1821–31, minister to Russia 1832–34, U.S. senator 1834–45, U.S. secretary of state 1845–49, and minister to Great Britain 1853–56. As president, his leanings toward the pro-slavery side in the developing dispute over slavery made the issue more fraught. He retired from politics in 1861.

Bu·cha·rest /ˈbo͞okəˌrest/ the capital of Romania, in the southeastern part of the country; pop. 2,343,800. Romanian name **BUCUREŞTI**.

Bu·chen·wald /ˈbo͞okənˌwôld/ a Nazi concentration camp in World War II, near the village of Buchenwald in central Germany.

Buch·ner /ˈbo͞oknər; ˈbo͞ok-/, Eduard (1860–1917), German organic chemist. He studied the chemistry of alcoholic fermentation and identified several enzymes, notably zymase. Nobel Prize for Chemistry (1907).

Buck /bək/, Pearl S. (1892–1973), U.S. writer; full name *Pearl Sydenstricker Buck*. Her upbringing and work in China inspired her earliest novels, including *The Good Earth* (1931) and *Dragon Seed* (1942). Nobel Prize for Literature (1938).

buck[1] /bək/ ▸*n.* **1** the male of some antlered animals, esp. the fallow deer, roe deer, reindeer, and antelopes. Compare with **DOE**. ■ a male hare, rabbit, ferret, rat, or kangaroo. **2** a vaulting horse. **3** a vertical jump performed by a horse, with the head lowered, back arched, and back legs thrown out behind. **4** a fashionable and typically hell-raising young man. **5** *informal, offensive* a black or American Indian man. **6** (**bucks**) an oxford shoe made of buckskin.
▸*v.* **1** [*intrans.*] (of a horse) to perform a buck: *he's got to get his head down to buck* | [*trans.*] *she* ***bucked*** *them* ***off*** *if they tried to get on her back.* ■ (of a vehicle) make sudden jerky movements: *the boat began to buck in the water.* **2** [*trans.*] oppose or resist (something that seems oppressive or inevitable): *the shares bucked the market trend.* **3** [*trans.*] *informal* make (someone) more cheerful: *Bella and Jim need me to* **buck** *them* **up** | [*intrans.*] (**buck up**) *buck up, kid, it's not the end of the world.*
▸*adj. military slang* lowest of a particular rank: *a buck private.* ▷Old English, partly from *buc* 'male deer' (of Germanic origin, related to Dutch *bok* and German *Bock*); reinforced by *bucca* 'male goat,' of the same ultimate origin.

buck[2] ▸*n. informal* a dollar: *a run-down hotel room for five bucks a night.* ▷mid 19th cent.: of unknown origin.
▸*PHRASES* □ **big bucks** a lot of money. □ **a fast** (or **quick**) **buck** easily and quickly earned money: *the pursuit of a fast buck is the cause of most losses.*

buck[3] ▸*n.* an article placed as a reminder before a player whose turn it is to deal at poker. ▷mid 19th cent.: from the use of a buck-handled knife to indicate the dealer in a poker game.
▸*PHRASES* □ **the buck stops here** (or **with someone**) *informal* the responsibility for something cannot or should not be passed to someone else. □ **pass the buck** *informal* shift the responsibility for something to someone else.

buck-and-wing ▸*n. chiefly historical* a lively solo tap dance, typically done in wooden-soled shoes.

buck·a·roo /ˌbəkəˈro͞o/ ▸*n.* a cowboy. ▷early 19th cent.: alteration of **VAQUERO**.

buck·bean /ˈbəkˌbēn/ ▸*n.* a plant of bogs and shallow water with creeping rhizomes, beanlike leaves that consist of three leaflets, and white or pinkish hairy flowers. Formerly used as a substitute for hops, it is now cultivated as an ornamental aquatic plant. Also called **BOGBEAN**. • *Menyanthes trifoliata*, family Menyanthaceae. ▷late 16th cent.: from Flemish *bocks boonen* 'goat's beans.'

buck·board /ˈbəkˌbôrd/ ▸*n.* an open, four-wheeled, horse-drawn carriage with seating that is attached to a plank stretching between the front and rear axles. ▷mid 19th cent.: from *buck* 'body of a cart' (perhaps a variant of obsolete *bouk* 'belly, body') + **BOARD**.

James Buchanan

buck·brush /ˈbəkˌbrəSH/ ▸*n.* coarse vegetation on which wild deer browse.

buck·e·roo ▸*n.* variant spelling of **BUCKAROO**.

buck·et /ˈbəkit/ ▸*n.* a roughly cylindrical open container, typically made of metal or plastic, with a handle, used to hold and carry liquids or other material. ■ the contents of such a container or the amount it can contain: *she emptied a* ***bucket of*** *water over them.* ■ (**buckets**) *informal* large quantities of liquid, typically rain or tears: *I wept buckets.* ■ *Basketball* a basket. ■ *Computing* a unit of data that can be transferred from a backing store in a single operation. ■ a compartment on the outer edge of a waterwheel. ■ the scoop of a dredger or grain elevator. ■ a scoop attached to the front of a loader, digger, or tractor.
▸*v.* (**buck·et·ed, buck·et·ing**) [*intrans.*] **1** (**it buckets, it is bucketing**, etc.) *informal* rain heavily: *it was still* ***bucketing down.*** **2** [with *adverbial of direction*] (of a vehicle) move quickly and jerkily: *the car came bucketing out of a side road.* ▷Middle English: from Anglo-Norman French *buquet* 'tub, pail,' perhaps from Old English *būc* 'belly, pitcher.' **—buck·et·ful** /-ˌfo͝ol/ *n.* (*pl.* **-fuls**) .
▸*PHRASES* □ **a drop in the bucket** see **DROP**. □ **kick the bucket** see **KICK**[1].

buck·et bri·gade ▸*n.* a line of people who pass buckets of water from one to another to put out a fire.

buck·et hat ▸*n.* a simple soft cloth hat with a brim.

buck·et·load /ˈbəkitˌlōd/ ▸*n. informal* a large quantity: *he scoops up business donations by the bucketload.*

buck·et seat ▸*n.* a seat in a car or aircraft with a rounded back to fit one person.

buck·et shop ▸*n. informal, derogatory* an unauthorized office for speculating in stocks or currency using the funds of unwitting investors.

buck·et·wheel /ˈbəkitˌ(h)wēl/ ▸*n.* a machine with a series of scoops or buckets on a rotating belt, used to excavate or move material.

buck·eye /ˈbəkˌī/ ▸*n.* **1** a North American tree or shrub related to the horse chestnut, with showy yellow, red, or white flowers. • Genus *Aesculus*, family Hippocastanaceae: several species, including the **Ohio buckeye** (*A. glabra*), with yellow flowers and prickly fruit husks. **2** (also **buckeye butterfly**) an orange and brown New World butterfly with conspicuous eyespots on the wings. • *Junonia coenia*, subfamily Nymphalinae, family Nymphalidae. **3** (**Buckeye**) *informal* a native of the state of Ohio. [from the name given to the state, with reference to the abundance of buckeye trees.] **4** (also **buckeye coupling**) a kind of automatic coupling for railroad rolling stock. [named after the *Buckeye* Steel Castings Company, Columbus, Ohio.]

buckeye butterfly

Buck·eye State a nickname for the state of **OHIO**.

buck fe·ver ▸*n.* nervousness felt by novice hunters when they first sight game.

buck·horn /ˈbəkˌhôrn/ ▸*n.* a horn of a deer. ■ such horn, used typically for knife handles, small containers, or rifle sights.

buckhound ▸*n.* a staghound of a small breed.

buck·jump /ˈbəkˌjəmp/ *Austral.* ▸*v.* [*intrans.*] (of a horse) jump vertically with the head lowered, back arched, and legs drawn together in an attempt to unseat the rider.
▸*n.* [often as *adj.*] an act or display of buckjumping: *a buckjump rider.* **—buck·jump·er** *n.*

buck·jump·ing /ˈbəkˌjəmpiNG/ ▸*n.* a rodeo event in which a rider attempts to stay in the saddle of a bucking horse for a period of eight seconds: [as *adj.*] *a buckjumping event.*

buck·le /ˈbəkəl/ ▸*n.* a flat, typically rectangular frame with a hinged pin, used for joining the ends of a belt or strap. ■ a similarly shaped ornament, esp. on a shoe.
▸*v.* **1** [*trans.*] fasten or decorate with a buckle: *he buckled his belt.* ■ [*intrans.*] (**buckle up**) fasten one's seat

belt in a car or aircraft. **2** [*intrans.*] bend and give way under pressure or strain: *the earth* ***buckled under*** *the titanic stress.* [from French *boucler* 'to bulge.'] ■ [*trans.*] bend (something) out of shape: *a giant oak buckles the sidewalk.* ■ *figurative* (of a person) yield or collapse under pressure: *a weaker person might have* ***buckled under*** *the strain.*

▶*phrasal v.* □ **buckle down** tackle a task with determination: *they will* ***buckle down to*** *negotiations over the next few months.* ▷Middle English: from Old French *bocle*, from Latin *buccula* 'cheek strap of a helmet,' from *bucca* 'cheek.'

buck·le bun·ny ▶*n. informal* a woman who is a follower or devotee of rodeos and cowboys.

buck·ler /ˈbək(ə)lər/ ▶*n. historical* a small, round shield held by a handle or worn on the forearm. ▷Middle English: from Old French *(escu) bocler*, literally '(shield) with a boss,' from *bocle* 'buckle, boss' (see BUCKLE).

Buck·ley /ˈbəklē/, William F(rank), Jr. (1925–), U.S. journalist and writer. Founder of the politically conservative *National Review* magazine (1955), he hosted the television discussion program "Firing Line" from 1966 until 1999.

buck·min·ster·ful·ler·ene /ˌbəkminstərˈfo͝oləˌrēn/ ▶*n. Chemistry* a form of carbon having molecules of 60 atoms arranged in a polyhedron resembling a geodesic sphere. See also FULLERENE. ▷1980s: named after Richard Buckminster Fuller (see FULLER3).

buck na·ked (also **buck-nak·ed**) ▶*adj. informal* completely naked.

buck·o /ˈbəkō/ ▶*n.* (*pl.* **-oes** or **-os**) *informal* a young man (often as a form of address): *now hold on a minute, bucko.* ▷late 19th cent. (originally nautical slang): from BUCK1 + -O.

buck-pass·ing ▶*n.* the practice of shifting the responsibility for something to someone else.

buck·ra /ˈbəkrə/ ▶*n.* (*pl.* same or **-ras**) *informal, offensive* a white person, typically a man. ▷mid 18th cent.: from Ibibio and Efik *(m)bakara* 'European, master.'

buck·ram /ˈbəkrəm/ ▶*n.* coarse linen or other cloth stiffened with gum or paste and used typically as interfacing and in bookbinding. ■ *figurative, archaic* stiffness of manner.

▶*adj.* [*attrib.*] of or like such material: *sturdy volumes in buckram bindings.* ■ *figurative, archaic* (of a person) starchy or formal. ▷Middle English (denoting a kind of fine linen or cotton cloth): from Old French *boquerant*, perhaps from BUKHORO in central Asia.

buck·saw /ˈbəkˌsô/ ▶*n.* a type of saw typically set in an H-shaped frame and used with both hands.

Bucks Coun·ty /bəks/ a county in southeastern Pennsylvania, on the Delaware River, noted for its affluent Philadelphia suburbs and its artists' colonies; pop. 541,174. Its seat is Doylestown.

buck·shee /bəkˈsʜē; ˈbəksʜē/ ▶*adj. informal, chiefly Brit.* free of charge: *a buckshee brandy.* ▷World War I (originally soldiers' slang): alteration of BAKSHEESH.

buck·shot /ˈbəkˌsʜät/ ▶*n.* coarse lead shot used in shotgun shells.

buck·skin /ˈbəkˌskin/ ▶*n.* **1** the skin of a male deer. ■ grayish leather with a suede finish, traditionally made from such skin but now more commonly made from sheepskin: [as *adj.*] *a pair of buckskin moccasins.* ■ (**buckskins**) clothes or shoes made from such leather. ■ thick, smooth cotton or woolen fabric. **2** a horse of a grayish-yellow color. —**buck·skinned** *adj.*

buck·thorn /ˈbəkˌᴛʜôrn/ ▶*n.* **1** a shrub or small tree of the buckthorn family, typically bearing thorns. Some kinds yield dyes, and others have been used medicinally. • Genus *Rhamnus*, family Rhamnaceae: several species, including the European **common buckthorn** (*R. cathartica*), now established in the northeastern and central U.S., and the **Carolina buckthorn** (*R. caroliniana*) of the southern U.S. **2** (also **buckthorn bumelia**) a shrub or small tree of the sapodilla family, with sharp thorns and clusters of small white flowers, commonly found in moist soils of the southern and central U.S. • *Bumelia lycioides*, family Sapotaceae. ▷late 16th cent.: from BUCK1 in the sense 'deer' + THORN, translating modern Latin *spina cervina*.

buck·tooth ▶*n.* an upper tooth that projects over the lower lip. —**buck·toothed** *adj.*

buck·wheat /ˈbəkˌ(h)wēt/ ▶*n.* **1** an Asian plant of the dock family that produces starchy seeds. The seeds are used for fodder and are also milled into flour that is widely used in the U.S. • *Fagopyrum esculentum*, family Polygonaceae. **2** (in full **buckwheat tree**) see TITI2. ▷mid 16th cent.: from Middle Dutch *boecweite* 'beech wheat,' its grains being shaped like beech mast.

buck·y·balls /ˈbəkēˌbôlz/ ▶*plural n. Chemistry, informal* spherical molecules of a fullerene, esp. buckminsterfullerene. Related cylindrical molecules are termed **buckytubes**.

buck·y·tube /ˈbəkēˌt(y)o͞ob/ ▶*n. informal* a carbon nanotube.

bu·col·ic /byo͞oˈkälik/ ▶*adj.* of or relating to the pleasant aspects of the countryside and country life: *the church is lovely for its bucolic setting.*

▶*n.* (usu. **bucolics**) a pastoral poem. ▷early 16th cent. (denoting a pastoral poem): via Latin from Greek *boukolikos*, from *boukolos* 'herdsman,' from *bous* 'ox.'

Bu·cu·reş·ti /ˌbo͞okəˈresʜt(y); -ˈresʜtē/ Romanian name for BUCHAREST.

bud1 /bəd/ ▶*n.* a compact knoblike growth on a plant that develops into a leaf, flower, or shoot. ■ *Biology* an outgrowth from an organism (e.g., a yeast cell) that separates to form a new individual without sexual reproduction taking place. ■ [with *adj.*] *Zoology* (of an animal) a rudimentary leg or other appendage that has not yet grown, or never will grow, to full size.

▶*v.* (**bud·ded, bud·ding**) [*intrans.*] *Biology* (of a plant or animal) form a bud: *new blood vessels bud out from the vascular bed* | [*trans.*] *tapeworms* ***bud off*** *egg-bearing sections from their tail end.* ■ [*trans.*] graft a bud of (a plant) on to another plant. ▷late Middle English: of unknown origin.

▶*PHRASE* □ **in bud** (of a plant) having newly formed buds.

bud2 ▶*n. informal* a form of address, usually to a boy or man, used esp. when the name of the one being addressed is not known: *listen, bud, I saw you there with my own eyes.* ▷mid 19th cent.: abbreviation of BUDDY.

Bu·da·pest /ˈbo͞odəˌpest; -ˌpesʜt/ the capital of Hungary, in the northern central part of the country; pop. 2,000,000. It was formed in 1873 by the union of the city of Buda on the right bank of the Danube River with the city of Pest on the left.

Bud·dha /ˈbo͞odə; ˈbo͝odə/ (often **the Buddha**) a title given to the founder of Buddhism, Siddartha Gautama (*c.*563–*c.*460 BC). Born an Indian prince, he renounced wealth and family to become an ascetic, and after achieving enlightenment while meditating, taught all who came to learn from him. ■ [as *n.*] (**a buddha**) *Buddhism* a person who has attained full enlightenment. ■ a statue or picture of the Buddha. ▷Sanskrit, literally 'enlightened,' past participle of *budh* 'know.'

Bud·dhism /ˈbo͞odizəm; ˈbo͝od-/ *n.* a widespread Asian religion or philosophy, founded by Siddartha Gautama in northeastern India in the 5th century BC. —**Bud·dhist** *n.* & *adj.* —**Bud·dhis·tic** /bo͞oˈdistik; bo͝od-/ *adj.* —**Bud·dhis·ti·cal** /bo͞oˈdistikəl; bo͝od-/ *adj.*

Buddhism has no creator god and gives a central role to the doctrine of karma. The 'four noble truths' of Buddhism state that all existence is suffering, that the cause of suffering is desire, that freedom from suffering is nirvana, and that this is attained through the 'eightfold' path of ethical conduct, wisdom, and mental discipline (including meditation). There are two major traditions, Theravada and Mahayana.

bud·ding /ˈbədiɴɢ/ ▶*adj.* [*attrib.*] (of a plant) having or developing buds: *a budding chrysanthemum.* ■ (of a part of the body) becoming larger as part of the process of normal growth. ■ (of a person) beginning and showing signs of promise in a particular career or field: *budding young actors.* ■ just beginning and showing promising signs of continuing: *their budding relationship.*

bud·dle /ˈbədl/ ▶*n.* a shallow inclined container in which ore is washed. ▷mid 16th cent.: of unknown origin.

bud·dle·ia /ˈbədlēə; bədˈlēə/ ▶*n.* a widely cultivated shrub with fragrant lilac, white, or yellow flowers. • Genus *Buddleia* (or *Buddleja*), family Loganiaceae: several species, esp. the butterfly bush. ▷modern Latin; named in honor of the English botanist Adam *Buddle* (died 1715), by Linnaeus, at the suggestion of Sir William Houston who introduced the plant to Europe from South America.

bud·dy /ˈbədē/ *informal* ▶*n.* (*pl.* **-dies**) a close friend. ■ a working companion with whom close cooperation is required.

▶*v.* (**-dies, -died**) [*intrans.*] become friendly and spend time with: *I decided to* ***buddy up to*** *them.* ▷mid 19th cent.: perhaps an alteration of BROTHER.

bud·dy-bud·dy ▶*adj. informal, chiefly derogatory* very friendly: *he's buddy-buddy with the ambassador.*

bud·dy mov·ie ▶*n. informal* a movie portraying a close friendship between two people, esp. between two men.

bud·dy sys·tem ▶*n.* a cooperative arrangement whereby individuals are paired or teamed up and assume responsibility for one another's instruction, productivity, welfare, or safety.

Budge /bəj/, Don (1915–2000), U.S. tennis player; born *John Donald Budge*. He was the first to win the four major singles championships, the "Grand Slam"—Australia, France, Wimbledon, and the U.S.—in one year, 1938.

budge /bəj/ ▶*v.* [usu. with *negative*] make or cause to make the slightest movement: [*intrans.*] *the line in the bank hasn't budged* | [*trans.*] *I couldn't budge the door.* ■ [*intrans.*] (**budge over**) *informal* make room for another person by moving: *budge over, boys, make room for your uncle.* ■ [usu. with *modal*] change or make (someone) change an opinion: [*intrans.*] *I tried to persuade him, but he wouldn't budge* | [*trans.*] *neither bribe nor threat will budge him.* ▷late 16th cent.: from French *bouger* 'to stir,' based on Latin *bullire* 'to boil.'

budg·er·i·gar /ˈbəjərēˌgär/ ▶*n.* a small gregarious Australian parakeet that in the wild is green with a yellow head. It is popular as a pet bird and has been bred in a variety of colors. • *Melopsittacus undulatus*, family Psittacidae. ▷mid 19th cent.: of Aboriginal origin, perhaps an alteration of Kamilaroi *gijirrigaa* (also in related languages).

budg·et /ˈbəjit/ ▶*n.* **1** an estimate of income and expenditure for a set period of time: *keep within the household budget.* | [as *adj.*] *a budget deficit.* ■ an annual or other regular estimate of national revenue and expenditure put forward by the government, often including details of changes in taxation. ■ the amount of money needed or available for a purpose: *they have a limited budget.* **2** *archaic* a quantity of material, typically that which is written or printed.

▶*v.* (**budg·et·ed, budg·et·ing**) [*intrans.*] allow or provide for in a budget: *the university is* ***budgeting for*** *a deficit* | [as *adj.*] (**budgeted**) *a budgeted figure of $31,000* | [as *n.*] (**budgeting**) *corporate planning and budgeting.* ■ [*trans.*] provide (a sum of money) for a particular purpose from a budget: *the council proposes to budget $100,000 to provide grants.*

▶*adj.* [*attrib.*] inexpensive: *a budget guitar.* ▷late Middle English: from Old French *bougette*, diminutive of *bouge* 'leather bag,' from Latin *bulga* 'leather bag, knapsack,' of Gaulish origin. Compare with BULGE. The word originally meant a pouch or wallet, and later its contents. In the mid 18th cent., the Chancellor of the Exchequer in the UK, in presenting his annual statement, was said "to open the budget." In the late 19th cent. the use of the term was extended from governmental to private or commercial finances. —**budg·et·ar·y** /-ˌterē/ *adj.*

▶*PHRASE* □ **on a budget** with a restricted amount of money: *we're traveling on a budget.*

budg·ie /ˈbəjē/ ▶*n.* (*pl.* **-ies**) informal term for BUDGERIGAR.

bud-graft ▶*v.* [*trans.*] graft a bud of (a plant) on to another plant.

▶*n.* a plant grown by this method.

Bud·weis /ˈbo͞otˌvīs/ German name for ČESKÉ BUDĚJOVICE.

bud·wood /ˈbədˌwo͝od/ ▶*n.* short lengths of young branches with buds prepared for grafting on to the rootstock of another plant.

bud·worm /ˈbədˌwərm/ ▶*n.* a moth caterpillar that is destructive to buds. See SPRUCE BUDWORM.

Bue·na Park /ˈbwānə; ˈbyo͞o-/ a city in southern California, southeast of Los Angeles; pop. 68,784. Its tourist attractions include Knott's Berry Farm, a theme park.

Bue·na·ven·tu·ra /ˌbwānəvenˈt(y)o͝orə; ˌbwenə-/ the chief Pacific Ocean port of Colombia; pop. 122,500.

Bue·na Vis·ta a village in northern Mexico, in Coahuila state, near Saltillo, where U.S. forces under Zachary Taylor won a major battle against Mexican forces under Santa Anna in February 1847.

Bue·nos Ai·res /ˌbwānəs ˈe(ə)rēz; ˈīriz/ the capital city and chief port of Argentina, in the eastern central part of the country, on the Plata River; pop. 2,961,000.

Buer·ger's dis·ease /ˈbərgərz/ ▸*n.* inflammation and thrombosis in small and medium-sized blood vessels, typically in the legs and leading to gangrene. It has been associated with smoking. ▷early 20th cent.: named after L. Buerger (1879–1943), American surgeon.

buff[1] /bəf/ ▸*n.* **1** a yellowish-beige color: **2** a stout, dull yellow leather with a velvety surface. ■ a stick, wheel, or pad used for polishing or smoothing.
▸*v.* [*trans.*] polish (something): *he buffed the glass until it gleamed.* ■ give (leather) a velvety finish by removing the surface of the grain.
▸*adj.* **1** yellowish beige: *a fortnight later the buff OHMS envelope had been delivered.* **2** *informal* being in good physical shape with fine muscle tone. ▷mid 16th cent.: probably from French *buffle*, from Italian *bufalo*, from late Latin *bufalus* (see BUFFALO). The original sense in English was 'buffalo,' later 'oxhide' or 'color of oxhide.'
▸*PHRASE* □ **in the buff** *informal* naked.

buff[2] ▸*n.* [with *adj.*] *informal* a person who is enthusiastically interested in and very knowledgeable about a particular subject: *a computer buff.* ▷early 20th cent.: from BUFF[1], originally applied to enthusiastic fire-watchers, because of the buff uniforms formerly worn by New York volunteer firemen.

Buf·fa·lo /ˈbəfəˌlō/ an industrial city in the northwestern part of the state of New York; pop. 292,648. Located at the eastern end of Lake Erie, it is a major port on the St. Lawrence Seaway.

buf·fa·lo /ˈbəfəˌlō/ ▸*n.* (*pl.* same, **-loes** or **-los**) **1** a heavily built wild ox with backswept horns, found mainly in the Old World tropics: • four species native to South Asia (genus *Bubalus*, family Bovidae). See also WATER BUFFALO, ANOA. • see AFRICAN BUFFALO. ■ the North American bison. **2** (also **buf·fa·lo fish**) a large grayish-olive freshwater fish with thick lips, common in North America. • Genus *Ictiobus*, family Catostomidae: several species.
▸*v.* (**-loes, -loed**) [*trans.*] (often **be buffaloed**) *informal* overawe or intimidate (someone): *she didn't like being buffaloed.* ■ baffle (someone): *the problem has buffaloed the advertising staff.* ▷mid 16th cent.: probably from Spanish or Portuguese *búfalo*, from late Latin *bufalus*, from earlier *bubalus*, from Greek *boubalos* 'antelope, wild ox.'

buf·fa·lo ber·ry ▸*n.* a North American shrub with silvery twigs and leaves and edible berries. See also SOAPBERRY. • Genus *Shepherdia*, family Elaeagnaceae: two species, the western **silver buffalo berry** (*S. argentea*), with bright red berries, and the northern **Canada buffalo berry** (*S. canadensis*), with reddish or yellow berries. ■ the berry of this shrub.

Buf·fa·lo Bill (1846–1917), U.S. showman; born *William Frederick Cody*. He gained his nickname for killing 4,280 buffalo in 8 months to feed the Union Pacific Railroad workers. He subsequently devoted his life to his traveling Wild West Show.

Buffalo Bill

buf·fa·lo gnat ▸*n.* another term for BLACK FLY (sense 2).

buf·fa·lo grass ▸*n.* any of a number of grasses, in particular: • a creeping grass of the North American plains, which is sometimes used for erosion control (*Buchloe dactyloides*, family Gramineae). • a grass native to Australia and New Zealand (*Stenotaphrum secundatum*, family Gramineae).

buf·fa·lo moz·za·rel·la ▸*n.* mozzarella cheese made in the traditional way, from the milk of the water buffalo.

Buf·fa·lo Riv·er a river that flows for 132 miles (213 km) through the Ozark Plateau in northwestern Arkansas and is a designated national preserve.

buf·fa·lo robe ▸*n.* a rug, cloak, or blanket made from the dressed hide of a North American bison.

buf·fa·lo sol·dier ▸*n.* (in U.S. history) an African-American cavalry soldier.

Buf·fa·lo wings (also **buf·fa·lo wings** or **Buffalo chicken wings**) ▸*plural n.* deep-fried chicken wings coated in a spicy sauce and usually served with blue cheese dressing.

buff·er /ˈbəfər/ ▸*n.* **1** a person or thing that prevents incompatible or antagonistic people or things from coming into contact with or harming each other: *family and friends can provide a buffer against stress.* **2** (also **buffer solution**) *Chemistry* a solution that resists changes in pH when acid or alkali is added to it. Buffers typically involve a weak acid or alkali together with one of its salts. **3** *Computing* a temporary memory area or queue used when transferring data between devices or programs operating at different speeds.
▸*v.* [*trans.*] **1** lessen or moderate the impact of (something): *the massage helped to buffer the strain.* **2** treat with a chemical buffer: *add organic matter to buffer the resulting alkalinity.* ▷mid 19th cent.: probably from obsolete *buff* (verb), imitative of the sound of a blow to a soft body.

buff·er state ▸*n.* a small neutral country, situated between two larger hostile countries, serving to prevent the outbreak of regional conflict.

buff·er zone ▸*n.* a neutral area serving to separate hostile forces or nations. ■ an area of land designated for environmental protection: *oyster harvesters are not allowed in certain buffer zones.*

buf·fet[1] /bəˈfā/ ▸*n.* **1** a meal consisting of several dishes from which guests serve themselves: [as *adj.*] *a cold buffet lunch.* **2** a room or counter in a station, hotel, or other public building selling light meals or snacks. **3** a cabinet with shelves and drawers for keeping dinnerware and table linens. ▷early 18th cent. (sense 3): from French, from Old French *bufet* 'stool,' of unknown origin.

buf·fet[2] /ˈbəfit/ ▸*v.* (**-fet·ed, -fet·ing**) [*trans.*] (esp. of wind or waves) strike repeatedly and violently; batter: *the rough seas buffeted the coast* | [*intrans.*] *the wind was* **buffeting at** *their bodies.* ■ knock (someone) over or off course: *he was buffeted from side to side.* ■ (often **be buffeted**) *figurative* (of misfortunes or difficulties) afflict or harm (someone) repeatedly or over a long period: *they were buffeted by a major recession.*
▸*n.* **1** *dated* a blow, typically of the hand or fist. ■ *figurative* a shock or misfortune: *the daily buffets of urban civilization.* **2** *Aeronautics* another term for BUFFETING. ▷Middle English: from Old French *buffeter* (verb), *buffet* (noun), diminutive of *bufe* 'a blow.'

buf·fet·ing /ˈbəfitiNG/ ▸*n.* the action of striking someone or something repeatedly and violently: *the roofs have survived the buffeting of worse winds than this.* ■ *figurative* the action or result of afflicting or harming someone, typically repeatedly or over a long period: *the buffeting that people are taking in lost job status.* ■ *Aeronautics* irregular oscillation of part of an aircraft, caused by turbulence.

Buf·fett /ˈbəfit/, Warren Edward (1930–), U.S. businessman and financier. He heads Berkshire Hathaway, Inc. and is an influential board member of Salomon Brothers.

buf·fle·head /ˈbəfəlˌhed/ ▸*n.* a small North American diving duck related to the goldeneye, with a large puffy head. The male has white plumage with a black back. • *Bucephala albeola*, family Anatidae. ▷mid 17th cent. (in the sense 'simpleton'): from obsolete *buffle* 'buffalo' + HEAD. The current sense (mid 18th cent.) may be an independent formation because of the duck's large square-shaped head.

buf·fo /ˈbo͞ofō/ ▸*n.* (*pl.* **-fos**) a comic actor in Italian opera or a person resembling such an actor.
▸*adj.* of or typical of Italian comic opera: *a buffo character.* ▷mid 18th cent.: Italian, 'puff of wind, buffoon,' from *buffare* 'to puff,' of imitative origin.

Buf·fon /byˈfôN/, Georges-Louis Leclerc, Comte de (1707–88), French naturalist. A founder of paleontology, he emphasized the unity of all living species, minimizing the apparent differences between animals and plants. His compilation of the animal kingdom, the *Histoire Naturelle*, reached 36 volumes by the time of his death.

buf·foon /bəˈfo͞on/ ▸*n.* a ridiculous but amusing person; a clown. ▷mid 16th cent.: from French *bouffon*, from Italian *buffone*, from medieval Latin *buffo* 'clown.' Originally recorded as a rare Scots word for a kind of pantomime dance, the term later (late 16th cent.) denoted a professional jester. —**buf·foon·ish** *adj.*

buf·foon·er·y /bəˈfo͞onərē/ ▸*n.* (*pl.* **-er·ies**) behavior that is ridiculous but amusing.

bug /bəg/ ▸*n.* **1** a small insect. ■ *informal* a harmful microorganism, as a bacterium or virus. ■ an illness caused by such a microorganism: *suffering from a flu bug.* ■ [with *adj.*] *figurative, informal* an enthusiastic, almost obsessive, interest in something: *they* **caught** *the sailing* **bug** | *Joe was* **bitten by the** *showbiz* **bug**. **2** (also **true bug**) *Entomology* an insect of a large order distinguished by having mouthparts that are modified for piercing and sucking. • Order Hemiptera: see HEMIPTERA. **3** a miniature microphone, typically concealed in a room or telephone, used for surveillance. **4** an error in a computer program or system.
▸*v.* (**bugged, bug·ging**) [*trans.*] **1** (often **be bugged**) conceal a miniature microphone in (a room or telephone) in order to monitor or record someone's conversations: *the telephones in the presidential palace were bugged.* ■ record or monitor (a conversation) in this way. **2** *informal* annoy or bother (someone): *a persistent reporter was bugging me.*
▸*phrasal v.* □ **bug off** *informal* go away. □ **bug out** *informal* **1** leave quickly: *if you see enemy troops, bug out.* **2** *chiefly figurative* bulge outward: *he did a double take and his eyes bugged out.* ▷early 17th cent.: of unknown origin. Current verb senses date from the early 20th cent.

bug·a·boo /ˈbəgəˌbo͞o/ ▸*n.* an object of fear or alarm; a bugbear. ▷mid 18th cent.: probably of Celtic origin and related to Welsh *bwci bo* 'bogey, the Devil,' *bwci* 'hobgoblin' and Cornish *bucca*.

bug·bane /ˈbəgˌbān/ ▸*n.* a tall plant with wandlike spikes of cream or yellow flowers. A member of the buttercup family, it is native to north temperate regions. • Genus *Cimicifuga*, family Ranunculaceae: several species, in particular the **American bugbane** (*C. americana*) of the eastern U.S. and the **black cohosh** (*C. racemosa*). ▷early 19th cent.: from BUG + BANE, with reference to the former use of the species *C. foetida* to drive away bedbugs.

bug·bear /ˈbəgˌbe(ə)r/ ▸*n.* a cause of obsessive fear, irritation, or loathing. ■ *archaic* an imaginary being invoked to frighten children, typically a sort of hobgoblin supposed to devour them. ▷late 16th cent.: probably from obsolete *bug* 'bogey' (of unknown origin) + BEAR[2].

bug-eyed ▸*adj.* & *adv.* with bulging eyes: [as *adj.*] *bug-eyed monsters* | [as *adv.*] *he stared bug-eyed at John.*

bug·ger /ˈbəgər; ˈbo͝og-/ *vulgar slang, chiefly Brit.* ▸*n.* **1** [with *adj.*] a contemptible or pitied person, typically a man. ■ a person with a particular negative quality or characteristic. ■ used as a term of affection or respect, typically grudgingly: *all right, let the* **little buggers** *come in.* **2** *derogatory* a person who commits buggery.
▸*v.* [*trans.*] penetrate the anus of (someone) during sexual intercourse; sodomize.
▸*phrasal v.* □ **bugger off** [usu. in *imperative*] go away.
▸*exclam.* used to express annoyance or anger. ▷Middle English (originally denoting a heretic, specifically an Albigensian): from Middle Dutch, from Old French *bougre*, originally in the sense 'heretic,' from medieval Latin *Bulgarus* 'Bulgarian,' particularly one belonging to the Orthodox Church and therefore regarded as a heretic by the Roman Church. The sense 'sodomite' (16th cent.) arose from an association of heresy with forbidden sexual practices; its use as a general insult dates from the early 18th cent. Compare with BULGAR.

bug·ger·y /ˈbəgərē; ˈbo͝og-/ ▸*n.* anal intercourse. ▷Middle English (in the sense 'heresy'): from Middle Dutch *buggerie*, from Old French *bougrerie*, from *bougre* (see BUGGER).

bug·gy[1] /ˈbəgē/ ▸*n.* (*pl.* **-gies**) a small or light vehicle, in particular: ■ a small motor vehicle, typically one with an open top: *a golf buggy.* ■ short for BABY BUGGY. ■ *historical* a light, horse-drawn vehicle for one or two people, with two or four wheels. ▷mid 18th cent.: of unknown origin.

bug·gy[2] ▸*adj.* (**-gi·er, -gi·est**) **1** infested with bugs. ■ (of a computer program or system) faulty in operation. **2** *informal* mad; insane.

bug·house /ˈbəgˌhous/ *informal* ▸*n.* *offensive* a mental hospital or asylum.
▸*adj.* crazy; insane.

bug juice ▸*n.* **1** whisky or other liquor, esp. when of poor quality. **2** a sweet, artificially colored, noncarbonated soft drink.

bu·gle[1] /ˈbyo͞ogəl/ ▸*n.* a brass instrument like a small

trumpet, typically without valves or keys and used for military signals. ■ a loud sound resembling that of a bugle, as the mating call of a bull elk: *the piercing bugle of adult bulls.*
▸*v.* [*intrans.*] sound a bugle. ■ [*trans.*] sound (a note or call) on a bugle: *he bugled a warning.* ■ issue a loud sound resembling that of a bugle, particularly the mating call of a bull elk. ▷Middle English: via Old French from Latin *buculus,* diminutive of *bos* 'ox.' The early English sense was 'wild ox,' hence the compound *bugle-horn,* being originally the horn of an ox used to give signals in hunting. **—bu·gler** /'byo͞og(ə)lər/ *n.*

bu·gle[2] ▸*n.* a creeping plant of the mint family with blue flowers held on upright stems. Also called **BUGLEWEED.** • Genus *Ajuga,* family Labiatae: several species, esp. the common *A. reptans.* ▷Middle English: from late Latin *bugula.*

bu·gle[3] ▸*n.* (also **bugle bead**) an ornamental tube-shaped glass or plastic bead sewn on to clothing. ▷late 16th cent.: of unknown origin.

bu·gle·weed /'byo͞ogəl,wēd/ ▸*n.* another term for **BUGLE**[2].

bu·gloss /'byo͞oglôs; -läs/ ▸*n.* a bristly plant of the borage family, with bright blue flowers. • *Anchusa, Lycopsis,* and other genera, family Boraginaceae: several species, including the **small bugloss** (*L. arvensis*) and the widespread **viper's bugloss.** ▷late Middle English: from Old French *buglosse* or Latin *buglossus,* from Greek *bouglōssos* 'ox-tongued,' from *bous* 'ox' + *glōssa* 'tongue.'

buhl /bo͞ol/ ▸*n.* brass, tortoiseshell, or other material cut to make a pattern and used for inlaying furniture: [as *adj.*] *buhl cabinets.* ■ work inlaid in such a way. ▷early 19th cent.: from French *boule,* from the name of André Charles *Boulle* (1642–1732), French cabinetmaker. The variant *buhl,* apparently a modern Germanized spelling, is standard in the U.S.

buhr·stone /'bər,stōn/ (also **bur·stone** or **burr·stone**) ▸a porous limestone formerly much used for millstones.

build /bild/ ▸*v.* (*past* and *past part.* **built** /bilt/) [*trans.*] (often **be built**) construct (something, typically something large) by putting parts or material together over a period of time: *the factory was built in 1936.* ■ commission, finance, and oversee the building of (something): *the city council plans to build a bridge.* ■ (**build something in/into**) incorporate (something) and make it a permanent part of a structure, system, or situation: *engineers want to build in extra traction.* ■ *Computing* compile (a program, database, index, etc.). ■ [*intrans.*] (of a program, database, index, etc.) be compiled. ■ establish and develop (a business, relationship, or situation) over a period of time: *he'd* ***built up*** *the store from nothing.* ■ [*intrans.*] (**build on**) use as a basis for further progress or development: *the nation should build on the talents of its workforce.* ■ increase the size, intensity, or extent of: *we* ***built up*** *confidence in our abilities* | [*intrans.*] *the air of excited anticipation builds.*
▸*n.* **1** the dimensions or proportions of a person's or animal's body: *she was of medium height and slim build* | [in *sing.*] *he has the ideal build for a sprinter.* ■ the style or form of construction of something, typically a vehicle. **2** *Computing* a compiled version of a program. ■ the process of compiling a program. ▷Old English *byldan,* from *bold, botl* 'dwelling,' of Germanic origin; related to **BOWER**[1].
▸*PHRASES* □ **build one's hopes up** become ever more hopeful or optimistic about something. □ **built upon/on sand** *figurative* without reliable foundations or any real substance: *what more could you expect from a relationship built upon sand?*

build·down /'bild,doun/ ▸*n.* a gradual, systematic reduction in numbers, esp. of nuclear weapons.

build·er /'bildər/ ▸*n.* a person who constructs something by putting parts or material together over a period of time: *a boat builder.* ■ a person whose job is to construct or repair houses, or to contract for their construction and repair. ■ [usu. in *combination*] a person or thing that creates or develops a particular thing: *breaking the record was a real confidence builder.*

build·ing /'bildiNG/ (abbr.: **bldg.**) ▸*n.* **1** a structure with a roof and walls, such as a house, school, store, or factory. **2** the process or business of constructing something: *the building of highways* | [as *adj.*] *building materials.* ■ the process of commissioning, financing, or overseeing the construction of something. ■ the process of creating or developing something, typically a system or situation, over a period of time: *the building of democracy in Guatemala.* ■ the process of increasing the intensity of a feeling: *a playwright's cunning in the building of suspense.*

-building ▸*comb. form* the process of constructing, shaping, developing, or forming a particular thing: *boat-building.* ■ the process of promoting something: *bridge-building (between the nations).* ■ able to build: *reef-building coral.*

build·ing block ▸*n.* a child's toy brick, typically made of wood or plastic. ■ *figurative* a basic unit from which something is built up: *sounds are the building blocks of language.*

build·ing site ▸*n.* an area where a structure is being constructed or repaired.

build-out /'bild,out/ ▸*n.* the growth, development, or expansion of something: *the rapid buildout of digital technology.*

build·up /'bild,əp/ ▸*n.* [usu. in *sing.*] **1** a gradual accumulation or increase, typically of something negative and typically leading to a problem or crisis: *the buildup of carbon dioxide in the atmosphere.* **2** a period of excitement and preparation in advance of a significant event: *the buildup to Christmas.* ■ a favorable description in advance; publicity: *a showbiz buildup before the album release.*

built /bilt/ ▸ past and past participle of **BUILD.**
▸*adj.* (of a person) having a specified physical size or build: *a slightly built woman.*

built-in ▸*adj.* [*attrib.*] forming an integral part of a structure or device: *a camera with a built-in zoom lens.* ■ (of a characteristic) inherent; innate: *the system has a built-in resistance to change.*

built-up ▸*adj.* **1** (of an area) densely covered by houses or other buildings. **2** increased in height by the addition of parts: *shoes with built-up heels.* ■ (of a feeling) increasing in intensity over a period of time: *built-up frustration.*

Bu·jum·bu·ra /bo͞o,jəm'bo͝orə/ the capital of Burundi, at the northeastern end of Lake Tanganyika; pop. 235,440. It was known as Usumbura until 1962.

Bu·kho·ro /bo͞o'KHôrō/ (also **Bu·kha·ra, Bo·kha·ra** /bo͞o'KHärə/) a city in southeastern Uzbekistan; pop. 246,200.

Bu·la·wa·yo /,bo͞olə'wā-ō; -'wī-ō/ an industrial city in western Zimbabwe; pop. 620,940.

bulb /bəlb/ ▸*n.* **1** a rounded underground storage organ present in some plants, notably those of the lily family, consisting of a short stem surrounded by fleshy scale leaves or leaf bases and resting over winter. Compare with **CORM, RHIZOME.** ■ a plant grown from an organ of this kind. ■ a similar underground organ such as a corm or a rhizome. **2** an object with a rounded or teardrop shape like a bulb, in particular: ■ a light bulb. ■ an expanded part of a glass tube such as that forming the reservoir of a thermometer. ■ a hollow flexible container with an opening through which the air can be expelled by squeezing, such as that used to fill a syringe. ■ a spheroidal dilated part at the end of an anatomical structure. ▷late Middle English: via Latin from Greek *bolbos* 'onion, bulbous root.'

bul·bar /'bəlbər; -,bär/ ▸*adj.* of or relating to a bulb, esp. the medulla oblongata.

bul·bil /'bəlbil/ ▸*n.* *Botany* a small bulblike structure, esp. in the axil of a leaf or at the base of a stem, that may form a new plant. ▷mid 19th cent.: from modern Latin *bulbillus,* diminutive of *bulbus* 'onion, bulbous root.'

bul·bous /'bəlbəs/ ▸*adj.* **1** fat, round, or bulging: *a bulbous nose.* **2** (of a plant) growing from a bulb.

bul·bul /'bo͝ol,bo͝ol/ ▸*n.* a tropical African and Asian songbird that typically has a melodious voice and drab plumage. Many kinds have a crest. • Family Pycnonotidae: several genera and numerous species. ▷mid 17th cent.: from Persian, of imitative origin.

Bul·ga·nin /bo͝ol'ganən/, Nikolai (Aleksandrovich) (1895–1975), Soviet statesman, chairman of the Council of Ministers (premier) 1955–58. He was vice-premier in the government of Georgi Malenkov in 1953 and shared the premiership with Khruschev in 1955.

Bul·gar /'bəlgər; 'bo͝ol-/ ▸*n.* a member of a Slavic people who settled in what is now Bulgaria in the 7th century. ▷from medieval Latin *Bulgarus,* from Old Church Slavic *Blŭgarinŭ.* Compare with **BUGGER.**

bul·gar /'bəlgər/ (also **bul·gur, bulgar wheat**) ▸*n.* a cereal food made from whole wheat partially boiled then dried: [as *adj.*] *bulgar wheat.* ▷1930s: from Turkish *bulgur* 'bruised grain.'

Bul·gar·i·a /,bəl'ge(ə)rēə/ a country in southeastern Europe, on the western shores of the Black Sea; pop. 7,517,000; capital, Sofia; official language, Bulgarian. ▷named after the Bulgars (see **BULGAR**).

Part of the Ottoman Empire from the 14th century, Bulgaria remained under Turkish rule until the late 19th century, becoming independent in 1908. A communist state was set up by the Soviet Union after World War II, and a multiparty democratic system was introduced in 1989. Bulgaria joined NATO in 2004.

Bul·gar·i·an /,bəl'ge(ə)rēən; ,bo͝ol-/ ▸*n.* **1** a native or national of Bulgaria. **2** the South Slavic language spoken in Bulgaria.
▸*adj.* of or relating to Bulgaria, its people, or their language.

bulge /bəlj/ ▸*n.* a rounded swelling or protuberance that distorts a flat surface. ■ (esp. in a military context) a piece of land that projects outward from an otherwise regular line: *the advance created an east-ward-facing bulge in the line.* ■ [in *sing.*] *informal* a temporary unusual increase in number or size: *a bulge in the birth rate.*
▸*v.* [*intrans.*] swell or protrude to an unnatural or incongruous extent: *the veins in his neck bulged* | [as *adj.*] (**bulging**) *he stared with bulging eyes.* ■ be full of and distended with: *a briefcase* ***bulging with*** *documents.* ■ ▷Middle English: from Old French *boulge,* from Latin *bulga* (see **BUDGET**). The original meaning was 'wallet or bag,' later 'a ship's bilge' (early 17th cent.); other senses presumably derived from association with the shape of a full bag. **—bulg·y** *adj.*

THE RIGHT WORD **bulge, project, protrude, protuberate**

While all of these verbs mean to extend outward, beyond the normal line or surface of something, it is almost impossible not to associate the word **bulge** with the human body (*a stomach that bulges over a waistband; muscles that bulge beneath a shirt*). *Bulge* suggests a swelling out that is quite noticeable or even abnormal, and that may be the result of internal pressure, although a brick wall can *bulge,* as can a bicep muscle.

Protuberate is a less common word meaning to swell or stick out, but it does not necessarily imply that anything is abnormal or radically wrong (*he was so thin that his knees protuberated*).

To **protrude** is to thrust forth in an unexpected way or to stick out in a way that is abnormal or disfiguring (*her eyes protruded from her skull*).

Project is the least upsetting of all these words, probably because it is used less often with reference to the human body. Anything that juts out abruptly beyond the rest of a surface is said to *project* (*the balcony projected from the south side of the house*).

bul·go·gi /bo͝ol'gōgē/ ▸*n.* a Korean dish of thin beef slices marinated and grilled on a barbecue.

bul·gur /'bəlgər/ ▸*n.* variant spelling of **BULGAR.**

bu·lim·a·rex·i·a /,bo͞olēmə'reksēə/ ▸*n.* another term for **BULIMIA NERVOSA** (see **BULIMIA**). ▷1970s: blend of **BULIMIA** and **ANOREXIA.** **—bu·lim·a·rex·ic** /-'reksik/ *adj.* & *n.*

bu·lim·i·a /bo͞o'limēə; -'lē-/ ▸*n.* insatiable overeating as a medical condition, in particular: ■ (also **bu·lim·i·a ner·vo·sa** /nər'vōsə/) an emotional disorder involving distortion of body image and an obsessive desire to lose weight, in which bouts of extreme overeating are followed by depression and self-induced vomiting, purging, or fasting. Also called **BINGE-PURGE SYNDROME.** ■ an eating disorder in which a large quantity of food is consumed in a short period of time, often followed by feelings of guilt or shame. Also called **BINGE-EATING SYNDROME.** ▷late Middle English (as *bolisme*, later *bulimy*): modern Latin, or from medieval Latin *bulismos*, from Greek *boulimia* 'ravenous hunger,' from *bous* 'ox' + *limos* 'hunger.' —**bu·lim·ic** /-ˈlēmik/ *adj.* & *n.*

bulk /bəlk/ ▸*n.* the mass or magnitude of something large: *the sheer bulk of the bags.* ■ a large mass or shape, for example of a building or a heavy body: *he moved quickly in spite of his bulk.* ■ [as *adj.*] large in quantity or amount: *bulk orders of more than 100 copies.* ■ (**the bulk**) the majority or greater part of something: *the bulk of the traffic had passed.* ■ roughage in food: *bread and potatoes supply energy, essential protein, and bulk.* ■ cargo that is an unpackaged mass such as grain, oil, or milk.
▸*v.* **1** [*intrans.*] be or seem to be of great size or importance: *territorial questions* **bulked large** *in diplomatic relations.* **2** [*trans.*] treat (a product) so that its quantity appears greater than it in fact is: *traders were* **bulking up** *their flour with chalk.* ■ [*intrans.*] (**bulk up**) build up body mass, typically in training for athletic events. ▷Middle English: the senses 'cargo as a whole' and 'heap, large quantity' (the earliest recorded) are probably from Old Norse *búlki* 'cargo'; the origin of other senses remains uncertain, perhaps arising by alteration of obsolete *bouk* 'belly, body.' The original senses are also reflected in the phrases *break bulk* and *in bulk.*
▸*PHRASE* □ **in bulk 1** (esp. of goods) in large quantities, usually at a reduced price: *buying tomatoes in bulk from a local farmer.* **2** (of a cargo or commodity) loose; not packaged: *sugar is imported in bulk and bagged on the island.*

bulk buy·ing ▸*n.* the purchase of goods in large amounts, typically at a discount. —**bulk-buy** *v.*

bulk car·ri·er ▸*n.* a ship that carries nonliquid cargoes such as grain or ore in bulk.

bulk·er /ˈbəlkər/ ▸*n. informal* another term for **BULK CARRIER.**

bulk·head /ˈbəlk,hed/ ▸*n.* a dividing wall or barrier between compartments in a ship, aircraft, or other vehicle. ▷late 15th cent.: from Old Norse *bálkr* 'partition' + **HEAD.**

bulk mail ▸*n.* a class of mail for sending out large numbers of identical items at a reduced rate.

bulk·y /ˈbəlkē/ ▸*adj.* (**bulk·i·er, bulk·i·est**) taking up much space, typically inconveniently; large and unwieldy: *a bulky piece of luggage.* ■ (of a person) heavily built. ■ (of clothing) made of a thick yarn or fabric: *a bulky sweater.* —**bulk·i·ly** /-kəlē/ *adv.* —**bulk·i·ness** *n.*

bull[1] /bŏŏl/ ▸*n.* **1** an uncastrated male bovine animal: [as *adj.*] *bull calves.* ■ a large male animal, esp. a whale or elephant. ■ (**the Bull**) the zodiacal sign or constellation Taurus. **2** *Stock Market* a person who buys shares hoping to sell them at a higher price later. Often contrasted with **BEAR**[2].
▸*adj.* [*attrib.*] (of a part of the body, esp. the neck) resembling the corresponding part of a male bovine animal in build and strength: *his bull neck and broad shoulders.*
▸*v.* **1** [*trans.*] push or drive powerfully or violently: *he bulled the motorcycle clear of the tunnel* | [*intrans.*] *he was* **bulling his way** *through a mob of admirers.* **2** [*intrans.*] (**be bulling**) (of a cow) behave in a manner characteristic of being in heat. ▷late Old English *bula* (recorded in place names), from Old Norse *boli.* Compare with **BULLOCK.**
▸*PHRASES* □ **like a bull in a china shop** behaving recklessly and clumsily in a place or situation where one is likely to cause damage or injury. □ **(like) a red rag to a bull** see **RED.** □ **take the bull by the horns** deal bravely and decisively with a difficult, dangerous, or unpleasant situation.

bull[2] ▸*n.* a papal edict. ▷Middle English: from Old French *bulle*, from Latin *bulla* 'bubble, rounded object' (in medieval Latin 'seal or sealed document').

bull[3] ▸*n. informal* stupid or untrue talk or writing; nonsense: *much of what he says is sheer bull.* ▷early 17th cent.: of unknown origin.

bul·la /ˈbŏŏlə/ ▸*n.* (*pl.* **bul·lae** /ˈbŏŏlē/) **1** *Medicine* a bubblelike cavity filled with air or fluid, in particular: ■ a large blister containing serous fluid. ■ an abnormal air-filled cavity in the lung. [early 19th cent.] **2** *Anatomy* a rounded prominence. [mid 19th cent.] **3** a round seal attached to a papal bull, typically made of lead. [Middle English] ▷Latin, literally 'bubble.'

bul·lace /ˈbŏŏlis/ ▸*n.* a thorny shrub or small tree of the rose family that bears purple-black fruits. It is a wild plum, of which the damson is the cultivated form. • *Prunus insititia* (or *Prunus domesticus* subsp. *insititia*), family Rosaceae. ▷Middle English: from Old French *buloce* 'sloe': of unknown origin.

bul·late /ˈbŏŏlāt/ ▸*adj. Botany* covered with rounded swellings like blisters. ▷mid 18th cent.: from Latin *bullatus*, from *bulla* 'bubble.'

bull·bait·ing /ˈbŏŏl,bātiNG/ ▸*n. historical* the practice of setting dogs to harass and attack a tethered bull, popular as a sport in medieval Europe.

bull·bat /ˈbŏŏl,bat/ ▸*n.* another term for **NIGHTHAWK** (sense 1).

bull·dog /ˈbŏŏl,dôg/ ▸*n.* a dog of a sturdy smooth-haired breed with a large head and powerful protruding lower jaw, a flat wrinkled face, and a broad chest. ■ a person noted for courageous or stubborn tenacity: [as *adj.*] *the bulldog spirit.* ■ *informal* (at Oxford and Cambridge Universities) an official who assists the proctors, esp. in disciplinary matters.
▸*v.* (**-dogged, -dog·ging**) [*trans.*] wrestle (a steer) to the ground by holding its horns and twisting its neck: [as *n.*] (**bulldogging**) *cowboys compete in bulldogging and bareback riding.* —**bull·dog·ger** *n.*

bulldog

bull·doze /ˈbŏŏl,dōz/ ▸*v.* [*trans.*] clear (ground) or destroy (buildings, trees, etc.) with a bulldozer: *developers are bulldozing the site.* ■ *figurative, informal* use insensitive force when dealing with (someone or something): *she believes that to build status you need to bulldoze everyone else.* ▷late 19th cent. (in the sense 'intimidate'): from **BULL**[1] + *-doze*, alteration of the noun **DOSE.**

bull·doz·er /ˈbŏŏl,dōzər/ ▸*n.* a powerful tractor with a broad upright blade at the front for clearing ground. ■ *figurative* a person, army, or other body exercising irresistible power, esp. in disposing of obstacles or opposition: *he was a political bulldozer* | *as president of the board, she was an insufferable bulldozer.*

bulldozer

bull·dyke /ˈbŏŏl,dīk/ (also **bull·dike** or **bull·dyk·er**) ▸*n. informal, offensive* a particularly masculine lesbian.

bul·let /ˈbŏŏlit/ ▸*n.* **1** a projectile for firing from a rifle, revolver, or other small firearms, typically of metal, cylindrical and pointed, and sometimes containing an explosive. ■ used in similes and comparisons to refer to someone or something that moves very fast: *the ball sped across the grass like a bullet.* ■ (in a sporting context) a very fast ball. **2** *Printing* a small solid circle printed just before a line of type, such as an item in a list, to emphasize it. ▷early 16th cent. (denoting a cannonball): from French *boulet*, *boulette* 'small ball,' diminutive of *boule*, from Latin *bulla* 'bubble.'

bul·let·head /ˈbŏŏlit,hed/ ▸*n. derogatory* a person's head that is small and round. ■ a person with this type of head. ■ a stupid, self-important, or obstinate person. —**bul·let·head·ed** *adj.*

bul·le·tin /ˈbŏŏlitn; -,tin/ ▸*n.* a short official statement or broadcast summary of news. ■ a regular newsletter or printed report issued by an organization or society. ▷mid 17th cent. (denoting an official warrant in some European countries): from French, from Italian *bullettino*, diminutive of *bulletta* 'passport,' diminutive of *bulla* 'seal, bull.'

bul·le·tin board ▸*n.* a board for displaying notices. ■ *Computing* (also **bulletin board system**) an information storage system designed to permit any authorized computer user to access and add to it from a remote terminal.

bul·let point ▸*n.* each of several items in a list, typically the ideas or arguments in an article or presentation and typically printed with a bullet before each for emphasis.

bul·let·proof /ˈbŏŏlit,prōōf/ ▸*adj.* designed to resist the penetration of bullets: *a bulletproof vest.*

bul·let train ▸*n. informal* a high-speed passenger train: *a bullet train that would whisk passengers at speeds of 150-250 mph along a Tampa-Miami route.*

bull fid·dle ▸*n. informal* a double bass.

bull·fight /ˈbŏŏl,fīt/ ▸*n.* a public spectacle, particularly in Spain, Portugal, and Latin America, at which a bull is baited in a highly stylized manner and then usually killed. —**bull·fight·er** *n.*

bull·fight·ing /ˈbŏŏl,fītiNG/ ▸*n.* the sport of baiting and killing a bull as a public spectacle in an outdoor arena.

> Bullfighting is the national spectator sport of Spain, and is found also in Latin America and Portugal. Typically, the bull is tormented with darts stuck into its neck, and the matador then baits it with a red cape and attempts to kill it with a sword-blow beneath the shoulder blade.

bull·finch /ˈbŏŏl,finCH/ ▸*n.* a stocky Eurasian finch with a short, thick bill, and typically with gray or pinkish plumage, dark wings, and a white rump. • Genus *Pyrrhula*, family Fringillidae: several species, in particular the common *P. pyrrhula*, the male of which has a black face and pink breast.

bull·frog /ˈbŏŏl,frôg; -,fräg/ ▸*n.* a very large frog that has a deep booming croak and is often a predator of smaller vertebrates. • Genera *Rana* and *Pyxicephalus*, family Ranidae: the **North American bullfrog** (*R. catesbeiana*), the **Asian bullfrog** (*R. tigrina*), and the **African bullfrog** (*P. adspersus*).

bull·head /ˈbŏŏl,hed/ ▸*n.* **1** (also **bullhead catfish**) an American freshwater catfish with four pairs of barbels around the mouth. • Family Ictaluridae: several genera and numerous species, including the **black bullhead** (*Ameiurus melas*). **2** a small, mainly freshwater Eurasian fish of the sculpin family, with a broad flattened head and spiny fins. • Genera *Cottus* and *Taurulus*, family Cottidae: three species. **3** (also **bullhead lily**) a North American water lily with globular yellow flowers. • *Nuphar variegatum*, family Nymphaeaceae.

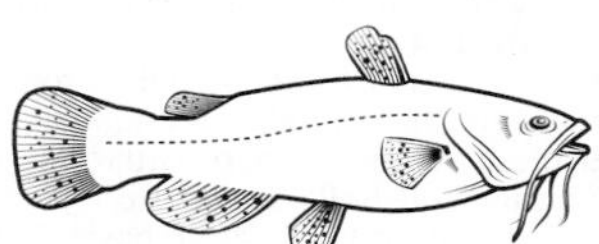
black bullhead

Bull·head Cit·y /ˈbŏŏl,hed/ a city in northwestern Arizona, on the Colorado River, a resort and casino center; pop. 21,951.

bull·head·ed /ˈbŏŏl,hedid/ ▸*adj.* determined in an obstinate or unthinking way: *a bullheaded belief that she is right.* —**bull·head·ed·ly** *adv.* —**bull·head·ed·ness** *n.*

bull·horn /ˈbŏŏl,hôrn/ ▸*n.* an electronic device for amplifying the sound of the voice so it can be heard at a distance.

bul·lion /ˈbŏŏlyən/ ▸*n.* **1** gold or silver in bulk before coining, or valued by weight. **2** (also **bullion fringe**) ornamental braid or trimming made with twists of gold or silver thread. ▷Middle English: from Anglo-Norman French, in the sense 'a mint,' variant of Old French *bouillon*, based on Latin *bullire* 'to boil.'

bul·lion knot ▸*n.* a decorative stitch in embroidery made by winding the thread several times around the needle before sewing a backstitch.

bull·ish /ˈbŏŏliSH/ ▸*adj.* **1** resembling a bull: *a sketch of his round, bullish head.* ■ stupid or oafish; bullheaded: *it's impossible to reason with such a bullish man.* ■ assertively masculine; macho: *surrounded by girls and the aura of bullish manhood.* ■ *chiefly Brit.* aggressively confident and self-assertive: *the team is at its most bullish.* **2** *Stock Market* characterized by rising share prices: *the market was bullish.* ■ (of a dealer) inclined to buy because of an anticipated rise in prices. **3** feeling especially hopeful; optimistic: *challenging those who are* **bullish on** *the nation's economic prospects.* —**bull·ish·ly** *adv.* —**bull·ish·ness** *n.*

bull kelp ▸*n.* a very large brown seaweed found in Pacific and Antarctic waters, growing up to 165 feet

(50 m) in length off the northwestern coasts of North America. • *Nereocystis* and other genera, class Phaeophyceae.

bull mar·ket ▸*n.* *Stock Market* a market in which share prices are rising, encouraging buying.

bull·mas·tiff /ˈbo͝olˈmastif/ ▸*n.* a dog of a crossbreed of bulldog and mastiff.

Bull Moose ▸*n.* a supporter or member of the Progressive Party.

Bull Moose Par·ty ▸*n.* another term for the **PROGRESSIVE PARTY**.

bull-necked ▸*adj.* having a short, thick neck: *a bull-necked man.*

bull·nose /ˈbo͝olˌnōz/ *technical* ▸*adj.* (also **bull·nosed**) [*attrib.*] (of the edge of a surface) rounded. ■ (of a surface or object) having a rounded edge or edges: *a bullnose tile.*
▸*n.* a rounded edge of this type.

Bul·lock /ˈbo͝olək/, Anna Mae see **TURNER**[2].

bul·lock ▸*n.* another term for **STEER**[2]. ▷late Old English *bulluc*, diminutive of *bula* (see **BULL**[1]).

bull of the woods ▸*n.* a sexually mature male of a large wild species, such as moose or elk. ■ *figurative* the supervisor of a logging camp.

bul·lous /ˈbo͝oləs/ ▸*adj.* *Medicine* characterized by blisters or bullae on the skin.

bull·pen /ˈbo͝olˌpen/ ▸*n.* (also **bull pen**) an enclosure for bulls. ■ an exercise area for baseball pitchers. ■ the relief pitchers of a baseball team. ■ an open-plan office area. ■ a large cell in which prisoners are held before a court hearing.

bull·ring /ˈbo͝olˌriNG/ ▸*n.* an arena where bullfights are held.

Bull Run a small river in eastern Virginia that was the scene of two Confederate victories—1861 and 1862—during the Civil War.

bull·rush ▸*n.* variant spelling of **BULRUSH**.

bull ses·sion ▸*n.* an informal, typically impromptu discussion, esp. among a small group. ▷1920s: *bull* from **BULL**[3].

bull's-eye ▸*n.* (also **bulls·eye**) **1** the center of a target in sports such as archery, shooting, and darts. ■ a shot that hits such a target center. ■ *figurative* used to refer to something that achieves exactly the intended effect: *the silence told him he'd* ***scored a bull's-eye.*** **2** a large, round, hard peppermint-flavored candy. **3** *dated* a hemisphere or thick disk of glass forming a small window in a ship or the glass of a lamp: [as *adj.*] *a bull's-eye lantern.* ■ a thick knob or boss of glass at the center of a blown glass sheet.

bull shark ▸*n.* a large, stout-bodied aggressive shark. Its widespread distribution, its habits of feeding close to shore, and its tendency to venture far into estuaries and rivers makes it a species particularly dangerous to humans. • *Carcharhinus leucas*, family Carcharhinidae.

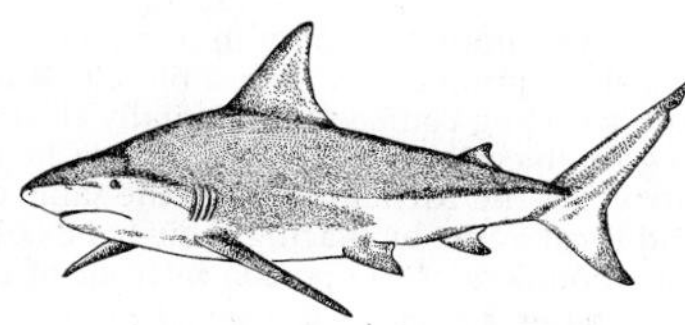

bull shark

bull·shit /ˈbo͝olˌSHit/ *vulgar slang* ▸*n.* stupid or untrue talk or writing; nonsense.
▸*v.* (**-shit·ted, -shit·ting**) [*trans.*] talk nonsense to (someone), typically to be misleading or deceptive. ▷early 20th cent.: from **BULL**[3] + **SHIT**. —**bull·shit·ter** *n.*

bull snake ▸*n.* (also **bull·snake**) a constrictor found commonly on the plains and prairies of North America. • Family Colubridae and genus *Pituophis*: several species, including the gopher snake *P. catenifer sayi.*

bull ter·ri·er ▸*n.* a short-haired dog of a breed that is a cross between a bulldog and a terrier.

bull trout ▸*n.* a North American trout that resembles the Dolly Varden, found in cold rivers and lakes. • *Salvelinus confluentus*, family Salmonidae.

bull·whip /ˈbo͝olˌ(h)wip/ ▸*n.* a whip with a long heavy lash.
▸*v.* (**-whipped, -whip·ping**) [*trans.*] strike or thrash with such a whip.

bul·ly[1] /ˈbo͝olē/ ▸*n.* (*pl.* **-lies**) a person who uses strength or power to harm or intimidate those who are weaker.
▸*v.* (**-lies, -lied**) [*trans.*] use superior strength or influence to intimidate (someone), typically to force him or her to do what one wants: *a local man was* ***bullied into*** *helping them.* ▷mid 16th cent.: probably from Middle Dutch *boele* 'lover.' The original usage was as a term of endearment applied to either sex; later becoming a familiar form of address to a male friend. The current sense dates from the late 17th cent.

bul·ly[2] *informal* ▸*adj.* very good; first-rate: *the statue really looked bully.*
▸*exclam.* (**bully for**) an expression of admiration or approval: *he got away—bully for him.* ▷late 16th cent. (originally of a person meaning 'admirable, gallant, jolly'): from **BULLY**[1]. The current sense dates from the mid 19th cent.

bul·ly[3] (also **bully beef**) *informal* ▸*n.* corned beef. ▷mid 18th cent.: from French *bouilli*, literally 'boiled.'

bul·ly boy ▸*n.* a tough or aggressive man: [as *adj.*] *bully-boy tactics.*

bul·ly pul·pit ▸*n.* [in *sing.*] a public office or position of authority that provides its occupant with an outstanding opportunity to speak out on any issue: *he could use the presidency as a bully pulpit to bring out the best in civic life.* ▷early 20th cent.: apparently originally used by President Theodore Roosevelt, explaining his personal view of the presidency.

bul·ly·rag /ˈbo͝olēˌrag/ ▸*v.* (**-ragged, -rag·ging**) [*trans.*] *informal* treat (someone) in a scolding or intimidating way: *he would* ***bullyrag*** *his staff* ***around*** *but then kiss up to his superiors.* ▷late 18th cent.: of unknown origin.

bul·rush /ˈbo͝olˌrəSH/ (also **bull·rush**) ▸*n.* **1** another term for **CATTAIL**. **2** a tall rushlike water plant of the sedge family. Native to temperate regions of the northern hemisphere, it has been widely used for weaving and is grown as an aid to water purification in some areas. • *Scirpus lacustris*, family Cyperaceae. **3** (in biblical use) a papyrus plant. ▷late Middle English: probably from **BULL**[1] in the sense 'large or coarse,' as in words such as *bullfrog.*

bul·wark /ˈbo͝olˌwərk/ ▸*n.* a defensive wall. ■ *figurative* a person, institution, or principle that acts as a defense: *the security forces are a* ***bulwark against*** *the breakdown of society.* ■ (usu. **bulwarks**) an extension of a ship's sides above the level of the deck. ▷late Middle English: from Middle Low German and Middle Dutch *bolwerk*; related to **BOLE**[1] and **WORK**.

Bul·wer-Lyt·ton /ˈbo͝olwər ˈlitn/ see **LYTTON**.

bum[1] /bəm/ *informal* ▸*n.* **1** a vagrant. ■ a lazy or worthless person: *you ungrateful bum.* **2** [in *combination*] a person who devotes a great deal of time to a specified activity: *a ski bum | a poker bum.*
▸*v.* (**bummed, bum·ming**) **1** [*intrans.*] travel, with no particular purpose or destination: *he* ***bummed around*** *Florida for a few months.* ■ pass one's time idly: *we spent most of the summer just* ***bumming around.*** **2** [*trans.*] get by asking or begging: *they tried to bum money off us.* **3** [*trans.*] make (someone) feel upset or disappointed: *it really* ***bummed*** *me* ***out*** *when he forgot my birthday.*
▸*adj.* [*attrib.*] of poor quality; bad or wrong: *not one bum note was played.* ▷mid 19th cent.: probably from **BUMMER**.
▸*PHRASES* □ **give someone** (or **get**) **the bum's rush** forcibly eject someone (or be forcibly ejected) from a place or gathering. ■ abruptly dismiss someone (or be abruptly dismissed) for a poor idea or performance. □ **on the bum** traveling with rough provisions and with no fixed home; a vagrant.

bum[2] ▸*n.* *Brit., informal* buttocks. ▷late Middle English: of unknown origin.

bum·bag /ˈbəmˌbag/ ▸*n.* British term for **FANNY PACK**.

bum-bail·iff ▸*n.* *historical, derogatory* a bailiff empowered to collect debts or arrest debtors for nonpayment. ▷early 17th cent.: from **BUM**[1], so named because of the association of an approach from behind.

bum·ber·shoot /ˈbəmbərˌSHo͞ot/ ▸*n.* *informal* an umbrella.

bum·ble /ˈbəmbəl/ ▸*v.* **1** [*intrans.*] move or act in an awkward or confused manner: *they* ***bumbled around*** *the house* | [as *adj.*] (**bumbling**) *his bumbling interventions.* **2** [*intrans.*] speak in a confused or indistinct way: *the succeeding speakers bumbled.* ■ [with *adverbial*] (of an insect) buzz or hum: *she watched a bee bumble among the flowers.* ▷late Middle English (in the sense 'hum, drone'): from **BOOM**[1] + **-LE**[4]. —**bum·bler** /-b(ə)lər/ *n.*

bum·ble·bee /ˈbəmbəlˌbē/ ▸*n.* a large hairy bee with a loud hum, living in small colonies in holes underground. • Genus *Bombus*, family Apidae: many species.

bum·boat /ˈbəmˌbōt/ ▸*n.* a small vessel carrying provisions for sale to ships in port. ▷late 17th cent.: from **BUM**[1] + **BOAT**. The term originally denoted a scavenger's boat removing refuse, etc., from ships, often also bringing produce for sale.

bumf /bəmf/ (also **bumph**) ▸*n.* *informal, chiefly Brit.* useless or tedious printed information or documents. ▷late 19th cent.: abbreviation of slang *bum-fodder*, in the same sense.

bum·ma·lo /ˈbəməˌlō/ ▸*n.* (*pl.* same) a small elongated fish of South Asian coasts that is dried and used as food. Also called **BOMBAY DUCK**. • *Harpodon nehereus*, family Harpadontidae. ▷late 17th cent.: perhaps from Marathi *bombīl.*

bum·mer /ˈbəmər/ ▸*n.* *informal* **1** (**a bummer**) a thing that is annoying or disappointing: *the party was* ***a real bummer.*** ■ an unpleasant reaction to a hallucinogenic drug. **2** a loafer or vagrant.
▸*exclam.* *informal* used to express frustration or disappointment, typically sympathetically: *You lost your wallet? Bummer!* ▷mid 19th cent.: perhaps from German *Bummler*, from *bummeln* 'stroll, loaf around.'

bump /bəmp/ ▸*n.* **1** a light blow or a jolting collision: *a nasty bump on the head.* ■ the dull sound of such a blow or collision. ■ *Aeronautics* a rising air current causing an irregularity in an aircraft's motion. **2** a protuberance on a level surface: *bumps in the road.* ■ a swelling on the skin, esp. one caused by illness or injury. ■ *dated* or *humorous* a prominence on a person's skull, formerly thought to indicate a particular mental faculty; such a faculty: *he was making the most of his bump of direction.* **3** a loosely woven fleeced cotton fabric used in upholstery and as lining material.
▸*v.* **1** [*intrans.*] knock or run into someone or something, typically with a jolt: *I almost* ***bumped into*** *him* | [*trans.*] *she bumped the girl with her hip.* ■ (**bump into**) meet by chance: *we might just bump into each other.* ■ [*trans.*] hurt or damage (something) by striking or knocking it against something else: *she* ***bumped*** *her head* ***on the sink.*** ■ [*trans.*] cause to collide with something: *she went through the door,* ***bumping*** *the bag* ***against it.*** **2** [*intrans.*] move or travel with much jolting and jarring: *the car* ***bumped along*** *the rutted track.* ■ [*trans.*] push (something) jerkily in a specified direction: *she had to bump the wheelchair down the steps.* **3** [*trans.*] refuse (a passenger) a reserved place on an airline flight, typically because of deliberate overbooking. ■ cause to move from a job or position, typically in favor of someone else; displace: *she was bumped for a youthful model.*
▸*phrasal v.* □ **bump someone off** *informal* murder someone. □ **bump someone up** *informal* move someone to a higher level or status; promote: *he was a writer for nine years before he was bumped up to editor.* □ **bump something up** *informal* **1** make larger, greater, or more numerous; increase: *they finally agreed to bump up her salary.* **2** make, complete, or release earlier than planned or expected: *the date of publication was bumped up to coincide with the grand jury investigation.* ▷mid 16th cent. (as a verb): imitative, perhaps of Scandinavian origin.

bump·er /ˈbəmpər/ ▸*n.* **1** a horizontal bar fixed across the front or back of a motor vehicle to reduce damage in a collision or as a trim. **2** *archaic* a generous glassful of an alcoholic drink, typically one drunk as a toast.
▸*adj.* exceptionally large, fine, or successful: *a bumper crop.*
▸*PHRASE* □ **bumper-to-bumper** very close together, as cars in a traffic jam.

bump·er car ▸*n.* a small electrically powered car with rubber bumpers all around, driven in an enclosure at an amusement park with the aim of bumping into other such cars.

bump·er stick·er ▸*n.* a label carrying a slogan or advertisement fixed to a vehicle's bumper.

bump·kin /ˈbəmpkin/ ▸*n.* *informal, often derogatory* an unsophisticated or socially awkward person from the countryside: *she thought Tom a bit of a* ***country bumpkin.*** ▷late 16th cent.. —**bump·kin·ish** *adj.*

bump run ▸*n.* a ski run with many small mounds on it, caused by skiers turning in the same places.

bump·tious /ˈbəmpSHəs/ ▸*adj.* self-assertive or proud to an irritating degree: *these bumptious young boys today.* See note at **BOLD**. ▷early 19th cent.:

Pronunciation Key ə *ago*; ər *over*; ˈə or ˌə *up*; ˈər or ˌər *fur*; a *hat*; ā *rate*; ä *car*; CH *chew*; e *let*; ē *see*; e(ə)r *air*; i *fit*; ī *by*; i(ə)r *ear*; NG *sing*; ō *go*; ô *for*; oi *boy*; o͝o *good*; o͞o *goo*; ou *out*; SH *she*; TH *thin*; T͟H *then*; (h)w *why*; ZH *vision*

humorously from **bump**, on the pattern of *fractious*. —**bump·tious·ly** *adv.* —**bump·tious·ness** *n.*

bump·y /ˈbəmpē/ ▶*adj.* (**bump·i·er**, **bump·i·est**) (of a surface) uneven, with many patches raised above the rest: *the bumpy road.* ■ (of a journey or other movement) involving sudden jolts and jerks, esp. caused by an uneven surface: *she took us all on a bumpy ride.* ■ *figurative* fluctuating and unreliable; subject to unexpected difficulties: *bumpy market conditions.* —**bump·i·ly** /-pəlē/ *adv.* —**bump·i·ness** *n.*

B

bum rap ▶*n.* [in *sing.*] *informal* a false charge, typically one leading to imprisonment: *he's been handed a bum rap for handling stolen goods.* ■ *figurative* an unfair punishment or scolding.

bum-rush ▶*v.* [*trans.*] suddenly force or barge one's way into: *fans bum-rushed record stores.*

bum steer ▶*n.* *informal* a piece of false information or guidance: *apparently, those who recommended your good service* **gave us a bum steer.** ▷1920s: from **bum**[2] + **steer**[1] in the sense 'advice, guidance.'

bun /bən/ ▶*n.* **1** a bread roll of various shapes and flavorings, typically sweetened and often containing dried fruit. **2** a hairstyle in which the hair is drawn back into a tight coil at the back of the head. **3** (**buns**) *informal* a person's buttocks. ▷late Middle English: of unknown origin.

▶*PHRASE* □ **have a bun in the oven** *informal* be pregnant.

bunch /bənCH/ ▶*n.* a number of things, typically of the same kind, growing or fastened together: ***a bunch of*** *grapes.* ■ [in *sing.*] *informal* a group of people. ■ *informal* a large number or quantity; a lot: *I had to turn down* ***a bunch of*** *well-paid jobs.*

▶*v.* [*trans.*] collect or fasten into a compact group: *she bunched the carnations together.* ■ gather (cloth) into close folds. ■ [*intrans.*] (of cloth) gather into close folds: *his pants bunched around his ankles.* ■ [*intrans.*] form into a tight group or crowd: *he halted, forcing the rest of the field to* ***bunch up*** *behind him.* ■ [*intrans.*] (of muscles) flex or bulge. ▷late Middle English: of unknown origin. —**bunch·y** *adj.*

▶*PHRASE* □ **the best** (or **the pick**) **of the bunch** the best in a particular group.

bunch·ber·ry /ˈbənCH,berē/ ▶*n.* (*pl.* **-ries**) a low-growing plant of the dogwood family that produces white flowers followed by red berries and bright red autumn foliage. It is native to North America, East Asia, and Greenland. • *Cornus canadensis*, family Cornaceae.

Bunche /bənCH/, Ralph Johnson (1904–71), U.S. diplomat and statesman. Instrumental in the settlement of the Israeli-Arab conflict in 1948, he was the first African American to receive a Nobel Prize. Nobel Peace Prize (1950).

bunch·flow·er /ˈbənCH,flou(-ə)r/ ▶*n.* a North American plant of the lily family that is sometimes cultivated for its yellowish-green flowers. • *Melanthium virginicum*, family Liliaceae.

bunch grass (also **bunch·grass**) ▶*n.* a grass that grows in clumps. • *Schizachyrium* and other genera, family Gramineae: several species, esp. *S. scoparium*, used for grazing and in erosion control, esp. on the Great Plains.

bun·co /ˈbəNGkō/ (also **bun·ko**) *informal* ▶*n.* (*pl.* **-cos**) [often as *adj.*] a swindle or confidence trick: *a bunco artist | he was out to make a buck using fraud or bunco.*

▶*v.* (**-coes**, **-coed**) [*trans.*] *dated* swindle or cheat: *he didn't propose to be buncoed without a fight.* ▷late 19th cent.: perhaps from Spanish *banca*, the name of a card game.

bun·combe ▶*n.* variant spelling of **bunkum**.

bund[1] /bənd/ ▶*n.* an embankment or causeway, particularly in India and other Asian countries. ▷early 19th cent.: from Urdu *band*, from Persian.

bund[2] /bŏŏnd; bənd/ ▶*n.* an association, esp. a politcal one. ■ (**Bund**) a pro-Nazi German-American organization of the 1930's. ■ (**Bund**) an Ashkenazi Jewish socialist movement founded in Russia in 1897.

Bun·des·tag /ˈbŏŏndəs,täg/ the Lower House of Parliament in Germany. ▷German, from *Bund* 'federation' + *tagen* 'confer.'

bun·dle /ˈbəndl/ ▶*n.* a collection of things, or a quantity of material, tied or wrapped up together: *a thick bundle of envelopes.* ■ *figurative* a large quantity or collection, typically a disorganized one: *a bundle of facts.* ■ [in *sing.*] *informal* a person displaying a specified characteristic to a very high degree: *he was an enthusiastic bundle of energy.* ■ *figurative* a person, esp. a child, huddled or wrapped up. ■ a set of nerve, muscle, or other fibers running close together in parallel. ■ *Computing* a set of software or hardware sold together. ■ (**a bundle**) *informal* a large amount of money: *the new printer* ***cost a bundle.***

▶*v.* **1** [*trans.*] tie or roll up (a number of things) together as though into a parcel: *she quickly* ***bundled up*** *her clothes.* ■ [*trans.*] wrap or pack (something): *the figure was bundled in furs.* ■ (usu. **be bundled up**) dress (someone) in many clothes to keep warm: *they were bundled up in thick sweaters | [intrans.] I bundled up in my parka.* ■ *Computing* sell (items of hardware and software) as a package. **2** [*trans.*] (often **be bundled**) *informal* push or carry forcibly: *he was bundled into a van.* ■ send (someone) away hurriedly or unceremoniously: *the old man was* ***bundled off*** *into exile.* ■ [*intrans.*] (esp. of a group of people) move clumsily or in a disorganized way: *they bundled out into the corridor.* **3** [*intrans.*] *dated* sleep fully clothed with another person, particularly during courtship, as a former local custom in New England and Wales: *he would dance at country frolics and bundle with the Yankee lasses.* ▷Middle English: perhaps originally from Old English *byndelle* 'a binding,' reinforced by Low German and Dutch *bundel* (to which *byndelle* is related).

▶*PHRASES* □ **a bundle of fun** (or **laughs**) [often with *negative*] *informal* something extremely amusing or pleasant: *the last year hasn't been a bundle of fun.* □ **a bundle of nerves** *informal* a person who is extremely timid or tense.

Bundt cake /ˈbənt/ ▶*n.* *trademark* a ring-shaped cake made in a fluted tube pan, called a **Bundt pan**.

bun·fight /ˈbən,fīt/ ▶*n.* *Brit., informal or humorous* a tea party or other function, typically of a grand or official kind. ■ a heated argument or exchange.

bun foot ▶*n.* (*pl.* **bun feet**) a foot in the shape of a flattened sphere, used for chairs, tables, or other furniture in the late 17th century.

bung /bəNG/ ▶*n.* a stopper for closing a hole in a container.

▶*v.* [*trans.*] close with a stopper: *the casks are bunged before delivery.* ■ (**bung something up**) block (something), typically by overfilling it: *you let vegetable peelings bung up the sink.* ▷late Middle English: from Middle Dutch *bonghe* (noun).

bun·ga·low /ˈbəNGgə,lō/ ▶*n.* a low house, with a broad front porch, having either no upper floor or upper rooms set in the roof, typically with dormer windows. ▷late 17th cent.: from Hindi *banglā* 'belonging to Bengal.'

bun·ga·ro·tox·in /,bəNGgərəˈtäksin/ ▶*n.* *Biochemistry* a powerful neurotoxin found in the venom of the krait. ▷1960s: from the modern Latin genus name *Bungarus* (perhaps from Sanskrit *bhangurā* 'bent') + **toxin**.

bun·gee /ˈbənjē/ ▶*n.* (also **bungee cord**) a long nylon-cased rubber band, used typically in bungee jumping or for securing luggage.

▶*v.* [*intrans.*] (as a sport) leap from a great height, typically a bridge or crane, while secured by such a band around the ankles. ▷1930s (denoting an elastic cord for launching a glider): of unknown origin.

bun·gee-jump·ing ▶*n.* the sport of leaping from a height while secured by a long nylon-cased rubber band from the ankles. —**bun·gee jump** *n.* —**bun·gee-jump·er** *n.*

bung·hole /ˈbəNG,hōl/ ▶*n.* an aperture through which a cask can be filled or emptied. ■ the anus.

bun·gle /ˈbəNGgəl/ ▶*v.* [*trans.*] carry out (a task) clumsily or incompetently, leading to failure or an unsatisfactory outcome: *she had bungled every attempt to help* | [as *adj.*] (**bungled**) *a bungled bank raid.* ■ [*intrans.*] [usu. as *adj.*] (**bungling**) make or be prone to making many mistakes: *the work of a bungling amateur.*

▶*n.* a mistake or failure, typically one resulting from mismanagement or confusion. ▷mid 16th cent.: of unknown origin; compare with **bumble**. —**bun·gler** /-g(ə)lər/ *n.*

Bu·nin /ˈbŏŏnyin/, Ivan (Alekseevich) (1870–1953), Russian poet and writer. An opponent of modernism, he concentrated on the themes of peasant life and love. Nobel Prize for Literature (1933).

bun·ion /ˈbənyən/ ▶*n.* a painful swelling on the first joint of the big toe. ▷early 18th cent.: from Old French *buignon*, from *buigne* 'bump on the head.'

bunk[1] /bəNGk/ ▶*n.* a narrow shelflike bed, typically one of two or more arranged one on top of the other.

▶*v.* [*intrans.*] sleep in a narrow berth or improvised bed, typically in shared quarters as a temporary arrangement: *they bunk together in the dormitory.* ▷mid 18th cent.: of unknown origin; perhaps related to **bunker**.

bunk[2] ▶*n.* *informal* nonsense: *anyone with a brain cell would never believe such bunk.* See note at **nonsense**. ▷early 20th cent.: abbreviation of **bunkum**.

bunk bed ▶*n.* a piece of furniture consisting of two beds, one above the other, that form a unit.

bun·ker /ˈbəNGkər/ ▶*n.* **1** a large container or compartment for storing fuel: *a coal bunker.* ■ (**bunkers**) fuel for a ship. **2** a reinforced underground shelter, typically for use in wartime. **3** a hollow filled with sand, used as an obstacle on a golf course.

▶*v.* [*trans.*] **1** fuel (a ship). **2** (**be bunkered**) *Golf* (of a player) have one's ball lodged in a bunker: *he was bunkered at the fifth hole.* ▷mid 16th cent. (originally Scots, denoting a seat or bench): perhaps related to **bunk**[1].

bun·ker bust·er (also **bun·ker-bust·er**) ▶*n.* a bomb designed to penetrate deep into the ground or rock before exploding.

Bun·ker Hill /ˈbəNGkər/ a hill in the Charlestown section of northern Boston in Massachusetts. It gave its name to the first pitched battle (1775) of the American Revolution, which was actually fought on nearby Breed's Hill. Although the British won, the good performance of the untrained Americans gave considerable impetus to the Revolution.

bunk·house /ˈbəNGk,hous/ ▶*n.* a building offering basic sleeping accommodations for workers, visitors, or campers.

bunk·mate /ˈbəNGk,māt/ ▶*n.* a person who sleeps in an adjoining bunk or who shares one's sleeping quarters.

bun·ko ▶*n.* variant spelling of **bunco**.

bun·kum /ˈbəNGkəm/ (also **bun·combe**) ▶*n.* *dated, informal* nonsense: *they talk a lot of bunkum about their products.* ▷mid 19th cent. (originally *buncombe*): named after *Buncombe* County in North Carolina, mentioned in an inconsequential speech made by its congressman solely to please his constituents (*c.*1820).

bun·ny /ˈbənē/ ▶*n.* (*pl.* **-nies**) *informal* (also **bunny rabbit**) a rabbit, esp. a young one. ■ [with *adj.*] *informal* a person of a specified type or in a specified mood: *ski slopes crawling with snow bunnies | that dumb bunny actually thought I was a famous writer.* ▷early 17th cent. (originally used as a term of endearment to a person, later as a pet name for a rabbit): from dialect *bun* 'squirrel, rabbit,' also used as a term of endearment, of unknown origin.

bun·ny-boil·er ▶*n.* *informal* a woman who acts vengefully after having been spurned by her lover. ▷with reference to the movie *Fatal Attraction* (1987), in which a rejected woman boils her lover's pet rabbit.

bun·ny-hop ▶*v.* [*intrans.*] jump forward in a crouched position: *he bunny-hopped around the stage.* ■ [*trans.*] move (a vehicle) forward jerkily. ■ move a bicycle forward by jumping in the air while standing on the pedals. ■ [*trans.*] jump (an obstacle) on a bicycle in this way.

▶*n.* (usu. **bun·ny hop**) **1** a jump in a crouched position. ■ a short jump forward on a bicycle. ■ an obstacle on a cycling course that is usually cleared by jumping the bicycle over it. **2** a dance of hopping steps in which the participants face the same direction and form a line by placing their hands on the waist or shoulders of the person in front of them.

bun·ny hug·ger ▶*n.* *informal, derogatory* an animal lover; a conservationist.

bun·ny slope ▶*n.* *Skiing* a gentle slope suitable for beginners.

Bun·sen /ˈbənsən/, Robert Wilhelm Eberhard (1811–99), German chemist. With Gustav Kirchhoff, he pioneered spectroscopy, detecting new elements (cesium and rubidium) and determining the composition of many substances and of the sun and stars. He also designed some chemical apparatuses, most notably the Bunsen burner (1855).

Bun·sen burn·er ▶*n.* a small adjustable gas burner used in laboratories.

Bun·shaft /ˈbən,SHaft/, Gordon (1909–90), U.S. architect. He is best known for his use of the International style in corporate architecture. He designed the Pepsi-Cola building 1960 in New York City and the Hirshhorn Museum and Sculpture Garden 1974 in Washington, DC.

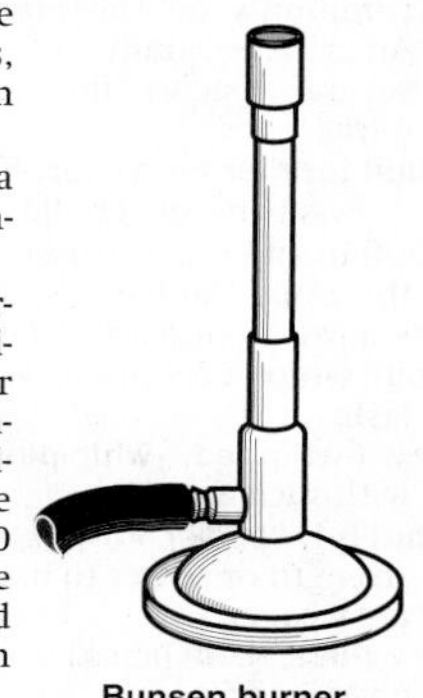

Bunsen burner

bunt[1] /bənt/ ▸*v.* [*trans.*] **1** *Baseball* (of a batter) gently tap (a pitched ball) without swinging in an attempt to make it more difficult to field: *the batter tried to bunt the ball down the first baseline* | [*intrans.*] *Phil bunted and got to first.* ■ (of a batter) help (a base runner) to progress to a further base by tapping a ball in such a way: *he* **bunted** *Davis* **to** *third.* **2** (of a person or animal) butt with the head or horns: *he bunted her with his head.*
▸*n.* **1** *Baseball* an act or result of tapping a pitched ball in such a way. **2** an act of flying an aircraft in part of an outside loop. ▹mid 18th cent.: probably related to the noun BUTT[1] (the original sense). The usage in aeronautics dates from the 1930s.

bunt[2] ▸*n.* the baggy center of a fishing net or a sail. ▹late 16th cent.: of unknown origin.

bunt[3] ▸*n.* a disease of wheat caused by a smut fungus, the spores of which give off a smell of rotten fish. Also called STINKING SMUT. • This disease is caused by *Tilletia caries*, class Teliomycetes. ▹early 17th cent. (denoting the puffball fungus): of unknown origin.

bunt·ing[1] /ˈbəntiNG/ ▸*n.* **1** an Old World seed-eating songbird related to the finches, typically with brown streaked plumage and a boldly marked head. • Family Emberizidae, subfamily Emberizinae (the **bunting family** and **subfamily**): several genera, in particular *Emberiza*, and numerous species. **2** a small New World songbird of the cardinal subfamily, the male of which is brightly colored. • Family Emberizidae, subfamily Cardinalinae: genera *Passerina* and *Cyanocompsa*, and several species, in particular the deep blue **indigo bunting** (*P. cyanea*) and the **painted bunting** (*P. ciris*). The painted bunting, with its violet head, red body, and green back, is the only such multicolored songbird in North America. ▹Middle English: of unknown origin.

bunt·ing[2] ▸*n.* flags and other colorful festive decorations. ■ a loosely woven fabric used for such decoration. ▹early 18th cent.: of unknown origin.

bunt·line /ˈbənt,līn/ ▸*n.* a line for restraining the loose center of a sail while it is furled.

Bu·ñuel /bo͞onˈwel/, Luis (1900–83), Spanish movie director. Influenced by surrealism, he wrote and directed his first movie *Un Chien andalou* (1928) jointly with Salvador Dali. Other notable movies: *Belle de jour* (1967) and *The Discreet Charm of the Bourgeoisie* (1972).

bun·ya /ˈbənyə/ (also **bunya pine** or **bun·ya-bun·ya**) ▸*n.* a tall coniferous Australian tree of the monkey puzzle family that bears large cones containing edible seeds. • *Araucaria bidwillii*, family Araucariaceae. ▹mid 19th cent.: from Wiradhuri.

Bun·yan /ˈbənyən/, John (1628–88), English writer. His major work, *The Pilgrim's Progress* (1678–84), is an allegory recounting the spiritual journey of its hero Pilgrim. **—Bun·yan·esque** /,bənyəˈnesk/ *adj.*

bun·yan·ize /ˈbənyə,nīz/ ▸*v.* [trans.] cause (someone) to appear heroic or larger than life: *How are you going to allow teachers to finish their work if you keep bunyanizing them?* ▹late 20th cent.: after Paul *Bunyan*, legendary American giant lumberjack.

bun·yip /ˈbənyip/ ▸*n.* *Austral.* **1** a fabulous amphibious monster inhabiting inland waterways. **2** [often as *adj.*] an impostor or pretender: *Australia's bunyip aristocracy.* ▹from Wemba-Wemba *banib.*

Buo·na·par·te /,bwōnäˈpärtā/ see BONAPARTE.

Buo·nar·ro·ti /,bwänəˈrôtē/, Michelangelo, see MICHELANGELO.

bu·oy /ˈbo͞o-ē; boi/ ▸*n.* an anchored float serving as a navigation mark, to show reefs or other hazards, or for mooring.
▸*v.* [*trans.*] **1** keep (someone or something) afloat: *I let the water* **buoy up** *my weight.* ■ (often **be buoyed**) cause to become cheerful or confident: *the party was buoyed by an election victory.* ■ (often **be buoyed**) cause (a price) to rise to or remain at a high level: *the price is* **buoyed up** *by investors.* **2** mark with a buoy: [as *adj.*] (**buoyed**) *a buoyed channel.* ▹Middle English: probably from Middle Dutch *boye, boeie*, from a Germanic base meaning 'signal.'

buoy·an·cy /ˈboi-ənsē; ˈbo͞oyənsē/ ▸*n.* the ability or tendency to float in water or air or some other fluid. ■ the power of a liquid to keep something afloat. ■ *figurative* an optimistic and cheerful disposition: *the happiness and buoyancy of his nature.* ■ *figurative* a high level of activity in an economy or stock market: *there is renewed buoyancy in the demand for steel.*

buoy·ant /ˈboi-ənt; ˈbo͞oyənt/ ▸*adj.* able or apt to stay afloat or rise to the top of a liquid or gas. ■ (of a liquid or gas) able to keep something afloat. ■ *figurative* (of an economy, business, or market) involving or engaged in much activity: *car sales were not buoyant.* ■ *figurative* cheerful and optimistic: *the conference ended with the party in a buoyant mood.* ▹late 16th cent.: from French *bouyant* or Spanish *boyante*, present participle of *boyar* 'to float' (see BUOY). **—buoy·ant·ly** *adv.*

bup·kis /ˈbo͝opkis; ˈbəp-/ ▸*n.* *informal* nothing at all: *you know bupkis about fund-raising.* ▹from Yiddish.

bup·pie /ˈbəpē/ ▸*n.* (*pl.* **-pies**) *informal* a young urban black professional; a black yuppie.

bu·pro·pi·on /byo͞oˈprōpēən/ ▸*n.* an antidepressant drug ($C_{13}H_{18}ClNO$) that is also given to relieve the symptoms of nicotine withdrawal. Also called ZYBAN (*trademark*). ▹1970s: from *butane* + *propionic.*

bur /bər/ (also **burr**) ▸*n.* **1** a prickly seed case or flowerhead that clings to animals and clothes. [Middle English] ■ [usu. as *adj.*] a plant that produces burs, e.g., bur reed. **2** [as *adj.*] denoting wood containing knots or other growths that show a pattern of dense swirls in the grain when sawn, used for veneers and other decorative woodwork: *bur walnut.* [late 19th cent.] **3** variant spelling of BURR (senses 2, 3, and 5). ▹possibly of Scandinavian origin, identical or related to Danish *burre* 'bur,' 'burdock.' See also BURR.

bur. ▸*abbr.* bureau.

burb /bərb/ ▸*n.* (usu. **the burbs**) *informal* short for SUBURB: *the leafy burbs of Connecticut.*

Bur·bank[1] /ˈbər,baNGk/ a city in southern California, a northern suburb of Los Angeles; pop. 93,640. It is a center of the movie and television industries.

Bur·bank[2], Luther (1849–1926), U.S. horticulturist. His experiments in cross-breeding led to new types and improved varieties of plants, esp. the Shasta daisy and the potato.

Bur·ber·ry /ˈbərbərē; -,berē/ ▸*n.* (*pl.* **-ries**) *trademark* a kind of lightweight belted raincoat, typically beige in color, with a distinctive tartan lining. ▹early 20th cent.: from *Burberrys*, the name of the manufacturer.

bur·ble /ˈbərbəl/ ▸*v.* [*intrans.*] make a continuous murmuring noise: *the wind burbled at his ear.* ■ speak in an unintelligible or silly way, typically at unnecessary length: *he* **burbled on** *about annuities* | [*trans.*] *he was burbling inanities.* ■ *Aeronautics* [often as *n.*] (**burbling**) (of an airflow) break up into turbulence.
▸*n.* continuous murmuring noise. ■ rambling speech: *an hour of boring burble.* ▹Middle English (in the sense 'to bubble'): imitative. Current senses date from the late 19th cent.

bur·bot /ˈbərbət/ ▸*n.* an elongated bottom-dwelling fish that is the only member of the cod family that lives in fresh water. It occurs in Eurasia and North America, but is almost extinct in Britain. • *Lota lota*, family Gadidae. ▹Middle English: from Old French *borbete*, probably from *borbe* 'mud, slime.'

bur·den /ˈbərdn/ ▸*n.* **1** a load, esp. a heavy one. ■ *figurative* a duty or misfortune that causes hardship, anxiety, or grief; a nuisance: *the burden of mental illness.* ■ the main responsibility for achieving a specified aim or task: *the burden of establishing that the cost was unreasonable.* ■ a ship's carrying capacity; tonnage: *the schooner* Wyoming, *of about 6,000 tons burden.* **2** (**the burden**) the main theme or gist of a speech, book, or argument: *the burden of his views.* ■ the refrain or chorus of a song.
▸*v.* [*trans.*] (usu. **be burdened**) load heavily: *she walked forward* **burdened with** *a wooden box.* ■ *figurative* cause (someone) hardship or distress: *they were not yet burdened with adult responsibility.* ▹Old English *byrthen*; related to BEAR[1]. **—bur·den·some** /ˈ-səm/ *adj.*
▸PHRASE □ **burden of proof** the obligation to prove one's assertion.

bur·dock /ˈbərdäk/ ▸*n.* a large herbaceous Old World plant of the daisy family. The hook-bearing flowers become woody burrs after fertilization and cling to animals' coats for seed dispersal. • Genus *Arctium*, family Compositae: several species, including the large-leaved **great burdock** (*A. lappa*), which has edible roots and is used in herbal medicine. ▹late 16th cent.: from BUR + DOCK[3].

bu·reau /ˈbyo͝orō/ ▸*n.* (*pl.* **bu·reaus** or **bu·reaux** /ˈbyo͝orōz/) **1** a chest of drawers. ■ *Brit.* a writing desk with drawers and typically an angled top opening downward to form a writing surface. **2** (abbr.: **bur.**) an office or department for transacting particular business: *a news bureau.* ■ the office in a particular place of an organization based elsewhere: *the London bureau of the* Washington Post. ■ a government department: *the intelligence bureau.* ▹late 17th cent.: from French, originally 'baize' (used to cover writing desks), from Old French *burel*, probably from *bure* 'dark brown,'.

bu·reauc·ra·cy /byo͝oˈräkrəsē/ ▸*n.* (*pl.* **-cies**) a system of government in which most of the important decisions are made by state officials rather than by elected representatives. ■ a state or organization governed or managed according to such a system. ■ the officials in such a system, considered as a group or hierarchy. ■ excessively complicated administrative procedure, seen as characteristic of such a system: *the unnecessary bureaucracy in local government.* ▹early 19th cent.: from French *bureaucratie*, from *bureau* (see BUREAU, -CRACY).

bu·reau·crat /ˈbyo͝orə,krat/ ▸*n.* an official in a government department. ■ an administrator concerned with procedural correctness at the expense of people's needs. ▹mid 19th cent.: from French *bureaucrate*, from *bureaucratie* (see BUREAUCRACY). **—bu·reau·crat·ic** /,byo͝orəˈkratik/ *adj.* **—bu·reau·crat·i·cal·ly** /,byo͝orəˈkratik(ə)lē/ *adv.*

bu·reau·crat·ese /byo͝o,räkrəˈtēz; -ˈtēs/ ▸*n.* a style of speech or writing characterized by jargon, euphemism, and abstractions, held to be typical of bureaucrats.

bu·reauc·ra·tize /byo͝oˈräkrə,tīz/ ▸*v.* [*trans.*] [usu. as *adj.*] (**bureaucratized**) endue (someone or something) with the characteristics of a bureaucracy: *impersonal and bureaucratized welfare systems.* **—bu·reauc·ra·ti·za·tion** /-,räkrətiˈzāSHən/ *n.*

bu·reau de change /ˈbyo͝orō də ˈSHänzH/ ▸*n.* (*pl.* **bu·reaux de change** *pronunc.* same) an establishment at which customers can exchange foreign money. ▹1950s: French, literally 'office of exchange.'

bu·rette /byo͝oˈret/ (also **bu·ret**) ▸*n.* a graduated glass tube with a tap at one end, for delivering known volumes of a liquid, esp. in titrations. ▹mid 19th cent.: from French, from *buire* 'jug,' of Germanic origin; related to German *Bauch* 'stomach.'

burg /bərg/ ▸*n.* an ancient or medieval fortress or walled town. [from late Latin *burgus* (see BURGESS).] ■ *informal* a town or city. [mid 19th cent.: from German *Burg* 'castle, city'; related to BOROUGH.]

bur·gage /ˈbərgij/ ▸*n.* *historical* (in England and Scotland) tenure of land in a town held in return for service or annual rent. ■ a house or other property held by such tenure. ▹late Middle English: from medieval Latin *burgagium*, from *burgus* 'fortified town,' of Germanic origin and related to BOROUGH.

Bur·gas /ˈbərgəs/ an industrial port and resort in eastern Bulgaria, on the coast of the Black Sea; pop. 226,120.

bur·gee /bərˈjē; ˈbərjē/ ▸*n.* a flag bearing the colors or emblem of a sailing club, typically triangular. ▹mid 18th cent.: perhaps from French *bourgeois* (see BURGESS) in the sense 'owner, master.'

bur·geon /ˈbərjən/ ▸*v.* [*intrans.*] [often as *adj.*] (**burgeoning**) begin to grow or increase rapidly; flourish: *manufacturers are keen to cash in on the burgeoning demand.* ■ put forth young shoots; bud. ▹Middle English: from Old French *bourgeonner* 'put out buds,' from *borjon* 'bud,' based on late Latin *burra* 'wool.'

Bur·ger /ˈbərgər/, Warren Earl (1907–95), U.S. chief justice 1969–86. Appointed to head the U.S. Supreme Court by President Richard Nixon, he was a conservative, except in matters of civil rights, and an advocate of judicial restraint.

burg·er /ˈbərgər/ ▸*n.* short for HAMBURGER. ■ [with *adj.*] a particular variation of a hamburger with additional or substitute ingredients: *a veggie burger.* ▹1930s (originally U.S.): abbreviation.

Bur·gess[1] /ˈbərjəs/, Anthony (1917–93), English novelist and critic; pseudonym of *John Anthony Burgess Wilson.* He wrote *A Clockwork Orange* (1962), a disturbing, futuristic vision of juvenile delinquency, violence, and high technology. Other notable works: *The Malayan Trilogy* (1956–59) and *Earthly Powers* (1980).

Bur·gess[2], Guy (Francis de Moncy) (1911–63), British foreign office official and spy. Acting as a Soviet agent from the 1930s, he was charged with espionage in 1951 and fled to the Soviet Union with Donald Maclean.

bur·gess /ˈbərjis/ ▸*n.* a person with municipal authority or privileges, in particular: ■ *Brit., archaic* an inhabitant of a town or borough with full rights of citizenship. ■ *Brit., historical* a member of Parliament for a borough, corporate town, or university. ■ (in the U.S. and also historically in the UK) a magistrate or member of the governing body of a town. ■ *historical* a member of the assembly of colonial Maryland or Virginia. ▹Middle English: from Anglo-

Norman French *burgeis*, from late Latin *burgus* 'castle, fort' (in medieval Latin 'fortified town'); related to **BOROUGH**.

Bur·gess Shale /ˈbərjis/ a bed of shale exposed in the Rocky Mountains in British Columbia, Canada. The bed, dated to the Cambrian period (about 530 million years ago), is rich in well-preserved fossils of early marine invertebrates, many of which represent evolutionary lineages unknown in later times. ▷named after the *Burgess* Pass, British Colombia, where the shale crops out.

burgh /bərg; ˈbərə/ ▸*n. archaic* or *Scottish* a borough or chartered town. ▷late Middle English: Scots form of **BOROUGH**. **—burgh·al** /ˈbərgəl/ *adj.*

burgh·er /ˈbərgər/ ▸*n. archaic* or *humorous* a citizen of a town or city, typically a member of the wealthy bourgeoisie. ▷Middle English: from **BURGH**, reinforced by Dutch *burger*, from *burg* 'castle' (see **BOROUGH**).

bur·glar /ˈbərglər/ ▸*n.* a person who commits burglary. ▷mid 16th cent.: from legal French *burgler* or Anglo-Latin *burgulator, burglator*; related to Old French *burgier* 'pillage.' **—bur·glar·i·ous** /bərˈgle(ə)rēəs/ *adj.* (*archaic*).

bur·glar·ize /ˈbərgləˌrīz/ ▸*v.* [*trans.*] (often **be burglarized**) enter (a building) illegally with intent to commit a crime, esp. theft: *our summer house has been burglarized.*

bur·glar·proof /ˈbərglərˌpro͞of/ ▸*adj.* protected against or providing protection against burglary.

bur·gla·ry /ˈbərglərē/ ▸*n.* (*pl.* **-ries**) entry into a building illegally with intent to commit a crime, esp. theft: *a two-year sentence for burglary | a series of burglaries.* ▷early 16th cent.: from legal French *burglarie*, from *burgler* (see **BURGLAR**).

bur·gle /ˈbərgəl/ ▸*v.* another term for **BURGLARIZE**. ▷late 19th cent.: originally a humorous and colloquial back-formation from **BURGLAR**.

bur·go·mas·ter /ˈbərgəˌmastər/ ▸*n.* the mayor of a Dutch, Flemish, German, Austrian, or Swiss town. ▷late 16th cent.: from Dutch *burgemeester*, from *burg* 'castle, citadel' (see **BOROUGH**) + *meester* 'master.' The change in the final element was due to association with **MASTER**[1].

bur·go·net /ˈbərgəˌnet; ˌbərgəˈnet/ ▸*n. historical* a kind of visored helmet. ▷late 16th cent.: from French *bourguignotte*, perhaps a use of the feminine of *bourguignot* 'Burgundian,' the ending being assimilated to **-ET**[1].

burgonet

bur·goo /bərˈgo͞o/ ▸*n.* a stew or thick soup, typically made for an outdoor meal. ■ an outdoor meal at which such food is served. ■ *chiefly Nautical* a thick porridge. ▷from Arabic *burġ ūl*

Bur·gos /ˈbo͝orgōs/ a town in northern Spain; pop. 169,280.

Bur·goyne /ˈbərˌgoin; bərˈgoin/, John (1722–92), English general and playwright; known as **Gentleman Johnny**. He surrendered to the Americans at Saratoga (1777) during the American Revolution. His plays include *The Maid of the Oaks* (1774) and *The Heiress* (1786).

bur·grave /ˈbərgrāv/ ▸*n. historical* the governor or hereditary ruler of a German town or castle. ▷mid 16th cent.: from German *Burggraf*, from *Burg* 'castle' (see **BOROUGH**) + *Graf* 'count, noble.'

Bur·gun·di·an /bərˈgəndēən/ ▸*n.* a native or inhabitant of Burgundy. ■ *historical* a member of a Germanic people that invaded Gaul from the east and established the kingdom of Burgundy in the 5th century AD.
▸*adj.* of or relating to Burgundy or the Burgundians.

Bur·gun·dy /ˈbərgəndē/ a region and former duchy of eastern central France, the center of which is Dijon. The region is noted for its wine. French name **BOURGOGNE**.

bur·gun·dy /ˈbərgəndē/ (also **Bur·gun·dy**) ▸*n.* (*pl.* **-dies**) a wine from Burgundy (usually taken to be red unless otherwise specified): *a glass of Burgundy | elegant red burgundies.* ■ a deep red color like that of burgundy wine: *warm shades of brown and burgundy |* [as *adj.*] *burgundy leather.*

bur·i·al /ˈberēəl/ ▸*n.* the action or practice of interring a dead body: *his remains were shipped home for burial.* ■ a ceremony at which someone's body is interred; a funeral: [as *adj.*] *burial rites.* ■ *Archaeology* a grave or the remains found in it: [as *adj.*] *burial mounds.* ▷Old English *byrgels* 'place of burial, grave' (interpreted as plural in Middle English, hence the loss of the final -*s*), of Germanic origin; related to **BURY**.

bur·i·al ground ▸*n.* (often as **burial grounds**) an area of ground set aside for the burying of human bodies. ■ a site at which the remains of once-living specimens can be found: *coral reefs are the burial grounds of untold organisms.*

bu·rin /ˈbyo͝orin/ ▸*n.* a steel tool used for engraving in copper or wood. ■ *Archaeology* a flint tool with a chisel point. ▷mid 17th cent.: from French; perhaps related to Old High German *bora* 'boring tool.'

bur·ka /ˈbo͝orkə/ (also **bur·kha, burqa**) ▸*n.* a long, loose garment covering the whole body, worn in public by many Muslim women. ▷from Urdu and Persian *burḳa'*, from Arabic *burḳu'*.

Burke[1] /bərk/, Edmund (1729–97), British politician and man of letters. He wrote on the issues of political emancipation and moderation, notably with respect to Roman Catholics and the American colonies.

Burke[2], John (1787–1848), Irish genealogical and heraldic writer. In 1826, he compiled the first edition of *Burke's Peerage*, still regarded as the authoritative guide to the British aristocracy.

Bur·ki·na Fa·so /bərˈkēnə ˈfäsō/ a landlocked country in western Africa, in the Sahel; pop. 13,574,000; capital, Ouagadougou; languages, French (official), indigenous languages of the Sudanic family. Former name (until 1984) **UPPER VOLTA**. **—Bur·ki·nan** /-ˈkēnən/ *adj.* & *n.*

A French protectorate from 1898, it became an autonomous republic within the French Community in 1958 and a fully independent republic in 1960.

Bur·kitt's lym·pho·ma /ˈbərkits/ ▸*n. Medicine* cancer of the lymphatic system, caused by the Epstein–Barr virus, chiefly affecting children in central Africa. ▷1960s: named after D. P. *Burkitt* (1911–93), the British surgeon who described it.

burl /bərl/ ▸*n.* a slub or lump in wool or cloth. ■ a rounded knotty growth on a tree, giving an attractive figure when polished and used esp. for handcrafted objects and veneers: *she used warty burls to construct her pieces | wooden coin banks made of elm burl |* [as *adj.*] *a burl bowl.* ▷late Middle English: from Old French *bourle* 'tuft of wool,' diminutive of *bourre* 'coarse wool,' from late Latin *burra* 'wool.'

bur·lap /ˈbərlap/ ▸*n.* coarse canvas woven from jute, hemp, or a similar fiber, used esp. for sacking. ■ lighter material of a similar kind used in dressmaking and furnishing: [as *adj.*] *a burlap shirt | fabrics ranging from hessians to burlaps.* ▷late 17th cent.: of unknown origin.

bur·lesque /bərˈlesk/ ▸*n.* **1** a parody or comically exaggerated imitation of something, esp. in a literary or dramatic work: *the funniest burlesque of opera |* [as *adj.*] *burlesque Shakespearean stanzas.* See note at **CARICATURE**. ■ humor that depends on comic imitation and exaggeration; absurdity: *the argument descends into burlesque.* **2** a variety show, typically including striptease: [as *adj.*] *burlesque clubs.*
▸*v.* (**-lesques, -lesqued, -lesqu·ing**) [*trans.*] cause to appear absurd by parodying or copying in an exaggerated form: *she struck a ridiculous pose that burlesqued her own vanity.* ▷mid 17th cent.: from French, from Italian *burlesco*, from *burla* 'mockery,' of unknown origin.

bur·ley /ˈbərlē/ ▸*n.* (also **burley tobacco**) a tobacco of a light-colored variety grown mainly in Kentucky. ▷late 19th cent.: of unknown origin.

Bur·lin·game /ˈbərlənˌgām; -liNG-/ a city in north central California, on San Francisco Bay, south of San Francisco; pop. 26,801.

Bur·ling·ton /ˈbərliNGtən/ **1** a city in southern Canada, on Lake Ontario, southwest of Toronto; pop. 129,600. **2** a city in north central North Carolina, noted as a textile center; pop. 39,498. **3** a city in northwestern Vermont, the largest in the state, on Lake Champlain; pop. 38,889.

bur·ly /ˈbərlē/ ▸*adj.* (**-li·er, -li·est**) (of a person) large and strong; heavily built. ▷Middle English (in the sense 'dignified, imposing'): probably from an unrecorded Old English word meaning 'stately, fit for the bower' (see **BOWER**[1], **-LY**[1]). **—bur·li·ness** *n.*

Bur·ma /ˈbərmə/, see **MYANMAR**.

bur mar·i·gold ▸*n.* another term for **BEGGAR TICKS**.

Bur·ma Road a route that links Lashio in Myanmar (Burma) to Kunming in China and covers 717 miles (1,154 km). Completed in 1939, it was built by the Chinese to serve as a supply route to the interior in response to the Japanese occupation of the Chinese coast.

Bur·mese /bərˈmēz; -ˈmēs/ ▸*n.* (*pl.* same) **1** a member of the largest ethnic group of Myanmar (Burma) in Southeast Asia. **2** a native or national of Myanmar. **3** the Tibeto-Burman language of the Burmese people, written in an alphabet derived from that of Pali and the official language of Myanmar. **4** (also **Burmese cat**) a cat of a short-haired breed originating in Asia.
▸*adj.* of or relating to Myanmar, its people, or their language.

burn[1] /bərn/ ▸*v.* (*past* and *past part.* **burned** or *chiefly Brit.* **burnt** /bərnt/) **1** [*intrans.*] (of a fire) flame or glow while consuming a material such as coal or wood: *a fire burned and crackled cheerfully in the grate.* ■ (of a candle or other source of light) be alight: *a light was burning in the hall.* ■ be or cause to be destroyed by fire: *he watched his restaurant* **burn to the ground** ■ [*trans.*] damage or injure by heat or fire: *I* **burned myself** *on the stove.* **2** [*intrans.*] (of a person, the skin, or a part of the body) become red and painful through exposure to the sun: *my skin tans easily but sometimes burns.* ■ feel or cause to feel sore, hot, or inflamed, typically as a result of illness or injury. ■ (of a person's face) feel hot and flushed from an intense emotion such as shame or indignation: *her face* **burned with** *the humiliation.* ■ (**be burning with**) be possessed by (a desire or an emotion): *Martha was burning with curiosity.* **3** [*trans.*] use (a type of fuel) as a source of heat or energy: *a diesel engine converted to burn natural gas.* ■ [*trans.*] (of a person) convert (calories) to energy: *the speed at which your body burns calories.* **4** [*trans.*] produce (a compact disc) by copying from an original or master copy. **5** [*intrans.*, with *adverbial of direction*] *informal* drive very fast: *he burned past us like a maniac.*
▸*phrasal v.* □ **burn something down** (or **burn down**) (of a building or structure) destroy or be destroyed completely by fire. □ **burn something in/into** brand or imprint by burning: *designs are burned into the skin | figurative a childhood incident that was burned into her memory.* ■ *Photography* expose one area of a print more than the rest: *the sky and bottom of the picture needed substantial burning in.* □ **burn something off** remove (a substance) using a flame: *using a blowtorch to burn off the paint.* □ **burn out** be completely consumed and thus no longer aflame: *the candle in the saucer had burned out | figurative his political ambitions had* **burned themselves out**. ■ cease to function as a result of excessive heat or friction: *the clutch had burned out.* □ **burn (oneself) out** ruin one's health or become completely exhausted through overwork. □ **burn someone out** make someone homeless by destroying their home by fire: *they were* **burned out of** *their homes.* □ **burn something out** completely destroy a building or vehicle by fire, so that only a shell remains. □ **burn up 1** (of a fire) produce brighter and stronger flames. **2** (of an object entering the earth's atmosphere) be destroyed by heat. □ **burn someone up** *informal* make someone angry: *his thoughtless remarks really burn me up.* □ **burn something up** ■ use up the calories or energy provided by food, rather than converting these to fat: *in the typical Western diet, all the energy in protein is burned up daily.*
▸*n.* **1** an injury caused by exposure to heat or flame: *he was treated in the hospital for* **burns to** *his hands.* ■ a mark left on something as a result of being burned: *the carpet was covered with cigarette burns.* ■ [with *adj.*] a feeling of heat and discomfort on the skin caused by friction, typically by a rope or razor: *a smooth shave without razor burn.* ■ a sensation of heat experienced on swallowing spicy food, hot liquid, or strong alcoholic drink: *Kate felt the burn as the curry hit her throat.* **2** consumption of a type of fuel as an en-

ergy source: *natural gas produces the cleanest burn of the lot.* ■ a firing of a rocket engine in flight. **3** an act of clearing vegetation by burning, intentionally or by accident. ■ an area of land cleared in this way. **4** a hot, painful sensation in the muscles experienced as a result of sustained vigorous exercise: *work up a burn.* **5** short for BURN RATE. ▷Old English *birnan* 'be on fire' and *bærnan* 'consume by fire,' both from the same Germanic base; related to German *brennen.*

▶*PHRASES* □ **be burned at the stake** *historical* be executed by being burned alive in public, typically for heresy or witchcraft. □ **burn one's bridges** do something that makes it impossible to return to an earlier state. □ **burn the candle at both ends** go to bed late and get up early, esp. to get work done. □ **burn the midnight oil** read, study, or work late into the night. □ **burn** (or **lay**) **rubber** *informal* drive very fast. □ **go for the burn** *informal* push one's body to the extremes when doing physical exercise. □ **money burns a hole in someone's pocket** someone has a strong urge to spend money as soon as they receive it. □ **slow burn** *informal* a state of slowly mounting anger or annoyance: *the medical community's shrugging acceptance is fueling a slow burn among women.*

THE RIGHT WORD **burn, cauterize, char, scald, scorch, sear, singe**

If you're not an experienced cook, you're likely to **burn** your vegetables and **char** your meat, and, if you put your face too close to the stove, you might even **singe** your eyebrows. All of these verbs mean to injure or bring about a change in something by exposing it to fire or intense heat.

Burn, which is the most comprehensive term, can mean to change only slightly (*she burned her face by staying out in the sun*) or to destroy completely (*the factory was burned to the ground*).

To *char* is to reduce a substance to carbon or charcoal (*the beams in the ceiling were charred by the fire*).

Like *char*, **singe** and **scorch** mean to burn only partially or superficially (*scorched the blouse while ironing it; singe the chicken before cooking it*). *Singeing* is often done deliberately to remove the hair, bristles, or feathers from the carcass of an animal or bird.

Scald refers specifically to burning with, or as if with, a hot liquid or steam (*the cook scalded herself when she spilled the boiling water*); it can also mean to parboil or heat to a temperature just below boiling (*scald the milk to make the sauce*).

Sear is also a term used in cooking, where it means to brown the outside of a piece of meat by subjecting it briefly to intense heat to seal in the juices.

When it's human flesh that's being seared in surgery, the correct verb is **cauterize**, which means to burn for healing purposes (*the doctor cauterized the wound to ward off infection*).

burn[2] ▶*n. chiefly Scottish & N. Engl.* a small stream; a brook. ▷Old English *burna, burn(e)*, of Germanic origin; related to Dutch *bron* and German *Brunnen* 'well.'

burned /bərnd/ (also **burnt**) ▶ past and past participle of BURN[1].

▶*adj.* [*attrib.*] having been burned: *burned wood | burned shoulders and peeling noses.* ■ (of a taste) like that of food that has been charred in cooking. ■ (of sugar) cooked or heated until caramelized. ■ (usu. **burnt**) (of a warm color) dark or deep: *burnt orange.*

burned-out (also **burnt-out**) ▶*adj.* (of a vehicle or building) destroyed or badly damaged by fire; gutted. ■ (of an electrical device or component) having failed through overheating. ■ (of a person) in a state of physical or mental collapse caused by overwork or stress: *she felt burned out, an empty shell | a burned-out undercover cop.* ■ *informal* (of a teenager or other person) having dropped out; drug-using.

Burne-Jones /ˈbərn ˈjōnz/, Sir Edward (Coley) (1833–98), English painter and designer. Notable paintings: *The Golden Stairs* (1880) and *The Mirror of Venus* (1898–99).

burn·er /ˈbərnər/ ▶*n.* a thing that burns something or is burned, in particular: ■ a part of a stove, lamp, etc., that emits and shapes a flame. ■ an apparatus in which a fuel is used or an aromatic substance is heated. ■ [with *adj.*] an activity that uses something of a specified kind as energy: *uphill walking is a great calorie burner.* ■ short for **CD** BURNER. ■ *informal* a handgun.

▶*PHRASE* □ **on the back** (or **front**) **burner** *informal* having low (or high) priority: *he wants the matter to* **be put on the back burner**.

bur·net /bərˈnet; ˈbərnit/ ▶*n.* **1** a herbaceous plant of the rose family, with globular pinkish flowerheads and leaves composed of many small leaflets. • Genus *Sanguisorba*, family Rosaceae: several species, including the edible **salad burnet** (*S. minor*), which is often cultivated, and the spiny shrublike **thorny burnet** (*S. spinosum*), common in the eastern Mediterranean. **2** a day-flying moth that typically has greenish-black wings marked with crimson spots. • *Zygaena* and other genera, family Zygaenidae. ▷Middle English (denoting a kind of dark brown woolen cloth): from Old French *brunete, burnete* (denoting brown cloth or a plant with brown flowers), diminutives of *brun* 'brown.'

Bur·nett[1] /bərˈnet/, Carol (1936–), U.S. comedienne and actress. She is best known for the television program "The Carol Burnett Show" (1966–77).

Bur·nett[2], Frances (Eliza) Hodgson (1849–1924), U.S. novelist; born in Britain. She is noted for her children's novels, which include *Little Lord Fauntleroy* (1886), *A Little Princess* (1905), and *The Secret Garden* (1911).

burn-in ▶*n.* damage to a computer or television screen, caused by being left on too long. ■ a reliability test in which a device is switched on for a long time.

burn·ing /ˈbərniNG/ ▶*adj.* [*attrib.*] on fire: *a burning building.* ■ very hot or bright: *burning desert sands.* ■ *figurative* very keenly or deeply felt; intense: *he had a* **burning ambition** *to climb to the upper reaches of management.* ■ *figurative* of urgent interest and importance; exciting or calling for debate: *democracy remains a* **burning issue** | *the* **burning question** *of independence.* —**burn·ing·ly** *adv.*

burn·ing bush ▶*n.* **1** any of a number of shrubs noted for their bright red autumn foliage, in particular: • the kochia. • the smoke tree. **2** any of a number of shrubs or trees with bright red leaves or fruits. • Several plants, in particular the purple-flowered North American *Euonymus atropurpurea* (family Celastraceae), a relative of the spindle tree. **3** another term for GAS PLANT. ▷mid 19th cent.: with biblical allusion to Exod. 3:2.

burn·ing glass ▶*n.* a lens for concentrating the sun's rays on an object so as to set fire to it.

bur·nish /ˈbərnish/ ▶*v.* [*trans.*] [usu. as *adj.*] (**burnished**) polish (something, esp. metal) by rubbing: *highly burnished armor.* ■ *figurative* enhance or perfect (something such as a reputation or a skill).

▶*n.* [in *sing.*] the shine on a highly polished surface. ▷Middle English: from Old French *burniss-*, lengthened stem of *burnir*, variant of *brunir* 'make brown,' from *brun* 'brown.' —**bur·nish·er** *n.*

bur·noose /bərˈnōōs/ (also **bur·nous**) ▶*n.* a long, loose hooded cloak worn by Arabs. ▷late 16th cent.: French, from Arabic *burnus*, from Greek *birros* 'cloak.'

burnoose

burn·out /ˈbərnˌout/ ▶*n.* **1** the reduction of a fuel or substance to nothing through use or combustion: *good carbon burnout* | [as *adj.*] *a burnout furnace.* **2** physical or mental collapse caused by overwork or stress: *high levels of professionalism that may result in burnout | you'll suffer a burnout.* ■ *informal* a dropout or drug abuser, esp. a teenage one. **3** failure of an electrical device or component through overheating: [with *adj.*] *an antistall mechanism prevents motor burnout.*

burn rate ▶*n.* the rate at which an enterprise spends money, especially venture capital, in excess of income: *the corporation lays off workers to cut burn rate.*

Burns[1] /bərnz/, George (1896–1996), U.S. comedian and movie actor; born *Nathan Birnbaum.* In 1922, he paired up with comedienne Gracie Allen (1902–64), whom he married in 1926. They had shows in vaudeville, on radio, and later on television. Notable movies: *The Sunshine Boys* (Academy Award, 1975) and *Oh God!* (1977).

Burns[2], Robert (1759–96), Scottish poet, noted for poems, such as "The Jolly Beggars" (1786) and "Tam o' Shanter" (1791), and for old Scottish songs that he collected, including "Auld Lang Syne."

Burn·side /ˈbərnˌsīd/, Ambrose Everett (1824–81), U.S. army officer. He was appointed General of the Army of the Potomac in 1862, but his incompetence at the Battle of Fredericksburg that same year led to his transfer to Ohio.

burn·side /ˈbərnˌsīd/ ▶*n.* (usu. **burnsides**) a mustache in combination with whiskers on the cheeks but no beard on the chin. ▷late 19th cent.: named after General Ambrose BURNSIDE.

burnsides

Burns·ville /ˈbərnzˌvil/ a city in southeastern Minnesota, south of Minneapolis; pop. 60,220.

burnt /bərnt/ ▶*adj.* variant spelling of BURNED.

burnt o·cher ▶*n.* a pigment made from ocher that has been darkened by heating, or resembling this in color. ■ the deep yellow-brown color of this pigment.

burnt of·fer·ing ▶*n.* **1** an offering burned on an altar as a religious sacrifice. **2** (usu. **burnt offerings**) *humorous* overcooked or charred food.

burnt si·en·na ▶*n.* a deep reddish-brown pigment made from sienna that has been darkened by heating, or resembling this in color. ■ the color of this pigment.

burnt um·ber ▶*n.* see UMBER (sense 1).

bur oak ▶*n.* a North American oak, with large fringed acorn cups. Its timber was formerly important in shipbuilding. Also called MOSSYCUP OAK. • *Quercus macrocarpa*, family Fagaceae.

burp /bərp/ *informal* ▶*v.* [*intrans.*] noisily release air from the stomach through the mouth; belch. ■ [*trans.*] make (a baby) belch after feeding, typically by patting its back.

▶*n.* a noise made by air released from the stomach through the mouth; a belch. ▷1930s): imitative.

burp gun ▶*n. informal* a lightweight submachine gun.

bur·qa /ˈbōōrkə/ ▶*n.* variant spelling of BURKA.

Burr /bər/, Aaron (1756–1836), U.S. statesman. In 1804, while U.S. vice-president, he killed Alexander Hamilton, his rival, in a duel. He then plotted to form an independent administration in Mexico and was tried for treason but was acquitted.

burr /bər/ ▶*n.* **1** [in *sing.*] a rough sounding of the sound *r*, esp. with a uvular trill (a "French *r*") as in certain Northern England accents. [mid 18th cent.] ■ (loosely) a regional accent charcterized by such a trill: *a soft Scottish burr.* ■ a whirring sound, such as a telephone ringing tone or the sound of cogs turning. [early 19th cent.] **2** (also **bur**) a rough edge or ridge left on an object (esp. of metal) by the action of a tool or machine. [early 17th cent.] **3** (also **bur**) a small rotary cutting tool with a shaped end, used chiefly in woodworking and dentistry. [mid 19th cent.] ■ a small surgical drill for making holes in bone, esp. in the skull. **4** a siliceous rock used for millstones. [mid 17th cent.] ■ a whetstone. **5** (also **bur**) a ring of bone at the base of a deer's antler. Also called CORONET. [late 16th cent.: possibly from French (cf. *bourre* 'vine-bud' or related to BURL.] **6** variant spelling of BUR.

▶*v.* **1** [*intrans.*] speak with an accent in which the sound *r* is trilled: [with *direct speech*] *"I like to have a purrrpose," she burrs.* [early 19th cent.] ■ make a whirring sound such as a telephone ringing tone or the sound of cogs turning. [late 18th cent.] **2** [*trans.*] form a rough edge on (metal): *the handles were fixed by rivets* **burred over** *on the shield's front.* [late 19th cent.]

George Burns

▷Sense 1 of the noun and verb is probably imitative, the word *burr* incorporating the uvular *r*, but it is also possibly a figurative use borrowed from senses 2, 3, and 4 of the noun and sense 2 of the verb, the *r* being a 'rough' sound. See also **BUR**.
▸*PHRASE* □ **a burr under one's saddle** *informal* a persistent source of irritation: *he had been a burr under the saddle of the government in his time.*

bur·ra·wang /ˈbərə,wang/ (also **bur·ra·wong**) ▸*n.* an Australian cycad with palmlike leaves and a sunken underground trunk. • *Macrozamia spiralis*, family Zamiaceae. ■ the poisonous nut of this tree, which loses its toxicity after prolonged soaking and becomes edible. ▷early 19th cent.: from Dharuk.

bur reed ▸*n.* an aquatic reedlike plant with rounded flowerheads. Its oily seeds are an important source of winter food for wildfowl. • Genus *Sparganium*, family Sparganiaceae.

burr·fish /ˈbər,fish/ ▸*n.* (*pl.* same or **-fish·es**) a porcupine fish with spines that are permanently erected, occurring in tropical waters of the Atlantic and Pacific. • Genus *Chilomycterus*, family Diodontidae: several species, including the common **striped burrfish** (*C. schoepfi*) of the western Atlantic.

bur·ri·to /bəˈrētō/ ▸*n.* (*pl.* **-tos**) a Mexican dish consisting of a tortilla rolled around a filling, typically of beans or ground or shredded beef. ▷Latin American Spanish, diminutive of Spanish *burro*, literally 'donkey' (see **BURRO**).

bur·ro /ˈbərō; ˈbo͝orō/ ▸*n.* (*pl.* **-ros**) a small donkey used as a pack animal. ▷early 19th cent.: from Spanish.

Bur·roughs[1] /ˈbərōz/, Edgar Rice (1875–1950), U.S. novelist and science fiction writer. Although he began his writing career with science fiction stories, he was most successful with an adventure series that began with *Tarzan of the Apes* (1914).

Bur·roughs[2], John (1837–1921), U.S. naturalist and author. At his home near the Hudson River at West Park, New York, he entertained friends such as John Muir, Theodore Roosevelt, and Walt Whitman. Among his works are *Wake-Robin* (1871), *Locusts and Wild Honey* (1879), and *The Summit of the Years* (1913).

Bur·roughs[3], William (Seward) (1914–97), U.S. novelist. In the 1940s, he became addicted to heroin, and his best-known writing, such as *Junkie* (1953) and *The Naked Lunch* (1959), deals in a unique, surreal style with life as a drug addict.

bur·row /ˈbərō/ ▸*n.* a hole or tunnel dug by a small animal, esp. a rabbit, as a dwelling.
▸*v.* [*intrans.*] (of an animal) make a hole or tunnel, esp. to use as a dwelling: *moles burrowing away underground* | [as *adj.*] (**burrowing**) *burrowing earthworms* | [*trans.*] *the fish can burrow a hiding place.* ■ [with *adverbial of direction*] advance into or through something solid by digging or making a hole: *worms that burrow through dead wood.* ■ [with *adverbial of direction*] move underneath or press close to something in order to hide oneself or in search of comfort: *the child* ***burrowed*** *deeper* ***into*** *the bed.* ■ [*trans.*] move (something) in this way: *she* ***burrowed*** *her face* ***into*** *the pillow.* ■ *figurative* make a thorough inquiry; investigate: *journalists are* ***burrowing into*** *the president's business affairs.* ▷Middle English. —**bur·row·er** *n.*

bur·ry /ˈbərē/ ▸*adj.* **1** having or containing burs; prickly. **2** (of speech) having a burr.

Bur·sa /ˈbərsə/ a city in northwestern Turkey; pop. 834,580. It was the capital of the Ottoman Empire 1326–1402.

bur·sa /ˈbərsə/ ▸*n.* (*pl.* **-sae** /-sē/ or **-sas**) *Anatomy* a fluid-filled sac or saclike cavity, esp. one countering friction at a joint. ▷early 19th cent.: from medieval Latin, 'bag, purse,' from Greek *bursa* 'leather.' —**bur·sal** *adj.*

bur·sa of Fa·bri·ci·us /fəˈbrēshəs/ ▸*n.* *Zoology* a glandular sac opening into the cloaca of a bird, producing B cells. ▷mid 19th cent. (in the Latin form *bursa Fabricii*): from **BURSA**, and a Latinized form of the name of Girolama *Fabrici* (1533–1619), Italian anatomist.

bur·sar /ˈbərsər/ ▸*n.* **1** a person who manages the financial affairs of a college or university. **2** *chiefly Scottish* a student attending a college or university on a scholarship. ▷late Middle English: from French *boursier* or (sense 1) medieval Latin *bursarius*, from *bursa* 'bag, purse' (see **BURSA**).

bur·sa·ry /ˈbərsərē/ ▸*n.* (*pl.* **-ries**) **1** *chiefly Brit.* a scholarship to attend a college or university. **2** the treasury of an institution, esp. a religious one. ▷late 17th cent. (sense 2): from medieval Latin *bursaria*, from *bursa* 'bag, purse' (see **BURSA**).

burse /bərs/ ▸*n.* a flat, square, fabric-covered case in which a folded corporal is carried to and from an altar in church.

bur·si·tis /bərˈsītis/ ▸*n.* *Medicine* inflammation of a bursa, typically one in the knee, elbow or shoulder.

burst /bərst/ ▸*v.* (*past* and *past part.* **burst**) [*intrans.*] (of a container) break suddenly and violently apart, spilling the contents, typically as a result of an impact or internal pressure: *we inflated dozens of balloons and only one burst.* ■ [*trans.*] cause to break, esp. by puncturing: *he burst the balloon in my face.* ■ [*trans.*] (of contents) break open (a container) from the inside by growing too large to be held: *the swollen river was expected to burst its banks.* ■ [*trans.*] suffer from the sudden breaking of (a bodily organ or vessel): *he burst a blood vessel during a fit of coughing.* ■ be so full as almost to break open: *the drawers were* ***bursting with*** *clothes.* ■ feel a very strong or irrepressible emotion or impulse: *he was* ***bursting with*** *joy and excitement* | [with *infinitive*] *she was bursting to say something.* ■ suddenly begin doing something as an expression of a strong feeling: *if anyone said anything to upset me, I'd* ***burst out crying*** | *she* ***burst into*** *a fresh flood of tears.* ■ issue suddenly and uncontrollably, as though from a splitting container: *the words* ***burst from*** *him in an angry rush* | *an aircraft crashed and* ***burst into flames.*** ■ be opened suddenly and forcibly: *a door burst open and a girl raced out.* ■ [with *adverbial of direction*] make one's way suddenly and typically violently: *he burst into the room without knocking.* ■ [*trans.*] separate (continuous stationery) into single sheets.
▸*n.* an instance of breaking or splitting as a result of internal pressure or puncturing; an explosion. ■ a sudden issuing forth: *her breath was coming in short bursts.* ■ a sudden outbreak, typically short and often violent or noisy: *a sudden burst of activity* | *he heard a burst of gunfire.* ■ a short, sudden, and intense effort: *he sailed 474 miles in one 24-hour burst.* ▷Old English *berstan*, of Germanic origin; related to Dutch *bersten, barsten*.
▸*PHRASE* □ **burst someone's bubble** shatter someone's illusions about something or destroy someone's sense of well-being.

burst·er /ˈbərstər/ ▸*n.* a thing that bursts, in particular: ■ *Astronomy* a cosmic source of powerful short-lived bursts of X-rays or other radiation. ■ a violent gale. ■ a machine that separates continuous stationery into single sheets.

burst·y /ˈbərstē/ ▸*adj.* *informal* or *technical* occurring at intervals in short sudden episodes or groups. ■ relating to or denoting the transmission of data in short separate bursts of signals.

bur·then /ˈbər*th*ən/ ▸*n.* archaic form of **BURDEN**.

Bur·ton[1] /ˈbərtn/, Harold Hitz (1888–1964), U.S. Supreme Court associate justice 1945–58. He was the mayor of Cleveland, Ohio 1935–40 and a U.S. senator 1941–45 before being appointed to the Court by President Truman. He held strongly to a constructionist view of the U.S. Constitution.

Bur·ton[2], Richard (1925–84), Welsh actor; born *Richard Jenkins*. He played a number of Shakespearean roles on stage before appearing in movies such as *The Spy Who Came in from the Cold* (1966) and *Who's Afraid of Virginia Woolf* (1966). He often costarred with Elizabeth Taylor, whom he married twice.

Bur·ton[3], Sir Richard (Francis) (1821–90), English explorer, anthropologist, and translator. In 1858, he and John Hanning Speke were the first Europeans to see Lake Tanganyika. Notable translations: *Arabian Nights* (1885–88), *Kama Sutra* (1883), and *The Perfumed Garden* (1886).

bur·ton /ˈbərtn/ (also **bur·ton-tack·le**) ▸*n.* *chiefly historical* a light two-block tackle for hoisting. ▷early 18th cent.: alteration of Middle English *Breton tackle*, a nautical term in the same sense (see **BRETON**[1]).

Bu·run·di /bəˈro͞ondē/ a central African country on the northeastern side of Lake Tanganyika, south of Rwanda; pop. 6,230,000; official languages, French and Kirundi; capital, Bujumbura. —**Bu·run·di·an** /-dēən/ *adj.* & *n.*

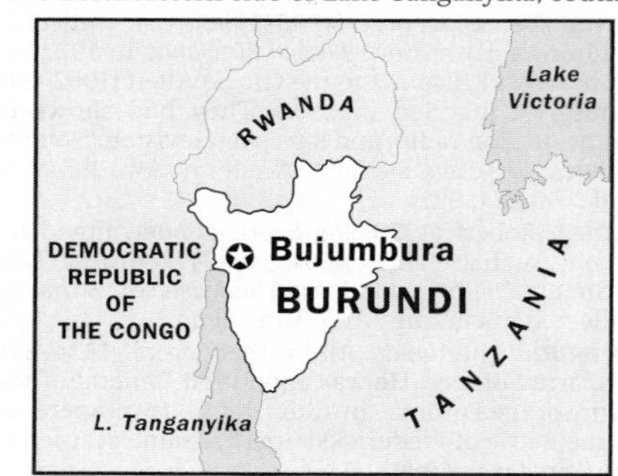

Inhabited mainly by Hutu and Tutsi peoples, the area formed part of German East Africa from the 1890s until World War I, after which it was administered by Belgium. The country became an independent monarchy in 1962 and a republic in 1966. Multiparty elections in 1993 resulted in the country's being led for the first time by a member of the Hutu majority rather than the traditionally dominant Tutsis; the assassination of the president within months, and the death in 1994 of the country's next leader, sparked large-scale ethnic violence. A new transitional government was formed in 2001, but a December 2002 cease-fire was not implemented.

bur·y /ˈberē/ ▸*v.* (**bur·ies, bur·ied**) [*trans.*] put or hide under ground: *he buried the box in the back garden* | [as *adj.*] (**buried**) *buried treasure.* ■ (usu. **be buried**) place (a dead body) in the earth, in a tomb, or in the sea, typically with funeral rites: *he was buried in Arlington National Cemetery.* ■ *figurative* lose (someone, typically a relative) through death: *she buried her sixty-year-old husband.* ■ completely cover; cause to disappear or become inconspicuous: *the countryside has been buried under layers of concrete* | *figurative the warehouse was buried in the faceless sprawl of the city.* ■ move or put out of sight: *she buried her face in her hands* | *with his hands buried in the pockets of his overcoat.* ■ *figurative* deliberately forget; conceal from oneself: *they had buried their feelings of embarrassment and fear.* ■ overwhelm (an opponent) beyond hope of recovery: *he boasted that socialism would bury capitalism.* ■ (**bury oneself**) involve oneself deeply in something to the exclusion of other concerns: *he* ***buried himself in*** *work.* ▷Old English *byrgan*; related to the verb **BORROW** and to **BOROUGH**.
▸*PHRASES* □ **bury the hatchet** end a quarrel or conflict and become friendly. □ **bury one's head in the sand** ignore unpleasant realities.

Bur·yat·ia /bo͝orˈyätēə/ (also **Bur·yat Re·pub·lic** /bo͝orˈyät; ˈbo͝or,yät/) an autonomous republic in southeastern Russia, between Lake Baikal and the Mongolian border; pop. 1,049,000; capital, Ulan-Ude.

bur·y·ing bee·tle ▸*n.* a black beetle that typically has broad orange bands on its wing cases. It buries small animal carcasses to provide a food store for its larvae. Also called **SEXTON BEETLE**. • *Nicrophorus* and other genera, family Silphidae.

bus /bəs/ ▸*n.* (*pl.* **bus·es** or **bus·ses**) **1** a large motor vehicle carrying passengers by road, esp. one serving the public on a fixed route and for a fare: [as *adj.*] *a bus service.* **2** *Computing* a distinct set of conductors carrying data and control signals within a computer system, to which pieces of equipment may be connected in parallel.
▸*v.* (**bus·es, bused, bus·ing** or **bus·ses, bus·sed, bus·sing**) **1** [*trans.*] (often **be bused**) transport in a communal road vehicle: *managerial staff was bused in and out of the factory.* ■ transport (a child of one race) to a school where another race is predominant, in an attempt to promote racial integration. **2** [*trans.*] remove (dirty tableware) from a table in a restaurant or cafeteria: *I'd never bused so many dishes in one night.* ■ remove dirty tableware from (a table): *Chad buses tables on weekends.* ▷early 19th cent.: shortening of **OMNIBUS**.

bus. ▸*abbr.* business.

bus·bar /ˈbəs,bär/ (also **bus bar**) ▸*n.* a system of electrical conductors in a generating or receiving station on which power is concentrated for distribution.

bus·boy /ˈbəs,boi/ ▸*n.* a young man who clears tables in a restaurant or cafeteria. ▷late 19th cent.: shortening of **OMNIBUS** + **BOY**.

bus·by /ˈbəzbē/ ▸*n.* (*pl.* **-bies**) a tall fur hat with a colored cloth flap hanging down on the right-hand side and often a plume on the top, worn by soldiers of certain regiments of hussars and artillerymen. ■ popular term for **BEARSKIN** (the cap). ▷mid 18th cent. (denoting a large bushy wig): of unknown origin.

busby

Bush[1] /bo͝osh/, George (Herbert Walker) (1924–), 41st president of the U.S. 1989–93. A

Texas Republican, he served in the U.S. House of Representatives 1967–71 and as director of the CIA 1975–76. His presidency was preceded by two terms as Ronald Reagan's vice president 1981–89. As president, Bush negotiated further arms reductions with the Soviet Union and organized international action to expel the Iraqis from Kuwait following the invasion in 1990.

George Herbert Walker Bush

Bush[2], George W(alker) (1946–), 43rd president of the U.S. 2001– . He is the son of President George Bush. A conservative Texas Republican, he served as governor of Texas 1994–2001 before he became president in one of the closest and most controversial presidential elections in U.S. history, when the accuracy of the vote count in the state of Florida was challenged by Democratic nominee Al Gore. As part of his war of terrorism and maintaining that Saddam Hussein was developing chemical, biological, and nuclear weapons, Bush ordered the invasion of Iraq in March 2003. The war became increasingly controversial as casualties mounted and as it became evident that U.S. troops would need to remain in Iraq for years to come.

George Walker Bush

bush /bŏŏsh/ ▸*n.* a shrub or clump of shrubs with stems of moderate length: *a rose bush | the plant will develop into a dense bush.* ■ a thing resembling such a shrub, esp. a clump of thick hair or fur: *a childish face with a bush of bright hair.* ■ *vulgar slang* a person's pubic hair, esp. that of a woman. ■ **(the bush)** (esp. in Australia, Africa, and Canada) wild or uncultivated country: *they have to spend a night camping in the bush.* ■ the vegetation growing in such a district: *the lowland country was covered in thick bush.*
▸*adj. informal* short for BUSH LEAGUE.
▸*v.* [*intrans.*] spread out into a thick clump: *her hair* ***bushed out*** *like a halo.* ▷Middle English: from Old French *bos, bosc,* variants of *bois* 'wood,' reinforced by Old Norse *buski,* of Germanic origin and related to obsolete Dutch *bosch* (now *bos*) and German *Busch.* The sense 'uncultivated country' is probably directly from Dutch *bos.*
▸*PHRASES* □ **beat around** (or **beat about**) **the bush** see BEAT. □ **beat the bushes** see BEAT.

bush ba·by (also **bush·ba·by**) ▸*n.* (*pl.* **-bies**) a small nocturnal tree-dwelling African primate with very large eyes. Also called GALAGO. • Genus *Galago,* family Lorisidae, suborder Prosimii: several species.

bush bean ▸*n.* a variety of bean plant whose bushy growth requires no support. Compare with POLE BEAN. ■ the edible bean from such a plant.

bush·buck /ˈbŏŏsh,bək/ ▸*n.* a small antelope with a reddish-brown coat with white markings, found in southern Africa. • *Tragelaphus scriptus,* family Bovidae. ▷mid 19th cent.: from BUSH[1] + BUCK[1], influenced by obsolete Dutch *boshbok* (now *bosbok).*

bush·craft /ˈbŏŏsh,kraft/ ▸*n.* skill at living in the bush.

bush dog ▸*n.* a small, stocky carnivorous mammal of the dog family, with short legs and small ears. It is native to the forests of Central and South America. • *Speothus venaticus,* family Canidae.

bushed /bŏŏsht/ ▸*adj. informal* tired out: *after three days of training, the rookies were totally bushed.*

bush·el /ˈbŏŏshəl/ (abbr.: **bu.**) ▸*n.* **1** a measure of capacity equal to 64 U.S. pints (equivalent to 35.2 liters), used for dry goods. ■ *figurative* a large amount: *we sold it for a bushel of money.* **2** *Brit.* a measure of capacity equal to 8 imperial gallons (equivalent to 36.4 liters), used for dry goods and liquids. **3** a container with the capacity of a bushel: [as *adj.*] *packing oysters into* ***bushel baskets.*** ▷Middle English: from Old French *boissel,* perhaps of Gaulish origin. **—bush·el·ful** /-,fŏŏl/ *n.* (*pl.* **-fuls**) .
▸*PHRASE* □ **hide one's light under a bushel** see HIDE[1].

bush fire (also **bush·fire**) ▸*n.* a fire in scrub or a forest, esp. one that spreads rapidly: *figurative news of discontent igniting a bush fire of revolt.*

bu·shi·do /ˈbŏŏshēdō/ ▸*n.* the code of honor and morals developed by the Japanese samurai. ▷Japanese, from *bushi* 'samurai' + *dō* 'way.'

bush·ing /ˈbŏŏshiNG/ ▸*n.* a metal lining for a round hole enclosing a revolving shaft. ■ more generally, a bearing for a revolving shaft. ■ a clamp that grips and protects an electric cable where it passes through a metal panel.

Bush·ism /ˈbŏŏsh,izəm/ ▸*n. informal* **1** a linguistic gaffe of President George H. W. Bush or President George W. Bush. **2** the policies or political philosophy of President George H. W. Bush or President George W. Bush: *Bushism is feel-good politics, adding self-satisfaction to the material comfort of the comfortable.*

bush jack·et ▸*n.* a belted cotton jacket with patch pockets.

bush league ▸*n.* a minor league of a professional sport, esp. baseball: [as *adj.*] *their bush league image.*
▸*adj.* (**bush-league**) *informal* not of the highest quality or sophistication; second-rate. **—bush lea·guer** *n.*

Bush·man /ˈbŏŏshmən/ ▸*n.* (*pl.* **-men**) **1** a member of any of several aboriginal peoples of southern Africa, esp. of the Kalahari Desert. They are traditionally nomadic hunter-gatherers. Also called SAN. [influenced by Dutch *boschjesman.*] **2** the language of these peoples, now usually called SAN. **3** (**bushman**) a person who lives, works, or travels in the Australian bush.

bush·mas·ter /ˈbŏŏsh,mastər/ ▸*n.* a pit viper that is the largest venomous snake in the New World, found in Central and South America. • *Lachesis muta,* family Viperidae. ▷early 19th cent.: perhaps from obsolete Dutch *boschmeester* (now *bosmeester*), from *bos* 'bush' + *meester* 'master.'

bush·meat /ˈbŏŏsh,mēt/ ▸*n.* the meat of African wild animals.

bush pig (also **African bush pig**) ▸*n.* a wild pig native to the forests and savannas of Africa and Madagascar. • *Potamochoerus porcus* and *P. larvatus,* family Suidae.

bush pi·lot ▸*n.* one who flies small aircraft into remote areas.

bush·rang·er /ˈbŏŏsh,rānjər/ ▸*n.* a person living far from civilization. ■ *Austral., historical* an outlaw living in the bush.

bush tea ▸*n.* a tea made from dried leaves and twigs of various shrubs, esp. in tropical countries.

bush tel·e·graph ▸*n.* [in *sing.*] a rapid informal network by which information or gossip is spread.

bush·tit /ˈbŏŏsh,tit/ (also **bush tit**) ▸*n.* a small American songbird of the long-tailed tit family, with mainly pale gray plumage and sometimes a black mask. • *Psaltriparus minimus,* family Aegithalidae (formerly Paridae); formerly regarded as two species.

bush·wa /ˈbŏŏshwä/ (also **bush·wah**) ▸*n. informal* rubbish; nonsense. ▷early 20th cent.: from French *bourgeois,* now used as a euphemism for BULLSHIT.

bush·walk·ing /ˈbŏŏsh,wôkiNG/ ▸*n. chiefly Austral./NZ* hiking or backpacking. **—bush·walk·er** /-,wôkər/ *n.*

bush·whack /ˈbŏŏsh,(h)wak/ ▸*v.* **1** [*intrans.*] [often as *n.*] (**bushwhacking**) live or travel in wild or uncultivated country: *I have not seen a bear yet after seven days of bushwhacking.* ■ [with *adverbial of direction*] cut or push one's way in a specified direction through dense vegetation: *he'd bushwhacked down the steep slopes.* **2** [*intrans.*] fight as a guerrilla in the bush. ■ [*trans.*] make a surprise attack on (someone) from a hidden place; ambush.

bush·whack·er /ˈbŏŏsh,(h)wakər/ ▸*n.* **1** a person who clears woods and bush country. ■ a person who lives or travels in bush country. **2** a guerrilla fighter (originally in the American Civil War).

bush·y /ˈbŏŏshē/ ▸*adj.* (**bush·i·er, bush·i·est**) **1** growing thickly into or so as to resemble a bush: *a dense, bushy plant | his eyebrows were thick and bushy.* **2** covered with bush or bushes: *bushy desert areas.* **—bush·i·ly** /ˈbŏŏshəlē/ *adv.* **—bush·i·ness** *n.*

busi·ness /ˈbiznis/ (**bus.**) ▸*n.* **1** a person's regular occupation, profession, or trade: *she had to do a lot of smiling in her business | are you here* ***on business?*** ■ an activity that someone is engaged in: *what is your business here?* ■ a person's concern: *this is none of your business | the neighbors make it their business to know all about you.* ■ work that has to be done or matters that have to be attended to: *government business | let's get down to business.* **2** the practice of making one's living by engaging in commerce: *the world of business | whom do you* ***do business with*** *in Manila?* | [as *adj.*] *the business community* | [with *adj.*] *the jewelry business.* ■ trade considered in terms of its volume or profitability: *how's business?* ■ a commercial house or firm: *a catering business.* **3** [in *sing.*] *informal* an affair or series of events, typically a scandalous or discreditable one: *they must be told about this blackmailing business.* ■ *informal* a group of related or previously mentioned things: *use carrots, cauliflower, and broccoli, and serve the whole business hot.* **4** *Theater* actions other than dialogue performed by actors: *a piece of business.* **5** *informal* a scolding; harsh verbal criticism: *the supervisor really* ***gave him the business.*** ▷Old English *bisignis* (see BUSY, -NESS). The sense in Old English was 'anxiety'; the sense 'the state of being busy' was used from Middle English down to the 18th cent., but is now differentiated as *busyness.* The sense 'an appointed task' dates from late Middle English, and from it all the other current senses have developed.
▸*PHRASES* □ **business as usual** an unchanging state of affairs despite difficulties or disturbances: *apart from being under new management, it's business as usual in the department.* □ **have no business** have no right to do something or be somewhere: *he had no business tampering with social services.* □ **in business** operating, esp. in commerce: *they will have to import from overseas to remain in business.* ■ *informal* able to begin operations: *if you'll contact the right people, I think we'll be in business.* □ **in the business of** engaged in or prepared to engage in: *I am not in the business of making accusations.* □ **like nobody's business** *informal* to an extraordinarily high degree or standard: *these weeds spread like nobody's business.* □ **mean business** be in earnest. □ **mind one's own business** refrain from meddling in other people's affairs: *he was yelling at her to get out and mind her own business.* □ **send someone about his/her business** *dated* tell someone to go away.

busi·ness card ▸*n.* a small card printed with one's name, professional occupation, company position, business address, and other contact information.

busi·ness cy·cle ▸*n.* a cycle or series of cycles of economic expansion and contraction.

busi·ness day ▸*n.* another term for WORKDAY.

busi·ness dou·ble ▸*n. Bridge* a double made with the intention of increasing the penalty points scored by a partnership if they defeat their opponents' contract. Often contrasted with TAKEOUT DOUBLE.

busi·ness end ▸*n. informal* (**the business end**) the functional part of a tool, device, or weapon: *he found himself facing the business end of six lethal-looking weapons.* ■ the essential or basic part of a process or operation: *the rigs are the business end of the oil industry.*

busi·ness hours ▸*plural n.* another term for OFFICE HOURS.

busi·ness·like /ˈbiznis,līk/ ▸*adj.* (of a person) carrying out tasks efficiently without wasting time or being distracted by personal or other concerns; systematic and practical. ■ (of clothing, furniture, etc.) designed or appearing to be practical rather than decorative. ■ excessively brisk or practical; severe or impersonal: *he was businesslike and unmoved.*

busi·ness·man /ˈbiznisˌman; -mən/ ▸*n.* (*pl.* **-men**) a man who works in business or commerce, esp. at an executive level. ▪ [with *adj.*] a person with a specified level of skill in financial matters: *his knowledge and talent were never in question, but he was a poor businessman.*

busi·ness mod·el ▸*n.* a design for the successful operation business, identifying revenue sources, customer base, products, and details of financing: *many of the free sites have either shifted their business model or have gone out of business completely.*

busi·ness park ▸*n.* an area where company offices and light industrial premises are built.

busi·ness per·son (also **busi·ness·per·son**) ▸*n.* a man or woman who works in business or commerce, esp. at an executive level.

busi·ness proc·ess re·en·gi·neer·ing (abbr.: **BPR**) ▸*n.* the process or activity of restructuring a company's organization and methods, esp. to exploit the capabilities of computers.

busi·ness stud·ies ▸*plural n.* [treated as *sing.*] the study of economics and management, esp. as an educational topic.

busi·ness·wom·an /ˈbiznisˌwŏŏmən/ ▸*n.* a woman who works in business or commerce, esp. at an executive level. ▪ [with *adj.*] a woman with a specified level of skill in financial affairs: *she has become quite the savvy* ***businesswoman.***

busk[1] /bəsk/ ▸*v.* [*intrans.*] play music or otherwise perform for voluntary donations in the street or in subways: *the group began by busking on Philadelphia sidewalks* | [as *n.*] (**busking**) *busking was a real means of living.* ▪ (**busk it**) *informal* improvise. ▷mid 17th cent.: from obsolete French *busquer* 'seek,' from Italian *buscare* or Spanish *buscar*, of Germanic origin. Originally in nautical use in the sense 'cruise about, tack,' the term later meant 'go around selling,' hence 'go around performing' (mid 19th cent.). **—busk·er** *n.*

busk[2] ▸*n. historical* a stay or stiffening strip for a corset. ▷late 16th cent.: from French *busc*, from Italian *busco* 'splinter' (related to French *bûche* 'log'), of Germanic origin.

bus·kin /ˈbəskin/ ▸*n. chiefly historical* a calf-high or knee-high boot of cloth or leather. ▪ a thick-soled laced boot worn by an ancient Athenian tragic actor to gain height. ▪ (**the buskin**) the style or spirit of tragic drama. ▷early 16th cent. (designating a calf-length boot): probably from Old French *bouzequin*, variant of *brousequin*, from Middle Dutch *broseken*, of unknown ultimate origin. **—bus·kined** *adj.*

bus lane /ˈbəs ˌlān/ ▸*n.* a division of a road marked off with painted lines for use by buses.

bus·man /ˈbəsmən/ ▸*n.* (*pl.* **-men**) a driver of a bus.
▸***PHRASE*** □ **a busman's holiday** a vacation or form of recreation that involves doing the same thing that one does at work.

buss /bəs/ *archaic or informal* ▸*n.* a kiss.
▸*v.* [*trans.*] kiss. ▷late 16th cent.: alteration of late Middle English *bass* (noun and verb), probably from French *baiser*, from Latin *basiare*.

bus shel·ter ▸*n.* a roofed structure for people to wait under at a bus stop.

bus sta·tion ▸*n.* a terminal where buses arrive and depart.

bus stop ▸*n.* a place where a bus regularly stops, typically marked by a sign.

bust[1] /bəst/ ▸*n.* **1** a woman's chest as measured around her breasts: *a 36-inch bust.* ▪ a woman's breasts, esp. considered in terms of their size: *selecting clothes that would minimize her big bust.* **2** a sculpture of a person's head, shoulders, and chest. ▷mid 17th cent. (denoting the upper part or torso of a large sculpture): from French *buste*, from Italian *busto*, from Latin *bustum* 'tomb, sepulchral monument.'

bust[2] *informal* ▸*v.* (*past* and *past part.* **bust·ed** or **bust**) [*trans.*] **1** break, split, or burst (something): *they bust the tunnel wide open* | *figurative the film busts every box-office record.* ▪ [*intrans.*] come apart or split open: *figurative he was laughing* ***fit to bust.*** ▪ cause to collapse; defeat utterly: *he promised to bust the mafia.* ▪ [*intrans.*] (**bust up**) (esp. of a married couple) separate, typically after a quarrel. ▪ (**bust something up**) cause (something) to break up: *men hired to bust up union rallies.* ▪ strike violently: *they wanted to bust me on the mouth.* ▪ [*intrans.*] (**bust out**) break out; escape: *she* ***busted out of*** *prison.* ▪ [*intrans.*] (in blackjack and similar card games) exceed the score of 21, losing one's stake. **2** raid or search (premises where illegal activity is suspected): *their house got busted.* ▪ arrest: *he was* ***busted for*** *drugs.* ▪ reduce (a soldier) to a lower rank; demote: *he was* ***busted to*** *private.*
▸*n.* **1** a period of economic difficulty or depression: *the boom was followed by the present bust.* **2** a police raid: *a drug bust.* **3** a worthless thing: *as a show it was a bust.*
▸*adj.* bankrupt: *firms will* ***go bust.*** ▷mid 18th cent. (originally as a noun in the sense 'an act of bursting or splitting'): variant of **BURST**.

bus·tard /ˈbəstərd/ ▸*n.* a large, heavily built, swift-running bird, found in open country in the Old World. The males of most bustards have a spectacular courtship display. • Family Otididae: several genera and species, including the **great bustard** (*Otis tarda*), which is the heaviest flying land bird. ▷late 15th cent.: perhaps an Anglo-Norman French blend of Old French *bistarde* and *oustarde*, both from Latin *avis tarda* 'slow bird': the name is unexplained, as the bustards are fast runners.

bus·tard quail ▸*n.* the barred button quail (see **BUTTON QUAIL**).

bus·tee /ˈbəstē/ ▸*n. Indian* a slum area or shanty town. ▷from Hindi *bastī* 'dwelling.'

bust·er /ˈbəstər/ ▸*n. chiefly informal* **1** a person or thing that breaks, destroys, or overpowers something: [in *combination*] *the drug's reputation as a flu-buster.* ▪ short for **BRONCOBUSTER**. **2** *informal* used as a mildly disrespectful or humorous form of address, esp. to a man or boy: *your parents' decisions affect you, like it or not, buster.*

bus·tier /bo͞osˈtyā/ ▸*n.* a close-fitting strapless top worn by women. ▷1970s: from French, from *buste* (see **BUST**[1]).

bus·tle[1] /ˈbəsəl/ ▸*v.* [*intrans.*] move in an energetic or noisy manner: *people clutching clipboards bustled about.* ▪ [*trans.*] make (someone) move hurriedly in a particular direction: *she bustled us into the kitchen.* ▪ [*intrans.*] (of a place) be full of activity: *the small harbor* ***bustled with*** *boats* | [as *adj.*] (**bustling**) *the bustling little town.*
▸*n.* excited activity and movement: *all the noise and the traffic and the bustle.* ▷late Middle English: perhaps a variant of obsolete *buskle*, frequentative of *busk* 'prepare,' from Old Norse.

bus·tle[2] ▸*n. historical* a pad or frame worn under a skirt and puffing it out behind. ▷late 18th cent.: of unknown origin.

bust·y /ˈbəstē/ ▸*adj.* (**bust·i·er**, **bust·i·est**) *informal* (of a woman) having large breasts. **—bust·i·ness** *n.*

bus·way /ˈbəsˌwā/ ▸*n.* a road, or section of a road, set apart exclusively for buses, typically with tracks or grooves for guiding them.

bus·y /ˈbizē/ ▸*adj.* (**bus·i·er**, **bus·i·est**) having a great deal to do: *he had been too busy to enjoy himself* | *there was enough work to keep two people busy.* ▪ occupied with or concentrating on a particular activity or object of attention: *the team members are busy raising money* | *he was* ***busy with*** *preparations.* ▪ (of a place) full of activity. ▪ excessively detailed or decorated; fussy: *they papered the bedroom with a busy pattern of satyrs and dryads.* ▪ (of a telephone line) engaged.
▸*v.* (**bus·ies**, **bus·ied**) [*trans.*] (**busy oneself**) keep occupied: *she* ***busied herself with*** *her new home.* ▷Old English *bisgian* (verb), *bisig* (noun); related to Dutch *bezig.* **—bus·i·ly** /-lē/ *adv.* **—bus·y·ness** *n.*

THE RIGHT WORD **assiduous, busy, diligent, engaged, industrious, sedulous**

There are varying degrees of busyness. **Busy** implies actively and attentively involved in work or a pastime (*too busy to come to the phone*). It can also be used to describe intensive activity of any kind (*a busy intersection; a busy day*).

Someone who is **engaged** is also *busy*, but in a more focused way (*engaged in compiling a dictionary*).

Diligent is used to describe earnest and constant effort, and it often connotes enjoyment of or dedication to what one is doing (*diligent efforts to rescue injured animals*).

To be **industrious** is to be more focused still, often with a definite goal in mind (*an industrious employee working for a promotion*).

Sedulous also applies to goal-oriented activity, but it suggests more close care and perseverance than *industrious* does (*a sedulous investigation of the accident*).

The award for concentrated effort goes to the person who is **assiduous**, which suggests painstaking preoccupation with a specific task (*an assiduous student is the one most likely to win his or her teacher's favor*).

bus·y bee ▸*n. informal* an industrious person.

bus·y·bod·y /ˈbizēˌbädē/ ▸*n.* (*pl.* **-bod·ies**) a meddling or prying person.

bus·y sig·nal ▸*n.* a sound indicating that a telephone line is engaged, typically a repeated single bleep.

bus·y·work /ˈbizēˌwərk/ ▸*n.* work that keeps a person busy but has little value in itself.

but /bət/ ▸*conj.* **1** used to introduce something contrasting with what has already been mentioned: ▪ nevertheless; however: *he stumbled but didn't fall* | *this is one principle, but it is not the only one.* ▪ on the contrary; in contrast: *I am clean but you are dirty* | *the problem is not that they are cutting down trees, but that they are doing it in a predatory way.* **2** [with *negative* or in *questions*] used to indicate the impossibility of anything other than what is being stated: *one* ***cannot but*** *sympathize* | *there was nothing they could do but swallow their pride* | *they had no alternative but to follow.* **3** used to introduce a response expressing a feeling such as surprise or anger: *but that's an incredible saving!* | *but why?* **4** used after an expression of apology for what one is about to say: *I'm sorry, but I can't pay you.* **5** [with *negative*] *archaic* without its being the case that: *it never rains but it pours.*
▸*prep.* except; apart from; other than: *in Texas, we were never anything but poor* | *I trusted no one but him* | *the last but one.* ▪ used with repetition of certain words to give emphasis: *nobody, but nobody, was going to stop her.*
▸*adv.* no more than; only: *he is but a shadow of his former self* | *choose from a colorful array of oranges, cherries, and raspberries, to name but a few.*
▸*n.* an argument against something; an objection: ***no buts****—just get out of here* | *as with all these proposals,* ***ifs and buts*** *abound.* ▷Old English *be-ūtan, būtan, būta* 'outside, without, except' (see **BY**, **OUT**).
▸***PHRASES*** □ **all but** see **ALL**. □ **anything but** see **ANYTHING**. □ **but for** except for: *I walked along Broadway, deserted but for the occasional cab.* ▪ if it were not for: *the game could be over but for you.* □ **but me no buts** do not raise objections. □ **but that** *archaic* other than that; except that: *who knows but that the pictures painted on air are eternal.* □ **but then** on the other hand; that being so: *it's a very hard exam, but then they all are.*

USAGE For advice about using **but** and other conjunctions to begin a sentence, see **usage** at **AND**.

bu·ta·di·ene /ˌbyo͞otəˈdīēn/ ▸*n. Chemistry* a colorless gaseous hydrocarbon made by catalytic dehydrogenation of butane and used in the manufacture of synthetic rubber. • Chem. formula: $CH_2{=}CHCH{=}CH_2$. ▷early 20th cent.: from **BUTANE** + **DI-**[1] + **-ENE**.

bu·tane /ˈbyo͞oˌtān/ ▸*n. Chemistry* a flammable hydrocarbon gas that is a constituent of petroleum and is used in bottled form as a fuel. It is a member of the alkane series. See also **ISOBUTANE**. • Chem. formula: $CH_3CH_2CH_2CH_3$. ▷late 19th cent.: from **BUTYL** + **-ANE**[2].

bu·ta·no·ic ac·id /ˌbyo͞otnˈōik/ ▸*n.* systematic chemical name for **BUTYRIC ACID**. **—bu·ta·no·ate** /ˌbyo͞otnˈōˌāt; byo͞oˈtanəˌwāt/ *n.*

bu·ta·nol /ˈbyo͞otnˌôl; -ˌäl/ ▸*n. Chemistry* each of two isomeric liquid alcohols used as solvents; butyl alcohol. • Chem. formula: $CH_3CH_2CH_2CH_2OH$ (**1-butanol, butan-1-ol**) and $CH_3CH_2CH(OH)CH_3$ (**2-butanol, butan-2-ol**).

Bu·ta·zo·li·din /ˌbyo͞otəˈzälidin/ ▸*n. trademark* a preparation of phenylbutazone used to reduce pain and inflammation.

butch /bo͝oCH/ *informal* ▸*adj.* manlike or masculine in appearance or behavior, typically aggressively or ostentatiously so.
▸*n.* a mannish lesbian, often contrasted with a more feminine partner. Compare with **FEMME**. ▷1940s: perhaps an abbreviation of **BUTCHER**.

butch·er /ˈbo͝oCHər/ ▸*n.* **1** a person whose trade is cutting up and selling meat in a shop. ▪ a person who slaughters and cuts up animals for food: [with *adj.*] *a pork butcher.* ▪ a person who kills or has people killed indiscriminately or brutally: *the Nazi death camp butcher.* **2** *informal* a person selling refreshments, newspapers, and other items on a train or in a stadium or theater.
▸*v.* [*trans.*] (often **be butchered**) slaughter or cut up (an animal) for food: *the meat will be butchered for the local market.* ▪ kill (someone) brutally: *they butchered 250 people.* ▪ *figurative* ruin (something) deliberately or through incompetence: *the film was butchered by the studio that released it.* ▷Middle English: from an Anglo-Norman French variant of Old French *bochier*, from *boc* 'he-goat,' probably of the same ultimate origin as **BUCK**[1].

butch·er·bird /ˈbo͝oCHərˌbərd/ ▸*n.* **1** a shrike (family Laniidae) that impales its prey on thorns. **2** a crow-like predacious Australasian songbird, with a heavy hook-tipped bill. Compare with MAGPIE (sense 2). • Family Cracticidae: three genera, in particular *Cracticus*, and several species. ▷mid 17th cent.: from its habit of impaling its prey on thorns.

butch·er block ▸*n.* a material used to make kitchen worktops and tables, consisting of strips of hardwood glued together: *a slab of butcher block* | [as *adj.*] *a butcher-block table.*

butch·er knife ▸*n.* a large, broad-bladed knife used for cutting meat.

butch·er's block /ˈbo͝ocHərz ˌbläk/ ▸*n.* a sturdy wooden kitchen table with a square top on which food may be chopped.

butch·er's broom ▸*n.* a low evergreen Eurasian shrub of the lily family, with flat shoots that give the appearance of stiff, spine-tipped leaves. • *Ruscus aculeatus*, family Liliaceae.

butch·er·y /ˈbo͝ocHərē/ ▸*n.* (*pl.* **-er·ies**) the savage killing of large numbers of people. ■ the work of slaughtering animals and preparing them for sale as meat. ▷Middle English (denoting a slaughterhouse or meat market): from Old French *boucherie*, from *bouchier* 'butcher.'

butch haircut ▸*n.* a haircut that is trimmed very close to the head; crewcut.

bute /byo͞ot/ ▸*n.* informal term for PHENYLBUTAZONE.

bu·te·o /ˈbyo͞otēō/ ▸*n.* a bird of prey of a group distinguished by broad wings that are used for soaring. • *Buteo* and related genera, family Accipitridae; many species, including the buzzards and the red-tailed and Harris's hawks. ▷from Latin *buteo* 'buzzard, hawk.'

Bu·tey·ko meth·od /bo͞oˈtākō / ▸*n.* a technique of controlled breathing that is claimed to alleviate asthma. ▷1990s: named after Ukrainian physiologist Konstantin *Buteyko* (1923–2003), who devised the technique.

Bu·the·le·zi /ˌbo͞otlˈäzē/, Chief Mangosuthu (Gatsha) (1928–), South African politician. He was elected leader of Zululand (later KwaZulu) in 1970 and was responsible for the revival of the Inkatha movement. He became minister of home affairs in 1994.

But·kus /ˈbətkis/, Dick (1942–), U.S. football player; full name *Richard Marvin Butkus*. A middle linebacker for the Chicago Bears 1965–73, he was named to the National Football League's (NFL) All-Pro team seven times. Football Hall of Fame (1979).

But·ler[1] /ˈbətlər/, Pierce (1866–1939), U.S. Supreme Court associate justice 1922–39. A conservative, he was appointed to the Court by President Harding.

But·ler[2], Samuel (1612–80), English poet, most notable for his three-part satirical poem *Hudibras* (1663–78).

But·ler[3], Samuel (1835–1902), English novelist. Notable works: *Erewhon* (1872), *Erewhon Revisited* (1901), and *The Way of All Flesh* (1903).

but·ler /ˈbətlər/ ▸*n.* the chief manservant of a house. ▷Middle English: from Old French *bouteillier* 'cupbearer,' from *bouteille* 'bottle.'

but·ler's pan·try ▸*n.* a small service and storage room between a kitchen and a dining room.

butt[1] /bət/ ▸*v.* [*trans.*] (of a person or animal) hit (someone or something) with the head or horns: *she* ***butted*** *him* ***in*** *the chest with her head.* ■ strike (the head) against something: *he* ***butts*** *his head* ***against*** *a wall.*

▸*phrasal v.* □ **butt in** take part in a conversation or activity, or enter somewhere, without being invited or expected: *sorry to* ***butt in*** *on you.* □ **butt out** *informal* stop interfering: *anyone who tries to cut across our policies should butt out.*

▸*n.* a push or blow, typically given with the head: *he would follow up with a butt from his head.* ▷Middle English: from Old French *boter*, of Germanic origin.

▸*PHRASE* □ **butt heads** engage in conflict or be in strong disagreement: *the residents continue to butt heads with the mall developers.*

butt[2] ▸*n.* the person or thing at which criticism or humor, typically unkind, is directed: *his singing is the butt of dozens of jokes.* ■ (usu. **butts**) an archery or shooting target or range. ■ a mound on or in front of which a target is set up for archery or shooting. ▷Middle English (in the archery sense): from Old French *but*, of unknown origin; perhaps influenced by French *butte* 'rising ground.'

butt[3] ▸*n.* **1** (also **butt end**) the thicker end, esp. of a tool or a weapon: *a rifle butt.* ■ the square end of a plank or plate meeting the end or side of another, as in the side of a ship. ■ the thicker or hinder end of a hide used for leather. **2** (also **butt end**) the stub of a cigar or a cigarette: *the ashtray was crammed with cigarette butts.* **3** *informal* the buttocks. ■ the anus. **4** the trunk of a tree, esp. the part just above the ground.

▸*v.* [*intrans.*] adjoin or meet end to end: *the church* ***butted up against*** *the row of houses* | *a garden that* ***butted up to*** *the neighbor's.* ■ [*trans.*] join (pieces of stone, lumber, and other building materials) with the ends or sides flat against each other: *the floorboards will be* ***butted up against*** *each other to make tight seams.* ▷late Middle English: the noun apparently related to Dutch *bot* 'stumpy,' also to BUTTOCK; the verb partly from BUTT[2], reinforced by ABUT.

butt[4] ▸*n.* a cask, typically used for wine, ale, or water. ■ a liquid measure equal to 2 hogsheads (equivalent to 126 U.S. gallons). ▷late Middle English: from Old French *bot*, from late Latin *buttis*.

Butte /byo͞ot/ a city in southwestern Montana, noted as a mining center; pop. 33,336.

butte /byo͞ot/ ▸*n.* *technical* an isolated hill with steep sides and a flat top (similar to but narrower than a mesa). ▷mid 19th cent.: from French, 'mound,' from Old French *but*, of unknown origin (compare with BUTT[2]).

but·ter /ˈbətər/ ▸*n.* a pale yellow edible fatty substance made by churning cream and used as a spread or in cooking. ■ [with *adj.*] a substance of a similar consistency: *cocoa butter.*

▸*v.* [*trans.*] spread (something) with butter: *she buttered the toast* | [as *adj.*] (**buttered**) *lavishly buttered bread.*

▸*phrasal v.* □ **butter someone up** *informal* flatter or otherwise ingratiate oneself with someone. ▷Old English *butere*, of West Germanic origin; related to Dutch *boter* and German *Butter*, based on Latin *butyrum*, from Greek *bouturon* 'cow cheese'.

▸*PHRASE* □ **look as if butter wouldn't melt in one's mouth** *informal* appear gentle or innocent while typically being the opposite.

but·ter-and-eggs ▸*n.* see TOADFLAX.

but·ter·ball /ˈbətərˌbôl/ ▸*n.* *informal derogatory* a fat person. ■ a plump bird, esp. a turkey or bufflehead.

but·ter bean ▸*n.* a lima bean, esp. one of a variety with large flat white seeds that are usually dried.

but·ter·bur /ˈbətərˌbər/ ▸*n.* a Eurasian waterside plant of the daisy family, the rounded flowerheads of which are produced before the leaves. The large soft leaves were formerly used to wrap butter, and extracts of the plant have long been used medicinally as a powerful anticonvulsant. • Genus *Petasites*, family Compositae: several species, in particular the common *P. hybridus*.

but·ter·cream /ˈbətərˌkrēm/ ▸*n.* a soft mixture of butter and powdered sugar used as a filling or topping for a cake.

but·ter·cup /ˈbətərˌkəp/ ▸*n.* a herbaceous plant with bright yellow cup-shaped flowers, common in grassland and as a garden weed. All kinds are poisonous and generally avoided by livestock. • Genus *Ranunculus*, family Ranunculaceae (the **buttercup family**): numerous species, including the very familiar **common buttercup** (*R. acris*). This large family also includes anemones, celandines, aconites, clematises, and hellebores, many of which have poisonous seeds.

but·ter·cup squash ▸*n.* a winter squash of a variety with dark green skin and orange flesh.

but·ter·fat /ˈbətərˌfat/ ▸*n.* the natural fat contained in milk and dairy products.

but·ter·fin·gers /ˈbətərˌfiNGgərz/ ▸*n.* (*pl.* same) *informal* a clumsy person, esp. one who fails to hold a catch. ■ clumsiness in handling something: *fumbling for the ball with butterfingers.* **—but·ter·fin·gered** *adj.*

but·ter·fish /ˈbətərˌfisH/ ▸*n.* (*pl.* same or **-fish·es**) any of a number of fishes with oily flesh or slippery skin, in particular: • a deep-bodied edible fish of temperate and tropical seas (family Stromateidae), in particular *Peprilus triacanthus* of eastern North America. • another term for GUNNEL[1]. • an Australasian reef fish (family Odacidae), in particular the edible *Odax pullus* of New Zealand, which has green bones and feeds on kelp. • a tropical freshwater or marine fish that is popular in aquariums (several families, including Scatophagidae).

but·ter·fly /ˈbətərˌflī/ ▸*n.* (*pl.* **-flies**) an insect with two pairs of large wings that are covered with tiny scales, usually brightly colored, and typically held erect when at rest. Butterflies fly by day, have clubbed or dilated antennae, and usually feed on nectar. • Superfamilies Papilionoidea and Hesperioidea, order Lepidoptera: several families. Formerly placed in a grouping known as the Rhopalocera. Compare with MOTH. ■ a showy or frivolous person: *a social butterfly.* ■ (**butterflies**) *informal* a fluttering and nauseated sensation felt in the stomach when one is nervous. ■ (in full **butterfly stroke**) [in *sing.*] a stroke in swimming in which both arms are raised out of the water and lifted forward together. ■ [as *adj.*] having a two-lobed shape resembling the spread wings of a butterfly: *a butterfly clip.*

▸*v.* (**-flies**, **-flied**) [*trans.*] split (a piece of meat) almost in two and spread it out flat: [as *adj.*] (**butterflied**) *butterflied shrimp.* ▷Old English, from BUTTER + FLY[2]; perhaps from the cream or yellow color of common species, or from an old belief that the insects stole butter.

but·ter·fly bush ▸*n.* a Chinese buddleia that is cultivated in the West for its large spikes of fragrant purplish-lilac or white flowers, which are highly attractive to butterflies. • *Buddleia davidii*, family Loganiaceae.

but·ter·fly ef·fect ▸*n.* (with reference to chaos theory) the phenomenon whereby a minute localized change in a complex system can have large effects elsewhere. ▷1980s: from the notion that a butterfly fluttering in Rio de Janeiro could change the weather in Chicago.

but·ter·fly·fish ▸*n.* **1** any of a number of typically brightly colored or boldly marked fish of warm waters, in particular: • a reef-dwelling fish that is popular in marine aquariums (*Chaetodon* and other genera, family Chaetodontidae). • a predatory marine fish that bears long venomous spines (genus *Pterois*, family Scorpaenidae). **2** a West African freshwater fish with large pectoral fins used in leaping out of the water and long fin rays used as stilts. • *Pantodon buchholzi*, the only member of the family Pantodontidae.

but·ter·fly knife ▸*n.* a long broad knife used in pairs in some forms of kung fu.

but·ter·fly net ▸*n.* a fine-meshed bag supported on a frame at the end of a handle for catching butterflies. ■ *figurative, humorous* such a net supposedly dropped over a person in order to take the person away to a mental hospital: *the men with the butterfly nets will be sitting on the foot of my bed.*

but·ter·fly nut ▸*n.* another term for WING NUT.

but·ter·fly or·chid ▸*n.* an epiphytic wild orchid of South America with large yellow and red flowers that somewhat resemble a butterfly in shape. • *Oncidium papilio*, family Orchidaceae.

but·ter·fly stroke ▸*n.* another term for BUTTERFLY (in swimming).

but·ter·fly valve ▸*n.* **1** a valve consisting of a disk rotating on an axis across the diameter of a pipe to regulate the flow, as in the throttles of many engines. **2** a valve consisting of a pair of semicircular plates that are attached to a spindle across a pipe and hinged to allow flow only one way.

but·ter·fly weed ▸*n.* a North American milkweed with bright orange flowers that are attractive to butterflies. • *Asclepias tuberosa*, family Asclepiadaceae.

but·ter·head let·tuce /ˈbətərˌhed ˈletəs/ ▸*n.* a class of lettuce varieties having soft leaves that grow in a loose head.

but·ter ic·ing ▸*n.* another term for BUTTERCREAM.

but·ter knife ▸*n.* a blunt knife used for cutting or spreading butter or other similar spreads.

but·ter·milk /ˈbətərˌmilk/ ▸*n.* the slightly sour liquid left after butter has been churned, used in baking or consumed as a drink. ■ a pale yellow color (used esp. to describe paint or wallpaper): [as *adj.*] *buttermilk paintwork.*

but·ter·nut /ˈbətərˌnət/ ▸*n.* **1** a North American walnut tree that bears oblong sticky fruits. Its light-colored, soft timber is useful primarily for making furniture and cabinetry. Also called WHITE WALNUT. • *Juglans cinerea*, family Juglandaceae. ■ the edible oily nut of this tree. **2** *historical, informal* a Confederate soldier or supporter (so called because the fabric of the Confederate uniform was typically homespun and dyed with butternut extract).

but·ter·nut squash ▸*n.* a popular winter squash of a variety that has a bell-shaped fruit with sweet orange-yellow flesh.

but·ter·scotch /ˈbətərˌskäcH/ ▸*n.* a flavor created originally by combining melted butter with brown sugar: [as *adj.*] *butterscotch syrup.* ■ a candy with this flavor.

but·ter·weed /ˈbətərˌwēd/ ▸*n.* a yellow-flowered plant of the daisy family, closely related to ragwort.

• Genus *Senecio*, family Compositae: several species, including the **common butterweed** (*S. vulgaris*) of the Pacific states and **Bolander's butterweed** (*S. bolanderi*), found esp. along the Pacific coast of North America.

but·ter·wort /ˈbətər,wərt; -,wôrt/ ▸*n.* a carnivorous bog plant that has violet flowers borne above a rosette of yellowish-green greasy leaves that trap and digest small insects. It is native to both Eurasia and North America. • Genus *Pinguicula*, family Lentibulariaceae: several species, in particular the **common butterwort** (*P. vulgaris*). ▷late 16th cent.

but·ter·y[1] /ˈbətərē/ ▸*adj.* containing or tasting like butter: *layers of flaky buttery pastry.* ■ covered with butter: *buttery fingers.* —**but·ter·i·ness** *n.*

but·ter·y[2] ▸*n.* (*pl.* **-ter·ies**) a pantry, or a room for storing wine and liquor. ■ *Brit.* a room, esp. in a college, where food is kept and sold to students. ▷Middle English: from Anglo-Norman French *boterie* 'storeroom for casks,' from Old French *bot* (see BUTT[4]).

butt hinge ▸*n.* a hinge attached to the abutting surfaces of a door and a door jamb.

butt·in·sky /bətˈinskē/ ▸*n.* (*pl.* **-skies**) a person who habitually butts in; an intruder or meddler.

butt joint ▸*n.* (of wood, metal, etc.) a joint formed by two surfaces abutting at right angles.

but·tle /ˈbətl/ ▸*v.* [*intrans.*] *humorous* work as a butler: *there is no one today worth* ***buttling for.*** ▷mid 19th cent.: back-formation from BUTLER.

but·tock /ˈbətək/ ▸*n.* either of the two round fleshy parts that form the lower rear area of a human trunk. ■ (**buttocks**) the rump of an animal. ▷Old English *buttuc*, probably from the base of BUTT[3] + -OCK.

but·ton /ˈbətn/ ▸*n.* a small disk or knob sewn on to a garment, either to fasten it by being pushed through a slit made for the purpose, or for decoration: *a blouse with five buttons in front* | [as *adj.*] *button thread.* ■ a knob on a piece of electrical or electronic equipment that is pressed to operate it. ■ a badge bearing a design or slogan and pinned to the clothing. ■ a small, round object resembling a button: *chocolate buttons.* ■ *Fencing* a knob fitted to the point of a foil to make it harmless.
▸*v.* [*trans.*] fasten (clothing) with buttons: *he* ***buttoned up*** *his jacket.* ■ (**button someone into**) fasten the buttons of a garment being worn by (someone): *he buttoned himself into the raincoat.* ■ [*intrans.*] (of a garment) be fastened with buttons: *a dress that buttons down the front.* ■ (**button it**) [often in *imperative*] *informal* stop talking.
▸*phrasal v.* □ **button something up 1** *informal* complete or conclude something satisfactorily: *trying to button up a deal.* **2** [often as *adj.*] (**buttoned up**) repress or contain something: *it was repressive enough to keep public opinion buttoned up.* ▷Middle English: from Old French *bouton*, of Germanic origin and related to BUTT[1]. —**but·ton·less** *adj.* —**but·toned** *adj.* [in *combination*] *a gold-buttoned blazer.*
▸*PHRASES* □ **button one's lip** *informal* stop or refrain from talking. □ **on the button** *informal* punctually: *it was nearly visiting hours and she would arrive on the button.* ■ exactly right: *his prediction was right on the button in terms of actual rainfall.* □ **press the button** *informal* initiate an action or train of events, esp. nuclear war. □ **push** (or **press**) **someone's buttons** *informal* arouse or provoke a reaction in someone: *stay cool and don't allow them to push your buttons.*

but·ton·ball tree /ˈbətn,bôl/ ▸*n.* another term for SYCAMORE (sense 1).

but·ton·bush /ˈbətn,bo͝osн/ ▸*n.* a low-growing North American aquatic shrub of the bedstraw family, with small tubular flowers that form globular flowerheads. • *Cephalanthus occidentalis*, family Rubiaceae.

but·ton-down ▸*adj.* [*attrib.*] (of a collar) having points that are buttoned to the garment. ■ (of a shirt) having such a collar. ■ (of a person) conservative or unimaginative.
▸*n.* a shirt with a button-down collar.

but·toned-up ▸*adj.* reserved and not inclined to reveal information: *Fleischer's buttoned-up style.*

but·ton·hole /ˈbətn,hōl/ ▸*n.* a slit made in a garment to receive a button for fastening. ■ *Brit.* a boutonnière.
▸*v.* [*trans.*] **1** *informal* attract the attention of and detain (someone) in conversation, typically against his or her will. **2** make slits for receiving buttons in (a garment).

but·ton·hol·er /ˈbətn,hōlər/ ▸*n.* an attachment for a sewing machine used to make buttonholes.

but·ton·hole stitch ▸*n.* a looped stitch used for edging buttonholes or pieces of material: *the edges are worked in buttonhole stitch.*

but·ton·hook /ˈbətn,ho͝ok/ ▸*n.* **1** a small hook with a long handle for fastening tight buttons (often formerly on buttoned boots or gloves). **2** *Football* a play in which a pass receiver runs straight downfield and then doubles back sharply toward the line of scrimmage.

but·ton man ▸*n. informal* a hired killer.

but·ton mush·room ▸*n.* a young unopened mushroom.

but·ton quail ▸*n.* a small quaillike Old World bird related to the rails, with only three toes. • Family Turnicidae and genus *Turnix*: several species, including the widespread **barred button quail** (*T. suscitator*) of Asia .

But·tons /ˈbətnz/ ▸*n. Brit., informal* a nickname for a liveried pageboy, esp. in pantomimes. ▷mid 19th cent.: from the rows of buttons on his jacket.

but·ton·wood /ˈbətn,wo͝od/ ▸*n.* **1** (also **buttonwood tree**) another term for SYCAMORE (sense 1). **2** either of two mangroves native mainly to tropical America, used in the production of tanbark and for charcoal. • *Conocarpus erectus* (the **button mangrove**) and *Laguncularia racemosa*, family Combretaceae.

but·tress /ˈbətris/ ▸*n.* a projecting support of stone or brick built against a wall. ■ a projecting portion of a hill or mountain. ■ *figurative* a source of defense or support: *there was a demand for a new stable order as a buttress against social collapse.*
▸*v.* [*trans.*] provide (a building or structure) with projecting supports built against its walls: [as *adj.*] (**buttressed**) *a buttressed wall.* ■ *figurative* increase the strength of or justification for; reinforce: *authority was buttressed by religious belief.* ▷Middle English: from Old French (*ars*) *bouterez* 'thrusting (arch),' from *boter* 'to strike, thrust' (see BUTT[1]).

but·tress root ▸ *n.* a tree root whose upper, exposed parts project from the trunk like a buttress.

bu·tut /ˈbo͞o,to͞ot/ ▸*n.* (*pl.* same or **-tuts**) a monetary unit of the Gambia, equal to one hundredth of a dalasi.

bu·tyl /ˈbyo͞otl/ ▸*n.* [as *adj.*] *Chemistry* an alkyl radical $-C_4H_9$, derived from butane: *butyl acetate.* ■ short for BUTYL RUBBER. ▷mid 19th cent.: from BUTYRIC ACID + -YL.

bu·tyl al·co·hol ▸*n.* any of four isomeric alcohols used as solvents and in organic synthesis.

bu·tyl·ate /ˈbyo͞otl,āt/ ▸*v.* [*trans.*] *Chemistry* to combine with a butyl group. —**bu·tyl·a·tion** /,byo͞otlˈāsнən/ *n.*

bu·tyl·at·ed hy·drox·y·an·i·sole /ˈbyo͞otl,ātid hī,drāksēˈanə,sōl/ (abbr.: **BHA**) ▸*n.* a synthetic antioxidant used to preserve fats and oils in food. • Chem. formula: $C_{11}H_{16}O_2$.

bu·tyl·at·ed hy·drox·y·tol·u·ene /hī,drāksēˈtälyo͞o,ēn/ (abbr. **BHT**) ▸*n.* a synthetic antioxidant used to preserve fats and oils in foods, medicinal drugs, and cosmetics. • Chem. formula: $C_{15}H_{24}O$.

bu·tyl·ene /ˈbyo͞otl,ēn/ ▸*n.* any of several isomeric hydrocarbons obtained from petroleum and used to make polymers and in organic synthesis. • Chem. formula: C_4H_8.

bu·tyl rub·ber ▸*n.* a synthetic rubber made by polymerizing isobutylene and isoprene.

bu·tyr·a·ceous /,byo͞otəˈrāsнəs/ ▸*adj.* of or like butter.

bu·tyr·ic ac·id /byo͞oˈtirik/ ▸*n. Chemistry* a colorless, syrupy liquid organic acid found in rancid butter and in arnica oil. • Alternative name: butanoic acid; chem. formula: C_3H_7COOH. ▷mid 19th cent.: *butyric* from Latin *butyrum* (see BUTTER) + -IC. —**bu·tyr·ate** /ˈbyo͞otə,rāt/ *n.*

bu·ty·rin /ˈbyo͞otərin/ ▸*n.* any of three glyceryl esters of butyric acid found naturally in butter. • Chem. formula: $C_3H_5(C_3H_4O_2)_3$.

bux·om /ˈbəksəm/ ▸*adj.* (of a woman) plump, esp. with large breasts. ▷Middle English: from the stem of Old English *būgan* 'to bend' (see BOW[2]) + -SOME[1]. The original sense was 'compliant, obliging,' later 'lively and good-tempered,' influenced by the traditional association of plumpness and good health with an easygoing nature. —**bux·om·ness** *n.*

buy /bī/ ▸*v.* (**buys, buy·ing**; *past* and *past part.* **bought** /bôt/) [*trans.*] **1** obtain in exchange for payment: *we had to find some money to buy a house* | *he had been able to* ***buy up*** *hundreds of acres* | [with *two objs.*] *he bought me a new dress* | [*intrans.*] *had no interest in* ***buying into*** *an entertainment company.* ■ (**buy someone out**) pay someone to give up an ownership, interest, or share. ■ procure the loyalty and support of (someone) by bribery: *here was a man who could not be bought* | *I'll* ***buy off*** *the investigators.* ■ [often with *negative*] be a means of obtaining (something) through exchange or payment: *money can't buy happiness.* ■ (often **be bought**) get by sacrifice or great effort: *greatness is* ***dearly bought.*** ■ [*intrans.*] make a profession of purchasing goods for a store or firm. **2** *informal* accept the truth of: *I am not prepared to buy the claim that the ends justify the means* | [*intrans.*] *I hate to* ***buy into*** *stereotypes.* **3** (**bought it**) *informal* used to say that someone has died: *his friends had bought it in the jungle.*
▸*n. informal* a purchase: *the wine is a good buy at $3.49.* ■ an act of purchasing something: *out on a produce buy for the restaurant.* ▷Old English *bycgan*, of Germanic origin.
▸*PHRASES* □ **buy the farm** *informal* die: *I refused to admit to my recklessness, even when I nearly bought the farm.* □ **buy time** delay an event temporarily so as to have longer to improve one's own position.

buy-back ▸*n.* the buying back of goods by the original seller. ■ the buying back by a company of its own shares. ■ a form of borrowing in which shares or bonds are sold with an agreement to repurchase them at a later date: [with *adj.*] *a share buy-back.*

buy·er /ˈbīər/ ▸*n.* a person who makes a purchase. ■ a person employed to select and purchase stock or materials for a large retail or manufacturing business, etc.
▸*PHRASE* □ **a buyer's market** an economic situation in which goods or shares are plentiful and buyers can keep prices down.

buy-in ▸*n.* **1** a purchase of shares by a broker after a seller has failed to deliver similar shares, the original seller being charged any difference in cost. **2** *informal* agreement to support a decision: *the CEO got a buy-in from all his vice presidents to launch the new product.*

buy·out /ˈbī,out/ ▸*n.* the purchase of a controlling share in a company, esp. by its own managers.

buzz /bəz/ ▸*n.* [in *sing.*] a low, continuous humming or murmuring sound, made by or similar to that made by an insect: *the buzz of the bees* | *a buzz of conversation.* ■ the sound of a buzzer or telephone. ■ *informal* a telephone call: *I'll give you a buzz.* ■ *informal* a rumor: *the buzz is that he's in big trouble.* ■ an atmosphere of excitement and activity: *there is a real buzz about the place.* ■ *informal* a feeling of excitement or euphoria: *I* ***got such a buzz out of*** *seeing the kids' faces.*
▸*v.* [*intrans.*] **1** make a humming sound: *mosquitoes were buzzing all around us.* ■ [often as *n.*] (**buzzing**) (of the ears) be filled with a humming sound: *I remember a buzzing in my ears.* ■ signal with a buzzer: *the electric bell began to buzz for closing time* | [*trans.*] *he buzzed the stewardesses every five minutes.* ■ [*trans.*] *informal* make a telephone call to (someone). **2** [with *adverbial of direction*] move quickly or busily: *she buzzed along the highway back into town.* ■ [*trans.*] *Aeronautics, informal* fly very close to (another aircraft, the ground, etc.) at a high speed. **3** (of a place) have an air of excitement or purposeful activity: *the club is* ***buzzing with*** *excitement.* ■ (of a person's mind or head) be filled with excited or confused thoughts: *her mind was* ***buzzing with*** *ideas.*
▸*phrasal v.* □ **buzz off** [often in *imperative*] *informal* go away. ▷late Middle English: imitative.

buz·zard /ˈbəzərd/ ▸*n.* a large hawklike bird of prey with broad wings and a rounded tail, typically seen soaring in wide circles. • Family Accipitridae: several genera, in particular *Buteo*, and including the common (**Eurasian**) **buzzard** (*B. buteo*). ■ a North American vulture, esp. a turkey vulture. ▷late Middle English: from Old French *busard*, based on Latin *buteo* 'falcon.'

Buz·zards Bay /ˈbəzərdz/ an inlet of the Atlantic Ocean in southeastern Massachusetts, just west of Cape Cod.

buzz bomb ▸*n. informal* a robot bomb, esp. the German V-1 used during World War II.

buzz cut ▸*n.* a haircut in which all the hair is cut very close to the scalp.

buzz·er /ˈbəzər/ ▸*n.* an electrical device, similar to a bell, that makes a buzzing noise and is used for signaling.
▸*PHRASE* □ **at the buzzer** *Sports* at the end of a game or period of play: *Smith missed another 3-pointer at the buzzer.*

buzz saw ▸*n.* another term for CIRCULAR SAW.

buzz·word /ˈbəz,wərd/ (also **buzz phrase**) ▸*n. informal* a technical word or phrase that has become fashionable, typically as a slogan.

buzz·y /ˈbəzē/ ▸*adj.* (**buzz·i·er, buzz·i·est**) *informal* (especially of a place or atmosphere) lively and exciting: *a buzzy bar with live music.*

BVDs ▶*plural n. trademark* a type of boxer shorts.

BVM ▶*abbr.* Blessed Virgin Mary.

b/w ▶*abbr.* black and white (used esp. to describe printing, movies, photographs, or television pictures).

bwa·na /ˈbwänə/ ▶*n.* (in East Africa) a boss or master. ■ used as a form of address: *he can't hear you, bwana.* ▷Kiswahili.

BWI *historical* ▶*abbr.* British West Indies.

BWR ▶*abbr.* boiling-water reactor.

by /bī/ ▶*prep.* **1** identifying the agent performing an action: ■ after a passive verb: *the door was opened by my cousin Annie | damage caused by fire.* ■ after a noun denoting an action: *further attacks by the mob | a clear decision by the electorate.* ■ identifying the author of a text, idea, or work of art: *a book by Ernest Hemingway.* **2** [often with *verbal n.*] indicating the means of achieving something: *malaria can be controlled by attacking the parasite | they plan to provide further working capital* **by means of** *borrowing.* ■ indicating a term to which an interpretation is to be assigned: *what is meant by "fair?"* ■ indicating a name according to which a person is known: *she mostly calls me by my last name.* ■ indicating the means of transport selected for a journey: *traveling by train to Boston.* ■ indicating the other parent of someone's child or children: *Richard is his son by his third wife.* ■ indicating the sire of a pedigree animal, esp. a horse: *a black filly by Goldfuerst.* ■ (followed by a noun without an adjective) in various phrases indicating how something happens: *I heard by chance that she has married again | Anderson, by contrast, rejects this view | she ate by candlelight.* **3** indicating the amount or size of a margin: *the shot missed her by miles | the raising of taxes by 2.5%.* ■ indicating a unit of measurement: *billing is by the minute.* ■ in phrases indicating something happening repeatedly or progressively, typically with repetition of a unit of time: *colors changing minute by minute | the risk becomes worse by the day.* ■ identifying a parameter: *a breakdown of employment figures by age and occupation.* ■ expressing multiplication, often in dimensions: *a map measuring 24 by 36 inches | she multiplied it by 89.* **4** indicating a deadline or the end of a particular time period: *I've got to do this report by Monday | by now Kelly needed extensive physiotherapy.* **5** indicating location of a physical object beside a place or object: *remains were discovered by the roadside | the lamp was by the door.* ■ past; beyond: *I drove by our house.* **6** indicating the period in which something happens: *this animal always hunts* **by night**. **7** concerning; according to: *anything you do is all right by me | she had done her duty by him.* **8** used in mild oaths: *it was the least he could do, by God.* [partly translating French *par* 'through the medium or agency of.']
▶*adv.* so as to go past: *a car flashed by on the other side of the road | he let only a moment go by.*
▶*n.* (*pl.* **byes**) variant spelling of **BYE**[1]. ▷Old English *bī, bi, be,* of Germanic origin; related to Dutch *bij* and German *bei.*
▶*PHRASES* □ **by and by** before long; eventually. □ **by the by** (or **bye**) incidentally; parenthetically: *where's Hector, by the by?* □ **by and large** on the whole; everything considered: *mammals have, by and large, bigger brains than reptiles.* [originally in nautical use, describing the handling of a ship both with the wind and against it.] □ **by oneself 1** alone: *living in that big house by himself.* **2** unaided: *the patient often learns to undress by himself.* □ **by way of** see **WAY**.

by- ▶*prefix* subordinate; incidental; secondary: *byform | byproduct.*

By·att /ˈbīət/, A. S. (1936–), English novelist and literary critic; born *Antonia Susan Byatt.* She is the sister of Margaret Drabble. Notable novels: *The Virgin in the Garden* (1978) and *Possession* (Booker Prize, 1990).

Byb·los /ˈbibləs/ an ancient Mediterranean seaport, located on the site of modern Jebeil, north of Beirut in Lebanon. It was a thriving Phoenician city in the 2nd millennium BC.

by-blow ▶*n. Brit.* **1** a side-blow not at the main target. **2** a man's illegitimate child.

by-catch ▶*n.* the unwanted fish and other marine creatures caught during commercial fishing for a different species.

Byd·goszcz /ˈbid,gôsh(ch)/ an industrial river port in northern central Poland; pop. 381,530. Twenty thousand of its citizens were massacred by Nazis in September 1939. German name **BROMBERG**.

bye[1] /bī/ ▶*n.* **1** the transfer of a competitor directly to the next round of a competition in the absence of an assigned opponent. **2** *Golf* one or more holes remaining unplayed after the match has been decided. ▷mid 16th cent. (denoting a side issue or incidental matter): from the noun **BY**.
▶*PHRASE* □ **by the bye** variant spelling of **BY THE BY** (see **BY**).

bye[2] ▶*exclam. informal* short for **GOODBYE**.

bye-bye ▶*exclam.* informal way of saying **GOODBYE**. ▷early 18th cent.: child's reduplication.

by-e·lec·tion ▶*n. chiefly Brit.* an election to fill a vacancy arising during a term of office.

Bye·lo·rus·sian ▶*adj.* & *n.* variant spelling of **BELORUSSIAN**.

by-form ▶*n.* a secondary form of a word: *historically, "inquire" is a by-form of "enquire."*

by·gone /ˈbī,gôn/ ▶*adj.* belonging to an earlier time: *relics of a bygone society.*
▶*n.* (usu. **bygones**) a thing dating from an earlier time.
▶*PHRASE* □ **let bygones be bygones** forget past offenses or causes of conflict and be reconciled.

by·law /ˈbī,lô/ (also **by-law**) ▶*n.* **1** a rule made by a company or society to control the actions of its members. **2** a regulation made by a local authority; an ordinance. ▷Middle English: probably from obsolete *byrlaw* 'local law or custom,' from Old Norse *býjar,* genitive singular of *býr* 'town,' but associated with **BY**.

by·line /ˈbī,līn/ ▶*n.* a line in a newspaper naming the writer of an article.

by·name /ˈbī,nām/ ▶*n.* (also **by-name**) a sobriquet or nickname, esp. one given to distinguish people with the same given name.

BYOB ▶*abbr.* bring your own bottle (or booze, or beer).

by·pass /ˈbī,pas/ ▶*n.* a road passing around a town or its center to provide an alternative route for through traffic. ■ a secondary channel, pipe, or connection to allow a flow when the main one is closed or blocked. ■ an alternative passage made by surgery, typically to aid the circulation of blood. ■ a surgical operation to make such a passage: *a heart bypass.*
▶*v.* [*trans.*] go past or around: *bypass the farm and continue to the road.* ■ provide (a town) with a route diverting traffic from its center: *the town has been bypassed.* ■ avoid or circumvent (an obstacle or problem): *a manager might bypass formal channels of communication.*

by·path /ˈbī,path/ ▶*n.* (also **by-path**) an indirect route. ■ *figurative* a minor or obscure branch or detail of a subject: *the bypaths of European political life.*

by·play /ˈbī,plā/ ▶*n.* (also **by-play**) secondary or subsidiary action or involvement in a play or movie.

by·prod·uct ▶*n.* (also **by-prod·uct**) an incidental or secondary product made in the manufacture or synthesis of something else: *zinc is a byproduct of the glazing process.* ■ a secondary result, unintended but inevitably produced in doing or producing something else: *he saw poverty as the byproduct of colonial prosperity.*

Byrd[1] /bərd/, Charlie (1925–99), U.S. guitarist; full name *Charles L. Byrd.* He was responsible for introducing and applying acoustic classical guitar techniques to jazz and popular music and for launching the samba and bossa nova movements of the 1960s in the U.S. with his album *Jazz Samba* (1962) with Stan Getz.

Byrd[2], Richard (Evelyn) (1888–1957), U.S. explorer, naval officer, and aviator. He claimed to have made the first aircraft flight over the North Pole 1926, although his actual course has been disputed. He was the first to fly over the South Pole 1929 and led further scientific expeditions to the Antarctic in 1933–34 and 1939–41.

Byrd[3], Robert (1917–), U.S. politician. From West Virginia, he served in the U.S. Senate 1950–52, 1959– in many leadership positions, including majority leader 1977–80, 1987–88 and chairman of the Appropriations Committee 1989–95.

byre /ˈbīr/ ▶*n. chiefly Brit.* a cowshed. ▷Old English *býre*; perhaps related to **BOWER**[1].

Byrnes /bərnz/, James Francis (1879–1972), U.S. Supreme Court associate justice 1941–42. A Democrat from South Carolina, he was a member of the U.S. House of Representatives 1911–25 and the U.S. Senate 1931–41 before being appointed to the Court by President Franklin D. Roosevelt. He resigned from the Court a year later to take several federal positions in the war effort.

by·road /ˈbī,rōd/ ▶*n.* (also **by-road**) a minor road.

By·ron /ˈbīrən/, George Gordon, 6th Baron (1788–1824), English poet. His poetry exerted considerable influence on the romantic movement, particularly on the Continent. Having joined the fight for Greek independence, he died of malaria before seeing serious action. Notable works: *Childe Harold's Pilgrimage* (1812–18) and *Don Juan* (1819–24).

By·ron·ic /bīˈränik/ ▶*adj.* characteristic of Lord Byron or his poetry. ■ (of a man) alluringly dark, mysterious, or moody.

bys·si·no·sis /,bisəˈnōsis/ ▶*n.* a lung disease caused by prolonged inhalation of textile fiber dust. ▷late 19th cent.: from Latin *byssinus* 'made of byssus' (from Greek *bussinos*) + **-OSIS**.

bys·sus /ˈbisəs/ ▶*n.* (*pl.* **bys·sus·es** or **bys·si** /ˈbisī/) **1** *historical* a fine textile fiber and fabric of flax. **2** *Zoology* a tuft of tough silky filaments by which mussels and some other bivalves adhere to rocks and other objects: [as *adj.*] *byssus threads.* ▷late Middle English: from Latin, from Greek *bussos*, of Semitic origin. **—bys·sal** /-səl/ *adj.*

by·stand·er /ˈbī,standər/ ▶*n.* a person who is present at an event or incident but does not take part.

by·street /ˈbī,strēt/ ▶*n.* a side street off the main thoroughfare.

byte /bīt/ ▶*n. Computing* a group of binary digits or bits (usually eight) operated on as a unit. Compare with **BIT**[4]. ■ such a group as a unit of memory size. ▷1960s: an arbitrary formation based on **BIT**[4] and **BITE**.

By·tom /ˈbi,tôm/ a city in southern Poland, northwest of Katowice; pop. 231,200. German name **BEUTHEN**.

by·town·ite /bīˈtounīt/ ▶*n.* a calcium-rich plagioclase present in many basic igneous rocks. ▷mid 19th cent.: from *Bytown*, the former name of Ottawa, Canada, + **-ITE**[1].

by·way /ˈbī,wā/ ▶*n.* a road or track not following a main route; a minor road or path. ■ a little-known area or detail: *byways of Russian music.*

by·word /ˈbī,wərd/ ▶*n.* a person or thing cited as a notorious and outstanding example or embodiment of something: *his name became a* **byword for** *luxury.* ■ a word or expression summarizing a thing's characteristics or a person's principles: *"Small is beautiful" may be the byword for most couturiers.*

by-your-leave ▶*n.* request for permission: *he borrowed my car without so much as a by-your-leave.* See also **LEAVE**[2]

Byz·an·tine /ˈbizən,tēn; bəˈzan-; -,tīn/ ▶*adj.* of or relating to Byzantium, the Byzantine Empire, or the Eastern Orthodox Church. ■ of an ornate artistic and architectural style that developed in the Byzantine Empire and spread esp. to Italy and Russia. The art is generally rich and stylized (as in religious icons) and the architecture typified by many-domed, highly decorated churches. ■ (of a system or situation) excessively complicated, typically involving a great deal of administrative detail: *Byzantine insurance regulations.* ■ characterized by deviousness or underhanded procedure: *Byzantine intrigues | he has the most Byzantine mind in politics.*
▶*n.* a citizen of Byzantium or the Byzantine Empire. ▷late 16th cent. (denoting a **BEZANT**, a Byzantine coin): from Latin *Byzantinus*, from **BYZANTIUM**. **—By·zan·tin·ism** /bəˈzantə,nizəm; bī-/ *n.*

Byz·an·tine Em·pire the empire in southeastern Europe and Asia Minor formed from the eastern part of the Roman Empire. It ended with the loss of Constantinople to the Ottoman Turks in 1453.

Byz·an·tin·ist /biˈzantənist; bī-/ ▶*n.* a historian or other scholar specializing in the study of the Byzantine Empire.

Byz·an·ti·um /bəˈzantēəm; -ˈzanchēəm/ an ancient Greek city, founded in the 7th century BC, at the southern end of the Bosporus, site of the modern city of Istanbul. It was rebuilt by Constantine the Great in AD 324–330 as Constantinople.

Cc

C

C[1] /sē/ (also **c**) ▸*n.* (*pl.* **Cs** or **C's**) **1** the third letter of the alphabet. ■ denoting the third in a set of items, categories, sizes, etc. ■ denoting the third of three or more hypothetical people or things. ■ the third highest class of academic grades. ■ (**c**) *Chess* denoting the third file from the left of a chessboard, as viewed from White's side of the board. ■ (usu. **c**) the third fixed constant to appear in an algebraic expression, or a known constant. ■ denoting the lowest soil horizon, comprising parent materials. **2** a shape like that of a letter C: [in *combination*] *C-springs.* **3** (usu. **C**) *Music* the first note of the diatonic scale of C major, the major scale having no sharps or flats. ■ a key based on a scale with C as its keynote. **4** the Roman numeral for 100. [abbreviation of Latin *centum* 'hundred.'] **5** (**C**) a high-level computer programming language originally developed for implementing the UNIX operating system. [formerly known as *B*, abbreviation of *BCPL*.]

C[2] ▸*abbr.* ■ (**C.**) Cape (chiefly on maps): *C. Hatteras.* ■ Celsius or centigrade: *it was 29°C at noon.* ■ (©) copyright. ■ (in personal ads) Christian. ■ a 1.5 volt dry cell battery size. ■ *Physics* coulomb(s).
▸*symbol* ■ *Physics* capacitance. ■ the chemical element carbon.
▸*PHRASE* □ **the Big C** *informal* cancer.

c ▸*abbr.* ■ cent(s). ■ [in *combination*] (in units of measurement) centi-: *centistokes (cS).* ■ (**c.**) century or centuries: *a watch case, 19th c.* ■ (preceding a date or amount) circa; approximately: *Isabella was born c 1759.* ■ (of water) cold: *all cabins have h & c.* ■ colt.
▸*symbol Physics* the speed of light in a vacuum: $E = mc^2$.

C8 ▸*n.* a popular designation for ammonium perfluorooctanoate, a detergentlike chemical used in the manufacture of fluoropolymers. It is the subject of litigation concerning its potentially harmful presence in some drinking water supplies.

CA ▸*abbr.* ■ California (in official postal use). ■ Central America. ■ chief accountant. ■ *Canadian & Scottish* chartered accountant.

Ca ▸*symbol* the chemical element calcium.

ca (also **ca.**) ▸*abbr.* (preceding a date or amount) circa.

Caa·ba variant spelling of **KAABA**.

CAB ▸*abbr.* Civil Aeronautics Board.

cab[1] /kab/ ▸*n.* **1** short for **TAXICAB**. ■ *historical* a horse-drawn vehicle for public hire. **2** the driver's compartment in a truck, bus, or train.
▸*v.* (**cabbed**, **cab·bing**) [*intrans.*] travel in a taxi: *Roger cabbed home.* ▷early 19th cent.: abbreviation of **CABRIOLET**.

cab[2] ▸*n. informal* a cabinet containing a speaker or speakers for a guitar amplifier. ▷late 20th cent.: abbreviation.

ca·bal /kə'bäl; -'bal/ ▸*n.* a secret political clique or faction: *a cabal of dissidents.* See note at **PLOT**. ▷late 16th cent. (denoting the cabbala): from French *cabale*, from medieval Latin *cabala* (see **KABBALAH**).

Cab·a·la ▸*n.* variant spelling of **KABBALAH**.

ca·ba·let·ta /ˌkabə'letə; ˌkäbə-/ ▸*n.* (*pl.* **-let·tas** or **-let·te** /-'leˌtā/) a simple aria with a repetitive rhythm. ■ the uniformly quick final section of an aria. ▷mid 19th cent.: from Italian, variant of *coboletta* 'short stanza,' diminutive of *cobola*, from Old Provençal *cobla*, from Latin *copula* 'connection.'

cab·a·lis·tic /ˌkabə'listik/ ▸*adj.* relating to or associated with mystical interpretation or esoteric doctrine. See also **KABBALAH**. ▷variant of *Kabbalistic*: see **KABBALAH**. —**cab·a·lism** /'kabəˌlizəm/ *n.* —**cab·a·list** /'kabəlist/ *n.*

ca·bal·le·ro /ˌkabə(l)'ye(ə)rō; -'le(ə)rō/ ▸*n.* (*pl.* **-ros**) **1** a Spanish or Mexican gentleman. **2** (in the southwestern U.S.) a horseman. ▷mid 19th cent.: Spanish, 'gentleman, horseman,' based on Latin *caballus* 'horse.' Compare with **CAVALIER, CHEVALIER**.

ca·ban·a /kə'ban(y)ə/ ▸*n.* a cabin, hut, or shelter, esp. one at a beach or swimming pool. ▷late 19th cent.: from Spanish *cabaña*, from late Latin *capana*, *cavana* 'cabin.'

cab·a·ret /ˌkabə'rā; 'kabəˌrā/ ▸*n.* entertainment held in a nightclub or restaurant while the audience eats or drinks at tables: *she was seen recently in cabaret* | [as *adj.*] *a cabaret act.* | ■ a nightclub or restaurant where such entertainment is performed. ▷mid-17th cent. (denoting a French inn): from Old French, literally 'wooden structure,' via Middle Dutch from Old Picard *camberet* 'little room.' Current senses date from the early 20th cent.

cab·bage /'kabij/ ▸*n.* a cultivated plant eaten as a vegetable, having thick green or purple leaves surrounding a spherical heart or head of young leaves. • *Brassica oleracea*, family Brassicaceae (the **cabbage family**). As well as the brassicas, the members of this family (known as crucifers) include the mustards and cresses together with many ornamentals (candytuft, alyssum, stocks, nasturtiums, wallflowers). ■ the leaves of this plant, eaten as a vegetable. ■ *informal* paper money: *I'd have cabbage galore in the bank if I were more frugal.* ▷late Middle English: from Old French (Picard) *caboche* 'head,' variant of Old French *caboce*, of unknown origin. —**cab·bage·y** *adj.*

cab·bage mag·got ▸*n.* a small fly whose larvae feed on the roots and stems of cabbages and related plants and can be a serious pest. • *Delia radicum*, family Anthomyiidae.

cab·bage moth ▸*n.* a brown moth whose caterpillars are pests of cabbages and related plants. • *Mamestra brassicae*, family Noctuidae.

cab·bage palm ▸*n.* any of a number of palms or palmlike plants that resemble a cabbage in some way, in particular: • a Caribbean palm with edible buds that resemble a cabbage (*Roystonea oleraceae*, family Palmae). • an evergreen plant occurring in warm regions and grown elsewhere as a greenhouse or indoor plant (genus *Cordyline*, family Agavaceae).

cab·bage pal·met·to ▸*n.* see **PALMETTO**.

cab·bage rose ▸*n.* a kind of rose with a large, round, compact double flower.

cab·bage white ▸*n.* a mainly white butterfly that has caterpillars that are pests of cabbages and related plants. • Genus *Pieris*, family Pieridae: several species, in particular the imported cabbageworm *P. rapae*.

cab·bage·worm /'kabijˌwərm/ ▸*n.* any caterpillar that is a pest of cabbages, esp. that of the cabbage white butterfly.

Cab·ba·la /kə'bälə; 'kabələ/ ▸*n.* variant spelling of **KABBALAH**.

cab·bie /'kabē/ (also **cab·by**) ▸*n.* (*pl.* **-bies**) *informal* a taxicab driver.

ca·ber /'kābər; 'käbər/ ▸*n.* a roughly trimmed tree trunk used in the Scottish Highland sport of **tossing the caber**. This involves holding the caber upright and running forward to toss it so that it lands on the opposite end. ▷early 16th cent.: from Scottish Gaelic *cabar* 'pole.'

Ca·ber·net /ˌkabər'nā/ ▸*n.* short for **CABERNET FRANC** or **CABERNET SAUVIGNON**.

Ca·ber·net Franc /'fräNGk/ ▸*n.* a variety of black wine grape grown chiefly in parts of the Loire valley and northeastern Italy. ■ a red wine made from this grape. ▷French.

Ca·ber·net Sau·vi·gnon /ˌsōvin'yôN; -vē'nyôN/ ▸*n.* a variety of black wine grape from the Bordeaux area of France, now grown throughout the world. ■ a red wine made from this grape. ▷French.

Ca·be·za Pri·e·ta /kə'bāzə prē'ātə/ a national wildlife refuge in southwestern Arizona, in the Sonoran Desert. The Cabeza Prieta Mountains give their name to the preserve, which is home to bighorn sheep and other species.

cab·e·zon /'kabəˌzän; -ˌzōn/ ▸*n.* a heavy-bodied fish with a broad tentacle above each eye and a green-brown body with white patches, found on the west coast of North America. • *Scorpaenichthys marmoratus*, family Cottidae. ▷Spanish.

cab-for·ward ▸*adj.* [*attrib.*] (of the design of car or truck) having the driver's or passenger compartment is placed so as to extend further forward than the standard position.

ca·bil·do /kə'bildō/ ▸*n.* (*pl.* **-dos**) (in Spain and Spanish-speaking countries) a town council or local government council. ■ a town hall. ▷Spanish, from late Latin *capitulum* 'chapter house.'

cab·in /'kabən/ ▸*n.* **1** a private room or compartment on a ship. ■ the area for passengers in an aircraft. **2** a small shelter or house, made of wood and situated in a wild or remote area.
▸*v.* (**cab·ined**, **cab·in·ing**) [*trans.*] [often as *adj.*] (**cabined**) *dated* confine in a small place. ▷Middle English: from Old French *cabane*, from Provençal *cabana*, from late Latin *capanna*, *cavanna*.

cab·in boy ▸*n. chiefly historical* a boy employed to wait on a ship's officers or passengers.

cab·in class ▸*n.* the intermediate class of accommodations on a passenger ship.

cab·in crew ▸*n.* [treated as *sing.* or *pl.*] the members of an aircraft crew who attend to passengers or cargo.

cab·in cruis·er ▸*n.* a recreational motorboat with sleeping accommodations.

Ca·bin·da /kə'bində/ an exclave of Angola at the mouth of the Congo River, separated from the rest of Angola by a wedge of the Democratic Republic of the Congo (formerly Zaire). ■ the capital of this area; pop. 163,000.

cab·i·net /'kabənit/ ▸*n.* **1** a cupboard with drawers or shelves for storing or displaying articles: *a medicine cabinet.* ■ a wooden box, container, or piece of furniture housing a radio, television set, or speaker. **2** (in the U.S.) a body of advisers to the President, composed of the heads of the executive departments of the government: [as *adj.*] *a cabinet meeting.* ■ (also **Cabinet**) (in the UK, Canada, and other Commonwealth countries) the committee of senior ministers responsible for controlling government policy. **3** *archaic* a small private room. ▷mid 16th cent.: from **CABIN** + **-ET**[1], influenced by French *cabinet*.

cab·i·net·mak·er /'kabənitˌmākər/ ▸*n.* a skilled joiner who makes furniture or similar high-quality woodwork. —**cab·i·net·mak·ing** /-ˌmākiNG/ *n.*

cab·i·net min·is·ter ▸*n.* (in the UK, Canada, and other Commonwealth countries) a member of a parliamentary cabinet.

cab·i·net·ry /'kabənitrē/ ▸*n.* cabinets collectively.

cab·in fe·ver ▸*n. informal* irritability, listlessness, and similar symptoms resulting from long confinement or isolation indoors during the winter.

ca·ble /'kābəl/ ▸*n.* **1** a thick rope of wire or nonmetallic fiber, typically used for construction, mooring ships, and towing vehicles. ■ the chain of a ship's anchor. ■ *Nautical* a length of 200 yards (182.9 m) or (in the U.S.) 240 yards (219.4 m). ■ short for **CABLE STITCH**. ■ (also **cable molding**) *Architecture* a molding resembling twisted rope. **2** an insulated wire or wires having a protective casing and used for transmitting electricity or telecommunication signals: *an underground cable* | *transatlantic phone calls went by cable.* ■ a cablegram. ■ short for **CABLE TELEVISION**.

▸*v.* [*trans.*] **1** contact or send a message to (someone) by cablegram. ■ transmit (a message) by cablegram. ■ [*intrans.*] send a cablegram: *we cabled to a boat at sea, asking it to stop.* **2** (often **be cabled**) provide (an area or community) with power lines or with the equipment necessary for cable television. **3** *Architecture* decorate (a structure) with rope-shaped moldings. ▷Middle English: from an Anglo-Norman French variant of Old French *chable,* from late Latin *capulum* 'halter.'

ca·ble car ▸*n.* **1** a transportation system, typically one traveling up and down a mountain, in which cabins are suspended on a continuous moving cable driven by a motor at one end of the route. ■ a cabin on such a system. **2** a car on a cable railroad.

ca·ble·gram /ˈkābəlˌgram/ ▸*n. historical* a telegraph message sent by cable: *Walter shot off a cablegram | we received the word of his death by cablegram.*

ca·ble-laid ▸*adj.* (of rope) made of three right-handed triple strands (or smaller ropes) twisted together left-handed, used originally of a very large rope of the type used for anchor cables.

ca·ble mo·dem ▸*n.* a type of modem that connects a computer or local network to broadband Internet service through the same cable that supplies cable television service: [as *adj.*] *a cable-modem connection.* ■ the service connection made via a cable modem: *a broadband Internet connection, such as DSL or cable modem.*

ca·ble rail·road ▸*n.* a railroad along which cars are drawn by a continuous cable, in particular: ■ a tramway on which the unpowered cars are attached, for as long as they are required to move, to a continuously moving cable running in a slot in the street. ■ a funicular.

ca·ble-read·y ▸*adj.* [*attrib.*] adapted for cable television.

ca·ble re·lease ▸*n. Photography* a cable attached to the shutter release of a camera, allowing the photographer to open the shutter without touching or moving the camera.

ca·ble-stayed bridge ▸*n.* a bridge in which the weight of the deck is supported by a number of cables running directly to one or more towers.

ca·ble stitch ▸*n.* a combination of knitted stitches done to resemble twisted rope.

ca·ble tel·e·vi·sion ▸*n.* a system in which television programs are transmitted to the sets of subscribers by cable rather than by a broadcast signal.

ca·ble tier ▸*n. historical Nautical* a place in a ship for stowing a coiled cable.

ca·ble·way /ˈkābəlˌwā/ ▸*n.* a transportation system in which goods are carried suspended from a continuous moving cable.

cab·man /ˈkabmən/ ▸*n.* (*pl.* **-men**) a taxicab driver. ■ *historical* the driver of a horse-drawn hackney carriage.

ca·boched ▸*adj.* variant spelling of **CABOSHED**.

cab·o·chon /ˈkabəˌshän/ ▸*n.* a gem polished but not faceted: [as *adj.*] *a necklace of cabochon rubies.* ▷mid 16th cent.: from French, diminutive of *caboche* 'head.'

▸*PHRASE* □ **en cabochon** /äɴ/ (of a gem) treated in this way.

ca·bo·clo /kəˈbôklo͞o; -klō/ ▸*n.* (*pl.* **-clos**) (in Brazil) an American Indian. ■ a Brazilian of mixed white and Indian or Indian and black ancestry. ▷Brazilian Portuguese, perhaps from Tupi *Kaa-boc* 'person having copper-colored skin.'

ca·boo·dle /kəˈbo͞odl/ (also **ka·boo·dle**) ▸*n.* (in phrase **the whole caboodle** or **the whole kit and caboodle**) *informal* the whole number or quantity of people or things in question. ▷mid 19th cent. (originally U.S.): perhaps from the phrase *kit and boodle,* in the same sense (see **KIT**[1], **BOODLE**).

ca·boose /kəˈbo͞os/ ▸*n.* **1** a railroad car with accommodations for the train crew, typically attached to the end of the train. ■ *informal* (typically referring to a woman) buttocks: *she got a sexy caboose.* **2** *archaic* a kitchen on a ship's deck. ▷mid 18th cent.: from Dutch *kabuis, kombuis,* of unknown origin.

Ca·bo·ra Bas·sa /kəˌbôrə ˈbäsə/ a lake on the Zambezi River in western Mozambique. Its waters are impounded by a dam and massive hydroelectric complex.

ca·boshed /kəˈbäsht/ (also **ca·boched** or **ca·bossed** /-ˈbäst/) ▸*adj.* [usu. *postpositive*] *Heraldry* (of the head of a stag, bull, etc.) shown full face with no neck visible. ▷late 16th cent.: from French *caboché,* in the same sense.

Cab·ot /ˈkabət/ the name of two Italian explorers and navigators. ■ **John** (*c.*1450–*c.*1498); Italian name *Giovanni Caboto.* An Italian in the service of England, he sailed from Bristol in 1497 in search of Asia, but in fact discovered the mainland of North America. ■ **Sebastian** (*c.*1475–1557), son of John. It is thought that he accompanied his father on his voyage in 1497 and that he made further voyages after the latter's death, most notably to explore the coast of Brazil and the Plate River in 1526.

cab·o·tage /ˈkabəˌtäzʜ; -bətij/ ▸*n.* the right to operate sea, air, or other transport services within a particular territory. ■ restriction of the operation of sea, air, or other transport services within or into a particular country to that country's own transport services. ▷mid 19th cent.: from French, from *caboter* 'sail along a coast,' perhaps from Spanish *cabo* 'cape, headland.'

Cab·ot Strait /ˈkabət/ an ocean passage between Newfoundland and Nova Scotia that links the Gulf of St. Lawrence with the Atlantic Ocean.

cab·o·ver /ˈkabˌōvər/ ▸*n.* a truck where the driver's cab is mounted directly above the engine.

Ca·bra·les /käˈbräläs/ ▸*n.* a pungent blue cheese from Spain. ▷Spanish, from *cabra* 'goat.'

Ca·bri·ni /kəˈbrēnē/, St. Frances Xavier (1850–1917), U.S. religious leader, born in Italy; born *Maria Francesca Cabrini;* known as **Mother Cabrini**. She founded the Missionary Sisters of the Sacred Heart in 1880 and was responsible for the establishment of many schools, hospitals, and orphanages in the U.S. and South America. She became the first American saint in 1946.

cab·ri·ole /ˈkabrēˌōl/ ▸*n. Ballet* a jump in which one leg is extended into the air forward or backward, the other is brought up to meet it, and the dancer lands on the second foot. ▷French, literally 'light leap,' from *cabrioler* (earlier *caprioler*), from Italian *capriolare* 'to leap in the air' (see **CAPRIOLE**).

cab·ri·ole leg ▸*n.* a kind of curved leg characteristic of Chippendale and Queen Anne furniture. ▷late 18th cent.: so named from the resemblance to the front leg of a leaping animal (see **CABRIOLE**).

cabriole leg

cab·ri·o·let /ˌkabrēəˈlā/ ▸*n.* **1** a car with a roof that folds down. **2** a light, two-wheeled carriage with a hood, drawn by one horse. ▷mid 18th cent.: from French, from *cabriole* 'goat's leap,' from *cabrioler* 'to leap in the air' (see **CABRIOLE**); so named because of the carriage's motion.

cabriolet 2

cab·stand /ˈkabˌstand/ ▸*n.* a place for taxis to wait for passengers.

ca'can·ny /käˈkanē/ ▸*n. Brit., dated* the policy of deliberately limiting output at work. ▷late 19th cent. (originally Scots in the sense 'proceed warily'): from *ca'* (variant of the verb **CALL**) and **CANNY**.

ca·ca·o /kəˈkou; kəˈkāō/ ▸*n.* (*pl.* **-os**) **1** beanlike seeds from which cocoa, cocoa butter, and chocolate are made. **2** the small tropical American evergreen tree that bears these seeds, which are contained in large, oval pods that grow on the trunk. The tree is now cultivated mainly in West Africa. • *Theobroma cacao,* family Sterculiaceae. ▷mid 16th cent.: via Spanish from Nahuatl *cacaua.*

cac·cia·to·re /ˌkäcʜəˈtôrē; ˌkacʜ-/ (also **cac·cia·to·ra** /-ˌtôrə/) ▸*adj.* [*postpositive*] prepared in a spicy tomato sauce with mushrooms and herbs: *chicken cacciatore.* ▷Italian, literally 'hunter' (because of the use of ingredients that a hunter might have to hand).

ca·cha·ca /kəˈsʜäsə/ (also **ca·cha·ça**) ▸*n.* a Brazilian white rum made from sugar cane. ▷mid 19th cent.: Brazilian Portuguese, from Portuguese *cacaça* '(white) rum.'

cach·a·lot /ˈkasʜəˌlät; -ˌlō/ ▸*n.* another term for **SPERM WHALE**. ▷mid 18th cent.: from French, from Spanish and Portuguese *cachalote,* from *cachola* 'big head.'

cache /kasʜ/ ▸*n.* a collection of items of the same type stored in a hidden or inaccessible place: *an arms cache | a cache of gold coins.* ■ a hidden or inaccessible storage place for valuables, provisions, or ammunition. ■ (also **cache memory**) *Computing* an auxiliary memory from which high-speed retrieval is possible.

▸*v.* [*trans.*] store away in hiding or for future use. ■ *Computing* store (data) in a cache memory. ■ *Computing* provide (hardware) with a cache memory. ▷late 18th cent.: from French, from *cacher* 'to hide.'

ca·chec·tic /kəˈkektik/ ▸*adj. Medicine* relating to or having the symptoms of cachexia.

cache·pot /ˈkasʜˌpät; ˈkasʜ(ə)ˌpō/ ▸*n.* (*pl.* same) an ornamental holder for a flowerpot. ▷late 19th cent.: from French *cache-pot,* from *cacher* 'to hide' + *pot* 'pot.'

cache-sexe /ˈkasʜˌseks/ ▸*n.* (*pl.* **cache-sexes** *pronunc.* same) a covering for a person's genitals, typically worn by erotic dancers or tribal peoples. ▷1920s: from French, from *cacher* 'to hide' and *sexe* 'genitals.'

ca·chet /kaˈsʜā/ ▸*n.* **1** the state of being respected or admired; prestige: *no other shipping company had quite the cachet of Cunard.* **2** a distinguishing mark or seal. ■ *Philately* a printed design added to an envelope to commemorate a special event. **3** a flat capsule enclosing a dose of unpleasant-tasting medicine. ▷early 17th cent.: from French, from *cacher* in the sense 'to press,' based on Latin *coactare* 'constrain.'

ca·chex·i·a /kəˈkeksēə/ ▸*n. Medicine* weakness and wasting of the body due to severe chronic illness. ▷mid 16th cent.: via late Latin from Greek *kakhexia,* from *kakos* 'bad' + *hexis* 'habit.'

cach·in·nate /ˈkakəˌnāt/ ▸*v.* [*intrans.*] *poetic/literary* laugh loudly. ▷early 19th cent.: from Latin *cachinnat-* 'laughed loudly,' from the verb *cachinnare,* of imitative origin. —**cach·in·na·tion** /ˌkakəˈnāsʜən/ *n.*

ca·chou /kaˈsʜo͞o; ˈkasʜo͞o/ ▸*n.* (*pl.* **-chous**) **1** *dated* a pleasant-smelling lozenge sucked to mask bad breath. **2** var. of **CATECHU**. ▷late 16th cent. (in the sense 'catechu'): from French, from Portuguese *cachu,* from Malay *kacu.* The 'lozenge' sense dates from the early 18th cent.

ca·chu·cha /kəˈcʜo͞ocʜə/ ▸*n.* a lively Spanish solo dance in triple time, accompanied by castanets. ▷Spanish.

ca·cique /kəˈsēk/ ▸*n.* **1** (in Latin America or the Spanish-speaking Caribbean) a native chief. **2** (in Spain or Latin America) a local political boss. ▷mid 16th cent.: from Spanish or French, from Taino.

cack·le /ˈkakəl/ ▸*v.* [*intrans.*] (of a bird, typically a hen or goose) give a raucous, clucking cry: *the hen was cackling as if demented* | [as *adj.*] (**cackling**) *cackling, whooping cries.* ■ make a harsh sound resembling such a cry when laughing: *she cackled with laughter* | [with *direct speech*] *"Ah ha!" he cackled.*

▸*n.* the raucous clucking cry of a bird such as a hen or a goose. ■ a harsh laugh resembling such a cry: *her delighted cackle.* ▷Middle English: probably from Middle Low German *kākelen,* partly imitative, reinforced by *kāke* 'jaw, cheek.'

cack·le·ber·ry /ˈkakəlˌberē/ ▸*n. humorous* a hen's egg.

cac·o·de·mon /ˌkakəˈdēmən/ ▸*n.* a malevolent spirit or person. ▷late 16th cent.: from Greek *kakodaimōn,* from *kakos* 'bad' + *daimōn* 'spirit.'

cac·o·dyl /ˈkakəˌdil/ ▸*n. Chemistry* a malodorous, toxic, spontaneously flammable liquid compound containing arsenic. • Chem. formula: $((CH_3)_2As)_2$. ■ [as *adj.*] of or denoting the radical $-As(CH_3)_2$, derived from this. ▷mid 19th cent.: from Greek *kakōdēs* 'stinking' (from *kakos* 'bad') + **-YL**.

cac·o·dyl·ic ac·id /ˌkakəˈdilik/ ▸*n. Chemistry* a toxic crystalline acid containing arsenic, used as a herbicide. • Chem. formula: $(CH_3)_2AsO(OH)$. —**cac·o·dyl·ate** /ˌkakəˈdilˌāt/ *n.*

cac·o·e·thes /ˌkakōˈwēᴛʜēz/ ▸*n.* [in *sing.*] *rare* an irresistible urge to do something inadvisable. ▷mid 16th cent.: via Latin from Greek *kakoēthes* 'ill-disposed,' from *kakos* 'bad' + *ēthos* 'disposition.'

ca·cog·ra·phy /kəˈkägrəfē/ ▸*n. archaic* bad handwriting or spelling. ▷late 16th cent.: from Greek *kakos* 'bad,' on the pattern of *orthography.* —**ca·cog·ra·pher** /-fər/ *n.*

C

ca·col·o·gy /kə'käləjē/ ▸*n. archaic* bad choice of words or poor pronunciation. ▷late 18th cent.: via late Latin from Greek *kakologia* 'vituperation,' from *kakos* 'bad.'

cac·o·mis·tle /'kakə,misəl/ ▸*n.* a nocturnal raccoon-like animal with a dark-ringed tail, found in North and Central America. • Genus *Bassariscus*, family Procyonidae: two species, in particular *B. sumichrasti* of Central America. See also RING-TAILED CAT. ▷mid 19th cent.: from Latin American Spanish *cacomixtle*, from Nahuatl *tlacomiztli*.

ca·coph·o·ny /kə'käfənē/ ▸*n.* (*pl.* **-nies**) a harsh, discordant mixture of sounds: *a cacophony of deafening alarm bells* | *figurative a cacophony of architectural styles* | *songs of unrelieved cacophony.* ▷mid 17th cent.: from French *cacophonie*, from Greek *kakophōnia*, from *kakophōnos* 'ill-sounding,' from *kakos* 'bad' + *phōnē* 'sound.' **—ca·coph·o·nous** /-nəs/ *adj.*

cac·tus /'kaktəs/ ▸*n.* (*pl.* **-ti** /-tī; -tē/ or **-tuses**) a succulent plant with a thick, fleshy stem that typically bears spines, lacks leaves, and has brilliantly colored flowers. Cacti are native to arid regions of the New World and are cultivated elsewhere, esp. as houseplants. • Family Cactaceae: numerous genera and species. ▷early 17th cent. (in the sense 'cardoon'): from Latin, from Greek *kaktos* 'cardoon.' **—cac·ta·ceous** /kak'tāsHəs/ *adj.*

cac·tus dahl·ia ▸*n.* a dahlia of a variety that has rolled petals, giving the flower a prickly appearance.

ca·cu·mi·nal /kə'kyoomənl/ ▸*adj. Phonetics* another term for RETROFLEX. ▷mid 19th cent.: from Latin *cacuminare* 'make pointed' (from *cacumen, cacumin-* 'top, summit') + -AL.

CAD /kad/ ▸*abbr.* computer-aided design.

cad /kad/ ▸*n. dated* or *humorous* a man who behaves dishonorably, esp. toward a woman: *her adulterous cad of a husband.* ▷late 18th cent. (denoting a passenger picked up by the driver of a horse-drawn coach for personal profit): abbreviation of CADDIE or CADET. **—cad·dish** *adj.* **—cad·dish·ly** *adv.* **—cad·dish·ness** *n.*

ca·das·tral /kə'dastrəl/ ▸*adj.* (of a map or survey) showing the extent, value, and ownership of land, esp. for taxation. ▷mid 19th cent.: from French, from *cadastre* 'register of property,' from Provençal *cadastro*, from Italian *catastro* (earlier *catastico*), from late Greek *katastikhon* 'list, register,' from *kata stikhon* 'line by line.'

ca·das·tre /kə'das,tər/ ▸*n.* a register of property showing the extent, value, and ownership of land for taxation.

ca·dav·er /kə'davər/ ▸*n. Medicine* or *poetic/literary* a corpse. See note at BODY. ▷late Middle English: from Latin, from *cadere* 'to fall.' **—ca·dav·er·ic** /-rik/ *adj.*

ca·dav·er·ine /kə'davə,rēn/ ▸*n.* a toxic liquid base, 1,5-diaminopentane, formed by the putrefaction of proteins. • Chem. formula: $H_2N(CH_2)_5NH_2$.

ca·dav·er·ous /kə'davərəs/ ▸*adj.* resembling a corpse in being very pale, thin, or bony: *he had a cadaverous appearance.* ▷late Middle English: from Latin *cadaverosus*, from *cadaver* 'corpse.'

CADCAM (also **CAD/CAM**) /'kad,kam/ ▸*abbr.* computer-aided design, computer-aided manufacturing.

cad·die /'kadē/ (also **cad·dy**) ▸*n.* (*pl.* **-dies**) a person who carries a golfer's clubs and provides other assistance during a match.
▸*v.* (**cad·died, cad·dy·ing**) [*intrans.*] work as a caddie. ▷mid 17th cent. (originally Scots): from French CADET. The original term denoted a gentleman who joined the army without a commission, intending to learn the profession and follow a military career, later coming to mean 'odd-job man.' The current sense dates from the late 18th cent.

cad·dis·fly /'kadis,flī/ (also **cad·dis fly**) ▸*n.* (*pl.* **-flies**) a small, mothlike insect with an aquatic larva that typically builds a protective, portable case of sticks, stones, and other particles. Some kinds have been traditionally used as bait by fishermen. • Order Trichoptera: several families. ▷mid 17th cent.: of unknown origin.

cad·dis-worm /'kadis ,wərm/ (also **cad·dis worm**) ▸*n.* the soft-bodied, aquatic larva of a caddisfly, often used as fishing bait.

Cad·do·an /'kadō-ən/ ▸*adj.* relating to or denoting a group of American Indian peoples formerly inhabiting the Midwest, or their languages.
▸*n.* **1** a member of any of these peoples. **2** the family of languages spoken by these peoples, which includes Pawnee and may be related to Siouan and Iroquoian. ▷from Caddo (a language of this family) *kaduhdacu*, denoting a band belonging to this group, + -AN.

cad·dy[1] /'kadē/ ▸*n.* (*pl.* **-dies**) [usu. with *adj.*] a small storage container, typically one with divisions: *a tool caddy.* See also TEA CADDY. ▷late 18th cent.: from earlier *catty*, denoting a unit of weight of $1^1/_3$ lb. (0.61 kg.), from Malay *kati*.

cad·dy[2] ▸*n.* & *v.* variant spelling of CADDIE.

Cade /kād/, Jack (died 1450), Irish rebel; full name *John Cade.* In 1450, he assumed the name of Mortimer and led the Kentish rebels against Henry VI. They occupied London for three days and executed the treasurer of England and the sheriff of Kent.

ca·delle /kə'del/ ▸*n.* a small, dark beetle that is frequently found in food storage, where it scavenges and preys on other insects. • *Tenebroides mauritanicus*, family Cleridae. ▷mid 19th cent.: from French, based on Latin *catella, catellus* 'young (of an animal), little dog.'

ca·dence /'kādns/ ▸*n.* **1** a modulation or inflection of the voice: *the measured cadences that he employed in the Senate.* ■ such a modulation in reading aloud as implied by the structure and ordering of words and phrases in written text: *the dry cadences of the essay.* ■ a fall in pitch of the voice at the end of a phrase or sentence. ■ rhythm: *the thumping cadence of the engines* | *try to vary your cadence during a run.* **2** *Music* a sequence of notes or chords comprising the close of a musical phrase: *the final cadences of the Prelude.* ▷late Middle English (in the sense 'rhythm or metrical beat'): via Old French from Italian *cadenza*, based on Latin *cadere* 'to fall.' **—ca·denced** *adj.*

ca·den·cy /'kādnsē/ ▸*n. chiefly Heraldry* the status of a younger branch of a family. ▷early 17th cent. (in the sense 'rhythm or metrical beat'): based on Latin *cadent-* 'falling,' from the verb *cadere*. The current sense is apparently by association with CADET.

ca·den·tial /kā'dencHəl/ ▸*adj.* of or relating to a cadenza or cadence. ▷mid 19th cent.: from CADENCE, on the pattern of pairs such as *essence, essential.*

ca·den·za /kə'denzə/ ▸*n. Music* a virtuoso solo passage inserted into a movement in a concerto or other work, typically near the end. ▷mid 18th cent.: from Italian (see CADENCE).

ca·det /kə'det/ ▸*n.* **1** a young trainee in the armed services or police force: *an air force cadet.* ■ a student in training at a military school. **2** *formal* or *archaic* a younger son or daughter. ■ [usu. as *adj.*] a junior branch of a family: *a cadet branch of the family.* ▷early 17th cent. (sense 2): from French, from Gascon dialect *capdet*, a diminutive based on Latin *caput* 'head.' The notion "little head" or "inferior head" gave rise to that of 'younger, junior.' **—ca·det·ship** /-,SHip/ *n.*

cadge /kaj/ ▸*v.* [*trans.*] *Brit. informal* ask for or obtain (something to which one is not strictly entitled): *he eats whenever he can cadge a meal.* | [*intrans.*] *they cadge, but timidly.*
▸*n. Falconry* a padded wooden frame on which hooded hawks are carried to the field. [apparently an alteration of CAGE, perhaps confused with the dialect verb *cadge* 'carry around.'] ▷early 17th cent. (in the dialect sense 'carry around'): back-formation from the noun *cadger*, which dates from the late 15th cent., denoting (in northern English and Scots) an itinerant dealer, whence the verb sense 'hawk, peddle,' giving rise to the current verb senses from the early 19th cent. **—cadg·er** *n.*
▸*PHRASE* □ **on the cadge** *Brit. informal* looking for an opportunity to obtain something without paying for it.

ca·di /'kädē; 'kā-/ (also **ka·di**) ▸*n.* (*pl.* **ca·dis**) (in Islamic countries) a judge. ▷late 16th cent.: from Arabic *ḳāḍī*, from *ḳaḍā* 'to judge.'

Ca·dil·lac /kädē'yäk; 'kadl,ak/, Antoine Laumet de La Mothe (1658–1730), French soldier and colonialist. He founded military posts at Mackinac 1694 and Detroit 1701; from 1713 to about 1716 or 1717 he served as governor of Louisiana.

Cad·il·lac Moun·tain /'kadl,ak/ a peak on Mount Desert Island in southeastern Maine, within Acadia National Park. At 1,532 feet (467 m), it is the highest point on the U.S. east coast.

Ca·diz /kə'diz; 'kādiz; 'kä-/ a city and port on the southwestern coast of Spain; pop. 156,560. Spanish name CÁDIZ.

Cad·me·an /kad'mēən; 'kadmēən/ ▸*adj.* of or relating to Cadmus.

cad·mi·um /'kadmēəm/ ▸*n.* the chemical element of atomic number 48, a silvery-white metal. (Symbol: **Cd**)

Cadmium occurs naturally in zinc ores and is obtained as a byproduct of zinc smelting. It is used as a component in low melting point alloys and as a corrosion-resistant coating on other metals.

▷early 19th cent.: from Latin *cadmia* 'calamine,' so named because it is found with calamine in zinc ore. Compare with CALAMINE.

cad·mi·um cell ▸*n.* a primary electric cell with a cathode of cadmium amalgam and an electrolyte of saturated cadmium sulfate solution, used in laboratories as a standard of electromotive force.

cad·mi·um yel·low ▸*n.* a bright yellow pigment containing cadmium sulfide. Deeper versions are called **cadmium orange**; the addition of cadmium selenide gives **cadmium red.** ■ a bright yellow color.

Cad·mus /'kadməs/ *Greek Mythology* the brother of Europa and traditional founder of Thebes in Boeotia. He killed a dragon that guarded a spring, and when (on Athena's advice) he sowed the dragon's teeth, there came up a harvest of armed men; he disposed of the majority by setting them to fight one another, and the survivors formed the ancestors of the Theban nobility.

ca·dre /'kadrē; 'käd-; -,rā/ ▸*n.* a small group of people specially trained for a particular purpose or profession: *a small cadre of scientists.* ■ a group of activists in a communist or other revolutionary organization. ■ a member of such a group. ▷mid 19th cent.: from French, from Italian *quadro*, from Latin *quadrus* 'square.'

ca·du·ce·us /kə'd(y)oosēəs; -SHəs/ ▸*n.* (*pl.* **-ce·i** /-sē,ī; -SHē,ī/) an ancient Greek or Roman herald's wand, typically one with two serpents twined around it, carried by the messenger god Hermes or Mercury. ■ a representation of this, traditionally associated with healing. ▷Latin, from Doric Greek *karukeion*, from Greek *kērux* 'herald.'

caduceus

ca·du·ci·ty /kə'd(y)oositē/ ▸*n. archaic* the infirmity of old age; senility. ■ *poetic/literary* frailty or transitory nature: *read these books and reflect on their caducity.* ▷mid 18th cent.: from French *caducité*, from *caduc*, from Latin *caducus* 'liable to fall,' from *cadere* 'to fall.'

ca·du·cous /kə'd(y)ookəs/ ▸*adj. chiefly Botany* (of an organ or part) easily detached and shed at an early stage. ▷late 17th cent. (in the sense 'epileptic'): from Latin *caducus* 'liable to fall' (from *cadere* 'to fall') + -OUS.

CAE ▸*abbr.* computer-aided engineering.

cae·cil·i·an /si'silyən/ (also **coe·cil·i·an**) ▸*n. Zoology* a burrowing wormlike amphibian of a tropical order distinguished by poorly developed eyes and the lack of limbs. • Order Gymnophiona (or Apoda): five families. ▷from modern Latin *Caecilia* (genus name), from Latin *caecilia* 'slow-worm' + -AN.

cae·cum ▸*n.* (*pl.* **-ca**) /-kə/ British spelling of CECUM.

Caed·mon /'kadmən/ (7th century), Anglo-Saxon monk and poet. He is said to have been an illiterate herdsman who was inspired in a vision to compose poetry on biblical themes.

Cae·lum /'sēləm/ *Astronomy* a small and faint southern constellation (the Chisel), next to Eridanus. ■ [as *genitive*] (**Caeli** /-lī; -lē/) used with a preceding letter or numeral to designate a star in this constellation: *the star Beta Caeli.* ▷Latin.

Caen /kän/ an industrial city and river port in northern France, in Normandy, on the Orne River, capital of the region of Basse-Normandie; pop. 115,620.

Caer·dydd /kär'dēTH/ Welsh name for CARDIFF.

Caer·phil·ly /kär'filē/ ▸*n.* a kind of mild white cheese, originally made in Caerphilly in Wales.

Cae·sar[1] /'sēzər/, Gaius Julius (100–44 BC), Roman general and statesman. He established the First Triumvirate with Pompey and Crassus in 60 and became consul in 59. Between 58 and 51 he fought the Gallic Wars, invaded Britain 55–54, and acquired immense power. After civil war with Pompey, which ended in Pompey's defeat at Pharsalus in 48, Caesar became dictator of the Roman Empire. He was murdered on the Ides (15th) of March in a conspiracy led by Brutus and Cassius.

Cae·sar[2], Sid (1922–), U.S. comedian and actor. One of the stars featured on television's "Your Show of

Shows" (1950–54), he was paired with comedienne Imogene Coca (1908–2001).

Cae·sar[3] ▸*n.* **1** a title used by Roman emperors, esp. those from Augustus to Hadrian. ■ an autocrat: *they complained that he was behaving like a Caesar.* **2** *informal Medicine* a Caesarean section. ▷Middle English: from Latin *Caesar*, family name of the Roman statesman Gaius **Julius Caesar**.

▸*PHRASE* □ **Caesar's wife** a person who is required to be above suspicion. [with reference to Plutarch's *Caesar* (x. 6) 'I thought my wife ought not even to be under suspicion.']

Caes·a·re·a /ˌsēzəˈrēə; ˌses-; ˌsez-/ an ancient port on the Mediterranean coast of Israel, one of the principal cities of Roman Palestine.

Cae·sa·re·a Maz·a·ca /ˈmazəkə/ former name for **Kayseri**.

cae·sar·e·an /siˈze(ə)rēən/ ▸*adj.* & *n.* **1** (also **Cae·sar·e·an**) variant spelling of **cesarean**. **2** (**Caesarean**) of or connected with Julius Caesar or the Caesars.

Caes·a·re·a Phi·lip·pi /ˈfiləˌpī; fəˈlipˌī/ a city in ancient Palestine, on the site of the present-day village of Baniyas in the Golan Heights.

Cae·sar sal·ad ▸*n.* a salad consisting of romaine lettuce and croutons served with a dressing of olive oil, lemon juice, raw egg, Worcestershire sauce, and seasoning. ▷named after *Caesar* Cardini, the Mexican restaurateur who invented it in 1924.

cae·si·um /ˈsēzēəm/ ▸*n.* British spelling of **cesium**.

cae·su·ra /siˈzhoorə; -ˈzoorə/ ▸*n.* (in Greek and Latin verse) a break between words within a metrical foot. ■ (in modern verse) a pause near the middle of a line. ■ any interruption or break: *an unaccountable caesura: no deaths were reported in the newspapers.* ▷mid 16th cent.: from Latin, from *caes-* 'cut, hewn,' from the verb *caedere.* **—cae·su·ral** *adj.*

CAF ▸*abbr.* cost and freight.

ca·fard /kaˈfär/ ▸*n.* depression; melancholia. ▷from French.

CAFE ▸*abbr.* Corporate Average Fuel Economy.

ca·fé /kaˈfā; kə-/ (also **ca·fe**) ▸*n.* **1** a small restaurant selling light meals and drinks. **2** a bar or nightclub. **3** a serving of coffee, esp. prepared European-style: [*in combination*] *an assortment of cappuccinos and café mochas.* ▷early 19th cent.: French, 'coffee or coffeehouse.'

ca·fé au lait /ˌkaˌfā ō ˈlā/ ▸*n.* coffee with milk. ■ the light brown color of this: [as *adj.*] *smooth café au lait skin.* ▷from French.

ca·fé con le·che /ˈkafā kän ˈlechā; kaˈfā-; kəˈfā-/ ▸*n.* coffee with milk. ▷Spanish, literally 'coffee with milk.'

ca·fé fil·tre /ˌkafā ˈfēlt(rə)/ ▸*n.* coffee made with a cafetière.

ca·fé noir /ˈkaˌfā ˈnwär/ ▸*n.* black coffee. ▷French.

caf·e·te·ri·a /ˌkafiˈti(ə)rēə/ ▸*n.* a restaurant or dining room in a school or a business in which customers serve themselves or are served from a counter and pay before eating. ▷mid 19th cent.: from Latin American Spanish *cafetería* 'coffee shop.'

caf·e·te·ri·a ben·e·fit ▸*n.* an employee benefit selected from a variety of offerings under a fringe-benefit plan that can be tailored to fit individual needs.

caf·fein·at·ed /ˈkafəˌnātid/ ▸*adj.* (of coffee or tea) containing the natural amount of caffeine, or with caffeine added.

caf·feine /kaˈfēn; ˈkafˌēn/ ▸*n.* a crystalline compound that is found esp. in tea and coffee plants and is a stimulant of the central nervous system. • An alkaloid, 1,3,7-trimethylxanthine; chem. formula: $C_8H_{10}N_4O_2$. ▷mid 19th cent.: from French *caféine*, from *café* 'coffee.'

caf·fè lat·te /ˌkafā ˈlätā/ ▸*n.* a drink made by adding a shot of espresso to a glass or cup of frothy steamed milk. ▷Italian, literally 'milk coffee.'

caf·tan ▸*n.* variant spelling of **kaftan**.

Ca·ga·yan Is·lands /ˌkägəˈyän/ a group of seven small islands in the western Philippines, in the Sulu Sea.

Cage /kāj/, John (Milton) (1912–92), U.S. composer, pianist, and writer. He was noted for his experimental approach, which included the use of aleatory music and periods of silence. He also experimented with musical instruments.

cage /kāj/ ▸*n.* a structure of bars or wires in which birds or other animals are confined: *she kept a canary in a cage* | *figurative his cage of loneliness.* ■ a prison cell or camp. ■ an open framework forming the compartment in an elevator. ■ a structure of crossing bars or wires designed to hold or support something. ■ *Baseball* a portable backstop situated behind the batter during batting practice. ■ (in hockey and other games) a goal made from a network frame. ■ an indoor athletic facility with areas fenced off for security.

▸*v.* [*trans.*] (usu. **be caged**) confine in or as in a cage: *the parrot screamed, furious at being caged* | [as *adj.*] (**caged**) *a caged bird.* ■ *informal* put in prison. ▷Middle English: via Old French from Latin *cavea.*

cag·ey /ˈkājē/ (also **cag·y**) ▸*adj. informal* reluctant to give information owing to caution or suspicion: *manufacturers are cagey about the recipes they use to create a wine.* ▷early 20th cent. (originally U.S.): of unknown origin. **—cag·i·ly** /ˈkājilē/ *adv.* **—cag·i·ness** (also **cag·ey·ness**) *n.*

Ca·glia·ri /ˈkälˌyärē/ the capital of the Italian island of Sardinia, a port on the southern coast; pop. 211,720.

Cag·ney /ˈkagnē/, James (1899–1986), U.S. actor. He is noted for playing gangster roles in movies such as *The Public Enemy* (1931) and *Angels with Dirty Faces* (1938). He was also a skilled dancer and comedian who received an Academy Award for his part in the musical *Yankee Doodle Dandy* (1942).

ca·goule /kəˈgool/ ▸*n.* a lightweight, hooded, thigh-length waterproof jacket. ▷1950s: from French, literally 'cowl.'

ca·hier /käˈyā/ ▸*n.* (*pl.* same) an exercise book or notebook. ▷mid 19th cent.: from French; compare with **quire**.

Ca·ho·kia /kəˈhōkēə/ a village in southwestern Illinois, across the Mississippi River from St. Louis in Missouri; pop. 17,550. The Cahokia Mounds, major pre-Columbian earthworks, are to the northeast.

ca·hoots /kəˈhoots/ ▸*plural n.* (in phrase **in cahoots**) *informal* colluding or conspiring together secretly: *the area is dominated by guerrillas* ***in cahoots with*** *drug traffickers.* ▷early 19th cent. (originally U.S.): of unknown origin.

ca·houn ▸*n.* variant spelling of **cohune**.

ca·how /kəˈhou/ ▸*n.* a large Atlantic petrel that breeds in Bermuda. It is an endangered species. • *Pterodroma cahow*, family Procellariidae. ▷early 17th cent.: imitative of its call.

CAI ▸*abbr.* computer-assisted (or -aided) instruction.

cai·man /ˈkāmən/ (also **cay·man**) ▸*n.* a semiaquatic reptile similar to the alligator but with a heavily armored belly, native to tropical America. • *Caiman* and other genera, family Alligatoridae: three species, in particular the **spectacled caiman** (*C. sclerops*). ▷late 16th cent.: from Spanish *caimán*, Portuguese *caimão*, from Carib *acayuman.*

Cain /kān/ ▸*n.* (in the Bible) the eldest son of Adam and Eve and murderer of his brother Abel.

▸*PHRASE* □ **raise Cain** *informal* create trouble or a commotion.

Caine /kān/, Sir Michael (1933–), English actor; born *Maurice Micklewhite.* He has appeared in a wide variety of movies that include *The Ipcress File* (1965) and *Educating Rita* (1983). He won Academy Awards for *Hannah and Her Sisters* (1986) and *The Cider House Rules* (1999).

Cai·no·zo·ic /ˌkānəˈzō-ik/ ▸*adj.* variant spelling of **Cenozoic**.

cai·pi·ri·nha /ˌkīpēˈrēnyä; ˌkīpəˈrinyə/ ▸*n.* a Brazilian cocktail made with cachaca, lime or lemon juice, sugar, and crushed ice. ▷Brazilian Portuguese, from *caipira* 'yokel.'

ca·ique /käˈēk; kīk/ ▸*n.* **1** a light rowboat used on the Bosporus. **2** a small eastern Mediterranean sailing ship. ▷early 17th cent.: from French *caïque*, from Italian *caicco*, from Turkish *kayık.*

cairn /ke(ə)rn/ ▸*n.* **1** a mound of rough stones built as a memorial or landmark, typically on a hilltop or skyline. ■ a prehistoric burial mound made of stones. **2** (also **cairn ter·ri·er**) a small terrier of a breed with short legs, a longish body, and a shaggy coat. [perhaps so named from being used to hunt among cairns.] ▷late Middle English: from Scottish Gaelic *carn.*

cairn·gorm /ˈke(ə)rnˈgôrm; kernˈgôrm/ ▸*n.* ■ another term for **smoky quartz**. ▷late 18th cent.: named after the **Cairngorm Mountains**.

Cairn·gorm Moun·tains /ˈke(ə)rnˈgôrm; kernˈgôrm/ (also **the Cairn·gorms**) a mountain range in northern Scotland. ▷from Scottish Gaelic *carn gorm* 'blue cairn.'

Cai·ro /ˈkīrō/ the capital of Egypt, a port on the Nile River near the head of its delta; pop. 13,300,000. Arabic name **Al Qahira**. **—Cai·rene** /kīˈrēn/ *adj.* & *n.*

cais·son /ˈkāˌsän; ˈkāsən/ ▸*n.* **1** a large watertight chamber, open at the bottom from which the water is kept out by air pressure and in which construction work may be carried out under water. ■ a floating vessel or watertight structure used as a gate across the entrance of a dry dock or basin. **2** *historical* a chest or wagon for holding or conveying ammunition. ▷late 17th cent.: from French, literally 'large chest,' from Italian *cassone*, the spelling having been altered in French by association with *caisse* 'case.'

cais·son dis·ease ▸*n.* another term for **decompression sickness**.

cai·tiff /ˈkātif/ ▸*n. archaic* a contemptible or cowardly person: [as *adj.*] *a caitiff knight.* ▷Middle English (denoting a captive or prisoner): from Old French *caitif* 'captive,' based on Latin *captivus* '(person) taken captive' (see **captive**).

ca·jole /kəˈjōl/ ▸*v.* [*trans.*] (often **cajole someone into doing something**) persuade someone to do something by sustained coaxing or flattery: *he hoped to cajole her into selling the house* | [*intrans.*] *she pleaded and cajoled as she tried to win his support.* ▷mid 17th cent.: from French *cajoler.* **—ca·jole·ment** *n.* **—ca·jol·er·y** *n.*

Ca·jun /ˈkājən/ ▸*n.* a member of any of the largely self-contained communities in the bayou areas of southern Louisiana formed by descendants of French Canadians, speaking an archaic form of French.

▸*adj.* of or relating to the Cajuns, esp. with reference to their folk music (typically featuring the concertina, accordion, and fiddle) or spicy cuisine. ▷alteration of **Acadian**.

Ca·jun Coun·try a region of southern Louisiana that is inhabited largely by Cajuns, who are descendants of 18th-century exiles from Acadia, now Nova Scotia.

caj·u·put /ˈkajəpət; -ˌpoot/ (also **caj·e·put**) ▸*n.* **1** (also **cajuput oil**) an aromatic medicinal oil that is similar to eucalyptus oil, obtained from a tree of the myrtle family. **2** a chiefly Australasian tree related to the bottlebrushes, having papery bark and yielding this aromatic oil. Also called **paperbark**. • Genus *Melaleuca*, family Myrtaceae: *M. cajuputi*, which produces cajuput oil, and *M. quinquenervia.* ▷late 18th cent.: from Malay *kayu putih*, literally 'white tree.'

cake /kāk/ ▸*n.* an item of soft, sweet food made from a mixture of flour, shortening, eggs, sugar, and other ingredients, baked and often decorated: *a carrot cake* | [as *adj.*] *cake pans* | *a mouthful of cake.* ■ an item of savory food formed into a flat, round shape, and typically baked or fried: *crab cakes.* ■ a flattish, compact mass of something, esp. soap: ***a cake of*** *soap.*

▸*v.* [*trans.*] (usu. **be caked**) (of a thick or sticky substance that hardens when dry) cover and become encrusted on (the surface of an object): *a pair of boots caked with mud.* ■ [*intrans.*] (of a thick or sticky substance) dry or harden into a solid mass: *the blood under his nose was beginning to cake.* ▷Middle English (denoting a small flat bread roll): of Scandinavian origin; related to Swedish *kaka* and Danish *kage.*

▸*PHRASES* □ **cakes and ale** *dated* merrymaking. □ **a piece of cake** *informal* something easily achieved: *I never said that training him would be a piece of cake.* □ **sell like hotcakes** *informal* be sold quickly and in large quantities. □ **take the cake** surpass or exceed all others: *of all the hard-hearted women, she takes the cake.* □ **you can't have your cake and eat it (too)** *proverb* you can't enjoy both of two desirable but mutually exclusive alternatives.

cake·box /ˈkākˌbäks/ ▸*n.* a storage container for a round layer cake, with a surrounding cover that protects and preserves the cake. ■ a similarly shaped package for blank, recordable compact discs, with a central spindle on which discs are stacked.

cake·walk /ˈkākˌwôk/ ▸*n.* **1** *informal* an absurdly or surprisingly easy task: *winning the game won't be a cakewalk.* **2** a strutting dance popular at the end of the 19th century, developed from a black-American contest in graceful walking that had a cake as a prize.

▸*v.* [*intrans.*] **1** *informal* achieve or win something easily: *he cakewalked to a 5-1 triumph.* **2** walk or dance in the manner of a cakewalk: *a troupe of clowns cakewalked by.*

CAL ▸*abbr.* computer-assisted (or -aided) learning.

Cal ▸*abbr.* large calorie(s).

cal (also **cal.**) ▸*abbr.* ■ calendar. ■ caliber. ■ calorie. ■ small calorie(s).

Cal. ▸*abbr.* California.

Cal·a·bar /ˈkaləˌbär; ˌkaləˈbär/ a seaport in southeastern Nigeria; pop. 126,000.

Cal·a·bar bean ▸*n.* the poisonous seed of a tropical West African climbing plant, containing physostigmine and formerly used for tribal ordeals. • The plant is *Physostigma venosum*, family Leguminosae. ▷late 19th cent.: named after **CALABAR**.

cal·a·bash /ˈkaləˌbash/ ▸*n.* (also **calabash tree**) an evergreen tropical American tree that bears fruit in the form of large woody gourds. • *Crescentia cujete*, family Bignoniaceae. ■ a gourd from this tree. ■ a water container, tobacco pipe, or other object made from the dried shell of this or a similar gourd. ▷mid 17th cent.: from French *calebasse*, from Spanish *calabaza*, perhaps from Persian *ḵarbuz* 'melon.'

cal·a·ba·za /ˌkaləˈbäzə/ ▸*n.* another term for **CALABASH**.

cal·a·boose /ˈkaləˌbo͞os/ ▸*n. informal* a prison. ▷late 18th cent.: from black French *calabouse*, from Spanish *calabozo* 'dungeon.'

Ca·la·bri·a /kəˈläbrēə; -ˈlā-/ a region of southwestern Italy, forming the "toe" of the Italian peninsula; capital, Reggio di Calabria. —**Ca·la·bri·an** *adj. & n.*

ca·la·di·um /kəˈlādēəm/ ▸*n.* (*pl.* **-ums**) a tropical South American plant of the arum family that is cultivated for its brilliantly colored ornamental foliage. • Genus *Caladium*, family Araceae. ▷modern Latin, from Malay *keladi*.

Cal·ais /kaˈlā; ˈkalā/ a ferry port in northern France; pop. 75,840.

cal·a·man·co /ˌkaləˈmaNGkō/ ▸*n.* (*pl.* **-coes**) *historical* a glossy woolen cloth checkered on one side only. ▷late 16th cent.: of unknown origin.

cal·a·man·der /ˈkaləˌmandər/ (also **calamander wood**) ▸*n.* another term for **COROMANDEL**. ▷early 19th cent.: from Sinhalese *kaḷu-madīriya*, perhaps from *Coromandel ebony* (see **COROMANDEL**), changed by association with Sinhalese *kaḷu* 'black.'

ca·la·ma·ri /ˌkäləˈmärē; ˌkalə-/ ▸ *n.* squid served as food. ▷Italian, plural of *calamaro*, from medieval Latin *calamarium* 'pen case,' from Greek *kalamos* 'pen' (with reference to the squid's long tapering internal shell and its ink). The variant *calamares* is Spanish, *calamaries* being its anglicized form.

cal·a·mi /ˈkaləˌmī; -ˌmē/ ▸*n.* plural form of **CALAMUS**.

cal·a·mine /ˈkaləˌmīn/ ▸*n.* a pink powder consisting of zinc carbonate and ferric oxide, used to make a soothing lotion or ointment. ■ *dated* smithsonite or a similar zinc ore. ▷late Middle English: via Old French from medieval Latin *calamina*, alteration of Latin *cadmia* 'calamine,' from Greek *kadmeia (gē)* 'Cadmean (earth),' from *Kadmos* 'Cadmus' (see **CADMUS**).

cal·a·mint /ˈkaləˌmint/ ▸*n.* an aromatic Eurasian herbaceous plant or shrub with blue or lilac flowers. • Genus *Calamintha*, family Labiatae. ▷Middle English: from Old French *calament*, from medieval Latin *calamentum*, from late Latin *calaminthe*, from Greek *kalaminthē*.

cal·a·mite /ˈkaləˌmīt/ ▸*n.* a jointed-stemmed swamp plant of an extinct group related to the horsetails, growing to a height of 60 feet (18 m). Calamites are characteristic fossils of the Carboniferous coal measures. • *Calamites* and other genera, family Calamitaceae, class Sphenopsida. ▷modern Latin, from **CALAMUS**.

ca·lam·i·ty /kəˈlamitē/ ▸*n.* (*pl.* **-ties**) an event causing great and often sudden damage or distress; a disaster. ■ disaster and distress: *the journey had led to calamity and ruin.* ▷late Middle English (in the sense 'disaster and distress'): from Old French *calamite*, from Latin *calamitas*. —**ca·lam·i·tous** /-itəs/ *adj.* —**ca·lam·i·tous·ly** *adv.*

Ca·lam·i·ty Jane /ˈjān/ (*c.*1852–1903), U.S. frontierswoman; noted for her skill at shooting and riding; born *Martha Jane Cannary*. She dressed as a man and was known for her wild behavior and heavy drinking. She later joined Buffalo Bill's Wild West Show.

cal·a·mon·din /ˌkaləˈmändən/ (also **calamondin orange**) ▸*n.* a small hybrid citrus plant that bears fragrant white flowers followed by small orange-yellow fruit, native to the Philippines and widely grown as a houseplant. • *Citrofortunella microcarpa* (formerly *Citrus mitis*), family Rutaceae. ▷early 20th cent.: from Tagalog *kalamunding*.

cal·a·mus /ˈkaləməs/ ▸*n.* (*pl.* **-mi** /-ˌmī; -ˌmē/) **1** another term for **SWEET FLAG**. ■ (also **calamus root**) a preparation of the aromatic root of the sweet flag. **2** *Zoology* the hollow lower part of the shaft of a feather, which lacks barbs; a quill. ▷late Middle English (denoting a reed or an aromatic plant mentioned in the Bible): from Latin, from Greek *kalamos*. Sense 1 dates from the mid 17th cent.

ca·lan·do /käˈländō/ ▸*adv. Music* (esp. as a direction) gradually decreasing in tempo and volume of sound. ▷Italian, literally 'slackening.'

ca·lan·dra /kəˈlandrə/ (also **calandra lark**) ▸*n.* a large Eurasian lark with a stout bill and a black patch on each side of the neck. • Genus *Melanocorypha*, family Alaudidae: two species, in particular *M. calandra*. ▷late 16th cent.: from Old French *calandre*, via medieval Latin from Greek *kalandros*.

ca·lash /kəˈlash/ ▸*n.* another term for **CALÈCHE**.

cal·a·the·a /ˌkaləˈTHēə/ ▸*n.* a tropical American plant that typically has variegated and ornamental leaves, widely grown as a greenhouse or indoor plant. • Genus *Calathea*, family Marantaceae: many species. ▷modern Latin, from Greek *kalathos* 'basket.'

Ca·la·ver·as Coun·ty /ˌkaləˈve(ə)rəs/ a largely rural county in east central California, in the Sierra Nevada, associated with the 1840s gold rush and the writings of Mark Twain.

calc- ▸*comb. form* (used chiefly in geological terms) of lime or calcium: *calcalkaline.* ▷from German *Kalk* 'lime,' with spelling influenced by Latin *calx* 'lime' (see **CALX**).

cal·cal·ka·line /kalˈkalkəlin; -ˌlīn/ ▸*adj. Geology* (chiefly of rocks) relatively rich in both calcium and alkali metals.

cal·ca·ne·us /kalˈkānēəs/ (also **cal·ca·ne·um** /-nēəm/) ▸*n.* (*pl.* **-ne·i** /-nēˌī; -nēˌē/ or **-ne·a** /-nēə/) *Anatomy* the large bone forming the heel. It articulates with the cuboid bone of the foot and the talus bone of the ankle, and the Achilles tendon (or *tendo calcaneus*) is attached to it. ▷mid 18th cent.: from Latin.

cal·car·e·ous /kalˈke(ə)rēəs/ ▸*adj.* containing calcium carbonate; chalky. ■ *Ecology* (of vegetation) occurring on chalk or limestone. ▷late 17th cent.: from Latin *calcarius* (from *calx, calc-* 'lime') + **-EOUS**.

cal·ce·o·lar·i·a /ˌkalsēəˈle(ə)rēə/ ▸*n.* a South American plant of the figwort family that is cultivated for its brightly colored slipper- or pouch-shaped flowers. Also called **POCKETBOOK PLANT**. • Genus *Calceolaria*, family Scrophulariaceae. ▷late 18th cent.: modern Latin, from Latin *calceolus*, diminutive of *calceus* 'shoe.'

cal·ces /ˈkalˌsēz/ ▸ plural form of **CALX**.

calci- ▸*comb. form* relating to calcium or its compounds: *calcifuge.* ▷from Latin *calx, calc-* 'lime.'

cal·cic /ˈkalsik/ ▸*adj.* (chiefly of minerals) containing or relatively rich in calcium.

cal·ci·cole /ˈkalsiˌkōl/ ▸*n. Botany* a plant that grows best in calcareous soil, occurring chiefly on chalk and limestone: [as *adj.*] *a rich calcicole flora.* ▷late 19th cent.: from **CALCI-** + Latin *colere* 'inhabit.' —**cal·cic·o·lous** /kalˈsikələs/ *adj.*

cal·cif·er·ol /kalˈsifəˌrôl; -ˌrōl/ ▸*n. Biochemistry* one of the D vitamins, a sterol that is formed when its isomer ergosterol is exposed to ultraviolet light, and that is routinely added to dairy products. Also called **ERGOCALCIFEROL**, **VITAMIN** D_2 (see **VITAMIN D**). ▷1930s: from **CALCIFEROUS** + **-OL**.

cal·cif·er·ous /kalˈsifərəs/ ▸*adj.* containing or producing calcium salts, esp. calcium carbonate.

cal·ci·fuge /ˈkalsəˌfyo͞oj/ ▸*n. Botany* a plant that is not suited to calcareous soil: [as *adj.*] *calcifuge plants such as heathers.*

Calamity Jane

cal·ci·fy /ˈkalsəˌfī/ ▸*v.* (**-fies**, **-fied**) [*trans.*] [usu. as *adj.*] (**calcified**) harden by deposition of or conversion into calcium carbonate or some other insoluble calcium compounds: *calcified cartilage.* —**cal·cif·ic** /kalˈsifik/ *adj.* —**cal·ci·fi·ca·tion** /ˌkalsəfiˈkāSHən/ *n.*

cal·ci·mine /ˈkalsəˌmīn/ (also **kal·so·mine**) ▸*n.* a kind of white or pale blue wash for walls and ceilings. ▸*v.* [*trans.*] whitewash with calcimine. ▷mid 19th cent.: of unknown origin.

cal·cine /ˈkalˌsīn/ ▸*v.* [*trans.*] [usu. as *adj.*] (**calcined**) reduce, oxidize, or desiccate by roasting or strong heat: *calcined bone ash.* ▷late Middle English: from medieval Latin *calcinare*, from late Latin *calcina* 'lime,' from Latin *calx, calc-* 'lime' (see **CALX**). —**cal·ci·na·tion** /kalsəˈnāSHən/ *n.*

cal·cite /ˈkalˌsīt/ ▸*n.* a white or colorless mineral consisting of calcium carbonate. It is a major constituent of sedimentary rocks such as limestone, marble, and chalk, can occur in crystalline form (as in Iceland spar), and may be deposited in caves to form stalactites and stalagmites. ▷mid 19th cent.: coined in German from Latin *calx, calc-* 'lime' (see **CALX**). —**cal·cit·ic** /kalˈsitik/ *adj.*

cal·ci·to·nin /ˌkalsəˈtōnən/ ▸*n. Biochemistry* a hormone secreted by the thyroid that has the effect of lowering blood calcium. ▷1960s: from **CALCI-** + **TONIC** + **-IN**[1].

cal·ci·um /ˈkalsēəm/ ▸*n.* the chemical element of atomic number 20, a soft gray metal. (Symbol: **Ca**)

Calcium is one of the alkaline earth metals. Its compounds occur naturally in limestone, fluorite, gypsum, and other minerals. Many physiological processes involve calcium ions, and calcium salts are an essential constituent of bone, teeth, and shells.

▷early 19th cent.: from Latin *calx, calc-* 'lime' (see **CALX**) + **-IUM**.

cal·ci·um an·tag·o·nist ▸*n. Medicine* a compound of a type that reduces the influx of calcium into the cells of cardiac and smooth muscle, reducing the strength of contractions. Such drugs are used to treat angina and high blood pressure.

cal·ci·um car·bide ▸*n.* see **CARBIDE**.

cal·ci·um car·bon·ate ▸*n.* a white, insoluble solid occurring naturally as chalk, limestone, marble, and calcite, and forming mollusk shells and stony corals. • Chem. formula: $CaCO_3$.

cal·ci·um chlo·ride ▸*n.* a white crystalline salt used to de-ice roads and as a drying agent. • Chem. formula: $CaCl_2$.

cal·ci·um hy·drox·ide ▸*n.* a soluble white crystalline solid commonly produced in the form of slaked lime. • Chem. formula: $Ca(OH)_2$.

cal·ci·um ox·ide ▸*n.* a white caustic alkaline solid, commonly produced in the form of quicklime. • Chem. formula: CaO.

cal·cu·la·ble /ˈkalkyələbəl/ ▸*adj.* able to be measured or assessed. —**cal·cu·la·bil·i·ty** /ˌkalkyələˈbilətē/ *n.* —**cal·cu·la·bly** /-blē/ *adv.*

cal·cu·late /ˈkalkyəˌlāt/ ▸*v.* [*trans.*] **1** determine (the amount or number of something) mathematically: *Japanese land value was calculated at 2.5 times that of the U.S.* | [with *clause*] *he calculated that Texas would gain four new seats in the House of Representatives.* ■ determine by reasoning, experience, or common sense; reckon or judge: *I was bright enough to calculate that she had been on vacation.* ■ [*intrans.*] (**calculate on**) include as an essential element in one's plans: *he may have calculated on maximizing pressure for policy revision.* **2** ■ (usu. **be calculated to do something**) intend (an action) to have a particular effect: *his last words were calculated to wound her.* ■ [with *clause*] suppose; believe. ▷late Middle English: from late Latin *calculat-* 'counted,' from the verb *calculare*, from *calculus* 'a small pebble (as used on an abacus).' —**cal·cu·la·tive** /-ˌlātiv/ *adj.*

cal·cu·lat·ed /ˈkalkyəˌlātid/ ▸*adj.* (of an action) done with full awareness of the likely consequences: *a calculated decision.* ■ carefully planned or intended: *victims of vicious and calculated assaults.* ■ (of an amount or number) mathematically worked out or measured. —**cal·cu·lat·ed·ly** *adv.*

cal·cu·lat·ing /ˈkalkyəˌlātiNG/ ▸*adj.* acting in a scheming and ruthlessly determined way: *he was a coolly calculating, ruthless man.* —**cal·cu·lat·ing·ly** *adv.*

cal·cu·la·tion /ˌkalkyəˈlāSHən/ ▸*n.* a mathematical determination of the size or number of something: *finding ways of saving money involves complicated calculations* | *calculation of depreciation.* ■ (often **calculations**) an assessment of the risks, possibilities, or effects of a situation or course of action: *decisions are shaped by* *political calculations.* ▷late Middle English: via Old French from late Latin *calculatio(n-)*, from the verb *calculare* (see CALCULATE).

cal·cu·la·tor /ˈkalkyəˌlātər/ ▶*n.* something used for making mathematical calculations, in particular a small electronic device with a keyboard and a visual display.

cal·cu·lus /ˈkalkyələs/ ▶*n.* **1** (*pl.* **-lus·es**) (also **infinitesimal calculus**) the branch of mathematics that deals with the finding and properties of derivatives and integrals of functions, by methods originally based on the summation of infinitesimal differences. The two main types are **differential calculus** and **integral calculus**. **2** (*pl.* **-lus·es**) *Mathematics & Logic* a particular method or system of calculation or reasoning. **3** (*pl.* **-li** /-ˌlī; -ˌlē/) *Medicine* a concretion of minerals formed within the body, esp. in the kidney or gallbladder. ■ another term for TARTAR. ▷mid 17th cent.: from Latin, literally 'small pebble (as used on an abacus).'

cal·cu·lus of var·i·a·tions ▶*n.* a form of calculus applied to expressions or functions in which the law relating the quantities is liable to variation, esp. to find what relation between the variables makes an integral a maximum or a minimum.

Cal·cut·ta /kalˈkətə/ a port and industrial center in eastern India, capital of the state of West Bengal, the second largest city in India; pop. 10,916,000. It is situated on the banks of the Hooghly River near the Bay of Bengal. **—Cal·cut·tan** /-ˈkətn/ *n.* & *adj.*

Cal·de·cott /ˈkôldikət; -ˌkät/, Randolph (1846–86), English graphic artist and watercolor painter. He is noted for his illustrations for children's books. A medal awarded annually for the illustration of U.S. children's books is named for him.

Cal·der /ˈkôldər/, Alexander (1898–1976), U.S. sculptor and painter. He was one of the first artists to introduce movement into sculpture, making mobiles incorporating abstract forms. His static sculptures are known as stabiles.

cal·de·ra /kalˈderə; kôl-; -ˈdi(ə)rə/ ▶*n.* a large volcanic crater, typically one formed by a major eruption leading to the collapse of the mouth of the volcano. ▷late 17th cent.: from Spanish, from late Latin *caldaria* 'boiling pot.'

Cal·de·rón de la Bar·ca /ˌkäldəˈrōn dā lä ˈbärkä/, Pedro (1600–81), Spanish playwright and poet. He wrote about 120 plays, more than 70 of them religious dramas.

cal·dron ▶*n.* variant spelling of CAULDRON.

Cald·well[1] /ˈkôldˌwel/, Erskine (Preston) (1903–87), U.S. novelist and short-story writer. Caldwell reproduced the dialect of the poor whites in his realistic, earthy, and popular novels. Notable works: *Tobacco Road* (1932) and *God's Little Acre* (1933).

Cald·well[2] a city in southwestern Idaho, west of Boise; pop. 25,967.

ca·lèche /kəˈlesн -ˈlasн/ (also **ca·leche** or **ca·lash**) ▶*n. historical* **1** a light low-wheeled carriage with a removable folding hood. **2** *Canadian* a two-wheeled one-horse vehicle with a seat for the driver on the splashboard. **3** a woman's hooped silk hood. ▷mid 17th cent.: French, from German *Kalesche*, from Polish *kołasa*, from *koło* 'wheel.'

Cal·e·do·ni·an /ˌkaləˈdōnēən/ ▶*adj.* **1** (chiefly in names or geographical terms) of or relating to Scotland or the Scottish Highlands: *the Caledonian Railway.* **2** *Geology* relating to or denoting a mountain-forming (orogenic) period in northwestern Europe and Greenland during the Early Paleozoic era, esp. the late Silurian.
▶*n.* **1** *humorous* or *poetic/literary* a person from Scotland. **2** (**the Caledonian**) *Geology* the Caledonian orogeny. ▷from *Caledonia*, the Latin name for northern Britain, + -AN.

Cal·e·do·ni·an Ca·nal a system of lochs and canals that cross Scotland from east to west.

cal·e·fa·cient /ˌkaləˈfāsнənt/ ▶*n. archaic Medicine* a drug or other agent causing a sensation of warmth. ▷mid 17th cent.: from Latin *calefacient-* 'making warm,' from the verb *calefacere*, from *calere* 'be warm' + *facere* 'make.'

cal·en·dar /ˈkaləndər/ (abbr.: **cal** or **cal.**) ▶*n.* a chart or series of pages showing the days, weeks, and months of a particular year, or giving particular seasonal information. ■ a datebook. ■ a system by which the beginning, length, and subdivisions of the year are fixed. See also JEWISH CALENDAR, JULIAN CALENDAR, GREGORIAN CALENDAR. ■ a timetable of special days or events of a specified kind or involving a specified group: *the college calendar.* ■ a list of people or events connected with particular dates, esp. canonized saints and cases for trial.
▶*v.* [*trans.*] enter (something) in a calendar or timetable. ▷Middle English: from Old French *calendier*, from Latin *kalendarium* 'account book,' from *kalendae* (see CALENDS). **—ca·len·dric** /kəˈlendrik/ *adj.* **—ca·len·dri·cal** /kəˈlendrikəl/ *adj.*

cal·en·dar month ▶*n.* see MONTH.

cal·en·dar year ▶*n.* see YEAR (sense 2).

cal·en·der /ˈkaləndər/ ▶*n.* a machine in which cloth or paper is pressed by rollers to glaze or smooth it.
▶*v.* [*trans.*] press in such a machine. ▷late 15th cent. (as a verb): from French *calendre* (noun), *calendrer* (verb), of unknown origin.

cal·ends /ˈkaləndz; ˈkā-/ (also **kal·ends**) ▶*plural n.* the first day of the month in the ancient Roman calendar. ▷Old English (denoting an appointed time): from Old French *calendes*, from Latin *kalendae*, *calendae* 'first day of the month' (when accounts were due and the order of days was proclaimed); related to Latin *calare* and Greek *kalein* 'call, proclaim.'

ca·len·du·la /kəˈlenjələ/ ▶*n.* a Mediterranean plant of a genus that includes the common (or pot) marigold. • Genus *Calendula*, family Compositae. ▷modern Latin, diminutive of *calendae* (see CALENDS); perhaps because it flowers for most of the year.

cal·en·ture /ˈkalənˌcнŏŏr/ ▶*n.* feverish delirium supposedly caused by the heat in the tropics. ▷late 16th cent.: from French, from Spanish *calentura* 'fever,' from *calentar* 'be hot,' based on Latin *calere* 'be warm.'

calf[1] /kaf/ ▶*n.* (*pl.* **calves** /kavz/) **1** a young bovine animal, esp. a domestic cow or bull in its first year. ■ the young of some other large mammals, such as elephants, rhinoceroses, large deer and antelopes, and whales. ■ short for CALFSKIN. **2** a floating piece of ice detached from an iceberg. ▷Old English *cælf*, of Germanic origin; related to Dutch *kalf* and German *Kalb*. **—calf·like** /-ˌlīk/ *adj.*
▶*PHRASES* □ **in** (or **with**) **calf** (of a cow) pregnant. □ **kill the fatted calf** see FAT.

calf[2] ▶*n.* (*pl.* **calves** /kavz/) the fleshy part at the back of a person's leg below the knee. ▷Middle English: from Old Norse *kálfi*, of unknown origin.

calf·skin /ˈkafˌskin/ ▶*n.* leather made from the hide or skin of a calf, used chiefly in bookbinding and shoemaking.

Cal·ga·ry /ˈkalgərē/ a city in southern Alberta, in southwestern Canada; pop. 710,680.

Cal·houn /kalˈhōōn/, John Caldwell (1782–1850) U.S. politician. A South Carolina Democrat, he served as U.S. vice president 1825–32 and in the U.S. Senate 1832–43, 1845–50. He was noted as a champion of states' rights and of slavery.

Ca·li /ˈkälē/ an industrial city in western Colombia; pop. 1,624,400.

cal·i·ber /ˈkaləbər/ (*Brit.* **cal·i·bre**) (abbr.: **cal** or **cal.**) ▶*n.* **1** the quality of someone's character or the level of someone's ability: *they could ill afford to lose a man of his caliber.* ■ the standard reached by something: *educational facilities of a very high caliber.* **2** the internal diameter or bore of a gun barrel: [*in combination*] *a .22 caliber repeater rifle.* ■ the diameter of a bullet, shell, or rocket. ■ the diameter of a body of circular section, such as a tube, blood vessel, or fiber. ▷mid 16th cent. (in the sense 'social standing or importance'): from French *calibre*, from Italian *calibro*, perhaps from Arabic *ḳālib* 'mold,' based on Greek *kalapous* 'shoemaker's last.' **—cal·i·bered** *adj.* [also *in combination*] .

cal·i·brate /ˈkaləˌbrāt/ ▶*v.* [*trans.*] (often **be calibrated**) mark (a gauge or instrument) with a standard scale of readings. ■ correlate the readings of (an instrument) with those of a standard in order to check the instrument's accuracy. ■ adjust (experimental results) to take external factors into account or to allow comparison with other data. ▷mid 19th cent.: from CALIBER + -ATE[3]. **—cal·i·bra·tor** /-ˌbrātər/ *n.*

cal·i·bra·tion /kaləˈbrāsнən/ ▶*n.* the action or process of calibrating an instrument or experimental readings: *the measuring devices require calibration* | *calibrations in the field of electronic measurements.* ■ each of a set of graduations on an instrument.

ca·li·che /kəˈlēsнē/ ▶*n.* a mineral deposit of gravel, sand, and nitrates, found esp. in dry areas of South America. ■ an area of calcium carbonate formed in the soils of semiarid regions. ▷mid 19th cent.: from Latin American Spanish.

cal·i·co /ˈkaliˌkō/ ▶*n.* (*pl.* **-coes** or **-cos**) printed cotton fabric: [as *adj.*] *a calico dress.* ■ *Brit.* a type of cotton cloth, typically plain white or unbleached.
▶*adj.* (of an animal, typically a cat) multicolored or mottled. ▷mid 16th cent. (originally also *calicut*): alteration of CALICUT, where the fabric originated.

Cal·i·cut /ˈkalikət/ a seaport in the state of Kerala in southwestern India, on the Malabar Coast; pop. 420,000. Also called KOZHIKODE.

Calif. ▶*abbr.* California.

Cal·i·for·nia /ˌkaləˈfôrnyə; -nēə/ a state in the western U.S., on the coast of the Pacific Ocean; pop. 33,871,648; capital, Sacramento; statehood, Sept. 9, 1850 (31). Formerly part of Mexico, it was ceded to the U.S. in 1847, having briefly been an independent republic. Large numbers of settlers were attracted to California in the 19th century, esp. during the gold rushes of the 1840s; it is now the most populous state. **—Cal·i·for·nian** *adj.* & *n.*

Cal·i·for·nia, Gulf of an arm of the Pacific Ocean that separates the Baja California peninsula from mainland Mexico.

Cal·i·for·nia Cur·rent a cold ocean current of the eastern Pacific Ocean that flows south along the western coast of North America.

Cal·i·for·nia pop·py ▶*n.* an annual poppy native to western North America that is cultivated for its brilliant yellow or orange flowers. • *Eschscholzia californica*, family Papaveraceae.

California poppy

Cal·i·for·nia sheeps·head ▶*n.* see SHEEPSHEAD.

cal·i·for·ni·um /ˌkaləˈfôrnēəm/ ▶*n.* the chemical element of atomic number 98, a radioactive metal of the actinide series, first produced by bombarding curium with helium ions. (Symbol: **Cf**) ▷1950s: named after *University of California at Berkeley* (where it was first made) + -IUM.

ca·lig·i·nous /kəˈlijənəs/ ▶*adj. archaic* misty, dim; obscure, dark. **—ca·lig·i·nos·i·ty** /kəˌlijəˈnäsitē/ *n.*

Ca·lig·u·la /kəˈligyələ/ (AD 12–41), Roman emperor 37–41; born *Gaius Julius Caesar Germanicus.* His reign was notorious for its tyrannical excesses.

cal·i·per /ˈkaləpər/ (also **cal·li·per**) ▶*n.* **1** (**calipers**) an instrument for measuring external or internal dimensions, having two hinged legs resembling a pair of compasses and in-turned or out-turned points. ■ (also **caliper rule**) an instrument performing a similar function but having one linear component sliding along another, with two parallel jaws and a vernier scale. ■ (also **brake caliper**) a motor-vehicle or bicycle brake consisting of two or more hinged components. See illustration on page 244. **2** (also **caliper splint**) a metal support for a person's leg. ▷late 16th cent.: apparently an alteration of CALIBER.

ca·liph /ˈkālif; ˈkal-/ ▶*n. historical* the chief Muslim civil and religious ruler, regarded as the successor of Muhammad. The caliph ruled in Baghdad until 1258 and then in Egypt until the Ottoman conquest of 1517; the title was then held by the Ottoman sultans until it was abolished in 1924 by Atatürk. ▷late Middle English: from Old French *caliphe*, from Arabic *ḵalīfa* meaning 'deputy (of God)' (from the title *ḵalīfat Allāh*), or meaning 'successor (of Muhammad)' (from the title *ḵalīfat rasūl Allāh* 'of the Messenger of God'), from *ḵalafa* 'succeed.' **—cal·iph·ate** /ˈkāləˌfāt; ˈkal-; -fit/ *n.*

cal·is·then·ics /ˌkaləsˈтнeniks/ (*Brit.* **cal·lis·then·ics**) ▶*plural n.* gymnastic exercises to achieve bodily fitness and grace of movement. ▷early 19th cent.: from Greek *kallos* 'beauty' + *sthenos* 'strength' + -ICS. **—cal·is·then·ic** *adj.*

ca·lix /ˈkāliks; ˈkal-/ ▶*n.* **1** variant spelling of CALYX. **2** a chalice.

calk ▶*n.* & *v.* variant spelling of CAULK.

call /kôl/ ▶*v.* **1** [*trans.*] cry out to (someone) in order to summon them or attract their attention: *she heard Terry calling her* | [*intrans.*] *I distinctly heard you call.* ■ cry out (a word or words): *he heard an insistent voice calling his name* | *Meredith was already* **calling out** *a greeting.* ■ shout out or chant (the steps and figures) to peo-

Pronunciation Key ə *ago*; ər *over*; ˈə or ˌə *up*; ˈər or ˌər *fur*; a *hat*; ā *rate*; ä *car*; cн *chew*; e *let*; ē *see*; e(ə)r *air*; i *fit*; ī *by*; i(ə)r *ear*; nɢ *sing*; ō *go*; ô *for*; oi *boy*; ŏŏ *good*; ōō *goo*; ou *out*; sн *she*; тн *thin*; T͟H *then*; (h)w *why*; zн *vision*

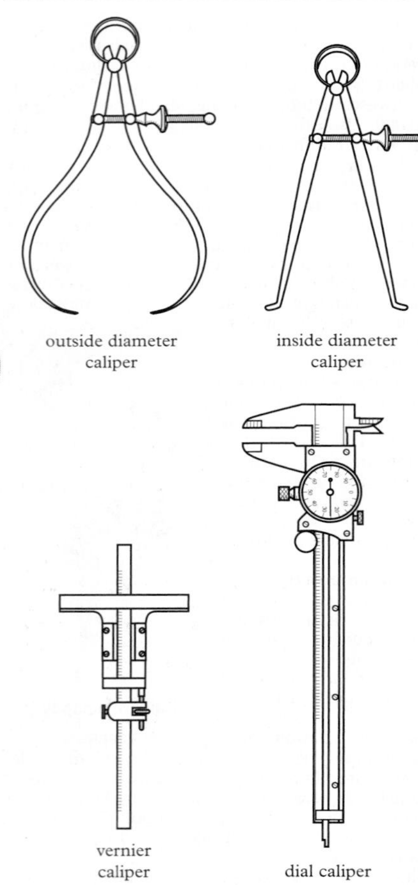

caliper 1

ple performing a square dance or country dance. ■ [*intrans.*] (of an animal, esp. a bird) make its characteristic cry. ■ telephone (a person or telephone number): *could I* **call** *you* **back**? ■ summon (something, esp. an emergency service or a taxicab) by telephone: *if you are suspicious, call the police.* ■ bring (a witness) into court to give evidence. ■ [*trans.*] *archaic* inspire or urge (someone) to do something: *I am called to preach the Gospel.* ■ fix a date or time for (a meeting, strike, or election). ■ [*intrans.*] guess the outcome of tossing a coin: *"You call," he said. "Heads or tails?"* ■ predict the result of (a future event, esp. an election or a vote): *in the Northeast, the race remains too close to call.* ■ *Computing* cause the execution of (a subroutine). **2** [*intrans.*] (of a person) pay a brief visit: *he* **called around** *last night looking for you.* ■ (**call for**) stop to pick up (someone) at the place where they are living or working: *I'll call for you around seven.* **3** [*trans.*] give (an infant or animal) a specified name: *they called their daughter Hannah.* ■ address or refer to (someone) by a specified name, title, endearment, or term of abuse: *please call me Lucy.* ■ refer to, consider, or describe (someone or something) as being: *he's the only person I would call a friend.* ■ (of an umpire or other official in a game) pronounce (a ball, stroke, or other action) to be the thing specified: *the linesman called the ball wide.*

▸*phrasal v.* □ **call for** make necessary: *desperate times call for desperate measures.* ■ draw attention to the need for: *the report calls for an audit of endangered species.* □ **call something forth** elicit a response: *few things call forth more compassion.* □ **call someone/something down 1** cause or provoke someone or something to appear or occur: *nothing called down the wrath of Nemesis quicker.* **2** *dated* reprimand someone. □ **call someone in** enlist someone's aid or services. □ **call something in** require payment of a loan or promise of money. □ **call someone/something off** order a person or dog to stop attacking someone. □ **call something off** cancel an event or agreement. □ **call on 1** pay a visit to (someone): *he's planning to call on Katherine today.* **2** (also **call upon**) have recourse to: *we are able to call on academic staff with a wide variety of expertise.* ■ [with *infinitive*] demand that (someone) do something: *he called on the government to hold a plebiscite.* □ **call someone out 1** summon someone, esp. to deal with an emergency or to do repairs. **2** order or advise workers to strike. **3** *archaic* challenge someone to a duel. □ **call something over** *dated* read out a list of names to determine those present. □ **call someone up 1** *informal* telephone someone. **2** summon someone to serve in the army: *they have called up more than 20,000 reservists.* ■ select someone to play in a team: *he was called up from Columbus to finish the season with the Yankees.* □ **call something up** summon for use something that is stored or kept available: *icons that allow you to call up a graphic.* ■ *figurative* evoke something: *the special effects that called up the Mars landscape were impressive.*

▸*n.* **1** a cry made as a summons or to attract someone's attention: *in response to the call, a figure appeared.* ■ the characteristic cry of a bird or other animal. ■ [with *adj.*] a series of notes sounded on a brass instrument as a signal to do something: *a bugle call to rise at 5:30.* ■ a telephone communication or conversation: *I'll give you a call at around five.* ■ (**a call for**) an appeal or demand for: *the call for action was welcomed.* ■ a summons: *a messenger arrived bringing news of his call to the throne.* ■ [in *sing.*] a vocation: *his call to be a disciple.* ■ [in *sing.*] a powerful force of attraction: *hikers can't resist the call of the Sierras.* ■ [usu. with *negative*] (**a call for**) a demand or need for (goods or services): *there was little call for Turkish food in Milltown.* ■ *Computing* a command to execute a subroutine. ■ a shout by an official in a game indicating whether the ball has gone out of play, if a rule has been breached, etc.; the decision or ruling so made: *the replay shows that the umpire made a bad call.* ■ *Bridge* a bid, response, or double. ■ a direction in a square dance given by the caller. ■ a demand for payment of lent or unpaid capital. ■ *Stock Market* short for CALL OPTION. ■ a player's right or turn to make a bid in a card game. **2** a brief visit: *we* **paid a call on** *Howard.* ■ a visit or journey made in response to an emergency appeal for help: *the doctor was out on a call.* ▷late Old English *ceallian*, from Old Norse *kalla* 'summon loudly.'

▸*PHRASES* □ **call attention to** cause people to notice: *he is seeking to call attention to himself by his crimes.* □ **call someone's bluff** see BLUFF[1]. □ **call collect** make a telephone call reversing the charges. □ **call something into play** cause or require something to start working so that one can make use of it: *our active participation as spectators is called into play.* □ **call something into** (or **in**) **question** cast doubt on something: *these findings call into question the legitimacy of the proceedings.* □ **call it a day** see DAY. □ **call someone names** see NAME. □ **call of nature** see NATURE. □ **call the shots** (or **tune**) take the initiative in deciding how something should be done. □ **call a spade a spade** see SPADE[1]. □ **call someone to account** see ACCOUNT. □ **call someone/something to mind** cause one to think of someone or something, esp. through similarity: *the still lifes call to mind certain of Cézanne's works.* ■ [with *negative*] remember someone or something: [with *clause*] *I cannot call to mind where I have seen you.* □ **call someone/something to order** ask those present at a meeting to be silent so that business may proceed. □ **don't call us, we'll call you** *informal* used as a dismissive way of saying that someone has not been successful in an audition or a job application. □ **on call 1** (of a person) able to be contacted in order to provide a professional service if necessary, but not formally on duty: *our technicians are on call around the clock.* **2** (of money lent) repayable on demand. □ **to call one's own** used to describe something that one can genuinely feel belongs to one: *I had not an item to call my own.* □ **within call** near enough to be summoned by calling: *she moved into the guest room,* **within call** *of her father's room.*

cal·la /'kalə/ ▸*n.* either of two plants of the arum family: • (usu. **calla lily**) Genus *Zantedeschia*, family Araceae: several species, in particular *Z. aethiopica*. • (also **wild calla**) another term for WATER ARUM. ▷early 19th cent.: modern Latin.

call·a·ble /'kôləbəl/ ▸*adj. Finance* designating a bond that can be paid off earlier than the maturity date.

Cal·la·ghan /'kalə,han/, (Leonard) James, Baron Callaghan of Cardiff (1912–), British statesman, prime minister 1976–79.

cal·la·loo /,kalə'lo͞o; 'kalə,lo͞o/ (also **cal·la·lou**) ▸*n.* **1** the spinachlike leaves of a tropical American plant, widely used in Caribbean cooking. ■ a soup or stew made with such leaves. **2** the plant of the arum family from which these leaves are obtained. • Genus *Xanthosoma*, family Araceae. ▷mid 18th cent.: from American Spanish *calalú*.

Cal·la·net·ics /kalə'netiks/ ▸*plural n.* [treated as *sing.* or *pl.*] *trademark* a system of physical exercises based on small repeated movements. ▷late 20th cent.: named after *Callan* Pinckney (born 1939), American deviser of the system, perhaps on the pattern of *athletics*.

Ca·llao /kə'yä-ō; kə'you/ the principal seaport of Peru, west of Lima; pop. 369,770.

Cal·las /'kaləs/, Maria (1923–77), U.S. opera singer; born *Maria Cecilia Anna Kalageropoulos*. She was a coloratura soprano whose bel canto style of singing was especially suited to early Italian opera.

call·back /'kôl,bak/ ▸*n.* **1** an invitation to return for a second audition or interview. **2** a telephone call made to return a call received. **3** a recall of a defective product: *ask which products have the most callbacks.* **4** an emergency call summoning an employee to work after hours: *uncontrolled air leakage results in increased callbacks.* **5** *Computing* a security feature used by systems accessed by telephone, in which a remote user must log on using a previously registered phone number, to which the system then places a return call.

call-board ▸*n.* a bulletin board in a theater on which announcements for the cast and crew are posted.

call box ▸*n.* **1** a roadside telephone for use only in an emergency. **2** *Brit.* a public telephone booth.

call boy ▸*n.* **1** a person in a theater who summons actors when they are due on stage. **2** a male prostitute who accepts appointments by telephone.

call cen·ter ▸*n.* an office set up to handle a large volume of telephone calls, esp. for taking orders and providing customer service.

call·er /'kôlər/ ▸*n.* **1** a person who makes a telephone call or pays a brief visit. **2** a person who calls out numbers in a game of bingo or directions in a dance.

call·er ID ▸*n.* a facility that identifies and displays the telephone numbers of incoming calls made to a particular line.

call for·ward·ing ▸*n.* a telephone feature that allows calls made to one number to be forwarded to another specified number.

call girl ▸*n.* a female prostitute who accepts appointments by telephone.

Cal·lic·ra·tes /kə'likrə,tēz/ (5th century BC), Greek architect. He was the leading architect in Periclean Athens and, with Ictinus, designed the Parthenon (447–438 BC).

cal·li·graph /'kali,graf/ ▸*v.* [*trans.*] (usu. **be calligraphed**) write in calligraphic style: *invitations meticulously calligraphed in black ink.* ▷mid 19th cent. (as a noun): from French *calligraphe*, via medieval Latin from Greek *kalligraphos* (see CALLIGRAPHY). The verb dates from the late 19th cent.

cal·li·graph·ic /,kali'grafik/ ▸*adj.* of or relating to calligraphy: *a calligraphic pen | calligraphic script.* ■ resembling lettering in shape.

cal·lig·ra·phy /kə'ligrəfē/ ▸*n.* decorative handwriting or handwritten lettering. ■ the art of producing decorative handwriting or lettering with a pen or brush. ▷early 17th cent.: from Greek *kalligraphia*, from *kalligraphos* 'person who writes beautifully,' from *kallos* 'beauty' + *graphein* 'write.' **—cal·lig·ra·pher** /-fər/ *n.* **—cal·lig·ra·phist** /-fist/ *n.*

Cal·lim·a·chus /kə'liməkəs/ (*c.*305–*c.*240 BC), Greek poet and scholar. He wrote hymns and epigrams and was head of the library at Alexandria.

call-in ▸*n.* a radio or television program during which the listeners or viewers telephone the studio and participate. ■ a telephone conversation that is broadcast during such a program: *Tuesday's show will include viewer call-ins.* ■ [as *adj.*] denoting something conducted by people leaving answers or messages by telephone: *a call-in poll.*

call·ing /'kôliNG/ ▸*n.* **1** the loud cries or shouts of an animal or person: *the calling of a cuckoo.* **2** [in *sing.*] a strong urge toward a particular way of life or career; a vocation: *those who have a special calling to minister to others' needs.* ■ a profession or occupation: *he considered engineering one of the highest possible callings.*

call·ing card ▸*n.* **1** a card bearing a person's name and address, sent or left in lieu of a formal social or business visit. ■ *figurative* an action or the result of an action by which someone or something can be identified: *a dog whose calling card is a savage nip at the nearest ankles.* **2** a card that allows the user to make telephone calls from any phone and charge the cost to their home telephone number. ■ a prepaid card that allows the user to make telephone calls up to a specified value.

Cal·li·o·pe /kə'līəpē/ *Greek & Roman Mythology* the

Muse of epic poetry. ▷from Greek *Kalliopē*, literally 'having a beautiful voice.'

cal·li·o·pe /kə'līəpē/ ▶*n. chiefly historical* a keyboard instrument resembling an organ but with the notes produced by steam whistles, used chiefly on showboats and in traveling fairs. ▷mid 19th cent.: from the Greek name *Kalliopē* (see **CALLIOPE**).

cal·li·per ▶*n.* variant spelling of **CALIPER**.

cal·li·pyg·i·an /,kalə'pijēən/ (also **cal·li·pyg·e·an**) ▶*adj.* having well-shaped buttocks. ▷late 18th cent.: from Greek *kallipūgos* (used to describe a famous statue of Venus), from *kallos* 'beauty' + *pūgē* 'buttocks,' + **-IAN**. —**cal·li·py·gous** /-'pīgəs/ *adj.*

cal·lis·then·ics /,kaləs'THeniks/ ▶*plural n.* British spelling of **CALISTHENICS**.

Cal·lis·to /kə'listō/ **1** *Greek Mythology* a nymph who was changed into a bear by Zeus. See also **URSA MAJOR**. **2** *Astronomy* one of the Galilean moons of Jupiter, the eighth closest satellite to the planet. Icy with a dark, cratered surface, it has a diameter of 2,938 miles (4,800 km).

cal·li·tri·chid /,kali'trikid; -'trī-/ ▶*n. Zoology* a primate of a family (Callitrichidae or Callithricidae) that comprises the marmosets and tamarins. ▷late 18th cent.: from modern Latin *Callitrichidae* (plural), from Greek *kallitrikhos* 'beautiful-haired.'

call let·ters ▶*plural n.* a sequence of letters used by a television or radio station as an identifying code.

call mon·ey ▶*n.* money lent by a bank or other institution that is repayable on demand.

call num·ber ▶*n.* a mark, esp. a number, on the spine of a library book, or listed in the library's catalog, indicating the book's location in the library.

call op·tion ▶*n. Stock Market* an option to buy assets at an agreed price on or before a particular date.

cal·los·i·ty /kə'läsitē/ ▶*n.* (*pl.* **-ties**) *technical* a thickened and hardened part of the skin; a callus. ▷late Middle English: from French *callosité*, from Latin *callositas*, from *callosus* 'hard-skinned,' from *callum*, *callus* 'hardened skin.'

cal·lous /'kaləs/ ▶*adj.* showing or having an insensitive and cruel disregard for others: *his callous comments about the murder made me shiver.*
▶*n.* variant spelling of **CALLUS**. ▷late Middle English (in the Latin sense): from Latin *callosus* 'hard-skinned.' —**cal·lous·ly** *adv.* —**cal·lous·ness** *n.*

cal·loused /'kaləst/ (also **cal·lused**) ▶*adj.* (of a part of the body) having an area of hardened skin: *a calloused palm.*

call-out ▶*n.* **1** an instance of being summoned, esp. in order to deal with an emergency or to do repairs: [as *adj.*] *a call-out charge.* **2** *Printing* a letter, word, number or other symbol identifying a specific part of an illustration.

cal·low /'kalō/ ▶*adj.* (esp. of a young person) inexperienced and immature: *earnest and callow undergraduates.* See notes at **GULLIBLE, RUDE, YOUTHFUL**. ▷Old English *calu* 'bald'; probably from Latin *calvus* 'bald.' This was extended to mean 'unfledged,' which led to the present sense 'immature.' —**cal·low·ly** *adv.* —**cal·low·ness** *n.*

Cal·lo·way /'kalə,wā/, Cab (1907–94), U.S. jazz singer and bandleader; full name *Cabell Calloway*. He was known for his style of scat singing and for his flamboyant appearance. He is associated with songs such as "Minnie the Moocher" (1931) and "Jumpin' Jive" (1939) and led a succession of outstanding big bands 1928–53.

call sign (also **call signal**) ▶*n.* a message, code, or tune that is broadcast by radio to identify the broadcaster or transmitter.

call to quar·ters ▶*n.* a bugle call summoning soldiers to their barracks.

call-up ▶*n.* [in *sing.*] an act of summoning someone or of being summoned to serve in the armed forces or on a sports team: [as *adj.*] *my call-up papers.*

cal·lus /'kaləs/ (also **cal·lous**) ▶*n.* a thickened and hardened part of the skin or soft tissue, esp. in an area that has been subjected to friction. ■ *Medicine* the bony healing tissue that forms around the ends of broken bone. ■ *Botany* a hard formation of tissue, esp. new tissue formed over a wound. ▷mid 16th cent.: from Latin *callus* (more commonly *callum*) 'hardened skin.'

cal·lused /'kaləst/ ▶*adj.* variant spelling of **CALLOUSED**.

call wait·ing ▶*n.* a service whereby someone making a telephone call is notified of an incoming call and is able to place the first call on hold while answering the second.

calm /kä(l)m/ ▶*adj.* **1** (of a person, action, or manner) not showing or feeling nervousness, anger, or other emotions: ***keep calm**, she told herself* | *his voice was calm.* ■ (of a place) peaceful, esp. in contrast to recent violent activity: *the city was reported to be calm, but army patrols remained.* **2** (of the weather) pleasantly free from wind: *the night was clear and calm.* ■ (of the sea) not disturbed by large waves.
▶*n.* **1** the absence of violent or confrontational activity within a place or group: *the elections proceeded in an atmosphere of relative calm* | [in *sing.*] *an edgy calm reigned in the capital.* ■ the absence of nervousness, agitation, or excitement in a person: *his usual calm deserted him.* **2** the absence of wind: *in the center of the storm calm prevailed.* ■ still air represented by force 0 on the Beaufort scale (less than 1 knot). ■ (often **calms**) an area of the sea without wind.
▶*v.* [*trans.*] make (someone) tranquil and quiet; soothe: *I took him inside and tried to **calm** him **down*** | *he lit a cigarette to calm his nerves* | [as *adj.*] (**calming**) *a cup of tea will have a calming effect.* ■ [*intrans.*] (**calm down**) (of a person) become tranquil and quiet: *gradually I calmed down and lost my anxiety.* ▷late Middle English: via one of the Romance languages from Greek *kauma* 'heat (of the day).' —**calm·ly** *adv.* —**calm·ness** *n.*
▶*PHRASE* □ **the calm before the storm** see **STORM**.

THE RIGHT WORD **calm, halcyon, peaceful, placid, serene, tranquil**

We usually speak of the weather or the sea as **calm**, meaning free from disturbance or storm. When applied to people and their feelings or moods, *calm* implies an unruffled state, often under disturbing conditions (*to remain calm in the face of disaster*).

Halcyon is another adjective associated with the weather (*the halcyon days of summer*); it comes from the name of a mythical bird, usually identified with the kingfisher, that builds its nest on the sea and possesses a magical power to calm the winds and waves.

Peaceful also suggests a lack of turbulence or disorder, although it is usually applied to situations, scenes, and activities rather than to people (*a peaceful gathering of protesters*; | *a peaceful resolution to their problems*).

Serene, tranquil, and **placid** are more often used to describe human states of being. *Serene* suggests a lofty and undisturbed calmness (*he died with a serene look on his face*), while *tranquil* implies an intrinsic calmness (*they led a tranquil life in the country*).

Placid usually refers to a prevailing tendency and is sometimes used disparagingly to suggest a lack of responsiveness or a dull complacency (*with her placid disposition, she seldom got involved in family arguments*).

calm·a·tive /'kä(l)mətiv/ ▶*adj.* (of a drug) having a sedative effect.
▶*n.* a calmative drug.

cal·mod·u·lin /kal'mäjələn/ ▶*n. Biochemistry* a protein that binds calcium and is involved in regulating a variety of activities in cells. ▷1970s: from *cal(cium)* + *modul(ate)* + **-IN**[1].

cal·o·mel /'kaləməl; -,mel/ ▶*n.* a white powder used as a purgative and a fungicide. Also called **MERCURIC CHLORIDE**. • Chem. formula: Hg_2Cl_2. ▷late 17th cent.: modern Latin, perhaps from Greek *kalos* 'beautiful' + *melas* 'black' (perhaps because it was originally obtained from a black mixture of mercury and mercuric chloride).

Ca·lo·o·can /,kalə'ōkän/ (also **Kalookan**) a city in the Philippines, on southern Luzon, northwest of Manila; pop. 763,000.

ca·lor·ic /kə'lôrik; -'lär-/ ▶*adj. technical* of or relating to heat; calorific: *a caloric value of 7 calories per gram.*
▶*n. historical Physics* (in the late 18th and early 19th centuries) a hypothetical fluid substance that was thought to be responsible for the phenomena of heat. ▷late 18th cent. (as a noun): from French *calorique*, from Latin *calor* 'heat.' —**ca·lor·i·cal·ly** *adv.*

cal·o·rie /'kal(ə)rē/ (abbr.: **cal.**) ▶*n.* (*pl.* **-ries**) either of two units of heat energy: ■ (also **small calorie**) (abbr.: **cal**) the energy needed to raise the temperature of 1 gram of water through 1 °C (now usually defined as 4.1868 joules). ■ (also **large calorie**) (abbr.: **Cal**) the energy needed to raise the temperature of 1 kilogram of water through 1 °C, equal to one thousand small calories and often used to measure the energy value of foods. ▷mid 19th cent.: from French, from Latin *calor* 'heat' + French suffix *-ie* (see **-Y**[3]).

cal·o·rif·ic /,kalə'rifik/ ▶*adj. chiefly Brit.* relating to the amount of energy contained in food or fuel: *she knew the calorific contents of every morsel.* ■ (of food or drink) containing many calories and so likely to be fattening: *there is fruit salad for those who can resist the more calorific concoctions.* ▷late 17th cent.: from Latin *calorificus*, from *calor* 'heat.' —**cal·o·rif·i·cal·ly** /-ik(ə)lē/ *adv.*

cal·o·rif·ic val·ue ▶*n.* the energy contained in a fuel or food, determined by measuring the heat produced by the complete combustion of a specified quantity of it. This is now usually expressed in joules per kilogram.

cal·o·rim·e·ter /,kalə'rimitər/ ▶*n.* an apparatus for measuring the amount of heat involved in a chemical reaction or other process. ▷late 18th cent.: from Latin *calor* 'heat' + **-METER**. —**cal·o·ri·met·ric** /,kalərə'metrik/ *adj.* —**cal·o·rim·e·try** /-'rimitrē/ *n.*

cal·o·type /'kalə,tīp/ (also **calotype process**) ▶*n. historical* an early photographic process in which negatives were made using paper coated with silver iodide. ▷mid 19th cent.: from Greek *kalos* 'beautiful' + **TYPE**.

calque /kalk/ *Linguistics* ▶*n.* another term for **LOAN TRANSLATION**.
▶*v.* (**be calqued on**) originate or function as a loan translation of. ▷1930s: from French, literally 'copy, tracing,' from *calquer* 'to trace,' via Italian from Latin *calcare* 'to tread.'

cal·trop /'kaltrəp; 'kôl-/ (also **cal·trap**) ▶*n.* **1** a spiked metal ball thrown on the ground to impede wheeled vehicles or (formerly) cavalry horses. **2** a creeping plant with woody carpels that typically have hard spines and resemble military caltrops. • Genus *Tribulus*, family Zygophyllaceae. **3** (also **water caltrop**) another term for **WATER CHESTNUT** (sense 3). ▷Old English *calcatrippe*, denoting any plant that tended to catch the feet, from medieval Latin *calcatrippa*, from *calx* 'heel' or *calcare* 'to tread' + a word related to **TRAP**[1]. Sense 1 was probably adopted from French.

cal·u·met /'kalyə,met; -mit; ,kalyə'met/ ▶*n.* a North American Indian peace pipe. ▷late 17th cent.: from French, from late Latin *calamellus* 'little reed,' diminutive of Latin *calamus* (referring to the pipe's reed stem).

calumet

Cal·u·met Cit·y /'kalyə,met/ a city in northeastern Illinois, south of Chicago, on the Indiana border; pop. 37,840. The surrounding industrial region, in both states, is called the Calumet.

ca·lum·ni·ate /kə'ləmnē,āt/ ▶*v.* [*trans.*] *formal* make false and defamatory statements about: *Ezra Pound calumniated the Jews over the airwaves.* See note at **MALIGN**. ▷mid 16th cent.: from Latin *calumniari*, from *calumnia* (see **CALUMNY**). —**ca·lum·ni·a·tion** /kə,ləmnē'āSHən/ *n.* —**ca·lum·ni·a·tor** /-,ātər/ *n.*

cal·um·ny /'kaləmnē/ ▶*n.* (*pl.* **-nies**) the making of false and defamatory statements in order to damage someone's reputation; slander. ■ a false and slanderous statement. ▷late Middle English: from Latin *calumnia*. —**ca·lum·ni·ous** /kə'ləmnēəs/ *adj.*

cal·u·tron /'kalyə,trän/ ▶*n.* a device that uses large electromagnets to separate uranium isotopes from uranium ore. It was developed in the 1940s to produce highly enriched weapons-grade uranium. ▷from *Cal(ifornia) U(niversity) (cyclo)tron.*

Cal·va·dos /,kalvə'dōs/ (also **cal·va·dos**) ▶*n.* apple brandy, traditionally made in the Calvados region of Normandy.

Cal·va·ry /'kalv(ə)rē/ the hill outside Jerusalem on which Jesus was crucified. ■ [as *n.*] (**a calvary**) a sculpture or picture representing the scene of the Crucifixion. ▷from late Latin *calvaria* 'skull,' translation of Greek *golgotha* 'place of a skull' (Matt. 27:33) (see **GOLGOTHA**).

calve /kav/ ▶*v.* **1** [*intrans.*] (of cows and certain other large animals) give birth to a calf. ■ [*trans.*] (of a person) help (a cow) give birth to a calf. **2** [*trans.*] (of an iceberg or glacier) split and shed (a smaller mass of ice). ■ [*intrans.*] (of a mass of ice) split off from an iceberg or glacier. ▷Old English *calfian*, from *cælf* 'calf.'

calves /kavz/ ▶ plural form of CALF[1], CALF[2].

Cal·vin[1] /'kalvin/, John (1509–64), French theologian and reformer. On becoming a Protestant, he fled to Switzerland, where he attempted to reorder society on reformed Christian principles. His *Institutes of the Christian Religion* (1536) was the first systematic account of reformed Christian doctrine.

Cal·vin[2], Melvin (1911–97), U.S. biochemist. He investigated photosynthesis and discovered the cycle of reactions (the **Calvin cycle**), which constitutes the dark reaction. Nobel Prize for Chemistry (1961).

Cal·vin·ism /'kalvə,nizəm/ ▶*n.* the Protestant theological system of John Calvin and his successors, which develops Luther's doctrine of justification by faith alone and emphasizes the grace of God and the doctrine of predestination. **—Cal·vin·ist** *n.* **—Cal·vin·is·tic** /,kalvə'nistik/ *adj.* **—Cal·vin·is·ti·cal** *adj.*

Cal·vi·no /käl'vēnō; kal-/, Italo (1923–87), Italian novelist and short-story writer; born in Cuba. Notable works: *The Path to the Nest of Spiders* (1947) and *If on a Winter's Night a Traveler* (1979).

calx /kalks/ ▶*n.* (*pl.* **cal·ces** /'kal,sēz/) *archaic Chemistry* a powdery metallic oxide formed when an ore or mineral has been heated. ▷late Middle English: from Latin, 'lime,' probably from Greek *khalix* 'pebble, limestone.'

Ca·lyp·so /kə'lipsō/ *Greek Mythology* a nymph who kept Odysseus on her island, Ogygia, for seven years. ▷Greek, literally 'she who conceals.'

ca·lyp·so /kə'lipsō/ ▶*n.* (*pl.* **-sos**) a kind of West Indian (originally Trinidadian) music in syncopated African rhythm, typically with words improvised on a topical theme. ■ a song in this style. ▷1930s: of unknown origin. **—ca·lyp·so·ni·an** /kə,lip'sōnēən; ,kalip-/ *adj.* & *n.*

ca·lyx /'kāliks; 'kal-/ (also **ca·lix**) ▶*n.* (*pl.* **ca·ly·ces** /'kālə,sēz; 'kal-/ or **ca·lyx·es**) **1** *Botany* the sepals of a flower, typically forming a whorl that encloses the petals and forms a protective layer around a flower in bud. Compare with COROLLA. **2** *Zoology* a cuplike cavity or structure, in particular: ■ a portion of the pelvis of a mammalian kidney. ■ the cavity in a calcareous coral skeleton that surrounds the polyp. ■ the plated body of a crinoid, excluding the stalk and arms. ▷late 17th cent.: from Latin, from Greek *kalux* 'case of a bud, husk,' related to *kaluptein* 'to hide.'

cal·zo·ne /kal'zōn(ē)/, ▶*n.* (*pl.* **-zo·ni** /-'zōnē/ or **-zo·nes** /-'zōn(ē)z/) a type of pizza that is folded in half before cooking to contain a filling. ▷Italian dialect, probably a special use of *calzone* 'trouser leg,' with reference to the shape of the pizza.

CAM /kam/ ▶*abbr.* computer-aided manufacturing.

cam /kam/ ▶*n.* a projection on a rotating part in machinery, designed to make sliding contact with another part while rotating and to impart reciprocal or variable motion to it. ■ short for CAMSHAFT. ■ short for CAMERA[1]. ▷late 18th cent.: from Dutch *kam* 'comb,' as in *kamrad* 'cogwheel.'

ca·ma /'kämə; 'kamə/ ▶*n.* a hybrid animal produced by crossing a camel with a llama.

ca·ma·ra·de·rie /,käm(ə)'rädərē; ,kam-; -'rad-/ ▶*n.* mutual trust and friendship among people who spend a lot of time together: *a genuine camaraderie on the hockey team.* ▷mid 19th cent.: from French, from *camarade* 'comrade.'

cam·a·ril·la /,kamə'rilə; -'rēə/ ▶*n.* a small group of people, esp. a group of advisers to a ruler or politician, with a shared, typically nefarious, purpose: *Stalin and his camarilla.* ▷mid 19th cent.: from Spanish, diminutive of *camara* 'chamber.'

Cam·a·ril·lo /,kamə'rilō; -'rēyō/ a city in southwestern California, west of Los Angeles; pop. 52,303.

cam·as /'kaməs/ (also **cam·ass** or **quam·ash**) ▶*n.* a North American plant of the lily family, cultivated for its starry blue or purple flowers. • Genera *Camassia* and *Zigadenus*, family Liliaceae: several species, including *C. quamash*, the large bulbs of which are edible. ▷mid 19th cent.: from Chinook Jargon *qamaš, qawaš*, perhaps from Nootka.

Cam·bay, Gulf of /kam'bā/ an inlet of the Arabian Sea on the Gujarat coast of western India, north of Bombay. Also called **Gulf of Khambhat**.

cam·ber /'kambər/ ▶*n.* a slightly convex or arched shape of a road or other horizontal surface: *the deck beams are curved for the camber of the deck.* ■ *Brit.* a tilt built into a road at a bend or curve, enabling vehicles to maintain speed. ■ the slight sideways inclination of the front wheels of a motor vehicle. ■ the extent of curvature of a section of an airfoil. ▷late Middle English: from Old French *cambre*, dialect variant of *chambre* 'arched,' from Latin *camurus* 'curved inward.' **—cam·bered** *adj.*

cam·bi·um /'kambēəm/ ▶*n.* (*pl.* **-bi·a** /-bēə/ or **-bi·ums**) *Botany* a cellular plant tissue from which phloem, xylem, or cork grows by division, resulting (in woody plants) in secondary thickening. ▷late 16th cent. (denoting one of the alimentary humors once supposed to nourish the body): from medieval Latin, 'change, exchange.' **—cam·bi·al** /-bēəl/ *adj.*

Cam·bo·di·a /kam'bōdēə/ a country in Southeast Asia between Thailand and southern Vietnam; pop. 13,363,000; capital, Phnom Penh; official language, Khmer. Also officially called the KHMER REPUBLIC (1970–75) and KAMPUCHEA (1976–89).

The country was made a French protectorate in 1863 and remained under French influence until it became fully independent in 1953. During the Vietnam War, it was the scene of fighting between the North Vietnamese army and South Vietnamese and U.S. forces. Following a civil war 1970–75, Cambodia came under the control of the Khmer Rouge led by Pol Pot; more than 2 million Cambodians died before the regime was toppled by a Vietnamese invasion in 1979. The Vietnamese withdrew in 1989, and the monarchy was restored in 1993. Elections were held in 1998 and again in 2003.

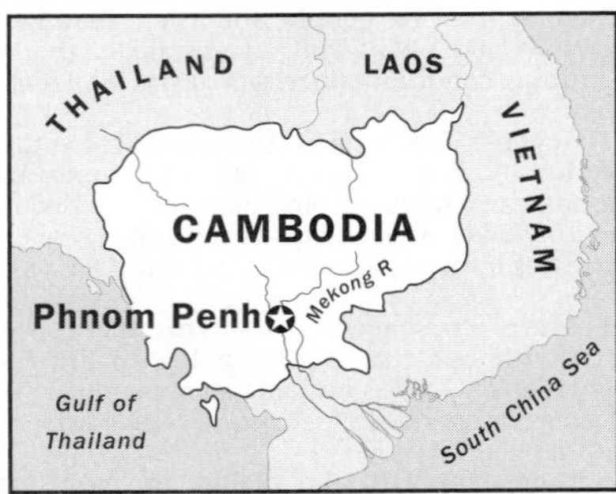

Cam·bo·di·an /kam'bōdēən/ ▶*adj.* of or relating to Cambodia, its people, or their language.
▶*n.* **1** a native or national of Cambodia, or a person of Cambodian descent. **2** another term for KHMER (the language).

cam·boy /'kam,boi/ ▶*n.* a boy or man who poses for a webcam.

cam·bo·zo·la /,kambə'zōlə/ (also **cam·ba·zo·la**) ▶*n.* *trademark* a type of German blue soft cheese with a rind like Camembert, produced using Gorgonzola blue mold. ▷an invented name, blend of CAMEMBERT and GORGONZOLA, with the insertion of *-bo-*.

Cam·brelle /kam'brel/ ▶*n.* *trademark* a synthetic fabric that absorbs perspiration, used as a lining material for climbing and hiking boots.

Cam·bri·an /'kambrēən; 'kām-/ ▶*adj.* **1** (chiefly in names or geographical terms) Welsh: *the Cambrian Railway.* **2** *Geology* of, relating to, or denoting the first period in the Paleozoic era, between the end of the Precambrian eon and the beginning of the Ordovician period. ■ [as *n.*] (**the Cambrian**) the Cambrian period or the system of rocks deposited during it.

The Cambrian lasted from about 570 million to 510 million years ago and was a time of widespread seas. It is the earliest period in which fossils, notably trilobites, can be used in geological dating.

▷mid 17th cent.: from Latin *Cambria* 'Wales,' variant of *Cumbria*, from Welsh *Cymry* 'Welshman' or *Cymru* 'Wales.'

cam·bric /'kāmbrik/ ▶*n.* a lightweight, closely woven white linen or cotton fabric. ▷late Middle English: from *Kamerijk*, Flemish form of *Cambrai*, a town in northern France, where it was originally made. Compare with CHAMBRAY.

Cam·bridge /'kāmbrij/ **1** a city in eastern England; pop. 101,000. Cambridge University is located here. **2** a city in eastern Massachusetts, across the Charles River from Boston; pop. 101,355. Harvard University and the Massachusetts Institute of Technology are located here.

Cam·bridge·shire /'kāmbrijshər; -,shi(ə)r/ a county in eastern England; county town, Cambridge.

Cam·by·ses /kam'bī,sēz/ (died 522 BC), king of Persia 529–522 BC, son of Cyrus. He is chiefly remembered for his conquest of Egypt in 525 BC.

cam·cord·er /'kam,kôrdər/ ▶*n.* a portable combined video camera and video recorder. ▷1980s: blend of CAMERA[1] and RECORDER.

Cam·den /'kamdən/ an industrial city in southwestern New Jersey, across the Delaware River from Philadelphia in Pennsylvania; pop. 79,904.

came /kām/ ▶ past tense of COME.

cam·el /'kaməl/ ▶*n.* **1** a large, long-necked ungulate mammal of arid country, with long slender legs, broad cushioned feet, and either one or two humps on the back. Camels can survive for long periods without food or drink, chiefly by using up the fat reserves in their humps. • Genus *Camelus*, family Camelidae (the **camel family**): two species (see ARABIAN CAMEL, BACTRIAN CAMEL). The camel family also includes the llama and its relatives. ■ a fabric made from camel hair. ■ a light yellowish-brown color like that of camel hair. **2** an apparatus for raising a sunken ship, consisting of one or more watertight chests to provide buoyancy. ■ a large floating fender used to keep a vessel off the dock. ▷Old English, from Latin *camelus*, from Greek *kamēlos*, of Semitic origin.

cam·el·back /'kaməl,bak/ ▶*n.* a back with a hump-shaped curve on a sofa or other piece of furniture: [as *adj.*] *a camelback sofa.*

cam·el crick·et ▶*n.* a wingless humpbacked insect related to the grasshoppers, typically living in caves or holes. Also called CAVE CRICKET. • Family Raphidophoridae: several genera.

cam·el·eer /,kamə'li(ə)r/ ▶*n.* a person who controls or rides a camel.

cam·el hair (also **cam·el's hair**) ▶*n.* **1** a fabric made from the hair of a camel: [as *adj.*] *a camel-hair coat.* **2** [usu. as *adj.*] fine, soft hair from a squirrel's tail, used in artists' brushes.

cam·e·lid /kə'mēlid; 'kaməlid/ ▶*n.* *Zoology* a mammal of the camel family (Camelidae). ▷late 20th cent.: from modern Latin *Camelidae* (plural), from Latin *camelus* 'camel,' from Greek *kamēlos*.

ca·mel·lia /kə'mēlyə/ ▶*n.* an evergreen eastern Asian shrub related to the tea plant, grown for its showy flowers and shiny leaves. • Genus *Camellia*, family Theaceae: several species, in particular the **common camellia** (*C. japonica*), which has numerous cultivars and hybrids. ▷modern Latin, named by Linnaeus after Joseph *Kamel* (Latinized as *Camellus*), Moravian botanist (1661–1706), who described the flora of Luzon, an island in the Philippines.

Ca·mel·lia State a nickname for the state of ALABAMA.

ca·mel·o·pard /kə'melə,pärd/ ▶*n.* *archaic* a giraffe. ▷late Middle English: via Latin from Greek *kamēlopardalis*, from *kamēlos* 'camel' + *pardalis* (see PARD).

Ca·mel·o·par·da·lis /kə,melə'pärdl-əs/ *Astronomy* a large but inconspicuous northern constellation (the Giraffe), between Polaris and Perseus. ■ [as *genitive*] (**Camelopardalis**) used with a preceding letter or numeral to designate a star in this constellation: *the star Alpha Camelopardalis.* ▷via Latin from Greek *kamēlopardalis* (see CAMELOPARD).

Cam·e·lot /'kamə,lät/ (in Arthurian legend) the place where King Arthur held his court. ■ [as *n.*] (**a Camelot**) a place associated with glittering romance and optimism.

ca·mel spi·der ▶*n.* another term for SUN SPIDER.

Cam·em·bert /'kaməm,be(ə)r/ ▶*n.* a kind of rich, soft, creamy cheese with a whitish rind, originally made near Camembert in Normandy.

cam·e·o /'kamē,ō/ ▶*n.* (*pl.* **-os**) **1** a piece of jewelry, typically oval in shape, consisting of a portrait in profile carved in relief on a background of a different color. **2** a short descriptive literary sketch that neatly encapsulates someone or something: *cameos of street life.* ■ a small character part in a play or movie, played by a distinguished actor or a celebrity: [as *adj.*] *he played numerous cameo roles.* ▷late Middle English: from Old French *camahieu, cama(h)u*; later influenced by Italian *cam(m)eo*, from medieval Latin *cammaeus*, related to the Old French word.

cam·er·a[1] /'kam(ə)rə/ ▶*n.* a device for recording visual images in the form of photographs, movie film, or video signals. ▷mid 19th cent.: from Latin (see CAMERA[2], CAMERA OBSCURA).
▶*PHRASE* □ **on** (or **off**) **camera** while being filmed or televised (or not being filmed or televised): *on camera, she was error-prone and nervous.*

cam·er·a[2] ▶*n.* [in *names*] a chamber or round building: *the Radcliffe Camera.* ▷late 17th cent. (denoting a council or legislative chamber in Italy or Spain): from Latin, 'vault, arched chamber,' from Greek *kamara* 'object with an arched cover.'

▸PHRASE □ **in camera** *chiefly Law* in private, in particular taking place in the private chambers of a judge, with the press and public excluded: *judges assess the merits of such claims in camera.* [late Latin, 'in the chamber.']

cam·er·a lu·ci·da /ˈlo͞osidə/ ▸n. an instrument in which rays of light are reflected by a prism to produce on a sheet of paper an image, from which a drawing can be made. ▷mid 18th cent.: from Latin, 'bright chamber,' on the pattern of *camera obscura.*

cam·er·a·man /ˈkam(ə)rəmən; -ˌman/ ▸n. (*pl.* **-men**) a man whose profession involves operating a television or movie camera.

cam·er·a ob·scu·ra /əbˈskyo͝orə/ ▸n. a darkened box with a convex lens or aperture for projecting the image of an external object onto a screen inside. It is important historically in the development of photography. ■ a small round building with a rotating angled mirror at the apex of the roof, projecting an image of the landscape on to a horizontal surface inside. ▷early 18th cent.: from Latin, 'dark chamber.'

cam·er·a·per·son /ˈkam(ə)rəˌpərsən/ ▸n. a cameraman or camerawoman (used as a neutral alternative).

cam·er·a-read·y ▸adj. *Printing* (of matter to be printed) in the right form and of good enough quality to be reproduced photographically onto a printing plate: *camera-ready copy.*

cam·er·a·wom·an /ˈkam(ə)rəˌwo͝omən/ ▸n. a woman whose profession involves operating a television or movie camera.

cam·er·a·work /ˈkam(ə)rəˌwərk/ ▸n. the way in which cameras are used in a movie or television program: *discreet camerawork and underplayed acting.*

Cam·e·roon /ˌkaməˈro͞on/ a country on the western coast of Africa, between Nigeria and Gabon; pop. 16,063,000; capital, Yaoundé; languages, French and English (official), many local languages, pidgin. French name **Cameroun** . —**Cam·e·roon·i·an** *adj.* & *n.*

A German protectorate from 1884 until 1916, it was subsequently administered by France and then by Britain as a League of Nations (later UN) trusteeship. In 1960, the French part became an independent republic and was joined in 1961 by part of British Cameroon; the remainder became part of Nigeria. Cameroon became a member of the Commonwealth of Nations in 1995.

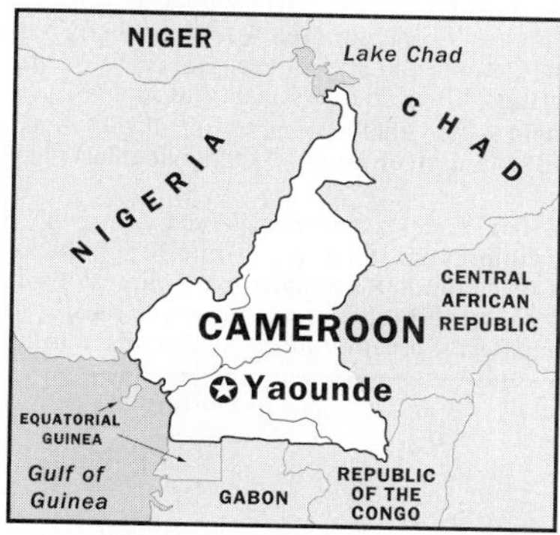

cam fol·low·er ▸n. the part of a machine in sliding or rolling contact with a rotating cam and given motion by it.

cam·girl /ˈkamˌgərl/ ▸n. a girl or woman who poses for a webcam.

cam·i /ˈkamē/ ▸n. a camisole.

cam·i·on /ˈkamēən/ ▸n. a large truck or a bus.

Cam·i·sard /ˌkaməˈzär(d)/ ▸n. a member of the French Protestant insurgents who rebelled against the persecution that followed the revocation of the Edict of Nantes. ▷French, from Provençal *camisa*, from late Latin *camisia* 'shirt,' because of the white shirts worn by the insurgents over their clothing for ease of recognition.

cam·i·sole /ˈkaməˌsōl/ ▸n. a woman's loose-fitting undergarment for the upper body, typically held up by shoulder straps and having decorative trimming. ▷early 19th cent.: from French, either from Italian *camiciola*, diminutive of *camicia*, or from Spanish *camisola*, diminutive of *camisa*, both from late Latin *camisia* 'shirt or nightgown.'

cam·lock /ˈkamˌläk/ ▸n. a fastening mechanism that incorporates a cam or tab that is turned to engage a catch or slot.

cam·o /ˈkamō/ ▸n. *informal* short for **camouflage**: [as *adj.*] *a camo jacket.*

Ca·mõ·es /kəˈmoinsh/ (also **Ca·mo·ëns** /ˈkamōˌens/), Luis (Vaz) de (*c.*1524–80), Portuguese poet. His most noted work, *The Lusiads* (1572), describes Vasco da Gama's discovery of the sea route to India.

cam·o·mile ▸n. variant spelling of **chamomile**.

Ca·mor·ra /kəˈmôrə/ (**the Camorra**) *n.* a secret criminal society originating in Naples and Neapolitan emigrant communities in the 19th century. Some members later moved to the U.S. and formed links with the Mafia. ▷Italian, perhaps from Spanish *camorra* 'dispute, quarrel.'

cam·ou·flage /ˈkaməˌfläzh; -ˌfläj/ ▸n. the disguising of military personnel, equipment, and installations by painting or covering them to make them blend in with their surroundings: *on the trenches were pieces of turf, which served for camouflage* | [as *adj.*] *camouflage nets.* ■ the clothing or materials used for such a purpose: *figures dressed in army camouflage.* ■ an animal's natural coloring or form that enables it to blend in with its surroundings: *the whiteness of polar bears provides camouflage.* ■ *figurative* actions or devices intended to disguise or mislead: *much of my apparent indifference was merely protective camouflage.*

▸v. [*trans.*] (often **be camouflaged**) hide or disguise the presence of (a person, animal, or object) by means of camouflage: *the war area had to be camouflaged with mud* | *figurative grievances should be discussed, not camouflaged.* ▷World War I: from French, from *camoufler* 'to disguise' (originally thieves' slang), from Italian *camuffare* 'disguise, deceive,' perhaps by association with French *camouflet* 'whiff of smoke in the face.'

Camp /kamp/, Walter Chauncey (1859–1925), U.S. football coach. One of the first to play U.S. football, he coached at Yale 1888–92 and was influential in shaping the rules of the sport. In 1889, he and a colleague initiated the annual selection of an All-American football team.

camp[1] /kamp/ ▸n. **1** a place with temporary accommodations of huts, tents, or other structures, typically used by soldiers, refugees, prisoners, or travelers: *the enemy camp* | *a detention camp.* ■ the people lodging in such a place: *the shot woke the whole camp.* ■ a recreational institution providing facilities for outdoor activities, sports, crafts, and other special interests and typically featuring rustic overnight accommodations: *a summer camp for children* | *drama camp.* ■ temporary overnight lodging out of doors, typically in tents: *we **made camp** at a bend in the creek* | *we **pitched camp** at a fine spot.* ■ a facility at which athletes train during the off-season: *football tryout camps.* **2** the supporters of a particular party or doctrine regarded collectively: *his views were firmly rooted in the conservative camp.*

▸v. [*intrans.*] live for a time in a camp, tent, or camper, as when on vacation: *parks in which you can camp or stay in a chalet* | [as *n.*] (**camping**) *camping attracts people of all ages.* ■ lodge temporarily, esp. in an inappropriate or uncomfortable place: *we **camped out** for the night in a mission schoolroom.* ■ remain persistently in one place: *the press will be camping on your doorstep once they get onto this story.* ▷early 16th cent.: from French *camp, champ*, from Italian *campo*, from Latin *campus* 'level ground,' specifically applied to the *Campus Martius* in Rome, used for games, athletic practice, and military drill.

▸PHRASE □ **break camp** take down a tent or the tents of an encampment ready to leave.

camp[2] *informal* ▸adj. deliberately exaggerated and theatrical in style, typically for humorous effect: *the movie seems more camp than shocking or gruesome.* ■ (of a man or his manner) ostentatiously and extravagantly effeminate: *a heavily made-up and highly camp actor.* ■ innocently idealistic, conventional, or sentimental: *straight camp is about the ongoing comedy of American straightness: the Mormon Tabernacle Choir, the Secret Service, the NRA.*

▸n. deliberately exaggerated and theatrical behavior or style: *Hollywood camp.*

▸v. [*intrans.*] (of a man) behave in an ostentatiously effeminate way: *he **camped it up** a bit for the cameras.* ▷early 20th cent.: of unknown origin. —**camp·i·ly** /ˈkampəlē/ *adv.* —**camp·i·ness** *n.* —**camp·y** *adj.*

cam·paign /kamˈpān/ ▸n. a series of military operations intended to achieve a particular objective, confined to a particular area, or involving a specified type of fighting: *a desert campaign* | *the air campaign* | *the army set off **on campaign**.* ■ an organized course of action to achieve a particular goal: *an advertising campaign* | *the **campaign for** a full inquiry into the regime* | [with *infinitive*] *his campaign to win the heart of a new woman.* ■ the organized actions that a political candidate undertakes in order to win an election.

▸v. [*intrans.*] work in an organized and active way toward a particular goal, typically a political or social one: *people who campaigned against child labor* | [with *infinitive*] *the services he had campaigned to protect.* ▷early 17th cent. (denoting a tract of open country): from French *campagne* 'open country,' via Italian from late Latin *campania*, from *campus* 'level ground' (see **camp**[1]). The change in sense arose from an army's practice of "taking the field" (i.e., moving from a fortress or town to open country) at the onset of summer. —**cam·paign·er** *n.*

Cam·pa·nel·la /ˌkampəˈnelə/, Roy (1921–93), U.S. baseball player; known as **Campy**. He was a catcher for the Brooklyn Dodgers 1948–58. Baseball Hall of Fame (1969).

cam·pa·ni·le /ˌkampəˈnēlē; -ˈnēl/ ▸n. an Italian bell tower, esp. a freestanding one. ▷mid 17th cent.: from Italian, from *campana* 'bell.'

cam·pa·nol·o·gy /ˌkampəˈnäləjē/ ▸n. the art or practice of bell-ringing. ▷mid 19th cent.: from modern Latin *campanologia*, from late Latin *campana* 'bell.' —**cam·pa·no·log·i·cal** /ˌkampənlˈäjikəl/ *adj.* —**cam·pa·nol·o·gist** /-jist/ *n.*

cam·pan·u·la /kamˈpanyələ/ ▸n. another term for **bellflower**. ▷modern Latin, diminutive of late Latin *campana* 'bell.'

cam·pan·u·late /kamˈpanyəlit; -ˌlāt/ ▸adj. *Botany* (of a flower) bell-shaped, as in a campanula.

Cam·pa·ri /kämˈpärē/ ▸n. *trademark* a pinkish aperitif flavored with bitters. ▷named after the manufacturer.

Camp·bell[1] /ˈkambəl/ a city in west central California, southwest of San Jose, part of the Silicon Valley research and industrial complex; pop. 36,048.

Camp·bell[2] /ˈkam(b)əl/, John Archibald (1811–89), U.S. Supreme Court associate justice 1853–61. Appointed to the Court by President Pierce, he resigned to serve as assistant secretary of war in the Confederate cabinet 1862–65.

Camp·bell[3], Mrs. Patrick (1865–1940), English actress; born *Beatrice Stella Tanner*. George Bernard Shaw wrote the part of Eliza Doolittle in *Pygmalion* (1914) for her.

Camp·bell-Ban·ner·man /ˈbanərmən/, Sir Henry (1836–1908), British statesman; prime minister 1905–08.

Camp Da·vid the country retreat of the President, in the Catoctin Mountains (part of the Blue Ridge Mountains) in northeastern Maryland. President Carter hosted talks there between the leaders of Israel and Egypt which resulted in the Camp David agreements (1978) and the Egypt–Israel peace treaty of 1979.

Cam·pe·che /kämˈpāchā; kamˈpēchē/ a state in southeastern Mexico, on the Yucatán Peninsula. ■ its capital, a seaport on the Gulf of Mexico; pop. 172,200.

camp·er /ˈkampər/ ▸n. **1** a person who spends a vacation in a tent or camp. **2** a large motor vehicle with facilities for sleeping and cooking while camping.

▸PHRASE □ **happy camper** a comfortable, contented person: *when I'm onstage, I'm really a happy camper.*

cam·pe·si·no /ˌkampəˈsēnō; ˌkäm-/ ▸n. (*pl.* **-nos**) (in Spanish-speaking regions) a peasant farmer. ▷Spanish.

camp·fire /ˈkampˌfī(ə)r/ ▸n. an open-air fire in a camp, used for cooking and as a focal point for social activity.

camp fol·low·er ▸n. a civilian who works in or is attached to a military camp. ■ a person who is nominally attached to a group but is not fully committed or does not make a substantial contribution to its activities: *cynical opportunists and camp followers.*

camp·ground /ˈkampˌground/ ▸n. a place used for camping, esp. one equipped with cooking grills, water, and bathrooms. ■ a place where a camp meeting is held.

cam·phor /ˈkamfər/ ▸n. a white, volatile, crystalline substance with an aromatic smell and bitter taste, occurring in certain essential oils. • A terpenoid ketone; chem. formula: $C_{10}H_{16}O$. ▷Middle English: from Old French *camphore* or medieval Latin *camphora*, from Arabic *kāfūr*, via Malay from Sanskrit *karpūra*.

cam·phor·ate /ˈkamfəˌrāt/ ▸*v.* [*trans.*] [usu. as *adj.*] (**camphorated**) impregnate or treat with camphor.

cam·phor tree ▸*n.* an eastern Asian tree that belongs to the laurel family and serves as the chief natural source of camphor. • *Cinnamomum camphora*, family Lauraceae.

Cam·pi·nas /kämˈpēnəs; käN-/ a city in southeastern Brazil, northwest of São Paulo; pop. 835,000.

Cam·pi·on[1] /ˈkampēən/, Jane (1954–), New Zealand movie director and screenwriter. She received an Academy Award for best screenplay for *The Piano* (1993).

Cam·pi·on[2], St. Edmund (1540–81), English Jesuit priest and martyr. Feast day, December 1.

cam·pi·on /ˈkampēən/ ▸*n.* a plant of the pink family, typically having pink or white flowers with notched petals, found in both Eurasia and North America. • Genera *Silene* and *Lychnis*, family Caryophyllaceae. ▷mid 16th cent.: perhaps related to **CHAMPION**. The name was originally used for the rose campion, whose name in Latin (*Lychnis coronaria*) and Greek (*lukhnis stephanōmatikē*) means 'campion fit for a crown,' and which was said in classical times to have been used for victors' garlands.

camp meet·ing ▸*n.* a religious meeting held in the open air or in a tent, often lasting several days.

cam·po /ˈkampō; ˈkämpō/ ▸*n.* (*pl.* **-pos**) **1** (usu. **the campo**) (in South America, esp. Brazil), a grass plain with occasional stunted trees. **2** a square in an Italian or Spanish town. ▷from Spanish, Portuguese, and Italian *campo*, literally 'field.'

Cam·po·bel·lo Is·land /ˌkampəˈbelō/ a resort island in southwestern New Brunswick, off Eastport in Maine, noted as the vacation home of Franklin D. Roosevelt.

Cam·po Gran·de /ˈkäN(m)pōō ˈgräN(n)də/ a city in southwestern Brazil; pop. 489,000.

camp·o·ree /ˌkampəˈrē/ ▸*n.* a local or regional camping event for Girl Scouts or Boy Scouts. ▷late 20th cent.: blend of **CAMP**[1] and **JAMBOREE**.

camp·site /ˈkampˌsīt/ ▸*n.* a place used for camping.

cam·pus /ˈkampəs/ ▸*n.* (*pl.* **-pus·es**) the grounds and buildings of a university or college: *for the first year I had a room* **on campus**. ■ the grounds of a school, hospital, or other institution. ▷late 18th cent. (originally U.S.): from Latin *campus* 'field' (see **CAMP**[1]).

cam·py·lo·bac·ter /ˈkampələˌbaktər; kamˈpilə-/ ▸*n.* *Medicine* a bacterium that sometimes causes abortion in animals and food poisoning in humans. • Genus *Campylobacter*: several species, in particular *C. jejuni*; curved or spiral Gram-negative bacteria. ▷1970s: modern Latin, from Greek *kampulos* 'bent' + **BACTERIUM**.

Cam Ranh Bay /ˈkam ˈrän/ an inlet of the South China Sea, in south central Vietnam. It has been a major base for France, Japan, the former Soviet Union, and the U.S., which had a major installation here during the Vietnam War.

cam·shaft /ˈkamˌsHaft/ ▸*n.* a shaft with one or more cams attached to it, esp. one operating the valves in an internal combustion engine.

Ca·mus /kaˈmōō/, Albert (1913–60), French novelist, playwright, and essayist; closely aligned with existentialism. Notable works: *The Stranger* (1942), *The Plague* (1947), and *The Rebel* (1951). Nobel Prize for Literature (1957).

can[1] /kan/ ▸*modal verb* (*3rd sing. present* **can**; *past* **could** /kŏŏd/) **1** be able to: *they can run fast | I could hear footsteps | he can't afford it.* ■ be able to through acquired knowledge or skill: *I can speak Italian.* ■ have the opportunity or possibility to: *there are many ways vacationers can take money abroad.* ■ [with *negative* or in *questions*] used to express doubt or surprise about the possibility of something's being the case: *he can't have finished | where can she have gone?* **2** be permitted to: *you can use the phone if you want to | nobody could legally drink on the premises.* ■ used to ask someone to do something: *can you open the window? | can't you leave me alone?* ■ used to make a suggestion or offer: *we can have another drink if you like.* **3** used to indicate that something is typically the case: *antique clocks can seem out of place in modern homes | he could be very moody.* ▷Old English *cunnan* 'know' (in Middle English 'know how to'), related to Dutch *kunnen* and German *können*; from an Indo-European root shared by Latin *gnoscere* 'know' and Greek *gignōskein* 'know.'

USAGE Is there any difference between **can** and **may** when used to request or express permission, as in **may** *I ask you a few questions?* or **can** *I ask you a few questions?* It is still widely held that using **can** for permission is somehow incorrect and that it should be reserved for expressions denoting capability, as in **can** *you swim?* Although the use of the 'permission' sense of **can** is not regarded as incorrect in standard English, there is a clear difference in formality between the two verbs: **may** is, generally speaking, a more polite way of asking for something and is the better choice in more formal contexts. The distinction is largely a matter of manners, and sometimes of authority.
See also **usage** at **MAY**[1].

can[2] ▸*n.* **1** a cylindrical metal container: *a garbage can | a can of paint.* ■ a small steel or aluminum container in which food or drink is hermetically sealed for storage over long periods: *soup cans.* ■ the quantity of food or drink held by such a container: *he drank two* **cans of** *beer.* **2** (**the can**) *informal* prison. **3** (**the can**) *informal* the toilet.
▸*v.* (**canned, can·ning**) [*trans.*] (often **be canned**) **1** preserve (food) in a can. **2** *informal* dismiss (someone) from their job: *he was canned because of a fight over promotion.* ■ reject (something) as inadequate: *the editorial team was so disappointed that they canned the project.* ▷Old English *canne*, related to Dutch *kan* and German *Kanne*; either of Germanic origin or from late Latin *canna*. **—can·ner** *n.*
▸*PHRASES* □ **a can of worms** a complicated matter likely to prove awkward or embarrassing: *to question the traditional model of education* **opens up a can of worms**. □ **in the can** *informal* on tape or film and ready to be broadcast or released.

Can. ▸*abbr.* Canada or Canadian.

Ca·na /ˈkānə/ an ancient small town in Galilee where Christ is said to have performed his first miracle by changing water into wine during a marriage feast (John 2:1–11).

Ca·naan /ˈkānən/ the biblical name for the area of ancient Palestine west of the Jordan River, the Promised Land of the Israelites, who conquered and occupied it during the latter part of the 2nd millennium BC. ▷early 17th cent.: via ecclesiastical Latin from ecclesiastical Greek *Khanaan*, from Hebrew *kĕna'an*. **—Ca·naan·ite** /-ˌnīt/ *n.* & *adj.*

Can·a·da /ˈkanədə/ a country in northern North America, the second largest country in the world; pop. 32,507,900; capital, Ottawa; official languages, English and French. **—Ca·na·di·an** /kəˈnādēən/ *n.* & *adj.*

Eastern Canada was colonized by the French in the 17th century, but the British emerged as the ruling colonial power in 1763 after the Seven Years War. Canada became a federation of provinces with dominion status in 1867. The signing of the Constitution Act of 1982 was the final step in attaining legal independence from the UK; however, Canada remains a member of the Commonwealth of Nations. French-speakers are largely concentrated in Quebec, the focal point for the French-Canadian separatist movement.

Can·a·da bal·sam ▸*n.* a yellowish resin obtained from the balsam fir and used for mounting preparations on microscope slides.

Can·a·da goose ▸*n.* a common North American goose with a black head and neck, a white chinstrap, and a loud, trumpeting call. • *Branta canadensis*, family Anatidae.

Can·a·da jay ▸*n.* another term for **GRAY JAY**.

Can·a·darm /ˈkanəˌdärm/ ▸*n.* the popular name for a robotic manipulation system designed for use in zero gravity. It has accompanied numerous space missions as a component on space shuttles. ▷1970s: blend of *Canada* (where it was manufactured) and *arm*.

Can·a·da this·tle ▸*n.* the European creeping or field thistle, which has become naturalized as a serious weed in North America. • *Cirsium arvense*, family Compositae.

Ca·na·di·an foot·ball /kəˈnādēən/ ▸*n.* a form of football played in Canada, derived from rugby but now resembling American football. There are twelve players on a side.

Ca·na·di·an French ▸*n.* the form of the French language written and spoken by French Canadians.

Ca·na·di·an goose ▸*n.* another term for **CANADA GOOSE**.

Ca·na·di·an Riv·er (also **South Canadian River**) a river that flows for 900 miles (1,450 km) from eastern New Mexico across the Texas Panhandle and Oklahoma. Oklahoma City lies on it.

Ca·na·di·an Shield a large plateau that occupies more than two fifths of the land area of Canada and is drained by rivers flowing into Hudson Bay. Also called **LAURENTIAN PLATEAU**.

ca·naille /kəˈnī; -ˈnāl/ ▸*n.* (**the canaille**) *derogatory* the common people; the masses: *the haughty contempt of a grandee sneering at the canaille.* ▷French, from Italian *canaglia* 'pack of dogs,' from *cane* 'dog.'

ca·nal /kəˈnal/ ▸*n.* an artificial waterway constructed to allow the passage of boats or ships inland or to convey water for irrigation. ■ a tubular duct in a plant or animal, serving to convey or contain food, liquid, or air: *the ear canal.* ■ *Astronomy* any of a number of linear markings formerly reported as seen by telescope on the planet Mars. [named *canali* ('channels') by G. V. Schiaparelli (1835–1910); the markings are now thought to have arisen from eye or lens defects.] ▷late Middle English: from Old French, alteration of *chanel* 'channel,' from Latin *canalis* 'pipe, groove, channel,' from *canna* 'cane.'

ca·nal boat ▸*n.* a long, narrow boat used on canals.

Ca·na·let·to /ˌkanlˈetō/ (1697–1768), Italian painter; born *Giovanni Antonio Canale*. He is noted for his paintings of Venetian festivals and scenery.

can·a·lic·u·lus /ˌkanlˈikyələs/ ▸*n.* (*pl.* **-li** /-ˌlī/) *Anatomy* a small channel or duct. **—can·a·lic·u·lar** /-ˈikyələr/ *adj.*

can·al·ize /ˈkanəlˌīz/ ▸*v.* [*trans.*] convert (a river) into a navigable canal. ■ convey (something) through a duct or channel. ■ *figurative* give a direction or purpose to (something): *his strategy was to canalize the enthusiasm of the diehards into party channels.* ▷mid 19th

cent.: from French *canaliser*, from *canal* 'channel' (see CANAL). —**ca·nal·i·za·tion** /ˌkanl-əˈzāSHən/ *n.*

Ca·nal Zone see PANAMA CANAL.

ca·na·pé /ˈkanəˌpā -pē/ ▸*n.* **1** a small piece of bread or pastry with a savory topping, often served with drinks at a reception or formal party. **2** a sofa, esp. a decorative French antique. ▷French, sense 1 being a figurative extension of the sense 'sofa' (as a "couch" on which to place toppings). See also CANOPY.

ca·nard /kəˈnär(d)/ ▸*n.* **1** an unfounded rumor or story: *the old canard that LA is a cultural wasteland.* **2** a small winglike projection attached to an aircraft forward of the main wing to provide extra stability or control, sometimes replacing the tail. ▷mid 19th cent.: from French, literally 'duck,' also 'hoax,' from Old French *caner* 'to quack.'

Ca·nar·sie /kəˈnärsē/ a residential section of southeastern Brooklyn in New York City, along Jamaica Bay. ▷named after the American Indian tribe who originally inhabited the area.

ca·nar·y /kəˈne(ə)rē/ ▸*n.* (*pl.* **-nar·ies**) **1** a mainly African finch with a melodious song, typically having yellowish-green plumage. One kind is popular as a pet bird and has been bred in a variety of colors, esp. bright yellow. • Genus *Serinus*, family Fringillidae: several species, esp. the **island canary** (*S. canaria*), which is native to the Canary Islands, the Azores, and Madeira, and from which the domestic canary was developed. **2** (also **canary yellow**) a bright yellow color resembling the plumage of a canary. **3** (also **canary wine**) *historical* a sweet wine from the Canary Islands, similar to Madeira. ▷late 16th cent.: from French *canari*, from Spanish *canario* 'canary' or 'person from the Canary Islands' (see CANARY ISLANDS).

ca·nar·y grass ▸*n.* a tall grass of northwestern Africa and the Canary Islands, grown for its seeds, which are fed to canaries and other caged finches. • Genus *Phalaris*, family Gramineae: several species, in particular *P. canariensis*.

Ca·nar·y Is·lands /kəˈne(ə)rē/ (also **the Ca·nar·ies**) a group of islands in the Atlantic Ocean, off the northwestern coast of Africa, that forms an autonomous region of Spain; capital, Las Palmas; pop. 1,557,530. ▷from French *Canarie*, via Spanish from Latin *Canaria (insula)* '(island) of dogs,' from *canis* "dog," one of the islands being noted in Roman times for large dogs.

ca·nas·ta /kəˈnastə/ ▸*n.* a card game resembling rummy, using two packs. It is usually played by two pairs of partners, and the aim is to collect sets (or melds) of cards. ■ a meld of seven cards in this game. ▷1940s: from Spanish (of Uruguayan origin), literally 'basket,' based on Latin *canistrum* 'basket' (see CANISTER).

Ca·nav·er·al, Cape /kəˈnav(ə)rəl/ a cape on the eastern coast of Florida, known as Cape Kennedy from 1963 until 1973. It is the site of the John F. Kennedy Space Center.

Can·ber·ra /ˈkanb(ə)rə; -ˌberə/ the capital of Australia and seat of the federal government, in Australian Capital Territory that is an enclave within New South Wales; pop. 310,000.

can·can /ˈkanˌkan/ ▸*n.* a lively, high-kicking stage dance originating in 19th-century Parisian music halls and performed by women in long skirts and petticoats: ▷mid 19th cent.: from French, child's word for *canard* 'duck,' from Old French *caner* 'to quack.'

can·cel /ˈkansəl/ ▸*v.* (**-celed, -cel·ing**; *Brit.* **-celled, -cel·ling**) [*trans.*] **1** decide or announce that (an arranged or planned event) will not take place: *he was forced to cancel his visit.* ■ annul or revoke (a formal arrangement which is in effect): *his visa had been canceled.* ■ abolish or make void (a financial obligation): *I intend to cancel your debt to me.* ■ mark, pierce, or tear (a ticket, check, or postage stamp) to show that it has been used or invalidated: [as *adj.*] *canceled checks.* **2** (of a factor or circumstance) neutralize or negate the force or effect of (another): *the electric fields may* **cancel each other out.** ■ *Mathematics* delete (an equal factor) from both sides of an equation or from the numerator and denominator of a fraction.
▸*n.* **1** a mark made on a postage stamp to show that it has been used. **2** *Printing* a new page or section inserted in a book to replace the original text, typically to correct an error: [as *adj.*] *a cancel title page.* ▷late Middle English (in the sense 'obliterate or delete writing by drawing or stamping lines across it'): from Old French *canceller*, from Latin *cancellare*, from *cancelli* 'crossbars.'

can·cel·bot /ˈkansəlˌbät/ ▸*n. Computing* a program that searches for and deletes specified postings from Internet newsgroups. ▷1990s: from CANCEL + BOT².

can·cel·er /ˈkansələr/ (also **can·cel·ler**) ▸*n.* a manual, mechanical, or electronic device used to cancel something, esp. one that makes a cancellation on a postage stamp.

can·cel·la·tion /ˌkansəˈlāSHən/ ▸*n.* the action of canceling something that has been arranged or planned: *train services are subject to cancellation at short notice | the project was threatened with cancellation by the government | the cancellation of the performance.* ■ a crossing out of something written: *all cancellations on documents must be made indelibly.* ■ a visible or electronic mark placed on a postage stamp to show that it has been used. ■ *Law* the annulling of a legal document: *the debtor can procure cancellation if satisfied within one month.*

can·cel·lous /ˈkansələs/ ▸*adj. Anatomy* of or denoting bone tissue with a meshlike structure containing many pores, typical of the interior of mature bones. ▷mid 19th cent.: from Latin *cancelli* 'crossbars' + -OUS.

Can·cer /ˈkansər/ **1** *Astronomy* a constellation (the Crab), said to represent a crab crushed under the foot of Hercules. It is most noted for the globular star cluster of Praesepe (the Beehive cluster). ■ [as *genitive*] (**Cancri** /ˈkaNGkrē/) used with a preceding letter or numeral to designate a star in this constellation: *the star Delta Cancri.* **2** *Astrology* the fourth sign of the zodiac, which the sun enters at the northern summer solstice (about June 21). ■ (**a Cancer**) a person born when the sun is in this sign. ▷Latin. —**Can·cer·i·an** /kanˈserēən; -ˈsi(ə)r-/ *n.* & *adj.* (in sense 2).
▸*PHRASE* □ **tropic of Cancer** see TROPIC¹.

can·cer /ˈkansər/ ▸*n.* the disease caused by an uncontrolled division of abnormal cells in a part of the body: *he's got cancer | smoking is the major cause of lung cancer.* ■ a malignant growth or tumor resulting from such a division of cells: *most skin cancers are curable.* ■ *figurative* a practice or phenomenon perceived to be evil or destructive and hard to contain or eradicate: *racism is a cancer sweeping across Europe.* ▷Old English, from Latin, 'crab or creeping ulcer,' translating Greek *karkinos*, said to have been applied to such tumors because the swollen veins around them resembled the limbs of a crab. CANKER was the usual form until the 17th cent. Compare with CANCER. —**can·cer·ous** /ˈkansərəs/ *adj.*

can·cer clus·ter ▸*n.* a geographic area with a statistically higher than average occurrence of cancer among its residents.

can·cer stick ▸*n. informal, humorous* a cigarette.

can·croid /ˈkaNGˌkroid/ ▸*adj.* **1** *Zoology* like a crab, esp. in structure. **2** *Medicine* (of a growth) resembling cancer.

Can·cún /kaNGˈkōōn; kan-/ a resort town in southeastern Mexico, on the northeastern coast of the Yucatán Peninsula; pop. 27,500.

can·de·la /kanˈdēlə; -ˈdelə/ (abbr.: **cd**) ▸*n. Physics* the SI unit of luminous intensity. One candela is the luminous intensity, in a given direction, of a source that emits monochromatic radiation of frequency 540×10^{12}Hz and has a radiant intensity in that direction of $1/683$ watt per steradian. ▷1950s: from Latin, 'candle.'

can·de·la·brum /ˌkandəˈläbrəm; -ˈlab-/ ▸*n.* (*pl.* **-la·bra** /-ˈläbrə; -ˈlabrə/) a large branched candlestick or holder for several candles or lamps. ▷early 19th cent.: from Latin, from *candela* (see CANDLE).

USAGE Based on the Latin forms, the correct singular is **candelabrum**, and the correct plural is **candelabra. Candelabra**, however, is often mistakenly thought to be the singular, resulting in the plural *candelabras* (as in Sir Walter Scott's *Ivanhoe*). Another false plural, *candelabrums*, is also sometimes found.

can·des·cent /kanˈdesənt/ ▸*adj.* glowing with, or as with, heat. —**can·des·cence** *n.* —**can·des·cent·ly** *adv.*

can·did /ˈkandid/ ▸*adj.* **1** truthful and straightforward; frank: *his responses were remarkably candid | a candid discussion.* **2** (of a photograph of a person) taken informally, esp. without the subject's knowledge. ▷mid 17th cent. (in the Latin sense): from Latin *candidus* 'white.' Subsequent early senses were 'pure, innocent,' 'unbiased,' and 'free from malice,' hence 'frank' (late 17th cent.). Compare with CANDOR. —**can·did·ly** *adv.* —**can·did·ness** *n.*

can·di·da /ˈkandidə/ ▸*n.* a yeastlike, parasitic fungus that can sometimes cause thrush. • Genus *Candida*, phylum Ascomycota, esp. *C. albicans*. ▷modern Latin, feminine of Latin *candidus* 'white.'

can·di·date /ˈkandiˌdāt; -dit/ ▸*n.* a person who applies for a job or is nominated for election: *candidates applying for this position should be computer-literate | the Republican candidate.* ■ a person taking an examination: *doctoral candidates in literature.* ■ a person or thing regarded as suitable for or likely to receive a particular fate, treatment, or position: *she was the perfect* **candidate for** *a biography | a leading* **candidate for** *the title of New York's ugliest building.* ▷early 17th cent.: from Latin *candidatus* 'white-robed,' also denoting a candidate for office (who traditionally wore a white toga), from *candidus* 'white.' —**can·di·da·cy** /ˈkandidəsē/ *n.* —**can·di·da·ture** /-ˌCHŏŏr; -CHər/ *n. Brit.*

can·di·di·a·sis /ˌkandiˈdīəsis/ ▸*n.* infection with candida, esp. as causing oral or vaginal thrush.

can·di·ru /ˌkandəˈrōō/ ▸*n.* a minute, slender catfish of the Amazon region that feeds by sucking blood from other fishes and sometimes enters the body orifices of mammals. It is notorious for its occasional habit of entering the urethra of human swimmers. • *Vandellia cirrhosa*, family Trichomycteridae. ▷mid 19th cent.: via Portuguese from Tupi *candirú*.

can·dle /ˈkandl/ ▸*n.* a cylinder or block of wax or tallow with a central wick that is lit to produce light as it burns. ■ (also **international candle**) *Physics* a unit of luminous intensity, superseded by the candela.
▸*v.* [*trans.*] (often **be candled**) (of a poultry breeder) test (an egg) for freshness or fertility by holding it to the light. ▷Old English *candel*, from Latin *candela*, from *candere* 'be white or glisten.' —**can·dler** /ˈkandlər; -dl-ər/ *n.*
▸*PHRASE* □ **be unable to hold a candle to** *informal* be not nearly as good as: *nobody in the final could hold a candle to her.*

can·dle·ber·ry /ˈkandlˌberē/ ▸*n.* (*pl.* **-ries**) any of a number of trees or shrubs whose berries or seeds yield a wax or oil that can be used for making candles, in particular: • a bayberry or related North American shrub (genus *Myrica*, family Myricaceae). • the candlenut.

can·dle·fish /ˈkandlˌfiSH/ ▸*n.* (*pl.* same or **-fish·es**) a small, edible marine fish with oily flesh, occurring on the west coast of North America. Also called EULACHON. • *Thaleichthys pacificus*, family Osmeridae. ▷so named because the Chinook Indians formerly burned the oily bodies of these fish as candles.

can·dle·hold·er /ˈkandlˌhōldər/ ▸*n.* a holder or support for a candle, typically one that is small or sturdy.

can·dle·light /ˈkandlˌlīt/ ▸*n.* dim light provided by a candle or candles: *we dined* **by candlelight**.

can·dle·lit /ˈkandlˌlit/ ▸*adj.* lit by a candle or candles: *a romantic candlelit dinner.*

Can·dle·mas /ˈkandlməs/ ▸*n.* a Christian festival held on February 2 to commemorate the purification of the Virgin Mary (after childbirth, according to Jewish law) and the presentation of Christ in the Temple. Candles were traditionally blessed at this festival. ▷Old English *Candelmæsse* (see CANDLE, MASS).

can·dle·nut /ˈkandlˌnət/ ▸*n.* an evergreen tree of the spurge family, with large seeds that yield an oil used for lighting and other purposes, native to Southeast Asia and the South Pacific islands. Also called CANDLEBERRY. • *Aleurites moluccana*, family Euphorbiaceae.

can·dle·pow·er /ˈkandlˌpou(ə)r/ ▸*n.* illuminating power expressed in candelas or candles: [as *adj.*] *a 16-candlepower lamp.*

can·dle·snuff·er /ˈkandlˌsnəfər/ ▸*n.* see SNUFFER.

can·dle·stick /ˈkandlˌstik/ ▸*n.* a support or holder for one or more candles, typically one that is tall and thin.

can·dle·wick /ˈkandlˌwik/ ▸*n.* a thick, soft cotton fabric with a raised, tufted pattern: [as *adj.*] *a candlewick dressing gown.* ■ the yarn used to make such a fabric. ■ tufted embroidery work made with heavy cotton yarn similar to that used to make wicks for candles.

can-do /ˈkan ˈdōō/ ▸*adj.* [*attrib.*] *informal* characterized by or exhibiting a determination or willingness to take action and achieve results: *I like his can-do attitude.*

can·dom·blé /ˌkan,dōmˈblā/ ▸*n.* Brazilian sect of the macumba cult. ▷Brazilian Portuguese.

Pronunciation Key ə *ago*; ər *over*; ˈə or ˌə *up*; ˈər or ˌər *fur*; a *hat*; ā *rate*; ä *car*; CH *chew*; e *let*; ē *see*; e(ə)r *air*; i *fit*; ī *by*; i(ə)r *ear*; NG *sing*; ō *go*; ô *for*; oi *boy*; ŏŏ *good*; ōō *goo*; ou *out*; SH *she*; TH *thin*; T͟H *then*; (h)w *why*; ZH *vision*

can·dor /ˈkandər; -ˌdôr/ (*Brit.* **can·dour**) ▸*n.* the quality of being open and honest in expression; frankness: *a man of refreshing candor.* ▷late Middle English (in the Latin sense): from Latin *candor* 'whiteness.' The current sense dates from the mid 18th cent.; the development of the senses paralleled that of CANDID.

CANDU /ˈkanˌdoo; -ˈdoo/ (also **Can·du**) ▸*n.* a nuclear reactor of a Canadian design in which the fuel is unenriched uranium oxide clad in zircaloy and the coolant and moderator is heavy water. ▷from *Can(ada)* + the initial letters of DEUTERIUM and URANIUM.

C&W ▸*abbr.* country and western (music).

can·dy /ˈkandē/ ▸*n.* (*pl.* **-dies**) a sweet food made with sugar or syrup combined with fruit, chocolate, or nuts: [as *adj.*] *a candy bar | pink and yellow candies.* ■ sugar crystallized by repeated boiling and slow evaporation.
▸*v.* (**-dies, -died**) [*trans.*] [often as *adj.*] (**candied**) preserve (fruit) by coating and impregnating it with a sugar syrup: *candied fruit.* ▷mid 17th cent. (as a verb): the noun use is from late Middle English *sugar-candy*, from French *sucre candi* 'crystallized sugar,' from Arabic *sukkar* 'sugar' + *ḳandī* 'candied,' based on Sanskrit *khaṇḍa* 'fragment.'

can·dy ap·ple ▸*n.* an apple coated with a thin layer of cooked sugar or caramel and fixed on a stick. ■ (also **candy-apple red**) a bright red color.

can·dy-ass ▸*n.* *informal* a timid, cowardly, or despicable person. **—can·dy-assed** *adj.*

can·dy cane ▸*n.* a cylindrical stick of striped, sweet candy with a curved end, resembling a walking stick.

can·dy corn ▸*n.* a form of chewy candy shaped like a large kernel of corn.

can·dy·man /ˈkandēˌman/ ▸*n.* (*pl.* **-men**) *informal* a person who sells illegal drugs. ▷mid 19th cent.: from CANDY + MAN, an earlier sense denoting a ragman who gave toffee in exchange for goods.

can·dy-striped ▸*adj.* (of material or a garment) patterned with alternating stripes of white and another color, typically pink. **—can·dy-stripe** *adj.* & *n.*

can·dy-strip·er /ˈstrīpər/ ▸*n.* *informal* a teenage girl who does volunteer nursing in a hospital. ▷so named because of the candy-striped uniforms of such nurses.

can·dy·tuft /ˈkandēˌtəft/ ▸*n.* a European plant with small heads of white, pink, or purple flowers, often cultivated as a garden plant. • Genus *Iberis*, family Brassicaceae. ▷early 17th cent.: from *Candy* (obsolete form of *Candia*, former name of Crete) + TUFT.

cane /kān/ ▸*n.* **1** the hollow, jointed stem of a tall grass, esp. bamboo or sugar cane, or the stem of a slender palm such as rattan. ■ any plant that produces such stems. ■ stems of bamboo, rattan, or wicker used as a material for making furniture or baskets: [as *adj.*] *a cane coffee table.* ■ short for SUGAR CANE. ■ a flexible, woody stem of the raspberry plant or any of its relatives. **2** a length of cane or a slender stick, esp. one used as a support for plants, as a walking stick, or as an instrument of punishment. ■ (**the cane**) *chiefly Brit.* a form of corporal punishment used in certain schools, involving beating with a cane: *wrong answers were rewarded by the cane.*
▸*v.* [*trans.*] **1** (often **be caned**) beat with a cane as a punishment. **2** [usu. as *adj.*] (**caned**) make or repair (furniture) with cane: *armchairs with caned seats.* ▷late Middle English: from Old French, via Latin from Greek *kanna, kannē*, of Semitic origin. **—can·er** *n.*

cane·brake /ˈkānˌbrāk/ ▸*n.* a piece of ground covered with a dense growth of canes.

cane chair ▸*n.* a chair with a seat made of woven cane strips.

cane rat ▸*n.* a large, ratlike, African rodent found in wetlands south of the Sahara. It is often a pest of sugar plantations. • Family Thryonomyidae and genus *Thryonomys*: two species.

cane sug·ar ▸*n.* sugar obtained from sugar cane.

Ca·nes Ve·nat·i·ci /ˈkānēz vəˈnatəsē; -ˌsī/ *Astronomy* a small northern constellation (the Hunting Dogs), said to represent two dogs (Asterion and Chara) held on a leash by Boötes. ■ [as *genitive*] (**Canum Venaticorum** /ˈkānəm veˌnatiˈkôrəm/) used with a preceding letter or numeral to designate a star in this constellation: *the star Beta Canum Venaticorum.* ▷Latin.

cane toad ▸*n.* a large brown toad native to tropical America. It has been introduced elsewhere as a pest control agent but can become a serious pest itself, partly because animals eating it are killed by its toxins. Also called MARINE TOAD, GIANT TOAD. • *Bufo marinus*, family Bufonidae.

Ca·net·ti /kəˈnetē/, Elias (1905–94), British writer; born in Bulgaria. Notable works: *Auto-da-Fé* (1936) and *Crowds and Power* (1960). Nobel Prize for Literature (1981).

Can·field /ˈkanˌfēld/ ▸*n.* a form of the card game solitaire. ▷early 20th cent.: named after Richard A. *Canfield* (1855–1914), an American gambler.

ca·nic·u·lar /kəˈnikyələr/ ▸*adj.* pertaining to a dog, in particular: ■ of or pertaining to the Dog Star, Sirius. ■ of or pertaining to the dog days.

can·id /ˈkanid; ˈkā-/ ▸*n.* *Zoology* a mammal of the dog family (Canidae). ▷late 19th cent.: from modern Latin *Canidae* (plural), from Latin *canis* 'dog.'

ca·nine /ˈkāˌnīn/ ▸*adj.* of, relating to, or resembling a dog or dogs: *canine distemper virus.* ■ *Zoology* of or relating to animals of the dog family.
▸*n.* **1** a dog. ■ *Zoology* another term for CANID. **2** (also **canine tooth**) a pointed tooth between the incisors and premolars of a mammal, often greatly enlarged in carnivores. ▷late Middle English (sense 2): from French, from Latin *caninus*, from *canis* 'dog.'

ca·nine dis·tem·per ▸*n.* see DISTEMPER[1] (sense 1).

Ca·nis Ma·jor /ˈkānis; ˈkan-/ *Astronomy* a small constellation (the Great Dog), said to represent one of the dogs following Orion. It is just south of the celestial equator and contains the brightest star, Sirius. ■ [as *genitive*] (**Canis Majoris** /məˈjôris/) used with a preceding letter or numeral to designate a star in this constellation: *the star Eta Canis Majoris.* ▷Latin.

Ca·nis Mi·nor *Astronomy* a small constellation (the Little Dog), said to represent one of the dogs following Orion. It is close to the celestial equator and contains the bright star Procyon. ■ [as *genitive*] (**Canis Minoris** /mīˈnôris/) used with a preceding letter or numeral to designate a star in this constellation: *the star Beta Canis Minoris.* ▷Latin.

can·is·ter /ˈkanəstər/ ▸*n.* a round or cylindrical container, typically one made of metal, used for storing such things as food, chemicals, or rolls of film. ■ a cylinder of pressurized gas, typically one that explodes when thrown or fired from a gun: *riot police fired tear-gas canisters into the crowd.* ■ *historical* small bullets packed in cases that fit the bore of an artillery piece or gun: *another deadly volley of canister.* ▷late 15th cent. (denoting a basket): from Latin *canistrum*, from Greek *kanastron* 'wicker basket,' from *kanna* 'cane, reed' (see CANE).

can·ker /ˈkaNGkər/ ▸*n.* **1** a necrotic, fungal disease of apple and other trees that results in damage to the bark. ■ an open lesion in plant tissue caused by infection or injury. ■ fungal rot in some fruits and vegetables, e.g., parsnips and tomatoes. **2** *Medicine* an ulcerous condition or disease, in particular: ■ (also **canker sore**) a small ulcer of the mouth or lips. ■ another term for THRUSH[2] (sense 2). ■ ulceration of the throat and other orifices of birds, typically caused by a protozoal infection. ■ (also **ear can·ker**) inflammation of the ear of a dog, cat, or rabbit, typically caused by a mite infestation. ■ *figurative* a malign and corrupting influence that is difficult to eradicate: [in *sing.*] *racism remains a canker at the heart of the nation.*
▸*v.* **1** [*intrans.*] (of woody plant tissue) become infected with canker: [as *n.*] (**cankering**) *we found some cankering of the wood.* **2** [*trans.*] [usu. as *adj.*] (**cankered**) infect with a pervasive and corrupting bitterness: *he hated her with a cankered, shameful abhorrence.* ▷Middle English (denoting a tumor): from Old French *chancre*, from Latin *cancer* 'crab' (see CANCER). **—can·ker·ous** /-kərəs/ *adj.*

can·ker·worm /ˈkaNGkərˌwərm/ ▸*n.* the caterpillar of a North American moth that has wingless females. Cankerworms consume the buds and leaves of trees and can be a major pest. • Several species in the family Geometridae, in particular *Paleacrita vernata* and *Alsophila pometaria.*

can·kle /ˈkaNGkəl/ ▸*n.* *informal* an unusually thick or stout ankle. ▷blend of *calf* and *ankle.*

Can·more /ˈkanˌmôr/, the nickname of Malcolm III of Scotland (see MALCOLM).

can·na /ˈkanə/ (also **canna lily**) ▸*n.* a lilylike, tropical American plant with bright flowers and ornamental straplike leaves. • Genus *Canna*, family Cannaceae: several species, in particular forms of Indian shot (*C. indica*), which are widely naturalized. ▷from modern Latin, from Latin *canna* 'cane, reed' (see CANE).

can·na·bin /ˈkanəbən/ ▸*n.* a poisonous resin extracted from cannabis.

can·nab·i·noid /ˈkanəbəˌnoid; kəˈnabə-/ ▸*n.* *Chemistry* any of a group of closely related compounds that include cannabinol and the active constituents of cannabis.

can·nab·i·nol /ˈkanəbəˌnôl; kəˈnabə-; -ˌnōl/ ▸*n.* *Chemistry* a crystalline compound whose derivatives, esp. THC, are the active constituents of cannabis. • A polycyclic phenol; chem. formula: $C_{21}H_{26}O_2$. ▷late 19th cent.: from CANNABIS + -OL.

can·na·bis /ˈkanəbəs/ ▸*n.* a tall plant with a stiff upright stem, divided serrated leaves, and glandular hairs. It is used to produce hemp fiber and as a psychotropic drug. Also called INDIAN HEMP, MARIJUANA. • *Cannabis sativa*, family Cannabaceae (or Cannabidaceae): two subspecies (sometimes considered two species), *C. s. sativa*, which is chiefly used for hemp, and *C. s. indica*, from which the drug is usually obtained. ■ a dried preparation of the flowering tops or other parts of this plant, or a resinous extract of it (**cannabis resin**), used (generally illegally) as a psychotropic drug, chiefly in cigarettes. ▷from Latin, from Greek *kannabis.*

canned /kand/ ▸*adj.* **1** (of food or drink) preserved or supplied in a sealed can: *canned beans.* **2** *informal, often derogatory* (of music, laughter, or applause) prerecorded and therefore considered to be lacking in freshness and spontaneity.

can·nel coal /ˈkanl/ ▸*n.* a hard, compact kind of bituminous coal. ▷mid 16th cent. (originally a northern English usage): of unknown origin.

can·nel·li·ni bean /ˌkanlˈēnē/ ▸*n.* a kidney-shaped bean of a medium-sized, creamy-white variety. ▷Italian *cannellini*, literally 'small tubes.'

can·nel·lo·ni /ˌkanlˈōnē/ ▸ *n.* rolls of pasta stuffed with a meat or vegetable mixture. ■ [treated as *sing.*] an Italian dish consisting of such rolls of pasta cooked in a cheese sauce. ▷Italian, literally 'large tubes,' from *cannello* 'tube.'

can·ne·lure /ˈkanlˌ(y)o͝or/ ▸*n.* a groove around the cylindrical part of a bullet. ▷mid 18th cent.: from French, from *canneler* 'provide with a channel,' from *canne* 'reed, cane.'

can·ner·y /ˈkanərē/ ▸*n.* (*pl.* **-ner·ies**) a factory where food is canned.

Cannes /kan; kän/ a resort on the Mediterranean coast of France; pop. 69,360. An international film festival is held here annually.

can·ni·bal /ˈkanəbəl/ ▸*n.* a person who eats the flesh of other human beings: [as *adj.*] *cannibal tribes.* ■ an animal that feeds on flesh of its own species. ▷mid 16th cent.: from Spanish *Canibales* (plural), variant (recorded by Columbus) of *Caribes*, the name of a West Indian people reputed to eat humans (see CARIB). **—can·ni·bal·ism** /-ˌlizəm/ *n.* **—can·ni·bal·is·tic** /ˌkanəbəˈlistik/ *adj.* **—can·ni·bal·is·ti·cal·ly** /ˌkanəbəˈlistik(ə)lē/ *adv.*

can·ni·bal·ize /ˈkanəbəˌlīz/ ▸*v.* [*trans.*] **1** use (a machine) as a source of spare parts for another, similar machine. ■ use (the creative work of others) in one's own art: *high culture should cannibalize mass culture.* ■ (of a company) reduce (the sales of one of its products) by introducing a similar, competing product. **2** (of an animal) eat (an animal of its own kind): *female spiders cannibalize courting males.* **—can·ni·bal·i·za·tion** /ˌkanəbələˈzāSHən/ *n.*

Can·niz·za·ro /ˌkänēdˈzärō/, Stanislao (1826–1910), Italian chemist. He revived Avogadro's law and used it to distinguish clearly between atoms and molecules and to introduce the unified system of atomic and molecular weights.

can·no·li /kəˈnōlē/ ▸*plural n.* Italian pastries in the form of hard tubular shells filled with sweetened ricotta cheese and often containing nuts, citron, or chocolate bits. ▷Italian, plural of *cannolo*, from *canna* 'reed,' from Greek *kanna*, of Semitic origin.

can·non /ˈkanən/ ▸*n.* **1** (*pl.* usu. same) a large, heavy piece of artillery, typically mounted on wheels, formerly used in warfare. ■ an automatic heavy gun that fires shells from an aircraft or tank. **2** *Billiards chiefly Brit.* a carom. [early 19th cent.: alteration of CAROM.] **3** *Engineering* a heavy cylinder or hollow drum that is able to rotate independently on a shaft.
▸*v.* [*intrans.*] *Billiards & Snooker* make a cannon shot. ▷late Middle English: from French *canon*, from Italian *cannone* 'large tube,' from *canna* 'cane, reed' (see CANE).

cannon 1

can·non·ade /ˌkanəˈnād/ ▸*n.* a period of continuous, heavy gunfire.
▸*v.* [*intrans.*] discharge heavy guns continuously: [as *n.*] (**cannonading**) *the daily cannonading continued.* ▷mid 16th cent.: from French, from Italian *cannonata*, from *cannone* (see CANNON).

can·non·ball /ˈkanənˌbôl/ ▸*n.* a round metal or stone projectile fired from a cannon in former times. ■ (also **cannonball dive**) a jump into water performed upright with the knees clasped to the chest.

can·non bone ▸*n.* a long, tube-shaped bone in the lower leg of a horse or other large quadruped, between the fetlock and the knee or hock.

can·non·eer /ˌkanəˈni(ə)r/ ▸*n. historical* an artilleryman who positioned and fired a cannon.

can·non fod·der ▸*n.* soldiers regarded merely as material to be expended in war.

can·non·ry /ˈkanənrē/ ▸*n.* (*pl.* **-ries**) the use or discharge of cannon; artillery.

can·not /kəˈnät; ˈkanˌät/ ▸*contraction of* can not.

USAGE Both the one-word form **cannot** and the two-word form **can not** are acceptable, but **cannot** is far more common in all contexts. Indeed, **can not** has come to be so unusual that it may be read as an error. The two-word form is advised only in a construction in which **not** is part of a set phrase, such as 'not only . . . but (also)': *Stevenson can not only sing well, but he paints brilliantly.*

can·nu·la /ˈkanyələ/ ▸*n.* (*pl.* **-lae** /-lē; -lī/ or **-las**) *Surgery* a thin tube inserted into a vein or body cavity to administer medicine, drain off fluid, or insert a surgical instrument. ▷late 17th cent.: from Latin, 'small reed,' diminutive of *canna* (see CANE).

can·nu·late /ˈkanyəˌlāt/ ▸*v.* [*trans.*] *Surgery* introduce a cannula or thin tube into (a vein or body cavity). —**can·nu·la·tion** /ˌkanyəˈlāsHən/ *n.*

can·ny /ˈkanē/ ▸*adj.* (**-ni·er**, **-ni·est**) **1** having or showing shrewdness and good judgment, esp. in money or business matters: *canny shoppers came early for a bargain.* **2** *Scottish & N. English* pleasant; nice: *she's a canny lass.* ▷late 16th cent. (originally Scots): from CAN1 (in the obsolete sense 'know') + -Y1. —**can·ni·ly** /ˈkanl-ē/ *adv.* —**can·ni·ness** *n.*

ca·noe /kəˈno͞o/ ▸*n.* a narrow, keelless boat with pointed ends, propelled by a paddle or paddles.
▸*v.* (**-noes**, **-noed**, **-noe·ing**) [*intrans.*] travel in or paddle a canoe: *he had once canoed down the Nile.* ▷mid 16th cent.: from Spanish *canoa*, from Arawak, from Carib *canaoua*. —**ca·noe·ist** /-ˈno͞oist/ *n.*

canoe

ca·noe·ing /kəˈno͞oiNG/ ▸*n.* the sport or activity of traveling in or paddling a canoe.

can·o·la /kəˈnōlə/ ▸*n.* oilseed rape of a variety developed in Canada and grown in North America. It yields a valuable culinary oil. ▷1970s: from CANADA + *-ola* (based on Latin *oleum* 'oil').

can·on1 /ˈkanən/ ▸*n.* **1** a general law, rule, principle, or criterion by which something is judged: *the appointment violated* **the canons of** *fair play and equal opportunity.* ■ a church decree or law: *a set of ecclesiastical canons.* **2** a collection or list of sacred books accepted as genuine: *the formation of the biblical canon.* ■ the works of a particular author or artist that are recognized as genuine: *the Shakespeare canon.* ■ a list of literary or artistic works considered to be permanently established as being of the highest quality: *Hopkins was firmly established in the canon of English poetry.* **3** (also **canon of the Mass**) (in the Roman Catholic Church) the part of the Mass containing the words of consecration. **4** *Music* a piece in which the same melody is begun in different parts successively, so that the imitations overlap. ▷Old English: from Latin, from Greek *kanōn* 'rule,' reinforced in Middle English by Old French *canon*.
▸***PHRASE*** □ **in canon** *Music* with different parts successively beginning the same melody.

can·on2 ▸*n.* a member of the clergy who is on the staff of a cathedral, esp. one who is a member of the chapter. The position is frequently conferred as an honorary one. ■ (also **canon regular** or **regular canon**) (in the Roman Catholic Church) a member of certain orders of clergy that live communally according to an ecclesiastical rule in the same way as monks. ▷Middle English (in the sense 'canon regular'): from Old French *canonie*, from Latin *canonicus* 'according to rule' (see CANONIC). The other sense dates from the mid 16th cent.

ca·ñon /ˈkanyən/ ▸*n.* archaic spelling of CANYON.

can·on can·cri·zans /ˈkaNGkrəˌzanz/ ▸*n. Music* a canon in which the theme or subject is repeated backward in the second part. Also called CRAB CANON. ▷late 19th cent.: from CANON1 + medieval Latin *cancrizans* 'walking backward' (from *cancer* 'crab').

can·on·ess /ˈkanənəs/ ▸*n.* (in the Roman Catholic Church) a member of certain religious orders of women living communally according to an ecclesiastical rule in the same way as nuns.

ca·non·ic /kəˈnänik/ ▸*adj.* **1** *Music* in canon form. **2** another term for CANONICAL. ▷Old English (as a noun): from Old French *canonique* or Latin *canonicus* 'canonical,' from Greek *kanonikos*, from *kanōn* 'rule' (see CANON1). The adjective dates from the late 15th cent. —**ca·non·i·cal·ly** /-ik(ə)lē/ *adv.*

ca·non·i·cal /kəˈnänikəl/ ▸*adj.* **1** according to or ordered by canon law: *the canonical rites of the Roman Church.* **2** included in the list of sacred books officially accepted as genuine: *the canonical Gospels of the New Testament.* ■ accepted as being accurate and authoritative: *the canonical method of comparative linguistics.* ■ (of an artist or work) belonging to the literary or artistic canon: *canonical writers like Jane Austen.* ■ according to recognized rules or scientific laws: *canonical nucleotide sequences.* ■ *Mathematics* of or relating to a general rule or standard formula. **3** of or relating to a cathedral chapter or a member of it.
▸*plural n.* (**canonicals**) the prescribed official dress of the clergy: *Cardinal Bea in full canonicals.* ▷late Middle English: from medieval Latin *canonicalis*, from Latin *canonicus* (see CANONIC). —**ca·non·i·cal·ly** /-ik(ə)lē/ *adv.*

ca·non·i·cal hours ▸*plural n.* the times of daily Christian prayer appointed in the breviary. ■ the offices set for these times, namely matins with lauds, prime, terce, sext, nones, vespers, and compline.

can·on·ic·i·ty /ˌkanəˈnisitē/ ▸*n.* the fact or status of being canonical: *established standards of canonicity.*

can·on·ist /ˈkanənəst/ ▸*n.* an expert in canon law. ▷mid 16th cent.: from French *canoniste* or medieval Latin *canonista*, from Latin *canon* (see CANON1). —**can·on·is·tic** /ˌkanəˈnistik/ *adj.*

can·on·ize /ˈkanəˌnīz/ ▸*v.* [*trans.*] (often **be canonized**) (in the Roman Catholic Church) officially declare (a dead person) to be a saint: *he was the last English saint to be canonized prior to the Reformation.* ■ *figurative* regard as being above reproach or of great significance: *we have canonized freedom of speech as an absolute value overriding all others.* ■ accept into the literary or artistic canon: [as *adj.*] *a familiar, canonized writer.* ■ sanction by Church authority. ▷late Middle English: from late Latin *canonizare* 'admit as authoritative' (in medieval Latin 'admit to the list of recognized saints'), from Latin *canon* (see CANON1). —**can·on·i·za·tion** /ˌkanənəˈzāsHən/ *n.*

can·on law ▸*n.* ecclesiastical law, esp. (in the Roman Catholic Church) that laid down by papal pronouncements.

can·on reg·u·lar ▸*n.* see CANON2.

can·on·ry /ˈkanənrē/ ▸*n.* (*pl.* **-ries**) the office or benefice of a canon.

ca·noo·dle /kəˈno͞odl/ ▸*v.* [*intrans.*] *informal* kiss and cuddle amorously: *she was caught* **canoodling with** *her boyfriend.* ▷mid 19th cent. (originally U.S.): of unknown origin.

Ca·no·pic jar /kəˈnōpik; -ˈnäpik/ (also **Canopic vase**) ▸*n.* a covered urn used in ancient Egyptian burials to hold the entrails from an embalmed body. ▷late 19th cent.: *Canopic* from Latin *Canopicus*, from *Canopus*, the name of a town in ancient Egypt.

Ca·no·pus /kəˈnōpəs/ *Astronomy* the second brightest star in the sky, and the brightest in the constellation Carina. It is a supergiant, visible only to observers in the southern hemisphere. ▷Latin, from Greek *Kanōpus*, the name of the pilot of the fleet of King Menelaus in the Trojan War.

can·o·py /ˈkanəpē/ ▸*n.* (*pl.* **-pies**) an ornamental cloth covering hung or held up over something, esp. a throne or bed. ■ *figurative* something hanging or perceived as hanging over a person or scene: *the canopy of twinkling stars.* ■ *Architecture* a rooflike projection or shelter: *they mounted the station steps under the concrete canopy.* ■ the transparent plastic or glass cover of an aircraft's cockpit. ■ the expanding, umbrellalike part of a parachute, made of silk or nylon. ■ [in *sing.*] the uppermost trees or branches of the trees in a forest, forming a more or less continuous layer of foliage: *monkeys spend hours every day sitting high in the canopy.*
▸*v.* (**-pies**, **-pied**) [*trans.*] [usu. as *adj.*] (**canopied**) cover or provide with a canopy: *a canopied bed | the river was canopied by overhanging trees.* ▷late Middle English: from medieval Latin *canopeum* 'ceremonial canopy,' alteration of Latin *conopeum* 'mosquito net over a bed,' from Greek *kōnōpeion* 'couch with mosquito curtains,' from *kōnōps* 'mosquito.'

ca·no·rous /kəˈnôrəs; ˈkanərəs/ ▸*adj. rare* (of song or speech) melodious or resonant. ▷mid 17th cent.: from Latin *canorus* (from *canere* 'sing') + -OUS.

canst /kanst/ ▸ archaic second person singular present of CAN1.

cant1 /kant/ ▸*n.* **1** hypocritical and sanctimonious talk, typically of a moral, religious, or political nature: *the liberal case against all censorship is often cant.* **2** [as *adj.*] denoting a phrase or catchword temporarily current or in fashion: *they are misrepresented as, in the cant word of our day, uncaring.* ■ language peculiar to a specified group or profession and regarded with disparagement: *thieves' cant.* See note at DIALECT.
▸*v.* [*intrans.*] *dated* talk hypocritically and sanctimoniously about something: *if they'd stop canting about "honest work," they might get somewhere.* ▷early 16th cent.: probably from Latin *cantare* 'to sing' (see CHANT). The early meaning was 'musical sound, singing'; in the mid 17th cent. this gave rise to the senses 'whining manner of speaking' and 'form of words repeated mechanically in such a manner' (for example a beggar's plea), hence 'jargon' (of beggars and other such groups).

cant2 ▸*v.* [*trans.*] cause (something) to be in a slanting or oblique position; tilt: *he canted his head to look at the screen.* ■ [*intrans.*] take or have a slanting position: *mismatched slate roofs canted at all angles.*
▸*n.* **1** [in *sing.*] a slope or tilt: *the outward cant of the curving walls.* **2** a wedge-shaped block of wood, esp. one remaining after the better-quality pieces have been cut off. ▷Middle English (denoting an edge or brink): from Middle Low German *kant, kante*, Middle Dutch *cant* 'point, side, edge,' based on a Romance word related to medieval Latin *cantus* 'corner, side.'

can't /kant/ ▸*contraction of* cannot.

Cant. ▸*abbr. Bible* Canticles.

can·ta·bi·le /känˈtäbəˌlā/ *Music* ▸*adv. & adj.* in a smooth singing style.
▸*n.* a cantabile passage or movement. ▷Italian, literally 'singable.'

Can·ta·brig·i·an /ˈkantəˌbrijēən/ ▸*adj.* of or relating to Cambridge (in England) or Cambridge University.
▸*n.* a student or faculty member of Cambridge University. ▷mid 16th cent.: from Latin *Cantabrigia* (see sense 1 of CAMBRIDGE) + -IAN.

can·tal /ˈkanˈtäl; kän-/ ▸*n.* a hard, strong cheese made chiefly in the Auvergne. ▷named after *Cantal*, a department of Auvergne, France.

can·ta·loupe /ˈkantlˌōp/ (also **cantaloupe melon**) ▸*n.* a small, round melon of a variety with orange flesh and ribbed skin. ▷late 18th cent.: from French *cantaloup*, from *Cantaluppi* near Rome, where it was first grown in Europe after being introduced from Armenia.

can·tan·ker·ous /kanˈtaNGkərəs/ ▸*adj.* bad-tempered, argumentative, and uncooperative: *a crusty, cantankerous old man.* ▷mid 18th cent.: of unknown origin; perhaps a blend of Anglo-Irish *cant* 'auction' and *rancorous* (see RANCOR). —**can·tan·ker·ous·ly** *adv.* —**can·tan·ker·ous·ness** *n.*

can·ta·ta /kənˈtätə/ ▸*n.* a medium-length narrative or descriptive piece of music with vocal solos and usually a chorus and orchestra. ▷early 18th cent.: from Italian *cantata (aria)* 'sung (air),' from *cantare* 'sing.'

cant dog ▸*n.* another term for CANT HOOK.

can·teen /kanˈtēn/ ▸*n.* **1** a restaurant provided by an organization such as a military camp, college, factory, or company for its students or staff. **2** a small water bottle, as used by soldiers or campers. ▷mid 18th cent. (originally denoting a type of shop in a barracks or garrison town): from French *cantine*, from Italian *cantina* 'cellar.'

can·ter /ˈkantər/ ▸*n.* [in *sing.*] a three-beat gait of a horse or other quadruped between a trot and a gallop: *he kicked his horse into a canter | I rode away* **at a**

Pronunciation Key ə *ago*; ər *over*; ˈə or ˌə *up*; ˈər or ˌər *fur*; a *hat*; ā *rate*; ä *car*; CH *chew*; e *let*; ē *see*; e(ə)r *air*; i *fit*; ī *by*; i(ə)r *ear*; NG *sing*; ō *go*; ô *for*; oi *boy*; o͝o *good*; o͞o *goo*; ou *out*; SH *she*; TH *thin*; T͟H *then*; (h)w *why*; ZH *vision*

canter. ■ a ride on a horse at such a speed: *we came back from one of our canters.*
▸*v.* [*intrans.*] (of a horse) move at a canter in a particular direction: *they cantered down into the village.* ■ [*trans.*] make (a horse) move at a canter: *Katharine cantered Benji in a smaller and smaller circle.* ▷early 18th cent. (as a verb): short for *Canterbury pace* or *Canterbury gallop*, from the supposed easy pace of medieval pilgrims to CANTERBURY.

Can·ter·bur·y /ˈkantərˌberē; -bərē/ a city in Kent, in southeastern England, the seat of the archbishop of Canterbury; pop. 39,700.

Can·ter·bur·y, Arch·bish·op of ▸*n.* the archbishop of the southern province of the Church of England, who is Primate of All England and plays a leading role in the worldwide Anglican Church.

Can·ter·bur·y bell ▸*n.* a tall, sturdy cultivated bellflower with large blue, pink, or white flowers. • *Campanula medium*, family Campanulaceae. ▷late 16th cent.: named after the bells on Canterbury pilgrims' horses (see CANTER).

can·thar·i·des /kanˈTHariˌdēz/ ▸*plural n.* see SPANISH FLY. ▷late Middle English: from Latin, plural of *cantharis*, from Greek *kantharis* 'Spanish fly.'

can·tha·rus /ˈkanTHərəs/ ▸*n.* (*pl.* **-ri** /-ˌrī; -rē/) (in ancient Greece and Rome) a large, two-handled drinking cup. ▷Latin, from Greek *kantharos.*

cant hook ▸*n.* a hinged metal hook at the end of a long handle, used for gripping and rolling logs.

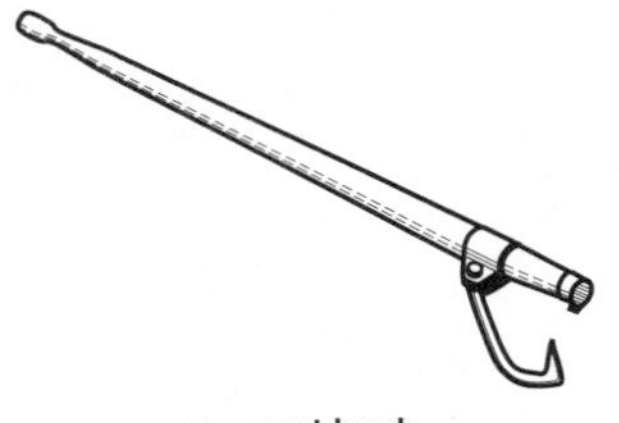

cant hook

can·thus /ˈkanTHəs/ ▸*n.* (*pl.* **-thi** /-ˌTHī; -ˌTHē/) the outer or inner corner of the eye, where the upper and lower lids meet. ▷mid 17th cent.: from Latin, from Greek *kanthos.* **—can·thic** /ˈkanTHik/ *adj.*

can·ti·cle /ˈkantikəl/ ▸*n.* **1** a hymn or chant, typically with a biblical text, forming a regular part of a church service. **2** (**Can·ti·cles** or **Can·ti·cle of Can·ti·cles**) another name for SONG OF SONGS (esp. in the Vulgate Bible). ▷Middle English: from Latin *canticulum* 'little song,' diminutive of *canticum*, from *canere* 'sing.'

can·ti·le·na /ˌkantlˈēnə/ ▸*n. Music* a lyrical vocal or instrumental melody in a composition. ▷mid 18th cent.: from Italian, from Latin, 'song.'

can·ti·le·ver /ˈkantlˌēvər; -ˌevər/ ▸*n.* a long projecting beam or girder fixed at only one end, used chiefly in bridge construction. ■ a long bracket or beam projecting from a wall to support a balcony, cornice, or similar structure.
▸*v.* [*trans.*] [usu. as *adj.*] (**cantilevered**) support by a cantilever or cantilevers: *a cantilevered deck.* ■ [*intrans.*] project as or like a cantilever: *a conveyor cantilevered out over the river.* ▷mid 17th cent.: of unknown origin.

can·ti·le·ver bridge ▸*n.* a bridge in which each span is constructed from cantilevers built out sideways from piers.

can·til·late /ˈkantlˌāt/ ▸*v.* [*trans.*] *rare* chant or intone (a passage of religious text). ▷mid 19th cent.: from Latin *cantillat-* 'hummed,' from the verb *cantillare*, from *cantare* (see CHANT). **—can·til·la·tion** /ˌkantlˈāSHən/ *n.*

can·ti·na /kanˈtēnə/ ▸*n.* (esp. in a Spanish-speaking country or the southwestern U.S.) a bar. ■ (in Italy) a wine shop. ▷late 19th cent.: from Spanish and Italian.

cant·ing arms ▸*plural n. Heraldry* arms containing an allusion to the name of the bearer. ▷early 17th cent.: *canting* from CANT[1], in the obsolete sense 'speak, say (in a particular way).'

can·tle /ˈkantl/ ▸*n.* the raised, curved part at the back of a horse's saddle. ▷Middle English (in the sense 'a corner'): from Anglo-Norman French *cantel*, variant of Old French *chantel*, from medieval Latin *cantellus*, from *cantus* 'corner, side.'

can·to /ˈkanˌtō/ ▸*n.* (*pl.* **-tos**) one of the sections into which certain long poems are divided. ▷late 16th cent.: from Italian, literally 'song,' from Latin *cantus.*

Can·ton[1] /kanˈtän/ variant of GUANGZHOU.

Can·ton[2] /ˈkantn/ an industrial city in northeastern Ohio; pop. 80,806. The Professional Football Hall of Fame is here.

can·ton /ˈkantn; ˈkanˌtän/ ▸*n.* **1** a subdivision of a country established for political or administrative purposes. ■ a state of the Swiss Confederation. **2** *Heraldry* a square charge smaller than a quarter and positioned in the upper (usually dexter) corner of a shield. ▷early 16th cent.: from Old French, literally 'corner,' from Provençal, based on a Romance word related to medieval Latin *cantus* (see CANT[2]). **—can·ton·al** /kanˈtänl; ˈkantnl/ *adj.*

Can·ton·ese /ˌkantnˈēz; -ˈēs/ ▸*adj.* of or relating to Canton (Guangzhou), its inhabitants, their dialect, or their cuisine.
▸*n.* (*pl.* same) **1** a native or inhabitant of Canton. **2** a form of Chinese spoken mainly in southeastern China (including Hong Kong). Also called YUE.

can·ton·ment /kanˈtōnmənt; -ˈtän-/ ▸*n.* a military camp. ■ *historical* a permanent military station in British India. ▷mid 18th cent.: from French *cantonnement*, from *cantonner* 'to quarter' (see CANTON).

Can·tor /ˈkantər/, Georg (1845–1918), German mathematician; born in Russia. His work on numbers laid the foundations for the theory of sets and stimulated 20th-century exploration of number theory.

can·tor /ˈkantər/ ▸*n.* **1** an official who sings liturgical music and leads prayer in a synagogue. Also called HAZZAN. **2** (in formal Christian worship) a person who sings solo verses or passages to which the choir or congregation responds. ▷mid 16th cent.: from Latin, 'singer,' from *canere* 'sing.'

can·to·ri·al /kanˈtôrēəl/ ▸*adj.* of or relating to a cantor. ■ relating to or denoting the north side of the choir of a church, the side on which the cantor sits. The opposite of DECANAL.

can·trip /ˈkantrip/ ▸*n. Scottish, archaic* a mischievous or playful act; a trick. ▷late 16th cent. (also in the sense 'witch's trick'): of unknown origin.

can·tus /ˈkantəs/ ▸*n.* the highest voice in polyphonic choral music. ▷late 16th cent.: from Latin.

can·tus fir·mus /ˈfərməs/ ▸*n.* (*pl.* **can·tus fir·mi** /ˈfərˌmī; -mē/) *Music* an existing melody used as the basis for a polyphonic composition. ▷mid 19th cent.: from Latin, literally 'firm song.'

Ca·nuck /kəˈnək/ ▸*n. informal* a Canadian, esp. a French Canadian (chiefly used by Canadians themselves and often derogatory in the U.S.). ▷apparently from CANADA.

Ca·nute /kəˈn(y)o͞ot/ (also **Cnut** or **Knut**) (died 1035), Danish king of England 1017–35, Denmark 1018–35, and Norway 1028–35; son of Sweyn I.

can·vas /ˈkanvəs/ ▸*n.* a strong, coarse unbleached cloth made from hemp, flax, cotton, or a similar yarn, used to make items such as sails and tents and as a surface for oil painting: [as *adj.*] *a canvas bag.* ■ a piece of such cloth prepared for use as the surface for an oil painting. ■ an oil painting: *Turner's late canvases.* ■ a variety of canvas with an open weave, used as a basis for tapestry and embroidery. ■ (**the canvas**) the floor of a boxing or wrestling ring, having a canvas covering. ■ either of a racing boat's tapering ends, originally covered with canvas.
▸*v.* (**-vased, -vas·ing**) [*trans.*] (usu. **be canvased**) cover with canvas: *the door had been canvased over.* ▷late Middle English: from Old Northern French *canevas*, based on Latin *cannabis* 'hemp,' from Greek *kannabis.*
▸***PHRASES*** □ **by a canvas** (in boat racing) by a small margin. [referring to the tapered front end of a racing boat (see above).] □ **under canvas** **1** in a tent or tents: *the family will be living under canvas.* **2** with sails spread.

can·vas·back /ˈkanvəsˌbak/ ▸*n.* a North American diving duck with a long, sloping black bill, related (and with similar coloring) to the pochard, common in Eurasia. • *Aythya valisineria*, family Anatidae. ▷late 16th cent.: so named because of the white back of the male.

can·vas duck ▸*n.* a lightweight cotton or linen fabric.

can·vass /ˈkanvəs/ ▸*v.* **1** [*trans.*] solicit votes from (electors in a constituency): *in each ward, two workers canvassed some 2,000 voters* | [*intrans.*] *she* ***canvassed for*** *votes.* ■ question (someone) in order to ascertain their opinion on something: *they promised to canvass all member clubs for their views.* ■ ascertain (someone's opinion) through questioning: *opinions on the merger were canvassed.* ■ try to obtain; request: *they're canvassing support among shareholders.* **2** [*trans.*] (often **be canvassed**) discuss thoroughly: *the issues that were canvassed are still unresolved.*
▸*n.* [usu. in *sing.*] an act or process of attempting to secure votes or ascertain opinions: *a house-to-house canvass.* ▷early 16th cent. (in the sense 'toss in a canvas sheet' (as a sport or punishment)): from CANVAS. Later extended senses include 'criticize, discuss' (mid 16th cent.) and 'propose for discussion'; hence 'seek support for.' **—can·vass·er** *n.*

can·yon /ˈkanyən/ ▸*n.* a deep gorge, typically one with a river flowing through it, as found in North America. ▷mid 19th cent.: from Spanish *cañón* 'tube,' based on Latin *canna* 'reed, cane.'

Can·yon de Chel·ly /də ˈSHā(lē)/ a national monument in northeastern Arizona, on the Navajo Indian Reservation, noted for cliff dwellings and other ruins.

can·yon·ing /ˈkanyəniNG/ (also **can·yon·eer·ing** /ˌkanyəˈni(ə)riNG/) ▸*n.* the sport of exploring a canyon by engaging in such activities as rappelling, rafting, and waterfall jumping.

Can·yon·lands /ˈkanyənˌlandz/ a region in southeastern Utah, many of whose rock formations are preserved in the Canyonlands National Park.

can·zo·na /kanˈzōnə; käntˈsōnə/ ▸*n. Music* an instrumental arrangement of a French or Flemish song, typical of 16th-century Italy. ▷late 19th cent.: from Italian, from CANZONE.

can·zo·ne /kanˈzōnē; käntˈsōnā/ ▸*n.* (*pl.* **can·zo·ni** /kanˈzōnē; käntˈsōnē/) an Italian or Provençal song or ballad. ■ a type of lyric resembling a madrigal. ▷late 16th cent.: from Italian, 'song,' from Latin *cantio(n-)* 'singing,' from *canere* 'sing.'

can·zo·net·ta /ˌkanzəˈnetə/ ▸*n.* (*pl.* **-net·tas** or **-net·te** /-ˈnetē/) a short, light vocal piece, esp. in the Italian style of the 17th century. ▷late 16th cent.: from Italian, 'little song,' diminutive of *canzone*, from Latin *cantio(n-)* 'singing,' from *canere* 'sing.'

caou·tchouc /ˈkouˌCHo͝ok; -ˌCHo͞o(k)/ ▸*n.* unvulcanized natural rubber. ▷late 18th cent.: from French, from obsolete Spanish *cauchuc*, from Quechua *kauchuk.*

CAP ▸*abbr.* Civil Air Patrol.

cap[1] /kap/ ▸*n.* **1** a kind of soft, flat hat without a brim, and sometimes having a visor. ■ [with *adj.*] a kind of soft, close-fitting head covering worn for a particular purpose or as a mark of a particular profession or status: *a nurse's cap* | *a bathing cap.* ■ an academic mortarboard: *graduates in cap and gown.* **2** a protective lid or cover for an object such as a bottle, the point of a pen, or a camera lens. ■ *Dentistry* an artificial protective covering for a tooth. ■ the top of a bird's head when distinctively colored. ■ the broad upper part of the fruiting body of most mushrooms and toadstools, at the top of a stem and bearing gills or pores. **3** an upper limit imposed on spending or other activities: *a cap on legal immigration.* **4** short for PERCUSSION CAP.
▸*v.* (**capped, cap·ping**) [*trans.*] **1** put a lid or cover on: *he capped his pen.* ■ (often **be capped**) form a covering layer or top part of: *several towers were capped by domes* | [as *adj.*, in *combination*] (**-capped**) *snow-capped mountains.* ■ put an artificial protective covering on (a tooth). ■ provide a fitting climax or conclusion to: *he capped a memorable season by becoming champion.* ■ follow or reply to (a story, remark, or joke) by producing a better or more apposite one: *they capped each other's stories.* **2** (often **be capped**) place a limit or restriction on (prices, expenditure, or other activity): *council budgets will be capped.* ▷Old English *cæppe* 'hood,' from late Latin *cappa*, perhaps from Latin *caput* 'head.' **—cap·ful** /-ˌfo͝ol/ *n.* (*pl.* **-fuls**) .
▸***PHRASES*** □ **cap** (or **hat**) **in hand** humbly asking for a favor: *we have to* ***go cap in hand*** *begging for funds.* □ **set one's cap for** (or **at**) *dated* (of a woman) try to attract (a particular man) as a suitor.

cap[2] /kap/ ▸*n. Finance* short for capitalization: [as *modifier*] *mid-cap companies* | *small-cap stocks.*

cap. ▸*abbr.* ■ capacity. ■ capital (city). ■ capital letter.

ca·pa·bil·i·ty /ˌkāpəˈbilitē/ ▸*n.* (*pl.* **-ties**) (often **capability of doing** (or **to do**) **something**) power or ability: *he had an intuitive* ***capability of*** *bringing the best out in people* | *the* ***capability to*** *increase productivity.* ■ (often **capabilities**) the extent of someone's or something's ability: *the job is* ***beyond my capabilities.*** ■ [usu. with *adj.*] a facility on a computer for performing a specified task: *a graphics capability.* ■ [usu. with *adj.*] forces or resources giving a country or state the ability to undertake a particular kind of military action: *their nuclear weapons capability.*

Ca·pa·bil·i·ty Brown see BROWN[4].

ca·pa·ble /ˈkāpəbəl/ ▸*adj.* [*predic.*] (**capable of doing something**) having the ability, fitness, or quality necessary to do or achieve a specified thing: *I'm quite capable of taking care of myself* | *the aircraft is capable of* *flying 5,000 miles nonstop.* ■ able to achieve efficiently whatever one has to do; competent: *she looked enthusiastic and capable | a highly capable man.* ■ open to or admitting of something: *the strange events are **capable of** rational explanation.* ■ ready or inclined to: *children **capable of** murder.* ▷mid 16th cent. (in the sense 'able to take in,' physically or mentally): from French, from late Latin *capabilis*, from Latin *capere* 'take or hold.' —**ca·pa·bly** /-blē/ *adv.*

ca·pa·cious /kə'pāsHəs/ ▸*adj.* having a lot of space inside; roomy: *she rummaged in her capacious handbag.* ▷early 17th cent.: from Latin *capax, capac-* 'capable' + -IOUS. —**ca·pa·cious·ly** *adv.* —**ca·pa·cious·ness** *n.*

ca·pac·i·tance /kə'pasitəns/ ▸*n. Physics* the ability of a system to store an electric charge. ■ the ratio of the change in an electric charge in a system to the corresponding change in its electric potential. (Symbol: **C**) ▷late 19th cent.: from CAPACITY + -ANCE.

ca·pac·i·tate /kə'pasi,tāt/ ▸*v.* [*trans.*] *formal* or *archaic* make (someone) capable of a particular action or legally competent to act in a particular way. ■ (**be capacitated**) *Physiology* (of spermatozoa) undergo changes inside the female reproductive tract enabling them to penetrate and fertilize an ovum. —**ca·pac·i·ta·tion** /kə,pasi'tāsHən/ *n.*

ca·pac·i·tor /kə'pasitər/ ▸*n.* a device used to store an electric charge, consisting of one or more pairs of conductors separated by an insulator.

ca·pac·i·ty /kə'pasitē/ ▸*n.* (*pl.* **-ties**) **1** [in *sing.*] the maximum amount that something can contain: *the capacity of the freezer is 1.1 cubic feet | the stadium's seating capacity | the room was **filled to capacity**.* ■ [as *adj.*] fully occupying the available area or space: *they played to a capacity crowd.* ■ the amount that something can produce: *the company aimed to double its electricity-generating capacity | when running **at full capacity**, the factory will employ 450 people.* ■ the total cylinder volume that is swept by the pistons in an internal combustion engine. ■ former term for CAPACITANCE. **2** the ability or power to do, experience, or understand something: *I was impressed by her **capacity for** hard work | [with infinitive] his capacity to inspire trust in others their intellectual capacities.* ■ [in *sing.*] a person's legal competence: *cases where a patient's testamentary capacity is in doubt.* **3** [in *sing.*] a specified role or position: *I was engaged in a voluntary capacity | writing **in his capacity as** legal correspondent.* ▷late Middle English: from French *capacité*, from Latin *capacitas*, from *capax, capac-* 'that can contain,' from *capere* 'take or hold.' —**ca·pac·i·tive** /-ətiv/ (also **ca·pac·i·ta·tive**) *adj.* (*chiefly Physics*).

cap and bells ▸*plural n. historical* the insignia of the professional jester.

ca·par·i·son /kə'parəsən/ ▸*n.* an ornamental covering spread over a horse's saddle or harness.
▸*v.* (**be caparisoned**) (of a horse) be decked out in rich decorative coverings. ▷early 16th cent.: from obsolete French *caparasson*, from Spanish *caparazón* 'saddlecloth,' from *capa* 'hood.'

cape[1] /kāp/ ▸*n.* a sleeveless cloak, typically a short one. ■ a part of a longer coat or cloak that falls loosely over the shoulders from the neckband. ■ the pelt from the head and neck of an animal, for preparation as a hunting trophy.
▸*v.* [*trans.*] skin the head and neck of (an animal) to prepare a hunting trophy. ▷mid 16th cent.: from French, from Provençal *capa*, from late Latin *cappa* 'covering for the head.' —**caped** *adj.*

cape[2] ▸*n.* **1** a headland or promontory. ■ (**the Cape**) the Cape of Good Hope. ■ (**the Cape**) Cape Cod, Massachusetts. ■ (**the Cape**) the former Cape Province of South Africa. **2** (**Cape**) short for CAPE COD (the style of house). ▷late Middle English: from Old French *cap*, from Provençal, based on Latin *caput* 'head.'

Cape A·gul·has, Cape Bon, etc. see AGULHAS, CAPE; BON, CAPE, etc.

Cape Bar·ren goose ▸*n.* a pale gray Australian goose related to the shelducks, with a short black bill that is almost covered by a waxy yellow cere, and a black tail. Also called CEREOPSIS GOOSE. • *Cereopsis novaehollandiae*, family Anatidae. ▷mid 19th cent.: named after *Cape Barren*, an island in the Bass Strait, Australia.

Cape Bret·on Is·land /,bretn/ an island that forms the northeastern part of the province of Nova Scotia in eastern Canada.

Cape buf·fa·lo ▸*n.* see AFRICAN BUFFALO.

cape·ci·ta·bine /kāp'sītə,bēn/ ▸*n. Medicine* an antimetabolite used to treat various metastatic cancers by inhibiting tumor growth while sparing most surrounding tissue.

Cape Cod /'käd/ (abbr.: **CC**) **1** a sandy peninsula in southeastern Massachusetts that forms a wide curve enclosing Cape Cod Bay. The Pilgrims landed on the northern tip of Cape Cod in November 1620. **2** (also **Cape**) a type of rectangular house with a deeply gabled roof.

Cape Col·o·ny early name (1814–1910) for the former CAPE PROVINCE.

Cape col·ored ▸*n.* (*pl.* same or **Cape col·oreds**) (in South Africa) a person of mixed ethnic descent resident in the Western Cape Province, speaking Afrikaans or English as their first language, and typically not a Muslim. Compare with CAPE MALAY.
▸*adj.* of or relating to Cape colored people.

Cape Cor·al a resort city in southwestern Florida, near the mouth of the Caloosahatchee River, southwest of Fort Myers; pop. 102,286.

ca·peesh /kə'pēsh/ ▸*exclam. informal* do you understand?: *Upstairs is off limits. Capeesh?* ▷1940s: from Italian *capisce* third person singular present tense of *capire* 'understand.'

Cape Fear Riv·er a river that flows for 200 miles (320 km) across eastern North Carolina to enter the Atlantic Ocean near Wilmington at Cape Fear.

Cape Gi·rar·deau /jə'rärdō/ a city in southeastern Missouri, on the Mississippi River; pop. 34,438.

cape goose·ber·ry ▸*n.* **1** a soft, edible, yellow berry enclosed in a husk that resembles a lantern in shape. **2** the tropical South American plant that has heart-shaped leaves and that bears this fruit. • *Physalis peruviana*, family Solanaceae.

Cape hunt·ing dog ▸*n.* see HUNTING DOG (sense 2).

Cape jas·mine (also **Cape jessamine**) ▸*n.* a fragrant Chinese gardenia, some kinds of which have flowers that are used to perfume tea. • Genus *Gardenia*, family Rubiaceae: several species, in particular *G. jasminoides*.

Ča·pek /'CHäpek/, Karel (1890–1938), Czech novelist and playwright. He is known for *R.U.R.* (*Rossum's Universal Robots*) (1920), which introduced the word *robot* to the English language, and for *The Insect Play* (1921), written with his brother **Josef** (1887–1945).

cap·e·lin /'kap(ə)lən/ (also **cap·lin** /'kaplən/) ▸*n.* a small fish of the North Atlantic, resembling a smelt. It is abundant in coastal waters and provides a staple food for humans and many animals. • *Mallotus villosus*, family *Osmeridae*. ▷early 17th cent.: from French, from Provençal *capelan*, from medieval Latin *cappellanus* 'custodian' (see CHAPLAIN).

Ca·pel·la /kə'pelə/ *Astronomy* the sixth brightest star in the sky, and the brightest in the constellation Auriga. It is a yellow giant. ▷Latin, 'she-goat,' diminutive of *caper* 'goat.'

cap·el·li·ni /,kapə'lēnē/ ▸*plural n.* pasta in the form of long, thin round strands, only slightly thicker than angel hair. ▷1950s: Italian, diminutive of *capello* 'hair.'

Cape Ma·lay (also **Cape Muslim**) ▸*n.* (in South Africa) a member of a predominantly Afrikaans-speaking and Muslim group resident mainly in the Western Cape Province. Compare with CAPE COLORED.
▸*adj.* of or relating to the Cape Malay people.

Cape May a resort city in extreme southern New Jersey, on the Atlantic Ocean; pop. 4,668.

Cape of Good Hope a mountainous promontory south of Cape Town, South Africa, near the southern extremity of Africa. Sighted toward the end of the 15th century by Bartolomeu Dias, it was sailed around for the first time by Vasco da Gama in 1497.

Cape pi·geon (also **Cape petrel**) ▸*n.* a common petrel of southern oceans that has black plumage with white markings. Also called PINTADO PETREL. • *Daption capense*, family Procellariidae.

Cape Prov·ince a former province of South Africa, containing the Cape of Good Hope. The area became a British colony in 1814: it was known as Cape Colony from then until 1910, when it joined the Union of South Africa. In 1994 it was divided into the provinces of Northern Cape, Western Cape, and Eastern Cape.

ca·per[1] /'kāpər/ ▸*v.* [*intrans.*] skip or dance about in a lively or playful way: *children were capering about the room.*
▸*n.* **1** a playful skipping movement: *she did a little caper.* **2** *informal* an activity or escapade, typically one that is illicit or ridiculous. ■ an amusing or far-fetched story, esp. one presented on film or stage: *a cop caper about intergalactic drug dealers.* ▷late 16th cent.: abbreviation of CAPRIOLE. —**ca·per·er** /'kāpərər/ *n.*
▸*PHRASE* □ **cut a caper** make a playful, skipping movement.

ca·per[2] ▸*n.* **1** (usu. **capers**) the cooked and pickled flower buds of a bramblelike southern European shrub, used to flavor food. **2** the shrub from which these buds are taken. • *Capparis spinosa*, family Capparidaceae. ▷late Middle English: from French *câpres* or Latin *capparis*, from Greek *kapparis*; later interpreted as plural, hence the loss of the final *-s* in the 16th cent.

cap·er·cail·lie /,kapər'kāl(y)ē/ (*Scottish* also **cap·er·cail·zie** /-'kālyē; -zē/) ▸*n.* (*pl.* **-lies**) a large, turkeylike Eurasian grouse of mature pine forests. The male has a courtship display in which it fans the tail and makes an extraordinary succession of sounds. • Genus *Tetrao*, family Tetraonidae (or Phasianidae): two species, in particular *T. urogallus*, which has been reestablished in the Scottish Highlands. ▷mid 16th cent.: from Scottish Gaelic *capull coille*, literally 'horse of the wood.'

cape·skin /'kāp,skin/ ▸*n.* a soft leather made from South African sheepskin.

Ca·pet /kä'pe; kä'pā; 'kāpit/, Hugh (938–996), king of France 987–996; founder of the Capetian dynasty.

Ca·pe·tian /kə'pēsHən/ ▸*adj.* relating to or denoting the dynasty ruling France 987–1328.
▸*n.* a member of this dynasty.

Cape Town a city in southwestern South Africa at the foot of Table Mountain, the legislative capital of the country and the administrative capital of the province of Western Cape; pop. 776,600.

Cape Verde /'vərd/ (also **Cape Verde Islands**) a country in Africa that consists of a group of islands in the Atlantic Ocean off the coast of Senegal, named after the most western cape in Africa; pop. 415,300; capital, Praia; languages, Portuguese (official) and Creole. —**Cape Ver·de·an** /'vərdēən/ *adj.* & *n.*

Previously uninhabited, the islands were settled by the Portuguese from the 15th century and later served as a trading center for African slaves. They remained a Portuguese colony until 1975, when an independent republic was established.

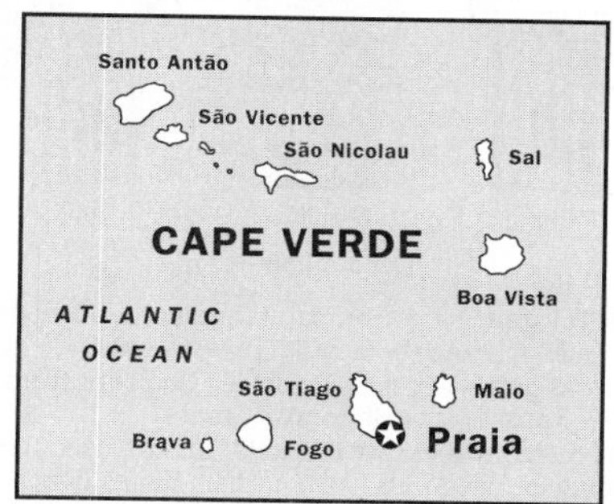

Cape York /'yôrk/ the northernmost point of Australia, on Torres Strait, at the tip of **Cape York Peninsula** in Queensland.

Cap-Ha·ï·tien /kăp 'hāsHən; ä-ē'syan/ a historic port city in northern Haiti; pop. 133,000. It is the former capital of Haiti and the second-largest city in the country.

ca·pi·as /'kāpēəs/ ▸*n.* (*pl.* **-as·es**) *Law* a writ ordering the arrest of a named person. ▷late Middle English: from Latin *capias (ad respondendum)*, literally 'you are to seize (until reply is made),' from *capere* 'take.'

cap·il·lar·i·ty /kapə'laritē/ ▸*n.* the tendency of a liquid in a capillary tube or absorbent material to rise or fall as a result of surface tension. Also called CAPILLARY ACTION. ▷mid 19th cent.: from French *capillarité*, from Latin *capillaris* 'like a hair' (see CAPILLARY).

cap·il·lar·y /'kapə,lerē/ ▸*n.* **1** *Anatomy* any of the fine branching blood vessels that form a network between the arterioles and venules. **2** (also **capillary tube**) a tube that has an internal diameter of hair-like thinness.
▸*adj.* [*attrib.*] of or relating to capillaries or capillarity. ▷mid 17th cent.: from Latin *capillaris*, from *capillus* 'hair,' influenced by Old French *capillaire*.

cap·il·lar·y ac·tion ▸*n.* another term for CAPILLARITY.

cap·il·lar·y at·trac·tion ▸*n.* the tendency of a liquid in a capillary tube to rise as a result of surface forces.

cap·i·tal[1] /ˈkapitl/ ▸*n.* **1** (also **capital city** or **town**) the most important city or town of a country or region, usually its seat of government and administrative center. ■ [with *adj.*] a place associated more than any other with a specified activity or product: *Milan is the fashion capital of the world.* **2** wealth in the form of money or other assets owned by a person or organization or available or contributed for a particular purpose such as starting a company or investing: *the senior partner would provide the initial capital* | *rates of return on invested capital were high.* ■ the excess of a company's assets over its liabilities. ■ people who possess wealth and use it to control a society's economic activity, considered collectively: *a conflict of interest between capital and labor.* ■ [with *adj.*] *figurative* a valuable resource of a particular kind: *there is insufficient investment in* ***human capital.*** **3** (also **capital letter**) a letter of the size and form used to begin sentences and names: *he wrote the name in capitals.*
▸*adj.* **1** [*attrib.*] (of an offense or charge) liable to the death penalty: *murder was a capital crime.* **2** of or relating to wealth: *capital losses.* **3** of greatest political importance: *the capital city.* **4** [*attrib.*] (of a letter of the alphabet) large in size and of the form used to begin sentences and names. **5** *Brit. informal, dated* excellent: *he's a really capital fellow.*
▸*exclam. Brit., informal dated* used to express approval, satisfaction, or delight: *That's splendid! Capital!* ▷Middle English (as an adjective in the sense 'relating to the head or top,' later 'standing at the head or beginning'): via Old French from Latin *capitalis*, from *caput* 'head.' —**cap·i·tal·ly** *adv.* (in sense 5).
▸*PHRASES* □ **make capital out of** use to one's own advantage: *trying to make political capital out of the weakness of his rival.* □ **with a capital ——** used to give emphasis to the word or concept in question: *he's trouble with a capital T.*

cap·i·tal[2] ▸*n. Architecture* the distinct, typically broader section at the head of a pillar or column. ▷Middle English: from Old French *capitel*, from late Latin *capitellum* 'little head,' diminutive of Latin *caput.*

Doric

Corinthian

Ionic

capitals

cap·i·tal gain ▸*n.* (often **capital gains**) a profit from the sale of property or of an investment.

cap·i·tal gains tax ▸*n.* a tax levied on profit from the sale of property or of an investment.

cap·i·tal goods ▸*plural n.* goods that are used in producing other goods, rather than being bought by consumers. Often contrasted with **CONSUMER GOODS.**

cap·i·tal-in·ten·sive ▸*adj.* (of a business or industrial process) requiring the investment of large sums of money.

cap·i·tal·ism /ˈkapətl,izəm/ ▸*n.* an economic and political system in which a country's trade and industry are controlled by private owners for profit, rather than by the state.

cap·i·tal·ist /ˈkapətlist/ ▸*n.* a wealthy person who uses money to invest in trade and industry for profit in accordance with the principles of capitalism: *the creation of the factory system by nineteenth-century capitalists.*
▸*adj.* practicing, supporting, or based on the principles of capitalism: *capitalist countries* | *the global economy is essentially capitalist.* —**cap·i·tal·is·tic** /,kapətlˈistik/ *adj.* —**cap·i·tal·is·ti·cal·ly** /,kapətlˈistik(ə)lē/ *adv.*

cap·i·tal·ize /ˈkapətl,īz/ ▸*v.* **1** [*intrans.*] (**capitalize on**) take the chance to gain advantage from: *an attempt by the opposition to capitalize on the government's embarrassment.* **2** [*trans.*] provide (a company or industry) with capital: [as *adj.*] (**capitalized**) *a highly capitalized industry.* **3** realize (the present value of an income); convert into capital. ■ reckon (the value of an asset) by setting future benefits against the cost of maintenance: *a trader will want to capitalize repairs expenditure.* **4** [*trans.*] write or print (a word or letter) in capital letters. ■ begin (a word) with a capital letter. —**cap·i·tal·i·za·tion** /,kapətl-əˈzāsʜən/ *n.*

cap·i·tal mar·ket ▸*n.* the part of a financial system concerned with raising capital by dealing in shares, bonds, and other long-term investments.

cap·i·tal pun·ish·ment ▸*n.* the legally authorized killing of someone as punishment for a crime.

cap·i·tal ship ▸*n.* a large warship such as a battleship or aircraft carrier.

cap·i·tal sum ▸*n.* a lump sum of money payable to an insured person or paid as an initial fee or investment.

cap·i·tal ter·ri·to·ry ▸*n.* a territory containing the capital city of a country, in Australia, Nigeria, Pakistan, and elsewhere.

ca·pi·ta·no /,kapiˈtänō/ ▸*n.* (*pl.* **-nos**) (in Italy or among Italian speakers) a captain or chief (used chiefly as a form of address). ▷Italian.

cap·i·tate /ˈkapi,tāt/ ▸*adj. Botany & Zoology* ending in a distinct compact head.
▸*n.* (also **capitate bone**) *Anatomy* the largest of the carpal bones, situated at the base of the palm of the hand and articulating with the third metacarpal. ▷mid 17th cent.: from Latin *capitatus*, from *caput, capit-* 'head.'

cap·i·ta·tion /,kapiˈtāsʜən/ ▸*n.* the payment of a fee or grant to a doctor, school, or other person or body providing services to a number of people, such that the amount paid is determined by the number of patients, pupils, or customers: *the increased capitation enabled schools to offer pupils an enhanced curriculum* | [as *adj.*] *income capitation fees.* ▷early 17th cent. (denoting the counting of heads): from late Latin *capitatio* 'poll tax,' from *caput* 'head.'

Cap·i·tol /ˈkapitl/ (usu. **the Capitol**) **1** the seat of the U.S. Congress in Washington, DC. ■ (**cap·i·tol**) a building housing a legislative assembly: *50,000 people marched on New Jersey's state capitol.* **2** the temple of Jupiter on the Capitoline Hill in ancient Rome. ▷from Old French *capitolie, capitoile*, later assimilated to Latin *Capitolium* (from *caput, capit-* 'head').

U.S. Capitol

Cap·i·tol Hill the region around the Capitol building in Washington, DC (often used as an allusive reference to the U.S. Congress itself).

Cap·i·tol Reef Na·tion·al Park a preserve in south central Utah, noted for its fossils and rock formations.

ca·pit·u·lar /kəˈpicʜələr/ ▸*adj.* **1** of or relating to a cathedral chapter. **2** *Anatomy & Biology* of or relating to a capitulum. ▷early 16th cent.: from late Latin *capitularis*, from Latin *capitulum* 'small head.'

ca·pit·u·lar·y /kəˈpicʜə,lerē/ ▸*n.* (*pl.* **-lar·ies**) *historical* a royal ordinance under the Merovingian dynasty. ▷mid 17th cent.: from late Latin *capitularius*, from Latin *capitulum* in the sense 'section of a law.'

ca·pit·u·late /kəˈpicʜə,lāt/ ▸*v.* [*intrans.*] cease to resist an opponent or an unwelcome demand; surrender: *the patriots had to* ***capitulate to*** *the enemy forces.* ▷mid 16th cent. (in the sense 'parley, draw up terms'): from French *capituler*, from medieval Latin *capitulare* 'draw up under headings,' from Latin *capitulum*, diminutive of *caput* 'head.' —**ca·pit·u·la·tor** /-ˈlātər/ *n.*

ca·pit·u·la·tion /kə,picʜəˈlāsʜən/ ▸*n.* the action of surrendering or ceasing to resist an opponent or demand: *the victor sees it as a sign of capitulation* | ***a capitulation to*** *wage demands.* ■ (**capitulations**) *historical* an agreement or set of conditions. ▷mid 16th cent.: from late Latin *capitulatio(n-)*, from the verb *capitulare* (see **CAPITULATE**).

ca·pit·u·lum /kəˈpicʜələm/ ▸*n.* (*pl.* **-la** /-lə/) *Anatomy & Biology* a compact head of a structure, in particular a dense, flat cluster of small flowers or florets, as in plants of the daisy family. ▷early 18th cent.: from Latin, diminutive of *caput* 'head.'

cap·let /ˈkaplit/ (*trademark* **Cap·let**) ▸*n.* a coated oral medicinal tablet. ▷1930s: blend of **CAPSULE** and **TABLET.**

cap·lin /ˈkaplən/ ▸*n.* variant spelling of **CAPELIN.**

cap'n /ˈkapm/ ▸*n.* informal contraction of **CAPTAIN**, used in representing speech.

ca·po[1] /ˈkāpō; ˈkäpō/ (also **ca·po tas·to**) ▸*n.* (*pl.* **-pos**) a clamp fastened across all the strings of a fretted musical instrument to raise their tuning by a chosen amount. ▷late 19th cent.: from Italian *capo tasto*, literally 'head stop.'

capo[1]

ca·po[2] ▸*n.* (*pl.* **-pos**) the head of a crime syndicate, esp. the Mafia, or a branch of one. ▷1950s: from Italian, from Latin *caput* 'head.'

ca·po·ei·ra /,käpōōˈārə/ ▸*n.* a system of physical discipline and movement originating among Brazilian slaves, treated as a martial art and dance form. ▷Portuguese.

cap of lib·er·ty ▸*n.* a soft conical cap given to Roman slaves on their emancipation and often used as a republican symbol in more recent times.

ca·pon /ˈkā,pän; -pən/ ▸*n.* a castrated domestic cock fattened for eating. ▷late Old English: from Old French, based on Latin *capo, capon-.* —**ca·pon·ize** /ˈkāpə,nīz/ *v.*

ca·po·na·ta /,käpəˈnätə/ ▸*n.* a dish of eggplant, olives, and onions seasoned with herbs, typically served as an appetizer. ▷Italian.

Ca·pone /kəˈpōn/, Al (1899–1947), U.S. gangster; full name *Alphonse Capone.* He was notorious for his domination of organized crime in Chicago in the 1920s. Although he was believed responsible for many murders, including the St. Valentine's Day Massacre, it was for federal income tax evasion that he was eventually imprisoned in 1931.

ca·po tas·to /,käpō ˈtästō/ ▸*n.* (*pl.* **-tos**) another term for **CAPO**[1].

Ca·pote /kəˈpōtē/, Truman (1924–84), U.S. writer; born *Truman Streckfus Persons.* Notable works: *Breakfast at Tiffany's* (1958) and *In Cold Blood* (1966).

Truman Capote

ca·pote /kəˈpōt/ ▸*n. historical* a long cloak or coat with a hood, typically part of an army or company uniform. ▷early 19th cent.: from French, diminutive of *cape* (see **CAPE**[1]).

Capp /kap/, Al (1909–79), U.S. cartoonist; full name *Alfred Gerald Caplin.* He was noted for his comic strip, "Li'l Abner," which appeared in the *New York Mirror* from 1934 to 1977.

Cap·pa·do·cia /,kapəˈdōsʜə/ an ancient region of central Asia Minor, between Lake Tuz and the Euphrates River, north of Cilicia. It was an important center of early Christianity. —**Cap·pa·do·cian** *adj.* & *n.*

cap·pel·let·ti /,kapəˈletē/ ▸ *n.* small pieces of pasta folded and stuffed with meat or cheese. ▷Italian, literally 'little hats.'

cap·per /ˈkapər/ ▸*n. informal* a more surprising, upsetting, or entertaining event or situation than all others that have gone before: *the capper was him accusing her of ripping off his car.*

cap·puc·ci·no /,käpəˈcʜēnō; ,kap-/ ▸*n.* (*pl.* **-nos**) coffee made with milk that has been frothed up with pressurized steam. ▷1940s: from Italian, literally 'Capuchin,' because its color resembles that of a Capuchin's habit.

Ca·pra /ˈkaprə/, Frank (1897–1991), U.S. movie director; born in Italy. He is known for movies such as *It Happened One Night* (Academy Award, 1934), *Mr. Deeds Goes to Town* (Academy Award, 1936), *You Can't Take It with You* (Academy Award, 1938), *Arsenic and Old Lace* (1944), and *It's a Wonderful Life* (1946).

Ca·pri /kəˈprē; ˈkaprē; ˈkäprē/ an island off the western coast of Italy, south of Naples.

ca·pric·ci·o /kəˈprēCHēˌō; -CHō/ ▸*n.* (*pl.* **-os**) a lively piece of music, typically one that is short and free in form. ■ a painting or other work of art representing a fantasy or a mixture of real and imaginary features. ▷early 17th cent. (denoting a sudden change of mind): from Italian, literally 'head with the hair standing on end,' hence 'horror,' later 'a sudden start' (influenced by *capra* 'goat,' associated with frisky movement), from *capo* 'head' + *riccio* 'hedgehog.'

ca·pric·ci·o·so /kəˌprēCHēˈōsō; -ˈōzō/ ▸*adv.* & *adj.* *Music* (esp. as a direction) in a free, playful, impulsive style. ▷Italian, literally 'capricious,' from CAPRICCIO.

ca·price /kəˈprēs/ ▸*n.* **1** a sudden and unaccountable change of mood or behavior: *her caprices had made his life impossible* | *a land where men were ruled by law and not by caprice.* **2** *Music* another term for CAPRICCIO. ▷mid 17th cent.: from French, from Italian (see CAPRICCIO).

ca·pri·cious /kəˈpriSHəs;-ˈprē-/ ▸*adj.* given to sudden and unaccountable changes of mood or behavior: *a capricious and often brutal administration* | *a capricious climate.* ▷early 17th cent.: from French *capricieux*, from Italian (see CAPRICCIOSO). **—ca·pri·cious·ly** *adv.* **—ca·pri·cious·ness** *n.*

Cap·ri·corn /ˈkapriˌkôrn/ *Astrology* the tenth sign of the zodiac (the Goat), which the sun enters at the northern winter solstice (about December 21). Compare with CAPRICORNUS. ■ (**a Capricorn**) a person born when the sun is in this sign. ▷Old English, from Latin *capricornus*, from *caper, capr-* 'goat' + *cornu* 'horn,' on the pattern of Greek *aigokerōs* 'goat-horned, Capricorn.' **—Cap·ri·corn·i·an** /ˌkapriˈkôrnēən/ *n.* & *adj.*

▸PHRASE □ **tropic of Capricorn** see TROPIC[1].

Cap·ri·cor·nus /ˌkapriˈkôrnəs/ *Astronomy* a constellation (the Goat), said to represent a goat with a fish's tail. It has few bright stars. Compare with CAPRICORN. ■ [as *genitive*] (**Capricorni** /-ˈkôrnē/) used with a preceding letter or numeral to designate a star in this constellation: *the star 41 Capricorni.* ▷Latin (see CAPRICORN).

cap·rine /ˈkapˌrīn/ ▸*adj.* of, relating to, or resembling goats. ▷late Middle English: from Latin *caprinus*, from *caper, capr-* 'goat.'

cap·ri·ole /ˈkaprēˌōl/ ▸*n.* a movement performed in classical riding, in which the horse leaps from the ground and kicks out with its hind legs. ■ a leap or caper in dancing, esp. a cabriole. ▷late 16th cent.: from obsolete French (now *cabriole*), from Italian *capriola* 'leap,' from *capriolo* 'roebuck,' from Latin *capreolus*, diminutive of *caper, capr-* 'goat.'

ca·pri pants /kəˈprē/ (also **ca·pris**) ▸*plural n.* close-fitting calf-length tapered trousers, usually worn by women and girls. ▷1950s (originally U.S.): named after the island of CAPRI.

Ca·pri·vi Strip /kəˈprēvē/ a narrow strip in Namibia that extends toward Zambia from the northeastern corner of Namibia and reaches the Zambezi River. ▷named after Leo Graf von *Caprivi*, German imperial Chancellor 1890–94 at the time when this region became part of the colony of German Southwest Africa.

cap rock ▸*n.* a layer of hard, impervious rock overlying and often sealing in a deposit of oil, gas, or coal.

ca·pro·ic ac·id /kəˈprō-ik/ ▸*n.* *Chemistry* a liquid fatty acid present in milk fat and coconut and palm oils. • Alternative name: **hexanoic acid**; chem. formula: $CH_3(CH_2)_4COOH$. ▷mid 19th cent.: *caproic* from Latin *caper, capr-* 'goat' (because of its smell) + -IC. **—cap·ro·ate** /ˈkaprōˌāt/ *n.*

cap·ro·lac·tam /ˌkaprōˈlakˌtam/ ▸*n.* *Chemistry* a synthetic crystalline compound that is an intermediate in nylon manufacture. • A lactam; chem. formula: $C_6H_{11}NO$. ▷1940s: from CAPROIC ACID + LACTAM.

ca·pryl·ic ac·id /kəˈprilik/ ▸*n.* *Chemistry* a liquid fatty acid present in butter and other fats. • Alternative name: ***n*-octanoic acid**; chem. formula: $CH_3(CH_2)_6COOH$. ▷mid 19th cent.: from Latin *caper, capr-* 'goat' + -YL + -IC. **—cap·ry·late** /ˈkaprəˌlāt/ *n.*

caps /kaps/ ▸*abbr.* capital letters.

cap·sa·i·cin /kapˈsāəsin/ ▸*n.* *Chemistry* a compound that is responsible for the pungency of capsicums. • A cyclic amide; chem. formula: $C_{18}H_{27}NO_3$. ▷late 19th cent.: alteration of *capsicine*, the name of a substance formerly thought to have the same property.

Cap·si·an /ˈkapsēən/ ▸*adj.* *Archaeology* of, relating to, or denoting a Paleolithic culture of North Africa and southern Europe, noted for its microliths. It is dated to *c.*8000–4500 BC. ■ [as *n.*] (**the Capsian**) the Capsian culture or period. ▷early 20th cent.: from Latin *Capsa* (now *Gafsa* in Tunisia), where objects from this culture were found, + -IAN.

cap·si·cum /ˈkapsikəm/ ▸*n.* (*pl.* **-cums**) a tropical American pepper plant of the nightshade family with fruits containing many seeds. Many cultivated varieties with edible, pungent fruits have been developed. • Genus *Capsicum*, family Solanaceae: several species and varieties, in particular *C. annuum* var. *annuum*, the cultivated forms of which include the '*grossum*' group (sweet peppers) and the '*longum*' group (chili peppers). ■ the fruit of any of these plants, varying in size, color, and pungency. ▷late 16th cent.: modern Latin, perhaps from Latin *capsa* (see CASE[2]).

cap·sid[1] /ˈkapsid/ ▸*n.* another term for MIRID. ▷late 19th cent.: from modern Latin *Capsidae* (plural), from *Capsus* (genus name).

cap·sid[2] ▸*n.* *Microbiology* the protein coat or shell of a virus particle, surrounding the nucleic acid or nucleoprotein core. ▷1960s: coined in French from Latin *capsa* (see CASE[2]).

cap·size /ˈkapˌsīz; kapˈsīz/ ▸*v.* (of a boat) overturn in the water: [*intrans.*] *the craft capsized in heavy seas* | [as *adj.*] (**capsized**) *a capsized dinghy.* | [*trans.*] *gale-force gusts capsized the dinghies.*
▸*n.* [in *sing.*] an instance of capsizing. ▷late 18th cent.: perhaps based on Spanish *capuzar* 'sink (a ship) by the head,' from *cabo* 'head' + *chapuzar* 'to dive or duck.'

cap sleeve ▸*n.* a sleeve extending only a short distance from the shoulder and tapering to nothing under the arm.

cap·stan /ˈkapstən/ ▸*n.* a revolving cylinder with a vertical axis used for winding a rope or cable, powered by a motor or pushed around by levers. ■ the motor-driven spindle on a tape recorder that makes the tape travel past the head at constant speed. ▷late Middle English: from Provençal *cabestan*, from *cabestre* 'halter,' from Latin *capistrum*, from *capere* 'seize.'

capstan

cap·stone /ˈkapˌstōn/ ▸*n.* a stone fixed on top of something, typically a wall. ■ *Archaeology* a large, flat stone forming a roof over the chamber of a megalithic tomb. ■ *figurative* a concluding achievement.

cap·sule /ˈkapsəl; ˈkapˌsoōl/ ▸*n.* a small case or container, esp. a round or cylindrical one. ■ a small, soluble case of gelatin containing a dose of medicine, swallowed whole. ■ a top or cover for a bottle, esp. the foil or plastic covering the cork of a wine bottle. ■ short for SPACE CAPSULE. ■ [as *adj.*] *figurative* (of a piece of writing) shortened but retaining the essence of the original; condensed: *a capsule review of the movie.* ■ *Anatomy* a tough sheath or membrane that encloses something in the body, such as a kidney, a lens, or a synovial joint. ■ *Biology* a gelatinous layer forming the outer surface of some bacterial cells. ■ *Botany* a dry fruit that releases its seeds by bursting open when ripe, such as a pea pod. ■ *Botany* the spore-producing structure of mosses and liverworts, typically borne on a stalk. ▷late Middle English (in the general sense 'small container'): via French from Latin *capsula*, diminutive of *capsa* (see CASE[2]). **—cap·su·lar** /ˈkapsələr/ *adj.* **—cap·su·late** /ˈkapsələt; -ˌlāt/ *adj.*

cap·sule en·do·scope ▸*n.* another term for VIDEO PILL. **—cap·sule en·dos·co·py** *n.*

cap·sul·ize /ˈkapsəˌlīz/ ▸*v.* [*trans.*] put (information) in compact form; summarize.

Capt. ▸*abbr.* Captain.

cap·tain /ˈkaptən/ ▸*n.* the person in command of a ship. ■ the pilot in command of a civil aircraft. ■ a naval officer of high rank, in particular (in the U.S. Navy or Coast Guard) an officer ranking above commander and below commodore. ■ an army officer of high rank, in particular (in the U.S. Army, Marine Corps, or Air Force) an officer ranking above first lieutenant and below major. ■ a police officer in charge of a precinct, ranking below a chief: *captain of the 20th precinct.* ■ the head of a precinct's fire department. ■ the leader of a team, esp. in sports. ■ a powerful or influential person in a particular field: *a captain of industry.* ■ a political party leader in a local district. ■ a supervisor of waiters or bellboys.
▸*v.* [*trans.*] be the captain of (a ship, aircraft, or sports team). ▷late Middle English (in the general sense 'chief or leader'): from Old French *capitain* (superseding earlier *chevetaigne* 'chieftain'), from late Latin *capitaneus* 'chief,' from Latin *caput, capit-* 'head.' **—cap·tain·cy** /-tənsē/ *n.*

cap·tain gen·er·al ▸*n.* an honorary rank of senior officer in the British army, most commonly in an artillery regiment.

cap·tain's chair ▸*n.* a wooden chair along whose side and back edges a row of vertical spindles supports a bar that forms the back and armrests.

captain's chair

cap·tain's mast ▸*n.* see MAST[1].

cap·tan /ˈkapˌtan/ ▸*n.* a synthetic fungicide derived from a mercaptan.

cap·tion /ˈkapSHən/ ▸*n.* a title or brief explanation appended to an article, illustration, cartoon, or poster. ■ a piece of text appearing on a movie or television screen as part of a movie or broadcast. ■ *Law* the heading of a legal document.
▸*v.* [*trans.*] (usu. **be captioned**) provide (an illustration) with a title or explanation: *the drawings were captioned with humorous texts* | [with *two objs.*] *the photograph was captioned "Three little maids."* ▷late Middle English (in the sense 'seizing, capture'): from Latin *caption-*, from *capere* 'take, seize.' Early senses 'arrest' and 'warrant for arrest' gave rise to 'statement of where, when, and by whose authority a warrant was issued' (late 17th cent.): this was usually appended to a legal document, hence the sense 'heading or appended wording' (late 18th cent.).

cap·tious /ˈkapSHəs/ ▸*adj.* *formal* (of a person) tending to find fault or raise petty objections. ▷late Middle English (also in the sense 'intended to deceive someone'): from Old French *captieux* or Latin *captiosus*, from *captio(n-)* 'seizing,' (figuratively) 'deceiving' (see CAPTION). **—cap·tious·ly** *adv.* **—cap·tious·ness** *n.*

cap·ti·vate /ˈkaptəˌvāt/ ▸*v.* [*trans.*] attract and hold the interest and attention of; charm: *he was captivated by her beauty* | [as *adj.*] (**captivating**) *a captivating smile.* ▷early 16th cent.: from late Latin *captivat-* 'taken captive,' from the verb *captivare*, from *captivus* (see CAPTIVE). **—cap·ti·vat·ing·ly** /-ˌvātiNGlē/ *adv.* **—cap·ti·va·tion** /ˌkaptəˈvāSHən/ *n.*

cap·tive /ˈkaptiv/ ▸*n.* a person who has been taken prisoner or an animal that has been confined.
▸*adj.* imprisoned or confined: *the farm was used to* ***hold*** *prisoners of war* ***captive*** | *a captive animal.* ■ [*attrib.*] having no freedom to choose alternatives or to avoid something: *advertisements at the movie theater reach a* ***captive audience.*** ■ (of a facility or service) controlled by, and typically for the sole use of, an establishment or company: *a captive power plant.* ▷late Middle English: from Latin *captivus*, from *capere* 'seize, take.'

cap·tive bal·loon ▸*n.* a lighter-than-air balloon secured by a rope to the ground, used to carry radar equipment or for parachute jumps.

cap·tiv·i·ty /kapˈtivitē/ ▸*n.* (*pl.* **-ties**) the condition of being imprisoned or confined: *he was released after*

865 days in captivity | the third month of their captivity. ■ (**the Captivity**) short for BABYLONIAN CAPTIVITY. ▷late Middle English: from Latin *captivitas*, from *captivus* 'taken captive' (see CAPTIVE).

cap·tor /ˈkaptər; -ˌtôr/ ▸*n.* a person or animal that catches or confines another. ▷mid 16th cent.: from Latin, from *capt-* 'seized, taken,' from the verb *capere*.

cap·ture /ˈkapCHər/ ▸*v.* [*trans.*] take into one's possession or control by force: *the Russians captured 13,000 men | figurative the appeal captured the imagination of thousands.* ■ record or express accurately in words or pictures: *she did a series of sketches, trying to capture all his moods.* ■ *Physics* absorb (an atomic or subatomic particle). ■ (in chess and other board games) make a move that secures the removal of (an opposing piece) from the board. ■ *Astronomy* (of a star, planet, or other celestial body) bring (a less massive body) permanently within its gravitational influence. ■ (of a stream) divert the upper course of (another stream) by encroaching on its catchment area. ■ cause (data) to be stored in a computer.
▸*n.* the action of capturing or of being captured: *the capture of the city marks the high point of his career | he was killed while resisting capture.* ■ a person or thing that has been captured. ■ *Physics* the absorption of an atomic or subatomic particle. ▷mid 16th cent. (as a noun): from French, from Latin *captura*, from *capt-* 'seized, taken,' from the verb *capere*. —**cap·tur·er** *n.*

cap·ture-the-flag ▸*n.* a game in which two teams each hide a colored cloth, representing the team's flag, and then try to find the other team's flag and return with it to their home base.

Cap·u·chin /ˈkap(y)əSHən; kəˈp(y)o͞o-/ ▸*n.* **1** a friar belonging to a branch of the Franciscan order that observes a strict rule drawn up in 1529. **2** (**capuchin**) a cloak and hood formerly worn by women. **3** (**capuchin** or **capuchin monkey**) a South American monkey with a cap of hair on the head that has the appearance of a cowl. • Genus *Cebus*, family Cebidae: four species, including the **brown capuchin** (*C. apella*). **4** (**capuchin**) a pigeon of a breed with head and neck feathers resembling a cowl. ▷late 16th cent.: from obsolete French, earlier form of *capucin*, from Italian *cappuccino*, from *cappuccio* 'hood, cowl,' from *cappa* (see CAPE[1]), the friars being so named because of their sharp-pointed hoods.

cap·y·ba·ra /ˈkapəˌberə; -ˌbärə/ ▸*n.* (*pl.* same or **-ras**) a South American mammal that resembles a giant, long-legged guinea pig. It lives in groups near water and is the largest living rodent. • *Hydrochoerus hydrochaeris*, the only member of the family Hydrochaeridae. ▷early 17th cent.: from Spanish *capibara* or Portuguese *capivara*, from Tupi *capiuára*, from *capī* 'grass' + *uára* 'eater.'

car /kär/ ▸*n.* a road vehicle, typically with four wheels, powered by an internal combustion engine and able to carry a small number of people: *we're going by car* | [as *adj.*] *a car crash.* ■ a vehicle that runs on rails, esp. a railroad car. ■ a railroad car of a specified kind: *the first-class cars.* ■ the passenger compartment of an elevator, cableway, airship, or balloon. ■ *poetic/literary* a chariot. ▷late Middle English (in the general sense 'wheeled vehicle'): from Old Northern French *carre*, based on Latin *carrum*, *carrus*, of Celtic origin. —**car·ful** /-ˌfo͝ol/ *n.* (*pl.* **-fuls**).

ca·ra·ba·o /ˌkarəˈbou; ˌkär-/ ▸*n.* (*pl.* same or **-os**) another term for WATER BUFFALO. ▷early 20th cent.: from Spanish, from a local word in the Philippines.

car·a·bid /ˈkarəbid; kəˈrabid/ ▸*n.* *Entomology* a fast-running beetle of a family (Carabidae) that comprises the predatory ground beetles. ▷late 19th cent.: from modern Latin *Carabidae* (plural), from Latin *carabus*, denoting a kind of crab.

car·a·bi·neer /ˌkarəbəˈni(ə)r/ (also **car·a·bi·nier**) ▸*n.* *historical* a cavalry soldier whose principal weapon was a carbine. ▷mid 17th cent.: from French *carabinier*, from *carabine* (see CARBINE).

car·a·bi·ner /ˌkarəˈbēnər/ (also **kar·a·bi·ner**) ▸*n.* a coupling link with a safety closure, used by rock climbers. ▷1930s: shortened from German *Karabiner-haken* 'spring hook.'

ca·ra·bi·ne·ro /ˌkarəbəˈne(ə)rō; ˌkär-/ ▸*n.* (*pl.* **-ros**) a Spanish or South American frontier guard or customs officer. ▷mid 19th cent.: Spanish, literally 'soldier armed with a carbine.'

ca·ra·bi·nie·re /ˌkarəbənˈye(ə)rē/ ▸*n.* (*pl.* **-ri** *pronunc.* same) a member of the Italian paramilitary police. ▷Italian, literally 'carabineer.'

car·a·cal /ˈkarəˌkal/ ▸*n.* a long-legged lynxlike cat with black tufted ears and a uniform brown coat, native to Africa and western Asia. Also called AFRICAN LYNX. • *Felis caracal*, family Felidae. ▷mid 19th cent.: from French or Spanish, from Turkish *karakulak*, from *kara* 'black' + *kulak* 'ear' (because of its black ear tufts).

Car·a·cal·la /ˌkarəˈkalə/ (188–217), Roman emperor 211–217; born *Septimius Bassanius*; later called *Marcus Aurelius Severus Antoninus Augustus*. In 212, he granted Roman citizenship to all free inhabitants of the Roman Empire.

ca·ra·ca·ra /ˌkarəˈkarə; ˌkärəˈkärə/ ▸*n.* (*pl.* same or **-ras**) a large New World bird of prey of the falcon family, with a bare face and a deep bill, feeding largely on carrion. • Family Falconidae: four genera and several species, in particular the **common caracara** (*Polyborus plancus*). ▷mid 19th cent.: from Spanish or Portuguese *caracará*, from Tupi-Guarani, imitating its cry.

Ca·ra·cas /kəˈräkəs; kəˈrakəs/ the capital of Venezuela, in the northern part of the country near the Caribbean Sea; pop. 1,824,890.

car·a·cole /ˈkarəˌkōl/ ▸*n.* a half turn to the right or left by a horse.
▸*v.* [*intrans.*] (of a horse) perform a caracole. ▷early 17th cent.: from French *caracole*, *caracol* 'snail's shell, spiral.'

car·a·cul ▸*n.* variant spelling of KARAKUL.

ca·rafe /kəˈraf; -ˈräf/ ▸*n.* an open-topped glass flask typically used for serving wine or water. ▷late 18th cent.: from French, from Italian *caraffa*, probably based on Arabic *garafa* 'draw water.'

car·a·ga·na /ˌkarəˈgänə; -ˈganə/ ▸*n.* a leguminous shrub or small tree native to central Asia and Siberia, widely planted as an ornamental. • Genus *Caragana*, family Leguminosae: several species, including the pea tree of Siberia. ▷modern Latin, of Turkic origin.

Ca·ra·jás /ˌkärəˈZHäs/ a mining region in northern Brazil, the site of one of the world's richest deposits of iron ore.

ca·ram·ba /kəˈrämbə/ ▸*exclam. informal, often humorous* an expression of surprise or dismay. ▷mid 19th cent.: from Spanish.

ca·ram·bo·la /ˌkarəmˈbōlə/ ▸*n.* **1** a golden-yellow juicy fruit with a star-shaped cross section. Also called STAR FRUIT. **2** the small tropical tree that bears this fruit. • *Averrhoa carambola*, family Oxalidaceae. ▷late 16th cent.: from Portuguese, probably from Marathi *karambal*.

car·a·mel /ˈkarəməl; -ˌmel; ˈkärməl/ ▸*n.* sugar or syrup heated until it turns brown, used as a flavoring or coloring for food or drink: *an apple dipped in caramel* | [as *adj.*] *caramel ice cream.* ■ the light brown color of this substance: *the liquid turns a pale caramel* | [as *adj.*] *a caramel sweater.* ■ a soft candy made with sugar and butter that have been melted and further heated. ▷early 18th cent.: from French, from Spanish *caramelo*.

car·a·mel·ize /ˈkarəməˌlīz; ˈkärmə-/ ▸*v.* [*intrans.*] (of sugar or syrup) be converted into caramel. ■ [*trans.*] [usu. as *adj.*] (**caramelized**) cook (food) with sugar so that it becomes coated with caramel. ▷mid 19th cent.: from French *caraméliser*, from *caramel* 'caramel.' —**car·a·mel·i·za·tion** /ˌkarəmələˌzāSHən/ *n.*

ca·ran·gid /kəˈranjid; -ˈraNGgid/ ▸*n.* *Zoology* a marine fish of the jack family (Carangidae), whose members typically have a sloping forehead and two dorsal fins. ▷late 19th cent.: from modern Latin *Carangidae* (plural), from the genus name *Caranx*.

car·a·pace /ˈkarəˌpās/ ▸*n.* the hard upper shell of a turtle or crustacean. ▷mid 19th cent.: from French, from Spanish *carapacho*, of unknown origin.

car·at /ˈkarət/ ▸*n.* **1** a unit of weight for precious stones and pearls, now equivalent to 200 milligrams: *a half-carat diamond ring.* **2** chiefly British spelling of KARAT. ▷late Middle English (sense 2): from French, from Italian *carato*, from Arabic *ķīrāţ* (a unit of weight), from Greek *keration* 'fruit of the carob' (also denoting a unit of weight), diminutive of *keras* 'horn,' with reference to the elongated seed-pod of the carob.

Ca·ra·vag·gio /ˌkarəˈväjō/, Michelangelo Merisi da (*c.*1571–1610), Italian painter. He was an influential figure in the transition from late mannerism to baroque.

car·a·van /ˈkarəˌvan/ ▸*n.* **1** *Brit.* a vehicle equipped for living in, typically towed by a car and used for vacations: [as *adj.*] *a caravan holiday.* ■ a covered horse-drawn wagon: *a gypsy caravan.* ■ a covered truck; a van. **2** *historical* a group of people, esp. traders or pilgrims, traveling together across a desert in Asia or North Africa. ■ any large group of people, typically with vehicles or animals traveling together, in single file: *a caravan of cars and trucks.* ▷late 15th cent. (sense 2): from French *caravane*, from Persian *kārwān*. The sense 'covered horse-drawn wagon' dates from the early 19th cent.

car·a·van·sa·ry /ˌkarəˈvansərē/ (*chiefly Brit.* also **car·a·van·se·rai** /-səˌrī/) ▸*n.* (*pl.* **-sa·ries** or **-se·rais** /-səˌrīz/) **1** *historical* an inn with a central courtyard for travelers in the desert regions of Asia or North Africa. **2** a group of people traveling together; a caravan. ▷late 16th cent.: from Persian *kārwānsarāy*, from *kārwān* 'caravan' + *sarāy* 'palace.'

car·a·vel /ˈkarəˌvel; -vəl/ (also **car·vel** /ˈkärvəl/) ▸*n.* *historical* a small, fast Spanish or Portuguese ship of the 15th–17th centuries. ▷early 16th cent.: from French *caravelle*, from Portuguese *caravela*, diminutive of *caravo*, via Latin from Greek *karabos* 'horned beetle' or 'light ship.'

car·a·way /ˈkarəˌwā/ ▸*n.* **1** (also **caraway seed**) the seeds of a plant of the parsley family, used for flavoring and as a source of oil. **2** the white-flowered Mediterranean plant that bears these seeds. • *Carum carvi*, family Umbelliferae. ▷Middle English: from medieval Latin *carui*, from Arabic *alkarāwiyā*, probably from Greek *karon* 'cumin.'

carb[1] /ˈkärb/ ▸*n.* short for CARBURETOR.

carb[2] ▸*n.* short for CARBOHYDRATE.

car·ba·mate /ˈkärbəˌmāt/ ▸*n.* *Chemistry* a salt or ester containing the anion NH_2COO^- or the group $-OOCNH_2$, derived from the hypothetical compound **carbamic acid**. ▷mid 19th cent.: from *carbamic* (from CARBO- + AMIDE + -IC) + -ATE[1].

car·ba·maz·e·pine /ˌkärbəˈmazəˌpēn/ ▸*n.* *Medicine* a synthetic compound of the benzodiazepine class, used as an anticonvulsant and analgesic drug. ▷1990s: from CARBO- + AMIDE, on the pattern of *benzodiazepine*.

car·ban·i·on /kärˈbanˌīən; -ˌīˌän/ ▸*n.* *Chemistry* an organic anion in which the negative charge is located on a carbon atom.

car·ba·ryl /ˈkärbəˌril/ ▸*n.* a synthetic insecticide used to protect crops and in the treatment of fleas and lice. • Alternative name: **1-naphthyl-N-methylcarbamate**; chem. formula: $C_{12}H_{11}NO_2$. ▷mid 20th cent.: from CARBAMATE + -YL.

car·ba·zole /ˈkärbəˌzōl/ ▸*n.* *Chemistry* a colorless crystalline substance obtained from coal tar, used in dye production. • A tricyclic heteroaromatic compound; chem. formula: $C_{12}H_9N$. ▷late 19th cent.: from CARBO- + AZO- + -OLE.

car·bene /ˈkärˌbēn/ ▸*n.* *Chemistry* a highly reactive molecule containing a divalent carbon atom, examples of which occur as intermediates in some organic reactions.

car·bide /ˈkärˌbīd/ ▸*n.* *Chemistry* a binary compound of carbon with an element of lower or comparable electronegativity. ■ calcium carbide (CaC_2), used to generate acetylene by reaction with water and formerly used in portable lamps: [as *adj.*] *a carbide lamp.*

car·bine /ˈkärˌbīn; -ˌbēn/ ▸*n.* a light automatic rifle. ■ *historical* a short rifle or musket used by cavalry. ▷early 17th cent.: from French *carabine*, from *carabin* 'mounted musketeer,' of unknown origin.

carbo- ▸*comb. form* representing CARBON.

car·bo·ca·tion /ˌkärbəˈkāSHən/ ▸*n.* *Chemistry* another term for CARBONIUM ION. ▷1950s: from CARBO- + CATION.

car·bo·hy·drate /ˌkärbəˈhīˌdrāt/ ▸*n.* *Biochemistry* any of a large group of organic compounds occurring in foods and living tissues and including sugars, starch, and cellulose. They contain hydrogen and oxygen in the same ratio as water (2:1) and typically can be broken down to release energy in the animal body.

car·bo·lat·ed /ˈkärbəˌlātid/ ▸*adj.* impregnated with carbolic acid.

car·bol·ic /kärˈbälik/ ▸*n.* short for CARBOLIC ACID or CARBOLIC SOAP.

car·bol·ic ac·id ▸*n.* phenol, esp. when used as a disinfectant.

car·bol·ic soap ▸*n.* disinfectant soap containing phenol.

car·bo-load /ˈkärbō ˌlōd/ ▸*verb* [*intrans.*] eat large amounts of carbohydrates, as in preparation for athletic endurance.

car·bo-load·ed /ˈkärbōˌlōdid/ ▸*adj.* (of a food, beverage, or meal) containing a relatively high amount of carbohydrates: *drink half a bottle of a carbo-loaded drink about 30 minutes before your workout.*

car bomb ▶*n.* a bomb concealed in or under a parked car, used esp. by terrorists.
▶*v.* (**car-bomb**) [*trans.*] attack with such a bomb. —**car bomb·er** *n.*

car·bon /ˈkärbən/ ▶*n.* the chemical element of atomic number 6, a nonmetal that has two main forms (diamond and graphite) and that also occurs in impure form in charcoal, soot, and coal. (Symbol: **C**) ■ *Chemistry* an atom of this element. ■ a rod of carbon in an arc light. ■ a piece of carbon paper or a carbon copy.

Compounds of carbon (organic compounds) form the physical basis of all living organisms. Carbon atoms are able to link with each other and with other atoms to form chains and rings, and an infinite variety of carbon compounds exist.

▷late 18th cent.: from French *carbone,* from Latin *carbo, carbon-* 'coal, charcoal.'

car·bon-12 ▶*n.* the commonest natural carbon isotope, of mass 12. It is the basis for the accepted scale of atomic mass units.

car·bon-14 ▶*n.* a long-lived naturally occurring radioactive carbon isotope of mass 14, used in carbon dating and as a tracer in biochemistry.

car·bo·na·ceous /ˌkärbəˈnāsнəs/ ▶*adj.* (chiefly of rocks or sediments) consisting of or containing carbon or its compounds.

car·bo·na·do /ˌkärbəˈnādō; -ˈnādō/ ▶*n.* (*pl.* **-dos**) a dark opaque diamond, used in abrasives and cutting tools. Compare with **BORT**. ▷mid 19th cent.: from Portuguese.

car·bo·na·ra /ˌkärbəˈnärə; -ˈnarə/ ▶*adj.* denoting a pasta sauce made with bacon or ham, egg, and cream: [*postpositive*] *spaghetti carbonara.* ▷Italian, literally 'charcoal kiln,' perhaps influenced by *carbonata,* a dish of charcoal-grilled salt pork.

car·bo·nate ▶*n.* /ˈkärbənət; -ˌnāt/ a salt of the anion CO_3^{2-}, typically formed by reaction of carbon dioxide with bases.
▶*v.* /ˈkärbəˌnāt/ [*trans.*] [usu. as *adj.*] (**carbonated**) dissolve carbon dioxide in (a liquid): *a carbonated soft drink.* ■ *Chemistry* convert into a carbonate, typically by reaction with carbon dioxide. —**car·bo·na·tion** /ˌkärbəˈnāsнən/ *n.*

car·bon black ▶*n.* a fine carbon powder used as a pigment, made by burning hydrocarbons in insufficient air.

car·bon cop·y ▶*n.* a copy of written or typed material made with carbon paper. ■ *figurative* a person or thing identical or very similar to another: *Karl was a carbon copy of his father.*

car·bon cy·cle ▶*n.* **1** the series of processes by which carbon compounds are interconverted in the environment, chiefly involving the incorporation of carbon dioxide into living tissue by photosynthesis and its return to the atmosphere through respiration, the decay of dead organisms, and the burning of fossil fuels. **2** *Astronomy* the cycle of thermonuclear reactions believed to occur in stars, in which carbon nuclei are repeatedly formed and broken down in the conversion of hydrogen into helium.

Car·bon·dale /ˈkärbənˌdāl/ a city in south central Illinois, a coal center and home to Southern Illinois University; pop. 27,033.

car·bon dat·ing ▶*n.* the determination of the age of an organic object from the relative proportions of the carbon isotopes carbon-12 and carbon-14 that it contains. The ratio between them changes as radioactive carbon-14 decays and is not replaced by exchange with the atmosphere.

car·bon di·ox·ide ▶*n.* a colorless, odorless gas produced by burning carbon and organic compounds and by respiration. It is naturally present in air (about 0.03 percent) and is absorbed by plants in photosynthesis. • Chem. formula: CO_2.

car·bon di·sul·fide ▶*n.* a colorless toxic flammable liquid used as a solvent, esp. for rubber and sulfur, and in the manufacture of viscose rayon, cellophane, and carbon tetrachloride. • Chem. formula: CS_2.

car·bon fi·ber ▶*n.* a material consisting of thin, strong crystalline filaments of carbon, used as a strengthening material, esp. in resins and ceramics: [as *adj.*] *a carbon-fiber chassis.*

car·bon·ic /kärˈbänik/ ▶*adj.* of or relating to carbon or its compounds, esp. carbon dioxide.

car·bon·ic ac·id ▶*n.* a very weak acid formed in solution when carbon dioxide dissolves in water. • Chem. formula: H_2CO_3.

car·bon·ic ac·id gas ▶*n.* archaic term for **CARBON DIOXIDE**.

car·bon·ic an·hy·drase /anˈhīˌdrās; -ˌdrāz/ ▶*n. Biochemistry* an enzyme that catalyzes the conversion of dissolved bicarbonates into carbon dioxide.

Car·bon·if·er·ous /ˌkärbəˈnifərəs/ ▶*adj. Geology* of, relating to, or denoting the fifth period of the Paleozoic era, between the Devonian and Permian periods. ■ (**the Carboniferous**) [as *n.*] the Carboniferous period or the system of rocks deposited during it.

The Carboniferous lasted from about 360 million to 286 million years ago. This period is subdivided into two periods, the **Older Carboniferous**, or **Mississippian Period** (about 360-320 million years ago), and the **Younger Carboniferous**, or **Pennsylvanian Period** (about 320-286 million years ago). During this time the first reptiles and seed-bearing plants appeared, and there were extensive coral reefs and coal-forming swamp forests.

car·bo·ni·um i·on /kärˈbōnēəm/ ▶*n. Chemistry* an organic cation in which the positive charge is located on a carbon atom. ▷early 20th cent.: *carbonium* from **CARBO-** 'carbon,' on the pattern of *ammonium.*

car·bon·ize /ˈkärbəˌnīz/ ▶*v.* [*trans.*] convert into carbon, typically by heating or burning, or during fossilization: *the steak was carbonized on the outside.* ■ [usu. as *adj.*] (**carbonized**) coat with carbon. —**car·bon·i·za·tion** /ˌkärbənəˈzāsнən/ *n.*

car·bon mon·ox·ide ▶*n.* a colorless, odorless toxic flammable gas formed by incomplete combustion of carbon. • Chem. formula: CO.

car·bon·nade /ˌkärbəˈnād/ ▶*n.* a rich beef stew made with onions and beer. ▷mid 17th cent. (denoting a piece of meat or fish cooked on hot coals): from French, from Latin *carbo, carbon-* 'coal, charcoal.'

car·bon pa·per ▶*n.* thin paper coated with carbon or another pigmented substance, used for making copies of written or typed documents.

car·bon proc·ess ▶*n.* a method of making photographic prints that uses a pigment, esp. carbon, contained in a sensitized tissue of gelatin.

car·bon sink ▶*n. Ecology* a forest, ocean, or other natural environment viewed in terms of its ability to absorb carbon dioxide from the atmosphere.

car·bon steel ▶*n.* steel in which the main alloying element is carbon, and whose properties are chiefly dependent on the percentage of carbon present.

car·bon tax ▶*n.* a tax on fossil fuels, esp. those used by motor vehicles, intended to reduce the emission of carbon dioxide.

car·bon tet·ra·chlo·ride /ˌtetrəˈklôrˌīd/ ▶*n.* a colorless toxic volatile liquid used as a solvent, esp. for fats and oils. • Chem. formula: CCl_4.

car·bon·yl /ˈkärbəˌnil/ ▶*n.* [as *adj.*] *Chemistry* of or denoting the divalent radical =C=O, present in such organic compounds as aldehydes, ketones, amides, and esters, and in organic acids as part of the carboxyl group: *carbonyl compounds.* ■ a coordination compound in which one or more carbon monoxide molecules are bonded as neutral ligands to a central metal atom: [with *adj.*] *nickel carbonyl.*

car·bon·yl chlo·ride ▶*n.* another term for **PHOSGENE**.

car·bo·run·dum /ˌkärbəˈrəndəm/ ▶*n.* a very hard black solid consisting of silicon carbide, used as an abrasive. ▷late 19th cent. (originally U.S., as a trademark): blend of **CARBON** and **CORUNDUM**.

car·box·y·he·mo·glo·bin /kärˌbäksēˈhēməˌglōbən/ ▶*n. Biochemistry* a compound formed in the blood by the binding of carbon monoxide to hemoglobin. It is stable and therefore cannot absorb or transport oxygen.

car·box·yl /kärˈbäksəl/ ▶*n.* [as *adj.*] *Chemistry* of or denoting the acid radical −COOH, present in most organic acids: *the carboxyl group.* ▷mid 19th cent.: from **CARBO-** + **OX-** 'oxygen' + **-YL**.

car·box·yl·ase /kärˈbäksəˌlās; -ˌlāz/ ▶*n. Biochemistry* an enzyme that catalyzes the addition of a carboxyl group to a specified substrate.

car·box·yl·ate /kärˈbäksəˌlāt; -lit/ *Chemistry* ▶*n.* a salt or ester of a carboxylic acid.
▶*v.* [*trans.*] add a carboxyl group to (a compound): [as *adj.*] (**carboxylated**) *carboxylated polysaccharides.* —**car·box·yl·a·tion** /kärˌbäksəˈlāsнən/ *n.*

car·box·yl·ic ac·id /ˈkärbäkˈsilik/ ▶*n. Chemistry* an organic acid containing a carboxyl group. The simplest examples are methanoic (or formic) acid and ethanoic (or acetic) acid.

car·boy /ˈkärˌboi/ ▶*n.* a large globular plastic bottle with a narrow neck, typically protected by a frame and used for holding acids or other corrosive liquids. ▷mid 18th cent.: from Persian *ḳarāba* 'large glass flagon.'

car bra ▶*n.* see **BRA**.

carbs /kärbz/ ▶*plural n. informal* dietary carbohydrates.

car·bun·cle /ˈkärˌbəngkəl/ ▶*n.* **1** a severe abscess or multiple boil in the skin, typically infected with staphylococcus bacteria. **2** a bright red gem, in particular a garnet cut en cabochon. ▷Middle English (sense 2): from Old French *charbuncle,* from Latin *carbunculus* 'small coal,' from *carbo* 'coal, charcoal.' —**car·bun·cu·lar** /kärˈbəngkyələr/ *adj.*

car·bu·ret·ed /ˈkärb(y)əˌrātəd; -ˌretid/ (*Brit.* **car·bu·ret·ted**) ▶*adj.* (of a vehicle or engine) having fuel supplied through a carburetor, rather than an injector. ▷early 19th cent.: from archaic *carburet* 'carbide' + **-ED**[2].

car·bu·re·tor /ˈkärb(y)əˌrātər/ (also **car·bu·ra·tor**, *Brit.* **car·bu·ret·tor** or **car·bu·ret·ter**) ▶*n.* a device in an internal combustion engine for mixing air with a fine spray of liquid fuel. ▷mid 19th cent.: from archaic *carburet* 'combine or charge with a hydrocarbon' + **-OR**[1].

car·bu·rize /ˈkärb(y)əˌrīz/ ▶*v.* [*trans.*] add carbon to (iron or steel), in particular by heating in the presence of carbon to harden the surface. ▷mid 19th cent.: from French *carbure* 'carbide' + **-IZE**. —**car·bu·ri·za·tion** /ˌkärb(y)ərəˈzāsнən/ *n.*

car·ca·jou /ˈkärkəˌjoō; ˌzнoō/ ▶*n.* another term for the North American **WOLVERINE**. ▷early 18th cent.: from Canadian French, from Montagnais *kwāhkwāčēw* (compare with **KINKAJOU**).

car·cass /ˈkärkəs/ (*Brit.* also **car·case**) ▶*n.* the dead body of an animal. See note at **BODY**. ■ the trunk of an animal such as a cow, sheep, or pig, for cutting up as meat. ■ the remains of a cooked bird after all the edible parts have been removed. ■ *derogatory* or *humorous* a person's body, living or dead: *my obsession will last while there's life in this old carcass.* ■ the structural framework of a building, ship, or piece of furniture. ■ *figurative* the remains of something being discarded, dismembered, or worthless: *the floor is littered with the carcasses of newspapers.* ▷Middle English: from Anglo-Norman French *carcois,* variant of Old French *charcois;* in later use from French *carcasse;* of unknown ultimate origin.

car·cin·o·gen /kärˈsinəjən; ˈkärsənəˌjen/ ▶*n.* a substance capable of causing cancer in living tissue. ▷mid 19th cent.: from an abbreviation of **CARCINOMA** + **-GEN**.

car·cin·o·gen·e·sis /ˌkärsənəˈjenəsis/ ▶*n.* the initiation of cancer formation.

car·cin·o·gen·ic /ˌkärsənəˈjenik/ ▶*adj.* having the potential to cause cancer. —**car·ci·no·ge·nic·i·ty** /-ˌnōjəˈnisitē/ *n.*

car·ci·noid /ˈkärsəˌnoid/ ▶*n. Medicine* a tumor of a type occurring in the glands of the intestine (esp. the appendix) or in the bronchi, and abnormally secreting hormones. ▷late 19th cent.: from an abbreviation of **CARCINOMA** + **-OID**.

car·ci·no·ma /ˌkärsəˈnōmə/ ▶*n.* (*pl.* **-no·mas** or **-no·ma·ta** /-ˈnōmətə/) a cancer arising in the epithelial tissue of the skin or of the lining of the internal organs. ▷early 18th cent.: via Latin from Greek *karkinōma,* from *karkinos* 'crab' (compare with **CANCER**). —**car·ci·no·ma·tous** /-ˈnōmətəs/ *adj.*

car coat ▶*n.* a short, square-cut style of coat designed to be worn when driving a car.

card[1] /kärd/ ▶*n.* **1** a piece of thick, stiff paper or thin pasteboard, in particular one used for writing or printing on: *some notes jotted down on a card.* ■ such a piece of thick paper printed with a picture and used to send a message or greeting: *a birthday card.* ■ a small piece of such paper with a person's name and other details printed on it for purposes of identification, for example a business card. **2** a small rectangular piece of plastic issued by a bank, containing personal data in a machine-readable form and used chiefly to obtain cash or credit. ■ a similar piece of plastic used for other purposes such as paying for a telephone call or gaining entry to a room or building. **3** a playing card: *a deck of cards.* ■ (**cards**) a game played with playing cards. **4** *Computing* short for **EXPANSION CARD**. **5** *informal* a person regarded as odd or amusing: *He laughed: "You're a card, you know."* **6** a program of events at a racetrack. ■ a record of scores in a sporting event; a scorecard. ■ a list of holes on a golf course, on which a player's scores are entered.

▸*v.* [*trans.*] **1** write (something) on a card, esp. for indexing. **2** check the identity card of (someone), in particular as evidence of legal drinking age. **3** *informal* (in golf and other sports) score (a certain number of points on a scorecard): *he carded 68 in the final round.* ▷late Middle English (sense 3 of the *noun*): from Old French *carte*, from Latin *carta, charta*, from Greek *khartēs* 'papyrus leaf.'

▸*PHRASES* □ **hold all the cards** be in a very strong or advantageous position. □ **in the cards** *informal* very possible or likely: *an overwhelming military triumph is in the cards.* □ **play the —— card** exploit the specified issue or idea mentioned, esp. for political advantage: *he saw an opportunity to play the peace card.* □ **play one's cards right** make the best use of one's assets and opportunities. □ **put** (or **lay**) **one's cards on the table** be completely open and honest in declaring one's resources, intentions, or attitude.

card[2] ▸*v.* [*trans.*] comb and clean (raw wool, hemp fibers, or similar material) with a sharp-toothed instrument in order to disentangle the fibers before spinning.

▸*n.* a toothed implement or machine for this purpose. ▷late Middle English: from Old French *carde*, from Provençal *carda*, from *cardar* 'tease, comb,' based on Latin *carere* 'to card.' —**card·er** *n.*

Card. ▸*abbr.* Cardinal.

car·da·mom /ˈkärdəməm/ (also **car·da·mon** /-mən/) ▸*n.* **1** the aromatic seeds of a plant of the ginger family, used as a spice and also medicinally. **2** the Southeast Asian plant that bears these seeds. • *Elettaria cardamomum*, family Zingiberaceae. ▷late Middle English: from Old French *cardamome* or Latin *cardamomum*, from Greek *kardamōmon*, from *kardamon* 'cress' + *amōmon*, the name of a kind of spice plant.

Car·da·mom Moun·tains /ˈkärdəməm/ a range of mountains in western Cambodia.

card·board /ˈkärd,bôrd/ ▸*n.* pasteboard or stiff paper: [as *adj.*] *a cardboard box.* ■ [as *adj.*] (of a character in a literary work) lacking depth and realism; artificial: *with its superficial, cardboard characters, the novel was typical of her work.*

card-car·ry·ing ▸*adj.* [*attrib.*] registered as a member of a political party or labor union. ■ *often humorous* confirmed in or dedicated to a specified pursuit or outlook: *a card-carrying pessimist.*

Cár·de·nas /ˈkärˈdä,näs; ˈkärdn-əs/ an industrial port in north central Cuba, east of Havana; pop. 63,000.

card·hold·er /ˈkärd,hōldər/ ▸*n.* a person who has a credit card or debit card.

car·di·a /ˈkärdēə/ ▸*n.* *Anatomy* the upper opening of the stomach, where the esophagus enters. ▷late 18th cent.: from Greek *kardia*.

car·di·ac /ˈkärdē,ak/ ▸*adj.* [*attrib.*] **1** of or relating to the heart: *a cardiac arrest.* **2** of or relating to the part of the stomach nearest the esophagus.

▸*n.* *informal Medicine* a person with heart disease. ▷late Middle English (as a noun denoting heart disease): from French *cardiaque* or Latin *cardiacus*, from Greek *kardiakos*, from *kardia* 'heart or upper opening of the stomach.' The adjective dates from the early 17th cent.

car·di·ac ar·rest ▸*n.* a sudden, sometimes temporary, cessation of function of the heart.

car·di·ac mas·sage ▸*n.* a procedure to resuscitate a patient suffering cardiac arrest or fibrillation by rhythmically compressing the chest and heart to restore circulation. Also called HEART MASSAGE.

car·di·ac mus·cle ▸*n.* another term for MYOCARDIUM.

car·di·ac tam·pon·ade ▸*n.* see TAMPONADE (sense 1).

car·di·al·gi·a /,kärdēˈalj(ē)ə/ ▸*n.* **1** heartburn. **2** another term for CARDIODYNIA.

Car·diff /ˈkärdif/ the capital of Wales, a seaport on the Bristol Channel, in the southern part of the country; pop. 272,600. Welsh name CAERDYDD.

car·di·gan /ˈkärdigən/ ▸*n.* a knitted sweater fastening down the front, typically with long sleeves. ▷mid 19th cent. (Crimean War): named after James Thomas Brudenel, 7th Earl of *Cardigan* (1797–1868), leader of the Charge of the Light Brigade, whose troops first wore such garments.

Car·din /kärˈdaN; -ˈdan/, Pierre (1922–), French couturier, the first designer in the field of haute couture to show a collection of clothes for men as well as for women.

car·di·nal /ˈkärd-nl; ˈkärdn-əl/ ▸*n.* **1** a leading dignitary of the Roman Catholic Church. Cardinals are nominated by the pope and form the Sacred College, which elects succeeding popes (now invariably from among their own number). ■ (also **cardinal red**) a deep scarlet color like that of a cardinal's cassock. **2** a New World songbird of the bunting family, with a stout bill and typically with a conspicuous crest. The male is partly or mostly red in color. • Family Emberizidae, subfamily Cardinalinae (the **cardinal grosbeak subfamily**): four genera and several species, esp. the **northern** (or **common**) **cardinal** (*Cardinalis cardinalis*), the male of which is scarlet with a black face. This subfamily also includes American grosbeaks, buntings, and saltators.

northern cardinal

▸*adj.* [*attrib.*] of the greatest importance; fundamental: *two cardinal points must be borne in mind.* ▷Old English, from Latin *cardinalis*, from *cardo, cardin-* 'hinge.' Sense 1 has arisen through the notion of the important function of such priests as "pivots" of church life. —**car·di·nal·ate** /ˈkärd-nl-it; ˈkärdn-əlit; -,lāt/ *n.* (in sense 1 of the *noun*) —**car·di·nal·ly** *adv.* —**car·di·nal·ship** /-,SHip/ *n.* (in sense 1 of the *noun*).

car·di·nal bee·tle ▸*n.* a mainly bright red beetle with feathery or comblike antennae. It typically lives under loose bark. • Family Pyrochroidae: several genera.

car·di·nal fish ▸*n.* a small brightly colored fish found in shallow tropical seas around reefs. The male often broods the eggs in his mouth. • Family Apogonidae: several genera, in particular *Apogon*, and numerous species.

car·di·nal flow·er ▸*n.* a tall scarlet-flowered lobelia found in North America. • *Lobelia cardinalis*, family Campanulaceae.

car·di·nal hu·mor ▸*n.* see HUMOR (sense 3).

car·di·nal·i·ty /,kärdnˈalitē/ ▸*n.* (*pl.* **-ties**) *Mathematics* the number of elements in a set or other grouping, as a property of that grouping.

car·di·nal num·ber ▸*n.* a number denoting quantity (one, two, three, etc.), as opposed to an ordinal number (first, second, third, etc.).

car·di·nal point ▸*n.* each of the four main points of the compass (north, south, east, and west).

car·di·nal sin ▸*n.* **1** another name for DEADLY SIN. **2** *chiefly humorous* a serious error of judgment: *the program was canceled for the biggest cardinal sin of them all—it dared to be intelligent.*

car·di·nal vir·tue ▸*n.* each of the chief natural virtues of justice, prudence, temperance, and fortitude, as defined by Plato and Aristotle and adopted by the Church Fathers. Compare with THEOLOGICAL VIRTUE.

card in·dex ▸*n.* a catalog or similar collection of information in which each item is entered on a separate card, and the cards are arranged in a particular order, typically alphabetical.

card·ing wool ▸*n.* short-stapled pieces of wool that result from the carding process, spun and woven to make standard-quality fabrics. Compare with COMBING WOOL.

cardio- ▸*comb. form* of or relating to the heart: *cardiograph | cardiopulmonary.* ▷from Greek *kardia* 'heart.'

car·di·o·dyn·i·a /,kärdēōˈdinēə/ ▸*n.* pain in the region of the heart.

car·di·o·gram /ˈkärdēə,gram/ ▸*n.* a record of muscle activity within the heart made by a cardiograph.

car·di·o·graph /ˈkärdēə,graf/ ▸*n.* an instrument for recording heart muscle activity, such as an electrocardiograph. —**car·di·og·ra·pher** /,kärdēˈägrəfər/ *n.* —**car·di·og·ra·phy** /-ˈägrəfē/ *n.*

car·di·oid /ˈkärdē,oid/ ▸*n.* *Mathematics* a heart-shaped curve traced by a point on the circumference of a circle as it rolls around another identical circle. ■ (also **cardioid microphone**) a directional microphone with a pattern of sensitivity of this shape.

cardioid

▸*adj.* of the shape of a cardioid. ▷mid 18th cent.: from Greek *kardioeidēs* 'heart-shaped,' from *kardia* 'heart' + *eidos* 'form.'

car·di·ol·o·gy /,kärdēˈäləjē/ ▸*n.* the branch of medicine that deals with diseases and abnormalities of the heart. —**car·di·o·log·i·cal** /,kärdēəˈläjikəl/ *adj.* —**car·di·ol·o·gist** /-jist/ *n.*

car·di·o·meg·a·ly /,kärdēōˈmegəlē/ ▸*n.* *Medicine* abnormal enlargement of the heart. ▷1960s: from CARDIO- + Greek *megas, megal-* 'great.'

car·di·o·my·op·a·thy /,kärdē,ō,mīˈäpəTHē/ ▸*n.* *Medicine* chronic disease of the heart muscle.

car·di·op·a·thy /,kärdēˈäpəTHē/ ▸*n.* heart disease.

car·di·o·pul·mo·nar·y /,kärdēōˈpo͝olmə,nerē; -ˈpəl-/ ▸*adj.* *Medicine* of or relating to the heart and the lungs.

car·di·o·pul·mo·nar·y re·sus·ci·ta·tion ▸*n.* emergency medical procedures for restoring normal heartbeat and breathing to victims of heart failure, drowning, etc.

car·di·o·res·pi·ra·to·ry /,kärdēōˈresp(ə)rə,tôrē; -rəˈspīrə-/ ▸*adj.* *Medicine* relating to the action of both heart and lungs.

car·di·o·vas·cu·lar /,kärdēōˈvaskyələr/ ▸*adj.* *Medicine* of or relating to the heart and blood vessels.

car·di·o·vas·cu·lar sys·tem ▸*n.* another term for CIRCULATORY SYSTEM.

car·di·tis /kärˈdītəs/ ▸*n.* *Medicine* inflammation of the heart.

card key ▸*n.* another term for KEY CARD.

card·mem·ber /ˈkärd,membər/ ▸*n.* a holder of a particular credit or charge card.

car·doon /kärˈdo͞on/ ▸*n.* a tall thistlelike southern European plant related to the globe artichoke, with leaves and roots that may be used as vegetables. • *Cynara cardunculus*, family Compositae. ▷early 17th cent.: from French *cardon*, from *carde* 'edible part of an artichoke,' from modern Provençal *cardo*, based on Latin *carduus, cardus* 'thistle, artichoke.'

Car·do·zo /kärˈdōzō/, Benjamin Nathan (1870–1938), U.S. Supreme Court associate justice 1932–38. Considered a liberal, he championed court involvement in the making of public policy.

card read·er ▸*n.* **1** an electronic sensor that reads a magnetic strip or bar code on a credit card, membership card, etc. **2** an electronic device that reads and transfers data from various portable memory storage devices. **3** a reader of tarot cards or other cards in fortune telling.

card sharp (also **card sharper** or **card shark**) ▸*n.* a person who cheats at cards in order to win money.

card ta·ble ▸*n.* a square table for playing cards on, typically having legs that fold flat for storage.

CARE /ke(ə)r/ ▸*abbr.* Cooperative for American Relief Everywhere, a large private organization that provides emergency and long-term assistance to people in need throughout the world.

care /ke(ə)r/ ▸*n.* **1** the provision of what is necessary for the health, welfare, maintenance, and protection of someone or something: *the care of the elderly | the child is safe* **in the care of** *her grandparents | health care.* **2** serious attention or consideration applied to doing something correctly or to avoid damage or risk: *he planned his departure with great care.* ■ an object of concern or attention: *the cares of family life.* ■ a feeling of or occasion for anxiety: *she was driving along without a care in the world.*

▸*v.* [*intrans.*] **1** [often with *negative*] feel concern or interest; attach importance to something: *they don't* **care about** *human life* | [with *clause*] *I don't care what she says.* ■ feel affection or liking: *you* **care** *very deeply* **for** *him.* ■ (**care for something/care to do something**) like or be willing to do or have something: *would you care for some tea? | I don't care to listen to him.* **2** (**care for**) look after and provide for the needs of: *he has numerous animals to care for.* ▷Old English *caru* (noun), *carian* (verb), of Germanic origin; related to Old High German *chara* 'grief, lament,' *charon* 'grieve,' and Old Norse *kǫr* 'sickbed.'

▸*PHRASES* □ **care of** at the address of: *write to me care of Anne.* □ **I** (or **he, she,** etc.) **couldn't** (or *informal* also **could**) **care less** *informal* used to express complete indifference: *he couldn't care less about football.* □ **for all you care** (or **he, she,** etc., **cares**) *informal* used to indicate that someone feels no interest or concern: *I could drown for all you care.* □ **have a care** [often in *imperative*] *dated* be cautious: *"Have a care!" she warned.* □ **take care 1** [often in *imperative*] be cautious; keep oneself safe: *take care if you're planning to go out tonight.* ■ said to someone on leaving them: *take care, see you soon.* **2** [with *infinitive*] make sure of doing something: *he would take care to provide himself with an escape clause.* □ **take care of 1** keep (someone or something) safe and provided for: *I can take care of myself.* **2** deal with (something): *he has the tools to take care of the electrical problem.*

ca·reen /kəˈrēn/ ▸*v.* **1** [*trans.*] turn (a ship) on its side for cleaning, caulking, or repair. ■ [*intrans.*] (of a ship) tilt; lean over: *a heavy flood tide caused my vessel to careen dizzily.* **2** [*intrans.*] move swiftly and in an uncontrolled way in a specified direction: *an electric golf cart careened around the corner.* [influenced by the verb CAREER.] ▷late 16th cent. (as a noun denoting the position of a careened ship): from French *carène*, from Italian *carena*, from Latin *carina* 'a keel.'

ca·reer /kə'ri(ə)r/ ▶*n.* an occupation undertaken for a significant period of a person's life and with opportunities for progress. ■ the time spent by a person in such an occupation or profession: *the end of a distinguished career in the navy.* ■ the progress through history of an institution or organization: *the court has had a* **checkered career**. ■ [as *adj.*] working permanently in or committed to a particular profession: *a career diplomat.* ■ [as *adj.*] (of a woman) interested in pursuing a profession rather than devoting all her time to child care and housekeeping.
▶*v.* [*intrans.*] move swiftly and in an uncontrolled way in a specified direction: *the car careered across the road and went through a hedge.* ▷mid 16th cent. (denoting a road or racecourse): from French *carrière*, from Italian *carriera*, based on Latin *carrus* 'wheeled vehicle.'
▶*PHRASE* □ **in full career** *archaic* at full speed.

ca·reer·ist /kə'ri(ə)rist/ ▶*n.* a person whose main concern is for professional advancement, esp. one willing to achieve this by any means: [as *adj.*] *a careerist politician.* **—ca·reer·ism** /-,izəm/ *n.*

care·free /'ke(ə)r,frē/ ▶*adj.* free from anxiety or responsibility: *she changed from a carefree girl into a woman* | *the carefree days of summer.* **—care·free·ness** *n.*

care·ful /'ke(ə)rfəl/ ▶*adj.* **1** making sure of avoiding potential danger, mishap, or harm; cautious: *I begged him to be more careful* | *be careful not to lose her address* | [as *exclam.*] *Careful! That stuff's worth a fortune!* ■ (**careful of/about**) anxious to protect (something) from harm or loss; solicitous: *he was very careful of his reputation.* See note at **VIGILANT**. ■ prudent in the use of something, esp. money: *Ali had always been* **careful with** *money.* **2** done with or showing thought and attention: *a careful consideration of the facts.* ▷Old English *carful* (see **CARE, -FUL**). **—care·ful·ly** *adv.* **—care·ful·ness** *n.*

care·giv·er /'ke(ə)r,givər/ ▶*n.* a family member or paid helper who regularly looks after a child or a sick, elderly, or disabled person. **—care·giv·ing** *n.* & *adj.*

care·less /'kerlis/ ▶*adj.* not giving sufficient attention or thought to avoiding harm or errors: *she had been careless and had left the window unlocked.* ■ (of an action or its result) showing or caused by a lack of attention: *he admitted careless driving* | *a careless error.* ■ [*predic.*] (**careless of/about**) not concerned or worried about: *he was careless about his own safety.* ■ showing no interest or effort; casual: *she gave a careless shrug.* ▷Old English *carlēas* 'free from care' (see **CARE, -LESS**). **—care·less·ly** *adv.* **—care·less·ness** *n.*

ca·ress /kə'res/ ▶*v.* [*trans.*] touch or stroke gently or lovingly: *she caressed the girl's forehead* | *figurative* [as *adj.*] (**caressing**) *the caressing warmth of the sun.*
▶*n.* a gentle or loving touch. ▷mid 17th cent.: from French *caresser* (verb), *caresse* (noun), from Italian *carezza*, based on Latin *carus* 'dear.' **—ca·ress·ing·ly** *adv.*

car·et /'karit/ ▶*n.* a mark (^, ‸) placed below the line to indicate a proposed insertion in a printed or written text. ▷late 17th cent.: from Latin, 'is lacking.'

care·tak·er /'ke(ə)r,tākər/ ▶*n.* **1** a person employed to look after a public building or a house in the owner's absence. ■ [as *adj.*] holding power temporarily: *his was a caretaker regime.* **2** a person employed to look after people or animals. **—care·take** *v.*

Ca·rew /kə'ro͞o/, Rod(ney Cline) (1945–), U.S. baseball player; born in Panama. A baseman for the Minnesota Twins 1967–79 and the California Angels 1979–85, he was a seven-time American League batting champion 1969, 1972–75, 1977–78. Baseball Hall of Fame (1991).

care work·er ▶*n. Brit.* a person employed to support and supervise vulnerable, infirm, or disadvantaged people, or those under the care of the state.

care·worn /'ke(ə)r,wôrn/ ▶*adj.* tired and unhappy because of prolonged worry: *a careworn expression.*

Car·ey[1] /'ke(ə)rē/, George (Leonard) (1935–), English Anglican churchman; archbishop of Canterbury 1991–2002.

Car·ey[2], Mariah (1970–), U.S. singer and songwriter. Noted for her wide vocal range, her albums include *Mariah Carey* (1990), *Merry Christmas* (1994), *Daydream* (1995), and *Butterfly* (1997).

car·fare /'kär,fe(ə)r/ ▶*n.* the fare for travel on a bus, subway, or similar mode of public transportation.

car·go /'kärgō/ ▶*n.* (*pl.* **-goes** or **-gos**) goods carried on a ship, aircraft, or motor vehicle: *transportation of bulk cargo* | *a cargo of oil.* ▷mid 17th cent.: from Spanish *cargo, carga*, from late Latin *carricare, carcare* 'to load,' from Latin *carrus* 'wheeled vehicle.'

car·go cult ▶*n.* (in the Melanesian Islands) a system of belief based around the expected arrival of ancestral spirits in ships bringing cargoes of food and other goods.

car·go pants ▶*n.* loose-fitting casual slacks with large patch pockets on the thighs.

car·hop /'kär,häp/ ▶*n. informal, dated* a waiter or waitress at a drive-in restaurant.

Car·i·a /'ke(ə)rēə/ an ancient region of southwestern Asia Minor, south of the Maeander River and northwest of Lycia. **—Car·i·an** *adj.* & *n.*

car·i·am·a /,karē'ämə/ ▶*n.* former term for **SERIEMA**.

Car·ib /'karib/ ▶*n.* **1** a member of an indigenous South American people living mainly in coastal regions of French Guiana, Suriname, Guyana, and Venezuela. **2** the Cariban language of this people. Also called **GALIBI**.

The Caribs were in the process of colonizing the Lesser Antilles from the mainland, displacing Arawak peoples, when their expansion was halted by the arrival of the Spaniards, who all but wiped them out; a few hundred remain on Dominica. Carib is now spoken by around 20,000 people in parts of northern South America. **Island Carib** is an extinct language of the entirely distinct Arawakan group, formerly used in the Lesser Antilles; **Black Carib**, spoken in parts of Central America, is derived from this.

▶*adj.* of or relating to the Caribs or their language. ■ of or relating to Island Carib or Black Carib. ▷from Spanish *caribe*, from Haitian Creole. Compare with **CANNIBAL**.

Car·i·ban /'karəbən; kə'rē-/ ▶*adj.* of, belonging to, or denoting a family of South American languages scattered widely throughout Brazil, Suriname, Guyana, Venezuela, and Colombia. With the exception of Carib, they are all extinct or nearly so.
▶*n.* this family of languages.

Car·ib·be·an /,karə'bēən; kə'ribēən/ ▶*n.* (**the Caribbean**) the region consisting of the Caribbean Sea, its islands (including the West Indies), and the surrounding coasts.
▶*adj.* of or relating to this region.

USAGE There are two possible pronunciations of the word **Caribbean**, and both are used widely and acceptably in the U.S. In the Caribbean itself, the preferred pronunciation puts the stress on the **-rib-**. In Britain, speakers more often put the stress on the **-be-**, although in recent years, the other pronunciation has gained ground in Britain as the more 'up-to-date' and, to some, the more 'correct' pronunciation.

Car·ib·be·an Sea the part of the Atlantic Ocean that lies between the Antilles and the mainland of Central and South America.

ca·ri·be /kə'rēbē/ ▶*n.* another term for **PIRANHA**.

Car·i·boo Moun·tains /'karə,bo͞o/ a range in east central British Columbia, part of the Rocky Mountains, scene of an 1860s gold rush.

car·i·bou /'karə,bo͞o/ ▶*n.* (*pl.* same or **-bous**) a large North American reindeer. • Genus *Rangifer*: several species, in particular the **woodland caribou** (*R. caribou*) and the **barren ground caribou** (*R. tarandus*). ▷mid 17th cent.: from Canadian French, from Micmac *γalipu*, literally 'snowshoveler' (because the caribou scrapes away snow to feed on the vegetation underneath).

barren ground caribou

car·i·ca·ture /'karikəCHər; -,CHo͝or/ ▶*n.* a picture, description, or imitation of a person or thing in which certain striking characteristics are exaggerated in order to create a comic or grotesque effect. ■ the art or style of such exaggerated representation: *there are elements of caricature in the portrayal of the hero.* ■ a ludicrous or grotesque version of someone or something: *he looked like a caricature of his normal self.*
▶*v.* [*trans.*] (usu. **be caricatured**) make or give a comically or grotesquely exaggerated representation of (someone or something): *he was caricatured on the cover of* TV Guide | *a play that caricatures the legal profession.* ▷mid 18th cent.: from French, from Italian *caricatura*, from *caricare* 'load, exaggerate,' from Latin *carricare* (see **CHARGE**). **—car·i·ca·tur·al** /,karikə'CHo͝orəl/ *adj.* **—car·i·ca·tur·ist** /-,CHo͝orist/ *n.*

THE RIGHT WORD **burlesque, caricature, lampoon, mimicry, parody, travesty**

Skilled writers and artists who want to poke fun at someone or something have a number of weapons at their disposal.

An artist might come up with a **caricature**, which is a drawing or written piece that exaggerates its subject's distinguishing features or peculiarities (*the cartoonist's caricature of the presidential candidate*).

A **parody** is similar to a caricature in purpose, but is used of written work or performances that ridicule an author or performer's work by imitating its language and style for comic effect (*a parody of the scene between Romeo and Juliet*).

While a *parody* concentrates on distorting the content of the original work, a **travesty** retains the subject matter but imitates the style in a grotesque or absurd way (*their version of the Greek tragedy was a travesty*).

A **lampoon** is a strongly satirical piece of writing that attacks or ridicules a person or an institution; it is more commonly used as a verb (*to lampoon the government in a local newspaper*).

While a *caricature*, a *parody*, and a *travesty* must have a specific original to imitate, a **burlesque** can be an independent creation or composition; it is a broad comic or satiric imitation, often a theatrical one, that treats a serious subject lightly or a trivial subject with mock seriousness (*the play was a burlesque of ancient Rome*).

Mimicry is something you don't have to be an artist, a writer, or an actor to be good at. Anyone who successfully imitates another person's speech or gestures is a good mimic or impressionist, whether the intent is playful or mocking (*he showed an early talent for mimicry, entertaining his parents with imitations of their friends*).

car·ies /'kerēz/ ▶*n.* decay and crumbling of a tooth or bone. ▷late 16th cent.: from Latin.

car·il·lon /'karə,län; -lən/ ▶*n.* a set of bells in a tower, played using a keyboard or by an automatic mechanism similar to a piano roll. ■ a tune played on such bells. ▷late 18th cent.: from French, from Old French *quarregnon* 'peal of four bells,' based on Latin *quattuor* 'four.' **—car·il·lon·neur** /,karələ'nər/ *n.*

Ca·ri·na /kə'rēnə; -'rī-/ *Astronomy* a southern constellation (the Keel) partly in the Milky Way, originally part of Argo. It contains the second brightest star in the sky, Canopus. ■ [as *genitive*] (**Carinae** /-nē/) used with a preceding letter or numeral to designate a star in this constellation: *the star Beta Carinae.* ▷Latin.

ca·ri·na /kə'rēnə; -'rī-/ ▶*n.* (*pl.* **-nae** /-,nē/ or **-nas**) *chiefly Biology* a keel-shaped structure, in particular: ■ *Zoology* the ridge of a bird's breastbone, to which the main flight muscles are attached. ■ *Anatomy* cartilage situated at the point where the trachea divides into the two bronchi. ▷early 18th cent.: from Latin, 'keel.' **—ca·ri·nal** *adj.*

car·i·nate /'karə,nāt; -nit/ ▶*adj.* having a keellike ridge. ■ (of a bird) having a deep ridge on the breastbone for the attachment of flight muscles. Contrasted with **RATITE**. ▷late 18th cent.: from Latin *carinatus* 'having a keel,' from *carina* 'keel.' **—car·i·nat·ed** /-,nātid/ *adj.* **—car·i·na·tion** /,karə'nāSHən/ *n.*

car·ing /'ke(ə)riNG/ ▶*adj.* displaying kindness and concern for others: *a caring and invaluable friend.*
▶*n.* the work or practice of looking after those unable to care for themselves, esp. the sick and the elderly: [as *adj.*] *the caring professions.*

Car·i·o·ca /,karē'ōkə/ ▶*n.* **1** a native of Rio de Janeiro. **2** (**carioca**) a Brazilian dance resembling the samba.

▷mid 19th cent.: from Portuguese, from Tupi *kari'oka* 'house of the white man.'

car·i·o·gen·ic /ˌkarēəˈjenik/ ▸*adj. technical* causing tooth decay.

car·i·ole ▸*n.* variant spelling of CARRIOLE.

car·i·ous /ˈkarēəs/ ▸*adj.* (of bones or teeth) decayed. ▷mid 16th cent.: from Latin *cariosus* (see CARIES).

ca·ri·tas /ˈkariˌtas; ˈkäriˌtäs/ ▸*n.* Christian love of humankind; charity. ▷mid 19th cent.: Latin.

car·jack·ing /ˈkärˌjakiNG/ ▸*n.* the action of violently stealing an occupied car. ▷1990s: blend of CAR and *hijacking* (see HIJACK). **—car·jack** *v.* **—car·jack·er** /-ˌjakər/ *n.*

cark·ing /ˈkärkiNG/ ▸*adj.* [*attrib.*] *archaic* causing distress or worry: *her carking doubts.* ▷mid 16th cent.: present participle of Middle English *cark* 'worry, burden,' from Old Northern French *carkier*, based on late Latin *carcare* (see CHARGE).

carl /kärl/ ▸*n. archaic* a peasant or man of low birth. ▷Old English (denoting a peasant or villein): from Old Norse *karl* 'man, freeman,' of Germanic origin; related to CHURL.

car·line /ˈkärˌlən/ (also **carline thistle**) ▸*n.* a thistlelike European plant with flowerheads that bear shiny persistent straw-colored bracts. • Genus *Carlina*, family Compositae: several species, in particular *C. vulgaris*. ▷late 16th cent.: from French, from medieval Latin *carlina*, perhaps an alteration of *cardina* (from Latin *carduus* 'thistle'), by association with *Carolus Magnus* (see CHARLEMAGNE), to whom its medicinal properties were said to have been revealed.

Car·lisle /kärˈlīl; ˈkärˌlīl/ a historic borough in southern Pennsylvania, southwest of Harrisburg; pop. 18,419. It is home to the Army War College.

Car·lism /ˈkärˌlizəm/ ▸*n. historical* a Spanish conservative political movement originating in support of Don Carlos, brother of Fernando VII (died 1833), who claimed the throne in place of Fernando's daughter Isabella. The movement supported the Catholic Church and opposed centralized government; it was revived in support of the Nationalist side during the Spanish Civil War. **—Car·list** *adj. & n.*

car·load /ˈkärˌlōd/ ▸*n.* the number of people that can travel in an automobile: ***a carload of** passengers.* ■ the quantity of goods that can be carried in a railroad freight car.

Car·lo·vin·gi·an /ˌkärləˈvinj(ē)ən/ ▸*adj. & n.* another term for CAROLINGIAN. ▷from French *carlovingien*, from *Karl* 'Charles,' on the pattern of *mérovingien* 'Merovingian.'

Car·low /ˈkärlō/ a county in the Republic of Ireland, in the province of Leinster.

Carls·bad /ˈkärlzˌbad/ **1** a city in southwestern California, on the Pacific coast, north of San Diego; pop. 63,126. **2** a city in southeastern New Mexico, on the Pecos River; pop. 25,625. To the southwest is Carlsbad Caverns, a vast cave complex.

Carls·bad plum ▸*n.* a dessert plum of a blue-black variety, that is often crystallized. ▷late 19th cent.: named after *Karlsbad* (now Karlovy Vary).

Carl·ton /ˈkärltən/, Steve (1944–), U.S. baseball player; born Steven Norman Carlton; nicknamed **Lefty**. He was the first pitcher to win four Cy Young awards 1972, 1977, 1980, 1982. He played for the St. Louis Cardinals 1965–72 and the Philadelphia Phillies 1972–88. Baseball Hall of Fame (1994).

Car·lyle /kärˈlīl; ˈkärˌlīl/, Thomas (1795–1881), Scottish historian and political philosopher. He wrote *History of the French Revolution* (1837).

car·mak·er /ˈkärˌmākər/ ▸*n.* a manufacturer of automobiles.

car·man /ˈkärmən/ ▸*n.* (*pl.* **-men**) *dated* a driver of a streetcar or horse-drawn carriage.

Car·mel /kärˈmel/ a city in west central California, a resort on the Pacific Ocean, south of Monterey; pop. 4,239.

Car·mel, Mount /ˈkärməl/ a group of mountains near the Mediterranean coast in northwestern Israel that shelter the port of Haifa. In the Bible it is the site of the defeat of the priests of Baal by the prophet Elijah (I Kings 18).

Car·mel·ite /ˈkärməˌlīt/ ▸*n.* a friar or nun of a contemplative Catholic order founded at Mount Carmel during the Crusades.
▸*adj.* of or relating to the Carmelites.

Car·mi·chael[1] /ˈkärˌmīkəl/ a community in north central California, northeast of Sacramento; pop. 48,702.

Car·mi·chael[2], Hoagy (1899–1981), U.S. jazz pianist, composer, and singer; born *Howard Hoagland Carmichael.* His best-known songs include "Stardust" (1929), "Georgia on My Mind" (1930), and "In the Cool, Cool, Cool of the Evening" (1951).

car·min·a·tive /kärˈminətiv; ˈkärməˌnātiv/ ▸*adj. Medicine* (chiefly of a drug) relieving flatulence.
▸*n.* a drug of this kind. ▷late Middle English: from Old French *carminatif, -ive*, or medieval Latin *carminat-* 'healed (by incantation),' from the verb *carminare*, from Latin *carmen* (see CHARM).

car·mine /ˈkärmən; -ˌmīn/ ▸*n.* a vivid crimson color: [as *adj.*] *carmine roses.* ■ a vivid crimson pigment made from cochineal. ▷early 18th cent.: from French *carmin*, based on Arabic *ḳirmiz* (see KERMES). Compare with CRIMSON.

Car·nac /ˈkärˌnak/ the site in Brittany of nearly 3,000 megalithic stones dating from the Neolithic period.

car·nage /ˈkärnij/ ▸*n.* the killing of a large number of people. ▷early 17th cent.: from French, from Italian *carnaggio*, from medieval Latin *carnaticum*, from Latin *caro, carn-* 'flesh.'

car·nal /ˈkärnl/ ▸*adj.* relating to physical, esp. sexual, needs and activities: *carnal desire.* ▷late Middle English: from Christian Latin *carnalis*, from *caro, carn-* 'flesh.' **—car·nal·i·ty** /kärˈnalitē/ *n.* **—car·nal·ly** *adv.*

car·nal knowl·edge ▸*n. dated, chiefly Law* sexual intercourse.

car·nall·ite /ˈkärnlˌīt/ ▸*n.* a white or reddish mineral consisting of a hydrated chloride of potassium and magnesium. ▷mid 19th cent.: named after Rudolf von *Carnall* (1804–74), German mining engineer, + -ITE[1].

Car·nap /ˈkärˌnap/, Rudolf (1891–1970), U.S. philosopher; born in Germany; a founding member of the logical positivist Vienna Circle. Notable works: *The Logical Structure of the World* (1928) and *The Logical Foundations of Probability* (1950).

car·nas·si·al /kärˈnasēəl/ ▸*adj. Zoology* denoting the large upper premolar and lower molar teeth of a carnivore, adapted for shearing flesh.
▸*n.* a tooth of this type. ▷mid 19th cent.: from French *carnassier* 'carnivorous,' based on Latin *caro, carn-* 'flesh.'

Car·nat·ic /kärˈnatik/ ▸*adj.* of or denoting the main style of classical music in southern India, as distinct from the Hindustani music of the north: *Carnatic music.* ▷Anglicization of KARNATAKA in southwestern India.

car·na·tion[1] /kärˈnāSHən/ ▸*n.* a double-flowered cultivated variety of clove pink, with gray-green leaves and showy pink, white, or red flowers. • *Dianthus caryophyllus*, family Caryophyllaceae: many cultivars. ▷late 16th cent.: perhaps based on a misreading of Arabic *ḳaranful* 'clove or clove pink,' from Greek *karyophullon*. The early forms suggest confusion with *carnation* 'rosy pink color,' with *incarnation*, and with *coronation*.

car·na·tion[2] ▸*adj.* of a rosy pink color: *sage and carnation throw pillows.*
▸*n.* a rosy pink color. ▷early 16th cent.: from French *carnation* 'color of one's flesh,' based on Latin *carn-* 'flesh.'

car·nau·ba /kärˈnôbə; -ˈnoubə/ ▸*n.* a northeastern Brazilian fan palm, the leaves of which exude a yellowish wax. Also called WAX PALM. • *Copernicia cerifera*, family Palmae. ■ (also **carnauba wax**) wax from this palm, formerly used as a polish and for making candles. ▷mid 19th cent.: from Portuguese, from Tupi.

Car·ne·gie /ˈkärnigē; kärˈnāgē/, Andrew (1835–1919), U.S. industrialist and philanthropist; born in Scotland. After building up a fortune in the steel industry, he retired in 1901 and devoted his wealth to charitable purposes, in particular to libraries, education, and the arts. He established the Carnegie Institute of Technology in 1900.

car·nel·ian /kärˈnēlyən/ (also **cor·nel·ian** /kôr-/) ▸*n.* a semiprecious stone consisting of an orange or orange-red variety of chalcedony. ▷late Middle English: from Old French *corneline*; the prefix *car-* being suggested by Latin *caro, carn-* 'flesh.'

car·net /kärˈnā/ ▸*n.* a permit, in particular: ■ a permit allowing use of certain campsites while traveling abroad. ■ a customs permit allowing a motor vehicle to be taken across an international border for a limited period. ■ a book of tickets for use on public transport in some countries. ▷1920s: from French, 'notebook.'

Car·ney /ˈkärnē/, Art (1918–2003), U.S. actor; born *Arthur William Matthew Carney.* Best known for his role as Ed Norton in the 1950s TV comedy "The Honeymooners," he also appeared in numerous films, winning an Academy Award for his performance in *Harry and Tonto* (1974). He also invented the role of Felix Unger in the stage production of *The Odd Couple* (1974).

Car·nic Alps /ˈkärnik/ (German name **Karnische Alpen**) a range of the Alps on the border of southern Austria and northeastern Italy that reaches 9,124 feet (2,781 m) at Monte Coglians (Hohe Warte).

car·ni·val /ˈkärnəvəl/ ▸*n.* **1** a period of public revelry at a regular time each year, typically during the week before Lent in Roman Catholic countries, involving processions, music, dancing, and the use of masquerade: *the culmination of the week-long carnival | Mardi Gras is the last day of carnival* | [as *adj.*] *a carnival parade.* ■ *figurative* an exciting or riotous mixture of something: *the whole evening was a carnival of fun.* **2** a traveling amusement show or circus. ▷mid 16th cent.: from Italian *carnevale, carnovale*, from medieval Latin *carnelevamen, carnelevarium* 'Shrovetide,' from Latin *caro, carn-* 'flesh' + *levare* 'put away.' **—car·ni·val·esque** /ˌkärnəvəˈlesk/ *adj.*

Car·niv·o·ra /kärˈnivərə/ *Zoology* an order of mammals that comprises the cats, dogs, bears, hyenas, weasels, civets, raccoons, and mongooses. They are distinguished by having powerful jaws and teeth adapted for stabbing, tearing, and eating flesh.

car·ni·vore /ˈkärnəˌvôr/ ▸*n.* an animal that feeds on flesh. ■ *Zoology* a mammal of the order Carnivora. ▷mid 19th cent.: from French, from Latin *carnivorus* (see CARNIVOROUS).

car·niv·o·rous /kärˈnivərəs/ ▸*adj.* (of an animal) feeding on other animals. ■ (of a plant) able to trap and digest small animals, esp. insects. ▷late 16th cent.: from Latin *carnivorus*, from *caro, carn-* 'flesh' + *-vorus* (see -VOROUS). **—car·niv·o·rous·ly** *adv.* **—car·niv·o·rous·ness** *n.*

car·no·saur /ˈkärnəˌsôr/ (also **car·no·sau·rus** /ˌkärnəˈsôrəs/) ▸*n.* a large bipedal carnivorous dinosaur, typically one with greatly reduced forelimbs. • Infraorder Carnosauria, suborder Theropoda, order Saurischia; includes tyrannosaurus, allosaurus, and megalosaurus. ▷1930s: from modern Latin, from Latin *caro, carn-* 'flesh' + Greek *sauros* 'lizard.' **—car·no·sau·ri·an** *adj.*

Car·not /kärˈnō/, Nicolas Léonard Sadi (1796–1832), French scientist. His work in analyzing the efficiency of steam engines was of crucial importance to the theory of thermodynamics.

car·no·tite /ˈkärnəˌtīt/ ▸*n.* a lemon-yellow radioactive mineral consisting of hydrated vanadate of uranium and potassium, often found near petrified trees. ▷late 19th cent.: named after Marie Adolphe *Carnot* (1839–1920), French inspector of mines, + -ITE[1].

car·ny[1] /ˈkärnē/ (also **car·nie** or **car·ney**) ▸*n.* [usu. as *adj.*] *informal* a carnival or amusement show: *a carny atmosphere.* ■ a person who works in a carnival or amusement show.

car·ny[2] (also **car·ney**) ▸*adj.* (**-ni·er, -ni·est**) *Brit., informal* artful; sly: *Finley's carny approach to baseball.* ▷late 19th cent.: of unknown origin.

car·ob /ˈkarəb/ ▸*n.* **1** a brown floury powder extracted from the carob bean, used as a substitute for chocolate. **2** (also **carob tree**) a small evergreen Arabian tree that bears long brownish-purple edible pods. Also called **locust tree.** • *Ceratonia siliqua*, family Leguminosae. ■ (also **carob bean**) the edible pod of this tree. Also called **locust bean.** ▷late Middle English (denoting the carob bean): from Old French *carobe*, from medieval Latin *carrubia*, from Arabic *ḵarrūba*.

car·ol /ˈkarəl/ ▸*n.* a religious folk song or popular hymn, particularly one associated with Christmas: *singing **Christmas carols** around the tree* | [as *adj.*] *a carol service.*
▸*v.* (**car·oled, car·ol·ing**; *chiefly Brit.* **car·ol·led, car·ol·ling**) [*intrans.*] sing Christmas songs or hymns, esp. in a group: *we caroled from door to door.* ■ [*trans.*] sing or say (something) happily: *she was cheerfully caroling the words of the song.* ▷Middle English: from Old French *carole* (noun), *caroler* (verb), of unknown origin. **—car·ol·er** *n.* **—car·ol·ing** *n. a night of **Christmas caroling** was traditional.*

Car·ol Cit·y /ˈkarəl/ a suburban community in southeastern Florida, north of Miami; pop. 53,331.

Car·o·li·na /ˌkarəˈlīnə/ a commercial and residential suburb in Puerto Rico, east of San Juan; pop. 162,404.

Car·o·li·na all·spice ▸*n.* see ALLSPICE.

Car·o·li·na duck ▸*n.* another term for WOOD DUCK.

Car·o·li·na par·a·keet ▸*n.* a small long-tailed parakeet with mainly green plumage and a yellow and orange head. It was formerly common in the eastern U.S. but was exterminated by about 1920. • *Conuropsis* (or **Aratinga**) *carolinensis*, family Psittacidae.

Car·o·li·na rose ▸*n.* another term for PASTURE ROSE.

Car·o·line /ˈkarəˌlīn; -lin/ ▸*adj.* **1** (also **Car·o·le·an** /ˌkarəˈlēən; ˌker-/) of or relating to the reigns of Charles I and II of England: *a Caroline poet.* **2** another term for CAROLINGIAN. ▷early 17th cent.: from medieval Latin *Carolus* 'Charles.'

Car·o·line Is·lands /ˈkerəˌlīn/ (also **the Car·o·lines**) a group of islands in the western Pacific Ocean, north of the equator, that form the Federated States of Micronesia.

Car·o·lin·gi·an /ˌkarəˈlinj(ē)ən/ (also **Car·lo·vin·gi·an**) ▸*adj.* of or relating to the Frankish dynasty, founded by Charlemagne's father (Pepin III), that ruled in western Europe from 750 to 987. ■ denoting or relating to a style of minuscule script developed in France during the time of Charlemagne, on which modern lower-case letters are largely based.
▸*n.* a member of the Carolingian dynasty. ▷alteration of earlier CARLOVINGIAN, by association with medieval Latin *Carolus* 'Charles.'

Car·o·lin·gi·an Ren·ais·sance a period during the reign of Charlemagne and his successors that was marked by achievements in art, architecture, learning, and music.

Car·ol Stream a village in northeastern Illinois, west of Chicago; pop. 31,716.

car·om /ˈkarəm/ ▸*n. Billiards* another term for BILLIARD (sense 2). ■ (also **carom billiards**) any of the billiard games played on a table without pockets.
▸*v.* [*intrans.*] make a carom; strike and rebound. ▷late 18th cent.: abbreviation of *carambole*, from Spanish *carambola*, apparently from *bola* 'ball.'

car·o·tene /ˈkarəˌtēn/ ▸*n. Chemistry* an orange or red plant pigment found in carrots and many other plant structures. It is a terpenoid hydrocarbon with several isomers, of which one (**beta carotene**) is important in the diet as a precursor of vitamin A. ▷mid 19th cent.: coined in German from Latin *carota* (see CARROT).

ca·rot·e·noid /kəˈrätnˌoid/ ▸*n. Chemistry* any of a class of mainly yellow, orange, or red fat-soluble pigments, including carotene, which give color to plant parts such as ripe tomatoes and autumn leaves. They are terpenoids based on a structure having the formula $C_{40}H_{56}$.

Ca·roth·ers /kəˈrəTHərz/, Wallace Hume (1896–1937), U.S. industrial chemist. He developed neoprene, the first successful synthetic rubber and also Nylon 6.6, a synthetic fiber.

ca·rot·id /kəˈrätid/ ▸*adj.* of, relating to, or denoting the two main arteries that carry blood to the head and neck, and their two main branches.
▸*n.* each of these arteries. ▷early 17th cent.: from French *carotide* or modern Latin *carotides*, from Greek *karōtides*, plural of *karōtis* 'drowsiness,' from *karoun* 'stupefy' (because compression of these arteries was thought to cause stupor).

ca·rot·id bod·y ▸*n.* a small mass of receptors in the carotid artery sensitive to chemical change in the blood.

ca·rouse /kəˈrouz/ ▸*v.* [*intrans.*] drink plentiful amounts of alcohol and enjoy oneself with others in a noisy, lively way: *they danced and caroused until the drink ran out* | [as *n.*] (**carousing**) *a night of carousing.*
▸*n.* a noisy, lively drinking party: *corporate carouses.* ▷mid 16th cent.: originally as an adverb meaning 'all out, completely' in the phrase *drink carouse*, from German *gar aus trinken*; hence 'drink heavily, have a drinking bout.' **—ca·rous·al** /-zəl/ *n.* **—ca·rous·er** *n.*

car·ou·sel /ˌkarəˈsel; ˈkarəˌsel/ (also **car·rou·sel**) ▸*n.* **1** a merry-go-round. ■ a rotating machine or device, in particular a conveyor system at an airport from which arriving passengers collect their luggage. **2** *historical* a tournament in which groups of knights took part in chariot races and other demonstrations of equestrian skills. ▷mid 17th cent.: from French *carrousel*, from Italian *carosello*.

carp[1] /kärp/ ▸*n.* (*pl.* same) a deep-bodied freshwater fish, typically with barbels around the mouth. Carp are farmed for food in some parts of the world and are widely kept in large ponds. • Family Cyprinidae (the **minnow family**): several genera and species, including the **common carp** (*Cyprinus carpio*) and **silver carp** (*Hypophthalmichthys molitrix*). The family includes the majority of freshwater fishes in Eurasia, Africa, and North and Central America. ▷late Middle English: from Old French *carpe*, from late Latin *carpa*.

carp[2] ▸*v.* [*intrans.*] complain or find fault continually, typically about trivial matters: *I don't want to carp about the way you did it* | *he was constantly carping at me.* ▷Middle English (in the sense 'talk, chatter'): from Old Norse *karpa* 'brag'; later influenced by Latin *carpere* 'pluck at, slander.' **—carp·er** *n.*

Car·pac·cio /kärˈpäCH(ē)ō/, Vittore (*c.*1455–1525), Italian painter.

car·pac·cio /kärˈpäCH(ē)ō/ ▸*n.* an Italian cold hors d'oeuvre consisting of thin slices of raw beef or fish served with a sauce. ▷Italian, named after Vittore CARPACCIO (from his use of red pigments, resembling raw meat).

car·pal /ˈkärpəl/ ▸*n.* any of the eight small bones forming the wrist. See CARPUS. ■ any of the equivalent bones in an animal's forelimb.
▸*adj.* of or relating to these bones. ▷mid 18th cent.: from CARPUS + -AL.

car·pal tun·nel syn·drome ▸*n.* a painful condition of the hand and fingers caused by compression of a major nerve where it passes over the carpal bones through a passage at the front of the wrist, alongside the flexor tendons of the hand. It may be caused by repetitive movements over a long period, or by fluid retention, and is characterized by sensations of tingling, numbness, or burning.

car park ▸*n. Brit.* a parking lot or parking garage.

Car·pa·thi·an Moun·tains /kärˈpāTHēən/ (also **the Car·p·ath·ians**) a mountain system that extends southeast from southern Poland and the Czech Republic into Romania.

car·pe di·em /ˌkärpā ˈdēˌem/ ▸*exclam.* used to urge someone to make the most of the present time and give little thought to the future. ▷early 19th cent.: Latin, 'seize the day!,' a quotation from Horace (*Odes* I.xi).

car·pel /ˈkärpəl/ ▸*n. Botany* the female reproductive organ of a flower, consisting of an ovary, a stigma, and usually a style. It may occur singly or as one of a group. ▷mid 19th cent.: from French *carpelle* or modern Latin *carpellum*, from Greek *karpos* 'fruit.' **—car·pel·lar·y** /-ˌlerē/ *adj.*

Car·pen·tar·i·a, Gulf of /ˌkärpənˈte(ə)rēə/ a large bay on the northern coast of Australia, between Arnhem Land and the Cape York Peninsula.

car·pen·ter /ˈkärpəntər/ ▸*n.* a person who makes and repairs wooden objects and structures.
▸*v.* [*trans.*] (usu. **be carpentered**) make by shaping wood: *the rails were carpentered very skillfully.* ■ [*intrans.*] do the work of a carpenter. ▷Middle English: from Anglo-Norman French, from Old French *carpentier*, *charpentier*, from late Latin *carpentarius (artifex)* 'carriage (maker),' from *carpentum* 'wagon,' of Gaulish origin; related to CAR.

car·pen·ter ant ▸*n.* a large ant that burrows into wood to nest. • Genus *Camponotus*, family Formicidae: numerous species.

car·pen·ter bee ▸*n.* a large solitary bee with purplish wings that nests in tunnels bored in dead wood or plant stems. • Genus *Xylocopa*, family Apidae: several species.

car·pen·ter pants ▸*plural n.* loose-fitting pants with many pockets of various sizes and loops for tools at the tops or sides of the legs.

car·pen·try /ˈkärpəntrē/ ▸*n.* the activity or occupation of making or repairing things in wood. ■ the work made or done by a carpenter: *the superb carpentry of the mahogany desk.* ▷late Middle English: from Anglo-Norman French *carpentrie*, Old French *charpenterie*, from *charpentier* (see CARPENTER).

car·pet /ˈkärpit/ ▸*n.* a floor or stair covering made from thick woven fabric, typically shaped to fit a particular room: *the house has fitted carpets throughout* | *the floor was covered with carpet.* ■ a large rug, typically an oriental one: *priceless Persian carpets.* ■ *figurative* a thick or soft expanse or layer of something: *carpets of snowdrops and crocuses.* ■ *informal* a carpetlike artificial playing surface on a tennis court or an athletic field.
▸*v.* (**-pet·ed**, **-pet·ing**) [*trans.*] **1** (usu. **be carpeted**) cover (a floor or stairs) with a carpet: *the stairs were carpeted in a lovely shade of red.* ■ *figurative* cover with a thick or soft expanse or layer of something: *the meadows are carpeted with flowers.* **2** *Brit., informal* reprimand severely. ▷Middle English (denoting a thick fabric used as a cover for a table or bed): from Old French *carpite* or medieval Latin *carpita*, from obsolete Italian *carpita* 'woolen bedspread,' based on Latin *carpere* 'pluck, pull to pieces.'
▸*PHRASE* □ **call someone on the carpet** *informal* severely reprimand someone below one in authority: *she might have called the accused person on the carpet.* [from *carpet* in the sense 'table covering,' referring to 'the carpet of the council table,' before which one would be summoned for reprimand.]

car·pet·bag /ˈkärpitˌbag/ ▸*n.* a traveling bag of a kind originally made of carpeting or carpetlike material.
▸*v.* [*intrans.*] act as a carpetbagger: [as *adj.*] (**carpetbagging**) *rich, carpetbagging developers.*

car·pet·bag·ger /ˈkärpitˌbagər/ ▸*n. derogatory* a political candidate who seeks election in an area where they have no local connections. ■ *historical* (in the U.S.) a person from the northern states who went to the South after the Civil War to profit from the Reconstruction. ■ a person perceived as an unscrupulous opportunist: *the organization is rife with carpetbaggers.*

car·pet bee·tle ▸*n.* a small beetle whose larva (a woolly bear) is destructive to carpets, fabrics, and other materials. • Genus *Anthrenus*, family Dermestidae.

car·pet-bomb ▸*v.* [*trans.*] [often as *n.*] (**carpet-bombing**) bomb (an area) intensively.

car·pet·ing /ˈkärpitiNG/ ▸*n.* carpets collectively: *offices with wall-to-wall carpeting.* ■ the fabric from which carpets are made.

car·pet moth ▸*n.* a drab moth related to the clothes moth, the larvae of which feed on coarse textiles and animal hair. • *Trichophaga tapetzella*, family Tineidae.

car·pet shark ▸*n.* a relatively small shallow-water shark with barbels around the nose or mouth and typically with a conspicuous color pattern. It is found in the Indo-Pacific region and the Red Sea. • Family Orectolobidae: *Orectolobus* and other genera, and several species.

car·pet shell ▸*n.* a burrowing bivalve mollusk of temperate and warm seas, with concentric growth rings and irregular colored markings. • Genus *Venerupis*, family Veneriidae.

car·pet slip·per ▸*n.* a soft slipper whose upper part is made of wool or thick cloth.

car·pet sweep·er ▸*n.* a manual household implement used for sweeping carpets, having a revolving brush or brushes and a receptacle for dust and dirt.

car·pet·weed /ˈkärpitˌwēd/ ▸*n.* any of various dicotyledonous, usually succulent plants that typically grow in warm, sandy regions. • Family Aizoaceae, order Caryophyllales: several genera and species, in particular *Mollugo verticillata*, a North American weed with small whitish flowers; like many of the carpetweeds, it is prostrate and forms a dense mat on the ground.

car·phol·o·gy /kärˈfäləjē/ ▸*n. rare* plucking at the bedclothes by a delirious patient. ▷mid 19th cent.: from Greek *karphologia*, from *karphos* 'straw' + *legein* 'collect.'

car phone ▸*n.* a cellular phone designed for use in a motor vehicle.

carpo- ▸*comb. form* fruit: *carpology* | *carpophore.*

car·pol·o·gy /kärˈpäləjē/ ▸*n. rare* the study of fruits and seeds. ▷early 19th cent.: from Greek *karpos* 'fruit' + -LOGY. **—car·po·log·i·cal** /ˌkärpəˈläjikəl/ *adj.*

car·pool /ˈkärˌpōōl/ ▸*n.* an arrangement between people to make a regular journey in a single vehicle, typically with each person taking turns to drive the others. ■ a group of people with such an arrangement.
▸*v.* [*intrans.*] form or participate in a carpool. **—car·pool·er** *n.*

car·po·phore /ˈkärpəˌfôr/ ▸*n. Botany* (in a flower) an elongated axis that raises the stem of the pistil above the stamens. ■ (in a fungus) the stem of the fruiting body. ▷late 19th cent.: from Greek *karpos* 'fruit' + -PHORE.

car·port /ˈkärˌpôrt/ ▸*n.* a shelter for a car consisting of a roof supported on posts, built beside a house.

car·pus /ˈkärpəs/ ▸*n.* (*pl.* **-pi** /-ˌpī; -ˌpē/) the group of small bones between the main part of the forelimb and the metacarpus in terrestrial vertebrates. The eight bones of the human carpus form the wrist and part of the hand, and are arranged in two rows. ▷late Middle English: from modern Latin, from Greek *karpos* 'wrist.'

Car·rac·ci /kärˈäCHē/ the name of a family of Italian painters comprised of brothers **Annibale** (1560–1609) and **Agostino** (1557–1602) and of their cousin **Ludovico** (1555–1619). Together they established a teaching academy at Bologna; while Annibale became famed for his frescoes on the ceiling of the Farnese Gallery in Rome and for his invention of the caricature.

car·rack /ˈkarək/ ▸*n.* a large merchant ship of a kind operating in European waters in the 14th to the 17th century. ▷late Middle English: from Old French *caraque*; perhaps from Spanish *carraca*, from Arabic, perhaps from *ḳarāḳir*, plural of *ḳurḳūra*, a type of merchant ship.

car·ra·geen /ˈkarə,gēn/ (also **car·ra·gheen** or **car·ra·geen moss**) ▸*n.* an edible red shoreline seaweed with flattened branching fronds, found in both Eurasia and North America and used to produce carrageenan. Also called **IRISH MOSS**. • *Chondrus crispus*, phylum Rhodophyta. ▷early 19th cent.: from Irish *carraigín*.

car·ra·gee·nan /,karəˈgēnən/ ▸*n.* a substance extracted from red and purple seaweeds, consisting of a mixture of polysaccharides. It is used as a thickening or emulsifying agent in food products. ▷1960s: from **CARRAGEEN** + **-AN**.

Car·ra·ra /kəˈrärə; -ˈre(ə)rə/ a town in northwestern Italy, in Tuscany, known for the white marble quarried here since Roman times; pop. 68,480.

car·re·four /ˈkarə,fo͝or; ,karəˈfo͝or/ ▸*n.* a crossroads. ■ a public square, plaza, or marketplace where roads converge.

Car·rel /käˈrel/, Alexis (1873–1944), French surgeon and biologist. He developed improved techniques for suturing arteries and veins and carried out some of the first organ transplants. Nobel Prize for Physiology or Medicine (1912).

car·rel /ˈkarəl/ ▸*n.* a small cubicle with a desk for the use of a reader or student in a library. ■ *historical* a small enclosure or study in a cloister. ▷late 16th cent.: apparently related to **CAROL** in the old sense 'ring.'

Car·re·ras /kəˈre(ə)rəs/, José (1946–), Spanish opera singer.

car·riage /ˈkarij/ ▸*n.* **1** a means of conveyance, in particular: ■ a four-wheeled passenger vehicle pulled by two or more horses: *a horse-drawn carriage.* ■ a baby carriage. ■ a shopping cart. ■ a wheeled support for moving a heavy object such as a gun. ■ *Brit.* a passenger car of a train: *the first-class carriages.* **2** the transporting of items or merchandise from one place to another. ■ the cost of such a procedure. **3** a moving part of a machine that carries other parts into the required position: *a typewriter carriage.* **4** [in *sing.*] a person's bearing or deportment: *her carriage was graceful, her movements quick and deft.* **5** the harboring of a potentially disease-causing organism by a person or animal that does not contract the disease. ▷late Middle English: from Old Northern French *cariage*, from *carier* (see **CARRY**).

car·riage bolt ▸*n.* a large bolt with a round head, used chiefly for fixing wooden panels to masonry or to one another.

car·riage dog ▸*n.* archaic term for **DALMATIAN**. ▷early 19th cent.: because Dalmatians were formerly trained to run behind a carriage as a guard dog.

car·riage house ▸*n.* a building for housing a horse-drawn carriage, typically such a building that has been converted into a dwelling.

car·riage re·lease ▸*n.* a function or lever that enables the carriage on a manual or electric typewriter to move freely, instead of only in one direction when the keys are pressed.

car·riage re·turn ▸*n.* another term for **RETURN** (sense 5).

car·riage trade ▸*n. archaic* those of sufficient wealth or social standing, esp. clientele who arrive by private carriage. ■ *informal* or *humorous* elite clientele.

car·riage·way /ˈkarij,wā/ ▸*n. Brit.* each of the two sides of a divided highway or expressway, each of which usually have two or more lanes. ■ the part of a road intended for vehicles rather than pedestrians.

car·rick bend /ˈkarik/ ▸*n.* a kind of knot used to join ropes, esp. hawsers, end to end, esp. so that they can go around a capstan without jamming. ▷early 19th cent.: from **BEND**2 : *carrick* perhaps an alteration of **CARRACK**.

car·ri·er /ˈkarēər/ ▸*n.* **1** a person or thing that carries, holds, or conveys something: *water carriers.* **2** a person or company that undertakes the professional conveyance of goods or people: *Pan Am was the third U.S. carrier to cease operations in 1991.* ■ a vessel or vehicle for transporting people or things, esp. goods in bulk: *the largest timber carrier ever to dock at a Malaysian port.* ■ an aircraft carrier. ■ a company that provides facilities for conveying telecommunications messages. **3** a person or animal that transmits a disease-causing organism to others. Typically, the carrier suffers no symptoms of the disease: *the black rat, best known as carrier of bubonic plague.* ■ a person or other organism that possesses a particular gene, esp. as a single copy whose effect is masked by a dominant allele, so that the associated characteristic (such as a hereditary disease) is not displayed but may be passed to offspring. **4** a substance used to support or convey another substance such as a pigment, catalyst, or radioactive material. ■ *Physics* short for **CHARGE CARRIER**. ■ *Biochemistry* a molecule that transfers a specified molecule or ion within the body, esp. across a cell membrane.

car·ri·er pig·eon ▸*n.* a homing pigeon trained to carry messages tied to its neck or leg.

car·ri·er wave ▸*n.* a high-frequency electromagnetic wave modulated in amplitude or frequency to convey a signal.

car·ri·ole /ˈkarē,ōl/ (also **car·i·ole**) ▸*n.* **1** *historical* a small open horse-drawn carriage for one person. ■ a light covered cart. **2** (in Canada) a kind of sledge pulled by a horse or dogs and with space for one or more passengers. ▷mid 18th cent.: from French, from Italian *carriuola*, diminutive of *carro*, from Latin *carrum* (see **CAR**).

car·ri·on /ˈkarēən/ ▸*n.* the decaying flesh of dead animals. ▷Middle English: from Anglo-Norman French and Old Northern French *caroine*, *caroigne*, Old French *charoigne*, based on Latin *caro* 'flesh.'

car·ri·on bee·tle ▸*n.* a beetle that feeds on decaying animal and plant matter and insect larvae. • Family Silphidae: many species, including the burying beetles.

car·ri·on crow ▸*n.* **1** a medium-sized, typically all-black crow that is common throughout much of Eurasia. • *Corvus corone*, family Corvidae. See also **HOODED CROW**. **2** another name for **BLACK VULTURE** (sense 1).

car·ri·on flow·er ▸*n.* **1** a North American climbing plant with small white flowers that smell of decaying flesh. • Genus *Smilax*: several species, in particular *S. herbacea*. **2** another term for **STAPELIA**.

Car·roll /ˈkarəl/, Lewis (1832–98), English writer; pseudonym of *Charles Lutwidge Dodgson*. He wrote the children's classics *Alice's Adventures in Wonderland* (1865) and *Through the Looking Glass* (1871), which were inspired by Alice Liddell, the young daughter of the dean at the Oxford college where Carroll was a mathematics lecturer.

Car·roll·ton /ˈkarəltən/ a city in northeastern Texas, north of Dallas; pop. 82,169.

car·ron·ade /,karəˈnād/ ▸*n. historical* a short large-caliber cannon, formerly in naval use. ▷late 18th cent.: from *Carron*, Scotland, where this kind of cannon was first made.

car·rot /ˈkarət/ ▸*n.* **1** a tapering orange-colored root eaten as a vegetable. **2** a cultivated plant of the parsley family with feathery leaves, which yields this vegetable. • *Daucus carota*, family Umbelliferae: two subspecies and many varieties; wild forms lack the swollen root. **3** an offer of something enticing as a means of persuasion (often contrasted with the threat of something punitive or unwelcome): *carrots will promote cooperation over the environment far more effectively than sticks.* [with allusion to the proverbial encouragement of a donkey to move by enticing it with a carrot.] ▷late 15th cent.: from French *carotte*, from Latin *carota*, from Greek *karōton*.

car·rot-and-stick ▸*adj. informal* (of a method, esp. for social change) characterized by both the offer of reward and the threat of punishment: *carrot-and-stick reforms intended to break long-term dependency on state and federal handouts.*

car·rot·wood /ˈkarət,wo͝od/ ▸*n.* a tree of the soapberry family, native to southeast Asia, that threatens mangrove swamps and other habitats in the U.S. because of its invasive habit. • *Cupaniopsis anacardioides*, family Sapindaceae.

car·rot·y /ˈkarətē/ ▸*adj.* (of a person's hair or whiskers) orange-red in color.

car·rou·sel ▸*n.* variant spelling of **CAROUSEL**.

car·ry /ˈkarē/ ▸*v.* (**-ries**, **-ried**) [*trans.*] **1** support and move (someone or something) from one place to another: *medics were carrying a wounded man on a stretcher.* ■ transport: *the train service carries 20,000 passengers daily.* ■ have on one's person and take with one wherever one goes: *the money he was carrying was not enough to pay the fine* | *figurative she had carried the secret all her life.* ■ conduct; transmit: *nerves carry visual information from the eyes.* ■ be infected with (a disease) and liable to transmit it to others: *ticks can carry Lyme disease.* ■ transfer (a figure) to an adjacent column during an arithmetical operation (e.g., when a column of digits adds up to more than ten). **2** support the weight of: *the bridge is capable of carrying even the heaviest loads.* ■ be pregnant with: *she was carrying twins.* ■ (**carry oneself**) stand and move in a specified way: *she carried herself straight and with assurance.* ■ assume or accept (responsibility or blame): *they must carry the responsibility for the mess they have gotten the company into.* ■ be responsible for the effectiveness or success of: *they relied on dialogue to carry the plot.* **3** have as a feature or consequence: *being a combat sport, karate* **carries with it** *the risk of injury* | *each bike carries a ten-year guarantee.* **4** take or develop (an idea or activity) to a specified point: *he carried the criticism much further.* ■ (of a gun or similar weapon) propel (a missile) to a specified distance. ■ (of a ball) move or be hit a specified distance: *the balls seem to carry well in that ballpark.* ■ *Golf* hit the ball over and beyond (a particular point). **5** (often **be carried**) approve (a proposed measure) by a majority of votes: *the resolution was carried by a two-to-one majority.* ■ persuade (colleagues or followers) to support one's policy: *he could not carry the cabinet.* ■ gain (a state or district) in an election. **6** (of a newspaper or a television or radio station) publish or broadcast: *the paper carried a detailed account of the current crisis.* ■ (of a retail outlet) keep a regular stock of (particular goods for sale): *this store no longer carries phonograph equipment.* ■ have visible on the surface: *the product does not carry the "UL" symbol.* ■ be known by (a name): *some products carry the same names as overseas beers.* **7** [*intrans.*] (of a sound or a person's voice) be audible at a distance: *his voice carried clearly across the room.*

▸*phrasal v.* □ **be/get carried away** lose self-control: *I got a bit carried away when describing the final game.* □ **carry something away** *Nautical* lose (a mast or other part of a ship) through breakage. □ **carry something forward** transfer figures to a new page or account. ■ keep something to use or deal with at a later time: *we carried forward a reserve, which allowed us to meet demands.* □ **carry someone/something off** take someone or something away by force: *bandits carried off his mule.* ■ (of a disease) kill someone: *Parkinson's disease carried him off in September.* □ **carry something off** win a prize: *she failed to carry off the gold medal.* ■ succeed in doing something difficult: *he could not have carried it off without government help.* □ **carry on 1** continue an activity or task: **carry on** *with what you were doing.* ■ *Brit.* continue to move in the same direction: *I knew I was going the wrong way, but I just carried on.* **2** *informal* behave in an extreme way: *she carries on about television programming.* **3** *informal* be engaged in a love affair, typically one of which the speaker disapproves: *she was* **carrying on with** *young Adam.* □ **carry something on** engage in an activity: *he could not carry on a logical conversation.* □ **carry something out** perform a task or planned operation: *we're carrying out a market-research survey.* □ **carry over** extend beyond the normal or original area of application: *his artistic practice is clearly carrying over into his social thought.* □ **carry something over** retain something and apply or deal with it in a new context: *much of the wartime economic planning was carried over into the next decade.* ■ postpone an event: *the match had to be carried over till Sunday.* ■ another way of saying **CARRY SOMETHING FORWARD**. □ **carry something through** bring a project to completion: *policy blueprints are rarely carried through perfectly.* ■ bring something safely out of difficulties: *he was the only person who could carry the country through.*

▸*n.* (*pl.* **-ries**) [usu. in *sing.*] **1** an act of lifting and transporting something from one place to another: *we did a carry of equipment from the camp.* ■ *Football* an act of running with the ball from scrimmage. ■ the action of keeping something, esp. a gun, on one's person: *this pistol is the right choice for on-duty or off-duty carry.* ■ *historical* a place or route between navigable waters over which boats or supplies had to be carried. ■ the transfer of a figure into an adjacent column (or the equivalent part of a computer memory) during an arithmetical operation. ■ *Finance* the maintenance of an investment position in a securities market, esp. with regard to the costs or profits accruing. **2** (in golf) the distance a ball travels before reaching the ground. ■ (in golf) the distance a ball must travel to reach a certain destination. ■ the range of a gun or similar weapon. ▷late Middle English: from Anglo-Norman French and Old Northern French *carier*, based on Latin *carrus* 'wheeled vehicle.'

▸*PHRASES* □ **carry conviction** be convincing. □ **carry**

the day be victorious or successful. □ **carry something into effect** act on a plan or proposal. □ **carry weight** be influential or important: *the report is expected to carry considerable weight with the administration.*

car·ry·all /ˈkarē,ôl/ ▸*n.* **1** a large bag or case. **2** *historical* a light carriage. [early 18th cent.: apparently altered by folk etymology from French *carriole*, denoting a small covered carriage.] ■ a large car or truck with seats facing each other along the sides.

car·ry·back note /ˈkarē,bak/ ▸*n. Finance* a negotiable promissory note representing the value of real estate when the seller has provided the financing.

car·ry·ing ca·pac·i·ty ▸*n.* the number or quantity of people or things that can be conveyed or held by a vehicle or container. ■ *Ecology* the number of people, other living organisms, or crops that a region can support without environmental degradation.

car·ry·ing charge ▸*n.* **1** *Finance* an expense or effective cost arising from unproductive assets such as stored goods or unoccupied premises. **2** a sum payable for the conveying of goods.

car·ry·ing-on ▸*n.* (*pl.* **car·ry·ings-on**) excited or overwrought behavior: *I'm fed up with your incessant carrying-on.* ■ salacious, improper, or immoral behavior: *the couple's public carrying-on embarrassed passersby.*

car·ry-on ▸*n.* a bag or suitcase suitable for taking onto an aircraft as hand-held luggage.

car·ry-out ▸*adj.* & *n.* another term for **TAKEOUT** (sense 1).

car·ry·o·ver ˈkarē,ōvər (also **car·ry-o·ver**) ▸*n.* [usu. in *sing.*] something transferred or resulting from a previous situation or context: *the slow trading was a carryover from the big losses of last week.*

car·sick /ˈkär,sik/ ▸*adj.* affected with nausea caused by the motion of a car or other vehicle in which one is traveling. **—car·sick·ness** *n.*

Car·son[1] /ˈkärsən/ a city in southwestern California, south of Los Angeles; pop. 83,995.

Car·son[2] /ˈkärsən/, Johnny (1925–), U.S. television personality and comedian; full name *John William Carson.* He hosted *The Tonight Show* 1962–92.

Car·son[3], Kit (1809–68), U.S. frontiersman and scout; full name *Christopher Carson.* He was a U.S. Indian agent in the Southwest 1853–61 and organized Union scouts in the West during the Civil War.

Car·son[4], Rachel Louise (1907–64), U.S. biologist and environmentalist. Her works include *The Sea Around Us* (1951) and *Silent Spring* (1962).

Car·son Cit·y the capital of Nevada, in the western part of the state, southeast of Reno; pop. 52,457.

cart /kärt/ ▸*n.* a strong open vehicle with two or four wheels, typically used for carrying loads and pulled by a horse. ■ a light two-wheeled open vehicle pulled by a single horse and used as a means of transport: *he drove them in a pony and cart.* ■ a shallow open container on wheels that may be pulled or pushed by hand. ■ a shopping cart.

▸*v.* [*trans.*] **1** (often **be carted**) convey or put in a cart or similar vehicle: *the produce was packed in crates and carted to Kansas City.* **2** [*trans.*] *informal* carry (a heavy or cumbersome object) somewhere with difficulty: *they carted the piano down three flights of stairs.* ■ remove or convey (someone) somewhere unceremoniously: *they carted off the refugees in the middle of the night.* ▷Middle English: from Old Norse *kartr*, probably influenced by Anglo-Norman French and Old Northern French *carete*, diminutive of *carre* (see **CAR**). **—cart·er** *n.*; **cart·ful** /-,fo͝ol/ *n.* (*pl.* **-fuls**) .

▸*PHRASE* □ **put the cart before the horse** reverse the proper order or procedure of something.

cart·age /ˈkärtij/ ▸*n.* the transporting of something in a cart or other vehicle. ■ the cost of such a procedure.

Car·ta·ge·na /,kärtəˈhānə; -ˈgānə/ **1** a port in southeastern Spain; pop. 172,150. Originally named Mastia, it was refounded as Carthago Nova (New Carthage) in *c.*225 BC as a base for the Carthaginian conquest of Spain. **2** a port, resort, and oil-refining center in northwestern Colombia, on the Caribbean Sea; pop. 688,300.

carte blanche /ˈkärt ˈblänsh; ˈblänch/ ▸*n.* complete freedom to act as one wishes or thinks best: *we were given carte blanche.* ▷late 17th cent.: French, literally 'blank paper' (i.e., a blank sheet on which to write whatever one wishes, particularly one's own terms for an agreement).

carte de vi·site /,kärt də vēˈzēt/ ▸*n.* (*pl.* **cartes de visite** *pronunc.* same) *historical* a small photographic portrait of someone, mounted on a piece of card. ▷mid 19th cent.: French, 'visiting card.'

car·tel /kärˈtel/ ▸*n.* an association of manufacturers or suppliers with the purpose of maintaining prices at a high level and restricting competition: *the Colombian drug cartels.* ■ *chiefly historical* a coalition or cooperative arrangement between political parties intended to promote a mutual interest. ▷late 19th cent.: from German *Kartell*, from French *cartel*, from Italian *cartello*, diminutive of *carta*, from Latin *carta* (see **CARD**[1]). It was originally used to refer to the coalition of the Conservatives and National Liberal parties in Germany (1887), and hence any political combination; later to denote a trade agreement (early 20th cent.).

car·tel·ize /kärˈtel,īz; ˈkärtl-/ ▸*v.* [*trans.*] (of manufacturers or suppliers) form a cartel in (an industry or trade).

Car·ter[1] /ˈkärtər/, Angela (1940–92), English novelist and short-story writer. Notable works: *The Magic Toyshop* (1967) and *Nights at the Circus* (1984).

Car·ter[2], Elliott (Cook) (1908–), U.S. composer. He is noted for his innovative approach to meter and his choice of sources, which are as diverse as modern jazz and Renaissance madrigals.

Car·ter[3], Howard (1874–1939), English archaeologist. In 1922, while excavating in the Valley of the Kings at Thebes, he discovered the tomb of Tutankhamen.

Car·ter[4], Jimmy (1924–), 39th president of the U.S. 1977–81; full name *James Earl Carter, Jr.* A Georgia Democrat, he served as a state senator 1962–66 and as governor 1971–74. As president, he hosted the talks that led to the Camp David agreements of 1978. The accomplishments of his administration were marred by the crisis caused by the seizure of 52 American hostages in Iran in 1979. After losing a bid for reelection, Carter remained politically active in world affairs, dedicated to the causes of peace and human rights. Nobel Peace Prize (2002).

Jimmy Carter

Car·te·sian /kärˈtēzhən/ ▸*adj.* of or relating to Descartes and his ideas.

▸*n.* a follower of Descartes. ▷mid 17th cent.: from modern Latin *Cartesianus*, from *Cartesius*, Latinized form of the name of *Descartes.* **—Car·te·sian·ism** /-,nizəm/ *n.*

Car·te·sian co·or·di·nates ▸*plural n. Mathematics* numbers that indicate the location of a point relative to a fixed reference point (the origin), being its shortest (perpendicular) distances from two fixed axes (or three planes defined by three fixed axes) that intersect at right angles at the origin.

Car·te·sian prod·uct ▸*n. Mathematics* the product of two sets: the product of set X and set Y is the set that contains all ordered pairs (*x*, *y*) for which *x* belongs to X and *y* belongs to Y.

Car·thage /ˈkärthij/ an ancient city on the coast of North Africa near present-day Tunis. Founded by the Phoenicians *c.*814 BC, it became a major force in the Mediterranean Sea area and fought with Rome during the Punic Wars. It was finally destroyed by the Romans in 146 BC. **—Car·tha·gin·i·an** /,kärthəˈjinēən/ *n.* & *adj.*

cart horse ▸*n. Brit.* a large, strong horse suitable for heavy work.

Car·thu·sian /kärˈth(y)o͞ozhən/ ▸*n.* a monk or nun of an austere contemplative order founded by St. Bruno in 1084.

▸*adj.* of or relating to this order. ▷from medieval Latin *Carthusianus*, from *Cart(h)usia*, Latin name of *Chartreuse*, near Grenoble, France, where the order was founded.

Car·tier /kärˈtyā; ˈkärtē,ā/, Jacques (1491–1557), French explorer. The first to establish France's claim to North America, he made three voyages to Canada between 1534 and 1541.

Car·tier-Bres·son /kärˈtyā brāˈsôN/, Henri (1908–2004), French photographer and movie director. He is known for his collection of photographs, *The Decisive Moment* (1952), and for his documentary about the Spanish Civil War, *Return to Life* (1937).

Car·tier Is·lands /ˈkärtē,ā/ see **ASHMORE AND CARTIER ISLANDS.**

car·ti·lage /ˈkärtl-ij/ ▸*n.* firm, whitish, flexible connective tissue found in various forms in the larynx and respiratory tract, in structures such as the external ear, and in the articulating surfaces of joints. It is more widespread in the infant skeleton, being replaced by bone during growth. ■ a particular structure made of this tissue. ▷late Middle English: from French, from Latin *cartilago, cartilagin-*. **—car·ti·lag·i·noid** /,kärtlˈajə,noid/ *adj.*

car·ti·lag·i·nous /,kärtlˈajənəs/ ▸*adj. Anatomy* (of a structure) made of cartilage. ■ *Zoology* (of a vertebrate animal) having a skeleton of cartilage. ▷late Middle English: from Old French, or from Latin *cartilaginosus*, from *cartilago, cartilagin-* 'cartilage.'

car·ti·lag·i·nous fish ▸*n.* a fish of a class distinguished by having a skeleton of cartilage rather than bone, including the sharks, rays, and chimeras. Compare with **BONY FISH.** • Class Chondrichthyes: subclasses Elasmobranchii (sharks and rays) and Hoplocephali (chimeras).

Cart·land /ˈkärtlənd/, Dame Barbara (1901–2000), English author of light romantic fiction; full name *Dame Mary Barbara Hamilton Cartland McCorquodale.*

cart·load /ˈkärt,lōd/ ▸*n.* the amount held by a cart.

car·to·gram /ˈkärtə,gram/ ▸*n.* a map on which statistical information is shown in diagrammatic form. ▷late 19th cent.: from French *cartogramme*, from *carte* 'map or card' + *-gramme* (from Greek *gramma* 'thing written').

car·tog·ra·phy /kärˈtägrəfē/ ▸*n.* the science or practice of drawing maps. ▷mid 19th cent.: from French *cartographie*, from *carte* 'map, card' (see **CARD**[1]) + *-graphie* (see **-GRAPHY**). **—car·tog·ra·pher** /-fər/ *n.* **—car·to·graph·ic** /,kärtəˈgrafik/ *adj.* **—car·to·graph·i·cal** /,kärtəˈgrafikəl/ *adj.* **—car·to·graph·i·cal·ly** /,kärtəˈgrafik(ə)lē/ *adv.*

car·to·man·cy /ˈkärtə,mansē/ ▸*n.* fortune-telling by interpreting a random selection of playing cards. ▷late 19th cent.: from French *cartomancie*, from *carte* 'card' + *-mancie* (see **-MANCY**).

car·ton /ˈkärtn/ ▸*n.* a light box or container, typically one made of waxed cardboard or plastic in which drinks or foodstuffs are packaged. ▷early 19th cent.: from French, from Italian *cartone* (see **CARTOON**).

car·toon /kärˈto͞on/ ▸*n.* **1** a simple drawing showing the features of its subjects in a humorously exaggerated way, esp. a satirical one in a newspaper or magazine. ■ a comic strip. ■ *figurative* a simplified or exaggerated version or interpretation of something: *this movie is a cartoon of rural life in America* | [as *adj.*] *Dolores becomes a cartoon housewife, reading glossy magazines in a bathrobe.* **2** a motion picture using animation techniques to photograph a sequence of drawings rather than real people or objects. **3** a full-size drawing made by an artist as a preliminary design for a painting or other work of art.

▸*v.* [*trans.*] (usu. **be cartooned**) make a drawing of (someone) in a simplified or exaggerated way: *she has a face with enough character to be cartooned.* ▷late 16th cent. (sense 3): from Italian *cartone*, from *carta*, from Latin *carta, charta* (see **CARD**[1]). Sense 1 dates from the mid 19th cent. **—car·toon·ish** *adj.* **—car·toon·ist** /-ist/ *n.* **—car·toon·y** *adj.*

car·toon·ing /kärˈto͞oniNG/ ▸*n.* the activity or occupation of drawing cartoons for newspapers or magazines.

car·top /ˈkär,täp/ ▸*adj.* designed to be used or carried on the top of an automobile.

car·touche /kärˈto͞osh/ ▸*n.* a carved tablet or drawing representing a scroll with rolled-up ends, used ornamentally or bearing an inscription. ■ *Archaeology* an oval or oblong enclosing a group of Egyptian hieroglyphs, typically representing the name and title of a monarch. ▷early 17th cent.: from French *cartouche* (masculine noun), earlier *cartoche*, from Italian *cartoccio*, from *carta*, from Latin *carta, charta* (see **CARD**[1]).

car·tridge /ˈkärtrij/ ▸*n.* a container holding a spool of photographic film, a quantity of ink, or other item or substance, designed for insertion into a mechanism. ■ a casing containing a charge and a bullet or shot for small arms or an explosive charge for blasting. ■ a component carrying the stylus on the pickup head of a record player. ▷late 16th cent.: from French *cartouche* (feminine noun), from Italian *cartoccio* (see CARTOUCHE).

car·tridge belt ▸*n.* a belt with pockets or loops for cartridges of ammunition, typically worn over the shoulder.

car·tridge clip ▸*n.* a metal frame or container that holds cartridges for loading into an automatic rifle or pistol.

cart·wheel /ˈkärt,(h)wēl/ ▸*n.* **1** the wheel of a cart. **2** a circular sideways handspring with the arms and legs extended.
▸*v.* [*intrans.*] perform such a handspring or handsprings: *he cartwheeled across the room.*

Cart·wright /ˈkärt,rīt/, Edmund (1743–1823), English engineer. He invented the power loom.

car·un·cle /kəˈrəNGkəl; ˈkar,əNG-/ ▸*n.* a fleshy outgrowth, in particular: ■ a wattle of a bird such as a turkey. ■ the red prominence at the inner corner of the eye. ■ any outgrowth from a seed near the micropyle, attractive to ants that aid the seed's dispersal. ▷late 16th cent.: obsolete French, from Latin *caruncula*, from *caro, carn-* 'flesh.' —**ca·run·cu·lar** /kəˈrəNGkyələr/ *adj.*

Ca·ru·so /kəˈro͞osō; -zō/, Enrico (1873–1921), Italian opera singer. He was the first major tenor to be recorded on phonograph records.

carve /kärv/ ▸*v.* [*trans.*] **1** (often **be carved**) cut (a hard material) in order to produce an aesthetically pleasing object or design: *the wood was carved with runes* | [as *adj.*] (**carved**) *bookcases of carved oak.* ■ produce (an object) by cutting and shaping a hard material: *the altar was carved from a block of solid jade.* ■ produce (an inscription or design) by cutting into hard material: *an inscription was carved over the doorway* | *figurative the river carved a series of gorges into the plain.* **2** cut (cooked meat) into slices for eating. ■ cut (a slice of meat) from a larger piece. **3** *Skiing* make (a turn) by tilting one's skis on to their edges and using one's weight to bend them so that they slide into an arc.
▸*phrasal v.* □ **carve something out 1** take something from a larger whole, esp. with difficulty: *carving out a 5 percent share of the overall vote.* **2** establish or create something through painstaking effort: *he managed to carve out a successful photographic career for himself.* □ **carve someone up** *informal* slash someone with a knife or other sharp object. □ **carve something up** divide something ruthlessly into separate areas or domains: *West Africa was carved up by the Europeans.* ▷Old English *ceorfan* 'cut, carve'; related to Dutch *kerven.*

car·vel ▸*n.* variant spelling of CARAVEL.

car·vel-built ▸*adj.* (of a boat or ship) having hull planks that do not overlap. Compare with LAPSTRAKE.

carv·en /ˈkärvən/ ▸ archaic past participle of CARVE.

carve·out /ˈkärv,out/ ▸*n.* **1** an entity separated from a larger one and given separate treatment, in particular: ■ a small company created from a larger one: *companies that are breaking up—through spin-offs, split-offs, and carveouts.* ■ a class of medical procedures treated separately with regard to insurance coverage. ■ a class of employees treated separately with regard to benefits. **2** the activity of effecting such a separation.

Car·ver /ˈkärvər/, George Washington (*c.*1864–1943), U.S. botanist. Born into slavery, he later became the director of agricultural research at Tuskegee Institute in 1896 and developed many products from soybeans, sweet potatoes, and peanuts.

George Washington Carver

car·ver /ˈkärvər/ ▸*n.* **1** a person who carves wood, stone, ivory, coral, etc., esp. professionally: *we watched a decoy carver at work.* **2** a knife designed for slicing meat. **3** a person who cuts and serves the meat at a meal.

carv·ing /ˈkärviNG/ ▸*n.* an object or design cut from a hard material as an artistic work.

carv·ing knife ▸*n.* a knife with a long blade used for carving cooked meat into slices.

car wash ▸*n.* **1** a building containing equipment for washing motor vehicles automatically. **2** an event, typically a fund-raiser, in which motor vehicles are washed: *the Teen Center will hold its third annual car wash on Saturday.*

Cary /ˈkarē; ˈke(ə)rē/ a town in east central North Carolina, a commercial and research center; pop. 94,536.

car·y·at·id /,karēˈatid; ˈkarēə,tid/ ▸*n.* (*pl.* **car·y·at·ids** or **car·y·at·i·des** /,karēˈatə,dēz/) *Architecture* a stone carving of a draped female figure, used as a pillar to support the entablature of a Greek or Greek-style building. ▷mid 16th cent.: via French and Italian from Latin *caryatides*, from Greek *karuatides*, plural of *karuatis* 'priestess of Artemis at Caryae,' from *Karuai* (Caryae) in Laconia.

caryatid

car·y·o·phyl·la·ceous /,karēōfəˈlāSHəs/ ▸*adj. Botany* of, relating to, or denoting plants of the pink family (Caryophyllaceae). ▷mid 19th cent.: from modern Latin *Caryophyllaceae* (plural), based on Greek *karuophullon* 'clove pink,' + -**ous**.

car·y·op·sis /,karēˈäpsis/ ▸*n.* (*pl.* **-ses** /-,sēz/) *Botany* a dry one-seeded fruit in which the ovary wall is united with the seed coat, typical of grasses and cereals. ▷early 19th cent.: from modern Latin, from Greek *karuon* 'nut' + *opsis* 'appearance.'

ca·sa·ba /kəˈsäbə/ (also **cas·sa·ba**) ▸*n.* a winter melon of a variety with a wrinkled yellow rind and sweet flesh. ▷early 20th cent.: named after *Kasaba* (now Turgutlu) in Turkey, from which the melons were first exported.

Ca·sa·blan·ca /,käsəˈbläNGkə; ,kasəˈblaNGkə/ the largest city in Morocco, a seaport on the Atlantic coast; pop. 2,943,000.

Ca·sals /kəˈsälz/, Pablo (1876–1973), Spanish cellist, conductor, and composer.

Ca·sa·no·va /,kazəˈnōvə; ,kasə-/, Giovanni Jacopo (1725–98), Italian adventurer; full name *Giovanni Jacopo Casanova de Seingalt.* He is known for his memoirs that describe his sexual encounters and other exploits.

cas·bah /ˈkas,bä/ (also **kas·bah**) ▸*n.* the citadel of a North African city. ■ (**the casbah**) the area surrounding such a citadel, typically the old part of a city. ▷mid 18th cent.: French, from Arabic *ḳaṣaba* 'citadel.'

cas·ca·bel /ˈkaskə,bel/ ▸*n.* a small red chile pepper of a mild-flavored variety. ▷mid 17th cent.: from Spanish, from Catalan *cascavel*, from medieval Latin *cascabellus* 'little bell.'

cas·cade /kasˈkād/ ▸*n.* **1** a small waterfall, typically one of several that fall in stages down a steep rocky slope. ■ a mass of something that falls or hangs in copious or luxuriant quantities: *a cascade of pink bougainvillea.* ■ a large number or amount of something occurring or arriving in rapid succession: *a cascade of antiwar literature.* **2** a process whereby something, typically information or knowledge, is successively passed on: [as *adj.*] *the greater the number of people who are well briefed, the wider the cascade effect.* ■ a succession of devices or stages in a process, each of which triggers or initiates the next.
▸*v.* **1** [*intrans.*] (of water) pour downward rapidly and in large quantities: *water was* ***cascading down*** *the stairs.* ■ fall or hang in copious or luxuriant quantities: *blonde hair* ***cascaded down*** *her back.* **2** [*trans.*] arrange (a number of devices or objects) in a series or sequence. ▷mid 17th cent.: from French, from Italian *cascata*, from *cascare* 'to fall,' based on Latin *casus* (see CASE[1]).

Cas·cade Range a range of volcanic mountains in western North America that extends from southern British Columbia through Washington and Oregon to northern California. Its highest peak is Mount Rainier. The range also includes an active volcano, Mount St. Helens.

cas·car·a /kasˈkarə/ (also **cascara sa·gra·da** /səˈgrädə/) ▸*n.* **1** a purgative made from the dried bark of an American buckthorn. **2** (also **cascara buckthorn**) the tree from which this bark is obtained, native to the Pacific Northwest. • *Rhamnus purshiana*, family Rhamnaceae. ▷late 19th cent.: from Spanish *cáscara (sagrada)*, literally '(sacred) bark.'

Cas·co Bay /ˈkaskō/ an inlet of the Atlantic in southern Maine, known for its hundreds of islands and protected anchorages. Portland lies on it.

case[1] /kās/ ▸*n.* **1** an instance of a particular situation; an example of something occurring: *a case of mistaken identity* | ***in many cases****, valid statistics are not available.* ■ [usu. in *sing.*] the situation affecting or relating to a particular person or thing; one's circumstances or position: *I'll make an exception* ***in your case.*** ■ an incident or set of circumstances under police investigation: *a murder case.* **2** an instance of a disease, or problem: *200,000 cases of hepatitis B.* ■ a person suffering from a disease or injury: *most breast cancer cases were older women.* ■ the circumstances or particular problem of a person who requires or receives professional attention: *the welfare office discussed Gerald's case* ■ [with *adj.*] *informal* a person whose situation is regarded as pitiable or as having no chance of improvement: *Vicky was a very* ***sad case.*** ■ *informal, dated* an amusing or eccentric person. **3** a legal action, esp. one to be decided in a court of law: *a libel case* | *a former employee brought the case against the council.* ■ a set of facts or arguments supporting one side in such a legal action: *the case for the defense.* ■ a legal action that has been decided and may be cited as a precedent. ■ a set of facts or arguments supporting one side of a debate or controversy: *the* ***case against*** *tobacco advertising.* **4** *Grammar* any of the inflected forms of a noun, adjective, or pronoun that express the semantic relation of the word to other words in the sentence: *the accusative case.* ■ such a relation whether indicated by inflection or not: *English normally expresses case by the use of prepositions.* ▷Middle English: from Old French *cas*, from Latin *casus* 'fall,' related to *cadere* 'to fall'; in sense 4 directly from Latin, translating Greek *ptōsis*, literally 'fall.'
▸*PHRASES* □ **as the case may be** according to the circumstances (used when referring to two or more possible alternatives): *the authorities will decide if they are satisfied or not satisfied, as the case may be.* □ **be the case** be so. □ **in any case** whatever happens or may have happened. ■ used to confirm or support a point or idea just mentioned: *he wasn't allowed out yet, and in any case he wasn't well enough.* □ (**just**) **in case 1** as a provision against something happening or being true: *we put on thick sweaters, in case it was cold.* **2** if it is true that: *in case you haven't figured it out, let me explain.* □ **in case of** in the event of (a particular situation): *instructions about what to do in case of fire.* □ **in no case** under no circumstances. □ **in that case** if that happens or has happened; if that is the situation: *"I'm free this evening." "In that case, why not have dinner with me?"* □ **on** (or **off**) **someone's case** *informal* continually (or no longer) criticizing or harassing someone: *the teacher will* ***get on your case*** *if you keep forgetting your homework.*

case[2] ▸*n.* a container designed to hold or protect something: *he placed the trumpet safely in its velvet-lined case.* ■ the outer protective covering of a natural or manufactured object: *a seed case.* ■ *Brit.* an item of luggage; a suitcase. ■ a box containing bottles or cans of a beverage, sold as a unit: *there are twelve bottles of champagne in a case.* ■ *Printing* a partitioned container for loose metal type. ■ each of the two forms, capital or minuscule, in which a letter of the alphabet may be written or printed. See also UPPERCASE, LOWERCASE.
▸*v.* [*trans.*] (usu. **be cased**) **1** surround in a material or substance: *the towers are of steel cased in granite.* ■ enclose in a protective container: [as *adj.*] (**cased**) *a cased pair of pistols.* **2** *informal* reconnoiter (a place) before carrying out a robbery: *I was* ***casing the joint.*** ▷late Middle English: from Old French *casse, chasse* (modern *caisse* 'trunk, chest,' *châsse* 'reliquary, frame'), from Latin *capsa*, related to *capere* 'to hold.'

ca·se·a·tion /,kāsēˈāSHən/ ▸*n. Medicine* a form of necrosis characteristic of tuberculosis, in which diseased tissue forms a firm, dry mass like cheese in appearance. ▷mid 19th cent.: from medieval Latin *caseatio(n-)*, from Latin *caseus* 'cheese.' **—ca·se·ate** /'kāsē,āt/ *v.*

case·book /'kās,bo͝ok/ ▸*n.* a book containing a selection of source materials on a particular subject, esp. one used as a reference work or in teaching.

case·bound /'kās,bound/ ▸*adj. technical* (of a book) in a hard cover.

case gram·mar ▸*n. Linguistics* a form of grammar in which the structure of sentences is analyzed in terms of the semantic roles of nouns in relation to predicates.

case-hard·en ▸*v.* [*trans.*] [often as *adj.*] (**case-hardened**) harden the surface of (a material): *case-hardened sandstones.* ■ give a hard surface to (iron or steel) by carburizing it: *a case-hardened steel anvil.* ■ *figurative* make (someone) callous or tough: *a case-hardened politician.*

case his·to·ry ▸*n.* a record of a person's background or medical history kept by a doctor or social worker.

ca·sein /kā'sēn; 'kāsēən/ ▸*n.* the main protein present in milk and (in coagulated form) in cheese. It is used in processed foods and in adhesives, paints, and other industrial products. ▷mid 19th cent.: from Latin *caseus* 'cheese.'

case knife ▸*n.* a type of dagger carried in a sheath.

case law ▸*n.* (also **caselaw**) the law as established by the outcome of former cases. Compare with COMMON LAW, STATUTORY LAW.

case·load /'kās,lōd/ ▸*n.* the amount of work (in terms of number of cases) with which a doctor, lawyer, or social worker is concerned at one time.

case·mate /'kās,māt/ ▸*n. historical* a small room in the thickness of the wall of a fortress, with embrasures from which guns or missiles can be fired. ■ an armored enclosure for guns on a warship. ▷mid 16th cent.: from French, from Italian *casamatta*, perhaps from Greek *khasma, khasmat-* (see CHASM).

case·ment /'kāsmənt/ ▸*n.* a window or part of a window set on a hinge so that it opens like a door: [as *adj.*] *casement windows.* ■ *chiefly poetic/literary* a window. ■ the sash of a sash window. ▷late Middle English (as an architectural term denoting a hollow molding): from Anglo-Latin *cassimentum*, from *cassa*, from Latin *capsa* (see CASE²).

case mod ▸*n. Computing* another term for MOD³.

ca·se·ous /'kāsēəs/ ▸*adj. Medicine* characterized by caseation. ▷mid 17th cent.: from Latin *caseus* 'cheese' + -OUS.

case-sen·si·tive ▸*adj. Computing* (of a program or function) differentiating between capital and lowercase letters. ■ (of input) treated differently depending on whether it is in capitals or lowercase text.

case shot ▸*n. historical* bullets or pieces of metal in an iron case fired from a cannon.

case stud·y ▸*n.* **1** a process or record of research in which detailed consideration is given to the development of a particular person, group, or situation over a period of time. **2** a particular instance of something used or analyzed in order to illustrate a thesis or principle: *airline deregulation provides a case study of the effects of the internal market.*

case sys·tem ▸*n.* a method of teaching or studying law that emphasizes the analysis and discussion of selected cases.

case·work¹ /'kās,wərk/ ▸*n.* social work directly concerned with individuals, esp. that involving a study of a person's family history and personal circumstances. **—case·work·er** *n.*

case·work² ▸*n.* the decorative outer case protecting the workings of a complex mechanism such as an organ or harpsichord.

Cash /kash/, Johnny (1932–2003), U.S. country music singer and songwriter. Notable songs: "I Walk the Line" (1956) and "A Boy Named Sue" (1969).

cash¹ /kash/ ▸*n.* money in coins or notes, as distinct from checks, money orders, or credit: *the staff were paid in cash | a discount for cash.* ■ money in any form, esp. that which is immediately available: *she was always short of cash.*

▸*v.* [*trans.*] give or obtain notes or coins for (a check or money order). ■ *Bridge* lead (a high card) so as to take the opportunity to win a trick.

▸*phrasal v.* □ **cash in** *informal* take advantage of or exploit (a situation): *the breweries were **cashing in on** the rediscovered taste for real ales.* □ **cash something in** convert an insurance policy, savings account, or other investment into money. □ **cash out** cost: *juicy baked chicken **cashed out at** $7.* □ **cash something out** another way of saying CASH SOMETHING IN. ▷late 16th cent. (denoting a box for money): from Old French *casse* or Italian *cassa* 'box,' from Latin *capsa* (see CASE²). **—cash·a·ble** *adj.*

▸PHRASE □ **cash in one's chips** *informal* die. [with reference to gambling in a casino.]

cash² ▸*n.* (*pl.* same) *historical* a coin of low value from China, southern India, or Southeast Asia. ▷late 16th cent.: from Portuguese *caixa*, from Tamil *kāsu*, influenced by CASH¹.

cash and car·ry ▸*n.* a system of wholesale trading whereby goods are paid for in full at the time of purchase and taken away by the purchaser. ■ a wholesale store operating this system.

cash-back ▸*adj.* denoting a form of incentive offered to buyers of certain products whereby they receive a cash refund after making their purchase.

cash bar ▸*n.* a bar at a social function at which guests buy drinks rather than having them provided free.

cash·box /'kash,bäks/ ▸*n.* a lockable metal box for keeping cash in.

cash cow ▸*n. informal* a business, investment, or product that provides a steady income or profit: *traditional cash cows like cars and VCRs.* ■ a person or organization that is a source of easy profit: *for the past 12 years, he's been nothing but her cash cow.*

cash crop ▸*n.* a crop produced for its commercial value rather than for use by the grower. **—cash crop·ping** *n.*

cash·ew /'kash,o͞o; kə'sho͞o/ ▸*n.* **1** (also **cashew nut**) an edible kidney-shaped nut, rich in oil and protein, which is roasted and shelled before it can be eaten. Oil is extracted from the shells and used as a lubricant and insecticide and in the production of plastics. **2** (also **cashew tree**) a bushy tropical American tree related to the mango, bearing cashew nuts singly at the tip of each swollen fruit. Also called ACAJOU. • *Anacardium occidentale*, family Anacardiaceae (the **cashew family**). ▷late 16th cent.: from Portuguese, from Tupi *acajú, cajú.*

cash·ew ap·ple ▸*n.* the swollen edible fruit of the cashew tree, from which the cashew nut hangs, sometimes used to make wine.

cash flow ▸*n.* the total amount of money being transferred into and out of a business, esp. as affecting liquidity.

cash·ier¹ /ka'shi(ə)r/ ▸*n.* a person handling payments and receipts in a store, bank, or other business. ▷late 16th cent.: from Dutch *cassier* or French *caissier*, from *caisse* 'cash.'

cash·ier² ▸*v.* [*trans.*] (usu. **be cashiered**) dismiss someone from the armed forces in disgrace because of a serious misdemeanor: *he was found guilty and cashiered* | [as *adj.*] (**cashiered**) *a cashiered National Guard major.* ■ *informal* suspend or dismiss someone from an office, position, or membership: *the team owner had been cashiered for consorting with a gambler.* ▷late 16th cent. (in the sense 'dismiss or disband troops'): from Flemish *kasseren* 'disband (troops)' or 'revoke (a will),' from French *casser* 'revoke, dismiss,' from Latin *quassare* (see QUASH).

cash·less /'kashləs/ ▸*adj.* characterized by the exchange of funds by check, debit or credit card, or various electronic methods rather than the use of cash: *the cashless society.*

cash ma·chine ▸*n.* another term for **ATM**.

cash·mere /'kazh,mi(ə)r; 'kash-/ ▸*n.* fine soft wool, originally that from the Kashmir goat. ■ woolen material made from or resembling such wool: [as *adj.*] *a cashmere sweater.* ▷late 17th cent.: an early spelling of KASHMIR.

cash·mere goat ▸*n.* variant spelling of KASHMIR GOAT.

cash nex·us ▸*n.* the relationship constituted by monetary transactions.

cash on de·liv·er·y (abbr.: **COD**) ▸*n.* the system of paying for goods when they are delivered.

cash·point /'kash,point/ ▸*n. Brit.* another term for AUTOMATED TELLER MACHINE.

cash reg·is·ter ▸*n.* a machine used in places of business for regulating money transactions with customers. It typically has a compartmental drawer for cash and totals, displays, and records the amount of each sale.

cas·ing /'kāsing/ ▸*n.* **1** a cover or shell that protects or encloses something: *a waterproof casing.* **2** the frame around a door or window.

ca·si·no /kə'sēnō/ ▸*n.* (*pl.* **-nos**) a public room or building where gambling games are played. ▷mid 18th cent.: from Italian, diminutive of *casa* 'house,' from Latin *casa* 'cottage.'

ca·si·ta /kə'sētə/ ▸*n.* (especially in the U.S. Southwest) a small house or other building. ▷early 19th cent.: from Spanish, diminutive of *casa* 'house.'

cask /kask/ ▸*n.* a large barrellike container made of wood, metal, or plastic, used for storing liquids, typically alcoholic drinks. ■ the quantity of liquid held in such a container: ***a cask of** cider.* ▷early 16th cent.: from French *casque* or Spanish *casco* 'helmet.' The current senses appear only in English; from the late 16th to the late 18th centuries the word also denoted a helmet (compare with CASQUE).

cas·ket /'kaskit/ ▸*n.* a small ornamental box or chest for holding jewels, letters, or other valuable objects. ■ a coffin. ▷late Middle English: perhaps an Anglo-Norman French form of Old French *cassette*, diminutive of *casse* (see CASE²).

Cas·lon /'kaz,län; -lən/ ▸*n.* a kind of roman typeface first introduced in the 18th century. ▷mid 19th cent.: named after William *Caslon* (1692–1766), English type founder.

Cas·ne·wydd /käs'ne-with/ Welsh name for NEWPORT.

Cas·par /'kaspər/ one of the three Magi.

Cas·per¹ /'kaspər/ a city in east central Wyoming, on the North Platte River; pop. 49,644. Oil is central to its economy.

Cas·per², Billy (1931–), U.S. golfer. He won the U.S. Open twice, in 1959 and in 1966.

Cas·pi·an Sea /'kaspēən/ a large landlocked salt lake, bounded by Russia, Kazakhstan, Turkmenistan, Azerbaijan, and Iran. The world's largest body of inland water, its surface lies 92 feet (28 m) below sea level.

casque /kask/ ▸*n.* **1** *historical* a helmet. **2** *Zoology* a helmetlike structure, such as that on the bill of a hornbill or the head of a cassowary. ▷late 17th cent.: from French, from Spanish *casco*. Compare with CASK.

cas·sa·ba ▸*n.* variant spelling of CASABA.

Cas·san·dra /kə'sandrə/ *Greek Mythology* a daughter of the Trojan king Priam, who was given the gift of prophecy by Apollo. When she cheated him, however, he turned this into a curse by causing her prophecies, though true, to be disbelieved. ■ [as *n.*] (**a Cassandra**) a prophet of disaster, esp. one who is disregarded.

cas·sa·reep /'kasə,rēp/ (also **cas·a·reep**) ▸*n. W. Indian* a thick brown syrup made by boiling down the juice of grated cassava with sugar and spices, and typically used as a flavoring for pepper pot (see PEPPER POT sense 2). ▷from Arawak *casiripe.*

cas·sa·ta /kə'sätə/ ▸*n.* a Neapolitan ice cream containing candied fruit and nuts. ▷from Italian, literally 'little case.'

cas·sa·tion /ka'sāshən/ ▸*n. Music* an informal instrumental composition of the 18th century, similar to a divertimento and originally often for outdoor performance. ▷late 19th cent.: from German *Kassation* 'serenade,' from Italian *cassazione.*

Cas·satt /kə'sat/, Mary (1844–1926), U.S. painter. Known for her draftmanship, etching, and dry-point studies, she was persuaded by Edgar Degas to exhibit with the Impressionists. She worked mostly in Paris, and her paintings, including *Lady at the Tea Table* (1885), display a close interest in everyday subject matter.

cas·sa·va /kə'sävə/ ▸*n.* **1** the starchy tuberous root of a tropical tree, used as food in tropical countries but requiring careful preparation to remove traces of cyanide from the flesh. Also called MANIOC. ■ a starch or flour obtained from such a root. **2** the shrubby tree from which this root is obtained, native to tropical America and cultivated throughout the tropics. • Genus *Manihot*, family Euphorbiaceae: several species, in particular **bitter cassava** (*M. esculenta*) and **sweet cassava** (*M. dulcis*). ▷mid 16th cent.: from Taino *casávi, cazábbi*, influenced by French *cassave.*

Cas·se·grain tel·e·scope /'kasə,grān/ ▸*n.* a reflecting telescope in which light reflected from a convex secondary mirror passes through a hole in the primary mirror. ▷late 19th cent.: named after N. *Cassegrain* (1625–1712), the French astronomer who devised it.

cas·se·role /'kasə,rōl/ ▸*n.* a kind of stew that is cooked slowly in an oven: *a chicken casserole.* ■ a large covered dish, typically of earthenware or glass, used for cooking such stews.

▸*v.* [*trans.*] cook (food) slowly in such a dish: [as *adj.*]

(**casseroled**) *casseroled chicken.* ▷early 18th cent.: from French, diminutive of *casse* 'spoonlike container,' from Old Provençal *casa*, from late Latin *cattia* 'ladle, pan,' from Greek *kuathion*, diminutive of *kuathos* 'cup.'

cas·sette /kə'set/ ▸*n.* a sealed plastic unit containing a length of audiotape wound on a pair of spools, for insertion into a recorder or playback device. ■ a similar unit containing videotape, film, or other material for insertion into a machine. ▷late 18th cent.: from French, diminutive of *casse* (see CASE²).

cas·sette deck ▸*n.* a unit in hi-fi equipment for playing or recording audiocassettes.

cas·sette play·er ▸*n.* a machine for playing audiocassettes. ■ another term for CASSETTE RECORDER.

cas·sette re·cord·er ▸*n.* a machine for recording and playing back audiocassettes.

cas·sette tape ▸*n.* a cassette of audiotape or videotape.

cas·sia /'kasHə/ ▸*n.* **1** a tree, shrub, or herbaceous plant of the pea family, native to warm climates. Cassias yield a variety of products, including fodder, timber, and medicinal drugs, and many are cultivated as ornamentals. [modern Latin.] • Genus *Cassia*, family Leguminosae: many species, including *C. fistula*, which provides much of the commercially produced senna. **2** (also **cassia bark**) the aromatic bark of an eastern Asian tree, yielding an inferior kind of cinnamon that is sometimes used to adulterate true cinnamon. [from Latin, probably denoting the wild cinnamon, via Greek from Hebrew *qĕṣī'āh*.] • *Cinnamomum aromaticum*, family Lauraceae.

cas·sin·gle /kə'siNGgəl/ ▸*n.* an audiocassette with a single piece of music, esp. popular music, on each side. ▷1970s: blend of CASSETTE and SINGLE.

Cas·si·ni /ka'sēnē/, Giovanni Domenico (1625–1712), French astronomer; born in Italy. He discovered the gap in the rings of Saturn known as Cassini's division.

Cas·si·o·pe·ia /,kasēə'pēə/ **1** *Greek Mythology* the wife of Cepheus, king of Ethiopia, and mother of Andromeda. **2** *Astronomy* a constellation near the north celestial pole, recognizable by the conspicuous "W" pattern of its brightest stars. ■ [as *genitive*] (**Cassiopeiae** /-'pē-ē/) used with a preceding letter or numeral to designate a star in this constellation: *the star Delta Cassiopeiae.*

cas·sis¹ /ka'sēs/ (also **crème de cas·sis** /,krem də ka'sēs/) ▸*n.* a syrupy liqueur flavored with black currants and produced mainly in Burgundy. ▷late 19th cent.: French, literally 'black currant,' apparently from Latin *cassia* (see CASSIA).

cas·sis² ▸*n.* a wine produced in the region of Cassis, a small town near Marseilles.

cas·sit·er·ite /kə'sitə,rīt/ ▸*n.* a reddish, brownish, or yellowish mineral consisting of tin dioxide. It is the main ore of tin. ▷mid 19th cent.: from Greek *kassiteros* 'tin' + -ITE¹.

Cas·sius /'kasēəs; 'kasHəs/, Gaius (died 42 BC), Roman general; full name *Gaius Cassius Longinus*. He was one of the leaders of the conspiracy in 44 BC to assassinate Julius Caesar.

cas·sock /'kasək/ ▸*n.* a full-length garment of a single color worn by certain Christian clergy, members of church choirs, acolytes, and others having some particular office or role in a church. ▷mid 16th cent.: from French *casaque* 'long coat,' from Italian *casacca* 'riding coat,' probably from Turkic *kazak* 'vagabond.' Compare with COSSACK. —**cas·socked** *adj.*

cassock

cas·sou·let /,kasə'lā/ ▸*n.* a stew made with meat and beans. ▷French, diminutive of dialect *cassolo* 'stewpan,' from Old Provençal *cassa* 'pan'; related to CASSEROLE.

cas·so·war·y /'kasə,werē/ ▸*n.* (*pl.* **-war·ies**) a very large flightless bird related to the emu, with a bare head and neck, a tall horny crest, and one or two colored wattles. It is native mainly to the forests of New Guinea. • Family Casuariidae and genus *Casuarius*: three species, in particular the **double-wattled** (or **Australian**) **cassowary** (*C. casuarius*). ▷early 17th cent.: from Malay *kesuari*.

cassowary

cast¹ /kast/ ▸*v.* (*past* **cast** /kast/) **1** [*trans.*] throw (something) forcefully in a specified direction: *lemmings cast themselves off the cliff* | *figurative individuals who do not accept the norms are **cast out** from the group.* ■ throw (something) so as to cause it to spread over an area: *the fishermen cast a large net around a school of tuna* | *figurative he cast his net far and wide in search of evidence.* ■ direct (one's eyes or a look) at something: *she cast down her eyes* | [with *two objs.*] *she cast him a desperate glance.* ■ [*trans.*] throw the hooked and baited end of (a fishing line) out into the water. ■ [*trans.*] register (a vote): *residents turned out in record numbers to cast their votes.* ■ [*trans.*] *Hunting* let loose (hounds) on a scent. ■ [*intrans.*] *Hunting* (of a dog) search in different directions for a lost scent: *the dog cast furiously for the vanished rabbit.* ■ [*trans.*] let down (an anchor or sounding line). **2** [*trans.*] cause (light or shadow) to appear on a surface: *the moon cast a pale light over the cottages* | *figurative running costs were already **casting a shadow** over the program.* ■ cause (uncertainty or disparagement) to be associated with something: *journalists **cast doubt on** the government's version of events* | *I do not wish to **cast aspersions on** your honesty.* ■ cause (a magic spell) to take effect: *the witch **cast a spell on** her to turn her into a beast* | *figurative the city casts a spell on the visitor.* **3** [*trans.*] discard: *the issue was cast from the list of concerns.* ■ shed (skin or horns) in the process of growth: *the antlers are cast each year.* ■ (of a horse) lose (a shoe). **4** [*trans.*] shape (metal or other material) by pouring it into a mold while molten. ■ make (a molded object) in this way: *a bell was cast for the church.* ■ arrange and present in a specified form or style: *he issued statements **cast in** tones of reason.* ■ calculate and record details of (a horoscope). **5** [*intrans.*] (in country dancing) change one's position by moving a certain number of places in a certain direction along the outside of the line in which one is dancing.

▸*phrasal v.* □ **cast about** (or **around**) search far and wide (physically or mentally): *he is restlessly casting about for novelties.* [from a hunting term meaning '(of a hound) go in all directions looking for game or a lost scent.'] □ **cast aside** discard or reject: *they cast aside the principles of their youth.* □ **be cast away** be stranded after a shipwreck. □ **be cast down** feel depressed: *she was greatly cast down by abusive criticism of her novels.* □ **cast off** (or **cast something off**) **1** *Knitting* take the stitches off the needle by looping each over the next to finish the edge. **2** set a boat or ship free from its moorings: *the boatmen cast off and rowed downriver* | *Jack cast off our moorings.* ■ (**cast off**) (of a boat or ship) be set free from its moorings: *the ferry cast off and made a beeline for the pier.* **3** let loose a hunting hound or hawk. **4** *Printing* estimate the space that will be taken in print by manuscript copy. □ **cast someone off** exclude someone from a relationship. □ **cast on** (or **cast something on**) *Knitting* make the first row of a specified number of loops on the needle: *cast on and knit a few rows of stockinette stitch.* □ **cast something up** **1** (of the sea) deposit something on the shore. **2** *dated* add up figures.

▸*n.* **1** an object made by shaping molten metal or similar material in a mold: *bronze casts of the sculpture.* ■ (also **plaster cast**) a mold used to make such an object. ■ (also **plaster cast**) a bandage stiffened with plaster of Paris, molded to the shape of a limb that is broken and used to support and protect it. **2** an act of throwing something forcefully: *he grabbed a spear for a third cast.* ■ *archaic* at dice, a throw or a number thrown. ■ *Fishing* a throw of a fishing line. **3** [in *sing.*] [with *adj.*] the form or appearance of something, esp. someone's features: *she had a somewhat masculine cast of countenance.* ■ the character of something: *this question is for minds of a more philosophical cast than mine.* ■ the overall appearance of someone's skin or hair as determined by a tinge of a particular color: *the colors he wore emphasized the olive cast of his skin.* **4** a slight squint: *he had a cast in one eye.* **5** a convoluted mass of earth or sand ejected onto the surface by a burrowing worm. ■ a pellet regurgitated by a hawk or owl. **6** a search made by a hound or pack of hounds over a wide area to find a trail. ▷Middle English: from Old Norse *kasta* 'to cast or throw.'

▸*PHRASES* □ **be cast in a —— mold** be of the type specified: *he was cast in a cautious mold.* □ **cast adrift** see ADRIFT. □ **cast one's bread upon the waters** see BREAD. □ **cast one's eyes over** have a quick appraising look at: *he was invited to cast his eyes over the exhibition.* □ **cast light on** see LIGHT¹. □ **cast lots** see LOT. □ **cast one's mind back** think back to a particular event or time: *he cast his mind back to the fatal evening.*

cast² ▸*n.* the actors taking part in a play, movie, or other production: *he draws sensitive performances from his inexperienced cast.*

▸*v.* (*past* and *past part.* **cast**) [*trans.*] assign a part in a play, movie, or other production to (an actor): *he was **cast as** the Spanish dancer* | *figurative a campaign for good nutrition, in which red meat is **cast as** the enemy.* ■ allocate parts in (a play, movie, or other production): *assembling a great baseball team is as tricky as casting a play.* ▷mid 17th cent.: a special use of CAST¹.

cas·ta·nets /,kastə'nets/ ▸*plural n.* small concave pieces of wood, ivory, or plastic, joined in pairs by a cord and clicked together by the fingers as a rhythmic accompaniment to Spanish dancing. ▷early 17th cent.: from Spanish *castañeta*, diminutive of *castaña*, from Latin *castanea* 'chestnut.'

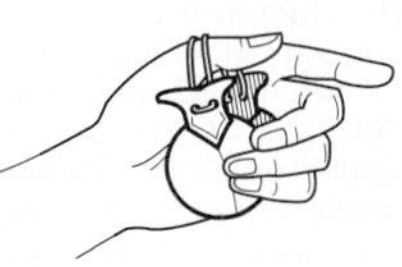
castanets

cast·a·way /'kastə,wā/ ▸*n.* a person who has been shipwrecked and stranded in an isolated place. ■ an outcast: *streets haunted by the city's castaways, layabouts, and panhandlers.*

caste /kast/ ▸*n.* each of the hereditary classes of Hindu society, distinguished by relative degrees of ritual purity or pollution and of social status: *members of the lower castes* | *a man of high caste.* ■ the system of dividing society into such classes. ■ any class or group of people who inherit exclusive privileges or are perceived as socially distinct: *those educated in private schools belong to a privileged caste.* ■ *Entomology* (in some social insects) a physically distinct individual with a particular function in the society.

There are four basic classes, or varnas, in Hindu society: Brahman (priest), Kshatriya (warrior), Vaishya (merchant or farmer), and Shudra (laborer).

▷mid 16th cent. (in the general sense 'race, breed'): from Spanish and Portuguese *casta* 'lineage, race, breed,' feminine of *casto* 'pure, unmixed,' from Latin *castus* 'chaste.'

caste Hin·du ▸*n.* a Hindu who belongs to one of the four main castes.

Cas·tel Gan·dol·fo /'käs,tel gän'dôlfō; -'dälfō/ the summer residence of the pope, located on the edge of Lake Albano near Rome.

cas·tel·lan /'kastələn/ ▸*n. historical* the governor of a castle. ▷late Middle English: from Old Northern French *castelain*, from medieval Latin *castellanus*, from Latin *castellum* (see CASTLE).

cas·tel·lat·ed /'kastə,lātid/ ▸*adj.* **1** having battlements: *a castellated tower.* ■ (of a nut or other mechanical part) having grooves or slots on its upper face. **2** having a castle or several castles: *the castellated hills along the east bank.* ▷late 17th cent.: from medieval Latin *castellatus*, from Latin *castellum* (see CASTLE).

cas·tel·la·tions /,kastə'lāsHənz/ ▸*plural n.* defensive or decorative parapets with regularly spaced notches; battlements. ■ (**castellation**) the use or building of such parapets. ▷early 19th cent.: based on medieval Latin *castellare* 'to build castles,' from *castellum* (see CASTLE).

caste mark ▸*n.* a symbol on the forehead denoting membership of a particular Hindu caste.

cast·er /'kastər/ ▸*n.* **1** a person who casts something or a machine for casting something. **2** *Fishing* a fly pupa used as bait. **3** each of a set of small wheels, free to swivel in any direction, fixed to the legs or base of a heavy piece of furniture so that it can be moved easily. **4** the angular inclination of a steering pivot or kingpin. **5** a small container with holes in the top, esp. one used for sprinkling sugar or pepper.

cas·ti·gate /ˈkastəˌgāt/ ▶*v.* [*trans.*] *formal* reprimand (someone) severely: *he was castigated for not setting a good example.* ▷early 17th cent.: from Latin *castigare* 'reprove,' from *castus* 'pure, chaste.' —**cas·ti·ga·tion** /ˌkastəˈgāSHən/ *n.* —**cas·ti·ga·tor** /-ˌgātər/ *n.* —**cas·ti·ga·to·ry** /-gəˌtôrē/ *adj.*

Cas·tile /kaˈstēl/ a region in central Spain, on the central plateau of the Iberian peninsula, formerly an independent Spanish kingdom. ▷from French *Castille*, from Spanish *Castilla*.

Cas·tile soap ▶*n.* fine, hard white or mottled soap made with olive oil and sodium hydroxide. ▷late Middle English: named after **CASTILE** in Spain, where it was originally made.

Cas·til·ian /kəˈstilyən/ ▶*n.* **1** a native of Castile. **2** the dialect of Spanish spoken in Castile, which is standard Spanish.

▶*adj.* of or relating to Castile, Castilians, or the Castilian form of Spanish.

Cas·til·la-La Man·cha /käˈstē(l)yä lä ˈmänCHə/ an autonomous region in central Spain; capital, Toledo.

Cas·til·la-Le·ón /käˈstē(l)yä läˈōn/ an autonomous region in northern Spain; capital, Valladolid.

cast·ing /ˈkastiNG/ ▶*n.* an object made by pouring molten metal or other material into a mold.

cast·ing couch ▶*n. informal* used in reference to the supposed practice whereby actors or actresses are awarded parts in movies, plays, or other productions in return for granting sexual favors to the casting director: *she was no stranger to the casting couch.*

cast·ing di·rec·tor ▶*n.* the person responsible for assigning roles in a movie, play, or other production.

cast·ing vote ▶*n.* an extra vote given by a chairperson to decide an issue when the votes on each side are equal. ▷early 17th cent.: from an obsolete sense of *cast* 'turn the scale.'

cast i·ron ▶*n.* a hard, relatively brittle alloy of iron and carbon that can be readily cast in a mold and contains a higher proportion of carbon than steel (typically 2.0–4.3 percent). ■ [as *adj.*] *figurative* firm and unchangeable: *there are no cast-iron guarantees.*

Cas·tle /ˈkasəl/, Vernon Blythe (1887–1918), British dancer; born *Vernon Blythe*. With his wife **Irene** (1893–1969), he originated the one-step, the turkey trot, the Castle walk, and the hesitation waltz. He also served as an aviator 1916–18 during World War I.

cas·tle /ˈkasəl/ ▶*n.* a large building or group of buildings fortified against attack with thick walls, battlements, towers, and in many cases a moat. ■ a magnificent and imposing mansion, esp. one that is the home or former home of a member of the nobility. [in *names*] Castle Howard. ■ *informal Chess* old-fashioned term for **ROOK**².

▶*v.* [*intrans.*] [often as *n.*] (**castling**) *Chess* make a special move (no more than once in a game by each player) in which the king is transferred from its original square two squares along the back rank toward the corner square of a rook, which is then transferred to the square passed over by the king. ■ [*trans.*] move (the king) in this way. ▷late Old English: from Anglo-Norman French and Old Northern French *castel*, from Latin *castellum*, diminutive of *castrum* 'fort.' —**cas·tled** /ˈkasəld/ *adj.* (*archaic*).

▶*PHRASE* □ **castles in the air** (or **in Spain**) visionary unattainable schemes; daydreams: *my father built castles in the air about owning a boat.*

cast net ▶*n. Fishing* a net that is thrown out and immediately drawn in again, as opposed to one that is set up and left.

cast·off /ˈkastˌôf/ ▶*adj.* no longer wanted; abandoned or discarded: *a pile of castoff clothes.*

▶*n.* (usu. **castoffs**) something, esp. a garment, that is no longer wanted: *I'm not going out in her castoffs!*

Cas·tor /ˈkastər/ **1** *Greek Mythology* the twin brother of Pollux. See **DIOSCURI**. **2** *Astronomy* the second brightest star in the constellation Gemini, close to Pollux. It is a multiple star system, the three components visible in a moderate telescope being close binaries.

cas·tor /ˈkastər/ ▶*n.* a reddish-brown oily substance secreted by beavers, used in medicine and perfumes. ▷late Middle English (in the sense 'beaver'): from Old French or Latin, from Greek *kastōr*.

cas·tor bean ▶*n.* the seed of the castor-oil plant. It contains a number of poisonous compounds, esp. ricin, as well as castor oil. ■ the castor-oil plant.

cas·tor oil ▶*n.* a pale yellow oil obtained from castor beans, used as a purgative and a lubricant and in manufacturing oil-based products. ▷mid 18th cent.: perhaps so named because it succeeded **CASTOR** in medicinal use.

cas·tor-oil plant ▶*n.* an African shrub with lobed serrated leaves, yielding the seeds from which castor oil is obtained and widely naturalized in warm countries. • *Ricinus communis*, family Euphorbiaceae.

cas·trate /ˈkasˌtrāt/ ▶*v.* [*trans.*] remove the testicles of (a male animal or man). ■ *figurative* deprive of power, vitality, or vigor: [as *adj.*] (**castrated**) *the nation is a castrated giant, afraid to really punish subversives.*

▶*n.* a man or male animal whose testicles have been removed. ▷mid 16th cent.: from Latin *castrare*. —**cas·tra·tion** /kaˈstrāSHən/ *n.* —**cas·tra·tor** /ˈkasˌtrātər/ *n.*

cas·tra·tion com·plex ▶*n. Psychoanalysis* (in Freudian theory) an unconscious anxiety arising during psychosexual development, represented in males as a fear that the penis will be removed by the father in response to sexual interest in the mother, and in females as a compulsion to demonstrate that they have an adequate symbolic equivalent to the penis, whose absence is blamed on the mother.

cas·tra·to /kasˈträˌtō/ ▶*n.* (*pl.* **-ti** /-tē/) *historical* a male singer castrated in boyhood so as to retain a soprano or alto voice. The practice of castration was banned in 1903. ▷mid 18th cent.: from Italian, past participle of *castrare* (see **CASTRATE**).

Cas·tries /kasˈtrē; ˈkästrēs/ the capital of the Caribbean island nation of St. Lucia, a seaport on the northwestern coast; pop. 14,055.

Cas·tro /ˈkastrō/, Fidel (1927–), Cuban statesman; prime minister 1959–76 and president from 1976. After overthrowing President Batista he set up a communist regime that survived the abortive Bay of Pigs invasion, the Cuban Missile Crisis, and the collapse of the Soviet bloc.

Fidel Castro

Cas·tro·ism /ˈkastrōˌizəm/ ▶*n.* the political principles or actions of Fidel Castro or his adherents or imitators. —**Cas·tro·ist** *n.* & *adj.* —**Cas·tro·ite** /-ˌīt/ *n.* & *adj.*

ca·su·al /ˈkaZHo͞oəl/ ▶*adj.* **1** relaxed and unconcerned: *she regarded his affairs with a casual indulgence | he tried to make his voice sound casual.* ■ made or done without much thought or premeditation: *a casual remark.* ■ done or acting in a desultory way: *to the casual observer, rugby looks something like soccer.* ■ done or acting without sufficient care or thoroughness: *the casual way in which victims were treated.* **2** not regular or permanent: *the tent is ideal for casual outdoor use | casual jobs.* ■ (of a worker) employed on a temporary or irregular basis: *casual staff.* ■ (of a sexual relationship or encounter) occurring between people who are not regular or established sexual partners. **3** [*attrib.*] happening by chance; accidental: *he pretended it was a casual meeting.* See note at **ACCIDENTAL**. **4** without formality of style, manner, or procedure, in particular: ■ (of clothes or a style of dress) suitable for everyday wear rather than formal occasions. ■ (of a social event) not characterized by particular social conventions. ■ (of a place or environment) relaxed and friendly: *the inn's casual atmosphere.*

▶*n.* **1** a person who does something irregularly: *a number of casuals became regular customers.* ■ a worker employed on an irregular or temporary basis. **2** (**casuals**) clothes or shoes suitable for everyday wear rather than formal occasions. ▷late Middle English (in senses 2 and 3 of the *adjective*): from Old French *casuel* and Latin *casualis*, from *casus* 'fall' (compare with **CASE**¹). —**ca·su·al·ly** *adv.* —**ca·su·al·ness** *n.*

cas·u·al Fri·day ▶*n.* Friday as a day when office workers are allowed to dress more casually than usual.

cas·u·al·ty /ˈkaZH(ə)wəltē; ˈkaZHəl-/ ▶*n.* (*pl.* **-ties**) a person killed or injured in a war or accident. ■ *figurative* a person or thing badly affected by an event or situation: *the building industry has been one of the casualties of the recession.* ■ (chiefly in insurance) an accident, mishap, or disaster. ▷late Middle English (in the sense 'chance, a chance occurrence'): from medieval Latin *casualitas*, from *casualis* (see **CASUAL**), on the pattern of words such as *penalty*.

ca·su·al wa·ter ▶*n. Golf* water that has accumulated temporarily and does not constitute a recognized hazard of the course. A player may move a ball from casual water without penalty.

ca·su·a·ri·na /ˌkaZHo͞oəˈrēnə/ ▶*n.* a tree with slender, jointed, drooping twigs that resemble horsetails and bear tiny scalelike leaves. It is native to Australia and Southeast Asia, and is a valuable source of timber and firewood. • Genus *Casuarina*, family Casuarinaceae. ▷from modern Latin *casuarius* 'cassowary' (from the resemblance of the branches to the bird's feathers).

cas·u·ist /ˈkaZHo͞oist/ ▶*n.* a person who uses clever but unsound reasoning, esp. in relation to moral questions; a sophist. ■ a person who resolves moral problems by the application of theoretical rules to particular instances. ▷early 17th cent.: from French *casuiste*, from Spanish *casuista*, from Latin *casus* (see **CASE**¹). —**cas·u·is·tic** /ˌkaZHo͞oˈistik/ *adj.* —**cas·u·is·ti·cal** /ˌkaZHo͞oˈistikəl/ *adj.* —**cas·u·is·ti·cal·ly** *adv.*

cas·u·ist·ry /ˈkaZH(ə)wəstrē/ ▶*n.* the use of clever but unsound reasoning, esp. in relation to moral questions; sophistry. ■ the resolving of moral problems by the application of theoretical rules to particular instances.

ca·sus bel·li /ˈkäsəs ˈbelē; ˈkāsəs ˈbelˌī/ ▶*n.* (*pl.* same) an act or situation provoking or justifying war. ▷Latin, from *casus* (see **CASE**¹) and *belli*, genitive of *bellum* 'war.'

CAT /ˈkat/ ▶*abbr.* ■ clear air turbulence. ■ computer-assisted (or -aided) testing. ■ *Medicine* computerized axial tomography: [as *adj.*] *a CAT scan.*

cat¹ /kat/ ▶*n.* **1** a small domesticated carnivorous mammal with soft fur, a short snout, and retractile claws. It is widely kept as a pet or for catching mice, and many breeds have been developed. • *Felis catus*, family Felidae (the **cat family**); probably domesticated in ancient Egypt from the local race of wildcat, and held in great reverence there. The cat family also includes the ocelot, serval, margay, lynx, and the big cats. ■ a wild animal of the cat family: *a marbled cat.* See also **BIG CAT**. ■ used in names of catlike animals of other families, e.g., **ring-tailed cat**. ■ *historical* short for **CAT-O'-NINE-TAILS**. ■ short for **CATFISH**. ■ short for **CATHEAD**. ■ short for **CATBOAT**. **2** *informal* (particularly among jazz enthusiasts) a person, esp. a man.

▶*v.* (**cat·ted**, **cat·ting**) [*trans.*] *Nautical* raise (an anchor) from the surface of the water to the cathead. ▷Old English *catt*, *catte*, of Germanic origin; related to Dutch *kat* and German *Katze*; reinforced in Middle English by forms from late Latin *cattus*.

▶*PHRASES* □ **cat and mouse** a series of cunning maneuvers designed to thwart an opponent: *their elite fighters are **playing cat and mouse** with U.S. troops.* □ **a cat may look at a king** *proverb* even a person of low status or importance has rights. □ **fight like cats and dogs** *informal* (of two people) be continually arguing with one another. □ **has the cat got your tongue?** said to someone who, when expected to speak, remains silent. □ **let the cat out of the bag** *informal* reveal a secret carelessly or by mistake. □ **like a cat on a hot tin roof** *informal* very agitated or anxious. □ **look like something the cat dragged in** (or **brought in**) *informal* (of a person) look very dirty or disheveled. □ **when** (or **while**) **the cat's away, the mice will play** *proverb* people will naturally take advantage of the absence of someone in authority to do as they like.

cat² ▶*n.* short for **CATALYTIC CONVERTER**.

cat³ ▶*n.* short for **CATAMARAN**.

cata- (also **cat-**) ▶*prefix* **1** down; downward: *catadromous | cataract.* **2** wrongly; badly: *catachresis | catastrophe* **3** completely; thoroughly: *catechize.* **4** against: *catapult.* ▷from Greek *kata* 'down.'

ca·tab·o·lism /kəˈtabəˌlizəm/ ▶*n. Biology* the breakdown of complex molecules in living organisms to form simpler ones, together with the release of energy; destructive metabolism. ▷late 19th cent.: from Greek *katabolē* 'throwing down,' from *kata-* 'down' + *ballein* 'to throw.' **—cat·a·bol·ic** /ˌkatə ˈbälik/ *adj.* **—ca·tab·o·lize** /-ˌlīz/ *v.*

ca·tab·o·lite /kəˈtabəˌlīt/ ▶*n. Biochemistry* a product of catabolism.

cat·a·chre·sis /ˌkatəˈkrēsis/ ▶*n.* (*pl.* **-ses** /-sēz/) the use of a word in a way that is not correct, for example, the use of *mitigate* for *militate.* ▷mid 16th cent.: from Latin, from Greek *katakhrēsis,* from *katakhrēsthai* 'misuse,' from *kata-* 'down' (expressing the sense 'wrongly') + *khrēsthai* 'use.' **—cat·a·chres·tic** /-ˈkrestik/ *adj.*

cat·a·clysm /ˈkatəˌklizəm/ ▶*n.* a large-scale and violent event in the natural world. ■ a sudden violent upheaval, esp. in a political or social context: *the cataclysm of the First World War.* ▷early 17th cent. (originally denoting the biblical Flood described in Genesis): from French *cataclysme,* via Latin from Greek *kataklusmos* 'deluge,' from *kata-* 'down' + *kluzein* 'to wash.'

cat·a·clys·mic /ˌkatəˈklizmik/ ▶*adj.* relating to or denoting a violent natural event. ■ *informal* denoting something unpleasant or unsuccessful on an enormous scale: *the concert was a cataclysmic failure.* **—cat·a·clys·mi·cal·ly** /-mik(ə)lē/ *adv.*

cat·a·comb /ˈkatəˌkōm/ ▶*n.* (usu. **catacombs**) an underground cemetery consisting of a subterranean gallery with recesses for tombs, as constructed by the ancient Romans. ■ an underground construction resembling or compared to such a cemetery. ▷Old English, from late Latin *catacumbas,* the name of the subterranean cemetery of St. Sebastian near Rome.

cat·a·di·op·tric /ˌkatəˌdīˈäptrik/ ▶*adj. Optics* denoting an optical system that involves both the reflecting and refracting of light, in order to reduce aberration.

ca·tad·ro·mous /kəˈtadrəməs/ ▶*adj. Zoology* (of a fish such as the eel) migrating down rivers to the sea to spawn. The opposite of **ANADROMOUS.** ▷late 19th cent.: from **CATA-** 'down' + Greek *dromos* 'running,' on the pattern of *anadromous.*

cat·a·falque /ˈkatəˌfô(l)k; -ˌfalk/ ▶*n.* a decorated wooden framework supporting the coffin of a distinguished person during a funeral or while lying in state. ▷mid 17th cent.: from French, from Italian *catafalco,* of unknown origin. Compare with **SCAFFOLD.**

Cat·a·lan /ˈkatlˌan; ˈkatl-ən/ ▶*n.* **1** a native of Catalonia. **2** a Romance language closely related to Castilian Spanish and Provençal, widely spoken in Catalonia (where it has official status alongside Castilian Spanish) and in Andorra, the Balearic Islands, and parts of southern France.
▶*adj.* of or relating to Catalonia, its people, or its language. ▷from French, from Spanish *catalán,* related to Catalan *català* 'Catalan,' *Catalunya* 'Catalonia.'

cat·a·lase /ˈkatlˌās; -ˌāz/ ▶*n. Biochemistry* an enzyme that catalyzes the reduction of hydrogen peroxide. ▷early 20th cent.: from **CATALYSIS** + **-ASE.**

cat·a·lec·tic /ˌkatlˈektik/ *Prosody* ▶*adj.* (of a metrical line of verse) lacking one syllable in the last foot.
▶*n.* a line lacking a syllable in the last foot. ▷late 16th cent.: from late Latin *catalecticus,* from Greek *katalēktikos,* from *katalēgein* 'leave off.'

cat·a·lep·sy /ˈkatlˌepsē/ ▶*n.* a medical condition characterized by a trance or seizure with a loss of sensation and consciousness accompanied by rigidity of the body. ▷late Middle English: from French *catalepsie* or late Latin *catalepsia,* from Greek *katalēpsis,* from *katalambanein* 'seize upon.' **—cat·a·lep·tic** /ˌkatlˈeptik/ *adj.* & *n.*

cat·a·lex·is /ˌkatlˈeksis/ ▶*n.* the absence of a syllable in the last foot of a line or verse.

cat·a·log /ˈkatlˌôg; -ˌäg/ (also **cat·a·logue**) ▶*n.* a complete list of items, typically one in alphabetical or other systematic order, in particular: ■ a list of all the books or resources in a library. ■ a publication containing details and often photographs of items for sale, esp. one produced by a mail-order company. ■ a descriptive list of works of art in an exhibition or collection giving detailed comments and explanations. ■ a list of courses offered by a university or college. ■ [in *sing.*] a series of unfortunate or bad things: *his life was a catalog of dismal failures.*
▶*v.* (**-logs, -loged, -log·ing**; also **-logues, -logued, -logu·ing**) [*trans.*] make a systematic list of (items of the same type). ■ enter (an item) in such a list: *the picture was withdrawn before being cataloged.* ■ list (similar situations, qualities, or events) in succession: *the report catalogs dangerous work practices in the company.* ▷late Middle English: via Old French from late Latin *catalogus,* from Greek *katalogos,* from *katalegein* 'pick out or enroll.' **—cat·a·log·er** (also **cat·a·logu·er**) *n.*

cat·a·logue rai·son·né /katlˌôg; ˌrāzəˈnā; -ˌäg/ ▶*n.* (*pl.* **cat·a·logues rai·son·nés** /ˈkatlˌôg(z) ˌrāzəˈnā; -ˌäg(z)/) a descriptive catalog of works of art with explanations and scholarly comments. ▷late 18th cent.: French, literally 'explained catalog.'

Cat·a·lo·ni·a /ˌkatlˈōnēə/ an autonomous region in northeastern Spain; capital, Barcelona. The region has a strong separatist tradition; the normal language for everyday purposes is Catalan, which has also won acceptance in recent years for various official purposes. Catalan name **CATALUNYA**; Spanish name **CATALUÑA**.

ca·tal·pa /kəˈtalpə/ ▶*n.* a tree with large heart-shaped leaves, clusters of trumpet-shaped flowers, and long, slender beanlike seedpods, native to North America and eastern Asia and cultivated as an ornamental. • Genus *Catalpa,* family Bignoniaceae: several species, including the **southern** (or **common**) **catalpa** (*C. bignonioides*). ▷from Creek.

cat·a·lu·fa /ˌkatlˈo͞ofə/ ▶*n.* another term for **BIGEYE** (sense 2). ▷from Spanish.

ca·tal·y·sis /kəˈtaləsis/ ▶*n. Chemistry* & *Biochemistry* the acceleration of a chemical reaction by a catalyst. ▷mid 19th cent.: from modern Latin, from Greek *katalusis,* from *kataluein* 'dissolve,' from *kata-* 'down' + *luein* 'loosen.'

cat·a·lyst /ˈkatl-ist/ ▶*n.* a substance that increases the rate of a chemical reaction without itself undergoing any permanent chemical change. ■ *figurative* a person or thing that precipitates an event: *the governor's speech acted as a catalyst for debate.* ▷early 20th cent.: from **CATALYSIS,** on the pattern of *analyst.*

cat·a·lyt·ic /ˌkatlˈitik/ ▶*adj.* relating to or involving the action of a catalyst. ▷mid 19th cent.: from **CATALYSIS,** on the pattern of pairs such as *analysis, analytic.* **—cat·a·lyt·i·cal·ly** /-ik(ə)lē/ *adv.*

cat·a·lyt·ic con·vert·er ▶*n.* a device incorporated in the exhaust system of a motor vehicle, containing a catalyst for converting pollutant gases into less harmful ones.

cat·a·lyze /ˈkatlˌīz/ (*Brit.* **cat·a·lyse**) ▶*v.* [*trans.*] cause or accelerate (a reaction) by acting as a catalyst. ■ *figurative* cause (an action or process) to begin: *the bank was set up to catalyze investment in the former communist countries.* ▷late 19th cent.: from **CATALYSIS,** on the pattern of *analyze.*

cat·a·ma·ran /ˌkatəməˈran; ˈkatəməˌran/ ▶*n.* a yacht or other boat with twin hulls in parallel. ▷early 17th cent.: from Tamil *kaṭṭumaram,* literally 'tied wood.'

catamaran

Cat·a·mar·ca /ˌkätäˈmärkä; ˌkatəˈmärkə/ a mining and commercial town in northwestern Argentina, the capital of Catamarca province; pop. 110,000.

cat·a·mite /ˈkatəˌmīt/ ▶*n. archaic* a boy kept for homosexual practices. ▷late 16th cent.: from Latin *catamitus,* via Etruscan from Greek *Ganumēdēs* (see **GANYMEDE**).

cat·a·mount /ˈkatəˌmount/ (also **cat·a·moun·tain** /-ˌmountən/) ▶*n.* a medium-sized or large wild cat, esp. a cougar. ▷late Middle English (as *catamountain*): from the phrase *cat of the mountain.*

Ca·ta·nia /kəˈtänyə; -ˈtān-; -ˈtänēə/ a seaport on the east coast of Sicily, in southern Italy, at the foot of Mount Etna; pop. 364,180.

Ca·tan·za·ro /ˌkätän(d)ˈzärō/ the chief town of the Calabria region of southern Italy; pop. 104,000.

cat·a·phat·ic /ˌkatəˈfatik/ ▶*adj. Theology* (of knowledge of God) obtained through affirmation. The opposite of **APOPHATIC.** ▷mid 19th cent.: from Greek *kataphatikos* 'affirmative,' from *kataphasis* 'affirmation,' from *kata-* (as an intensifier) + *phanai* 'speak.'

cat·a·phor /ˈkatəfər; -ˌfôr/ ▶*n. Grammar* a word or phrase that refers to or stands for a later word or phrase (e.g., in *when they saw Ruth, the men looked slightly abashed,* the word *they* is used as a cataphor for *the men*). ▷late 20th cent.: back-formation from **CATAPHORA.**

ca·taph·o·ra /kəˈtafərə/ ▶*n. Grammar* the use of a word or phrase that refers to or stands for a later word or phrase (e.g., the pronoun *he* in *he may be 37, but Jeff behaves like a teenager*). Compare with **ANAPHORA.** ▷1970s: from **CATA-** on the pattern of *anaphora.* **—cat·a·phor·ic** /ˌkatəˈfôrik/ *adj.* **—cat·a·phor·i·cal·ly** /ˌkatəˈfôrik(ə)lē/ *adv.*

cat·a·pho·re·sis /ˌkatəfəˈrēsis/ ▶*n.* another term for **ELECTROPHORESIS.**

cat·a·phract /ˈkatəˌfrakt/ ▶*n. archaic* a soldier in full armor. ▷late 17th cent.: via Latin from Greek *kataphraktos* 'clothed in full armor.'

cat·a·plasm /ˈkatəˌplazəm/ ▶*n.* another term for **POULTICE.**

cat·a·plex·y /ˈkatəˌpleksē/ ▶*n.* a medical condition in which strong emotion or laughter causes a person to suffer sudden physical collapse though remaining conscious. ▷late 19th cent.: from Greek *kataplēxis* 'stupefaction,' from *kataplessein,* from *kata-* 'down' + *plēssein* 'strike.' **—cat·a·plec·tic** /ˌkatəˈplektik/ *adj.*

cat·a·pult /ˈkatəˌpəlt; -ˌpo͝olt/ ▶*n.* a device in which accumulated tension is suddenly released to hurl an object some distance, in particular: ■ *historical* a military machine worked by a lever and ropes for hurling large stones or other missiles. ■ a mechanical device for launching a glider or other aircraft, esp. from the deck of a ship. ■ *chiefly Brit.* a slingshot.
▶*v.* [*trans.*] hurl or launch (something) in a specified direction with or as if with a catapult: *the plane was refueled and catapulted back into the air again* | *the explosion catapulted the car 30 yards along the road* | *figurative their music catapulted them to the top of the charts.* ■ [*intrans.*] move suddenly or at great speed as though hurled by a catapult: *the horse catapulted away from the fence.* ▷late 16th cent.: from French *catapulte* or Latin *catapulta,* from Greek *katapeltēs,* from *kata-* 'down' + *pallein* 'hurl.'

cat·a·ract /ˈkatəˌrakt/ ▶*n.* **1** a large waterfall. ■ a sudden rush of water; a downpour: *the rain enveloped us in a deafening cataract.* **2** a medical condition in which the lens of the eye becomes progressively opaque, resulting in blurred vision: *she had cataracts in both eyes.* ▷late Middle English: from Latin *cataracta* 'waterfall, floodgate,' also 'portcullis' (medical sense 2 probably being a figurative use of this), from Greek *kataraktēs* 'down-rushing,' from *katarassein,* from *kata-* 'down' + *arassein* 'strike, smash.'

ca·tarrh /kəˈtär/ ▶*n.* excessive discharge or buildup of mucus in the nose or throat, associated with inflammation of the mucous membrane. ▷early 16th cent.: from French *catarrhe,* from late Latin *catarrhus,* from Greek *katarrhous,* from *katarrhein* 'flow down,' from *kata-* 'down' + *rhein* 'flow.' **—ca·tarrh·al** /kəˈtärəl/ *adj.*

cat·ar·rhine /ˈkatəˌrīn/ *Zoology* ▶*adj.* of or relating to primates of a group that comprises the Old World monkeys, gibbons, great apes, and humans. They are distinguished by having nostrils that are close together and directed downward. Compare with **PLATYRRHINE.**
▶*n.* a catarrhine primate. • Infraorder Catarrhini, order Primates: four families. ▷mid 19th cent.: from **CATA-** 'down' + Greek *rhis, rhin-* 'nose.'

ca·tas·ta·sis /kəˈtastəsis/ ▶*n.* (*pl.* **-ses** /-ˌsēz/) the third part of the ancient drama, in which the action is heightened for the catastrophe.

ca·tas·tro·phe /kəˈtastrəfē/ ▶*n.* an event causing great and often sudden damage or suffering; a disaster: *a national economic catastrophe* | *leading the world to catastrophe.* ■ the denouement of a drama, esp. a classical tragedy. ▷mid 16th cent. (in the sense 'denouement'): from Latin *catastropha,* from Greek *katastrophē* 'overturning, sudden turn,' from *kata-* 'down' + *strophē* 'turning' (from *strephein* 'to turn').

ca·tas·tro·phe the·o·ry ▶*n.* a branch of mathematics concerned with systems displaying abrupt discontinuous change.

cat·a·stroph·ic /ˌkatəˈsträfik/ ▶*adj.* **1** involving or causing sudden great damage or suffering: *a catastrophic earthquake.* ■ involving a sudden and large-scale alteration in the state of something: *the body undergoes catastrophic collapse toward the state of a black hole.* ■ of or relating to geological catastrophism. **2** extremely unfortunate or unsuccessful: *catastrophic mismanagement of the economy.* **—cat·a·stroph·i·cal·ly** /-ik(ə)lē/ *adv.*

ca·tas·tro·phism /kəˈtastrəˌfizəm/ *n.* ▶*Geology* the theory that changes in the earth's crust during geological history have resulted chiefly from sudden violent and unusual events. Often contrasted with UNIFORMITARIANISM. **—ca·tas·tro·phist** *n.* & *adj.*

cat·a·to·ni·a /ˌkatəˈtōnēə/ ▸*n. Psychiatry* abnormality of movement and behavior arising from a disturbed mental state (typically schizophrenia). It may involve repetitive or purposeless overactivity, or catalepsy, resistance to passive movement, and negativism. ■ *informal* a state of immobility and stupor. ▷late 19th cent.: from CATA- 'badly' + Greek *tonos* 'tone or tension.'

cat·a·ton·ic /ˌkatəˈtänik/ ▸*adj. Psychiatry* of, relating to, or characterized by catatonia: *catatonic schizophrenia.* ■ *informal* of or in an immobile or unresponsive stupor.

Ca·taw·ba /kəˈtôbə/ ▸*n.* a North American variety of grape. ■ a white wine made from this grape. ▷named after the *Catawba* River in North and South Carolina.

Ca·taw·ba Riv·er /kəˈtôbə; -ˈtäbə/ a river that flows for 300 miles (480 km) from the Blue Ridge Mountains in North Carolina across much of South Carolina.

cat·bird /ˈkatˌbərd/ ▸*n.* **1** a long-tailed American songbird of the mockingbird family, with mainly dark gray or black plumage and catlike calls. • Two genera and species, family Mimidae, in particular the **gray catbird** (*Dumetella carolinensis*) of North America. **2** a thickset Australasian bird of the bowerbird family, typically with a loud call like a yowling cat. It does not generally construct bowers. • Genus *Ailuroedus* (and *Scenopoeetes*), family Ptilonorhynchidae: several species, in particular the **green catbird** (*A. crassirostris*).
▸*PHRASE* □ **in the catbird seat** *informal* in a superior or advantageous position. [said to be an allusion to a baseball player in the fortunate position of having no strikes and therefore three balls still to play (a reference made in James Thurber's short story *The Catbird Seat*).]

cat·boat /ˈkatˌbōt/ ▸*n.* a sailboat with a single mast placed well forward and carrying only one sail. ▷mid 19th cent.: perhaps from *cat* (denoting a type of merchant ship formerly used in the coal and timber trades in northeastern England) + BOAT.

cat·bri·er /ˈkatˌbrī(ə)r/ (also **cat·bri·ar**) ▸*n.* another term for GREENBRIER.

cat bur·glar ▸*n.* a thief who enters a building by climbing to an upper story.

cat·call /ˈkatˌkôl/ ▸*n.* a shrill whistle or shout of disapproval, typically one made at a public meeting or performance. ■ a loud whistle or a comment of a sexual nature made by a man to a passing woman.
▸*v.* [*intrans.*] make such a whistle, shout, or comment: *they were fired for catcalling at women.* ▷mid 17th cent.: from CAT[1] + CALL, originally denoting a kind of whistle or squeaking instrument used to express disapproval at a theater.

catch /kacH; kecH/ ▸*v.* (*past* **caught** /kôt/) [*trans.*] **1** intercept and hold (something that has been thrown, propelled, or dropped): *she threw the bottle into the air and caught it again.* ■ intercept the fall of (someone). ■ seize or take hold of: *he **caught hold of** her arm as she tried to push past him.* ■ [*intrans.*] (**catch at**) grasp or try to grasp: *his hands caught at her arms as she tried to turn away.* **2** capture (a person or animal that tries or would try to escape): *we hadn't caught a single rabbit.* ■ [*intrans.*] (of an object) accidentally become entangled or trapped in something: *the charm bracelet always caught on her clothing.* ■ [*trans.*] (of a person) have (a part of one's body or clothing) become entangled or trapped in something: *she caught her foot in the bedspread* | *figurative companies face increased risks of being caught in a downward spiral.* ■ [*trans.*] (usu. **be caught**) fix or fasten in place: *her hair was caught back in a scrunchie.* **3** reach in time and board (a train, bus, or aircraft): *they caught the 12:15 from Chicago.* ■ reach or be in a place in time to see (a person, performance, program, etc.): *she was hurrying downstairs to catch the news.* ■ come upon (someone) unexpectedly: *unexpected snow **caught us by surprise**.* ■ (**be caught in**) (of a person) unexpectedly find oneself in (an unwelcome situation): *my sister was caught in a thunderstorm.* ■ (**catch it**) *informal* be punished or told off. ■ (often **be caught**) surprise (someone) in an incriminating situation or in the act of doing something wrong: *he was caught with bomb-making equipment in his home.* **4** engage (a person's interest or imagination). ■ perceive fleetingly: *she **caught a glimpse of** herself in the mirror.* ■ hear or understand (something said), esp. with effort: *he bellowed something Jess couldn't catch.* ■ succeed in evoking or representing: *the program caught something of the flavor of Minoan culture.* **5** [*trans.*] strike (someone) on a part of the body: *Ben caught him on the chin with an uppercut.* ■ accidentally strike (a part of one's body) against something: *she fell and caught her head on the corner of the hearth.* **6** contract (an illness) through infection or contagion. **7** [*intrans.*] become ignited, due to contact with flame, and start burning: *the rafters have caught.* ■ (of an engine) fire and start running.
▸*phrasal v.* □ **catch on** *informal* **1** (of a practice or fashion) become popular: *his music never caught on in the South.* **2** understand what is meant or how to do something: *I **caught on to** what it was the guy was saying.* □ **catch up** succeed in reaching a person who is ahead of one: *O'Hara **caught up with** Stella at the bottom of the hill.* ■ do work or other tasks that one should have done earlier: *he normally used the afternoons to **catch up on** paperwork.* □ **catch up with 1** talk to (someone) whom one has not seen for some time in order to find out what he or she has been doing in the interim: *a chance to catch up with old friends.* **2** begin to have a damaging effect on: *the physical exertions began to catch up with Sue.* **3** succeed in reaching a person who is ahead of one: *you go with Stasia and Katie, and I'll catch up with you.* □ **be/get caught up in** become involved in (something that one had not intended to become involved in): *he had no desire to be caught up in political activities.*
▸*n.* **1** an act of catching something, typically a ball. ■ an amount of fish caught: *a record catch of 6.9 billion pounds of fish.* ■ [in *sing.*] *informal* a person considered attractive, successful, or prestigious and so desirable as a partner or spouse: *I mistakenly thought he would be a good catch.* **2** a device for securing something such as a door, window, or box: *the window catch was rusty.* **3** a hidden problem or disadvantage in an apparently ideal situation: *there's a catch in it somewhere.* **4** [in *sing.*] an unevenness in a person's voice caused by emotion: *there was a catch in Anne's voice.* **5** *Music* a round, typically one with words arranged to produce a humorous effect. ▷Middle English (also in the sense 'chase'): from Anglo-Norman French and Old Northern French *cachier*, variant of Old French *chacier*, based on Latin *captare* 'try to catch,' from *capere* 'take.' **—catch·a·ble** *adj.*
▸*PHRASES* □ **catch someone napping** see NAP[1]. □ **be caught short** see SHORT. □ **catch at straws** see STRAW. □ **catch one's breath 1** draw one's breath in sharply as a reaction to an emotion. **2** recover one's breath after exertion. □ **catch one's death (of cold)** see DEATH. □ **catch someone's eye 1** be noticed by someone: *a vase on a side table caught his eye.* **2** attract someone's attention by making eye contact: *I caught Rhoda's eye and gave her a friendly wave.* □ **catch fire** become ignited and burn. □ **catch someone in the act** see ACT. □ **catch the light** shine or glint in the light. □ **catch sight of** suddenly notice; glimpse. □ **you wouldn't catch —— doing something** *informal* used to indicate that there is no possibility of the person mentioned doing what is specified: *you wouldn't catch me walking back to the house alone at night.*

catch-22 ▸*n.* a dilemma or difficult circumstance from which there is no escape because of mutually conflicting or dependent conditions: [as *adj.*] *a catch-22 situation.* ▷1970s: title of a novel by Joseph Heller (1961), in which the main character feigns madness in order to avoid dangerous combat missions, but his desire to avoid them is taken to prove his sanity.

catch-all ▸*n.* [usu. as *adj.*] a term or category that includes a variety of different possibilities: *the stigmatizing catch-all term "schizophrenia."*

catch-as-catch-can ▸*n. archaic* wrestling in which all holds are permitted.
▸*adj.* [*attrib.*] using whatever methods or materials are available: *our catch-as-catch-can repair of fences.*

catch·er /ˈkacHər; ˈkecH-/ ▸*n.* a person or thing that catches something. ■ *Baseball* a fielder positioned behind home plate to catch pitches not hit by the batter and to execute other defensive plays.

catch·fly /ˈkacHˌflī; ˈkecH-/ ▸*n.* (*pl.* **-flies**) a campion or similar plant of the pink family, with a sticky stem. • *Silene*, *Lychnis*, and other genera, family Caryophyllaceae.

catch·ing /ˈkacHiNG; ˈkecH-/ ▸*adj.* [*predic.*] *informal* (of a disease) infectious: *Huntington's chorea isn't catching* | *figurative her enthusiasm is catching.*

catch·light /ˈkacHˌlīt; ˈkecH-/ ▸*n.* a gleam of reflected light in the eye of a person or animal in a photograph.

catch·line /ˈkacHˌlīn; ˈkecH-/ ▸*n. Printing* a short, eye-catching line of type, typically one at the top of a page such as a running head. ■ an advertising slogan.

catch·ment /ˈkacHmənt; ˈkecH-/ ▸*n.* the action of collecting water, esp. the collection of rainfall over a natural drainage area.

catch·ment ar·e·a ▸*n.* **1** (also **catch·ment**) the area of a city, town, etc., from which a hospital's patients or school's students are drawn. **2** the area from which rainfall flows into a river, lake, or reservoir.

catch·pen·ny /ˈkacHˌpenē; ˈkecH-/ ▸*adj.* [*attrib.*] having a cheap superficial attractiveness designed to encourage quick sales.

catch·phrase /ˈkacHˌfrāz; ˈkecH-/ ▸*n.* a well-known sentence or phrase, typically one that is associated with a particular famous person.

catch-up (also **catch·up**) ▸*n. informal* an act of catching someone up in a particular activity.
▸*PHRASE* □ **play catch-up 1** fall behind continually with work or financial matters: *I'm always playing catch-up with my homework.* **2** try to equal a competitor in a sport or game.

catch·weight /ˈkacHˌwāt; ˈkecH-/ ▸*n.* [usu. as *adj.*] *chiefly historical* unrestricted weight in a wrestling match or other sporting contest: *a catchweight contest.*

catch·word /ˈkacHˌwərd; ˈkecH-/ ▸*n.* **1** a briefly popular or fashionable word or phrase used to encapsulate a particular concept: *"motivation" is a great catchword.* **2** a word printed or placed so as to attract attention. ■ *chiefly historical Printing* the first word of a page given at the foot of the previous one.

catch·y /ˈkacHē; ˈkecHē/ ▸*adj.* (**catch·i·er**, **catch·i·est**) (of a tune or phrase) instantly appealing and memorable: *a catchy recruiting slogan.* **—catch·i·ly** /ˈkacHəlē; ˈkecH-/ *adv.* **—catch·i·ness** *n.*

cate /kāt/ ▸*n.* (usu. **cates**) *archaic* a choice food; a delicacy. ▷late Middle English (in the sense 'selling, a bargain'): from obsolete *acate* 'purchasing, things purchased,' from Old French *acat*, *achat*, from *acater*, *achater* 'buy,' based on Latin *captare* 'seize,' from *capere* 'take.'

cat·e·che·sis /ˌkatəˈkēsis/ ▸*n.* religious instruction given to a person in preparation for Christian baptism or confirmation, typically using a catechism. ▷mid 18th cent.: via ecclesiastical Latin from Greek *katēkhēsis* 'oral instruction.'

cat·e·chet·i·cal /ˌkatəˈketikəl/ ▸*adj.* of or relating to religious instruction given to a person in preparation for Christian baptism or confirmation. ■ of or relating to religious teaching by means of questions and answers. ▷early 17th cent.: from ecclesiastical Greek *katēkhētikos*, from *katēkhētēs* 'catechist,' from *katēkhein* 'instruct orally' (see CATECHIZE). **—cat·e·chet·ic** *adj.* **—cat·e·chet·i·cal·ly** /-ik(ə)lē/ *adv.*

cat·e·chet·ics /ˌkatəˈketiks/ ▸*plural n.* [treated as *sing.*] the branch of theology that deals with the instruction given to Christians before baptism or confirmation. ■ religious teaching in general, typically that given to children in the Roman Catholic Church.

cat·e·chin /ˈkatəˌkin/ ▸*n. Chemistry* a crystalline compound that is the major constituent of catechu. • A phenol; chem. formula: $C_{15}H_{14}O_6$; several isomers. ▷mid 19th cent.: from CATECHU + -IN[1].

cat·e·chism /ˈkatəˌkizəm/ ▸*n.* a summary of the principles of Christian religion in the form of questions and answers, used for the instruction of Christians. ■ a series of fixed questions, answers, or precepts used for instruction in other situations. ▷early 16th cent.: from ecclesiastical Latin *catechismus*, from ecclesiastical Greek, from *katēkhizein* (see CATECHIZE). **—cat·e·chis·mal** /ˌkatəˈkizməl/ *adj.*

cat·e·chist /ˈkatəkist/ ▸*n.* a teacher of the principles of Christian religion, esp. one using a catechism. ▷mid 16th cent.: via ecclesiastical Latin from ecclesiastical Greek *katēkhistēs*, from *katēkhein* 'instruct orally.'

cat·e·chize /ˈkatəˌkīz/ ▸*v.* [*trans.*] instruct (someone) in the principles of Christian religion by means of question and answer, typically by using a catechism. ■ *figurative* put questions to or interrogate (someone). ▷late Middle English: via late Latin from ecclesiastical Greek *katēkhizein*, from *katēkhein* 'instruct orally, make hear.' **—cat·e·chiz·er** *n.*

cat·e·chol /ˈkatəˌkôl; -ˌkōl/ ▸*n. Chemistry* a crystalline compound obtained by distilling catechu.

• Alternative name: **benzene-1,2-diol**; chem. formula: $C_6H_4(OH)_2$. ▷late 19th cent.: from CATECHU + -OL.

cat·e·chol·a·mine /katəˈkōlə,mēn; -ˈkôlə-/ ▸n. *Biochemistry* any of a class of aromatic amines that includes a number of neurotransmitters such as epinephrine and dopamine.

cat·e·chu /ˈkatə,CHōō; -,SHōō/ (also **ca·chou**) ▸n. a vegetable extract containing tannin, esp. one (also called CUTCH) obtained from the heartwood of an Indian acacia tree, used chiefly for tanning and dyeing. • The chief source of this is *Acacia catechu*, family Leguminosae. ▷late 17th cent.: modern Latin, from Malay *kacu*. Compare with CACHOU.

cat·e·chu·men /,katəˈkyōōmən/ ▸n. a Christian convert under instruction before baptism. ■ a young Christian preparing for confirmation. ▷late Middle English: via ecclesiastical Latin from Greek *katēkhoumenos* 'being instructed,' present participle of *katēkhein* 'instruct orally' (see CATECHIZE).

C

cat·e·go·ri·cal /,katəˈgôrikəl/ ▸adj. unambiguously explicit and direct: *a categorical assurance.* ▷late 16th cent.: from late Latin *categoricus* (from Greek *katēgorikos*, from *katēgoria* 'statement': see CATEGORY) + -AL. —**cat·e·gor·ic** *adj.* —**cat·e·gor·i·cal·ly** /-ik(ə)lē/ *adv.*

cat·e·go·ri·cal im·per·a·tive ▸n. *Philosophy* (in Kantian ethics) an unconditional moral obligation that is binding in all circumstances and is not dependent on a person's inclination or purpose.

cat·e·go·rize /ˈkatəgə,rīz/ ▸v. [*trans.*] (often **be categorized**) place in a particular class or group: *odors have been categorized into only seven basic groups.* —**cat·e·go·ri·za·tion** /,katəgərəˈzāSHən/ *n.*

cat·e·go·ry /ˈkatə,gôrē/ ▸n. (*pl.* **-ries**) **1** a class or division of people or things regarded as having particular shared characteristics: *five categories of intelligence.* **2** *Philosophy* one of a possibly exhaustive set of classes among which all things might be distributed. ■ one of the a priori conceptions applied by the mind to sense impressions. ■ a relatively fundamental philosophical concept. ▷late Middle English (sense 2): from French *catégorie* or late Latin *categoria*, from Greek *katēgoria* 'statement, accusation,' from *katēgoros* 'accuser.' —**cat·e·go·ri·al** /,katəˈgôrēəl/ *adj.*

cat·e·go·ry kill·er ▸n. a large store, typically one of a chain, that specializes in a particular type of discounted merchandise and becomes the dominant retailer in that category.

cat·e·go·ry mis·take ▸n. *Logic* the error of assigning to something a quality or action that can properly be assigned to things only of another category, for example, treating abstract concepts as though they had a physical location.

ca·te·na /kəˈtēnə/ ▸n. (*pl.* **-nae** /-nē; -,nī/ or **-nas**) *technical* a connected series or chain. ■ a connected series of texts written by early Christian theologians. ▷mid 17th cent.: from Latin, 'chain,' originally in *catena patrum* 'chain of the (Church) Fathers.'

cat·e·nar·y /ˈkatə,nerē; ˈkatn,erē/ ▸n. (*pl.* **-nar·ies**) a curve formed by a wire, rope, or chain hanging freely from two points that are on the same horizontal level. ■ a wire, rope, or chain forming such a curve.
▸adj. [*attrib.*] having the form of, involving, or denoting a curve of this type. ▷mid 18th cent.: from Latin *catenarius* 'relating to a chain,' from *catena* 'chain.'

cat·e·nat·ed /ˈkatə,nātid; ˈkatn,ātid/ ▸adj. *technical* connected in a chain or series: *catenated molecules.* ▷late 19th cent.: past participle of the rare verb *catenate*, from Latin *catenat-* 'chained, fettered,' from the verb *catenare*, from *catena* 'chain.' —**cat·e·na·tion** /,katəˈnāSHən; ,katnˈāSHən/ *n.*

cat·e·na·tive /ˈkatə,nātiv; ˈkatn,ātiv/ *Grammar* ▸adj. denoting a verb that governs a nonfinite form of another verb, for example, *like* in *I like swimming.*
▸n. a catenative verb. ▷late 20th cent.: from Latin *catena* 'chain' + -ATIVE.

cat·e·noid /ˈkatə,noid; ˈkatn,oid/ ▸n. *Geometry* the surface generated by rotating a catenary about its axis of symmetry. ▷late 19th cent.: from Latin *catena* 'chain' + -OID.

ca·ter /ˈkātər/ ▸v. [*trans.*] provide (food and drink), typically at social events and in a professional capacity: *he catered a lunch for 20 people* | [as *adj.*] (**catered**) *planning another catered affair.* ■ [*intrans.*] (**cater for**) *chiefly Brit.* provide with food and drink, in this way: *my mother helped to cater for the party.* ■ (**cater to**) provide with what is needed or required: *the school caters to children with learning difficulties.* ■ (**cater to**) try to satisfy (a particular need or demand): *he catered to her every whim.* ▷late 16th cent.: from obsolete *cater* 'caterer,' from Old French *acateor* 'buyer,' from *acater* 'buy' (see CATE). —**ca·ter·er** *n.*

cat·er·an /ˈkatərən/ ▸n. *historical* a warrior or raider from the Scottish Highlands. ▷Middle English (originally in the plural or as a collective singular denoting the peasantry as fighters): from Scottish Gaelic *ceathairne* 'peasantry.'

cat·er-cor·nered /ˈkatē ,kôrnərd; ˈkatər/ (also **cat·er-cor·ner** or **cat·ty-cor·nered** or **kit·ty-cor·ner**) ▸adj. & adv. situated diagonally opposite someone or something: [as *adj.*] *a restaurant **cater-cornered from** the movie theater* | [as *adv.*] *motorcyclists cut **cater-cornered across** his yard.* ▷mid 19th cent.: from dialect *cater* 'diagonally,' from *cater* denoting the four on dice, from French *quatre* 'four,' from Latin *quattuor.*

cat·er·pil·lar /ˈkatə(r),pilər/ ▸n. **1** the larva of a butterfly or moth, having a segmented wormlike body with three pairs of true legs and several pairs of leglike appendages. Caterpillars may be hairy, have warning coloration, or be colored to resemble their surroundings. ■ (in general use) any similar larva of various insects, esp. sawflies. **2** (also **caterpillar track** or **tread**) *trademark* an articulated steel band passing around the wheels of a vehicle for travel on rough ground. ■ a vehicle with such tracks. ▷late Middle English: perhaps from a variant of Old French *chatepelose*, literally 'hairy cat,' influenced by obsolete *piller* 'ravager.' The association with "cat"is found in other languages, e.g., Swiss German *Teufelskatz* (literally 'devil's cat'), Lombard *gatta* (literally 'cat'). Compare with French *chaton*, English CATKIN, resembling hairy caterpillars.

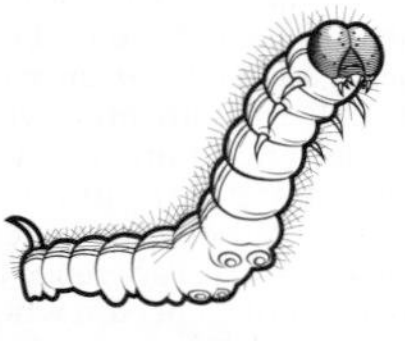
caterpillar 1

cat·er·waul /ˈkatər,wôl/ ▸v. [*intrans.*] [often as *n.*] (**caterwauling**) (of a cat) make a shrill howling or wailing noise: *the caterwauling of a pair of bobcats* | [as *adj.*] (**caterwauling**) *figurative a caterwauling guitar.*
▸n. a shrill howling or wailing noise. ▷late Middle English: from CAT[1] + imitative WAUL.

cat·fish /ˈkat,fiSH/ ▸n. (*pl.* same or **-fish·es**) **1** a freshwater or marine fish with whiskerlike barbels around the mouth, typically bottom-dwelling. • Order Siluriformes: many families, including the Eurasian family Siluridae and the large North American family Ictaluridae. **2** another term for WOLFFISH.

cat·gut /ˈkat,gət/ ▸n. a material used for the strings of musical instruments and for surgical sutures, made of the dried twisted intestines of sheep or horses, but not cats. ▷late 16th cent.: the association with CAT[1] remains unexplained.

Cath. ▸abbr. ■ Cathedral. ■ Catholic.

Cath·ar /ˈkaTH,är/ ▸n. (*pl.* **Cath·ars** or **Cath·a·ri** /ˈkaTHə,rī; -,rē/) a member of a heretical medieval Christian sect which professed a form of Manichaean dualism and sought to achieve great spiritual purity. ▷mid 17th cent.: from medieval Latin *Cathari* (plural), from Greek *katharoi* 'the pure.' —**Cath·a·rism** /ˈkaTHərizəm/ *n.* —**Cath·a·rist** /ˈkaTHərist/ *n.* & *adj.*

ca·thar·sis /kəˈTHärsis/ ▸n. **1** the process of releasing, and thereby providing relief from, strong or repressed emotions. **2** *rare Medicine* purgation. ▷early 19th cent. (sense 2): from Greek *katharsis*, from *kathairein* 'cleanse,' from *katharos* 'pure.' The notion of "release" through drama (sense 1) derives from Aristotle's *Poetics.*

ca·thar·tic /kəˈTHärtik/ ▸adj. **1** providing psychological relief through the open expression of strong emotions; causing catharsis: *crying is a cathartic release.* **2** *Medicine* (chiefly of a drug) purgative.
▸n. *Medicine* a purgative drug. ▷early 17th cent. (in medical use): via late Latin from Greek *kathartikos*, from *katharsis* 'cleansing' (see CATHARSIS). —**ca·thar·ti·cal·ly** *adv.*

Ca·thay /kəˈTHā; ka-/ the name by which China was known to medieval Europe. Also called KHITAI. ▷from medieval Latin *Cataya, Cathaya*, from Turkic *Khitāy.*

cat·head /ˈkat,hed/ ▸n. a horizontal beam extending from each side of a ship's bow, used for raising and carrying an anchor.

ca·thec·tic /kəˈTHektik/ ▸adj. *Psychoanalysis* of or relating to cathexis. ▷1920s: from Greek *kathektikos* 'capable of holding.'

ca·the·dra /kəˈTHēdrə/ ▸n. (*pl.* **-drae** /-drē/) **1** a seat, specifically the chair of a bishop in his church. **2** a bishop's see. See also EX CATHEDRA.

ca·the·dral /kəˈTHēdrəl/ ▸n. the principal church of a diocese, with which the bishop is officially associated: [in *names*] *St. Paul's Cathedral.* ▷Middle English (as an adjective, the noun being short for *cathedral church* 'the church that contains the bishop's throne'): from late Latin *cathedralis*, from Latin *cathedra* 'seat,' from Greek *kathedra.*

ca·the·dral ceil·ing ▸n. a pointed or slanting ceiling of a room that rises through more than one floor.

Ca·the·dral Cit·y a city in southern California, southeast of Palm Springs; pop. 30,085.

Cath·er /ˈkaTHər/, Willa (Sibert) (1876–1974), U.S. novelist and short-story writer. Her home state of Nebraska provides the setting for some of her best writing. Notable works: *O Pioneers!* (1913), *My Antonia* (1918), and *Death Comes for the Archbishop* (1927).

Cath·er·ine, St. (died *c.*307), early Christian martyr; known as **St. Catherine of Alexandria**. According to tradition, she opposed the persecution of Christians under the emperor Maxentius and refused to recant or to marry the emperor. Feast day, November 25.

Cath·er·ine II /ˈkaTH(ə)rən/ (1729–96), empress of Russia; reigned 1762–96; known as **Catherine the Great**. She became empress after her husband, Peter III, was deposed. She formed alliances with Prussia and Austria and made territorial advances at the expense of the Turks and Tartars.

Cath·er·ine de Mé·di·cis /ˈkaTH(ə)rən də ˈmedəCHē/ (1519–89), queen of France; wife of Henry II; Italian name **Catherine de' Medici**. She ruled as regent 1560–74 during the minority reigns of her three sons: Francis II, Charles IX, and Henry III.

Cath·er·ine of Ar·a·gon (1485–1536), first wife of Henry VIII; youngest daughter of Ferdinand and Isabella of Castile; mother of Mary I. Henry's wish to annul his marriage to Catherine (due to her failure to produce a male heir) led eventually to England's break with the Roman Catholic Church.

Cath·er·ine wheel ▸n. a firework in the form of a flat coil that spins when fixed to something solid and lit. ■ *Heraldry* a wheel with curved spikes projecting around the circumference. ▷late 16th cent. (as a heraldic term): named after St. *Catherine* (see CATHERINE, ST.), with reference to her martyrdom.

cath·e·ter /ˈkaTHətər/ ▸n. *Medicine* a flexible tube inserted through a narrow opening into a body cavity, particularly the bladder, for removing fluid. ▷early 17th cent.: from late Latin, from Greek *kathetēr*, from *kathienai* 'send or let down.'

cath·e·ter·ize /ˈkaTHitə,rīz/ ▸v. [*trans.*] *Medicine* insert a catheter into (a patient or body cavity). —**cath·e·ter·i·za·tion** /,kaTHitərəˈzāSHən/ *n.*

ca·thex·is /kəˈTHeksis/ ▸n. *Psychoanalysis* the concentration of mental energy on one particular person, idea, or object (esp. to an unhealthy degree). ▷1920s: from Greek *kathexis* 'retention,' translating German *Libidobesetzung*, coined by Freud.

cath·ode /ˈkaTH,ōd/ ▸n. the negatively charged electrode by which electrons enter an electrical device. The opposite of ANODE. ■ the positively charged electrode of an electrical device, such as a primary cell, that supplies current. ▷mid 19th cent.: from Greek *kathodos* 'way down,' from *kata-* 'down'+ *hodos* 'way.' —**cath·o·dal** /ˈkaTH,ōdl/ *adj.* —**ca·thod·ic** /kaˈTHädik/ *adj.*

cath·ode ray ▸n. a beam of electrons emitted from the cathode of a high-vacuum tube.

cath·ode-ray tube (abbr.: **CRT**) (also **cath·ode ray tube**) ▸n. a high-vacuum tube in which cathode rays produce a luminous image on a fluorescent screen, used chiefly in televisions and computer terminals.

cath·o·lic /ˈkaTH(ə)lik/ ▸adj. **1** (esp. of a person's tastes) including a wide variety of things; all-embracing. See note at UNIVERSAL. **2** (**Catholic**) of the Roman Catholic faith. ■ of or including all Christians. ■ of or relating to the historic doctrine and practice of the Western Church.
▸n. (**Catholic**) a member of the Roman Catholic Church. ▷late Middle English (sense 2): from Old French *catholique* or late Latin *catholicus*, from Greek *katholikos* 'universal,' from *kata* 'with respect to' + *holos* 'whole.' —**cath·o·lic·i·ty** /,kaTH(ə)ˈlisətē/ *n.* —**ca·thol·ic·ly** *adv.*

Cath·o·lic Church ▸n. short for ROMAN CATHOLIC CHURCH.

Ca·thol·i·cism /kəˈTHälə,sizəm/ ▸n. the faith, practice, and church order of the Roman Catholic Church. ■ adherence to the forms of Christian doctrine and practice which are generally regarded as Catholic rather than Protestant or Eastern Orthodox.

Ca·thol·i·cize /kəˈTHälə,sīz/ ▸*v.* [*trans.*] make Roman Catholic; convert to Catholicism.

Cath·o·lic League see **HOLY LEAGUE**.

ca·thol·i·con /kəˈTHäli,kän; -ikən/ ▸*n.* **1** a comprehensive treatise. **2** a universal remedy; a panacea.

Ca·thol·i·cos /kəˈTHäləkəs; -,käs/ ▸*n.* (*pl.* **Ca·thol·i·cos·es** /kə,THäləˈkō,sēz/ or **Ca·thol·i·coi** /kəˈTHälə,koi/) the Patriarch of the Armenian or the Nestorian Church. ▷early 17th cent.: from medieval Greek *katholikos* 'universal' (see **CATHOLIC**).

cat·house /ˈkat,hous/ ▸*n. informal* a brothel.

cat·i·on /ˈkat,īən; -,ī,än/ ▸*n. Chemistry* a positively charged ion, i.e., one that would be attracted to the cathode in electrolysis. The opposite of **ANION**. ▷mid 19th cent.: from **CATA-** 'alongside' or from **CATHODE**, + **ION**. —**cat·i·on·ic** /,katīˈänik/ *adj.*

cat·kin /ˈkatkin/ ▸*n.* a flowering spike of trees such as willow and hazel. Catkins are typically downy, pendulous, composed of flowers of a single sex, and wind-pollinated. ▷late 16th cent.: from obsolete Dutch *katteken* 'kitten.'

cat·like /ˈkat,līk/ ▸*adj.* resembling a cat in appearance, action, or character, esp. by moving gracefully or stealthily.

cat·lin·ite /ˈkatlə,nīt/ ▸*n.* a red clay of the Upper Missouri region, the sacred pipestone of the American Indians. ▷mid 19th cent.: from the name of George *Catlin* (1796–1872), American artist, + **-ITE**[1].

cat lit·ter ▸*n.* see **LITTER** (sense 3).

cat·mint /ˈkat,mint/ ▸*n.* another term for **CATNIP**.

cat·nap /ˈkat,nap/ ▸*n.* a short, light sleep; a doze. ▸*v.* (**-napped**, **-nap·ping**) [*intrans.*] have such a sleep.

cat·nip /ˈkat,nip/ ▸*n.* a plant of the mint family, with downy leaves, purple-spotted white flowers, and a pungent smell attractive to cats. Also called **CATMINT**. • Genus *Nepeta*, family Labiatae: several species, including the Eurasian *N. cataria*. ▷late 18th cent. (originally U.S.): from **CAT**[1] + *nip*, variant of dialect *nep*, *nept*, from medieval Latin *nepta*, from Latin *nepeta* 'catmint.'

Ca·to /ˈkātō/, Marcus Porcius (234–149 BC), Roman statesman, orator, and writer; known as **Cato the Elder** or **Cato the Censor**. As censor, he initiated a vigorous program of reform and attempted to stem the growing influence of Greek culture.

cat-o'-nine-tails ▸*n. historical* a rope whip with nine knotted cords, formerly used (esp. at sea) to flog offenders.

Ca·tons·ville /ˈkātnz,vil/ a community in central Maryland, southwest of Baltimore; pop. 35,233.

ca·top·tric /kəˈtäptrik/ ▸*adj. Physics* of or relating to a mirror, a reflector, or reflection. ▷early 18th cent.: from Greek *katoptrikos*, from *katoptron* 'mirror.'

ca·top·trics /kəˈtäptriks/ ▸*plural n.* [treated as *sing.*] *Physics* the branch of optics that deals with reflection. ▷mid 16th cent. (originally *catoptric*): from Greek *katoptrikos* 'reflecting,' from *katoptron* 'mirror.'

cat rig ▸*n.* the rig of a catboat with the single mast placed far forward.

Ca·tron /ˈkātrən/, John (c.1786–1865), U.S. Supreme Court associate justice 1837–65. Appointed to the Court by President Jackson, he was an advocate of states' rights.

CAT scan ▸*n* an X-ray image made using computerized axial tomography. —**CAT scan·ner** *n.*

cat's cra·dle ▸*n.* a child's game in which a loop of string is put around and between the fingers and complex patterns are formed. ■ [in *sing.*] a complex pattern made of string in such a game.

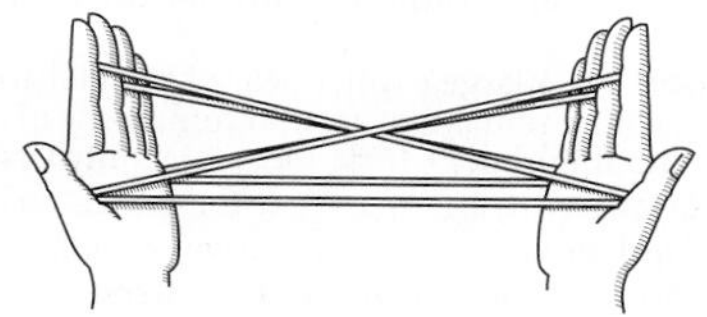

cat's cradle

cat scratch fe·ver (also **cat scratch disease**) ▸*n.* an infectious disease occurring after a scratch by a cat's claw, a splinter, or a thorn. Symptoms include mild fever and inflammation of the injury site and of the lymph glands.

cat's ear (also **cat's ears**) ▸*n.* a plant that resembles the dandelion, with yellow flowers and rosettes of leaves. • Genus *Hypochaeris*, family Compositae: several species, in particular the Old World *H. radicata*, naturalized in North America.

cat's-eye ▸*n.* a semiprecious stone, esp. chalcedony or chrysoberyl, with a chatoyant luster.

cat shark ▸*n.* a small bottom-dwelling shark that has catlike eyes and small dorsal fins set well back. It is typically strikingly marked and lives in warmer waters. • *Apristurus* and other genera, family Scyliorhinidae: several species, including the **brown cat shark** (*A. brunneus*).

Cats·kill Moun·tains /ˈkat,skil/ (also **the Cats·kills**) a range of mountains in the state of New York, part of the Appalachian system.

cat's me·ow ▸*n.* (**the cat's meow**) another term for **THE CAT'S PAJAMAS** (see **CAT'S PAJAMAS**).

cat's pa·ja·mas ▸*n.* (**the cat's pajamas**) *informal, dated* an excellent person or thing: *this car is the cat's pajamas.*

cat's-paw ▸*n.* a person who is used by another, typically to carry out an unpleasant or dangerous task.

cat·suit /ˈkat,so͞ot/ ▸*n.* a woman's jumpsuit, typically close-fitting and covering the body from the neck to the feet.

cat·sup /ˈkeCHəp; ˈkaCHəp; ˈkatsəp/ ▸*n.* variant spelling of **KETCHUP**.

cat's whisk·er ▸*n.* a fine adjustable wire in a crystal radio receiver.
▸*PHRASE* □ **the cat's whiskers** *informal* another term for **THE CAT'S PAJAMAS** (see **CAT'S PAJAMAS**).

Catt /kat/, Carrie Clinton Chapman Lane (1859–1947), U.S. suffragist. As president of the National American Woman Suffrage Association 1900–04, 1915–47 and of the International Woman Suffrage Alliance 1904–23, she was instrumental in the adoption of the 19th amendment to the Constitution in 1920.

cat·tail /ˈkat,tāl/ ▸*n.* a tall, reedlike marsh plant with straplike leaves and a dark brown, velvety cylindrical head of numerous tiny flowers. Also called **REED MACE**, **BULRUSH**. • Genus *Typha*, family Typhaceae: several species, in particular the **common cattail** (*T. latifolia*).

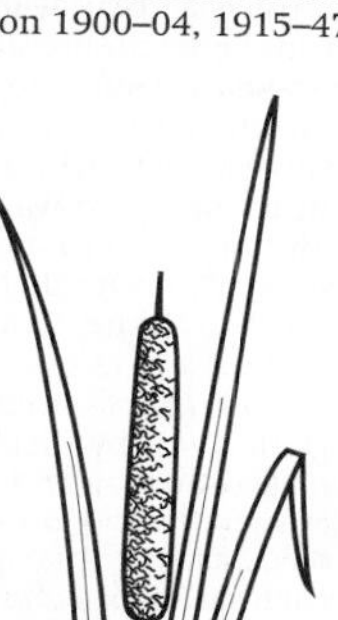

common cattail

cat·te·ry /ˈkatərē/ ▸*n.* (*pl.* **-ries**) a boarding or breeding establishment for cats.

cat·tish /ˈkatiSH/ ▸*adj.* another term for **CATTY**. —**cat·tish·ly** *adv.* —**cat·tish·ness** *n.*

cat·tle /ˈkatl/ ▸*plural n.* **1** large ruminant animals with horns and cloven hoofs, domesticated for meat or milk, or as beasts of burden; cows. • *Bos taurus* (including the zebu, *B. indicus*), family Bovidae; descended from the extinct aurochs. **2** similar animals of a group related to domestic cattle, including yak, bison, and buffalo. • Tribe Bovini, family Bovidae (the **cattle family**): four genera, in particular *Bos*. The cattle family also includes the sheep, goats, goat-antelopes, and antelopes. ▷Middle English (also denoting personal property or wealth): from Anglo-Norman French *catel*, variant of Old French *chatel* (see **CHATTEL**).

cat·tle call ▸*n. informal* an open audition for parts in a play, movie, or other production.

cat·tle e·gret ▸*n.* a small white heron with long buff feathers on the head, back, and chest in the breeding season, and normally feeding around grazing cattle and game herds. It is native to southern Eurasia and Africa, and has colonized North and South America and Australasia in the 20th century. • *Bubulcus* (or **Ardeola**) *ibis*, family Ardeidae.

cat·tle guard ▸*n.* a metal grid covering a ditch, allowing vehicles and pedestrians to pass over but not cattle and other animals.

cat·tle·man /ˈkatlmən; -,man/ ▸*n.* (*pl.* **-men**) a person who tends or rears cattle.

catt·ley·a /ˈkatlēə; katˈlāə; katˈlēə/ ▸*n.* a tropical American orchid with brightly colored showy flowers and thick leaves, typically growing as an epiphyte. It is a popular greenhouse plant, with many hybrids. • Genus *Cattleya*, family Orchidaceae. ▷early 19th cent.: modern Latin, named after William *Cattley* (died 1832), English patron of botany.

cat-train ▸*n. Canadian* a crawler tractor pulling a train of sleighs across snow or ice. ▷*cat* from **CATERPILLAR**.

cat·ty /ˈkatē/ ▸*adj.* (**cat·ti·er**, **cat·ti·est**) **1** deliberately hurtful in one's remarks; spiteful. **2** of or relating to cats; catlike. —**cat·ti·ly** /ˈkatl-ē/ *adv.* —**cat·ti·ness** *n.*

cat·ty-cor·nered ▸*adj.* another term for **CATER-CORNERED**.

Ca·tul·lus /kəˈtələs/, Gaius Valerius (*c.*84–*c.*54 BC), Roman poet, known for his love poems.

CATV ▸*abbr.* community antenna television (i.e., cable television).

cat·walk /ˈkat,wôk/ ▸*n.* a narrow walkway or platform extending into an auditorium, esp. in an industrial installation, along which models walk to display clothes in fashion shows. ■ a narrow platform or stage.

Cau·ca Riv·er /ˈkoukə/ a river in western Colombia that flows north for 800 miles (1,300 km) from the Andes to the Magdalena River.

Cau·ca·sian /kôˈkāZHən/ ▸*adj.* **1** *often offensive* of or relating to one of the traditional divisions of humankind, covering a broad group of peoples from Europe, western Asia, and parts of India and North Africa. [so named because the German physiologist Blumenbach believed that it originated in the Caucasus region of southeastern Europe.] ■ white-skinned; of European origin. **2** of or relating to the Caucasus. **3** of or relating to a group of languages spoken in the region of the Caucasus, of which thirty-eight are known, many not committed to writing. The most widely spoken is Georgian, of the small **South Caucasian** family, not related to the three **North Caucasian** families.
▸*n. often offensive* a Caucasian person. ■ a white person; a person of European origin.

USAGE In the racial classification as developed by anthropologists in the 19th century, **Caucasian** (or **Caucasoid**) included peoples whose skin color ranged from light (in northern Europe) to dark (in parts of North Africa and India). Although the classification is outdated and the categories are now not generally accepted as scientific (see **usage** at **AUSTRALOID** and **MONGOLOID**), the term **Caucasian** has acquired a more restricted meaning. It is now used, esp. in the U.S., as a synonym for 'white or of European origin,' as in the following citation: *the police are looking for a **Caucasian** male in his forties.*

Cau·ca·soid /ˈkôkə,soid/ ▸*adj. sometimes offensive* of or relating to the Caucasian division of humankind.

USAGE See usage at **CAUCASIAN**.

Cau·ca·sus /ˈkôkəsəs/ (also **Cau·ca·sia** /kôˈkāZHə/) a mountainous region in southeastern Europe that lies between the Black and Caspian seas in Georgia, Armenia, Azerbaijan, and southeastern Russia.

Cau·chy /kôˈSHē/, Augustin Louis, Baron (1789–1857), French mathematician. He transformed the theory of complex functions, founded the modern theory of elasticity, and contributed substantially to the founding of group theory and analysis.

cau·cus /ˈkôkəs/ ▸*n.* (*pl.* **-cus·es**) **1** a meeting of the members of a legislative body who are members of a particular political party, to select candidates or decide policy. ■ the members of such a body. **2** a group of people with shared concerns within a political party or larger organization. ■ a meeting of such a group.
▸*v.* (**-cused**, **-cus·ing**) [*intrans.*] hold or form such a group or meeting. ▷mid 18th cent. (originally U.S.): perhaps from Algonquian *cau'-cau'-as'u* 'adviser.'

cau·dal /ˈkôdl/ ▸*adj.* of or like a tail. ■ at or near the tail or the posterior part of the body. ▷mid 17th cent.: from modern Latin *caudalis*, from Latin *cauda* 'tail.' —**cau·dal·ly** *adv.*

cau·dal fin ▸*n. Zoology* another term for **TAIL FIN**.

Cau·da·ta /kôˈdātə; kouˈdātə/ *Zoology* another term for **URODELA**. ▷modern Latin (plural), from Latin *cauda* 'tail.'

cau·date /ˈkô,dāt/ ▸*adj.* **1** *Anatomy* relating to or denoting the caudate nucleus. **2** *Zoology* (of an animal) having a tail.
▸*n.* short for **CAUDATE NUCLEUS**. ▷early 17th cent.: from medieval Latin *caudatus*, from *cauda* 'tail.'

cau·date nu·cle·us ▸*n. Anatomy* the upper of the two gray nuclei of the corpus striatum in the cerebrum of the brain.

cau·dex /ˈkô,deks/ ▸*n.* (*pl.* **-di·ces** /-də,sēz/ or **-dex·es**) *Botany* the axis of a woody plant, esp. a palm or tree fern, comprising the stem and root. ▷late 18th cent.: from Latin, earlier form of CODEX.

cau·dil·lo /kô'dēlyō; -'dēō; kou'dē,(y)ō/ ▸*n.* (*pl.* **-los**) (in Spanish-speaking regions) a military or political leader. ▷Spanish, from late Latin *capitellum*, diminutive of *caput* 'head.' The title *El Caudillo* 'the leader' was assumed by General Franco of Spain in 1938.

caught /kôt/ ▸ past and past participle of CATCH.

caul /kôl/ ▸*n.* **1** the amniotic membrane enclosing a fetus. ■ part of this membrane occasionally found on a child's head at birth, thought to bring good luck. **2** *historical* a woman's close-fitting indoor headdress or hairnet. **3** *Anatomy* the omentum. ▷Middle English: perhaps from Old French *cale* 'head covering,' but recorded earlier.

caul·dron /'kôldrən/ (also **cal·dron**) ▸*n.* a large metal pot with a lid and handle, used for cooking over an open fire. ■ *figurative* a situation characterized by instability and strong emotions: *a cauldron of repressed anger.* ▷Middle English: from Anglo-Norman French *caudron*, based on Latin *caldarium, calidarium* 'cooking pot,' from *calidus* 'hot.'

cau·li·flow·er /'kôli,flou(-ə)r; 'käli-/ ▸*n.* a cabbage of a variety that bears a large immature flowerhead of small creamy-white flower buds. ■ the flowerhead of this plant eaten as a vegetable. ▷late 16th cent.: from obsolete French *chou fleuri* 'flowered cabbage,' probably from Italian *cavolfiore* or modern Latin *cauliflora*. The original English form *colieflorie* or *cole-flory* had its first element influenced by COLE; the second element was influenced by FLOWER during the 17th cent.

cauliflower

cau·li·flow·er ear ▸*n.* an ear that has become thickened or deformed as a result of repeated blows, typically in boxing.

cau·li·flow·er fun·gus (also **cauliflower mushroom**) ▸*n.* an edible fungus that forms a distinctive fruiting body with a yellowish lobed surface, growing on wood and other plant debris in both Eurasia and North America. • Genus *Sparassis* and family Sparassidaceae, class Basidiomycetes: several species, in particular *S. crispa*.

caulk /kôk/ (also **calk**) ▸*n.* (also **caulk·ing**) a waterproof filler and sealant, used in building work and repairs.
▸*v.* [*trans.*] seal (a gap or seam) with such a substance. ■ stop up (the seams of a boat) with oakum and waterproofing material, or by driving plate-junctions together; make (a boat) watertight by this method. ▷late Middle English (in the sense 'copulate,' used of birds): from Old Northern French *cauquer, caukier*, variant of *cauchier* 'tread, press with force,' from Latin *calcare* 'tread,' from *calx, calc-* 'heel.' **—caulk·er** *n.*

caus·al /'kôzəl/ ▸*adj.* of, relating to, or acting as a cause: *the causal factors associated with illness.* ■ *Grammar & Logic* expressing or indicating a cause: *a causal conjunction.* ▷late Middle English (as a noun denoting a causal conjunction or particle): from late Latin *causalis*, from Latin *causa* 'cause.' **—caus·al·ly** *adv.*

cau·sal·gi·a /kô'zalj(ē)ə; -'sal-/ ▸*n.* severe burning pain in a limb caused by injury to a peripheral nerve. ▷mid 19th cent.: from Greek *kausos* 'heat, fever' + -ALGIA.

cau·sal·i·ty /kô'zalətē/ ▸*n.* **1** the relationship between cause and effect. **2** the principle that everything has a cause. ▷late 15th cent.: from French *causalité* or medieval Latin *causalitas*, from Latin *causa* 'cause.'

cau·sa·tion /kô'zāsнən/ ▸*n.* the action of causing something: *investigating the role of nitrate in the causation of cancer.* ■ the relationship between cause and effect; causality. ▷late 15th cent.: from Latin *causatio(n-)* 'pretext' (in medieval Latin 'the action of causing'), from *causare* 'to cause.'

caus·a·tive /'kôzətiv/ ▸*adj.* acting as a cause: *a causative factor.* ■ *Grammar* expressing causation: *a causative verb.*
▸*n.* a causative verb. ▷late Middle English: from Old French *causatif, -ive*, or late Latin *causativus*, from *causare* 'to cause.'

cause /kôz/ ▸*n.* **1** a person or thing that gives rise to an action, phenomenon, or condition: *the cause of the accident is not clear.* ■ reasonable grounds for doing, thinking, or feeling something: *Faye's condition had given no **cause for concern** | [with infinitive] the government had good cause to avoid war | class size is a cause for complaint in some schools.* **2** a principle, aim, or movement that, because of a deep commitment, one is prepared to defend or advocate: *she devoted her life to the cause of deaf people.* ■ [with *adj.*] something deserving of one's support, typically a charity: *I'm raising money for **a good cause**.* **3** a matter to be resolved in a court of law. ■ an individual's case offered at law.
▸*v.* [*trans.*] make (something) happen: *this disease can cause blindness | [trans.] we have no idea what has happened to cause people to stay away.* ▷Middle English: from Old French, from Latin *causa* (noun), *causare* (verb). **—cause·less** *adj.* **—caus·er** *n.*
▸*PHRASES* □ **cause and effect** the principle of causation. ■ the operation or relation of a cause and its effect. □ **cause of action** *Law* a fact or facts that enable a person to bring an action against another. □ **in the cause of** so as to support, promote, or defend something. □ **make common cause** unite in order to achieve a shared aim: *nationalist movements **made common cause with** the reformers.* □ **a rebel without a cause** a person who is dissatisfied with society but does not have a specific aim to fight for. [from the title of a U.S. film, released in 1955.]

'cause /kəz/ ▸*conj. informal* short for BECAUSE.

cause cé·lè·bre /'kôz sə'leb(rə); 'kōz/ ▸*n.* (*pl.* **causes cé·lè·bres** *pronunc.* same) a controversial issue that attracts a great deal of public attention. ▷mid 18th cent.: French, literally 'famous case.'

cau·se·rie /,kōz(ə)'rē/ ▸*n.* (*pl.* **-ries** *pronunc.* same) an informal article or talk, typically one on a literary subject. ▷French, from *causer* 'to talk.'

cause·way /'kôz,wā/ ▸*n.* a raised road or track across low or wet ground. ▷late Middle English: from *causey* (from Anglo-Norman French *causee*, based on Latin *calx* 'lime, limestone' (used for paving roads)) + WAY.

caus·tic /'kôstik/ ▸*adj.* **1** able to burn or corrode organic tissue by chemical action: *a caustic cleaner.* ■ *figurative* sarcastic in a scathing and bitter way: *the players were making caustic comments about the refereeing.* ■ *figurative* (of an expression or sound) expressive of such sarcasm: *a caustic smile.* **2** *Physics* formed by the intersection of reflected or refracted parallel rays from a curved surface.
▸*n.* **1** a caustic substance. **2** *Physics* a caustic surface or curve. ▷late Middle English: via Latin from Greek *kaustikos*, from *kaustos* 'combustible,' from *kaiein* 'to burn.' **—caus·ti·cal·ly** /-ik(ə)lē/ *adv.* **—caus·tic·i·ty** /kô'stisətē/ *n.*

caus·tic pot·ash ▸*n.* another term for POTASSIUM HYDROXIDE.

caus·tic so·da ▸*n.* another term for SODIUM HYDROXIDE.

cau·ter·ize /'kôtə,rīz/ ▸*v.* [*trans.*] *Medicine* burn the skin or flesh of (a wound) with a heated instrument or caustic substance, typically to stop bleeding or prevent the wound from becoming infected. ▷late Middle English: from Old French *cauteriser*, from late Latin *cauterizare*, from Greek *kautēriazein*, from *kautērion* 'branding iron,' from *kaiein* 'to burn.' **—cau·ter·i·za·tion** /,kôtərə'zāsнən/ *n.*

cau·ter·y /'kôtərē/ ▸*n.* (*pl.* **-ter·ies**) *Medicine* an instrument or a caustic substance used for cauterizing. ■ the action of cauterizing something. ▷late Middle English: via Latin from Greek *kautērion* 'branding iron' (see CAUTERIZE).

Cau·then /'kôтнən; 'kä-/, Steve (1960–), U.S. jockey. In 1978, riding Affirmed, he became the youngest jockey to win the Triple Crown. He retired in 1992 with a total of 2,794 career victories. Horse Racing Hall of Fame (1994).

cau·tion /'kôsнən/ ▸*n.* **1** care taken to avoid danger or mistakes: *anyone receiving a suspect package should exercise extreme caution.* ■ warning: *business advisers have sounded a note of caution.* **2** *informal, dated* an amusing or surprising person.
▸*v.* [*reporting verb*] say something as a warning: [with *clause*] *the secretary cautioned that economic uncertainties remained* | [with *direct speech*] *"Be careful now," I cautioned.* ■ [*intrans.*] (**caution against**) warn or advise against (doing something): *advisers have cautioned against tax increases* ▷Middle English (denoting bail or a guarantee): from Latin *caution-*, from *cavere* 'take heed.'

cau·tion·ar·y /'kôsнə,nerē/ ▸*adj.* serving as a warning: *a cautionary tale.*

cau·tious /'kôsнəs/ ▸*adj.* attentive to potential problems or dangers: *a cautious driver.* See note at VIGILANT. ■ (of an action) characterized by such an attitude: *the plan received a cautious welcome.* ▷mid 17th cent.: from CAUTION, on the pattern of pairs such as *ambition, ambitious.* **—cau·tious·ly** *adv.* **—cau·tious·ness** *n.*

Cau·ver·y /'kôvərē/ (also **Ka·ver·i** *pronunc.* same or /'kä-/) a river in southern India that rises in northern Kerala and flows east for 475 miles (765 km) to the Bay of Bengal, south of Pondicherry. It is held sacred by Hindus.

ca·va /'kävə/ ▸*n.* a Spanish sparkling wine made in the same way as champagne. ▷Spanish.

cav·al·cade /,kavəl'kād/ ▸*n.* a formal procession of people walking, on horseback, or riding in vehicles. ▷late 16th cent. (denoting a ride or raid on horseback): from French, from Italian *cavalcata*, from *cavalcare* 'to ride,' based on Latin *caballus* 'horse.'

cav·a·lier /,kavə'li(ə)r/ ▸*n.* **1** (**Cavalier**) *historical* a supporter of King Charles I in the English Civil War. ■ *archaic* or *poetic/literary* a courtly gentleman, esp. one acting as a lady's escort. ■ *archaic* a horseman, esp. a cavalryman. **2** (also **Cavalier King Charles**) a small spaniel of a breed with a moderately long, noncurly, silky coat.
▸*adj.* showing a lack of proper concern; offhand: *Anne was irritated by his cavalier attitude.* ▷mid 16th cent.: from French, from Italian *cavaliere*, based on Latin *caballus* 'horse': Compare with CABALLERO and CHEVALIER. **—cav·a·lier·ly** *adv.*

cav·al·ry /'kavəlrē/ ▸*n.* (*pl.* **-ries**) [usu. treated as *pl.*] *historical* soldiers who fought on horseback. ■ *historical* a branch of an army made up of such soldiers. ■ modern soldiers who fight in armored vehicles. ▷mid 16th cent.: from French *cavallerie*, from Italian *cavalleria*, from *cavallo* 'horse,' from Latin *caballus.* **—cav·al·ry·man** /-mən/ *n.* (*pl.* **-men**) .

cav·al·ry twill ▸*n.* strong woolen twill used typically for making pants and sportswear.

Cav·an /'kavən/ a county in the Republic of Ireland, part of the old province of Ulster.

ca·va·quin·ho /,kävə'kēnyō/ ▸*n.* (*pl.* **-hos**) a small, four-stringed guitar resembling a ukulele, popular in Brazil and Portugal. ▷Portuguese.

cav·a·ti·na /,kavə'tēnə/ ▸*n.* (*pl.* **-ti·ne** /-'tēnā/) *Music* a short operatic aria in simple style without repeated sections. ■ a similar piece of lyrical instrumental music. ▷early 19th cent.: from Italian.

cave /kāv/ ▸*n.* a large underground chamber, typically of natural origin, in a hillside or cliff.
▸*v.* [*intrans.*] **1** explore caves as a sport. **2** short for CAVE IN below.
▸*phrasal v.* □ **cave in** (or **cave something in**) (with reference to a roof or similar structure) subside or collapse or cause something to do this: *the tunnel walls caved in | mudstorms caved the roof in.* ■ *figurative* yield or submit under pressure: *the manager **caved in to** his demands.* ▷Middle English: from Old French, from Latin *cava*, from *cavus* 'hollow' (compare with CAVERN). The usage *cave in* may be from the synonymous dialect expression *calve in*, influenced by obsolete *cave* 'excavate, hollow out.' **—cave·like** /-,līk/ *adj.* **—cav·er** *n.*

ca·ve·at /'kavē,ät; 'käv-/ ▸*n.* a warning or proviso of specific stipulations, conditions, or limitations. ■ *Law* a notice, esp. in a probate, that certain actions may not be taken without informing the person who gave the notice. ▷mid 16th cent.: from Latin, literally 'let a person beware.'

ca·ve·at emp·tor /'emp,tôr/ ▸*n.* the principle that the buyer alone is responsible for checking the quality and suitability of goods before a purchase is made. ▷early 16th cent.: Latin, literally 'let the buyer beware.'

cave bear ▸*n.* a large extinct bear of the Pleistocene epoch, whose remains are found commonly in caves throughout Europe. • *Ursus spelaeus*, family Ursidae.

cave crick·et ▸*n.* another term for CAMEL CRICKET.

cave dwell·er ▸*n.* a caveman or cavewoman.

cave·fish /'kāv,fisн/ ▸*n.* (*pl.* same or **-fish·es**) a small colorless fish that lives only in limestone caves in North America. It has reduced or absent eyes, and the head and body are covered with papillae that are sensitive to vibration. Also called BLINDFISH. • Family Amblyopsidae: four genera, in particular *Amblyopsis* and *Typhlichthys*.

cave-in ▸*n.* a collapse of a roof or similar structure, typically underground: *a mine cave-in.* ■ [in *sing.*] *figurative* an instance of yielding or submitting under pressure: *the government's cave-in to industry pressure.*

cave·man /'kāv,man/ ▸*n.* (*pl.* **-men**) a prehistoric man who lived in caves. ■ a man whose behavior is uncivilized or violent: [as *adj.*] *you can't change my mind by caveman tactics.*

Cav·en·dish /ˈkavəndisʜ/, Henry (1731–1810), English chemist and physicist. He identified hydrogen, studied carbon dioxide, and determined their densities relative to atmospheric air.

cav·en·dish /ˈkavədisʜ/ ▸*n.* tobacco softened, sweetened, and formed into cakes. ▷mid 19th cent.: probably from the surname *Cavendish.*

cave paint·ing ▸*n.* a prehistoric picture on the interior of a cave, often depicting animals.

cav·ern /ˈkavərn/ ▸*n.* a cave, or a chamber in a cave, typically a large one. ■ used in similes and comparisons to refer to a vast, dark space: *the dark cavern of the main performance hall | rouses me from the cavern of sleep.* ▷late Middle English: from Old French *caverne* or from Latin *caverna,* from *cavus* 'hollow.' Compare with **CAVE.**

cav·ern·ous /ˈkavərnəs/ ▸*adj.* like a cavern in size, shape, or atmosphere: *a cavernous warehouse.* ■ *figurative* giving the impression of vast, dark depths: *his cavernous eyes.* ▷late Middle English: from Old French *caverneux* or Latin *cavernosus* (from *caverna* 'cavern'). **—cav·ern·ous·ly** *adv.*

cave sal·a·man·der ▸*n.* a cave-dwelling salamander with pinkish to brown skin. • Several genera and species in the family Plethodontidae, including the North American *Eurycea lucifuga* and the European genus *Hydromantes.*

cav·es·son /ˈkavəsən/ ▸*n.* (also **lunging cavesson**) a type of heavy bridle, which lacks a bit and has a thick noseband fitted with rings to which a lunge rein may be attached. ▷late 16th cent.: from French *caveçon,* Italian *cavezzone,* based on Latin *caput* 'head.'

cave·wom·an /ˈkāv,wŏŏmən/ ▸*n.* (*pl.* **-wom·en**) a prehistoric woman who lived in caves.

cav·i·ar /ˈkavē,är/ (also **caviare**) ▸*n.* the pickled roe of sturgeon or other large fish, eaten as a delicacy. ▷mid 16th cent.: from Italian *caviale* (earlier *caviaro*) or French *caviar,* probably from medieval Greek *khaviari.*

cav·il /ˈkavəl/ ▸*v.* [*intrans.*] make petty or unnecessary objections: *they* ***caviled at*** *the cost.* ▸*n.* an objection of this kind. ▷mid 16th cent.: from French *caviller,* from Latin *cavillari,* from *cavilla* 'mockery.' **—cav·il·er** *n.*

cav·ing /ˈkāviɴɢ/ ▸*n.* another term for **SPELUNKING.**

cav·i·ta·tion /,kavəˈtāsʜən/ ▸*n.* *Physics* the formation of an empty space within a solid object or body. ■ the formation of bubbles in a liquid, typically by the movement of a propeller through it.

cav·i·ty /ˈkavitē/ ▸*n.* (*pl.* **-ties**) an empty space within a solid object, in particular the human body: *the abdominal cavity | a body cavity.* ■ a decayed part of a tooth. ▷mid 16th cent.: from French *cavité* or late Latin *cavitas,* from Latin *cavus* 'hollow.' **—cav·i·tar·y** /-i,terē/ *adj.*

cav·i·ty wall ▸*n.* a wall formed from two thicknesses of masonry with a space between them.

cav·o·lo ne·ro /ˈkävə,lō ˈne(ə)rō/ ▸*n.* an Italian variety of kale with very dark-colored leaves. ▷Italian, from *cavolo* 'cabbage' + *nero* 'black.'

cav·ort /kəˈvôrt/ ▸*v.* [*intrans.*] jump or dance around excitedly: *spider monkeys leap and cavort in the branches.* ■ *informal* apply oneself enthusiastically to sexual or disreputable pursuits: *he spent his nights cavorting with the glitterati.* ▷late 18th cent. (originally U.S.): perhaps an alteration of **CURVET.**

Ca·vou·ki·an /kəˈvōōkēən/, Raffi see **RAFFI.**

Ca·vour /kəˈvŏŏr/, Camillo Benso, Conte di (1810–61), Italian statesman. In 1861, he became the first premier of a unified Italy.

ca·vy /ˈkāvē/ ▸*n.* (*pl.* **-vies**) a South American rodent with a sturdy body and vestigial tail. • Family Caviidae: five genera and several species, in particular the guinea pig. ▷late 18th cent.: from modern Latin *cavia,* from Galibi *cabiai.*

caw /kô/ ▸*n.* the harsh cry of a crow or similar bird. ▸*v.* [*intrans.*] utter such a cry. ▷late 16th cent.: imitative.

Caw·ley /ˈkôlē/, Evonne (1951–), Australian tennis player; born *Evonne Fay Goolagong.* She won two Wimbledon 1971, 1980, four Australian 1974–77, and one French 1971 singles titles.

Cawn·pore /kônˈpôr/ variant spelling of **KANPUR.**

Cax·ton /ˈkakstən/, William (*c.*1422–91), English printer. He printed the first book in English in 1474.

cay /kē; kā/ ▸*n.* a low bank or reef of coral, rock, or sand. Compare with **KEY**2. ▷late 17th cent.: from Spanish *cayo* 'shoal, reef,' from French *quai* 'quay.'

Cay·enne /kīˈen; kāˈen/ the capital and chief port of French Guiana; pop. 41,600.

cay·enne /kīˈen; kā-/ (also **cayenne pepper**) ▸*n.* a pungent hot-tasting red powder prepared from ground dried chili peppers. ▷early 18th cent.: from Tupi *kyynha, quiynha,* later associated with **CAYENNE.**

Cay·ley /ˈkālē/, Arthur (1821–95), English mathematician and attorney. The **Cayley numbers,** a generalization of complex numbers, are named after him.

cay·man ▸*n.* variant spelling of **CAIMAN.**

Cay·man Is·lands /ˈkāmən/ (also **the Cay·mans**) a group of three islands in the Caribbean Sea, south of Cuba; pop. 31,930; capital, George Town. The Cayman Islands are a British dependency.

Ca·yu·ga /kāˈ(y)ōōgə; kī-/ ▸*n.* (*pl.* same or **-gas**) **1** a member of an American Indian people, one of the Five Nations, formerly inhabiting New York. **2** the Iroquoian language of this people. ▸*adj.* of or relating to this people or their language. ▷from an Iroquoian place name.

Cay·u·ga, Lake /kəˈyōōgə; kāˈ(y)ōō-/ one of the Finger Lakes, in west central New York. Ithaca lies at its southern end.

Cay·use /ˈkī,(y)ōōs; kīˈ(y)ōōs/ ▸*n.* (*pl.* same or **-us·es**) **1** a member of an American Indian people of Washington State and Oregon. **2** the language of this people, of unknown affinity. **3** (**cayuse**) an American Indian pony. ■ *informal* a horse. ▸*adj.* of or relating to this people or their language. ▷probably from Chinook Jargon from Spanish *caballos,* 'horses,' for which the Cayuse were especially known.

CB ▸*abbr.* Citizens' Band (radio frequencies).

CBC ▸*abbr.* Canadian Broadcasting Corporation.

CBS ▸*abbr.* Columbia Broadcasting System.

CC ▸*abbr.* ■ closed-captioned. ■ Cape Cod.

cc (also **c.c.**) ▸*abbr.* ■ carbon copy (used as an indication that a duplicate has been or should be sent to another person). ■ cubic centimeter(s).

CCD ▸*abbr.* ■ *Electronics* charge-coupled device, a high-speed semiconductor used chiefly in image detection. ■ Confraternity of Christian Doctrine.

CCK ▸*abbr. Biochemistry* cholecystokinin.

C clef ▸*n.* the soprano, alto, or tenor clef.

CCTV ▸*abbr.* closed-circuit television.

CCU ▸*abbr.* ■ cardiac care unit. ■ coronary care unit. ■ critical care unit.

CD ▸*abbr.* ■ certificate of deposit. ■ civil defense. ■ compact disc. ■ corps diplomatique.

Cd ▸*symbol* the chemical element cadmium.

cd ▸*abbr.* ■ candela. ■ cord.

CD burn·er ▸*n.* a device for producing a compact disc by copying from an original or master copy.

CDC ▸*abbr.* Centers for Disease Control.

CD-I ▸*abbr.* compact disc (interactive).

CDM ▸*abbr.* cold dark matter.

CDMA ▸*abbr. Electronics* Code Division Multiple Access, a generic term denoting a wireless interface based on code division multiple access technology.

cDNA ▸*abbr.* complementary DNA.

Cdr. (also **CDR**) ▸*abbr.* Commander.

Cdre. ▸*abbr.* Commodore.

CD-ROM /,sē ,dē ˈräm/ ▸*n.* a compact disc used as a read-only optical memory device for a computer system. ▷1980s: acronym from *compact disc read-only memory.*

CD-RW ▸*abbr.* compact disc rewritable, a blank CD that can be recorded, erased, and rerecorded many times ■ a disk drive that can read and record CDs

CDT ▸*abbr.* Central Daylight Time (see **CENTRAL TIME**).

CD vid·e·o (abbr.: **CDV**) ▸*n.* a video system in which both sound and picture are recorded on compact disc.

CE ▸*abbr.* ■ Chemical Engineer. ■ Church of England. ■ civil engineer. ■ Common Era. ■ Corps of Engineers.

Ce ▸*symbol* the chemical element cerium.

ce·a·no·thus /,sēəˈnōтʜəs/ ▸*n.* a North American shrub of the buckthorn family, cultivated for its dense clusters of small blue or white flowers. • Genus *Ceanothus,* family Rhamnaceae: numerous species, esp. in the western U.S., including the **blueblossom ceanothus** of the Pacific coast. ▷modern Latin, from Greek *keanōthos,* denoting a kind of thistle.

Ce·a·rá /,sāəˈrä/ a state in northeastern Brazil, on the Atlantic coast; capital, Fortaleza.

cease /sēs/ ▸*v.* [*intrans.*] come to an end: *the hostilities had ceased and normal life was resumed* | [with *infinitive*] *on his retirement the job will cease to exist.* ■ [*trans.*] bring (a specified action) to an end: *they were asked to cease all military activity.* ▷Middle English: from Old French *cesser,* from Latin *cessare* 'stop,' from *cedere* 'to yield.'

▸*PHRASES* □ **never cease to** (in hyperbolic use) do something very frequently: *her exploits never cease to amaze me.* □ **without cease** without stopping.

cease-fire ▸*n.* a temporary suspension of fighting, typically one during which peace talks take place; a truce. ■ an order or signal to stop fighting.

cease·less /ˈsēslis/ ▸*adj.* constant and unending: *the fort was subjected to ceaseless bombardment.* **—cease·less·ly** *adv.*

Ceau·şes·cu /cʜou'sʜeskōō/, Nicolae (1918–89), Romanian communist statesman; first president of the Socialist Republic of Romania 1974–89. His regime became increasingly totalitarian and corrupt; a popular uprising in December 1989 resulted in its downfall and in his execution.

Ce·bu /sāˈbōō/ an island in southern central Philippines. ■ its chief city and port; pop. 610,000.

Ce·cil·ia, St. /səˈsilyə; -ˈsēlyə/ (2nd or 3rd century), Roman martyr. According to legend, she took a vow of celibacy but, when forced to marry, converted her husband to Christianity and both were martyred. She is the patron saint of church music. Feast day, November 22.

ce·cro·pi·a /siˈkrōpēə/ ▸*n.* **1** a fast-growing tropical American tree, typically among the first to colonize a cleared area. Many cecropias have a symbiotic relationship with ants. • Genus *Cecropia,* family Cecropiaceae. **2** (also **cecropia moth**) a very large North American silkworm moth with boldly marked reddish-brown wings. The caterpillars feed on a variety of forest trees. • *Hyalophora cecropia,* family Saturniidae. ▷early 19th cent.: modern Latin, from the name *Cecrops,* a king of Attica.

cecropia moth

ce·cum /ˈsēkəm/ (*Brit.* **cae·cum**) ▸*n.* (*pl.* **-ca** /-kə/) *Anatomy* a pouch connected to the junction of the small and large intestines. ▷late Middle English: from Latin (*intestinum*) *caecum* 'blind (gut),' translation of Greek *tuphlon enteron.* **—ce·cal** /-kəl/ *adj.*

ce·dar /ˈsēdər/ ▸*n.* any of a number of conifers that typically yield fragrant, durable timber, in particular: • a large tree of the pine family (genus *Cedrus,* family Pinaceae), in particular the **cedar of Lebanon** (*C. libani*), with spreading branches, and the deodar. • a tall slender North American or Asian tree (genus *Thuja,* family Cupressaceae), in particular the **western red cedar** (*T. plicata*) and the **northern white cedar** (*T. occidentalis*). ▷Old English, from Old French *cedre* or Latin *cedrus,* from Greek *kedros.* **—ce·darn** /-dərn/ *adj.* (*poetic/literary*).

Ce·dar Falls a city in northeastern Iowa, on the Cedar River; pop. 36,145.

Ce·dar Ra·pids an industrial and commercial city in east central Iowa, on the Cedar River; pop. 120,758.

ce·dar wax·wing ▸*n.* a North American waxwing. • *Bombycilla cedrorum.*

cede /sēd/ ▸*v.* [*trans.*] give up (power or territory): *they have had to* ***cede*** *control of the schools* ***to*** *the government.* See note at **RELINQUISH.** ▷early 16th cent.: from French *céder* or Latin *cedere* 'to yield.'

cedar waxwing

ce·di /ˈsādē/ ▸*n.* (*pl.* same or **-dis**) the basic monetary unit of Ghana, equal to 100 pesewas. ▷of Ghanaian origin, perhaps an alteration of **SHILLING.**

ce·dil·la /səˈdilə/ ▸*n.* a mark (̧) written under the letter *c,* esp. in French, to show that it is pronounced

Pronunciation Key ə ago; ər over; ˈə or ,ə up; ˈər or ,ər fur; a hat; ā rate; ä car; cʜ chew; e let; ē see; e(ə)r air; i fit; ī by; i(ə)r ear; ɴɢ sing; ō go; ô for; oi boy; ŏŏ good; ōō goo; ou out; sʜ she; тʜ thin; тʜ then; (h)w why; zʜ vision

like an *s* rather than a *k* (e.g., *façade*). ■ a similar mark under *s* in Turkish and other oriental languages. ▷late 16th cent.: from obsolete Spanish, earlier form of *zedilla*, diminutive of *zeda* (the letter Z), from Greek *zēta*.

cei·ba /ˈsābə/ ▶*n.* a very tall tropical American tree from which kapok is obtained, with lightweight yellowish or pinkish timber. It is pollinated by bats and was held sacred by the Maya. Also called **KAPOK**. • *Ceiba pentandra*, family Bombacaceae. ▷early 19th cent.: via Spanish from Taino, literally 'giant tree.'

ceil /sēl/ ▶*v.* [*trans.*] (usu. **be ceiled**) *archaic* line or plaster the roof of (a building). ▷late Middle English (in the sense 'line (the interior of a room) with plaster or paneling': perhaps related to Latin *celare*, French *céler* 'conceal.'

cei·lidh /ˈkālē/ ▶*n.* a social event at which there is Scottish or Irish folk music and singing, traditional dancing, and storytelling. ▷late 19th cent.: from Scottish Gaelic *ceilidh* and Irish *céilidhe* (earlier form of *céilí*), from Old Irish *céilide* 'visit, visiting,' from *céile* 'companion.'

ceil·ing /ˈsēliNG/ ▶*n.* **1** the upper interior surface of a room or other similar compartment. ■ *figurative* an upper limit, typically one set on prices, wages, or expenditure. See also **GLASS CEILING**. ■ the maximum altitude that a particular aircraft can reach. ■ the altitude of the base of a cloud layer. **2** the inside planking of a ship's bottom and sides. ▷Middle English (denoting the action of lining the interior of a room with plaster or paneling): from **CEIL** + **-ING**[1]. Sense 1 dates from the mid 16th cent.

ceil·om·e·ter /sēˈlämitər/ ▶*n.* a device for measuring and recording the height of clouds.

cel /sel/ ▶*n.* a transparent sheet of celluloid or similar film material that can be drawn on, used in the production of cartoons. ▷mid 20th cent.: abbreviation of **CELLULOID**.

cel·a·don /ˈseləˌdän/ ▶*n.* a willow-green color: [as *adj.*] *paneling painted in* **celadon green**. ■ a gray-green glaze used on pottery, esp. that from China. ■ pottery made with this glaze. ▷mid 18th cent.: from French *céladon*, a color named after the hero in d'Urfé's pastoral romance *L'Astrée* (1607–27).

cel·an·dine /ˈselənˌdīn; -ˌdēn/ (also **lesser celandine**) ▶*n.* a common plant of the buttercup family that produces yellow flowers in the early spring, reproducing either by seed or by bulbils at the base of the stems. See also **GREATER CELANDINE**. • *Ranunculus ficaria*, family Ranunculaceae. ▷Middle English, from Old French *celidoine*, from medieval Latin *celidonia*, based on Greek *khelidōn* 'swallow' (the flowering of the plant being associated with the arrival of swallows).

-cele ▶*comb. form* variant spelling of **-COELE**.

ce·leb /səˈleb/ ▶*n. informal* a celebrity: *a TV celeb.* ▷early 20th cent. (originally U.S.): abbreviation.

Cel·e·bes /ˈseləˌbēz; səˈlēbēz/ former name of **SULAWESI**.

Cel·e·bes sail·fish ▶*n.* see **SAILFISH**.

Cel·e·bes Sea a part of the western Pacific Ocean between the Philippines and the island of Sulawesi and is bounded on the west by Borneo. It is linked to the Java Sea by the Makassar Strait.

Ce·leb·ra /səˈlebrə/ ▶*n. trademark* a synthetic drug (a COX-2 inhibitor) used in the management of arthritic pain. ▷1990s: an invented word.

cel·e·brant /ˈseləbrənt/ ▶*n.* **1** a person who performs a rite, esp. a priest at the Eucharist. **2** a person who celebrates something. ▷mid 19th cent.: from French *célébrant* or Latin *celebrant-* 'celebrating,' from the verb *celebrare* (see **CELEBRATE**).

cel·e·brate /ˈseləˌbrāt/ ▶*v.* [*trans.*] **1** mark (a significant or happy day or event), typically with a social gathering. ■ [*intrans.*] do something enjoyable to mark such an occasion: *she celebrated with a glass of champagne.* ■ reach (a birthday or anniversary). **2** perform (a religious ceremony) publicly and duly, in particular officiate at (the Eucharist): *he celebrated holy communion.* **3** honor or praise publicly: *a film celebrating the actor's career* | [as *adj.*] (**celebrated**) *a celebrated mathematician.* ▷late Middle English (sense 2): from Latin *celebrat-* 'celebrated,' from the verb *celebrare*, from *celeber*, *celebr-* 'frequented or honored.' **—cel·e·bra·tor** /-ˌbrātər/ *n.* **—cel·e·bra·to·ry** /səˈlebrəˌtôrē; ˈseləbrə-/ *adj.*

cel·e·bra·tion /ˌseləˈbrāSHən/ ▶*n.* the action of marking one's pleasure at an important event or occasion by engaging in enjoyable, typically social, activity: *the birth of his son was a cause for celebration* | *a birthday celebration.* ▷early 16th cent.: from Latin *celebratio(n-)*, from the verb *celebrare* (see **CELEBRATE**).

ce·leb·ri·ty /səˈlebrətē/ ▶*n.* (*pl.* **-ties**) a famous person. ■ the state of being well known: *his prestige and celebrity grew.* ▷late Middle English (in the sense 'solemn ceremony'): from Old French *celebrite* or Latin *celebritas*, from *celeber*, *celebr-* 'frequented or honored.'

ce·ler·i·ac /səˈlerēˌak/ ▶*n.* celery of a variety that forms a large swollen turniplike root that can be eaten cooked or raw. Also called **CELERY ROOT**. • *Apium graveolens rapaceum.* ▷mid 18th cent.: from **CELERY** + an arbitrary use of **-AC**.

ce·ler·i·ty /səˈleritē/ ▶*n. archaic* or *poetic/literary* swiftness of movement. ▷late 15th cent.: from Old French *celerite*, from Latin *celeritas*, from *celer* 'swift.'

cel·er·y /ˈsel(ə)rē/ ▶*n.* a cultivated plant of the parsley family, with closely packed succulent leafstalks that are eaten raw or cooked. • *Apium graveolens* var. *dulce*, family Umbelliferae. ▷mid 17th cent.: from French *céleri*, from Italian dialect *selleri*, based on Greek *selinon* 'parsley.'

cel·er·y root ▶*n.* another term for **CELERIAC**.

cel·er·y salt ▶*n.* a mixture of salt and ground celery seed used for seasoning.

cel·er·y seed ▶*n.* the seed of a plant related to the celery plant, with a celerylike flavor and aroma.

ce·les·ta /səˈlestə/ ▶*n.* (also **ce·leste**) a small keyboard instrument in which felted hammers strike a row of steel plates suspended over wooden resonators, giving an ethereal bell-like sound. ▷late 19th cent.: pseudo-Latin, based on French *céleste* 'heavenly.'

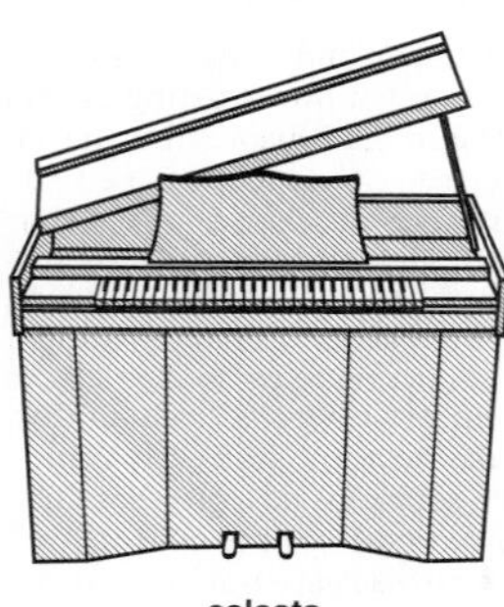

celesta

ce·les·tial /səˈlesCHəl/ ▶*adj.* [*attrib.*] positioned in or relating to the sky, or outer space as observed in astronomy: *a celestial body.* ■ belonging or relating to heaven: *the celestial city.* ■ supremely good: *the celestial beauty of music.* ▷late Middle English: via Old French from medieval Latin *caelestialis*, from Latin *caelestis*, from *caelum* 'heaven.' **—ce·les·tial·ly** *adv.*

ce·les·tial bam·boo ▶*n.* another term for **NANDINA**.

ce·les·tial e·qua·tor ▶*n.* the projection into space of the earth's equator; an imaginary circle equidistant from the celestial poles.

ce·les·tial globe ▶*n.* a spherical representation of the sky showing the constellations.

ce·les·tial ho·ri·zon ▶*n.* see **HORIZON** (sense 1).

ce·les·tial lat·i·tude ▶*n. Astronomy* the angular distance of a point north or south of the ecliptic. Compare with **DECLINATION** (sense 1).

ce·les·tial lon·gi·tude ▶*n. Astronomy* the angular distance of a point east of the vernal equinox, measured along the ecliptic. Compare with **RIGHT ASCENSION**.

ce·les·tial me·chan·ics ▶*plural n.* [treated as *sing.*] the branch of theoretical astronomy that deals with the calculation of the motions of celestial objects such as planets.

ce·les·tial nav·i·ga·tion ▶*n.* the action of finding one's way by observing the sun, moon, and stars.

ce·les·tial pole ▶*n. Astronomy* the point on the celestial sphere directly above either of the earth's geographic poles, around which the stars and planets appear to rotate during the course of the night. The north celestial pole is currently within one degree of the star Polaris.

ce·les·tial sphere ▶*n.* an imaginary sphere of which the observer is the center and on which all celestial objects are considered to lie.

ce·li·ac /ˈsēlēˌak/ (*Brit.* **coe·li·ac**) ▶*adj.* **1** *Anatomy* of or relating to the abdomen. **2** *Medicine* of, relating to, or affected by celiac disease: *a celiac child.*
▶*n.* a person with celiac disease. ▷mid 17th cent.: from Latin *coeliacus*, from Greek *koiliakos*, from *koilia* 'belly.'

ce·li·ac dis·ease ▶*n.* a disease in which chronic failure to digest food is triggered by hypersensitivity of the small intestine to gluten.

cel·i·bate /ˈseləbət/ ▶*adj.* abstaining from marriage and sexual relations, typically for religious reasons: *a celibate priest.* ■ having or involving no sexual relations: *I'd rather stay single and celibate.*
▶*n.* a person who abstains from marriage and sexual relations. ▷early 19th cent.: from *celibacy*, on the pattern of pairs such as *magistracy*, *magistrate*. **—cel·i·ba·cy** /-bəsē/ *n.*

cell /sel/ ▶*n.* **1** a small room in which a prisoner is locked up or in which a monk or nun sleeps. ■ a small compartment in a larger structure such as a honeycomb. ■ *historical* a small monastery or nunnery dependent on a larger one. **2** *Biology* the smallest structural and functional unit of an organism, typically microscopic and consisting of cytoplasm and a nucleus enclosed in a membrane. Microscopic organisms typically consist of a single cell, which is either eukaryotic or prokaryotic. ■ an enclosed cavity in an organism. ■ *figurative* a small group forming a nucleus of political activity, typically a secret, subversive one: *the weapons may be used to arm terrorist cells.* ■ the local area covered by one of the short-range transmitters in a cellular telephone system. **3** a device containing electrodes immersed in an electrolyte, used for current-generation or electrolysis. ■ a unit in a device for converting chemical or solar energy into electricity. ▷Old English, from Old French *celle* or Latin *cella* 'storeroom or chamber.' **—celled** *adj.* [in *combination*] *a single-celled organism.* **—cell-like** /-ˌlīk/ *adj.*

cel·la /ˈselə/ ▶*n.* (*pl.* **cel·lae** /ˈselē/) the inner area of an ancient temple, esp. one housing the hidden cult image in a Greek or Roman temple. ▷late 17th cent.: Latin, literally 'storeroom, shrine,' from *celare* 'hide.' (See **CONCEAL**).

cel·lar /ˈselər/ ▶*n.* a room below ground level in a house, typically one used for storing wine or coal. ■ a stock of wine.
▶*v.* [*trans.*] store (wine) in a cellar. ▷Middle English (in the general sense 'storeroom'): from Old French *celier*, from late Latin *cellarium* 'storehouse,' from *cella* 'storeroom or chamber.'

cel·lar·age /ˈseləriј/ ▶*n.* cellars collectively. ■ cellar space. ■ money charged for the use of a cellar or storehouse.

cel·lar·er /ˈselərər/ ▶*n.* the person in a monastery who is responsible for the provisioning of food and drink.

cel·lar·et /ˌseləˈret/ (also **cel·lar·ette**) ▶*n. historical* a cabinet for keeping bottles of wine and liquor.

cell block ▶*n.* a large single building or part of a complex subdivided into separate prison cells.

cell di·vi·sion ▶*n. Biology* the division of a cell into two daughter cells with the same genetic material.

Cel·li·ni /CHəˈlēnē/, Benvenuto (1500–71), Italian goldsmith and sculptor.

cell line ▶*n. Biology* a cell culture developed from a single cell and therefore consisting of cells with a uniform genetic makeup.

cell-me·di·at·ed ▶*adj. Physiology* denoting the aspect of an immune response involving the action of white blood cells, rather than that of circulating antibodies. Often contrasted with **HUMORAL**.

cell mem·brane ▶*n.* the semipermeable membrane surrounding the cytoplasm of a cell. Also called **CYTOMEMBRANE**.

cel·lo /ˈCHelō/ ▶*n.* (*pl.* **-los**) a bass instrument of the violin family, held upright on the floor between the legs of the seated player. ▷late 19th cent.: shortening of **VIOLONCELLO**. **—cel·list** /ˈCHelist/ *n.*

cello

cel·lo·phane /ˈseləˌfān/ ▶*n.* a thin transparent wrapping material made from viscose. ▷early 20th cent.: originally a trademark.

cell phone ▶*n.* (also **cell·phone**) short for **CELLULAR PHONE**.

cel·lu·lar /ˈselyələr/ ▶*adj.* **1** of, relating to, or consisting of living cells: *cellular proliferation.* **2** denoting or relating to a mobile telephone system that uses a number of short-range radio stations to cover the area that it serves, the signal being automatically switched from one station to another as the user travels about. **3** (of a fabric item, such as a blanket or vest) knitted so as to form holes or hollows that trap air and provide extra insulation. **4** consisting of small compartments or rooms: *cellular accommodations.* ▷mid 18th cent.: from French *cellulaire,* from modern Latin *cellularis,* from *cellula* 'little chamber,' diminutive of *cella.* —**cel·lu·lar·i·ty** /ˌselyəˈlaritē/ *n.*

cel·lu·lar au·tom·a·ton ▸*n.* (*pl.* **cel·lu·lar au·tom·a·ta**) *Computing* one of a set of units in a mathematical model that have simple rules governing their replication and destruction. They are used to model complex systems composed of simple units such as living things or parallel processors.

cel·lu·lar blind ▸*n.* a window blind with a single or double layer of collapsible voids that provide insulation when the blind is extended.

cel·lu·lar phone (also **cellular telephone**) ▸*n.* a telephone with access to a cellular radio system so it can be used over a wide area, without a physical connection to a network.

cel·lu·lase /ˈselyəˌlās; -ˌlāz/ ▸*n. Biochemistry* an enzyme that converts cellulose into glucose or a disaccharide. ▷early 20th cent.: from CELLULOSE + -ASE.

cel·lu·lite /ˈselyəˌlīt/ ▸*n.* persistent subcutaneous fat causing dimpling of the skin, esp. on women's hips and thighs. Not in technical use. ▷1960s: from French, from *cellule* 'small cell.'

cel·lu·li·tis /ˌselyəˈlītis/ ▸*n. Medicine* inflammation of subcutaneous connective tissue.

cel·lu·loid /ˈselyəˌloid/ ▸*n.* a transparent flammable plastic made in sheets from camphor and nitrocellulose, formerly used for cinematographic film. ■ motion pictures as a genre: *having made the leap from theater to celluloid, she can now make more money.* ▷mid 19th cent.: from CELLULOSE + -OID.

cel·lu·lose /ˈselyəˌlōs; -ˌlōz/ ▸*n.* **1** an insoluble substance that is the main constituent of plant cell walls and of vegetable fibers such as cotton. It is a polysaccharide consisting of chains of glucose monomers. **2** paint or lacquer consisting principally of cellulose acetate or nitrate in solution. ▷mid 19th cent.: from French, from *cellule* 'small cell' + -OSE[2]. —**cel·lu·lo·sic** /ˌselyəˈlōsik; -ˈlōzik/ *adj.*

cel·lu·lose ac·e·tate ▸*n. Chemistry* a nonflammable thermoplastic polymer made by acetylating cellulose, used as the basis of artificial fibers and plastic.

cel·lu·lose ni·trate ▸*n.* another term for NITROCELLULOSE.

cel·lu·lose tri·ac·e·tate ▸*n.* see TRIACETATE.

cell wall ▸*n. Biology* a rigid layer of polysaccharides lying outside the plasma membrane of the cells of plants, fungi, and bacteria. In the algae and higher plants, it consists mainly of cellulose.

cell·y /ˈselē/ (also **cell·ie**) ▸*n.* (*pl.* **cell·ies**) *informal* **1** a cellular phone: *Timmy whips out his celly to beep White Mike.* ■ a person who uses a cellular phone. **2** (among prisoners) cellmate. ▷by shortening and alteration.

ce·lom ▸*n.* variant spelling of COELOM.

ce·lo·sia /siˈlōzʜ(ē)ə/ ▸*n.* a plant of a genus that includes cockscomb. • Genus *Celosia,* family Amaranthaceae. ▷modern Latin, from Greek *kēlos* 'burned or dry' (from the burned appearance of the flowers in some species).

Cel·si·us[1] /ˈselsēəs; ˈselsʜəs/, Anders (1701–44), Swedish astronomer; best known for his temperature scale.

Cel·si·us[2] (abbr.: **C**) ▸*adj.* [*postpositive* when used with a numeral] of or denoting a scale of temperature on which water freezes at 0° and boils at 100° under standard conditions.
▸*n.* (also **Celsius scale**) this scale of temperature.

USAGE **Celsius**, rather than **centigrade**, is the standard accepted term when giving temperatures: use *25° Celsius* rather than *25° centigrade.*

Celt /kelt; selt/ ▸*n.* a member of a group of peoples inhabiting much of Europe and Asia Minor in pre-Roman times. Their culture developed in the late Bronze Age around the upper Danube, and reached its height in the La Tène culture (5th to 1st centuries BC) before being overrun by the Romans and various Germanic peoples. ■ a native of any of the modern nations or regions in which Celtic languages are (or were until recently) spoken; a person of Irish, Highland Scottish, Manx, Welsh, or Cornish descent. ▷from Latin *Celtae* (plural), from Greek *Keltoi;* in later use from French *Celte* 'Breton' (taken as representing the ancient Gauls).

USAGE See usage at CELTIC.

celt /selt/ ▸*n. Archaeology* a prehistoric stone or metal implement with a beveled cutting edge, probably used as a tool or weapon. ▷early 18th cent.: from medieval Latin *celtis* 'chisel.'

Celt·i·ber·i·an /ˌkelˌtiˈbirēən; ˌsel-/ ▸*n.* another term for IBERIAN (sense 3).

Celt·ic /ˈkeltik; ˈsel-/ ▸*adj.* of or relating to the Celts or their languages, which constitute a branch of the Indo-European family and include Irish, Scottish Gaelic, Welsh, Breton, Manx, Cornish, and several extinct pre-Roman languages such as Gaulish.
▸*n.* the Celtic language group. See also P-CELTIC, Q-CELTIC. ▷late 16th cent.: from Latin *Celticus* (from *Celtae* 'Celts'), or from French *Celtique* (from *Celte* 'Breton'). —**Celt·i·cism** /ˈkeltəˌsizəm; ˈsel-/ *n.* —**Celt·i·cist** /ˈkeltəˌsist; ˈsel-/ *n.*

USAGE **Celt** and **Celtic** can be pronounced either with an initial **k-** or **s-** sound. In standard English, the normal pronunciation is with a **k-** sound, except in the name of the Boston basketball team.

Celt·ic Church the Christian Church in the British Isles from its foundation in the 2nd or 3rd century until its assimilation into the Roman Catholic Church (664 in England; 12th century in Wales, Scotland, and Ireland).

Celt·ic cross ▸*n.* a Latin cross with a circle around the center.

Celt·ic fringe ▸*n.* the Highland Scots, Irish, Welsh, and Cornish in relation to the rest of Britain. ■ the land inhabited by these peoples.

Celt·ic harp ▸*n.* a small harp with wire strings, used in the folk and early music of Scotland and Ireland.

Celt·ic Sea the part of the Atlantic Ocean that is between southern Ireland and southwestern England.

cem·ba·lo /ˈcʜembəˌlō/ ▸*n.* (*pl.* **-los**) another term for HARPSICHORD. ▷mid 19th cent.: from Italian, shortening of *clavicembalo,* from medieval Latin *clavicymbalum,* from Latin *clavis* 'key' + *cymbalum* 'cymbal.' —**cem·ba·list** /-bəlist/ *n.*

ce·ment /siˈment/ ▸*n.* a powdery substance made by calcining lime and clay, mixed with water to form mortar or mixed with sand, gravel, and water to make concrete. ■ a soft glue that hardens on setting: *rubber cement.* ■ *figurative* an element that unites a group of people: *traditional entertainment was a form of community cement.* ■ another term for CONCRETE. ■ a substance for filling cavities in teeth. ■ (also **cementum**) *Anatomy* a thin layer of bony material that fixes teeth to the jaw. ■ *Geology* the material that binds particles together in sedimentary rock.
▸*v.* [*trans.*] attach with cement: *wooden posts were cemented into the ground.* ■ *figurative* settle or establish firmly: *the two firms are expected to cement an agreement soon.* ■ *Geology* (of a material) bind (particles) together in sedimentary rock. ▷Middle English: from Old French *ciment* (noun), *cimenter* (verb), from Latin *caementum* 'quarry stone,' from *caedere* 'hew.' —**ce·ment·er** *n.*

ce·men·ta·tion /ˌsēˌmenˈtāsʜən/ ▸*n.* **1** *chiefly Geology* the binding together of particles or other things by cement. **2** *Metallurgy* a process of altering a metal by heating it in contact with a powdered solid, esp. a former method of making steel by heating iron in contact with charcoal.

ce·ment·ite /siˈmenˌtīt/ ▸*n. Metallurgy* a hard, brittle iron carbide present in cast iron and most steels. • Chem. formula: Fe_3C. ▷late 19th cent.: from CEMENT + -ITE[1].

ce·men·ti·tious /ˌsēˌmenˈtisʜəs/ ▸*adj.* of the nature of cement.

ce·ment mix·er (also **concrete mixer**) ▸*n.* a machine with a revolving drum used for mixing cement with sand, gravel, and water to make concrete.

cem·e·ter·y /ˈseməˌterē/ ▸*n.* (*pl.* **-ter·ies**) a burial ground; a graveyard. ▷late Middle English: via late Latin from Greek *koimētērion* 'dormitory,' from *koiman* 'put to sleep.'

cen·a·cle /ˈsenikəl/ ▸*n.* **1** a group of people, such as a discussion group or literary clique. **2** the room in which the Last Supper was held. ▷late Middle English: from Old French *cenacle,* from Latin *cenaculum,* from *cena* 'dinner.'

ce·no·bite /ˈsenəˌbīt/ (also **coe·no·bite**) ▸*n.* a member of a monastic community. ▷late Middle English: from Old French *cenobite* or ecclesiastical Latin *coenobita,* via late Latin from Greek *koinobion* 'convent,' from *koinos* 'common' + *bios* 'life.' —**ce·no·bit·ic** /ˌsenəˈbitik/ *adj.* —**ce·no·bit·i·cal** /ˌsenəˈbitikəl/ *adj.*

ce·no·spe·cies /ˈsēnəˌspēsēz; -ˌspēsʜēz/ ▸*n.* a group of species whose members produce partially fertile hybrids when crossbred.

ce·no·taph /ˈsenəˌtaf/ ▸*n.* a tomblike monument to someone buried elsewhere, esp. one commemorating people who died in a war. ▷early 17th cent.: from French *cénotaphe,* from late Latin *cenotaphium,* from Greek *kenos* 'empty' + *taphos* 'tomb.'

Ce·no·zo·ic /ˌsenəˈzōik/ (also **Cai·no·zo·ic** /ˌkīnə-/) ▸*adj. Geology* relating to or denoting the most recent era, following the Mesozoic era and comprising the Tertiary and Quaternary periods. ■ [as *n.*] (**the Cenozoic**) the Cenozoic era, or the system of rocks deposited during it.

The Cenozoic has lasted from about 65 million years ago to the present day. It has seen the rapid evolution and rise to dominance of mammals, birds, and flowering plants.

▷mid 19th cent.: from Greek *kainos* 'new' + *zōion* 'animal' + -IC.

cense /sens/ ▸*v.* [*trans.*] perfume (something) ritually with the odor of burning incense. ▷late Middle English: from Old French *encenser.*

cen·ser /ˈsensər/ ▸*n.* a container in which incense is burned, typically during a religious ceremony. ▷Middle English: from Old French *censier,* from *encensier,* from *encens* (see INCENSE[1]).

cen·sor /ˈsensər/ ▸*n.* **1** an official who examines material that is about to be released, such as books, movies, news, and art, and suppresses any parts that are considered obscene, politically unacceptable, or a threat to security. ■ *Psychoanalysis* an aspect of the superego that is said to prevent certain ideas and memories from emerging into consciousness. [from a mistranslation of German *Zensur* 'censorship,' coined by Freud.] **2** (in ancient Rome) either of two magistrates who held censuses and supervised public morals.
▸*v.* [*trans.*] (often **be censored**) examine (a book, movie, etc.) officially and suppress unacceptable parts of it: *my mail was being censored.* ▷mid 16th cent. (in sense 2): from Latin, from *censere* 'assess.' —**cen·so·ri·al** /senˈsôrēəl/ *adj.*

USAGE Both **censor** and **censure** are both verbs and nouns, but **censor** means ' scrutinize, revise, or cut unacceptable parts (from a book, movie, etc.)' or 'a person who does this,' while **censure** means 'criticize harshly' or 'harsh criticism:' *the inmates received their mail only after prison officials had censored all the contents; some senators considered a resolution of censure to express strong disapproval of the president's behavior.*

cen·so·ri·ous /senˈsôrēəs/ ▸*adj.* severely critical of others: *modest, charitable in his judgments, never censorious, Jim carried tolerance almost too far.* ▷mid 16th cent.: from Latin *censorius* (from *censor* 'magistrate') + -IOUS. —**cen·so·ri·ous·ly** *adv.* —**cen·so·ri·ous·ness** *n.*

cen·sor·ship /ˈsensərˌsʜip/ ▸*n.* the practice of officially examining books, movies, etc., and suppressing unacceptable parts: *details of the visit were subject to military censorship.*

cen·sure /ˈsensʜər/ ▸*v.* [*trans.*] (often **be censured**) express severe disapproval of (someone or something), typically in a formal statement: *a judge was censured in 1983 for a variety of types of injudicious conduct.* See note at REBUKE.
▸*n.* the expression of formal disapproval: *angry delegates offered a resolution of censure against the offenders they paid the price in social ostracism and family censure.* ▷late Middle English (in the sense 'judicial sentence'): from Old French *censurer* (verb), *censure* (noun), from Latin *censura* 'judgment, assessment,' from *censere* 'assess.' —**cen·sur·a·ble** *adj.*

USAGE On the difference in meaning between **censure** and **censor**, see **usage** at CENSOR.

cen·sus /ˈsensəs/ ▸*n.* (*pl.* **-sus·es**) an official count or survey of a population, typically recording various details of individuals: *population estimates extrapolated from the 1981 census* | [as *adj.*] *census data.* ▷early 17th cent. (denoting a poll tax): from Latin, applied

Pronunciation Key ə *ago;* ər *over;* ˈə *or* ˌə *up;* ˈər *or* ˌər *fur;* a *hat;* ā *rate;* ä *car;* cʜ *chew;* e *let;* ē *see;* e(ə)r *air;* i *fit;* ī *by;* i(ə)r *ear;* ɴɢ *sing;* ō *go;* ô *for;* oi *boy;* o͝o *good;* o͞o *goo;* ou *out;* sʜ *she;* tʜ *thin;* t̲ʜ̲ *then;* (h)w *why;* zʜ *vision*

to the registration of citizens and property in ancient Rome, usually for taxation, from *censere* 'assess.' The current sense dates from the mid 18th cent.

cent /sent/ ▸*n.* **1** a monetary unit of the U.S., Canada, and various other countries, equal to one hundredth of a dollar. ■ a coin of this value. ■ *informal* a small sum of money: *she saved every cent possible.* ■ [in *sing.*] [with *negative*] *informal* used for emphasis to denote any money at all: *he hadn't yet earned a cent.* **2** a monetary unit of some states of the European Union, equal to one hundredth of a euro. **3** *Music* one hundredth of a half step. ▷late Middle English (in the sense 'a hundred'): from French *cent*, Italian *cento*, or Latin *centum* 'hundred.'
▸*PHRASE* □ **one's two cents' worth** one's opinion.

cent. ▸*abbr.* ■ centigrade. ■ century.

cen·tas /'sen,täs/ ▸*n.* (*pl.* same) a monetary unit of Lithuania, equal to one hundredth of a litas. ▷Lithuanian.

centaur

cen·taur /'sen,tôr/ ▸*n.* *Greek Mythology* a creature with the head, arms, and torso of a man and the body and legs of a horse. ▷via Latin from Greek *kentauros*, the Greek name for a Thessalonian tribe of expert horsemen; of unknown ultimate origin.

cen·tau·re·a /sen'tôrēə/ ▸*n.* a plant of a Eurasian genus that includes the cornflower and knapweed. Several kinds are cultivated for their bright flowers. • Genus *Centaurea*, family Compositae. ▷modern Latin based on Greek *kentauros* 'centaur' (see CENTAURY).

Cen·tau·rus /sen'tôrəs/ *Astronomy* a large southern constellation (the Centaur). It lies in the Milky Way and contains the stars Alpha and Proxima Centauri. ■ [as *genitive*] (**Centauri** /-'tôrī/) used with a preceding letter or numeral to designate a star in this constellation: *the star Lambda Centauri.* ▷Latin.

cen·tau·ry /'sen,tôrē/ ▸*n.* (*pl.* **-ries**) a widely distributed herbaceous plant of the gentian family, typically having pink petals atop long calyx tubes. • *Centaurium* and related genera, family Gentianaceae: many species, including the wild *C. pulchellum* and the cultivated ornamental *C. scilloides.* ▷late Middle English: from late Latin *centaurea*, based on Greek *kentauros* 'centaur' (because its medicinal properties were said to have been discovered by the centaur Chiron).

cen·ta·vo /sen'tävō/ ▸*n.* (*pl.* **-vos**) a monetary unit of Mexico, Brazil, and certain other countries (including Portugal until the introduction of the euro), equal to one hundredth of the basic unit. ▷Spanish and Portuguese, from Latin *centum* 'a hundred.'

CENTCOM (also **CentCom**) ▸*abbr.* the unified armed forces command organization that oversees U.S. military operations in the Middle East. ▷acronym from *Central Command.*

cen·te·nar·i·an /,sentn'e(ə)rēən/ ▸*n.* a person who is one hundred or more years old.
▸*adj.* [*attrib.*] one hundred or more years old.

cen·ten·ar·y /sen'tenərē; 'sentn,erē/ *chiefly Brit.* ▸*n.* (*pl.* **-ar·ies**) the hundredth anniversary of a significant event; a centennial. ■ a celebration of such an anniversary.
▸*adj.* of or relating to a hundredth anniversary; centennial. ▷early 17th cent. (denoting a century): from Latin *centenarius* 'containing a hundred,' based on Latin *centum* 'a hundred.'

cen·ten·ni·al /sen'tenēəl/ ▸*adj.* of or relating to a hundredth anniversary: *centennial celebrations.*
▸*n.* a hundredth anniversary: *the museum's centennial.* ■ a celebration of such an anniversary. ▷late 18th cent.: from Latin *centum* 'a hundred,' on the pattern of *biennial.*

Cen·ten·ni·al State a nickname for the state of COLORADO.

cen·ter /'sentər/ (*Brit.* **cen·tre**) ▸*n.* **1** the middle point of a circle or sphere, equidistant from every point on the circumference or surface. ■ a point or part that is equally distant from all sides, ends, or surfaces of something; the middle: *the center of the ceiling | the center of a vast territory.* ■ a pivot or axis of rotation: *the galactic rotation of the solar system around the galactic center.* ■ a political party or group holding moderate opinions. ■ *Sports* the middle player in a line or group in many games: *Terry played center on the basketball team.* ■ *Baseball* short for CENTER FIELD: *he flied out to center.* ■ a core, such as the filling in a piece of chocolate: *truffles with liqueur centers.* ■ a conical adjustable support for a workpiece in a lathe or similar machine. **2** a place or group of buildings where a specified activity is concentrated: *a* ***center for*** *medical research | a shopping center.* ■ a point at which an activity or quality is at its most intense and from which it spreads: *the city was* ***a center of*** *discontent.* ■ the point on which an activity or process is focused: *two issues* ***at the center of*** *the health-care debate.* ■ the most important place in the respect specified: *Geneva was then the center of the international world.*
▸*v.* **1** [*intrans.*] (**center around/on**) have (something) as a major concern or theme: *the case centers around the couple's adopted children | the plot centers on two young men.* ■ [*trans.*] (**center something around/on**) cause an argument or discussion to focus on (a specified issue): *he is centering his discussion on an analysis of patterns of mortality.* ■ (**be centered in**) (of an activity) occur mainly in or around (a specified place): *the mercantile association was centered in northern Germany.* **2** [*trans.*] place in the middle: *to center the needle, turn the knob.* ■ *Football* pass the ball back from the ground to another player to begin a down; snap. ▷late Middle English *centre*, from Old French, or from Latin *centrum*, from Greek *kentron* 'sharp point, stationary point of a pair of compasses,' related to *kentein* 'to prick.' **—cen·ter·most** /-,mōst/ *adj.*
▸*PHRASE* □ **the center of attention** a person or thing that draws general attention.

USAGE The construction **center around** (as opposed to *center on*, or *revolve around*) has been denounced as incorrect and illogical since it first appeared in the mid 19th century. Although the phrase is common, it defies geometry by confusing the orbit with the fixed point: *the earth revolves around (or its revolution centers on) the sun.* A careful writer will use a precise expression, such as *centers on, revolves around, concerns,* or *involves.*

cen·ter back ▸*n.* *Sports* a player in the middle of the back line in some sports, such as volleyball.

cen·ter bit ▸*n.* a tool for boring cylindrical holes.

cen·ter·board /'sentər,bôrd/ ▸*n.* a pivoted board that can be lowered through the keel of a sailboat to reduce sideways movement. Compare with DAGGERBOARD.

cen·tered /'sentərd/ (*Brit.* **cen·tred**) ▸*adj.* **1** in the center: *a centered oval window.* **2** [in *combination*] having the specified subject as the focal element: *a computer-centered industry.* **3** (of a person) well balanced and confident or serene. **4** [in *combination*] having a center or filling of a specified type: *a soft-centered chocolate.* **—cen·tered·ness** *n.*

cen·ter field (also **cen·ter·field**) ▸*n.* *Baseball* the central part of the outfield, behind second base: *a single to center field.* ■ the position of an outfielder in this area: *Amaro played some center field when Dykstra went on the disabled list.* **—cen·ter field·er** *n.*

cen·ter·fire /'sentər,fīr/ ▸*adj.* [*attrib.*] (of a gun cartridge) having the primer in the center of the base. ■ (of a gun) using such cartridges.
▸*n.* a gun using such a cartridge.

cen·ter·fold /'sentər,fōld/ ▸*n.* the two middle pages of a magazine, typically taken up by a single illustration or feature. ■ an illustration on such pages, typically a picture of a naked or scantily clad model.

cen·ter for·ward ▸*n.* *Soccer* an attacker who plays in the middle of the field.

cen·ter half·back ▸*n.* *Soccer* another term for CENTER BACK.

cen·ter·ing /'sentəriNG/ ▸*n.* *Architecture* framing used to support an arch or dome while it is under construction.

cen·ter·line /'sentər,līn/ (also **center line**) ▸*n.* a real or imaginary line through the center of something, esp. one following an axis of symmetry. ■ a painted line running down the middle of a road, dividing traffic traveling in opposite directions.

cen·ter of buoy·an·cy ▸*n.* *Physics* the centroid of the immersed part of a ship or other floating body.

cen·ter of cur·va·ture ▸*n.* *Mathematics* the center of a circle that passes through a curve at a given point and has the same tangent and curvature at that point.

cen·ter of grav·i·ty ▸*n.* a point from which the weight of a body or system may be considered to act. In uniform gravity it is the same as the center of mass.

cen·ter of mass ▸*n.* a point representing the mean position of the matter in a body or system.

cen·ter·piece /'sentər,pēs/ ▸*n.* a decorative piece or display placed in the middle of a dining or serving table. ■ an item or issue intended to be a focus of attention: *the tower is the centerpiece of the park.*

cen·ter punch ▸*n.* a tool with a conical point for making an indentation in an object, to allow a drill to make a hole at the same spot without slipping.

cen·ter spread ▸*n.* the two facing middle pages of a newspaper or magazine.

cen·ter stage ▸*n.* [in *sing.*] the center of a stage. ■ the most prominent position: *oil remains at center stage, with demands for expanded drilling.*
▸*adv.* at or toward the middle of a stage: *at the play's opening she stands center stage.* ■ in or toward a prominent position: *Asian countries have moved center stage for world business.*

cen·ter-weight·ed me·ter·ing ▸*n.* *Photography* a mode of automatic light metering in a camera that compensates for differences in the brightness of the central and peripheral portions of the image.

cen·tes·i·mal /sen'tesəməl/ ▸*adj.* of or relating to division into hundredths. ▷early 19th cent.: from Latin *centesimus* 'hundredth,' from *centum* 'a hundred.' **—cen·tes·i·mal·ly** *adv.*

cen·tes·i·mo /sen'tesə,mō; CHen'tez-/ ▸*n.* (*pl.* **-mos** or **-mi** /-mē/) a monetary unit of Italy until the introduction of the euro, worth one hundredth of a lira (used only in calculations). ▷Italian.

cen·té·si·mo /sen'tesə,mō/ ▸*n.* (*pl.* **-mos**) a monetary unit of Uruguay and Panama, equal to one hundredth of a peso in Uruguay and one hundredth of a balboa in Panama. ▷Spanish.

centi- ▸*comb. form* used commonly in units of measurement: **1** one hundredth: *centiliter.* **2** hundred: *centigrade | centipede.* ▷from Latin *centum* 'hundred.'

cen·ti·grade /'sentə,grād/ ▸*adj.* [*postpositive* when used with a numeral] another term for CELSIUS[2]. ■ having a scale of a hundred degrees. ▷early 19th cent.: from French, from Latin *centum* 'a hundred' + *gradus* 'step.'

USAGE See usage at CELSIUS.

cen·ti·gram /'sentə,gram/ (abbr.: **cg**) ▸*n.* a metric unit of mass, equal to one hundredth of a gram.

cen·ti·li·ter /'sentə,lētər/ (*Brit.* **cen·ti·li·tre**) (abbr.: **cl**) ▸*n.* a metric unit of capacity, equal to one hundredth of a liter.

cen·time /'sän,tēm; 'sent-/ ▸*n.* a monetary unit of Switzerland and certain other countries (including France, Belgium, and Luxembourg until the introduction of the euro), equal to one hundredth of a franc or other decimal currency unit. ■ a coin of this value. ▷French, from Latin *centesimus* 'hundredth,' from *centum* 'a hundred.'

cen·ti·me·ter /'sentə,mētər; 'sän-/ (*Brit.* **cen·ti·me·tre**) (abbr.: **cm**) ▸*n.* a metric unit of length, equal to one hundredth of a meter.

cen·ti·me·ter-gram-sec·ond sys·tem ▸*n.* a system of measurement using the centimeter, the gram, and the second as basic units of length, mass, and time.

cen·ti·mo /'sentəmō/ ▸*n.* (*pl.* **-mos**) a monetary unit of Spain (until the introduction of the euro) and a number of Latin American countries, equal to one hundredth of the basic unit. ▷Spanish.

cen·ti·pede /'sentə,pēd/ ▸*n.* a predatory myriapod invertebrate with a flattened elongated body composed of many segments. Most segments bear a single pair of legs. • Class Chilopoda: several orders. ▷mid 17th cent.: from French *centipède* or Latin *centipeda*, from *centum* 'a hundred' + *pes, ped-* 'foot.'

centipede

cen·to /'sentō/ ▸*n.* (*pl.* **-tos**) *rare* a literary work made up of quotations from other authors. ▷early 17th cent.: Latin, 'patchwork garment,' the original sense in English.

cen·tra /'sentrə/ ▸ a plural form of CENTRUM.

cen·tral /'sentrəl/ ▸*adj.* **1** of, at, or forming the center: *the station has a central courtyard.* ■ accessible from a variety of places: *coaches met at a central location.* ■ *Phonetics* (of a vowel) articulated in the center of the mouth. **2** of the greatest importance; principal or essential: *his preoccupation with American history* *is central to his work | the rising crime rate remained the central campaign issue.* ■ [*attrib.*] (of a group or organization) having controlling power over a country or another organization: *central government | the central office.* ■ [*attrib.*] (of power or authority) in the hands of such a group: *local councils are increasingly subject to central control.* ▷mid 17th cent.: from French, or from Latin *centralis*, from *centrum* (see CENTER). **—cen·tral·i·ty** /sen'tralətē/ *n.* **—cen·tral·ly** *adv.*

Cen·tral Af·ri·can Re·pub·lic a country in central Africa; pop. 3,742,000; capital, Bangui; languages, French (official) and Sango. Former name (until 1958) UBANGHI SHARI.

Formerly a French colony, it became a republic within the French Community in 1958 and a fully independent state in 1960. Some stability was achieved when a civilian government was elected in 1993.

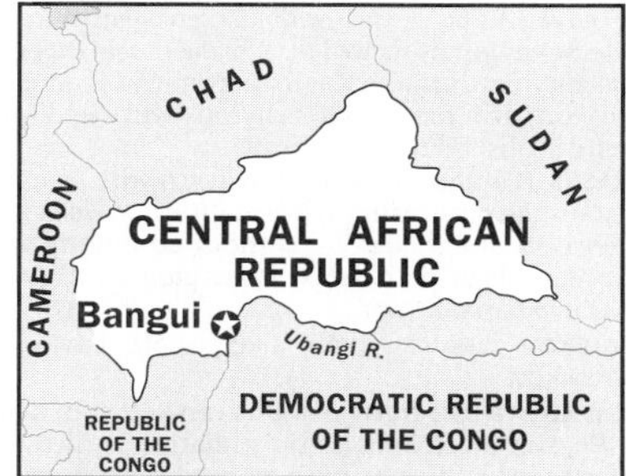

Cen·tral A·mer·i·ca the southernmost part of North America that links the continent to South America and consists of the countries of Guatemala, Belize, Honduras, El Salvador, Nicaragua, Costa Rica, and Panama. **—Cen·tral A·mer·i·can** *adj. & n.*

cen·tral bank ▸*n.* a national bank that provides financial and banking services for its country's government and commercial banking system, as well as implementing the government's monetary policy and issuing currency.

cen·tral cast·ing ▸*n.* a department at a movie or television studio that hires actors for smaller parts.

cen·tral cit·y ▸*n.* a heavily populated city at the center of a large metropolitan area.

Cen·tral Com·mand (abbr.: **Centcom**) a military strike force consisting of units from the U.S. Army, Air Force, and Navy, established in 1979 (as the Rapid Deployment Force) to operate in the Middle East and North Africa.

cen·tral heat·ing ▸*n.* a system for warming a building by heating water or air in one place and circulating it through pipes and radiators or vents.

Cen·tral In·tel·li·gence A·gen·cy (abbr.: **CIA**) a U.S. federal agency responsible for coordinating government intelligence activities.

cen·tral·ism /'sentrə,lizəm/ ▸*n.* a system that centralizes, esp. an administration. **—cen·tral·ist** *n. & adj.*

cen·tral·ize /'sentrə,līz/ ▸*v.* [*trans.*] [often as *adj.*] (**centralized**) concentrate (control of an activity or organization) under a single authority: *a vast superstructure of centralized control.* ■ bring (activities) together in one place: *the ultimate goal is to centralize boxing under one umbrella.* **—cen·tral·i·za·tion** /,sentrələ'zāsʜən/ *n.*

cen·tral lock·ing ▸*n.* a locking system in a motor vehicle that enables the locks of all doors to be operated simultaneously by a single person.

cen·tral nerv·ous sys·tem ▸*n. Anatomy* the complex of nerve tissues that controls the activities of the body. In vertebrates it comprises the brain and spinal cord.

Cen·tral Park a large public park in the center of Manhattan in New York City.

Cen·tral Pow·ers the alliance of Germany, Austria–Hungary, Turkey, and Bulgaria during World War I. ■ the alliance of Germany, Austria–Hungary, and Italy between 1882 and 1914.

cen·tral proc·ess·ing u·nit (also **cen·tral proc·es·sor**) (abbr.: **CPU**) ▸*n. Computing* the part of a computer in which operations are controlled and executed.

Cen·tral time the standard time in a zone that includes the central states of the U.S. and parts of central Canada, specifically: • (**Central Standard Time** abbrev.: **CST**) standard time based on the mean solar time at longitude 90° W., six hours behind GMT. • (**Central Daylight Time** abbrev.: **CDT**) Central time during daylight saving, five hours behind GMT.

Cen·tral Val·ley a lowland in central California that is drained in the north by the Sacramento River and also is called the Sacramento Valley. In the south, it is called the San Joaquin Valley.

cen·tre ▸*n.* British spelling of CENTER.

cen·trex /'sen,treks/ (*trademark* **Cen·trex**) ▸*n.* a telephone service in which a group of phone lines can be joined by part of the local exchange acting as a private exchange. ▷late 20th cent.: blend of CENTRAL and EXCHANGE.

cen·tric /'sentrik/ ▸*adj.* **1** in or at the center; central: *centric and peripheral forces.* **2** *Botany* (of a diatom) radially symmetrical. Compare with PENNATE. ▷late 16th cent.: from Greek *kentrikos*, from *kentron* 'sharp point' (see CENTER). **—cen·tri·cal** /-trikəl/ *adj.* **—cen·tric·i·ty** /sen'trisətē/ *n.*

-centric ▸*comb. form* having a specified center: *geocentric.* ■ forming an opinion or evaluation originating from a specified viewpoint: *Eurocentric | ethnocentric.* ▷from Greek *kentrikos*, on the pattern of words such as *(con)centric.*

-centricity ▸*comb. form* in nouns corresponding to adjectives ending in *-centric* (such as *ethnocentricity* corresponding to *ethnocentric*).

cen·trif·u·gal /sen'trif(y)əgəl/ ▸*adj. Physics* moving or tending to move away from a center. The opposite of CENTRIPETAL. ▷early 18th cent.: from modern Latin *centrifugus*, from Latin *centrum* (see CENTER) + *-fugus* 'fleeing' (from *fugere* 'flee'). **—cen·trif·u·gal·ly** *adv.*

cen·trif·u·gal force ▸*n. Physics* an apparent force that acts outward on a body moving around a center, arising from the body's inertia.

cen·trif·u·gal pump ▸*n.* a pump that uses an impeller to move water or other fluids.

cen·tri·fuge /'sentrə,fyōōj/ ▸*n.* a machine with a rapidly rotating container that applies centrifugal force to its contents, typically to separate fluids of different densities (e.g., cream from milk) or liquids from solids.
▸*v.* [*trans.*] (usu. **be centrifuged**) subject to the action of a centrifuge. ■ separate by centrifuge: *the black liquid is centrifuged into oil and water.* **—cen·trif·u·ga·tion** /,sentrə,fyōō'gāsʜən; sen,trif(y)ə-/ *n.*

cen·tri·ole /'sentrē,ōl/ ▸*n. Biology* a minute cylindrical organelle near the nucleus in animal cells, occurring in pairs and involved in the development of spindle fibers in cell division. ▷late 19th cent.: from modern Latin *centriolum*, diminutive of *centrum* (see CENTER).

cen·trip·e·tal /sen'tripətl/ ▸*adj. Physics* moving or tending to move toward a center. The opposite of CENTRIFUGAL. ▷early 18th cent.: from modern Latin *centripetus*, from Latin *centrum* (see CENTER) + *-petus* 'seeking' (from *petere* 'seek'). **—cen·trip·e·tal·ly** *adv.*

cen·trip·e·tal force ▸*n. Physics* a force that acts on a body moving in a circular path and is directed toward the center around which the body is moving.

cen·trist /'sentrəst/ ▸*adj.* having moderate political views or policies.
▸*n.* a person who holds moderate political views. ▷late 19th cent.: from French *centriste*, from Latin *centrum* (see CENTER). **—cen·trism** /-,trizəm/ *n.*

cen·troid /'sen,troid/ ▸*n. Mathematics* the center of mass of a geometric object of uniform density.

cen·tro·mere /'sentrə,mi(ə)r/ ▸*n. Biology* the point on a chromosome by which it is attached to a spindle fiber during cell division. ▷1920s: from Latin *centrum* (see CENTER) + Greek *meros* 'part.' **—cen·tro·mer·ic** /,sentrə'mi(ə)rik; -'merik/ *adj.*

cen·tro·some /'sentrə,sōm/ ▸*n. Biology* an organelle near the nucleus of a cell that contains the centrioles (in animal cells) and from which the spindle fibers develop in cell division. ▷late 19th cent.: from Latin *centrum* (see CENTER) + Greek *sōma* 'body.'

cen·tro·sphere /'sentrə,sfi(ə)r/ ▸*n.* **1** *Biology* a region of clear, differentiated cytoplasm from which the asters extend during cell division and containing the centriole(s) if present. **2** *Geology* the central or inner part of the earth.

cen·trum /'sentrəm/ ▸*n.* (*pl.* **-trums** or **-tra** /-trə/) *Anatomy* the solid central part of a vertebra, to which the arches and processes are attached. ▷mid 19th cent.: from Latin.

cen·tu·ple /sen't(y)ōōpəl; 'sen,t(y)ōōpəl/ ▸*v.* [*trans.*] multiply by a hundred or by a large amount: *they were centupling the national debt.* ▷early 17th cent.: from French, or from ecclesiastical Latin *centuplus*, alteration of Latin *centuplex*, from *centum* 'hundred.'

cen·tu·ri·on /sen't(y)ōōrēən/ ▸*n.* the commander of a century in the ancient Roman army. ▷Middle English: from Latin *centurion-*, from *centuria* (see CENTURY).

cen·tu·ry /'sencʜ(ə)rē/ ▸*n.* (*pl.* **-ries**) **1** a period of one hundred years: *a century ago most people walked to work.* ■ a period of one hundred years reckoned from the traditional date of the birth of Jesus Christ: *the fifteenth century | [as adj., in combination] (-century) a twentieth-century lifestyle.* **2** a group of one hundred things. **3** a company in the ancient Roman army, originally of one hundred men. ■ an ancient Roman political division for voting. **4** a bicycle race of one hundred miles: [as *adj.*] *the nation's largest single-day century ride.* ■ a score of one hundred in a sporting event. ▷late Middle English (sense 3): from Latin *centuria*, from *centum* 'hundred.' Sense 1 dates from the early 17th cent. **—cen·tu·ri·al** /sen't(y)ōōrēəl/ *adj.*

USAGE **1** In contemporary use, a **century** is popularly calculated as beginning in a year that ends with '00,' whereas the traditional system designates the '00' year as the final year of a century. This discrepancy was particularly apparent on January 1, 2000, which was commercially celebrated worldwide as the first day of the 21st century, even though January 1, 2001, was regarded as the more proper date for this milestone.
2 Since the 1st century ran from the year 1 to the year 100, the ordinal number (i.e., second, third, fourth, etc.) used to denote the century will always be one digit higher than the corresponding cardinal digit(s). Thus, 1492 is a date in the 15th century, 1776 is in the 18th century, and so on.

cen·tu·ry plant ▸*n.* a stemless agave with long spiny leaves, which produces a tall flowering stem after many years of growth and then dies. Also called AMERICAN ALOE. • *Agave americana*, family Agavaceae.

CEO ▸*abbr.* chief executive officer.

cep /sep/ (also **cèpe**) ▸*n.* an edible European and North American mushroom with a smooth brown cap, a stout white stalk, and pores rather than gills, growing in dry woodland and much sought after as a delicacy. Also called KING BOLETE, PORCINI. • *Boletus edulis*, family Boletaceae, class Basidiomycetes. ▷mid 19th cent.: from French *cèpe*, from Gascon *cep* 'tree trunk, mushroom,' from Latin *cippus* 'stake.'

cèpe /sep/ ▸*n.* another term for CEP.

ce·phal·ic /sə'falik/ ▸*adj. technical* of, in, or relating to the head. ▷late Middle English: from Old French *cephalique*, from Latin *cephalicus*, from Greek *kephalikos*, from *kephalē* 'head.'

-cephalic ▸*comb. form* equivalent to -CEPHALOUS.

ce·phal·ic in·dex ▸*n. Anthropology* a number expressing the ratio of the maximum breadth of a skull to its maximum length.

ceph·a·lin /'sefəlin/ ▸*n. Biochemistry* any of a group of phospholipids present in cell membranes, esp. in the brain. ▷late 19th cent.: from Greek *kephalē* 'brain' + -IN[1].

ceph·a·li·za·tion /,sefələ'zāsʜən/ ▸*n. Zoology* the concentration of sense organs, nervous control, etc., at the anterior end of the body, forming a head and brain, both during evolution and in the course of an embryo's development.

cephalo- ▸*comb. form* relating to the head or skull: *cephalometry.* ▷from Greek *kephalē* 'head.'

Ceph·a·lo·chor·da·ta /,sefəlō,kôr'dätə -'dātə/ *Zoology* a small group of marine invertebrates comprising the lancelets. • Subphylum Cephalochordata, phylum Chordata. ▷modern Latin (plural), from CEPHALO- 'head' + Latin *khorda* 'cord.' **—ceph·a·lo·chor·date** /-'kôr,dāt/ *n. & adj.*

ceph·a·lom·e·ter /sefə'lämitər/ ▸*n.* a device for measuring the human head.

ceph·a·lom·e·try /,sefə'lämətrē/ ▸*n. Medicine* measurement and study of the proportions of the head and face, esp. during development and growth. **—ceph·a·lo·met·ric** /-lō'metrik/ *adj.*

ceph·a·lon /'sefə,län; -lən/ ▸*n. Zoology* (in some arthropods, esp. trilobites) the region of the head, composed of fused segments. ▷late 19th cent.: from Greek *kephalē* 'head.'

Ceph·a·lop·o·da /,sefə'läpədə/ *Zoology* a class of active predatory mollusks comprising octopuses, squids, and cuttlefish. They have a distinct head with large eyes and a ring of tentacles around a beaked mouth and are able to release a cloud of inky fluid to confuse predators. ▷modern Latin (plural), from Greek *kephalē* 'head' + *pous, pod-* 'foot.' **—ceph·a·lo·pod** /ˈsefələ,päd/ *n.*

ceph·a·lo·spo·rin /,sefəlōˈspôrən/ ▸*n.* any of a group of semisynthetic broad-spectrum antibiotics resembling penicillin. ▷1950s: from modern Latin *Cephalosporium* (genus providing molds for this) + **-IN**[1].

ceph·a·lo·tho·rax /,sefəlōˈTHôraks/ ▸*n.* (*pl.* **-tho·ra·ces** /-ˈTHôrə,sēz/ or **-tho·rax·es**) *Zoology* the fused head and thorax of spiders and other chelicerate arthropods.

-cephalous ▸*comb. form* -headed (used commonly in medical, zoological, and botanical terms): *macrocephalous.* ▷based on Greek *kephalē* 'head' + **-OUS**.

ce·pheid /ˈsēfēəd; ˈsef-/ (also **cepheid variable**) ▸*n. Astronomy* a variable star having a regular cycle of brightness with a frequency related to its luminosity, so allowing estimation of its distance from the earth. ▷early 20th cent.: from the name of the variable star *Delta Cephei*, which typifies this class of stars.

Ce·phe·us /ˈsēfēəs; ˈsefēəs; ˈsē,fyo͞os/ *Astronomy* a constellation near the north celestial pole. ■ [as *genitive*] (**Cephei** /-fē,ī/) used with a preceding letter or numeral to designate a star in this constellation: *the star Beta Cephei.* ▷from the name of a king of Ethiopia, the husband of Cassiopeia.

'cept /sep(t)/ ▸*prep., conj.,* & *v.* nonstandard contraction of **EXCEPT** used in representing speech: *everyone else had visitors—'cept for Captain.*

ce·ram·ic /səˈramik/ ▸*adj.* made of clay and hardened by heat: *a ceramic bowl.* ■ of or relating to the manufacture of such articles.

▸*n.* (**ceramics**) pots and other articles made from clay hardened by heat: *handmade pottery and imaginative ceramics for the table.* ■ [usu. treated as *sing.*] the art of making such articles: *sculpting, drawing, ceramics, and fiber art.* ■ (**ceramic**) the material from which such articles are made: *tableware in ceramic.* ■ (**ceramic**) any nonmetallic solid that remains hard when heated. ▷early 19th cent.: from Greek *keramikos*, from *keramos* 'pottery.' **—ce·ram·i·cist** /səˈraməsist/ *n.*

Ce·ram Sea /ˈsā,räm/ (also **Se·ram Sea**) the part of the western Pacific Ocean that is at the center of the Molucca Islands in Indonesia.

ce·ras·tes /səˈras,tēz/ ▸*n.* a North African viper that has a spike over each eye. • Genus *Cerastes*, family Viperidae: two species, in particular the horned viper. ▷late Middle English: from Latin, from Greek *kerastēs* 'horned,' from *keras* 'horn.'

ce·rat·ed /ˈsi(ə)r,ātid/ ▸*adj.* **1** covered with wax or resin. **2** *Ornithology* having a cere.

cer·a·tite /ˈserə,tīt/ ▸*n.* an ammonoid fossil of an intermediate type found chiefly in the Permian and Triassic periods, typically with partly frilled and partly lobed suture lines. Compare with **AMMONITE** and **GONIATITE**. • Typified by the genus *Ceratites*, order Ceratida. ▷mid 19th cent.: from modern Latin *Ceratites* (from Greek *keras, kerat-* 'horn') + **-ITE**[1].

cer·a·top·si·an /,serəˈtäpsēən/ *Paleontology* ▸*n.* a gregarious quadrupedal herbivorous dinosaur of a group found in the Cretaceous period, including triceratops. It had a large beaked and horned head and a bony frill protecting the neck. • Infraorder Ceratopsia, order Ornithischia.

▸*adj.* of or relating to the ceratopsians. ▷early 20th cent.: from modern Latin *Ceratopsia* (plural) (from Greek *keras, kerat-* 'horn' + *ops* 'face') + **-AN**.

Cer·ber·us /ˈsərbərəs/ *Greek Mythology* a monstrous watchdog with three (or in some accounts fifty) heads that guarded the entrance to Hades.

cer·car·i·a /sərˈke(ə)rēə/ ▸*n.* (*pl.* **-car·i·ae** /-ˈke(ə)rē,ē/) *Zoology* a free-swimming larval stage in which a parasitic fluke passes from an intermediate host (typically a snail) to another intermediate host or to the final vertebrate host. ▷mid 19th cent.: modern Latin, formed irregularly from Greek *kerkos* 'tail.'

cer·clage /sərˈkläZH/ ▸*n. Medicine* the use of a ring or loop to bind together the ends of an obliquely fractured bone or to encircle the opening of a malfunctioning cervix. ▷early 20th cent.: from French, literally 'encirclement.'

cer·co·pi·the·cine /,sərkōˈpiTHə,sīn; -,sēn/ ▸*n. Zoology* an Old World monkey of a group that includes the macaques, mangabeys, baboons, and guenons. • Subfamily Cercopithecinae, family Cercopithecidae. ▷from modern Latin *Cercopithecinae* (plural), based on Greek *kerkopithēkos* 'long-tailed monkey,' from *kerkos* 'tail' + *pithēkos* 'ape.'

cer·co·pi·the·coid /,sərkəˈpiTHə,koid/ *Zoology* ▸*n.* a primate of a group that comprises the Old World monkeys. • Superfamily Cercopithecoidea and family Cercopithecidae.

▸*adj.* of or relating to monkeys of this group. ▷late 19th cent.: from modern Latin *Cercopithecoidea*, based on Greek *kerkopithēkos*, a long-tailed monkey (from *kerkos* 'tail' + *pithēkos* 'ape').

cer·cus /ˈsərkəs/ ▸*n.* (*pl.* **cer·ci** /ˈsər,sī; -,kī/) *Zoology* a small appendage at the end of the abdomen of some insects and other arthropods, occurring in pairs. ▷early 19th cent.: from modern Latin, from Greek *kerkos* 'tail.'

cere /si(ə)r/ ▸*n. Ornithology* a waxy, fleshy covering at the base of the upper beak in some birds. ▷late 15th cent.: from Latin *cera* 'wax.'

ce·re·al /ˈsi(ə)rēəl/ ▸*n.* a grain used for food, such as wheat, oats, or corn. ■ (usu. **cereals**) a grass producing such grain, grown as an agricultural crop: [as *adj.*] *low yields for cereal crops.* ■ a breakfast food made from roasted grain, typically eaten with milk: *a bowl of cereal* | [as *adj.*] *a cereal box.* ▷early 19th cent. (as an adjective): from Latin *cerealis*, from *Ceres*, the name of the Roman goddess of agriculture.

cer·e·bel·lum /,serəˈbeləm/ ▸*n.* (*pl.* **-bel·lums** or **-bel·la** /-ˈbelə/) *Anatomy* the part of the brain at the back of the skull in vertebrates. Its function is to coordinate and regulate muscular activity. ▷mid 16th cent.: from Latin, diminutive of **CEREBRUM**. **—cer·e·bel·lar** *adj.*

ce·re·bral /səˈrēbrəl; ˈserəbrəl/ ▸*adj.* **1** of the cerebrum of the brain: *a cerebral hemorrhage* | *the cerebral cortex.* ■ intellectual rather than emotional or physical: *photography is a cerebral process.* **2** *Phonetics* another term for **RETROFLEX**. ▷early 19th cent.: from Latin *cerebrum* 'brain' + **-AL**. **—ce·re·bral·ly** *adv.*

ce·re·bral aq·ue·duct ▸*n. Anatomy* a fluid-filled canal that runs through the midbrain connecting the third and fourth ventricles.

ce·re·bral dom·i·nance ▸*n.* the normal tendency for one side of the brain to control particular functions, such as handedness and speech.

ce·re·bral e·de·ma ▸*n. Medicine* a swelling in the brain caused by the presence of escessive fluid. See **ALTITIUDE SICKNESS**.

ce·re·bral pal·sy ▸*n.* a condition marked by impaired muscle coordination (spastic paralysis) and/or other disabilities, typically caused by damage to the brain before or at birth. See also **SPASTIC**.

cer·e·bra·tion /,serəˈbrāSHən/ ▸*n. technical* or *formal* the working of the brain; thinking. **—cer·e·brate** /ˈserə,brāt/ *v.*

cerebro- ▸*comb. form* of or relating to the brain: *cerebrospinal.* ▷from Latin *cerebrum* 'brain.'

ce·re·bro·side /səˈrēbrə,sīd; ˈserəbrə-/ ▸*n. Biochemistry* any of a group of complex lipids present in the sheaths of nerve fibers. ▷late 19th cent.: from Latin *cerebrum* 'brain' + **-OSE**[2] + **-IDE**.

ce·re·bro·spi·nal /sə,rēbrōˈspīnl; ,serəbrō-/ ▸*adj. Anatomy* of or relating to the brain and spine.

ce·re·bro·spi·nal flu·id ▸*n. Anatomy* clear watery fluid that fills the space between the arachnoid membrane and the pia mater.

ce·re·bro·vas·cu·lar /sə,rēbrōˈvaskyələr; ,serəbrō-/ ▸*adj. Anatomy* of or relating to the brain and its blood vessels.

ce·re·brum /səˈrēbrəm; ˈserə-/ ▸*n.* (*pl.* **-bra** /-brə/) *Anatomy* the principal and most anterior part of the brain in vertebrates, located in the front area of the skull and consisting of two hemispheres, left and right, separated by a fissure. It is responsible for the integration of complex sensory and neural functions and the initiation and coordination of voluntary activity in the body. See also **TELENCEPHALON**. ▷early 17th cent.: from Latin, 'brain.'

cere·cloth /ˈsi(ə)r,klôTH/ ▸*n. historical* waxed cloth typically used for wrapping a corpse. ▷late Middle English: from earlier *cered cloth*, from *cere* 'to wax,' from Latin *cerare*, from *cera* 'wax.'

cere·ment /ˈserəmənt; ˈsi(ə)rmənt/ ▸*n.* (usu. **cerements**) *historical* waxed cloth for wrapping a corpse. ▷early 17th cent. (first used by Shakespeare in *Hamlet*, 1602): from *cere* (see **CERECLOTH**).

cer·e·mo·ni·al /,serəˈmōnēəl/ ▸*adj.* **1** relating to or used for formal events of a religious or public nature: *a ceremonial Buddhist headpiece* | *the solemn, ceremonial air of a procession of monks* | *presented at ceremonial occasions.* See note at **FORMAL**. **2** (of a position or role) involving only nominal authority or power: *originally a ceremonial post, it is now a position with executive power.*

▸*n.* the system of rules and procedures to be observed at a formal or religious occasion: *the procedure was conducted with all due ceremonial.* ■ a rite or ceremony: *a ceremonial called the ghost dance.* ▷late Middle English: from late Latin *caerimonialis*, from *caerimonia* 'religious worship' (see **CEREMONY**). **—cer·e·mo·ni·al·ism** *n.* **—cer·e·mo·ni·al·ist** *n.* **—cer·e·mo·ni·al·ly** *adv.*

cer·e·mo·ni·ous /,serəˈmōnēəs/ ▸*adj.* relating or appropriate to grand and formal occasions: *a Great Hall where ceremonious and public appearances were made.* See note at **FORMAL**. ■ excessively polite; punctilious: *he accepted the gifts with ceremonious dignity.* ▷mid 16th cent.: from French *cérémonieux* or late Latin *caerimoniosus*, from *caerimonia* (see **CEREMONY**). **—cer·e·mo·ni·ous·ly** *adv.* **—cer·e·mo·ni·ous·ness** *n.*

cer·e·mo·ny /ˈserə,mōnē/ ▸*n.* (*pl.* **-nies**) **1** a formal religious or public occasion, typically one celebrating a particular event or anniversary. ■ an act or series of acts performed according to a traditional or prescribed form. **2** the ritual observances and procedures performed at grand and formal occasions: *the new Queen was proclaimed with due ceremony.* ■ formal polite behavior: *he showed them to their table with great ceremony.* ▷late Middle English: from Old French *ceremonie* or Latin *caerimonia* 'religious worship,' (plural) 'ritual observances.'

▸*PHRASES* □ **stand on ceremony** [usu. with *negative*] insist on the observance of formalities: *we don't stand on ceremony in this house.* □ **without ceremony** without preamble or politeness: *he was pushed without ceremony into the bathroom.*

Ce·ren·kov /CHəˈreNG,kôv; -,kôf; -kəf/, Pavel, see **CHERENKOV**.

Ce·ren·kov ra·di·a·tion (also **Che·ren·kov ra·di·a·tion**) ▸*n. Physics* electromagnetic radiation emitted by particles moving through a medium at speeds greater than that of light in the same medium.

ce·re·ol·o·gy /,si(ə)rēˈäləjē/ ▸*n.* the study or investigation of crop circles. ▷late 20th cent.: from **CERES** + **-LOGY**. **—ce·re·ol·o·gist** /-jist/ *n.*

ce·re·op·sis goose /,si(ə)rēˈäpsəs/ ▸*n.* another term for **CAPE BARREN GOOSE**. ▷late 19th cent.: from modern Latin *Cereopsis* (genus name), from Greek *kerinos* 'waxen' + *opsis* 'face' (because of its cere).

Ce·res /ˈsi(ə)rēz/ **1** *Roman Mythology* the goddess of grain and agriculture. Greek equivalent **DEMETER**. **2** *Astronomy* the first asteroid to be discovered, found by G. Piazzi of Palermo in 1801. It is also the largest, with a diameter of 567 miles (913 km).

cer·e·sin /ˈserəsin/ ▸*n.* a hard whitish paraffin wax used with or instead of beeswax. ▷late 19th cent.: from modern Latin *ceres* (from Latin *cera* 'wax') + **-IN**[1].

ce·re·us /ˈsi(ə)rēəs/ ▸*n.* one of numerous neotropical cacti now or formerly included in the genus *Cereus*.

ce·ric /ˈsi(ə)rik/ ▸*adj.* of cerium in its higher valency (4).

cer·i·man /ˈserəmən; ,serəˈman; -ˈmän/ ▸*n.* a large monstera with perforated leaves, popularly grown as a houseplant while young, and with creamy arumlike spathes followed by pineapple-flavored fruit when mature. • *Monstera deliciosa*, family Araceae.

ce·rise /səˈrēs; -ˈrēz/ ▸*n.* a bright or deep red color: *a shade of vivid cerise.*

▸*adj.* of a bright or deep red color. ▷mid 19th cent.: from French, literally 'cherry.'

ce·ri·um /ˈsi(ə)rēəm/ ▸*n.* the chemical element of atomic number 58, a silvery white metal. It is the most abundant of the lanthanide elements and is the main component of the alloy misch metal. (Symbol: **Ce**) ▷early 19th cent.: named after the asteroid **CERES**, discovered shortly before.

cer·met /ˈsər,met/ ▸*n.* any of a class of heat-resistant materials made of ceramic and sintered metal. ▷1950s: blend of **CERAMIC** and **METAL**.

CERN /sərn/ ▸*abbr.* European Organization for Nuclear Research. ▷initial letters of French *Conseil Européen pour la Recherche Nucléaire*, its former title.

ce·ro /ˈsi(ə)rō/ ▸*n.* (*pl.* same or **-ros**) a large fish of the mackerel family, serving as an important food fish in the tropical western Atlantic. • *Scomberomorus regalis*, family Scombridae. ▷late 19th cent.: from Spanish *sierra* 'saw or sawfish.'

cero- ▸*comb. form* of or relating to wax: *ceroplastic.* ▷from Latin *cera* or Greek *kēros* 'wax.'

ce·roc /səˈräk/ ▸*n. chiefly Brit.* a type of modern social dance having elements of rock and roll, jive, and salsa. ▷1990s: invented word, apparently coined in English from French *ce* 'this' + *roc* 'rock.'

ce·ro·plas·tic /,si(ə)rōˈplastik; ,serō-/ ▸*adj.* of or relating to modeling in wax.

ce·rous /ˈsi(ə)rəs/ ▸*adj.* of cerium in its lower valency (3).

Cer·ri·tos /sə'rētəs/ a city in southwestern California, southeast of Los Angeles; pop. 53,240.

Cer·ro Gor·do /'serō 'gôrdō/ a mountain pass in eastern Mexico, between Veracruz and Jalapa, scene of an 1847 victory by U.S. forces in the Mexican War.

cert. ▸*abbr.* ■ certificate. ■ certified.

cer·tain /'sərtn/ ▸*adj.* **1** known for sure; established beyond doubt: *it's certain that more changes are in the offing she looks certain to win an Oscar.* ■ having complete conviction about something; confident: *are you absolutely* ***certain about*** *this? | true and certain knowledge of the essence of existence.* **2** [*attrib.*] specific but not explicitly named or stated: *he raised certain personal problems with me | the exercise was causing him a certain amount of pain.* ■ used when mentioning the name of someone not known to the reader or hearer: *a certain General Percy captured the town.*
▸*pron.* (**certain of**) some but not all: *certain of his works have been edited.* ▷Middle English: from Old French, based on Latin *certus* 'settled, sure.'
▸*PHRASES* □ **for certain** without any doubt: *I don't know for certain.* □ **make certain** [with *clause*] take action to ensure that something happens or is the case: *I made certain that our paths would never cross again.* ■ establish whether something is definitely correct or true: *he probably knew her, but it didn't do any harm to make certain.*

cer·tain·ly /'sərtnlē/ ▸*adv.* [*sentence adverb*] undoubtedly; definitely; surely: *the prestigious address certainly adds to the firm's appeal | it certainly isn't worth risking your life.* ■ (in answer to a question or command) yes; by all means: *"A good idea," she agreed. "Certainly!"*

cer·tain·ty /'sərtntē/ ▸*n.* (*pl.* **-ties**) firm conviction that something is the case: *she knew* ***with absolute certainty*** *that they were dead.* ■ the quality of being reliably true: *there is a bewildering lack of certainty and clarity in the law.* ■ a fact that is definitely true or an event that is definitely going to take place: *an immediate transfer would be a certainty.* ■ a person or thing that may be relied on: *he was expected to be a certainty for a gold medal.* ▷Middle English: from Old French *certainete*, from *certain* (see **CERTAIN**).
▸*PHRASE* □ **for a certainty** beyond the possibility of doubt.

cer·tes /'sərtēz; sərts/ ▸*adv. archaic* assuredly; I assure you. ▷Middle English: from Old French, based on Latin *certus* 'settled, sure.'

cer·ti·fi·a·ble /,sərtə'fīəbəl/ ▸*adj.* **1** able or needing to be certified: *encephalitis was a certifiable condition | little hope for certifiable progress.* **2** officially recognized as needing treatment for a mental disorder. ■ *informal* crazy: *the world of fashion is almost entirely insane, the people who work in it mainly certifiable.* **—cer·ti·fi·a·bly** /-blē/ *adj.*

cer·tif·i·cate ▸*n.* /sər'tifikit/ an official document attesting a certain fact, in particular: ■ a document recording a person's birth, marriage, or death. ■ a document describing a medical condition: *certificate of immunization.* ■ a document attesting a level of achievement in a course of study or training: *graduate certificate in information technology.* ■ a document attesting ownership of a certain item: *a stock certificate.*
▸*v.* /-'tifəkāt/ [*trans.*] (usu. **be certificated**) provide with or attest in an official document. ▷late Middle English (in the sense 'certification, attestation'): from French *certificat* or medieval Latin *certificatum*, from *certificare* (see **CERTIFY**). **—cer·ti·fi·ca·tion** /,sərtəfi'kāsHən/ *n.*

cer·tif·i·cate of de·pos·it (abbr.: **CD**) ▸*n.* a certificate issued by a bank to a person depositing money for a specified length of time.

cer·ti·fied check ▸*n.* a check that is guaranteed by a bank.

cer·ti·fied mail ▸*n.* a postal service in which the sending and receipt of a letter or package are recorded.

cer·ti·fied milk ▸*n.* *historical* milk guaranteed free from the tubercle bacillus.

cer·ti·fied pub·lic ac·count·ant (abbr.: **CPA**) ▸*n.* a member of an officially accredited professional body of accountants.

cer·ti·fy /'sərtə,fī/ ▸*v.* (**-fies, -fied**) [*trans.*] (often **be certified**) attest or confirm in a formal statement: *the profits for the year had been certified by the auditors |* [with *clause*] *the medical witness certified that death was due to cerebral hemorrhage.* See note at **APPROVE**. ■ [often as *adj.*] (**certified**) officially recognize (someone or something) as possessing certain qualifications or meeting certain standards: *a certified scuba instructor |* ***board certified*** *in obstetrics and gynecology.* ■ officially declare insane. ▷Middle English: from Old French *certifier*, from late Latin *certificare*, from Latin *certus* 'certain.'

cer·ti·o·ra·ri /,sərsH(ē)ə'rārē; -'re(ə)rī/ ▸*n. Law* a writ or order by which a higher court reviews a decision of a lower court: *an order of certiorari.* ▷late Middle English: from Law Latin, 'to be informed,' a phrase originally occurring at the start of the writ, from *certiorare* 'inform,' from *certior*, comparative of *certus* 'certain.'

cer·ti·tude /'sərtə,t(y)o͞od/ ▸*n.* absolute certainty or conviction that something is the case: *the question may never be answered with certitude.* ■ something that someone firmly believes is true: *his certitude that "we're number one."* ▷late Middle English: from late Latin *certitudo*, from *certus* 'certain.'

ce·ru·le·an /sə'ro͞olēən/ *poetic/literary* ▸*adj.* deep blue in color like a clear sky: *cerulean waters and golden sands.*
▸*n.* a deep sky-blue color. ▷mid 17th cent.: from Latin *caeruleus* 'sky blue,' from *caelum* 'sky.'

ce·ru·men /sə'ro͞omən/ ▸*n.* technical term for **EARWAX**. ▷late 17th cent.: modern Latin, from Latin *cera* 'wax.'

ce·ruse /sə'ro͞os; 'si(ə)r,o͞os/ ▸*n.* archaic term for **WHITE LEAD**. ▷late Middle English: via Old French from Latin *cerussa*, perhaps from Greek *kēros* 'wax.'

Cer·van·tes /sər'vantēz; ser'väntās/, Miguel de (1547–1616), Spanish novelist and playwright; full name *Miguel de Cervantes Saavedra*. His most well-known work is *Don Quixote* (1605–15), a satire on chivalric romances that greatly influenced the development of the novel.

cer·vi·cal /'sərvikəl/ ▸*adj. Anatomy* **1** of or relating to the narrow necklike passage forming the lower end of the uterus: *cervical cancer.* **2** of or relating to the neck: *the fifth cervical vertebra.* ▷late 17th cent.: from French, or from modern Latin *cervicalis*, from Latin *cervix, cervic-* 'neck.'

cer·vi·ci·tis /sərvə'sītis/ ▸*n. Medicine* inflammation of the cervix.

cer·vid /'sərvəd/ ▸*n. Zoology* a mammal of the deer family (Cervidae). ▷late 19th cent.: from modern Latin *Cervidae* (plural), from Latin *cervus* 'deer.'

cer·vine /'sər,vin; -vin/ ▸*adj.* of or relating to deer; deerlike. ▷mid 19th cent.: from Latin *cervinus*, from *cervus* 'deer.'

cer·vix /'sərviks/ ▸*n.* (*pl.* **-vices** /-və,sēz/) the narrow necklike passage forming the lower end of the uterus. ■ *technical* the neck. ■ a part of other bodily organs resembling a neck. ▷mid 18th cent.: Latin.

ce·sar·e·an /si'ze(ə)rēən/ (also **cae·sar·e·an**, **Cae·sar·e·an**, or *chiefly Brit.* **Cae·sar·i·an**) ▸*adj.* of or effected by cesarean section: *a cesarean delivery.*
▸*n.* a cesarean section: *I had to have a cesarean | two sons both born by cesarean.* ▷early 16th cent. (as a noun denoting a supporter of an emperor or imperial system): from Latin *Caesareus* 'of Caesar' + **-AN**

ce·sar·e·an sec·tion ▸*n.* a surgical operation for delivering a child by cutting through the wall of the mother's abdomen. ▷early 17th cent.: *cesarean* from the story that Julius Caesar was delivered by this method.

ce·si·um /'sēzēəm/ (*Brit.* **cae·si·um**) ▸*n.* the chemical element of atomic number 55, a soft, silvery, extremely reactive metal. It belongs to the alkali metal group and occurs as a trace element in some rocks and minerals. (Symbol: **Cs**) ▷mid 19th cent.: from Latin *caesius* 'grayish-blue' (because it has characteristic lines in the blue part of the spectrum).

Čes·ké Bu·dě·jo·vi·ce /'CHeske 'bo͝odyə-yôvitse/ a city in the southern Czech Republic, on the Vltava River; pop. 173,400. It is noted for the production of lager. German name **BUDWEIS**.

ces·pi·tose /'sespi,tōs/ ▸*adj. Botany* forming mats or growing in dense tufts or clumps.

cess[1] /ses/ (also **sess**) ▸*n.* (in Scotland, Ireland, and India) a tax or levy. ▷late 15th cent. (denoting the obligation placed on the Irish to supply the Lord Deputy's household and garrison with provisions at prices "assessed" by the government): shortened from the obsolete noun *assess* 'assessment.'

cess[2] ▸*n.* (in phrase **bad cess to**) *chiefly Irish* a curse on: *bad cess to the day I joined that band!* ▷mid 19th cent. (originally Anglo-Irish): perhaps from **CESS**[1].

ces·sa·tion /se'sāsHən/ ▸*n.* a ceasing; an end: *the cessation of hostilities | a cessation of animal testing of cosmetics.* ■ a pause or interruption: *a cessation of respiration requiring resuscitation.* ▷late Middle English: from Latin *cessatio(n-)*, from *cessare* 'cease.'

ces·ser /'sesər/ ▸*n. Law* termination or cessation, esp. of a period of tenure or legal liability. ▷mid 16th cent.: from Old French *cesser* 'cease,' used as a noun.

ces·sion /'sesHən/ ▸*n.* the formal giving up of rights, property, or territory, esp. by a state: *the cession of twenty important towns.* ▷late Middle English: from Latin *cession-*, from *cedere* 'cede.'

cess·pit /'ses,pit/ ▸*n.* a pit for the disposal of liquid waste and sewage. ■ *figurative* a disgusting or corrupt place or situation: *the affair threatened to be a cesspit of scandal.* ▷mid 19th cent.: from *cess* (the supposed base of **CESSPOOL**) + **PIT**[1].

cess·pool /'ses,po͞ol/ ▸*n.* an underground container for the temporary storage of liquid waste and sewage. ■ *figurative* a disgusting or corrupt place: *they should clean out their own political cesspool.* ▷late 17th cent. (denoting a trap under a drain to catch solids): probably an alteration, influenced by **POOL**[1], of archaic *suspiral* 'vent, water pipe, settling tank,' from Old French *souspirail* 'air hole,' based on Latin *sub-* 'from below' + *spirare* 'breathe.'

ces·ta /'sestə/ ▸a wicker basket used in jai alai to catch and throw the ball.

c'est la vie /,sā lä 'vē/ ▸*exclam.* that's life; such is life: *if you get thwarted, c'est la vie.* ▷early 20th cent.: French.

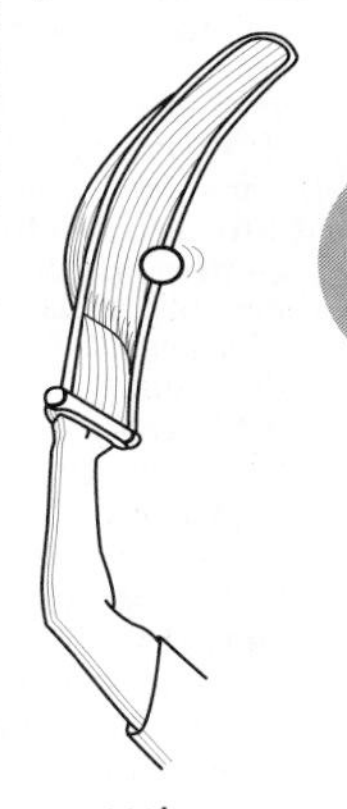

cesta

Ces·to·da /ses'tōdə/ (also **Ces·toi·de·a** /-'toidēə/) *Zoology* a class of parasitic flatworms that comprises the tapeworms. ▷modern Latin (plural), from Latin *cestus*, from Greek *kestos*, literally 'stitched,' used as a noun in the sense 'girdle.' **—ces·tode** /'ses,tōd/ *n.*

Ce·ta·cea /si'tāsH(ē)ə/ *Zoology* an order of marine mammals that comprises the whales, dolphins, and porpoises. These have a streamlined hairless body, no hind limbs, a horizontal tail fin, and a blowhole on top of the head for breathing. See also **MYSTICETI**, **ODONTOCETI**. ▷modern Latin (plural), from Latin *cetus*, from Greek *kētos* 'whale.' **—ce·ta·cean** /si'tāsHən/ *n. & adj.*

ce·tane /'sē,tān/ ▸*n. Chemistry* a colorless liquid hydrocarbon of the alkane series, used as a solvent. • Alternative name: ***n*-hexadecane**; chem. formula: $C_{16}H_{34}$. ▷late 19th cent.: from Latin *cetus* 'whale,' from Greek *kētos* (because related compounds were first derived from spermaceti) + **-ANE**[2].

ce·tane num·ber ▸*n.* a measure of the ignition properties of diesel fuel relative to cetane as a standard.

ce·te·ris pa·ri·bus /,kātəris 'parəbəs/ ▸*adv. formal* with other conditions remaining the same: *shorter hours of labor will, ceteris paribus, reduce the volume of output.* ▷early 17th cent.: modern Latin.

ce·tol·o·gy /sē'täləjē/ ▸*n.* the branch of zoology that deals with whales, dolphins, and porpoises.

Cetsh·wa·yo /keCH'wī-ō/ (also **Cet·e·wa·yo** /,setə'wī-ō/) (*c.*1826–84), Zulu king. He became ruler of Zululand in 1873 and was involved in a series of battles with the Afrikaners and British; he was deposed as leader after the capture of his capital by the British in 1879.

Ce·tus /'sētəs/ *Astronomy* a large northern constellation (the Whale), said to represent the sea monster that threatened Andromeda. It contains the variable star Mira. ■ [as *genitive*] (**Ceti** /-tē/) used with a preceding letter or numeral to designate a star in this constellation: *the star Tau Ceti.* ▷Latin.

ce·tyl al·co·hol /'sētl/ ▸*n.* a waxy alcohol occurring in feces and esterified in spermaceti and wool wax. It is used in cosmetics and as an emulsifier. • Chem. formula: $CH_3(CH_2)_{15}OH$.

Ceu·ta /'THā,o͞otə; 'sā-/ a Spanish enclave, consisting of a port and a military post, on the coast of Morocco in northern Africa; pop. 67,615. It overlooks the Mediterranean approach to the Strait of Gibraltar and with Melilla forms a community of Spain.

Cé·vennes /sā'ven/ a mountain range in France, on the southeastern edge of the Massif Central.

ce·vi·che /sə'vēCHā; -CHē/ (also **se·viche**) ▸*n.* a South American dish of marinated raw fish or seafood, typically garnished and served as an appetizer. ▷South American Spanish.

Cey·lon /si'län; sā'län/ former name (until 1972) of **SRI LANKA**.

Cey·lon moss ▸*n.* a red seaweed of the Indian

Pronunciation Key ə *ago*; ər *over*; 'ə *or* ,ə *up*; 'ər *or* ,ər *fur*; a *hat*; ā *rate*; ä *car*; CH *chew*; e *let*; ē *see*; e(ə)r *air*; i *fit*; ī *by*; i(ə)r *ear*; NG *sing*; ō *go*; ô *for*; oi *boy*; o͝o *good*; o͞o *goo*; ou *out*; SH *she*; TH *thin*; TH *then*; (h)w *why*; ZH *vision*

subcontinent, the main source of agar. • *Gracilaria lichenoides,* phylum Rhodophyta.

Cey·lon sat·in·wood ▸*n.* see SATINWOOD (sense 2).

Cé·zanne /sā'zän/, Paul (1839–1906), French painter. He is closely identified with post-Impressionism, and his later work had an important influence on cubism. Notable works: *Still Life with Cupid* (1895) and *Bathers* (sequence of paintings, 1890–1905).

CF ▸*abbr.* ■ carried forward. ■ cost and freight. ■ cystic fibrosis.

Cf ▸*symbol* the chemical element californium.

cf. ▸*abbr.* compare with (used to refer a reader to another written work or another part of the same written work). ▷from Latin *confer* 'compare.'

c.f. ▸*abbr.* carried forward (used to refer to figures transferred to a new page or account).

CFA[1] (also **CFA franc**) ▸*n.* the basic monetary unit of Cameroon, Congo, Gabon, and the Central African Republic, equal to 100 centimes. ▷*CFA* from French *Communauté Financière Africaine* 'African Financial Community.'

CFA[2] ▸*abbr.* chartered financial analyst.

CFC ▸*abbr. Chemistry* chlorofluorocarbon.

cfm ▸*abbr.* cubic feet per minute.

CFO ▸*abbr.* chief financial officer.

CFS ▸*abbr.* chronic fatigue syndrome.

cfs ▸*abbr.* cubic feet per second.

CG ▸*abbr.* ■ Coast Guard. ■ commanding general.

cg ▸*abbr.* centigram(s).

cgi ▸*abbr. Computing* common gateway interface, a script standard for writing interactive programs (such as forms and searches) generated by visitors to Web pages.

cgi-bin /'sē,jē'ī ,bin/ ▸*n. Computing* a server directory where cgi programs are stored: [as *modifier*] *cgi-bin files.*

cGMP ▸*abbr.* cyclic GMP.

cgs ▸*abbr.* centimeter-gram-second.

CGT ▸*abbr.* capital gains tax.

CH ▸*abbr.* ■ courthouse. ■ custom house.

ch. ▸*abbr.* ■ chaplain. ■ chapter. ■ (of a horse) chestnut in color. ■ church.

c.h. (also **C.H.**) ▸*abbr.* clearinghouse.

chab·a·zite /'kabə,zīt/ ▸*n.* a colorless, pink, or yellow zeolite mineral, typically occurring as rhombohedral crystals. ▷early 19th cent.: from French *chabazie,* from Greek *khabazie,* a misreading of *khalazie,* vocative form of *khalazios* 'hailstone' (from *khalaza* 'hail,' because of its form and color), + -ITE[1].

Cha·blis /SHa'blē; SHə-; SHä-/ ▸*n.* a dry white burgundy wine from Chablis in eastern France.

Cha·brol /SHä'brōl/, Claude (1930–), French movie director; a member of the *nouvelle vague.*

cha-cha /'CHä ,CHä/ (also **cha-cha-cha** /-'CHä/) ▸*n.* a ballroom dance with small steps and swaying hip movements, performed to a Latin American rhythm. ■ music for or in the rhythm of such a dance.

▸*v.* (**cha-chas, cha-chaed** or **cha-cha'd, cha-cha·ing**) [*intrans.*] dance the cha-cha. ▷1950s: Latin American Spanish.

cha·cha·la·ca /,CHäCHə'läkə/ ▸*n.* a pheasantlike tree-dwelling bird of the guan family, with a loud harsh call. It is found mainly in the forests of tropical America. • Genus *Ortalis,* family Cracidae: several species, in particular the **plain chachalaca** (*O. vetula*). ▷late 19th cent.: via South American Spanish from Nahuatl, of imitative origin.

cha·cham /KHä'KHäm/ (also **ha·ham**) /'hähəm/ ▸*n.* a spiritual leader among Sephardic Jews, or, more generally, a person learned in Jewish law. ▷from Hebrew *ḥāḵām* 'wise.'

chac·ma ba·boon /'CHäkmə/ ▸*n.* a dark gray baboon that lives on the savanna of southern Africa. • *Papio ursinus,* family Cercopithecidae. ▷mid 19th cent.: from Khoikhoi.

Cha·co /'CHäkō/ another name for GRAN CHACO.

cha·conne /SHä'kôn; -'kän; -'kən/ ▸*n. Music* a composition in a series of varying sections in slow triple time, typically over a short repeated bass theme. Compare with PASSACAGLIA. ■ a stately dance performed to such music, popular in the 18th century. ▷late 17th cent.: from French, from Spanish *chacona.*

Cha·co War a boundary dispute in 1932–35 between Bolivia and Paraguay, in which Paraguay eventually gained most of the disputed territory.

cha·cun à son goût /SHä,kœN nä SON 'goo/ ▸*exclam.* each to one's own taste. ▷late 19th cent.: French.

Chad /CHad/ a landlocked country in northern central Africa; pop. 9,538,000; capital, N'Djamena; official languages, French and Arabic. **—Chad·i·an** *adj. & n.*

Much of the country lies in the Sahel, as well as the Sahara Desert in the north. A French colony from 1913, Chad became autonomous within the French Community in 1958 and fully independent as a republic in 1960. The country has been troubled by rebellions in the north since 1998.

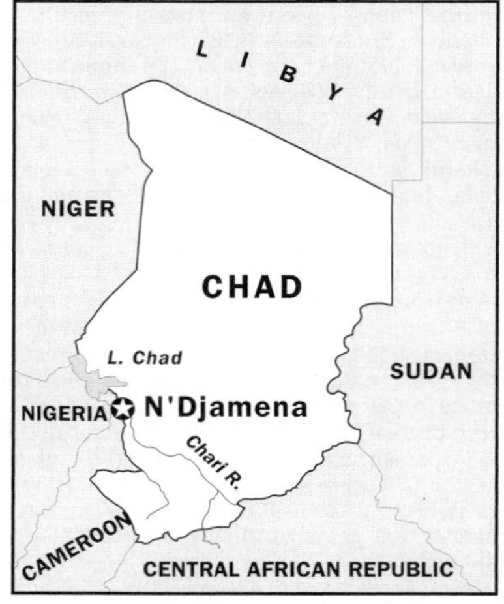

Chad, Lake a shallow lake on the borders of Chad, Niger, and Nigeria in north central Africa. Its size varies seasonally from about 4,000 square miles (10,360 sq km) to about 10,000 square miles (25,900 sq km).

chad /CHad/ ▸*n.* a piece of waste material created by punching cards or tape. ■ a small piece of paper punched out of a ballot. ▷1930s: possibly from Scots *chad* 'gravel; small stones' or dialect *chat* 'chip of wood.' It is not, as suggested, from the name of Mr. Chadless, inventor of a *Chadless Keypunch,* no such person has been found. Nor is it formed as an acronym from 'card hole aggregate debris.'

Chad·ic /'CHadik/ ▸*n.* a group of Afro-Asiatic languages spoken in the region of Lake Chad, of which the most important is Hausa.

▸*adj.* of or relating to this group of languages.

chad·or /'CHədər; 'CHäd,ôr/ (also **chad·ar** or **chud·dar**) ▸*n.* a large piece of dark-colored cloth, typically worn by Muslim women, wrapped around the head and upper body to leave only the face exposed. ▷early 17th cent.: from Urdu *chādar, chaddar,* from Persian *čādar* 'sheet or veil.'

Chad·wick /'CHadwik/, Sir James (1891–1974), English physicist who discovered the neutron. Nobel Prize for Physics (1935).

chae·bol /'kī,bäl; -,bôl/ ▸*n.* (*pl.* same or **-bols**) (in South Korea) a large business conglomerate, typically a family-owned one. ▷1980s: Korean, literally 'money clan.'

chae·ta /'kētə/ ▸*n.* (*pl.* **-tae** /-tē/) *Zoology* a stiff bristle made of chitin, esp. in an annelid worm. ▷mid 19th cent.: modern Latin, from Greek *khaitē* 'long hair.'

Chae·tog·na·tha /kē'tägnəTHə/ *Zoology* a small phylum of marine invertebrates that comprises the arrow worms. ▷modern Latin (plural), from Greek *khaitē* 'long hair' + *gnathos* 'jaw.' **—chae·tog·nath** /'kētäg,naTH/ *n.*

chafe /CHāf/ ▸*v.* **1** [*trans.*] (of something restrictive or too tight) make (a part of the body) sore by rubbing against it: *the collar chafed his neck.* ■ [*intrans.*] (of a part of the body) be or become sore as a result of such rubbing. ■ [*intrans.*] (of an object) rub abrasively against another object: *the grommet stops the cable from chafing on the metal.* **2** [*trans.*] rub (a part of the body) to restore warmth or sensation. ■ restore (warmth or sensation) in this way: *he* **chafed** *some feeling* **into** *his frozen hands.* **3** become or make annoyed or impatient because of a restriction or inconvenience: [*intrans.*] *the bank chafed at the restrictions imposed upon it* | [*trans.*] *it chafed him to be confined like this.*

▸*n.* **1** wear or damage caused by rubbing: *to prevent chafe the ropes should lie flat.* **2** *archaic* a state of annoyance. ▷late Middle English (in the sense 'make warm'): from Old French *chaufer* 'make hot,' based on Latin *calefacere,* from *calere* 'be hot' + *facere* 'make.'

▸*PHRASE* □ **chafe at the bit** see CHOMP AT THE BIT at CHOMP.

chaf·er /'CHāfər/ ▸*n.* a flying beetle, the adult and larva of which can be very destructive to foliage and plant roots respectively. • Several subfamilies of the family Scarabaeidae. See also COCKCHAFER. ▷Old English *ceafor, cefer,* of Germanic origin; related to Dutch *kever.*

chaff[1] /CHaf/ ▸*n.* the husks of corn or other seed separated by winnowing or threshing. ■ chopped hay and straw used as fodder. ■ *figurative* worthless things; trash. ■ strips of metal foil or metal filings released in the atmosphere from aircraft, or deployed as missiles, to obstruct radar detection or confuse radar-tracking missiles. ▷Old English *cæf, ceaf,* probably from a Germanic base meaning 'gnaw'; related to Dutch *kaf,* also to CHAFER. **—chaff·y** *adj.*

▸*PHRASE* □ **separate the wheat from the chaff** distinguish valuable people or things from worthless ones.

chaff[2] ▸*n.* lighthearted joking; banter.

▸*v.* [*trans.*] tease. ▷early 19th cent.: perhaps from CHAFE.

chaff-cut·ter ▸*n. chiefly historical* a machine for chopping hay and straw for use as fodder.

Chaf·fee /'CHafē/ Roger B., see GRISSOM.

chaf·fer /'CHafər/ ▸*v.* [*intrans.*] haggle about the terms of an agreement or price of something.

▸*n. archaic* haggling about the price of something. ▷Middle English (in the sense 'trade or trading'): from Old English *cēap* 'a bargain' + *faru* 'journey'; probably influenced by Old Norse *kaupfor.* **—chaff·er·er** *n.*

chaf·finch /'CHaf,inCH/ ▸*n.* a Eurasian and North African finch, typically with a bluish top to the head and dark wings and tail. • Genus *Fringilla,* family Fringillidae: two species, in particular *F. coelebs,* which (in the male of the typical European form) has a pinkish face and breast. ▷Old English *ceaffinc* 'chaff finch' (because it forages around barns, picking seeds out of the chaff).

chaff·weed /'CHaf,wēd/ ▸*n.* a tiny European pimpernel with pink or white flowers. • *Anagallis minima,* family Primulaceae. ▷mid 16th cent.: probably from the verb CHAFE + WEED.

chaf·ing dish /'CHāfiNG/ ▸*n.* a metal pan with an outer pan of hot water, used for keeping food warm. ■ a metal pan, typically one containing an alcohol lamp, used for cooking at the table. ▷late 15th cent.: from the original (now obsolete) sense of CHAFE 'become warm, warm up.'

Cha·gall /SHə'gäl/, Marc (1887–1985), French painter and graphic artist; born in Russia. His work was characterized by the use of rich emotive color and dream imagery and had a significant influence on surrealism.

Cha·gas' dis·ease /'SHägəs/ ▸*n.* a disease caused by trypanosomes transmitted by bloodsucking bugs, endemic in South America and causing damage to the heart and central nervous system. ▷early 20th cent.: named after Carlos *Chagas* (1879–1934), the Brazilian physician who first described it.

Cha·gos Ar·chi·pel·a·go /'CHägəs/ an island group in the Indian Ocean that forms the British Indian Ocean Territory.

cha·grin /SHə'grin/ ▸*n.* distress or embarrassment at having failed or been humiliated: *Jeff, much* **to his chagrin,** *wasn't invited.*

▸*v.* (**be chagrined**) feel distressed or humiliated: *he was chagrined when his friend poured scorn on him.* ▷mid 17th cent. (in the sense 'melancholy'): from French *chagrin* (noun), literally 'rough skin, shagreen,' *chagriner* (verb), of unknown origin.

chai /CHī/ ▸*n. Indian* tea, esp. when made by boiling the tea leaves with milk, sugar, and cardamom. ▷a term in various Indian languages.

Chain /CHān/, Sir Ernst Boris (1906–79), British biochemist; born in Germany. With Howard Florey he isolated and purified penicillin. Nobel Prize for Physiology or Medicine (1945, shared with Florey and Alexander Fleming).

chain /CHān/ ▸*n.* **1** a connected flexible series of metal links used for fastening or securing objects and pulling or supporting loads. ■ (**chains**) such a series of links, or a set of them, used to confine a prisoner: *the drug dealer is being kept* **in chains.** ■ such a series of links worn as a decoration; a necklace. ■ *chiefly Brit.* such a series of links worn as a badge of office. ■ (**chains**) *figurative* a force or factor that binds or restricts someone: *the chains of illness.* ■ (**chains**) short for SNOW CHAINS. **2** a sequence of items of the same type forming a line: *he kept the chain of buckets supplied with water.* ■ a sequence or series of connected elements: *a chain of events | the food chain.* ■ a group of establishments, such as hotels, stores, or restaurants, owned by the same company: *the nation's largest hotel chain.* ■ a range of mountains: *a chain of volcanic ridges.* ■ a part of a molecule consisting of a number of atoms (typically carbon) bonded together in a linear sequence. ■ a figure in a quadrille or similar dance, in which dancers meet and pass each other in a continuous sequence. **3** a jointed measuring line consisting of linked metal rods. ■ the length of such a measuring line (66 ft.). ■ *Football* a measuring chain of ten yards, used in the determination of first downs. **4** (**chains**) a structure of planks projecting horizontally from a sailing ship's sides abreast of the masts, used to widen the basis for the shrouds. [formed earlier of iron plates.]

▸*v.* [*trans.*] fasten or secure with a chain: *she chained her bicycle to the railing.* ■ confine with a chain: *he had been* ***chained up*** | *figurative as an actuary you will not be chained to a desk.* ▷Middle English: from Old French *chaine, chaeine,* from Latin *catena* 'a chain.'

▸*PHRASE* □ **pull** (or **yank**) **someone's chain** *informal* tease someone, typically by leading them to believe something untrue.

chain bridge ▸*n.* a suspension bridge supported by chains rather than cables.

chain drive ▸*n.* a mechanism in which power is transmitted from an engine, typically to the wheels of a vehicle or a boat's propeller, by means of a moving endless chain. **—chain-driv·en** *adj.*

chain gang ▸*n.* a group of convicts chained together while working outside the prison.

chain gear ▸*n.* a gear transmitting motion by means of a moving endless chain, esp. on a bicycle.

chain har·row ▸*n.* a harrow consisting of a net made of chains in a metal frame.

chain let·ter ▸*n.* one of a sequence of letters, each recipient in the sequence being requested to send copies to a specific number of other people.

chain-link ▸*adj.* [*attrib.*] made of wire in a diamond-shaped mesh: *a chain-link fence.*

chain mail ▸*n. historical* armor made of small metal rings linked together.

chain·plate /'CHān,plāt/ ▸*n.* a strong link or plate on a sailing ship's side, to which the shrouds are secured.

chain re·ac·tion ▸*n.* a chemical reaction or other process in which the products themselves promote or spread the reaction, which under certain conditions may accelerate dramatically. ■ the self-sustaining fission reaction spread by neutrons that occurs in nuclear reactors and bombs. ■ *figurative* a series of events, each caused by the previous one: *an article in one publication sets off a chain reaction in the media.*

chain·ring /'CHān,riNG/ ▸*n.* a large cog carrying the chain on a bicycle, which is attached to the crank.

chain·saw /'CHān,sô/ ▸*n.* a mechanical power-driven cutting tool with teeth set on a chain that moves around the edge of a blade.

chain shot ▸*n. historical* pairs of cannonballs or half balls joined by a chain, fired from cannons in sea battles in order to damage masts and rigging.

chain-smoke ▸*v.* [*intrans.*] smoke continually, esp. by lighting a new cigarette from the butt of the last one smoked. **—chain-smok·er** *n.*

chain stitch ▸*n.* an ornamental stitch in which loops are crocheted or embroidered in a chain.

chain store ▸*n.* one of a series of stores owned by one company and selling the same merchandise.

chain wheel ▸*n.* a toothed wheel transmitting power by means of a chain fitted to its edges.

chair /CHe(ə)r/ ▸*n.* **1** a separate seat for one person, typically with a back and four legs. ■ *historical* a sedan chair. ■ short for **CHAIRLIFT**. **2** the person in charge of a meeting or organization (used as a neutral alternative to chairman or chairwoman): *the deputy chair of the Supreme Soviet.* ■ an official position of authority, for example on a board of directors: *the editorial chair.* ■ (also **chair umpire**) *Tennis* another term for **UMPIRE**. **3** a professorship: *he held a chair in physics.* **4** a particular seat in an orchestra: [as *adj.*, in *combination*] *she was fourth-chair trumpet.* **5** (**the chair**) short for **ELECTRIC CHAIR**. **6** *chiefly Brit.* a metal socket holding a railroad rail in place.

▸*v.* [*trans.*] **1** act as chairperson of or preside over (an organization, meeting, or public event). **2** *Brit.* carry (someone) aloft in a chair or in a sitting position to celebrate a victory. ▷Middle English: from Old French *chaiere* (modern *chaire* 'bishop's throne, etc.,' *chaise* 'chair'), from Latin *cathedra* 'seat,' from Greek *kathedra*. Compare with **CATHEDRAL**.

▸*PHRASE* □ **take the chair** act as chairperson.

chair·borne /'CHe(ə)r,bôrn/ ▸*adj. military slang* assigned to a desk job rather than field duty.

chair car ▸*n.* a railroad car with individual seats instead of long benches; a parlor car.

chair·la·dy /'CHe(ə)r,lādē/ ▸*n.* (*pl.* **-dies**) another term for **CHAIRWOMAN**.

chair·lift /'CHe(ə)r,lift/ ▸*n.* **1** a series of chairs hung from a moving cable, typically used for carrying passengers up and down a mountain. **2** a device for carrying people in wheelchairs from one floor of a building to another.

chair·man /'CHe(ə)rmən/ ▸*n.* (*pl.* **-men**) **1** a person, esp. a man, designated to preside over a meeting. ■ the permanent or long-term president of a committee, company, or other organization. ■ (**Chairman**) (since 1949) the leading figure in the Chinese Communist Party. **2** a person, esp. a man, who is the administrative head of a department of instruction at a college or university. **3** *historical* a sedan-bearer. **—chair·man·ship** /-,SHip/ *n.*

chair·per·son /'CHe(ə)r,pərsən/ ▸*n.* a chairman or chairwoman (used as a neutral alternative).

chair·wom·an /'CHe(ə)r,wŏŏmən/ ▸*n.* (*pl.* **-wom·en**) **1** a woman designated to preside over committee or board meetings. **2** a woman who is the administrative head of a department of instruction at a college or university.

chaise /SHāz/ ▸*n.* **1** *chiefly historical* a horse-drawn carriage for one or two people, typically one with an open top and two wheels. ■ another term for **POST-CHAISE**. **2** short for **CHAISE LONGUE**. ▷mid 17th cent.: from French, variant of *chaire* (see **CHAIR**).

chaise longue /'SHāz 'lôNG/ ▸*n.* (*pl.* **chaises longues** /'SHāz 'lôNG(z)/) a reclining chair with a lengthened seat forming a leg rest. ▷early 19th cent.: French, literally 'long chair.'

chaise lounge /'SHāz 'lounj; 'CHās/ ▸*n.* variant of **CHAISE LONGUE**. ▷early 20th cent.: alteration by association with **LOUNGE**.

Cha·ka variant spelling of **SHAKA**.

chak·ra /'CHäkrə/ ▸*n.* (in Indian thought) each of the centers of spiritual power in the human body, usually considered to be seven in number. ▷from Sanskrit *cakra* 'wheel or circle,' from an Indo-European base meaning 'turn,' shared by **WHEEL**.

cha·la·za /kə'lāzə; -'lazə/ ▸*n.* (*pl.* **-la·zae** /-'lāzē; -'lazē; -,zī/) *Zoology* (in a bird's egg) each of two twisted membranous strips joining the yolk to the ends of the shell. ▷early 18th cent.: modern Latin, from Greek *khalaza* 'small knot.' **—cha·la·zal** *adj.*

Chal·ce·don /'kalsə,dän; kal'sēdn/ a former city on the Bosporus in Asia Minor, now part of Istanbul. Turkish name **KADIKÖY**.

Chal·ce·don, Coun·cil of /kal'sēdn; 'kalsə,dän/ the fourth ecumenical council of the Christian Church, held at Chalcedon in 451. It condemned the Monophysite position and affirmed the dual but united nature of Christ as god and man. **—Chal·ce·do·ni·an** /,kalsə'dōnēən/ *n.* & *adj.*

chal·ced·o·ny /kal'sedn,ē; CHal-; 'kalsə,dōnē; 'CHalsə-/ ▸*n.* (*pl.* **-nies**) a microcrystalline type of quartz occurring in several different forms, including onyx, agate, and jasper. ▷late Middle English: from Latin *calcedonius, chalcedonius* (often believed to mean 'stone of Chalcedon,' but this is doubtful), from Greek *khalkēdōn*. **—chal·ce·don·ic** /,kalsə'dänik/ *adj.*

chal·cid /'kalsid/ (also **chalcid wasp**) ▸*n.* a minute parasitic wasp of a large group whose members lay eggs inside the eggs of other insects. They typically have bright metallic coloration. • Superfamily Chalcidoidea, order Hymenoptera. ▷late 19th cent.: from modern Latin *Chalcis* (genus name), from Greek *khalkos* 'copper, brass,' + **-ID**[3].

chal·co·cite /'kalkə,sīt/ ▸*n.* cuprous sulfide, an ore of copper, usu. occurring as black, fine-grained masses. • Chem. formula: Cu_2S.

chal·co·py·rite /,kalkə'pī,rīt/ ▸*n.* a yellow crystalline mineral consisting of a sulfide of copper and iron. It is the principal ore of copper. • Chem. formula $CuFeS_2$. ▷mid 19th cent.: from modern Latin *chalcopyrites*, from Greek *khalkos* 'copper' + *puritēs* (see **PYRITE**).

Chal·de·a /kal'dēə/ an ancient country in what is now southern Iraq, inhabited by the Chaldeans. ▷from Greek *Khaldaia*, from Akkadian *Kaldû*, the name of a Babylonian tribal group.

Chal·de·an /kal'dēən/ ▸*n.* **1** a member of an ancient people who lived in Chaldea *c.*800 BC and ruled Babylonia 625–539 BC. They were renowned as astronomers and astrologers. **2** the Semitic language of the ancient Chaldeans. ■ a language related to Aramaic and spoken in parts of Iraq. **3** a member of a Syrian Uniate (formerly Nestorian) Church based mainly in Iran and Iraq.

▸*adj.* **1** of or relating to ancient Chaldea or its people or language. ■ *poetic/literary* of or relating to astrology. **2** of or relating to the East Syrian Uniate Church.

Chal·dee /'kal,dē/ ▸*n.* **1** the Semitic language of the ancient Chaldeans. ■ *dated* the Aramaic language as used in some books of the Old Testament. **2** a native of ancient Chaldea. ▷from Latin *Chaldaei* 'Chaldeans,' from Greek *Khaldaioi*, from *Khaldaia* (see **CHALDEA**).

chal·dron /'CHôldrən/ ▸*n.* a chiefly British unit of dry measure, esp. a unit of approximately 36 bushels (of coal).

cha·let /SHa'lā; 'SHa,lā/ ▸*n.* a wooden house or cottage with overhanging eaves, typically found in the Swiss Alps. ■ a similar building used as a ski lodge. ▷late 18th cent.: from Swiss French, diminutive of Old French *chasel* 'farmstead,' based on Latin *casa* 'hut, cottage.'

chalet

chal·ice /'CHaləs/ ▸*n. historical* a large cup or goblet, typically used for drinking wine. ■ the wine cup used in the Christian Eucharist. ▷Middle English: via Old French from Latin *calix, calic-* 'cup.'

chal·i·co·there /'kalikō,THir/ ▸*n.* a horselike fossil mammal of the late Tertiary period, with stout claws on the toes instead of hooves. • Family Chalicotheriidae, order Perissodactyla: several genera, in particular *Moropus*. ▷early 20th cent.: from modern Latin *Chalicotherium* (genus name), from Greek *khalix, khalik-* 'gravel' + *thērion* 'wild animal.'

chalk /CHôk/ ▸*n.* **1** a soft white limestone (calcium carbonate) formed from the skeletal remains of sea creatures. ■ a similar substance (calcium sulfate), made into white or colored sticks used for drawing or writing. ■ *Geology* a series of strata consisting mainly of chalk. **2** short for **FRENCH CHALK**.

▸*v.* [*trans.*] **1** draw or write with chalk. ■ draw or write on (a surface) with chalk: *blackboards chalked with Japanese phrases.* **2** rub (something, esp. a pool cue) with chalk. **3** *Brit.* charge (drinks bought in a bar) to a person's account.

▸*phrasal v.* □ **chalk something out** sketch or plan something. □ **chalk something up** **1** achieve something noteworthy: *he has chalked up a box-office success.* **2** ascribe something to a particular cause: *I* ***chalked*** *my sleeplessness* ***up to*** *nerves.* ▷Old English *cealc* (also denoting lime), related to Dutch *kalk* and German *Kalk*, from Latin *calx* (see **CALX**).

▸*PHRASES* □ **as different as** (or **like**) **chalk and cheese** *Brit.* fundamentally different or incompatible. □ **by a long chalk** *Brit.* by far.

chalk·board /'CHôk,bôrd/ ▸*n.* another term for **BLACKBOARD**.

chalk·face /'CHôk,fās/ ▸*n.* [in *sing.*] *Brit.* the day-to-day work of teaching in a school: *teachers* ***at the chalkface.***

chalk·stone /'CHôk,stōn/ ▸*n. dated Medicine* a chalky deposit of sodium urate formed in the hands and feet of sufferers from severe gout.

chalk-stripe ▸*adj.* [*attrib.*] (of a garment or material) having a pattern of thin white stripes on a dark background.

Pronunciation Key ə *ago;* ər *over;* 'ə or ,ə *up;* 'ər or ,ər *fur;* a *hat;* ā *rate;* ä *car;* CH *chew;* e *let;* ē *see;* e(ə)r *air;* i *fit;* ī *by;* i(ə)r *ear;* NG *sing;* ō *go;* ô *for;* oi *boy;* ŏŏ *good;* ōō *goo;* ou *out;* SH *she;* TH *thin;* TH *then;* (h)w *why;* ZH *vision*

▸*n.* (**chalk stripe**) a pattern of this kind. —**chalk-striped** *adj.*

chalk talk ▸*n.* a talk or lecture in which the speaker uses blackboard and chalk.

chalk·y /ˈCHôkē/ ▸*adj.* (**chalk·i·er**, **chalk·i·est**) **1** consisting of or rich in chalk: *a chalky, powdery soil.* **2** resembling chalk in texture or paleness of color: *patches of creamy or chalky white.* —**chalk·i·ness** *n.*

chal·lah /ˈhälə; ˈKHälə/ ▸*n.* (*pl.* **chal·lahs** /ˈhäləz; ˈKHäləz/ or **cha·lot(h)** /häˈlōt; KHä-; -ˈlōs/) a loaf of white leavened bread, typically plaited in form, traditionally baked to celebrate the Jewish sabbath. ▷1920s: from Hebrew *ḥallah.*

chal·lenge /ˈCHalənj/ ▸*n.* **1** a call to take part in a contest or competition, esp. a duel: *he accepted the challenge.* ■ a task or situation that tests someone's abilities: *the ridge is a challenge for experienced climbers.* ■ an attempt to win a contest or championship in a sport: *a world title challenge.* **2** an objection or query as to the truth of something, often with an implicit demand for proof: *a* **challenge to** *the legality of the order.* ■ a sentry's call for a password or other proof of identity. ■ *Law* an objection regarding the eligibility or suitability of a jury member. **3** *Medicine* exposure of the immune system to pathogenic organisms or antigens: *recently vaccinated calves should be protected from challenge.*
▸*v.* [*trans.*] **1** invite (someone) to engage in a contest: *he challenged one of my men to a duel.* ■ enter into competition with or opposition against: *incumbent Democrats are being challenged in the 29th district.* ■ make a rival claim to or threaten someone's hold on (a position): *they were challenging his leadership.* ■ [*trans.*] invite (someone) to do something that one thinks will be difficult or impossible; dare: *I challenged them to make up their own minds.* ■ [usu. as *adj.*] (**challenging**) test the abilities of: *challenging and rewarding employment.* **2** dispute the truth or validity of: *employees challenged the company's requirement.* ■ *Law* object to (a jury member). ■ (of a sentry) call on (someone) for proof of identity. **3** *Medicine* expose (the immune system) to pathogenic organisms or antigens. ▷Middle English (in the senses 'accusation' and 'accuse'): from Old French *chalenge* (noun), *chalenger* (verb), from Latin *calumnia* 'calumny,' *calumniari* 'calumniate.' —**chal·lenge·a·ble** *adj.* —**chal·leng·er** *n.* —**chal·leng·ing·ly** *adv.*

chal·lenged /ˈCHalənjd/ ▸*adj.* [with *submodifier* or in *combination*] (used euphemistically) impaired or disabled in a specified respect: *physically challenged.* ■ *informal* lacking or deficient in a specified respect: *vertically challenged | today's attention-challenged teens.*

USAGE The use with a preceding adverb, e.g., **physically challenged**, originally intended to give a more positive tone than such terms as **disabled** or **handicapped**, arose in the U.S. in the 1980s. Despite the originally serious intention, the term rapidly became stalled by uses whose intention was to make fun of the attempts at euphemism and whose tone was usually clearly ironic: examples include **cerebrally challenged**, **follicularly challenged**, etc.

Chal·leng·er /ˈCHalənjər/ ▸*n.* a U.S. space shuttle that exploded 1.5 minutes after launch on January 28, 1986, killing its crew of seven.

Chal·leng·er Deep /ˈCHalənjər/ the deepest part (36,201 feet, 11,034 m) of the Mariana Trench in the North Pacific, discovered by HMS *Challenger II* in 1948.

chal·lis /ˈSHalē/ ▸*n.* a soft lightweight clothing fabric made from silk and worsted. ▷mid 19th cent.: origin uncertain; perhaps from the surname *Challis.*

chal·u·meau /ˌSHaləˈmō/ ▸*n.* (*pl.* **-meaux** /-ˈmō(z)/) a reed instrument of the early 18th century from which the clarinet was developed. ■ (also **chalumeau register**) the lowest octave of the clarinet's range. ▷early 18th cent.: from French, from Latin *calamellus* 'little reed,' diminutive of *calamus.*

cha·lu·pa /cHəˈlo͞opə/ ▸*n.* a fried tortilla in the shape of a boat, with a spicy filling. ▷late 19th cent.: Spanish, ultimately related to Dutch *sloep* 'sloop.'

cha·lyb·e·ate /kəˈlēbēət; -ˈlib-/ ▸*adj.* [*attrib.*] of or denoting natural mineral springs containing iron salts. ▷mid 17th cent.: from modern Latin *chalybeatus*, from Latin *chalybs*, from Greek *khalups, khalub-* 'steel.'

Cham /kam/ ▸*n.* (*pl.* same or **Chams**) **1** a member of an indigenous people of Vietnam and Cambodia, who formed an independent kingdom from the 2nd to 17th centuries AD, and whose culture is strongly influenced by that of India. **2** either of two Austronesian languages of this people.
▸*adj.* of or relating to this people, their culture, or their language.

Cha·mae·le·on /kəˈmēlyən; -lēən/ *Astronomy* a small and faint southern constellation (the Chameleon), close to the south celestial pole. ■ [as *genitive*] (**Chamaeleontis** /kəˌmēlēˈäntis/) used with a preceding letter or numeral to designate a star in this constellation: *the star Delta Chamaeleontis.* ▷from Greek.

cha·mae·le·on ▸*n.* *chiefly Brit.* variant spelling of **CHAMELEON**.

cham·ae·phyte /ˈkaməˌfīt/ ▸*n.* *Botany* a woody plant whose resting buds are on or near the ground. ▷early 20th cent.: from Greek *khamai* 'on the ground' + **-PHYTE**.

cham·ber /ˈCHāmbər/ ▸*n.* **1** a hall used by a legislative or judicial body. ■ the body that meets in such a hall. ■ any of the houses of a legislature: *the Senate chamber.* **2** *poetic/literary or archaic* a private room, typically a bedroom: *he had his meals brought to his chamber.* ■ (**chambers**) *Law* a judge's room used for official proceedings not required to be held in open court. ■ (**chambers**) *Brit. Law* rooms used by a lawyer or lawyers. **3** an enclosed space or cavity: *an echo chamber.* ■ a large underground cavern. ■ the part of a gun bore that contains the charge or bullet. ■ *Biology* a cavity in a plant, animal body, or organ: *the four chambers of the heart.* **4** [as *adj.*] *Music* of or for a small group of instruments: *a chamber concert.*
▸*v.* [*trans.*] place (a bullet) into the chamber of a gun. ▷Middle English (in the sense 'private room'): from Old French *chambre*, from Latin *camera* 'vault, arched chamber,' from Greek *kamara* 'object with an arched cover.' —**cham·bered** *adj.*

cham·bered nau·ti·lus ▸*n.* see **NAUTILUS**.

Cham·ber·lain[1] /ˈCHāmbərlən/, (Arthur) Neville (1869–1940), British statesman; prime minister 1937–40. He pursued a policy of appeasement with Nazi Germany and signed the Munich Agreement in 1938, but was forced to abandon this policy following Hitler's invasion of Czechoslovakia in 1939.

Cham·ber·lain[2], Sir Austin, see **DAWES**.

Cham·ber·lain[3], Owen (1920–), U.S. physicist. He investigated subatomic particles and in 1955 discovered the antiproton with **E. G. Segrè** (1905–89). Nobel Prize for Physics (1959, shared with Segrè).

Cham·ber·lain[4], Richard (1934–), U.S. actor; born *George Richard Chamberlain.* Most famous for his starring role in the TV series "Dr. Kildare" (1961–66), he also played leading roles in numerous other Hollywood and TV productions, including the miniseries "Shogun" (1980) and "The Thorn Birds" (1983). He has appeared on the stage in Britain and in the U.S.

Cham·ber·lain[5], Wilt (1936–99), U.S. basketball player; full name *Wilton Norman Chamberlain*; known as **Wilt the Stilt**. He played for the Philadelphia Warriors (later the Golden State Warriors), the Philadelphia 76ers, and the Los Angeles Lakers from 1959 until 1973. Basketball Hall of Fame (1978).

cham·ber·lain /ˈCHāmbərlən/ ▸*n.* *historical* an officer who manages the household of a monarch or noble. ■ *Brit.* the treasurer of a corporation or public body. ▷Middle English (denoting a servant in a bedchamber): via Old French from Old Saxon *kamera*, from Latin *camera* 'vault'(see **CHAMBER**). —**cham·ber·lain·ship** /-ˌSHip/ *n.*

cham·ber·maid /ˈCHāmbərˌmād/ ▸*n.* a maid who cleans bedrooms and bathrooms, esp. in a hotel.

cham·ber mu·sic ▸*n.* instrumental music played by a small ensemble, with one player to a part, the most important form being the string quartet which developed in the 18th century.

cham·ber of com·merce (abbr.: **C. of C.**) ▸*n.* a local association to promote and protect the interests of the business community in a particular place.

Cham·ber of Dep·u·ties ▸*n.* the lower legislative assembly in some parliaments.

cham·ber of hor·rors ▸*n.* an exhibit containing instruments or scenes of torture or execution. ▷mid 19th cent.: from the name given to a room in Madame Tussaud's waxworks exhibition in London.

cham·ber or·ches·tra ▸*n.* a small orchestra.

cham·ber pot ▸*n.* a bowl kept in a bedroom and used as a toilet, esp. at night.

Cham·bers /ˈCHāmbərz/, Whittaker (1901–61), U.S. journalist; full name *Jay Vivian Chambers.* In 1948, he accused Alger Hiss of Communist party membership and of passing State Department documents to Soviet agents.

Cham·ber·tin /ˌSHänberˈtaN/ ▸*n.* a dry red burgundy wine of high quality from Gevrey Chambertin in eastern France.

cham·bray /ˈSHamˌbrā; -brē/ ▸*n.* a linen-finished gingham cloth with a white weft and a colored warp, producing a mottled appearance. ▷early 19th cent. (originally U.S.): formed irregularly from *Cambrai*, the name of a town in northern France, where it was originally made. Compare with **CAMBRIC**.

cham·bré /ˈSHamˌbrā; SHamˈbrā/ ▸*adj.* [*predic.*] (of red wine) at room temperature: *Cabernet tastes best chambré.* ▷1950s: French, past participle of *chambrer* 'bring to room temperature,' from *chambre* 'room' (see **CHAMBER**).

common chameleon

cha·me·le·on /kəˈmēlyən; -lēən/ (*chiefly Brit.* also **cha·mae·le·on**) ▸*n.* a small slow-moving Old World lizard with a prehensile tail, long extensible tongue, protruding eyes that rotate independently, and a highly developed ability to change color. • Family Chamaeleonidae: four genera, in particular *Chamaeleo*, and numerous species, including the **European chameleon** (*C. vulgaris*) and the **common chameleon** (*C. chamaeleon*). ■ (also **American chameleon**) an anole. ■ *figurative* a changeable or inconstant person. ▷Middle English: via Latin *chamaeleon* from Greek *khamaileōn*, from *khamai* 'on the ground' + *leōn* 'lion.' —**cha·me·le·on·ic** /kəˌmēlēˈänik/ *adj.*

cha·metz /KHôˈmäts; ˈKHôˌmets/ (also **cho·metz**) ▸*n.* *Judaism* leaven, or food mixed with leaven, prohibited during Passover. ▷mid 19th cent.: from Hebrew *ḥāmēṣ.*

cham·fer /ˈCHamfər/ ▸*v.* [*trans.*] in carpentry, cut away (a right-angled edge or corner) to make a symmetrical sloping edge.
▸*n.* a symmetrical sloping surface at an edge or corner. ▷mid 16th cent. (in the sense 'flute or furrow'): back-formation from *chamfering*, from French *chamfrain*, from *chant* 'edge' (see **CANT**[2]) + *fraint* 'broken' (from Old French *fraindre* 'break,' from Latin *frangere*).

cha·mise /SHəˈmēz/ ▸*n.* an evergreen shrub with small narrow leaves, common in the chaparral of California. Also called **GREASEWOOD**. • *Adenostoma fasciculatum*, family Rosaceae. ▷mid 19th cent.: from Mexican Spanish *chamiso.*

cham·ois /ˈSHamē/ ▸*n.* **1** (*pl.* same /ˈSHamēz/) an agile goat-antelope with short hooked horns, found in mountainous areas of Europe from Spain to the Caucasus. • Genus *Rupicapra*, family Bovidae: *R. rupicapra* (of the Alps, East, and southeastern Europe), and *R. pyrenaica* (of the Pyrenees and Apennines, also called **IZARD**). **2** (*pl.* same) (also **chamois leather**) soft pliable leather made from the skin of sheep, goats, or deer. ■ a piece of such leather, used typically for washing windows or cars. ▷mid 16th cent.: from French, of unknown ultimate origin.

cham·o·mile /ˈkaməˌmēl; -ˌmīl/ (also **cam·o·mile**) ▸*n.* an aromatic European plant of the daisy family, with white and yellow daisylike flowers. • The perennial **sweet** (or **Roman**) **chamomile** (*Chamaemelum nobile* (or *Anthemis nobilis*), family Compositae), used, esp. formerly, for lawns and herbal medicine, the annual **German chamomile** (*Matricaria recutita*), used medicinally, and the yellow-flowered **dyer's chamomile** (*Anthemis tinctoria*), used to produce a yellow-brown dye. ▷Middle English: from Old French *camomille*, from late Latin *chamomilla*, from Greek *khamaimēlon* 'earth apple' (because of the applelike smell of its flowers).

cham·o·mile tea (also **cam·o·mile**) ▸*n.* an infusion of dried flowers of sweet chamomile.

Cha·mor·ro /CHəˈmôrō/ ▸*n.* **1** a member of the native people of the Mariana Islands (including Guam). **2** the Austronesian language of this people.

champ[1] /CHamp/ ▸*v.* another term for **CHOMP**. ▷late Middle English: imitative.

champ[2] ▸*n.* *informal* a champion. ▷mid 19th cent.: abbreviation.

Cham·pagne /SHänˈpänyə; SHamˈpān/ a region and former province in northeastern France that now corresponds to the Champagne-Ardenne administrative region. It is noted for the white sparkling wine first produced here in about 1700.

cham·pagne /SHamˈpān/ ▸*n.* a white sparkling wine associated with celebration and regarded as a symbol of luxury, typically that made in the Champagne region of France. ■ a pale cream or straw color.

Cham·pagne-Ar·denne /SHän'pän yär'den/ a region of northeastern France that consists of part of the Ardennes forest and the vine-growing area of Champagne.

cham·pagne so·cial·ist ▸*n. Brit., derogatory* a person who espouses socialist ideals while enjoying a wealthy and luxurious lifestyle. —**cham·pagne so·cial·ism** *n.*

Cham·paign /SHam'pān/ a city in east central Illinois, home to the University of Illinois; pop. 67,518.

cham·paign /SHam'pān/ ▸*n. poetic/literary* open level countryside. ▷late Middle English: from Old French *champagne*, from late Latin *campania*, based on Latin *campus* 'level ground.' Compare with CAMPAIGN.

cham·pak /'CHəmpək; 'CHam-/ ▸*n.* an Asian evergreen tree of the magnolia family, bearing fragrant orange flowers and sacred to Hindus and Buddhists. • *Michelia champaca*, family Magnoliaceae. ▷from Sanskrit *campaka*.

cham·per·ty /'CHampərtē/ ▸*n. Law* an illegal agreement in which a person with no previous interest in a lawsuit finances it with a view to sharing the disputed property if the suit succeeds. ▷late Middle English: from Anglo-Norman French *champartie*, from Old French *champart* 'feudal lord's share of produce,' from Latin *campus* 'field' + *pars* 'part.' —**cham·per·tous** /-təs/ *adj.*

cham·pi·gnon /SHam'pinyən; CHam-/ ▸*n.* a small edible mushroom with a light brown cap, growing in short grass in both Eurasia and North America and widely grown commercially. Also called MEADOW MUSHROOM, FIELD MUSHROOM. • *Agaricus campestris*, family Agaricaceae, class Basidiomycetes. ▷late 16th cent.: from French, diminutive of Old French *champagne* 'open country' (see CHAMPAIGN).

Cham·pi·on /'CHampēən/, Gower (1921–80), U.S. choreographer, dancer, and director. He danced with his wife **Marge** (1923–) on stage and in movies such as *Jupiter's Darling* (1955), and he choreographed Broadway musicals such as *42nd Street* (1980).

cham·pi·on /'CHampēən/ ▸*n.* **1** a person who has defeated or surpassed all rivals in a competition, esp. in sports: [as *adj.*] *a champion hurdler.* **2** a person who fights or argues for a cause or on behalf of someone else: *a* **champion of** *women's rights.* ■ *historical* a knight who fought in single combat on behalf of the monarch.
▸*v.* [*trans.*] support the cause of; defend: *priests who championed human rights.* ▷Middle English (denoting a fighting man): from Old French, from medieval Latin *campio(n-)* 'fighter,' from Latin *campus* (see CAMP[1]).

cham·pi·on·ship /'CHampēən,SHip/ ▸*n.* **1** a contest for the position of champion in a sport, often involving a series of games or matches. ■ the position or title of the winner of such a contest. **2** the vigorous support or defense of someone or something: *Alan's championship of his estranged wife.*

Cham·plain /SHam'plān/, Samuel de (1567–1635), French explorer and colonial statesman. He established a settlement at Quebec in Canada in 1608 and developed alliances with the native peoples. He was appointed lieutenant governor in 1612.

Cham·plain, Lake /SHam'plān/ a lake in North America, east of the Adirondack Mountains. It forms part of the border between the states of New York and Vermont, and its northern tip extends into Quebec, Canada. ▷named after Samuel de CHAMPLAIN, who reached it in 1609.

champ·le·vé /,SHänlə'vā/ ▸*n.* enamelwork in which hollows made in a metal surface are filled with colored enamel. ▷French, from *champ* 'field' + *levé* 'raised.'

Cham·pol·lion /,SHänpôl'yôN/, Jean-François (1790–1832), French Egyptologist. He is noted for his success in deciphering some of the hieroglyphic inscriptions on the Rosetta Stone in 1822.

Champs É·ly·sées /'SHänz ,ālē'zā/ an avenue in Paris, France, that extends from the Place de la Concorde to the Arc de Triomphe.

chance /CHans/ ▸*n.* **1** a possibility of something happening: *a chance of victory | there is little chance of his finding a job.* ■ (**chances**) the probability of something happening: *he played down his chances of becoming chairman.* ■ [in *sing.*] an opportunity to do or achieve something: *I gave her a chance to answer.* ■ a ticket in a raffle or lottery. ■ *Baseball* an opportunity to make a defensive play, which if missed counts as an error: *541 straight chances without an error.* **2** the occurrence and development of events in the absence of any obvious design: *he met his brother* **by chance** | *what a lucky chance that you are here.* ■ the unplanned and unpredictable course of events regarded as a power: *chance was offering me success.*
▸*adj.* fortuitous; accidental: *a chance meeting.*
▸*v.* **1** [*intrans.*] do something by accident or without design: *if they chanced to meet.* See note at HAPPEN. ■ (**chance upon/on**) find or see by accident: *he chanced upon an interesting advertisement.* **2** [*trans.*] *informal* do (something) despite its being dangerous or of uncertain outcome: *she waited a few seconds and chanced another look.* ▷Middle English: from Old French *cheance*, from *cheoir* 'fall, befall,' based on Latin *cadere*.
▸*PHRASES* □ **by any chance** possibly (used in tentative inquiries or suggestions): *were you looking for me by any chance?* □ **no chance** *informal* there is no possibility of that: *I asked if we could leave early and she said, "No chance."* □ **on the (off) chance** just in case: *Joan phoned at noon on the off chance that he'd be home.* □ **stand a chance** [usu. with *negative*] have a prospect of success or survival: *his rivals don't stand a chance.* □ **take a chance** (or **chances**) behave in a way that leaves one vulnerable to danger or failure. ■ (**take a chance on**) put one's trust in (something or someone) knowing that it may not be safe or certain. □ **take one's chances** do something risky with the hope of success.

chan·cel /'CHansəl/ ▸*n.* the part of a church near the altar, reserved for the clergy and choir, and typically separated from the nave by steps or a screen. ▷Middle English: from Old French, from Latin *cancelli* 'crossbars.'

chan·cel·ler·y /'CHans(ə)lərē/ ▸*n.* (*pl.* **-ler·ies**) **1** the position, office, or department of a chancellor. ■ the official residence of a chancellor. **2** an office attached to an embassy or consulate. ▷Middle English: from Old French *chancellerie*, from *chancelier* 'secretary' (see CHANCELLOR).

chan·cel·lor /'CHans(ə)lər/ ▸*n.* a senior state or legal official. ■ the head of the government in some European countries, such as Germany. ■ the presiding judge of a chancery court. ■ the president or chief administrative officer of a college or university. ■ *chiefly Brit.* the nonresident honorary head of a university. ■ a bishop's law officer. ■ (**Chancellor**) short for CHANCELLOR OF THE EXCHEQUER. ▷late Old English, from Old French *cancelier*, from late Latin *cancellarius* 'porter, secretary' (originally a court official stationed at the grating separating public from judges), from *cancelli* 'crossbars.' —**chan·cel·lor·ship** /-,SHip/ *n.*

Chan·cel·lor of the Ex·cheq·uer ▸*n.* the finance minister of the United Kingdom, responsible for preparing the nation's annual budgets.

Chan·cel·lors·ville /'CHans(ə)lərz,vil/ a historic locality in east central Virginia, west of Fredericksburg, site of a Civil War battle in May 1863.

chance-med·ley ▸*n. rare Law* the killing of a person accidentally in self-defense in a fight. ▷late 15th cent.: from Anglo-Norman French *chance medlee*, literally 'mixed chance,' from *chance* 'luck' + *medlee*, feminine past participle of *medler* 'to mix' (based on Latin *miscere*).

chan·cer·y /'CHans(ə)rē/ ▸*n.* (*pl.* **-cer·ies**) **1** a court of equity. ■ equity. ■ *historical* the court of a bishop's chancellor. ■ (**Chancery**) *Brit. Law* the Lord Chancellor's court, a division of the High Court of Justice. **2** (in the Roman Catholic Church) the office of a diocese. **3** *chiefly Brit.* an office attached to an embassy or consulate. **4** a public records office. ▷late Middle English: contraction of CHANCELLERY.
▸*PHRASE* □ **in chancery** *informal* (of a boxer or wrestler) with their head held, contrary to the rules, between the opponent's arm and body and unable to avoid blows.

Chan-chi·ang /'jän jē'äNG/ variant of ZHANJIANG.

chan·cre /'kaNGkər; 'SHaNG-/ ▸*n. Medicine* a painless ulcer, particularly one developing on the genitals as a result of venereal disease. ▷late 16th cent.: from French, from Latin *cancer* 'creeping ulcer.'

chan·croid /'kaNG,kroid; 'SHaNG-/ ▸*n.* a venereal infection causing ulceration of the lymph nodes in the groin. Also called SOFT CHANCRE.

chanc·y /'CHansē/ ▸*adj.* (**chanc·i·er**, **chanc·i·est**) *informal* subject to unpredictable changes and circumstances: *the screening process was likely to be chancy and unreliable.* —**chanc·i·ly** /-səlē/ *adv.* —**chanc·i·ness** *n.*

chan·de·lier /,SHandə'li(ə)r/ ▸*n.* a decorative hanging light with branches for several light bulbs or candles. ▷mid 18th cent.: from French, from *chandelle* 'candle,' from Latin *candela*, from *candere* 'be white, glisten.'

chan·delle /SHan'del; SHän-/ ▸*n.* a steep climbing turn executed in an aircraft to gain height while changing the direction of flight. ▷1970s: from French, literally 'candle.'

Chan·di·garh /'CHəndēgər/ **1** a Union Territory in northwestern India, created in 1966. **2** a city in this territory; pop. 503,000. The present city was designed in 1950 by Le Corbusier as a new capital for the Punjab and is now the capital of the states of Punjab and Haryana.

Chan·dler[1] /'CHandlər/ a city in south central Arizona, a suburb and resort southeast of Phoenix; pop. 176,581.

Chan·dler[2], Raymond (Thornton) (1888–1959), U.S. novelist; the creator of private detective Philip Marlowe. Many of his novels, written in a tough and realistic style, were made into movies. Notable novels: *The Big Sleep* (1939), *Farewell, My Lovely* (1940), and *The Long Goodbye* (1953).

chan·dler /'CHan(d)lər/ ▸*n.* **1** (also **ship chandler**) a dealer in supplies and equipment for ships and boats. **2** *historical* a dealer in household items such as oil, soap, paint, and groceries. ■ a person who makes and sells candles. ▷Middle English (denoting a candlemaker or candle seller): from Old French *chandelier*, from *chandelle* 'candle' (see CHANDELIER).

chan·dler·y /'CHan(d)lərē/ ▸*n.* (*pl.* **-dler·ies**) the warehouse or store of a chandler. ■ goods sold by a chandler.

Chan·dra·gup·ta Mau·ry·a /,CHəndrə'gŏoptə 'mourēə/ (c.325–297 BC), Indian emperor. He founded the Mauryan empire and annexed provinces in Afghanistan from Alexander's Greek successors.

Chan·dra·se·khar /,CHəndrə'sākər/, Subrahmanyan (1910–95), U.S. astronomer; born in India. He suggested that some stars could eventually collapse to form a dense white dwarf, provided that their mass does not exceed an upper limit (the **Chandrasekhar limit**).

Cha·nel /SHə'nel/, Coco (1883–1971), French couturière; born *Gabrielle Bonheur Chanel*. Her simple but sophisticated garments were a radical departure from the stiff corseted styles of the day.

Cha·ney /'CHānē/, Lon (1883–1930), U.S. actor; born *Alonso Chaney*. He played a wide variety of deformed villains and macabre characters in more than 150 movies, including *The Hunchback of Notre Dame* (1923) and *The Phantom of the Opera* (1925). He became known as "the Man of a Thousand Faces."

Chang·an /'CHäNG'än/ former name of XIAN.

Chang-chia·kow /'jäNG jē'ä'kou/ variant of ZHANGJIAKOU.

Chang·chun /'CHäNG'CHŏon/ an industrial city in northeastern China, capital of Jilin province; pop. 2,070,000.

change /CHānj/ ▸*v.* **1** make or become different: [*trans.*] *a proposal to change the law* | [*intrans.*] *a Virginia creeper just beginning to* **change from** *green* **to** *gold.* ■ make or become a different substance entirely; transform: [*trans.*] *filters* **change** *the ammonia* **into** *nitrate* | [*intrans.*] *computer graphics can show cars changing into cheetahs.* ■ [*intrans.*] alter in terms of: *the ferns began to* **change shape**. ■ [*intrans.*] (of traffic lights) move from one color of signal to another. ■ (of a boy's voice) become deeper with the onset of puberty. ■ [*intrans.*] (of the moon) arrive at a fresh phase; become new. **2** [*trans.*] take or use another instead of: *she decided to change her name.* ■ move from one to another: *she changed jobs incessantly* | *change sides.* ■ exchange; trade: *the sun and moon* **changed places**. ■ [*intrans.*] move to a different train, airplane, or subway line. ■ give up (something) in exchange for something else: *we* **changed** *the shades* **for** *vertical blinds.* ■ remove (something dirty or faulty) and replace it with another of the same kind: *change a light bulb.* ■ put a clean diaper on (a baby or young child). ■ engage a different gear in a motor vehicle: [*trans.*] *wait for a gap and then change gears* | *figurative with business concluded, the convention changes gear and a gigantic circus takes over the town.* ■ exchange (a sum of money) for the same amount in smaller denominations or in coins, or for different currency. ■ [*intrans.*] put different clothes on: *he changed for dinner.*
▸*phrasal v.* □ **change over** move from one system or situation to another: *crop farmers have to* **change over to** *dairy farming.*

▸*n.* **1** the act or instance of making or becoming different: *the* **change from** *a nomadic* **to** *an agricultural society | environmental change.* ■ the substitution of one thing for another: *a change of venue.* ■ an alteration or modification: *a change came over Eddie's face.* ■ a new or refreshingly different experience: *couscous makes an interesting change from rice.* ■ [in *sing.*] a clean garment or garments as a replacement for clothes one is wearing: ***a change of*** *socks.* ■ (**the change** or **the change of life**) *informal* menopause. ■ the moon's arrival at a fresh phase, typically at the new moon. ■ *Baseball* another term for **CHANGE-UP**. **2** coins as opposed to paper currency: *a handful of loose change.* ■ money given in exchange for the same amount in larger denominations. ■ money returned to someone as the balance of the amount paid for something: *I watched him pocket the change.* **3** (usu. **changes**) an order in which a peal of bells can be rung. **4** (**Change** or **'Change**) *Brit., historical* a place where merchants met to do business. ▷Middle English: from Old French *change* (noun), *changer* (verb), from late Latin *cambiare*, from Latin *cambire* 'barter,' probably of Celtic origin. **—change·ful** /'CHānjfəl/ *adj.*

▸*PHRASES* □ **change color** blanch or flush. □ **change hands** (of a business or building) pass to a different owner. ■ (of money or a marketable commodity) pass to another person during a business transaction: *no money has changed hands.* □ **change one's mind** adopt a different opinion or plan. □ **change off** take turns. □ **a change of heart** a move to a different opinion or attitude. □ **change step** (in marching) alter one's step so that the opposite leg marks time. □ **change the subject** begin talking about something different, esp. to avoid embarrassment or the divulgence of confidences. □ **change one's tune 1** express a different opinion or behave in a different way. **2** change one's style of language or manner, esp. from an insolent to a respectful tone. □ **for a change** contrary to how things usually happen; for variety: *it's nice to be pampered for a change.* □ **ring the changes** vary the ways of expressing, arranging, or doing something. [with allusion to bell-ringing and the different orders in which a peal of bells may be rung.]

change·a·ble /'CHānjəbəl/ ▸*adj.* **1** irregular; inconstant: *the weather will be changeable, with rain at times.* **2** able to change or be changed. **—change·a·bil·i·ty** /,CHānjə'bilətē/ *n.* **—change·a·ble·ness** *n.* **—change·a·bly** /-blē/ *adv.*

change·less /'CHānjlis/ ▸*adj.* remaining the same. **—change·less·ly** *adv.* **—change·less·ness** *n.*

change·ling /'CHānjliNG/ ▸*n.* a child believed to have been secretly substituted by fairies for the parents' real child in infancy.

change·out /'CHānj,out/ ▸*n.* the replacement of a spent, used, dysfunctional or otherwise inferior part or object with a new one.

change·o·ver /'CHānj,ōvər/ ▸*n.* a change from one system or situation to another.

change purse ▸*n.* a small strapless purse used for carrying money.

chang·er /'CHānjər/ ▸*n.* a person or thing that changes something. ■ a device that holds several computer disks or compact disks and is able to switch between them.

change-ring·ing ▸*n.* the ringing of sets of church bells or handbells in a constantly varying order. **—change-ring·er** *n.*

change-up ▸*n.* *Baseball* a deceptively slow pitch intended to throw off the batter's timing.

Chang Jiang /'CHäNG jē'äNG/ another name for **YANGTZE**.

Chang·sha /'CHäNG'SHä/ the capital of Hunan province in eastern central China; pop. 1,300,000.

Chang·zhou /'CHäNG'jō/ a city in Jiangsu province in eastern China, on the Grand Canal, north of Shanghai; pop. 670,000.

chan·nel /'CHanl/ ▸*n.* **1** a length of water wider than a strait, joining two larger areas of water, esp. two seas. ■ the navigable part of a waterway: *buoys marked the safe limits of the channel.* ■ a hollow bed for a natural or artificial waterway. ■ (**the Channel**) the English Channel. ■ a narrow gap or passage: *a channel opened up between two lines of cars.* ■ a tubular passage or duct for liquid. ■ an electric circuit that acts as a path for a signal: *an audio channel.* ■ a groove or flute, esp. in a column. ■ *Electronics* the semiconductor region in a field-effect transistor that forms the main current path between the source and the drain. **2** a band of frequencies used in radio and television transmission, esp. as used by a particular station. ■ a service or station using such a band: *a shopping channel.* **3** a medium for communication or the passage of information: *they didn't apply through the proper channels.*

▸*v.* (**-neled**, **-nel·ing**; *Brit.* **-nelled**, **-nel·ling**) [*trans.*] **1** direct toward a particular end or object: *advertisers channel money into radio.* ■ guide along a particular route or through a specified medium: *many countries* ***channel*** *their aid* ***through*** *charities.* ■ (of a person) serve as a medium for (a spirit). **2** [usu. as *adj.*] (**channeled**) form channels or grooves in: *the lower jawbone is deeply channeled.* ▷Middle English: from Old French *chanel*, from Latin *canalis* 'pipe, groove, channel,' from *canna* 'reed' (see **CANE**). Compare with **CANAL**.

chan·nel cat (also **channel catfish**) ▸*n.* a common North American freshwater catfish that has a pale blue to olive back with dark spots. • *Ictalurus punctatus*, family Ictaluridae.

chan·nel-hop ▸*v.* [*intrans.*] *informal* **1** another term for **CHANNEL-SURF**. **2** travel across the English Channel and back frequently or for only a brief trip. **—chan·nel-hop·per** *n.*

Chan·nel Is·lands 1 a group of islands in the English Channel off the northwestern coast of France; pop. 146,000. The largest are Jersey, Guernsey, and Alderney. **2** another name for the **SANTA BARBARA ISLANDS** in California.

chan·nel·ize /'CHanl,īz/ ▸*v.* [*trans.*] another term for **CHANNEL** (senses 1 and 2).

chan·nel-surf ▸*v.* *informal* change frequently from one television channel to another, using a remote control device. **—chan·nel-surf·er** *n.* **—chan·nel-surf·ing** *n.*

Chan·nel Tun·nel a railroad tunnel under the English Channel that extends for 31 miles (49 km) and links England and France. The tunnel (popularly called the Chunnel) opened in 1994 after eight years of construction to link Holywell, near Folkestone, England, and Sangatte, near Calais, France.

chan·son /SHän'sôn/ ▸*n.* a French song. ▷French, from Latin *cantio(n-)* 'singing,' from *canere* 'sing.'

chan·son de geste /SHän'sôn də 'ZHest/ ▸*n.* (*pl.* **chansons de geste** /SHän'sôN(z)/) a medieval historical romance in French verse, typically one connected with Charlemagne. ▷mid 19th cent.: French, literally 'song of heroic deeds,' from *chanson* 'song' (see **CHANSON**) and *geste* from Latin *gesta* 'actions, exploits'.

chant /CHant/ ▸*n.* **1** a repeated rhythmic phrase, typically one shouted or sung in unison by a crowd. ■ a monotonous or repetitive song, typically an incantation or part of a ritual. **2** *Music* a short musical passage in two or more phrases used for singing unmetrical words; a psalm or canticle sung to such music. ■ the style of music consisting of such passages: *Gregorian chant.*

▸*v.* [*trans.*] say or shout repeatedly in a sing-song tone: *protesters were chanting slogans* | [with *direct speech*] *the crowd chanted "No violence!"* ■ sing or intone (a psalm, canticle, or sacred text). ▷late Middle English (in the sense 'sing'): from Old French *chanter* 'sing,' from Latin *cantare*, frequentative of *canere* 'sing.'

chant·er /'CHantər/ ▸*n.* **1** a person who chants something. **2** *Music* the pipe of a bagpipe with finger holes, on which the melody is played. ▷late Middle English: from Old French *chanteor*, from Latin *cantator*, from *cantare* (see **CHANT**).

chan·te·relle /,SHantə'rel; ,SHänt-/ ▸*n.* an edible woodland mushroom with a yellow funnel-shaped cap and a faint smell of apricots, found in both Eurasia and North America. • *Cantharellus cibarius*, family Cantharellaceae, class Basidiomycetes. ▷late 18th cent.: from French, from modern Latin *cantharellus*, diminutive of *cantharus*, from Greek *kantharos*, denoting a kind of drinking container.

chan·teuse /,SHän'to͞oz; 'tœz/ ▸*n.* a female singer of popular songs, esp. in a nightclub. ▷French, from *chanter* 'sing.'

chant·ey /'SHantē/ (also **chant·y**, **shant·y**, or **sea chant·ey**) ▸*n.* a song with alternating solo and chorus, of a kind originally sung by sailors while performing physical labor together. ▷mid 19th. cent.: probably from French *chantez!* 'sing!,' imperative plural of *chanter.*

chan·ti·cleer /'CHantə,kli(ə)r; 'SHant-/ ▸*n.* *poetic/literary* a name given to a rooster, esp. in fairy tales. ▷Middle English: from Old French *Chantecler*, the name of the cock in the fable *Reynard the Fox*, from *chanter* 'sing, crow' (see **CHANT**) + *cler* 'clear.'

Chan·til·ly lace ▸*n.* a delicate kind of bobbin lace. ▷mid 19th cent.: named after *Chantilly*, a town near Paris.

chant·ing gos·hawk ▸*n.* a long-legged African hawk with pale gray upper parts, throat, and breast, noted for its prolonged musical fluting call delivered from a treetop perch. • Genus *Melierax*, family Accipitridae: three species.

chan·try /'CHantrē/ ▸*n.* (*pl.* **-tries**) an endowment for a priest or priests to celebrate masses for the founder's soul. ■ a chapel, altar, or other part of a church endowed for such a purpose. ▷late Middle English: from Old French *chanterie*, from *chanter* 'to sing.'

chant·y ▸*n.* (*pl.* **chant·ies**) variant spelling of **CHANTEY**.

Cha·nu·kah ▸*n.* variant spelling of **HANUKKAH**.

Cha·nute /SHə'no͞ot/, Octave (1832–1910), U.S. aviation pioneer; born in France. From 1898, he produced a number of gliders, including a biplane that made over 700 flights. He assisted the Wright brothers in making the world's first controlled powered flight.

Chao Phra·ya /CHou 'prīə/ a major waterway in central Thailand that is formed by the junction of the Ping and Nan rivers.

cha·os /'kā,äs/ ▸*n.* complete disorder and confusion: *snow caused chaos in the region.* ■ *Physics* behavior so unpredictable as to appear random, owing to great sensitivity to small changes in conditions. ■ the formless matter supposed to have existed before the creation of the universe. ■ (**Chaos**) *Greek Mythology* the first created being, from which came the primeval deities Gaia, Tartarus, Erebus, and Nyx. ▷late 15th cent. (denoting a gaping void or chasm, later formless primordial matter): via French and Latin from Greek *khaos* 'vast chasm, void.'

cha·os the·o·ry ▸*n.* the branch of mathematics that deals with complex systems whose behavior is highly sensitive to slight changes in conditions, so that small alterations can give rise to strikingly great consequences.

cha·ot·ic /kā'ätik/ ▸*adj.* in a state of complete confusion and disorder: *a chaotic jumble of spools, tapes, and books.* ■ *Physics* of or relating to systems that exhibit chaos. ▷early 18th cent.: from **CHAOS**, on the pattern of words such as *hypnotic.* **—cha·ot·i·cal·ly** /-ik(ə)lē/ *adv.*

cha·ot·ic at·trac·tor ▸*n.* *Mathematics* another term for **STRANGE ATTRACTOR**.

chap[1] /CHap/ ▸*v.* (**chapped**, **chap·ping**) [*intrans.*] (of the skin) become cracked, rough, or sore, typically through exposure to cold weather: ■ [*trans.*] [usu. as *adj.*] (**chapped**) (of the wind or cold) cause (skin) to crack in this way: *chapped lips.*

▸*n.* a cracked or sore patch on the skin. ▷late Middle English: of unknown origin.

chap[2] ▸*n.* *informal, chiefly Brit.* a man or a boy. ■ *dated* a friendly form of address between men and boys: *best of luck, old chap.* ▷late 16th cent. (denoting a buyer or customer): abbreviation of **CHAPMAN**. The current sense dates from the early 18th cent.

chap. ▸*abbr.* chapter.

cha·pa·ra·jos /,SHapə'rā-ōs; -'rəs/ (also **cha·pa·re·jos**) ▸*plural n.* full form of **CHAPS**. ▷mid 19th cent.: from Mexican Spanish *chaparreras*, from *chaparra* (with reference to protection from thorny vegetation: see **CHAPARRAL**); probably influenced by Spanish *aparejo* 'equipment.'

chap·ar·ral /,SHapə'ral/ ▸*n.* vegetation consisting chiefly of tangled shrubs and thorny bushes. ▷mid 19th cent.: from Spanish, from *chaparra* 'dwarf evergreen oak.'

cha·pa·ti /CHə'pätē/ (also **cha·pat·ti**) ▸*n.* (*pl.* **-tis**) (in Indian cooking) a thin pancake of unleavened wholegrain bread cooked on a griddle. ▷from Hindi *capātī*, from *capānā* 'flatten, roll out.'

chap·book /'CHap,bo͝ok/ ▸*n.* *historical* a small pamphlet containing tales, ballads, or tracts, sold by peddlers. ■ a small paperback booklet, typically containing poems or fiction. ▷early 19th cent.: from **CHAPMAN** + **BOOK**.

chape /CHāp/ ▸*n.* **1** *historical* the metal point of a scabbard. **2** the metal pin of a buckle. ▷Middle English (in the general sense 'plate of metal overlaying or trimming something'): from Old French, literally 'cape, hood,' from late Latin *cappa* 'cap.'

cha·peau /SHa'pō/ ▸*n.* (*pl.* **-peaux** /-'pō(z)/) a hat. ▷late 15th cent.: from French, from Latin *cappellum*, diminutive of *cappa* 'cap.'

chap·el /'CHapəl/ ▸*n.* **1** a small building for Christian worship, typically one attached to an institution or private house. ■ regular services held in such a building: *attendance* **at chapel** *was compulsory.* ■ a part of a large church or cathedral with its own altar and dedication. ■ a room or building in which funeral services are held. ■ *Brit.* a place of worship for certain Protestant denominations. **2** *Brit. Printing* the members or branch of a labor union at a particular place of work. ▷Middle English: from Old French *chapele*, from medieval Latin *cappella*, diminutive of *cappa* 'cap or cape' (the first chapel being a sanctuary in which St. Martin's cloak was preserved).

Chap·el Hill a town in north central North Carolina, home to the University of North Carolina as well as many research facilities; pop. 38,719.

chap·el of ease ▶*n.* a chapel situated for the convenience of parishioners living a long distance from the parish church.

chap·er·one /ˈSHapəˌrōn/ (also **chap·er·on**) ▶*n.* a person who accompanies and looks after another person or group of people, in particular: ■ *dated* an older woman responsible for the decorous behavior of a young unmarried girl at social occasions. ■ a person who takes charge of a child or group of children in public.

▶*v.* [*trans.*] accompany and look after or supervise. ▷late Middle English (denoting a hood or cap, regarded as giving protection): from French, feminine of *chaperon* 'hood,' diminutive of *chape* (see **CHAPE**). The current sense dates from the early 18th cent. —**chap·er·on·age** /-ˌrōnij; ˌSHapəˈrōnij/ *n.*

chap·er·o·nin /ˌSHapəˈrōnin/ ▶*n. Biochemistry* a protein that aids the assembly and folding of other protein molecules in living cells. ▷late 20th cent.: from **CHAPERONE** + **-IN**[1].

chap·fall·en /ˈCHapˌfôlən/ (also **chop·fall·en** /ˈCHäp-/) ▶*adj. archaic* with one's lower jaw hanging due to extreme exhaustion or dejection. ▷late 16th cent.: from **CHAP**[3].

chap·lain /ˈCHaplən/ ▶*n.* a member of the clergy attached to a private chapel, institution, ship, branch of the armed forces, etc. ▷Middle English: from Old French *chapelain*, from medieval Latin *cappellanus*, originally denoting a custodian of the cloak of St. Martin, from *cappella*, originally 'little cloak' (see **CHAPEL**). —**chap·lain·cy** /ˈCHaplənsē/ *n.*

chap·let /ˈCHaplət/ ▶*n.* **1** a garland or wreath for a person's head. **2** a string of 55 beads (one third of the rosary number) for counting prayers, or as a necklace. **3** a metal support for the core of a hollow casting mold. ▷late Middle English: from Old French *chapelet*, diminutive of *chapel* 'hat,' based on late Latin *cappa* 'cap.' —**chap·let·ed** *adj.*

Chap·lin /ˈCHaplən/, Charlie (1889–1977), English movie actor and director; full name *Sir Charles Spencer Chaplin*. He directed and starred in many short silent comedies, mostly playing a bowler-hatted tramp, a character that was his trademark for more than 25 years. Notable movies: *The Kid* (1921) and *The Gold Rush* (1925).

Charlie Chaplin

Chap·man /ˈCHapmən/, John, see **APPLESEED**.

chap·man /ˈCHapmən/ ▶*n.* (*pl.* **-men**) *archaic* a peddler. ▷Old English *cēapman*, from *cēap* 'bargaining, trade' (see **CHEAP**) + **MAN**.

Chap·pa·quid·dick Is·land /ˌCHapəˈkwidik/ a small island in southern Massachusetts, just off the southeastern coast of Martha's Vineyard, the scene of a car accident in 1969 that involved Senator Edward Kennedy in which his assistant Mary Jo Kopechne drowned.

chap·pie /ˈCHapē/ ▶*n.* (*pl.* **-pies**) *Brit., informal* another term for **CHAP**[2].

chaps /CHaps; SHaps/ ▶*plural n.* leather pants without a seat, worn by a cowboy over ordinary pants to protect the legs. ▷mid 19th cent.: short for **CHAPARAJOS**.

chaps

Chap Stick ▶*n. trademark* a small stick of a cosmetic substance used to prevent chapping of the lips.

chap·tal·i·za·tion /ˌSHaptələˈzāSHən/ ▶*n.* (in winemaking) the correction or improvement of must by the addition of calcium carbonate to neutralize acid, or of sugar to increase alcoholic strength. ▷late 19th cent.: from the name of Jean A. *Chaptal* (1756–1832), the French chemist who invented the process, + *-ization* (see **-IZE**). —**chap·tal·ize** /ˈSHaptəˌlīz/ *v.*

chap·ter /ˈCHaptər/ ▶*n.* **1** a main division of a book, typically with a number or title. ■ *figurative* a period of time or an episode in a person's life, a nation's history, etc.: *a tragic chapter in European history.* **2** a local branch of a society: *the local chapter of the American Cancer Society.* **3** the governing body of a religious community, esp. a cathedral or a knightly order. **4** a series or sequence: *the latest episode in a chapter of problems.* ▷Middle English: from Old French *chapitre*, from Latin *capitulum*, diminutive of *caput* 'head.'

▶*PHRASE* □ **chapter and verse** an exact reference or authority: *she can give chapter and verse on current legislation.*

Chap·ter 7 ▶*n.* protection from creditors granted to individuals or companies who legally file for bankruptcy, providing for liquidation of certain assets to pay debts. ▷with allusion to chapter 7 of the U.S. bankruptcy code.

Chap·ter 11 ▶*n.* protection from creditors given to a company in financial difficulties for a limited period to allow it to reorganize. ▷with allusion to chapter 11 of the U.S. bankruptcy code.

Chap·ter 13 ▶*n.* protection from creditors granted to individuals who legally file for bankruptcy, providing for repayment of debts by a court-approved plan. ▷with allusion to chapter 13 of the U.S. bankruptcy code.

chap·ter house ▶*n.* a building used for the meetings of the canons of a cathedral or other religious community. ■ a place where a college fraternity or sorority meets.

Cha·pul·te·pec /CHəˈpo͝oltəˌpek/ a hill ("Grasshopper Hill") in the major park of Mexico City in Mexico. It is the ancient seat of Aztec emperors and is surmounted by a castle that was captured by U.S. forces in September 1847.

char[1] /CHär/ ▶*v.* (**charred**, **char·ring**) [*trans.*] (usu. **be charred**) partially burn (an object) so as to blacken its surface: *their bodies were badly charred in the fire* | [as *adj.*] (**charred**) *charred remains.* See note at **BURN**. ■ [*intrans.*] (of an object) become burned and discolored in such a way.

▶*n.* material that has been charred. ▷late 17th cent.: apparently a back-formation from **CHARCOAL**.

char[2] *Brit., informal* ▶*n.* a charwoman.

▶*v.* (**charred**, **char·ring**) [*intrans.*] work as a charwoman.

char[3] (also **cha** /CHä/ or **chai** /CHī/) ▶*n. Brit., informal* tea. ▷late 16th cent. (as *cha*; rare before the early 20th cent.): from Chinese (Mandarin dialect) *chá*.

char[4] (also **charr**) ▶*n.* (*pl.* same) a troutlike freshwater or marine fish of northern countries, widely valued as a food and game fish. • Genus *Salvelinus*, family Salmonidae: several species, in particular the North American **brook trout** (*S. fontinalis*), which has been introduced widely elsewhere, and the red-bellied **Arctic char** (*S. alpinus*), which occurs in Arctic waters as well as landlocked lakes.

char·a·banc /ˈSHarəˌbaNG; -ˌbaNGk/ ▶*n. Brit.* an early form of bus, used typically for pleasure trips. ▷early 19th cent.: from French *char-à-bancs* 'carriage with benches' (the original horse-drawn charabancs having rows of bench seats).

char·a·cin /ˈkarəsən/ ▶*n.* a small and brightly colored freshwater fish native to Africa and tropical America. • Family Characidae: numerous species, including the piranhas and popular aquarium fishes such as the tetras. ▷late 19th cent.: from modern Latin *Characinus* (genus name), from Greek *kharax*, literally 'pointed stake,' denoting a kind of fish.

char·ac·ter /ˈkariktər/ ▶*n.* **1** the mental and moral qualities distinctive to an individual: *running away was not in keeping with her character.* ■ the distinctive nature of something: *gas lamps give the area its character.* ■ the quality of being individual, typically in an interesting or unusual way: *the island is full of character.* ■ strength and originality in a person's nature: *she had character as well as beauty.* ■ a person's good reputation: *to what do I owe this attack on my character?* ■ *dated* a written statement of someone's good qualities; a recommendation. **2** a person in a novel, play, or movie. ■ a part played by an actor. ■ [with *adj.*] a person seen in terms of a particular aspect of character: *he was a larger-than-life character* | *shady characters.* ■ *informal* an interesting or amusing individual: *he's a real character.* **3** a printed or written letter or symbol. ■ *Computing* a symbol representing a letter or number. ■ *Computing* the bit pattern used to store such a symbol. **4** *chiefly Biology* a characteristic, esp. one that assists in the identification of a species.

▶*v.* [*trans.*] *archaic* inscribe; engrave. ■ describe; characterize: *you have well charactered him.* ▷Middle English: from Old French *caractere*, via Latin from Greek *kharaktēr* 'a stamping tool.' From the early sense 'distinctive mark' arose 'token, feature, or trait' (early 16th cent.), and from this 'a description, esp. of a person's qualities,' giving rise to 'distinguishing qualities.' —**char·ac·ter·ful** /-fəl/ *adj.* —**char·ac·ter·ful·ly** *adv.* —**char·ac·ter·less** *adj.*

▶*PHRASE* □ **in** (or **out of**) **character** in keeping (or not in keeping) with someone's usual pattern of behavior.

char·ac·ter ac·tor ▶*n.* an actor who specializes in playing eccentric or unusual people rather than leading roles.

char·ac·ter as·sas·si·na·tion ▶*n.* the malicious and unjustified harming of a person's good reputation.

char·ac·ter code ▶*n. Computing* the binary code used to represent a letter or number.

char·ac·ter dance ▶*n.* a style of ballet deriving inspiration from national or folk dances, or interpreting and representing a particular profession, mode of living, or personality. The movements used tend to be less stylized than in classical ballet, allowing greater individual expression and diversity. —**char·ac·ter danc·er** *n.*

char·ac·ter·is·tic /ˌkariktəˈristik/ ▶*adj.* typical of a particular person, place, or thing: *large farms are characteristic of this area.*

▶*n.* **1** a feature or quality belonging typically to a person, place, or thing and serving to identify it: *inherited characteristics such as blood groups.* **2** *Mathematics* the whole number or integral part of a logarithm, which gives the order of magnitude of the original number. ▷mid 17th cent.: from French *caractéristique* or medieval Latin *characteristicus*, from Greek *kharaktēristikos*, from *kharaktēr* 'a stamping tool.' —**char·ac·ter·is·ti·cal·ly** *adv.*

char·ac·ter·is·tic curve ▶*n.* a graph showing the relationship between two variable but interdependent quantities.

char·ac·ter·is·tic func·tion ▶*n. Mathematics* a function whose result is one for the members of a given set and zero for all nonmembers.

char·ac·ter·ize /ˈkariktəˌrīz/ ▶*v.* [*trans.*] **1** describe the distinctive nature or features of: *the historian characterized the period as the decade of revolution.* **2** (often **be characterized**) (of a feature or quality) be typical or characteristic of: *the disease is* **characterized by** *weakening of the immune system.* ▷late 16th cent. (in the sense 'engrave, inscribe'): from French *caractériser* or medieval Latin *characterizare*, from Greek *kharaktērizein*, from *kharaktēr* 'a stamping tool.' —**char·ac·ter·i·za·tion** /ˌkariktərəˈzāSHən/ *n.*

char·ac·ter part ▶*n.* a part played by a character actor.

char·ac·ter rec·og·ni·tion ▶*n.* the identification by electronic means of printed or written characters.

char·ac·ter string ▶*n.* a linear sequence of characters, typically one stored in or processed by a computer.

Pronunciation Key ə *ago*; ər *over*; ˈə or ˌə *up*; ˈər or ˌər *fur*; a *hat*; ā *rate*; ä *car*; CH *chew*; e *let*; ē *see*; e(ə)r *air*; i *fit*; ī *by*; i(ə)r *ear*; NG *sing*; ō *go*; ô *for*; oi *boy*; o͝o *good*; o͞o *goo*; ou *out*; SH *she*; TH *thin*; T͟H *then*; (h)w *why*; ZH *vision*

char·ac·ter wit·ness ▸*n.* a person who attests to another's moral conduct and good reputation in a court of law.

char·ac·ter·y /'kariktərē/ ▸*n. poetic/literary* the expression of thought by symbols or characters; the symbols or characters collectively.

cha·rade /SHə'räd/ ▸*n.* an absurd pretense intended to create a pleasant or respectable appearance: *talk of unity was nothing more than a charade.* ■ (**charades**) a game in which players guess a word or phrase from pantomimed clues. ▷late 18th cent.: from French, from modern Provençal *charrado* 'conversation,' from *charra* 'chatter,' perhaps of imitative origin.

cha·ran·go /CHə'raNGgō/ ▸*n.* a small Andean guitar, traditionally made from an armadillo shell. ▷1920s: from South American Spanish.

cha·ras /'CHärəs/ ▸*n.* a psychoactive resin from the flowerheads of hemp; cannabis resin. ▷from Hindi *caras.*

char·broil /'CHär,broil/ ▸*v.* [*trans.*] [usu. as *adj.*] (**charbroiled**) grill (food, esp. meat) on a rack over charcoal: *charbroiled steak.* ▷1950s: blend of CHARCOAL and BROIL[1].

char·coal /'CHär,kōl/ ▸*n.* a porous black solid, consisting of an amorphous form of carbon, obtained as a residue when wood, bone, or other organic matter is heated in the absence of air. ■ briquettes of charcoal used for barbecueing: *lamb grilled on charcoal.* ■ a crayon made of charcoal and used for drawing. ■ a drawing made using charcoal. ■ a dark gray color: *his charcoal sweater* | [as *adj.*] *charcoal gray.*
▸*v.* [usu. as *adj.*] (**charcoaled**) cook over charcoal: *charcoaled lobster.* ■ *figurative* darken or blacken as if with charcoal: *drifts of snow charcoaled from soot.* ▷late Middle English: probably related to COAL in the early sense 'charcoal.'

char·coal burn·er ▸*n.* **1** a small stove using charcoal as fuel. **2** a person who makes charcoal.

char·coal fil·ter ▸*n.* a filter containing charcoal to absorb impurities.

Char·cot /SHär'kō/, Jean-Martin (1825–93), French neurologist; regarded as one of the founders of modern neurology. His work on hysteria was adopted by his student Sigmund Freud.

char·cu·te·rie /SHär,kōōtə'rē; -'kōōtərē/ ▸*n.* (*pl.* **-ries**) cold cooked meats collectively. ■ a store selling such meats. ▷French, from obsolete *char* (earlier form of *chair*) 'flesh' + *cuite* 'cooked.'

chard /CHärd/ ▸*n.* (also **Swiss chard**) a beet of a variety with broad white leaf stalks that may be prepared and eaten separately from the green parts of the leaf. ■ the blanched shoots of other plants, eaten as a vegetable, e.g., globe artichoke. ▷mid 17th cent.: from French *carde,* perhaps influenced by *chardon* 'thistle.'

Char·don·nay /,SHärdn'ā/ ▸*n.* a variety of white wine grape used for making champagne and other wines. ■ a wine made from this grape. ▷French.

Char·en·tais /,SHarən'tā/ (also **Charentais melon**) ▸*n.* a small melon with a pale green rind and orange flesh. ▷French, literally 'from the Charentes region.'

Cha·rente /SHä'ränt/ a river in western France that rises in the Massif Central and flows west for 225 miles (360 km) to the Bay of Biscay at Rochefort.

charge /CHärj/ ▸*v.* [*trans.*] **1** demand (an amount) as a price from someone for a service rendered or goods supplied: *the restaurant charged $15 for dinner* | [with *two objs.*] *he charged me 20,000 lire for the postcard* | [*intrans.*] *museums should* **charge for** *admission.* ■ (**charge something to**) record the cost of something as an amount payable by (someone) or on (an account): *they charge the calls to their credit-card accounts.* **2** accuse (someone) of something, esp. an offense under law: *they were* **charged with** *assault.* ■ [with *clause*] make an accusation or assertion that: *opponents* **charged that** *below-cost pricing would reduce safety.* ■ *Law* accuse someone of (an offense). **3** entrust (someone) with a task as a duty or responsibility: *the committee was* **charged with** *reshaping the educational system.* **4** store electrical energy in (a battery or battery-operated device): *the shaver can be* **charged up** *and used while traveling.* ■ [*intrans.*] (of a battery or battery-operated device) receive and store electrical energy. ■ *technical formal* load or fill (a container, gun, etc.) to the full or proper extent: *will you see to it that your glasses are charged?* ■ (usu. **be charged with**) *figurative* fill or pervade (something) with a quality or emotion: *the air was charged with menace.* **5** [*intrans.*] rush forward in attack: *the plan is to charge headlong at the enemy.* See note at ATTACK. ■ [*trans.*] rush aggressively toward (someone or something) in attack. ■ [with *adverbial of direction*] move quickly and with impetus: *Henry charged up the staircase.* **6** (usu. **be charged with**) *Heraldry* place a heraldic bearing on: *a pennant argent, charged with a cross gules.*
▸*n.* **1** a price asked for goods or services: *an admission charge.* ■ a financial liability or commitment: *an asset of $550,000 should have been taken as* **a charge on** *earnings.* **2** an accusation, typically one formally made against a prisoner brought to trial: *he appeared in court* **on a charge of** *attempted murder* | *three people were arrested but released* **without charge**. **3** the responsibility of taking care or control of someone or something: *the people* **in her charge** *are pupils and not experimental subjects.* ■ a person or thing entrusted to the care of someone: *the babysitter watched over her charges.* ■ *dated* a responsibility or onerous duty assigned to someone. ■ an official instruction, esp. one given by a judge to a jury regarding points of law. **4** the property of matter that is responsible for electrical phenomena, existing in a positive or negative form. ■ the quantity of this carried by a body. ■ energy stored chemically for conversion into electricity. ■ the process of storing electrical energy in a battery. ■ [in *sing.*] *informal* a thrill: *I* **get a** *real* **charge out of** *working hard.* **5** a quantity of explosive to be detonated, typically in order to fire a gun or similar weapon. **6** a headlong rush forward, typically one made by attacking soldiers in battle: *a cavalry charge.* ■ the signal or call for such a rush: *he yelled to his bugler to sound the charge.* **7** *Heraldry* a device or bearing placed on a shield or crest. ▷Middle English (in the general senses 'to load' and 'a load'): from Old French *charger* (verb), *charge* (noun), from late Latin *carricare, carcare* 'to load,' from Latin *carrus* 'wheeled vehicle.' —**charge·a·ble** *adj.*
▸PHRASES □ **free of charge** without any payment due. □ **in charge** in control or with overall responsibility: *he was* **in charge of** *civil aviation matters.* □ **press** (or **prefer**) **charges** accuse someone formally of a crime so that they can be brought to trial. □ **take charge** assume control or responsibility: *the candidate must* **take charge of** *an actual flight.*

charge ac·count ▸*n.* an account to which goods and services may be charged on credit.

charge·back /'CHärj,bak/ ▸*n.* a demand by a credit-card provider for a retailer to make good the loss on a fraudulent or disputed transaction. ■ (in business use) an act or policy of allocating the cost of an organization's centrally located resources to the individuals or departments that use them.

charge card ▸*n.* a credit card for use with an account that must be paid when a statement is issued.

charge car·ri·er ▸*n. Physics* a particle that carries an electric charge. ■ a mobile electron or hole by which an electric charge passes through a semiconductor.

charge con·ju·ga·tion ▸*n. Physics* the operation of changing every particle into its antiparticle.

charge-cou·pled de·vice ▸*n.* see **CCD**.

charged /CHärjd/ ▸*adj.* having an electric charge. ■ *figurative* filled with excitement, tension, or emotion: *the highly charged atmosphere created by the boycott.*

char·gé d'af·faires /SHär,ZHā dä'fer/ (also **char·gé**) ▸*n.* (*pl.* **char·gés d'af·faires** /SHär'zā(z)/) a diplomatic official who temporarily takes the place of an ambassador. ■ a state's diplomatic representative in a minor country. ▷mid 18th cent.: French, '(a person) in charge of affairs.'

charge den·si·ty ▸*n. Physics* the electric charge per unit area of a surface, or per unit volume of a field or body.

charge nurse ▸*n. Brit.* a nurse in charge of a ward in a hospital.

Charge of the Light Bri·gade a British cavalry charge in 1854 during the Battle of Balaclava in the Crimean War. A misunderstanding between the commander of the Light Brigade and his superiors led to the British cavalry being destroyed. The charge was immortalized in verse by Alfred Tennyson.

charg·er[1] /'CHärjər/ ▸*n.* **1** a horse trained for battle; a cavalry horse. **2** a device for charging a battery or battery-powered equipment. **3** a person who charges forward.

charg·er[2] (also **charger plate**) ▸*n.* a large, flat dish; a platter. ■ a large plate placed under a dinner plate in some formal table settings. ▷Middle English: from Anglo-Norman French *chargeour,* from *chargier* 'to load,' from late Latin *carricare, carcare* 'to load' (see CHARGE).

charge sheet ▸*n. Brit.* a record made in a police station of the charges against a person.

char·grill /'CHär,gril/ ▸*v.* [usu. as *adj.*] (**chargrilled**) grill (food, typically meat or fish) quickly at a high heat. ▷late 20th cent.: on the pattern of *charbroil.*

Cha·ri Riv·er /SHä'rē/ (also **Shari**) a river that flows for 660 miles (1,060 km) through the Central African Republic, Chad, and Cameroon. Emptying into Lake Chad, it is the longest river in the African continent that drains internally.

char·i·ot /'CHarēət/ ▸*n. historical* a two-wheeled horse-drawn vehicle used in ancient warfare and racing. ■ *historical* a four-wheeled carriage with back seats and a coachman's seat. ■ *poetic/literary* a stately or triumphal carriage.
▸*v.* [*trans.*] *poetic/literary* convey in or as in a chariot. ▷late Middle English: from Old French, augmentative of *char* 'cart,' based on Latin *carrus* 'wheeled vehicle.'

two-wheeled chariot

char·i·ot·eer /,CHarēə'ti(ə)r/ ▸*n.* a chariot driver. ■ (**the Charioteer**) the constellation Auriga. ▷Middle English: from Old French *charieter,* from *chariot* 'large cart' (see CHARIOT). The sense in astronomy dates from the early 20th cent.

char·ism /'kar,izəm/ ▸*n. Theology* another term for CHARISMA (sense 2).

cha·ris·ma /kə'rizmə/ ▸*n.* **1** compelling attractiveness or charm that can inspire devotion in others: *she enchanted guests with her charisma.* **2** (*pl.* **-ma·ta** /-,mətə/) (also **char·ism** /'kar,izəm/) a divinely conferred power or talent. ▷mid 17th cent. (sense 2): via ecclesiastical Latin from Greek *kharisma,* from *kharis* 'favor, grace.'

char·is·mat·ic /,kariz'matik/ ▸*adj.* **1** exercising a compelling charm that inspires devotion in others: *a charismatic leader.* **2** of or relating to the charismatic movement in the Christian Church. ■ (of a power or talent) divinely conferred: *charismatic prophecy.*
▸*n.* an adherent of the charismatic movement. ■ a person who claims divine inspiration. ▷late 19th cent.: from Greek *kharisma, kharismat-* 'charisma' + -IC. —**char·is·mat·i·cal·ly** *adv.*

char·is·mat·ic move·ment ▸*n.* a movement within some Christian churches that emphasizes gifts believed to be conferred by the Holy Spirit, such as speaking in tongues and healing of the sick.

char·i·ta·ble /'CHaritəbəl/ ▸*adj.* **1** of or relating to the assistance of those in need: *charitable works such as care of the sick.* ■ (of an organization or activity) officially recognized as devoted to the assistance of those in need. ■ generous in giving to those in need. **2** apt to judge others leniently or favorably: *those who were less charitable called for his resignation.* ▷Middle English (in the sense 'showing Christian love to God and man'): from Old French, from *charite* (see CHARITY). —**char·i·ta·ble·ness** *n.* —**char·i·ta·bly** *adv.*

char·i·ty /'CHaritē/ ▸*n.* (*pl.* **-ties**) **1** the voluntary giving of help, typically in the form of money, to those in need. ■ help or money given in this way: *an unemployed teacher living on charity.* **2** an organization set up to provide help and raise money for those in need. ■ such organizations viewed collectively as the object of fund-raising or donations: *the proceeds of the sale will go to charity.* **3** kindness and tolerance in judging others: *she found it hard to look on her mother with much charity.* See note at MERCY. ■ *archaic* love of humankind, typically in a Christian context: *faith, hope, and charity.* ▷late Old English (in the sense 'Christian love of one's fellows'): from Old French *charite,* from Latin *caritas,* from *carus* 'dear.'
▸PHRASE □ **charity begins at home** *proverb* one's first responsibility is for the needs of one's own family and friends.

char·i·ty school ▸*n. historical* a school supported by charitable contributions.

chari·va·ri /,SHivə'rē; 'SHivə,rē/ (also **shiv·a·ree**) ▸*n.* (*pl.* **-va·ris**) *chiefly historical* a cacophonous mock serenade, typically performed by a group of people in derision of an unpopular person or in celebration of a marriage. ■ a series of discordant noises. ▷mid 17th cent.: from French, of unknown origin.

char·kha /ˈCHərkə; ˈCHär-/ (also **char·ka**) ▸*n.* (in the Indian subcontinent) a domestic spinning wheel used chiefly for cotton. ▷from Urdu *charḵa* 'spinning wheel,' from Persian; related to Sanskrit *cakra* 'wheel.'

char·la·dy /ˈCHärˌlādē/ ▸*n.* (*pl.* **-dies**) *Brit.* a charwoman.

char·la·tan /ˈSHärlətən; ˈSHärlətn/ ▸*n.* a person falsely claiming to have a special knowledge or skill; a fraud. See note at QUACK. ▷early 17th cent. (denoting an itinerant seller of supposed remedies): from French, from Italian *ciarlatano*, from *ciarlare* 'to babble.' **—char·la·tan·ism** /-ləˌnizəm; -lətnˌizəm/ *n.* **—char·la·tan·ry** /ˈSHärlətənrē; -lətnrē/ *n.*

Char·le·magne /ˈSHärləˌmān/ (742–814), king of the Franks 768–814 and Holy Roman Emperor (as Charles I) 800–814; Latin name *Carolus Magnus*; known as **Charles the Great**. As the first Holy Roman emperor, Charlemagne promoted the arts and education, and his court became the cultural center of the Carolingian Renaissance.

Char·le·roi /ˌSHärləˈrwä; -ˈroi/ an industrial city in southwestern Belgium; pop. 206,200.

Charles[1] /CHärlz/ the name of two kings of England, Scotland, and Ireland: ■ **Charles I** (1600–49), son of James I; reigned 1625–49. His reign was dominated by the deepening religious and constitutional crisis that resulted in the English Civil War 1642–49. After the battle of Naseby, Charles tried to regain power in alliance with the Scots, but his forces were defeated in 1648; he was tried by a special Parliamentary court and beheaded. ■ **Charles II** (1630–85), son of Charles I; reigned 1660–85. Charles was restored to the throne after the collapse of Oliver Cromwell's regime. Although he displayed considerable adroitness in handling the difficult constitutional situation, religious and political strife continued during his reign.

Charles[2] the name of four kings of Spain: ■ **Charles I** (1500–58), son of Philip I; reigned 1516–56; Holy Roman Emperor (as Charles V) 1519–56. His reign was characterized by the struggle against Protestantism in Germany, rebellion in Castile, and war with France 1521–44. Exhausted by these struggles, Charles handed Naples, the Netherlands, and Spain over to his son Philip II and the imperial Crown to his brother Ferdinand before retiring to a monastery. ■ **Charles II** (1661–1700), reigned 1665–1700. He inherited a kingdom already in a decline that he was unable to halt. His choice of Philip of Anjou, grandson of Louis XIV of France, as his successor gave rise to the War of the Spanish Succession. ■ **Charles III** (1716–88), reigned 1759–88. He improved Spain's position as an international power by increasing foreign trade, and he brought a brief cultural and economic revival to Spain. ■ **Charles IV** (1748–1819), reigned 1788–1808. During the Napoleonic Wars he suffered the loss of the Spanish fleet, destroyed along with that of France at Trafalgar in 1805. Following the French invasion of Spain in 1807, he was forced to abdicate.

Charles[3] the name of two European kings: ■ **Charles VII** (1403–61), king of France 1422–61. At the time of his accession, much of northern France was under English occupation. After the intervention of Joan of Arc, however, the French experienced a dramatic military revival, and the defeat of the English ended the Hundred Years War. ■ **Charles XII** (also **Karl XII** /kärl/) (1682–1718), king of Sweden 1697–1718. In 1700, he initiated a war against Denmark, Poland-Saxony, and Russia. Initially successful, he embarked on an expedition into Russia in 1709 that ended in the destruction of his army and his internment.

Charles[4] the name of seven Holy Roman Emperors: ■ **Charles I** see CHARLEMAGNE. ■ **Charles II** (823–877), reigned 875–877. ■ **Charles III** (839–888), reigned 881–887. ■ **Charles IV** (1316–78), reigned 1355–78. ■ **Charles V** Charles I of Spain (see CHARLES[2]). ■ **Charles VI** (1685–1740), reigned 1711–40. His claim to the Spanish throne instigated the War of the Spanish Succession, but he was ultimately unsuccessful. He drafted the Pragmatic Sanction in an attempt to ensure that his daughter Maria Theresa succeeded to the Habsburg dominions; this triggered the War of the Austrian Succession after his death. ■ **Charles VII** (1697–1745), reigned 1742–45.

Charles[5], **Prince** (1948–), son of Elizabeth II; full name *Charles Philip Arthur George, Prince of Wales*; heir apparent to Elizabeth II. He married Lady Diana Spencer in 1981; the couple had two children, Prince William Arthur Philip Louis (1982–) and Prince Henry Charles Albert David (known as Prince Harry) (1984–), and were divorced in 1996.

Charles[6], **Ray** (1930–2004), U.S. pianist and singer; born *Ray Charles Robinson*. Totally blind from the age of six, he drew on blues, jazz, and country music for songs such as "What'd I Say" (1959), "Georgia On My Mind" (1960), and "Busted" (1963).

Charles' law (also **Charles's law**) *Chemistry* a law stating that the volume of an ideal gas at constant pressure is directly proportional to the absolute temperature. ▷late 19th cent.: named after Jacques A. C. Charles (1746–1823), the French physicist who first formulated it.

Charles Mar·tel /ˈCHärlz märˈtel/ (*c.*688–741), Frankish ruler of the eastern part of the Frankish kingdom from 715 and the whole kingdom from 719; grandfather of Charlemagne. His rule marked the beginning of Carolingian power.

Charles Riv·er /CHärlz/ a river that flows for 60 miles (100 km) through eastern Massachusetts, between Cambridge and Boston, to Boston Harbor.

Charles's Wain *archaic, chiefly Brit.* the Big Dipper. ▷Old English *Carles wægn* 'the wain of Carl (Charlemagne),' perhaps because the star Arcturus was associated with King Arthur, with whom Charlemagne was connected in legend.

Charles·ton[1] /ˈCHärlstən/ **1** the capital of West Virginia, in the southwestern part of the state; pop. 53,421. **2** a city and port in South Carolina; pop. 96,650. The bombardment of Fort Sumter in 1861 by Confederate troops marked the beginning of the Civil War.

Charles·ton[2] (also **charles·ton**) ▸*n.* a lively dance of the 1920s that involved turning the knees inward and kicking out the lower legs.
▸*v.* [*intrans.*] dance the Charleston. ▷1920s: named after CHARLESTON[1] in South Carolina.

Charles·town /ˈCHärlzˌtoun/ a neighborhood in northern Boston in Massachusetts, north of the Charles River. Bunker Hill is here.

char·ley horse /ˈCHärlē/ ▸*n.* [in *sing.*] *informal* a cramp or feeling of stiffness in an arm or leg. ▷late 19th cent.: of unknown origin.

Char·lie /ˈCHärlē/ ▸*n.* **1** a code word representing the letter C, used in radio communication. **2** *informal* cocaine. **3** *historical military slang* a member of the Vietcong or the Vietcong collectively. [shortening of *Victor Charlie*, radio code for *VC*, representing *Vietcong*.] ▷late 19th cent.: diminutive of the male given name *Charles*.

Char·lie Hust·le see ROSE.

char·lock /ˈCHärˌläk; -lək/ ▸*n.* a wild mustard with yellow flowers, commonly found as a weed in fields and along roadsides. • *Brassica kaber* (or *Sinapis arvensis*), family Brassicaceae. ▷Old English *cerlic, cyrlic*, of unknown origin.

Char·lotte /ˈSHärlət/ a commercial city and transportation center in southern North Carolina; pop. 540,828.

char·lotte /ˈSHärlət/ ▸*n.* a dessert made of stewed fruit or mousse with a casing or covering of bread, sponge cake, ladyfingers, or breadcrumbs. ▷French, from the female given name *Charlotte*.

Char·lotte A·ma·li·e /əˈmälyə/ the capital of the U.S. Virgin Islands, a resort on the island of St. Thomas; pop. 52,660. ▷named after the wife of King Christian V of Denmark.

char·lotte russe /ˈro͞os/ ▸*n.* a dessert consisting of custard enclosed in sponge cake or a casing of ladyfingers. ▷mid 19th cent.: French, literally 'Russian charlotte.'

Char·lottes·ville /ˈSHärləts,vil/ a city in central Virginia, in the Blue Ridge Mountains, home to the University of Virginia; pop. 45,049. Monticello, the home of Thomas Jefferson, is nearby.

Char·lotte·town /ˈSHärlətˌtoun/ the capital and chief port of Prince Edward Island, in eastern Canada; pop. 33,150.

charm /CHärm/ ▸*n.* **1** the power or quality of giving delight or arousing admiration: *he was captivated by her youthful charm.* ■ (usu. **charms**) an attractive or alluring characteristic: *the hidden charms of the city.* **2** a small ornament worn on a necklace or bracelet. **3** an object, act, or saying believed to have magic power: *the dreamcatcher is a charm used to prevent bad dreams.* ■ an object kept or worn to ward off evil and bring good luck: *a good luck charm.* **4** *Physics* one of six flavors of quark.
▸*v.* [*trans.*] **1** delight greatly: *the books have charmed children the world over.* ■ gain or influence by charm: *he charmed her into going out.* **2** control or achieve by or as if by magic: *pretending to charm a cobra* | [with *adverbial*] *she will charm your warts away.* ▷Middle English (in the senses 'incantation or magic spell' and 'to use spells'): from Old French *charme* (noun), *charmer* (verb), from Latin *carmen* 'song, verse, incantation.'
▸*PHRASES* □ **turn on the charm** use one's ability to charm in order to influence someone. □ **work like a charm** be completely successful or effective.

charm brace·let ▸*n.* a bracelet hung with small trinkets or ornaments.

charmed /CHärmd/ ▸*adj.* **1** (of a person's life) unusually lucky or happy as though protected by magic: *I felt that I had a charmed life.* **2** *Physics* (of a particle) possessing the property charm: *a charmed quark.*
▸*exclam. dated* expressing polite pleasure at an introduction: *charmed, I'm sure.*

charm·er /ˈCHärmər/ ▸*n.* a person with an attractive, engaging personality. ■ a person who habitually seeks to impress or manipulate others by exploiting an ability to charm.

char·meuse /SHärˈm(y)o͞oz/ ▸*n.* a soft, silky dress fabric. ▷early 20th cent.: from French, feminine of *charmeur* 'charmer,' from *charmer* 'to charm.'

charm·ing /ˈCHärmiNG/ ▸*adj.* pleasant or attractive: *a charming country cottage.* ■ (of a person or manner) polite, friendly, and likable: *he was a charming, affectionate colleague.* **—charm·ing·ly** *adv.*

charm·less /ˈCHärmlis/ ▸*adj.* unattractive or unpleasant. **—charm·less·ly** *adv.* **—charm·less·ness** *n.*

charm of·fen·sive ▸*n.* a campaign of flattery and friendliness designed to achieve the support or agreement of others: *a charm offensive aimed at winning the confidence of Russia.*

char·mo·ni·um /CHärˈmōnēəm/ ▸*n.* (*pl.* **-ni·a** /-nēə/) *Physics* a combination of a charmed quark and an antiquark. ▷1970s: from CHARM (sense 4).

charm school ▸*n.* a school where young women are taught social graces such as etiquette.

char·nel /ˈCHärnl/ ▸*n.* short for CHARNEL HOUSE.
▸*adj.* associated with death: *I gagged on the charnel stench of the place.* ▷late Middle English: from Old French, from medieval Latin *carnale*, neuter (used as a noun) of *carnalis* 'relating to flesh' (see CARNAL).

char·nel house ▸*n.* *historical* a building or vault in which corpses or bones are piled. ■ *figurative* a place associated with violent death: *Europe in the immediate postwar period had become a charnel house.* ▷mid 16th cent.: from Middle English *charnel* 'burying place,' from Old French, from medieval Latin *carnale*, from late Latin *carnalis* 'relating to flesh,' from *caro, carn-* 'flesh.'

Cha·ro·lais /ˌSHärəˈlā/ ▸*n.* (*pl.* same) one of a breed of large white beef cattle. ▷late 19th cent.: named after the *Monts du Charollais*, hills in eastern France where the breed originated.

Char·on /ˈkarən; ˈke(ə)r-/ **1** *Greek Mythology* an old man who ferried the souls of the dead across the Styx and Acheron rivers to Hades. **2** *Astronomy* the only satellite of Pluto, discovered in 1978. Its diameter of 789 miles (1,270 km) is more than half that of Pluto.

Cha·roph·y·ta /kəˈräfitə/ *Botany* a phylum that includes the stoneworts, which are frequently treated as a class (Charophyceae) of the green algae. ▷modern Latin (plural), former name of the family Characeae, from *Chara* (genus name) + Greek *phuton* 'a plant.' **—char·o·phyte** /ˈkarəˌfit/ *n.*

charr /CHär/ (also **char**) ▸*n.* variant spelling of CHAR[4]. ▷mid 17th cent.: perhaps of Celtic origin.

char·ro /ˈCHärō/ ▸*n.* (*pl.* **-ros**) a Mexican horseman or cowboy, typically one in elaborate traditional dress. ▷early 20th cent.: Mexican Spanish, from Spanish, literally 'rustic.'

chart /CHärt/ ▸*n.* a sheet of information in the form of a table, graph, or diagram: *a chart showing how much do-it-yourself costs compared with retail.* ■ (usu. **the charts**) a weekly listing of the current best-selling pop records: *she topped the charts for eight weeks.* ■ a geographical map or plan, esp. one used for navigation by sea or air. ■ *Medicine* a written record of information about a patient: *scribbled on a patient's chart.* ■ (also **birth chart** or **natal chart**) *Astrology* a map, typically circular, showing the positions of the planets at the time of someone's birth, from which astrologers are said to be able to deduce character or potential.

▸*v.* **1** [*trans.*] make a map of (an area). ■ plot (a course) on a chart: *the pilot found his craft taking a route he had not charted* | *figurative the poems chart his descent into madness.* ■ (usu. **be charted**) record on a chart. **2** [*intrans.*] (of a record) enter the weekly music charts at a particular position: *the record will probably chart at about No. 74.* ▷late 16th cent.: from French *charte*, from Latin *charta* 'paper, papyrus leaf' (see **CARD**[1]).

chart·bust·er /ˈCHärtˌbəstər/ ▸*n. informal* a popular singer or group that makes a best-selling recording. ■ a best-selling recording.

char·ter /ˈCHärtər/ ▸*n.* **1** a written grant by a country's legislative or sovereign power, by which an institution such as a company, college, or city is created and its rights and privileges defined. ■ a written constitution or description of an organization's functions. **2** the reservation of an aircraft, boat, or bus for private use: *a plane on charter to a multinational company.* ■ an aircraft, boat, or bus that is reserved for private use. ■ a trip made by an aircraft, boat, or bus under charter: *he liked to see the boat sparkling clean before each charter.*

▸*v.* [*trans.*] **1** grant a charter to (a city, university, or other institution): *the company was chartered in 1553.* **2** reserve (an aircraft, boat, or bus) for private use: *he chartered a plane to take him to Paris.* ▷Middle English: from Old French *chartre*, from Latin *chartula*, diminutive of *charta* 'paper' (see **CARD**[1]).

char·tered /ˈCHärtərd/ ▸*adj.* [*attrib.*] *Brit.* (of an accountant, engineer, librarian, etc.) qualified as a member of a professional body that has a royal charter.

char·ter·er /ˈCHärtərər/ ▸*n.* a person or organization that charters an aircraft, boat, or bus.

char·ter flight ▸*n.* a flight by an aircraft chartered for a specific trip, not part of an airline's regular schedule.

char·ter mem·ber ▸*n.* an original or founding member of an organization.

char·ter school ▸*n.* (in North America) a publicly funded independent school established by teachers, parents, or community groups under the terms of a charter with a local or national authority.

Chart·ism /ˈCHärtˌizəm/ ▸*n.* a UK parliamentary reform movement of 1837–48, the principles of which were set out in a manifesto called *The People's Charter*. —**Chart·ist** *n.* & *adj.*

char·tist /ˈCHärtəst/ ▸*n.* a person who uses charts of financial data to predict future trends and to guide investment strategies. —**char·tism** /ˈCHärtˌizəm/ *n.*

chart·let /ˈCHärtlit/ ▸*n.* a small chart, as for navigation, highlighting a particular feature.

Char·tres /ˈSHärt(rə)/ a city in northern France, noted for its Gothic cathedral; pop. 41,850.

Chartres Cathedral

char·treuse /SHärˈtro͞oz; -ˈtro͞os/ ▸*n.* **1** a pale green or yellow liqueur made from brandy and aromatic herbs. ■ a pale yellow or green color resembling this liqueur. **2** a dish made in a mold using pieces of meat, vegetables, or (now most often) fruit in jelly. ▷named after *La Grande Chartreuse*, the Carthusian monastery near Grenoble, France, where the liqueur (sense 1) was first made; sense 2 is an extended use.

chart-top·ping ▸*adj. informal* (of a popular singer, group, or recording) having reached the top of the music charts. —**chart-top·per** *n.*

char·wom·an /ˈCHärˌwo͝omən/ ▸*n.* (*pl.* **-wom·en**) *Brit.*, *dated* a woman employed to clean houses or offices. ▷late 16th cent.: from obsolete *char* or *chare* 'a turn of work, an odd job, chore' (obscurely related to **CHORE**) + **WOMAN**.

char·y /ˈCHe(ə)rē/ ▸*adj.* (**char·i·er**, **char·i·est**) cautious; wary: *most people are* **chary of** *allowing themselves to be photographed.* ■ cautious about the amount one gives or reveals: *he was chary with specifics about the script.* ▷Old English *cearig* 'sorrowful, anxious'; related to **CARE**. The current sense arose in the mid 16th cent. —**char·i·ly** /ˈCHe(ə)rəlē/ *adv.*

Cha·ryb·dis /kəˈribdis; CHə-/ *Greek Mythology* a dangerous whirlpool in a narrow channel of the sea, opposite the cave of the sea monster Scylla.

Chas. /CHaz/ ▸*abbr.* Charles.

Chase[1] /CHās/, Salmon Portland (1808–73), U.S. chief justice 1864–73. He served in the U.S. Senate 1849–55, as governor of Ohio 1855–59, and as U.S. secretary of the treasury 1861–64 during which time he established the national banking system and issued the first "greenbacks."

Chase[2], Samuel (1741–1811), U.S. Supreme Court associate justice 1796–1811. A delegate to the Continental Congresses 1774–78, 1784, 1785 and a signer of the Declaration of Independence, he stressed national supremacy.

chase[1] /CHās/ ▸*v.* [*trans.*] **1** pursue in order to catch or catch up with: *police chased the stolen car through the city* | [*intrans.*] *the dog* **chased after** *the stick.* ■ seek to attain: *seventy candidates chasing a single job.* ■ seek the company of (a member of the opposite sex) in an obvious way: *playing football by day and chasing women by night.* ■ [*trans.*] drive or cause to go in a specified direction: *she* **chased** *him* **out of** *the house.* **2** try to make contact with (someone) in order to get something owed or required: *chasing customers who had not paid their bills.* ■ make further investigation of (an unresolved matter): *investigators got a warrant, but they didn't have time to* **chase down** *the case.*

▸*n.* an act of pursuing someone or something: *they captured the youths after a brief chase* | *a chase for limited supplies of hard currency* | [with *adj.*] *a car chase.* ■ (**the chase**) hunting as a sport: *she was an ardent follower of the chase.* ■ short for **STEEPLECHASE**. ■ *Brit.* an area of unenclosed land formerly reserved for hunting. ■ *archaic* a hunted animal. ▷Middle English: from Old French *chacier* (verb), *chace* (noun), based on Latin *captare* 'continue to take,' from *capere* 'take.'

▸*PHRASE* □ **give chase** go in pursuit: *a patrol car gave chase and finally overtook him.*

chase[2] ▸*v.* [*trans.*] [usu. as *adj.*] (**chased**) engrave (metal, or a design on metal): *a miniature container with a delicately chased floral design.* ▷late Middle English: apparently from earlier *enchase*, from Old French *enchasser*.

chase[3] ▸*n.* (in letterpress printing) a metal frame for holding the composed type and blocks being printed at one time. ▷late 16th cent.: from French *châsse*, from Latin *capsa* 'box' (see **CASE**[2]).

chase[4] ▸*n.* **1** the part of a gun enclosing the bore. **2** a groove or furrow cut in the face of a wall or other surface to receive a pipe. ▷early 17th cent.: from French *chas* 'enclosed space,' from Provençal *cas*, *caus*, from medieval Latin *capsum* 'thorax or nave of a church.'

chas·er /ˈCHāsər/ ▸*n.* **1** a person or thing that chases: [*in combination*] *promotion-chasers.* **2** *informal* a drink taken after another of a different kind, typically a weak alcoholic drink after a stronger one: *bourbon on the rocks with a beer chaser.* **3** a horse for steeplechasing.

Cha·sid ▸*n.* variant spelling of **HASID**.

Cha·sid·ism ▸*n.* variant spelling of **HASIDISM**.

chasm /ˈkazəm/ ▸*n.* a deep fissure in the earth, rock, or another surface. ■ *figurative* a profound difference between people, viewpoints, feelings, etc.: *the* **chasm between** *rich and poor.* ▷late 16th cent. (denoting an opening up of the sea or land, as in an earthquake): from Latin *chasma*, from Greek *khasma* 'gaping hollow.' —**chas·mic** /ˈkazmik/ *adj.* (*rare*).

chas·sé /SHaˈsā/ ▸*n.* a gliding step in dancing in which one foot displaces the other.

▸*v.* (**chas·séd**, **chas·sé·ing**) [*intrans.*] make such a step. ▷early 19th cent.: French, literally 'chased.'

chasse·pot /ˈSHasˌpō/ ▸*n.* a type of bolt-action breech-loading rifle used by the French army between 1866 and 1874. ▷named for Antoine A. Chassepot (1833–1905), its French designer.

chas·seur /SHaˈsər/ ▸*n.* (*pl.* same) *historical* a soldier, usually in the light cavalry, equipped and trained for rapid movement, esp. in the French army. ▷mid 18th cent.: French, from *chasser* 'to chase.'

Chas·sid ▸*n.* variant spelling of **HASID**.

Chas·sid·ism ▸*n.* variant spelling of **HASIDISM**.

chas·sis /ˈCHasē; ˈSHasē/ ▸*n.* (*pl.* same) the base frame of a motor vehicle or other wheeled conveyance. ■ the outer structural framework of a piece of audio, radio, or computer equipment. ▷early 20th cent.: from French *châssis* 'frame,' based on Latin *capsa* 'box' (see **CASE**[2]).

chaste /CHāst/ ▸*adj.* abstaining from extramarital, or from all, sexual intercourse. ■ not having any sexual nature or intention: *a chaste, consoling embrace.* ■ without unnecessary ornamentation; simple or restrained: *the dark, chaste interior was lightened by tilework.* ▷Middle English: from Old French, from Latin *castus*. —**chaste·ly** *adv.* —**chaste·ness** *n.*

chas·ten /ˈCHāsən/ ▸*v.* [*trans.*] (usu. **be chastened**) (of a reproof or misfortune) have a restraining or moderating effect on: *the director was somewhat chastened by his recent flops* | [as *adj.*] (**chastening**) *a chastening experience.* ■ *archaic* (esp. of God) discipline; punish. ▷early 16th cent.: from an obsolete verb *chaste*, from Old French *chastier*, from Latin *castigare* 'castigate,' from *castus* 'morally pure, chaste.' —**chas·ten·er** /ˈCHās(ə)nər/ *n.*

chaste tree ▸*n.* a southern European shrub with blue or white flowers, grown as an ornamental. It is also highly valued for its dark purple berries, which yield medicinal preparations used to treat gynecological conditions. Also called **VITEX**. • *Vitex agnus-castus*, family Verbenaceae. ▷mid 16th cent.: so named because of its association with chastity in sacrifices to Ceres.

chas·tise /CHasˈtīz/ ▸*v.* [*trans.*] rebuke or reprimand severely: *he chastised his colleagues for their laziness.* ■ *dated* punish, esp. by beating. ▷Middle English: apparently formed irregularly from the obsolete verb *chaste* (see **CHASTEN**). —**chas·tise·ment** /CHasˈtīzmənt; ˈCHastəz-/ *n.* —**chas·tis·er** /ˈCHasˌtīzər/ *n.*

chas·ti·ty /ˈCHastətē/ ▸*n.* the state or practice of refraining from extramarital, or esp. from all, sexual intercourse: *vows of chastity.* ▷Middle English: from Old French *chastete*, from Latin *castitas*, from *castus* 'morally pure' (see **CHASTE**).

chas·ti·ty belt ▸*n. historical* a garment or device designed to prevent a woman from having sexual intercourse.

chas·u·ble /ˈCHazəbəl; ˈCHazh-; ˈCHas-/ ▸*n.* a sleeveless outer vestment worn by a Catholic or High Anglican priest when celebrating Mass, typically ornate and having a simple hole for the head. ▷Middle English: from Old French *chesible*, later *chasuble*, from late Latin *casubla*, alteration of Latin *casula* 'hooded cloak or little cottage,' diminutive of *casa* 'house.'

chasuble

chat[1] /CHat/ ▸*v.* (**chat·ted**, **chat·ting**) [*intrans.*] talk in a friendly and informal way: *she chatted to her mother on the phone every day.*

▸*phrasal v.* □ **chat someone up** *informal* engage someone in flirtatious conversation. ■ talk persuasively to someone, esp. with a particular motive: *I chatted up the editor at the press club.*

▸*n.* an informal conversation: *he dropped in for a chat.* See note at **CONVERSATION**. ▷Middle English: shortening of **CHATTER**.

chat[2] ▸*n.* **1** [often in *combination*] a small Old World songbird of the thrush subfamily, with a harsh call and typically with bold black, white, and buff or chestnut coloration. • *Saxicola* and other genera, subfamily Turdinae, family Muscicapidae: numerous species. See also **STONECHAT**, **WHINCHAT**. **2** [with *adj.*] any of a number of small songbirds with harsh calls: • a New World warbler that typically has a yellow or pink breast (genera *Icteria* and *Granatellus*, subfamily Parulinae, family Emberizidae). • an Australian songbird related to the honeyeaters, the male of which is either mainly yellow or boldly marked (genera *Ephthianura* and *Ashbyia*, family Ephthianuridae). ▷late 17th cent.: probably imitative of its call.

châ·teau /SHaˈtō/ (also **cha·teau**) ▸*n.* (*pl.* **-teaux** /-ˈtō(z)/) a large French country house or castle often giving its name to wine made in its neighborhood: [*in names*] *Château Margaux.* ▷mid 18th cent.: French, from Old French *chastel* (see **CASTLE**).

Cha·teau·bri·and /SHaˌtōbrēˈän/, François-René, Vicomte de (1768–1848), French writer and diplomat. Notable works: *Le Génie du Christianisme* (1802) and *Mémoires d'outre-tombe* (autobiography, 1849–50).

cha·teau·bri·and /SHaˌtōbrēˈōn/ ▸*n.* a thick tenderloin of beef, typically served with Béarnaise sauce. ▷late 19th cent.: named after François-René,

Vicomte de CHATEAUBRIAND, whose chef is said to have created the dish.

Cha·teau-Thierr·y /SHa,tō tye'rē/ a town in the Picardy region of northern France, on the Marne River; pop. 15,000. It was a major battlefield during World War I; there is a monument to the U.S. soldiers who took the town from German occupiers in 1918 and a military cemetery.

chat·e·lain /'SHatl,ān/ ▸*n.* another term for CASTELLAN. ▷late Middle English: from Old French *chastelain*, from medieval Latin *castellanus* 'castellan,' from Latin *castellum* (see CASTLE).

chat·e·laine /'SHatl,ān/ ▸*n. dated* a woman in charge of a large house. ■ *historical* a set of short chains attached to a woman's belt, used for carrying keys or other items. ▷mid 19th cent.: from French *châtelaine*, feminine of *châtelain* 'castellan,' from medieval Latin *castellanus* (see CHATELAIN).

chat group ▸*n.* a group of people who communicate regularly via the Internet, usually in real time but also by e-mail.

Chat·ham /'CHatəm/, 1st Earl of, see PITT.

Chat·ham Is·lands /'CHatəm/ two islands, Pitt and Chatham, in the southwestern Pacific Ocean, east of New Zealand.

chat line (also **chat·line**) ▸*n.* a telephone service that allows conversation among a number of people who call into it separately. ■ the access to, or connection with, a chat room.

cha·toy·ant /SHə'toi-ənt/ ▸*adj.* (of a gem, esp. when cut en cabochon) showing a band of bright reflected light caused by aligned inclusions in the stone. ▷late 18th cent.: French, present participle of *chatoyer* 'to shimmer.' **—cha·toy·ance** *n.* **—cha·toy·an·cy** /-ənsē/ *n.* .

chat room ▸*n.* an area on the Internet or other computer network where users can communicate, typically limiting communication to a particular topic.

chat show ▸*n.* British term for TALK SHOW.

Chat·ta·hoo·chee Riv·er /,CHatə'hōōCHē/ a river that flows for 435 miles (700 km) through Georgia to the Florida border, where it continues as the Apalachicola River into the Gulf of Mexico.

Chat·ta·noo·ga /,CHatn'ōōgə/ a city in southeastern Tennessee, on the Tennessee River, near the Georgia border, a rail and industrial center; pop. 155,554.

chat·tel /'CHatl/ ▸*n.* (in general use) a personal possession. ■ *Law* an item of property other than real estate. See also GOODS AND CHATTELS. ▷Middle English: from Old French *chatel*, from medieval Latin *capitale*, from Latin *capitalis*, from *caput* 'head.' Compare with CAPITAL[1] and CATTLE.

chat·ter /'CHatər/ ▸*v.* [*intrans.*] talk rapidly or incessantly about trivial matters: *the kids chattered and splashed at the edge of the lagoon.* ■ (of a bird, monkey, or machine) make a series of quick high-pitched sounds. ■ (of a person's teeth) click repeatedly together, typically from cold or fear.
▸*n.* incessant trivial talk: *a stream of idle chatter.* ■ a series of quick high-pitched sounds: *the chatter of a typewriter.* ■ undesirable vibration in a mechanism: *the wipers should operate without chatter.* ▷Middle English: imitative. **—chat·ter·y** *adj.*
▸*PHRASE* □ **the chattering classes** *derogatory* educated people, esp. those in academic, artistic, or media circles.

chat·ter·bot /'CHatər,bät/ ▸*n.* a computer program designed to interact with people by simulating human conversation. ▷1990s: blend of *chatter* and *(ro)bot*.

chat·ter·box /'CHatər,bäks/ ▸*n. informal* a person who talks at length about trivial matters.

chat·ter·er /'CHatərər/ ▸*n.* **1** another term for CHATTERBOX. **2** *informal* any of a number of birds with chattering calls, esp. a babbler, a waxwing, or a cotinga.

Chat·tis·garh /'CHətēs,gär/ a state in central India, formed in 2000 from the southeastern part of Madhya Pradesh; capital, Raipur.

chat·ty /'CHatē/ ▸*adj.* (**chat·ti·er**, **chat·ti·est**) (of a person) fond of talking in an easy, informal way. ■ (of a conversation, letter, etc.) informal and lively. **—chat·ti·ly** /'CHatl-ē/ *adv.* **—chat·ti·ness** *n.*

Chau·bu·na·gun·ga·maug, Lake /CHô,bənə'gəNGgə-,môg/ a small lake in southern Massachusetts, south of Worcester, in the town of Webster. The full form of its name, Chargoggagoggmanchaugagoggchaubunagungamaugg, is said to be the longest American place name.

Chau·cer /'CHôsər/, Geoffrey (*c.*1342–1400), English poet. His *Canterbury Tales* (*c.*1387–1400) is a cycle of linked tales told by a group of pilgrims. His skills of characterization, humor, and versatility established him as the first great English poet. Chaucer also wrote *Troilus and Criseyde* (1385).

Chau·ce·ri·an /CHô'si(ə)rēən/ ▸*adj.* of or relating to Chaucer or his style.
▸*n.* an admirer, imitator, or student of Chaucer or his writing.

Chau·diere Riv·er /SHō'dyer/ a river that flows north for 120 miles (190 km) from the Maine border through Quebec and empties into the St. Lawrence River opposite Quebec City.

chauf·feur /'SHōfər; SHō'fər/ ▸*n.* a person employed to drive a private or rented automobile.
▸*v.* [*trans.*] drive (a car or a passenger in a car), typically as part of one's job: *she insisted on being* **chauffeured around**. ▷late 19th cent. (in the general sense 'motorist'): from French, literally 'stoker' (by association with steam engines), from *chauffer* 'to heat.'

chauf·feuse /SHō'fə(r)z/ ▸*n. rare* a female chauffeur.

chaul·moo·gra /CHôl'mōōgrə/ ▸*n.* a tropical Asian evergreen tree with narrow leathery leaves and oil-rich seeds. • Genus *Hydnocarpus*, family Flacourtiaceae: several species, in particular *H. kurzii*, a principal source of the oil. ■ (also **chaulmoogra oil**) the oil obtained from the seeds of this tree. It is used medically and as a preservative, and was formerly used in the treatment of leprosy. ▷early 19th cent.: from Bengali *cāul-mugrā*.

chausses /SHōs/ ▸*plural n. historical* pantaloons or close-fitting coverings for the legs and feet, in particular those forming part of a knight's armor. ▷late 15th cent.: French, literally 'clothing for the legs.'

Chau·tau·qua /SHə'tôkwə/ ▸*n.* a resort town in southwestern New York, on Chautauqua Lake, noted as the birthplace of a 19th-century popular education movement; pop. 4,554. ■ (also **chautauqua**) an institution offering popular adult education courses and entertainment, typically held outdoors in the summer in the late 19th and early 20th centuries: *some sophisticate who had attended Chautauquas in other parts of the country.* ▷late 19th cent.: named after *Chautauqua*, a county in New York State, where such an institution was first set up.

chau·vin·ism /'SHōvə,nizəm/ ▸*n.* exaggerated or aggressive patriotism: *public opinion was easily moved to chauvinism and nationalism.* ■ excessive or prejudiced loyalty or support for one's own cause, group, or gender: *a bastion of male chauvinism.* ▷late 19th cent.: named after Nicolas *Chauvin*, a Napoleonic veteran noted for his extreme patriotism, popularized as a character by the Cogniard brothers in *Cocarde Tricolore* (1831).

chau·vin·ist /'SHōvənist/ ▸*n.* a person displaying aggressive or exaggerated patriotism. ■ a person displaying excessive or prejudiced loyalty or support for a particular cause, group, or gender: *what a male chauvinist that man is.*
▸*adj.* showing or relating to such excessive or prejudiced support or loyalty: *a chauvinist slur.* **—chau·vin·is·tic** /,SHōvə'nistik/ *adj.* **—chau·vin·is·ti·cal·ly** /,SHōvə'nistik(ə)lē/ *adv.*

Cha·vez /'CHävez; 'SHä-/, Cesar Estrata (1927–93), U.S. labor leader. In 1962, he founded the organization that became the United Farm Workers, and he used nonviolent tactics to gain union contracts with California vineyard owners in 1970.

chaw /CHô/ *informal* ▸*n.* an act of chewing something, esp. something not intended to be swallowed: *enjoying a good chaw.* ■ something chewed, esp. a wad of tobacco: *a chaw of tobacco.*
▸*v.* [*trans.*] chew (something, esp. tobacco). ▷late Middle English (as a verb): variant of CHEW.

Cha·yef·sky /CHī'efskē; -'ev-/, Paddy (1923–81), U.S. writer; real name *Sidney Chayefsky*. He wrote television dramas, movie screenplays, stage plays, and a science fiction novel, *Altered States* (1978). He received three Academy Awards for his screenplays for *Marty* (1955), *Hospital* (1971), and *Network* (1976).

cha·yo·te /CHä'yōtē/ ▸*n.* **1** a green pear-shaped tropical fruit that resembles cucumber in flavor. **2** the tropical American vine that yields this fruit, also producing an edible yamlike tuberous root. • *Sechium edule*, family Cucurbitaceae. ▷late 19th cent.: from Spanish, from Nahuatl *chayotli*.

CHD ▸*abbr.* coronary heart disease.

Ch.E ▸*abbr.* Chemical Engineer.

cheap /CHēp/ ▸*adj.* (of an item for sale) low in price; worth more than its cost: *they bought some cheap fruit* | *local buses were reliable and cheap.* ■ charging low prices: *a cheap restaurant.* ■ (of prices or other charges) low: *my rent was pretty cheap.* ■ inexpensive because of inferior quality: *cheap, shoddy goods.* ■ *informal* miserly; stingy: *she's too cheap to send me a postcard.* ■ of little worth because achieved in a discreditable way requiring little effort: *her moment of cheap triumph.* ■ deserving of contempt: *a cheap trick.*
▸*adv.* at or for a low price: *a house that was* **going cheap**. ▷late 15th cent.: from an obsolete phrase *good cheap* 'a good bargain,' from Old English *cēap* 'bargaining, trade,' based on Latin *caupo* 'small trader, innkeeper.' **—cheap·ish** *adj.* **—cheap·ly** *adv.* **—cheap·ness** *n.*
▸*PHRASES* □ **dirt cheap** very cheap or cheaply: *the auctioneers let us have it dirt cheap.* □ **on the cheap** *informal* at a low cost: *in search of symbols of prestige, but on the cheap.*

cheap·en /'CHēpən/ ▸*v.* [*trans.*] reduce the price of: *the depreciation of the dollar would cheapen U.S. exports.* ■ degrade: *the mass media simplify and cheapen the experience of art.*

cheap·jack /'CHēp,jak/ ▸*n.* a seller of cheap inferior goods, typically a hawker at a fair or market.
▸*adj.* of inferior quality. ▷mid 19th cent.: from CHEAP + JACK[1].

cheap·o /'CHēpō/ (also **cheap·ie**) ▸*adj.* [*attrib.*] *informal* inexpensive and of poor quality: *a cheapo guitar.*
▸*n.* (*pl.* **-os**) an inexpensive thing of poor quality.

cheap·skate /'CHēp,skāt/ ▸*n. informal* a stingy person. ▷late 19th cent. (originally U.S.): from CHEAP + *skate* 'a worn-out horse' or 'a mean, contemptible, or dishonest person,' of unknown origin.

cheat /CHēt/ ▸*v.* **1** [*intrans.*] act dishonestly or unfairly in order to gain an advantage, esp. in a game or examination: *she always* **cheats at** *cards.* ■ [*trans.*] deceive or trick: *he had* **cheated** *her* **out of** *everything she had.* ■ use inferior materials or methods unobtrusively in order to save time or money: *they cheat by photographing mashed potatoes instead of ice cream.* ■ *informal* be sexually unfaithful: *his wife was* **cheating on** *him.* **2** [*trans.*] avoid (something undesirable) by luck or skill: *she* **cheated death** *in a spectacular crash.* ■ *archaic* help (time) pass: *the tuneless rhyme with which the warder cheats the time.*
▸*n.* a person who behaves dishonestly in order to gain an advantage: *a liar and a cheat.* ■ an act of cheating; a fraud or deception. ▷late Middle English: shortening of ESCHEAT (the original sense).

cheat·er /CHētər/ ▸*n.* **1** a person who acts dishonestly in order to gain an advantage. **2** (**cheaters**) *informal* a pair of glasses or sunglasses.

cheat grass (also **cheat·grass**) ▸*n.* a tough wild grass of open land, sometimes growing as a weed among cereal crops and in pasture. • Genus *Bromus*, family Gramineae: several species, in particular *B. tectorum*. ▷late 18th cent.: a local word for various wild plants, perhaps from their resemblance to the cereals among which they grew.

cheat sheet ▸*n. informal* a piece of paper bearing written notes intended to aid one's memory, typically one used surreptitiously in an examination.

Che·bo·ksa·ry /,CHebäk'sär(y)ē/ a city in western central Russia, on the Volga River, west of Kazan, capital of the autonomous republic of Chuvashia; pop. 429,000.

Che·chen /'CHeCHən/ ▸*n.* (*pl.* same or **-chens**) **1** a member of the largely Muslim people inhabiting Chechnya. **2** the North Caucasian language of this people.
▸*adj.* of or relating to this people or their language. ▷from obsolete Russian *chechen* (earlier form of *chechenets*).

Chech·ny·a /'CHeCHnēə; CHeCH'nyä/ (also **Che·che·nia** /CHeCHə'nyə/) an autonomous republic in the Caucasus in southwestern Russia, on the border with Georgia; pop. 1,290,000; capital, Grozny. The republic declared itself independent of Russia in 1991; Russian troops invaded the republic in 1994, but withdrew after the signing of a peace treaty in 1996. Also called CHECHEN REPUBLIC.

check[1] /CHek/ ▸*v.* [*trans.*] **1** examine (something) in order to determine its accuracy, quality, or condition, or to detect the presence of something: *customs officers have the right to check all luggage* | [*intrans.*] *a simple blood test to* **check for** *anemia.* ■ verify or establish to one's satisfaction: *check the expiration date on your passport* [with *clause*] *she glanced over her shoulder to*

C

check that the door was shut. ■ examine with a view to rectifying any fault or problem discovered: *check the oil and fluid levels again.* ■ (**check against**) verify the accuracy of something by comparing it with (something else): *keep your receipt to check against your statement.* ■ another way of saying **CHECK SOMETHING OFF.** ■ another way of saying **CHECK SOMETHING IN.** ■ [*intrans.*] agree or correspond when compared. **2** stop or slow down the progress of (something undesirable): *efforts were made to check the disease.* ■ curb or restrain (a feeling or emotion): *he learned to check his excitement.* ■ (**check oneself**) master an involuntary reaction: *Chris took one step backward then checked himself.* ■ *Hockey* hamper or neutralize (an opponent) with one's body or stick. ■ [*intrans.*] (**check against**) provide a means of preventing: *processes to check against deterioration in the quality of the data held.* ■ [*intrans.*] (of a hound) pause to make sure of or regain a scent. ■ [*intrans.*] (of a trained hawk) abandon the intended quarry and fly after other prey. **3** [*trans.*] *Chess* move a piece or pawn so that (the opposing king) is under attack. **4** [*intrans.*] (in poker) choose not to make a bet when called upon, allowing the action to move to another player.

▸*phrasal v.* □ **check in** (or **check someone in**) arrive and register at a hotel or airport: *you must check in at least one hour before takeoff* | *they check in the passengers.* □ **check something in** have one's baggage weighed and put aside for consignment to the hold of an aircraft on which one is booked to travel. ■ register and leave baggage in a left-luggage department. □ **check into** register one's arrival at (a hotel). □ **check something off** tick or otherwise mark an item on a list to show that it has been dealt with. □ **check on 1** verify, ascertain, or monitor the state or condition of: *the doctor had come to check on his patient.* **2** another way of saying **CHECK UP ON.** □ **check out** settle one's hotel bill before leaving. ■ *informal* die. □ **check someone/something out 1** establish the truth or inform oneself about someone or something: *they decided to go and check out a local restaurant.* **2** (**check something out**) enter the price of goods in a supermarket into a cash machine for addition and payment by a customer. ■ register something as having been borrowed. □ **check something over** inspect or examine something thoroughly. □ **check through** inspect or examine thoroughly. □ **check up on** investigate in order to establish the truth about or accuracy of.

▸*n.* **1** an examination to test or ascertain accuracy, quality, or satisfactory condition: *a campaign calling for regular checks on gas appliances* | *a health check.* **2** a stopping or slowing of progress: *there was no check to the expansion of the market.* ■ a means of control or restraint: *a permanent check upon the growth or abuse of central authority.* ■ *Hockey* an act of hampering or neutralizing an opponent with one's body or stick. ■ a temporary loss of the scent in hunting. ■ *Falconry* a false stoop when a hawk abandons its intended quarry and pursues other prey. ■ a part of a piano that catches the hammer and prevents it from retouching the strings. **3** *Chess* a move by which a piece or pawn directly attacks the opponent's king. If the defending player cannot counter the attack, the king is checkmated. **4** the bill in a restaurant. ■ (also **baggage/luggage check**) a token of identification for left luggage. ■ a counter used as a stake in a gambling game. **5** short for **CHECK MARK. 6** a crack or flaw in timber.

▸*exclam.* **1** *informal* expressing assent or agreement. **2** used by a chess player to announce that the opponent's king has been placed in check. ▷Middle English (originally as used in the game of chess): the noun and exclamation from Old French *eschec,* from medieval Latin *scaccus,* via Arabic from Persian *šāh* 'king'; the verb from Old French *eschequier* 'play chess, put in check.' The sense 'stop, restrain, or control' arose from the use in chess, and led (in the late 17th cent.) to 'examine the accuracy of, verify.' **—check·a·ble** *adj.*

▸**PHRASES** □ **in check 1** under control: *a way of keeping inflation in check.* **2** *Chess* (of a king) directly attacked by an opponent's piece or pawn; (of a player) having the king in this position. □ **keep a check on** monitor: *keep a regular check on your score.*

check2 (*Brit.* **cheque**) ▸*n.* a written order to a bank to pay a stated sum from the drawer's account: *awarded* **a check for** *$1,000.* ■ the printed form on which such an order is written. ▷early 18th cent. (originally denoting a check stub): variant of **CHECK**1, in the sense 'device for checking the amount of an item.'

check3 ▸*n.* a pattern of small squares: *a fine black-and-white check.* ■ a garment or fabric with such a pattern.

▸*adj.* [*attrib.*] having such a pattern: *a blue check T-shirt.* ▷late Middle English: probably from **CHECKER**2.

check·book /ˈCHek,bo͝ok/ ▸*n.* a book of blank checks with a register for recording checks written.

check·book jour·nal·ism ▸*n. chiefly derogatory* the practice of paying large amounts of money for exclusive rights to material for newspaper stories, esp. personal ones.

check·box /ˈCHek,bäks/ ▸*n. Computing* a small box on a computer screen that, when selected by the user, is filled with an X to show that the feature described alongside it has been enabled.

checked /CHekt/ ▸*adj.* **1** (of clothes or fabric) having a pattern of small squares: *a checked shirt.* **2** *Phonetics* (of a vowel) followed by one or more consonants in the same syllable.

Check·er /ˈCHekər/, Chubby (1941–), U.S. singer; born Ernest Evans. He popularized dance crazes such as "The Twist" 1960.

check·er1 /ˈCHekər/ ▸*n.* **1** a person or thing that verifies or examines something: *a spelling checker.* **2** a cashier in a supermarket.

check·er2 (*Brit.* **cheq·uer**) ▸*n.* **1** (often **checkers**) a pattern of squares, typically alternately colored: *a geometric shape bordered by checkers* | [as *adj.*] (**checker**) *a checker design.* **2** (**checkers**) [treated as *sing.*] a game for two players, with twelve pieces each, played on a checkerboard. ■ (**checker**) a round flat piece, usually red or black, used to play checkers. ▷Middle English: from **EXCHEQUER.** The original sense 'chessboard' gave rise to *checkered* meaning 'marked like a chessboard'; hence sense 1 (early 16th cent.).

check·er·ber·ry /ˈCHekər,berē/ ▸*n.* (*pl.* **-ries**) a creeping evergreen North American shrub of the heath family, with spiny scented leaves and waxy white flowers. Also called **WINTERGREEN.** • *Gaultheria procumbens,* family Ericaceae. ■ the edible red fruit of this plant. ▷late 18th cent.: from *checkers* or *chequers* 'berries of the service tree' (so named from their color) + **BERRY.**

check·er·board /ˈCHekər,bôrd/ ▸*n.* a board for playing checkers and certain other games, with a regular pattern of squares in alternating colors, typically black and white. ■ a pattern resembling such a board.

check·ered /ˈCHekərd/ ▸*adj.* having a pattern of alternating squares of different colors. ■ *figurative* marked by periods of varied fortune or discreditable incidents: *his* **checkered past** *might hurt his electability.*

check·ered flag ▸*n.* **1** *Auto Racing* a flag with a black-and-white checkered pattern, displayed to drivers as they finish a race. **2** victory in a race: *Unser took the checkered flag four times this spring.*

check·er·spot /ˈCHekər,spät/ ▸*n.* a North American butterfly with pale markings on the wings that typically form a checkered pattern. • *Euphydryas* and other genera, subfamily Melitaeinae, family Nymphalidae: several species, in particular the **Baltimore checkerspot** (*E. phaeton*).

Baltimore checkerspot

check-in ▸*n.* [often as *adj.*] the act of reporting one's presence and registering, typically at an airport or hotel: *the check-in counter.* ■ the point at which such registration takes place.

check·ing ac·count (*Canadian* **cheq·uing ac·count**) ▸*n.* an account at a bank against which checks can be drawn by the account depositor. ▷1920s: from **CHECK**3.

check·list /ˈCHek,list/ ▸*n.* a list of items required, things to be done, or points to be considered, used as a reminder.

check mark ▸*n.* a mark (√) used to indicate that a textual item is correct or has been chosen or verified.

check·mate /ˈCHek,māt/ ▸*n. Chess* a check from which a king cannot escape. ■ [as *exclam.*] (by a player) announcing that the opponent's king is in such a position. ■ *figurative* a final defeat or deadlock: *if the rebel forces succeed in cutting off the road, they will have achieved checkmate.*

▸*v.* [*trans.*] *Chess* put into checkmate. ■ *figurative* defeat or frustrate totally: *U.S. aid would help them to checkmate communist invasion.* ▷Middle English: from Old French *eschec mat,* from Arabic *šāh māta,* from Persian *šāh manad* 'the king is helpless.'

check·out /ˈCHek,out/ ▸*n.* **1** a point at which goods are paid for in a supermarket or other store: [as *adj.*] *packaging that is scanned at the checkout counter.* **2** the administrative procedure followed when a guest leaves a hotel at the end of a stay: [as *adj.*] *checkout time.*

check·point /ˈCHek,point/ ▸*n.* a barrier or manned entrance, typically at a border, where travelers are subject to security checks. ■ a place along the route of a long-distance race where the time for each competitor is recorded. ■ a location whose exact position can be verified visually or electronically, used by pilots to aid navigation.

check rein ▸*n.* a bearing rein.

check·room /ˈCHek,ro͞om; -,ro͝om/ ▸*n.* a room in a public building where coats, hats, luggage, etc., may be left temporarily.

checks and bal·anc·es ▸*plural n.* counterbalancing influences by which an organization or system is regulated, typically those ensuring that political power is not concentrated in the hands of individuals or groups.

check·sum /ˈCHek,səm/ ▸*n.* a digit representing the sum of the correct digits in a piece of stored or transmitted digital data, against which later comparisons can be made to detect errors in the data.

check·up /ˈCHek,əp/ ▸*n.* a thorough examination, esp. a medical or dental one.

check valve ▸*n.* a valve that closes to prevent backward flow of liquid.

ched·dar /ˈCHedər/ ▸*n.* a kind of firm smooth cheese, originally made in Cheddar in southern England.

che·der /ˈKHedər; ˈKHā-/ (also **he·der**) ▸*n.* (*pl.* **che·da·rim** /KHeˈdärim/, **che·ders**) a school for Jewish children in which Hebrew and religious knowledge are taught. ▷late 19th cent.: from Hebrew *ḥeder* 'room.'

chee·cha·ko /CHiˈCHäkō; -ˈCHôkō/ ▸*n.* (*pl.* **-kos**) *informal* a person newly arrived in the mining districts of Alaska or northwestern Canada. ▷late 19th cent.: Chinook Jargon, 'newcomer.'

cheek /CHēk/ ▸*n.* **1** either side of the face below the eye: *tears rolled down her cheeks.* ■ either of the inner sides of the mouth: *Sam had to bite his cheeks to keep from laughing.* ■ *informal* either of the buttocks. ■ either of two side pieces or parts in a structure. **2** [in *sing.*] impertinent talk or behavior: *he* **had the cheek** *to complain* | *that's enough of your cheek!* ▷Old English *cē(a)ce, cēoce* 'cheek, jaw'; related to Dutch *kaak.* **—cheeked** *adj.* [in *combination*] *rosy-cheeked.*

▸**PHRASES** □ **cheek by jowl** close together; side by side: *the houses were packed cheek by jowl along the coast.* [from a use of *jowl* in the sense 'cheek'; the phrase was originally *cheek by cheek.*] □ **cheek to cheek** (of two people dancing) with their heads close together in an intimate way. □ **turn the other cheek** refrain from retaliating when one has been attacked or insulted. [with biblical allusion to Matt. 5:39.]

cheek·bone /ˈCHēk,bōn/ ▸*n.* the bone below the eye.

cheek·piece /ˈCHēk,pēs/ ▸*n.* a part of an object that covers or rests on the cheek, in particular: ■ the portion of the stock of a rifle or shotgun that rests against the face when aiming from the shoulder. ■ either of the two straps of a horse's bridle joining the bit and the headpiece. ■ a bar on a horse's bit that lies outside the mouth.

cheek pouch ▸*n.* a saclike fold of skin on either side of the mouth, esp. in squirrels, monkeys, and gophers, used for carrying food.

Cheek·to·wa·ga /,CHēktəˈwägə/ a town in western New York, an industrial suburb east of Buffalo; pop. 99,314.

cheek·y /ˈCHēkē/ ▸*adj.* (**cheek·i·er, cheek·i·est**) impudent or irreverent, typically in an endearing or amusing way: *a cheeky grin.* **—cheek·i·ly** /-kəlē/ *adv.* **—cheek·i·ness** *n.*

cheep /CHēp/ ▸*n.* a shrill squeaky cry made by a bird, typically a young one. ■ a sound resembling such a cry: *an electronic cheep from the alarm.*

▸*v.* [*intrans.*] make a shrill squeaky sound. ▷early 16th cent. (originally Scots): imitative (compare with **PEEP**2).

cheer /CHi(ə)r/ ▸*v.* **1** [*intrans.*] shout for joy or in praise or encouragement: *she cheered from the sidelines.* ■ [*trans.*] praise or encourage with shouts: *they cheered his emotional speech | the cyclists were* **cheered on** *by the crowds.* **2** [*trans.*] give comfort or support to: *he seemed greatly cheered by my arrival.* ■ (**cheer someone up** or **cheer up**) make or become less miserable: [*trans.*] *I asked her out to lunch to cheer her up* | [*intrans.*] *he cheered up at the sight of the food.*

▸*n.* **1** a shout of encouragement, praise, or joy: *a tremendous cheer from the audience.* ■ a brief phrase shouted in unison by a crowd, typically led by cheerleaders, in support of an athletic team. **2** (also **good cheer**) cheerfulness, optimism, or confidence: *an attempt to inject a little cheer into this gloomy season.* ■ something that causes such feelings: *the sunset provided some cheer for rush-hour motorists.* ■ food and drink provided for a festive occasion: *they had partaken heartily of the Christmas cheer.* ▷Middle English: from Old French *chiere* 'face,' from late Latin *cara*, from Greek *kara* 'head.' The original sense was 'face,' hence 'expression, mood,' later specifically 'a good mood.'

▸*PHRASES* □ **of good cheer** *archaic* cheerful; optimistic. □ **three cheers** three successive hurrahs shouted to express appreciation or congratulation: ***three cheers for** the winners!* □ **what cheer?** *archaic* how are you?

cheer·ful /ˈCHi(ə)rfəl/ ▸*adj.* noticeably happy and optimistic: *how can she be so cheerful at six o'clock in the morning? | a cheerful voice.* ■ causing happiness by its nature or appearance: *a chatty, cheerful letter | the room was painted in cheerful colors.* —**cheer·ful·ness** *n.*

cheer·ful·ly /ˈCHi(ə)rfəlē/ ▸*adv.* in a way that displays happiness or optimism: *he was whistling cheerfully.* ■ in a way that inspires feelings of happiness: *cheerfully decorated rooms.* ■ readily and willingly: *I could cheerfully have strangled her.*

cheer·i·o /ˌCHi(ə)rēˈō/ ▸*exclam. Brit., informal* used as an expression of good wishes on parting; goodbye. ■ *dated* used as a toast.

cheer·lead·er /ˈCHi(ə)rˌlēdər/ ▸*n.* a person who leads cheers and applause, esp. at a sports event. ■ an enthusiastic and vocal supporter: *he was a cheerleader for individual initiative.* —**cheer·lead** *v.* (*past* and *past part.* **-led**)

cheer·less /ˈCHi(ə)rlis/ ▸*adj.* gloomy; depressing: *the corridors were ill-lit and cheerless.* —**cheer·less·ly** *adv.* —**cheer·less·ness** *n.*

cheer·ly /ˈCHi(ə)rlē/ ▸*adv. archaic* heartily (used as a cry of encouragement among sailors).

cheers /CHi(ə)rz/ ▸*exclam. informal* expressing good wishes, in particular: ■ good wishes before drinking: *"Cheers," she said, raising her glass.* ■ *Brit.* good wishes on parting or ending a conversation: *"Cheers, Jack, see you later."* ■ *chiefly Brit.* gratitude or acknowledgment for something: *Billy tossed him the key. "Cheers, pal."*

cheer·y /ˈCHi(ə)rē/ ▸*adj.* (**cheer·i·er**, **cheer·i·est**) happy and optimistic: *a cheery smile.* —**cheer·i·ly** /ˈCHi(ə)rəlē/ *adv.* —**cheer·i·ness** *n.*

cheese[1] /CHēz/ ▸*n.* **1** a food made from the pressed curds of milk: *grated cheese | a slice of cheese |* [as *adj.*] *a cheese sandwich.* ■ a molded mass of such food with its rind, often in a round flat shape: *a 50-pound, muslin-wrapped cheese.* ■ a round flat object resembling a cheese. **2** *informal* the quality of being too obviously sentimental: *the conversations tend too far toward cheese.* ▷Old English *cēse, cȳse*; related to Dutch *kaas* and German *Käse*; from Latin *caseus*.

▸*PHRASES* □ **hard cheese** *Brit., informal* used to express sympathy over a petty matter. □ **say cheese** said by a photographer to encourage the subject to smile.

cheese[2] (also **big cheese**) ▸*n. informal* an important person: *he was a big cheese in the business world.* ▷early 19th cent. (originally in the sense 'the right thing or something excellent'): probably from Urdu, from Persian *čīz* 'thing.' The current sense dates from the 1920s.

cheese[3] ▸*v. informal, chiefly Brit.*, exasperate, frustrate, or bore: *that really* **cheesed off** *Ricky.* ▷early 19th cent. (in sense 1 of *cheese it*): of unknown origin.

▸*PHRASE* □ **cheese it** **1** *Brit., archaic* look out. **2** *dated* run away: *cheese it, here comes Mr. Madigan!*

cheese·board /ˈCHēzˌbôrd/ ▸*n.* a board on which cheese is served and cut. ■ a selection of cheeses.

cheese·burg·er /ˈCHēzˌbərgər/ ▸*n.* a hamburger with a slice of cheese on it.

cheese·cake /ˈCHēzˌkāk/ ▸*n.* **1** a kind of rich dessert cake made with cream and soft cheese on a graham cracker, cookie, or pastry crust, typically topped with a fruit sauce. **2** *informal* photography, a movie, or art that portrays women in a manner emphasizing stereotypical sexual attractiveness: [as *adj.*] *a cheesecake photo of herself wearing a silly hat and little else.*

cheese·cloth /ˈCHēzˌklôTH/ ▸*n.* thin, loosely woven cloth of cotton, used originally for making and wrapping cheese.

cheese-cut·ter ▸*n.* **1** an implement for cutting cheese, esp. by means of a wire that can be pulled through the cheese. **2** (also **cheese-cutter cap**) *informal* a cap with a broad, square brim.

cheese fly ▸*n.* another term for CHEESE-SKIPPER.

cheese·head /ˈCHēzˌhed/ ▸*n.* **1** *informal* a resident of Wisconsin, esp. a fan of the Green Bay Packers football team. [so called because Wisconsin is noted for the production of cheese.] **2** *informal* a blockhead; an idiot.

cheese·mon·ger /ˈCHēzˌmäNGgər; -ˌməNGgər/ ▸*n. Brit.* a person who sells cheese, butter, and other dairy products.

cheese·par·ing /ˈCHēzˌpe(ə)riNG/ ▸*adj.* careful or stingy with money.

▸*n.* stinginess.

cheese-skip·per ▸*n.* a small shiny black fly whose larvae frequently infest cheese. Also called CHEESE FLY. • *Piophila casei*, family Piophilidae.

cheese·steak /ˈCHēzˌstāk/ ▸*n.* (also **Philly cheesesteak**) a sandwich containing thin-sliced sautéed beef, melted cheese, and typically sautéed onions, served in a long roll.

cheese straw ▸*n.* a thin strip of pastry, flavored with cheese and eaten as a snack.

chees·y /ˈCHēzē/ ▸*adj.* (**chees·i·er**, **chees·i·est**) **1** like cheese in taste, smell, or consistency: *a pungent, cheesy sauce.* **2** *informal* cheap, unpleasant, or blatantly inauthentic: *a big cheesy grin | cheesy motel rooms.* —**chees·i·ness** *n.*

chee·tah /ˈCHētə/ ▸*n.* a large spotted cat found in Africa and parts of Asia. It is the fastest animal on land. • *Acinonyx jubatus*, family Felidae. ▷late 18th cent.: from Hindi *cītā*, perhaps from Sanskrit *citraka* 'leopard.'

Chee·ver /CHēvər/, John (1912–82), U.S. novelist and short-story writer. His stories frequently satirize affluent residents of the suburbs of Westchester County and New England. Notable works: *The Wapshot Chronicle* (1957), *The Wapshot Scandal* (1964), *Bullet Park* (1969), and *The Stories of John Cheever* (1978).

chef /SHef/ ▸*n.* a professional cook, typically the chief cook in a restaurant or hotel.

▸*v.* (**cheffed**, **chef·fing**) [*intrans.*] *informal* work as a chef: *when they finish cheffing, they gather themselves together and they drink their owners' best wines.* ▷early 19th cent.: French, literally 'head.'

chef-d'œu·vre /SHā ˈdœv(rə); ˈdə(r)v/ ▸*n.* (*pl.* **chefs-d'œu·vre** /SHā(z) ˈdœv(rə); ˈdə(r)v/) a masterpiece. ▷early 17th cent.: French, literally 'chief work.'

Che·foo /ˈjəˈfo͞o/ former name of **YANTAI**.

chef's sal·ad ▸*n.* a large salad of lettuce topped with strips of meat (usu. turkey and ham) and cheese, and large pieces of tomato and hard-boiled egg, typically served as a main course.

cheiro- ▸*comb. form* variant spelling of CHIRO-.

Che·ka /ˈCHekə/ an organization under the Soviet regime for the investigation of counterrevolutionary activities. It executed many real and alleged enemies of Lenin's regime from its formation in 1917 until 1922 when it was replaced by the OGPU. ▷Russian, from *che, ka*, the initial letters of *Chrezvychaĭnaya komissiya* 'Extraordinary Commission (for combating Counterrevolution, Sabotage, and Speculation).'

Che·khov /ˈCHekˌôv; ˈCHekˌôf/, Anton (Pavlovich) (1860–1904), Russian playwright and short-story writer. His work, which portrays upper-class life in prerevolutionary Russia with a blend of naturalism and symbolism, had a considerable influence on 20th-century drama. Notable plays: *The Seagull* (1895), *Uncle Vanya* (1900), *The Three Sisters* (1901), and *The Cherry Orchard* (1904).

Che·kiang /ˈjəkēˈäNG/ variant of **ZHEJIANG**.

che·la[1] /ˈkēlə/ ▸*n.* (*pl.* **-lae** /-lē; -lī/) *Zoology* a pincerlike claw, esp. of a crab or other crustacean. Compare with CHELICERA. ▷mid 17th cent.: modern Latin, from Latin *chele* or Greek *khēlē* 'claw.'

che·la[2] /ˈCHālā/ ▸*n.* a follower and student of a guru. ▷from Hindi *celā*.

che·late /ˈkēˌlāt/ ▸*n. Chemistry* a compound containing a ligand (typically organic) bonded to a central metal atom at two or more points.

▸*adj. Zoology* (of an appendage) bearing chelae.

▸*v.* [*trans.*] *Chemistry* form a chelate with. —**che·la·tion** /kēˈlāSHən/ *n.* —**che·la·tor** /-ˌlātər/ *n.*

che·la·tion ther·a·py ▸*n.* a therapy for mercury or lead poisoning that binds the toxins in the bloodstream by circulating a chelating solution. ■ a therapy that attempts to remove calcium deposits from the arteries on the same principle.

che·lic·er·a /kəˈlisərə/ ▸*n.* (*pl.* **-lic·er·ae** /-ˈlisəˌrē/) *Zoology* either of a pair of appendages in front of the mouth in arachnids and some other arthropods, usually modified as pincerlike claws. Compare with CHELA[1]. ▷mid 19th cent.: modern Latin, from Greek *khēlē* 'claw' + *keras* 'horn.' —**che·lic·er·al** *adj.*

Che·lic·er·at·a /kəˌlisəˈrätə/ *Zoology* a large group of arthropods that comprises the arachnids, sea spiders, and horseshoe crabs. They lack antennae, but possess a pair of chelicerae, a pair of pedipalps, and (typically) four pairs of legs. • Subphylum Chelicerata, phylum Arthropoda. ▷modern Latin (plural), from Greek *khēlē* 'claw' + *keras* 'horn.' —**che·lic·er·ate** /kəˈlisəˌrāt; -rət/ *n.* & *adj.*

Chel·le·an /ˈSHelēən/ ▸*adj.* & *n.* former term for **ABBEVILLIAN**. ▷late 19th cent.: from French *Chelléen*, from *Chelles*, near Paris, where tools from this period were discovered.

Chelms·ford /ˈCHelmsfərd/ a city in southeastern England, noted for its cathedral; the county town of Essex; pop. 152,418.

Che·lo·ni·a /kəˈlōnēə/ *Zoology* former term for **TESTUDINES**. ▷modern Latin (plural), from Greek *khelōnē* 'tortoise.' —**che·lo·ni·an** *n.* & *adj.*

Chel·sea /ˈCHelsē/ **1** an industrial and commercial city in northeastern Massachusetts, just north of Boston; pop. 28,710. **2** a residential district of London, on the northern bank of the Thames River. **3** a fashionable residential section of southern Manhattan in New York City, on the west side of the city.

Chel·sea boot ▸*n.* an elastic-sided boot, typically with a high heel.

Chel·ya·binsk /CHelˈyäbinsk/ an industrial city in southern Russia, on the eastern slopes of the Ural Mountains; pop. 1,148,000.

chem. ▸*abbr.* ■ chemical. ■ chemist. ■ chemistry.

chemi- ▸*comb. form* representing CHEMICAL. See also CHEMO-.

chem·i·cal /ˈkemikəl/ (abbr.: **chem.**) ▸*adj.* of or relating to chemistry or the interactions of substances as studied in chemistry: *the chemical composition of the atmosphere.* ■ of or relating to chemicals: *chemical treatments for killing fungi.* ■ relating to, involving, or denoting the use of poison gas or other chemicals as weapons of war: *the manufacture of chemical weapons.*

▸*n.* a compound or substance that has been purified or prepared, esp. artificially: *never mix disinfectant with other chemicals | controversy arose over treatment of apples with this chemical.* ▷late 16th cent.: from French *chimique* or modern Latin *chimicus, chymicus*, from medieval Latin *alchymicus*, from *alchimia* (see ALCHEMY). —**chem·i·cal·ly** /-ik(ə)lē/ *adv.*

chem·i·cal a·buse ▸*n.* another term for SUBSTANCE ABUSE.

chem·i·cal bond ▸*n.* see BOND (sense 3).

chem·i·cal com·pound ▸*n.* see COMPOUND[1].

chem·i·cal de·pend·en·cy ▸*n.* addiction to a mood- or mind-altering drug, such as alcohol or cocaine.

chem·i·cal en·gi·neer·ing ▸*n.* the branch of engineering concerned with the design and operation of industrial chemical plants. —**chem·i·cal en·gi·neer** *n.*

chem·i·cal for·mu·la ▸*n.* see FORMULA (sense 1).

chem·i·cal po·ten·tial ▸*n.* the change in Gibbs free energy with respect to change in amount of the component, with pressure, temperature, and amounts of other components being constant. Components are in equilibrium if their chemical potentials are equal.

chem·i·cal re·ac·tion ▸*n.* a process that involves rearrangement of the molecular or ionic structure of a substance, as opposed to a change in physical form or a nuclear reaction.

chem·i·cal weath·er·ing ▸*n.* the erosion or disintegration of rocks, building materials, etc., caused by chemical reactions (chiefly with water and substances dissolved in it) rather than by mechanical processes.

chemico- ▸*comb. form* representing CHEMICAL.

chem·i·lum·i·nes·cence /ˌkemiˌlo͞oməˈnesəns/ ▸*n.* the emission of light during a chemical reaction that does not produce significant quantities of heat. **—chem·i·lum·i·nes·cent** *adj.*

chem·in de fer /sHə,man də 'fe(ə)r/ ▶*n.* a form of the card game baccarat. ▷late 19th cent.: French, literally 'railroad.'

che·mise /sHə'mēz; -'mēs/ ▶*n.* a dress hanging straight from the shoulders and giving the figure a uniform shape, popular in the 1920s. ■ a woman's loose-fitting undergarment or nightdress, typically of silk or satin with a lace trim. ■ a priest's alb or surplice. ■ *historical* a smock. ▷Middle English: from Old French, from late Latin *camisia* 'shirt or nightgown.'

chem·i·sette /,sHemi'zet/ ▶*n.* a woman's undergarment similar to a camisole, typically worn so as to be visible beneath an open-necked blouse or dress. ▷early 19th cent.: French, diminutive of *chemise.*

chem·i·sorp·tion /,kemi'sôrpsHən; -'zôrp-/ ▶*n. Chemistry* adsorption in which the adsorbed substance is held by chemical bonds. ▷1930s: from **CHEMI-** + a shortened form of **ADSORPTION** (see **ADSORB**). **—chem·i·sorbed** /'kemi,sôrbd/ *adj.* .

chem·ist /'kemist/ (abbr.: **chem.**) ▶*n.* **1** an expert in chemistry; a person engaged in chemical research or experiments. **2** *Brit.* a drugstore. ■ a pharmacist. ▷late Middle English (denoting an alchemist): from French *chimiste,* from modern Latin *chimista,* from *alchimista* 'alchemist,' from *alchimia* (see **ALCHEMY**).

chem·is·try /'kemәstrē/ (abbr.: **chem.**) ▶*n.* (*pl.* **-tries**) **1** the branch of science that deals with the identification of the substances of which matter is composed; the investigation of their properties and the ways in which they interact, combine, and change; and the use of these processes to form new substances. ■ the chemical composition and properties of a substance or body: *the chemistry of soil* | [*count noun*] *the chemistries of other galaxies.* ■ *figurative* a complex entity or process: *the chemistry of politics.* **2** the emotional or psychological interaction between two people, esp. when experienced as a powerful mutual attraction: *their affair was triggered by intense sexual chemistry.*

Chem·nitz /'KHemnits/ an industrial city in eastern Germany, on the Chemnitz River; pop. 310,000. Former name (from 1953) **KARL-MARX-STADT**.

che·mo /'kēmō/ ▶*n. informal* chemotherapy.

chemo- ▶*comb. form* representing **CHEMICAL**. See also **CHEMI-**.

che·mo·at·tract·ant /,kēmōə'traktənt; ,kemō-/ ▶*n. Biology* a substance that attracts motile cells of a particular type: *a fibroblast chemoattractant.*

che·mo·au·to·troph /,kēmō'ôtə,trōf; ,kemō-/ ▶*n. Biology* an organism, typically a bacterium, that derives energy from the oxidation of inorganic compounds. **—che·mo·au·to·tro·phic** /-,ôtə'trōfik/ *adj.* **—che·mo·au·tot·ro·phy** /-'ôtə,trōfē/ *n.*

che·mo·kine /'kēmō,kīn; 'kemō-/ ▶*n.* any of a class of cytokines with various immunoregulatory functions, including attracting white blood cells to sites of infection.

che·mo·pro·phy·lax·is /,kēmō,prōfə'laksis; ,kemō-/ ▶*n.* the use of drugs to prevent disease. **—che·mo·pro·phy·lac·tic** *adj.*

che·mo·re·cep·tor /,kēmōri'septər; ,kemō-/ ▶*n. Physiology* a sensory cell or organ responsive to chemical stimuli. **—che·mo·re·cep·tion** /-ri'sepsHən/ *n.*

che·mo·stat /'kēmō,stat; 'kemō-/ ▶*n.* a system in which the chemical composition is kept at a controlled level, esp. for the culture of microorganisms.

che·mo·syn·the·sis /,kēmō'sinTHəsəs; ,kemō-/ ▶*n. Biology* the synthesis of organic compounds by bacteria or other living organisms using energy derived from reactions involving inorganic chemicals, typically in the absence of sunlight. Compare with **PHOTOSYNTHESIS**. **—che·mo·syn·thet·ic** /-sin'THetik/ *adj.*

che·mo·tax·is /,kēmō'taksis; ,kemō-/ ▶*n. Biology* movement of a motile cell or organism, or part of one, in a direction corresponding to a gradient of increasing or decreasing concentration of a particular substance. **—che·mo·tac·tic** /-'taktik/ *adj.*

che·mo·ther·a·py /,kēmō'THerəpē; ,kemō-/ ▶*n.* the treatment of disease by the use of chemical substances, esp. the treatment of cancer by cytotoxic and other drugs. **—che·mo·ther·a·pist** /-pist/ *n.*

che·mot·ro·pism /ki'mätrə,pizəm/ ▶*n.* a tropism, esp. of a plant, in response to a particular substance. **—che·mo·trop·ic** /,kēmō'träpik; ,kemō-; -'trō-/ *adj.* **—che·mo·trop·i·cal·ly** /-ik(ə)lē/ *adv.*

chempaka ▶*n.* variant spelling of **CHAMPAK**.

chem·ur·gy /'kemərjē/ ▶*n.* the chemical and industrial use of organic raw materials. ▷1930s: from **CHEMO-**, on the pattern of *metallurgy.* **—chem·ur·gic** /kə'mərjik; ke-/ *adj.*

Che·nab /cHə'näb/ a river in northern India and Pakistan that rises in the Himalayas and flows through Himachal Pradesh and Jammu and Kashmir to join the Sutlej River in Punjab. It is one of the five rivers that gave Punjab its name.

Chenai /'cHin,ī/ official name (since 1995) for **MADRAS**.

che·nar ▶*n.* variant spelling of **CHINAR**.

Chen-chiang /'jən jē'NG/ variant of **ZHENJIANG**.

Che·ney /'cHānē/, Dick (1941–), U.S. vice president 2001–; full name *Richard Bruce Cheney.* A conservative Republican from Wyoming, he served as President Ford's chief of staff 1975–76, in the U.S. House of Representatives 1979–89, and as secretary of defense under President George H. W. Bush 1989–93 before assuming the duties of vice president under President George W. Bush. He was a major proponent of the U.S. invasion of Iraq in 2003.

Cheng·chow /'jəNG'jō/ variant of **ZHENGZHOU**.

Cheng·du /'cHəNG'dōō/ the capital of Sichuan province in western central China; pop. 2,780,000.

che·nille /sHə'nēl/ ▶*n.* a tufted velvety cord or yarn, used for trimming furniture and making carpets and clothing. ■ fabric made from such yarn. ▷mid 18th cent.: French, literally 'hairy caterpillar'.

Chen·nault /sHə'nôlt/, Claire Lee (1890–1958), U.S. military pilot and officer. During World War II, he formed the "Flying Tigers," a U.S. volunteer group, to aid China.

cheong·sam /'cHông,säm/ ▶*n.* a straight, close-fitting silk dress with a high neck, short sleeves, and a slit skirt, worn traditionally by Chinese and Indonesian women. ▷Chinese (Cantonese dialect).

cheongsam

Che·ops /'kē,äps/ (*fl.* early 26th century BC), Egyptian pharaoh of the 4th dynasty; Egyptian name **Khufu**. He commissioned the building of the Great Pyramid at Giza.

cheque ▶*n.* British spelling of **CHECK**[3].

cheq·uer ▶*n.* & *v.* British spelling of **CHECKER**[2].

cheq·uer·board ▶*n.* British spelling of **CHECKERBOARD**.

Cher[1] /sHe(ə)r/ a river in central France that rises in the Massif Central and flows north for 220 miles (350 km) to meet the Loire River near Tours.

Cher[2] /sHe(ə)r/ (1946–), U.S. actress and singer; born *Cherilyn LaPiere Sarkisian.* She was married to Sonny Bono, with whom she starred on a television show 1971–74, and to musician Gregg Allman. Her notable movies include *Silkwood* (1983), *Moonstruck* (1987), for which she won an Academy Award, and *Tea With Mussolini* (1999).

Cher·bourg /'sHer,bŏŏr(g); 'sHər-/ a seaport and naval base in Normandy, in northern France; pop. 28,770.

Che·ren·kov /cHə'reNG,kôv; -,kôf; -kəf/, Pavel (Alekseevich) (also **Ce·ren·kov**) (1904–90), Soviet physicist. He investigated the effects of high-energy particles and discovered the cause of blue light (now called **CERENKOV RADIATION**) emitted by radioactive substances underwater. Nobel Prize for Physics (1958, shared with Ilja Mikhailovich Frank 1908–90 and Igor Yevgenyevich Tamm 1895–1971)

Che·ren·kov ra·di·a·tion ▶*n.* variant spelling of **CERENKOV RADIATION**.

Che·re·po·vets /,cHerəpə'v(y)ets/ a city in northwestern Russia, on the Rybinsk Reservoir; pop. 313,000.

cher·i·moy·a /,cHerə'moiə; ,cHir-/ (also **chir·i·moy·a**) ▶*n.* **1** a tropical American fruit with a flavor like pineapple and scaly green skin. **2** the small tree that bears this fruit, native to the Andes of Peru and Ecuador. • *Annona cherimola,* family Annonaceae. ▷mid 18th cent.: from Spanish, from Quechua, from *chiri* 'cold or refreshing' + *muya* 'circle.'

cher·ish /'cHerisH/ ▶*v.* [*trans.*] protect and care for (someone) lovingly: *he cared for me beyond measure and cherished me in his heart.* ■ hold (something) dear: *I cherish the letters she wrote* | [as *adj.*] (**cherished**) *cherished possessions.* ■ (of a hope, idea, or memory) think of longingly or lovingly: *we will cherish your memory.* ▷Middle English (in the sense 'treat with affection'): from Old French *cheriss-,* lengthened stem of *cherir,* from *cher* 'dear,' from Latin *carus.*

Cher·kas·sy /cHir'käsē/ Russian for **CHERKASY**.

Cher·ka·sy /cHir'käsē/ a port in central Ukraine, on the Dnieper River; pop. 297,000. Russian name **CHERKASSY**.

Cher·kessk /cHir'k(y)esk/ a city in the Caucasus in southern Russia, capital of the republic of Karachai-Cherkessia; pop 113,000.

Cher·nen·ko /cHə'reNGkō/, Konstantin (Ustinovich) (1911–85), Soviet statesman, general secretary of the Communist Party of the Soviet Union and president 1984–85. He died after only thirteen months in office and was succeeded by Mikhail Gorbachev.

Cher·ni·gov /cHi(ə)r'n(y)ēgəf/ Russian for **CHERNIHIV**.

Cher·ni·hiv /cHir'n(y)ēhəf/ a port in northern Ukraine, on the Desna River; pop. 301,000. Russian name **CHERNIGOV** .

Cher·niv·tsi /,cHirnift'sē/ a city in western Ukraine, in the foothills of the Carpathian Mountains, close to the border with Romania; pop. 257,000. It was part of Romania between 1918 and 1940. Russian name **CHERNOVTSY** .

Cher·no·byl /cHir'nōbil; cHər'nōbəl/ a town near Kiev in Ukraine where an accident at a nuclear power station in April 1986 resulted in serious radioactive contamination in Ukraine, Belarus, and other parts of Europe.

Cher·no·rech·ye /,cHernə'recHə/ former name (until 1919) for **DZERZHINSK**.

cher·no·zem /'cHernə,zHôm; -,zem/ ▶*n. Soil Science* a fertile black soil rich in humus, with a lighter lime-rich layer beneath. Such soils typically occur in temperate grasslands such as the Russian steppes and North American prairies. ▷mid 19th cent.: from Russian, from *chërnyĭ* 'black' + *zemlya* 'earth.'

Cher·o·kee /'cHerəkē/ ▶*n.* (*pl.* same or **-kees**) **1** a member of an American Indian people of the southeastern U.S., now living on reservations in Oklahoma and North Carolina. **2** the Iroquoian language of this people, which has had its own script since 1820.
▶*adj.* of or relating to this people or their language. ▷from Cherokee *tsaraki.*

Cher·o·kee rose ▶*n.* a climbing rose with fragrant white flowers, native to China and naturalized in the southern U.S. • *Rosa laevigata,* family Rosaceae.

che·root /sHə'rōōt/ ▶*n.* a cigar with both ends open and untapered. ▷late 17th cent.: from French *cheroute,* from Tamil *curuṭṭu* 'roll of tobacco.'

cher·ry /'cHerē/ ▶*n.* (*pl.* **-ries**) **1** a small, round stone fruit that is typically bright or dark red. See also **MARASCHINO CHERRY**. **2** (also **cherry tree**) the tree that bears such fruit. • Genus *Prunus,* family Rosaceae: several species, the edible fruits being derived from the **mazzard** (or **sweet**) **cherry** (*P. avium*) and the **morello** (or **sour**) **cherry** (*P. cerasus*). ■ the wood of this tree. ■ used in names of unrelated plants with similar fruits, e.g., **cornelian cherry**. **3** a bright or deep red color: [as *adj.*] *her mouth was a bright cherry red.* **4** [in *sing.*] *vulgar slang* the hymen, as representing a woman's virginity. ▷Middle English: from Old Northern French *cherise,* from medieval Latin *ceresia,* based on Greek *kerasos* 'cherry tree, cherry.' The final *-s* was lost because *cherise* was interpreted as plural (compare with **CAPER**[2] and **PEA**).
▶*PHRASES* □ **a bowl of cherries** [usu. with *negative*] a pleasant or enjoyable situation or experience: *being in the band isn't a bowl of cherries.* □ **pop someone's cherry** *vulgar slang* have sexual intercourse with a girl or woman who is a virgin.

Cher·ry Hill a township in southwestern New Jersey, southeast of Philadelphia in Pennsylvania; pop. 69,965.

cher·ry lau·rel ▶*n.* an evergreen shrub or small tree of the rose family, with leathery leaves, white flowers, and cherrylike fruits, native to the Balkans and widely cultivated. • *Prunus laurocerasus,* family Rosaceae.

cher·ry-pick ▶*v.* **1** [*trans.*] selectively choose (the most beneficial items) from what is available: *the company should buy the whole airline and not just cherry-pick its best assets.* **2** [*intrans.*] *Sports* in a game such as basketball, wait near the goal for a pass, which can be converted to an easy score. **—cher·ry-pick·ing** *n.*

cher·ry pick·er ▶*n. informal* **1** a hydraulic crane with a railed platform at the end for raising and lowering people, for instance to work on overhead cables. **2** a person who cherry-picks.

cher·ry to·ma·to ▶*n.* a spherical miniature tomato.

The fruit is glossy red, or occasionally yellow, and typically eaten in salad. • Many varieties, in particular *Lycopersicon lycopersicum cerasiforme*.

Cher·so·nese /ˈkərsəˌnēz; ˌkərsəˌnēz/ ancient name for the Gallipoli peninsula. ▷from Latin *chersonesus*, from Greek *khersonēsos*, from *khersos* 'dry' + *nēsos* 'island.'

chert /CHərt; CHat/ ▸*n.* a hard, dark, opaque rock composed of silica (chalcedony) with an amorphous or microscopically fine-grained texture. It occurs as nodules (flint) or, less often, in massive beds. ▷late 17th cent. (originally dialect): of unknown origin. **—chert·y** *adj.*

cher·ub /ˈCHerəb/ ▸*n.* (*pl.* **cher·u·bim**) /ˈCHer(y)əbim/ a winged angelic being described in biblical tradition as attending on God. It is represented in ancient Middle Eastern art as a lion or bull with eagles' wings and a human face, and regarded in traditional Christian angelology as an angel of the second highest order of the ninefold celestial hierarchy. ■ (*pl.* **cher·u·bim** /ˈCHer(y)əˌbim/ or **cher·ubs**) a representation of a cherub in art, depicted as a chubby, healthy-looking child with wings. ■ (*pl.* **cher·ubs**) a beautiful or innocent-looking child. ▷Old English *cherubin*, ultimately (via Latin and Greek) from Hebrew *kĕrûḇ*, plural *kĕrûḇîm*. A rabbinic folk etymology, which explains the Hebrew singular form as representing Aramaic *kĕ-raḇyā* 'like a child,' led to the representation of the cherub as a child.

che·ru·bic /CHəˈro͞obik/ ▸*adj.* having the childlike innocence or plump prettiness of a cherub: *a round, cherubic face.* **—che·ru·bi·cal·ly** /-bik(ə)lē/ *adv.*

Che·ru·bi·ni /ˌkero͞oˈbēnē/, (Maria) Luigi (Carlo Zenobio Salvatore) (1760–1842), Italian composer. He is principally known for his church music and operas.

cher·vil /ˈCHərvəl/ ▸*n.* a plant of the parsley family, with small white flowers and delicate fernlike leaves that are used as a culinary herb. • *Anthriscus cerefolium*, family Umbelliferae. ▷Old English, from Latin *chaerephylla*, from Greek *khairephullon*.

Ches·a·peake /ˈCHesəˌpēk/ a port city in central Virginia, in the Hampton Roads area; pop. 199,184.

Ches·a·peake Bay /ˈCHesəˌpēk/ a large inlet of the North Atlantic Ocean on the U.S. coast that extends north for 200 miles (320 km) through the states of Virginia and Maryland.

Chesh·ire[1] /ˈCHesHər; ˈCHesHˌir/ a county in western central England; county town, Chester.

Chesh·ire[2] /ˈCHesHər/ (also **Cheshire cheese**) ▸*n.* a kind of firm crumbly cheese, originally made in Cheshire, England.

Chesh·ire cat ▸*n.* a cat depicted with a broad fixed grin, as popularized through Lewis Carroll's *Alice's Adventures in Wonderland* (1865). ▷late 18th cent.: of unknown origin, but it is said that cheeses made in *Cheshire*, England, used to be marked with the face of a smiling cat.

chess /CHes/ ▸*n.* a board game of strategic skill for two players, played on a checkered board. Each player begins the game with sixteen pieces that are moved and used to capture opposing pieces according to precise rules. The object is to put the opponent's king under a direct attack from which escape is impossible (*checkmate*). ▷Middle English: from Old French *esches*, plural of *eschec* 'a check' (see **CHECK**[1]).

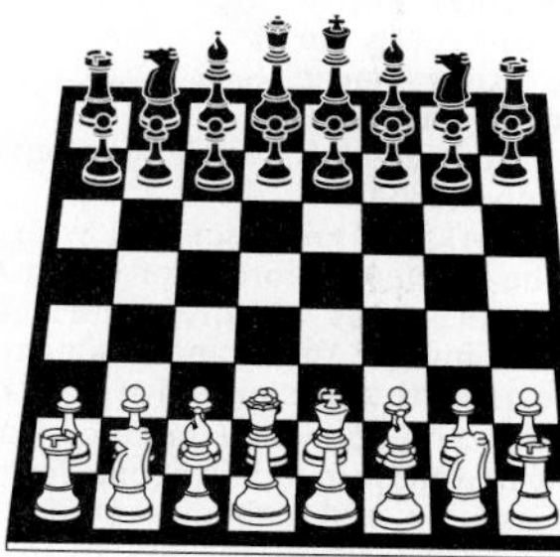

chessboard and pieces

chess·board /ˈCHesˌbôrd/ ▸*n.* a square board divided into sixty-four alternating dark and light squares, used for playing chess or checkers.

chess·man /ˈCHesˌman; -mən/ ▸*n.* (*pl.* **-men**) a solid figure used as a chess piece.

chess pie ▸*n.* a type of pie filled with a mixture of eggs, butter, and sugar, to which nuts and fruits may be added.

chess set ▸*n.* a chessboard and a set of chessmen.

chest /CHest/ ▸*n.* **1** the front surface of a person's or animal's body between the neck and the abdomen. ■ the whole of a person's upper trunk, esp. with reference to physical size: *a 42-inch chest.* ■ *informal* a woman's breasts. **2** a large strong box, typically made of wood and used for storage or shipping: *an oak chest.* ■ a small cabinet for medicines, toiletries, etc.: *the medicine chest.* ■ short for **CHEST OF DRAWERS**. ■ *Brit.* the treasury or financial resources of some institutions: *the university chest.* ▷Old English *cest, cyst*, related to Dutch *kist* and German *Kiste*, based on Greek *kistē* 'box.' **—chest·ed** *adj.* [in *combination*] *a bare-chested youth.*

▸*PHRASES* □ **get something off one's chest** *informal* say something that one has wanted to say for a long time, resulting in a feeling of relief. □ **play** (or **keep**) **one's cards close to one's chest** (or **vest**) *informal* be secretive and cautious about one's intentions.

Ches·ter /ˈCHestər/ **1** a town in western England, the county town of Cheshire; pop. 115,000. **2** a city in southeastern Pennsylvania, on the Delaware River, southwest of Philadelphia; pop. 41,856.

Ches·ter·field /ˈCHestərˌfēld/ a city in eastern Missouri, on the Missouri River, a suburb of St. Louis; pop. 46,802.

ches·ter·field /ˈCHestərˌfēld/ ▸*n.* **1** a sofa with padded arms and back of the same height and curved outward at the top. ■ *chiefly Canadian* any sofa or couch. **2** a man's plain straight overcoat, typically with a velvet collar. ▷mid 19th cent. (sense 2): named after a 19th-cent. Earl of Chesterfield.

Ches·ter·ton /ˈCHestərtən/, G. K. (1874–1936), English essayist, novelist, and critic; full name *Gilbert Keith Chesterton*. His novels include *The Napoleon of Notting Hill* (1904) and a series of detective stories featuring Father Brown, a priest with a talent for crime detection.

Ches·ter White ▸*n.* a pig of a prolific white breed with drooping ears, developed in Pennsylvania.

chest freez·er ▸*n.* a freezer with a hinged lid that opens from the top, rather than a front-opening door.

chest·nut /ˈCHes(t)ˌnət/ ▸*n.* **1** (also **sweet chestnut**) a glossy brown nut that may be roasted and eaten. **2** (also **chestnut tree, sweet chestnut,** or **Spanish chestnut**) the large European tree that produces the edible chestnut, which develops within a bristly case, with serrated leaves and heavy timber. • *Castanea sativa*, family Fagaceae. ■ (also **American chestnut**) a related tree (*C. dentata*), which succumbed to a fungus bark disease in the early 1900s. Once prolific in the eastern U.S., very few large specimens survived. ■ (also **Chinese chestnut**) a related tree (*C. mollissima*) native to China and Korea, cultivated elsewhere for its edible nut. The flowers have a putrid odor. ■ short for **HORSE CHESTNUT**. ■ used in names of trees and plants that are related to the sweet chestnut or that produce similar nuts, e.g., **water chestnut**. **3** a deep reddish-brown color: [as *adj.*] *chestnut hair.* ■ a horse of a reddish-brown color, with a brown mane and tail. **4** a small horny patch on the inside of each of a horse's legs. ▷early 16th cent.: from Old English *chesten* (from Old French *chastaine*, via Latin from Greek *kastanea*) + **NUT**.

▸*PHRASES* □ **an old chestnut** a joke or story that has become tedious because of its age and constant repetition. □ **pull someone's chestnuts out of the fire** succeed in a hazardous undertaking for someone else's benefit. [with reference to the fable of a monkey using a cat's paw to extract roasting chestnuts from a fire.]

Chest·nut Hill **1** an affluent suburban area west of Boston in Massachusetts, partly in Brookline and partly in Newton. **2** an affluent residential section in northern Philadelphia in Pennsylvania.

chest·nut oak ▸*n.* a North American oak that has leaves resembling those of the chestnut. • Genus *Quercus*, family Fagaceae: several species, in particular *Q. montana* (or *Q. prinus*) of the eastern U.S.

chest of drawers ▸*n.* a piece of furniture consisting of a set of drawers in a frame, typically used for storing clothes.

chest pro·tec·tor ▸*n.* *Baseball* a padded covering worn over the chest by a catcher or umpire as protection against fouled-off or errant pitches.

chest voice ▸*n.* [in *sing.*] the lowest register of the voice in singing or speaking.

chest·y /ˈCHestē/ ▸*adj.* *informal* **1** (of a sound) produced deep in the chest: *a chesty chuckle* | *a chesty growl.* **2** (of a woman) having large or prominent breasts. **3** conceited and arrogant. **4** *Brit.* having a lot of mucus in the lungs: *a chesty cough.* **—chest·i·ly** /ˈCHestəlē/ *adv.* **—chest·i·ness** *n.*

Ches·van variant spelling of **HESVAN**.

Chet·nik /ˈCHetnik/ ▸*n.* a member of a Slavic nationalist guerrilla force in the Balkans, esp. one active during World War II. ▷early 20th cent.: from Serbo-Croat *četnik*, from *četa* 'band, troop.'

che·trum /ˈCHētrəm; ˈCHe-/ ▸*n.* (*pl.* same or **-trums**) a monetary unit of Bhutan, equal to one hundredth of a ngultrum. ▷Dzongkha.

che·val-de-frise /SHəˈval də ˈfrēz/ ▸*n.* **1** a portable obstacle, consisting of a wooden frame covered with spikes or barbed wire, used by the military to close off a passage or block enemy advancement. **2** shards of glass or spikes set into masonry along the top of a wall.

che·val glass /SHəˈval/ (also **cheval mirror**) ▸*n.* a tall mirror fitted at its middle to an upright frame so that it can be tilted. ▷mid 19th cent.: *cheval* from French, in the sense 'frame.'

Chev·a·lier /SHəˈvalˌyā; SHəvalˈyā/, Maurice (1888–1972), French singer and actor. Notable movies: *Innocents of Paris* (1929), *Love Me Tonight* (1932), and *Gigi* (1958).

chev·a·lier /ˌSHevəˈli(ə)r/ ▸*n.* *historical* a knight. ■ a chivalrous man. ■ a member of certain orders of knighthood or of modern French orders such as the Legion of Honor. ■ (**Chevalier**) *Brit., historical* the title of James and Charles Stuart, pretenders to the British throne. ▷late Middle English (denoting a horseman or mounted knight): from Old French, from medieval Latin *caballarius*, from Latin *caballus* 'horse.' Compare with **CABALLERO** and **CAVALIER**.

Chev·i·ot /ˈSHevēət/ ▸*n.* a sheep of a breed with short thick wool. ■ (**cheviot**) the wool or tweed cloth obtained from this breed.

Chev·i·ot Hills /ˈCHēvēət; ˈCHev-; ˈCHiv-; ˈSHev-/ (also **the Chev·i·ots**) a range of hills on the border between England and Scotland.

chev·on /ˈSHevən/ ▸*n.* the flesh of goats as food; goat meat: *the entree was crisp-on-the-outside, succulent-inside haunch of spring chevon.* ▷from French *chèvre*, 'goat,' on the pattern of *mutton*.

chè·vre /ˈSHev(rə)/ ▸*n.* cheese made with goat's milk. ▷1960s: French, literally 'goat, she-goat,' from Latin *capra*.

chev·ron /ˈSHevrən/ ▸*n.* a line or stripe in the shape of a V or an inverted V, esp. one on the sleeve of a uniform indicating rank or length of service. ■ *Heraldry* an ordinary in the form of a broad inverted V-shape. ■ *Architecture* a molding of continuous V-shaped patterns, common in Norman architecture. ▷late Middle English (in heraldic use): from Old French, based on Latin *caper* 'goat'; compare with Latin *capreoli* (diminutive of *caper*) used to mean 'pair of rafters.'

chevron

chev·ro·tain /ˈSHevrəˌtān/ ▸*n.* a small deerlike mammal with short tusks, typically nocturnal and found in the tropical rain forests of Africa and South Asia. Also called **MOUSE DEER**. • Family Tragulidae: genera *Moschiola* (one Asian species), *Tragulus* (two Asian species) and *Hyemoschus* (one African species). ▷late 18th cent.: from French, diminutive of Old French *chevrot*, diminutive of *chèvre* 'goat.'

Chev·y /ˈSHevē/ ▸*n.* (*pl.* **chev·ys**) *informal* a Chevrolet car.

chev·y /ˈCHivē/ ▸*v.* variant spelling of **CHIVVY**.

Chevy Chase /ˈCHevē ˈCHās/ a fashionable suburb north of Washington, DC, in Montgomery County in Maryland; pop. 8,559.

chew /CHo͞o/ ▸*v.* [*trans.*] bite and work (food) in the mouth with the teeth, esp. to make it easier to swallow: *he was chewing a mouthful of toast* | [*intrans.*] *he chewed for a moment, then swallowed.* ■ gnaw at (something) persistently, typically as a result of worry or anxiety: *he chewed his lip reflectively* | [*intrans.*] *she chewed at a fingernail.*

▸*phrasal v.* □ **chew someone out** *informal* reprimand

Pronunciation Key ə *ago*; ər *over*; ˈə or ˌə *up*; ˈər or ˌər *fur*; a *hat*; ā *rate*; ä *car*; CH *chew*; e *let*; ē *see*; e(ə)r *air*; i *fit*; ī *by*; i(ə)r *ear*; NG *sing*; ō *go*; ô *for*; oi *boy*; o͝o *good*; o͞o *goo*; ou *out*; SH *she*; TH *thin*; T͟H *then*; (h)w *why*; ZH *vision*

someone severely: *he chewed me out for being late.* □ **chew something over** discuss or consider something at length: *executives met to chew over the company's future.* □ **chew something up** chew food until it is soft or in small pieces. ■ damage or destroy something as if by chewing: *the bikes were chewing up the paths.*
▸*n.* a repeated biting or gnawing of something. ■ something other than food that is meant for chewing: *a dog chew | a chew of tobacco.* ▷Old English *cēowan*; related to Dutch *kauwen* and German *kauen.* **—chew·a·ble** *adj.* **—chew·er** *n.* [usu. in *combination*] *a tobacco-chewer.*
▸*PHRASES* □ **chew the cud** see CUD. □ **chew the fat** (or **rag**) *informal* chat in a leisurely way, esp. at length.

C

chew·ing gum ▸*n.* flavored gum for chewing, typically sold in packets of individually wrapped thin strips.

chew·y /'CHōōē/ ▸ **1** *adj.* (**chew·i·er, chew·i·est**) (of food) needing to be chewed hard or for some time: *the bread was never quite fresh, always pretty chewy.* **2** suitable for chewing: *pasta should be chewy, never soft.* **—chew·i·ness** *n.*

Chey·enne[1] /SHī'an; SHī'en/ the capital of Wyoming, in the southeastern part of the state; pop. 53,011.

Chey·enne[2] ▸*n.* (*pl.* same or **-ennes**) **1** a member of an American Indian people formerly living between the Missouri and Arkansas rivers but now on reservations in Montana and Oklahoma. **2** the Algonquian language of this people.
▸*adj.* of or relating to the Cheyenne or their language. ▷Canadian French, from Dakota *šahíyena,* 'little Cree'.

Chey·enne Riv·er /SHī'an; -'en/ a river that flows for 530 miles (850 km) from northeastern Wyoming into western South Dakota to join the Missouri River at Lake Oahe.

Chey·ne-Stokes breath·ing /'CHān 'stōks 'brēTHiNG; 'CHānē / ▸*n. Medicine* a cyclical pattern of breathing in which movement gradually decreases to a complete stop and then returns to normal. It occurs in various medical conditions, and at high altitudes. ▷late 19th cent.: named after John *Cheyne* (1777–1836), Scottish physician, and William *Stokes* (1804–78), Irish physician.

chez /SHā/ ▸*prep.* at the home of (used in imitation of French, often humorously): *I spent one summer chez Grandma.* ▷mid 18th cent.: French, from Old French *chiese*, from Latin *casa* 'cottage.'

chi[1] /kī/ ▸*n.* the twenty-second letter of the Greek alphabet (**Χ, χ**), transliterated in the traditional Latin style as 'ch' (as in *Christ*) or in the modern style as 'kh' (as in *Khaniá* and in the etymologies of this dictionary). ■ (**Chi**) [followed by Latin genitive] *Astronomy* the twenty-second star in a constellation: *Chi Ophiuchi.*

chi[2] /CHē/ (also **qi** or **ki**) ▸*n.* variant spelling of QI.

chi·a /'CHēə/ ▸*n.* a plant of the mint family with clusters of small two-lipped purple flowers. Chia is common throughout California and the Great Basin. • *Salvia columbariae*, family Labiatae.

Chiang Kai-shek /ˌCHaNG ˌkī'SHek/ (also **Jiang Jie Shi** /jē'äNG jē'e 'SHē/) (1887–1975), Chinese statesman and general; president of China 1928–31 and 1943–49 and of Taiwan 1950–75. He tried to unite China by military means in the 1930s but was defeated by the Communists. Forced to abandon mainland China in 1949, he set up a separate Nationalist Chinese State in Taiwan.

Chiang Kai-shek

Chiang·mai /jē'äNG'mī/ a city in northwestern Thailand; pop. 164,900.

Chi·a·ni·na /ˌkēə'nēnə/ ▸*n.* an animal of a large white breed of cattle, raised for its lean meat. ▷from Italian.

Chi·an·ti /kē'äntē; -'antē/ (also **chi·an·ti**) ▸*n.* (*pl.* **-tis**) a dry red wine, originally produced in Tuscany, Italy. ▷named after the *Chianti* Mountains, Italy.

Chi·a·pas /CHē'äpəs; 'CHäpəs/ a state in southern Mexico that borders on Guatemala; capital, Tuxtla Gutiérrez.

chi·a·ro·scu·ro /kēˌärə'sk(y)ŏŏrō; kēˌarə-/ ▸*n.* the treatment of light and shade in drawing and painting. ■ an effect of contrasted light and shadow created by light falling unevenly or from a particular direction on something: *the chiaroscuro of cobbled streets.* ▷mid 17th cent.: from Italian, from *chiaro* 'clear, bright' (from Latin *clarus*) + *oscuro* 'dark, obscure' (from Latin *obscurus*).

chi·as·ma /kī'azmə/ ▸*n.* (*pl.* **-ma·ta** /-mətə/) *Biology* a point at which paired chromosomes remain in contact during the first metaphase of meiosis, and at which crossing over and exchange of genetic material occur between the strands. See also OPTIC CHIASMA. ▷mid 19th cent.: modern Latin, from Greek *chiasma* 'crosspiece, cross-shaped mark,' from *khiazein* 'mark with the letter chi.'

chi·as·mus /kī'azməs/ ▸*n.* a rhetorical or literary figure in which words, grammatical constructions, or concepts are repeated in reverse order, in the same or a modified form; e.g. 'Poetry is the record of the best and happiest moments of the happiest and best minds.' ▷mid 17th cent. (in the general sense 'crosswise arrangement'): modern Latin, from Greek *khiasmos* 'crosswise arrangement,' from *khiazein* 'mark with the letter chi,' from *khi* 'chi.' **—chi·as·tic** /kī'astik/ *adj.*

chi·as·to·lite /kī'astəˌlīt/ ▸*n.* a form of the mineral andalusite containing carbonaceous inclusions that cause some sections of the mineral to show the figure of a cross. ▷early 19th cent.: from Greek *khiastos* 'arranged crosswise' + -LITE.

Chi·ba /'CHēbə/ a city in Japan, on the island of Honshu, east of Tokyo; pop. 829,470.

Chib·cha /'CHibCHä/ ▸*n.* (*pl.* same) **1** a member of a native people of Colombia whose well-developed political structure was destroyed by Europeans. **2** the Chibchan language of this people.
▸*adj.* of or relating to the Chibcha or their language. ▷American Spanish, from Chibcha *zipa* 'chief, hereditary leader.'

Chib·chan /'CHibCHən/ ▸*n.* a language family of Colombia and Central America, most members of which are extinct or nearly so.
▸*adj.* of or relating to this language family.

chi·bouk /CHə'bŏŏk; SHə-/ (also **chi·bouque**) ▸*n.* a long Turkish tobacco pipe. ▷early 19th cent.: French *chibouque*, from Turkish *çubuk*, literally 'tube.'

chic /SHēk/ ▸*adj.* (**chic·er, chic·est**) elegantly and stylishly fashionable.
▸*n.* stylishness and elegance, typically of a specified kind: *French chic | biker chic.* ▷mid 19th cent.: from French, probably from German *Schick* 'skill.' **—chic·ly** *adv.*

Chi·ca·go /SHi'kôgō; -'kägō/ a city in northeastern Illinois, on Lake Michigan; pop. 2,896,016. Chicago developed during the 19th century as a major grain market and food-processing center. **—Chi·ca·go·an** /-'kôgō-ən; -'käg-/ *n.* & *adj.*

Chi·ca·go Board of Trade ▸*n.* see BOARD OF TRADE (sense 1).

Chi·ca·go·land /SHi'kägōˌland/ ▸*n.* Chicago and its suburbs, considered as a unit: [often as *modifier*] *a thoughtful unpretentious matchmaking service for Chicagoland singles.*

Chi·ca·na /CHi'känə; SHi-/ ▸*n.* (in North America) a girl or woman of Mexican origin or descent. ▷Mexican Spanish, alteration of Spanish *mejicana* (feminine) 'Mexican.'

USAGE See usage at CHICANO.

chi·cane /SHi'kān; CHi-/ ▸*n.* **1** an artificial narrowing or turn on a road or auto-racing course. **2** *dated* (in card games) a hand without cards of one particular suit; a void. **3** *archaic* chicanery.
▸*v. archaic* employ trickery or chicanery. ■ [*trans.*] deceive or trick (someone). ▷late 17th cent. (in the senses 'chicanery' and 'use chicanery'): from French *chicane* (noun), *chicaner* (verb) 'quibble,' of unknown origin.

chi·can·er·y /SHi'kānərē; CHi-/ ▸*n.* the use of trickery to achieve a political, financial, or legal purpose: *an underhanded person who schemes corruption and political chicanery behind closed doors.* ▷late 16th cent.: from French *chicanerie*, from *chicaner* 'to quibble' (see CHICANE).

Chi·ca·no /CHi'känō; SHi-/ ▸*n.* (*pl.* **-nos**) (in North America) a person of Mexican origin or descent. See also CHICANA. ▷Mexican Spanish, alteration of Spanish *mejicano* (masculine) 'Mexican.'

USAGE The term **Chicano** (derived from Mexican Spanish), and the feminine form **Chicana**, became current in the early 1960s, first used by politically active groups. **Chicano** and **Chicana** are still in frequent use and have become less politicized. However, Mexican-Americans with less militant political views might find the terms offensive. **Hispanic** is a more generic term denoting persons in the U.S. of Latin-American or Spanish descent. See also **usage** at HISPANIC.

chi·cha·rron /ˌCHēCHə'rōn/ ▸*n.* (*pl.* **-rron·es** /-'rōnēz/) (in Mexican cooking) a piece of fried pork crackling. ▷from American Spanish *chicharrón.*

Chi·chén It·zá /CHiˌCHen it'sä 'CHiCHən 'ētsə/ a site in northern Yucatán, Mexico, the center of the Mayan empire after AD 918 until about 1200. Its pyramids, temples, and other structures have been partly restored.

Chi·ches·ter /'CHiCHəstər/, Sir Francis (Charles) (1901–72), English sailor. He was the first person to sail alone around the world 1966–67 with only one stop.

Chi·che·wa /CHi'CHäwə/ ▸*n.* another term for NYANJA (the language).

chi·chi[1] /'SHēSHē; 'CHēCHē/ ▸*adj.* attempting stylish elegance but achieving only an overelaborate affectedness: *the chichi world of Manhattan cultural privilege.*
▸*n.* pretentious and overelaborate refinement: *the relentless chichi of late-eighties dining.* ▷early 20th cent. (in the sense 'showiness or pretentious object'): from French, of imitative origin.

chi·chi[2] /'CHēˌCHē/ ▸*n. informal* a woman's breast. ▷late 20th cent.: military slang, of Japanese origin.

Chi·chi·mec /'CHēCHəˌmek/ ▸*n.* (*pl.* same or **-mecs**) **1** a member of a group of native peoples, including the Toltecs and the Aztecs, dominant in central Mexico from the 10th to the 16th centuries. **2** the Uto-Aztecan language of these peoples. ▷Spanish, from Nahuatl.

chick /CHik/ ▸*n.* **1** a young bird, esp. one newly hatched. ■ a newly hatched domestic fowl. **2** *informal, chiefly derogatory* a young woman: *she's a great-looking chick.* ▷Middle English: abbreviation of CHICKEN.
▸*PHRASE* □ **neither chick nor child** *dialect* no children at all.

chick·a·dee /'CHikədē/ ▸*n.* a North American titmouse, in particular: the **black-capped chickadee** (*Parus atricapillus*), with distinctive black cap and throat, and the similar but smaller **Carolina chickadee** (*P. carolinensis*). ▷mid 19th cent.: imitative of its call.

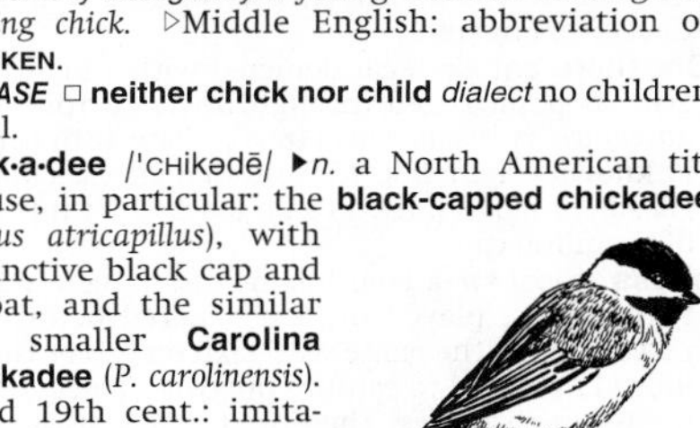
black-capped chickadee

Chick·a·mau·ga Creek /ˌCHikə'môgə/ a stream that flows from northwestern Georgia into the Tennessee River, near Chattanooga in Tennessee. A brutal Civil War battle was fought along it in September 1863.

chick·a·ree /'CHikəˌrē/ ▸*n.* a squirrel with red fur, found in the coniferous forests of North America. • Genus *Tamiasciurus*, family Sciuridae: three species, including the American red squirrel (*T. hudsonicus*). ▷early 19th cent.: imitative of its call.

Chick·a·saw /'CHikəˌsô/ ▸*n.* (*pl.* same or **-saws**) **1** a member of an American Indian people formerly resident in Mississippi and Alabama, and now in Oklahoma. **2** the Muskogean language of this people.
▸*adj.* of or relating to this people or their language. ▷the name in Chickasaw.

chick·en /'CHikən/ ▸*n.* **1** a domestic fowl kept for its eggs or meat, esp. a young one. ■ meat from such a bird: *roast chicken.* **2** *informal* a game in which the first person to lose nerve and withdraw from a dangerous situation is the loser. ■ a coward. **3** *informal* (among homosexuals) an adolescent male.
▸*adj.* [*predic.*] *informal* cowardly: *they were too chicken to follow the murderers into the mountains.*
▸*v.* [*intrans.*] (**chicken out**) *informal* withdraw from or fail in something through lack of nerve: *the referee*

chickened out of giving a penalty. ▷Old English *cīcen, cȳcen*, of Germanic origin; related to Dutch *kieken* and German *Küchlein*, and probably also to COCK[1].

▸PHRASE □ **don't count your chickens before they're hatched** see COUNT[1].

chick·en à la king ▸*n.* cooked breast of chicken in a cream sauce with mushrooms and peppers. ▷said to be named after E. Clark *King*, proprietor of a New York hotel.

chick·en-and-egg ▸*adj.* [*attrib.*] denoting a situation in which each of two things appears to be necessary to the other, making it impossible to say which came first.

chick·en breast ▸*n. Medicine* another term for PIGEON BREAST. —**chick·en-breast·ed** (also **chick·en-chest·ed**) *adj.*

chick·en feed ▸*n.* food for poultry. ■ *figurative, informal* an insignificant amount of money: *the pay was chicken feed for the work I put in.*

chick·en-fried steak ▸*n.* a thin piece of beef that is lightly battered and fried until crisp.

chick·en hawk ▸*n.* a hawk of a type that is reputed to prey on domestic fowl. ■ (also **chicken queen**) *informal, figurative* an older man who seeks young boys as sexual partners.

chick·en-heart·ed (also **chick·en-liv·ered**) ▸*adj.* easily frightened; cowardly.

Chick·en Lit·tle ▸*n.* an alarmist or doomsayer. *my beloved capital sounds more and more these days like a barnyard filled with Chicken Littles.* ▷1990s: from the name of a character in a children's story who repeatedly warns that the sky is falling.

chick·en pox (also **chick·en·pox**) ▸*n.* an infectious disease causing a mild fever and a rash of itchy inflamed blisters. It is caused by the herpes zoster virus and mainly affects children, who are afterward usually immune. Also called VARICELLA. ▷early 18th cent.: probably so named because of its mildness, as compared to smallpox.

chick·en·shit /ˈCHikən,SHit/ *vulgar slang* ▸*adj.* worthless or contemptible (used as a general term of deprecation): *no more chickenshit excuses.* ■ cowardly.

▸*n.* a worthless or contemptible person. ■ something worthless or petty: *names are chickenshit; they didn't need any names.*

chick·en wire ▸*n.* light wire netting with a hexagonal mesh.

chick flick ▸*n. informal* a movie that appeals mainly to women.

chick·ling pea /ˈCHikliNG/ (also **chickling vetch**) ▸*n.* another term for GRASS PEA. ▷mid 16th cent.: based on obsolete *chich* 'chickpea.'

chick lit ▸*n. informal, chiefly derogatory* literature that appeals mainly to women.

chick·pea /ˈCHik,pē/ ▸*n.* **1** a round yellowish seed, used widely as food. Also called GARBANZO. **2** the leguminous Old World plant that bears these seeds. • *Cicer arietinum*, family Leguminosae. ▷early 18th cent. (earlier as *chiche-pease*): from late Middle English *chiche* (from Old French *chiche, cice*, from Latin *cicer* 'chickpea') + PEASE.

chick·weed /ˈCHik,wēd/ ▸*n.* a small plant of the pink family with deeply cleft white petals, often growing as a garden weed and sometimes eaten by poultry. • *Stellaria, Cerastium*, and other genera, family Caryophyllaceae: several species, including **common chickweed** (*S. media*), with smooth leaves and stems, and **mouse-ear chickweed** (*C. vulgatum*), with hairy leaves and stems.

chic·le /ˈCHikəl; ˈCHiklē/ ▸*n.* the milky latex of the sapodilla tree, used to make chewing gum. ■ another term for SAPODILLA. ▷via Latin American Spanish, from Nahuatl *tzictli*.

Chi·co /ˈCHēkō/ a city in northern California, at the north end of the Sacramento Valley; pop. 40,079.

Chic·o·pee /ˈCHikə,pē/ a city in south central Massachusetts, an industrial center on the northern side of Springfield; pop. 56,632.

chic·o·ry /ˈCHikərē/ ▸*n.* (*pl.* **-ries**) **1** a blue-flowered Mediterranean plant of the daisy family, cultivated for its edible salad leaves and carrot-shaped root. • *Cichorium intybus*, family Compositae. ■ the root of this plant, which is roasted and ground for use as an additive to or substitute for coffee. **2** another term for ENDIVE. ▷late Middle English: from obsolete French *cicorée* (earlier form of *chicorée*) 'endive,' via Latin from Greek *kikhorion*.

chicory 1

chide /CHīd/ ▸*v.* (*past* **chid·ed** or *archaic* **chid** /CHid/; *past part.* **chid·ed** or *archaic* **chid·den** /ˈCHidn/) [*trans.*] scold or rebuke: *she* **chided** *him* **for** *not replying to her letters* | [with *direct speech*] *"You mustn't speak like that," she chided gently.* See note at SCOLD. ▷Old English *cīdan*, of unknown origin. —**chid·er** *n.* —**chid·ing·ly** *adv.*

chief /CHēf/ ▸*n.* **1** a leader or ruler of a people or clan: *the chief of the village* | *the Tlingit chief* | [as *title*] *an island where Chief Seattle was born.* ■ the person with the highest rank in an organization: *a bureau chief* | *the chief of police.* ■ an informal form of address, esp. to someone of superior rank or status: *it's quite simple, chief.* **2** *Heraldry* an ordinary consisting of a broad horizontal band across the top of the shield. ■ the upper third of the field.

▸*adj.* most important: *the chief reason for the spending cuts* | *chief among her concerns is working alone at night.* ■ having or denoting the highest rank or authority: *the government's chief adviser.* ▷Middle English: from Old French *chief, chef*, based on Latin *caput* 'head.' —**chief·dom** /-dəm/ *n.* —**chief·ship** /-,SHip/ *n.*

▸PHRASES □ **chief cook and bottle-washer** *informal* a person who performs a variety of important but routine tasks. □ **in chief** *Heraldry* at the top; in the upper part. □ **too many chiefs and not enough Indians** too many people giving orders and not enough people to carry them out.

chief jus·tice ▸*n.* (the title of) the presiding judge in a supreme court. ■ (**Chief Justice of the United States**) (the formal title of) the chief justice of the U.S. Supreme Court.

chief·ly /ˈCHēflē/ ▸*adv.* above all; mainly: *he is remembered chiefly for his sonatas.* ■ for the most part; mostly: *a faction that consisted chiefly of communists.*

chief mas·ter ser·geant ▸*n.* a noncommissioned officer in the U.S. Air Force ranking above senior master sergeant and below warrant officer.

chief of staff ▸*n.* the senior staff officer of a service or command.

chief of state ▸*n.* the titular head of a nation as distinct from the head of the government.

chief pet·ty of·fi·cer ▸*n.* a senior noncommissioned officer in a navy, in particular an NCO in the U.S. Navy or Coast Guard ranking above petty officer and below senior chief petty officer.

chief rab·bi ▸*n.* (in the UK and some other countries) the preeminent rabbi of a national Jewish community.

chief·tain /ˈCHēftən/ ▸*n.* the leader of a people or clan. ■ *informal* a powerful member of an organization. ▷Middle English and Old French *chevetaine*, from late Latin *capitaneus* (see CAPTAIN). The spelling was altered by association with CHIEF. —**chief·tain·cy** /-sē/ *n.* (*pl.* **-cies**) —**chief·tain·ship** /-,SHip/ *n.*

chief war·rant of·fi·cer ▸*n.* a member of the U.S. armed forces ranking above warrant officer and below the lowest-ranking commissioned officer.

chiff·chaff /ˈCHif,CHaf/ ▸*n.* a migratory Eurasian and North African leaf warbler with drab plumage. • Genus *Phylloscopus*, family Sylviidae: two species, in particular the common *P. collybita.* ▷late 18th cent.: imitative of its call.

chif·fon /SHiˈfän; ˈSHif,än/ ▸*n.* a light, sheer fabric typically made of silk or nylon: [as *adj.*] *a chiffon blouse.* ■ [as *adj.*] (of a cake or dessert) made with beaten egg whites to give a light consistency: *chiffon cake.* ▷mid 18th cent. (originally plural, denoting trimmings or ornaments on a woman's dress): from French, from *chiffe* 'rag.'

chif·fo·nade /,SHifəˈnäd; -ˈnäd/ (also **chif·fon·nade**) ▸*n.* (*pl.* same) a preparation of shredded or finely cut leaf vegetables, used as a garnish for soup. ▷French, from *chiffonner* 'to crumple.'

chif·fo·nier /,SHifəˈni(ə)r/ ▸*n.* **1** a tall chest of drawers, often with a mirror on top. **2** *Brit.* a low cupboard, sometimes with a raised bookshelf on top. ▷mid 18th cent.: from French *chiffonnier, chiffonnière*, literally 'ragpicker,' also denoting a chest of drawers for odds and ends.

chif·fo·robe /ˈSHifə,rōb/ ▸*n.* a piece of furniture with drawers on one side and hanging space on the other. ▷early 20th cent.: blend of CHIFFONIER and WARDROBE.

chig·ger /ˈCHigər/ (also **jig·ger**) ▸*n.* **1** a tiny mite whose parasitic larvae live on or under the skin of warm-blooded animals, where they cause irritation and dermatitis and sometimes transmit scrub typhus. Also called HARVEST MITE. • Genus *Trombicula*, family Trombiculidae: many species. **2** another term for CHIGOE. ▷mid 18th cent.: variant of CHIGOE.

chigger

chi·gnon /ˈSHēn,yän; SHēnˈyän/ ▸*n.* a knot or coil of hair arranged on the back of a woman's head. ▷late 18th cent.: from French, originally 'nape of the neck,' based on Latin *catena* 'chain.'

chig·oe /ˈCHigō; ˈCHēgō/ ▸*n.* a tropical flea, the female of which burrows and lays eggs beneath the host's skin, causing painful sores. Also called CHIGGER, SAND FLEA. • *Tunga penetrans*, family Tungidae. ▷mid 17th cent.: from French *chique*, from a West African language.

Chih·li, Gulf of /ˈjirˈlē; ˈCHēˈlē/ another name for **Bo Hai**.

Chi·hua·hua /CHəˈwäwə; SHə-/ a state in northern Mexico. ■ its capital, the principal city of northern central Mexico; pop. 530,490.

chi·hua·hua /CHəˈwäwä; SHə-; -wə/ ▸*n.* a small dog of a smooth-haired, large-eyed breed originating in Mexico. ▷early 19th cent.: named after CHIHUAHUA.

chihuahua

chi·la·qui·les /,CHēläˈkēläs/ ▸*n.* (in Mexican cooking) a dish of fried tortilla strips typically topped with a spicy tomato sauce and cheese. ▷from Nahuatl.

chil·blain /ˈCHil,blān/ ▸*n.* a painful, itching swelling on the skin, typically on a hand or foot, caused by poor circulation in the skin when exposed to cold. ▷mid 16th cent.: from CHILL + BLAIN. —**chil·blained** *adj.*

Child[1] /CHīld/, Julia (1912–2004), U.S. chef and cookbook author. Her cookbooks, beginning with *Mastering the Art of French Cooking* (written in 1961 with Simone Beck and Louisette Bertholle), and her television cooking show "The French Chef," which began on PBS in 1963, revolutionized American cooking.

Child[2] /CHīld/, Lydia Marie (1802–80), U.S. abolitionist and writer; born *Lydia Marie Francis.* She was editor of the National Anti-Slavery Standard 1841–43 and the author of novels, children's books, and the poem "Thanksgiving Day" that begins "Over the river and through the woods."

child /CHīld/ ▸*n.* (*pl.* **chil·dren** /ˈCHildrən/) a young human being below the age of full physical development or below the legal age of majority. ■ a son or daughter of any age. ■ an immature or irresponsible person: *she's such a child!* ■ a person who has little or no experience in a particular area: *he's a child in financial matters.* ■ (**children**) the descendants of a family or people: *the children of Abraham.* ■ (**child of**) a person or thing influenced by a specified environment: *a child of the sixties* | *OPEC was in a sense a child of the Cold War.* ▷Old English *cild*, of Germanic origin. The Middle English plural *childer* or *childre* became *childeren* or *children* by association with plurals ending in *-en*, such as *brethren.* —**child·less** *adj.* —**child·less·ness** *n.*

▸PHRASES □ **child's play** a task that is easily accomplished. □ **from a child** since childhood. □ **with child** *formal* pregnant.

child a·buse ▸*n.* physical maltreatment or sexual molestation of a child.

child·bear·ing /ˈCHīld,be(ə)riNG/ ▸*n.* the process of giving birth to children: [as *adj.*] *women of childbearing age.*

child·bed /ˈCHīld,bed/ ▸*n.* archaic term for CHILDBIRTH.

child·bed fe·ver ▸*n.* another term for PUERPERAL FEVER.

child·birth /ˈCHīld,bərTH/ ▸*n.* the action of giving birth to a child: *she died* **in childbirth.**

child care ▸*n.* the action or skill of looking after children. ■ the care of children by a day-care center, babysitter, or other provider while parents are working.

child-cen·tered ▸*adj.* giving priority to the interests and needs of children: *child-centered teaching methods.*

Childe /CHīld/ ▸*n.* [in *names*] *archaic* or *poetic/literary* a youth of noble birth: *Childe Harold.* ▷late Old English, variant of **CHILD**.

Chil·der·mas /'CHildər,mas/ ▸*n. archaic* the feast of the Holy Innocents, December 28. ▷Old English *cildramæsse*, from *cildra* 'of children,' genitive plural of *cild* (see **CHILD**) + *mæsse* (see **MASS**).

child·hood /'CHīld,ho͝od/ ▸*n.* the state of being a child: *the idealized world of childhood.* ■ the period during which a person is a child: *she spent her childhood in Pennsylvania* | [as *adj.*] *a childhood friend.* ▷Old English *cildhād* (see **CHILD**, **-HOOD**).

child·ish /'CHīldiSH/ ▸*adj.* of, like, or appropriate to a child: *childish enthusiasm.* ■ silly and immature: *a childish outburst.* —**child·ish·ly** *adv.* —**child·ish·ness** *n.*

child la·bor ▸*n.* the use of children in industry or business, esp. when illegal or considered inhumane.

child·like /'CHīld,līk/ ▸*adj.* (of an adult) having good qualities associated with a child: *she speaks with a childlike directness.*

child·mind·er /'CHīld,mīndər/ ▸*n. Brit.* a child-care worker or babysitter. —**child-mind·ing** *n.*

child·proof /'CHīld,pro͞of/ ▸*adj.* designed to prevent children from injuring themselves or doing damage: *disinfectants that are fitted with childproof caps.*
▸*v.* [*trans.*] make inaccessible to children: *childproof those cabinets with safety latches.*

chil·dren /'CHildrən/ ▸ plural form of **CHILD**.

chil·dren of Is·ra·el see **ISRAEL**[1] (sense 1).

Chil·dren's Cru·sade a crusade to the Holy Land in 1212 by tens of thousands of children, chiefly from France and Germany. Most of the children never reached their destination, and were sold into slavery.

child re·straint ▸*n.* a device used to control and protect a child in a motor vehicle.

child sup·port ▸*n.* court-ordered payments, typically made by a noncustodial divorced parent, to support one's minor child or children.

Chil·e /'CHilē/ a country in South America that occupies a long coastal strip that runs down the western coast of Bolivia and Argentina, on the Pacific Ocean; pop. 15,823,000; capital, Santiago; official language, Spanish. —**Chil·e·an** /'CHilēən; CHə'lāən/ *adj.* & *n.*

Most of Chile was part of the Inca empire and became part of Spanish Peru after Pizarro's conquest. Independence was achieved in 1818 with help from Argentina. After the overthrow of the Marxist democrat Salvador Allende in 1973, Chile was ruled by the right-wing military dictatorship of General Pinochet until a democratically elected president took office in 1990. The economy grew through the 1990s.

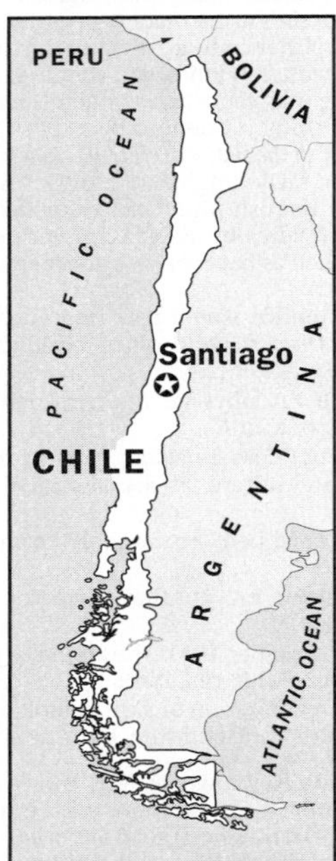

chil·e[1] /'CHilē/ ▸*n.* variant spelling of **CHILI**.

chile[2] /CHīl/ ▸*n.* nonstandard spelling of **CHILD**, used in representing chiefly southern U.S. dialect: *where you been, honey chile?*

Chil·e·an sea bass /bas/ ▸*n.* see **PATAGONIAN TOOTHFISH**.

Chil·e·an wine palm ▸*n.* another term for **COQUITO**.

chil·e re·lle·no /rə(l)'yānō/ ▸*n.* (*pl.* **chil·es re·lle·nos**) (in Mexican cuisine) a stuffed chili pepper, typically battered and deep-fried. ▷early 20th cent.: Spanish, literally 'stuffed chili.'

Chil·e salt·pe·ter ▸*n.* another term for **SODIUM NITRATE**, esp. as a commercial product mined in Chile and other arid parts of the world.

chil·i /'CHilē/ (also **chil·i pep·per** or **chil·e** or *Brit.* **chil·li**) ▸*n.* (*pl.* **chil·ies** or **chil·es** or *Brit.* **chil·lies**) a small hot-tasting pod of a variety of capsicum, used chopped (and often dried) in sauces, relishes, and spice powders. There are various forms with pods of differing size, color, and strength of flavor, such as cascabels and jalapeños. • *Capsicum annuum* var. *annuum*, *'longum'* group (or var. *longum*). ■ short for **CHILI POWDER**. ■ short for **CHILI CON CARNE**. ▷early 17th cent.: from Spanish *chile*, from Nahuatl *chilli*.

chil·i·ast /'kilē,ast/ ▸*n.* another term for **MILLENARIAN**. ▷late 16th cent.: via late Latin from Greek *khiliastēs*, from *khilias* 'a thousand years,' from *khilioi* 'thousand.' —**chil·i·asm** /-,azəm/ *n.* —**chil·i·as·tic** /,kilē'astik/ *adj.*

chil·i·burg·er /'CHilē,bərgər/ ▸*n.* a hamburger with a topping of chili con carne.

chil·i con car·ne /kän 'kärnē; kən/ ▸*n.* a spicy stew of beef and red chilies or chili powder, often with beans and tomatoes. ▷mid 19th cent.: from Spanish *chile con carne*, literally 'chili pepper with meat.'

chil·i dog ▸*n.* a hot dog garnished with chili con carne.

chil·i pow·der ▸*n.* a hot-tasting mixture of ground dried red chilies and other spices.

chil·i sauce ▸*n.* a hot sauce made with tomatoes, chilies, and spices.

chill /CHil/ ▸*n.* [in *sing.*] a moderate but unpleasant coldness: *there was a chill in the air.* ■ (often **chills**) a lowered body temperature, often accompanied by shivering: *the disease begins abruptly with chills, headaches, and dizziness.* ■ a feverish cold. ■ *figurative* a coldness of manner: *the sudden chill in China's relations with the West.* ■ *figurative* a depressing influence: *his statements have cast a chill over this whole country.* ■ a sudden and powerful unpleasant feeling, esp. of fear: *his words sent* **a chill of** *apprehension down my spine.* ■ a metal mold or part of a mold, often cooled, designed to ensure rapid or even cooling of metal during casting.
▸*v.* [*trans.*] **1** (often **be chilled**) make (someone) cold: *I'm* **chilled to the bone.** ■ cool (food or drink) in a refrigerator: [as *adj.*] (**chilled**) *chilled white wine.* **2** (often **be chilled**) horrify or frighten (someone): *the city was chilled by the violence* | [as *adj.*] (**chilling**) *a chilling account of the prisoners' fate.* **3** (also **chill out**) [*intrans.*] *informal* calm down and relax: *I can lean back and chill* | *chill out, okay?* ■ pass time without a particular aim or purpose, esp. with other people: *we had a week at home and we chilled out.*
▸*adj.* chilly: *the chill gray dawn* | *figurative the chill winds of public censure.* ▷Old English *cele*, *ciele* 'cold, coldness,' of Germanic origin; related to **COLD**. —**chill·ing·ly** *adv.* —**chill·ness** *n.* —**chill·some** /-səm/ *adj.* (*poetic/literary*).
▸PHRASES □ **chill someone's blood** horrify or terrify someone. □ **take the chill off** warm slightly.

chill·er /'CHilər/ ▸*n.* **1** a machine for cooling something, esp. a cold cabinet or refrigerator for keeping stored food a few degrees above freezing. **2** short for **SPINE-CHILLER**.

chill fac·tor ▸*n.* another term for **WINDCHILL**.

chil·li ▸*n.* (*pl.* **chil·lies**) British spelling of **CHILI**.

Chil·li·cothe /,CHilə'käTHē; -'kôTHē/ a historic city in south central Ohio, an early capital of the state; pop. 21,921.

chil·lum /'CHiləm/ ▸*n.* (*pl.* **-lums**) a hookah. ■ a pipe used for smoking marijuana. ▷from Hindi *cilam*.

chill·y /'CHilē/ ▸*adj.* (**chill·i·er**, **chill·i·est**) uncomfortably cool or cold: *it had turned chilly* | *a chilly day.* ■ (of a person) feeling cold: *I felt a bit chilly.* ■ unfriendly: *a chilly reception.* —**chill·i·ness** *n.*

Chi·lop·o·da /kī'läpədə/ *Zoology* a class of myriapod arthropods that comprises the centipedes. ▷modern Latin (plural), from Greek *kheilos* 'lip' + *pous*, *pod-* 'foot.' —**chi·lo·pod** /'kīlə,päd/ *n.*

Chil·pan·cin·go /,CHēlpän'siNGgō/ a city in southwestern Mexico, capital of the state of Guerrero; pop. 120,000.

Chil·tern Hun·dreds /'CHiltərn 'həndrədz/ (in the UK) a Crown manor, whose administration is a nominal office for which a member of Parliament applies as a way of resigning from the House of Commons. ▷from **CHILTERN HILLS** and *Hundreds* (see the noun **HUNDRED**).

Chi·lu·ba /CHə'lo͞obə/ ▸*n.* another term for **LUBA** (the language).

Chi·lung /'jē'lo͝oNG/ (also **Chi-lung**, **Kee·lung**) a chief port and naval base in Taiwan, at the northern tip of the island; pop. 357,000.

chi·mae·ra ▸*n.* variant spelling of **CHIMERA**.

chim·bley ▸*n.* (*pl.* **-bleys**) dialect form of **CHIMNEY**.

Chim·bo·ra·zo /,CHimbə'räzō; ,SHim-/ the highest peak in the Andes in Ecuador. It rises to 20,487 ft. (6,310 m.).

Chim·bo·te /CHēm'bō,tā/ an industrial port city in west central Peru, on the Pacific Ocean north of Lima; pop. 297,000.

chime[1] /CHīm/ ▸*n.* (often **chimes**) a bell or a metal bar or tube, typically one of a set tuned to produce a melodious series of ringing sounds when struck. ■ a sound made by such an instrument: *I hear the chimes of the hour from the courthouse.* ■ (**chimes**) a set of tuned metal rods used as an orchestral instrument. ■ (**chimes**) a set of tuned bells used as a doorbell. ■ *Bell-ringing* a stroke of the clapper against one or both sides of a scarcely moving bell.
▸*v.* [*intrans.*] **1** (of a bell or clock) make melodious ringing sounds, typically to indicate the time. ■ [*trans.*] (of a clock) make such sounds in order to indicate (the time): *the clock chimed eight.* **2** be in agreement; harmonize: *his poem* **chimes with** *our modern experience of loss.*
▸*phrasal v.* □ **chime in 1** interject a remark: *"Yes, you do that," Doreen chimed in eagerly.* **2** join in harmoniously. ▷Middle English (in the senses 'cymbal' and 'ring out'): probably from Old English *cimbal* (see **CYMBAL**), later interpreted as *chime bell.* —**chim·er** *n.*

chime[2] (also **chimb**) ▸*n.* the projecting rim at the end of a cask. ▷late Middle English: probably from an Old English word related to Dutch *kim* and German *Kimme*. Compare with **CHINE**[3].

chi·me·ra /kī'mi(ə)rə; kə-/ (also **chi·mae·ra**) ▸*n.* **1** (**Chimera**) (in Greek mythology) a fire-breathing female monster with a lion's head, a goat's body, and a serpent's tail. ■ any mythical animal with parts taken from various animals. **2** a thing that is hoped or wished for but in fact is illusory or impossible to achieve: *the economic sovereignty you claim to defend is a chimera.* **3** *Biology* an organism containing a mixture of genetically different tissues, formed by processes such as fusion of early embryos, grafting, or mutation: *the sheeplike goat chimera.* ■ a DNA molecule with sequences derived from two or more different organisms, formed by laboratory manipulation. **4** (usu. **chimaera**) a cartilaginous marine fish with a long tail, an erect spine before the first dorsal fin, and typically a forward projection from the snout. • Subclass Holocephali: three families, in particular Chimaeridae. See also **RABBITFISH**, **RATFISH**. ▷late Middle English: via Latin from Greek *khimaira* 'she-goat or chimera.' —**chi·mer·ic** /kī'mi(ə)rik; kə-; -'merik/ *adj.* —**chi·mer·i·cal** *adj.* —**chi·mer·i·cal·ly** *adv.*

chi·mer·ism /kī'mi(ə)r,izəm; 'kīmə,rizəm/ ▸*n. Biology* the state of being a genetic chimera.

chi·mi·chan·ga /,CHimi'CHäNGgə; -'CHaNGgə/ ▸*n.* a tortilla wrapped around a filling, typically of meat, and deep-fried. ▷Mexican Spanish, literally 'trinket.'

chi·mi·ne·a /CHimə'nēə/ (also **chi·me·ne·a**) ▸*n.* an earthenware outdoor fireplace shaped like a lightbulb, with the bulbous end housing the fire and typically supported by a wrought-iron stand.

chiminea

chim·ney /'CHimnē/ ▸*n.* (*pl.* **-neys**) a vertical channel or pipe that conducts smoke and combustion gases up from a fire or furnace and typically through the roof of a building. ■ the part of such a structure that extends above the roof. ■ a glass tube that protects the flame of a lamp. ■ a steep narrow cleft by which a rock face may be climbed. ▷Middle English (denoting a fireplace or furnace): from Old French *cheminee* 'chimney, fireplace,' from late Latin *caminata*, perhaps from *camera caminata* 'room with a fireplace,' from Latin *caminus* 'forge, furnace,' from Greek *kaminos* 'oven.'

chim·ney breast ▸*n.* a part of an interior wall that projects to surround a chimney.

chim·ney cor·ner ▸*n.* a warm seat at the side of an old-fashioned fireplace.

chim·ney piece ▸*n. Brit.* a mantelpiece.

chim·ney pot ▸*n.* an earthenware or metal pipe at the top of a chimney, narrowing the aperture and increasing the updraft.

chim·ney stack ▸*n.* the part of a chimney that projects above a roof.

chim·ney sweep ▸*n.* a person whose job is cleaning out the soot from chimneys.

chim·ney swift ▸*n.* the common swift found over the eastern part of North America, with mainly dark gray plumage. • *Chaetura pelagica*, family Apodidae.

chimney swift

chimp /CHimp/ ▸*n. informal* term for CHIMPANZEE.

chim·pan·zee /ˌCHimˌpan'zē; -pən'zē; -'panzē/ ▸*n.* a great ape with large ears, mainly black coloration, and lighter skin on the face, native to the forests of western and central Africa. Chimpanzees show advanced behavior such as the making and using of tools. • Genus *Pan*, family Pongidae: the **common chimpanzee** (*P. troglodytes*) and the bonobo. ▷mid 18th cent.: from French *chimpanzé*, from Kikongo.

Chin variant spelling of JIN.

Ch'in variant spelling of QIN.

chin /CHin/ ▸*n.* the protruding part of the face below the mouth, formed by the apex of the lower jaw.
▸*v.* [*trans.*] draw one's body up so as to bring one's chin level with or above (a horizontal bar) with one's feet off the ground, as an exercise. ▷Old English *cin, cinn*, of Germanic origin; related to Dutch *kin*, from an Indo-European root shared by Latin *gena* 'cheek' and Greek *genus* 'jaw.' **—chinned** *adj.* [*in combination*] *square-chinned.*
▸*PHRASES* □ **keep one's chin up** *informal* remain cheerful in difficult circumstances: *keep your chin up, we're not lost yet.* □ **take it on the chin** endure or accept misfortune courageously or stoically.

Chi·na /'CHīnə/ a country in eastern Asia, the third largest and most populous in the world; pop. 1,298,847,000; capital, Beijing; language, Chinese (Mandarin is the official form). Official name PEOPLE'S REPUBLIC OF CHINA.

Chinese civilization stretches back until at least the 3rd millennium BC, the country being ruled by a series of dynasties until the Qing (or Manchu) dynasty was overthrown by Sun Yat-sen in 1911; China was proclaimed a republic the following year. After World War II, the Kuomintang government of Chiang Kai-shek was overthrown by the Communists under Mao Zedong, and the People's Republic of China was declared in 1949. Market-oriented reforms were introduced in the last quarter of the twentieth century.

Chi·na, Republic of official name for TAIWAN.

chi·na /'CHīnə/ ▸*n.* a fine white or translucent vitrified ceramic material: *a plate made of china* | [as *adj.*] *a china cup.* Also called PORCELAIN. ■ household tableware or other objects made from this or a similar material: *the breakfast china.* ▷late 16th cent. (as an adjective): from Persian *chīnī* used attributively relating to China, where it was originally made.

Chi·na as·ter ▸*n.* a Chinese plant of the daisy family, cultivated for its bright showy flowers. • *Callistephus chinensis*, family Compositae.

chi·na·ber·ry /'CHīnəˌberē/ (also **Chi·na·ber·ry**) ▸*n.* (*pl.* **-ries**) (also **chinaberry tree**) a tall tree of the mahogany family native to Asia and Australasia, bearing fragrant lilac flowers and yellow berries. It has become naturalized in parts of North America. • *Melia azedarach*, family Meliaceae. ■ the fruit of this tree, used as beads and to make insecticides: *a rosary made of chinaberries.*

chi·na blue ▸*n.* a pale grayish blue.

chi·na clay ▸*n.* another term for KAOLIN.

Chi·na·man /'CHīnəmən/ ▸*n.* (*pl.* **-men**) *informal, dated, offensive* a native of China.

chi·na mark·er ▸*n.* a waxy pencil used to write on china, glass, or other hard surfaces.

chi·nar /CHi'när/ (also **chinar tree**) ▸*n.* the oriental plane tree, native from southeastern Europe to northern Iran. • *Platanus orientalis*, family Platanaceae. ▷from Persian *chinār*.

Chi·na rose ▸*n.* **1** a Chinese rose that was introduced into Europe in the 19th century. • *Rosa chinensis*, family Rosaceae. ■ any of a number of garden rose varieties derived from crosses of this plant. **2** a tropical shrubby evergreen hibiscus, cultivated for its large showy flowers. • *Hibiscus rosa-sinensis*, family Malvaceae.

Chi·na Sea the part of the Pacific Ocean off the coast of China, divided by the island of Taiwan into the **East China Sea** in the north and the **South China Sea** in the south.

chi·na stone ▸*n.* partly kaolinized granite containing plagioclase feldspar, ground and mixed with kaolin to make porcelain.

Chi·na syn·drome ▸*n.* a hypothetical sequence of events following the meltdown of a nuclear reactor, in which the core melts through its containment structure and deep into the earth. ▷1970s: from CHINA (as being on the opposite side of the earth from a reactor in the U.S.).

Chi·na tea ▸*n.* tea made from a small-leaved type of tea plant grown in China, typically flavored by smoke curing or the addition of flower petals.

Chi·na·town /'CHīnəˌtoun/ ▸*n.* a district of any non-Chinese town, esp. a city or seaport, in which the population is predominantly of Chinese origin.

chi·na tree (also **Chi·na tree**) ▸*n.* another term for CHINABERRY.

chi·na·ware /'CHīnəˌwər/ ▸*n.* dishes made of china.

chinch /CHinCH/ (also **chinch bug** /sinCH/) ▸*n.* a plant-eating ground bug that forms large swarms on grasses and rushes. • Two species in the family Lygaeidae, suborder Heteroptera: the American *Blissus leucopterus*, which is a major pest of cereal crops, and the European *Ischnodemus sabuleti.* ▷early 17th cent. (in the sense 'bedbug'): from Spanish *chinche*, from Latin *cimex, cimic-*.

chin·che·rin·chee /ˌCHinCHə'rinCHē; -rin'CHē/ ▸*n.* a white-flowered South African lily. • *Ornithogalum thyrsoides*, family Liliaceae. ▷early 20th cent.: imitative of the squeaky sound made by rubbing its stalks together.

chin·chil·la /CHin'CHilə/ ▸*n.* a small South American rodent with soft gray fur and a long bushy tail. • Genus *Chinchilla*, family Chinchillidae: two species, in particular *C. lanigera.* ■ a cat or rabbit of a breed with silver-gray or gray fur. ■ the highly valued fur of the chinchilla, or of the chinchilla rabbit. ▷early 17th cent.: from Spanish, from Aymara or Quechua.

Chin·co·teague Is·land /ˌSHiNGkə'tēg; ˌCHiNG-/ an island in eastern Virginia, west of Assateague Island, noted for its wild horses.

Chin·co·teague po·ny /'SHiNGkəˌtēg; 'CHiNG-/ ▸*n.* a small, hardy horse found running wild on the islands of Chincoteague and Assateague off the Virginia and Maryland coasts.

Chin·dit /'CHindit/ ▸*n.* a member of the Allied forces behind the Japanese lines in Burma (now Myanmar) in 1943–45. ▷World War II: from Burmese *chinthé*, a mythical creature.

Chin·dwin /'CHin'dwin/ a river that rises in northern Myanmar (Burma) and flows south for 550 miles (885 km) to meet the Irrawaddy River.

chine[1] /CHīn/ ▸*n.* a backbone, esp. that of an animal as it appears in a cut of meat. ■ a cut of meat containing all or part of this. ■ a mountain ridge or arête.
▸*v.* [*trans.*] cut (meat) across or along the backbone. ▷Middle English: from Old French *eschine*, based on a blend of Latin *spina* 'spine' and a Germanic word meaning 'narrow piece,' related to SHIN.

chine[2] ▸*n. Brit.* a deep, narrow ravine formed by running water. ▷Old English *cinu* 'cleft, chink,' of Germanic origin; related to Dutch *keen*, also to CHINK[1].

chine[3] ▸*n.* the angle where the bottom of a boat or ship meets the side. ▷late Middle English: variant of CHIME[2] (the original sense).

Chi·nese /CHī'nēz; -'nēs/ ▸*adj.* of or relating to China or its language, culture, or people. ■ belonging to or relating to the people forming the dominant ethnic group of China and widely dispersed elsewhere. Also called HAN.
▸*n.* (*pl.* same) **1** the Chinese language. **2** a native or national of China, or a person of Chinese descent.

Chinese, a member of the Sino-Tibetan language family, is the world's most commonly spoken first language, with an estimated 1.2 billion native speakers worldwide. The script is logographic, using characters that originated as stylized pictographs but now also represent abstract concepts and the sounds of syllables. Though complex, it permits written communication between speakers of the many dialects, most of which are mutually incomprehensible in speech. About 8,000 characters are in everyday use, some having been simplified during the 20th century. For transliteration into the Roman alphabet, the Pinyin system is now usually used.

chinchilla

Chi·nese an·ise ▸*n.* another term for STAR ANISE.

Chi·nese ar·ti·choke ▸*n.* an Asian plant of the mint family, cultivated for its edible tubers. • Genus *Stachys*, family Labiatae: several species, esp. *S. sieboldii* and *S. affinis*.

Chi·nese black mush·room ▸*n.* another term for SHIITAKE MUSHROOM

Chi·nese box ▸*n.* each of a series of nested boxes.

Chi·nese cab·bage ▸*n.* an oriental cabbage that does not form a firm heart. • Genus *Brassica*, family Brassicaceae: two species, bok choy (*B. chinensis*), which has smooth tapering leaves, and pe-tsai (*B. pekinenis*), which resembles lettuce; they are often treated as varieties of *B. rapa*.

Chi·nese check·ers ▸*plural n.* [usu. treated as *sing.*] a board game for two to six players who attempt to move marbles or counters from one corner to the opposite one on a star-shaped board.

Chi·nese chest·nut ▸*n.* see CHESTNUT.

Chi·nese chives ▸*plural n.* an Asian relative of chives, with a garliclike flavor. Also called GARLIC CHIVES. • *Allium tuberosum*, family Liliaceae (or Alliaceae).

Chi·nese date ▸*n.* another term for JUJUBE.

Chi·nese fire drill ▸*n. informal, often offensive* a state of disorder or confusion. ■ a game in which the passengers of a motor vehicle that is stopped at an intersection get out of the vehicle, circle it, and return to their seats.

Chi·nese goose·ber·ry ▸*n.* another term for KIWI FRUIT.

Chi·nese kale ▸*n.* a leafy green Asian plant of the cabbage family, closely related to broccoli but with more leaf and stem and much smaller florettes. It is commonly used in Asian cooking. • *Brassica alboglabra*, family Brassicaceae.

Chi·nese lan·tern ▸*n.* **1** a collapsible paper lantern. **2** a Eurasian plant with white flowers and globular orange fruits enclosed in an orange-red papery calyx. The stems bearing these are dried and used for decoration. • *Physalis alkekengi*, family Solanaceae.

Chinese lantern 2

Chi·nese pars·ley ▸*n.* another term for CORIANDER.

Chi·nese pear ▸*n.* another term for ASIAN PEAR.

Chi·nese puz·zle ▸*n.* an intricate puzzle consisting of many interlocking pieces. ■ a very complicated or perplexing situation: *it's turning out to be a regular Chinese puzzle.*

Chi·nese rad·ish ▸*n.* another term for DAIKON.

Chi·nese red ▸*n.* a vivid orange-red.

Chi·nese res·tau·rant syn·drome ▸*n.* an illness marked by short attacks of weakness, numbness, palpitations, and headaches, often attributed to overconsumption of monosodium glutamate (commonly used as a seasoning in Chinese cooking).

Chi·nese rhu·barb ▸*n.* a tall perennial plant with palmate leaves, whitish flowers, and winged fruits. The dried rhizomes and roots are used medicinally. • *Rheum longifolia*, family Polygonaceae.

Chi·nese wall ▸*n.* an insurmountable barrier, esp. to the passage of information or communication: *she'd built a Chinese wall between them.* ▷early 20th cent.: with allusion to the GREAT WALL OF CHINA.

Chi·nese whis·pers ▸*plural n.* [treated as *sing.*] a game in which a message is distorted by being passed around in a whisper. Also called TELEPHONE.

Chi·nese white ▸*n.* white pigment made from zinc oxide.

Chi·nese wind·lass ▸*n.* another term for DIFFERENTIAL WINDLASS.

Ch'ing variant spelling of QING.

ching /CHiNG/ ▸*n.* an abrupt high-pitched ringing sound, typically one made by a cash register. ▷imitative.

Chink /CHiNGk/ ▸*n. informal, offensive* a Chinese person. ▷late 19th cent.: irregular formation from CHINA.

chink[1] /CHiNGk/ ▸*n.* a narrow opening or crack, typically one that admits light: *a chink in the curtains.* ■ a narrow beam or patch of light admitted by such an opening: *I noticed a* **chink of light** *under the door.* ▷mid 16th cent.: related to CHINE[2].

▸*PHRASE* □ **a chink in someone's armor** a weak point in someone's character, arguments, or ideas, making them vulnerable to attack or criticism.

chink[2] ▸*v.* make or cause to make a light and high-pitched ringing sound, as of glasses or coins striking together: [*intrans.*] *the chain joining the handcuffs chinked* | [*trans.*] *they chinked glasses and kissed.*

▸*n.* a high-pitched ringing sound: *the chink of glasses.* ▷late 16th cent.: imitative.

chin·ka·pin ▸*n.* variant spelling of CHINQUAPIN.

chin·ka·ra /CHiNG'kärə; CHin-/ ▸*n.* (*pl.* same) (in the Indian subcontinent) the Indian gazelle, which occurs from Iran to central India. • *Gazella bennettii*, family Bovidae. ▷mid 19th cent.: from Hindi *cikārā*, from Sanskrit *chikkāra*.

Chin·kiang /'jinjē'äNG/ variant of ZHENJIANG.

Chink·y /'CHiNGkē/ *informal, offensive* ▸*n.* (*pl.* **Chink·ies**) a Chinese person.

▸*adj.* Chinese.

chin·less /'CHinlis/ ▸*adj.* (of a person) lacking a well-defined chin. ■ *informal* lacking strength of character; ineffectual.

chin mu·sic ▸*n. informal* **1** idle chatter. **2** *Baseball* used to refer to a pitched ball that passes very close to the batter's chin: *Clemens delivered some wicked chin music to Hernandez.*

Chi·no /'CHēnō/ a city in southwestern California, east of Los Angeles; pop. 59,682.

chi·no /'CHēnō/ ▸*n.* (*pl.* **-nos**) a cotton twill fabric, typically khaki-colored. ■ (**chinos**) casual pants made from such fabric. ▷1940s: from Latin American Spanish, literally 'toasted' (referring to the typical color).

Chino- ▸*comb. form* equivalent to SINO-.

chi·nois /SHin'wä; SHēn-/ ▸*n.* a cone-shaped sieve with a closely woven mesh for straining sauces.

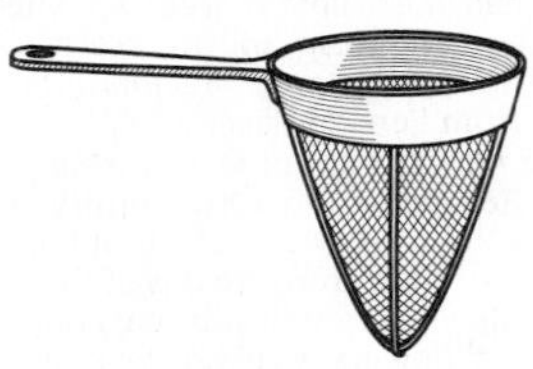

chinois

chi·noi·se·rie /ˌSHēnˌwäz(ə)'rē; ˌSHēn'wäzərē/ ▸*n.* (*pl.* **-ries**) the imitation or evocation of Chinese motifs and techniques in Western art, furniture, and architecture, esp. in the 18th century. ■ objects or decorations in this style: *a piece of chinoiserie* | *one room has red velvet and chinoiseries.* ▷late 19th cent.: from French, from *chinois* 'Chinese.'

Chi·nook /SHə'nŏŏk; CHə-/ ▸*n.* (*pl.* same or **-nooks**) **1** a member of an American Indian people originally inhabiting the region around the lower Columbia River in Oregon and Washington. **2** the language of this people.

▸*adj.* of or relating to the Chinook or their language. ▷from *c'inúk*, a Salishan word for the name of a Chinook village.

chi·nook /SHə'nŏŏk; CHə-/ ▸*n.* **1** (also **chinook wind**) a warm dry wind that blows down the east side of the Rocky Mountains at the end of winter. **2** (also **chinook salmon**) a large North Pacific salmon that is an important commercial food fish. • *Oncorhynchus tshawytscha*, family Salmonidae. ▷mid 19th cent.: from attributive use of CHINOOK.

Chi·nook Jar·gon ▸*n.* an extinct pidgin composed of elements from Chinook, Nootka, English, French, and other languages, formerly used in the Pacific Northwest.

chin·qua·pin /'CHiNGkiˌpin/ (also **chin·ka·pin**) ▸*n.* a North American chestnut tree. • Several species in the family Fagaceae, in particular the **Allegheny** (or **eastern**) **chinquapin** (*Castanea pumila*). ■ the edible nut of one of these trees. ▷early 17th cent.: from Virginia Algonquian.

chin·strap /'CHinˌstrap/ ▸*n.* a strap attached to a hat, helmet, or other headgear, designed to hold it in place by fitting under the wearer's chin.

chintz /CHints/ ▸*n.* printed multicolored cotton fabric with a glazed finish, used esp. for curtains and upholstery: *a sofa upholstered in chintz* | [as *adj.*] *floral chintz curtains.* ▷early 17th cent. (as *chints*, plural of *chint*, denoting a stained or painted calico cloth imported from India): from Hindi *chīṃṭ* 'spattering, stain.'

chintz·y /'CHintsē/ ▸*adj.* (**chintz·i·er**, **chintz·i·est**) **1** of, like, or decorated with chintz: *brighten the room with fresh paint and chintzy fabrics.* ■ brightly colorful but gaudy and tasteless. **2** *informal* miserly: *a chintzy salary increase.* —**chintz·i·ly** /'CHintsəlē/ *adv.* —**chintz·i·ness** *n.*

chin-up ▸*n.* another term for PULL-UP (sense 1).

chin·wag /'CHinˌwag/ (also **chin wag**) *informal* ▸*n.* a chat.

▸*v.* (**-wagged**, **-wag·ging**) [*intrans.*] have a chat.

Chi·os /'kēˌäs; 'kī-; -ˌôs/ a Greek island in the Aegean Sea; pop. 52,690. Greek name KHIOS. —**Chi·an** /'kēən; 'kī-/ *n.* & *adj.*

chip /CHip/ ▸*n.* **1** a small piece of something removed in the course of chopping, cutting, or breaking something, esp. a hard material such as wood or stone: *mulch the shrubs with cedar chips.* ■ a hole or flaw left by the removal of such a piece: *a chip on his tooth.* ■ *Brit.* wood or woody fiber split into thin strips and used for weaving hats or baskets. **2** a thin slice of food made crisp by being fried, baked, or dried and typically eaten as a snack: *tortilla chips dipped in salsa* | *banana chips.* ■ a small chunk of candy added to desserts or sweet snacks, esp. of chocolate. ■ (**chips**) *chiefly Brit.* French fries: *an order of* **fish and chips**. **3** short for MICROCHIP. **4** a counter used in certain gambling games to represent money: *a poker chip.* **5** (in golf, soccer, and other sports) a short lofted kick or shot with the ball. ■ *Tennis* a softly sliced return intended to land between the net and the opponent's service line.

▸*v.* (**chipped**, **chip·ping**) [*trans.*] **1** cut or break (a small piece) from the edge or surface of a hard material: *we had to chip ice off the upper deck.* ■ [*intrans.*] (of a material or object) break at the edge or on the surface: *the paint had* **chipped off** *the gate.* ■ cut pieces off (a hard material) to alter its shape or break it up: *it required a craftsman to chip the blocks of flint to the required shape* | [*intrans.*] *she* **chipped away at** *the ground outside the door.* **2** (in golf, soccer, and other sports) kick or strike (a ball or shot) to produce a short lobbed shot or pass: *he chipped a superb shot.*

▸*phrasal v.* □ **chip away** gradually and relentlessly make something smaller or weaker: *rivals may* **chip away at** *one's profits by undercutting product prices.* □ **chip in** (or **chip something in**) contribute something as one's share of a joint activity, cost, etc.: *the rookie pitcher* **chipped in with** *nine saves and five wins* | *the council will chip in a further $30,000 a year.* ▷Middle English: related to Old English *forcippian* 'cut off.'

▸*PHRASES* □ **a chip off the old block** *informal* someone who resembles his or her parent, esp. in character. □ **a chip on one's shoulder** *informal* a deeply ingrained grievance, typically about a particular thing. □ **when the chips are down** *informal* when a very serious and difficult situation arises.

chip·board /'CHipˌbôrd/ ▸*n.* another term for PARTICLEBOARD.

Chip·e·wy·an /ˌCHipə'wīən/ ▸*n.* (*pl.* same or **-ans**) **1** a member of a Dene people of northwestern Canada. Do not confuse with CHIPPEWA. **2** the Athabaskan language of this people.

▸*adj.* of or relating to this people or their language. ▷from Cree *čīpwayān*, literally '(wearing) pointed-skin (garments).'

chip·mak·er /'CHipˌmākər/ ▸*n.* a company that manufactures microchips.

chip·munk /'CHipˌməNGk/ ▸*n.* a burrowing ground squirrel with cheek pouches and light and dark stripes running down the body, found in North America and northern Eurasia. • Genus *Tamias*, family Sciuridae: many species, including the **eastern chipmunk** (*T. striatus*), common in the eastern U.S. ▷mid 19th cent.: from Ojibwa.

eastern chipmunk

chi·pot·le /CHi'pōtlā/ ▸*n.* a smoked hot chili pepper used esp. in Mexican cooking. ▷Mexican Spanish, from Nahuatl.

Chip·pen·dale[1] /ˈCHipən,dāl/, Thomas (1718–79), English furniture-maker and designer. He produced furniture in a neoclassical vein, with elements of the French rococo, chinoiserie, and Gothic revival styles.

Chip·pen·dale[2] ▶*adj.* (of furniture) designed, made by, or in the style of Thomas Chippendale.

chip·per[1] /ˈCHipər/ ▶*adj. informal* cheerful and lively. ▷mid 19th cent.: perhaps from northern English dialect *kipper* 'lively.'

chip·per[2] ▶*n.* a person or thing that turns something into chips. ■ a machine for chipping the trunks and limbs of trees.

Chip·pe·wa /ˈCHipə,wä; -,wä; -wə/ (also **Chip·pe·way** /-,wā/) ▶*n.* (*pl.* same) another term for **OJIBWA**. Do not confuse with **CHIPEWYAN**. ▷alteration of **OJIBWA**.

chip·pie /ˈCHipē/ ▶*n.* (*pl.* **-pies**) variant spelling of **CHIPPY**.

chip·ping spar·row ▶*n.* a common American songbird related to the buntings, with a chestnut crown and a white stripe over the eye. • *Spizella passerina*, family Emberizidae (subfamily Emberizinae). ▷early 19th cent.: *chipping* from *chip* 'chirp,' with reference to the bird's repetitive chirping song.

chip·py /ˈCHipē/ *informal* ▶*n.* (also **chip·pie**) (*pl.* **-pies**) **1** a promiscuous young woman, esp. a prostitute. **2** *Brit.* a fish-and-chip shop. **3** *Brit.* a carpenter.
▶*adj.* touchy and irritable. ■ (of an ice-hockey game or player) rough and belligerent, with or incurring numerous penalties.

chip·set /ˈCHip,set/ ▶*n.* a collection of integrated circuits that form the set needed to make an electronic device such as a computer motherboard or portable telephone.

chip shot ▶*n. Golf* a stroke at which the ball is or must be chipped into the air.

Chi·rac /SHēˈräk/, Jacques (René) (1932–), French statesman; prime minister 1974–76 and 1986–88; president (1995–).

chi·ral /ˈkīrəl/ ▶*adj. Chemistry* asymmetric in such a way that the structure and its mirror image are not superimposable. Chiral compounds are typically optically active; large organic molecules often have one or more **chiral centers** where four different groups are attached to a carbon atom. ▷late 19th cent.: from Greek *kheir* 'hand' + **-AL**. —**chi·ral·i·ty** /kīˈralitē/ *n.*

chi-rho /ˈkī ˈrō/ ▶*n.* a monogram of chi (X) and rho (P) as the first two letters of Greek *Khristos* Christ, used as a Christian symbol.

Chir·i·ca·hua /,CHi-riˈkä-wə/ ▶*n.* **1** a member of an Apache people, formerly located in southern New Mexico, southeastern Arizona, and northern Mexico, now living primarily in Oklahoma and New Mexico. **2** the Athabaskan language of this people.
▶*adj.* of or relating to this people or their language.

Chi·ri·ca·hua Moun·tains /,CHiriˈkäwə/ a range in southeastern Arizona, on the Mexican border, controlled by Cochise and other Apache leaders during the 19th century.

chir·i·moy·a ▶*n.* variant spelling of **CHERIMOYA**.

chiro- (also **cheiro-**) ▶*comb. form* of the hand or hands: *chiromancy.* ▷from Greek *kheir* 'hand.'

chi·rog·ra·phy /kīˈrägrəfē/ ▶*n.* handwriting, esp. as distinct from typography. —**chi·ro·graph·ic** /,kīrəˈgrafik/ *adj.*

chi·ro·man·cy /ˈkīrə,mansē/ ▶*n.* the prediction of a person's future from the lines on the palms of his or her hands; palmistry.

Chi·ron /ˈkīrən/ **1** *Greek Mythology* a learned centaur who acted as teacher to Jason, Achilles, and many other heroes. **2** *Astronomy* asteroid 2060, discovered in 1977, which is unique in having an orbit lying mainly between the orbits of Saturn and Uranus. It is believed to have a diameter of 370 km.

chi·ron·o·mid /kīˈränəmid/ ▶*n. Entomology* an insect of a family (Chironomidae) that comprises the nonbiting midges. ▷late 19th cent.: from modern Latin *Chironomidae* (plural), from the genus name *Chironomus*, from Greek *kheironomos* 'pantomime dancer.'

chi·rop·o·dy /kəˈräpədē; SHə-/ ▶*n.* another term for **PODIATRY**. ▷late 19th cent.: from **CHIRO-** 'hand' + Greek *pous, pod-* 'foot.' —**chi·rop·o·dist** /kəˈräpədist/ *n.*

chi·ro·prac·tic /,kīrəˈpraktik/ ▶*n.* a system of complementary medicine based on the diagnosis and manipulative treatment of misalignments of the joints, esp. those of the spinal column, which are held to cause other disorders by affecting the nerves, muscles, and organs. ▷late 19th cent.: from **CHIRO-** 'hand' + Greek *praktikos* 'practical,' from *prattein* 'do.' —**chi·ro·prac·tor** /ˈkīrə,praktər/ *n.*

Chi·rop·ter·a /kīˈräptərə/ *Zoology* an order of mammals that comprises the bats. There are over 900 living species of bats, and they are found on every continent except Antarctica. See also **MEGACHIROPTERA**, **MICROCHIROPTERA**. ▷modern Latin (plural), from **CHIRO-** 'hand' + Greek *pteron* 'wing.' —**chi·rop·ter·an** *n. & adj.*

chirp /CHərp/ ▶*v.* [*intrans.*] (typically of a small bird or an insect) utter a short, sharp, high-pitched sound: *outside, the crickets chirped monotonously.* ■ [with *direct speech*] (of a person) say something in a lively and cheerful way: *"Good morning!" chirped Alex.*
▶*n.* a short, sharp, high-pitched sound. ▷late Middle English: imitative. —**chirp·er** *n.*

chirp·y /ˈCHərpē/ ▶*adj.* (**chirp·i·er**, **chirp·i·est**) *informal* cheerful and lively. —**chirp·i·ly** /ˈCHərpəlē/ *adv.* —**chirp·i·ness** *n.*

chirr /CHər/ (also **churr**) ▶*v.* [*intrans.*] (esp. of an insect) make a prolonged low trilling sound.
▶*n.* a low trilling sound. ▷early 17th cent.: imitative.

chir·rup /ˈCHi(ə)rəp; ˈCHərəp/ ▶*v.* (**-ruped**, **-ruping**) [*intrans.*] (esp. of a small bird) make repeated short high-pitched sounds; twitter. ■ [with *direct speech*] (of a person) say something in a high-pitched voice: *"Yes, Miss Honey," chirruped eighteen voices.*
▶*n.* a short, high-pitched sound. ▷late 16th cent.: alteration of **CHIRP**, by trilling the *-r-*. —**chir·rup·y** *adj.*

chir·u /ˈCHir,o͞o/ ▶*n.* (*pl.* same) a sandy-colored gazelle with black horns, found on the Tibetan plateau. Also called **TIBETAN ANTELOPE**. • *Pantholops hodgsoni*, family Bovidae. ▷late 19th cent.: probably from Tibetan.

chis·el /ˈCHizəl/ ▶*n.* a long-bladed hand tool with a beveled cutting edge and a plain handle that is struck with a hammer or mallet, used to cut or shape wood, stone, metal, or other hard materials.
▶*v.* (**-eled**, **-el·ing**; *Brit.* **-elled**, **-el·ling**) [*trans.*] **1** cut or shape (something) with a chisel: *carefully* ***chisel out*** *a groove for the hinge.* **2** *informal* cheat or swindle (someone) out of something: *he's chiseled me out of my dues.* ▷late Middle English: from Old Northern French, based on Latin *cis-* (as in late Latin *cisorium*), variant of *caes-*, stem of *caedere* 'to cut.' Compare with **SCISSORS**. —**chis·el·er** /ˈCHiz(ə)lər/ *n.*

chis·eled /ˈCHizəld/ ▶*adj.* (of wood or stone) shaped or cut with a chisel. ■ (of a facial feature, typically a man's) strongly and clearly defined: *the chiseled features of a male model.*

Chis·holm /ˈCHizəm/, Shirley Anita St. Hill (1924–), U.S. politician, social activist, and educator. The first African-American woman elected to Congress, she was a member of the House of Representatives from New York 1968–83.

Chis·holm Trail a historic route over which 19th-century cowboys drove cattle for 1,500 miles (2,400 km) north from Texas to Abilene and other Kansas cities that had been reached by developing railroads.

Chi·şi·nă·u /,kēSHəˈnou/ the capital of Moldova; pop. 665,000. Russian name **KISHINYOV**.

chi-square /kī/ ▶*n.* [as *adj.*] relating to or denoting a statistical method assessing the goodness of fit between observed values and those expected theoretically. (Symbol: χ^2)

chit[1] /CHit/ ▶*n.* a short official note, memorandum, or voucher, typically recording a sum owed. ▷late 18th cent.: Anglo-Indian, from Hindi *ciṭṭhī* 'note, pass.'

chit[2] ▶*n.* a young woman regarded with disapproval for her immaturity or lack of respect: *a mere chit of a girl.* ▷late Middle English (denoting a whelp, cub, or kitten): perhaps related to dialect *chit* 'sprout.'

Chi·ta /CHiˈtä/ a city in southeastern Siberia in Russia, on the Trans-Siberian Railway; pop. 349,000.

chi·tal /ˈCHētl/ ▶*n.* (*pl.* same) another term for **AXIS DEER**. ▷late 19th cent.: from Hindi *cītal*, from Sanskrit *citrala* 'spotted,' from *citra* 'spot, mark.'

chit·chat /ˈCHit,CHat/ *informal* ▶*n.* inconsequential conversation.
▶*v.* [*intrans.*] talk about trivial matters: *I can't stand around chitchatting.* ▷late 17th cent.: reduplication of **CHAT**[1].

chi·tin /ˈkītn/ ▶*n. Biochemistry* a fibrous substance consisting of polysaccharides and forming the major constituent in the exoskeleton of arthropods and the cell walls of fungi. ▷mid 19th cent.: from French *chitine*, formed irregularly from Greek *khitōn* (see **CHITON**). —**chi·tin·ous** /ˈkītn-əs/ *adj.*

chi·ton /ˈkītn; ˈkī,tän/ ▶*n.* **1** a long woolen tunic worn in ancient Greece. [from Greek *khitōn* 'tunic.'] **2** a marine mollusk that has an oval flattened body with a shell of overlapping plates. [modern Latin (genus name).] • Class Polyplacophora.

Chit·ta·gong /ˈCHitə,gäNG; -,gôNG/ a seaport in southeastern Bangladesh, on the Bay of Bengal; pop. 1,566,070.

chit·ter /ˈCHitər/ ▶*v.* [*intrans.*] make a twittering or chattering sound. ▷Middle English: imitative; compare with **CHATTER**.

chit·ter·lings /ˈCHitlənz/ ▶*plural n.* the smaller intestines of a pig, cooked for food. ▷Middle English: perhaps related to synonymous German *Kutteln*.

Chi·tun·gwi·za /,CHēto͞oNGˈgwēzə/ a city in northeastern Zimbabwe, southeast of Harare; pop. 274,000.

chiv·al·rous /ˈSHivəlrəs/ ▶*adj.* (of a man or his behavior) courteous and gallant, esp. toward women. ■ of or relating to the historical notion of chivalry. ▷late Middle English (in the sense 'characteristic of a medieval knight'): from Old French *chevalerous*, from *chevalier* (see **CHEVALIER**). —**chiv·al·rous·ly** *adv.*

chiv·al·ry /ˈSHivəlrē/ ▶*n.* the medieval knightly system with its religious, moral, and social code. ■ *historical* knights, noblemen, and horsemen collectively: *I fought against the cream of French chivalry.* ■ the combination of qualities expected of an ideal knight, esp. courage, honor, courtesy, justice, and a readiness to help the weak. ■ courteous behavior, esp. that of a man toward women: *their relations with women were models of chivalry and restraint.* ▷Middle English: from Old French *chevalerie*, from medieval Latin *caballerius*, from late Latin *caballarius* 'horseman' (see **CHEVALIER**). —**chi·val·ric** /SHəˈvalrik/ *adj.*

chives /CHīvz/ ▶*plural n.* a widely cultivated small Eurasian plant related to the onion, with purple-pink flowers and dense tufts of long tubular leaves that are used as a culinary herb. • *Allium schoenoprasum*, family Liliaceae (or Alliaceae). ■ the leaves from this plant: *freshly chopped chives* | [as *adj.*] (**chive**) *chive and garlic dressing.* ▷Middle English: from Old French, dialect variant of *cive*, from Latin *cepa* 'onion.'

chiv·vy /ˈCHivē/ (also **chiv·y** or **chev·y** /ˈCHevē/) ▶*v.* (**-vies**, **-vied**) [*trans.*] tell (someone) repeatedly to do something: *an association that chivvies government* ***into*** *action.* ▷late 18th cent.: probably from the ballad *Chevy Chase*, celebrating a skirmish (probably the battle of Otterburn, 1388) on the Scottish border (but often mistakenly thought to be a place name). Originally a noun denoting a hunting cry, the term later meant 'a pursuit,' hence the verb 'to chase, worry' (mid 19th cent.).

Chka·lov /CHəˈkäləf/ former name (1938–57) for **ORENBURG**.

Chlad·ni fig·ures /ˈklädnē; ˈkladnē/ (also **Chlad·ni pat·terns** or **Chlad·ni's fig·ures**) ▶*plural n.* the patterns formed when a sand-covered surface is made to vibrate. The sand collects in the regions of least motion. ▷early 19th cent.: named after Ernst *Chladni* (1756–1827), German physicist.

chlam·y·date /ˈklami,dāt/ ▶*adj. Zoology* having a mantle or pallium like that of a mollusk.

chla·myd·e·ous kləˈmidēəs ▶*adj. Botany* having or pertaining to a perianth or floral envelope.

chla·myd·i·a /kləˈmidēə/ ▶*n.* (*pl.* same or **-myd·i·ae** /-ˈmidē,ē/) a very small parasitic bacterium that, like a virus, requires the biochemical mechanisms of another cell in order to reproduce. Bacteria of this type cause various diseases including trachoma, psittacosis, and nonspecific urethritis. • Genus *Chlamydia* and order Chlamydiales. ▷1960s: modern Latin (plural), from Greek *khlamus, khlamud-* 'cloak.' —**chla·myd·i·al** *adj.* .

chlam·y·dom·o·nas /,klaməˈdämənəs/ ▶*n. Biology* a common single-celled green alga that lives in water and moist soil and typically has two flagella for swimming. • Genus *Chlamydomonas*, phylum Chlorophyta, kingdom or Plantae (or Protista). ▷late 19th cent.: modern Latin, from Greek *khlamus, khlamud-* 'cloak' + *monas* (see **MONAD**).

chla·myd·o·spore /kləˈmidə,spôr/ ▶*n. Botany* (in certain fungi) a thick-walled hyphal cell that functions as a spore. ▷late 19th cent.: from Greek *khlamus, khlamud-* 'mantle' + **SPORE**.

chla·mys /ˈklaməs; ˈklā-/ ▶*n.* (*pl.* **chla·mys·es** or **chla·my·des** /ˈklamə,dēz/) a short cloak worn by men in ancient Greece. ▷late 17th cent.: from Greek *khlamus* 'mantle.'

Pronunciation Key ə ago; ər over; ˈə or ,ə up; ˈər or ,ər fur; a hat; ā rate; ä car; CH chew; e let; ē see; e(ə)r air; i fit; ī by; i(ə)r ear; NG sing; ō go; ô for; oi boy; o͝o good; o͞o goo; ou out; SH she; TH thin; T͟H then; (h)w why; ZH vision

chlo·as·ma /klō'azmə/ ▸*n.* a temporary condition, typically caused by hormonal changes, in which large brown patches form on the skin, mainly on the face. ▷mid 19th cent.: from Greek *khloazein* 'become green.'

chlor- ▸*comb. form* variant spelling of **CHLORO-** before a vowel (as in *chloracne*).

chlor·ac·ne /klôr'aknē/ ▸*n. Medicine* a skin disease resembling severe acne, caused by exposure to chlorinated chemicals.

chlo·ral /'klôrəl/ ▸*n. Chemistry* a colorless, viscous liquid made by chlorinating acetaldehyde. • Alternative name: **trichloroethanal**; chem. formula: CCl_3CHO. ■ short for **CHLORAL HYDRATE**. ▷mid 19th cent.: from French, blend of *chlore* 'chlorine' and *alcool* 'alcohol.'

chlo·ral hy·drate ▸*n. Chemistry* a colorless crystalline solid made from chloral and used as a sedative. • Chem. formula: $CCl_3CH(OH)_2$.

chlo·ram·bu·cil /klôr'ambyə,sil/ ▸*n. Medicine* a cytotoxic drug used in the treatment of cancer. It belongs to the class of nitrogen mustards. ▷1950s: from *chlor(oethyl)am(inophenyl)bu(tyric acid)*, the systematic name, + *-cil*.

chlo·ra·mine /'klôrə,mēn/ ▸*n. Chemistry* an organic compound containing a chlorine atom bonded to nitrogen, esp. any of a group of sulfonamide derivatives used as antiseptics and disinfectants.

chlo·ram·phen·i·col /,klôr,am'fenə,kôl; -,kōl/ ▸*n. Medicine* an antibiotic used against serious infections such as typhoid fever. • This antibiotic is obtained from the bacterium *Streptomyces venezuelae* or produced synthetically. ▷1940s: from **CHLORO-** (representing **CHLORINE**) + *am(ide)* + **PHENO-** + *ni(tro-)* + *(gly)col*.

chlor·dane /'klôr,dān/ ▸*n.* a synthetic viscous toxic compound used as an insecticide. • A chlorinated derivative of indene; chem. formula: $C_{10}H_6Cl_8$. ▷1940s: from **CHLOR-** (representing **CHLORINE**) + *(in)dene* + **-ANE**[2].

chlor·di·az·e·pox·ide /,klôrdī,azə'päk,sīd/ ▸*n. Medicine* a tranquilizer of the benzodiazepine group, used chiefly to treat anxiety and alcoholism. Also called **LIBRIUM** (*trademark*).

chlo·rel·la /klə'relə/ ▸*n. Biology* a common single-celled green alga of both terrestrial and aquatic habitats, frequently turning stagnant water an opaque green. • Genus *Chlorella*, phylum Chlorophyta, kingdom Plantae (or Protista). ▷modern Latin, diminutive of Greek *khlōros* 'green.'

chlo·ric /'klôrik/ ▸*adj.* of, relating to, or containing chlorine in the pentavalent state.

chlo·ric ac·id /'klôrik/ ▸*n. Chemistry* a colorless liquid acid with strong oxidizing properties. • Chem. formula: $HClO_3$. ■ any acid containing chlorine and oxygen. ▷early 19th cent.: *chloric* from **CHLORINE** + **-IC**.

chlo·ride /'klôr,īd/ ▸*n. Chemistry* a compound of chlorine with another element or group, esp. a salt of the anion Cl^- or an organic compound with chlorine bonded to an alkyl group. ▷early 19th cent.: from **CHLORINE** + **-IDE**.

chlo·ri·nate /'klôrə,nāt/ ▸*v.* [*trans.*] [usu. as *adj.*] (**chlorinated**) impregnate or treat with chlorine: *chlorinated water*. ■ *Chemistry* introduce chlorine into (a compound). —**chlo·ri·na·tion** /,klôrə'nāsHən/ *n.* —**chlo·ri·na·tor** /-,nātər/ *n.*

chlo·rine /'klôr,ēn/ ▸*n.* the chemical element of atomic number 17, a toxic, irritant, pale green gas. (Symbol: **Cl**)

A member of the halogen group, chlorine occurs in nature mainly as sodium chloride in seawater and salt deposits. The gas was used as a poison gas in World War I. Chlorine is added to water supplies as a disinfectant.

▷early 19th cent.: named by Sir Humphrey Davy, from Greek *khlōros* 'green' + **-INE**[4].

chlo·rite[1] /'klôr,īt/ ▸*n.* a dark green mineral consisting of a basic hydrated aluminosilicate of magnesium and iron. It occurs as a constituent of many metamorphic rocks, typically forming flat crystals resembling mica. ▷late 18th cent.: via Latin from Greek *khlōritis*, a green precious stone. —**chlo·rit·ic** /klôr'itik/ *adj.*

chlo·rite[2] ▸*n. Chemistry* a salt of chlorous acid, containing the anion ClO_2^-. ▷mid 19th cent.: from **CHLORINE** + **-ITE**[1].

chlo·ri·toid /'klôrə,toid/ ▸*n.* a greenish-gray or black mineral resembling chlorite, found in metamorphosed clay sediments. It consists of a basic aluminosilicate of iron, often with magnesium.

chloro- (usu. **chlor-** before a vowel) ▸*comb. form* **1** *Biology & Mineralogy* green. **2** *Chemistry* representing **CHLORINE**: *chloroquine*. ▷from Greek *khlōros* 'green.'

chlo·ro·car·bon /'klôrō,kärbən/ ▸*n.* a chemical compound that contains carbon and chlorine or carbon, chlorine, and hydrogen.

chlo·ro·fluor·o·car·bon /,klôrō,flŏŏrō'kärbən/ (abbr.: **CFC**) ▸*n.* any of a class of compounds of carbon, hydrogen, chlorine, and fluorine, typically gases used chiefly in refrigerants and aerosol propellants. They are harmful to the ozone layer in the earth's atmosphere owing to the release of chlorine atoms upon exposure to ultraviolet radiation.

chlo·ro·form /'klôrə,fôrm/ ▸*n.* a colorless, volatile, sweet-smelling liquid used as a solvent and formerly as a general anesthetic. • Alternative name: **trichloromethane**; chem. formula: $CHCl_3$.

▸*v.* [*trans.*] render (someone) unconscious with this substance. ▷mid 19th cent.: from **CHLORO-** (representing **CHLORINE**) + *form-* from **FORMIC ACID**.

chlo·ro·mel·a·nite /,klôrō'melə,nīt/ ▸*n.* a greenish-black variety of jadeite containing a high proportion of iron.

chlo·ro·my·ce·tin /,klôrōmī'sētn/ ▸*n.* trademark for **CHLORAMPHENICOL**. ▷1940s: from **CHLORO-** 'green' + Greek *mukēs*, *mukēt-* 'fungus' + **-IN**[1].

chlo·ro·phyll /'klôrə,fil/ ▸*n.* a green pigment, present in all green plants and in cyanobacteria, responsible for the absorption of light to provide energy for photosynthesis. Its molecule contains a magnesium atom held in a porphyrin ring. ▷early 19th cent.: coined in French from Greek *khlōros* 'green' + *phullon* 'leaf.' —**chlo·ro·phyl·lous** /,klôrə'filəs/ *adj.*

Chlo·roph·y·ta /klôr'äfətə/ *Botany* a phylum that comprises the green algae. They are more recently treated as a phylum of the kingdom Protista. ▷modern Latin (plural), from Greek *khlōros* 'green' + *phuton* 'plant.' —**chlo·ro·phyte** /'klôrə,fīt/ *n.*

chlo·ro·plast /'klôrə,plast/ ▸*n. Botany* (in green plant cells) a plastid that contains chlorophyll and in which photosynthesis takes place. ▷late 19th cent.: coined in German from Greek *khlōros* 'green' + *plastos* 'formed.'

chlo·ro·prene /'klôrə,prēn/ ▸*n. Chemistry* a colorless liquid made from acetylene and hydrochloric acid and polymerized to form neoprene. • Chem. formula: $CH_2{=}CClCH{=}CH_2$. ▷1930s: from **CHLORO-** + a shortened form of **ISOPRENE**.

chlo·ro·quine /'klôrə,kwēn/ ▸*n. Medicine* a synthetic drug related to quinoline, chiefly used against malaria. ▷1940s: from **CHLORO-** + *quin(olin)e*.

chlo·ro·sis /klə'rōsəs/ ▸*n.* **1** *Botany* abnormal reduction or loss of the normal green coloration of leaves of plants, typically caused by iron deficiency in lime-rich soils, or by disease or lack of light. **2** *Medicine* anemia caused by iron deficiency, esp. in adolescent girls, causing a pale, faintly greenish complexion. It was a common diagnosis in the 19th century. —**chlo·rot·ic** /klôr'ätik/ *adj.*

chlo·ro·thi·a·zide /,klôrō'THīə,zīd/ ▸*n. Medicine* a synthetic drug used to treat fluid retention and high blood pressure. It is one of the thiazide diuretics.

chlo·rous ac·id /'klôrəs/ ▸*n. Chemistry* a weak acid with oxidizing properties, formed when chlorine dioxide dissolves in water. • Chem. formula: $HClO_2$.

chlor·prom·a·zine /,klôr'prämə,zēn/ ▸*n. Medicine* a synthetic drug used as a tranquilizer, sedative, and antiemetic. It is a phenothiazine derivative. ▷1950s: from **CHLORO-** + *prom(eth)azine*.

chlor·pyr·i·fos /klôr'pirə,fäs/ ▸*n.* a broad-spectrum organophosphate insecticide, widely used in food and crop agriculture and as a termiticide.

chlor·tet·ra·cy·cline /,klôr,tetrə'sī,klēn/ ▸*n. Medicine* an antibiotic of the tetracycline group, active against many bacterial and fungal infections. • This antibiotic is obtained from the bacterium *Streptomyces aureofaciens* or produced synthetically.

cho·a·no·cyte /kō'anə,sīt/ ▸*n. Zoology* a flagellated cell with a collar of protoplasm at the base of the flagellum, numbers of which line the internal chambers of sponges. ▷late 19th cent.: from Greek *khoanē* 'funnel' + **-CYTE**.

choc·a·hol·ic ▸*n.* variant spelling of **CHOCOHOLIC**.

chock /CHäk/ ▸*n.* **1** a wedge or block placed against a wheel or rounded object, to prevent it from moving. ■ a support on which a rounded structure, such as a cask or the hull of a boat, may be placed to keep it steady. **2** a fitting with a gap at the top, through which a rope or line is run.

▸*v.* [*trans.*] (often **be chocked**) prevent the forward movement of (a wheel or vehicle) with a chock. ■ support (a boat, cask, etc.) on chocks. ▷Middle English: probably from an Old Northern French variant of Old French *çouche*, *çoche* 'block, log,' of unknown ultimate origin.

chock·a·block /'CHäkə,bläk/ (also **chock-a-block**) ▸*adj.* [*predic.*] *informal* crammed full of people or things: *the manual is* **chockablock with** *information*. ▷mid 19th cent. (originally in nautical use, with reference to tackle having the two blocks run close together): from *chock* (in **CHOCK-FULL**) and **BLOCK**.

chock-full /'CHäk 'fŏŏl; 'CHək-/ ▸*adj.* [*predic.*] *informal* filled to overflowing: *my briefcase is chock-full of notes*. ▷late Middle English: of unknown origin; later associated with **CHOCK**.

chock·stone /'CHäk,stōn/ ▸*n. Climbing* a stone that has become wedged in a vertical cleft.

choc·o·hol·ic /,CHäkə'hôlik; ,CHô-; -'hälik/ (also **choc·a·hol·ic**) ▸*n. informal* a person who is addicted to or excessively fond of chocolate.

choc·o·late /'CHäk(ə)lit; 'CHôk-/ ▸*n.* a food preparation in the form of a paste or solid block made from roasted and ground cacao seeds, typically sweetened: *a bar of chocolate* | [as *adj.*] *a chocolate cookie*. ■ a candy made of or covered with this: *a box of chocolates*. ■ a drink made by mixing milk with chocolate: *sipping on* **hot chocolate**. ■ a deep brown color: [as *adj.*] *huge spiders, yellow and* **chocolate brown**. ▷early 17th cent. (in the sense 'a drink made with chocolate'): from French *chocolat* or Spanish *chocolate*, from Nahuatl *chocolatl* 'food made from cacao seeds,' influenced by unrelated *cacaua-atl* 'drink made from cacao.' —**choc·o·lat·y** (also **choc·o·lat·ey**) *adj.*

choc·o·late chip ▸*n.* [usu. as *adj.*] a small piece of chocolate used in making cookies and other sweet foods: *chocolate-chip ice cream*.

choc·o·late mousse ▸*n.* see **MOUSSE**.

choc·o·late spot ▸*n.* a fungal disease affecting field and broad beans, characterized by dark brown spots on all parts of the plant. • This is caused by the fungus *Botrytis fabae* (sometimes the gray mold *B. cinerea*), phylum Ascomycota.

choc·o·late vine ▸*n.* a fast-growing, shade-tolerant woody twining vine, native to Asia and introduced as an ornamental in the U.S. It has escaped cultivation and threatens native plants in some woodland habitats. • *Akebia quinata*, family Lardizabalaceae.

cho·co·la·tier /,CHôk(ə)lə'ti(ə)r; ,SHôkəlä'tyā/ ▸*n.* a maker or seller of chocolate. ▷late 19th cent.: French.

Choc·taw /'CHäk,tô/ ▸*n.* (*pl.* same or **-taws**) **1** a member of a native people now living mainly in Mississippi. **2** the Muskogean language of this people, closely related to Chickasaw. **3** *Figure Skating* a step from one edge of a skate to the other edge of the other skate in the opposite direction.

▸*adj.* of or relating to the Choctaw or their language. ▷from Choctaw *čahta*.

choice /CHois/ ▸*n.* an act of selecting or making a decision when faced with two or more possibilities: *the* **choice between** *good and evil*. ■ the right or ability to make, or possibility of making, such a selection: *I had to do it, I had no choice*. ■ a range of possibilities from which one or more may be selected: *you can have a sofa made to order in a choice of over forty fabrics*. ■ a course of action, thing, or person that is selected or decided upon: *this CD drive is the perfect choice for your computer*.

▸*adj.* **1** (esp. of food) of very good quality: *he picked some choice early plums*. **2** (of words, phrases, or language) rude and abusive: *he had a few choice words at his command*. ▷Middle English: from Old French *chois*, from *choisir* 'choose,' of Germanic origin and related to **CHOOSE**. —**choice·ly** *adv.* —**choice·ness** *n.*

▸*PHRASES* □ **by choice** of one's own volition. □ **of choice** selected as one's favorite or the best: *champagne was his drink of choice*. □ **of one's choice** that one chooses or has chosen: *the college of her choice*.

choil /CHoil/ ▸*n.* the end of a knife's cutting edge that is nearer to the handle. ▷late 19th cent.: of unknown origin.

choir /'kwīr/ ▸*n.* an organized group of singers, typically one that takes part in church services or performs regularly in public: *a church choir*. ■ one of two or more subdivisions of such a group performing together: *his famous* Spem in alium *for eight five-part choirs*. ■ the part of a cathedral or large church between the altar and the nave, used by the choir and clergy. ■ a group of instruments of one family playing together: *a clarinet choir*. ▷Middle English *quer*, *quere*, from Old French *quer*, from Latin *chorus* (see CHORUS). The spelling change in the 17th cent. was due to association with Latin *chorus* and modern French *choeur*.

choir·boy /ˈkwīrˌboi/ ▸*n.* a boy who sings in a church or cathedral choir.

choir·girl /ˈkwīrˌgərl/ ▸*n.* a girl who sings in a church or cathedral choir.

choir·mas·ter /ˈkwīrˌmastər/ ▸*n.* the conductor of a choir.

choir or·gan ▸*n.* a separate division of many large organs, played using a third manual (keyboard), and typically having distinctively toned stops.

choir stall ▸*n.* (usu. **choir stalls**) a fixed seat for one or more people in the choir of a church or chapel.

choi·sy·a /SHwäˈzēə/ ▸*n.* an evergreen Mexican shrub with sweet-scented white flowers, widely grown as an ornamental. • *Choisya ternata*, family Rutaceae. ▷named after Jacques D. *Choisy* (1799–1859), Swiss botanist.

choke[1] /CHōk/ ▸*v.* **1** [*intrans.*] (of a person or animal) have severe difficulty in breathing because of a constricted or obstructed throat or a lack of air: *Willie* ***choked on*** *a mouthful of soda.* ■ [*trans.*] hinder or obstruct the breathing of (a person or animal) in such a way. ■ [*trans.*] retard the growth of or kill (a plant) by depriving it of light, air, or nourishment: *the bracken will choke the wild gladiolus.* ■ [*trans.*] (often **be choked with**) fill (a passage or space), esp. so as to make movement difficult or impossible: *the roads were choked with traffic.* ■ [*trans.*] prevent or suppress (the occurrence of something): *higher rates of interest* ***choke off*** *investment demand.* **2** [*trans.*] (often **be choked**) overwhelm and make (someone) speechless with a strong and typically negative feeling or emotion: *she was choked with angry emotion* | [*intrans.*] *I just* ***choked up*** *reading it.* ■ [*intrans.*] *informal* (in sports) fail to perform at a crucial point of a game or contest owing to a failure of nerve: *we were the only team not to choke when it came to the crunch.* **3** [*trans.*] enrich the fuel mixture in (a gasoline engine) by reducing the intake of air.

▸*phrasal v.* □ **choke something back** suppress a strong emotion or the expression of such an emotion: *Liz was choking back her anger.* □ **choke something down** swallow something with difficulty: *I attempted to choke down supper.* □ **choke up** (in sports) grip (a bat, racket, etc.) further from the narrow end than is usual: *he* ***choked up on*** *the bat a few inches.*

▸*n.* **1** a valve in the carburetor of a gasoline engine that is used to reduce the amount of air in the fuel mixture when the engine is started. ■ a knob that controls such a valve. ■ a narrowed part of a shotgun bore, typically near the muzzle and serving to restrict the spread of the shot. ■ *informal* an electrical inductor, esp. an inductance coil used to smooth the variations of an alternating current or to alter its phase. **2** an action or sound of a person or animal having or seeming to have difficulty in breathing: *a little choke of laughter.* ▷Middle English: from Old English *ācēocian* (verb), from *cēoce* (see CHEEK).

choke[2] ▸*n.* the inedible mass of silky fibers at the center of a globe artichoke. ▷late 17th cent.: probably a confusion of the ending of *artichoke* with CHOKE[1].

choke·ber·ry /ˈCHōkˌberē/ ▸*n.* a North American shrub of the rose family, with white flowers and red autumn foliage, cultivated as an ornamental. • Genus *Aronia*, family Rosaceae: several species, esp. the **red chokeberry** (*A. arbutifolia*), **purple chokeberry** (*A. floribunda*), and **black chokeberry** (*A. melanocarpa*), each named for the color of its fruits. ■ the berrylike fruit of this shrub, which is bitter and unpalatable.

choke chain ▸*n.* a chain formed into a loop by passing one end through a ring on the other, placed around a dog's neck to exert control by causing pressure on the windpipe when the dog pulls.

choke·cher·ry /ˈCHōkˌCHerē/ ▸*n.* a North American cherry with an edible astringent fruit that is more palatable when cooked. • *Prunus virginiana*, family Rosaceae.

choke·damp /ˈCHōkˌdamp/ ▸*n.* another term for BLACKDAMP.

choke·hold /ˈCHōkˌhōld/ ▸*n.* a tight grip around a person's neck, used to restrain him or her by restricting breathing: *the police have banned chokeholds* | *figurative the southern delegates had the convention in a chokehold.*

choke point ▸*n.* a point of congestion or blockage: *the tunnel is a choke point at rush hour.*

chok·er /ˈCHōkər/ ▸*n.* **1** a close-fitting necklace or ornamental neckband. ■ a clerical or other high collar. **2** a cable looped around a log to drag it.

cho·ki·dar /ˈCHōkiˌdär/ ▸*n.* variant spelling of CHOWKIDAR.

Chok·we /ˈCHäkwē/ ▸*n.* (*pl.* same) **1** a member of a people living in the Democratic Republic of the Congo (formerly Zaire) and northern Angola. **2** the Bantu language of this people.

▸*adj.* of or relating to this people or their language.

chok·y /ˈCHōkē/ ▸*adj.* (**chok·i·er**, **chok·i·est**) having or causing difficulty in breathing: *the whole place was choky with tear gas.* ■ breathless and overwhelmed with emotion: *"Nick," she said, suddenly choky.*

cho·la /ˈCHōlə/ ▸*n.* a Latin American woman or girl with Indian blood; a mestiza: [as *adj.*] *a couple of chola girls.* ■ the girlfriend of a cholo. ▷mid 19th cent.: American Spanish (see CHOLO).

cho·lan·gi·og·ra·phy /kəˌlanjēˈägrəfē/ ▸*n.* *Medicine* X-ray examination of the bile ducts, used to locate and identify an obstruction. ▷1930s: coined in Spanish from Greek *kholē* 'bile' + *angeion* 'vessel' + *-graphia* (see -GRAPHY). —**cho·lan·gi·o·gram** /kəˈlanjēəˌgram/ *n.*

chole- (also **chol-** before a vowel) ▸*comb. form* *Medicine & Chemistry* relating to bile or the bile ducts: *cholelithiasis* | *cholesterol.* ▷from Greek *kholē* 'gall, bile.'

cho·le·cal·cif·er·ol /ˌkōləˌkalˈsifəˌrôl; -ˌrōl/ ▸*n.* *Biochemistry* one of the D vitamins, a sterol that is formed by the action of sunlight on dehydrocholesterol in the skin. Deficiency of this vitamin affects calcium levels, causing rickets in children and osteomalacia in adults. Also called VITAMIN D_3.

cholecyst- ▸*comb. form* relating to the gallbladder: *cholecystectomy.* ▷from modern Latin *cholecystis* 'gallbladder.'

cho·le·cys·tec·to·my /ˌkōləˌsisˈtektəmē/ ▸*n.* (*pl.* **-mies**) surgical removal of the gallbladder.

cho·le·cys·ti·tis /kōləˌsisˈtītis/ ▸*n.* *Medicine* inflammation of the gallbladder.

cho·le·cys·tog·ra·phy /ˌkōləˌsisˈtägrəfē/ ▸*n.* *Medicine* X-ray examination of the gallbladder, esp. used to detect the presence of gallstones.

cho·le·cys·to·ki·nin /ˌkōləˌsistōˈkīnən/ ▸*n.* *Biochemistry* a hormone that is secreted by cells in the duodenum and stimulates the release of bile into the intestine and the secretion of enzymes by the pancreas.

cho·le·li·thi·a·sis /ˌkōləˌləˈTHīəsəs/ ▸*n.* *Medicine* the formation of gallstones.

cho·lent /ˈCHôlənt; ˈCHəl-/ ▸*n.* a Jewish Sabbath dish of slowly baked meat and vegetables, prepared on a Friday and cooked overnight. ▷from Yiddish *tsholnt*.

chol·er /ˈkälər/ ▸*n.* (in medieval science and medicine) one of the four bodily humors, identified with bile, believed to be associated with a peevish or irascible temperament. Also called YELLOW BILE. ■ *poetic/literary* or *archaic* anger or irascibility. ▷late Middle English (also denoting diarrhea): from Old French *colere* 'bile, anger,' from Latin *cholera* 'diarrhea' (from Greek *kholera*), which in late Latin acquired the senses 'bile or anger,' from Greek *kholē* 'bile.'

chol·er·a /ˈkälərə/ ▸*n.* an infectious and often fatal bacterial disease of the small intestine, typically contracted from infected water supplies and causing severe vomiting and diarrhea. • The disease is caused by the bacterium *Vibrio cholerae*. See VIBRIO. ▷late Middle English (originally denoting bile and later applied to various ailments involving vomiting and diarrhea): from Latin (see CHOLER). The current sense dates from the early 19th cent.

chol·e·ra·ic /ˌkäləˈrā-ik/ ▸*adj.* *archaic* infected with cholera.

chol·er·ic /ˈkälərik; kəˈlerik/ ▸*adj.* bad-tempered or irritable. ■ *historical* influenced by or predominating in the humor called choler: *a choleric disposition.* ▷Middle English (in the sense 'bilious'): from Old French *cholerique*, via Latin from Greek *kholerikos*, from *kholera* (see CHOLER). —**chol·er·i·cal·ly** *adv.*

cho·les·ter·ol /kəˈlestəˌrôl; -ˌrōl/ ▸*n.* a compound of the sterol type found in most body tissues, including the blood and the nerves. Cholesterol and its derivatives are important constituents of cell membranes and precursors of other steroid compounds, but high concentrations in the blood (mainly derived from animal fats in the diet) are thought to promote atherosclerosis. • Chem. formula: $C_{27}H_{45}OH$. ▷late 19th cent.: from Greek *kholē* 'bile' + *stereos* 'stiff' + -OL.

cho·lic ac·id /ˈkōlik/ ▸*n.* *Biochemistry* a compound produced by oxidation of cholesterol. It is a steroidal fatty acid and its salts are present in bile. ▷mid 19th cent.: from Greek *kholikos*, from *kholē* 'bile.'

cho·line /ˈkōˌlēn/ ▸*n.* *Biochemistry* a strongly basic compound occurring widely in living tissues and important in the synthesis and transport of lipids. • Chem. formula: $HON(CH_3)_3CH_2CH_2OH$. ▷mid 19th cent.: coined in German from Greek *kholē* 'bile.'

cho·lin·er·gic /ˌkōləˈnərjik/ ▸*adj.* *Physiology* **1** relating to or denoting nerve cells in which acetylcholine acts as a neurotransmitter. Contrasted with ADRENERGIC. **2** releasing or responding to acetylcholine. ▷1930s: from CHOLINE + Greek *ergon* 'work' + -IC.

cho·lin·es·ter·ase /ˌkōləˈnestəˌrās; -ˌrāz/ ▸*n.* *Biochemistry* an enzyme, esp. acetylcholinesterase, that hydrolyzes esters of choline.

chol·la /ˈCHoi(y)ə/ ▸*n.* a cactus with a cylindrical stem, native to Mexico and the southwestern U.S. • Genus *Opuntia*, family Cactaceae. ▷mid 19th cent.: Mexican Spanish use of Spanish *cholla* 'skull, head,' of unknown origin.

cho·lo /ˈCHōlō/ ▸*n.* (*pl.* **-los**) a Latin American with Indian blood; a mestizo. ■ *informal, offensive* a lower-class Mexican, esp. in an urban area. ■ a teenage boy, esp. in a Mexican-American community, who is a member of a street gang. ▷mid 19th cent.: American Spanish, from *Chololl*án (now *Cholula*), in Mexico.

cho·metz ▸*n.* variant spelling of CHAMETZ.

chomp /CHämp; CHômp/ ▸*v.* [*intrans.*] **1** munch or chew vigorously and noisily: *he* ***chomped on*** *his sandwich.* ■ (of a horse) make a noisy biting or chewing action. **2** fret impatiently: *he waited, chomping at her nonappearance.*

▸*n.* [in *sing.*] a chewing noise or action. ▷mid 17th cent.: probably imitative.

▸*PHRASE* □ **chomp** (or **champ** or **chafe**) **at the bit** be restless and impatient to start doing something.

Chom·sky /ˈCHäm(p)skē/, (Avram) Noam (1928–), U.S. theoretical linguist, noted for expounding the theory of generative grammar. He also theorized that linguistic behavior is innate, not learned, and that all languages share the same underlying grammatical base. Chomsky opposed U.S. involvement in the Vietnam and Gulf Wars. Notable works: *Syntactic Structures* (1957) and *Aspects of the Theory of Syntax* (1965).

Chon·drich·thy·es /känˈdrikTHēˌēz/ *Zoology* a class of fishes that includes those with a cartilaginous skeleton. Compare with OSTEICHTHYES. ▷modern Latin, from Greek *khondros* 'cartilage' + *ikhthus* 'fish.'

chon·drite /ˈkänˌdrīt/ ▸*n.* a stony meteorite containing small mineral granules (chondrules). ▷mid 19th cent.: from Greek *khondros* 'granule' + -ITE[1]. —**chon·drit·ic** /känˈdritik/ *adj.*

chondro- ▸*comb. form* of or relating to cartilage: *chondrocyte.* ▷from Greek *khondros* 'grain or cartilage.'

chon·dro·cra·ni·um /ˌkändrōˈkrānēəm/ ▸*n.* *Zoology & Embryology* the primary skull of vertebrates, composed of cartilage, which in humans and most other vertebrates is replaced by bone during development.

chon·dro·cyte /ˈkändrəˌsīt/ ▸*n.* *Biology* a cell that has secreted the matrix of cartilage and become embedded in it.

chon·dro·i·tin /känˈdroitn; -ˈdrōətn/ ▸*n.* *Biochemistry* a compound that is a major constituent of cartilage and other connective tissue. It is a glycosaminoglycan and occurs mainly in the form of sulfate esters. ▷late 19th cent.: from CHONDRO- + -ITE[1] + -IN[1].

chon·drule /ˈkändrōōl/ ▸*n.* a spheroidal mineral grain present in large numbers in some stony meteorites.

Chong·jin /ˈCHəNGˈjēn/ a port on the northeastern coast of North Korea; pop. 754,100.

Chong·qing /ˈCHəNGˈkiNG/ (also **Chung·king**) a city in Sichuan province, in central China, on the Yangtze River; pop. 2,960,000. It was the capital of China from 1938 to 1946.

choo-choo /ˈCHōō ˌCHōō/ (also **choo-choo train**) ▸*n.* a child's word for a railroad train or locomotive, esp. a steam engine. ▷early 20th cent.: imitative.

choose /CHōōz/ ▸*v.* (*past* **chose** /CHōz/; *past part.* **cho·sen** /ˈCHōzən/) [*trans.*] pick out or select (someone or something) as being the best or most appropriate of two or more alternatives: *he chose a seat facing the door* | [*intrans.*] *now it's my turn to choose.* ■ [*intrans.*] decide on a course of action, typically after rejecting alternatives: [with *infinitive*] *he chose to go I'll stay as long as I choose.* ▷Old English *cēosan*, of Germanic origin; related to Dutch *kiezen*. **—choos·er** *n.*

▸*PHRASES* □ **cannot choose but do something** *formal* have no alternative to doing something. □ **there is little** (or **nothing**) **to choose between** there is little or no difference between.

choos·y /'CHo͞ozē/ ▸*adj.* (**choos·i·er**, **choos·i·est**) *informal* overly fastidious in making a choice. **—choos·i·ly** /-zəlē/ *adv.* **—choos·i·ness** *n.*

chop /CHäp/ ▸*v.* (**chopped**, **chop·ping**) [*trans.*] cut (something) into small pieces with repeated sharp blows using an ax or knife: *they* ***chopped up*** *the pulpit for firewood | finely chop the parsley.* ■ (**chop something off**) remove by cutting: *they chopped off all her hair.* ■ cut through the base of (something, esp. a tree) with blows from an ax or similar implement, in order to fell it: *the boy* ***chopped down*** *eight trees* | [*intrans.*] *the men were* ***chopping at*** *the undergrowth with machetes.* ■ strike (a ball) with a short heavy blow, as if cutting at something. ■ (usu. **be chopped**) abolish or reduce the size or extent of (something) in a way regarded as brutally sudden: *their training courses are to be chopped.*

▸*n.* **1** a downward cutting blow or movement, typically with the hand: *an effective chop to the back of the neck.* **2** a thick slice of meat, esp. pork or lamb, adjacent to, and typically including, a rib. **3** crushed or ground grain used as animal feed. **4** [in *sing.*] the broken motion of water, typically due to the action of the wind against the tide: *we started our run into a two-foot chop.* ▷late Middle English: variant of **CHAP**[1].

▸*PHRASE* □ **chop logic** argue in a tiresomely pedantic way; quibble. [mid 16th cent.: from a dialect use of *chop* meaning 'bandy words.']

chop-chop /'CHäp 'CHäp/ ▸*adv.* & *exclam.* quickly; quick: *"Two beers, chop-chop," Jimmy called.* ▷mid 19th cent.: pidgin English, based on Chinese dialect *kuai-kuai*. Compare with **CHOPSTICK**.

chop·fall·en /'CHäp,fôlən/ ▸*adj.* variant spelling of **CHAPFALLEN**.

chop·house /'CHäp,hous/ ▸*n.* a restaurant that specializes in steaks, chops, and similar fare.

Cho·pin[1] /'SHō,pan; SHō'pan/, Frédéric (François) (1810–49), French composer and pianist; born in Poland; Polish name *Fryderyk Franciszek Szopen*. Writing almost exclusively for the piano, he composed numerous mazurkas and polonaises inspired by Polish folk music, as well as nocturnes, preludes, and two piano concertos (1829; 1830).

Cho·pin[2] /'SHō,pan; SHō'pan/, Kate (O'Flaherty) (1851–1904), U.S. novelist and short-story writer. Notable works: *Bayou Folk* (1894), *A Night in Acidie* (1897), and *The Awakening* (1899).

chop·per /'CHäpər/ ▸*n.* **1** a person, tool, or machine that chops. ■ a butcher's cleaver. ■ a device for regularly interrupting an electric current or a beam of light or particles. ■ (**choppers**) *informal* teeth. **2** *informal* a helicopter. **3** *informal* a motorcycle, esp. one with high handlebars and the front-wheel fork extended forward. **4** *Baseball* a batted ball that makes a high bounce after hitting the ground in fair territory: *Bell followed with a high chopper to the third baseman.*

chop·ping block ▸*n.* a block for chopping something on, in particular: ■ a block for chopping wood. ■ a block for chopping food such as meat, vegetables, and herbs. ■ *historical* an executioner's block.

▸*PHRASE* □ **on the chopping block** likely to be abolished or drastically reduced.

chop·py /'CHäpē/ ▸*adj.* (**chop·pi·er**, **chop·pi·est**) (of a sea or river) having many small waves. ▷early 17th cent. (in the sense 'full of chaps or clefts'): from **CHOP** + **-Y**[1]. **—chop·pi·ly** /'CHäpəlē/ *adv.* **—chop·pi·ness** *n.*

chops /CHäps/ ▸*plural n. informal* **1** a person's or animal's mouth or jaws: *a smack in the chops.* ■ a person's cheeks; jowls. **2** the technical skill of a musician, esp. one who plays jazz: *when I'm on tour, my chops go down.* ▷late Middle English: variant of **CHAP**[3].

▸*PHRASES* □ **bust one's chops** *informal* exert oneself. □ **bust someone's chops** *informal* nag or criticize someone.

chop shop ▸*n. informal* a place where stolen vehicles are dismantled so that the parts can be sold or used to repair other stolen vehicles.

chop·sock·y /'CHäp,säkē/ ▸*n.* [usu. as *adj.*] *informal* kung fu or a similar martial art, esp. as depicted in violent action movies: *chopsocky epics from Hong Kong.* ▷1970s: perhaps humorously, suggested by **CHOP SUEY**.

chop·stick /'CHäp,stik/ ▸*n.* (usu. **chopsticks**) each of a pair of small, thin, tapered sticks of wood, ivory, or plastic, held together in one hand and used as eating utensils, esp. by the Chinese, the Japanese, and other people in eastern Asia. ▷late 17th cent.: pidgin English, from *chop* 'quick' + **STICK**[1], translating Chinese dialect *kuaizi*, literally 'nimble ones.' Compare with **CHOP-CHOP**.

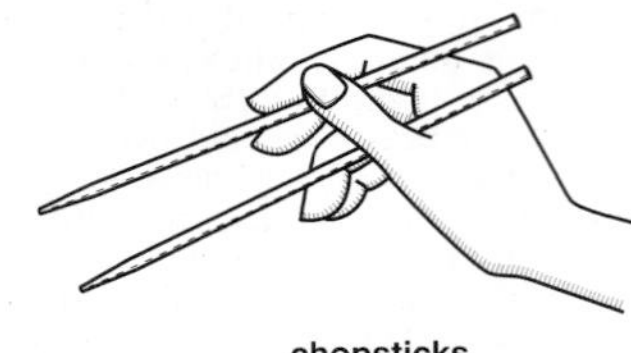

chopsticks

chop su·ey /,CHäp 'so͞oē/ ▸*n.* a Chinese-style dish of meat stewed and fried with bean sprouts, bamboo shoots, and onions, and often served with rice. ▷late 19th cent.: from Chinese (Cantonese dialect) *tsaâp suì* 'mixed bits.'

cho·ral /'kôrəl/ ▸*adj.* composed for or sung by a choir or chorus: *a choral work | choral singing.* ■ engaged in or concerned with singing: *a choral scholar.* ▷late 16th cent.: from medieval Latin *choralis*, from Latin *chorus* (see **CHORUS**). **—cho·ral·ly** *adv.*

cho·rale /kə'ral; -'räl/ ▸*n.* **1** a musical composition (or part of one) consisting of or resembling a harmonized version of a simple, stately hymn tune. **2** a choir or choral society. ▷mid 19th cent.: from German *Choral(gesang)*, translating medieval Latin *cantus choralis*.

cho·rale pre·lude ▸*n.* an organ piece based on a chorale.

cho·ral speak·ing ▸*n.* the recitation of poetry or prose by a chorus or ensemble.

chord[1] /kôrd/ ▸*n.* a group of (typically three or more) notes sounded together, as a basis of harmony: *the triumphal opening chords | a G major chord.*

▸*v.* [*intrans.*] [usu. as *n.*] (**chording**) play, sing, or arrange notes in chords. ▷Middle English *cord*, from **ACCORD**. The spelling change in the 18th cent. was due to confusion with **CHORD**[2]. The original sense was 'agreement, reconciliation,' later 'a musical concord or harmonious sound'; the current sense dates from the mid 18th cent. **—chord·al** /'kôrdl/ *adj.*

chord[2] ▸*n.* **1** *Mathematics* a straight line joining the ends of an arc. ■ *Aeronautics* the width of an airfoil from leading to trailing edge. ■ *Engineering* each of the two principal members of a truss. **2** *Anatomy* variant spelling of **CORD**: *spinal chord.* **3** *poetic/literary* a string on a harp or other instrument. ▷mid 16th cent. (in the anatomical sense): a later spelling (influenced by Latin *chorda* 'rope') of **CORD**.

▸*PHRASES* □ **strike** (or **touch**) **a chord** affect or stir someone's emotions: *the issue of food safety strikes a chord with almost everyone.* [with figurative reference to the emotions being the 'strings' of the mind visualized as a musical instrument.] □ **strike** (or **touch**) **the right chord** skillfully appeal to or arouse a particular emotion in others: *Dickens knew how to strike the right chord in the hearts of his readers.*

Chor·da·ta /kôr'dätə; -'dātə/ *Zoology* a large phylum of animals that includes the vertebrates together with the sea squirts and lancelets. They are distinguished by the possession of a notochord at some stage during their development. ▷modern Latin (plural), from Latin *chorda* (see **CHORD**[2]), on the pattern of words such as *Vertebrata*. **—chor·date** /'kôrdət; -,dāt/ *n.* & *adj.*

chor·do·phone /'kôrdə,fōn/ ▸*n. technical Music* a stringed instrument.

chor·do·to·nal /,kôrdə'tōnl/ ▸*adj. Entomology* (in insects) denoting sense organs that are responsive to mechanical and sound vibrations. ▷late 19th cent.: from **CHORD**[2] + **TONAL**.

chore /CHôr/ ▸*n.* a routine task, esp. a household one. ■ an unpleasant but necessary task: *he sees interviews as a chore.* ▷mid 18th cent. (originally dialect and U.S.): variant of obsolete *char* or *chare* (see **CHARWOMAN**).

cho·re·a /kə'rēə/ ▸*n. Medicine* a neurological disorder characterized by jerky involuntary movements affecting esp. the shoulders, hips, and face. See also **HUNTINGTON'S CHOREA**, **SYDENHAM'S CHOREA**. ▷late 17th cent.: via Latin from Greek *khoreia* 'dancing in unison,' from *khoros* 'chorus.'

cho·re·o·graph /'kôrēə,graf/ ▸*v.* [*trans.*] compose the sequence of steps and moves for (a performance of dance or ice skating): *he is now choreographing a ballet.* ■ *figurative* plan and control (an event or operation): *the committee choreographs the movement of troops.* ▷1940s: back-formation from **CHOREOGRAPHY**. **—cho·re·og·ra·pher** /,kôrē'ägrəfər/ *n.*

cho·re·og·ra·phy /,kôrē'ägrəfē/ ▸*n.* the sequence of steps and movements in dance or figure skating, esp. in a ballet or other staged dance: *the lively choreography reflects the themes of the original play.* ■ the art or practice of designing such sequences. ■ the written notation for such a sequence. ▷late 18th cent. (in the sense 'written notation of dancing'): from Greek *khoreia* 'dancing in unison' (from *khoros* 'chorus') + **-GRAPHY**. **—cho·re·o·graph·ic** /,kôrēə'grafik/ *adj.* **—cho·re·o·graph·i·cal·ly** /,kôrēə'grafik(ə)lē/ *adv.*

cho·re·ol·o·gy /,kôrē'äləjē/ ▸*n.* the notation of dance movement. ▷1960s: from Greek *khoreia* 'dancing in unison' (from *khoros* 'chorus') + **-LOGY**. **—cho·re·ol·o·gist** /-jist/ *n.*

cho·ri·am·bus /,kôrē'ambəs/ (also **cho·ri·amb** /'kôrē,am(b)/) ▸*n.* (*pl.* **-bi** /-bī; -bē/) a metrical foot consisting of two short (or unstressed) syllables between two long (or stressed) ones. ▷late 18th cent.: via late Latin from Greek *khoriambos*, from *khoreios* 'of the dance' + *iambos* (see **IAMBUS**). **—cho·ri·am·bic** /-'ambik/ *adj.*

cho·ric /'kôrik/ ▸*adj.* belonging to, spoken by, or resembling a chorus in drama or recitation. ▷mid 19th cent.: via late Latin from Greek *khorikos*, from *khoros* 'chorus.'

cho·rine /'kôr,ēn/ ▸*n.* a chorus girl. ▷1920s (originally U.S.): from **CHORUS** + **-INE**[3].

chorio- ▸*comb. form* representing **CHORION** or **CHOROID**.

cho·ri·o·al·lan·to·ic /,kôrēō,alən'tō-ik/ ▸*adj. Embryology* relating to or denoting fused chorionic and allantoic membranes around a fetus.

cho·ri·o·car·ci·no·ma /,kôrēō,kärsə'nōmə/ ▸*n.* (*pl.* **-no·mas** or **-no·ma·ta** /-'nōmətə/) *Medicine* a malignant tumor of the uterus that originates in the cells of the chorion of a fetus.

cho·ri·oid /'kôrē,oid/ ▸*adj.* another term for **CHOROID**.

cho·ri·on /'kôrē,än/ ▸*n. Embryology* the outermost membrane surrounding an embryo of a reptile, bird, or mammal. In mammals (including humans), it contributes to the formation of the placenta. ▷mid 16th cent.: from Greek *khorion*. **—cho·ri·on·ic** /,kôrē'änik/ *adj.*

cho·ri·on·ic vil·lus sam·pling (abbr.: **CVS**) ▸*n. Medicine* a test made in early pregnancy to detect congenital abnormalities in the fetus. A tiny tissue sample is taken from the villi of the chorion, which forms the fetal part of the placenta.

chor·is·ter /'kôrəstər; 'kär-/ ▸*n.* **1** a member of a choir, esp. a child or young person singing the treble part in a church choir. **2** a person who leads the singing of a church choir or congregation. ▷late Middle English *queristre*, from an Anglo-Norman French variant of Old French *cueriste*, from *quer* (see **CHOIR**). The change in the first syllable in the 16th cent. was due to association with obsolete *chorist* 'member of a choir or chorus,'but the older form *quirister* long survived.

cho·ri·zo /CHə'rēzō; -sō/ ▸*n.* (*pl.* **-zos**) a spicy Spanish pork sausage. ▷Spanish.

cho·rog·ra·phy /kə'rägrəfē/ ▸*n. chiefly historical* the systematic description and mapping of regions or districts. ▷mid 16th cent.: via Latin from Greek *khōrographia*, from *khōra* or *khōros* 'region.' **—cho·rog·ra·pher** /-fər/ *n.* **—cho·ro·graph·ic** /,kôrə'grafik/ *adj.*

cho·roid /'kôr,oid/ (also **cho·ri·oid** /'kôrē,oid/) ▸*adj.* resembling the chorion, particularly in containing many blood vessels.

▸*n.* (also **choroid coat**) the pigmented vascular layer of the eyeball between the retina and the sclera. ▷mid 17th cent.: from Greek *khoroeidēs* (adjective), alteration of *khorioeidēs*, from *khorion* (see **CHORION**). **—cho·roi·dal** /kə'roidl/ *adj.* .

cho·roid plex·us ▸*n.* (*pl.* same or **plex·uses**) a network of blood vessels in each ventricle of the brain. It is derived from the pia mater and produces the cerebrospinal fluid.

chor·o·pleth map /'kôrə,pleTH/ ▸*n.* a map that uses differences in shading, coloring, or the placing of symbols within predefined areas to indicate the average values of a property or quantity in those areas. Compare with **ISOPLETH**. ▷1930s: *choropleth* from Greek *khōra* 'region' + *plēthos* 'multitude.'

Chor·ril·los /CHō'rē-ōs/ a town in west central Peru, a resort and suburb south of Lima; pop. 213,000.

chor·tle /ˈCHôrtl/ ▸*v.* [*intrans.*] laugh in a breathy, gleeful way; chuckle: *he **chortled at** his own pun.*
▸*n.* a breathy, gleeful laugh: *Thomas gave a chortle.* ▷1871: coined by Lewis Carroll in *Through the Looking Glass*; probably a blend of CHUCKLE and SNORT.

cho·rus /ˈkôrəs/ ▸*n.* (*pl.* **-rus·es**) **1** a large organized group of singers, esp. one that performs together with an orchestra or opera company. ■ a group of singers or dancers performing together in a supporting role in a stage musical or opera. ■ a piece of choral music, esp. one forming part of a larger work such as an opera or oratorio. ■ a part of a song that is repeated after each verse, typically by more than one singer. ■ a simple song for group singing, esp. in informal Christian worship. **2** (in ancient Greek tragedy) a group of performers who comment on the main action, typically speaking and moving together. ■ a simultaneous utterance of something by many people: *a growing **chorus of** complaint | "Good morning," we replied **in chorus**.* ■ a single character who speaks the prologue and other linking parts of the play, esp. in Elizabethan drama. ■ a section of text spoken by the chorus in drama. ■ a device used with an amplified musical instrument to give the impression that more than one instrument is being played: [as *adj.*] *a chorus pedal.*
▸*v.* (**-rused**, **-rus·ing**) [*trans.*] (of a group of people) say the same thing at the same time: *they chorused a noisy amen* | [with *direct speech*] *"Morning, Father," the children chorused.* ▷mid 16th cent. (denoting a character speaking the prologue and epilogue in a play and serving to comment on events): from Latin, from Greek *khoros.*

cho·rus girl ▸*n.* a young woman who sings or dances in the chorus of a musical.

Cho·rzów /ˈhô,ZHōōf; ˈkô-/ a transportation and industrial center in southern Poland; pop. 133,000.

chose /CHōz/ ▸ past of CHOOSE.

cho·sen /ˈCHōzən/ ▸ past participle of CHOOSE.
▸*adj.* [*attrib.*] having been selected as the best or most appropriate: *music is his chosen vocation.*
▸PHRASES □ **chosen few** a group of people who are special or different, typically in a way thought to be unfair: *why have they kept this secret to themselves, the chosen few?* □ **chosen people** those selected by God for a special relationship with him, esp. the people of Israel; the Jews. ■ those destined to be saved by God; believing Christians.

Chou variant spelling of ZHOU.

chou·croute /SHōōˈkrōōt/ ▸*n.* pickled cabbage; sauerkraut. ▷French, from German dialect *Surkrut* 'sauerkraut,' influenced by French *chou* 'cabbage.'

chou·croute gar·ni /SHōōˈkrōōt gärˈnē/ ▸*n.* a French dish consisting of sauerkraut flavored with juniper and served with assorted meats. ▷French, literally 'garnished sauerkraut.'

Chou En-lai /ˈjō ˈen ˈlī/ variant of ZHOU ENLAI.

chough /CHəf/ ▸*n.* a black Eurasian and North African bird of the crow family, with a down-curved bill and broad rounded wings, typically frequenting mountains and sea cliffs. • Genus *Pyrrhocorax,* family Corvidae: three species, esp. the **red-billed chough** (*P. pyrrhocorax*), with a long red bill, and the **alpine chough** (*P. graculus*), with a shorter yellow bill. ▷Middle English (originally denoting the jackdaw): probably imitative.

choux pastry /SHōō/ ▸*n.* very light pastry made with egg, typically used for eclairs and profiteroles. ▷late 19th cent.: from *choux* or *chou,* denoting a round cream-filled pastry cake (from French *chou* (plural *choux*) 'cabbage, rosette,' from Latin *caulis*) + PASTRY.

chow /CHou/ ▸*n.* **1** *informal* food. **2** (also **chow chow**) a dog of a sturdy Chinese breed with a broad muzzle, a tail curled over the back, a bluish-black tongue, and typically a dense thick coat. ▷late 19th cent.: shortened from CHOW CHOW.

chow 2

▸*phrasal v.* □ **chow down** (or **chow something down**) *informal* eat: *he chowed down on lobster | lions chow down their kills.*

chow chow /ˈCHou ,CHou/ ▸*n.* **1** another term for CHOW (sense 2). **2** (also **chow-chow**) a Chinese preserve of ginger, orange peel, and other ingredients, in syrup. **3** (also **chow-chow**) a mixed vegetable pickle. ▷late 18th cent.: pidgin English, of unknown ultimate origin.

chow·der /ˈCHoudər/ ▸*n.* a rich soup typically containing fish, clams, or corn with potatoes and onions: *clam chowder.* ▷mid 18th cent.: perhaps from French *chaudière* 'stew pot,' related to Old Northern French *caudron* (see CAULDRON).

chow·der·head /ˈCHoudər,hed/ ▸*n.* *informal* a stupid person. ▷mid 19th cent.: probably a variant form of early 17th-cent. *jolter-head* 'thick-headed person.' —**chow·der·head·ed** *adj.*

chow·ki·dar /ˈCHôki,där/ (also **cho·ki·dar**) ▸*n.* (in India) a watchman or gatekeeper. ▷from Urdu *caukīdār,* from *caukī* 'toll house' + *-dār* 'keeper.'

chow mein /ˈCHou ˈmān/ ▸*n.* a Chinese-style dish of fried noodles with shredded meat or seafood and vegetables. ▷late 19th cent.: from Chinese *chǎo miàn* 'fried noodles.'

CHP ▸*abbr.* combined heat and power, a system in which steam produced in a power station as a byproduct of electricity generation is used to heat nearby buildings.

Chr. ▸*abbr. Bible* Chronicles.

chres·tom·a·thy /kreˈstäməTHē/ ▸*n.* (*pl.* **-thies**) *formal* a selection of passages from an author or authors, designed to help in learning a language. ▷mid 19th cent.: from Greek *khrēstomatheia,* from *khrēstos* 'useful' + *-matheia* 'learning.'

Chré·tien /kräˈtyeN -ˈtyen/, (Joseph-Jacques) Jean (1934–), Canadian statesman; prime minister 1993–2003.

Chré·tien de Troyes /kräˈtyeN də ˈtrwä/ (12th century), French poet. His courtly romances on Arthurian themes include *Lancelot* (*c.*1177–81) and *Perceval* (1181–90, unfinished).

chrism /ˈkrizəm/ ▸*n.* a mixture of oil and balsam, consecrated and used for anointing at baptism and in other rites of Catholic, Orthodox, and Anglican Churches. ▷Old English, from medieval Latin *crisma,* ecclesiastical Latin *chrisma,* from Greek *khrisma* 'anointing,' from *khriein* 'anoint.'

Chris·ma·tion /krizˈmāSHən/ ▸*n.* a rite in the Orthodox and Eastern Catholic churches that is comparable and similar to confirmation in the Roman Catholic Church. ▷*chrism* (holy oil) + *-ation*

chris·om /ˈkrizəm/ ▸*n.* *historical* a white robe put on a child at baptism. ▷Middle English: alteration of CHRISM, representing a popular pronunciation with two syllables.

Chris·sake /krī(s)ˈsāk/ (also **chris·sake,Chris·sakes,chris·sakes**) ▸*n.* (in phrase **for Chrissake**) *informal* for Christ's sake (used as an exclamation, typically of annoyance or exasperation): *for Chrissake, listen to me!* ▷1920s: representing a pronunciation.

Christ /krīst/ ▸*n.* the title, also treated as a name, given to Jesus of Nazareth (see JESUS).
▸*exclam.* an oath used to express irritation, dismay, or surprise. ▷Old English *Crīst,* from Latin *Christus,* from Greek *Khristos,* noun use of an adjective meaning 'anointed,' from *khriein* 'anoint,' translating Hebrew *māšīaḥ* 'Messiah.' —**Christ·hood** /-,hōōd/ *n.* —**Christ·like** /-,līk/ *adj.* —**Christ·ly** *adj.*
▸PHRASE □ **before Christ** full form of **BC**.

Chris·ta·del·phi·an /,kristəˈdelfēən/ ▸*n.* a member of a Christian sect, founded in the U.S. in 1848, that claims to return to the beliefs and practices of the earliest disciples and holds that Christ will return in power to set up a worldwide theocracy beginning at Jerusalem.
▸*adj.* of or adhering to this sect and its beliefs. ▷from late Greek *Khristadelphos* 'in brotherhood with Christ' (from *Khristos* 'Christ' + *adelphos* 'brother') + -IAN.

Christ·church /ˈkris(t),CHərCH/ a city in New Zealand, on the eastern coast of South Island; pop. 303,400.

chris·ten /ˈkrisən/ ▸*v.* [*trans.*] (often **be christened**) give (a baby) a Christian name at baptism as a sign of admission to a Christian Church: [*trans.*] *their second daughter was christened Jeanette.* ■ give to (someone or something) a name that reflects a notable quality or characteristic: [*trans.*] *a person so creepy that his colleagues christened him "Millipede."* ■ dedicate (a vessel, building, etc.) ceremonially: *their first garbage truck was christened with a bottle of champagne.* ■ *informal* use for the first time: *let's get steaks and christen the new grill.* ▷Old English *crīstnian* 'make Christian,' from *crīsten* 'Christian,' from Latin *Christianus,* from *Christus* 'Christ.' —**chris·ten·er** /ˈkris(ə)nər/ *n.*

Chris·ten·dom /ˈkrisəndəm/ ▸*n.* *dated* the worldwide body or society of Christians. ■ the Christian world: *the greatest church in Christendom.* ▷Old English *crīstendōm,* from *crīsten* (see CHRISTEN) + *-dōm* (see -DOM).

Christ·er /ˈkrīstər/ ▸*n.* *informal* a sanctimonious or ostentatiously pious Christian.

Chris·tian[1] /ˈkrisCHən/, Fletcher (*c.*1764–93), English seaman and mutineer. In April 1789, as first mate under Captain Bligh on the HMS *Bounty,* he seized the ship and cast Bligh and others adrift. In 1790, the mutineers settled on Pitcairn Island, where Christian was probably killed by Tahitians.

Chris·tian[2] ▸*adj.* of, relating to, or professing Christianity or its teachings: *the Christian Church.* ■ *informal* having or showing qualities associated with Christians, esp. those of decency, kindness, and fairness.
▸*n.* a person who has received Christian baptism or is a believer in Jesus Christ and his teachings. ▷late Middle English: from Latin *Christianus,* from Greek *Christianos* (see CHRIST). —**Chris·tian·i·za·tion** /,krisCHənəˈzāSHən/ *n.* —**Chris·tian·ize** /-,nīz/ *v.* —**Chris·tian·ly** *adv.*

Chris·tian Broth·ers a Roman Catholic lay teaching order founded in France in 1684.

Chris·tian e·ra ▸*n.* (**the Christian era**) the period of time that begins with the traditional date of Christ's birth.

Chris·ti·an·i·a /,kristēˈanēə; ,krisCHē-/ (also **Kris·ti·an·i·a**) former name (1624–1924) of OSLO.

Chris·ti·an·i·ty /,krisCHēˈanitē/ ▸*n.* the religion based on the person and teachings of Jesus of Nazareth, or its beliefs and practices. ■ Christian quality or character: *you may know a man by his Christianity.*

Christianity is today the world's most widespread religion, with more than a billion members, mainly divided between the Roman Catholic, Protestant, and Eastern Orthodox Churches. It originated among the Jewish followers of Jesus of Nazareth, who believed that he was the promised Messiah (or 'Christ'), but the Christian Church soon became an independent organization, largely through the missionary efforts of St. Paul. In 313 Constantine ended official persecution in the Roman Empire and in 380 Theodosius I recognized it as the state religion. Most Christians believe in one God in three Persons (the Father, the Son, and the Holy Spirit) and that Jesus is the Son of God who rose from the dead after being crucified; a Christian hopes to attain eternal life after death through faith in Jesus Christ and tries to live by his teachings as recorded in the New Testament.

▷Middle English: from Old French *crestiente,* from *crestien* 'Christian,' influenced by late Latin *christianitas,* from Latin *Christianus,* from *Christus* 'Christ.'

Chris·tian name ▸*n.* a name given to an individual that distinguishes him or her from other members of the same family and is used as an address of familiarity; a forename, esp. one given at baptism.

USAGE In recognition of the fact that English-speaking societies have many religions and cultures, not just Christian ones, the term **Christian name** has largely given way, at least in official contexts, to alternative terms such as **given name**, **first name**, or **forename**.

Chris·tian Sci·ence ▸*n.* the beliefs and practices of the Church of Christ Scientist, a Christian sect founded by Mary Baker Eddy in 1879. Members hold that only God and the mind have ultimate reality, and that sin and illness are illusions that can be overcome by prayer and faith. —**Chris·tian Sci·en·tist** *n.*

Chris·tian·sted /ˈkrisCHən,sted/ a resort town on Saint Croix Island in the U.S. Virgin Islands, once the capital of the Danish West Indies; pop. 2,555.

Chris·tie[1] /ˈkristē/, Dame Agatha (1890–1976), English writer of detective fiction and plays. Many of her novels feature the Belgian detective Hercule Poirot or the resourceful Miss Marple. Her play *The Mousetrap* (1952) has had a run of more than 40 years on the London stage. Other notable works: *Murder on the Orient Express* (1934) and *Death on the Nile* (1937).

Chris·tie[2], Linford (b.1960), Jamaican-born British sprinter who won the Olympic gold medal in the 100 meters in 1992 and the world championship title at this distance in 1993.

Chris·tie[3] (also **chris·tie**) ▶*n.* (*pl.* **-ties**) *dated Skiing* a sudden turn in which the skis are kept parallel, used for changing direction fast or stopping short. ▷1920s (earlier as *Christiania*): named after CHRISTIANIA in Norway.

Chris·tin·gle /ˈkristiNGgəl/ ▶*n.* a lighted candle symbolizing Christ as the light of the world, held by children esp. at a special Advent service originating in the Moravian Church. ▷1950s: probably from German dialect *Christkindl* 'Christ child, Christmas gift.'

Christ·mas /ˈkrisməs/ ▶*n.* (*pl.* **-mas·es**) the annual Christian festival celebrating Christ's birth, held on December 25. ■ the period immediately before and after December 25: *we had guests over Christmas.*
▶*exclam. informal* expressing surprise, dismay, or despair. ▷Old English *Crīstes mæsse* (see CHRIST, MASS). —**Christ·mas·sy** /-məsē/ *adj.*

Christ·mas cac·tus ▶*n.* a Brazilian cactus with branching stems of glossy green, flat, broad, toothedged sections, the tips of which bear long flowers, typically red or pink, with recurved outer petals. Christmas cacti are widely cultivated as houseplants. • *Schlumbergera bridgesii* (or *Zygocactus bridgesii*), family Cactaceae.

Christ·mas card ▶*n.* a greeting card sent at Christmas.

Christ·mas Day ▶*n.* the day on which the festival of Christmas is celebrated, December 25.

Christ·mas Eve the day or the evening before Christmas Day, December 24.

Christ·mas fern ▶*n.* an evergreen fern with dark green leathery fronds that grow in circular clumps from a central rootstock. • *Polystichum acrostichoides*, family Polypodiaceae.

Christ·mas Is·land **1** an island in the Indian Ocean, 200 miles (350 km) south of Java, administered as an external territory of Australia since 1958; pop. 1,275. **2** former name (until 1981) of KIRITIMATI.

Christ·mas stock·ing ▶*n.* a real or ornamental stocking hung up by children on Christmas Eve for Santa Claus to fill with presents.

Christ·mas tree ▶*n.* a real or artificial evergreen tree set up and decorated with lights and ornaments as part of Christmas celebrations.

Christo- ▶*comb. form* of or relating to Christ: *Christocentric* | *Christology.* ▷from Latin *Christus* or Greek *Khristos* 'Christ.'

Chris·to·cen·tric /ˈkristəˈsentrik; ˌkrī-/ ▶*adj.* having Christ as its center: *a thoroughly Christocentric theology.*

Chris·to·gram /ˈkristəˌgram/ ▶*n.* a symbol for Christ, consisting of the Greek letters chi (X) and rho (P).

Chris·tol·o·gy /krisˈtäləjē/ ▶*n.* the branch of Christian theology relating to the person, nature, and role of Christ. —**Chris·to·log·i·cal** /ˌkristlˈäjikəl/ *adj.* —**Chris·to·log·i·cal·ly** /ˌkristlˈäjik(ə)lē/ *adv.*

Chris·to·pher /ˈkristəfər/, Warren (1925–), U.S. statesman and lawyer. He served as secretary of state 1993–97 in President Bill Clinton's administration.

Chris·to·pher, St. /ˈkristəfər/ a legendary Christian martyr, adopted as the patron saint of travelers, since it is said that he once carried Christ in the form of a child across a river.

chris·to·phine /ˈkristəˌfēn/ (also **chris·to·phene**) ▶*n.* another term for CHAYOTE (sense 1). ▷probably based on the French given name *Christophe.*

Christ's thorn ▶*n.* a thorny shrub popularly supposed to have formed Christ's crown of thorns, in particular: • either of two shrubs related to the buckthorn: *Paliurus spina-christi* (also called JERUSALEM THORN) and *Ziziphus spina-christi* (also called CROWN OF THORNS), family Rhamnaceae.

chro·ma /ˈkrōmə/ ▶*n.* purity or intensity of color. ▷late 19th cent.: from Greek *khrōma* 'color.'

chro·maf·fin /krōˈmafin/ ▶*adj.* [*attrib.*] *Physiology* denoting granules or vesicles containing epinephrine and norepinephrine, and the secretory cells of the adrenal medulla in which they are found. ▷early 20th cent.: from CHROMO-[1] 'chromium' + Latin *affinis* 'akin' (because readily stained brown by chromates).

chro·ma·key /ˈkrōməkē/ ▶*n.* a technique by which a block of a particular color in a video image can be replaced either by another color or by a separate image, enabling, for example, a weather forecaster to appear against a background of a computer-generated weather map.
▶*v.* (**-keys**, **-keyed**) [*trans.*] manipulate (an image) using this technique.

chro·mate /ˈkrōˌmāt/ ▶*n. Chemistry* a salt in which the anion contains both chromium and oxygen, esp. one of the anion $CrO_4{}^{2-}$. ▷early 19th cent.: from CHROMIC + -ATE[1].

chro·mat·ic /krōˈmatik/ ▶*adj.* **1** *Music* relating to or using notes not belonging to the diatonic scale of the key in which a passage is written. ■ (of a scale) ascending or descending by semitones. ■ (of an instrument) able to play all the notes of the chromatic scale. **2** of, relating to, or produced by color. ▷early 17th cent.: from French *chromatique* or Latin *chromaticus*, from Greek *khrōmatikos*, from *khrōma*, *khrōmat-* 'color, chromatic scale.' —**chro·mat·i·cal·ly** /-ik(ə)lē/ *adv.* —**chro·mat·i·cism** /-əˌsizəm/ *n.*

chro·mat·ic ab·er·ra·tion ▶*n. Optics* the material effect produced by the refraction of different wavelengths of electromagnetic radiation through slightly different angles, resulting in a failure to focus. It causes colored fringes in the images produced by uncorrected lenses.

chro·ma·tic·i·ty /ˌkrōməˈtisətē/ ▶*n.* the quality of color, independent of brightness.

chro·ma·tid /ˈkrōməˌtid/ ▶*n. Biology* each of the two threadlike strands into which a chromosome divides longitudinally during cell division. Each contains a double helix of DNA. ▷early 20th cent.: from Greek *khrōma*, *khrōmat-* 'color' + -ID[2].

chro·ma·tin /ˈkrōmətən/ ▶*n. Biology* the material of which the chromosomes of organisms other than bacteria (i.e., eukaryotes) are composed. It consists of protein, RNA, and DNA. ▷late 19th cent.: coined in German from Greek *khrōma*, *khrōmat-* 'color.'

chromato- (also **chromo-**) ▶*comb. form* color; of or in colors: *chromatopsia* | *chromosome.* ▷from Greek *khrōma*, *khrōmat-* 'color.'

chro·mat·o·gram /krōˈmatəˌgram/ ▶*n.* a visible record (such as a series of colored bands, or a graph) showing the result of separation of the components of a mixture by chromatography.

chro·mat·o·graph /krōˈmatəˌgraf/ ▶*n.* an apparatus for performing chromatography. ■ another term for CHROMATOGRAM.

chro·ma·tog·ra·phy /ˌkrōməˈtägrəfē/ ▶*n. Chemistry* the separation of a mixture by passing it in solution or suspension or as a vapor (as in gas chromatography) through a medium in which the components move at different rates. ▷1930s: from German *Chromatographie* (see CHROMATO-, -GRAPHY). The name alludes to the earliest separations when the result was displayed as a number of colored bands or spots. —**chro·mat·o·graph·ic** /krōˌmatəˈgrafik/ *adj.*

chro·mat·o·phore /krəˈmatəˌfôr; ˈkrōmətə-/ ▶*n.* a cell or plastid that contains pigment. —**chro·mat·o·phor·ic** /krəˌmatəˈfôrik; ˌkrōmətə-/ *adj.*

chro·ma·top·si·a /ˌkrōməˈtäpsēə/ ▶*n. Medicine* abnormally colored vision, a rare symptom of varied cause. ▷mid 19th cent.: from CHROMATO- 'color' + Greek *-opsia* 'seeing.'

chrome /krōm/ ▶*n.* chromium plate as a decorative or protective finish on motor-vehicle fittings and other objects: [as *adj.*] *a chrome bumper.* ■ [as *adj.*] denoting compounds or alloys of chromium: *chrome dyes.* ■ short for CHROME YELLOW. ▷early 19th cent.: from French, from Greek *khrōma* 'color' (because of the brilliant colors of chromium compounds).

chrome al·um ▶*n.* a reddish-purple crystalline compound used in solution in photographic processing and as a mordant in dyeing. • Chem. formula: $K_2SO_4Cr_2(SO_4)_3.24H_2O$.

chromed /krōmd/ ▶*adj.* chromium-plated.

chrome leath·er ▶*n.* leather tanned with chromium salts.

chrome-mol·y /ˈkrōm ˈmōlē/ (also **chro·mol·y**) ▶*n.* a strong steel alloy made principally of chromium and molybdenum: *the bicycle is made lighter and stronger with chrome-moly tubing.* ▷1980s: blend of CHROMIUM and MOLYBDENUM.

chrome red ▶*n.* a bright red pigment consisting of lead chromate with varying amounts of lead oxide.

chrome steel ▶*n.* a hard fine-grained steel containing chromium, used for making tools.

chrome yel·low ▶*n.* a bright yellow pigment made from lead chromate, now little used.

chro·mic /ˈkrōmik/ ▶*adj. Chemistry* of chromium with a higher valence, usually three. Compare with CHROMOUS.

chro·mic ac·id ▶*n. Chemistry* a corrosive and strongly oxidizing acid existing only in solutions of chromium trioxide. • Chem. formula: H_2CrO_4.

chro·mi·nance /ˈkrōmənəns/ ▶*n.* the colorimetric difference between a given color in a television picture and a standard color of equal luminance. ▷1950s: from Greek *khrōma* 'color,' on the pattern of *luminance.*

chro·mite /ˈkrōˌmīt/ ▶*n.* a brownish-black mineral that consists of a mixed oxide of chromium and iron and is the principal ore of chromium. ▷mid 19th cent.: from CHROME or CHROMIUM + -ITE[1].

chro·mi·um /ˈkrōmēəm/ ▶*n.* the chemical element of atomic number 24, a hard white metal used in stainless steel and other alloys. (Symbol: **Cr**) ▷early 19th cent.: from CHROME + -IUM.

chro·mi·um plate ▶*n.* a decorative or protective coating of metallic chromium. ■ metal with such a coating.
▶*v.* (**chro·mi·um-plate**) [*trans.*] coat with chromium, typically by electrolytic deposition.

chro·mi·um steel ▶*n.* another term for CHROME STEEL.

chro·mo /ˈkrōmō/ ▶*n.* (*pl.* **-mos**) **1** shortened form of CHROMOLITHOGRAPH. **2** *informal* chromoly.

chromo-[1] ▶*comb. form Chemistry* representing CHROMIUM.

chromo-[2] ▶*comb. form* variant spelling of CHROMATO-.

chro·mo·dy·nam·ics /ˌkrōmōdīˈnamiks/ ▶*plural n.* see QUANTUM CHROMODYNAMICS.

chro·mo·gen /ˈkrōməjən/ ▶*n.* a substance that can be readily converted into a dye or other colored compound.

chro·mo·gen·ic /ˌkrōməˈjenik/ ▶*adj.* involving the production of color or pigments, in particular: ■ *Photography* denoting a modern process of film developing that uses couplers to produce black-and-white or color images of very high definition. ■ *Photography* denoting any of a number of similar developing processes. ■ *Microbiology* (of a bacterium) producing a pigment.

chro·mo·lith·o·graph /ˌkrōmōˈliTHəˌgraf/ *historical* ▶*n.* a colored picture printed by lithography, esp. in the late 19th and early 20th centuries.
▶*v.* [*trans.*] print or produce (a picture) by this process. —**chro·mo·li·thog·ra·pher** /-liˈTHägrəfər/ *n.* —**chro·mo·lith·o·graph·ic** /-ˌliTHəˈgrafik/ *adj.* —**chro·mo·li·thog·ra·phy** /-liˈTHägrəfē/ *n.*

chro·mo·ly /krōˈmälē/ ▶ variant spelling of CHROMEMOLY.

chro·mo·phore /ˈkrōməˌfôr/ ▶*n. Chemistry* an atom or group whose presence is responsible for the color of a compound. —**chro·mo·phor·ic** /ˌkrōməˈfôrik/ *adj.*

chro·mo·plast /ˈkrōməˌplast/ ▶*n. Botany* a colored plastid other than a chloroplast, typically containing a yellow or orange pigment. ▷late 19th cent.: from CHROMO-[2] 'color' + Greek *plastos* 'formed.'

chro·mo·some /ˈkrōməˌsōm/ ▶*n. Biology* a threadlike structure of nucleic acids and protein found in the nucleus of most living cells, carrying genetic information in the form of genes.

Each chromosome consists of a DNA double helix bearing a linear sequence of genes, coiled and recoiled around aggregated proteins (histones). Their number varies from species to species: humans have 22 pairs plus the two sex chromosomes (two X chromosomes in females, one X and one Y in males). During cell division, each DNA strand is duplicated, and the chromosomes condense to become visible as distinct pairs of chromatids joined at the centromere. Bacteria and viruses lack a nucleus and have a single chromosome without histones.

▷late 19th cent.: coined in German from Greek *khrōma* 'color' + *sōma* 'body.' —**chro·mo·so·mal** /ˌkrōməˈsōməl/ *adj.*

chro·mo·some map ▶*n. Genetics* a diagram showing the relative positions of genes along the length of a chromosome.

chro·mo·some num·ber ▶*n. Genetics* the characteristic number of chromosomes found in the cell nuclei of organisms of a particular species.

chro·mo·sphere /ˈkrōməˌsfi(ə)r/ ▶*n. Astronomy* a reddish gaseous layer immediately above the photosphere of the sun or another star. Together with the corona, it constitutes the star's outer atmosphere. ▷mid 19th cent.: from CHROMO-[2] 'color' + SPHERE. —**chro·mo·spher·ic** /ˌkrōməˈsfi(ə)rik; -ˈsferik/ *adj.*

chro·mo·ther·a·py /ˌkrōməˈTHerəpē/ ▶*n.* another term for COLOR THERAPY. —**chro·mo·ther·a·pist** *n.*

chro·mous /ˈkrōməs/ ▶*adj. Chemistry* of chromium with a valence of two; of chromium(II). Compare with CHROMIC.

Chron. ▶*abbr.* *Bible* Chronicles.

chro·nax·ie /ˈkrō,naksē; ˈkrä-/ ▶*n.* *Physiology* the minimum amount of time needed to stimulate a muscle or nerve fiber, using an electric current twice the strength required to elicit a threshold response.

chron·ic /ˈkränik/ ▶*adj.* (of an illness) persisting for a long time or constantly recurring: *chronic bronchitis.* Often contrasted with ACUTE. ■ (of a person) having such an illness: *a chronic asthmatic.* ■ (of a problem) long-lasting and difficult to eradicate: *the school suffers from chronic overcrowding.* ■ (of a person) having a particular bad habit: *a chronic liar.* ▷late Middle English: from French *chronique,* via Latin from Greek *khronikos* 'of time,' from *khronos* 'time.' **—chron·i·cal·ly** /-ik(ə)lē/ *adv.* **—chro·nic·i·ty** /krä'nisətē/ *n.*

USAGE **Chronic** is often used to mean 'habitual, inveterate,' e.g., *a chronic liar.* Some consider this use incorrect. The precise meaning of **chronic** is 'persisting for a long time,' and it is used chiefly of illnesses or other problems: *more than one million people in the U.S. have chronic bronchitis.*

chron·ic fa·tigue syn·drome (abbr.: **CFS**) ▶*n.* a medical condition of unknown cause, with fever, aching, and prolonged tiredness and depression, typically occurring after a viral infection.

chron·i·cle /ˈkränikəl/ ▶*n.* a factual written account of important or historical events in the order of their occurrence. ■ a work of fiction or nonfiction that describes a particular series of events.
▶*v.* [*trans.*] record (a related series of events) in a factual and detailed way: *his work chronicles 20th-century displacement and migration.* ▷Middle English: from Anglo-Norman French *cronicle,* variant of Old French *cronique,* via Latin from Greek *khronika* 'annals,' from *khronikos* (see CHRONIC). **—chron·i·cler** /-iklər/ *n.*

chron·i·cle play ▶*n.* a historical drama consisting of a series of short episodes arranged chronologically. Also called **chronicle history**.

Chron·i·cles /ˈkränikəlz/ the name of two books of the Bible, recording the history of Israel and Judah until the return from Exile (536 BC). See also PARALIPOMENA.

chrono- ▶*comb. form* relating to time: *chronometry.* ▷from Greek *khronos* 'time.'

chron·o·bi·ol·o·gy /,kränō,bīˈäləjē; ,krō-/ ▶*n.* the branch of biology concerned with natural physiological rhythms and other cyclical phenomena. **—chron·o·bi·ol·o·gist** /-,bīˈäləjist/ *n.*

chron·o·graph /ˈkränə,graf; ˈkrō-/ ▶*n.* an instrument for recording time with great accuracy. ■ a stopwatch. **—chron·o·graph·ic** /,kränəˈgrafik; ,krō-/ *adj.*

chron·o·log·i·cal /,kränlˈäjikəl/ ▶*adj.* relating to the establishment of dates and time sequences: *the diary provided a chronological framework for the events.* ■ (of a record of several events) starting with the earliest and following the order in which they occurred: *the entries are in **chronological order**.* ■ calculated in terms of the passage of time rather than some other criterion: *ratings are calculated by dividing a child's mental age by his or her chronological age.* **—chron·o·log·i·cal·ly** /-ik(ə)lē/ *adv.*

chro·nol·o·gy /krəˈnäləjē/ ▶*n.* (*pl.* **-gies**) the study of historical records to establish the dates of past events. ■ the arrangement of events or dates in the order of their occurrence: *the novel abandons the conventions of normal chronology | a diary recording a chronology of events.* ■ a table or document displaying such an arrangement. ▷late 16th cent.: from modern Latin *chronologia,* from Greek *khronos* 'time' + *-logia* (see -LOGY). **—chro·nol·o·gist** /-jist/ *n.*

chro·nom·e·ter /krəˈnämətər/ ▶*n.* an instrument for measuring time, esp. one designed to keep accurate time in spite of motion or variations in temperature, humidity, and air pressure. Chronometers were first developed for marine navigation, being used in conjunction with astronomical observation to determine longitude.

chro·nom·e·try /krəˈnämətrē/ ▶*n.* the science of accurate time measurement. **—chron·o·met·ric** /,kränəˈmetrik; ,krō-/ *adj.* **—chron·o·met·ri·cal** /,kränəˈmetrikəl; ,krō-/ *adj.* **—chron·o·met·ri·cal·ly** /,kränəˈmetrik(ə)lē/ *adv.*

chron·o·scope /ˈkränə,skōp/ ▶*n.* a device for measuring short time intervals, esp. in determining the velocity of projectiles, or a person's reaction time.

chron·o·stra·tig·ra·phy /,kränə,strəˈtigrəfē; ,krō-/ ▶*n.* the branch of geology concerned with establishing the absolute ages of strata. **—chron·o·strat·i·graph·ic** /-,stratəˈgrafik/ *adj.*

chron·o·ther·a·py /,kränəˈTHerəpē/ ▶*n.* treatment of an illness or disorder that takes into account the body's natural rhythms and cycles.

chrys·a·lis /ˈkrisələs/ (also **chrys·a·lid** /ˈkrisə,lid/) ▶*n.* (*pl.* **-lis·es**) a quiescent insect pupa, esp. of a butterfly or moth. ■ the hard outer case of this, esp. after being discarded. ■ *figurative* a preparatory or transitional state: *she emerged from the chrysalis of self-conscious adolescence.* ▷early 17th cent.: from Latin *chrysal(l)is, chrysal(l)id-,* from Greek *khrusallis,* from *khrusos* 'gold' (because of the gold color or metallic sheen of the pupae of some species).

chry·san·the·mum /kriˈsanTHəməm/ ▶*n.* (*pl.* **-mums**) a popular plant of the daisy family, having brightly colored ornamental flowers and existing in many cultivated varieties. • Genera *Chrysanthemum* or (most cultivated species) *Dendranthema,* family Compositae. ■ a flower or flowering stem of this plant. ▷(originally denoting the corn marigold): from Latin, from Greek *khrusanthemon,* from *khrusos* 'gold' + *anthemon* 'flower.'

chrys·el·e·phan·tine /,kris,eləˈfan,tēn; -ˈeləfən,tēn; -,tīn/ ▶*adj.* (of ancient Greek sculpture) overlaid with gold and ivory. ▷early 19th cent.: from Greek *khruselephantinos,* from *khrusos* 'gold' + *elephas, elephant-* 'elephant' or 'ivory.'

Chrys·ler /ˈkrīslər/, Walter Percy (1875–1940), U.S. automobile manufacturer. He was president and general manager of Buick Motor Co. 1916–21 and introduced the Chrysler automobile in 1924.

chrys·o·ber·yl /ˈkrisə,berəl/ ▶*n.* a greenish or yellowish-green mineral consisting of an oxide of beryllium and aluminum. It occurs as tabular crystals, sometimes of gem quality. ▷mid 17th cent.: from Latin *chrysoberyllus,* from Greek *khrusos* 'gold' + *bērullos* 'beryl.'

chrys·o·col·la /,krisəˈkälə/ ▶*n.* a greenish-blue mineral consisting of hydrated copper silicate, typically occurring as opaline crusts and masses. ▷late 16th cent. (in the Greek sense): from Latin, from Greek *khrusokolla,* denoting a mineral used in ancient times for soldering gold.

chrys·o·lite /ˈkrisə,līt/ ▶*n.* a yellowish-green or brownish variety of olivine, used as a gemstone. ▷late Middle English: from Old French *crisolite,* from medieval Latin *crisolitus,* from Latin *chrysolithus,* based on Greek *khrusos* 'gold' + *lithos* 'stone.'

chrys·o·mel·id /,krisəˈmelid; -ˈmēlid/ ▶*n.* *Entomology* a beetle of a family (Chrysomelidae) that comprises the leaf beetles and their relatives. ▷late 19th cent.: from modern Latin *Chrysomelidae* (plural), from *Chrysomela* (genus name), from Greek *khrusomēlon,* literally 'golden apple,' influenced by *khrusomēlolonthion* 'little golden chafer.'

chrys·o·prase /ˈkrisə,prāz/ ▶*n.* an apple-green variety of chalcedony containing nickel, used as a gemstone. ■ (in the New Testament) a golden-green precious stone, perhaps a variety of beryl. ▷Middle English (in the New Testament sense): from Old French *crisopace,* via Latin from Greek *khrusoprasos,* from *khrusos* 'gold' + *prason* 'leek.'

Chrys·os·tom, St. John /ˈkrisəstəm; krisˈästəm/ (*c.*347–407), doctor of the Church; bishop of Constantinople. His attempts to reform the corrupt state of the court, clergy, and people caused him to be banished in 403. Feast day, January 27.

chrys·o·tile /ˈkrisə,tīl/ ▶*n.* a fibrous form of the mineral serpentine. Also called WHITE ASBESTOS (see ASBESTOS). ▷mid 19th cent.: from Greek *khrusos* 'gold' + *tilos* 'fiber.'

chthon·ic /ˈTHänik/ (also **chtho·ni·an** /ˈTHōnēən/) ▶*adj.* concerning, belonging to, or inhabiting the underworld: *a chthonic deity.* ▷late 19th cent.: from Greek *khthōn* 'earth' + -IC.

chub /CHəb/ ▶*n.* a thick-bodied European river fish with a gray-green back and white underparts, popular with anglers. • *Leuciscus cephalus,* family Cyprinidae. ▷late Middle English: of unknown origin.

chub·by /ˈCHəbē/ ▶*adj.* (**-bi·er, -bi·est**) plump and rounded: *a pretty child with chubby cheeks.* ▷early 17th cent. (in the sense 'short and thickset, like a chub'): from CHUB. **—chub·bi·ly** /ˈCHəbəlē/ *adv.* **—chub·bi·ness** *n.*

chuck1 /CHək/ *informal* ▶*v.* [*trans.*] throw (something) carelessly or casually: *someone chucked a brick through the window | figurative he was chucking his money around.* ■ throw (something) away: *they make a living out of stuff people **chuck out**.* ■ give up (a job or activity) suddenly: *Richard chucked his cultural studies course.* ■ break off a relationship with (a partner): *Mary chucked him for another guy.*
▶*phrasal v.* □ **chuck someone out** force someone to leave a building: *the tenants have been chucked out of the cottages.* ▷late 17th cent. (as a verb): from CHUCK2. **—chuck·er** *n.*
▶*PHRASE* □ **chuck it all in** abandon a course of action or way of life, esp. for another that is radically different.

chuck2 ▶*v.* [*trans.*] touch (someone) playfully or gently under the chin.
▶*n.* a playful touch under the chin. ▷early 17th cent. (as a noun): probably from Old French *chuquer,* later *choquer* 'to knock, bump,' of unknown ultimate origin.

chuck3 ▶*n.* **1** a device for holding a workpiece in a lathe or a tool in a drill, typically having three or four jaws that move radially in and out. **2** a cut of beef that extends from the neck to the ribs, typically used for stewing. ▷late 17th cent., as a variant of CHOCK; see also CHUNK1.

chuck4 ▶*n.* *informal* food or provisions. ▷mid 19th cent.: perhaps the same word as CHUCK3.

chuck5 ▶*n.* short for WOODCHUCK.

chuck-a-luck /ˈCHək ə ,lək/ ▶*n.* a gambling game played with three dice.

chuck·hole /ˈCHək,hōl/ ▶*n.* a hole or rut in a road or track.

chuck key ▶*n.* a small metal device for tightening the chuck of a drill so that it holds the drill bit securely.

chuck·le /ˈCHəkəl/ ▶*v.* [*intrans.*] laugh quietly or inwardly: *I chuckled at the astonishment on her face* | [with *direct speech*] *"That's a bit strong, isn't it?" he chuckled.*
▶*n.* [in *sing.*] a quiet or suppressed laugh. ▷late 16th cent. (in the sense 'laugh convulsively'): from *chuck* meaning 'to cluck' in late Middle English. **—chuck·ler** /ˈCHəklər/ *n.*

chuck·le·head /ˈCHəkəl,hed/ ▶*n.* *informal* a stupid person. ▷mid 18th cent.: from early 18th-cent. *chuckle* 'big and clumsy,' probably related to CHUCK3. **—chuck·le·head·ed** *adj.*

chuck wag·on ▶*n.* a wagon with cooking facilities providing food on a ranch, worksite, or campsite. ▷late 19th cent.: *chuck,* colloquial in the sense 'food, provisions.'

chuck·wal·la /ˈCHək,wälə/ ▶*n.* a large dark-bodied lizard, the male of which has a light yellow tail, native to the deserts of the southwestern U.S. and Mexico. When threatened, it inflates itself with air to wedge itself into a crevice. • *Sauromalus obesus,* family Iguanidae. ▷late 19th cent.: from Mexican Spanish *chacahuala,* from American Indian.

chuck-will's-wid·ow /,CHək ,wilz ˈwidō; ˈwidə/ ▶*n.* a large nightjar native to eastern North America. • *Caprimulgus carolinensis,* family Caprimulgidae. ▷late 18th cent.: imitative of its call.

chud·dar /ˈCHədər/ ▶*n.* variant spelling of CHADOR.

chu·fa /ˈCHo͞ofə/ ▶*n.* an Old World sedge that yields an edible tuber. It is cultivated on a small scale, particularly in some marshy regions of Spain and Italy. Also called EARTH ALMOND. • *Cyperus esculentus* var. *sativus,* family Cyperaceae. ■ the tuber of this plant, which may be roasted, made into flour, or turned into juice. ▷mid 19th cent.: from Spanish.

chuff /CHəf/ ▶*v.* [*intrans.*] (of a steam engine) move with a regular sharp puffing sound. ▷early 20th cent.: imitative.

chuffed /CHəft/ ▶*adj.* [*predic.*] *Brit., informal* very pleased: *I'm dead chuffed to have won.* ▷1950s: from dialect *chuff* 'plump or pleased.'

chug1 /CHəg/ ▶*v.* (**chugged, chug·ging**) [*intrans.*] emit a series of regular muffled explosive sounds, as of an engine running slowly: *he could hear the pipes chugging.* ■ [*intrans.*] (of a vehicle or boat) move slowly making such sounds: *a cabin cruiser was chugging down the river.*
▶*n.* a muffled explosive sound or a series of such sounds: *the chug of a motorboat.* ▷mid 19th cent. (as a noun): imitative.

chug2 (also **chug·a·lug** or **chug-a-lug** /ˈCHəgə,ləg/) ▶*v.* (**chugged, chug·ging**) [*trans.*] *informal* consume (a drink) in large gulps without pausing: *Avery chugged a cup of coffee.* ▷1980s: imitative.

Chu·gach Moun·tains /ˈCHo͞o,gaCH; -,gaSH/ a range of mountains, part of the Coast Ranges, in southern Alaska. Anchorage lies at its base, and it is noted for glaciers that flow south into the Gulf of Alaska.

chu·kar /ˈCHo͝ok,är; CHo͝okˈär/ (also **chukar partridge**) ▶*n.* a Eurasian partridge similar to the red-legged partridge, but with a call like a clucking domestic hen. • Genus *Alectoris*, family Phasianidae: two species, in particular *A. chukar*. ▷early 19th cent.: from Sanskrit *cakora*.

Chuk·chi /ˈCHŏŏkCHē; ˈCHək-/ (also **Chuk·chee**) ▸*n.* (*pl.* same or **-chis**) **1** a member of an indigenous people of extreme northeastern Siberia. **2** the language of this people, which belongs to a small, isolated language family.
▸*adj.* of or relating to this people or their language. ▷Russian (plural).

Chuk·chi Sea /ˈCHəkCHē; ˈCHŏŏk-/ part of the Arctic Ocean that lies between North America and Asia and north of the Bering Strait.

chuk·ker /ˈCHəkər/ (also **chuk·ka**) ▸*n.* each of a number of periods (typically six) into which play in a game of polo is divided. A chukker lasts 7½ minutes. ▷late 19th cent.: from Hindi *cakkar*, from Sanskrit *cakra* 'circle or wheel.'

Chu·la Vis·ta /ˌCHōōlə ˈvistə/ a city in southwestern California, south of San Diego, near the Mexican border; pop. 135,163.

chum[1] /CHəm/ *informal, dated* ▸*n.* a close friend. ■ a form of address expressing familiarity or friendliness: *it's your own fault, chum.*
▸*v.* (**chummed**, **chum·ming**) [*intrans.*] be friendly to or form a friendship with someone: *they started* ***chumming around*** *in high school.* ▷late 17th cent. (originally Oxford University slang, denoting a roommate): probably short for *chamber-fellow*. Compare with COMRADE and CRONY. —**chum·mi·ly** /ˈCHəmәlē/ *adv.* —**chum·mi·ness** *n.* —**chum·my** *adj.*

chum[2] ▸*n.* chopped fish, fish fluids, and other material thrown overboard as angling bait. ■ refuse from fish, esp. that remaining after expressing oil.
▸*v.* [*intrans.*] use chum as bait when fishing. ▷mid 19th cent.: of unknown origin.

chum[3] (also **chum salmon**) ▸*n.* (*pl.* same or **chums**) a large North Pacific salmon that is commercially important as a food fish. • *Oncorhyncus keta*, family Salmonidae. ▷early 20th cent.: from Chinook Jargon *tzum (samun)*, literally 'spotted (salmon).'

Chu·mash /ˈCHōō,masH/ ▸*n.* (*pl.* same or **-mash·es**) **1** a member of an American Indian people inhabiting coastal parts of southern California. **2** the Hokan language of this people.
▸*adj.* of or relating to this people or their language. ▷Chumash, literally 'islander.'

chump /CHəmp/ ▸*n. informal* a foolish person: *how can this chump be a detective?* ■ an easily deceived person; a sucker. ▷early 18th cent. (in the sense 'thick lump of wood'): probably a blend of CHUNK[1] and LUMP[1] or STUMP.

chump change ▸*n. informal* a small or insignificant amount of money. ▷1960s: originally black English.

Chün /jōōn; jyn; CHōōn/ ▸*n.* a type of thickly glazed, typically bluish or purplish gray stoneware originally made at Chün Chou in Honan province, China, during the Song dynasty.

Chun·chon /ˈCHōōnˈCHən/ an industrial city in northeastern South Korea, the capital of Kangwon province; pop. 179,000.

Chung·king /ˈCHŏŏNGˈkiNG/ variant of CHONGQING.

Chung·shan /ˈCHŏŏNG ˈSHän/ variant of ZHONGSHAN.

chunk[1] /CHəNGk/ ▸*n.* a thick, solid piece of something: *huge* ***chunks of*** *masonry littered the street.* ■ [in *sing.*] an amount or part of something: *fuel takes a large* ***chunk of*** *their small income.*
▸*v.* [*trans.*] divide (something) into chunks: *chunk four pounds of pears.* ■ (in psychology or linguistic analysis) group together (connected items or words) so that they can be stored or processed as single concepts. ▷late 17th cent.: apparently an alteration of CHUCK[3].

chunk[2] ▸*v.* [*intrans.*] move with or make a muffled, metallic sound: *the door chunked behind them.* ▷late 19th cent.: imitative.

chunk·y /ˈCHəNGkē/ ▸*adj.* (**chunk·i·er**, **chunk·i·est**) **1** (of a person) short and sturdy. ■ bulky and solid: *a chunky bracelet.* ■ (of wool or a woolen garment) thick and bulky. **2** (of food) containing chunks: *fresh chunky salsa* | *a chunky soup.* —**chunk·i·ly** /-kәlē/ *adv.* —**chunk·i·ness** *n.*

Chun·nel /ˈCHənl/ ▸*n. informal* short for CHANNEL TUNNEL. ▷1920s (but rare before the 1950s): blend.

chup·pah /ˈKHŏŏpə/ (also **chup·pa**) ▸*n.* (*pl.* **chup·pot** /ˈKHŏŏpōt; -ōs/) a canopy beneath which Jewish marriage ceremonies are performed. ▷late 19th cent.: from Hebrew *ḥuppāh* 'cover, canopy.'

Chu·qui·sa·ca /ˌCHŏŏkēˈsäkə/ former name (1539–1840) of SUCRE[1].

Church /CHərCH/, Frederick Edwin (1826–1900), U.S. painter. A student of Thomas Cole and a leader of the Hudson River School, he was known for his landscapes.

church /CHərCH/ ▸*n.* a building used for public Christian worship: *they came* ***to church*** *with me.* ■ (usu. **Church**) a particular Christian organization, typically one with its own clergy, buildings, and distinctive doctrines: *the Church of England.* ■ (**the Church**) the hierarchy of clergy of such an organization, esp. the Roman Catholic Church or the Church of England. ■ institutionalized religion as a political or social force: *the separation of church and state.* ■ the body of all Christians.
▸*v.* [*trans.*] *archaic* take (a woman who has recently given birth) to church for a service of thanksgiving. ▷Old English *cir(i)ce, cyr(i)ce*, related to Dutch *kerk* and German *Kirche*, based on medieval Greek *kurikon*, from Greek *kuriakon (dōma)* 'Lord's (house),' from *kurios* 'master or lord.' Compare with KIRK.

Church·es of Christ a number of Protestant denominations, chiefly in the U.S., originating in the Disciples of Christ but later separated over doctrinal issues.

Church Fa·thers ▸*n.* see FATHER (sense 3).

church·go·er /ˈCHərCH,gōər/ ▸*n.* a person who goes to church, esp. one who does so regularly. —**church·go·ing** /-,gō-iNG/ *n.* & *adj.*

Church·ill /ˈCHər,CHil; ˈCHərCH,hil/, Sir Winston (Leonard Spencer) (1874–1965), British statesman; prime minister 1940–45 and 1951–55. A consistent opponent of appeasement during the 1930s, he replaced Neville Chamberlain as British prime minister in 1940 and led Britain throughout World War II. Notable works: *The Second World War* (1948–53) and *A History of the English-Speaking Peoples* (1956–58). Nobel Prize for Literature (1953).

Winston Churchill

Church·ill Downs a horse-racing facility in Louisville in Kentucky, the site of the annual Kentucky Derby.

Church·ill Riv·er[1] a river that flows for 1,000 miles (1,600 km) from northern Saskatchewan across Manitoba to Hudson Bay at Churchill.

Church·ill Riv·er[2] a river that flows for 600 miles (1,000 km) from the Canadian Shield across eastern Labrador to the Labrador Sea. Its high falls generate hydroelectric power. Formerly called the HAMILTON RIVER.

church·man /ˈCHərCHmən/ ▸*n.* (*pl.* **-men**) a male member of the Christian clergy or of a church.

Church Mil·i·tant ▸*n.* (**the Church Militant**) the whole body of living Christian believers. ▷mid 16th cent.: contrasted with the *Church Triumphant* in heaven.

Church of Christ, Sci·en·tist ▸*n.* the Christian Science Church.

Church of Eng·land the English branch of the Western Christian Church, which combines Catholic and Protestant traditions, rejects the pope's authority, and has the monarch as its titular head.

Church of Je·sus Christ of Lat·ter-Day Saints ▸*n.* the church of the Mormons.

Church of Rome ▸*n.* another term for ROMAN CATHOLIC CHURCH.

Church of Scot·land the national Christian Church in Scotland, established as Presbyterian in 1690.

church plant·ing ▸*n.* the practice of establishing a core of Christian worshipers in a parish, with the intention that they should develop into a thriving congregation.

Church Slav·ic (also **Church Sla·von·ic**) ▸*n.* the liturgical language used in the Orthodox Church in Russia, Serbia, and some other countries. It is a modified form of Old Church Slavic.

church·ward·en /ˈCHərCH,wôrdn/ ▸*n.* **1** either of the two elected lay representatives in an Anglican parish, formally responsible for movable church property and for keeping order in church. ■ a church administrator. **2** *chiefly Brit.* a long-stemmed clay pipe.

church·wom·an /ˈCHərCH,wŏŏmən/ ▸*n.* (*pl.* **-wom·en**) a female member of the Christian clergy or of a church.

church·y /ˈCHərCHē/ ▸*adj.* **1** (of a person) excessively pious and consequently narrow-minded or intolerant. **2** resembling a church: *Gothic design looks too churchy.* —**church·i·ness** *n.*

church·yard /ˈCHərCH,yärd/ ▸*n.* an enclosed area surrounding a church, esp. as used for burials.

churl /CHərl/ ▸*n.* an impolite and mean-spirited person. ■ *archaic* a miser. ■ *archaic* a person of low birth; a peasant. ▷Old English *ceorl*; related to Dutch *kerel* and German *Kerl* 'fellow,' also to CARL.

churl·ish /ˈCHərlisH/ ▸*adj.* rude in a mean-spirited and surly way: *it seems churlish to complain.* ▷Old English *cierlisc, ceorlisc* (see CHURL, -ISH[1]). —**churl·ish·ly** *adv.* —**churl·ish·ness** *n.*

churn /CHərn/ ▸*n.* a machine or container in which butter is made by agitating milk or cream.
▸*v.* **1** [*trans.*] (often **be churned**) agitate or turn (milk or cream) in a machine in order to produce butter: *the cream is ripened before it is churned.* ■ produce (butter) in such a way. **2** [*intrans.*] (of liquid) move about vigorously: *the seas churned* | *figurative her stomach was churning at the thought of the ordeal.* ■ [*trans.*] (often **be churned**) cause (liquid) to move in this way: *in high winds most of the lake is* ***churned up.*** ■ [*trans.*] break up the surface of (an area of ground): *the earth had been* ***churned up*** *where vehicles had passed through.* **3** [*trans.*] (of a broker) encourage frequent turnover of (investments) in order to generate commission.
▸*phrasal v.* □ **churn something out** produce something routinely or mechanically, esp. in large quantities: *artists continued to churn out insipid works.* ▷Old English *cyrin*, of Germanic origin; related to Middle Low German *kerne* and Old Norse *kirna*.

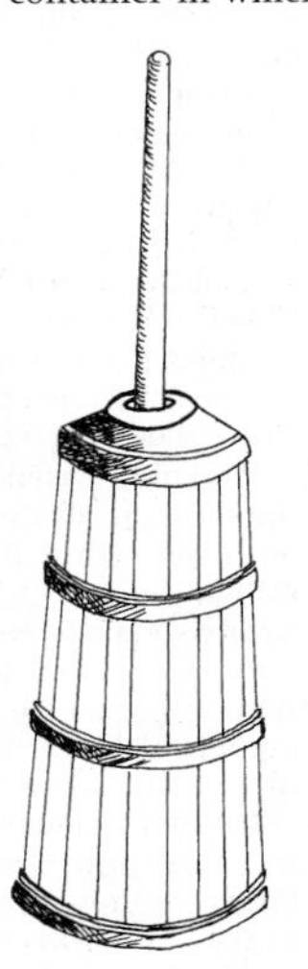

butter churn

churn rate ▸*n.* the annual percentage rate at which customers discontinue using a service, in particular cable and satellite television.

churr ▸*v.* & *n.* variant spelling of CHIRR.

chur·ri·gue·resque /ˌCHŏŏrigəˈresk/ (also **Chur·ri·gue·resque**) ▸*adj.* *Architecture* of or relating to the lavishly ornamented late Spanish baroque style: *a Churrigueresque church.* ▷mid 19th cent.: from the name José Benito de *Churriguera* (1665–1725), a Spanish architect who worked in this style.

chur·ro /ˈCHŏŏrō/ ▸*n.* (*pl.* **chur·ros**) a Latin American fried pastry in ridged cigar shapes, very similar to funnel cake.

chute[1] /SHōōt/ (also **shoot**) ▸*n.* a sloping channel or slide for conveying things to a lower level. ■ a water slide into a swimming pool. ■ short for CHUTE-THE-CHUTE. ▷early 19th cent.: from French, 'fall' (of water or rocks), from Old French *cheoite*, feminine past participle of *cheoir* 'to fall,' from Latin *cadere*; influenced by SHOOT.

chute[2] ▸*n. informal* a parachute. ■ *Sailing* informal term for SPINNAKER. ▷1920s: shortened form. —**chut·ist** /ˈSHōōtist/ *n.*

chute-the-chute (also **chute-the-chutes**) ▸*n.* a steep slide or roller coaster, esp. with water at the foot.
▸*v.* (**chute the chute** or **chute the chutes**) slide down or ride on a chute-the-chute.

chut·ney /ˈCHətnē/ ▸*n.* (*pl.* **-neys**) a spicy condiment made of fruits or vegetables with vinegar, spices, and sugar, originating in India. ▷early 19th cent.: from Hindi *caṭnī*.

chutz·pah /ˈhŏŏtspə; ˈKHŏŏtspə; -spä/ (also **chutz·pa** or **hutz·pah** or **hutz·pa**) ▸*n. informal* shameless audacity; impudence. ▷late 19th cent.: Yiddish, from Aramaic *ḥu ṣpā.*

Chu·vash /ˈCHo͞oˌväSH; CHo͞oˈväSH/ ▸*n.* (*pl.* same) **1** a member of a people living mainly in Chuvashia. **2** the language of this people, usually classified as Turkic.
▸*adj.* of or relating to this people or their language.

Chu·vash·ia /CHo͞oˈväSHēə/ an autonomous republic in Russia, in Europe east of Nizhni Novgorod; pop. 1,340,000; capital, Cheboksary.

chyle /kīl/ ▸*n. Physiology* a milky fluid consisting of fat droplets and lymph. It drains from the lacteals of the small intestine into the lymphatic system during digestion. ▷late Middle English: from late Latin *chylus*, from Greek *khūlos* 'juice' (see CHYME). **—chy·lous** /ˈkīləs/ *adj.*

chy·lo·mi·cron /ˌkīlōˈmīˌkrän/ ▸*n. Physiology* a droplet of fat present in the blood or lymph after absorption from the small intestine. ▷1920s: from *chylo-* (combining form of CHYLE) + MICRON.

chyme /kīm/ ▸*n. Physiology* the pulpy acidic fluid that passes from the stomach to the small intestine, consisting of gastric juices and partly digested food. ▷late Middle English: from late Latin *chymus*, from Greek *khūmos* 'juice' (compare with CHYLE). The Greek words *khūlos* and *khūmos* are from the same root and more or less identical in sense; however, *khūlos* came to be used for juice in a raw or natural state, *khūmos* for juice produced by decoction or digestion. **—chy·mous** /ˈkīməs/ *adj.*

chy·mo·tryp·sin /ˌkīmōˈtripsən/ ▸*n. Biochemistry* a digestive enzyme that breaks down proteins in the small intestine. It is secreted by the pancreas and converted into an active form by trypsin. ▷1930s: from *chymo-* (combining form of CHYME) + TRYPSIN.

chy·ron /ˈkīˌrän/ ▸*n. trademark* an electronically generated caption superimposed on a television or movie screen. ▷1970s: from *Chyron* Corporation, its manufacturer.

CI ▸*abbr.* ■ certificate of insurance. ■ Channel Islands. ■ cost and insurance.

Ci ▸*abbr.* ■ cirrus. ■ curie.

CIA ▸*abbr.* Central Intelligence Agency.

cia·bat·ta /CHəˈbätə/ (also **ciabatta bread**) ▸*n.* a type of flattish, open-textured Italian bread with a floury crust, made with olive oil. ▷Italian, literally 'slipper' (from its shape).

ciao /CHou/ ▸*exclam. informal* used as a greeting at meeting or parting. ▷1920s: Italian, dialect alteration of *schiavo* '(I am your) slave,' from medieval Latin *sclavus* 'slave.'

ci·bo·ri·um /səˈbôrēəm/ ▸*n.* (*pl.* **-bo·ri·a** /-ˈbôrēə/) **1** a receptacle shaped like a shrine or a cup with an arched cover, used in the Christian Church for the reservation of the Eucharist. **2** a canopy over an altar in a church, standing on four pillars. ▷mid 16th cent.: via medieval Latin from Greek *kibōrion* 'seed vessel of the water lily or a cup made from it.' Sense 1 is probably influenced by Latin *cibus* 'food.'

ci·ca·da /səˈkādə; səˈkädə/ ▸*n.* a large homopterous insect with long transparent wings, occurring chiefly in warm countries. The male cicada makes a loud shrill droning noise after dark by vibrating two membranes on its abdomen. • Family Cicadidae, suborder Homoptera: many genera. ▷late Middle English: from Latin *cicada, cicala.*

cicada

cic·a·trix /ˈsikəˌtriks/ (also **cic·a·trice** /-ˌtris/) ▸*n.* (*pl.* **cic·a·tri·ces** /ˌsikəˈtrīsēz; səˈkātrəˌsēz/) the scar of a healed wound. ■ a scar on the bark of a tree. ■ *Botany* a mark on a stem left after a leaf or other part has become detached. ▷late Middle English (as *cicatrice*): from Latin *cicatrix* or Old French *cicatrice.* **—cic·a·tri·cial** /ˌsikəˈtriSHəl/ *adj.*

cic·a·trize /ˈsikəˌtrīz/ ▸*v.* (with reference to a wound) heal by scar formation: [*trans.*] *it was used to cicatrize certain types of wounds* | [*intrans.*] *his wound had cicatrized.* ▷late Middle English: from Old French *cicatriser*, from *cicatrice* 'scar' (see CICATRIX). **—cic·a·tri·za·tion** /ˌsikətrəˈzāSHən/ *n.*

cic·e·ly /ˈsisilē/ (also **sweet cicely**) ▸*n.* (*pl.* **-lies**) an aromatic white-flowered plant of the parsley family, with fernlike leaves. • Genera *Myrrhis* and *Osmorhiza*, family Umbelliferae: several species, in particular the European *M. odorata*, grown as a pot herb and used in herbal medicine, and the North American *O. claytoni.* ▷late 16th cent.: from Latin *seselis*, from Greek. The spelling change was due to association with the given name *Cicely.*

Cic·e·ro[1] /ˈsisəˌrō/ a town in northeastern Illinois, just west of Chicago; pop. 85,616.

Cic·e·ro[2] /ˈsisərō/, Marcus Tullius (106–43 BC), Roman statesman, orator, and writer. He established a model for Latin prose. A supporter of Pompey against Julius Caesar, he attacked Mark Antony in the *Philippics* (43 BC). For this offense, Mark Antony had him put to death.

cic·e·ro·ne /ˌsisəˈrōnē; ˌCHēCHə-/ ▸*n.* (*pl.* **-ro·ni** *pronunc.* same) a guide who gives information about antiquities and places of interest to sightseers. ▷early 18th cent.: from Italian, from Latin *Cicero, Ciceron-* (see CICERO[2]), apparently alluding humorously to his eloquence and learning.

Cic·e·ro·ni·an /ˌsisəˈrōnēən/ ▸*adj.* characteristic of the work and thought of Cicero. ■ (of a piece of speech or writing) in an eloquent and rhythmic style similar to that of Cicero.

cich·lid /ˈsiklid/ ▸*n. Zoology* a perchlike freshwater fish of a family (Cichlidae) that is widely distributed in tropical countries. Cichlids provide a valuable source of food in some areas, and many are popular in aquariums. ▷late 19th cent.: from modern Latin *Cichlidae* (plural), from Greek *kikhlē*, denoting a kind of fish.

CID ▸*abbr.* (in the UK) Criminal Investigation Department.

Cid /el ˈsid/ (**El Cid**) (also **the Cid**), Count of Bivar (*c.*1043–99), Spanish soldier; born *Rodrigo Díaz de Vivar.* A champion of Christianity against the Moors, he captured Valencia in 1094 and went on to rule it. He is immortalized in *Poema del Cid* (12th century) and in Pierre Corneille's play, *Le Cid* (1637).

-cide ▸*comb. form* **1** denoting a person or substance that kills: *insecticide* | *regicide.* **2** denoting an act of killing: *homicide* | *suicide.* ▷via French; sense 1 from Latin *-cida*; sense 2 from Latin *-cidium*, both from *caedere* 'kill.'

ci·der /ˈsīdər/ ▸*n.* (also **sweet cider**) an unfermented drink made by crushing fruit, typically apples. ■ (also **hard cider**) an alcoholic drink made from fermented crushed fruit, typically apples. ▷Middle English: from Old French *sidre*, via ecclesiastical Latin from ecclesiastical Greek *sikera*, from Hebrew *šēkār* 'strong drink.'

ci·der press ▸*n.* a press for crushing fruit, typically apples, to make cider.

ci·der vin·e·gar ▸*n.* a vinegar made from fermented cider.

ci-de·vant /ˌsē dəˈväN/ ▸*adj.* [*attrib.*] from or in an earlier time (used to indicate that someone or something once possessed a specified characteristic but no longer does so): *her ci-devant pupil, now her lover.* ▷early 18th cent.: French, literally 'heretofore.'

Cien·fue·gos /sē-enˈfwāgōs/ a port city in south central Cuba, on Cienfuegos Bay in the Caribbean Sea, the capital of Cienfuegos province; pop. 124,000.

CIF (also **C.I.F.**) ▸*abbr.* cost, insurance, freight (as included in a price).

cig /sig/ ▸*n. informal* a cigarette. ▷late 19th cent.: abbreviation.

ci·gar /siˈgär/ ▸*n.* a cylinder of tobacco rolled in tobacco leaves for smoking. ▷early 18th cent.: from French *cigare*, or from Spanish *cigarro*, probably from Mayan *sik'ar* 'smoking.'
▸**PHRASE** □ **close, but no cigar** *informal* (of an attempt) almost, but not quite successful. [referring to a cigar received in congratulation.]

cig·a·rette /ˌsigəˈret; ˈsigəˌret/ (also **cig·a·ret**) ▸*n.* a thin cylinder of finely cut tobacco rolled in paper for smoking. ■ a similar cylinder containing a narcotic, herbs, or a medicated substance. ▷mid 19th cent.: from French, diminutive of *cigare* (see CIGAR).

cig·a·rette pants ▸*plural n.* women's pants with straight, very narrow legs.

cig·a·rette pa·per ▸*n.* a piece of thin paper with a gummed edge in which tobacco can be rolled to make a cigarette.

cig·a·ril·lo /ˌsigəˈrilō; -ˈrē(y)ō/ ▸*n.* (*pl.* **-los**) a small cigar. ▷mid 19th cent.: from Spanish, diminutive of *cigarro* (see CIGAR).

ci·gua·te·ra /ˌsēgwəˈterə/ ▸*n.* poisoning by neurotoxins as a result of eating the flesh of a tropical marine fish that carries a toxic dinoflagellate. • This is caused by *Gambierdiscus toxicus*, phylum Dinophyta. ▷mid 19th cent.: from American Spanish, from *cigua* 'sea snail.'

ci·lan·tro /siˈlanˌtrō; -ˈlän-/ ▸*n.* another term for CORIANDER (esp. the leaves). ▷1920s: from Spanish, from Latin *coliandrum* 'coriander.'

cil·i·a /ˈsilēə/ ▸ plural form of CILIUM.

cil·i·ar·y /ˈsilēˌerē/ ▸*adj.* **1** *Biology* of, relating to, or involving cilia: *ciliary action.* **2** *Anatomy* of or relating to the eyelashes or eyelids. ■ of or relating to the ciliary body of the eye.

cil·i·ar·y bod·y ▸*n. Anatomy* the part of the eye that connects the iris to the choroid. It consists of the **ciliary muscle** (which alters the curvature of the lens), a series of radial **ciliary processes** (from which the lens is suspended by ligaments), and the **ciliary ring** (which adjoins the choroid).

cil·i·ate /ˈsilēˌāt; -ēət/ ▸*n. Zoology* a single-celled animal of a phylum distinguished by the possession of cilia or ciliary structures. The ciliates are a large and diverse group of advanced protozoans. • Phylum Ciliophora, kingdom Protista (formerly class Ciliata, phylum Protozoa).
▸*adj. Zoology* (of an organism, cell, or surface) bearing cilia. ■ *Botany* (of a margin) having a fringe of hairs. **—cil·i·at·ed** /ˈsilēātid/ *adj.*

cil·ice /ˈsiləs/ ▸*n.* haircloth. ■ a garment made of such cloth. ▷late 16th cent.: from French, from Latin *cilicium*, from Greek *kilikion*, from *Kilikia*, the Greek name for CILICIA in Asia Minor (because the cloth was originally made of Cilician goats' hair).

Ci·li·cia /səˈliSHə/ an ancient region on the coast of southeastern Asia Minor. **—Ci·li·cian** *adj.* & *n.*

Ci·li·cian Gates /səˈliSHən/ a mountain pass in the Taurus Mountains in southern Turkey. Historically, it forms part of a route that linked Anatolia with the Mediterranean coast.

cil·i·o·late /ˈsilēəlit; -ˌlāt/ ▸*adj.* having cilia.

cil·i·um /ˈsilēəm/ ▸*n.* (usu. in *pl.* **cil·i·a** /ˈsilēə/) *Biology & Anatomy* a short, microscopic, hairlike vibrating structure. Cilia occur in large numbers on the surface of certain cells, either causing currents in the surrounding fluid, or, in some protozoans and other small organisms, providing propulsion. ■ an eyelash, or a delicate hairlike structure that resembles one. ▷early 18th cent. (in the sense 'eyelash'): from Latin. **—cil·i·at·ed** /ˈsilēˌātid/ *adj.* **—cil·i·a·tion** /ˌsilēˈāSHən/ *n.*

Cim·ar·ron Riv·er /ˈsiməˌrän; -ˌrōn/ a river that flows for 600 miles (1,000 km) from New Mexico across Oklahoma to the Arkansas River near Tulsa. The western part of Oklahoma's panhandle was once known as the Territory of Cimarron.

ci·met·i·dine /sīˈmetəˌdēn/ ▸*n. Medicine* an antihistamine drug used to treat stomach acidity and peptic ulcers. It is a sulfur-containing derivative of imidazole. ▷1970s: from *ci-* (alteration of *cy-* in *cyano-*) + *met(hyl)* + -IDE + -INE[4].

Cim·me·ri·an /səˈmi(ə)rēən; -ˈmer-/ ▸*adj.* **1** relating to or denoting members of an ancient nomadic people who overran Asia Minor in the 7th century BC. **2** *Greek Mythology* relating to or denoting members of a mythical people who lived in perpetual mist and darkness near the land of the dead.
▸*n.* a member of the historical or mythological Cimmerian people. ▷via Latin from Greek *Kimmerios* + -AN.

CINC ▸*abbr.* Commander in Chief.

cinch /sinCH/ ▸*n.* **1** *informal* an extremely easy task: *the program was a cinch to use.* ■ a sure thing; a certainty: *he was a cinch to take a prize.* **2** a girth for a Western saddle or pack.
▸*v.* [*trans.*] **1** secure (a garment) with a belt. ■ fix (a saddle) securely by means of a girth; girth up (a horse). **2** *informal* make certain of: *his advice cinched her decision to accept the offer.* ▷mid 19th cent. (sense 2 of the *noun*): from Spanish *cincha* 'girth.'

cinch bug ▸*n.* another term for CHINCH.

cin·cho·na /siNGˈkōnə; sinˈCHōnə/ ▸*n.* an evergreen South American tree or shrub of the bedstraw family, with fragrant flowers and cultivated for its bark. • Genus *Cinchona*, family Rubiaceae: several species. ■ (also **cinchona bark**) the dried bark of this tree, which is a source of quinine and other medicinal alkaloids. ■ a drug made from this bark, formerly used as a tonic and to stimulate the appetite. ▷mid 18th cent.: modern Latin, named after the Countess

Pronunciation Key ə *ago*; ər *over*; ˈə *or* ˌə *up*; ˈər *or* ˌər *fur*; a *hat*; ā *rate*; ä *car*; CH *chew*; e *let*; ē *see*; e(ə)r *air*; i *fit*; ī *by*; i(ə)r *ear*; NG *sing*; ō *go*; ô *for*; oi *boy*; o͝o *good*; o͞o *goo*; ou *out*; SH *she*; TH *thin*; T͟H *then*; (h)w *why*; ZH *vision*

of *Chinchón* (died 1641), who introduced the drug into Spain.

cin·cho·nine /ˈsiNGkə,nēn; ˈsinCHə-/ ▸*n. Chemistry* a compound with antipyretic properties, derived from cinchona bark and used as a substitute for quinine. • An alkaloid; chem. formula: $C_{19}H_{22}ON_2$.

cin·chon·ism /ˈsiNGkə,nizəm; ˈsin-/ ▸*n.* poisoning due to excessive ingestion of cinchona alkaloids.

Cin·cin·nat·i /,sinsəˈnatē/ an industrial city in southwestern Ohio, on the Ohio River; pop. 331,285.

cinc·ture /ˈsiNGkCHər/ ▸*n.* **1** *poetic/literary* a girdle or belt. **2** *Architecture* a ring at either end of a column shaft. ▷late 16th cent. (in the sense 'encircling or enclosure'): from Latin *cinctura*, from *cinct-* 'encircled,' from the verb *cingere*.

cin·der /ˈsindər/ ▸*n.* a small piece of partly burned coal or wood that has stopped giving off flames but still has combustible matter in it. ▷Old English *sinder* 'slag,' of Germanic origin; related to German *Sinter*. The similar but unconnected French *cendre* (from Latin *cinis* 'ashes') has influenced both the sense development and the spelling. Compare with SINTER. **—cin·der·y** *adj.*

cin·der block ▸*n.* a lightweight building brick made from small cinders mixed with sand and cement.

cin·der cone ▸*n.* a cone formed around a volcanic vent by fragments of lava thrown out during eruptions.

Cin·der·el·la /,sindəˈrelə/ a girl in various traditional European fairy tales. In the version by Charles Perrault she is exploited as a servant by her family but enabled by a fairy godmother to attend a royal ball. She meets and captivates Prince Charming but has to flee at midnight, leaving the prince to identify her by the glass slipper that she leaves behind. ■ [as *n.*] a person or thing of unrecognized or disregarded merit or beauty. ■ [as *n.*] a neglected aspect of something: *is research into breast cancer to remain the Cinderella of medicine?* ■ *Philately* any stamplike label that is not valid as postage. ▷from CINDER + the diminutive suffix *-ella*, on the pattern of French *Cendrillon*, from *cendre* 'cinders.'

cin·der track (also **cinder path**) ▸*n.* a footpath or running track laid with fine cinders.

cin·e /ˈsinē/ ▸*adj. chiefly Brit.* cinematographic: *a cine camera.*

cine- ▸*comb. form* representing CINEMATOGRAPHIC (see CINEMATOGRAPHY).

cin·e·ast /ˈsinē,ast/ (also **cin·é·aste** or **cin·e·aste**) ▸*n.* a filmmaker. ■ an enthusiast for or devotee of movies or filmmaking. ▷1920s: from French *cinéaste*, from *ciné* (from *cinéma*), on the pattern of *enthousiaste* 'enthusiast.'

cin·e·ma /ˈsinəmə/ ▸*n. chiefly Brit.* a movie theater. ■ the production of movies as an art or industry: *the history of American cinema.* ▷early 20th cent.: from French *cinéma*, abbreviation of *cinématographe* (see CINEMATOGRAPH).

Cin·e·ma·Scope /ˈsinəmə,skōp/ ▸*n. trademark* a cinematographic process in which special lenses are used to compress a wide image into a standard frame and then expand it again during projection. It results in an image that is almost two and a half times as wide as it is high. **—Cin·e·ma·Scop·ic** /,sinəməˈskäpik/ *adv.*

cin·e·ma·theque /ˈsinəmə,tek/ ▸*n.* **1** a motion-picture library or archive. **2** a small movie theater, esp. one that shows avant-garde or classic movies. ▷1960s: from French *cinémathèque*, from *cinéma* 'cinema,' on the pattern of *bibliothèque* 'library.'

cin·e·mat·ic /,sinəˈmatik/ ▸*adj.* of or relating to motion pictures: *cinematic output.* ■ having qualities characteristic of motion pictures: *the cinematic feel of their video.* **—cin·e·mat·i·cal·ly** /-ik(ə)lē/ *adv.*

cin·e·ma·tize /ˈsinəmə,tīz/ ▸*v.* [*trans.*] adapt (a play, story, etc.) to the cinema; make a movie of.

cin·e·mat·o·graph /,sinəˈmatəgraf/ (also **kin·e·mat·o·graph** /,kinə-/) ▸*n. chiefly Brit., historical* an early motion-picture projector. ▷late 19th cent.: from French *cinématographe*, from Greek *kinēma*, *kinēmat-* 'movement,' from *kinein* 'to move.'

cin·e·ma·tog·ra·phy /,sinəməˈtägrəfē/ ▸*n.* the art of making motion pictures. **—cin·e·ma·tog·ra·pher** /-fər/ *n.* **—cin·e·mat·o·graph·ic** /-,matəˈgrafik/ *adj.* **—cin·e·mat·o·graph·i·cal·ly** /-,matəˈgrafik(ə)lē/ *adv.*

ci·né·ma vé·ri·té /ˈsinəmə ,veriˈtā/ ▸*n.* a style of filmmaking characterized by realistic, typically documentary motion pictures that avoid artificiality and artistic effect and are generally made with simple equipment. ■ motion pictures of this style collectively. ▷mid 20th cent.: French, literally 'cinema truth.'

cin·e·phile /ˈsini,fīl/ ▸*n.* a person who is fond of motion pictures.

cin·e·plex /ˈsini,pleks/ (also **Cin·e·plex**) ▸*n. trademark* a movie theater with several separate screens; a multiplex. ▷1970s: blend of CINEMA and COMPLEX.

cin·e·rar·i·a /,sinəˈre(ə)rēə/ ▸*n.* a plant of the daisy family with compact masses of bright flowers, often cultivated as a houseplant. • Genus *Pericallis* (formerly *Senecio* or *Cineraria*), family Compositae. ▷modern Latin, feminine of Latin *cinerarius* 'of ashes,' from *cinis*, *ciner-* 'ashes' (because of the ash-colored down on the leaves).

cin·e·rar·i·um /,sinəˈre(ə)rēəm/ ▸*n.* (*pl.* **-ums**) a place where the ashes of the cremated dead are kept. ▷late 19th cent.: from late Latin, neuter (used as a noun) of *cinerarius* 'of ashes.' **—cin·e·rar·y** /ˈsinə,rerē/ *adj.*

ci·ne·re·ous /səˈni(ə)rēəs/ ▸*adj.* (esp. of hair or feathers) ash-gray. ▷late Middle English: from Latin *cinereus* 'similar to ashes' (from *cinis*, *ciner-* 'ashes') + -OUS.

ci·ne·re·ous vul·ture ▸*n.* another term for BLACK VULTURE (sense 2).

ci·né·vé·ri·té /,sinə ,veriˈtā; siˈnā/ ▸*n.* another term for CINÉMA-VÉRITÉ.

cin·gu·lum /ˈsiNGgyələm/ ▸*n.* (*pl.* **-la** /-lə/) *Anatomy* an encircling structure, in particular: ■ a curved bundle of nerve fibers in each hemisphere of the brain. ■ a ridge of enamel on the base or margin of the crown of a tooth. ▷mid 19th cent.: from Latin, 'belt,' from *cingere* 'gird.' **—cin·gu·late** /-lit/ *adj.*

cin·na·bar /ˈsinə,bär/ ▸*n.* a bright red mineral consisting of mercury sulfide. It is the only important ore of mercury and is sometimes used as a pigment. ■ the bright red color of this; vermilion: [as *adj.*] *the blood coagulated in cinnabar threads.* ▷Middle English: from Latin *cinnabaris*, from Greek *kinnabari*, of obscure origin.

cin·nam·ic /səˈnamik/ ▸*adj.* of cinnamon. ■ denoting an acidic crystalline powder (**cinnamic acid**), $C_9H_8O_2$, derived from cinnamon or produced synthetically and used in medicine and perfumery.

cin·na·mon /ˈsinəmən/ ▸*n.* **1** an aromatic spice made from the peeled, dried, and rolled bark of a Southeast Asian tree. ■ flavored with cinnamon, or having a similar flavor: *cinnamon candy.* ■ a reddish- or yellowish-brown color resembling that of cinnamon. **2** (also **cinnamon tree**) the tree that yields this spice. • Genus *Cinnamomum*, family Lauraceae: several species, in particular *C. zeylanicum*, native to southern India and Sri Lanka. ▷late Middle English: from Old French *cinnamome* (from Greek *kinnamōmon*), and Latin *cinnamon* (from Greek *kinnamon*), both from a Semitic language and perhaps based on Malay.

cin·na·mon stick ▸*n.* a piece, typically several inches long, of the peeled, dried, and rolled bark of a cinnamon tree, used decoratively or to flavor mulled drinks.

cin·na·mon bear ▸*n.* a North American black bear of a variety with reddish-brown hair.

cin·na·mon fern ▸*n.* a large North American fern whose fertile fronds are cinnamon-colored in spring. • *Osmunda cinnamomea*, family Osmundaceae.

cinque /siNGk; saNGk/ (also **cinq**) ▸*n.* the five on dice. ▷late Middle English: from Old French *cinc*, *cink*, from Latin *quinque* 'five.'

cin·que·cen·to /,CHiNGkwiˈCHentō/ ▸*n.* (**the cinquecento**) the 16th century as a period of Italian art, architecture, or literature, with a reversion to classical forms. ▷Italian, literally '500' (shortened from *milcinquecento* '1500') used with reference to the years 1500–99.

cinque·foil /ˈsiNGk,foil; ˈsaNGk-/ ▸*n.* **1** a widely distributed herbaceous plant of the rose family, with compound leaves of five leaflets and five-petaled yellow flowers. • Genus *Potentilla*, family Rosaceae: numerous species, including the small-flowered creeping **common cinquefoil** (*P. simplex*) and the larger-flowered erect **rough-fruited cinquefoil** (*P. recta*). **2** *Art* an ornamental design of five lobes arranged in a circle, e.g., in architectural tracery or heraldry. ▷Middle English: from Latin *quinquefolium*, from *quinque* 'five' + *folium* 'leaf.'

rough-fruited cinquefoil

Cin·za·no /CHinˈzänō; sin-/ ▸*n. trademark* a type of vermouth produced in Italy. ▷from the name of the producers.

CIO ▸*abbr.* Congress of Industrial Organizations.

ci·on ▸*n.* variant spelling of SCION (sense 1).

ci·pher /ˈsīfər/ (also **cy·pher**) ▸*n.* **1** a secret or disguised way of writing; a code: *he was writing cryptic notes in a cipher | the information may be given in cipher.* ■ a thing written in such a code. ■ a key to such a code. **2** *dated* a zero; a figure 0. ■ *figurative* a person or thing of no importance, esp. a person who does the bidding of others and seems to have no will of their own. **3** a monogram. **4** a continuous sounding of an organ pipe, caused by a mechanical defect.
▸*v.* **1** [*trans.*] put (a message) into secret writing; encode. **2** [*intrans.*] *archaic* do arithmetic. ▷late Middle English (in the senses 'symbol for zero' and 'Arabic numeral'): from Old French *cifre*, based on Arabic *ṣifr* 'zero.' Sense 4 is perhaps a different word.

cir. (also **circ.**) ▸*abbr.* ■ circle. ■ circuit. ■ circular. ■ circulation. ■ circumference.

cir·ca /ˈsərkə/ ▸*prep.* (often preceding a date) approximately: *built circa 1935.* ▷mid 19th cent.: Latin.

cir·ca·di·an /sərˈkādēən/ ▸*adj. Physiology* (of biological processes) recurring naturally on a twenty-four-hour cycle, even in the absence of light fluctuations: *a circadian rhythm.* ▷1950s: formed irregularly from Latin *circa* 'around' + *dies* 'day.'

Cir·cas·sian /sərˈkaSHən/ ▸*adj.* relating to or denoting a group of mainly Sunni Muslim peoples of the northwest Caucasus.
▸*n.* **1** a member of this people. **2** either of two North Caucasian languages of these peoples. ▷from *Circassia*, Latinized form of Russian *Cherkes*, denoting a district in the northern Caucasus.

Cir·ce /ˈsərsē/ *Greek Mythology* an enchantress who lived with her wild animals on the island of Aeaea. When Odysseus visited the island, his companions were changed into pigs by her potions, but he protected himself with the mythical herb *moly* and forced her to restore his men into human form. ▷via Latin from Greek *Kirkē*.

cir·ci·nate /ˈsərsə,nāt/ ▸*adj. Botany* rolled up with the tip in the center, for example the young frond of a fern. ■ *Medicine* circular in appearance. ▷early 19th cent.: from Latin *circinatus*, past participle of *circinare* 'make round,' from *circinus* 'pair of compasses.'

Cir·ci·nus /ˈsərsənəs/ *Astronomy* a small and faint southern constellation (the Compasses), in the Milky Way next to Centaurus. ■ [as *genitive*] (**Circini** /-nī/) used with a preceding letter or numeral to designate a star in this constellation: *the star Alpha Circini.* ▷Latin.

cir·cle /ˈsərkəl/ (abbr.: **cir.** or **circ.**) ▸*n.* **1** a round plane figure whose boundary (the circumference) consists of points equidistant from a fixed point (the center). ■ the line enclosing such a figure. ■ something in the shape of such a figure: *the lamp spread a circle of light.* ■ a group of people or things arranged to form such a figure: *they all sat around in a circle.* ■ a movement or series of movements that follows the approximate circumference of such a figure: *the astrological houses rotate in a circle.* ■ a dark circular mark below each eye, typically caused by illness or tiredness. ■ a curved upper tier of seats in a theater. See also DRESS CIRCLE. **2** a group of people with a shared profession, interests, or acquaintances: *she did not normally move in such exalted circles.*
▸*v.* [*trans.*] move all the way around (someone or something), esp. more than once: *the two dogs circle each other with hackles raised | [intrans.] we circled around the island.* ■ [*trans.*] (from the air) move in a ring-shaped path above (someone or something), esp. more than once: *they were circling the airport |* [as *adj.*] (**circling**) *a circling helicopter.* ■ [*intrans.*] (**circle back**) move in a wide loop back toward one's starting point. ■ (often **be circled**) form a ring around: *the monastery was circled by a huge wall.* ■ draw a line around: *circle the correct answers.* ▷Old English, from Old French *cercle*, from Latin *circulus* 'small ring,' diminutive of *circus* 'ring.'
▸*PHRASES* □ **circle the wagons** *informal* (of a group) unite in defense of a common interest. [with reference to the defensive position of a wagon train under attack.] □ **come** (or **turn**) **full circle** return to a past position or situation, esp. in a way considered to be inevitable. □ **go around** (or **around and around**) **in circles** *informal* do something for a long time without achieving anything but purposeless repetition: *the discussion went around and around in*

circles. □ **run around in circles** *informal* be fussily busy with little result. □ **the wheel has turned** (or **come**) **full circle** the situation has returned to what it was in the past, as if completing a cycle. [with reference to Shakespeare's *King Lear*, by association with the wheel fabled to be turned by Fortune and representing mutability.]

cir·cle dance ▶*n.* a country dance or folk dance, typically following a traditional set of steps, in which dancers form a circle.

cir·cle graph ▶*n.* another term for PIE CHART.

cir·clet /ˈsərklət/ ▶*n.* a circular band, typically one made of precious metal, worn on the head as an ornament. ■ a small circular arrangement or object. ▷late Middle English: from CIRCLE + -ET[1], perhaps reinforced by archaic French *cerclet*.

cir·cuit /ˈsərkət/ (abbr.: **cir.** or **circ.**) ▶*n.* **1** a roughly circular line, route, or movement that starts and finishes at the same place: *I ran a circuit of the village.* ■ a complete and closed path around which a circulating electric current can flow. ■ a system of electrical conductors and components forming such a path. **2** an established itinerary of events or venues used for a particular activity, typically involving public performance: *the alternative cabaret circuit.* ■ a series of sporting events in which the same players regularly take part: *his first season on the professional circuit.* ■ a series of athletic exercises performed consecutively in one training session: [as *adj.*] *circuit training.* ■ a regular journey made by a judge around a particular district to hear cases in court: [as *adj.*] *a circuit judge.* ■ a district of this type. ■ a judicial region formerly administered by traveling judges. ■ a group of local Methodist churches forming an administrative unit. ■ a chain of theaters or nightclubs under a single management.
▶*v.* [*trans.*] move all the way around (a place or thing): *the trains will follow the northern line, circuiting the capital.* ▷late Middle English: via Old French from Latin *circuitus*, from *circuire*, variant of *circumire* 'go around,' from *circum* 'around' + *ire* 'go.'

cir·cuit board ▶*n.* a thin rigid board containing an electric circuit; a printed circuit.

cir·cuit break·er ▶*n.* an automatic device for stopping the flow of current in an electric circuit as a safety measure.

cir·cu·i·tous /sərˈkyo͞oətəs/ ▶*adj.* (of a route or journey) longer than the most direct way: *the canal followed a circuitous route* | *figurative a circuitous line of reasoning.* ▷mid 17th cent.: from medieval Latin *circuitosus*, from *circuitus* 'a way around'(see CIRCUIT). —**cir·cu·i·tous·ly** *adv.* —**cir·cu·i·tous·ness** *n.*

cir·cuit rid·er ▶*n. historical* a clergyman who traveled on horseback from church to church, esp. within a rural Methodist circuit.

cir·cuit·ry /ˈsərkətrē/ ▶*n.* (*pl.* **-ries**) electric circuits collectively: *solid state circuitry.* ■ a circuit or system of circuits performing a particular function in an electronic device: *switching circuitry.*

cir·cu·lar /ˈsərkyələr/ (abbr.: **cir.** or **circ.**) ▶*adj.* **1** having the form of a circle: *the building features a circular atrium.* See note at ROUND. ■ (of a movement or journey) starting and finishing at the same place and often following roughly the circumference of an imaginary circle: *a circular walk.* **2** *Logic* (of an argument) already containing an assumption of what is to be proved, and therefore fallacious. **3** [*attrib.*] (of a letter or advertisement) for distribution to a large number of people.
▶*n.* a letter or advertisement that is distributed to a large number of people. ▷late Middle English: from Old French *circulier*, from late Latin *circularis*, from Latin *circulus* 'small ring' (see CIRCLE). —**cir·cu·lar·i·ty** /ˌsərkyəˈlaritē/ *n.* —**cir·cu·lar·ly** *adv.*

cir·cu·lar breath·ing ▶*n.* a technique of inhaling through the nose while blowing air through the lips from the cheeks, used to maintain constant exhalation esp. by players of certain wind instruments.

cir·cu·lar func·tion ▶*n. Mathematics* another term for TRIGONOMETRIC FUNCTION.

cir·cu·lar·ize /ˈsərkyələˌrīz/ ▶*v.* [*trans.*] **1** distribute a large number of letters, leaflets, or questionnaires to (a group of people) in order to advertise something or canvas opinion. **2** *Biochemistry* make (a stretch of DNA) into a circular loop. —**cir·cu·lar·i·za·tion** /ˌsərkyələrəˈzāSHən/ *n.*

cir·cu·lar po·lar·i·za·tion ▶*n. Physics* polarization of an electromagnetic wave in which either the electric or the magnetic vector executes a circle perpendicular to the path of propagation with a frequency equal to that of the wave. It is frequently used in satellite communications.

cir·cu·lar saw ▶*n.* a power saw with a rapidly rotating toothed disk.

cir·cu·late /ˈsərkyəˌlāt/ ▶*v.* **1** move or cause to move continuously or freely through a closed system or area: [*intrans.*] *antibodies circulate in the bloodstream* | [*trans.*] *the fan circulates hot air around the oven.* ■ [*intrans.*] move around a social function in order to talk to many different people. **2** pass or cause to pass from place to place or person to person: [*intrans.*] *rumors of his arrest circulated* | [*trans.*] *they were circulating the list to conservation groups.* ▷late 15th cent. (as an alchemical term meaning 'distill something in a closed container, allowing condensed vapor to return to the original liquid'): from Latin *circulat-* 'moved in a circular path,' from the verb *circulare*, from *circulus* 'small ring' (see CIRCLE). Sense 1 dates from the mid 17th cent. —**cir·cu·la·tive** /-ˌlātiv; -lətiv/ *adj.* —**cir·cu·la·tor** /-ˌlātər/ *n.*

cir·cu·lat·ing dec·i·mal ▶*n.* another term for REPEATING DECIMAL.

cir·cu·lat·ing li·brar·y ▶*n. historical* a small library with books lent for a small fee to subscribers.

cir·cu·la·tion /ˌsərkyəˈlāSHən/ (abbr.: **cir.** or **circ.**) ▶*n.* **1** movement to and fro or around something, esp. that of fluid in a closed system: *an extra pump for good water circulation.* ■ the continuous motion by which the blood travels through all parts of the body under the action of the heart. ■ the movement of sap through a plant. **2** the public availability or knowledge of something: *his music has achieved wide circulation.* ■ the movement, exchange, or availability of money in a country: *the new coins go into circulation today.* ■ [in *sing.*] the number of copies sold of a newspaper or magazine: *the magazine had a large circulation.* ▷late Middle English (denoting continuous distillation of a liquid): from Latin *circulatio(n-)*, from the verb *circulare* (see CIRCULATE).
▶*PHRASE* □ **in** (or **out of**) **circulation** available (or unavailable) to the public; in (or not in) general use: *there is a huge volume of video material in circulation.* ■ used of a person who is seen (or not seen) in public: *Anne had made a good recovery and was back in circulation.*

cir·cu·la·to·ry /ˈsərkyələˌtôrē/ ▶*adj.* of or relating to the circulation of blood or sap.

cir·cu·la·to·ry sys·tem ▶*n. Biology* the system that circulates blood and lymph through the body, consisting of the heart, blood vessels, blood, lymph, and the lymphatic vessels and glands. Also called CARDIOVASCULAR SYSTEM.

circum. ▶*abbr.* circumference.

circum- ▶*prefix* about; around: *circumambulate* | *circumpolar.* ▷from Latin *circum* 'around.'

cir·cum·am·bi·ent /ˌsərkəmˈambēənt/ ▶*adj. chiefly poetic/literary* surrounding: *he could not see them clearly by reason of the circumambient water.* —**cir·cum·am·bi·ence** *n.* —**cir·cum·am·bi·en·cy** *n.*

cir·cum·am·bu·late /ˌsərkəmˈambyəˌlāt/ ▶*v.* [*trans.*] *formal* walk all the way around (something): *they used to circumambulate the perimeter wall.* —**cir·cum·am·bu·la·tion** /-ˌambyəˈlāSHən/ *n.* —**cir·cum·am·bu·la·to·ry** /-ˈambyələˌtôrē/ *adj.*

cir·cum·cise /ˈsərkəmˌsīz/ ▶*v.* [*trans.*] cut off the foreskin of (a young boy or man, esp. a baby) as a religious rite, esp. in Judaism and Islam, or as a medical treatment. ■ cut off the clitoris, and sometimes the labia, of (a girl or young woman) as a traditional practice among some peoples. ▷Middle English: from Old French *circonciser*, or from Latin *circumcis-* 'cut around,' from the verb *circumcidere*, from *circum* 'around, about' + *caedere* 'to cut.'

cir·cum·ci·sion /ˌsərkəmˈsiZHən; ˈsərkəmˌsiZHən/ ▶*n.* the action or practice of circumcising a young boy or man. See also FEMALE CIRCUMCISION. ■ (**Circumcision**) (in church use) the feast of the Circumcision of Jesus, January 1. ▷Middle English: from late Latin *circumcisio(n-)*, from the verb *circumcidere* (see CIRCUMCISE).

cir·cum·fer·ence /sərˈkəmf(ə)rəns/ (abbr.: **cir.**, **circ.**, or **circum.**) ▶*n.* the enclosing boundary of a curved geometric figure, esp. a circle. ■ the distance around something: *babies who have small head circumferences* | *two inches in circumference.* ■ the edge or region that entirely surrounds something: *petals on the circumference are larger than those in the center.* ▷late Middle English: from Old French *circonference*, from Latin *circumferentia*, from *circum* 'around, about' + *ferre* 'carry, bear.' —**cir·cum·fer·en·tial** /sərˌkəmfəˈrenCHəl/ *adj.* —**cir·cum·fer·en·tial·ly** *adv.*

cir·cum·flex /ˈsərkəmˌfleks/ ▶*n.* (also **circumflex accent**) a mark (^) placed over a vowel in some languages to indicate contraction, length, or pitch or tone.
▶*adj. Anatomy* bending around something else; curved: *circumflex coronary arteries.* ▷late 16th cent.: from Latin *circumflexus* (from *circum* 'around, about' + *flectere* 'to bend'), translating Greek *perispōmenos* 'drawn around.'

cir·cum·flu·ent /sərˈkəmflo͞oənt; ˌsərkəmˈflo͞oənt/ ▶*adj.* flowing around; surrounding. ▷late 16th cent.: from Latin *circumfluent-* 'flowing around,' from the verb *circumfluere*, from *circum* 'around, about' + *fluere* 'to flow.' —**cir·cum·flu·ence** *n.*

cir·cum·fuse /ˌsərkəmˈfyo͞oz/ ▶*v.* [*trans.*] (usu. **be circumfused**) *archaic* pour (a liquid) so as to cause it to surround something: *Earth with her nether Ocean circumfused.* ▷late 16th cent.: from Latin *circumfus-* 'poured around,' from the verb *circumfundere*, from *circum* 'around' + *fundere* 'pour.'

cir·cum·ja·cent /ˌsərkəmˈjāsənt/ ▶*adj. archaic* surrounding: *the circumjacent parts of the mouth.* ▷late 15th cent.: from Latin *circumjacent-* 'lying around, bordering upon,' from the verb *circumjacere*, from *circum* 'around' + *jacere* 'to lie.'

cir·cum·lo·cu·tion /ˌsərkəmˌlōˈkyo͞oSHən/ ▶*n.* the use of many words where fewer would do, esp. in a deliberate attempt to be vague or evasive: *his admission came after years of circumlocution* | *he used a number of poetic circumlocutions.* ▷late Middle English: from Latin *circumlocutio(n-)* (translating Greek *periphrasis*), from *circum* 'around' + *locutio(n-)* from *loqui* 'speak.' —**cir·cum·loc·u·to·ry** /-ˈläkyəˌtôrē/ *adj.*

cir·cum·lu·nar /ˌsərkəmˈlo͞onər/ ▶*adj.* moving or situated around the moon: *a circumlunar flight.*

cir·cum·nav·i·gate /ˌsərkəmˈnavəˌgāt/ ▶*v.* [*trans.*] sail all the way around (something, esp. the world). ■ *humorous* go around or across (something): *he helped her to circumnavigate a frozen puddle.* —**cir·cum·nav·i·ga·tion** /-ˌnavəˈgāSHən/ *n.* —**cir·cum·nav·i·ga·tor** /-ˌgātər/ *n.*

cir·cum·po·lar /ˌsərkəmˈpōlər/ ▶*adj.* situated around or inhabiting one of the earth's poles: *the eight circumpolar countries met in 1991.* ■ *Astronomy* (of a star or motion) above the horizon at all times in a given latitude: *the Big Dipper is circumpolar at Mediterranean latitudes.*

cir·cum·ro·tate /ˌsərkəmˈrōtāt/ ▶*v.* [*intrans.*] to revolve or turn like a wheel.

cir·cum·scribe /ˈsərkəmˌskrīb/ ▶*v.* [*trans.*] (often **be circumscribed**) **1** restrict (something) within limits: *their movements were strictly monitored and circumscribed.* **2** *Geometry* draw (a figure) around another, touching it at points but not cutting it. Compare with INSCRIBE. ▷late Middle English: from Latin *circumscribere*, from *circum* 'around' + *scribere* 'write.' —**cir·cum·scrib·er** *n.* —**cir·cum·scrip·tion** /ˌsərkəmˈskripSHən/ *n.*

THE RIGHT WORD **circumscribe, encircle, enclose, encompass, envelop, surround**

Strictly speaking, to **circumscribe** is to draw a line around something to mark its limits or boundary (*a square circumscribed by a circle*).

Beyond the realm of geometry, however, it suggests something that is hemmed in on all sides (*a lake circumscribed by mountains*).

Encompass is used when something is set within a circle or within limits (*a road that encompassed the grounds of the estate;* | *a view that encompassed the harbor*).

Surround is a less formal word for *circumscribe*, but it can also refer to an undesirable, threatening, or dangerous situation (*surrounded by angry demonstrators;* | *surrounded by skyscrapers*).

Encircle is similar to *surround* in meaning, but it suggests a tight or quite circular clustering around a central object (*a bowl of fruit encircled by flowers*) or a deliberate attempt to surround someone or something for a definite reason (*to encircle the enemy camp*).

Envelop is the right word if something is surrounded to the point where it can barely be seen (*a lonely figure enveloped in fog*) or if it is surrounded by layers or folds of an amorphous material (*enveloped in soft cotton to prevent breakage*).

Enclose is very similar to *envelop*, but it suggests that something has been especially designed to fit around something else for protection or containment (*a ship model enclosed in a glass case*).

cir·cum·so·lar /ˌsərkəm'sōlər/ ▸*adj.* moving or situated around the sun.

cir·cum·spect /'sərkəmˌspekt/ ▸*adj.* wary and unwilling to take risks: *the officials were very circumspect in their statements.* See note at **VIGILANT**. ▷late Middle English: from Latin *circumspectus*, from *circumspicere* 'look around,' from *circum* 'around, about' + *specere* 'look.' —**cir·cum·spec·tion** /ˌsərkəm'spekSHən/ *n.* —**cir·cum·spect·ly** *adv.*

cir·cum·stance /'sərkəmˌstans; -stəns/ ▸*n.* **1** (usu. **circumstances**) a fact or condition connected with or relevant to an event or action: *we wanted to marry but circumstances didn't permit.* ■ an event or fact that causes or helps to cause something to happen, typically something undesirable: *he was found dead but there were no suspicious circumstances | they were thrown together by circumstance.* **2** one's state of financial or material welfare: *the artists are living in reduced circumstances.* ▷Middle English: from Old French *circonstance* or Latin *circumstantia*, from *circumstare* 'encircle, encompass,' from *circum* 'around' + *stare* 'stand.' —**cir·cum·stanced** *adj.*

▸*PHRASES* □ **under no circumstances** never, whatever the situation is or might be: *under no circumstances may the child be identified.* □ **under** (or **in**) **the circumstances** given the difficult nature of the situation: *she had every right to be angry under the circumstances.*

cir·cum·stan·tial /ˌsərkəm'stanCHəl/ ▸*adj.* **1** (of evidence or a legal case) pointing indirectly toward someone's guilt but not conclusively proving it. **2** (of a description) containing full details: *the picture was circumstantial and therefore convincing.* ▷late 16th cent.: from Latin *circumstantia* (see **CIRCUMSTANCE**) + **-AL**. —**cir·cum·stan·ti·al·i·ty** /-ˌstanCHē'alətē/ *n.* —**cir·cum·stan·tial·ly** *adv.*

cir·cum·stan·ti·ate /ˌsərkəm'stansHēˌāt/ ▸*v.* [*trans.*] *rare* set forth or support with circumstances or details. —**cir·cum·stan·ti·a·tion** /ˌsərkəmˌstansHē'āsHən/ *n.*

cir·cum·ter·res·tri·al /ˌsərkəmtə'restrēəl; -tə'resCHəl/ ▸*adj.* moving or situated around the earth: *circumterrestrial space.*

cir·cum·val·late /ˌsərkəm'valˌāt/ ▸*v.* [*trans.*] *poetic/literary* surround with or as if with a rampart: *the walls were circumvallated with a ditch.*

▸*adj. poetic/literary* surrounded as if by a rampart: *we looked at the circumvallate mountains.* ■ *Anatomy* denoting certain papillae near the back of the tongue, surrounded by taste receptors. ▷mid 17th cent. (as an adjective): from Latin *circumvallat-* 'surrounded with a rampart,' from the verb *circumvallare*, from *circum* 'around' + *vallare*, from *vallum* 'rampart.' The verb dates from the early 19th cent.

cir·cum·vent /ˌsərkəm'vent/ ▸*v.* [*trans.*] find a way around (an obstacle). ■ overcome (a problem or difficulty), typically in a clever and surreptitious way: *terrorists found the airport checks easy to circumvent.* ■ *archaic* deceive; outwit: *he's circumvented her with some of his stories.* ▷late Middle English: from Latin *circumvent-* 'skirted around,' from the verb *circumvenire*, from *circum* 'around' + *venire* 'come.' —**cir·cum·ven·tion** /-'venCHən/ *n.*

cir·cum·vo·lu·tion /ˌsərkəmvə'lo͞osHən; sərˌkəm-/ ▸*n.* a winding movement, esp. of one thing around another. ▷late Middle English: from Latin *circumvolut-* 'rolled around,' from the verb *circumvolvere*, from *circum* 'around' + *volvere* 'roll.'

cir·cum·volve /'sərkəmˌvälv/ ▸*v. rare* rotate; revolve. ■ wind, fold, or twist around; enwrap.

cir·cus /'sərkəs/ ▸*n.* (*pl.* **-cus·es**) **1** a traveling company of acrobats, trained animals, and clowns that gives performances, typically in a large tent, in a series of different places: [as *adj.*] *a circus elephant.* ■ (in ancient Rome) a rounded or oblong arena lined with tiers of seats, used for equestrian and other sports and games. ■ *informal* a group of people involved in a particular sport who travel around to compete against one another in a series of different places: *the Formula One circus.* ■ *informal* a public scene of frenetic and noisily intrusive activity: *a media circus.* **2** [in *place names*] *Brit.* a rounded open space in a city where several streets converge: *Piccadilly Circus.* ▷late Middle English (with reference to the arena of Roman antiquity): from Latin, 'ring or circus.' The sense 'traveling company of performers' dates from the late 18th cent.

ci·ré /sə'rā/ (also **ci·re**) ▸*n.* a fabric with a smooth shiny surface obtained by waxing and heating. ▷1920s: French, literally 'waxed.'

cire per·due /'si(ə)r per'd(y)o͞o/ ▸*n.* another term for **LOST WAX**. ▷late 19th cent.: French, literally 'lost wax.'

cirque /sərk/ ▸*n.* **1** *Geology* a half-open steep-sided hollow at the head of a valley or on a mountainside, formed by glacial erosion. Also called **CORRIE** or **CWM**. **2** *poetic/literary* a ring, circlet, or circle. ▷late 17th cent. (sense 2): from French, from Latin *circus*.

cir·rho·sis /sə'rōsəs/ ▸*n.* a chronic disease of the liver marked by degeneration of cells, inflammation, and fibrous thickening of tissue. It is typically a result of alcoholism or hepatitis. ▷early 19th cent.: modern Latin, from Greek *kirrhos* 'tawny' (because this is the color of the liver in many cases). —**cir·rhot·ic** /sə'rätik/ *adj.*

Cir·ri·pe·di·a /ˌsirə'pēdēə; -'pedēə/ *Zoology* a class of crustaceans that comprises the barnacles. ▷modern Latin (plural), from Latin *cirrus* 'a curl' (because of the form of the legs) + *pes, ped-* 'foot.' —**cir·ri·ped** /'sirəˌped/ *n.* —**cir·ri·pede** /'sirəˌpēd/ *n.*

cir·ro·cu·mu·lus /ˌsirō'kyo͞omyələs/ ▸*n.* cloud forming a broken layer of small fleecy clouds at high altitude, usually 16,500–45,000 feet (5–13 km), typically with a rippled or granulated appearance (as in a mackerel sky).

cir·ro·stra·tus /ˌsirō'stratəs; -'strātəs/ ▸*n.* cloud forming a thin, more or less uniform, semitranslucent layer at high altitude, usually 16,500–45,000 feet (5–13 km).

cir·rus /'sirəs/ ▸*n.* (*pl.* **cir·ri** /'sirˌī; 'sirē/) **1** cloud forming wispy filamentous tufted streaks ("mare's tails") at high altitude, usually 16,500–45,000 feet (5–13 km). **2** *Zoology* a slender tendril or hairlike filament, such as the appendage of a barnacle, the barbel of a fish, or the intromittent organ of an earthworm. ■ *Botany* a tendril. ▷early 18th cent. (in the sense 'tendril'): from Latin, literally 'a curl.'

CIS ▸*abbr.* Commonwealth of Independent States.

cis /sis/ ▸*adj. Chemistry* denoting or relating to a molecular structure in which two particular atoms or groups lie on the same side of a given plane in the molecule, in particular denoting an isomer in which substituents at opposite ends of a carbon–carbon double bond are on the same side of the bond: *the cis isomer of stilbene.* Compare with **TRANS**. ▷independent usage of **CIS-**.

cis- ▸*prefix* **1** on this side of; on the side nearer to the speaker: *cisatlantic | cislunar.* ■ *historical* on the side nearer to Rome: *cisalpine.* ■ (of time) closer to the present: *cis-Elizabethan.* Often contrasted with **TRANS-** or **ULTRA-**. **2** *Chemistry* (usu. *cis-*) denoting molecules with cis arrangements of substituents: cis-*1,2-dichloroethylene.* ▷from Latin *cis* 'on this side of.'

cis·al·pine /sis'alpīn/ ▸*adj.* on the southern side of the Alps. ▷mid 16th cent.: from Latin *cisalpinus*.

Cis·al·pine Gaul /sis'alˌpīn/ see **GAUL**[1].

cis·at·lan·tic /ˌsisət'lantik/ ▸*adj.* on the same side of the Atlantic as the speaker.

cis·co /'siskō/ ▸*n.* (*pl.* **-coes**) a freshwater whitefish of northern countries. Most species are migratory and are important food fishes. • Genus *Coregonus*, family Salmonidae: several species, including the **lake cisco** (*C. artedii*) of North America, and the **Arctic cisco** (*C. autumnalis*) of northern Eurasia and northern North America. ▷mid 19th cent.: of unknown origin.

cis·lu·nar /sis'lo͞onər/ ▸*adj.* between the earth and the moon: *the darkness of cislunar space.*

cis·mon·tane /sis'mänˌtān/ ▸*adj.* on this side of the mountains, esp. the Alps. Compare with **CISALPINE**.

cis·plat·in /sis'platn/ ▸*n. Medicine* a cytotoxic drug used in cancer chemotherapy. • A coordination compound of platinum; chem. formula: $Pt(NH_3)_2Cl_2$. ▷late 20th cent.: from **CIS-** + **PLATINUM**.

cis·sus /'sisəs/ ▸*n.* a woody climbing vine of the grape family, with trifoliate leaves that are sometimes evergreen. • Genus *Cissus*, family Vitaceae: several species, esp. *C. incisa* of the central and southeastern U.S. ▷modern Latin: from Greek *kissos* 'ivy.'

cist /sist; kist/ (also **kist**) ▸*n. Archaeology* a coffin or burial chamber made from stone or a hollowed tree. ▷early 19th cent.: Welsh, literally 'chest,' from Latin *cista*, from Greek *kistē* 'basket.'

Cis·ter·cian /sis'tərsHən/ ▸*n.* a monk or nun of an order founded in 1098 as a stricter branch of the Benedictines. The monks are now divided into two observances, the strict observance, whose adherents are known popularly as Trappists, and the common observance, which has certain relaxations.

▸*adj.* of or relating to this order: *a Cistercian abbey.* ▷from French *cistercien*, from *Cistercium*, the Latin name of *Cîteaux* near Dijon in France, where the order was founded.

cis·tern /'sistərn/ ▸*n.* a tank for storing water, esp. one supplying taps or as part of a flushing toilet. ■ an underground reservoir for rainwater. ▷Middle English: from Old French *cisterne*, from Latin *cisterna*, from *cista* 'box.'

cis·tron /'sisˌträn/ ▸*n. Biochemistry* a section of a DNA or RNA molecule that codes for a specific polypeptide in protein synthesis. ▷1950s: from **CIS-** + **TRANS-** (because of the possibility of two genes being on the same or different chromosomes) + **-ON**.

cit. ▸*abbr.* ■ citation. ■ cited. ■ citizen.

cit·a·del /'sitədl; -ˌdel/ ▸*n.* a fortress, typically on high ground, protecting or dominating a city. ▷mid 16th cent.: from French *citadelle*, or from Italian *cittadella*, based on Latin *civitas* 'city' (see **CITY**).

ci·ta·tion /sī'tāsHən/ (abbr.: **cit.**) ▸*n.* **1** a quotation from or reference to a book, paper, or author, esp. in a scholarly work: *there were dozens of citations from the works of Byron | recognition through citation is one of the principal rewards in science.* ■ a mention of a praiseworthy act or achievement in an official report, esp. that of a member of the armed forces in wartime. ■ a note accompanying an award, describing the reasons for it: *the Nobel citation noted that his discovery would be useful for energy conversion technology.* ■ *Law* a reference to a former tried case, used as guidance in the trying of comparable cases or in support of an argument. **2** *Law* a summons: *a traffic citation.* ▷Middle English (sense 2): from Old French, from Latin *citation-*, from *citare* 'cite.'

cite /sīt/ ▸*v.* [*trans.*] (often **be cited**) **1** quote (a passage, book, or author) as evidence for or justification of an argument or statement, esp. in a scholarly work. ■ mention as an example: *medics have been cited as a key example of a modern breed of technical expert.* ■ praise (someone, typically a member of the armed forces) for a courageous act in an official dispatch. ■ *Law* adduce a former tried case as a guide to deciding a comparable case or in support of an argument. **2** *Law* summon (someone) to appear in a court of law: *the summons cited four of defendants.*

▸*n.* a citation. ▷late Middle English (sense 2, originally with reference to a court of ecclesiastical law): from Old French *citer*, from Latin *citare*, from *ciere*, *cire* 'to call.' —**cit·a·ble** *adj.*

CITES /'sītˌēz/ ▸*abbr.* Convention on International Trade in Endangered Species.

cith·a·ra /'siTHərə; 'kiTH-/ (also **kith·a·ra** /'kiTH-/) ▸*n.* an ancient Greek and Roman stringed musical instrument similar to the lyre, having two arms rising vertically from the soundbox.

cith·ern /'siTHərn; 'siT͟H-/ ▸*n.* variant spelling of **CITTERN**.

cit·ied /'sitēd/ ▸*adj.* made into or like a city; occupied by a city or cities.

cit·i·fied /'sitiˌfīd/ (also **cit·y·fied**) ▸*adj. often derogatory* characteristic of or adjusted to an urban environment: *black-hatted, citified cowboys.* —**cit·i·fi·ca·tion** /ˌsitifi'kāsHən/ *n.* —**cit·i·fy** /-fī/ (**-fies**, **-fied**) *v.*

cit·i·zen /'sitizən; -sən/ (abbr.: **cit.**) ▸*n.* a legally recognized subject or national of a state or commonwealth, either native or naturalized: *a Polish citizen | the rights of every citizen.* ■ an inhabitant of a particular town or city: *the* **citizens of** *Los Angeles.* ▷Middle English: from Anglo-Norman French *citezein*, alteration (probably influenced by *deinzein* 'denizen') of Old French *citeain*, based on Latin *civitas* 'city' (see **CITY**). —**cit·i·zen·ry** /-rē/ *n.* —**cit·i·zen·ship** /-ˌSHip/ *n.*

▸*PHRASE* □ **citizen of the world** a person who is at home in any country.

cit·i·zen's ar·rest ▸*n.* an arrest by an ordinary person without a warrant, allowable in certain cases.

Cit·i·zens' Band (abbr.: **CB**) ▸*n.* a range of radio frequencies that are allocated for local communication by private individuals, esp. by hand-held or vehicle radio.

Ci·tlal·té·petl /sētˌläl'tāˌpetl/ the highest peak in Mexico, in the eastern part of the country, north of Orizaba. It is 18,503 feet (5,699 m) high and is an extinct volcano. Spanish name **PICO DE ORIZABA**. ▷Aztec, literally 'star mountain.'

cit·ral /'sitrəl/ ▸*n. Chemistry* a fragrant liquid occurring in citrus and lemongrass oils and used in flavorings and perfumes. • A terpene; chem. formula: $C_{10}H_{16}O$.

cit·rate /'siˌtrāt/ ▸*n.* a salt or ester of citric acid.

cit·ric /'sitrik/ ▸*adj.* derived from or related to citrus fruit: *lemongrass gives a slightly sweet citric flavor.* ▷late 18th cent.: from Latin *citrus* 'citron tree' + **-IC**.

cit·ric ac·id ▸*n. Chemistry* a sharp-tasting crystalline acid present in the juice of lemons and other sour fruits. It is made commercially by the fermentation of sugar and used as a flavoring and setting agent. • A tribasic acid; chem. formula: $C_6H_8O_7$.

cit·ric ac·id cy·cle ▸*n.* another term for **KREBS CYCLE**.

cit·ri·cul·ture /ˈsitriˌkəlCHər/ ▸*n.* the cultivation of citrus fruit trees.

cit·rin /ˈsitrən/ ▸*n.* another term for **BIOFLAVONOID**.

cit·rine /siˈtrēn; ˈsiˌtrēn/ ▸*n.* (also **citrine quartz**) a glassy yellow variety of quartz. Also called **FALSE TOPAZ**. ■ a light greenish-yellow. ▷late Middle English: from Old French *citrin* 'lemon-colored,' from medieval Latin *citrinus*, from Latin *citrus* 'citron tree.'

cit·ron /ˈsitrən/ ▸*n.* a shrubby Asian tree that bears large fruits similar to lemons, but with flesh that is less acid and peels that are thicker and more fragrant. • *Citrus medica*, family Rutaceae; one of the ancestors of modern commercial citrus fruits. ■ the fruit of this tree. ▷early 16th cent. (denoting the fruit): from French, from Latin *citrus* 'citron tree,' on the pattern of *limon* 'lemon.'

cit·ron·el·la /ˌsitrəˈnelə/ ▸*n.* **1** (also **citronella oil**) a fragrant natural oil used as an insect repellent and in perfume and soap manufacture. **2** the South Asian grass from which this oil is obtained. • *Cymbopogon nardus*, family Gramineae. ▷mid 19th cent.: modern Latin, from **CITRON** + the diminutive suffix *-ella*.

cit·ron·el·lal /ˌsitrəˈnelal/ ▸*n.* a terpenoid aldehyde found esp. in citronella, rose, and geranium oils. • Chem. formula: $C_{10}H_{18}O$.

cit·rus /ˈsitrəs/ ▸*n.* (*pl.* **-rus·es**) a tree of a genus that includes citron, lemon, lime, orange, and grapefruit. Native to Asia, citrus trees are widely cultivated in warm countries for their fruit, which has juicy flesh and a pulpy rind. • Genus *Citrus*, family Rutaceae. ■ (also **citrus fruit**) a fruit from such a tree. ▸*adj.* (also **cit·rous**) of or relating to these trees or their fruits: *citrus extracts.* ▷early 19th cent.: Latin, literally 'citron tree, thuja.' **—cit·rus·y** *adj.*.

Cit·rus Heights a community in north central California, northeast of Sacramento; pop. 107,439.

cit·tern /ˈsitərn/ (also **cith·ern** /ˈsiTHərn; ˈsiT͟H-/) ▸*n.* a stringed instrument similar to a lute, with a flattened back and wire strings, used in 16th- and 17th-century Europe. ▷mid 16th cent.: from Latin *cithara*, from Greek *kithara*, denoting a kind of harp. The spelling has been influenced by **GITTERN**.

cit·y /ˈsitē/ ▸*n.* (*pl.* **cit·ies**) **1** a large town: [as *adj.*] *the city center.* ■ an incorporated municipal center. **2** [with *modifier*] *informal* a place or situation characterized by a specified attribute: *panic city.* **3** (**the City**) the financial and commercial district of London, England. ▷Middle English: from Old French *cite*, from Latin *civitas*, from *civis* 'citizen.' Originally denoting a town, and often used as a Latin equivalent to Old English *burh* 'borough,' the term was later applied to foreign and ancient cities and to the more important English boroughs. **—cit·y·ward** /-wərd/ *adj.* & *adv.* **—cit·y·wards** /-wərdz/ *adv.* **—cit·y·wide** /-ˌwīd/ *adj.*

cit·y desk ▸*n.* the department of a newspaper dealing with local news.

cit·y ed·i·tor ▸*n.* an editor dealing with local news in a newspaper or magazine.

cit·y fa·ther ▸*n.* (usu. **city fathers**) a person concerned with or experienced in the administration of a city: *the city fathers decided to build a museum.*

cit·y·fied ▸*adj.* variant spelling of **CITIFIED**.

cit·y hall (often **City Hall**) ▸*n.* the administration building of a municipal government. ■ [treated as *sing.*] municipal offices or officers collectively: *they cultivated close ties with City Hall.*

cit·y man·ag·er ▸*n.* an appointed official who directs the administration of a city.

Cit·y of God Paradise, perceived as an ideal community in Heaven. ■ the Christian Church. [from *The City of God* by St. Augustine.]

Cit·y of Lon·don the part of London that is within the ancient boundaries and governed by the Lord Mayor and the Corporation.

cit·y plan·ning ▸*n.* the planning and control of the construction, growth, and development of a city or town. Also called **TOWN PLANNING**. **—cit·y plan·ner** *n.*

cit·y·scape /ˈsitēˌskāp/ ▸*n.* the visual appearance of a city or urban area; a city landscape: *shades of red brick which once colored the cityscape.* ■ a picture of a city.

cit·y slick·er /ˈslikər/ ▸*n. chiefly derogatory* a person with the sophistication and tastes or values generally associated with urban dwellers, typically regarded as unprincipled and untrustworthy.

cit·y-state ▸*n. chiefly historical* a city that with its surrounding territory forms an independent state.

Ciu·dad Bo·lí·var /syo͞oˈdä(d) bōˈlēvär/ a city in southeastern Venezuela, on the Orinoco River; pop. 225,850. Formerly called Angostura, its name was changed in 1846 to honor Simón Bolívar, the country's liberator.

Ciu·dad del Es·te /syo͞oˈdäd del ˈestā/ a port city in southeastern Paraguay, on the Paraná River, near the Itaipu Dam; pop. 134,000. Called (before 1989) **Puerto Presidente Stroessner.**

Ciu·dad Gua·ya·na /syo͞oˈdäd gīˈänə/ (also **Santo Tomé; de Guayana**) an industrial city in eastern Venezuela, at the junction of the Caroní and Orinoco rivers; pop. 543,000.

Ciu·dad Juá·rez /syo͞oˈdäd ˈhwäres/ (also **Juárez**) a commercial and industrial city in Chihuahua state, in northern Mexico, across the Rio Grande from El Paso in Texas; pop. 790,000.

Ciu·dad Re·al /syo͞oˈdäd rāˈäl/ an agricultural market town in central Spain, between the Guadiana and Jablón rivers, capital of Ciudad Real province; pop. 475,000.

Ciu·dad Tru·jil·lo /syo͞oˈdä(d) tro͞oˈhē(l)yō/ former name (1936–61) for **SANTO DOMINGO**.

Ciu·dad Vic·to·ri·a /syo͞oˈdä(d) vēkˈtôryə/ a city in northeastern Mexico, capital of the state of Tamaulipas; pop. 207,830.

civ·et /ˈsivət/ ▸*n.* (also **civet cat**) **1** a slender nocturnal carnivorous mammal with a barred and spotted coat and well-developed anal scent glands, native to Africa and Asia. • Family Viverridae (the **civet family**): several genera and species, in particular the **African civet** (*Viverra civetta*). The civet family also includes the genets, linsang, and fossa, and formerly included the mongooses. ■ a strong musky perfume obtained from the secretions of the civet's scent glands. **2** another term for **CACOMISTLE**. ■ the fur of the cacomistle. ▷mid 16th cent.: from French *civette*, from Italian *zibetto*, from medieval Latin *zibethum*, from Arabic *zabād*, denoting the perfume.

civ·ic /ˈsivik/ ▸*adj.* [*attrib.*] of or relating to a city or town, esp. its administration; municipal: *civic and business leaders.* ■ of or relating to the duties or activities of people in relation to their town, city, or local area: *they could not be denied access to education, the vote, and other civic rights.* ▷mid 16th cent.: from French *civique* or Latin *civicus*, from *civis* 'citizen.' The original use was in *civic garland, crown*, etc., translating Latin *corona civica*, denoting a garland of oak leaves and acorns given in ancient Rome to a person who saved a fellow citizen's life. **—civ·i·cal·ly** /-ik(ə)lē/ *adv.*

civ·ic cen·ter ▸*n.* a municipal building or building complex, often publicly financed, with space for conventions, sports events, and theatrical entertainment.

civ·ics /ˈsiviks/ ▸*plural n.* [usu. treated as *sing.*] the study of the rights and duties of citizenship.

civ·ies ▸*plural n.* variant spelling of **CIVVIES**.

civ·il /ˈsivəl/ ▸*adj.* **1** [*attrib.*] of or relating to ordinary citizens and their concerns, as distinct from military or ecclesiastical matters: *civil aviation.* ■ (of disorder or conflict) occurring between citizens of the same country. ■ *Law* relating to private relations between members of a community; noncriminal: *a civil action.* ■ *Law* of or relating to aspects the civil (or code) law derived from European systems. **2** courteous and polite: *we tried to be* **civil to** *him.* **3** (of time measurement or a point in time) fixed by custom or law rather than being natural or astronomical: *civil twilight starts at sunset.* ▷late Middle English: via Old French from Latin *civilis*, from *civis* 'citizen.' **—civ·il·ly** *adv.*

civ·il com·mit·ment /ˈsivəl kəˈmitmənt/ ▸*n.* post-sentence institutional detention of a sex offender with the intention of preventing a reoffense: *a 75-year-old convicted sex offender being held in civil commitment.*

civ·il con·vic·tion ▸*n.* (in military use) a current or former criminal conviction, under civil law, of an enlisted person.

civ·il court ▸*n.* a court dealing with noncriminal cases.

civ·il death ▸*n. rare* or *chiefly historical* the loss of a citizen's privileges through life imprisonment, banishment, etc.

civ·il de·fense ▸*n.* the organization and training of civilians for the protection of lives and property during and after attacks in wartime.

civ·il dis·o·be·di·ence ▸*n.* the refusal to comply with certain laws or to pay taxes and fines, as a peaceful form of political protest.

civ·il en·gi·neer ▸*n.* an engineer who designs and maintains roads, bridges, dams, and similar structures. **—civ·il en·gi·neer·ing** *n.*

ci·vil·ian /səˈvilyən/ ▸*n.* a person not in the armed services or the police force.
▸*adj.* of, denoting, or relating to a person not belonging to the armed services or police: *military agents in civilian clothes.* ▷late Middle English (denoting a practitioner of civil law): from Old French *civilien*, in the phrase *droit civilien* 'civil law.' The current sense arose in the early 19th cent.

ci·vil·ian·ize /səˈvilyəˌnīz/ ▸*v.* [*trans.*] make (something) nonmilitary in character or function. **—ci·vil·ian·i·za·tion** /səˌvilyənəˈzāSHən/ *n.*

ci·vil·i·ty /səˈvilətē/ ▸*n.* (*pl.* **-ties**) formal politeness and courtesy in behavior or speech: *I hope we can treat each other with civility and respect.* ■ (**civilities**) polite remarks used in formal conversation: *she was exchanging civilities with his mother.* ▷late Middle English: from Old French *civilite*, from Latin *civilitas*, from *civilis* 'relating to citizens' (see **CIVIL**). In early use the term denoted the state of being a citizen and hence good citizenship or orderly behavior. The sense 'politeness' arose in the mid 16th cent.

civ·i·li·za·tion /ˌsivələˈzāSHən/ ▸*n.* the stage of human social development and organization that is considered most advanced: *they equated the railroad with progress and civilization.* ■ the process by which a society or place reaches this stage. ■ the society, culture, and way of life of a particular area: *the great books of Western civilization | the early civilizations of Mesopotamia and Egypt.* ■ the comfort and convenience of modern life, regarded as available only in towns and cities: *the fur traders moved further and further from civilization.*

civ·i·lize /ˈsivəˌlīz/ ▸*v.* [*trans.*] [usu. as *adj.*] (**civilized**) bring (a place or people) to a stage of social, cultural, and moral development considered to be more advanced: *a civilized society.* ■ [as *adj.*] (**civilized**) polite and well-mannered: *such an affront to civilized behavior will no longer be tolerated.* ▷early 17th cent.: from French *civiliser*, from *civil* 'civil.' **—civ·i·liz·a·ble** *adj.* **—civ·i·liz·er** *n.*

civ·il law ▸*n.* the system of law concerned with private relations between members of a community rather than criminal, military, or religious affairs. Contrasted with **CRIMINAL LAW**. ■ the system of law predominant on the European continent and of which a form is in force in Louisiana, historically influenced by the codes of ancient Rome. Compare with **COMMON LAW**.

civ·il lib·er·ty ▸*n.* the state of being subject only to laws established for the good of the community, esp. with regard to freedom of action and speech. ■ (**civil liberties**) individual rights protected by law from unjust governmental or other interference. **—civ·il lib·er·tar·i·an** *n.*

civ·il mar·riage ▸*n.* a marriage solemnized as a civil contract without religious ceremony.

civ·il rights ▸*plural n.* the rights of citizens to political and social freedom and equality.

civ·il serv·ant ▸*n.* a member of the civil service.

civ·il serv·ice ▸*n.* the permanent professional branches of a government's administration, excluding military and judicial branches and elected politicians. ▷late 18th cent.: originally applied to the part of the service of the British East India Company conducted by staff who did not belong to the army or navy.

civil un·ion ▸*n.* a legally recognized union of a same-sex couple, with rights similar to those of marriage.

civ·il war ▸*n.* a war between citizens of the same country. See also **AMERICAN CIVIL WAR, ENGLISH CIVIL WAR, SPANISH CIVIL WAR**.

civ·il wrong ▸*n. Law* an infringement of a person's rights, such as a tort or breach of contract.

civ·il year ▸*n.* see **YEAR** (sense 2).

civ·vies /ˈsivēz/ *informal* ▸*plural n.* civilian clothes, as opposed to a uniform: *he showered and changed into civvies.*
▸*adj.* [*attrib.*] (**civvy**) of or relating to civilians: *I learned a good trade for civvy life.* ▷late 19th cent.: abbreviation.

CJ ▸*abbr.* chief justice.

Pronunciation Key ə *ago*; ər *over*; ˈə or ˌə *up*; ˈər or ˌər *fur*; a *hat*; ā *rate*; ä *car*; CH *chew*; e *let*; ē *see*; e(ə)r *air*; i *fit*; ī *by*; i(ə)r *ear*; NG *sing*; ō *go*; ô *for*; oi *boy*; o͝o *good*; o͞o *goo*; ou *out*; SH *she*; TH *thin*; T͟H *then*; (h)w *why*; ZH *vision*

CJD ▸*abbr.* Creutzfeldt–Jakob disease.

CL ▸*abbr.* chemiluminescence.

Cl ▸*symbol* the chemical element chlorine.

cl ▸*abbr.* centilitre: *70 cl bottles.*

clab·ber /ˈklabər/ ▸*n.* milk that has naturally clotted on souring.
▸*v.* curdle or cause to curdle. ▷early 19th cent.: shortening of BONNY CLABBER.

cla·chan /ˈklaKHən/ ▸*n.* (in Scotland or Northern Ireland) a small village or hamlet. ▷late Middle English: from Scottish Gaelic and Irish *clachán.*

clack /klak/ ▸*v.* make or cause to make a sharp sound or series of such sounds as a result of a hard object striking another: [*intrans.*] *he heard the sound of her heels clacking across flagstones* | [*trans.*] *he clacked the castanets in fine syncopation.* ■ [*intrans.*] *archaic* chatter loudly: *he will sit clacking for hours.*
▸*n.* a sharp sound or series of sounds made in such a way: *the clack of her high heels.* ■ *archaic* loud chatter: *her clack would go all day.* ▷Middle English: imitative. **—clack·er** *n.*

Clac·to·ni·an /klakˈtōnēən/ ▸*adj. Archaeology* of, relating to, or denoting a Lower Paleolithic culture represented by flint implements found at Clacton-on-Sea in southeastern England, dated to about 250,000–200,000 years ago. ■ [as *n.*] (**the Clactonian**) the Clactonian culture or period.

clad[1] /klad/ ▸ past participle of CLOTHE.
▸*adj.* **1** clothed: *they were* **clad in** *T-shirts and shorts* [in *combination*] *a leotard-clad instructor.* **2** provided with cladding: [in *combination*] *copper-clad boards.*

clad[2] ▸*v.* (**clad·ding**; *past* and *past part.* **clad·ded** or **clad**) [*trans.*] provide or encase with a covering or coating: *he cladded the concrete-frame structure in stainless steel.* ▷mid 16th cent. (in the sense 'clothe'): apparently from CLAD[1].

clad·ding /ˈkladiNG/ ▸*n.* a covering or coating on a structure or material: [as *adj.*] *a range of roofing and cladding products.*

clade /klād/ ▸*n. Biology* a group of organisms believed to have evolved from a common ancestor, according to the principles of cladistics. ▷1950s: from Greek *klados* 'branch.'

cla·dis·tics /kləˈdistiks/ ▸*plural n.* [treated as *sing.*] *Biology* a method of classification of animals and plants according to the proportion of measurable characteristics that they have in common. It is assumed that the higher the proportion of characteristics that two organisms share, the more recently they diverged from a common ancestor. ▷1960s: from CLADE + -IST + -ICS. **—clad·ism** /ˈklādˌizəm/ *n.* **—cla·dis·tic** *adj.*

clado- ▸*comb. form* relating to a branch or branching: *cladogram.* ▷from Greek *klados* 'branch or shoot.'

Cla·doc·er·a /kləˈdäsərə/ *Zoology* an order of minute branchiopod crustaceans that includes the water fleas. They typically have a transparent shell enclosing the trunk, and large antennae that are used for swimming. ▷modern Latin (plural), from Greek *klados* 'branch or root' + *keras* 'horn' (because of the branched antennae). **—cla·doc·er·an** *n.* & *adj.*

clad·ode /ˈkladˌōd/ (also **clad·o·phyll** /ˈkladəˌfil/) ▸*n. Botany* a flattened leaflike stem. ▷late 19th cent.: from Greek *kladōdēs* 'with many shoots,' from *klados* 'shoot.'

clad·o·gen·e·sis /ˌkladəˈjenəsəs/ ▸*n. Biology* the formation of a new group of organisms or higher taxon by evolutionary divergence from an ancestral form. Compare with ANAGENESIS. **—clad·o·ge·net·ic** /ˌkladōjəˈnetik/ *adj.*

clad·o·gram /ˈkladəˌgram/ ▸*n. Biology* a branching diagram showing the cladistic relationship between a number of species.

cla·fou·tis /klaˈfo͞otē/ ▸*n.* (*pl.* same) a tart made of fruit, typically cherries, baked in a sweet batter. ▷French, from dialect *clafir* 'to stuff.'

Clai·borne /ˈklābôrn/, Craig (1920–2000), U.S. food editor and critic. He was the food editor for the *New York Times* 1957–70, 1974–88. He wrote *The New York Times Cookbook* (1961), *Classic French Cuisine* (1970), and *Elements of Etiquette* (1992).

claim /klām/ ▸*v.* [*reporting verb*] state or assert that something is the case, typically without providing evidence or proof: [with *clause*] *he* **claimed that** *he came from a wealthy, educated family* | [with *direct speech*] *"I'm entitled to be conceited," he claimed* | [*trans.*] *these sunblocks claim protection factors as high as 34.* ■ [*trans.*] assert that one has gained or achieved (something): *his supporters claimed victory in the presidential elections.* ■ [*trans.*] formally request or demand; say that one owns or has earned (something): *if no one claims the items, they will become government property.* ■ [*trans.*] make a demand for (money) under the terms of an insurance policy: *she could have claimed the cost through her insurance.* ■ call for (someone's notice and thought): *a most unwelcome event* **claimed his attention.** ■ cause the loss of (someone's life).
▸*n.* **1** an assertion of the truth of something, typically one that is disputed or in doubt: [with *clause*] *he was dogged by the* **claim that** *he had CIA links history belies statesmen's claims to be in charge of events.* **2** a demand or request for something considered one's due: *the court had denied their* **claims to** *asylum.* ■ an application for compensation under the terms of an insurance policy. ■ a right or title to something: *they have first* **claim on** *the assets of the trust.* ■ (also **mining claim**) a piece of land allotted to or taken by someone in order to be mined. ▷Middle English: from Old French *claime* (noun), *clamer* (verb), from Latin *clamare* 'call out.' **—claim·a·ble** *adj.*
▸PHRASE □ **claim to fame** a reason for being regarded as unusual or noteworthy: *his claim to fame was bringing Garbo to Hollywood.*

claim·ant /ˈklāmənt/ ▸*n.* a person making a claim, esp. in a lawsuit or for a government-sponsored benefit.

clair·au·di·ence /kle(ə)rˈôdēəns/ ▸*n.* the supposed faculty of perceiving, as if by hearing, what is inaudible. ▷mid 19th cent.: from French *clair* 'clear' + AUDIENCE, on the pattern of *clairvoyance.* **—clair·au·di·ent** *adj.* & *n.*

clair de lune /ˌkle(ə)r dl ˈo͞on; ˌkle(ə)r də ˈlo͞on/ ▸*n.* a pale blue-gray or pale green color. ■ a Chinese porcelain glaze of this color. ▷late 19th cent.: French, literally 'moonlight.'

clair·voy·ance /kle(ə)rˈvoiəns/ ▸*n.* the supposed faculty of perceiving things or events in the future or beyond normal sensory contact: *she stared at the card as if she could contact its writer by clairvoyance.* ▷mid 19th cent.: from French, from *clair* 'clear' + *voir* 'to see.'

clair·voy·ant /kle(ə)rˈvoiənt/ ▸*n.* a person who claims to have a supernatural ability to perceive events in the future or beyond normal sensory contact.
▸*adj.* having or exhibiting such an ability: *he didn't tell me about it and I'm not clairvoyant.* ▷late 17th cent. (in the sense 'clear-sighted, perceptive'): from French, from *clair* 'clear' + *voyant* 'seeing' (from *voir* 'to see'). The current sense dates from the mid 19th cent. **—clair·voy·ant·ly** *adv.*

clam /klam/ ▸*n.* **1** a marine bivalve mollusk with shells of equal size. • Subclass Heterodonta: several families and numerous species, including the edible North American **hard-shell clam** (see QUAHOG) and **soft-shell clam.** See also GIANT CLAM. ■ *informal* any of a number of edible bivalve mollusks, e.g., a scallop. **2** *informal* a dollar: *all I got for the job was 50 lousy clams.* **3** *informal* a shy or withdrawn person.

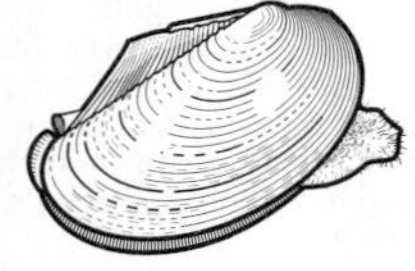
common Washington clam

▸*v.* (**clammed, clamming**) [*intrans.*] **1** dig for or collect clams: [as *n.*] (**clamming**) *it was one of the worst times for clamming.* **2** (**clam up**) *informal* abruptly stop talking, either for fear of revealing a secret or from shyness. ▷early 16th cent.: apparently from earlier *clam* 'a clamp,' from Old English *clam, clamm* 'a bond or bondage,' of Germanic origin; related to Dutch *klemme,* German *Klemme,* also to CLAMP.

cla·mant /ˈklāmənt; ˈklam-/ ▸*adj.* forcing itself urgently on the attention: *the proper use of biotechnology has become a clamant question.* ▷mid 17th cent.: from Latin *clamant-* 'crying out,' from the verb *clamare.* **—cla·mant·ly** *adv.*

clam·bake /ˈklamˌbāk/ ▸*n.* an outdoor social gathering at which clams and other seafood (and often chicken, potatoes, and sweet corn) are baked or steamed, traditionally in a pit, over heated stones and under a bed of seaweed.

clam·ber /ˈklambər; ˈklamər/ ▸*v.* [*intrans.*] climb, move, or get in or out of something in an awkward and laborious way, typically using both hands and feet: *I clambered out of the trench.*
▸*n.* [in *sing.*] a difficult climb or movement of this sort: *a clamber up the cliff path.* ▷Middle English: probably from *clamb,* obsolete past tense of CLIMB.

clam·dig·gers /ˈklamˌdigərz/ ▸*n.* close-fitting women's casual pants hemmed at mid-calf.

clam·my /ˈklamē/ ▸*adj.* (**clam·mi·er, clam·mi·est**) unpleasantly damp and sticky or slimy to touch: *his skin felt cold and clammy.* ■ (of air or atmosphere) damp and unpleasant: *the clammy atmosphere of the cave.* ▷late Middle English: from dialect *clam* 'to be sticky or adhere,' of Germanic origin; related to CLAY. **—clam·mi·ly** /ˈklaməlē/ *adv.* **—clam·mi·ness** *n.*

clam·or /ˈklamər/ (*Brit.* **clam·our**) ▸*n.* [in *sing.*] a loud and confused noise, esp. that of people shouting vehemently: *the questions rose to a clamor.* ■ a strongly expressed protest or demand, typically from a large number of people: *the growing public* **clamor for** *more policemen on the beat.*
▸*v.* [*intrans.*] (of a group of people) shout loudly and insistently: *the surging crowds* **clamored** *for attention.* ■ make a vehement protest or demand: *scientists are* **clamoring for** *a ban on all chlorine substances.* ▷late Middle English: via Old French from Latin *clamor,* from *clamare* 'cry out.' **—clam·or·ous** /-ərəs/ *adj.* **—clam·or·ous·ly** /-ərəslē/ *adv.* **—clam·or·ous·ness** /-ərəsnəs/ *n.*

clamp /klamp/ ▸*n.* a brace, band, or clasp used for strengthening or holding things together. ■ an electric circuit that serves to maintain the voltage limits of a signal at prescribed levels.
▸*v.* [*trans.*] (often **be clamped**) fasten (something) in place with a clamp: *the sander is clamped onto the edge of a workbench.* ■ fasten (two things) firmly together: *the two frames are* **clamped together.** ■ hold (something) tightly against or in another thing: *Maggie had to clamp a hand over her mouth to stop herself from laughing.* ■ [*trans.*] maintain the voltage limits of (an electrical signal) at prescribed values.
▸*phrasal v.* □ **clamp down** suppress or prevent something, typically in an oppressive or harsh manner: *police* **clamped down on** *a pro-democracy demonstration.* ▷Middle English: probably of Dutch or Low German origin and related to CLAM. **—clamp·er** *n.*

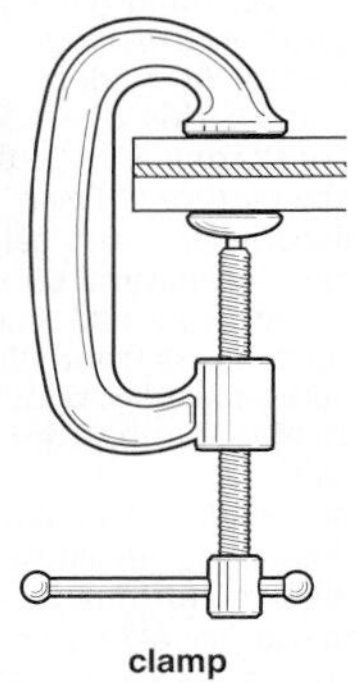
clamp

clamp·down /ˈklampˌdoun/ ▸*n. informal* a severe or concerted attempt to suppress something: *a* **clampdown on** *crime.*

clam·shell /ˈklamˌSHel/ ▸*n.* the shell of a clam, formed of two roughly equal valves with a hinge. ■ a thing with hinged parts that open and shut in a manner resembling the parts of such a shell, such as a kind of mechanical digger, a portable computer, or a box for takeout food: *some clamshells offer full desktop power* | [as *adj.*] *a clamshell lid.*

clan /klan/ ▸*n.* a group of close-knit and interrelated families (esp. associated with families in the Scottish Highlands). ■ *often informal* a family, esp. a large one: *the Kennedy clan gathered for the celebration.* ■ a group of people with a strong common interest: *New York's garrulous clan of artists.* ■ *informal* a family or group of plants or animals: *the lily family is a clan noted for its spectacular springtime emergences.* ▷late Middle English: from Scottish Gaelic *clann* 'offspring, family,' from Old Irish *cland,* from Latin *planta* 'sprout.'

Clan·cy /ˈklansē/, Tom (1947–), U.S. novelist. His works, usually techno-military thrillers, include *Hunt for Red October* (1985), *Patriot Games* (1987), *Rainbow Six* (1998), and *The Bear and the Dragon* (2000).

clan·des·tine /klanˈdestən; -ˌtīn; -ˌtēn; ˈklandəs-/ ▸*adj.* kept secret or done secretively, esp. because illicit: *she deserved better than these clandestine meetings.* See note at SECRET. ▷mid 16th cent.: from French *clandestin* or Latin *clandestinus,* from *clam* 'secretly.' **—clan·des·tine·ly** *adv.* **—clan·des·tin·i·ty** /ˌklandesˈtinitē/ *n.*

clang /klaNG/ ▸*n.* a loud, resonant metallic sound or series of sounds: *the steel door slammed shut with a clang.*
▸*v.* make or cause to make such a sound: [*intrans.*] *she turned the faucet on and the plumbing clanged* | [*trans.*] *the belfry still clangs its bell at 9 p.m.* ▷late 16th cent.: imitative, influenced by Latin *clangere* 'resound.'

clang·or /ˈklaNGər/ (*Brit.* **clang·our**) ▸*n.* [in *sing.*] a continuous loud banging or ringing sound: *he went deaf because of the clangor of the steam hammers.* ▷late 16th cent.: from Latin *clangor,* from *clangere* 'resound.' **—clang·or·ous** /ˈklaNGərəs/ *adj.* **—clang·or·ous·ly** /ˈklaNGərəslē/ *adv.*

clank /klaNGk/ ▸*n.* a loud, sharp sound or series of sounds, typically made by pieces of metal meeting or being struck together: *the groan and clank of a winch.*
▸*v.* make or cause to make such a sound: [*intrans.*]

I could hear the chain clanking | [*trans.*] *Cassie bounced on the bed, clanking the springs.* ▷late Middle English (but rare before the mid 17th cent.): imitative. **—clank·ing·ly** *adv.*

clan·nish /ˈklanisн/ ▶*adj. chiefly derogatory* (of a group or their activities) tending to exclude others outside the group. **—clan·nish·ly** *adv.* **—clan·nish·ness** *n.*

clans·man /ˈklanzmən/ ▶*n.* (*pl.* **-men**) a member of a clan, esp. a male member.

clans·wom·an /ˈklanz,wo͝omən/ ▶*n.* (*pl.* **-wom·en**) a female member of a clan.

clap[1] /klap/ ▶*v.* (**clapped, clap·ping**) [*trans.*] strike the palms of (one's hands) together repeatedly, typically in order to applaud: *Agnes clapped her hands in glee* | [*intrans.*] *the crowd was clapping and cheering.* ■ show approval of (a person or action) in this way. ■ strike the palms of (one's hands) together once, esp. as a signal: *the designer clapped his hands and the other girls exited the room.* ■ slap (someone) encouragingly on the back or shoulder: *as they parted, he clapped Owen on the back.* ■ place (a hand) briefly against or over one's mouth or forehead as a gesture of dismay or regret: *he swore and clapped a hand to his forehead.* ■ (of a bird) flap (its wings) audibly.

▶*phrasal v.* □ **clap (something) on** abruptly impose (a restrictive or punitive measure): *most countries clapped on tariffs to protect their farmers.*

▶*n.* **1** an act of striking together the palms of the hands, either once or repeatedly. ■ a friendly slap or pat on the back or shoulder. **2** an explosive sound, esp. of thunder: *a clap of thunder echoed through the valley.* ▷Old English *clappan* 'throb, beat,' of imitative origin. Sense 1 dates from late Middle English.

▶*PHRASES* □ **clap eyes on** see EYE. □ **clap (someone) in jail** (or **irons**) put (someone) in prison (or in chains).

clap[2] ▶*n.* (usu. **the clap**) *informal* a venereal disease, esp. gonorrhea. ▷late 16th cent.: from Old French *clapoir* 'venereal bubo.'

clap·board /ˈklabərd; ˈklap,bôrd/ ▶*n.* a long, thin, flat piece of wood with edges horizontally overlapping in series, used to cover the outer walls of buildings: [as *adj.*] *neat clapboard houses.* ■ *informal* a house with outer walls covered in such pieces of wood. ▷early 16th cent. (denoting a piece of oak used for barrel staves or wainscot): partial translation of Low German *klappholt* 'barrel stave,' from *klappen* 'to crack' + *holt* 'wood.' **—clap·board·ed** *adj.*

clapped-out ▶*adj. informal, chiefly Brit.* (of a vehicle, machine, or person) worn out from age or heavy use and unable to work or operate: *a clapped-out old van.*

clap·per /ˈklapər/ ▶*n.* the free-swinging metal piece inside a bell that is made to strike the bell to produce the sound.

clap·per·board /ˈklapər,bôrd/ ▶*n.* a device of hinged boards that are struck together before filming as a signal to synchronize the starting of picture and sound machinery.

clap·per rail ▶*n.* a large grayish rail of American coastal marshes. It has a distinctive clattering rattlelike call. • *Rallus longirostris*, family Rallidae. ▷from *clapper*, denoting a device for making a loud clattering sound, with reference to the bird's cry.

Clap·ton /ˈklaptən/, Eric (1945–), English blues and rock guitarist, singer, and composer.

clap·trap /ˈklap,trap/ (also **clap-trap**) ▶*n.* absurd or nonsensical talk or ideas: *such sentiments are just pious claptrap.* ▷mid 18th cent. (denoting something designed to elicit applause): from CLAP[1] + TRAP[1].

claque /klak/ ▶*n.* a group of people hired to applaud (or heckle) a performer or public speaker. ■ a group of sycophantic followers: *the president was surrounded by a claque of scheming bureaucrats.* ▷mid 19th cent.: French, from *claquer* 'to clap.' The practice of paying members of an audience for their support originated at the Paris opera.

cla·queur /klaˈkər/ ▶*n.* a member of a claque. ▷mid 19th cent.: French, from *claquer* 'to clap.'

clar·a·bel·la /,klarəˈbelə/ ▶*n.* an organ stop with the quality of a flute. ▷mid 19th cent.: from the feminine forms of Latin *clarus* 'clear' and *bellus* 'pretty.'

Clare /kle(ə)r/ a county in the Republic of Ireland, on the western coast in the province of Munster; county town, Ennis.

Clare·mont /ˈkle(ə)r,mänt/ a city in southwestern California, east of Los Angeles; pop. 32,503.

clar·ence /ˈklarəns/ (also **Clar·ence**) ▶*n. historical* a closed horse-drawn carriage with four wheels, seating four inside and two outside next to the coachman. ▷mid 19th cent.: named in honor of the Duke of *Clarence*, later William IV.

Clar·en·don /ˈklarəndən/, Edward Hyde, Earl of (1609–74), English statesman and historian; chief adviser to Charles II and chancellor of Oxford University 1660–67.

Clare of As·si·si, St. /kle(ə)r/ (1194–1253), Italian saint and abbess. With St. Francis, she founded the order of Poor Ladies of San Damiano ("Poor Clares"). Feast day, August 11 (formerly 12).

clar·et /ˈklarit/ ▶*n.* a red wine from Bordeaux, or wine of a similar character made elsewhere. ■ a deep purplish-red color. ▷late Middle English (originally denoting a light red or yellowish wine, as distinct from a red or white): from Old French *(vin) claret* and medieval Latin *claratum (vinum)* 'clarified (wine),' from Latin *clarus* 'clear.'

clar·i·fy /ˈklarə,fī/ ▶*v.* (**-fies, -fied**) [*trans.*] **1** make (a statement or situation) less confused and more clearly comprehensible: *the report managed to clarify the government's position.* **2** [often as *adj.*] (**clarified**) melt (butter) in order to separate out the impurities. ▷Middle English (in the senses 'set forth clearly' and 'make pure and clean'): from Old French *clarifier*, from late Latin *clarificare*, from Latin *clarus* 'clear.' **—clar·i·fi·ca·tion** /,klarəfiˈkāsнən/ *n.* **—clar·i·fi·er** *n.*

THE RIGHT WORD **clarify, construe, elucidate, explain, explicate, interpret**

When a biology teacher gets up in front of a class and tries to **explain** how two brown-eyed parents can produce a blue-eyed child, the purpose is to make an entire process or sequence of events understandable. In a less formal sense, to *explain* is to make a verbal attempt to justify certain actions or to make them understood (*she tried to explain why she was so late*).

That same teacher might **clarify** a particular exam question that almost everyone in the class got wrong—a word that means to make an earlier event, situation, or statement clear.

Elucidate is a more formal word meaning to *clarify*, but where the root of the latter refers to clearness, the root of the former refers to light. To *elucidate* is to shed light on something through explanation, illustration, etc. (*the principal's comments were an attempt to elucidate the school's policy on cheating*).

A teacher who **explicates** something discusses a complex subject in a point-by-point manner (*to explicate a poem*).

If a personal judgment is inserted in making such an explication, the correct word is **interpret** (*to interpret a poem's symbolic meanings*).

To **construe** is to make a careful interpretation of something, especially where the meaning is ambiguous. For example, when a class misbehaves in front of a visitor, the teacher is likely to *construe* that behavior as an attempt to cause embarrassment or ridicule.

clar·i·net /,klarəˈnet/ ▶*n.* a woodwind instrument with a single-reed mouthpiece, a cylindrical tube of dark wood with a flared end, and holes stopped by keys. The most common forms are tuned in B flat, A, and E flat. ■ an organ stop with a tone resembling that of a clarinet. ▷mid 18th cent.: from French *clarinette*, diminutive of *clarine*, denoting a kind of bell; related to CLARION. **—clar·i·net·ist** /-ˈnetist/ (*Brit.* **clar·i·net·tist**) *n.*

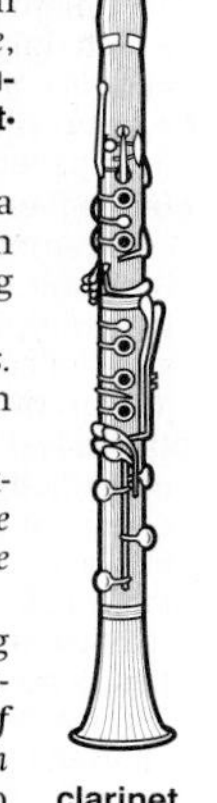
clarinet

clar·i·on /ˈklarēən/ ▶*n. chiefly historical* a shrill, narrow-tubed war trumpet. ■ an organ stop with a quality resembling that of such a trumpet.

▶*adj.* loud and clear: *clarion trumpeters.* ▷Middle English: from medieval Latin *clario(n-)*, from Latin *clarus* 'clear.'

▶*PHRASE* □ **clarion call** a strongly expressed demand or request for action: *he issued a clarion call to young people to join the party.*

clar·i·ty /ˈklaritē/ ▶*n.* the quality of being clear, in particular: ■ the quality of coherence and intelligibility: ***for the sake of clarity**, each of these strategies is dealt with separately.* ■ the quality of being easy to see or hear; sharpness of image or sound: *the clarity of the picture.* ■ the quality of being certain or definite: *it was clarity of purpose that he needed.* ■ the quality of transparency or purity: *the crystal clarity of water.* ▷Middle English (in the sense 'glory, divine splendor'): from Latin *claritas*, from *clarus* 'clear.' The current sense dates from the early 17th cent.

Clark[1] /klärk/, George Rogers (1752–1818), American Revolution war leader and frontiersman. He defended the Illinois frontier against the British.

Clark[2], Mark Wayne (1896–1984), U.S. army officer. He served as chief of staff of the U.S. Army ground forces in 1942 and as UN commander and commander in chief of the U.S. Far East command 1952–53. He signed the Korean armistice.

Clark[3], Tom Campbell (1899–1977), U.S. Supreme Court associate justice 1949–67. He was U.S. attorney general 1945–49 before being appointed to the Court by President Truman. Considered somewhat conservative, he tended to be more liberal regarding civil rights issues.

Clark[4], Wesley (1944–), U.S. Army general and politician. A commander in the Vietnam War and the first Gulf War, he served as Commander in Chief, U.S. European Command and Supreme Allied Commander Europe 1997–2000 during the Kosovo conflict. In 2004 he ran for the Democratic presidential nomination.

Clark[5], William (1770–1838), U.S. explorer. With Meriwether Lewis, he commanded an expedition 1804–06 across the North American continent.

Clarke[1] /klärk/, Sir Arthur C. (1917–), English science fiction writer; full name *Arthur Charles Clarke*. He wrote, with Stanley Kubrick, the screenplay for the movie *2001: A Space Odyssey* (1968).

Clarke[2], John Hessin (1857–1945), U.S. Supreme Court associate justice 1916–22. Appointed to the Court by President Wilson, he was considered a liberal. He later headed the League of Nations Non-Partisan Committee 1922–28.

Clark Fork Riv·er /ˈklärk/ a river that flows for 360 miles (580 km) from western Montana into eastern Idaho into the Columbia River.

clark·i·a /ˈklärkēə/ ▶*n.* a North American plant with showy white, pink, or purple flowers, cultivated as a border plant in gardens. • Genus *Clarkia*, family Onagraceae. ▷modern Latin, named after W. CLARK, who discovered it.

Clarks·ville /ˈklärks,vil; -vəl/ an industrial and commercial city in north central Tennessee, on the Cumberland River; pop. 103,445.

clar·y /ˈkle(ə)rē/ ▶*n.* an aromatic herbaceous plant of the mint family, some kinds of which are used as culinary and medicinal herbs. • Genus *Salvia*, family Labiatae: several species, in particular the southern European *S. sclarea*, which is used in perfumery and from which an essential oil (**clary sage**) is obtained. ▷late Middle English: from obsolete French *clarie*, from medieval Latin *sclarea*.

clash /klasн/ ▶*n.* **1** a violent confrontation: *there have been minor **clashes with** security forces.* ■ an incompatibility leading to disagreement: *a personality clash.* **2** a mismatch of colors: *a clash of tweeds and a striped shirt.* ■ an inconvenient coincidence of the timing of events or activities: *it is hoped that clashes of dates will be avoided.* **3** a loud jarring sound made by or resembling that made by metal objects being struck together: *a clash of cymbals.*

▶*v.* **1** [*intrans.*] meet and come into violent conflict: *protesters demanding self-rule **clashed with** police.* ■ have a forceful disagreement: *Clarke has frequently **clashed with** his colleagues.* ■ be incompatible or at odds: *his thriftiness **clashed with** Ross's largesse.* **2** [*intrans.*] (of colors) appear discordant or ugly when placed close to each other: [as *adj.*] (**clashing**) *suits in clashing colors.* ■ inconveniently occur at the same time: *the date of the wedding **clashes with** Sean's graduation.* **3** [*trans.*] strike (cymbals) together, producing a loud discordant sound. ▷early 16th cent.: imitative. **—clash·er** *n.*

clasp /klasp/ ▶*v.* [*trans.*] **1** grasp (something) tightly with one's hand: *he clasped her arm.* ■ place (one's arms) around something so as to hold it tightly: *Kate's arms were **clasped around** her knees.* ■ hold (someone) tightly: *he clasped Joanne in his arms.* ■ (**clasp one's hands**) press one's hands together with the fingers interlaced: *he lay on his back with his hands clasped behind his head.* **2** *archaic* fasten (something) with a small device, typically a metal one: *one modest emerald clasped her robe.*

▶*n.* **1** a device with interlocking parts used for fastening things together: *a handbag with a golden clasp.* ■ a silver bar on a medal ribbon, inscribed with the name of the battle at which the wearer was present.

2 [in *sing.*] an embrace. ■ a grasp or handshake: *he took her hand in a firm clasp.* ▷Middle English: of unknown origin.

▸*PHRASE* □ **clasp hands** shake hands with fervor or affection.

clasp·ers /ˈklaspərz/ ▸*plural n. Zoology* a pair of appendages under the abdomen of a male shark or ray, or at the end of the abdomen of a male insect, used to hold the female during copulation. ▷mid 19th cent.: from CLASP.

clasp knife ▸*n.* a knife with a blade that folds into the handle.

class /klas/ ▸*n.* **1** a set or category of things having some property or attribute in common and differentiated from others by kind, type, or quality: *the accommodations were good for a hotel of this class | a new class of heart drug.* ■ *Biology* a principal taxonomic grouping that ranks above order and below phylum or division, such as Mammalia or Insecta. **2** the system of ordering a society in which people are divided into sets based on perceived social or economic status: *people who are socially disenfranchised by class |* [as *adj.*] *the class system.* ■ a set in a society ordered in such a way: *the ruling class.* ■ (**the classes**) *archaic* the rich or educated. ■ *informal* impressive stylishness in appearance or behavior: *she's got class—she looks like a princess.* **3** a group of students who are taught together. ■ an occasion when students meet with their teacher for instruction; a lesson: *I was late for a class.* ■ a course of instruction: *I took classes in Indian music.* ■ all those graduating from a school or college in a particular year: *the class of 1907.*

▸*v.* [*trans.*] (often **be classed as**) assign or regard as belonging to a particular category: *conduct that is classed as criminal.*

▸*adj.* [*attrib.*] *informal* showing stylish excellence: *he's a class player.* ▷mid 16th cent. (sense 3): from Latin *classis* 'a division of the Roman people, a grade, or a class of pupils.'

▸*PHRASES* □ **class act** a person or thing displaying impressive and stylish excellence. □ **in a class of** (or **on**) **its** (or **one's**) **own** unequaled, esp. in excellence or performance: *the delicacy of English roses puts them in a class of their own.*

class ac·tion ▸*n. Law* a lawsuit filed or defended by an individual or small group acting on behalf of a large group.

class con·scious·ness ▸*n.* awareness of one's place in a system of social classes, esp. (in Marxist terms) as it relates to the class struggle. **—class-con·scious** *adj.*

clas·sic /ˈklasik/ ▸*adj.* judged over a period of time to be of the highest quality and outstanding of its kind: *a classic novel | a classic car.* ■ (of a garment or design) of a simple elegant style not greatly subject to changes in fashion: *this classic navy blazer.* ■ remarkably and instructively typical: *I had all the classic symptoms of flu.*

▸*n.* **1** a work of art of recognized and established value: *his books have become classics.* ■ a garment of a simple, elegant, and long-lasting style. ■ a thing that is memorable and a very good example of its kind: *he's hoping that tomorrow's game will be a classic.* **2** (usu. **Classics**) a school subject that involves the study of ancient Greek and Latin literature, philosophy, and history. ■ (usu. **the classics**) the works of ancient Greek and Latin writers and philosophers. ■ *dated* a scholar of ancient Greek and Latin. **3** a major sports tournament or competition, as in golf or tennis: *dozens of celebrity golfers attended the Bob Hope Desert Classic.* ▷early 17th cent.: from French *classique* or Latin *classicus* 'belonging to a class or division,' later 'of the highest class,' from *classis* (see CLASS).

USAGE Traditionally, **classic** means 'typical, excellent as an example, timeless,' and **classical** means 'of (esp. Greek or Roman) antiquity.' Thus: *John Ford directed many classic Westerns; the museum was built in the classical style.* Great art is considered **classic**, not **classical**, unless it is created in the forms of antiquity. *Classical music* is formal and sophisticated music adhering to certain stylistic principles, esp. those of the late 18th century, but *a classic folk song* is one that well expresses its culture. A *classical education* exposes a student to *classical* literature, history, and languages (esp. Latin and Greek), but the study of Greek and Latin languages and their literatures is also referred to as *classics*, as in *he majored in classics at college.*

clas·si·cal /ˈklasikəl/ ▸*adj.* **1** of or relating to ancient Greek or Latin literature, art, or culture: *classical mythology.* ■ (of art or architecture) influenced by ancient Greek or Roman forms or principles. ■ (of language) having the form used by the ancient standard authors: *classical Latin.* ■ based on the study of ancient Greek and Latin: *a classical education.* **2** (typically of a form of art) regarded as representing an exemplary standard; traditional and long-established in form or style: *a classical ballet.* **3** of or relating to the first significant period of an area of study: *classical Marxism.* ■ *Physics* relating to or based upon concepts and theories that preceded the theories of relativity and quantum mechanics; Newtonian: *classical physics.* ▷late 16th cent. (in the sense 'outstanding for its kind'): from Latin *classicus* 'belonging to a class' (see CLASSIC) + -AL. **—clas·si·cal·ism** /-ˌlizəm/ *n.* **—clas·si·cal·i·ty** /ˌklasəˈkalətē/ *n.* **—clas·si·cal·ly** /-ik(ə)lē/ *adv.*

USAGE See usage at CLASSIC.

clas·si·cal con·di·tion·ing ▸*n. Psychology* a learning process that occurs when two stimuli are repeatedly paired: a response that is at first elicited by the second stimulus is eventually elicited by the first stimulus alone.

clas·si·cal mu·sic ▸*n.* serious or conventional music following long-established principles rather than a folk, jazz, or popular tradition. ■ (more specifically) music written in the European tradition during a period lasting approximately from 1750 to 1830, when forms such as the symphony, concerto, and sonata were standardized. Often contrasted with BAROQUE and ROMANTIC.

clas·si·cism /ˈklasəˌsizəm/ ▸*n.* the following of ancient Greek or Roman principles and style in art and literature, generally associated with harmony, restraint, and adherence to recognized standards of form and craftsmanship, esp. from the Renaissance to the 18th century. Often contrasted with ROMANTICISM. ■ the following of traditional and long-established theories or styles.

clas·si·cist /ˈklasəsist/ ▸*n.* **1** a person who studies Classics (ancient Greek and Latin). **2** a follower of classicism in the arts.

clas·si·cize /ˈklasəˌsīz/ ▸*v.* [*intrans.*] [usu. as *adj.*] (**classicizing**) imitate a classical style: *the classicizing strains in Guercino's art.*

Clas·si·co /ˈklasikō/ ▸*adj.* [*postpositive*] used in the classification of Italian wines to designate a wine produced in the region from which the type takes its name: *Chianti Classico.* ▷Italian.

clas·si·fi·ca·tion /ˌklasəfəˈkāshən/ ▸*n.* the action or process of classifying something according to shared qualities or characteristics: *the classification of disease according to symptoms.* ■ *Biology* the arrangement of animals and plants in taxonomic groups according to their observed similarities (including at least kingdom and phylum in animals, division in plants, and class, order, family, genus, and species). ■ another term for TAXONOMY. ■ a category into which something is put.

clas·si·fied /ˈklasəˌfīd/ ▸*adj.* arranged in classes or categories: *a classified catalog of books.* ■ [*attrib.*] (of newspaper or magazine advertisements or the pages on which these appear) organized in categories according to what is being advertised. ■ (of information or documents) designated as officially secret and to which only authorized people may have access: *classified information on nuclear experiments.*

▸*n.* (**classifieds**) small advertisements placed in a newspaper and organized in categories.

clas·si·fi·er /ˈklasəˌfīər/ ▸*n.* a person or thing that classifies something. ■ *Linguistics* an affix or word that indicates the semantic class to which a noun belongs, typically used in numerals or other expressions of counting, esp. in Chinese and Japanese, e.g. *head* in *two head of cattle.*

clas·si·fy /ˈklasəˌfī/ ▸*v.* (**-fies**, **-fied**) [*trans.*] (often **be classified**) arrange (a group of people or things) in classes or categories according to shared qualities or characteristics: *mountain peaks are classified according to their shape.* ■ assign (someone or something) to a particular class or category: *elements are usually classified as metals or nonmetals.* ■ designate (documents or information) as officially secret or to which only authorized people may have access: *government officials classified 6.3 million documents in 1992.* ▷late 18th cent.: back-formation from CLASSIFICATION, from French, from *classe* 'class,' from Latin *classis* 'division.' **—clas·si·fi·a·ble** /ˌklasəˈfīəbəl/ *adj.* **—clas·si·fi·ca·to·ry** /-fikəˌtôrē/ *adj.*

clas·si·fy·ing /ˈklasəˌfī-iNG/ ▸*adj. Grammar* denoting an adjective that describes the class that a head noun belongs to and characterized by not having a comparative or superlative (for example *American, mortal*). Contrasted with GRADABLE, QUALITATIVE.

class in·ter·val ▸*n. Statistics* the size of each class into which a range of a variable is divided, as represented by the divisions of a histogram or bar chart.

class·ism /ˈklasˌizəm/ ▸*n.* prejudice against or in favor of people belonging to a particular social class. **—class·ist** *adj.* & *n.*

class·less /ˈklasləs/ ▸*adj.* (of a society) not divided into social classes. ■ not showing obvious signs of belonging to a particular social class: *his voice was classless.* **—class·less·ness** *n.*

class·mate /ˈklasˌmāt/ ▸*n.* a fellow member of a class at school or college. ■ a schoolmate.

class·room /ˈklasˌro͞om; -ˌro͝om/ ▸*n.* a room, typically in a school, in which a class of students is taught.

class strug·gle ▸*n.* (in Marxist ideology) the conflict of interests between the workers and the ruling class in a capitalist society, regarded as inevitably violent.

class war (also **class war·fare**) ▸*n.* another term for CLASS STRUGGLE.

class·y /ˈklasē/ ▸*adj.* (**class·i·er**, **class·i·est**) *informal* stylish and sophisticated: *the hotel is classy but relaxed.* **—class·i·ly** /ˈklasəlē/ *adv.* **—class·i·ness** *n.*

clast /klast/ ▸*n. Geology* a constituent fragment of a clastic rock. ▷mid 20th cent.: back-formation from CLASTIC.

clas·tic /ˈklastik/ ▸*adj. Geology* denoting rocks composed of broken pieces of older rocks. ▷late 19th cent.: from French *clastique*, from Greek *klastos* 'broken in pieces.'

clath·rate /ˈklaTHˌrāt/ ▸*n. Chemistry* a compound in which molecules of one component are physically trapped within the crystal structure of another. ▷1940s: from Latin *clathratus*, from *clathri* 'lattice bars,' from Greek *klēthra.*

clat·ter /ˈklatər/ ▸*n.* [in *sing.*] a continuous rattling sound as of hard objects falling or striking each other: *the horse spun around with a clatter of hooves | she dropped her knife and fork with a clatter.* ■ noisy rapid talk: *I could hear the clatter from the next table.*

▸*v.* make or cause to make a continuous rattling sound: [*intrans.*] *her coffee cup clattered in the saucer |* [*trans.*] *she clattered cups and saucers onto a tray.* ■ [*intrans.*] fall or move with such a sound: *the knife clattered to the floor.* ▷Old English (as a verb), of imitative origin.

Claude glass /klôd; klōd/ ▸*n.* a convex dark or colored glass that reflects a small image in subdued colors, used by landscape painters to show the tonal values of a scene.

Claude Lor·raine /ˌklôd ləˈrān; ˌklōd ləˈren/ (also **Lorrain**) (1600–82), French painter; born *Claude Gellée*. He is noted for the use of light in his landscapes. His works include *Ascanius and the Stag* (1682).

clau·di·ca·tion /ˌklôdəˈkāshən/ ▸*n. Medicine* limping. ■ (also **intermittent claudication**) a condition in which cramping pain in the leg is induced by exercise, typically caused by obstruction of the arteries. ▷late Middle English: from Latin *claudicatio(n-)*, from the verb *claudicare* 'to limp,' from *claudus* 'lame.'

Clau·di·us /ˈklôdēəs/ (10 BC–AD 54), Roman emperor 41–54; full name *Tiberius Claudius Drusus Nero Germanicus*. He restored order after Caligula's decadence and expanded the empire, in particular by invading Britain in AD 43.

clause /klôz/ ▸*n.* **1** a unit of grammatical organization next below the sentence in rank and in traditional grammar said to consist of a subject and predicate. See also MAIN CLAUSE, SUBORDINATE CLAUSE. **2** a particular and separate article, stipulation, or proviso in a treaty, bill, or contract. ▷Middle English: via Old French *clause*, based on Latin *claus-* 'shut, closed,' from the verb *claudere*. **—claus·al** /ˈklôzəl/ *adj.*

Clau·se·witz /ˈklouzəˌvits/, Karl von (1780–1831), Prussian general and military theorist. He wrote *On War* (1833), which had a marked influence on strategic studies in the 19th and 20th centuries.

Clau·si·us /ˈklouzēəs/, Rudolf (1822–88), German physicist. He was one of the founders of modern thermodynamics.

claus·tral /ˈklôstrəl/ ▸*adj.* of or relating to a cloister or religious house: *claustral buildings.* ■ *figurative* enveloping; confining: *this claustral heat.* ▷late Middle English: from late Latin *claustralis*, from Latin *claustrum* 'lock, enclosed place' (see CLOISTER).

claus·tra·tion /klôˈstrāshən/ ▸*n.* confinement as if in a cloister. ▷mid 19th cent.: from Latin *claustrum* 'lock, bolt' + -ATION.

claus·tro·pho·bi·a /ˌklôstrəˈfōbēə/ ▸*n.* extreme or irrational fear of confined places. ▷late 19th cent.: modern Latin, from Latin *claustrum* 'lock, bolt' + **-PHOBIA**. **—claus·tro·phobe** /ˈklôstrəˌfōb/ *n.*

claus·tro·pho·bic /ˌklôstrəˈfōbik/ ▸*adj.* (of a person) suffering from claustrophobia: *crowds made him feel claustrophobic.* ■ (of a place or situation) inducing claustrophobia: *the claustrophobic interior of the cruiser.* ▸*n.* a person who suffers from claustrophobia. **—claus·tro·pho·bi·cal·ly** /-ik(ə)lē/ *adv.*

claus·trum /ˈklôstrəm; ˈkloustrəm/ ▸*n.* (*pl.* **-tra** /-trə/) *Anatomy* a thin layer of gray matter in each cerebral hemisphere between the lentiform nucleus and the insula. ▷mid 19th cent.: Latin.

cla·vate /ˈklāˌvāt/ ▸*adj. Botany & Zoology* club-shaped; thicker at the apex than at the base. ▷mid 17th cent.: from modern Latin *clavatus*, from Latin *clava* 'club.'

clave[1] /kläv/ ▸*n.* (usu. **claves**) *Music* one of a pair of hardwood sticks used to make a hollow sound when struck together. ▷1920s: from Latin American Spanish, from Spanish *clave* 'keystone,' from Latin *clavis* 'key.'

clave[2] ▸ archaic past of **CLEAVE**[2].

clav·i·chord /ˈklavəˌkôrd/ ▸*n.* a small, rectangular keyboard instrument producing a soft sound by means of metal blades attached to the ends of key levers that gently press the strings, popular from the early 15th to early 19th centuries. ▷late Middle English: from medieval Latin *clavichordium*, from Latin *clavis* 'key' + *chorda* 'string.'

clav·i·cle /ˈklavikəl/ ▸*n. Anatomy* technical term for **COLLARBONE**. ▷early 17th cent.: from Latin *clavicula* 'small key,' diminutive of *clavis* (because of its shape). **—cla·vic·u·lar** /kləˈvikyələr; klə-/ *adj.*

cla·vier /kləˈvi(ə)r; ˈklävēər; ˈklavēər/ ▸*n.* **1** the keyboard of a musical instrument. **2** a keyboard instrument, esp. one with strings, such as the harpsichord. ▷early 18th cent.: from German *Klavier*, from French *clavier*, from medieval Latin *claviarius* 'key bearer,' from Latin *clavis* 'key.'

clav·i·form /ˈklavəˌfôrm/ ▸*adj. technical* another term for **CLAVATE**. ▷early 19th cent.: from Latin *clava* 'club' + **-IFORM**.

claw /klô/ ▸*n.* a curved pointed horny nail on each digit of the foot in birds, lizards, and some mammals. ■ either of a pair of small hooked appendages on an insect's leg. ■ the pincer of a crab, scorpion, or other arthropod. ■ a mechanical device resembling a claw, used for gripping or lifting.
▸*v.* **1** [*intrans.*] (of an animal or person) scratch or tear something with the claws or the fingernails: *the kitten was **clawing at** Lowell's trouser leg* | *figurative bitter jealousy **clawed at** her* | [*trans.*] *her hands clawed his shoulders.* ■ clutch at something with the hands: *his fingers **clawed at** the air.* ■ (**claw one's way**) make one's way with difficulty by hauling oneself forward with one's hands: *he clawed his way over a pile of bricks.* ■ [*trans.*] (**claw something away**) try desperately to move or remove something with the hands: *rescuers clawed away rubble with their bare hands.* **2** [*intrans.*] (of a sailing ship) beat to windward: *the ability to **claw off** a lee shore.* ▷Old English *clawu* (noun), *clawian* (verb); related to Dutch *klauw* and German *Klaue*. **—clawed** *adj.* [often in *combination*] *a short-clawed otter.* **—claw·less** *adj.*
▸*PHRASE* □ **get one's claws into** *informal* enter into a possessive relationship with.

claw·back /ˈklôˌbak/ ▸*n.* the recovery of money already disbursed: *funds that are not subject to any clawback by the government.*
▸*v.* [*trans.*] retrieve or recover (funds) already allocated or dispersed: *all three plans would clawback benefits at retirement.*

clawed toad ▸*n.* an aquatic toad with a flattened body and claws on the hind toes, related to the Surinam toad. • *Xenopus* and other genera, family Pipidae: several species. See also **XENOPUS**.

claw foot ▸*n.* (*pl.* **claw feet**) **1** a foot on a piece of furniture or a standing fixture, shaped to resemble a claw. **2** *Medicine* an excessively arched foot with an unnaturally high instep. ■ a disease causing such a distortion of the foot. **—claw-foot·ed** *adj.*

claw foot 1

claw ham·mer ▸*n.* **1** a hammer with one side of the head split and curved, used for extracting nails. **2** (**clawhammer**) a style of banjo playing in which the thumb and fingers strum or pluck the strings in a downward motion.

Clay[1] /klā/, Cassius, see **ALI**[2].

Clay[2], Henry (1777–1852), U.S. politician, statesman, and orator; nicknamed **the Great Pacificator** and **the Great Compromiser**. He was a leader of the "War Hawks" 1811 and championed the Missouri Compromise 1820. He served as secretary of state 1825–29 and as a senator from Kentucky 1831–42.

clay /klā/ ▸*n.* a stiff, sticky fine-grained earth, typically yellow, red, or bluish-gray in color and often forming an impermeable layer in the soil. It can be molded when wet, and is dried and baked to make bricks, pottery, and ceramics. ■ *technical* sediment with particles smaller than silt, typically less than 0.00016 inch (0.004 mm). ■ a hardened clay surface for a tennis court. ■ *poetic/literary* the substance of the human body: *this lifeless clay.* ▷Old English *clǣg*; related to Dutch *klei*, also to **CLEAVE**[2] and **CLIMB**. **—clay·ey** /ˈklā-ē/ *adj.* **—clay·ish** *adj.* **—clay·like** /-ˌlīk/ *adj.*
▸*PHRASE* □ **feet of clay** see **FOOT**.

clay·ma·tion /klāˈmāsHən/ (also **Clay·ma·tion**) ▸*n.* a method of animation in which clay figures are filmed using stop-motion photography. ▷1980s: from **CLAY** + **ANIMATION**.

clay min·er·al ▸*n.* any of a group of minerals that occur as minute sheetlike or fibrous crystals in clay. They are all hydrated aluminosilicates having layered crystal structures.

clay·more /ˈklāˌmôr/ ▸*n.* **1** *historical* a two-edged broadsword used by Scottish Highlanders. ■ a single-edged broadsword having a hilt with a basketwork design, introduced in Scotland in the 16th century. **2** a type of antipersonnel mine. ▷early 18th cent.: from Scottish Gaelic *claidheamh* 'sword' + *mór* 'great.'

clay pig·eon ▸*n.* a saucer-shaped piece of baked clay or other material thrown up in the air from a trap as a target for shooting.

-cle ▸*suffix* forming nouns such as *article, particle*, which were originally diminutives. ▷via French from Latin *-culus, -cula, -culum*.

clean /klēn/ ▸*adj.* **1** free from dirt, marks, or stains: *the room was spotlessly clean* | *keep the wound clean.* ■ having been washed since last worn or used: *a clean blouse.* ■ [*attrib.*] (of paper) not yet marked by writing or drawing: *he copied the directions onto a clean sheet of paper.* ■ (of a person) attentive to personal hygiene: *by nature he was clean and neat.* ■ free from pollutants or unpleasant substances: *we will create a cleaner, safer environment.* ■ free from or producing relatively little radioactive contamination. **2** morally uncontaminated; pure; innocent: *clean living.* ■ not sexually offensive or obscene: *it's all **good clean fun*** | *even when clean, his verses are very funny.* ■ showing or having no record of offenses or crimes: *a clean driving license is essential for the job.* ■ played or done according to the rules: *it was a good clean fight.* ■ [*predic.*] *informal* not possessing or containing anything illegal, esp. drugs or stolen goods: *I searched him and his luggage, and he was clean.* ■ [*predic.*] *informal* (of a person) not taking or having taken drugs or alcohol. ■ free from ceremonial defilement, according to Mosaic Law and similar religious codes. ■ (of an animal) not prohibited under such codes and fit to be used for food. **3** free from irregularities; having a smooth edge or surface: *a clean fracture of the leg.* ■ having a simple, well-defined, and pleasing shape: *the clean lines and pared-down planes of modernism.* ■ (of an action) smoothly and skillfully done: *I still hadn't made a clean takeoff.* ■ (of a taste, sound, or smell) giving a clear and distinctive impression to the senses; sharp and fresh: *clean, fresh, natural flavors.* ■ (of timber) free from knots.
▸*adv.* **1** so as to be free from dirt, marks, or unwanted matter: *the room had been washed clean.* **2** *informal* used to emphasize the completeness of a reported action, condition, or experience: *he was knocked clean off his feet* | *I clean forgot her birthday.*
▸*v.* [*trans.*] make (something or someone) free of dirt, marks, or mess, esp. by washing, wiping, or brushing: *clean your teeth properly after meals* | *chair covers should be easy to clean* | *we **cleaned** Uncle Jim **up** and made him presentable* | [*intrans.*] *he always expected other people to **clean up after** him* | [as *n.*] (**cleaning**) *Anne will help with the cleaning.* ■ remove the innards of (fish or poultry) prior to cooking.
▸*phrasal v.* □ **clean someone out** *informal* use up or take all someone's money: *they were cleaned out by the Englishman at the baccarat table.* □ **clean up** ■ make things or an area clean or neat: *he was in the kitchen, cleaning up.* ■ *informal* make a substantial gain or profit. ■ win all the prizes available in a sporting competition or series of events: *the Germans cleaned up at Wimbledon.* □ **clean something up** restore order or morality to: *the police chief was given the job of cleaning up a notorious district.* ▷Old English *clǣne*; related to Dutch and German *klein* 'small.' **—clean·a·ble** *adj.* **—clean·ish** *adj.* **—clean·ness** *n.*
▸*PHRASES* □ (**as**) **clean as a whistle** see **WHISTLE**. □ **clean bill of health** see **BILL OF HEALTH**. □ **clean someone's clock** *informal* give someone a beating: *he went wild and cleaned everybody's clock down there in the dugout.* ■ defeat or surpass someone decisively. □ **clean house** do housework. ■ eliminate corruption or inefficiency: *unless our organization cleans house, it will be difficult to raise funds.* □ **clean one's plate** eat up all the food put on one's plate. □ **a clean sweep** **1** the removal of all unwanted people or things in order to start afresh: *the new leaders wanted to **make a clean sweep of** the discredited old order.* **2** the winning of all of a group of similar or related competitions, events, or matches: *he was in reach of the nomination after a clean sweep of Tuesday's primaries.* □ **clean up one's act** *informal* begin to behave in a better way, esp. by giving up alcohol, drugs, or illegal activities: *the casino industry is bent on cleaning up its act.* □ **come clean** *informal* be completely honest; keep nothing hidden: *the company has refused to come clean about its pollution record.* □ **have clean hands** be uninvolved and blameless with regard to an immoral act: *no one involved in the conflict has clean hands.* □ **keep one's hands clean** not involve oneself in an immoral act. □ **keep one's nose clean** see **NOSE**. □ **make a clean breast of something** (or **make a clean breast of it**) confess fully one's mistakes or wrongdoings. □ **make a clean job of something** *informal* do something thoroughly. □ **wipe the slate clean** see **WIPE**.

clean and jerk ▸*n.* [in *sing.*] a two-movement weightlifting exercise in which a weight is raised above the head following an initial lift to shoulder level.

clean-cut ▸*adj.* sharply outlined: *the normally clean-cut edge between sea and land has become blurred.* ■ giving the appearance of neatness and respectability: *the ad featured two clean-cut teenagers.* ■ evoking or suggesting such respectability: *a scandal that threatens her clean-cut image.*

clean·er /ˈklēnər/ ▸*n.* a person or thing that cleans something, in particular: ■ a person employed to clean the interior of a building. ■ (**the cleaners**) a place of business where clothes and fabrics are dry-cleaned: *my suit's at the cleaners.* ■ a device for cleaning, such as a vacuum cleaner. ■ a chemical substance used for cleaning: *an oven cleaner.*
▸*PHRASE* □ **take someone to the cleaners** *informal* take all someone's money or possessions in a dishonest or unfair way. ■ inflict a crushing defeat on someone: *the Blue Jays went home and were taken to the cleaners by the Red Sox.*

clean·er fish ▸*n.* a small fish, esp. a striped wrasse, that is permitted to remove parasites from the skin, gills, and mouth of larger fishes, to their mutual benefit. • Genus *Labroides*, family Labridae: several species, in particular *L. dimidiatus*.

clean-limbed ▸*adj.* (esp. of the human figure) slim; well formed and shapely.

clean·ly ▸*adv.* /ˈklēnlē/ **1** in a way that produces no dirt, noxious gases, or other pollutants: *the engine burns very cleanly.* **2** without difficulty or impediment; smoothly and efficiently: *he vaulted cleanly through the open window.* [Old English *clǣnlīce* (see **CLEAN**, **-LY**[2]).]
▸*adj.* /ˈklenlē/ (**-li·er**, **-li·est**) *archaic* (of a person or animal) habitually clean and careful to avoid dirt. [Old English *clǣnlīc* (see **CLEAN**, **-LY**[1]).] **—clean·li·ness** /ˈklenlēnis/ *n.*

clean room ▸*n.* an environment free from dust and other contaminants, used chiefly for the manufacture of electronic components.

cleanse /klenz/ ▸*v.* [*trans.*] make (something, esp. the skin) thoroughly clean: *this preparation will cleanse and tighten the skin* | [as *adj.*] (**cleansing**) *a cleansing cream.* ■ rid (a person, place, or thing) of something seen as unpleasant, unwanted, or defiling: *the mission to **cleanse** the nation **of** subversives.* ■ free (someone) from sin or guilt. ■ *archaic* (in biblical translations) cure (a leper). ▷Old English *clǣnsian*, from *clǣne* (see **CLEAN**).

cleans·er /ˈklenzər/ ▸*n.* [often with *adj.*] a substance that cleanses, in particular: ■ a powder or liquid for

Pronunciation Key ə *ago*; ər *over*; ˈə or ˌə *up*; ˈər or ˌər *fur*; a *hat*; ā *rate*; ä *car*; CH *chew*; e *let*; ē *see*; e(ə)r *air*; i *fit*; ī *by*; i(ə)r *ear*; NG *sing*; ō *go*; ô *for*; oi *boy*; o͝o *good*; o͞o *goo*; ou *out*; SH *she*; TH *thin*; T̲H̲ *then*; (h)w *why*; ZH *vision*

scouring sinks, toilets, and bathtubs: *harsh cleansers will scratch the basin.* ■ a cosmetic product for cleansing the skin.

clean-shav·en ▸*adj.* (of a man) without a beard or mustache.

clean slate ▸*n.* an absence of existing restraints or commitments: *no government starts with a clean slate.*

clean·up /ˈklēnˌəp/ (also **clean-up**) ▸*n.* **1** an act of making a place clean or tidy: *an environmental cleanup.* ■ an act of removing or putting an end to disorder, immorality, or crime. **2** [usu. as *adj.*] *Baseball* the fourth position in a team's batting order, typically reserved for a power hitter likely to clear the bases by enabling any runners to score: *L.A.'s cleanup hitter smacked a fastball over the left-field fence* | [as *adverb*] *he garnered a certain amount of attention while playing right field and batting cleanup.*

clear /ˈkli(ə)r/ ▸*adj.* **1** easy to perceive, understand, or interpret: *the voice on the telephone was clear and strong* | *clear and precise directions* | *her handwriting was clear* | *am I **making myself clear**?* ■ leaving no doubt; obvious or unambiguous: *it was **clear that** they were in a trap* | *a clear case of poisoning.* ■ having or feeling no doubt or confusion: *every student must be clear about what is expected.* **2** free of anything that marks or darkens something, in particular: ■ (of a substance) transparent: *the clear glass of the French windows* | *a stream of clear water.* ■ free of cloud, mist, or rain: *the day was fine and clear.* ■ (of a person's skin) free from blemishes. ■ (of a person's eyes) unclouded; shining: *I looked into her clear gray eyes.* ■ (of a color) pure and intense: *clear blue delphiniums.* ■ *archaic* (of a fire) burning with little smoke: *a bright, clear flame.* **3** free of any obstructions or unwanted objects: *with a clear road ahead, he shifted into high gear* | *I had a clear view in both directions* | *his desktop was almost clear.* ■ (of a period of time) free of any appointments or commitments: *the following Saturday Mattie had a clear day.* ■ [*predic.*] (of a person) free of something undesirable or unpleasant: *after 18 months of treatment he was **clear of** TB.* ■ (of a person's mind) free of something that impairs logical thought: *in the morning, with a clear head, she would tackle all her problems.* ■ (of a person's conscience) free of guilt. **4** [*predic.*] (**clear of**) not touching; away from: *the truck was wedged in the ditch, one wheel clear of the ground.* **5** [*attrib.*] (of a sum of money) net: *a clear profit of $1,100.* **6** *Phonetics* denoting a palatalized form of *l* (as in *salad* or *willing*) in some southern U.S. accents or as in *leaf* in Irish accents. Often contrasted with DARK.

▸*adv.* **1** so as to be out of the way of or away from: *he leapt **clear of** the car* | *stand clear, I'll start the plane up.* ■ so as not to be obstructed or cluttered: *the floor had been swept **clear of** litter.* **2** with clarity; distinctly: *she had to toss her head to see the lake clear again.* **3** completely: *he had time to get clear away.* ■ (**clear to**) all the way to: *you could see clear to the bottom of the lagoon.*

▸*v.* **1** [*intrans.*] become free of something that marks, darkens, obstructs, or covers something, in particular: ■ (of the sky or weather) become free of cloud or rain: *we'll go out if the weather clears.* ■ (of a liquid) become transparent: *a wine that refuses to clear.* ■ become free of obstructions: *the boy's lungs cleared and he began to breathe more easily.* ■ gradually go away or disappear: *the fever clears in two to four weeks* | *the mist had **cleared away**.* ■ (of a person's face or expression) assume a happier aspect following previous confusion or distress: *for a moment, Sam was confused; then his expression cleared.* ■ (of a person's mind) regain the capacity for logical thought; become free of confusion: *his mind cleared and he began to reflect.* **2** [*trans.*] make (something) free of marks, obstructions, or unwanted items, in particular: ■ remove an obstruction or unwanted item or items from: *the driveway had been **cleared of** snow* | *Carolyn cleared the table.* ■ free (land) for cultivation or building by removing vegetation or existing structures. ■ free (one's mind) of unpleasantness or confusion: *even the final clue failed to clear his mind.* ■ cause people to leave (a building or place): *the police shouted a warning and cleared the streets.* **3** [*trans.*] remove (an obstruction or unwanted item) from somewhere: *snow was cleared from the storm drains* | *park staff **cleared away** dead trees.* ■ *chiefly Soccer* send (the ball) away from the area near one's goal. ■ discharge (a debt). **4** [*trans.*] get past or over (something) safely or without touching it: *the plane rose high enough to clear the trees.* ■ jump (a specified height) in a competition: *she cleared 1.50 meters in the high jump.* **5** [*trans.*] show or declare (someone) officially to be innocent: *the commission had **cleared** the weightlifter **of** cheating.* **6** [*trans.*] give official approval or authorization to: *I cleared him to return to his squadron.* ■ get official approval for (something): *the press releases had to be **cleared with** the White House.* ■ (of a person or goods) satisfy the necessary requirements to pass through (customs): *I can help her to clear customs quickly.* ■ pass (a check) through a clearinghouse so that the money goes into the payee's account: *the check could not be cleared until Monday.* ■ [*intrans.*] (of a check) pass through a clearinghouse in such a way. **7** [*trans.*] earn or gain (an amount of money) as a net profit: *I would hope to clear $50,000 profit.*

▸*phrasal v.* □ **clear off** [usu. in *imperative*] *informal* go away: *"Clear off!" he yelled.* □ **clear out** *informal* leave quickly. □ **clear something out** remove the contents from something so as to tidy it or free it for alternative use: *they told her to clear out her desk by the next day.* □ **clear up 1** (of an illness or other medical condition) become cured: *all my health problems cleared up.* **2** (of the weather) become brighter. ■ (of rain) stop. □ **clear something up 1** (also **clear up**) tidy something up by removing trash or other unwanted items: *he decided to clear up his garage* | *I keep meaning to come down here and clear up.* ■ remove trash or other unwanted items to leave something tidy: *he asked the boys to clear up their mess.* **2** solve or explain something: *he wanted to clear up some misconceptions.* **3** cure an illness or other medical condition: *folk customs prescribed sage tea to clear up measles.* ▷Middle English: from Old French *cler*, from Latin *clarus*. —**clear·a·ble** *adj.* —**clear·ness** *n.*

▸*PHRASES* □ **as clear as mud** see MUD. □ **clear the air** make the air less sultry. ■ defuse or clarify an angry, tense, or confused situation by frank discussion: *it's time a few things were said to clear the air.* □ **(as) clear as a bell** see BELL[1]. □ **(as) clear as day** very easy to see or understand. □ **clear the decks** prepare for a particular event or goal by dealing with anything beforehand that might hinder progress. □ **clear the name of** show to be innocent: *the spokesman released a statement attempting to clear his client's name.* □ **clear one's throat** cough slightly so as to speak more clearly, attract attention, or to express hesitancy before saying something awkward. □ **clear the way** remove an obstacle or hindrance to allow progress: *the ruling could be enough to clear the way for impeachment proceedings.* ■ [in *imperative*] stand aside: *Stand back, there! Clear the way!* □ **in clear** not encrypted; not in code: *the Russian staff practice of sending radio messages and orders in clear.* □ **in the clear** no longer in danger or suspected of something: *the latest information put her in the clear.* □ **out of a** (or **the**) **clear blue sky** as a complete surprise: *his moods blew up suddenly out of a clear blue sky.*

clear·ance /ˈkli(ə)rəns/ ▸*n.* **1** the action or process of removing or getting rid of something or of something's dispersing: *cleaning of the machine should include clearance of blockages* | *there will be sunny intervals after clearance of any early mist.* ■ [often with *adj.*] the removal of buildings, people, or trees from land so as to free it for alternative uses: *slum clearance accelerated during the 1960s* | *forest clearances.* ■ (in soccer and other games) a kick or hit that sends the ball out of a defensive zone. **2** official authorization for something to proceed or take place: *there was a delay in obtaining diplomatic clearance to overfly Israel.* ■ (also **security clearance**) official permission for someone to have access to classified information: *these people don't have clearance.* ■ permission for an aircraft to take off or land at an airport: *he took off without air traffic clearance.* ■ the clearing of a person or ship by customs. ■ a certificate showing that such clearance has been granted. ■ the process of clearing checks through a clearinghouse. **3** clear space allowed for a thing to move past or under another: *always give cyclists plenty of clearance.*

clear·ance sale ▸*n.* a sale of goods at reduced prices to get rid of superfluous stock or because the store is closing down.

clear-cut ▸*adj.* **1** sharply defined; easy to perceive or understand: *we now had a clear-cut objective.* **2** (of an area) from which every tree has been cut down and removed.

▸*v.* [*trans.*] cut down and remove every tree from (an area): *colonizers who clear-cut large jungle tracts.*

clear-eyed ▸*adj.* having unclouded, bright eyes: *a handsome, clear-eyed young man.* ■ *figurative* having a shrewd understanding and no illusions: *clear-eyed about human nature.*

Clear·field /ˈkli(ə)rˌfēld/ a city in northern Utah, southwest of Ogden and of Hill Air Force Base, which is central to its economy; pop. 21,435.

clear·head·ed /ˈkli(ə)rˌhedid/ (also **clear-head·ed**) ▸*adj.* alert and thinking logically and coherently. —**clear·head·ed·ly** *adv.* —**clear·head·ed·ness** *n.*

clear·ing /ˈkli(ə)riNG/ ▸*n.* an open space in a forest, esp. one cleared for cultivation.

clear·ing·house /ˈkli(ə)riNGˌhous/ (also **clear·ing house**) (abbr.: **c.h.** or **C.H.**) ▸*n.* a bankers' establishment where checks and bills from member banks are exchanged, so that only the balances need be paid in cash. ■ an agency or organization that collects and distributes something, esp. information.

clear·ly /ˈkli(ə)rlē/ ▸*adv.* in such a way as to allow easy and accurate perception or interpretation: *the ability to write clearly* | [as *submodifier*] *on white paper, the seeds are clearly visible.* ■ [*sentence adverb*] without doubt; obviously: *clearly, there have been disasters and reversals here.*

clear-sight·ed ▸*adj.* thinking clearly and sensibly; perspicacious and discerning: *a clear-sighted sense of what is possible and appropriate.* —**clear-sight·ed·ly** *adv.* —**clear-sight·ed·ness** *n.*

clear·sto·ry ▸*n.* (*pl.* **-ries**) variant spelling of CLERESTORY.

Clear·wa·ter /ˈkli(ə)rˌwôtər; -ˌwätər/ a city in west central Florida, on the Gulf of Mexico, west of Tampa; pop. 108,787.

Clear·wa·ter Moun·tains a range in northern Idaho, part of the Rocky Mountains.

clear·wing /ˈkli(ə)rˌwiNG/ (also **clearwing moth**) ▸*n.* a day-flying moth that has narrow mainly transparent wings and mimics a wasp or bee in appearance. • Family Sesiidae: several genera and many species, including the hornet moth.

cleat /klēt/ ▸*n.* a T-shaped piece of metal or wood, esp. on a boat or ship, to which ropes are attached. ■ one of a number of projecting pieces of metal, rubber, or other material on the sole of a shoe, designed to prevent the wearer from losing their footing. ■ (**cleats**) athletic shoes with a cleated sole, typically used when playing football. ■ a projection on a spar or other part of a ship, to prevent slipping. ■ a small wedge, esp. one on a plow or scythe. ▷Middle English (in the sense 'wedge'); related to Dutch *kloot* 'ball, sphere' and German *Kloss* 'clod, dumpling,' also to CLOT and CLOUT. —**cleat·ed** *adj.*

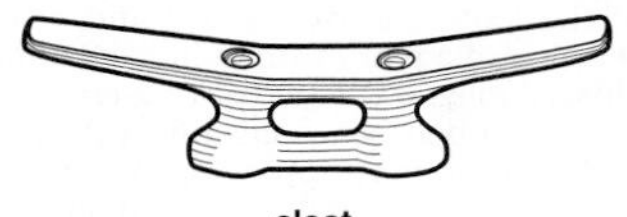

cleat

cleav·age /ˈklēvij/ ▸*n.* a sharp division; a split: *a system dominated by the class cleavage.* ■ the hollow between a woman's breasts when supported, esp. as exposed by a low-cut garment. ■ *Biology* cell division, esp. of a fertilized egg cell. ■ the splitting of rocks or crystals in a preferred plane or direction.

cleave[1] /klēv/ ▸*v.* (*past* **clove** /klōv/ or **cleft** /kleft/ or **cleaved** /klēvd/; *past part.* **clo·ven** /ˈklōvən/ or **cleft** or **cleaved**) [*trans.*] split or sever (something), esp. along a natural line or grain: *the large ax his father used to cleave wood for the fire.* ■ split (a molecule) by breaking a particular chemical bond. ■ make a way through (something) forcefully, as if by splitting it apart: *they watched a coot cleave the smooth water* | *Stan was off, **cleaving a path through** the traffic* | [*intrans.*] *an unstoppable warrior **clove through** their ranks.* ■ [*intrans.*] *Biology* (of a cell) divide: *the egg cleaves to form a mulberry-shaped cluster of cells.* ▷Old English *clēofan*, of Germanic origin; related to Dutch *klieven* and German *klieben*. —**cleav·a·ble** *adj.*

cleave[2] ▸*v.* [*intrans.*] (**cleave to**) *poetic/literary* stick fast to: *Rose's mouth was dry, her tongue cleaving to the roof of her mouth.* ■ adhere strongly to (a particular pursuit or belief): *part of why we cleave to sports is that excellence is so measurable.* ■ become very strongly involved with or emotionally attached to (someone): *it was his choice to cleave to the Brownings.* ▷Old English *cleofian*, *clifian*, *clīfan*; related to Dutch *kleven* and German *kleben*, also to CLAY and CLIMB.

Clea·ver /ˈklēvər/, Eldridge (1935–98), U.S. civil rights activist. He converted to the Nation of Islam and wrote *Soul on Ice* (1968) about the black experience.

cleav·er /ˈklēvər/ ▸*n.* a tool with a heavy broad blade, used by butchers for chopping meat.

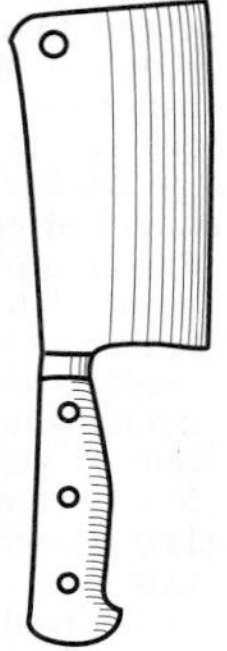

cleaver

cleav·ers /ˈklēvərz/ ▸*plural n.* [treated as *sing.* or *pl.*] a widely distributed scrambling plant related to bedstraws, with hooked bristles on the stem, leaves, and seeds that cling to fur and clothing. Also called GOOSEGRASS. • *Galium aparine*, family Rubiaceae. ▷Old English *clīfe*, related to CLEAVE².

Cleese /klēz/, John (Marwood) (1939–), English comic actor and writer, noted for "Monty Python's Flying Circus" (1969–74) and for the situation comedy "Fawlty Towers" (1975–79).

clef /klef/ ▸*n. Music* any of several symbols placed at the left-hand end of a stave, indicating the pitch of the notes written on it. ▷late 16th cent.: from French, from Latin *clavis* 'key.'

cleft¹ /kleft/ ▸ past and past participle of CLEAVE¹. ▸*adj.* split, divided, or partially divided into two: *a cleft chin.*

cleft² ▸*n.* a fissure or split, esp. one in rock or the ground. ■ a vertical indentation in the middle of a person's forehead or chin. ■ a deep division between two parts of the body. ▷Middle English *clift*: of Germanic origin; related to Dutch *kluft* and German *Kluft*, also to CLEAVE¹. The form of the word was altered in the 16th cent. by association with CLEFT¹.

cleft lip ▸*n.* a congenital split in the upper lip on one or both sides of the center, often associated with a cleft palate.

USAGE **Cleft lip** is the standard, accepted term and should be used instead of **harelip**, which can cause offense.

cleft pal·ate ▸*n.* a congenital split in the roof of the mouth.

cleft sen·tence ▸*n. Grammar* a sentence in which an element is emphasized by being put in a separate clause with the use of an empty introductory word such as *it* or *that*, e.g., *it's money we want; it was today that I saw him; that was the King you were talking to.*

cleg ▸*n. Brit.* another term for HORSEFLY. ▷late Middle English: from Old Norse *kleggi*.

cleis·tog·a·my /klīˈstägəmē/ ▸*n. Botany* self-fertilization that occurs within a permanently closed flower. ▷late 19th cent.: from Greek *kleistos* 'closed' + *-gamy* (from *gamos* 'marriage'). **—cleis·tog·a·mous** /-əməs/ *adj.*

clem·a·tis /ˈklemətəs; kləˈmatəs/ ▸*n.* a climbing plant of the buttercup family that bears white, pink, or purple flowers and feathery seeds. Several kinds are cultivated as ornamentals. • Genus *Clematis*, family Ranunculaceae. ▷Latin (also denoting the periwinkle), from Greek *klēmatis*, from *klēma* 'vine branch.'

Cle·men·ceau /ˌklemənˈsō; ˌkläˌmänˈsō/, Georges (Eugène Benjamin) (1841–1929), French statesman, prime minister 1906–09 and 1917–20. At the Versailles peace talks he pushed hard for a punitive settlement with Germany, but failed to obtain all that he demanded.

clem·en·cy /ˈklemənsē/ ▸*n.* mercy; lenience: *an appeal for clemency.* See note at MERCY. ▷late Middle English: from Latin *clementia*, from *clemens*, *clement-* 'clement.'

Clem·ens¹ /ˈklemənz/, (William) Roger (1962–), U.S. baseball player; known as **the Rocket**. In 2004, he became the first pitcher to have won seven Cy Young awards (1986, 1987, 1991, 1997, 1998, 2001, 2004). He had previously set another major league record by twice (1986, 1996) striking out 20 batters during a nine-inning game. He played for the Boston Red Sox 1983–96, the Toronto Blue Jays 1997–98, the New York Yankees 1999–2003, and the Houston Astros from 2004.

Clem·ens², Samuel Langhorne, see TWAIN.

Clem·ent, St. (1st century AD), pope (bishop of Rome) *c.*88–*c.*97, probably the third after St. Peter; known as **St. Clement of Rome**. Feast day, November 23.

clem·ent /ˈklemənt/ ▸*adj.* **1** (of weather) mild. **2** (of a person or a person's actions) merciful. ▷late Middle English (sense 2): from Latin *clemens*, *clement-*.

Cle·men·te /kləˈmentā; -tē/, Roberto Walker (1934–72), U.S. baseball player; born in Puerto Rico. An outfielder for the Pittsburgh Pirates 1955–72, he was a four-time National League batting champion. He was killed in an airplane crash. Baseball Hall of Fame (1973).

clem·en·tine /ˈkleménˌtīn; -ˌtēn/ ▸*n.* a tangerine of a deep orange-red North African variety that is grown around the Mediterranean and in South Africa. ▷1920s: from French *clémentine*, from the male given name *Clément*.

Clem·ent of Al·ex·an·dri·a, St. /ˈklemənt/ (*c.*150–*c.*215), Greek theologian; Latin name *Titus Flavius Clemens*. He related the ideas of Greek philosophy to the Christian faith. Feast day, December 5.

Clem·son /ˈklemsən/ a city in northwestern South Carolina, home to Clemson University; pop. 11,096.

clen·bu·te·rol /klenˈbyoōtəˌrôl; -ˌrōl/ ▸*n. Medicine* a synthetic drug used in the treatment of asthma and other respiratory diseases and also in veterinary obstetrics. It also promotes the growth of muscle and has been used illegally by athletes to enhance performance. ▷1970s: from *c(h)l(oro-)* + *(ph)en(yl)* + *but(yl)* + *er* + -OL.

clench /klenCH/ ▸*v.* (with reference to the fingers or hand) close into a tight ball, esp. when feeling extreme anger: [*trans.*] *she clenched her fists, struggling for control* | [*intrans.*] *John's right hand* **clenched into** *a fist* | [as *adj.*] (**clenched**) *he struck the wall with his clenched fist.* ■ (with reference to the teeth) press or be pressed tightly together, esp. with anger or determination or so as to suppress a strong emotion: [*intrans.*] *her teeth clenched in anger.* ■ [*trans.*] grasp (something) tightly, esp. with the hands or between the teeth: *he clenched the steering wheel so hard that the car wobbled.* ■ [*intrans.*] (of a muscular part of the body) tighten or contract sharply, esp. with strong emotion: *Mark felt his stomach clench in alarm.*
▸*n.* [in *sing.*] a contraction or tightening of part of the body: *she saw the anger rise, saw the clench of his fists.* ■ the state of being tightly closed or contracted. ▷Old English (in the sense of *clinch* 'fix securely'): of Germanic origin; related to CLING.

cle·o·me /klēˈōmē/ ▸*n.* a plant of a chiefly tropical genus that includes the spider flower. Cleomes are noted for their long stamens. • Genus *Cleome*, family Capparidaceae. ▷modern Latin, from Greek, denoting a different plant.

Cle·o·pa·tra /ˌklēəˈpatrə/ (69–30 BC), queen of Egypt 47–30; the last Ptolemaic (Macedonian dynasty) ruler; also known as **Cleopatra VII**. After a brief liaison with Julius Caesar, she formed a political and romantic alliance with Mark Antony. Their ambitions ultimately brought them into conflict with Rome, and they were defeated at the battle of Actium in 31. She is reputed to have committed suicide by allowing herself to be bitten by an asp.

cle·o·pa·tra /ˌklēəˈpatrə/ ▸*n.* a European butterfly related to the brimstone, with wings that vary from pale cream to orange-yellow. • *Gonepteryx cleopatra*, family Pieridae.

Cle·o·pa·tra's Needle /klēəˈpatrəz/ a popular name for either of two ancient Egyptian obelisks, one on the Victoria Embankment in London, England; the other in Central Park, New York City.

Cle·o·pa·tra's Nee·dles a pair of granite obelisks erected at Heliopolis by Tuthmosis III *c.*1475 BC. They were taken from Egypt in 1878, one being set up on the Thames Embankment in London and the other in Central Park, New York. They have no known historical connection with Cleopatra.

clep·sy·dra /ˈklepsədrə/ ▸*n.* (*pl.* **-dras** or **-drae** /-ˌdrē; -ˌdrī/) an ancient time-measuring device worked by a flow of water. ▷late Middle English: via Latin from Greek *klepsudra*, based on *kleptein* 'steal' + *hudōr* 'water.'

clere·sto·ry /ˈkli(ə)rˌstôrē/ (also **clear·sto·ry**) ▸*n.* (*pl.* **-ries**) the upper part of the nave, choir, and transepts of a large church, containing a series of windows. It is clear of the roofs of the aisles and admits light to the central parts of the building. ■ such a series of windows in a church or similar windows in another building. ■ a raised section of roof running down the center of a railroad car, with small windows or ventilators. ▷late Middle English: from CLEAR + STORY².

cler·gy /ˈklərjē/ ▸*n.* (*pl.* **-gies**) [usu. treated as *pl.*] the body of all people ordained for religious duties, esp. in the Christian Church: *all marriages were to be solemnized by* **the clergy**. ▷Middle English: from Old French, based on ecclesiastical Latin *clericus* 'clergyman' (see CLERIC).

cler·gy·man /ˈklərjēmən/ ▸*n.* (*pl.* **-men**) a male priest or minister of a Christian church.

cler·gy·wom·an /ˈklərjēˌwoŏmən/ ▸*n.* (*pl.* **-wom·en**) a female priest or minister of a Christian church.

cler·ic /ˈklerik/ ▸*n.* a priest or minister of a Christian church. ■ a priest or religious leader in any religion. ▷early 17th cent.: from ecclesiastical Latin *clericus* 'clergyman,' from Greek *klērikos* 'belonging to the Christian clergy,' from *klēros* 'lot, heritage' (Acts 1:26).

cler·i·cal /ˈklerikəl/ ▸*adj.* **1** (of a job or person) concerned with or relating to work in an office, esp. routine documentation and administrative tasks: *temps are always needed for clerical work.* **2** of or relating to the clergy: *he was still attired in his clerical outfit.* ▷late 15th cent. (sense 2): from ecclesiastical Latin *clericalis*, from *clericus* 'clergyman' (see CLERIC). **—cler·i·cal·ism** *n.* (in sense 2). **—cler·i·cal·ist** *n.* (in sense 2). **—cler·i·cal·ly** *adv.*

cler·i·cal col·lar ▸*n.* a stiff upright white collar that fastens at the back, worn by the clergy in some churches.

cler·i·hew /ˈklerəˌhyoō/ ▸*n.* a short comic or nonsensical verse, typically in two rhyming couplets with lines of unequal length and referring to a famous person. ▷1920s: named after Edmund *Clerihew* Bentley (1875–1956), the English writer who invented it.

cler·i·sy /ˈklerəsē/ ▸*n.* [usu. treated as *pl.*] a distinct class of learned or literary people: *the clerisy are those who read for pleasure.* ▷early 19th cent.: apparently influenced by German *Klerisei*, based on Greek *klēros* 'heritage' (see CLERIC).

clerk /klərk/ ▸*n.* **1** a person employed in an office or bank to keep records and accounts and to undertake other routine administrative duties: *a bank clerk.* ■ an official in charge of the records of a local council or court: *a clerk to the court.* ■ a person employed by a judge, or being trained by a lawyer, who does legal research, etc. ■ a lay officer of a cathedral, parish church, college chapel, etc.: *a chapter clerk.* **2** (also **desk clerk**) a receptionist in a hotel. ■ an assistant in a store; a salesclerk. **3** (also **clerk in holy orders**) *formal* a member of the clergy.
▸*v.* [*intrans.*] work as a clerk: *eleven of those who left college this year are clerking in auction houses.* ▷Old English *cleric, clerc* (in the sense 'ordained minister, literate person'), from ecclesiastical Latin *clericus* 'clergyman' (see CLERIC); reinforced by Old French *clerc*, from the same source. Sense 1 dates from the early 16th cent. **—clerk·ish** *adj.*

clerk·ly /ˈklərklē/ ▸*adj. archaic* of, relating to, or appropriate to a clerk: *a list drawn up in a clerkly hand.* ■ scholarly; learned.

clerk·ship /ˈklərkˌSHip/ ▸*n.* the position or status of a clerk, esp. in the legal profession.

Cler·mont-Fer·rand /klerˈmôN fəˈräN/ an industrial city in central France, capital of the Auvergne region, at the center of the Massif Central; pop. 140,170.

C-lev·el (also **c-lev·el**) ▸*adj.* denoting the executive level of a corporation: *a c-level corporate officer.* ▷early 2000s: from the fact that initialisms for jobs at this level begin with C (for *chief*).

Cleve·land¹ /ˈklēvlənd/ **1** a major port and industrial city in northeastern Ohio, on Lake Erie and the Cuyahoga River; pop. 478,403. **2** a city in southeastern Tennessee, northeast of Chattanooga; pop. 37,192.

Cleve·land², (Stephen) Grover (1837–1908), 22nd and 24th president of the U.S. 1885–89 and 1893–97. A New York Democrat, he served as governor of his state 1883–85 before being elected to the presidency. During his first term, he championed civil service reform and revision of the tariff system. Although he was defeated for reelection by Benjamin Harrison in 1888, he was again elected in 1892. His second term was marked by his application of the Monroe Doctrine to Britain's border dispute with Venezuela in 1895.

Grover Cleveland

Cleve·land Heights a city in northeastern Ohio, northeast of Cleveland; pop. 54,052.

clev·er /ˈklevər/ ▸*adj.* (**clev·er·er, clev·er·est**) quick to understand, learn, and devise or apply ideas; intelligent: *a clever and studious young woman | how **clever of** him to think of this!* ■ skilled at doing or achieving something; talented: *he was **clever at** getting what he wanted | she is **clever with** her hands.* ■ (of a thing, action, or idea) showing intelligence or skill; ingenious: *a simple but clever idea for helping people learn computing.* ■ superficially ingenious or witty: *a story too clever and tidy to be real.* ■ *dated* [usu. with *negative*] *informal* sensible; well-advised: *it wasn't too clever, leaving Dolly alone.* ▷Middle English (in the sense 'quick to catch hold,' only recorded in this period): perhaps of Dutch or Low German origin, and related to CLEAVE². In the late 16th cent. the term came to mean (probably through dialect use) 'manually skillful'; the sense 'possessing mental agility' dates from the early 18th cent. **—clev·er·ly** *adv.* **—clev·er·ness** *n.*

▸*PHRASE* □ **too clever by half** *informal* annoyingly proud of one's intelligence or skill and in danger of overreaching oneself.

clev·is /ˈklevəs/ ▸*n.* a U-shaped or forked metal connector within which another part can be fastened by means of a bolt or pin passing through the ends of the connector. ▷late 16th cent.: perhaps related to CLEAVE¹.

clew /klo͞o/ ▸*n.* **1** the lower or after corner of a sail. **2** (**clews**) *Nautical* the cords by which a hammock is suspended. ■ (**clew**) a ball of thread (used esp. with reference to the thread supposedly used by Theseus to mark his way out of the Cretan labyrinth). **3** archaic variant of CLUE.

▸*v.* [*trans.*] (**clew a sail up**) *Sailing* haul up the clews of a sail to the yard or into the mast ready for furling. ■ (**clew a sail down**) lower an upper square sail by hauling down on the clew lines while slacking away on the halyard. ▷Old English *cliwen, cleowen* (denoting a rounded mass, also a ball of thread), of Germanic origin; related to Dutch *kluwen.* All senses are also recorded for the form CLUE.

CLI ▸*abbr.* COST-OF-LIVING INDEX.

cli·ché /klēˈSHā kli-; ˈklē,SHā/ (also **cli·che**) ▸*n.* **1** a phrase or opinion that is overused and betrays a lack of original thought: *the old cliché "one man's meat is another man's poison."* ■ a very predictable or unoriginal thing or person: *each building is a mishmash of tired clichés.* **2** *Printing chiefly Brit.* a stereotype or electrotype. ▷mid 19th cent.: French, past participle (used as a noun) of *clicher* 'to stereotype.'

cli·chéd /klēˈSHād; kli-; ˈklē,SHād/ (also **cli·ched**) ▸*adj.* showing a lack of originality; based on frequently repeated phrases or opinions: *people have a clichéd view of the Middle East.*

click /klik/ ▸*n.* a short, sharp sound as of a switch being operated or of two hard objects coming quickly into contact: *she heard the click of the door.* ■ *Phonetics* an ingressive consonantal stop produced by sudden withdrawal of the tongue from the soft palate, front teeth, or back teeth and hard palate, occurring in some southern African and other languages. ■ *Computing* an act of pressing a mouse button.

▸*v.* **1** make or cause to make a short, sharp sound: [*intrans.*] *the key clicked in the lock and the door opened* | [*trans.*] *she clicked off the light | Martha clicked her tongue* | [as *adj.*] (**clicking**) *the clicking cameras outside the church.* ■ [*intrans.*] move with such a sound: *Louise turned on her three-inch heels and clicked away.* ■ [*trans.*] *Computing* press (a mouse button): *click the left mouse button twice.* ■ [*intrans.*] (**click on**) *Computing* select (an item represented on the screen or a particular function) by pressing one of the buttons on the mouse when the cursor is over the appropriate symbol. **2** [*intrans.*] *informal* become suddenly clear or understandable: *finally **it clicked** what all the fuss had been about.* ■ become very comfortable with someone at the first meeting: *we just clicked, and I found myself falling in love.* ■ become successful or popular: *I don't think this issue has **clicked with** the voters.* ▷late 16th cent. (as a verb): imitative.

▸*PHRASE* □ **click into place** (of an object, esp. part of a mechanism) fall smoothly into its allotted position. ■ *figurative* become suddenly clear and understandable: *everything has clicked into place for the organization.*

click·a·ble /ˈklikəbəl/ ▸*adj.* *Computing* (of text or images on a computer screen) such that clicking on them with a mouse will produce a reaction.

click bee·tle ▸*n.* a long, narrow beetle that can spring up with a click as a means of startling predators and escaping. Its larva is the wireworm. Also called SKIPJACK. • Family Elateridae: numerous genera.

click·er /ˈklikər/ ▸*n.* a device that clicks. ■ a remote control keypad.

click·e·ty-clack /ˈklikətē ˈklak/ (also **clickety-click**) ▸*n.* a repeated clicking sound as of shoe heels on a hard surface.

▸*v.* [*intrans.*, with *adverbial of direction*] move with such a sound: *the train clickety-clacked along the tracks.*

click lan·guage ▸*n.* a language in which clicks are used.

click rate (also **click-through rate**) ▸*n.* *Computing* the percentage of people downloading a Web page who access a hypertext link to a particular advertisement.

clicks and mor·tar ▸*n.* used to refer to a traditional business that has expanded its activities to operate also on the Internet: [*as modifier*] *a clicks-and-mortar strategy.* Compare with BRICKS AND MORTAR.

click stop ▸*n.* a control for the aperture of a camera lens that clicks into position at certain standard settings.

click·stream /ˈklik,strēm/ ▸*n.* a series of mouse clicks made while using a Web site or in linking to multiple Web sites.

click·wrap /ˈklik,rap/ ▸*adj.* denoting a legal agreement for which acceptance is confirmed by clicking on a screen icon, such as for software use: *do the clickwrap contracts adequately advise me of what the adware and spyware does?*

cli·ent /ˈklīənt/ ▸*n.* **1** a person or organization using the services of a lawyer or other professional person or company: *insurance tailor-made to a client's specific requirements.* ■ a person receiving social or medical services: *a client referred for counseling.* ■ (also **client state**) a nation that is dependent on another, more powerful nation. **2** *Computing* (in a network) a desktop computer or workstation that is capable of obtaining information and applications from a server. ■ (also **client application** or **program**) a program that is capable of obtaining a service provided by another program. **3** (in ancient Rome) a plebeian under the protection of a patrician. ■ *archaic* a dependent; a hanger-on. ▷late Middle English: from Latin *cliens, client-,* variant of *cluens* 'heeding,' from *cluere* 'hear or obey.' The term originally denoted a person under the protection and patronage of another, hence a person "protected" by a legal adviser (sense 1). **—cli·ent·ship** /-,SHip/ *n.*

cli·en·tele /,klīənˈtel; ,klē-/ ▸*n.* [treated as *sing.* or *pl.*] clients collectively: *an upscale clientele.* ■ the customers of a shop, bar, or place of entertainment: *the dancers don't mix with the clientele.* ▷mid 16th cent. (in the sense 'clientship, patronage'): via French from Latin *clientela* 'clientship,' from *cliens, client-* (see CLIENT).

cli·en·tel·ism /,klīənˈtel,izəm; ,klē-/ (also **cli·ent·ism** /ˈklīən,tizəm/) ▸*n.* a social order that depends upon relations of patronage; in particular, a political approach that emphasizes or exploits such relations. ▷1970s: from Italian *clientelismo* 'patronage system.' **—cli·en·tel·is·tic** /-telˈistik/ *adj.*

cli·ent-serv·er ▸*adj.* *Computing* denoting a computer system in which a central server provides data to a number of networked workstations.

cliff /klif/ ▸*n.* a steep rock face, esp. at the edge of the sea: *a path along the top of rugged cliffs* | [as *adj.*] *the cliff face.* ▷Old English *clif,* of Germanic origin; related to Dutch *klif.* **—cliff-like** /-,līk/ *adj.* **—cliff·y** *adj.*

cliff·hang·er /ˈklif,haNGər/ ▸*n.* an ending to an episode of a serial drama that leaves the audience in suspense. ■ a story or event with a strong element of suspense: *the game was a cliffhanger right up to the final buzzer.* **—cliff·hang·ing** /-,haNGiNG/ *adj.*

Clif·ford¹ /ˈklifərd/, Clark M. (1906–98), U.S. attorney and public official. A key adviser to four Democratic presidents, he helped draft the legislation that established the Central Intelligence Agency (CIA).

Clif·ford², Nathan (1803–81), U.S. Supreme Court associate justice 1858–81. He was the U.S. attorney general 1846–48 before being appointed to the Court by President Buchanan. He was an advocate of states' rights.

CliffsNotes /ˈklifs,nōts/ ▸*n.* *trademark* a brand name for a series of prepared notes used as study guides for literary works and other school and college subject matter. ▷for Cliff Hillegass (1918–2001), U.S. developer of the series.

Clift /klift/, (Edward) Montgomery (1920–66), U.S. actor. He received four Academy Award nominations for movies that included *From Here to Eternity* (1953) and *Judgment at Nuremberg* (1961).

Clif·ton /ˈkliftən/ an industrial city in northeastern New Jersey, immediately west of Passaic; pop. 78,672.

cli·mac·ter·ic /klīˈmaktərik; ,klīmakˈterik/ ▸*n.* a critical period or event: *the first major climacteric in twentieth-century poetry.* ■ *Medicine* the period of life when fertility and sexual activity are in decline; (in women) menopause. ■ *Botany* the ripening period of certain fruits such as apples, involving increased metabolism and only possible while still on the tree.

▸*adj.* having extreme and far-reaching implications or results; critical: *Britain must possess so climacteric a weapon in order to deter an atomically armed enemy.* ■ *Medicine* occurring at, characteristic of, or undergoing the climacteric; (in women) menopausal. ■ *Botany* (of a fruit) undergoing a climacteric. ▷mid 16th cent. (in the sense 'constituting a critical period in life'): from French *climactérique* or via Latin from Greek *klimaktērikos,* from *klimaktēr* 'critical period,' from *klimax* 'ladder, climax.'

cli·mac·tic /klīˈmaktik; klə-/ ▸*adj.* (of an action, event, or scene) exciting or thrilling and acting as a climax to a series of events: *the film's climactic scenes.* ▷late 19th cent.: formed irregularly from CLIMAX + -IC, probably influenced by CLIMACTERIC. **—cli·mac·ti·cal·ly** /-ik(ə)lē/ *adv.*

cli·mate /ˈklīmit/ ▸*n.* the weather conditions prevailing in an area in general or over a long period: *our cold, wet climate | agricultural development is constrained by climate.* ■ a region with particular prevailing weather conditions: *vacationing in a warm climate.* ■ the prevailing trend of public opinion or of another aspect of public life: *the current economic climate.* ▷late Middle English: from Old French *climat* or late Latin *clima, climat-,* from Greek *klima* 'slope, zone,' from *klinein* 'to slope.' The term originally denoted a zone of the earth between two lines of latitude, then any region of the earth, and later, a region considered with reference to its atmospheric conditions. Compare with CLIME. **—cli·mat·ic** /klīˈmatik/ *adj.* **—cli·mat·i·cal** /klīˈmatikəl/ *adj.* **—cli·mat·i·cal·ly** /klīˈmatik(ə)lē/ *adv.*

cli·mate change ▸*n.* long-term, significant change in the climate of an area or of the earth, usually seen as resulting from human activity. Often used as a synonym for GLOBAL WARMING.

cli·mate con·trol ▸*n.* another term for AIR CONDITIONING.

cli·ma·tol·o·gy /,klīməˈtäləjē/ ▸*n.* the scientific study of climate. **—cli·ma·to·log·i·cal** /,klīmətlˈäjikəl/ *adj.* **—cli·ma·tol·o·gist** /-jist/ *n.*

cli·max /ˈklī,maks/ ▸*n.* the most intense, exciting, or important point of something; a culmination or apex: *the climax of her speech | a thrilling climax to the game.* ■ an orgasm. ■ *Ecology* the final stage in a succession in a given environment, at which a plant community reaches a state of equilibrium: [as *adj.*] *a mixed hardwood climax forest.* ■ *Rhetoric* a sequence of propositions or ideas in order of increasing importance, force, or effectiveness of expression.

▸*v.* [*intrans.*] culminate in an exciting or impressive event; reach a climax: *the day **climaxed with** a gala concert.* ■ [*trans.*] bring (something) to a climax: *the sentencing climaxed a seven-month trial.* ■ have an orgasm. ▷mid 16th cent. (in rhetoric): from late Latin, from Greek *klimax* 'ladder, climax.' The sense 'culmination' arose in the late 18th cent.

climb /klīm/ ▸*v.* **1** [*trans.*] go or come up (a slope, incline, or staircase), esp. by using the feet and sometimes the hands; ascend: *we began to climb the hill* | [*intrans.*] *the air became colder as they climbed higher | he **climbed up** the steps slowly.* ■ [*intrans.*] (of an aircraft or the sun) go upward: *we decided to climb to 6,000 feet.* ■ [*intrans.*] (of a road or track) slope upward or up: *the track climbed steeply up a narrow, twisting valley.* ■ (of a plant) grow up (a wall, tree, or trellis) by clinging with tendrils or by twining: *when ivy climbs a wall, it infiltrates any crack* | [*intrans.*] *there were roses **climbing up** the walls.* ■ [*intrans.*] grow in scale, value, or power: *the stock market climbed 24 points | he climbed from a job as office messenger to president of the bank.* ■ move to a higher position in (a chart or table): *the song is climbing the adult-contemporary chart.* **2** [*intrans.*, with *adverbial of direction*] move with effort, esp. into or out of a confined space; clamber: *Howard started to climb out of the front seat | I climbed down a narrow ladder | he climbed to a high bough.* ■ (**climb into**) put on (clothes): *he climbed into his suit.*

▸*n.* an ascent, esp. of a mountain or hill, by climbing: *the rigorous climb up the mountain | figurative his long climb from poverty.* ■ a mountain, hill, or slope that is climbed or is to be climbed: *the mountain is no easy climb.* ■ a recognized route up a mountain or cliff:

this may be the hardest rock climb in the world. ■ an aircraft's flight upward: *we leveled out from the climb at 600 feet* | *rate of climb.* ■ a rise or increase in value, rank, or power: *an above-average climb in prices.* ▷Old English *climban*; related to Dutch and German *klimmen*, also to CLAY and CLEAVE[2]. —**climb·a·ble** *adj.*

▸*PHRASE* □ **be climbing the walls** *informal* feel frustrated, helpless, and trapped: *his job soon had him climbing the walls.*

climb·er /ˈklīmər/ ▸*n.* a person or animal that climbs: *leopards are great tree climbers.* ■ a mountaineer. ■ a climbing plant. ■ see SOCIAL CLIMBER.

climb·ing /ˈklīmiNG/ ▸*n.* the sport or activity of ascending mountains or cliffs.

climb·ing eu·on·y·mus ▸*n.* another name for WINTER CREEPER.

climb·ing i·rons ▸*plural n.* a set of spikes attached to boots for climbing trees or ice slopes.

climb·ing perch ▸*n.* a small, edible freshwater fish that is able to breathe air and move over land, native to Africa and Asia. • Family Anabantidae: three genera and several species, including *Anabas testudineus.*

climb·ing wall ▸*n.* a wall at a sports center or in a gymnasium fitted with attachments to simulate a rock face for climbing practice.

climb-out ▸*n.* the part of a flight of an aircraft after takeoff and before it reaches a level altitude.

clime /klīm/ ▸*n.* (usu. **climes**) *chiefly poetic/literary* a region considered with reference to its climate: *the Continent and its sunnier climes.* ▷late Middle English: from late Latin *clima* 'zone' (see CLIMATE).

clin- ▸*comb. form* variant spelling of CLINO- shortened before a vowel.

clinch /klinCH/ ▸*v.* [*trans.*] **1** confirm or settle (a contract or bargain): *to clinch a business deal.* ■ conclusively settle (an argument or debate): *these findings clinched the matter.* ■ confirm the winning or achievement of (a game, competition, or victory): *his team clinched the title.* ■ secure (a nail or rivet) by driving the point sideways when it has penetrated. ■ fasten (a rope or fishing line) with a clinch knot. **2** [*intrans.*] grapple at close quarters, esp. (of boxers) so as to be too closely engaged for full-arm blows. ■ (of two people) embrace.

▸*n.* **1** a struggle or scuffle at close quarters, esp. (in boxing) one in which the fighters become too closely engaged for full-arm blows. ■ an embrace, esp. an amorous one: *we went into a passionate clinch on the sofa.* **2** a knot used to fasten a rope to a ring or cringle, using a half hitch with the end seized back on its own part. ▷late 16th cent. (in the senses 'something that grips' and 'fix securely'): variant of CLENCH.

clinch·er /ˈklinCHər/ ▸*n.* **1** a fact, argument, or event that settles a matter conclusively: *his two-run double was the clincher.* **2** (in full **clincher tire**) a bicycle or automobile tire that has flange beads that fit into the wheel rim.

Clinch Riv·er /klinCH/ a river that flows for 300 miles (480 km) from southwestern Virginia into Tennessee where it passes the Norris Dam and Oak Ridge before joining the Tennessee River.

Cline /klīn/, Patsy (1932–63), U.S. country singer; born *Virginia Petterson Hensley.* She had hits with "Crazy" (1961) and "Sweet Dreams of You" (1963) before dying in an air crash.

cline /klīn/ ▸*n.* a continuum with an infinite number of gradations from one extreme to the other: *a point along a cline of activity.* ■ *Biology* a gradation in one or more characteristics within a species or other taxon, esp. between different populations. See also ECOCLINE. ▷1930s: from Greek *klinein* 'to slope.' —**clin·al** /ˈklīnl/ *adj.*

cling /kliNG/ ▸*v.* (*past* and *past part.* **clung** /kləNG/) [*intrans.*] (**cling to/onto/on**) (of a person or animal) hold on tightly to: *she clung to Joe's arm* | *they clung together* | *figurative she clung onto life.* ■ (**cling to**) adhere or stick firmly or closely to; be hard to part or remove from: *the smell of smoke clung to their clothes* | *the fabric clung to her smooth skin.* ■ (**cling to**) remain very close to: *the fish cling to the line of the weed.* ■ remain persistently or stubbornly faithful to something: *she clung resolutely to her convictions.* ■ be overly dependent on someone emotionally: *you are clinging to him for security.*

▸*n.* (also **cling peach**) a clingstone peach. ▷Old English *clingan* 'stick together,' of Germanic origin; related to Middle Dutch *klingen* 'adhere,' Middle High German *klingen* 'climb,' also to CLENCH. —**cling·er** *n.*

cling film ▸*n.* British term for PLASTIC WRAP.

cling·fish /ˈkliNG,fiSH/ ▸*n.* (*pl.* same or **-fish·es**) a small fish occurring mainly in shallow or intertidal water, with a sucker for attachment to rocks and other surfaces. • Family Gobiesocidae: several genera and species, including the **shore clingfish** (*Lepadogaster lepadogaster*) of Europe and West Africa.

cling·ing /ˈkliNGiNG/ ▸*adj.* **1** (of a garment) fitting closely to the body and showing its shape: *she was wearing a clinging black dress.* **2** overly dependent on someone emotionally: *she wasn't the clinging type.*

▸*PHRASE* □ **clinging vine** a person who is submissively dependent on another.

cling·stone /ˈkliNG,stōn/ ▸*n.* a peach or nectarine of a variety in which the flesh adheres to the stone. Contrasted with FREESTONE (sense 2).

cling·y /ˈkliNGē/ ▸*adj.* (**cling·i·er**, **cling·i·est**) (of a person or garment) liable to cling; clinging: *at about 18 months my son became very clingy* | *clingy leggings.* —**cling·i·ness** *n.*

clin·ic /ˈklinik/ ▸*n.* **1** a place or hospital department where outpatients are given medical treatment or advice, esp. of a specialist nature: *a mental health clinic.* ■ an occasion or time when such treatment or advice is given: *we're now holding regular clinics.* ■ a gathering at a hospital bedside for the teaching of medicine or surgery. **2** a conference or short course on a particular subject: *a ski clinic.* ▷mid 19th cent. (in the sense 'teaching of medicine at the bedside'): from French *clinique*, from Greek *klinikē (tekhnē)* 'bedside (art),' from *klinē* 'bed.'

clin·i·cal /ˈklinikəl/ ▸*adj.* **1** of or relating to a clinic: *an annual clinical examination* ■ of or relating to the observation and treatment of actual patients rather than theoretical or laboratory studies: *clinical medicine* | *clinical drug trials.* ■ (of a disease or condition) causing observable and recognizable symptoms: *clinical depression.* **2** efficient and unemotional; coldly detached: *the clinical detail of a textbook.* ■ (of a room or building) bare, functional, and clean. ▷late 18th cent.: from Greek *klinikē* 'bedside' (see CLINIC) + -AL.

clin·i·cal death ▸*n.* death as judged by the medical observation of cessation of vital functions. It is typically identified with the cessation of heartbeat and respiration, though modern resuscitation methods and life-support systems have required the introduction of the alternative concept of brain death.

clin·i·cal e·col·o·gy ▸*n.* an earlier name for ENVIRONMENTAL MEDICINE.

clin·i·cal·ly /ˈklinik(ə)lē/ ▸*adv.* **1** as regards clinical medicine; in clinical terms: *the first clinically useful antibiotics* | *clinically dead.* **2** efficiently and without emotion: *he scrutinized her clinically.* ■ [usu. as *submodifier*] in a very functional and clean manner: *a clinically clean kitchen.*

clin·i·cal psy·chol·o·gy ▸*n.* the branch of psychology concerned with the assessment and treatment of mental illness and disability. —**clin·i·cal psy·chol·o·gist** *n.*

clin·i·cal ther·mom·e·ter ▸*n.* a small medical thermometer with a short but finely calibrated range, for taking a person's temperature.

cli·ni·cian /kləˈniSHən/ ▸*n.* a doctor having direct contact with and responsibility for patients, rather than one involved with theoretical or laboratory studies.

clink[1] /kliNGk/ ▸*n.* a sharp ringing sound, such as that made when metal or glass are struck: *a clink of keys* | *the clink of ice in tall glasses.*

▸*v.* [*intrans.*] make such a sound: *his ring clinked against the crystal* | [as *n.*] (**clinking**) *the clinking of glasses* | [as *adj.*] (**clinking**) *clinking chains.* ■ [*trans.*] cause (something) to make such a sound: *I heard Suzie clink a piece of crockery.* ■ [*trans.*] strike (a glass or glasses) with another to express friendly feelings toward one's companions before drinking: *she* **clinked** *her glass* **on** *mine.* ▷Middle English (as a verb): probably from Middle Dutch *klinken.*

clink[2] ▸*n.* [in *sing.*] *informal* prison: *he was put in the clink for six days.* ▷early 16th cent. (originally denoting a prison in Southwark, London): of unknown origin.

clink·er[1] /ˈkliNGkər/ ▸*n.* the stony residue from burned coal or from a furnace. ■ (also **clinker brick**) a brick with a vitrified surface. ▷mid 17th cent.: from obsolete Dutch *klinckaerd* (earlier form of *klinker*), from *klinken* 'to clink.'

clink·er[2] ▸*n.* *informal* something that is unsatisfactory, of poor quality, or a failure: *marketing couldn't save such clinkers as these films.* ■ a wrong musical note. ▷late 17th cent. (denoting a person or thing that clinks): from CLINK[1] + -ER[1]. The current sense (with depreciatory reference) dates from the 1930s.

clink·er-built ▸*adj.* (of a boat) having external planks secured with clinched nails such that the bottom edge of an upper plank overlaps the upper edge of a lower plank. Compare with CARVEL-BUILT. ▷mid 18th cent.: *clinker* from *clink* (northern English variant of CLINCH).

clino- (usu. **clin-** before a vowel) ▸*comb. form* slant; slope: *clinometer.*

cli·nom·e·ter /klīˈnämətər/ ▸*n.* *Surveying* an instrument used for measuring the angle or elevation of slopes. ▷early 19th cent.: from Greek *klinein* 'to slope' + -METER.

cli·no·py·rox·ene /,klīnō,pīˈräk,sēn/ ▸*n.* a mineral of the pyroxene group crystallizing in the monoclinic system. ▷early 20th cent.: from *clino-* in the sense 'monoclinic' + PYROXENE.

clin·quant /ˈkliNGkənt/ ▸*adj.* glittering with gold and silver; tinseled.

▸*n.* imitation gold leaf. ■ *figurative* literary or artistic tinsel; false glitter.

Clin·ton[1] /ˈklintən/ **1** a city in east central Iowa, on the Mississippi River; pop. 27,772. **2** a city in southwest central Mississippi, west of Jackson; pop. 23,347

Clin·ton[2], Bill (1946–), 42nd President of the U.S. 1993–2001; full name *William Jefferson Blythe Clinton.* An Arkansas Democrat, he served as governor of his state 1979–81, 1983–93 before becoming president. During his first term, he worked with a Republican-controlled Congress to balance the budget. His second term brought economic prosperity as well as international crises in the Middle East and Yugoslavia. Problems that included contested allegations of financial and sexual misconduct escalated, and in 1998 he became the second president ever to be impeached, in his case, on charges of perjury and obstruction of justice. He was acquitted by the Senate in 1999.

William Jefferson Clinton

Clin·ton[3], DeWitt (1769–1828), U.S. politician. Among his political positions, he was a member of the New York legislature 1798–1802, a U.S. senator 1802–03, and mayor of New York City 1803–07, 1808–10, 1811–15. As governor of New York 1817–23, 1825–28, he was a champion of the Erie Canal.

Clin·ton[4], George (1739–1812), U.S. politician. He was governor of New York 1777–95, 1801–04 and vice president of the U.S. 1805–12.

Clin·ton[5], Hillary Rodham (1947–), U.S. lawyer, first lady 1993–2001, and senator 2001– . As first lady during Bill Clinton's administration, she worked on health care reform and wrote *It Takes a Village* (1996)

Hillary Rodham Clinton

about raising the children of the world. In 2000, she was elected to the U.S. Senate as a Democrat from the state of New York.

Cli·o /ˈklīō; ˈklēō/ **1** *Greek & Roman Mythology* the Muse of history. **2** an award given annually for advertising achievement in television, radio, billboards, and other media. ▷from Greek *kleiein* 'celebrate.'

cli·o·met·rics /ˌklīəˈmetriks/ ▶*plural n.* [treated as *sing.*] a technique for the interpretation of economic history, based on the statistical analysis of large-scale numerical data from population censuses, parish registers, and similar sources. ▷1960s (originally U.S.): from CLIO, on the pattern of words such as *econometrics*. **—cli·o·met·ric** *adj.* **—cli·o·me·tri·cian** /-meˈtrisHən/ *n.*

clip[1] /klip/ ▶*n.* a device, typically flexible or worked by a spring, for holding an object or objects together or in place. ■ a device such as this used to hold paper currency. ■ a piece of jewelry fastened by a clip. ■ a metal holder containing cartridges for an automatic firearm.

▶*v.* (**clipped**, **clip·ping**) [with *adverbial of place*] fasten or be fastened with a clip or clips: [*trans.*] *she clipped on a pair of diamond earrings* | [*intrans.*] *the panels simply clip on to the framework.* ▷Old English *clyppan* (verb). The noun use dates from the late 15th cent.

clip[2] ▶*v.* (**clipped**, **clip·ping**) [*trans.*] **1** cut short or trim (hair, wool, nails, or vegetation) with shears or scissors: *clipping the hedge.* ■ trim or remove the hair or wool of (an animal): *how to clip your horse.* ■ (**clip something off**) cut off a thing or part of a thing with shears or scissors: *he clipped off a piece of wire* | *figurative she clipped nearly two seconds off the old record.* ■ cut (a section) from a newspaper or magazine: *a photograph clipped from a magazine.* ■ pare the edge of (a coin), esp. illicitly: *they clipped the edges of gold coins and melted the clippings down.* ■ speak (words) in a quick, precise, staccato manner: *"Yes?" The word was clipped short* | [as *adj.*] (**clipped**) *cold, clipped tones.* ■ *Computing* process (an image) so as to remove the parts outside a certain area. ■ *Electronics* truncate the amplitude of (a signal) above or below predetermined levels. **2** strike briskly or with a glancing blow: *the steamroller clipped some parked cars* | *branches clipped his face.* ■ [*trans.*] strike or kick (something, esp. a ball) briskly in a specified direction: *he clipped a right-field double.* **3** *informal* swindle or rob (someone): *in all the years he ran the place, he was clipped only three times.* **4** [*intrans.*] *informal* move quickly in a specified direction: *we clip down the track.*

▶*n.* **1** an act of clipping or trimming something: *I gave him a full clip.* ■ a short sequence taken from a movie or broadcast: *clips from earlier shows.* ■ (also **wool clip**) the quantity of wool clipped from a sheep or flock. **2** *informal* a quick or glancing blow: *you need a clip on the jaw.* **3** [in *sing.*] *informal* a specified speed or rate of movement, esp. when rapid: *we crossed the dance floor at a fast clip.* ▷Middle English: from Old Norse *klippa*, probably imitative.

▶*PHRASES* □ **at a clip** *informal* at a time; all at once: *I spent several days with him, eight hours at a clip.* □ **clip the wings of** trim the feathers of (a bird) so as to disable it from flight. ■ prevent (someone) from acting freely; check the aspirations of: *he finally clipped the wings of his high-flying chief of staff.*

clip art ▶*n. Computing* predrawn pictures and symbols that computer users can add to their documents, often provided with word-processing software and drawing packages.

clip·board /ˈklipˌbôrd/ ▶*n.* a small board with a spring clip at the top, used for holding papers and providing support for writing. ■ *Computing* a temporary storage area where text or other data cut or copied from a file is kept until it is pasted into another file.

clip-clop /ˈklip ˌkläp/ (also **clippety-clop**) ▶*n.* [in *sing.*] the sound as of a horse's hoofs beating on a hard surface.

▶*v.* [*intrans.*] move with such a sound: *the horses clip-clopped slowly along the street.* ▷late 19th cent.: imitative.

clip joint ▶*n. informal* a nightclub or bar that charges exorbitant prices.

clip-on ▶*adj.* attached by a clip so as to be easy to fasten or remove: *a clip-on bow tie.*

▶*n.* (usu. **clip-ons**) things, esp. sunglasses or earrings, that are attached by clips.

clip·per /ˈklipər/ ▶*n.* **1** (usu. **clippers**) an instrument for cutting or trimming small pieces off things: *hedge clippers.* **2** a person who clips or cuts: *a coupon clipper.* **3** *Electronics* another term for LIMITER. **4** (also **clip·per chip**) a microchip that inserts an identifying code into encrypted transmissions, allowing them to be deciphered by a third party having access to a government-held key. **5** (also **clip·per ship**) a fast sailing ship, esp. one of 19th-century design with concave bows and raked masts.

clip·ping /ˈklipiNG/ ▶*n.* (often **clippings**) a small piece trimmed from something: *hedge clippings and grass cuttings.* ■ an article cut from a newspaper or magazine.

clique /klēk; klik/ ▶*n.* a small group of people, with shared interests or other features in common, who spend time together and do not readily allow others to join them. ▷early 18th cent.: from French, from Old French *cliquer* 'make a noise'; the modern sense is related to CLAQUE. **—cli·quish** *adj.* **—cli·quish·ness** *n.*

cli·quey /ˈklēkē; ˈklikē/ ▶*adj.* (**cli·qui·er**, **cli·qui·est**) (of a group or place) tending to form or hold exclusive groups and so not welcoming to outsiders: *a cliquey school.* ■ (of music or art) appealing only to a small group or minority: *the music was very cliquey.*

clit /klit/ ▶*n. vulgar slang* short for CLITORIS.

cli·tel·lum /klīˈteləm/ ▶*n.* (*pl.* **-tel·la** /-ˈtelə/) a raised band encircling the body of oligochaete worms and some leeches, made up of reproductive segments.

clit·ic /ˈklitik/ ▶*n. Grammar* an unstressed word that normally occurs only in combination with another word, for example *'m* in *I'm.* ▷1940s: from *(en)clitic* and *(pro)clitic.* **—clit·i·ci·za·tion** /ˌklitəsəˈzāsHən/ *n.*

clit·o·ri·dec·to·my /ˌklitərəˈdektəmē/ ▶*n.* (*pl.* **-mies**) excision of the clitoris; female circumcision.

clit·o·ris /ˈklitərəs/ ▶*n.* a small sensitive and erectile part of the female genitals at the anterior end of the vulva. ▷early 17th cent.: modern Latin, from Greek *kleitoris.* **—clit·o·ral** /ˈklitərəl/ *adj.*

clit·ter /ˈklitər/ ▶*v.* [*intrans.*] make a thin, vibratory, rattling sound: *a coded message clittered over the radio speakers.* ▷early 16th cent.: imitative.

Clive /klīv/, Robert, 1st Baron Clive of Plassey (1725–74), British general and colonial administrator; known as **Clive of India**. He served as governor of Bengal, India, 1765–67, but was implicated in the East India Company's corruption scandals and committed suicide.

cli·vi·a /ˈklīvēə/ ▶*n.* a southern African plant of the lily family, with dark green, straplike leaves and trumpet-shaped orange, red, or yellow flowers. Also called KAFFIR LILY. • Genus *Clivia*, family Liliaceae (or Amaryllidaceae). ▷modern Latin, from *Clive*, the maiden name of Charlotte, Duchess of Northumberland (1787–1866).

clo·a·ca /klōˈākə/ ▶*n.* (*pl.* **-cae** /-ˌkē; -ˌsē/) *Zoology* a common cavity at the end of the digestive tract for the release of both excretory and genital products in vertebrates (except most mammals) and certain invertebrates. Specifically, the cloaca is present in birds, reptiles, amphibians, most fish, and monotremes. ■ *archaic* a sewer. ▷late 16th cent. (in the sense 'sewer'): from Latin, related to *cluere* 'cleanse.' The current sense dates from the mid 19th cent. **—clo·a·cal** *adj.*

cloak /klōk/ ▶*n.* an outdoor overgarment, typically sleeveless, that hangs loosely from the shoulders. ■ *figurative* something serving to hide or disguise something: *lifting **the cloak of secrecy** on the arms trade.*

▶*v.* [*trans.*] dress in a cloak: *she cloaked herself in black.* ■ *figurative* hide, cover, or disguise (something): *the horror of war was cloaked in the trappings of chivalry.* ▷Middle English: from Old French *cloke*, dialect variant of *cloche* 'bell, cloak' (from its bell shape), from medieval Latin *clocca* 'bell.' Compare with CLOCK[1].

cloak-and-dag·ger ▶*adj.* involving or characteristic of mystery, intrigue, or espionage: *a cloak-and-dagger operation.*

cloak·room /ˈklōkˌro͝om; -ˌro͞om/ ▶*n.* a room in a public building where coats and other belongings may be left temporarily.

clob·ber[1] /ˈkläbər/ ▶*v.* [*trans.*] *informal* hit (someone) hard: *if he does that I'll clobber him!* ■ treat or deal with harshly: *the recession clobbered other parts of the business.* ■ defeat heavily: [*trans.*] *the Braves clobbered the Cubs 23–10.* ▷World War II (apparently British air-force slang): of unknown origin.

clob·ber[2] ▶*v.* [*trans.*] add enameled decoration to (porcelain). ▷late 19th cent.: of unknown origin.

clo·chard /ˈklōsHərd; klōˈsHär/ ▶*n.* (*pl.* same) (in France) a beggar; a vagrant. ▷French, from *clocher* 'to limp.'

cloche /klōsH/ ▶*n.* a small translucent cover for protecting or forcing outdoor plants. ■ (also **cloche hat**) a woman's close-fitting, bell-shaped hat. ▷late 19th cent.: from French, literally 'bell' (see CLOAK).

cloche hat

clock[1] /kläk/ ▶*n.* a mechanical or electrical device for measuring time, indicating hours, minutes, and sometimes seconds, typically by hands on a round dial or by displayed figures. ■ (**the clock**) time taken as a factor in an activity, esp. in competitive sports: *they play **against the clock** | her life is ruled by the clock.* ■ *informal* a measuring device resembling a clock for recording things other than time, such as a speedometer, taximeter, or odometer. ■ see TIME CLOCK.

▶*v.* [*trans.*] *informal* **1** attain or register (a specified time, distance, or speed): *Thomas has **clocked up** forty years service* | [*intrans.*] *the book **clocks in at** 989 pages.* ■ achieve (a victory): *he **clocked up** his first win of the year.* ■ record as attaining a specified time or rate: *the tower operators clocked a gust of 185 mph.* **2** *informal* hit (someone), esp. on the head: *someone clocked him for no good reason.*

▶*phrasal v.* □ **clock in** (or **out**) (of an employee) punch in (or out). ▷late Middle English: from Middle Low German and Middle Dutch *klocke*, based on medieval Latin *clocca* 'bell.'

▶*PHRASES* □ **around** (or **round**) **the clock** all day and all night: *working around the clock.* □ **run out the clock** *Sports* deliberately use as much time as possible in order to preserve one's own team's advantage: *facing a tie, he decided to run out the clock in the final moments.* □ **stop the clock** allow extra time by temporarily ceasing to count the time left before a deadline arrives: *he agreed to stop the clock as negotiations continued.* □ **turn** (or **put**) **back the clock** return to the past or to a previous way of doing things. □ **watch the clock** (of an employee) be overly strict or zealous about not working more than one's required hours.

clock[2] ▶*n. dated* an ornamental pattern woven or embroidered on the side of a stocking or sock near the ankle. ▷mid 16th cent.: of unknown origin.

clock·er /ˈkläkər/ ▶*n. informal* a drug dealer, esp. one who sells cocaine or crack.

clock·mak·er /ˈkläkˌmākər/ ▶*n.* a person who makes and repairs clocks and watches. **—clock·mak·ing** /-ˌmākiNG/ *n.*

clock ra·di·o ▶*n.* a combined radio and alarm clock that can be set so that the radio will come on at the desired time.

clock speed ▶*n.* the operating speed of a computer or its microprocessor, defined as the rate at which it performs internal operations and expressed in cycles per second (megahertz).

clock tow·er ▶*n.* a tower typically forming part of a church or civic building, with a large clock at the top.

clock-watch·er (also **clock watch·er**) ▶*n.* an employee who is overly strict or zealous about not working more than the required hours: *his lamp burned throughout the night; he was no clock-watcher.* **—clock-watch** *v.*

clock·wise /ˈkläkˌwīz/ ▶*adv.* & *adj.* in a curve corresponding in direction to the movement of the hands of a clock: [as *adv.*] *turn the knob clockwise* | [as *adj.*] *a clockwise direction.*

clock·work /ˈkläkˌwərk/ ▶*n.* a mechanism with a spring and toothed gearwheels, used to drive a mechanical clock, toy, or other device.

▶*adj.* [*attrib.*] driven by clockwork: *a clockwork motor* | *a clockwork toy.* ■ very smooth and regular: *the clockwork precision of the galaxy.* ■ repetitive and predictable: *it was a clockwork existence for the children.*

▶*PHRASES* □ **as regular as clockwork** very regularly; repeatedly and predictably. □ **like clockwork** very smoothly and easily: *the event **ran like clockwork**.* ■ with mechanical regularity: *these hens lay like clockwork.*

clod /kläd/ ▶*n.* **1** a lump of earth or clay. **2** *informal* a stupid person (often used as a general term of abuse). ▷late Middle English: variant of CLOT.

clod·dish /ˈklädisH/ ▶*adj.* foolish, awkward, or clumsy. **—clod·dish·ly** *adv.* **—clod·dish·ness** *n.*

clod·hop·per /ˈklädˌhäpər/ ▶*n.* **1** a large, heavy shoe. **2** *informal* a foolish, awkward, or clumsy person.

clod·hop·ping /ˈklädˌhäpiNG/ ▶*adj. informal* foolish, awkward, or clumsy.

clog /kläg; klôg/ ▸*n.* **1** a shoe with a thick wooden sole. **2** an encumbrance or impediment: *a clog in the system.*
▸*v.* (**clogged, clog·ging**) [*trans.*] fill or block with an accumulation of thick, wet matter: *the gutters were* **clogged up** *with leaves* | [as *adj.*] (**clogged**) *clogged drains.* ■ [*intrans.*] become blocked in this way: *too much fatty food makes your arteries* **clog up**. ■ fill up or crowd (something) so as to obstruct passage: *tourists clog the roads in summer.* ▷Middle English (in the sense 'block of wood to impede an animal's movement'): of unknown origin.

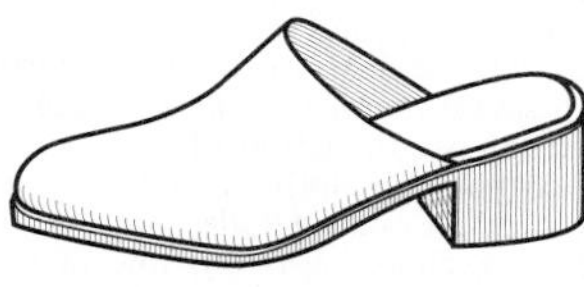
clog 1

clog dance ▸*n.* a dance performed in clogs with rhythmic beating of the feet, esp. as a traditional dance in Ireland, Scotland, and the north of England. ■ a North American country tap dance of similar style. **—clog danc·er** *n.* **—clog danc·ing** *n.*
clog·ger /ˈklägər; ˈklôgər/ ▸*n.* **1** a person who performs a clog dance. **2** someone or something that clogs: *pore-cloggers.*
clog·ging /kläging; ˈklôg-/ ▸*n.* clog dancing.
cloi·son·né /ˌkloizəˈnā; ˌklwäz-/ (also **cloisonné enamel**) ▸*n.* enamel work in which the different colors are separated by strips of flattened wire placed edgeways on a metal backing. ▷mid 19th cent.: French, literally 'partitioned,' past participle of *cloisonner*, from *cloison* 'a partition or division.'
clois·ter /ˈkloistər/ ▸*n.* a covered walk in a convent, monastery, college, or cathedral, typically with a wall on one side and a colonnade open to a quadrangle on the other. ■ (**the cloister**) monastic life: *he was inclined more to the cloister than the sword.* ■ a convent or monastery. ■ any place or position of seclusion: *college is a cloister apart from the cares of the world.*
▸*v.* [*trans.*] seclude or shut up in or as if in a convent or monastery: *the monastery was where the Brothers would cloister themselves to meditate* | *she cloisters herself at home.* ▷Middle English (in the sense 'place of religious seclusion'): from Old French *cloistre*, from Latin *claustrum*, *clostrum* 'lock, enclosed place,' from *claudere* 'to close.' **—clois·tral** /ˈkloistrəl/ *adj.*

cloister

clois·tered /ˈkloistərd/ ▸*adj.* **1** kept away from the outside world; sheltered: *a cloistered upbringing.* **2** having or enclosed by a cloister, as in a monastery: *a cloistered walkway bordered the courtyard.*
clomb /klōm/ ▸ archaic past and past participle of CLIMB.
clom·i·phene /ˈkläməˌfēn; ˈklō-/ ▸*n. Medicine* a synthetic nonsteroidal drug used to treat infertility in women by stimulating ovulation.
clomp /klämp; klômp/ ▸*v.* [*intrans.*] walk with a heavy tread: *she clomped down the steps.* ▷early 19th cent.: imitative; compare with CLUMP.
clon·al·i·ty /klōˈnalitē/ ▸*n.* the fact or condition of being genetically identical, as to a parent, sibling, or other biological source: *the lack of genetic diversity may be a combination of both isolation and clonality.*
clone /klōn/ ▸*n. Biology* a group of organisms or cells produced asexually from one ancestor or stock, to which they are genetically identical. ■ an individual organism or cell so produced. ■ a person or thing regarded as identical to another: *successful women don't want to be male clones.* ■ a microcomputer designed to simulate exactly the operation of another, typically more expensive, model: *an IBM PC clone.*
▸*v.* [*trans.*] propagate (an organism or cell) as a clone: *of the hundreds of new plants cloned, the best ones are selected.* ■ make an identical copy of. ■ *Biochemistry* replicate (a fragment of DNA placed in an organism) so that there is enough to analyze or use in protein production. ■ illegally copy the security codes from (a mobile phone) to one or more others as a way of obtaining free calls. ▷early 20th cent.: from Greek *klōn* 'twig.' **—clon·al** /ˈklōnl/ *adj.*
clonk /klängk; klôngk/ another term for CLUNK. ▸*v.* **1** [*intrans.*] move with or make such a sound: *the horses clonked and snorted softly.* **2** [*trans.*] *informal* hit: *I'll clonk you on the head.* ▷mid 19th cent.: imitative. **—clonk·y** *adj.*
clo·nus /ˈklōnəs/ ▸*n. Medicine* muscular spasm involving repeated, often rhythmic, contractions. ▷early 19th cent.: from Greek *klonos* 'turmoil.' **—clon·ic** /ˈklänik/ *adj.*
clop /kläp/ ▸*n.* [in *sing.*] a sound or series of sounds made by a horse's hooves on a hard surface.
▸*v.* (**clopped, clop·ping**) [*intrans.*] (of a horse) move with such a sound: *the animal clopped on at a steady pace.* ▷mid 19th cent.: imitative.
clo·qué /klōˈkā/ ▸*n.* a fabric with an irregularly raised or embossed surface. ▷French, literally 'blistered.' It was first recorded (1920s) in the anglicized form *cloky*; use of the French form dates from the 1950s.
Close /klōs/, Glenn (1947–), U.S. actress. She received Academy Award nominations for her roles in *The Big Chill* (1983), *Fatal Attraction* (1987), and *Dangerous Liaisons* (1988). She has also received three Tony Awards for her stage performances.
close[1] /klōs/ ▸*adj.* **1** a short distance away or apart in space or time: *the hotel is* **close to** *the sea* | *her birthday and her wedding date were* **close together** | *why don't we go straight to the shops, as we're so close?* | *the months of living* **in close proximity to** *her were taking their toll.* ■ with very little or no space in between; dense: *cloth with a closer weave* | *this work occupies over 1,300 pages of close print.* ■ [*predic.*] (**close to**) very near to (being or doing something): *on a good day the climate in LA is close to perfection* | *she was close to tears.* ■ (of a competitive situation) won or likely to be won by only a small amount or distance: *the race will be a close contest.* ■ [*attrib.*] (of a final position in a competition) very near to the competitor immediately in front: *she finished a close second.* ■ narrowly enclosed: *animals in close confinement.* ■ (of hair or grass) very short or near the surface: *the ground will need to be level enough to allow close mowing.* ■ *Phonetics* another term for HIGH (sense 7). **2** [*attrib.*] denoting a family member who is part of a person's immediate family, typically a parent or sibling: *the family history of cancer in close relatives.* ■ (of a person or relationship) on very affectionate or intimate terms: *they had always been very close, with no secrets at all.* ■ (of a connection or resemblance) strong: *the college has close links with many other institutions.* **3** (of observation, examination, etc.) done in a careful and thorough way: *we need to* **keep a close eye on** *this project* | **pay close attention to** *what your body is telling you about yourself.* ■ carefully guarded: *his whereabouts are a close secret.* ■ not willing to give away money or information; secretive: *you're very close about your work, aren't you?* ■ following faithfully an original or model: *the debate about close or free translation.* **4** uncomfortably humid or airless: *a close, hazy day* | *it was very close in the dressing room.*
▸*adv.* in a position so as to be very near to someone or something; with very little space between: *they stood close to the door* | *he was holding her close.* ▷Middle English: from Old French *clos* (as noun and adjective), from Latin *clausum* 'enclosure' and *clausus* 'closed,' past participle of *claudere.* **—close·ly** *adv.* **—close·ness** *n.* **—clos·ish** *adj.*
▸*PHRASES* □ **close by** very near; nearby: *her father lives quite close by.* □ **close to** (or **close on**) (of an amount) almost; very nearly: *he spent close to 30 years in jail.* □ **close to the bone** see BONE. □ **close to one's heart** see HEART. □ **close to home** see HOME. □ **close up** very near: *close up she was no less pretty.* □ **close to the wind** *Sailing* (of a sailing vessel) pointed as near as possible to the direction from which the wind is blowing while still making headway. □ **come close** almost achieve or do: *he* **came close to** *calling the President a liar.* □ **too close for comfort** dangerously or uncomfortably near: *the friendly stranger who suddenly comes too close for comfort.*
close[2] /klōz/ ▸*v.* **1** move or cause to move so as to cover an opening: [*intrans.*] *she jumped into the train just as the doors were closing* | [*trans.*] *they had to close the window because of the insects.* ■ [*trans.*] block up (a hole or opening): *glass doors* **close off** *the living room from the hall* | *figurative Stephen closed his ears to the sound.* ■ [*trans.*] bring two parts of (something) together so as to block its opening or bring it into a folded state: *Loretta closed her mouth* | *Ron closed the book.* ■ [*intrans.*] gradually get nearer to someone or something: *they plotted a large group of aircraft about 130 miles away and closing fast.* ■ [*intrans.*] (**close around/over**) come into contact with (something) so as to encircle and hold it: *my fist closed around the weapon.* ■ [*trans.*] make (an electric circuit) continuous: *this will cause a relay to operate and close the circuit.* **2** bring or come to an end: [*trans.*] *the members were thanked for attending, and the meeting was closed* | [*intrans.*] *the concert* **closed with** *"Silent Night"* | [as *adj.*] (**closing**) *the closing stages of the election campaign.* ■ [*intrans.*] (of a business, organization, or institution) cease to be in operation or accessible to the public, either permanently or at the end of a working day or other period of time: *the factory is to close with the loss of 150 jobs* | [*trans.*] *the country has been* **closed to** *outsiders for almost 50 years.* ■ [*intrans.*] finish speaking or writing: *we* **close with** *a point about truth* | [as *adj.*] (**closing**) *Nellie's closing words.* ■ [*trans.*] bring (a business transaction) to a satisfactory conclusion: *he closed a deal with a metal dealer.* ■ [*trans.*] remove all the funds from (a bank account) and cease to use it. ■ [*trans.*] *Computing* make (a data file) inaccessible after use, so that it is securely stored until required again.
▸*phrasal v.* □ **close something down** (or **close down**) cause to cease or cease business or operation, esp. permanently: *the government promised to close down the nuclear plants within twenty years.* □ **close in (on)** come nearer to someone being pursued: *the police were* **closing in on** *them.* ■ gradually surround, esp. with the effect of hindering movement or vision: *the weather has now closed in, so an attempt on the summit is unlikely.* ■ (of days) get successively shorter with the approach of the winter solstice: *November was closing in.* □ **close something out** bring something to an end: *Steve tried to close out the conversation.* □ **close up** (of a person's face) become blank and emotionless or hostile: *he didn't like her laughter and his face closed up angrily.* □ **close something up** (or **close up**) **1** cause to cease or cease operation or being used: *the broker advised me to close the house up for the time being.* **2** (**close up**) (of an opening) grow smaller or become blocked by something: *she felt her throat close up.* □ **close with** come near, esp. so as to engage with (an enemy force).
▸*n.* [in *sing.*] **1** the end of an event or of a period of time or activity: *the afternoon* **drew to a close**. ■ (**the close**) the end of a day's trading on a stock market: *at the close the Dow Jones average was down 13.52 points.* ■ *Music* the conclusion of a phrase; a cadence. **2** the shutting of something, esp. a door: *the door jerked to a close behind them.* ▷Middle English: from Old French *clos-*, stem of *clore*, from Latin *claudere* 'to shut.' **—clos·a·ble** *adj.* **—clos·er** *n.*
▸*PHRASES* □ **close the door on** (or **to**) see DOOR. □ **close one's eyes to** see EYE. □ **close one's mind to** see MIND. □ **close ranks** see RANK[1]. □ **close up shop** see SHOP.
close call /klōs/ ▸*n.* a narrow escape from danger or disaster.
close-cropped /klōs/ (also **close·ly cropped**) ▸*adj.* (typically of hair or grass) cut very short.
closed /klōzd/ ▸*adj.* not open: *rooms with closed doors lined the hallway* | *he sat with his eyes closed.* ■ (of a business) having ceased trading, esp. for a short period: *he put the "Closed" sign up on the door.* ■ no longer under discussion or investigation; concluded: *closed cases of alleged contract irregularities.* ■ (of a society or system) not communicating with or influenced by others; independent: *the perception of the Soviet Union as a closed society* | *a closed system in which income and expenditure must balance.* ■ limited to certain people; not open or available to all: *the UN Security Council met* **in closed session**. ■ unwilling to accept new ideas: *you're facing the situation with a closed mind.* ■ *Mathematics* (of a set) having the property that the result of a specified operation on any element of the set is itself a member of the set. ■ *Mathematics* (of a set) containing all its limit points. ■ *Geometry* of or pertaining to a curve whose ends are joined.
▸*PHRASES* □ **behind closed doors** taking place secretly or without public knowledge. □ **closed book** a subject or person about which one knows nothing: *accounting has always been* **a closed book to** *me.*

closed cap·tion ▸*n.* one of a series of subtitles to a television program, accessible through a decoder.
▸*v.* (**closed-cap·tion**) [*trans.*] [usually as *noun* **closed-captioning**] provide (a program) with closed captions.
closed chain ▸*n Chemistry* a number of atoms bonded together to form a closed loop in a molecule.
closed-cir·cuit tel·e·vi·sion (abbr.: **CCTV**) ▸*n.* a television system in which the video signals are transmitted from one or more cameras by cable to a restricted set of monitors.
closed cou·plet ▸*n.* a rhyming couplet with end-stopped lines that is logically or grammatically complete: *Instruct the planets in what orbs to run,/Correct old Time, and regulate the Sun.*
closed-door ▸*adj.* restricted; obstructive; secret: *the senior staff went into closed-door sessions.*
closed-end ▸*adj.* having a predetermined and fixed extent: *a closed-end contract.* ■ denoting an investment trust or company that issues a fixed number of shares.
closed sea·son ▸*n.* a period between specified dates when fishing or the killing of particular game is officially forbidden.
closed shop ▸*n.* a place of work where membership in a union is a condition for being hired and for continued employment. Compare with OPEN SHOP, UNION SHOP. ■ [in *sing.*] a system whereby such an arrangement applies: *the outlawing of the closed shop.*
closed u·ni·verse ▸*n. Astronomy* the condition in which there is sufficient matter in the universe to halt the expansion driven by the big bang and cause eventual recollapse. The amount of visible matter is only a tenth of the total required for closure, but there may be large quantities of dark matter.
close en·coun·ter /ˈklōs enˈkountər/ ▸*n.* a supposed encounter with a UFO or with aliens.
▸*PHRASE* □ **close encounter of the first** (or **second,** etc.) **kind** used to describe encounters involving increasing degrees of complexity and apparent exposure of the witness to aliens, with the first kind being a mere sighting and the fourth kind being abduction.
close-fist·ed /klōs/ ▸*adj.* unwilling to spend money; stingy.
close-fit·ting /klōs/ ▸*adj.* (of a garment) fitting tightly and showing the contours of the body.
close-grained /klōs/ ▸*adj.* (of wood, stone, or other material) having tightly packed fibers, crystals, or other structural elements.
close har·mo·ny /klōs/ ▸*n. Music* harmony in which the notes of the chord are close together, typically in vocal music.
close-hauled /klōs/ ▸*adj.* & *adv. Sailing* (of a ship) close to the wind.
close-in /klōs/ ▸*adj.* only a short distance away: *a close-in shot.* ■ near to the center of a town or city: *close-in parking.*
close-knit /klōs/ ▸*adj.* (of a group of people) united or bound together by strong relationships and common interests: *a close-knit community.*
close-mouthed /ˈklōs ˈmouTHd; ˈmouTHt/ ▸*adj.* reticent; discreet: *the candidates have been close-mouthed about their fund-raising goals.*
close quar·ters /klōs/ ▸*plural n.* a situation of being very or uncomfortably close to someone or something: *living in close quarters with people* | *engaging the enemy* ***at close quarters.***
clos·er /ˈklōzər/ ▸*n. Baseball* a relief pitcher who specializes in pitching to the final batters of a game if the pitcher's team has the lead.
close range /klōs/ ▸*n.* a short distance between someone or something and a target: *two bullets fired* ***at close range*** | *watching a bird at close range.*
close-ra·tio /klōs/ ▸*adj.* (of a vehicle's gearbox) having gear ratios that are set at values not very different from each other.
close reach /klōs/ *Sailing* ▸*n.* a point of sailing in which the wind blows from slightly forward of the beam: *we sailed* ***on a close reach*** *directly for Sharp's Island.*
▸*v.* (**close-reach**) [*intrans.*] sail with the wind in this position.
close sea·son /klōz/ ▸*n.* British term for CLOSED SEASON.
close-set /klōs/ ▸*adj.* (of two or more things) placed or occurring with little space in between: *her eyes were too close-set for beauty.*
close shave /klōs/ ▸*n.* **1** a shave in which the hair is cut very short. **2** *informal* another term for CLOSE CALL.
clos·et /ˈkläzit/ ▸*n.* **1** a small room or cupboard used for storing things. ■ *archaic* a small, private room used for prayer or study. **2** *archaic* a toilet. **3** (**the closet**) a state of secrecy or concealment, esp. about one's homosexuality: *lesbians who had* ***come out of the closet.***
▸*adj.* [*attrib.*] secret; covert: *a closet socialist.*
▸*v.* (**clos·et·ed**, **clos·et·ing**) [*trans.*] (often **be closeted**) shut (someone) away, esp. in private conference or study: *he was closeted with the king* | *he returned home and closeted himself in his room.* ■ in a state of concealment, esp. about one's homosexuality. ▷late Middle English (denoting a private or small room): from Old French, diminutive of *clos* 'closed' (see CLOSE[1]).
clos·et dra·ma (also **closet play**) ▸*n.* a play to be read rather than acted.
close-up /ˈklōs ˌəp/ ▸*n.* a photograph, movie, or video taken at close range and showing the subject on a large scale: *a close-up of her face* | *they see themselves* ***in close-up*** | [as *adj.*] *a close-up view.* ■ an intimate and detailed description or study: [as *adj.*] *the book's close-up account of the violence.*
clos·ing date ▸*n.* the last date by which something must be submitted for consideration, esp. a job application.
clos·ing price ▸*n.* the price of a security at the end of the day's business in a financial market.
clos·ing time ▸*n.* the regular time at which a restaurant, store, or other place closes to the public each day.
clos·trid·i·um /kläˈstridēəm/ ▸*n.* (*pl.* **clos·trid·i·a** /kläˈstridēə/) *Biology* an anaerobic bacterium of a large genus that includes many pathogenic species, e.g., those causing tetanus, gas gangrene, botulism, and other forms of food poisoning. • Genus *Clostridium*: typically rod-shaped and Gram-positive. ▷modern Latin, based on Greek *klōstēr* 'spindle.' —**clos·trid·i·al** /-ˈstridēəl/ *adj.*
clo·sure /ˈklōZHər/ ▸*n.* an act or process of closing something, esp. an institution, thoroughfare, or frontier, or of being closed: *road closures* | *hospitals that face closure.* ■ a thing that closes or seals something, such as a cap or zipper. ■ a resolution or conclusion to a work or process: *he brings modernistic closure to his narrative.* ▷late Middle English: from Old French, from late Latin *clausura*, from *claus-* 'closed,' from the verb *claudere.*
clot /klät/ ▸*n.* **1** a thick mass of coagulated liquid, esp. blood, or of material stuck together: *a flat, wet* ***clot of*** *dead leaves* | *figurative a clot of people arguing in the doorway.* **2** *Brit., informal* a foolish or clumsy person: *"Watch where you're going, you clot!"*
▸*v.* (**clot·ted**, **clot·ting**) form or cause to form into clots: [*intrans.*] *drugs that help blood to clot* | [*trans.*] *a blood protein known as factor VIII clots blood.* ■ [*trans.*] cover (something) with sticky matter: *its nostrils were clotted with blood.* ▷Old English *clott, clot*, of Germanic origin; related to German *Klotz.*
clot·bur /ˈklätˌbər/ ▸*n.* a herbaceous plant of the daisy family, with burred fruits. It originated in tropical America but is now cosmopolitan. See also COCKLEBUR. • Genus *Xanthium*, family Compositae: two or three species, in particular **spiny clotbur** (*X. spinosum*). ■ a burdock. ▷mid 16th cent.: from dialect *clote* 'burdock' + BURR.
cloth /klôTH/ ▸*n.* (*pl.* **cloths** /klôTHz; klôTHs/) **1** woven or felted fabric made from wool, cotton, or a similar fiber: *shelves covered with bright red cloth* | [as *adj.*] *a cloth bag.* ■ a piece of cloth for a particular purpose, such as a dishcloth or a tablecloth: *wipe clean with a damp cloth.* ■ a variety of cloth. **2** (**the cloth**) the clergy; the clerical profession: *a man of the cloth.* ▷Old English *clāth*, related to Dutch *kleed* and German *Kleid*, of unknown ultimate origin.
clothe /klōTH/ ▸*v.* (*past* and *past part.* **clothed** or **clad** /klad/) [*trans.*] (often **be clothed in**) put clothes on (oneself or someone); dress: *she was clothed all in white* | *she lay down* ***fully clothed*** | [as *adj.*, with *submodifier*] (**clothed**) *a partially clothed body.* ■ provide (someone) with clothes: *they already had eight children to feed and clothe.* ■ *figurative* cover (something) as if with clothes: *luxuriant tropical forests clothed the islands.* ■ *figurative* endow (someone) with a particular quality: *he is clothed with the personality and character of Jesus.* ▷Old English (only recorded in the past participle *geclāded*), from *clāth* (see CLOTH).
clothes /klō(TH)z/ ▸*plural n.* **1** items worn to cover the body: *he stripped off his clothes* | *baby clothes* | [as *adj.*] *a clothes shop.* **2** bedclothes. ▷Old English *clāthas*, plural of *clāth* (see CLOTH).
clothes horse ▸*n.* a frame on which washed clothes are hung to air indoors. ■ *informal, often derogatory* a determinedly fashionable person.
clothes·line /ˈklō(TH)zˌlīn/ ▸*n.* a rope or wire on which washed clothes are hung to dry.
▸*v.* [*trans.*] (chiefly in football and other games) knock down (a runner) by placing one's outstretched arm in the runner's path at neck level.
clothes moth ▸*n.* a small, drab moth whose larvae feed on a range of animal fibers and can be destructive to clothing and other domestic textiles. • Family Tineidae: several species, in particular the **common clothes moth** (*Tineola bisselliella*).
clothes·pin /ˈklō(TH)zˌpin/ (*Brit.* also **clothes peg**) ▸*n.* a wooden or plastic clip for securing clothes to a clothes line.
cloth·ier /ˈklōTHyər; -THēər/ ▸*n.* a person or company that makes, sells, or deals in clothes or cloth. ▷Middle English *clother*, from CLOTH. The change in the ending was due to association with -IER.
cloth·ing /ˈklōTHiNG/ ▸*n.* clothes collectively: *an item of clothing* | [as *adj.*] *the clothing trade.*
Clo·tho /ˈklōTHō/ *Greek Mythology* one of the three Fates. ▷Greek, literally 'she who spins.'
cloth of gold ▸*n.* fabric made of gold threads interwoven with silk or wool.
cloth yard ▸*n.* a unit for measuring cloth, formerly 37 inches but now equivalent to a standard yard (36 inches).
clot·ted cream ▸*n. chiefly Brit.* thick cream obtained by heating milk slowly and then allowing it to cool while the cream content rises to the top in coagulated lumps.
clot·ting fac·tor ▸*n. Physiology* any of a number of substances in blood plasma that are involved in the clotting process, such as factor VIII.
clo·ture /ˈklōCHər/ ▸*n.* (in a legislative assembly) a procedure for ending a debate and taking a vote: [as *adj.*] *a cloture motion.*
▸*v.* [*trans.*] apply the cloture to (a debate or speaker) in a legislative assembly. ▷late 19th cent.: from French *clôture*, from Old French *closure* (see CLOSURE).
cloud /kloud/ ▸*n.* **1** a visible mass of condensed water vapor floating in the atmosphere, typically high above the ground: *the sun had disappeared behind a cloud* | *the full moon, hidden by veils of cloud.* ■ an indistinct or billowing mass, esp. of smoke or dust: ***a cloud of*** *dust.* ■ a large number of insects or birds moving together: ***clouds of*** *orange butterflies.* ■ a vague patch of color in or on a liquid or transparent surface. **2** *figurative* a state or cause of gloom, suspicion, trouble, or worry: *the only cloud to appear on the horizon was Leopold's unexpected illness* | *a black cloud hung over their lives.* ■ a frowning or depressed look: *a cloud passed over Jessica's face.*
▸*v.* **1** [*intrans.*] (of the sky) become overcast with clouds: *the blue skies* ***clouded over*** *abruptly.* ■ [*trans.*] (usu. **be clouded**) darken (the sky) with clouds: *the western sky was still clouded.* ■ make or become less clear or transparent: [*trans.*] *blood pumped out, clouding the water* | [*intrans.*] *her eyes clouded with tears.* **2** *figurative* make or become darkened or overshadowed, in particular: ■ [*intrans.*] (of someone's face or eyes) show worry, sorrow, or anger: *his expression* ***clouded over.*** ■ [*trans.*] (of such an emotion) show in (someone's face): *suspicion clouded her face.* ■ [*trans.*] make (a matter or mental process) unclear or uncertain; confuse: *don't allow your personal feelings to cloud your judgment.* ■ [*trans.*] spoil or mar (something): *the general election was clouded by violence.* ▷Old English *clūd* 'mass of rock or earth'; probably related to CLOT. Sense 1 dates from Middle English. —**cloud·less** *adj.* —**cloud·less·ly** *adv.* —**cloud·let** /-lət/ *n.*
▸*PHRASES* □ **every cloud has a silver lining** see SILVER. □ **have one's head in the clouds** (of a person) be out of touch with reality; be daydreaming. □ **in the clouds** out of touch with reality: *this clergyman was in the clouds.* □ **on cloud nine** extremely happy. [with reference to a ten-part classification of clouds in which "nine" was next to the highest.] □ **under a cloud** under suspicion; discredited: *he left under something of a cloud, accused of misappropriating funds.*
cloud base ▸*n.* [in *sing.*] the level or altitude of the lowest part of a general mass of clouds.
cloud·ber·ry /ˈkloudˌberē/ ▸*n.* (*pl.* **-ries**) a dwarf bramble that has white flowers and edible orange fruit and that grows on the mountains and moorlands of northern Eurasia and northern North America. • *Rubus chamaemorus*, family Rosaceae. ▷late 16th cent.: apparently from the noun CLOUD in the obsolete sense 'hill' + BERRY.
cloud·burst /ˈkloudˌbərst/ ▸*n.* a sudden, violent rainstorm.
cloud cham·ber ▸*n. Physics* a device that contains air or gas supersaturated with water vapor and that is

used to detect charged particles, X-rays, and gamma rays by the condensation trails that they produce.

cloud cov·er ▸*n.* [in *sing.*] a mass of cloud covering all or most of the sky.

cloud deck ▸*n. Meteorology* a bank of clouds of a particular type forming a layer at a certain altitude.

cloud·ed leop·ard ▸*n.* a large spotted cat that hunts in trees at twilight and is found in forests in Southeast Asia. • *Neofelis nebulosa,* family Felidae.

cloud hop·ping ▸*n.* the flying of an aircraft from cloud to cloud, typically for concealment.

cloud·scape /ˈkloudˌskāp/ ▸*n.* a large cloud formation considered in terms of its visual effect. ▷mid 19th cent.: from the noun CLOUD, on the pattern of words such as *landscape.*

cloud seed·ing ▸*n.* the dropping of crystals into clouds to cause rain.

cloud·y /ˈkloudē/ ▸*adj.* (**cloud·i·er, cloud·i·est**) **1** (of the sky or weather) covered with or characterized by clouds; overcast: *next morning was cloudy.* **2** (of a liquid) not transparent or clear: *the pond water is slightly cloudy.* ■ (of a color) opaque; having white as a constituent: *cloudy reds and blues and greens.* ■ (of marble) variegated with cloudlike markings. ■ (of someone's eyes) misted with tears: *she stared at him, her eyes cloudy.* ■ uncertain; unclear: *the issue becomes more cloudy.* —**cloud·i·ly** /ˈkloudl-ē/ *adv.* —**cloud·i·ness** *n.*

Clou·et /klo͞oˈā; klo͞oˈe/ two French court portrait painters, **Jean** (*c.*1485–1541) and his son **François** (*c.*1516–72).

clout /klout/ ▸*n.* **1** *informal* a heavy blow with the hand or a hard object: *a clout on the ear.* **2** *informal* influence or power, esp. in politics or business: *I knew he carried a lot of clout.* **3** *archaic* a piece of cloth or clothing, esp. one used as a patch. **4** *Archery* a target used in long-distance shooting, placed flat on the ground with a flag marking its center. ■ a shot that hits such a target.
▸*v.* [*trans.*] **1** *informal* hit hard with the hand or a hard object: *I clouted him on the head.* **2** *archaic* mend with a patch. ▷Old English *clūt* (in the sense 'a patch or metal plate'); related to Dutch *kluit* 'lump, clod,' also to CLEAT and CLOT. The shift of sense to 'heavy blow,' which dates from late Middle English, is difficult to explain; possibly the change occurred first in the verb (from 'put a patch on' to 'hit hard').

clove[1] /klōv/ ▸*n.* **1** the dried flower bud of a tropical tree, used as a pungent aromatic spice: *a teaspoon of ground cloves.* ■ (**oil of cloves**) aromatic analgesic oil extracted from these buds and used medicinally, esp. for the relief of dental pain. **2** the Indonesian tree from which these buds are obtained. • *Syzygium aromaticum* (also called *Eugenia caryophyllus*), family Myrtaceae. **3** (also **clove pink**) a clove-scented pink that is the original type from which the carnation and other double pinks have been bred. • *Dianthus caryophyllus,* family Caryophyllaceae. ▷Middle English: from Old French *clou de girofle,* literally 'nail of gillyflower' (from its shape), GILLYFLOWER being originally the name of the spice and later applied to the similarly scented pink.

clove[2] ▸*n.* any of the small bulbs making up a compound bulb of garlic, shallot, etc. ▷Old English *clufu,* of Germanic origin, corresponding to the first element of German *Knoblauch* (altered from Old High German *klovolouh*), and the base of CLEAVE[1].

clove[3] ▸ past of CLEAVE[1].

clove hitch ▸*n.* a knot by which a rope is secured by passing it twice around a spar or another rope that it crosses at right angles in such a way that both ends pass under the loop of rope at the front. ▷mid 18th cent.: *clove,* past tense of CLEAVE[1] (because the rope appears as separate parallel lines at the back of the knot).

clo·ven /ˈklōvən/ ▸ past participle of CLEAVE[1].
▸*adj.* split or divided in two.

clo·ven hoof (also **cloven foot**) ▸*n.* the divided hoof or foot of ruminants such as cattle, sheep, goats, antelopes, and deer. ■ a similar foot ascribed to a satyr, the god Pan, or to the Devil, sometimes used as a symbol or mark of the Devil. —**clo·ven-hoofed** *adj.* —**clo·ven-foot·ed** *adj.*

white clover

clove pink ▸*n.* see CLOVE[1] (sense 3).

clo·ver /ˈklōvər/ ▸*n.* a herbaceous plant of the pea family that has dense, globular flowerheads and leaves that are typically three-lobed. It is an important and widely grown fodder and rotational crop. • Genus *Trifolium,* family Leguminosae: many species, in particular **red clover** (*T. pratense*) and the creeping **white clover** (*T. repens*). ▷Old English *clāfre,* of Germanic origin; related to Dutch *klaver* and German *Klee.*
▸PHRASE □ **in clover** in ease and luxury: *if your sister married the old codger, we could be in clover.*

clo·ver·leaf /ˈklōvərˌlēf/ ▸*n.* a junction of roads intersecting at different levels with connecting sections forming the pattern of a four-leaf clover.
▸*adj.* having a shape or pattern resembling a leaf of clover, esp. a four-leaf clover: *cloverleaf rolls.*

Clo·vis[1] /ˈklōvis/ **1** a city in central California, in the San Joaquin Valley, northeast of Fresno; pop. 50,323. **2** an agricultural city in eastern New Mexico; pop. 32,667. The Clovis culture of 11,000 years ago is named for artifacts found nearby.

Clo·vis[2] (465–511), king of the Franks 481–511. He extended Merovingian rule to Gaul and Germany, making Paris his capital. After his conversion to Christianity, he championed orthodoxy against the Arian Visigoths, finally defeating them in the battle of Poitiers 507.

Clo·vis[3] ▸*n.* [usu. as *adj.*] *Archaeology* a Paleo-Indian culture of Central and North America, dated to about 11,500–11,000 years ago and earlier. The culture is distinguished by heavy, leaf-shaped stone spearheads. Compare with FOLSOM. ▷first found near CLOVIS[1], New Mexico.

clown /kloun/ ▸*n.* **1** a comic entertainer, esp. one in a circus, wearing a traditional costume and exaggerated makeup. ■ a comical, silly, playful person: *I was always the class clown.* ■ a foolish or incompetent person: *we need a serious government, not a bunch of clowns.* **2** *archaic* an unsophisticated country person; a rustic.
▸*v.* [*intrans.*] behave in a comical way; act playfully: *Harvey* ***clowned around*** *pretending to be a dog.* ▷mid 16th cent. (sense 2): perhaps of Low German origin. —**clown·ish** *adj.* —**clown·ish·ly** *adv.* —**clown·ish·ness** *n.*

clown·fish /ˈklounˌfish/ ▸*n.* (*pl.* same or **-fish·es**) a small, tropical marine fish with bold vertical stripes or other bright coloration. It lives in close association with anemones and is protected from their stings by mucus. Also called ANEMONE FISH. • Genera *Amphiprion* and *Premnas,* family Pomacentridae: several species, including *A. percula.*

cloy /kloi/ ▸*v.* [*trans.*] [usu. as *adj.*] (**cloying**) disgust or sicken (someone) with an excess of sweetness, richness, or sentiment: *a romantic, rather cloying story* | *a curious bittersweetness that cloyed her senses* | [*intrans.*] *the first long sip gives a malty taste that never cloys.* ▷late Middle English: shortening of obsolete *accloy* 'stop up, choke,' from Old French *encloyer* 'drive a nail into,' from medieval Latin *inclavare,* from *clavus* 'a nail.' —**cloy·ing·ly** *adv.*

clo·za·pine /ˈklōzəˌpēn/ ▸*n. Medicine* a sedative drug of the benzodiazepine group, used to treat schizophrenia. ▷mid 20th cent.: from *c(h)lo(ro)-* + elements of BENZODIAZEPINE.

cloze test /klōz/ ▸*n.* a test in which one is asked to supply words that have been removed from a passage in order to measure one's ability to comprehend text. ▷1950s: *cloze* representing a spoken abbreviation of CLOSURE.

CLU ▸*abbr.* Civil Liberties Union.

club[1] /kləb/ ▸*n.* [treated as *sing.* or *pl.*] an association or organization dedicated to a particular interest or activity: *a photography club* | [as *adj.*] *the club secretary.* ■ the building or facilities used by such an association. ■ an organization or facility offering members social amenities, meals, and temporary residence: *dinner at his club.* ■ a nightclub, esp. one playing fashionable dance music. ■ [treated as *sing.* or *pl.*] an organization constituted to play games in a particular sport: *a football club* | [as *adj.*] *the club captain.* ■ [usu. with *adj.*] a commercial organization offering subscribers special benefits: *a shopping club.* ■ [usu. with *adj.*] a group of people, organizations, or nations having something in common: *in cocktail lounges all over town convenes the daily meeting of the ain't-it-awful club.*
▸*v.* (**clubbed, club·bing**) [*intrans.*] *informal* go out to nightclubs: *she enjoys* ***going clubbing*** *in Orlando.* ▷early 17th cent. (as a verb): formed obscurely from CLUB[2].
▸PHRASE □ **join the club** [in *imperative*] *informal often humorous* used as an observation that someone else is in a difficult or unwelcome situation to one's own: *if you're confused, join the club!*

club[2] ▸*n.* **1** a heavy stick with a thick end, esp. one used as a weapon. ■ short for GOLF CLUB. **2** (**clubs**) one of the four suits in a conventional pack of playing cards, denoted by a black trefoil. ■ a card of such a suit.
▸*v.* (**clubbed, club·bing**) [*trans.*] beat (a person or animal) with a club or similar implement: *the islanders clubbed whales to death.* ▷Middle English: from Old Norse *clubba,* variant of *klumba;* related to CLUMP.

club·ba·ble /ˈkləbəbəl/ ▸*adj.* suitable for membership of a club because of one's sociability or popularity. —**club·ba·bil·i·ty** /ˌkləbəˈbilətē/ *n.*

club·by /ˈkləbē/ ▸*adj.* (**-bi·er, -bi·est**) *informal* friendly and sociable with fellow members of a group or organization but not with outsiders.

club car ▸*n.* a railroad car equipped with a lounge and other amenities.

club chair ▸*n.* a thickly upholstered armchair of the type often found in clubs.

club face ▸*n.* the side of the head of a golf club that strikes the ball.

club foot ▸*n.* **1** a deformed foot that is twisted so that the sole cannot be placed flat on the ground. It is typically congenital or a result of polio. Also called TALIPES. **2** a woodland toadstool with a grayish-brown cap, primrose-yellow gills, and a stem with a swollen woolly base, found in both Eurasia and North America. • *Clitocybe clavipes,* family Tricholomataceae, class Basidiomycetes. —**club-foot·ed** *adj.*

club·house /ˈkləbˌhous/ ▸*n.* **1** a building or part of a building used by a sports team, esp. a baseball team, as a locker room. **2** a building or room used by a club. **3** a building in a sporting area, esp. a golf course, used for socializing and recreation.

club·land /ˈkləbˌland/ ▸*n.* the world of nightclubs and of people who frequent them.

club·man /ˈkləbmən; -ˌman/ ▸*n.* (*pl.* **-men**) a man who is a member of one or more clubs, esp. a member of a gentleman's club.

club moss (also **club·moss**) ▸*n.* a low-growing green plant that resembles a large moss, having branching stems with undivided leaves. Relatives of the club mosses were the first plants to colonize the land during the Silurian period. • Class Lycopodiopsida, phylum Lycopodiophyta: one living family, Lycopodiaceae.

club·root /ˈkləbˌro͞ot; -ˌro͝ot/ ▸*n.* a fungal disease of cabbages, turnips, and related plants, in which the root becomes swollen and distorted by a single large gall or groups of smaller galls. • The fungus is *Plasmodiophora brassicae,* phylum Plasmodiophoromycota.

club sand·wich ▸*n.* a sandwich of meat (usually chicken and bacon), tomato, lettuce, and mayonnaise, with two layers of filling between three slices of toast or bread.

club so·da ▸*n. trademark* another term for SODA (sense 1).

club steak ▸*n.* another term for DELMONICO STEAK.

cluck /klək/ ▸*n.* **1** the characteristic short, guttural sound made by a hen. ■ a similar sound made by a person to express annoyance: *Loretta gave a cluck of impatience.* **2** *informal* a stupid or foolish person: *a cluck too lazy to put up a clothesline.*
▸*v.* (also **cluck-cluck**) [*intrans.*] (of a hen) make a short, guttural sound. ■ [*trans.*] (of a person) make such a sound with (one's tongue) to express concern or disapproval: *Michael clucked his tongue irritably.* ■ [*intrans.*] (**cluck over/at/about**) express fussy concern about: *they were cluck-clucking over the dishonor he brought to the office.* ▷late 15th cent. (as a verb): imitative, corresponding to Danish *klukke,* Swedish *klucka.*

clue /klo͞o/ ▸*n.* **1** a piece of evidence or information used in the detection of a crime or solving of a mystery: *police officers are still searching for clues.* ■ a fact or idea that serves as a guide or aid in a task or problem: *archaeological evidence can give clues about the past.* **2** a verbal formula giving an indication as to what is to be inserted in a particular space in a crossword or other puzzle.
▸*v.* (**clues, clued, clue·ing**) [*trans.*] (**clue someone in**) *informal* inform someone about a particular matter: *Stella had clued her in about Peter.* ▷late Middle English: variant of CLEW. The original sense was 'a ball of thread'; hence one used to guide a person out of a labyrinth (literally or figuratively). Sense 1 dates from the early 17th cent.

▸PHRASE □ **not have a clue** *informal* know nothing about something or about how to do something.

clued-in ▸*adj. informal* well-informed about a particular subject.

clue·ful /ˈklo͞ofəl/ ▸*adj. informal* well-informed; competently intelligent: *clueful implementors are aware of the issues and are looking out for you.*

clue·less /ˈklo͞oləs/ ▸*adj. informal* having no knowledge, understanding, or ability: *you're clueless about how to deal with the world.* **—clue·less·ly** *adv.* **—clue·less·ness** *n.*

Cluj–Na·po·ca /ˈklo͞ozʜ ˈnäpōkə; näˈpōkə/ a city in western central Romania; pop. 321,850. The name was changed from Cluj in the mid 1970s to incorporate the name of a nearby ancient settlement. Also called **Cluj**; Hungarian name **Kolozsvár**; original name **Klausenburg**.

Clum·ber span·iel /ˈkləmbər/ ▸*n.* a spaniel of a slow, heavily built breed. ▷mid 19th cent.: from the name of *Clumber* Park, an estate in Nottinghamshire, England.

clump /kləmp/ ▸*n.* **1** a compacted mass or lump of something: ***clumps of** earth.* ■ a small, compact group of people: *they sat on the wall in **clumps of** two and three.* ■ a small group of trees or plants growing closely together: ***a clump of** ferns.* ■ *Physiology* an agglutinated mass of blood cells or bacteria, esp. as an indicator of the presence of an antibody to them. **2** a thick extra sole on a boot or shoe. **3** the sound of heavy footsteps.
▸*v.* [*intrans.*] **1** form into a clump or mass: *the particles tend to **clump together**.* **2** (also **clomp**) walk with a heavy tread. ▷Middle English (denoting a heap or lump): partly imitative, reinforced by Middle Low German *klumpe* and Middle Dutch *klompe*; related to **club**[2].

clump·y /ˈkləmpē/ ▸*adj.* (**clump·i·er**, **clump·i·est**) **1** (of shoes or boots) heavy and inelegant. **2** forming or showing a tendency to form clumps.

clum·sy /ˈkləmzē/ ▸*adj.* (**-si·er**, **-si·est**) awkward in movement or in handling things: *a terribly clumsy fellow | the cold made his fingers clumsy.* ■ done awkwardly or without skill or elegance: *a clumsy attempt to park | a clumsy remake of an old movie.* ■ difficult to handle or use; unwieldy: *chairs with clumsy wooden armrests | the legal procedure is far too clumsy.* ■ lacking social skills and graces: *his choice of words was clumsy.* ▷late 16th cent.: from obsolete *clumse* 'make numb, be numb,' probably of Scandinavian origin and related to Swedish *klumsig*. **—clum·si·ly** /-zəlē/ *adv.* **—clum·si·ness** *n.*

clung /kləɴɢ/ ▸ past and past participle of **cling**.

Clu·ni·ac /ˈklo͞onēˌak/ ▸*adj.* of or relating to a reformed Benedictine monastic order founded at Cluny in eastern France in 910.
▸*n.* a monk of this order.

clunk /kləɴɢk/ ▸*n.* **1** a heavy, dull sound such as that made by thick pieces of metal striking together. **2** *informal* a stupid or foolish person.
▸*v.* [*intrans.*] move with or make such a sound: *the machinery clunked into life.* ▷late 18th cent. (originally Scots, as a verb): imitative; compare with **clank**, **clink**[1], and **clonk**.

clunk·er /ˈkləɴɢkər/ ▸*n. informal* an old, run-down vehicle or machine. ■ a thing that is totally unsuccessful: *novel after novel and not a clunker among them.*

clunk·y /ˈkləɴɢkē/ ▸*adj.* (**clunk·i·er**, **clunk·i·est**) *informal* **1** awkwardly solid, heavy, and outdated: *even last year's laptops look clunky | clunky brown shoes | figurative surprisingly clunky comedy.* **2** making a clunking sound: *clunky conveyor belts.*

clu·pe·oid /ˈklo͞opēˌoid/ *Zoology* ▸*n.* a marine fish of a group that includes the herring family together with the anchovies and related fish. • Order Clupeiformes or suborder Clupeoidei.
▸*adj.* of or relating to fish of this group. ▷mid 19th cent.: from modern Latin *Clupeoidei* (plural), from Latin *clupea*, the name of a river fish.

clus·ter /ˈkləstər/ ▸*n.* a group of similar objects growing closely together: ***clusters of** creamy-white flowers.* ■ a group of people or similar objects positioned or occurring close together: ***a cluster of** antique shops.* ■ *Astronomy* a group of stars or galaxies forming a relatively close association. ■ *Linguistics* (also **consonant cluster**) a group of consonants pronounced in immediate succession, as *str* in *strong*. ■ a natural subgroup of a population, used for statistical sampling or analysis. ■ *Chemistry* a group of atoms of the same element, typically a metal, bonded closely together in a molecule.
▸*v.* [*intrans.*] be or come into a cluster or close group; congregate: *the children **clustered around** her skirts.* ■ *Statistics* (of data points) have similar numerical values: *students tended to have scores clustering around 70 percent.* ▷Old English *clyster*; probably related to **clot**.

clus·ter bean ▸*n.* another term for **guar**.

clus·ter bomb ▸*n.* a bomb that releases a number of projectiles on impact to injure or damage personnel and vehicles.

clus·tered /ˈkləstərd/ ▸*adj.* [*attrib.*] growing or situated in a group: *the spires and clustered roofs of the old town.* ■ *Architecture* (of pillars, columns, or shafts) positioned close together, or disposed around or half-detached from a pier.

clus·ter fly ▸*n.* a fly that often enters buildings in large numbers during the autumn while looking for a place to overwinter. • *Pollenia rudis* (family Calliphoridae), whose larvae parasitize earthworms, and the smaller *Thaumatomyia notata* (family Chloropidae).

clus·ter head·ache ▸*n.* a type of severe headache that tends to recur over a period of several weeks and in which the pain is usually limited to one side of the head.

clutch[1] /kləcʜ/ ▸*v.* [*trans.*] grasp or seize (something) tightly or eagerly: *he stood clutching a microphone | [intrans.] figurative Mrs. Longhill clutched at the idea.* ■ (also *Brit.* **clutch up**) become nervous and panicked: *doctors could clutch up and lose control as easily as anyone.*
▸*n.* **1** a tight grasp or an act of grasping something: *she made a **clutch at** his body.* ■ (**someone's clutches**) a person's power or control, esp. when perceived as cruel or inescapable: *he had narrowly escaped the clutches of the Nazis.* **2** a slim, flat handbag without handles or a strap. **3** (**the clutch**) an emergency or critical moment: *he came through for us in the clutch* [as *adj.*] *they were among the best clutch hitters in baseball.* **4** a mechanism for connecting and disconnecting a vehicle engine from its transmission system. ■ the pedal operating such a mechanism. ■ an arrangement for connecting and disconnecting the working parts of any machine. ▷Middle English (in the sense 'bend, crook'): variant of obsolete *clitch* 'close the hand,' from Old English *clyccan* 'crook, clench,' of Germanic origin.
▸PHRASE □ **clutch at straws** see **straw**.

clutch[2] ▸*n.* a group of eggs fertilized at the same time, typically laid in a single session and (in birds) incubated together. ■ a brood of chicks. ■ a small group of people or things: ***a clutch of** young girls on roller skates.* ▷early 18th cent.: probably a southern variant of northern English dialect *cletch*, related to Middle English *cleck* 'to hatch,' from Old Norse *klekja*.

Clu·tha /ˈklo͞otʜə/ a gold-bearing river at the southern end of South Island, in New Zealand. It flows for 213 miles (338 km) to the Pacific Ocean.

clut·ter /ˈklətər/ ▸*n.* a collection of things lying about in an untidy mass: *the attic is full of clutter.* ■ [in *sing.*] an untidy state: *the room was in a clutter of smelly untidiness.*
▸*v.* [*trans.*] crowd (something) untidily; fill with clutter: *his apartment was cluttered with paintings and antiques | luggage **cluttered up** the hallway.* ▷late Middle English (as a verb): variant of dialect *clotter* 'to clot,' influenced by **cluster** and **clatter**.

Clyde /klīd/ a river in western central Scotland that flows for 106 miles (170 km) from the southern uplands to the Firth of Clyde.

Clyde, Firth of the estuary of the Clyde River in western Scotland that separates southern Scotland on the east from the southern end of the Highlands on the northwest.

Clydes·dale /ˈklīdzˌdāl/ ▸*n.* **1** a horse of a heavy, powerful breed, used for pulling heavy loads. **2** a dog of a small breed of terrier. ▷from the name of the area around the river **Clyde** in Scotland, where they were originally bred.

Clydesdale 1

clyp·e·us /ˈklipēəs/ ▸*n.* (*pl.* **clyp·e·i** /ˈklipēˌī; -ēˌē/) *Entomology* a broad plate at the front of an insect's head. ▷mid 19th cent.: from Latin, literally 'round shield.' **—clyp·e·al** /-pēəl/ *adj.*

clys·ter /ˈklistər/ ▸*n.* archaic term for **enema**. ▷late Middle English: from Old French *clystere* or Latin *clyster*, from Greek *klustēr* 'syringe,' from *kluzein* 'wash out.'

Cly·tem·nes·tra /ˌklītəmˈnestrə/ *Greek Mythology* wife of Agamemnon. She conspired with her lover Aegisthus to murder Agamemnon on his return from the Trojan War and was murdered in retribution by her son Orestes and her daughter Electra.

CM ▸*abbr.* ■ command module. ■ common meter or measure.

Cm ▸*symbol* the chemical element curium.

cm ▸*abbr.* centimeter(s).

Cmdr. ▸*abbr.* Commander.

Cmdre. ▸*abbr.* Commodore.

CMEA ▸*abbr.* Council for Mutual Economic Assistance.

c'mon /kəˈmän/ ▸*contraction of* come on: *C'mon, it'll be fun!*

CMOS ▸*n.* [often as *adj.*] *Electronics* a technology for making low power integrated circuits. ■ a chip built using such technology. ▷1980s: from *Complementary Metal Oxide Semiconductor*.

CMSgt ▸*abbr.* chief master sergeant.

CMV ▸*abbr.* cytomegalovirus.

CMYK ▸*abbr.* cyan, magenta, yellow, and black, the four colors used in most color printers, usually in two ink cartridges, one of black ink and the other containing cyan, magenta, and yellow inks in separate reservoirs. ▷the final 'k' in *black* is used to differentiate black from blue; the color scheme RGB (red, green, blue) is used for color computer display screens.

cne·mi·al crest /ˈnēmēəl/ ▸*n. Zoology* (in the legs of many mammals, birds, and dinosaurs) a ridge at the front of the head of the tibia or tibiotarsus to which the main extensor muscle of the thigh is attached. It is particularly well developed in running species. ▷late 19th cent.: *cnemial*, from Greek *knēmē* 'tibia' + **-al**.

CNG ▸*abbr.* compressed natural gas.

Cni·dar·i·a /nīdˈe(ə)rēə/ *Zoology* a phylum of aquatic invertebrate animals that comprises the coelenterates. ▷modern Latin (plural), from Greek *knidē* 'nettle.' **—cni·dar·i·an** *n.* & *adj.*

CNN ▸*abbr.* Cable News Network.

CNR *historical* ▸*abbr.* Canadian National Railways.

CNS ▸*abbr.* central nervous system.

Cnut /kəˈno͞ot/ variant of **Canute**.

CO ▸*abbr.* ■ Colorado (in official postal use). ■ Commanding Officer. ■ conscientious objector.

Co ▸*symbol* the chemical element cobalt.

Co. ▸*abbr.* ■ company: *the Consett Iron Co.* ■ county: *Hudson Co.*
▸PHRASE □ **and Co.** used as part of the titles of commercial businesses to designate the partner or partners not named. ■ (also **and co.**) *informal* and the rest of them: *I got there at 12.30 and waited for Mark and Co. to arrive.*

c/o ▸*abbr.* ■ care of. ■ carried over.

co- ▸*prefix* **1** (forming nouns) joint; mutual; common: *coeducation.* **2** (forming adjectives) jointly; mutually: *coequal.* **3** (forming verbs) together with another or others: *coproduce | co-own.* **4** *Mathematics* of the complement of an angle: *cosine.* ■ the complement of: *colatitude | coset.* ▷from Latin, originally a form of **com-**.

USAGE 1 In modern American English, the tendency increasingly is to write compound words beginning with **co-** without hyphenation, as in *costar*, *cosignatory*, and *coproduce*. British usage generally tends more often to show a preference for the older, hyphenated, spelling, but even in Britain the trend seems to be in favor of less hyphenation than in the past. In both the U.S. and the UK, for example, the spellings of *coordinate* and *coed* are encountered with or without hyphenation, but the more common choice for either word in either country is without the hyphen.
2 **Co-** with the hyphen is often used in compounds that are not yet standard (*co-golfer*), or to prevent ambiguity (*co-driver*—because *codriver* could be mistaken for *cod river*), or simply to avoid an awkward spelling (*co-own* is clearly preferable to *coown*). There are also some relatively less common

coown). There are also some relatively less common terms, such as *co-respondent* (in a divorce suit), where the hyphenated spelling distinguishes the word's meaning and pronunciation from that of the more common *correspondent*.

CoA *Biochemistry* ▸*abbr.* coenzyme A.

co·ac·er·vate /kōˈasərˌvāt/ ▸*n. Chemistry* a colloid-rich viscous liquid phase that may separate from a colloidal solution on addition of a third component. ▷early 20th cent.: back-formation from *coacervation*, based on Latin *cum* '(together) with' + *acervus* 'heap.'

coach¹ /kōCH/ ▸*n.* **1** a horse-drawn carriage, esp. a closed one. **2** a railroad car. ■ [as *adj.*] denoting economy class seating in an aircraft or train: *the cheapest coach-class fare.* **3** a bus, esp. one that is comfortably equipped and used for longer journeys. [as *adj.*]
▸*v.* [*intrans.*] travel by coach: *they coached to Claude's dwelling.*
▸*adv.* in economy class accommodations in an aircraft or train: *flying coach.* ▷mid 16th cent. (sense 1): from French *coche*, from Hungarian *kocsi (szekér)* '(wagon) from *Kocs*,' a town in Hungary.

coach² ▸*n.* an athletic instructor or trainer. ■ a tutor who gives private or specialized teaching.
▸*v.* [*trans.*] train or instruct (a team or player): *he has coached Little League baseball.* ■ give (someone) extra or private teaching: *he was coached to speak more slowly and curb his hand gestures.* ■ teach (a subject or sport) as a coach: *a Washington realtor who coaches soccer.* ■ prompt or urge (someone) with instructions: *he had improperly coached the witness to testify more credibly.* ▷early 18th cent. (as a verb): figuratively from COACH¹.

coach house ▸*n.* an outbuilding in which a carriage is or was kept.

coach·man /ˈkōCHmən/ ▸*n.* (*pl.* **-men**) a driver of a horse-drawn carriage.

coach·roof /ˈkōCHˌro͞of; -ˌro͝of/ ▸*n.* a raised part of the cabin roof of a yacht.

coach screw ▸*n.* another term for LAG SCREW.

coach·whip /ˈkōCHˌ(h)wip/ ▸*n.* (also **coachwhip snake**) a harmless, fast-moving North American snake. The pattern of scales on its slender body is said to resemble a braided whip. • *Masticophis flagellum*, family Colubridae.

coach·wood /ˈkōCHˌwo͝od/ ▸*n.* a slender tree of the rain forests of Australia and New Guinea, with close-grained timber that has a characteristic caramel scent and is used for cabinetmaking and veneers. • *Ceratopetalum apetalum*, family Cunoniaceae.

co·ac·tion /kōˈakSHən/ ▸*n.* **1** compulsion; restraint; coercion. **2** concerted action; acting together.

co·a·dapt·ed /ˌkōəˈdaptid/ ▸*adj. Biology* mutually adapted; mutually accommodating. —**co·a·dap·ta·tion** /ˌkōadəpˈtāSHən/ *n.*

co·ad·ju·tant /kōˈajətənt/ ▸*adj.* helping another or others, or with another or others.
▸*n.* a person who thus helps.

co·ad·ju·tor /ˌkōəˈjo͞otər; kōˈajətər/ ▸*n.* a bishop appointed to assist a diocesan bishop, and often also designated as his successor. ▷late Middle English: via Old French from late Latin *coadjutor*, from *co-* (from Latin *cum* 'together with') + *adjutor* 'assistant' (from *adjuvare* 'to help').

co·ag·u·lant /kōˈagyələnt/ ▸*n.* a substance that causes blood or another liquid to coagulate. ▷late 18th cent.: from Latin *coagulant-* 'curdling,' from the verb *coagulare* (see COAGULATE).

co·ag·u·lase /kōˈagyəˌlās; -ˌlāz/ ▸*n. Biochemistry* a bacterial enzyme that brings about the coagulation of blood or plasma and is produced by disease-causing forms of staphylococcus.

co·ag·u·late /kōˈagyəˌlāt/ ▸*v.* [*intrans.*] (of a fluid, esp. blood) change to a solid or semisolid state: *blood had coagulated around the edges of the wound.* ■ [*trans.*] cause (a fluid) to change to a solid or semisolid state: *epinephrine coagulates the blood.* ▷late Middle English: from Latin *coagulat-* 'curdled,' from the verb *coagulare*, from *coagulum* 'rennet.' —**co·ag·u·la·ble** /-ləbəl/ *adj.* —**co·ag·u·la·tion** /kōˌagyəˈlāSHən/ *n.* —**co·ag·u·la·tive** /-ˌlātiv/ *adj.* —**co·ag·u·la·tor** /-ˌlātər/ *n.*

co·ag·u·lum /kōˈagyələm/ ▸*n.* (*pl.* **-u·la** /-yələ/) a mass of coagulated matter. ▷mid 16th cent. (denoting a coagulant): from Latin, literally 'rennet.'

Co·a·hui·la /ˌkōəˈwēlə/ a state in northern Mexico, on the U.S. border; capital, Saltillo.

coal /kōl/ ▸*n.* a combustible black or dark brown rock consisting mainly of carbonized plant matter, found mainly in underground deposits and widely used as fuel: [as *adj.*] *a coal fire.* ■ a red-hot piece of coal or other material in a fire: *the glowing coals.*
▸*v.* [*trans.*] provide with a supply of coal: [as *n.*] (**coaling**) *the coaling and watering of the engine.* ▷Old English *col* (in the senses 'glowing ember' and 'charred remnant'), of Germanic origin; related to Dutch *kool* and German *Kohle*. The sense 'combustible mineral used as fuel' dates from Middle English. —**coal·y** *adj.*
▸*PHRASES* □ **coals to Newcastle** something brought or sent to a place where it is already plentiful. □ **rake** (or **haul**) **someone over the coals** reprimand someone severely.

coal-black ▸*adj.* as black as coal; utterly black.

coal·er /ˈkōlər/ ▸*n.* **1** a ship that transports coal. **2** a large mechanized structure for loading coal on to a ship, railroad car, or steam locomotive.

co·a·lesce /ˌkōəˈles/ ▸*v.* [*intrans.*] come together and form one mass or whole: *the puddles had* **coalesced into** *shallow streams | the separate details coalesce to form a single body of scientific thought.* ■ [*trans.*] combine (elements) in a mass or whole: *to help coalesce the community, they established an office.* ▷mid 16th cent. (in the sense 'bring together, unite'): from Latin *coalescere*, from *co-* (from *cum* 'with') + *alescere* 'grow up' (from *alere* 'nourish'). —**co·a·les·cence** /-ˈlesəns/ *n.* —**co·a·les·cent** /-ˈlesənt/ *adj.*

coal·field /ˈkōlˌfēld/ ▸*n.* an extensive area containing a number of underground coal deposits.

coal-fired ▸*adj.* heated, driven, or produced by the burning of coal: *a coal-fired power station.*

coal gas ▸*n.* a mixture of gases (chiefly hydrogen, methane, and carbon monoxide) obtained by the destructive distillation of coal and formerly used for lighting and heating. ■ gas given off when coal is burned

coal·i·fi·ca·tion /ˌkōləfiˈkāSHən/ ▸*n.* the process by which plant remains become coal.

co·a·li·tion /ˌkōəˈliSHən/ ▸*n.* an alliance for combined action, especially a temporary alliance of political parties forming a government or of states: *a coalition of conservatives and disaffected Democrats | he governed* **in coalition with** *the socialist Labor Party |* [as *adj.*] *a coalition government.* ▷early 17th cent. (in the sense 'fusion'): from medieval Latin *coalitio(n-)*, from the verb *coalescere* (see COALESCE). Usage in politics dates from the late 18th cent. —**co·a·li·tion·ist** /-nist/ *n.*

coal meas·ures ▸*plural n. Geology* a series of strata of the Carboniferous period, including coal seams.

coal oil ▸*n.* another term for KEROSENE.

Coal·port /ˈkōlˌpôrt/ ▸*n.* a kind of porcelain, frequently decorated with floral designs, produced at Coalport, England, from the late 18th century.

Coal·sack /ˈkōlˌsak/ (**the Coalsack**) *Astronomy* a dark nebula of dust near the Southern Cross that gives the appearance of a gap in the stars of the Milky Way.

coal tar ▸*n.* a thick black liquid produced by the destructive distillation of bituminous coal. It contains benzene, naphthalene, phenols, aniline, and many other organic chemicals.

coam·ing /ˈkōmiNG/ (also **coam·ings**) ▸*n.* a raised border around a ship's hatch serving to support the hatch covers and to keep out water. ■ a similar structure around the cockpit of a boat. ▷early 17th cent.: of unknown origin.

co·ap·ta·tion /ˌkōˌapˈtāSHən/ ▸*n.* the adaptation or adjustment of things, parts, or people to each other. ■ *Medicine* the drawing together of the separated tissue in a wound or fracture. ▷mid 16th cent.: from late Latin *coaptatio(n-)*, from the verb *coaptare*, from *co-* (from Latin *cum* 'with, together') + *aptare* (from *aptus* 'apt').

co·arc·tate /kōˈärkˌtāt/ ▸*adj. chiefly Anatomy Biology* pressed close together; contracted; confined. ■ *Entomology* (of the pupa of certain flies) formed within and remaining concealed by the larval cuticle or puparium. ▷late Middle English: from Latin *coarctatus*, past participle of *coarctare* 'press or draw together.'

co·arc·ta·tion /ˌkōˌärkˈtāSHən/ ▸*n. Medicine* congenital narrowing of a short section of the aorta. ▷late Middle English: from Latin *coarctatio(n-)*, from the verb *coarctare* (see COARCTATE).

coarse /kôrs/ ▸*adj.* **1** rough or loose in texture or grain: *a coarse woolen cloth.* ■ made of large grains or particles: *dry, coarse sand.* ■ (of grains or particles) large. ■ (of a person's features) not elegantly formed or proportioned. ■ (of food or drink) of inferior quality. **2** (of a person or a person's speech) rude, crude, or vulgar. ▷late Middle English (in the sense 'ordinary or inferior'): origin uncertain; until the 17th cent. identical in spelling with COURSE, and possibly derived from the latter in the sense 'habitual or ordinary manner.' —**coarse·ness** *n.* —**coars·ish** *adj.*

coarse-grained ▸*adj.* **1** coarse in texture or grain: *a coarse-grained flour.* ■ (of photographic film) having a noticeably grainy appearance. **2** coarse in manner or speech: *a coarse-grained man.*

coars·en /ˈkôrsən/ ▸*v.* make or become rough: [*trans.*] *her hands were coarsened by outside work |* [*intrans.*] *his facial features appeared to coarsen with age.* ■ make or become crude, vulgar, or unpleasant: [*trans.*] [as *adj.*] *people with coarsened characters |* [*intrans.*] *the voice coarsened.*

co·ar·tic·u·la·tion /ˌkō-ärˌtikyəˈlāSHən/ ▸*n. Phonetics* the articulation of two or more speech sounds together, so that one influences the other.

coast /kōst/ ▸*n.* **1** the part of the land near the sea; the edge of the land: *the west coast of Africa | they sailed further up the coast |* [as *adj.*] *the coast road.* ■ (**the Coast**) the Pacific coast of North America. **2** a run or movement in or on a vehicle without the use of power.
▸*v.* **1** [*intrans.*] (of a person or vehicle) move easily without using power: *the engines stopped, and the craft coasted along.* ■ act or make progress without making much effort: *he* **coasted to** *victory.* ■ slide down a snowy hill on a sled. **2** [*intrans.*] sail along the coast, esp. in order to carry cargo: [as *adj.*] (**coasting**) *a coasting schooner.* ▷Middle English (in the sense 'side of the body'), from Old French *coste* (noun), *costeier* (verb), from Latin *costa* 'rib, flank, side.' Sense 1 arose from the phrase *coast of the sea* 'side of the sea.'
▸*PHRASE* □ **the coast is clear** there is no danger of being observed or caught.

coast·al /ˈkōstəl/ ▸*adj.* of, relating to, or near a coast: *coastal erosion | coastal waters.*

coast·eer·ing /ˈkōstˌi(ə)riNG/ ▸*n. chiefly Brit.* the sport of exploring a shoreline that does not have a continuous pedestrian route.

coast·er /ˈkōstər/ ▸*n.* **1** a ship used to carry cargo along the coast. ■ [with *adj.*] a person who inhabits a specified coast: *a West coaster.* **2** a small tray or mat placed under a bottle or glass to protect the table underneath. **3** a toboggan. ■ short for ROLLER COASTER.

coast guard /ˈkōstˌgärd/ (also **coast·guard**) ▸*n.* (**Coast Guard**) a branch of the U.S. armed forces, under the Department of Transportation since 1967, responsible for the enforcement of maritime law and for the protection of life and property at sea. In time of war, or at the direction of the president, the Coast Guard serves as part of the U.S. Navy. ■ (**the coastguard**) a civilian or volunteer organization keeping watch on the sea near a coast in order to assist people or ships in danger and to prevent smuggling. ■ a member of a federal or civilian organization.

coast·guards·man /ˈkōstˌgärdzmən/ ▸*n.* a member of a coastguard, esp. the U.S. Coast Guard.

coast·land /ˈkōstˌland/ ▸*n.* (usu. **coastlands**) an expanse of land near the sea.

coast·line /ˈkōstˌlīn/ ▸*n.* the outline of a coast, esp. with regard to its shape and appearance: *the hotel has wonderful views of the rugged coastline.*

Coast Moun·tains a range that curves northwest for 1,000 miles (1,600 km) from British Columbia to Alaska and extends the line of the Cascade Mountains. Mount Waddington at 13,104 feet (3,994 m) is the high point.

Coast Rang·es the name for various ranges that extend from southern California along the Pacific coast to Alaska. Parallel to and west of the Coast Mountains, they reach 19,524 feet (5,951 m) at Mount Logan in the Yukon Territory.

coast to coast ▸*adj.* & *adv.* all the way across an island or continent: [as *adv.*] *retail stores from coast to coast |* [as *adj.*] (**coast-to-coast**) *a coast-to-coast journey.*

coast·ward /ˈkōstwərd/ (also **coast·wards**) ▸*adv.* & *adj.* toward the coast.

coast·wise /ˈkōstˌwīz/ ▸*adj.* & *adv.* along, following, or connected with the coast: [as *adj.*] *a small coastwise steamer |* [as *adv.*] *the cargo was ferried coastwise.*

coat /kōt/ ▸*n.* **1** an outer garment worn outdoors, having sleeves and typically extending below the hips: *a winter coat |* [as *adj.*] *his coat pocket.* ■ a similar item worn indoors as a protective garment: *a laboratory coat.* ■ a man's jacket or tunic, esp. as worn when hunting or by soldiers. ■ a man's or woman's tailored jacket. **2** an animal's covering of fur or

hair. **3** a structure, esp. a membrane, enclosing or lining an organ.■ a skin, rind, or husk. ■ a layer of a plant bulb. ■ an outer layer or covering of a specified kind: *the protein coat of the virus.* **4** a covering of paint or similar material laid on a surface at one time: *a protective coat of varnish.*
▸*v.* [*trans.*] (often **be coated**) provide with a layer or covering of something; apply a coat to: *his boots were* ***coated with*** *mud* | *coat each part with a thin oil* ■ (of a substance) form a covering to: *a film of dust coated the floor.* ▷Middle English: from Old French *cote,* of unknown ultimate origin. **—coat·ed** *adj.* [in *combination*] *plastic-coated wire.*

coat ar·mor ▸*n.* heraldic arms.

coat check ▸*n.* a cloakroom with an attendant.

coat check·er ▸*n.* a cloakroom attendant.

coat dress ▸*n.* a woman's tailored dress, typically fastening down the front and resembling a coat.

coat hang·er ▸*n.* see **HANGER** (sense 2).

co·a·ti /kō'ätē/ ▸*n.* (*pl.* **-tis**) a raccoonlike animal found mainly in Central and South America, with a long, flexible snout and a ringed tail. Also called **COATIMUNDI.** • Genera *Nasua* and *Nasuella,* family Procyonidae: three or four species, in particular *Nasua nasua,* whose range reaches the southern U.S. ▷early 17th cent.: from Spanish and Portuguese, from Tupi *kua'ti,* from *cua* 'belt' + *tim* 'nose.'

co·a·ti·mun·di /kō,äti'məndē/ ▸*n.* (*pl.* **-dis**) another term for **COATI.** ▷late 17th cent.: from Portuguese, from Tupi *kuatimu'ne,* from *kua'ti* (see **COATI**) + *mu'ne* 'snare or trick.' The *coatimundi* was originally thought to be a different species from the coati, but then discovered to be the male of the same species.

coat·ing /'kōtiNG/ ▸*n.* a thin layer or covering of something: *a coating of paint.* ■ material used for making coats.

coat of arms ▸*n.* the distinctive heraldic bearings or shield of a person, family, corporation, or country.

coat of mail ▸*n. historical* a jacket covered with or composed of metal rings or plates, serving as armor.

coat·rack /'kōt,rak/ ▸*n.* a rack or stand with hooks on which to hang coats, hats, etc.

coat·room /'kōt,ro͞om; -,ro͝om/ ▸*n.* another term for **CLOAKROOM.**

Coats Land /'kōts/ a region of Antarctica, east of the Antarctic Peninsula.

coat stand ▸*n.* another term for **COAT RACK.**

coat·tail /'kōt,tāl/ ▸*n.* (usu. **coattails**) each of the flaps formed by the lower back of a coat, esp. a tailcoat.
▸*PHRASE* □ **on someone's coattails** benefiting from another's success, sometimes undeservedly: *he was elected on the coattails of his predecessor.*

co·au·thor /kō'ôTHər/ ▸*n.* a joint author.
▸*v.* [*trans.*] be a joint author of (a book, paper, or report).

coax[1] /kōks/ ▸*v.* [*trans.*] [*trans.*] persuade (someone) gradually or by flattery to do something: *the trainees were* ***coaxed into*** *doing hard, boring work* | *"Come on now," I coaxed.* ■ (**coax something from/out of**) use such persuasion to obtain something from: *we coaxed money out of my father* | *figurative coaxing more speed from the car.* ■ manipulate (something) carefully into a particular shape or position: *her lovely hair had been coaxed into ringlets.* ▷late 16th cent.: from obsolete *cokes* 'simpleton,' of unknown origin. The original sense was 'pet, fondle,' hence 'persuade by caresses or flattery,' the underlying sense being 'make a simpleton of.' **—coax·er** *n.* **—coax·ing·ly** *adv.*

coax[2] /'kō-aks; kō'aks/ *informal* ▸*n.* coaxial cable.
▸*adj.* coaxial: *coax connectors.*

co·ax·i·al /kō'aksēəl/ ▸*adj.* having a common axis. ■ (of a cable or line) consisting of two concentric conductors separated by an insulator. **—co·ax·i·al·ly** *adv.*

COB ▸*abbr.* close of business: *you have until COB today to show us why you should not be disconnected.*

cob[1] /käb/ ▸*n.* **1** (also **corn·cob**) the central, cylindrical, woody part of the corn ear to which the grains, or kernels, are attached. **2** (also **cob·nut**) a hazelnut or filbert, esp. one of a large variety. ■ a hazel or filbert bush. **3** a powerfully built, short-legged horse. **4** a male swan. **5** *Brit.* a roundish lump of coal. ▷late Middle English (denoting a strong man or leader): of unknown origin. The underlying general sense appears to be 'stout, rounded, sturdy.'

cob[2] ▸*n. Brit.* a mixture of compressed clay and straw used, esp. in former times, for building walls: [as *adj.*] *cob and thatch cottages.* ▷early 17th cent.: of unknown origin.

Co·bain, Kurt (Donald) (1967–94), U.S. rock singer, guitarist, and songwriter. As leader of the Seattle band Nirvana, his style helped characterize the alternative music scene. His notoriety reached cult status, undiminished by his suicide in April 1994.

co·bal·a·min /kō'baləmin/ ▸*n. Biochemistry* any of a group of cobalt-containing substances including cyanocobalamin (vitamin B_{12}). ▷1950s: blend of **COBALT** and **VITAMIN.**

co·balt /'kō,bôlt/ ▸*n.* the chemical element of atomic number 27, a hard silvery-white magnetic metal. (Symbol: **Co**) ■ short for **COBALT BLUE:** [as *adj.*] *a cobalt sky.*

> Cobalt is chiefly obtained as a byproduct from nickel and copper ores. It is a transition metal similar in many respects to nickel. Its main use is as a component of magnetic alloys and those designed for use at high temperatures.

▷late 17th cent.: from German *Kobalt* 'imp, demon' (from the belief that cobalt was harmful to the ores with which it occurred). **—co·bal·tic** /kō'bôltik/ *adj.* **—co·bal·tous** /kō'bôltəs/ *adj.*

co·balt blue ▸*n.* a deep blue pigment containing cobalt and aluminum oxides. ■ the deep blue color of this.

Cobb /käb/, Ty (1886–1961), U.S. baseball player; full name *Tyrus Raymond Cobb;* also known as **the Georgia Peach.** His lifetime batting average (.367) is the highest in baseball history. An outfielder, he played for the Detroit Tigers 1905–26 and the Philadelphia Athletics 1927–28. Baseball Hall of Fame (1936).

Cobb Coun·ty /käb/ a county in northwestern Georgia that contains many northwestern suburbs of Atlanta; pop. 447,745. Its seat is Marietta.

cob·ble[1] /'käbəl/ ▸*n.* (usu. **cobbles**) a cobblestone. ■ (**cobbles**) *Brit.* coal in lumps of such a size. ▷late Middle English: from **COB**[1] + **-LE**[2].

cob·ble[2] ▸*v.* [*trans.*] **1** *dated* repair (shoes). **2** (**cobble something together**) roughly assemble or put together something from available parts or elements: *the mayor cobbled together a budget.* ▷late 15th cent.: back-formation from **COBBLER.**

cob·bled /'käbəld/ ▸*adj.* (of an area or roadway) paved with cobbles: *a cobbled courtyard.*

cob·bler /'käblər/ ▸*n.* **1** a person who mends shoes as a job. **2** an iced drink made with wine or sherry, sugar, and lemon. **3** a fruit pie with a rich crust on top. ▷Middle English: of unknown origin.
▸*PHRASE* □ **let the cobbler stick to his last** *proverb* people should only concern themselves with things they know something about. [translating Latin *ne sutor ultra crepidam.*]

cob·ble·stone /'käbəl,stōn/ ▸*n.* a small, round stone of a kind formerly used to cover road surfaces.

cob·by /'käbē/ ▸*adj.* (of horses, dogs, and other animals) shortish and thickset; stocky.

cob coal ▸*n.* see **COB**[1] (sense 5).

Cob·den /'käbdən/, Richard (1804–65), English political reformer. From 1838, with John Bright, he led the Anti-Corn Law League in its successful campaign for the repeal of the Corn Laws 1846.

COBE /'kōbē/ a NASA satellite launched in 1989 to map the background microwave radiation from space in a search for evidence of the big bang. ▷abbreviation of *Cosmic Background Explorer.*

co-bel·lig·er·ent /kōbə'lijərənt/ ▸*n.* any of two or more nations engaged in war as allies. **—co-bel·lig·er·ence** *n.*

co·bi·a /'kōbēə/ ▸*n.* (*pl.* same) a large, edible game fish that lives in open waters of the Atlantic, Indian, and western Pacific oceans. Also called **SERGEANT FISH.** • *Rachycentron canadum,* family Rachycentridae. ▷mid 19th cent.: of unknown origin.

cob·nut /'käb,nət/ ▸*n.* see **COB**[1] (sense 2).

COBOL /'kō,bôl/ ▸*n.* a computer programming language designed for use in commerce. ▷1960s: from *co(mmon) b(usiness) o(riented) l(anguage).*

co·bot /'kō,bät; -bət/ ▸*n.* a computer-controlled robotic device designed to assist a person: *a cobot and a UAW member working together to install a large truck instrument panel.* ▷blend of *collaborative* and *robot.*

co·bra /'kōbrə/ ▸*n.* a highly venomous snake native to Africa and Asia that spreads the skin of its neck into a hood when disturbed. • *Naja* and two other genera, family Elapidae: several species, in particular the **king cobra** and the **spectacled cobra.** ▷mid 17th cent.: from Portuguese *cobra de capello,* literally 'snake with hood,' based on Latin *colubra* 'snake.'

co-brand /'kō ,brand/ ▸*v.* [*trans.*] designate (a product or service) with the brands of joint manufacturers or sponsors: *E-Truck Leasing co-brands services with Truck Wash Guys.*
▸*n.* a product or service jointly offered by two manufacturers or sponsors: [as *modifier*] *we can easily set up a co-brand version of Small Business IS Here with your logo in the top right hand corner of every page.* **—co-brand·ing** *n.*

cob·web /'käb,web/ ▸*n.* (usu. **cobwebs**) a spider's web, esp. when old and covered with dust. ■ *Zoology* a tangled three-dimensional spider's web. ■ something resembling a cobweb in delicacy or intricacy: *white* ***cobwebs of*** *frost.* ▷Middle English *coppeweb, copweb,* from obsolete *coppe* 'spider' + **WEB. —cob·webbed** *adj.* **—cob·web·by** *adj.*
▸*PHRASE* □ **blow** (or **clear**) **away the cobwebs** banish a state of sluggishness; enliven or refresh oneself.

cob·web spi·der ▸*n.* a spider that builds tangled three-dimensional webs. • Family Theridiidae: many species, class Arachnida.

co·ca /'kōkə/ ▸*n.* a tropical American shrub that is widely grown for its leaves, which are the source of cocaine. • *Erythroxylum coca,* family Erythroxylaceae. ■ the dried leaves of this shrub, which are mixed with lime and chewed as a stimulant by the native people of western South America. ▷late 16th cent.: from Spanish, from Aymara *kuka* or Quechua *koka.*

co·caine /kō'kān; 'kō,kān/ ▸*n.* an addictive drug derived from coca or prepared synthetically, used as an illegal stimulant and sometimes medicinally as a local anesthetic. • An alkaloid; chem. formula: $C_{17}H_{21}NO_4$. ▷mid 19th cent.: from **COCA** + **-INE**[4].

co·cain·ism /kō'kānizəm; 'kōkə,nizəm/ ▸*n.* (the condition due to) excessive use of or addiction to cocaine.

co·cain·ize /kō'kā,nīz; 'kōkə,nīz/ ▸*v.* [*trans.*] treat or anesthetize with cocaine.

coc·cid /'käksid/ ▸*n.* a homopteran insect of the family Coccidae; a scale insect.

coc·cid·i·a /käk'sidēə/ ▸*plural n.* (*sing.* **-cid·i·um** /-'sidēəm/) *Biology* parasitic protozoa of a group that includes those that cause diseases such as coccidiosis and toxoplasmosis. • Suborder Eimeriorina (formerly order or subclass Coccidia), phylum Sporozoa. **—coc·cid·i·an** *adj.* & *n.*

coc·cid·i·oi·do·my·co·sis /käk,sidē,oidōmī'kōsəs/ ▸*n.* a serious fungal disease of the lungs and other tissues, endemic in the warmer, arid regions of America. • The fungus is *Coccidioides immitis,* phylum Ascomycota. ▷1930s: from modern Latin *Coccidioides* (part of the binomial of the fungus) + **MYCOSIS.**

coc·cid·i·o·sis /käk,sidē'ōsəs/ ▸*n.* a disease of birds and mammals that chiefly affects the intestines, caused by coccidia. • The coccidia belong to the genera *Eimeria, Isopora,* and others. ▷late 19th cent.: from *coccidium* (singular of modern Latin *Coccidia,* from Greek *kokkis,* diminutive of *kokkos* 'berry') + **-OSIS.**

coc·cid·i·o·stat /käk'sidēō,stat/ ▸*n. Veterinary Medicine* a substance administered to poultry, cattle, puppies, and kittens to retard the growth and reproduction of coccidian parasites.

coc·cid·i·um /käk'sidēəm/ ▸*n.* singular form of **COCCIDIA.**

coc·ci·nel·lid /,käksə'nelid/ ▸*n. Entomology* a beetle of a family (Coccinellidae) that includes the ladybugs. ▷late 19th cent.: from modern Latin *Coccinellidae* (plural), from the genus name *Coccinella,* from Latin *coccineus* 'scarlet.'

coc·co·lith /'käkə,liTH/ ▸*n. Biology* a minute, rounded, calcareous platelet, numbers of which form the spherical shells of coccolithophores. ▷mid 19th cent.: from Greek *kokkos* 'grain or berry' + *lithos* 'stone.'

coc·co·lith·o·phore /,käkə'liTHə,fôr/ ▸*n. Biology* a single-celled marine flagellate that secretes a calcareous shell, forming an important constituent of the phytoplankton. • Order Coccolithophorida, phylum Haptophyta. **—coc·co·lith·o·phor·id** /,käkəli'THäfərid/ *n.* & *adj.*

coc·cus /'käkəs/ ▸*n.* (*pl.* **coc·ci** /'käk,(s)ī; 'käk,(s)ē/) *Biology* any spherical or roughly spherical bacterium. ▷mid 18th cent. (denoting a scale insect): modern Latin, from Greek *kokkos* 'berry.' Compare with **COCHINEAL. —coc·cal** /'käkəl/ *adj.* **—coc·coid** /'käk,oid/ *adj.*

coc·cyx /'käksiks/ ▸*n.* (*pl.* **coc·cy·ges** /'käksə,jēz/ or **coc·cyx·es** /'käksiksiz/) a small, triangular bone at the base of the spinal column in humans and some apes, formed of fused vestigial vertebrae. ▷late 16th cent.: via Latin from Greek *kokkux* 'cuckoo' (because the shape of the human bone resembles the cuckoo's bill). **—coc·cyg·e·al** /käk'sijēəl/ *adj.*

Co·cha·bam·ba /ˌkōchəˈbämbə/ a city in western central Bolivia, at the center of a rich agricultural region; pop. 404,100.

co·chair ▸*n.* /ˈkōˌcher/ a person who is in charge of a meeting or organization jointly with another or others.
▸*v.* ˌkōˈche(ə)r [*trans.*] chair (a meeting) in this way.

Co·chin[1] /kōˈchin/ a seaport and naval base on the Malabar Coast of southwestern India, in the state of Kerala; pop. 504,000.

Co·chin[2] /ˈkōchin; ˈkächin/ (also **Cochin China**) ▸*n.* a chicken of an Asian breed with feathery legs.

Co·chin-Chi·na /ˈkōˌchin/ the former name for the southern region of what is now Vietnam. Part of French Indo-China from 1862, it became a French overseas territory in 1946 and then merged officially with Vietnam in 1949.

coch·i·neal /ˈkächəˌnēl; ˈkō-/ ▸*n.* **1** a scarlet dye used chiefly for coloring food. ■ the dried bodies of a female scale insect, which are crushed to yield this dye. ■ a similar dye or preparation made from the oak kermes insect (see KERMES). **2** (**cochineal insect**) the scale insect that is used for cochineal, native to Mexico and formerly widely cultivated on cacti. • *Dactylopius coccus*, family Dactylopiidae, suborder Homoptera. ▷late 16th cent.: from French *cochenille* or Spanish *cochinilla*, from Latin *coccinus* 'scarlet,' from Greek *kokkos* 'berry' (because the insect bodies were originally mistaken for grains or berries). Compare with COCCUS and KERMES.

Co·chise /kōˈchēs/ (c.1812–74), American Indian leader, chief of the Apache Indians. With a band of followers, he resisted white encroachment on Indian lands.

coch·le·a /ˈkōklēə; ˈkäk-/ ▸*n.* (*pl.* **-le·ae** /-lēˌē; -lēˌī/) the spiral cavity of the inner ear containing the organ of Corti, which produces nerve impulses in response to sound vibrations. ▷mid 16th cent. (used to denote spiral objects such as a spiral staircase and an Archimedean screw): from Latin, 'snail shell or screw,' from Greek *kokhlias*. The current sense dates from the late 17th cent. —**coch·le·ar** *adj.*

coch·le·ate /ˈkäklēit; -ˌāt/ (also **coch·le·at·ed**) ▸*adj.* *chiefly Botany* formed like a spiral shell; twisted.

Coch·ran[1] /ˈkäkrən/, Eddie (1938–60), U.S. rock-and-roll singer and songwriter; born *Edward Cochrane*. Notable songs: "Summertime Blues" (1958), "C'mon Everybody" (1959), and "Three Steps to Heaven" (1960).

Coch·ran[2], Jacqueline (*c.*1910–80), U.S. aviator. The first woman to break the sound barrier 1953, she set many speed and altitude records.

Coch·ran[3], Margaret, see CORBIN.

cock[1] /käk/ ▸*n.* **1** a male bird, esp. a rooster. ■ [in *combination*] used in names of birds, esp. game birds, e.g., **moorcock**. ■ *Brit.* a male lobster, crab, or salmon. **2** *vulgar slang* a penis. **3** *Brit., informal* nonsense: *that's all a lot of cock.* **4** a firing lever in a gun which can be raised to be released by the trigger. **5** a stopcock.
▸*v.* [*trans.*] **1** tilt (something) in a particular direction: *she cocked her head slightly to one side.* ■ bend a (limb or joint) at an angle: [as *adj.*] (**cocked**) *she listened, her little finger cocked as she held her coffee cup.* ■ (of a male dog) lift (a back leg) in order to urinate. **2** raise the cock of (a gun) in order to make it ready for firing. ▷Old English *cocc*, from medieval Latin *coccus*; reinforced in Middle English by Old French *coq*.
▸*PHRASES* □ **at full cock** (of a gun) with the cock lifted to the position at which the trigger will act. □ **cock one's ear** (of a dog) raise its ears to an erect position. ■ (of a person) listen attentively to or for something. □ **cock one's eye** (or **eyebrow**) glance in a quizzical or knowing manner with a raised eyebrow. □ **cock of the walk** someone who dominates others within a group. □ **cock a snook** see SNOOK[2].

cock[2] ▸*n.* *dated* a small pile of hay, straw, or other material, with vertical sides and a rounded top.
▸*v.* [*trans.*] *archaic* pile (hay, straw, or other material) into such a shape. ▷late Middle English: perhaps of Scandinavian origin and related to Norwegian *kok* 'heap, lump,' Danish *kok* 'haycock,' and Swedish *koka* 'clod.'

cock·ade /käˈkād/ ▸*n.* a rosette or knot of ribbons worn in a hat as a badge of office or party, or as part of a livery. ▷mid 17th cent.: from French *cocarde*, originally in *bonnet à la coquarde*, from the feminine of obsolete *coquard* 'saucy.' —**cock·ad·ed** *adj.*

cock-a-doo·dle-doo /ˌkäk ə ˌdo͞odl ˈdo͞o/ ▸*n.* used to represent the sound made by a cock when it crows.

cock-a-hoop /ˌkäk ə ˈho͞op; ˈho͝op/ ▸*adj.* [*predic.*] extremely and obviously pleased, esp. about a triumph or success. ▷mid 17th cent.: from the phrase *set cock a hoop*, of unknown origin, apparently denoting the action of turning on the tap and allowing liquor to flow (prior to a drinking session).

cock-a-leek·ie /ˌkäk ə ˈlēkē/ ▸*n.* a Scottish soup traditionally made with chicken and leeks. ▷mid 18th cent.: from COCK[1] and LEEK.

cock·a·lo·rum /ˌkäkəˈlôrəm/ ▸*n.* (*pl.* **-rums**) *informal, dated* a self-important little man. ▷early 18th cent.: an arbitrary formation from COCK[1].

cock·a·ma·mie /ˈkäkəˌmāmē; ˌkäkəˈmāmē/ (also **cock·a·ma·my**) ▸*adj.* *informal* ridiculous; implausible: *a cockamamie theory.* ▷1940s (originally denoting a design left by a transfer): probably an alteration of DECALCOMANIA.

cock and bull sto·ry ▸*n.* *informal* a ridiculous and implausible story.

cock·a·tiel /ˈkäkəˌtēl/ ▸*n.* a slender, long-crested Australian parrot related to the cockatoos, with a mainly gray body, white shoulders, and a yellow and orange face. • *Nymphicus hollandicus*, family Cacatuidae (or Psittacidae). ▷late 19th cent.: from Dutch *kaketielje*, probably a diminutive of *kaketoe* 'cockatoo.'

cock·a·too /ˈkäkəˌto͞o/ ▸*n.* a parrot with an erectile crest, found in Australia, eastern Indonesia, and neighboring islands. • Family Cacatuidae (or Psittacidae): several genera and numerous species, including the **sulfur-crested cockatoo** (*Cacatua galerita*). ▷mid 17th cent.: from Dutch *kaketoe*, from Malay *kakatua*, the spelling influenced by COCK[1].

sulfur-crested cockatoo

cock·a·trice /ˈkäkətris; -ˌtrīs/ ▸*n.* another term for BASILISK (sense 1). ■ *Heraldry* a mythical animal depicted as a two-legged dragon (or wyvern) with a cock's head. ▷late Middle English: from Old French *cocatris*, from Latin *calcatrix* 'tracker' (from *calcare* 'to tread or track'), translating Greek *ikhneueinōn* (see ICHNEUMON).

cock·bead ▸*n.* a projecting wooden molding used to decorate furniture. —**cock·bead·ed** *adj.* —**cock·bead·ing** *n.*

cock·chaf·er /ˈkäkˌchāfər/ ▸*n.* a large brown European beetle that flies at dusk and often crashes into lighted windows. The adults are damaging to foliage and flowers, and the larvae are a pest of cereal and grass roots. • *Melolontha melolontha*, family Scarabaeidae. ▷early 18th cent.: from COCK[1] (expressing size or vigor) + CHAFER.

Cock·croft /ˈkäkˌkrôft/, Sir John Douglas (1897–1967), English physicist. In 1932, working with E. T. S. Walton, he succeeded in splitting the atom. Nobel Prize for Physics (1951, shared with Walton).

cock·crow /ˈkäkˌkrō/ (also **cock-crow** or **cock crow**) ▸*n.* *poetic/literary* dawn: *the hour of cockcrow was still far off.*

cocked hat ▸*n.* a brimless triangular hat pointed at the front, back, and top. ■ *historical* a hat with a wide brim permanently turned up toward the crown, such as a tricorne.
▸*PHRASE* □ **knock something into a cocked hat** utterly defeat or outdo something.

cock·er·el /ˈkäkərəl/ ▸*n.* a young domestic cock. ▷Middle English: diminutive of COCK[1].

cock·er span·iel /ˈkäkər/ (also **cock·er**) ▸*n.* a small spaniel of a breed with a silky coat. ▷early 19th cent.: from COCK[1] + -ER[1] (because the dog was bred to flush game birds such as woodcock, for shooting).

cocker spaniel

cock·eye /ˈkäkˌī/ ▸*n.* an eye that squints or is affected by strabismus.

cock·eyed /ˈkäkˈīd/ ▸*adj.* *informal* crooked or askew; not level: *cockeyed camera angles.* ■ absurd; impractical: *do you expect us to believe a cockeyed story like that?* ■ drunk: *I got cockeyed.* ■ (of a person or a person's eyes) having a squint. ■ cross-eyed. ▷early 19th cent.: apparently from the verb COCK[1] and EYE. The sense 'drunk' (originally U.S.) dates from the 1920s.

cock·fight·ing /ˈkäkˌfītiNG/ ▸*n.* the sport (illegal in certain countries) of setting two cocks to fight each other. Fighting cocks often have had their legs fitted with metal spurs. —**cock·fight** /ˈkäkˌfīt/ *n.*

cock·le[1] /ˈkäkəl/ ▸*n.* **1** an edible, burrowing bivalve mollusk with a strong ribbed shell. • Genus *Cardium*, family Cardiidae. **2** (also **cock·le·shell**) *poetic/literary* a small shallow boat. ▷Middle English: from Old French *coquille* 'shell,' based on Greek *konkhulion*, from *konkhē* 'conch.'
▸*PHRASE* □ **warm the cockles of one's heart** give one a comforting feeling of pleasure or contentment.

cock·le[2] ▸*v.* [*intrans.*] (of paper) bulge out in certain places so as to present a wrinkled or creased surface; pucker. ▷mid 16th cent.: from French *coquiller* 'blister (bread in cooking),' from *coquille* 'shell' (see COCKLE[1]).

cock·le·bur /ˈkäkəlˌbər/ ▸*n.* a herbaceous plant of the daisy family, with broad leaves and burred fruits. It originated in tropical America but is now cosmopolitan. See also CLOTBUR. • Genus *Xanthium*, family Compositae: two or three species, in particular *X. strumarium*. ▷mid 19th cent.: from COCKLE[2] + BURR.

cock·loft /ˈkäkˌlôft/ ▸*n.* a small loft or attic.

cock·ney /ˈkäknē/ ▸*n.* (*pl.* **-neys**) a native of East London, traditionally one born within hearing of Bow Bells. ■ the dialect or accent typical of such people.
▸*adj.* of or characteristic of cockneys or their dialect or accent: *cockney humor.* ▷early 17th century, originally in the sense 'a town dweller regarded as affected or puny.'

cock·ney·ism /ˈkäknēˌizəm/ ▸*n.* a feature or style of speech or idiom characteristic of cockneys.

cock-of-the-rock ▸*n.* (*pl.* **cocks-of-the-rock**) a crested cotinga found in the tropical forests of South America. The male has brilliant orange or red plumage used in communal display. • Genus *Rupicola*, family Cotingidae: two species.

cock·pit /ˈkäkˌpit/ ▸*n.* **1** a compartment for the pilot and sometimes also the crew in an aircraft or spacecraft. ■ a similar compartment for the driver in a racing car. ■ a sunken area in the after deck of a boat providing space for members of the crew. **2** a place where a battle or other conflict takes place: *the cockpit of capitalist conflict in Europe.* ■ a place where cockfights are held. ▷late 16th cent. (sense 2): from COCK[1] + PIT[1]. In the early 18th cent. the term was in nautical use, denoting an area in the aft lower deck of a man-of-war where the wounded were taken, later coming to mean 'the "pit" or well in a sailing yacht from which it was steered'; hence the place housing the controls of other vehicles (sense 1, early 20th cent.).

cock·roach /ˈkäkˌrōch/ ▸*n.* a beetlelike insect with long antennae and legs, feeding by scavenging. Several tropical species have become established worldwide as pests in homes and food service establishments. • Suborder Blattodea, order Dictyoptera: many genera and species, including the **oriental cockroach** (*Blatta orientalis*) and the **American cockroach** (*Periplaneta americana*); some, esp. in the genus *Ectobius*, are small temperate species that live outdoors. ▷early 17th cent. (as *cacaroch*): from Spanish *cucaracha*. The spelling change was due to association with COCK[1] and ROACH[2].

American cockroach

cocks·comb /ˈkäksˌkōm/ ▸*n.* **1** the crest or comb of a domestic cock. **2** a

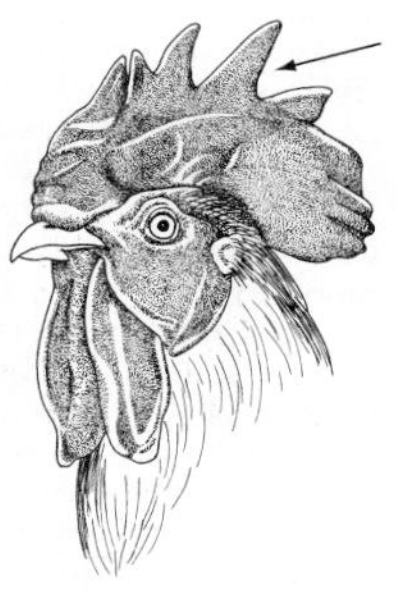
cockscomb 1

tropical plant with a crest or plume of tiny yellow, orange, or red flowers, widely cultivated as a garden annual or a houseplant. • *Celosia cristata,* family Amaranthaceae. **3** an orchid related to the coralroots but with more colorful flowers, native to southern North America. Also called CORALROOT. • Genus *Hexalectris,* family Orchidaceae.

cocks·foot /ˈkäks,fo͝ot/ ▸*n.* British term for ORCHARD GRASS.

cock·shy /ˈkäk,SHī/ ▸*n.* (*pl.* **-shies**) *Brit., dated* a target for throwing sticks or stones at as a game. ■ an act of throwing something at such a target. ■ *figurative* an object of ridicule or criticism. ▷from the original use of a cockerel, or a replica of a cockerel, as a target.

cocks·man /ˈkäksmən/ ▸*n.* (*pl.* **-men**) *vulgar slang* a man reputed to be extremely virile or sexually accomplished. **—cocks·man·ship** /-,SHip/ *n.*

cock·spur thorn ▸*n.* a North American hawthorn that is often cultivated for its rich orange autumn foliage. • *Crataegus crus-galli,* family Rosaceae. ■ any of a number of trees bearing long spiny thorns.

cock·suck·er /ˈkäk,səkər/ ▸*n. vulgar slang* a fellator. ■ a generalized term of abuse.

cock·sure /ˈkäkˈSHo͝or/ ▸*adj.* presumptuously or arrogantly confident. ▷early 16th cent.: from archaic *cock* (a euphemism for *God*) + SURE; later associated with COCK[1]. **—cock·sure·ly** *adv.* **—cock·sure·ness** *n.*

cock·tail /ˈkäk,tāl/ ▸*n.* **1** an alcoholic drink consisting of a spirit or several spirits mixed with other ingredients, such as fruit juice, lemonade, or cream: [as *adj.*] *cocktail parties | a cocktail bar.* ■ a mixture of substances or factors, esp. when dangerous or unpleasant in its effects: *financial pressure plus isolation can be a deadly cocktail for some people | a cocktail of drugs that inhibits replication of HIV.* **2** a dish consisting of small pieces of seafood or fruits, typically served cold at the beginning of a meal as an hors d'oeuvre: *a shrimp cocktail.* ▷early 17th cent.: from COCK[1] + TAIL[1]. The original use was as an adjective describing a creature with a tail like that of a cock, specifically a horse with a docked tail; hence (because hunters and coach horses were generally docked) a racehorse that was not a thoroughbred, having a cocktailed horse in its pedigree (early 19th cent.). Sense 1 (originally U.S., also early 19th cent.) is perhaps analogous, from the idea of an adulterated spirit.

cock·tail dress ▸*n.* an elegant dress suitable for semiformal social occasions.

cock·tail lounge ▸*n.* a bar, typically in a hotel, restaurant, or airport, where alcoholic drinks are served.

cock·tail nap·kin ▸*n.* a small napkin designed to be placed under a drink when it is served.

cock·tail ta·ble ▸*n.* another term for COFFEE TABLE.

cock·teas·er /ˈkäk,tēzər/ (also **cock·tease**) ▸*n. vulgar slang* a woman who leads a man to the mistaken belief that she is likely to have sexual intercourse with him.

cock-up ▸*n. Brit., informal* something done badly or inefficiently: *we've made a total cock-up of it.*

cock·y /ˈkäkē/ ▸*adj.* (**cock·i·er, cock·i·est**) conceited or arrogant, esp. in a bold or impudent way. ▷mid 16th cent. (in the sense 'lecherous'): from COCK[1] + -Y[1]. **—cock·i·ly** /ˈkäkəlē/ *adv.* **—cock·i·ness** *n.*

co·co /ˈkōkō/ ▸*n.* (*pl.* **-cos**) **1** [usu. as *adj.*] coconut: *coco matting | coco palm.* **2** *W. Indian* the root of the taro. ▷mid 16th cent. (originally denoting the nut): from Spanish and Portuguese, literally 'grinning face' (because of the appearance of the base of the coconut).

co·coa /ˈkōkō/ ▸*n.* **1** a chocolate powder made from roasted and ground cacao seeds. ■ a hot drink made from such a powder mixed with sugar and milk or water. **2** variant spelling of COCO, usu. regarded as a misspelling. ▷early 18th cent. (denoting cacao seed): alteration of CACAO.

co·coa bean ▸*n.* a cacao seed.

co·coa but·ter ▸*n.* a fatty substance obtained from cocoa beans and used esp. in the manufacture of confectionery and cosmetics.

co·co·bo·lo /,kōkōˈbōlō/ ▸*n.* (*pl.* **-los**) a tropical American tree with hard, reddish timber that is used chiefly to make cutlery handles. • *Dalbergia retusa,* family Leguminosae. ▷mid 19th cent.: via Spanish from Arawak *kakabali.*

co·co de mer /ˈkōkō də ˈmer/ ▸*n.* a tall palm tree that is native to the Seychelles and has an immense, seaborne nut in a hard, woody shell, which is the largest known seed. • *Lodoicea maldivica,* family Palmae. ■ the large nut of this palm. ▷early 19th cent.: from French *coco-de-mer,* literally 'coco from the sea' (because the tree was first known from nuts found floating in the sea).

co·co·nut /ˈkōkə,nət/ (also **cocoanut**) ▸*n.* **1** the large, oval, brown seed of a tropical palm, consisting of a hard shell lined with edible white flesh and containing a clear liquid. It grows inside a woody husk, surrounded by fiber. ■ the flesh of a coconut, esp. when used as food. **2** (also **coconut palm** or **tree**) the tall palm tree that yields this nut, which grows mainly by coastal beaches and has become naturalized throughout the tropics. Many tropical economies are dependent upon its products, which include copra and coir. • *Cocos nucifera,* family Palmae.

co·co·nut but·ter ▸*n.* a solid fat obtained from the flesh of the coconut, and used in the manufacture of soap, candles, ointment, etc.

co·co·nut crab ▸*n.* a large terrestrial crablike crustacean that climbs coconut palms to feed on the nuts, found on islands in the Indo-Pacific area. Also called ROBBER CRAB. • *Birgus latro,* family Paguridae. ▷so named because it climbs trees to reach coconuts.

Co·co·nut Creek a city in southeastern Florida, northwest of Fort Lauderdale; pop. 27,485.

Co·co·nut Grove a district in southwestern Miami in Florida, noted as an arts colony and a thriving tourist destination.

co·co·nut mat·ting ▸*n.* matting made of fiber from coconut husks.

co·co·nut milk ▸*n.* the watery liquid found inside a coconut.

co·co·nut oil ▸*n.* the fatty oil obtained from the coconut and used in candies and confections and in cosmetics.

co·co·nut palm ▸*n.* see COCONUT (sense 2).

co·coon /kəˈko͞on/ ▸*n.* a silky case spun by the larvae of many insects for protection as pupae. ■ a similar structure made by other animals. ■ a covering that prevents the corrosion of metal equipment. ■ something that envelops or surrounds, esp. in a protective or comforting way: *the* **cocoon of** *her kimono | figurative a warm* **cocoon of** *love.*
▸*v.* [*trans.*] (usu. **be cocooned**) envelop or surround in a protective or comforting way: *we began to feel cold even though we were* **cocooned in** *our sleeping bags.* ■ spray with a protective coating. ■ [*intrans.*] retreat from the stressful conditions of public life into the cozy private world of the family: *the movers and shakers are now cocooning.* ▷late 17th cent.: from French *cocon,* from medieval Provençal *coucoun* 'eggshell, cocoon,' diminutive of *coca* 'shell.' The verb dates from the mid 19th cent. **—co·coon·er** *n.* (in the last sense of the *verb*).

Co·cos Is·lands /ˈkōkəs/ a group of 27 small coral islands in the Indian Ocean, administered as an external territory of Australia since 1955; pop. 603. Also called KEELING ISLANDS.

co·cotte /kôˈkôt; kəˈkät/ ▸*n.* **1** (usu. **en cocotte**) a covered, heatproof dish or casserole in which food can be both cooked and served; a Dutch oven. [early 20th cent.: from French *cocasse,* from Latin *cucuma* 'cooking container.'] **2** *dated* a fashionable prostitute. [mid 19th cent.: French, from a child's name for a hen.]

co-coun·sel·ing /ˈkō,kounsəliNG; kōˈkoun-/ (also **co-coun·sel·ing**) ▸*n.* a form of personal or psychological counseling in which two or more people alternate the roles of therapist and patient.

Coc·teau /kākˈtō/, Jean (1889–1963), French playwright, novelist, and movie director. His films include *Beauty and the Beast* (1945) and *Orpheus* (1949).

co·cus wood /ˈkōkəs/ ▸*n.* hard, heavy timber that blackens with age and is used for musical instruments. • This timber is obtained from the Jamaican ebony (*Brya ebenus,* family Leguminosae). ▷mid 17th cent.: *cocus,* of unknown origin.

COD ▸*abbr.* ■ cash on delivery. ■ collect on delivery.

cod[1] /käd/ (also **cod·fish**) ▸*n.* (*pl.* same) a large marine fish with a small barbel on the chin. • Family Gadidae (the **cod family**): many genera and species, in particular the North Atlantic *Gadus morhua,* of great commercial importance as a food fish and as a source of cod liver oil. The cod family also includes the haddock, ling, pollack, whiting, and other food fishes. ■ used in names of similar or related fishes, e.g., **rock cod, tomcod.** ▷Middle English: of unknown origin; one suggestion is that the word is the same as Old English *cod(d)* 'bag,' because of the fish's appearance.

co·da /ˈkōdə/ ▸*n. Music* the concluding passage of a piece or movement, typically forming an addition to the basic structure. ■ the concluding section of a dance, esp. of a pas de deux or the finale of a ballet in which the dancers parade before the audience. ■ a concluding event, remark, or section: *his new novel is a kind of* **coda to** *his previous books.* ▷mid 18th cent.: Italian, from Latin *cauda* 'tail.'

cod·dle /ˈkädl/ ▸*v.* [*trans.*] **1** treat in an indulgent or overprotective way: *I was coddled and cosseted.* **2** cook (an egg) in water below the boiling point. ▷late 16th cent. (in the sense 'boil (fruit) gently'): origin uncertain; sense 1 is probably a dialect variant of obsolete *caudle* 'administer invalids' gruel,' based on Latin *caldum* 'hot drink,' from *calidus* 'warm.' **—cod·dler** /ˈkädlər; ˈkädl-ər/ *n.*

code /kōd/ ▸*n.* **1** a system of words, letters, figures, or other symbols substituted for other words, letters, etc., esp. for the purposes of secrecy: *the Americans cracked their diplomatic code | sending messages* **in code.** ■ a system of signals, such as sounds, light flashes, or flags, used to send messages: *Morse code.* ■ a series of letters, numbers, or symbols assigned to something for the purposes of classification or identification: *the genetic code | calls with either code will work in the 201 area.* **2** *Computing* program instructions: *hundreds of lines of code | assembly code.* **3** a systematic collection of laws or regulations: *the criminal code.* ■ a set of conventions governing behavior or activity in a particular sphere *a dress code.* ■ a set of rules and standards adhered to by a society, class, or individual: *a stern code of honor.*
▸*v.* **1** [*trans.*] (usu. **be coded**) convert (the words of a message) into a particular code in order to convey a secret meaning: *only Mitch knew how to read the message—even the name was coded.* ■ express the meaning of (a statement or communication) in an indirect or euphemistic way: [as *adj.*] (**coded**) *a national campaign against "playing by ear," a coded phrase that meant jazz.* ■ assign a code to (something) for purposes of classification, analysis, or identification: *she coded the samples and sent them down for dissection.* **2** [*intrans.*] (**code for**) *Biochemistry* specify the genetic sequence for (an amino acid or protein): *genes that code for human growth hormone.* ■ be the genetic determiner of (a characteristic): *one pair of homologous chromosomes that codes for eye color.* ▷Middle English: via Old French from Latin *codex, codic-* (see CODEX). The term originally denoted a systematic collection of statutes made by one of the later Roman emperors, particularly that of Justinian; compare with sense 3 (mid 18th cent.), the earliest modern sense. **—cod·er** *n.*
▸*PHRASE* □ **bring something up to code** renovate an old building or update its features in line with the latest building regulations.

co·dec /ˈkō,dek/ ▸*n. Electronics* a microchip that compresses data to enable faster transmission or decompresses received data. ▷1960s: blend of *coder* (see CODE) and DECODER.

co·de·fend·ant /,kōdiˈfendənt/ ▸*n.* a joint defendant.

co·deine /ˈkō,dēn/ ▸*n. Medicine* a sleep-inducing and analgesic drug derived from morphine. • An alkaloid; chem. formula: $C_{18}H_{21}NO_3$. ▷mid 19th cent.: from Greek *kōdeia* 'poppy head' + -INE[4].

code mon·key ▸*n. informal* a computer programmer, especially an inexperienced or plodding one.

code name ▸*n.* a word used for secrecy or convenience instead of the usual name. **—code-named** *adj.*

co·de·pend·en·cy /,kōdəˈpendənsē/ ▸*n.* excessive emotional or psychological reliance on a partner, typically a partner who requires support due to an illness or addiction. **—co·de·pend·ence** /-dəns/ *n.* **—co·de·pend·ent** /-dənt/ *adj.* & *n.*

cod·er /ˈkōdər/ ▸*n.* a computer programmer: *flaws that could be used by malicious coders to create new worms.*

code·share /ˈkōd,SHe(ə)r/ *n.* ▸a marketing arrangement in which two airlines sell seats on a flight that one of them operates: [as adj.] *Qantas is a codeshare partner with both American Airlines and Alaska Airlines in North America.* ■ a flight or aircraft in which such an arrangement is in effect. **—code-shar·ing** *n.*

code-shar·ing ▸*n.* agreement between two or more airlines to list certain flights in a reservation system under each other's names.

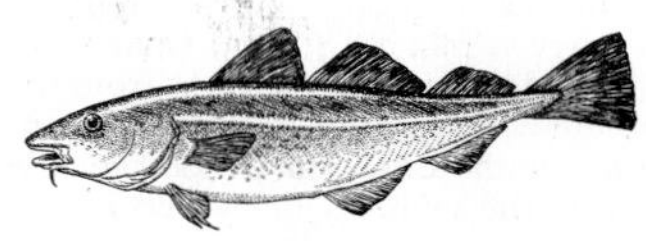

cod[1]

co·de·ter·mi·na·tion /ˌkōdiˌtərmə'nāSHən/ ▸n. cooperation between management and workers in decision-making, esp. by the representation of workers on boards of directors. ▷1950s: from **co-** 'together' + **DETERMINATION** (translating German *Mitbestimmung*).

co·dex /'kōˌdeks/ ▸n. (pl. **co·di·ces** /'kōdəˌsēz; 'kād-/ or **co·dex·es**) an ancient manuscript text in book form. ■ an official list of medicines, chemicals, etc. ▷late 16th cent. (denoting a collection of statutes or set of rules): from Latin, literally 'block of wood,' later denoting a block split into leaves or tablets for writing on, hence a book.

cod·fish /'kädˌfiSH/ ▸n. (pl. same or **-fish·es**) another term for **COD**[1].

codg·er /'käjər/ ▸n. *often derogatory* an elderly man, esp. one who is old-fashioned or eccentric: ***old codgers*** *always harp on about yesteryear.* ▷mid 18th cent.: perhaps a variant of *cadger* (see **CADGE**).

co·di·ces /'kōdəˌsēz; 'kād-/ ▸ plural form of **CODEX**.

cod·i·cil /'kädəsəl; -ˌsil/ ▸n. an addition or supplement that explains, modifies, or revokes a will or part of one. ▷late Middle English: from Latin *codicillus*, diminutive of *codex, codic-* (see **CODEX**). **—cod·i·cil·la·ry** /ˌkädə'silərē/ *adj.*

cod·i·fy /'kädəˌfī; 'kōd-/ ▸v. (**-fies, -fied**) [*trans.*] arrange (laws or rules) into a systematic code. ■ arrange according to a plan or system: *Verdi helped codify an international operatic culture.* **—cod·i·fi·ca·tion** /ˌkädəfə'kāSHən; ˌkōd-/ *n.* **—cod·i·fi·er** /'kädəˌfīər; 'kōd-/ *n.*

cod·ing /'kōdiNG/ ▸n. the process of assigning a code to something for the purposes of classification or identification. ■ a code assigned for such a purpose: *text type codings.* ■ *Biochemistry* the process of coding genetically for an amino acid, protein, or characteristic.

cod·ling /'kädliNG/ ▸n. an immature cod.

cod·ling moth (also **cod·lin moth**) ▸n. a small, grayish moth whose larva feeds on apples. • *Cydia pomonella*, family Tortricidae. ▷late Middle English: *codling* from Anglo-Norman French *quer de lion* 'lionheart.'

cod liv·er oil ▸n. oil pressed from the fresh liver of cod, which is rich in vitamins D and A.

co·do·main /'kōdōˌmān; ˌkōdō'mān/ ▸n. *Mathematics* a set that includes all the possible values of a given function.

co·don /'kōˌdän/ ▸n. *Biochemistry* a sequence of three nucleotides which together form a unit of genetic code in a DNA or RNA molecule. ▷1960s: from **CODE** + **-ON**.

cod·piece /'kädˌpēs/ ▸n. a pouch, esp. a conspicuous and decorative one, attached to a man's breeches or close-fitting hose to cover the genitals, worn in the 15th and 16th centuries. ▷from earlier *cod* 'scrotum' (from Old English *codd* 'bag, pod') + **PIECE**.

cods·wal·lop /'kädzˌwäləp/ ▸n. *Brit., informal* nonsense. ▷1960s: sometimes said to be named after Hiram Codd, who invented a bottle for carbonated beverages (1875); the derivation remains unconfirmed.

Co·dy[1] /'kōdē/ a city in northwestern Wyoming, associated with Buffalo Bill Cody, who lived here; pop. 7,897.

Co·dy[2], William Frederick, see **BUFFALO BILL**.

Coe /kō/, Sebastian (1956–), British middle-distance runner and politician. He won an Olympic gold medal in the 1,500 meters in 1980 and in 1984. After his retirement from athletics, he became a member of Parliament in 1992.

coe·cil·i·an ▸n. variant spelling of **CAECILIAN**.

co·ed /'kōˌed/ *informal* ▸n. *dated* a female student at a co-educational institution.

▸adj. (of an institution or system) co-educational. ▷late 19th cent.: abbreviation.

co·ed·u·ca·tion /ˌkōˌejə'kāSHən/ ▸n. the education of students of both sexes together. **—co·ed·u·ca·tion·al** /-SHənl/ *adj.*

co·ef·fi·cient /ˌkōə'fiSHənt/ ▸n. **1** *Mathematics* a numerical or constant quantity placed before and multiplying the variable in an algebraic expression (e.g., 4 in *4x*^{y}). **2** *Physics* a multiplier or factor that measures some property: *coefficients of elasticity | the drag coefficient.* ▷mid 17th cent. (in the sense 'cooperating to produce a result'): from modern Latin *coefficient-*, from *com-* 'together' + *efficient-* 'accomplishing' (see **EFFICIENT**).

co·ef·fi·cient of fric·tion ▸n. the ratio between the force necessary to move one surface horizontally over another and the pressure between the two surfaces.

co·ef·fi·cient of vis·cos·i·ty ▸n. *Physics* the degree to which a fluid resists flow under an applied force, expressed as the ratio of the shearing stress to the velocity gradient. The coefficient of viscosity of liquids decreases as temperature increases because the bonds between molecules are weakened.

coe·la·canth /'sēləˌkanTH/ ▸n. a large, bony marine fish with a three-lobed tail fin and fleshy pectoral fins, found chiefly around the Comoro Islands near Madagascar. It is thought to be related to the ancestors of land vertebrates and was known only from fossils until one was found alive in 1938. • *Latimeria chalumnae*, family Latimeriidae (or Coelacanthidae), subclass Crossopterygii. ▷mid 19th cent.: from modern Latin *Coelacanthus* (genus name), from Greek *koilos* 'hollow' + *akantha* 'spine' (because its fins have hollow spines).

-coele (also **-cele**) ▸*comb. form Medicine* denoting a swelling or hernia in a specified part: *meningocele.* ▷from Greek *kēlē* 'tumor.'

coe·len·ter·ate /si'lentəˌrāt; -rət/ ▸n. *Zoology* an aquatic invertebrate animal of a phylum that includes jellyfishes, corals, and sea anemones. They are distinguished by having a tube- or cup-shaped body and a single opening ringed with tentacles. Also called **CNIDARIAN**. • Phylum Cnidaria (formerly Coelenterata): four classes. ▷late 19th cent.: from modern Latin *Coelenterata*, from Greek *koilos* 'hollow' + *enteron* 'intestine.'

coe·len·ter·on /si'lentəˌrän/ ▸n. (pl. **-ter·a** /-tərə/) the central gastric cavity of a coelenterate.

coe·li·ac ▸n. British spelling of **CELIAC**.

coe·lom /'sēləm/ (also **ce·lom**) ▸n. (pl. **coe·loms** or **coe·lom·a·ta** /si'lōmətə/) *Zoology* the body cavity in metazoans, located between the intestinal canal and the body wall. ▷late 19th cent.: from Greek *koilōma* 'cavity.' **—coe·lo·mate** /'sēləˌmāt/ *adj.* & *n.*

coe·lo·stat /'sēləˌstat/ ▸n. *Astronomy* an advanced version of a heliostat, having a rotating mirror that continuously reflects the light from the same area of sky, allowing the path of a celestial object to be monitored. ▷late 19th cent.: formed irregularly from Latin *caelum* 'sky' + **-STAT**.

coe·lur·o·saur /si'lŏŏrəˌsôr; sē-/ (also **coe·lur·o·sau·rus** /siˌlŏŏrə'sôrəs/) ▸n. a small, slender, bipedal, carnivorous dinosaur with long forelimbs, from which the birds are believed to have evolved. • Infraorder Coelurosauria, suborder Theropoda, order Saurischia: many genera. ▷1950s: from Greek *koilos* 'hollow' + *oura* 'tail' + *sauros* 'lizard.' **—coe·lur·o·sau·ri·an** /-ˌlŏŏrə'sôrēən/ *adj.*

coe·no·bite ▸n. *chiefly Brit.* variant spelling of **CENOBITE**.

coe·no·cyte /'sēnəˌsīt/ ▸n. *Botany* a body of algal or fungal cytoplasm containing several nuclei enclosed in a single membrane. ▷early 20th cent.: from Greek *koinos* 'common' + **-CYTE**. **—coe·no·cyt·ic** /ˌsēnə'sitik/ *adj.*

co·en·zyme /kō'enˌzīm/ ▸n. *Biochemistry* a nonprotein compound that is necessary for the functioning of an enzyme.

co·en·zyme A ▸n. *Biochemistry* a coenzyme derived from pantothenic acid, important in respiration and many other biochemical reactions. ▷*A* from *acylation* (see **ACYLATE**).

co·en·zyme Q ▸n. another term for **UBIQUINONE**. ▷*Q* from **QUINONE**.

co·e·qual /kō'ēkwəl/ ▸adj. equal with one another; having the same rank or importance: *coequal partners.*

▸n. a person or thing equal with another. ▷late Middle English: from Latin *coaequalis* 'of the same age,' from *co-* 'jointly' + *aequalis* (see **EQUAL**). **—co·e·qual·i·ty** /ˌkō-i'kwälitē/ *n.*

co·erce /kō'ərs/ ▸v. [*trans.*] persuade (an unwilling person) to do something by using force or threats: *they were* ***coerced into*** *silence.* See note at **COMPEL**. ■ obtain (something) by such means: *their confessions were allegedly coerced by torture.* ▷late Middle English: from Latin *coercere* 'restrain,' from *co-* 'jointly, together' + *arcere* 'restrain.' **—co·er·ci·ble** *adj.* **—co·er·cion** /kō'ərZHən; -SHən/ *n.*

co·er·cive /kō'ərsiv/ ▸adj. relating to or using force or threats: *coercive measures.* **—co·er·cive·ly** *adv.* **—co·er·cive·ness** *n.*

co·er·cive force ▸n. *Physics* another term for **COERCIVITY**.

co·er·civ·i·ty /ˌkōər'sivitē/ ▸n. *Physics* the resistance of a magnetic material to changes in magnetization. ■ the field intensity necessary to demagnetize it when fully magnetized.

co·es·sen·tial /ˌkō-i'senSHəl/ ▸adj. united or inseparable in essence or being. ■ having the same substance or essence. **—co·es·sen·ti·al·i·ty** /kōiˌsenSHē'alitē/ *n.* **—co·es·sen·tial·ly** *adv.* **—co·es·sen·tial·ness** *n.*

co·e·ta·ne·ous /ˌkō-i'tānēəs/ ▸adj. another term for **COEVAL**.

co·e·ter·nal /ˌkō-i'tərnl/ ▸adj. equally eternal; existing with something else eternally: *creation is not* ***coeternal with*** *God.* **—co·e·ter·nal·ly** *adv.*

Coet·zee /kŏŏt'sēə/, J. M. (1940–), South African novelist; full name *John Maxwell Coetzee.* Notable works: *In the Heart of the Country* (1977), *Life and Times of Michael K* (1983), *White Writing* (1988), and *Age of Iron* (1990). Nobel Prize for Literature (2003).

Coeur d'Alene /ˌkôr dl'ān/ a commercial and resort city in northwestern Idaho, on Coeur d'Alene Lake, which is fed by the Coeur d'Alene River; pop. 34,514.

co·e·val /kō'ēvəl/ ▸adj. having the same age or date of origin; contemporary: *these lavas were* ***coeval with*** *the volcanic activity.*

▸n. a person of roughly the same age as oneself; a contemporary: *like so many of his coevals, he yearned for stability.* ▷early 17th cent. (as a noun): from late Latin *coaevus*, from *co-* 'jointly, in common' + Latin *aevum* 'age.' **—co·e·val·i·ty** /ˌkō-ē'valitē/ *n.* **—co·e·val·ly** *adv.*

co·ev·o·lu·tion /ˌkōevə'lŏŏSHən; -ēvə-/ ▸n. *Biology* the influence of closely associated species on each other in their evolution. **—co·ev·o·lu·tion·ar·y** /-SHəˌnerē/ *adj.* **—co·e·volve** /ˌkō-i'välv/ *v.*

co·ex·ist /ˌkō-ig'zist/ ▸v. [*intrans.*] exist at the same time or in the same place: *traditional and modern values coexist in Africa.* ■ (of nations or peoples) exist in mutual tolerance despite different ideologies or interests: *the task of diplomacy was to help different states to coexist.* ▷mid 17th cent.: from late Latin *coexistere*, from *co-* 'together' + *existere* 'exist,' from *ex-* 'out' + *sistere* 'take a stand.' **—co·ex·ist·ence** /-'zistəns/ *n.* **—co·ex·ist·ent** /-'zistənt/ *adj.*

co·ex·tend /ˌkō-ik'stend/ ▸v. extend equally through the same space or period of time.

co·ex·ten·sive /ˌkō-ik'stensiv/ ▸adj. extending over the same space or time; corresponding exactly in extent: *the Caliphate, a Muslim state more or less* ***coextensive with*** *the Muslim world of its day.* ■ (of a term) denoting the same referent as another.

co·fac·tor /'kōˌfaktər/ ▸n. **1** a contributory cause of a disease. **2** *Biochemistry* a substance (other than the substrate) whose presence is essential for the activity of an enzyme. **3** *Mathematics* the quantity obtained from a determinant or a square matrix by removal of the row and column containing a specified element.

C. of C. ▸abbr. Chamber of Commerce.

C. of E. ▸abbr. Church of England.

cof·fee /'kôfē; 'käfē/ ▸n. **1** a drink made from the roasted and ground beanlike seeds of a tropical shrub, served hot or iced: *a cup of coffee* | [as *adj.*] *a coffee pot.* ■ a cup of this drink: *she'll buy you a coffee.* ■ these seeds raw, roasted and ground, or processed into a powder that dissolves in hot water: *a jar of instant coffee.* ■ a pale brown color like that of coffee mixed with milk. ■ a party or reception at which coffee is served: *going to coffees and answering questions.* **2** the shrub of the bedstraw family that yields these seeds, two of which are contained in each red berry. Native to the Old World tropics, most coffee is grown in tropical America. • Genus *Coffea*, family Rubiaceae: several species. See also **ARABICA** and **ROBUSTA**. ▷late 16th cent.: from Turkish *kahveh*, from Arabic *ḳahwa*, probably via Dutch *koffie*.

cof·fee bar ▸n. a bar or cafe serving coffee and light refreshments.

cof·fee bean ▸n. a beanlike seed of the coffee shrub.

cof·fee cake ▸n. a cake often cinnamon-flavored, with a drizzled white icing or crumb topping, and usually eaten with coffee.

cof·fee grind·er ▸n. a small machine for grinding roasted coffee beans.

cof·fee·house /'kôfēˌhous; 'käfē-/ ▸n. a place where coffee is served and people gather for conversation, music, poetry readings, and other informal entertainment.

cof·fee klatsch (also **cof·fee klatch**) ▸n. variant spelling of **KAFFEEKLATSCH**.

cof·fee mak·er (also **cof·fee·mak·er**) ▸n. a machine or pot for brewing coffee.

cof·fee mill ▸*n.* another term for COFFEE GRINDER.
cof·fee pot ▸*n.* a covered container with a spout, in which coffee is made or served.
cof·fee shop ▸*n.* a small, informal restaurant, as may be found in a hotel. ■ a shop serving coffee and light refreshments.
cof·fee ta·ble ▸*n.* a low table, typically placed in front of a sofa.
cof·fee-ta·ble book ▸*n.* a large, expensive, lavishly illustrated book, esp. one intended only for casual reading.
cof·fer /ˈkôfər; ˈkäfər/ ▸*n.* **1** a strongbox or small chest for holding valuables. ■ (**coffers**) the funds or financial reserves of a group or institution: *the federal government's empty coffers.* **2** a recessed panel in a ceiling. ▷Middle English: from Old French *coffre* 'chest,' via Latin from Greek *kophinos* 'basket.' **—cof·fered** *adj.* (in sense 2).
cof·fer·dam /ˈkôfərˌdam; ˈkäfərˌdam/ ▸*n.* a watertight enclosure pumped dry to permit construction work below the waterline, as when building bridges or repairing a ship.
Cof·fin /ˈkôfən; ˈkäf-/, William Sloan (1924–), U.S. Presbyterian minister. As Yale University chaplain 1958–75, he was a leader of antiwar protests. He served as senior minister of Riverside Church in New York 1977–1987.
cof·fin /ˈkôfən; ˈkäfən/ ▸*n.* a long, narrow box, typically of wood, in which a corpse is buried or cremated. ■ *informal* an old and unsafe aircraft or vessel. ▸*v.* (**-fined, -fin·ing**) [*trans.*] put (a dead body) in a coffin. ▷Middle English (in the general sense 'box, chest, casket'): from Old French *cofin* 'little basket or case,' from Latin *cophinus* (see COFFER).
cof·fin bone ▸*n.* the terminal bone in a horse's hoof (the distal phalanx).
cof·fin joint ▸*n.* the joint at the top of a horse's hoof.
cof·fin nail ▸*n. informal* a cigarette.
cof·fle /ˈkôfəl; ˈkäfəl/ ▸*n.* a line of animals or slaves fastened or driven along together. ▷mid 18th cent.: from Arabic *ḳāfila* 'caravan.'
co·found·er /ˈkōˈfoundər; ˈkōˌfoun-/ ▸*n.* a joint founder. **—co·found** /kōˈfound/ *v.*
co·func·tion /ˈkōˌfəNGkSHən/ ▸*n. Mathematics* the trigonometric function of the complement of an angle or arc.
cog /käg/ ▸*n.* a wheel or bar with a series of projections on its edge that transfers motion by engaging with projections on another wheel or bar: *figurative she was only a very small cog in a big machine.* ■ each of such a series of projections. ▷Middle English: probably of Scandinavian origin and related to Swedish *kugge* and Norwegian *kug.* **—cogged** *adj.*
co·gen·er·a·tion /ˌkōˌjenəˈrāSHən/ ▸*n.* the generation of electricity and other energy jointly, esp. the utilization of the steam left over from electricity generation to produce heat.
co·gent /ˈkōjənt/ ▸*adj.* (of an argument or case) clear, logical, and convincing. See note at BELIEVABLE. ▷mid 17th cent.: from Latin *cogent-* 'compelling,' from the verb *cogere,* from *co-* 'together' + *agere* 'drive.' **—co·gen·cy** *n.* **—co·gent·ly** *adv.*
cog·i·ta·ble /ˈkäjətəbəl/ ▸*adj. rare* able to be grasped by the mind; conceivable. ▷late Middle English: from Latin *cogitabilis,* from the verb *cogitare* (see COGITATE).
cog·i·tate /ˈkäjəˌtāt/ ▸*v.* [*intrans.*] *formal* or *humorous* think deeply about something; meditate or reflect: *he stroked his beard and retired to cogitate.* ▷late 16th cent.: from Latin *cogitat-* 'considered,' from the verb *cogitare,* from *co-* 'together' + *agitare* 'turn over, consider.' **—cog·i·ta·tion** /ˌkäjəˈtāSHən/ *n.* **—cog·i·ta·tive** /-ˌtātiv/ *adj.* **—cog·i·ta·tor** /-ˌtātər/ *n.*
co·gi·to /ˈkägiˌtō; ˈkāj-/ ▸*n.* (usu. **the cogito**) *Philosophy* the principle establishing the existence of a being from the fact of its thinking or awareness. ▷mid 19th cent.: Latin, literally 'I think,' in Descartes's formula (1641) *cogito, ergo sum* 'I think therefore I am.'
co·gnac /ˈkōnˌyak; ˈkän-; ˈkôn-/ ▸*n.* a high-quality brandy, properly that distilled in Cognac in western France.
cog·nate /ˈkägˌnāt/ ▸*adj.* **1** *Linguistics* (of a word) having the same linguistic derivation as another; from the same original word or root (e.g., English *is,* German *ist,* Latin *est* from Indo-European *esti*). **2** *formal* related; connected: *cognate subjects such as physics and chemistry.* ■ related to or descended from a common ancestor. Compare with AGNATE. ▸*n.* **1** *Linguistics* a cognate word. **2** *Law* a blood relative. ▷early 17th cent.: from Latin *cognatus,* from *co-* 'together with' + *natus* 'born.' **—cog·nate·ly** *adv.* **—cog·nate·ness** *n.*
cog·nate ob·ject ▸*n. Grammar* a direct object that has the same linguistic derivation as the verb that governs it, as in "sing a song," "live a good life." ■ a direct object that makes explicit a semantic concept that is already wholly present in the semantics of the verb which governs it, as in "ask a question," "eat some food."
cog·ni·tion /ˌkägˈniSHən/ ▸*n.* the mental action or process of acquiring knowledge and understanding through thought, experience, and the senses. ■ a result of this; a perception, sensation, notion, or intuition. ▷late Middle English: from Latin *cognitio(n-),* from *cognoscere* 'get to know.' **—cog·ni·tion·al** /-SHənl/ *adj.*
cog·ni·tive /ˈkägnətiv/ ▸*adj.* of or relating to cognition. ▷late 16th cent.: from medieval Latin *cognitivus,* from *cognit-* 'known,' from the verb *cognoscere.* **—cog·ni·tive·ly** *adv.*
cog·ni·tive dis·so·nance ▸*n. Psychology* the state of having inconsistent thoughts, beliefs, or attitudes, esp. as relating to behavioral decisions and attitude change.
cog·ni·tive gram·mar ▸*n.* a theory of language that seeks to characterize knowledge of grammar in terms of symbolic conceptual and semantic categories and general cognitive processes.
cog·ni·tive map ▸*n.* a mental representation of one's physical environment.
cog·ni·tive pros·the·sis ▸*n.* an electronic computational device that extends the capability of human cognition or sense perception.
cog·ni·tive sci·ence ▸*n.* the study of thought, learning, and mental organization, which draws on aspects of psychology, linguistics, philosophy, and computer modeling. **—cog·ni·tive sci·en·tist** *n.*
cog·ni·tive ther·a·py ▸*n.* a type of psychotherapy in which negative patterns of thought about the self and the world are challenged in order to alter unwanted behavior patterns or treat mood disorders such as depression.
cog·ni·tiv·ist /ˈkägnətivist/ ▸*n.* a person who believes or works in cognitive grammar. ▸*adj.* of or relating to cognitive grammar. ▷1950s (in the sense 'believing that moral judgments are true or false statements about moral facts'): from COGNITIVE + -IST. **—cog·ni·tiv·ism** /-ˌvizəm/ *n.*
cog·ni·za·ble /ˈkägnəzəbəl; kägˈnīz-/ ▸*adj.* **1** *formal* perceptible; clearly identifiable. **2** *Law* within the jurisdiction of a court. ▷late 17th cent.: from COGNIZANCE + -ABLE.
cog·ni·zance /ˈkägnəzəns/ (also **cog·ni·sance**) ▸*n.* **1** *formal* knowledge, awareness, or notice: *he was deputed to bring the affair to the cognizance of the court.* ■ *Law* the action of taking jurisdiction. ■ the action of taking judicial notice (of a fact beyond dispute). **2** *Heraldry* a distinctive device or mark, esp. an emblem or badge formerly worn by retainers of a noble house. ▷Middle English *conisance,* from Old French *conoisance,* based on Latin *cognoscere* 'get to know.' The spelling with g, influenced by Latin, arose in the 15th cent. and gradually affected the pronunciation.
▸*PHRASE* □ **take cognizance of** *formal* attend to; take account of.
cog·ni·zant /ˈkägnəzənt/ (also **cog·ni·sant**) ▸*adj.* [*predic.*] *formal* having knowledge or being aware of: *statesmen must be* ***cognizant of*** *the political boundaries within which they work* ▷early 19th cent.: probably directly from COGNIZANCE.
cog·nize /kägˈnīz; ˈkägˌnīz/ ▸*v.* [*trans.*] *formal* perceive, know, or become aware of: *what the novel cognizes, discerns, knows.* ▷early 19th cent.: from COGNIZANCE, on the pattern of words such as *recognize.*
cog·no·men /kägˈnōmən; ˈkägnəmən/ ▸*n.* an extra personal name given to an ancient Roman citizen, functioning rather like a nickname and typically passed down from father to son. ■ a name; a nickname. ▷Latin, from *co-* 'together with' + *gnomen, nomen* 'name.'
co·gno·scen·te /ˌkänyəˈSHentē; ˌkägnə-/ ▸*n.* (*pl.* **-ti** /-tē/) a connoisseur; a discerning expert.
co·gno·scen·ti /ˌkänyōˈSHentē; ˌkägnə-/ ▸*plural n.* people who are considered to be especially well informed about a particular subject: *it was hailed by* ***the cognoscenti*** *as one of the best golf courses in Europe.* ▷late 18th cent.: from Italian *conoscenti,* literally 'people who know.' The g was added under the influence of Latin *cognoscent-* 'getting to know,' from the verb *cognoscere* (Italian *conoscere*).
co·gon grass /kōˈgōn/ ▸*n.* a perennial, rhizomatous grass of Asian origin, used for thatching and as a packing material; identified as a noxious weed in much of the southeastern U.S. • *Imperata cylindrica* , family Poaceae.
cog rail·way ▸*n.* a railroad with a toothed central rail between the bearing rails that engages with a cogwheel under the locomotive, providing traction for ascending very steep slopes.
cog·wheel /ˈkägˌ(h)wēl/ ▸*n.* another term for COG.
co·hab·it /kōˈhabit/ ▸*v.* (**-hab·it·ed, -hab·it·ing**) [*intrans.*] live together and have a sexual relationship without being married. ■ coexist: *animals that can* ***cohabit with*** *humans thrive.* ▷mid 16th cent.: from Latin *cohabitare,* from *co-* 'together' + *habitare* 'dwell.' **—co·hab·it·ant** *n.* **—co·hab·i·ta·tion** /kōˌhabəˈtāSHən/ *n.* **—co·hab·it·er** *n.*
Co·han /ˈkōˌhan/, George Michael (1878–1942), U.S. composer, playwright, actor, and producer. Among his most well-known songs are "Yankee Doodle Dandy" (1904) and "Give My Regards to Broadway" (1904).
co·heir /kōˈe(ə)r/ ▸*n.* a joint heir.
co·heir·ess /kōˈe(ə)ris/ ▸*n.* a joint heiress.
co·hen ▸*n.* variant spelling of KOHEN.
co·here /kōˈhi(ə)r/ ▸*v.* [*intrans.*] **1** be united; form a whole: *our mixed physical and spiritual natures cohere and mature.* **2** (of an argument or theory) be logically consistent: *this view does not* ***cohere with*** *their other beliefs.* ▷mid 16th cent.: from Latin *cohaerere,* from *co-* 'together' + *haerere* 'to stick.'
co·her·ent /kōˈhi(ə)rənt/ ▸*adj.* **1** (of an argument, theory, or policy) logical and consistent: *they failed to develop a coherent economic strategy.* ■ (of a person) able to speak clearly and logically: *she was lucid and coherent and did not appear to be injured.* **2** united as or forming a whole: *divided into a number of geographically coherent kingdoms.* **3** *Physics* (of waves) having a constant phase relationship. ▷mid 16th cent. (in the sense 'logically related to'): from Latin *cohaerent-* 'sticking together,' from the verb *cohaerere* (see COHERE). **—co·her·ence** *n.* **—co·her·en·cy** *n.* (*rare*) **—co·her·ent·ly** *adv.*
co·he·sion /kōˈhēZHən/ ▸*n.* the action or fact of forming a united whole: *the work at present lacks cohesion.* ■ *Physics* the sticking together of particles of the same substance. ▷mid 17th cent.: from Latin *cohaes-* 'cleaved together,' from the verb *cohaerere* (see COHERE), on the pattern of *adhesion.*
co·he·sive /kōˈhēsiv; -ziv/ ▸*adj.* characterized by or causing cohesion. **—co·he·sive·ly** *adv.* **—co·he·sive·ness** *n.*
Cohn /kōn/, Ferdinand Julius (1828–98), German botanist. A founder of bacteriology, he was the first to devise a systematic classification of bacteria into genera and species.
co·ho /ˈkōhō/ (also **co·ho salmon** or **co·hoe**) ▸*n.* (*pl.* same, **-hos,** or **-hoes**) a deep-bodied North Pacific salmon with small black spots. Also called SILVER SALMON. • *Oncorhynchus kisutch,* family Salmonidae. ▷mid 19th cent.: probably from Salish *k'wəxwəϑ.*
co·hort /ˈkōˌhôrt/ ▸*n.* **1** [treated as *sing.* or *pl.*] an ancient Roman military unit, comprising six centuries, equal to one tenth of a legion. **2** [treated as *sing.* or *pl.*] a group of people banded together or treated as a group: ***a cohort of*** *civil servants patiently drafting legislation.* ■ a group of people with a common statistical characteristic: *the 1940–44 birth cohort of women.* **3** a supporter or companion. ■ an accomplice or conspirator: *his three cohorts each had pled guilty.* ▷late Middle English: from Old French *cohorte,* or from Latin *cohors, cohort-* 'yard, retinue.' Compare with COURT.

USAGE The *co-* in **cohort** is not a prefix signifying a joint or auxiliary relationship (as in *coauthor* or *codependency*). The word derives from the Latin *cohors,* an ancient Roman military unit, and also 'band of people with a common interest.' In the mid 20th century a new sense developed in the U.S., meaning 'a companion or colleague,' as in *young Jack arrived with three of his cohorts.* Although this use is well established, there are still some people who object to it on the grounds that **cohort** should only be used for groups of people, never for individuals. The use of **cohort** to refer to a group of people with a common characteristic, as in a demographic context (*the 1946–60 birth cohort*), is generally considered acceptable.

co·hosh /ˈkōˌhäSH/ ▸*n.* either of two medicinal plants native to North America: • (also **black cohosh**) a plant of the buttercup family, with small white flowers (*Cimicifuga racemosa,* family Ranunculaceae).

• (also **blue cohosh**) a plant of the barberry family (*Caulophyllum thalictroides*, family Berberidaceae). ▷late 18th cent.: from Eastern Abnaki.

co·host /ˈkō,hōst/ ▶*n.* a joint host.
▶*v.* [*trans.*] act as a joint host.

co·hune /kəˈho͞on; kō-/ (also **ca·houn**) ▶*n.* a Central American palm that is a valuable source of oil. • *Orbignya cohune*, family Palmae. ■ (also **cohune nut**) the oil-rich nut of this palm. ▷mid 18th cent.: from Miskito.

coif ▶*n.* **1** /koif/ a woman's close-fitting cap, now only worn under a veil by nuns. ■ *historical* a protective metal skullcap worn under armor. **2** /kwäf; koif/ *informal* short for **COIFFURE**.
▶*v.* /kwäf; koif/ (**coiffed, coif·fing**; also **coifed, coif·ing**) [*trans.*] style or arrange (someone's hair), typically in an elaborate way: [as *adj.*] (**coiffed**) *her elaborately coiffed hair.* ■ style or arrange the hair of (someone): *she was sent to Paris to be groomed and coiffed.* ▷Middle English: from Old French *coife* 'headdress,' from late Latin *cofia* 'helmet.'

coif·feur /kwäˈfər/ ▶*n.* a hairdresser. ▷mid 19th cent.: French, from *coiffer* 'arrange the hair,' in Old French 'cover with a coif' (see **COIF**).

coif·feuse /kwäˈf(y)o͞oz; -ˈfə(r)z/ ▶*n.* a female hairdresser.

coif·fure /kwäˈfyo͝or/ ▶*n.* a person's hairstyle, typically an elaborate one. ▷mid 17th cent.: French, from *coiffer* 'arrange the hair,' in Old French 'cover with a coif' (see **COIF**). **—coif·fured** *adj.*

coign /koin/ ▶*n.* a projecting corner or angle of a wall or building. ▷late Middle English: variant of **COIN**. The phrase *coign of vantage* was first used by Shakespeare (*Macbeth* I. iv. 7), and later popularized by Sir Walter Scott.
▶*PHRASE* □ **coign of vantage** a favorable position for observation or action.

coil[1] /koil/ ▶*n.* a length of something wound or arranged in a spiral or sequence of rings: *a coil of rope.* ■ a single ring or loop in such a sequence: *the snake wrapped its coils around her.* ■ a roll of postage stamps, esp. one for use in a vending machine. ■ a slow-burning spiral made with the dried paste of pyrethrum powder, which produces a smoke that inhibits mosquitoes from biting. ■ (often **the coil**) an intrauterine contraceptive device in the form of a coil. ■ an electrical device consisting of a length of wire arranged in a coil for converting the level of a voltage, producing a magnetic field, or adding inductance to a circuit: *a relay coil.* ■ such a device used for transmitting high voltage to the spark plugs of an internal combustion engine. ■ a length of wire or piping wound in circles or spirals.
▶*v.* [*trans.*] arrange or wind (something long and flexible) in a joined sequence of concentric circles or rings: *he began to* **coil up** *the heavy ropes* | *he* **coiled** *a lock of her hair* **around** *his finger.* ■ [*intrans.*] move or twist into such an arrangement or shape: *smoke coiled lazily toward the ceiling.* ▷early 16th cent. (as a verb): from Old French *coillir*, from Latin *colligere* 'gather together' (see **COLLECT**[1]).

coil[2] ▶*n. archaic* or *dialect* a confusion or turmoil. ▷mid 16th cent.: of unknown origin.
▶*PHRASE* □ **shuffle off this mortal coil** *chiefly humorous* die. [from Shakespeare's *Hamlet* (III. i. 67).]

coil spring ▶*n.* a helical spring made from metal wire or a metal band.

Co·im·ba·tore /ˈkōimbə,to͝or/ a city in southern India, in the state of Tamil Nadu; pop. 853,000.

coin /koin/ ▶*n.* a flat, typically round piece of metal with an official stamp, used as money. ■ money in the form of coins: *large amounts of coin and precious metal.* ■ *informal* money: *he showed me how we could make a lot of coin.* ■ (**coins**) one of the suits in some tarot packs, corresponding to pentacles in others.
▶*v.* [*trans.*] **1** make (coins) by stamping metal. ■ make (metal) into coins. **2** invent or devise (a new word or phrase): *he coined the term "desktop publishing."* ▷Middle English: from Old French *coin* 'wedge, corner, die,' *coigner* 'to mint,' from Latin *cuneus* 'wedge.' The original sense was 'cornerstone,' later 'angle or wedge' (senses now spelled **QUOIN**); in late Middle English the term denoted a die for stamping money, or a piece of money produced by such a die.
▶*PHRASES* □ **the other side of the coin** the opposite or contrasting aspect of a matter. □ **pay someone back in his or her own coin** retaliate with similar behavior. □ **to coin a phrase** said ironically when introducing a banal remark or cliché: *I had to find out the hard way—to coin a phrase.* ■ said when introducing a new expression or a variation on a familiar one.

coin·age /ˈkoinij/ ▶*n.* **1** coins collectively: *the volume of coinage in circulation.* ■ the action or process of producing coins from metal. ■ a system or type of coins in use: *decimal coinage.* **2** the invention of a new word or phrase. ■ a newly invented word or phrase. ▷late Middle English: from Old French *coigniage*, from *coignier* 'to mint' (see **COIN**).

co·in·cide /,kōənˈsīd; ˈkōən,sīd/ ▶*v.* [*intrans.*] occur at or during the same time: *publication is timed to* **coincide with** *a major exhibition* | *the two events coincided.* ■ correspond in nature; tally: *the interests of employers and employees do not always coincide.* ■ correspond in position; meet or intersect: *the two long-distance walks briefly coincide here.* ■ be in agreement: *the members of the College* **coincide in** *this opinion.* ▷early 18th cent. (in the sense 'occupy the same space'): from medieval Latin *coincidere*, from *co-* 'together with' + *incidere* 'fall upon or into.'

co·in·ci·dence /kōˈinsədəns; -,dens/ ▶*n.* **1** a remarkable concurrence of events or circumstances without apparent causal connection: *it's no coincidence that this new burst of innovation has occurred in the free nations* | *they met* **by coincidence***.* **2** correspondence in nature or in time of occurrence: *the coincidence of interest between the mining companies and certain politicians.* **3** *Physics* the presence of ionizing particles or other objects in two or more detectors simultaneously, or of two or more signals simultaneously in a circuit. ▷early 17th cent. (in the sense 'occupation of the same space'): from medieval Latin *coincidentia*, from *coincidere* 'coincide, agree' (see **COINCIDE**). Sense 3 dates from the 1930s.

co·in·ci·dent /kōˈinsədənt; -,dent/ ▶*adj.* occurring together in space or time: *liberty is an idea* **coincident with** *the spread of Christianity.* ■ in agreement or harmony: *the stake of defense attorneys is not always* **coincident with** *that of their clients.* ▷mid 16th cent.: from medieval Latin *coincident-* 'coinciding, agreeing,' from the verb *coincidere* (see **COINCIDE**). **—co·in·ci·dent·ly** /kō,insəˈdentlē/ *adv.*

co·in·ci·den·tal /kō,insəˈdentl/ ▶*adj.* **1** resulting from a coincidence; done or happening by chance: *any resemblance between their reports is purely coincidental* | *it cannot be* **coincidental that** *these years were a time of important new developments.* **2** happening or existing at the same time: *it's convenient that his plan is* **coincidental with** *the group's closure.* **—co·in·ci·den·tal·ly** /kō,insəˈdentlē; -ˈdentl-ē/ *adv.* [*sentence adverb*] *coincidentally, we had both left our previous jobs on the same day.*

coin·er /ˈkoinər/ ▶*n.* **1** *historical* a person who coins money, in particular a maker of counterfeit coins. **2** a person who invents or devises a new word, sense, or phrase.

coin-op·er·at·ed (also **coin-op**) ▶*adj.* operated by inserting coins in a slot: *coin-operated telephones.*
▶*n.* a machine that is coin-operated.

co·in·sur·ance ▶*n.* a type of insurance in which the insured pays a share of the payment made against a claim.

Coin·treau /kwänˈtrō/ ▶*n. trademark* a colorless orange-flavored liqueur. ▷named after the *Cointreau* family, liqueur producers based in Angers, France.

coir /ˈkoi(ə)r/ ▶*n.* fiber from the outer husk of the coconut, used for making ropes and matting. ▷late 16th cent.: from Malayalam *kayaṟu* 'cord, coir.'

co·i·tion /kōˈisнən/ ▶*n.* another term for **COITUS**. ▷mid 16th cent. (in the sense 'meeting or uniting'): from Latin *coitio(n-)*, from the verb *coire*, from *co-* 'together' + *ire* 'go.'

co·i·tus /ˈkōətəs; kōˈētəs/ ▶*n. formal* sexual intercourse. ▷mid 19th cent.: from Latin, from *coire* 'go together' (see **COITION**). **—co·i·tal** /ˈkōətl; kōˈētl/ *adj.*

co·i·tus in·ter·rup·tus /intəˈrəptəs/ ▶*n.* sexual intercourse in which the penis is withdrawn before ejaculation. ▷from **COITUS** + Latin *interruptus* 'interrupted.'

co·i·tus re·ser·va·tus /,rezərˈvätəs; -ˈvätəs/ ▶*n.* the postponement or avoidance of ejaculation, to prolong sexual intercourse. ▷from **COITUS** + Latin *reservatus* 'reserved, kept.'

co·jo·nes /kəˈhō,näz; -,näs/ ▶*plural n. informal* a man's testicles. ■ *figurative* courage; guts: *he does not have the cojones to kill a flea.* ▷Spanish.

coke[1] /kōk/ ▶*n.* a solid fuel made by heating coal in the absence of air so that the volatile components are driven off. ■ carbon residue left after the incomplete combustion of gasoline or other fuels.
▶*v.* [*trans.*] [usu. as *n.*] (**coking**) convert (coal) into coke. ▷late Middle English (in the sense 'charcoal'): of unknown origin. The current sense dates from the mid 17th cent.

coke[2] ▶*n.* informal term for **COCAINE**. ▷early 20th cent.: abbreviation.

Coke-bot·tle ▶*n.* [as *adj.*] *informal* denoting very thick lenses for glasses or glasses with such lenses.

coked /kōkt/ ▶*adj. informal* having taken a large amount of cocaine: *a druggie coked so far out of his mind that he'd torn the furniture apart.*

col /käl/ ▶*n.* the lowest point of a ridge or saddle between two peaks, typically affording a pass from one side of a mountain range to another. ■ *Meteorology* a region of slightly elevated pressure between two anticyclones. ▷mid 19th cent.: from French, literally 'neck,' from Latin *collum*.

Col. ▶*abbr.* ■ colonel. ■ *Bible* Colossians.

col. ▶*abbr.* ■ collected. ■ college. ■ colony. ■ column.

col- ▶*prefix* variant spelling of **COM-** assimilated before *l* (as in *collocate, collude*).

COLA ▶*abbr.* cost-of-living adjustment, an increase made to wages or Social Security benefits to keep them in line with inflation.

co·la /ˈkōlə/ ▶*n.* **1** a brown carbonated drink that is flavored with an extract of cola nuts, or with a similar flavoring. [shortening of **COCA-COLA**.] **2** (also **ko·la**) a small evergreen African tree that is cultivated in the tropics for its seeds (cola nuts). [from Temne *k'ola* 'cola nut.'] • Genus *Cola*, family Sterculiaceae: several species, in particular *C. acuminata*.

col·an·der /ˈkələndər; ˈkäl-/ ▶*n.* a perforated bowl used to strain off liquid from food, esp. after cooking. ▷Middle English: based on Latin *colare* 'to strain.'

co·la nut (also **kola nut**) ▶*n.* the seed of the cola tree, which contains caffeine and is chewed or made into a drink.

co·lat·i·tude /kōˈlatə,t(y)o͞od/ ▶*n. Astronomy* the complement of the latitude; the difference between latitude and 90°.

col·can·non /kälˈkanən/ ▶*n.* an Irish and Scottish dish of cabbage and potatoes boiled and pounded. ▷late 18th cent.: from **COLE**; the origin of the second element is uncertain but it is said that cannonballs were used to pound such vegetables as spinach.

col·chi·cine /ˈkälcнə,sēn; ˈkälkə-/ ▶*n. Chemistry* a yellow compound present in the corms of colchicums, used to relieve pain in cases of gout. • An alkaloid; chem. formula: $C_{22}H_{25}NO_6$.

col·chi·cum /ˈkälcнikəm; ˈkälki-/ ▶*n.* (*pl.* **-cums**) a plant of a genus that includes the autumn crocuses. • Genus *Colchicum*, family Liliaceae. ■ the dried corm or seed of meadow saffron, which has analgesic properties and is used medicinally, esp. as a tincture. ▷from Latin, from Greek *kolkhikon* 'of Colchis' (see **COLCHIS**), alluding to the skills as a poisoner of the sorceress Medea of Colchis in classical mythology.

Col·chis /ˈkälkis/ an ancient region south of the Caucasus Mountains at the eastern end of the Black Sea. In classical mythology it was the goal of Jason's expedition for the Golden Fleece. Greek name **KOLKHIS**.

cold /kōld/ ▶*adj.* **1** of or at a low or relatively low temperature, esp. when compared with the human body: *a freezing cold day* | *it's cold outside* | *a sharp, cold wind.* ■ (of food or drink) served or consumed without being heated or after cooling: *a cold drink* | *serve hot or cold.* ■ (of an engine) not having been warmed up properly. ■ (of a person) feeling uncomfortably cold: *she was cold, and I put some more wood on the fire.* ■ feeling or characterized by fear or horror: *he suddenly went cold with a dreadful certainty* | *a cold shiver of fear.* ■ *informal* unconscious: *she was* **out cold***.* ■ dead: *lying cold and stiff in a coffin.* **2** lacking affection or warmth of feeling; unemotional: *how cold and calculating he was* | *cold black eyes* | *cold politeness.* ■ not affected by emotion; objective: *cold statistics.* ■ sexually unresponsive; frigid. ■ depressing or dispiriting; not suggestive of warmth: *the cold, impersonal barrack-room* | *a cold light streamed through the window.* ■ (of a color) containing pale blue or gray. ■ ineffective in playing a game: *Butler capitalized on Xavier's cold shooting.* **3** (of the scent or trail of a hunted person or animal) no longer fresh and easy to follow: *the trail went cold.* ■ (in children's games) far from finding or guessing what is sought, as opposed to warm or nearing success. **4** without preparation or rehearsal; unawares: *going into the test cold.*
▶*n.* **1** a low temperature, esp. in the atmosphere;

cold weather; a cold environment: *my teeth chattered with **the cold** | they nearly died **of cold**.* **2** a common viral infection in which the mucous membrane of the nose and throat becomes inflamed, typically causing running at the nose, sneezing, a sore throat, and other similar symptoms.
▸*adv. informal* completely; entirely: *she knew world capitals cold by age nine.* ▷Old English *cald*, of Germanic origin; related to Dutch *koud* and German *kalt*, also to Latin *gelu* 'frost.' **—cold·ish** /ˈkōldisн/ *adj.* **—cold·ness** /ˈkōl(d)nəs/ *n.*
▸*PHRASES* □ **as cold as ice** (or **stone** or **the grave**, etc.) very cold. □ **catch** (or **take**) **cold** become infected with a cold. □ **cold comfort** poor or inadequate consolation: *another drop in the inflation rate was cold comfort for the 2.74 million jobless.* □ **cold feet** loss of nerve or confidence: *some investors **got cold feet** and backed out.* □ **the cold light of day** the objective realities of a situation: ***in the cold light of day** it all seemed so ridiculous.* □ **the cold shoulder** a show of intentional unfriendliness; rejection: *why is even his own family **giving** him **the cold shoulder**?* □ **cold-shoulder someone** reject or be deliberately unfriendly to someone. □ **down cold** see DOWN[1]. □ **in cold blood** without feeling or mercy; ruthlessly: *the government forces killed them in cold blood.* □ **out in the cold** ignored; neglected: *the talks **left** the French **out in the cold**.* □ **throw** (or **pour**) **cold water on** be discouraging or negative about.

cold-blood·ed ▸*adj.* **1** (of a kind of animal) having a body temperature varying with that of the environment; poikilothermic. **2** without emotion or pity; deliberately cruel or callous: *a cold-blooded murder.* **—cold-blood·ed·ly** *adv.* **—cold-blood·ed·ness** *n.*

cold-call ▸*v.* [*trans.*] make an unsolicited call on (someone), by telephone or in person, in an attempt to sell goods or services: [as *n.*] (**cold-calling**) *severe new regulations against cold-calling.*
▸*n.* (**cold call**) an unsolicited call of this kind.

cold cash ▸*n.* another term for HARD CASH.

cold cath·ode ▸*n. Electronics* a cathode that emits electrons without being heated.

cold chis·el ▸*n.* a chisel used for cutting metal.

cold cream ▸*n.* a cosmetic preparation used for cleansing and softening the skin.

cold cuts /ˈkōld ˌkəts/ ▸*plural n.* slices of cold cooked or processed meats. See LUNCHMEAT.

cold dark mat·ter (abbr.: **CDM**) ▸*n.* see DARK MATTER.

cold deck ▸*n.* **1** *informal* a deck of cards that has been dishonestly arranged beforehand. **2** a pile of logs stored away from the immediate area where logging is taking place.

cold-drawn ▸*adj.* (of metal) drawn out into a wire or bar while cold. **—cold-draw·ing** *n.*

cold duck ▸*n.* a type of sparkling wine made from burgundy and champagne.

cold frame ▸*n.* a four-sided frame of boards with a removable glass or plastic top. The frame is placed on the ground and is used to house, protect, and harden off seedlings and small plants, without artificial heat.

cold front ▸*n. Meteorology* the boundary of an advancing mass of cold air, in particular the trailing edge of the warm sector of a low-pressure system.

cold fu·sion ▸*n.* nuclear fusion occurring at or close to room temperature. Claims for its discovery in 1989 are generally held to have been mistaken.

cold-heart·ed ▸*adj.* lacking affection or warmth; unfeeling. **—cold-heart·ed·ly** *adv.* **—cold-heart·ed·ness** *n.*

cold light ▸*n. Physics* light accompanied by little or no heat; luminescence.

cold·ly /ˈkōldlē/ ▸*adv.* without affection or warmth of feeling; unemotionally: *Derek looked at her coldly | a coldly contemptuous tone.*

cold-mold·ed ▸*adj.* (of an object) molded from a resin that hardens without being heated. **—cold-mold·ing** *n.*

cold-rolled ▸*adj. Metallurgy* (of metal) having been rolled into sheets while cold, resulting in a smooth hard finish. **—cold-roll·ing** *n.*

cold snap ▸*n.* a sudden, brief spell of cold weather.

cold sore ▸*n.* an inflamed blister in or near the mouth, caused by infection with the herpes simplex virus.

Cold Spring Harbor a village on the north shore of Long Island in New York, in the town of Huntington, noted as a center for biological research; pop. 4,789.

cold stor·age ▸*n.* the keeping of something in a refrigerator or other cold place for preservation. ■ *figurative* the temporary postponement of something: *the project went **into cold storage**.*

cold store ▸*n.* a large refrigerated room for preserving food stocks at very low temperatures.

cold sweat ▸*n.* a state of sweating induced by fear, nervousness, or illness: *he used to **break into a cold sweat** when he was called on in class.*

cold tur·key *informal* ▸*n.* the abrupt and complete cessation of taking a drug to which one is addicted: *cold turkey, with no medication, is not recommended for those with medical conditions.*
▸*adv.* in a sudden and abrupt manner: *many banks have cut commercial builders off cold turkey.*

cold war ▸*n.* a state of political hostility existing between countries, characterized by threats, violent propaganda, subversive activities, and other measures short of open warfare, in particular: ■ (**the Cold War**) the state of political hostility that existed between the Soviet bloc countries and the U.S.-led Western powers from 1945 to 1990.

cold wave ▸*n.* **1** a spell of cold weather over a wide area. **2** a kind of permanent wave for the hair created by applying chemicals at room temperature.

cold-weld ▸*v.* [*trans.*] join (a piece of metal) to another without the use of heat, by forcing them together so hard that the surface oxide films are disrupted and adhesion occurs.

cold-work ▸*v.* [*trans.*] shape (metal) while it is cold.
▸*n.* (**cold work**) the shaping of metal while it is cold.

Cole[1] /kōl/, Nat King (1919–65), U.S. singer and pianist; born *Nathaniel Adams Coles*. He became the first African American to have his own radio 1948–49 and television 1956–57 series. Notable songs: "Mona Lisa" (1950) and "Ramblin' Rose" (1962).

Nat King Cole

Cole[2], Thomas (1801–48), U.S. artist. He was one of the founders of the Hudson River School of painting.

cole /kōl/ ▸*n. chiefly archaic* a brassica, esp. cabbage, kale, or rape. ▷Old English *cāwel, caul*, related to Dutch *kool* and German *Kohl*, from Latin *caulis* 'stem, cabbage'; reinforced in Middle English by forms from Old Norse *kál*. Compare with KALE.

co·lec·to·my /kōˈlektəmē/ ▸*n.* (*pl.* **-mies**) surgical removal of all or part of the colon.

Cole·man /ˈkōlmən/, Ornette (1930–), U.S. jazz saxophonist, trumpeter, violinist, and composer. His music is noted for its lack of harmony and chordal structure.

cole·man·ite /ˈkōlməˌnīt/ ▸*n.* a white crystalline mineral, typically occurring as glassy prisms, consisting of hydrated calcium borate. ▷named after William T. *Coleman* (1824–93) + -ITE[1].

Cole·man lan·tern /ˈkōlmən/ (also **Coleman lamp**) ▸*n. trademark* a type of bright gasoline lamp used by campers.

Co·le·op·ter·a /ˌkōlēˈäptərə/ *Entomology* an order of insects that comprises the beetles (including weevils), forming the largest order of animals on the earth. ■ [as *plural n.*] (**coleoptera**) insects of this order; beetles. ▷modern Latin (plural), from Greek *koleopteros*, from *koleos* 'sheath' + *pteron* 'wing.' **—co·le·op·ter·an** *n.* & *adj.* **—co·le·op·ter·ous** /-tərəs/ *adj.*

co·le·op·ter·ist /ˌkōlēˈäptərist/ ▸*n.* a person who studies or collects beetles. ▷mid 19th cent.: from COLEOPTERA + -IST.

co·le·op·tile /ˌkōlēˈäpˌtīl/ ▸*n. Botany* a sheath protecting a young shoot tip in a grass or cereal. ▷mid 19th cent.: from Greek *koleon* 'sheath' + *ptilon* 'feather.'

co·le·o·rhi·za /ˌkōlēˌəˈrīzə/ ▸*n.* (*pl.* **-zae** /-zē/) *Botany* a sheath protecting the root of a germinating grass or cereal grain. ▷mid 19th cent.: from *koleos* 'sheath' + *rhiza* 'root.'

Cole·ridge /ˈkōl(ə)rij/, Samuel Taylor (1772–1834), English poet, critic, and philosopher. His *Lyrical Ballads* (1798), written with William Wordsworth, marked the start of English romanticism and included "The Rime of the Ancient Mariner." Other notable poems: "Christabel" and "Kubla Khan" (both 1816).

cole·seed /ˈkōlˌsēd/ ▸*n.* old-fashioned term for RAPE[2]. ▷late 17th cent.: from Dutch *koolzaad* 'cabbage or rape seed.'

cole·slaw /ˈkōlˌslô/ ▸*n.* sliced raw cabbage mixed with mayonnaise and other vegetables, eaten as a salad. ▷late 18th cent. (originally U.S.): from Dutch *koolsla*, from *kool* 'cabbage' + *sla* (see SLAW).

Co·lette /kəˈlet/ (1873–1954), French novelist; born *Sidonie Gabrielle Claudine*. Notable works *Chéri* (1920), *La Fin de Chéri* (1926), and *Gigi* (1945).

co·le·us /ˈkōlēəs/ ▸*n.* a tropical Southeast Asian plant of the mint family that has brightly colored variegated leaves and is popular as a houseplant. • Genus *Solenostemon* (formerly *Coleus*), family Labiatae. ▷modern Latin, from Greek *koleos* 'sheath' (because of the way the stamens are joined together, resembling a sheath).

cole·wort /ˈkōlˌwərt; -ˌwôrt/ ▸*n. chiefly archaic* another term for COLE.

col·ic /ˈkälik/ ▸*n.* severe, often fluctuating pain in the abdomen caused by intestinal gas or obstruction in the intestines and suffered esp. by babies. ▷late Middle English: from Old French *colique*, from late Latin *colicus*, from *colon* (see COLON[2]). **—col·ick·y** *adj.*

col·i·cin /ˈkäləsin; -ˌsēn/ ▸*n. Biology* a bacteriocin produced by a coliform bacterium. ▷1940s: from French *colicine* (from *coli*, denoting a bacterium) + -IN.

col·ic·root /ˈkälikˌro͞ot; -ˌro͝ot/ ▸*n.* a North American plant of the lily family, with a rosette of leaves and a spike of small goblet-shaped white or cream flowers. It was formerly used in the treatment of colic. • *Aletris farinosa*, family Liliaceae.

col·i·form bac·te·ri·um /ˈkōləˌfôrm; ˈkäl-/ ▸*adj.* a rod-shaped bacterium, esp. *Escherichia coli* and members of the genus *Aerobacter*, found in the intestinal tract of humans and other animals. Its presence in water indicates fecal contamination and can cause diarrhea and other dysenteric symptoms Also called COLON BACILLUS. ▷early 20th cent.: from modern Latin *coli*, specific epithet in the sense 'of the colon' + -IFORM + BACTERIUM.

Co·li·ma /kəˈlēmə/ **1** a state in southwestern Mexico, on the Pacific coast. **2** the capital city of this state; pop. 58,000.

co·lin·e·ar /ˌkōˈlinēər/ (also **col·lin·e·ar**) ▸*adj.* lying in the same straight line or linear sequence.

col·i·se·um /ˌkäləˈsēəm/ (also **col·os·se·um**) ▸*n.* [*in names*] a large theater or stadium: *the Charlotte Coliseum.* ▷late 19th cent.: from medieval Latin, alteration of Latin *colosseum* (see COLOSSEUM).

co·li·tis /kəˈlītis; kō-/ ▸*n. Medicine* inflammation of the lining of the colon.

Coll /kôl/ an island in the Inner Hebrides, west of Mull.

Coll. ▸*abbr.* ■ Collateral. ■ Collected or Collection (used in written references to published works or sources). ■ College. ■ Colloquial.

col·lab·o·rate /kəˈlabəˌrāt/ ▸*v.* [*intrans.*] work jointly on an activity, esp. to produce or create something: *he **collaborated with** a distinguished painter **on** the designs.* ■ cooperate traitorously with an enemy: *during the last war they **collaborated with** the Nazis.* ▷late 19th cent.: from Latin *collaborat-* 'worked with,' from the verb *collaborare*, from *col-* 'together' + *laborare* 'to work.' **—col·lab·o·ra·tor** /-ˌrātər/ *n.*

col·lab·o·ra·tion /kəˌlabəˈrāsнən/ ▸*n.* **1** the action of working with someone to produce or create something: *he wrote on art and architecture **in collaboration with** John Betjeman.* ■ something produced or created in this way: *his recent opera was a collaboration with Lessing.* **2** traitorous cooperation with an enemy: *he faces charges of collaboration.* ▷mid 19th cent.: from Latin *collaboratio(n-)*, from *collaborare* 'work together.' **—col·lab·o·ra·tion·ist** /-nist/ *n.* & *adj.* (sense 2).

col·lab·o·ra·tive /kəˈlabərətiv/ ▸*adj.* produced or conducted by two or more parties working together: *collaborative research.* **—col·lab·o·ra·tive·ly** *adv.*

col·lage /kəˈläzн; kô-; kō-/ ▸*n.* a form of art in which various materials such as photographs and pieces of paper or fabric are arranged and stuck to a backing. ■ a composition made in this way. ■ a combination or collection of various things. ▷early 20th cent.: from French, literally 'gluing.' **—col·lag·ist** /-läzнist/ *n.*

col·la·gen /ˈkäləjən/ ▸*n.* *Biochemistry* the main structural protein found in animal connective tissue, yielding gelatin when boiled. ▷mid 19th cent.: from French *collagène*, from Greek *kolla* 'glue' + French *-gène* (see **-GEN**).

col·lap·sar /kəˈlap,sär/ ▸*n.* *Astronomy* an old star that has collapsed under its own gravity to form a white dwarf, neutron star, or black hole. ▷late 20th cent.: from **COLLAPSE**, on the pattern of words such as *pulsar*.

col·lapse /kəˈlaps/ ▸*v.* [*intrans.*] **1** (of a structure) fall down or in; give way: *the roof collapsed on top of me.* ■ [*trans.*] cause (something) to fall in or give way: *it feels as if the slightest pressure would collapse it* | *figurative many people tend to collapse the distinction between the two concepts.* ■ (of a lung or blood vessel) fall inward and become flat and empty: [as *adj.*] (**collapsed**) *a collapsed lung.* ■ [*trans.*] cause (a lung or blood vessel) to do this. ■ fold or be folded to fit into a small space: [*intrans.*] *some cots collapse down to fit into a bag.* **2** (of a person) fall down and become unconscious, typically through illness or injury: *he collapsed from loss of blood.* ■ *informal* sit or lie down as a result of tiredness or prolonged exertion: *exhausted, he collapsed on the bed.* **3** (of an institution or undertaking) fail suddenly and completely: *in the face of such resolve his opposition finally collapsed.* ■ (of a price or currency) drop suddenly in value.
▸*n.* an instance of a structure falling down or in: *the collapse of a railroad bridge* | *the church roof is in danger of collapse.* ■ a sudden failure of an institution or undertaking: *the collapse of communism.* ■ a physical or mental breakdown: *he suffered a collapse from overwork* | *she's lying there in a state of collapse.* ▷early 17th cent. (as *collapsed*): from medical Latin *collapsus*, past participle of *collabi*, from *col-* 'together' + *labi* 'to slip.'

col·laps·i·ble /kəˈlapsəbəl/ ▸*adj.* (of an object) able to be folded into a small space: *a collapsible bed.* —**col·laps·i·bil·i·ty** /kə,lapsəˈbilitē/ *n.*

col·lar /ˈkälər/ ▸*n.* **1** a band of material around the neck of a shirt, dress, coat, or jacket, either upright or turned over and generally an integral part of the garment: *we turned our collars up against the chill.* ■ short for **CLERICAL COLLAR**. ■ a band of leather or other material put around the neck of a domestic animal, esp. a dog or cat. ■ a colored marking resembling a collar around the neck of a bird or other animal. ■ a heavy rounded part of the harness worn by a draft animal, which rests at the base of its neck on the shoulders. **2** a restraining or connecting band, ring, or pipe in machinery. **3** *Brit.* a piece of meat rolled up and tied. ■ a cut of bacon taken from the neck of a pig. **4** *Botany* the part of a plant where the stem joins the roots.
▸*v.* **1** [*trans.*] put a collar on: *biologists who were collaring polar bears.* **2** [*trans.*] *informal* seize, grasp, or apprehend (someone): *police collared the culprit.* ■ approach aggressively and talk to (someone who wishes to leave): *he collared a departing guest for some last words.* ▷Middle English: from Old French *colier*, from Latin *collare* 'band for the neck, collar,' from *collum* 'neck.' —**col·lared** *adj.* [in *combination*] *a fur-collared jacket.* —**col·lar·less** *adj.*

col·lar beam ▸*n.* a horizontal wooden joist or beam connecting two rafters and forming with them an A-shaped roof truss.

col·lar·bone /ˈkälər,bōn/ ▸*n.* either of the pair of bones joining the breastbone to the shoulder blades. Also called **CLAVICLE**.

col·lards /ˈkälərdz/ (also **col·lard greens**) ▸*n.* a cabbage of a variety that does not develop a heart. ▷mid 18th cent.: reduced form of *colewort*, in the same sense, from **COLE** + **WORT**.

col·lared dove /dəv/ ▸*n.* an Old World dove related to the ringed turtle dove, with buff, gray, or brown plumage and a narrow black band around the back of the neck. • Genus *Streptopelia*, family Columbidae: several species, in particular the sandy gray *S. decaocto*, which originated in Asia, and has recently been found breeding widely in southeastern Florida.

col·lared liz·ard ▸*n.* a lizard that is typically marked with spots and bands and has a distinctive black-and-white collar. It is found in dry rocky areas in the southern U.S. and Mexico. • *Crotaphytus collaris*, family Iguanidae.

col·lar stud ▸*n.* a stud used to fasten a detachable collar to a shirt.

col·lar tie ▸*n.* another term for **COLLAR BEAM**.

col·late /kəˈlāt; ˈkō,lāt; ˈkäl,āt/ ▸*v.* [*trans.*] **1** collect and combine (texts, information, or sets of figures) in proper order. ■ compare and analyze (texts or other data): *these accounts he* ***collated with*** *his own experience.* ■ *Printing* verify the order of (sheets of a book) by their signatures. **2** appoint (a clergyman) to a benefice. ▷mid 16th cent. (in the sense 'confer (a benefice) upon'): from Latin *collat-* 'brought together,' from the verb *conferre* (see **CONFER**).

col·lat·er·al /kəˈlatərəl; kəˈlatrəl/ ▸*n.* **1** something pledged as security for repayment of a loan, to be forfeited in the event of a default. **2** a person having the same descent in a family as another but by a different line.
▸*adj.* **1** descended from the same stock but by a different line: *a collateral descendant of George Washington.* **2** additional but subordinate; secondary: *the collateral meanings of a word.* ■ situated side by side; parallel: *collateral veins.* ▷late Middle English (as an adjective): from medieval Latin *collateralis*, from *col-* 'together with' + *lateralis* (from *latus, later-* 'side'). Sense 1 (originally U.S.) is from the phrase *collateral security*, denoting something pledged in addition to the main obligation of a contract. —**col·lat·er·al·i·ty** /kə,latəˈralitē/ *n.* —**col·lat·er·al·ly** *adv.*

col·lat·er·al con·tract ▸*n.* *Law* a subsidiary contract that induces a person to enter into a main contract or that depends upon the main contract for its existence.

col·lat·er·al dam·age ▸*n.* used euphemistically to refer to inadvertent casualties among civilians and destruction in civilian areas in the course of military operations.

col·lat·er·al·ize /kəˈlatərə,līz; kəˈlatrə-/ ▸*v.* [*trans.*] provide something as collateral for (a loan): *these loans are collateralized by property.*

col·la·tion /kəˈlāsʜən; kō-; kä-/ ▸*n.* **1** the action of collating something: *data management and collation.* **2** a light, informal meal. ■ (in the Roman Catholic Church) a light meal allowed during a fast. ▷Middle English: via Old French from Latin *collation-*, from *conferre* (see **CONFER**). Originally (in the plural) the term denoted John Cassian's *Collationes Patrum in Scetica Eremo Commorantium* 'Conferences of, or with, the Egyptian Hermits' (AD 415–20), from which a reading would be given in Benedictine communities prior to a light meal (see sense 2).

col·la·tor /-tər/ ▸*n.* a person or machine that collates.

col·league /ˈkäl,ēg/ ▸*n.* a person with whom one works, esp. in a profession or business. ▷early 16th cent.: from French *collègue*, from Latin *collega* 'partner in office,' from *col-* 'together with' + *legare* 'depute.'

col·lect[1] /kəˈlekt/ ▸*v.* [*trans.*] **1** bring or gather together (things, typically when scattered or widespread): *he went around the office collecting old coffee cups* | *he* ***collected up*** *all his clothing.* ■ accumulate and store over a period of time: *collect rainwater to use on the garden.* ■ systematically seek and acquire (items of a particular kind) as a hobby: *I've started collecting stamps.* [*intrans.*] *the urge to collect, to have the full set, is in us all.* ■ [*intrans.*] come together and form a group or mass: *worshipers* ***collected together*** *in a stadium* | *dust and dirt collect so quickly.* See note at **GATHER**. **2** call for and take away; fetch: *the children were collected from school.* ■ go somewhere and accept or receive (something), esp. as a right or due: *she went to Oxford to collect her honorary degree.* ■ solicit and receive (donations), esp. for charity: *collecting money for the war effort* | [*intrans.*] *we* ***collected for*** *the United Way.* ■ receive (money that is due); be paid: [*trans.*] *they called to collect a debt* [*intrans.*] *he'd come to collect.* **3** (**collect oneself**) regain control of oneself, typically after a shock. ■ bring together and concentrate (one's thoughts). **4** *archaic* conclude; infer: *by all best conjectures, I collect Thou art to be my fatal enemy.* **5** cause (a horse) to bring its hind legs further forward as it moves, thereby shortening the stride and increasing balance and impulsion.
▸*adv.* & *adj.* (with reference to a telephone call) to be paid for by the person receiving it: [as *adv.*] *I called my mother collect* | [as *adj.*] *a collect call.* ▷late Middle English: from Old French *collecter* or medieval Latin *collectare*, from Latin *collect-* 'gathered together,' from the verb *colligere*, from *col-* 'together' + *legere* 'choose or collect.'

col·lect[2] /ˈkäl,ekt; -likt/ ▸*n.* (in church use) a short prayer, esp. one assigned to a particular day or season. ▷Middle English: from Old French *collecte*, from Latin *collecta* 'gathering,' feminine past participle of *colligere* 'gather together' (see **COLLECT**[1]).

col·lec·ta·ne·a /,käl,ekˈtānēə/ ▸*plural n.* [also treated as *sing.*] passages, remarks, and other pieces of text collected from various sources. ▷mid 17th cent.: Latin, neuter plural of *collectaneus* 'gathered together,' used as an adjective in Caesar's *Dicta collectanea* and as a noun in Solinus' *Collectanea.*

col·lect·ed /kəˈlektid/ ▸*adj.* **1** (of a person) not perturbed or distracted: *outwardly they are cool, calm, and collected.* **2** (of individual works) brought together in one volume or edition: *Lenin's collected works.* ■ (of a volume or edition) containing all the works of a particular person or category. **3** (of a horse) moving with a shortened stride and with its hind legs correctly placed to achieve balance and impulsion. —**col·lect·ed·ly** *adv.* (in sense 1).

col·lect·i·ble /kəˈlektəbəl/ (also *chiefly Brit.* **col·lect·a·ble**) ▸*adj.* **1** (of an item) worth collecting; of interest to a collector. **2** able to be collected: *a surplus collectible as rent by the landowner.*
▸*n.* (usu. **collectibles**) an item valued and sought by collectors. —**col·lect·i·bil·i·ty** /kə,lektəˈbilitē/ *n.*

col·lec·tion /kəˈleksʜən/ ▸*n.* **1** the action or process of collecting someone or something: *the collection of maple sap* | *tax collection* ■ a regular removal of mail for dispatch or of trash for disposal. ■ an instance of collecting money in a church service or for a charitable cause: *when she died, they* ***took up a collection*** *for her burial.* ■ a sum collected in this way. **2** a group of things or people: *a rambling* ***collection of*** *houses.* ■ an assembly of items such as works of art, pieces of writing, or natural objects, esp. one systematically ordered: *paintings from the permanent collection* | *a record collection.* ■ (**collections**) an art museum's holdings organized by medium, such as sculpture, painting, or photography. ■ a book or recording containing various texts, poems, songs, etc.: *a collection of essays.* ■ a range of new clothes produced by a fashion house: *a preview of their autumn collection.* ▷late Middle English: via Old French from Latin *collectio(n-)*, from *colligere* 'gather together' (see **COLLECT**[1]).

col·lec·tive /kəˈlektiv/ ▸*adj.* done by people acting as a group: *a collective protest.* ■ belonging or relating to all the members of a group: *ministers who share collective responsibility.* ■ (esp. of feelings or memories) common to the members of a group: *a collective sigh of relief from parents.* ■ taken as a whole; aggregate: *the collective power of the workforce.*
▸*n.* a cooperative enterprise. ■ a collective farm. ▷late Middle English (in the sense 'representing many individuals'): from Old French *collectif, -ive* or Latin *collectivus*, from *collect-* 'gathered together,' from the verb *colligere* (see **COLLECT**[1]). —**col·lec·tive·ly** *adv.* —**col·lec·tive·ness** *n.* —**col·lec·tiv·i·ty** /kə,lekˈtivitē; ,käl,ek-/ *n.*

col·lec·tive bar·gain·ing ▸*n.* negotiation of wages and other conditions of employment by an organized body of employees.

col·lec·tive farm ▸*n.* a jointly operated amalgamation of several small farms, esp. one owned by the government.

col·lec·tive mark ▸*n.* a trademark or service mark that identifies members of a union, cooperative, or other collective organization.

col·lec·tive mem·o·ry ▸*n.* the memory of a group of people, typically passed from one generation to the next.

col·lec·tive noun ▸*n.* *Grammar* a count noun that denotes a group of individuals (e.g., *assembly, family, crew*).

> **USAGE** Examples of collective nouns include *group, crowd, family, committee, class, crew*, and the like. In the U.S., collective nouns are usually followed by a singular verb (*the crowd was nervous*), while in Britain it is more common to follow a collective noun with a plural verb (*the band were late for their own concert*). Notice that if the verb is singular, any following pronouns must also be singular: *the council is prepared to act, but not until it has taken a poll.* When preceded by the definite article *the*, the collective noun *number* is usually treated as a singular (*the number of applicants was beyond belief*), whereas it is treated as a plural when preceded by the indefinite article *a* (*a number of proposals were considered*). See also usage at **NUMBER**.

col·lec·tive se·cu·ri·ty ▸*n.* the cooperation of several countries in an alliance to strengthen the security of each.

col·lec·tive un·con·scious ▸*n.* (in Jungian psychology) the part of the unconscious mind that is derived from ancestral memory and experience and is

Pronunciation Key ə *ago*; ər *over*; ˈə or ,ə *up*; ˈər or ,ər *fur*; a *hat*; ā *rate*; ä *car*; ch *chew*; e *let*; ē *see*; e(ə)r *air*; i *fit*; ī *by*; i(ə)r *ear*; ng *sing*; ō *go*; ô *for*; oi *boy*; o͝o *good*; o͞o *goo*; ou *out*; sh *she*; th *thin*; t͟h *then*; (h)w *why*; zh *vision*

common to all humankind, as distinct from the individual's unconscious.

col·lec·tiv·ism /kə'lektə,vizəm/ ▸*n.* the practice or principle of giving a group priority over each individual in it. ■ the theory and practice of the ownership of land and the means of production by the people or the state. —**col·lec·tiv·ist** *adj.* & *n.* —**col·lec·tiv·is·tic** /-,lektə'vistik/ *adj.*

col·lec·ti·vize /kə'lektə,vīz/ ▸*v.* [*trans.*] [usu. as *adj.*] (**collectivized**) organize (something) on the basis of ownership by the people or the state, abolishing private ownership or involvement: *collectivized agriculture.* —**col·lec·ti·vi·za·tion** /kə,lektəvə'zāsHən/ *n.*

col·lec·tor /kə'lektər/ ▸*n.* a person or thing that collects something, in particular: ■ a person who collects things of a specified type, professionally or as a hobby: *book collectors.* ■ an official who is responsible for collecting money owed to an organization or body: *a tax collector.* ■ *Electronics* the region in a bipolar transistor that absorbs charge carriers.

C

col·lec·tor's i·tem ▸*n.* an object of interest to collectors, esp. because it is rare, beautiful, or associated with someone famous.

col·leen /kə'lēn; 'käl,ēn/ ▸*n.* an Irish term for a girl or young woman. ■ an Irish girl or young woman. ▷early 19th cent.: from Irish *cailín*, diminutive of *caile* 'countrywoman.'

col·lege /'kälij/ ▸*n.* **1** an educational institution or establishment, in particular: ■ one providing higher education or specialized professional or vocational training: *my brother wanted to* **go to college** | *I'm* **at college** *studying graphic design.* ■ (within a university) a school offering a general liberal arts curriculum leading only to a bachelor's degree. ■ (in Britain) any of a number of independent institutions within certain universities, each having its own teaching staff, students, and buildings. ■ *Brit.* a private secondary school: [in *names*] *Eton College.* ■ the teaching staff and students of a college considered collectively: *the college was shocked by his death.* ■ the buildings and campus of a college. **2** an organized group of professional people with particular aims, duties, and privileges: [in *names*] *the electoral college.* ▷late Middle English: from Old French, from Latin *collegium* 'partnership, association,' from *collega* 'partner in office,' from *col-* 'together with' + *legare* 'depute.'

Col·lege Board ▸*n.* an organization that prepares and administers standardized tests that are used in college admission and placement.

Col·lege of Arms (also **College of Heralds**) (in the UK) a corporation that officially records and grants armorial bearings. Formed in 1484, it comprises three Kings of Arms, six heralds, and four pursuivants. Also called **HERALDS' COLLEGE**.

Col·lege of Car·di·nals the body of cardinals of the Roman Catholic Church, founded in the 11th century and since 1179 responsible for the election of the pope. Also called **SACRED COLLEGE**.

Col·lege Park a city in central Maryland, just northeast of Washington, DC, home to the University of Maryland; pop. 24,657.

Col·lege Station a city in east central Texas, home to Texas A&M University; pop. 52,456.

col·lege try ▸*n.* a sincere effort or attempt at performing a difficult, or seemingly impossible, task: *the chances of overturning this decision are slim, but the Democrats will* **give it the old college try**.

col·le·gi·a /kə'legēə/ ▸ plural form of **COLLEGIUM**.

col·le·gi·al /kə'lēj(ē)əl/ ▸*adj.* **1** relating to or involving shared responsibility, as among a group of colleagues. **2** another term for **COLLEGIATE** (sense 1). ▷late Middle English: from Old French *collegial* or late Latin *collegialis*, from *collegium* 'partnership, association' (see **COLLEGE**). —**col·le·gi·al·i·ty** /kə,lējē'alitē/ *n.*

col·le·gian /kə'lējən/ ▸*n.* a member of a college, esp. within a university.■ a college student ▷late Middle English: from medieval Latin *collegianus*, from *collegium* 'partnership, association' (see **COLLEGE**).

col·le·giate /kə'lējət/ ▸*adj.* **1** belonging or relating to a college or its students: *collegiate life.* **2** (of a university) composed of different colleges. ▷late Middle English: from late Latin *collegiatus*, from *collegium* 'partnership, association' (see **COLLEGE**).

col·le·giate church ▸*n.* a church endowed for a chapter of canons but without a bishop's see. ■ a church or group of churches established under two or more pastors.

col·le·giate Goth·ic ▸*n.* a style of Gothic revival architecture used for many college and university buildings.
▸*adj.* of or built in such a style.

col·le·gi·um /kə'lējēəm/ ▸*n.* (*pl.* **-le·gi·a** /-'legēə/) **1** (in full **col·le·gi·um mu·si·cum** /'m(y)ōōzikəm/) (*pl.* **col·le·gi·a mu·si·ca** /'m(y)ōōzikə/) a society of amateur musicians, esp. one attached to a German or U.S. college. **2** *historical* an advisory or administrative board in Russia. ▷late 19th cent.: from Latin, literally 'association.'

col le·gno /kō(l)'lānyō/ ▸*adv.* (of a passage of music for a bowed instrument) played by hitting the strings with the back of the bow. ▷Italian, 'with the wood (of the bow).'

Col·lem·bo·la /kə'lembələ/ *Entomology* an order of insects that comprises the springtails. ■ [as *plural n.*] (**collembola**) insects of this order; springtails. ▷modern Latin (plural), from Greek *kolla* 'glue' + *embolon* 'peg, stopper' (with reference to the sticky substance secreted by the ventral tube of the insects). —**col·lem·bo·lan** /-bələn/ *n.* & *adj.*

col·len·chy·ma /kə'lengkəmə/ ▸*n.* *Botany* tissue strengthened by the thickening of cell walls, as in young shoots. ▷mid 19th cent.: from Greek *kolla* 'glue' + *enkhuma* 'infusion.'

Colles' frac·ture /kälz/ ▸*n.* *Medicine* a fracture of the lower end of the radius in the wrist with a characteristic backward displacement of the hand. ▷late 19th cent.: named after Abraham *Colles* (1773–1843), Irish surgeon.

col·let /'kälət/ ▸*n.* a ring or lining that holds something, in particular: ■ a segmented band or sleeve put around a shaft or spindle and tightened so as to grip it. ■ a small collar in a clock to which the inner end of a balance spring is attached. ■ a flange or socket for setting a gem in jewelry. ▷late Middle English (denoting a piece of armor to protect the neck): from Old French, diminutive of *col* 'neck,' from Latin *collum*.

col·lic·u·lus /kə'likyələs/ ▸*n.* (*pl.* **-li** /-,lī; -,lē/) *Anatomy* a small protuberance, esp. one of two pairs in the roof of the midbrain, involved respectively in vision and hearing. ▷mid 19th cent.: from Latin, diminutive of *collis* 'hill.' —**col·lic·u·lar** /-lər/ *adj.*

col·lide /kə'līd/ ▸*v.* [*intrans.*] hit with force when moving: *she* **collided with** *someone* | *two suburban trains collided.* ■ come into conflict or opposition: *in his work, politics and metaphysics collide.* ▷early 17th cent. (in the sense 'cause to collide'): from Latin *collidere*, from *col-* 'together' + *laedere* 'to strike or damage.'

col·lid·er /kə'līdər/ ▸*n.* *Physics* an accelerator in which two beams of particles are made to collide.

col·lie /'kälē/ ▸*n.* (*pl.* **-lies**) a sheepdog of a breed originating in Scotland, having a long, pointed nose and thick, long hair. ▷mid 17th cent.: perhaps from **COAL** (the breed originally being black).

collie

col·lier /'kälyər/ ▸*n.* *chiefly Brit.* **1** a coal miner. **2** a ship carrying coal. ▷Middle English: from **COAL** + **-IER**. The original sense was 'maker of charcoal,' who usually brought it to market, hence 'person selling charcoal,' later 'person selling coal,' whence current senses.

col·lier·y /'kälyərē/ ▸*n.* (*pl.* **-ler·ies**) a coal mine and the buildings and equipment associated with it.

col·li·gate /'kälə,gāt/ ▸*v.* **1** *Linguistics* be or cause to be juxtaposed or grouped in a syntactic relation: [*intrans.*] *the two grammatical items are said to colligate* | [*trans.*] *pronouns are regularly colligated with verbal forms.* **2** [*trans.*] connect; unite.■ *Logic* join or relate (apparently unrelated facts) into a pattern, esp. to reveal a general principle. ▷mid 16th cent. (in the literal Latin sense): from Latin *colligat-* 'bound together,' from the verb *colligare*, from *col-* 'together' + *ligare* 'bind.' The current sense dates from the 1960s. —**col·li·ga·tion** /,kälə'gāsHən/ *n.*

col·li·ga·tive /'kälə,gātiv/ ▸*adj.* *Chemistry* of or relating to the binding together of molecules: *the colligative properties of dilute solutions.*

col·li·mate /'kälə,māt/ ▸*v.* [*trans.*] make (rays of light or particles) accurately parallel: [as *adj.*] (**collimated**) *a collimated electron beam.* ■ accurately align (an optical or other system). ▷mid 19th cent.: from Latin *collimare*, an erroneous reading (in some editions of Cicero) of *collineare* 'align or aim,' from *col-* 'together with' + *linea* 'line.' —**col·li·ma·tion** /,kälə'māsHən/ *n.*

col·li·ma·tor /'kälə,mātər/ ▸*n.* a device for producing a parallel beam of rays or radiation. ■ a small fixed telescope used for adjusting the line of sight of an astronomical telescope.

col·lin·e·ar /kə'linēər; kä-/ ▸*adj.* *Geometry* (of points) lying in the same straight line. —**col·lin·e·ar·i·ty** /kə,linē'aritē; kä-/ *n.*

Col·lins[1] /'kälənz/, Joan (Henrietta) (1933–), English actress, a sex symbol in movies such as *Our Girl Friday* (1953) and known for the television series *Dynasty* (1981–89).

Col·lins[2], Michael (1890–1922), Irish nationalist leader and politician. A member of Parliament for Sinn Fein, he was one of the negotiators of the Anglo-Irish Treaty of 1921. He commanded the Irish Free State forces in the civil war and became head of state but was assassinated ten days later.

Col·lins[3], Phil (1951–), British rock musician and singer; full name *Phillip David Charles Collins*. His many hits include "You Can't Hurry Love" (1982) and "Sussudio" (1985).

Col·lins[4], (William) Wilkie (1824–89), English novelist. He is noted for his detective stories *The Woman in White* (1860) and *The Moonstone* (1868).

Col·lins[5] ▸*n.* short for **TOM COLLINS**.

col·li·sion /kə'lizHən/ ▸*n.* **1** an instance of one moving object or person striking violently against another: *a midair* **collision between** *two aircraft* | *the device increases the chances of collision.* ■ an instance of conflict between opposing ideas, interests, or factions: *a* **collision between** *experience and theory* | *cultures in collision.* **2** *Computing* an event of two or more records being assigned the same location in memory. ■ an instance of simultaneous transmission by more than one node of a network. ▷late Middle English: from late Latin *collisio(n-)*, from Latin *collidere* 'strike together' (see **COLLIDE**). —**col·li·sion·al** /-zHənl/ *adj.*
▸*PHRASE* □ **on** (**a**) **collision course** going in a direction that will lead to a collision with another moving object or person. ■ adopting an approach that is certain to lead to conflict with another person or group: *the strikers are on a collision course with the government.*

col·lo·cate /'kälə,kāt/ ▸*v.* **1** [*intrans.*] *Linguistics* (of a word) be habitually juxtaposed with another with a frequency greater than chance: *"maiden" collocates with "voyage."* **2** [*trans.*] *rare* place side by side or in a particular relation: [as *adj.*] (**collocated**) *McAndrew was a collocated facility with Argentia Naval Station.*
▸*n.* *Linguistics* a word that is habitually juxtaposed with another with a frequency greater than chance: *collocates for the word "mortgage" include "lend" and "property."* ▷early 16th cent. (sense 2): from Latin *collocat-* 'placed together,' from the verb *collocare*, from *col-* 'together' + *locare* 'to place.' Sense 1 dates from the 1950s.

col·lo·ca·tion /,kälə'kāsHən/ ▸*n.* **1** *Linguistics* the habitual juxtaposition of a particular word with another word or words with a frequency greater than chance: *the words have a similar range of collocation.* ■ a pair or group of words that are juxtaposed in such a way: *"strong coffee" and "heavy drinker" are typical English collocations.* **2** the action of placing things side by side or in position: *the collocation of the two pieces.* ▷late Middle English: from Latin *collocatio(n-)*, from *collocare* 'place together' (see **COLLOCATE**).

col·lo·di·on /kə'lōdēən/ ▸*n.* a syrupy solution of nitrocellulose in a mixture of alcohol and ether, used for coating things, chiefly in surgery and in a former photographic process. ▷mid 19th cent.: from Greek *kollōdēs* 'gluelike,' from *kolla* 'glue.'

col·logue /kə'lōg/ ▸*v.* (**-logues, -logued, -logu·ing**) [*intrans.*] *archaic* talk confidentially or conspiratorially. ▷early 17th cent. (in the sense 'flatter, pretend to agree with or believe'): probably an alteration of obsolete *colleague* 'conspire,' by association with Latin *colloqui* 'to converse.'

col·loid /'käl,oid/ ▸*n.* a homogeneous, noncrystalline substance consisting of large molecules or ultramicroscopic particles of one substance dispersed through a second substance. Colloids include gels, sols, and emulsions; the particles do not settle and cannot be separated out by ordinary filtering or centrifuging like those in a suspension. ■ *Anatomy & Medicine* a substance of gelatinous consistency.
▸*adj.* [*attrib.*] of the nature of, relating to, or characterized by a colloid or colloids. ▷mid 19th cent.:

from Greek *kolla* 'glue' + **-OID.** **—col·loi·dal** /kəˈloidl/ *adj.*

col·lop /ˈkäləp/ *dialect* ▸*n.* a slice of meat: *three collops of bacon.* ▷late Middle English: of Scandinavian origin and related to Swedish *kalops* 'meat stew.'

col·lo·qui·al /kəˈlōkwēəl/ ▸*adj.* (of language) used in ordinary or familiar conversation; not formal or literary. ▷mid 18th cent.: from Latin *colloquium* 'conversation' + **-AL.** **—col·lo·qui·al·ly** *adv.*

col·lo·qui·al·ism /kəˈlōkwēəˌlizəm/ ▸*n.* a word or phrase that is not formal or literary, typically one used in ordinary or familiar conversation. ▪ the use of such words or phrases.

col·lo·qui·um /kəˈlōkwēəm/ ▸*n.* (*pl.* **-qui·ums** or **-qui·a** /-kwēə/) an academic conference or seminar. ▷late 16th cent. (denoting a conversation or dialogue): from Latin, from *colloqui* 'to converse,' from *col-* 'together' + *loqui* 'to talk.'

col·lo·quy /ˈkäləkwē/ ▸*n.* (*pl.* **-quies**) **1** *formal* a conversation: *they broke off their colloquy at once | an evening of sophisticated colloquy.* See note at **CONVERSATION.** **2** a gathering for discussion of theological questions. ▷late Middle English: from Latin *colloquium* 'conversation.'

col·lo·type /ˈkäləˌtīp/ ▸*n. Printing* a process for making high-quality prints from a sheet of light-sensitive gelatin exposed photographically to the image without using a screen: [as *adj.*] *collotype printing.* ▪ a print made by such a process. ▷late 19th cent.: from Greek *kolla* 'glue' + **TYPE.**

col·lude /kəˈlo͞od/ ▸*v.* [*intrans.*] come to a secret understanding for a harmful purpose; conspire: *university leaders* **colluded in** *price-rigging | the president accused his opponents of* **colluding with** *foreigners.* ▷early 16th cent.: from Latin *colludere* 'have a secret agreement,' from *col-* 'together' + *ludere* 'to play.' **—col·lud·er** *n.*

col·lu·sion /kəˈlo͞oZHən/ ▸*n.* secret or illegal cooperation or conspiracy, esp. in order to cheat or deceive others: *the armed forces were working* **in collusion with** *drug traffickers |* **collusion between** *media owners and political leaders.* ▪ *Law* such cooperation or conspiracy, esp. between ostensible opponents in a lawsuit. ▷late Middle English: from Latin *collusion-*, from *colludere* 'have a secret agreement' (see **COLLUDE**). **—col·lu·sive** /-siv; -ziv/ *adj.* **—col·lu·sive·ly** /-sivlē; -zivlē/ *adv.*

col·lu·vi·um /kəˈlo͞ovēəm/ ▸*n. Geology* material that accumulates at the foot of a steep slope. ▷mid 20th cent.: from Latin *colluvies* 'confluence or collection of matter,' from *colluere* 'to rinse,' from *col-* 'together' + *luere* 'to wash.' **—col·lu·vi·al** /-vēəl/ *adj.*

col·lyr·i·um /kəˈli(ə)rēəm/ ▸*n.* (*pl.* **-i·a** /-ēə/) a medicated eyewash. ▪ a kind of dark eyeshadow, used esp. in Eastern countries. ▷late Middle English: Latin, from Greek *kollurion* 'poultice,' from *kollura* 'coarse bread roll.'

col·ly·wob·bles /ˈkälēˌwäbəlz/ ▸*plural n. informal, chiefly humorous* stomach pain or queasiness: *an attack of collywobbles.* ▪ intense anxiety or nervousness, esp. with such symptoms: *such organizations give him the collywobbles.* ▷early 19th cent.: fanciful formation from **COLIC** and **WOBBLE.**

Col·man /ˈkōlmən/, Ronald (1891–1958), British actor. Among his notable movies were *A Tale of Two Cities* (1935), *The Prisoner of Zenda* (1937), and *Random Harvest* (1942).

Colo. ▸*abbr.* Colorado.

col·o·bine /ˈkäləˌbīn; -bin/ ▸*n. Zoology* an Old World monkey of a mainly leaf-eating group that includes the colobus monkeys, langurs, and leaf monkeys. • Subfamily Colobinae, family Cercopithecidae. ▷1950s: from modern Latin *Colobinae*, based on Greek *kolobos* 'curtailed.'

col·o·bo·ma /ˌkäləˈbōmə/ ▸*n. Medicine* a congenital malformation of the eye causing defects in the lens, iris, or retina. ▷mid 19th cent.: modern Latin, from Greek *kolobōma* 'part removed in mutilation,' from *kolobos* 'cut short.'

col·o·bus /ˈkäləbəs/ (also **colobus monkey**) ▸*n.* (*pl.* same) a slender, leaf-eating African monkey with silky fur, a long tail, and very small or absent thumbs. • Genera *Colobus* and *Procolobus*, family Cercopithecidae: several species. ▷modern Latin, from Greek *kolobos* 'curtailed.'

co·lo·cate /kōˈlōˌkāt; ˈkō-/ (also **co-lo·cate**) ▸*v.* (**be colocated**) share a location or facility with someone (or something) else: *a woman officer can often be* **colocated with** *her husband.*

col·o·cynth /ˈkäləˌsinTH/ ▸*n.* a tropical Old World climbing plant of the gourd family, which bears a pulpy fruit and has long been cultivated. Also called **BITTER APPLE.** • *Citrullus colocynthis*, family Cucurbitaceae. ▪ the fruit of this plant. ▪ a bitter purgative drug obtained from this fruit. ▷mid 16th cent.: via Latin from Greek *kolokunthis.*

Co·logne /kəˈlōn/ an industrial and university city in western Germany, in North Rhine-Westphalia, on the Rhine River; pop. 956,690. German name **KÖLN.**

co·logne /kəˈlōn/ ▸*n.* eau de cologne or scented toilet water. ▷early 19th cent.: named after **COLOGNE** in Germany.

Co·lo·ma /kəˈlōmə/ a historic locality in northeastern California, on the American River, northeast of Sacramento, where gold was discovered in 1848 on John (Johann) Sutter's mill site that led to the California gold rush.

Co·lom·bi·a /kəˈləmbēə/ a country in extreme northwestern South America that has a coastline on both the Atlantic and the Pacific oceans; pop. 42,310,000; capital, Bogotá; official language, Spanish. **—Co·lom·bi·an** *adj.* & *n.*

Colombia was conquered by the Spanish in the early 16th century and achieved independence in the early 19th century, although the resulting Republic of Great Colombia lasted only until 1830, when first Venezuela and then Ecuador broke away to become independent states in their own right. Since the civil war of 1949–53, the country has struggled with poverty and social problems. During the 1990s, guerrilla warfare, partly funded by the growing drug trade, dominated Colombia's countryside.

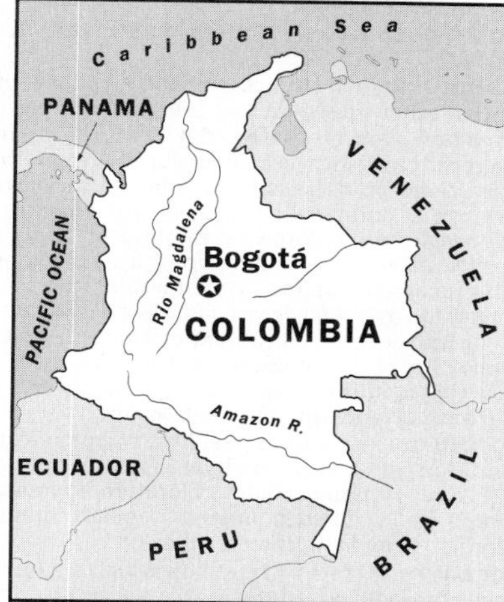

Co·lom·bo /kəˈləmbō/ the capital and chief port of Sri Lanka, on the southwestern coast of the country; pop. 615,000.

Co·lón /kəˈlōn/ the chief port of Panama, at the Caribbean Sea end of the Panama Canal; pop. 140,900.

co·lon¹ /ˈkōlən/ ▸*n.* a punctuation mark (:) indicating: ▪ that a writer is introducing a quotation or a list of items. ▪ that a writer is separating two clauses of which the second expands or illustrates the first. ▪ a statement of proportion between two numbers: *a ratio of 10:1.* ▪ the separation of hours from minutes (and minutes from seconds) in a statement of time given in numbers: *4:30 p.m.* ▪ the number of the chapter and verse respectively in biblical references: *Exodus 3:2.* ▷mid 16th cent. (as a term in rhetoric denoting a section of a complex sentence, or a pause before it): via Latin from Greek *kōlon* 'limb, clause.'

co·lon² ▸*n. Anatomy* the main part of the large intestine, which passes from the cecum to the rectum and absorbs water and electrolytes from food that has remained undigested. Its parts are called the ascending, transverse, descending, and sigmoid colon. ▷late Middle English: via Latin from Greek *kolon.*

co·lón /kəˈlōn/ ▸*n.* (*pl.* **-lo·nes** /-ˈlōˌnās/) the basic monetary unit of Costa Rica and El Salvador, equal to 100 centimos in Costa Rica and 100 centavos in El Salvador. ▷from Cristóbal *Colón*, the Spanish name of Christopher Columbus (see **COLUMBUS**²).

co·lon ba·cil·lus ▸*n.* another term for **COLIFORM BACTERIUM.**

colo·nel /ˈkərnl/ ▸*n.* an army officer of high rank, in particular (in the U.S. Army, Air Force, and Marine Corps) an officer above a lieutenant colonel and below a brigadier general. ▪ *informal* short for **LIEUTENANT COLONEL.** ▷mid 16th cent.: from obsolete French *coronel* (earlier form of *colonel*), from Italian *colonnello* 'column of soldiers,' from *colonna* 'column,' from Latin *columna.* The form *coronel*, source of the modern pronunciation, was usual until the mid 17th cent. **—colo·nel·cy** /ˈkərnlsē/ *n.* (*pl.* **-cies**).

Colo·nel Blimp ▸*n.* another term for **BLIMP** (sense 2).

colo·nel-in-chief ▸*n.* (*pl.* **colo·nels-in-chief**) a title given to the honorary head of a regiment in the British army.

co·lo·ni·al /kəˈlōnyəl; -nēəl/ ▸*adj.* **1** of, relating to, or characteristic of a colony or colonies: *British colonial rule | colonial expansion.* ▪ relating to the period of the British colonies in America before independence. ▪ (esp. of architecture or furniture) made during or in the style of this period. **2** (of animals or plants) living in colonies.
▸*n.* **1** a native or inhabitant of a colony. **2** a house built in colonial style. **—co·lo·ni·al·ly** *adv.*

co·lo·ni·al·ism /kəˈlōnēəˌlizəm; kəˈlōnyəˌlizəm/ ▸*n.* the policy or practice of acquiring full or partial political control over another country, occupying it with settlers, and exploiting it economically. **—co·lo·ni·al·ist** /-list/ *n.* & *adj.*

co·lon·ic /kōˈlänik; kə-/ ▸*adj. Anatomy* of, relating to, or affecting the colon.
▸*n. informal* an act or instance of colonic irrigation, performed for its supposed therapeutic benefits.

co·lon·ic ir·ri·ga·tion ▸*n.* a water enema given to flush out the colon.

col·o·nist /ˈkälənist/ ▸*n.* a settler in or inhabitant of a colony.

col·o·nize /ˈkäləˌnīz/ ▸*v.* [*trans.*] (of a country or its citizens) send a group of settlers to (a place) and establish political control over it: *the Greeks colonized Sicily and southern Italy.* ▪ come to settle among and establish political control over (the indigenous people of an area): *a white family that tries to colonize a Caribbean island.* ▪ appropriate (a place or domain) for one's own use. ▪ *Ecology* (of a plant or animal) establish itself in an area: *mussels can colonize even the most inhospitable rock surfaces* [*intrans.*] *insect borers colonize in rotted shoreline deadfalls.* **—col·o·ni·za·tion** /ˌkälənəˈzāSHən/ *n.* **—col·o·niz·er** *n.*

col·on·nade /ˌkäləˈnād/ ▸*n.* a row of columns supporting a roof, an entablature, or arcade. ▪ a row of trees or other tall objects. ▷early 18th cent.: from French, from *colonne* 'column,' from Latin *columna.* **—col·on·nad·ed** *adj.*

co·lon·o·scope /kəˈlänəˌskōp/ ▸*n. Medicine* a flexible fiber-optic instrument inserted through the anus in order to examine the colon. **—co·lon·os·co·py** /ˌkōləˈnäskəpē/ *n.*

co·lon ther·a·py ▸ another term for **COLONIC IRRIGATION.**

col·o·ny /ˈkälənē/ ▸*n.* (*pl.* **-nies**) **1** a country or area under the full or partial political control of another country, typically a distant one, and occupied by settlers from that country. ▪ a group of people living in such a country or area, consisting of the original settlers and their descendants and successors. ▪ (**the Colonies**) chiefly British term for **THIRTEEN COLONIES.** ▪ (**the colonies**) all the foreign countries or areas formerly under British political control. **2** a group of people of one nationality or ethnic group living in a foreign city or country: *the British colony in New York.* ▪ a place where a group of people with similar interests live together: *an artists' colony.* **3** *Biology* a community of animals or plants of one kind living close together or forming a physically connected structure: *a colony of seals.* ▪ a group of fungi or bacteria grown from a single spore or cell on a culture medium. ▷late Middle English (denoting a settlement formed mainly of retired soldiers, acting as a garrison in newly conquered territory in the Roman Empire): from Latin *colonia* 'settlement, farm,' from *colonus* 'settler, farmer,' from *colere* 'cultivate.'

col·o·ny-stim·u·lat·ing fac·tor ▸*n. Biochemistry* a substance secreted by bone marrow that promotes the growth and differentiation of stem cells into colonies of specific blood cells.

col·o·phon /ˈkäləfən; -ˌfän/ ▸*n.* a publisher's emblem or imprint, esp. one on the title page or spine of a book. ▪ *historical* a statement at the end of a book, typically with a printer's emblem, giving information about its authorship and printing. ▷early 17th cent. (denoting a finishing touch): via late Latin from Greek *kolophōn* 'summit or finishing touch.'

col·o·pho·ny /kəˈläfənē; ˈkälə,fōnē/ ▸*n.* another term for ROSIN. ▷Middle English: from Latin *colophonia (resina)* '(resin) from *Colophon*,' a town in Lydia, Asia Minor.

col·or /ˈkələr/ (*Brit.* **col·our**) ▸*n.* **1** the property possessed by an object of producing different sensations on the eye as a result of the way the object reflects or emits light: *the lights flickered and changed color.* ■ one, or any mixture, of the constituents into which light can be separated in a spectrum or rainbow, sometimes including (loosely) black and white: *a rich brown color | a range of bright colors.* ■ the use of all colors, not only black, white, and gray, in photography or television: *he has shot the whole film* **in color** | [as *adj.*] *color television.* ■ a substance used to give something a particular color: *lip color.* ■ *figurative* a shade of meaning: *many events in her past had taken on a different color.* ■ *figurative* character or general nature: *the hospitable color of his family.* ■ *Heraldry* any of the major conventional colors used in coats of arms (gules, vert, sable, azure, purpure), esp. as opposed to the metals, furs, and stains. **2** the appearance of someone's skin; in particular: ■ pigmentation of the skin, esp. as an indication of someone's race: *discrimination on the basis of color.* ■ a group of people considered as being distinguished by skin pigmentation: *all colors and nationalities.* ■ rosiness of the complexion, esp. as an indication of someone's health: *there was some color back in his face.* ■ redness of the face as a manifestation of an emotion, esp. embarrassment or anger: *color flooded her skin as she realized what he meant.* **3** vividness of visual appearance resulting from the presence of brightly colored things: *for color, plant groups of winter-flowering pansies.* ■ *figurative* picturesque or exciting features that lend a particularly interesting quality to something: *a town full of color and character.* ■ *figurative* variety of musical tone or expression: *orchestral color.* **4** (**colors**) an item or items of a particular color or combination of colors worn to identify an individual or a member of a school, group, or organization; in particular: ■ the clothes or accoutrements worn by a jockey or racehorse to indicate the horse's owner. ■ the flag of a regiment or ship. ■ a national flag. ■ the armed forces of a country, as symbolized by its flag: *he was* **called to the colors** *during the war.* **5** *Physics* a quantized property of quarks which can take three values (designated blue, green, and red) for each flavor. **6** *Mining* a particle of gold remaining in a mining pan after most of the mud and gravel have been washed away.

▸*v.* **1** [*trans.*] change the color of (something) by painting or dyeing it with crayons, paints, or dyes. ■ [*intrans.*] take on a different color: *the foliage will not color well if the soil is too rich.* ■ use crayons to fill (a particular shape or outline) with color: *color the head, eyes, and bill with crayons.* ■ *figurative* make vivid or picturesque: *he has colored the dance with gestures from cabaret and vaudeville.* **2** [*intrans.*] (of a person or their skin) show embarrassment or shame by becoming red; blush: *everyone stared at him, and he colored slightly.* ■ [*trans.*] cause (a person or their skin) to change in color: *rage colored his pale complexion.* ■ [*trans.*] (of a particular color) imbue (a person's skin): *a faint pink flush colored her cheeks.* ■ [*trans.*] *figurative* (of an emotion) imbue (a person's voice) with a particular tone: *surprise colored her voice.* **3** [*trans.*] influence, esp. in a negative way; distort: *the experiences had colored her whole existence.* ■ misrepresent by distortion or exaggeration: *witnesses might color evidence to make a story saleable.* ▷Middle English (as *colo(u)r*): from Old French *colour* (noun), *colourer* (verb), from Latin *color* (noun), *colorare* (verb).

▸*PHRASES* □ **lend** (or **give**) **color to** make something seem true or probable: *this lent color and credibility to his defense.* □ **person of color** see PERSON OF COLOR. □ **show one's true colors** reveal one's real character or intentions, esp. when these are disreputable or dishonorable. □ **under color of** under the pretext of. □ **with flying colors** see FLYING.

col·or·a·ble /ˈkələrəbəl/ (*Brit.* **col·our·able**) ▸*adj.* **1** apparently correct or justified: *a colorable legal claim.* ■ counterfeit. **2** capable of being colored: *colorable illustrations.*

Col·o·rad·o /,käləˈrädō; -ˈradō/ **1** a river that rises in the Rocky Mountains of northern Colorado and flows southwest for 1,468 miles (2,333 km) to the Gulf of California. It passes through the Grand Canyon. **2** a river that flows east for 900 miles (1,450 km) across Texas, from the Llano Estacado to the Gulf of Mexico. Austin is situated on it. **3** a state in the central U.S.; pop. 4,301,261; capital, Denver; statehood, Aug. 1, 1876 (38). Part of Colorado was acquired by the U.S. with the Louisiana Purchase in 1803 and the rest was ceded by Mexico in 1848. —**Col·o·rad·an** /-ˈrädn; -ˈradn/ *n.* & *adj.*

Col·o·rad·o blue spruce ▸*n.* another term for BLUE SPRUCE.

Col·o·ra·do Desert a region in southern California and northern Baja California in Mexico. The Salton Sea, the Imperial Valley, and the city of Palm Springs are here.

Col·o·ra·do Plateau a region of arid uplands in the southwestern U.S.; along the Colorado River in Colorado, Utah, New Mexico, and Arizona; noted for its scenery.

Col·o·rad·o po·ta·to bee·tle ▸*n.* a yellow- and black-striped leaf beetle native to North America. The larvae are highly destructive to potato plants and have occurred in many countries. • *Leptinotarsa decemlineata*, family Chrysomelidae. ▷late 19th cent.: named after the state of COLORADO.

Colorado potato beetle

Col·o·ra·do Springs a city in central Colorado, south of Denver, at the foot of the Front Range of the Rocky Mountains, home to the U.S. Air Force Academy; pop. 360,890.

Col·o·rad·o spruce ▸*n.* another term for BLUE SPRUCE.

col·or·ant /ˈkələrənt/ (*Brit.* **col·our·ant**) ▸*n.* a dye, pigment, or other substance that colors something.

col·or·a·tion /,kələˈrāSHən/ ▸*n.* **1** a visual appearance with regard to color: *some bacterial structures take on a purple coloration.* ■ the natural color or variegated markings of animals or plants: *the red coloration of many maples* ■ a scheme or method of applying color: *the coloration of the drawing.* **2** a specified pervading character or tone of something: *the movement has taken on a fundamentalist coloration.* ■ a variety of musical or vocal expression: *the subtle colorations of big-box speakers | a skillful singer can do much with coloration.* ▷early 17th cent.: from late Latin *coloratio(n-)*, from *colorare* 'to color.'

col·o·ra·tu·ra /,kələrəˈto͝orə; ,käl-/ ▸*n.* elaborate ornamentation of a vocal melody, esp. in operatic singing by a soprano. ■ (also **coloratura soprano**) a soprano skilled in such singing. ▷Italian, literally 'coloring,' from Latin *colorare* 'to color.'

col·or bar ▸*n.* **1** a social system in which a group of people (typically nonwhite) are denied access to the same rights, opportunities, and facilities as other people (typically white) on the basis of skin color. **2** a strip on printed material or a screen display showing a range of colors, used to ensure that all colors are printed or displayed correctly.

col·or-blind (also **col·or·blind**) ▸*adj.* **1** unable to distinguish certain colors, or (rarely in humans) any colors at all. See PROTANOPIA. **2** not influenced by racial prejudice: *a color-blind society.* —**col·or-blind·ness** *n.*

col·or code ▸*n.* a system of marking things with different colors as a means of identification.

▸*v.* (**col·or-code**) [*trans.*] (usu. **be color-coded**) mark (things) with different colors as a means of identification: *each unit is color-coded for clarity.* ■ mark different features of (something) with different colors: *the map is color-coded.*

co·lo·rec·tal /,kōlōˈrektəl/ ▸*adj.* relating to or affecting the colon and the rectum.

col·ored /ˈkələrd/ (*Brit.* **col·oured**) ▸*adj.* **1** having or having been given a color or colors, esp. as opposed to being black, white, or neutral: *brightly colored birds are easier to see* | [in *combination*] *a peach-colored sofa.* ■ *figurative* imbued with an emotive or exaggerated quality: ***highly colored** examples were used by both sides.* **2** (also **Colored**) wholly or partly of nonwhite descent (now usually offensive in the U.S.). ■ (also **Coloured**) *S. African* used as an ethnic label for people of mixed ethnic origin, including African slave, Malay, Chinese, and white. ■ relating to people who are wholly or partly of nonwhite descent: *a colored club.*

▸*n.* **1** (also **Colored**) *dated, usually offensive* a person who is wholly or partly of nonwhite descent. ■ *S. African* a person of mixed ethnic origin speaking Afrikaans or English as their mother tongue. **2** (**coloreds**) clothes, sheets, etc., that are any color but white (used esp. in the context of washing and color fastness).

USAGE **Colored** referring to skin color is first recorded in the early 17th century and was adopted in the U.S. by emancipated slaves as a term of racial pride after the end of the Civil War. The word is still used in the National Association for the Advancement of Colored People (NAACP), but otherwise **colored** sounds old-fashioned at best, and is usually offensive.

In South Africa, the term **colored** (normally written **Coloured**) has a different history. It is used to refer to people of mixed-race parentage rather than, as elsewhere, to refer to African peoples and their descendants, i.e., as a synonym for **black**. In modern use in this context, the term is not considered offensive or derogatory.

See also **usage** at BLACK and PERSON OF COLOR.

col·or·fast /ˈkələr,fast/ ▸*adj.* dyed in colors that will not fade or be washed out. —**col·or·fast·ness** *n.*

col·or-field paint·ing (also **col·or-field**) ▸*n.* a style of American abstract painting prominent from the late 1940s to the 1960s that features large expanses of unmodulated color covering the greater part of the canvas. Barnett Newman and Mark Rothko were considered its chief exponents.

col·or fil·ter ▸*n.* a photographic filter that absorbs light of certain colors.

col·or·ful /ˈkələrfəl/ (*Brit.* **col·our·ful**) ▸*adj.* **1** having much or varied color; bright: *a colorful array of fruit.* **2** full of interest; lively and exciting: *a controversial and colorful character | a colorful account of the meeting.* ■ (of a person's life or background) involving variously disreputable activities: *he gained a playboy reputation during a colorful bachelorhood.* ■ (of language) vulgar or rude: *colorful words usually impolite in public meetings.* —**col·or·ful·ly** /-f(ə)lē/ *adv.* —**col·or·ful·ness** *n.*

col·or guard ▸*n.* a uniformed group, esp. of soldiers, police officers, or school representatives, who parade or present their institution's flag (and sometimes their national flag) on ceremonial occasions.

col·or·if·ic /,kələˈrifik/ ▸*adj. rare* having much color: *the colorific radiance of costume.* ▷late 17th cent.: from French *colorifique* or modern Latin *colorificus*, from Latin *color* 'color.'

col·or·im·e·ter /,kələˈrimitər/ ▸*n.* an instrument for measuring the intensity of color. ▷mid 19th cent.: from Latin *color* 'color' + -METER. —**col·or·i·met·ric** /,kələrəˈmetrik/ *adj.* —**col·or·im·e·try** /,kələˈrimitrē/ *n.*

col·or·ing /ˈkələriNG/ (*Brit.* **col·our·ing**) ▸*n.* **1** the process or skill of applying a substance to something so as to change its original color. ■ the process of filling in a particular shape or outline with crayons: [as *adj.*] *a coloring book.* ■ a drawing produced in this way. **2** visual appearance with regard to color, in particular: ■ the arrangement of colors and markings on an animal. ■ the natural hues of a person's skin, hair, and eyes: *her fair coloring.* ■ *figurative* the pervading character or tone of something: *the chorus is given oriental coloring by the use of exotic instruments.* **3** a substance used to give a particular color to something, esp. food.

col·or·ist /ˈkələrist/ (*Brit.* **col·our·ist**) ▸*n.* an artist or designer who uses color in a special or skillful way. ■ a person who tints black-and-white prints, photographs, or movies. ■ a hairdresser who specializes in dyeing people's hair.

col·or·is·tic /,kələˈristik/ (*Brit.* **col·our·is·tic**) ▸*adj.* showing or relating to a special use of color: *his great coloristic wallpapers.* ■ having or showing a variety of musical or vocal expression: *the choir's coloristic resources.* —**col·or·is·ti·cal·ly** /-ik(ə)lē/ *adv.*

col·or·ize /ˈkələ,rīz/ (*Brit.* also **col·our·ize**) ▸*v.* [*trans.*] add color to (a black-and-white movie) by means of computer technology. —**col·or·i·za·tion** /,kələrəˈzāSHən/ *n. trademark* —**col·or·iz·er** *n. trademark* .

col·or·less /ˈkələrləs/ (*Brit.* **col·our·less**) ▸*adj.* **1** (esp. of a gas or liquid) without color. ■ dull or pale in hue: *colorless cheeks.* **2** lacking distinctive character or interest; dull: *the book is rather colorless, like its author.* —**col·or·less·ly** *adv.*

color line ▸*n.* another term for COLOR BAR (sense 1).

col·or phase ▸*n.* a genetic or seasonal variation in the color of the skin, pelt, or feathers of an animal.

col·or·point /ˈkələr,point/ (also **col·our·point**) ▸*n.* chiefly British term for HIMALAYAN.

col·or re·ver·sal ▸*n.* [usu. as *adj.*] *Photography* the process of producing a positive image directly from another positive: *color reversal films.*

col·or sat·u·ra·tion ▶*n.* see SATURATION.

col·or scheme ▶*n.* an arrangement or combination of colors, esp. as used in interior decoration: *a cool, simple color scheme.*

col·or sep·a·ra·tion ▶*n.* *Photography & Printing* any of three negative images of the same subject taken through green, red, and blue filters and combined to reproduce the full color of the original. ■ the production of such images.

col·or tem·per·a·ture ▶*n.* *Astronomy & Physics* the temperature at which a black body would emit radiation of the same color as a given object.

col·or ther·a·py ▶*n.* a system of alternative medicine based on the use of color, esp. projected colored light.

col·or wash ▶*n.* colored calcimine or tempera. ▶*v.* (**col·or-wash**) [*trans.*] paint (something) with colored calcimine or tempera.

col·or·way /ˈkələrˌwā/ (*Brit.* **col·our·way**) ▶*n.* any of a range of combinations of colors in which a style or design is available: *wallpaper books show coordinating patterns and colorways.*

col·or wheel ▶*n.* a circle with different colored sectors used to show the relationship between colors.

co·los·sal /kəˈläsəl/ ▶*adj.* extremely large: *a colossal amount of mail | a colossal mistake.* ■ *Architecture* (of a giant order) having more than one story of columns. ■ *Sculpture* (of a statue) at least twice life size. ▷early 18th cent.: from French, from *colosse,* from Latin *colossus* (see COLOSSUS). **—co·los·sal·ly** *adv.*

Col·os·se·um /ˌkäləˈsēəm/ ▶*n.* the name since medieval times of the *Amphitheatrum Flavium,* a vast amphitheater in Rome, begun by Vespasian *c.*AD 75. It held 50,000 spectators, its sections connected by an elaborate network of stairs, and was the scene of various kinds of combat. ▷from Latin, neuter of *colosseus* 'gigantic,' from *colossus* (see COLOSSUS).

Colosseum

Co·los·sians /kəˈläsHənz/ a book of the New Testament, an epistle of St. Paul to the Church at Colossae in Phrygia.

co·los·sus /kəˈläsəs/ ▶*n.* (*pl.* **-los·si** /-ˈläsˌī/ or **-los·sus·es**) a statue that is much bigger than life size. ■ *figurative* a person or thing of enormous size, importance, or ability: *the Russian Empire was the colossus of European politics.* ▷late Middle English: via Latin from Greek *kolossos* (applied by Herodotus to the statues of Egyptian temples).

Co·los·sus of Rhodes a huge bronze statue of the sun god Helios, one of the Seven Wonders of the World. Built *c.*292–280 BC, it stood beside the harbor entrance at Rhodes for about fifty years.

co·los·to·my /kəˈlästəmē/ ▶*n.* (*pl.* **-mies**) a surgical operation in which a piece of the colon is diverted to an artificial opening in the abdominal wall so as to bypass a damaged part of the colon. ■ an opening so formed: [as *adj.*] *a colostomy bag.* ▷late 19th cent.: from COLON[2] + Greek *stoma* 'mouth.'

co·los·trum /kəˈlästrəm/ ▶*n.* the first secretion from the mammary glands after giving birth, rich in antibodies. ▷late 16th cent.: from Latin.

col·our ▶*n.* & *v.* British spelling of COLOR.

col·por·teur /ˈkälˌpôrtər; ˌkälpôrˈtər/ ▶*n.* a peddler of books, newspapers, and similar literature. ■ someone employed by a religious society to distribute Bibles and other religious tracts. ▷late 18th cent.: French, from the verb *colporter,* probably an alteration of *comporter,* from Latin *comportare* 'carry with one.' **—col·por·tage** *n.*

col·po·scope /ˈkälpəˌskōp/ ▶*n.* a surgical instrument used to examine the vagina and the cervix of the uterus. ▷mid 20th cent.: from Greek *kolpos* 'womb, uterus' + -SCOPE. **—col·pos·co·py** /kälˈpäskəpē/ *n.*

Colt[1] /kōlt/, Samuel (1814–62), U.S. inventor. He is remembered chiefly for the revolver named after him, which he originally patented in 1836. It was adopted by the U.S. Army in 1846. His armory at Hartford, Connecticut, advanced the manufacturing techniques of interchangeable parts and the production line.

Colt[2] ▶*n. trademark* a type of revolver.

colt /kōlt/ ▶*n.* a young, uncastrated male horse, in particular one less than four years old. ▷Old English; perhaps related to Swedish *kult,* applied to boys or half-grown animals.

col·tan /ˈkältan/ ▶*n.* a dull metallic mineral composed of columbite and tantalite, and refined to produce tantalum. ▷early 21st cent.: from *col(umbite)* + *tan(talite).*

col·ter /ˈkōltər/ ▶*n.* variant spelling of COULTER.

colt·ish /ˈkōltisH/ ▶*adj.* energetic but awkward in one's movements or behavior. **—colt·ish·ly** *adv.* **—colt·ish·ness** *n.*

Col·ton /ˈkōltn/ a city in southwestern California, just southwest of San Bernardino; pop. 40,213.

Col·trane /ˈkōlˌtrān; kōlˈtrān/, John (William) (1926–67), U.S. jazz saxophonist. He was a leading figure in avant-garde jazz, bridging the gap between the harmonically dense jazz of the 1950s and the free jazz that evolved in the 1960s.

colts·foot /ˈkōltsˌfo͝ot/ ▶*n.* (*pl.* **-foots**) a Eurasian plant of the daisy family, with yellow flowers that appear in early spring, followed by large, heart-shaped leaves. It is used in herbal medicine for the treatment of coughs and respiratory disorders. • *Tussilago farfara,* family Compositae. ▷mid 16th cent.: translating medieval Latin *pes pulli* 'foal's foot,' with reference to the shape of the leaves.

col·u·brid /ˈkäl(y)əbrid/ ▶*n.* *Zoology* a snake of a very large family (Colubridae) that includes the majority of harmless species, such as grass snakes and garter snakes. The few venomous species have grooved fangs in the rear of the upper jaw. ▷late 19th cent.: from modern Latin *Colubridae* (plural), from Latin *coluber* 'snake.'

col·u·brine /ˈkäl(y)əˌbrīn/ ▶*adj. rare, chiefly figurative* of or belonging to a snake; snakelike: *he had played a game of subtle, colubrine misdirection.* ▷early 16th cent.: from Latin *colubrinus,* from *coluber* 'snake.'

co·lu·go /kəˈlo͞ogō/ ▶*n.* (*pl.* **-gos**) another term for FLYING LEMUR. ▷late 18th cent.: of unknown origin.

Co·lum·ba /kəˈləmbə/ *Astronomy* a small and faint southern constellation (the Dove), near Canis Major. It is sometimes said to represent the dove that Noah sent out from the Ark. ■ [as *genitive*] (**Columbae** /-bē/) used with a preceding letter or numeral to designate a star in this constellation: *the star Beta Columbae.* ▷Latin.

Co·lum·ba, St. (*c.*521–597), Irish abbot and missionary. He established a monastery at Iona *c.*563 and converted the Picts to Christianity. Feast day, June 9.

col·um·bar·i·um /ˌkäləmˈbe(ə)rēəm/ ▶*n.* (*pl.* **-bar·i·a** /-ˈbe(ə)rēə/) a room or building with niches for funeral urns to be stored. ■ a niche to hold a funeral urn. ■ a stone wall or walk within a garden for burial of funeral urns, esp. attached to a church. ▷mid 18th cent.: from Latin, literally 'pigeon house'.

Co·lum·bi·a /kəˈləmbēə/ **1** a river in northwestern North America that rises in the Rocky Mountains of southeastern British Columbia, Canada, and flows for 1,230 miles (1,953 km), first south into the U.S. and then west to enter the Pacific Ocean south of Seattle. **2** a residential community in central Maryland, between Baltimore and Washington, DC, planned and established in the 1960s; pop. 75,883. **3** a city in central Missouri, home to the University of Missouri; pop. 84,531. **4** the capital of South Carolina, in the central part of the state; pop. 116,278. **5** a city in west central Tennessee, on the Tennessee River, southwest of Nashville; pop. 33,055

Co·lum·bi·a, District of see DISTRICT OF COLUMBIA.

Co·lum·bine /ˈkäləmˌbīn/ a character in Italian *commedia dell'arte,* the mistress of Harlequin. ▷from French *Colombine,* from Italian *Colombina,* feminine of *colombino* 'dovelike,' from *colombo* 'dove.'

co·lum·bine /ˈkäləmˌbīn/ ▶*n.* an aquilegia with long-spurred flowers. • Genus *Aquilegia,* family Ranunculaceae: several species, including the white-flowered **Colorado blue columbine** (*A. coerulea*) with blue sepals, and the red-flowered *A. canadensis.* ▷late Middle English: from Old French *colombine,* from medieval Latin *colombina (herba)* 'dovelike (plant),' from Latin *columba* 'dove' (from the supposed resemblance of the flower to a cluster of five doves).

Colorado blue columbine

co·lum·bite /ˈkäləmˌbīt/ ▶*n.* a black mineral, typically occurring as dense, tabular crystals, consisting of an oxide of iron, manganese, niobium, and tantalum. It is the chief ore of niobium. ▷early 19th cent.: from COLUMBIUM + -ITE[1].

co·lum·bi·um /kəˈləmbēəm/ ▶*n.* old-fashioned term for NIOBIUM. ▷early 19th cent.: modern Latin, from *Columbia,* a poetic name for America from the name of Christopher *Columbus* (see COLUMBUS[2]).

Co·lum·bus[1] /kəˈləmbəs/ **1** an industrial city in western Georgia, on the Chattahoochee River, noted as a textile center; pop. 188,291. **2** an industrial city in south central Indiana; pop. 31,802. **3** a city in eastern Mississippi, on the Tombigbee River; pop. 25,944. **4** a city in eastern Nebraska, southwest of Lincoln, where the Loup and Platte rivers meet; pop: 20,971. **5** the capital of Ohio, in the central part of the state; pop. 711,470.

Co·lum·bus[2], Christopher (1451–1506), Spanish explorer; born in Italy; Italian name *Cristoforo Colombo;* Spanish name *Cristóbal Colón.* Columbus persuaded the Spanish monarchs, Ferdinand and Isabella, to sponsor an expedition to sail across the Atlantic in search of Asia and to prove that the world was round. In 1492, he set sail with three small ships (the *Niña,* the *Pinta,* the *Santa Maria*) and discovered the New World (in fact, various Caribbean islands). He made three further voyages between 1493 and 1504, landing on the South American mainland in 1498.

Co·lum·bus Day ▶*n.* a legal holiday commemorating the discovery of the New World by Christopher Columbus in 1492. It is observed by most states on the second Monday of October.

col·u·mel·la /ˌkäl(y)əˈmelə/ ▶*n.* (*pl.* **-mel·lae** /-ˈmelˌī; -ˈmelē/) *Biology* a structure resembling a small column and typically forming a central axis; in particular: ■ *Zoology* the axis of a spiral shell. ■ *Zoology* an ossicle of the middle ear of birds, reptiles, and amphibians. ■ *Anatomy* the pillar around which the cochlea spirals. ■ *Botany* the axis of the spore-producing body of some lower plants. ▷late 16th cent.: from Latin, 'small column.' **—col·u·mel·lar** /-ˈmelər/ *adj.*

col·umn /ˈkäləm/ ▶*n.* **1** an upright pillar, typically cylindrical and made of stone or concrete, supporting an entablature, arch, or other structure or standing alone as a monument. ■ a similar vertical, roughly cylindrical thing: *a great column of smoke.* ■ an upright shaft forming part of a machine and typically used for controlling it: *a Spitfire control column.* **2** a vertical division of a page or text. ■ a vertical arrangement of figures or other information. ■ a section of a newspaper or magazine regularly devoted to a particular subject or written by a particular person. **3** one or more lines of people or vehicles moving in the same direction: *a column of tanks moved northwest | we walked in a column.* ■ *Military* a narrow-fronted deep formation of troops in successive lines. ■ a military force deployed in such a formation. ■ a similar formation of ships in a fleet or convoy. ▷late Middle English: partly from Old French *columpne,* reinforced by its source, Latin *columna* 'pillar.' **—co·lum·nar** /kəˈləmnər/ *adj.* **—col·umned** /ˈkäləmd/ *adj.* [often in *combination*] *a four-columned portico.*

col·um·nat·ed /ˈkäləmˌnātid/ ▶*adj.* *Architecture* supported on or having columns: *a columnated church interior.*

co·lum·ni·a·tion /kəˌləmnēˈāsHən/ ▶*n.* *Architecture* the use or arrangement of columns.

col·umn inch ▶*n.* a one-inch length of a column in a newspaper or magazine.

col·um·nist /ˈkäləmnist/ ▶*n.* a journalist contributing regularly to a newspaper or magazine.

co·lure /kəˈlo͝or/ ▶*n.* *Astronomy* either of two great circles intersecting at right angles at the celestial poles and passing through the ecliptic at either the equinoxes or the solstices. ▷late Middle English: from late Latin *coluri* (plural), from Greek *kolourai* *(grammai)* 'truncated (lines),' from *kolouros* 'truncated,' so named because the lower part is permanently cut off from view.

co·ly /ˈkōlē/ ▸*n.* (*pl.* **-lies**) another term for MOUSEBIRD. ▷mid 19th cent.: from modern Latin *Colius*, from Greek *kolios*, denoting a type of woodpecker.

col·za /ˈkälzə; ˈkōlzə/ ▸*n.* another term for RAPE[2]. ▷early 18th cent.: from Walloon French *kolza*, from Low German *kōlsāt*, Dutch *koolzaad*, from *kool* 'cole' + *zaad* 'seed.'

COM /käm/ ▸*abbr.* ■ computer output on microfilm or microfiche. ■ (also **Com.**) Commodore.

com- (also **co-**, **col-**, **con-**, or **cor-**) ▸*prefix* with; together; jointly; altogether: *combine* | *command* | *collude.* ▷from Latin *cum* 'with.'

USAGE Com- is used before **b**, **m**, **p**, also occasionally before vowels and **f**. The following variant forms occur: **co-** esp. before vowels, **h**, and **gn**; **col-** before **l**; **cor-** before **r**; and **con-** before other consonants.

co·ma[1] /ˈkōmə/ ▸*n.* a state of deep unconsciousness that lasts for a prolonged or indefinite period, caused esp. by severe injury or illness: *a road crash left him in a coma* | *figurative a victim of a legislative coma.* ▷mid 17th cent.: modern Latin, from Greek *kōma* 'deep sleep'; related to *koitē* 'bed' and *keisthai* 'lie down.'

co·ma[2] ▸*n.* (*pl.* **co·mae** /ˈkōmē/) *Astronomy* a diffuse cloud of gas and dust surrounding the nucleus of a comet. ■ *Optics* aberration that causes the image of an off-axis point to be flared like a comet. ▷early 17th cent. (as a botanical term): via Latin from Greek *komē* 'hair of the head.'

Co·ma Ber·e·ni·ces /ˈkōmə ˌberəˈnīsēz/ *Astronomy* an inconspicuous northern constellation (Berenice's Hair), said to represent the tresses of Queen Berenice. It contains a large number of galaxies. ■ [as *genitive*] (**Comae Berenices** /ˈkōm ́/) used with a preceding letter or numeral to designate a star in this constellation: *the star Beta Comae Berenices.* ▷Latin.

Co·man·che /kəˈmanCHē/ ▸*n.* (*pl.* same or **-ches**) **1** a member of an American Indian people of the southwestern U.S. The Comanche were among the first to acquire horses (from the Spanish) and resisted white settlers fiercely. **2** the Uto-Aztecan language of this people.
▸*adj.* of or relating to this people or their language. ▷Spanish, from Ute *kimmanči* 'strangers'.

Co·ma·ne·ci /ˌkōməˈnēCH; -ˈnäCH/, Nadia (1961–), Romanian gymnast; emigrated to the U.S. in 1989. In 1976, she became the first Olympic gymnast to be awarded the maximum score of 10.00.

com·a·tose /ˈkōməˌtōs; ˈkämə-/ ▸*adj.* of or in a state of deep unconsciousness for a prolonged or indefinite period, esp. as a result of severe injury or illness: *she had been comatose for seven months* | *lying in a comatose state.* ■ *humorous* (of a person or thing) extremely exhausted, lethargic, or sleepy: *the economy remains almost comatose.* ▷late 17th cent.: from Greek *kōma*, *kōmat-* 'deep sleep' + -OSE[1].

comb /kōm/ ▸*n.* **1** a strip of plastic, metal, or wood with a row of narrow teeth, used for untangling or arranging the hair. ■ [in *sing.*] an instance of untangling or arranging the hair with such a device: *she gave her hair a comb.* ■ a short curved device of this type, worn by women to hold hair in place or as an ornament. **2** something resembling a comb in function or structure, in particular: ■ a device for removing loose hair from an animal, esp. a dog or cat. ■ a device for separating and dressing textile fibers. ■ a row of brass points for collecting the electricity in an electrostatic generator. **3** the red fleshy crest on the head of a domestic fowl, esp. a rooster. **4** short for HONEYCOMB (sense 1).
▸*v.* [*trans.*] **1** untangle or arrange (the hair) by drawing a comb through it: [as *adj.*] (**combed**) *neatly combed hair.* ■ (**comb something out**) remove something from the hair by drawing a comb through it: *she combed the burrs out of the dog's coat.* ■ curry (a horse). **2** prepare (wool, flax, or cotton) for manufacture with a comb. ■ [usu. as *adj.*] (**combed**) treat (a fabric) in such a way: *the socks are made of soft combed cotton.* **3** search carefully and systematically: *police combed the area for the murder weapon* | [*intrans.*] *his mother* ***combed through*** *the cardboard boxes.* ▷Old English *camb*, of Germanic origin; related to Dutch *kam* and German *Kamm.* —**comb·like** /-ˌlīk/ *adj.*

com·bat ▸*n.* /ˈkämˌbat/ fighting between armed forces: *killed* ***in combat*** | *pilots reenacted the aerial combats of yesteryear* | [as *adj.*] *a combat zone.* ■ nonviolent conflict or opposition: *intellectual combat.*
▸*v.* /kəmˈbat; ˈkämˌbat/ (**-bat·ed** or **-bat·ted**, **-bat·ing** or **-bat·ting**) [*trans.*] take action to reduce, destroy, or prevent (something undesirable): *an effort to combat drug trafficking.* ■ *archaic* engage in a fight with; oppose in battle: [*intrans.*] *your men combated against the first of ours.* ▷mid 16th cent. (originally denoting a fight between two persons or parties): from French *combattre* (verb), from late Latin *combattere*, from *com-* 'together with' + *battere*, variant of Latin *batuere* 'to fight.'

com·bat·ant /kəmˈbatnt; ˈkämbətənt/ ▸*n.* a person engaged in fighting during a war. ■ a nation at war with another. ■ a person engaged in conflict or competition with another.
▸*adj.* engaged in fighting during a war: *all the combatant armies went to war with machine guns.* ▷late Middle English (as an adjective used in heraldry to describe two lions facing one another with raised forepaws): from Old French, present participle of *combatre* 'to fight' (see COMBAT).

com·bat boots ▸*plural n.* boots of a type worn by soldiers in combat, typically black with laces and thick rubber soles.

com·bat fa·tigue ▸*n.* **1** psychological disturbance caused by prolonged exposure to active warfare, esp. being under bombardment. **2** (**combat fatigues**) a uniform of a type to be worn into combat.

com·bat·ive /kəmˈbativ/ ▸*adj.* ready or eager to fight; pugnacious: *he made some enemies with his combative style.* —**com·bat·ive·ly** *adv.* —**com·bat·ive·ness** *n.*

comb-back ▸*n.* a high-backed Windsor chair with a straight top rail: [as *adj.*] *a comb-back rocker.*

combe /ko͞om; kōm/ (also **coomb** or **coombe**) ▸*n. Brit.* a short valley or hollow on a hillside or coastline. ■ *Geology* a dry valley in a limestone or chalk escarpment. ▷Old English *cumb*, occurring in charters in the names of places in southern England, many of which survive; of Celtic origin, related to CWM. The current general use dates from the late 16th cent.

comb·er /ˈkōmər/ ▸*n.* **1** a long curling sea wave. **2** a person or machine that separates and straightens the fibers of cotton or wool.

comb·fish /ˈkōmˌfiSH/ ▸*n.* (*pl.* same or **-fish·es**) a fish of the northeastern Pacific, with small rough scales and long spines in the comblike dorsal fin. • Family Zaniolepididae and genus *Zaniolepis*: several species.

com·bi·na·tion /ˌkämbəˈnāSHən/ ▸*n.* **1** the act or an instance of combining; the process of being combined: *the combination of hot water and cold air can produce heart attacks.* ■ [as *adj.*] uniting different uses, functions, or ingredients: *a combination garment bag and backpack.* ■ the state of being joined or united in such a way: *these four factors work together* ***in combination.*** ■ *Chemistry* the joining of substances in a compound with new properties. ■ *Chemistry* the state of being in a compound. **2** a set of people or things that have been combined: *a combination of blackberries, raspberries, and rhubarb* | *a combination of beauty and utility.* ■ an arrangement of elements: *the canvases may be arranged in any number of combinations.* ■ a sequence of numbers or letters used to open a combination lock: [as *adj.*] *a combination briefcase.* ■ (in various sports and games) a coordinated and effective sequence of moves: *a good uppercut/hook combination.* ■ (in equestrian sports) a jump consisting of two or more elements. **3** *Mathematics* a selection of a given number of elements from a larger number without regard to their arrangement. ▷late Middle English: from late Latin *combinatio(n-)*, from the verb *combinare* 'join two by two' (see COMBINE[1]). —**com·bi·na·tion·al** /-SHənl/ *adj.* —**com·bi·na·tive** /ˈkämbəˌnātiv; kəmˈbīnətiv/ *adj.* —**com·bi·na·to·ri·al** /ˌkämbənəˈtôrēəl; kəmˌbīnə-/ *adj.* (*Mathematics*) —**com·bi·na·to·ri·al·ly** *adv.* (*Mathematics*) —**com·bi·na·to·ry** /kəmˈbīnəˌtôre; ˈkämbənə-/ *adj.*

com·bi·na·tion lock ▸*n.* a lock that is opened by rotating a dial or set of dials, marked with letters or numbers, through a specific sequence.

com·bi·na·tion ov·en ▸*n.* an oven operating by both conventional heating and microwaves.

com·bi·na·tion ther·a·py ▸*n.* treatment in which a patient is given two or more drugs (or other therapeutic agents) for a single disease.

com·bi·na·tor·ics /ˌkämbənəˈtôriks; kəmˌbīnə-/ ▸*plural n.* [treated as *sing.*] the branch of mathematics dealing with combinations of objects belonging to a finite set in accordance with certain constraints, such as those of graph theory. ▷1940s: from *combinatorial* (see COMBINATION), influenced by German *Kombinatorik.*

com·bine[1] ▸*v.* /kəmˈbīn/ [*trans.*] unite; merge: *the band combines a variety of musical influences* | ***combine*** *the flour* ***with*** *the margarine and salt* | [*intrans.*] *high tides and winds combined to bring chaos to the East Coast.* ■ [*intrans.*] *Chemistry* unite to form a compound: *oxygen and hydrogen do not combine at room temperatures.* ■ [*intrans.*] unite for a common purpose: *groups of teachers combined to tackle a variety of problems.* ■ engage in simultaneously: *combine shopping and sightseeing.* See note at JOIN.
▸*n.* /ˈkämˌbīn/ a group of people or companies acting together for a commercial purpose: *a powerful industrial combine.* ▷late Middle English: from Old French *combiner* or late Latin *combinare* 'join two by two,' from *com-* 'together' + Latin *bini* 'two together.' —**com·bin·a·ble** /kəmˈbīnəbəl/ *adj.*

com·bine[2] /ˈkämˌbīn/ ▸*n.* (in full **combine harvester**) an agricultural machine that cuts, threshes, and cleans a grain crop in one operation.
▸*v.* [*trans.*] harvest (a crop) by means of a combine. ▷early 20th cent..

com·bin·er[1] /kəmˈbīnər/ ▸*n.* any of various electronic devices that combine signals, in particular: ■ a device that couples different frequencies to a single antenna. ■ a component of a cipher that combines two data sources to encrypt text. ■ an electrical transformer comprising several smaller ones.

com·bin·er[2] /ˈkämˌbīnər/ ▸*n.* an operator of a combine harvester.

comb·ings /ˈkōmiNGz/ ▸*plural n.* hairs or other material removed with a comb.

comb·ing wool ▸*n.* long-stapled wool with straight, parallel fibers, suitable for combing and making into high-quality fabrics, in particular worsted. Compare with CARDING WOOL.

com·bin·ing form /kəmˈbīniNG/ ▸*n. Grammar* a linguistic element used in combination with another element to form a word (e.g., *Anglo-* 'English' in *Anglo-American*, *bio-* 'life' in *biology*, *-graphy* 'writing' in *biography*).

USAGE In this dictionary, **combining form** is used to denote an element that contributes to the particular sense of words (as with **bio-** and **-graphy** in **biography**), as distinct from a prefix or suffix that adjusts the sense of or determines the function of words (as with **un-**, **-able**, and **-ation**).

comb jel·ly ▸*n.* a marine animal with a jellyfishlike body bearing rows of fused cilia for propulsion. They are typically small planktonic animals and are noted for their luminescence. • Phylum Ctenophora: two classes.

com·bo /ˈkämbō/ ▸*n.* (*pl.* **-bos**) *informal* **1** a small jazz, rock, or pop band. **2** a combination, typically of different foods: [as *adj.*] *the combo platter.* ▷1920s (originally U.S.): abbreviation of COMBINATION + -O.

com·bo box ▸*n. informal Computing* a type of dialogue box containing a combination of controls, such as sliders, text boxes, and drop-down lists.

com·bo drive ▸*n. Computing* an optical disk drive that can read and record CDs and can also read DVDs.

comb·over /ˈkōmˌōvər/ (also **comb-o·ver**) ▸*n.* hair that is combed over a bald spot in an attempt to cover it.

com·bust /kəmˈbəst/ ▸*v.* [*trans.*] consume by fire. ■ [*intrans.*] be consumed by fire. ▷late 15th cent.: from obsolete *combust* 'burned, calcined,' from Latin *combustus*, past participle of *comburere* 'burn up.'

com·bus·ti·ble /kəmˈbəstəbəl/ ▸*adj.* able to catch fire and burn easily: *highly combustible paint thinner.* ■ *figurative* excitable; easily annoyed: *two combustible personalities.*
▸*n.* a combustible substance. ▷early 16th cent.: from Old French, from late Latin *combustibilis*, from Latin *combust-* 'burned up,' from the verb *comburere.* —**com·bus·ti·bil·i·ty** /kəmˌbəstəˈbilitē/ *n.*

com·bus·tion /kəmˈbəsCHən/ ▸*n.* the process of burning something: *the combustion of fossil fuels.* ■ *Chemistry* rapid chemical combination of a substance with oxygen, involving the production of heat and light. ▷late Middle English: from late Latin *combustio(n-)*, from Latin *comburere* 'burn up.' —**com·bus·tive** /-ˈbəstiv/ *adj.*

com·bus·tion cham·ber ▸*n.* an enclosed space in which combustion takes place, esp. in an engine or furnace.

Comdr. ▸*abbr.* commander.

come /kəm/ ▸*v.* (*past* **came** /kām/; *past part.* **come**) [*intrans.*] **1** move or travel toward or into a place thought of as near or familiar to the speaker: *Jessica came into the kitchen | they came here as immigrants | he came rushing out.* ■ arrive at a specified place: *we walked along till we* **came to** *a stream | it was very late when she* **came back** *| my trunk hasn't come yet.* ■ (of a thing) reach or extend to a specified point: *women in slim dresses that came all the way to their shoes | the path comes straight down.* ■ (**be coming**) approach: *someone was coming | she heard the train coming.* ■ travel in order to be with a specified person, to do a specified thing, or to be present at an event: *the police came |* **come and** *live with me | the electrician came to fix the stove | figurative we have certainly come a long way since Aristotle.* ■ join someone in participating in a specified activity or course of action: *do you want to come fishing tomorrow?* ■ (**come along/on**) make progress; develop: *he's coming along nicely | she asked them how their garden was coming on.* ■ [*in imperative*] (also **come, come!**) said to someone when correcting, reassuring, or urging them on: *"Come, come, child, no need to thank me."* **2** occur; happen; take place: *twilight had not yet come | waiting for a crash that never came | a chance like this doesn't* **come along** *every day.* ■ be heard, perceived, or experienced: *a voice came from the kitchen | "No," came the reply | it* **came as** *a great shock.* ■ (of a quality) become apparent or noticeable through actions or performance: *as an actor your style and personality must* **come through**. ■ (**come across** or **off** or *Brit.* **over**) (of a person) appear or sound in a specified way; give a specified impression: *he'd always* **come across as** *a decent guy.* ■ (of a thought or memory) enter one's mind: *the basic idea* **came to** *me while reading an article | a passage from a novel* **came back to** *Adam.* **3** take or occupy a specified position in space, order, or priority: *prisons come far down the list of priorities | I make sure my kids come first.* ■ achieve a specified place in a race or contest: *she came second among sixty contestants.* **4** pass into a specified state, esp. one of separation or disunion: *his shirt had come undone.* ■ (**come to/into**) reach or be brought to a specified situation or result: *you will come to no harm | staff who come into contact with the public.* ■ reach eventually a certain condition or state of mind: *he had come to realize she was no puppet.* **5** be sold, available, or found in a specified form: *the cars* **come with** *a variety of extras | they* **come in** *three sizes.* **6** *informal* have an orgasm.

▸*phrasal v.* □ **come about 1** happen; take place: *the relative speed with which emancipation came about.* **2** (of a ship) change direction. □ **come across 1** meet or find by chance: *I came across these old photos recently.* **2** *informal* hand over or provide what is wanted: *she has* **come across with** *some details.* ■ (of a woman) agree to have sexual intercourse with a man. □ **come along** [*in imperative*] said when encouraging someone or telling them to hurry up. □ **come around** (*chiefly Brit.* also **round**) **1** recover consciousness: *I'd just come around from a drunken stupor.* **2** be converted to another person's opinion: *I came around to her point of view.* **3** (of a date or regular occurrence) recur; be imminent again: *Friday had come around so quickly.* □ **come at** launch oneself at (someone); attack. □ **come away** be left with a specified feeling, impression, or result after doing something: *she came away feeling upset.* □ **come back 1** (in sports) recover from a deficit: *the Mets* **came back from** *a 3–0 deficit.* **2** reply or respond to someone, esp. vigorously: *he* **came back at** *Judy with a vengeance.* □ **come before** be dealt with by (a judge or court): *it is the most controversial issue to come before the Supreme Court.* □ **come between** interfere with or disturb the relationship of (two people): *I let my stupid pride come between us.* □ **come by 1** call casually and briefly as a visitor: *his friends came by | she came by the house.* **2** manage to acquire or obtain (something). □ **come down 1** (of a building or other structure) collapse or be demolished. ■ (of an aircraft) crash or crash-land. **2** be handed down by tradition or inheritance: *the name has* **come down from** *the last century.* **3** reach a decision or recommendation in favor of one side or another: *advisers and inspectors came down on our side.* **4** *Brit.* leave a university, esp. Oxford or Cambridge, after finishing one's studies. **5** *informal* experience the lessening of an excited or euphoric feeling, esp. one produced by a narcotic drug. □ **come down on** criticize or punish (someone) harshly: *she came down on me like a ton of bricks.* □ **come down to** (of a situation or outcome) be dependent on (a specified factor): *it came down to her word against Guy's.* □ **come down with** begin to suffer from (a specified illness): *I came down with influenza.* □ **come for** (of police or other officials) arrive to arrest or detain (someone). □ **come forward** volunteer oneself for a task or post or to give evidence about a crime. □ **come from** originate in; have as its source: *the word caviar comes from the Italian caviale.* ■ be the result of: *a dignity that comes from being in control.* ■ have as one's place of birth or residence: *I come from the Bronx.* ■ be descended from: *she comes from a family of Muslim scholars.* □ **come in 1** join or become involved in an enterprise: *that's where Jack comes in | I agreed to* **come in on** *the project.* ■ have a useful role or function: *this is where grammar comes in.* ■ prove to have a specified good quality: *the money came in handy for treating his cronies at the tavern.* **2** finish a race in a specified position: *the favorite came in first.* **3** (of money) be earned or received regularly. **4** [*in imperative*] begin speaking or make contact, esp. in radio communication: *come in, London.* **5** (of a tide) rise; flow. □ **come in for** receive or be the object of (a reaction), typically a negative one: *he has come in for a lot of criticism.* □ **come into** suddenly receive (money or property), esp. by inheriting it. □ **come of** result from: *no good will come of it.* ■ be descended from: *she came of Neapolitan stock.* □ **come off 1** (of an action) succeed; be accomplished. ■ fare in a specified way in a contest: *Jeff always came off worse in an argument.* **2** become detached or be detachable from something. □ **come on 1** (of a state or condition) start to arrive or happen: *she felt a mild case of the sniffles coming on | it was coming on to rain.* **2** (also **come upon**) meet or find by chance. **3** [*in imperative*] said when encouraging someone to do something or to hurry up or when one feels that someone is wrong or foolish: *Come on! We must hurry!* ■ said or shouted to express support, for example for a sports team. □ **come on to** *informal* make sexual advances toward. □ **come out 1** (of a fact) emerge; become known: *it* **came out that** *the accused had illegally registered to vote.* ■ happen as a result: *something good can* **come out of** *something that went wrong.* ■ (of a photograph) be produced satisfactorily or in a specified way: *I hope my photographs come out all right.* ■ (of the result of a calculation or measurement) emerge at a specified figure: *rough cider usually* **comes out at** *about eight percent alcohol.* **2** (of a book or other work) appear; be released or published. **3** declare oneself as being for or against something: *residents have* **come out against** *the proposals.* **4** achieve a specified placing in an examination or contest: *he deservedly came out the winner on points | she came out victorious.* ■ acquit oneself in a specified way: *surprisingly, it's Penn who comes out best.* **5** (of a stain) be removed or able to be removed. **6** *informal* openly declare that one is homosexual. [from the phrase *come out of the closet* (see **CLOSET** (sense 3)).] **7** *dated* (of a young upper-class woman) make one's debut in society. □ **come out in** *Brit.* (of a person's skin) break out in (pimples or a similar condition). □ **come out with** say (something) in a sudden, rude, or incautious way. □ **come over 1** (of a feeling or manner) begin to affect (someone). **2** change to another side or point of view. □ **come round** see **COME AROUND** above. □ **come through 1** succeed in surviving or dealing with (an illness or ordeal): *she's come through the operation very well.* **2** (of a message) be sent and received. ■ (of an official decree) be processed and notified. □ **come to 1** (also **come to oneself**) recover consciousness. **2** (of an expense) reach in total; amount to: *he hasn't the least idea of how much it will come to.* **3** (of a ship) come to a stop. □ **come under 1** be classified as or among: *they all come under the general heading of opinion polls.* **2** be subject to (an influence or authority). ■ be subjected to (pressure or aggression): *his vehicle came under mortar fire.* □ **come up 1** (of an issue, situation, or problem) occur or present itself, esp. unexpectedly. ■ (of a specified time or event) approach or draw near: *she's got exams coming up.* ■ (of a legal case) reach the time when it is scheduled to be dealt with. **2** *Brit.* begin one's studies at a university, esp. Oxford or Cambridge. □ **come up against** be faced with or opposed by (something such as an enemy or problem). □ **come up with** produce (something), esp. when pressured or challenged. □ **come upon 1** attack by surprise. **2** see **COME ON** (sense 2).

▸*prep. informal* when a specified time is reached or event happens: *I don't think that they'll be far away from honors come the new season.*

▸*n. informal* semen ejaculated at orgasm. ▷Old English *cuman*, of Germanic origin; related to Dutch *komen* and German *kommen*.

▸*PHRASES* □ **as —— as they come** used to describe someone or something that is a supreme example of the quality specified: *Smith is as tough as they come.* □ **come again?** *informal* used to ask someone to repeat or explain something they have said. □ **come and go** arrive and then depart again; move around freely. ■ exist or be present for a limited time; be transitory: *health fads come and go.* □ **come from behind** win after lagging. □ **come off it** [*in imperative*] *informal* said when vigorously expressing disbelief. □ **come to nothing** have no significant or successful result in the end. □ **come to pass** *chiefly poetic/literary* happen; occur: *it* **came to pass that** *she had two sons.* □ **come to rest** eventually cease moving. □ **come to that** (or **if it comes to that**) *informal* in fact (said to introduce an additional point): *there isn't a clock on the mantelpiece—come to that, there isn't a mantelpiece!* □ **come to think of it** on reflection (said when an idea or point occurs to one while one is speaking). □ **come what may** no matter what happens. □ **have it coming (to one)** *informal* be due for retribution on account of something bad that one has done: *his uppity sister-in-law had it coming to her.* □ **how come?** *informal* said when asking how or why something happened or is the case: *how come you never married, Jimmy?* □ **to come** (following a noun) in the future: *films that would inspire generations to come | in years to come.* □ **where someone is coming from** *informal* someone's meaning, motivation, or personality.

USAGE The use of **come** followed by **and**, as in ***come and*** *see for yourself*, dates back to Old English, but is seen by some as incorrect or only suitable for informal English.
For more details see **usage** at **AND**.

come·a·long ▸*n. informal* a hand-operated winch.

come·back /ˈkəmˌbak/ ▸*n.* **1** a return by a well-known person, esp. an entertainer or sports player, to the activity in which they have formerly been successful: *the heavyweight champion is set to* **make his comeback** *| [as adj.] his career died after a couple of comeback attempts.* ■ a return to fashion of an item, activity, or style: *stirrup pants have* **made a comeback**. **2** *informal* a quick reply to a critical remark. ■ the opportunity to seek redress: *there's no comeback if he messes up your case.*

Com·e·con /ˈkäməˌkän/ an economic association of eastern European countries founded in 1949 and analogous to the European Economic Community. With the collapse of communism in eastern Europe, the association was dissolved in 1991. ▷contraction of **COUNCIL FOR MUTUAL ECONOMIC ASSISTANCE**.

co·me·di·an /kəˈmēdēən/ ▸*n.* an entertainer whose act is designed to make an audience laugh. ■ *often ironic* an amusing or entertaining person. ■ a comic actor. ▷late 16th cent. (denoting a comic playwright): from French *comédien*, from Old French *comedie* (see **COMEDY**). The sense 'entertainer' dates from the late 19th cent.

Co·mé·die Fran·çaise /ˌkômādē fränˈsez/ the French national theater (used for both comedy and tragedy), in Paris, founded in 1680 by Louis XIV.

co·me·di·enne /kəˌmēdēˈen/ ▸*n.* a female comedian. ▷mid 19th cent.: from French *comédienne*, feminine of *comédien* (see **COMEDIAN**).

com·e·do /ˈkäməˌdō/ ▸*n.* (*pl.* **com·e·do·nes** /ˌkäməˈdōnēz/) technical term for **BLACKHEAD** (sense 1). ▷mid 19th cent.: from Latin, literally 'glutton,' from *comedere* 'eat up,' from *com-* 'altogether' + *edere* 'eat.' Used formerly as a name for parasitic worms, the term here alludes to the wormlike matter that can be squeezed from a blackhead.

com·e·do·gen·ic /ˌkäməˌdōˈjenik/ ▸*adj.* tending to cause blackheads by blocking the pores of the skin.

come·down /ˈkəmˌdoun/ ▸*n. informal* **1** a loss of status or importance: *patrol duty? A* **comedown for** *a sergeant.* **2** a feeling of disappointment or depression: *it's such a comedown after Christmas is over.* ■ [*in sing.*] a lessening of the sensations generated by a narcotic drug as its effects wear off.

com·e·dy /ˈkämədē/ ▸*n.* (*pl.* **-dies**) professional entertainment consisting of jokes and satirical sketches, intended to make an audience laugh. ■ a movie, play, or broadcast program intended to make an audience laugh: *a rollicking new comedy.* ■ the style or genre of such types of entertainment. ■ the humorous or amusing aspects of something: *advertising people see the comedy in their work.* ■ a play characterized by its humorous or satirical tone and its depiction of amusing people or incidents, in which the characters ultimately triumph over adversity: *Shakespeare's* *comedies.* ■ the dramatic genre represented by such plays: *satiric comedy.* Compare with TRAGEDY (sense 2). ▷late Middle English (as a genre of drama, also denoting a narrative poem with a happy ending, as in Dante's *Divine Comedy*): from Old French *comedie,* via Latin from Greek *kōmōidia,* from *kōmōidos* 'comic poet,' from *kōmos* 'revel' + *aoidos* 'singer.' **—co·me·dic** /kə'mēdik/ *adj.*

▸*PHRASE* □ **comedy of errors** a situation made amusing by bungling and incompetence: *the comedy of errors that is Medicare's physician payment schedule.*

com·e·dy of man·ners ▸*n.* a comedy that satirizes behavior in a particular social group, esp. the upper classes.

come-hith·er *informal, dated* ▸*adj.* flirtatious; sexually inviting: *nymphs with come-hither looks.*

▸*n.* [in *sing.*] a flirtatious or enticing manner.

C

come·ly /'kəmlē/ ▸*adj.* (**-li·er, -li·est**) (typically of a woman) pleasant to look at; attractive. ■ agreeable; suitable. ▷Middle English: probably shortened from *becomely* 'fitting, becoming,' from BECOME. **—come·li·ness** *n.*

come-on ▸*n. informal* a thing that is intended to lure or entice. ■ a gesture or remark that is intended to attract someone sexually: *she was* ***giving*** *me* ***the come-on.*** ■ a marketing ploy, such as a free or cheap offer: [as *adj.*] *introductory come-on rates.*

come-out·er ▸*n. chiefly historical* a person who dissociates himself or herself from an organization.

com·er /'kəmər/ ▸*n.* **1** a person who arrives somewhere: *feeding every comer is still a sacred duty.* See also ALL COMERS at ALL; LATECOMER; NEWCOMER. **2** [in *sing.*] *informal* a person or thing likely to succeed: *many in the party see tax relief as a comer.*

co·mes·ti·ble /kə'mestəbəl/ ▸*n.* (usu. **comestibles**) an item of food: *a fridge groaning with comestibles.*

▸*adj.* edible: *comestible plants.* ▷late 15th cent.: from Old French, from medieval Latin *comestibilis,* from Latin *comest-* 'eaten up,' from the verb *comedere,* from *com-* 'altogether' + *edere* 'eat.'

com·et /'kämit/ ▸*n.* a celestial object consisting of a nucleus of ice and dust and, when near the sun, a "tail" of gas and dust particles pointing away from the sun.

Originating in the remotest regions of the solar system, most comets follow regular eccentric orbits and appear in the inner solar system as periodic comets, some of which break up and can be the origin of annual meteor showers. They were formerly considered to be supernatural omens.

▷late Old English, from Latin *cometa,* from Greek *komētēs* 'long-haired (star),' from *komē* 'hair'; reinforced by Old French *comete.* **—com·et·ar·y** /'kämi,terē/ *adj.*

come·up·pance /kə'məpəns/ ▸*n.* [usu. in *sing.*] *informal* a punishment or fate that someone deserves: *he* ***got his comeuppance.***

com·fit /'kəmfit; 'kämfit/ ▸*n. dated* a candy consisting of a nut, seed, or other center coated in sugar. ▷Middle English: from Old French *confit,* from Latin *confectum* 'something prepared,' neuter past participle of *conficere* 'put together' (see CONFECT).

com·fort /'kəmfərt/ ▸*n.* **1** a state of physical ease and freedom from pain or constraint: *room for four people to travel in comfort.* ■ (**comforts**) things that contribute to physical ease and well-being: *the low upholstered chair was one of the room's few comforts.* ■ prosperity and the pleasant lifestyle secured by it: *my father left us enough to live in comfort.* **2** consolation for grief or anxiety: *a few words of comfort.* ■ reassurance: *they should* ***take comfort*** *that help is available.* ■ [in *sing.*] a person or thing that gives consolation: *his friendship was a great comfort.* ■ a person or thing that gives satisfaction: *I felt a great comfort in the relationship of the moon to my astrological sign.* **3** *dialect* a warm quilt.

▸*v.* [*trans.*] soothe in grief; console: *she broke down in tears and her friend tried to comfort her.* ■ help (someone) feel at ease; reassure: *her strength comforted and protected me* | [as *adj.*] (**comforting**) *his comforting presence.* ▷Middle English (as a noun, in the senses 'strengthening, support, consolation'; as a verb, in the senses 'strengthen, give support, console'): from Old French *confort* (noun), *conforter* (verb), from late Latin *confortare* 'strengthen,' from *com-* (expressing intensive force) + Latin *fortis* 'strong.' The sense 'something producing physical ease' arose in the mid 17th cent. **—com·fort·ing·ly** *adv.* **—com·fort·less** *adj.*

▸*PHRASE* □ **too — for comfort** causing physical or mental unease by an excess of the specified quality: *it can be too hot for comfort in July and August.*

com·fort·a·ble /'kəmfərtəbəl; 'kəmftərbəl/ ▸*adj.* **1** (esp. of clothes or furnishings) providing physical ease and relaxation: *invitingly comfortable beds.* ■ (of a person) physically relaxed and free from constraint: *he would not be comfortable in any other clothes.* ■ not in pain (used esp. of a hospital patient). ■ free from stress or fear: *they appear very comfortable in each other's company* | *few of us are* ***comfortable with*** *confrontations.* ■ free from financial worry; having an adequate standard of living. **2** as large as is needed or wanted: *a comfortable income.* ■ with a wide margin: *a comfortable victory.*

▸*n. dialect* a warm quilt. ▷Middle English (in the sense 'pleasant, pleasing'): from Anglo-Norman French *confortable,* from *conforter* 'to comfort' (see COMFORT). **—com·fort·a·ble·ness** *n.* **—com·fort·a·bly** /-blē/ *adv.*

com·fort·er /'kəmfərtər/ ▸*n.* **1** a warm quilt. **2** a person or thing that provides consolation. ■ (**Comforter**) the Holy Spirit. **3** *dated* a woolen scarf. ▷late Middle English: from Old French *comforteor,* from *conforter* 'to comfort' (see COMFORT).

com·fort food ▸*n.* food that provides consolation or a feeling of well-being, typically any with a high sugar or other carbohydrate content and associated with childhood or home cooking.

com·fort sta·tion ▸*n.* a public restroom for travelers or campers.

com·fort zone ▸*n.* a place or situation where one feels safe or at ease and without stress: *times when we must act beyond our comfort zones* | *if you stay within your comfort zone, you will never improve.*

com·frey /'kəmfrē/ ▸*n.* (*pl.* **-freys**) a Eurasian plant of the borage family, with large hairy leaves and clusters of purplish or white bell-shaped flowers. • Genus *Symphytum,* family Boraginaceae: several species, in particular the **common comfrey** (*S. officinale*), which is used in herbal medicine (see BONESET). ▷Middle English: from Anglo-Norman French *cumfirie,* based on Latin *conferva,* from *confervere* 'heal' (literally 'boil together,' referring to the plant's medicinal use).

com·fy /'kəmfē/ ▸*adj.* (**-fi·er, -fi·est**) *informal* comfortable. ▷early 19th cent.: abbreviation. **—com·fi·ly** /-fəlē/ *adv.* **—com·fi·ness** *n.*

com·ic /'kämik/ ▸*adj.* causing or meant to cause laughter: *comic and fantastic exaggeration.* ■ relating to or in the style of comedy: *a comic actor* | *comic drama.*

▸*n.* **1** a comedian, esp. a professional one: *a stand-up comic.* **2** (**comics**) comic strips. ▷late 16th cent.: via Latin from Greek *kōmikos,* from *kōmos* 'revel.'

com·i·cal /'kämikəl/ ▸*adj.* amusing: *a series of comical misunderstandings.* ▷late Middle English (in the sense 'relating to or in the style of comedy'): from Latin *comicus* (see COMIC) + -AL. **—com·i·cal·i·ty** /,kämə'kalitē/ *n.* **—com·i·cal·ly** /-ik(ə)lē/ *adv.*

Co·mice /'kämәs/ (in full **Doyenne du Comice**) ▸*n.* a large yellow dessert pear. ▷mid 19th cent.: from French, literally 'association, cooperative,' referring to the *Comice Horticole* of Angers, France, where this variety was developed.

com·ic op·er·a ▸*n.* an opera that portrays humorous situations and characters, enhanced by spoken dialogue. ■ the genre of such opera.

com·ic re·lief ▸*n.* comic episodes in a dramatic or literary work that offset more serious sections. ■ a character or characters providing this. ■ comical episodes that serve to release tension in real life.

com·ic strip ▸*n.* a sequence of drawings in boxes that tell an amusing story, typically printed in a newspaper or comic book.

com·ing /'kəmiNG/ ▸*adj.* **1** due to happen or just beginning: *work is due to start in the coming year.* **2** likely to be important or successful in the future: *he was the coming man of French racing.*

▸*n.* [in *sing.*] an arrival or an approach: *the coming of a new age.*

▸*PHRASES* □ **comings and goings** the busy movements of a person or group of people, esp. in and out of a place. □ **not know if one is coming or going** *informal* be confused, esp. as a result of being very busy.

Co·mi·no /kə'mēnō/ the smallest of the three main islands of Malta.

COMINT /'käm,int/ ▸*abbr.* communications intelligence.

Com·in·tern /'kämin,tərn/ the Third International, a communist organization (1919–43). See INTERNATIONAL (sense 2). ▷from Russian *Komintern,* blend of *kom(munisticheskiĭ)* 'communist' and *intern(atsional)* 'international.'

com·i·tal /'kämətl/ ▸*adj. chiefly historical* of or relating to a count or earl. ▷mid 19th cent.: from medieval Latin *comitalis,* from *comes, comit-* 'a count.'

com·i·ty /'kämitē/ ▸*n.* (*pl.* **-ties**) **1** courtesy and considerate behavior toward others. **2** an association of nations for their mutual benefit. ■ (also **comity of nations**) the mutual recognition by nations of the laws and customs of others. ▷mid 16th cent. (sense 1): from Latin *comitas,* from *comis* 'courteous.'

com·ix /'kämiks/ ▸*plural n.* comic books and comic strips, esp. ones written for adults or of an underground or alternative nature. ▷alteration of *comics.*

comm /käm/ ▸*n.* short for COMMUNICATION: [as *adj.*] *a comm link.*

comm. ▸*abbr.* ■ commerce. ■ commercial. ■ commission. ■ commissioner. ■ committee. ■ common.

com·ma /'kämə/ ▸*n.* **1** a punctuation mark (,) indicating a pause between parts of a sentence. It is also used to separate items in a list and to mark the place of thousands in a large numeral. **2** *Music* a minute interval or difference of pitch. **3** (also **comma butterfly**) a butterfly that has wings with irregular, ragged edges and typically a white or silver comma-shaped mark on the underside of each hind wing. • Genus *Polygonia,* subfamily Nymphalinae, family Nymphalidae: numerous species, in particular the common **eastern comma** (*P. comma*) of eastern North America. ▷late 16th cent. (originally as a term in rhetoric denoting a group of words shorter than a colon; see COLON[1]): via Latin from Greek *komma* 'piece cut off, short clause,' from *koptein* 'cut.'

comma 3

Com·ma·ger /'kämijər/, Henry Steele (1902–98), U.S. educator and writer. Among his notable works are *The Growth of the American Republic* (co-authored with Samuel Eliot Morison, 1931), *The American Mind* (1951), and *The Empire of Reason* (1977).

com·mand /kə'mand/ ▸*v.* **1** [*reporting verb*] give an authoritative order: [*trans.*] *a gruff voice commanded us to enter* | [with *direct speech*] *"Stop arguing!" he commanded* | [with *clause*] *he commanded that work should cease* | [*trans.*] *my mother commands my presence.* ■ [*intrans.*] give orders: *she commands and we obey.* ■ [*intrans.*] have authority: *someone born to command.* ■ [*trans.*] *Military* have authority over; be in charge of (a unit): *he commanded a battalion at Normandy.* ■ [*trans.*] dominate (a strategic position) from a superior height: *the two castles commanded the harbor.* ■ [*trans.*] *archaic* control or restrain (oneself or one's feelings): *he commanded himself with an effort.* **2** [*trans.*] be in a strong enough position to secure: *no party commanded a majority.* ■ deserve and receive: *a moral force that commanded respect.*

▸*n.* an authoritative order: *it's unlikely they'll obey your commands.* ■ *Computing* an instruction or signal that causes a computer to perform one of its basic functions. ■ authority, esp. over armed forces: *an officer* ***took command*** | *who's* ***in command?*** | *we will have nearly thirty thousand people* ***under our command.*** ■ [in *sing.*] the ability to use or control something: *he had a brilliant command of English.* ■ [treated as *sing.* or *pl.*] *Military* a group of officers exercising control over a particular group or operation. ■ *Military* a body of troops or a district under the control of a particular officer. See note at JURISDICTION. ▷Middle English: from Old French *comander* 'to command,' from late Latin *commandare,* from *com-* (expressing intensive force) + *mandare* 'commit, command.' Compare with COMMEND.

▸*PHRASE* □ **at someone's command** at someone's disposal; available: *he had at his command a vast number of ready-made phrases.*

com·mand and con·trol ▸*n.* [usu. as *adj.*] *chiefly Military* the running of an armed force or other organization: *a command-and-control bunker.*

com·man·dant /'kämən,dant; -,dänt/ ▸*n.* an officer in charge of a particular force or institution: *the West Point commandant of cadets.* ▷late 17th cent.: from French *commandant,* or Italian or Spanish *commandante*, all from late Latin *commandare* 'to command' (see **COMMAND**).

com·mand-driv·en ▸*adj. Computing* (of a program or computer) operated by means of commands keyed in by the user or issued by another program or computer.

com·mand e·con·o·my ▸*n.* an economy in which production, investment, prices, and incomes are determined centrally by a government.

com·man·deer /ˌkämənˈdi(ə)r/ ▸*v.* [*trans.*] officially take possession or control of (something), esp. for military purposes: *telegraph and telephone lines were commandeered by the generals.* ■ take possession of (something) without authority: *he hoisted himself onto a table, commandeering it as a speaker's platform.* ■ enlist (someone) to help in a task, typically against the person's will: *he commandeered the men to find a table.* ▷early 19th cent.: from Afrikaans *kommandeer*, from Dutch *commanderen*, from French *commander* 'to command' (see **COMMAND**).

com·mand·er /kəˈmandər/ (abbr.: **Comdr.**) ▸*n.* **1** a person in authority, esp. over a body of troops or a military operation: *the commander of a paratroop regiment.* ■ a naval officer of high rank, in particular (in the U.S. Navy or Coast Guard) an officer ranking above lieutenant commander and below captain. ■ (in certain metropolitan police departments) the officer in charge of a division, district, precinct, or squad. **2** a member of a higher class in some orders of knighthood. ▷Middle English: from Old French *comandeor*, from late Latin *commandare* 'to command' (see **COMMAND**). —**com·mand·er·ship** /-ˌSHip/ *n.*

com·mand·er in chief (also **Com·mand·er in Chief**) ▸*n.* (*pl.* **com·mand·ers in chief**) a head of state or officer in supreme command of a country's armed forces. ■ an officer in charge of a major subdivision of a country's armed forces, or of its forces in a particular area.

Com·mand·er of the Faith·ful ▸*n.* one of the titles of a caliph.

com·mand·ing /kəˈmandiNG/ ▸*adj.* [*attrib.*] (in military contexts) having a position of authority: *a commanding officer.* ■ (of an advantage or position) controlling; superior: *a commanding 13-6 lead.* ■ indicating or expressing authority; imposing: *a man of commanding presence | her style is commanding.* ■ (of a place or position) dominating physically; giving a wide view: *a commanding position looking out over the sea.* —**com·mand·ing·ly** *adv.*

com·mand lan·guage ▸*n. Computing* a computer programming language composed chiefly of a set of commands or operators, used esp. for communicating with the operating system of a computer.

com·mand·ment /kəˈmandmənt/ ▸*n.* a divine rule, esp. one of the Ten Commandments. ■ a rule to be observed as strictly as one of the Ten Commandments. ▷Middle English: from Old French *comandement*, from *comander* 'to command' (see **COMMAND**).

com·mand mod·ule (abbr.: **CM**) ▸*n.* the detachable control portion of a manned spacecraft.

com·man·do /kəˈmandō/ ▸*n.* (*pl.* **-dos**) a soldier specially trained to carry out raids. ■ a unit of such troops. ■ a group forming part of a larger organization, typically an illegal or secret one, and carrying out attacks on its behalf. ▷late 18th cent. (denoting a militia, originally consisting of Boers in South Africa): from Portuguese (earlier form of *comando*), from *commandar* 'to command,' from late Latin *commandare* (see **COMMAND**).

▸*PHRASE* □ **go commando** *humorous* wear no underpants.

com·mand per·for·mance ▸*n.* a presentation of a play, concert, opera, or other show at the request of royalty.

com·mand post ▸*n.* the place from which a military unit is commanded.

com·mand ser·geant ma·jor ▸*n.* a noncommissioned officer in the U.S. Army ranking above first sergeant.

comme ci, comme ça /kôm ˈsē kôm ˈsä/ ▸*adv.* (in answer to a question) neither very good nor very bad; so-so. ▷mid 20th cent.: French, literally 'like this, like that.'

com·me·dia dell'ar·te /kəˈmādēə dəl ˈärtē/ ▸*n.* an improvised kind of popular comedy in Italian theaters in the 16th–18th centuries, based on stock characters. Actors adapted their comic dialogue and action according to a few basic plots (commonly love intrigues) and to topical issues. ▷Italian, 'comedy of art.'

comme il faut /ˌkôm ēl ˈfō/ ▸*adj.* [*predic.*] correct in behavior or etiquette. ▷mid 18th cent.: French, literally 'as is necessary.'

com·mem·o·ra·to·ry /kəˈmemərəˌtôrē/ ▸*adj.* serving to commemorate; commemorative.

com·mem·o·rate /kəˈmeməˌrāt/ ▸*v.* [*trans.*] recall and show respect for (someone or something) in a ceremony: *a wreath-laying ceremony to commemorate the war dead.* ■ serve as a memorial to: *a stone commemorating a boy who died at sea.* ■ mark (a significant event): *the City of Boston commemorated the 400th anniversary of the discovery of America.* ■ (often **be commemorated**) celebrate (an event, a person, or a situation) by doing or building something: *it was a night commemorated in a song.* ▷late 16th cent.: from Latin *commemorat-* 'brought to remembrance,' from the verb *commemorare*, from *com-* 'altogether' + *memorare* 'relate' (from *memor* 'mindful'). —**com·mem·o·ra·tor** /-ˌrātər/ *n.*

com·mem·o·ra·tion /kəˌmeməˈrāSHən/ ▸*n.* remembrance, typically expressed in a ceremony: *solemn ceremonies of commemoration.* ■ a ceremony or celebration in which a person or event is remembered: *VJ-Day commemorations in August.* ▷late Middle English: from Latin *commemoratio(n-)*, from the verb *commemorare* 'bring to remembrance' (see **COMMEMORATE**).

▸*PHRASE* □ **in commemoration** as a reminder, esp. a ritual or official one: *the window was ordered by the duchess in commemoration of her son.*

com·mem·o·ra·tive /kəˈmem(ə)rətiv; kəˈmeməˌrātiv/ ▸*adj.* acting as a memorial or mark of an event or person: *a commemorative plaque.*

▸*n.* an object such as a stamp or coin made to mark an event or honor a person. Compare with **DEFINITIVE**.

com·mence /kəˈmens/ ▸*v.* begin; start: [*trans.*] *his design team commenced work* | [*intrans.*] *a public inquiry is due to commence on the 16th.* ▷Middle English: from Old French *commencier*, *comencier*, based on Latin *com-* (expressing intensive force) + *initiare* 'begin.'

com·mence·ment /kəˈmensmənt/ ▸*n.* **1** [usu. in *sing.*] a beginning or start: *at the commencement of training.* **2** a ceremony in which degrees or diplomas are conferred on graduating students: [as *adj.*] *a commencement address.* ▷Middle English: from Old French, from the verb *commencier* (see **COMMENCE**).

com·mend /kəˈmend/ ▸*v.* [*trans.*] **1** (often **be commended**) praise formally or officially: *he was commended by the judge for his courageous actions.* See notes at **APPROVE, PRAISE.** ■ present as suitable for approval or acceptance; recommend: *I* **commend** *her* **to** *you without reservation.* ■ cause to be acceptable or pleasing: *this recording has a lot to commend it.* **2** (**commend someone/something to**) entrust someone or something to: *I commend them to your care.* ▷Middle English: from Latin *commendare*, from *com-* (expressing intensive force) + *mandare* 'commit, entrust.' Compare with **COMMAND**.

▸*PHRASE* □ **commend me to** *archaic* remember me kindly to (someone): *commend me to my son, and bid him rule better than I.*

com·mend·a·ble /kəˈmendəbəl/ ▸*adj.* deserving praise: *commendable restraint.* ▷late Middle English: via Old French from Latin *commendabilis*, from *commendare* (see **COMMEND**). —**com·mend·a·bly** /-blē/ *adv.*

com·men·da·tion /ˌkämənˈdāSHən; -ˌen-/ ▸*n.* praise: *the film deserved the highest commendation | commendations for their kindness.* ■ an award involving special praise: *the detectives received commendations for bravery.* ▷Middle English: from Old French, from Latin *commendatio(n-)*, from *commendare* 'commit to the care of' (see **COMMEND**). Originally (in the plural) the term denoted a liturgical office ending with a prayer commending the souls of the dead to God.

com·mend·a·to·ry /kəˈmendəˌtôrē/ ▸*adj. archaic* serving to commend; recommending. ▷mid 16th cent.: from late Latin *commendatorius*, from Latin *commendare* 'commit to the care of' (see **COMMEND**).

com·men·sal /kəˈmensəl/ ▸*adj. Biology* of, relating to, or exhibiting commensalism.

▸*n. Biology* a commensal organism, such as many bacteria. ▷late 19th cent.: from medieval Latin *commensalis*, from *com-* 'sharing' + *mensa* 'a table.' —**com·men·sal·i·ty** /ˌkämenˈsalitē/ *n.*

com·men·sal·ism /kəˈmensəˌlizəm/ ▸*n. Biology* an association between two organisms in which one benefits and the other derives neither benefit nor harm.

com·men·su·ra·ble /kəˈmensərəbəl; kəˈmenSHərəbəl/ ▸*adj.* **1** measurable by the same standard: *the finite is not* **commensurable with** *the infinite.* **2** (**commensurable to**) *rare* proportionate to. **3** *Mathematics* (of numbers) in a ratio equal to a ratio of integers. ▷mid 16th cent.: from late Latin *commensurabilis*, from *com-* 'together' + *mensurabilis*, from *mensurare* 'to measure.' —**com·men·su·ra·bil·i·ty** /kəˌmensərəˈbilətē; -ˌmenSHə-/ *n.* —**com·men·su·ra·bly** /-blē/ *adv.*

com·men·su·rate /kəˈmensərət; -ˈmenSHə-/ ▸*adj.* corresponding in size or degree; in proportion: *salary will be* **commensurate with** *experience | such heavy responsibility must receive commensurate reward.* ▷mid 17th cent.: from late Latin *commensuratus*, from *com-* 'together' + *mensuratus*, past participle of *mensurare* 'to measure.' —**com·men·su·rate·ly** *adv.*

com·ment /ˈkämˌent/ ▸*n.* a remark expressing an opinion or reaction: *you asked for* **comments on** *the new proposals.* ■ discussion, esp. of a critical nature, of an issue or event: *the plans were not sent to the council for comment.* ■ an indirect expression of the views of the creator of an artistic work: *their second single is a comment on the commercial nature of raves.* ■ an explanatory note in a book or other written text. ■ *archaic* a written explanation or commentary. ■ *Computing* a piece of specially tagged text placed within a program to help other users to understand it, which the computer ignores when running the program.

▸*v.* [*trans.*] express (an opinion or reaction): *the review commented that the book was agreeably written* | [*intrans.*] *the company would not* **comment on** *the venture | "He's an independent soul," she commented.* ■ [*trans.*] *Computing* place a piece of specially tagged explanatory text within (a program) to assist other users. ■ *Computing* turn (part of a program) into a comment so that the computer ignores it when running the program: *you could try* **commenting out** *that line.* ▷late Middle English (in the senses 'expository treatise' and 'explanatory note'): from Latin *commentum* 'contrivance' (in late Latin also 'interpretation'), neuter past participle of *comminisci* 'devise.' —**com·ment·er** *n.*

▸*PHRASE* □ **no comment** used in refusing to answer a question, esp. in a sensitive situation.

com·men·tar·i·at /ˌkämənˈte(ə)rēət/ ▸*n.* members of the news media considered as a class. ▷late 20th cent.: blend of *commentary* and *proletariat*.

com·men·tar·y /ˈkämənˌterē/ ▸*n.* (*pl.* **-tar·ies**) the expression of opinions or explanations about an event or situation: *an editorial commentary | narrative overlaid with commentary.* ■ opinion, either written or spoken. ■ a descriptive spoken account (esp. on radio or television) of an event or a performance as it happens. ■ a set of explanatory or critical notes on a text: *a commentary on the Old Testament.* ▷late Middle English: from Latin *commentarius*, *commentarium* (adjective, used as a noun), from *commentari*, frequentative of *comminisci* 'devise.'

com·men·tate /ˈkämənˌtāt/ ▸*v.* [*intrans.*] report on an event as it occurs, esp. for a news or sports broadcast; provide a commentary. ▷mid 19th cent.: back-formation from **COMMENTATOR**.

com·men·ta·tor /ˈkämənˌtātər/ ▸*n.* a person who comments on events, esp. on television or radio. ■ a person who writes a commentary on a text.

com·merce /ˈkämərs/ (abbr.: **comm.**) ▸*n.* **1** the activity of buying and selling, esp. on a large scale: *the possible increase of commerce by a great railroad.* **2** *dated* social dealings between people: *outside the normal commerce of civilized life.* **3** *archaic* sexual intercourse. ▷mid 16th cent. (sense 2): from French, or from Latin *commercium* 'trade, trading,' from *com-* 'together' + *mercium* (from *merx, merc-* 'merchandise').

com·mer·cial /kəˈmərSHəl/ (abbr.: **comm.**) ▸*adj.* **1** concerned with or engaged in commerce: *a commercial agreement.* **2** making or intended to make a profit: *commercial products.* ■ having profit, rather than artistic or other value, as a primary aim: *their work is too commercial.* **3** (of television or radio) funded by the revenue from broadcast advertisements. **4** (of chemicals) supplied in bulk and not of the highest purity.

▸*n.* a television or radio advertisement. —**com·mer·ci·al·i·ty** /kəˌmərSHēˈalitē/ *n.* —**com·mer·cial·ly** *adv.*

com·mer·cial art ▸*n.* art used in advertising and selling.

com·mer·cial bank ▸*n.* a bank that offers services to the general public and to companies.

com·mer·cial break ▸*n.* an interruption in the transmission of broadcast programming during which advertisements are broadcast.

com·mer·cial·ism /kəˈmərSHəˌlizəm/ ▸*n.* emphasis on

the maximizing of profit: *deficits prompted efforts for greater commercialism.* ■ *derogatory* practices and attitudes that are concerned with the making of profit at the expense of quality: *the issue of creeping commercialism in schools.*

com·mer·cial·ize /kəˈmərsʜəˌlīz/ ▸*v.* [*trans.*] (usu. **be commercialized**) make (an organization or activity) commercial: *the museum has been commercialized.* ■ exploit or spoil for the purpose of gaining profit: [as *adj.*] (**commercialized**) *commercialized resort areas.* —**com·mer·cial·i·za·tion** /kəˌmərsʜələˈzāsʜən/ *n.*

com·mer·cial pa·per ▸*n.* short-term unsecured promissory notes issued by companies.

com·mer·cial space ▸*n.* see SPACE (sense 1).

com·mer·cial trav·el·er ▸*n. dated* a traveling sales representative.

com·mer·cial ve·hi·cle ▸*n.* a vehicle used for carrying goods or fare-paying passengers.

com·mie /ˈkämē/ (also **Com·mie**) *informal, derogatory* ▸*n.* (*pl.* **-mies**) a communist.
▸*adj.* communist. ▷1940s: abbreviation.

com·mi·na·tion /ˌkäməˈnāsʜən/ ▸*n.* the action of threatening divine vengeance. ■ the recital of divine threats against sinners in the Anglican Liturgy for Ash Wednesday. ▷late Middle English: from Latin *comminatio(n-)*, from the verb *comminari*, from *com-* (expressing intensive force) + *minari* 'threaten.'

com·min·a·to·ry /ˈkämənəˌtôrē; kəˈminə-/ ▸*adj.* threatening, punitive, or vengeful. ▷early 16th cent.: from medieval Latin *comminatorius*, from *comminat-* 'threatened,' from the verb *comminari* (see COMMINATION).

com·min·gle /kəˈmiNGgəl; kä-/ ▸*v.* mix; blend: [*intrans.*] *the dust had* **commingled with** *the rain* | [*trans.*] *publicly reproved for commingling funds.* ▷early 17th cent.: from COM- 'together' + MINGLE.

com·mi·nut·ed /ˈkäməˌn(y)o͞otəd/ ▸*adj. technical* reduced to minute particles or fragments. ■ *Medicine* (of a fracture) producing multiple bone splinters. ▷early 17th cent.: past participle of *comminute*, from Latin *comminut-* 'broken into pieces,' from the verb *comminuere*, from *com-* 'together' + *minuere* 'lessen.'

com·mi·nu·tion /ˌkäməˈn(y)o͞osʜən/ ▸*n. technical* the action of reducing a material, an ore, to minute particles or fragments.

com·mis /kəˈmē; kô-/ (also **commis chef**) ▸*n.* (*pl.* same) a junior chef. ▷1930s: from French, 'deputy, clerk,' past participle of *commettre* 'entrust,' from Latin *committere* (see COMMIT).

com·mis·er·ate /kəˈmizəˌrāt/ ▸*v.* [*intrans.*] express or feel sympathy or pity; sympathize: *she went over to* **commiserate with** *Rose on her unfortunate circumstances.* ■ [*trans.*] *archaic* feel, show, or express pity for (someone): *she did not exult in her rival's fall, but, on the contrary, commiserated her.* ▷late 16th cent.: from Latin *commiserat-* 'commiserated,' from the verb *commiserari*, from *com-* 'with' + *miserari* 'to lament' (from *miser* 'wretched'). —**com·mis·er·a·tion** /kəˌmizəˈrāsʜən/ *n.* —**com·mis·er·a·tive** /-rətiv/ *adj.*

com·mish /kəˈmisʜ/ ▸*n. informal* **1** short for COMMISSIONER. **2** short for COMMISSION: *out of commish.*

com·mis·saire /ˌkômiˈse(ə)r/ ▸*n.* a senior police officer in France. ■ an official at a bicycle race or other sporting event. ▷mid 18th cent.: French.

com·mis·sar /ˈkäməˌsär; ˌkäməˈsär/ ▸*n.* an official of the Communist Party, esp. in the former Soviet Union or present-day China, responsible for political education and organization. ■ a head of a government department in the former Soviet Union before 1946. ■ *figurative* a strict or prescriptive figure of authority: *our academic commissars.* ▷early 20th cent. (Russian Revolution): from Russian *komissar*, from French *commissaire*, from medieval Latin *commissarius* (see COMMISSARY).

com·mis·sar·i·at /ˌkäməˈse(ə)rēit/ ▸*n.* **1** *chiefly Military* a department for the supply of food and equipment. **2** a government department of the USSR before 1946. ▷late 16th cent. (as a Scots legal term denoting the jurisdiction of a commissary, often spelled *commissariot*): from French *commissariat*, reinforced by medieval Latin *commissariatus*, both from medieval Latin *commissarius* 'person in charge,' from Latin *committere* 'entrust.'

com·mis·sar·y /ˈkäməˌserē/ ▸*n.* (*pl.* **-sar·ies**) **1** a restaurant in a movie studio, military base, prison, or other institution. ■ a store that sells food and drink to members of an organization, esp. a large grocery store on a military base. **2** a deputy or delegate. ▷late Middle English: from medieval Latin *commissarius* 'person in charge,' from Latin *commiss-* 'joined, entrusted,' from the verb *committere* (see COMMIT). —**com·mis·sar·i·al** /ˌkäməˈse(ə)rēəl/ *adj.*

com·mis·sion /kəˈmisʜən/ (abbr.: **comm.**) ▸*n.* **1** the authority to perform a task or certain duties. ■ an instruction, command, or duty given to a person or group of people: *his commission to redesign the building* | *he received a commission to act as an informer.* ■ an order for something, esp. a work of art, to be produced: *Mozart at last received a commission to write an opera.* ■ a work produced in response to such an order. **2** a group of people officially charged with a particular function: *the United Nations High Commission for Refugees.* **3** an amount of money, typically a set percentage of the value involved, paid to an agent in a commercial transaction: *foreign banks may charge a commission* | *he sold cosmetics* **on commission.** **4** a warrant conferring the rank of officer in an army, navy, or air force: *he has resigned his commission.* **5** the action of committing a crime or offense: *use of a deadly weapon in the commission of a felony.*
▸*v.* [*trans.*] **1** give an order for or authorize the production of (something such as a building, piece of equipment, or work of art). ■ order or authorize (a person or organization) to do or produce something: *they commissioned an architect to manage the building project.* ■ give (an artist) an order for a piece of work: *he was commissioned to do a series of drawings.* **2** bring (something newly produced, such as a factory or machine) into working condition: *we had a few hiccups getting the heating equipment commissioned.* ■ bring (a warship) into readiness for active service: *the aircraft carrier* Midway *was commissioned in 1945.* **3** (usu. **be commissioned**) appoint (someone) to the rank of officer in the armed services: *he was commissioned after attending midshipman school* | [as *adj.*] (**commissioned**) *a commissioned officer.* ▷Middle English: via Old French from Latin *commissio(n-)*, from *committere* 'entrust' (see COMMIT). —**com·mis·sion·a·ble** *adj.*
▸PHRASES □ **in commission** (of a ship, vehicle, machine, etc.) in use or in service. □ **out of commission** not in service; not in working order. ■ (of a person) unable to work or function normally, esp. through illness or injury.

com·mis·sion·aire /kəˌmisʜəˈne(ə)r/ ▸*n. chiefly Brit.* a uniformed door attendant at a hotel, theater, or other building. ■ a retired member of the armed services. ▷mid 17th cent.: from French, from medieval Latin *commissarius* 'person in charge,' from Latin *committere* 'entrust' (see COMMIT).

com·mis·sion·er /kəˈmisʜ(ə)nər/ (abbr.: **comm.**) ▸*n.* a person appointed by a commission to perform a specific task: *the traffic commissioner.* ■ a person appointed as a member of a government commission: *the New York State Health Commissioner.* ■ a person appointed to regulate a particular sport: *the baseball commissioner.* ■ a representative of the supreme authority in an area. ▷late Middle English: from medieval Latin *commissionarius*, from Latin *commissio* (see COMMISSION). —**com·mis·sion·er·ship** /-ˌsʜip/ *n.*

com·mis·sure /ˈkäməˌsʜo͝or/ ▸*n. technical* a junction, joint, or seam, in particular: ■ *Anatomy* the joint between two bones. ■ *Anatomy* a band of nerve tissue connecting the hemispheres of the brain, the two sides of the spinal cord, etc. ■ *Anatomy* the line where the upper and lower lips or eyelids meet. ▷late Middle English: from Latin *commissura* 'junction,' from *committere* 'join' (see COMMIT). —**com·mis·su·ral** /ˌkäməˈsʜo͝orəl/ *adj.*

com·mit /kəˈmit/ ▸*v.* (**-mit·ted**, **-mit·ting**) [*trans.*] **1** carry out or perpetrate (a mistake, crime, or immoral act): *he committed an uncharacteristic error.* **2** pledge or bind (a person or an organization) to a certain course or policy: *they were reluctant to* **commit themselves to** *an opinion* | *the treaty commits each party to defend the other* | *try it out before you* **commit to** *a purchase.* ■ pledge or set aside (resources) for future use: *manufacturers will have to* **commit** *substantial funds* **to** *developing new engines.* ■ (**be committed to**) be in a long-term emotional relationship with (someone). ■ (**be committed to**) be dedicated to (something): *it is a modern Marxist party committed to democratic socialism.* **3** send, entrust, or consign, in particular: ■ consign (someone) officially to prison, esp. on remand: *he was* **committed to** *prison for contempt of court.* ■ send (a person or case) for trial. ■ send (someone) to be confined in a psychiatric hospital: *he had been committed for treatment.* ■ (**commit something to**) transfer something to (a state or place): *he composed a letter but didn't commit it to paper* | *she committed each tiny feature to memory* | *committed to the flames.* ■ refer (a legislative bill) to a committee. ▷late Middle English: from Latin *committere* 'join, entrust' (in medieval Latin 'put into custody'), from *com-* 'with' + *mittere* 'put or send.' —**com·mit·ta·ble** *adj.* —**com·mit·ter** *n.*

com·mit·ment /kəˈmitmənt/ ▸*n.* **1** the act of committing or the state of being committed. ■ dedication; application: *the company's* **commitment to** *quality.* ■ a pledge or undertaking: *I cannot make such a commitment at the moment.* ■ an act of pledging or setting aside something: *there must be a major commitment of money and time.* **2** (usu. **commitments**) an engagement or obligation that restricts freedom of action: *business commitments* | *young people delay major commitments including marriage and children.*

com·mit·ment cer·e·mo·ny ▸*n.* a ceremony to mark the spousal union of two people who are not legally allowed to marry, such as gay people.

com·mit·ment or·der ▸*n.* an order authorizing the admission and detention of a patient in a psychiatric hospital.

com·mit·tal /kəˈmitl/ ▸*n.* **1** the action of sending a person to an institution, esp. prison or a psychiatric hospital: *his* **committal to** *prison* | [as *adj.*] *committal proceedings.* **2** the burial of a corpse.

com·mit·ted /kəˈmitid/ ▸*adj.* feeling dedication and loyalty to a cause, activity, or job; wholeheartedly dedicated: *a committed Christian.*

com·mit·tee /kəˈmitē/ ▸*n.* **1** [treated as *sing.* or *pl.*] a group of people appointed for a specific function, typically consisting of members of a larger group: *the housing committee* | [as *adj.*] *a committee meeting.* ■ such a body appointed by a legislature to consider the details of proposed legislation: *there was much scrutiny* **in committee.** **2** *Law* a person who has been judicially committed to the charge of another because of insanity or mental retardation. ■ *Brit.* a person entrusted with the charge of another person or another person's property. ▷late 15th cent. (in the general sense 'person to whom something has been entrusted'): from COMMIT + -EE.

com·mit·tee·man /kəˈmitēmən; -ˌman/ ▸*n.* (*pl.* **-men**) (in the U.S.) a male local political party leader.

com·mit·tee of the whole the entire membership of a legislative body when sitting as a committee.

com·mit·tee·wom·an /kəˈmitēˌwo͝omən/ ▸*n.* (*pl.* **-wom·en**) (in the U.S.) a female local political party leader.

com·mix /kəˈmiks/ ▸*v.* [*trans.*] *archaic* mix; mingle: *beat them till they be thoroughly commixed.* ▷late Middle English (as the past participle *commixt*): from Latin *commixtus*, from *com-* 'together with' + *mixtus* 'mixed.' —**com·mix·ture** /kəˈmiksCHər/ *n.*

com·mo /ˈkämō/ ▸*n. informal* communication, esp. as a departmental function in an organization.

com·mode /kəˈmōd/ ▸*n.* **1** a piece of furniture containing a concealed chamber pot. ■ a toilet. ■ *historical* a movable washstand. **2** a chest of drawers or chiffonier of a decorative type popular in the 18th century. ▷mid 18th cent. (sense 2): from French, literally 'convenient, suitable,' from Latin *commodus*. Sense 1 dates from the early 19th cent.

com·mod·i·fy /kəˈmädəˌfī/ ▸*v.* (**-fies**, **-fied**) [*trans.*] turn into or treat as a commodity: [as *adj.*] (**commodified**) *art has become commodified.* ▷1980s: from COMMODITY + -FY. —**com·mod·i·fi·ca·tion** /kəˌmädəfəˈkāsʜən/ *n.*

com·mo·di·ous /kəˈmōdēəs/ ▸*adj.* **1** *formal* (esp. of furniture or a building) roomy and comfortable. **2** *archaic* convenient. ▷late Middle English (in the sense 'beneficial, useful'): from French *commodieux* or medieval Latin *commodiosus*, based on Latin *commodus* 'convenient.' —**com·mo·di·ous·ly** *adv.* —**com·mo·di·ous·ness** *n.*

com·mod·i·tize /kəˈmädiˌtīz/ ▸*v.* another term for COMMODIFY. —**com·mod·i·ti·za·tion** /kəˌmäditəˈzāsʜən/ *n.*

com·mod·i·ty /kəˈmäditē/ ▸*n.* (*pl.* **-ties**) a raw material or primary agricultural product that can be bought and sold, such as copper or coffee. ■ a useful or valuable thing, such as water or time. ▷late Middle English: from Old French *commodite* or Latin *commoditas*, from *commodus* (see COMMODIOUS).

com·mo·dore /ˈkäməˌdôr/ ▸*n.* a naval officer of high rank, in particular an officer in the U.S. Navy or Coast Guard ranking above captain and below rear admiral. ■ the president of a yacht club. ■ the senior captain of a shipping line. ▷late 17th cent.: probably from Dutch *komandeur*, from French *commandeur* 'commander.'

com·mon /ˈkämən/ ▸*adj.* (**-mon·er**, **-mon·est**) **1** occurring, found, or done often; prevalent: *salt and pepper are the two most common seasonings* | *it's* **common for** *a woman to be depressed after giving birth.* See notes at PREVALENT, UNIVERSAL. ■ (of an animal or plant) found or living in relatively large numbers; not rare. ■ ordinary; of ordinary qualities; without special rank or position: *the dwellings of common people | a common soldier.* ■ (of a quality) of a sort or level to be generally expected: *common decency.* ■ of the most familiar type: *the common or vernacular name.* ■ denoting the most widespread or typical species of an animal or plant: *the common blue spruce.* **2** showing a lack of taste and refinement; vulgar. **3** shared by, coming from, or done by more than one: *the two republics' common border | problems* ***common to*** *both communities.* ■ belonging to, open to, or affecting the whole of a community or the public: *common land.* ■ *Mathematics* belonging to two or more quantities. **4** *Grammar* (in Latin and certain other languages) of or denoting a gender of nouns that are conventionally regarded as masculine or feminine, contrasting with neuter. ■ (in English) denoting a noun that refers to individuals of either sex (e.g., *teacher*). **5** *Prosody* (of a syllable) able to be either short or long. **6** *Law* (of a crime) of relatively minor importance: *common assault.*

▸*n.* **1** a piece of open land for public use, esp. in a village or town. **2** (in the Christian Church) a form of service used for each of a group of occasions. ▷Middle English: from Old French *comun* (adjective), from Latin *communis.* **—com·mon·ness** *n.*

▸*PHRASES* □ **the common good** the benefit or interests of all: *it is time our elected officials stood up for the common good.* □ **common ground** a point or argument accepted by both sides in a dispute. ■ ideas or interests shared by different people: *artists from different cultural backgrounds found common ground.* □ **common knowledge** something known by most people. □ **common or garden** *Brit., informal* of the usual or ordinary type: *a yak is your basic common or garden cow, only bigger, hairier, and wilder.* □ **common property** a thing or things held jointly. ■ something known by most people. □ **the common touch** the ability to get along with or appeal to ordinary people. □ **in common 1** in joint use or possession; shared: *car engines have nothing in common with aircraft engines.* **2** of joint interest: *the two men had little in common.* See also TENANCY IN COMMON. □ **in common with** in the same way as: *in common with other officers, I had to undertake guard duties.*

com·mon·a·ble /ˈkämənəbəl/ ▸*adj. Brit., chiefly historical* (of land) allowed to be jointly used or owned. ■ (of an animal) allowed to be pastured on public land: *these Acts exclude the deer and commonable cattle.* ▷early 17th cent.: from obsolete *common* 'to exercise right of common' + -ABLE.

com·mon·age /ˈkämənij/ ▸*n.* **1** *chiefly Brit.* the right of pasturing animals on common land. ■ land held in common. **2** the common people; the commonalty.

Com·mon Ag·ri·cul·tur·al Pol·i·cy (abbr.: **CAP**) the system in the EU for establishing common prices for most agricultural products within the European Union, a single fund for price supports, and levies on imports.

com·mon·al·i·ty /ˌkämənˈalitē/ ▸*n.* (*pl.* **-ties**) **1** [in *sing.*] the state of sharing features or attributes: *a commonality of interest ensures cooperation.* ■ a shared feature or attribute: *we discern the commonalities between these writers.* **2** (**the commonality**) another term for COMMONALTY. ▷late Middle English (sense 2): variant of COMMONALTY. Sense 1 dates from the mid 16th cent., but was rarely used before the 1950s.

com·mon·al·ty /ˈkämənl-tē/ ▸*n.* [treated as *pl.*] (**the commonalty**) *chiefly historical* people without special rank or position; common people: *a petition by the earls, barons, and commonalty of the realm.* ■ the general body of a group. ▷Middle English: from Old French *comunalte*, from medieval Latin *communalitas*, from Latin *communis* 'common, general' (see COMMON).

com·mon car·ri·er ▸*n.* a person or company that transports goods or passengers on regular routes at set rates. ■ a company providing public telecommunications facilities.

com·mon chord ▸*n. Music* a triad containing a root, a major or minor third, and a perfect fifth.

com·mon cold ▸*n.* (**the common cold**) another term for COLD (sense 2).

com·mon coun·cil ▸*n.* a town or city council in some parts of the U.S. and Canada, and in London.

com·mon de·nom·i·na·tor ▸*n. Mathematics* a shared multiple of the denominators of several fractions. See also LOWEST COMMON DENOMINATOR. ■ *figurative* a feature shared by all members of a group: *the common denominator for the fevers was the bite of a tick.*

com·mon di·vi·sor ▸*n. Mathematics* a number that can be divided into all of the other numbers of a given set without any remainder. Also called **common factor**.

com·mon·er /ˈkämənər/ ▸*n.* **1** an ordinary person, without rank or title. **2** a person who has the right of common (commonage). **3** (at some British universities) an undergraduate who does not have a scholarship. ▷Middle English (denoting a citizen or burgess): from medieval Latin *communarius*, from *communa, communia* 'community,' based on Latin *communis* (see COMMON).

Com·mon E·ra ▸*n.* (**the Common Era**) another term for CHRISTIAN ERA.

com·mon frac·tion ▸*n.* a fraction expressed by a numerator and a denominator, not decimally.

com·mon gen·der ▸*n.* **1** the gender of those nouns in English that are not limited to either sex, such as cousin or spouse. **2** in some languages, such as Latin, the gender of those nouns that may be either masculine or feminine but not neuter. **3** in some languages, such as modern Danish, the gender of those nouns derived from the earlier masculine and feminine genders that do not belong to the neuter gender.

com·mon law ▸*n.* the part of English law that is derived from custom and judicial precedent rather than statutes. Often contrasted with STATUTORY LAW. ■ the body of English law as adopted and modified separately by the different states of the U.S. and by the federal government. Compare with CIVIL LAW. ■ [as *adj.*] denoting a partner in a marriage by common law (which recognized unions created by mutual agreement and public behavior), not by a civil or ecclesiastical ceremony: *a common-law husband.* ■ [as *adj.*] denoting a partner in a long-term relationship of cohabitation.

com·mon log·a·rithm ▸*n.* a logarithm to the base 10.

com·mon·ly /ˈkämənlē/ ▸*adv.* very often; frequently: *BSE, commonly called mad cow disease | a commonly used industrial chemical.*

com·mon mar·ket ▸*n.* a group of countries imposing few or no duties on trade with one another and a common tariff on trade with other countries. ■ (**the Common Market**) a name for the European Economic Community or European Union, used esp. in the 1960s and 1970s.

com·mon me·ter (also **common measure**) (abbr.: **CM**) ▸*n.* a metrical pattern for hymns in which the stanzas have four lines containing eight and six syllables alternately rhyming *abcb* or *abab.*

com·mon mul·ti·ple ▸*n. Mathematics* a number into which each number in a given set may be evenly divided.

com·mon noun ▸*n. Grammar* a noun denoting a class of objects or a concept as opposed to a particular individual. Often contrasted with PROPER NOUN.

com·mon·place /ˈkämənˌplās/ ▸*adj.* not unusual; ordinary: *unemployment was commonplace in his profession.* ■ not interesting or original; trite: *the usual commonplace remarks.*

▸*n.* **1** a usual or ordinary thing: *bombing has become almost a commonplace of public life there.* ■ a trite saying or topic; a platitude: *it is a commonplace to talk of the young being alienated.* **2** a notable quotation copied into a commonplace book. ▷mid 16th cent. (originally *common place*): translation of Latin *locus communis*, rendering Greek *koinos topos* 'general theme.' **—com·mon·place·ness** *n.*

com·mon·place book ▸*n.* a book into which notable extracts from other works are copied for personal use.

Com·mon Pleas (in full **Court of Common Pleas**) *Law* (in some jurisdictions) a court for hearing civil cases between citizens.

com·mon por·poise ▸ another term for HARBOR PORPOISE.

Com·mon Prayer the liturgy of the Anglican Communion, originally set forth in the *Book of Common Prayer* of Edward VI (1549).

com·mon rat ▸*n.* another term for BROWN RAT.

com·mon room ▸*n.* a room in a school, college, or other educational institution for use of students or staff outside teaching hours. ■ a room in a residential facility for the recreational use of all residents.

com·mons /ˈkämənz/ ▸*plural n.* **1** a dining hall in a residential school or college. **2** [treated as *sing.*] land or resources belonging to or affecting the whole of a community. ■ a public park of a town or city. **3** (**the Commons**) short for HOUSE OF COMMONS. ■ *historical* the common people regarded as a part of a political system, esp. in Britain. **4** *archaic* provisions shared in common; rations. ▷Middle English: plural of COMMON.

▸*PHRASE* □ **short commons** *archaic* insufficient allocation of food: *for two weeks we have been on short commons.*

com·mon salt ▸*n.* see SALT (sense 1).

com·mon sense ▸*n.* good sense and sound judgment in practical matters: *use your common sense | [as adj.] a common-sense approach.* **—com·mon·sen·si·cal** /ˌkämənˈsensikəl/ *adj.*

com·mon sol·dier ▸*n.* see SOLDIER (sense 1).

com·mon stock ▸*plural n.* (also **com·mon stocks**) shares entitling their holder to dividends that vary in amount and may even be missed, depending on the fortunes of the company: *the company announced a public offering of 3.5 million shares of common stock.* Compare with PREFERRED STOCK.

com·mon time ▸*n. Music* a rhythmic pattern in which there are four beats, esp. four quarter notes, in a measure. This pattern occurs often in classical music and is the norm in rock, jazz, country, and bluegrass.

com·mon·weal /ˈkämənˌwēl/ ▸*n.* (**the commonweal**) the welfare of the public.

com·mon·wealth /ˈkämənˌwelTH/ ▸*n.* **1** an independent country or community, esp. a democratic republic. ■ an aggregate or grouping of countries or other bodies. ■ a community or organization of shared interests in a nonpolitical field: *the Christian commonwealth | the commonwealth of letters.* ■ a self-governing unit voluntarily grouped with the U.S., such as Puerto Rico. ■ a formal title of some of the states of the U.S., esp. Kentucky, Massachusetts, Pennsylvania, and Virginia. ■ the title of the federated Australian states. ■ (**the Commonwealth**) the republican period of government in Britain between the execution of Charles I in 1649 and the Restoration of Charles II in 1660. **2** (**the Commonwealth**) (in full **the Commonwealth of Nations**) an international association consisting of the UK together with states that were previously part of the British Empire, and dependencies. The British monarch is the symbolic head of the Commonwealth. **3** (**the commonwealth**) *archaic* the general good. ▷late Middle English (originally as two words, denoting public welfare; compare with COMMONWEAL): from COMMON + WEALTH.

Com·mon·wealth Games an amateur sports competition held every four years between member countries of the Commonwealth of Nations.

Com·mon·wealth of In·de·pend·ent States (abbr.: **CIS**) a confederation of independent states that were formerly constituent republics of the Soviet Union, established in 1991. Member states are Armenia, Belarus, Kazakhstan, Kyrgyzstan, Moldova, Russia, Tajikistan, Turkmenistan, Ukraine, and Uzbekistan.

com·mo·tion /kəˈmōSHən/ ▸*n.* a state of confused and noisy disturbance: *she was distracted by a commotion across the street | figure out what all the commotion is about.* ■ civil insurrection: *damage caused by civil commotion.* ▷late Middle English: from Latin *commotio(n-)*, from *com-* 'altogether' + *motio* (see MOTION).

com·move /kəˈmo͞ov/ ▸*v.* [*trans.*] move violently; agitate or excite.

com·mu·nal /kəˈmyo͞onl/ ▸*adj.* **1** shared by all members of a community; for common use: *a communal bathroom and kitchen.* ■ of, relating to, or done by a community: *communal achievement.* ■ involving the sharing of work and property: *communal living.* **2** (of conflict) between different communities, esp. those having different religions or ethnic origins: *violent communal riots.* ▷early 19th cent. (in the sense 'relating to a commune, esp. the Paris Commune'): from French, from late Latin *communalis*, from *communis* (see COMMON). **—com·mu·nal·i·ty** /ˌkämyəˈnalitē/ *n.* **—com·mu·nal·ly** *adv.*

com·mu·nal·ism /kəˈmyo͞onlˌizəm/ ▸*n.* **1** a principle of political organization based on federated communes. ■ the principle or practice of living together and sharing possessions and responsibilities. **2** allegiance to one's own ethnic group rather than to the wider society. **—com·mu·nal·ist** *adj.* & *n.* **—com·mu·nal·is·tic** /kəˌmyo͞onlˈistik/ *adj.*

com·mu·nal·ize /kəˈmyo͞onlˌīz/ ▸*v.* [*trans.*] *rare* organize (something) on the basis of shared ownership:

attempts to communalize farming. —**com·mu·nal·i·za·tion** /kəˌmyo͞onl-əˈzāsʜən/ *n.*

com·mu·nard /ˌkämyəˈnär(d)/ ▸*n.* a member of a commune. ■ (**Communard**) *historical* a supporter of the Paris Commune. ▷late 19th cent.: from French, from COMMUNE[1].

com·mune[1] /ˈkämˌyo͞on/ ▸*n.* **1** a group of people living together and sharing possessions and responsibilities. ■ a communal settlement in a communist country. **2** the smallest French territorial division for administrative purposes. ■ a similar division elsewhere. **3** (**the Commune**) the group that seized the municipal government of Paris in the French Revolution and played a leading part in the Reign of Terror until suppressed in 1794. ■ (also **the Paris Commune**) the municipal government organized on communalistic principles elected in Paris in 1871. It was soon brutally suppressed by government troops. ▷late 17th cent. (sense 2): from French, from medieval Latin *communia*, neuter plural of Latin *communis* (see COMMON).

com·mune[2] /kəˈmyo͞on/ ▸*v.* [*intrans.*] **1** (**commune with**) share one's intimate thoughts or feelings with (someone or something), esp. when the exchange is on a spiritual level: *the purpose of praying is to commune with God.* ■ feel in close spiritual contact with: *he spent an hour communing with nature on the bank of a stream.* **2** *Christian Church* receive Holy Communion. ▷Middle English: from Old French *comuner* 'to share,' from *comun* (see COMMON).

com·mu·ni·ca·ble /kəˈmyo͞onikəbəl/ ▸*adj.* able to be communicated to others: *the value of the product must be communicable to the potential consumers.* ■ (of a disease) able to be transmitted from one sufferer to another; contagious or infectious. ▷late Middle English (in the sense 'communicating, having communication'): from Old French, from late Latin *communicabilis*, from the verb *communicare* 'to share' (see COMMUNICATE). —**com·mu·ni·ca·bil·i·ty** /kəˌmyo͞onikəˈbilitē/ *n.* —**com·mu·ni·ca·bly** /-blē/ *adv.*

com·mu·ni·cant /kəˈmyo͞onikənt/ ▸*n.* **1** *Christian Church* a person who receives Holy Communion. **2** *archaic* a person who imparts information. ▷mid 16th cent.: from Latin *communicant-* 'sharing,' from the verb *communicare* (see COMMUNICATE).

com·mu·ni·cate /kəˈmyo͞onəˌkāt/ ▸*v.* **1** [*intrans.*] share or exchange information, news, or ideas: *the prisoner was forbidden to* ***communicate with*** *his family.* ■ [*trans.*] impart or pass on (information, news, or ideas): *he* ***communicated*** *his findings* ***to*** *the inspector.* ■ [*trans.*] convey or transmit (an emotion or feeling) in a nonverbal way: *the ability of good teachers to communicate their own enthusiasm | his sudden fear* ***communicated itself.*** ■ succeed in conveying one's ideas or in evoking understanding in others: *a politician must have the ability to communicate.* ■ (of two people) be able to share and understand each other's thoughts and feelings. ■ [*trans.*] (usu. **be communicated**) pass on (an infectious disease) to another person or animal. ■ [*trans.*] transmit (heat or motion): *the heat is communicated through a small brass grating.* ■ [often as *adj.*] (**communicating**) (of two rooms) have a common connecting door: *he went into the communicating room to pick up the phone.* **2** [*intrans.*] *Christian Church* receive Holy Communion. ▷early 16th cent.: from Latin *communicat-* 'shared,' from the verb *communicare*, from *communis* (see COMMON). —**com·mu·ni·ca·tor** /-ˌkātər/ *n.* —**com·mu·ni·ca·to·ry** /-kəˌtôrē/ *adj.*

com·mu·ni·ca·tion /kəˌmyo͞onəˈkāsʜən/ ▸*n.* **1** the imparting or exchanging of information or news: *direct communication between the two countries will produce greater understanding | at the moment I am* ***in communication with*** *London.* ■ a letter or message containing such information or news. ■ the successful conveying or sharing of ideas and feelings: *there was a lack of* ***communication between*** *Pamela and her parents.* ■ social contact: *she gave him some hope of her return, or at least of their future communication.* **2** (**communications**) means of connection between people or places, in particular: ■ the means of sending or receiving information, such as telephone lines or computers: *satellite communications |* [as *adj.*] *a communications network.* ■ the means of traveling or of transporting goods, such as roads or railroads: *a city providing excellent road and rail communications.* ■ [treated as *sing.*] the field of study concerned with the transmission of information by various means. ▷late Middle English: from Old French *comunicacion*, from Latin *communicatio(n-)*, from the verb *communicare* 'to share' (see COMMUNICATE). —**com·mu·ni·ca·tion·al** /-ˈkāsʜənl/ *adj.*

▸*PHRASE* □ **lines of communication** the connections between an army in the field and its bases. ■ any system for communicating information or ideas: *bureaucracies are characterized by established lines of communication.*

com·mu·ni·ca·tions sat·el·lite (also **com·mu·ni·ca·tion sat·el·lite**) ▸*n.* a satellite placed in orbit around the earth in order to relay television, radio, and telephone signals.

com·mu·ni·ca·tion the·o·ry (also **com·mu·ni·ca·tions the·o·ry**) ▸*n.* the branch of knowledge dealing with the principles and methods by which information is conveyed.

com·mu·ni·ca·tive /kəˈmyo͞onəˌkātiv; -nikətiv/ ▸*adj.* ready to talk or impart information: *the patient was alert and communicative.* ■ relating to the conveyance or exchange of information: *the communicative process in literary texts.* ▷late Middle English: from late Latin *communicativus*, from *communicat-* 'shared,' from the verb *communicare* (see COMMUNICATE). —**com·mu·ni·ca·tive·ly** *adv.*

com·mun·ion /kəˈmyo͞onyən/ ▸*n.* **1** the sharing or exchanging of intimate thoughts and feelings, esp. when the exchange is on a mental or spiritual level: *in this churchyard* ***communion with*** *the dead was almost palpable.* See note at CONVERSATION. ■ common participation in a mental or emotional experience: *popular festivals where all take part in joyous communion.* **2** (often **Communion** or **Holy Communion**) the service of Christian worship at which bread and wine are consecrated and shared. See EUCHARIST. ■ the consecrated bread and wine so administered and received: *the priests gave him Holy Communion.* ■ reception of the consecrated bread and wine at such a service. **3** a relationship of recognition and acceptance between Christian churches or denominations, or between individual Christians or Christian communities and a church (signified by a willingness to give or receive the Eucharist): *the Eastern Churches are not* ***in communion with*** *Rome.* ■ a group of Christian communities or churches that recognize one another's ministries or that of a central authority: *the Anglican communion.* ▷late Middle English: from Latin *communio(n-)*, from *communis* (see COMMON).

▸*PHRASE* □ **make one's communion** receive bread and wine that has been consecrated at a Eucharist, as a sacramental, spiritual, or symbolic act of receiving the presence of Christ.

com·mun·ion of saints ▸*n.* [in *sing.*] a fellowship between Christians living and dead.

com·mu·ni·qué /kəˌmyo͞onəˈkā; kəˈmyo͞onəˌkā/ (also **com·mu·ni·que**) ▸*n.* an official announcement or statement, esp. one made to the media. ▷mid 19th cent.: from French, past participle of *communiquer* 'communicate.'

com·mu·nism /ˈkämyəˌnizəm/ (often **Communism**) ▸*n.* a political theory derived from Karl Marx, advocating class war and leading to a society in which all property is publicly owned and each person works and is paid according to their abilities and needs. See also MARXISM.

> The most familiar form of communism is that established by the Bolsheviks after the Russian Revolution of 1917, and it has generally been understood in terms of the system practiced by the former USSR and its allies in eastern Europe, in China since 1949, and in some developing countries such as Cuba, Vietnam, and North Korea. Communism embraced a revolutionary ideology in which the state would wither away after the overthrow of the capitalist system. In practice, however, the state grew to control all aspects of communist society. Communism in eastern Europe collapsed in the late 1980s and early 1990s against a background of failure to meet people's economic expectations, a shift to more democracy in political life, and increasing nationalism such as that which led to the breakup of the USSR.

▷mid 19th cent.: from French *communisme*, from *commun* (see COMMON). —**com·mu·nist** *n.* & *adj.* —**com·mu·nis·tic** /ˌkämyəˈnistik/ *adj.*

Com·mu·nism Peak one of the principal peaks in the Pamir Mountains of Tajikistan, rising to 24,590 feet (7,495 m). It was the highest mountain in the former Soviet Union. Former names MOUNT GARMO (until 1933) and STALIN PEAK (until 1962).

com·mu·ni·tar·i·an·ism /kəˌmyo͞oniˈte(ə)rēəˌnizəm/ ▸*n.* a theory or system of social organization based on small self-governing communities. ■ an ideology that emphasizes the responsibility of the individual to the community and the social importance of the family unit. ▷mid 19th cent.: from COMMUNITY + -ARIAN, on the pattern of words such as *unitarian.* —**com·mu·ni·tar·i·an** *adj.* & *n.* .

com·mu·ni·ty /kəˈmyo͞onitē/ ▸*n.* (*pl.* **-ties**) **1** a group of people living together in one place, esp. one practicing common ownership: *a community of nuns.* ■ all the people living in a particular area or place: *local communities.* ■ a particular area or place considered together with its inhabitants: *a rural community.* ■ (**the community**) the people of a district or country considered collectively, esp. in the context of social values and responsibilities; society: *preparing prisoners for life back in the community.* ■ [as *adj.*] denoting a worker or resource designed to serve the people of a particular area: *community health services.* **2** [usu. with *adj.*] a group of people having a religion, race, profession, or other particular characteristic in common: *Rhode Island's Japanese community | the scientific community.* ■ a body of nations or states unified by common interests: [in *names*] *the European Community | the African Economic Community.* **3** a feeling of fellowship with others, as a result of sharing common attitudes, interests, and goals: *the sense of community that organized religion can provide.* ■ [in *sing.*] a similarity or identity: *writers who shared a community of interests.* ■ joint ownership or liability: *a commitment to the community of goods.* **4** *Ecology* a group of interdependent organisms of different species growing or living together in a specified habitat: *communities of insectivorous birds.* ■ a set of species found in the same habitat or ecosystem at the same time. ▷late Middle English: from Old French *comunete*, reinforced by its source, Latin *communitas*, from *communis* (see COMMON).

▸*PHRASE* □ **the international community** the countries of the world considered collectively.

com·mu·ni·ty an·ten·na tel·e·vi·sion (abbr.: **CATV**) ▸*n.* another term for CABLE TELEVISION.

com·mu·ni·ty ar·chi·tect ▸*n.* an architect working in consultation with local inhabitants in designing housing and other amenities. —**com·mu·ni·ty ar·chi·tec·ture** *n.*

com·mu·ni·ty bank ▸*n.* a commercial bank that derives funds from and lends to the community where it operates, and is not affiliated with a multibank holding company.

com·mu·ni·ty cen·ter ▸*n.* a place where people from a particular community can meet for social, educational, or recreational activities.

com·mu·ni·ty chest ▸*n.* a fund for charitable activities among the people in a particular area.

com·mu·ni·ty col·lege ▸*n.* a nonresidential junior college offering courses to people living in a particular area.

com·mu·ni·ty po·lic·ing ▸*n.* the system of allocating police officers to particular areas so that they become familiar with the local inhabitants.

com·mu·ni·ty pro·per·ty ▸*n.* property owned jointly by a husband and wife.

com·mu·ni·ty serv·ice ▸*n.* voluntary work intended to help people in a particular area. ■ *Law* unpaid work, intended to be of social use, that an offender is required to do instead of going to prison: *sentenced to 600 hours of community service.*

com·mu·ni·ver·si·ty /kəˌmyo͞onəˈvərsitē/ ▸*n.* an organization representing a liaison between a college and the community where it is located: [as *modifier*] *a communiversity theater.* ▷1990s: blend of *community* and *university.*

com·mu·nize /ˈkämyəˌnīz/ ▸*v.* [*trans.*] cause (a country, people, or economic activity) to be organized on the principles of communism. ▷late 19th cent.: from Latin *communis* (see COMMON) + -IZE. —**com·mu·ni·za·tion** /ˌkämyənəˈzāsʜən/ *n.*

com·mut·a·ble /kəˈmyo͞otəbəl/ ▸*adj.* **1** (of a place or home) sufficiently close to one's place of work that one can travel between the two on a regular basis. ■ (of a distance) sufficiently short that it can be traveled on a regular basis. [1970s from sense 1 of COMMUTE.] **2** *rare* capable of being exchanged or converted. ▷mid 17th cent.: from Latin *commutabilis*, from *commutare* 'exchange, interchange' (see COMMUTE). —**com·mut·a·bil·i·ty** /kəˌmyo͞otəˈbilitē/ *n.*

com·mu·tate /ˈkämyəˌtāt/ ▸*v.* [*trans.*] regulate or reverse the direction of (an alternating electric current), esp. to make it a direct current. ▷late 19th cent.: from Latin *commutat-* 'changed altogether, exchanged, interchanged,' from the verb *commutare* (see COMMUTE).

com·mu·ta·tion /ˌkämyəˈtāsʜən/ ▸*n.* **1** action or the process of commuting a judicial sentence. ■ the conversion of a legal obligation or entitlement into another form, e.g., the replacement of an annuity or series of payments by a single payment. **2** the process of commutating an electric current. **3** *Mathematics* the property of having a commutative relation. ▷late Middle English (in the sense 'exchange, barter,' later 'alteration'): from Latin *commutatio(n-)*, from *commutare* 'exchange, interchange' (see COMMUTE). Sense 1 dates from the late 16th cent.

com·mu·ta·tion tick·et ▸*n.* a ticket issued at a reduced rate by a railroad or bus company, entitling the holder to travel a given route a fixed number of times or during a specified period.

com·mu·ta·tive /ˈkämyəˌtātiv; kəˈmyo͞otətiv/ ▸*adj.* *Mathematics* involving the condition that a group of quantities connected by operators gives the same result whatever the order of the quantities involved, e.g., $a \times b = b \times a$. ■ *rare* relating to or involving substitution or exchange. ▷mid 16th cent. (in the sense 'relating to transactions between people'): from French *commutatif, -ive* or medieval Latin *commutativus*, from *commutat-* 'exchanged,' from the verb *commutare* (see COMMUTE).

com·mu·ta·tor /ˈkämyəˌtātər/ ▸*n.* an attachment, connected to the armature of a motor or generator, through which electrical connection is made and which ensures that the current flows as direct current. ■ a device for reversing the direction of flow of electric current.

com·mute /kəˈmyo͞ot/ ▸*v.* **1** [*intrans.*] travel some distance between one's home and place of work on a regular basis: *she* ***commuted from*** *Westport* ***in to*** *Grand Central Station.* **2** [*trans.*] reduce (a judicial sentence, esp. a sentence of death) to one less severe: *the governor recently commuted the sentences of dozens of women convicted of killing their husbands.* ■ (**commute something for/into**) change one kind of payment or obligation for (another). ■ replace (an annuity or other series of payments) with a single payment: *if he had commuted some of his pension, he would have received $330,000.* **3** [*intrans.*] *Mathematics* (of two operations or quantities) have a commutative relationship.
▸*n.* a regular journey of some distance to and from one's place of work. ▷late Middle English (in the sense 'interchange (two things)'): from Latin *commutare*, from *com-* 'altogether' + *mutare* 'to change.' Sense 1 originally meant to buy and use a *commutation ticket*, a dated term for 'a season ticket' (because the daily fare is commuted to a single payment). **—com·mut·er** *n.* (in sense 1).

com·mut·er belt ▸*n.* the area surrounding a city from which a large number of people travel to work each day.

Co·mo, Lake /ˈkōmō/ a lake in the foothills of the Alps in northern Italy.

Co·mo·do·ro Ri·va·da·vi·a /ˌkōmōˈdôrō ˌrēvāˈdävēə/ a port in southeastern Argentina, on the Atlantic coast of Patagonia; pop. 124,000.

co·mon·o·mer /kōˈmänəmər/ ▸*n.* *Chemistry* one of the monomers that constitutes a copolymer.

co·mor·bid·i·ty /ˌkōmôrˈbiditē/ ▸*n.* the simultaneous presence of two chronic diseases or conditions in a patient: *the comorbidity of anxiety and depression in Parkinson's disease.*

Com·o·ros /ˈkäməˌrōz; kəˈmôrōz; -ōs/ a country in Africa that consists of a group of islands in the Indian Ocean, north of Madagascar; pop. 651,000; capital, Moroni; languages, French (official), Arabic (official), and Shikomore (a blend of Swahili and Arabic). **—Com·o·ran** /ˈkämərən; kəˈmôrən/ *adj.* & *n.*

The islands were first visited by the English at the end of the 16th century. At that time and for long afterward, Arab influence was dominant. In the mid 19th century they came under French protection until 1974 when all but one of the four major islands voted for independence.

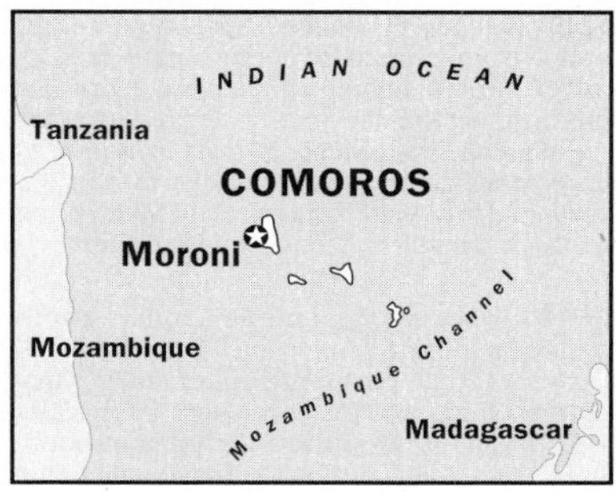

comp /kämp/ *informal* ▸*n.* short for: ■ a composition. ■ a complimentary ticket or voucher. ■ compensation. ■ (also **comp time**) compensatory. ■ a musical accompaniment. ■ a comprehensive examination.
▸*v.* [*trans.*] **1** play (music) as an accompaniment, esp. in jazz or blues: *if someone is comping chord changes, there are more textured harmonies* | [*intrans.*] *he comps with an open, jangly sound.* **2** give (something) away free, esp. as part of a promotion: *the management did graciously comp our wine selection.* **3** short for COMPOSITE.
▸*adj.* [*attrib.*] complimentary; free: *the average fan was unable to get comp press tickets.*

comp. ▸*abbr.* ■ companion. ■ comparative. ■ compensation. ■ compilation. ■ compiled. ■ compiler. ■ complete. ■ composite. ■ composition. ■ compositor. ■ comprehensive.

com·pact[1] ▸*adj.* /kəmˈpakt; käm-; ˈkämˌpakt/ **1** closely and neatly packed together; dense: *a compact cluster of houses.* ■ having all the necessary components or features neatly fitted into a small space: *a compact car.* ■ (of a person or animal) small, solid, and well-proportioned. ■ (of speech or writing) concise in expression: *a compact summary of the play.* **2** [*predic.*] (**compact of**) *archaic* composed or made up of: *towns compact of wooden houses.*
▸*v.* /kəmˈpakt; käm-/ [*trans.*] (often **be compacted**) exert force on (something) to make it more dense; compress: *the soil may be compacted by iron oxide* | [as *adj.*] (**compacted**) *compacted paper waste.* ■ [*intrans.*] (of a substance) become compressed in this way: *the snow hardened and compacted.* ■ *archaic* form (something) by pressing its component parts firmly together. ■ express in fewer words; condense: *the ideas are* ***compacted into*** *two sentences.*
▸*n.* /ˈkämˌpakt/ **1** a small flat case containing face powder, a mirror, and a powder puff. **2** something that is a small and conveniently shaped example of its kind, in particular: ■ short for COMPACT CAR. **3** *Metallurgy* a mass of powdered metal compacted together in preparation for sintering. ▷late Middle English: from Latin *compact-* 'closely put together, joined,' from the verb *compingere*, from *com-* 'together' + *pangere* 'fasten.' **—com·pac·tion** /kəmˈpakshən/ *n.* **—com·pact·ly** *adv.* **—com·pact·ness** *n.* **—com·pac·tor** /kəmˈpaktər; käm-; ˈkämˌpaktər/ (also **com·pact·er**) *n.*

com·pact[2] ▸*n.* /ˈkämˌpakt/ a formal agreement or contract between two or more parties.
▸*v.* /kəmˈpakt; käm-; ˈkämˌpakt/ [*trans.*] make or enter into (a formal agreement) with another party or parties: *the Democratic Party compacted an alliance with dissident groups.* ▷late 16th cent.: from Latin *compactum*, past participle of *compacisci*, from *com-* 'with' + *pacisci* 'make a covenant.' Compare with PACT.

com·pact car ▸*n.* a medium-sized car.

com·pact disc (also **com·pact disk**) (abbr.: **CD**) ▸*n.* a small plastic disc on which music or other digital information is stored, and from which the information can be read using reflected laser light. See also **CD-ROM**.

com·pa·dre /kəmˈpädrā/ ▸*n.* (*pl.* **-pa·dres**) *informal* a way of addressing or referring to a friend or companion. ▷mid 19th cent.: Spanish, literally 'godfather,' hence 'benefactor, friend.' Compare with COMPÈRE and GOSSIP.

com·pand /kəmˈpand/ ▸*v.* [*trans.*] reduce the signal-to-noise ratio of (a signal) using a compander. ▷1950s: back-formation from COMPANDER.

com·pand·er /kəmˈpandər/ (also **com·pan·dor**) ▸*n.* a device that improves the signal-to-noise ratio of an electrical signal by compressing the range of amplitudes of the signal before transmission, and then expanding it on reproduction or reception. ▷1930s: blend of COMPRESSOR and *expander* (see EXPAND).

com·pan·ion[1] /kəmˈpanyən/ ▸*n.* **1** a person or animal with whom one spends a lot of time or with whom one travels: *his traveling companion* | *figurative fear became my constant companion.* ■ a person who shares the experiences of another, esp. when these are unpleasant or unwelcome: *my* ***companions in*** *misfortune.* ■ a person with similar tastes and interests to one's own and with whom one has a friendly relationship: *drinking companions.* ■ a person's long-term sexual partner outside marriage. ■ a person, esp. an unmarried or widowed woman, employed to live with and assist another. ■ *Astronomy* a star, galaxy, or other celestial object that is close to or associated with another. **2** one of a pair of things intended to complement or match each other: [as *adj.*] *a companion volume.* ■ [usu. in *names*] a book that provides information about a particular subject: *the Oxford Companion to English Literature.* ■ *Brit., dated* a piece of equipment containing objects used in a particular activity: *a traveler's companion.* **3** (**Companion**) a member of the lowest grade of certain orders of knighthood.
▸*v.* [*trans.*] *formal* accompany: *he is companioned by a pageboy.* ▷Middle English: from Old French *compaignon*, literally 'one who breaks bread with another,' based on Latin *com-* 'together with' + *panis* 'bread.'

com·pan·ion[2] ▸*n.* *Nautical* a covering over the hatchway leading below decks. ■ *archaic* a raised frame with windows on the quarterdeck of a ship to allow light into the decks below. ■ short for COMPANIONWAY. ▷mid 18th cent.: from obsolete Dutch *kompanje* (earlier form of *kampanje*) 'quarterdeck,' from Old French *compagne*, from Italian *(camera della) compagna* '(storeroom for) provisions.'

com·pan·ion·a·ble /kəmˈpanyənəbəl/ ▸*adj.* (of a person) friendly and sociable: *a companionable young man.* ■ (of a shared situation) relaxed and pleasant: *they walked in companionable silence.* ▷early 17th cent.: alteration of obsolete *companiable*, influenced by COMPANION[1]. **—com·pan·ion·a·ble·ness** *n.* **—com·pan·ion·a·bly** /-blē/ *adv.*

com·pan·ion an·i·mal ▸*n.* a pet or other domestic animal.

USAGE **Companion animal** is a somewhat more formal term for **pet** and is generally restricted to larger animals such as dogs and cats.

com·pan·ion·ate /kəmˈpanyənət/ ▸*adj.* *formal* (of a marriage or relationship) between partners or spouses as equal companions. ■ (of a person) acting as a companion.

com·pan·ion plant·ing ▸*n.* the close planting of different plants that enhance each other's growth or protect each other from pests. **—com·pan·ion plant** *n.* **—com·pan·ion-plant** *v.*

com·pan·ion·ship /kəmˈpanyənˌship/ ▸*n.* a feeling of fellowship or friendship.

com·pan·ion·way /kəmˈpanyənˌwā/ ▸*n.* a set of steps leading from a ship's deck down to a cabin or lower deck.

com·pa·ny /ˈkəmpənē/ ▸*n.* (*pl.* **-nies**) **1** a commercial business: *a shipping company* | [in *names*] *the Ford Motor Company* | [as *adj.*] *a company director.* **2** the fact or condition of being with another or others, esp. in a way that provides friendship and enjoyment: *I could do with some company.* ■ a person or people seen as a source of such friendship and enjoyment: *she is excellent company.* ■ the person or group of people whose society someone is currently sharing: *he was silent among such distinguished company.* ■ a visiting person or group of people: *I'm expecting company.* **3** a number of individuals gathered together, esp. for a particular purpose: *the mayor addressed the assembled company.* ■ a body of soldiers, esp. the smallest subdivision of an infantry battalion, typically commanded by a major or captain: *the troops of C Company.* ■ a group of actors, singers, or dancers who perform together: *a touring opera company.* **4** (**the Company**) *informal* the Central Intelligence Agency.
▸*v.* (**-nies, -nied**) [*intrans.*] (**company with**) *poetic/literary* associate with; keep company with: *these men which have companied with us all this time.* ■ [*trans.*] *archaic* accompany (someone): *the fair dame, companied by Statius and myself.* ▷Middle English (in senses 2 and 3): from Old French *compainie*; related to *compaignon* (see COMPANION[1]).
▸*PHRASES* □ **and company** used after a person's name to denote those people usually associated with them: *the psycholinguistics of Jacques Lacan and company.* ■ used in the name of a business to denote other unspecified partners: *Little, Brown and Company.* □ **be in good company** be in the same situation as someone important or respected: *if you spot the ghost, you are in good company: King George V saw it too.* □ **in company** with another person or a group of people: *you were never to mention in company your father's uncle.* □ **in company with** together with: *the U.S. dollar went through a bad patch in 1986, in company with the oil market.* □ **keep someone company** accompany or spend time with someone in order to prevent them from feeling lonely or bored. ■ engage in the same activity as someone else in order to be sociable: *I'll have a drink myself, just to keep you company.*

Pronunciation Key ə *ago*; ər *over*; ˈə or ˌə *up*; ˈər or ˌər *fur*; a *hat*; ā *rate*; ä *car*; CH *chew*; e *let*; ē *see*; e(ə)r *air*; i *fit*; ī *by*; i(ə)r *ear*; NG *sing*; ō *go*; ô *for*; oi *boy*; o͝o *good*; o͞o *goo*; ou *out*; SH *she*; TH *thin*; T͟H *then*; (h)w *why*; ZH *vision*

□ **keep company with** associate with habitually: *we don't especially care for the people he's been keeping company with.*■ have a social or romantic relationship with; date: *are you keeping company with anyone special these days?* □ **part company** see PART.

com·pa·ny car ▸*n.* a car provided by a company for the business and sometimes private use of an employee.

com·pa·ny of·fi·cer ▸*n.* an army officer serving within an infantry company.

com·pa·ra·ble /ˈkämp(ə)rəbəl/ ▸*adj.* (of a person or thing) able to be likened to another; similar: *flaked stone and bone tools* ***comparable to*** *Neanderthal man's tools.* ■ of equivalent quality; worthy of comparison: *nobody is comparable with this athlete.* ▷late Middle English: from Old French, from Latin *comparabilis*, from the verb *comparare* (see COMPARABLE). **—com·pa·ra·bil·i·ty** /ˌkämp(ə)rəˈbilitē/ *n.*

USAGE The correct pronunciation in standard English is with the stress on the first syllable rather than the second: **com**parable, not com**par**able.

com·pa·ra·bly /ˈkämp(ə)rəblē; kəmˈparəblē/ ▸*adv.* in a similar way or to a similar degree: *a comparably priced CD player.*

com·par·a·tist /kəmˈparətist/ ▸*n.* a person who carries out comparative study, esp. of language or literature. ▷1930s: from COMPARATIVE + -IST.

com·par·a·tive /kəmˈparətiv/ ▸*adj.* **1** perceptible by comparison; relative: *he returned to the comparative comfort of his own home.* **2** of or involving comparison between two or more branches of science or subjects of study: *comparative religion.* **3** *Grammar* (of an adjective or adverb) expressing a higher degree of a quality, but not the highest possible (e.g., *braver; more fiercely*). Contrasted with POSITIVE, SUPERLATIVE. ■ (of a clause) involving comparison (e.g., *their memory is not as good as it used to be*).
▸*n. Grammar* a comparative adjective or adverb. ■ (**the comparative**) the middle degree of comparison. ▷late Middle English (sense 3): from Latin *comparativus*, from *comparare* 'to pair, match' (see COMPARE).

com·par·a·tive ad·van·tage ▸*n.* the ability of an individual or group to carry out a particular economic activity (such as making a specific product) more efficiently than another activity.

com·par·a·tive lin·guis·tics ▸*plural n.* [treated as *sing.*] the study of similarities and differences between languages, in particular the comparison of related languages with a view to reconstructing forms in their lost parent languages.

com·par·a·tive·ly /kəmˈparətivlē/ ▸*adv.* [as *submodifier*] to a moderate degree as compared to something else; relatively: *inflation was comparatively low.*

com·par·a·tor /kəmˈparətər/ ▸*n.* a device for comparing a measurable property or thing with a reference or standard. ■ an electronic circuit for comparing two electrical signals. ■ something used as a standard for comparison. ▷late 19th cent.: from Latin *comparat-* 'paired, matched,' from the verb *comparare* (see COMPARE), + -OR[1].

com·pare /kəmˈpe(ə)r/ ▸*v.* [*trans.*] **1** estimate, measure, or note the similarity or dissimilarity between: *individual schools* ***compared*** *their facilities* ***with*** *those of others in the area | the survey compares prices in different countries | total attendance figures were 28,000,* ***compared to*** *40,000 at last year's event.* ■ (**compare something to**) point out the resemblances to; liken to: *her novel was compared to the work of Daniel Defoe.* ■ (**compare something to**) draw an analogy between one thing and (another) for the purposes of explanation or clarification: *he compared the religions to different paths toward the peak of the same mountain.* ■ [*intrans.*] have a specified relationship with another thing or person in terms of nature or quality: *salaries* ***compare*** *favorably* ***with*** *those of other professions.* ■ [*intrans.*] be of an equal or similar nature or quality: *sales were modest and cannot* ***compare with*** *the glory days of 1989.* **2** (usu. **be compared**) *Grammar* form the comparative and superlative degrees of (an adjective or an adverb): *words of one syllable are usually compared by "-er" and "-est."* ▷late Middle English: from Old French *comparer*, from Latin *comparare*, from *compar* 'like, equal,' from *com-* 'with' + *par* 'equal.'
▸*PHRASES* □ **beyond** (or **without**) **compare** of a quality or nature surpassing all others of the same kind: *a diamond beyond compare.* □ **compare notes** (of two or more people) exchange ideas, opinions, or information about a particular subject.

USAGE Traditionally, **compare to** is used when similarities are noted in dissimilar things: *shall I compare thee to a summer's day?* To **compare with** is to look for either differences or similarities, usually in similar things: *compare the candidate's claims with his actual performance.* In practice, however, this distinction is rarely maintained.
See also **usage** at CONTRAST.

com·par·i·son /kəmˈparəsən/ ▸*n.* **1** the act or instance of comparing: *they* ***drew a comparison between*** *Gandhi's teaching and that of other teachers | the two books invite comparison with one another.* ■ an analogy: *perhaps the best comparison is that of seasickness.* ■ the quality of being similar or equivalent: *if you want a thrill, there's no comparison to climbing on a truck and going out there on the expressway.* **2** *Grammar* the formation of the comparative and superlative forms of adjectives and adverbs. ▷Middle English: from Old French *comparesoun*, from Latin *comparatio(n-)*, from *comparare* 'to pair, match' (see COMPARE).
▸*PHRASES* □ **bear** (or **stand**) **comparison** be of sufficient quality to be likened favorably to someone or something of the same kind: *it can* ***stand comparison with*** *any publishing house.* □ **beyond comparison** another way of saying BEYOND COMPARE (see COMPARE). □ **by/in comparison** when compared: *computer-based communication is extremely fast* ***in comparison with*** *telephone or postal services.*

com·part·ment /kəmˈpärtmənt/ ▸*n.* **1** a separate section or part of something, in particular: ■ a division of a railroad car marked by partitions: *a first-class compartment.* ■ a section of a container in which certain items can be kept separate from others: *there's some ice cream in the freezer compartment.* ■ a watertight section of a ship: *the aft cargo compartment.* ■ *figurative* an area in which something can be considered in isolation from other things: *religion and politics should be kept in different compartments.* **2** *Heraldry* a grassy mound or other support depicted below a shield.
▸*v.* [*trans.*] (usu. **be compartmented**) divide (something) into separate parts or sections: *the buildings are to be compartmented by fire walls.* ▷mid 16th cent.: from French *compartiment*, from Italian *compartimento*, from *compartire*, from late Latin *compartiri* 'divide.' **—com·part·men·ta·tion** /kəmˌpärtˌmenˈtāshən; -mən-/ *n.*

com·part·men·tal /kəmˌpärtˈmentl/ ▸*adj.* characterized by division into separate sections: *the compartmental interior of the church.* **—com·art·men·tal·ly** *adv.*

com·part·men·tal·ize /kəmˌpärtˈmentlˌīz/ ▸*v.* [*trans.*] divide into sections or categories: *he had the ability to compartmentalize his life.* **—com·part·men·tal·ism** /-ˌizəm/ *n.* **—com·part·men·tal·i·za·tion** /kəmˌpärtˌmentl-əˈzāshən/ *n.*

com·pass /ˈkəmpəs/ ▸*n.* **1** (also **magnetic compass**) an instrument containing a magnetized pointer that shows the direction of magnetic north and bearings from it.

The use of the compass for navigation at sea was reported from China *c.*1100, western Europe 1187, Arabia *c.*1220, and Scandinavia *c.*1300, although it probably dates from much earlier. Since the early 20th century the magnetic compass has been superseded by the gyrocompass as primary equipment for ships and aircraft.

2 (also **pair of compasses**) an instrument for drawing circles and arcs and measuring distances between points, consisting of two arms linked by a movable joint, one arm ending in a point and the other usually carrying a pencil or pen. **3** [in *sing.*] the range or scope of something: *the event had political repercussions that are* ***beyond the compass of*** *this book.* See note at RANGE. ■ the enclosing limits of an area: *this region had within its compass many types of agriculture.* ■ the range of notes that can be produced by a voice or a musical instrument: *the cellos were playing in a rather somber part of their compass.*
▸*v.* [*trans.*] *archaic* **1** go around (something) in a circular course: *the ship wherein Magellan compassed the world.* ■ surround or enclose on all sides: *they were compassed with numerous fierce and cruel tribes.* **2** contrive to accomplish (something): *he compassed his end only by the exercise of violence.* ▷Middle English: from Old French *compas* (noun), *compasser* (verb), based on Latin *com-* 'together' + *passus* 'a step or pace.' Several senses ('measure,' 'artifice,' 'circumscribed area,' and 'pair of compasses') that appeared in Middle English are also found in Old French, but their development and origin are uncertain. The transference of sense to the magnetic compass is held to have occurred in the related Italian word *compasso*, from the circular shape of the compass box.

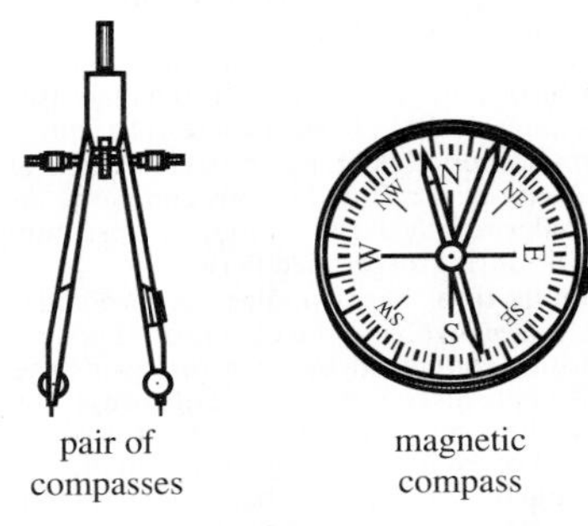

pair of compasses
magnetic compass
compass

com·pass card ▸*n.* a circular rotating card showing the 32 principal bearings, forming the indicator of a magnetic compass.

com·pas·sion /kəmˈpashən/ ▸*n.* sympathetic pity and concern for the sufferings or misfortunes of others: *the victims should be treated with compassion.* See note at MERCY. ▷Middle English: via Old French from ecclesiastical Latin *compassio(n-)*, from *compati* 'suffer with.'

com·pas·sion·ate /kəmˈpashənət/ ▸*adj.* feeling or showing sympathy and concern for others. ▷late 16th cent.: from COMPASSION + -ATE[2], influenced by archaic French *compassioné* 'feeling pity.' **—com·pas·sion·ate·ly** *adv.*

com·pas·sion·ate leave ▸*n.* a period of absence from work granted to someone as the result of particular personal circumstances, esp. the death of a close relative.

com·pas·sion fa·tigue ▸*n.* indifference to charitable appeals on behalf of those who are suffering, experienced as a result of the frequency or number of such appeals.

com·pass rose ▸*n.* a circle showing the principal directions printed on a map or chart.

com·pass saw ▸*n.* a handsaw with a narrow blade for cutting curves.

com·pat·i·ble /kəmˈpatəbəl/ ▸*adj.* (of two things) able to exist or occur together without conflict: *the fruitiness of Beaujolais is* ***compatible with*** *a number of meat dishes.* ■ (of two people) able to have a harmonious relationship: well-suited: *it's a pity we're not compatible.* ■ (of one thing) consistent with another: *the symptoms were compatible with gastritis or a peptic ulcer.* ■ (of a computer, a piece of software, or other device) able to be used with a specified piece of equipment or software without special adaptation or modification: *the printer is fully compatible with all leading software.*
▸*n.* a computer that can use software designed for another make or type. ▷late Middle English: from French, from medieval Latin *compatibilis*, from *compati* 'suffer with.' **—com·pat·i·bil·i·ty** /kəmˌpatəˈbilitē/ *n.* **—com·pat·i·bly** /-blē/ *adv.*

com·pa·tri·ot /kəmˈpātrēət/ ▸*n.* a fellow citizen or national of a country: *Stich defeated his compatriot Boris Becker in the quarterfinals.* ▷late 16th cent.: from French *compatriote*, from late Latin *compatriota* (translating Greek *sumpatriōtēs*), from *com-* 'together with' + *patriota* (see PATRIOT).

com·peer /ˈkämˌpi(ə)r; kämˈpi(ə)r/ ▸*n. formal* a person of equal rank, status, or ability: *he was better versed in his profession than his compeers.* ■ *archaic* a companion or associate. ▷late Middle English: from Old French *comper*, from *com-* 'with' + *per*, from Latin *par* 'equal' (compare with PEER[2]).

com·pel /kəmˈpel/ ▸*v.* (**-pelled, -pel·ling**) [*trans.*] force or oblige (someone) to do something: *a sense of duty compelled Harry to answer her questions.* ■ bring about (something) by the use of force or pressure: *they may compel a witness's attendance at court by issue of a summons.* ■ *poetic/literary* drive forcibly: *by heav'n's high will compell'd from shore to shore.* ▷late Middle English: from Latin *compellere*, from *com-* 'together' + *pellere* 'drive.'

THE RIGHT WORD **coerce, compel, constrain, force, necessitate, oblige**
A parent faced with a rebellious teenager may try to **compel** him to do his homework by threatening to take away his allowance. *Compel* commonly implies the exercise of authority, the exertion of great

effort, or the impossibility of doing anything else (*compelled to graduate from high school by her eagerness to leave home*). It typically requires a personal object, although it is possible to *compel* a reaction or response (*she compels admiration*).

Force is a little stronger, suggesting the exertion of power, energy, or physical strength to accomplish something or to subdue resistance (*his mother forced him to confess that he'd broken the basement window*).

Coerce can imply the use of force, but often stops short of using it (*she was coerced into obedience by the threat of losing her telephone privileges*).

Constrain means *compel*, but by means of restriction, confinement, or limitation (*constrained from dating by his parents' strictness*).

Necessitate and **oblige** make an action necessary by imposing certain conditions that demand a response (*her mother's illness obliged her to be more cooperative; it also necessitated her giving up her social life*).

com·pel·la·ble /kəm'peləbəl/ ▸*adj.* *Law* (of a witness) able to be made to attend court or testify.

com·pel·ling /kəm'peliNG/ ▸*adj.* evoking interest, attention, or admiration in a powerfully irresistible way: *his eyes were strangely compelling | a compelling film.* ■ not able to be refuted; inspiring conviction: *compelling evidence | a compelling argument.* ■ not able to be resisted; overwhelming: *the temptation to give up was compelling.* —**com·pel·ling·ly** *adv.*

com·pen·di·ous /kəm'pendēəs/ ▸*adj. formal* containing or presenting the essential facts of something in a comprehensive but concise way: *a compendious study.* ▷late Middle English: from Old French *compendieux*, from Latin *compendiosus* 'advantageous, brief,' from *compendium* 'profit, saving, abbreviation.' —**com·pen·di·ous·ly** *adv.* —**com·pen·di·ous·ness** *n.*

com·pen·di·um /kəm'pendēəm/ ▸*n.* (*pl.* **-di·ums** or **-di·a** /-dēə/) a collection of concise but detailed information about a particular subject, esp. in a book or other publication. ■ a collection of things, esp. one systematically gathered: *the program is a compendium of outtakes from our archives.* ▷late 16th cent.: from Latin, 'profit, saving' (literally 'what is weighed together'), from *compendere*, from *com-* 'together' + *pendere* 'weigh.'

com·pen·sa·ble /kəm'pensəbəl/ ▸*adj.* (of a loss or hardship) for which compensation can be obtained. ▷mid 17th cent.: French, from *compenser*, from Latin *compensare* 'weigh (something) against (another).'

com·pen·sate /'kämpən,sāt/ ▸*v.* **1** [*trans.*] recompense (someone) for loss, suffering, or injury, typically by the award of a sum of money: *payments were made to farmers to* ***compensate*** *them* ***for*** *cuts in subsidies.* ■ pay (someone) for work performed: *he will be richly compensated for his efforts.* **2** [*intrans.*] (**compensate for**) make up for (something unwelcome or unpleasant) by exerting an opposite force or effect: *officials have boosted levies to compensate for huge deficits.* ■ act to neutralize or correct (a deficiency or abnormality in a physical property or effect): *the output voltage rises, compensating for the original fall.* ■ *Psychology* attempt to conceal or offset (a disability or frustration) by development in another direction: *they identified with radical movements to compensate for their inability to relate to individual human beings.* **3** [*trans.*] *Mechanics* provide (a pendulum) with extra or less weight to neutralize the effects of temperature, etc. ▷mid 17th cent. (in the sense 'counterbalance'): from Latin *compensat-* 'weighed against,' from the verb *compensare*, from *com-* 'together' + *pensare* (frequentative of *pendere* 'weigh'). —**com·pen·sa·tive** /kəm'pensətiv; 'kämpən,sātiv/ *adj.* —**com·pen·sa·tor** /-,sātər/ *n.*

com·pen·sa·tion /,kämpən'sāSHən/ ▸*n.* something, typically money, awarded to someone as a recompense for loss, injury, or suffering: *seeking compensation for injuries suffered at work* | [as *adj.*] *a compensation claim.* ■ the action or process of making such an award: *the compensation of victims.* ■ the money received by an employee from an employer as a salary or wages. ■ something that counterbalances or makes up for an undesirable or unwelcome state of affairs: *the gray streets of London were small compensation for the loss of her beloved Africa | getting older has some compensations.* ■ *Psychology* the process of concealing or offsetting a psychological difficulty by developing in another direction. ▷late Middle English: via Old French from Latin *compensatio(n-)*, from the verb *compensare* 'weigh against' (see COMPENSATE). —**com·pen·sa·tion·al** /-SHənl/ *adj.*

com·pen·sa·tion pen·du·lum ▸*n.* *Physics* a pendulum constructed from metals with differing coefficients of expansion in order to neutralize the effects of temperature variation.

com·pen·sa·to·ry /kəm'pensə,tôrē/ ▸*adj.* providing, effecting, or aiming at compensation, in particular: ■ (of a payment) intended to recompense someone who has experienced loss, suffering, or injury: *$50 million in compensatory damages.* ■ reducing or offsetting the unpleasant or unwelcome effects of something: *the government is taking compensatory actions to keep the interest rate constant.*

com·père /'käm,per/ *Brit.* ▸*n.* a person who introduces the performers or contestants in a variety show; host.
▸*v.* [*trans.*] act as a compère for (such a show). ▷early 20th cent.: French, literally 'godfather'.

com·pete /kəm'pēt/ ▸*v.* [*intrans.*] strive to gain or win something by defeating or establishing superiority over others who are trying to do the same: *universities are* ***competing for*** *applicants | he* ***competed with*** *a number of other candidates* | [as *adj.*] (**competing**) *competing political ideologies.* ■ take part in a contest: *he competed in numerous track meets as a child.* ▷early 17th cent.: from Latin *competere*, in its late sense 'strive or contend for (something),' from *com-* 'together' + *petere* 'aim at, seek.'

com·pe·tence /'kämpətəns/ (also **com·pe·ten·cy** /-tənsē/) ▸*n.* **1** the ability to do something successfully or efficiently: *the players displayed varying degrees of competence.* ■ the scope of a person's or group's knowledge or ability: *the music is within the competence of an average choir.* ■ a skill or ability. ■ the legal authority of a court or other body to deal with a particular matter: *the court's competence has been accepted to cover these matters.* ■ the ability of a criminal defendant to stand trial, as gauged by their mental ability to understand the proceedings and to assist defense lawyers. ■ (also **linguistic** or **language competence**) *Linguistics* a speaker's subconscious, intuitive knowledge of the rules of their language. Often contrasted with PERFORMANCE. ■ *Biology & Medicine* effective performance of the normal function. **2** *dated* an income large enough to live on, typically unearned: *he found himself with an ample competence and no obligations.*

com·pe·tent /'kämpətənt/ ▸*adj.* having the necessary ability, knowledge, or skill to do something successfully: *a highly competent surgeon | make sure the firm* ***is competent to*** *carry out the work.* ■ (of a person) efficient and capable: *an infinitely competent mother of three.* ■ acceptable and satisfactory, though not outstanding: *she spoke quite competent French.* ■ (chiefly of a court or other body) accepted as having legal authority to deal with a particular matter: *the governor was not the* ***competent authority*** *to deal with the matter.* ■ (of a criminal defendant) able to understand the charges and to aid in defending themselves. ■ *Biology & Medicine* capable of performing the normal function effectively. ▷late Middle English (in the sense 'suitable, adequate'): from Latin *competent-*, from the verb *competere* in its earlier sense 'be fit or proper' (see COMPETE). —**com·pe·tent·ly** *adv.*

com·pe·ti·tion /,kämpə'tiSHən/ ▸*n.* the activity or condition of competing: *there is fierce* ***competition between*** *banks | at this conservatory,* ***competition for*** *admissions is stiff.* ■ an event or contest in which people compete: *a beauty competition.* ■ the action of participating in such an event or contest: *in the heat of competition.* ■ [in *sing.*] the person or people with whom one is competing, esp. in a commercial or sporting arena; the opposition: *I walked around to check out the competition.* ■ *Ecology* interaction between organisms, populations, or species, in which birth, growth and death depend on gaining a share of a limited environmental resource. ▷early 17th cent.: from late Latin *competitio(n-)* 'rivalry,' from *competere* 'strive for' (see COMPETE).

com·pet·i·tive /kəm'petətiv/ ▸*adj.* **1** of, relating to, or characterized by competition: *a competitive sport | the intensely competitive newspaper industry.* ■ having or displaying a strong desire to be more successful than others: *she had a competitive streak.* **2** as good as or better than others of a comparable nature: *a car industry competitive with any in the world.* ■ (of prices) low enough to compare well with those of rival merchants: *we offer prompt service at competitive rates.* ▷early 19th cent.: from Latin *competit-* 'striven for,' from the verb *competere* (see COMPETE), + -IVE. —**com·pet·i·tive·ness** *n.*

com·pet·i·tive ex·clu·sion ▸*n.* *Ecology* the inevitable elimination from a habitat of one of two different species with identical needs for resources.

com·pet·i·tive·ly /kəm'petətivlē/ ▸*adv.* in a competitive way, in particular: ■ in a way that strives to gain or win something by defeating others engaged in the same attempt: *their father rowed competitively.* ■ (of a product) priced in a way that compares favorably with others of the same nature: *our exports remained competitively priced.*

com·pet·i·tor /kəm'petətər/ ▸*n.* an organization or country that is engaged in commercial or economic competition with others: *our main industrial competitors.* ■ a person who takes part in an athletic contest.

com·pi·la·tion /,kämpə'lāSHən/ ▸*n.* **1** the action or process of producing something, esp. a list, book, or report, by assembling information collected from other sources: *great care has been taken in the compilation of this guidebook.* **2** a thing, esp. a book, record, or broadcast program, that is put together by assembling previously separate items: *there are thirty-three stories in this compilation* | [as *adj.*] *a compilation album.* ▷late Middle English: via Old French from Latin *compilatio(n-)*, from *compilare* 'to plunder' (see COMPILE).

com·pile /kəm'pīl/ ▸*v.* [*trans.*] **1** produce (something, esp. a list, report, or book) by assembling information collected from other sources: *the local authority must compile a list of taxpayers.* ■ collect (information) in order to produce something: *the figures were compiled from a survey of 2,000 schoolchildren.* ■ accumulate (a specified score): *the 49ers have compiled a league-leading 14–2 record.* **2** *Computing* (of a computer) convert (a program) into a machine-code or lower-level form in which the program can be executed. ▷Middle English: from Old French *compiler* or its apparent source, Latin *compilare* 'plunder or plagiarize.' —**com·pil·er** *n.*

comp·ing /'kämpiNG/ ▸*n.* **1** the process of making composite images, esp. electronically. **2** the action of playing a musical accompaniment, esp. in jazz or blues. **3** *Brit., informal* the practice of entering competitions, esp. those promoting consumer products. —**comp·er** /-pər/ *n. Brit.* (in sense 3).

com·pla·cen·cy /kəm'plāsənsē/ (also **com·pla·cence**) ▸*n.* a feeling of smug or uncritical satisfaction with oneself or one's achievements: *the figures are better, but there are no grounds for complacency.* ▷mid 17th cent.: from medieval Latin *complacentia*, from Latin *complacere* 'to please.'

com·pla·cent /kəm'plāsənt/ ▸*adj.* showing smug or uncritical satisfaction with oneself or one's achievements: *you can't afford to be complacent about security.* ▷mid 17th cent. (in the sense 'pleasant'): from Latin *complacent-* 'pleasing,' from the verb *complacere.* —**com·pla·cent·ly** *adv.*

USAGE **Complacent** and **complaisant** are two words that are similar in pronunciation and that both come from the Latin verb *complacere* 'to please', but which in English do not mean the same thing. **Complacent** is the more common word and means 'smug and self-satisfied': *after four consecutive championships, the team became complacent.* **Complaisant**, on the other hand, means 'willing to please': *the local people proved* ***complaisant*** *and cordial.*

com·plain /kəm'plān/ ▸*v.* [*trans.*] express dissatisfaction or annoyance about a state of affairs or an event: *local authorities complained that they lacked sufficient resources* | [intrans.] *"You never listen to me," Larry complained.* | [*intrans.*] *we all* ***complained*** *bitterly* ***about*** *the food.* ■ [*intrans.*] (**complain of**) state that one is suffering from (a pain or other symptom of illness): *her husband began to complain of headaches.* ■ [*intrans.*] state a grievance: *they* ***complained to*** *the French government.* ■ [*intrans.*] *poetic/literary* make a mournful sound: *let the warbling flute complain.* ■ [*intrans.*] (of a structure or mechanism) groan or creak under strain. ▷late Middle English: from Old French *complaindre*, from medieval Latin *complangere* 'bewail,' from *com-* (expressing intensive force) + *plangere* 'to lament.' —**com·plain·er** *n.* —**com·plain·ing·ly** *adv.*

com·plain·ant /kəm'plānənt/ ▸*n.* *Law* a plaintiff in certain lawsuits. ▷late Middle English: from French *complaignant*, present participle of *complaindre* 'to lament' (see COMPLAIN).

com·plaint /kəm'plānt/ ▸*n.* **1** a statement that a situation is unsatisfactory or unacceptable: *I intend to make an official complaint | there were complaints that the* *building was an eyesore.* ■ a reason for dissatisfaction: *I have no complaints about the hotel.* ■ the expression of dissatisfaction: *a letter of complaint* | *he hasn't any cause for complaint.* ■ *Law* the plaintiff's reasons for proceeding in a civil action. **2** an illness or medical condition, esp. a relatively minor one: *she is receiving treatment for her skin complaint.* ▷late Middle English: from Old French *complainte*, feminine past participle of *complaindre* 'to lament' (see COMPLAIN).

com·plai·sant /kəm'plāsənt/ ▸*adj.* willing to please others; obliging; agreeable: *when unharnessed, Northern dogs are peaceful and complaisant.* ▷mid 17th cent.: French, from *complaire* 'acquiesce in order to please,' from Latin *complacere* 'to please.' **—com·plai·sance** *n.* **—com·plai·sant·ly** *adv.*

USAGE See usage at COMPLACENT.

C

com·pleat /kəm'plēt/ ▸*adj.* & *v.* archaic spelling of COMPLETE.

com·plect·ed /kəm'plektəd/ ▸*adj.* [in *combination*] having a specified complexion: *lighter-complected invaders from the north.* ▷early 19th cent.: apparently from COMPLEXION.

com·ple·ment ▸*n.* /'kämpləmənt/ **1** a thing that completes or brings to perfection: *the libretto proved a perfect* ***complement to*** *the music.* **2** [in *sing.*] a number or quantity of something required to make a group complete: *at the moment we have* ***a full complement of*** *staff.* ■ the number of people required to crew a ship: *almost half the ship's complement of 322 were wounded.* ■ *Geometry* the amount in degrees by which a given angle is less than 90°. ■ *Mathematics* the members of a set that are not members of a given subset. **3** *Grammar* one or more words, phrases, or clauses governed by a verb (or by a nominalization or a predicative adjective) that complete the meaning of the predicate. ■ (in systemic grammar) an adjective or noun that has the same reference as either the subject (as *mad* in *he is mad*) or the object (as *mad* in *he drove her mad*). **4** *Physiology* a group of proteins present in blood plasma and tissue fluid that combine with an antigen–antibody complex to bring about the lysis of foreign cells.

▸*v.* /-ˌment; -mənt/ [*trans.*] add to (something) in a way that enhances or improves it; make perfect: *a classic blazer complements a look that's stylish or casual.* ■ add to or make complete: *the proposals complement the incentives already available.* ▷late Middle English (in the sense 'completion'): from Latin *complementum*, from *complere* 'fill up' (see COMPLETE). Compare with COMPLIMENT. **—com·ple·men·tal** /ˌkämplə'mentl/ *adj.*

USAGE **Complement** and **compliment** (and the related words **complementary** and **complimentary**) are frequently confused. Although pronounced alike, they have quite different meanings. As a verb, **complement** means 'add to (something) in a way that completes, enhances, or improves,' as in *Janet's new necklace complemented her pearl earrings nicely.* **Compliment** means 'admire and praise (someone) for something,' as in *they complimented Janet on her new necklace.*

Complementary means 'forming a complement or addition, completing,' as in *I purchased a suit with a complementary tie and handkerchief.* This can be confused with **complimentary**, for which one sense is 'given freely, as a courtesy': *you must pay for the suit, but the tie and handkerchief are complimentary.*

com·ple·men·tar·i·ty /ˌkämpləmen'taritē/ ▸*n.* (*pl.* **-ties**) a complementary relationship or situation: *a culture based on the complementarity of men and women.* ■ *Physics* the concept that two contrasted theories, such as the wave and particle theories of light, may be able to explain a set of phenomena, although each separately only accounts for some aspects. ■ *Law* the principle that jurisdictions will not overlap in legislation, administration, or prosecution of crime.

com·ple·men·ta·ry /ˌkämplə'ment(ə)rē/ ▸*adj.* **1** completing; forming a complement: *backyard satellite dishes and the complementary electronic components.* ■ (of two or more different things) combining in such a way as to enhance or emphasize each other's qualities: *three guitarists playing interlocking, complementary parts.* ■ *Biochemistry* (of gene sequences, nucleotides, etc.) related by the rules of base pairing. **2** [*attrib.*] of or relating to complementary medicine. **—com·ple·men·ta·ri·ly** /ˌkämplə'mentrəlē; -men'terəlē/ *adv.* **—com·ple·men·ta·ri·ness** *n.*

com·ple·men·ta·ry an·gle ▸*n.* either of two angles whose sum is 90°.

com·ple·men·ta·ry col·ors ▸*plural n.* colors directly opposite each other in the color spectrum, such as red and green or blue and orange, that when combined in the right proportions, produce white light. The effect is not the same when mixing paints.

com·ple·men·ta·ry dis·tri·bu·tion ▸*n. Linguistics* the occurrence of speech sounds in mutually exclusive contexts.

com·ple·men·ta·ry DNA ▸*n. Biochemistry* synthetic DNA in which the sequence of bases is complementary to that of a given example of DNA.

com·ple·men·ta·ry func·tion ▸*n. Mathematics* the part of the general solution of a linear differential equation that is the general solution of the associated homogeneous equation obtained by substituting zero for the terms not containing the dependent variable.

com·ple·men·ta·ry med·i·cine ▸*n.* any of a range of medical therapies that fall beyond the scope of scientific medicine but may be used alongside it in the treatment of disease and ill health. Examples include acupuncture and osteopathy. See also ALTERNATIVE MEDICINE.

com·ple·men·ta·tion /ˌkämpləmen'tāsʜən/ ▸*n.* the action of complementing something. ■ *Grammar* all the clause constituents that are governed by a verb, nominalization, or adjective. ■ *Genetics* the phenomenon by which the effects of two different nonallelic mutations in a gene are partly or entirely canceled out when they occur together.

com·ple·ment fix·a·tion test ▸*n. Medicine* a test for infection with a microorganism that involves measuring the amount of complement available in serum to bind with an antibody–antigen complex.

com·ple·men·tiz·er /'kämpləˌmenˌtīzər; -mən-/ ▸*n. Grammar* a word or morpheme that marks an embedded clause as functioning as a complement, typically a subordinating conjunction or infinitival *to.*

com·plete /kəm'plēt/ ▸*adj.* **1** having all the necessary or appropriate parts: *a complete list of courses offered by the college* | *no wardrobe is complete this year without culottes.* ■ (of all the works of a particular author) collected together in one volume or edition: *the complete works of Shakespeare.* ■ entire; full: *I only managed one complete term at school.* ■ having run its full course; finished: *the restoration of the chapel is complete.* **2** (often used for emphasis) to the greatest extent or degree; total: *a complete ban on smoking* | *their marriage came as a complete surprise to me.* ■ (also **com·pleat**) *chiefly humorous* skilled at every aspect of a particular activity; consummate: *these articles are for the compleat mathematician.* [the spelling *compleat* is a revival of the 17th cent. use as in Walton's *The Compleat Angler.*]

▸*v.* [*trans.*] **1** finish making or doing: *he completed his Ph.D. in 1983.* ■ *Football* (esp. of a quarterback) successfully throw (a forward pass) to a receiver: *he completed 12 of 16 passes for 128 yards.* ■ [*intrans.*] *Brit.* conclude the sale of a property. **2** make (something) whole or perfect: *he only needed one thing to complete his happiness* | *more recent box cameras complete the collection.* ■ write the required information on (a form or questionnaire): *please complete the attached forms.* ▷late Middle English: from Old French *complet* or Latin *completus*, past participle of *complere* 'fill up, finish, fulfill,' from *com-* (expressing intensive force) + *plere* 'fill.' **—com·plete·ness** *n.* **—com·plet·er** *n.*

▸*PHRASE* □ **complete with** having something as an additional part or feature: *the detachable keyboard* ***comes complete with*** *numeric keypad.*

USAGE On the use of adjectives like **complete**, **equal**, and **unique** with submodifiers such as **very** or **more**, see **usage** at UNIQUE.

com·plete game ▸*n. Baseball* a game in which one pitcher pitches all innings without relief.

com·plete·ly /kəm'plētlē/ ▸*adv.* totally; utterly: *the fire completely destroyed the building* | [as *submodifier*] *no code can be completely secure.*

com·ple·tion /kəm'plēsʜən/ ▸*n.* the action or process of finishing something: *funds for the completion of the new building.* ■ the state of being finished: *work on the new golf course is nearing completion* | [as *adj.*] *the completion date is early next year.* ■ *Football* a successful forward pass: *21 completions in 26 attempts for 233 yards.* ■ *Law* the final stage in the sale of a property, at which point it legally changes ownership: *the risk stays with the seller until completion.* ■ the action of writing the required information on a form. ▷late 15th cent.: from Latin *completion-*, from *complere* 'fill up' (see COMPLETE).

com·ple·tist /kəm'plētist/ ▸*n.* an obsessive, typically indiscriminate, collector or fan of something.

com·ple·tive /kəm'plētiv/ ▸*n. Grammar* a word or morpheme that adds a sense of completeness to a word or phrase (e.g., *up* in the phrase *break up*).

com·plex ▸*adj.* /käm'pleks; kəm'pleks; 'kämˌpleks/ **1** consisting of many different and connected parts: *a complex network of water channels.* ■ not easy to analyze or understand; complicated or intricate: *a complex personality* | *the situation is more complex than it appears.* **2** *Mathematics* denoting or involving numbers or quantities containing both a real and an imaginary part. **3** *Chemistry* denoting an ion or molecule in which one or more groups are linked to a metal atom by coordinate bonds.

▸*n.* /'kämˌpleks/ **1** a group of similar buildings or facilities on the same site: *a new apartment complex* | *a complex of hotels.* ■ a group or system of different things that are linked in a close or complicated way; a network: *a complex of mountain roads.* **2** *Psychoanalysis* a related group of emotionally significant ideas that are completely or partly repressed and that cause psychic conflict leading to abnormal mental states or behavior. ■ *informal* a disproportionate concern or anxiety about something: *there's no point having a* ***complex about*** *losing your hair.* **3** *Chemistry* an ion or molecule in which one or more groups are linked to a metal atom by coordinate bonds. ■ any loosely bonded species formed by the association of two molecules: *cross-linked protein—DNA complexes.*

▸*v.* /käm'pleks; kəm'pleks; 'kämˌpleks/ [*trans.*] (usu. **be complexed**) *Chemistry* make (an atom or compound) form a complex with another: *the DNA was* ***complexed with*** *the nuclear extract* | [as *adj.*] (**complexed**) *the complexed metal ion.* ■ [*intrans.*] form a complex: *these proteins are capable of complexing with VP16.* ▷mid 17th cent. (in the sense 'group of related elements'): from Latin *complexus*, past participle (used as a noun) of *complectere* 'embrace, comprise,' later associated with *complexus* 'plaited'; the adjective is partly via French *complexe*. **—com·plex·a·tion** /kämˌplek'sāsʜən; kəm-/ *n.* (*Chemistry*) **—com·plex·ly** *adv.*

com·plex plane ▸*n.* an infinite two-dimensional space representing the set of complex numbers, esp. one in which Cartesian coordinates represent the real and imaginary parts of the complex numbers.

com·plex con·ju·gate ▸*n. Mathematics* each of two complex numbers having their real parts identical and their imaginary parts of equal magnitude but opposite sign.

com·plex·ion /kəm'pleksʜən/ ▸*n.* **1** the natural color, texture, and appearance of a person's skin, esp. of the face: *an attractive girl with a pale complexion.* **2** the general aspect or character of something: *Congress's new complexion became boldly apparent last summer* | *wind, rain, and road construction have gradually changed Baja's complexion.* ▷Middle English: via Old French from Latin *complexio(n-)* 'combination' (in late Latin 'physical constitution'), from *complectere* 'embrace, comprise.' The term originally denoted physical constitution or temperament determined by the combination of the four bodily humors, hence sense 1 (late 16th cent.) as a visible sign of this. **—com·plex·ioned** *adj.* [often in *combination*] *they were both fair-complexioned.*

com·plex·i·ty /kəm'pleksitē/ ▸*n.* (*pl.* **-ties**) the state or quality of being intricate or complicated: *an issue of great complexity.* ■ (usu. **complexities**) a factor involved in a complicated process or situation: *the complexities of family life.*

com·plex sen·tence ▸*n. Grammar* a sentence containing a subordinate clause or clauses.

com·pli·ance /kəm'plīəns/ (also **com·pli·an·cy** /-'plīənsē/) ▸*n.* **1** the action or fact of complying with a wish or command: *they must secure each other's cooperation or compliance.* ■ (**compliance with**) the state or fact of according with or meeting rules or standards: *all imports of timber are* ***in compliance with*** *regulations.* ■ unworthy or excessive acquiescence: *the appalling compliance with government views shown by the commission.* **2** *Physics* the property of a material of undergoing elastic deformation or (of a gas) change in volume when subjected to an applied force. It is equal to the reciprocal of stiffness. ■ *Medicine* the ability of an organ to distend in response to applied pressure.

▸*adj.* undertaken or existing mainly in order to comply with an earlier treaty, order, or law: *WTO compliance legislation that ignores skyrocketing drug costs.*

com·pli·ant /kəm'plīənt/ ▸*adj.* **1** inclined to agree with others or obey rules, esp. to an excessive degree; acquiescent: *good-humored, eagerly compliant* girls. See note at OBEDIENT. ■ meeting or in accordance with rules or standards: *the systems are Y2K compliant.* **2** *Physics & Medicine* having the property of compliance. —**com·pli·ant·ly** *adv.*

com·pli·cate /ˈkämplə,kāt/ ▸*v.* [*trans.*] make (something) more difficult or confusing by causing it to be more complex: *middlemen can complicate the process* | [as *adj.*] (**complicating**) *a complicating factor.* ■ *Medicine* introduce complications in (an existing condition): *smoking may complicate pregnancy.* ▷early 17th cent. (in the sense 'combine, entangle, intertwine'): from Latin *complicat-* 'folded together,' from the verb *complicare*, from *com-* 'together' + *plicare* 'to fold.'

com·pli·cat·ed /ˈkämplə,kātid/ ▸*adj.* **1** consisting of many interconnecting parts or elements; intricate: *a complicated stereo system.* ■ involving many different and confusing aspects: *a long and complicated saga.* **2** *Medicine* involving complications: *complicated appendicitis.* —**com·pli·cat·ed·ly** *adv.*

com·pli·ca·tion /,kämpləˈkāSHən/ ▸*n.* **1** a circumstance that complicates something; a difficulty: *there is a complication concerning ownership of the site.* ■ an involved or confused condition or state: *to add further complication, English speakers use a different name.* **2** *Medicine* a secondary disease or condition aggravating an already existing one: *she developed complications after the surgery.* ▷late Middle English: from late Latin *complicatio(n-)*, from Latin *complicare* 'fold together' (see COMPLICATE).

com·plic·it /kəmˈplisit/ ▸*n.* involved with others in an illegal activity or wrongdoing: *all of these people are* **complicit in** *some criminal conspiracy.* ▷1940s: back-formation from COMPLICITY.

com·plic·i·ty /kəmˈplisitē/ ▸*n.* the state of being involved with others in an illegal activity or wrongdoing: *they were accused of* **complicity in** *the attempt to overthrow the government.* ▷mid 17th cent.: from Middle English *complice* 'an associate,' from Old French, from late Latin *complex, complic-* 'allied,' from Latin *complicare* 'fold together' (see COMPLICATE). Compare with ACCOMPLICE.

com·pli·ment ▸*n.* /ˈkämpləmənt/ a polite expression of praise or admiration: *she paid me an enormous compliment..* ■ an act or circumstance that implies praise or respect: *it's a compliment to the bride to dress up on her special day.* ■ (**compliments**) congratulations or praise expressed to someone: **my compliments on** *your cooking.* ■ (**compliments**) greetings or regards, esp. when sent as a message: *carry my compliments to your kinsmen.*

▸*v.* /ˈkämplə,ment/ [*trans.*] politely congratulate or praise (someone) for something: *he* **complimented** *Erica* **on** *her appearance.* ■ praise (something) politely: *complimenting the other team's good play.* ■ (**compliment someone with**) *archaic* present someone with (something) as a mark of courtesy: *Prince George expected to be complimented with a seat in the royal coach.* ▷mid 17th cent.: from French *compliment* (noun), *complimenter* (verb), from Italian *complimento* 'fulfillment of the requirements of courtesy,' from Latin *complementum* 'completion, fulfillment' (reflected in the earlier English spelling *complement*, gradually replaced by the French form between 1655 and 1715).

▸*PHRASES* □ **compliments of the season** used as a seasonal greeting at Christmas or the New Year. □ **pay one's compliments** send or express formal greetings. □ **return the compliment** give a compliment in return for another. ■ retaliate or respond in kind. □ **with someone's compliments** (or **the compliments of**) used to express the fact that what one is giving is free: *all drinks will be supplied with our compliments.*

USAGE **Compliment** (together with **complimentary**) is quite different in meaning from **complement** (and **complementary**). See **usage** at COMPLEMENT.

com·pli·men·ta·ry /,kämpləˈmentərē; -ˈmentrē/ ▸*adj.* **1** expressing a compliment; praising or approving: *Jennie was very complimentary about Kathy's riding* | *complimentary remarks.* **2** given or supplied free of charge: *a complimentary bottle of wine.*

com·pli·men·tary close (also **complimentary closing**) ▸*n.* the part of a letter that immediately precedes the writer's signature, consisting of words such as *Sincerely, Cordially, Very truly yours,* etc.

com·pline /ˈkämplin; -,plīn/ ▸*n.* a service of evening prayers forming part of the Divine Office of the Western Christian Church, traditionally said (or chanted) before retiring for the night. ▷Middle English: from Old French *complie*, feminine past participle of obsolete *complir* 'to complete,' from Latin *complere* 'fill up' (see COMPLETE). The ending *-ine* was probably influenced by Old French *matines* 'matins.'

com·ply /kəmˈplī/ ▸*v.* (**-plies, -plied**) [*intrans.*] (of a person or group) act in accordance with a wish or command: *we are unable to* **comply with** *your request.* ■ (of an article) meet specified standards: *all secondhand furniture must* **comply with** *the new standards.* ▷late 16th cent.: from Italian *complire*, Catalan *complir*, Spanish *cumplir*, from Latin *complere* 'fill up, fulfill' (see COMPLETE). The original sense was 'fulfill, accomplish,' later 'fulfill the requirements of courtesy,' hence 'to be agreeable, to oblige or obey.' Compare with COMPLIMENT.

com·po·nent /kəmˈpōnənt/ ▸*n.* a part or element of a larger whole, esp. a part of a machine or vehicle: *stereo components.* ■ *Physics* each of two or more forces, velocities, or other vectors acting in different directions that are together equivalent to a given vector.

▸*adj.* constituting part of a larger whole; constituent: *light passed through a prism breaks up into its component colors.* ▷mid 17th cent.: from Latin *component-* 'putting together,' from the verb *componere*, from *com-* 'together' + *ponere* 'put.' Compare with COMPOUND[1].

com·po·nen·tial a·nal·y·sis /,kämpəˈnenCHəl/ ▸*n. Linguistics* the analysis of the meaning of an expression into discrete semantic components.

com·po·ny /kəmˈpōnē/ ▸*adj.* [usu. *postpositive*] *Heraldry* divided into a single row of squares in alternating tinctures: *a bordure compony.* ▷late 16th cent.: from French *componé*, from Old French *compondre*, from Latin *componere* 'put together.'

com·port[1] /kəmˈpôrt/ ▸*v.* **1** (**comport oneself**) *formal* conduct oneself; behave: *articulate students who comported themselves well in television interviews.* **2** [*intrans.*] (**comport with**) accord with; agree with: *the actions that comport with her own liberal views* ▷late Middle English (in the sense 'tolerate'): from Latin *comportare*, from *com-* 'together' + *portare* 'carry, bear.'

com·port[2] /ˈkäm,pôrt/ ▸*n.* another term for COMPOTE (sense 2). ▷late 19th cent.: apparently an abbreviation of French *comportier*, variant of *compotier* 'dessert dish.'

com·port·ment /kəmˈpôrtmənt/ ▸*n.* behavior; bearing: *he displayed the comportment expected of the rightful king.* ▷late 16th cent.: from French *comportement*, from the verb *comporter*, from Latin *comportare* (see COMPORT[1]).

com·pose /kəmˈpōz/ ▸*v.* [*trans.*] **1** write or create (a work of art, esp. music or poetry): *he composed the First Violin Sonata four years earlier.* ■ write or phrase (a letter or piece of writing) with care and thought: *the first sentence is so hard to compose.* ■ form (a whole) by ordering or arranging the parts, esp. in an artistic way: *compose and draw a still life.* ■ order or arrange (parts) to form a whole, esp. in an artistic way: *make an attempt to compose your images.* **2** (usu. **be composed**) (of elements) constitute or make up (a whole): *the system is* **composed of** *a group of machines.* ■ be (a specified number or amount) of a whole: *Christians compose 40 percent of the state's population.* **3** calm or settle (oneself or one's features or thoughts): *she tried to* **compose herself.** ■ *archaic* settle (a dispute): *the king, with some difficulty, composed this difference.* **4** prepare (a text) for printing by manually, mechanically, or electronically setting up the letters and other characters in the order to be printed. ■ set up (letters and characters) in this way. ▷late Middle English (in the general sense 'put together, construct'): from Old French *composer*, from Latin *componere* (see COMPONENT), but influenced by Latin *compositus* 'composed' and Old French *poser* 'to place.'

USAGE On the differences between **comprise** and **compose**, see **usage** at COMPRISE.

com·posed /kəmˈpōzd/ ▸*adj.* having one's feelings and expression under control; calm. —**com·pos·ed·ly** /-ˈpōzədlē/ *adv.*

com·pos·er /kəmˈpōzər/ ▸*n.* a person who writes music, esp. as a professional occupation.

com·pos·ite /kəmˈpäzət; käm-/ ▸*adj.* **1** made up of various parts or elements. ■ (esp. of a construction-al material) made up of recognizable constituents: *a new composite material—a blend of plastic and ceramic resins.* ■ (of a railroad car) having compartments of more than one class or function. ■ *Mathematics* (of an integer) being the product of two or more factors greater than one; not prime. **2** (**Composite**) relating to or denoting a classical order of architecture consisting of elements of the Ionic and Corinthian orders. **3** *Botany* relating to or denoting plants of the daisy family (Compositae).

▸*n.* **1** a thing made up of several parts or elements: *the English legal system is a composite of legislation and judicial precedent.* ■ a composite photograph. ■ a composite constructional material. **2** *Botany* a plant of the daisy family (Compositae). **3** (**Composite**) the Composite order of architecture.

▸*v.* [*trans.*] [usu. as *n.*] (**compositing**) combine (two or more images) to make a single picture, esp. electronically: *photographic compositing by computer.* ■ ■ amalgamate (two or more similar resolutions). ▷late Middle English (describing a number having more than one digit): via French from Latin *compositus*, past participle of *componere* 'put together.' —**com·pos·ite·ly** *adv.* —**com·pos·ite·ness** *n.*

com·pos·ite pho·to·graph ▸*n.* a photograph made by overlapping or juxtaposing two or more separate images.

com·po·si·tion /,kämpəˈziSHən/ ▸*n.* **1** the nature of something's ingredients or constituents; the way in which a whole or mixture is made up: *the social composition of villages.* ■ the action of putting things together; formation or construction: *the composition of a new government was announced.* ■ a thing composed of various elements: *a theory is a composition of interrelated facts.* ■ *archaic* mental constitution; character: *persons who have a touch of madness in their composition.* ■ [often as *adj.*] a compound artificial substance, esp. one serving the purpose of a natural one: *composition flooring.* ■ *Linguistics* the formation of words into a compound word. ■ *Mathematics* the successive application of functions to a variable, the value of the first function being the argument of the second, and so on: *composition of functions, when defined, is associative.* ■ *Physics* the process of finding the resultant of a number of forces. **2** a work of music, literature, or art: *Chopin's most romantic compositions.* ■ the action or art of producing such a work: *the technical aspects of composition.* ■ an essay, esp. one written by a school or college student. ■ the artistic arrangement of the parts of a picture: *spoiling the composition of many of the pictures.* **3** the preparing of text for printing by setting up the characters in order. See COMPOSE (sense 4). **4** a legal agreement to pay an amount of money in lieu of a larger debt or other obligation. ■ an amount of money paid in this way. ▷late Middle English: via Old French from Latin *composition-*, from *componere* 'put together.' —**com·po·si·tion·al** /-SHənl/ *adj.* —**com·po·si·tion·al·ly** /-SHənl-ē/ *adv.*

com·pos·i·tor /kəmˈpäzitər/ ▸*n. Printing* a person who arranges type for printing or keys text into a composing machine. ▷late Middle English (originally Scots, denoting an umpire or arbiter): from Anglo-Norman French *compositour*, from Latin *compositor*, from *composit-* 'put together,' from the verb *componere* (see COMPOSITION).

com·pos men·tis /,kämpəs ˈmentəs/ ▸*adj.* [*predic.*] having full control of one's mind; sane: *are you sure he was totally compos mentis?* ▷early 17th cent.: Latin.

com·pos·si·ble /kəmˈpäsəbəl; käm-/ ▸*adj. rare* (of one thing) compatible or possible in conjunction with another. ▷mid 17th cent.: from Old French, from medieval Latin *compossibilis*, from *com-* 'together with' + *possibilis* (see POSSIBLE).

com·post /ˈkäm,pōst/ ▸*n.* decayed organic material used as a plant fertilizer. ■ a mixture of this with loam and/or other ingredients, used as a growing medium.

▸*v.* [*trans.*] make (vegetable matter or manure) into compost: *don't compost heavily infested plants.* ■ treat (soil) with compost: *we turned clay soil into almost workable soil by composting it.* ▷late Middle English: from Old French *composte*, from Latin *composita, compositum* 'something put together,' feminine and neuter past participle of *componere*.

com·post heap (also **compost pile**) ▸*n.* a pile of garden and organic kitchen refuse that decomposes to produce compost.

com·po·sure /kəmˈpōZHər/ ▸*n.* the state or feeling of being calm and in control of oneself: *she was struggling to regain her composure.* ▷late 16th cent. (in the sense 'composing, composition'): from COMPOSE + -URE.

com·pote /ˈkäm,pōt/ ▸*n.* **1** fruit preserved or cooked in syrup. ■ a dish consisting of fruit salad or stewed

Pronunciation Key ə *ago*; ər *over*; ˈə or ,ə *up*; ˈər or ,ər *fur*; a *hat*; ā *rate*; ä *car*; CH *chew*; e *let*; ē *see*; e(ə)r *air*; i *fit*; ī *by*; i(ə)r *ear*; NG *sing*; ō *go*; ô *for*; oi *boy*; o͝o *good*; o͞o *goo*; ou *out*; SH *she*; TH *thin*; T͟H *then*; (h)w *why*; ZH *vision*

fruit, often with syrup. **2** a bowl-shaped dessert dish with a stem. ▷late 17th cent.: from French, from Old French *composte* 'mixture' (see COMPOST).

com·pound1 ▸*n.* /ˈkämˌpound/ a thing that is composed of two or more separate elements; a mixture: *the air smelled like a compound of diesel and gasoline fumes.* ■ (also **chemical compound**) a substance formed from two or more elements chemically united in fixed proportions: *a compound of hydrogen and oxygen.* ■ a word made up of two or more existing words, such as *steamship.*
▸*adj.* /ˈkämˌpound; kämˈpound; kəmˈpound/ [*attrib.*] made up or consisting of several parts or elements, in particular: ■ (of a word) made up of two or more existing words or elements: *a compound noun.* ■ (of interest) payable on both capital and the accumulated interest: *compound interest.* Compare with SIMPLE. ■ *Biology* (esp. of a leaf, flower, or eye) consisting of two or more simple parts or individuals in combination.
▸*v.* /kəmˈpound; kämˈpound; ˈkämˌpound/ [*trans.*] **1** (often **be compounded**) make up (a composite whole); constitute: *a dialect* ***compounded of*** *Spanish and Dutch.* ■ mix or combine (ingredients or constituents): *yellow pastas compounded with lemon zest or saffron.* ■ calculate (interest) on previously accumulated interest: *the yield at which the interest is compounded.* ■ (of a sum of money invested) increase by compound interest: *let your money compound for five years.* **2** make (something bad) worse; intensify the negative aspects of: *I compounded the problem by trying to make wrong things right.* **3** *Law* forbear from prosecuting (a felony) in exchange for money or other consideration. ■ settle (a debt or other matter) in this way: *he compounded the case with the defendant for a cash payment.* ▷late Middle English *compoune* (verb), from Old French *compoun-*, present tense stem of *compondre*, from Latin *componere* 'put together.' The final *-d* was added in the 16th cent. on the pattern of *expound* and *propound.* —**com·pound·a·ble** /kəmˈpoundəbəl; kämˈ-/ *adj.*

USAGE The sense of the verb **compound** that means 'worsen,' as in *this* ***compounds*** *their problems,* has an interesting history. It arose through a misinterpretation of the phrase **compound a felony**, which, strictly speaking, means 'forbear from prosecuting a felony in exchange for money or other consideration.' The 'incorrect' sense has become the usual one in legal uses and, by extension, in general senses too, and is now accepted as part of standard English.

com·pound2 /ˈkämˌpound/ ▸*n.* an area enclosed by a fence, in particular: ■ an open area in which a factory or large house stands. ■ an open area in a prison, prison camp, or work camp. ▷late 17th cent. (referring to such an area in Southeast Asia): from Portuguese *campon* or Dutch *kampoeng*, from Malay *kampong* 'enclosure, hamlet'; compare with KAMPONG.

com·pound-com·plex sen·tence ▸*n.* a sentence having two or more coordinate independent clauses and one or more dependent clauses.

com·pound·er /kämˈpoundər; kəmˈpoundər; ˈkämˌpoundər/ ▸*n.* a person who mixes or combines ingredients in order to produce an animal feed, medicine, or other substance.

com·pound eye ▸*n.* an eye consisting of an array of numerous small visual units, as found in insects and crustaceans. Contrasted with SIMPLE EYE.

com·pound frac·tion ▸*n.* a fraction in which either the numerator or the denominator, or both, contain one or more fractions. Also called COMPLEX FRACTION.

com·pound frac·ture ▸*n.* an injury in which a broken bone pierces the skin, causing a risk of infection. Compare with SIMPLE FRACTURE.

com·pound in·ter·val ▸*n. Music* an interval greater than an octave.

com·pound leaf ▸*n.* a leaf of a plant consisting of several or many distinct parts (leaflets) joined to a single stem.

com·pound num·ber ▸*n.* a quantity expressed in terms of more than one unit or denomination, such as 5 feet 7 inches or 2 pounds 3 ounces.

com·pound sen·tence ▸*n.* a sentence with more than one subject or predicate.

com·pound time ▸*n. Music* musical rhythm or meter in which each beat in a bar is subdivided into three smaller units, so having the value of a dotted note. Compare with SIMPLE TIME.

com·pra·dor /ˌkämprəˈdôr/ (also **com·pra·dore**) ▸*n.* a person within a country who acts as an agent for foreign organizations engaged in investment, trade, or economic or political exploitation. ▷early 17th cent. (denoting a local person employed in a European household in Southeast Asia or India to make small purchases and keep the household accounts): from Portuguese, 'buyer,' from late Latin *comparator*, from Latin *comparare* 'to purchase,' from *com-* 'with' + *parare* 'provide.'

com·pre·hend /ˌkämpriˈhend/ ▸*v.* [*trans.*] **1** grasp mentally; understand: *he couldn't comprehend her reasons for marrying Lovat* | *I simply couldn't comprehend what had happened.* **2** *formal* include, comprise, or encompass: *a divine order comprehending all men.* ▷Middle English: from Old French *comprehender*, or Latin *comprehendere*, from *com-* 'together' + *prehendere* 'grasp.' —**com·pre·hend·er** *n.*

com·pre·hen·si·ble /ˌkämpriˈhensəbəl/ ▸*adj.* able to be understood; intelligible: *clear and comprehensible English.* ▷late 15th cent.: from French *compréhensible* or Latin *comprehensibilis*, from *comprehens-* 'seized, comprised,' from the verb *comprehendere* (see COMPREHEND). —**com·pre·hen·si·bil·i·ty** /-ˌhensəˈbilitē/ *n.* —**com·pre·hen·si·bly** /-blē/ *adv.*

com·pre·hen·sion /ˌkämpriˈhenCHən/ ▸*n.* **1** the action or capability of understanding something: *some won't have the least comprehension of what I'm trying to do* | *the comprehension of spoken language.* **2** *archaic* inclusion. ▷late Middle English: from French *compréhension* or Latin *comprehensio(n-)*, from the verb *comprehendere* 'seize, comprise' (see COMPREHEND).

com·pre·hen·sive /ˌkämpriˈhensiv/ ▸*adj.* **1** complete; including all or nearly all elements or aspects of something: *a comprehensive list of sources.* ■ of large content or scope; wide-ranging: *a comprehensive collection of photographs.* ■ (of automobile insurance) providing coverage for most risks, including damage to the policyholder's own vehicle: *comprehensive and collision insurance.* ■ (also **comprehensive examination** or **comp**) an examination testing a student's command of a special field of knowledge. **2** *archaic* of or relating to understanding.
▸*n.* (in full **comprehensive school**) *Brit.* a secondary school catering to children of all abilities from a given area. ▷early 17th cent.: from French *compréhensif, -ive*, from late Latin *comprehensivus*, from the verb *comprehendere* 'grasp mentally.' —**com·pre·hen·sive·ly** *adv.* —**com·pre·hen·sive·ness** *n.*

com·press ▸*v.* /kəmˈpres/ [*trans.*] (often **be compressed**) flatten by pressure; squeeze; press: *the skirt can be folded and* ***compressed into*** *a small bag* | [as *adj.*] (**compressed**) *compressed gas.* ■ [*intrans.*] be squeezed or pressed together or into a smaller space: *the land is sinking as the soil compresses.* ■ squeeze or press (two things) together: *Violet compressed her lips together grimly.* ■ express in a shorter form; abridge: *in this chapter we* ***compress into*** *summary form the main findings.* ■ *Computing* alter the form of (data) to reduce the amount of storage necessary. ■ [as *adj.*] (**compressed**) *chiefly Biology* having a narrow shape as if flattened, esp. sideways: *most sea snakes have a compressed tail.*
▸*n.* /ˈkämˌpres/ a pad of absorbent material pressed onto part of the body to relieve inflammation or stop bleeding: *a cold compress.* ▷late Middle English: from Old French *compresser* or late Latin *compressare*, frequentative of Latin *comprimere*, from *com-* 'together' + *premere* 'to press'; or directly from *compress-* 'pressed together,' from the verb *comprimere.* —**com·press·i·bil·i·ty** /kəmˌpresəˈbilitē/ *n.* —**com·press·i·ble** *adj.* —**com·pres·sive** /-ˈpresiv/ *adj.*

com·pressed air ▸*n.* air that has been compressed to a pressure higher than atmospheric pressure.

com·pres·sion /kəmˈpresHən/ ▸*n.* the action of compressing or being compressed. ■ the reduction in volume (causing an increase in pressure) of the fuel mixture in an internal combustion engine before ignition. ▷late Middle English: via Old French from Latin *compressio(n-)*, from *comprimere* 'press together' (see COMPRESS). —**com·pres·sion·al** /-SHənl/ *adj.*

com·pres·sion ra·tio ▸*n.* the ratio of the maximum to minimum volume in the cylinder of an internal combustion engine.

com·pres·sive strength ▸*n.* the resistance of a material to breaking under compression. Compare with TENSILE STRENGTH.

com·pres·sor /kəmˈpresər/ ▸*n.* an instrument or device for compressing something. ■ a machine used to supply air or other gas at increased pressure, e.g., to power a gas turbine. ■ an electrical amplifier that reduces the dynamic range of a signal.

com·prise /kəmˈprīz/ ▸*v.* [*trans.*] consist of; be made up of: *the country comprises twenty states.* ■ make up; constitute: *this single breed comprises 50 percent of the Swiss cattle population* | (**be comprised of**) *documents are comprised of words.* ▷late Middle English: from French, 'comprised,' feminine past participle of *comprendre*, from Old French *comprehender* (see COMPREHEND).

USAGE 1 According to traditional usage, **comprise** means 'consist of,' as in *the country comprises twenty states*, and should not be used to mean 'constitute or make up (a whole),' as in *this single breed comprises 50 percent of the Swiss cattle population.* But confusion has arisen because of uses in the passive, which have been formed by analogy with words like **compose**: when **comprise** is used in the active (as in *the country comprises twenty states*) it is, oddly, more or less synonymous with the passive use of the second sense (as in *the country is comprised of twenty states*). Such passive uses of **comprise** are common and are fast becoming part of standard English.

2 On the differences between **comprise** and **include**, see **usage** at INCLUDE.

com·pro·mise /ˈkämprəˌmīz/ ▸*n.* an agreement or a settlement of a dispute that is reached by each side making concessions: *an ability to listen to two sides in a dispute, and devise a compromise acceptable to both* | *the secret of a happy marriage is compromise.* ■ a middle state between conflicting opinions or actions reached by mutual concession or modification: *a* ***compromise between*** *communism and private enterprise.* ■ the acceptance of standards that are lower than is desirable: *sexism should be tackled without compromise.*
▸*v.* **1** [*intrans.*] settle a dispute by mutual concession: *in the end we compromised and deferred the issue.* ■ [*trans.*] *archaic* settle (a dispute) by mutual concession: *I should compromise the matter with my father.* **2** [*trans.*] weaken (a reputation or principle) by accepting standards that are lower than is desirable: *commercial pressures could compromise safety.* ■ [*intrans.*] accept standards that are lower than is desirable: *we were not prepared to* ***compromise on*** *safety.* ■ bring into disrepute or danger by indiscreet, foolish, or reckless behavior: *situations in which his troops could be compromised.* ▷late Middle English (denoting mutual consent to arbitration): from Old French *compromis*, from late Latin *compromissum* 'a consent to arbitration,' neuter past participle of *compromittere*, from *com-* 'together' + *promittere* (see PROMISE). —**com·pro·mis·er** *n.*

com·pro·mis·ing /ˈkämprəˌmīzing/ ▸*adj.* (of information or a situation) revealing an embarrassing or incriminating secret about someone: *to cover up compromising evidence of malpractice.*

compte ren·du /ˈkônt räNˈdy; räNˈd(y)o͞o/ ▸*n.* (*pl.* **comptes ren·dus** *pronunc.* same) a formal report or review. ▷early 19th cent.: French, literally 'account rendered.'

Comp·ton1 /ˈkämptən/ an industrial city in southwestern California, just south of Los Angeles; pop. 90,454.

Comp·ton2, Arthur Holly (1892–1962), U.S. physicist. He observed the Compton effect and thus demonstrated the dual particle and wave properties of electromagnetic radiation and matter, as predicted by quantum theory. Nobel Prize for Physics (1927, shared with C. Wilson).

Comp·ton ef·fect ▸*n. Physics* an increase in wavelength of X-rays or gamma rays that occurs when they are scattered. ▷early 20th cent.: named after A. H. *Compton* (see COMPTON2).

comp·trol·ler /kənˈtrōlər; ˌkäm(p)ˈtrōlər; ˈkäm(p)ˌtrōlər/ ▸*n.* a controller (used in the title of some financial officers). ▷late 15th cent.: variant of CONTROLLER, by erroneous association with French *compte* 'calculation' or its source, late Latin *computus.*

com·pul·sion /kəmˈpəlSHən/ ▸*n.* **1** the action or state of forcing or being forced to do something; constraint: *the payment was made* ***under compulsion.*** **2** an irresistible urge to behave in a certain way, esp. against one's conscious wishes: *he felt a compulsion to babble on about what had happened.* ▷late Middle English: via Old French from late Latin *compulsio(n-)*, from *compellere* 'to drive, force' (see COMPEL).

com·pul·sive /kəmˈpəlsiv/ ▸*adj.* **1** resulting from or relating to an irresistible urge, esp. one that is against one's conscious wishes: *compulsive eating.* ■ (of a person) acting as a result of such an urge: *a compulsive liar.* **2** irresistibly interesting or exciting; compelling: *this play is compulsive viewing.* ▷late 16th cent. (in the sense 'compulsory'): from medieval

Latin *compulsivus*, from *compuls-* 'driven, forced,' from the verb *compellere* (see COMPEL). Sense 1 (originally a term in psychology) dates from the early 20th cent. **—com·pul·sive·ly** *adv.* **—com·pul·sive·ness** *n.*

com·pul·so·ry /kəmˈpəlsərē/ ▸*adj.* required by law or a rule; obligatory: *compulsory military service | it was compulsory to attend Mass.* ■ involving or exercising compulsion; coercive: *the abuse of compulsory powers.* ▷early 16th cent. (as a noun denoting a legal mandate that had to be obeyed): from medieval Latin *compulsorius*, from *compuls-* 'driven, forced,' from the verb *compellere* (see COMPEL). **—com·pul·so·ri·ly** /-sərəlē/ *adv.* **—com·pul·so·ri·ness** *n.*

com·punc·tion /kəmˈpəNG(k)SHən/ ▸*n.* [usu. with *negative*] a feeling of guilt or moral scruple that follows the doing of something bad: *spend the money* ***without compunction.*** See note at QUALM. ■ a pricking of the conscience: *he had no compunction about behaving blasphemously.* ▷Middle English: from Old French *componction*, from ecclesiastical Latin *compunctio(n-)*, from Latin *compungere* 'prick sharply,' from *com-* (expressing intensive force) + *pungere* 'to prick.' **—com·punc·tion·less** *adj.* **—com·punc·tious** /-SHəs/ *adj.* **—com·punc·tious·ly** /-SHəslē/ *adv.*

com·pur·ga·tion /ˌkämpərˈgāSHən/ ▸*n. historical Law* acquittal from a charge or accusation, obtained by statements of innocence given by witnesses under oath. ▷mid 17th cent.: from medieval Latin *compurgation-*, from Latin *compurgare*, from *com-* (expressing intensive force) + *purgare* 'purify' (from *purus* 'pure').

com·pur·ga·tor /ˈkämpərˌgātər/ ▸*n. historical Law* a sworn witness to the innocence or good character of an accused person. ▷mid 16th cent.: medieval Latin, from Latin *com-* 'together with' + *purgator*, from *purgare* 'purify' (see COMPURGATION).

com·pu·ta·tion /ˌkämpyo͞oˈtāSHən/ ▸*n.* the action of mathematical calculation: *months of computation carried out on more than 200 computers | statistical computations.* ■ the use of computers, esp. as a subject of research or study. ▷late Middle English: from Latin *computatio(n-)*, from the verb *computare* (see COMPUTE).

com·pu·ta·tion·al /ˌkämpyo͞oˈtāSHənl/ ▸*adj.* using computers: *the computational analysis of English.* ■ of or relating to computers: *computational power.* ■ of or relating to the process of mathematical calculation: *the exam only really tested computational ability.* **—com·pu·ta·tion·al·ly** /-SHənl-ē/ *adv.*

com·pu·ta·tion·al lin·guis·tics ▸*plural n.* [treated as *sing.*] the branch of linguistics in which the techniques of computer science are applied to the analysis and synthesis of language and speech.

com·pute /kəmˈpyo͞ot/ ▸*v.* [*trans.*] (often **be computed**) calculate or reckon (a figure or amount): *we can compute the exact increase | depreciation is computed by applying the straight-line method.* ■ [*intrans.*] make a calculation, esp. using a computer: *modern circuitry can compute faster than any chess player.* ■ [*intrans.*, with *negative*] *informal* seem reasonable; make sense: *the idea of an ethic governing what goes on in cyberspace simply does not compute.* [from the phrase *does not compute*, once used as an error message in computing.] ▷early 17th cent.: from French *computer* or Latin *computare*, from *com-* 'together' + *putare* 'to settle (an account).' **—com·put·a·bil·i·ty** /kəmˌpyo͞otəˈbilitē/ *n.* **—com·put·a·ble** *adj.* **—com·put·a·bly** /-blē/ *adv.* **—com·put·ist** /-ˈpyo͞otist/ *n.*

com·put·er /kəmˈpyo͞otər/ ▸*n.* an electronic device for storing and processing data, typically in binary form, according to instructions given to it in a variable program. ■ a person who makes calculations, esp. with a calculating machine.

com·put·er an·i·ma·tion ▸*n.* see ANIMATION.

com·put·er con·fer·enc·ing ▸*n.* the use of computer and telecommunications technology to hold discussions between three or more people operating computers in separate locations.

com·put·er dat·ing ▸*n.* the use of computer databases to identify potentially compatible partners for people.

com·put·er·ese /kəmˌpyo͞otəˈrēz; -ˈrēs/ ▸*n. chiefly derogatory* the jargon associated with computers. ■ the symbols and rules of a computer programming language.

com·put·er-friend·ly ▸*adj.* **1** suitable for use with computers; compatible with computers: *present the data in computer-friendly form.* **2** (of a person) well disposed toward computers: *a computer-friendly politician.*

com·put·er game ▸*n.* a game played using a computer, typically a video game.

com·put·er graph·ics ▸*plural n.* another term for GRAPHICS (sense 3).

com·put·er·ist /kəmˈpyo͞otərist/ ▸*n.* a (frequent) user of computers.

com·put·er·ize /kəmˈpyo͞otəˌrīz/ ▸*v.* [*trans.*] [often as *adj.*] (**computerized**) convert to a system that is operated or controlled by computer: *the advantages of computerized accounting.* ■ convert (information) to a form that is stored or processed by computer: *a computerized register of dogs.* **—com·put·er·i·za·tion** /kəmˌpyo͞otərəˈzāSHən/ *n.*

com·put·er-lit·er·ate ▸*adj.* (of a person) having sufficient knowledge and skill to be able to use computers; familiar with the operation of computers. **—com·put·er lit·er·a·cy** *n.*

com·put·er pro·gram·mer ▸*n.* a person who writes programs for the operation of computers, esp. as an occupation.

com·put·er sci·ence ▸*n.* the study of the principles and use of computers.

com·put·er vi·rus ▸*n.* see VIRUS.

com·put·ing /kəmˈpyo͞otiNG/ ▸*n.* the use or operation of computers: *developments in mathematics and computing |* [as *adj.*] *computing facilities.*

com·rade /ˈkämˌrad; ˈkämrəd/ ▸*n.* a companion who shares one's activities or is a fellow member of an organization. ■ (also **com·rade-in-arms**) a fellow soldier or serviceman. ■ a fellow socialist or communist (often as a form of address): [as *title*] *Comrade Lenin.* ▷mid 16th cent. (originally also *camerade*): from French *camerade*, *camarade* (originally feminine), from Spanish *camarada* 'roommate,' from Latin *camera* 'chamber.' Compare with CHUM[1]. **—com·rade·ly** *adj.* **—com·rade·ship** /-ˌSHip/ *n.*

Com·sat /ˈkämˌsat/ ▸*n. trademark* the Communications Satellite Corporation, a private corporation authorized by Congress to develop commercial communications satellite systems. ■ (**comsat**) *informal* a communications satellite. ▷1960s: blend.

Com·stock·er·y /ˈkämˌstäkərē; ˈkəm-/ ▸*n.* excessive opposition to supposed immorality in the arts; prudery. ▷named for Anthony Comstock (1844–1915), U.S. author and reformer.

Com·stock Lode /ˈkämˌstäk/ a historic gold and silver source in the Virginia Mountains of western Nevada, south of Reno, the basis of a boom that lasted from the 1850s through the late-19th century.

Comte /kônt/, Auguste (1798–1857), French philosopher; one of the founders of sociology. His positivist philosophy attempted to define the laws of social evolution and to found a genuine social science that could be used for social reconstruction. **—Comt·ism** /ˈkônˌtizəm/ *n.*

con[1] /kän/ *informal* ▸*v.* (**conned**, **con·ning**) [*trans.*] persuade (someone) to do or believe something, typically by use of a deception: *I* ***conned*** *him* ***into*** *giving me your home number | she was jailed for* ***conning*** *her aunt* ***out of*** *$500,000.*
▸*n.* an instance of deceiving or tricking someone: *when depositors, realizing that the whole thing is a con, demand repayment |* [as *adj.*] *a con artist.* ▷late 19th cent. (originally U.S.): abbreviation of CONFIDENCE, as in *confidence trick.*

con[2] ▸*n.* a disadvantage: *borrowers have to weigh up* ***the pros and cons of*** *each mortgage offer.* ▷late 16th cent.: from Latin *contra* 'against.'

con[3] ▸*n. informal* a convict. ▷late 19th cent.: abbreviation.

con[4] ▸ variant spelling of CONN.

con[5] ▸*v.* (**conned**, **con·ning**) [*trans.*] *archaic* study attentively or learn by heart (a piece of writing): *the girls conned their pages with a great show of industry.* ▷Middle English *cunne*, *conne*, *con*, variants of CAN[1].

con[6] ▸*n. informal* a convention, esp. one for science-fiction enthusiasts. ▷1970s: abbreviation.

con- ▸*prefix* variant spelling of COM- assimilated before *c, d, f, g, j, n, q, s, t, v*, and sometimes before vowels (as in *concord, condescend, confide*, etc.). ▷Latin variant of *com-*.

Co·na·kry /ˈkänəkrē/ the capital and chief port of Guinea, in the western part of the county, on the Atlantic coast; pop. 950,000.

con a·mo·re /ˌkän əˈmôrā/ ▸*adv. Music* (esp. as a direction) with tenderness. ▷Italian, 'with love.'

Co·nan Doyle /ˈkōnən ˈdoil/ see DOYLE.

co·na·tion /kōˈnāSHən/ ▸*n. Philosophy & Psychology* the mental faculty of purpose, desire, or will to perform an action; volition. ▷early 17th cent. (denoting an attempt or endeavor): from Latin *conatio(n-)*, from *conari* 'to try.'

con bri·o /kän ˈbrēō; kōn/ ▸*adv. Music* (esp. as a direction) with vigor. ▷Italian.

con·cat·e·nate /kənˈkatnˌāt/ ▸*v.* [*trans.*] *formal* or *technical* link (things) together in a chain or series: *some words may be concatenated, such that certain sounds are omitted.* ▷late 15th cent. (as an adjective): from late Latin *concatenat-* 'linked together,' from the verb *concatenare*, from *con-* 'together' + *catenare*, from *catena* 'chain.'

con·cat·e·na·tion /kənˌkatnˈāSHən/ ▸*n.* a series of interconnected things or events: *a singular concatenation of events unlikely to recur.* ■ the action of linking things together in a series. ■ the condition of being linked in such a way.

con·cave /känˈkāv; ˈkänˌkāv/ ▸*adj.* having an outline or surface that curves inward like the interior of a circle or sphere. Compare with CONVEX (sense 1). ▷late Middle English: from Latin *concavus*, from *con-* 'together' + *cavus* 'hollow.' **—con·cave·ly** *adv.*

con·cav·i·ty /känˈkavitē/ ▸*n.* (*pl.* **-ties**) the state or quality of being concave. ■ a concave surface or thing.

con·ca·vo-con·cave /känˈkāvō ˌkänˈkāv/ ▸*adj.* another term for BICONCAVE.

con·ca·vo-con·vex /känˈkāvō ˌkänˈveks/ ▸*adj.* (of a lens) concave on one side and convex on the other and thickest at the periphery.

con·ceal /kənˈsēl/ ▸*v.* [*trans.*] keep from sight; hide: *a line of sand dunes concealed the distant sea |* [as *adj.*] (**concealed**) *he pressed a concealed button.* ■ keep (something) secret; prevent from being known or noticed: *love that they had to* ***conceal from*** *others.* ▷Middle English: from Old French *conceler*, from Latin *concelare*, from *con-* 'completely' + *celare* 'hide.' **—con·ceal·a·ble** *adj.* **—con·ceal·ment** *n.*

con·ceal·er /kənˈsēlər/ ▸*n.* a flesh-toned cosmetic used to cover facial blemishes and dark circles under the eyes.

con·cede /kənˈsēd/ ▸*v.* **1** [*reporting verb*] admit that something is true or valid after first denying or resisting it: [with *clause*] *I had to concede that I'd overreacted |* [*trans.*] *that principle now seems to have been conceded.* ■ [*trans.*] admit (defeat) in a contest: *he conceded defeat.* ■ [*trans.*] admit defeat in (a contest): *ready to concede the gold medal.* **2** [*trans.*] surrender or yield (something that one possesses): *to concede all the territory he'd won.* ■ grant (a right, privilege, or demand): *their rights to redress of grievances were conceded once more.* ■ (in sports) fail to prevent the scoring of (a goal or point) by an opponent: *the coach conceded three safeties rather than kick into the wind.* ■ allow (a lead or advantage) to slip: *he took an early lead that he never conceded.* ■ [*intrans.*] make a concession: *Zoie conceded with a grin and went with Jay.* ▷late 15th cent.: from French *concéder* or Latin *concedere*, from *con-* 'completely' + *cedere* 'yield.' **—con·ced·er** *n.*

con·ceit /kənˈsēt/ ▸*n.* **1** excessive pride in oneself: *he was puffed up with conceit.* See notes at EGOTISM, PRIDE. **2** . a fanciful expression in writing or speech; an elaborate metaphor: *the idea of the wind's singing is a prime romantic conceit.* ■ an artistic effect or device: *the director's brilliant conceit was to film this tale in black and white.* ■ a fanciful notion: *he is alarmed by the widespread conceit that he spent most of the 1980s drunk.* ▷late Middle English (in the sense 'idea or notion,' also 'quaintly decorative article'): from CONCEIVE, on the pattern of pairs such as *deceive, deceit.*

con·ceit·ed /kənˈsētid/ ▸*adj.* excessively proud of oneself; vain. **—con·ceit·ed·ly** *adv.* **—con·ceit·ed·ness** *n.*

con·ceiv·a·ble /kənˈsēvəbəl/ ▸*adj.* capable of being imagined or grasped mentally: *a mass uprising was entirely conceivable | it was photographed from every conceivable angle.* **—con·ceiv·a·bil·i·ty** /kənˌsēvəˈbilitē/ *n.*

con·ceiv·a·bly /kənˈsēvəblē/ ▸*adv.* [*sentence adverb*] it is conceivable or imaginable that: *it may conceivably cause liver disease.*

con·ceive /kənˈsēv/ ▸*v.* [*trans.*] (often **be conceived**) **1** become pregnant with (a child): *she was conceived when her father was 49.* ■ [*intrans.*] (of a woman) become pregnant: *five months ago Wendy conceived.* **2** form or devise (a plan or idea) in the mind: *the dam project was originally conceived in 1977 |* [as *adj.*] (**conceived**) *a brilliantly conceived and executed robbery.* ■ form a mental representation of; imagine: *without society an individual cannot be* ***conceived as*** *having rights |* [*intrans.*] *we could not* ***conceive of*** *such things happening to us.* ■ become affected by (a feeling): *he conceived a passion for football.* ▷Middle English: from Old French

Pronunciation Key ə *ago*; ər *over*; ˈə *or* ˌə *up*; ˈər *or* ˌər *fur*; a *hat*; ā *rate*; ä *car*; CH *chew*; e *let*; ē *see*; e(ə)r *air*; i *fit*; ī *by*; i(ə)r *ear*; NG *sing*; ō *go*; ô *for*; oi *boy*; o͝o *good*; o͞o *goo*; ou *out*; SH *she*; TH *thin*; TH *then*; (h)w *why*; ZH *vision*

concevoir, from Latin *concipere*, from *com-* 'together' + *capere* 'take.'

con·cel·e·brate /kän'selə,brāt/ ▸*v.* [*trans.*] *Christian Church* officiate jointly at (a Mass): *to* ***concelebrate*** *a Mass* ***with*** *other priests.* ▷late 19th cent.: from Latin *concelebrat-* 'celebrated together,' from the verb *concelebrare*, from *con-* 'together' + *celebrare* (see CELEBRATE). —**con·cel·e·brant** /-brənt/ *n.* —**con·cel·e·bra·tion** /kän,selə'brāsHən/ *n.*

con·cen·ter /kən'sentər; kän-/ ▸*v.* [*trans.*] concentrate (something) in a small space or area. ■ [*intrans.*] come together or collect at a common center: *his thoughts concenter there monotonously.* ■ *archaic* bring or draw (two or more things) toward a common center. ▷late 16th cent.: from French *concentrer*, from Latin *con-* 'together' + *centrum* 'center.'

con·cen·trate /'känsən,trāt/ ▸*v.* **1** [*intrans.*] focus one's attention or mental effort on a particular object or activity: *she couldn't* ***concentrate on*** *the movie.* ■ (**concentrate on/upon**) do or deal with (one particular thing) above all others: *Luke wants to concentrate on his film career.* **2** [*trans.*] (often **be concentrated**) gather (people or things) together in numbers or in a mass to one point: *power was* ***concentrated*** *in the hands of the ruling Politburo.* ■ [*intrans.*] come together in this way: *troops were concentrating at the western front.* ■ increase the strength or proportion of (a substance or solution) by removing or reducing the water or any other diluting agent or by selective accumulation of atoms or molecules.
▸*n.* a substance made by removing water or other diluting agent; a concentrated form of something, esp. food: *apple juice concentrate.* ▷mid 17th cent. (in the sense 'bring toward a center'): Latinized form of CONCENTER, 'concenter' or from French *concentrer* 'to concentrate.' Sense 1 dates from the early 20th cent. —**con·cen·tra·tive** /-,trātiv/ *adj.* —**con·cen·tra·tor** /-,trātər/ *n.*

con·cen·trat·ed /'känsən,trātid/ ▸*adj.* **1** wholly directed to one thing; intense: *a concentrated campaign.* **2** gathered in one place: *concentrated accumulations of fossilized remains | the remains of Antony's defeated fleet concentrated 2 miles off the coast of Greece.* ■ (of a substance or solution) present in a high proportion relative to other substances; having had water or other diluting agent removed or reduced: *concentrated fruit juice.* —**con·cen·trat·ed·ly** *adv.*

con·cen·tra·tion /,känsən'trāsHən/ ▸*n.* **1** the action or power of focusing one's attention or mental effort: *frowning in concentration | the worker needs total concentration.* ■ (**concentration on/upon**) dealing with one particular thing above all others: *concentration on the needs of the young can mean that the elderly are forgotten.* **2** a close gathering of people or things: *the largest concentration of Canada geese on earth.* ■ the action of gathering together closely: *the concentration of power.* **3** the relative amount of a given substance contained within a solution or in a particular volume of space; the amount of solute per unit volume of solution: *the gas can collect in dangerous concentrations.* ■ the action of strengthening a solution by the removal of water or other diluting agent or by the selective accumulation of atoms or molecules.

con·cen·tra·tion camp ▸*n.* a place where large numbers of people, esp. political prisoners or members of persecuted minorities, are deliberately imprisoned in a relatively small area with inadequate facilities, sometimes to provide forced labor or to await mass execution. The term is most strongly associated with the several hundred camps established by the Nazis in Germany and occupied Europe in 1933–45, among the most infamous being Dachau, Belsen, and Auschwitz.

con·cen·tric /kən'sentrik; kän-/ ▸*adj.* of or denoting circles, arcs, or other shapes that share the same center, the larger often completely surrounding the smaller: *concentric circles indicate distances of 1 km, 2 km, and 3 km from the center.* ▷late Middle English: from Old French *concentrique* or medieval Latin *concentricus*, from *con-* 'together' + *centrum* 'center.' —**con·cen·tri·cal·ly** /-(ə)lē/ *adv.* —**con·cen·tric·i·ty** /,kän,sen'trisitē/ *n.*

concentric circles

Con·cep·ción /,kän,sepsē'ōn/ an industrial city in southern central Chile; pop. 294,000.

con·cept /'kän,sept/ ▸*n.* an abstract idea; a general notion: *structuralism is a difficult concept | the concept of justice.* See note at IDEA. ■ a plan or intention; a conception: *the center has kept firmly to its original concept.* ■ an idea or invention to help sell or publicize a commodity: *a new concept in corporate hospitality.* ■ *Philosophy* an idea or mental picture of a group or class of objects formed by combining all their aspects. ■ [as *adj.*] (of a car or other vehicle) produced as an experimental model to test the viability of new design features. ▷mid 16th cent. (in the sense 'thought, frame of mind, imagination'): from Latin *conceptum* 'something conceived,' from *concept-* 'conceived,' from *concipere* (see CONCEIVE).

con·cept al·bum ▸*n.* a rock album featuring a cycle of songs expressing a particular theme or idea.

con·cep·tion /kən'sepsHən/ ▸*n.* **1** the action of conceiving a child or of a child being conceived: *an unfertilized egg before conception | a rise in premarital conceptions.* ■ the forming or devising of a plan or idea: *the time between a product's conception and its launch.* **2** the way in which something is perceived or regarded: *our conception of how language relates to reality.* ■ a general notion; an abstract idea: *the conception of a balance of power.* See note at IDEA. ■ a plan or intention: *reconstructing Bach's original conceptions.* ■ understanding; ability to imagine: *he* ***had no conception of*** *politics.* ▷Middle English: via Old French from Latin *conceptio(n-)*, from the verb *concipere* (see CONCEIVE). —**con·cep·tion·al** /-sHənl/ *adj.*

con·cep·tu·al /kən'sepCHōōəl/ ▸*adj.* of, relating to, or based on mental concepts: *philosophy deals with conceptual difficulties.* ▷mid 17th cent.: from medieval Latin *conceptualis*, from Latin *concept-* 'conceived,' from the verb *concipere* (see CONCEPT).

con·cep·tu·al art (also **con·cept art**) ▸*n.* art in which the idea presented by the artist is considered more important than the finished product, if there is one.

con·cep·tu·al·ism /kən'sepCHōōə,lizəm/ ▸*n.* *Philosophy* the theory that universals can be said to exist, but only as concepts in the mind. —**con·cep·tu·al·ist** *n.*

con·cep·tu·al·ize /kən'sepCHōōə,līz/ ▸*v.* [*trans.*] form a concept or idea of (something): *we can more easily conceptualize speed in miles per hour.* —**con·cep·tu·al·i·za·tion** /kən,sepCHōōələ'zāsHən/ *n.* —**con·cep·tu·al·iz·er** *n.*

con·cep·tu·al·ly /kən'sepCHōōəlē/ ▸*adv.* in terms of a concept or abstract idea: *a conceptually simple task | conceptually, this is a complex process.*

con·cep·tus /kən'septəs/ ▸*n.* (*pl.* **-tus·es**) *technical* the embryo in the uterus, esp. during the early stages of pregnancy. ▷mid 18th cent.: from Latin, literally 'conception, embryo'.

con·cern /kən'sərn/ ▸*v.* [*trans.*] **1** relate to; be about: *the story concerns a friend of mine* (**be concerned with**) *this fable is concerned with forgiveness and redemption.* ■ be relevant or important to; affect or involve: *they should not pry into what does not concern them | many thanks to* ***all concerned.*** ■ (**be concerned with**) regard it as important or interesting to do something: *I was mainly concerned with making something that children could enjoy.* ■ (**be concerned in**) *formal* have a specific connection with or responsibility for: *the organs concerned in digestion and in blood-making.* ■ (**concern oneself with**) interest or involve oneself in: *we need not concern ourselves with the semantics of this language.* **2** worry (someone); make anxious: *the roof of the barn concerns me because eventually it will fall in | you must not* ***concern yourself*** *about me.*
▸*n.* **1** anxiety; worry: *such unsatisfactory work gives cause for concern.* ■ a cause of anxiety or worry: *the new techniques raise some safety concerns.* **2** a matter of interest or importance to someone: *oil reserves are the concern of the Energy Department | the survival of an endangered species is* ***of concern to*** *wildlife biologists.* ■ (**concerns**) affairs; issues: *public awareness of Aboriginal concerns.* **3** a business; a firm: *a small, debt-ridden concern.* **4** *informal, dated* a complicated or awkward object or structure. ▷late Middle English: from French *concerner* or late Latin *concernere* (in medieval Latin 'be relevant to'), from *con-* (expressing intensive force) + *cernere* 'sift, discern.'
▸*PHRASES* □ **as** (or **so**) **far as —— is concerned** as regards the interests or case of ——: *the measures are irrelevant as far as inflation is concerned.* □ **have no concern with** *formal* have nothing to do with: *drama seemed to have no concern with "truth" at all.* □ **to whom it may concern** a formula placed at the beginning of a letter or document when the identity of the reader or readers is unknown.

con·cerned /kən'sərnd/ ▸*adj.* worried, troubled, or anxious: *the villagers are* ***concerned about*** *burglaries.* —**con·cern·ed·ly** /-'sərnədlē/ *adv.*

con·cern·ing /kən'sərniNG/ ▸*prep.* on the subject of or in connection with; about: *dreadful stories concerning a horrible beast.*

con·cern·ment /kən'sərnmənt/ ▸*n.* *archaic* importance: *matters of great public concernment.* ■ a matter of interest or importance to someone; a concern: *a family or any absorbing concernment of that sort.*

con·cert ▸*n.* /'kän,sərt; 'känsərt/ **1** a musical performance given in public, typically by several performers or of several separate compositions: *symphony concerts |* [as *adj.*] *a concert pianist.* ■ [as *adj.*] of, relating to, or denoting the performance of music written for opera, ballet, or theater on its own without the accompanying dramatic action: *the concert version of the fourth interlude from the opera.* See also CONCERT PERFORMANCE. **2** *formal* agreement, accordance, or harmony: *critics' inability to describe with any precision and concert the characteristics of literature.*
▸*v.* /kən'sərt/ [*trans.*] *formal* arrange (something) by mutual agreement or coordination: *they started meeting regularly to concert their tactics.* ▷late 16th cent. (in the sense 'unite, cause to agree'): from French *concerter*, from Italian *concertare* 'harmonize.' The noun use, dating from the early 17th cent. (in the sense 'a combination of voices or sounds'), is from French *concert*, from Italian *concerto*, from *concertare*.
▸*PHRASE* □ **in concert** **1** acting jointly: *he made his decision* ***in concert with*** *his son and son-in-law.* **2** (of music or a performer) giving a public performance; live: *they saw Pink Floyd in concert.*

con·cer·tan·te /,käsər'täntē; ,känCHər-; -,tā/ ▸*adj.* **1** denoting a piece of music containing one or more solo parts, typically of less prominence or weight than in a concerto. See also SINFONIA CONCERTANTE. **2** *chiefly historical* denoting prominent instrumental parts present throughout a piece of music, esp. in baroque and early classical compositions. ▷Italian, 'harmonizing,' from *concertare* 'harmonize.'

con·cert band ▸*n.* a relatively large group of brass, woodwind, and percussion players that performs in a concert hall, as distinguished from a marching band.

con·cert·ed /kən'sərtəd/ ▸*adj.* **1** jointly arranged, planned, or carried out; coordinated: *determined to begin a concerted action against them.* ■ strenuously carried out; done with great effort: *it would take* ***a concerted effort*** *for a burglar to break into my home.* **2** (of music) arranged in several parts of equal importance: *concerted secular music for voices.*

con·cert·go·er /'känsərt,gōər/ ▸*n.* a person who attends a concert, esp. one who does so regularly.

con·cert grand ▸*n.* the largest size of grand piano, up to 12 feet (2.75 m) long, that produces enough sound to be used for concerts in large halls.

con·cer·ti·na /,känsər'tēnə/ ▸*n.* a small musical instrument, typically polygonal in form, played by stretching and squeezing between the hands, to work a central bellows that blows air over reeds, each note being sounded by a button. Compare with ACCORDION. ■ [as *adj.*] opening or closing in multiple folds: *concertina doors.*
▸*v.* (**-ti·nas, -ti·naed** /-'tēnəd/) [*trans.*] extend, compress, or collapse in folds like those of a concertina: [as *adj.*] (**concertinaed**) *big rolls of concertinaed wire | figurative a request that the negotiations be concertinaed into a week-long session.* ▷mid 19th cent.: from CONCERT + -INA.

concertina

con·cer·ti·no /,känCHər'tēnō/ ▸*n.* (*pl.* **-nos**) **1** a simple or short concerto. **2** a solo instrument or solo instruments playing with an orchestra. ▷late 18th cent.: Italian, diminutive of *concerto* (see CONCERTO).

con·cert·ize /'känsər,tīz/ ▸*v.* [*intrans.*] give a concert or concerts.

con·cert·mas·ter /'känsərt,mastər/ ▸*n.* (*fem.* **con·cert·mis·tress**) the leading first-violin player in some orchestras.

con·cer·to /kən'CHertō/ ▶*n.* (*pl.* **-tos** or **-ti** /-tē/) a musical composition for a solo instrument or instruments accompanied by an orchestra, esp. one conceived on a relatively large scale. ▷early 18th cent.: Italian, from *concertare* 'harmonize.'

con·cer·to gros·so /'grōsō; 'grôsō/ ▶*n.* (*pl.* **con·cer·ti gros·si** /'grōsē; 'grôsē/) a musical composition for a group of solo instruments accompanied by an orchestra. The term is used mainly of baroque works. ▷early 18th cent.: Italian, literally 'big concerto.'

con·cert o·ver·ture ▶*n.* a piece of music in the style of an overture but intended for independent performance.

con·cert per·for·mance ▶*n.* **1** a performance of a piece of music written for an opera, ballet, religious service, etc., at a concert without the accompanying dramatic action, dance, or liturgy. **2** a performance of a piece of music at a live concert.

con·cert pitch ▶*n.* *Music* a standard for the tuning of musical instruments, internationally agreed upon in 1960, in which the note A above middle C has a frequency of 440 Hz. ■ *figurative* a state of readiness, efficiency, and keenness: *slightly unnerved by the contretemps, I was not at concert pitch.*

con·ces·sion /kən'seSHən/ ▶*n.* **1** a thing that is granted, esp. in response to demands; a thing conceded: *the strikers returned to work having won some concessions.* ■ the action of conceding, granting, or yielding something. ■ (**a concession to**) a gesture, esp. a token one, made in recognition of a demand or prevailing standard: *her only concession to fashion was her ornate silver ring.* **2** a preferential allowance or rate given by an organization: *tax concessions.* **3** the right to use land or other property for a specified purpose, granted by a government, company, or other controlling body: *new logging concessions.* ■ a commercial operation within the premises of a larger concern, typically selling refreshments: *operates the concessions at the stadium* | [as *adj.*] *public restrooms and concession stands.* ■ *Canadian* a piece of land into which surveyed land is divided, itself further divided into lots. ▷late Middle English: from Latin *concessio(n-)*, from the verb *concedere* (see **CONCEDE**).

con·ces·sion·aire /kən,seSHə'ne(ə)r/ (also **con·ces·sion·er**) ▶*n.* the holder of a concession or grant, esp. for the use of land or commercial premises. ▷mid 19th cent.: from French *concessionnaire*, from Latin *concessio* (see **CONCESSION**).

con·ces·sion·al /kən'seSHənl/ ▶*adj.* [*attrib.*] (of a rate or allowance) constituting a concession: *concessional and commercial types of loans.*

con·ces·sion road (also **concession line**) ▶*n.* *Canadian* a rural road separating concessions.

con·ces·sive /kən'sesiv/ ▶*adj.* **1** characterized by, or tending to concession: *we must look for a more concessive approach.* **2** *Grammar* (of a preposition or conjunction) introducing a phrase or clause denoting a circumstance that might be expected to preclude the action of the main clause, but does not (e.g., *in spite of, although*). ■ (of a phrase or clause) introduced by a concessive preposition or conjunction. ▷early 18th cent. (sense 2): from late Latin *concessivus*, from *concess-* 'withdrawn, yielded' (see **CONCESSION**).

conch /käNGk; känCH; kôNGk/ ▶*n.* (*pl.* **conchs** or **conches** /käNGks; 'känCHiz; kôNGks/) **1** (also **conch shell**) a tropical marine mollusk with a spiral shell that may bear long projections and have a flared lip. • *Strombus* and other genera, family Strombidae, class Gastropoda. ■ a shell of this kind blown like a trumpet to produce a musical note, often depicted as played by Tritons and other mythological figures. **2** *Architecture* the roof of a semicircular apse, shaped like half a dome. **3** another term for **CONCHA**. ▷late Middle English: from Latin *concha* 'shellfish, shell,' from Greek *konkhē* 'mussel, cockle, or shell-like cavity.'

con·cha /'käNGkə/ ▶*n.* (*pl.* **-chae** /-kē; -,kī/) *Anatomy & Zoology* **1** a body part that resembles a spiral shell, in particular: ■ the depression in the external ear leading to its central opening. ■ (also **nasal concha**) any of several thin, scroll-like (turbinate) bones in the sides of the nasal cavity. **2** a round or oval hammered metal disk used as decoration on jewelry, belts, harnesses, etc. ▷late 16th cent.: from Latin (see **CONCH**).

con·chie /'känCHē/ ▶*n.* (*pl.* **-chies**) *Brit., informal* or *derogatory* a conscientious objector. ▷World War I: abbreviation.

con·chif·er·ous /käNG'kifərəs/ ▶*adj.* producing, bearing, or characterized by the presence of shells.

con·chi·o·lin /käNG'kīəlin/ ▶*n.* *Zoology* a tough, insoluble protein secreted by mollusks, forming the organic matrix of the shell within which calcium carbonate is deposited. ▷late 19th cent.: from Latin *concha* 'shell' + the diminutive suffix *-iola* + **-IN**[1].

conch·o belt /'känCHō/ ▶*n.* a belt decorated with conchas or representations of them.

con·choid /'käNG,koid/ ▶*n.* *Mathematics* a plane quartic curve consisting of two separate branches either side of and asymptotic to a central straight line (the asymptote), such that if a line is drawn from a fixed point (the pole) to intersect both branches, the part of the line falling between the two branches is of constant length and is exactly bisected by the asymptote. • Such curves are represented by the general equation $(x - a)^2(x^2 + y^2) = b^2x^2$, where a is the distance between the pole and the asymptote, and b is the constant length. The branch on the same side of the asymptote as the pole typically has a cusp or loop. ▷early 18th cent.: from **CONCH** + **-OID**.

con·choi·dal /käNG'koidl/ ▶*adj.* *chiefly Mineralogy* denoting a type of fracture in a solid (such as flint or quartz) that results in a smooth rounded surface resembling the shape of a scallop shell.

con·chol·o·gy /käNG'käləjē/ ▶*n.* the scientific study or collection of mollusk shells. Compare with **MALACOLOGY**. ▷late 18th cent.: from Greek *konkhē* 'shell' + **-LOGY**. —**con·cho·log·i·cal** /,käNGkə'läjikəl/ *adj.* —**con·chol·o·gist** /-jist/ *n.*

con·cierge /kôN'syerZH; ,känsē'erZH/ ▶*n.* **1** (esp. in France) a caretaker of an apartment complex or a small hotel, typically one living on the premises. **2** a hotel employee whose job is to assist guests by arranging tours, making theater and restaurant reservations, etc. ▷mid 16th cent. (denoting the warden of a house, castle, prison, or royal palace): French, probably based on Latin *conservus* 'fellow slave.'

con·cil·i·ar /kən'silēər/ ▶*adj.* of, relating to, or proceeding from a council, esp. an ecclesiastical one: *conciliar decrees.* ▷late 17th cent.: from medieval Latin *consiliarius* 'counselor,' from Latin *concilium* (see **COUNCIL**).

con·cil·i·ate /kən'silē,āt/ ▶*v.* [*trans.*] **1** stop (someone) from being angry or discontented; placate; pacify: *concessions were made to conciliate the peasantry.* See note at **PACIFY**. ■ [*intrans.*] act as a mediator: *he sought to conciliate in the dispute.* ■ *formal* reconcile; make compatible: *all complaints about charges will be conciliated if possible.* **2** *archaic* gain (esteem or goodwill).: *the arts which conciliate popularity.* ▷mid 16th cent. (sense 2): from Latin *conciliat-* 'combined, gained,' from the verb *conciliare*, from *concilium* (see **COUNCIL**). —**con·cil·i·a·tion** /kən,silē'āSHən/ *n.* —**con·cil·i·a·tive** /-'silēətiv; -ē,ātiv/ *adj.* —**con·cil·i·a·tor** /-,ātər/ *n.*

con·cil·i·a·to·ry /kən'silēə,tôrē/ ▶*adj.* intended or likely to placate or pacify: *a conciliatory approach.* —**con·cil·i·a·to·ri·ness** *n.*

con·cin·ni·ty /kən'sinitē/ ▶*n.* *rare* the skillful and harmonious arrangement or fitting together of the different parts of something. ■ studied elegance of literary or artistic style. ▷mid 16th cent.: from Latin *concinnitas*, from *concinnus* 'skillfully put together.'

con·cise /kən'sīs/ ▶*adj.* giving a lot of information clearly and in a few words; brief but comprehensive: *a concise account of the country's history.* See note at **TERSE**. ▷late 16th cent.: from French *concis* or Latin *concisus*, past participle of *concidere* 'cut up, cut down,' from *con-* 'completely' + *caedere* 'to cut.' —**con·cise·ly** *adv.* —**con·cise·ness** *n.* —**con·ci·sion** /-'siZHən/ *n.*

con·clave /'kän,klāv/ ▶*n.* a private meeting. ■ (in the Roman Catholic Church) the assembly of cardinals for the election of a pope. ■ the meeting place for such an assembly. ▷late Middle English (denoting a private room): via French from Latin *conclave* 'lockable room,' from *con-* 'with' + *clavis* 'key.'

con·clude /kən'klo͞od/ ▶*v.* **1** [*trans.*] bring (something) to an end: *they conclude their study with these words* | [*intrans.*] *we concluded by singing carols.* ■ [*intrans.*] come to an end: *the talk concluded with slides.* ■ formally and finally settle or arrange (a treaty or agreement): *an attempt to conclude a cease-fire.* **2** arrive at a judgment or opinion by reasoning: *the doctors* **concluded that** *Esther had suffered a stroke* | *what do you conclude from all this?* ■ say in conclusion: *"It's a wicked old world," she concluded.* ■ with *dated* decide to do something: *I concluded to go without his knowledge.* ▷Middle English (in the sense 'convince'): from Latin *concludere*, from *con-* 'completely' + *claudere* 'to shut.'

con·clu·sion /kən'klo͞oZHən/ ▶*n.* **1** the end or finish of an event or process: *the conclusion of World War Two.* ■ the summing-up of an argument or text. ■ the settling or arrangement of a treaty or agreement: *the conclusion of a free-trade accord.* **2** a judgment or decision reached by reasoning: *each research group came to a similar conclusion.* ■ *Logic* a proposition that is reached from given premises. ▷late Middle English: from Latin *conclusio(n-)*, from the verb *concludere* (see **CONCLUDE**).

▶*PHRASES* □ **in conclusion** lastly; to sum up: *in conclusion it is clear that the market is maturing.* □ **jump** (or **leap**) **to conclusions** make a hasty judgment before learning or considering all the facts.

con·clu·sive /kən'klo͞osiv; -ziv/ ▶*adj.* (of evidence or argument) serving to prove a case; decisive or convincing: *conclusive evidence* | *the findings were by no means conclusive.* ■ (of a victory) achieved easily or by a large margin. ▷late 16th cent. (in the sense 'summing up, concluding'): from late Latin *conclusivus*, from Latin *conclus-* 'closed up,' from the verb *concludere* (see **CONCLUSION**). —**con·clu·sive·ly** *adv.* —**con·clu·sive·ness** *n.*

con·coct /kən'käkt/ ▶*v.* [*trans.*] make (a dish or meal) by combining various ingredients: *they concoct relish from corn that is so naturally sweet no extra sugar is needed.* ■ create or devise (said esp. of a story or plan): *they concocted a preposterous but entertaining story.* ▷mid 16th cent.: from Latin *concoct-*, literally 'cooked together,' from *concoquere*. The original sense was 'refine or purify metals or minerals by heating,' later 'cook.' —**con·coct·er** *n.*

con·coc·tion /kən'käkSHən/ ▶*n.* a mixture of various ingredients or elements: *a concoction of gables, shingles, stained glass, and towers inspired by English medieval houses.* ■ an elaborate story, esp. a fabrication: *her story is an improbable concoction.*

con·com·i·tance /kən'kämitəns/ ▶*n.* (also **con·com·i·tan·cy** /-tənsē/) the fact of existing or occurring together with something else. ■ *Theology* the doctrine that the body and blood of Christ are each present in both the bread and the wine of the Eucharist. ▷mid 16th cent.: from medieval Latin *concomitantia*, from the verb *concomitari* 'accompany' (see **CONCOMITANT**).

con·com·i·tant /kən'kämitənt/ *formal* ▶*adj.* naturally accompanying or associated: *she loved travel, with all its concomitant worries* | **concomitant with** *his obsession with dirt was a desire for order.*

▶*n.* a phenomenon that naturally accompanies or follows something: *some of us look on pain and illness as concomitants of the stresses of living.* ▷early 17th cent.: from late Latin *concomitant-* 'accompanying,' from *concomitari*, from *con-* 'together with' + *comitari*, from Latin *comes* 'companion.' —**con·com·i·tant·ly** *adv.*

Con·cord[1] /'käNGkərd; -,kôrd/ **1** a city in north central California, northeast of Oakland; pop. 111,348. **2** a town in northeastern Massachusetts; pop. 17,080. Battles here and at Lexington in April 1775 marked the start of the American Revolution. **3** the capital of New Hampshire, in the southern part of the state, on the Merrimack River; pop. 40,687. **4** an industrial city in south central North Carolina, a textile center; pop. 55,977.

Con·cord[2] ▶*n.* a variety of dessert grape developed at Concord, Massachusetts.

con·cord /'käNG,kôrd; 'kän-/ ▶*n.* **1** *formal* agreement or harmony between people or groups: *a pact of peace and concord.* ■ a treaty. **2** *Grammar* agreement between words in gender, number, case, person, or any other grammatical category that affects the forms of the words. **3** *Music* a chord that is pleasing or satisfactory in itself. ▷Middle English: from Old French *concorde*, from Latin *concordia*, from *concors* 'of one mind,' from *con-* 'together' + *cor, cord-* 'heart.'

con·cord·ance /kən'kôrdns/ ▶*n.* **1** an alphabetical list of the words (esp. the important ones) present in a text, usually with citations of the passages concerned: *a concordance to the Bible.* **2** *formal* agreement: *the concordance between the teams' research results.* ■ *Medicine* the inheritance by two related individuals (esp. twins) of the same genetic characteristic, such as susceptibility to a disease.

▶*v.* [*trans.*] [often as *adj.*] (**concordanced**) make a concordance of: *the value of concordanced information.* ▷late Middle English: from Old French, from medieval Latin *concordantia*, from *concordant-* 'being of one mind' (see **CONCORDANT**).

con·cord·ant /kən'kôrdnt/ ▶*adj.* in agreement; consistent: *the answers were roughly concordant.* ■ *Geology* corresponding in direction with the planes of adjacent or underlying strata. ■ *Medicine* (of twins) inheriting the same genetic characteristic, such as susceptibility to a disease. ■ *Music* in harmony. ▷late 15th cent.: via Old French from Latin *concordant-* 'being of one mind,' from the verb *concordare* (see CONCORD). **—con·cord·ant·ly** *adv.*

con·cor·dat /kən'kôr,dat/ ▸*n.* an agreement or treaty, esp. one between the Vatican and a secular government relating to matters of mutual interest. ▷early 17th cent.: from French, or from Latin *concordatum* 'something agreed upon,' neuter past participle of *concordare* 'be of one mind' (see CONCORD).

Con·corde /'käNG,kôrd; 'kän-/ a supersonic airliner able to cruise at twice the speed of sound. Produced through Anglo-French cooperation, it made its maiden flight in 1969 and its last in 2003.

Con·cord grape ▸*n.* a cultivated variety of fox grape, used to make wine, juice, and jellies.

Con·cor·di·a /kän'kôrdēə/ a port city in northeastern Argentina, in a farming region of Entre Ríos province, on the Uruguay River and the border with Uruguay; pop. 139,000.

con·cours /kôN'ko͝or/ (also **con·cours d'é·lé·gance** /dālā'gäNs/) ▸*n.* (*pl.* same) an exhibition or contest, esp. a parade of vintage or classic motor vehicles in which prizes are awarded for those in the best original condition. ▷mid 20th cent.: French, literally 'contest (of elegance).'

con·course /'kän,kôrs; 'käNG-/ ▸*n.* **1** a large open area inside or in front of a public building, as in an airport or train station: *the domestic arrivals concourse.* **2** *formal* a crowd or assembly of people: *a vast **concourse of** learned men.* ■ the action of coming together or meeting: *the attracted concourse of the beauty and wealth of modern civilization.* ■ another term for CONCOURS. ▷late Middle English (sense 2): from Old French *concours,* from Latin *concursus,* from *concurs-* 'run together, met,' from the verb *concurrere* (see CONCUR). Sense 1 (originally U.S.) dates from the mid 19th cent.

con·cres·cence /kən'kresəns/ ▸*n. Biology* the coalescence or growing together of parts originally separate. ▷early 17th cent. (in the senses 'growth by assimilation' and 'a concretion'): from CON- 'together' + *-crescence,* on the pattern of words such as *excrescence.* The current sense dates from the late 19th cent. **—con·cres·cent** /-'kresənt/ *adj.*

con·crete ▸*adj.* /kän'krēt; 'kän,krēt; kən'krēt/ existing in a material or physical form; real or solid; not abstract: *concrete objects like stones | it exists as a physically concrete form.* ■ specific; definite: *I haven't got any concrete proof.* ■ (of a noun) denoting a material object as opposed to an abstract quality, state, or action.
▸*n.* /'kän,krēt; kän'krēt/ a heavy, rough building material made from a mixture of broken stone or gravel, sand, cement, and water, that can be spread or poured into molds and that forms a stonelike mass on hardening: *slabs of concrete* | [as *adj.*] *the concrete sidewalk.*
▸*v.* /'kän,krēt; kän'krēt/ [*trans.*] (often **be concreted**) **1** cover (an area) with concrete: *the precious English countryside may soon be **concreted over**.* ■ [*trans.*] fix in position with concrete: *the post is concreted into the ground.* **2** *archaic* form (something) into a mass; solidify: *the juices of the plants are concreted upon the surface.* ■ make real or concrete instead of abstract: *concreting God into actual form of man.* ▷late Middle English (in the sense 'formed by cohesion, solidified'): from French *concret* or Latin *concretus,* past participle of *concrescere* 'grow together.' Early use was also as a grammatical term designating a quality belonging to a substance (usually expressed by an adjective such as *white* in *white paper*) as opposed to the quality itself (expressed by an abstract noun such as *whiteness*); later *concrete* came to be used to refer to nouns embodying attributes (e.g., *fool, hero*), as opposed to the attributes themselves (e.g., *foolishness, heroism*), and this is the basis of the modern use as the opposite of 'abstract.' The noun sense 'building material' dates from the mid 19th cent. **—con·crete·ly** *adv.* **—con·crete·ness** *n.*
▸*PHRASE* □ **be set in concrete** (of a policy or idea) be fixed and unalterable: *I do not regard the Constitution as set in concrete.*

con·crete jun·gle ▸*n.* a city or area of a city that has a high density of large, unattractive, modern buildings and that is perceived as an unpleasant living environment.

con·crete mix·er ▸*n.* a cement mixer.

con·crete mu·sic ▸*n.* another term for MUSIQUE CONCRÈTE.

con·crete po·et·ry ▸*n.* poetry in which the meaning or effect is conveyed partly or wholly by visual means, using patterns of words or letters and other typographical devices.

con·crete u·ni·ver·sal ▸*n.* (in idealist philosophy) an abstraction that is manifest in a developing or organized set of instances, so having the qualities of both the universal and the particular.

con·cre·tion /kən'krēSHən; kän-/ ▸*n.* a hard solid mass formed by the local accumulation of matter, esp. within the body or within a mass of sediment: *a mass of small concretions, each built up layer upon layer around some small nucleus.* ■ the formation of such a mass. ▷mid 16th cent.: from Latin *concretio(n-),* from *concrescere* 'grow together.' **—con·cre·tion·ar·y** /-SHə,nerē/ *adj.*

con·cret·ism /kän'krē,tizəm; 'känkrē-/ ▸*n.* the theory or practice of concrete poetry, in which the visual arrangement of words in patterns or forms on the page takes precedence over the semantic or phonetic elements involved.

con·cre·tize /'känkrə,tīz; kän'krēt,īz/ ▸*v.* [*trans.*] make (an idea or concept) real; give specific or definite form to: *the theme park is an attempt to concretize our fantasies.* **—con·cret·i·za·tion** /,kän,krētə'zāSHən; ,käNGkrətə-/ *n.*

con·cu·bi·nage /kən'kyo͞obənij; kän-/ ▸*n. chiefly historical* the practice of keeping a concubine. ■ the state of being a concubine. ▷late Middle English: from French, from Old French *concubine* (see CONCUBINE).

con·cu·bine /'käNGkyo͞o,bīn/ ▸*n. chiefly historical* (in polygamous societies) a woman who lives with a man but has lower status than his wife or wives. ■ *archaic* a mistress. ▷Middle English: from Old French, from Latin *concubina,* from *con-* 'with' + *cubare* 'to lie.' **—con·cu·bi·nar·y** /kən'kyo͞obə,nerē; kän-/ *adj.*

con·cu·pis·cence /kän'kyo͞opisəns; kən-/ ▸*n. formal* strong sexual desire; lust. ▷Middle English: via Old French from late Latin *concupiscentia,* from Latin *concupiscent-* 'beginning to desire,' from the verb *concupiscere,* from *con-* (expressing intensive force) + *cupere* 'to desire.'

con·cu·pis·cent /kän'kyo͞opisənt; kən-/ ▸*adj. formal* filled with sexual desire; lustful: *concupiscent dreams.*

con·cur /kən'kər/ ▸*v.* (**-curred, -cur·ring**) [*intrans.*] **1** be of the same opinion; agree: *the authors **concurred with** the majority | they **concurred in** the creation of the disciplinary procedures | "That's right," the chairman concurred.* ■ (**concur with**) agree with (a decision, opinion, or finding): *we strongly concur with this recommendation.* **2** happen or occur at the same time; coincide: *in tests, cytogenetic determination has been found to **concur with** enzymatic determination.* ▷late Middle English (also in the senses 'collide' and 'act in combination'): from Latin *concurrere* 'run together, assemble in crowds,' from *con-* 'together with' + *currere* 'to run.' **—con·cur·rence** /-'kərəns/ *n.* **—con·cur·ren·cy** /-'kərənsē/ *n.*

con·cur·rent /kən'kərənt; -'kæ-rənt/ ▸*adj.* existing, happening, or done at the same time: *there are three concurrent art fairs around the city.* ■ (of two or more prison sentences) to be served at the same time. ■ *Mathematics* (of three or more lines) meeting at or tending toward one point. ▷late Middle English: from Latin *concurrent-* 'running together, meeting,' from the verb *concurrere* (see CONCUR). **—con·cur·rent·ly** *adv.*

con·cur·rent res·o·lu·tion ▸*n.* a resolution adopted by both houses of a legislative assembly that does not require the signature of the chief executive and that does not have the force of law.

con·cuss /kən'kəs/ ▸*v.* [*trans.*] [usu. as *adj.*] (**concussed**) hit the head of (a person or animal), causing temporary unconsciousness or confusion: *she was shaken, slightly concussed, and in no state to carry on.* ▷late 16th cent. (in the sense 'shake violently'): from Latin *concuss-* 'dashed together, violently shaken,' from the verb *concutere,* from *con-* 'together' + *quatere* 'shake.' **—con·cus·sive** /-'kəsiv/ *adj.*

con·cus·sion /kən'kəSHən/ ▸*n.* **1** temporary unconsciousness caused by a blow to the head. The term is also used loosely of the aftereffects such as confusion or temporary incapacity. **2** a violent shock as from a heavy blow: *the ground shuddered with the concussion of the blast.* ▷late Middle English: from Latin *concussio(n-),* from the verb *concutere* 'dash together, shake' (see CONCUSS).

con·demn /kən'dem/ ▸*v.* [*trans.*] **1** express complete disapproval of, typically in public; censure: *fair-minded people declined to condemn her on mere suspicion.* **2** find (someone) guilty of a criminal act or wrong. ■ sentence (someone) to a particular punishment, esp. death: *the rebels had been **condemned to** death* | [as *adj.*] (**condemned**) *the condemned men.* ■ (usu. **be condemned**) officially declare (something, esp. a building) to be unfit for use: *the pool has been condemned as a health hazard.* ■ prove or show the guilt of: *she could see in his eyes that her stumble had condemned her.* ■ (of circumstances) force (someone) to endure something unpleasant or undesirable: *the physical ailments that **condemned** him **to** a lonely childhood.* ▷Middle English (sense 2): from Old French *condemner,* from Latin *condemnare,* from *con-* (expressing intensive force) + *damnare* 'inflict loss on' (see DAMN). **—con·dem·na·ble** /-'dem(n)əbəl/ *adj.* **—con·dem·na·tion** /,kändem'nāSHən; -dəm-/ *n.* **—con·dem·na·to·ry** /-'demnə,tôrē/ *adj.*

con·den·sate /'kändən,sāt; 'kän,den-; kən'den-/ ▸*n.* liquid formed by condensation. ■ *Chemistry* a compound produced by a condensation reaction.

con·den·sa·tion /,kän,den'sāSHən; -dən-/ ▸*n.* **1** water that collects as droplets on a cold surface when humid air is in contact with it. **2** the process of becoming more dense, in particular: ■ the conversion of a vapor or gas to a liquid. ■ (also **condensation reaction**) *Chemistry* a reaction in which two molecules combine to form a larger molecule, producing a small molecule such as H_2O as a byproduct. ■ *Psychology* the fusion of two or more images, ideas, or symbolic meanings into a single composite or new image, as a primary process in unconscious thought exemplified in dreams. **3** a concise version of something, esp. a text: *a readable condensation of the recent literature.* ▷early 17th cent.: from late Latin *condensatio(n-),* from *condensare* 'press close together' (see CONDENSE).

con·dense /kən'dens/ ▸*v.* **1** [*trans.*] make (something) denser or more concentrated: *the limestones of the Jurassic age are condensed into a mere 11 feet* | [as *adj.*] (**condensed**) *check that your printer can cope with wide text or condensed characters.* ■ [usu. as *adj.*] (**condensed**) thicken (a liquid) by reducing the water content, typically by heating: *condensed soup.* ■ express (a piece of writing or speech) in fewer words; make concise: *he **condensed** the three plays **into** a three-hour drama.* ■ (in word processing) (of character spacing) reduced. **2** [*intrans.*] be changed from a gas or vapor to a liquid: *the moisture vapor in the air **condenses into** droplets of water.* ■ [*trans.*] cause (a gas or vapor) to be changed to a liquid: *the cold air was condensing his breath.* ▷late Middle English: from Old French *condenser* or Latin *condensare,* from *condensus* 'very thick,' from *con-* 'completely' + *densus* 'dense.' **—con·den·sa·ble** *adj.*

con·densed milk ▸*n.* canned milk that has been thickened by evaporation and sweetened.

con·densed tan·nin ▸*n.* any of various tannins with antioxidant properties occuring naturally in plants, comprising polymers of flavonoids linked by a carbon-to-carbon bond.

con·dens·er /kən'densər/ ▸*n.* a person or thing that condenses something, in particular: ■ an apparatus or container for condensing vapor. ■ a lens or system of lenses for collecting and directing light. ■ another term for CAPACITOR.

con·de·scend /,kändə'send/ ▸*v.* [*intrans.*] show feelings of superiority; patronize: *take care not to **condescend to** your reader.* ■ do something in a haughty way, as though it is below one's dignity or level of importance: *we'll be waiting for twenty minutes before she condescends to appear.* ▷Middle English (in the sense 'give way, defer'): from Old French *condescendre,* from ecclesiastical Latin *condescendere,* from *con-* 'together' + *descendere* 'descend.' **—con·de·scend·ence** /-'sendəns/ *n.* (*rare*). **—con·de·scen·sion** /-'senCHən/ *n.*

con·de·scend·ing /,kändə'sendiNG/ ▸*adj.* acting in a way that betrays a feeling of patronizing superiority: *she thought the teachers were arrogant and condescending.* ■ (of an action) demonstrating such an attitude: *a condescending smile.* **—con·de·scend·ing·ly** *adv.*

con·dign /kən'dīn/ ▸*adj. formal* (of punishment or retribution) appropriate to the crime or wrongdoing; fitting and deserved. ▷late Middle English (in the general sense 'worthy, appropriate'): from Old French *condigne,* from Latin *condignus,* from *con-* 'altogether' + *dignus* 'worthy.' **—con·dign·ly** *adv.*

con·di·ment /'kändəmənt/ ▸*n.* a substance such as salt or ketchup that is used to add flavor to food. ▷late Middle English: from Latin *condimentum,* from *condire* 'to pickle.'

con·di·tion /kən'diSHən/ ▸*n.* **1** the state of something, esp. with regard to its appearance, quality, or working order: *the wiring is in good condition* | [in *sing.*] *the bridge is in an extremely dangerous condition.* ■ a person's or animal's state of health or physical fitness: *he is in fairly good condition considering what he has been through* | [in *sing.*] *she was in a serious condition.* ■ an illness or other medical problem: *a heart condition.* ■ [in *sing.*] a particular state of existence: *a condition of misery.* ■ *archaic* social position or rank: *those of humbler condition.* **2** (**conditions**) the circumstances affecting the way in which people live or work, esp. with regard to their safety or well-being: *harsh working and living conditions.* ■ the factors or prevailing situation influencing the performance or the outcome of a process: *present market conditions.* ■ the prevailing state of the weather, ground, sea, or atmosphere at a particular time, esp. as it affects a sporting event: *the appalling conditions determined the style of play.* **3** a state of affairs that must exist or be brought about before something else is possible or permitted: *for a member to borrow money, three conditions have to be met* | *all personnel should comply with this policy as* **a condition of** *employment* | *I'll accept your offer* **on one condition.**

▸*v.* [*trans.*] **1** (often **be conditioned**) have a significant influence on or determine (the manner or outcome of something): *national choices are conditioned by the international political economy.* ■ train or accustom (someone or something) to behave in a certain way or to accept certain circumstances: *we have all been conditioned to the conventional format of TV* | *the child is conditioned to dislike food* | [as *n.*] (**conditioning**) *the program examines aspects of social conditioning.* **2** bring (something) into the desired state for use: *a product for conditioning leather.* ■ [often as *adj.*] (**conditioned**) make (a person or animal) fit and healthy: *he was six feet two of perfectly conditioned muscle and bone.* ■ apply something to (the skin or hair) to give it a healthy or attractive look or feel: *I condition my hair regularly.* ■ [often as *adj.*] (**conditioned**) bring (beer or stout) to maturation after fermentation while the yeast is still present: *cask-conditioned real ales.* ■ [*intrans.*] (of a beer or stout) undergo such a process: *brews that are allowed to condition in the bottle.* **3** set prior requirements on (something) before it can occur or be done: *Congressmen have sought to limit and condition military and economic aid.* ▷Middle English: from Old French *condicion* (noun), *condicionner* (verb), from Latin *condicio(n-)* 'agreement,' from *condicere* 'agree upon,' from *con-* 'with' + *dicere* 'say.'

▸*PHRASES* □ **in** (or **out of**) **condition** in a fit (or unfit) physical state. □ **in no condition to do something** certainly not fit or well enough to do something: *you're in no condition to tackle the stairs.* □ **on condition that** with the stipulation that: *he proposed deep cuts in offensive forces, on condition that an agreement be reached.*

con·di·tion·al /kən'disHənl/ ▸*adj.* **1** subject to one or more conditions or requirements being met; made or granted on certain terms: *Western aid was only granted conditional on further reform* | *the consortium has made a conditional offer.* **2** *Grammar* (of a clause, phrase, conjunction, or verb form) expressing a condition.

▸*n.* **1** *Grammar & Philosophy* a conditional clause or conjunction. ■ a statement or sentence containing a conditional clause. **2** *Grammar* the conditional mood of a verb, for example *should die* in *if I should die.* ▷late Middle English: from Old French *condicionel* or late Latin *condicionalis*, from *condicio(n-)* 'agreement' (see CONDITION). **—con·di·tion·al·i·ty** /kən,disHə'nalitē/ *n.* **—con·di·tion·al·ly** *adv.*

con·di·tion·al prob·a·bil·i·ty ▸*n.* *Statistics* the probability of an event (*A*), given that another (*B*) has already occurred.

con·di·tion·al sale ▸*n.* the sale of goods according to a contract containing conditions, typically that ownership does not pass to the buyer until after a set time, usually after payment of the last installment of the purchase price, although the buyer has possession and is committed to acquiring ownership.

con·di·tioned re·sponse (also **conditioned reflex**) ▸*n.* *Psychology* an automatic response established by training to an ordinarily neutral stimulus. See also CLASSICAL CONDITIONING.

con·di·tion·er /kən'disH(ə)nər/ ▸*n.* a substance or appliance used to improve or maintain something's condition: *add a water conditioner to neutralize chlorine.* ■ a liquid applied to the hair after shampooing to improve its condition: *conditioner will protect your hair from damage.*

con·do /'kändō/ ▸*n.* (*pl.* **-dos**) *informal* short for CONDOMINIUM (sense 1): *a high-rise condo.*

con·dole /kən'dōl/ ▸*v.* [*intrans.*] (**condole with**) express sympathy for (someone); grieve with: *the priest came to condole with Madeleine.* ▷late 16th cent.: from Christian Latin *condolere*, from *con-* 'with' + *dolere* 'grieve, suffer.'

con·do·lence /kən'dōləns/ ▸*n.* (usu. **condolences**) an expression of sympathy, esp. on the occasion of a death: *we offer our sincere condolences to his widow* | *letters of condolence.* ▷early 17th cent.: from CONDOLE, influenced by French *condoléance.*

con·dom /'kändəm; 'kən-/ ▸*n.* a thin rubber sheath worn on a man's penis during sexual intercourse as a contraceptive or as protection against infection. ▷early 18th cent.: of unknown origin; often said to be named after a physician who invented it, but no such person has been traced.

con·do·min·i·um /,kändə'minēəm/ ▸*n.* (*pl.* **-ums**) **1** a building or complex of buildings containing a number of individually owned apartments or houses. ■ each of the individual apartments or houses in such a building or complex. ■ the system of ownership by which these operate, in which owners have full title to the individual apartment or house and an undivided interest in the shared parts of the property. **2** the joint control of a country's or territory's affairs by other countries. ■ a state so governed. ▷early 18th cent.: modern Latin, from *con-* 'together with' + *dominium* 'right of ownership' (see DOMINION). Sense 1 dates from the 1960s.

con·done /kən'dōn/ ▸*v.* [*trans.*] accept and allow (behavior that is considered morally wrong or offensive) to continue: *the college cannot condone any behavior that involves illicit drugs.* ■ approve or sanction (something), esp. with reluctance: *the practice is not officially condoned by any airline.* ▷mid 19th cent.: from Latin *condonare* 'refrain from punishing,' from *con-* 'altogether' + *donare* 'give.' **—con·don·a·ble** *adj.* **—con·do·na·tion** /-'nāsHən; -dō-/ *n.* **—con·don·er** *n.*

con·dor /'kän,dôr; -dər/ ▸*n.* a large New World vulture with a bare head and mainly black plumage, living in mountainous country and spending much time soaring. • Two species in the family Cathartidae: the **Andean condor** (*Vultur gryphus*) of South America, and the **California condor** (*Gymnogyps californianus*), which is close to extinction in the wild. ▷early 17th cent.: from Spanish *cóndor*, from Quechua *kuntur.*

California condor

con·dot·ti·e·re /,kändätē'erē; ,kändə'tyerē/ ▸*n.* (*pl.* **-ti·e·ri** *pronunc.* same) *historical* a leader or a member of a troop of mercenaries, esp. in Italy. ▷Italian, from *condotto* 'troop under contract,' from *condotta* 'a contract,' from *condurre* 'conduct,' from Latin *conducere* (see CONDUCT).

con·duce /kən'd(y)o͞os/ ▸*v.* [*intrans.*] (**conduce to**) *formal* help to bring about (a particular situation or outcome): *every possible care was taken that could conduce to their health and comfort.* ▷late Middle English (in the sense 'lead or bring'): from Latin *conducere* 'bring together' (see CONDUCT).

con·du·cive /kən'd(y)o͞osiv/ ▸*adj.* making a certain situation or outcome likely or possible: *the harsh lights and cameras were hardly* **conducive to** *a relaxed atmosphere.* ▷mid 17th cent.: from CONDUCE, on the pattern of words such as *conductive.*

con·duct ▸*n.* /'kän,dəkt/ **1** the manner in which a person behaves, esp. on a particular occasion or in a particular context: *the conduct of the police during the riot* | *members are bound by a* **code of conduct.** **2** the action or manner of managing an activity or organization: *his conduct of the campaign.* ■ *archaic* the action of leading; guidance: *traveling through the world under the conduct of chance.*

▸*v.* /kən'dəkt/ [*trans.*] **1** organize and carry out: *in the second trial he conducted his own defense* | *surveys conducted among students.* ■ direct the performance of (a piece of music or a musical ensemble): *my first attempt to conduct a great work* | [*intrans.*] *Toscanini is coming to conduct.* ■ lead or guide (someone) to or around a particular place: *he conducted us through his personal gallery of the Civil War.* ■ *Physics* transmit (a form of energy such as heat or electricity) by conduction: *heat is conducted to the surface.* **2** (**conduct oneself**) behave in a specified way: *he conducted himself with the utmost propriety.* ▷Middle English: from Old French, from Latin *conduct-* 'brought together,' from the verb *conducere*. The term originally denoted some provision for safe passage, such as an escort or pass, surviving in SAFE CONDUCT; later the verb sense 'lead, guide' arose, hence 'manage' and 'management' (late Middle English), later 'management of oneself, behavior' (mid 16th cent.). The original form of the word was *conduit*, which was preserved only in the sense 'channel' (see CONDUIT); in all other uses the spelling was influenced by Latin. **—con·duct·i·ble** /kən'dəktəbəl/ *adj.* **—con·duct·i·bil·i·ty** /kən-,dəktə'bilitē/ *n.*

con·duct·ance /kən'dəktəns/ ▸*n.* the degree to which an object conducts electricity, calculated as the ratio of the current that flows to the potential difference present. This is the reciprocal of the resistance, and is measured in siemens or mhos. (Symbol: **G**)

con·duct dis·or·der ▸*n.* a range of antisocial types of behavior displayed in childhood or adolescence.

con·duc·tion /kən'dəksHən/ ▸*n.* the process by which heat or electricity is directly transmitted through a substance when there is a difference of temperature or of electrical potential between adjoining regions, without movement of the material. ■ the process by which sound waves travel through a medium. ■ the transmission of impulses along nerves. ■ the conveying of fluid through a pipe or other channel. ▷mid 16th cent. (in the senses 'provision for safe passage' and 'leadership'): from Latin *conductio(n-)*, from the verb *conducere* (see CONDUCT).

con·duc·tion band ▸*n.* *Physics* a delocalized band of energy partly filled with electrons in a crystalline solid. These electrons have great mobility and are responsible for electrical conductivity.

con·duc·tive /kən'dəktiv/ ▸*adj.* having the property of conducting something (esp. heat or electricity): *to induce currents in conductive coils.* ■ of or relating to conduction. **—con·duc·tive·ly** *adv.*

con·duc·tiv·i·ty /,kän,dək'tivitē; kən-/ ▸*n.* (*pl.* **-ties**) (also **electrical conductivity**) the degree to which a specified material conducts electricity, calculated as the ratio of the current density in the material to the electric field that causes the flow of current. It is the reciprocal of the resistivity. ■ (also **thermal conductivity**) the rate at which heat passes through a specified material, expressed as the amount of heat that flows per unit time through a unit area with a temperature gradient of one degree per unit distance.

con·duc·tor /kən'dəktər/ ▸*n.* **1** a person who directs the performance of an orchestra or choir: *he was appointed principal conductor of the Berlin Philharmonic Orchestra.* **2** a person in charge of a train, streetcar, or other public conveyance, who collects fares and sells tickets. **3** *Physics* a material or device that conducts or transmits heat, electricity, or sound, esp. when regarded in terms of its capacity to do this: *graphite is a reasonably good conductor of electricity.* ■ another term for LIGHTNING ROD. ▷late Middle English (denoting a military leader): via Old French from Latin *conductor*, from *conducere* 'bring together' (see CONDUCT). **—con·duc·to·ri·al** /,kän,dək'tôrēəl; kən-/ *adj.* **—con·duc·tor·ship** /-,sHip/ *n.* (in sense 1).

con·duc·tress /kən'dəktrəs/ ▸*n.* a female conductor, esp. in a bus or other passenger vehicle.

con·duc·tus /kən'dəktəs/ ▸*n.* (*pl.* **-ti** /-,tī; -,tē/) a musical setting of a metrical Latin text, of the 12th or 13th century. ▷from medieval Latin, from Latin *conducere* 'bring together' (see CONDUCT).

con·duit /'kän,d(y)o͞oət; 'känd(w)ət/ ▸*n.* a channel for conveying water or other fluid: *a conduit for conveying water to the power plant* | *figurative the office acts as a conduit for ideas to flow throughout the organization.* ■ a tube or trough for protecting electric wiring: *the gas pipe should not be close to any electrical conduit.* ▷Middle English: from Old French, from medieval Latin *conductus*, from Latin *conducere* 'bring together' (see CONDUCT).

con·dy·larth /'kändə,lärTH/ ▸*n.* a fossil herbivorous mammal of the early Tertiary period, ancestral to the ungulates. • Order Condylarthra: several families. ▷late 19th cent.: from modern Latin *Condylarthra* (plural), from Greek *kondulus* 'knuckle' + *arthron* 'joint.'

con·dyle /'kän,dīl/ ▸*n.* *Anatomy* a rounded protuberance at the end of some bones, forming an articulation with another bone. ▷mid 17th cent.: from

French, from Latin *condylus*, from Greek *kondulos* 'knuckle.' **—con·dy·lar** /ˈkändələr/ *adj.* **—con·dy·loid** /ˈkändəˌloid/ *adj.*

con·dy·lo·ma /ˌkändəˈlōmə/ ▸*n.* (*pl.* **-mas** or **-ma·ta** /-mətə/) *Medicine* a raised growth on the skin resembling a wart, typically in the genital region, caused by viral infection or syphilis and transmissible by contact. ▷late Middle English: via Latin from Greek *kondulōma* 'callous lump,' from *kondulos* 'knuckle.' **—con·dy·lom·a·tous** /-mətəs/ *adj.*

cone /kōn/ ▸*n.* **1** a solid or hollow object that tapers from a circular or roughly circular base to a point. ■ *Mathematics* a surface or solid figure generated by the straight lines that pass from a circle or other closed curve to a single point (the vertex) not in the same plane as the curve. A cone with the vertex perpendicularly over the center of a circular base is a **right circular cone**. ■ (also **traffic cone**) a plastic cone-shaped object that is used to separate off or close sections of a road. ■ an edible wafer container shaped like a cone in which ice cream is served. ■ a conical mountain or peak, esp. one of volcanic origin. ■ (also **pyrometric cone**) a ceramic pyramid that melts at a known temperature and is used to indicate the temperature of a kiln. ■ short for **CONE SHELL**. **2** the dry fruit of a conifer, typically tapering to a rounded end and formed of a tight array of overlapping scales on a central axis that separate to release the seeds. ■ a flower resembling a pine cone, esp. that of the hop plant. **3** *Anatomy* a light-sensitive cell of one of the two types present in the retina of the eye, responding mainly to bright light and responsible for sharpness of vision and color perception. Compare with **ROD** (sense 5). ▷late Middle English (denoting an apex or vertex): from French *cône*, via Latin from Greek *kōnos*.

coned /kōnd/ ▸*adj.* conical. ■ having cones: [in *combination*] *the big-coned southern California pine.*

cone·flow·er /ˈkōnˌflou(-ə)r/ ▸*n.* a North American plant of the daisy family that has flowers with conelike disks that appear to consist of soft spines. • *Rudbeckia*, *Echinacea*, and other genera, family Compositae: numerous species, including the yellow-flowered **sweet coneflower** (*R. subtomentosa*), the **purple coneflower** (*E. purpurea*) with swept-back reddish-purple petals, and the tall **green-headed coneflower** (*R. laciniata*) with yellow petals and greenish disks.

purple coneflower

cone of si·lence ▸*n.* **1** an imaginary device that prevents eavesdropping on a private conversation. ■ an electronic device or isolated room intended for the same purpose. **2** a directive that prohibits oral communication about a specified subject. ■ an agreement or conspiracy to maintain secrecy about a subject. ▷1960s: originally a fantasy prop in the television series *Get Smart*.

cone shell ▸*n.* shell a predatory mollusk of warm seas, with a conical shell that typically displays intricate patterns. It captures prey by injecting venom, which can be lethal to humans, and the shells are popular with collectors. • Genus *Conus*, family Conidae, class Gastropoda: numerous species.

Con·es·to·ga wag·on /ˌkänəˈstōgə/ ▸*n.* *historical* a large covered wagon used for long-distance travel, typically carrying pioneers in the westward migration. ▷early 18th cent.: named after *Conestoga*, a town in Pennsylvania.

con·ex ▸*n.* a large, steel-reinforced reusable container for shipping military cargo or, when modified, for use as temporary accommodation: *they told us we'd be staying in luxury air-conditioned conexes.* ▷acronym from *container express*.

co·ney /ˈkōnē/ (also **co·ny**) ▸*n.* (*pl.* **-neys**) **1** *Brit.* & *Heraldry* a pika. ■ a rabbit. ■ rabbit fur. ■ (in biblical use) a hyrax. **2** a small grouper (fish) found on the coasts of the tropical western Atlantic, with variable coloration. • *Epinephelus fulvus*, family Serranidae. ▷Middle English: from Old French *conin*, from Latin *cuniculus*.

Co·ney Is·land1 /ˈkōnē/ a resort and amusement park in the Brooklyn borough of New York City, on the southern shore of Long Island.

Co·ney Is·land2 ▸*n. informal* a hot dog. ▷named after **CONEY ISLAND**, New York.

con·fab *informal* ▸*n.* /ˈkänˌfab; kənˈfab/ an informal private conversation or discussion: *they wandered off to the woods for a private confab.* ■ a meeting or conference of members of a particular group: *this year's annual American Booksellers Association confab.*

▸*v.* /kənˈfab; ˈkänˌfab/ (**-fabbed**, **-fab·bing**) [*intrans.*] engage in informal private Fconversation: *Peter was confabbing with a curly-haired guy.* ▷early 18th cent.: abbreviation of *confabulation* (see **CONFABULATE**).

con·fab·u·late /kənˈfabyəˌlāt/ ▸*v.* [*intrans.*] **1** *formal* engage in conversation; talk: *she could be heard on the telephone confabulating with someone.* **2** *Psychiatry* fabricate imaginary experiences as compensation for loss of memory. ▷early 17th cent.: from Latin *confabulat-* 'chatted together,' from the verb *confabulari*, from *con-* 'together' + *fabulari* (from *fabula* 'fable'). **—con·fab·u·la·tion** /-ˌfabyəˈlāshən/ *n.* **—con·fab·u·la·to·ry** /-ləˌtôrē/ *adj.*

con·fect /kənˈfekt/ ▸*v.* [*trans.*] *poetic/literary* make (something) by putting together various elements: *together they had confected a valiseful of show tunes.* ▷late Middle English: from Latin *confect-* 'put together,' from the verb *conficere*, from *con-* 'together' + *facere* 'make.'

con·fec·tion /kənˈfekshən/ ▸*n.* **1** a dish or delicacy made with sweet ingredients: *a whipped chocolate and cream confection.* ■ an elaborately constructed thing, esp. a frivolous one: *the city is a classical confection of shimmering gold.* ■ a fashionable or elaborate article of women's dress: *she was wearing some white confection with an enormous satin bow.* **2** the action of mixing or compounding something. ▷Middle English (in the general sense 'something made by mixing,' esp. a medicinal preparation): via Old French from Latin *confectio(n-)*, from *conficere* 'put together' (see **CONFECT**). **—con·fec·tion·ar·y** /-ˌnerē/ *adj.*

con·fec·tion·er /kənˈfekshənər/ ▸*n.* a person whose occupation is making or selling candy and other sweets.

con·fec·tion·ers' sug·ar (also **con·fec·tion·er's sug·ar**) ▸*n.* finely powdered sugar with cornstarch added, used for making icings and candy.

con·fec·tion·er·y /kənˈfekshəˌnerē/ ▸*n.* (*pl.* **-er·ies**) candy and other sweets considered collectively. ■ a shop that sells such items.

con·fed·er·a·cy /kənˈfedərəsē/ ▸*n.* (*pl.* **-cies**) a league or alliance, esp. of confederate states. ■ (**the Confederacy**) another term for **CONFEDERATE STATES OF AMERICA**. ■ an alliance formed for an unlawful purpose; a conspiracy. ▷late Middle English: from Old French *confederacie*, based on Latin *confoederare* 'join together in league' (see **CONFEDERATION**).

con·fed·er·al /kənˈfedərəl/ ▸*adj.* relating to or denoting a confederation. ▷late 18th cent.: from **CONFEDERATION**, on the pattern of *federal*.

con·fed·er·ate ▸*adj.* /kənˈfedərət/ joined by an agreement or treaty: *some local groups united to form confederate councils.* ■ (**Confederate**) of or relating to the Confederate States of America: *the Confederate flag.*

▸*n.* /kənˈfedərət/ **1** a person one works with, esp. in something secret or illegal; an accomplice: *where was his confederate, the girl who had stolen Richard's wallet?* **2** (**Confederate**) a supporter of the Confederate States of America.

▸*v.* /-ˌrāt/ [*trans.*] [usu. as *adj.*] (**confederated**) bring (states or groups of people) into an alliance: *Switzerland is a model for the new confederated Europe.* ▷late Middle English: from late (ecclesiastical) Latin *confoederatus*, from *con-* 'together' + *foederatus* (see **FEDERATE**).

Con·fed·er·ate States of A·mer·i·ca (also **the Con·fed·er·a·cy**) the 11 Southern states (Alabama, Arkansas, Florida, Georgia, Louisiana, Mississippi, North Carolina, South Carolina, Tennessee, Texas, and Virginia) that seceded from the U.S. in 1860–61, thus precipitating the Civil War.

con·fed·er·a·tion /kənˌfedəˈrāshən/ ▸*n.* an organization that consists of a number of parties or groups united in an alliance or league: *a confederation of trade unions.* ■ a more or less permanent union of countries with some or most political power vested in a central authority: *Canada became a confederation in 1867.* ■ the action of confederating or the state of being confederated: *a referendum on confederation.* ▷late Middle English: from Old French *confederacion* or late Latin *confederatio(n-)*, from Latin *confoederare*, from *con-* 'together' + *foederare* 'join in league with' (from *foedus* 'league, treaty').

con·fer /kənˈfər/ ▸*v.* (**-ferred**, **-fer·ring**) **1** [*trans.*] grant or bestow (a title, degree, benefit, or right): *moves were made to **confer** an honorary degree **on** her.* See note at **GIVE**. **2** [*intrans.*] have discussions; exchange opinions: *the officials were **conferring with** allies.* ▷late Middle English (in the general sense 'bring together,' also in sense 2): from Latin *conferre*, from *con-* 'together' + *ferre* 'bring.' **—con·fer·ment** *n.* (in sense 1). **—con·fer·ra·ble** *adj.* **—con·fer·ral** /-ˈfərəl/ *n.* (in sense 1).

con·fer·ee /ˌkänfəˈrē/ ▸*n.* **1** a person who attends a conference. **2** a person on whom something is conferred.

con·fer·ence /ˈkänf(ə)rəns/ ▸*n.* **1** a formal meeting for discussion: *he gathered all the men around the table for a conference.* ■ a formal meeting that typically takes place over a number of days and involves people with a shared interest, esp. one held regularly by an association or organization: *an international conference on the environment | the third annual National Wilderness Conference.* ■ [usu. as *adj.*] a linking of several telephones or computers, so that each user may communicate with the others simultaneously: *a **conference call**.* **2** an association of sports teams that play each other. **3** the governing body of some Christian churches, esp. the Methodist Church.

▸*v.* [*intrans.*] [usu. as *n.*] (**conferencing**) take part in a conference or conference call: *video conferencing.* ▷early 16th cent. (in the general sense 'conversation, talk'): from French *conférence* or medieval Latin *conferentia*, from Latin *conferre* 'bring together' (see **CONFER**).

▸*PHRASE* □ **in conference** in a meeting; engaged in discussions.

Con·fer·ence on Dis·ar·ma·ment a committee with forty nations as members that seeks to negotiate multilateral disarmament.

con·fess /kənˈfes/ ▸*v.* [*reporting verb*] admit or state that one has committed a crime or is at fault in some way: [with *clause*] *he confessed that he had attacked the old man* | [*intrans.*] *he wants to **confess to** Caroline's murder* | [with *direct speech*] *"I damaged your car," she confessed* | [*trans.*] *once apprehended, they would confess their guilt.* ■ admit or acknowledge something reluctantly, typically because one feels slightly ashamed or embarrassed: [with *clause*] *I must confess that I was slightly surprised* | [*intrans.*] *he **confessed to** a lifelong passion for food* | [with *direct speech*] *"I needed to see you, too," he confessed.* ■ [*trans.*] declare (one's religious faith): *150 people confessed faith in Christ.* ■ declare one's sins formally to a priest: [*trans.*] *I could not confess all my sins to the priest* | [*intrans.*] *he gave himself up after **confessing to** a priest.* ■ [*trans.*] (of a priest) hear the confession of (someone) in such a way: *St. Ambrose would weep bitter tears when confessing a sinner.* ▷late Middle English: from Old French *confesser*, from Latin *confessus*, past participle of *confiteri* 'acknowledge,' from *con-* (expressing intensive force) + *fateri* 'declare, avow.'

con·fes·sant /kənˈfesənt/ ▸*n.* a person who confesses to a priest; a penitent.

con·fess·ed·ly /kənˈfesədlē/ ▸*adv.* by one's own admission: *many therapists have had clients who, confessedly or otherwise, have fallen in love with them.*

con·fes·sion /kənˈfeshən/ ▸*n.* **1** a formal statement admitting that one is guilty of a crime: *he signed a confession to the murders.* ■ an admission or acknowledgment that one has done something that one is ashamed or embarrassed about: *by his own confession, he had strayed perilously close to alcoholism.* ■ a formal admission of one's sins with repentance and desire of absolution, esp. privately to a priest as a religious duty: *she still had not been **to confession**.* See also **SACRAMENT OF RECONCILIATION**. ■ (**confessions**) *often humorous* intimate revelations about a person's private life or occupation, esp. as presented in a sensationalized form in a book, newspaper, or movie: *confessions of a driving instructor.* **2** (also **confession of faith**) a statement setting out essential religious doctrine. ■ (also **Confession**) the religious body or church sharing a confession of faith. ■ a statement of one's principles: *his words are a political confession of faith.* ▷late Middle English: via Old French from Latin *confessio(n-)*, from *confiteri* 'acknowledge' (see **CONFESS**). **—con·fes·sion·ar·y** /-ˌnerē/ *adj.*

con·fes·sion·al /kənˈfeshənl/ ▸*n.* **1** an enclosed stall in a church divided by a screen or curtain in which a priest sits to hear people confess their sins. **2** an admission or acknowledgment that one has done something that one is ashamed or embarrassed about; a confession.

▶*adj.* **1** (esp. of speech or writing) in which a person reveals or admits to private thoughts or past incidents, esp. ones that cause shame or embarrassment: *the autobiography is remarkably confessional* | *his confessional outpourings.* ■ of or relating to religious confession: *the priest leaned forward in his best confessional manner.* **2** of or relating to confessions of faith or doctrinal systems: *the confessional approach to religious education.* ▷late Middle English (as an adjective): the adjective from CONFESSION + -AL; the noun via French from Italian *confessionale*, from medieval Latin, neuter of *confessionalis*, from Latin *confessio(n-)*, from *confiteri* 'acknowledge' (see CONFESS).

con·fes·sor /kən'fesər/ ▶*n.* **1** /kōn'fesər; 'kän,fesər; 'känfə,sôr/ a priest who hears confessions and gives absolution and spiritual counsel. ■ a person to whom another confides personal problems. **2** /kən'fesər; 'kän,fesər/ a person who avows religious faith in the face of opposition, but does not suffer martyrdom. **3** /kən'fesər/ a person who makes a confession. ▷Old English (sense 2): from Old French *confessour*, from ecclesiastical Latin *confessor*, from Latin *confess-* 'acknowledged' (see CONFESS).

con·fet·ti /kən'fetē/ ▶*n.* small pieces of colored paper thrown during a celebration such as a wedding. ▷early 19th cent. (originally denoting the real or imitation sweets thrown during Italian carnivals): from Italian, literally 'sweets,' from Latin *confectum* 'something prepared,' neuter past participle of *conficere* 'put together' (see CONFECT).

con·fi·dant /'känfə,dant; -,dänt/ ▶*n.* (*fem.* **con·fi·dante** *pronunc.* same) a person with whom one shares a secret or private matter, trusting them not to repeat it to others. ▷mid 17th cent.: alteration of CONFIDENT (as a noun in the same sense in the early 17th cent.), probably to represent the pronunciation of French *confidente* 'having full trust.'

con·fide /kən'fīd/ ▶*v.* [*trans.*] tell someone about a secret or private matter while trusting them not to repeat it to others: *he* ***confided*** *his fears* ***to*** *his mother* | *"I have been afraid," she confided* | *the judge confided that he had been swayed by the sister of the accused.* ■ [*intrans.*] (**confide in**) trust (someone) enough to tell them of such a secret or private matter: *he confided in friends that he and his wife planned to separate.* ■ (**confide something to**) *dated* entrust something to (someone) for safekeeping: *the property of others confided to their care was unjustifiably risked.* ▷late Middle English (in the sense 'place trust (in)'): from Latin *confidere* 'have full trust.' The sense 'impart as a secret' dates from the mid 18th cent. —**con·fid·ing·ly** *adv.*

con·fi·dence /'känfədəns; -fə,dens/ ▶*n.* the feeling or belief that one can rely on someone or something; firm trust: *we had every* ***confidence in*** *the staff* | *he had gained the young man's confidence.* ■ the state of feeling certain about the truth of something: *it is not possible to say with confidence how much of the increase in sea levels is due to melting glaciers.* ■ a feeling of self-assurance arising from one's appreciation of one's own abilities or qualities: *she's brimming with confidence* | [*in sing.*] *he would walk up those steps with a confidence he didn't feel.* ■ the telling of private matters or secrets with mutual trust: *someone with whom you may raise your suspicions* ***in confidence.*** ■ (often **confidences**) a secret or private matter told to someone under such a condition of trust: *the girls exchanged confidences about their parents.* ▷late Middle English: from Latin *confidentia*, from *confidere* 'have full trust' (see CONFIDENT).

▶**PHRASES** □ **in someone's confidence** in a position of trust with someone. □ **take someone into one's confidence** tell someone one's secrets.

con·fi·dence game (*Brit.* also **confidence trick**) ▶*n.* a swindle in which the victim is persuaded to trust the swindler in some way. —**con·fi·dence trick·ster** *n. Brit.*

con·fi·dence in·ter·val ▶*n.* *Statistics* a range of values so defined that there is a specified probability that the value of a parameter lies within it.

con·fi·dence lev·el ▶*n.* *Statistics* the probability that the value of a parameter falls within a specified range of values.

con·fi·dence lim·it ▶*n.* *Statistics* either of the extreme values of a confidence interval.

con·fi·dence man ▶*n.* old-fashioned term for CON MAN.

con·fi·dent /'känfədənt; -fə,dent/ ▶*adj.* feeling or showing confidence in oneself; self-assured: *she was a confident, outgoing girl* | *a confident smile.* ■ feeling or showing certainty about something: *this time they're* ***confident of*** *a happy ending* | *I am not very* ***confident about*** *tonight's game.*

▶*n. archaic* a confidant. ▷late 16th cent.: from French *confident(e)*, from Italian *confidente*, from Latin *confident-* 'having full trust,' from the verb *confidere*, from *con-* (expressing intensive force) + *fidere* 'trust.' —**con·fi·dent·ly** *adv.*

con·fi·den·tial /,känfə'denCHəl/ ▶*adj.* intended to be kept secret: *confidential information* | *knowledge that was privileged and confidential.* ■ (of a person's tone of voice) indicating that what one says is private or secret: *he dropped his voice to a confidential whisper.* ■ entrusted with private or restricted information: *a confidential secretary.* —**con·fi·den·ti·al·i·ty** /-,denCHē'alitē/ *n.* —**con·fi·den·tial·ly** *adv.*

con·fig·u·ra·tion /kən,fig(y)ə'rāSHən/ ▶*n.* an arrangement of elements in a particular form, figure, or combination: *the broad configuration of the economy remains capitalist* | *the arena is equipped to stage indoor sports with various configurations of seating.* ■ *Chemistry* the fixed three-dimensional relationship of the atoms in a molecule, defined by the bonds between them. Compare with CONFORMATION. ■ *Computing* the arrangement in which items of computer hardware or software are interconnected: *it comes with a removable hard disk drive as part of the standard configuration.* ■ *Psychology* another term for GESTALT. ▷mid 16th cent. (denoting the relative position of celestial objects): from late Latin *configuratio(n-)*, from Latin *configurare* 'shape after a pattern' (see CONFIGURE). —**con·fig·u·ra·tion·al** /-SHənl/ *adj.* —**con·fig·u·ra·tion·al·ly** /-SHənl-ē/ *adv.* —**con·fig·u·ra·tive** /-'fig(y)ərətiv/ *adj.*

con·fig·ure /kən'figyər/ ▶*v.* [*trans.*] (often **be configured**) shape or put together in a particular form or configuration: *two of the aircraft will be configured as VIP transports.* ■ *Computing* arrange or order (a computer system or an element of it) so as to fit it for a designated task: *expanded memory can be configured as a virtual drive.* ▷late Middle English (in the Latin sense): from Latin *configurare* 'shape after a pattern,' from *con-* 'together' + *figurare* 'to shape' (from *figura* 'shape or figure'). —**con·fig·ur·a·ble** *adj.*

con·fine ▶*v.* /kən'fīn/ [*trans.*] (**confine someone/something to**) keep or restrict someone or something within certain limits of (space, scope, quantity, or time): *he does not confine his message to politics* | *your boating will mostly be confined to a few hours at weekends* | *you've* ***confined yourself*** *to what you know.* ■ (**confine someone to/in**) restrain or forbid someone from leaving (a place): *the troops were confined to their barracks.* ■ (**be confined to**) (of a person) be unable to leave (one's bed, home, or a wheelchair) because of illness or disability: *he had been confined to a wheelchair for some time.* ■ (**be confined**) *dated* (of a woman) remain in bed for a period before, during, and after the birth of a child: *she was confined for nearly a month.*

▶*n.* /'kän,fīn/ (**confines**) the borders or boundaries of a place, esp. with regard to their restricting freedom of movement: *they were cramped within* ***the confines of*** *a little cabin.* ■ *figurative* the limits or restrictions of something abstract, esp. a subject or sphere of activity: *the narrow confines of political life.* ▷late Middle English (as a noun): from French *confins* (plural noun), from Latin *confinia*, from *confinis* 'bordering,' from *con-* 'together' + *finis* 'end, limit' (plural *fines* 'territory'). The verb senses are from French *confiner*, based on Latin *confinis*. —**con·fine·ment** *n.*

con·fined /kən'fīnd/ ▶*adj.* (of a space) restricted in area or volume; cramped: *wear a dust mask and goggles when soldering in confined spaces.*

con·firm /kən'fərm/ ▶*v.* [*trans.*] **1** establish the truth or correctness of (something previously believed, suspected, or feared to be the case): *if these fears are confirmed, the outlook for the economy will be dire* | *the report confirms that a diet rich in vitamin C can help to prevent cataracts.* ■ state with assurance that a report or fact is true: *he confirmed that the general was in the hands of the rebels* | *"It is indeed real coffee," I confirmed.* ■ (**confirm someone in**) reinforce someone in (an opinion, belief, or feeling): *he fueled his misogyny by cultivating women who confirmed him in this view.* ■ make (a provisional arrangement or appointment) definite: *Mr. Baker's assistant telephoned to confirm his appointment with the chairman.* ■ make (something, esp. a person's appointment to a position or an agreement) formally valid; ratify: *the organization has confirmed the appointment of Mr. Collins as managing director.* ■ formally declare (someone) to be appointed to a particular position: *he was* ***confirmed as*** *the new peace envoy.* **2** administer the religious rite of confirmation to: *he had been baptized and confirmed.* ▷Middle English: from Old French *confermer*, from Latin *confirmare*, from *con-* 'together' + *firmare* 'strengthen' (from *firmus* 'firm'). —**con·firm·a·tive** /-mətiv/ *adj.* —**con·firm·a·to·ry** /-mə,tôrē/ *adj.*

con·fir·mand /'känfər,mand; ,känfər'mand/ ▶*n.* a person who is to undergo the religious rite of confirmation.

con·fir·ma·tion /,känfər'māSHən/ ▶*n.* **1** the action of confirming something or the state of being confirmed: *Sylvia received official confirmation of the instructorship.* **2** (in the Christian Church) the rite at which a baptized person, esp. one baptized as an infant, affirms Christian belief and is admitted as a full member of the church. ■ the Jewish ceremony of bar mitzvah or bat mitzvah. ▷Middle English: via Old French from Latin *confirmatio(n-)*, from *confirmare* 'make firm, establish' (see CONFIRM).

con·firmed /kən'fərmd/ ▶*adj.* (of a person) firmly established in a particular habit, belief, or way of life and unlikely to change: *a confirmed bachelor* | *a confirmed teetotaler.*

con·fis·cate /'känfə,skāt/ ▶*v.* [*trans.*] take or seize (someone's property) with authority: *the guards confiscated his camera* | [as *adj.*] (**confiscated**) *confiscated equipment.* ■ take (a possession, esp. land) as a penalty and give it to the public treasury: *the government confiscated his property.* ▷mid 16th cent.: from Latin *confiscat-* 'put away in a chest, consigned to the public treasury,' from the verb *confiscare*, based on *con-* 'together' + *fiscus* 'chest, treasury.' —**con·fis·ca·tion** /,känfə'skāSHən/ *n.* —**con·fis·ca·tor** /-,skātər/ *n.* —**con·fis·ca·to·ry** /kən'fiskə,tôrē/ *adj.*

con·fit /kôN'fē/ ▶*n.* duck or other meat cooked slowly in its own fat. ▷French, 'conserved,' from *confire* 'prepare.'

Con·fit·e·or /kän'fitē,ôr/ ▶*n.* a form of prayer confessing sins, used in the Roman Catholic Mass and some other sacraments. ▷Middle English: Latin, literally 'I confess,' from the formula *Confiteor Deo Omnipotenti* 'I confess to Almighty God.'

con·fi·ture /'känfi,CHŏŏr/ ▶*n.* a preparation of preserved fruit. ■ a confection.

con·fla·grant /kən'flāgrənt/ ▶*adj.* on fire; blazing.

con·fla·gra·tion /,känflə'grāSHən/ ▶*n.* an extensive fire that destroys a great deal of land or property. ▷late 15th cent. (denoting consumption by fire): from Latin *conflagratio(n-)*, from the verb *conflagrare*, from *con-* (expressing intensive force) + *flagrare* 'to blaze.'

con·flate /kən'flāt/ ▶*v.* [*trans.*] combine (two or more texts, ideas, etc.) into one: *the urban crisis conflates a number of different economic and social issues.* ▷late Middle English (in the sense 'fuse or melt down metal'): from Latin *conflat-* 'kindled, fused,' from the verb *conflare*, from *con-* 'together' + *flare* 'to blow.' —**con·fla·tion** /-'flāSHən/ *n.*

con·flict ▶*n.* /'kän,flikt/ a serious disagreement or argument, typically a protracted one: *the eternal* ***conflict between*** *the sexes* | *doctors often* ***come into conflict with*** *politicians.* ■ a prolonged armed struggle: *overseas conflicts.* ■ an incompatibility between two or more opinions, principles, or interests: *there was a* ***conflict between*** *his business and domestic life.* ■ *Psychology* a condition in which a person experiences a clash of opposing wishes or needs.

▶*v.* /kən'flikt; 'kän,flikt/ [*intrans.*] be incompatible or at variance; clash: *parents' and children's interests sometimes conflict* | *those tournament dates would have* ***conflicted with*** *Memorial Day* | [as *adj.*] (**conflicting**) *there are conflicting accounts of what occurred.* ■ [as *adj.*] (**conflicted**) having or showing confused and mutually inconsistent feelings: *my feelings are so conflicted that I hardly know how to answer.* ▷late Middle English: from Latin *conflict-* 'struck together, fought,' from the verb *confligere*, from *con-* 'together' + *fligere* 'to strike'; the noun is via Latin *conflictus* 'a contest.' —**con·flic·tive** /kən'fliktiv; 'kän,flik-/ *adj.* —**con·flic·tu·al** /kən'flikCHŏŏəl/ *adj.*

con·flict dia·mond ▶*n.* a rough diamond mined in an area controlled by insurgent forces whose sale is used to finance antigovernment military action.

con·flu·ence /'kän,flŏŏəns; kən'flŏŏəns/ ▶*n.* the junction of two rivers, esp. rivers of approximately equal width: *here at* ***the confluence of*** *the Laramie and North Platte Rivers.* ■ an act or process of merging: *a major confluence of the world's financial markets.* ▷late Middle

English: from late Latin *confluentia*, from Latin *confluere* 'flow together' (see **CONFLUENT**).

con·flu·ent /ˈkänˌflo͞oənt; kənˈflo͞oənt/ ▸*adj.* flowing together or merging: *warm confluent smells.* ▷late 15th cent.: from Latin *confluent-* 'flowing together,' from *confluere*, from *con-* 'together' + *fluere* 'to flow.'

con·flux /ˈkänˌfləks/ ▸*n.* another term for **CONFLUENCE.** ▷early 17th cent.: from late Latin *confluxus*, from *con-* 'together' + *fluxus* (see **FLUX**).

con·fo·cal /känˈfōkəl/ ▸*adj.* having a common focus or foci: *confocal ellipses.* ■ denoting or using a microscope whose imaging system only collects light from a small spot on the specimen, giving greater resolution.

con·form /kənˈfôrm/ ▸*v.* [*intrans.*] comply with rules, standards, or laws: *the kitchen does not* ***conform to*** *hygiene regulations | the changes were introduced to* ***conform with*** *international classifications.* ■ (of a person) behave according to socially acceptable conventions or standards: *the pressure to conform.* ■ be similar in form or type; agree: *the countryside should* ***conform to*** *a certain idea of the picturesque.* ▷Middle English (in the sense 'make (something) like another thing'): from Old French *conformer*, from Latin *conformare*, from *con-* 'together' + *formare* 'to form.'

con·form·a·ble /kənˈfôrməbəl/ ▸*adj.* (usu. **conformable to**) (of a person) disposed or accustomed to conform to what is acceptable or expected. ■ similar in form or nature; consistent: *this proposition might be conformable to the original conjecture.* ■ *Geology* (of strata in contact) deposited in a continuous sequence, and typically having the same direction of stratification. ▷late 15th cent. (in the sense 'compliant (to) or tractable'): from medieval Latin *conformabilis*, from Latin *conformare* 'to form, fashion' (see **CONFORM**). **—con·form·a·bil·i·ty** /-ˌfôrməˈbilitē/ *n.* **—con·form·a·bly** /-blē/ *adv.*

con·for·mal /kənˈfôrməl/ ▸*adj.* (of a map projection or a mathematical mapping) preserving the correct angles between directions within small areas, though distorting distances. Also called **ORTHOMORPHIC.** ▷mid 17th cent. (in the sense 'conformable'): from late Latin *conformalis*, from *con-* 'together' + *formalis* 'formal.' The current sense was coined in German. **—con·for·mal·ly** *adv.*

con·form·ance /kənˈfôrməns/ ▸*n.* another term for **CONFORMITY.**

con·for·ma·tion /ˌkänfôrˈmāshən; -fər-/ ▸*n.* the shape or structure of something, esp. an animal: *the judges run their hands over the dog's body and legs, checking its conformation.* ■ *Chemistry* any of the spatial arrangements that the atoms in a molecule may adopt and freely convert between, esp. by rotation about individual single bonds. Compare with **CONFIGURATION.** ▷early 16th cent. (in the sense 'conforming, adaptation'): from Latin *conformatio(n-)*, from *conformare* 'to shape, fashion' (see **CONFORM**). **—con·for·ma·tion·al** /-shənl/ *adj.*

con·form·er /kənˈfôrmər/ ▸*n. Chemistry* a form of a compound having a particular molecular conformation: *changing the temperature alters the relative proportions of the conformers.* ▷1960s: blend of *conformational* (see **CONFORMATION**) and **ISOMER.**

con·form·ist /kənˈfôrmist/ ▸*n.* a person who conforms to accepted behavior or established practices. ■ *Brit., chiefly historical* a person who conforms to the practices of the Church of England.
▸*adj.* (of a person or activity) conforming to accepted behavior or established practices; conventional. **—con·form·ism** /-ˌmizəm/ *n.*

con·form·i·ty /kənˈfôrmitē/ ▸*n.* compliance with standards, rules, or laws: ***conformity to*** *regulations | the goods were* ***in conformity with*** *the contract.* ■ behavior in accordance with socially accepted conventions or standards: *loyalty to one's party need not imply unquestioning conformity.* ■ *Brit., chiefly historical* compliance with the practices of the Church of England. ■ similarity in form or type; agreement in character: *these changes are intended to ensure* ***conformity between*** *all schemes.* ■ *Geology* (of strata in contact) a continuous sequence of deposits, typically in parallel strata. ▷late Middle English: from Old French *conformite* or late Latin *conformitas*, from *conformare* 'to form, fashion' (see **CONFORM**).

con·found /kənˈfound/ ▸*v.* [*trans.*] **1** cause surprise or confusion in (someone), esp. by acting against their expectations: *the inflation figure confounded economic analysts.* ■ prove (a theory, expectation, or prediction) wrong: *the rise in prices confounded expectations.* ■ defeat (a plan, aim, or hope): *we will confound these tactics by the pressure groups.* ■ *archaic* overthrow (an enemy). **2** (often **be confounded with**) mix up (something) with something else so that the individual elements become difficult to distinguish: *'nuke' is now a cooking technique, as microwave radiation is confounded with nuclear radiation.*
▸*exclam. dated* used to express anger or annoyance: *oh, confound it, where is the thing?* ▷Middle English: from Old French *confondre*, from Latin *confundere* 'pour together, mix up.' Compare with **CONFUSE.**

con·found·ed /kənˈfoundəd; kän-/ ▸*adj. informal, dated* used for emphasis, esp. to express anger or annoyance: *he was a confounded nuisance.* **—con·found·ed·ly** *adv.*

con·fra·ter·ni·ty /ˌkänfrəˈtərnitē/ ▸*n.* (*pl.* **-ties**) a brotherhood, esp. with a charitable or religious purpose. ▷late Middle English: from Old French *confraternite*, from medieval Latin *confraternitas*, from *confrater* (see **CONFRÈRE**).

con·frère /ˈkänˌfrer; känˈfrer; kônˈfrer/ (also **con·frere**) ▸*n.* a fellow member of a profession; a colleague: *executives from the four broadcast television networks, along with their cable confreres.* ▷mid 18th cent.: French, from medieval Latin *confrater*, from *con-* 'together with' + *frater* 'brother.'

con·front /kənˈfrənt/ ▸*v.* [*trans.*] meet (someone) face to face with hostile or argumentative intent: *300 policemen confronted an equal number of union supporters.* ■ face up to and deal with (a problem or difficult situation): *we knew we couldn't ignore the race issue and decided we'd confront it head on.* ■ compel (someone) to face or consider something, esp. by way of accusation: *Tricia* ***confronted*** *him* ***with*** *her suspicions.* ■ (often **be confronted**) (of a problem, difficulty, etc.) present itself to (someone) so that dealing with it cannot be avoided: *post-czarist Russia was* ***confronted with*** *a Ukrainian national movement.* ■ (usu. **be confronted**) appear or be placed in front of (someone) so as to unsettle or threaten: *we were* ***confronted with*** *pictures of moving skeletons.* ▷mid 16th cent.: from French *confronter*, from medieval Latin *confrontare*, from Latin *con-* 'with' + *frons, front-* 'face.'

con·fron·ta·tion /ˌkänfrənˈtāshən/ ▸*n.* a hostile or argumentative meeting or situation between opposing parties: *a* ***confrontation with*** *the legislature | four months of violent confrontation between government and opposition forces.* **—con·fron·ta·tion·al** /-shənl/ *adj.*

Con·fu·cian /kənˈfyo͞oshən/ ▸*adj.* of or relating to Confucius or Confucianism.
▸*n.* an adherent of Confucianism.

Con·fu·cian·ism /kənˈfyo͞oshəˌnizəm/ ▸*n.* a system of philosophical and ethical teachings founded by Confucius and developed by Mencius. **—Con·fu·cian·ist** *n.* & *adj.*

Con·fu·cius /kənˈfyo͞oshəs/ (551–479 BC), Chinese philosopher; Latinized name of *Kongfuze* (*K'ung Futzu*) "Kong the master." His ideas about the importance of practical moral values, collected by his disciples in the *Analects*, formed the basis of the philosophy known as Confucianism.

con·fus·a·ble /kənˈfyo͞ozəbəl/ ▸*adj.* able or liable to be confused with something else.
▸*n.* a word or phrase that is easily confused with another in meaning or usage, such as *mitigate*, which is often confused with *militate*. **—con·fus·a·bil·i·ty** /kənˌfyo͞ozəˈbilitē/ *n.*

con·fuse /kənˈfyo͞oz/ ▸*v.* [*trans.*] cause (someone) to become bewildered or perplexed: *past and present blurred together, confusing her still further.* ■ make (something) more complex or less easy to understand: *the points made by the authors confuse rather than clarify the issue.* ■ identify wrongly; mistake: *a lot of people* ***confuse*** *a stroke* ***with*** *a heart attack | purchasers might confuse the two products.* ▷Middle English (in the sense 'rout, bring to ruin'): from Old French *confus*, from Latin *confusus*, past participle of *confundere* 'mingle together' (see **CONFOUND**). Originally all senses of the verb were passive, and therefore appeared only as the past participle *confused*; the active voice occurred rarely until the 19th cent. when it began to replace *confound*. **—con·fus·ing·ly** *adv.*

con·fused /kənˈfyo͞ozd/ ▸*adj.* (of a person) unable to think clearly; bewildered: *she was utterly* ***confused about*** *what had just happened | a very confused and unhappy boy.* ■ showing bewilderment: *a confused expression crossed her face.* ■ not in possession of all one's mental faculties, esp. because of old age: *interviewing confused old people does take longer.* ■ lacking order and thus difficult to understand: *the confused information supplied by authorities | reports about the incident were rather confused.* ■ lacking clear distinction of elements; jumbled: *the sound of a sort of confused hammering and shouting.* **—con·fus·ed·ly** /-ˈfyo͞ozədlē/ *adv.*

con·fu·sion /kənˈfyo͞ozhən/ ▸*n.* **1** lack of understanding; uncertainty: *there seems to be some* ***confusion about*** *which system does what | he cleared up the* ***confusion over*** *the party's policy.* ■ a situation of panic; a breakdown of order: *the shaken survivors retreated* ***in confusion.*** ■ a disorderly jumble: *all I can see is* ***a confusion of*** *brown cardboard boxes.* See note at **JUMBLE.** **2** the state of being bewildered or unclear in one's mind about something: *she looked about her* ***in confusion.*** ■ the mistaking of one person or thing for another: *there is some confusion between "unlawful" and "illegal" | most of the errors are reasonable confusions between similar words or sequences of words.* ▷Middle English: from Latin *confusio(n-)*, from the verb *confundere* 'mingle together' (see **CONFUSE**).

con·fute /kənˈfyo͞ot/ ▸*v.* [*trans.*] *formal* prove (a person or an assertion) to be wrong: *restorers who sought to confute this view were accused of ignorance.* ▷early 16th cent.: from Latin *confutare* 'restrain, answer conclusively,' from *con-* 'altogether' + the base of *refutare* 'refute.' **—con·fu·ta·tion** /ˌkänfyo͞oˈtāshən/ *n.*

Cong. ▸*abbr.* ■ Congress. ■ Congressional. ■ Congregational.

con·ga /ˈkänggə/ ▸*n.* **1** a Latin American dance of African origin, usually with several people in a single line, one behind the other. **2** (also **conga drum**) a tall, narrow, low-toned drum beaten with the hands.
▸*v.* (**-gas, -gaed** /-gəd/ or **-ga'd, -ga·ing** /-gə-ing/) [*intrans.*] dance the conga. ▷1930s: from Latin American Spanish, from Spanish, feminine of *congo* 'Congolese.'

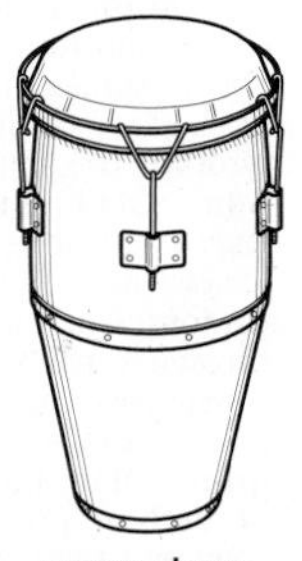
conga drum

con game ▸*n.* informal term for **CONFIDENCE GAME.**

con·gé /kônˈzhā ˈkänˌjā/ ▸*n.* [in *sing.*] an unceremonious dismissal of someone; a leavetaking: *the woman who gave you your congé when she wanted to marry Mr. Sugar.* ▷late Middle English (in the general sense 'permission to do something'): from Old French *congie*, from Latin *commeatus* 'leave of absence,' from *commeare* 'go and come.' The word is now usually treated as equivalent to modern French.

con·geal /kənˈjēl/ ▸*v.* [*intrans.*] solidify or coagulate, esp. by cooling: *the blood had* ***congealed into*** *blobs* | [as *adj.*] (**congealed**) *congealed egg white.* ■ *figurative* take shape or coalesce, esp. to form a satisfying whole: *the ballet failed to congeal as a single oeuvre.* ▷late Middle English: from Old French *congeler*, from Latin *congelare*, from *con-* 'together' + *gelare* 'freeze' (from *gelu* 'frost'). **—con·geal·a·ble** *adj.* **—con·geal·ment** *n.* (*archaic*).

con·gee /ˈkänjē; kônˈzhā/ ▸*n.* (in Chinese cooking) broth or porridge made from rice. ▷from Tamil *kañci*.

con·ge·la·tion /ˌkänjəˈlāshən/ ▸*n.* the process of congealing or the state of being congealed: *the component of metals that causes their congelation.* ▷late Middle English: from Latin *congelatio(n-)*, from the verb *congelare* 'freeze together' (see **CONGEAL**).

con·ge·ner /kənˈjēnər/ ▸*n.* **1** a thing or person of the same kind or category as another. ■ an animal or plant of the same genus as another: *these birds or their congeners may be found in East Africa.* **2** a minor chemical constituent, esp. one that gives a distinctive character to a wine or liquor or is responsible for some of its physiological effects. ▷mid 18th cent.: from Latin, from *con-* 'together with' + *genus, gener-* 'race, stock.'

con·ge·ner·ic /ˌkänjəˈnerik/ ▸*adj. Biology* (of an animal or plant species) belonging to the same genus: *this animal is* ***congeneric with*** *the later species.* ■ of a related nature or origin: *the two sets were congeneric.* ▷mid 17th cent.: from Latin *congener* (see **CONGENER**) + **-IC.** **—con·gen·er·ous** /kənˈjenərəs; kän-; -ˈjēnərəs/ *adj.*

con·gen·ial /kənˈjēnyəl/ ▸*adj.* (of a person) pleasant because of a personality, qualities, or interests that are similar to one's own: *his need for some congenial company.* See note at **PLEASANT.** ■ (of a thing) pleasant or agreeable because suited to one's taste or inclination: *he went back to a climate more* ***congenial to*** *his cold stony soul.* **—con·ge·ni·al·i·ty** /-ˌjēnēˈalitē/ *n.* **—con·gen·ial·ly** *adv.*

con·gen·i·tal /kənˈjenətl/ ▸*adj.* (esp. of a disease or physical abnormality) present from birth: *a congenital malformation of the heart.* ■ (of a person) having a particular trait from birth or by firmly established habit: *a congenital liar.* See note at **INHERENT.** ▷late 18th cent.: from Latin *congenitus*, from *con-* 'together' + *genitus* (past participle of *gignere* 'beget') + **-AL.** **—con·gen·i·tal·ly** *adv.*

con·ger /'käNGgər/ (also **conger eel**) ▸*n.* a large edible predatory eel of shallow coastal waters. • *Conger* and other genera, family Congridae: several species, in particular the European *C. conger* and the American *C. oceanicus.* ▷Middle English: from Old French *congre,* via Latin from Greek *gongros.*

con·ge·ries /'känjərēz/ ▸*n.* (*pl.* same) a disorderly collection; a jumble: *whiffs of ground coffee and a congeries of smells.* ▷mid 16th cent.: from Latin *congeries* 'heap, pile,' from *congerere* 'heap up.'

con·gest·ed /kən'jestid/ ▸*adj.* blocked up with or too full of something, in particular: ■ (of a road or place) so crowded with traffic or people as to hinder freedom of movement: *one of the most congested airports in the world | the road was* ***congested with*** *refugees.* ■ (of the respiratory tract) blocked with mucus so as to hinder breathing: *his nose was congested.* ■ (of a part of the body) abnormally full of blood: *congested arteries.* ▷mid 19th cent.: past participle of *congest,* from Latin *congest-* 'heaped up,' from the verb *congerere,* from *con-* 'together' + *gerere* 'bring.'

con·ges·tion /kən'jesCHən/ ▸*n.* the state of being congested: *the new bridge should ease congestion in the area.* ▷late Middle English: via Old French from Latin *congestio(n-),* from *congere* 'heap up,' from *con-* 'together' + *gerere* 'bring.'

con·ges·tive /kən'jestiv/ ▸*adj. Medicine* involving or produced by congestion of a part of the body. ▷mid 19th cent.: from *congest* (see CONGESTED) + -IVE.

con·ges·tive heart fail·ure ▸*n.* a weakness of the heart that leads to a buildup of fluid in the lungs and surrounding body tissues.

con·gi·us /'känjēəs/ ▸*n.* (*pl.* **-gi·i** /-jē,ī/) an ancient Roman liquid measure of one eighth of an amphora, equal in modern terms to about 6.4 pints (3.6 liters). ▷late Middle English: Latin, from Greek *konkhion, konkhē.* (See CONCH).

con·glob·u·late /kən'gläbyələt/ ▸*v.* [*intrans.*] *rare* join closely together: *a group of tourists conglobulating in a close mass.* ▷mid 18th cent.: from Latin *globulus* 'globule,' on the pattern of earlier *conglobate* 'make into a ball.'

con·glom·er·ate ▸*n.* /kən'glämərət/ **1** a number of different things or parts that are put or grouped together to form a whole but remain distinct entities: *the Earth is a specialized conglomerate of organisms.* ■ a large corporation formed by the merging of separate and diverse firms: *a media conglomerate.* **2** *Geology* a coarse-grained sedimentary rock composed of rounded fragments (> 2 mm) within a matrix of finer grained material: *the sediments vary from coarse conglomerate to fine silt and clay.*
▸*adj.* /kən'glämərət/ of or relating to a conglomerate, esp. a large corporation: *conglomerate businesses.*
▸*v.* /-,rāt/ [*intrans.*] gather together into a compact mass: *atoms that conglomerate at the center.* ■ form a conglomerate by merging diverse businesses. ▷late Middle English (as an adjective describing something gathered up into a rounded mass): from Latin *conglomeratus,* past participle of *conglomerare,* from *con-* 'together' + *glomus, glomer-* 'ball.' The geological sense dates from the early 19th cent.; the other noun senses are later. **—con·glom·er·a·tion** /kən,glämə'rāsHən/ *n.*

Con·go /'käNGgō/ a major river in central Africa that rises as the Lualaba River south of Kisangani in northern Democratic Republic of the Congo (formerly Zaire). It flows for 2,880 miles (4,630 km) in a great curve to the west and then turns southwest to form the border between the Congo and the Democratic Republic of the Congo before emptying into the Atlantic Ocean. Also called ZAIRE RIVER.

Con·go, Democratic Republic of the a large country in central Africa with a short coastline on the Atlantic Ocean; pop. 58,317,000; capital, Kinshasa; languages, French (official), Kongo, Lingala, Swahili, and others. Formerly called (until 1997) ZAIRE.

The Democratic Republic of the Congo (formerly Zaire) was a Belgian colony known as the Congo Free State 1885–1908 and the Belgian Congo 1908–60. Independence in 1960 was followed by civil war and UN intervention. General Mobutu seized control in a coup in 1965, changed the name of the country from the Republic of the Congo to Zaire in 1971, and remained in power until he was overthrown in 1997 by Laurent Kabila, who changed the country's name again—back to the Democratic Republic of the Congo.The country experienced a huge influx of refugees following the violence in Rwanda in 1994.

Con·go, Republic of the ▸a country in western Africa, with a short coastline on the Atlantic Ocean; pop. 2,998,000; capital, Brazzaville; languages, French (official), Kikongo, and other Bantu languages.

The region was colonized in the 19th century by France and, as Middle Congo, formed part of the larger territory of French Congo (later, French Equatorial Africa). After becoming independent in 1960, the Congo was the scene of civil war for nearly two decades. A peace accord was signed in 2003.

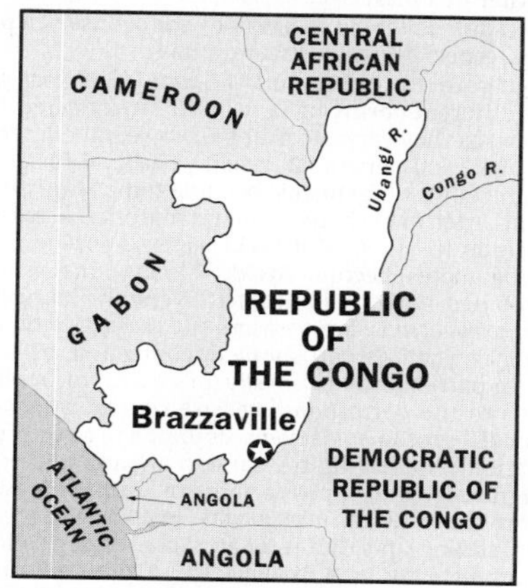

Con·go·lese /,käNGgə'lēz; -'lēs/ ▸*adj.* of or relating to the Congo or the Democratic Republic of the Congo (formerly Zaire).
▸*n.* (*pl.* same) **1** a native or inhabitant of the Congo or the Democratic Republic of the Congo. **2** any of the Bantu languages spoken in the Congo region, in particular Kikongo. ▷from French *Congolais.*

Con·go red ▸*n.* a red-brown azo dye that becomes blue in acidic conditions, used as a chemical indicator and as a stain in histology.

con·grats /kən'grats/ ▸*plural n. informal* congratulations: [as *exclam.*] *"Congrats on your promotion, Cal!"* ▷late 19th cent.: abbreviation.

con·grat·u·late /kən'graCHə,lāt; -'grajə-/ ▸*v.* [*trans.*] give (someone) one's good wishes when something special or pleasant has happened to them: *I went into the living room to* ***congratulate*** *Bill* ***on*** *his marriage.* ■ praise (someone) for a particular achievement: *the operators are to be* ***congratulated for*** *the excellent service that they now provide.* ■ (**congratulate oneself**) feel pride or satisfaction: *she* ***congratulated herself on*** *her powers of deduction | the Director was congratulating himself that nothing could go wrong.* ▷mid 16th cent.: from Latin *congratulat-* 'congratulated,' from the verb *congratulari,* from *con-* 'with' + *gratulari* 'show joy' (from *gratus* 'pleasing'). **—con·grat·u·la·tor** /-,lātər/ *n.* **—con·grat·u·la·to·ry** /-lə,tôrē/ *adj.*

con·grat·u·la·tion /kən,graCHə'lāsHən; -,grajə-/ ▸*n.* an expression of praise for an achievement or good wishes on a special occasion; the act of congratulating: *he began pumping the hand of his son in congratulation.* ■ (**congratulations**) words expressing congratulation: *our congratulations to the winners |* [as *exclam.*] *congratulations on a job well done!* ▷late Middle English: from Latin *congratulatio(n-),* from the verb *congratulari* (see CONGRATULATE).

con·gre·gant /'käNGgrəgənt/ ▸*n.* a member of a congregation, esp. that of a church or synagogue. ▷late 19th cent.: from Latin *congregant-* 'collecting (into a flock), uniting,' from the verb *congregare* (see CONGREGATE).

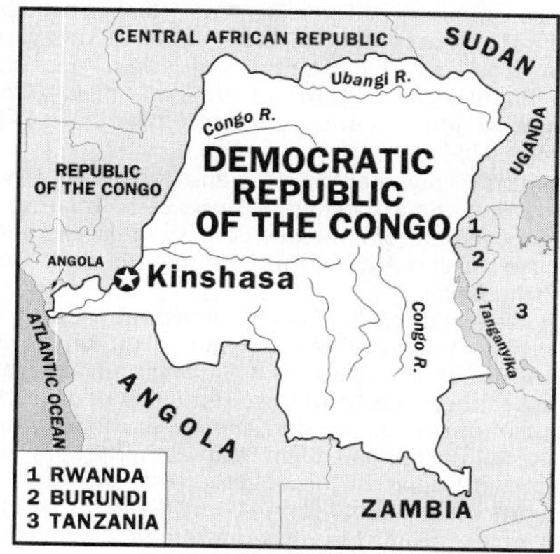

con·gre·gate ▸*v.* /'käNGgrə,gāt/ [*intrans.*] gather into a crowd or mass: *some 4000 demonstrators had congregated at a border point.* See note at GATHER.
▸*adj.* /-gət; -,gāt/ communal: *nursing homes and adult congregate living facilities.* ▷late Middle English: from Latin *congregat-* 'collected (into a flock), united,' from the verb *congregare,* from *con-* 'together' + *gregare* (from *grex, greg-* 'a flock').

con·gre·ga·tion /,käNGgrə'gāsHən/ ▸*n.* **1** a group of people assembled for religious worship. ■ a group of people regularly attending a particular place of worship: *that church took the place of the storefront the congregation had used before the war.* **2** a gathering or collection of people, animals, or things: *large congregations of birds may cause public harm.* ■ the action of gathering together in a crowd: *drought conditions lead to congregation of animals around watering points.* **3** (often **Congregation**) a council or deliberative body. ■ (in the Roman Catholic Church) a permanent committee of the College of Cardinals: *the Congregation for the Doctrine of the Faith.* ■ *Brit.* (in some universities) a general assembly of resident senior members. **4** a group of people obeying a common religious rule but under less solemn vows than members of the older religious orders: *the sisters of the Congregation of Our Lady.* ■ a group of communities within a religious order sharing particular historical or regional links. ▷late Middle English (in senses 2, 3, and 4): from Latin *congregatio(n-),* from *congregare* 'collect (into a flock)' (see CONGREGATE).

con·gre·ga·tion·al /,käNGgrə'gāsHənl/ ▸*adj.* **1** of or relating to a congregation: *congregational singing.* **2** (**Congregational**) of or adhering to Congregationalism: *the Congregational Church.*

Con·gre·ga·tion·al·ism /,käNGgrə'gāsHənl,izəm/ ▸*n.* a system of organization among Christian churches whereby individual local churches are largely self-governing. **—Con·gre·ga·tion·al·ist** *n. & adj.*

con·gress /'käNGgrəs; 'kän-/ ▸*n.* **1** the national legislative body of a country. ■ (**Congress**) the national legislative body of the U.S., meeting at the Capitol in Washington, DC. It was established by the Constitution of 1787 and is composed of the Senate and the House of Representatives: *changes in taxation required the approval of Congress.* ■ a particular session of the U.S. Congress: *the 104th Congress.* **2** a formal meeting or series of meetings for discussion between delegates, esp. those from a political party or trade union or from within a particular discipline: *an international congress of mathematicians.* **3** a society or organization, esp. a political one: *the National Congress of American Indians.* **4** the action of coming together: *sexual congress.* ▷late Middle English (denoting an encounter during battle): from Latin *congressus,* from *congredi* 'meet,' from *con-* 'together' + *gradi* 'walk.' **—con·gres·sion·al** /kən'gresHənl/ *adj.*

con·gress boot ▸*n. dated* a high boot with elastic sides.

Con·gres·sion·al Med·al of Hon·or ▸*n.* see MEDAL OF HONOR.

con·gress·man /'käNGgrəsmən; 'kän-/ ▸*n.* (*pl.* **-men**) a member of the U.S. Congress (also used as a form of address), usually specifically a member of the U.S. House of Representatives.

Con·gress of In·dus·tri·al Or·gan·i·za·tions (abbr.: **CIO**) a federation of North American trade unions, organized largely by industry rather than craft. In 1955 it merged with the American Federation of Labor to form the AFL-CIO.

con·gress·per·son /'käNGgrəs,pərsən; 'kän-/ (*pl.* **congress·peo·ple** or **con·gress·per·sons**) ▸*n.* a member of a legislative congress, esp. the U.S. House of Representatives.

con·gress·wom·an /'käNGgrəs,wŏŏmən; 'kän-/ ▸*n.* (*pl.* **-wom·en**) a female member of the U.S. Congress (also used as a form of address).

Con·greve /'käNG,grēv; 'kän,grēv/, William (1670–1729), English playwright. His plays, such as *Love for Love* (1695) and *The Way of the World* (1700), epitomize the wit and satire of Restoration comedy.

con·gru·ent /kən'grōōənt; 'käNGgrōōənt/ ▸*adj.* **1** in agreement or harmony: *institutional and departmental objectives are largely congruent | the rules may not be*

congruent with *the requirements of the law.* **2** Geometry (of figures) identical in form; coinciding exactly when superimposed. ▷late Middle English: from Latin *congruent-* 'agreeing, meeting together,' from the verb *congruere,* from *con-* 'together' + *ruere* 'fall or rush.' —**con·gru·ence** *n.* —**con·gru·en·cy** *n.* —**con·gru·ent·ly** *adv.*

con·gru·ous /ˈkäNGgro͞oəs/ ▶*adj.* in agreement or harmony: *this explanation is* ***congruous with*** *earlier observations.* ▷late 16th cent.: from Latin *congruus,* from *congruere* 'agree' (see CONGRUENT), + -OUS. —**con·gru·i·ty** /kənˈgro͞oitē/ *n.* —**con·gru·ous·ly** *adv.*

con·ic /ˈkänik/ *chiefly Mathematics* ▶*adj.* of or like a cone.
▶*n.* short for CONIC SECTION. See also CONICS. ▷late 16th cent.: from modern Latin *conicus,* from Greek *kōnikos,* from *kōnos* 'cone.'

con·i·cal /ˈkänikəl/ ▶*adj.* having the shape of a cone. —**con·i·cal·ly** /-ik(ə)lē/ *adv.*

con·i·cal pro·jec·tion (also **con·ic pro·jec·tion**) ▶*n.* a map projection in which an area of the earth is projected onto a cone whose vertex is usually above one of the poles, then unrolled onto a flat surface.

con·ics /ˈkäniks/ ▶*plural n.* [treated as *sing.*] the branch of mathematics concerned with conic sections.

con·ic sec·tion ▶*n.* a figure formed by the intersection of a plane and a right circular cone. Depending on the angle of the plane with respect to the cone, a conic section may be a circle, an ellipse, a parabola, or a hyperbola.

co·nid·i·o·phore /kəˈnidēəˌfôr/ ▶*n.* Botany (in certain fungi) a conidium-bearing hypha or filament. ▷late 19th cent.: from *conidio-* (combining form of CONIDIUM) + -PHORE.

co·nid·i·um /kəˈnidēəm/ ▶*n.* (*pl.* **-nid·i·a** /-ˈnidēə/) Botany a spore produced asexually by various fungi at the tip of a specialized hypha. ▷late 19th cent.: modern Latin, from Greek *konis* 'dust' + the diminutive suffix *-idium.*

co·ni·fer /ˈkänəfər; kō-/ ▶*n.* a tree that bears cones and evergreen needlelike or scalelike leaves. Conifers are of major importance as the source of softwood, and also supply resins and turpentine. • Order Coniferales, class Coniferopsida, subdivision Gymnospermae: several families, including the pines and firs (Pinaceae) and the cypresses (Cupressaceae). ▷mid 19th cent.: from Latin, literally 'cone-bearing,' from *conus* (see CONE). —**co·nif·er·ous** /kəˈnifərəs/ *adj.*

co·ni·form /ˈkōnəˌfôrm; ˈkänə-/ ▶*adj.* *rare* having the shape of a cone. ▷late 18th cent.: from Latin *conus* 'cone' + -IFORM.

co·ni·ine /ˈkōnēˌēn; -ˈnē-in/ ▶*n.* Chemistry a volatile poisonous compound found in hemlock and other plants. It affects the motor nerves, causing paralysis and asphyxia. • An alkaloid, 2-propylpiperidine; chem. formula: $C_8H_{17}N$. ▷mid 19th cent.: from Latin *conium* (from Greek *kōneion* 'hemlock') + -INE[4].

conj. ▶*abbr.* conjunction.

con·jec·tur·al /kənˈjekCHərəl/ ▶*adj.* based on or involving conjecture: *much of the racial history of Madagascar remains conjectural.* ▷mid 16th cent.: via French from Latin *conjecturalis,* from *conjectura* 'inference' (see CONJECTURE). —**con·jec·tur·al·ly** *adv.*

con·jec·ture /kənˈjekCHər/ ▶*n.* an opinion or conclusion formed on the basis of incomplete information: ***conjectures about*** *the newcomer were many and varied | the purpose of the opening in the wall is open to conjecture.* ■ an unproven mathematical or scientific theorem: *the Goldbach conjecture.* ■ (in textual criticism) the suggestion or reconstruction of a reading of a text not present in the original source.
▶*v.* [*trans.*] form an opinion or supposition about (something) on the basis of incomplete information: *he conjectured the existence of an otherwise unknown feature | many conjectured that she had a second husband in mind.* ■ (in textual criticism) propose (a reading). ▷late Middle English (in the senses 'to divine' and 'divination'): from Old French, or from Latin *conjectura,* from *conicere* 'put together in thought,' from *con-* 'together' + *jacere* 'throw.' —**con·jec·tur·a·ble** *adj.*

con·join /kənˈjoin; kän-/ ▶*v.* [*trans.*] *formal* join; combine: *an approach that conjoins theory and method.* ▷late Middle English: from Old French *conjoindre,* from Latin *conjungere,* from *con-* 'together' + *jungere* 'to join.'

con·joined twin ▶ *n.* either of a pair of congenitally fused twins.

USAGE This more accurate and correct term has supplanted the older term **Siamese twin** in all contexts other than informal conversation.

con·joint /kənˈjoint; kän-/ ▶*adj.* [*attrib.*] combining all or both people or things involved: *conjoint family therapy.* ▷Middle English: from Old French, past participle of *conjoindre* (see CONJOIN). —**con·joint·ly** *adv.*

con·ju·gal /ˈkänjəgəl/ ▶*adj.* of or relating to marriage or the relationship between husband and wife: *conjugal loyalty.* ▷early 16th cent.: from Latin *conjugalis,* from *conjux, conjug-* 'spouse,' from *con-* 'together'+ *jugum* 'a yoke.' —**con·ju·gal·i·ty** /ˌkänjəˈgalitē/ *n.* —**con·ju·gal·ly** *adv.*

con·ju·gal rights ▶*plural n.* the rights, esp. to sexual relations, regarded as exercisable in law by each partner in a marriage.

con·ju·gal vis·it ▶*n.* Law a visit by the spouse of a prisoner, especially for sexual relations.

con·ju·gate ▶*v.* /ˈkänjəˌgāt/ **1** [*trans.*] Grammar give the different forms of (a verb in an inflected language) as they vary according to voice, mood, tense, number, and person. **2** [*intrans.*] Biology (of bacteria or unicellular organisms) become temporarily united in order to exchange genetic material: *E. coli only conjugate when one of the cells possesses fertility genes.* ■ (of gametes) become fused. **3** [*trans.*] Chemistry be combined with or joined to reversibly: *bilirubin is then conjugated by liver enzymes and excreted in the bile.*
▶*adj.* /ˈkänjigət; -jəˌgāt/ coupled, connected, or related, in particular: ■ Chemistry (of an acid or base) related to the corresponding base or acid by loss or gain of a proton. ■ Mathematics joined in a reciprocal relation, esp. having the same real parts and equal magnitudes but opposite signs of imaginary parts. Short for COMPLEX CONJUGATE. ■ Geometry (of angles) adding up to 360°; (of arcs) combining to form a complete circle. ■ Biology (esp. of gametes) fused.
▶*n.* /ˈkänjigət; -jəˌgāt/ a thing that is conjugate or conjugated, in particular: ■ *chiefly* Biochemistry a substance formed by the reversible combination of two or more others. ■ a mathematical value or entity having a reciprocal relation with another. See also COMPLEX CONJUGATE. ▷late 15th cent. (as an adjective): from Latin *conjugat-* 'yoked together,' from the verb *conjugare,* from *con-* 'together' + *jugum* 'yoke.' —**con·ju·ga·cy** /ˈkänjəgəsē/ *n.* —**con·ju·ga·tive** /ˈkänjəˌgātiv/ *adj.*

con·ju·gat·ed /ˈkänjəˌgātid/ ▶*adj.* [*attrib.*] another term for CONJUGATE, in particular: ■ Chemistry relating to or denoting double or triple bonds in a molecule that are separated by a single bond, across which some sharing of electrons occurs. ■ (of a substance) reversibly combined with another: *conjugated bile salts.*

con·ju·gate di·am·e·ter ▶*n.* Anatomy the distance between the front and rear of the pelvis.

con·ju·ga·ted pro·tein ▶*n.* a complex protein, such as hemoglobin, consisting of amino acids combined with other substances.

con·ju·ga·tion /ˌkänjəˈgāSHən/ ▶*n.* **1** the formation or existence of a link or connection between things, in particular: ■ Biology the temporary union of two bacteria or unicellular organisms for the exchange of genetic material. ■ Biology the fusion of two gametes, esp. when they are of a similar size. ■ *chiefly* Biochemistry the combination of two substances: *toxic compounds eliminated from the body by conjugation with glutathione.* ■ Chemistry the sharing of electron density between nearby multiple bonds in a molecule. ■ Mathematics the solution of a problem by transforming it into an equivalent problem of a different form, solving this, and then reversing the transformation. **2** Grammar the variation of the form of a verb in an inflected language such as Latin, by which are identified the voice, mood, tense, number, and person. ■ the class in which a verb is put according to the manner of this variation: *a past participle of the first conjugation.* ▷late Middle English (sense 2): from Latin *conjugatio(n-),* from *conjugare* 'join together' (see CONJUGATE). —**con·ju·ga·tion·al** /-SHənl/ *adj.*

con·junct ▶*adj.* /kənˈjəNGkt; kän-/ joined together, combined, or associated. ■ Music of or relating to the movement of a melody between adjacent notes of the scale. ■ Astrology in conjunction with: *Moon conjunct Jupiter.*
▶*n.* /ˈkänjəNGkt/ each of two or more things that are joined or associated. ■ Logic each of the terms of a conjunctive proposition. ■ Grammar an adverbial whose function is to join two sentences or other discourse units (e.g., *however, anyway, in the first place*). ▷late Middle English: from Latin *conjunctus,* past participle of *conjungere* 'join together' (see CONJOIN).

con·junc·tion /kənˈjəNGkSHən/ ▶*n.* **1** the act of joining or the condition of being joined: *he postulated that the Americas were formed by the conjunction of floating islands.* ■ an instance of two or more events or things occurring at the same point in time or space: *a conjunction of favorable political and economic circumstances.* ■ Astronomy & Astrology an alignment of two planets or other celestial objects so that they appear to be in the same, or nearly the same, place in the sky. **2** Grammar a word used to connect clauses or sentences or to coordinate words in the same clause (e.g., *and, but, if*). ▷late Middle English: via Old French from Latin *conjunctio(n-),* from the verb *conjungere* (see CONJOIN). —**con·junc·tion·al** /-SHənl/ *adj.*
▶*PHRASE* □ **in conjunction** together: *herbal medicine was used* ***in conjunction with*** *acupuncture and massage.*

con·junc·ti·va /ˌkänˌjəNG(k)ˈtīvə; kən-/ ▶*n.* Anatomy the mucous membrane that covers the front of the eye and lines the inside of the eyelids. ▷late Middle English: from medieval Latin *(membrana) conjunctiva* 'conjunctive (membrane),' from late Latin *conjunctivus,* from *conjungere* 'join together' (see CONJOIN). —**con·junc·ti·val** *adj.*

con·junc·tive /kənˈjəNG(k)tiv/ ▶*adj.* serving to join; connective: *the conjunctive tissue.* ■ involving the combination or co-occurrence of two or more conditions or properties: *conjunctive hypotheses are simpler to process than negative or disjunctive ones.* ■ Grammar of the nature of or relating to a conjunction.
▶*n.* Grammar a word or expression acting as a conjunction. ▷late Middle English: from late Latin *conjunctivus,* from *conjungere* 'join together' (see CONJUNCT). —**con·junc·tive·ly** *adv.*

con·junc·ti·vi·tis /kənˌjəNG(k)təˈvītis/ ▶*n.* Medicine inflammation of the conjunctiva of the eye. Also called PINKEYE.

con·junc·ture /kənˈjəNGkCHər/ ▶*n.* a combination of events: *the peculiar political conjunctures that led to war.* ■ a state of affairs: *the wider political conjuncture.* ▷early 17th cent.: from CONJUNCTION, by substitution of the suffix; influenced by obsolete French *conjuncture,* from Italian *congiuntura,* based on Latin *conjungere* 'join together' (see CONJOIN).

con·jun·to /känˈho͞ontō; -ˈhəntō/ ▶*n.* (*pl.* **-tos**) (in Latin America or Hispanic communities) a small musical group or band: [as *modifier*] *Texas' leading female conjunto accordionist.* ▷Spanish, literally 'an ensemble, group.'

con·jur·a·tion /ˌkänjo͝orˈāSHən/ ▶*n.* a magic incantation or spell. ■ the performance of something supernatural by means of a magic incantation or spell. ▷late Middle English (also in the sense 'conspiracy, the swearing of an oath together'): via Old French from Latin *conjuratio(n-),* from *conjurare* (see CONJURE).

con·jure ▶*v.* **1** /ˈkänjər; ˈkən-/ [*trans.*] make (something) appear unexpectedly or seemingly from nowhere as if by magic: *Anne* ***conjured up*** *a most delicious homemade stew.* ■ call (an image) to mind: *she had forgotten how to* ***conjure up*** *the image of her mother's face.* ■ (of a word, sound, smell, etc.) cause someone to feel or think of (something): *one scent can* ***conjure up*** *a childhood summer beside a lake.* ■ call upon (a spirit or ghost) to appear, by means of a magic ritual: *they hoped to* ***conjure up*** *the spirit of their dead friend.* **2** /kənˈjo͝or/ [*trans.*] *archaic* implore (someone) to do something. ▷Middle English (also in the sense 'oblige by oath'): from Old French *conjurer* 'to plot or exorcize,' from Latin *conjurare* 'band together by an oath, conspire' (in medieval Latin 'invoke'), from *con-* 'together' + *jurare* 'swear.'
▶*PHRASE* □ **a name to conjure with** the name of an important person within a particular sphere of activity: *on the merger scene his is a name to conjure with.*

con·jure wom·an /ˈkänjər; ˈkən-/ ▶*n.* (*masc.* **con·jure man**) a sorceress, esp. one who practices voodoo.

con·jur·ing /ˈkänjəriNG; ˈkən-/ ▶*n.* [often as *adj.*] the performance of tricks that are seemingly magical, typically involving sleight of hand: *a conjuring trick.*

con·ju·ror /ˈkänjərər; ˈkən-/ (also **con·jur·er**) ▶*n.* a person who conjures. ■ *chiefly Brit.* a performer of conjuring tricks; a magician. ▷Middle English: partly from CONJURE, partly from Old French *conjureor, conjurere,* from medieval Latin *conjurator,* from Latin *conjurare* 'conspire' (see CONJURE).

conk[1] /käNGk; kôNGk/ ▶*v.* [*intrans.*] (**conk out**) *informal* (of a machine) break down: *my car conked out.* ■ (of a person) faint or go to sleep: *he conked out on the rear seat.* ■ die. ▷World War I: of unknown origin.

conk[2] *informal* ▶*v.* [*trans.*] hit (someone) on the head: *the clown conked him and sent him to the hospital with a concussion.*
▶*n.* *Brit.* a person's nose. ■ *dated* a person's head. ▷early 19th cent.: perhaps an alteration of CONCH.

conk[3] ▸*n.* a hairstyle in which curly or kinky hair is straightened.
▸*v.* [*trans.*] straighten curly or kinky hair.

conk·er /ˈkäNGkər/ ▸*n. Brit.* the hard shiny dark brown nut of a horse chestnut tree. ■ (**conkers**) [treated as *sing.*] a children's game in which each child has a conker on the end of a string and takes turns trying to break another's with it. ▹mid 19th cent. (a dialect word denoting a snail shell, with which the game, or a similar form of it, was originally played): perhaps from CONCH, but associated with (and frequently spelled) CONQUER in the 19th and early 20th centuries: an alternative name was *conquerors*.

con man ▸*n. informal* a man who cheats or tricks someone by means of a confidence game.

con mo·to /kän ˈmōtō/ ▸*adv. Music* (esp. as a direction) with movement: *andante con moto.* ▹Italian.

conn /kän/ (also **con**) *Nautical* ▸*v.* [*trans.*] direct the steering of (a ship): *he hadn't conned anything bigger than a Boston whaler.*
▸*n.* (**the conn**) the action or post of conning a ship: *I quickly took the conn and restored the channel course.* ▹early 17th cent.: apparently a weakened form of obsolete *cond* 'conduct, guide,' from Old French *conduire*, from Latin *conducere* (see CONDUCE).

Conn. ▸*abbr.* Connecticut.

Con·nacht /ˈkänôt; kəˈnôt/ (also **Con·naught**) a province in southwestern Republic of Ireland.

con·nate /ˈkän,āt; käˈnāt/ ▸*adj.* **1** (esp. of ideas or principles) existing in a person or thing from birth; innate: *are our ethical values connate?* ■ of the same or similar nature; allied; congenial: *the mother's role is not connate with death and absence.* **2** *Biology* (of parts) united so as to form a single part. **3** *Geology* (of water) trapped in sedimentary rock during its deposition. ▹mid 17th cent.: from late Latin *connatus*, past participle of *connasci*, from *con-* 'together' + *nasci* 'be born.'

con·nat·u·ral /kəˈnaCH(ə)rəl; kä-/ ▸*adj.* belonging naturally; innate: *religion is connatural with man.* ▹late 16th cent.: from late Latin *connaturalis*, from *con-* 'together'+ Latin *naturalis* 'natural.' —**con·nat·u·ral·ly** *adv.*

Con·naught variant spelling of CONNACHT.

con·nect /kəˈnekt/ ▸*v.* [*trans.*] (often **be connected**) bring together or into contact so that a real or notional link is established: *the electrodes were* **connected to** *a recording device | a modem connects computers over a telephone line.* See note at JOIN. ■ join together so as to provide access and communication: *all the buildings are connected by underground passages |* [*intrans.*] *the highway* **connects with** *major routes from all parts of the country.* ■ link to a power or water supply: *your house* **is connected to** *the main cable TV network.* ■ put (someone) into contact by telephone: *I was quickly* **connected to** *the police.* ■ [*intrans.*] (of a train, bus, aircraft, etc.) be timed to arrive at its destination before another train, aircraft, etc., departs so that passengers can transfer from one to the other: *the bus* **connects with** *trains from Union Station.* ■ associate or relate in some respect: *employees are rewarded with bonuses* **connected to** *their firm's performance | a variety of physical complaints* **connected with** *stress.* ■ think of as being linked or related: *I didn't connect the two incidents at the time.* ■ (of a thing) provide or have a link or relationship with (someone or something): *there was no evidence to* **connect** *Jeff* **with** *the theft.* ■ [*intrans.*] form a relationship or feel an affinity: *I taught in a reading program and I* **connected with** *kids individually.* ■ [*intrans.*] *informal* (of a blow) hit the intended target: *the blow connected and he felt a burst of pain.* ▹late Middle English (in the sense 'be united physically'; rare before the 18th cent.): from Latin *connectere*, from *con-* 'together' + *nectere* 'bind.' —**con·nect·a·ble** *adj.* —**con·nect·ed·ly** *adv.* —**con·nect·ed·ness** *n.*

Con·nect·i·cut /kəˈnetəkət/ a state in the northeastern U.S., on the coast of the Atlantic Ocean's Long Island Sound, one of the six New England states; pop. 3,405,565; capital, Hartford; statehood, Jan. 9, 1788 (5). One of the original thirteen states. The Fundamental Orders, adopted by the Connecticut Colony in 1639, is often considered the first democratic constitution in America.

Con·nect·i·cut Riv·er the longest river in New England, flows south for 407 miles (655 km), from northern New Hampshire on the Quebec border, between New Hampshire and Vermont, through western Massachusetts and central Connecticut to Long Island Sound.

con·nect·ing rod ▸*n.* a rod connecting two moving parts in a mechanism, esp. that between the piston and the crankpin (or equivalent parts) in an engine or pump.

con·nec·tion /kəˈnekSHən/ (*Brit.* also **con·nex·ion**) ▸*n.* **1** a relationship in which a person, thing, or idea is linked or associated with something else: *the* **connections between** *social attitudes and productivity | sufferers deny that their problems have any* **connection with** *drugs.* ■ the action of linking one thing with another: *connection to the Internet.* ■ the placing of parts of an electric circuit in contact so that a current may flow. ■ a link between pipes or electrical components: *it is important to ensure that all connections between the wires are properly made.* ■ a link between two telephones: *she replaced the receiver before the connection was made.* ■ an arrangement or opportunity for catching a connecting train, bus, aircraft, etc.: *ferry connections are sporadic in the off season.* ■ such a train, bus, etc.: *we had to wait for our connection to Frankfurt.* ■ (**connections**) people with whom one has social or professional contact or to whom one is related, esp. those with influence and able to offer one help: *he had connections with the music industry.* **2** *informal* a supplier of narcotics: *she introduced Jean to a number of her male drug connections.* ■ a narcotics sale or purchase. **3** *chiefly historical* an association of Methodist churches. ▹late Middle English: from Latin *connexio(n-)*, from *connectere* (see CONNECT). The spelling *-ct* (18th cent.) is from *connect*, on the pattern of pairs such as *collect, collection.* —**con·nec·tion·al** /-SHənl/ *adj.* .
▸*PHRASES* □ **in connection with** with reference to; concerning: *detectives are questioning two men in connection with alleged criminal damage.* □ **in this** (or **that**) **connection** with reference to this (or that): *of value in this connection was the work done by the state police.*

con·nec·tion·ism /kəˈnekSHə,nizəm/ ▸*n.* an artificial intelligence approach to cognition in which multiple connections between nodes (equivalent to brain cells) form a massive interactive network in which many processes take place simultaneously. Certain processes in this network, operating in parallel, are grouped together in hierarchies that bring about results such as thought or action. Also called PARALLEL DISTRIBUTED PROCESSING.

con·nec·tive /kəˈnektiv/ ▸*adj.* connecting: *connective words and phrases.*
▸*n.* something that connects, in particular: ■ *Grammar* a word or phrase whose function is to link linguistic units together. ■ *Zoology* a bundle of nerve fibers connecting two nerve centers or ganglia, esp. in invertebrate animals.

con·nec·tive tis·sue ▸*n. Anatomy* tissue that connects, supports, binds, or separates other tissues or organs, typically having relatively few cells embedded in an amorphous matrix, often with collagen or other fibers, and including cartilaginous, fatty, and elastic tissues.

con·nec·tiv·i·ty /kə,nekˈtivitē/ ▸*n.* the state or extent of being connected or interconnected. ■ *Computing* capacity for the interconnection of platforms, systems, and applications: *connectivity between Sun and Mac platforms.*

con·nect·or /kəˈnektər/ ▸*n.* [often with *adj.*] a thing that links two or more things together: *a pipe connector.* ■ a device for keeping two parts of an electric circuit in contact. ■ a short road or highway that connects two longer roads or highways.

Con·ne·ma·ra /,känəˈmärə; -ˈmarə/ a mountainous coastal region in Galway, in western Republic of Ireland.

Con·ne·ma·ra po·ny (also **Con·ne·ma·ra**) ▸*n.* a pony of a hardy breed originally from Ireland, typically gray.

Con·ne·ry /ˈkänərē/, Sean (1930–), Scottish movie actor; born *Thomas Connery.* He is best known for his portrayal of British agent James Bond in several movies. He won an Academy Award for his role in *The Untouchables* (1987).

con·nex·ion /kəˈnekSHən/ ▸*n.* British spelling of CONNECTION.

conn·ing tow·er ▸*n.* the superstructure of a submarine, from which it can be commanded when on the surface, and containing the periscope.

con·nip·tion /kəˈnipSHən/ ▸*n. informal* a fit of rage or hysterics: *the casting choice gave the writers a conniption.* ▹mid 19th cent.: probably an invented word.

con·niv·ance /kəˈnīvəns/ ▸*n.* willingness to secretly allow or be involved in wrongdoing, esp. an immoral or illegal act: *this infringement of the law had taken place with* **the connivance of** *officials.* ▹late 16th cent. (also in the Latin sense 'winking'): from French *connivence* or Latin *conniventia*, from *connivere* 'shut the eyes (to)' (see CONNIVE).

con·nive /kəˈnīv/ ▸*v.* [*intrans.*] (**connive at/in**) secretly allow (something considered immoral, illegal, wrong, or harmful) to occur: *you have it in your power to connive at my escape.* ■ conspire to do something considered immoral, illegal, or harmful: *the government had* **connived with** *security forces in permitting murder* | [as *adj.*] (**conniving**) *a heartless and conniving woman.* ▹early 17th cent.: from French *conniver* or Latin *connivere* 'shut the eyes (to),' from *con-* 'together' + an unrecorded word related to *nictare* 'to wink.' —**con·niv·er** *n.*

con·niv·ent /kəˈnīvənt/ ▸*adj. Botany* coming into contact; converging and touching but not fused together.

con·nois·seur /,känəˈsər; -ˈsŏŏr/ ▸*n.* an expert judge in matters of taste: *a* **connoisseur of** *music.* ▹early 18th cent.: from obsolete French, from *conoistre* 'know.' —**con·nois·seur·ship** /-,SHip/ *n.*

Con·nol·ly /ˈkän(ə)lē/, Maureen Catherine (1934–69), U.S. tennis player; known as **Little Mo**. She was 16 when she first won the U.S. singles title and 17 when she took the Wimbledon title. In 1953, she became the first woman to win the tennis Grand Slam before being forced to retire in 1954 after a riding accident.

Con·nor /ˈkänər/, Dennis (1942–), U.S. yachtsman. Three-time winner of the America's Cup 1980, 1987, 1988, he is also the first U.S. skipper to lose the cup 1983.

Con·nors /ˈkänərz/, Jimmy (1952–), U.S. tennis player; full name *James Scott Connors.* He won the men's singles title at Wimbledon in 1974 and 1982, at the Australian Open in 1974, and at the U.S. Open five times: 1974, 1976, 1978, 1982, and 1983.

con·no·ta·tion /,känəˈtāSHən/ ▸*n.* an idea or feeling that a word invokes person in addition to its literal or primary meaning: *the word "discipline" has unhappy connotations of punishment and repression.* ■ the implication of such ideas or feelings: *the work functions both by analogy and by connotation.* ■ *Philosophy* the abstract meaning or intension of a term, which forms a principle determining which objects or concepts it applies to. Often contrasted with DENOTATION. ▹mid 16th cent.: from medieval Latin *connotatio(n-)*, from *connotare* 'mark in addition' (see CONNOTE).

con·note /kəˈnōt/ ▸*v.* [*trans.*] (of a word) imply or suggest (an idea or feeling) in addition to the literal or primary meaning: *the term "modern science" usually connotes a complete openness to empirical testing.* ■ (of a fact) imply as a consequence or condition: *in that period a log cabin connoted hard luck.* ▹mid 17th cent.: from medieval Latin *connotare* 'mark in addition,' from *con-* 'together with' + *notare* 'to note' (from *nota* 'a mark'). —**con·no·ta·tive** /ˈkänə,tātiv/ *adj.*

USAGE **Connote** does not mean the same as **denote. Denote** refers to the literal, primary meaning of something; **connote** refers to other characteristics suggested or implied by that thing. Thus, one might say that the word 'mother' **denotes** 'a woman who is a parent' but **connotes** qualities such as 'protection' and 'affection.'

con·nu·bi·al /kəˈn(y)ōōbēəl/ ▸*adj. poetic/literary* of or relating to marriage or the relationship of husband and wife; conjugal: *their connubial bed.* ▹mid 17th cent.: from Latin *connubialis*, from *connubium* 'marriage,' from *con-* 'with' + *nubere* 'marry.' —**con·nu·bi·al·i·ty** /kə,n(y)ōōbēˈalitē/ *n.* —**con·nu·bi·al·ly** *adv.*

co·no·dont /ˈkōnə,dänt/ ▸*n.* (also **conodont animal**) an extinct marine animal of the Cambrian to Triassic periods, having a long wormlike body, numerous small teeth, and a pair of eyes. It is now believed to be the earliest vertebrate. • Class Conodonta, phylum Chordata: numerous families. ■ (also **conodont element**) a tooth of this animal, often found as a fossil. ▹mid 19th cent.: from modern Latin *Conodonta* (plural), from Greek *kōnos* 'cone' + *odous, odont-* 'tooth.'

co·noid /ˈkō,noid/ ▸*adj.* (also **co·noi·dal** /kōˈnoidl/) *chiefly Zoology* approximately conical in shape.
▸*n.* a conoid object.

con·quer /ˈkäNGkər/ ▸*v.* [*trans.*] overcome and take control of (a place or people) by use of military force: *the Magyars conquered Hungary in the Middle Ages.* ■ successfully overcome (a problem or weakness): *a* *fear she never managed to conquer.* ■ climb (a mountain) successfully: *the second American to conquer Everest.* ■ gain the love, admiration, or respect of (a person or group of people): *the Beatles were to leave Liverpool and conquer the world.* ▷Middle English (also in the general sense 'acquire, attain'): from Old French *conquerre*, based on Latin *conquirere* 'gain, win,' from *con-* (expressing completion) + *quaerere* 'seek.' **—con·quer·a·ble** /-k(ə)rəbəl/ *adj.* **—con·quer·or** /-kərər/ *n.*

con·quest /ˈkän,kwest; ˈkäNG-/ ▶*n.* the subjugation and assumption of control of a place or people by use of military force: *the conquest of the Aztecs by the Spanish.* ■ a territory that has been gained in such a way: *colonial conquests.* ■ (**the Conquest**) the invasion and assumption of control of England by William of Normandy in 1066. See also **Norman Conquest**. ■ the overcoming of a problem or weakness: *the conquest of inflation.* ■ a person whose affection or favor has been won: *someone he could display before his friends as his latest conquest.* ▷Middle English: from Old French *conquest(e)*, based on Latin *conquirere* (see **conquer**).

con·quis·ta·dor /kôNGˈkēstə,dôr; känˈk(w)istə-; kən-/ ▶*n.* (*pl.* **-quis·ta·do·res** /-,kēstəˈdôrēz; -ās; -,k(w)istə-/ or **-quis·ta·dors**) a conqueror, esp. one of the Spanish conquerors of Mexico and Peru in the 16th century. ▷mid 19th cent.: Spanish.

Con·rad[1] /ˈkän,rad/, Charles, Jr. (1930–99), U.S. astronaut 1962–73; nickname **Pete**. He commanded the *Apollo 12* lunar mission in 1969, becoming the third man to set foot on the Moon. He was one of a few astronauts that flew four space missions (*Gemini V*, 1965; *Gemini XI*, 1966; *Apollo 12*; and *Skylab*, 1973).

Con·rad[2], Joseph (1857–1924), British novelist; born in Poland; born *Józef Teodor Konrad Korzeniowski*. Much of his work, including his novella *Heart of Darkness* (1902) and the novel *Nostromo* (1904), explores the darkness within human nature. Other notable works include *Lord Jim* (1900) and *Chance* (1913).

Con·roe /ˈkänrō/ a city in eastern Texas, north of Houston; pop. 27,610.

con·san·guine /känˈsaNGgwin/ ▶*adj.* another term for **consanguineous**. **—con·san·guin·e·al** /-,saNGgwəˈnēəl/ *adj.*

con·san·guin·e·ous /,kän,saNGˈgwinēəs/ ▶*adj.* relating to or denoting people descended from the same ancestor: *consanguineous marriages.* ▷early 17th cent.: from Latin *consanguineus* 'of the same blood' (from *con-* 'together' + *sanguis* 'blood') + **-ous**. **—con·san·guin·i·ty** /-ˈgwinitē/ *n.*

con·science /ˈkänCHəns/ ▶*n.* an inner feeling or voice viewed as acting as a guide to the rightness or wrongness of one's behavior: *he had a* ***guilty conscience*** *about his desires | Ben was suffering a pang of conscience.* ▷Middle English (also in the sense 'inner thoughts or knowledge'): via Old French from Latin *conscientia*, from *conscient-* 'being privy to,' from the verb *conscire*, from *con-* 'with' + *scire* 'know.' **—con·science·less** *adj.*

▶*PHRASES* □ **in (good) conscience** by any reasonable standard; by all that is fair: *they have in conscience done all they could.* □ **on one's conscience** weighing heavily and guiltily on one's mind: *an act of providence had prevented him from having a death on his conscience.*

con·science clause ▶*n.* a clause that makes concessions to the consciences of those affected by a law: *Congress passed a "conscience clause" bill, which permitted any individual opposed to abortion to refuse to perform the procedure.*

con·science mon·ey ▶*n.* money paid because of feelings of guilt, esp. about a payment that one has evaded.

con·science-strick·en ▶*adj.* made uneasy by a guilty conscience: *she was still conscience-stricken over her outburst.*

con·sci·en·tious /,känCHēˈenCHəs/ ▶*adj.* (of a person) wishing to do what is right, esp. to do one's work or duty well and thoroughly: *a conscientious and hardworking clerk.* ■ (of work or a person's manner) showing such an attitude: *a conscientious and purposeful look on her face.* ■ relating to a person's conscience: *the act does not provide exemption from service on the basis of personal conscientious beliefs.* ▷early 17th cent.: from French *consciencieux*, from medieval Latin *conscientiosus*, from Latin *conscientia* (see **conscience**). **—con·sci·en·tious·ly** *adv.* **—con·sci·en·tious·ness** *n.*

con·sci·en·tious ob·jec·tor ▶*n.* a person who for reasons of conscience objects to serving in the armed forces. **—con·sci·en·tious ob·jec·tion** *n.*

con·scious /ˈkänCHəs/ ▶*adj.* aware of and responding to one's surroundings; awake. ■ having knowledge of something; aware: *we are* ***conscious of*** *the extent of the problem.* ■ (**conscious of**) painfully aware of; sensitive to: *he was very conscious of his appearance.* ■ concerned with or worried about a particular matter: *they were growing increasingly security-conscious.* ■ (of an action or feeling) deliberate and intentional: *a conscious effort to walk properly.* ■ (of the mind or a thought) directly perceptible to and under the control of the person concerned. ▷late 16th cent. (in the sense 'being aware of wrongdoing'): from Latin *conscius* 'knowing with others or in oneself' (from *conscire* 'be privy to') + **-ous**. **—con·scious·ly** *adv.*

con·scious·ness /ˈkänCHəsnəs/ ▶*n.* the state of being awake and aware of one's surroundings: *she failed to regain consciousness and died two days later.* ■ the awareness or perception of something by a person: *her acute consciousness of Mike's presence.* ■ the fact of awareness by the mind of itself and the world: *consciousness emerges from the operations of the brain.*

con·scious·ness-rais·ing ▶*n.* the activity of seeking to make people more aware of personal, social, or political issues: [as *adj.*] *a consciousness-raising group.*

con·script ▶*v.* /kənˈskript/ [*trans.*] (often **be conscripted**) enlist (someone) compulsorily, typically into the armed services: *they were* ***conscripted into*** *the army.*
▶*n.* /ˈkän,skript/ a person enlisted compulsorily. ▷late 18th cent. (as a noun): from French *conscrit*, from Latin *conscriptus*, past participle of *conscribere* 'enroll.' The verb is a back-formation from **conscription**.

con·scrip·tion /kənˈskripSHən/ ▶*n.* compulsory enlistment for state service, typically into the armed forces. ▷early 19th cent.: via French (conscription was introduced in France in 1798), from late Latin *conscriptio(n-)* 'levying of troops,' from Latin *conscribere* 'write down together, enroll,' from *con-* 'together' + *scribere* 'write.'

con·se·crate /ˈkänsi,krāt/ ▶*v.* [*trans.*] (usu **be consecrated**) make or declare (something, typically a church) sacred; dedicate formally to a religious or divine purpose: *the present Holy Trinity church was consecrated in 1845* | [as *adj.*] (**consecrated**) *consecrated ground.* ■ (in Christian belief) make (bread or wine) into the body or blood of Christ: [as *adj.*] (**consecrated**) *they received the host but not the consecrated wine.* ■ ordain (someone) to a sacred office, typically that of bishop: *in 1969 he was consecrated bishop of Northern Uganda.* ■ *informal* devote (something) exclusively to a particular purpose: *they'd decided to* ***consecrate*** *all their energies* ***to*** *this purposeful act.* ▷late Middle English: from Latin *consecrat-* 'dedicated, devoted as sacred,' from the verb *consecrare*, from *con-* (expressing intensive force) + *sacrare* 'dedicate,' from *sacer* 'sacred.' **—con·se·cra·tion** /,känsiˈkrāSHən/ *n.* **—con·se·cra·tor** /-,krātər/ *n.* **—con·se·cra·to·ry** /-krə,tôrē/ *adj.*

con·sec·u·tive /kənˈsekyətiv/ ▶*adj.* following continuously: *five consecutive months of serious decline.* ■ in unbroken or logical sequence. ■ *Grammar* expressing consequence or result: *a consecutive clause.* ■ *Music* denoting intervals of the same kind (esp. fifths or octaves) occurring in succession between two parts or voices. ▷early 17th cent.: from French *consécutif, -ive*, from medieval Latin *consecutivus*, from Latin *consecut-* 'followed closely,' from the verb *consequi*. **—con·sec·u·tive·ly** *adv.* **—con·sec·u·tive·ness** *n.*

con·sen·su·al /kənˈsenCHo͞oəl/ ▶*adj.* relating to or involving consent, esp. mutual consent: *he admitted to having consensual sex with two women.* ■ relating to or involving consensus: *decision-making was consensual.* ▷mid 18th cent.: from Latin *consensus* 'agreement' (from *consens-* 'felt together, agreed,' from the verb *consentire*) + **-al**. **—con·sen·su·al·ly** *adv.*

con·sen·sus /kənˈsensəs/ ▶*n.* [usu. in *sing.*] general agreement: *a consensus of opinion among judges* | [as *adj.*] *a consensus view.* ▷mid 17th cent.: from Latin, 'agreement,' from *consens-* 'agreed,' from the verb *consentire*.

con·sen·sus se·quence ▶*n.* *Biochemistry* a sequence of DNA having similar structure and function in different organisms.

con·sent /kənˈsent/ ▶*n.* permission for something to happen or agreement to do something: *no change may be made without the consent of all the partners.*
▶*v.* [*intrans.*] give permission for something to happen: *he* ***consented to*** *a search by a detective.* ■ agree to do something: *he had consented to serve on the panel.* ▷Middle English: from Old French *consente* (noun), *consentir* (verb), from Latin *consentire*, from *con-* 'together' + *sentire* 'feel.'

▶*PHRASES* □ **by common consent** with the agreement of all: *it was, by common consent, our finest performance.* □ **informed consent** permission granted in the knowledge of the possible consequences, typically that which is given by a patient to a doctor for treatment with full knowledge of the possible risks and benefits.

con·sen·tient /kənˈsenCHənt/ ▶*adj.* *archaic* of the same opinion in a matter; in agreement. ▷early 17th cent.: from Latin *consentient-* 'agreeing,' from the verb *consentire* (see **consent**).

con·sent·ing a·dult ▶*n.* an adult who willingly agrees to engage in an act, esp. a sexual act.

con·se·quence /ˈkänsikwəns; -,kwens/ ▶*n.* **1** a result or effect of an action or condition: *many have been laid off from work* ***as a consequence*** *of the administration's policies.* **2** [often with *negative*] importance or relevance: *the past is* ***of no consequence*** | *he didn't say anything* ***of great consequence.*** ■ *dated* social distinction: *a woman* ***of consequence.*** ▷late Middle English: via Old French from Latin *consequentia*, from *consequent-* 'following closely,' from the verb *consequi*.

▶*PHRASES* □ **in consequence** as a result. □ **take the consequences** accept responsibility for the negative results of one's action.

con·se·quent /ˈkänsikwənt; -,kwent/ ▶*adj.* following as a result or effect: *labor shortages would be created with a consequent increase in wages.* ■ *Geology* (of a stream or valley) having a direction or character determined by the original slope of the land before erosion. ■ *archaic* logically consistent.
▶*n.* a thing that follows another. ■ *Logic* the second part of a conditional proposition, whose truth is stated to be conditional upon that of the antecedent. ■ *Mathematics* the second term of a ratio. ▷late Middle English: via Old French from Latin *consequent-* 'overtaking, following closely,' from the verb *consequi*.

con·se·quen·tial /,känsəˈkwenCHəl/ ▶*adj.* **1** following as a result or effect: *a loss of confidence and a consequential withdrawal of funds.* ■ *Law* resulting from an act, but not immediately and directly: *consequential damages.* **2** important; significant: *perhaps the most consequential discovery of the eighteenth century.* ▷early 17th cent.: from Latin *consequentia* (see **consequence**) + **-al**. **—con·se·quen·ti·al·i·ty** /,känsə,kwenCHēˈalitē/ *n.* **—con·se·quen·tial·ly** *adv.*

con·se·quen·tial·ism /,känsəˈkwenCHəlizəm/ ▶*n.* *Philosophy* the doctrine that the morality of an action is to be judged solely by its consequences. **—con·se·quen·tial·ist** *adj.* & *n.*

con·se·quent·ly /ˈkänsikwəntlē; -,kwentlē/ ▶*adv.* as a result: *flexible workers find themselves in great demand, and consequently earn high salaries.*

con·serv·an·cy /kənˈsərvənsē/ ▶*n.* (*pl.* **-cies**) **1** [in *names*] a body concerned with the preservation of nature, specific species, or natural resources: *the Nature Conservancy.* ■ *Brit.* a commission or group of officials controlling a port, river, or drainage basin. **2** the conservation of something, esp. wildlife and the environment. ▷mid 18th cent.: alteration of obsolete *conservacy*, from Anglo-Norman French *conservacie*, via Anglo-Latin from Latin *conservation-* (see **conservation**).

con·ser·va·tion /,känsərˈvāSHən/ ▶*n.* the action of conserving something, in particular: ■ preservation, protection, or restoration of the natural environment, natural ecosystems, vegetation, and wildlife. ■ preservation, repair, and prevention of deterioration of archaeological, historical, and cultural sites and artifacts. ■ prevention of excessive or wasteful use of a resource. ■ *Physics* the principle by which the total value of a physical quantity (such as energy, mass, or linear or angular momentum) remains constant in a system. ▷late Middle English (in the general sense 'conserving, preservation'): from Latin *conservatio(n-)*, from the verb *conservare* (see **conserve**). **—con·ser·va·tion·al** /-SHənl/ *adj.*

con·ser·va·tion·ist /,känsərˈvāSHənist/ ▶*n.* a person who advocates or acts for the protection and preservation of the environment and wildlife.

con·ser·va·tion of charge ▶*n.* a principle stating that the total electric charge of an isolated system is fixed.

con·ser·va·tion of en·er·gy ▶*n.* a principle stating that energy cannot be created or destroyed, but can be altered from one form to another.

con·ser·va·tion of mass ▶*n.* a principle stating that mass cannot be created or destroyed.

con·serv·a·tive /kənˈsərvətiv; -və,tiv/ ▶*adj.* holding to traditional attitudes and values and cautious about change or innovation, typically in relation to politics or religion. ■ (of dress or taste) sober and conventional: *a conservative suit.* ■ (of an estimate)

purposely low for the sake of caution: *the film was not cheap—$30,000 is a conservative estimate.* ■ (of surgery or medical treatment) intended to control rather than eliminate a condition, with existing tissue preserved as far as possible. ■ (**Conservative**) of or relating to the Conservative Party of Great Britain or a similar party in another country.
▸*n.* a person who is averse to change and holds to traditional values and attitudes, typically in relation to politics. ■ (**Conservative**) a supporter or member of the Conservative Party of Great Britain or a similar party in another country. ▷late Middle English (in the sense 'aiming to preserve'): from late Latin *conservativus*, from *conservat-* 'conserved,' from the verb *conservare* (see CONSERVE). Current senses date from the mid 19th century onward. —**con·serv·a·tism** /kən'sərvə,tizəm/ *n.* —**con·serv·a·tive·ly** *adv.* —**con·serv·a·tive·ness** *n.*

Con·serv·a·tive Ju·da·ism ▸*n.* a form of Judaism, particularly prevalent in North America, that seeks to preserve Jewish tradition and ritual but has a more flexible approach to the interpretation of the law than Orthodox Judaism.

Con·serv·a·tive Par·ty ▸*n.* a political party promoting free enterprise and private ownership, in particular a major British party that emerged from the old Tory Party in the 1830s and 1840s.

con·ser·va·toire /kən'sərvə,twär/ ▸*n.* another term for CONSERVATORY (sense 1). ▷late 18th cent.: French, from Italian *conservatorio*, from late Latin *conservatorium*, from *conservare* 'to preserve' (see CONSERVE). Compare with CONSERVATORY.

con·ser·va·tor /kən'sərvətər; -,tôr; 'känsər,vātər/ ▸*n.* a person responsible for the repair and preservation of works of art, buildings, or other things of cultural or environmental interest. ■ a guardian or protector: *the court does not need to appoint a conservator to handle an incapacitated person's affairs.*

con·serv·a·to·ry /kən'sərvə,tôrē/ ▸*n.* (*pl.* **-ries**) **1** a college for the study of classical music or other arts. **2** a room with a glass roof and walls, attached to a house at one side and used as a greenhouse or a sun parlor. ▷mid 16th cent. (denoting something that preserves): from late Latin *conservatorium*, from *conservare* 'to preserve' (see CONSERVE).

con·serve ▸*v.* /kən'sərv/ [*trans.*] protect (something, esp. an environmentally or culturally important place or thing) from harm or destruction: *the funds raised will help conserve endangered meadowlands.* ■ prevent the wasteful or harmful overuse of (a resource): *industry should conserve more water.* ■ *Physics* maintain (a quantity such as energy or mass) at a constant overall total. ■ (usu. **be conserved**) *Biochemistry* retain (a particular amino acid, nucleotide, or sequence of these) unchanged in different protein or DNA molecules. ■ preserve (food, typically fruit) with sugar.
▸*n.* /'kän,sərv/ a sweet food made by preserving fruit with sugar; jam. ▷late Middle English: from Old French *conserver* (verb), *conserve* (noun), from Latin *conservare* 'to preserve,' from *con-* 'together' + *servare* 'to keep.'

con·sid·er /kən'sidər/ ▸*v.* [*trans.*] (often **be considered**) think carefully about (something), typically before making a decision: *each application is considered on its merits* | [as *adj.*] (**considered**) *it is my considered opinion that we should await further developments.* ■ think about and be drawn toward (a course of action): *he had considered giving up his job.* ■ regard (someone or something) as having a specified quality: *I consider him irresponsible.* ■ believe; think: *at first women were considered to be at low risk from HIV* | *I don't consider that I'm to blame.* ■ take (something) into account when making an assessment or judgment: *one service area is not enough when you consider the number of cars using this highway.* ■ look attentively at: *he considered the women around the table with wariness.* ▷late Middle English: from Old French *considerer*, from Latin *considerare* 'examine,' perhaps based on *sidus, sider-* 'star.'
▸PHRASE □ **all things considered** taking everything into account.

con·sid·er·a·ble /kən'sidər(ə)bəl; -'sidrəbəl/ ▸*adj.* notably large in size, amount, or extent: *a position of considerable influence.* ■ (of a person) having merit or distinction: *he was a limited, but still considerable, novelist.* ▷late Middle English (in the sense 'capable of being considered'): from medieval Latin *considerabilis* 'worthy of consideration,' from Latin *considerare* (see CONSIDER). —**con·sid·er·a·bly** /-blē/ *adv.*

con·sid·er·ate /kən'sidərət/ ▸*adj.* careful not to cause inconvenience or hurt to others: *the quietest and most considerate tenants possible.* ■ *archaic* showing careful thought: *be considerate over your handwriting.* ▷late 16th cent. (in the sense 'showing careful thought'): from Latin *consideratus*, past participle of *considerare* 'examine' (see CONSIDER). —**con·sid·er·ate·ly** *adv.* —**con·sid·er·ate·ness** *n.*

con·sid·er·a·tion /kən,sidə'rāsHən/ ▸*n.* **1** careful thought, typically over a period of time: *a long process involving a great deal of careful consideration.* ■ a fact or a motive taken into account in deciding or judging something: *the idea was motivated by political considerations.* ■ thoughtfulness and sensitivity toward others: *companies should show more consideration for their employees.* **2** a payment or reward: *you can buy the books for a small consideration.* ■ *Law* (in a contractual agreement) anything given or promised or forborne by one party in exchange for the promise or undertaking of another. **3** *archaic* importance; consequence. ▷late Middle English: via Old French from Latin *consideration-*, from *considerare* 'examine.'
▸PHRASES □ **in consideration of** on account of: *a nightlight burned in consideration of Ernie's phobia.* ■ in return for: *he paid them in consideration of their services.* □ **take into consideration** take into account. □ **under consideration** being thought about: *a bird under consideration for being listed as endangered.*

con·sid·er·ing /kən'sidəriNG/ ▸*prep.* & *conj.* taking into consideration: [as *prep.*] *considering the conditions, it's very good* | [as *conj.*] ***considering that** he was the youngest on the field, he played well.*
▸*adv. informal* taking everything into account: *they weren't feeling too bad, considering.*

con·si·glie·re /,kônsē'lye-re/ ▸*n.* (*pl.* **-ri** /-rē/) an adviser, esp. to a crime boss.

con·sign /kən'sīn/ ▸*v.* [*trans.*] deliver (something) to a person's custody, typically in order for it to be sold: *he **consigned** three paintings **to** Sotheby's.* ■ send (goods) by a public carrier. ■ (**consign someone/something to**) assign; commit decisively or permanently: *she consigned the letter to the wastebasket.* ▷late Middle English (in the sense 'mark with the sign of the cross,' esp. at baptism or confirmation, as a sign of dedication to God): from French *consigner* or Latin *consignare* 'mark with a seal.' —**con·sign·ee** /,känsə'nē; ,kän,sī-'nē; kən,sī'nē/ *n.* —**con·sign·or** /kən'sīnər/ *n.*

con·sign·ment /kən'sīnmənt/ ▸*n.* a batch of goods destined for or delivered to someone: *a consignment of beef.* ■ the action of consigning or delivering something. ■ agreement to pay a supplier of goods after the goods are sold: *new and used children's clothing **on consignment**.*

con·sign·ment shop (or **consignment store**) ▸*n.* a store that sells secondhand items (typically clothing and accessories) on behalf of the original owner, who receives a percentage of the selling price.

con·sil·i·ence /kən'silēəns/ ▸*n.* agreement between the approaches to a topic of different academic subjects, especially science and the humanities. ▷mid 19th cent.: from *con(current)* + Latin *-silient-*, *-siliens* 'jumping' (as in *resilience*). —**con·sil·i·ent** *adj.*

USAGE Though first attested in the 19th century, this word has been largely ignored by smaller dictionaries. The publication in 1998 of Edward O. Wilson's *Consilience* has given it new life.

con·sist ▸*v.* /kən'sist/ [*intrans.*] **1** (**consist of**) be composed or made up of: *the exhibition consists of 180 drawings.* ■ (**consist in**) have as an essential feature: *his duties consist in taking the condition of the barometer.* **2** (**consist with**) *archaic* be consistent with: *the information perfectly consists with our friend's account.*
▸*n. Railroad* ▷late Middle English (in the sense 'be located or inherent in'): from Latin *consistere* 'stand firm or still, exist,' from *con-* 'together' + *sistere* 'stand (still).'

con·sist·ence /kən'sistəns/ ▸*n.* another term for CONSISTENCY.

con·sist·en·cy /kən'sistənsē/ (also **con·sist·ence** /-təns/) ▸*n.* (*pl.* **-cies**) **1** conformity in the application of something, typically that which is necessary for the sake of logic, accuracy, or fairness: *the grading system is to be streamlined to ensure greater consistency.* ■ the achievement of a level of performance that does not vary greatly in quality over time: *his principal problem in tennis has been consistency.* **2** the way in which a substance, typically a liquid, holds together; thickness or viscosity: *the sauce has the consistency of creamed butter.* ▷late 16th cent. (denoting permanence of form): from late Latin *consistentia*, from *consistent-* 'standing firm' (see CONSISTENT).

con·sist·ent /kən'sistənt/ ▸*adj.* (of a person, behavior, or process) unchanging in achievement or effect over a period of time: *manufacturing processes require a consistent approach.* ■ compatible or in agreement with something: *the injuries are **consistent with** falling from a great height.* ■ (of an argument or set of ideas) not containing any logical contradictions: *a consistent explanation.* ▷late 16th cent. (in the sense 'consisting or composed of'): from Latin *consistent-* 'standing firm or still, existing,' from the verb *consistere* (see CONSIST). —**con·sist·ent·ly** *adv.*

con·sis·to·ry /kən'sistərē/ ▸*n.* (*pl.* **-ries**) a church council or court, in particular: ■ (in the Roman Catholic Church) the council of cardinals, with or without the pope. ■ (also **consistory court**) (in the Church of England) a court presided over by a bishop, for the administration of ecclesiastical law in a diocese. ■ (in other churches) a local administrative body. ▷Middle English (originally denoting a nonecclesiastical council): from Anglo-Norman French *consistorie*, from late Latin *consistorium*, from *consistere* 'stand firm' (see CONSIST). —**con·sis·to·ri·al** /,kän,sis'tôrēəl; kən-/ *adj.*

con·so·ci·a·tion /,kän,sōsHē'āsHən; -,sōsē-/ ▸*n.* **1** a group or association of a distinctive type, in particular: ■ a political system formed by the cooperation of different, esp. antagonistic, social groups on the basis of shared power. ■ *Zoology* a group of animals of the same species that interact more or less equally with each other. ■ *dated* an association of Congregational Churches. **2** *dated* close association or fellowship. ▷late 16th cent. (in the sense 'associating, combination'): from Latin *consociatio(n-)*, from the verb *consociare*, from *con-* 'together' + *sociare* 'to associate' (from *socius* 'fellow'). —**con·so·ci·a·tion·al** /-sHənl/ *adj.* —**con·so·ci·a·tion·al·ism** /-sHənl,izəm/ *n.*

con·so·la·tion /,känsə'lāsHən/ ▸*n.* comfort received by a person after a loss or disappointment: *there was consolation in knowing that others were worse off.* ■ a person or thing providing such comfort: *the church was the main consolation in a short and hard life.* ■ *Sports* a round or contest for tournament entrants who have been eliminated before the finals, often to determine third and fourth place. ▷late Middle English: via Old French from Latin *consolatio(n-)*, from the verb *consolari* (see CONSOLE[1]). —**con·sol·a·to·ry** /kən-'sōlə,tôrē/ *adj.*

con·so·la·tion prize ▸*n.* a prize given to a competitor who narrowly fails to win or who finishes last: *two hundred runners-up will get a consolation prize.*

con·sole[1] /kən'sōl/ ▸*v.* [*trans.*] comfort (someone) at a time of grief or disappointment: *she tried to console him but he pushed her gently away* | *you can **console** yourself **with** the thought that you did your best.* ▷mid 17th cent. (replacing earlier *consolate*): from French *consoler*, from Latin *consolari*, from *con-* 'with' + *solari* 'soothe.' —**con·sol·a·ble** *adj.* —**con·sol·er** *n.* —**con·sol·ing·ly** *adv.*

con·sole[2] /'kän,sōl/ ▸*n.* **1** a panel or unit accommodating a set of controls for electronic or mechanical equipment. ■ a cabinet for television or radio equipment. ■ the cabinet or enclosure containing the keyboards, stops, pedals, etc., of an organ. ■ a monitor and keyboard in a multiuser computer system. **2** an ornamented bracket with scrolls or corbel supporting a cornice, shelf, or tabletop. **3** a support between the seats of an automobile that has indentations for holding small items. ▷mid 17th cent. (sense 2): from French, perhaps from *consolider*, from Latin *consolidare* (see CONSOLIDATE).

con·sole ta·ble /'kän,sōl/ ▸*n.* a table supported by ornamented brackets, either movable or fixed against a wall.

con·sol·i·date /kən'sälə,dāt/ ▸*v.* **1** [*trans.*] make (something) physically stronger or more solid: *the first phase of the project is to consolidate the outside walls.* ■ reinforce or strengthen (one's position or power): *the company consolidated its position in the international market.* ■ combine (a number of things) into a single more effective or coherent whole: *all manufacturing activities have been consolidated in new premises.* See note at JOIN. ■ combine (a number of financial accounts or funds) into a single overall account or set of accounts. ■ combine (two or more legal actions involving similar questions) into one for action by a court. **2** [*intrans.*] become stronger or more solid: *the limy sands consolidate to sandy textured limestone.* ▷early 16th cent. (in the sense 'combine into a single whole'): from Latin *consolidare*, from *con-*

Pronunciation Key ə *ago*; ər *over*; 'ə or ,ə *up*; 'ər or ,ər *fur*; a *hat*; ā *rate*; ä *car*; CH *chew*; e *let*; ē *see*; e(ə)r *air*; i *fit*; ī *by*; i(ə)r *ear*; NG *sing*; ō *go*; ô *for*; oi *boy*; o͝o *good*; o͞o *goo*; ou *out*; SH *she*; TH *thin*; <u>TH</u> *then*; (h)w *why*; ZH *vision*

'together' + *solidare* 'make firm' (from *solidus* 'solid'). **—con·sol·i·da·tion** /-,säləˈdāSHən/ *n.* **—con·sol·i·da·tor** /-,dātər/ *n.*

con·som·mé /,känsəˈmā/ ▶*n.* a clear soup made with concentrated stock. ▷French, past participle of *consommer* 'consume or consummate,' from Latin *consummare* 'make complete' (see CONSUMMATE).

con·so·nance /ˈkänsənəns/ ▶*n.* agreement or compatibility between opinions or actions: *consonance between conservation measures and existing agricultural practice.* ■ the recurrence of similar sounds, esp. consonants, in close proximity (chiefly as used in prosody). ■ *Music* the combination of notes that are in harmony with each other due to the relationship between their frequencies. ▷late Middle English: from Old French, or from Latin *consonantia*, from *consonant-* 'sounding together,' from the verb *consonare* (see CONSONANT).

con·so·nant /ˈkänsənənt/ ▶*n.* a basic speech sound in which the breath is at least partly obstructed and which can be combined with a vowel to form a syllable. Contrasted with VOWEL. ■ a letter representing such a sound.
▶*adj.* **1** denoting or relating to such a sound or letter: *a consonant phoneme.* **2** (**consonant with**) in agreement or harmony with: *the findings are consonant with other research.* ■ *Music* making a harmonious interval or chord: *the bass is consonant with all the upper notes.* ▷Middle English (in the sense 'letter representing a consonantal sound'): via Old French from Latin *consonare* 'sound together,' from *con-* 'with' + *sonare* 'to sound' (from *sonus* 'sound'). **—con·so·nan·tal** /,känsəˈnantl/ *adj.* **—con·so·nant·ly** *adv.*

con sor·di·no /kän ,sôrˈdēnō; kōn/ ▶*adv. Music* (esp. as a direction) with the use of a mute. ▷Italian.

con·sort[1] ▶*n.* /ˈkän,sôrt/ a wife, husband, or companion, in particular the spouse of a reigning monarch. ■ a ship sailing in company with another.
▶*v.* /kənˈsôrt; ˈkän,sôrt/ [*intrans.*] (**consort with**) habitually associate with (someone), typically with the disapproval of others: *you chose to consort with the enemy.* ■ (**consort with/to**) *archaic* agree or be in harmony with. ▷late Middle English (denoting a companion or colleague): via French from Latin *consors* 'sharing, partner,' from *con-* 'together with' + *sors, sort-* 'lot, destiny.' The verb senses are probably influenced by similar senses (now obsolete) of the verb *sort*.

con·sort[2] /ˈkän,sôrt/ ▶*n.* a small group of musicians performing together, typically playing instrumental music of the Renaissance period: *a consort of viols.* ▷late 16th cent.: earlier form of CONCERT.

con·sor·ti·um /kənˈsôrSH(ē)əm; -ˈsôrtēəm/ ▶*n.* (*pl.* **-ti·a** /-tēə; -SH(ē)ə/ or **-ti·ums**) **1** an association, typically of several business companies. **2** *Law* the right of association and companionship with one's husband or wife. ▷early 19th cent. (in the sense 'partnership'): from Latin, from *consors* 'sharing, partner' (see CONSORT[1]).

con·spe·cif·ic /,känspəˈsifik/ *Biology* ▶*adj.* (of animals or plants) belonging to the same species.
▶*n.* (usu. **conspecifics**) a member of the same species: *the rabbit was isolated from male conspecifics.* **—con·spec·i·fic·i·ty** /,kän,spesəˈfisitē/ *n.*

con·spec·tus /kənˈspektəs/ ▶*n.* a summary or overview of a subject: *five of his works give a rich conspectus of his art.* ▷mid 19th cent.: from Latin, past participle (used as a noun) of *conspicere* 'look at attentively.'

con·spic·u·ous /kənˈspikyo͞oəs/ ▶*adj.* standing out so as to be clearly visible: *he was very thin, with a conspicuous Adam's apple.* See note at NOTICEABLE. ■ attracting notice or attention: *he showed conspicuous bravery.* ▷mid 16th cent.: from Latin *conspicuus* (from *conspicere* 'look at attentively,' from *con-* (expressing intensive force) + *specere* 'look at') + -OUS. **—con·spi·cu·i·ty** /,känspiˈkyo͞oitē/ *n.* **—con·spic·u·ous·ly** *adv.* **—con·spic·u·ous·ness** *n.*
▶PHRASE □ **conspicuous by one's absence** obviously not present in a place where one should be. [from a speech made by Lord John Russell in an address to electors (1859): taken from Tacitus (*Annals* iii. 76).]

con·spir·a·cist /kənˈspirəsist/ ▶*n.* a person who supports a conspiracy theory.

con·spir·a·cy /kənˈspirəsē/ ▶*n.* (*pl.* **-cies**) a secret plan by a group to do something unlawful or harmful: *a conspiracy to destroy the government.* See note at PLOT. ■ the action of plotting or conspiring: *they were cleared of conspiracy to pervert the course of justice.* ▷late Middle English: from Anglo-Norman French *conspiracie*, alteration of Old French *conspiration*, based on Latin *conspirare* 'agree, plot' (see CONSPIRE).
▶PHRASE □ **a conspiracy of silence** an agreement to say nothing about an issue that should be generally known.

con·spir·a·cy the·o·ry ▶*n.* a belief that some covert but influential organization is responsible for an unexplained event.

con·spir·a·tor /kənˈspirətər/ ▶*n.* a person who takes part in a conspiracy. ▷late Middle English: from Old French *conspirateur*, from Latin *conspirator*, from *conspirat-* 'agreed, plotted,' from the verb *conspirare* (see CONSPIRE). **—con·spir·a·to·ri·al** /kən,spirəˈtôrēəl/ *adj.* **—con·spir·a·to·ri·al·ly** /kən,spirəˈtôrēəlē/ *adv.*

con·spire /kənˈspīr/ ▶*v.* [*intrans.*] make secret plans jointly to commit an unlawful or harmful act: *they* ***conspired against*** *him | they deny conspiring to defraud the Internal Revenue Service.* ■ (of events or circumstances) seem to be working together to bring about a particular result, typically to someone's detriment: *everything conspires to exacerbate the situation.* ▷late Middle English: from Old French *conspirer*, from Latin *conspirare* 'agree, plot,' from *con-* 'together with' + *spirare* 'breathe.'

con spi·ri·to /kän ˈspiri,tō; ˈkōn-/ ▶*adv. Music* (as a direction) vigorously; in a spirited manner.

Con·sta·ble /ˈkänstəbəl/, John (1776–1837), English painter. His early paintings were inspired by the landscape of his native Suffolk.

con·sta·ble /ˈkänstəbəl/ ▶*n.* **1** a peace officer with limited policing authority, typically in a small town. ■ *Brit.* a police officer. **2** the governor of a royal castle. ■ *historical* the highest-ranking official in a royal household. ▷Middle English (sense 2): from Old French *conestable*, from late Latin *comes stabuli* 'count (head officer) of the stable.'

con·stab·u·lar·y /kənˈstabyə,lerē/ ▶*n.* (*pl.* **-lar·ies**) the constables of a district, collectively. ■ an armed police force organized as a military unit. ■ *Brit.* a police force covering a particular area or city.
▶*adj.* of or relating to a constabulary. ▷late 15th cent. (denoting the district under the charge of a constable): from medieval Latin *constabularia (dignitas)* '(rank) of constable,' from *constabulus*, based on Latin *comes stabuli* (see CONSTABLE).

Con·stance, Lake /ˈkänstəns/ a lake in southeastern Germany, on the northern side of the Swiss Alps where Germany, Switzerland, and Austria meet. It forms part of the course of the Rhine River. German name BODENSEE.

con·stan·cy /ˈkänstənsē/ ▶*n.* the quality of being faithful and dependable. ■ the quality of being enduring and unchanging: *the trade winds are noted for constancy in speed and direction.* ▷late 15th cent.: from Latin *constantia*, from *constant-* 'standing firm' (see CONSTANT).

con·stant /ˈkänstənt/ ▶*adj.* occurring continuously over a period of time: *the pain is constant.* ■ remaining the same over a period of time: *the company has kept its prices fairly constant.* ■ (of a person) unchangingly faithful and dependable. See note at RESOLUTE.
▶*n.* a situation or state of affairs that does not change: *the condition of struggle remained a constant.* ■ *Mathematics* a quantity or parameter that does not change its value whatever the value of the variables, under a given set of conditions. ■ *Physics* a number expressing a relation or property that remains the same in all circumstances, or for the same substance under the same conditions. ▷late Middle English (in the sense 'staying resolute or faithful'): from Old French, from Latin *constant-* 'standing firm,' from the verb *constare*, from *con-* 'with' + *stare* 'stand.' The noun senses date from the mid 19th cent. **—con·stant·ly** *adv.*

Con·stan·ţa /kōnˈstäntsə; kôn-/ (also **Con·stan·za**) the chief port of Romania, in the southeastern part of the country, on the Black Sea; pop. 349,000. Formerly called Tomis, it was renamed for Constantine I in the 4th century.

con·stant·an /ˈkänstən,tan/ ▶*n.* a copper–nickel alloy used in electrical work for its high resistance. ▷early 20th cent.: from CONSTANT + -AN.

Con·stan·tine[1] /ˈkänstən,tēn/ a city in northeastern Algeria; pop. 449,000. The capital of the Roman province of Numidia, it was destroyed in 311 but was rebuilt by Constantine the Great and given his name.

Con·stan·tine[2] /ˈkänstən,tēn; -,tīn/ (*c.*274–337), Roman emperor; known as **Constantine the Great**. He was the first Roman emperor to be converted to Christianity and in 324 made Christianity the empire's state religion. In 330, he moved his capital from Rome to Byzantium, renaming it Constantinopolis (Constantinople). He is venerated as a saint in the Orthodox Church.

Con·stan·ti·no·ple /,kän,stantnˈōpəl/ the former name of Istanbul from AD 330 (when it was given its name by Constantine the Great) until the capture of the city by the Turks in 1453.

con·sta·tive /ˈkänstətiv; kənˈstātiv/ *Linguistics* ▶*adj.* denoting a speech act or sentence that is a statement declaring something to be the case. Often contrasted with PERFORMATIVE.
▶*n.* a constative speech act or sentence. ▷early 20th cent.: from Latin *constat-* 'established' (from the verb *constare*) + -IVE.

con·stel·late /ˈkänstəlāt/ ▶*v. poetic/literary* form or cause to form into a cluster or group; gather together: [*intrans.*] *the towns and valleys where people constellate |* [*trans.*] *their stories were never constellated.* ▷mid 17th cent.: from late Latin *constellatus*, from *con-* 'together' + *stellatus* 'arranged like a star.'

con·stel·la·tion /,känstəˈlāSHən/ ▶*n.* a group of stars forming a recognizable pattern that is traditionally named after its apparent form or identified with a mythological figure. Modern astronomers divide the sky into eighty-eight constellations with defined boundaries. ■ a group or cluster of related things: *no two patients ever show exactly the same* ***constellation of*** *symptoms.* ▷Middle English (as an astrological term denoting the relative positions of the "stars" (planets), supposed to influence events): via Old French from late Latin *constellatio(n-)*, based on Latin *stella* 'star.'

con·ster·nate /ˈkänstər,nāt/ ▶*v.* [*trans.*] fill (someone) with anxiety: [as *adj.*] (**consternated**) *you'll probably be consternated by all this talk.* ▷mid 17th cent.: from Latin *consternat-* 'terrified, prostrated,' from the verb *consternare*.

con·ster·na·tion /,känstərˈnāSHən/ ▶*n.* feelings of anxiety or dismay, typically at something unexpected: *I always welcomed clover, much* ***to the consternation of*** *the neighbors.* ▷early 17th cent.: from Latin *consternatio(n-)*, from the verb *consternare* 'lay prostrate, terrify' (see CONSTERNATE).

con·sti·pat·ed /ˈkänstə,pātid/ ▶*adj.* (of a person or animal) affected with constipation. ■ *figurative* slow-moving; restricted or inhibited in some way: *spontaneous girls like Ellen are never going to be intimate with constipated deadpan fellows like me.* ▷mid 16th cent.: from Latin *constipat-* 'crowded or pressed together,' from the verb *constipare*, from *con-* 'together' + *stipare* 'press, cram.' **—con·sti·pate** /-,pāt/ *v.*

con·sti·pa·tion /,känstəˈpāSHən/ ▶*n.* a condition in which there is difficulty in emptying the bowels, usually associated with hardened feces. ■ *figurative* a high level of constraint or restriction; a pronounced lack of ease: *literary constipation.* ▷late Middle English (in the sense 'contraction of body tissues'): from late Latin *constipatio(n-)*, from the verb *constipare* (see CONSTIPATED).

con·stit·u·en·cy /kənˈstiCHo͞oənsē/ ▶*n.* (*pl.* **-cies**) a body of voters in a specified area who elect a representative to a legislative body: *the politician who wishes to remain in the good graces of his constituency.* ■ *chiefly Brit.* the area represented in this way. ■ a body of customers or supporters: *a constituency of racing fans.*

con·stit·u·ent /kənˈstiCHo͞oənt/ ▶*adj.* **1** being a part of a whole: *the constituent minerals of the rock.* **2** being a voting member of a community or organization and having the power to appoint or elect: *the constituent body has a right of veto.* ■ able to make or change a political constitution: *a constituent assembly.*
▶*n.* **1** a member of a constituency. **2** a component part of something: *the essential constituents of the human diet.* ■ *Linguistics* the common part of two or several more complex forms, e.g., *gentle* in *gentleman, gentlemanly, ungentlemanly.* ■ *Linguistics* a word or construction that is part of a larger construction. ▷late 15th cent. (in the legal sense of the noun): from Latin *constituent-* (partly via French *constituant*) 'establishing, appointing,' from the verb *constituere* (see CONSTITUTE).

con·sti·tute /ˈkänstə,t(y)o͞ot/ ▶*v.* [*trans.*] **1** be (a part) of a whole: *single parents constitute a great proportion of the poor.* ■ (of people or things) combine to form (a whole): *there were enough members present to constitute a quorum.* ■ be or be equivalent to (something): *his failure to act constituted a breach of duty.* **2** (usu. **be constituted**) give legal or constitutional form to (an institution); establish by law. ▷late Middle English: from Latin *constitut-* 'established, appointed,' from the verb *constituere*, from *con-* 'together' + *statuere* 'set up.'

con·sti·tu·tion /,känstəˈt(y)o͞oSHən/ ▶*n.* **1** a body of fundamental principles or established precedents according to which a state or other organization is acknowledged to be governed. ■ a written record of this: *the preamble to the constitution of UNESCO.* ■ (**the Constitution**) the basic written set of principles and precedents of federal government in the U.S., which came into operation in 1789 and has since been modified by twenty-seven amendments. **2** the composition of something: *the genetic constitution of a species.* ■ the forming or establishing of something: *the constitution of a police authority.* **3** a person's physical state with regard to vitality, health, and strength: *pregnancy had weakened her constitution.* ■ a person's mental or psychological makeup. ▷Middle English (denoting a law, or a body of laws or customs): from Latin *constitutio(n-)*, from *constituere* 'establish, appoint' (see CONSTITUTE).

con·sti·tu·tion·al /ˌkänstəˈt(y)o͞oSHənl/ ▸*adj.* **1** of or relating to an established set of principles governing a state: *a constitutional amendment.* ■ in accordance with or allowed by such principles: *a constitutional monarchy.* **2** of or relating to someone's physical or mental condition: *a constitutional weakness.*
▸*n. dated* a walk, typically one taken regularly to maintain or restore good health. —**con·sti·tu·tion·al·i·ty** /-ˌt(y)o͞oSHəˈnalitē/ *n.* —**con·sti·tu·tion·al·ly** *adv.*

con·sti·tu·tion·al·ism /ˌkänstəˈt(y)o͞oSHənl-izəm/ ▸*n.* constitutional government. ■ adherence to such a system of government. —**con·sti·tu·tion·al·ist** *n.*

con·sti·tu·tion·al·ize /ˌkänstəˈt(y)o͞oSHənl-īz/ ▸*v.* [*trans.*] make subject to explicit provisions of a country's constitution: *divorce is not constitutionalized.*

Con·sti·tu·tion State a nickname for the state of CONNECTICUT.

con·sti·tu·tive /ˈkänstəˌt(y)o͞otiv; kənˈstiCHətiv/ ▸*adj.* **1** having the power to establish or give organized existence to something: *the state began to exercise a new and constitutive function.* **2** forming a part or constituent of something; component: *poverty is a constitutive element of a particular form of economic growth.* ■ forming an essential element of something: *language is* ***constitutive of*** *thought.* **3** *Biochemistry* relating to an enzyme or enzyme system that is continuously produced in an organism, regardless of the needs of cells. —**con·sti·tu·tive·ly** *adv.*

con·strain /kənˈstrān/ ▸*v.* [*trans.*] (often **be constrained**) severely restrict the scope, extent, or activity of: *agricultural development is considerably constrained by climate | we can constrain data access.* ■ compel or force (someone) toward a particular course of action: *children are constrained to work in the way the book dictates.* ■ [usu. as *adj.*] (**constrained**) cause to appear unnaturally forced, typically because of embarrassment: *he was acting in a constrained manner.* ■ *poetic/literary* confine forcibly; imprison. ■ *archaic* bring about (something) by compulsion: *Calypso in her caves constrained his stay.* See note at COMPEL. ▷Middle English: from Old French *constraindre*, from Latin *constringere* 'bind tightly together.' —**con·strain·ed·ly** /-nədlē/ *adv.*

con·straint /kənˈstrānt/ ▸*n.* a limitation or restriction: *the availability of water is the main* ***constraint on*** *food production | time constraints make it impossible to do everything.* ■ stiffness of manner and inhibition in relations between people: *they would be able to talk without constraint.* ▷late Middle English (in the sense 'coercion'): from Old French *constreinte*, feminine past participle of *constraindre* (see CONSTRAIN).

con·strict /kənˈstrikt/ ▸*v.* [*trans.*] make narrower, esp. by encircling pressure: *chemicals that constrict the blood vessels |* [as *adj.*] (**constricted**) *constricted air passages.* ■ [*intrans.*] become narrower: *he felt his throat constrict.* ■ (of a snake) coil around (prey) in order to asphyxiate it. ■ *figurative* restrict: *the fear and the reality of crime constrict many people's lives.* ▷mid 18th cent.: from Latin *constrict-* 'bound tightly together,' from the verb *constringere* (see CONSTRAIN). —**con·stric·tion** /-ˈstrikSHən/ *n.* —**con·stric·tive** /-tiv/ *adj.*

con·stric·tor /kənˈstriktər/ ▸*n.* **1** a snake that kills by coiling around its prey and asphyxiating it. • Families Boidae and Pythonidae, and some members of other families (in particular Colubridae). **2** (also **constrictor muscle**) *Anatomy* a muscle whose contraction narrows a vessel or passage. ■ each of the muscles that constrict the pharynx. ▷early 18th cent.: modern Latin, from *constrict-* 'bound tightly together,' from the verb *constringere* (see CONSTRAIN).

con·struct ▸*v.* /kənˈstrəkt/ [*trans.*] build or erect (something, typically a building, road, or machine): *a company that constructs oil rigs.* ■ form (an idea or theory) by bringing together various conceptual elements, typically over a period of time: *Ptolemy combined his interests to construct a theory in support of Aristotle.* ■ *Grammar* form (a sentence) according to grammatical rules. ■ *Geometry* draw or delineate (a geometric figure) accurately to given conditions.
▸*n.* /ˈkänˌstrəkt/ an idea or theory containing various conceptual elements, typically one considered to be subjective and not based on empirical evidence: *history is largely an ideological construct.* ■ *Linguistics* a group of words forming a phrase. ■ a physical thing that is deliberately built or formed. ▷late Middle English: from Latin *construct-* 'heaped together, built,' from the verb *construere*, from *con-* 'together' + *struere* 'pile, build.' —**con·struct·i·ble** *adj.* —**con·struc·tor** /-tər/ *n.*

con·struc·tion /kənˈstrəkSHən/ ▸*n.* the building of something, typically a large structure: *there was a skyscraper* ***under construction.*** ■ such activity considered as an industry. ■ the style or method used in the building of something: *the mill is of brick construction.* ■ a building or other structure. ■ the creation or formation of an abstract entity: *language plays a large part in our construction of reality.* ■ an interpretation or explanation: *you could* ***put*** *an honest* ***construction upon*** *their conduct.* ■ *Grammar* the arrangement of words according to syntactical rules: *sentence construction.* ▷late Middle English: via Old French from Latin *constructio(n-)*, from *construere* 'heap together' (see CONSTRUCT). —**con·struc·tion·al** /-SHənl/ *adj.* —**con·struc·tion·al·ly** /-SHənl-ē/ *adv.*

con·struc·tion·ism /kənˈstrəkSHəˌnizəm/ ▸*n.* another term for CONSTRUCTIVISM.

con·struc·tion·ist /kənˈstrəkSHənist/ ▸*n.* **1** another term for CONSTRUCTIVIST (see CONSTRUCTIVISM). **2** a person who puts a particular construction upon a legal document, esp. the U.S. Constitution. —**con·struc·tion·ism** *n.*

con·struc·tive /kənˈstrəktiv/ ▸*adj.* **1** serving a useful purpose; tending to build up: *constructive criticism.* **2** *Law* derived by inference; implied by operation of law; not obvious or explicit: *constructive liability.* **3** *Mathematics* relating to, based on, or denoting mathematical proofs that show how an entity may in principle be constructed or arrived at in a finite number of steps. ▷mid 17th cent. (sense 2): from late Latin *constructivus*, from Latin *construct-* 'heaped together,' from the verb *construere* (see CONSTRUCT). —**con·struc·tive·ly** *adv.* —**con·struc·tive·ness** *n.*

con·struc·tiv·ism /kənˈstrəktiˌvizəm/ ▸*n.* **1** *Art* a style or movement in which assorted mechanical objects are combined into abstract mobile structural forms. The movement originated in Russia in the 1920s and has influenced many aspects of modern architecture and design. [transliterating Russian *konstruktivizm*.] **2** *Mathematics* a view which admits as valid only constructive proofs and entities demonstrable by them, implying that the latter have no independent existence. —**con·struc·tiv·ist** *n.*

con·strue /kənˈstro͞o/ ▸*v.* (**-strues, -strued, -stru·ing**) [*trans.*] (often **be construed**) interpret (a word or action) in a particular way: *his words could hardly be* ***construed as*** *an apology.* See note at CLARIFY. ■ *dated* analyze the syntax of (a text, sentence, or word): *both verbs can be* ***construed with*** *either infinitive.* ■ *dated* translate (a passage or author) word for word, typically aloud. ▷late Middle English: from Latin *construere* (see CONSTRUCT), in late Latin 'analyze the construction of a sentence.' —**con·stru·a·ble** *adj.* —**con·stru·al** /-ˈstro͞oəl/ *n.*

con·sub·stan·tial /ˌkänsəbˈstanCHəl/ ▸*adj.* of the same substance or essence (used esp. of the three persons of the Trinity in Christian theology): *Christ is* ***consubstantial with*** *the Father.* ▷late Middle English: from ecclesiastical Latin *consubstantialis* (translating Greek *homoousios* 'of one substance'), from *con-* 'with' + *substantialis* (see SUBSTANTIAL). —**con·sub·stan·ti·al·i·ty** /-ˌstanCHēˈalətē/ *n.*

con·sub·stan·ti·a·tion /ˌkänsəbˌstanCHēˈāSHən/ ▸*n.* *Christian Theology* the doctrine, esp. in Lutheran belief, that the substance of the bread and wine coexists with the body and blood of Christ in the Eucharist. Compare with TRANSUBSTANTIATION. ▷late 16th cent.: from modern Latin *consubstantiatio(n-)*, from *con-* 'together,' on the pattern of *transubstantiation-* 'transubstantiation.'

con·sue·tude /ˈkänswiˌt(y)o͞od/ ▸*n.* an established custom, esp. one having legal force. ▷late Middle English: from Old French, or from Latin *consuetudo* (see CUSTOM). —**con·sue·tu·di·nar·y** /ˌkänswiˈt(y)o͞odn-ˌerē/ *adj.*

con·sul /ˈkänsəl/ ▸*n.* **1** an official appointed by a government to live in a foreign city and protect and promote the government's citizens and interests there. **2** (in ancient Rome) one of the two annually elected chief magistrates who jointly ruled the republic. ■ any of the three chief magistrates of the first French republic (1799–1804). ▷late Middle English (denoting an ancient Roman magistrate): from Latin, related to *consulere* 'take counsel.' —**con·su·lar** /ˈkäns(y)ələr/ *adj.* —**con·sul·ship** /-ˌSHip/ *n.*

con·su·late /ˈkänsələt/ ▸*n.* **1** the place or building in which a consul's duties are carried out. ■ the office, position, or period of office of a consul. **2** *historical* the period of office of a Roman consul. ■ (**the consulate**) the system of government by consuls in ancient Rome. **3** (**the Consulate**) the government of the first French republic (1799–1804) by three consuls. ▷late Middle English (denoting the government of Rome by consuls, or their office or dignity): from Latin *consulatus*, from *consul* (see CONSUL).

con·sul gen·er·al ▸*n.* (*pl.* **con·suls gen·er·al**) a consul of the highest status, stationed in a major city and supervising other consuls in the district..

con·sult /kənˈsəlt/ ▸*v.* [*trans.*] seek information or advice from (someone with expertise in a particular area): *you should consult a financial advisor.* ■ have discussions or confer with (someone), typically before undertaking a course of action: *patients are entitled to be consulted about their treatment |* [*intrans.*] *they've got to* ***consult with*** *their board of directors.* ■ refer for information to (a book, watch, etc.) in order to ascertain something: *consult the index at the back of the brochure.* ▷early 16th cent. (in the sense 'deliberate together, confer'): from French *consulter*, from Latin *consultare*, frequentative of *consulere* 'take counsel.' —**con·sul·ta·tive** /-ˈsəltətiv/ *adj.*

con·sult·an·cy /kənˈsəltnsē/ ▸*n.* (*pl.* **-cies**) a professional practice that gives expert advice within a particular field, esp. business:| *a management consultancy firm.* ■ the work of giving such advice.

con·sult·ant /kənˈsəltnt/ ▸*n.* **1** a person who provides expert advice professionally. **2** [usu. as *adj.*] *Brit.* a hospital doctor of senior rank within a specific field: *a consultant pediatrician.* ▷late 17th cent. (in the sense 'a person who consults'): probably from French, from Latin *consultare* (see CONSULT).

con·sul·ta·tion /ˌkänsəlˈtāSHən/ ▸*n.* the action or process of formally consulting or discussing: *they improved standards* ***in consultation with*** *consumer representatives | consultations between the two governments.* ■ a meeting with an expert or professional, such as a medical doctor, in order to seek advice. ▷late Middle English: from Latin *consultatio(n-)*, from the verb *consultare* (see CONSULT).

con·sult·ing /kənˈsəltiNG/ ▸*adj.* (of a senior person in a professional or technical field) engaged in the business of giving advice to others working in the same field: *a consulting engineer.* ■ (of a business or company) giving specialist advice: *an environmental consulting company.*
▸*n.* the business of giving specialist advice to other professionals, typically in financial and business matters.

con·sult·ing room ▸*n.* a room in which a doctor or other therapeutic practitioner examines patients.

con·sum·a·ble /kənˈso͞oməbəl/ ▸*adj.* (of an item for sale) intended to be used up and then replaced.
▸*n.* (usu. **consumables**) a commodity that is intended to be used up relatively quickly: *drugs and other medical consumables.*

con·sume /kənˈso͞om/ ▸*v.* [*trans.*] eat, drink, or ingest (food or drink): *people consume a good deal of sugar in drinks.* ■ buy (goods or services). ■ use up (a resource): *these machines consume 5 percent of the natural gas in the U.S.* ■ (esp. of a fire) completely destroy: *the fire spread rapidly, consuming many homes.* ■ (usu. **be consumed**) (of a feeling) absorb all of the attention and energy of (someone): *Carolyn was consumed with guilt |* [as *adj.*] (**consuming**) *a consuming passion.* ▷late Middle English: from Latin *consumere*, from *con-* 'altogether' + *sumere* 'take up'; reinforced by French *consumer.* —**con·sum·ing·ly** *adv.*

con·sum·er /kənˈso͞omər/ ▸*n.* a person who purchases goods and services for personal use: [as *adj.*] *consumer demand.* ■ a person or thing that eats or uses something: *Scandinavians are the largest consumers of rye.*

con·sum·er goods ▸*plural n.* goods bought and used by consumers, rather than by manufacturers for producing other goods. Often contrasted with CAPITAL GOODS.

Pronunciation Key ə *ago*; ər *over*; ˈə *or* ˌə *up*; ˈər *or* ˌər *fur*; a *hat*; ā *rate*; ä *car*; CH *chew*; e *let*; ē *see*; e(ə)r *air*; i *fit*; ī *by*; i(ə)r *ear*; NG *sing*; ō *go*; ô *for*; oi *boy*; o͝o *good*; o͞o *goo*; ou *out*; SH *she*; TH *thin*; T͟H *then*; (h)w *why*; ZH *vision*

C

con·sum·er·ism /kən'so͞omə,rizəm/ ▶*n.* **1** the protection or promotion of the interests of consumers. **2** *often derogatory* the preoccupation of society with the acquisition of consumer goods. —**con·sum·er·ist** *adj.* & *n.* —**con·sum·er·is·tic** /kən,so͞omə'ristik/ *adj.*

con·sum·er price in·dex (abbr.: **CPI**) ▶*n.* an index of the variation in prices paid by typical consumers for retail goods and other items.

con·sum·er re·search ▶*n.* the investigation of the needs and opinions of consumers, esp. with regard to a particular product or service.

con·sum·er so·ci·e·ty ▶*n. often derogatory* a society in which the buying and selling of goods and services is the most important social and economic activity.

con·sum·er sov·er·eign·ty ▶*n. Economics* the situation in an economy where the desires and needs of consumers control the output of producers.

con·sum·mate ▶*v.* /'känsə,māt/ [*trans.*] make (a marriage or relationship) complete by having sexual intercourse: *his first wife refused to consummate their marriage.* ■ complete (a transaction or attempt); make perfect: *his scheme of colonization was consummated through bloodshed.*
▶*adj.* /'känsəmət; kən'səmət/ showing a high degree of skill and flair; complete or perfect: *she dressed with consummate elegance.* ▷late Middle English (as an adjective in the sense 'completed, accomplished'): from Latin *consummat-* 'brought to completion,' from the verb *consummare*, from *con-* 'altogether' + *summa* 'sum total,' feminine of *summus* 'highest, supreme.' —**con·sum·mate·ly** /'känsəmətlē; kən 'səmətlē/ *adv.* —**con·sum·ma·tor** /'känsə,mātər/ *n.*

con·sum·ma·tion /,känsə'māsнən/ ▶*n.* the point at which something is complete or finalized: ***the consummation of** a sale.* ■ the action of making a marriage or relationship complete by having sexual intercourse: *the eager consummation that follows a long and passionate seduction.* ▷late Middle English: from Latin *consummatio(n-)*, from the verb *consummare* (see **CONSUMMATE**).

con·sump·tion /kən'səm(p)sнən/ ▶*n.* **1** the using up of a resource: *industrialized countries should reduce their energy consumption.* ■ the eating, drinking, or ingesting of something: *liquor is sold for consumption off the premises.* ■ an amount of something that is used up or ingested: *a daily consumption of 15 cigarettes.* ■ the purchase and use of goods and services by the public: *an article for mass consumption.* ■ the reception of information or entertainment, esp. by a mass audience: *his confidential speech was not meant for public consumption.* **2** *dated* a wasting disease, esp. pulmonary tuberculosis. ▷late Middle English: from Latin *consumptio(n-)*, from the verb *consumere* (see **CONSUME**).

con·sump·tive /kən'səm(p)tiv/ ▶*adj.* **1** *dated* affected with a wasting disease, esp. pulmonary tuberculosis: *from birth he was sickly and consumptive.* **2** *chiefly derogatory* of or relating to the using up of resources: *tourism represents an insidious form of consumptive activity.*
▶*n. dated* a person with a wasting disease, esp. pulmonary tuberculosis. ▷mid 17th cent.: from medieval Latin *consumptivus*, from Latin *consumpt-* 'consumed,' from the verb *consumere* (see **CONSUME**). —**con·sump·tive·ly** *adv.*

cont. ▶*abbr.* ■ contents. ■ continued.

con·tact ▶*n.* /'kän,takt/ **1** the state or condition of physical touching: *the tennis ball is **in contact with** the court surface for as little as 5 milliseconds.* ■ the state or condition of communicating or meeting: *Lewis and Clark **came into contact with** numerous river tribes | he had **lost contact with** his friends.* ■ [as *adj.*] activated by or operating through physical touch: *contact dermatitis.* ■ a connection for the passage of an electric current from one thing to another, or a part or device by which such a connection is made: *a one-way electrical contact between a metal and a semiconductor.* ■ (**contacts**) contact lenses. **2** a meeting, communication, or relationship with someone: *they have forged contacts with key people in business.* ■ a person who may be communicated with for information or assistance, esp. with regard to one's job: *Francie had good contacts.* ■ a person who has associated with a patient with a contagious disease (and so may carry the infection).
▶*v.* /'kän,takt; kən'takt/ [*trans.*] communicate with (someone), typically in order to give or receive specific information. ▷early 17th cent.: from Latin *contactus*, from *contact-* 'touched, grasped, bordered on,' from the verb *contingere*, from *con-* 'together with' + *tangere* 'to touch.' —**con·tact·a·ble** /'kän,taktəbəl; kən'tak-/ *adj.*

con·tact cen·ter ▶*n.* an integrated and usually automated communications system that coordinates all telephone and electronic contacts between an organization and the public.

con·tact·ee /,kän,tak'tē; kən-/ ▶*n.* a person who claims to have been contacted by alien beings, esp. through an abduction.

con·tact flight (also **contact flying**) ▶*n.* navigation of an aircraft by the observation of landmarks.

con·tact lens ▶*n.* a thin plastic lens placed directly on the surface of the eye to correct visual defects.

con·tact met·a·mor·phism ▶*n. Geology* metamorphism due to contact with or proximity to an igneous intrusion.

con·tac·tor /'kän,taktər; kən'tak-/ ▶*n.* a device for making and breaking an electric circuit.

con·tact per·son ▶*n.* a person who provides a link for information or representation between two parties.

con·tact print ▶*n.* a photographic print made by placing a negative directly onto sensitized paper, glass, or film and illuminating it.
▶*v.* (**con·tact-print**) [*trans.*] make a photograph from (a negative) in this way.

con·tact proc·ess ▶*n.* the major industrial process used to make sulfuric acid, by oxidizing sulfur dioxide in the presence of a solid catalyst and absorbing the resulting sulfur trioxide in water.

con·tact sheet ▶*n.* a piece of photographic paper onto which several or all of the negatives on a roll of film have been contact printed.

con·tact sport ▶*n.* a sport in which the participants necessarily come into bodily contact with one another.

con·ta·di·na /,käntə'dēnə/ ▶*n.* (*pl.* **-di·ne** /-'dē,nā/ or **-di·nas**) an Italian peasant girl or peasant woman. ▷Italian.

con·ta·di·no /,käntə'dēnō/ ▶*n.* (*pl.* **-di·ni** /-'dēnē/ or **-di·nos**) an Italian peasant or rustic. ▷Italian, from *contado*, denoting the peasant population around a city.

Con·ta·gem /,kōntə'zнäm/ a city in Minas Gerais state in southeastern Brazil, west of Belo Horizonte; pop. 491,000.

con·ta·gion /kən'tājən/ ▶*n.* the communication of disease from one person to another by close contact: *the rooms held no risk of contagion.* ■ a disease spread in such a way. ■ *figurative* the spreading of a harmful idea or practice: *the contagion of disgrace.* ■ a contagium. ▷late Middle English (denoting a contagious disease): from Latin *contagio(n-)*, from *con-* 'together with' + the base of *tangere* 'to touch.'

con·ta·gious /kən'tājəs/ ▶*adj.* (of a disease) spread from one person or organism to another by direct or indirect contact: *a contagious infection.* ■ (of a person or animal) likely to transmit a disease by contact with other people or animals. ■ *figurative* (of an emotion, feeling, or attitude) likely to spread to and affect others: *her enthusiasm is contagious.* ▷late Middle English: from late Latin *contagiosus*, from *contagio* (see **CONTAGION**). —**con·ta·gious·ly** *adv.* —**con·ta·gious·ness** *n.*

USAGE In practice, there is little or no difference in meaning between **contagious** and **infectious** when applied to disease: both mean, roughly, 'communicable.' There is, however, a difference in emphasis or focus between the two words. **Contagious** tends to be focused on the person or animal affected by the disease (*precautions are taken with anyone who seems contagious*), while **infectious** emphasizes the agent or organism that carries the disease. In figurative, nontechnical senses, **contagious** may describe the spread of things good or bad, such as laughter and merriment, or corruption, violence, panic, etc.: *the chief's paranoia had a contagious effect on the officers.* **Infectious**, in figurative senses, usually refers to the spread of only pleasant, positive things, such as good humor or optimism: *Sharon's infectious enthusiasm for the project attracted many volunteers.*

con·ta·gium /kən'tājəm; -jēəm/ ▶*n.* (*pl.* **-gi·a** /-jə; -jēə/) a substance or agent, such as a virus, by which a contagious disease is transmitted.

con·tain /kən'tān/ ▶*v.* [*trans.*] **1** have or hold (someone or something) within: *coffee cans that once contained a full pound of coffee.* ■ be made up of (a number of things); consist of: *borscht can contain mainly beets or a number of vegetables.* ■ (of a number) be divisible by (a factor) without a remainder. **2** control or restrain (oneself or a feeling): *she was scarcely able to contain herself as she waited to spill the beans.* ■ prevent (a severe problem) from increasing in extent or intensity: *a new western policy to contain the conflict in Bosnia.* ▷Middle English: from Old French *contenir*, from Latin *continere*, from *con-* 'altogether' + *tenere* 'to hold.' —**con·tain·a·ble** *adj.*

con·tain·er /kən'tānər/ ▶*n.* an object that can be used to hold or transport something: *a microwaveable glass container.* ■ a large metal box of a standard design and size used for the transportation of goods by road, rail, sea, or air: *a container ship.*

con·tain·er·ize /kən'tānə,rīz/ ▶*v.* [*trans.*] [usu. as *adj.*] (**containerized**) pack into or transport by container: *containerized cargo.* —**con·tain·er·i·za·tion** /-,tānərə'zāsнən/ *n.*

con·tain·er port ▶*n.* a port that specializes in handling goods transported in containers.

con·tain·er ship ▶*n.* a ship that is designed to carry goods stowed in containers.

con·tain·ment /kən'tānmənt/ ▶*n.* the action of keeping something harmful under control or within limits: *the containment of the AIDS epidemic.* ■ the action or policy of preventing the expansion of a hostile country or influence: *the U.S. government saw the containment of communism as a global task.*

con·tam·i·nate /kən'tamə,nāt/ ▶*v.* [*trans.*] (often **be contaminated**) make (something) impure by exposure to or addition of a poisonous or polluting substance: *the site was found to be contaminated by radioactivity | figurative the entertainment industry is able to contaminate the mind of the public |* [as *adj.*] (**contaminated**) *contaminated blood products.* See note at **POLLUTE**. ▷late Middle English: from Latin *contaminat-* 'made impure,' from the verb *contaminare*, from *contamen* 'contact, pollution,' from *con-* 'together with' + the base of *tangere* 'to touch.' —**con·tam·i·nant** /-'tamənənt/ *n.* —**con·tam·i·na·tion** /-,tamə'nāsнən/ *n.* —**con·tam·i·na·tor** /-,nātər/ *n.*

con·te /kônt/ ▶*n.* a short story as a form of literary composition. ■ a medieval narrative tale. ▷French, based on Latin *computare* 'reckon, sum up.'

con·té /kôn'tā/ (also *trademark* **Con·té**) ▶*n.* a kind of hard, grease-free crayon used as a medium for artwork: *powerful drawings in rough red conté.* ▷mid 19th cent.: named after Nicolas J. Conté (1755–1805), the French inventor who developed it.

con·temn /kən'tem/ ▶*v.* [*trans.*] *archaic* treat or regard with contempt. ▷late Middle English: from Latin *contemnere*, from *con-* (expressing intensive force) + *temnere* 'despise.' —**con·temn·er** /-'tem(n)ər/ *n.*

con·tem·plate /'käntəm,plāt/ ▶*v.* [*trans.*] look thoughtfully for a long time at: *he sat on the carpet contemplating his image in the mirrors.* ■ think about: *the results of a trade war are too horrifying to contemplate.* ■ [*intrans.*] think profoundly and at length; meditate: *he sat morosely contemplating.* ■ have in mind as a probable though not certain intention: *she was contemplating a gold mining venture.* ▷late 16th cent.: from Latin *contemplat-* 'surveyed, observed, contemplated,' from the verb *contemplari*, based on *templum* 'place for observation.' —**con·tem·pla·tor** /-,plātər/ *n.*

con·tem·pla·tion /,käntəm'plāsнən/ ▶*n.* the action of looking thoughtfully at something for a long time: *the road is too busy for leisurely contemplation of the scenery.* ■ deep reflective thought: *he would retire to his room for study or contemplation.* ■ the state of being thought about or planned. ■ religious meditation. ■ (in Christian spirituality) a form of prayer or meditation in which a person seeks to pass beyond mental images and concepts to a direct experience of the divine. ▷Middle English: from Old French, from Latin *contemplatio(n-)*, from the verb *contemplari* (see **CONTEMPLATE**).

con·tem·pla·tive /kən'templətiv/ ▶*adj.* expressing or involving prolonged thought: *she regarded me with a contemplative eye.* ■ involving or given to deep silent prayer or religious meditation: *contemplative knowledge of God.*
▶*n.* a person whose life is devoted primarily to prayer, esp. in a monastery or convent. —**con·tem·pla·tive·ly** *adv.*

con·tem·po·ra·ne·ous /kən,tempə'rānēəs/ ▶*adj.* existing or occurring in the same period of time: *Pythagoras was **contemporaneous with** Buddha.* ▷mid 17th cent.: from Latin, from *con-* 'together with' + *temporaneus* (from *tempus, tempor-* 'time') + **-OUS**. —**con·tem·po·ra·ne·i·ty** /-rə'nēitē; -rə'nāitē/ *n.* —**con·tem·po·ra·ne·ous·ly** *adv.* —**con·tem·po·ra·ne·ous·ness** *n.*

con·tem·po·rar·y /kən'tempə,rerē/ ▶*adj.* **1** living or occurring at the same time: *the event was recorded by a contemporary historian.* ■ dating from the same time: *this series of paintings is **contemporary with** other works in an early style.* **2** belonging to or occurring in the present: *the tension and complexities of our*

contemporary society. ■ following modern ideas or fashion in style or design: *contemporary art.*
▸*n.* (*pl.* **-rar·ies**) a person or thing living or existing at the same time as another: *he was a contemporary of Darwin.* ■ a person of roughly the same age as another: *my contemporaries at school.* ▷mid 17th cent.: from medieval Latin *contemporarius,* from *con-* 'together with' + *tempus, tempor-* 'time' (on the pattern of Latin *contemporaneus* and late Latin *contemporalis*). **—con·tem·po·rar·i·ly** /kən,tempə're(ə)rəlē/ *adv.* **—con·tem·po·rar·i·ness** *n.*

con·tempt /kən'tem(p)t/ ▸*n.* the feeling that a person or a thing is beneath consideration, worthless, or deserving scorn: *he showed his contempt for his job by doing it very badly.* ■ disregard for something that should be taken into account: *this action displays an arrogant* ***contempt for*** *the wishes of the majority.* ■ (also **contempt of court**) the offense of being disobedient to or disrespectful of a court of law and its officers: *several unions were* ***held to be in contempt*** *and were fined.* ■ the offense of being similarly disobedient to or disrespectful of the lawful operation of a legislative body (e.g., its investigations). ▷late Middle English: from Latin *contemptus,* from *contemnere* (see **CONTEMN**).
▸*PHRASES* □ **beneath contempt** utterly worthless or despicable. □ **hold someone/something in contempt** consider someone or something to be unworthy of respect or attention: *the speed limit is held in contempt by many drivers.*

con·tempt·i·ble /kən'tem(p)təbəl/ ▸*adj.* deserving contempt; despicable: *a display of contemptible cowardice.* ▷late Middle English: from Old French, or from late Latin *contemptibilis,* from Latin *contemnere* (see **CONTEMN**). **—con·tempt·i·bly** /-blē/ *adv.*

con·temp·tu·ous /kən'tem(p)CHōōəs/ ▸*adj.* showing contempt; scornful: *she was intolerant and* ***contemptuous of*** *the majority of the human race.* ▷mid 16th cent. (in the sense 'despising law and order'): from medieval Latin *contemptuosus,* from Latin *contemptus* 'contempt,' from *contemnere* (see **CONTEMN**). **—con·temp·tu·ous·ly** *adv.* **—con·temp·tu·ous·ness** *n.*

con·tend /kən'tend/ ▸*v.* **1** [*intrans.*] (**contend with/against**) struggle to surmount (a difficulty or danger): *she had to contend with his uncertain temper.* ■ (**contend for**) engage in a competition or campaign in order to win or achieve (something): *the local team should contend for a division championship* | [as *adj.*] (**contending**) *disputes continued between the contending parties.* **2** assert something as a position in an argument: *he contends that the judge was wrong.* ▷late Middle English (in the sense 'compete for (something)'): from Old French *contendre* or Latin *contendere,* from *con-* 'with' + *tendere* 'stretch, strive.' **—con·tend·er** *n.*

con·tent[1] /kən'tent/ ▸*adj.* in a state of peaceful happiness: *he seemed more content, less bitter.* ■ satisfied with a certain level of achievement, good fortune, etc., and not wishing for more: *he had to be* ***content with*** *third place* | *the duke was content to act as Regent.*
▸*v.* [*trans.*] satisfy (someone): *nothing would content her.* ■ (**content oneself with**) accept as adequate despite wanting more or better: *we contented ourselves with a few small purchases.*
▸*n.* **1** a state of satisfaction: *the greater part of the century was a time of content.* **2** a member of the British House of Lords who votes for a particular motion. ▷late Middle English: via Old French from Latin *contentus* 'satisfied,' past participle of *continere* (see **CONTAIN**).
▸*PHRASE* □ **to one's heart's content** to the full extent of one's desires: *the children could run and play to their heart's content.*

con·tent[2] /'kän,tent/ ▸*n.* **1** (usu. **contents**) the things that are held or included in something: *he unscrewed the top of the flask and drank the contents* | *he picked up the correspondence and scanned the contents.* ■ [usu. in *sing.*] the amount of a particular constituent occurring in a substance: *milk with a low-fat content.* ■ (**contents** or **table of contents**) a list of the titles of chapters or sections contained in a book or periodical: *the contents page.* ■ information made available by a Web site or other electronic medium: *online content providers.* **2** the substance or material dealt with in a speech, literary work, etc., as distinct from its form or style: *the outward form and precise content of the messages.* ▷late Middle English: from medieval Latin *contentum* (plural *contenta* 'things contained'), neuter past part. of *continere* (see **CONTAIN**). **—con·tent·less** *adj.*

con·tent·ed /kən'tentəd/ ▸*adj.* happy and at ease: *I felt warm and contented.* ■ expressing happiness and satisfaction: *she gave a contented little smile.* ■ willing to accept something; satisfied: *I was never* ***contented with*** *half measures.* **—con·tent·ed·ly** *adv.* **—con·tent·ed·ness** *n.*

con·ten·tion /kən'tenCHən/ ▸*n.* **1** heated disagreement: *the captured territory was one of the main areas of contention between the two countries.* **2** an assertion, esp. one maintained in argument: *statistics bear out his contention that many runners are undertrained for this event.* ▷late Middle English: from Latin *contentio(n-),* from *contendere* 'strive with' (see **CONTEND**).
▸*PHRASE* □ **in contention** having a good chance of success in a contest: *he was* ***in contention for*** *the batting title in September.*

con·ten·tious /kən'tenCHəs/ ▸*adj.* causing or likely to cause an argument; controversial: *a contentious issue.* ■ involving heated argument: *the socioeconomic plan had been the subject of contentious debate.* ■ (of a person) given to arguing or provoking argument: *a contentious amateur politician who has offended minority groups.* ■ *Law* relating to or involving differences between contending parties. ▷late Middle English: from Old French *contentieux,* from Latin *contentiosus,* from *content-* 'striven,' from the verb *contendere.* **—con·ten·tious·ly** *adv.* **—con·ten·tious·ness** *n.*

con·tent·ment /kən'tentmənt/ ▸*n.* a state of happiness and satisfaction: *he found contentment in living a simple life in the country.* ▷late Middle English (denoting the payment of a claim): from French *contentement,* from Latin *contentus* (see **CONTENT**[1]).

con·tent pro·vid·er ▸*n.* a person or organization who supplies information for use on a Web site: *the content provider for short law and practice news updates* | *he worked for an Internet content provider.*

con·ter·mi·nous /kän'tərmənəs; kən-/ ▸*adj.* sharing a common boundary: *the forty-eight conterminous United States.* ■ having the same area, context, or meaning: *a genealogy conterminous with the history of the USA.* ▷mid 17th cent.: from Latin *conterminus* (from *con-* 'with' + *terminus* 'boundary') + **-OUS**. Compare with **COTERMINOUS**. **—con·ter·mi·nous·ly** *adv.*

con·tes·sa /kən'tesə/ ▸*n.* an Italian countess. ▷Italian, from late Latin *comitissa* (see **COUNTESS**).

con·test ▸*n.* /'kän,test/ an event in which people compete for supremacy in a sport, activity, or particular quality: *a gigantic air rifle shooting contest* | *a beauty contest.* ■ a competition for a political position: *the presidential contest.* ■ a dispute or conflict: *a contest between traditional and liberal views.*
▸*v.* /kən'test; 'kän,test/ [*trans.*] **1** engage in competition to attain (a position of power): *she declared her intention to contest the presidency.* ■ take part in (a competition or election): *a coalition was formed to contest the presidential elections.* **2** oppose (an action, decision, or theory) as mistaken or wrong: *the former chairman contests his dismissal.* ■ engage in dispute about: *the issues have been hotly contested.* ▷late 16th cent. (as a verb in the sense 'swear to, attest'): from Latin *contestari* 'call upon to witness, initiate an action (by calling witnesses),' from *con-* 'together' + *testare* 'to witness.' The senses 'wrangle, strive, struggle for' arose in the early 17th cent., whence the current noun and verb senses. **—con·test·a·ble** /kən'testəbəl/ *adj.* **—con·test·er** /kən'testər; 'kän,tes-/ *n.*
▸*PHRASE* □ **no contest** **1** another term for **NOLO CONTENDERE**: *he pleaded no contest to two misdemeanor counts.* **2** a competition, comparison, or choice of which the outcome is a foregone conclusion: *when the two teams faced each other it was no contest.* ■ a decision by the referee to declare a boxing match invalid on the grounds that one or both of the boxers are not making serious efforts.

con·test·ant /kən'testənt/ ▸*n.* a person who takes part in a contest or competition. ▷mid 17th cent.: from French, present participle of *contester,* from Latin *contestari* 'call upon to witness' (see **CONTEST**).

con·tes·ta·tion /,kän,təs'tāSHən/ ▸*n. formal* the action or process of disputing or arguing. ▷mid 16th cent. (in the sense 'solemn appeal or protest'): from Latin *contestatio(n-),* from *contestari* 'call upon to witness' (see **CONTEST**); reinforced by French *contestation.*

con·text /'kän,tekst/ ▸*n.* the circumstances that form the setting for an event, statement, or idea, and in terms of which it can be fully understood and assessed: *the decision was taken within the context of planned cuts in spending.* ■ the parts of something written or spoken that immediately precede and follow a word or passage and clarify its meaning: *word processing is affected by the context in which words appear.* ▷late Middle English (denoting the construction of a text): from Latin *contextus,* from *con-* 'together' + *texere* 'to weave.' **—con·text·less** *adj.* **—con·tex·tu·al** /kən'teksCHōōəl/ *adj.* **—con·tex·tu·al·ly** *adv.*
▸*PHRASES* □ **in context** considered together with the surrounding words or circumstances: *it is difficult now to view these masterpieces in context.* □ **out of context** without the surrounding words or circumstances and so not fully understandable: *comments that aides have long insisted were taken out of context.*

con·tex·tu·al·ism /kən'teksCHōōə,lizəm/ ▸*n. Philosophy* a doctrine that emphasizes the importance of the context of inquiry in a particular question. **—con·tex·tu·al·ist** *n.*

con·tex·tu·al·ize /kən'teksCHōōə,līz/ ▸*v.* [*trans.*] place or study in context: *the book contextualizes Melville's short fiction and poetry.* **—con·tex·tu·al·i·za·tion** /kən-,teksCHōōələ'zāSHən/ *n.*

con·tex·ture /kən'teks,CHər/ ▸*n.* the fact or manner of being woven or linked together to form a connected whole. ■ a mass of things interwoven together; a fabric. ■ the putting together of words and sentences in connected composition; the construction of a text. ■ a connected literary structure; a continuous text.

con·ti·gu·i·ty /,käntə'gyōōitē/ ▸*n.* the state of bordering or being in direct contact with something: *nations bound together by geographical contiguity.* ■ *Psychology* the sequential occurrence or proximity of stimulus and response, causing their association in the mind. ▷early 16th cent.: from late Latin *contiguitas,* from Latin *contiguus* 'touching' (see **CONTIGUOUS**).

con·tig·u·ous /kən'tigyōōəs/ ▸*adj.* sharing a common border; touching: *the 48 contiguous states.* ■ next or together in sequence: *five hundred contiguous dictionary entries.* ▷early 16th cent.: from Latin *contiguus* 'touching,' from the verb *contingere* 'be in contact, befall' (see **CONTINGENT**), + **-OUS**. **—con·tig·u·ous·ly** *adv.*

con·ti·nent[1] /'käntn-ənt; 'käntnənt/ ▸*n.* any of the world's main continuous expanses of land (Africa, Antarctica, Asia, Australia, Europe, North America, South America). ■ (also **the Continent**) the mainland of Europe as distinct from the British Isles. ■ a mainland contrasted with islands: *the maritime zone is richer in varieties of plant than the continent.* ▷mid 16th cent. (denoting a continuous tract of land): from Latin *terra continens* 'continuous land.'

con·ti·nent[2] ▸*adj.* **1** able to control movements of the bowels and bladder. **2** exercising self-restraint, esp. sexually. ▷late Middle English (in the sense 'characterized by self-restraint'): from Latin *continent-* 'holding together, restraining oneself,' from *continere* (see **CONTAIN**). **—con·ti·nence** *n.* **—con·ti·nent·ly** *adv.*

con·ti·nen·tal /,käntn'entl/ ▸*adj.* **1** forming or belonging to a continent: *continental Antarctica.* **2** coming from or characteristic of mainland Europe: *traditional continental cuisine.* **3** (also **Continental**) pertaining to the 13 original colonies of the US: *in 1783 the officers and men of the Continental forces had little to celebrate.*
▸*n.* **1** an inhabitant of mainland Europe. **2** (**Continental**) a member of the colonial army in the American Revolution: *22 Continentals were killed and scalped.* **3** (also **Continental**) a piece of paper currency used at the time of the American Revolution: *the redemption of Continentals by the government.* **—con·ti·nen·tal·ly** *adv.*

Con·ti·nen·tal Ar·my the army raised by the Continental Congress of 1775, with George Washington as commander.

con·ti·nen·tal break·fast ▸*n.* a light breakfast, typically consisting of coffee and rolls with butter and jam.

con·ti·nen·tal cli·mate ▸*n.* a relatively dry climate with very hot summers and very cold winters, characteristic of the central parts of Asia and North America.

Con·ti·nen·tal Con·gress each of the three congresses held by the American colonies (in 1774, 1775, and 1776, respectively) in revolt against British rule. The second Congress, convened in the wake of the battles at Lexington and Concord, created a Continental Army, which fought and eventually won the American Revolution.

con·ti·nen·tal crust ▸*n. Geology* the relatively thick part of the earth's crust that forms the large landmasses. It is generally older and more complex than the oceanic crust.

Con·ti·nen·tal Di·vide the main series of mountain ridges in North America, chiefly the crests of the Rocky Mountains that form a watershed that separates the rivers flowing east into the Atlantic Ocean or the Gulf of Mexico from those flowing west into the Pacific Ocean. Also called GREAT DIVIDE.

con·ti·nen·tal drift ▸*n.* the gradual movement of the continents across the earth's surface through geological time.

The theory of "continental drift," proposed in 1912, suggested that continents and continental crust drifted over denser oceanic crust. The mechanisms by which the original theory explained the drift, however, could not be substantiated and were proven wrong. The theory of continental drift has been replaced by the theory of plate tectonics. It is believed that a single supercontinent called Pangaea broke up to form Gondwana and Laurasia, which further split to form the present-day continents. South America and Africa, for example, are moving apart at a rate of a few centimeters per year.

See PLATE TECTONICS

con·ti·nen·tal shelf ▸*n.* the area of seabed around a large landmass where the sea is relatively shallow compared with the open ocean. The continental shelf is geologically part of the continental crust.

con·ti·nen·tal slope ▸*n.* the slope between the outer edge of the continental shelf and the deep ocean floor.

con·tin·gence /kən'tinjəns/ ▸*n.* touching; contact. ■ connection; affinity.

con·tin·gen·cy /kən'tinjənsē/ ▸*n.* (*pl.* **-cies**) a future event or circumstance that is possible but cannot be predicted with certainty: *a detailed contract that attempts to provide for all possible contingencies.* ■ a provision for such an events or circumstance: *a contingency reserve.* ■ an incidental expense: *allow an extra fifteen percent in the budget for contingencies.* ■ the absence of certainty in events: *the island's public affairs can be invaded by contingency.* ■ *Philosophy* the absence of necessity; the fact of being so without having to be so. ▷mid 16th cent. (in the philosophical sense): from late Latin *contingentia* (in its medieval Latin sense 'circumstance'), from *contingere* 'befall' (see CONTINGENT).

con·tin·gen·cy fund ▸*n.* a reserve of money set aside to cover possible unforeseen future expenses.

con·tin·gen·cy plan ▸*n.* a plan designed to take a possible future event or circumstance into account: *contingency plans for dealing with oil spills.*

con·tin·gen·cy ta·ble ▸*n.* *Statistics* a table showing the distribution of one variable in rows and another in columns, used to study the association between the two variables.

con·tin·gent /kən'tinjənt/ ▸*adj.* **1** subject to chance: *the contingent nature of the job.* See note at ACCIDENTAL. ■ (of losses, liabilities, etc.) that can be anticipated to arise if a particular event occurs: *businesses need to be aware of their liabilities, both actual and contingent.* ■ *Philosophy* true by virtue of the way things in fact are and not by logical necessity: *that men are living creatures is a contingent fact.* **2** (**contingent on/upon**) occurring or existing only if (certain other circumstances) are the case; dependent on: *resolution of the conflict was contingent on the signing of a cease-fire agreement.*
▸*n.* a group of people united by some common feature, forming part of a larger group: *a contingent of Japanese businessmen attending a conference.* ■ a body of troops or police sent to join a larger force in an operation: *a contingent of 2,000 marines.* ▷late Middle English (in the sense 'of uncertain occurrence'): from Latin *contingere* 'befall,' from *con-* 'together with' + *tangere* 'to touch.' The noun sense was originally 'something happening by chance,' then 'a person's share resulting from a division, a quota'; the current sense dates from the early 18th cent. —**con·tin·gent·ly** *adv.*

con·tin·u·al /kən'tinyo͞oəl/ ▸*adj.* frequently recurring; always happening: *his plane went down after continual attacks.* ■ having no interruptions: *some patients need continual safeguarding.* ▷Middle English: from Old French *continuel*, from *continuer* 'continue,' from Latin *continuare*, from *continuus* (see CONTINUOUS). —**con·tin·u·al·ly** *adv.*

USAGE For an explanation of the difference between **continual** and **continuous**, see **usage** at CONTINUOUS.

con·tin·u·ance /kən'tinyo͞oəns/ ▸*n.* **1** *formal* the state of remaining in existence or operation: *his interests encouraged him to favor the continuance of war.* ■ the time for which a situation or action lasts: *the trademarks shall be used only during the continuance of this agreement.* ■ the state of remaining in a particular position or condition: *the king's ministers depended on his favor for their continuance in office.* **2** *Law* a postponement or adjournment: *if this man's testimony is important, I will grant a continuance.* ▷late Middle English: from Old French, from *continuer* 'continue,' from Latin *continuare*, from *continuus* (see CONTINUOUS).

con·tin·u·ant /kən'tinyo͞oənt/ ▸*n.* **1** *Phonetics* a consonant that is sounded with the vocal tract only partly closed, allowing the breath to pass through and the sound to be prolonged (as with *f, l, m, n, r, s, v*). **2** *Philosophy & Psychology* a thing that retains its identity even though its states and relations may change.
▸*adj.* of, relating to, or denoting a continuant. ▷early 17th cent. (as an adjective in the general sense 'continuing'): from French, from *continuer*, reinforced by Latin *continuant-* 'continuing,' from the verb *continuare*, from *continuus* (see CONTINUOUS). Current senses date from the 19th cent.

con·tin·u·a·tion /kən,tinyə'wāsʜən/ ▸*n.* [usu. in *sing.*] the action of carrying something on over a period of time or the process of being carried on: *the continuation of discussions about a permanent peace.* ■ the state of remaining in a particular position or condition: *the administration's continuation in office.* ■ a part that is attached to and an extension of something else: *once a separate village, it is now a continuation of the suburbs.* ▷late Middle English: via Old French from Latin *continuatio(n-)*, from *continuare* 'continue,' from *continuus* (see CONTINUOUS).

con·tin·u·a·tive /kən'tinyo͞oətiv; -,ātiv/ *Linguistics* ▸*adj.* (of a word or phrase) having the function of moving a discourse or conversation forward.
▸*n.* a word or phrase of this type (e.g., *yes, well, as I was saying*). ▷mid 16th cent. (as a noun denoting something that brings about continuity): from late Latin *continuativus*, from *continuat-* 'continued,' from the verb *continuare* (see CONTINUE).

con·tin·u·a·tor /kən'tinyə,wātər/ ▸*n.* a person or thing that continues something or maintains continuity. ■ a person who writes a continuation of another's work.

con·tin·ue /kən'tinyo͞o/ ▸*v.* (**-ues, -ued, -u·ing**) **1** [*intrans.*] persist in an activity or process: *he was unable to continue with his job | prices continued to fall during April.* ■ remain in existence or operation: *discussions continued throughout the year.* ■ [*trans.*] carry on with (something that one has begun): *I continued my stroll* [as *adj.*] (**continued**) *he asked for their continued support.* ■ remain in a specified position or state: *they have indicated their willingness to continue in office | the weather continued warm and pleasant.* carry on traveling in the same direction: *he hummed to himself as they continued northward.* ■ (of a road, river, etc.) extend farther in the same direction: *the main path continued through a tunnel.* **2** recommence or resume after interruption: [*trans.*] *we continue the story from the point reached in Chapter 1* | [*intrans.*] *the trial continues tomorrow.* ■ [*intrans.*] carry on speaking after a pause or interruption: *I told him he was obstructing the inquiry and he let me continue.* ■ [*trans.*] *Law* postpone or adjourn (a legal proceeding): *the case was continued without a finding until August 2.* ▷Middle English: from Old French *continuer*, from Latin *continuare*, from *continuus* (see CONTINUOUS). —**con·tin·u·er** *n.*

con·tin·ued frac·tion ▸*n.* *Mathematics* a fraction of infinite length whose denominator is a quantity plus a fraction, which latter fraction has a similar denominator, and so on.

con·tin·u·ing ed·u·ca·tion ▸*n.* education provided for adults after they have left the formal education system, consisting typically of short or part-time courses.

con·ti·nu·i·ty /,käntn'(y)o͞oətē/ ▸*n.* (*pl.* **-ties**) **1** the unbroken and consistent existence or operation of something over a period of time: *pension rights accruing through continuity of employment.* ■ a state of stability and the absence of disruption: *they have provided the country with a measure of continuity.* ■ (often **continuity between/with**) a connection or line of development with no sharp breaks: *the Church stands in direct continuity with the Old Testament people of God.* **2** the maintenance of continuous action and self-consistent detail in the various scenes of a movie or broadcast: [as *adj.*] *a continuity error.* ■ the linking of broadcast items, esp. by a spoken commentary.
▷late Middle English: from Old French *continuite*, from Latin *continuitas*, from *continuare* 'continue,' from *continuus* (see CONTINUOUS).

con·tin·u·o /kən'tinyə,wō/ (also **bas·so con·tin·u·o**) ▸*n.* (*pl.* **-os**) (in baroque music) an accompanying part that includes a bass line and harmonies, typically played on a keyboard instrument and with other instruments such as cello or bass viol. ▷early 18th cent.: Italian *basso continuo* 'continuous bass.'

con·tin·u·ous /kən'tinyo͞oəs/ ▸*adj.* **1** forming an unbroken whole; without interruption: *the whole performance is enacted in one continuous movement.* ■ forming a series with no exceptions or reversals: *there are continuous advances in design and production.* ■ *Mathematics* (of a function) of which the graph is a smooth unbroken curve, i.e., one such that as the value of *x* approaches any given value *a*, the value of *f(x)* approaches that of *f(a)* as a limit. **2** *Grammar* another term for PROGRESSIVE (sense 3). ▷mid 17th cent.: from Latin *continuus* 'uninterrupted,' from *continere* 'hang together' (from *con-* 'together with' + *tenere* 'hold') + **-ous**. —**con·tin·u·ous·ly** *adv.* —**con·tin·u·ous·ness** *n.*

USAGE In precise usage, **continual** means 'frequent, repeating at intervals' and **continuous** means 'going on without pause or interruption': *we suffered from the* **continual** *attacks of mosquitoes; the waterfall's* **continuous** *flow creates an endless roar.* The most common error is the use of **continuous** where **continual** is meant: **continual** (that is, 'intermittent') *rain or tantrums can be tolerated;* **continuous** (that is, 'uninterrupted') *rain or tantrums cannot be tolerated.* To prevent misunderstanding, some careful writers use *intermittent* instead of **continual**, and *uninterrupted* in place of **continuous**. **Continuous** is the word to use in describing spatial relationships, as in *a* **continuous** *series of rooms* or *a* **continuous** *plain of arable land.* Avoid using **continuous** or **continuously** as a way of describing something that occurs at regular or seasonal intervals: in the sentence, *our synagogue's Hanukkah candle-lighting ceremony has been held* **continuously** *since 1925*, the word *continuously* should be replaced with *annually*.

con·tin·u·ous cre·a·tion ▸*n.* the creation of matter as a continuing process throughout time, esp. as postulated in steady state theories of the universe.

con·tin·u·ous spec·trum ▸*n.* *Physics* an emission spectrum that consists of a continuum of wavelengths.

con·tin·u·ous wave ▸*n.* an electromagnetic wave, esp. a radio wave, having a constant amplitude.

con·tin·u·um /kən'tinyo͞oəm/ ▸*n.* (*pl.* **-u·a** /-yo͞oə/) [usu. in *sing.*] a continuous sequence in which adjacent elements are not perceptibly different from each other, although the extremes are quite distinct: *at the fast end of the fast-slow continuum.* ■ *Mathematics* the set of real numbers. ▷mid 17th cent.: from Latin, neuter of *continuus* (see CONTINUOUS).

con·tin·u·um hy·poth·e·sis ▸*n.* *Mathematics* the assertion that there is no transfinite cardinal between the cardinal of the set of positive integers and that of the set of real numbers.

con·tort /kən'tôrt/ ▸*v.* twist or bend out of its normal shape: [*trans.*] *a spasm of pain contorted his face* | [*intrans.*] *her face contorted with anger* | [as *adj.*] (**contorted**) *contorted limbs | figurative a contorted version of the truth.* ▷late Middle English: from Latin *contort-* 'twisted around, brandished,' from the verb *contorquere*, from *con-* 'together' + *torquere* 'twist.' —**con·tor·tion** /kən'tôrsʜən/ *n.*

con·tor·tion·ist /kən'tôrsʜənist/ ▸*n.* an entertainer who twists and bends their body into strange and unnatural positions.

con·tour /'kän,to͝or/ ▸*n.* (usu. **contours**) an outline, esp. one representing or bounding the shape or form of something: *she traced the contours of his face with her finger.* | *figurative the contours of American life.* ■ an outline of a natural feature such as a hill or valley: *cliffs with grassy rounded contours.* ■ short for CONTOUR LINE. ■ a line joining points on a diagram at which some property has the same value: *the map shows contours of every 10-foot difference in elevation.* ■ a way in which something varies, esp. the pitch of music or the pattern of tones in an utterance: *the movement tends to place more emphasis on rhythm than melodic contour.*
▸*v.* [*trans.*] **1** (usu. **be contoured**) mold into a specific shape, typically one designed to fit into something else: *the compartment has been contoured with smooth rounded corners* | [as *adj.*] (**contoured**) *the contoured*

leather seats. **2** mark (a map or diagram) with contour lines: [as *adj.*] (**contoured**) *a huge contoured map.* **3** (of a road or railroad) follow the outline of (a topographical feature), esp. along a contour line: *the road contours the hillside.* ▷mid 17th cent.: from French, from Italian *contorno,* from *contornare* 'draw in outline,' from *con-* 'together'+ *tornare* 'to turn.'

con·tour feath·er ▶*n.* any of the mainly small feathers that form the outline of an adult bird's plumage.

con·tour line ▶*n.* a line on a map joining points of equal height above or below sea level.

con·tour map ▶*n.* a map marked with contour lines.

con·tour plow·ing ▶*n.* plowing along the contours of the land in order to minimize soil erosion.

con·tra /ˈkäntrə/ (also **Con·tra**) ▶*n.* a member of a guerrilla force in Nicaragua that opposed the left-wing Sandinista government 1979–90, and was supported by the U.S. for much of that time. It was officially disbanded in 1990, after the Sandinistas' electoral defeat. ▷abbreviation of Spanish *contrarevolucionario* 'counterrevolutionary.'

contra- ▶*prefix* **1** against; opposite; contrasting: *contradict | contraflow | contralateral.* **2** *Music* (of instruments or organ stops) pitched an octave below: *contralto | contrabass.* ▷from Latin *contra* 'against.'

con·tra·band /ˈkäntrəˌband/ ▶*n.* goods that have been imported or exported illegally: *the police looked for drugs, guns, and other contraband.* ■ trade in smuggled goods: *the government has declared a nationwide war on contraband.* ■ (also **contraband of war**) goods forbidden to be supplied by neutrals to those engaged in war. ■ during the U.S. Civil War, a black slave who escaped or was transported across Union lines.

▶*adj.* imported or exported illegally, either in defiance of a total ban or without payment of duty: *contraband drug shipments.* ■ relating to traffic in illegal goods: *the contraband market.* ▷late 16th cent.: from Spanish *contrabanda,* from Italian *contrabando,* from *contra-* 'against' + *bando* 'proclamation, ban.' —**con·tra·band·ist** /-ist/ *n.*

con·tra·bass /ˈkäntrəˌbās/ ▶*n.* another term for DOUBLE BASS.

▶*adj.* [*attrib.*] denoting a musical instrument with a range an octave lower than the normal bass range: *a contrabass clarinet.* ▷late 18th cent.: from Italian *contrabasso,* from *contra-* 'pitched an octave below' + *basso* (see BASS[1]).

con·tra·bas·soon /ˌkäntrəbəˈso͞on; -ba-/ ▶*n.* a bassoon that is larger and longer than the normal type and sounds an octave lower in pitch.

con·tra·cep·tion /ˌkäntrəˈsepSHən/ ▶*n.* the deliberate use of artificial methods or other techniques to prevent pregnancy as a consequence of sexual intercourse. The major forms of artificial contraception are: barrier methods, of which the commonest is the condom; the contraceptive pill, which contains synthetic sex hormones that prevent ovulation in the female; intrauterine devices, such as the coil, which prevent the fertilized ovum from implanting in the uterus; and male or female sterilization. ▷late 19th cent.: from CONTRA- 'against' + a shortened form of CONCEPTION.

con·tra·cep·tive /ˌkäntrəˈseptiv/ ▶*adj.* (of a method or device) serving to prevent pregnancy: *the contraceptive pill.* ■ of or relating to contraception: *a book popularizing contraceptive knowledge.*

▶*n.* a device or drug serving to prevent pregnancy.

con·tract ▶*n.* /ˈkänˌtrakt/ a written or spoken agreement, esp. one concerning employment, sales, or tenancy, that is intended to be enforceable by law: *both parties must sign employment contracts | a network of doctors and hospitals* ***under contract*** *to provide services.* ■ the branch of law concerned with the making and observation of such agreements. ■ *informal* an arrangement for someone to be killed by a hired assassin: *smuggling bosses routinely put out contracts on witnesses.* ■ *Bridge* the declarer's undertaking to win the number of tricks bid with a stated suit as trump: *South can* ***make the contract*** *with correct play.* ■ *dated* a formal agreement to marry.

▶*v.* **1** /kənˈtrakt/ [*intrans.*] decrease in size, number, or range: *glass contracts as it cools.* ■ (of a muscle) become shorter or tighter in order to effect movement of part of the body: *the heart is a muscle that contracts about seventy times a minute* | [*trans.*] *then contract your lower abdominal muscles.* ■ [*trans.*] shorten (a word or phrase) by combination or elision: *"quasistellar objects" was soon contracted to "quasar."* **2** /ˈkänˌtrakt; kənˈtrakt/ [*intrans.*] enter into a formal and legally binding agreement: *the local authority will* ***contract with*** *a wide range of agencies to provide services.* ■ secure specified rights or undertake specified obligations in a formal and legally binding agreement: *a buyer may* ***contract for*** *the right to withhold payment | the paper had contracted to publish extracts from the diaries.* ■ impose an obligation on (someone) to do something by means of a formal agreement: *health authorities contract a hospital to treat a specific number of patients.* ■ [*trans.*] (**contract something out**) arrange for work to be done by another organization: *local authorities will have to contract out waste management.* ■ [*trans.*] *dated* formally enter into (a marriage): *before Fanny met him, he had contracted a disastrous liaison and marriage.* ■ [*trans.*] enter into (a friendship or other relationship): *the patterns of social relationships contracted by men and women differ.* **3** /kənˈtrakt/ [*trans.*] catch or develop (a disease or infectious agent): *three people contracted a killer virus.* **4** /kənˈtrakt/ [*trans.*] become liable to pay (a debt): *he contracted a debt of $3,300.* ▷Middle English: via Old French from Latin *contractus,* from *contract-* 'drawn together, tightened,' from the verb *contrahere,* from *con-* 'together' + *trahere* 'draw.' —**con·tract·ee** /ˌkänˌtrakˈtē/ *n.* —**con·trac·tive** /kənˈtraktiv; ˈkänˌtraktiv/ *adj.*

con·tract·a·ble /kənˈtraktəbəl/ ▶*adj.* (of a disease) able to be caught.

con·tract bridge /ˈkänˌtrakt/ ▶*n.* the standard form of the card game bridge, in which only tricks bid and won count toward the game, as opposed to auction bridge.

con·tract·i·ble /kənˈtraktəbəl/ ▶*adj.* able to be shrunk or capable of contracting.

con·trac·tile /kənˈtraktəl; -ˌtīl/ ▶*adj. Biology & Physiology* capable of or producing contraction: *the contractile activity of the human colon.* —**con·trac·til·i·ty** /ˌkänˌtrakˈtilitē/ *n.*

con·trac·tile vac·u·ole ▶*n. Zoology* a vacuole in some protozoans that expels excess liquid on contraction.

con·trac·tion /kənˈtrakSHən/ ▶*n.* the process of becoming smaller: *the general contraction of the industry did further damage to morale.* ■ the process in which a muscle becomes or is made shorter and tighter: *neurons control the contraction of muscles | repeat the exercise, holding each contraction for one second.* ■ (usu. **contractions**) a shortening of the uterine muscles occurring at intervals before and during childbirth. ■ a word or group of words resulting from shortening an original form: *"goodbye" is a contraction of "God be with you."* ■ the process of shortening a word by combination or elision. ▷late Middle English: via Old French from Latin *contractio(n-),* from *contrahere* 'draw together' (see CONTRACT).

con·trac·tor /ˈkänˌtraktər/ ▶*n.* a person or company that undertakes a contract to provide materials or labor to perform a service or do a job.

con·trac·tu·al /kənˈtrakCHo͞oəl/ ▶*adj.* agreed in a contract: *a contractual obligation.* ■ having similar characteristics to a contract: *the contractual nature of the shareholder's rights.* —**con·trac·tu·al·ly** *adv.*

con·trac·ture /kənˈtrakCHər/ ▶*n. Medicine* a condition of shortening and hardening of muscles, tendons, or other tissue, often leading to deformity and rigidity of joints. ▷mid 17th cent.: from French, or from Latin *contractura,* from Latin *contract-* 'drawn together,' from the verb *contrahere.* —**con·trac·tur·al** /-CHərəl/ *adj.*

con·tra·dance /ˈkäntrəˌdans/ ▶*n.* a country dance in which the couples form lines facing each other. ▷early 19th cent.: variant of CONTREDANSE.

con·tra·dict /ˌkäntrəˈdikt/ ▶*v.* [*trans.*] deny the truth of (a statement), esp. by asserting the opposite: *the survey appears to contradict the industry's claims | he did not contradict what he said last week.* ■ assert the opposite of a statement made by (someone): *he did not contradict her but just said nothing | within five minutes he had contradicted himself twice.* ■ be in conflict with: *that evaporation seems to contradict one of the most fundamental principles of physics.* ▷late 16th cent.: from Latin *contradict-* 'spoken against,' from the verb *contradicere,* originally *contra dicere* 'speak against.' —**con·tra·dic·tor** /-ˈdiktər/ *n.*

con·tra·dic·tion /ˌkäntrəˈdikSHən/ ▶*n.* a combination of statements, ideas, or features of a situation that are opposed to one another: *the proposed new system suffers from a set of internal contradictions.* ■ a person, thing, or situation in which inconsistent elements are present: *the paradox of using force to overcome force is a real contradiction.* ■ the statement of a position opposite to one already made: *the second sentence appears to be in flat contradiction of the first | the experiment provides a contradiction of the hypothesis.* ▷late Middle English: via Old French from Latin *contradictio(n-),* from the verb *contradicere* (see CONTRADICT).

▶*PHRASE* □ **contradiction in terms** a statement or group of words associating objects or ideas that are incompatible: *"true fiction" is a contradiction in terms.*

con·tra·dic·to·ry /ˌkäntrəˈdikt(ə)rē/ ▶*adj.* mutually opposed or inconsistent: *the two attitudes are contradictory.* See note at OPPOSITE. ■ containing elements which are inconsistent or in conflict: *the committee rejected the policy as too vague and internally contradictory.* ■ *Logic* (of two propositions) so related that one and only one must be true. Compare with CONTRARY.

▶*n.* (*pl.* **-ries**) *Logic* a contradictory proposition. ▷late Middle English (as a term in logic denoting a proposition or principle that contradicts another): from late Latin *contradictorius,* from Latin *contradict-* 'spoken against,' from the verb *contradicere* (see CONTRADICT). —**con·tra·dic·to·ri·ly** /-ˈdikt(ə)rəlē/ *adv.* —**con·tra·dic·to·ri·ness** *n.*

con·tra·dis·tinc·tion /ˌkäntrədəˈstiNGkSHən/ ▶*n.* distinction made by contrasting the different qualities of two things: *the bacterium is termed "rough"* ***in contradistinction to*** *its ordinary smooth form.*

con·tra·dis·tin·guish /ˌkäntrədəˈstiNGgwiSH/ ▶*v.* [*trans.*] (often **be contradistinguished**) *archaic* distinguish between (two things) by contrasting them.

con·tra·fac·tive /ˌkäntrəˈfaktiv/ ▶*adj. Linguistics* denoting a verb that assigns to its object (normally a clausal object) the status of not being true, e.g., *pretend* and *wish.* Contrasted with FACTIVE, NONFACTIVE.

con·tra·fac·tu·al /ˌkäntrəˈfakCHo͞oəl/ ▶*adj.* another term for COUNTERFACTUAL.

con·trail /ˈkänˌtrāl/ ▶*n.* a trail of condensed water from an aircraft or rocket at high altitude, seen as a white streak against the sky. ▷1940s: abbreviation of *condensation trail.*

con·tra·in·di·cate /ˌkäntrəˈindəˌkāt/ ▶*v.* [*trans.*] (usu. **be contraindicated**) *Medicine* (of a condition or circumstance) suggest or indicate that (a particular technique or drug) should not be used in the case in question. —**con·tra·in·di·ca·tion** /-ˌindəˈkāSHən/ *n.*

con·tra·lat·er·al /ˌkäntrəˈlatərəl; -ˈlatrəl/ ▶*adj. Medicine* relating to or denoting the side of the body opposite to that on which a particular structure or condition occurs: *the symptom develops in the hand* ***contralateral to*** *the lesion.*

con·tral·to /kənˈtraltō/ ▶*n.* (*pl.* **-tos**) the lowest female singing voice: *she sang in a high contralto.* ■ a singer with such a voice. ■ a part written for such a voice. ▷mid 18th cent.: Italian, from *contra-* (in the sense 'counter to') + ALTO. Compare with COUNTERTENOR.

con·tra mun·dum /ˌkäntrə ˈmo͝ondəm; ˈməndəm/ ▶*adv.* defying or opposing everyone else. ▷Latin, 'against the world.'

con·tra·po·si·tion /ˌkäntrəpəˈziSHən/ ▶*n. Logic* conversion of a proposition from *all A is B* to *all not-B is not-A.* ▷mid 16th cent.: from late Latin *contrapositio(n-),* from the verb *contraponere,* from *contra-* 'against' + *ponere* 'to place.' —**con·tra·pos·i·tive** /-ˈpäzətiv/ *adj.* & *n.*

con·trap·pos·to /ˌkōntrəˈpästō/ ▶*n.* (*pl.* **-trap·pos·ti** /-trəˈpästē/) *Sculpture* an asymmetrical arrangement of the human figure in which the line of the arms and shoulders contrasts with while balancing those of the hips and legs. ▷Italian, past participle of *contrapporre,* from Latin *contraponere* 'place against.'

con·trap·tion /kənˈtrapSHən/ ▶*n.* a machine or device that appears strange or unnecessarily complicated, and often badly made or unsafe. ▷early 19th cent.: perhaps from CONTRIVE (on the pattern of pairs such as *conceive, conception*), by association with TRAP[1].

con·tra·pun·tal /ˌkäntrəˈpəntl/ ▶*adj. Music* of or in counterpoint. ■ (of a piece of music) with two or more independent melodic lines. ▷mid 19th cent.: from Italian *contrapunto* (see COUNTERPOINT) + -AL. —**con·tra·pun·tal·ly** *adv.* —**con·tra·pun·tist** /-tist/ *n.*

con·trar·i·an /kənˈtre(ə)rēən; kän-/ ▶*n.* a person who opposes or rejects popular opinion, esp. in stock exchange dealing.

▶*adj.* opposing or rejecting popular opinion; going against current practice: *the comment came more from a contrarian disposition than moral conviction.* —**con·trar·i·an·ism** /-ˌnizəm/ *n.*

con·tra·ri·e·ty /ˌkäntrəˈrīətē/ ▶*n.* **1** opposition or inconsistency between two or more things: *questions that involved much contrariety of opinion.* **2** *Logic* contrary opposition. ▷late Middle English: from Old French *contrariete,* from late Latin *contrarietas,* from *contrarius* (see CONTRARY).

con·trar·i·ous /kən'tre(ə)rēəs/ ▸*adj. archaic* **1** perverse; refractory. **2** opposed; unfavorable.

con·trar·i·wise /'kän,trerē,wīz; kən'tre(ə)rē-/ ▸*adv.* in the opposite way or order. ■ in contrast to something that has just been stated or mentioned: *contrariwise, a registered person may vote, even if not entitled to be registered.*

con·trar·y ▸*adj.* /'kän,tre(ə)rē/ **1** opposite in nature, direction, or meaning: *he ignored contrary advice and agreed on the deal.* See note at OPPOSITE. ■ (of two or more statements, beliefs, etc.) opposed to one another: *his mother had given him contrary messages.* ■ (of a wind) blowing in the opposite direction to one's course; unfavorable. ■ *Logic* (of two propositions) so related that one or neither but not both must be true. Compare with CONTRADICTORY. **2** kən'tre(ə)rē perversely inclined to disagree or to do the opposite of what is expected or desired: *she is sulky and contrary where her work is concerned.*
▸*n.* /'kän,tre(ə)rē/ (*pl.* **-trar·ies**) **1** (**the contrary**) the opposite: *the magazine has proved that the contrary is true.* **2** *Logic* a contrary proposition. ▷Middle English: from Anglo-Norman French *contrarie*, from Latin *contrarius*, from *contra* 'against.' —**con·trar·i·ly** /-əlē/ *adv.* —**con·trar·i·ness** *n.*
▸*PHRASES* □ **contrary to** conflicting with; counter to: *contrary to his expectations, he found the atmosphere exciting | the restrictions were not contrary to the public interest.* □ **on** (or **quite**) **the contrary** used to intensify a denial of what has just been implied or stated: *there was no malice in her; on the contrary, she was very kind.* □ **to the contrary** with the opposite meaning or implication: *he continued to drink despite medical advice to the contrary.*

con·trast ▸*n.* /'kän,trast/ the state of being strikingly different from something else, typically something in juxtaposition or close association: *the day began cold and blustery, **in contrast to** almost two weeks of uninterrupted sunshine | a **contrast between** rural and urban trends.* ■ the degree of difference between tones in a television picture, photograph, or other image. ■ enhancement of the apparent brightness or clarity of a design provided by the juxtaposition of different colors or textures. ■ the action of calling attention to notable differences: *use knowledge of other languages for **contrast** and comparison **with** English.* ■ [in *sing.*] a thing or person having qualities noticeably different from another: *the castle is quite a **contrast to** other places where the singer has performed.*
▸*v.* /'kän,trast; kən'trast/ [*intrans.*] differ strikingly: *his friend's success **contrasted with** his own failure* | [as *adj.*] (**contrasting**) *a contrasting view.* ■ [*trans.*] compare in such a way as to emphasize differences: *people **contrasted** her **with** her sister.* ▷late 17th cent. (as a term in fine art, in the sense 'juxtapose so as to bring out differences in form and color'): from French *contraste* (noun), *contraster* (verb), via Italian from medieval Latin *contrastare*, from Latin *contra-* 'against' + *stare* 'stand.' —**con·trast·ing·ly** /'kän,trastiNGlē; kən'tras-/ *adv.* —**con·tras·tive** /kən'trastiv; 'kän,tras-/ *adj.*

USAGE **Contrast** means 'note the differences,' whereas **compare** means 'note the similarities' (or, in some cases, inconsistencies).
See also **usage** at COMPARE.

con·trast me·di·um /'kän,trast/ ▸*n. Medicine* a substance introduced into a part of the body in order to improve the visibility of internal structure during radiography.

con·trast·y /'kän,trastē/ ▸*adj. informal* (of a photograph, movie, or television picture) showing a high degree of contrast.

con·tra·sug·gest·i·ble /,käntrə sə(g)'jestəbəl/ ▸*adj. Psychology* tending to respond to a suggestion by believing or doing the contrary.

con·tra·vene /,käntrə'vēn/ ▸*v.* [*trans.*] violate the prohibition or order of (a law, treaty, or code of conduct): *this would contravene the rule against hearsay.* ■ conflict with (a right, principle, etc.), esp. to its detriment: *this contravened Washington's commitment to its own proposal.* ▷mid 16th cent.: from late Latin *contravenire*, from Latin *contra-* 'against' + *venire* 'come.' —**con·tra·ven·er** *n.*

con·tra·ven·tion /,käntrə'venCHən/ ▸*n.* an action that violates a law, treaty, or other ruling: *young persons who commit offenses bear responsibility for their contraventions.* ▷mid 16th cent.: via French from medieval Latin *contraventio(n-)*, from late Latin *contravenire* (see CONTRAVENE).
▸*PHRASE* □ **in contravention of** in a manner contrary and disobedient to (a law or other ruling).

con·tre·danse /'käntrə,dans; ,kôntrə'däNs/ ▸*n.* (*pl.* same) a French form of country dance, originating in the 18th century and related to the quadrille. ■ a piece of music for such a dance. ■ another term for CONTRADANCE. ▷French, alteration of English COUNTRY DANCE, by association with *contre* 'against, opposite.'

con·tre-jour /,kôntrə 'ZHŏŏr/ ▸*adj. & adv. Photography* having or involving the sun or other light source behind the subject: [as *adj.*] *a glorious contre-jour effect* | [as *adv.*] *it is recommended not to use the film contre-jour.* ▷early 20th cent.: French, from *contre* 'against' + *jour* 'daylight.'

con·tre·temps /'käntrə,tän; ,kôntrə'täN/ ▸*n.* (*pl.* same /-,tän(z); -'täN(z)/) an unexpected and unfortunate occurrence: *the hotel had to deal with more than one contretemps before the end of the night.* ■ a minor dispute or disagreement: *she had occasional contretemps with her staff.* ▷late 17th cent. (originally as a fencing term, denoting a thrust made at an inopportune moment): French, originally 'motion out of time,' from *contre-* 'against' + *temps* 'time.'

con·trib·ute /kən'tribyōōt; -byət/ ▸*v.* [*trans.*] give (something, esp. money) in order to help achieve or provide something: *he **contributed** more than $500,000 **to** the center* | [*intrans.*] *she contributed to a private pension.* ■ [*intrans.*] (**contribute to**) help to cause or bring about: *gases that contribute to global warming.* ■ supply (an article) for publication: *he **contributed** articles **to** the magazine* | [*intrans.*] *the staff who **contribute to** your sports pages are doing a splendid job.* ■ [*intrans.*] give one's views in a discussion: *he did not **contribute to** the meetings.* ▷mid 16th cent.: from Latin *contribut-* 'brought together, added,' from the verb *contribuere*, from *con-* 'with' + *tribuere* 'bestow.' —**con·trib·u·tive** /-yətiv/ *adj.*

con·tri·bu·tion /,käntrə'byōōSHən/ ▸*n.* a gift or payment to a common fund or collection: *charitable contributions.* ■ the part played by a person or thing in bringing about a result or helping something to advance: *he made a lasting contribution by designing the modern radio telescope.* ■ an article or other piece of writing submitted for publication in a collection. ▷late Middle English (denoting a tax or levy): from late Latin *contributio(n-)*, from Latin *contribuere* 'bring together, add' (see CONTRIBUTE).

con·trib·u·tor /kən'tribyətər/ ▸*n.* a person or thing that contributes something, in particular: ■ a person who writes articles for a magazine or newspaper. ■ a person who donates money to a cause. ■ a causal factor in the existence or occurrence of something: *stress is a major contributor to most diseases.*

con·trib·u·to·ry /kən'tribyə,tôrē/ ▸*adj.* **1** playing a part in bringing something about: *smoking may be a contributory cause of lung cancer.* **2** (of or relating to a pension or insurance plan) operated by means of a fund into which people pay: *contributory benefits.* ▷late Middle English (in the sense 'contributing to a fund'): from medieval Latin *contributorius*, from Latin *contribut-* 'added' (see CONTRIBUTION).

con·trib·u·to·ry neg·li·gence ▸*n. Law* failure of an injured plaintiff to act prudently, considered to be a contributory factor in the injury suffered, and sometimes reducing the amount recovered from the defendant.

con·trite /kən'trīt/ ▸*adj.* feeling or expressing remorse or penitence; affected by guilt: *a broken and a contrite heart.* ▷Middle English: from Old French *contrit*, from Latin *contritus*, past participle of *conterere* 'grind down, wear away,' from *con-* 'together' + *terere* 'rub.' —**con·trite·ly** *adv.* —**con·trite·ness** *n.*

con·tri·tion /kən'triSHən/ ▸*n.* the state of feeling remorseful and penitent. ■ (in the Roman Catholic Church) the repentance of past sins during or after confession: *prayers of contrition.* ▷Middle English: via Old French from late Latin *contritio(n-)*, from *contrit-* 'ground down,' from the verb *conterere* (see CONTRITE).

con·triv·ance /kən'trīvəns/ ▸*n.* a thing that is created skillfully and inventively to serve a particular purpose: *an assortment of electronic equipment and mechanical contrivances.* ■ the use of skill to bring something about or create something: *the requirements of the system, by happy chance and some contrivance, can be summed up in an acronym.* ■ a device, esp. in literary or artistic composition, that gives a sense of artificiality.

con·trive /kən'trīv/ ▸*v.* [*trans.*] create or bring about (an object or a situation) by deliberate use of skill and artifice: *his opponents contrived a crisis | you contrived to be alone with me despite the supervision.* ■ manage to do something foolish or create an undesirable situation: *the poor guy in some way contrived to hang himself.* ▷Middle English: from Old French *controeve-*, stressed stem of *controver* 'imagine, invent,' from medieval Latin *contropare* 'compare.' —**con·triv·a·ble** *adj.* —**con·triv·er** *n.*

con·trived /kən'trīvd/ ▸*adj.* deliberately created rather than arising naturally or spontaneously: *the carefully contrived image of party unity.* ■ giving a sense of artificiality: *the ending of the novel is too pat and contrived.*

con·trol /kən'trōl/ ▸*n.* **1** the power to influence or direct people's behavior or the course of events: *the whole operation is **under the control of** a production manager | the situation was slipping **out of** her **control**.* ■ the ability to manage a machine or other moving object: *he lost control of his car | improve your ball control.* ■ the restriction of an activity, tendency, or phenomenon: *pest control.* ■ the power to restrain something, esp. one's own emotions or actions: *give children time to get control of their emotions.* ■ (often **controls**) a means of limiting or regulating something: *growing **controls on** local spending.* ■ a switch or other device by which a machine is regulated: *the volume control.* ■ the place where a particular item is verified: *passport control.* ■ the base from which a system or activity is directed: *communications could be established with central control | mission control.* ■ *Bridge* a high card that will prevent opponents from establishing a particular suit. ■ *Computing* short for CONTROL KEY. **2** *Statistics* a group or individual used as a standard of comparison for checking the results of a survey or experiment: *they saw no difference between the cancer patients and the controls.* **3** a member of an intelligence organization who personally directs the activities of a spy.
▸*v.* (**-trolled**, **-trol·ling**) **1** [*trans.*] determine the behavior or supervise the running of: *he was appointed to control the company's marketing strategy.* ■ maintain influence or authority over: *you shouldn't have dogs if you can't control them.* ■ limit the level, intensity, or numbers of: *he had to control his temper.* ■ (**control oneself**) remain calm and reasonable despite provocation: *he made an effort to control himself.* ■ regulate (a mechanical or scientific process): *the airflow is controlled by a fan.* ■ [as *adj.*] (**controlled**) (of a drug) restricted by law with respect to use and possession: *a sentence for possessing controlled substances.* **2** *Statistics* [*intrans.*] (**control for**) take into account (an extraneous factor that might affect results) when performing an experiment: *no attempt was made to control for variations* | [as *adj.*] (**controlled**) *a controlled trial.* ■ check; verify. ▷late Middle English (as a verb in the sense 'check or verify accounts,' esp. by referring to a duplicate register): from Anglo-Norman French *contreroller* 'keep a copy of a roll of accounts,' from medieval Latin *contrarotulare*, from *contrarotulus* 'copy of a roll,' from *contra-* 'against' + *rotulus* 'a roll.' The noun is perhaps via French *contrôle*. —**con·trol·la·bil·i·ty** /kən-,trōlə'bilitē/ *n.* —**con·trol·la·ble** *adj.* —**con·trol·la·bly** /-əblē/ *adv.*
▸*PHRASES* □ **in control** able to direct a situation, person, or activity: *I felt calm and in control.* □ **out of control** no longer possible to manage: *fires burning out of control.* □ **under control** (of a danger or emergency) being dealt with successfully and competently: *it took two hours to bring the blaze under control.*

con·trol ac·count ▸*n.* an account used to record the balances on a number of subsidiary accounts and to provide a cross-check on them.

con·trol char·ac·ter ▸*n. Computing* a character that does not represent a printable character but serves to initiate a particular action.

con·trol freak ▸*n. informal* a person who feels an obsessive need to exercise control over themselves and others and to take command of any situation.

con·trol key ▸*n. Computing* a key that alters the function of another key if both are pressed at the same time.

con·trol·ler /kən'trōlər/ ▸*n.* a person or thing that directs or regulates something: *the power controller on a subway train.* ■ a person in charge of an organization's finances. ▷Middle English (denoting a person who kept a duplicate register of accounts): from Anglo-Norman *contrerollour*, from *contreroller* 'keep a copy of a roll of accounts' (see CONTROL). Compare with COMPTROLLER. —**con·trol·ler·ship** /-,SHip/ *n.*

con·trol·ling in·ter·est ▸*n.* the holding by one person or group of a majority of the stock of a business, giving the holder a means of exercising control: *the purchase of a **controlling interest in** a company in California.*

con·trol rod ▸*n.* a rod of a neutron-absorbing substance used to vary the output power of a nuclear reactor.

con·trol tow·er ▶*n.* a tall building at an airport from which the movements of air and runway traffic are controlled.

con·tro·ver·sial /ˌkäntrəˈvərsHəl; -ˈvərsēəl/ ▶*adj.* giving rise or likely to give rise to public disagreement: *years of wrangling over a controversial bypass.* ▷late 16th cent.: from late Latin *controversialis,* from *controversia* (see **CONTROVERSY**). **—con·tro·ver·sial·ist** /-list/ *n.* **—con·tro·ver·sial·ly** *adv.*

con·tro·ver·sy /ˈkäntrəˌvərsē/ ▶*n.* (*pl.* **-sies**) disagreement, typically when prolonged, public, and heated: *security laws passed to tackle terrorism caused controversy* | *the announcement ended a protracted controversy.* ▷late Middle English: from Latin *controversia,* from *controversus* 'turned against, disputed,' from *contro-* (variant of *contra-* 'against') + *versus,* past participle of *vertere* 'to turn.'

USAGE There are two possible pronunciations of the word **controversy**: one puts the stress on the **con-** and the other puts it on the **-trov-**. The second pronunciation, though common in Britain, is still held to be incorrect in standard American and British English.

con·tro·vert /ˈkäntrəˌvərt; ˌkäntrəˈvərt/ ▶*v.* [*trans.*] deny the truth of (something): *subsequent work from the same laboratory controverted these results.* ■ argue about (something): *the views in the article have been controverted.* ▷mid 16th cent.: from Latin *controversus* (see **CONTROVERSY**), on the pattern of pairs such as *adversus* (see **ADVERSE**), *advertere* (see **ADVERT**2). **—con·tro·vert·i·ble** *adj.*

con·tu·ma·cious /ˌkänt(y)əˈmāsHəs/ ▶*adj. archaic* or *Law* (esp. of a defendant's behavior) stubbornly or willfully disobedient to authority. ▷late 16th cent.: from Latin *contumax, contumac-* (perhaps from *con-* 'with' + *tumere* 'to swell') + **-IOUS**. **—con·tu·ma·cious·ly** *adv.*

con·tu·ma·cy /kənˈt(y)o͞oməsē; ˈkänt(y)əməsē/ ▶*n. archaic* or *Law* stubborn refusal to obey or comply with authority, esp. a court order or summons. ▷Middle English: from Latin *contumacia* 'inflexibility,' from *contumax* (see **CONTUMACIOUS**).

con·tu·me·li·ous /ˌkänt(y)əˈmēlēəs/ ▶*adj. archaic* (of behavior) scornful and insulting; insolent. ▷late Middle English: from Old French *contumelieus,* from Latin *contumeliosus,* from *contumelia* 'abuse, insult' (see **CONTUMELY**). **—con·tu·me·li·ous·ly** *adv.*

con·tu·me·ly /kənˈt(y)o͞oməlē; ˈkänt(y)əˌmēlē; ˈkänˌt(y)o͞omlē/ ▶*n.* (*pl.* **-lies**) insolent or insulting language or treatment: *the church should not be exposed to gossip and contumely.* ▷late Middle English: from Old French *contumelie,* from Latin *contumelia,* perhaps from *con-* 'with' + *tumere* 'to swell.'

con·tuse /kənˈto͞oz/ ▶*v.* [*trans.*] (usu. **be contused**) injure (a part of the body) without breaking the skin, forming a bruise: *the whole region beneath the rib cage was contused.* ▷late Middle English: from Latin *contus-* 'bruised, crushed,' from the verb *contundere,* from *con-* 'together' + *tundere* 'beat, thump.'

con·tu·sion /kənˈto͞ozHən/ ▶*n.* a region of injured tissue or skin in which blood capillaries have been ruptured; a bruise. ▷late Middle English: from French, from Latin *contusio(n-),* from the verb *contundere* (see **CONTUSE**).

co·nun·drum /kəˈnəndrəm/ ▶*n.* (*pl.* **-drums**) a confusing and difficult problem or question: *one of the most difficult conundrums for the experts.* ■ a question asked for amusement, typically one with a pun in its answer; a riddle. See note at **RIDDLE**. ▷late 16th cent.: of unknown origin, but first recorded in a work by Thomas Nashe, as a term of abuse for a crank or pedant, later coming to denote a whim or fancy, also a pun. Current senses date from the late 17th cent.

con·ur·ba·tion /ˌkänərˈbāsHən/ ▶*n.* an extended urban area, typically consisting of several towns merging with the suburbs of one or more cities. ▷early 20th cent.: from **CON-** 'together' + Latin *urbs, urb-* 'city' + **-ATION**.

con·ure /ˈkänyər; -ˌyo͝or/ ▶*n.* a Central and South American parakeet that typically has green plumage with patches of other colors. • *Aratinga, Pyrrhura,* and other genera, family Psittacidae: numerous species. ▷mid 19th cent.: from modern Latin *conurus* (former genus name), from Greek *kōnos* 'cone' + *oura* 'tail.'

co·nus /ˈkōnəs/ ▶*n.* (*pl.* **co·ni** /ˈkōˌnī/) *Anatomy* **1** (in full **co·nus ar·te·ri·o·sus** /ärˌti(ə)rēˈōsis/) the upper front part of the right ventricle of the heart. **2** (in full **co·nus me·dul·lar·is** /ˌmedəˈle(ə)ris/) the conical lower extremity of the spinal cord. ▷late 19th cent.: from Latin, literally 'cone.'

con·va·lesce /ˌkänvəˈles/ ▶*v.* [*intrans.*] recover one's health and strength over a period of time after an illness or operation: *he spent eight months convalescing after the stroke.* ▷late 15th cent.: from Latin *convalescere,* from *con-* 'altogether' + *valescere* 'grow strong' (from *valere* 'be well').

con·va·les·cent /ˌkänvəˈlesənt/ ▶*adj.* (of a person) recovering from an illness or operation. ■ relating to convalescence: *a convalescent home.*
▶*n.* a person who is recovering after an illness or operation. ▷mid 17th cent.: from Latin *convalescent-* 'growing strong, recovering,' from the verb *convalescere* (see **CONVALESCE**). **—con·va·les·cence** *n.*

con·vect /kənˈvekt/ ▶*v.* [*trans.*] transport (heat or material) by convection: *this wood stove convects heat efficiently* | [as *adj.*] (**convected**) *convected warmth.* ■ [*intrans.*] (of a fluid or fluid body) undergo convection: *the fluid starts to convect* | [as *adj.*] (**convecting**) *the convecting layer.* ▷late 19th cent.: back-formation from **CONVECTION**.

con·vec·tion /kənˈveksHən/ ▶*n.* the movement caused within a fluid by the tendency of hotter and therefore less dense material to rise, and colder, denser material to sink under the influence of gravity, which consequently results in transfer of heat. ▷mid 19th cent.: from late Latin *convectio(n-),* from Latin *convehere,* from *con-* 'together' + *vehere* 'carry.' **—con·vec·tion·al** /-sHənl/ *adj.* **—con·vec·tive** /-ˈvektiv/ *adj.*

con·vec·tion cell ▶*n.* a self-contained convective zone in a fluid in which upward motion of warmer fluid in the center is balanced by downward motion of cooler fluid at the periphery.

con·vec·tion cur·rent ▶*n.* a current in a fluid that results from convection.

con·vec·tion ov·en ▶*n.* a cooking device that heats food by the circulation of hot air.

con·vec·tor /kənˈvektər/ ▶*n.* a heating appliance that circulates warm air by convection.

con·ve·nance /ˈkänvənəns/ ▶*n.* (also **convenances**) *archaic* conventional propriety. ▷French, from *convenir* 'be fitting,' from Latin *convenire* (see **CONVENE**).

con·vene /kənˈvēn/ ▶*v.* [*trans.*] call people together for (a meeting): *he had convened a secret meeting of military personnel.* ■ assemble or cause to assemble for a common purpose: [*trans.*] *he convened a group of well-known scientists and philosophers* | [*intrans.*] *the committee had convened for its final plenary session.* See note at **GATHER**. ▷late Middle English: from Latin *convenire* 'assemble, agree, fit,' from *con-* 'together' + *venire* 'come.' **—con·ven·a·ble** *adj.* **—con·ven·er** *n.* **—con·ve·nor** /-ˈvēnər/ *n.*

con·ven·ience /kənˈvēnyəns/ ▶*n.* **1** the state of being able to proceed with something with little effort or difficulty: *the museum has a cafeteria for your convenience.* ■ the quality of contributing to such a state: *the convenience of a portable phone.* ■ a thing that contributes to an easy and effortless way of life: *voice mail was seen as one of the desktop conveniences of the electronic office.* **2** *Brit.* a public toilet. ▷late Middle English: from Latin *convenientia,* from *convenient-* 'assembling, agreeing,' from the verb *convenire* (see **CONVENE**).
▶***PHRASES*** □ **at one's convenience** at a time or place that suits one. □ **at one's earliest convenience** as soon as one can without difficulty.

con·ven·ience food ▶*n.* a food, typically a complete meal, that has been preprepared commercially and so requires little preparation by the consumer.

con·ven·ience store ▶*n.* a store with extended opening hours and in a convenient location, stocking a limited range of household goods and groceries.

con·ven·ien·cy /kənˈvēnyənsē/ ▶*n.* archaic term for **CONVENIENCE** (sense 1).

con·ven·ient /kənˈvēnyənt/ ▶*adj.* fitting in well with a person's needs, activities, and plans: *I phoned your office to confirm that this date is convenient.* ■ involving little trouble or effort: *the new parking lot will make shopping much more convenient.* ■ (**convenient to**) situated so as to allow easy access to: *the 34-story building is convenient to downtown.* ■ occurring in a place or at a time that is useful: *put the blame on a convenient scapegoat.* ▷late Middle English (in the sense 'befitting, becoming, suitable'): from Latin *convenient-* 'assembling, agreeing, fitting,' from the verb *convenire* (see **CONVENE**). **—con·ven·ient·ly** *adv.* [*sentence adverb*] *he lived, conveniently, in Paris.*

con·vent /ˈkänˌvent/ ▶*n.* a Christian community under monastic vows, esp. one of nuns. ■ (also **convent school**) a school, esp. one for girls, attached to and run by such a community. ■ the building or buildings occupied by such a community. ▷Middle English: from Old French, from Latin *conventus* 'assembly, company,' from the verb *convenire* (see **CONVENE**). The original spelling was *covent* (surviving in the place name *Covent Garden*); the modern form dates from the 16th cent.

con·ven·ti·cle /kənˈventikəl/ ▶*n. historical* a secret or unlawful religious meeting, typically of people with nonconformist views. ▷late Middle English (in the general sense 'assembly, meeting,' particularly a clandestine or illegal one): from Latin *conventiculum* '(place of) assembly,' diminutive of *conventus* 'assembly, company,' from the verb *convenire* (see **CONVENE**).

con·ven·tion /kənˈvencHən/ ▶*n.* **1** a way in which something is usually done, esp. within a particular area or activity: *the woman who overturned so many conventions of children's literature.* ■ behavior that is considered acceptable or polite to most members of a society: *he was an upholder of convention and correct form* | *social conventions.* ■ *Bridge* an artificial bid by which a bidder tries to convey specific information about the hand to their partner. **2** an agreement between countries covering particular matters, esp. one less formal than a treaty. **3** a large meeting or conference, esp. of members of a political party or a particular profession: *a convention of retail merchants.* ■ (in the U.S.) an assembly of the delegates of a political party to select candidates for office. ■ an organized meeting of enthusiasts for a television program, movie, or literary genre: *a Star Trek convention.* ■ a body set up by agreement to deal with a particular issue: *the convention is a UN body responsible for the regulation of sea dumping.* ▷late Middle English (sense 3): via Old French from Latin *conventio(n-)* 'meeting, covenant,' from the verb *convenire* (see **CONVENE**). Sense 1 dates from the late 18th cent.

con·ven·tion·al /kənˈvencHənl/ ▶*adj.* based on or in accordance with what is generally done or believed: *a conventional morality had dictated behavior.* ■ (of a person) concerned with what is generally held to be acceptable at the expense of individuality and sincerity. ■ (of a work of art or literature) following traditional forms and genres: *conventional love poetry.* ■ (of weapons or power) nonnuclear: *agreement on reducing conventional forces in Europe.* ■ *Bridge* (of a bid) intended to convey a particular meaning according to an agreed upon convention. Often contrasted with **NATURAL**. ▷late 15th cent. (in the sense 'relating to a formal agreement or convention'): from French *conventionnel* or late Latin *conventionalis,* from Latin *conventio(n-)* 'meeting, covenant,' from the verb *convenire* (see **CONVENE**). **—con·ven·tion·al·ism** /-ˌizəm/ *n.* **—con·ven·tion·al·ist** /-ist/ *n.* **—con·ven·tion·al·i·ty** /-ˌvencHəˈnalitē/ *n.* **—con·ven·tion·al·ize** /-ˌīz/ *v.* **—con·ven·tion·al·ly** *adv.*

con·ven·tion·al mem·o·ry ▶*n. Computing* (in a personal computer running DOS) the first 640k of memory where programs to be run must be loaded.

con·ven·tion·eer /kənˌvencHəˈni(ə)r/ ▶*n.* a person attending a convention.

con·ven·tu·al /kənˈvencHo͞oəl/ ▶*adj.* relating or belonging to a convent: *the conventual life.* ■ relating to the less strict order of the Franciscans, living in large convents.
▶*n.* a person who lives in or is a member of a convent. ▷late Middle English: from medieval Latin *conventualis,* from Latin *conventus* 'assembly, company' (see **CONVENT**).

con·verge /kənˈvərj/ ▶*v.* [*intrans.*] (of several people or things) come together from different directions so as eventually to meet: *convoys from America and the UK traversed thousands of miles to converge in the Atlantic* | *figurative two separate people whose lives converge briefly from time to time.* ■ (**converge on/upon**) come from different directions and meet at (a place): *half a million sports fans will converge on the capital.* ■ (of a number of things) gradually change so as to become similar or develop something in common: *two cultures converged as the French settled Vermont.* ■ (of lines) tend to meet at a point: *a pair of lines of longitude are parallel at the equator but converge toward the poles.* ■ *Mathematics* (of a series) approximate in the sum of its terms toward a definite limit: *the powers of e therefore converge very slowly.* ▷late 17th cent.: from late Latin *convergere*, from *con-* 'together' + Latin *vergere* 'incline.'

con·ver·gence /kən'vərjəns/ (also **con·ver·gen·cy** /-jənsē/) ▸*n.* the process or state of converging: *the convergence of lines in the distance.* ■ *Biology* the tendency of unrelated animals and plants to evolve superficially similar characteristics under similar environmental conditions. ■ (also **convergence zone**) a location where airflows or ocean currents meet, characteristically marked by upwelling (of air) or downwelling (of water).

con·ver·gent /kən'vərjənt/ ▸*adj.* coming closer together, esp. in characteristics or ideas: *convergent changes in languages.* ■ relating to convergence: *a convergent boundary.* ■ *Mathematics* (of a series) approaching a definite limit as more of its terms are added. ■ *Biology* relating to or denoting evolutionary convergence. ■ (of thought) tending to follow well-established patterns. ▷early 18th cent.: from late Latin *convergent-* 'inclining together,' from the verb *convergere* (see CONVERGE).

con·ver·sant /kən'vərsənt/ ▸*adj.* familiar with or knowledgeable about something: *many ladies are* ***conversant with*** *the merits of drill-eyed needles.* ▷Middle English: from Old French, present participle of *converser* (see CONVERSE[1]). The original sense was 'habitually spending time in a particular place or with a particular person.' **—con·ver·sance** *n.* **—con·ver·san·cy** /-sənsē/ *n.*

con·ver·sa·tion /,känvər'sāSHən/ ▸*n.* the informal exchange of ideas by spoken words: *the two men were deep* ***in conversation.*** ■ an instance of this: *she picked up the phone and* ***held a conversation*** *in French.* ▷Middle English (in the sense 'living among, familiarity, intimacy'): via Old French from Latin *conversatio(n-)*, from the verb *conversari* (see CONVERSE[1]).

▸*PHRASE* □ **make conversation** talk for the sake of politeness without having anything to say.

THE RIGHT WORD **chat, colloquy, communion, conversation, dialogue, parley, tête-à-tête**

It is nearly impossible for most people to get through a day without having a **conversation** with someone, even if it's only a **chat** with the mailman.

Although *conversation* can and does take place in all sorts of contexts, both formal and informal, the word usually implies a relaxed, casual exchange.

A *chat* is the least formal of all conversations, whether it's a father talking to his son about girls or two women having a **tête-à-tête** (French for "head to head," meaning a confidential conversation) about their wayward husbands. Both men and women often complain that their partners don't understand the meaning of **dialogue**, which is a two-way conversation that may involve opposing points of view.

Argument is even more likely to play a role in a **parley**, which formally is a discussion between enemies regarding the terms of a truce.

A **colloquy** is the most formal of all conversations (*a colloquy on nuclear disarmament*); it can also be used to jocularly describe a guarded exchange (*a brief colloquy with the arresting officer*).

Communion may be form of conversation as well, but sometimes it takes place on such a profound level that no words are necessary (*communion with nature*).

con·ver·sa·tion·al /,känvər'sāSHənl/ ▸*adj.* appropriate to an informal conversation: *his tone was casual and conversational.* ■ consisting of or relating to conversation: *conversational skills.* **—con·ver·sa·tion·al·ly** *adv.*

con·ver·sa·tion·al·ist /,känvər'sāSHənl-ist/ ▸*n.* a person who is good at or fond of engaging in conversation.

con·ver·sa·tion piece ▸*n.* **1** a type of genre painting in which a group of figures are posed in a landscape or domestic setting, popular esp. in the 18th century. **2** an object whose unusual quality makes it a topic of conversation.

con·ver·sa·tion-stop·per ▸*n. informal* an unexpected or outrageous remark that cannot easily be answered.

con·ver·sa·zi·o·ne /,känvər,sätsē'ōnē; -'ō,nā/ ▸*n.* (*pl.* **-nes** or **-ni** /-nē/) a scholarly social gathering held for discussion of literature and the arts. ▷Italian, from Latin *conversatio* (see CONVERSATION).

con·verse[1] ▸*v.* /kən'vərs/ [*intrans.*] engage in conversation: *he fell in beside her and they began to converse amicably.*

▸*n.* /'kän,vərs/ *archaic* conversation. ▷late Middle English (in the sense 'live among, be familiar with'): from Old French *converser*, from Latin *conversari* 'keep company (with),' from *con-* 'with' + *versare*, frequentative of *vertere* 'to turn.' The current sense of the verb dates from the early 17th cent. **—con·vers·er** /kən'vərsər/ *n.*

con·verse[2] /'kän,vərs/ ▸*n.* a situation, object, or statement that is the reverse of another, or that corresponds to it but with certain terms transposed: *if spirituality is properly political, the converse is also true: politics is properly spiritual.* ■ *Mathematics* a theorem whose hypothesis and conclusion are the conclusion and hypothesis of another.

▸*adj.* /'kän,vərs; kən'vərs/ having characteristics that are the reverse of something else already mentioned: *the slow process of growth and the converse process of decay.* ▷late Middle English: from Latin *conversus* 'turned around,' past participle of *convertere* (see CONVERT).

con·verse·ly /'kän,vərslē; kən'vərslē/ ▸*adv.* introducing a statement or idea that reverses one that has just been made or referred to: *he would have preferred his wife not to work, although conversely he was also proud of what she did.*

con·ver·sion /kən'vərZHən/ ▸*n.* **1** the act or an instance of converting or the process of being converted: *the conversion of food into body tissues.* ■ the fact of changing one's religion or beliefs or the action of persuading someone else to change theirs: *my conversion to the Catholic faith.* ■ *Christian Theology* repentance and change to a godly life. ■ the adaptation of a building for a new purpose: *the conversion of a house into apartments* ■ *Brit.* a building or part of a building that has been adapted in this way. ■ *Law* the changing of real into personal property, or of joint into separate property, or vice versa. ■ *Psychiatry* the manifestation of a mental disturbance as a physical disorder or disease: [as *adj.*] *conversion disorders.* ■ *Logic* the transposition of the subject and predicate of a proposition according to certain rules to form a new proposition by inference. **2** *Football* the act of scoring an extra point or points after having scored a touchdown. ■ the act of gaining a first down. **3** *Law* the action of wrongfully dealing with goods in a manner inconsistent with the owner's rights: *he was found guilty of the fraudulent conversion of clients' monies.* **4** *Physics* the change in a quantity's numerical value as a result of using a different unit of measurement. ▷Middle English (in the sense 'turning of sinners to God'): via Old French from Latin *conversio(n-)*, from *convers-* 'turned around,' from the verb *convertere* (see CONVERT).

con·ver·sion fac·tor ▸*n.* **1** an arithmetical multiplier for converting a quantity expressed in one set of units into an equivalent expressed in another. **2** *Economics* the manufacturing cost of a product relative to the cost of raw materials.

con·ver·sion van ▸*n.* a van in which the cargo space has been converted to a special purpose, such as a living space.

con·vert ▸*v.* /kən'vərt/ **1** [*trans.*] cause to change in form, character, or function: *production processes that* ***converted*** *raw material* ***into*** *useful forms.* ■ [*intrans.*] change or be able to change from one form to another: *the seating* ***converts to*** *a double or two single beds.* ■ [*intrans.*] change one's religious faith or other beliefs: *at sixteen he converted to Catholicism.* ■ persuade (someone) to do this: *he was* ***converted*** *in his later years* ***to*** *the socialist cause.* ■ change (money, stocks, or units in which a quantity is expressed) into others of a different kind: *the figures have been converted at $0.545 to the Dutch guilder.* ■ adapt (a building) to make it suitable for a new purpose: *the space can be easily converted into a home office* | [as *adj.*] (**converted**) *they lived in a converted chicken house.* ■ *Logic* transpose the subject and predicate of (a proposition) according to certain rules to form a new proposition by inference. **2** [*trans.*] score from (a penalty kick, pass, or other opportunity) in a sport or game. ■ [*intrans.*] *Football* score an extra point or points after having scored a touchdown by kicking a goal (one point) or running another play into the end zone (two points). ■ [*intrans.*] *Football* advance the ball far enough during a down to earn a first down: *the Oilers converted on over half of their third downs.*

▸*n.* /'kän,vərt/ a person who has been persuaded to change their religious faith or other beliefs: *he is a recent* ***convert to*** *the church.* ▷Middle English (in the sense 'turn around, send in a different direction'): from Old French *convertir*, based on Latin *convertere* 'turn around,' from *con-* 'altogether' + *vertere* 'turn.'

con·vert·ed rice ▸*n. trademark* white rice prepared from brown rice that has been soaked, steamed under pressure, and then dried and milled.

con·vert·er /kən'vərtər/ (also **con·ver·tor**) ▸*n.* a person or thing that converts something: *the converter of a building to domestic use.* ■ a device for altering the nature of an electric current or signal, esp. from AC to DC or vice versa, or from analog to digital or vice versa. ■ a retort used in steelmaking. ■ short for CATALYTIC CONVERTER. ■ *Computing* a program that converts data from one format to another. ■ a camera lens that changes the focal length of another lens by a set amount: *a camera fitted with a x2 converter.*

con·vert·i·ble /kən'vərtəbəl/ ▸*adj.* able to be changed in form, function, or character: *a living room that is miraculously* ***convertible into*** *a bedroom.* ■ (of a car) having a folding or detachable roof: *his white convertible Mercedes.* ■ (of currency) able to be converted into other forms, esp. into gold or U.S. dollars. ■ (of a bond or stock) able to be converted into ordinary or preference shares. ■ *Logic* (of terms) synonymous.

▸*n.* **1** a car with a folding or detachable roof. **2** (usu. **convertibles**) a convertible security. ▷late Middle English (in the sense 'interchangeable'): from Old French, from Latin *convertibilis*, from *convertere* 'turn around' (see CONVERT). **—con·vert·i·bil·i·ty** /-,vərtə'bilitē/ *n.*

con·vex /kän'veks; 'kän,veks; kən'veks/ ▸*adj.* **1** having an outline or surface curved like the exterior of a circle or sphere. Compare with CONCAVE. **2** (of a polygon) not having any interior angles greater than 180°. ▷late 16th cent.: from Latin *convexus* 'arched, vaulted.' **—con·vex·i·ty** /kän'veksitē; kən-/ *n.* **—con·vex·ly** *adv.*

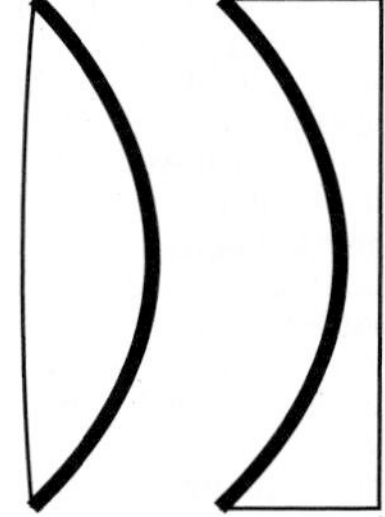
convex and concave

con·vex·o-con·cave /kən-,veksō'kän,kāv; -kän'kāv/ ▸*adj.* (of a lens) convex on one side and concave on the other and thickest in the center.

con·vex·o-con·vex /kən ,veksō'kän,veks; -kän'veks/ ▸*adj.* another term for BICONVEX.

con·vey /kən'vā/ ▸*v.* [*trans.*] transport or carry to a place: *pipes were laid to* ***convey*** *water* ***to*** *the house.* ■ make (an idea, impression, or feeling) known or understandable to someone: *the real virtues and diversity of America had never been conveyed in the movies* | *it's impossible to convey how lost I felt.* ■ communicate (a message or information): *Mr. Harvey and his daughter have asked me to convey their very kind regards.* ■ *Law* transfer the title to (property). ▷Middle English (in the sense 'escort'; compare with CONVOY): from Old French *conveier*, from medieval Latin *conviare*, from *con-* 'together' + Latin *via* 'way.' **—con·vey·a·ble** *adj.*

con·vey·ance /kən'vāəns/ ▸*n.* **1** the action or process of transporting someone or something from one place to another: *he was building vessels for the conveyance of live cod.* ■ a means of transportation; a vehicle: *adventurers attempt the trail using all manner of conveyances, including mountain bikes and motorcycles.* ■ the action of making an idea, feeling, or impression known or understandable to someone: *art's conveyance of meaning is complicated.* **2** *Law* the legal process of transferring property from one owner to another: *protective measures that might be taken before the conveyance is concluded.* ■ a legal document effecting such a process.

con·vey·anc·ing /kən'vāənsiNG/ ▸*n.* the branch of law concerned with the preparation of documents for the transferring of property. ■ the action of preparing documents for the transfer of property. **—con·vey·anc·er** /-sər/ *n.*

con·vey·or /kən'vāər/ (also **con·vey·er**) ▸*n.* a person or thing that transports or communicates something: *a conveyor of information.* ■ a conveyor belt.

con·vey·or belt ▸*n.* a continuous moving band of fabric, rubber, or metal used for moving objects from one place to another.

con·vict ▸*v.* /kən'vikt/ [*trans.*] (often **be convicted**) declare (someone) to be guilty of a criminal offense by the verdict of a jury or the decision of a judge in a court of law: *her former boyfriend was* ***convicted of*** *assaulting her* | [as *adj.*] (**convicted**) *a convicted murderer.*

▸*n.* /'kän,vikt/ a person found guilty of a criminal offense and serving a sentence of imprisonment. ▷Middle English: from Latin *convict-* 'demonstrated, refuted, convicted,' from the verb *convincere* (see CONVINCE). The noun is from obsolete *convict* 'convicted.'

con·vic·tion /kən'vikSHən/ ▸*n.* **1** a formal declaration that someone is guilty of a criminal offense, made by the verdict of a jury or the decision of a judge in a court of law: *she had a previous conviction for a similar offense.* **2** a firmly held belief or opinion: *his conviction that the death was no accident | she takes pride in stating her political convictions.* See note at **OPINION**. ■ the quality of showing that one is firmly convinced of what one believes or says: *his voice lacked conviction.* ▷late Middle English: from Latin *convictio(n-)*, from the verb *convincere* (see **CONVINCE**).

con·vince /kən'vins/ ▶*v.* [*trans.*] cause (someone) to believe firmly in the truth of something: *Robert's expression had obviously* ***convinced*** *her* ***of*** *his innocence | you couldn't convince him that a floppy disk was as good as a manuscript.* ■ persuade (someone) to do something: *she convinced my father to branch out on his own.* ▷mid 16th cent. (in the sense 'overcome, defeat in argument'): from Latin *convincere*, from *con-* 'with' + *vincere* 'conquer.' Compare with **CONVICT**. **—con·vinc·er** *n.* **—con·vin·ci·ble** *adj.*

USAGE Although it is common to see **convince** and **persuade** used interchangeably, there are distinctions in meaning that careful writers and speakers try to preserve. **Convince** derives from a Latin word meaning 'conquer, overcome.' **Persuade** derives from a Latin word meaning 'advise, make appealing, sweeten.' One can **convince** or **persuade** someone with facts or arguments, but, in general, *convincing* is limited to the mind, while *persuasion* results in action (just as *dissuasion* results in nonaction): *the prime minister convinced the council that delay was pointless; the senator persuaded her colleagues to pass the legislation.*

con·vinced /kən'vinst/ ▶*adj.* completely certain about something: *she was not entirely* ***convinced of*** *the soundness of his motives | I am convinced the war will be over in a matter of months.* ■ firm in one's belief, esp. with regard to a particular cause or issue: *a convinced pacifist.*

con·vinc·ing /kən'vinsiNG/ ▶*adj.* capable of causing someone to believe that something is true or real: *there is no convincing evidence that advertising influences total alcohol consumption | to make the detective's character convincing, she did extensive research.* See note at **BELIEVABLE**. ■ (of a victory or a winner) leaving no margin of doubt; clear: *the team cruised to a convincing win.* **—con·vinc·ing·ly** *adv.*

con·viv·i·al /kən'vivēəl; kən'vivyəl/ ▶*adj.* (of an atmosphere or event) friendly, lively, and enjoyable. ■ (of a person) cheerful and friendly; jovial. ▷mid 17th cent. (in the sense 'fit for a feast, festive'): from Latin *convivialis*, from *convivium* 'a feast,' from *con-* 'with' + *vivere* 'live.' **—con·viv·i·al·i·ty** /kən,vivē'alitē/ *n.* **—con·viv·i·al·ly** *adv.*

con·vo·ca·tion /,känvə'kāsHən/ ▶*n.* **1** a large formal assembly of people. ■ a formal ceremony at a college or university, as for the conferring of awards. **2** the action of calling people together for a large formal assembly. ▷late Middle English: from Latin *convocatio(n-)*, from the verb *convocare* (see **CONVOKE**). **—con·vo·ca·tion·al** /-sHənl/ *adj.*

con·voke /kən'vōk/ ▶*v.* [*trans.*] *formal* call together or summon (an assembly or meeting): *she sent messages convoking a Council of Ministers.* ▷late 16th cent.: from Latin *convocare*, from *con-* 'together' + *vocare* 'call.'

con·vo·lute /'känvə,lo͞ot/ ▶*adj Biology* rolled longitudinally upon itself, as a leaf in the bud.

con·vo·lut·ed /'känvə,lo͞otid/ ▶*adj.* (esp. of an argument, story, or sentence) extremely complex and difficult to follow: *its convoluted narrative encompasses all manner of digressions.* ■ *chiefly technical* intricately folded, twisted, or coiled: *walnuts come in hard and convoluted shells.* ▷late 18th cent.: past participle of *convolute*, from Latin *convolutus*, past participle of *convolvere* 'roll together, intertwine' (see **CONVOLVE**). **—con·vo·lut·ed·ly** *adv.*

con·vo·lu·tion /,känvə'lo͞osHən/ ▶*n.* **1** (often **convolutions**) a coil or twist, esp. one of many: *crosses adorned with elaborate convolutions.* ■ a thing that is complex and difficult to follow: *the convolutions of farm policy.* ■ a sinuous fold in the surface of the brain. ■ the state of being coiled or twisted, or the process of becoming so: *the flexibility of the polymer chain allows extensive convolution.* **2** (also **convolution integral**) *Mathematics* a function derived from two given functions by integration that expresses how the shape of one is modified by the other. ■ a method of determination of the sum of two random variables by integration or summation. ▷mid 16th cent.: from medieval Latin *convolutio(n-)*, from *convolvere* 'roll together' (see **CONVOLVE**). **—con·vo·lu·tion·al** /-sHənl/ *adj.*

con·volve /kən'välv; -'vôlv/ ▶*v.* [*trans.*] *rare* roll or coil together; entwine. ■ *Mathematics* combine (one function or series) with another by forming their convolution. ▷late 16th cent. (in the sense 'enclose in folds'): from Latin *convolvere* 'roll together,' from *con-* 'together' + *volvere* 'roll.'

con·vol·vu·lus /kən'välvyələs; -'vôl-/ ▶*n.* (*pl.* **-lus·es**) a twining plant with trumpet-shaped flowers, some kinds of which are invasive weeds (see also **BINDWEED**), while others, esp. morning glories, are cultivated for their bright flowers. • Genus *Convolvulus*, family Convolvulaceae. ▷mid 16th cent.: Latin, literally 'bindweed,' from *convolvere* 'roll together' (see **CONVOLVE**).

con·voy /'kän,voi/ ▶*n.* a group of ships or vehicles traveling together, typically accompanied by armed troops, warships, or other vehicles for protection.
▶*v.* /'kän,voi; kən'voi/ [*trans.*] (of a warship or armed troops) accompany (a group of ships or vehicles) for protection. ▷late Middle English (originally Scots, as a verb in the senses 'convey,' 'conduct,' and 'act as escort'): from French *convoyer*, from medieval Latin *conviare* (see **CONVEY**).
▶*PHRASE* □ **in convoy** (of traveling vehicles) as a group; together: *the army trucks had passed through in convoy the previous evening.*

con·vul·sant /kən'vəlsənt/ ▶*adj.* (chiefly of drugs) producing sudden and involuntary muscle contractions.
▶*n.* a convulsant drug. ▷late 19th cent.: from French, from *convulser*, from Latin *convuls-* 'pulled violently, wrenched,' from the verb *convellere* (see **CONVULSE**).

con·vulse /kən'vəls/ ▶*v.* [*intrans.*] (of a person) suffer violent involuntary contraction of the muscles, producing contortion of the body or limbs: *she convulsed, collapsing to the floor with the pain.* ■ [*trans.*] (usu. **be convulsed**) (of an emotion, laughter, or physical stimulus) cause (someone) to make sudden, violent, uncontrollable movements: *Carlos was convulsed by a second bout of sneezing | she rocked backward and forward,* ***convulsed with*** *helpless mirth.* ■ [*trans.*] *figurative* throw (a country) into violent social or political upheaval: *a wave of mass strikes convulsed the Ruhr, Berlin, and central Germany.* ▷mid 17th cent.: from Latin *convuls-* 'pulled violently, wrenched,' from the verb *convellere*, from *con-* 'together' + *vellere* 'to pull.'

con·vul·sion /kən'vəlsHən/ ▶*n.* (often **convulsions**) a sudden, violent, irregular movement of a limb or of the body, caused by involuntary contraction of muscles and associated esp. with brain disorders such as epilepsy, the presence of certain toxins or other agents in the blood, or fever in children. ■ (**convulsions**) uncontrollable laughter: *the audience collapsed in convulsions.* ■ an earthquake or other violent or major movement of the earth's crust: *the violent convulsions of tectonic plates.* ■ *figurative* a violent social or political upheaval: *the convulsions of 1939–45.* ▷mid 16th cent. (originally in the sense 'cramp, spasm'): from Latin *convulsio(n-)*, from the verb *convellere* (see **CONVULSE**).

con·vul·sive /kən'vəlsiv/ ▶*adj.* producing or consisting of convulsions: *a convulsive disease | she gave a convulsive sob.* **—con·vul·sive·ly** *adv.*

Con·way /'kän,wā/ a city in central Arkansas; pop. 43,167.

co·ny ▶*n.* (*pl.* **-nies**) variant spelling of **CONEY**.

coo[1] /ko͞o/ ▶*v.* (**coos, cooed**) [*intrans.*] (of a pigeon or dove) make a soft murmuring sound: *ringdoves cooed among the branches.* ■ (of a baby) make a soft murmuring sound similar to this, expressing contentment: *he gurgled and cooed in her arms.* ■ (of a person) speak in a soft gentle voice, typically to express affection: *I cruised the room, cooing at toddlers | "I knew I could count on you," she cooed.*
▶*n.* [in *sing.*] a soft murmuring sound made by a dove or pigeon. ▷mid 17th cent.: imitative.
▶*PHRASE* □ **bill and coo** see **BILL**[2].

coo[2] ▶*exclam. Brit., informal* used to express surprise: *"Coo, ain't it high!" Mary squeaked.* ▷early 20th cent.: imitative.

co-oc·cur /,kō ə'kər/ ▶*v.* [*intrans.*] occur together or simultaneously. **—co-oc·cur·rence** /ə'kərəns/ *n.*

Cook[1] /ko͝ok/, Captain James (1728–79), English explorer. On his first expedition to the Pacific 1768–71, he charted the coasts of New Zealand and New Guinea and explored the east coast of Australia, claiming it for Britain. He made two more voyages to the Pacific before being killed in a skirmish with the Hawaiians.

Cook[2], Thomas (1808–92), English founder of the travel agency, Thomas Cook. In 1841, he organized the first publicly advertised excursion train in England; the success of this venture led him to organize further excursions both in Britain and abroad, laying the foundations for the tourist and travel-agent industry.

Cook, Mount the highest peak in New Zealand, in the Southern Alps on South Island, that rises to a height of 12,349 feet (3,764 m). It is named after Captain James Cook. Maori name **AORANGI**.

cook /ko͝ok/ ▶*v.* **1** [*trans.*] prepare (food, a dish, or a meal) by combining and heating the ingredients in various ways: *shall I cook dinner tonight? |* [*intrans.*] *I told you I could cook |* [as *adj.*] (**cooked**) *a cooked breakfast.* ■ [*intrans.*] (of food) be heated so that the condition required for eating is reached: *while the rice is cooking, add the saffron to the stock.* ■ (**cook something down**) heat food and cause it to thicken and reduce in volume: *cooking down the chutney can take up to 45 minutes.* ■ [*intrans.*] (**cook down**) (of food being cooked) be reduced in volume in this way. ■ (**be cooking**) *informal* be happening or planned: *what's cooking on the alternative fuels front?* **2** [*trans.*] *informal* alter dishonestly; falsify: *a narcotics team who cooked the evidence.* ■ (**be cooked**) be in an inescapably bad situation: *if I can't talk to him, I'm cooked.* **3** [*intrans.*] *informal* perform or proceed vigorously or well: *the band used to get up on the bandstand and really cook.*
▶*phrasal v.* □ **cook something up** concoct a story, excuse, or plan, esp. an ingenious or devious one.
▶*n.* [often with *adj.*] a person who prepares and cooks food, esp. as a job or in a specified way: *a short order cook | I'm a good cook.* ▷Old English *cōc* (noun), from popular Latin *cocus*, from Latin *coquus*. **—cook·a·ble** *adj.*
▶*PHRASES* □ **cook the books** *informal* alter facts or figures dishonestly or illegally. □ **cook someone's goose** *informal* cause someone's downfall: *I've got enough on you to cook your goose.* □ **too many cooks spoil the broth** *proverb* if too many people are involved in a task, it will not be done well.

cook·book /'ko͝ok,bo͝ok/ ▶*n.* a book containing recipes and other information about the preparation and cooking of food.

Cook Coun·ty /ko͝ok/ a county in northeastern Illinois that includes Chicago and most of its closer suburbs; pop. 5,105,067.

Cooke[1] /ko͝ok/, Alastair (1908–2004), British journalist and broadcaster; in the U.S. from 1937. His BBC broadcasts of "Letter from America" began in 1946 and continued until shortly before his death. He hosted "Omnibus" on CBS 1952–60 and "Masterpiece Theater" on PBS 1971–92.

Cooke [2] /ko͝ok/, Jay (1821–1905), U.S. financier. He was the founder of Jay Cooke and Co., a leading Philadelphia bank, in 1861; his sale of bonds helped to finance the Civil War, and his financing of western railroads precipitated the Panic of 1873.

cook·er /'ko͝okər/ ▶*n. chiefly Brit.* an appliance used for cooking food.

cook·er·y /'ko͝okərē/ ▶*n.* (*pl.* **-er·ies**) **1** the practice or skill of preparing and cooking food. **2** a place in which food is cooked; a kitchen.

cook·house /'ko͝ok,hous/ ▶*n.* **1** a kitchen or dining hall in a military camp. **2** an outdoor kitchen in a warm country.

cook·ie /'ko͝okē/ ▶*n.* (*pl.* **-ies**) **1** a small sweet cake, typically round, flat, and crisp. **2** *informal* a person of a specified kind: *a* ***tough cookie*** *with one eye on her bank account.* **3** *Computing* a packet of data sent by an Internet server to a browser, which is returned by the browser each time it subsequently accesses the same server, used to identify the user or track their access to the server. ▷early 18th cent.: from Dutch *koekje* 'little cake,' diminutive of *koek*.
▶*PHRASE* □ **that's the way the cookie crumbles** *informal* that's how things turn out (often used of an undesirable but unalterable situation).

cook·ie cut·ter ▶*n.* a device with sharp edges for cutting cookie dough into a particular shape. ■ [as *adj.*] denoting something mass-produced or lacking any distinguishing characteristics: *a cookie-cutter apartment in a high-rise building.*

cook·ie jar ▶*n.* a jar to hold cookies.
▶*PHRASE* □ **with one's hand in the cookie jar** engaged in surreptitious theft from one's employer: *they got* ***caught with their hands in the cookie jar.***

cook·ie sheet ▶*n.* a flat metal tray on which cookies are baked.

C

cook·ing /ˈko͝okiNG/ ▸*n.* the process of preparing food by heating it: *frozen food must be fully defrosted before cooking.* ■ the practice or skill of preparing food: *he developed an interest in cooking.* ■ food that has been prepared in a particular way: *authentic Italian cooking.* ■ [as *adj.*] suitable for or used in cooking: *cooking oil.*

Cook In·let an inlet of the Gulf of Alaska, west of the Kenai Peninsula in southern Alaska. Anchorage lies at its northern end.

Cook Is·lands a group of 15 islands in the southwestern Pacific Ocean between Tonga and French Polynesia that have the status of a self-governing territory in free association with New Zealand; pop. 18,000; capital, Avarua, on Rarotonga. ▷named after Captain J. Cook (see **Cook**[1]), who visited them in 1773.

cook·out /ˈko͝okˌout/ ▸*n.* a party or gathering where a meal is cooked and eaten outdoors.

Cook·son /ˈko͝oksən/, Dame Catherine (Anne) (1906–98), English writer. A prolific author of light romantic fiction, she is best known for the Mary Ann series (1956–67), the Mallen trilogy (1973–74), and the Tilly Trotter series (1980–82).

Cook's tour ▸*n. informal* a rapid tour of many places: *figurative he then took me on a Cook's tour of his neuroscientific theories.* ▷early 20th cent.: from the name of the travel agent Thomas Cook (see **Cook**[2]).

Cook Strait the strait that separates North and South islands of New Zealand. It was named after Captain James Cook, who visited it in 1770.

cook·top /ˈko͝okˌtäp/ ▸*n.* a cooking unit, usually with hot plates or burners, built into or fixed on the top of a cabinet or other surface.

cook·ware /ˈko͝okˌwe(ə)r/ ▸*n.* pots, pans, or dishes for cooking food: *cast-iron cookware.*

cool /ko͞ol/ ▸*adj.* **1** of or at a fairly low temperature: *it'll be a cool afternoon | the wind kept them cool.* ■ soothing or refreshing because of its low temperature: *a cool drink in the leafy shade | figurative the bathroom was all glass and cool, muted blues.* ■ (esp. of clothing) keeping one from becoming too hot: *wear your cool, comfortable shirts.* ■ showing no friendliness toward a person or enthusiasm for an idea or project: *he gave a cool reception to the suggestion for a research center.* ■ free from excitement or anxiety: *he prided himself on* ***keeping a cool head*** *| she seems* ***cool, calm, and collected.*** ■ calmly audacious: *such an expensive strategy requires cool nerves.* ■ (of jazz, esp. modern jazz) restrained and relaxed. **2** *informal* fashionably attractive or impressive: *I always wore sunglasses to look cool.* ■ excellent: [as *exclam.*] *a computer you didn't even have to plug in. Cool!* **3** (**a cool ——**) *informal* used to emphasize a specified quantity or amount, esp. of money: *a cool $15,000 to buy the franchise.*
▸*n.* **1** (**the cool**) a fairly low temperature: *the cool of the night air.* ■ a time or place at which the temperature is pleasantly low: *the cool of the evening.* ■ calmness; composure: *he recovered his cool and then started laughing at us.* **2** the quality of being fashionably attractive or impressive: *all the cool of high fashion.*
▸*v.* become or cause to become less hot: [*intrans.*] *we dived into the river to* ***cool off*** *| figurative his feelings for her took a long time to cool |* [*trans.*] *cool the pastry for five minutes.* ■ become or cause to become calm or less excited: [*intrans.*] *after I'd* ***cooled off,*** *I realized I was being irrational |* [*trans.*] *George was trying to* ***cool*** *him* ***down.*** ■ [usu. in *imperative*] (**cool it**) *informal* behave in a less excitable manner: *"Cool it and tell me why you're so ecstatic."* ▷Old English *cōl* (noun), *cōlian* (verb), of Germanic origin; related to Dutch *koel*, also to **cold**.
—cooled *adj. a water-cooled engine.* **—cool·ish** *adj.* **—cool·ly** *adv.* **—cool·ness** *n.*
▸*PHRASES* □ **cool down** recover from strenuous physical exertion by doing gentle stretches and exercises; warm down. □ **cool one's heels** be kept waiting. □ **keep** (or **lose**) **one's cool** *informal* maintain (or fail to maintain) a calm and controlled attitude. □ **play it cool** see **play**.

coo·la·bah /ˈko͞oləˌbä/ ▸*n.* variant spelling of **coolibah**.

cool·ant /ˈko͞olənt/ ▸*n.* a liquid or gas that is used to remove heat from something. ▷1930s: from **cool**, on the pattern of *lubricant*.

cool·er /ˈko͞olər/ ▸*n.* **1** a device or container for keeping things cool, in particular: ■ an insulated container for keeping food and drink cool. ■ a refrigerated room. **2** a tall drink, esp. a mixture of wine, fruit juice, and soda water. **3** (**the cooler**) *informal* prison or a prison cell.

Coo·ley's a·ne·mi·a /ˈko͞olēz/ ▸*n.* another term for **thalassemia**. ▷1930s: named after Thomas B. Cooley (1871–1945), American pediatrician.

cool·head·ed /ˈko͞olˌhedəd/ ▸*adj.* not easily worried or excited.

coo·li·bah /ˈko͞oləˌbä/ (also **coo·la·bah**) ▸*n.* a northern Australian gum tree that typically grows near watercourses and yields strong, hard timber. • *Eucalyptus microtheca*, family Myrtaceae. ▷late 19th cent.: from Kamilaroi (and related languages) *gulubaa*.

Cool·idge /ˈko͞olij/, (John) Calvin (1872–1933), 30th president of the U.S. 1923–29. A Republican, he served as Massachusetts's lieutenant governor 1916–18 and governor 1919–20. He became the U.S. vice president in 1921, succeeding to the presidency upon the death of President Harding in 1923. Elected in 1924 to serve a full term, Coolidge was committed to reducing income taxes and the national debt, and was noted for his policy of noninterference in foreign affairs, which culminated in the Kellogg Pact in 1928.

Calvin Collidge

coo·lie /ˈko͞olē/ ▸*n.* (*pl.* **-lies**) *offensive* an unskilled native laborer in India, China, and some other Asian countries. ▷mid 17th cent.: from Hindi and Telugu *kūlī* 'day-laborer,' probably associated with Urdu *ḳulī* 'slave.'

coo·lie hat ▸*n.* a broad conical straw hat as worn by laborers in some Asian countries.

cool·ing-off pe·ri·od ▸*n.* an interval during which two people or groups who are in disagreement can try to settle their differences before taking further action. ■ an interval after a sales contract is agreed upon during which the purchaser can decide to cancel without loss.

cool·ing tow·er ▸*n.* a tall, open-topped, cylindrical concrete tower, used for cooling water or condensing steam from an industrial process.

Cool·Max /ˈko͞olˌmaks/ ▸*n. trademark* a polyester fabric that draws perspiration along its fibers away from the skin, used chiefly in sportswear. ▷1980s: an invented name, probably from *cool* + *max(imum)*.

coolth /ko͞olTH/ ▸*n. chiefly humorous* **1** pleasantly low temperature: *the coolth of the evening.* **2** articles, activities, or people perceived as fashionable: *the pinnacle of 1960s coolth.* ▷mid 16th cent. (but rare before the 20th cent.): from **cool** + **-th**[2].

coombe (also **coomb**) ▸*n.* variant spelling of **combe**.

coon /ko͞on/ ▸*n.* **1** short for **raccoon**. **2** *informal, offensive* a black person. [slang use of sense 1, from an earlier sense '(sly) fellow'.]
▸*PHRASE* □ **a coon's age** *informal* a long time: *I haven't seen you* ***in a coon's age!***

coon·can /ˈko͞onˌkan/ ▸*n.* a card game for two players, originally from Mexico, similar to rummy. ▷late 19th cent.: probably from Spanish *con quién* 'with whom?'

coon·hound /ˈko͞onˌhound/ ▸*n.* a dog of an American breed, used to hunt raccoons. There are several breeds, including the **black and tan coonhound** and the **bluetick coonhound**.

Coon Rap·ids a city in southeastern Minnesota, on the Mississippi River, north of Minneapolis; pop. 61,607.

coon·skin /ˈko͞onˌskin/ ▸*n.* the pelt of a raccoon: *a coonskin hat.*

coop /ko͞op; ko͝op/ ▸*n.* a cage or pen for confining poultry: *a chicken coop.*
▸*v.* [*trans.*] (usu. **be cooped up**) confine in a small space: *being cooped up indoors all day makes him fidgety.* ■ put or keep (a fowl) in a cage or pen. ▷Middle English *cowpe*; related to Dutch *kuip* 'vat' and German *Kufe* 'cask,' based on Latin *cupa*. Compare with **cooper**.
▸*PHRASE* □ **fly the coop** see **fly**[1].

co-op /ˈkōˌäp; kōˈäp/ ▸*n. informal* a cooperative society, business, or enterprise. ▷mid 19th cent.: abbreviation.

Coop·er[1] /ˈko͞opər/, Gary (1901–61), U.S. actor; born *Frank James Cooper*. He is noted for his Academy-Award–winning performances in *Sergeant York* (1941) and *High Noon* (1952). Other notable movies: *The Virginian* (1929) and *For Whom the Bell Tolls* (1943).

Coop·er[2], James Fenimore (1789–1851), U.S. novelist. He is renowned for his tales of Native Americans and frontier life, in particular the Leatherstocking tales—*The Pioneers* (1823), *The Last of the Mohicans* (1826), and *The Prairie* (1827).

Coo·per[3], Leon N., see **Bardeen**.

coop·er /ˈko͞opər; ˈko͝opər/ ▸*n.* a maker or repairer of casks and barrels.
▸*v.* [*trans.*] make or repair (a cask or barrel). ▷Middle English *cowper*, from Middle Dutch, Middle Low German *kūper*, from *kūpe* 'tub, vat,' based on Latin *cupa*. Compare with **coop**.

coop·er·age /ˈko͞opərij; ˈko͝op-/ ▸*n.* a cooper's business or premises. ■ the making of barrels and casks.

co·op·er·ate /kōˈäpəˌrāt/ (also **co-op·er·ate**) ▸*v.* [*intrans.*] act jointly; work toward the same end: *the leaders promised to* ***cooperate in*** *ending the civil war.* ■ assist someone or comply with their requests: *I was the villain for not* ***cooperating with*** *the FBI.* ▷late 16th cent.: from ecclesiastical Latin *cooperat-* 'worked together,' from the verb *cooperari*, from *co-* 'together' + *operari* 'to work.' **—co·op·er·ant** /-rənt/ *n.* **—co·op·er·a·tor** /-ˌrātər/ *n.*

co·op·er·a·tion /kōˌäpəˈrāSHən/ (also **co-op·er·a·tion**) ▸*n.* the process of working together to the same end: *they worked* ***in close cooperation with*** *the AAA.* ■ assistance, esp. by ready compliance with requests: *we would like to ask for your cooperation in the survey.* ■ *Economics* the formation and operation of cooperatives. ▷late Middle English: from Latin *cooperatio(n-)*, from the verb *cooperari* (see **cooperate**); later reinforced by French *coopération*.

co·op·er·a·tive /kōˈäp(ə)rətiv/ (also **co-op·er·a·tive**) ▸*adj.* involving mutual assistance in working toward a common goal: *every member has clearly defined tasks in a cooperative enterprise.* ■ willing to be of assistance: *they have been extremely considerate, polite, and cooperative.* ■ (of a farm, business, etc.) owned and run jointly by its members, with profits or benefits shared among them.
▸*n.* a farm, business, or other organization that is owned and run jointly by its members, who share the profits or benefits. ▷early 17th cent.: from late Latin *cooperativus*, from Latin *cooperat-* 'worked together,' from the verb *cooperari* (see **cooperate**). **—co·op·er·a·tive·ly** *adv.* **—co·op·er·a·tive·ness** *n.*

Co·op·er·a·tive Re·pub·lic of Guy·a·na official name for **Guyana**.

Coo·per pair /ˈko͞opər; ˈko͝opər/ ▸*n. Physics* a loosely bound pair of electrons with opposite spins and moving with the same speed in opposite directions, held to be responsible for the phenomenon of superconductivity. ■ a similar bound pair of atoms in a superfluid. ▷1960s: named after Leon N. *Cooper* (born 1930), American physicist.

Coo·per's hawk ▸*n.* a North American bird of prey resembling but smaller than the goshawk. • *Accipiter cooperii*, family Accipitridae. ▷early 19th cent.: named after William *Cooper* (1798–1864), American naturalist.

Coo·pers·town /ˈko͞opərzˌtoun; ˈko͝op-/ a resort village in central New York, on Otsego Lake, site of the Baseball Hall of Fame; pop. 2,180.

coop·e·ry /ˈko͞opərē; ˈko͝op-/ ▸*n.* (*pl.* **-ries**) another term for **cooperage**.

co·op·e·ti·tion /kōˌäpiˈtiSHən/ ▸*n.* collaboration between business competitors, in the hope of mutually beneficial results. ▷1980s: blend of *cooperative* and *competition*.

co-opt /kōˈäpt; ˈkōˌäpt/ ▸*v.* [*trans.*] (often **be co-opted**) appoint to membership of a committee or other body by invitation of the existing members. ■ divert to or use in a role different from the usual or original one: *social scientists were co-opted to work with the development agencies.* ■ adopt (an idea or policy) for one's own use: *the green parties have had most of their ideas co-opted by bigger parties.* ▷mid 17th cent.: from Latin *cooptare*, from *co-* 'together' + *optare* 'choose.' **—co-op·ta·tion** /kōˌäpˈtāSHən/ *n.* **—co-op·tion** /ˌkōˈäpSHən/ *n.* **—co-op·tive** /-ˈäptiv/ *adj.*

co·or·di·nate (also **co-or·di·nate**) ▸*v.* [*trans.*] /kōˈôrdəˌnāt/ **1** bring the different elements of (a complex activity or organization) into a relationship that will ensure efficiency or harmony: *he had responsibility for*

coordinating Chicago's transportation services. ■ [*intrans.*] negotiate with others in order to work together effectively: *you will coordinate with consultants and other departments on a variety of projects.* ■ [*intrans.*] match or harmonize attractively: *the stud fastenings are colored to coordinate with the shirt* | [as *adj.*] (**coordinating**) *a variety of coordinating colors.* **2** *Chemistry* form a coordinate bond to (an atom or molecule): *the sodium atom is coordinated to two oxygen atoms.*
▸*adj.* /kō'ôrdn-ət/ **1** equal in rank or importance: *cross references in the catalog link subjects that may be coordinate.* ■ *Grammar* (of parts of a compound sentence) equal in rank and fulfilling identical functions. **2** *Chemistry* denoting a type of covalent bond in which one atom provides both the shared electrons.
▸*n.* /kō'ôrdənət/ **1** *Mathematics* each of a group of numbers used to indicate the position of a point, line, or plane. **2** (**coordinates**) matching items of clothing. ▷mid 17th cent. (in the senses 'of the same rank' and 'place in the same rank'): from **co-** 'together' + Latin *ordinare* (from *ordo* 'order'), on the pattern of *subordinate.* —**co·or·di·na·tive** /kō'ôrdn-ətiv; 'ôrdn,ātiv/ *adj.* —**co·or·di·na·tor** /-'ôrdn,ātər/ *n.*

Co·or·di·nat·ed U·ni·ver·sal Time (abbr.: **UTC**) another term for **GREENWICH MEAN TIME.**

co·or·di·nat·ing con·junc·tion ▸*n.* a conjunction placed between words, phrases, clauses, or sentences of equal rank, e.g., *and, but, or.* Contrasted with **SUBORDINATING CONJUNCTION.**

co·or·di·na·tion /kō,ôrdn'āsHən/ ▸*n.* **1** the process or state of coordinating or being coordinated. ■ the organization of the different elements of a complex body or activity so as to enable them to work together effectively: *both countries agreed to intensify efforts at economic policy coordination.* ■ cooperative effort resulting in an effective relationship: *action groups work* ***in coordination with*** *local groups to end rain forest destruction.* ■ the ability to use different parts of the body together smoothly and efficiently: *changing from one foot position to another requires coordination and balance.* **2** *Chemistry* the linking of atoms by coordinate bonds. ▷mid 17th cent. (in the sense 'placing in the same rank'): from French or from late Latin *coordinatio(n-)*, based on Latin *ordo, ordin-* 'order.'

co·or·di·na·tion num·ber ▸*n.* *Chemistry* the number of atoms or ions immediately surrounding a central atom in a complex or crystal.

coot /ko͞ot/ ▸*n.* **1** (*pl.* same) an aquatic bird of the rail family, with blackish plumage, lobed feet, and a bill that extends back onto the forehead as a horny shield. • Genus *Fulica*, family Rallidae: several species, in particular the widespread *F. atra*, which has a white bill and frontal shield. **2** *informal* a foolish or eccentric person, typically an old man. ▷Middle English: probably of Dutch or Low German origin and related to Dutch *koet.*

coot·er /'ko͞otər/ ▸*n.* a North American river turtle with a dull brown shell and typically having yellow stripes on the head. • Genus *Pseudemys*, family Emydidae: several species, in particular *P. concinna*, some races of which are known as sliders. ▷early 19th cent.: of unknown origin.

coot·ie /'ko͞otē/ ▸*n.* *informal* a body louse. ■ a children's term for an imaginary germ or repellent quality transmitted by obnoxious or slovenly people. ▷World War I: perhaps from Malay *kutu*, denoting a parasitic biting insect.

co-own /'kō 'ōn/ ▸*v.* [*trans.*] own (something) jointly. —**co-own·er** *n.* —**co-own·er·ship** /'ōnər,sHip/ *n.*

cop[1] /käp/ *informal* ▸*n.* a police officer.
▸*v.* (**copped, cop·ping**) [*trans.*] **1** catch or arrest (an offender): *he was copped for speeding.* ■ incur (something unwelcome): *the team's captain copped most of the blame.* ■ obtain (an illegal drug): *he copped some hash for me.* ■ steal: *he watched her cop a pair of earrings and then nabbed her at the door.* ■ receive or attain (something welcome): *she copped an award for her role in the film.* **2** strike (an attitude or pose): *I copped an attitude—I acted real tough.*
▸*phrasal v.* □ **cop out** avoid doing something that one ought to do: *he copped out at the last moment.* □ **cop to** accept or admit to: *there are a lot of people who don't cop to their past.* ▷early 18th cent. (as a verb): perhaps from obsolete *cap* 'arrest,' from Old French *caper* 'seize,' from Latin *capere.* The noun is from **COPPER**[2].
▸*PHRASES* □ **cop a feel** *informal* fondle someone sexually, esp. in a surreptitious way or without their permission. □ **cop hold of** [usu. in *imperative*] *Brit.* take hold of: *cop hold of the suitcase, I'm off.* □ **cop a plea** engage in plea bargaining. □ **it's a fair cop** see **FAIR**[1].

cop[2] ▸*n.* a conical or cylindrical roll of thread wound onto a spindle. ▷late 18th cent.: possibly from Old English *cop* 'summit, top.'

Co·pa·ca·ba·na Beach /,kōpəkə'banə/ a resort on the Atlantic coast of Brazil near Rio de Janeiro.

co·pa·cet·ic /,kōpə'setik/ (also **co·pa·set·ic**) ▸*adj. informal* in excellent order. ▷early 20th cent.: of unknown origin.

co·pal /'kōpəl/ ▸*n.* resin from any of a number of tropical trees, used to make varnish. • The resin is obtained from trees in the families Leguminosae (genera *Guibourtia, Copaifera,* and *Trachylobium*) and Araucariaceae (genus *Agathis*). ▷late 16th cent.: via Spanish from Nahuatl *copalli* 'incense.'

Co·pán /kō'pän/ an ancient Mayan city, the ruins of which are in western Honduras near the Guatemalan frontier.

co·part·ner /'kō,pärtnər/ ▸*n.* a partner or associate, esp. an equal partner in a business. —**co·part·ner·ship** /-,sHip/ *n.*

co·pay /'kō,pā/ ▸*n.* short for **COPAYMENT.**

co·pay·ment /kō'pāmənt/ ▸*n.* (also **co·pay**) (of insurance policies) a payment owed by the person insured at the time a covered service is rendered, covering part of the cost of the service.

COPD *Medicine* ▸*abbr.* chronic obstructive pulmonary disease, involving constriction of the airways and difficulty or discomfort in breathing.

cope[1] /kōp/ ▸*v.* [*intrans.*] (of a person) deal effectively with something difficult: *his ability to* ***cope with*** *stress* | *it all got too much for me and I couldn't cope.* ■ (of a machine or system) have the capacity to deal successfully with: *the roads are barely adequate to* ***cope with*** *the present traffic.* ▷Middle English (in the sense 'meet in battle, come to blows'): from Old French *coper, colper*, from *cop, colp* 'a blow,' via Latin from Greek *kolaphos* 'blow with the fist.' —**cop·er** *n.*

cope[2] ▸*n.* a long, loose cloak worn by a priest or bishop on ceremonial occasions. ■ *technical* or *poetic/literary* a thing resembling or likened to a cloak: *the bay and the square were a seamless cope.*
▸*v.* [*trans.*] [usu. as *adj.*] (**coped**) (in building) cover (a joint or structure) with a coping. ▷Middle English (denoting a long outdoor cloak): from medieval Latin *capa*, variant of late Latin *cappa* (see **CAP** and **CAPE**[1]).

cope[2]

co·peck /'kō,pek/ ▸*n.* chiefly British variant spelling of **KOPEK.**

Co·pen·ha·gen /'kōpən,hägən; -,hāgən/ the capital and chief port of Denmark, a city that occupies the eastern part of Zealand and northern part of the island of Amager; pop. 466,700. Danish name **KØBENHAVN.**

Co·pep·o·da /kō'pepədə/ *Zoology* a large class of small aquatic crustaceans, many of which occur in plankton and some of which are parasitic on larger aquatic animals. ▷modern Latin, from Greek *kōpē* 'handle, oar' + *pous, pod-* 'foot' (because of its paddlelike feet). —**co·pe·pod** /'kōpə,päd/ *n.*

Co·per·ni·can sys·tem /kə'pərnikən/ (also **Copernican theory**) ▸*n.* *Astronomy* the theory that the sun is the center of the solar system, with the planets (including the earth) orbiting around it. Compare with **PTOLEMAIC SYSTEM.** ▷mid 17th cent.: named after **COPERNICUS.**

Co·per·ni·cus /kə'pərnikəs/, Nicolaus (1473–1543), Polish astronomer; Latinized name of *Mikołaj Kopernik.* He proposed a model of the solar system in which the planets orbit in perfect circles around the sun; his work ultimately led to rejection of the established geocentric cosmology.

cope·stone /'kōp,stōn/ ▸*n.* a flat stone forming part of a coping. ■ *figurative* a finishing touch or crowning achievement. ▷mid 16th cent.: from **COPE**[2] + **STONE.**

cop·i·a·ble /'käpēəbəl/ ▸*adj.* able to be copied, esp. legitimately photocopied.

cop·i·er /'käpēər/ ▸*n.* a machine that makes exact copies of something, esp. documents, video or audio recordings, or software.

co·pi·lot /'kō,pīlət/ ▸*n.* a second pilot in an aircraft. ▸*v.* [*trans.*] act as the copilot of (an aircraft).

cop·ing /'kōpiNG/ ▸*n.* the top, typically sloping, course of a brick or stone wall. ▷mid 16th cent.: from the verb **COPE**[2], originally meaning 'dress in a cope,' hence 'to cover.'

cop·ing saw ▸*n.* a saw with a very narrow blade stretched across a U-shaped frame, used for cutting curves in wood. ▷1920s: *coping* from **COPE**[2], used to describe likeness to a vault, arch, canopy, etc., based on Latin *cappa* 'cap or cape.'

cop·ing stone ▸*n.* chiefly British term for **COPESTONE.**

co·pi·ous /'kōpēəs/ ▸*adj.* abundant in supply or quantity: *she took copious notes.* See note at **PREVALENT.** ■ *archaic* profuse in speech or ideas: *I had been a little too copious in talking of my country.* ▷late Middle English: from Old French *copieux* or Latin *copiosus*, from *copia* 'plenty.' —**co·pi·ous·ly** *adv.* —**co·pi·ous·ness** *n.*

co·pla·nar /kō'plānər; -,när/ ▸*adj.* *Geometry* in the same plane. —**co·pla·nar·i·ty** /,kō,plā'ne(ə)ritē/ *n.*

Cop·land /'kōplənd/, Aaron (1900–90), U.S. composer, pianist, and conductor. He established a distinctive American style in his compositions, borrowing from jazz, folk, and other traditional music. Notable works: *Music for the Theater* (1925), *Appalachian Spring* (1944), and *Fanfare for the Common Man* (1942).

Cop·ley /'käplē/, John Singleton (1738–1815), U.S. painter. He is noted for his portraits and for paintings such as *The Death of Chatham* (1779–80), one of the first large-scale paintings of contemporary events.

co·pol·y·mer /kō'päləmər/ ▸*n.* *Chemistry* a polymer made by reaction of two different monomers, with units of more than one kind.

co·po·lym·er·ize /kō'päləmə,rīz/ ▸*v.* [*trans.*] *Chemistry* polymerize together to form a copolymer. —**co·pol·y·mer·i·za·tion** /kō,päləmərə'zāsHən/ *n.*

cop-out ▸*n.* *informal* an instance of avoiding a commitment or responsibility: *being 'average' is the lazy person's cop-out.*

cop·per[1] /'käpər/ ▸*n.* **1** a red-brown metal, the chemical element of atomic number 29. (Symbol: **Cu**)

Copper was the earliest metal to be used by humans, first by itself and then later alloyed with tin to form bronze. A ductile, easily worked metal, it is a very good conductor of heat and electricity and is used esp. for electrical wiring.

2 *dated* a copper coin, esp. a penny: *you could hire a raft for a few coppers.* **3** a reddish-brown color like that of copper. **4** [with *adj.*] a small butterfly of North America and Eurasia. The upper surface of its wings is typically bright reddish-orange or purple. • Genus *Lycaena*, family Lycaenidae: numerous species, including the **American copper** (*L. phlaeas*) of the eastern U.S. and arctic North America.
▸*v.* [*trans.*] cover or coat (something) with copper. ▷Old English *copor, coper* (related to Dutch *koper* and German *Kupfer*), based on late Latin *cuprum*, from Latin *cyprium aes* 'Cyprus metal' (so named because Cyprus was the chief source).

copper[1] 4

cop·per[2] ▸*n.* *informal* a police officer. ▷mid 19th cent.: from **COP**[1] + **-ER**[1].

cop·per·as /'käpərəs/ ▸*n.* green crystals of hydrated ferrous sulfate, esp. as an industrial product. ▷late Middle English *coperose*, from Old French *couperose*, from medieval Latin *cuperosa*, literally 'flower of copper,' from late Latin *cuprum* (see **COPPER**[1]) + *rosa* 'rose,' translating Greek *khalkanthon.*

cop·per beech ▸*n.* a variety of European beech tree with purplish-brown leaves.

C

Cop·per·belt /ˈkäpər,belt/ a mining region in central Zambia that has rich deposits of copper, cobalt, and uranium; chief town, Ndola.

cop·per·head /ˈkäpər,hed/ ▸n. any of a number of stout-bodied venomous snakes with coppery-pink or reddish-brown coloration, in particular: • a North American pit viper (*Agkistrodon contortrix*, family Viperidae). Also called HIGHLAND MOCCASIN. • an Australian snake of the cobra family (genus *Austrelaps*, family Elapidae, in particular *A. superbus*).

cop·per·plate /,käpərˈplāt; ˈkäpər,plāt/ ▸n. **1** a polished copper plate with a design engraved or etched into it. ■ a print made from such a plate. **2** a style of neat, round handwriting, usually slanted and looped, the thick and thin strokes being made by pressure with a flexible metal nib. [the copybooks for this round hand were originally printed from copperplates.]
▸adj. of or in copperplate writing.

cop·per·smith /ˈkäpər,smiTH/ ▸n. **1** a person who makes things out of copper. **2** (also **coppersmith barbet**) the crimson-breasted barbet of Southeast Asia, which has a red breast band, a streaked belly, and a repetitive metallic call. • *Megalaima haemacephala*, family Capitonidae.

cop·per sul·fate ▸n. a blue crystalline solid used in electroplating and as a fungicide. • Chem. formula: $CuSO_4.5H_2O$.

cop·per·y /ˈkäpərē/ ▸adj. like copper, esp. in color: *his hair was fine and coppery.*

cop·pice /ˈkäpəs/ *chiefly Brit.* ▸n. an area of woodland in which the trees or shrubs are, or formerly were, periodically cut back to ground level to stimulate growth and provide firewood or timber.
▸v. [*trans.*] cut back (a tree or shrub) to ground level periodically to stimulate growth: [as *adj.*] (**coppiced**) *coppiced timber.* ▷late Middle English: from Old French *copeiz*, based on medieval Latin *colpus* 'a blow' (see COPE[1]). Compare with COPSE.

Cop·po·la /ˈkäpələ/, Francis Ford (1939–), U.S. movie director, writer, and producer. He is known for *The Godfather* (1972) and its two sequels, which chart the fortunes of a New York Mafia family over several generations; these movies earned him three Academy Awards. Other notable movies include *Apocalypse Now* (1979).

cop·ra /ˈkäprə/ ▸n. dried coconut kernels, from which oil is obtained. ▷late 16th cent.: via Portuguese and Spanish from Malayalam *koppara* 'coconut.'

copro- ▸*comb. form* of or relating to dung or feces: *coprophagia* | *coprophilia.* ▷from Greek *kopros* 'dung.'

co·proc·es·sor /kōˈprä,sesər; ,kōˈpräsesər/ ▸n. *Computing* a microprocessor designed to supplement the capabilities of the primary processor.

co·pro·duce /,kōprəˈd(y)o͞os/ ▸v. [*trans.*] produce (a theatrical work or a radio or television program) jointly. —**co·pro·duc·er** n. —**co·pro·duc·tion** /-ˈdəkSHən/ n.

cop·ro·la·li·a /,käprəˈlālēə/ ▸n. *Psychiatry* the involuntary and repetitive use of obscene language, as a symptom of mental illness or organic brain disease. ▷late 19th cent.: from Greek *kopros* 'dung' + *lalia* 'speech, chatter.'

cop·ro·lite /ˈkäprə,līt/ ▸n. *Paleontology* a piece of fossilized dung.

cop·rol·o·gy /kəˈpräləjē/ ▸n. another term for SCATOLOGY.

cop·roph·a·gy /kəˈpräfəjē/ (also **cop·ro·pha·gia** /,käprəˈfāj(ē)ə/) ▸n. *Zoology* the eating of feces or dung. —**cop·ro·phag·ic** /,käprəˈfajik/ *adj.* —**cop·roph·a·gous** /-ˈpräfəgəs/ *adj.* (*chiefly Zoology*).

cop·ro·phil·i·a /,käprəˈfilēə/ ▸n. abnormal interest and pleasure in feces and defecation.

cops and rob·bers ▸*plural n.* a children's game of hiding and chasing, in which the participants pretend to be police and criminals. ■ *figurative* a simplistic polarization of the conflict between criminals and police, seen virtually as a game; a lifestyle centered around this: *to him this could be a lark, a bit of cops and robbers.*

copse /käps/ ▸n. a small group of trees. ▷late 16th cent.: shortened from COPPICE.

cop shop ▸n. *informal* a police station.

Copt /käpt/ ▸n. **1** a native Egyptian in the Hellenistic and Roman periods. **2** a member of the Coptic Church. ▷from French *Copte* or modern Latin *Coptus*, from Arabic *al-ḳibṭ*, *al-ḳubṭ* 'Copts,' from Coptic *Gyptios*, from Greek *Aiguptios* 'Egyptian.'

cop·ter /ˈkäptər/ ▸n. informal term for HELICOPTER.

Cop·tic /ˈkäptik/ ▸n. the language of the Copts, which represents the final stage of ancient Egyptian. It now survives only as the liturgical language of the Coptic Church.
▸adj. of or relating to the Copts or their language.

Cop·tic Church the native Christian Church in Egypt, traditionally founded by St. Mark, and adhering to the Monophysite doctrine rejected by the Council of Chalcedon. Long persecuted after the Muslim Arab conquest of Egypt in the 7th century, the Coptic community now make up about 5 percent of Egypt's population.

cop·u·la /ˈkäpyələ/ ▸n. *Logic & Grammar* a connecting word, in particular a form of the verb *be* connecting a subject and complement. ▷early 17th cent.: from Latin, 'connection, linking of words,' from *co-* 'together' + *apere* 'fasten.' —**cop·u·lar** /ˈkäpyələr/ *adj.*

cop·u·late /ˈkäpyə,lāt/ ▸v. [*intrans.*] have sexual intercourse. ▷late Middle English (in the sense 'join'): from Latin *copulat-* 'fastened together,' from the verb *copulare*, from *copula* (see COPULA). —**cop·u·la·tion** /,käpyəˈlāSHən/ n. —**cop·u·la·to·ry** /-lə,tôrē/ *adj.*

cop·u·la·tive /ˈkäpyə,lātiv; -,lətiv/ ▸adj. **1** *Grammar* (of a word) connecting words or clauses linked in sense. Compare with DISJUNCTIVE. ■ connecting a subject and predicate. **2** of or relating to sexual intercourse. ▷late Middle English: from Old French *copulatif, -ive* or late Latin *copulativus*, from *copulat-* 'coupled,' from the verb *copulare* (see COPULATE). —**cop·u·la·tive·ly** *adv.*

cop·y /ˈkäpē/ ▸n. (*pl.* **cop·ies**) **1** a thing made to be similar or identical to another: *the problem is telling which is the original document and which the copy.* **2** a single specimen of a particular book, record, or other publication or issue: *the record has sold more than a million copies.* **3** matter to be printed: *copy for the next issue must be submitted by the beginning of the month.* ■ material for a newspaper or magazine article: *it is an unfortunate truth of today's media that bad news makes good copy.* ■ the text of an advertisement: *"No more stubble—no more trouble," trumpeted their ad copy.*
▸v. (**cop·ies, cop·ied**) [*trans.*] make a similar or identical version of; reproduce: *each form had to be copied and sent to a different department.* ■ *Computing* reproduce (data stored in one location) in another location: *the command will* **copy** *a file* **from** *one disc* **to** *another.* ■ write out information that one has read or heard: *he copied the details into his notebook* | *I began to* **copy out** *the addresses.* ■ behave in a similar way to; do the same as: *she was such fun that everybody wanted to copy her.* ■ imitate or reproduce (an idea or style) rather than creating something original: *lifestyles* **copied from** *Miami and Fifth Avenue* | [*intrans.*] *art students* **copied from** *approved old masters.* See note at IMITATE. ■ (**copy something to**) send a copy of a letter to (a third party). ▷Middle English (denoting a transcript or copy of a document): from Old French *copie* (noun), *copier* (verb), from Latin *copia* 'abundance' (in medieval Latin 'transcript,' from such phrases as *copiam describendi facere* 'give permission to transcribe').

cop·y·book /ˈkäpē,bo͝ok/ ▸n. a book containing models of handwriting for learners to imitate.
▸adj. exactly in accordance with established criteria; perfect. ■ tritely conventional: *out come the copybook maxims.*

cop·y·cat /ˈkäpē,kat/ ▸n. *informal, derogatory* (esp. in children's use) a person who copies another's behavior, dress, or ideas. ■ [as *adj.*] denoting an action, typically a crime, carried out in imitation of another: *copycat killings.*

cop·y·desk /ˈkäpē,desk/ ▸n. a desk in a newspaper office at which copy is edited for printing.

cop·y·ed·it /ˈkäpē,edit/ (also **cop·y-ed·it**) ▸v. [*trans.*] edit (text to be printed) by checking its consistency and accuracy. —**cop·y·ed·i·tor** /-,edətər/ (also **cop·y ed·i·tor**) n.

cop·y·hold /ˈkäpē,hōld/ ▸n. *Brit., historical* tenure of land based on manorial records.

cop·y·hold·er /ˈkäpē,hōldər/ ▸n. **1** (also **cop·y hold·er**) a clasp or stand for holding sheets of text while it is keyed or typed. **2** *Brit., historical* a person who holds land in copyhold.

cop·y·ist /ˈkäpē-ist/ ▸n. a person who makes copies, esp. of handwritten documents or music. ■ a person who imitates the styles of others, esp. in art. ▷mid 17th cent.: from COPY + -IST; replacing earlier *copist*, from French *copiste* or medieval Latin *copista*, from *copiare* 'to copy,' from *copia* (see COPY).

cop·y·left /ˈkäpē,left/ ▸n. an arrangement whereby software or artistic work may be used, modified, and distributed freely on condition that anything derived from it is bound by the same condition. ▷1980s: on the pattern of *copyright.* —**cop·y·left·ed** *adj.*

cop·y·right /ˈkäpē,rīt/ ▸n. the exclusive legal right, given to an originator or an assignee to print, publish, perform, film, or record literary, artistic, or musical material, and to authorize others to do the same.
▸v. [*trans.*] secure copyright for (such material).

cop·y·right li·brar·y ▸n. *Brit.* a library entitled to receive one free copy of each book, pamphlet, map, music sheet or score, and periodical published in the UK. See also BODLEIAN LIBRARY.

cop·y·writ·er /ˈkäpi,rītər/ ▸n. a person who writes the text of advertisements or publicity material. —**cop·y·writ·ing** /-,rītiNG/ n.

coq au vin /,kōk ō ˈvan; ,käk/ ▸n. a casserole of chicken pieces cooked in red wine. ▷mid 20th cent.: French, literally 'cock in wine.'

co·quet /kōˈket/ ▸v. flirt, or flirt with.
▸n. *dated* a man who flirts.

co·quet·ry /ˈkōkətrē; kōˈketrē/ ▸n. flirtatious behavior or a flirtatious manner. ▷mid 17th cent.: from French *coquetterie*, from *coqueter* 'to flirt,' from *coquet* 'wanton' (see COQUETTE).

co·quette /kōˈket/ ▸n. **1** a woman who flirts. **2** a crested Central and South American hummingbird, typically with green plumage, a reddish crest, and elongated cheek feathers. • *Lophornis* and two other genera, family Trochilidae: several species. ▷mid 17th cent.: French, feminine of *coquet* 'wanton,' diminutive of *coq* 'cock.' —**co·quet·tish** *adj.* —**co·quet·tish·ly** *adv.* —**co·quet·tish·ness** *n.*

co·qui /ˈkōkē/ *n.* ▸a singing tree frog (*Eleutherodactylus coqui*), native to Puerto Rico, that has become an invasive pest in Hawaii. ▷imitative of the male's call.

co·qui·na /kōˈkēnə/ ▸n. **1** a soft limestone of broken shells, used in road-making in the Caribbean and Florida. **2** (also **coquina clam**) a small bivalve mollusk with a wedge-shaped shell that has a wide variety of colors and patterns. • Genus *Donax*, family Donacidae: several species, including the edible **American coquina** (*D. variabilis*). ▷mid 19th cent.: from Spanish, literally 'cockle,' based on Latin *concha* (see CONCH).

co·qui·to /kōˈkētō/ ▸n. (*pl.* **-tos**) a thick-trunked Chilean palm tree that yields large amounts of sweet sap (palm honey) and fiber. Also called CHILEAN WINE PALM. • *Jubaea chilensis*, family Palmae. ▷mid 19th cent.: from Spanish, diminutive of *coco* 'coconut.'

Cor. ▸*abbr.* ■ coroner. ■ *Bible* Corinthians.

cor /kôr/ ▸*exclam. Brit., informal* expressing surprise, excitement, admiration, or alarm: *"Cor! That's a beautiful black eye you've got!"* ▷1930s: alteration of GOD.
▸PHRASE □ **cor blimey** /,kôr ˈblīmē/ see BLIMEY.

cor- ▸*prefix* variant spelling of COM- assimilated before *r* (as in *corrode*, *corrugate*).

Co·ra /ˈkôrə/ ▸n. **1** a member of an American Indian people of western Mexico. **2** the Uto-Aztecan language of this people.
▸adj. of or relating to this people or their language.

cor·a·cle /ˈkôrəkəl; ˈkär-/ ▸n. (esp. in Wales and Ireland) a small, round boat made of wickerwork covered with a watertight material, propelled with a paddle. ▷mid 16th cent.: from Welsh *corwgl, cwrwgl*, related to Scottish Gaelic and Irish *curach* 'small boat'; compare with CURRACH.

cor·a·coid /ˈkôrə,koid/ ▸n. (also **coracoid process**) *Anatomy* a short projection from the shoulder blade in mammals, to which part of the biceps is attached. ▷mid 18th cent.: from modern Latin *coracoides*, from Greek *korakoeidēs* 'ravenlike,' from *korax* 'raven' (because of the resemblance to a raven's beak).

cor·al /ˈkôrəl; ˈkär-/ ▸n. **1** a hard stony substance secreted by certain marine coelenterates as an external skeleton, typically forming large reefs in warm seas: [as *adj.*] *a coral reef.* ■ precious red coral, used in jewelry. ■ the pinkish-red color of red coral. **2** a sedentary coelenterate of warm and tropical seas, with a calcareous, horny, or soft skeleton. Most corals are colonial and many rely on the presence of green algae in their tissues to obtain energy from sunlight. • Several orders in the class Anthozoa, including the 'true' or **stony corals** (order Scleractinia or Madreporaria), which form reefs, the **soft corals** (order Alcyonacea), and the **horny corals** (order Gorgonacea). **3** the unfertilized roe of a lobster or scallop, which is used as food and becomes reddish when cooked. ▷Middle English: via Old French from Latin *corallum*, from Greek *korallion, kouralion.* —**cor·al·loid** /-,loid/ *adj.* (*chiefly Biology Zoology*).

cor·al bells ▸*n.* a red-flowered heuchera (*Heuchera sanguinea*) native to the southwestern U.S., but established elsewhere with many ornamental cultivars.

cor·al·ber·ry /ˈkôrəlˌberē; ˈkär-/ ▸*n.* (*pl.* **-ries**) an evergreen North American shrub of the honeysuckle family, which has fragrant white flowers followed by deep red berries. • *Symphoricarpos orbiculatus*, family Caprifoliaceae.

cor·al fun·gus ▸*n.* a widely distributed fungus that produces a fruiting body composed of upright branching fingerlike projections that resemble coral, found in both Eurasia and North America. • *Clavulina*, *Ramaria*, and other genera, several families, class Basidiomycetes.

Cor·al Ga·bles a resort and commercial city in southeastern Florida, just southwest of Miami, on Biscayne Bay; pop. 40,091.

cor·al·i·ta /ˌkôrəˈlētə; ˌkärə-/ ▸*n.* a pink-flowered climbing vine native to Mexico and the Caribbean, grown as an ornamental. • *Antigonon leptopus*, family Polygonaceae. ▷late 19th cent.: from American Spanish *coralito*, diminutive of Spanish *coral* 'coral.'

cor·al·line /ˈkôrəˌlin/ ▸*n.* (also **coralline alga** or **coralline seaweed**) a branching reddish seaweed with a calcareous jointed stem. • Family Corallinaceae, phylum Rhodophyta, in particular *Corallina officinalis*, which is common on the coasts of the North Atlantic. ■ (in general use) a sedentary colonial marine animal, esp. a bryozoan.
▸*adj. chiefly Geology* derived or formed from coral: *the islands were volcanic rather than coralline in origin.* ■ of the pinkish-red color of precious red coral. ■ resembling coral: *coralline sponges.* ▷mid 16th cent.: the noun from Italian *corallina*, diminutive of *corallo* 'coral,' the adjective (mid 17th cent.) from French *corallin* or late Latin *corallinus*, both based on Latin *corallum* 'coral.'

cor·al·lite /ˈkôrəˌlīt; ˈkär-/ ▸*n. Paleontology* the cuplike calcareous skeleton of a single coral polyp. ■ a fossil coral. ▷early 19th cent.: from Latin *corallum* 'coral' + **-ITE**[1].

cor·al·root /ˈkôrəlˌro͞ot; ˈkärəl-; -ˌro͞ot/ ▸*n.* (also **coral-root orchid**) a leafless orchid that has inconspicuous flowers and lacks chlorophyll. It has a pale knobbly rhizome that obtains nourishment from decaying organic matter. • Genus *Corallorhiza*, family Orchidaceae: several species, including the widespread *C. trifida*. ■ another term for **COCKSCOMB** (sense 3).

Cor·al Sea a part of the western Pacific Ocean that is surrounded by Australia, New Guinea, and Vanuatu, the scene of a naval battle between U.S. and Japanese carriers in 1942 during World War II.

cor·al snake ▸*n.* a brightly colored venomous snake of the cobra family, typically having conspicuous bands of red, yellow, white, and black. Compare with **FALSE CORAL SNAKE**. • *Micrurus* and other genera in the family Elapidae: numerous species.

cor·al spot (also **coral spot disease**) ▸*n.* a common fungal disease of trees and shrubs, appearing as numerous minute pink or dark red cushionlike bodies on the twigs and branches and causing dieback. • *Nectria cinnabarina*, family Hypocreaceae, phylum Ascomycota.

Cor·al Springs a residential city in southeastern Florida; pop. 117,549.

cor·al tree ▸*n.* a tropical or subtropical thorny shrub or tree with showy red or orange flowers that are pollinated by birds. • Genus *Erythrina*, family Leguminosae.

cor·beil /ˈkôrbəl; kôrˈbā/ ▸*n. Architecture* a representation in stone of a basket of flowers. ▷early 18th cent.: from French *corbeille* 'basket,' from late Latin *corbicula* 'small basket,' diminutive of *corbis*.

cor·beille /ˈkôrbəl; kôrˈbā/ ▸*n.* an elegant basket of flowers or fruit. ▷early 19th cent.: French, 'basket' (see also **CORBEIL**).

cor·bel /ˈkôrbəl/ ▸*n.* a projection jutting out from a wall to support a structure above it.
▸*v.* (**-beled**, **-bel·ing**; *chiefly Brit.* **-belled**, **-bel·ling**) [*trans.*] (often **be corbeled out**) support (a structure such as an arch or balcony) on corbels. ▷late Middle English: from Old French, diminutive of *corp* 'crow,' from Latin *corvus* 'raven' (perhaps because of the shape of a corbel, resembling a crow's beak).

cor·bel ta·ble ▸*n.* a projecting course of bricks or stones resting on corbels.

Cor·bett /ˈkôrbit/, James John (1866–1933), U.S. boxer; known as **Gentleman Jim**. He won two world heavyweight championships 1892, 1897.

cor·bic·u·la /kôrˈbikyələ/ ▸*n.* (*pl.* **-u·lae** /-yəlē; -yəˌlī/) *Entomology* another term for **POLLEN BASKET**. ▷early 19th cent.: from late Latin.

cor·bie /ˈkôrbē/ ▸*n.* (*pl.* **-bies**) *Scottish* a raven, crow, or rook. ▷late Middle English: from Old French *corb*, variant of *corp* 'crow' (see **CORBEL**).

cor·bie·steps /ˈkôrbēˌsteps/ (also **cor·bie steps**) ▸*n.* the steplike projections on the sloping part of a gable, common in Flemish architecture and 16- and 17th-century Scottish buildings. Also called **CROW STEPS**.

Cor·bin /ˈkôrbin/, Margaret (1751–1800), American Revolution heroine; born *Margaret Cochran*. After her husband's death in the attack on Fort Washington in 1776, she took his place at his cannon until becoming severely wounded. She was the first woman to be pensioned by the U.S. government.

Cor·co·va·do /ˌkôrkōˈvädō/ a peak that rises to 2,310 feet (711 m) on the south side of Rio de Janeiro. A statue of Jesus Christ (named "Christ the Redeemer"), 131 feet (40 m) high, stands on its summit.

Christ the Redeemer Statue on Corcovado

Cor·cy·ra /kôrˈsīrə/ ancient Greek name for **CORFU**.

cord /kôrd/ ▸*n.* **1** long thin flexible string or rope made from several twisted strands: *hang the picture from a rail on a length of cord.* ■ a length of such material, typically one used to fasten or move a specified object: *a dressing-gown cord.* ■ an anatomical structure resembling a length of cord (e.g., the spinal cord, the umbilical cord): *the baby was still attached to its mother by the cord.* ■ a flexible insulated cable used for carrying electric current to an appliance. **2** ribbed fabric, esp. corduroy: [as *adj.*] *cord jackets.* ■ (**cords**) *informal* corduroy pants: *he was dressed in faded black cords.* ■ a cordlike rib on fabric. **3** a measure of cut wood, usually 128 cubic feet (3.62 cu m).
▸*v.* [*trans.*] attach a cord to. ▷Middle English: from Old French *corde*, from Latin *chorda*, from Greek *khordē* 'gut, string of a musical instrument.' —**cord·like** /-ˌlīk/ *adj.*
▸*PHRASE* □ **cut the (umbilical) cord** *figurative* cease to rely on someone or something protective or supportive and begin to act independently.

cord·age /ˈkôrdij/ ▸*n.* cords or ropes, esp. in a ship's rigging. ▷late 15th cent.: from Old French, from *corde* 'rope' (see **CORD**).

cor·date /ˈkôrˌdāt/ ▸*adj. Botany & Zoology* heart-shaped. ▷mid 17th cent. (in the sense 'wise, prudent'): from Latin *cordatus* 'wise' (in modern Latin 'heart-shaped'), from *cor*, *cord-* 'heart.'

Cor·day /kôrˈdā/, Charlotte (1768–93), French political assassin; full name *Marie Anne Charlotte Corday d'Armont*. In 1793, she assassinated revolutionary leader Jean Paul Marat in his bath; she was found guilty of treason and guillotined four days later.

cord blood ▸*n.* blood from the human umbilical cord, a source of stem cells.

cord·ed /ˈkôrdəd/ ▸*adj.* **1** (of cloth) ribbed. ■ (of a tensed muscle) standing out so as to resemble a piece of cord. **2** equipped with a cord: *a corded waistband | corded and cordless phones.*

cord·grass /ˈkôrdˌgras/ ▸*n.* a coarse wiry coastal grass that is sometimes used to stabilize mudflats. • Genus *Spartina*, family Gramineae.

cor·dial /ˈkôrjəl/ ▸*adj.* warm and friendly: *the atmosphere was cordial and relaxed.* ■ strongly felt: *I earned his cordial loathing.*
▸*n.* **1** another term for **LIQUEUR**. **2** a comforting or pleasant-tasting medicine. ▷Middle English (also in the sense 'belonging to the heart'): from medieval Latin *cordialis*, from Latin *cor*, *cord-* 'heart.' —**cor·dial·i·ty** /ˌkôrjēˈalitē/ *n.* —**cor·dial·ly** *adv.*

cor·di·er·ite /ˈkôrdēəˌrīt/ ▸*n.* a dark blue mineral occurring chiefly in metamorphic rocks. It consists of an aluminosilicate of magnesium, and also occurs as a dichroic gem variety. ▷early 19th cent.: named after Pierre L. A. *Cordier* (1777–1861), French geologist, + **-ITE**[1].

cor·di·form /ˈkôrdəˌfôrm/ ▸*adj.* heart-shaped.

cor·dil·le·ra /ˌkôrdlˈ(y)erə/ ▸*n.* a system or group of parallel mountain ranges together with the intervening plateaus and other features, esp. in the Andes or the Rockies. ▷early 18th cent.: from Spanish, from *cordilla*, diminutive of *cuerda* 'cord,' from Latin *chorda* (see **CORD**).

cord·ing /ˈkôrdiNG/ ▸*n.* cord or braid, esp. that used as a decorative fabric trimming.

cord·ite /ˈkôrˌdīt/ ▸*n.* a smokeless explosive made from nitrocellulose, nitroglycerine, and petroleum jelly, used in ammunition. ▷late 19th cent.: from **CORD** (because of its stringlike appearance) + **-ITE**[1].

cord·less /ˈkôrdləs/ ▸*adj.* (of an electrical appliance or telephone) working without connection to a main supply or central unit.
▸*n.* (usu. **the cordless**) a cordless telephone: *I keep the cordless with me at all times.*

Cor·do·ba /ˈkôrdəbə; -dəvə/ (also **Cor·do·va**) **1** a city in Andalusia, in southern Spain; pop. 309,200. Founded by the Carthaginians, it was under Moorish rule from 711 to 1236 and was renowned for its architecture, particularly the Great Mosque. Spanish name **CÓRDOBA** . **2** a city in central Argentina; pop. 1,198,000.

cor·do·ba /ˈkôrdəbə; -dəvə/ ▸*n.* the basic monetary unit of Nicaragua, equal to 100 centavos. ▷named after F. Fernández de *Córdoba*, a 16th-cent. Spanish governor of Nicaragua.

cor·don /ˈkôrdn/ ▸*n.* **1** a line or circle of police, soldiers, or guards preventing access to or from an area or building: *troops threw a cordon around the headquarters.* **2** an ornamental cord or braid. **3** *Architecture* another term for **STRINGCOURSE**.
▸*v.* [*trans.*] (**cordon off**) prevent access to or from (an area or building) by surrounding it with police or other guards: *the city center was cordoned off after fires were discovered in two stores.* ▷late Middle English (denoting an ornamental braid worn on the person): from Italian *cordone*, augmentative of *corda*, and French *cordon*, diminutive of *corde*, both from Latin *chorda* 'string, rope' (see **CORD**). Sense 3, the earliest of the current noun senses, dates from the early 18th cent.

cor·don bleu /ˌkôrdôN ˈblœ/ ▸*adj. Cooking* of the highest class: *a cordon bleu chef.* ■ denoting a dish consisting of an escalope of veal or chicken rolled, filled with cheese and ham, and then fried in breadcrumbs.
▸*n.* a cook of the highest class. ▷mid 18th cent. (as a noun, often specifically denoting a first-class cook): French, literally 'blue ribbon.' The blue ribbon once signified the highest order of chivalry in the reign of the Bourbon kings.

cor·don sa·ni·taire /kôrdôN ˌsänēˈter/ ▸*n.* (*pl.* **cor·dons sa·ni·taires** *pronunc.* same) a guarded line preventing anyone from leaving an area infected by a disease and thus spreading it. ■ a measure designed to prevent communication or the spread of undesirable influences: *these rules help to reinforce the cordon sanitaire around the Pentagon.* ■ a series or chain of small neutral buffer states around a larger, potentially dangerous or hostile state. ▷mid 19th cent.: French, from *cordon* 'line, border' (see **CORDON**) + *sanitaire* 'sanitary.'

Cor·do·va /ˈkôrdəvə/ English name for **CORDOBA**.

cor·do·van /ˈkôrdəvən/ ▸*n.* a kind of soft leather made originally from goatskin and now from horsehide. ▷late 16th cent.: from Spanish *cordován*, former spelling of *cordobán* 'of Cordoba' (see sense 1 of **CORDOBA**), where it was originally made.

Cor·du·ra /kôrˈd(y)o͝orə/ ▸*n. trademark* a durable synthetic fabric.

cor·du·roy /ˈkôrdəˌroi/ ▸*n.* a thick cotton fabric with velvety ribs. ■ (**corduroys**) pants made of corduroy. ▷late 18th cent.: probably from **CORD** 'ribbed fabric' + *duroy*, denoting a kind of lightweight worsted formerly made in the West of England; of unknown origin.

cor·du·roy road ▸*n. historical* a road made of tree trunks laid across a swamp.

cord·wood /ˈkôrdˌwo͝od/ ▸*n.* wood that has been cut into uniform lengths, used esp. as firewood.

CORE /kôr/ ▸*abbr.* Congress of Racial Equality.

Pronunciation Key ə *ago*; ər *over*; ˈə or ˌə *up*; ˈər or ˌər *fur*; a *hat*; ā *rate*; ä *car*; CH *chew*; e *let*; ē *see*; e(ə)r *air*; i *fit*; ī *by*; i(ə)r *ear*; NG *sing*; ō *go*; ô *for*; oi *boy*; o͝o *good*; o͞o *goo*; ou *out*; SH *she*; TH *thin*; TH *then*; (h)w *why*; ZH *vision*

core /kôr/ ▸*n.* **1** the tough central part of various fruits, containing the seeds: *an apple core.* **2** the central or most important part of something, in particular: ■ [often as *adj.*] the part of something that is central to its existence or character: *managers can concentrate on their core activities | the plan has the interests of children at its core.* ■ an important or unchanging group of people forming the central part of a larger body. ■ the dense central region of a planet, esp. the nickel–iron inner part of the earth. ■ the central part of a nuclear reactor, which contains the fissile material. ■ a tiny ring of magnetic material used in a computer memory to store one bit of data, now superseded by semiconductor memories. ■ the inner strand of an electrical cable or rope. ■ a piece of soft iron forming the center of an electromagnet or an induction coil. ■ an internal mold filling a space to be left hollow in a casting. ■ a cylindrical sample of rock, ice, or other material obtained by boring with a hollow drill. ■ *Archaeology* a piece of flint from which flakes or blades have been removed.
▸*v.* [*trans.*] remove the tough central part and seeds from (a fruit): *peel and core the pears.* ▷Middle English: of unknown origin. **—cor·er** *n.*
▸*PHRASE* □ **to the core** to the depths of one's being: *she was shaken to the core by his words.* ■ used to indicate that someone possesses a characteristic to a very high degree: *he is a politician to the core.*

-core ▸*comb. form* (used as the second element of various compounds) denoting types of rock or dance music that have an aggressive presentation: *queercore.* ▷from CORE, on the pattern of *hard-core.*

core as·set ▸*n.* an asset of an enterprise considered to be essential to its success.

core com·pe·ten·cy ▸*n.* a defining capability or advantage that distinguishes an enterprise from its competitors. ■ a defined level of competence in a particular job or academic program.

core dump ▸*n. Computing* a dump of the contents of main memory, carried out typically as an aid to debugging.

co·ref·er·en·tial /ˌkōˌrefəˈrenCHəl/ ▸*adj. Linguistics* (of two elements or units) having the same reference. **—co·ref·er·ence** /kōˈref(ə)rəns; ˈkō-/ *n.*

co·re·li·gion·ist /ˌkō riˈlijənist/ ▸*n.* an adherent of the same religion as another person.

co·rel·la /kəˈrelə/ ▸*n.* a white Australasian cockatoo with some pink feathers on the face, bare blue skin around the eye, and typically a long bill. • Genus *Cacatua*, family Cacatuidae (or Psittacidae): three species, in particular the widespread **little corella** (*C. sanguinea*). ▷late 19th cent.: from Wiradhuri.

Co·rel·li /kəˈrelē/, Arcangelo (1653–1713), Italian violinist and composer, known for his Concerti grossi and sonatas for violin.

co·re·op·sis /ˌkôrēˈäpsəs/ ▸*n.* a plant of the daisy family, cultivated for its rayed, typically yellow, flowers. Also called TICKSEED. • Genus *Coreopsis*, family Compositae. ▷modern Latin, from Greek *koris* 'bug' + *opsis* 'appearance' (because of the shape of the seed).

co·re·spond·ent (also **co·re·spond·ent**) ▸*n.* **1** a joint defendant in a lawsuit, esp. one on appeal. **2** a person cited in a divorce case as having committed adultery with the respondent.

Cor·fu /kôrˈfo͞o; ˈkôrf(y)o͞o/ a Greek island, one of the largest of the Ionian Islands, off the west coast of mainland Greece. It was known in ancient times as Corcyra; pop. 105,350. Greek name KÉRKIRA.

cor·gi /ˈkôrgē/ ▸*n.* (*pl.* **cor·gis**) short for WELSH CORGI.

co·ri·a·ceous /ˌkôrēˈāSHəs/ ▸*adj. technical* resembling or having the texture of leather: *coriaceous leaves.* ▷late 17th cent.: from late Latin *coriaceus* (from Latin *corium* 'leather') + -OUS.

co·ri·an·der /ˈkôrēˌandər; ˌkôrēˈandər/ ▸*n.* an aromatic Mediterranean plant of the parsley family, the leaves and seeds of which are used as culinary herbs. • *Coriandrum sativum*, family Umbelliferae. ▷Middle English: from Old French *coriandre*, from Latin *coriandrum*, from Greek *koriannon.*

Cor·inth /ˈkôrinTH; ˈkär-/ a city on the northern coast of the Peloponnese, in Greece; pop. 27,400. The modern city, built in 1858, is slightly northeast of the site of an ancient city of the same name that was a prominent city-state in ancient Greece. Greek name KÓRINTHOS.

Cor·inth, Gulf of an inlet of the Ionian Sea that extends between the Peloponnese and central Greece. Also called LEPANTO, GULF OF.

Cor·inth, Isthmus of a narrow neck of land that links the Peloponnese with central Greece and separates the Gulf of Corinth from the Saronic Gulf.

Cor·inth Ca·nal a man-made shipping channel that crosses the narrowest part of the Isthmus of Corinth (a distance of 4 miles or 6.4 km). Opened in 1893, it links the Gulf of Corinth and the Saronic Gulf.

Co·rin·thi·an /kəˈrinTHēən/ ▸*adj.* **1** belonging or relating to Corinth, esp. the ancient city. ■ relating to or denoting the lightest and most ornate of the classical orders of architecture (used esp. by the Romans), characterized by flared capitals with rows of acanthus leaves. **2** involving or displaying the highest standards of sportsmanship: *a club embodying the Corinthian spirit.*
▸*n.* **1** a native of Corinth. ■ *historical* a wealthy amateur of sport. **2** the Corinthian order of architecture.

Co·rin·thi·ans /kəˈrinTHēənz/ either of two books of the New Testament, epistles of St. Paul to the Church at Corinth.

Cor·i·o·la·nus /ˌkôrēəˈlānəs/, Gaius (or Gnaeus) Marcius (5th century BC), Roman general who acquired his name from the capture of the Volscian town of Corioli.

Co·ri·o·lis ef·fect /ˌkôrēˈōləs/ ▸*n. Physics* an effect whereby a mass moving in a rotating system experiences a force (the **Coriolis force**) acting perpendicular to the direction of motion and to the axis of rotation. On the earth, the effect tends to deflect moving objects to the right in the northern hemisphere and to the left in the southern and is important in the formation of cyclonic weather systems. ▷early 20th cent.: named after Gaspard *Coriolis* (1792–1843), French engineer.

co·ri·um /ˈkôrēəm/ ▸*n. chiefly Zoology* another term for DERMIS. ▷early 19th cent.: from Latin, 'skin.'

Cork /kôrk/ a county in the Republic of Ireland, in the province of Munster, on the Celtic Sea. ■ its county town, a port on the Lee River; pop. 127,000.

cork /kôrk/ ▸*n.* the buoyant, light brown substance obtained from the outer layer of the bark of the cork oak: [as *adj.*] *cork tiles.* ■ a bottle stopper, esp. one made of cork. ■ a piece of cork used as a float for a fishing line or net. ■ *Botany* a protective layer of dead cells immediately below the bark of woody plants.
▸*v.* [*trans.*] (often **be corked**) **1** close or seal (a bottle) with a cork. ■ [as *adj.*] (**corked**) (of wine) spoiled by tannin from the cork. **2** draw with burnt cork. **3** illicitly hollow out (a baseball bat) and fill it with cork to make it lighter. ▷Middle English: from Dutch and Low German *kork*, from Spanish *alcorque* 'cork-soled sandal,' from Arabic *al-* 'the' and (probably) Spanish Arabic *ḳurḳ*, *ḳorḳ*, based on Latin *quercus* 'oak, cork oak.' **—cork·like** /-ˌlīk/ *adj.*

cork·age /ˈkôrkij/ ▸*n.* a charge made by a restaurant or hotel for serving wine that has been brought in by a customer.

cork cam·bi·um ▸*n. Botany* tissue in the stem of a plant that gives rise to cork on its outer surface and a layer of cells containing chlorophyll on its inner surface.

cork·er /ˈkôrkər/ ▸*n.* **1** an excellent or astonishing person or thing: *it was the season's first goal, and a corker.* **2** a device that places a cork into a bottle: *it's a great wine corker.*

cork oak ▸*n.* an evergreen Mediterranean oak, the outer layer of the bark of which is the source of cork, which can be stripped without harming the tree. • *Quercus suber*, family Fagaceae.

cork·screw /ˈkôrkˌskro͞o/ ▸*n.* a device for pulling corks from bottles, consisting of a spiral metal rod that is inserted into the cork and a handle that extracts it. ■ [usu. as *adj.*] a thing with a spiral shape or movement: *a girl with corkscrew curls.*
▸*v.* [*intrans.*] move or twist in a spiral motion: *the plane was corkscrewing toward the earth.*

cork tree (also **cork·tree**) ▸*n.* **1** another term for CORK OAK. **2** an Asian citrus tree with a corky bark. • Genus *Phellodendron*, family Rutaceae: several species, including *P. sachalinense*, often cultivated as on ornamental.

cork·wood /ˈkôrkˌwo͝od/ ▸*n.* a shrub or tree that yields light porous timber, in particular: • a small American tree that produces timber used for fishing floats (*Leitneria floridana*, family Leitneriaceae). • a similar tree native to New Zealand (*Entelea arborescens*, family Tiliaceae).

cork·y /ˈkôrkē/ ▸*adj.* (**cork·i·er**, **cork·i·est**) **1** corklike. **2** (of wine) corked.

corm /kôrm/ ▸*n.* a rounded underground storage organ present in plants such as crocuses, gladioli, and cyclamens, consisting of a swollen stem base covered with scale leaves. Compare with BULB (sense 1), RHIZOME. ▷mid 19th cent.: from modern Latin *cormus*, from Greek *kormos* 'trunk stripped of its boughs.'

cor·mel /ˈkôrməl; kôrˈmel/ ▸*n.* a small corm growing at the side of a mature corm.

corm·let /ˈkôrmlət/ ▸*n.* a small corm growing at the base of a mature corm.

cor·mo·rant /ˈkôrmərənt/ ▸*n.* a large diving bird with a long neck, long hooked bill, short legs, and mainly dark plumage. It typically breeds on coastal cliffs and is noted for its voracious appetite. • Genus *Phalacrocorax* (and *Nannopterum*), family Phalacrocoracidae: numerous species, in particular the widespread **great** (or **European**) **cormorant** (*P. carbo*) and the North American **double-crested cormorant** (*P. auritus*). ■ *figurative* an insatiably greedy person or thing. ▷Middle English: from Old French *cormaran*, from medieval Latin *corvus marinus* 'sea raven.' The final *-t* is on the pattern of words such as *peasant.*

double-crested cormorant

corn[1] /kôrn/ ▸*n.* **1** a North American cereal plant that yields large grains, or kernels, set in rows on a cob. Its many varieties yield numerous products, highly valued for both human and livestock consumption. Also called INDIAN CORN. • *Zea mays*, family Gramineae; it was domesticated before 5000 BC, although the wild ancestor is unidentified. ■ the grains of this: *creamed corn | two ears of corn.* ■ *Brit.* the chief cereal crop of a district, esp. (in England) wheat or (in Scotland) oats. **2** *informal* something banal or sentimental: *the movie is pure corn.* ▷Old English, of Germanic origin; related to Dutch *koren* and German *Korn.*
▸*PHRASE* □ **corn on the cob** corn when cooked and eaten straight from the cob; an ear of corn.

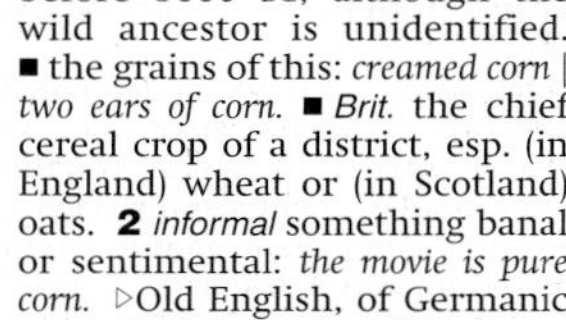

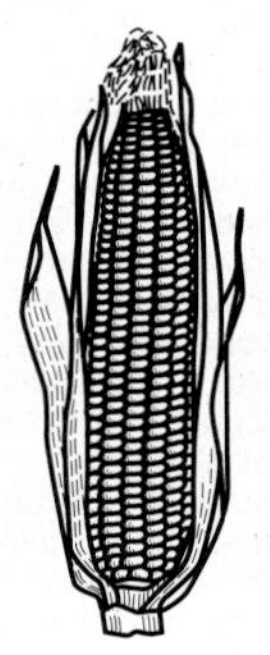
corn[1] **1**

corn[2] ▸*n.* a small, painful area of thickened skin on the foot, esp. on the toes, caused by pressure. ▷late Middle English: via Anglo-Norman French from Latin *cornu* 'horn.'

Cor·na·ro Pis·co·pi·a /kôrˈnärō pisˈkōpēə/, Elena Lucrezia (1646–1684), Venetian philosopher and mathematician. The first woman to be awarded a college degree, she received the doctorate of philosophy from the University of Padua on June 25, 1678.

corn·ball /ˈkôrnˌbôl/ *informal* ▸*adj.* trite and sentimental: *a cornball movie.*
▸*n.* a person with trite or sentimental ideas.

corn beef ▸*n.* corned beef.

Corn Belt name for parts of the U.S. Midwest, esp. Illinois and Iowa, where corn is a major crop.

corn bor·er ▸*n.* a moth whose larvae feed upon and bore into corn. • Several species in the family Pyralidae, in particular the **European corn borer** (*Ostrinia nubilalis*), which was accidentally introduced into North America, and *Diatraea* (or **Zeadiatraea**) *grandiosella* of the southern U.S.

corn·bread /ˈkôrnˌbred/ (also **corn bread**) ▸*n.* a type of bread made from cornmeal and typically leavened without yeast.

corn cake (also **corn·cake**) ▸*n.* cornbread made in the form of flat cakes.

corn·cob /ˈkôrnˌkäb/ (also **corn cob**) ▸*n.* see COB[1] (sense 1).

corn·cob pipe ▸*n.* a tobacco pipe with a bowl made from a dried corncob.

corn cock·le (also **corn·cock·le**) ▸*n.* a Mediterranean plant with bright pink or purple flowers and poisonous seeds, introduced into Britain and North America. If unchecked, it can be a prolific weed in fields of grain. It is often cultivated as a showy annual. • *Agrostemma githago*, family Caryophyllaceae. ▷early 18th cent.: from CORN[1] + *cockle* (from Old English *coccul* 'corn cockle,' perhaps via Latin from Greek *kokkos* 'berry').

corn crake (also **corn·crake**) ▸*n.* a secretive Eurasian crake inhabiting coarse grasslands, with mainly brown streaked plumage and a distinctive double rasping call. Also called **LAND RAIL**. • *Crex crex*, family Rallidae.

corn crib (also **corn·crib**) ▸*n.* a bin or ventilated building for storing unhusked ears of corn.

corn dodg·er ▸*n.* a small, hard fried or baked cornmeal cake. ■ a boiled cornmeal dumpling.

corn dog ▸*n.* a hot dog covered in cornmeal batter, fried, and served on a stick.

cor·ne·a /ˈkôrnēə/ ▸*n.* the transparent layer forming the front of the eye. ▷late Middle English: from medieval Latin *cornea tela* 'horny tissue,' from Latin *cornu* 'horn.' **—cor·ne·al** *adj.*

corn ear·worm ▸*n.* an American moth caterpillar that is a pest of corn, cotton, and tomatoes. Also called **BOLLWORM, COTTON BOLLWORM, TOMATO FRUITWORM**. • *Heliothis zea*, family Noctuidae.

corned /kôrnd/ ▸*adj.* (of food) preserved in salt water: *corned beef.*

corned beef (also **corn beef**) ▸*n.* beef brisket cured in brine and boiled, served hot typically with cabbage, or cold, sliced for sandwiches. ▷*corned*, in the sense 'preserved in salt water.'

Cor·neille /kôrˈnā(l)/, Pierre (1606–84), French playwright; regarded as the founder of classical French tragedy. Notable plays: *Le Cid* (1637), *Cinna* (1641), and *Polyeucte* (1643).

cor·ne·i·tis /ˌkôrnēˈītis/ ▸*n. Medicine* inflammation of the cornea.

cor·nel /ˈkôrnl; -ˌnel/ ▸*n.* a dogwood, esp. of a dwarf variety. • Genus *Cornus*, family Cornaceae: several species, including the dwarf *C. suecica*. ▷late Middle English (denoting the wood of the cornelian cherry): from Old French *corneille*, from Latin *cornus*.

cor·nel·ian /kôrˈnēlyən/ ▸*n.* variant spelling of **CARNELIAN**.

cor·nel·ian cher·ry ▸*n.* a Eurasian flowering shrub or small tree of the dogwood family, cultivated as an ornamental. • *Cornus mas*, family Cornaceae. ■ the edible oval red berry of this plant. ▷early 17th cent.: *cornelian* from **CORNEL** + **-IAN**.

cor·ne·ous /ˈkôrnēəs/ ▸*adj. formal* hornlike; horny: *the skeleton is formed of a corneous substance.* ▷mid 17th cent.: from Latin *corneus* (from *cornu* 'horn') + **-OUS**.

cor·ner /ˈkôrnər/ ▸*n.* **1** a place or angle where two or more sides or edges meet: *Jan sat at one corner of the table.* ■ an area inside a room, box, or square-shaped space, near the place where two or more edges or surfaces meet: *he drove the ball into the corner of the net.* ■ a place where two streets meet: *an apartment on the corner of 199th Street and Amsterdam Avenue* | [as *adj.*] *the corner house.* ■ *figurative* a difficult or awkward situation: *he found himself* ***backed into a corner.*** ■ first or third base on a baseball diamond: *two outs, with runners on the corners.* ■ a sharp bend in a road: *serious racers want a car that is fast going into and out of the corners.* **2** a part, region, or area, esp. one regarded as secluded or remote: *they descended on the college* ***from all corners of the world*** | *his wisdom was disseminated to* ***the four corners*** *of the earth* | *figurative she couldn't bear journalists prying into every corner of her life.* ■ a position in which one dominates the supply of a particular commodity. **3** short for **CORNER KICK**. **4** *Boxing & Wrestling* each of the diagonally opposite ends of the ring, where a contestant rests between rounds. ■ a contestant's supporters or seconds: *Hodkinson was encouraged by his corner.* **5** *Baseball* each of the two parallel sides of home plate, which are perceived as defining the vertical edges of the strike zone.

▸*v.* [*trans.*] **1** (often **be cornered**) force (a person or animal) into a place or situation from which it is hard to escape: *the man was eventually cornered by police dogs.* ■ detain (someone) in conversation, typically against their will: *I managed to corner Gary for fifteen minutes.* **2** control (a market) by dominating the supply of a particular commodity: *whether they will* ***corner the market*** *in graphics software remains to be seen.* ■ establish a corner in (a commodity): *you cornered vanadium and made a killing.* **3** [*intrans.*] (of a vehicle or driver) go around a bend in a road: *no squeal is evident from the tires when cornering fast.* ▷Middle English: from Anglo-Norman French, based on Latin *cornu* 'horn, tip, corner.'

▸*PHRASES* □ **(just) around** (or **round**) **the corner** very near: *there's a pharmacy around the corner.* □ **cut corners** see **CUT**. □ **in someone's corner** acting as a second, to a boxer. ■ on someone's side; giving someone support and encouragement. □ **on** (or **at** or **in**) **every corner** everywhere: *there were saloons on every corner* | *it's difficult to readjust when the past assaults you at every corner* | *young executives sprouted in every corner.* □ **see someone/something out of** (or **from**) **the corner of one's eye** see someone or something at the edge of one's field of vision. □ **turn the corner** see **TURN**.

cor·ner·back /ˈkôrnərˌbak/ ▸*n. Football* a defensive back positioned to the outside of the linebackers.

cor·nered /ˈkôrnərd/ ▸*adj.* having a specified number of places or angles where the edges or sides meet: *young boys in six-cornered hats.* ■ having a specified number of parties involved: *a three-cornered meeting was being arranged in Hong Kong.*

cor·ner kick (also **cor·ner**) ▸*n. Soccer* a free kick taken by the attacking side from a corner of the field after the ball has been sent over the end line outside the goal by a defender: *Kavanagh lofted a corner kick.*

cor·ner·man /ˈkôrnərˌman/ ▸*n.* (*pl.* **-men**) a person whose job is to assist a boxer or wrestler at the corner between rounds.

cor·ner·stone /ˈkôrnərˌstōn/ ▸*n.* a stone that forms the base of a corner of a building, joining two walls.■ a stone ceremonially laid usually at the corner of a foundation to mark the occasion of a building being erected. ■ an important quality or feature on which a particular thing depends or is based: *a national minimum wage remained the cornerstone of policy.*

cor·ner·wise /ˈkôrnərˌwīz/ ▸*adv.* at an angle of approximately 45°; diagonally: *he laid the cloth cornerwise on the polished table.*

cor·net /kôrˈnet/ ▸*n.* **1** *Music* a brass instrument resembling a trumpet but shorter and wider, played chiefly in bands. ■ a compound organ stop with a powerful treble sound. **2** *Brit.* a cone-shaped wafer, esp. one filled with ice cream. ▷late Middle English (originally denoting a wind instrument made of a horn): from Old French, diminutive of a variant of Latin *cornu* 'horn.' **—cor·net·ist** /-ˈnetəst/ (also **cor·net·tist**) *n.*

cor·net·fish /kôrˈnetˌfisн; ˈkôrnət-/ ▸*n.* (*pl.* same or **-fish·es**) a large marine fish with a long, narrow, flutelike snout, an elongated body, and a whiplike extension to the tail. It is common in shallow tropical waters of the Atlantic and Indo-Pacific region. • Family Fistularidae and genus *Fistularia*: several species.

cor·net·to /kôrˈnetō/ (also **cor·nett** /-ˈnet/) ▸*n.* (*pl.* **-net·ti** /-ˈnetē/ or **-netts**) a woodwind instrument of the 16th and 17th centuries, typically curved, with finger holes and a cup-shaped mouthpiece. ▷late 19th cent.: from Italian, diminutive of *corno* 'horn,' from Latin *cornu*. Compare with **CORNET**.

corn-fed (also **corn·fed**) ▸*adj.* fed on corn: *corn-fed chickens.* ■ *informal* plump; well fed. ■ *informal* provincial; unsophisticated: *a backward, corn-fed Heartland city.*

corn·field /ˈkôrnˌfēld/ ▸*n.* a field in which corn is grown.

corn·flakes /ˈkôrnˌflāks/ ▸*plural n.* a breakfast cereal consisting of toasted flakes made from corn.

corn flour ▸*n.* flour made from corn: *the fish were coated with corn flour and fried.* ■ (usu. **corn·flour**) British term for **CORNSTARCH**.

corn·flow·er /ˈkôrnˌflouər/ ▸*n.* a slender Eurasian plant related to the knapweeds, with flowers that are typically a deep, vivid blue. • Genus *Centaurea*, family Compositae: several species, including the annual *Centaurea cyanus* (also called **BLUEBOTTLE**), formerly a common weed of cornfields, and the perennial *C. montana*, grown in gardens. ■ (also **cornflower blue**) a deep, vivid blue color.

Corn·husk·er State /ˈkôrnˌhəskər/ a nickname for the state of **NEBRASKA**.

corn·husk·ing /ˈkôrnˌhəskiNG/ ▸*n.* the removal of husks from ears of corn. ■ the husking of corn by several people as a social event. Also called **HUSKING BEE**. **—corn·husk·er** *n.*

cor·nice /ˈkôrnis/ ▸*n.* **1** an ornamental molding around the wall of a room just below the ceiling. ■ a horizontal molded projection crowning a building or structure, esp. the uppermost member of the entablature of an order, surmounting the frieze. **2** an overhanging mass of hardened snow at the edge of a mountain precipice. ▷mid 16th cent.: from French *corniche*, from Italian *cornice*, perhaps from Latin *cornix* 'crow' (compare with **CORBEL**), but influenced by Greek *korōnis* 'copestone.' **—cor·niced** *adj.* **—cor·nic·ing** *n.*

cor·niche /ˈkôrnisн; kôrˈnēsн/ ▸*n.* a road cut into the edge of a cliff, esp. one running along a coast. ▷mid 19th cent.: from French (see **CORNICE**).

Cor·nish /ˈkôrnisн/ ▸*adj.* of or relating to Cornwall, or its people or language.

▸*n.* **1** [as *plural n.*] (**the Cornish**) the people of Cornwall collectively. **2** the extinct Brythonic language of Cornwall ▷late Middle English: from the first element of **CORNWALL** + **-ISH**[1]. **—Cor·nish·man** /-mən/ *n.* (*pl.* **-men**) **—Cor·nish·wom·an** /-ˌwo͝omən/ *n.* (*pl.* **-wom·en**) .

Cor·nish hen (also **Cornish game hen**) ▸*n.* another term for **ROCK CORNISH**.

Corn Laws (in the UK) a series of 19th-century laws introduced to protect British farmers from foreign competition. They were repealed in 1846.

corn mar·i·gold ▸*n.* a daisylike yellow-flowered Eurasian plant. • *Chrysanthemum segetum*, family Compositae.

corn·meal /ˈkôrnˌmēl/ ▸*n.* meal made from ground, dried corn.

corn oil ▸*n.* an oil obtained from the germ of corn, used in cooking and salad dressings.

corn pone ▸*n.* see **PONE**.

▸*adj.* (**corn-pone**) *often derogatory* rustic; unsophisticated: *corn-pone humor.*

corn roast ▸*n. Canadian* an oudoor party at which fresh ears of sweet corn are roasted and eaten.

corn·rows /ˈkôrnˌrōz/ ▸*plural n.* a style of braiding and plaiting the hair in narrow strips to form geometric patterns on the scalp.

corn sal·ad ▸*n.* a small blue-flowered herbaceous plant of dry soils, native to Europe and the Mediterranean. Widely cultivated in North America, its narrow leaves are used in salad. Also called **LAMB'S LETTUCE, MACHE**. • *Valerianella locusta*, family Valerianaceae.

corn·silk /ˈkôrnˌsilk/ ▸*n.* each of the long silklike filiform styles of the female flower of corn.

corn snake ▸*n.* a long North American rat snake with a spear-shaped mark between the eyes. • *Elaphe guttata*, family Colubridae. ▷late 17th cent.: so named because often found in cornfields.

corn snow ▸*n.* snow with a rough granular surface resulting from alternate thawing and freezing. ▷from *corn* in the dialect sense 'granule.'

corn spur·rey ▸ see **SPURREY**.

corn·stalk /ˈkôrnˌstôk/ ▸*n.* the stem of a corn plant.

corn·starch /ˈkôrnˌstärcн/ ▸*n.* finely ground corn flour, used as a thickener in cooking.

Corn State a nickname for the state of **IOWA**.

corn sug·ar ▸*n.* dextrose, esp when made from cornstarch.

corn syr·up ▸*n.* syrup made from cornstarch, consisting of dextrose, maltose, and dextrins.

cor·nu /ˈkôrn(y)o͞o/ ▸*n.* (*pl.* **-nu·a** /-n(y)o͞oə/) *Anatomy* a structure with a shape likened to a horn, in particular: ■ a horn-shaped projection of the thyroid cartilage or of certain bones (such as the hyoid and the coccyx). ■ either of the two lateral cavities of the uterus, into which the Fallopian tubes pass. ■ each of three elongated parts of the lateral ventricles of the brain. ▷late 17th cent.: from Latin, 'horn.' **—cor·nu·al** /-n(y)o͞oəl/ *adj.*

cor·nu·co·pi·a /ˌkôrn(y)əˈkōpēə/ ▸*n.* a symbol of plenty consisting of a goat's horn overflowing with flowers, fruit, and corn. ■ an ornamental container shaped like such a horn. ■ an abundant supply of good things of a specified kind: *the festival offers* ***a cornucopia of*** *pleasures.* ▷early 16th cent.: from late Latin, from Latin *cornu copiae* 'horn of plenty' (a mythical horn able to provide whatever is desired). **—cor·nu·co·pi·an** *adj.*

Corn·wall /ˈkôrnˌwôl; -wəl/ **1** a county occupying the extreme southwestern peninsula of England; county town, Truro. **2** a city in eastern Ontario in Canada, a port on the St. Lawrence River, across from Massena, New York; pop. 47,137.

Corn·wal·lis /kôrnˈwäləs/, Charles, 1st Marquis (1738–1805), English soldier. He surrendered the British forces at Yorktown in 1781, ending the fighting in the American Revolution.

corn·y /ˈkôrnē/ ▸*adj.* (**corn·i·er, corn·i·est**) *informal* trite, banal, or mawkishly sentimental: *it sounds corny, but as soon as I saw her I knew she was the one.* ▷1930s: from an earlier sense 'rustic, appealing to country folk.' **—corn·i·ly** /'kôrnl-ē/ *adv.* **—corn·i·ness** *n.*

co·rol·la /kə'rälə; kə'rōlə/ ▸*n. Botany* the petals of a flower, typically forming a whorl within the sepals and enclosing the reproductive organs. Compare with CALYX. ▷late 17th cent. (in the sense 'little crown'): from Latin, diminutive of *corona* 'wreath, crown, chaplet.'

cor·ol·lar·y /'kôrə,lerē; 'kärə-/ ▸*n.* (*pl.* **-lar·ies**) a proposition that follows from (and is often appended to) one already proved. ■ a direct or natural consequence or result: *the huge increases in unemployment were the corollary of expenditure cuts.*
▸*adj.* forming a proposition that follows from one already proved. ■ associated; supplementary. ▷late Middle English: from Latin *corollarium* 'money paid for a garland or chaplet; gratuity' (in late Latin 'deduction'), from *corolla*, diminutive of *corona* 'wreath, crown, chaplet.'

cor·o·man·del /,kôrə'mandəl; ,kär-/ ▸*n.* **1** (also **coromandel wood** or **coromandel ebony**) a fine-grained, grayish-brown wood streaked with black, used in furniture. Also called CALAMANDER. **2** the Sri Lankan tree that yields this wood. • *Diospyros quaesita*, family Ebenaceae.
▸*adj.* denoting a form of Asian lacquerware with intaglio designs. ▷from COROMANDEL COAST, from which Asian lacquerware was originally transshipped.

Cor·o·man·del Coast /,kôrə'mandəl/ the southern part of the eastern coast of India, from Point Calimere to the mouth of the Krishna River.

Co·ro·na /kə'rōnə/ a city in southwestern California, southwest of Riverside; pop. 76,095.

co·ro·na1 /kə'rōnə/ ▸*n.* (*pl.* **-nae** /-nē; -nī/) **1** *Astronomy* the rarefied gaseous envelope of the sun and other stars. The sun's corona is normally visible only during a total solar eclipse when it is seen as an irregularly shaped pearly glow surrounding the darkened disk of the moon. ■ (also **corona discharge**) *Physics* the glow around a conductor at high potential. ■ a small circle of light seen around the sun or moon, due to diffraction by water droplets. **2** *Anatomy* a crown or crownlike structure. ■ *Botany* the cup-shaped or trumpet-shaped outgrowth at the center of a daffodil or narcissus flower. **3** a circular chandelier in a church. **4** *Architecture* a part of a cornice having a broad vertical face. ▷mid 16th cent. (sense 4): from Latin, 'wreath, crown.'

co·ro·na2 ▸*n.* a long, straight-sided cigar. ▷late 19th cent.: from Spanish *La Corona*, literally 'the crown,' originally a proprietary name.

Co·ro·na Aus·tra·lis /kə'rōnə ô'strāləs; ä'strā-/ *Astronomy* a small southern constellation (the Southern Crown), with no bright stars. ■ [as *genitive*] (**Coronae Australis** /kə'rōnē/) used with a preceding letter or numeral to designate a star in this constellation: *the star Theta Coronae Australis.* ▷Latin.

Co·ro·na Bo·re·al·is /bôrē'aləs/ *Astronomy* a northern constellation (the Northern Crown), in which the main stars form a small but prominent arc. ■ [as *genitive*] (**Coronae Borealis** /kə'rōnē/) used with a preceding letter or numeral to designate a star in this constellation: *the star R Coronae Borealis.* ▷Latin.

cor·o·nach /'kôrənəKH; 'kär-/ ▸*n.* (in Scotland or Ireland) a funeral song. ▷early 16th cent. (originally Scots, denoting the outcry of a crowd): from Scottish Gaelic *corranach* (Irish *coranach*), from *comh-* 'together' + *rànach* 'outcry.'

co·ro·na dis·charge ▸*n.* see CORONA1 (sense 1).

Co·ro·na·do /,kôrə'nädō; ,kär-/, Francisco Vásquez de (*c.*1510–54), Spanish explorer. His explorations into Arizona and New Mexico from Mexico opened the Southwest to Spanish colonization.

co·ro·na·graph /kə'rōnə,graf/ ▸*n.* an instrument that blocks out light emitted by the sun's actual surface so that the corona can be observed.

cor·o·nal1 /'kôrənl; 'kär-/ ▸*adj.* **1** of or relating to the crown or corona of something, in particular: ■ *Astronomy* of or relating to the corona of the sun or another star. ■ *Anatomy* of or relating to the crown of the head. **2** *Anatomy* of or in the coronal plane: *coronal imaging.* **3** *Phonetics* (of a consonant) formed by raising the tip or blade of the tongue toward the hard palate.
▸*n. Phonetics* a coronal consonant. ▷late Middle English (in the sense 'relating to the crown of the head'): from Latin *coronalis*, from *corona* 'crown.'

cor·o·nal2 /'kôrənl; 'kär-; kə'rōnl/ ▸*n.* a garland or wreath for the head: *her eyes sparkled beneath a coronal of flowers.* ■ *poetic/literary* a small crown; a coronet. ▷Middle English: apparently from Anglo-Norman French, from *corune* 'crown, wreath' (see CROWN).

cor·o·nal plane ▸*n. Anatomy* an imaginary plane dividing the body into dorsal and ventral parts.

cor·o·nal su·ture ▸*n. Anatomy* the transverse suture in the skull separating the frontal bone from the parietal bones.

cor·o·nar·y /'kôrə,nerē; 'kär-/ ▸*adj. Anatomy* relating to or denoting the arteries that surround and supply the heart. ■ relating to or denoting a structure that encircles a part of the body.
▸*n.* (*pl.* **-nar·ies**) short for CORONARY THROMBOSIS. ▷mid 17th cent. (in the sense 'resembling a crown'): from Latin *coronarius*, from *corona* 'wreath, crown.'

cor·o·nar·y ar·ter·y ▸*n.* an artery supplying blood to the heart.

cor·o·nar·y care unit (abbr. **CCU**) ▸*n.* a hospital department that provides special care and monitoring for heart patients.

cor·o·nar·y oc·clu·sion ▸*n.* partial or total obstruction of a coronary artery, usually resulting in a myocardial infarction (heart attack).

cor·o·nar·y si·nus ▸*n.* a wide venous channel about 2.25 centimeters in length that receives blood from the coronary veins and empties into the right atrium of the heart.

cor·o·nar·y throm·bo·sis ▸*n.* a blockage of the flow of blood to the heart, caused by a blood clot in a coronary artery.

cor·o·nar·y vein ▸*n.* any of several veins that drain blood from the heart wall and empty into the coronary sinus.

cor·o·na·tion /,kôrə'nāSHən; ,kär-/ ▸*n.* the ceremony of crowning a sovereign or a sovereign's consort. ▷late Middle English: via Old French from medieval Latin *coronatio(n-)*, from *coronare* 'to crown, adorn with a garland,' from *corona* (see CROWN).

co·ro·na·vi·rus /kə'rōnə,vīrəs/ ▸*n. Medicine* any of a group of RNA viruses that cause a variety of diseases in humans and other animals.

cor·o·ner /'kôrənər; 'kär-/ ▸*n.* an official who investigates violent, sudden, or suspicious deaths. ■ *historical* in England, an official responsible for safeguarding the private property of the Crown. ▷Middle English: from Anglo-Norman French *coruner*, from *corune* 'a crown' (see CROWN); reflecting the Latin title *custos placitorum coronae* 'guardian of the pleas of the crown.' **—cor·o·ner·ship** /-,SHip/ *n.*

cor·o·net /,kôrə'net; ,kär-/ ▸*n.* **1** a small or relatively simple crown, esp. as worn by lesser royalty and peers or peeresses. ■ a circular decoration for the head, esp. one made of flowers. **2** the band of tissue on the lowest part of a horse's pastern, containing the horn-producing cells from which the hoof grows. ■ another term for BURR sense 5. ▷late Middle English: from Old French *coronete* 'small crown or garland,' diminutive of *corone* (see CROWN). **—cor·o·net·ed** *adj.*

co·ro·ni·al /kə'rōnēəl/ ▸*adj. Austral.* relating to a coroner: *a coronial hearing.*

cor·o·noid /'kôrə,noid; 'kär-/ ▸*adj. Anatomy* relating to or denoting a hooked projection of bone. See CORONOID PROCESS.
▸*n.* (also **coronoid bone**) *Zoology* a slender bone forming part of the lower jaw in primitive vertebrates. ▷mid 18th cent.: from Greek *korōnē*, denoting something hooked, + -OID.

cor·o·noid proc·ess ▸*n. Anatomy* **1** a flattened triangular projection above the angle of the jaw where the temporalis muscle is attached. **2** a projection from the front of the ulna forming part of the articulation of the elbow. ▷mid 18th cent.: *coronoid* from Greek *korōnē* (denoting something hooked) + -OID.

Corp. ▸*abbr.* ■ (**Corp**) *informal* corporal: *been abroad before, Corp?* ■ corporation: *IBM Corp.*

cor·po·ra /'kôrpərə/ ▸ plural form of CORPUS.

cor·po·ral1 /'kôrp(ə)rəl/ ▸*n.* a low-ranking noncommissioned officer in the armed forces, in particular (in the U.S. Army) an NCO ranking above private first class and below sergeant or (in the U.S. Marine Corps) an NCO ranking above lance corporal and below sergeant. ▷mid 16th cent.: from French, obsolete variant of *caporal*, from Italian *caporale*, probably based on Latin *corpus, corpor-* 'body (of troops),' with a change of spelling in Italian due to association with *capo* 'head.'

cor·po·ral2 ▸*adj.* of or relating to the human body. ▷late Middle English: via Old French from Latin *corporalis*, from *corpus, corpor-* 'body.' **—cor·po·ral·ly** *adv.*

cor·po·ral3 ▸*n.* a cloth on which the chalice and paten are placed during the celebration of the Eucharist. ▷Middle English: from medieval Latin *corporale (pallium)* 'body (cloth),' from Latin *corpus, corpor-* 'body.'

cor·po·ral·i·ty /,kôrpə'ralitē/ ▸*n. rare* material or corporeal existence. ▷late Middle English: from late Latin *corporalitas*, from Latin *corporalis* 'relating to the body' (see CORPORAL2).

cor·po·ral pun·ish·ment ▸*n.* physical punishment, such as caning or flogging. ■ punishment under law that includes imprisonment and death.

cor·po·rate /'kôrp(ə)rət/ ▸*adj.* of or relating to a corporation, esp. a large company or group: *airlines are very keen on their corporate identity.* ■ *Law* (of a company or group of people) authorized to act as a single entity and recognized as such in law. ■ of or shared by all the members of a group: *the service emphasizes the corporate responsibility of the congregation.*
▸*n.* a corporate company or group. ▷late 15th cent.: from Latin *corporatus*, past participle of *corporare* 'form into a body,' from *corpus, corpor-* 'body.' **—cor·po·rate·ly** *adv.*

cor·po·rate raid·er ▸*n.* a financier who makes a practice of making hostile takeover bids for companies, either to control their policies or to resell them for a profit.

cor·po·rate wel·fare ▸*n.* government support or subsidy of private business, such as by tax incentives.

cor·po·ra·tion /,kôrpə'rāSHən/ ▸*n.* a company or group of people authorized to act as a single entity (legally a person) and recognized as such in law. ■ (also **municipal corporation**) a group of people elected to govern a city, town, or borough. ■ *dated, humorous* a paunch. ▷late Middle English: from late Latin *corporatio(n-)*, from Latin *corporare* 'combine in one body' (see CORPORATE).

cor·po·rat·ism /'kôrp(ə)rə,tizəm/ ▸*n.* the control of a state or organization by large interest groups. **—cor·po·rat·ist** *adj.* & *n.*

cor·po·ra·tize /'kôrp(ə)rə,tīz/ ▸*v.* [*trans.*] convert (a state organization) into an independent commercial company.

cor·po·re·al /kôr'pôrēəl/ ▸*adj.* of or relating to a person's body, esp. as opposed to their spirit: *he was frank about his corporeal appetites.* ■ having a body: *a corporeal God.* ■ *Law* consisting of material objects; tangible: *corporeal property.* See note at TANGIBLE. ▷late Middle English (in the sense 'material'): from late Latin *corporealis*, from Latin *corporeus* 'bodily, physical,' from *corpus, corpor-* 'body.' **—cor·po·re·al·i·ty** /kôr,pôrē'alitē/ *n.* **—cor·po·re·al·ly** *adv.*

cor·po·re·i·ty /,kôrpə'rēitē; -'rāitē/ ▸*n. rare* the quality of having a physical body or existence. ▷early 17th cent.: from French *corporéité* or medieval Latin *corporeitas*, from Latin *corporeus* 'composed of flesh,' from *corpus, corpor-* 'body.'

cor·po·sant /'kôrpə,sant; -zant/ ▸*n. archaic* an appearance of St. Elmo's fire on a mast, rigging, or other structure. ▷mid 16th cent.: from Old Spanish, Portuguese, and Italian *corpo santo* 'holy body.'

corps /kôr/ ▸*n.* (*pl.* **corps** /kôrz/) a main subdivision of an armed force in the field, consisting of two or more divisions: *the 5th Army Corps.* ■ a branch of a military organization assigned to a particular kind of work: *the U.S. Army Medical Corps.* ■ a body of people engaged in a particular activity: *the press corps.* ■ short for CORPS DE BALLET. ▷late 16th cent.: from French, from Latin *corpus* 'body.'

corps de bal·let /,kôr də ba'lā/ ▸*n.* [treated as *sing.* or *pl.*] the members of a ballet company who dance together as a group. ■ the members of the lowest rank of dancers in a ballet company. ▷early 19th cent.: French.

corpse /kôrps/ ▸*n.* a dead body, esp. of a human being rather than an animal. See note at BODY. ▷Middle English (denoting the living body of a person or animal): alteration of CORSE by association with Latin *corpus*, a change that also took place in French (Old French *cors* becoming *corps*). The *p* was originally silent, as in French; the final *e* was rare before the 19th cent., but now distinguishes *corpse* from *corps*.

corps·man /'kôrmən/ ▸*n.* an enlisted member of a military medical unit. ■ a member of a civilian corps, esp. a paramedical corps.

cor·pu·lent /'kôrpyələnt/ ▸*adj.* (of a person) fat. ▷late Middle English: from Latin *corpulentus*, from *corpus* 'body.' **—cor·pu·lence** *n.* **—cor·pu·len·cy** *n.*

cor pul·mo·na·le /,kôr ,po͝olmə'nalē; -'nälē/ ▸*n. Medicine* abnormal enlargement of the right side of the heart as a result of disease of the lungs or the pulmonary blood vessels. ▷mid 19th cent.: from Latin *cor* 'heart' and modern Latin *pulmonalis* (from Latin *pulmo(n-)* 'lung').

cor·pus /ˈkôrpəs/ ▶*n.* (*pl.* **-po·ra** /-pərə/ or **-pus·es**) **1** a collection of written texts, esp. the entire works of a particular author or a body of writing on a particular subject: *the Darwinian corpus.* ■ a collection of written or spoken material in machine-readable form, assembled for the purpose of studying linguistic structures, frequencies, etc. **2** *Anatomy* the main body or mass of a structure. ■ the central part of the stomach, between the fundus and the antrum. ▷late Middle English (denoting a human or animal body): from Latin, literally 'body.' Sense 1 dates from the early 18th cent.

cor·pus cal·lo·sum /kaˈlōsəm/ ▶*n.* (*pl.* **cor·po·ra cal·lo·sa** /ˈkôrpərə kaˈlōsə/) *Anatomy* a broad band of nerve fibers joining the two hemispheres of the brain. ▷early 18th cent.: from CORPUS and Latin *callosum*, neuter of *callosus* 'tough.'

cor·pus ca·ver·no·sum /ˌkavərˈnōsəm/ ▶*n.* (*pl.* **cor·po·ra ca·ver·no·sa** /-ˈnōsə/) *Anatomy* either of two masses of erectile tissue forming the bulk of the penis and the clitoris. ▷from CORPUS and Latin *cavernosum*, neuter of *cavernosus* 'containing hollows.'

Cor·pus Chris·ti[1] /ˌkôrpəs ˈkristē/ a city and port in southern Texas, on Corpus Christi Bay; pop. 277,454.

Cor·pus Chris·ti[2] a feast of the Western Christian Church commemorating the institution of the Eucharist, observed on the Thursday after Trinity Sunday. ▷Latin, literally 'body of Christ.'

cor·pus·cle /ˈkôrˌpəsəl/ ▶*n. Biology* a minute body or cell in an organism, esp. a red or white cell in the blood of vertebrates. ■ *historical* a minute particle regarded as the basic constituent of matter or light. ▷mid 17th cent.: from Latin *corpusculum* 'small body,' diminutive of *corpus.* —**cor·pus·cu·lar** /kôr ˈpəskyələr/ *adj.*

cor·pus de·lic·ti /dəˈlikˌtī; -tē/ ▶*n. Law* the facts and circumstances constituting a breach of a law. ■ concrete evidence of a crime, such as a corpse. ▷Latin, literally 'body of offense.'

cor·pus lu·te·um /ˈlōōtēəm/ ▶*n.* (*pl.* **cor·po·ra lu·te·a** /ˈlōōtēə/) *Anatomy* a hormone-secreting structure that develops in an ovary after an ovum has been discharged but degenerates after a few days unless pregnancy has begun. ▷late 18th cent.: from CORPUS and Latin *luteum*, neuter of *luteus* 'yellow.'

cor·pus spon·gi·o·sum /ˌspənjēˈōsəm/ ▶*n.* (*pl.* **cor·po·ra spon·gi·o·sa** /ˌspənjēˈōsə/) *Anatomy* a mass of erectile tissue alongside the corpora cavernosa of the penis and terminating in the glans. ▷from CORPUS and Latin *spongiosum*, neuter of *spongiosus* 'porous.'

cor·pus stri·a·tum /strīˈātəm/ ▶*n.* (*pl.* **cor·po·ra stri·a·ta** /strīˈātə/) *Anatomy* part of the basal ganglia of the brain, comprising the caudate and lentiform nuclei. ▷from CORPUS and Latin *striatum*, neuter of *striatus* 'grooved.'

corr. ▶*abbr.* ■ correction. ■ correspondence.

cor·ral /kəˈral/ ▶*n.* a pen for livestock, esp. cattle or horses, on a farm or ranch. ■ *historical* a defensive enclosure of wagons in an encampment.
▶*v.* (**-ralled, -ral·ling**) [*trans.*] put or keep (livestock) in a corral. ■ *figurative* gather (a group of people or things) together: *the organizers were corralling the crowd into marching formation.* ■ *historical* form (wagons) into a corral. ▷late 16th cent.: from Spanish and Old Portuguese (now *curral*), perhaps based on Latin *currere* 'to run.' Compare with KRAAL.

cor·rect /kəˈrekt/ ▶*adj.* free from error; in accordance with fact or truth: *make sure you have been given the correct information.* ■ not mistaken in one's opinion or judgment; right: *the government was correct to follow a course of defeating inflation.* ■ (of a thing or course of action) meeting the requirements of or most appropriate for a particular situation or activity: *cut the top and bottom tracks to the correct length with a hacksaw.* ■ (of a person or their appearance or behavior) conforming to accepted social standards; proper: *he was a polite man, invariably correct and pleasant with Mrs. Collins.* ■ conforming to a particular political or ideological orthodoxy. See also POLITICALLY CORRECT.
▶*v.* [*trans.*] put right (an error or fault): *the council issued a statement correcting some points in the press reports.* ■ mark the errors in (a written or printed text): *he corrected Dixon's writing for publication.* ■ tell (someone) that they are mistaken: *he had assumed she was married and she had not corrected him* | [as *adj.*] (**corrected**) *sorry, I stand corrected.* ■ counteract or rectify: *the problem of diminished sight can be reduced or corrected by wearing eyeglasses.* ■ adjust (an instrument) to function accurately or in accord with a standard: *motorists can have their headlights tested and corrected at a reduced price on Saturday.* ■ adjust (a numerical result or reading) to allow for departure from standard conditions: *data were* ***corrected for*** *radionuclide decay.* ▷Middle English (as a verb): from Latin *correct-* 'made straight, amended,' from the verb *corrigere*, from *cor-* 'together' + *regere* 'guide.' The adjective is via French. —**cor·rect·a·ble** *adj.* —**cor·rect·ly** *adv.* —**cor·rect·ness** *n.*

cor·rec·tion /kəˈrekshən/ ▶*n.* the action or process of correcting something: *I checked the typing for errors and sent it back for correction.* ■ a change that rectifies an error or inaccuracy: *he made a few corrections to my homework.* ■ used to introduce an amended version of something one has just said: *after today—correction, she thought grimly, after tonight—she'd never see him again.* ■ a quantity adjusting a numerical result to allow for a departure from standard conditions. ■ a temporary reversal in an overall trend of stock market prices, esp. a brief fall during an overall increase: *they're still looking for the market to go up and believe we are just going through a correction.* ■ punishment, esp. that of criminals in prison intended to rectify their behavior. ▷Middle English: via Old French from Latin *correctio(n-)*, from *corrigere* 'make straight, bring into order' (see CORRECT).

cor·rec·tion·al /kəˈrekshənl/ ▶*adj.* of or relating to the punishment of criminals in a way intended to rectify their behavior: *a correctional institution.*

cor·rec·tion flu·id ▶*n.* an opaque liquid painted over a typed or written error so as to leave a blank space for the insertion of the correct character.

cor·rec·ti·tude /kəˈrektəˌt(y)ōōd/ ▶*n.* correctness, esp. conscious correctness in one's behavior. ▷late 19th cent.: blend of CORRECT and RECTITUDE.

cor·rec·tive /kəˈrektiv/ ▶*adj.* designed to correct or counteract something harmful or undesirable: *management was informed so that corrective action could be taken.*
▶*n.* a thing intended to correct or counteract something else: *the move might be a* ***corrective to*** *some inefficient practices within hospitals.* ▷mid 16th cent.: from French *correctif, -ive* or late Latin *correctivus*, from Latin *correct-* 'brought into order,' from the verb *corrigere* (see CORRECT). —**cor·rec·tive·ly** *adv.*

cor·rec·tor /kəˈrektər/ ▶*n.* a person or thing that corrects something, esp. a computer program or electronic device with a specified function: *a spelling corrector.*

Cor·reg·gio /kəˈrej(ē)ō/, Antonio Allegri da (*c.*1494–1534), Italian painter; born *Antonio Allegri*. The soft, sensual style of his devotional and mythological paintings influenced the rococo style of the 18th century.

Cor·reg·i·dor /kəˈregəˌdôr/ an island in the Philippines, just south of the Bataan Peninsula on Luzon Island, scene of World War II battles and now a national shrine.

cor·re·late ▶*v.* /ˈkôrəˌlāt; ˈkär-/ [*intrans.*] have a mutual relationship or connection, in which one thing affects or depends on another: *the study found that success in the educational system* ***correlates*** *highly* ***with*** *class.* ■ [*trans.*] establish such a relationship or connection between: *we should* ***correlate*** *general trends in public opinion* ***with*** *trends in the content of television news.*
▶*n.* /-lət/ each of two or more related or complementary things: *strategies to promote health should pay greater attention to financial hardship and other correlates of poverty.* ▷mid 17th cent. (as a noun): back-formation from CORRELATION and CORRELATIVE.

cor·re·la·tion /ˌkôrəˈlāshən/ ▶*n.* a mutual relationship or connection between two or more things: *research showed a clear* ***correlation between*** *recession and levels of property crime.* ■ *Statistics* interdependence of variable quantities. ■ *Statistics* a quantity measuring the extent of such interdependence. ■ the process of establishing a relationship or connection between two or more measures. ▷mid 16th cent.: from medieval Latin *correlatio(n-)*, from *cor-* 'together' + *relatio* (see RELATION). —**cor·re·la·tion·al** /-shənl/ *adj.*

cor·re·la·tion co·ef·fi·cient ▶*n. Statistics* a number between −1 and +1 calculated so as to represent the linear dependence of two variables or sets of data. (Symbol: **r.**)

cor·rel·a·tive /kəˈrelətiv/ ▶*adj.* having a mutual relationship; corresponding: *rights, whether moral or legal, can involve correlative duties.* ■ *Grammar* (of words such as *neither* and *nor*) corresponding to each other and regularly used together.
▶*n.* a word or concept that has a mutual relationship with another word or concept: *the child's right to education is a correlative of the parent's duty to send the child to school.* ▷mid 16th cent.: from medieval Latin *correlativus*, from *cor-* 'together' + late Latin *relativus* (see RELATIVE). —**cor·rel·a·tive·ly** *adv.* —**cor·rel·a·tiv·i·ty** /kəˌreləˈtivitē/ *n.*

cor·re·spond /ˌkôrəˈspänd; ˌkär-/ ▶*v.* [*intrans.*] **1** have a close similarity; match or agree almost exactly: *the carved heads described in the poem* ***correspond to*** *those in the drawing* | *communication is successful when the ideas in the minds of the speaker and hearer correspond.* ■ be analogous or equivalent in character, form, or function: *the Inuit month* ***corresponding to*** *December was called Aagjulirvik.* ■ represent: *digits that* ***correspond to*** *certain letters of the alphabet.* **2** communicate by exchanging letters: *Margaret* ***corresponded with*** *him until his death* | *the doctor and I corresponded for more than two decades.* ▷late Middle English: from Old French *correspondre*, from medieval Latin *correspondere*, from *cor-* 'together' + Latin *respondere* (see RESPOND).

cor·re·spond·ence /ˌkôrəˈspändəns; ˌkär-/ ▶*n.* **1** a close similarity, connection, or equivalence: *there is a simple* ***correspondence between*** *the distance of a focused object from the eye and the size of its image on the retina.* **2** communication by exchanging letters with someone: *the organization engaged in detailed* ***correspondence with*** *local congressmen.* ■ letters sent or received: *his wife dealt with his private correspondence.* ▷late Middle English: via Old French from medieval Latin *correspondentia*, from *correspondent-* 'corresponding' (see CORRESPONDENT). —**cor·re·spond·en·cy** /-dənsē/ *n.* (*rare*).

cor·re·spond·ence course ▶*n.* a course of study in which student and teachers communicate by mail.

cor·re·spond·ence prin·ci·ple *Physics* ▶*n.* the principle that states that for very large quantum numbers the laws of quantum theory merge with those of classical physics.

cor·re·spond·ence school ▶*n.* a school offering correspondence courses.

cor·re·spond·ence the·o·ry *Philosophy* ▶*n.* the theory that states that the definition or criterion of truth is that true propositions correspond to the facts.

cor·re·spond·ent /ˌkôrəˈspändənt; ˌkär-/ ▶*n.* a person who writes letters to a person or a newspaper, esp. on a regular basis: *she wasn't much of a correspondent.* ■ a person employed to report for a newspaper or broadcasting organization, typically on a particular subject or from a particular country: *a White House correspondent.*
▶*adj.* corresponding. ▷late Middle English (as an adjective): from Old French *correspondant* or medieval Latin *correspondent-* 'corresponding,' from the verb *correspondere* (see CORRESPOND).

cor·re·spond·ing /ˌkôrəˈspändiNG; ˌkär-/ ▶*adj.* **1** similar in character, form, or function: *we discussed our corresponding viewpoints.* ■ able to be matched, joined, or interlocked: *he dovetailed the corresponding pieces.* **2** dealing with written communication; having this responsibility: *the corresponding secretary.* ■ having an honorary association with a group, esp. at a distance (from the group's headquarters): *at the last meeting, 255 academicians and lesser-ranking corresponding members were elected.* —**cor·re·spond·ing·ly** *adv.*

cor·re·spond·ing an·gles ▶*plural n. Mathematics* the angles that occupy the same relative position at each intersection where a straight line crosses two others. If the two lines are parallel, the corresponding angles are equal.

cor·ri·da /kôˈrēdə/ ▶*n.* a bullfight. ▷late 19th cent.: from Spanish *corrida de toros* 'running of bulls.'

cor·ri·dor /ˈkôrədər; ˈkär-; -ˌdôr/ ▶*n.* a long passage in a building from which doors lead into rooms. ■ *Brit.* a passage along the side of a railroad car, from which doors lead into compartments. ■ a belt of land between two other areas, typically having a particular feature or giving access to a particular area: *the valley provides the principal wildlife corridor between the uplands and the central urban area.* ■ a belt of land following a road, river, or other route of passage: *the Boston-to-Washington corridor.* ▷late 16th cent. (as a military term denoting a strip of land along the outer edge of a ditch, protected by a parapet): from French, from Italian *corridore*, alteration (by association with *corridore* 'runner') of *corridoio* 'running place,' from *correre* 'to run,' from Latin *currere*. The current sense dates from the early 19th cent.

Pronunciation Key ə *ago*; ər *over*; ˈə or ˌə *up*; ˈər or ˌər *fur*; a *hat*; ā *rate*; ä *car*; CH *chew*; e *let*; ē *see*; e(ə)r *air*; i *fit*; ī *by*; i(ə)r *ear*; NG *sing*; ō *go*; ô *for*; oi *boy*; ŏŏ *good*; ōō *goo*; ou *out*; SH *she*; TH *thin*; T͟H *then*; (h)w *why*; ZH *vision*

▸*PHRASE* □ **the corridors of power** the senior levels of government or administration, where covert influence is regarded as being exerted and significant decisions are made. [from the name of C. P. Snow's novel *The Corridors of Power (1964)*.]

cor·rie /ˈkôrē; ˈkärē/ ▸*n.* (*pl.* **-ries**) a cirque, esp. one in the mountains of Scotland. ▷mid 16th cent.: from Scottish Gaelic and Irish *coire* 'cauldron, hollow.'

Cor·rie·dale /ˈkôrē,dāl; ˈkär-/ ▸*n.* a sheep of a New Zealand breed kept for both wool and meat. ▷early 20th cent.: named after an estate in New Zealand.

cor·ri·gen·dum /,kôriˈjendəm; ,kär-/ ▸*n.* (*pl.* **-gen·da** /-ˈjendə/) a thing to be corrected, typically an error in a printed book. ▷early 19th cent.: Latin, neuter gerundive of *corrigere* 'bring into order' (see CORRECT).

cor·ri·gi·ble /ˈkôrijəbəl; ˈkär-/ ▸*adj.* capable of being corrected, rectified, or reformed. ▷late Middle English (in the sense 'liable to or deserving punishment'): via French from medieval Latin *corrigibilis*, from Latin *corrigere* 'to correct.' —**cor·ri·gi·bil·i·ty** /,kôrijəˈbilitē; ,kär-/ *n.*

cor·rob·o·rant /kəˈräbərənt/ ▸*adj.* **1** corroborating; confirming. **2** *archaic* (of a medicine) invigorating; producing strength.
▸*n.* **1** something that corroborates. **2** *archaic* an invigorating medicine.

cor·rob·o·rate /kəˈräbə,rāt/ ▸*v.* [*trans.*] confirm or give support to (a statement, theory, or finding): *the witness had corroborated the boy's account of the attack.* ▷mid 16th cent. (in the sense 'make physically stronger'): from Latin *corroborat-* 'strengthened,' from the verb *corroborare*, from *cor-* 'together' + *roborare*, from *robur* 'strength.' —**cor·rob·o·ra·tion** /kə,räbəˈrāsʜən/ *n.* —**cor·rob·o·ra·tive** /-ˈräb(ə)rətiv/ *adj.* —**cor·rob·o·ra·tor** /-,rātər/ *n.* —**cor·rob·o·ra·to·ry** /-ˈräb(ə)rə,tôrē/ *adj.*

cor·rob·o·ree /kəˈräbərē/ ▸*n.* an Australian Aboriginal dance ceremony that may take the form of a sacred ritual or an informal gathering. ■ *chiefly Austral.* a party or other social gathering, esp. a lively one. ▷from Dharuk *garaabara*, denoting a style of dancing.

cor·rode /kəˈrōd/ ▸*v.* [*trans.*] destroy or damage (metal, stone, or other materials) slowly by chemical action: *acid rain poisons fish and corrodes buildings.* ■ [*intrans.*] (of metal or other materials) be destroyed or damaged in this way: *over the years copper tubing corrodes.* ■ *figurative* destroy or weaken (something) gradually: *the self-centered climate corrodes ideals and concerns about social justice.* ▷late Middle English: from Latin *corrodere*, from *cor-* (expressing intensive force) + *rodere* 'gnaw.' —**cor·rod·i·ble** *adj.*

cor·ro·sion /kəˈrōzʜən/ ▸*n.* the process of corroding metal, stone, or other materials: *each aircraft part is sprayed with oil to prevent corrosion.* ■ damage caused by such a process: *engineers found the corrosion when checking the bridge.* ▷late Middle English: from Old French, or from late Latin *corrosio(n-)*, from Latin *corrodere* 'gnaw through' (see CORRODE).

cor·ro·sive /kəˈrōsiv; -ziv/ ▸*adj.* tending to cause corrosion.
▸*n.* a corrosive substance. ▷late Middle English: from Old French *corosif*, *-ive*, from medieval Latin *corrosivus*, from Latin *corros-* 'gnawed through,' from the verb *corrodere* (see CORRODE). —**cor·ro·sive·ly** *adv.* —**cor·ro·sive·ness** *n.*

cor·ro·sive sub·li·mate ▸*n.* *rare* another term for MERCURIC CHLORIDE.

cor·ru·gate /ˈkôrə,gāt; ˈkär-/ ▸*v.* contract or cause to contract into wrinkles or folds: [*intrans.*] *Micky's brow corrugated in a simian frown.* ▷late Middle English: from Latin *corrugat-* 'wrinkled,' from the verb *corrugare*, from *cor-* (expressing intensive force) + *rugare* (from *ruga* 'a wrinkle').

cor·ru·gat·ed /ˈkôrə,gātid; ˈkär-/ ▸*adj.* (of a material, surface, or structure) shaped into alternate ridges and grooves: *the roof was made of corrugated iron.* —**cor·ru·ga·tion** /,kôrəˈgāsʜən; ,kär-/ *n.*

cor·ru·gat·ed pa·per ▸*n.* packaging material made from layers of thick paper, the top layer of which is alternately grooved and ridged for added strength and rigidity.

cor·rupt /kəˈrəpt/ ▸*adj.* **1** having or showing a willingness to act dishonestly in return for money or personal gain: *unscrupulous logging companies assisted by corrupt officials.* ■ evil or morally depraved: *the play can do no harm since its audience is already corrupt.* See note at DEPRAVED. ■ *archaic* (of organic or inorganic matter) in a state of decay; rotten or putrid: *a corrupt and rotting corpse.* **2** (of a text or manuscript) debased or made unreliable by errors or alterations. ■ (of a computer database or program) having errors introduced.
▸*v.* [*trans.*] **1** cause to act dishonestly in return for money or personal gain: *there is a continuing fear of firms corrupting politicians in the search for contracts.* ■ cause to become morally depraved: *he has corrupted the boy.* ■ *archaic* infect; contaminate: [as *adj.*] (**corrupting**) *the corrupting smell of death.* **2** (often **be corrupted**) change or debase by making errors or unintentional alterations: *Epicurus's teachings have since been much corrupted.* ■ cause errors to appear in (a computer program or database): *a program that has somehow corrupted your system files.* ▷Middle English: from Latin *corruptus*, past participle of *corrumpere* 'mar, bribe, destroy,' from *cor-* 'altogether' + *rumpere* 'to break.' —**cor·rupt·er** *n.* —**cor·rupt·i·bil·i·ty** /kə,rəptəˈbilitē/ *n.* —**cor·rupt·i·ble** *adj.* —**cor·rup·tive** /-tiv/ *adj.* —**cor·rupt·ly** *adv.*

cor·rup·tion /kəˈrəpsʜən/ ▸*n.* **1** dishonest or fraudulent conduct by those in power, typically involving bribery: *the journalist who wants to expose corruption in high places.* ■ the action of making someone or something morally depraved or the state of being so: *the word "addict" conjures up evil and corruption.* ■ *archaic* decay; putrefaction: *the potato turned black and rotten with corruption.* **2** the process by which something, typically a word or expression, is changed from its original use or meaning to one that is regarded as erroneous or debased. ■ the process of causing errors to appear in a computer program or database. ▷Middle English: via Old French from Latin *corruptio(n-)*, from *corrumpere* 'mar, bribe, destroy' (see CORRUPT).

cor·rup·tion·ist /kəˈrəpsʜənist/ ▸*n.* one who practices or endorses corruption, esp. in politics.

cor·rupt prac·tice ▸*n.* (often **corrupt practices**) a fraudulent activity, esp. an attempt to rig an election.

cor·sage /kôrˈsäzʜ; -ˈsäj/ ▸*n.* **1** a spray of flowers worn pinned to a woman's clothes. **2** the upper part of a woman's dress. ▷early 19th cent. (sense 2): French, from Old French *cors* 'body,' from Latin *corpus*.

cor·sair /ˈkôr,se(ə)r/ ▸*n.* *archaic* **1** a pirate. ■ a privateer, esp. one operating along the southern coast of the Mediterranean in the 17th century. **2** a pirate ship. ▷mid 16th cent.: from French *corsaire*, from medieval Latin *cursarius*, from *cursus* 'a raid, plunder,' special use of Latin *cursus* 'course,' from *currere* 'to run.'

Corse /kôrs/ French name for CORSICA.

corse /kôrs/ ▸*n.* *archaic* a corpse. ▷Middle English: from Old French *cors* 'body,' from Latin *corpus*. Compare with CORPSE.

corse·let /ˈkôrslət/ ▸*n.* **1** *historical* a piece of armor covering the trunk. **2** variant spelling of CORSELETTE. ▷late 15th cent.: from Old French *corslet*, diminutive of *cors* 'body.'

cor·se·lette /ˈkôrslət/ (also **cor·se·let**) ▸*n.* a woman's foundation garment combining corset and brassière. ▷1920s: from *corselet* (see CORSELET).

cor·set /ˈkôrsət/ ▸*n.* a woman's tightly fitting undergarment extending from below the chest to the hips, worn to shape the figure. ■ a similar garment worn by men or women to support a weak or injured back. ■ *historical* a tightly fitting laced or stiffened outer bodice or dress. ▷Middle English: from Old French, diminutive of *cors* 'body,' from Latin *corpus*. The sense 'close-fitting undergarment' dates from the late 18th cent., by which time the sense 'bodice' had mainly historical reference. —**cor·set·ed** *adj.* —**cor·set·ry** /-trē/ *n.*

cor·se·tière /,kôrsəˈti(ə)r; -ˈtyer/ ▸*n.* a woman who makes or fits corsets. ▷mid 19th cent.: French, feminine of *corsetier*, from *corset* (see CORSET).

Cor·si·ca /ˈkôrsikə/ a mountainous island off the western coast of Italy that forms an administrative region of France; pop. 249,740; chief towns, Bastia (northern department) and Ajaccio (southern department). It was the birthplace of Napoleon I. French name CORSE.

Cor·si·can /ˈkôrsikən/ ▸*adj.* of or relating to Corsica, its people, or their language.
▸*n.* **1** a native of Corsica. **2** the language of Corsica, which originated as a dialect of Italian.

Cor·si·ca·na /,kôrsiˈkanə/ a city in east central Texas, an oil center; pop. 22,911.

cor·tège /kôrˈtezʜ; ˈkôr,tezʜ/ ▸*n.* a solemn procession, esp. for a funeral. ■ a person's entourage or retinue. ▷mid 17th cent.: from French, from Italian *corteggio*, from *corteggiare* 'attend court,' from *corte* 'court,' from Latin *cohors*, *cohort-* 'retinue.'

Cor·tes /ˈkôr,tes/ the legislative assembly of Spain and formerly of Portugal. ▷Spanish and Portuguese, plural of *corte* 'court,' from Latin *cohors*, *cohort-* 'yard, retinue.'

Cor·tés /kôrˈtez/ (also **Cor·tez**), Hernando (1485–1547), first of the Spanish conquistadors. He overthrew the Aztec empire by conquering its capital, Tenochtitlán, in 1519 and by deposing its emperor, Montezuma. In 1521, he destroyed Tenochtitlán completely, established Mexico City as the capital of New Spain (now Mexico), and served briefly as its governor.

cor·tex /ˈkôr,teks/ ▸*n.* (*pl.* **-ti·ces** /-tə,sēz/) *Anatomy* the outer layer of the cerebrum (the **cerebral cortex**), composed of folded gray matter and playing an important role in consciousness. ■ an outer layer of another organ or body part such as a kidney (the **renal cortex**), the cerebellum, or a hair. ■ *Botany* an outer layer of tissue immediately below the epidermis of a stem or root. ▷late Middle English: from Latin, literally 'bark.' —**cor·ti·cal** /ˈkôrtikəl/ *adj.*

cor·ti·cate /ˈkôrtə,kāt; -kət/ ▸*adj.* *Botany* having a cortex, bark, or rind. ▷mid 19th cent.: from Latin *corticatus*, from *cortex*, *cortic-* 'bark.' —**cor·ti·ca·tion** /,kôrtəˈkāsʜən/ *n.*

cortico- ▸*comb. form* representing CORTEX, used esp. with reference to the adrenal and cerebral cortices: *corticosterone.* ▷from Latin *cortex*, *cortic-* 'bark.'

cor·ti·co·fu·gal /,kôrtikōˈfyoōgəl/ (also **cor·ti·cif·u·gal** /-ˈsifyəgəl/) ▸*adj.* *Anatomy* (of a nerve fiber) originating in and running from the cerebral cortex. ▷late 19th cent.: from CORTICO- 'cortex' + Latin *fugere* 'run from.'

cor·ti·coid /ˈkôrti,koid/ ▸*n.* another term for CORTICOSTEROID.

cor·ti·co·ster·oid /,kôrtikōˈster,oid; -ˈsti(ə)r,oid/ ▸*n.* *Biochemistry* any of a group of steroid hormones produced in the adrenal cortex or made synthetically. There are two kinds: glucocorticoids and mineralocorticoids. They have various metabolic functions and some are used to treat inflammation.

cor·ti·cos·ter·one /kôrtəˈkästə,rōn/ ▸*n.* *Biochemistry* a hormone secreted by the adrenal cortex, one of the glucocorticoids.

cor·ti·co·tro·pin /,kôrtikōˈtrōpin/ (also **cor·ti·co·troph·in** /-ˈtrāfən/) ▸*n.* *Biochemistry* another term for ADRENOCORTICOTROPIC HORMONE.

cor·ti·le /kôrˈtē,lā/ ▸*n.* (*pl.* **-ti·li** /-ˈtēlē/ or **-ti·les** /-ˈtē,lāz/) (in Italy) an enclosed area, typically roofless and arcaded, within or attached to a building. ▷Italian, derivative of *corte* 'court.'

cor·ti·na /kôrˈtīnə; -ˈtēnə/ ▸*n.* (*pl.* **-ti·nae** /-ˈtinē; -ˈtē,nī/) *Botany* (in some toadstools) a thin weblike veil extending from the edge of the cap to the stalk. ▷mid 19th cent.: from late Latin, literally 'curtain.' —**cor·ti·nate** /ˈkôrtn,āt/ *adj.*

cor·ti·sol /ˈkôrtə,sôl; -,sōl/ ▸*n.* *Biochemistry* another term for HYDROCORTISONE.

cor·ti·sone /ˈkôrtə,sōn/ ▸*n.* *Biochemistry* a hormone produced by the adrenal cortex. One of the glucocorticoids, it is also made synthetically for use as an anti-inflammatory and anti-allergy agent. ▷1940s: from elements of its chemical name *17-hydroxy-11-dehydrocorticosterone*.

co·run·dum /kəˈrəndəm/ ▸*n.* extremely hard aluminum oxide, used as an abrasive. Ruby and sapphire are varieties of corundum. ▷early 18th cent.: from Tamil *kuruntam* and Telugu *kuruvindam*.

Co·run·na /kəˈrənə/ a port in northwestern Spain; pop. 251,300. It was the point of departure for the armada in 1588. Spanish name LA CORUÑA.

co·rus·cant /kəˈrəskənt/ ▸*adj.* *poetic/literary* glittering; sparkling. ▷late 15th cent.: from Latin *coruscant-* 'vibrating, glittering,' from the verb *coruscare*.

cor·us·cate /ˈkôrə,skāt; ˈkär-/ ▸*v.* [*intrans.*] *poetic/literary* (of light) flash or sparkle: *the light was coruscating from the walls.* ▷early 18th cent.: from Latin *coruscat-* 'glittered,' from the verb *coruscare*. —**cor·us·ca·tion** /,kôrəˈskāsʜən/ *n.*

cor·us·cat·ing /ˈkôrə,skātiɴɢ/ ▸*adj.* flashing; sparkling: *a coruscating kaleidoscope of colors.* ■ brilliant or striking in content or style: *the play's coruscating wit.*

Cor·val·lis /kôrˈvalis/ a city in western Oregon, on the Willamette River, home to Oregon State University; pop. 49,322.

cor·vée /ˈkôr,vā; kôrˈvā/ ▸*n.* *historical* a day's unpaid labor owed by a vassal to his feudal lord. ■ forced labor exacted in lieu of taxes, in particular that on public roads. ▷Middle English: from Old French, based on Latin *corrogare* 'ask for, collect.' Rare in English before the late 18th cent.

cor·vette /kôr'vet/ ▶*n.* a small warship designed for convoy escort duty. ■ *historical* a sailing warship with one tier of guns. ▷mid 17th cent.: from French, from Dutch *korf*, denoting a kind of ship, + the diminutive suffix *-ette*.

cor·vid /'kôrvid/ ▶*n. Ornithology* a bird of the crow family (Corvidae); a crow. ▷mid 20th cent.: from modern Latin *Corvidae* (plural), from Latin *corvus* 'raven.'

cor·vi·na[1] /kôr'vēnə/ ▶*n.* a variety of wine grape native to the Veneto region of northeastern Italy, used to make Valpolicella and Bardolino. ▷Italian (feminine adjective), literally 'raven-black.'

cor·vi·na[2] ▶*n.* a marine food and game fish of the drum family, found on the Pacific coasts of California and Mexico and sometimes living in fresh water. • Genus *Cynoscion*, family Sciaenidae: two species, in particular the **shortfin corvina** (*C. parvipennis*). ▷late 18th cent.: from Spanish and Portuguese.

cor·vine /'kôr,vīn/ ▶*adj.* of or like a raven or crow, esp. in color. ▷mid 17th cent.: from Latin *corvinus*, from *corvus* 'raven.'

Cor·vus /'kôrvəs/ *Astronomy* a small southern constellation (the Crow or Raven), south of Virgo. ■ (**Corvi** /-vī/) used with a preceding letter or numeral to designate a star in this constellation: *the star Gamma Corvi.* ▷Latin.

cor·y·ban·tic /,kôrə'bantik/ ▶*adj.* wild; frenzied. ▷mid 17th cent.: from *Corybantes*, Latin name of the priests of Cybele, a Phrygian goddess of nature who performed wild dances, from Greek *Korubantes* + **-IC**.

co·ryd·a·lis /kə'ridl-əs/ ▶*n.* a herbaceous plant of the poppy family with spurred tubular flowers, closely related to bleeding heart and found in north temperate regions. • Genus *Corydalis*, family Fumariaceae: many species, including **yellow corydalis** (*C. flavula*) of the eastern U.S. ▷modern Latin, from Greek *korudallis* 'crested lark,' alluding to a similarity between the flower and the bird's spur.

cor·ymb /'kôr,im(b); 'kär-/ ▶*n. Botany* a flower cluster whose lower stalks are proportionally longer so that the flowers form a flat or slightly convex head. ▷early 18th cent.: from French *corymbe* or Latin *corymbus*, from Greek *korumbos* 'cluster.' **—co·rym·bose** /'kôrəm,bōs; 'kär-; -,bōz/ *adj.*

cor·y·ne·bac·te·ri·um /,kôrənēbak'ti(ə)rēəm; kə,rinə-/ ▶*n.* (*pl.* **-te·ri·a** /-'ti(ə)rēə/) a bacterium that sometimes causes disease in humans and other animals, including diphtheria. • Genus *Corynebacterium*; Gram-positive nonmotile club-shaped rods. ▷modern Latin, from Greek *korunē* 'club' + **BACTERIUM**.

cor·y·phée /,kôrə'fā/ ▶*n.* a leading dancer in a corps de ballet. ▷French, via Latin from Greek *koruphaios* 'leader of a chorus,' from *koruphē* 'head.'

co·ry·za /kə'rīzə/ ▶*n. Medicine* catarrhal inflammation of the mucous membrane in the nose, caused esp. by a cold or by hay fever. ▷early 16th cent.: from Latin, from Greek *koruza* 'nasal mucus.'

cos[1] /käs; kôs/ (also **cos lettuce**) ▶*n.* another term for **ROMAINE**. ▷late 17th cent.: named after the Aegean island of *Cos*, where it originated.

cos[2] ▶*abbr.* cosine.

Co·sa Nos·tra /,kōsə 'nōstrə; ,kōzə/ a U.S. criminal organization resembling and related to the Mafia. ▷Italian, literally 'our affair.'

Cos·by /'kôzbē; 'käz-/, Bill (1937–), U.S. comedian, actor, and writer; full name *William Henry Cosby, Jr.* He was the first African American to star in a weekly television drama ("I Spy"; 1965–68). His comedy series "The Cosby Show" 1984–92 was one of the most successful programs in television history. He wrote *Fatherhood* (1987) and *Love and Marriage* (1989).

cos·co·ro·ba swan /,käskə'rōbə/ ▶*n.* a small South American swan with white plumage and bright pink legs and feet. • *Coscoroba coscoroba*, family Anatidae. ▷early 19th cent.: *coscoroba* from the modern Latin taxonomic name, of unknown origin.

co·sec /'kōsek/ ▶*abbr.* cosecant.

co·se·cant /kō'sē,kant; -kənt/ ▶*n. Mathematics* the ratio of the hypotenuse (in a right-angled triangle) to the side opposite an acute angle; the reciprocal of sine. ▷early 18th cent.: from modern Latin *cosecant*, from **co-** 'mutually' + Latin *secant-* 'cutting' (from the verb *secare*). Compare with **SECANT**.

co·seis·mal /kō'sīzməl; -'sīsməl/ ▶*adj.* relating to points on the earth's surface affected by an earthquake simultaneously.
▶*n.* a line on a map connecting such points. ▷mid 19th cent.: from **co-** 'jointly' + *seismal* (from Greek *seismos* 'earthquake,' from *seien* 'to shake').

co·set /'kō,set/ ▶*n. Mathematics* a set composed of all the products obtained by multiplying each element of a subgroup in turn by one particular element of the group containing the subgroup.

cosh[1] /käsн/ *chiefly Brit., informal* ▶*n.* a thick heavy stick or bar used as a weapon; a bludgeon.
▶*v.* [*trans.*] hit (someone) on the head with a cosh. ▷mid 19th cent.: of unknown origin.

cosh[2] *Mathematics* ▶*abbr.* hyperbolic cosine. ▷from **COS**[2] + *-h* for *hyperbolic*. Compare with **COTH**.

co-sign /'kō,sīn/ ▶*v.* **1** sign (a document) in order to guarantee a loan or other obligation: [*trans.*] *co-sign a loan* [*intrans.*] *see if your parents will co-sign for you.* **2** [*trans.*] designate with two different labels or signs: *original interchange numbers will be co-signed with new numbers for two years after the conversion | U.S. 400 is co-signed with U.S. 166 for about 8 miles.*

co·sig·na·to·ry /kō'signə,tôrē/ (also **co-sig·na·to·ry**) ▶*n.* a person or state signing a treaty or other document jointly with others.

Cos·i·mo de' Me·di·ci /'kôzē,mō də 'medəcнē/ (1389–1464), Italian statesman and banker; known as **Cosimo the Elder**. He laid the foundations for the Medici family's power in Florence, becoming the city's ruler in 1434 and using his considerable wealth to promote the arts and learning.

co·sine /'kō,sīn/ ▶*n. Mathematics* the trigonometric function that is equal to the ratio of the side adjacent to an acute angle (in a right-angled triangle) to the hypotenuse.

co-sleep·ing /,kō'slēpiNG/ ▶*n.* the practice of sleeping in the same bed with one's infant or young child: *co-sleeping often facilitates a good breastfeeding relationship.* **—co-sleep** *v.* (**-slept**) [*intrans.*] *a more contemporary approach would be to teach parents who choose to co-sleep to do it safely.*

cos·me·ceu·ti·cal /,käzmə'sōōtikəl/ ▶*n.* a cosmetic that has or is claimed to have medicinal properties, esp. anti-aging ones. ▷1980s: blend of *cosmetic* and *pharmaceutical.*

cos·met·ic /käz'metik/ ▶*adj.* involving or relating to treatment intended to restore or improve a person's appearance: *cosmetic surgery.* ■ designed or serving to improve the appearance of the body, esp. the face: *lens designs can improve the cosmetic effect of your glasses.* ■ affecting only the appearance of something rather than its substance: *the reform package was merely a cosmetic exercise.*
▶*n.* (usu. **cosmetics**) a product applied to the body, esp. the face, to improve its appearance. ▷early 17th cent. (as a noun denoting the art of beautifying the body): from French *cosmétique*, from Greek *kosmētikos*, from *kosmein* 'arrange or adorn,' from *kosmos* 'order or adornment.' **—cos·met·i·cal·ly** /-(ə)lē/ *adv.*

cos·me·ti·cian /,käzmə'tisнən/ ▶*n.* a person who sells or applies cosmetics as an occupation.

cos·me·tol·o·gy /,käzmə'täləjē/ ▶*n.* the professional skill or practice of beautifying the face, hair, and skin. **—cos·me·to·log·i·cal** /-tə'läjikəl/ *adj.* **—cos·me·tol·o·gist** /-jist/ *n.*

cos·mic /'käzmik/ ▶*adj.* of or relating to the universe or cosmos, esp. as distinct from the earth: *cosmic matter.* ■ inconceivably vast. **—cos·mi·cal** *adj.* **—cos·mi·cal·ly** /-(ə)lē/ *adv.*

cos·mic dust ▶*n.* small particles of matter distributed throughout space.

cos·mic ra·di·a·tion ▶*n.* radiation consisting of cosmic rays.

cos·mic ray ▶*n.* a highly energetic atomic nucleus or other particle traveling through space at a speed approaching that of light.

cos·mic string ▶*n.* another term for **STRING** (sense 5).

cosmo- ▶*comb. form* of or relating to the world or the universe: *cosmodrome | cosmography.* ▷from Greek *kosmos* 'order, world.'

cos·mo·drome /'käzmə,drōm/ ▶*n.* (in the countries of the former USSR) a launching site for spacecraft. ▷1950s: from **COSMO-** + **-DROME**, on the pattern of *aerodrome.*

cos·mo·gen·e·sis /,käzmə'jenəsis/ ▶*n.* the origin or evolution of the universe. **—cos·mo·ge·net·ic** /-jə-'netik/ *adj.* **—cos·mo·gen·ic** /-'jenik/ *adj.*

cos·mog·o·ny /käz'mägənē/ ▶*n.* (*pl.* **-nies**) the branch of science that deals with the origin of the universe, esp. the solar system. ■ a theory regarding this: *in their cosmogony, the world was thought to be a square, flat surface.* ▷late 17th cent.: from Greek *kosmogonia*, from *kosmos* 'order or world' + *-gonia* '-begetting.' **—cos·mo·gon·ic** /,käzmə'gänik/ *adj.* **—cos·mo·gon·i·cal** /,käzmə'gänikəl/ *adj.* **—cos·mog·o·nist** /-nist/ *n.*

cos·mog·ra·phy /käz'mägrəfē/ ▶*n.* (*pl.* **-phies**) the science that deals with the general features of the universe, including the earth. The branches of cosmography include astronomy, geography, and geology. ■ a description or representation of the universe or the earth. ▷late Middle English: from French *cosmographie*, or via late Latin from Greek *kosmographia*, from *kosmos* (see **COSMOS**[1]) + *-graphia* 'writing.' **—cos·mog·ra·pher** /-fər/ *n.* **—cos·mo·graph·ic** /,käzmə'grafik/ *adj.* **—cos·mo·graph·i·cal** /,käzmə'grafikəl/ *adj.*

cos·mo·log·i·cal ar·gu·ment /,käzmə'läjikəl/ ▶*n. Philosophy* an argument for the existence of God that claims that all things in nature depend on something else for their existence (i.e., are contingent), and that the whole cosmos must therefore itself depend on a being that exists independently or necessarily. Compare with **ONTOLOGICAL ARGUMENT** and **TELEOLOGICAL ARGUMENT**.

cos·mo·log·i·cal con·stant ▶*n. Physics* an arbitrary constant in the field equations of general relativity.

cos·mol·o·gy /käz'mäləjē/ ▶*n.* (*pl.* **-gies**) the science of the origin and development of the universe. Modern astronomy is dominated by the big bang theory, which brings together observational astronomy and particle physics. ■ an account or theory of the origin of the universe. ▷mid 17th cent.: from French *cosmologie* or modern Latin *cosmologia*, from Greek *kosmos* 'order or world' + *-logia* 'discourse.' **—cos·mo·log·i·cal** /,käzmə'läjikəl/ *adj.* **—cos·mol·o·gist** /-jist/ *n.*

cos·mo·naut /'käzmə,nôt; -,nät/ ▶*n.* a Russian astronaut. ▷1950s: from **COSMOS**[1], on the pattern of *astronaut* and Russian *kosmonavt*.

cos·mop·o·lis /käz'mäpələs/ ▶*n.* a city inhabited by people from many different countries. ▷mid 19th cent.: from Greek *kosmos* 'world' + *polis* 'city.'

cos·mo·pol·i·tan /,käzmə'pälitn/ ▶*adj.* familiar with and at ease in many different countries and cultures: *his knowledge of French, Italian, and Spanish made him genuinely cosmopolitan.* ■ including people from many different countries: *immigration transformed the city into a cosmopolitan metropolis.* ■ having an exciting and glamorous character associated with travel and a mixture of cultures: *their designs became a byword for cosmopolitan chic.* See note at **URBANE**. ■ (of a plant or animal) found all over the world.
▶*n.* **1** a cosmopolitan person. ■ a cosmopolitan organism or species. **2** a cocktail typically made with vodka, Cointreau, cranberry juice, and lime juice. ▷mid 17th cent. (as a noun): from **COSMOPOLITE** + **-AN**. **—cos·mo·pol·i·tan·ism** /-,izəm/ *n.* **—cos·mo·pol·i·tan·ize** /-,īz/ *v.*

cos·mop·o·lite /käz'mäpə,līt/ ▶*n.* a cosmopolitan person. ▷early 17th cent.: from French, from Greek *kosmopolitēs*, from *kosmos* 'world' + *politēs* 'citizen.'

cos·mos[1] /'käzməs; -,mōs; -,mäs/ ▶*n.* (**the cosmos**) the universe seen as a well-ordered whole: *he sat staring deep into the void, reminding himself of his place in the cosmos.* ■ a system of thought: *the new gender-free intellectual cosmos.* ▷Middle English: from Greek *kosmos* 'order or world.'

cos·mos[2] ▶*n.* an ornamental plant of the daisy family with single dahlialike flowers. Native to tropical America, it is widely grown as an ornamental. • Genus *Cosmos*, family Compositae. ▷from Greek *kosmos* in the sense 'ornament.'

COSPAR /'kō,spär/ ▶*abbr.* Committee on Space Research.

Cos·sack /'käs,ak; -ək/ ▶*n.* a member of a people of southern Russia, Ukraine, and Siberia, noted for their horsemanship and military skill. ■ a member of a Cossack military unit.

> The Cossacks had their origins in the 15th century when refugees from religious persecution, outlaws, adventurers, and escaped serfs banded together in settlements for protection. Under the tsars they were allowed considerable autonomy in return for protecting the frontiers; with the collapse of Soviet rule, Cossack groups have reasserted their identity in both Russia and Ukraine.

▶*adj.* of, relating to, or characteristic of the Cossacks. ▷late 16th cent.: from Russian *kazak* from Turkic, 'vagabond, nomad'; later influenced by French *Cosaque* (see also **KAZAKH**).

cos·set /'käsət/ ▶*v.* (**-set·ed**, **-set·ing**) [*trans.*] care for and protect in an overindulgent way: *all her life she'd been cosseted by her family.* ▷mid 16th cent. (as a noun denoting a lamb brought up by hand, later a spoiled child): probably from Anglo-Norman French *coscet* 'cottager,' from Old English *cotsǣta* 'cottar.'

cost /kôst/ ▸*v.* (*past* and *past part.* **cost**) [*trans.*] **1** (of an object or an action) require the payment of (a specified sum of money) before it can be acquired or done: *each issue of the magazine costs $2.25.* ■ cause the loss of: *driving at more than double the speed limit cost the woman her driving license.* ■ involve (someone) in (an effort or unpleasant action): *the accident cost me a visit to the doctor.* ■ *informal* be expensive for (someone): *if you want to own an island, it'll cost you.* **2** (*past* and *past part.* **cost·ed**) estimate the price of: *it is their job to plan and cost a media schedule for the campaign.*
▸*n.* an amount that has to be paid or spent to buy or obtain something: *we are able to* **cover the cost** *of the event | health care costs | the tunnel has been built* **at no cost** *to the state.* ■ the effort, loss, or sacrifice necessary to achieve or obtain something: *she averted a train accident* **at the cost of** *her life.* ■ (**costs**) legal expenses, esp. those allowed in favor of the winning party or against the losing party in a suit. ▷Middle English: from Old French *coust* (noun), *couster* (verb), based on Latin *constare* 'stand firm, stand at a price.'
▸*PHRASES* □ **at all costs** (or **at any cost**) regardless of the price to be paid or the effort needed: *he was anxious to avoid war at all costs.* □ **at cost** at cost price; without profit to the seller. □ **cost an arm and a leg** see ARM[1]. □ **cost someone dearly** (or **dear**) involve someone in a serious loss or a heavy penalty: *they were really bad mistakes on my part and they cost us dearly.*

Cos·ta /'kôstə/, Lúcio (1902–63), Brazilian architect, town planner, and architectural historian; born in France. He designed Brasilia, the capital of Brazil, in 1956.

cos·ta /'kästə/ ▸*n.* (*pl.* **-tae** /-tē; -tī/) *Botany & Zoology* a rib, midrib, or riblike structure. ■ *Entomology* the main vein running along the leading edge of an insect's wing. ▷mid 19th cent.: from Latin.

Cos·ta Blan·ca /,kôstə 'blängkə/ a resort region on the Mediterranean coast of southeastern Spain. ▷Spanish, literally 'white coast.'

Cos·ta Bra·va /,kôstə 'brävə/ a resort region on the Mediterranean coast of northeastern Spain, north of Barcelona. ▷Spanish, literally 'wild coast.'

cost ac·count·ing ▸*n.* the recording of all the costs incurred in a business in a way that can be used to improve its management. —**cost ac·count·ant** *n.*

Cos·ta del Sol /,kôstə del 'sōl/ a resort region on the Mediterranean coast of southern Spain. ▷Spanish, 'coast of the sun.'

cos·tal /'kästəl/ ▸*adj.* of or relating to the ribs. ■ *Anatomy & Zoology* of or relating to a costa. ▷mid 17th cent.: from French, from modern Latin *costalis*, from Latin *costa* 'rib.'

Cos·ta Me·sa /,kōstə 'māsə; ,kästə/ a city in southwestern California, on the Pacific Ocean, south of Los Angeles; pop. 96,357.

co·star /'kō,stär; kō'stär/ (also **co-star**) ▸*n.* a leading actor or actress appearing in a movie, on stage, etc., with another or others of equal importance.
▸*v.* [*intrans.*] appear in a production as a costar: *she* **costarred with** *Robert De Niro in the movie version.* ■ [*trans.*] (of a production) include as a costar: *his latest movie costars Meryl Streep.*

cos·tard /'kästərd/ (also **Cos·tard**) ▸*n. Brit.* a cooking apple of a large ribbed variety. ■ *archaic, humorous* a person's head. ▷Middle English: from Anglo-Norman French, from *coste* 'rib,' from Latin *costa*.

Cos·ta Ri·ca /,kōstə 'rēkə; ,kôstə; ,kästə/ a republic in Central America on the Isthmus of Panama, with coastlines on the Pacific Ocean and the Caribbean Sea; pop. 3,956,000; capital, San José; language, Spanish. ▷Spanish, 'rich coast.' —**Cos·ta Ri·can** /'rēkən/ *adj.* & *n.*

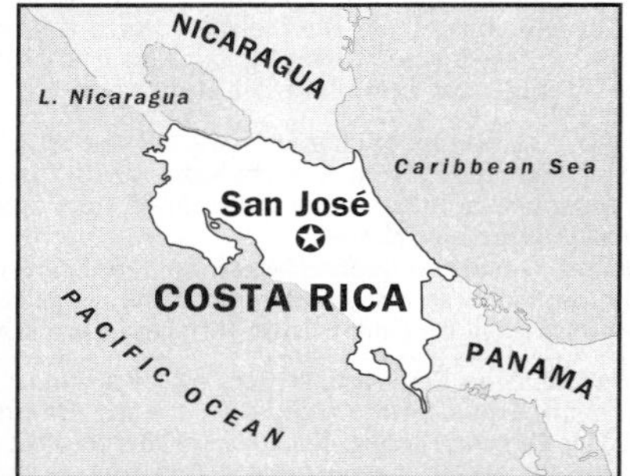

Colonized by Spain in the early 16th century, Costa Rica achieved independence in 1823 and emerged as a separate country in 1838.

cos·tate /'käs,tāt; 'kästət/ ▸*adj. Botany & Zoology* ribbed; possessing a costa. ▷early 19th cent.: from Latin *costatus*, from *costa* 'rib.'

cost-ben·e·fit ▸*adj.* relating to or denoting a process that assesses the relation between the cost of an undertaking and the value of the resulting benefits: *a cost-benefit analysis.*

cost cen·ter ▸*n.* a department or other unit within an organization to which costs may be charged for accounting purposes.

cost-ef·fec·tive ▸*adj.* effective or productive in relation to its cost: *the most cost-effective way to invest in the stock market.* —**cost-ef·fec·tive·ly** *adv.* —**cost-ef·fec·tive·ness** *n.*

cost-ef·fi·cient ▸*adj.* another term for COST-EFFECTIVE. —**cost-ef·fi·cien·cy** *n.*

cos·ter·mon·ger /'kästər,mənggər; -,mänggər/ ▸*n. Brit., dated* a person who sells goods, esp. fruit and vegetables, from a handcart in the street. ▷early 16th cent. (denoting an apple seller): from COSTARD + -MONGER.

cos·tive /'kästiv; 'kôstiv/ ▸*adj.* constipated. ■ slow or reluctant in speech or action; unforthcoming: *if he did ask her she would become costive.* ▷late Middle English: via Old French from Latin *constipatus* 'pressed together' (see CONSTIPATED). —**cos·tive·ly** *adv.* —**cos·tive·ness** *n.*

cost·ly /'kôstlē/ ▸*adj.* (**-li·er**, **-li·est**) costing a lot; expensive: *major problems requiring costly repairs.* ■ causing suffering, loss, or disadvantage: *the government's biggest and most costly mistake.* —**cost·li·ness** *n.*

cost·mar·y /'kôst,me(ə)rē; 'käst-/ ▸*n.* (*pl.* **-mar·ies**) an aromatic plant of the daisy family, formerly used in medicine and for flavoring ale prior to the use of hops. • *Balsamita major*, family Compositae. ▷late Middle English: from obsolete *cost* (via Latin from Greek *kostos*, via Arabic from Sanskrit *kuṣṭha*, denoting an aromatic plant) + *Mary*, the mother of Jesus Christ (with whom it was associated in medieval times because of its medicinal qualities).

Cost·ner /'kästnər/, Kevin (1955–), U.S. actor, director, and producer. His movies include *Field of Dreams* (1989), *Dances with Wolves* (Academy Award, 1990), *JFK* (1991), and *Message in a Bottle* (1999).

cost of liv·ing ▸*n.* the level of prices relating to a range of everyday items.

cost-of-liv·ing in·dex (abbr.: **CLI**) ▸*n.* former term for CONSUMER PRICE INDEX.

cost-plus ▸*adj.* relating to or denoting a method of pricing a service or product in which a fixed profit factor is added to the costs.

cos·tume ▸*n.* /'käs,t(y)o͞om; -təm/ a set of clothes in a style typical of a particular country or historical period: *authentic Elizabethan costumes | a Chinese woman in national costume.* ■ a set of clothes worn by an actor or other performer for a particular role or by someone attending a masquerade: *a nun's costume.* ■ a set of clothes, esp. a woman's ensemble, for a particular occasion or purpose; an outfit.
▸*v.* /käs't(y)o͞om; 'käst(y)o͞om; 'kästəm/ [*trans.*] dress (someone) in a particular set of clothes: *an all-woman troupe elaborately costumed in clinging silver lamé.* ▷early 18th cent.: from French, from Italian *custume* 'custom, fashion, habit,' from Latin *consuetudo* (see CUSTOM).

cos·tume dra·ma (also **costume play**) ▸*n.* a television or film production set in a particular historical period, in which the actors wear costumes typical of that period.

cos·tume jew·el·ry ▸*n.* jewelry made with inexpensive materials or imitation gems.

cos·tum·er /'käs,t(y)o͞omər; käs't(y)o͞o-/ (also *chiefly Brit.* **cos·tu·mi·er**) /käs't(y)o͞omēər/ ▸*n.* a person or company that makes or supplies theatrical or fancy-dress costumes. ▷mid 19th cent.: from French *costumier*, from *costumer* 'dress in a costume' (see COSTUME).

co·sy ▸*adj.* British spelling of COZY.

cot[1] /kät/ ▸*n.* a type of bed, in particular: ■ a camp bed, particularly a portable, collapsible one. ■ a plain narrow bed. ■ *Brit.* a baby's crib. ▷mid 17th cent. (originally Anglo-Indian, denoting a light bedstead): from Hindi *khāṭ* 'bedstead, hammock.'

cot[2] ▸*n.* a small shelter for livestock. ■ *archaic* a small, simple cottage. ▷Old English, of Germanic origin; compare with Old Norse *kytja* 'hovel'; related to COTE.

cot[3] *Mathematics* ▸*abbr.* cotangent.

co·tan·gent /kō'tanjənt/ ▸*n. Mathematics* (in a right-angled triangle) the ratio of the side (other than the hypotenuse) adjacent to a particular acute angle to the side opposite the angle.

cot death ▸*n. Brit.* informal term for SUDDEN INFANT DEATH SYNDROME.

cote /kōt; kät/ ▸*n.* a shelter for mammals or birds, esp. pigeons. ▷Old English (in the sense 'cottage'), of Germanic origin; related to COT[2].

Côte d'Azur /,kōtdä'zyr; -də'zo͝or/ a coastal area of southeastern France, along the Mediterranean Sea, roughly coterminous with the French Riviera. It includes the towns of Cannes, Saint Tropez, Juan-les-Pins, and Antibes and the city of Nice, as well as the principality of Monaco.

Côte d'I·voire /,kōt dēv'wär/ a country in West Africa, on the Gulf of Guinea; pop. 17,327,000; capital, Yamoussoukro; languages, French (official) and West African languages.

The area was explored by the Portuguese in the late 15th century. Subsequently, it was disputed over by traders from various European countries, who mainly sought ivory and slaves. Made a French protectorate in 1842, it became a fully independent republic in 1960. There was a military coup in 1999; a peace accord was signed in 2003, but the country remained unstable.

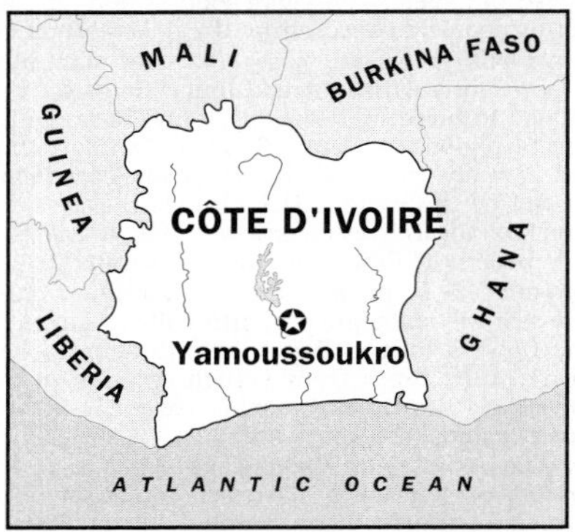

cote-har·die /,kōt 'ärdē; 'här-/ ▸*n.* (*pl.* **cote-har·dies**) *historical* a medieval close-fitting tunic with sleeves, worn by both sexes. ▷Middle English: from Old French, from *cote* 'coat' + *hardie* (feminine) 'bold.'

co·te·rie /'kōtərē; ,kōtə'rē/ ▸*n.* (*pl.* **-ries**) a small group of people with shared interests or tastes, esp. one that is exclusive of other people: *a coterie of friends and advisers.* ▷early 18th cent.: from French, earlier denoting an association of tenants, based on Middle Low German *kote* 'cote.'

co·ter·mi·nous /kō'tərmənəs/ ▸*adj.* having the same boundaries or extent in space, time, or meaning: *the southern frontier was coterminous with the French Congo colony.* ▷late 18th cent.: alteration of CONTERMINOUS. —**co·ter·mi·nous·ly** *adv.*

coth /käth/ ▸*abbr.* hyperbolic cotangent. ▷from COT[3] + *-h* for *hyperbolic*.

co·thur·nus /kō'thərnəs/ ▸*n.* **1** a thick-soled boot or buskin worn by actors in Greek tragedy. **2** an elevated style of acting in classical tragic drama.

co·tid·al line /kō'tīdl/ ▸*n.* a line on a map connecting points at which a tidal level, esp. high tide, occurs simultaneously.

co·til·lion /kə'tilyən/ ▸*n.* **1** a dance with elaborate steps and figures, in particular: ■ an 18th-century French dance based on the contredanse. ■ a quadrille. **2** a formal ball, esp. one at which debutantes are presented. ▷early 18th cent.: from French *cotillon*, literally 'petticoat dance,' diminutive of *cotte*, from Old French *cote*.

co·tin·ga /kō'tinggə; kə-/ ▸*n.* a perching bird found in the forests of Central and South America, the male of which is frequently brilliantly colored. • Family Cotingidae (the **cotinga family**): several genera, esp. *Cotinga*, and numerous species. The cotinga family also includes the bellbirds, umbrellabirds, and cocks-of-the-rock, and is sometimes placed within the family Tyrannidae. ▷via French from Tupi *cutinga*.

co·to·ne·as·ter /kə'tōnē,astər; 'kätn,ēstər/ ▸*n.* a small-leaved shrub of the rose family, cultivated as a hedging plant or for its bright red berries, which often remain on the plant throughout the winter. • Genus *Cotoneaster*, family Rosaceae. ▷mid 18th cent.: modern Latin, from Latin *cotoneum* (see QUINCE) + -ASTER.

Co·to·nou /ˌkōtnˈo͞o/ the largest city, chief port, and commercial and political center of Benin, on the coast of West Africa; pop. 536,830.

Co·to·pax·i /ˌkōtəˈpäksē; -ˈpaksē/ the highest active volcano in the world, in the Andes in central Ecuador, that rises to 19,142 feet (5,896 m). Its name is Quechuan and means "shining peak."

co·tri·mox·a·zole /ˌkō,trīˈmäksəˌzōl/ ▶*n.* *Medicine* a mixture of the drugs sulfamethoxazole and trimethoprim, used to treat bacterial infections synergistically.

Cots·wold /ˈkätˌswōld/ ▶*n.* a sheep of a breed with fine wool, often used to produce crossbred lambs. ▶*adj.* of or relating to the Cotswolds.

Cots·wold Hills /ˈkätswəld; -ˌswōld/ (also **the Cots·wolds**) a range of limestone hills in southwestern England.

cot·ta /ˈkätə/ ▶*n.* a short garment resembling a surplice, worn typically by Catholic priests and servers. ▷mid 19th cent.: from Italian; ultimately related to COAT.

cot·tage /ˈkätij/ ▶*n.* a small simple house, typically one near a lake or beach. ■ a dwelling forming part of a farm establishment, used by a worker: *farm cottages.* ▷late Middle English: from Anglo-Norman French *cotage* and Anglo-Latin *cotagium*, from COT[2] or COTE.

cot·tage cheese ▶*n.* soft, lumpy white cheese made from the curds of slightly soured milk.

cot·tage in·dus·try ▶*n.* a business or manufacturing activity carried on in a person's home.

cot·tag·er /ˈkätijər/ ▶*n.* a person living in a cottage. ■ a person vacationing in a cottage.

cot·tar /ˈkätər/ (also **cot·ter**) ▶*n.* *historical* (in Scotland and Ireland) a farm laborer or tenant occupying a cottage in return for labor. ▷late Old English, from COT[2] + -AR[4].

Cott·bus /ˈkätˌbo͝os/ an industrial city in southeastern Germany, in the state of Brandenburg, on the Spree River; pop. 123,320.

Cot·ten /ˈkätn/, Joseph (1905–94), U.S. actor. A star of Broadway, Hollywood, and television, his credits include over 60 movies, which include *Citizen Kane* (1941), *Gaslight* (1944), *The Third Man* (1949), and *Heaven's Gate* (1980).

cot·ter pin /ˈkätər/ (also **cot·ter**) ▶*n.* a metal pin used to fasten two parts of a mechanism together. ■ a split pin that is opened out after being passed through a hole. ▷mid 17th cent.: of unknown origin.

cot·ti·er /ˈkätēər/ ▶*n.* **1** *Brit., archaic* a rural laborer living in a cottage. **2** *historical* an Irish peasant holding land by cottier tenure. ▷Middle English: from Old French *cotier*, ultimately of Germanic origin and related to COT[2].

cot·ti·er ten·ure ▶*n.* *historical* (in Ireland) the renting of land in small portions direct to the laborers, at a rent fixed by competition.

cot·tise /ˈkätis/ (also **cot·ise**) ▶*n.* *Heraldry* a narrow band adjacent and parallel to an ordinary such as a bend or chevron. ▷late 16th cent.: from French *cotice* 'leather thong.' **—cot·tised** *adj.*

cot·ton /ˈkätn/ ▶*n.* **1** a soft white fibrous substance that surrounds the seeds of a tropical and subtropical plant and is used as textile fiber and thread for sewing: *a cargo of cotton and wheat | a white cotton blouse | an Indian hammock woven in colored cottons.* ■ a thread of this fiber. ■ absorbent cotton. **2** (also **cotton plant**) the plant that is commercially grown for this product. Oil and a protein-rich flour are also obtained from the seeds. • Genus *Gossypium*, family Malvaceae: many species and forms, including *G. barbadense*, which is grown in the southern U.S. ▶*v.* [*intrans.*] *informal* **1** (**cotton on**) begin to understand: *he **cottoned on to** what I was trying to say.* **2** (**cotton to**) have a liking for: *his rivals didn't cotton to all the attention he was getting.* ▷late Middle English: from Old French *coton*, from Arabic *ḳuṭn*. **—cot·ton·y** *adj.*

cot·ton bat·ting ▶*n.* light, soft cotton fibers formed into layers, used esp. for filling quilts, cushions, etc.

Cot·ton Belt ▶*n.* (**the Cotton Belt**) *informal* a region of the U.S. South where cotton is the historic main crop, esp. in parts of Georgia, Alabama, and Mississippi.

cot·ton cake ▶*n.* compressed cotton seed, used as food for cattle.

cot·ton can·dy ▶*n.* a mass of fluffy spun sugar, usually pink or white, wrapped around a stick or a paper cone.

cot·ton gin ▶*n.* a machine for separating cotton from its seeds.

cot·ton grass ▶*n.* a sedge that typically grows on swampy land in the northern hemisphere, producing tufts of long white silky hairs, which aid in the dispersal of the seeds. • Genus *Eriophorum*, family Cyperaceae.

cot·ton lav·en·der ▶*n.* chiefly British term for LAVENDER COTTON.

cot·ton-leaf worm ▶*n.* the larva of a migratory tropical moth that feeds on the leaves of the cotton plant and was formerly a major pest in North America. • *Alabama argillacea*, family Noctuidae.

cot·ton·mouth /ˈkätnˌmouTH/ ▶*n.* a large, dangerous semiaquatic pit viper that inhabits lowland swamps and waterways of the southeastern U.S. When threatening, it opens its mouth wide to display the white interior. Also called WATER MOCCASIN. • *Agkistrodon piscivorus*, family Viperidae.

cot·ton-pick·ing (also **cot·ton-pick·in'**) ▶*adj.* *informal* used for emphasis, esp. with disapproval or reproach: *just a cotton-picking minute! | he's a cotton-pickin' liar!*

cot·ton rat ▶*n.* a short-tailed rat found in grassland and scrub from North America to Guyana. • Genus *Sigmodon*, family Muridae: several species.

cot·ton·seed /ˈkätnˌsēd/ ▶*n.* the seed of the cotton plant, yielding cottonseed oil.

cot·ton stain·er ▶*n.* a North American bug that feeds on cotton bolls, causing reddish staining of the fibers. • Genus *Dysdercus*, family Pyrrhocoridae, suborder Heteroptera: several species, in particular *D. suturellus.*

Cot·ton State a nickname for the state of ALABAMA.

cot·ton swab ▶*n.* a small wad of absorbent cotton on a short thin stick, used for cosmetic or hygienic purposes.

cot·ton·tail /ˈkätnˌtāl/ ▶*n.* an American rabbit that has a speckled brownish coat and a white underside to the tail. • Genus *Sylvilagus*, family Leporidae: several species.

cot·ton·wood /ˈkätnˌwo͝od/ ▶*n.* a North American poplar with seeds covered in white cottony hairs. • Genus *Populus*, family Salicaceae: several species, including *P. deltoides.*

cot·ton wool ▶*n.* **1** raw cotton. **2** British term for ABSORBENT COTTON.

cot·y·le·don /ˌkätlˈēdn/ ▶*n.* *Botany* an embryonic leaf in seed-bearing plants, one or more of which are the first leaves to appear from a germinating seed. ▷mid 16th cent. (denoting a patch of villi on the placenta of mammals): from Latin, 'navelwort' (which has cup-shaped leaves), from Greek *kotulēdōn* 'cup-shaped cavity,' from *kotulē* 'cup.' **—cot·y·le·don·ar·y** /-ˈēdnˌerē/ *adj.*

cou·cal /ˈko͞okəl/ ▶*n.* an ungainly long-tailed Old World bird that is a large ground-dwelling member of the cuckoo family. • Genus *Centropus* (and *Coua*), family Cuculidae: numerous species, including the Australasian **pheasant coucal** (*Centropus phasianinus*). ▷early 19th cent.: from French, perhaps a blend of *coucou* 'cuckoo' and *alouette* 'lark.'

couch /kouCH/ ▶*n.* a long upholstered piece of furniture for several people to sit on. ■ a reclining seat with a headrest at one end on which a psychoanalyst's subject or doctor's patient lies while undergoing treatment. ▶*v.* [*trans.*] **1** (usu. **be couched in**) express (something) in language of a specified style: *many false claims are couched in scientific jargon.* **2** [*intrans.*] *poetic/literary* lie down: *two creatures, couched side by side in the deep grass.* ■ [*trans.*] lay down; spread out: *pieces of eel couched on a bed of steaming rice.* **3** *archaic* lower (a spear) to the position for attack. **4** [usu. as *n.*] (**couching**) *chiefly historical* treat (a cataract) by pushing the lens of the eye downward and backward, out of line with the pupil. **5** (in embroidery) fix (a thread) to a fabric by stitching it down flat with another thread: *gold and silver threads couched by hand.* ▷Middle English (as a noun denoting something to sleep on; as a verb in the sense 'lay something down'): from Old French *couche* (noun), *coucher* (verb), from Latin *collocare* 'place together' (see COLLOCATE).

▶PHRASE □ **on the couch** undergoing psychoanalysis or psychiatric treatment.

couch·ant /ˈkouCHənt/ ▶*adj.* [usu. *postpositive*] *Heraldry* (of an animal) lying with the body resting on the legs and the head raised: *two lions couchant.* ▷late Middle English: French, 'lying,' present participle of *coucher* (see COUCH).

cou·chette /ko͞oˈSHet/ ▶*n.* a European railroad car with seats convertible into sleeping berths. ■ a berth in such a car. ▷1920s: French, literally 'little bed,' diminutive of *couche* 'a couch.'

couch grass /kouCH; ko͞oCH/ ▶*n.* a coarse grass with long creeping roots, which can be troublesome in lawns and gardens. • Genera *Elymus* and *Agropyron*, family Gramineae: several species, in particular the **common couch** (*A. repens*). ▷late 16th cent.: variant of QUITCH.

couch po·ta·to /ˈkouCH/ ▶*n.* *informal* a person who spends little or no time exercising and a great deal of time watching television.

cou·dé /ko͞oˈdā/ ▶*adj.* relating to or denoting a telescope in which the rays are bent to a focus at a fixed point off the axis. ▶*n.* a telescope constructed in this way. ▷late 19th cent.: French, literally 'bent at right angles,' past participle of *couder*, from *coude* 'elbow,' from Latin *cubitum*.

cou·gar /ˈko͞ogər/ ▶*n.* a large American wild cat with a plain tawny to grayish coat, found from Canada to Patagonia. Also called MOUNTAIN LION, PUMA, PANTHER, PAINTER, and CATAMOUNT. • *Felis concolor*, family Felidae. ▷late 18th cent.: from French *couguar*, abbreviation of modern Latin *cuguarcarana*, from Guarani *guaçuarana*.

cough /kôf/ ▶*v.* [*intrans.*] expel air from the lungs with a sudden sharp sound. ■ (of an engine) make a sudden harsh noise, esp. as a sign of malfunction. ■ [*trans.*] force (something, esp. blood) out of the lungs or throat by coughing: *he **coughed up** blood-stained fluid.* ■ [*trans.*] (**cough something out**) say something in a harsh, abrupt way: *he coughed out his orders.*

▶*phrasal v.* □ **cough something up** (or **cough up**) give something reluctantly, esp. money or information that is due or required.

▶*n.* an act or sound of coughing: *she gave a discreet cough.* ■ a condition of the respiratory organs causing coughing: *he looked feverish and had a bad cough.* ▷Middle English: of imitative origin; related to Dutch *kuchen* 'to cough' and German *keuchen* 'to pant.'

cough drop ▶*n.* a medicated lozenge sucked to relieve a cough or sore throat.

cough syr·up ▶*n.* liquid medicine taken either to suppress or expectorate a cough.

could /ko͝od/ ▶*modal verb* past of CAN[1]. ■ used to indicate possibility: *they could be right | I would go if I could afford it.* ■ used in making polite requests: *could I use the phone?* ■ used in making suggestions: *you could always phone him.* ■ used to indicate annoyance because of something that has not been done: *they could have told me!* ■ used to indicate a strong inclination to do something: *he irritates me so much that I could scream.*

could·n't /ˈko͝odnt/ ▶*contraction of* could not.

couldst /ko͝odst/ (also **could·est** /ˈko͝odist/) ▶*auxiliary v.* *archaic* second person singular of COULD.

cou·lee /ˈko͞olē/ ▶*n.* **1** a deep ravine. **2** a lava flow. ▷early 19th cent.: from French *coulée* '(lava) flow,' from *couler* 'to flow,' from Latin *colare* 'to strain or flow,' from *colum* 'strainer.'

cou·li·biac /ko͞oˈlēbyäk/ ▶*n.* a Russian fish pie typically made with salmon or sturgeon, hard-boiled eggs, mushrooms, and herbs, in a puff pastry shell. ▷from Russian *kulebyaka*.

cou·lis /ˈko͞olē/ ▶*n.* (*pl.* same) a thin fruit or vegetable purée, used as a sauce. ▷French, from *couler* 'to flow.'

cou·lisse /ko͞oˈlēs/ ▶*n.* **1** a flat piece of scenery at the side of the stage in a theater. ■ (**the coulisses**) the spaces between these pieces of scenery; the wings. **2** a groove, or a grooved timber, in which a movable partition slides up and down. ▷early 19th cent.: French, feminine of *coulis* 'sliding,' based on Latin *colare* 'to flow.'

cou·loir /ko͞olˈwär/ ▶*n.* a steep, narrow gully on a mountainside. ▷early 19th cent.: French, 'gully or corridor,' from *couler* 'to flow.'

cou·lomb /ˈko͞oˌläm; -ˌlōm/ (abbr.: **C**) ▶*n.* *Physics* the SI unit of electric charge, equal to the quantity of electricity conveyed in one second by a current of one ampere. ▷late 19th cent.: named after

Charles-Augustin de *Coulomb* (1736–1806), French military engineer.

Cou·lomb's law *Physics* a law stating that like charges repel and opposite charges attract, with a force proportional to the product of the charges and inversely proportional to the square of the distance between them. ▷late 18th cent.: named after C.-A. de *Coulomb* (see COULOMB).

coul·ter /ˈkōltər/ (also **col·ter**) ▸*n.* a vertical cutting blade fixed in front of a plowshare. ■ the part of a seed drill that makes the furrow for the seed.

cou·ma·rin /ˈko͞omərən/ ▸*n. Chemistry* a vanilla-scented compound found in many plants, formerly used for flavoring food. • A bicyclic ketone; chem. formula: $C_9H_6O_2$. ■ any derivative of this. ▷mid 19th cent.: from French *coumarine*, from *coumarou*, via Portuguese and Spanish from Tupi *cumarú* 'tonka bean.'

cou·ma·rone /ˈko͞oməˌrōn/ ▸*n. Chemistry* an organic compound present in coal tar, used to make thermoplastic resins chiefly for paints and varnishes. • A bicyclic compound with fused benzene and furan rings; chem. formula: C_8H_6O. ▷late 19th cent.: from COUMARIN + -ONE.

coun·cil /ˈkounsəl/ ▸*n.* an advisory, deliberative, or legislative body of people formally constituted and meeting regularly: *an official human rights council.* ■ a body of people elected to manage the affairs of a city, county, or other municipal district. ■ an ecclesiastical assembly. ■ an assembly or meeting for consultation or advice: *that evening, she held a family council.* ▷Old English (in the sense 'ecclesiastical assembly'): from Anglo-Norman French *cuncile*, from Latin *concilium* 'convocation, assembly,' from *con-* 'together' + *calare* 'summon.' Compare with COUNSEL.

Coun·cil Bluffs an industrial and commercial city in southwestern Iowa, on the Missouri River, opposite Omaha in Nebraska; pop. 58,268.

Coun·cil for Mu·tu·al Ec·o·nom·ic As·sis·tance *historical* fuller form of COMECON. ▷translating Russian *Sovet ékonomicheskoĭ vzaimopomoshchi.*

coun·cil·man /ˈkounsəlmən/ ▸*n.* (*pl.* **-men**) a person, esp. a man, who is a member of a council, esp. a municipal one.

Coun·cil of Chal·ce·don, Coun·cil of Eu·rope, etc. see CHALCEDON, COUNCIL OF; EUROPE, COUNCIL OF, etc.

coun·cil of min·is·ters ▸*n.* an administrative body that advises the chief executive or head of state. ■ (**Council of Ministers**) the policymaking body of the European Economic Community.

coun·cil of war ▸*n.* a gathering of military officers in wartime. ■ a meeting held to plan a response to an emergency.

coun·ci·lor /ˈkouns(ə)lər/ (also *chiefly Brit.* **coun·cil·lor**) ▸*n.* a member of a council. ▷late Middle English: alteration of COUNSELOR, by association with COUNCIL. —**coun·ci·lor·ship** /-ˌSHip/ *n.*

USAGE On the difference between **councilor** and **counselor**, see **usage** at COUNSELOR.

coun·cil·wom·an /ˈkounsəlˌwo͝omən/ ▸*n.* (*pl.* **-wom·en**) a woman who is a member of a council, esp. a municipal one.

coun·sel /ˈkounsəl/ ▸*n.* **1** advice, esp. that given formally. ■ consultation, esp. to seek or give advice. **2** (*pl.* same) the lawyer or lawyers conducting a case: *the counsel for the defense.*

▸*v.* (**-seled, -sel·ing**; *chiefly Brit.* **-selled, -sel·ling**) [*trans.*] give advice to (someone): *he was counseled by his supporters to return to Germany.* ■ give professional psychological help and advice to (someone): *he was being counseled for depression.* ■ recommend (a course of action): *the athlete's coach counseled caution.* ▷Middle English: via Old French *counseil* (noun), *conseiller* (verb), from Latin *consilium* 'consultation, advice,' related to *consulere* (see CONSULT). Compare with COUNCIL.

▸*PHRASES* □ **keep one's own counsel** say nothing about what one believes, knows, or plans: *she doubted what he said but kept her own counsel.* □ **take counsel** discuss a problem: *the party leader and chairman took counsel together.*

coun·sel·ing /ˈkouns(ə)liNG/ (also *chiefly Brit.* **coun·sel·ling**) ▸*n.* the provision of assistance and guidance in resolving personal, social, or psychological problems and difficulties, esp. by a professional: *bereavement counseling.*

coun·se·lor /ˈkouns(ə)lər/ (also *chiefly Brit.* **coun·sel·lor**) ▸*n.* **1** a person trained to give guidance on personal, social, or psychological problems: *a marriage counselor.* ■ [often with *adj.*] a person who gives advice on a specified subject: *a debt counselor.* **2** a person who supervises children at a camp. **3** a trial lawyer. **4** a senior officer in the diplomatic service. ▷Middle English (in the general sense 'adviser'): from Old French *conseiller*, from Latin *consiliarius*, and Old French *conseillour*, from Latin *consiliator*, both from *consilium* 'consultation or advice.'

USAGE A **counselor** is someone who gives advice or counsel, esp. an attorney. A **councilor** is a member of a council, such as a town or city council. Confusion arises because many *counselors* sit on councils, and *councilors* are often called on to give counsel.

count[1] /kount/ ▸*v.* **1** [*trans.*] determine the total number of (a collection of items): *I started to count the stars I could see | they **counted up** their change.* ■ [*intrans.*] recite numbers in ascending order, usually starting at the number one: *hold the position as you **count to** five.* ■ [*intrans.*] (**count down**) recite or display numbers backward to zero to indicate the time remaining before the launch of a rocket or the start of an operation: *the floor manager pointed at the camera and counted down.* ■ [*intrans.*] (**count down**) prepare for a significant event in the short time remaining before it: *with more orders expected, the company is **counting down to** a bumper Christmas.* **2** [*trans.*] take into account; include: *the staff has shrunk to four, or five if you count the summer intern.* ■ (**count someone in**) include someone in an activity or the plans for it: *if the project gets started, count me in.* ■ consider (someone or something) to possess a specified quality or fulfill a specified role: *she met some rebuffs from people she had **counted as** her friends | I count myself fortunate to have known him.* ■ [*intrans.*] be regarded as possessing a specified quality or fulfilling a specified role: *the rebate **counts as** taxable income.* **3** [*intrans.*] be significant: *it did not matter what the audience thought—it was the critics that counted.* ■ (of a factor) play a part in influencing opinion for or against someone or something: *he hopes his sportsmanlike attitude will **count in his favor**.* ■ (**count for**) be worth (a specified amount): *he has no power base and his views count for little.* ■ (**count toward**) be included in an assessment of (a final result or amount): *reduced rate contributions do not count toward your pension.* ■ (**count on/upon**) rely on: *whatever you're doing, you can count on me.*

▸*phrasal v.* □ **count someone out** **1** complete a count of ten seconds over a fallen boxer to indicate defeat. **2** *informal* exclude someone from an activity or the plans for it: *if this is a guessing game, you can count me out.* **3** (in children's games) select a player for dismissal or a special role by using a counting rhyme. □ **count something out** take items one by one from a stock of something, esp. money, keeping a note of how many one takes: *opening the wallet, I counted out 19 dollars.*

▸*n.* **1** an act of determining the total number of something: *at the last **count**, fifteen applications were still outstanding | the party's only candidate was eliminated at the first count.* ■ the total determined by such an action: *there was a moderate increase in the white cell count in both patients.* **2** an act of reciting numbers in ascending order, up to the specified number: *hold the position for five counts | hold it for a count of seven.* ■ *Boxing* an act of reciting numbers up to ten by the referee when a boxer is knocked down, the boxer being considered knocked out if still down when ten is reached. ■ *Baseball* the number of balls and strikes that have been charged to the batter, as recalculated with each pitch: *the count on Gwynn is 1 ball and 2 strikes.* **3** a point for discussion or consideration: *the program remained vulnerable **on a number of counts**.* ■ *Law* a separate charge in an indictment: *he pleaded guilty to five counts of murder.* **4** the measure of the fineness of a yarn expressed as the weight of a given length or the length of a given weight. ■ a measure of the fineness of a woven fabric expressed as the number of warp or weft threads in a given length. ▷Middle English (as a noun): from Old French *counte* (noun), *counter* (verb), from the verb *computare* 'calculate' (see COMPUTE).

▸*PHRASES* □ **beat the count** (of a boxer who has been knocked down) get up before the referee counts to ten. □ **count one's blessings** be grateful for what one has. □ **count the cost** calculate the consequences of something, typically a careless or foolish action. □ **count the days** (or **hours**) be impatient for time to pass: *they counted the days until they came home on leave.* □ **count (something) on the fingers of one hand** used to emphasize the small number of a particular thing: *I could count on the fingers of one hand the men I know who are desperate to experience fatherhood.* □ **count (one's) pennies** see PENNY. □ **count sheep** see SHEEP. □ **don't count your chickens before they're hatched** *proverb* don't be too confident in anticipating success or good fortune before it is certain: *I wouldn't count your chickens—I've agreed to sign the contract but that's all I've agreed to.* □ **down** (or *Brit.* **out**) **for the count** *Boxing* defeated by being knocked to the canvas and unable to rise within ten seconds. ■ unconscious or soundly asleep. ■ defeated. □ **keep count** (or **a count**) take note of the number or amount of something: *you can protect yourself by keeping a count of what you drink.* □ **lose count** forget how many of something there are, esp. because the number is so high: *I've lost count of the hundreds of miles I've covered.* □ **take the count** *Boxing* be knocked out.

count[2] ▸*n.* a European nobleman whose rank corresponds to that of an English earl. ▷late Middle English: from Old French *conte*, from Latin *comes, comit-* 'companion, overseer, attendant' (in late Latin 'person holding a state office'), from *com-* 'together with' + *it-* 'gone' (from the verb *ire* 'go'). —**count·ship** /-ˌSHip/ *n.*

count·a·ble /ˈkountəbəl/ ▸*adj.* able to be counted.

count·down /ˈkountˌdoun/ ▸*n.* [usu. in *sing.*] an act of counting numerals in reverse order to zero, esp. to time the last seconds before the launching of a rocket or missile: *the launch crews would begin their final countdown.* ■ (often **countdown to**) the final moments before a significant event and the procedures carried out during this time: *it is hard to imagine the countdown to war continuing without an intensification of diplomacy.* ■ a digital display that counts down.

coun·te·nance /ˈkountn-əns/ ▸*n.* **1** a person's face or facial expression: *his impenetrable eyes and inscrutable countenance give little away.* **2** support: *she was giving her specific countenance to the occasion.*

▸*v.* [*trans.*] admit as acceptable or possible: *he was reluctant to countenance the use of force.* ▷Middle English: from Old French *contenance* 'bearing, behavior,' from *contenir* (see CONTAIN). The early sense was 'bearing, demeanor,' also 'facial expression,' hence 'the face.'

▸*PHRASES* □ **keep one's countenance** maintain one's composure, esp. by refraining from laughter. □ **keep someone in countenance** help someone to remain calm and confident: *to keep herself in countenance she opened her notebook.* □ **out of countenance** disconcerted or unpleasantly surprised: *I **put** him clean **out of countenance** just by looking at him.*

coun·ter[1] /ˈkountər/ ▸*n.* **1** a long flat-topped fixture in a store or bank across which business is conducted with customers. ■ a similar structure used for serving food and drinks in a cafeteria or bar. ■ a countertop. **2** an apparatus used for counting: *the counter tells you how many pictures you have taken.* ■ a person who counts something, for example votes in an election. ■ *Physics* an apparatus used for counting individual ionizing particles or events. **3** a small disk used as a place marker or for keeping the score in board games. ■ a token representing a coin. ▷Middle English (sense 3): from Old French *conteor*, from medieval Latin *computatorium*, from Latin *computare* (see COMPUTE).

▸*PHRASES* □ **behind the counter** serving in a store or bank: *ask the young man behind the counter.* □ **over the counter** by ordinary retail purchase, with no need for a prescription or license: [as *adj.*] *over-the-counter medicines.* ■ (of share transactions) taking place outside the stock exchange system. □ **under the counter** (or **table**) (with reference to goods bought or sold) surreptitiously and typically illegally: *certain labs have been peddling this drug under the counter* | [as *adj.*] *an under-the-counter deal.*

coun·ter[2] ▸*v.* [*trans.*] speak or act in opposition to: *the second argument is more difficult to counter.* ■ [*intrans.*] respond to hostile speech or action: *"What would you like me to do about it ?" she countered* ■ [*intrans.*] *Boxing* give a return blow while parrying: *he countered with a left hook.*

▸*adv.* (**counter to**) in the opposite direction to or in conflict with: *some actions by the authorities **ran counter to** the call for leniency.*

▸*adj.* responding to something of the same kind, esp. in opposition. See also COUNTER-.

▸*n.* **1** [usu. in *sing.*] a thing that opposes or prevents something else: *the stimulus to employers' organization was partly a **counter to** growing union power.* ■ an answer to an argument or criticism: *he anticipates an objection and plans his counter.* ■ *Boxing* a blow given while parrying; a counterpunch. **2** the curved part of the stern of a ship projecting aft above the waterline. **3** *Printing* the white space enclosed by a letter such as *O* or *c.* ▷late Middle English: from Old French *contre,* from Latin *contra* 'against,' or directly from COUNTER-.

coun·ter[3] ▸*n.* the back part of a shoe or boot, enclosing the heel. ▷mid 19th cent.: abbreviation of *counterfort* 'buttress,' from French *contrefort.*

coun·ter- ▸*prefix* denoting opposition, retaliation, or rivalry: *counterattack | counterespionage.* ■ denoting movement or effect in the opposite direction: *counterbalance | counterpoise.* ■ denoting correspondence, duplication, or substitution: *counterpart | counterpoint.* ▷from Anglo-Norman French *countre-,* Old French *contre,* from Latin *contra* 'against.'

coun·ter·act /ˈkountər,akt/ ▸*v.* [*trans.*] act against (something) in order to reduce its force or neutralize it: *should we deliberately intervene in the climate system to counteract global warming?* **—coun·ter·ac·tion** /ˌkountərˈaksHən/ *n.* **—coun·ter·ac·tive** /kountərˈaktiv/ *adj.*

coun·ter·at·tack /ˈkountərə,tak/ ▸*n.* an attack made in response to one by an enemy or opponent.

▸*v.* [*intrans.*] attack in response: *as deputies tried to dislodge him, he counterattacked by forcing through elections.* **—coun·ter·at·tack·er** *n.*

coun·ter·bal·ance ▸*n.* /ˈkountər,baləns/ a weight that balances another weight. ■ a factor having the opposite effect to that of another and so preventing it from exercising a disproportionate influence: *his restoration to power was intended as a* **counterbalance to** *his rival's influence.*

▸*v.* /ˌkountərˈbaləns/ [*trans.*] (of a weight) balance (another weight). ■ neutralize or cancel by exerting an opposite influence: *the extra cost of mail order may be counterbalanced by its convenience.*

coun·ter·blow /ˈkountər,blō/ ▸*n.* a blow given in return.

coun·ter·bore /ˈkountər,bôr/ ▸*n.* a drilled hole that has a flat-bottomed enlargement at its mouth. ■ a drill whose bit has a uniform smaller diameter near the tip, for drilling counterbores in one operation.

▸*v.* [*trans.*] drill a counterbore in (an object).

coun·ter·change /ˈkountər,CHānj/ ▸*v.* [*trans.*] **1** change (places or parts); interchange. **2** *poetic/literary* checker with contrasting colors. ■ *Heraldry* interchange the tinctures of (a charge) with that of a divided field.

▸*n.* change that is equivalent in degree but opposite in effect to a previous change. ▷late Middle English (as a heraldic term): from French *contrechanger,* from *contre* (expressing substitution) + *changer* 'to change.'

coun·ter·charge /ˈkountər,CHärj/ ▸*n.* an accusation made in turn by someone against their accuser: *charges and countercharges concerning producers, quotas, and affidavits.* ■ a charge by police or an armed force in response to one made against them.

count·er·check /ˈkountər,CHek/ ▸*n.* **1** a second check for security or accuracy. **2** a restraint.

▸*v.* [*trans.*] *archaic* stop (something) by acting to cancel or counteract it: *the king with his own hand wrote to countercheck his former decree.*

coun·ter·claim /ˈkountər,klām/ ▸*n.* a claim made to rebut a previous claim. ■ *Law* a claim made by a defendant against the plaintiff.

▸*v.* [*intrans.*] *chiefly Law* make a counterclaim for something.

coun·ter·clock·wise /ˌkountərˈkläk,wīz/ ▸*adv.* & *adj.* in the opposite direction to the way in which the hands of a clock move around.

coun·ter·con·di·tion·ing /ˌkountərkənˈdisH(ə)niNG/ ▸*n.* a technique employed in animal training, and in the treatment of phobias and similar conditions in humans, in which behavior incompatible with a habitual undesirable pattern is induced. Compare with DECONDITION (sense 2).

coun·ter·cul·ture /ˈkountər,kəlCHər/ ▸*n.* a way of life and set of attitudes opposed to or at variance with the prevailing social norm: *the idealists of the 60s counterculture.*

coun·ter·cur·rent ▸*n.* /ˈkountər,kərənt/ a current flowing in an opposite direction to another.

▸*adv.* /ˌkountərˈkərənt/ in or with opposite directions of flow.

coun·ter·es·pi·o·nage /ˌkountərˈespēə,näzH; -,näj/ ▸*n.* activities designed to prevent or thwart spying by an enemy.

coun·ter·fac·tu·al /ˌkountərˈfakCHo͞oəl/ *Philosophy* ▸*adj.* relating to or expressing what has not happened or is not the case.

▸*n.* a counterfactual conditional statement (e.g., *If kangaroos had no tails, they would topple over*).

coun·ter·feit /ˈkountər,fit/ ▸*adj.* made in exact imitation of something valuable or important with the intention to deceive or defraud: *two men were remanded on bail on a charge of passing counterfeit $10 bills.* See note at SPURIOUS. ■ pretended; sham: *the filmmakers created a counterfeit world using smoke and mirrors.*

▸*n.* a fraudulent imitation of something else; a forgery: *he knew the tapes to be counterfeits.*

▸*v.* [*trans.*] imitate fraudulently: *my signature is extremely hard to counterfeit.* ■ pretend to feel or possess (an emotion or quality): *no pretense could have counterfeited such terror.* ■ *poetic/literary* resemble closely: *sleep counterfeited Death so well.* ▷Middle English (as a verb): from Anglo-Norman French *countrefeter,* from Old French *contrefait,* past participle of *contrefaire,* from Latin *contra-* 'in opposition' + *facere* 'make.' **—coun·ter·feit·er** *n.*

coun·ter·foil /ˈkountər,foil/ ▸*n.* *chiefly Brit.* the part of a check, receipt, ticket, or other document that is torn off and kept as a record by the person issuing it.

coun·ter·in·sur·gen·cy /ˌkountərinˈsərjənsē/ ▸*n.* [usu. as *adj.*] military or political action taken against the activities of guerrillas or revolutionaries: *a counterinsurgency force.*

coun·ter·in·tel·li·gence /ˌkountərinˈteləjəns/ ▸*n.* activities designed to prevent or thwart spying, intelligence gathering, and sabotage by an enemy or other foreign entity.

coun·ter·in·tu·i·tive /ˌkountərinˈt(y)o͞oitiv/ ▸*adj.* contrary to intuition or to common-sense expectation (but often nevertheless true). **—coun·ter·in·tu·i·tive·ly** *adv.*

coun·ter·ir·ri·tant /ˌkountərˈiritənt/ ▸*n.* *chiefly historical* something such as heat or an ointment that is used to produce surface irritation of the skin, thereby counteracting underlying pain or discomfort. **—coun·ter·ir·ri·ta·tion** /-,iriˈtāsHən/ *n.*

coun·ter·mand /ˌkountərˈmand; ˈkountər,mand/ ▸*v.* [*trans.*] revoke (an order): *an order to arrest the strike leaders had been countermanded.* ■ cancel an order for (goods): *she decided she had been extravagant and countermanded the cream.* ■ revoke an order issued by (another person): *he was already countermanding her.* ■ declare (voting) invalid: *the election commission has countermanded voting on the grounds of intimidation.* ▷late Middle English: from Old French *contremander* (verb), *contremand* (noun), from medieval Latin *contramandare,* from *contra-* 'against' + *mandare* 'to order.'

coun·ter·march /ˈkountər,märCH/ ▸*v.* [*intrans.*] march in the opposite direction or back along the same route.

▸*n.* an act or instance of marching in this way.

coun·ter·mark /ˈkountər,märk/ ▸*n.* *chiefly Brit.* an additional mark placed on something already marked, typically for increased security. ■ a second watermark.

coun·ter·meas·ure /ˈkountər,mezHər/ ▸*n.* an action taken to counteract a danger or threat.

coun·ter·mel·o·dy /ˈkountər,melədē/ ▸*n.* (*pl.* **-dies**) a subordinate melody accompanying a principal one.

coun·ter·mine /ˈkountər,mīn/ *Military* ▸*n.* an excavation dug to intercept another dug by an enemy.

▸*v.* [*trans.*] dig a countermine against.

coun·ter·move /ˈkountər,mo͞ov/ ▸*n.* a move or other action made in opposition to another. **—coun·ter·move·ment** *n.*

coun·ter·of·fen·sive /ˈkountərə,fensiv/ ▸*n.* an attack made in response to one from an enemy, typically on a large scale or for a prolonged period.

coun·ter·of·fer /ˈkountər,ôfər; -,äfər/ ▸*n.* an offer made in response to another.

coun·ter·pane /ˈkountər,pān/ ▸*n.* *dated* a bedspread. ▷early 17th cent.: alteration of COUNTERPOINT, from Old French *contrepointe,* based on medieval Latin *culcitra puncta* 'quilted mattress' (*puncta,* literally meaning 'pricked,' from the verb *pungere*). The change in the ending was due to association with PANE in an obsolete sense 'cloth.'

coun·ter·part /ˈkountər,pärt/ ▸*n.* **1** a person or thing holding a position or performing a function that corresponds to that of another person or thing in another place: *the minister held talks with his French counterpart.* **2** *Law* one of two or more copies of a legal document.

coun·ter·plot /ˈkountər,plät/ ▸*n.* a plot intended to thwart another plot.

▸*v.* (**-plot·ted, -plot·ting**) [*intrans.*] devise a counterplot.

coun·ter·point /ˈkountər,point/ ▸*n.* **1** *Music* the art or technique of setting, writing, or playing a melody or melodies in conjunction with another, according to fixed rules. ■ a melody played in conjunction with another. **2** an argument, idea, or theme used to create a contrast with the main element: *I have used my interviews with parents as a counterpoint to a professional judgment*

▸*v.* [*trans.*] **1** *Music* add counterpoint to (a melody): *the orchestra counterpoints the vocal part.* **2** (often **be counterpointed**) emphasize by contrast: *the cream walls and maple floors are counterpointed by black accents.* ■ compensate for: *the story's fanciful excesses are counterpointed with some sharp and unsentimental dialogue.* ▷late Middle English: from Old French *contrepoint,* from medieval Latin *contrapunctum* '(song) pricked or marked over against (the original melody),' from *contra-* 'against' + *punctum,* from *pungere* 'to prick.'

coun·ter·poise /ˈkountər,poiz/ ▸*n.* a factor, force, or influence that balances or neutralizes another: *money is a good counterpoise to beauty | they see the power of Brussels as a counterpoise to that of London.* ■ *archaic* a state of equilibrium. ■ a counterbalancing weight.

▸*v.* [*trans.*] have an opposing and balancing effect on: *our ideal of what God can do in our lives is counterpoised by the actual human condition we are in.* ■ bring into contrast: *the stories counterpoise a young recruit with an old-timer.* ▷late Middle English: from Old French *contrepois,* from *contre* 'against' + *pois* from Latin *pensum* 'weight.' Compare with POISE[1]. The verb, originally *counterpeise,* from Old French *contrepeser,* was altered under the influence of the noun in the 16th cent.

coun·ter·pose /ˌkountərˈpōz/ ▸*v.* [*trans.*] set against or in opposition to. **—coun·ter·po·si·tion** /-pəˈzisHən/ *n.*

coun·ter·pro·duc·tive /ˌkountərprəˈdəktiv/ ▸*adj.* having the opposite of the desired effect: *they believe they are helping animals but their extremist behavior is actually counterproductive.*

coun·ter·punch /ˈkountər,pənCH/ *Boxing* ▸*n.* a punch thrown in return for one received.

▸*v.* [*intrans.*] throw a counterpunch. **—coun·ter·punch·er** *n.*

Coun·ter-Ref·or·ma·tion the reform of the Church of Rome in the 16th and 17th centuries that was stimulated by the Protestant Reformation.

Measures to oppose the spread of the Reformation were decided on at the Council of Trent (1545–63), and the Jesuit order became the spearhead of the Counter-Reformation, both within Europe and abroad. Although most of northern Europe remained Protestant, southern Germany and Poland were brought back to the Roman Catholic Church.

coun·ter·rev·o·lu·tion /ˈkountər,revəˈlo͞osHən/ ▸*n.* a revolution opposing a former one or reversing its results. **—coun·ter·rev·o·lu·tion·ar·y** /-,nerē/ *adj.* & *n.*

coun·ter·ro·tate /ˌkountərˈrō,tāt/ ▸*v.* [*intrans.*] rotate in opposite directions, esp. about the same axis. **—coun·ter·ro·ta·tion** /-rōˈtāsHən/ *n.*

coun·ter·scarp /ˈkountər,skärp/ ▸*n.* the outer wall of a ditch in a fortification. Compare with SCARP. ▷late 16th cent.: from French *contrescarpe,* from Italian *controscarpa;* compare with SCARP.

coun·ter·shad·ing /ˈkountər,SHādiNG/ ▸*n.* *Zoology* protective coloration of some animals in which parts normally in shadow are light and those exposed to the sky are dark. **—coun·ter·shad·ed** /-,SHādid/ *adj.*

coun·ter·shaft /ˈkountər,SHaft/ ▸*n.* a machine driveshaft that transmits motion from the main shaft to where it is required, such as the drive axle in a vehicle.

coun·ter·sign /ˈkountər,sīn/ ▸*v.* [*trans.*] add a signature to (a document already signed by another person): *each check had to be signed and countersigned.*

▸*n.* *archaic* a signal or password given in reply to a soldier on guard. ▷late 16th cent. (as a noun): from French *contresigner* (verb), *contresigne* (noun), from Italian *contrassegno,* based on Latin *signum* 'sign.' **—coun·ter·sig·na·ture** /ˌkountərˈsignəCHər; -,CHo͝or/ *n.*

coun·ter·sink /ˈkountər,siNGk/ ▸*v.* (*past* and *past part.* **-sunk** /-,səNGk/) [*trans.*] enlarge and bevel the rim of (a drilled hole) so that a screw, nail, or bolt can be inserted flush with the surface. ■ drive (a screw, nail, or bolt) into such a hole.

coun·ter·spy /ˈkountər,spī/ ▸*n.* (*pl.* **-spies**) a spy engaged in counterespionage.

coun·ter·stain /ˈkountərˌstān/ *Biology* ▸*n.* an additional dye used in a microscopy specimen to produce a contrasting background or to make clearer the distinction between different kinds of tissue.
▸*v.* [*trans.*] treat (a specimen) with a counterstain.

coun·ter·sto·ry /ˈkountərˌstôrē/ ▸*n.* an alternative or opposing narrative or explanation.

coun·ter·sub·ject /ˈkountərˌsəbjikt; -ˌjekt/ ▸*n. Music* a second or subsidiary subject, esp. accompanying the subject or its answer in a fugue.

coun·ter·ten·or /ˈkountərˌtenər/ ▸*n. Music* the highest male adult singing voice (sometimes distinguished from the male alto voice by its strong, pure tone). ■ a singer with such a voice. ▷late Middle English: from French *contre-teneur*, from obsolete Italian *contratenore*, based on Latin *tenor* (see TENOR[1]). Compare with CONTRALTO.

C

coun·ter·ter·ror·ism /ˌkountərˈterəˌrizəm/ ▸*n.* political or military activities designed to thwart terrorism. **—coun·ter·ter·ror·ist** /ˌkountərˈterərist/ *n. & adj.*

coun·ter·top /ˈkountərˌtäp/ ▸*n.* a flat surface for working on, esp. in a kitchen.

coun·ter·trade /ˈkountərˌtrād/ ▸*n.* international trade by exchange of goods rather than by currency purchase.

coun·ter·trans·fer·ence /ˌkountərˌtransˈfərəns; -ˌtranz-/ ▸*n. Psychoanalysis* the emotional reaction of the analyst to the subject's contribution. Compare with TRANSFERENCE.

coun·ter·vail /ˌkountərˈvāl/ ▸*v.* [*trans.*] [usu. as *adj.*] (**countervailing**) offset the effect of (something) by countering it with something of equal force: *the dominance of the party was mediated by a number of countervailing factors.* ▷late Middle English (in the sense 'be equivalent to in value, compensate for'): from Anglo-Norman French *contrevaloir*, from Latin *contra valere* 'be of worth against.'

coun·ter·vail·ing du·ty ▸*n.* an import tax imposed on certain goods in order to prevent dumping or counter export subsidies.

coun·ter·weight /ˈkountərˌwāt/ ▸*n.* another term for COUNTERBALANCE.

count·ess /ˈkountəs/ ▸*n.* the wife or widow of a count or earl. ■ a woman holding the rank of count or earl in her own right. ▷Middle English: from Old French *contesse*, from late Latin *comitissa*, feminine of *comes* (see COUNT[2]).

coun·ti·an /ˈkountēən/ ▸*n.* an inhabitant of a particular county: *a Sussex Countian.*

count·ing /ˈkountiNG/ ▸*prep.* taking account of when reaching a total; including: *there were three of us in the family, or four counting my pet rabbit | the college had 139 employees,* **not counting** *those engaged in routine clerical work.*

count·ing·house /ˈkountiNGˌhous/ ▸*n. historical* an office or building in which the accounts and money of a person or company were kept.

count·less /ˈkountləs/ ▸*adj.* too many to be counted; very many: *she'd apologized countless times before.*

count noun ▸*n. Grammar* a noun that can form a plural and, in the singular, can be used with the indefinite article (e.g., *books, a book*). Contrasted with MASS NOUN.

count pal·a·tine ▸*n.* (*pl.* **counts pal·a·tine**) *historical* a feudal lord having royal authority within a region of a kingdom. ■ a high official of the Holy Roman Empire with royal authority within his domain. ▷see PALATINE[1].

coun·tri·fied /ˈkəntriˌfīd/ (also **coun·try·fied**) ▸*adj.* reminiscent or characteristic of the country, esp. in being unsophisticated: *a countrified cottage garden | her tweeds were far too countrified.* ▷mid 17th cent.: past participle of *countrify* 'make rural.'

coun·try /ˈkəntrē/ ▸*n.* (*pl.* **-tries**) **1** a nation with its own government, occupying a particular territory: *the country's increasingly precarious economic position.* ■ (**the country**) the people of a nation: *the whole country took to the streets.* ■ the land of a person's birth or citizenship: *both my native and adopted countries are at war with yours.* **2** (often **the country**) districts and small settlements outside large towns, cities, or the capital: *the airfield is right out in the country* | [as *adj.*] *a country lane.* **3** an area or region with regard to its physical features: *a tract of wild country.* ■ a region associated with a particular person, esp. a writer, or with a particular work: *Steinbeck country includes the Monterey Peninsula.* **4** short for COUNTRY MUSIC. ▷Middle English: from Old French *cuntree*, from medieval Latin *contrata (terra)* '(land) lying opposite,' from Latin *contra* 'against, opposite.'
▸PHRASE □ **across country** not keeping to roads: *their route was across country, through fields of corn.*

coun·try and west·ern ▸*n.* another term for COUNTRY MUSIC [as *adj.*] *country-and-western singer.*

coun·try blues ▸*n.* a simple form of blues in which the singer is accompanied by an acoustic guitar.

coun·try club ▸*n.* a club with sporting and social facilities, set in a suburban area.

coun·try cous·in ▸*n.* a person with an unsophisticated and provincial appearance or manners.

coun·try dance ▸*n.* a traditional type of social English dance, in particular one performed by couples facing each other in long lines.

coun·try·fied ▸*adj.* variant spelling of COUNTRIFIED.

coun·try gen·tle·man ▸*n. chiefly Brit.* a rich man of good social standing who owns and lives on an estate in a rural area. ■ an Englishman who owns land in the countryside and is considered a member of the gentry.

coun·try ham ▸*n.* a ham that is dry-cured with salt before smoking.

coun·try house ▸*n. chiefly Brit.* a large house in the country, typically the home of a wealthy or aristocratic family.

coun·try·man /ˈkəntrēmən/ ▸*n.* (*pl.* **-men**) **1** *Brit.* a person living or born in a rural area, esp. one engaged in a typically rural occupation. **2** a person from the same country or region as someone else: *she followed in the tradition of her countrymen | they trust a fellow countryman.*

coun·try mile ▸*n. informal* a very long way: *he hit the ball a country mile.*

coun·try mu·sic ▸*n.* a form of popular music originating in the rural southern U.S. It is traditionally a mixture of ballads and dance tunes played characteristically on fiddle, guitar, steel guitar, drums, and keyboard. Also called COUNTRY AND WESTERN.

coun·try·pol·i·tan /ˌkəntriˈpälitn/ (also **Coun·try·pol·i·tan**) ▸*n.* a type of country music that resembles pop music, usually characterized by orchestrated arrangements: [usu. as *modifier*] *a slick countrypolitan ballad.*
▸*adj.* relating to or denoting an architectural style that combines country charm with sophistication. ▷on the pattern of *cosmopolitan.*

coun·try rock[1] ▸*n. Geology* the rock that encloses a mineral deposit, igneous intrusion, or other feature.

coun·try rock[2] ▸*n.* a type of popular music that is a blend of rock and country music.

coun·try seat ▸*n. Brit.* a large country house and estate belonging to an aristocratic family.

coun·try·side /ˈkəntrēˌsīd/ ▸*n.* the land and scenery of a rural area: *they explored the surrounding countryside.* ■ the inhabitants of such an area: *the political influence of the countryside remains strong.*

coun·try·wide /ˈkəntrēˈwīd/ ▸*adj. & adv.* extending throughout a nation: [as *adj.*] *a countrywide tour* | [as *adv.*] *traveling countrywide.*

coun·try·wom·an /ˈkəntrēˌwo͝omən/ ▸*n.* (*pl.* **-wom·en**) **1** a woman living or born in a rural area, esp. one engaged in a typically rural occupation. **2** a woman from the same country or district as someone else: *a fellow countrywoman from Ohio.*

coun·ty /ˈkountē/ ▸*n.* (*pl.* **-ties**) (in the U.S.) a political and administrative division of a state, providing certain local governmental services. ■ a territorial division of some countries, forming the chief unit of local administration. ■ [treated as *sing.* or *pl.*] the people of such a territorial division collectively. ■ ▷Middle English: from Old French *conte*, from Latin *comitatus*, from *comes, comit-* (see COUNT[2]). The word seems earliest to have denoted a meeting held periodically to transact the business of a shire. **—coun·ty·wide** *adj. & adv.*

coun·ty bor·ough ▸*n.* (in England, Wales, and Northern Ireland) a large town formerly having the administrative status of a county.

coun·ty court ▸*n.* a court in some states with civil and criminal jurisdiction for a given county.

coun·ty crick·et ▸*n.* first-class cricket played in the UK between the eighteen professional teams contesting the County Championship.

Coun·ty Pal·a·tine *historical* (in England and Ireland) a county in which royal privileges and exclusive rights of jurisdiction were held by its earl or lord. ▷see PALATINE[1].

coun·ty seat ▸*n.* the town that is the governmental center of a county.

coup /ko͞o/ ▸*n.* (*pl.* **coups** /ko͞oz/) **1** (also **coup d'é·tat**) a sudden, violent, and illegal seizure of power from a government: *he was overthrown in an army coup.* **2** a notable or successful stroke or move: *it was a major coup to get such a prestigious contract.* ■ an unusual or unexpected but successful tactic in card play. **3** *historical* (among North American Indians) an act of touching an armed enemy in battle as a deed of bravery, or an act of first touching an item of the enemy's in order to claim it. ▷late 18th cent.: from French, from medieval Latin *colpus* 'blow' (see COPE[1]).

coup de fou·dre /ˌko͞o də ˈfo͞od(rə)/ ▸*n.* (*pl.* **coups de fou·dre** *pronunc.* same) a sudden unforeseen event, in particular an instance of love at first sight. ▷late 18th cent.: French, literally 'stroke of lightning.'

coup de grâce /ˌko͞o də ˈgräs/ ▸*n.* (*pl.* **coups de grâce** *pronunc.* same) a final blow or shot given to kill a wounded person or animal: *he administered the* coup de grâce *with a knife | figurative the party won another term and delivered the* coup de grâce *to socialism.* ▷late 17th cent.: French, literally 'stroke of grace.'

coup de main /ˌko͞o də ˈmaN/ ▸*n.* (*pl.* **coups de main** *pronunc.* same) a sudden surprise attack, esp. one made by an army during war. ▷mid 18th cent.: French, literally 'stroke of hand.'

coup de maî·tre /ˌko͞o də ˈmet(rə)/ ▸*n.* (*pl.* **coups de maî·tre** *pronunc.* same) a master stroke. ▷French.

coup d'é·tat /ˌko͞o dāˈtä/ ▸*n.* (*pl.* **coups d'é·tat** /ˌko͞o dāˈtä(z)/) another term for COUP (sense 1). ▷mid 17th cent.: French, literally 'blow of state.'

coup de thé·â·tre /ˌko͞o də tāˈät(rə)/ ▸*n.* (*pl.* **coups de thé·â·tre** *pronunc.* same) a sensational or dramatically sudden action or turn of events, esp. in a play. ▷mid 18th cent.: French, literally 'blow of theater.'

coup d'œil /ˌko͞o ˈdœē/ ▸*n.* (*pl.* **coups d'œil** *pronunc.* same) a glance that takes in a comprehensive view. ▷mid 18th cent.: French, literally 'stroke of eye.'

coupe[1] /ko͞op/ (also **cou·pé** /ko͞oˈpā/) ▸*n.* **1** a car with a fixed roof and two doors. **2** *historical* a four-wheeled enclosed carriage for two passengers and a driver. **3** *historical* an end compartment in a railroad car, with seats on only one side. ▷mid 19th cent. (sense 2): from French *carrosse coupé*, literally 'cut carriage.' Sense 1 dates from the early 20th cent.

coupe[2] ▸*n.* a shallow glass or glass dish, typically with a stem, in which desserts or champagne are served. ■ a dessert served in such a dish. ▷late 19th cent.: French, literally 'goblet.'

cou·ple /ˈkəpəl/ ▸*n.* **1** two individuals of the same sort considered together: ***a couple of*** *girls were playing marbles.* ■ *informal* an indefinite small number: *he hoped she'd be better in* ***a couple of*** *days* [as *pron.*] *we got some eggs—would you like a couple?* | [as *adj.*] *just a couple more questions | clean the stains with a couple squirts of dishwashing liquid.* **2** [treated as *sing.* or *pl.*] two people who are married, engaged, or otherwise closely associated romantically or sexually. ■ a pair of partners in a dance or game. ■ *Mechanics* a pair of equal and parallel forces acting in opposite directions, and tending to cause rotation about an axis perpendicular to the plane containing them.
▸*v.* [*trans.*] (often **be coupled to/with**) combine: *a sense of hope is coupled with a palpable sense of loss.* ■ connect (a railroad vehicle or a piece of equipment) to another: *a cable is* ***coupled up*** *to one of the wheels.* ■ [*intrans.*] (**couple up**) join to form a pair. ■ [*intrans.*] *dated* have sexual intercourse. ■ connect (two electrical components) using electromagnetic induction, electrostatic charge, or an optical link: [as *adj.*] (**coupled**) *networks of coupled oscillators.* ▷Middle English: from Old French *cople* (noun), *copler* (verb), from Latin *copula* (noun), *copulare* (verb), from *co-* 'together' + *apere* 'fasten.' Compare with COPULA and COPULATE. **—cou·ple·dom** /-dəm/ *n.*

cou·pler /ˈkəp(ə)lər/ ▸*n.* something that connects two things, esp. mechanical components or systems: *a hydraulic coupler* | [as *adj.*] *coupler rod.* ■ *Music* a device in an organ for connecting two manuals, or a manual with pedals, so that they both sound when only one is played. ■ *Music* (also **octave coupler**) a similar device for connecting notes with their octaves above or below. ■ *Photography* a compound in a developer or an emulsion that combines with the products of development to form an insoluble dye, part of the image. ■ (also **acoustic coupler**) a modem that converts digital signals from a computer into audible sound signals and vice versa, so that the former can be transmitted and received over telephone lines.

cou·plet /ˈkəplət/ ▸*n.* two lines of verse, usually in the same meter and joined by rhyme, that form a unit. ▷late 16th cent.: from French, diminutive of *couple*, from Old French *cople* (see COUPLE).

cou·pling /ˈkəp(ə)liNG/ ▸*n.* **1** a device for connecting parts of machinery. ■ a fitting on the end of a railroad vehicle for connecting it to another. **2** the pairing of two items: *the coupling of Christian ideals with Marxist principles.* ■ sexual intercourse. ■ the arrangement of items on a musical recording: *this coupling of two of the greatest works of Haydn.* ■ each such item: *one of the more interesting couplings for the B minor Sonata.* ■ an interaction between two electrical components by electromagnetic induction, electrostatic charge, or optical link.

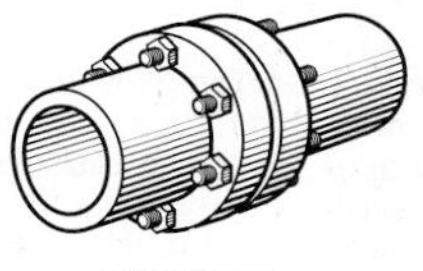
coupling 1

cou·pling con·stant ▸*n. Physics* a measure of the strength of interaction between two particles, or between a particle and a field.

cou·pon /ˈk(y)o͞oˌpän/ ▸*n.* **1** a voucher entitling the holder to a discount for a particular product. ■ a detachable portion of a bond that is given up in return for a payment of interest. **2** a form in a newspaper or magazine that may be filled in and sent as an application for a purchase or information. ▷early 19th cent. (denoting a detachable portion of a bond to be given up in return for payment of interest): from French, literally 'piece cut off,' from *couper* 'cut,' from Old French *colper* (see **COPE**[1]).

cou·pon bond ▸*n.* an investment bond on which interest is paid by presenting coupons.

cou·pon clip·per ▸*n. informal* a person with a large number of coupon bonds.

coup stick /ko͞o/ ▸*n.* (among North American Indians) a decorated stick recording coups attained by the warrior.

cour·age /ˈkərij; ˈkə-rij/ ▸*n.* the ability to do something that frightens one: *she called on all her courage to face the ordeal.* ■ strength in the face of pain or grief: *he fought his illness with great courage.* ▷Middle English (denoting the heart, as the seat of feelings): from Old French *corage,* from Latin *cor* 'heart.'

▸*PHRASES* □ **have the courage of one's convictions** act on one's beliefs despite danger or disapproval. □ **pluck up** (or **screw up** or **take**) **courage** make an effort to do something that frightens one. □ **take one's courage in both hands** nerve oneself to do something that frightens one.

THE RIGHT WORD **courage, fortitude, guts, nerve, pluck, resolution, tenacity**

Courage is what makes someone capable of facing extreme danger and difficulty without retreating (*the courage to confront the enemy head-on*). It implies not only bravery and a dauntless spirit but the ability to endure in times of adversity (*a mother's courage in the face of her loss*).

Someone who has **guts**, a slang word indicating an admirable display of courage when it really counts (*having the guts to stand up to one's boss*), might also be described as having "intestinal fortitude," a cliché that is more formal and means the same thing.

Fortitude is the most formal of any of these words; it suggests firmness or strength of mind rather than physical bravery (*the fortitude to stand up for his beliefs*).

Resolution also implies firmness of mind rather than fearlessness, but the emphasis is on the determination to achieve a goal in spite of opposition or interference (*a woman of strong resolution, not easily held back by her male superiors*).

Tenacity goes one step beyond *resolution*, adding stubborn persistence and unwillingness to acknowledge defeat (*the tenacity of a bulldog*).

Nerve and **pluck** are informal words. *Pluck* connotes high spirits, conviction, and eagerness (*the pluck to volunteer her time even after she'd been laid off*), while *nerve* is the cool, unflappable daring with which someone takes a calculated risk (*the nerve to take over the controls and land the plane safely*).

Nerve can also refer to brashness or even rudeness in social situations (*She had the nerve to go to his house without calling first*).

cou·ra·geous /kəˈrājəs/ ▸*adj.* not deterred by danger or pain; brave: *her courageous human rights work.* ▷Middle English: from Old French *corageus,* from *corage* (see **COURAGE**). —**cou·ra·geous·ly** *adv.* —**cou·ra·geous·ness** *n.*

cou·rant /ˈko͝orənt; ko͞oˈrant; ko͞oˈränt/ ▸*adj.* [usu. *postpositive*] *Heraldry* represented as running: *white horse courant.* ▷early 17th cent.: French, 'running,' present participle of *courir.*

cou·rante /ko͞oˈränt; -ˈrant/ ▸*n.* a 16th-century court dance consisting of short advances and retreats. ■ a piece of music written for or in the style of such a dance, typically one forming a movement of a suite. ▷late 16th cent.: French, literally 'running,' feminine present participle of *courir.*

Cour·bet /ko͝orˈbā/, Gustave (1819–77), French painter. A leader of the 19th-century realist school of painting, his works include *Burial at Ornans* (1850) and *Painter in His Studio* (1855).

cou·reur de bois /ko͞oˌrər də ˈbwä/ ▸*n.* (*pl.* **cou·reurs de bois** *pronunc.* same) *historical* (in Canada and the northern U.S.) a woodsman or trader of French origin. ▷early 18th cent.: French, literally 'wood runner.'

cour·gette /ˌko͝orˈzhet/ ▸*n. Brit.* a zucchini. ▷1930s: from French, diminutive of *courge* 'gourd,' from Latin *cucurbita.*

cour·i·er /ˈko͝orēər; ˈkərēər/ ▸*n.* **1** a messenger who transports goods or documents, in particular: ■ a company or employee of a company that transports commercial packages and documents: *the check was dispatched by courier* | [as *adj.*] *a courier service.* ■ a messenger for an underground or espionage organization. **2** a person employed to guide and assist a group of tourists.

▸*v.* [*trans.*] (often **be couriered**) send or transport (goods or documents) by courier. ▷late Middle English (denoting a person sent to run with a message): originally from Old French *coreor;* later from French *courier* (now *courrier*), from Italian *corriere;* based on Latin *currere* 'to run.'

Cour·règes /ko͝orˈezh/, André (1923–), French fashion designer. He is noted for his futuristic and youth-oriented styles, in particular, the use of plastic and metal, and for unisex fashion such as trouser suits for women.

course /kôrs/ ▸*n.* **1** [in *sing.*] the route or direction followed by a ship, aircraft, road, or river: *the road adopts a tortuous course along the coast* | *the new fleet* **changed course** *to join the other ships.* ■ the way in which something progresses or develops: *the course of history.* ■ a procedure adopted to deal with a situation: *the wisest* **course of action** *is to tackle the problem at its source.* ■ the route of a race or similar sporting event. ■ an area of land set aside and prepared for racing, golf, or another sport. **2** a dish, or a set of dishes served together, forming one of the successive parts of a meal: *guests are offered a choice of main course* | [in *combination*] *a four-course meal.* **3** a series, in particular: ■ a series of lectures or lessons in a particular subject, typically leading to a qualification: *a business studies course.* ■ *Medicine* a series of repeated treatments or doses of medication: *the doctor prescribed a course of antibiotics.* **4** *Architecture* a continuous horizontal layer of brick, stone, or other material in a building. **5** a pursuit of game (esp. hares) with greyhounds by sight rather than scent. **6** the lowest sail on a square-rigged mast. **7** a set of adjacent strings on a guitar, lute, etc., tuned to the same note.

▸*v.* **1** [*intrans.*] (of liquid) move without obstruction; flow: *tears were coursing down her cheeks* | *figurative exultation coursed through him.* **2** [*trans.*] pursue (game, esp. hares) with greyhounds using sight rather than scent: *many of the hares coursed escaped unharmed* | [*intrans.*] *she would course for hares with her greyhounds.* ▷Middle English: from Old French *cours,* from Latin *cursus,* from *curs-* 'run,' from the verb *currere.*

▸*PHRASES* □ **a matter of course** see **MATTER**. □ **the course of nature** events or processes that are normal and to be expected: *each man would, in the course of nature, have his private opinions.* □ **in the course of — 1** undergoing the specified process: *a new text book was in the course of preparation.* **2** during the specified period: *he was a friend to many people in the course of his life.* ■ during and as a part of the specified activity: *they became friends in the course of their long walks.* □ **in the course of time** as time goes by. □ **in due course** see **DUE**. □ **of course** used to introduce an idea or turn of events as being obvious or to be expected: *the point is, of course, that the puzzle itself is misleading.* ■ used to give or emphasize agreement or permission: *"Can I see you for a minute?" "Of course."* ■ introducing a qualification or admission: *of course we've been in touch by phone, but I wanted to see things for myself.* □ **off course** not following the intended route: *the car went careering off course.* □ **on course** following the intended route: *he battled to keep the ship on course* | *figurative to get back on course, I relied on one of my stock questions.* □ **run** (or **take**) **its course** complete its natural development without interference: *his illness had to run its course.*

cours·er[1] /ˈkôrsər/ ▸*n. dated or poetic/literary* a swift horse. ▷Middle English: from Old French *corsier,* based on Latin *cursus* (see **COURSE**).

cours·er[2] ▸*n.* a fast-running ploverlike bird related to the pratincoles, typically found in open country in Africa and Asia. • Genera *Cursorius* and *Rhinoptilus,* family Glareolidae: several species, in particular the desert-dwelling **cream-colored courser** (*C. cursor*). ▷mid 18th cent.: from modern Latin *Cursorius* 'adapted for running,' from *cursor* 'runner,' from the verb *currere* (see **COURSE**).

cours·er[3] ▸*n.* a person who hunts animals such as hares with greyhounds using sight rather than scent. ▷early 17th cent.: from **COURSER**[1].

course·ware /ˈkôrsˌwe(ə)r/ ▸*n.* computer programs or other material designed for use in an educational or training course.

course·work /ˈkôrsˌwərk/ (also **course work**) ▸*n.* written or practical work done by a student during a course of study, usually assessed in order to count toward a final mark or grade: *the graduate program combines coursework and internship.*

cours·ing /ˈkôrsiNG/ ▸*n.* the sport of hunting game animals such as hares with greyhounds using sight rather than scent.

Court /kôrt/, Margaret Smith (1942–), Australian tennis player. She won more Grand Slam events (66) than any other player.

court /kôrt/ ▸*n.* **1** (also **court of law**) a tribunal presided over by a judge, judges, or a magistrate in civil and criminal cases: *a settlement was reached during the first sitting of the court* | *she will* **take** *the matter* **to court** | [as *adj.*] *a court case.* ■ any of various other tribunals, such as military courts. ■ the place where such a tribunal meets. ■ (**the court**) the judge or judges presiding at such a tribunal. **2** a quadrangular area, either open or covered, marked out for ball games such as tennis or basketball: *an indoor tennis court.* ■ a quadrangular area surrounded by a building or group of buildings. ■ a subdivision of a building, usually a large hall extending to the ceiling with galleries and staircases. **3** the establishment, retinue, and courtiers of a sovereign: *the emperor is shown with his court.* ■ a sovereign and his or her councilors, constituting a ruling power: *relations between the king and the imperial court.* ■ a sovereign's residence.

▸*v.* [*trans.*] *dated* be involved with romantically, typically with the intention of marrying: *he was courting a girl from the neighboring farm* | [*intrans.*] *we went to the movies when we were courting.* ■ (of a male bird or other animal) try to attract (a mate). ■ pay special attention to (someone) in an attempt to win their support or favor: *Western politicians courted the leaders of the newly independent states.* ■ go to great lengths to win (favorable attention): *he never had to court the approval of the political elite.* ■ risk incurring (misfortune) because of the way one behaves: *he has often courted controversy.* ▷Middle English: from Old French *cort,* from Latin *cohors, cohort-* 'yard or retinue.' The verb is influenced by Old Italian *corteare,* Old French *courtoyer.* Compare with **COHORT**.

▸*PHRASES* □ **go to court** take legal action. □ **hold court** see **HOLD**[1]. □ **in court** appearing as a party or an attorney in a court of law. □ **out of court 1** before a legal hearing can take place: *they are trying to settle the squabble out of court* | [as *adj.*] *an out-of-court settlement.* **2** treated as impossible or not worthy of consideration: *the price would put it out of court for most private buyers.* □ **pay court to** pay flattering attention to someone in order to win favor.

court bouil·lon /ko͝or ˈbo͞o(l)ˌyän; ˌko͝or bēˈôn/ ▸*n.* a stock made from wine and vegetables, typically used in fish dishes. ▷French, from *court* 'short' and **BOUILLON**.

court card ▸*n.* British term for **FACE CARD**. ▷mid 17th cent.: alteration of 16th-cent. *coat card,* so named because of the decorative dress of the figures depicted.

court dress ▸*n. historical* formal clothing worn at a royal court.

cour·te·ous /ˈkərtēəs/ ▸*adj.* polite, respectful, or considerate in manner. ▷Middle English (meaning 'having manners fit for a royal court'): from Old French *corteis,* based on Latin *cohors* 'yard, retinue' (see **COURT**). The change in the ending in the 16th cent. was due to association with words ending in **-EOUS**. —**cour·te·ous·ly** *adv.* —**cour·te·ous·ness** *n.*

cour·te·san /ˈkôrtəzən; ˈkər-/ ▸*n.* a prostitute, esp. one with wealthy or upper-class clients. ▷mid 16th cent.: from French *courtisane*, from obsolete Italian *cortigiana*, feminine of *cortigiano* 'courtier,' from *corte* (see COURT).

cour·te·sy /ˈkərtəsē/ ▶*n.* (*pl.* **-sies**) the showing of politeness in one's attitude and behavior toward others: *he had been treated with a degree of courtesy not far short of deference.* ■ (often **courtesies**) a polite speech or action, esp. one required by convention: *the superficial courtesies of diplomatic exchanges.* ■ [as *adj.*] (esp. of transport) supplied free of charge to people who are already paying for another service: *he traveled from the hotel in a courtesy car.* ■ *archaic* a curtsy. ▷Middle English: from Old French *cortesie*, from *corteis* (see COURTEOUS).

▶*PHRASES* □ **by courtesy** as a favor rather than by right: *he was not at the conference only by courtesy.* □ **(by) courtesy of** given or allowed by: *photograph courtesy of the Evening Star.* ■ *informal* as a result of; thanks to.

cour·te·sy light ▶*n.* a small light in a car, automatically switched on when one of the doors is opened.

cour·te·sy ti·tle ▶*n.* a title given to someone, esp. the son or daughter of a peer, that has no legal validity.

court hand ▶*n. Brit.* a notoriously illegible style of handwriting used in English courts of law until banned in 1731.

court·house /ˈkôrtˌhous/ ▶*n.* **1** a building in which a judicial court is held. **2** a building containing the administrative offices of a county.

cour·ti·er /ˈkôrtēər; ˈkôrCHər/ ▶*n.* a person who attends a royal court as a companion or adviser to the king or queen. ■ a person who fawns and flatters in order to gain favor or advantage. ▷Middle English: via Anglo-Norman French from Old French *cortoyer* 'be present at court,' from *cort* (see COURT).

court·ly /ˈkôrtlē/ ▶*adj.* (**-li·er**, **-li·est**) **1** polished or refined, as befitting a royal court: *he gave a courtly bow.* **2** given to flattery; obsequious. —**court·li·ness** *n.*

court·ly love ▶*n.* a highly conventionalized medieval tradition of love between a knight and a married noblewoman, first developed by the troubadours of Southern France and extensively employed in European literature of the time. The love of the knight for his lady was regarded as an ennobling passion and the relationship was typically unconsummated.

court-mar·tial ▶*n.* (*pl.* **courts-mar·tial** or **court-mar·tials**) a judicial court for trying members of the armed services accused of offenses against military law: *they appeared before a court-martial | he was found guilty by court-martial.*

▶*v.* (**-mar·tialed**, **-mar·tial·ing**; *Brit.* **-mar·tialled**, **-mar·tial·ling**) [*trans.*] try (someone) by such a court.

court of ap·peals ▶*n.* a court to which appeals are taken in a federal circuit or a state.

court of claims ▶*n.* a court in which claims against the government are adjudicated.

court of in·quir·y ▶*n.* in the armed forces, a tribunal appointed to investigate a complaint against a member of the military to decide whether a court-martial is called for.

court of law ▶*n.* see COURT (sense 1).

court of rec·ord ▶*n.* a court whose proceedings are recorded and available as evidence of fact.

Court of St. James's the British sovereign's court.

court or·der ▶*n.* a direction issued by a court or a judge requiring a person to do or not do something.

court plas·ter ▶*n. historical* sticking plaster made of silk or other cloth with an adhesive such as isinglass. ▷late 18th cent.: so named because it was formerly used by ladies at court for beauty spots.

court rec·ord ▶*n.* see RECORD (sense 1).

court·room /ˈkôrtˌro͞om; -ˌro͝om/ ▶*n.* the place or room in which a court of law meets.

court·ship /ˈkôrtˌSHip/ ▶*n.* a period during which a couple develop a romantic relationship, esp. with a view to marriage. ■ behavior designed to persuade someone to marry one. ■ the behavior of male birds and other animals aimed at attracting a mate. ■ the process of attempting to win a person's favor or support: *the country's courtship of foreign investors.*

court ten·nis ▶*n.* the original form of tennis, played with a solid ball on an enclosed court divided into equal but dissimilar halves, the service side (from which service is always delivered) and the hazard side (on which service is received).

court·yard /ˈkôrtˌyärd/ ▶*n.* an unroofed area that is completely or mostly enclosed by the walls of a large building.

cous·cous /ˈko͞oˌsko͞os/ ▶*n.* a type of North African semolina in granules made from crushed durum wheat. ■ a spicy dish made by steaming or soaking such granules and adding meat, vegetables, or fruit. ▷early 17th cent.: from French, from Arabic *kuskus*, from *kaskasa* 'to pound,' probably of Berber origin.

cous·in /ˈkəzən/ ▶*n.* (also **first cousin**) a child of one's uncle or aunt. ■ a person belonging to the same extended family. ■ a thing related or analogous to another: *the new motorbikes are not proving as popular as their four-wheeled cousins.* ■ (usu. **cousins**) a person of a kindred culture, race, or nation: *the Russians and their Slavic cousins.* ■ *historical* a title formerly used by a sovereign in addressing another sovereign or a noble of their own country. ▷Middle English: from Old French *cosin*, from Latin *consobrinus* 'mother's sister's child,' from *con-* 'with' + *sobrinus* 'second cousin' (from *soror* 'sister'). —**cous·in·hood** /-ˌho͝od/ *n.* —**cous·in·ly** *adj.* —**cous·in·ship** /-ˌSHip/ *n.*

▶*PHRASES* □ **first cousin once removed 1** a child of one's first cousin. **2** one's parent's first cousin. □ **first cousin twice removed 1** a grandchild of one's first cousin. **2** one's grandparent's first cousin. □ **second cousin** a child of one's parent's first cousin. □ **second cousin once removed 1** a child of one's second cousin. **2** one's parent's second cousin. □ **third cousin** a child of one's parent's second cousin.

cous·in-ger·man ▶*n.* (*pl.* **cous·ins-ger·man**) old-fashioned term for COUSIN. ▷Middle English: from French *cousin germain* (see COUSIN, GERMAN).

Cous·teau /ko͞oˈstō/, Jacques-Yves (1910–97), French oceanographer and documentary movie director. He devised the scuba apparatus, but is known primarily for several documentaries and popular television series on marine life.

Cou·sy /ˈko͞ozē/, Bob (1928–), U.S. basketball player; full name *Robert Joseph Cousy*. He played for the Boston Celtics from 1950 until 1963. Basketball Hall of Fame (1970).

couth /ko͞oTH/ *humorous* ▶*adj.* cultured, refined, and well mannered: *it is more couth to hold your shrimp by the tail.*

▶*n.* good manners; refinement: *their hockey team had more talent but less couth.* ▷late 19th cent.: back-formation from UNCOUTH.

cou·ture /ko͞oˈto͝o(ə)r; -ˈtyr/ ▶*n.* the design and manufacture of fashionable clothes to a client's specific requirements and measurements. See also HAUTE COUTURE. ■ the business of designing and making such clothes. ■ such clothes: *they were dressed in size eight printed-silk couture.* ▷1920s: French, 'sewing, dressmaking.'

cou·tu·ri·er /ko͞oˈto͝orēər; -ˈto͝orēˌā/ ▶*n.* a fashion designer who manufactures and sells clothes that have been tailored to a client's specific requirements and measurements. ▷late 19th cent.: French, from COUTURE.

cou·tu·ri·ère /ko͞oˈto͝orēər; -ˌto͝orēˈe(ə)r/ ▶*n.* a female couturier.

cou·vade /ko͞oˈväd/ ▶*n.* the custom in some cultures in which a man takes to his bed and goes through certain rituals when his child is being born, as though he were physically affected by the birth. ▷mid 19th cent.: French, from *couver* 'to hatch,' from Latin *cubare* 'lie down.' The adoption of the term in French was due to a misunderstanding of the phrase *faire la couvade* 'sit doing nothing,' used by earlier writers.

cou·vert /ko͞oˈver/ ▶*n.* **1** another term for COVER (sense 4). **2** another term for COVER CHARGE: *there is a $1.50 couvert weekdays and $2.00 Saturdays and holidays.* ▷mid 18th cent.: French, past participle (used as a noun) of *couvrir* 'to cover.'

cou·ver·ture /ˌko͞overˈt(y)o͝or/ ▶*n.* chocolate made with extra cocoa butter to give a high gloss, used for covering sweets and cakes. ▷1930s: French, literally 'covering'.

co·va·lent /ˌkōˈvālənt/ ▶*adj. Chemistry* of, relating to, or denoting chemical bonds formed by the sharing of electrons between atoms. Often contrasted with IONIC. —**co·va·lence** *n.* —**co·va·lent·ly** *adv.*

co·var·i·ance /ˌkōˈve(ə)rēəns/ ▶*n.* **1** *Mathematics* the property of a function of retaining its form when the variables are linearly transformed. **2** *Statistics* the mean value of the product of the deviations of two variates from their respective means.

co·var·i·ant /kōˈve(ə)rēənt/ *Mathematics* ▶*n.* a function of the coefficients and variables of a given function that is invariant under a linear transformation except for a factor equal to a power of the determinant of the transformation.

▶*adj.* changing in such a way that mathematical interrelations with another simultaneously changing quantity or set of quantities remain unchanged. ■ of, having the properties of, or relating to a covariant.

co·var·i·a·tion /ˌkōve(ə)rēˈāSHən/ ▶*n. Mathematics* correlated variation.

cove[1] /kōv/ ▶*n.* **1** a small sheltered bay. **2** a sheltered recess, esp. one in a mountain. **3** *Architecture* a concave arched molding, esp. one formed at the junction of a wall with a ceiling.

▶*v.* [*trans.*] [usu. as *adj.*] (**coved**) *Architecture* provide (a room, ceiling, etc.) with a cove. ▷Old English *cofa* 'chamber, cave,' of Germanic origin; related to German *Koben* 'pigpen, pen.' Sense 1 dates from the late 16th cent.

cove[2] ▶*n. Brit., informal, dated* a man: *he is a perfectly amiable cove.* ▷mid 16th cent.: perhaps from Romany *kova* 'thing or person.'

co·vel·lite /kōˈvelˌīt; ˈkōvəˌlīt/ ▶*n.* a blue mineral consisting of copper sulfide, typically occurring as a coating on other copper minerals. ▷mid 19th cent.: named after Nicolò *Covelli* (1790–1829), Italian chemist, + -ITE[1].

cov·en /ˈkəvən/ ▶*n.* a group or gathering of witches who meet regularly. ■ *figurative, often derogatory* a secret or close-knit group of associates: *covens of militants within the party.* ▷mid 17th cent.: variant of COVIN.

cov·e·nant /ˈkəvənənt/ ▶*n.* an agreement. ■ *Law* a contract drawn up by deed. ■ *Law* a clause in a contract. ■ *Theology* an agreement that brings about a relationship of commitment between God and his people. The Jewish faith is based on the biblical covenants made with Abraham, Moses, and David. See also ARK OF THE COVENANT.

▶*v.* [*intrans.*] agree, esp. by lease, deed, or other legal contract: *the landlord covenants to repair the property.* ▷Middle English: from Old French, present participle of *covenir* 'agree,' from Latin *convenire* (see CONVENE). —**cov·e·nan·tal** /ˌkəvəˈnantl/ *adj.* —**cov·e·nant·er** (also *chiefly Law* **cov·e·nan·tor**) *n.*

▶*PHRASES* □ **Old Covenant** *Christian Theology* the covenant between God and Israel in the Old Testament. □ **New Covenant** *Christian Theology* the covenant between God and the followers of Jesus Christ.

cov·e·nan·tee /ˌkəvənənˈtē; -nan-/ ▶*n. Law* the person to whom a promise by covenant is made.

Cov·e·nant·er /ˈkəvənantər; -ənəntər/ ▶*n.* an adherent of the National Covenant (1638) or of the Solemn League and Covenant (1643), upholding the organization of the Scottish Presbyterian Church.

cov·e·nant of grace *n.* (in Calvinist theology) the covenant between God and humanity that was established by Jesus Christ at the Atonement.

cov·e·nant of works ▶*n.* (in Calvinist theology) the covenant between God and humanity that was broken by Adam's sin at the Fall.

Cov·ent Gar·den /ˈkəvənt/ a district in central London.

Cov·en·try /ˈkəvəntrē; ˈkäv-/ **1** an industrial city in central England; pop. 292,600. **2** a city in central Rhode Island, a southwestern suburb of Providence; pop. 33,668.

cov·er /ˈkəvər/ ▶*v.* [*trans.*] **1** (often **be covered**) put something such as a cloth or lid on top of or in front of (something) in order to protect or conceal it: *the table had been **covered with** a checked tablecloth | she **covered** her face **with** a pillow.* ■ envelop in a layer of something, esp. dirt: *he was covered in mud | figurative she was covered in confusion.* ■ scatter a layer of loose material over (a surface, esp. a floor), leaving it completely obscured: *the barn floor was covered in straw.* ■ lie over or adhere to (a surface), as decoration or to conceal something: *masonry paint will cover hairline cracks.* ■ protect (someone) with a garment or hat: [as *adj.*] (**covered**) *keep children covered with T-shirts.* ■ extend over (an area): *the grounds covered eight acres.* ■ travel (a specified distance): *it took them four days to cover 150 miles.* **2** deal with (a subject) by describing or analyzing its most important aspects or events: *a sequence of novels that will cover the period from 1968 to the present.* ■ investigate, report on, or publish or broadcast pictures of (an event): *NBC is covering the Olympics.* ■ work in, have responsibility for, or provide services to (a particular area): *development officers whose work would cover a large area.* ■ (of a rule or law) apply to (a person or situation). **3** (of a sum of money) be enough to pay (a bill or cost): *there are grants to cover the cost of materials for loft insulation.* ■ (of insurance) protect against a liability, loss, or accident involving financial consequences: *your contents are now **covered against** accidental loss or damage in transit.* ■ (**cover oneself**) take precautionary measures so as to protect oneself against future blame or liability: *one reason doctors take temperatures is to* **cover** *themselves* **against** *negligence claims.* **4** disguise the sound or fact of (something) with another sound or action: *Louise laughed to cover her embarrassment.* ■ [*intrans.*] (**cover for**) disguise the illicit absence or wrongdoing of (someone) in order to spare them punishment: *if the sergeant wants to know where you are, I'll cover for you.* ■ [*intrans.*] (**cover for**) temporarily take over the job of (a colleague) in their absence: *during August ministers cover for other ministers.* **5** aim a gun at (someone) in order to prevent them from moving or escaping. ■ protect (an exposed person) by shooting at an enemy: [as *adj.*] (**covering**) *the jeeps retreated behind spurts of* **covering** *fire.* ■ (of a fortress, gun, or cannon) have (an area) within range. ■ (in team games) take up a position ready to defend against (an opposing player). ■ *Baseball* be in position at (a base) ready to catch a thrown ball. **6** *Bridge* play a higher card on (a high card) in a trick: *the ploy will fail if the ten is covered* | [*intrans.*] *East covered with his queen.* **7** record or perform a new version of (a song) originally performed by someone else: *other artists who have covered the song include U2.* **8** (of a male animal, esp. a stallion) copulate with (a female animal), esp. as part of a commercial transaction between the owners of the animals.

▸*phrasal v.* □ **cover something up** put something on, over, or around something, esp. in order to conceal or disguise it. ■ try to hide or deny the fact of an illegal or illicit action or activity.

▸*n.* **1** a thing that lies on, over, or around something, esp. in order to protect or conceal it: *a seat cover.* ■ a thin solid object that seals a container or hole; a lid: *a manhole cover.* ■ a thick protective outer part or page of a book or magazine: *her life was captured between hard covers in her 1986 autobiography.* ■ *Philately* a card or envelope that has traveled through the mail or that contains postal markings. ■ (**the covers**) bedclothes: *she burrowed down beneath the covers.* **2** physical shelter or protection sought by people in danger: *the sirens wailed and people ran for cover* | *store seats* **under cover** *before the bad weather sets in.* ■ undergrowth, trees, or other vegetation used as a shelter by hunted animals: *the standing crops of game cover* | *a landscape bare of woodland except for neat little fox covers.* See also **COVERT** (sense 1). ■ an activity or organization used as a means of concealing an illegal or secret activity: *the organizations often use their philanthropy as a* **cover for** *subsidies to terrorists.* ■ [in *sing.*] an identity or activity adopted by a person, typically a spy, to conceal their true activities: *he was worried that their cover was blown.* ■ military support given when someone is in danger from or being attacked by an enemy: *they agreed to provide additional naval cover.* ■ *Ecology* the amount of ground covered by a vertical projection of the vegetation, usually expressed as a percentage. **3** short for **COVER CHARGE**. **4** a place setting at a table in a restaurant. [rendering French *couvert.*] **5** (also **cover version**) a recording or performance of a previously recorded song made esp. to take advantage of the original's success. ▷Middle English: from Old French *covrir*, from Latin *cooperire*, from *co-* (expressing intensive force) + *operire* 'to cover.' The noun is partly a variant of **COVERT**. —**cov·er·a·ble** *adj.*

▸**PHRASES** □ **break cover** suddenly leave a place of shelter, esp. vegetation, when being hunted or pursued. □ **cover one's ass** (or **back**) *informal* foresee and avoid the possibility of attack or criticism. □ **cover all bases** (or **cover all the bases**) include all relevant information: *for the prospective homebuilder, this book covers all bases.* ■ prepare for all likely circumstances. □ **cover a multitude of sins** conceal or gloss over many problems or defects: *stucco could cover a multitude of sins, including poor brickwork.* □ **cover one's position** purchase securities in order to be able to fulfill a commitment to sell. □ **cover one's tracks** conceal evidence of what one has done. □ **cover the waterfront** *informal* include a wide range of things; cover every aspect of something: *while half the dishes are Italian, the kitchen covers the waterfront from Greece to Morocco.* □ **from cover to cover** from beginning to end of a book or magazine. □ **take cover** protect oneself from attack by ducking down into or under a shelter: *if the bombing starts, take cover in the basement.* □ **under cover of** concealed by: *the yacht made landfall under cover of darkness.* ■ while pretending to do something: *Moran watched every move under cover of reading the newspaper.* □ **under plain cover** in an envelope or parcel without any marks to identify the sender. □ **under separate cover** in a separate envelope.

cov·er·age /ˈkəv(ə)rij/ ▸*n.* the extent to which something deals with or applies to something else: *the grammar did not offer total coverage of the language.* ■ the treatment of an issue by the media: *the program won an award for its news coverage.* ■ the amount of protection given by an insurance policy. ■ the area reached by a particular broadcasting station or advertising medium: *a network of eighty transmitters would give nationwide coverage.* ■ *Football* the manner in which a defender or a defensive team covers a player, an area, or a play.

cov·er·all /ˈkəvərˌôl/ ▸*n.* (usu. **coveralls**) a full-length protective outer garment often zipped up the front. ■ [as *adj.*] inclusive: *a coverall term.*

cov·er charge ▸*n.* a flat fee paid for admission to a restaurant, bar, club, etc.

cov·er crop ▸*n.* a crop grown for the protection and enrichment of the soil.

Cov·er·dale /ˈkəvərˌdāl/, Miles (1488–1568), English biblical scholar. He translated the first complete printed English Bible in 1535.

cov·ered wag·on ▸*n.* a horse- or mule-drawn wagon topped with a spacious, arched canvas-covered framework. Covered wagons were the common transport for the western-moving North American pioneers of the 19th century. See also **CONESTOGA WAGON, PRAIRIE SCHOONER**.

covered wagon

cov·er girl ▸*n.* a female model whose picture appears on magazine covers.

cov·er glass ▸*n.* another term for **COVERSLIP**.

cov·er·ing /ˈkəv(ə)riNG/ ▸*n.* a thing used to cover something else, typically in order to protect or conceal it: *a vinyl floor covering.* ■ [usu. in *sing.*] a layer of something that covers something else: *the sky was obscured by a covering of cloud.*

cov·er·ing let·ter ▸*n.* British term for **COVER LETTER**.

cov·er·let /ˈkəvərlət/ ▸*n.* a bedspread, typically less than floor-length. ▷Middle English: from Anglo-Norman French *covrelet*, from Old French *covrir* 'to cover' + *lit* 'bed.'

cov·er let·ter ▸*n.* a letter sent with, and explaining the contents of, another document or a parcel of goods.

cov·er sheet ▸*n.* **1** a page sent as the first page of a fax transmission, identifying the sender, number of pages, etc. **2** a page placed before a manuscript or report, typically with the name of the author, title of the book or report, and date.

cov·er·slip /ˈkəvərˌslip/ (also **cov·er slip**) ▸*n.* a small, thin piece of glass used to cover and protect a specimen on a microscope slide.

cov·er sto·ry ▸*n.* **1** a magazine article that is illustrated or advertised on the front cover. **2** a fictitious account invented to conceal a person's identity or reasons for doing something.

co·vert ▸*adj.* /ˈkōvərt; kōˈvərt; ˈkəvərt/ **1** not openly acknowledged or displayed: *covert operations against the dictatorship.* See note at **SECRET**. **2** *Law* (of a woman) married and under the authority and protection of her husband.

▸*n.* /ˈkəvər(t); ˈkōvərt/ **1** a shelter or hiding place. ■ a thicket in which game can hide. **2** *Ornithology* any of the feathers covering the bases of the main flight or tail feathers of a bird. ▷Middle English (in the general senses 'covered' and 'a cover'): from Old French, 'covered,' past participle of *covrir* (see **COVER**). —**co·vert·ly** /ˈkōvərtlē; kōˈvərtlē; ˈkəvərtlē/ *adv.* —**co·vert·ness** *n.*

cov·er·ture /ˈkəvərˌCHo͝or; -CHər/ ▸*n.* **1** *poetic/literary* protective or concealing covering. **2** *historical Law* the legal status of a married woman, considered to be under her husband's protection and authority. ▷Middle English: from Old French, from *covrir* 'to cover.' It originally denoted a coverlet or a garment, later various kinds of covering or shelter.

cov·er-up (also **cov·er·up**) ▸*n.* **1** an attempt to prevent people's discovering the truth about a serious mistake or crime. **2** a loose outer garment, typically worn over a swimsuit or exercise outfit.

cov·er ver·sion ▸*n.* see **COVER** (sense 5).

cov·et /ˈkəvət/ ▸*v.* (**cov·et·ed**, **cov·et·ing**) [*trans.*] yearn to possess or have (something): *the president-elect covets time for exercise and fishing* | [as *adj.*] (**coveted**) *he won the coveted Booker Prize for fiction.* ▷Middle English: from Old French *cuveitier*, based on Latin *cupiditas* (see **CUPIDITY**). —**cov·et·a·ble** *adj.*

cov·et·ous /ˈkəvətəs/ ▸*adj.* having or showing a great desire to possess something, typically something belonging to someone else: *she fingered the linen with covetous hands.* See note at **GREEDY**. ▷Middle English: from Old French *coveitous*, based on Latin *cupiditas* (see **CUPIDITY**). —**cov·et·ous·ly** *adv.* —**cov·et·ous·ness** *n.*

cov·ey /ˈkəvē/ ▸*n.* (*pl.* **-eys**) a small party or flock of birds, esp. partridge. ■ *figurative* a small group of people or things: *coveys of actors rushed through the rooms.* ▷Middle English: from Old French *covee*, feminine past participle of *cover*, from Latin *cubare* 'lie down.'

C

cov·in /ˈkəvən; ˈkō-/ (also **cov·ine**) ▸*n. archaic* fraud; deception. ▷Middle English (denoting a company or band): from Old French, from medieval Latin *convenium*, from Latin *convenire* (see **CONVENE**). Compare with **COVEN**.

Co·vi·na /kōˈvēnə/ a city in southwestern California, east of Los Angeles; pop. 43,207.

Cov·ing·ton a city in northern Kentucky, where the Licking River flows into the Ohio River; pop. 43,370.

cow[1] /kou/ ▸*n.* a fully grown female animal of a domesticated breed of ox, used as a source of milk or beef: *a dairy cow.* See **CATTLE**. ■ (loosely) a domestic bovine animal, regardless of sex or age. ■ (in farming) a female domestic bovine animal that has borne more than one calf. Compare with **HEIFER**. ■ the female of certain other large animals, for example elephant, rhinoceros, whale, seal, or reindeer. ■ *informal, derogatory* a woman, esp. a fat or stupid one: *what does he see in that cow?* ▷Old English *cū*, of Germanic origin; related to Dutch *koe* and German *Kuh*, from an Indo-European root shared by Latin *bos* and Greek *bous*.

▸**PHRASES** □ **have a cow** *informal* become angry, excited, or agitated: *don't have a cow—it's no big deal.* □ **till the cows come home** *informal* for an indefinitely long time: *those two could talk till the cows came home.*

cow[2] ▸*v.* [*trans.*] (usu. **be cowed**) cause (someone) to submit to one's wishes by intimidation: *the intellectuals had been* **cowed into** *silence.* ▷late 16th cent.: probably from Old Norse *kúga* 'oppress.'

cow·a·bun·ga /ˌkou-əˈbəNGgə/ ▸*exclam. informal* used to express delight or satisfaction: *Cowabunga! It's an actor's dream.* ▷1940s: originally *cowabonga*, an exclamation frequently used by the character Chief Thunderthud on the "Howdy Doody Show."

cow·age /ˈkouij/ (also **cow·hage**) ▸*n.* a leguminous climbing plant, *Mucuna pruriens*, with hairy pods that cause stinging and itching. ▷mid 17th cent.: from Hindi *kāuñc*.

Cow·ard /ˈkou-ərd/, Sir Noel (Pierce) (1899–1973), English playwright, actor, and composer. He is remembered for witty, satirical plays, such as *Hay Fever* (1925) and *Private Lives* (1930), as well as for revues and musicals featuring songs such as "Mad Dogs and Englishmen" (1932).

cow·ard /ˈkou-ərd/ ▸*n.* a person who lacks the courage to do or endure dangerous or unpleasant things.

▸*adj.* **1** *poetic/literary* excessively afraid of danger or pain. **2** *Heraldry* (of an animal) depicted with the tail between the hind legs. ▷Middle English: from Old French *couard*, based on Latin *cauda* 'tail,' possibly with reference to a frightened animal with its tail between its legs, reflected in sense 2 (early 16th cent.).

cow·ard·ice /ˈkou-ərdəs/ ▸*n.* lack of bravery. ▷Middle English: from Old French *couardise*, from *couard* (see **COWARD**).

cow·ard·ly /ˈkou-ərdlē/ ▸*adj.* lacking courage. ■ (of an action) carried out against a person who is unable to retaliate: *a cowardly attack on a helpless victim.*

▸*adv. archaic* in a way that shows a lack of courage. —**cow·ard·li·ness** *n.*

cow·bane /ˈkouˌbān/ ▸*n.* any of a number of tall poisonous plants of the parsley family, growing in swampy or wet habitats: • another term for **WATER HEMLOCK**. • a North American plant (*Oxypolis rigidior*, family Umbelliferae). ▷late 18th cent.: from **cow**[1] + **BANE**, because it is poisonous to grazing cattle.

cow·bell /ˈkouˌbel/ ▸*n.* a bell hung around a cow's neck in order to help locate the animal by the noise it makes. ■ a similar bell used as a percussion instrument, typically without a clapper and struck with a stick.

cow·ber·ry /ˈkouˌberē/ ▸*n.* (*pl.* **-ries**) another term for **MOUNTAIN CRANBERRY**.

cow·bird /ˈkouˌbərd/ ▸*n.* a New World songbird with dark plumage and a relatively short bill, typically laying its eggs in other birds' nests. • Genus *Molothrus* (and *Scaphidura*), family Icteridae: several species, in particular the widespread **brown-headed** (or **common**) **cowbird** (*M. ater*).

cow·boy /ˈkouˌboi/ ▸*n.* **1** a man, typically one on horseback, who herds and tends cattle, esp. in the western U.S. and as represented in westerns and novels: *they are always playing* ***cowboys and Indians****.* **2** *informal* a person who is reckless or careless, esp. when driving an automobile.
▸*v.* [*intrans.*] work as a cowboy: *Sonora, Mexico, where he learned to cowboy.*
▸*PHRASE* □ **cowboy up** *informal* mount a brave effort to overcome a formidable obstacle: *Millar cowboyed up, but couldn't he have flipped the Enrique grounder to Pedro?*

cow·boy boot ▸*n.* a style of boot with a pointed toe and a moderately high heel, extending to mid-calf.

Cow·boy State a nickname for the state of **WYOMING**.

cow camp ▸*n.* a seasonal camp apart from the main buildings of a ranch, used during a cattle roundup.

cow·catch·er /ˈkouˌkaCHər; -ˌkeCHər/ ▸*n.* a metal frame at the front of a locomotive for pushing aside cattle or other obstacles on the line.

cow chip ▸*n. informal* a dried cowpat.

cow·er /ˈkou(-ə)r/ ▸*v.* [*intrans.*] crouch down in fear: *children cowered in terror as the shoot-out erupted.* See note at **WINCE**. ▷Middle English: from Middle Low German *kūren* 'lie in wait,' of unknown ultimate origin.

cow·fish /ˈkouˌfiSH/ ▸*n.* (*pl.* same or **-fish·es**) a boxfish with spines that resemble horns on the head, and typically with other spines on the back and sides. • Several genera and species in the family Ostraciontidae, in particular *Lactoria diaphana*.

cow flop (also **cow·flop** or *chiefly Canadian* **cow flap** or **cow·flap**) ▸*n. informal* a cowpat.

cow·girl /ˈkouˌgərl/ ▸*n.* a female equivalent of a cowboy, esp. as represented in westerns and novels.

cow·hage ▸*n.* variant spelling of **COWAGE**.

cow·hand /ˈkouˌhand/ ▸*n.* a person employed to tend or ranch cattle; a cowboy or cowgirl.

cow·herd /ˈkouˌhərd/ ▸*n.* a person who tends grazing cattle. ▷Old English, from **cow**[1] + obsolete *herd* 'herdsman.'

cow·hide /ˈkouˌhīd/ ▸*n.* a cow's hide. ■ leather made from such a hide. ■ a whip made from such leather.

cowl /koul/ ▸*n.* a large loose hood, esp. one forming part of a monk's habit. ■ a monk's hooded, sleeveless habit. ■ a cloak with wide sleeves worn by members of Benedictine orders. ■ the hood-shaped covering of a chimney or ventilation shaft. ■ the part of a motor vehicle that supports the windshield and houses the dashboard. ■ another term for **COWLING**. ▷Old English *cugele*, *cūle*, from ecclesiastical Latin *cuculla*, from Latin *cucullus* 'hood of a cloak.' —**cowled** *adj.*

cow·lick /ˈkouˌlik/ ▸*n.* a lock of hair that grows in a direction different from the rest and that resists being combed flat: *a little sprig of a cowlick stood up on the back of her head.*

cowl·ing /ˈkouliNG/ ▸*n.* the removable cover of a vehicle or aircraft engine.

cowl neck ▸*n.* a neckline on a woman's garment that hangs in draped folds: [as *adj.*] *a cowl-neck sweater.*

cow·man /ˈkoumən; -ˌman/ ▸*n.* (*pl.* **-men**) a person who owns or is in charge of a cattle ranch. ■ a cowboy.

co·work·er /ˈkōˌwərkər; kōˈwərkər/ ▸*n.* a fellow worker.

cow pars·nip ▸*n.* a very large, bad-smelling hogweed. Cow parsnips prefer moist ground and can reach a height of 10 feet (3 m). • *Heracleum maximum*, family Umbelliferae.

cow·pat /ˈkouˌpat/ ▸*n.* a flat, round piece of cow dung.

cow·pea /ˈkouˌpē/ ▸*n.* a plant of the pea family native to the Old World tropics. It is an important pulse for animal feed and human consumption, both the pod and the seed being edible. • *Vigna unguiculata*, family Leguminosae. ■ the seed of this plant as food.

Cow·per /ˈko͞opər; ˈko͝opər; ˈkoupər/, William (1731–1800), English poet, noted for the poem *The Task* (1785) and for the comic ballad *John Gilpin* (1782).

Cow·per's gland /ˈkoupərz; ˈko͞opərz; ˈko͝opərz/ ▸*n. Anatomy* either of a pair of small glands that open into the urethra at the base of the penis and secrete a constituent of seminal fluid. ▷mid 18th cent.: named after William *Cowper* (1666–1709), English anatomist.

cow·poke /ˈkouˌpōk/ ▸*n. informal* a cowboy.

cow po·ny ▸*n.* a small horse trained for use in cattle ranching.

cow·pox /ˈkouˌpäks/ ▸*n.* a viral disease of cows' udders which, when contracted by humans through contact, resembles mild smallpox, and was the basis of the first smallpox vaccines.

cow·punch·er /ˈkouˌpənCHər/ ▸*n. informal* a cowboy.

cow·punk /ˈkouˌpəNGk/ ▸*n.* a type of popular music combining elements of country and western with those of punk rock. ■ a singer or musician who performs this type of music: *she burst on to the scene as a cowpunk.*

cow·rie /ˈkourē/ (also **cow·ry**) ▸*n.* (*pl.* **-ries**) a marine mollusk that has a smooth, glossy, domed shell with a long narrow opening, typically brightly patterned and popular with collectors. • Genus *Cypraea*, family Cypraeidae, class Gastropoda: numerous species, including the small **money cowrie** (*C. moneta*). ■ the flattened yellowish shell of the money cowrie, formerly used as money in parts of Africa and the Indo-Pacific area. ▷mid 17th cent.: from Hindi *kauṛī*.

co·write /kōˈrīt; ˈkōˌrīt/ ▸*v.* [*trans.*] write (something) with another person: *the movie is based on a story he cowrote with his wife.* —**co·writ·er** *n.*

cow shark ▸*n.* a dull gray or brown shark that lives mainly in deep water, esp. in the North Atlantic and Mediterranean. • *Hexanchus griseus*, family Hexanchidae.

cow·shed /ˈkouˌSHed/ ▸*n.* a farm building in which cattle are kept when not in a pasture, or in which they are milked.

cow·slip /ˈkouˌslip/ ▸*n.* **1** a European primula with clusters of drooping fragrant yellow flowers in spring, growing on dry grassy banks and in pasture. • *Primula veris*, family Primulaceae. **2** any of a number of herbaceous plants, in particular: • another term for **MARSH MARIGOLD**. • (also **Virginia bluebell**) a North American plant with blue flowers (*Mertensia virginica*, family Boraginaceae). ▷Old English *cūslyppe*, from *cū* 'cow' + *slipa*, *slyppe* 'slime,' i.e., cow slobber or dung.

cow·town /ˈkouˌtoun/ (also **cow town**) ▸*n.* a town or city in a cattle-raising area of western North America. ■ *figurative* a small, isolated, or unsophisticated town.

cow wheat ▸*n.* a yellowish-flowered plant of the figwort family, partly parasitic on the roots of other plants and found in both Eurasia and North America. • Genus *Melampyrum*, family Scrophulariaceae: several species, including *M. lineare*.

cox /käks/ ▸*n.* a coxswain, esp. of a racing boat.
▸*v.* [*trans.*] act as a coxswain for (a racing boat or crew): *the winning eight was coxed by a woman* | [as *adj.*] (**coxed**) *the coxed pairs* | [*intrans.*] *he once coxed for Harvard.* ▷mid 19th cent.: abbreviation. —**cox·less** *adj.*

cox·a /ˈkäksə/ ▸*n.* (*pl.* **cox·ae** /ˈkäksē; -sī/) *Anatomy* the hipbone or hip joint. ■ *Entomology* the first or basal segment of the leg of an insect. ▷late 17th cent.: from Latin, 'hip.' —**cox·al** *adj.*

cox·al·gi·a /käkˈsalj(ē)ə/ ▸*n.* pain in the hip joint.

cox·comb /ˈkäksˌkōm/ ▸*n.* **1** *dated* a vain and conceited man; a dandy. **2** variant spelling of **COCKSCOMB** (sense 2). ▷mid 16th cent. (denoting a simpleton): variant of **COCKSCOMB**, in the sense 'jester's cap' (resembling a cock's comb), hence 'a jester, a fool.' —**cox·comb·ry** *n.* (*pl.* **-ries**) (in sense 1). —**cox·comb·er·y** /-ˌkōm(ə)rē/ *n.*

cox·op·o·dite /käkˈsäpəˌdīt/ ▸*n. Zoology* the segment nearest the body in the leg of an arthropod, esp. a crustacean. ▷late 19th cent.: from Latin *coxa* 'hip' + Greek *pous*, *pod-* 'foot' + **-ITE**[1].

Cox·sack·ie vi·rus /käkˈsakē; ko͝ok-/ (also **cox·sack·ie virus** or **cox·sack·ie·vi·rus**) ▸*n. Medicine* any of a group of enteroviruses that cause various respiratory, neurological, and muscular diseases in humans. ▷1940s: named after *Coxsackie*, New York, where the first cases were diagnosed.

cox·swain /ˈkäksən/ ▸*n.* the steersman of a ship's boat, lifeboat, racing boat, or other boat. ▷Middle English: from obsolete *cock* + **SWAIN**. Compare with **BOATSWAIN**. —**cox·swain·ship** /-ˌSHip/ *n.*

COX-2 in·hib·i·tor /ˈkäks ˈto͞o/ ▸*n.* a painkiller that works by inhibiting the enzyme cyclooxygenase-2 (COX-2), which triggers the release of prostaglandins.

coy /koi/ ▸*adj.* (**coy·er**, **coy·est**) (esp. of a woman) making a pretense of shyness or modesty that is intended to be alluring but is often regarded as irritating: *she treated him to a coy smile of invitation.* ■ reluctant to give details, esp. about something regarded as sensitive: *he is* ***coy about*** *his age.* ■ *dated* quiet and reserved; shy. ▷Middle English: from Old French *coi*, *quei*, from Latin *quietus* (see **QUIET**). The original sense was 'quiet, still' (esp. in behavior), later 'modestly retiring,' and hence (of a woman) 'affecting to be unresponsive to advances.' —**coy·ly** *adv.* —**coy·ness** *n.*

coy·dog /ˈkoiˌdôg/ ▸*n.* the hybrid offspring of a coyote and a dog.

Co·yo·a·cán /ˌkoi-ōəˈkän/ a municipality within the Federal District of Mexico, a suburb of Mexico City; pop. 640,000.

coy·o·te /ˈkīˌōt; kīˈōtē/ ▸*n.* **1** (*pl.* same or **-tes**) a wolflike wild dog native to North America. Also called **BRUSH WOLF** or **PRAIRIE WOLF**. • *Canis latrans*, family Canidae. **2** *informal* a person who smuggles Latin Americans across the U.S. border, typically for a high fee: *at the bus station, there were coyotes offering to drive us to Los Angeles.* ▷mid 18th cent.: from Mexican Spanish, from Nahuatl *coyotl*.

Coy·o·te State a nickname for the state of **SOUTH DAKOTA**.

coy·pu /ˈkoiˌpo͞o/ ▸*n.* (*pl.* **-pus**) another term for **NUTRIA**. ▷late 18th cent.: from Araucanian.

coz /kəz/ ▸*n.* an informal word for 'cousin,' used esp. as a term of address. ▷mid 16th cent.: abbreviation.

coz·en /ˈkəzən/ ▸*v.* [*trans.*] trick or deceive: *do not think to cozen your contemporaries.* ■ obtain by deception: *he was able to cozen a profit.* ▷late 16th cent.: perhaps from obsolete Italian *cozzonare* 'to cheat,' from *cozzone* 'middleman, broker,' from Latin *cocio* 'dealer.' —**coz·en·age** /-nij/ *n.* —**coz·en·er** *n.*

Co·zu·mel /ˌkōzo͞oˈmel/ a resort island in the Caribbean Sea, off the northeastern coast of the Yucatán Peninsula in Mexico.

co·zy /ˈkōzē/ (*Brit.* **co·sy**) ▸*adj.* (**-zi·er**, **-zi·est**) giving a feeling of comfort, warmth, and relaxation: *a cozy cabin tucked away in the trees.* ■ (of a relationship or conversation) intimate and relaxed. ■ avoiding or not offering challenge or difficulty; complacent: *a rather cozy assumption among automakers that they would never actually go bust.* ■ (of a transaction or arrangement) working to the mutual advantage of those involved (used to convey a suspicion of corruption): *a cozy deal.*
▸*n.* (*pl.* **-zies**) a cover to keep a teapot hot.
▸*v.* (**-zies**, **-zied**) [*trans.*] *informal* impart a feeling or quality of comfort to (something): *the wood stove really* ***cozies up*** *the house.* ■ [*trans.*] *informal* give (someone) a feeling of comfort or complacency: *she cozied him, pretending to find him irresistibly attractive.* ■ [*intrans.*] (**cozy up to**) snuggle up to: *he cozied up to the heater.* ■ [*intrans.*] (**cozy up to**) ingratiate oneself with: *he decided to resign rather than cozy up to hard-liners in the party.* ▷early 18th cent. (originally Scots): of unknown origin. —**co·zi·ly** /-zəlē/ *adv.* —**co·zi·ness** *n.*

CP ▸*abbr.* ■ cerebral palsy. ■ Command Post. ■ *Finance* commercial paper. ■ Common Pleas. ■ Communist Party. ■ (also **cp**) candlepower.

cp. ▸*abbr.* compare.

CPA ▸*abbr.* certified public accountant.

cpd. ▸*abbr.* compound.

CPI ▸*abbr.* consumer price index.

Cpl. ▸*abbr.* corporal.

CPO ▸*abbr.* Chief Petty Officer.

CPR ▸*abbr.* cardiopulmonary resuscitation.

cps (also **c.p.s.**) ▸*abbr.* ■ *Computing* characters per second. ■ cycles per second.

Cpt. ▸*abbr.* Captain.

CPU ▸*abbr. Computing* central processing unit.

CPUSA ▸*abbr.* Communist Party USA.

CPVC ▸*abbr.* chlorinated polyvinyl chloride, a plastic material used to make water pipes.

CR ▸*abbr.* ■ Conditioned reflex. ■ Conditioned response.

Cr ▸*symbol* the chemical element chromium.

cr ▸*abbr.* ■ credit. ■ creditor.

crab[1] /krab/ ▸*n.* **1** a crustacean with a broad carapace, stalked eyes, and five pairs of legs, the first pair of which are modified as pincers. Crabs are

abundant on many shores, esp. in the tropics, where some have become adapted to life on land. • Many families in the order Decapoda, class Malacostraca. ■ the flesh of a crab as food. ■ (**the Crab**) the zodiacal sign or constellation Cancer. **2** (also **crab louse**) a louse that infests human body hair, esp. in the genital region, causing extreme irritation. Also called PUBIC LOUSE. • *Phthirus pubis*, family Pediculidae, order Anoplura. ■ (**crabs**) *informal* an infestation of crab lice. **3** a machine for picking up and lifting heavy weights.
▸*v.* **1** [*intrans.*] move sideways or obliquely: *he began crabbing sideways across the roof.* ■ [*trans.*] steer (an aircraft or ship) slightly sideways to compensate for a crosswind or current. **2** [*intrans.*] fish for crabs. ▷Old English *crabba*, of Germanic origin; related to Dutch *krabbe*, and more distantly to Dutch *kreeft* and German *Krebs*; also to CRAB[3]. —**crab·ber** *n.* —**crab·like** /-ˌlīk/ *adj. & adv.*
▸*PHRASE* □ **catch a crab** *Rowing* make a faulty stroke in which the oar is under water too long or misses the water altogether.

crab[2] ▸*n.* short for CRAB APPLE.

crab[3] ▸*n. informal* an irritable person.
▸*v.* (**crabbed**, **crab·bing**) *informal* **1** [*intrans.*] grumble, typically about something petty: *on picnics, I would crab about sand in my food.* **2** [*trans.*] act so as to spoil: *you're trying to crab my act.* ▷late 16th cent. (referring to hawks, meaning 'claw or fight each other'): from Low German *krabben*; related to CRAB[1].

crab ap·ple (also **crab·ap·ple**) ▸*n.* (also **crab**) **1** a small, sour apple. **2** (also **crab tree**, **crab·ap·ple tree**, or **crab·ap·ple tree**) the small tree that bears this fruit. • Genus *Malus*, family Rosaceae: several species and hybrids, in particular the wild **Eurasian crab apple** (*M. sylvestris*), which is one of the possible ancestors of cultivated apples. ▷late Middle English: *crab* perhaps an alteration (influenced by CRAB[1] or CRABBED) of Scots and northern English *scrab*, in the same sense, probably of Scandinavian origin.

crab·bed /ˈkrabəd/ ▸*adj.* **1** (of handwriting) ill-formed and hard to decipher. ■ (of style) contorted and difficult to understand: *crabbed legal language.* **2** ill-humored: *a crabbed, unhappy middle age.* ▷Middle English (in the sense 'perverse, wayward'): from CRAB[1], because of the crab's sideways gait and habit of snapping, thought to suggest a perverse or irritable disposition. —**crab·bed·ly** *adv.* —**crab·bed·ness** *n.*

crab·by /ˈkrabē/ ▸*adj.* (**crab·bi·er**, **crab·bi·est**) irritable. —**crab·bi·ly** /ˈkrabəlē/ *adv.* —**crab·bi·ness** *n.*

crab can·on ▸*n.* another term for CANON CANCRIZANS.

crab·eat·er seal /ˈkrabˌētər/ ▸*n.* a slender, gray Antarctic seal that lives on the pack ice, feeding mainly on krill. • *Lobodon carcinophagus*, family Phocidae.

crab·grass /ˈkrabˌgras/ ▸*n.* a creeping grass that can become a serious weed. • *Digitaria* and other genera, family Gramineae: several species, in particular *D. sanguinalis* and *D. ciliaris*.

crab louse ▸*n.* see CRAB[1] (sense 2).

crab·meat /ˈkrabˌmēt/ ▸*n.* the flesh of a crab as food.

Crab Neb·u·la *Astronomy* an irregular patch of luminous gas in the constellation Taurus, believed to be the remnant of a supernova explosion seen by Chinese astronomers in 1054. At its center is the first pulsar to be observed visually, and the nebula is a strong source of high-energy radiation.

crab pot ▸*n.* a wicker trap for crabs.

crab spi·der ▸*n.* a spider with long front legs, moving with a crablike sideways motion and typically lying in wait in vegetation and flowers for passing prey. • Family Thomisidae: several genera.

crab stick ▸*n.* a rectangular stick of mixed, compressed fish pieces flavored with crab.

crab tree ▸*n.* see CRAB APPLE (sense 2).

crab·wise /ˈkrabˌwīz/ ▸*adv. & adj.* (of movement) sideways, typically in an awkward way: [as *adv.*] *supermarket carts that only go crabwise* | [as *adj.*] *crabwise steps.*

crack /krak/ ▸*n.* **1** a line on the surface of something along which it has split without breaking into separate parts: *a hairline crack down the middle of the glass.* ■ a narrow space between two surfaces, esp. ones that have broken or been moved apart: *he climbed into a crack between two rocks* | *the door opened a tiny crack.* ■ *figurative* a vulnerable point; a flaw: *the company spotted a crack in their rival's defenses.* **2** a sudden sharp or explosive noise: *a loud crack of thunder.* ■ a sharp blow, esp. one that makes a noise: *she gave the thief a crack over the head with her rolling pin.* ■ a sudden harshness or change in pitch in a person's voice: *the boy's voice had an uncertain crack in it.* **3** *informal* a joke, typically a critical or unkind one. **4** [in *sing.*] *informal* an attempt to gain or achieve something: *I thought I **had a crack at** winning.* ■ a chance to attack or compete with someone: *he wanted to **have a crack at** the enemy.* **5** (also **crack cocaine**) a hard, crystalline form of cocaine broken into small pieces and smoked.
▸*v.* **1** break or cause to break without a complete separation of the parts: [*intrans.*] *the ice all over the lake had cracked* | [*trans.*] *a stone cracked the headlight glass on his car.* ■ break or cause to break open or apart: [*intrans.*] *you can see how the landmasses have **cracked up** and moved around* | *figurative* [*intrans.*] *his face cracked into a smile* | [*trans.*] *she cracked an egg into the frying pan.* ■ [*trans.*] break (wheat or corn) into coarse pieces. ■ [*trans.*] open slightly: *gingerly, he cracks open his door.* ■ *figurative* give way or cause to give way under torture, pressure, or strain: [*intrans.*] *the witnesses cracked and the truth came out* | [*trans.*] *no one can crack them—they believe their story.* ■ [*intrans.*] (**crack up**) *informal* suffer an emotional breakdown under pressure. ■ (**crack up**) *informal* burst or cause to burst into laughter. **2** make or cause to make a sudden sharp or explosive sound: [*intrans.*] *a shot cracked across the ridge* | [*trans.*] *he **cracked** his **whip** and galloped away.* ■ [*intrans.*] knock against something, making a noise on impact: *she winced as her knees cracked against metal.* ■ [*trans.*] hit (someone or something) hard, making a sharp noise: *she cracked him across the forehead.* ■ [*intrans.*] (of a person's voice, esp. that of an adolescent boy or a person under strain) suddenly change in pitch: *"I want to get away," she said, her voice cracking.* **3** [*trans.*] *informal* find a solution to; decipher or interpret: *a hacker cracked the codes used in Internet software.* ■ break into (a safe). ■ succeed in achieving: *he cracked a brilliant goal.* **4** [*trans.*] tell (a joke): *he cracked jokes which she didn't find very funny.* **5** [*trans.*] decompose (hydrocarbons) by heat and pressure with or without a catalyst to produce lighter hydrocarbons, esp. in oil refining: [as *n.*] (**cracking**) *catalytic cracking.*
▸*phrasal v.* □ **crack down on** *informal* take severe measures against: *we need to crack down hard on workplaces that break safety regulations.* □ **crack on** (of a sailing vessel) sail in high winds with all sails unfurled.
▸*adj.* [*attrib.*] very good, esp. at a specified activity or in a specified role: *he is a crack shot* | *crack troops.* ▷Old English *cracian* 'make an explosive noise'; of Germanic origin; related to Dutch *kraken* and German *krachen*.
▸*PHRASES* □ **crack a book** *informal* open a book and read it; study. □ **crack of dawn** a time very early in the morning; daybreak. □ **crack of doom** a thunder peal announcing the Day of Judgment. □ **cracked up to be** [with *negative*] *informal* asserted to be (used to indicate that someone or something has been described too favorably): *life on tour is not as glamorous as it's cracked up to be.* □ **crack wise** *informal* make jokes; wisecrack. □ **fall** (or **slip**) **through the cracks** escape from or be missed by something organized to catch or deal with one: *fatherless kids were not allowed to fall through the cracks.* □ **get cracking** *informal* act quickly and energetically: *most tickets have been snapped up, so get cracking if you want one.*

crack·a·jack /ˈkrakəˌjak/ ▸*adj.* variant spelling of CRACKERJACK.

crack·brained /ˈkrakˌbrānd/ ▸*adj. informal* extremely foolish; crazy: *a crackbrained idea.*

crack·down /ˈkrakˌdoun/ ▸*n.* [usu. in *sing.*] severe measures to restrict or discourage undesirable or illegal people or behavior: *a **crackdown on** crime and corruption.*

cracked /krakt/ ▸*adj.* **1** damaged and showing lines on the surface from having split without coming apart: *the old pipes were cracked and leaking.* ■ (of a person's voice) having an unusual harshness or pitch, often due to distress. **2** [*predic.*] *informal* crazy; insane: *you must think my family is cracked.*

cracked wheat ▸*n.* grains of wheat that have been crushed into small pieces.

crack·er /ˈkrakər/ ▸*n.* **1** a thin, crisp wafer often eaten with cheese or other savory toppings. **2** a person or thing that cracks. ■ an installation for cracking hydrocarbons: *a catalytic cracker.* ■ a person who breaks into a computer system, typically for an illegal purpose: *computer crackers will push the outer limits of network security.* **3** *often offensive* another term for POOR WHITE. **4** *Brit., informal* a fine example of something: *don't miss this **cracker of a** CD.* **5** *chiefly Brit.* a paper cylinder that is pulled apart at Christmas or other celebrations, making a sharp noise and releasing a small toy or other novelty. ■ a firework exploding with a sharp noise.

crack·er-bar·rel ▸*adj.* [*attrib.*] (esp. of a philosophy) plain, simple, and unsophisticated: *his cracker-barrel fascism.* ▷late 19th cent.: with reference to the barrels of soda crackers once found in country stores, around which informal discussions would take place between customers.

crack·er·jack /ˈkrakərˌjak/ *informal* ▸*adj.* exceptionally good: *a crackerjack eye surgeon.*
▸*n.* an exceptionally good person or thing.

crack·ers /ˈkrakərz/ ▸*adj. informal, chiefly Brit.* insane: *if Luke wasn't here I'd go crackers.*

crack·head /ˈkrakˌhed/ ▸*n. informal* a person who habitually takes crack cocaine.

crack house ▸*n.* a place where crack cocaine is traded.

crack·ing /ˈkrakiNG/ *Brit., informal* ▸*adj.* excellent: *he is in cracking form to win this race* | *a cracking good war story.*

crack·le /ˈkrakəl/ ▸*v.* [*intrans.*] make a rapid succession of slight cracking noises: *the fire suddenly crackled and spat sparks.* ■ *figurative* give a sense of great tension or animation: *attraction and antagonism were crackling between them.*
▸*n.* **1** a sound made up of a rapid succession of slight cracking sounds: *there was a crackle and a whine from the microphone.* **2** a pattern of minute surface cracks on painted or varnished surfaces, glazed ceramics, or glass. ▷late Middle English: from CRACK + -LE[4]. —**crack·ly** /ˈkrak(ə)lē/ *adj.*

crack·ling /ˈkraklən; -liNG/ ▸*n.* the crisp, fatty skin of roast pork.

crack·nel /ˈkraknəl/ ▸*n.* **1** a light, crisp, savory biscuit. **2** small pieces of crackling. ▷late Middle English: alteration of Old French *craquelin*, from Middle Dutch *krākelinc*, from *krāken* 'to crack.'

crack·pot /ˈkrakˌpät/ *informal* ▸*n.* an eccentric or foolish person.
▸*adj.* eccentric; impractical: *his head's full of crackpot ideas.*

cracks·man /ˈkraksmən/ ▸*n.* (*pl.* **-men**) *informal, dated* a burglar, esp. a safecracker.

crack-up (also **crackup**) ▸*n.* [usu. in *sing.*] *informal* **1** a collapse under strain: *he had a complete mental crack-up.* **2** an act of breaking up or splitting apart: *the crack-up of the Soviet Union.* **3** a car crash: *motorists were asked to report minor crack-ups later.*

crack wil·low ▸*n.* a large Eurasian willow with long, glossy leaves, growing typically in damp or riverside habitats. The brittle branches break off easily, often taking root and producing new growth. • *Salix fragilis*, family Salicaceae.

crack·y /ˈkrakē/ ▸*n.* (in phrase **by cracky**) *dated, informal* an exclamation used for emphasis.

Crac·ow /ˈkräkˌou; ˈkräˌko͞of/ an industrial and college city in southern Poland, on the Vistula River; pop 750,540. It was the capital of Poland from 1320 until it was replaced by Warsaw in 1609. Polish name **Kraków**.

-cracy ▸*comb. form* denoting a particular form of government, rule, or influence: *autocracy* | *democracy.* ▷from French *-cratie*, via medieval Latin from Greek *-kratia* 'power, rule.'

cra·dle /ˈkrādl/ ▸*n.* **1** an infant's bed or crib, typically one mounted on rockers. ■ *figurative* a place, process, or event in which something originates or flourishes: *he saw Greek art as the cradle of European civilization.* ■ *figurative* infancy; childhood: *a society that would secure the welfare of its citizens **from cradle to grave**.* **2** a framework resembling a cradle, in particular: ■ a framework on which a ship or boat rests during construction or repairs. ■ the part of a telephone on which the receiver rests when not in use. ■ a frame put over a hospital bed to prevent the bedclothes from touching a patient's injury. ■ *Mining* a trough on rockers in which auriferous earth or sand is shaken in water to separate the gold.
▸*v.* [*trans.*] **1** hold gently and protectively: *she cradled his head in her arms.* ■ *figurative* be the place of origin of: *the northeastern states cradled an American industrial revolution.* **2** place (a telephone receiver) in its cradle. ▷Old English *cradol*, of uncertain origin; perhaps related to German *Kratte* 'basket.'

cra·dle·board /ˈkrādlˌbôrd/ ▸*n.* (among North American Indians) a board to which an infant is strapped.

cra·dle cap ▸*n.* a skin condition sometimes seen in

babies caused by excessive production of sebum, characterized by areas of yellowish or brownish scales on the top of the head.

cra·dle-rob·ber ▸*n. derogatory* a person who marries or has a sexual relationship with a much younger person.

cra·dle song ▸*n.* a lullaby.

cra·dling /ˈkrādliNG; ˈkrādl-iNG/ ▸*n. Architecture* a wooden or iron framework, typically one used as a structural support in a ceiling.

craft /kraft/ ▸*n.* **1** an activity involving skill in making things by hand: *the craft of bookbinding* | *pewter craft.* ■ (**crafts**) work or objects made by hand: *the shop sells local crafts* | [as *adj.*] (**craft**) *a craft fair.* ■ a skilled activity or profession: *the historian's craft.* ■ skill in carrying out one's work: *a player with plenty of craft.* ■ skill used in deceiving others: *her cousin was not her equal in guile and evasive craft.* ■ the members of a skilled profession. ■ (**the Craft**) the brotherhood of Freemasons. **2** (*pl.* same) a boat or ship: *sailing craft.* ■ an airplane or spaceship.
▸*v.* [*trans.*] exercise skill in making (something): *he crafted the chair lovingly* | [as *adj.*] (**crafted**) *a beautifully crafted object.* ▹Old English *cræft* 'strength, skill,' of Germanic origin; related to Dutch *kracht*, German *Kraft*, and Swedish *kraft* 'strength' (the change of sense to 'skill' occurring only in English). Sense 2, originally in the expression *small craft* 'small trading vessels or lighters,' may be elliptical, referring to vessels requiring a small amount of "craft" or skill to handle, as opposed to large oceangoing ships. —**craft·er** *n.*

craft brew (also **craft beer**) ▸*n.* a beer with a distinctive flavor, produced in small quantities and distributed in a particular region. —**craft-brewed** *adj.* —**craft brew·er** *n.* —**craft brew·ing** *n.*

craft guild ▸*n. historical* an association of workers of the same trade for mutual benefit.

crafts·man /ˈkraf(t)smən/ ▸*n.* (*pl.* **-men**) a person who is skilled in a particular craft. ■ an artist. —**crafts·man·ship** /-ˌSHip/ *n.*

crafts·per·son /ˈkraf(t)sˌpərsən/ ▸*n.* (*pl.* **-peo·ple** /-ˌpēpəl/) a person who is skilled in a particular craft (used as a neutral alternative).

crafts·wom·an /ˈkraf(t)sˌwo͝omən/ ▸*n.* (*pl.* **-wom·en**) a woman who is skilled in a particular craft. ■ a woman artist.

craft un·ion ▸*n.* a labor union of people of the same skilled craft.

craft·work /ˈkraftˌwərk/ ▸*n. chiefly Brit.* the making of things, esp. decorative objects, by hand as a profession or leisure activity. ■ work produced in such a way. —**craft·work·er** *n.*

craft·y /ˈkraftē/ ▸*adj.* (**craft·i·er, craft·i·est**) **1** clever at achieving one's aims by indirect or deceitful methods: *a crafty crook faked an injury to escape from prison.* ■ of, involving, or relating to indirect or deceitful methods: *a shameless and crafty trick to mislead public opinion.* **2** *informal* of, involving, or relating to the making of decorative objects and other things by hand: *a market full of crafty pots and interesting earrings.* ▹Old English *cræftig* 'strong, powerful,' later 'skillful' (see CRAFT, -Y[1]). —**craft·i·ly** /-təlē/ *adv.* —**craft·i·ness** *n.*

crag /krag/ ▸*n.* a steep or rugged cliff or rock face. ▹Middle English: of Celtic origin. Sense 2, dating from the mid 18th cent., may have been a different word originally.

crag·gy /ˈkragē/ ▸*adj.* (**-gi·er, -gi·est**) (of a landscape) having many crags: *a craggy coastline.* ■ (of a cliff or rock face) rough and uneven. ■ (of a person's face, typically a man's) rugged and rough-textured in an attractive way. —**crag·gi·ly** /ˈkragəlē/ *adv.* —**crag·gi·ness** *n.*

crags·man /ˈkragzmən/ ▸*n.* (*pl.* **-men**) a skilled rock climber.

Cra·io·va /krīˈōvə/ a city in southwestern Romania; pop. 300,030.

crake /krāk/ ▸*n.* a bird of the rail family, esp. one with a short bill like the corn crake. • Family Rallidae: several genera, in particular *Porzana*, and numerous species. ■ the rasping cry of the corn crake. ▹Middle English (originally denoting a crow or raven): from Old Norse *kráka*, *krákr*, of imitative origin.

cram /kram/ ▸*v.* (**crammed, cram·ming**) [*trans.*] (often **be crammed**) completely fill (a place or container) to the point that it appears to be overflowing: *the ashtray by the bed was* **crammed with** *cigarette butts* | *it's amazing how you've managed to* **cram** *everyone* **in.** ■ [*intrans.*] (of a number of people) enter a place or space that is or seems to be too small to accommodate all of them: *they all crammed into the car.* ■ put (something) quickly or roughly into something that is or appears to be too small to contain it: *he* **crammed** *the sandwiches* **into** *his mouth* | *figurative he had* **crammed** *so much* **into** *his short life.* ■ [*intrans.*] study intensively over a short period of time just before an examination: *lectures were called off so students could cram for finals.* ▹Old English *crammian*, of Germanic origin; related to Dutch *krammen* 'to cramp or clamp.'

cram·bo /ˈkrambō/ ▸*n.* a game in which a player gives a word or line of verse to which each of the other players must find a rhyme. ▹early 17th cent. (denoting a particular fashion in drinking): from earlier *crambe* 'cabbage,' used figuratively to denote something distasteful that is repeated, apparently from Latin *crambe repetita* 'cabbage served up again,' applied by Juvenal to any distasteful repetition.

cram·mer /ˈkramər/ ▸*n. Brit.* a person or institution that prepares pupils for an examination intensively over a short period of time.

cram·ming /ˈkramiNG/ ▸*n.* the fraudulent practice of adding unauthorized charges to a customer's phone bill.

cramp /kramp/ ▸*n.* **1** a painful, involuntary contraction of a muscle or muscles, typically caused by fatigue or strain: *he suffered severe cramps in his foot.* ■ (**cramps**) abdominal pain caused by menstruation. **2** a tool, typically shaped like a capital G, for clamping two objects together for gluing or other work. ■ (also **cramp-iron**) a metal bar with bent ends for holding masonry together.
▸*v.* **1** [*trans.*] restrict or inhibit the development of: *tighter rules will cramp economic growth.* **2** [*trans.*] fasten with a cramp or cramps: *cramp the gates to the posts.* **3** [*intrans.*] suffer from sudden and painful contractions of a muscle or muscles. ▹late Middle English: from Middle Low German and Middle Dutch *krampe*; sense 1 of the *noun* is via Old French *crampe*.
▸*PHRASE* □ **cramp someone's style** *informal* prevent a person from acting freely or naturally.

cramped /kram(p)t/ ▸*adj.* **1** feeling or causing someone to feel uncomfortably confined or hemmed in by lack of space: *the staff had to work in cramped conditions.* ■ restricting or inhibiting the development of someone or something: *he felt cramped in a large organization.* ■ (of handwriting) small and difficult to read. **2** suffering from a cramp: *cramped muscles.*

cram·pon /ˈkramˌpän/ ▸*n.* (usu. **crampons**) **1** a metal plate with spikes fixed to a boot for walking on ice or rock climbing. **2** archaic term for GRAPPLING HOOK. ▹Middle English (sense 2): from Old French, of Germanic origin.

Cra·nach /ˈkränəKH/ two German painters. **Lucas** (1472–1553), known as **Cranach the Elder**, was a member of the Danube School, noted for his early religious pictures. His son **Lucas** (1515–86), known as **Cranach the Younger**, continued working in the same tradition as his father.

cran·ber·ry /ˈkranˌberē; -bərē/ ▸*n.* (*pl.* **-ries**) **1** a small, red, acid berry used in cooking. **2** the evergreen dwarf shrub of the heath family that yields this fruit. • Genus *Vaccinium*, family Ericaceae: several species, in particular the North American *V. macrocarpon*, which thrives in boggy places and from which most commercial varieties originate. ▹mid 17th cent. (originally North American): from German *Kranbeere* or Low German *kranebeere* 'crane-berry.'

cran·ber·ry sauce ▸*n.* a jellied sauce made from cranberries, a traditional accompaniment to turkey.

Crane[1] /krān/, (Harold) Hart (1899–1932), U.S. poet. He published only two books—*White Buildings* (1926), a collection, and *The Bridge* (1930), a mystical epic poem concerned with American life and consciousness—before committing suicide by jumping from a ship.

Crane[2], Stephen (1871–1900), U.S. writer. He is well known for the novel, *The Red Badge of Courage* (1895), a study of an inexperienced soldier during the Civil War. It was hailed as a masterpiece of psychological realism, even though Crane himself had no personal war experience.

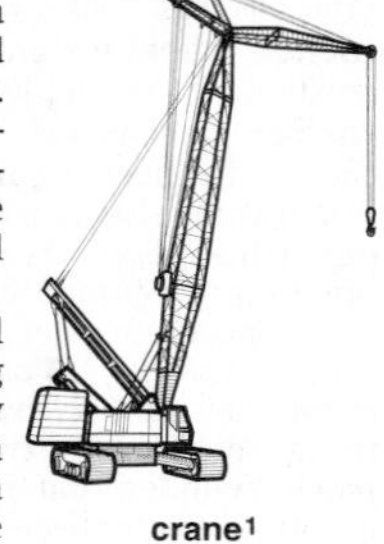
crane1

crane[1] /krān/ ▸*n.* a large, tall machine used for moving heavy objects, typically by suspending them from a projecting arm or beam. ■ a metal arm fastened inside a fireplace for holding cooking pots. ■ a moving platform supporting a television or movie camera.
▸*v.* **1** [*intrans.*] stretch out one's neck in order to see something: *she craned forward to look more clearly.* ■ [*trans.*] stretch out (one's neck) in this way. **2** [*trans.*] move (a heavy object) with a crane: *the wheelhouse module is craned into position on the hull.* ▹Middle English: figuratively from CRANE[2] (the same sense development occurred in the related German *Kran* and Dutch *kraan* (see CRANE[2]), and in French *grue*). The verb dates from the late 16th cent.

crane[2] ▸*n.* a tall, long-legged, long-necked bird, typically with white or gray plumage and often with tail plumes and patches of bare red skin on the head. Cranes are noted for their elaborate courtship dances. • Family Gruidae: four genera, in particular *Grus*, and several species, including the Eurasian **common crane** (*G. grus*). ▹Old English, of Germanic origin; related to Dutch *kraan* and German *Kran*, from an Indo-European root shared by Latin *grus* and Greek *geranos*.

crane fly ▸*n.* a slender, two-winged fly with very long legs. The larva of some kinds is the leatherjacket. • Family Tipulidae: many genera and species, in particular the large and common *Tipula maxima*.

cranes·bill /ˈkrānzˌbil/ ▸*n.* a herbaceous plant that typically has lobed leaves and purple, violet, or pink five-petaled flowers. • Genus *Geranium*, family Geraniaceae: several species, including the common **meadow cranesbill** (*G. pratense*), with deeply toothed leaves and bluish-purple flowers. ▹mid 16th cent.: so named because of the long spur on the fruit, thought to resemble a crane's beak.

cra·ni·al /ˈkrānēəl/ ▸*adj. Anatomy* of or relating to the skull or cranium. ▹early 19th cent.: from CRANIUM + -AL.

cra·ni·al in·dex ▸*n.* another term for CEPHALIC INDEX.

cra·ni·al nerve ▸*n. Anatomy* each of twelve pairs of nerves that arise directly from the brain, not from the spinal cord, and pass through separate apertures in the skull.

They are (with conventional roman numbering) the olfactory (I), optic (II), oculomotor (III), trochlear (IV), trigeminal (V), abducens (VI), facial (VII), vestibulocochlear (VIII), glossopharyngeal (IX), vagus (X), accessory (XI), and hypoglossal (XII) nerves.

cra·ni·ate /ˈkrānēˌāt; -nēət/ *Zoology* ▸*n.* an animal that possesses a skull. Compare with VERTEBRATE. • Subphylum Craniata, phylum Chordata; used instead of Vertebrata in some classification schemes.
▸*adj.* of or relating to the craniates. ▹late 19th cent.: from modern Latin *craniatus*, from medieval Latin *cranium* (see CRANIUM).

cranio- ▸*comb. form* relating to the skull: *craniotomy.* ▹from Greek *kranion* 'skull.'

cra·ni·o·ce·re·bral /ˌkrānēōsəˈrēbrəl; -ˈserəbrəl/ ▸*adj.* relating to or involving both the cranium and the cerebrum.

cra·ni·ol·o·gy /ˌkrānēˈäləjē/ ▸*n. historical* the scientific study of the shape and size of the skulls of different human races. ■ another term for PHRENOLOGY. —**cra·ni·o·log·i·cal** /-nēəˈläjikəl/ *adj.* —**cra·ni·ol·o·gist** /-jist/ *n.*

cra·ni·om·e·ter /ˌkrānēˈämitər/ ▸*n.* a device for measuring the external dimensions of the skull.

cra·ni·om·e·try /ˌkrānēˈämətrē/ ▸*n. historical* the scientific measurement of skulls, esp. in relation to craniology. —**cra·ni·o·met·ric** /ˌkrānēəˈmetrik/ *adj.*

cra·ni·op·a·gus /ˌkrānēˈäpəgəs/ ▸*n.* (of conjoined twins) the condition of being joined at the head: [as *modifier*] *the first time that surgeons had tried to separate adult craniopagus twins.* ▹based on *cranio-* 'skull' + Greek *pagos*'something that has become solid.'

cra·ni·o·sa·cral ther·a·py /ˌkrānēōˈsakrəl; -ˈsākrəl/ ▸*n.* a system of alternative medicine intended to relieve pain and tension by gentle manipulations of the skull regarded as harmonizing with a natural rhythm in the central nervous system.

cra·ni·ot·o·my /ˌkrānēˈätəmē/ ▸*n.* surgical opening into the skull. ■ surgical perforation of the skull of a dead fetus to ease delivery.

cra·ni·um /ˈkrānēəm/ ▸*n.* (*pl.* **-ni·ums** or **-ni·a** /-nēə/) *Anatomy* the skull, esp. the part enclosing the brain. ▹late Middle English: via medieval Latin from Greek *kranion* 'skull.'

crank[1] /kraNGk/ ▸*v.* [*trans.*] **1** turn the crankshaft of (an internal combustion engine), typically in order to start the engine. ■ turn (a handle), typically in order to start an engine. ■ (**crank something up**)

informal increase the intensity of something: *he cranked up the foghorn to full volume.* ■ (**crank something out**) *informal* produce something regularly and routinely: *an army of researchers cranked out worthy studies.* **2** [usu. as *adj.*] (**cranked**) give a bend to (a shaft, bar, etc.).
▸*n.* **1** a part of an axle or shaft bent out at right angles, for converting reciprocal to circular motion and vice versa. **2** *informal* methamphetamine. ▷Old English *cranc* (recorded in *crancstæf*, denoting a weaver's implement), related to *crincan* (see CRINGE).

crank[2] ▸*n.* **1** an eccentric person, esp. one who is obsessed by a particular subject or theory: *when he first started to air his views, they labeled him a crank.* ■ a bad-tempered person: *she was so sweet and forbearing that I came off as a crank.* [mid 19th cent.: back-formation from CRANKY.] **2** *poetic/literary* a fanciful turn of speech. [late 16th cent.: perhaps from a base meaning 'bent together, curled up,' shared by Old English *cranc* (see CRANK[1]).]
▸*adj.* originating from or denoting a malicious or mischievous person: *she was the target of a rash of crank calls.*

crank[3] ▸*adj. archaic Nautical* (of a sailing ship) easily keeled over, esp. by wind or sea through improper design or loading. ▷early 17th cent.: perhaps from dialect *crank* 'weak, shaky' (compare with CRANKY or CRANK[1]).

crank·case /'kraNGk,kās/ ▸*n.* a case or covering enclosing a crankshaft.

crank·pin /'kraNGk,pin/ ▸*n.* a pin by which a connecting rod is attached to a crank.

crank·shaft /'kraNGk,SHaft/ ▸*n.* a shaft driven by a crank.

crank·y /'kraNGkē/ ▸*adj.* (**crank·i·er**, **crank·i·est**) *informal* ill-tempered; irritable: *he was bored and cranky after eight hours of working.* ■ eccentric or strange, typically because highly unorthodox: *a cranky scheme to pipe ground-level ozone into the stratosphere.* ■ (of a machine) working badly; shaky: *the cranky elevator breaks down periodically.* ▷late 18th cent. (in the sense 'sickly, in poor health'): perhaps from obsolete (*counterfeit*) *crank* 'a rogue feigning sickness,' from Dutch or German *krank* 'sick.' —**crank·i·ly** /-kəlē/ *adv.* —**crank·i·ness** *n.*

Cran·mer /'kranmər/, Thomas (1489–1556), English cleric and martyr. A leader in the English Reformation, he was appointed the first Protestant archbishop of Canterbury in 1532 and was responsible for liturgical reform and the compilation of the Book of Common Prayer (1549).He was convicted of treason and heresy under Mary Tudor and burned at the stake.

cran·nog /'kran,ôg; -əg/ ▸*n.* an ancient fortified dwelling constructed in a lake or marsh in Scotland or Ireland. ▷early 17th cent.: from Irish *crannóg*, Scottish Gaelic *crannag* 'timber structure,' from *crann* 'tree, beam.'

cran·ny /'kranē/ ▸*n.* (*pl.* **-nies**) a small, narrow space or opening. ▷late Middle English: from Old French *crane* 'notched,' from *cran*, from popular Latin *crena* 'notch.' —**cran·nied** /'kranēd/ *adj.*

Cran·ston /'kranstən/ an industrial city in central Rhode Island, south of Providence; pop. 79,269.

Cran·ston /'kranstən/, Alan (1914–2000), U.S. politician. A Democrat from California, he was a member of the U.S. Senate 1969–93. From 1993 he worked toward the abolishment of nuclear weapons.

crap[1] /krap/ *vulgar slang* ▸*n.* **1** something that is of extremely poor quality. ■ nonsense. ■ rubbish; junk. **2** excrement. ■ [in *sing.*] an act of defecation.
▸*v.* (**crapped**, **crap·ping**) [*intrans.*] defecate. ▷Middle English: related to Dutch *krappe*, from *krappen* 'pluck or cut off,' and perhaps also to Old French *crappe* 'siftings,' Anglo-Latin *crappa* 'chaff.' The original sense was 'chaff,' later 'residue from rendering fat,' also 'dregs of beer.' Current senses date from the late 19th cent.

crap[2] ▸*n.* a losing throw of 2, 3, or 12 in craps.
▸*v.* [*intrans.*] (**crap out**) *informal* make a losing throw at craps. ■ withdraw from or give up on a game or activity because of fear or fatigue: *when entrepreneurs get to $1 billion they crap out and turn their companies over to others.* ■ fail in what one is attempting to do: *the Rams almost crapped out late in the game.* ■ (of a machine) break down: *his TelePrompTer crapped out.* ▷early 20th cent.: from CRAPS.

crape /krāp/ ▸*n.* archaic spelling of CREPE. ▷early 16th cent.: from French *crêpe* (see CREPE). —**crap·y** *adj.*

crape myr·tle (also **crepe myr·tle**) ▸*n.* an ornamental Asian shrub or small tree with pink, white, or purplish crinkled petals. • Genus *Lagerstroemia*, family Lythraceae: several species, in particular **common crape myrtle** (*L. indica*) and **queen's crape myrtle** (*L. speciosa*).

crap game ▸*n.* a game of craps.

crap·per /'krapər/ ▸*n. vulgar slang* a toilet.

crap·pie /'kräpē; 'krapē/ ▸*n.* (*pl.* **-pies**) a North American freshwater fish of the sunfish family, the male of which builds a nest and guards the eggs and young. • Genus *Pomoxis*, family Centrarchidae: several species, including the **black crappie** (*P. nigromaculatus*) and the **white crappie** (*P. annularis*). ▷mid 19th cent.: of unknown origin.

crap·py /'krapē/ ▸*adj.* (**-pi·er**, **-pi·est**) *vulgar slang* of extremely poor quality: *crappy wine.* ■ disgusting or unpleasant; worthless: *Phil's room is the crappiest.* ■ ill; in poor physical condition: *I feel really crappy today.*

craps /kraps/ ▸*plural n.* [treated as *sing.*] a gambling game played with two dice, chiefly in North America. A throw of 7 or 11 is a winning throw, 2, 3, or 12 is a losing throw; any other throw must be repeated. See also CRAP[2]. ▷early 19th cent.: perhaps from CRAB[1] or *crab's eyes*, denoting the lowest throw (two ones) at dice.

crap·shoot /'krap,SHōōt/ ▸*n.* a crap game. ■ *informal* a risky or uncertain matter: *predicting any extreme weather event is a scientific crapshoot.* —**crap·shoot·er** *n.*

crap·u·lent /'krapyələnt/ ▸*adj. poetic/literary* of or relating to the drinking of alcohol or drunkenness. ▷mid 17th cent.: from late Latin *crapulentus* 'very drunk,' from Latin *crapula* 'inebriation,' from Greek *kraipalē* 'drunken headache.' —**crap·u·lence** *n.* —**crap·u·lous** /-yələs/ *adj.*

cra·que·lure /kra'klŏŏr; 'krak,lŏŏr/ ▸*n.* a network of fine cracks in the paint or varnish of a painting. ▷early 20th cent.: French, from *craqueler* 'to crackle.'

crash[1] /kraSH/ ▸*v.* **1** [*intrans.*] (of a moving object) collide violently with an obstacle or another moving object: *the coffin slipped out the back door, slid down the hill, and crashed.* ■ [*trans.*] cause (a moving object) to collide in this way. ■ (of an aircraft) fall from the sky and violently hit the land or sea: *a jet crashed 200 yards from the school.* ■ [*trans.*] cause (an aircraft) to fall from the sky in this way. ■ *informal* (of a business, a market, or a price) fall suddenly and disastrously in value: *silver prices crashed in early 1980.* ■ *Computing* [*intrans.*] (of a machine, system, or software) fail suddenly: *the project was postponed because the computer crashed.* ■ *informal* [*intrans.*] go to sleep, esp. suddenly or in an improvised setting: *I'll crash in the back of the van for a couple of hours.* **2** [*intrans.*] move with force, speed, and sudden loud noise: *huge waves crashed down on us.* ■ [*trans.*] move (something) in this way: *she crashed down the telephone receiver.* ■ make a sudden loud, deep noise: *the thunder crashed.* **3** [*trans.*] *informal* enter (a party) without an invitation or permission.
▸*n.* **1** a violent collision, typically of one moving object with another or with an obstacle: *a car crash.* ■ an instance of an aircraft falling from the sky to hit the land or sea. ■ a sudden loud noise as of something breaking or hitting another object: *he slammed the phone down with a crash.* **2** a sudden disastrous drop in the value or price of something, esp. shares of stock: *a stock market crash* | *the crash of 1987.* ■ the sudden collapse of a business. ■ *Computing* a sudden failure which puts a system out of action.
▸*adj.* done rapidly or urgently and involving a concentrated effort: *a crash course in Italian* | *a crash diet.*
▸*adv.* with a sudden loud sound: *crash went the bolt.* ▷late Middle English: imitative, perhaps partly suggested by CRAZE and DASH.
▸*PHRASE* □ **crash and burn** *informal* come to grief or fail spectacularly.

crash[2] ▸*n. dated* a coarse plain linen, woolen, or cotton fabric, used for curtains and towels. ▷early 19th cent.: from Russian *krashenina* 'dyed coarse linen.'

crash-dive ▸*v.* [*intrans.*] (of a submarine) dive rapidly and steeply to a deeper level in an emergency. ■ (of an aircraft) plunge steeply downward into a crash.
▸*n.* (**crash dive**) a steep dive of this kind by a submarine or aircraft.

crash hel·met ▸*n.* a helmet worn by a motorcyclist or a race car driver to protect the head in case of a crash.

crash·ing /'kraSHiNG/ ▸*adj. informal* complete; total (used for emphasis): *a crashing bore.* —**crash·ing·ly** *adv.*

crash-land ▸*v.* [*intrans.*] (of an aircraft) land roughly in an emergency, typically without lowering the landing gear: [as *n.*] (**crash landing**) *a plane made a crash landing near the airport.*

crash pad ▸*n.* **1** *informal* a place to sleep, esp. for a single night or in an emergency. **2** a thick piece of shock-absorbing material for the protection of the occupants of an aircraft cockpit or motor vehicle.

crash-test ▸*v.* [*trans.*] deliberately crash (a new vehicle) under controlled conditions in order to evaluate and improve its ability to withstand impact.
▸*n.* (**crash test**) a test of this kind.

crash·wor·thy /'kraSH,wər<u>TH</u>ē/ ▸*adj.* (of a vehicle or an aircraft) relatively well able to withstand a crash. —**crash·wor·thi·ness** *n.*

crass /kras/ ▸*adj.* lacking sensitivity, refinement, or intelligence: *the crass assumptions that men make about women.* ▷late 15th cent. (in the sense 'dense or coarse (in constitution or texture)'): from Latin *crassus* 'solid, thick.' —**cras·si·tude** /'krasə,t(y)ōōd/ *n.* —**crass·ly** *adv.* —**crass·ness** *n.*

Cras·sus /'krasəs/, Marcus Licinius (*c.*115–53 BC), Roman politician. After defeating Spartacus in 71 BC, he joined Caesar and Pompey in the First Triumvirate in 60.

-crat ▸*comb. form* denoting a member or supporter of a particular form of government or rule: *plutocrat* | *technocrat.* ▷from French *-crate*, from adjectives ending in *-cratique* (see -CRATIC).

crate /krāt/ ▸*n.* **1** a slatted wooden case used for transporting or storing goods: *a crate of bananas.* ■ a square metal or plastic container divided into small individual units, used for transporting or storing bottles: *a milk crate* | *a crate of beer.* **2** *informal, dated* an old and dilapidated vehicle.
▸*v.* [*trans.*] (often **be crated**) pack (something) in a crate for transportation. ▷late Middle English: perhaps related to Dutch *krat* 'tailboard of a wagon,' earlier 'box of a coach,' of unknown origin. —**crate·ful** /'krāt,fŏŏl/ *n.* (*pl.* **-fuls**) .

Cra·ter /'krātər/ *Astronomy* a small and faint southern constellation (the Cup), between Hydra and Leo, said to represent the goblet of Apollo. ■ [as *genitive*] (**Crateris** /krā'tēris/) used with a preceding letter or numeral to designate a star in this constellation: *the star Delta Crateris.* ▷Latin, from Greek, 'mixing bowl.'

cra·ter /'krātər/ ▸*n.* **1** a large, bowl-shaped cavity in the ground or on the surface of a planet or the moon, typically one caused by an explosion or the impact of a meteorite or other celestial body. ■ a large pit or hollow forming the mouth of a volcano. ■ a cavity or hole in any surface. **2** a large bowl used in ancient Greece for mixing wine.
▸*v.* [*trans.*] form a crater in (the ground or a planet): *he has the offensive power to crater the enemy's runways* | [as *adj.*] (**cratered**) *the heavily cratered areas of the moon.* ▷early 17th cent. (denoting the hollow forming the mouth of a volcano): via Latin from Greek *kratēr* 'mixing bowl,' from *krasis* 'mixture.'

Cra·ter Lake a lake that fills a volcanic crater in the Cascade Mountains in southwestern Oregon. With a depth of more than 1,968 feet (600 m), it is the deepest lake in the U.S.

-cratic ▸*comb. form* relating to a particular kind of government or rule: *bureaucratic* | *democratic.* ▷from French *-cratique*, from *-cratie* (see -CRACY).

-cratically ▸*suffix* forming adverbs corresponding to adjectives ending in *-cratic*: *democratically.* ▷from -CRATIC + -ALLY. (See -CRACY).

C rations ▸*plural n.* a type of canned food formerly used by U.S. soldiers. ▷*C* for *combat*.

cra·ton /'krā,tän; 'kra-/ ▸*n. Geology* a large, stable block of the earth's crust forming the nucleus of a continent. ▷1930s: alteration of *kratogen* in the same sense, from Greek *kratos* 'strength.' —**cra·ton·ic** /krā'tänik; kra-; krə-/ *adj.*

cra·vat /krə'vat/ ▸*n.* a short, wide strip of fabric worn by men around the neck and tucked inside an open-necked shirt.■ a necktie. ▷mid 17th cent.: from French *cravate*, from *Cravate* 'Croat' (from German *Krabat*, from Serbo-Croat *Hrvat*), because of the scarf worn by Croatian mercenaries in France. —**cra·vat·ted** *adj.*

crave /krāv/ ▸*v.* [*trans.*] feel a powerful desire for (something): *a program to give the infants the human touch they crave.* ■ *dated* beg for (something): *I must crave your indulgence.* ▷Old English *crafian* (in the sense 'demand, claim as a right'), of Germanic origin; related to Swedish *kräva*, Danish *kræve* 'demand.' The current sense dates from late Middle English. —**crav·er** *n.*

cra·ven /ˈkrāvən/ ▸*adj.* contemptibly lacking in courage; cowardly: *a craven abdication of his moral duty.*

▸*n. archaic* a cowardly person. ▷Middle English *cravant* 'defeated,' perhaps via Anglo-Norman French from Old French *cravante*, past participle of *cravanter* 'crush, overwhelm,' based on Latin *crepare* 'burst.' The change in the ending in the 17th cent. was due to association with past participles ending in *-en* (see **-EN**[3]). —**cra·ven·ly** *adv.* —**cra·ven·ness** *n.*

crav·ing /ˈkrāviNG/ ▸*n.* a powerful desire for something: *a* **craving for** *chocolate.*

craw /krô/ ▸*n. dated* the crop of a bird or insect. ■ *chiefly humorous* the stomach of a person or animal. ▷late Middle English: from or related to Middle Dutch *crāghe* or Middle Low German *krage* 'neck, throat.'

▸*PHRASE* □ **stick in one's craw** see **STICK**[2].

craw·dad /ˈkrô,dad/ ▸*n.* a freshwater crayfish. ▷early 20th cent.: fanciful alteration of **CRAWFISH**.

craw·fish /ˈkrô,fiSH/ ▸*n.* (*pl.* same or **-fish·es**) a freshwater crayfish. ■ another term for **SPINY LOBSTER**.

▸*v.* [*intrans.*] *informal* retreat from a position: *the three networks, intimidated by the public outcry, had begun to crawfish.* ▷early 17th cent.: variant of **CRAYFISH**.

Craw·ford /ˈkrôfərd/, Joan (1908–77), U.S. actress; born *Lucille Le Sueur*. Her movie career lasted for over 40 years, during which time she played the female lead in movies such as *Mildred Pierce* (1945), for which she was awarded an Academy Award. She later appeared in mature roles, such as her part in the horror movie *Whatever Happened to Baby Jane?* (1962).

Joan Crawford

crawl /krôl/ ▸*v.* [*intrans.*] **1** (of a person) move forward on the hands and knees or by dragging the body close to the ground: *they crawled out from under the table.* ■ (of an insect or small animal) move slowly along a surface: *the tiny spider was crawling up Nicky's arm.* ■ (of a vehicle) move at an unusually slow pace: *the traffic was crawling along.* ■ swim using the crawl. ■ *informal* behave obsequiously or ingratiatingly in the hope of gaining someone's favor: *don't come crawling back to me later when you realize your mistake.* ■ *technical* (of paint or other liquid) move after application to form an uneven layer over the surface below: *glazes can crawl away from a crack in the piece.* **2** (**be crawling with**) be covered or crowded with insects or people, to an extent that is disgusting or objectionable: *the place was crawling with soldiers.*

▸*n.* [in *sing.*] **1** an act of moving on one's hands and knees or dragging one's body along the ground: *they began the crawl back to their own lines.* ■ a slow rate of movement, typically that of a vehicle: *he reduced his speed to a crawl.* **2** a swimming stroke involving alternate overarm movements and rapid kicks of the legs. ▷Middle English: of unknown origin; possibly related to Swedish *kravla* and Danish *kravle*. —**crawl·ing·ly** *adv.* —**crawl·y** *adj.*

▸*PHRASE* □ **make someone's skin crawl** see **SKIN**.

crawl·er /ˈkrôlər/ ▸*n.* a thing that crawls or moves at a slow pace, esp. an insect. ■ (in full **crawler tractor**) a tractor or other vehicle moving on an endless caterpillar track. ■ *Computing* a program that searches the World Wide Web, typically in order to create an index of data.

crawl·ing peg ▸*n.* a point on a scale of exchange rates in which a currency's value is allowed to go up or down frequently by small amounts within overall limits.

crawl space ▸*n.* an area of limited height under a floor or roof, giving access to wiring and plumbing.

cray·fish /ˈkrā,fiSH/ ▸*n.* (*pl.* same or **-fish·es**) (also **freshwater crayfish**) a nocturnal freshwater crustacean that resembles a small lobster and inhabits streams and rivers. • Several genera in the infraorder Astacidea, class Malacostraca, including *Astacus* of Europe and *Cambarus* of North America. ■ (also **marine crayfish**) another term for **SPINY LOBSTER**. ▷Middle English: from Old French *crevice*, of Germanic origin and related to German *Krebs* (see **CRAB**[1]). In the 16th cent. or earlier the second syllable was altered by association with **FISH**[1].

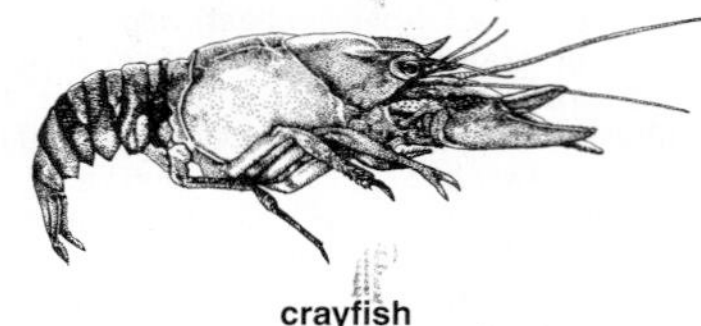

crayfish

cray·on /ˈkrā,än; ˈkrāən/ ▸*n.* a pencil or stick of colored chalk or wax, used for drawing.

▸*v.* [*trans.*] draw with a crayon or crayons: *Jeff crayoned a picture on a legal pad* | [*intrans.*] *a child crayoning in a coloring book.* ▷mid 17th cent.: from French, from *craie* 'chalk,' from Latin *creta*.

craze /krāz/ ▸*n.* an enthusiasm for a particular activity or object that typically appears suddenly and achieves widespread but short-lived popularity: *the latest* **craze for** *bungee jumping.*

▸*v.* [*trans.*] **1** [usu. as *adj.*] (**crazed**) wildly insane or excited: *a crazed killer* | *power-crazed tinpot dictators.* **2** (often **be crazed**) produce a network of fine cracks on (a surface): *the lake was frozen over but crazed with cracks.* ■ [*intrans.*] develop such cracks. ▷late Middle English (in the sense 'break, shatter, produce cracks'): perhaps of Scandinavian origin and related to Swedish *krasa* 'crunch.'

cra·zy /ˈkrāzē/ *informal* ▸*adj.* (**-zi·er**, **-zi·est**) **1** mentally deranged, esp. as manifested in a wild or aggressive way: *Stella* **went crazy** *and assaulted a visitor* | *a crazy grin.* ■ extremely annoyed or angry: *the noise they made was* **driving me crazy**. ■ foolish: *it was* **crazy to** *hope that good might come out of this mess.* **2** extremely enthusiastic: *I'm* **crazy about** *Cindy* | *a football-crazy bunch of boys.* **3** (of an angle) appearing absurdly out of place or in an unlikely position: *the monument leaned at a crazy angle.* ■ *archaic* (of a ship or building) full of cracks or flaws; unsound or shaky.

▸*n.* (*pl.* **-zies**) a mentally deranged person. —**cra·zi·ly** /-zilē/ *adv.* —**cra·zi·ness** *n.*

▸*PHRASE* □ **like crazy** to a great degree: *I was laughing like crazy.*

cra·zy bone ▸*n.* another term for **FUNNY BONE**.

Cra·zy Horse (*c.*1849–77), Sioux chief; Sioux name *Ta-Sunko-Witko*. A leading figure in the resistance to white settlement on Native-American land, he was at the center of the confederation that defeated General Custer at Little Bighorn in 1876. He surrendered in 1877 and was killed while in custody.

cra·zy quilt ▸*n.* a patchwork quilt of a type traditionally made in North America, with patches of randomly varying sizes, shapes, colors, and fabrics.

CRC ▸*abbr.* ■ *Printing* camera-ready copy. ■ Civil Rights Commission. ■ *Computing* cyclic redundancy check (or code).

creak /krēk/ ▸*v.* [*intrans.*] (of an object, typically a wooden one) make a harsh, high-pitched sound when being moved or when pressure or weight is applied: *the stairs creaked as she went up them* | *the garden gate creaked open.* ■ *figurative* show weakness or frailty under strain: *stock prices creaked to a mixed finish today.*

▸*n.* a harsh scraping or squeaking sound: *the creak of a floorboard broke the silence.* ▷Middle English (as a verb in the sense 'croak'): imitative. —**creak·ing·ly** *adv.*

creak·y /ˈkrēkē/ ▸*adj.* (**creak·i·er**, **creak·i·est**) (of an object, typically a wooden one) making or liable to make a harsh, high-pitched sound when being moved or when pressure or weight is applied: *I climbed the creaky stairs.* ■ (of a voice) producing such a sound. ■ *figurative* appearing old-fashioned; decrepit: *the country's creaky legal system.* —**creak·i·ly** /-kəlē/ *adv.* —**creak·i·ness** *n.*

cream /krēm/ ▸*n.* **1** the thick white or pale yellow fatty liquid that rises to the top when milk is left to stand and that can be eaten as an accompaniment to desserts or used as a cooking ingredient: *strawberries and cream* | [as *adj.*] *a cream sauce.* ■ the part of a liquid that gathers at the top. ■ *figurative* the very best of a group of people or things: *the paper's readership is* **the cream of** *American society.* ■ a sauce, soup, dessert, or similar food containing cream or milk or having the consistency of cream: *a can of* **cream of** *mushroom* **soup**. ■ a candy of a specified flavor that is creamy in texture, typically covered with chocolate: *a peppermint cream.* **2** a thick liquid or semisolid cosmetic or medical preparation applied to the skin: *shaving cream* | *moisturizing creams.* **3** a very pale yellow or off-white color: *the dress is available in white or cream* | [as *adj.*] *a cream linen jacket.*

▸*v.* [*trans.*] **1** work (butter, typically with sugar) to form a smooth soft paste. ■ [usu. as *adj.*] (**creamed**) mash (a cooked vegetable) and mix with milk or cream: *creamed turnips.* ■ add cream to (coffee). **2** rub a cosmetic cream into (the skin): *Madge was creaming her face in front of the mirror.* **3** *informal* defeat (someone) heavily, esp. in a sports contest. ■ (often **be creamed**) hit or collide heavily and violently with (someone), esp. in a car: *she got creamed by a speeding car.* **4** [*intrans.*] *vulgar slang* (of a person) be sexually aroused, esp. to the point of producing sexual secretions. ■ [*trans.*] moisten (one's underpants) due to such arousal.

▸*phrasal v.* □ **cream something off** take the best of a group of people or things, esp. in a way that is considered unfair: *the schools cream off some of the better students.* ■ make a disproportionate or excessive profit on a transaction. ▷Middle English: from Old French *cresme*, from a blend of late Latin *cramum* (probably of Gaulish origin) and ecclesiastical Latin *chrisma* (see **CHRISM**).

cream cheese ▸*n.* soft, rich cheese made from unskimmed milk and cream.

cream·er /ˈkrēmər/ ▸*n.* **1** a cream or milk substitute for adding to coffee or tea. **2** a small jug for cream. **3** *historical* a flat dish used for skimming the cream off milk. ■ a machine used for separating cream from milk.

cream·er·y /ˈkrēm(ə)rē/ ▸*n.* (*pl.* **-er·ies**) a place where butter and cheese are produced. ■ *dated* a shop where dairy products are sold. ▷mid 19th cent.: from **CREAM**, on the pattern of French *crémerie*.

cream of tar·tar ▸*n.* a white, crystalline, acidic compound obtained as a byproduct of wine fermentation and used chiefly in baking powder. • Alternative name: **potassium hydrogen tartrate**; chem. formula: $HOOC(CHOH)_2COOK$.

cream puff ▸*n.* **1** a cake made of light pastry filled with cream. **2** *informal* a weak or ineffectual person. ■ [as *adj.*] denoting something of little consequence or difficulty: *a cream-puff assignment.* **3** *informal* a secondhand car or other item maintained in excellent condition.

cream so·da ▸*n.* a carbonated, vanilla-flavored soft drink.

cream·ware /ˈkrēm,we(ə)r/ ▸*n.* glazed earthenware pottery of a rich cream color, developed by Josiah Wedgwood in about 1760.

cream·y /ˈkrēmē/ ▸*adj.* (**cream·i·er**, **cream·i·est**) resembling cream in consistency or color: *beat the sugar and egg yolks together until thick and creamy* | *creamy white flowers.* ■ containing a lot of cream: *a thick, creamy dressing.* —**cream·i·ly** /-məlē/ *adv.* —**cream·i·ness** *n.*

cre·ance /ˈkrēəns/ ▸*n. Falconry* a long, fine cord attached to a hawk's leash to prevent escape during training. ▷late 15th cent.: from French *créance* 'faith,' also denoting a cord to retain a bird of *peu de créance* ('of little faith,' i.e., which cannot yet be relied upon).

crease /krēs/ ▸*n.* **1** a line or ridge produced on paper or cloth by folding, pressing, or crushing it: *khaki trousers with knife-edge creases.* ■ a wrinkle or furrow in the skin, typically of the face, caused by age or a particular facial expression. **2** (usu. **the crease**) an area around the goal in ice hockey or lacrosse that attacking players may not normally enter unless the puck or ball has already done so. ■ *Cricket* any of a number of lines marked on the pitch at specified places, esp. the position of a batsman.

▸*v.* [*trans.*] **1** make a crease in (cloth or paper): *he sank into the chair, careful not to crease his dinner jacket* | [as *adj.*] (**creased**) *a creased piece of paper.* ■ cause a crease to appear temporarily in (the face or its features), typically as a result of the expression of an emotion or feeling: *a small frown creased her forehead.* **2** (of a bullet) graze (someone or something), causing little damage: *a bullet creased his thigh.* ▷late 16th cent.: probably a variant of **CREST**.

cre·ate /krēˈāt/ ▸*v.* [*trans.*] bring (something) into existence: *he created a thirty-acre lake* | *over 170 jobs were* *created.* ■ cause (something) to happen as a result of one's actions: *divorce only created problems for children.* ■ (of an actor) originate (a role) by playing a character for the first time. ■ invest (someone) with a new rank or title: *he was created a baronet.* ▷late Middle English (in the sense 'form out of nothing,' used of a divine or supernatural being): from Latin *creat-* 'produced,' from the verb *creare.*

cre·a·tine /'krēə,tēn; 'krēətn/ ▶*n. Biochemistry* a compound formed in protein metabolism and present in much living tissue. It is involved in the supply of energy for muscular contraction. • A guanidine derivative, usually present as a phosphate; chem. formula: $C_4H_9N_3O_2$. ▷mid 19th cent.: formed irregularly from Greek *kreas* 'meat' + -INE[4].

cre·a·tine phos·phate ▶*n.* another term for PHOSPHOCREATINE.

cre·at·i·nine /krē'atn,ēn; -'atn-in/ ▶*n. Biochemistry* a compound that is produced by metabolism of creatine and excreted in the urine. • An anhydride of creatine; chem. formula: $C_7H_4N_3O$.

cre·a·tion /krē'āshən/ ▶*n.* **1** the action or process of bringing something into existence: *the creation of a coalition government | job creation.* ■ a thing that has been made or invented, esp. something showing artistic talent: *she treats fictional creations as if they were real people.* **2** (**the Creation**) the bringing into of existence of the universe, esp. when regarded as an act of God. ■ everything so created; the universe: *our alienation from the rest of Creation.* **3** the action or process of investing someone with a new rank or title. ▷late Middle English: via Old French from Latin *creatio(n-),* from the verb *creare* (see CREATE).

cre·a·tion·ism /krē'āshə,nizəm/ ▶*n.* the belief that the universe and living organisms originate from specific acts of divine creation, as in the biblical account, rather than by natural processes such as evolution. ■ another term for CREATION SCIENCE. —**cre·a·tion·ist** *n.* & *adj.*

cre·a·tion sci·ence ▶*n.* the interpretation of scientific knowledge in accord with belief in the literal truth of the Bible, esp. regarding the creation of matter, life, and humankind in six days.

cre·a·tive /krē'ātiv/ ▶*adj.* relating to or involving the imagination or original ideas, esp. in the production of an artistic work: *change unleashes people's creative energy | creative writing.* ■ (of a person) having good imagination or original ideas: *Homer, the creative genius of Greek epic.*
▶*n.* a person who is creative, typically in a professional context. —**cre·a·tive·ly** *adv.* —**cre·a·tive·ness** *n.*

THE RIGHT WORD **creative, imaginative, ingenious inventive, original, resourceful,**

Everyone likes to think that he or she is **creative**, which is used to describe the active, exploratory minds possessed by artists, writers, and inventors (*a creative approach to problem-solving*). Today, however, *creative* has become an advertising buzzword (*creative cooking, | creative hairstyling*) that simply means new or different.

Original is more specific and limited in scope. Someone who is *original* comes up with things that no one else has thought of (*an original approach to constructing a doghouse*), or thinks in an independent and creative way (*| a highly original filmmaker*).

Imaginative implies having an active and creative imagination, which often means that the person visualizes things quite differently than the way they appear in the real world (*imaginative illustrations for a children's book*).

The practical side of *imaginative* is **inventive**; the *inventive* person figures out how to make things work (*an inventive solution to the problem of getting a wheelchair into a van*).

But where an *inventive* mind tends to comes up with solutions to problems it has posed for itself, a **resourceful** mind deals successfully with externally imposed problems or limitations (*A resourceful child can amuse herself with simple wooden blocks*).

Someone who is **ingenious** is both *inventive* and *resourceful*, with a dose of cleverness thrown in (*the ingenious idea of using recycled plastic to create a warm, fleecelike fabric*).

cre·a·tive ac·count·an·cy (also **cre·a·tive ac·count·ing**) ▶*n. informal* the exploitation of loopholes in financial regulation in order to gain advantage or present figures in a misleadingly favorable light.

cre·a·tiv·i·ty /,krē-ā'tivitē/ ▶*n.* the use of the imagination or original ideas, esp. in the production of an artistic work.

cre·a·tor /krē'ātər/ ▶*n.* a person or thing that brings something into existence. ■ (**the Creator**) used as a name for God.

crea·ture /'krēchər/ ▶*n.* an animal, as distinct from a human being: *night sounds of birds and other creatures.* ■ an animal or person: *as fellow creatures on this planet, animals deserve respect.* ■ a fictional or imaginary being, typically a frightening one: *a creature from outer space.* ■ *archaic* anything living or existing: *dress, jewels, and other transitory creatures.* ■ a person of a specified kind, typically one viewed with pity, contempt, or desire: *you heartless creature!* ■ a person or organization considered to be under the complete control of another: *the village teacher was expected to be the creature of his employer.* ▷Middle English (in the sense 'something created'): via Old French from late Latin *creatura,* from the verb *creare* (see CREATE). —**crea·ture·ly** *adj.*
▶***PHRASE*** □ **creature of habit** a person who follows an unvarying routine.

crea·ture com·forts ▶*plural n.* material comforts that contribute to physical ease and well-being, such as good food and accommodations.

crèche /kresh/ ▶*n.* **1** a model or tableau representing the scene of Jesus Christ's birth, displayed in homes or public places at Christmas. **2** *Brit.* a nursery where babies and young children are cared for during the working day. ▷late 18th cent. (sense 1): French.

Cré·cy, Battle of /krā'sē/ a battle between the English and the French in 1346 near the village of Crécy-en-Ponthieu in Picardy, at which the forces of Edward III defeated those of Philip VI. It was the first major English victory of the Hundred Years War.

cred /kred/ ▶*n.* informal term for STREET CREDIBILITY.

cred·al /'krēdl/ (also **creed·al**) ▶*adj.* of or relating to a statement of Christian or other religious belief.

cre·dence /'krēdns/ ▶*n.* **1** belief in or acceptance of something as true: *psychoanalysis finds little credence among laymen.* ■ the likelihood of something being true; plausibility: *being called upon by the media as an expert* ***lends credence*** *to one's opinions.* **2** [usu. as *adj.*] a small side table, shelf, or niche in a church for holding the elements of the Eucharist before they are consecrated: *a credence table.* ▷Middle English: via Old French from medieval Latin *credentia,* from Latin *credent-* 'believing,' from the verb *credere.*
▶***PHRASE*** □ **give credence to** accept as true.

cre·den·tial /krə'denchəl/ ▶*n.* (usu. **credentials**) a qualification, achievement, personal quality, or aspect of a person's background, typically when used to indicate that they are suitable for something: *recruitment is based mainly on academic credentials.* ■ a document or certificate proving a person's identity or qualifications. ■ a letter of introduction given by a government to an ambassador before a new posting. ▷late Middle English: from medieval Latin *credentialis,* from *credentia* (see CREDENCE). The original use was as an adjective in the sense 'giving credence to, recommending,' frequently in *credential letters* or *papers,* hence *credentials* (mid 17th cent.).

cre·den·tialed /krə'denshəld/ ▶*adj.* awarded or in possession of credentials: *impeccably credentialed professionals.*

cre·den·za /krə'denzə/ ▶*n.* a sideboard or cupboard. ▷late 19th cent.: Italian, from medieval Latin *credentia* (see CREDENCE).

cred·i·bil·i·ty /,kredə'bilitē/ ▶*n.* the quality of being trusted and believed in: *the government's loss of credibility.* ■ the quality of being convincing or believable: *the book's anecdotes have scant regard for credibility.* ■ another term for STREET CREDIBILITY. ▷mid 16th cent.: from medieval Latin *credibilitas,* from Latin *credibilis* (see CREDIBLE).

cred·i·bil·i·ty gap ▶*n.* an apparent difference between what is said or promised and what happens or is true. ■ a lack of trust in a person's or institution's statements and motives: *the* Times*'s worst enemy is a continuing credibility gap.*

cred·i·ble /'kredəbəl/ ▶*adj.* able to be believed; convincing: *few people found his story credible | a credible witness.* See note at BELIEVABLE. ■ capable of persuading people that something will happen or be successful: *a credible threat.* ▷late Middle English: from Latin *credibilis,* from *credere* 'believe.' —**cred·i·bly** /-blē/ *adv.*

cred·it /'kredit/ ▶*n.* **1** the ability of a customer to obtain goods or services before payment, based on the trust that payment will be made in the future: *I've got unlimited credit.* ■ the money lent or made available under such an arrangement: *the bank refused to extend their credit |* [as *adj.*] *he was exceeding his credit limit.* **2** an entry recording a sum received, listed on the right-hand side or column of an account. The opposite of DEBIT. ■ a payment received: *you need to record debits or credits made to your account.* **3** public acknowledgment or praise, typically that given or received when a person's responsibility for an action or idea becomes or is made apparent: *the president claims credit for each accomplishment.* ■ [in *sing.*] a source of pride, typically someone or something that reflects well on another person or organization: *he's* ***a credit to*** *his mother.* ■ (usu. **credits**) an acknowledgment of a contributor's services to a movie or a television program, typically one of a list that is scrolled down the screen at the beginning or end of a movie or program: *the closing credits finished rolling.* **4** the acknowledgment of a student's completion of a course that counts toward a degree or diploma as maintained in a school's records: *a student can earn one unit of academic credit.* ■ a unit of study counting toward a degree or diploma: *in his first semester he earned 17 credits.* ■ acknowledgment of merit in an examination which is reflected in the grades awarded: *students will receive credit for accuracy and style.* **5** *archaic* the quality of being believed or credited: *the abstract philosophy of Cicero has lost its credit.* ■ favorable estimation; good reputation: *John Gilpin was a citizen of credit and renown.*
▶*v.* (**cred·it·ed, cred·it·ing**) [*trans.*] (often **be credited**) **1** publicly acknowledge someone as a participant in the production of (something published or broadcast): *the screenplay is* ***credited to*** *one American and two Japanese writers.* ■ (**credit someone with**) ascribe (an achievement or good quality) to someone: *he is credited with painting one hundred and twenty-five canvases.* **2** add (an amount of money) to an account: *this deferred tax can be* ***credited to*** *the profit and loss account.* **3** believe (something surprising or unlikely): *you would hardly credit it—but it was true.* ▷mid 16th cent. (originally in the senses 'belief,' 'credibility'): from French *crédit,* probably via Italian *credito* from Latin *creditum,* neuter past participle of *credere* 'believe, trust.'
▶***PHRASES*** □ **credit where credit is due** praise given when it is deserved, even if one is reluctant to give it. □ **do someone credit** (or **do credit to someone**) make someone worthy of praise or respect: *your concern does you credit.* □ **give someone credit for** commend someone for (a quality or achievement), esp. with reluctance or surprise: *please give me credit for some sense.* □ **have something to one's credit** have achieved something notable: *he has 65 tournament wins to his credit.* □ **on credit** with an arrangement to pay later. □ **on the credit side** as a good aspect of the situation: *on the credit side, the text is highly readable.* □ **to one's credit** used to indicate that something praiseworthy has been achieved, esp. despite difficulties: *to her credit, she had never betrayed a confidence.*

cred·it·a·ble /'kreditəbəl/ ▶*adj.* (of a performance, effort, or action) deserving public acknowledgment and praise but not necessarily outstanding or successful: *a very creditable 2–4 defeat.* See note at BELIEVABLE. —**cred·it·a·bil·i·ty** /,kreditə'bilitē/ *n.* —**cred·it·a·bly** /'kreditəblē/ *adv.*

cred·it an·a·lyst ▶*n.* a person employed to assess the credit rating of people or companies.

cred·it bu·reau ▶*n.* a company that collects information relating to the credit ratings of individuals and makes it available to credit card companies, financial institutions, etc.

cred·it card ▶*n.* a small plastic card issued by a bank, business, etc., allowing the holder to purchase goods or services on credit.

cred·it line ▶*n.* another term for LINE OF CREDIT (see LINE[1]).

cred·i·tor /'kreditər/ ▶*n.* a person or company to whom money is owed.

cred·it rat·ing ▶*n.* an estimate of the ability of a person or organization to fulfill their financial commitments, based on previous dealings. ■ the process of assessing this.

cred·it score ▶*n. Finance* a number assigned to a person that indicates to lenders their capacity to repay a loan.

cred·it un·ion ▶*n.* a nonprofit-making money cooperative whose members can borrow from pooled deposits at low interest rates.

cred·it·worth·y /'kredit,wərthē/ ▶*adj.* (of a person or company) considered suitable to receive credit, esp.

because of being reliable in paying money back in the past. **—cred·it·wor·thi·ness** *n.*

cre·do /ˈkrēdō; ˈkrādō/ ▸*n.* (*pl.* **-dos**) a statement of the beliefs or aims that guide someone's actions: *he announced his credo in his first editorial.* ■ (**Credo**) a creed of the Christian Church in Latin. ■ (**Credo**) a musical setting of the Nicene Creed, typically as part of a mass. ▷Middle English: Latin, 'I believe.' Compare with CREED.

cre·du·li·ty /krəˈd(y)o͞olitē/ ▸*n.* a tendency to be too ready to believe that something is real or true.

cred·u·lous /ˈkrejələs/ ▸*adj.* having or showing too great a readiness to believe things. See note at GULLIBLE. ▷late 16th cent. (in the general sense 'inclined to believe'): from Latin *credulus* (from *credere* 'believe') + -OUS. **—cred·u·lous·ly** *adv.* **—cred·u·lous·ness** *n.*

Cree /krē/ ▸*n.* (*pl.* same or **Crees**) **1** a member of a American Indian people living in a vast area of central Canada. **2** the Algonquian language of this people, closely related to Montagnais.
▸*adj.* of or relating to the Cree or their language. ▷from Canadian French *Cris*, abbreviation of *Cristinaux*, from Algonquian *kiristinō*.

creed /krēd/ ▸*n.* a system of Christian or other religious belief; a faith: *people of many creeds and cultures.* ■ (often **the Creed**) a formal statement of Christian beliefs, esp. the Apostles' Creed or the Nicene Creed. ■ a set of beliefs or aims that guide someone's actions: *liberalism was more than a political creed.* ▷Old English, from Latin CREDO.

creed·al /ˈkrēdl/ ▸*adj.* variant spelling of CREDAL.

Creek /krēk/ ▸*n.* (*pl.* same) **1** a member of a confederacy of native peoples of the southeastern U.S. in the 16th to 19th centuries whose descendants now live mainly in Oklahoma. **2** the Muskogean language of this confederacy.
▸*adj.* of, relating to, or denoting this confederacy. ▷from CREEK, because they lived beside the waterways of the flatlands of Georgia and Alabama.

creek /krēk; krik/ ▸*n.* a stream, brook, or minor tributary of a river. ■ an inlet in a shoreline, a channel in a marsh, or another narrow, sheltered waterway. ▷Middle English: from Old French *crique* or from Old Norse *kriki* 'nook'; perhaps reinforced by Middle Dutch *krēke*; of unknown ultimate origin.
▸*PHRASES* □ **be up the creek** *informal* (also **be up the creek without a paddle**) be in severe difficulty or trouble, esp. with no means of extricating oneself from it. □ **be up shit creek** see SHIT.

creel /krēl/ ▸*n.* **1** a large wicker basket for carrying fish. ■ an angler's fishing basket. **2** a rack holding bobbins or spools for spinning. ▷Middle English (sense 1; originally Scots and northern English): of unknown origin. Sense 2 (perhaps the same word) dates from the mid 19th cent.

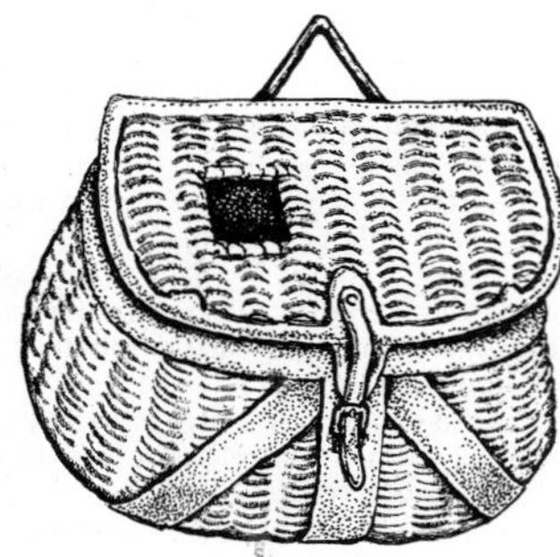

creel 1

creep /krēp/ ▸*v.* (*past* and *past part.* **crept** /krept/) [*intrans.*] **1** move slowly and carefully, esp. in order to avoid being heard or noticed: *he crept downstairs, hardly making any noise | they were taught how to* ***creep up on*** *an enemy.* ■ (of a thing) move very slowly at an inexorably steady pace: *the fog was creeping up from the marsh.* ■ (of a plant) grow along the ground or other surface by means of extending stems or branches: [as *adj.*] (**creeping**) *tufts of fine leaves grow on creeping rhizomes.* ■ (of a plastic solid) undergo gradual deformation under stress. **2** (**creep in/into**) (of an unwanted and negative characteristic or fact) occur or develop gradually and almost imperceptibly: *errors crept into his game |* [as *adj.*] (**creeping**) *the creeping centralization of power.* ■ (**creep up**) increase slowly but steadily in number or amount: *interest rates have been creeping up in the past few weeks.*
▸*n.* **1** *informal* a detestable person. ■ a person who behaves in an obsequious way in the hope of advancement. **2** slow movement, esp. at a steady but almost imperceptible pace: *an attempt to prevent this slow creep of costs.* ■ the tendency of a car with automatic transmission to move when in gear without the accelerator being pressed. ■ the gradual downward movement of disintegrated rock or soil due to gravitational forces: *stones and earth slowly slip down the slopes by soil creep.* ■ the gradual deformation of a plastic solid under stress. ■ gradual bulging of the floor of a mine owing to pressure on the pillars. ▷Old English *crēopan* 'move with the body close to the ground,' of Germanic origin; related to Dutch *kruipen*. Sense 1 of the *verb* dates from Middle English.
▸*PHRASES* □ **give someone the creeps** *informal* induce a feeling of revulsion or fear in someone. □ **make one's flesh creep** feel disgust or revulsion and have a sensation like that of something crawling over the skin.

creep·er /ˈkrēpər/ ▸*n.* **1** *Botany* any plant that grows along the ground, around another plant, or up a wall by means of extending stems or branches. **2** any of a number of small birds that creep around in trees, vegetation, etc.: • (**brown creeper**) the American treecreeper (*Certhia americana*, family Certhiidae). • (**brown creeper**) *NZ* a New Zealand songbird (*Mohoua* (or **Finschia**) *novaeseelandiae*, family Pachycephalidae or Acanthizidae). • a Philippine songbird (family Rhabdornithidae and genus *Rhabdornis*: two species). • a Hawaiian honeycreeper (genus *Paroreomyza*, family Drepanididae: three species). **3** a low, wheeled platform on which a mechanic lies while working on the underside of a motor vehicle.

creep·ing Char·lie ▸*n.* a creeping or trailing plant, in particular: ■ another term for MONEYWORT. ■ another term for GROUND IVY.

creep·ing Jen·ny ▸*n.* another term for MONEYWORT.

creep·y /ˈkrēpē/ ▸*adj.* (**creep·i·er, creep·i·est**) *informal* causing an unpleasant feeling of fear or unease: *the creepy feelings one often gets in a strange house.* **—creep·i·ly** /-pəlē/ *adv.* **—creep·i·ness** *n.*

creep·y-crawl·y /ˈkrôlē/ *informal* ▸*n.* (*pl.* **-crawl·ies**) a spider, worm, or other small, flightless creature, esp. when considered unpleasant or frightening.
▸*adj.* causing an unpleasant feeling of fear or unease: *creepy-crawly stories.*

creese ▸*n.* archaic spelling of KRIS.

cre·mas·ter /kriˈmastər/ ▸*n.* **1** (also **cre·mas·ter mus·cle**) *Anatomy* the muscle of the spermatic cord, by which the testicle can be partially raised. **2** *Entomology* the hooklike tip of a butterfly pupa, serving as an anchorage point. ▷late 17th cent.: from Greek *kremastēr*, from *krema-* 'hang.'

cre·mate /ˈkrēˌmāt; kriˈmāt/ ▸*v.* [*trans.*] (usu. **be cremated**) dispose of (a dead person's body) by burning it to ashes, typically after a funeral ceremony. ■ to burn (something), typically food. ▷late 19th cent. (as *cremation*): from Latin *cremare* 'burn.' **—cre·ma·tion** /kriˈmāsHən/ *n.* **—cre·ma·tor** /-mātər/ *n.*

cre·ma·to·ri·um /ˌkrēməˈtôrēəm; ˌkrem-/ ▸*n.* (*pl.* **-to·ri·a** /-ˈtôrēə/ or **-to·ri·ums**) another term for CREMATORY. ▷late 19th cent.: modern Latin, from *cremare* 'burn.'

cre·ma·to·ry /ˈkrēməˌtôrē; ˈkrem-/ ▸*n.* (*pl.* **-ries**) a place where a dead person's body is cremated.
▸*adj.* of or relating to cremation.

crème an·glaise /ˌkrem äNGˈglez; -ˈglāz/ ▸*n.* a rich egg custard. ▷French, literally 'English cream.'

crème brû·lée /ˌkrem bro͞oˈlā/ ▸*n.* (*pl.* **crèmes brû·lées** *pronunc.* same, or **crème brû·lées** /bro͞oˈlāz/) a dessert of custard topped with caramelized sugar. ▷late 19th cent.: French, literally 'burned cream.'

crème car·a·mel /ˌkrem karəˈmel; ˈkarəˌmel/ ▸*n.* (*pl.* **crèmes car·a·mel** *pronunc.* same, or **crème car·a·mels** /-ˈmelz; -ˌmelz/) a custard dessert made with whipped cream and eggs and topped with caramel. ▷early 20th cent.: French, literally 'caramel custard.'

crème de ca·ca·o /ˌkrem də kəˈkou; ˈkōkō/ ▸*n.* a chocolate-flavored liqueur. ▷mid 20th cent.: French, literally 'cream of cacao.'

crème de cas·sis /ˌkrem də kaˈsēs/ ▸*n.* see CASSIS[1]. ▷French, literally 'cream of black currant.'

crème de la crème /ˌkrem də lə ˈkrem/ ▸*n.* the best person or thing of a particular kind: *the crème de la crème of the dancers have left the country.* ▷mid 19th cent.: French, literally 'cream of the cream.'

crème de menthe /ˌkrēm də ˈmenTH ˌkrēm; ˈmint/ ▸*n.* a peppermint-flavored liqueur. ▷early 20th cent.: French, literally 'cream of mint.'

crème fraiche /ˌkrem ˈfresH/ ▸*n.* a type of thick cream made from heavy cream with the addition of buttermilk, sour cream, or yogurt. ▷from French *crème fraîche*, literally 'fresh cream.'

Cre·mo·na /krəˈmōnə/ a city in northern Italy, in Lombardy; pop. 75,160. Between the 16th and the 18th century the city was home to three renowned families of violin-makers: the Amati, the Guarneri, and the Stradivari.

cre·nate /ˈkrēˌnāt/ ▸*adj. Botany & Zoology* (esp. of a leaf or shell) having a round-toothed or scalloped edge. Compare with CRENULATE. ▷late 18th cent. (earlier as *crenated*): from modern Latin *crenatus*, from popular Latin *crena* 'notch.' **—cre·nat·ed** *adj.* **—cre·na·tion** /kriˈnāsHən/ *n.*

cren·el /ˈkrenl/ (also **cre·nelle** /krəˈnel/) ▸*n.* an indentation in the battlements of a fort or castle, used for shooting or firing missiles through. ▷late 15th cent.: from Old French, based on popular Latin *crena* 'notch.'

cren·el·late /ˈkrenlˌāt/ (also **cren·e·late**) ▸*v.* [*trans.*] [usu. as *adj.*] (**crenellated**) *chiefly historical* provide (a wall of a building) with battlements. ▷early 19th cent.: from French *créneler*, from Old French *crenel* (see CRENEL).

cren·el·la·tions /ˌkrenlˈāsHənz/ ▸*plural n.* the battlements of a castle or other building.

cren·u·late /ˈkrenyəlit; -yəˌlāt/ ▸*adj. technical* (esp. of a leaf, shell, or shoreline) having a finely scalloped or notched outline or edge. Compare with CRENATE. ▷late 18th cent.: from modern Latin *crenulatus*, from *crenula*, diminutive of *crena* 'notch.' **—cren·u·lat·ed** *adj.* **—cren·u·la·tion** /ˌkrenyəˈlāsHən/ *n.*

cre·o·dont /ˈkrēəˌdänt/ ▸*n.* an extinct carnivorous mammal of the early Tertiary period, ancestral to modern carnivores. • Order Creodonta: several families. ▷late 19th cent.: from modern Latin *Creodonta* (plural), from Greek *kreas* 'flesh' + *odous, odont-* 'tooth.'

Cre·ole /ˈkrēˌōl/ (also **cre·ole**) ▸*n.* **1** a person of mixed European and black descent, esp. in the Caribbean. ■ a descendant of Spanish or other European settlers in the Caribbean or Central or South America. ■ a white descendant of French settlers in Louisiana and other parts of the southern U.S. **2** a mother tongue formed from the contact of two languages through an earlier pidgin stage: *a Portuguese-based Creole.*
▸*adj.* of or relating to a Creole or Creoles. ▷from French *créole, criole*, from Spanish *criollo*, probably from Portuguese *crioulo* 'black person born in Brazil, home-born slave,' from *criar* 'to breed,' from Latin *creare* 'produce, create.'

cre·o·lize /ˈkrēəˌlīz/ ▸*v.* [*trans.*] form (a Creole language) from the contact of two languages: [as *adj.*] (**creolized**) *a creolized variety of French.* **—cre·o·li·za·tion** /ˌkrēələˈzāsHən/ *n.*

cre·o·sol /ˈkrēəˌsôl; -ˌsōl/ ▸*n. Chemistry* a colorless liquid that is the chief constituent of wood-tar creosote. • Alternative name: **2-methoxy-4-methylphenol**; chem. formula: $C_8H_{10}O_2$. ▷mid 19th cent.: from CREOSOTE + -OL.

cre·o·sote /ˈkrēəˌsōt/ ▸*n.* (also **creosote oil**) a dark brown oil distilled from coal tar and used as a wood preservative. It contains a number of phenols, cresols, and other organic compounds. ■ a colorless, pungent, oily liquid, containing creosol and other compounds, distilled from wood tar and used as an antiseptic.
▸*v.* [*trans.*] treat (wood) with creosote. ▷mid 19th cent.: coined in German from Greek *kreas* 'flesh' + *sōtēr* 'preserver,' with reference to its antiseptic properties.

cre·o·sote bush ▸*n.* a shrub native to arid parts of Mexico and the western U.S. Its leaves smell of creosote and when steeped in boiling water, they yield an antiseptic lotion. • *Larrea tridentata*, family Zygophyllaceae.

crepe (also **crêpe**) ▸*n.* **1** /krāp/ a light, thin fabric with a wrinkled surface: [as *adj.*] *a silk crepe blouse.* ■ (also **crepe rubber**) hard-wearing wrinkled rubber, used esp. for the soles of shoes. **2** /krāp/ black silk or imitation silk, formerly used for mourning clothes. ■ a band of such fabric formerly worn around a person's hat as a sign of mourning. **3** /krāp; krep/ a thin pancake. ▷late 18th cent.: French, from Old French *crespe* 'curled, frizzed,' from Latin *crispus*. **—crep·ey** *adj.*

crepe de chine /ˌkrāp də ˈsHēn/ (also **crepe de Chine**) ▸*n.* a fine crepe of silk or similar fiber. ▷late 19th cent.: French, literally 'crêpe of China.'

crepe myr·tle ▸*n.* variant spelling of CRAPE MYRTLE.

crepe pa·per ▸*n.* thin, crinkled paper resembling crepe, used esp. for making decorations.

crêp·er·ie /ˌkrep(ə)ˈrē ˈkrāpərē/ ▸*n.* (*pl.* **-er·ies**) a small restaurant, typically one in France, in which a variety of crêpes are served. ▷French.

crêpe su·zette /ˌkrāp so͞oˈzet/ ▸*n.* (*pl.* **crêpes su·zette** *pronunc.* same) a thin dessert pancake with a brandy and citrus sauce, usually set aflame when served.

crépinette /ˌkrāpəˈnet; ˌkrep-/ ▸*n.* a flat sausage consisting of minced meat and savory stuffing wrapped in pieces of pork caul. ▷French, diminutive of *crêpine* 'caul.'

crep·i·tate /ˈkrepəˌtāt/ ▸*v.* [*intrans.*] make a crackling sound: *the night crepitates with an airy, whistling cacophony* | [as *adj.*] (**crepitating**) *spidery fingers of crepitating electricity.* ▷early 17th cent. (in the sense 'break wind'): from Latin *crepitat-* 'crackled, rustled,' from the verb *crepitare,* from *crepare* 'to rattle.' **—crep·i·tant** /ˈkrepətənt/ *adj.*

crep·i·ta·tion /ˌkrepəˈtāsHən/ ▸*n.* a crackling or rattling sound: *pistollike crepitations.* ■ *Medicine* a crackling sound made in breathing by a person with an inflamed lung, detected using a stethoscope. ■ *Entomology* the explosive ejection of irritant fluid from the abdomen of a bombardier beetle. ▷mid 17th cent.: from French *crépitation* or Latin *crepitatio(n-),* from the verb *crepitare* (see CREPITATE).

crep·i·tus /ˈkrepətəs/ ▸*n. Medicine* a grating sound or sensation produced by friction between bone and cartilage or the fractured parts of a bone. ■ the production of crepitations in the lungs; rale. ▷early 19th cent.: from Latin, from *crepare* 'rattle.'

cré·pon /ˈkrāˌpän/ ▸*n.* a fabric resembling crepe, but heavier and with a more pronounced crinkled effect. ▷late 19th cent.: French.

crept /krept/ ▸ past and past participle of CREEP.

cre·pus·cu·lar /krəˈpəskyələr/ ▸*adj.* of, resembling, or relating to twilight. ■ *Zoology* (of an animal) appearing or active in twilight. ▷mid 17th cent.: from Latin *crepusculum* 'twilight' + -AR[1].

cre·pus·cule /kriˈpəsˌkyo͞ol/ ▸*n.* the period of partial darkness at the beginning or end of the day; twilight.

cresc. (also **cres.**) *Music* ▸*abbr.* crescendo.

cre·scen·do /krəˈSHendō/ ▸*n.* (*pl.* **-dos** or **-di** /-dē/) *Music* a gradual increase in loudness in a piece of music. ■ *Music* a passage of music marked to be performed in this way. ■ the loudest point reached in a gradually increasing sound: *Deborah's voice was rising* ***to a crescendo.*** ■ a progressive increase in force or intensity: *a crescendo of misery.* ■ the most intense point reached in this; a climax: *the negative reviews* ***reached a crescendo*** *in mid-February.*
▸*adv.* & *adj. Music* with a gradual increase in loudness: [as *adj.*] *a short crescendo kettledrum roll.*
▸*v.* (**-does, -doed**) [*intrans.*] increase in loudness or intensity: *the reluctant cheers began to crescendo.* ▷late 18th cent.: Italian, present participle of *crescere* 'to increase,' from Latin *crescere* 'grow.'

cres·cent /ˈkresənt/ ▸*n.* **1** the curved sickle shape of the waxing or waning moon. ■ a representation of such a shape used as an emblem of Islam or of Turkey. ■ (**the Crescent**) *chiefly historical* the political power of Islam or of the Ottoman Empire. **2** a thing that has has the shape of a single curve, esp. one that is broad in the center and tapers to a point at each end: *a three-mile crescent of golden sand* | *a crescent-shaped building.* ■ a street or row of houses forming an arc: *we lived at Westway Crescent.* ■ *Heraldry* a charge in the form of a crescent, typically with the points upward (also a mark of cadency for a second son). **3** a moth or butterfly that bears crescent-shaped markings on the wings, in particular: • an orange or brown American butterfly with a silvery mark on the underside of the hind wing (genus *Phyciodes,* subfamily Melitaeinae, family Nymphalidae). • a brownish European moth with a pale mark on the forewing (several species in the family Noctuidae, in particular *Celaena leucostigma*).
▸*adj.* **1** having the shape of a crescent: *a crescent moon.* **2** *poetic/literary* growing, increasing, or developing. ▷late Middle English *cressant,* from Old French *creissant,* from Latin *crescere* 'grow.' The spelling change in the 17th century was due to the influence of the Latin. **—cres·cen·tic** /krəˈsentik/ *adj.*

cres·cent wrench ▸*n.* an adjustable wrench designed to grip hexagonal nuts, with an adjusting screw fitted in the crescent-shaped head of the wrench.

cre·sol /ˈkrēˌsôl; -ˌsōl/ ▸*n. Chemistry* each of three isomeric crystalline compounds present in coal-tar creosote, used as disinfectants. • The *ortho-, meta-,* and *para-*methyl derivatives of phenol; chem. formula: $CH_3C_6H_4OH$. ▷mid 19th cent.: from CREOSOTE + -OL.

cress /kres/ ▸*n.* a plant of the cabbage family, typically having small white flowers and pungent leaves. Some kinds are edible and are eaten raw as salad. • *Barbarea* and other genera, family Brassicaceae: several species, including **garden cress** and **watercress.** ▷Old English *cresse, cærse;* related to Dutch *kers* and German *Kresse.*

cres·set /ˈkresit/ ▸*n. historical* a metal container of oil, grease, wood, or coal burned as a torch and typically mounted on a pole. ▷late Middle English: from Old French, from *craisse,* variant of *graisse* 'oil, grease.'

Cres·si·da /ˈkresədə/ (in medieval legends of the Trojan War) the daughter of Calchas, a priest. She was unfaithful to her lover Troilus, a son of Priam.

crest /krest/ ▸*n.* **1** a comb or tuft of feathers, fur, or skin on the head of a bird or other animal. ■ a thing resembling such a tuft, esp. a plume of feathers on a helmet. **2** the top of something, esp. a mountain or hill: *she reached the crest of the hill.* ■ the curling foamy top of a wave. ■ *Anatomy* a ridge along the surface of a bone. ■ the upper line of the neck of a horse or other mammal. **3** *Heraldry* a distinctive device borne above the shield of a coat of arms (originally as worn on a helmet), or separately reproduced, for example on writing paper or silverware, to represent a family or corporate body.
▸*v.* [*trans.*] reach the top of (something such as a hill or wave): *she crested a hill and saw the valley spread out before her.* ■ [*intrans.*] (of a river) rise to its highest level: *the river was expected to crest at eight feet above flood stage.* ■ [*intrans.*] (of a wave) form a curling foamy top. ■ (**be crested**) have attached or affixed at the top: *his helmet was* ***crested with*** *a fan of spikes.* ▷Middle English: from Old French *creste,* from Latin *crista* 'tuft, plume.' **—crest·less** *adj.*

crest·ed /ˈkrestid/ ▸*adj.* **1** (of a bird or other animal) having a comb or tuft of feathers, fur, or skin on the head: *the crested drake mandarin duck* | *a plush-crested jay.* **2** emblazoned with a coat of arms or other emblem: *crested notepaper.*

crest·ed tit ▸*n.* a small European tit (songbird) with a short crest, living chiefly in coniferous woodland. • *Parus cristatus,* family Paridae.

crest·ed wood i·bis ▸*n.* see WOOD IBIS (sense 2).

crest·fal·len /ˈkrestˌfôlən/ ▸*adj.* sad and disappointed: *he came back empty-handed and crestfallen.* ▷late 16th cent.: figuratively, from the original use referring to a mammal or bird having a fallen or drooping crest.

crest·fish /ˈkrestˌfiSH/ ▸*n.* (*pl.* same or **-fish·es**) a very elongated silvery marine fish with a crimson dorsal fin running the full length of its body and a forehead that projects forward into a long filament. • *Lophotus lacepedei,* family Lophotidae.

crest·ing /ˈkrestiNG/ ▸*n.* an ornamental decoration at the ridge of a roof or top of a wall or screen.

cres·yl /ˈkresəl; ˈkrēˌsil/ ▸*n.* [as *adj.*] *Chemistry* of or denoting a radical $-OC_6H_4CH_3$, derived from a cresol.

Cre·ta·ceous /krəˈtāsHəs/ ▸*adj. Geology* of, relating to, or denoting the last period of the Mesozoic era, between the Jurassic and Tertiary periods. ■ [as *n.*] (**the Cretaceous**) the Cretaceous period or the system of rocks deposited during it.

The Cretaceous lasted from about 146 million to 65 million years ago. The climate was warm, and the sea level rose; the period is characterized esp. in northwestern Europe and parts of North America by the deposition of chalk. The first flowering plants emerged, and the domination of the dinosaurs continued although they died out quite abruptly toward the end of it.

▷late 17th cent.: from Latin *cretaceus* (from *creta* 'chalk') + -OUS.

Cre·ta·ceous–Ter·ti·ar·y bound·a·ry (also **K/T boundary**) *Geology* the division between the Cretaceous and Tertiary periods, about 65 million years ago.

A widespread layer of sediment dating from this time has been shown since 1980 to be enriched in iridium and other elements and carbon deposits indicative of extensive fires. This appears to indicate the catastrophic impact of one or more large meteorites, and geologists have identified a formation at Chicxulub in the Yucatán Peninsula, Mexico, as a probable impact site. A resulting drastic climate change has been suggested as the cause of the extinction of dinosaurs and many other organisms at this time, but this remains controversial.

Crete /krēt/ a Greek island in the eastern Mediterranean Sea; pop. 536,980; capital, Heraklion. It is noted for the remains of the Minoan civilization that flourished here in the 2nd millennium BC. Crete played an important role in the Greek struggle for independence from the Turks in the late 19th and early 20th centuries that resulted in it becoming administratively part of an independent Greece in 1913. Greek name **KRÍTI.** **—Cre·tan** /ˈkrētn/ *adj.* & *n.*

cre·tic /ˈkrētik/ ▸*n. Prosody* a metrical foot containing one short or unstressed syllable between two long or stressed ones. ▷late 16th cent.: from Latin *Creticus,* from Greek *Krētikos,* from *Krētē* 'Crete.'

cre·tin /ˈkrētn/ ▸*n.* a stupid person (used as a general term of abuse). ■ *dated Medicine* a person who is deformed and mentally handicapped because of congenital thyroid deficiency. ▷late 18th cent.: from French *crétin,* from Swiss French *crestin* 'Christian' (from Latin *Christianus*), here used to mean 'human being,' apparently as a reminder that, though deformed, cretins were human and not beasts. **—cre·tin·ism** /-ˌizəm/ *n.* **—cre·tin·ous** /-əs/ *adj.*

cre·tonne /ˈkrēˌtän; kriˈtän/ ▸*n.* a heavy cotton fabric, typically with a floral pattern printed on one or both sides, used for upholstery. ▷late 19th cent.: from French, of unknown origin.

Creutz·feldt–Ja·kob dis·ease /ˈkroitsˌfelt ˈyäkôb/ ▸*n.* a fatal degenerative disease affecting nerve cells in the brain, causing mental, physical, and sensory disturbances such as dementia and seizures. It is believed to be caused by prions and hence to be related to BSE and other spongiform encephalopathies such as kuru and scrapie. ▷1930s: named after H. G. *Creutzfeldt* (1885–1964) and A. *Jakob* (1882–1927), the German neurologists who first described cases of the disease in 1920–21. Creutzfeldt is credited with the first description of the disease in 1920, although the case is atypical by current diagnostic criteria; a year later Jakob described four cases, at least two of whom had clinical features suggestive of CJD as it is currently described.

cre·vasse /krəˈvas/ ▸*n.* a deep open crack, esp. one in a glacier. ■ a breach in the embankment of a river or canal. ▷early 19th cent.: from French, from Old French *crevace* (see CREVICE).

crev·ice /ˈkrevəs/ ▸*n.* a narrow opening or fissure, esp. in a rock or wall. ▷Middle English: from Old French *crevace,* from *crever* 'to burst,' from Latin *crepare* 'to rattle, crack.'

crew[1] /kro͞o/ ▸*n.* [treated as *sing.* or *pl.*] a group of people who work on and operate a ship, boat, aircraft, spacecraft, or train. ■ such a group other than the officers: *the ship's captain and crew may be brought to trial.* ■ the group that rows a racing shell. ■ the sport of rowing a racing shell. ■ a group of people who work closely together, in a job that is technically difficult or dangerous: *an ambulance crew.* | *crews of firefighters from neighboring towns were called in.* ■ *informal, often derogatory* a group of people associated in some way: *a crew of assorted computer geeks.* ■ *informal* a group of rappers, breakdancers, or graffiti artists performing or operating together. ■ *informal* a criminal gang.
▸*v.* [*trans.*] (often **be crewed**) provide (a craft or vehicle) with a group of people to operate it: *normally the boat is crewed by 5 people.* ■ [*intrans.*] act as a member of a crew, subordinate to a captain: *I've never* ***crewed for*** *a world-famous yachtsman before.* ▷late Middle English: from Old French *creue* 'augmentation, increase,' feminine past participle of *croistre* 'grow,' from Latin *crescere.* The original sense was 'band of soldiers serving as reinforcements'; hence it came to denote any organized armed band or, generally, a company of people (late 16th cent.). **—crew·man** /ˈkro͞omən/ *n.* (*pl.* **-men**) .

crew[2] ▸*chiefly Brit.* past of CROW[2].

crew cut ▸*n.* a very short haircut for men and boys. ▷1940s: apparently first adopted as a style by boat crews of Harvard and Yale universities.

crew·el /ˈkro͞oəl/ ▸*n.* a thin, loosely twisted, worsted yarn used for tapestry and embroidery. ▷late 15th cent.: of unknown origin.

crew·el work ▸*n.* embroidery or tapestry done with crewel yarn on linen cloth.

crew neck ▸*n.* a close-fitting, round neckline, esp. on

Pronunciation Key ə *ago;* ər *over;* ˈə or ˌə *up;* ˈər or ˌər *fur;* a *hat;* ā *rate;* ä *car;* CH *chew;* e *let;* ē *see;* e(ə)r *air;* i *fit;* ī *by;* i(ə)r *ear;* NG *sing;* ō *go;* ô *for;* oi *boy;* o͝o *good;* o͞o *goo;* ou *out;* SH *she;* TH *thin;* T͟H *then;* (h)w *why;* ZH *vision*

C

a sweater or T-shirt: [as *adj.*] *a crew-neck sweater.* ■ a sweater with such a neckline.

crib /krib/ ▸*n.* **1** a young child's bed with barred or latticed sides. ■ a barred container or rack for animal fodder; a manger. **2** *informal* unfair use of notes on an examination or schoolwork. ■ *informal Brit.* a trot: *an English crib of Caesar's Gallic Wars.* ■ a thing that has been plagiarized: *is the song a crib from Mozart's "Don Giovanni?"* **3** *informal* an apartment or house. **4** short for CRIBBAGE. ■ the cards discarded by the players at cribbage, counting to the dealer. **5** (also **crib·work**) a heavy timber framework used in foundations for a building or to line a mine shaft.
▸*v.* (**cribbed, crib·bing**) [*trans.*] **1** *informal* copy (another person's work) illicitly or without acknowledgment: *he was doing an exam and didn't want anybody to crib the answers from him* | [*intrans.*] *he often* **cribbed from** *other researchers.* ■ *archaic* steal. **2** *archaic* restrain: *he had been so cabined, cribbed, and confined by office.* ▷Old English (in the sense 'manger'), of Germanic origin; related to Dutch *krib, kribbe* and German *Krippe.* **—crib·ber** /'kribər/ *n.*

crib·bage /'kribij/ ▸*n.* a card game for two to four players, in which the objective is to play so that the value of one's cards played reaches exactly 15 or 31. ▷mid 17th cent.: related to CRIB; according to John Aubrey, the game was invented by the English poet Sir John Suckling (1609–42); it seems to have been developed from an older game called Noddy.

crib·bage board ▸*n.* a board with pegs and holes, used for scoring at cribbage.

crib-bit·ing ▸*n.* a repetitive habit of some horses that involves biting and chewing of wood, esp. that of doors and mangers, in the stable, causing excessive wear to the front teeth.

crib death ▸*n.* informal term for SUDDEN INFANT DEATH SYNDROME.

cri·bel·lum /kri'beləm/ ▸*n.* (*pl.* **-bel·la** /-'belə/) *Zoology* (in some spiders) an additional spinning organ with numerous fine pores, situated in front of the spinnerets. ▷late 19th cent.: from late Latin, diminutive of *cribrum* 'sieve.' **—cri·bel·late** /'kribələt; -,lāt/ *adj.*

cri·bo /'krē,bō/ ▸*n.* (*pl.* **-bos**) another term for INDIGO SNAKE. ▷late 19th cent.: of unknown origin.

crib·ri·form /'kribrə,fôrm/ ▸*adj. Anatomy* denoting an anatomical structure that is pierced by numerous small holes, in particular the plate of the ethmoid bone through which the olfactory nerves pass. ▷mid 18th cent.: from Latin *cribrum* 'sieve' + -IFORM.

crib·work /'krib,wərk/ ▸*n.* see CRIB (sense 5).

Crich·ton[1] /'krītn/, James (1560–*c.*1585), Scottish adventurer; known as **the Admirable Crichton**. He was an accomplished swordsman, poet, and scholar and served in the French army.

Crich·ton[2] /'krītn/ ▸, Michael (1942–), U.S. novelist. Notable works: *The Andromeda Strain*(1969), *The Great Train Robbery* (1975), and *Jurassic Park* (1990).

Crick /krik/, Francis Harry Compton (1916–2004), English biophysicist. With J. D. Watson, he proposed the double helix structure of the DNA molecule, thus broadly explaining how genetic information is carried in living organisms and how genes replicate. Nobel Prize for Physiology or Medicine (1962, shared with Watson and M. H. F. Wilkins).

Francis Crick

crick[1] /krik/ ▸*n.* a painful stiff feeling in the neck or back.
▸*v.* [*trans.*] twist or strain (one's neck or back), causing painful stiffness: [as *adj.*] (**cricked**) *he suffered a cricked neck during tackling practice.* ▷late Middle English: of unknown origin.

crick[2] ▸*n. dialect* creek.

crick·et[1] /'krikit/ ▸*n.* an insect related to the grasshoppers. The male produces a characteristic rhythmical chirping sound. • Family Gryllidae: many genera and species, including the **field cricket** and the **house cricket**. ▷Middle English: from Old French *criquet*, from *criquer* 'to crackle,' of imitative origin.

crick·et[2] ▸*n.* an open-air game played on a large grass field with ball, bats, and two wickets, between teams of eleven players, the object of the game being to score more runs than the opposition.

Cricket is played mainly in Britain and in territories formerly under British rule, including Australia, South Africa, the West Indies, New Zealand, and the Indian subcontinent. The full game with two innings per side can last several days; shorter matches are usual at the amateur level and have become popular at professional level since the 1960s.

▷late 16th cent.: of unknown origin. **—crick·et·er** *n.* **—crick·et·ing** *adj.*
▸*PHRASE* □ **not cricket** *Brit., informal* a thing contrary to traditional standards of fairness or rectitude.

crick·et[3] ▸*n.* a low stool, typically with a rectangular or oval seat and four legs splayed out.

cri·coid /'krī,koid/ ▸*n.* (also **cricoid cartilage**) *Anatomy* the ring-shaped cartilage of the larynx. ▷mid 18th cent.: from modern Latin *cricoides* 'ring-shaped,' from Greek *krikoeidēs*, from *krikos* 'ring.'

cri de cœur /,krē də 'kər/ ▸*n.* (*pl.* **cris de cœur** /,krē(z)/) a passionate appeal, complaint, or protest. ▷early 20th cent.: French, literally 'cry from the heart.'

cried /krīd/ ▸ past and past participle of CRY.

cri·er /'krīər/ ▸*n.* an officer who makes public announcements in a court of justice. ■ short for TOWN CRIER. ■ a person who shouts out announcements about their wares; a hawker. ▷late Middle English: from Old French *criere*, from *crier* 'to shout.'

cri·key /'krīkē/ ▸*exclam. Brit., informal* an expression of surprise: *Crikey! I never thought I'd see you again.* ▷mid 19th cent.: euphemism for CHRIST.

crime /krīm/ ▸*n.* an action or omission that constitutes an offense that may be prosecuted by the state and is punishable by law: *shoplifting was a serious crime.* ■ illegal activities: *the victims of crime.* ■ an action or activity that, although not illegal, is considered to be evil, shameful, or wrong: *they condemned apartheid as a* **crime against** *humanity* | *it's a crime to keep a creature like Willy in a tank.* See note at SIN. ▷Middle English (in the sense 'wickedness, sin'): via Old French from Latin *crimen* 'judgment, offense,' based on *cernere* 'to judge.'

Cri·me·a /krī'mēə/ (usu. **the Crimea**) a peninsula in Ukraine that lies between the Sea of Azov and the Black Sea. The Crimean War was fought here in the 1850s. **—Cri·me·an** *adj.*

Cri·me·an War /krī'mēən/ a war (1853–56) between Russia and an alliance of Great Britain, France, Sardinia, and Turkey. Russian aggression against Turkey led to war, with Turkey's European allies intervening to destroy Russian naval power in the Black Sea in 1854; eventually the allies captured the fortress city of Sebastopol in 1855 after a lengthy siege.

crime-fight·ing ▸*n.* the action of working to reduce the incidence of crime. **—crime-fight·er** *n.*

crime pas·si·on·nel /,krēm ,pasyə'nel/ ▸*n.* (*pl.* **crimes pas·si·on·nels** *pronunc.* same) a crime, typically a murder, committed in a fit of sexual jealousy. ▷early 20th cent.: French, literally 'crime of passion.'

crime wave ▸*n.* a sudden increase in the number of crimes committed in a country or area.

crime writ·er ▸*n.* a writer of detective stories or thrillers.

crim·i·nal /'krimənl/ ▸*n.* a person who has committed a crime: *these men are dangerous criminals.*
▸*adj.* of or relating to a crime: *he is charged with conspiracy to commit criminal damage.* ■ *Law* of or relating to crime as opposed to civil matters: *a criminal court.* ■ *informal* (of an action or situation) deplorable and shocking: *he may never fulfill his potential, and that would be a criminal waste.* ▷late Middle English (as an adjective): from late Latin *criminalis*, from Latin *crimen, crimin-* (see CRIME). **—crim·i·nal·i·ty** /,krimə'nalitē/ *n.* **—crim·i·nal·ly** *adv.*

crim·i·nal con·ver·sa·tion ▸*n. historical* adultery, esp. as formerly constituting grounds for the recovery of legal damages by a husband from his adulterous wife's partner.

crim·i·nal·is·tics /,krimənl'istiks/ ▸*plural n.* [treated as sing.] another term for FORENSICS (see FORENSIC). **—crim·i·nal·ist**

crim·i·nal·ize /'krimənl,īz/ ▸*v.* [*trans.*] turn (an activity) into a criminal offense by making it illegal: *the law that criminalizes assisted suicide.* ■ turn (someone) into a criminal by making their activities illegal: *these punitive measures would further criminalize travelers for their way of life.* **—crim·i·nal·i·za·tion** /,krimənlə'zāshən/ *n.*

crim·i·nal jus·tice sys·tem ▸*n.* the system of law enforcement that is directly involved in apprehending, prosecuting, defending, sentencing, and incarcerating those who are suspected of or have been charged with criminal offenses.

crim·i·nal law ▸*n.* a system of law concerned with the punishment of those who commit crimes. Contrasted with CIVIL LAW. ■ a law belonging to this system.

crim·i·nal li·bel ▸*n. Law* a malicious, defamatory statement in a permanent form, rendering the maker liable to criminal prosecution.

crim·i·nal re·cord ▸*n.* a history of being convicted for crime: *he admits he has a criminal record.* ■ a list of a person's previous criminal convictions: *the court said his criminal record would be expunged at the end of the year.*

crim·i·no·gen·ic /,krimənə'jenik/ ▸*adj.* (of a system, situation, or place) causing or likely to cause criminal behavior: *the criminogenic nature of homelessness.*

crim·i·nol·o·gy /,krimə'näləjē/ ▸*n.* the scientific study of crime and criminals. ▷late 19th cent.: from Latin *crimen, crimin-* 'crime' + -LOGY. **—crim·i·no·log·i·cal** /,krimənl'äjikəl/ *adj.* **—crim·i·nol·o·gist** /-jist/ *n.*

crimp /krimp/ ▸*v.* [*trans.*] compress (something) into small folds or ridges: *she crimped the edge of the pie.* ■ squeeze (metal) so as to bend or corrugate it. ■ connect (a wire or cable) in this way. ■ [often as *adj.*] (**crimped**) make waves in (someone's hair) with a curling iron: *crimped blond hair.* ■ *informal* have a limiting or adverse effect on (something): *farmers complain that the drought could crimp their income potential.*
▸*n.* a curl, wave, or folded or compressed edge: *this cascade of delicate crimps depends on a perm* | *the wool had too much crimp to be used in weaving.* ■ a small connecting piece for crimping wires or lines together. ■ *informal* a restriction or limitation: *the crimp on take-home pay has been even tighter since taxes were raised.* ▷Old English *gecrympan*, of Germanic origin; related to Dutch *krimpen* 'shrink, wrinkle.' Of rare occurrence before the 18th cent., the word was perhaps reintroduced from Low German or Dutch. **—crimp·er** *n.* **—crimp·y** *adj.*
▸*PHRASE* □ **put a crimp in** *informal* have an adverse effect on: *well, that puts a crimp in my theory.*

crim·son /'krimzən/ ▸*adj.* of a rich deep red color inclining to purple: *she blushed crimson with embarrassment.*
▸*n.* a rich deep red color inclining to purple.
▸*v.* [*intrans.*] (of a person's face) become flushed, esp. through embarrassment: *my face crimsoned and my hands began to shake.* ▷late Middle English: from obsolete French *cramoisin* or Old Spanish *cremesin*, based on Arabic *ḳirmizī*, from *ḳirmiz* (see KERMES). Compare with CARMINE.

cringe /krinj/ ▸*v.* (**cring·ing**) [*intrans.*] bend one's head and body in fear or in a servile manner: *he* **cringed away** *from the blow* | [as *adj.*] (**cringing**) *we are surrounded by cringing yes-men and sycophants.* ■ experience an inward shiver of embarrassment or disgust: *I* **cringed at** *the fellow's stupidity.* See note at WINCE.
▸*n.* an act of cringing in fear. ■ a feeling of embarrassment or disgust. ▷Middle English *crenge, crenche*, related to Old English *cringan, crincan* 'bend, yield, fall in battle,' of Germanic origin and related to Dutch *krengen* 'heel over' and German *krank* 'sick,' also to CRANK[1]. **—cring·er** *n.*

cringe-mak·ing ▸*adj.* another term for CRINGEWORTHY.

cringe·wor·thy /'krinj,wər*th*ē/ ▸*adj. informal* causing feelings of embarrassment or awkwardness: *the play's cast was excellent, but the dialogue was unforgivably cringeworthy.*

crin·gle /'kriNGgəl/ ▸*n. Sailing* a ring of rope formed in the edge of a sail and containing a thimble, for another rope to pass through. ▷early 17th cent.: from Low German *kringel*, diminutive of *kring* 'ring.'

crin·kle /'kriNGkəl/ ▸*v.* [*intrans.*] form small creases or wrinkles in the surface of something, esp. the skin of the face as the result of a facial expression: *Rose's face crinkled in bewilderment* | *his face* **crinkled up** *in a smile* | [as *adj.*] (**crinkled**) *plants with crinkled foliage.* ■ [*trans.*] cause to form such creases or wrinkles:

Burney crinkled his eyes in a smile. ■ [*trans.*] cause (something) to make a crackling or rustling sound: *we tried hard not to crinkle the plastic as we unwrapped the pies.* ▸*n.* a wrinkle or crease found on the surface of something: *there was a crinkle of suspicion on her forehead.* ■ the sound of crinkling: *I heard the crinkle of clothing.* ▷late Middle English: related to Old English *crincan* (see CRINGE). **—crin·kly** /-k(ə)lē/ *adj.*

crin·kle-cut ▸*adj.* (esp. of French fries) cut with wavy edges.

crin·kum-cran·kum /ˈkriNGkəm ˈkraNGkəm/ ▸*n. archaic* elaborate decoration or detail. ▷mid 17th cent.: fanciful reduplication of the nouns CRANK[1] and CRANK[2].

Cri·noid·e·a /krīˈnoidēə/ *Zoology* a class of echinoderms that comprises the sea lilies and feather stars. They have slender, feathery arms and (in some kinds) a stalk for attachment, and were abundant in the Paleozoic era. ▷modern Latin (plural), from Greek *krinoeidēs* 'lilylike,' from *krinon* 'lily.' **—cri·noid** /ˈkrīˌnoid/ *n.* & *adj.* **—cri·noi·dal** /ˈkrīˌnoidl/ *adj.*

crin·o·line /ˈkrinl-in/ ▸*n.* **1** *historical* a stiffened or hooped petticoat worn to make a long skirt stand out. **2** a stiff fabric made of horsehair and cotton or linen thread, typically used for stiffening petticoats or as a lining. ▷mid 19th cent. (originally in sense 2, early crinolines being made of such material): from French, formed irregularly from Latin *crinis* 'hair' + *linum* 'thread.'

cri·ol·lo /krēˈō(l)yō/ (also **Cri·ol·lo**) ▸*n.* (*pl.* **-los**) **1** a person from Spanish South or Central America, esp. one of pure Spanish descent. ■ a horse or other domestic animal of a South or Central American breed. **2** (also **criollo tree**) a cacao tree of a variety producing thin-shelled beans of high quality. ▷late 19th cent.: Spanish, literally 'native to the locality' (see CREOLE).

crip /krip/ ▸*n. informal* **1** *derogatory* a disabled person. [early 20th cent.: abbreviation of CRIPPLE.] **2** (usu. **Crip**) a member of a Los Angeles street gang.

cripes /krīps/ ▸*exclam. informal* used as a euphemism for Christ. ▷early 20th cent.: alteration of CHRIST.

crip·ple /ˈkripəl/ ▸*n.* **1** *dated, offensive* a person who is unable to walk or move properly because of disability or injury to their back or legs. **2** a person who is disabled in a specified way: *an emotional cripple.*
▸*v.* [*trans.*] (often **be crippled**) cause (someone) to become unable to move or walk properly: *a writer who was crippled by polio at the age of eleven* | [as *adj.*] (**crippling**) *a crippling disease.* ■ cause severe and disabling damage to (a machine): [as *adj.*] (**crippled**) *the pilot displayed skill and nerve in landing the crippled plane.* ■ cause a severe and almost insuperable problem for: *developing countries are crippled by their debts.* ▷Old English: from two words, *crypel* and *crēopel*, both of Germanic origin and related to CREEP. **—crip·pler** /ˈkrip(ə)lər/ *n.*

USAGE The word **cripple** has long been in use to refer to 'a person unable to walk due to illness or disability' and is recorded as early as AD 950. In the 20th century, the term acquired offensive connotations and has now been largely replaced by broader terms such as 'disabled person.'

crip·ple·ware /ˈkripəlˌwe(ə)r/ ▸*n. informal Computing* software distributed with reduced functionality with a view to attracting payment for a fully functional version.

cri·sis /ˈkrīsis/ ▸*n.* (*pl.* **-ses** /-ˌsēz/) a time of intense difficulty, trouble, or danger: *the current economic crisis* | *a family in crisis a crisis of semiliteracy among high school graduates.* ■ a time when a difficult or important decision must be made: [as *adj.*] *a crisis point of history.* ■ the turning point of a disease when an important change takes place, indicating either recovery or death. ■ the point in a play or story when a crucial conflict takes place, determining the outcome of the plot. ▷late Middle English (denoting the turning point of a disease): medical Latin, from Greek *krisis* 'decision,' from *krinein* 'decide.' The general sense 'decisive point' dates from the early 17th cent.

cri·sis cen·ter ▸*n.* a facility, telephone answering system, etc., where individuals going through personal crises can obtain help or advice. ■ an office or agency that serves as a clearinghouse for information and coordinates action during an emergency or disaster.

cri·sis man·age·ment ▸*n.* the use of expert managers by a business or government to limit damage or danger from a crisis. ■ the tendency to take action only after a crisis has developed.

crisp /krisp/ ▸*adj.* **1** (of a substance) firm, dry, and brittle, esp. in a way considered pleasing or attractive: *crisp bacon* | *the snow is lovely and crisp.* ■ (of a fruit or vegetable) firm, indicating freshness: *crisp lettuce.* ■ (of the weather) cool, fresh, and invigorating: *a crisp autumn day.* ■ (of paper or cloth) smoothly and attractively stiff and uncreased: *a crisp $5 bill.* ■ (of hair) having tight curls, giving an impression of rigidity. **2** (of a way of speaking or writing) briskly decisive and matter-of-fact, without hesitation or unnecessary detail: *they were cut off with a crisp "Thank you."*
▸*n.* **1** a dessert of fruit baked with a crunchy topping of brown sugar, butter, and flour: *rhubarb crisp.* **2** (also **potato crisp**) British term for POTATO CHIP.
▸*v.* [*trans.*] give (something, esp. food) a crisp surface by placing it in an oven or grill: *crisp the pita rounds in the oven.* ■ [*intrans.*] (of food) acquire a crisp surface in this way: *open the foil so that the bread browns and crisps.* ■ *archaic* curl into short, stiff, wavy folds or crinkles. ▷Old English (referring to hair in the sense 'curly'): from Latin *crispus* 'curled.' Other senses may result from symbolic interpretation of the sound of the word. **—crisp·ly** *adv.* **—crisp·ness** *n.*
▸***PHRASE*** □ **burn something to a crisp** burn something completely, leaving only a charred remnant.

cris·pate /ˈkrisˌpāt; -pət/ ▸*adj. Botany* (esp. of a leaf) having a wavy or curly edge. ▷mid 19th cent.: from Latin *crispatus*, past participle of *crispare* 'to curl.'

crisp·er /ˈkrispər/ ▸*n.* a compartment at the bottom of a refrigerator for storing fruit and vegetables.

crisp·y /ˈkrispē/ ▸*adj.* (**crisp·i·er**, **crisp·i·est**) (of food, typically cooked food) having a pleasingly firm, dry, and brittle surface or texture: *crispy fried bacon.* **—crisp·i·ness** *n.*

cris·sal thrash·er /ˈkrisəl/ ▸*n.* a large gray thrasher (songbird) with a red patch under the tail, found in the southwestern U.S. and Mexico. • *Toxostoma dorsale* (or **crissale**), family Mimidae. ▷late 19th cent.: *crissal* from modern Latin *crissum* (denoting the vent region of a bird) + -AL.

criss·cross /ˈkrisˌkrôs/ ▸*n.* a pattern of intersecting straight lines or paths: *the crisscross of wrinkles on his face.*
▸*adj.* (of a pattern) containing a number of straight lines or paths that intersect each other: *the streets ran in a regular crisscross pattern.*
▸*adv.* in a pattern of intersecting straight lines: *the swords were strung crisscross on his back.*
▸*v.* [*trans.*] (usu. **be crisscrossed**) form a pattern of intersecting lines or paths on (a place): *the green hill was crisscrossed with a network of sheep tracks.* ■ [*intrans.*] (of straight lines or paths) intersect repeatedly: *the smaller streets crisscrossed in a grid pattern.* ■ move or travel around (a place) by going back and forth repeatedly: *the President crisscrossed America.* ▷early 17th cent. (denoting a figure of a cross preceding the alphabet in a hornbook): from *Christ-cross* (in the same sense in late Middle English), from *Christ's cross.* The form was later treated as a reduplication of CROSS.

cris·ta /ˈkristə/ ▸*n.* (*pl.* **-tae** /-tē; -tī/) **1** *Anatomy & Zoology* a ridge or crest. **2** *Biology* each of the partial partitions in a mitochondrion formed by infolding of the inner membrane. ▷mid 19th cent.: from Latin, 'tuft, plume, crest.' **—cris·tate** /ˈkrisˌtāt/ *adj.*

cris·to·bal·ite /kriˈstōbəˌlīt/ ▸*n.* a form of silica that is the main component of opal and also occurs as small octahedral crystals. ▷late 19th cent.: named after *Cerro San Cristóbal* in Mexico, where it was discovered, + -ITE[1].

crit /krit/ ▸*n. informal* short for CRITICISM or CRITIC.

cri·te·ri·on /krīˈti(ə)rēən/ ▸*n.* (*pl.* **-te·ri·a** /-ˈti(ə)rēə/) a principle or standard by which something may be judged or decided: *the launch came too close to violating safety criteria.* ▷early 17th cent.: from Greek *kritērion* 'means of judging,' from *kritēs* (see CRITIC). **—cri·te·ri·al** /-ˈti(ə)rēəl/ *adj.*

USAGE Strictly speaking, the singular form (following the original Greek) is **criterion** and the plural form is **criteria**. It is a common mistake, however, to use **criteria** as if it were a singular, as in *a further **criteria** needs to be considered.*

cri·te·ri·um /krīˈti(ə)rēəm/ ▸*n.* a one-day bicycle race on a circuit road course.

crit·ic /ˈkritik/ ▸*n.* **1** a person who expresses an unfavorable opinion of something: *critics say many schools are not prepared to handle the influx of foreign students.* **2** a person who judges the merits of literary, artistic, or musical works, esp. one who does so professionally: *a film critic.* ▷late 16th cent.: from Latin *criticus*, from Greek *kritikos*, from *kritēs* 'a judge,' from *krinein* 'judge, decide.'

crit·i·cal /ˈkritikəl/ ▸*adj.* **1** expressing adverse or disapproving comments or judgments: *he was **critical of** many U.S. welfare programs.* **2** expressing or involving an analysis of the merits and faults of a work of literature, music, or art: *she never won the critical acclaim she sought.* ■ (of a published literary or musical text) incorporating a detailed and scholarly analysis and commentary: *a critical edition of a Bach sonata.* **3** (of a situation or problem) having the potential to become disastrous; at a point of crisis: *the flood waters had not receded, and the situation was still critical.* ■ (of a person) extremely ill and at risk of death: *he had been **in critical condition** since undergoing surgery.* ■ having a decisive or crucial importance in the success or failure of something: *temperature is a critical factor in successful fruit storage.* See note at CRUCIAL. **4** *Mathematics & Physics* relating to or denoting a point of transition from one state to another. ■ (of a nuclear reactor or fuel) maintaining a self-sustaining chain reaction: *the reactor is due to **go critical** in October.* ▷mid 16th cent. (in the sense 'relating to the crisis of a disease'): from late Latin *criticus* (see CRITIC). **—crit·i·cal·i·ty** /ˌkritəˈkalitē/ *n.* (in senses 3 and 4). **—crit·i·cal·ly** /ˈkritik(ə)lē/ *adv.* [as *submodifier*] *he's critically ill.* **—crit·i·cal·ness** *n.*

crit·i·cal an·gle ▸*n. Optics* the angle of incidence beyond which rays of light passing through a denser medium to the surface of a less dense medium are no longer refracted but totally reflected.

crit·i·cal ap·pa·ra·tus ▸*n.* see APPARATUS (sense 3).

crit·i·cal damp·ing ▸*n. Physics* damping just sufficient to prevent oscillations.

crit·i·cal list ▸*n.* [in *sing.*] a list of those who are critically ill in the hospital.

crit·i·cal mass ▸*n. Physics* the minimum amount of fissile material needed to maintain a nuclear chain reaction. ■ *figurative* the minimum size or amount of something required to start or maintain a venture: *a communication system is of no value unless there is a critical mass of users.*

crit·i·cal path ▸*n.* the sequence of stages determining the minimum time needed for an operation, esp. when analyzed on a computer for a large organization.

crit·i·cal path a·nal·y·sis ▸*n.* the mathematical network analysis technique of planning complex working procedures with reference to the critical path of each alternative system.

crit·i·cal pe·ri·od ▸*n. Psychology* a period during someone's development in which a particular skill or characteristic is believed to be most readily acquired.

crit·i·cal point ▸*n.* **1** *Chemistry* a point on a phase diagram at which both the liquid and gas phases of a substance have the same density, and are therefore indistinguishable. **2** *Mathematics* a point on a curve where the gradient is zero.

crit·i·cal pres·sure ▸*n. Chemistry* the pressure of a gas or vapor in its critical state.

crit·i·cal state ▸*n. Chemistry* the state of a substance when it is at the critical point, i.e., at critical temperature and pressure.

crit·i·cal tem·per·a·ture ▸*n. Chemistry* the temperature of a gas or vapor in its critical state. Above this temperature, a gas cannot be liquefied by pressure alone.

crit·i·cal the·o·ry ▸*n.* a philosophical approach to culture, and esp. to literature, that seeks to confront the social, historical, and ideological forces and structures that produce and constrain it. The term is applied particularly to the work of the Frankfurt School.

crit·i·cal vol·ume ▸*n. Chemistry* the volume occupied by a unit mass of a gas or vapor in its critical state.

crit·ic·as·ter /ˈkritəˌkastər/ ▸*n. rare* a minor or inferior critic. ▷late 17th cent.: from CRITIC + -ASTER.

crit·i·cism /ˈkritəˌsizəm/ ▸*n.* **1** the expression of disapproval of someone or something based on perceived faults or mistakes: *he received a lot of criticism* | *he ignored the criticisms of his friends.* **2** the analysis and judgment of the merits and faults of a literary or artistic work: *alternative methods of criticism supported by well-developed literary theories.* ■ an article, book, or comment containing such analysis: *I only read poetry and criticism.* ■ the scholarly investigation of literary or historical texts to determine their origin or intended form. ▷early 17th cent.: from CRITIC or Latin *criticus* + -ISM.

crit·i·cize /ˈkritəˌsīz/ ▶*v.* [*trans.*] **1** indicate the faults of (someone or something) in a disapproving way: *they criticized the failure of Western nations to adequately resettle Indochinese refugees* | *technicians were* **criticized** *for defective workmanship.* **2** form and express a sophisticated judgment of (a literary or artistic work): *a literary text may be criticized on two grounds: the semantic and the expressive.* —**crit·i·ciz·a·ble** *adj.* —**crit·i·ciz·er** *n.*

cri·tique /kriˈtēk/ ▶*n.* a detailed analysis and assessment of something, esp. a literary, philosophical, or political theory.
▶*v.* (**-tiques, -tiqued, -tiqu·ing**) [*trans.*] evaluate (a theory or practice) in a detailed and analytical way: *the authors critique the methods and practices used in the research.* ▷mid 17th cent. (as a noun): from French, based on Greek *kritikē tekhnē* 'critical art.'

crit·ter /ˈkritər/ ▶*n. informal* or *dialect* a living creature; an animal. ■ a person of a particular kind: *the old critter used to live in a shack.* ▷early 19th cent.: variant of CREATURE.

CRM ▶*abbr.* customer relationship management, denoting strategies and software that enable a company to organize and optimize its customer relations.

croak /krōk/ ▶*n.* a deep hoarse sound made by a frog or a crow. ■ a sound resembling this, esp. one made by a person: *Lorton tried to laugh—it came out as a croak.*
▶*v.* [*intrans.*] **1** (of a frog or crow) make a characteristic deep hoarse sound. ■ (of a person) make a similar sound when speaking or laughing: *"Thank you," I croaked.* ■ *archaic* prophesy evil or misfortune, esp. unjustifiably and to the irritation of others: *without croaking, it may be observed that our government is upon a dangerous experiment.* **2** *informal* die: *the dog finally croaked in 1987.* ■ [*trans.*] kill (someone): *Scissors Haggerty's mob croaked two messengers.* ▷Middle English (as a verb): imitative.

croak·er /ˈkrōkər/ ▶*n.* **1** an animal or fish that makes a deep, hoarse sound. ■ another term for DRUM[3]. **2** *archaic* a person who habitually prophesies evil or misfortune unjustifiably and to the irritation of others.

croak·y /ˈkrōkē/ ▶*adj.* (**croak·i·er, croak·i·est**) (of a person's voice) deep and hoarse. —**croak·i·ly** /-kəlē/ *adv.*

Cro·at /ˈkrōˌat; ˈkrōˌät; krōt/ ▶*n.* **1** a native or national of Croatia, or a person of Croatian descent. **2** the South Slavic language of the Croats, almost identical to Serbian but written in the Roman alphabet. See SERBO-CROAT.
▶*adj.* of or relating to the Croats or their language. ▷from modern Latin *Croatae* (plural), from Serbo-Croat *Hrvat*.

Cro·a·tia /krōˈāshə/ a country in southeastern Europe, formerly a constituent republic of Yugoslavia; pop. 4,760,000; capital, Zagreb; language, Croatian. Croatian name HRVATSKA.

Apart from a period of Turkish rule in the 16th–17th centuries, Croatia largely remained linked with Hungary until 1918, when it joined the Kingdom of the Serbs, Croats, and Slovenes (later Yugoslavia). After a period during World War II as a Nazi puppet state (1941–45), it became part of Yugoslavia once more and remained a constituent republic until it declared itself independent in 1991. The secession of Croatia led to war between Croats and the Serb minority, and with Serbia; a cease-fire was called for in 1992 but it was not until 1998 that peace came about.

Cro·a·tian /krōˈāshən/ ▶*n.* & *adj.* another term for CROAT.

croc /kräk/ ▶*n. informal* a crocodile. ▷late 19th cent.: abbreviation.

Cro·ce /ˈkrōchā/, Benedetto (1866–1952), Italian philosopher and politician. In his "Philosophy of Spirit," he denied the physical reality of a work of art and identified philosophical endeavor with a methodological approach to history.

cro·chet /krōˈshā/ ▶*n.* a handicraft in which yarn is made up into a patterned fabric by looping yarn with a hooked needle: [as *adj.*] *a crochet hook.* ■ fabric or items made in such a way: *the bikini is tiny, three triangles of cotton crochet.*
▶*v.* (**-cheted** /-ˈshād/, **-chet·ing** /-ˈshāiNG/) [*trans.*] make (a garment or piece of fabric) in such a way: *she had crocheted the shawl herself* | [*intrans.*] *her mother had stopped crocheting.* ▷mid 19th cent.: from French, diminutive of *croc* 'hook,' from Old Norse *krókr*. —**cro·chet·er** /-ˈshāər/ *n.*

cro·ci /ˈkrōˌkī; -ˌsī/ ▶ plural form of CROCUS.

cro·cid·o·lite /krōˈsidlˌīt/ ▶*n.* a fibrous blue or green mineral consisting of a silicate of iron and sodium. Also called BLUE ASBESTOS (see ASBESTOS). ▷mid 19th cent.: from Greek *krokis, krokid-* 'nap of cloth' + -LITE.

crock[1] /kräk/ ▶*n.* **1** an earthenware pot or jar. ■ a broken piece of earthenware. **2** (also *vulgar slang* **crock of shit**) a thing that is considered to be complete nonsense. ▷Old English *croc, crocca*, of Germanic origin; related to Old Norse *krukka* and probably to Dutch *kruik* and German *Krug*.

crock[2] *informal* ▶*n.* an old person who is feeble and useless.
▶*v.* [*trans.*] *Brit.* cause an injury to (a person or part of the body): *he crocked a shoulder.* ▷late Middle English: perhaps from Flemish, and probably related to CRACK. Originally a Scots term for an old ewe, it came in the late 19th cent. to denote an old or broken-down horse.

crocked /kräkt/ ▶*adj. informal* drunk: *his party guests were pretty crocked.*

crock·er·y /ˈkräkərē/ ▶*n.* plates, dishes, cups, and other similar items, esp. ones made of earthenware or china. ▷early 18th cent.: from obsolete *crocker* 'potter,' from CROCK[2].

crock·et /ˈkräkit/ ▶*n.* (in Gothic architecture) a small carved ornament, typically a bud or curled leaf, on the inclined side of a pinnacle or gable. ▷Middle English (denoting a curl or roll of hair): from Old Northern French, variant of Old French *crochet* (see CROTCHET). The current sense dates from the late 17th cent., but *crotchet* was used in the same sense from late Middle English until the 19th cent.

Crock·ett /ˈkräkit/, Davy (1786–1836), U.S. frontiersman, soldier, and politician; full name *David Crockett*. While a member of the House of Representatives 1827–35, he cultivated the image of a rough backwoods legislator. When he left politics, he returned to the frontier, where he fought for the cause of Texan independence. He was killed at the siege of the Alamo.

Crock·pot /ˈkräkˌpät/ ▶*n. trademark* a large electric cooking pot used to cook stews and other dishes slowly.

croc·o·dile /ˈkräkəˌdīl/ ▶*n.* **1** a large predatory semiaquatic reptile with long jaws, long tail, short legs, and a horny textured skin, using submersion and stealth to approach prey unseen. The crocodile has been extensively hunted for its valuable skin. • Family Crocodylidae: three genera, in particular *Crocodylus*, and several species. ■ leather made from crocodile skin, used esp. to make bags and shoes. **2** *Brit., informal* a line of schoolchildren walking in pairs. ▷Middle English *cocodrille, cokadrill*, from Old French *cocodrille*, via medieval Latin from Latin *crocodilus*, from Greek *krokodilos* 'worm of the stones,' from *krokē* 'pebble' + *drilos* 'worm.' The spelling was changed in the 16th cent. to conform with the Latin and Greek forms.

croc·o·dile bird ▶*n.* the Egyptian plover, which is said to feed on insects parasitic on crocodiles.

croc·o·dile clip ▶*n.* British term for ALLIGATOR CLIP.

croc·o·dile tears ▶*plural n.* tears or expressions of sorrow that are insincere. ▷mid 16th cent.: said to be so named from a belief that crocodiles wept while devouring or luring their prey.

croc·o·dil·i·an /ˌkräkəˈdilēən/ ▶*n. Zoology* a large, predatory, semiaquatic reptile of an order that comprises the crocodiles, alligators, caimans, and gharial. Crocodilians are distinguished by long jaws, short legs, and a powerful tail. • Order Crocodylia: three families.
▶*adj.* of or relating to such reptiles.

cro·co·ite /ˈkräkəˌwīt/ ▶*n.* a rare, bright orange mineral consisting of lead chromate. ▷mid 19th cent.: originally as French *crocoise*, from Greek *krokoeis* 'saffron-colored,' from *krokos* 'crocus.' The spelling was altered to *crocoisite*, then *crocoite*.

cro·cus /ˈkrōkəs/ ▶*n.* (*pl.* **-cus·es** or **-ci** /-kī; -sī/) a small, spring-flowering plant of the iris family, which grows from a corm and bears bright yellow, purple, or white flowers. See also AUTUMN CROCUS. • Genus *Crocus*, family Iridaceae. ▷late Middle English (also denoting saffron, obtained from a species of crocus): via Latin from Greek *krokos*, of Semitic origin and related to Hebrew *karkōm* and Arabic *kurkum*.

Croe·sus /ˈkrēsəs/ (6th century BC), last king of Lydia *c.*560–546 BC. Renowned for his great wealth, he subjugated the Greek cities on the coast of Asia Minor before being overthrown by Cyrus the Great of Persia.

croft /krôft/ *Brit.* ▶*n.* a small rented farm, esp. one in Scotland, comprising a plot of arable land attached to a house and with a right of pasturage held in common with other such farms. ■ an enclosed field used for tillage or pasture, typically attached to a house and worked by the occupier.
▶*v.* [*trans.*] farm (land) as a croft or crofts. ▷Old English: of unknown origin. —**croft·er** *n.*

Crohn's dis·ease /ˈkrōnz/ ▶*n.* a chronic inflammatory disease of the intestines, esp. the colon and ileum, associated with ulcers and fistulae. ▷1930s: named after Burrill B. *Crohn* (1884–1983), American pathologist, who was among the first to describe it.

crois·sant /k(r)wäˈsänt; -ˈsäN/ ▶*n.* a French crescent-shaped roll made of sweet flaky pastry, often eaten for breakfast. ▷late 19th cent.: French (see CRESCENT). The term had occasionally been recorded earlier as a variant of *crescent*.

Cro-Mag·non man /krō ˈmagnən; ˈmanyən/ ▶*n.* the earliest form of modern human in Europe, associated with the Aurignacian flint industry. Their appearance *c.*35,000 years ago marked the beginning of the Upper Paleolithic and the apparent decline and disappearance of Neanderthal man; the group persisted at least into the Neolithic period. ▷*Cro-Magnon*, the name of a hill in the Dordogne, France, where remains were found in 1868.

crom·bec /ˈkrämˌbek/ ▶*n.* a small African warbler with a very short tail, and gray or green upper parts with rufous or white underparts. • Genus *Sylvietta*, family Sylviidae: several species, in particular the (**northern**) **crombec** (*S. brachyura*). ▷early 20th cent.: from French, from Dutch *krom* 'crooked' + *bek* 'beak.'

Crome /krōm/, John (1768–1821), English painter; founder and leading member of the Norwich School.

crom·lech /ˈkrämˌlek; -ˌlekh/ ▶*n.* (in Wales) a megalithic tomb consisting of a large flat stone laid on upright ones. Also called DOLMEN. [Welsh, from *crom*, feminine of *crwm* 'arched' + *llech* 'flat stone.'] ■ (in Brittany) a circle of standing stones. [via French from Breton *krommlec'h*.]

Crom·well[1] /ˈkrämwəl; -ˌwel/, Oliver (1599–1658), English general and statesman; lord protector of the Commonwealth 1653–58. He was the leader of the victorious Parliamentary forces (or Roundheads) in the English Civil War. As head of state, he instituted many puritan reforms in the Church of England. He was briefly succeeded by his son **Richard** (1626–1712), who was forced into exile in 1659.

Crom·well[2], Thomas (*c.*1485–1540), English statesman, chief minister to Henry VIII 1531–40. He presided over the king's divorce from Catherine of Aragon (1533) and his break with the Roman Catholic Church.

crone /krōn/ ▶*n.* an old woman who is thin and ugly. ▷late Middle English: via Middle Dutch *croonje, caroonje* 'carcass, old ewe' from Old Northern French *caroigne* 'carrion, cantankerous woman' (see CARRION).

Cro·nin /ˈkrōnən/, A. J. (1896–1981), Scottish novelist; full name *Archibald Joseph Cronin*. His novels, including *The Citadel* (1937), often reflect his early experiences as a doctor.

cron·ing /ˈkrōniNG/ ▶*n.* (especially among feminists in the U.S. and Australasia) a celebration or ceremony to honor older women. ▷1990s: blend of *crone* + *crowning*.

Cron·kite /ˈkräNG,kīt; ˈkrän-/, Walter Leland, Jr. (1916–), U.S. television journalist. He anchored the "The CBS News with Walter Cronkite" 1962–81, ending each broadcast with "And that's the way it is."

Walter Cronkite

Cro·nus /ˈkrōnəs/ (also **Kro·nos**) *Greek Mythology* the supreme god until dethroned by Zeus. The youngest son of Uranus (Heaven) and Gaia (Earth), Cronus overthrew and castrated his father and then married his sister Rhea. Because he was fated to be overcome by one of his male children, Cronus swallowed all of them as soon as they were born, but when Zeus was born, Rhea deceived him and hid the baby away. Roman equivalent **SATURN**.

cro·ny /ˈkrōnē/ ▸*n.* (*pl.* **-nies**) *informal, often derogatory* a close friend or companion: *he went gambling with his cronies.* ▷mid 17th cent. (originally Cambridge University slang): from Greek *khronios* 'long-lasting' (here used to mean 'contemporary'), from *khronos* 'time.' Compare with **CHUM**[1].

cro·ny·ism /ˈkrōnē,izəm/ ▸*n. derogatory* the appointment of friends and associates to positions of authority, without proper regard to their qualifications.

Cro·nyn /ˈkrōnin/, Hume (Blake) (1911–2003), Canadian actor; husband of Jessica Tandy. He often teamed with his wife on the stage and also appeared in movies such as *Sunrise at Campobello* (1960), *Cocoon* (1985), and *Batteries Not Included* (1987).

Crook /kro͝ok/, George (1829–90), U.S. army officer. He served during the Civil War and then fought against the Indians in the northwest. He was defeated by Crazy Horse in 1876 but went on to fight against the Apaches under Geronimo 1882–85.

crook /kro͝ok/ ▸*n.* **1** the hooked staff of a shepherd. ■ a bishop's crozier. ■ a bend in something, esp. at the elbow in a person's arm: *her head was cradled in* **the crook of** *Luke's left arm.* ■ a piece of extra tubing that can be fitted to a brass instrument to lower the pitch by a set interval. ■ a metal tube on which the reed of some wind instruments (such as the bassoon) is set. **2** *informal* a person who is dishonest or a criminal.
▸*v.* [*trans.*] bend (something, esp. a finger as a signal): *he crooked a finger for the waitress.*
▸*adj. Austral./NZ, informal* (esp. of a situation) bad, unpleasant, or unsatisfactory: *it was pretty crook on the land in the early 1970s.* ■ (of a person or a part of the body) unwell or injured: *a crook knee.* ■ dishonest; illegal: *some pretty crook things went on there.* [late 19th cent.: abbreviation of **CROOKED**.] ▷Middle English (in the sense 'hooked tool or weapon'): from Old Norse *krókr* 'hook.' A noun sense 'deceit, guile, trickery' (compare with **CROOKED**) was recorded in Middle English but was obsolete by the 17th cent. —**crook·er·y** /ˈkro͝okərē/ *n.*

crook·back /ˈkro͝ok,bak/ ▸*n. archaic* a person with a hunchback. —**crook-backed** /-,bakt/ *adj.*

crook·ed /ˈkro͝okəd/ ▸*adj.* (**crook·ed·er**, **crook·ed·est**) bent or twisted out of shape or out of place: *his teeth were yellow and crooked.* ■ (of a smile or grin) with the mouth sloping down on one side; lopsided. ■ *informal* dishonest; illegal: *a crooked business deal.* ▷Middle English: from **CROOK**, probably modeled on Old Norse *krókóttr* 'crooked, cunning.' —**crook·ed·ly** *adv.* —**crook·ed·ness** *n.*

crook·neck /ˈkro͝ok,nek/ (also **crookneck squash**) ▸*n.* a squash of a club-shaped variety with a curved neck and warty skin.

croon /kro͞on/ ▸*v.* [*intrans.*] hum or sing in a soft, low voice, esp. in a sentimental manner: *she was crooning to the child* | [*trans.*] *the female vocalist crooned smoky blues into the microphone.* ■ say in a soft, low voice: *"Goodbye, you lovely darling," she crooned.*
▸*n.* [in *sing.*] a soft, low voice or tone: *he sang in a gentle, highly expressive croon.* ▷late 15th cent. (originally Scots and northern English): from Middle Low German and Middle Dutch *krōnen* 'groan, lament.' The use of *croon* in standard English was probably popularized by Robert Burns.

croon·er /ˈkro͞onər/ ▸*n.* a singer, typically a male one, who sings sentimental songs in a soft, low voice.

crop /kräp/ ▸*n.* **1** a cultivated plant that is grown as food, esp. a grain, fruit, or vegetable: *the main crops were oats and barley.* ■ an amount of such plants or their produce harvested at one time: *a heavy crop of fruit.* ■ an abundance of something, esp. a person's hair: *he had a thick* **crop of** *wiry hair.* ■ the total number of young farm animals born in a particular year on one farm. ■ a group or amount of related people or things appearing or occurring at one time: *the current* **crop of** *politicians.* ■ the entire tanned hide of an animal. **2** a hairstyle in which the hair is cut very short. **3** short for **RIDING CROP**. **4** a pouch in a bird's gullet where food is stored or prepared for digestion. ■ a similar organ in an insect or earthworm.
▸*v.* (**cropped**, **crop·ping**) [*trans.*] **1** cut (something, esp. a person's hair) very short: [as *adj.*] (**cropped**) *cropped blond hair.* ■ (of an animal) bite off and eat the tops of (plants): *the horse was gratefully cropping the grass.* ■ cut the edges of (a photograph) in order to produce a better picture or to fit a given space. **2** (often **be cropped**) harvest (plants or their produce) from a particular area: *hay would have been cropped several times through the summer.* ■ sow or plant (land) with plants that will produce food or fodder, esp. on a large commercial scale: *the southern areas are cropped in cotton* | [as *adj.*] (**cropped**) *intensively cropped areas.*
▸*phrasal v.* □ **crop out** (of rock) appear or be exposed at the surface of the earth. □ **crop up** appear, occur, or come to one's notice unexpectedly: *some urgent business had cropped up.* ▷Old English, of Germanic origin; related to German *Kropf*. From Old English to the late 18th cent. there existed a sense 'flowerhead, ear of corn,' giving rise to sense 1 and senses referring to the top of something, whence sense 3.

crop cir·cle ▸*n.* an area of standing crops that has been flattened in the form of a circle or more complex pattern. No general cause of crop circles has been identified although various natural and unorthodox explanations have been put forward; many of the circles are known to have been hoaxes.

crop dust·ing ▸*n.* the spraying of powdered or liquid insecticide or fertilizer on crops, esp. from the air.

crop-eared ▸*adj. historical* (esp. of an animal) having the tops of the ears cut off. ■ (esp. of a Roundhead in the English Civil War) having the hair cut very short.

crop·per /ˈkräpər/ ▸*n.* **1** a plant that yields a crop of a specified kind or in a specified way: *the white-fleshed varieties are the heaviest croppers.* **2** a machine or person that cuts or trims something, such as wool off a sheep or the pile of a carpet during manufacture. **3** a person who raises a crop, esp. as a sharecropper.
▸PHRASE □ **come a cropper** *informal* fall heavily. ■ suffer a defeat or disaster: *the club's challenge for the championship has come a cropper.*

crop ro·ta·tion ▸*n.* see **ROTATION**.

crop top ▸*n.* a woman's casual garment or undergarment for the upper body, cut short so that it reveals the stomach.

cro·quem·bouche /,krôk,änˈbo͞osh/ ▸*n.* a decorative dessert consisting of cream puff pastry and crystallized fruit or other confectionery items arranged in a cone and held together by a caramel sauce. ▷French, literally 'crunch in the mouth.'

cro·quet /krōˈkā/ ▸*n.* a game played on a lawn, in which colored wooden balls are driven through a series of wickets by means of mallets: [as *adj.*] *a croquet lawn.* ■ an act of croqueting a ball.
▸*v.* (**-queted** /-ˈkād/, **-quet·ing** /-ˈkāiNG/) [*trans.*] drive away (an opponent's ball) by holding one's own ball against it and striking this with the mallet. A player is entitled to do this after their ball has struck an opponent's ball. ▷mid 19th cent.: perhaps a dialect form of French *crochet* 'hook.'

cro·quette /krōˈket/ ▸*n.* a small roll of chopped vegetables, meat, or fish, fried in breadcrumbs: *a potato croquette.* ▷French, from *croquer* 'to crunch.'

crore /krôr/ ▸*n. Indian* ten million; one hundred lakhs, esp. of rupees, units of measurement, or people. ▷from Hindi *karoṛ*, based on Sanskrit *koṭi* 'ten million.'

Cros·by /ˈkrôzbē/, Bing (1904–77), U.S. singer and actor; born *Harry Lillis Crosby*. His songs include "Pennies from Heaven," "Blue Skies," and, in particular, "White Christmas" (from the movie *Holiday Inn*, 1942), one of the best selling songs of all time. He also starred in the series of *Road* movies from 1940 to 1962 with Bob Hope and Dorothy Lamour.

Bing Crosby

cro·sier ▸*n.* variant spelling of **CROZIER**.

cross /krôs/ ▸*n.* **1** a mark, object, or figure formed by two short intersecting lines or pieces (+ or ×): *cut a cross in the bark with a sharp knife.* ■ a mark of this type (×) made to represent a signature by a person who cannot write. ■ *Brit.* a mark of this type (×) used to show that something is incorrect or unsatisfactory. **2** an upright post with a transverse bar, as used in antiquity for crucifixion. ■ (**the Cross**) the cross on which Jesus was crucified. ■ this, or a representation of it, as an emblem of Christianity: *she wore a cross around her neck.* ■ *figurative* a thing that is unavoidable and has to be endured: *she's just a cross we have to bear.* ■ short for **SIGN OF THE CROSS** (see **SIGN**). ■ a staff surmounted by a cross carried in religious processions. ■ a cross-shaped decoration awarded for personal valor or indicating rank in some orders of knighthood: *the Military Cross.* ■ (**the Cross**) the constellation Southern Cross. Also called **CRUX**. **3** an animal or plant resulting from crossbreeding; a hybrid: *a Devon and Holstein cross.* ■ (**a cross between**) a mixture or compromise of two things: *the system is a cross between a monorail and a conventional railroad.* **4** a sideways or transverse movement or pass, in particular: ■ *Soccer* a pass of the ball across the field toward the center close to one's opponents' goal. ■ *Boxing* a blow delivered across and over the opponent's lead: *a right cross.*
▸*v.* [*trans.*] **1** go or extend across or to the other side of (a path, road, stretch of water, or area): *he has*

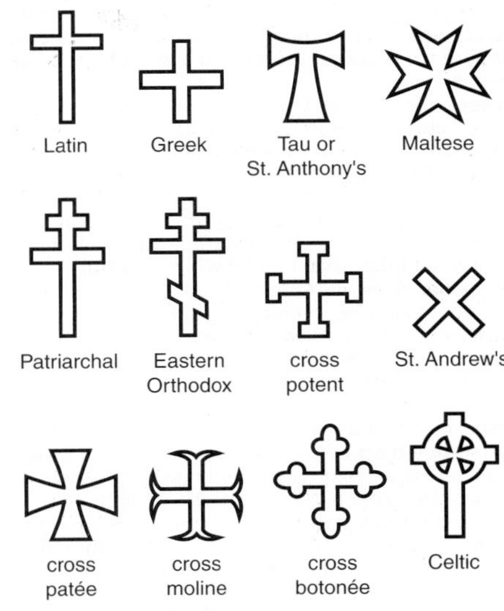

cross 2
types of crosses

crossed the Atlantic twice | two paths crossed the field | figurative a shadow of apprehension crossed her face | [*intrans.*] *we* **crossed over** *the bridge.* ■ go across or climb over (an obstacle or boundary): *he attempted to cross the border into Jordan* | [*intrans.*] *we* **crossed over** *a fence.* ■ [*intrans.*] (**cross over**) (esp. of an artist or an artistic style or work) begin to appeal to a different audience, esp. a wider one: *a talented animator who crossed over to live action.* **2** [*intrans.*] pass in an opposite or different direction; intersect: *the two lines cross at 90°.* ■ [*trans.*] cause (two things) to intersect: *cross the cables in opposing directions.* ■ [*trans.*] place (something) crosswise: *Michele sat back and crossed her arms.* ■ (of a letter) be sent before receipt of another from the person being written to: *our letters crossed.* **3** draw a line or lines across; mark with a cross: *cross the t's.* ■ *Brit.* mark or annotate (a check), typically by drawing a pair of parallel lines across it, to indicate that it must be paid into a named bank account. ■ (**cross someone/something off**) delete a name or item on a list as being no longer required or involved: *Liz crossed off the days on the calendar.* ■ (**cross something out**) delete an incorrect or inapplicable word or phrase by drawing a line through it. **4** (**cross oneself**) (of a person) make the sign of the cross in front of one's chest as a sign of Christian reverence or to invoke divine protection. **5** *Soccer* pass (the ball) across the field toward the center when attacking. **6** cause (an animal of one species, breed, or variety) to interbreed with one of another species, breed, or variety: *many animals of the breed were* **crossed with** *the closely related Guernsey | figurative he behaved like an old regular officer* **crossed with** *a mathematician.* ■ cross-fertilize (a plant): *a hybrid tea was* **crossed with** *a polyantha rose.* **7** oppose or stand in the way of (someone): *no one dared cross him.*

▸*adj.* annoyed: *he seemed to be very cross about something.* ▷late Old English (in the sense 'monument in the form of a cross'): from Old Norse *kross*, from Old Irish *cros*, from Latin *crux*. —**cross·er** *n.* —**cross·ly** *adv.* —**cross·ness** *n.*

▸*PHRASES* □ **at cross purposes** misunderstanding or having different aims from one another: *we had been talking at cross purposes.* □ **cross one's fingers** (or **keep one's fingers crossed**) put one finger across another as a sign of hoping for good luck. ■ hope that someone or something will be successful. □ **cross the floor** *Brit.* join the opposing side in Parliament. □ **cross my heart** (**and hope to die**) used to emphasize the truthfulness and sincerity of what one is saying, and sometimes reinforced by making a sign of the cross over one's chest. □ **cross one's mind** (of a thought) occur to one, esp. transiently: *it never crossed my mind to leave the tent and live in a house.* □ **cross someone's palm with silver** *often humorous* pay someone for a favor or service, esp. before having one's fortune told. □ **cross someone's path** meet or encounter someone. □ **cross swords** have an argument or dispute. □ **get one's wires** (or **lines**) **crossed** become wrongly connected by telephone. ■ have a misunderstanding. □ **the way of the Cross** see **WAY**.

cross- ▸*comb. form* **1** denoting movement or position across something: *cross-channel.* ■ denoting interaction: *cross-pollinate.* ■ passing from side to side; transverse: *crosspiece.* **2** describing the form or figure of a cross: *crossbones.* ▷from **CROSS**.

cross-as·sem·bler ▸*n. Computing* an assembler that can convert instructions into machine code for a computer other than that on which it is run.

cross·bar /ˈkrôs,bär/ ▸*n.* a horizontal bar fixed across another bar or between two upright bars, in particular: ■ (in sports) the bar between the two upright posts of a goal. ■ the horizontal metal bar between the handlebars and saddle on a man's or boy's bicycle.

cross·beam /ˈkrôs,bēm/ ▸*n.* a transverse beam.

cross-bed·ding ▸*n. Geology* layering within a stratum and at an angle to the main bedding plane.

cross·bill /ˈkrôs,bil/ ▸*n.* a thickset finch with a crossed bill adapted for extracting seeds from the cones of conifers. The plumage is typically red in the male and olive green in the female. • Genus *Loxia*, family Fringillidae: four species, in particular the widespread **red** (or **common**) **crossbill** (*L. curvirostra*).

cross·bones /ˈkrôs,bōnz/ ▸*n.* see **SKULL AND CROSSBONES** at **SKULL**.

cross-bor·der ▸*adj.* passing, occurring, or performed across a border between two countries: *cross-border trade.*

cross·bow /ˈkrôs,bō/ ▸*n.* a medieval bow of a kind that is fixed across a wooden support and has a groove for the bolt and a mechanism for drawing and releasing the string. —**cross·bow·man** /-,bōmən/ *n.* (*pl.* **-men**) .

cross·breed /ˈkrôs,brēd/ ▸*n.* an animal or plant produced by mating or hybridizing two different species, breeds, or varieties: [as *adj.*] *a crossbreed Labrador.*

▸*v.* [*trans.*] produce (an animal or plant) in this way: [as *adj.*] (**crossbred**) *a crossbred puppy.* ■ hybridize (a breed, species, or variety) with another. ■ [*intrans.*] (of an animal or plant) breed with a different breed, species, or variety.

cross-check ▸*v.* [*trans.*] **1** verify (figures or information) by using an alternative source or method: *always try to cross-check your bearings* | [as *n.*] (**cross-checking**) *no cross-checking has been done.* **2** *Ice Hockey* obstruct (an opponent) illegally with the stick held horizontally in both hands.

▸*n.* **1** an instance of verifying something by using an alternative source or method: *as a cross-check, they were also asked to give their date of birth.* **2** *Ice Hockey* an illegal obstruction using the stick held horizontally in both hands.

cross-claim ▸*Law* a claim brought by one defendant against another in the same proceeding.

cross-col·or ▸*n.* colored flashes of interference in a color television receiver caused by the misinterpretation of high-frequency luminance detail as color information.

cross-com·pil·er ▸*n. Computing* a compiler that can convert instructions into machine code or low level code for a computer other than that on which it is run.

cross-con·nec·tion ▸*n.* a connection made between two or more distinct things, typically parts of different networks or circuits.

cross-con·tam·i·na·tion ▸*n.* the process by which bacteria or other microorganisms are unintentionally transferred from one substance or object to another, with harmful effect. —**cross-con·tam·i·nate** *v.*

cross-cor·re·late ▸*v.* [*trans.*] compare (a sequence of data) against another. —**cross-cor·re·la·tion** *n.*

cross-coun·try ▸*adj.* **1** across fields or countryside, as opposed to on roads or tracks: *cross-country walking.* ■ of, relating to, or denoting the sport of running, riding, or driving along a course in the countryside, as opposed to around a track. ■ of, relating to, or denoting skiing over relatively flat or mountainous terrain, as opposed to skiing only downhill. **2** across a region or country, in particular: ■ not keeping to main or direct roads, routes, or railroad lines: *mine shafts camouflaged by vegetation have swallowed up more than one cross-country hiker* | [as *adv.*] *if you are traveling cross-country, choose where you walk with care.* ■ traveling to many different parts of a country: *a whirlwind cross-country tour.*

▸*n.* a cross-country race or competition. ■ the sport of cross-country running, riding, skiing, or driving: *skiing in the Rockies is a pleasant mix of downhill and cross-country.*

cross·court /ˈkrôs,kôrt/ ▸*adv.* & *adj.* (of a stroke in tennis and other racket sports) hit diagonally across the court: [as *adj.*] *a crosscourt volley.*

▸*n.* a stroke of this type.

cross cous·in ▸*n.* each of two cousins who are children of a brother and sister.

cross-cul·tur·al ▸*adj.* of or relating to different cultures or comparison between them: *cross-cultural understanding.*

cross·cur·rent /ˈkrôs,kərənt/ ▸*n.* a current in a river or sea that flows across another. ■ *figurative* a process or tendency that is in conflict with another: *strong crosscurrents of debate.*

cross·cut /ˈkrôs,kət/ ▸*v.* [*trans.*] **1** cut (wood or stone) across its main grain or axis. **2** alternate (one sequence) with another when editing a movie.

▸*n.* **1** a diagonal cut, esp. one across the main grain or axis of wood or stone. ■ short for **CROSSCUT SAW**. ■ *Mining* a cutting made across the course of a vein or the general direction of the workings. **2** an instance of alternating between two or more sequences when editing a movie.

cross·cut saw ▸*n.* a saw with a handle at each end, used by two people for cutting across the grain of timber.

cross-dress ▸*v.* [*intrans.*] wear clothing typical of the opposite sex. —**cross-dress·er** *n.*

crosse /krôs/ ▸*n.* the stick used in lacrosse. ▷mid 19th cent.: from French, from Old French *croce* 'bishop's crook,' ultimately of Germanic origin and related to **CRUTCH**.

cross-ex·am·ine ▸*v.* [*trans.*] question (a witness called by the other party) in a court of law to discredit or undercut testimony already given. Compare with **DIRECT EXAMINATION**. ■ question (someone) aggressively or in great detail: *I was cross-examined over the breakfast table.* —**cross-ex·am·i·na·tion** *n.* —**cross-ex·am·in·er** *n.*

cross-eyed ▸*adj.* having one or both eyes turned inward toward the nose, either from focusing on something very close, through temporary loss of control of focus, or as a permanent condition (convergent strabismus).

cross-fade ▸*v.* [*intrans.*] (in sound or movie editing) make a picture or sound appear or be heard gradually as another disappears or becomes silent.

▸*n.* an act or instance of cross-fading.

cross-fer·ti·lize ▸*v.* [*trans.*] fertilize (a plant) using pollen from another plant of the same species. ■ [*intrans.*] (of two plants) fertilize each other. ■ *figurative* stimulate the development of (something) with an exchange of ideas or information: *sessions between the two groups cross-fertilize ideas and provide insights.* —**cross-fer·ti·li·za·tion** *n.*

cross·fire /ˈkrôs,fīr/ ▸*n.* gunfire from two or more directions passing through the same area, often killing or wounding noncombatants: *a photographer was killed in the crossfire.* ■ *figurative* used to refer to a situation in which two or more groups are attacking or arguing with each other: *grape growers have been* ***caught in the crossfire*** *of the boycott.*

cross·flow /ˈkrôs,flō/ ▸*n.* a type of engine cylinder head where the intake ports are on the opposite side of the engine from the exhaust ports.

cross-grain ▸*adj.* running across the regular grain in timber: *cross-grain swelling.*

cross-grained ▸*adj.* (of timber) having a grain that runs across the regular grain. ■ stubbornly contrary or bad-tempered: *Bruce was a cross-grained and boastful individual.*

cross·hairs /ˈkrôs,he(ə)rz/ ▸*plural n.* a pair of fine wires or lines crossing at right angles at the focus of an optical instrument or gun sight, for use in positioning, aiming, or measuring. ■ a representation of this on a computer screen.

cross·hatch /ˈkrôs,hach/ ▸*v.* [*trans.*] [often as *n.*] (**crosshatching**) (in drawing or graphics) shade (an area) with intersecting sets of parallel lines.

cross·head /ˈkrôs,hed/ ▸*n.* a bar or block between the piston rod and connecting rod in a steam engine.

cross in·dex ▸*n.* a note or cross reference in a book or list that refers the reader to other material.

▸*v.* (**cross-in·dex**) [*trans.*] index (something) under another heading as a cross reference: [as *adj.*] *a cross-indexed file.*

cross in·fec·tion ▸*n.* the transfer of infection, esp. to a hospital patient with a different infection or between different species of animal or plant.

cross·ing /ˈkrôsiNG/ ▸*n.* **1** a place where two roads, two railroad lines, or a road and a railroad line cross. ■ the action of moving across or over something: *the crossing of the Pyrenees.* ■ a journey across water in a ship: *a short ferry crossing.* ■ a place at which one may safely cross something, esp. a street. ■ a place at which one can cross a border between countries. ■ *Architecture* the intersection of a church nave and the transepts. **2** crossbreeding.

cross·ing guard ▸a person whose job it is to help pedestrians, esp. schoolchildren, to cross intersections safely.

cross·ing o·ver ▸*n. Genetics* the exchange of genes between homologous chromosomes, resulting in a mixture of parental characteristics in offspring.

cross-leg·ged /ˈleg(ə)d/ ▸*adj.* & *adv.* (of a seated person) with the legs crossed at the ankles and the knees bent outward: [as *adv.*] *John sat cross-legged on the floor.*

cross·light /ˈkrôs,līt/ ▸*n.* a light positioned to illuminate the parts of a photographic subject that the main lighting leaves in shade.

cross-link ▸*n.* a chemical bond between different chains of atoms in a polymer or other complex molecule.

▸*v.* make or become linked with such a bond. ■ [*trans.*] connect (something) by a series of transverse links. —**cross-link·age** *n.*

cross·match /ˈkrôs,mach/ *Medicine* ▸*v.* [*trans.*] [often

as *n.*] (**crossmatching**) test the compatibility of (a donor's and a recipient's blood or tissue).
▸*n.* an instance of such testing.

cross·mem·ber /ˈkrôs,membər/ ▸*n.* a transverse structural piece that adds support to a motor-vehicle chassis or other construction.

cross of Lor·raine ▸*n.* another term for LORRAINE CROSS.

cros·sop·te·ryg·i·an /,krô,säptəˈrijēən/ *Zoology* ▸*n.* a lobe-finned fish, such as the coelacanth.
▸*adj.* of or relating to such fishes. ▷mid 19th cent.: from modern Latin *Crossopterygii*, from Greek *krossos* 'tassel' + *pterux, pterug-* 'fin.'

cross·o·ver /ˈkrôs,ōvər/ ▸*n.* **1** a point or place of crossing from one side to the other. ■ a short length of track joining two adjacent railroad lines. **2** the process of achieving success in a different field or style, esp. in popular music: [as *adj.*] *a jazz-classical crossover album.* **3** a person who votes for a candidate in a different political party than the one they usually support: [as *adj.*] *crossover votes.* **4** [as *adj.*] relating to or denoting trials of medical treatment in which experimental subjects and control groups are exchanged after a set period: *a crossover study.*

cross·o·ver dis·tor·tion ▸*n.* *Electronics* distortion occurring where a signal changes from positive to negative or vice versa.

cross·o·ver net·work ▸*n.* a filter in a loudspeaker unit that divides the signal and delivers different parts to bass and treble speakers.

cross own·er·ship ▸*n.* the ownership by one corporation of different companies with related interests or commercial aims.

cross-par·ty ▸*adj.* involving or relating to two or more political parties.

USAGE Though appearing occasionally in American writing to denote cooperation between the two main political parties, this term does not compete very effectively with **bipartisan** the default term. Cross-party is far more common in other English dialects, and in American English to describe political cooperation in other countries.

cross·patch /ˈkrôs,pach/ ▸*n.* *informal* a bad-tempered person. ▷early 18th cent.: from the adjective CROSS + obsolete *patch* 'fool, clown,' perhaps from Italian *pazzo* 'madman.'

cross peen (also **cross pein**) ▸*n.* a hammer having a peen that lies crossways to the length of the shaft.

cross·piece /ˈkrôs,pēs/ ▸*n.* a beam or bar fixed or placed across something else.

cross-plat·form ▸*adj.* *Computing* able to be used on different types of computers or with different software packages: *a cross-platform game.*

cross-pol·li·nate ▸*v.* [*trans.*] pollinate (a flower or plant) with pollen from another flower or plant. —**cross-pol·li·na·tion** *n.*

cross-post (also **cross·post**) *Computing* ▸*v.* [*trans.*] post a single message to multiple Internet newsgroups or reading lists. ■ repost a message appearing on one list or newsgroup to another: *please do not cross-post this vacancy.*
▸*n.* a message posted to more than one newsgroup or reading list: *we strongly recommend that crossposts be to relevant newsgroups only.*

cross-post·ing ▸*n.* the simultaneous sending of a message to more than one newsgroup or other distribution system on the Internet in such a way that the receiving software at individual sites can detect and ignore duplicates.

cross-pres·sure ▸*v.* [*trans.*] expose (someone) to different, incompatible opinions: *the executive has been cross-pressured by the interests of the states and the electorate.*

cross prod·uct ▸*n.* another term for VECTOR PRODUCT.

cross-ques·tion ▸*v.* [*trans.*] question (someone) in great detail; cross-examine: *it seemed ungrateful to cross-question him* | [as *n.*] (**cross-questioning**) *the cross-questioning of Lopez.*

cross-rate ▸*n.* *Finance* an exchange rate between two currencies computed by reference to a third currency, usually the U.S. dollar.

cross-re·ac·tion ▸*n.* *Biochemistry* the reaction of an antibody with an antigen other than the one that gave rise to it. —**cross-re·act** *v.* —**cross-re·ac·tive** *adj.* —**cross-re·ac·tiv·i·ty** *n.*

cross-re·fer ▸*v.* [*intrans.*] (of a text) refer to another text or part of a text, typically in order to elaborate on a point: *the database* **cross-refers to** *the printed book.* ■ [*trans.*] refer (someone) to another text: *the entry cross-refers readers to "Style."* ■ (of a person) follow a cross reference from one part of a text to another, or one text to another: *students should be shown how to cross-refer between texts.*

cross ref·er·ence ▸*n.* a reference to another text or part of a text, typically given in order to elaborate on a point.
▸*v.* [*trans.*] (usu. **be cross-referenced**) provide with cross references to another text or part of a text: *entries are fully cross-referenced.*

cross-rhythm ▸*n.* *Music* a rhythm used simultaneously with another rhythm or rhythms. ■ the use of two or more rhythms simultaneously.

cross·roads /ˈkrôs,rōdz/ ▸*n.* an intersection of two or more roads. ■ a point at which a crucial decision must be made that will have far-reaching consequences: *we stand again* ***at a*** *historic* ***crossroads.*** ■ (**crossroad**) a road that crosses a main road or joins two main roads.

cross·ruff /ˈkrôs,rəf; -ˈrəf/ ▸*n.* a sequence of play in bridge or whist in which partners alternately trump each other's leads.
▸*v.* [*intrans.*] alternately trump particular suits in such a way.

cross sec·tion ▸*n.* a surface or shape that is or would be exposed by making a straight cut through something, esp. at right angles to an axis: *the cross section of an octahedron is a square* | ***in cross section*** *the sailfish's body looks like a tapering spear.* ■ a thin strip of organic tissue or other material removed by making two such cuts. ■ a diagram representing what such a cut would reveal. ■ a typical or representative sample of a larger group, esp. of people: *a cross section of our senior managers.* ■ *Physics* a quantity having the dimensions of an area which expresses the probability of a given interaction between particles.
▸*v.* (**cross-sec·tion**) [*trans.*] make a cross section of (something): [as *n.*] (**cross-sectioning**) *complex triangular terrain models for contour cross-sectioning.* —**cross-sec·tion·al** *adj.*

cross-sell ▸*v.* [*trans.*] sell (a different product or service) to an existing customer: *their database is used to cross-sell financial services.*

cross-slide ▸*n.* a sliding part on a lathe or planing machine that is supported by the saddle and carries the tool in a direction at right angles to the bed of the machine.

cross-stitch *Needlework* ▸*n.* a stitch formed of two stitches crossing each other. ■ needlework done using such stitches.
▸*v.* [*trans.*] sew or embroider using such stitches: [as *adj.*] (**cross-stitched**) *a cross-stitched pillow.*

cross street ▸*n.* a street crossing another or connecting two streets.

cross-sub·si·dize ▸*v.* [*trans.*] subsidize (a business or activity) out of the profits of another business or activity. —**cross-sub·si·di·za·tion** *n.* —**cross-sub·si·dy** *n.*

cross·talk /ˈkrôs,tôk/ ▸*n.* **1** unwanted transfer of signals between communication channels. **2** casual conversation.

cross·tie /ˈkrôs,tī/ ▸*n.* a wooden or concrete beam laid transversely under the rails of a railroad track to support it.

cross-tol·er·ance ▸*n.* resistance to the effects of a substance because of exposure to a pharmacologically similar substance: *cross-tolerance of barbiturates with alcohol was observed.*

cross·town /ˈkrôs,toun/ ▸*adj.* & *adv.* running or leading across a town: [as *adj.*] *the crosstown traffic* | [as *adv.*] *she drove us crosstown.*

cross-train ▸*v.* [*intrans.*] learn another skill, esp. one related to one's current job.

cross-train·ing ▸*n.* training in two or more sports in order to improve fitness and performance, esp. in a main sport.

cross·trees /ˈkrôs,trēz/ ▸*plural n.* a pair of horizontal struts attached to a sailing ship's mast to spread the rigging, esp. at the head of a topmast.

cross vault ▸*n.* a vault formed by the intersection of two or more vaults.

cross·walk /ˈkrôs,wôk/ ▸*n.* a marked part of a road where pedestrians have right of way to cross.

cross·ways /ˈkrôs,wāz/ ▸*adv.* another term for CROSSWISE.

cross·wind /ˈkrôs,wind/ ▸*n.* a wind blowing across one's direction of travel.

cross·wise /ˈkrôs,wīz/ ▸*adv.* in the form of a cross: *their arms were held out crosswise.* ■ diagonally; transversely: *wash the potatoes and halve them crosswise.*

cross·word /ˈkrôswərd/ (also **crossword puzzle**) ▸*n.* a puzzle consisting of a grid of squares and blanks into which words crossing vertically and horizontally are written according to clues. ▷said to have been invented by the journalist Arthur Wynne, whose puzzle (called a "word-cross") appeared in a Sunday newspaper, the *New York World*, on December 21, 1913.

cros·ti·ni /krôˈstēnē/ ▸*plural n.* small pieces of toasted or fried bread served with a topping as an appetizer or canapé. ▷Italian, plural of *crostino* 'little crust.'

crot·al ▸*n.* variant spelling of CROTTLE.

cro·tale /ˈkrō,täl; ˈkrōtl/ ▸*n.* (usu. **crotales**) a small tuned cymbal. ▷1930s: French, from Latin *crotalum*, denoting an ancient type of castanet, from Greek *krotalon*.

crotch /kräch/ ▸*n.* the part of the human body between the legs where they join the torso. ■ the part of a garment that passes between the legs. ■ a fork in a tree, road, or river. ▷mid 16th cent. (denoting an agricultural or garden fork, also a crutch): perhaps related to Old French *croche* 'crozier, shepherd's crook,' based on Old Norse *krókr* 'hook'; partly also a variant of CRUTCH.

crotch·et /ˈkrächət/ ▸*n.* **1** *Music chiefly Brit.* a quarter note. **2** a perverse or unfounded belief or notion: *the natural crotchets of inveterate bachelors.* ▷Middle English (in the sense 'hook'): from Old French *crochet*, diminutive of *croc* 'hook,' from Old Norse *krókr*.

crotch·et·y /ˈkrächətē/ ▸*adj.* irritable: *he was tired and crotchety.* ▷early 19th cent.: from of CROTCHET + -Y[1]. —**crotch·et·i·ness** *n.*

crotch·less /ˈkrächləs/ ▸*adj.* (of a garment) having a hole cut so as to leave the genitals uncovered.

cro·ton /ˈkrōtn/ ▸*n.* **1** a strong-scented tree, shrub, or herbaceous plant of the spurge family, native to tropical and warm regions. Several kinds yield timber and other commercially important products. • Genus *Croton*, family Euphorbiaceae: numerous species, including *C. laccifer*, the host plant for the lac insect. **2** a small evergreen tree or shrub of the Indo-Pacific region, which is grown for its colorful ornamental foliage. • Genus *Codiaeum*, family Euphorbiaceae: several species, in particular *C. variegatum*, many varieties of which are popular houseplants. ▷modern Latin, from Greek *krotōn* 'sheep tick' (from the shape of the seeds of the croton in sense 1).

cro·ton oil ▸*n.* a foul-smelling oil, formerly used as a purgative, obtained from the seeds of a tropical Asian croton tree. • The tree is *Croton tiglium* (family Euphorbiaceae).

Cro·ton Riv·er /ˈkrōtn/ a short river in eastern New York that flows into the Hudson River. It was dammed to form part of New York City's water system.

crot·tle /ˈkrätl/ (also **crot·al**) ▸*n.* a common lichen found on rocks, used in Scotland to make a golden-brown or reddish-brown dye for staining wool for making tweed. • *Parmelia saxatilis* (order Parmeliales) and other species. ▷mid 18th cent.: from Scottish Gaelic and Irish *crotal, crotan*.

crouch /krouch/ ▸*v.* [*intrans.*] adopt a position where the knees are bent and the upper body is brought forward and down, sometimes to avoid detection or to defend oneself: *we* ***crouched down*** *in the trench* | (**be crouched**) *Leo was crouched before the fire.* ■ (**crouch over**) bend over in this wayso as to be close to (someone or something): *she was crouching over some flower bed.*
▸*n.* [in *sing.*] a crouching stance or posture. ▷late Middle English: perhaps from Old French *crochir* 'be bent,' from *croche* (see CROTCH).

croup[1] /kro͞op/ ▸*n.* inflammation of the larynx and trachea in children, associated with infection and causing breathing difficulties. ▷mid 18th cent.: from dialect *croup* 'to croak,' of imitative origin. —**croup·y** *adj.*

croup[2] ▸*n.* the rump or hindquarters, esp. of a horse. ▷Middle English: from Old French *croupe*, ultimately of Germanic origin and related to CROP.

croup·i·er /ˈkro͞opē,ā; -pēər/ ▸*n.* **1** the person in charge of a gaming table, gathering in and paying out money or tokens. **2** *historical* the assistant chairman at a public dinner, seated at the lower end of the table. ▷early 18th cent. (denoting a person standing behind a gambler to give advice): French, from Old French *cropier* 'pillion rider, rider on the croup,' related to Old French *croupe* (see CROUP2). Compare with CRUPPER.

crous·tade /kro͞o'städ/ ▸*n.* a crisp piece of bread or pastry hollowed to receive a savory filling. ▷French, from Old French *crouste* or Italian *crostata* 'tart' (from *crosta* 'crust').

croute /kro͞ot/ ▸*n.* a piece of toasted bread on which savory snacks can be served. See also EN CROUTE. ▷French *croûte* (see CRUST).

crou·ton /'kro͞o,tän; kro͞o'tän/ ▸*n.* a small piece of fried or toasted bread served with soup or used as a garnish. ▷from French *croûton*, from *croûte* (see CRUST).

Crow /krō/ ▸*n.* (*pl.* same or **Crows**) **1** a member of an American Indian people inhabiting eastern Montana. **2** the Siouan language of this people.
▸*adj.* of or relating to this people or their language. ▷suggested by French *(gens des) corbeaux* '(people of the) crows', translating Siouan *apsáaloke* 'crow people.'

crow1 /krō/ ▸*n.* **1** a large perching bird with mostly glossy black plumage, a heavy bill, and a raucous voice. • Genus *Corvus*, family Corvidae (the **crow family**): several species, including the **American crow** (*C. brachyrhynchos*) and the **carrion crow** (*C. corone*). The crow family also includes the ravens, jays, magpies, choughs, and nutcrackers. **2** *derogatory* a woman, esp. an old or ugly one. **3** (**the Crow**) the constellation Corvus. ▷Old English *crāwe*; related to Dutch *kraai* and German *Krähe*, also to CROW2.

crow 1

▸*PHRASES* □ **as the crow flies** in a straight line: *Easingwold was 22 miles away as the crow flies.* □ **eat crow** *informal* be humiliated by having to admit one's defeats or mistakes.

crow2 ▸*v.* (*past* **crowed** or *Brit.* **crew** /kro͞o/) [*intrans.*] (of a cock) utter its characteristic loud cry. ■ (of a person) make a sound expressing a feeling of happiness or triumph: *Ruby crowed with delight.* ■ say something in a tone of gloating satisfaction: *avoid crowing about your success | "I knew you'd be back," she crowed.*
▸*n.* [usu. in *sing.*] the cry of a cock. ■ a sound made by a person expressing triumph or happiness: *she gave a little crow of triumph.* ▷Old English *crāwan*; related to German *krähen*, also to CROW1; ultimately imitative.

crow·bait /'krō,bāt/ ▸*n. informal, derogatory* an old horse.

crow·bar /'krō,bär/ ▸*n.* an iron bar with a flattened end, used as a lever.
▸*v.* (**-barred**, **-bar·ring**) [*trans.*] use a crowbar to open (something): *he crowbarred the box open.*

crow·ber·ry /'krō,berē/ ▸*n.* (*pl.* **-ries**) a creeping heatherlike dwarf shrub with small, needle-shaped leaves and black or reddish berries. • Genus *Empetrum*, family Empetraceae: several species, in particular the **black crowberry** (*E. nigrum*), with pea-sized black berries. ■ the edible but flavorless berry of this plant.

crowd /kroud/ ▸*n.* a large number of people gathered together, typically in a disorganized or unruly way: *a huge crowd gathered in the street outside.* ■ an audience: *a* **crowd of** *500 filled the synagogue.* ■ *informal, often derogatory* a group of people who are linked by a common interest or activity: *I've broken away from that whole junkie crowd.* ■ (**the crowd**) the mass or multitude of people, esp. those considered to be drearily ordinary or anonymous: *make yourself* **stand out from the crowd.** ■ a large number of things regarded collectively: *the* **crowd of** *tall buildings.*
▸*v.* [*trans.*] (often **be crowded**) (of a number of people) fill (a space) almost completely, leaving little or no room for movement: *the dance floor was crowded with revelers* | [as *adj.*] (**crowded**) *the crowded streets of Chicago.* ■ [*intrans.*] (**crowd into**) (of a number of people) move into (a space, esp. one that seems too small): *they crowded into the cockpit.* ■ [*intrans.*] (**crowd around**) (of a group of people) form a tightly packed mass around (someone or something): *photographers crowded around him.* ■ move too close to (someone), either aggressively or in a way that causes discomfort or harm: *don't crowd her, she needs air.* ■ (**crowd someone/something out**) exclude someone or something by taking their place: *grass invading the canyon has crowded out native plants.* ■ [*intrans.*] (**crowd in on**) *figurative* overwhelm and preoccupy (someone): *as demands crowd in on you it becomes difficult to keep things in perspective.* ■ *Baseball* (of a batter) stand very close to (the plate) when batting. ▷Old English *crūdan* 'press, hasten,' of Germanic origin; related to Dutch *kruien* 'push in a wheelbarrow.' In Middle English the senses 'move by pushing' and 'push one's way' arose, leading to the sense 'congregate,' and hence (mid 16th cent.) to the noun. —**crowd·ed·ness** *n.*

crowd·ie /'kroudē/ (also **crowd·y**) ▸*n.* a soft Scottish cheese made from buttermilk or sour milk. ▷early 19th cent.: from CRUD + -IE.

crowd-pleas·er ▸*n.* a person or thing with great popular appeal. —**crowd-pleas·ing** *adj.*

crowd-pull·er ▸*n. informal* an event, person, or thing that attracts a large audience.

crowd-surf·ing ▸*n.* the activity of being passed in a prone position over the heads of the audience at a rock concert, typically after having jumped from the stage. —**crowd-surf** *v.*

crow·foot /'krō,fo͝ot/ ▸*n.* a herbaceous plant related to the buttercups, typically having lobed or divided leaves and white or yellow flowers. Many kinds are aquatic with flowers held above the water. • Genus *Ranunculus*, family Ranunculaceae: many species, in particular the European **water crowfoot** (*R. aquatilis*).

crown /kroun/ ▸*n.* **1** a circular ornamental headdress worn by a monarch as a symbol of authority, usually made of or decorated with precious metals and jewels. ■ (**the Crown**) the reigning monarch, representing a country's government: *their loyalty to the Church came before their loyalty to the Crown.* ■ (usu. **the Crown**) the power or authority residing in the monarchy: *they claimed immunity on behalf of the Crown.* ■ an ornament, emblem, or badge shaped like a crown. ■ a wreath of leaves or flowers, esp. that worn as an emblem of victory in ancient Greece or Rome. ■ an award or distinction gained by a victory or achievement, esp. in sports: *the world heavyweight crown.* **2** the top or highest part of something: *the crown of the hill.* ■ the top part of a person's head or a hat. ■ the part of a plant just above and below the ground from which the roots and shoots branch out. ■ the upper branching or spreading part of a tree or other plant. ■ the upper part of a cut gem, above the girdle. ■ the part of a tooth projecting from the gum. ■ an artificial replacement or covering for the upper part of a tooth. ■ the point of an anchor at which the arms reach the shaft. **3** (also **crown piece**) a British coin with a face value of five shillings or 25 pence, now minted only for commemorative purposes. ■ a foreign coin with a name meaning 'crown,' esp. the krona or krone. **4** (in full **metric crown**) a paper size, now standardized at 384 × 504 mm. ■ (in full **crown octavo**) a book size, now standardized at 186 × 123 mm. ■ (in full **crown quarto**) a book size, now standardized at 246 × 189 mm.
▸*v.* [*trans.*] **1** (usu. **be crowned**) ceremonially place a crown on the head of (someone) in order to invest them as a monarch: *he went to Rome to be crowned | she was crowned queen in 1953.* ■ declare or acknowledge (someone) as the best, esp. at a sport: *he was crowned world champion last September.* ■ (in checkers) promote (a piece) to king by placing another on top of it. ■ rest on or form the top of: *the distant knoll was crowned with trees.* ■ fit a crown to (a tooth). ■ *informal* hit on the head: *she contained the urge to crown him.* **2** be the triumphant culmination of (an effort or endeavor, esp. a prolonged one): *years of struggle were crowned by a state visit to Paris* | [as *adj.*] (**crowning**) *the crowning moment of a worthy career.* **3** [*intrans.*] (of a baby's head during labor) fully appear in the vaginal opening prior to emerging. ▷Middle English: from Anglo-Norman French *corune* (noun), *coruner* (verb), Old French *corone* (noun), *coroner* (verb), from Latin *corona* 'wreath, chaplet.'
▸*PHRASES* □ **crowning glory** the best and most notable aspect of something: *the scene is the crowning glory of this marvelously entertaining show.* ■ *chiefly humorous* a person's hair. □ **to crown it all** as the final event in a series of particularly fortunate or unfortunate events: *it was cold and raining, and, to crown it all, we had to walk home.*

Crown at·tor·ney ▸*n.* In Canada, a government prosecutor in criminal cases.

crown col·o·ny a British colony whose legislature and administration is controlled by the Crown, represented by a governor. Some British dependencies within the Commonwealth still retain the designation, with varying degrees of self-government.

Crown Der·by ▸*n.* a kind of soft-paste porcelain made at Derby, England, and often marked with a crown above the letter "D."

crowned crane ▸*n.* an African crane with a yellowish bristly crest, a mainly black or dark gray body, much white on the wings, and pink and white cheeks. • Genus *Balearica*, family Gruidae: two species, in particular the (**black**) **crowned crane** (*B. pavonina*).

crowned head ▸*n.* (usu. **crowned heads**) a king or queen.

crowned pi·geon ▸*n.* the largest known pigeon, which has mainly bluish plumage and a tall, erect crest, and is found in New Guinea. • Genus *Goura*, family Columbidae: three species, including the **Victoria crowned pigeon** (*G. victoria*).

crown e·ther ▸*n. Chemistry* any of a class of organic compounds whose molecules are large rings containing a number of ether linkages.

crown fire ▸*n.* a forest fire that spreads from treetop to treetop.

crown gall ▸*n.* a bacterial disease of plants, esp. fruit bushes and trees, that is characterized by large tumorlike galls on the roots and lower trunk. • This disease is caused by the soil bacterium *Agrobacterium tumefaciens.* ■ a gall of this type.

crown glass ▸*n.* glass made without lead or iron, originally in a circular sheet. Formerly used in windows, it is now used as optical glass of low refractive index.

Crown Heights a neighborhood in northern Brooklyn in New York City, noted for its West Indian and Orthodox Jewish communities.

crown im·pe·ri·al ▸*n.* an Asian fritillary (plant) with a cluster of bell-like flowers at the top of a tall, largely bare stem. • *Fritillaria imperialis*, family Liliaceae.

crown jew·els ▸*plural n.* the crown and other ornaments and jewelry worn or carried by the sovereign on certain state occasions. ■ (**crown jewel**) a prized asset, achievement, or person: *the new stadium will be the crown jewel of sporting arenas.*

Crown land ▸*n.* (also **Crown lands**) land belonging to the British Crown. ■ land belonging to the state in some parts of the Commonwealth.

crown lens ▸*n.* a lens made of crown glass and usu. forming one component of an achromatic lens.

crown mold·ing ▸*n.* another term for CORNICE (sense 1).

crown of thorns ▸*n.* **1** (also **crown-of-thorns-star·fish**) a large spiky starfish of the tropical Indo-Pacific, feeding on coral and sometimes causing great damage to reefs. • *Acanthaster planci*, class Asteroidea. **2** a Madagascan shrub of the spurge family, with bright red flowers and many slender thorns. It is a popular houseplant and is sometimes used for hedges in the tropics. • *Euphorbia milii*, family Euphorbiaceae. ■ any of a number of other thorny plants, esp. Christ's thorn. ▷by association with Christ's crown of thorns.

crown piece ▸*n.* see CROWN (sense 3).

Crown Point a resort town in northeastern New York, on Lake Champlain, scene of much military action during the 18th century.

crown prince ▸*n.* (in some countries) a male heir to a throne.

crown prin·cess ▸*n.* the wife of a crown prince. ■ (in some countries) a female heir to a throne.

crown roast ▸*n.* a roast of rib sections of pork or lamb arranged like a crown in a circle with the bones pointing upward.

crown saw ▸*n.* another term for HOLE SAW.

crown wheel ▸*n.* a gearwheel or cogwheel with teeth that project from the face of the wheel at right angles, used esp. in the gears of motor vehicles.

crow-pheas·ant ▸*n.* a coucal, esp. the greater coucal, which has black plumage with chestnut wings and back and is found in South Asia. • Genus *Centropus*, family Cuculidae, esp. *C. sinensis*.

crow's-foot ▸*n.* (*pl.* **-feet**) **1** (usu. **crow's-feet**) a branching wrinkle at the outer corner of a person's eye. **2** a mark, symbol, or design formed of lines diverging from a point, resembling a bird's footprint. **3** *historical* a caltrop.

crow's-nest ▸*n.* a shelter or platform fixed near the top of the mast of a vessel as a place for a lookout to stand.

crow steps ▸*plural n.* another term for CORBIESTEPS. —**crow-stepped** *adj.*

croze /krōz/ ▸*n.* a groove at the end of a cask or barrel to receive the edge of the head. ■ a cooper's tool for making such grooves. ▷early 17th cent.: perhaps from French *creux*, *creuse* 'hollow.'

Cro·zet Is·lands /krō'zā/ a group of five small islands in the southern Indian Ocean, under French administration.

cro·zier /ˈkrōzhər/ (also **cro·sier**) ▸*n.* a hooked staff carried by a bishop as a symbol of pastoral office. ■ the curled top of a young fern. ▷Middle English (originally denoting the person who carried a processional cross in front of an archbishop): partly from Old French *croisier* 'cross bearer,' from *crois* 'cross,' based on Latin *crux*; reinforced by Old French *crocier* 'bearer of a bishop's crook,' from *croce* (see CROSSE).

CRT ▸*abbr.* cathode-ray tube.

cru /kro͞o; kry/ ▸*n.* (*pl.* **crus** *pronunc.* same) (in France) a vineyard or group of vineyards, esp. one of recognized quality. See also GRAND CRU, PREMIER CRU. ▷French, from *crû*, literally 'growth,' past participle of *croître*.

cru·ces /ˈkro͞oˌsēz/ ▸ plural form of CRUX.

cru·cial /ˈkro͞oshəl/ ▸*adj.* decisive or critical, esp. in the success or failure of something: *negotiations were at a crucial stage.* ■ of great importance: *this game is* ***crucial to*** *our survival.* ▷early 18th cent. (in the sense 'cross-shaped'): from French, from Latin *crux, cruc-* 'cross.' The sense 'decisive' is from Francis Bacon's Latin phrase *instantia crucis* 'crucial instance,' which he explained as a metaphor from a *crux* or fingerpost marking a fork at a crossroad; Newton and Boyle took up the metaphor in *experimentum crucis* 'crucial experiment.' —**cru·ci·al·i·ty** /ˌkro͞oshēˈalitē/ *n.* —**cru·cial·ly** *adv.*

USAGE **Crucial** is used in formal contexts to mean 'decisive, critical': *the testimony of the only eyewitness was crucial to the case.* Its broader use to mean 'very important' should be restricted to informal contexts: *it is crucial to get good light for your photographs.*

THE RIGHT WORD **acute, critical, crucial, deciding, pressing, urgent**

In any emergency or crisis situation, there is usually a turning point. Such an event is called **critical** if it determines the outcome of a situation (*a critical point in the nuclear disarmament negotiations;* | *a critical election for the Democratic Party*).

Crucial can also refer to a turning point, but it emphasizes the necessity of something happening before a result can be achieved (*the battle was crucial to their victory*), while *critical* suggests more of a balance between positive and negative outcomes (*a critical debate on foreign policy*).

Acute describes the intensification of a situation that is rapidly approaching a climax (*an acute shortage of O-negative blood*), while **deciding** refers to something that forces a certain outcome (*a deciding factor in his recovery*).

Pressing and **urgent** are milder words. A situation that is *pressing* may be chronic rather than acute (*a pressing need for changes in the political system*), while an *urgent* situation may be approaching a crisis without reference to a specific turning point (*an urgent meeting between the two presidents*).

While *urgent* expresses more intensity than *pressing*, neither adjective conveys the same sense of intensity as *crucial, critical,* or *acute.*

cru·cian /ˈkro͞oshən/ (also **crucian carp**) ▸*n.* a small olive-green to reddish-brown European carp of still or slow-moving waters, important as a farmed fish in eastern Europe. • *Carassius carassius*, family Cyprinidae. ▷mid 18th cent.: from Low German *karusse, karutze*, perhaps based on Latin *coracinus*, from Greek *korax* 'raven,' also denoting a black fish found in the Nile.

cru·ci·ate /ˈkro͞osh(ē)ət; -shēˌāt/ ▸*adj. Anatomy & Botany* cross-shaped. ▷early 19th cent.: from Latin *cruciatus*, from *crux, cruc-* 'cross.'

cru·ci·ate lig·a·ment ▸*n. Anatomy* either of a pair of ligaments in the knee that cross each other and connect the femur to the tibia.

cru·ci·ble /ˈkro͞osəbəl/ ▸*n.* a ceramic or metal container in which metals or other substances may be melted or subjected to very high temperatures. ■ a place or occasion of severe test or trial: *the crucible of combat.* ■ a place or situation in which different elements interact to produce something new: *the crucible of the new Romantic movement.* ▷late Middle English: from medieval Latin *crucibulum* 'night lamp, crucible' (perhaps originally a lamp hanging in front of a crucifix), from Latin *crux, cruc-* 'cross.'

cru·ci·fer /ˈkro͞osəfər/ ▸*n.* **1** *Botany* a cruciferous plant, with four petals arranged in a cross. **2** a person carrying a cross or crucifix in a procession. ▷mid 16th cent.: from Christian Latin, from Latin *crux, cruc-* 'cross.'

cru·cif·er·ous /kro͞oˈsifərəs/ ▸*adj. Botany* of, relating to, or denoting plants of the cabbage family (Brassicaceae). ▷mid 19th cent.: from modern Latin *Cruciferae* (plural), from Latin *crux, cruc-* 'cross' + *-fer* 'bearing' (because the flowers have four equal petals arranged crosswise), + -OUS.

cru·ci·fix /ˈkro͞osəˌfiks/ ▸*n.* a representation of a cross with a figure of Jesus Christ on it. ▷Middle English: via Old French from ecclesiastical Latin *crucifixus*, from Latin *cruci fixus* 'fixed to a cross.' Compare with CRUCIFY.

cru·ci·fix·ion /ˌkro͞osəˈfikshən/ ▸*n. chiefly historical* the execution of a person by nailing or binding them to a cross. ■ (**the Crucifixion**) the killing of Jesus Christ in such a way. ■ (**Crucifixion**) [in *sing.*] an artistic representation or musical composition based on this event. ▷late Middle English: from ecclesiastical Latin *crucifixio(n-)*, from the verb *crucifigere* (see CRUCIFY).

cru·ci·form /ˈkro͞osəˌfôrm/ ▸*adj.* having the shape of a cross: *a cruciform sword.* ■ of or denoting a church having a cross-shaped plan with a nave and transepts.

▸*n.* a thing shaped like a cross. ▷mid 17th cent.: from Latin *crux, cruc-* 'cross' + -IFORM.

cru·ci·fy /ˈkro͞osəˌfī/ ▸*v.* (**-fies, -fied**) [*trans.*] (often **be crucified**) *chiefly historical* put (someone) to death by nailing or binding them to a cross: *two thieves were crucified with Jesus.* ■ criticize (someone) severely and unrelentingly: *our fans would crucify us if we lost.* ■ cause anguish to (someone): *she'd been crucified by his departure.* ▷Middle English: from Old French *crucifier*, from late Latin *crucifigere*, from Latin *crux, cruc-* 'cross' + *figere* 'fix.' Compare with CRUCIFIX. —**cru·ci·fi·er** *n.*

cruck /krək/ ▸*n. Brit.* either of a pair of curved timbers extending to the ground in the roof framework of a type of medieval house: [as *adj.*] *a cruck barn.* ▷late 16th cent.: variant of CROOK.

crud /krəd/ ▸*n. informal* a substance that is disgusting or unpleasant, typically because of its dirtiness. ■ snow that is not packed down or groomed, on which it is difficult to ski. ■ nonsense: *they just want the simple truth without any religious crud.* ■ a contemptible person. ▷late Middle English: variant of CURD (the original sense). The earliest modern senses, 'filth' and 'nonsense' (originally U.S.), date from the 1940s. —**crud·dy** /ˈkrədē/ *adj.*

crude /kro͞od/ ▸*adj.* **1** in a natural or raw state; not yet processed or refined: *crude oil.* ■ *Statistics* (of figures) not adjusted or corrected: *the crude mortality rate.* ■ (of an estimate or guess) likely to be only approximately accurate. **2** constructed in a rudimentary or makeshift way: *a relatively crude nuclear weapon.* ■ (of an action) showing little finesse or subtlety and as a result unlikely to succeed: *the measure was condemned by economists as crude and ill-conceived.* **3** (of language, behavior, or a person) offensively coarse or rude, esp. in relation to sexual matters: *a crude joke.* See note at RUDE.

▸*n.* natural petroleum: *the ship was carrying 80,000 tons of crude.* ▷late Middle English: from Latin *crudus* 'raw, rough.' —**crude·ly** *adv.* —**crude·ness** *n.* —**cru·di·ty** /ˈkro͞oditē/ *n.*

crude tur·pen·tine ▸*n.* see TURPENTINE (sense 1).

cru·di·tés /ˌkro͞odəˈtā/ ▸*plural n.* assorted raw vegetables served as an hors d'oeuvre, typically with a sauce into which they may be dipped. ▷plural of French *crudité* 'rawness, crudity,' from Latin *crudus* 'raw, rough.'

cru·el /ˈkro͞oəl/ ▸*adj.* (**-el·er, -el·est**; *Brit.* **-el·ler, -el·lest**) causing pain or suffering: *I can't stand people who are cruel to animals.* ■ having or showing a sadistic disregard for the pain or suffering of others: *the girl had a cruel face.* ▷Middle English: via Old French from Latin *crudelis*, related to *crudus* (see CRUDE). —**cru·el·ly** *adv.*

cru·el·ty /ˈkro͞oəltē/ ▸*n.* (*pl.* **-ties**) callous indifference to or pleasure in causing pain and suffering: *he has treated her with extreme cruelty.* ■ behavior that causes pain or suffering to a person or animal: *we can't stand cruelty to animals* | *the cruelties of forced assimilation and genocide.* ■ *Law* behavior that causes physical or mental harm to another, esp. a spouse, whether intentionally or not. ▷Middle English: from Old French *crualte*, based on Latin *crudelitas*, from *crudelis* (see CRUEL).

cru·el·ty-free ▸*adj.* (of cosmetics or other commercial products) manufactured or developed by methods that do not involve experimentation on animals.

cru·et /ˈkro͞oət/ ▸*n.* **1** a small container for salt, pepper, oil, or vinegar for use at a dining table. **2** (in church use) a small container for the wine or water to be used in the celebration of the Eucharist. ▷Middle English (sense 2): from Anglo-Norman French, diminutive of Old French *crue* 'pot,' from Old Saxon *krūka*; related to CROCK[2].

Cruik·shank /ˈkro͝okˌshangk/, George (1792–1878), English painter, illustrator, and caricaturist.

Cruise /kro͞oz/, Tom (1962–), U.S. actor. He achieved success in *Risky Business* (1983) and went on to star in movies such as *Top Gun* (1986), *Born on the Fourth of July* (1989), *Jerry McGuire* (1996), and *Eyes Wide Shut* (1999).

cruise /kro͞oz/ ▸*v.* [*intrans.*] sail about in an area without a precise destination, esp. for pleasure: *they were cruising off the California coast* | [*trans.*] *she cruised the canals of France in a barge.* ■ take a vacation on a ship or boat following a predetermined course, usually calling in at several ports. ■ (of a vehicle or person) travel or move slowly around without a specific destination in mind: *a police van cruised past us* | [*trans.*] *teenagers were aimlessly cruising the mall.* ■ (of a motor vehicle or aircraft) travel smoothly at a moderate or economical speed. ■ achieve an objective with ease, esp. in sports: *he* ***cruised to*** *an easy victory in Tuesday's primary.* ■ [*trans.*] *informal* wander about (a place) in search of a sexual partner: *he cruised the gay bars of Los Angeles.* ■ [*trans.*] *informal* attempt to pick up (a sexual partner): *he was cruising a pair of sailors.*

▸*n.* a voyage on a ship or boat taken for pleasure or as a holiday and usually calling in at several places: *a cruise down the Nile* | [as *adj.*] *a cruise liner.* ▷mid 17th cent. (as a verb): probably from Dutch *kruisen* 'to cross,' from *kruis* 'cross,' from Latin *crux*.

▸***PHRASE*** □ **cruising for a bruising** *informal* heading or looking for trouble.

cruise con·trol ▸*n.* an electronic device in a motor vehicle that can be switched on to maintain a selected constant speed without the use of the accelerator.

cruise mis·sile ▸*n.* a low-flying missile that is guided to its target by an on-board computer.

cruis·er /ˈkro͞ozər/ ▸*n.* **1** a relatively fast warship larger than a destroyer and less heavily armed than a battleship. **2** a yacht or motorboat with passenger accommodations, designed for leisure use. ■ a person who goes on a pleasure cruise. **3** an automobile that can be driven smoothly at high speed. ■ a police patrol car. ▷late 17th cent.: from Dutch *kruiser*, from *kruisen* (see CRUISE).

cruis·er·weight /ˈkro͞ozərˌwāt/ ▸*n. chiefly Brit.* **1** another term for LIGHT HEAVYWEIGHT. **2** in professional boxing, a weight between light heavyweight and heavyweight, ranging from 175 to 190 pounds (79 to 85 kg). ■ a boxer of this weight.

cruis·ing range ▸*n.* the maximum distance a ship or aircraft can travel at a given speed without refueling.

cruis·ing speed ▸*n.* a speed for a particular vehicle, ship, or aircraft, usually somewhat below maximum, that is comfortable and economical.

crul·ler /ˈkrələr/ ▸*n.* a small cake made of rich, sweetened dough twisted or curled and fried in deep fat. ▷early 19th cent.: from Dutch *kruller*, from *krullen* 'to curl.'

crumb /krəm/ ▸*n.* **1** a small fragment of bread, cake, or cracker. ■ a very small amount of something: *the budget provided few crumbs of comfort.* ■ the soft inner part of a loaf of bread. ■ a dessert topping made of brown sugar, butter, flour, and spices and crumbled over a pie or cake: [as *adj.*] *apple crumb pie.* ■ (usu. **crumb rubber**) granulated rubber, made from recycled tires. **2** *informal* an objectionable or contemptible person: *he's an absolute crumb.*

▸*v.* [*trans.*] cover (food) with breadcrumbs: [as *adj.*] (**crumbed**) *crispy crumbed mushrooms with garlic dip.* ▷Old English *cruma*, of Germanic origin; related to Dutch *kruim* and German *Krume*. The final *-b* was added in the 16th cent., perhaps from CRUMBLE but also influenced by words such as *dumb*, where the original final *-b* is retained although no longer pronounced.

▸***PHRASE*** □ **crumbs from someone's** (or **a rich man's**) **table** an unfair and inadequate or unsatisfactory share of something.

crum·ble /ˈkrəmbəl/ ▸*v.* [*intrans.*] break or fall apart into small fragments, esp. over a period of time as part of a process of deterioration: *the plaster started to crumble* | [as *adj.*] (**crumbling**) *their crumbling ancestral home.* ■ [*trans.*] cause (something) to break apart into

Pronunciation Key ə *ago*; ər *over*; ˈə or ˌə *up*; ˈər or ˌər *fur*; a *hat*; ā *rate*; ä *car*; ch *chew*; e *let*; ē *see*; e(ə)r *air*; i *fit*; ī *by*; i(ə)r *ear*; ng *sing*; ō *go*; ô *for*; oi *boy*; o͝o *good*; o͞o *goo*; ou *out*; sh *she*; th *thin*; t͟h *then*; (h)w *why*; zh *vision*

small fragments: *the easiest way to crumble blue cheese.* ■ (of an organization, relationship, or structure) disintegrate gradually over a period of time: *the party's fragile unity began to crumble.*

▸*n. Brit.* a mixture of flour and butter that is rubbed to the texture of breadcrumbs and cooked as a topping for fruit. ■ a dessert made with such a topping and a particular fruit: *rhubarb crumble.* ▷late Middle English: probably from an Old English word related to CRUMB.

crum·bly /ˈkrəmblē/ ▸*adj.* (**-blier, -bli·est**) consisting of or easily breaking into small fragments: *the cheese is crumbly and moist.* —**crum·bli·ness** *n.*

crumb struc·ture ▸*n.* the porous structure or condition of soil when its particles are moderately aggregated.

crumb·y /ˈkrəmē/ ▸*adj.* (**crumb·i·er, crumb·i·est**) **1** like or covered in crumbs. **2** variant spelling of CRUMMY.

crum·horn ▸*n.* variant spelling of KRUMMHORN.

crum·my /ˈkrəmē/ (also **crumb·y**) *informal* ▸*adj.* (**-mi·er, -mi·est**) dirty, unpleasant, or of poor quality: *a crummy little room.* ■ unwell; ill: *I'm feeling crummy and want to get better.*

▸*n.* an old or converted truck used to transport loggers to and from work. ■ another term for CABOOSE (sense 1) . ▷mid 19th cent. (earlier in the literal senses 'crumbly' and 'like or covered with crumbs'): variant of CRUMBY. —**crum·mi·ly** /ˈkrəməlē/ *adv.* —**crum·mi·ness** *n.*

crump /krəmp/ ▸*n.* a loud thudding sound, esp. one made by an exploding bomb or shell.

▸*v.* [*intrans.*] make such a sound. ▷mid 17th cent.: imitative. The original sense (as a verb) was 'munch, crunch,' later 'hit hard' (used initially as a term in the game of cricket), hence the military sense 'bombard' (World War I).

crum·pet /ˈkrəmpət/ ▸*n.* a thick, flat, savory cake with a soft, porous texture, made from a yeast mixture cooked on a griddle and eaten toasted and buttered. ▷late 17th cent.: of unknown origin.

crum·ple /ˈkrəmpəl/ ▸*v.* [*trans.*] crush (something, typically paper or cloth) so that it becomes creased and wrinkled: *he* ***crumpled up*** *the paper bag* | [as *adj.*] (**crumpled**) *a crumpled sheet.* ■ [*intrans.*] become bent, crooked, or creased: *they heard the jetliner crumple moments before it crashed.* ■ [*intrans.*] (of a person) suddenly flop down to the ground so that their body appears bent or broken: *she crumpled to the floor in a dead faint.* ■ [*intrans.*] (of a person's face) suddenly sag and show an expression of desolation: *the child's face crumpled and he began to howl.* ■ [*intrans.*] suddenly lose force or effectiveness: *her composure crumpled.*

▸*n.* a crushed fold, crease, or wrinkle. ▷Middle English: from obsolete *crump* 'make or become curved,' from Old English *crump* 'bent, crooked'; related to German *krumm.* —**crum·ply** /ˈkrəmp(ə)lē/ *adj.*

crum·ple zone ▸*n.* a part of a motor vehicle, esp. the extreme front and rear, designed to crumple easily in a crash and absorb the main force of an impact.

crunch /krənCH/ ▸*v.* **1** [*trans.*] crush (a hard or brittle foodstuff) with the teeth, making a loud but muffled grinding sound: *she paused to crunch a ginger snap.* ■ [*intrans.*] make such a sound, esp. when walking or driving over gravel or an icy surface. ■ strike or crush noisily: *two cab drivers who had just crunched fenders.* **2** process large amounts of information or perform operations of great complexity, esp. by computer: *computers crunch data from real-world observations.*

▸*n.* **1** [usu. in *sing.*] a loud muffled grinding sound made when crushing, moving over, or hitting something: *Marco's fist struck Brian's nose with a crunch.* **2** (**the crunch**) *informal* a crucial point or situation, typically one at which a decision with important consequences must be made: *when it comes to the crunch, you chicken out.* ■ a severe shortage of money or credit: *the Fed would do what it could to ease America's* ***credit crunch.*** **3** a physical exercise designed to strengthen the abdominal muscles; a sit-up. ▷early 19th cent. (as a verb): variant of 17th-cent. *cranch* (probably imitative), by association with CRUSH and MUNCH.

crunch·er /ˈkrənCHər/ ▸*n. informal* **1** a critical or vital point; a crucial or difficult question. **2** a computer, system, or person able to perform operations of great complexity or to process large amounts of information: *a global information cruncher.* See also NUMBER CRUNCHER.

crunch·y /ˈkrənCHē/ ▸*adj.* (**crunch·i·er, crunch·i·est**) **1** making a sharp noise when bitten or crushed and (of food) pleasantly crisp: *bake until the topping is crunchy.* **2** *informal* politically and environmentally liberal: *a song that incorporates whale-singing seems pretty crunchy.* —**crunch·i·ly** /-CHəlē/ *adv.* —**crunch·i·ness** *n.*

crup·per /ˈkrəpər/ ▸*n.* a strap buckled to the back of a saddle and looped under the horse's tail to prevent the saddle or harness from slipping forward. ▷Middle English: from Old French *cropiere,* related to *croupe* (see CROUP[2]). Compare with CROUPIER.

cru·ra /ˈkro͝orə/ ▸ plural form of CRUS.

cru·ra ce·re·bri /ˈkro͝orə ˈserəˌbrī; ˈkerəˌbrē/ ▸ plural form of CRUS CEREBRI.

cru·ral /ˈkro͝o(ə)rəl/ ▸*adj. Anatomy & Zoology* of or relating to the leg or the thigh. ■ of or relating to any part called "crus," for example, the crura cerebri. ▷late 16th cent.: from Latin *cruralis,* from *crus, crur-* 'leg.'

crus /kro͞os; krəs/ ▸*n.* (*pl.* **cru·ra** /kro͝orə/) *Anatomy* an elongated part of an anatomical structure, esp. one that occurs in the body as a pair. See CRUS CEREBRI. ▷early 18th cent.: Latin, literally 'leg.'

cru·sade /kro͞oˈsād/ ▸*n.* (often **Cru·sade**) a medieval military expedition, one of a series made by Europeans to recover the Holy Land from the Muslims in the 11th, 12th, and 13th centuries. ■ a war instigated by the Church for alleged religious ends. ■ an organized campaign concerning a political, social, or religious issue, typically motivated by a fervent desire for change: *a* ***crusade against*** *crime.*

▸*v.* [*intrans.*] lead or take part in an energetic and organized campaign concerning a social, political, or religious issue: *he crusaded against gambling in the 1950s.* ▷late 16th cent. (originally as *croisade*): from French *croisade,* an alteration (influenced by Spanish *cruzado*) of earlier *croisée,* literally 'the state of being marked with the cross,' based on Latin *crux, cruc-* 'cross'; in the 17th cent. the form *crusado,* from Spanish *cruzado,* was introduced; the blending of these two forms led to the current spelling, first recorded in the early 18th cent. —**cru·sad·er** *n.*

crus ce·re·bri /ˈserəˌbrī; ˈkerəˌbrē/ ▸*n.* (*pl.* **cru·ra ce·re·bri** /ˈkro͝orə/) *Anatomy* either of two symmetrical tracts of nerve fibers at the base of the midbrain, linking the pons and the cerebral hemispheres. ▷early 18th cent.: from Latin, literally 'leg of the brain.'

cruse /kro͞oz/ ▸*n. archaic* an earthenware pot or jar. ▷Old English *crūse,* of Germanic origin; related to Dutch *kroes* and German *Krause*; reinforced in Middle English by Low German *krūs.*

crush /krəSH/ ▸*v.* [*trans.*] press or squeeze (someone or something) with force or violence, typically causing serious damage or injury: *he was crushed to death by a subway train* | [as *adj.*] (**crushed**) *the crushed remains of a Ford Bronco.* ■ reduce (something) to a powder or pulp by exerting strong pressure on it: *you can crush a pill between two spoons.* ■ crease or crumple (cloth or paper): [as *adj.*] (**crushed**) *crushed trousers and a crumpled jacket.* ■ (of a government or state) violently subdue (opposition or a rebellion): *the government had taken elaborate precautions to crush any resistance.* ■ bring about a feeling of overwhelming disappointment or embarrassment in (someone): *his defeat crushed a lot of left-wing supporters* | [as *adj.*] (**crushing**) *the news came as a crushing blow.*

▸*n.* **1** [usu. in *sing.*] a crowd of people pressed closely together, esp. in an enclosed space: *a number of youngsters fainted in the crush.* **2** *informal* a brief but intense infatuation for someone, esp. someone unattainable or inappropriate: *she did* ***have a crush on*** *Dr. Russell.* **3** a drink made from the juice of pressed fruit: *lemon crush.* ▷Middle English: from Old French *cruissir* 'gnash (teeth) or crack,' of unknown origin. —**crush·a·ble** *adj.* —**crush·er** *n.* —**crush·ing·ly** *adv.*

crushed vel·vet ▸*n.* velvet that has its nap pointing in different directions in irregular patches.

crush space *n.* ▸ **1** space in a motor vehicle between occupants and a point of impact that can absorb some of the shock of collision. **2** space in the common area of a performance venue that can accommodate the largest crowd expected.

crush zone ▸*n.* another term for CRUMPLE ZONE.

crust /krəst/ ▸*n.* the tough outer part of a loaf of bread: *a sandwich with the crusts cut off* | *I tore off several pieces of crust from the loaf.* ■ a hard, dry scrap of bread: *a kindly old woman might give her a crust.* ■ a slice of bread from the end of the loaf. ■ a layer of pastry covering a pie. ■ a hardened layer, coating, or deposit on the surface of something, esp. something soft: *a crust of snow.* ■ the outermost layer of rock of which a planet consists, esp. the part of the earth above the mantle: *the earth's crust* | *at the midocean ridge new crust is formed.* ■ a deposit of tartrates and other substances formed in wine aged in the bottle, esp. port.

▸*v.* [*intrans.*] form into a hard outer layer: *the blisters eventually crust over.* ■ [*trans.*] cover with a hard outer layer: *the burns crusted his cheek.* ▷Middle English: from Old French *crouste,* from Latin *crusta* 'rind, shell, crust.' —**crus·tal** /ˈkrəstəl/ *adj.* (in the geological sense of the *noun*).

Crus·ta·cea /krəˈstāSHə/ *Zoology* a large group of mainly aquatic arthropods that include crabs, lobsters, shrimps, wood lice, barnacles, and many minute forms. They are very diverse, but most have four or more pairs of limbs and several other appendages. • Subphylum (or phylum) Crustacea. ■ [as *plural n.*] (**crustacea**) arthropods of this group. ▷modern Latin (plural), from *crusta* (see CRUST). —**crus·ta·cean** *n. & adj.* —**crus·ta·ceous** /-SHəs/ *adj.*

crust·ed /ˈkrəstəd/ ▸*adj.* **1** having or forming a hard top layer or covering: *she washed away the crusted blood.* ■ denoting a style of unfiltered, blended port that deposits a sediment in the bottle. **2** old-fashioned; venerable: *a crusted establishment figure.*

crus·tose /ˈkrəsˌtōs/ ▸*adj. Botany* (of a lichen or alga) forming or resembling a crust. ▷late 19th cent.: from Latin *crustosus,* from *crusta* (see CRUST).

crust·y /ˈkrəstē/ ▸*adj.* (**crust·i·er, crust·i·est**) **1** having a crisp or hard outer layer or covering: *crusty bread.* ■ (of a substance) acting as a hard outer layer or covering: *Lake Manyara was ringed by crusty salt deposits.* **2** (esp. of an old person) outspoken and irritable: *a crusty old grandfather.* —**crust·i·ly** /ˈkrəstəlē/ *adv.* —**crust·i·ness** *n.*

crutch /krəCH/ ▸*n.* **1** a long stick with a crosspiece at the top, used as a support under the armpit by a lame person. ■ [in *sing.*] *figurative* a thing used for support or reassurance: *they use the Internet as a crutch for their loneliness.* **2** *archaic* another term for CROTCH (of the body or a garment).

▸*v.* [*intrans.*] move by means of or as if by means of crutches: *I was crutching down a long corridor.* ▷Old English *crycc, cryc,* of Germanic origin; related to Dutch *kruk* and German *Krücke.*

Crux /krəks; kro͝oks/ *Astronomy* another term for the SOUTHERN CROSS. ■ [as *genitive*] (**Crucis** /ˈkro͞osis/) used with a preceding letter or numeral to designate a star in this constellation: *the star Beta Crucis.* ▷Latin.

crux /krəks; kro͝oks/ ▸*n.* (*pl.* **crux·es** or **cru·ces** /ˈkro͞oˌsēz/) (**the crux**) the decisive or most important point at issue: *the crux of the matter is that attitudes have changed.* ■ a particular point of difficulty: *both cruces can be resolved by a consideration of the manuscripts.* ▷mid 17th cent. (denoting a representation of a cross, chiefly in *crux ansata* 'ankh,' literally 'cross with a handle'): from Latin, literally 'cross.'

cru·za·do /kro͞oˈzädō/ ▸*n.* (*pl.* **-dos**) the basic monetary unit of Brazil from 1988 to 1990, equal to 100 centavos. ▷from Portuguese *cruzado, crusado* 'marked with the cross.'

cru·zei·ro /kro͞oˈze(ə)rō/ ▸*n.* (*pl.* **-ros**) the basic monetary unit of Brazil from 1990 to 1993, equal to 100 centavos. ▷Portuguese, literally 'large cross.'

cry /krī/ ▸*v.* (**cries, cried**) [*intrans.*] shed tears, esp. as an expression of distress or pain: *don't cry—it'll be all right* | [*trans.*] *you'll cry tears of joy.* ■ shout or scream, esp. to express one's fear, pain, or grief: *the little girl fell down and cried for her mommy.* ■ say something in an excited or anguished tone of voice: *"Where will it end?" he* ***cried out.*** ■ (**cry out for**) *figurative* demand as a self-evident requirement or solution: *the present system cries out for reform.* ■ (of a bird or other animal) make a loud characteristic call: *the wild birds* ***cried out*** *over the water.* ■ [*trans.*] (of a hawker) proclaim (wares) for sale in the street.

▸*phrasal v.* □ **cry someone/something down** *dated* disparage or belittle someone or something. □ **cry off** *informal* go back on a promise or fail to keep to an arrangement: *we were going to Spain together and he cried off at the last moment.* □ **cry someone/something up** *dated* praise or extol someone or something.

▸*n.* (*pl.* **cries**) a spell of weeping: *I still* ***have a cry,*** *sometimes, when I realize that my mother is dead.* ■ a loud inarticulate shout or scream expressing a powerful feeling or emotion: *a cry of despair.* ■ a distinctive call of a bird or other animal. ■ a loud excited utterance of a word or words: *there was a cry of "Silence!"* ■ the call of a hawker selling wares on the street. ■ an urgent appeal or entreaty: *fund-raisers have issued a cry for help.* ■ a demand or opinion expressed by many people: *peace became the popular cry.* ▷Middle English (in the sense 'ask for earnestly or loudly'): from Old

French *crier* (verb), *cri* (noun), from Latin *quiritare* 'raise a public outcry,' literally 'call on the *Quirites* (Roman citizens) for help.'

▸*PHRASES* □ **cry one's eyes** (or **heart**) **out** weep bitterly and at length. □ **cry for the moon** ask for what is unattainable or impossible. □ **cry foul** protest strongly about a real or imagined wrong or injustice. □ **cry from the heart** a passionate and honest appeal or protest. □ **cry wolf** see WOLF. □ **for crying out loud** *informal* used to express one's irritation or impatience: *why do you have to take everything so personally, for crying out loud?* □ **in full cry** used to describe hounds baying in keen pursuit. □ **it's no use crying over spilt** (or **spilled**) **milk** see MILK.

cry·ba·by /ˈkrī,bābē/ ▸*n.* (*pl.* **-bies**) a person, esp. a child, who sheds tears frequently or readily.

cry·er /ˈkrīər/ ▸*n.* archaic spelling of CRIER.

cry·ing /ˈkrī-iNG/ ▸*adj.* very great: *it would be **a crying shame** to let some other woman have it.*

cryo- ▸*comb. form* involving or producing cold, esp. extreme cold: *cryostat* | *cryosurgery.* ▷from Greek *kruos* 'frost.'

cry·o·bi·ol·o·gy /,krīō,bīˈäləjē/ ▸*n.* the branch of biology that deals with the properties of organisms and tissues at low temperatures. **—cry·o·bi·o·log·i·cal** /-,bīəˈläjəkəl/ *adj.* **—cry·o·bi·ol·o·gist** /-jist/ *n.*

cry·o·gen /ˈkrīəjən/ ▸*n.* a substance used to produce very low temperatures.

cry·o·gen·ics /,krīəˈjeniks/ ▸*plural n.* [treated as *sing.*] the branch of physics dealing with the production and effects of very low temperatures. ■ another term for CRYONICS. **—cry·o·gen·ic** *adj.* **—cry·o·gen·i·cal·ly** /-ik(ə)lē/ *adv.*

cry·og·e·ny /krīˈäjənē/ ▸*n.* another term for CRYOGENICS.

cry·o·glob·u·lin /,krīəˈgläbyələn/ ▸*n. Biochemistry* a protein that occurs in the blood in certain disorders. It can be precipitated out of solution below 10°C, causing obstruction in the fingers and toes.

cry·o·lite /ˈkrīə,līt/ ▸*n.* a white or colorless mineral consisting of a fluoride of sodium and aluminum. It is added to bauxite as a flux in aluminum smelting. ▷early 19th cent.: from CRYO- 'cold, frost' (because the main deposits are found in Greenland) + -LITE.

cry·om·e·ter /krīˈämitər/ ▸*n.* a thermometer for measuring very low temperatures.

cry·on·ics /krīˈäniks/ ▸*plural n.* [treated as *sing.*] the practice or technique of deep-freezing the bodies of those who have died of an incurable disease, in the hope of a future cure. ▷1960s: contraction of CRYOGENICS. **—cry·on·ic** *adj.*

cry·o·pre·cip·i·tate /,krīōpriˈsipətət; -ˈsipə,tāt/ ▸*n. chiefly Biochemistry* a substance precipitated from a solution, esp. from the blood, at low temperatures. ■ *Medicine* an extract rich in a blood-clotting factor obtained as a residue when frozen blood plasma is thawed.

cry·o·pre·serve /,krīōpriˈzərv/ ▸*v.* [*trans.*] *Biology & Medicine* preserve (cells or tissues) by cooling them below the freezing point of water. **—cry·o·pres·er·va·tion** /-,prezərˈvāSHən/ *n.*

cry·o·pro·tect·ant /,krīōprəˈtektənt/ ▸*n. Physiology* a substance that prevents the freezing of tissues, or prevents damage to cells during freezing.

cry·o·scope /ˈkrīə,skōp/ ▸*n.* an instrument used to determine the freezing point of a liquid or a solution.

cry·o·stat /ˈkrīə,stat/ ▸*n.* an apparatus for maintaining a very low temperature. ■ an apparatus for taking very fine slices of tissue while it is kept very cold.

cry·o·sur·ger·y /,krīōˈsərjərē/ ▸*n.* surgery using the local application of intense cold to destroy unwanted tissue.

cry·o·ther·a·py /,krīōˈTHerəpē/ ▸*n.* the use of extreme cold in surgery or other medical treatment.

crypt /kript/ ▸*n.* **1** an underground room or vault beneath a church, used as a chapel or burial place. **2** *Anatomy* a small tubular gland, pit, or recess. ▷late Middle English (in the sense 'cavern'): from Latin *crypta*, from Greek *kruptē* 'a vault,' from *kruptos* 'hidden.'

crypt·a·nal·y·sis /,kriptəˈnaləsəs/ ▸*n.* the art or process of deciphering coded messages without being told the key. ▷1920s: from CRYPTO- + ANALYSIS. **—crypt·an·a·lyst** /kripˈtanl-əst/ *n.* **—crypt·an·a·lyt·ic** /-,tanlˈitik/ *adj.* **—crypt·an·a·lyt·i·cal** /-,tanlˈitikəl/ *adj.*

cryp·tic /ˈkriptik/ ▸*adj.* **1** having a meaning that is mysterious or obscure: *he found his boss's utterances too cryptic.* ■ (of a crossword) having difficult clues that indicate the solutions indirectly. **2** *Zoology* (of coloration or markings) serving to camouflage an animal in its natural environment. ▷early 17th cent.: from late Latin *crypticus*, from Greek *kruptikos*, from *kruptos* 'hidden.' Sense 2 dates from the late 19th cent. **—cryp·ti·cal·ly** /-ik(ə)lē/ *adv.*

cryp·to /ˈkriptō/ ▸*n.* **1** short for CRYPTOGRAPHY. **2** (*pl.* **-tos**) *informal* a person having a secret allegiance to a political creed, esp. communism.

crypto- ▸*comb. form* concealed; secret: *cryptogram.* ▷from Greek *kruptos* 'hidden.'

cryp·to·bi·ont /,kriptəˈbī,änt/ ▸*n. Biology* an organism capable of cryptobiosis.

cryp·to·bi·o·sis /,kriptə,bīˈōsis/ ▸*n. Biology* a physiological state in which metabolic activity is reduced to an undetectable level without disappearing altogether. It is known in certain plant and animal groups adapted to survive periods of extremely dry conditions.

cryp·to·bi·ot·ic /,kriptə,bīˈätik/ ▸*adj. Biology* **1** of, relating to, or capable of cryptobiosis. **2** of or denoting primitive organisms of the kind presumed to have existed in earlier geological periods but to have left no trace of their existence.

cryp·to·clas·tic /,kriptōˈklastik/ ▸*adj. Geology* composed of microscopic fragments.

cryp·to·coc·co·sis /,kriptəkäˈkōsəs/ ▸*n. Medicine* infestation with a yeastlike fungus, resulting in tumors in the lungs and sometimes spreading to the brain. • The fungus is *Cryptococcus neoformans*, phylum Basidiomycota, class Basidiomycetes). ▷1930s: from modern Latin *Cryptococcus* (part of the binomial of the fungus) + -OSIS. **—cryp·to·coc·cal** /-ˈkäkəl/ *adj.*

cryp·to·crys·tal·line /,kriptōˈkristə,lin; -,līn; -,lēn/ ▸*adj.* having a crystalline structure visible only when magnified.

cryp·to·gam /ˈkriptə,gam/ ▸*n. dated Botany* a plant that has no true flowers or seeds, including ferns, mosses, liverworts, lichens, algae, and fungi. ▷mid 19th cent.: from French *cryptogame*, from modern Latin *cryptogamae (plantae)*, denoting nonflowering plants, from Greek *kruptos* 'hidden' + *gamos* 'marriage' (because the means of reproduction was not apparent). **—cryptogamous** /kripˈtägəməs/ *adj.*

cryp·to·gam·ic /,kriptəˈgamik/ ▸*adj. Botany* of, relating to, or denoting cryptogams. ■ *Ecology* (of a desert soil or surface crust) covered with or consisting of a fragile black layer of cyanobacteria, mosses, and lichens, which is often important in preventing erosion.

cryp·to·gen·ic /,kriptəˈjenik/ ▸*adj.* (of a disease) of obscure or uncertain origin.

cryp·to·gram /ˈkriptə,gram/ ▸*n.* **1** a text written in code. **2** a symbol or figure with secret or occult significance.

cryp·tog·ra·phy /kripˈtägrəfē/ ▸*n.* the art of writing or solving codes. **—cryp·tog·ra·pher** /-fər/ *n.* **—cryp·to·graph·ic** /,kriptəˈgrafik/ *adj.* **—cryp·to·graph·i·cal·ly** /,kriptəˈgrafik(ə)lē/ *adv.*

cryp·tol·o·gy /kripˈtäləjē/ ▸*n.* the study of codes, or the art of writing and solving them. **—cryp·to·log·i·cal** /,kriptəˈläjikəl/ *adj.* **—cryp·tol·o·gist** /-jist/ *n.*

cryp·to·me·ri·a /,kriptəˈmi(ə)rēə/ ▸*n.* a tall, conical, coniferous tree with long, curved, spirally arranged leaves and short cones. Native to China and Japan, it is grown for timber in Japan. Also called JAPANESE CEDAR. • *Cryptomeria japonica*, family Taxodiaceae. ▷modern Latin, from CRYPTO- 'hidden' + Greek *meros* 'part' (because the seeds are concealed by scales).

cryp·to·nym /ˈkriptə,nim/ ▸*n.* a code name. ▷late 19th cent.: from CRYPTO- 'hidden' + Greek *onuma* 'name.' **—cryp·ton·y·mous** /kripˈtänəməs/ *adj.*

cryp·tor·chid /kripˈtôrkid/ ▸*n. Medicine* a person suffering from cryptorchidism.

cryp·tor·chi·dism /kripˈtôrki,dizəm/ ▸*n. Medicine* a condition in which one or both of the testes fail to descend from the abdomen into the scrotum. ▷late 19th cent.: from CRYPTO- 'hidden' + Greek *orkhis, orkhid-* 'testicle' + -ISM.

cryp·to·spor·i·di·um /,kriptəspəˈridēəm/ ▸*n.* a parasitic coccidian protozoan found in the intestinal tract of many vertebrates, where it sometimes causes disease. • Genus *Cryptosporidium*, phylum Sporozoa. ▷early 20th cent.: from CRYPTO- 'concealed' + modern Latin *sporidium* 'small spore.'

Cryp·to·zo·ic /,kriptəˈzō-ik/ ▸*adj. Geology* of, relating to, or denoting the period (the Precambrian) in which rocks contain no, or only slight, traces of living organisms. Compare with PHANEROZOIC. ▷early 20th cent.: from Greek *kruptos* 'hidden' + *zōē* 'life' + -IC.

cryp·to·zo·ic /,kriptəˈzō-ik/ ▸*adj. Ecology* (of small invertebrates) living on the ground but hidden in the leaf litter, under stones or pieces of wood. ▷late 19th cent.: from Greek *kruptos* 'hidden' + *zōē* 'life' + -IC. **—cryp·to·zo·a** /-ˈzōə/ *plural n.*

cryp·to·zo·ol·o·gy /,kriptəzōˈäləjē; -zōō-/ ▸*n.* the search for and study of animals whose existence or survival is disputed or unsubstantiated, such as the Loch Ness monster and the yeti. **—cryp·to·zo·o·log·i·cal** /-,zōəˈläjikəl; -,zōōə-/ *adj.* **—cryp·to·zo·ol·o·gist** /-jist/ *n.*

crys·tal /ˈkristl/ ▸*n.* **1** a piece of a homogeneous solid substance having a natural geometrically regular form with symmetrically arranged plane faces. ■ *Chemistry* any solid consisting of a symmetrical, ordered, three-dimensional aggregation of atoms or molecules. ■ *Electronics* a crystalline piece of semiconductor used as an oscillator or transducer. ■ a clear transparent mineral, esp. quartz. ■ a piece of crystalline substance believed to have healing powers. ■ *informal* short for CRYSTAL METH (methamphetamine). **2** (also **crystal glass**) highly transparent glass with a high refractive index: [as *adj.*] *a crystal chandelier.* ■ articles made of such glass: *a collection of crystal.* ■ the glass over a watch face.

▸*adj.* clear and transparent like crystal: *the clean crystal waters of the lake.* ▷late Old English (denoting ice or a mineral resembling it), from Old French *cristal*, from Latin *crystallum*, from Greek *krustallos* 'ice, crystal.' The chemistry sense dates from the early 17th cent.

▸*PHRASE* □ **crystal clear** completely transparent and unclouded. ■ unambiguous; easily understood: *the house rules are crystal clear.*

crys·tal ax·is ▸*n.* each of three axes used to define the edges of the unit cell of a crystal.

crys·tal ball ▸*n.* a solid globe of glass or rock crystal, used by fortune-tellers and clairvoyants for crystal-gazing.

crys·tal form ▸*n.* a set of crystal faces defined according to their relationship to the crystal axes.

crys·tal-gaz·ing ▸*n.* looking intently into a crystal ball with the aim of seeing images relating to future or distant events. ■ *figurative* attempting to forecast the future.

crys·tal heal·ing (also **crystal therapy**) ▸*n.* the use of the healing powers of crystals in alternative medicine.

crys·tal lat·tice ▸*n.* the symmetrical three-dimensional arrangement of atoms inside a crystal.

crys·tal·lif·er·ous /,kristlˈifərəs/ (also **crys·tal·lig·er·ous** /-ˈijərəs/) ▸*adj.* bearing, containing, or producing crystals.

crys·tal·lin /ˈkristəlin/ ▸*n. Biochemistry* a protein of the globulin class present in the lens of the eye. ▷mid 19th cent.: from Latin *crystallum* 'crystal' + -IN[1].

crys·tal·line /ˈkristl-in; -tl-,in; -tl-,ēn/ ▸*adj.* having the structure and form of a crystal; composed of crystals: *a crystalline rock.* ■ *poetic/literary* very clear: *he writes a crystalline prose.* ▷Middle English: from Old French *cristallin*, via Latin from Greek *krustallinos*, from *krustallos* (see CRYSTAL). **—crys·tal·lin·i·ty** /,kristlˈinitē/ *n.*

crys·tal·line lens ▸*n.* the transparent elastic structure behind the iris by which light is focused onto the retina of the eye.

crys·tal·line sphere ▸*n. historical* (in ancient and medieval astronomy) a transparent sphere of the heavens postulated to lie between the fixed stars and the *primum mobile* and to account for the precession of the equinox and other motions.

crys·tal·lite /ˈkristə,līt/ ▸*n.* an individual perfect crystal or region of regular crystalline structure in the substance of a material, typically of a metal or a partly crystalline polymer. ■ a very small crystal.

crys·tal·lize /ˈkristə,līz/ ▸*v.* form or cause to form crystals: [intrans.] *when most liquids freeze they crystallize.* ■ *figurative* [intrans.] make or become definite and clear: *vague feelings of unrest **crystallized into** something more concrete* | [*trans.*] *writing can help to crystallize your thoughts.* ■ [usu. as *adj.*] (**crystallized**) coat and impregnate (fruit or petals) with sugar as a means of preserving them: *a box of crystallized fruits.* **—crys·tal·liz·a·ble** /ˈkristə,līzəbəl; ,kristəˈlīzəbəl/ *adj.* **—crys·tal·li·za·tion** /,kristələˈzāSHən/ *n.*

C

Pronunciation Key ə *ago*; ər *over*; ˈə *or* ,ə *up*; ˈər *or* ,ər *fur*; a *hat*; ā *rate*; ä *car*; CH *chew*; e *let*; ē *see*; e(ə)r *air*; i *fit*; ī *by*; i(ə)r *ear*; NG *sing*; ō *go*; ô *for*; oi *boy*; o͝o *good*; o͞o *goo*; ou *out*; SH *she*; TH *thin*; T͟H *then*; (h)w *why*; ZH *vision*

crys·tal·log·ra·phy /ˌkristəˈlägrəfē/ ▸*n.* the branch of science concerned with the structure and properties of crystals. —**crys·tal·log·ra·pher** /-fər/ *n.* —**crys·tal·lo·graph·ic** /-ləˈgrafik/ *adj.* —**crys·tal·lo·graph·i·cal·ly** /-ləˈgrafik(ə)lē/ *adv.*

crys·tal·loid /ˈkristəˌloid/ ▸*adj.* resembling a crystal in shape or structure.
▸*n.* **1** *Botany* a small, crystallike mass of protein in a plant cell. **2** *Chemistry* a substance that, when dissolved, forms a true solution rather than a colloid and is able to pass through a semipermeable membrane.

crys·tal meth ▸*n.* see METH (sense 1).

Crys·tal Pal·ace a large building of prefabricated iron and glass resembling a giant greenhouse, designed by Joseph Paxton for the Great Exhibition of 1851 in Hyde Park, London, and reerected at Sydenham near Croydon; it was accidentally burned down in 1936.

crys·tal set (also **crystal radio**) ▸*n.* a simple early form of radio receiver with a crystal touching a metal wire as the rectifier (instead of a tube or transistor), and no amplifier or loudspeaker, necessitating headphones or an earphone.

crys·tal sys·tem ▸*n.* each of seven categories of crystals (cubic, tetragonal, orthorhombic, trigonal, hexagonal, monoclinic, and triclinic) classified according to the possible relations of the crystal axes.

crys·tal ther·a·py ▸*n.* another term for CRYSTAL HEALING.

crys·tal vi·o·let ▸*n.* a synthetic violet dye, related to rosaniline, used as a stain in microscopy and as an antiseptic in the treatment of skin infections.

Cs ▸*symbol* the chemical element cesium.

c/s ▸*abbr.* cycles per second.

CSA ▸*abbr.* Confederate States of America.

csar·das /ˈCHärˌdäSH; -ˌdäs/ (also **czar·das**) ▸*n.* (*pl.* same) a Hungarian dance with a slow introduction and a fast, wild finish. ▷mid 19th cent.: from Hungarian *csárdás*, from *csárda* 'inn.'

CSC ▸*abbr.* Civil Service Commission.

CSF ▸*abbr.* cerebrospinal fluid.

CS gas ▸*n.* a powerful form of tear gas used particularly in the control of riots. ▷1960s: from the initials of Ben B. *Corson* (born 1896) and Roger W. *Stoughton* (1906–57), the American chemists who discovered the properties of the chemical in 1928.

CSM ▸*abbr.* ■ command and service modules (see COMMAND MODULE). ■ command sergeant major.

CST ▸*abbr.* Central Standard Time (see CENTRAL TIME).

CT ▸*abbr.* ■ computerized (or computed) tomography. ■ Connecticut (in official postal use).

ct. ▸*abbr.* ■ carat: *18 ct. gold.* ■ cent. ■ county. ■ court.

cte·nid·i·um /təˈnidēəm/ ▸*n.* (*pl.* **-nid·i·a** /-ˈnidēə/) *Zoology* a comblike structure, esp. a respiratory organ or gill in a mollusk, consisting of an axis with a row of projecting filaments. ▷late 19th cent.; modern Latin, from Greek *ktenidion*, diminutive of *kteis, kten-* 'comb.'

cte·noid /ˈtēˌnoid; ˈtenˌoid/ ▸*adj. Zoology* (of fish scales) having many tiny projections on the edge like the teeth of a comb, as in many bony fishes. Compare with GANOID and PLACOID. ▷mid 19th cent.: from Greek *kteis, kten-* 'comb' + -OID.

Cte·noph·o·ra /tiˈnäfərə/ *Zoology* a small phylum of aquatic invertebrates that comprises the comb jellies. ▷modern Latin (plural), from Greek *kteis, kten-* 'comb' + *pherein* 'to bear.' —**cten·o·phore** /ˈtenəˌfôr/ *n.*

ctn. ▸*abbr.* ■ carton. ■ *Mathematics* cotangent.

C2C ▸*abbr.* consumer-to-consumer, denoting transactions conducted via the Internet between consumers.

CTS ▸*abbr.* carpal tunnel syndrome.

CT scan ▸*n* another term for **CAT SCAN**. —**CT scan·ner** *n.*

CTT ▸*abbr.* capital transfer tax.

Cu ▸*symbol* the chemical element copper. ▷from late Latin *cuprum*.

cu. ▸*abbr.* cubic (in units of measurement: for example, cu. ft. = cubic feet).

cua·dril·la /kwäˈdrē(l)yə/ ▸*n.* a matador's team of assistants, including picadors and banderilleros. ▷mid 19th cent.: Spanish.

cua·tro /ˈkwätrō/ ▸*n.* (*pl.* **-tros**) a small guitar, typically with four (or five) single or paired strings, used in Latin American and Caribbean folk music, esp. in Puerto Rico. ▷Latin American Spanish, literally 'four.'

cub /kəb/ ▸*n.* the young of a fox, bear, lion, or other carnivorous mammal. ■ *archaic* a young man, esp. one who is awkward or ill-mannered.
▸*v.* (**cubbed, cub·bing**) [*intrans.*] give birth to cubs: *both share the same earth during the first ten days after cubbing.* ▷mid 16th cent.: of unknown origin.

Cu·ba /ˈkyo͞obə/ a country in the western West Indies, the largest and furthest west of the islands, in the Caribbean Sea at the mouth of the Gulf of Mexico; pop. 11,308,000; capital, Havana; official language, Spanish. —**Cu·ban** *adj.* & *n.*

A Spanish colony, Cuba became nominally independent after the Spanish–American War of 1898 and achieved full autonomy in 1934. Since a communist revolution in 1959, it has been under the presidency of Fidel Castro. The country has suffered under a U.S. trade embargo and, since the collapse of the Soviet Union and the Eastern bloc, has lost much of its trade.

cub·age /ˈkyo͞obij/ ▸*n.* cubic content or capacity.

Cu·ba li·bre /ˌk(y)o͞obə ˈlēbrā/ ▸*n.* (*pl.* **Cu·ba li·bres**) a cocktail typically containing cola, lime juice, rum, and a garnish of lime. ▷late 19th cent.: American Spanish, literally 'free Cuba.'

Cu·ban·go /ko͞oˈbäNGgō/ another name for **OKAVANGO**.

Cu·ban heel /ˈkyo͞obən/ ▸*n.* a moderately high, straight-sided heel on a shoe or boot.

Cu·ban Mis·sile Cri·sis an international crisis in October 1962, the closest approach to nuclear war at any time between the U.S. and the USSR. When the U.S. discovered Soviet nuclear missiles on Cuba, President John F. Kennedy demanded their removal and announced a naval blockade of the island; the Soviet leader Khrushchev acceded to the U.S. demands a week later.

Cu·ban sand·wich ▸*n.* a type of submarine sandwich, typically grilled, esp. with ham, roast pork, Swiss cheese, mustard, and pickles.

cu·ba·ture /ˈkyo͞obəˌCHər/ ▸*n.* the determination of the volume of a solid. ▷late 17th cent.: from the verb CUBE, on the pattern of *quadrature*.

cub·by /ˈkəbē/ ▸*n.* (*pl.* **-bies**) a cubbyhole. ▷mid 17th cent. (originally Scots, denoting a straw basket): related to dialect *cub* 'stall, pen, hutch,' of Low German origin.

cub·by·hole /ˈkəbēˌhōl/ ▸*n.* a small, enclosed compartment or room.

cube /kyo͞ob/ ▸*n.* a symmetrical three-dimensional shape, either solid or hollow, contained by six equal squares. ■ short for CUBICLE. ■ a block of something with six sides: *a sugar cube.* ■ *Mathematics* the product of a number multiplied by its square, represented by a superscript figure 3: *a body increasing in weight by the cube of its length.*
▸*v.* [*trans.*] **1** *Mathematics* raise (a number or value) to its cube. **2** cut (food) into small cubes: *I bought sirloin from the butcher and cubed it myself.* **3** tenderize (meat) by scoring a pattern of small squares into its surface: [as *adj.*] (**cubed**) *cubed steaks.* ▷mid 16th cent.: from Old French, or via Latin from Greek *kubos*.

cu·beb /ˈkyo͞oˌbeb/ ▸*n.* a tropical shrub of the pepper family that bears pungent berries. • Genus *Piper*, family Piperaceae: several species, including the Asian *P. cubeba*. ■ the dried unripe berries of this shrub, used medicinally and to flavor cigarettes. ▷Middle English: from Old French *cubebe*, from Spanish Arabic *kubēba*, from Arabic *kubāba*.

cube farm ▸*n.* a large open-plan office divided into cubicles for individual workers.

cube root ▸*n.* the number that produces a given number when cubed.

cu·bic /ˈkyo͞obik/ ▸*adj.* having the shape of a cube: *a cubic room.* ■ denoting a unit of measurement equal to the volume of a cube whose side is one of the linear unit specified: *15 billion cubic meters of water.* ■ measured or expressed in such units. ■ involving the cube (and no higher power) of a quantity or variable: *a cubic equation.* ■ of or denoting a crystal system or three-dimensional geometric arrangement having three equal axes at right angles.
▸*n. Mathematics* a cubic equation, or a curve described by one. ▷late 15th cent. (in the sense 'involving the cube (and no higher power)'): from Old French *cubique*, or via Latin from Greek *kubikos*, from *kubos* 'cube.' —**cu·bi·cal** *adj.* —**cu·bi·cal·ly** /-ik(ə)lē/ *adv.*

cu·bic ca·pac·i·ty ▸*n.* the volume contained by a hollow structure, expressed in liters, cubic centimeters, or other cubic units.

cu·bic con·tent ▸*n.* the volume of a solid, often expressed in cubic meters.

cu·bi·cle /ˈkyo͞obikəl/ ▸*n.* a small partitioned-off area of a room, for example one containing a bed in a dwelling or one containing a desk in an office: *each cubicle is equipped with a PC and printer, and there are two fax machines in the east alcove.* ▷late Middle English (in the sense 'bedroom'): from Latin *cubiculum*, from *cubare* 'lie down.'

cu·bic zir·co·ni·a ▸*n.* a colorless form of zirconia that is very similar to diamond in refractivity and appearance.

cu·bi·form /ˈkyo͞obiˌfôrm/ ▸*adj. technical* cube-shaped: *the columns are thick and have cubiform capitals.*

cub·ism /ˈkyo͞oˌbizəm/ ▸*n.* an early 20th-century style and movement in art, esp. painting, in which perspective with a single viewpoint was abandoned and use was made of simple geometric shapes, interlocking planes, and, later, collage.

Cubism was a reaction against traditional modes of representation and Impressionist concerns with light and color. The style, created by Picasso and Braque and first named by the French critic Louis Vauxcelles in 1908, was inspired by the later work of Cézanne and by African sculpture.

▷early 20th cent.: from French *cubisme*, from *cube* (see CUBE). —**cub·ist** *n.* & *adj.* —**cub·is·tic** /kyo͞oˈbistik/ *adj.*

cu·bit /ˈkyo͞obit/ ▸*n.* an ancient measure of length, approximately equal to the length of a forearm. It was typically about 18 inches or 44 cm, though there was a **long cubit** of about 21 inches or 52 cm. ▷Middle English: from Latin *cubitum* 'elbow, forearm, cubit.'

cu·bi·tal /ˈkyo͞obitl/ ▸*adj.* **1** *Anatomy* of the forearm or the elbow: *the cubital vein.* **2** *Entomology* of the cubitus. ▷late Middle English: from Latin *cubitalis*, from *cubitus* 'cubit.'

cu·bi·tus /ˈkyo͞obitəs/ ▸*n. Entomology* the fifth longitudinal vein from the anterior edge of an insect's wing. ▷early 19th cent.: from Latin.

cu·boid /ˈkyo͞oˌboid/ ▸*adj.* more or less cubic in shape: *the school was a hideous cuboid erection of brick and glass.*
▸*n.* **1** *Geometry* a solid that has six rectangular faces at right angles to each other. **2** (also **cuboid bone**) *Anatomy* a squat tarsal bone on the outer side of the foot, articulating with the heel bone and the fourth and fifth metatarsals. ▷early 19th cent.: from modern Latin *cuboides*, from Greek *kuboeidēs*, from *kubos* (see CUBE). —**cu·boi·dal** /-ˌboidl/ *adj.*

cub re·port·er ▸*n. informal* a young or inexperienced newspaper reporter.

Cub Scout ▸*n.* a member of the junior branch of the Boy Scouts, for boys aged about 8 to 10.

cuck·ing stool /ˈkəkiNG/ ▸*n. historical* a chair to which a disorderly person was tied and then ducked into water or subjected to public ridicule as a punishment. ▷Middle English: from obsolete *cuck* 'defecate,' of Scandinavian origin; so named because a stool containing a chamber pot was often used for the purpose.

cuck·old /ˈkəkəld; -ōld/ ▸*n. archaic* the husband of an adulteress, often regarded as an object of derision.
▸*v.* [*trans.*] (of a man) make (another man) a cuckold by having a sexual relationship with his wife. ■ (of a man's wife) make (her husband) a cuckold. ▷late Old English, from Old French *cucuault*, from *cucu* 'cuckoo' (from the cuckoo's habit of laying its egg in another bird's nest). The equivalent words in French and other languages applied to both the bird and the adulterer; *cuckold* has never been applied to the bird in English. —**cuck·old·ry** /-drē/ *n.*

cuck·oo /ˈko͞okoo; ˈko͝oko͞o/ ▸*n.* **1** a medium-sized long-tailed bird, typically with a gray or brown back and barred or pale underparts. Many cuckoos lay their eggs in the nests of small songbirds. • Family Cuculidae (the **cuckoo family**): numerous genera and species, esp. the (**Eurasian**) **cuckoo** (*Cuculus canorus*), the male of which has a well-known two-note call. The cuckoo family also includes the

coucals, roadrunners, and anis. **2** *informal* a crazy person.
▸*adj. informal* crazy: *people think you're cuckoo.* ▷Middle English: from Old French *cucu*, imitative of its call.
▸*PHRASE* □ **cuckoo in the nest** an unwelcome intruder in a place or situation.

cuck·oo bee ▸*n.* a bee that lays its eggs in the nest of another species of bee, the young being raised and fed by the host. • *Nomada* and related genera (which parasitize solitary bees), and *Psithyrus* (which parasitize bumblebees), family Apidae.

cuck·oo clock ▸*n.* a clock that strikes the hour with a sound like a cuckoo's call and typically has a mechanical cuckoo that emerges with each note.

cuck·oo·flow·er /ˈko͝oko͞oˌflou(-ə)r; ˈko͝oko͞o-/ ▸*n.* a spring-flowering, herbaceous plant with pale lilac flowers, growing in damp meadows and by streams. • *Cardamine pratensis*, family Brassicaceae. ▷late 16th cent.: so named because it flowers at the time of year when the cuckoo is first heard calling.

cuck·oo·pint /ˈko͝oko͞oˌpīnt; ˈko͝oko͞o-/ ▸*n.* the common European wild arum of woodland and hedgerows, with a pale spathe and a purple or green spadix followed by bright red berries. Also called LORDS-AND-LADIES or JACK-IN-THE-PULPIT. • *Arum maculatum*, family Araceae. ▷late Middle English: from earlier *cuckoo-pintle*, from PINTLE in the obsolete sense 'penis' (because of the shape of the spadix).

cuck·oo spit ▸*n.* whitish froth found in compact masses on leaves and plant stems, exuded by the nymphs of froghoppers.

cuck·oo wasp ▸*n.* a wasp that lays its eggs in the nest of a bee or another species of wasp, in particular: • a true wasp lacking a worker caste, whose larvae are fed by the social wasp host (several species in the family Vespidae, including *Vespula austriaca*).

cu·cum·ber /ˈkyo͞oˌkəmbər/ ▸*n.* **1** a long, green-skinned fruit with watery flesh, usually eaten raw in salads or pickled. **2** the climbing plant of the gourd family that yields this fruit, native to the Chinese Himalayan region. It is widely cultivated but very rare in the wild. • *Cucumis sativus*, family Cucurbitaceae. ▷late Middle English: from Old French *cocombre, coucombre*, from Latin *cucumis, cucumer-*.
▸*PHRASE* □ **(as) cool as a cucumber** untroubled by heat, stress, or exertion. ■ calm and relaxed.

cu·cum·ber mo·sa·ic ▸*n.* a viral disease affecting plants of the gourd family, spread by beetles and aphids and causing mottling and stunting.

cu·cur·bit /kyo͞oˈkərbət/ ▸*n.* a plant of the gourd family (Cucurbitaceae), which includes melon, pumpkin, squash, and cucumber. ■ a gourd-shaped vessel forming the lower part of an alembic. ▷late Middle English: from Old French *cucurbite*, from Latin *cucurbita*. —**cu·cur·bi·ta·ceous** /kyo͞oˌkərbəˈtāsʜəs/ *adj.*

Cú·cu·ta /ˈko͞oko͞oˌtä/ an industrial and commercial city in northern Colombia, near the Venezuelan border, in the Andes; pop. 450,000.

cud /kəd/ ▸*n.* partly digested food returned from the first stomach of ruminants to the mouth for further chewing. ▷Old English *cwidu, cudu*, of Germanic origin; related to German *Kitt* 'cement, putty' and Swedish *kåda* 'resin.'
▸*PHRASE* □ **chew the cud** **1** (of a ruminant animal) further chew partly digested food. **2** think or talk reflectively.

cud·dle /ˈkədl/ ▸*v.* [*trans.*] hold close in one's arms as a way of showing love or affection: *he cuddles the baby close | they were cuddling each other in the back seat.* | [*intrans.*] *the pair have been spotted kissing and cuddling.* ■ [*intrans.*] lie or sit close and snug: *I love* **cuddling up** *in front of a fire | they cuddled together to keep out the cold.*
▸*n.* a prolonged and affectionate hug. ▷early 16th cent. (rare before the 18th cent.): of unknown origin. —**cud·dle·some** /-səm/ *adj.*

cud·dly /ˈkədlē; ˈkədl-ē/ ▸*adj.* (**-dli·er, -dli·est**) attractive, endearing, and pleasant to cuddle, esp. as a result of being soft or plump: *she was short and cuddly.*

cud·dy[1] /ˈkədē/ ▸*n.* a small room or compartment on a boat. ■ a small room or closet.

cud·dy[2] ▸*n.* (*pl.* **-dies**) *dialect, chiefly Scottish* **1** a donkey. **2** a stupid person: *you great soft cuddy!* ▷early 18th cent.: perhaps a nickname for the given name *Cuthbert*, once popular in Scotland and northern England.

cudg·el /ˈkəjəl/ ▸*n.* a short thick stick used as a weapon.
▸*v.* (**cudg·eled, cudg·el·ing**; *Brit.* **cudg·el·led, cudg·el·ling**) [*trans.*] beat with a cudgel. ▷Old English *cycgel*, of unknown origin.
▸*PHRASES* □ **cudgel one's brain** (or **brains**) think hard about a problem. □ **take up the cudgels** start to defend or support someone or something strongly: *there was no one else to* **take up the cudgels on their behalf.**

cue[1] /kyo͞o/ ▸*n.* a thing said or done that serves as a signal to an actor or other performer to enter or to begin their speech or performance. ■ a signal for action: *any conversational lull was my* **cue for** *asking a question.* ■ a piece of information or circumstance that aids the memory in retrieving details not recalled spontaneously. ■ *Psychology* a feature of something perceived that is used in the brain's interpretation of the perception: *expectancy is communicated both by auditory and visual cues.* ■ a hint or indication about how to behave in particular circumstances: *my teacher joked about such attitudes and I followed her cue.* ■ a facility for playing through an audio or video recording very rapidly until a desired starting point is reached.
▸*v.* (**cues, cued, cue·ing** or **cu·ing**) [*trans.*] give a cue to or for: *curious pedestrians are cued by the arrival of stretch limousines.* ■ act as a prompt or reminder: *have a list of needs and questions on paper to cue you.* ■ set a piece of audio or video equipment in readiness to play (a particular part of the recorded material): *features make it easier to* **cue up** *a tape for editing.* ▷mid 16th cent.: of unknown origin.
▸*PHRASES* □ **on cue** at the correct moment: *right on cue the door opened.* □ **take one's cue from** follow the example or advice of: *McGee did not move and Julia took her cue from him.*

cue[2] ▸*n.* a long, straight, tapering wooden rod for striking the ball in pool, billiards, snooker, etc.
▸*v.* (**cues, cued, cue·ing** or **cu·ing**) [*intrans.*] use such a rod to strike the ball. ▷mid 18th cent. (denoting a long plait or pigtail): variant of QUEUE.

cue ball ▸*n.* the ball, usually a white one, that is to be struck with the cue in pool, billiards, snooker, etc.

cue bid ▸*n. Bridge* a bid intended to give specific information about the content of the hand to the bidder's partner, for example, possession of a control in the opponents' suit.

cue·ca /ˈkwākə/ ▸*n.* a lively South American dance. ▷early 20th cent.: American Spanish, from *zamacueca*, also denoting a dance performed esp. in Chile.

cue card ▸*n.* a card held beside a camera for a television broadcaster to read from while appearing to look into the camera.

cued speech /kyo͞od/ ▸*n.* a type of sign language that uses hand movements combined with mouth shapes to communicate to the hearing impaired.

Cuen·ca /ˈkwengkə/ a city in the Andes in southern Ecuador; pop. 239,900. Founded in 1557, it is known as the "marble city" because of its many fine buildings.

Cuer·na·va·ca /ˌkwernəˈväkə/ a resort town in central Mexico, at an altitude of 5,060 feet (1,542 m), capital of the state of Morelos; pop. 400,000.

cues·ta /ˈkwestə/ ▸*n. Geology* a ridge with a gentle slope (dip) on one side and a steep slope (scarp) on the other. ▷early 19th cent. (originally a U.S. term for a steep slope at the edge of a plain): from Spanish, 'slope,' from Latin *costa* 'rib, flank.'

cuff[1] /kəf/ ▸*n.* **1** the end part of a sleeve, where the material of the sleeve is turned back or a separate band is sewn on. ■ the part of a glove covering the wrist. ■ the turned-up end of a trouser leg. ■ the top part of a boot, typically padded or turned down. ■ an inflatable bag wrapped around the arm when blood pressure is measured. **2** (**cuffs**) *informal* handcuffs.
▸*v.* [*trans.*] *informal* secure with handcuffs: *the man's hands were cuffed behind his back.* ▷late Middle English (denoting a glove or mitten): of unknown origin. —**cuffed** *adj.* [in *combination*] *a double-cuffed striped shirt.*
▸*PHRASE* □ **off the cuff** *informal* without preparation: *they posed some difficult questions to answer off the cuff* | [as *adj.*] *an off-the-cuff remark.* [as if from impromptu notes made on one's shirt cuffs.]

cuff[2] ▸*v.* [*trans.*] strike (someone) with an open hand, esp. on the head: *he cuffed him playfully on the ear.*
▸*n.* [usu. in *sing.*] a blow given with an open hand. ▷mid 16th cent.: of unknown origin.

cuff link ▸*n.* (usu. **cuff links**) a device for fastening together the sides of a shirt cuff, often decorative.

Cu·fic /ˈk(y)o͞ofik/ ▸*n.* & *adj.* variant spelling of KUFIC.

Cu·ia·bá /ˌko͞oyəˈbä/ **1** a river port in west central Brazil, on the Cuiabá River; pop. 389,070. **2** a river in western Brazil that rises in the Mato Grosso plateau and flows for 300 miles (483 km) to join the São Lourenço River near the border with Bolivia.

cui bo·no? /kwē ˈbōnō/ ▸*exclam.* who stands, or stood, to gain (from a crime, and so might have been responsible for it)? ▷early 17th cent.: Latin, literally 'to whom (is it) a benefit?'

cuirass 1

cui·rass /kwiˈras; kyo͝or-ˈas/ ▸*n.* **1** *historical* a piece of armor consisting of breastplate and backplate fastened together. ■ a hard protective cover on an animal. **2** *Medicine* an artificial ventilator that encloses the body, leaving the limbs free, and forces air in and out of the lungs by changes in pressure. ▷late Middle English: from Old French *cuirace*, based on late Latin *coriaceus* (adjective), from *corium* 'leather' (of which a cuirass was originally made).

cui·ras·sier /ˌkwi(ə)rəˈsi(ə)r; ˌkyo͝or-/ ▸*n. historical* a cavalry soldier wearing a cuirass. ▷mid 16th cent.: French, from *cuirasse*, from Old French *cuirace* (see CUIRASS).

cui·sine /kwiˈzēn/ ▸*n.* a style or method of cooking, esp. as characteristic of a particular country, region, or establishment: *much Venetian cuisine is based on seafood.* ■ food cooked in a certain way: *we spent the evening sampling the local cuisine.* ▷late 18th cent.: French, literally 'kitchen'.

cuisse /kwis/ (also **cuish** /kwisʜ/) ▸*n.* (usu. **cuisses** or **cuishes**) *historical* a piece of armor for the thigh. ▷Middle English (originally in the plural): from Old French *cuisseaux*, plural of *cuissel*, from late Latin *coxale*, from *coxa* 'hip.'

cuke /kyo͞ok/ ▸*n.* informal term for CUCUMBER.

Cul·bert·son /ˈkəlbərtsən/, Ely (1891–1955), U.S. bridge player. He revolutionized the game of contract bridge by formalizing a system of bidding.

culch ▸*n.* variant spelling of CULTCH.

Cul·dee /ˈkəlˌdē/ ▸*n.* an Irish or Scottish monk of the 8th to 12th centuries, living as a recluse usually in a group of thirteen (on the analogy of Jesus Christ and his Apostles). The tradition ceased as the Celtic Church was brought under Roman Catholic rule. ▷late Middle English: from medieval Latin *culdeus*, alteration, influenced by Latin *cultores Dei* 'worshipers of God,' of *kelledei* (plural, found in early Scottish records), from Old Irish *céle dé*, literally 'companion of God.'

cul-de-sac /ˈkəl di ˌsak/ ▸*n.* (*pl.* **cul-de-sacs** or **culs-de-sac** /ˈkəl(z)/) a street or passage closed at one end. ■ *figurative* a route or course leading nowhere: *the pro-democracy forces found themselves in a political cul-de-sac.* ■ *Anatomy* a vessel, tube, or sac, e.g., the cecum, open at only one end. ▷mid 18th cent. (originally in anatomy): French, literally 'bottom of a sack.'

-cule ▸*suffix* forming nouns such as *molecule, reticule*, which were originally diminutives. ▷from French *-cule* or Latin *-culus, -cula, -culum*.

cu·lex /ˈkyo͞oˌleks/ (also **culex mosquito**) ▸*n.* (*pl.* **-li·ces** /-ləˌsēz/) a mosquito of a genus that includes a number of kinds commonly found in cooler regions. They do not transmit malaria, but can pass on a variety of other parasites including those causing filariasis. Compare with ANOPHELES. • Genus *Culex*, subfamily Culicinae, family Culicidae. ▷late 19th cent.: Latin, literally 'gnat.' —**cu·li·cine** /ˈkyo͞oləˌsin/ *adj.* & *n.*

Cu·lia·cán Ro·sa·les /ˌko͞olyəˈkän rōˈsäləs; rōˈzäləs/ a city in northwestern Mexico, capital of the state of Sinaloa; pop. 662,110.

cu·li·nar·y /ˈkələˌnerē; ˈkyo͞olə-/ ▸*adj.* of or for cooking: *culinary skills | savor the culinary delights of the region.* ▷mid 17th cent.: from Latin *culinarius*, from *culina* 'kitchen.' —**cu·li·nar·i·ly** *adv.*

cull /kəl/ ▸*v.* [*trans.*] (usu. **be culled**) select from a large quantity; obtain from a variety of sources: *anecdotes culled from Greek and Roman history.* ■ reduce the population of (a wild animal) by selective slaughter: *he sees culling deer as a necessity* | [as *n.*] (**culling**) *kangaroo culling.* ■ send (an inferior or surplus animal on a farm) to be slaughtered. ■ *poetic/literary* pick (flowers or fruit): [as *adj.*] (**culled**) *fresh culled daffodils.*
▸*n.* a selective slaughter of wild animals. ■ [usu. as *adj.*] an inferior or surplus livestock animal selected

Pronunciation Key ə *ago*; ər *over*; ˈə or ˌə *up*; ˈər or ˌər *fur*; a *hat*; ā *rate*; ä *car*; cʜ *chew*; e *let*; ē *see*; e(ə)r *air*; i *fit*; ī *by*; i(ə)r *ear*; ɴɢ *sing*; ō *go*; ô *for*; oi *boy*; o͝o *good*; o͞o *goo*; ou *out*; sʜ *she*; tʜ *thin*; ᴛʜ *then*; (h)w *why*; zʜ *vision*

for killing: *a cull cow.* ▷Middle English: from Old French *coillier*, based on Latin *colligere* (see COLLECT[1]). —**cull·er** *n.*

Cul·len /ˈkələn/, Countee (1903–46), U.S. poet and leader of the Harlem Renaissance. His works include *Color* (1925), *The Black Christ* (1929), and *The Medea and Some Poems* (1935).

cul·let /ˈkələt/ ▶*n.* recycled broken or waste glass used in glassmaking. ▷early 19th cent.: variant of COLLET, in the obsolete sense 'glass left on the blowing iron when the finished article is removed.'

Cul·lo·den, Battle of /kəˈlädn/ the final engagement of the Jacobite uprising of 1745–6, fought on a moor near Inverness, the last pitched battle on British soil. The Hanoverian army under the Duke of Cumberland crushed the small and poorly supplied Jacobite army of Charles Edward Stuart, and a ruthless pursuit after the battle effectively prevented any chance of saving the Jacobite cause.

C

cul·ly /ˈkəlē/ ▶*n.* (*pl.* **-lies**) *Brit., informal* (often as a form of address) a man; a friend. ▷mid 17th cent. (denoting a person who is imposed upon): of unknown origin.

Culm /kəlm/ ▶*n. Geology* a series of Carboniferous strata in southwestern England, mainly shale and limestone with some thin coal seams. ■ (**culm**) *archaic* coal dust or slack. ▷Middle English (in the sense 'soot, smut,' now only Scots): probably related to COAL.

culm /kəlm/ ▶*n.* the hollow stem of a grass or cereal plant, esp. that bearing the flower. ▷mid 17th cent.: from Latin *culmus* 'stalk.'

cul·men /ˈkəlmən/ ▶*n.* (*pl.* **-mi·na** /-mənə/) **1** *Ornithology* the upper ridge of a bird's bill. **2** *Anatomy* a small region in the brain on the anterior surface of the cerebellum. ▷mid 17th cent. (in the sense 'top, summit'): from Latin, contraction of *columen* 'top, summit.'

cul·mi·nant /ˈkəlmənənt/ ▶*adj.* at or forming the top or highest point.

cul·mi·nate /ˈkəlməˌnāt/ ▶*v.* [*intrans.*] reach a climax or point of highest development: *the tensions and disorders which* ***culminated in*** *World War II.* ■ [*trans.*] be the climax or point of highest development of: *her book culminated a research project on the symmetry studies of Escher.* ■ *Astronomy Astrology* (of a celestial body) reach the highest point at the meridian. ▷mid 17th cent. (in astronomy and astrology): from late Latin *culminat-* 'exalted,' from the verb *culminare*, from *culmen* 'summit.'

cul·mi·na·tion /ˌkəlməˈnāSHən/ ▶*n.* [in *sing.*] the highest or climactic point of something, esp. as attained after a long time: *the product was the culmination of 13 years of research.* ■ *Astronomy Astrology* the reaching of the meridian by a celestial body.

cu·lottes /ˈk(y)o͞oˌläts; k(y)o͞oˈläts/ ▶*plural n.* women's knee-length trousers, cut with very full legs to resemble a skirt. ▷mid 19th cent.: French, 'breeches,' diminutive of *cul* 'rump,' from Latin *culus*.

culottes

cul·pa·ble /ˈkəlpəbəl/ ▶*adj.* deserving blame: *sometimes you're just as culpable when you watch something as when you actually participate.* ▷Middle English (in the sense 'deserving punishment'): from Old French *coupable, culpable*, from Latin *culpabilis*, from *culpare* 'to blame,' from *culpa* 'fault, blame.' —**cul·pa·bil·i·ty** /ˌkəlpəˈbilitē/ *n.* —**cul·pa·bly** /-blē/ *adv.*

cul·prit /ˈkəlprət; ˈkəlˌprit/ ▶*n.* a person who is responsible for a crime or other misdeed. ■ the cause of a problem or defect: *viruses could turn out to be the culprit.* ▷late 17th cent. (originally in the formula *Culprit, how will you be tried?*, said by the Clerk of the Crown in England to a prisoner pleading not guilty): perhaps from a misinterpretation of the written abbreviation *cul. prist*, for Anglo-Norman French *Culpable: prest d'averrer notre bille* '(You are) guilty: (We are) ready to prove our indictment'; in later use influenced by Latin *culpa* 'fault, blame.'

cult /kəlt/ ▶*n.* a system of religious veneration and devotion directed toward a particular figure or object: *the cult of St. Olaf.* ■ a relatively small group of people having religious beliefs or practices regarded by others as strange or sinister: *a network of Satan-worshiping cults.* ■ a misplaced or excessive admiration for a particular person or thing: ***a cult of personality*** *surrounding the leaders.* ■ [usu. as *adj.*] a person or thing that is popular or fashionable, esp. among a particular section of society: *a cult film.* ▷early 17th cent. (originally denoting homage paid to a divinity): from French *culte* or Latin *cultus* 'worship,' from *cult-* 'inhabited, cultivated, worshiped,' from the verb *colere*. —**cult·tic** /-tik/ *adj.* —**cult·ish** *adj.* —**cult·ish·ness** *n.* —**cult·ism** /-ˌtizəm/ *n.* —**cult·ist** /-tist/ *n.*

cultch /kəlCH/ (also **culch**) ▶*n.* the mass of stones, broken shells, and grit of which an oyster bed is formed. ▷mid 17th cent.: of unknown origin.

cul·ti·gen /ˈkəltəjən/ ▶*n. Botany* a plant species or variety known only in cultivation, esp. one with no known wild ancestor. ▷early 20th cent.: from *cultivated* (past participle of CULTIVATE) + -GEN.

cul·ti·var /ˈkəltəˌvär/ ▶*n. Botany* a plant variety that has been produced in cultivation by selective breeding. Cultivars are usually designated in the style *Taxus baccata* "Variegata." See also VARIETY (sense 2). ▷1920s: blend of CULTIVATE and VARIETY.

cul·ti·vate /ˈkəltəˌvāt/ ▶*v.* [*trans.*] **1** prepare and use (land) for crops or gardening. ■ break up (soil) in preparation for sowing or planting. ■ raise or grow (plants), esp. on a large scale for commercial purposes. ■ *Biology* grow or maintain (living cells or tissue) in culture. **2** try to acquire or develop (a quality, sentiment, or skill): *he cultivated an air of indifference.* ■ try to win the friendship or favor of (someone): *it helps if you go out of your way to cultivate the local people.* ■ [usu. as *adj.*] (**cultivated**) apply oneself to improving or developing (one's mind or manners): *he was a remarkably cultivated and educated man.* ▷mid 17th cent.: from medieval Latin *cultivat-* 'prepared for crops,' from the verb *cultivare*, from *cultiva (terra)* 'arable (land),' from *colere* 'cultivate, inhabit.' —**cul·ti·va·ble** /-vəbəl/ *adj.* —**cul·ti·vat·a·ble** /-ˌvātəbəl/ *adj.* —**cul·ti·va·tion** /ˌkəltəˈvāSHən/ *n.*

cul·ti·va·tor /ˈkəltəˌvātər/ ▶*n.* a person or thing that cultivates something: *they were herders of cattle and cultivators of corn.* ■ a mechanical implement for breaking up the soil and uprooting weeds.

cul·tur·al /ˈkəlCHərəl/ ▶*adj.* of or relating to the ideas, customs, and social behavior of a society: *the cultural diversity of the world's peoples.* ■ of or relating to the arts and to intellectual achievements: *a cultural festival.* ▷mid 19th cent.: from Latin *cultura* 'tillage' + -AL. —**cul·tur·al·ly** *adv.*

cul·tur·al an·thro·pol·o·gy ▶*n.* see ANTHROPOLOGY.

cul·tur·al at·ta·ché ▶*n.* an embassy official whose function is to promote cultural relations between the home country and the foreign country.

Cul·tur·al Rev·o·lu·tion a political upheaval in China 1966–68 intended to bring about a return to revolutionary Maoist beliefs. Largely carried forward by the Red Guard, it resulted in attacks on intellectuals, a large-scale purge in party posts, and the appearance of a personality cult around Mao Zedong. It led to considerable economic dislocation and was gradually brought to a halt by premier Zhou Enlai.

cul·tu·ra·ti /ˌkəlCHəˈrätē/ ▶*plural n.* well-educated people who appreciate the arts: *avant-garde enough to please the culturati but not there long enough to scare the old guard.* ▷1980s: blend of *culture* and *literati*.

cul·ture /ˈkəlCHər/ ▶*n.* **1** the arts and other manifestations of human intellectual achievement regarded collectively: *20th century popular culture.* ■ a refined understanding or appreciation of this: *men of culture.* ■ the customs, arts, social institutions, and achievements of a particular nation, people, or other social group: *Caribbean culture | people from many different cultures.* ■ [with *adj.*] the attitudes and behavior characteristic of a particular social group: *the emerging drug culture.* **2** *Biology* the cultivation of bacteria, tissue cells, etc., in an artificial medium containing nutrients: *the cells proliferate readily* ***in culture.*** ■ a preparation of cells obtained in such a way: *the bacterium was isolated in two blood cultures.* ■ the cultivation of plants: *this variety of lettuce is popular for its ease of culture.*

▶*v.* [*trans.*] *Biology* maintain (tissue cells, bacteria, etc.) in conditions suitable for growth. ▷Middle English (denoting a cultivated piece of land): the noun from French *culture* or directly from Latin *cultura* 'growing, cultivation'; the verb from obsolete French *culturer* or medieval Latin *culturare*, both based on Latin *colere* 'tend, cultivate' (see CULTIVATE). In late Middle English the sense was 'cultivation of the soil' and from this (early 16th cent.) arose 'cultivation (of the mind, faculties, or manners)'; sense 1 dates from the early 19th cent.

cul·ture-bound ▶*adj.* restricted in character or outlook by belonging or referring to a particular culture.

cul·tured /ˈkəlCHərd/ ▶*adj.* **1** characterized by refined taste and manners and good education: *Muslim Spain was the most cultured society in western Europe.* **2** *Biology* (of tissue cells, bacteria, etc.) grown or propagated in an artificial medium. ■ (of a pearl) formed around a foreign body inserted into an oyster.

cul·ture shock ▶*n.* the feeling of disorientation experienced by someone who is suddenly subjected to an unfamiliar culture, way of life, or set of attitudes.

cul·ture vul·ture ▶*n. informal* a person who is very interested in the arts, esp. to an obsessive degree.

cul·ture war ▶*n.* a conflict between groups with different ideals, beliefs, and philosophies: *a persisting culture war between religious and nonobservant Jews.*

cul·tus /ˈkəltəs/ ▶*n. technical* a system or variety of religious worship. ▷mid 19th cent.: Latin (see CULT).

Cul·ver Cit·y /ˈkəlvər/ a city in southwestern California, west of Los Angeles, an industrial and filmmaking center; pop. 38,793.

cul·ver·in /ˈkəlvərin/ ▶*n.* **1** a 16th- or 17th- century cannon with a relatively long barrel for its bore, typically about 10 to 13 feet long. **2** a kind of handgun of the 15th and 16th centuries. ▷late 15th cent. (sense 2): from Old French *coulevrine*, from *couleuvre* 'snake,' based on Latin *colubra*.

cul·vert /ˈkəlvərt/ ▶*n.* a tunnel carrying a stream or open drain under a road or railroad.

▶*v.* [*trans.*] (usu. **be culverted**) channel (a stream or drain) through a culvert. ▷late 18th cent.: of unknown origin.

cum[1] /ko͝om; kəm/ ▶*prep.* [usu. in *combination*] combined with; also used as (used to describe things with a dual nature or function): *a study-cum-bedroom.* ▷late 19th cent.: Latin.

cum[2] ▶*n. informal* variant spelling of COME.

cum. ▶*abbr.* cumulative.

Cu·ma·ná /ˌko͞omäˈnä/ a historic port city in northeastern Venezuela, capital of Sucre state, on the Manzanares River; pop. 212,000. It is said to be the oldest European settlement in South America.

cum·ber /ˈkəmbər/ ▶*v.* [*trans.*] *dated* hamper or hinder (someone or something): *they were cumbered with greatcoats and swords.* ■ obstruct (a path or space): *the road was clean and dry and not still cumbered by slush.*

▶*n. archaic* a hindrance, obstruction, or burden: *a cumber of limestone rocks.* ▷Middle English (in the sense 'overthrow, destroy'): probably from ENCUMBER.

Cum·ber·land /ˈkəmbərlənd/ **1** a city in northwestern Maryland, on the northern banks of the Potomac River; pop. 21,518. **2** a city in northeastern Rhode Island, north of Providence; pop. 31,840.

Cum·ber·land Gap /ˈkəmbərlənd/ a historic pass through the Appalachian Mountains, from southwestern Virginia into southeastern Kentucky.

Cum·ber·land Riv·er a river that flows for 690 miles (1,110 km) from the Cumberland Plateau in southeastern Kentucky across northern Tennessee and back into Kentucky, where it joins the Ohio River near Paducah.

Cum·ber·land sauce ▶*n.* a piquant sauce served as a relish with game and cold meats. It is typically made from red currant jelly flavored with orange, mustard, and port.

cum·ber·some /ˈkəmbərsəm/ ▶*adj.* large or heavy and therefore difficult to carry or use; unwieldy: *cumbersome diving suits.* See note at HEAVY. ■ slow or complicated and therefore inefficient: *organizations with cumbersome hierarchical structures.* ▷late Middle English (in the sense 'difficult to get through'): from CUMBER + -SOME[1]. —**cum·ber·some·ly** *adv.* —**cum·ber·some·ness** *n.*

cum·bi·a /ˈko͞ombēə/ ▶*n.* a kind of dance music of Colombian origin, similar to salsa. ■ a dance performed to this music. ▷1940s: from Colombian Spanish, perhaps from Spanish *cumbé*.

Cum·bri·a /ˈkəmbrēə/ a county in northwestern England; county town, Carlisle. Cumbria was an ancient British kingdom, and the name continued to be used for the hilly northwestern region of England that contains the Lake District and much of the northern Pennines. The county of Cumbria was formed in 1974. ▷from medieval Latin, from Welsh *Cymry* 'Welshman.' —**Cum·bri·an** *adj.* & *n.*

cum·brous /ˈkəmbrəs/ ▶*adj.* poetic or literary term for CUMBERSOME. ▷late Middle English (in the sense 'difficult to get through'): from CUMBER + -OUS. —**cum·brous·ly** *adv.* —**cum·brous·ness** *n.*

cum div·i·dend ▶*adv.* (of stocks) with a dividend.

cu·mec /ˈkyo͞oˌmek/ ▶*n.* a unit of flow equal to one cubic meter of water per second: *minimum flows proposed would vary seasonally between 80 cumecs in winter and 140 cumecs in summer.* ▷on the model of *cusec*.

cu·mene /ˈkyo͞oˌmēn/ ▶*n. Chemistry* a liquid hydrocarbon made catalytically from benzene, chiefly as an intermediate in phenol synthesis. • Alternative name: **isopropyl benzene**; chem. formula: $C_6H_5CH(CH_3)_2$. ▷mid 19th cent.: from Latin *cuminum* 'cumin' + **-ENE**.

cum gra·no sal·is /ko͝om ˌgränō ˈsälis/ ▶*adv.* (in phrase **take something cum grano salis**) another way of saying **TAKE SOMETHING WITH A PINCH OF SALT** (see **SALT**). ▷Latin, literally 'with a grain of salt.'

cum·in /ˈkəmən; ˈk(y)o͞o-/ (also **cum·min**) ▶*n.* **1** the aromatic seeds of a plant of the parsley family, used as a spice, esp. ground and used in curry powder. **2** the small, slender plant that bears this fruit and grows from the Mediterranean to central Asia. • *Cuminum cyminum*, family Umbelliferae. ▷Old English *cymen*, from Latin *cuminum*, from Greek *kuminon*, probably of Semitic origin and related to Hebrew *kammōn* and Arabic *kammūn*; superseded in Middle English by forms from Old French *cumon*, *comin*, also from Latin.

cum·mer·bund /ˈkəmərˌbənd/ ▶*n.* a sash worn around the waist, esp. as part of a man's evening clothes. ▷early 17th cent.: from Urdu and Persian *kamar-band*, from *kamar* 'waist, loins' and *-bandi* 'band.' The sash was formerly worn in the Indian subcontinent by domestic workers and low-status office workers.

cummerbund

cum·mings /ˈkəmiNGz/, e. e. (1894–1962), U.S. poet and novelist; full name *Edward Estlin Cummings*. His poems are characterized by their experimental typography (most notably by the avoidance of capital letters), technical skill, frank vocabulary, and sharp satire. Notable works: *The Enormous Room* (1922) and *95 Poems* (1956).

cum·ming·ton·ite /ˈkəmiNGtəˌnīt/ ▶*n.* a mineral occurring typically as brownish fibrous crystals in some metamorphic rocks. It is a magnesium-rich iron silicate of the amphibole group. ▷early 19th cent.: named after *Cummington*, a town in Massachusetts, + **-ITE**[1].

cum·quat /ˈkəmˌkwät/ ▶*n.* variant spelling of **KUMQUAT**.

cu·mu·late ▶*v.* /ˈkyo͞omyəˌlāt/ [*trans.*] gather together and combine: *the systems cumulate data over a period of years.* ■ [*intrans.*] be gathered together and combined: *all unpaid dividend payments cumulate and are paid when earnings are sufficient.* ■ [as *adj.*] (**cumulated**) *Chemistry* denoting two double bonds attached to the same carbon atom.
▶*n.* /ˈkyo͞omyəˌlit/ *Geology* an igneous rock formed by gravitational settling of particles in a magma. ▷mid 16th cent. (as a verb in the sense 'gather in a heap'): from Latin *cumulat-* 'heaped,' from the verb *cumulare*, from *cumulus* 'a heap.' Current senses date from the early 20th cent. —**cu·mu·la·tion** /ˌkyo͞omyəˈlāSHən/ *n.*

cu·mu·la·tive /ˈkyo͞omyələtiv; -ˌlātiv/ ▶*adj.* increasing or increased in quantity, degree, or force by successive additions: *the cumulative effect of two years of drought.* —**cu·mu·la·tive·ly** *adv.* —**cu·mu·la·tive·ness** *n.*

cu·mu·la·tive dis·tri·bu·tion func·tion ▶*n. Statistics* a function whose value is the probability that a corresponding continuous random variable has a value less than or equal to the argument of the function.

cu·mu·la·tive er·ror ▶*n. Statistics* an error consistently in the same direction for all observations.

cu·mu·la·tive pre·ferred stock ▶*n.* a preferred stock whose annual fixed-rate dividend, if it cannot be paid in any year, accrues until it can and is paid before common dividends.

cu·mu·la·tive vot·ing ▶*n.* a system of voting in an election in which each voter is allowed as many votes as there are candidates and may give all to one candidate or varying numbers to several.

cu·mu·li·form /ˈkyo͞omyələˌfôrm/ ▶*adj.* (of a cloud) developed in a predominantly vertical direction.

cu·mu·lo·nim·bus /ˌkyo͞omyəlōˈnimbəs/ ▶*n.* (*pl.* **-nim·bi** /-ˈnimbī; -bē/) *Meteorology* a cloud forming a towering mass with a flat base at fairly low altitude and often a flat top, as in thunderstorms.

cu·mu·lus /ˈkyo͞omyələs/ ▶*n.* (*pl.* **-li** /-ˌlī; -lē/) *Meteorology* a cloud forming rounded masses heaped on each other above a flat base at fairly low altitude. ▷mid 17th cent. (denoting a heap or an accumulation): from Latin, 'heap.' —**cu·mu·lous** /-ləs/ *adj.*

Cu·na ▶*n.* & *adj.* variant spelling of **KUNA**.

Cu·nard /k(y)o͞oˈnärd/, Sir Samuel (1787–1865), British shipowner; born in Canada. He founded the steamship company that still bears his name with the aid of a contract that began in 1840 to carry the mail between Britain and Canada.

cunc·ta·tion /kəNGkˈtāSHən/ ▶*n.* the action or an instance of delaying; tardy action.

cu·ne·ate /ˈkyo͞onēˌāt; -nēət/ ▶*adj. chiefly Anatomy Botany* wedge-shaped. ▷early 19th cent.: from Latin *cuneus* 'wedge' + **-ATE**[2].

cu·ne·i·form /kyo͞oˈnēəˌfôrm; ˈkyo͞on(ē)ə-/ ▶*adj.* denoting or relating to the wedge-shaped characters used in the ancient writing systems of Mesopotamia, Persia, and Ugarit, surviving mainly impressed on clay tablets: *a cuneiform inscription.* ■ *Anatomy* denoting three bones of the tarsus (ankle) between the navicular bone and the metatarsals. ■ *chiefly Biology* wedge-shaped: *the eggs are cuneiform.*
▶*n.* cuneiform writing. ▷late 17th cent.: from French *cunéiforme* or modern Latin *cuneiformis*, from Latin *cuneus* 'wedge.'

Cu·ne·ne /ko͞oˈnānə/ a river in Angola that rises near the city of Huambo and flows south and then west for 156 miles (250 km) to the Atlantic Ocean.

cun·ner /ˈkənər/ ▶*n.* an edible greenish-gray wrasse (fish) that lives along the Atlantic coast of North America. • *Tautogolabrus adspersus*, family Labridae. ▷early 17th cent.: perhaps associated with archaic *conder*, denoting a lookout who alerts the crew of fishing boats to the direction taken by shoals of herring.

cun·ni·lin·gus /ˌkənlˈiNGgəs/ ▶*n.* stimulation of the female genitals using the tongue or lips. ▷late 19th cent.: from Latin, from *cunnus* 'vulva' + *lingere* 'lick.'

cun·ning /ˈkəniNG/ ▶*adj.* **1** having or showing skill in achieving one's ends by deceit or evasion: *a cunning look came into his eyes.* ■ ingenious: *plants have evolved cunning defenses.* **2** attractive; quaint: *the baby will look cunning in that pink print.*
▶*n.* skill in achieving one's ends by deceit: *a statesman to whom cunning had come as second nature.* ■ ingenuity: *what resources of energy and cunning it took just to survive.* ▷Middle English: perhaps from Old Norse *kunnandi* 'knowledge,' from *kunna* 'know' (related to **CAN**[1]), or perhaps from Middle English *cunne*, an obsolete variant of **CAN**[1]. The original sense was '(possessing) erudition or skill' and had no implication of deceit; the sense 'deceitfulness' dates from late Middle English. —**cun·ning·ly** *adv.* —**cun·ning·ness** *n.*

Cun·ning·ham /ˈkəniNGˌham/, Merce (1919–), U.S. dancer and choreographer. As a dancer with the Martha Graham dance company 1939–45, he experimented with choreography and collaborated with composer John Cage in solo performances in 1944. He formed his own company in 1953.

Cu·no·be·li·nus /ˌk(y)o͞onōbəˈlīnəs; -ˈlē-/ variant of **CYMBELINE**.

cunt /kənt/ ▶*n. vulgar slang* a woman's genitals. ■ *offensive* a woman. ▷Middle English: of Germanic origin; related to Norwegian and Swedish dialect *kunta*, and Middle Low German, Middle Dutch, and Danish dialect *kunte*.

cup /kəp/ ▶*n.* **1** a small, bowl-shaped container for drinking from, typically having a handle and used with a matching saucer for hot drinks. ■ the contents of such a container: *a strong* ***cup of tea.*** ■ a measure of capacity used in cooking, equal to half a pint—that is, 8 ounces (0.237 l): ***one cup of butter.*** ■ (in church use) a chalice used at the Eucharist. ■ the wine of the Eucharist. ■ one's portion or share, as of sorrow or joy: *I submit to God's will and drink this cup for his satisfaction.* ■ an ornamental trophy in the form of a cup, usually made of gold or silver and having a stem and two handles, awarded as a prize in a contest. ■ (**Cup**) such a contest: *playing in the Cup is the best thing ever.* ■ (**cups**) one of the suits in a tarot pack. **2** a cup-shaped thing, in particular: ■ either of the two parts of a bra shaped to contain or support one breast. ■ this as a measure of breast size: *she had grown from an A to a C cup in just six months.* ■ a jockstrap having a protective reinforcement of rigid plastic or metal. ■ *Golf* the hole on a putting green or the metal container in it. ■ *Canadian* a receptacle forming part of a liquidizer. **3** a mixed drink served at parties, typically flavored with fruit juices and containing wine or cider.
▶*v.* (**cupped**, **cup·ping**) [*trans.*] **1** form (one's hand or hands) into the curved shape of a cup: *"Hey!" Dad shouted, with his hands cupped around his mouth.* ■ place the curved hand or hands around: *he* ***cupped*** *her face* ***in his hands.*** **2** *historical, Medicine* bleed (someone) by using a glass in which a partial vacuum is formed by heating: *Dr. Ross ordered me to be cupped.* ▷Old English: from popular Latin *cuppa*, probably from Latin *cupa* 'tub.'
▶*PHRASES* □ **in one's cups** *informal* drunk. □ **not one's cup of tea** *informal* not what one likes or is interested in: *cats were not her cup of tea.*

cup-and-ring ▶*adj.* denoting marks cut in megalithic monuments consisting of a circular depression surrounded by concentric rings.

cup·bear·er ˈkəpˌbe(ə)rər ▶*n. chiefly historical* or *poetic/literary* a person who serves wine, esp. in a royal or noble household.

cup·board /ˈkəbərd/ ▶*n.* a cabinet or closet, usually with a door and shelves, used for storage: *a kitchen cupboard.* ▷late Middle English (denoting a table or sideboard on which cups, plates, etc., were displayed): from **CUP** + **BOARD**.

cup·cake /ˈkəpˌkāk/ ▶*n.* **1** a small cake baked in a cup-shaped container and typically iced. **2** an attractive woman (often as a term of address). ■ a weak or effeminate man.

cup cor·al ▶*n.* a small, brightly colored, solitary coral with tentacles that end in small knobs, sometimes found in colder seas. • Genus *Caryophyllia*, order Scleractinia (or Madreporaria): several species, including the **Devonshire cup coral** (*C. smithi*), of European waters.

cu·pel /kyo͞oˈpel; ˈkyo͞opəl/ ▶*n.* a shallow, porous container in which gold or silver can be refined or assayed by melting with a blast of hot air, which oxidizes lead or other base metals.
▶*v.* (**-peled**, **-pel·ing**; *Brit.* **-pel·led**, **-pel·ling**) [*trans.*] assay or refine (a metal) in such a container. ▷early 17th cent. (as a noun): from French *coupelle*, diminutive of *coupe* 'goblet.' —**cu·pel·la·tion** /ˌkyo͞opəˈlāSHən/ *n.*

Cu·per·ti·no /ˌko͞opərˈtēnō/ a city in north central California, west of San Jose, part of the Silicon Valley complex; pop. 40,263.

Cup Fi·nal ▶*n.* the final match in a sports competition in which the winners are awarded a cup.

cup·ful /ˈkəpˌfo͝ol/ ▶*n.* (*pl.* **-fuls**) the amount held by a cup: *a* ***cupful of*** *water.* ■ another term for **CUP** as a measure in cooking: *add 1* ***cupful of*** *flour.*

cup fun·gus ▶*n.* a fungus in which the spore-producing layer forms the lining of a shallow cup. • Several families in the orders Helotiales and Pezizales, phylum Ascomycota.

Cu·pid /ˈkyo͞opəd/ *Roman Mythology* the god of love. He is represented as a naked, winged boy with a bow and arrows, with which he wounds his victims. Greek equivalent **EROS**. ■ [as *n.*] (also **cupid**) a representation of a naked winged child, typically carrying a bow. ▷from Latin *Cupido*, personification of *cupido* 'love, desire,' from *cupere* 'to desire.'

cu·pid·i·ty /kyo͞oˈpiditē/ ▶*n.* greed for money or possessions. ▷late Middle English: from Old French *cupidite* or Latin *cupiditas*, from *cupidus* 'desirous,' from *cupere* 'to desire.' Compare with **COVET**.

Cu·pid's bow ▶*n.* a shape like that of the double-curved bow often shown carried by Cupid, esp. at the top edge of a person's upper lip.

cup li·chen ▶*n.* a greenish-gray lichen that has small, cuplike structures arising from its spreading lobes and is found typically on heathland and moorland. • Genus *Cladonia*, order Cladoniales: many species.

cu·po·la /ˈkyo͞opələ/ ▶*n.* a small dome, esp. a small dome on a drum on top of a larger dome, adorning a roof or ceiling. ■ a gun turret; a small domed

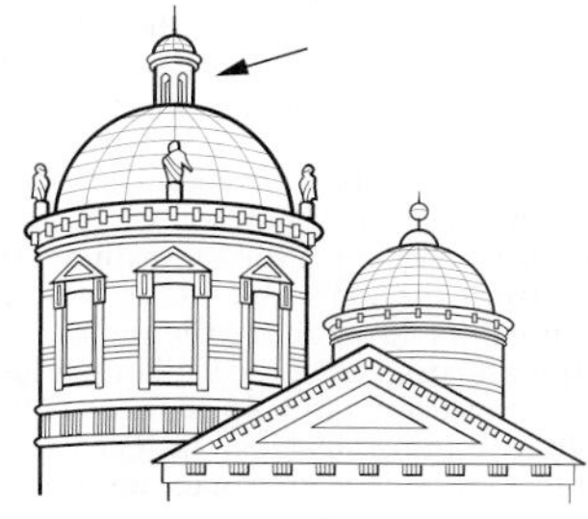
cupola

Pronunciation Key ə *ago*; ər *over*; ˈə or ˌə *up*; ˈər or ˌər *fur*; a *hat*; ā *rate*; ä *car*; CH *chew*; e *let*; ē *see*; e(ə)r *air*; i *fit*; ī *by*; i(ə)r *ear*; NG *sing*; ō *go*; ô *for*; oi *boy*; o͝o *good*; o͞o *goo*; ou *out*; SH *she*; TH *thin*; T͟H *then*; (h)w *why*; ZH *vision*

hatch above a gun turret on some tanks. ■ (also **cupola furnace**) a cylindrical furnace for refining metals, with openings at the bottom for blowing in air and originally with a dome leading to a chimney above. ▷mid 16th cent.: Italian, from late Latin *cupula* 'small cask or burying vault,' diminutive of *cupa* 'cask.' —**cu·po·laed** *adj.*

cup·pa /ˈkəpə/ *Brit., informal* ▸*n.* a cup of tea: *a good strong cuppa.*
▸*contraction of* cup of: *let's have another cuppa coffee.* ▷1920s: alteration.

cup·ping /ˈkəpiNG/ ▸*n.* (in Chinese medicine) a therapy in which heated glass cups are applied to the skin along the meridians of the body, creating suction as a way of stimulating the flow of energy.

cup·py /ˈkəpē/ ▸*adj.* (**-pi·er**, **-pi·est**) (of ground) full of shallow depressions.

cupr- ▸*comb. form* variant spelling of **CUPRO-** shortened before a vowel (as in *cuprammonium*).

cu·pram·mo·ni·um /ˌk(y)o͝oprəˈmōnēəm/ ▸*n.* [as *adj.*] *Chemistry* a complex ion, $Cu(NH_3)_4^{2+}$, formed in solution when ammonia is added to copper salts. The solution is deep blue and is used to dissolve cellulose.

cu·pre·ous /ˈk(y)o͞oprēəs/ ▸*adj. dated or poetic/literary* of or like copper. ▷mid 17th cent.: from late Latin *cupreus* (from *cuprum* 'copper') + **-OUS**.

cu·pric /ˈk(y)o͞oprik/ ▸*adj. Chemistry* of copper with a valence of two; of copper(II). Compare with **CUPROUS**. ▷late 18th cent.: from late Latin *cuprum* 'copper' + **-IC**.

cu·prite /ˈk(y)o͞oˌprīt/ ▸*n.* a dark red or brownish black mineral consisting of cuprous oxide.

cupro- (also **cupr-**) ▸*comb. form* of or relating to copper: *cupronickel.* ▷from late Latin *cuprum*.

cu·pro /ˈk(y)o͞oprō/ ▸*n.* a type of rayon made by dissolving cotton cellulose with cuprammonium salts and spinning the resulting solution into filaments. ▷1980s: an invented word, probably from *cuprammonium*.

cu·pro·nick·el /ˌk(y)o͞oprō ˈnikəl/ ▸*n.* an alloy of copper and nickel, esp. in the proportions 3:1 as used in "silver" coins.

cu·prous /ˈk(y)o͞oprəs/ ▸*adj. Chemistry* of copper with a valence of one; of copper(I). ▷mid 17th cent.: partly directly from late Latin *cuprum* 'copper' (reinforced by **CUPRIC**) + **-OUS**.

cu·pule /ˈkyo͞opyo͞ol/ ▸*n. Botany & Zoology* a cup-shaped organ, structure, or receptacle in a plant or animal. ▷late Middle English: from late Latin *cupula* (see **CUPOLA**).

cur /kər/ ▸*n.* an aggressive dog or one that is in poor condition, esp. a mongrel. ■ *informal* a contemptible man. ▷Middle English (in the general sense 'dog'): probably originally in *cur-dog*, perhaps from Old Norse *kurr* 'grumbling.'

cur. ▸*abbr.* ■ currency. ■ current.

cur·a·ble /ˈkyo͝orəbəl/ ▸*adj.* (of a disease or condition) able to be cured: *most skin cancers are completely curable.* ■ (of plastic, varnish, etc.) able to be hardened by some additive or other agent: *a radiation-curable coating.* ▷late Middle English: from Old French, or from late Latin *curabilis*, from Latin *curare* (see **CURE**). —**cur·a·bil·i·ty** /ˌkyo͝orəˈbilitē/ *n.*

Cu·ra·çao /ˌk(y)o͝orəˈsō; -ˈsou/ the largest island in the Netherlands Antilles, in the Caribbean Sea, 37 miles (60 km) north of the Venezuelan coast; pop. 144,100; chief town, Willemstad.

cu·ra·çao /ˈkyo͝orəˌsō; -ˌsou/ ▸*n.* (*pl.* **-çaos**) a liqueur flavored with the peel of bitter oranges. ▷early 19th cent.: named after **CURAÇAO**, where the oranges are grown.

cu·ra·cy /ˈkyo͝orəsē/ ▸*n.* (*pl.* **-cies**) the office, position, or work of a curate: *I was in England serving my curacy.*

cu·ran·de·ro /ˌkyo͝orənˈderō/ ▸*n.* (*pl.* **-de·ros**) (*fem.* **cu·ran·de·ra** /-ˈderə/) (in Spain and Latin America) a healer who uses folk remedies. ▷Spanish, from *curar* 'to cure,' from Latin *curare.*

cu·ra·re /k(y)o͝oˈrärē/ ▸*n.* a bitter, resinous substance obtained from the bark and stems of some South American plants. It paralyzes the motor nerves and is traditionally used by some Indian peoples to poison their arrows and blowpipe darts. • Curare is obtained from *Curarea* species and *Chondodendron tomentosum* (family Menispermaceae), and *Strychnos toxifera* (family Loganiaceae). ▷late 18th cent.: from a Carib word, partly via Spanish and Portuguese.

cu·ras·sow /ˈk(y)o͝orəˌsou; -ˌsō/ ▸*n.* a large, crested, pheasantlike bird of the guan family, found in tropical American forests. The male is typically black in color. • Genus *Crax* (and *Nothocrax*), family Cracidae: several species. ▷late 17th cent.: anglicized form of **CURAÇAO**.

cu·rate[1] /ˈkyo͝orət; -ˌrāt/ ▸*n.* (also **assistant curate**) a member of the clergy engaged as assistant to a vicar, rector, or parish priest. ■ *archaic* a minister with pastoral responsibility. ▷Middle English: from medieval Latin *curatus*, from Latin *cura* 'care.'

cu·rate[2] /ˈkyo͝oˌrāt/ ▸*v.* [*trans.*] (usu. **be curated**) select, organize, and look after the items in (a collection or exhibition): *both exhibitions are curated by the museum's director.* ▷late 19th cent.: back-formation from **CURATOR**. —**cu·ra·tion** /kyəˈrāSHən/ *n.*

cu·rate's egg ▸*n. Brit.* a thing that is partly good and partly bad: *this book is a bit of a curate's egg.* ▷early 20th cent.: from a cartoon in *Punch* (1895) depicting a meek curate who, given a stale egg at the bishop's table, assures his host that "parts of it are excellent."

cur·a·tive /ˈkyo͝orətiv/ ▸*adj.* able to cure something, typically disease: *the curative properties of herbs.*
▸*n.* a medicine or remedy. ▷late Middle English (in the sense 'relating to cures'): from French *curatif, -ive*, from medieval Latin *curativus*, from Latin *curare* (see **CURE**). —**cur·a·tive·ly** *adv.*

cu·ra·tor /ˈkyo͝orˌātər; kyo͝oˈrātər; ˈkyo͝orətər/ ▸*n.* a keeper or custodian of a museum or other collection. ▷late Middle English (denoting an ecclesiastical pastor, also (still a Scots legal term) the guardian of a minor): from Old French *curateur* or, in later use, directly from Latin *curator*, from *curare* (see **CURE**). The current sense dates from the mid 17th cent. —**cu·ra·to·ri·al** /ˌkyo͝orəˈtôrēəl/ *adj.* —**cu·ra·tor·ship** /-ˌSHip/ *n.*

curb /kərb/ ▸*n.* **1** a stone or concrete edging to a street or path. **2** a check or restraint on something: *curbs on the powers of labor unions.* **3** (also **curb bit**) a type of bit that is widely used in western riding. In English riding it is usually only used with a snaffle as part of a double bridle. **4** a swelling on the back of a horse's hock, caused by spraining a ligament.
▸*v.* [*trans.*] **1** restrain or keep in check: *she promised she would curb her temper.* ■ restrain (a horse) by means of a curb. **2** lead (a dog being walked) near the curb to urinate or defecate. ▷late 15th cent. (denoting a strap fastened to the bit): from Old French *courber* 'bend, bow,' from Latin *curvare* (see **CURVE**).

curb chain ▸*n.* a small chain which is attached to a curb bit and lies in the groove on a horse's chin.

curb·ing /ˈkərbiNG/ ▸*n.* the concrete or stones collectively forming a curb.

curb mar·ket ▸*n.* a market for selling shares not dealt with on the normal stock exchange.

curb roof ▸*n.* another term for **GAMBREL**.

curb serv·ice ▸*n.* service, esp. at a restaurant, extended to customers remaining in their parked vehicles.

curb·side /ˈkərbˌsīd/ ▸*n.* [usu. as *adj.*] the side of a road or sidewalk that is nearer to the curb: *curbside collection of trash.*

curb·stone /ˈkərbˌstōn/ ▸*n.* a long, narrow stone or concrete block, laid end to end with others to form a curb. ■ [as *adj.*] *informal* unqualified; amateur: *curbstone commentators.*

curb weight ▸*n.* the weight of an automobile without occupants or baggage.

cur·cu·li·o /kərˈkyo͞olēˌō/ ▸*n.* (*pl.* **-os**) a beetle of the weevil family, esp. one that is a pest of fruit trees. • Several genera and species in the family Curculionidae, including the **plum curculio** (*Conotrachelus nenuphar*). ▷modern Latin, used as the genus name for weevils in the 18th cent., now restricted to the nut weevils.

cur·cu·ma /ˈkərkyəmə/ ▸*n.* a tropical Asian plant of a genus that includes turmeric, zedoary, and other species that yield spices, dyes, and medicinal products. • Genus *Curcuma*, family Zingiberaceae. ▷modern Latin, from Arabic *kurkum* 'saffron,' from Sanskrit *kuṅkuma* (so named because the color of turmeric resembles that of saffron).

curd /kərd/ ▸*n.* **1** (also **curds**) a soft, white substance formed when milk sours, used as the basis for cheese. ■ a fatty substance found between the flakes of poached salmon. **2** the edible head of a cauliflower or similar plant. ▷late Middle English: of unknown origin. —**curd·y** *adj.*

curd cheese ▸*n. chiefly Brit.* a mild, soft, smooth cheese made from skimmed milk curd.

cur·dle /ˈkərdl/ ▸*v.* separate or cause to separate into curds or lumps: [*intrans.*] *take care not to let the soup boil or it will curdle* | [*trans.*] *making cheese by curdling milk.* ▷late 16th cent.: frequentative of obsolete *curd* 'congeal.' —**cur·dler** /ˈkərdlər; ˈkərdl-ər/ *n.*
▸*PHRASE* □ **make one's blood curdle** fill one with horror.

cure /kyo͝or/ ▸*v.* [*trans.*] **1** relieve (a person or animal) of the symptoms of a disease or condition: *he was* **cured of** *the disease* | *figurative centuries of science have not* **cured** *us* **of** *our superstitions.* ■ eliminate (a disease, condition, or injury) with medical treatment: *this technology could be used to cure diabetes.* ■ solve (a problem): *stopping foreign investment is no way to cure the fundamental problem.* **2** preserve (meat, fish, tobacco, or an animal skin) by various methods such as salting, drying, or smoking: *some farmers cured their own bacon* | [as *adj.*] (**cured**) *home-cured ham.* ■ harden (rubber, plastic, concrete, etc.) after manufacture by a chemical process such as vulcanization. ■ [*intrans.*] undergo this process.
▸*n.* **1** a substance or treatment that cures a disease or condition: *the search for a cure for the common cold.* ■ restoration to health: *he was beyond cure.* ■ a solution to a problem: *the cure is to improve the clutch operation.* **2** the process of curing rubber, plastic, or other material. **3** a Christian minister's pastoral charge or area of responsibility for spiritual ministry: *a benefice involving the* **cure of souls**. ■ a parish. ▷Middle English (as a noun): from Old French *curer* (verb), *cure* (noun), both from Latin *curare* 'take care of,' from *cura* 'care.' The original noun senses were 'care, concern, responsibility,' in particular spiritual care (hence sense 3). In late Middle English the senses 'medical care' and 'successful medical treatment' arose, and hence 'remedy.' —**cur·er** *n.*

cu·ré /kyo͞oˈrā; ˈkyo͝orˌā/ ▸*n.* a parish priest in a French-speaking country or region. ▷French, from medieval Latin *curatus* (see **CURATE**[1]).

cure-all ▸*n.* a medicine or other remedy that will supposedly cure any ailment. ■ a solution to any problem: *unfortunately, the new output circuitry is not a cure-all.*

cu·ret·tage /ˌkyo͝orəˈtäZH/ ▸*n. Surgery* the use of a curette, esp. on the lining of the uterus. See **DILATION AND CURETTAGE**. ▷late 19th cent.: from French, from **CURETTE**.

cu·rette /kyo͞oˈret/ ▸*n.* a surgical instrument used to remove material by a scraping action, esp. from the uterus.
▸*v.* [*trans.*] clean or scrape with a curette. ▷mid 18th cent. (as a noun): from French, from *curer* 'cleanse,' from Latin *curare* (see **CURE**).

cur·few /ˈkərˌfyo͞o/ ▸*n.* a regulation requiring people to remain indoors between specified hours, typically at night: *a dusk-to-dawn curfew* | *the whole area was immediately placed* **under curfew**. ■ the hour designated as the beginning of such a restriction: *to be out after curfew without permission was to risk punishment.* ■ the daily signal indicating this. ▷Middle English (denoting a regulation requiring people to extinguish fires at a fixed hour in the evening, or a bell rung at that hour): from Old French *cuevrefeu*, from *cuvrir* 'to cover' + *feu* 'fire.' The current sense dates from the late 19th cent.

Cu·ri·a /ˈkyo͝orēə/ the papal court at the Vatican, by which the Roman Catholic Church is governed. It comprises various Congregations, Tribunals, and other commissions and departments. ▷mid 19th cent.: from Latin *curia*, denoting a division of an ancient Roman tribe, also (by extension) the senate of cities other than Rome; later the term came to denote a feudal or Roman Catholic court of justice, whence the current sense. —**Cu·ri·al** *adj.*

Cu·rie /kyo͞oˈrē; ˈkyo͝orē/, Marie (1867–1934) and Pierre (1859–1906), French physicists; (Marie was born *Maria Sklodowska* in Poland); pioneers in

Marie Curie

Pierre Curie

radioactivity. Working together on the mineral pitchblende, they discovered the elements polonium and radium. After her husband's accidental death, Marie isolated radium. She died of leukemia, caused by prolonged exposure to radioactive materials. Nobel Prize for Physics (1903, both; shared with Becquerel); Nobel Prize for Chemistry (1911, Marie).

cu·rie /ˈkyo͝orē; kyo͝oˈrē/ (abbr.: **Ci**) ▸*n.* (*pl.* **-ries**) a unit of radioactivity, corresponding to 3.7×10^{10} disintegrations per second. ■ the quantity of radioactive substance that has this amount of activity. ▷early 20th cent.: named after Pierre and Marie CURIE.

cu·ri·o /ˈkyo͝orē,ō/ ▸*n.* (*pl.* **-os**) a rare, unusual, or intriguing object. ▷mid 19th cent.: abbreviation of CURIOSITY.

cu·ri·o·sa /ˌkyo͝orēˈōsə; -ˈōzə/ ▸*plural n.* curiosities, esp. erotic or pornographic books or articles. ▷late 19th cent.: from Latin, neuter plural of *curiosus* (see CURIOUS).

cu·ri·os·i·ty /ˌkyo͝orēˈäsitē/ ▸*n.* (*pl.* **-ties**) **1** a strong desire to know or learn something: *filled with curiosity, she peered through the window.* **2** a strange or unusual object or fact: *he showed them some of the curiosities of the house.* ▷late Middle English: from Old French *curiousete*, from Latin *curiositas*, from *curiosus* (see CURIOUS).
▸*PHRASE* □ **curiosity killed the cat** *proverb* being inquisitive about other people's affairs may get you into trouble.

cu·ri·ous /ˈkyo͝orēəs/ ▸*adj.* **1** eager to know or learn something: *I began to be curious about the whereabouts of the bride and groom | she was* ***curious to know*** *what had happened.* ■ expressing curiosity: *a curious stare.* **2** strange; unusual: *a curious sensation overwhelmed her.* ▷Middle English: from Old French *curios*, from Latin *curiosus* 'careful,' from *cura* 'care.' Sense 2 dates from the early 18th cent. **—cu·ri·ous·ly** *adv.* [*sentence adverb*] *curiously, I find snooker riveting.* **—cu·ri·ous·ness** *n.*

Cu·ri·ti·ba /ˌko͝orəˈtēbə/ a city in southern Brazil, capital of the state of Paraná; pop. 1,315,035.

cu·ri·um /ˈkyo͝orēəm/ ▸*n.* the chemical element of atomic number 96, a radioactive metal of the actinide series. Curium does not occur naturally and was first made by bombarding plutonium with helium ions. (Symbol: **Cm**) ▷1940s: modern Latin, from the name of Marie and Pierre CURIE.

curl /kərl/ ▸*v.* **1** form or cause to form into a curved or spiral shape: [*intrans.*] *her fingers curled around the microphone | a slice of ham had begun to* ***curl up*** *at the edges |* [*trans.*] *she used to curl her hair with rags.* ■ [*intrans.*] (**curl up**) sit or lie with the knees drawn up: *she curled up and went to sleep.* ■ move or cause to move in a spiral or curved course: [*intrans.*] *a wisp of smoke curling across the sky.* ■ (with reference to one's mouth or upper lip) raise or cause to raise slightly on one side as an expression of contempt or disapproval: [*intrans.*] *Maria saw his lip curl sardonically.* ■ (in weight training) lift (a weight) using only the hands, wrists, and forearms. **2** [*intrans.*] play at the game of curling.
▸*n.* **1** a lock of hair having a spiral or coiled form: *her blond hair was a mass of tangled curls.* ■ a thing having a spiral or inwardly curved form: *a curl of blue smoke.* ■ a curling movement: *the sneering curl of his lip.* ■ (with reference to a person's hair) a state or condition of being curled: *your hair has a natural curl | large perm rods give volume and control rather than lots of curl.* ■ see LEAF CURL. ■ a weightlifting exercise involving movement of only the hands, wrists, and forearms: *a dumbbell curl.* **2** *Mathematics* the vector product of the operator del and a given vector. ▷late Middle English: from obsolete *crulle* 'curly,' from Middle Dutch *krul.*
▸*PHRASE* □ **make someone's hair curl** *informal* shock or horrify someone.

curl·er /ˈkərlər/ ▸*n.* **1** (usu. **curlers**) a roller or clasp around which a lock of hair is wrapped to curl it. **2** a player in the game of curling.

cur·lew /ˈkər,lo͞o; ˈkərl,yo͞o/ ▸*n.* (*pl.* same or **-lews**) a large wading bird of the sandpiper family, with a long downcurved bill, brown streaked plumage, and frequently a distinctive ascending two-note call. See also STONE CURLEW. • Genus *Numenius*, family Scolopacidae: several species, including the common Eurasian *N. arquata* and the North American **long-billed curlew** (*N. americanus*). ▷Middle English: from Old French *courlieu*, alteration (by association with *courliu* 'courier,' from *courre* 'run' + *lieu* 'place') of imitative *courlis.*

long-billed curlew

Cur·ley /ˈkərlē/, James Michael (1874–1958), U.S. politician. An urban political boss, he was a member of the U.S. House of Representatives 1911–14, 1943–47, mayor of Boston for four terms between 1914 and 1950, and governor of Massachusetts 1935–37.

curl·i·cue /ˈkərlē,kyo͞o/ (also **curl·y·cue**) ▸*n.* a decorative curl or twist in calligraphy or in the design of an object. ▷mid 19th cent.: from CURLY + CUE[2] (in the sense 'pigtail'), or *-cue* representing the letter *q.*

curl·ing /ˈkərliNG/ ▸*n.* a game played on ice, esp. in Scotland and Canada, in which large, round, flat stones are slid across the surface toward a mark. Members of a team use brooms to sweep the surface of the ice in the path of the stone to control its speed and direction.

curl·ing i·ron ▸*n.* a heated rod used for rolling a person's hair into curls.

curl·ing stone ▸*n.* a large, polished, circular stone with an iron handle on top, used in the game of curling.

curl·y /ˈkərlē/ ▸*adj.* (**curl·i·er, curl·i·est**) made, grown, or arranged in curls or curves: *my hair is just naturally thick and curly.* **—curl·i·ness** *n.*

curl·y·cue ▸*n.* variant spelling of CURLICUE.

curl·y en·dive ▸*n.* see ENDIVE.

curl·y kale ▸*n.* kale of a variety with dark green, tightly curled leaves.

cur·ly top (also **curly top disease**) ▸*n.* a viral disease affecting plants, esp. beets and members of the gourd family, spread by beetles, particularly the beet leafhopper. Infected plants become dwarfed and have puckered, distorted foliage.

curl·y-wurl·y ▸*adj. informal* twisting and curling. ▷late 18th cent.: reduplication of CURLY.

cur·mudg·eon /kərˈməjən/ ▸*n.* a bad-tempered or surly person. ▷late 16th cent.: of unknown origin. **—cur·mudg·eon·li·ness** *n.* **—cur·mudg·eon·ly** *adj.*

cur·rach /ˈkərə(KH); kə-rə(KH)/ (also **cur·ragh**) ▸*n.* Irish and Scottish term for CORACLE. ▷late Middle English: from Irish and Scottish Gaelic *curach* 'small boat.' Compare with CORACLE.

cur·ragh ▸*n.* variant spelling of CURRACH.

cur·ra·jong ▸*n.* variant spelling of KURRAJONG.

cur·rant /ˈkərənt; ˈkə-rənt/ ▸*n.* **1** a small dried fruit made from a seedless variety of grape originally grown in the eastern Mediterranean region, now widely produced in California, and much used in cooking: [as *adj.*] *a currant bun.* **2** a Eurasian shrub that produces small edible black, red, or white berries. • Genus *Ribes*, family Grossulariaceae: numerous species, including **black currant** and **red currant**. ■ a berry from such a shrub. ▷Middle English *raisons of Corauntz*, translating Anglo-Norman French *raisins de Corauntz* 'grapes of Corinth' (the original source).

cur·rant gall ▸*n.* a spherical red or purple gall that forms on the leaves or male catkins of oak trees in response to the developing larva of a gall wasp. It results from eggs laid in the spring and alternates with the spangle gall. • The wasp is *Neuroterus quercusbaccarum*, family Cynipidae.

cur·rant to·ma·to ▸*n.* a kind of tomato with tiny fruits, native to the Andes. • *Lycopersicon pimpinellifolium*, family Solanaceae.

cur·ren·cy /ˈkərənsē; ˈkə-rənsē/ ▸*n.* (*pl.* **-cies**) **1** a system of money in general use in a particular country: *the dollar was a strong currency | travelers checks in foreign currency | figurative he was rich in the currency of love.* **2** the fact or quality of being generally accepted or in use: *since the Gulf War, the term has gained new currency.* ■ the time during which something is in use or operation: *no claim had been made during the currency of the policy.*

cur·rent /ˈkərənt; ˈkə-rənt/ ▸*adj.* belonging to the present time; happening or being used or done now: *keep abreast of current events | I started my current job last year.* ■ in common or general use: *the other meaning of the word is still current.*
▸*n.* a body of water or air moving in a definite direction, esp. through a surrounding body of water or air in which there is less movement: *ocean currents.* ■ a flow of electricity which results from the ordered directional movement of electrically charged particles. ■ a quantity representing the rate of flow of electric charge, usually measured in amperes. ■ the general tendency or course of events or opinion: *the student movement formed a distinct current of protest.* ▷Middle English (in the adjective sense 'running, flowing'): from Old French *corant* 'running,' from *courre* 'run,' from Latin *currere* 'run.'

cur·rent af·fairs ▸*plural n.* events of political or social interest and importance happening in the world at the present time.

cur·rent as·sets ▸*plural n.* cash and other assets that are expected to be converted to cash within a year. Compare with FIXED ASSETS.

cur·rent cost ac·count·ing ▸*n.* a method of accounting in which assets are valued on the basis of their current replacement cost, and increases in their value as a result of inflation are excluded from calculations of profit.

cur·rent den·si·ty ▸*n. Physics* the amount of electric current flowing per unit cross-sectional area of a material.

cur·rent li·a·bil·i·ties ▸*plural n.* amounts due to be paid to creditors within twelve months.

cur·rent·ly /ˈkərəntlē; ˈkə-rəntlē/ ▸*adv.* at the present time: *the price is currently at a premium.*

cur·ri·cle /ˈkərikəl/ ▸*n. historical* a light, open, two-wheeled carriage pulled by two horses side by side. ▷mid 18th cent.: from Latin *curriculum* 'course, racing chariot,' from *currere* 'to run.'

cur·ric·u·lum /kəˈrikyələm/ ▸*n.* (*pl.* **-la** /-lə/ or **-lums**) the subjects comprising a course of study in a school or college. ▷early 19th cent.: from Latin (see CURRICLE). **—cur·ric·u·lar** /-lər/ *adj.*

cur·ric·u·lum vi·tae /kəˈrik(y)ələm ˈvē,tī; ˈvītē/ (abbr.: **CV**) ▸*n.* (*pl.* **cur·ric·u·la vi·tae** /kəˈrik(y)ələ/) a brief account of a person's education, qualifications, and previous experience, typically sent with a job application. ▷early 20th cent.: Latin, literally 'course of life.'

Cur·ri·er /ˈkərēər; ˈkə-rēər/, Nathaniel (1813–88), U.S. lithographer. He partnered with James Ives in 1857 to establish the company of Currier & Ives, which produced hand-colored prints of American scenes.

cur·ri·er /ˈkərēər; ˈkə-rēər/ ▸*n.* a person who curries leather. ▷late Middle English: from Old French *corier*, from Latin *coriarius*, from *corium* 'leather.'

cur·rish /ˈkəriSH/ ▸*adj.* **1** like a cur; snappish. **2** ignoble. **—cur·rish·ly** *adv.* **—cur·rish·ness** *n.*

cur·ry[1] /ˈkərē; ˈkə-rē/ ▸*n.* **1** (*pl.* **-ries**) a dish of meat, vegetables, etc., cooked in an Indian-style sauce of strong spices and turmeric and typically served with rice. **2** curry powder.
▸*v.* (**-ries, -ried**) [*trans.*] [usu. as *adj.*] (**curried**) prepare or flavor with a sauce of hot-tasting spices: *curried chicken.* ▷late 16th cent.: from Tamil *kari.*

cur·ry[2] ▸*v.* (**-ries, -ried**) [*trans.*] **1** groom (a horse) with a rubber or plastic curry-comb. **2** *historical* treat (tanned leather) to improve its properties. ■ *archaic* thrash; beat. ▷Middle English: from Old French *correier*, ultimately of Germanic origin.
▸*PHRASE* □ **curry favor** ingratiate oneself with someone through obsequious behavior: *a wimpish attempt to* ***curry favor with*** *the new bosses.* [alteration of Middle English *curry favel*, from the name (*Favel* or *Fauvel*) of a chestnut horse in a 14th-cent. French romance who became a symbol of cunning and duplicity; hence 'to rub down Favel' meant to use the cunning that he personified.]

cur·ry-comb ▸*n.* a hand-held metal device with serrated ridges, used for removing dirt out of a horse's coat or for cleaning brushes with which a horse is being groomed. ■ (also **rubber curry-comb**) a similar device of flexible rubber, used for grooming horses.

curry-comb

cur·ry leaf ▸*n.* a shrub or small tree native to India and Sri Lanka, the leaves of which are widely used in Indian cooking. • *Murraya koenigii*, family Rutaceae.

cur·ry plant ▸*n.* a small, shrubby plant of the daisy family, which has narrow, silver-gray leaves and small yellow flowers and emits a strong smell of curry. • *Helichrysum angustifolium*, family Compositae.

cur·ry pow·der ▸*n.* a mixture of finely ground spices, such as turmeric, ginger, and coriander, used for making curry.

curse /kərs/ ▸*n.* **1** a solemn utterance intended to invoke a supernatural power to inflict harm or punishment on someone or something: *she'd* ***put a curse on*** *him.* ■ [usu. in *sing.*] a cause of harm or misery: *impatience is the curse of our day and age.* ■ (**the curse**) *informal* menstruation. **2** an offensive word or phrase used to express anger or annoyance: *his mouth was spitting vile oaths and curses.*
▸*v.* **1** [*trans.*] invoke or use a curse against: *it often seemed as if the family had been cursed.* ■ (**be cursed with**) be afflicted with: *many owners have been cursed with a series of bankruptcies.* **2** [*intrans.*] utter offensive words in anger or annoyance: *drivers were cursing and sounding their horns.* ■ [*trans.*] address with such words: *I* ***cursed myself*** *for my carelessness.* ▷Old English, of unknown origin. —**curs·er** *n.*

curs·ed /ˈkərsid; kərst/ ▸*adj. informal, dated* used to express annoyance or irritation: *he didn't whine about his cursed fate.* —**curs·ed·ly** /ˈkərsidlē/ *adv.* —**curs·ed·ness** /ˈkərsidnəs/ *n.*

cur·sil·lo /kərˈsē(l)yō/ ▸*n.* (*pl.* **-los**) a short informal spiritual retreat by a group of Roman Catholics, organized mainly by lay people and originally developed in Spain. ▷1950s: Spanish, literally 'little course.'

cur·sive /ˈkərsiv/ ▸*adj.* written with the characters joined: *cursive script.*
▸*n.* writing with such a style. ▷late 18th cent.: from medieval Latin *cursivus*, from Latin *curs-* 'run,' from the verb *currere*. —**cur·sive·ly** *adv.*

cur·sor /ˈkərsər/ ▸*n.* a movable indicator on a computer screen identifying the point that will be affected by input from the user, for example showing where typed text will be inserted. ■ *chiefly historical* the transparent slide engraved with a hairline that is part of a slide rule and is used for marking a point on the rule while bringing a point on the central sliding portion up to it. ▷Middle English (denoting a runner or running messenger): from Latin, 'runner,' from *curs-* (see **CURSIVE**). The sense 'sliding part of an instrument' dates from the late 16th cent.

cur·so·ri·al /kərˌsôrēəl/ ▸*adj. Zoology* having limbs adapted for running. ▷mid 19th cent.: from Latin *cursor* (see **CURSOR**) + **-IAL**.

cur·so·ry /ˈkərsərē/ ▸*adj.* hasty and therefore not thorough or detailed: *a cursory glance at the figures.* See note at **SUPERFICIAL**. ▷early 17th cent.: from Latin *cursorius* 'of a runner,' from *cursor* (see **CURSOR**). —**cur·so·ri·ly** /ˈkərsərəlē/ *adv.* —**cur·so·ri·ness** *n.*

curst /kərst/ ▸*adj.* archaic spelling of **CURSED**.

curt /kərt/ ▸*adj.* rudely brief: *his reply was curt.* See note at **BRUSQUE**. ▷late Middle English (in the sense 'short, shortened'): from Latin *curtus* 'cut short, abridged.' —**curt·ly** *adv.* —**curt·ness** *n.*

cur·tail /kərˈtāl/ ▸*v.* [*trans.*] (often **be curtailed**) reduce in extent or quantity; impose a restriction on: *civil liberties were further curtailed.* ■ (**curtail someone of**) *archaic* deprive someone of (something): *I that am curtailed of this fair proportion.* ▷late 15th cent.: from obsolete *curtal* 'horse with a docked tail,' from French *courtault*, from *court* 'short,' from Latin *curtus*. The change in the ending was due to association with **TAIL**[1] and perhaps also with French *tailler* 'to cut.' —**cur·tail·ment** /kərˈtālmənt/ *n.*

cur·tain /ˈkərtn/ ▸*n.* a piece of material suspended at the top to form a covering or screen, typically one of a pair at a window: *she drew the curtains and lit the fire* | *figurative through the curtain of falling snow, she could just make out gravestones.* ■ (**the curtain**) a screen of heavy cloth or other material that can be raised or lowered at the front of a stage. ■ a raising or lowering of such a screen at the beginning or end of an act or scene: *the art is to hold your audience right from the opening curtain.* ■ (**curtains**) *informal* a disastrous outcome: *it looked like* ***curtains for*** *me.*
▸*v.* [*trans.*] [often as *adj.*] (**curtained**) provide with a curtain or curtains: *a curtained window.* ■ conceal or screen with a curtain: *a* ***curtained-off*** *side room* | *figurative her unbound hair curtaining her face.* ▷Middle English: from Old French *cortine*, from late Latin *cortina*, translation of Greek *aulaia*, from *aulē* 'court.'
▸*PHRASE* □ **bring down the curtain on** bring to an end: *her decision brought down the curtain on a glittering 30-year career.*

cur·tain call ▸*n.* the appearance of one or more performers on stage after a performance to acknowledge the audience's applause.

cur·tain lec·ture ▸*n. dated* an instance of a wife reprimanding her husband in private. ▷mid 17th cent.: originally a reprimand given behind bed curtains.

cur·tain rais·er ▸*n.* an entertainment or other arts event happening just before a longer or more important one: *Bach's Sinfonia in B flat was an ideal* ***curtain-raiser*** *to Mozart's last piano concerto.* ▷late 19th cent.: originally used in the theater to denote a short opening piece performed before a play.

cur·tain speech ▸*n.* a speech of thanks or appreciation to an audience, made after a performance by an actor playing a leading role, typically from the front of the stage with the curtains closed.

cur·tain time ▸*n.* [in *sing.*] the beginning of a stage performance: *curtain time is at 8 p.m.*

cur·tain wall ▸*n.* a fortified wall around a medieval castle, typically one linking towers together. ■ a wall that encloses the space within a building but does not support the roof, typically on a modern high-rise.

cur·tal /ˈkərtl/ ▸*adj. archaic* shortened, abridged, or curtailed.
▸*n. historical* a dulcian or bassoon of the late 16th to early 18th century. ▷late 15th cent. (denoting a short-barreled cannon): from French *courtault*, from *court* 'short' + the pejorative suffix *-ault*. In both English and French the noun denoted various items characterized by something short, esp. an animal with a docked tail, which probably gave rise to the adjective sense.

cur·ta·na /kərˈtänə; -ˈtānə/ ▸*n. Brit.* the unpointed sword carried in front of English sovereigns at their coronation to represent mercy. ▷Middle English: from Anglo-Latin *curtana (spatha)* 'shortened (sword),' from Old French *cortain*, the name of the sword belonging to **ROLAND** (the point of which was damaged when it was thrust into a block of steel), from *cort* 'short,' from Latin *curtus* 'cut short.'

cur·te·sy /ˈkərtəsē/ ▸*n.* (*pl.* **-sies**) *historical Law* a tenure by which a husband, after his wife's death, held certain kinds of property that she had inherited.

cur·ti·lage /ˈkərtl-ij/ ▸*n. Law* an area of land attached to a house and forming one enclosure with it: *the roads* ***within the curtilage of*** *the development site.* ▷Middle English: from Anglo-Norman French, variant of Old French *courtillage*, from *courtil* 'small court,' from *cort* 'court.'

Cur·tis /ˈkərtis/, Benjamin Robbins (1809–74), U.S. Supreme Court associate justice 1851–57. He resigned in protest over the Court's handling of the Dred Scott case 1857. He served as chief counsel to Andrew Johnson during Johnson's impeachment in 1868. His brother, George Ticknor Curtis (1812–94), a lawyer and writer, argued for the plaintiff before the U.S. Supreme Court in the Dred Scott case.

Cur·tiss /ˈkərtəs/, Glenn (Hammond) (1878–1930), U.S. air pioneer and aircraft designer. In 1908, Curtiss made the first public U.S. flight, traversing 0.6 miles (1.0 km). He built his first airplane in 1909 and invented the aileron and then demonstrated the first practical seaplane two years later.

curt·sy /ˈkərtsē/ (also **curt·sey**) ▸*n.* (*pl.* **-sies** or **-seys**) a woman's or girl's formal greeting made by bending the knees with one foot in front of the other: *she* ***bobbed a curtsy*** *to him.*
▸*v.* (**-sies**, **-sied** or **-seys**, **-seyed**) [*intrans.*] perform such an action: *she curtsied onto the stage.* ▷early 16th cent.: variant of **COURTESY**. Both forms were used to denote the expression of respect or courtesy by a gesture, esp. in phrases such as *do courtesy, make courtesy*, and from this arose the current use (late 16th cent.).

cu·rule /ˈkyo͝orˌo͞ol/ ▸*adj. historical* denoting or relating to the authority exercised by the senior magistrates in ancient Rome, chiefly the consul and praetor, who were entitled to use the *sella curulis* ('curule seat,' a kind of folding chair). ▷early 17th cent.: from Latin *curulis*, from *currus* 'chariot' (in which the chief magistrate was conveyed to the seat of office), from *currere* 'to run.'

cur·va·ceous /kərˈvāSHəs/ ▸*adj.* (esp. of a woman or a woman's figure) having an attractively curved shape. —**cur·va·ceous·ness** *n.*

cur·va·ture /ˈkərvəCHər; -ˌCHo͝or/ ▸*n.* the fact of being curved or the degree to which something is curved: *spinal curvature* | *the curvature of the earth* | *it has a distinct curvature near the middle.* ■ *Geometry* the degree to which a curve deviates from a straight line, or a curved surface deviates from a plane. ■ a numerical quantity expressing this. ▷late Middle English: via Old French from Latin *curvatura*, from *curvare* (see **CURVE**).

curve /kərv/ ▸*n.* a line or outline that gradually deviates from being straight for some or all of its length: *the parapet wall sweeps down in a bold curve.* ■ a place where a road deviates from a straight path: *the vehicle rounded a curve.* ■ (**curves**) a curving contour of a woman's figure. ■ a line on a graph (whether straight or curved) showing how one quantity varies with respect to another: *the population curve.* ■ a system in which grades are assigned to students based on their performance relative to other students, regardless of their actual knowledge of the subject: *grades were marked on a curve.* ■ *Baseball* another term for **CURVEBALL**.
▸*v.* form or cause to form a curve: [*intrans.*] *her mouth curved in a smile* | [as *adj.*] (**curved**) *birds with long curved bills* | [*trans.*] *starting with arms outstretched, curve the body sideways.* ▷late Middle English: from Latin *curvare* 'to bend,' from *curvus* 'bent.' The noun dates from the late 17th cent.

curve·ball /ˈkərvˌbôl/ ▸*n. Baseball* a ball that is pitched with a snap of the wrist and a strong downward spin, which causes the ball to drop suddenly and deceptively veer away from home plate.

cur·vet /kərˈvet/ ▸*n.* (of a horse) a graceful or energetic leap.
▸*v.* (**-vet·ted**, **-vet·ting** or **-vet·ed**, **-vet·ing**) [*intrans.*] *rare* (of a horse) leap gracefully or energetically. ▷late 16th cent.: from Italian *corvetta*, diminutive of *corva*, earlier form of *curva* 'a curve,' from Latin *curvus* 'bent.'

cur·vi·lin·e·ar /ˌkərvəˈlinēər/ ▸*adj.* contained by or consisting of a curved line or lines: *these designs employ flowing, curvilinear forms.* ▷early 18th cent.: from *curvi-* 'curved,' from Latin *curvus*, on the pattern of *rectilinear*. —**cur·vi·lin·e·ar·ly** *adv.*

cur·vi·ros·tral /ˌkərvəˈrästrəl/ ▸*adj.* with a curved beak.

curv·y /ˈkərvē/ ▸*adj.* (**curv·i·er**, **curv·i·est**) having many curves: *a curvy stretch of road.* ■ *informal* (esp. of a woman's figure) shapely and voluptuous. —**curv·i·ness** *n.*

cus·cus /ˈkəskəs; ˈko͞osko͞os/ ▸*n.* a tree-dwelling marsupial with a rounded head and prehensile tail, native to New Guinea and northern Australia. • Four genera in the family Phalangeridae: several species, including the **spotted cuscus** (*Spilocuscus maculatus*) and the **grey cuscus** (*Phalanger orientalis*). See also **PHALANGER**. ▷mid 17th cent.: via French and Dutch from a local name in the Molucca Islands.

cu·sec /ˈkyo͞oˌsek/ ▸*n.* a unit of flow (esp. of water) equal to one cubic foot per second. ▷early 20th cent.: abbreviation of *cubic foot per second*.

Cush /ko͝oSH/ **1** (in the Bible) the eldest son of Ham and grandson of Noah (Gen. 10:6). **2** the southern part of ancient Nubia, first mentioned in Egyptian records of the Middle Kingdom. In the Bible it is the country of the descendants of Cush.

cush·at /ˈkəSHət/ ▸*n. dialect, chiefly Scottish* a wood pigeon. ▷Old English, of unknown origin.

cu·shaw /ko͞oˈSHô; ˈko͞oˌSHô/ (also **cushaw squash**) ▸*n.* a large winter squash of a variety with a curved neck. ▷late 16th cent.: of unknown origin.

cush-cush /ˈko͝oSH ˌko͝oSH/ (also **cush-cush yam**) ▸*n.* a tropical American yam that produces a number of tubers on each plant. Also called **YAMPEE**. • *Dioscorea trifida*, family Dioscoreaceae. ■ the edible tuber of this plant, eaten as a vegetable. ▷late 19th cent.: perhaps ultimately of African origin.

Cush·ing /ˈko͝oSHiNG/, William (1732–1810), U.S. Supreme Court associate justice 1789–1810. After serving as chief justice of the Massachusetts Supreme Court 1780–89, he was the first person to be nominated by President Washington to serve as an associate justice on the U.S. Supreme Court.

Cush·ing's dis·ease /ˈko͝oSHiNGz/ ▸*n.* Cushing's syndrome as caused by a tumor of the pituitary gland.

Cush·ing's syn·drome ▸*n. Medicine* a metabolic disorder caused by overproduction of corticosteroid hormones by the adrenal cortex and often involving obesity and high blood pressure. ▷1930s: named after Harvey W. *Cushing* (1869–1939), American surgeon.

cush·ion /ˈko͝oSHən/ ▸*n.* a pillow or pad stuffed with a mass of soft material, used as a comfortable support for sitting or leaning on. ■ something providing support or protection against impact: *the pad forms a cushion between carpet and floor* | *figurative a poll showed the candidate with a 14-point cushion.* ■ the elastic lining of the sides of a billiard table, from which the ball rebounds. ■ the layer of air supporting a hovercraft or similar vehicle.
▸*v.* [*trans.*] soften the effect of an impact on: *the bag cushions equipment from inevitable knocks.* ■ *figurative* mitigate the adverse effects of: *he called for federal assistance to* **cushion the blow** *for farmers.* ▷Middle English: from Old French *cuissin*, based on a Latin word meaning 'cushion for the hip,' from *coxa* 'hip, thigh'. —**cush·ioned** *adj.* —**cush·ion·y** *adj.*

cush·ion cap·i·tal ▸*n. Architecture* a capital resembling a cushion pressed down by a weight, seen particularly in Romanesque churches.

Cush·it·ic /ko͝oSHˈitik; ˌkəSH-/ ▸*n.* a group of East African languages of the Afro-Asiatic family spoken mainly in Ethiopia and Somalia, including Somali and Oromo.
▸*adj.* of or relating to this group of languages. ▷early 20th cent.: from **CUSH** + **-ITIC**.

cush·y /ˈko͝oSHē/ ▸*adj.* (**cush·i·er**, **cush·i·est**) *informal* **1** (of a job, task, or situation) undemanding, easy, or secure: *cushy jobs that pay you to ski.* **2** (of furniture) comfortable. ▷World War I (originally Anglo-Indian): from Urdu *ḵušī* 'pleasure,' from Persian *ḵuš*. —**cush·i·ness** *n.*

cusk /kəsk/ ▸*n.* another term for **TORSK**. ▷early 17th cent.: of unknown origin.

cusk-eel ▸*n.* a small, eellike fish with a tapering body and fins that form a pointed tail, typically found in deep water. • Family Ophidiidae: numerous genera.

cusp /kəsp/ ▸*n.* **1** a pointed end where two curves meet, in particular: ■ *Architecture* a projecting point between small arcs in Gothic tracery. ■ a cone-shaped prominence on the surface of a tooth, esp. of a molar or premolar. ■ *Anatomy* a pocket or fold in the wall of the heart or a major blood vessel that fills and distends if the blood flows backward, so forming part of a valve. ■ *Mathematics* a point at which the direction of a curve is abruptly reversed. ■ each of the pointed ends of a crescent, esp. of the moon. **2** *Astrology* the initial point of an astrological sign or house: *he was Aries* **on the cusp** *with Taurus.* ■ *figurative* a point between two different situations or states, when a person or thing is poised between the two or just about to move from one to the other: *those* **on the cusp of** *adulthood.* ▷late 16th cent. (sense 2): from Latin *cuspis* 'point or apex.' —**cus·pate** /ˈkəspət; -ˌpāt/ *adj.* —**cusped** *adj.* —**cus·pi·date** /ˈkəspəˌdāt/ *adj.*

cus·pid /ˈkəspid/ ▸*n.* a tooth with a single cusp or point; a canine tooth. ▷mid 18th cent.: from Latin *cuspis, cuspid-* 'point or apex.'

cus·pi·dor /ˈkəspəˌdôr/ ▸*n.* a spittoon. ▷mid 18th cent.: from Portuguese, literally 'spitter'.

cusp·ing /ˈkəspiNG/ ▸*n.* **1** formation of a cusp or cusps: *if you use the incorrect pressure there will be serious cusping and uneven wear on the tire.* **2** *Architecture* a decorative feature consisting of cusps.

cuss /kəs/ *informal* ▸*n.* **1** an annoying or stubborn person or animal: *he was certainly an unsociable cuss.* **2** another term for **CURSE** (sense 2).
▸*v.* another term for **CURSE** (sense 2).

cuss·ed /ˈkəsəd/ ▸*adj. informal* stubborn; annoying: *why do you have to be so cussed?* ▷mid 19th cent. (originally U.S.): variant of **CURSED**. —**cuss·ed·ly** *adv.* —**cuss·ed·ness** *n.*

cuss word ▸*n. informal* a swear word.

cus·tard /ˈkəstərd/ ▸*n.* a dessert or sweet sauce made with milk, eggs, and sugar. ▷late Middle English *crustarde, custarde* (denoting an open pie containing meat or fruit in a spiced or sweetened sauce thickened with eggs), from Old French *crouste* (see **CRUST**).

cus·tard ap·ple ▸*n.* **1** a large, fleshy, tropical fruit with a sweet yellow pulp. See also **CHERIMOYA** and **SWEETSOP**. **2** the tree that bears this fruit, native to Central and South America. • Genus *Annona*, family Annonaceae: several species.

Cus·ter /ˈkəstər/, George (Armstrong) (1839–76), U.S. cavalry officer. He served with distinction during the Civil War. In 1876, he was killed, along with all of his men (266) in a clash (popularly known as Custer's Last Stand) with the Sioux Indians at Little Bighorn in Montana.

cus·to·di·an /kəsˈtōdēən/ ▸*n.* a person who has responsibility for or looks after something, such as a museum, financial assets, or a culture or tradition: *the custodians of pension and insurance funds.* ■ a person employed to clean and maintain a building. ▷late 18th cent.: from **CUSTODY**, on the pattern of *guardian*. —**cus·to·di·an·ship** /-ˌSHip/ *n.*

cus·to·dy /ˈkəstədē/ ▸*n.* the protective care or guardianship of someone or something: *the property was placed in the custody of a trustee.* ■ imprisonment: *my father was being* **taken into custody**. ■ *Law* parental responsibility, esp. as allocated to one of two divorcing parents: *he was trying to get* **custody** *of their child.* ▷late Middle English: from Latin *custodia*, from *custos* 'guardian.' —**cus·to·di·al** /ˌkəˈstōdēəl/ *adj.*

cus·tom /ˈkəstəm/ ▸*n.* **1** a traditional and widely accepted way of behaving or doing something that is specific to a particular society, place, or time: *the old English custom of dancing around the maypole* | *custom demanded that a person should have gifts for the child.* ■ [in *sing.*] a thing that one does habitually: *it was my custom to nap for an hour every day.* ■ *Law* established practice or usage having the force of law or right. **2** *chiefly Brit.* regular dealings with a shop or business by customers: *if you keep me waiting, I will take my custom elsewhere.*
▸*adj.* made or done to order for a particular customer: *a custom guitar.* ▷Middle English: from Old French *coustume*, based on Latin *consuetudo*, from *consuetus*, past participle of *consuescere* 'accustom,' from *con-* (expressing intensive force) + *suescere* 'become accustomed.'

cus·tom·al ▸*n.* variant spelling of **CUSTUMAL**.

cus·tom·ar·y /ˈkəstəˌmerē/ ▸*adj.* according to the customs or usual practices associated with a particular society, place, or set of circumstances: *it is* **customary** *to mark an occasion like this with a toast.* ■ according to a person's habitual practice: *I put the kettle on for our customary cup of tea.* ■ *Law* established by or based on custom rather than common law or statute.
▸*n.* (*pl.* **-ar·ies**) *historical* another term for **CUSTUMAL**. ▷late Middle English (as a noun): from medieval Latin *custumarius*, from *custuma*, from Anglo-Norman French *custume* (see **CUSTOM**). —**cus·tom·ar·i·ly** /ˌkəstəˈme(ə)rəlē/ *adv.* —**cus·tom·ar·i·ness** *n.*

cus·tom-built ▸*adj.* another term for **CUSTOM-MADE**.

cus·tom·er /ˈkəstəmər/ ▸*n.* **1** a person or organization that buys goods or services from a store or business: *Mr. Harrison was a regular customer at the Golden Lion* | [as *adj.*] *customer service.* **2** a person or thing of a specified kind that one has to deal with: *the fish is a slippery customer and very hard to catch* | *Jon won over Lucie's father, but her mother is a tough customer.*

cus·tom house (also **cus·toms house**) ▸*n. chiefly historical* the office at a port or frontier where customs duty is collected.

cus·tom·ize /ˈkəstəˌmīz/ ▸*v.* [*trans.*] (often **be customized**) modify (something) to suit a particular individual or task: *the suit can be customized for every skydiving need.*

cus·tom-made ▸*adj.* made to a particular customer's order.

cus·toms /ˈkəstəmz/ ▸*plural n.* the official department that administers and collects the duties levied by a government on imported goods: *cocaine seizures by customs have risen this year* | [as *adj.*] *a customs officer.* ■ the place at a port, airport, or frontier where officials check incoming goods, travelers, or luggage: *arriving refugees were whisked through customs.* ■ (usu. **customs duties**) the duties levied by a government on imported goods. ▷late Middle English: originally in the singular, denoting a customary due paid to a ruler, later duty levied on goods on their way to market.

cus·toms un·ion ▸*n.* a group of countries that have agreed to charge the same import duties as each other and usually to allow free trade between themselves.

cus·tu·mal /ˈkəstəməl; ˈkəsCHə-/ (also **cus·to·mal**) ▸*n. historical* a written account of the customs of a manor or other local community or large establishment. ▷late 16th cent.: from medieval Latin *custumale* 'customs book,' neuter of *custumalis*, from *custuma* 'custom.'

cut /kət/ ▸*v.* (**cut·ting**; *past* and *past part.* **cut**) [*trans.*] **1** make an opening, incision, or wound in (something) with a sharp-edged tool or object: *he cut his big toe on a sharp stone* | *he* **cut open** *MacKay's face with the end of his hockey stick* | [*intrans.*] *figurative his scorn cut deeper than knives.* **2** remove (something) from something larger by using a sharp implement: *I* **cut** *his photograph* **out of** *the paper* | *some prisoners had their right hands* **cut off**. ■ *informal* castrate (an animal, esp. a horse). ■ remove the foreskin of a penis; circumcise. ■ (**cut something out**) make something by cutting: *I cut out some squares of paper.* ■ (**cut something out**) remove, exclude, or stop eating or doing something undesirable: *start today by cutting out fatty foods.* ■ (**cut something out**) separate an animal from the main herd. **3** divide into pieces with a knife or other sharp implement: **cut** *the beef* **into** *thin slices* | *he* **cut** *his food* **up** *into teeny pieces.* ■ make divisions in (something): *land that has been* **cut up** *by streams into forested areas.* ■ separate (something) into two; sever: *they cut the rope before he choked.* ■ (**cut something down**) make something, esp. a tree, fall by cutting it through at the base. ■ (**cut someone down**) (of a weapon, bullet, or disease) kill or injure someone: *Barker had been cut down by a sniper's bullet.* **4** make or form (something) by using a sharp tool to remove material: *workmen* **cut a hole in** *the pipe.* ■ make or design (a garment) in a particular way: [as *adj.*] (**cut**) *an impeccably cut chalk-stripe suit.* ■ make (a path, tunnel, or other route) by excavation, digging, or chopping: *plans to cut a road through a rain forest* | [*intrans.*] *investigators called for a machete to* **cut through** *the bush* | *figurative a large woman with a voice that* **cut through** *crowds.* **5** trim or reduce the length of (something, esp. grass or a person's hair or fingernails) by using a sharp implement: *cutting the lawn* | **cut back** *all the year's growth to about four leaves.* **6** reduce the amount or quantity of: *buyers will bargain hard to* **cut the cost of** *the house they want* | *I should* **cut down** *my sugar intake* | [*intrans.*] *they've* **cut back on** *costs* | *the state passed a law to* **cut down on** *drunk-driving* | *the paper glut* **cuts into** *profits.* ■ abridge (a text, movie, or performance) by removing material: *he had to cut unnecessary additions made to the opening scene.* ■ *Computing* delete (part of a text or other display) completely or so as to insert a copy of it elsewhere. See also **CUT AND PASTE**. ■ (in sports) remove (a player) from a team's roster. ■ end or interrupt the provision of (something, esp. power or food supplies): *we resolved to cut oil supplies to territories controlled by the rebels* | *if the pump develops a fault, the electrical supply is immediately* **cut off**. ■ (**cut something off**) block the usual means of access to a place: *the caves were* **cut off from** *the outside world by a landslide.* ■ absent oneself deliberately from (something one should normally attend, esp. school): *Robert was cutting class.* ■ switch off (an engine or a light). **7** (of a line) cross or intersect (another line): *the point where the line cuts the vertical axis.* ■ [*intrans.*] (**cut across**) pass or traverse, esp. so as to shorten one's route: *the following aircraft cut across to join him.* ■ [*intrans.*] (**cut across**) have an effect regardless of (divisions or boundaries between groups): *subcultures that cut across national and political boundaries.* ■ [*intrans.*] (**cut along**) *informal, dated* leave or move hurriedly: *you can cut along now.* **8** *dated* ignore or refuse to recognize (someone). **9** [*intrans.*, often in *imperative*] stop filming or recording. ■ move to another shot in a movie: **cut to** *a dentist's surgery.* ■ [*trans.*] make (a movie) into a coherent whole by removing parts or placing them in a different order. **10** make (a sound recording). **11** divide (a pack of playing cards) by lifting a portion from the top, either to reveal or draw a card at random or to place the top portion under the bottom portion. **12** *Golf* slice (the ball). **13** adulterate (a drug) or dilute (alcohol) by mixing it with another substance: *speed* **cut with** *rat poison.* **14** (**cut it**) *informal* come up to expectations; meet requirements: *this CD player doesn't quite cut it.* [shortened form of the idiom *cut the mustard*.]
▸*phrasal v.* □ **cut in 1** interrupt someone while they are speaking: *"It's urgent," Raoul cut in.* ■ *dated* interrupt a dancing couple to take over from one partner. **2** pull in too closely in front of another vehicle after having overtaken it: *she* **cut in on** *a station wagon, forcing the driver to brake.* **3** (of a motor or other mechanical device) begin operating, esp. when

C

triggered automatically by an electrical signal: *emergency generators cut in.* **4** □ **cut someone in** *informal* include someone in a deal and give them a share of the profits. □ **cut into** interrupt the course of: *Victoria's words cut into her thoughts.* □ **cut someone off** interrupt someone while they are speaking. ■ interrupt someone during a telephone call by breaking the connection: *I listened to prerecorded messages for twenty-three minutes before being cut off.* ■ prevent someone from receiving or being provided with something, esp. power or water: *consumers cut off for nonpayment.* ■ reject someone as one's heir; disinherit someone: *Gabrielle's family* ***cut her off without a penny***. ■ prevent someone from having access to somewhere or someone; isolate someone from something they previously had connections with: *we were cut off from reality.* ■ *informal* (of a driver) overtake someone and pull in too closely in front of them. □ **cut out 1** (of a motor or engine) suddenly stop operating. **2** *informal* (of a person) leave quickly, esp. so as to avoid a boring or awkward situation. □ **cut someone out** exclude someone: *his mother cut him out of her will.* □ **cut up 1** *informal* behave in a mischievous or unruly manner: *kids cutting up in a classroom.* **2** *informal* (of a horse race) have a particular selection of runners: *the race has* ***cut up badly*** *with no other opposition from England.* □ **cut someone up** *informal* criticize someone severely: *my kids cut him up about his appetite all the time.*

▶*n.* **1** an act of cutting, in particular: ■ [in *sing.*] a haircut: *his hair was in need of a cut.* ■ a stroke or blow given by a sharp-edged implement or by a whip or cane: *he could skin an animal with a single cut of the knife.* ■ *figurative* a wounding remark or act: *his unkindest cut at Elizabeth was to call her heartless.* ■ a reduction in amount or size: *she took a 20% pay cut | a* ***cut in*** *interest rates.* ■ (in sports) a removal of a player from a team's roster. ■ an act of removing part of a play, movie, or book, esp. to shorten the work or to delete offensive material: *they would not publish the book unless the author was willing to* ***make cuts***. ■ an immediate transition from one scene to another in a movie. ■ *Golf* the halfway point of a golf tournament where half of the players are eliminated. ■ *Tennis* a stroke made with a sharp horizontal or downward action of the racket, imparting spin. **2** a result of cutting something, in particular: ■ a long narrow incision in the skin made by something sharp. ■ a long narrow opening or incision made in a surface or piece of material: *make a single cut along the top of each potato.* ■ a piece of meat cut from a carcass: *a good lean cut of beef.* ■ [in *sing.*] *informal* a share of the profits from something: *the directors are demanding their cut.* ■ a recording of a piece of music: *a cut from his forthcoming album.* ■ a version of a movie after editing: *the director's cut.* ■ a passage cut or dug out, as a railroad cutting or a new channel made for a river or other waterway. ■ a woodcut. **3** [in *sing.*] the way or style in which something, esp. a garment or someone's hair, is cut: *the elegant cut of his dinner jacket.* ▷Middle English (probably existing, although not recorded, in Old English); probably of Germanic origin and related to Norwegian *kutte* and Icelandic *kuta* 'cut with a small knife,' *kuti* 'small blunt knife.'

▶*PHRASES* □ **be cut out for** (or **to be**) [usu. with *negative*] *informal* have exactly the right qualities for a particular role, task, or job: *I'm just not cut out to be a policeman.* □ **a cut above** *informal* noticeably superior to: *she's a cut above the rest.* □ **cut and dried** [often with *negative*] (of a situation) completely settled or decided: *the championship is not as cut and dried as everyone thinks.* [early 18th cent.: originally used to distinguish the herbs of herbalists' shops from growing herbs.] □ **cut and run** *informal* make a speedy or sudden departure from an awkward or hazardous situation rather than deal with it. [originally a nautical phrase, meaning 'cut the anchor cable because of some emergency and make sail immediately.'] □ **cut and thrust** *Fencing* the use of both the edge and the point of one's sword while fighting. ■ a spirited and rapid interchange of views: *the cut and thrust of political debate.* ■ a situation or sphere of activity regarded as carried out under adversarial conditions: *the ruthless cut and thrust of the business world.* □ **cut both ways** (of a point or statement) serve both sides of an argument. ■ (of an action or process) have both good and bad effects: *the triumphs of civilization cut both ways.* □ **cut the corner** take the shortest course by going across and not around a corner. □ **cut corners** undertake something in what appears to be the easiest, quickest, or cheapest way, esp. by omitting to do something important or ignoring rules. □ **cut the crap** [often in *imperative*] *vulgar slang* get to the point; state the real situation. □ **cut someone dead** completely ignore someone. □ **cut a deal** *informal* come to an arrangement, esp. in business; make a deal. □ **cut someone down to size** *informal* deflate someone's exaggerated sense of self-worth. □ **cut something down to size** reduce the size or power of something, for example an organization, that is regarded as having become too large or powerful. □ **cut a —— figure** present oneself or appear in a particular way: *David has cut a dashing figure on the international social scene.* □ **cut someone free** free someone from something in which they are trapped. □ **cut from the same cloth** of the same nature; similar: *don't assume all women are cut from the same cloth.* □ **cut in line** push into a line of people in order to be served or dealt with before one's turn. □ **cut it fine** see FINE[1]. □ **cut it out** [usu. in *imperative*] *informal* used to ask someone to stop doing or saying something that is annoying or offensive: *I'm sick of that joke; cut it out, can't you?* □ **cut loose** distance oneself from a person, group, or system by which one is unduly influenced or on which one is overdependent: *Poland* ***cut loose from*** *communism.* ■ act without restraint: *consumers want to cut loose and have secret bacchanals.* □ **cut someone/something loose** free someone or something from something that holds or restricts them; untie: *he'd cut loose the horses.* □ **cut one's losses** abandon an enterprise or course of action that is clearly going to be unprofitable or unsuccessful before one suffers too much loss or harm. □ **cut the mustard** *informal* come up to expectations; reach the required standard: *I didn't cut the mustard as a hockey player.* □ **cut no ice** *informal* have no influence or effect: *your holier-than-thou attitude* ***cuts no ice with*** *me.* □ **cut someone off** (or **down**) **in their prime** bring someone's life or career to an abrupt end while they are at the peak of their abilities. □ **cut someone/something short** interrupt someone or something; bring an abrupt or premature end to something said or done: *Peter cut him short rudely.* □ **cut someone to pieces** kill or severely injure someone. ■ *figurative* totally defeat someone. □ **cut a** (or **the**) **rug** *informal* dance, typically in an energetic or accomplished way: *you can cut a rug when dance bands and singers take to the stage.* □ **cut one's teeth** acquire initial practice or experience of a particular sphere of activity or with a particular organization: *the brothers cut their professional teeth at Lusardi's before starting their own restaurant.* □ **cut a tooth** (usu.of a baby or child) have a tooth appear through the gum. □ **cut to the chase** *informal* come to the point: *cut to the chase—what is it you want us to do?* [cut in the sense 'move to another part of the movie,' expressing the notion of ignoring any preliminaries.] □ **cut your coat according to your cloth** *proverb* undertake only what you have the money or ability to do and no more. □ **have one's work cut out** see WORK. □ **make the cut** *Golf* equal or better a required score, thus avoiding elimination from the last two rounds of a four-round tournament. □ **miss the cut** *Golf* fail to equal or better a required score, thus being eliminated from the last two rounds of a four-round tournament.

cut-and-come-a·gain ▶*n.* [usu. as *adj.*] a garden plant, esp. a green vegetable or a flower, that can be repeatedly cut or harvested: *cut-and-come-again spinach.*

cut-and-cov·er ▶*n.* a method of building a tunnel by making a cutting, which is then lined and covered over.

cut and paste ▶*n.* a process used in assembling text on a word processor or computer, in which items are removed from one part and inserted elsewhere.
▶*v.* [*trans.*] move (an item of text) using this technique.

cu·ta·ne·ous /kyo͞oˈtānēəs/ ▶*adj.* of, relating to, or affecting the skin: *cutaneous pigmentation.* ▷late 16th cent.: from modern Latin *cutaneus* (from Latin *cutis* 'skin') + -OUS.

cut·a·way /ˈkətəˌwā/ ▶*n.* [often as *adj.*] **1** a thing made or designed with a part cut out or absent, in particular: ■ a coat or jacket with the front cut away below the waist so as to curve back to the tails. ■ a diagram or drawing with some external parts left out to reveal the interior. **2** a shot in a movie that is of a different subject from those to which it is joined in editing.

cutaway jacket

cut·back /ˈkətˌbak/ ▶*n.* an act or instance of reducing something, typically expenditures: ***cutbacks in*** *defense spending.*

cutch /kəCH/ ▶*n.* see CATECHU.

cut·down /ˈkətˌdoun/ ▶*n.* **1** a decrease or reduction: [as *adj.*] *left with a cutdown staff.* **2** *Surgery* a procedure of cutting into a vein in order to insert a needle or cannula.

cute /kyo͞ot/ ▶*adj.* **1** attractive in a pretty or endearing way: *a cute kitten.* ■ *informal* sexually attractive. **2** *informal* affectedly or superficially clever: *I don't want to be cute with you.* ▷early 18th cent. (in the sense 'clever, shrewd'): shortening of ACUTE. **—cute·ly** *adv.* **—cute·ness** *n.*

cute·sy /ˈkyo͞otsē/ ▶*adj. informal* cute to a sentimental or mawkish extent: *hair pulled back in cutesy little bows.*

cut·ey ▶*n.* variant spelling of CUTIE.

cut glass ▶*n.* glass that has been ornamented by having patterns cut into it by grinding and polishing: [as *adj.*] *a cut-glass vase.*

Cuth·bert, St. /ˈkəTHbərt/ (died 687), English monk. Feast day, March 20.

cu·ti·cle /ˈkyo͞otikəl/ ▶*n.* **1** the outer layer of living tissue, in particular: ■ *Botany & Zoology* a protective and waxy or hard layer covering the epidermis of a plant, invertebrate, or shell. ■ the outer cellular layer of a hair. ■ *Zoology* another term for EPIDERMIS. **2** the dead skin at the base of a fingernail or toenail. ▷late 15th cent. (denoting a membrane of the body): from Latin *cuticula*, diminutive of *cutis* 'skin.' **—cu·tic·u·lar** /kyo͞oˈtikyələr/ *adj.*

cut·ie /ˈkyo͞otē/ (also **cutie pie**) ▶*n. informal* an attractive or endearing person.

cut·in /ˈkyo͞otn/ ▶*n. Biochemistry* a waxy, water-repellent substance occurring in the cuticle of plants and consisting of highly polymerized esters of fatty acids. ▷mid 19th cent.: from CUTIS + -IN[1].

cut-in ▶*n.* a shot in a movie that is edited into another shot or scene.

cu·tis /ˈkyo͞otəs/ ▶*n. Anatomy* the true skin or dermis. ▷early 17th cent.: from Latin, 'skin.'

cut·lass /ˈkətləs/ ▶*n.* a short sword with a slightly curved blade, formerly used by sailors. ▷late 16th cent.: from French *coutelas*, based on Latin *cultellus* 'small knife' (see CUTLER).

cutlass

cut·lass·fish /ˈkətləsˌfiSH/ ▶*n.* (*pl.* same or **-fish·es**) a long, slender marine fish with sharp teeth and a dorsal fin running the length of the back. • Family Trichiuridae: several species, including the Atlantic *Trichiurus lepturus* (also called SNAKEFISH), an important food fish in the tropics.

cut·ler /ˈkətlər/ ▶*n.* a person who makes or sells cutlery. ▷Middle English: from Old French *coutelier*, from *coutel* 'knife,' from Latin *cultellus*, diminutive of *culter* 'knife, plowshare.' Compare with COULTER.

cut·ler·y /ˈkətlərē/ ▶*n.* **1** cutting utensils, esp. knives for cutting food. **2** knives, forks, and spoons used for eating or serving food. ▷Middle English: from Old French *coutellerie*, from *coutelier* (see CUTLER).

cut·let /ˈkətlət/ ▶*n.* a portion of sliced meat breaded and served either grilled or fried. ■ a flat croquette of minced meat, nuts, or pulses, typically covered in breadcrumbs and fried. ▷early 18th cent.: from French *côtelette*, earlier *costelette*, diminutive of *coste* 'rib,' from Latin *costa*.

cut·line /ˈkətˌlīn/ ▶*n.* **1** the caption to a photograph or other illustration. **2** (in squash) the line above which a served ball must strike the front wall.

cut·off /ˈkətˌôf/ (also **cut-off**) ▶*adj.* **1** of or constituting a limit: *the cutoff date to register is July 2.* **2** (of a device) producing an interruption or cessation of a power or fuel supply: *a cutoff valve.* **3** (of an item of clothing) having been cut short: *a cutoff T-shirt.* **4** (of a person) isolated from or no longer having access to someone or something: *aid to the cutoff troops in the north.*

▶*n.* **1** a point or level that is a designated limit of something: *1 p.m. is the cutoff for being out of the woods.* **2** an act of stopping or interrupting the supply or provision of something: *a cutoff of aid would be a dis-*

aster. ■ a device for producing an interruption or cessation of a power or fuel supply. ■ a sudden drop in amplification or responsiveness of an electric device at a certain frequency: [as *adj.*] *a cutoff frequency of 8 Hz.* ■ the stopping of the supply of steam to the cylinders of a steam engine when the piston has traveled a set percentage of its stroke. **3** (**cutoffs**) shorts made by cutting off the legs of a pair of jeans or other trousers above or at the knee and leaving the edges unhemmed. **4** a shortcut. **5** *Geology* a pattern of a meandering stream in which a channel cuts a new course to bypass a meander bend.

cut·out /ˈkət,out/ (also **cut-out**) ▶*n.* **1** a shape of a person or thing cut out of cardboard or another material. ■ *figurative* a person perceived as characterless or as lacking in individuality: *this film's protagonists are cardboard cutouts.* **2** a hole cut in something for decoration or to allow the insertion of something else. **3** a device that automatically breaks an electric circuit for safety and either resets itself or can be reset.

cut·o·ver /ˈkət,ōvər/ ▶*n.* a rapid transition from one phase of a business enterprise or project to another. ▶*adj.* (of land) having had its saleable timber felled and removed.

cut·purse /ˈkət,pərs/ ▶*n.* archaic term for PICKPOCKET. ▷late Middle English: with reference to stealing by cutting purses suspended from a waistband.

cut-rate (also **cut-price**) ▶*adj.* for sale at a reduced or unusually low price: *cut-rate tickets.* ■ offering goods at such prices: *a cut-rate furniture store.*

cut·scene /ˈkət,sēn/ ▶*n.* (in computer games) a scene that develops the story line and is often shown on completion of a certain level, or when the player's character dies.

cut·ter /ˈkətər/ ▶*n.* **1** a person or thing that cuts something, in particular: ■ [often with *adj.*] a tool for cutting something, esp. one intended for cutting a particular thing or for producing a particular shape: *a glass cutter* | (**cutters**) *a pair of bolt cutters.* ■ a person who cuts or edits movies. ■ a person in a tailoring establishment who takes measurements and cuts the cloth. ■ a person who reduces or cuts down on something, esp. expenditures: *a determined cutter of costs.* **2** a light, fast coastal patrol boat. ■ a ship's boat used for carrying light stores or passengers. ■ *historical* a small fore-and-aft-rigged sailing ship with one mast, more than one headsail, and a running bowsprit, used as a fast auxiliary. ■ a yacht with a gaff-rigged mainsail and two foresails. **3** *Baseball* (also **cut fastball**) a fastball that breaks somewhat on being pitched. **4** a light horse-drawn sleigh.

cut·throat /ˈkət,THrōt/ ▶*n.* **1** *dated* a murderer or other violent criminal. **2** (also **cutthroat trout**) a trout of western North America, with red or orange markings under the jaw. • *Salmo clarki*, family Salmonidae. ▶*adj.* (of a competitive situation or activity) fierce and intense; involving the use of ruthless measures: *cutthroat competition led to a lot of bankruptcies* | *the cutthroat world of fashion.* ■ (of a person) using ruthless methods in a competitive situation: *the greedy cutthroat manufacturers he worked for.* ■ *Sports* relating to or being a game or contest in which each of three players scores individually against the other two. ■ denoting a form of whist (or other card game normally for four) played by three players.

cut·throat ra·zor ▶*n.* British term for STRAIGHT RAZOR.

cut·throat weav·er (also **cut·throat** or **cutthroat finch**) ▶*n.* a small, finchlike African bird of the waxbill family, with speckled brown plumage, a conspicuous crimson throat band, and a rufous belly. • *Amadina fasciata*, family Estrildidae.

cut·ting /ˈkətiNG/ ▶*n.* **1** (often **cuttings**) a piece cut off from something, esp. what remains when something is being trimmed or prepared: *grass cuttings.* ■ a piece cut from a plant for propagation. ■ *Brit.* a clipping from a newspaper or periodical. **2** the action of someone or something that cuts: *the cutting of the cake* | *tax-cutting.* **3** an open passage excavated through higher ground for a railroad, road, or canal. ▶*adj.* capable of cutting something: *the cutting blades of the hedge trimmer.* ■ *figurative* (esp. of a comment) causing emotional pain; hurtful: *a cutting remark.* ■ *figurative* (of the wind) bitterly cold. —**cut·ting·ly** *adv.*

cut·ting edge ▶*n.* edge of a tool's blade. ■ [in *sing.*] the latest or most advanced stage in the development of something: *researchers* ***at the cutting edge of*** *molecular biology.* ■ [in *sing.*] a person or factor that contributes a dynamic or invigorating quality to a situation and thereby puts one at an advantage over one's rivals: *the campaign began to lose its cutting edge.* ■ *figurative* incisiveness and directness of expression: *his wit retains its cutting edge.* ▶*adj.* (**cut·ting-edge**) at the latest or most advanced stage of development; innovative or pioneering: *cutting-edge technology.*

cut·ting horse ▶*n.* a horse trained in separating cattle from a herd.

cut·ting·ly /ˈkətiNGlē/ ▶*adv.* in an unkind or hurtful way: *he can be cuttingly rude.*

cut·ting room ▶*n.* a room in a production studio where film or videotape is cut and edited: [as *adj.*] *such a scene would end up* ***on the cutting-room floor.***

cut·tle /ˈkətl/ ▶*n.* a cuttlefish. ▷Old English *cudele* 'cuttlefish,' of Germanic origin; related to *codd* 'bag,' with reference to its ink bag.

cut·tle·bone /ˈkətl,bōn/ ▶*n.* the flattened oval internal skeleton of the cuttlefish, which is made of white, lightweight, chalky material. It is used as a dietary supplement for caged birds and for making casts for precious metal items.

cut·tle·fish /ˈkətl,fiSH/ ▶*n.* (*pl.* same or **-fish·es**) a swimming marine mollusk that resembles a broad squid, having eight arms and two long tentacles that are used for grabbing prey. Its internal skeleton is cuttlebone, which it uses for adjusting buoyancy. • Order Sepioidea, class Cephalopoda: *Sepia* and other genera. ▷late 16th cent.: from CUTTLE + FISH[1].

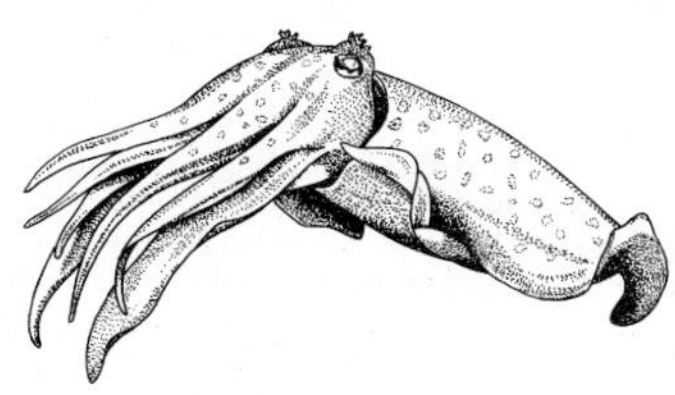

cuttlefish

Cut·ty Sark /särk/ the only survivor of the British tea clippers, launched in 1869 and now preserved as a museum ship at Greenwich, London. ▷from Robert Burns's *Tam o' Shanter*, a poem about a Scottish farmer chased by a young witch who wore only her "cutty sark" (= short shift).

cut·ty-stool ▶*n. Scottish, historical* a stool on which an offender was publicly rebuked during a church service.

cut-up (also **cut up**) ▶*adj.* **1** divided into pieces by cutting: *cut-up vegetables.* ■ (of a soft piece of ground) having an uneven surface after the passage of heavy vehicles or animals: *the ground was deeply cut up where the cattle had strayed.* **2** *informal* (of a person) very distressed: *his girlfriend is dying and he's really* ***cut up about*** *it.* ▶*n.* **1** a film or sound recording made by cutting and editing material from preexisting recordings. **2** (**cutup**) *informal* a person who is fond of making jokes or playing pranks.

cut·wa·ter /ˈkət,wôtər; -,wätər/ ▶*n.* **1** the forward edge of a ship's prow. **2** a wedge-shaped projection on the pier of a bridge, which divides the flow of water and prevents debris from becoming trapped against the pier.

cut·work /ˈkət,wərk/ ▶*n.* embroidery or lace with parts cut out and the edges oversewn or filled with needlework designs. ■ appliqué work in which the pattern is cut out and sewn on.

cut·worm /ˈkət,wərm/ ▶*n.* a moth caterpillar that lives in the upper layers of the soil and eats through the stems of young plants at ground level. • Several species in the family Noctuidae.

cu·vée /k(y)o͞oˈvā/ ▶*n.* a type, blend, or batch of wine, esp. champagne. ▷mid 19th cent.: French, 'vatful,' from *cuve* 'cask,' from Latin *cupa.*

cu·vette /kyo͞oˈvet/ ▶*n. Biochemistry* a straight-sided, optically clear container for holding liquid samples in a spectrophotometer or other instrument. ▷early 18th cent.: from French, diminutive of *cuve* 'cask,' from Latin *cupa.*

Cu·vi·er /ko͞oˈvyā/, Georges Léopold Chrétien Frédéric Dagobert, Baron (1769–1832), French naturalist. Cuvier founded the science of paleontology.

cuz /kəz/ (also **'cuz** or **coz**) ▶*conj. informal* short for BECAUSE.

Cuz·co /ˈko͞oskō/ a city in the Andes in southern Peru; pop. 275,000. It was the capital of the Inca empire until the Spanish conquest in 1533.

CV ▶*abbr.* ■ cardiovascular. ■ curriculum vitae.

cv ▶*abbr.* cultivated variety.

CVS ▶*abbr.* chorionic villus sampling.

CVT ▶*abbr.* continuously variable transmission.

cwm /ko͝om; ko͞om/ ▶*n.* a cirque, esp. one in the mountains of Wales. ▷mid 19th cent.: Welsh; related to COMBE.

CWO ▶*abbr.* Chief Warrant Officer.

c.w.o. ▶*abbr.* cash with order.

cwr ▶*abbr.* continuous welded rail; railroad track laid in long unbroken strips rather than as short fixed lengths with gaps.

cwt. ▶*abbr.* hundredweight.

CY ▶*abbr.* calendar year.

-cy ▶*suffix* **1** denoting state or condition: *bankruptcy.* **2** denoting rank or status: *baronetcy.* ▷from Latin *-cia, -tia* and Greek *-k(e)ia, -t(e)ia.*

cy·an /ˈsī,an; ˈsīən/ ▶*n.* a greenish-blue color, which is one of the primary subtractive colors, complementary to red. ▷late 19th cent.: from Greek *kuaneos* 'dark blue.'

cy·an·a·mide /sīˈanəməd; -,mīd/ ▶*n. Chemistry* a weakly acidic crystalline compound made as an intermediate in the industrial production of ammonia. • Alternative name: **cyanogen amide**; chem. formula: CH_2N_2. ■ a salt of this containing the anion CN_2^{2-} esp. the calcium salt (**calcium cyanamide**) used as a fertilizer. ▷mid 19th cent.: blend of CYANOGEN and AMIDE.

cy·an·ic /sīˈanik/ ▶*adj. rare* blue; azure. ▷early 19th cent.: from CYAN + -IC.

cy·an·ic ac·id ▶*n. Chemistry* a colorless, poisonous, volatile, strongly acidic liquid. • Chem. formula: HOCN. See also FULMINIC ACID. ▷early 19th cent.: from CYANOGEN. —**cy·a·nate** /ˈsīə,nāt; -nət/ *n.*

cy·a·nide /ˈsīə,nīd/ ▶*n. Chemistry* a salt or ester of hydrocyanic acid, containing the anion CN^- or the group $-CN$. The salts are generally extremely toxic. Compare with NITRILE. ■ sodium or potassium cyanide used as a poison or in the extraction of gold and silver. ▷early 19th cent.: from CYANOGEN + -IDE.

cy·a·nine /ˈsīə,nēn; -nin/ ▶*n.* a blue pigment that is a mixture of cobalt blue and Prussian blue.

cy·a·nite /ˈsīə,nīt/ ▶*n.* variant of KYANITE.

cyano- ▶*comb. form* **1** relating to the color blue, esp. dark blue: *cyanosis.* **2** representing CYANIDE. ▷from Greek *kuan(e)os* 'dark blue.'

cy·a·no·ac·ry·late /,sīənōˈakrə,lāt; sīˈanō-/ ▶*n. Chemistry* any of a class of compounds that are cyanide derivatives of acrylates. They are easily polymerized and are used to make quick-setting adhesives.

Cy·a·no·bac·te·ri·a /,sīənōbakˈtirēə; sī,anō-/ *Biology* a division of microorganisms that are related to the bacteria but are capable of photosynthesis. They are prokaryotic and represent the earliest known form of life on the earth. • Class Cyanophyceae, kingdom Eubacteria. ■ [as *plural n.*] (**cyanobacteria**) microorganisms of this division. Also called BLUE-GREEN ALGAE. ▷modern Latin (plural), from Greek *kuaneos* 'dark blue' + plural of BACTERIUM.

cy·a·no·co·bal·a·min /,sīənō,kōˈbaləmin; sī,anō-/ ▶*n.* a vitamin found in foods of animal origin such as liver, fish, and eggs, a deficiency of which can cause pernicious anemia. It contains a cyanide group bonded to the central cobalt atom of a cobalamin molecule. Also called VITAMIN B_{12}. ▷1950s: from CYANOGEN and *cobalamin* (blend of COBALT and VITAMIN).

cy·a·no·gen /sīˈanəjən/ ▶*n. Chemistry* a colorless, flammable, highly poisonous gas made by oxidizing hydrogen cyanide. One of the pseudohalogens, cyanogen is an intermediate in fertilizer manufacture. • Chem. formula: C_2N_2. ▷early 19th cent.: from French *cyanogène*, from Greek *kuanos* 'dark blue mineral' + *-gène* (see -GEN), so named because it is a constituent of Prussian blue.

cy·a·no·gen·e·sis /,sīənōˈjenəsis; sī,anō-/ ▶*n. Botany* the production of hydrogen cyanide by certain plants, such as cherry laurel, bracken, and some legumes, as a response to wounding or a deterrent to herbivores.

cy·a·no·gen·ic /,sīənōˈjenik; sī,anō-/ ▶*adj. Botany* (of a plant) capable of cyanogenesis: *cyanogenic forms.* ■ *Biochemistry* containing a cyanide group in the molecule.

cy·a·no·hy·drin /,sīənōˈhīdrin; sī,anō-/ ▶*n. Chemistry* an organic compound containing a carbon atom linked to both a cyanide group and a hydroxyl group.

cy·a·no·phyte /'sīənə,fīt; sī'anə-/ ▸*n. Biology* a microorganism of the division Cyanobacteria.

cy·a·no·sis /,sīə'nōsəs/ ▸*n. Medicine* a bluish discoloration of the skin resulting from poor circulation or inadequate oxygenation of the blood. ▹mid 19th cent.: modern Latin, from Greek *kuanōsis* 'blueness,' from *kuaneos* 'dark blue.' —**cy·a·not·ic** /,sīə'nätik/ *adj.*

cy·an·o·type /'sīənə,tīp; sī'anə-/ ▸*n.* a photographic blueprint.

cy·ath·i·um /sī'aTHēəm/ ▸*n.* (*pl.* **-ath·i·a** /-'aTHēə/) *Botany* the characteristic inflorescence of the spurges, resembling a single flower. It consists of a cup-shaped involucre of fused bracts enclosing several greatly reduced male flowers and a single female flower. ▹late 19th cent.: modern Latin, from Greek *kuathion*, diminutive of *kuathos* 'cup.'

Cyb·e·le /'sibəlē/ *Mythology* a mother goddess worshiped esp. in Phrygia and later in Greece (where she was associated with Demeter), Rome, and the Roman provinces, with her consort Attis.

cy·ber /'sībər/ ▸*adj.* of, relating to, or characteristic of the culture of computers, information technology, and virtual reality: *the cyber age.* ▹1980s: abbreviation of CYBERNETICS.

cyber- ▸*comb. form* relating to electronic communication networks and virtual reality: *cyberpunk | cyberspace.* ▹back-formation from CYBERNETICS.

cy·ber·at·tack /'sībərə,tak/ ▸*n.* an effort by hackers to damage or destroy a computer network or system. —**cy·ber·at·tack·er** *n.*

cy·ber·ca·fé /,sībərka'fā/ ▸*n.* a café that offers internet access on computers that it owns, or via Wi-Fi on patrons' computers.

cy·ber·cash /'sībər,kaSH/ ▸*n.* **1** funds used in electronic financial transactions, especially over the Internet. **2** money stored on an electronic smart card or in an online credit account.

cy·ber·crime /'sībər,krīm/ ▸*n.* crime conducted via the Internet or some other computer network.

cy·ber·law /'sībər,lô/ ▸*n.* laws, or a specific law, relating to Internet and computer offenses, especially fraud or copyright infringement.

cy·ber·mall /'sībər,môl/ ▸*n.* a commercial Web site through which a range of goods may be purchased; a virtual shopping mall on the Internet: *a cybermall, where a user might move from store to store and acquire various merchandise along the way.*

cy·ber·naut /'sībər,nôt; -,nät/ ▸*n. Computing* a person who wears sensory devices in order to experience virtual reality. ■ a person who uses the Internet. ▹1990s: from CYBER-, on the pattern of *astronaut* and *aeronaut*.

cy·ber·net·ics /,sībər'netiks/ ▸*plural n.* [treated as *sing.*] the science of communications and automatic control systems in both machines and living things. ▹1940s: from Greek *kubernētēs* 'steersman,' from *kubernan* 'to steer.' —**cy·ber·net·ic** *adj.* —**cy·ber·ne·ti·cian** /-nə'tiSHən/ *n.* —**cy·ber·net·i·cist** /-'netəsəst/ *n.*

cy·ber·pet /'sībər,pet/ ▸*n.* an electronic toy that simulates a real pet and with which human interaction is possible. Also called DIGIPET or VIRTUAL PET.

cy·ber·pho·bi·a /,sībər'fōbēə/ ▸*n.* extreme or irrational fear of computers or technology. —**cy·ber·phobe** /'sībər,fōb/ *n.* —**cy·ber·pho·bic** /-'fōbik/ *adj.* & *n.*

cy·ber·porn /'sībər,pôrn/ ▸*n.* pornography viewable on a computer screen, especially accessed via the Internet.

cy·ber·punk /'sībər,pəNGk/ ▸*n.* a genre of science fiction set in a lawless subculture of an oppressive society dominated by computer technology. ■ a writer of such science fiction. ■ a person who accesses computer networks illegally, esp. with malicious intent.

cy·ber·sex /'sībər,seks/ ▸*n.* sexual arousal using computer technology, esp. by wearing virtual reality equipment or by exchanging messages with another person via the Internet.

cy·ber·shop /'sībər,SHäp/ ▸*v.* (**-shopped, -shop·ping**) [*intrans.*, often as *noun*] (**cybershopping**) purchase or shop for goods and services on a Web site: *more than half of American workers cybershop on company time.* ▸*n.* a Web site that sells or provides information about retail goods or services: *the retailer's cybershop sometimes has different prices than in its mail-order catalog.* Also called CYBERSTORE. —**cy·ber·shop·per** *n.*

cy·ber·slack·er /'sībər,slakər/ ▸*n. informal* a person who uses their employer's Internet and e-mail facilities for personal activities during working hours: *cyberslackers who download and distribute pornography.* —**cy·ber·slack·ing** *n.*

cy·ber·space /'sībər,spās/ ▸*n.* the notional environment in which communication over computer networks occurs.

cy·ber·squat·ting /'sībər,skwätiNG/ ▸*n.* the practice of registering names, especially well-known company or brand names, as Internet domains, in the hope of reselling them at a profit. —**cy·ber·squat·ter** *n.*

cy·ber·stalk·ing /'sībər,stôkiNG/ ▸*n.* the repeated use of electronic communications to harass or frighten someone, for example by sending threatening e-mails. —**cy·ber·stalk·er** *n.*

cy·ber·store /-,stôr/ ▸*n.* another term for CYBERSHOP.

cy·ber·surf·ing /'sībər,sərfiNG/ ▸*n.* the practice of using and browsing the Internet, especially as a habitual pastime. —**cy·ber·surf·er** *n.*

cy·ber·ter·ror·ism /,sībər'terə,rizəm/ ▸*n.* the politically motivated use of computers and information technology to cause severe disruption or widespread fear in society: *a bill that would make it easier for law enforcement to wiretap computers and combat cyberterrorism.* —**cy·ber·ter·ror·ist** *n.*

cy·ber·war /'sībər,wôr/ ▸*n.* acts of hostility carried out on the Internet against national interests or ethnic groups.

cy·borg /'sī,bôrg/ ▸*n.* a fictional or hypothetical person whose physical abilities are extended beyond normal human limitations by mechanical elements built into the body. ▹1960s: blend of CYBER- and ORGANISM.

cy·brar·i·an /sī'bre(ə)rēən/ ▸*n.* a librarian or researcher who uses the Internet as an information resource. ▹blend of *cyber-* and *librarian*.

cy·cad /'sīkəd; 'sī,kad/ ▸*n.* a palmlike plant of tropical and subtropical regions, bearing large male or female cones. Cycads were abundant during the Triassic and Jurassic eras, but have since been in decline. • Class Cycadopsida, subdivision Gymnospermae: twenty species in the genus *Cycas* and family Cycadaceae. ▹mid 19th cent.: from modern Latin *Cycas, Cycad-* (order name), from supposed Greek *kukas*, scribal error for *koikas*, plural of *koix* 'Egyptian palm.'

Cyc·la·des /'siklə,dēz/ a large group of islands in the southern Aegean Sea, regarded in antiquity as circling around the sacred island of Delos. Greek name KIKLÁDHES. ▹Latin, based on Greek *kuklos* 'circle.'

Cy·clad·ic /sī'kladik; sə-/ ▸*adj.* of or relating to the Cyclades. ■ *Archaeology* of, relating to, or denoting a Bronze Age civilization that flourished in the Cyclades, dated to *c.*3000–1050 BC. ■ [as *n.*] (**the Cycladic**) the Cycladic culture or period.

cy·cla·mate /'sīklə,māt; -mət/ ▸*n. Chemistry* a salt of a synthetic acid which is a cyclohexyl derivative of sulfamic acid. Sodium and calcium cyclamates were formerly used as artificial sweeteners. ▹1950s: contraction of *cyclohexylsulphamate*.

cy·cla·men /'sīkləmən; 'sik-/ ▸*n.* (*pl.* same or **-mens**) a European plant of the primrose family, having pink, red, or white flowers with backward-curving petals and widely grown as a winter-flowering houseplant. • Genus *Cyclamen*, family Primulaceae: several species. ■ a pinkish-purple color. ▹modern Latin, from Latin *cyclaminos*, from Greek *kuklaminos*, perhaps from *kuklos* 'circle,' with reference to its bulbous roots.

cy·cle /'sīkəl/ ▸*n.* **1** [often with *adj.*] a series of events that are regularly repeated in the same order: *the boom and slump periods of a trade cycle.* ■ the period of time taken to complete a single sequence of such events: *the cells are shed over a cycle of twenty-eight days* ■ *technical* a recurring series of successive operations or states, as in the working of an internal combustion engine, or in the alternation of an electric current or a wave: *the familiar four cycles of intake, combustion, ignition, and exhaust.* ■ *Biology* a recurring series of events or metabolic processes in the lifetime of a plant or animal: *the storks' breeding cycle.* ■ *Biochemistry* a series of successive metabolic reactions in which one of the products is regenerated and reused. ■ *Ecology* the movement of a simple substance through the soil, rocks, water, atmosphere, and living organisms of the earth. See CARBON CYCLE, NITROGEN CYCLE. ■ *Computing* a single set of hardware operations, esp. that by which memory is accessed and an item is transferred to or from it, to the point at which the memory may be accessed again. ■ *Physics* a cycle per second; one hertz. **2** a complete set or series: *the painting is one of a cycle of seven.* ■ a series of songs, stories, plays, or poems composed around a particular theme and usually intended to be performed or read in sequence: *Wagner's Ring Cycle.* **3** a bicycle or tricycle. ■ [in *sing.*] a ride on a bicycle: *a 112-mile cycle.* ▸*v.* [*intrans.*] **1** ride a bicycle: *she cycled to work every day.* **2** move in or follow a regularly repeated sequence of events: *economies cycle regularly between boom and slump.* ▹late Middle English: from Old French, from late Latin *cyclus*, from Greek *kuklos* 'circle.'

cy·cle of e·ro·sion ▸*n. dated Geology* an idealized course of landscape evolution, passing from youthful stages, which are marked by steep gradients, to old age, when the landscape is reduced to a peneplain.

cy·clic /'sīklik; 'sik-/ ▸*adj.* **1** occurring in cycles; regularly repeated: *nature is replete with cyclic processes | the cyclic pattern of the last two decades.* ■ *Mathematics* (of a group) having the property that each element of the group can be expressed as a power of one particular element. ■ relating to or denoting a musical or literary composition with a recurrent theme or structural device. **2** *Mathematics* of or relating to a circle or other closed curve. ■ *Geometry* (of a polygon) having all its vertices lying on a circle. ■ *Chemistry* (of a compound) having a molecular structure containing one or more closed rings of atoms. ■ *Botany* (of a flower) having its parts arranged in whorls. ▹late 18th cent.: from French *cyclique* or Latin *cyclicus*, from Greek *kuklikos*, from *kuklos* 'circle.' —**cy·cli·cal** *adj.* (in sense 1). —**cy·cli·cal·ly** /-ik(ə)lē/ *adv.*

cy·cli·cals /'sīklikəlz; 'sik-/ ▸*plural n.* stocks in cyclical companies (those whose success varies with the seasonal or economic cycle).

cy·clic AMP ▸*n. Biochemistry* a cyclic form of adenosine monophosphate (adenylic acid) that plays a major role in controlling many enzyme-catalyzed processes in living cells.

cy·clic GMP (abbr. **cGMP**) ▸*n.* a cyclic version of the nucleotide guanosine monophosphate. In cellular metabolism, it is a secondary messenger affecting cell growth and division..

cy·clic re·dun·dan·cy check (also **cyclic redundancy code**) (abbr.: **CRC**) ▸*n. Computing* a code added to data that is used to detect errors occurring during transmission, storage, or retrieval.

cy·clin /'sīklən/ ▸*n. Biochemistry* any of a number of proteins associated with the cycle of cell division that are thought to initiate certain processes of mitosis. ▹1980s: from CYCLE + -IN[1].

cy·cling /'sīk(ə)liNG/ ▸*n.* the sport or activity of riding a bicycle. Bicycle racing has three main forms: road racing (typically over long distances), track racing (on an oval track), and cyclocross (over rough, open country).

Cy·cli·oph·o·ra /,siklē'äfərə; ,sī-/ *Zoology* a new phylum that has been proposed for a minute marine invertebrate (*Symbion pandora*) that was discovered in 1996 attached to the mouthparts of lobsters. It is related to the phyla Bryozoa and Entoprocta. ▹modern Latin (plural), from Greek *kuklios* 'circular' + *pherein* 'to bear.'

cy·clist /'sīk(ə)list/ ▸*n.* a person who rides a bicycle.

cy·clize /'sīk(ə),līz/ ▸*v. Chemistry* undergo or cause to undergo a reaction in which one part of a molecule becomes linked to another to form a closed ring. —**cy·cli·za·tion** /,sīk(ə)lə'zāSHən/ *n.*

cyclo- ▸*comb. form* **1** circular: *cyclorama.* **2** relating to a cycle or cycling: *cyclocross.* **3** cyclic: *cycloparaffin.* ▹from Greek *kuklos* 'circle,' or directly from CYCLE or CYCLIC.

cy·clo·ad·di·tion /,sīklōə'diSHən/ ▸*n. Chemistry* an addition reaction in which a cyclic molecule is formed.

cy·clo·al·kane /,sīklō'al,kān/ ▸*n. Chemistry* another term for CYCLOPARAFFIN.

cy·clo·cross /'sīklə,krôs/ (also **cy·clo-cross**) ▸*n.* cross-country racing on bicycles.

cy·clo·hex·ane /,sīklō'hek,sān/ ▸*n. Chemistry* a colorless, flammable liquid cycloparaffin obtained from petroleum or by hydrogenating benzene, and used as a solvent and paint remover. • Chem. formula: C_6H_{12}.

cy·clo·hex·yl /,sīklə'heksəl/ ▸*n.* [as *adj.*] *Chemistry* of or denoting the cyclic hydrocarbon radical $-C_6H_{11}$, derived from cyclohexane.

cy·cloid /'sī,kloid/ ▸*n. Mathematics* a curve (resembling a series of arches) traced by a point on a circle being rolled along a straight line. ▹mid 17th cent.: from Greek *kukloeidēs* 'circular,' from *kuklos* 'circle.' —**cy·cloi·dal** /sī'kloidl/ *adj.*

cy·clom·e·ter /sī'klämətər/ ▸*n.* **1** an instrument for measuring circular arcs. **2** an instrument attached to a bicycle for measuring the distance it travels.

cy·clone /ˈsīˌklōn/ ▸*n. Meteorology* a system of winds rotating inward to an area of low atmospheric pressure, with a counterclockwise (northern hemisphere) or clockwise (southern hemisphere) circulation; a depression. ■ another term for TROPICAL STORM. ▷mid 19th cent.: probably from Greek *kuklōma* 'wheel, coil of a snake,' from *kuklos* 'circle.' The change of spelling from *-m* to *-n* is unexplained. —**cy·clon·ic** /sīˈklänik/ *adj.* —**cy·clon·i·cal·ly** /sīˈklänik(ə)lē/ *adv.*

cy·clo·par·af·fin /ˌsīklōˈparəfin/ ▸*n. Chemistry* a hydrocarbon with a molecule containing a ring of carbon atoms joined by single bonds.

cy·clo·pe·an /ˌsīkləˈpēən; sīˈklōpēən/ (also **cy·clo·pi·an**) ▸*adj.* **1** denoting a type of ancient masonry made with massive irregular blocks: *cyclopean stone walls.* [by association with the great size of the Cyclops.] **2** of or resembling a Cyclops: *a cyclopean eye.*

cy·clo·pe·di·a /ˌsīkləˈpēdēə/ (also **cy·clo·pae·di·a**) ▸*n. archaic (except in book titles)* an encyclopedia: *Bailey's Cyclopedia of Horticulture.* ▷late 17th cent.: shortening of ENCYCLOPEDIA. —**cy·clo·pe·dic** /-ˈpēdik/ *adj.*

cy·clo·pen·ta·di·ene /ˌsīkləˌpentəˈdīēn; ˌsiklə-/ ▸*n.* a colorless toxic liquid derived from the distillation of coal tar, insoluble in water, soluble in alcohol, and used in the manufacture of insecticides and resins.

cy·clo·phos·pha·mide /ˌsīklōˈfäsfəˌmīd/ ▸*n. Medicine* a synthetic cytotoxic drug used in treating leukemia and lymphoma and as an immunosuppressive agent.

cy·clo·ple·gia /ˌsīkləˈplēj(ē)ə/ ▸*n.* paralysis of the ciliary muscle of the eye.

cy·clo·pro·pane /ˌsīklōˈprōˌpān/ ▸*n. Chemistry* a flammable, gaseous synthetic compound whose molecule contains a ring of three carbon atoms. It has some use as a general anesthetic. • Chem. formula: C_3H_6.

Cy·clops /ˈsīˌkläps/ ▸*n.* **1** (*pl.* **Cy·clops** or **Cy·clops·es** or **Cy·clo·pes** /sīˈklōpēz/) *Greek Mythology* a member of a race of savage one-eyed giants. In the Odyssey, Odysseus escaped death by blinding the Cyclops Polyphemus. **2** (**cyclops**) a minute predatory freshwater crustacean which has a cylindrical body with a single central eye. • Genus *Cyclops* and other genera, order Cyclopoida. ▷via Latin from Greek *Kuklōps*, literally 'round-eyed,' from *kuklos* 'circle' + *ōps* 'eye.'

cy·clo·ram·a /ˌsīkləˈramə; -ˈrämə/ ▸*n.* a circular picture of a 360° scene, viewed from inside. ■ a cloth stretched tight in an arc around the back of a stage set, often used to depict the sky. ▷mid 19th cent.: from CYCLO-, on the pattern of words such as *panorama.* —**cy·clo·ram·ic** /-ˈramik/ *adj.*

cy·clo·spo·rine /ˌsīkləˈspôrin; -ˌēn/ (also **cy·clo·spo·rin A**, **cy·clo·spo·rin**) ▸*n. Medicine* a drug with immunosuppressive properties used to prevent the rejection of grafts and transplants. A cyclic peptide, it is obtained from a fungus. • This drug is obtained from the fungus *Trichoderma polysporum.* ▷1970s: from CYCLO- + *-sporin* (from Latin *spora* 'spore') + -IN[1].

cy·clo·stome /ˈsīkləˌstōm/ ▸*n. Zoology* an eellike, jawless vertebrate with a round sucking mouth, formerly included in a group with the lampreys and hagfishes. • Subclass Cyclostomata, now incorporated in the superclass Agnatha. ▷mid 19th cent.: from CYCLO- + Greek *stoma* 'mouth.'

cy·clo·style /ˈsīkləˌstīl/ ▸*n.* an early device for duplicating handwriting, in which a pen with a small toothed wheel pricks holes in a sheet of waxed paper, which is then used as a stencil.
▸*v.* [*trans.*] [usu. as *adj.*] (**cyclostyled**) duplicate with such a device: *a cyclostyled leaflet.* ▷late 19th cent.: from CYCLO- 'circular' + the noun STYLE.

cy·clo·thy·mi·a /ˌsīkləˈTHīmēə/ ▸*n. dated Psychiatry* a mental state characterized by marked swings of mood between depression and elation; manic-depressive tendency. ▷1920s: from CYCLO- + Greek *thumos* 'temper.' —**cy·clo·thy·mic** /-ˈTHīmik/ *adj.*

cy·clo·tron /ˈsīkləˌträn/ ▸*n. Physics* an apparatus in which charged atomic and subatomic particles are accelerated by an alternating electric field while following an outward spiral or circular path in a magnetic field.

cy·der ▸*n.* archaic spelling of CIDER.

cyg·net /ˈsignət/ ▸*n.* a young swan. ▷late Middle English: from Anglo-Norman French *cignet*, diminutive of Old French *cigne* 'swan,' based on Latin *cycnus*, from Greek *kuknos*.

Cyg·nus /ˈsignəs/ *Astronomy* a prominent northern constellation (the Swan), said to represent a flying swan that was the form adopted by Zeus on one occasion. It contains the bright star Deneb. ■ [as *genitive*] (**Cygni** /-nī/) used with a preceding letter or numeral to designate a star in this constellation: *the star Delta Cygni.* ▷Latin.

cyl. ▸*abbr.* cylinder.

cyl·in·der /ˈsiləndər/ ▸*n.* a solid geometric figure with straight parallel sides and a circular or oval section. ■ a solid or hollow body, object, or part with such a shape. ■ a piston chamber in a steam or internal combustion engine. ■ a cylindrical container for liquefied gas under pressure. ■ a rotating metal roller in a printing press. ■ *Archaeology* a cylinder seal. ▷late 16th cent.: from Latin *cylindrus*, from Greek *kulindros* 'roller,' from *kulindein* 'to roll.' —**cy·lin·dric** /səˈlindrik/ *adj.* —**cy·lin·dri·cal** /səˈlindrikəl/ *adj.* —**cy·lin·dri·cal·ly** /səˈlindrik(ə)lē/ *adv.*

cyl·in·der block ▸*n.* see BLOCK (sense 1).

cyl·in·der head ▸*n.* the end cover of a cylinder in an internal combustion engine, against which the piston compresses the cylinder's contents.

cyl·in·der lin·er ▸*n.* see LINER[2].

cyl·in·der lock ▸*n.* a lock with the keyhole and tumbler mechanism contained in a cylinder.

cyl·in·der seal ▸*n. Archaeology* a small, barrel-shaped stone object with a hole down the center and an incised design or cuneiform inscription. It was originally rolled on clay when soft to indicate ownership or to authenticate a document and was used chiefly in Mesopotamia from the late 4th to the 1st millennium BC.

cyl·in·droid /ˈsilənˌdroid/ ▸*n.* a figure or body resembling a cylinder.
▸*adj.* resembling a cylinder in shape.

cy·ma /ˈsīmə/ ▸*n.* (*pl.* **-mas** or **-mae** /-mē; -mī/) **1** *Architecture* a cornice molding with an S-shaped cross section. Compare with OGEE. **2** *Botany* variant spelling of CYME. ▷mid 16th cent.: modern Latin, from Greek *kuma* 'wave or wavy molding.'

cym·bal /ˈsimbəl/ ▸*n.* a musical instrument consisting of a slightly concave round brass plate that is either struck against another one or struck with a stick to make a ringing or clashing sound. ▷Old English, from Latin *cymbalum*, from Greek *kumbalon*, from *kumbē* 'cup'; readopted in Middle English from Old French *cymbale.* —**cym·bal·ist** /-ist/ *n.*

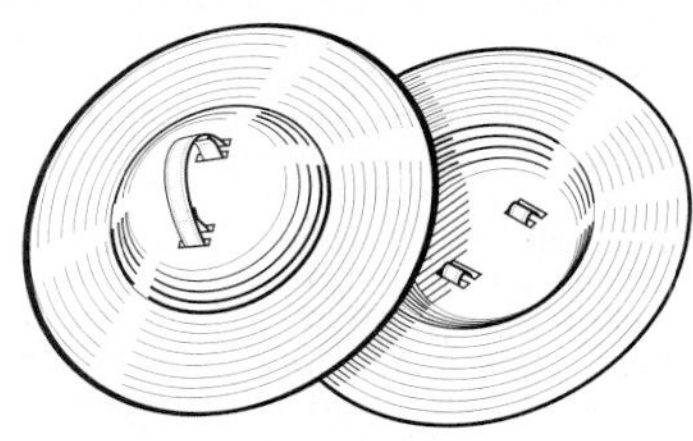
cymbals

cym·ba·lom /ˈsimbələm/ (also **cim·ba·lom**) ▸*n.* a large Hungarian dulcimer. ▷late 19th cent.: from Hungarian, from Italian *cembalo, cimbalo*, from Latin *cymbalum* (see CYMBAL).

Cym·be·line /ˈsimbəˌlēn/ (also **Cu·no·be·li·nus** /ˌk(y)o͞onōbəˈlīnəs/) (died c.AD 42), English chieftain. A powerful ruler, he made the town of Camulodunum (Colchester) his capital and established a mint.

cym·bid·i·um /ˌsimˈbidēəm/ ▸*n.* (*pl.* **-ums**) a tropical orchid with long, narrow leaves and arching stems bearing several flowers, growing chiefly as an epiphyte from Asia to Australasia and widely cultivated for boutonnières. • Genus *Cymbidium*, family Orchidaceae. ▷modern Latin, from Greek *kumbē* 'cup.'

cyme /sīm/ ▸*n. Botany* a flower cluster with a central stem bearing a single terminal flower that develops first, the other flowers in the cluster developing as terminal buds of lateral stems. Compare with RACEME. ▷early 18th cent. (denoting the unopened head of a plant): from French, literally 'summit,' from a popular variant of Latin *cyma.* —**cy·mose** /ˈsīˌmōs/ *adj.*

cy·moid /ˈsīˌmoid/ ▸*adj.* resembling a cyma or a cyme.

Cym·ric /ˈkəmrik/ ▸*adj.* Welsh in language or culture.
▸*n.* the Welsh language. ▷mid 19th cent.: from Welsh *Cymru* 'Wales,' *Cymry* 'the Welsh,' + -IC.

Cym·ru /ˈkəmrē/ Welsh name for **WALES**.

Cyn·e·wulf /ˈkinəˌwo͝olf; ˈko͞on-/ (late 8th–9th centuries), Anglo-Saxon poet. Four poems are attributed to him: *Juliana, Elene, The Fates of the Apostles*, and *Christ II.*

cyn·ic /ˈsinik/ ▸*n.* **1** a person who believes that people are motivated purely by self-interest rather than acting for honorable or unselfish reasons: *some cynics thought that the controversy was all a publicity stunt.* ■ a person who questions whether something will happen or whether it is worthwhile: *the cynics were silenced when the factory opened.* **2** (**Cynic**) a member of a school of ancient Greek philosophers founded by Antisthenes, marked by an ostentatious contempt for ease and pleasure. The movement flourished in the 3rd century BC and revived in the 1st century AD. ▷mid 16th cent. (sense 2): from Latin *cynicus*, from Greek *kunikos*; probably originally from *Kunosarges*, the name of a gymnasium where Antisthenes taught, but popularly taken to mean 'doglike, churlish,' *kuōn, kun-* 'dog' becoming a nickname for a Cynic. —**cyn·i·cism** /ˈsinəˌsizəm/ *n.*

cyn·i·cal /ˈsinikəl/ ▸*adj.* **1** believing that people are motivated by self-interest; distrustful of human sincerity or integrity: *her cynical attitude.* ■ doubtful as to whether something will happen or whether it is worthwhile: *most residents are* **cynical about** *efforts to clean mobsters out of their city.* ■ contemptuous; mocking: *he gave a cynical laugh.* **2** concerned only with one's own interests and typically disregarding accepted or appropriate standards in order to achieve them: *Stalin had struck a cynical deal with Hitler.* —**cyn·i·cal·ly** /-ik(ə)lē/ *adv.*

cyno- ▸*comb. form* of or relating to dogs: *cynodont.* ▷from Greek *kuōn, kun-* 'dog.'

cyn·o·dont /ˈsīnəˌdänt/ ▸*n.* a carnivorous, mammallike fossil reptile of the late Permian and Triassic periods, with well-developed, specialized teeth. • Suborder Cynodontia, order Therapsida: several families. ▷late 19th cent.: from Greek *kuōn, kun-* 'dog' + *odous, odont-* 'tooth.'

cy·no·sure /ˈsīnəˌSHo͝or; ˈsin-/ ▸*n.* [in *sing.*] a person or thing that is the center of attention or admiration: *the Queen was the cynosure of all eyes.* ▷late 16th cent.: from French, or from Latin *cynosura*, from Greek *kunosoura* 'dog's tail' (also 'Ursa Minor'), from *kuōn, kun-* 'dog' + *oura* 'tail.' The term originally denoted the constellation Ursa Minor, or the star Polaris that it contains, long used as a guide by navigators.

cy·pher ▸*n.* variant spelling of CIPHER.

cy·pher·punk /ˈsīfərˌpəNGk/ ▸*n.* a person who uses encryption when accessing a computer network in order to ensure privacy, esp. from government authorities. ▷1990s: on the pattern of *cyberpunk.*

cy·pres /sēˈprā/ ▸*adv. & adj. Law* as near as possible to the testator's or donor's intentions when these cannot be precisely followed. ▷early 19th cent.: from a late Anglo-Norman French variant of French *si près* 'so near.'

Cy·press /ˈsīprəs/ a city in south central California, southeast of Los Angeles; pop. 42,655.

cy·press /ˈsīprəs/ ▸*n.* (also **cypress tree**) an evergreen coniferous tree with small, rounded, woody cones and flattened shoots bearing small, scalelike leaves. • *Cupressus, Chamaecyparis*, and other genera, family Cupressaceae: many species, including the columnar **Italian cypress** (*Cupressus sempervirens*), common throughout southern Europe. See also **LAWSON CYPRESS**. ■ a tree of this type, or branches from it, as a symbol of mourning. ■ used in names of similar coniferous trees of other families, e.g., **bald cypress**. ▷Middle English: from Old French *cipres*, from late Latin *cypressus*, from Greek *kuparissos.*

cy·press knees ▸*plural n.* the cone-shaped exposed growths on the buttress roots of a bald cypress.

Cyp·ri·an, St. /ˈsiprēən/ (died 258), Carthaginian bishop and martyr. Feast day, September 16 or 26.

cy·pri·nid /ˈsiprənid/ ▸*n. Zoology* a fish of the minnow (or carp) family (Cyprinidae). ▷late 19th cent.: from modern Latin *Cyprinidae* (plural), based on Greek *kuprinos* 'carp.'

cyp·ri·noid /ˈsiprəˌnoid/ *Zoology* ▸*n.* a fish of a large group that includes the carps, suckers, and loaches, and (in some classification schemes) the characins. • Order Cypriniformes or superfamily Cyprinoidea.
▸*adj.* of or relating to fish of this group. ▷mid 19th cent.: from modern Latin *Cyprinoidea*, based on Latin *cyprinus* 'carp' (from Greek *kuprinos*).

Cyp·ri·ot /ˈsiprēət; -ˌät/ ▸*n.* **1** a native or national of Cyprus. **2** the dialect of Greek used in Cyprus.

Pronunciation Key ə *ago*; ər *over*; ˈə or ˌə *up*; ˈər or ˌər *fur*; a *hat*; ā *rate*; ä *car*; CH *chew*; e *let*; ē *see*; e(ə)r *air*; i *fit*; ī *by*; i(ə)r *ear*; NG *sing*; ō *go*; ô *for*; oi *boy*; o͝o *good*; o͞o *goo*; ou *out*; SH *she*; TH *thin*; T͟H *then*; (h)w *why*; ZH *vision*

▶*adj.* of or relating to Cyprus or its people or the Greek dialect used there. ▷from Greek *Kupriōtes*, from *Kupros* 'Cyprus.'

cyp·ri·pe·di·um /ˌsiprəˈpēdēəm/ ▶*n.* (*pl.* **-ums**) an orchid of a genus that comprises the lady's slippers. • Genus *Cypripedium*, family Orchidaceae. ▷modern Latin, from Greek *Kupris* 'Aphrodite' + *pedilon* 'slipper.'

Cy·prus /ˈsīprəs/ an island country in southeastern Europe, in the eastern Mediterranean Sea, about 50 miles (80 km) south of the Turkish coast; pop. 775,000; capital, Nicosia; official languages, Greek and Turkish.

A Greek colony in ancient times, Cyprus was held by the Turks from 1571 until 1878, when it was placed under British administration. After virtual civil war between the Greek Cypriots (some of whom favor enosis or union with Greece) and the Turkish Cypriots, Cyprus became an independent Commonwealth of Nations republic in 1960. In 1974, Turkish forces took over the northern part of the island, which proclaimed itself the independent Turkish Republic of Northern Cyprus in 1983 and effectively divided the island between the Greek and Turkish communities. It is now under UN supervision. The Greek Cypriot–controlled Republic of Cyprus joined the EU in May 2004.

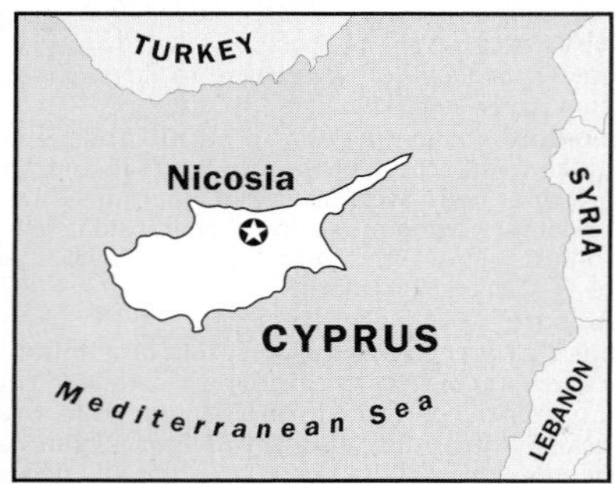

cyp·se·la /ˈsipsələ/ ▶*n.* (*pl.* **-lae** /-lē/) *Botany* a dry, single-seeded fruit formed from a double ovary, of which only one develops into a seed, as in the daisy family. ▷late 19th cent.: modern Latin, from Greek *kupselē* 'hollow vessel.'

Cyr·a·no de Ber·ge·rac /ˈsirənō də ˈbərzhəˌrak; ˈberzhˌrak/, Savinien (1619–55), French soldier, duelist, and writer. He is chiefly remembered for the large number of duels that he fought (many because of his proverbially large nose) as immortalized in *Cyrano de Bergerac* (1897), a play by Edmond Rostand.

Cyr·e·na·ic /ˌsirəˈnāik/ ▶*adj.* of or denoting the hedonistic school of philosophy, whichwas founded *c.*400 BC by Aristippus the Elder of Cyrene and which holds that pleasure is the highest good and that virtue is to be equated with the ability to enjoy.
▶*n.* a follower of this school of philosophy. **—Cyr·e·na·i·cism** /-ˈnāəˌsizəm/ *n.*

Cyr·e·na·i·ca /ˌsirəˈnāəkə/ a region in northeastern Libya that borders on the Mediterranean Sea and was settled by the Greeks *c.*640 BC.

Cy·re·ne /sīˈrēnē/ an ancient Greek city in North Africa, near the coast in Cyrenaica.

Cyr·il, St. /ˈsirəl/ (826–869), Greek missionary. The invention of the Cyrillic alphabet is ascribed to him. Feast day (in the Eastern Church) May 11; (in the Western Church) February 14.

Cy·ril·lic /səˈrilik/ ▶*adj.* denoting the alphabet used by many Slavic peoples, chiefly those with a historical allegiance to the Orthodox Church. Ultimately derived from Greek uncials, it is now used for Russian, Bulgarian, Serbian, Ukrainian, and some other Slavic languages.
▶*n.* the Cyrillic alphabet. ▷early 19th cent.: named after St. *Cyril* (see **CYRIL, ST.**).

Cyr·il of Al·ex·an·dri·a, St. (died 444), doctor of the Church and patriarch of Alexandria. He is best known for his vehement opposition to the views of Nestorius, the patriarch of Constantinople. Feast day, February 9.

Cy·rus[1] /ˈsīrəs/ (died *c.*530 BC), king of Persia 559–530 BC; founder of the Achaemenid dynasty; father of Cambyses; known as **Cyrus the Great**. He defeated the Median empire in 550 BC and went on to conquer Asia Minor, Babylonia, Syria, Palestine, and most of the Iranian plateau. He is said to have ruled with wisdom and moderation, maintaining good relations with the Jews (whom he freed from the Babylonian Captivity) and the Phoenicians.

Cy·rus[2] (died 401 BC), Persian prince; known as **Cyrus the Younger**. On the death of his father, Darius II, in 405 BC, Cyrus led an army of mercenaries against his elder brother, who had succeeded to the throne as Artaxerxes II.

cyst /sist/ ▶*n. Biology* in an animal or plant, a thin-walled, hollow organ or cavity containing a liquid secretion; a sac, vesicle, or bladder. ■ *Medicine* in the body, a membranous sac or cavity of abnormal character containing fluid. ■ a tough protective capsule enclosing the larva of a parasitic worm or the resting stage of an organism. ▷early 18th cent.: from late Latin *cystis*, from Greek *kustis* 'bladder.'

cys·tec·to·my /sisˈtektəmē/ ▶*n.* **1** (*pl.* **-mies**) a surgical operation to remove the urinary bladder. **2** a surgical operation to remove an abnormal cyst: *an ovarian cystectomy.*

cys·te·ine /ˈsistəˌēn; ˈsisˌtēn/ ▶*n. Biochemistry* a sulfur-containing amino acid that occurs in keratins and other proteins, often in the form of cystine, and is a constituent of many enzymes. • Chem. formula: $HSCH_2CH(NH_2)COOH$. ▷late 19th cent.: from **CYSTINE** + *-eine* (variant of **-INE**[4]).

cys·tic /ˈsistik/ ▶*adj.* **1** *chiefly Medicine* of, relating to, or characterized by cysts. ■ *Zoology* (of a parasite or other organism) enclosed in a cyst: *the cystic stage.* **2** of or relating to the urinary bladder or the gallbladder: *the cystic artery.* ▷mid 17th cent. (originally referring to the gallbladder): from French *cystique* or modern Latin *cysticus*, from late Latin *cystis* (see **CYST**).

cys·ti·cer·cus /ˌsistəˈsərkəs; -ˈkərkəs/ ▶*n.* (*pl.* **-cer·ci** /-ˈsərˌsī; -ˈsərˌkī/) *Zoology* a larval tapeworm that is at a stage in which the scolex is inverted in a sac, and that is typically found encysted in the muscle tissue of the host. ▷mid 19th cent.: modern Latin (originally the name of a supposed genus), from Greek *kustis* 'bladder' + *kerkos* 'tail.' **—cys·ti·cer·coid** /-ˈsərˌkoid/ *adj.* & *n.*

cys·tic fi·bro·sis ▶*n.* a hereditary disorder affecting the exocrine glands. It causes the production of abnormally thick mucus, leading to the blockage of the pancreatic ducts, intestines, and bronchi and often resulting in respiratory infection.

cys·tine /ˈsisˌtēn/ ▶*n. Biochemistry* a compound that is an oxidized dimer of cysteine and is the form in which cysteine often occurs in organic tissue. • Chem. formula: $C_6H_{12}N_2O_4S_2$. ▷mid 19th cent.: from Greek *kustis* 'bladder' (because it was first isolated from urinary calculi) + **-INE**[4].

cys·ti·tis /sisˈtītis/ ▶*n. Medicine* inflammation of the urinary bladder. It is often caused by infection and is usually accompanied by frequent, painful urination.

cysto- ▶*comb. form* of or relating to the urinary bladder: *cystotomy.* ▷from Greek *kustis* 'bladder.'

cyst·oid /ˈsistoid/ ▶*adj.* of the nature of a cyst.
▶*n.* a cystoid formation.

cys·to·scope /ˈsistəˌskōp/ ▶*n. Medicine* an instrument inserted into the urethra for examining the urinary bladder. **—cys·to·scop·ic** /ˌsistəˈskäpik/ *adj.* **—cys·tos·co·py** /sisˈtäskəpē/ *n.*

cys·tot·o·my /sisˈtätəmē/ ▶*n.* (*pl.* **-mies**) a surgical incision into the urinary bladder.

-cyte ▶*comb. form Biology* denoting a mature cell: *lymphocyte.* Compare with **-BLAST**. ▷from Greek *kutos* 'vessel.'

Cyth·er·e·a /ˌsithəˈrēə/ ▶*n.* another name for **APHRODITE**. ▷from Latin *Cythera* 'Kithira,' the name of an Ionian island.

Cyth·er·ean /ˌsithəˈrēən/ ▶*adj. Astronomy* of or relating to the planet Venus: *the Cytherean atmosphere.* ■ of or relating to the goddess Cytherea.

cyt·i·dine /ˈsitəˌdēn; ˈsit-/ ▶*n. Biochemistry* a nucleoside composed of cytosine linked to ribose, obtained from RNA by hydrolysis. ▷early 20th cent.: from **CYTO-** + **-IDE** + **-INE**[4].

cyto- ▶*comb. form Biology* of a cell or cells: *cytology* | *cytoplasm.* ▷from Greek *kutos* 'vessel.'

cy·to·ar·chi·tec·ton·ics /ˌsītōˌärkəˌtekˈtäniks/ ▶*plural n.* [treated as *sing.* or *pl.*] another term for **CYTOARCHITECTURE**. **—cy·to·ar·chi·tec·ton·ic** *adj.*

cy·to·ar·chi·tec·ture /ˌsītōˈärkiˌtekchər/ ▶*n. Anatomy* the arrangement of cells in a tissue, esp. in specific areas of the cerebral cortex characterized by the arrangement of their cells and each associated with particular functions. Also called **CYTOARCHITECTONICS**. ■ the study of this. **—cy·to·ar·chi·tec·tur·al** /-ˌärkiˈtekchərəl/ *adj.* **—cy·to·ar·chi·tec·tur·al·ly** /-ˌärkiˈtekchərəlē/ *adv.*

cy·to·cen·tri·fuge /ˌsītəˈsentrəˌfyo͞oj/ *Biology* ▶*n.* a centrifuge used for depositing cells suspended in a liquid onto a slide for microscopic examination.
▶*v.* [*trans.*] deposit (cells) on a slide using such a centrifuge.

cy·to·cha·la·sin /ˌsītəkəˈlāsən/ ▶*n. Biochemistry* any of a group of polycyclic compounds produced by fungi and used experimentally in research for their property of interfering with cell processes. ▷1960s: from **CYTO-** 'cell' + Greek *khalasis* 'dislocation.'

cy·to·chem·is·try /ˌsītəˈkeməstrē/ ▶*n.* the chemistry of living cells, esp. as studied microscopically. **—cy·to·chem·i·cal** /-ˈkemikəl/ *adj.*

cy·to·chrome /ˈsītəˌkrōm/ ▶*n. Biochemistry* any of a number of compounds consisting of heme bonded to a protein. Cytochromes function as electron transfer agents in many metabolic pathways, esp. cellular respiration.

cy·to·gen·e·sis /ˌsītəˈjenəsis/ (also **cy·tog·e·ny** /sīˈtäjənē/) ▶*n.* the formation and development of cells.

cy·to·ge·net·ics /ˌsītōjəˈnetiks/ ▶*plural n.* [treated as *sing.*] *Biology* the study of inheritance in relation to the structure and function of chromosomes. **—cy·to·ge·net·ic** *adj.* **—cy·to·ge·net·i·cal** /-ikəl/ *adj.* **—cy·to·ge·net·i·cal·ly** /-ik(ə)lē/ *adv.* **—cy·to·ge·net·i·cist** /-jəˈnetəsist/ *n.*

cy·to·kine /ˈsītəˌkīn/ ▶*n. Physiology* any of a number of substances, such as interferon, interleukin, and growth factors, that are secreted by certain cells of the immune system and have an effect on other cells.

cy·to·ki·ne·sis /ˌsītōkəˈnēsis; -kī-/ ▶*n. Biology* the cytoplasmic division of a cell at the end of mitosis or meiosis, bringing about the separation into two daughter cells.

cy·to·ki·nin /ˌsītəˈkīnin/ ▶*n.* another term for **KININ** (sense 2).

cy·tol·o·gy /sīˈtäləjē/ ▶*n.* the branch of biology concerned with the structure and function of plant and animal cells. **—cy·to·log·i·cal** /ˌsītlˈäjikəl/ *adj.* **—cy·to·log·i·cal·ly** /ˌsītlˈäjik(ə)lē/ *adv.* **—cy·tol·o·gist** /-jist/ *n.*

cy·tol·y·sis /sīˈtäləsəs/ ▶*n. Biology* the dissolution or disruption of cells, esp. by an external agent. **—cy·to·lyt·ic** /ˌsītlˈlitik/ *adj.*

cy·to·me·gal·ic /ˌsītəmiˈgalik/ ▶*adj. Medicine* characterized by enlarged cells, esp. with reference to a disease caused by a cytomegalovirus.

cy·to·meg·a·lo·vi·rus /ˌsītəˌmegəlōˈvīrəs/ (abbr.: **CMV**) ▶*n. Medicine* a kind of herpesvirus that usually produces very mild symptoms in an infected person but may cause severe neurological damage in people with weakened immune systems and in the newborn.

cy·to·mem·brane /ˌsītəˈmembrān/ ▶*n.* another term for **CELL MEMBRANE**.

cy·to·path·ic /ˌsītəˈpathik/ (also **cy·to·path·o·gen·ic** /ˌsītəˌpathəˈjenik/) ▶*adj.* of, pertaining to, or producing damage to living cells.

cy·to·phil·ic /ˌsītəˈfilik/ ▶*adj.* having an affinity for living cells.

cy·to·pho·tom·e·try /ˌsītəfōˈtämətrē/ ▶*n. Biology* the investigation of the contents of cells by measuring the light they allow through after staining. **—cy·to·pho·tom·e·ter** /-ˈtämətər/ *n.* **—cy·to·pho·to·met·ric** /-ˌfōtəˈmetrik/ *adj.*

cy·to·plasm /ˈsītəˌplazəm/ ▶*n. Biology* the material or protoplasm within a living cell, excluding the nucleus. **—cy·to·plas·mic** /ˌsītəˈplazmik/ *adj.*

cy·to·plast /ˈsītəˌplast/ ▶*n.* the intact cytoplasmic content of a single cell.

cy·to·sine /ˈsītəˌsēn/ ▶*n. Biochemistry* a compound found in living tissue as a constituent base of nucleic acids. It is paired with guanine in double-stranded DNA. • A pyrimidine derivative; chem. formula: $C_4H_5N_3O$.

cy·to·skel·e·ton /ˌsītəˈskelitn/ ▶*n. Biology* a microscopic network of protein filaments and tubules in the cytoplasm of many living cells, giving them shape and coherence. **—cy·to·skel·e·tal** /-ˈskelitl/ *adj.*

cy·to·sol /ˈsītəˌsäl; -ˌsôl/ ▶*n. Biology* the aqueous component of the cytoplasm of a cell, within which various organelles and particles are suspended. **—cy·to·sol·ic** /ˌsītəˈsälik; -ˈsôlik/ *adj.*

cy·to·stat·ic /ˌsītəˈstatik/ ▶*adj.* inhibiting cell growth and division.
▶*n.* any substance that inhibits cell growth and division.

cy·to·tax·on·o·my /ˌsītətak'sänəmē/ ▸*n.* taxonomy based on cytological (and esp. cytogenetic) study.

cy·to·tox·ic /ˌsītə'täksik/ ▸*adj.* toxic to living cells. **—cy·to·tox·ic·i·ty** /-täk'sisətē/ *n.*

cy·to·tox·ic T cell ▸*n.* another term for KILLER CELL.

cy·to·tox·in /ˌsītə'täksin/ ▸*n.* a substance toxic to cells.

Cy Young A·ward ▸*n. Baseball* an annual award to the outstanding pitcher in each of the major leagues. ▷named in honor of Cy Young.

czar /zär; (t)sär/ (also **tsar** or **tzar**) ▸*n.* **1** variant spelling of TSAR **2** a person with great authority or power in a particular area: *America's new drug czar.* ▷from Russian *tsar'*, representing Latin *Caesar*. **—czar·dom** /-dəm/ *n.* **—czar·ism** /-ˌizəm/ *n.* **—czar·ist** /-ist/ *n.* & *adj.*

czar·das ▸*n.* variant spelling of CSARDAS.

czar·e·vich /'zärəˌvich; '(t)sär-/ ▸ variant spelling of TSAREVICH

cza·rev·na /zä'revnə; (t)sä-/ ▸ variant spelling of TSAREVNA

cza·ri·na /zä'rēnə; (t)sä-/ ▸ variant spelling of TSARINA

Czech /chek/ ▸*n.* **1** a native or national of the Czech Republic or (formerly) Czechoslovakia, or a person of Czech descent. **2** the West Slavic language spoken in the Czech Republic, closely related to Slovak. ▸*adj.* of or relating to the Czechs or their language. ▷Polish spelling of Czech *Čech.*

Czech·o·slo·va·ki·a /ˌchekəslə'väkēə; -'vakēə/ a former country in central Europe, now divided between the Czech Republic and Slovakia; capital, Prague. Created out of the northern part of the Austro-Hungarian empire at the end of World War I, it was crushed by the Nazi takeover of the Sudetenland in 1938 and the rest of the country in 1939. After World War II, it fell under Soviet domination. The two parts separated on January 1, 1993. **—Czech·o·slo·vak** /-'slōˌväk; -ˌvak/ *n.* & *adj.* **—Czech·o·slo·va·ki·an** *adj.* & *n.*

Czech Re·pub·lic a country in central Europe; pop. 10,298,700; capital, Prague; official language, Czech.

The Czech Republic was formerly one of the two constituent republics of Czechoslovakia. When Czechoslovakia was partitioned on January 1, 1993, the Czech Republic became independent. It includes the former provinces of Bohemia, Silesia, and Moravia. In 2004 the Czech Republic joined both NATO and the EU.

Czę·sto·cho·wa /ˌchenstə'khōvə/ an industrial city in south central Poland; pop. 258,000. It is known for the statue of the black Madonna in its church.

Dd

D

D1 /dē/ (also **d**) ▸*n.* (*pl.* **Ds**or **D's**) **1** the fourth letter of the alphabet. ■ denoting the fourth in a set of items, categories, sizes, etc. ■ the fourth highest category of academic mark. ■ (**d**) *Chess* denoting the fourth file from the left, as viewed from White's side of the board. ■ denoting the second-lowest-earning socioeconomic category for marketing purposes, including semiskilled and unskilled personnel. **2** (**D**) a shape like that of a capital D: [in *combination*] *the D-shaped handle.* ■ a loop or ring of this shape. **3** (usu. **D**) *Music* the second note of the diatonic scale of C major. ■ a key based on a scale with D as its keynote. **4** the Roman numeral for 500. [understood as half of CIↃ, an earlier form of M (= 1,000).]

D2 ▸*abbr.* ■ Democrat or Democratic. ■ depth (in the sense of the dimension of an object from front to back). ■ *Chemistry* dextrorotatory: *D-glucose.* ■ (with a numeral) dimension(s) or dimensional: *a 3-D model.* ■ (in tables of sports results) drawn. ■ (on an automatic gearshift) drive. ■ (in personal ads) divorced.
▸*symbol* ■ *Physics* electric flux density. ■ *Chemistry* the hydrogen isotope deuterium.

d ▸*abbr.* ■ date. ■ (in genealogies) daughter. ■ day(s): *orbital period (Mars): 687.0d.* ■ deceased. ■ deep. ■ [in *combination*] (in units of measurement) deci-. ■ (in travel timetables) departs. ■ (**d.**) died (used to indicate a date of death): *Barents, Willem (d.1597).* ■ divorced. ■ *Brit.* penny or pence (of predecimal currency): *£20 10s 6d.* [from Latin *denarius* 'penny.'] ■ *Chemistry* denoting electrons and orbitals possessing two units of angular momentum: *d-electrons.* [*d* from *diffuse*, originally applied to lines in atomic spectra.]
▸*symbol* ■ *Mathematics* diameter. ■ *Mathematics* denoting a small increment in a given variable: *dy/dx.*

'd ▸*contraction of* ■ had: *they'd already gone.* ■ would: *I'd expect that.*

DA ▸*abbr.* ■ district attorney. ■ Doctor of Arts. ■ *informal* duck's ass.

da ▸*abbr.* [in *combination*] (in units of measurement) deca-.

da /də/ ▸*adj.* nonstandard spelling of *the*, used in representing informal speech.

D/A *Electronics* ▸*abbr.* digital to analog.

DAB ▸*abbr.* digital audio broadcasting.

dab1 /dab/ ▸*v.* (**dabbed, dab·bing**) [*trans.*] **1** press against (something) lightly with a piece of absorbent material in order to clean or dry it: *he dabbed his mouth with his napkin* | [*intrans.*] *she* **dabbed at** *her eyes with a handkerchief.* ■ apply (a substance) with light quick strokes: *she* **dabbed** *disinfectant* **on** *the cut.* **2** aim at or strike with a light blow.
▸*n.* a small amount of something: *she licked* **a dab of** *chocolate from her finger.* ■ a brief application of cosmetic, paint, or the like to a surface: *apply concealer with light dabs.* ▷Middle English: symbolic of a light striking movement; compare with DABBLE and DIB.

dab2 ▸*n.* a small, commercially important flatfish that is found chiefly in the North Atlantic. • *Limanda* and other genera, family Pleuronectidae (several species, in particular the European *L. limanda*), and genus *Citharichthys*, family Bothidae (see also SAND DAB). ▷late Middle English: of unknown origin.

dab·ber /'dabər/ ▸*n.* a rounded pad used in printing to apply ink to a surface.

dab·ble /'dabəl/ ▸*v.* [*trans.*] immerse (one's hands or feet) partially in water and move them around gently: *they dabbled their feet in the rock pools.* ■ [*intrans.*] (of a duck or other waterbird) move the bill around in shallow water while feeding: *teal dabble in the shallows.* ■ [*intrans.*] *figurative* take part in an activity in a casual or superficial way: *he* **dabbled in** *writing as a young man.* ▷mid 16th cent.: from obsolete Dutch *dabbelen*, or a frequentative of the verb DAB1. —**dab·bler** /'dab(ə)lər/ *n.*

dab·bling duck /'dab(ə)liNG/ ▸*n.* a freshwater duck that typically feeds in shallow water by dabbling and upending, such as the mallard, teal, shoveler, and pintail. Compare with DIVING DUCK. • Tribe Anatini, family Anatidae: genus *Anas* (numerous species), and perhaps some other genera.

dab·chick /'dab,CHik/ ▸*n.* a small grebe, esp. the little grebe. • Genera *Tachybaptus* and *Podilymbus*, family Podicipedidae: several species. ▷mid 16th cent. (as *dapchick* or *dopchick*): the first element is perhaps related to DIP and DEEP.

dab hand ▸*n. Brit., informal* a person who is an expert at a particular activity: *Tony is a* **dab hand at** *golf.* ▷early 19th cent.: of unknown origin.

D'A·bruz·zo, Alphonso, see ALDA.

DAC *Electronics* ▸*abbr.* digital to analog converter.

da ca·po /dä 'käpō/ *Music* ▸*adv.* (esp. as a direction) repeat from the beginning. Compare with DAL SEGNO.
▸*adj.* [*attrib.*] including the repetition of a passage at the beginning: *da capo arias.* ▷Italian, literally 'from the head.'

Dac·ca /'däkä/ variant spelling of DHAKA.

dace /dās/ ▸*n.* (*pl.* same) a small freshwater fish of the minnow family, typically living in running water. • *Leuciscus* and numerous other genera, family Cyprinidae: several species, including the **longfin dace** (*Agosia chrysogaster*) of western North America and the widely distributed *L. leuciscus* of northern Eurasia. ▷late Middle English: from Old French *dars* (see DART).

da·cha /'däCHə/ ▸*n.* a country house or cottage in Russia, typically used as a second or vacation home. ▷mid 19th cent.: Russian, originally 'grant (of land).'

Da·chau /'dä,KHou/ a city in Bavaria in southwestern Germany, on the Amper River, near Munich, site of a Nazi concentration camp from 1933 until 1945; pop. 33,000.

dachs·hund /'däksənd; 'däks,hŏŏnt/ ▸*n.* a dog of a short-legged, long-bodied breed. ▷late 19th cent.: from German, literally 'badger dog' (the breed being originally used to dig badgers out of their setts).

Da·ci·a /'dāSH(ē)ə/ an ancient country in southeastern Europe in what is now northwestern Romania. It was annexed by Trajan in AD 106 as a province of the Roman Empire. —**Da·ci·an** /'dāSH(ē)ən/ *adj.* & *n.*

da·cite /'dā,sīt/ ▸*n. Geology* a volcanic rock resembling andesite but containing free quartz. ▷late 18th cent.: from the name of the Roman province of DACIA (as it was first found in the Carpathian Mountains) + -ITE1. —**da·cit·ic** /dā'sitik/ *adj.*

da·coit /də'koit/ ▸*n.* a member of a band of armed robbers in India or Myanmar (Burma). ▷from Hindi *ḍakait*, from *ḍakaitī* 'robbery by a gang.'

da·coit·y /də'koitē/ ▸*n.* (*pl.* **-coit·ies**) an act of armed robbery committed by a gang in India or Myanmar (Burma). ▷from Hindi *ḍakaitī*.

Da·cron /'dā,krän; 'dak,rän/ ▸*n. trademark* a synthetic polyester (polyethylene terephthalate) with tough, elastic properties, used as a textile fabric. ▷1950s: an invented name.

dac·tyl /'daktl/ ▸*n. Prosody* a metrical foot consisting of one stressed syllable followed by two unstressed syllables or (in Greek and Latin) one long syllable followed by two short syllables. ▷late Middle English: via Latin from Greek *daktulos*, literally 'finger' (the three bones of the finger corresponding to the three syllables).

dac·tyl·ic /dak'tilik/ *Prosody* ▸*adj.* of or using dactyls: *dactylic rhythm.*
▸*n.* (usu. **dactylics**) dactylic verse. ▷late 16th cent.: via Latin from Greek *daktulikos*, from *daktulos*, literally 'finger' (see DACTYL).

dad /dad/ ▸*n. informal* one's father: *his dad was with him* | *what are you making, Dad?* ▷mid 16th cent.: perhaps imitative of a young child's first syllables *da, da.*

Da·da /'dädä/ ▸*n.* an early 20th-century international movement in art, literature, music, and film, repudiating and mocking artistic and social conventions and emphasizing the illogical and absurd.

Dada was launched in Zurich in 1916 by Tristan Tzara and others, soon merging with a similar group in New York. It favored montage, collage, and the ready-made. Leading figures: Jean Arp, André Breton, Max Ernst, Man Ray, and Marcel Duchamp.

▷French, literally 'hobbyhorse,' the title of a review that appeared in Zurich in 1916. —**Da·da·ism** /-,izəm/ *n.* —**Da·da·ist** /-ist/ *n.* & *adj.* —**Da·da·is·tic** /,dädä'istik/ *adj.*

da·da /'dada; -də/ ▸*n. informal* one's father. ▷late 17th cent.: perhaps imitative of a young child's first syllables (see DAD).

dad·dy /'dadē/ ▸*n.* (*pl.* **-dies**) *informal* one's father. ■ the oldest, best, or biggest example of something: ***the daddy of** all potholes.* ▷early 16th cent.: from DAD + -Y2.

dad·dy long·legs ▸*n.* **1** an arachnid with a globular body and long thin legs, typically living in leaf litter and on tree trunks. Also called HARVESTMAN. • Order Phalangida: numerous genera and species, including the common *Phalangium opilio.* **2** *Brit.* a crane fly.

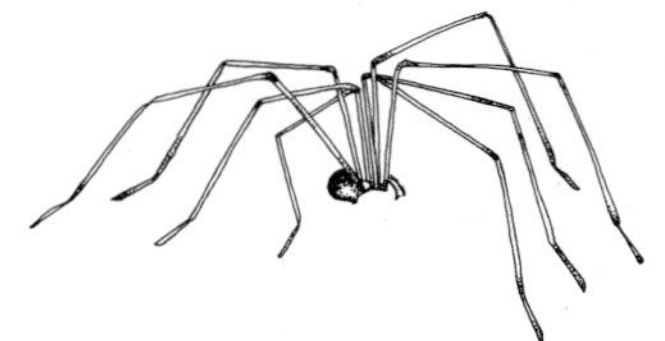

daddy longlegs 1

Dade Coun·ty /dād/ a county in southeastern Florida, on the Atlantic coast, that includes Miami and many suburbs as well as much of the Everglades; pop. 2,253,362. Formally **Miami-Dade County**.

da·do /'dādō/ ▸*n.* (*pl.* **-dos**) the lower part of the wall of a room, below about waist height, if it is a different color or has a different covering than the upper part. ■ a groove cut in the face of a board, into which the edge of another board is fixed. ■ *Architecture* the part of a pedestal between the base and the cornice. ▷mid 17th cent. (denoting the main part of a pedestal, above the base): from Italian, literally 'dice or cube,' from Latin *datum* 'something given, starting point' (see DATUM).

Da·dra and Na·gar Ha·ve·li /də'drä and ,nəgər ə'velē/ a union territory in western India, on the Arabian Sea; pop. 138,500; capital, Silvassa.

Daed·a·lus /'dedl-əs/ *Greek Mythology* a craftsman, considered the inventor of carpentry, who is said to have built the labyrinth for Minos, king of Crete. Minos imprisoned him and his son Icarus, but they escaped using wings that Daedalus made and fastened with wax. Icarus, however, flew too near the sun and was killed.

dae·mon1 /'dēmən/ (also **dai·mon**) ▸*n.* **1** (in ancient Greek belief) a divinity or supernatural being of a nature between gods and humans. ■ an inner or attendant spirit or inspiring force. **2** *archaic* spelling of DEMON1. ▷mid 16th cent.: common spelling of

DEMON1 until the 19th cent. —**dae·mon·ic** /di'mänik/ *adj.*

dae·mon2 (also **de·mon**) ▸*n. Computing* a background process that handles requests for services such as print spooling and file transfers, and is dormant when not required. ▷1980s: perhaps from *d(isk) a(nd) e(xecution) mon(itor)* or from *de(vice) mon(itor)*, or merely a transferred use of DEMON1.

daf·fo·dil /'dafə,dil/ ▸*n.* a bulbous plant that typically bears bright yellow flowers with a long trumpet-shaped center (corona). • Genus *Narcissus*, family Liliaceae (or Amaryllidaceae): several species, in particular the common *N. pseudonarcissus* and its varieties. See also NARCISSUS. ▷mid 16th cent.: from late Middle English *affodill*, from medieval Latin *affodilus*, variant of Latin *asphodilus* (see ASPHODEL). The initial *d-* is unexplained.

daffodil

daf·fy /'dafē/ ▸*adj.* (**-fi·er**, **-fi·est**) *informal* silly; mildly eccentric: *daffy anecdotes.* ■ crazy: *you must both be daffy.* ▷late 19th cent.: from northern English dialect *daff* 'simpleton' + -Y1; perhaps related to DAFT. —**daf·fi·ness** *n.*

daft /daft/ ▸*adj. informal,* silly; foolish: *don't ask such daft questions.* ■ crazy: *have you gone daft?* ■ [*predic.*] (**daft about**) infatuated with: *we were all daft about him.* ▷Old English *gedæfte* 'mild, meek,' of Germanic origin; related to Gothic *gadaban* 'become or be fitting.'

dag /dag/ ▸*n. Austral./NZ informal* an unfashionable or socially conservative person. ▷late Middle English (in the sense 'a hanging part of something'): of unknown origin.

da Ga·ma /də 'gämə/, Vasco (*c.*1469–1524), Portuguese explorer. He led the first European expedition around the Cape of Good Hope in 1497, sighting and naming Natal on Christmas Day before crossing the Indian Ocean and arriving in Calicut (Kozhikode, in India) in 1498.

Da·ge·stan /,dägə'stän; ,dagə'stan/ an autonomous republic in southwestern Russia, on the western shore of the Caspian Sea; pop. 1,823,000; capital, Makhachkala.

dag·ga /'dagə/ ▸*n. chiefly S. African* marijuana. ▷late 17th cent.: from Afrikaans, from Khoikhoi *dachab.*

dag·ger /'dagər/ ▸*n.* **1** a short knife with a pointed and edged blade, used as a weapon. ■ *Printing* another term for OBELUS. **2** a moth with a dark dagger-shaped marking on the forewing. • Genus *Acronicta*, family Noctuidae: several species. ▷late Middle English: perhaps from obsolete *dag* 'pierce, stab,' influenced by Old French *dague* 'long dagger.'

▸*PHRASES* □ **at daggers drawn** in bitter enmity. □ **look daggers at** glare angrily or venomously at.

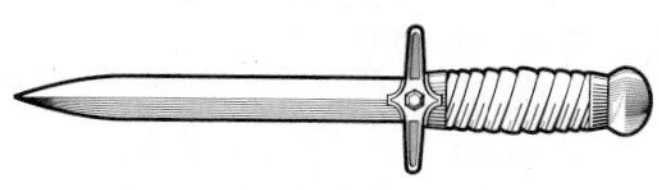
dagger 1

dag·ger·board /'dagər,bôrd/ ▸*n.* a board that slides vertically through the keel of a sailboat to reduce sideways movement. Compare with CENTERBOARD.

da·go /'dāgō/ ▸*n.* (*pl.* **-gos** or **-goes**) *informal, offensive* an Italian, Spanish, or Portuguese-speaking person. ▷mid 19th cent.: from the Spanish given name *Diego* (equivalent to *James*).

Da·gon /'dā,gän/ (in the Bible) a national deity of the ancient Philistines, represented as a fish-tailed man. ▷via Latin and Greek from Hebrew *dāgōn*, perhaps from *dāgān* 'corn,' but said (according to folk etymology) to be from *dāg* 'fish.'

da·go red ▸*n. offensive* cheap red wine, typically from Italy.

Da·guerre /də'ger(ə)r; dä'ger/, Louis-Jacques-Mandé (1789–1851), French physicist. He invented the first practical photographic process, which became known as the daguerreotype process.

da·guerre·o·type /də'ge(ə)rə,tīp/ (also **da·guer·ro·type**) ▸*n.* a photograph taken by an early photographic process employing an iodine-sensitized silvered plate and mercury vapor. ▷mid 19th cent.: from French *daguerréotype*, named after L.-J.-M. DAGUERRE, its French inventor.

Dag·wood sand·wich /'dag,wŏŏd/ (also **Dag·wood**) ▸*n.* a thick sandwich with a variety of different fillings. ▷1970s: named after *Dagwood* Bumstead, a comic-strip character who makes and eats this type of sandwich.

dah /dä/ ▸*n.* (in Morse code) another term for DASH. ▷World War II: imitative.

da·ha·be·ah /,dähə'bēə/ (also **da·ha·bee·yah**) ▸*n.* a passenger boat used on the Nile, typically with lateen sails. ▷mid 19th cent.: from Arabic, literally 'golden,' denoting the gilded state barge formerly used by the Muslim rulers of Egypt.

Dahl /däl/, Roald (1916–90), British writer. His fiction and drama, such as the short-story collection *Tales of the Unexpected* (1979), typically include macabre plots and unexpected outcomes. Notable works for children include *James and the Giant Peach* (1961) and *Charlie and the Chocolate Factory* (1964).

dahl ▸*n.* variant spelling of DHAL.

dahl·ia /'dalyə; 'däl-/ ▸*n.* a tuberous-rooted Mexican plant of the daisy family, cultivated for its brightly colored single or double flowers. • Genus *Dahlia*, family Compositae. ▷modern Latin, named in honor of Andreas *Dahl* (1751–89), Swedish botanist.

Da·ho·mey /də'hōmē/ former name (until 1975) of BENIN.

dai·kon /'dī,kän; -kən/ ▸*n.* a radish of a variety with a large slender white root that is typically eaten cooked, esp. in Eastern cuisine, and is also used for fodder. ▷Japanese, from *dai* 'large' + *kon* 'root.'

dai·ly /'dālē/ ▸*adj.* [*attrib.*] done, produced, or occurring every day or every weekday: *a daily newspaper | daily flights to Prague.* ■ relating to the period of a single day: *boats can be rented for a daily rate.*
▸*adv.* every day: *the museum is open daily.*
▸*n.* (*pl.* **-lies**) *informal* **1** a newspaper published every day except Sunday. **2** (**dailies**) the first prints from cinematographic takes, made rapidly for movie producers or editors; the rushes. **3** (also **dai·ly help**) *Brit., dated* a woman who is employed to clean someone's house each day. ▷late Middle English: from DAY + -LY1, -LY2.
▸*PHRASE* □ **daily life** the activities and experiences that constitute a person's normal existence.

dai·ly dou·ble ▸*n. Horse Racing* a single bet on the winners of two named races in a day.

dai·ly doz·en ▸*n.* [in *sing.*] *informal, dated* regular exercises, esp. those done first thing in the morning.

Daim·ler /'dīmlər/, Gottlieb (1834–1900), German engineer and engine manufacturer. In 1884 he produced a small internal combustion engine using gasoline as a fuel and made it propel a bicycle. In 1890 he formed a company to produce these engines.

dai·mon /'dī,mōn/ ▸*n.* (*pl.* **-mons** or **-mo·nes** /-mə,nēz/) variant spelling of DAEMON1. —**dai·mon·ic** /dī'mänik/ *adj.*

dai·myo /'dīmyō/ (also **dai·mio**) ▸*n.* (*pl.* **-myos**) *historical* (in feudal Japan) one of the great lords who were vassals of the shogun. ▷Japanese, from *dai* 'great' + *myō* 'name.'

dain·ty /'dāntē/ ▸*adj.* (**-ti·er**, **-ti·est**) **1** delicately small and pretty: *a dainty lace handkerchief.* ■ (of a person) delicate and graceful in build or movement. ■ (of food) particularly good to eat: *a dainty morsel.* **2** fastidious or difficult to please, typically concerning food: *a dainty appetite.*
▸*n.* (*pl.* **-ties**) (usu. **dainties**) something good to eat; a delicacy. ▷Middle English (in the sense 'tidbit, [something] pleasing to the palate'): from Old French *daintie, deintie* 'choice morsel, pleasure,' from Latin *dignitas* 'worthiness or beauty,' from *dignus* 'worthy.' —**dain·ti·ly** /'dāntəlē/ *adv.* —**dain·ti·ness** *n.*

dai·qui·ri /'dakərē; 'dīkə-/ ▸*n.* (*pl.* **-ris**) a cocktail containing rum and lime juice. ▷named after *Daiquiri*, a rum-producing district in Cuba.

Dai·ren /'dī'rən; -'ren/ former name of DALIAN.

dair·y /'de(ə)rē/ ▸*n.* (*pl.* **dair·ies**) a building, room, or establishment for the storage, processing, and distribution of milk and milk products. ■ a store where milk and milk products are sold. ■ food made from or containing milk.
▸*adj.* [*attrib.*] containing or made from milk: *dairy products.* ■ concerned with or involved in the production of milk: *a dairy farmer.* ▷Middle English *deierie*, from *deie* 'dairymaid' (in Old English *dǣge* 'female servant'), of Germanic origin; related to Old Norse *deigja*, also to DOUGH and to the second element of Old English *hlǣfdige* (see LADY).

dair·y·ing /'de(ə)rē-ING/ ▸*n.* the business of producing, storing, and distributing milk and its products.

dair·y·maid /'de(ə)rē,mād/ ▸*n. archaic* a woman employed in a dairy.

dair·y·man /'de(ə)rēmən; -,man/ ▸*n.* (*pl.* **-men**) a man who is employed in a dairy or sells dairy products.

da·is /'dāis; 'dī-/ ▸*n.* a low platform for a lectern, seats of honor, or a throne. ▷Middle English (originally denoting a raised table for distinguished guests): from Old French *deis*, from Latin *discus* 'disk or dish' (later 'table'). Little used after the Middle English period, the word was revived by antiquarians in the early 19th cent. with the disyllabic pronunciation.

dai·sy /'dāzē/ ▸*n.* (*pl.* **-sies**) a small grassland plant that has flowers with a yellow disk and white rays. It has given rise to many ornamental garden varieties. • *Bellis perennis*, family Compositae (or Asteraceae; the **daisy family**). The plants of this large family (known as composites) are distinguished by having composite flowerheads consisting of numerous disk florets, ray florets, or both; they include many weeds (dandelions, thistles, ragworts) and garden flowers (asters, chrysanthemums, dahlias, marigolds). ■ used in names of other plants of this family with similar flowers, e.g., **Michaelmas daisy**, **Shasta daisy**. ▷Old English *dæges ēage* 'day's eye' (because the flower opens in the morning and closes at night).
▸*PHRASES* □ (**as**) **fresh as a daisy** healthy and full of energy. □ **pushing up** (**the**) **daisies** *informal* dead and buried.

dai·sy chain ▸*n.* a string of daisies threaded together by their stems. ■ *figurative* a string of associated people or things: *we can all make daisy chains of blame.* ■ *informal* a sexual activity in which participants serve as partners to different people simultaneously.
▸*v.* (**dai·sy-chain**) [*trans.*] *Computing* connect (several devices) together in a linear series. —**dai·sy-chain·a·ble** *adj.*

dai·sy-cut·ter ▸*n. informal* an immensely powerful aerial bomb that derives its destructive power from the mixture of ammonium nitrate and aluminum powder with air. ▷early 20th cent.: so named because the bomb explodes just above ground level.

dai·sy wheel ▸*n.* a device used as a printer in word processors and typewriters, consisting of a disk of spokes extending radially from a central hub, each terminating in a printing character.

Dak. ▸*abbr.* Dakota.

Da·kar /dä'kär; 'dak,är/ the capital of Senegal, a port on the Atlantic coast of West Africa; pop. 1,641,350.

Da·ko·ta1 /də'kōtə/ a former territory of the U.S. that was organized in 1889 into the states of North Dakota and South Dakota. —**Da·ko·tan** *n.* & *adj.*

Da·ko·ta2 ▸*n.* (*pl.* same or **-tas**) **1** a member of a North American Indian people of the upper Mississippi valley and the surrounding plains. **2** the Siouan language of this people. Also called SIOUX.
▸*adj.* of or relating to this people or their language. ▷early 19th cent.: the name in Dakota, literally 'allies.'

Da·ko·ta Riv·er another name for JAMES RIVER (sense 1).

dal1 ▸*abbr.* decaliter(s).

dal2 ▸*n.* variant spelling of DHAL.

Da·lai La·ma /'dälī 'lämə/ ▸*n.* the spiritual head of Tibetan Buddhism and, until the establishment of Chinese communist rule, the spiritual and temporal ruler of Tibet.

Each Dalai Lama is believed to be the reincarnation of the bodhisattva Avalokiteshvara, reappearing in a child when the incumbent Dalai Lama dies. The present Dalai Lama, the fourteenth incarnation, escaped to India in 1959 following the invasion of Tibet by the Chinese and was awarded the Nobel Peace Prize in 1989.

▷late 17th cent.: from Tibetan, literally 'ocean guru,' so named because he is regarded as "the ocean of compassion" (see LAMA).

da·la·si /də'läsē/ ▸*n.* (*pl.* same or **-sis** /-sēz/) the basic monetary unit of Gambia, equal to 100 butut. ▷a local word.

Dal·croze /dal'krōz/ see JAQUES-DALCROZE.

Dale /dāl/, Sir Henry Hallett (1875–1968), English physiologist and pharmacologist. He investigated the role of histamine in anaphylactic shock and allergy and the role of acetylcholine as a natural neurotransmitter. Nobel Prize for Physiology or Medicine (1936, shared with Loewi).

dale /dāl/ ▸*n.* a valley, esp. a broad one. ▷Old English *dæl*, of Germanic origin; related to Old Norse *dalr*, Dutch *dal*, and German *Tal*, also to DELL.

Da·ley /'dālē/, Richard Joseph (1902–76), U.S. politician. As mayor of Chicago 1955–76, he was known as a big-city boss. He also led the national Democratic Party.

Da·li /'dälē; dä'lē/, Salvador (1904–89), Spanish painter. A surrealist, he portrayed dream images with almost photographic realism against backgrounds of arid Catalan landscapes. Notable works: *The Persistence of Memory* (1931) and *Christ of St. John of the Cross* (1951).

Salvador Dali

Da·lian /'dä'lyan/ a port and shipbuilding center on the Liaodong Peninsula in northeastern China, now part of the urban complex of Luda. Former name DAIREN.

Da·lit /'dälit/ ▸*n.* (in the traditional Indian caste system) a member of the lowest caste. See also UNTOUCHABLE, SCHEDULED CASTE. ▷via Hindi from Sanskrit *dalita* 'oppressed.'

Dal·las /'daləs/ a city in northeastern Texas, noted as a center of the oil industry; pop. 1,188,580. Pres. John F. Kennedy was assassinated here in November 1963.

dal·li·ance /'dalēəns; 'dalyəns/ ▸*n.* a casual romantic or sexual relationship. ■ brief or casual involvement with something: *Berkeley was my last* ***dalliance with*** *the education system.* ▷Middle English (in the sense 'conversation'): from DALLY + -ANCE.

Dall sheep /dôl/ (also **Dall's sheep**) ▸*n.* a wild North American sheep found in mountainous country from Alaska to British Columbia. • *Ovis dalli*, family Bovidae. ▷early 20th cent.: named after William H. Dall (1845–1927), U.S. naturalist.

dal·ly /'dalē/ ▸*v.* (**-lies**, **-lied**) [*intrans.*] **1** act or move slowly: *workers were loafing, dallying, or goofing off.* See note at LOITER. **2** have a casual romantic or sexual liaison with someone: *he should stop* ***dallying with*** *movie stars.* ■ show a casual interest in something, without committing oneself seriously: *the company has been* ***dallying with*** *the idea of opening a new office.* ▷Middle English: from Old French *dalier* 'to chat' (commonly used in Anglo-Norman French), of unknown origin.

Dal·ma·tia /dal'māsн(ē)ə/ an ancient region in what is now southwestern Croatia that is composed of mountains and a narrow coastal plain along the Adriatic Sea, together with offshore islands. It once formed part of the Roman province of Illyricum.

Dal·ma·tian /dal'māsнən/ ▸*n.* **1** a dog of a white, short-haired breed with dark spots. **2** a native or inhabitant of Dalmatia. ▷late 16th cent. (sense 2): the dog is believed to have originated in Dalmatia in the 18th cent.

Dalmation 1

dal·mat·ic /dal'matik/ ▸*n.* a wide-sleeved, long, loose vestment open at the sides, worn by deacons and bishops, and by some monarchs at their coronation. ▷late Middle English: from Old French *dalmatique* or late Latin *dalmatica*, from *dalmatica (vestis)* '(robe) of (white) Dalmatian wool,' from *Dalmaticus* 'of Dalmatia.'

dal se·gno /däl 'sānyō/ ▸*adv. Music* (esp. as a direction) repeat from the point marked by a sign. Compare with DA CAPO. ▷Italian, 'from the sign.'

Dal·ton[1] /'dôltn/ a city in northwestern Georgia; pop. 21,761.

Dal·ton[2], John (1766–1844), English chemist; father of the modern atomic theory. He defined an atom as the smallest part of a substance that could participate in a chemical reaction and argued that elements are composed of atoms. He produced the first table of comparative atomic weights.

dal·ton /'dôltn/ ▸*n. Chemistry* a unit used in expressing the molecular weight of proteins, equivalent to atomic mass unit. ▷1930s: named after John DALTON.

dal·ton·ism /'dôltn,izəm; -tə,niz-/ ▸*n.* another term for PROTANOPIA, a form of color-blindness. ▷mid 19th cent.: from the name of J. DALTON + -ISM.

Dal·ton's law /'dôltnz/ *Chemistry* a law stating that the pressure exerted by a mixture of gases in a fixed volume is equal to the sum of the pressures that would be exerted by each gas alone in the same volume.

Da·ly Cit·y /'dālē/ a city in north central California, southwest of San Francisco; pop. 92,311.

dam[1] ▸*abbr.* decameter(s).

dam[2] /dam/ ▸*n.* a barrier, typically of concrete, constructed to hold back water and raise its level, the resulting reservoir being used in the generation of electricity or as a water supply. ■ a barrier of branches in a stream, constructed by a beaver to provide a deep pool and a lodge. ■ any barrier resembling a dam. ■ a rubber sheet used to keep saliva from the teeth during dental operations.

▸*v.* (**dammed**, **dam·ming**) [*trans.*] build a dam across (a river or lake). ■ hold back or obstruct (something): *the closed lock gates* ***dammed up*** *the canal.* ▷Middle English: from Middle Low German or Middle Dutch; related to Dutch *dam* and German *Damm*, also to Old English *fordemman* 'close up.'

dam[3] ▸*n.* the female parent of an animal, esp. a domestic mammal. ▷late Middle English (denoting a human mother): alteration of DAME.

dam·age /'damij/ ▸*n.* **1** physical harm caused to something in such a way as to impair its value, usefulness, or normal function. ■ unwelcome and detrimental effects: *the* ***damage to*** *his reputation was considerable.* **2** (**damages**) a sum of money claimed or awarded in compensation for a loss or an injury: *she was awarded $284,000 in damages.*

▸*v.* [*trans.*] inflict physical harm on (something) so as to impair its value, usefulness, or normal function: *the car was badly damaged in the accident* | [as *adj.*] (**damaged**) *damaged ligaments* | [as *adj.*] (**damaging**) *extreme heat can be very* ***damaging to*** *color film.* ■ have a detrimental effect on: *the scandal could seriously damage his career.* ▷Middle English: from Old French, from *dam, damne* 'loss or damage,' from Latin *damnum* 'loss or hurt'; compare with DAMN. —**dam·ag·ing·ly** *adv.*

▸*PHRASE* □ **what's the damage?** *informal, humorous* used to ask the cost of something.

dam·age con·trol (also *Brit.* **damage limitation**) ▸*n.* action taken to limit the damaging effects of an accident or error: *the cost of doing damage control after problems reach the crisis stage.*

dam·aged goods ▸*plural n.* merchandise that has deteriorated in quality. ■ *figurative* a person regarded as inadequate or impaired in some way: *I was just damaged goods, another misfit.*

Dam·an and Di·u /də'män and 'dē-o͞o/ a union territory in India, on the western coast, north of Bombay; pop. 101,400; capital, Daman.

dam·ar ▸*n.* & *adj.* variant spelling of DAMMAR.

Dam·a·scene /'damə,sēn; ,damə'sēn/ ▸*adj.* of or relating to the city of Damascus. ■ of, relating to, or resembling the conversion of St. Paul on the road to Damascus: *a transformation of Damascene proportions.* ■ *historical* of or relating to Damascus steel or its manufacture. ■ (often **damascene**) relating to or denoting a process of inlaying a metal object with gold or silver decoration.

▸*n.* a native or inhabitant of Damascus. ▷late Middle English (as a noun): via Latin from Greek *Damaskēnos* 'of *Damascus*.'

dam·a·scened /'damə,sēnd; ,damə'sēnd/ ▸*adj.* (of iron or steel) given a wavy pattern by hammer-welding and repeated heating and forging. ■ (of a metal object) inlaid with gold or silver decoration.

Da·mas·cus /də'maskəs/ the capital of Syria since the country's independence in 1946; pop. 1,497,000. It has existed as a city for over 4,000 years.

Da·mas·cus steel ▸*n. historical* steel made with a wavy surface pattern produced by hammer-welding strips of steel and iron followed by repeated heating and forging, used chiefly for knife and sword blades. Such items were often marketed, but not necessarily made, in Damascus during the medieval period.

dam·ask /'daməsk/ ▸*n.* **1** a figured woven fabric with a pattern visible on both sides, typically used for table linen and upholstery. ■ a tablecloth made of this material. **2** short for DAMASK ROSE. **3** (also **dam·ask steel**) *historical* another term for DAMASCUS STEEL.

▸*adj.* made of or resembling damask: *the satinlike finish of these damask napkins.* ■ *poetic/literary* having the velvety pink or light red color of a damask rose.

▸*v.* [*trans.*] weave with figured designs. ■ *poetic/literary* decorate with or as if with a variegated pattern. ▷late Middle English: from *Damaske*, early form of the name of *Damascus*, where the fabric was first produced.

dam·ask rose ▸*n.* a sweet-scented rose of an old variety (or hybrid) that is typically pink or light red in color. The petals are soft and velvety and are used to make attar. • *Rosa damascena*, family Rosaceae.

dame /dām/ ▸*n.* **1** (**Dame**) (in the UK) the title given to a woman equivalent to the rank of knight. ■ a woman holding this title. **2** *informal* a woman. ■ *archaic or humorous* an elderly or mature woman. ▷Middle English (denoting a female ruler): via Old French from Latin *domina* 'mistress.'

dam·fool /'dam'fo͞ol/ *informal, dated* ▸*adj.* (also **dam·fool·ish**) [*attrib.*] (of a person) thoroughly foolish and stupid.

▸*n.* a stupid or foolish person.

dam·i·an·a /,damē'anə/ ▸*n.* a small shrub native to Mexico whose leaves are used in herbal medicine and in the production of a liqueur. It is reputed to possess aphrodisiac qualities. • *Turnera diffusa*, family Turneraceae. ▷American Spanish.

Dam·i·et·ta /,damē'etə/ the eastern branch of the Nile delta. Arabic name DUMYAT. ■ a port at the mouth of this delta; pop. 113,000.

da·min·o·zide /də'minə,zīd/ ▸*n.* a growth retardant sprayed on vegetables and fruit, esp. apples, to enhance the quality of the crop. In the U.S., the application of daminozide is now restricted to ornamental plants due to the potential health risks of consuming the chemical. • Chem. formula: $C_6H_{12}N_2O_3$.

dam·mar /'damər/ (also **dam·ar**) ▸*n.* resin obtained from any of a number of tropical and mainly Indo-Malaysian trees, used to make varnish. • The resin is obtained from trees in the families Araucariaceae (genus *Agathis*), Dipterocarpaceae (genera *Hopea*, *Shorea*, and *Vatica*), and Burseraceae (genus *Canarium*). ▷late 17th cent.: from Malay *damar* 'resin.'

dam·mit /'damit/ ▸*exclam.* used to express anger and frustration. ▷mid 19th cent.: alteration of *damn it*.

damn /dam/ ▸*v.* [*trans.*] (in Christian belief) (of God) condemn (a person) to suffer eternal punishment in hell: *be forever damned with Lucifer.* ■ (**be damned**) be doomed to misfortune or failure: *the enterprise was damned.* ■ condemn, esp. by the public expression of disapproval: *intellectuals whom he damns as rigid doctrinaire idealists.* ■ curse (someone or something): *she cleared her throat, damning it for its huskiness* | *damn him for making this sound trivial.*

▸*exclam. informal* expressing anger, surprise, or frustration: *Damn! I completely forgot!*

▸*adj.* [*attrib.*] *informal* used for emphasis, esp. to express anger or frustration: *turn that damn thing off!* | [as *submodifier*] *don't be so damn silly!* ▷Middle English: from Old French *dam(p)ner*, from Latin *dam(p)nare* 'inflict loss on,' from *damnum* 'loss, damage.'

▸*PHRASES* □ **—— be damned** used to express rejection of someone or something previously mentioned: *"Glory be damned!"* □ **damn all** *Brit., informal* nothing at all. □ **damn well** *informal* used to emphasize a statement, esp. when the speaker is angry: *this is your mess and you can damn well clear it up!* □ **damn someone/something with faint praise** praise someone or something so unenthusiastically as to imply condemnation. □ **I'll be** (or **I'm**) **damned if** *informal* used to express a strong negative: *I'll be damned if I'll call her.* □ **not be worth a damn** *informal* have no value or validity at all. □ **not give a damn** see GIVE. □ **well I'll be** (or **I'm**) **damned** *informal* used as an expression of surprise.

dam·na·ble /ˈdamnəbəl/ ▸*adj.* **1** extremely bad or unpleasant: *leave this damnable place behind.* **2** subject to or worthy of divine condemnation: *suicide was thought damnable in the Middle Ages.* ▷Middle English (in the sense 'worthy of condemnation'): from Old French *dam(p)nable,* from Latin *dam(p)nabilis,* from *dam(p)nare* 'inflict loss on' (see DAMN). **—dam·na·bly** /-blē/ *adv.*

dam·na·tion /damˈnāSHən/ ▸*n.* (in Christian belief) condemnation to eternal punishment in hell.
▸*exclam.* expressing anger or frustration. ▷Middle English: via Old French from Latin *dam(p)natio(n-),* from the verb *dam(p)nare* 'inflict loss on' (see DAMN).

dam·na·to·ry /ˈdamnəˌtôrē/ ▸*adj.* conveying or causing censure or damnation: *the case against you was most damnatory.* ▷late 17th cent.: from Latin *damnatorius,* from *dam(p)nat-* 'caused to suffer loss,' from the verb *dam(p)nare* (see DAMN).

damned /damd/ ▸*adj.* **1** (in Christian belief) condemned by God to suffer eternal punishment in hell: [as *plural n.*] (**the damned**) *the spirits of the damned.* **2** [*attrib.*] *informal* used for emphasis, esp. to express anger or frustration: *it's none of your damned business* | [as *submodifier*] *she's too damned arrogant.* ■ (**damnedest**) used to emphasize the surprising nature of something: *the damnedest thing I ever saw.*
▸*adv.* extremely; exceedingly: *called her one damned fine pilot.*
▸*PHRASES* □ **damned well** *informal* used for emphasis when the speaker is angry or irritated: *you can damned well tell him yourself!* □ **do** (or **try**) **one's damnedest** do or try one's utmost.

dam·ni·fy /ˈdamnəˌfī/ ▸*v.* (**-fies, -fied**) [*trans.*] *rare, Law* cause injury to. ▷early 16th cent.: from Old French *damnefier, dam(p)nifier,* from late Latin *damnificare* 'injure, condemn,' from Latin *damnificus* 'hurtful,' from *damnus* 'loss, damage.' **—dam·ni·fi·ca·tion** /ˌdamnəfiˈkāSHən/ *n.*

damn·ing /ˈdamiNG/ ▸*adj.* (of a circumstance or piece of evidence) strongly suggesting guilt or error: *presented with damning affidavits.* ■ extremely critical: *last year's damning report on the industry.* **—damn·ing·ly** *adv.*

Dam·o·cles /ˈdaməˌklēz/ a legendary courtier who extravagantly praised the happiness of Dionysius I, ruler of Syracuse. To show him how precarious this happiness was, Dionysius seated him at a banquet with a sword hung by a single hair over his head.
▸*PHRASE* □ **sword of Damocles** used to refer to a precarious situation.

Da·mon /ˈdāmən/ a legendary Syracusan of the 4th century BC whose friend Pythias was sentenced to death by Dionysius I. Damon stood bail for Pythias, who returned just in time to save him, and was himself reprieved.

damp /damp/ ▸*adj.* slightly wet: *her hair was still damp from the shower.*
▸*n.* **1** moisture diffused through the air or a solid substance or condensed on a surface, typically with detrimental or unpleasant effects. ■ foul, stifling, or poisonous gas, esp. in a mine. ■ (**damps**) *archaic* damp air or atmosphere. **2** *archaic* a check or discouragement: *shame gave a damp to her triumph.*
▸*v.* [*trans.*] **1** make (something) slightly wet: *damp a small area with water.* **2** control or restrain (a feeling or a state of affairs): *she tried to **damp down** her feelings of despair.* ■ make (a fire) burn less strongly by reducing the flow of air to it. **3** restrict the amplitude of vibrations on (a piano or other musical instrument) so as to reduce the volume of sound: *rapidly damping the cymbals after repeatedly clashing them together.* ■ *Physics* progressively reduce the amplitude of (an oscillation or vibration): *concrete structures **damp out** any vibrations.* ■ reduce the level of (a noise or sound): *the ground mist clung to the hedgerows, **damping down** all sound.* ▷Middle English (in the noun sense 'noxious inhalation'); related to a Middle Low German word meaning 'vapor, steam, smoke.' **—damp·ish** *adj.* **—damp·ly** *adv.* **—damp·ness** *n.*

damp-dry ▸*v.* [*intrans.*] dry (something) until it is only damp: *the machine automatically washes, rinses, and damp-dries.*

damp·en /ˈdampən/ ▸*v.* [*trans.*] **1** make slightly wet: *the fine rain dampened her face.* **2** make less strong or intense: *nothing could dampen her enthusiasm.* ■ reduce the amplitude of (a sound source): *slider switches on the mixers can dampen the drums.* **—damp·en·er** *n.*

damp·er /ˈdampər/ ▸*n.* a person or thing that has a depressing, subduing, or inhibiting effect: *another damper on reactor development was the problem of safeguards.* ■ *Music* a pad that silences a piano string except when removed by means of a pedal or by the note being struck. ■ a device for reducing mechanical vibration, in particular a shock absorber on a motor vehicle. ■ a conductor used to reduce hunting in an electric motor or generator. ■ a movable metal plate in a flue or chimney, used to regulate the draft and so control the rate of combustion.
▸*PHRASE* □ **put a damper on** have a depressing, subduing, or inhibiting effect on: *he put a damper on her youthful excitement.*

damp·ing /ˈdampiNG/ ▸*n.* **1** *technical* a decrease in the amplitude of an oscillation as a result of energy being drained from the system to overcome frictional or other resistive forces. ■ a mechanism or system for bringing about such a decrease. ■ a method of bringing about a decrease in oscillatory peaks in an electric current or voltage using an energy-absorbing or resistance circuit. **2** short for DAMPING-OFF.

damp·ing-off ▸*n.* a plant disease occurring in excessively damp conditions, in particular the collapse and death of young seedlings as a result of a fungal infection. • The disease is commonly caused by fungi of the genera *Pythium* (phylum Oomycota) or *Fusarium* (phylum Ascomycota).

dam·sel /ˈdamzəl/ ▸*n.* *archaic* or *poetic/literary* a young unmarried woman. ▷Middle English: from Old French *dameisele, damisele,* based on Latin *domina* 'mistress.'
▸*PHRASE* □ **damsel in distress** *often humorous* a young woman in trouble (with the implication that the woman needs to be rescued, as by a prince in a fairy tale).

dam·sel bug ▸*n.* a slender long-legged bug that is a predator of other insects. • Family Nabidae, suborder Heteroptera: several genera.

dam·sel·fish /ˈdamzəlˌfiSH/ ▸*n.* (*pl.* same or **-fish·es**) a small brightly colored tropical fish that lives in or near coral reefs. • *Chromis* and other genera, family Pomacentridae: numerous species, in particular *C. chromis.*

dam·sel·fly /ˈdamzəlˌflī/ ▸*n.* (*pl.* **-flies**) a slender insect related to the dragonflies, having weak flight and typically resting with the wings folded back along the body. • Suborder Zygoptera, order Odonata: several families.

dam·son /ˈdamzən; -sən/ ▸*n.* **1** a small purple-black plumlike fruit. ■ a dark purple color. **2** (also **damson tree**) the small deciduous tree that bears this fruit, probably derived from the bullace. • *Prunus domestica* subsp. *insititia* (or *P. damascena*), family Rosaceae. ▷late Middle English *damascene,* from Latin *damascenum (prunum)* '(plum) of Damascus.' Compare with DAMASCENE and DAMASK.

Dan /dan/ (in the Bible) a Hebrew patriarch, son of Jacob and Bilhah (Gen. 30:6). ■ the tribe of Israel traditionally descended from him. ■ an ancient town in the north of Canaan, where the tribe of Dan settled. It marked the northern limit of the ancient Hebrew kingdom of Israel (Judges 20).

dan[1] /dän; dan/ ▸*n.* any of ten degrees of advanced proficiency in judo or karate. ■ a person who has achieved such a degree. ▷1940s: from Japanese.

dan[2] /dan/ (also **dan buoy**) ▸*n.* a small marker buoy with a lightweight flagpole. ▷late 17th cent.: of unknown origin.

Dan. ▸*abbr. Bible* Daniel.

Da·na[1] /ˈdānə/, Charles Anderson (1819–97), U.S. newspaper editor. He was a resident of the Brook Farm commune near Boston 1841–46, an experimental community, and the owner and editor of the *New York Sun* 1868–97.

Da·na[2], James Dwight (1813–95), U.S. naturalist, geologist, and mineralogist. He founded a classification of minerals based on chemistry and physics and viewed the earth as a unit.

Da·na[3], Richard Henry (1815–82), U.S. adventurer, lawyer, and writer. An expert in maritime law and an editor of an international law journal, he is most noted for the account of his voyage from Boston around Cape Horn to California in *Two Years before the Mast* (1840).

Dan·a·e /ˈdanəˌē/ *Greek Mythology* the daughter of Acrisius, king of Argos. An oracle foretold that she would bear a son who would kill her father. Attempting to evade this, Acrisius imprisoned her, but Zeus visited her in the form of a shower of gold and she conceived Perseus, who killed Acrisius by accident.

da·na·id /ˈdanē-id; ˈdanā-/ ▸*n.* a large strikingly marked butterfly of a group that includes the monarch, found chiefly in the tropics of Africa and the Far East. • Subfamily Danainae, family Nymphalidae (formerly family Danaidae). ▷late 19th cent.: from modern Latin *Danaidae,* arbitrary use of the Latin name of the daughters of Danaus.

Da·na·ids /dəˈnā-idz; ˈdanē-idz/ *Greek Mythology* the daughters of Danaus, king of Argos, who were compelled to marry the sons of his brother Aegyptus but murdered their husbands on the wedding night, except for one, Hypermnestra, who helped her husband to escape. The remaining Danaids were punished in Hades by being sent to fill a leaky jar with water.

Da Nang /ˈdä ˈnäNG; də ˈnaNG/ a port and city in central Vietnam, on the South China Sea; pop. 382,670. It served as a U.S. military base during the Vietnam War. Former name TOURANE.

Da·na Point a city in southwestern California, on the Pacific coast; pop. 31,896.

Dan·bury /ˈdanˌberē; -b(ə)rē/ a city in west central Connecticut, formerly noted for its hat industry; pop. 74,848.

dance /dans/ ▸*v.* [*intrans.*] **1** move rhythmically to music, typically following a set sequence of steps: *their cheeks were pressed together as they danced.* ■ [*trans.*] perform (a particular dance or a role in a ballet): *they danced a tango.* ■ [*trans.*] lead (someone) in a particular direction while dancing: *I danced her out of the room.* **2** [with *adverbial of direction*] (of a person) move in a quick and lively way: *Sheila danced in gaily.* ■ [with *adverbial of place*] move up and down lightly and quickly: *midges danced over the stream.* ■ (of someone's eyes) sparkle brightly with pleasure or excitement.
▸*n.* a series of movements that match the speed and rhythm of a piece of music. ■ a particular sequence of steps and movements constituting a particular form of dancing. ■ steps and movements of this type considered as an activity or art form: *she has studied dance with Martha Graham.* ■ a social gathering at which people dance: *she met her husband at a dance.* ■ a set of lively movements resembling a dance: *he gesticulated comically and did a little dance.* ■ a piece of music for dancing to: *the last dance had been played.* ■ (also **dance music**) music for dancing to, esp. in a nightclub. ■ a set of stylized movements performed by certain animals: *the waggle dances of honeybees convey the direction, distance, and desirability of food sources.* ▷Middle English: from Old French *dancer* (verb), *dance* (noun), of unknown origin. **—dance·a·bil·i·ty** *n.* **—dance·a·ble** *adj.*
▸*PHRASES* □ **dance attendance on** do one's utmost to please someone by attending to all possible needs or requests. □ **dance to someone's tune** comply completely with someone's demands and wishes. □ **lead someone a dance** (or **a merry dance**) *Brit.* cause someone a great deal of trouble or worry.

dance band ▸*n.* a band that plays music suitable for dancing, esp. swing.

dance card ▸*n.* *dated* a card bearing the names of a woman's prospective partners at a formal dance.

dance floor ▸*n.* an area of uncarpeted floor, typically in a nightclub or restaurant, reserved for dancing. ■ [as *adj.*] denoting a recording or type of music particularly popular as an accompaniment to dancing: *a current dance-floor hit.*

dance hall ▸*n.* **1** a large public hall or building where people pay to enter and dance. **2** (**dance·hall**) an uptempo style of dance music originating in Jamaica and derived from reggae, in which a DJ improvises lyrics over a recorded instrumental backing track or to the accompaniment of live musicians.

dance of death ▸*n.* a medieval allegorical representation in which a personified Death leads people to the grave, designed to emphasize the equality of all before death. Also called DANSE MACABRE.

danc·er /ˈdansər/ ▸*n.* a person who dances or whose profession is dancing.

dan·cer·cise /ˈdansərˌsīz/ (also **dan·cer·cize**) ▸*n.* a system of aerobic exercise using dance movements. ▷1960s: blend of DANCE and EXERCISE.

Pronunciation Key ə *ago;* ər *over;* ˈə or ˌə *up;* ˈər or ˌər *fur;* a *hat;* ā *rate;* ä *car;* CH *chew;* e *let;* ē *see;* e(ə)r *air;* i *fit;* ī *by;* i(ə)r *ear;* NG *sing;* ō *go;* ô *for;* oi *boy;* o͝o *good;* o͞o *goo;* ou *out;* SH *she;* TH *thin;* T͟H *then;* (h)w *why;* ZH *vision*

danc·ing girl ▸*n.* a female professional dancer, esp. an erotic dancer or a member of the chorus in a musical.

D and C ▸*abbr.* dilatation and curettage.

dan·de·li·on /ˈdandlˌīən/ ▸*n.* a widely distributed weed of the daisy family, with a rosette of leaves, bright yellow flowers followed by globular heads of seeds with downy tufts, and stems containing a milky latex. • Genus *Taraxacum*, family Compositae: several species, in particular the common *T. officinale*, which has edible leaves. ▷late Middle English: from French *dent-de-lion*, translation of medieval Latin *dens leonis* 'lion's tooth' (because of the jagged shape of the leaves).

dan·de·li·on greens ▸*plural n.* fresh dandelion leaves used as a salad vegetable or herb.

dan·der[1] /ˈdandər/ ▸*n.* (in phrase **get/have one's dander up**) *informal* lose one's temper. ▷mid 19th cent.: of unknown origin.

dan·der[2] ▸*n.* skin flakes in an animal's fur or hair. ▷late 18th cent.: related to DANDRUFF.

dan·di·a·cal /danˈdīəkəl/ ▸*adj. dated, humorous* relating to or characteristic of a dandy. ▷mid 19th cent.: from DANDY, on the pattern of words such as *hypochondriacal*.

Dan·die Din·mont /ˈdandē ˈdinˌmänt/ ▸*n.* a terrier of a breed with short legs, a long body, and a rough coat. ▷early 19th cent.: named after a farmer who owned a special breed of terriers, portrayed in Sir Walter Scott's *Guy Mannering*.

dan·di·fied /ˈdandiˌfīd/ ▸*adj.* (of a man) showing excessive concern about his clothes or appearance. ■ self-consciously sophisticated or elaborate: *he writes a dandified prose.*

dan·di·prat /ˈdandēˌprat/ ▸*n. archaic, informal* a small boy. ■ an insignificant person. ▷early 16th cent. (denoting a coin worth three halfpence): of unknown origin.

dan·dle /ˈdandl/ ▸*v.* [*trans.*] move (a baby or young child) up and down in a playful or affectionate way. ■ move (something) lightly up and down: *dandling the halter rope, he gently urged the pony's head up.* ▷mid 16th cent.: of unknown origin.

Dan·dong /ˈdänˈdo͝ong/ a port in Liaoning province, in northeastern China, near the mouth of the Yalu River, on the border with North Korea; pop. 660,500. Former name ANTUNG.

dan·druff /ˈdandrəf/ ▸*n.* small pieces of dead skin in a person's hair. ▷mid 16th cent.: the first element is unknown; the second (*-ruff*) is perhaps related to Middle English *rove* 'scurfiness.' **—dan·druff·y** *adj.*

D&X ▸*abbr.* dilation and extraction. See PARTIAL-BIRTH ABORTION.

dan·dy /ˈdandē/ ▸*n.* (*pl.* **-dies**) **1** a man unduly devoted to style, neatness, and fashion in dress and appearance. **2** *informal, dated* an excellent thing of its kind: *this umbrella is a dandy.*

▸*adj.* (**-di·er, -di·est**) **1** *informal* excellent: *upgrading seemed a dandy idea* | *things are all* ***fine and dandy.*** **2** relating to or characteristic of a dandy. ▷late 18th cent.: perhaps a shortened form of 17th-cent. *Jack-a-dandy* 'conceited fellow' (the last element representing *Dandy*, a nickname for the given name *Andrew*). **—dan·dy·ish** *adj.* **—dan·dy·ism** /-ˌizəm/ *n.*

dan·dy brush ▸*n.* a coarse brush used for grooming a horse.

dan·dy roll (also **dandy roll·er**) ▸*n.* a roller that is used to solidify partly formed paper during its manufacture, and to impress the water mark.

Dane /dān/ ▸*n.* a native or national of Denmark, or a person of Danish descent. ■ *historical* one of the Viking invaders of the British Isles in the 9th–11th centuries. ▷Old English *Dene*; superseded in Middle English by forms influenced by Old Norse *Danir* and late Latin *Dani* (both plural).

Dane·geld /ˈdānˌgeld/ ▸*n. historical* a land tax levied in medieval England, originally to raise funds for protection against Danish invaders. ▷late Old English, from Old Norse *Danir* 'Danes' + *gjald* 'payment.'

Dan·forth an·chor /ˈdanˌfôrTH/ ▸*n.* a type of stockless lightweight anchor with flat flukes.

dang /daNG/ ▸*adj., exclam. & v. informal* euphemism for DAMN: [as *adj.*] *just get the dang car started!* | [as *exclam.*] *dang it, Phil, stop snoring!* | [as *v.*] *I'll be danged.*

dan·ger /ˈdānjər/ ▸*n.* the possibility of suffering harm or injury: *his life was* ***in danger.*** ■ a person or thing that is likely to cause harm or injury: *infertile soils where drought is a danger.* ■ the possibility of something unwelcome or unpleasant: *there was no danger of the champagne running out.* ■ *Brit.* the status of a railroad signal indicating that the line is not clear and that a train should not proceed. ▷Middle English: from Old French *dangier*, based on Latin *dominus* 'lord.' The original sense was 'jurisdiction or power,' specifically 'power to harm,' hence the current meaning 'liability to be harmed.'

▸*PHRASES* □ **in danger of** likely to incur or to suffer from: *the animal is in danger of extinction.* □ **out of danger** (of a person who has suffered a serious injury or illness) not expected to die.

dan·ger·ous /ˈdānjərəs/ ▸*adj.* able or likely to cause harm or injury: *a dangerous animal* | *ice was making the roads dangerous.* ■ likely to have adverse or unfortunate consequences; risky: *it is dangerous to underestimate an enemy.* ■ likely to cause problems or difficulty: *our most dangerous opponents in the playoffs.* ■ (of a drug) addictive or otherwise harmful or illegal. ▷Middle English (in the senses 'arrogant,' 'fastidious,' and 'difficult to please'): from Old French *dangereus*, from *dangier* (see DANGER). **—dan·ger·ous·ness** *n.*

dan·gle /ˈdaNGgəl/ ▸*v.* [*intrans.*] hang or swing loosely: *saucepans dangled from a rail* | [*trans.*] *they were dangling their legs over the water.* ■ [*trans.*] *figurative* offer (an enticing incentive) to someone: *two rich commissions that had been dangling so sweetly in front of me.* ▷late 16th cent.: symbolic of something loose and pendulous, corresponding to Danish *dangle*, Swedish *dangla*, but the origin is not clear. **—dan·gler** /-glər/ *n.* **—dan·gly** /-glē/ *adj.*

▸*PHRASE* □ **keep someone dangling** keep someone in an uncertain position.

dan·gling par·ti·ci·ple /ˈdaNGg(ə)liNG/ ▸*n. Grammar* a participle intended to modify a noun that is not actually present in the text.

USAGE A **participle** is a word formed as an inflection of the verb, such as *arriving* or *arrived*. A **dangling participle** is one left "hanging" because, in the grammar of the clause, it does not relate to the noun it should. In the sentence ***arriving*** *at the station,* ***she*** *picked up her case,* the construction is correct because the participle *arriving* and the subject *she* relate to each other (*she* is the one doing the *arriving*). But in the following sentence, a **dangling participle** has been created: ***arriving*** *at the station,* ***the sun*** *came out.* We know, logically, that it is not *the sun* that is *arriving*, but grammatically that is exactly the link that has been created. Such errors are frequent in written English and can give rise to confusion.

Dan·iel[1] /ˈdanyəl/ a Hebrew prophet (6th century BC), who spent his life as a captive at the court of Babylon. In the Bible he interpreted the dreams of Nebuchadnezzar and was delivered by God from the lions' den into which he had been thrown as the result of a trick; in the apocryphal Book of Susanna he is portrayed as a wise judge (Sus. 45–64). ■ a book of the Bible containing his prophecies. It was probably written at the outbreak of the persecution of the Jews under Seleucid rule *c.*167 BC.

Dan·iel[2], Peter Vivian (1784–1860), U.S. Supreme Court associate justice 1841–60. Appointed to the Court by President Van Buren, he advocated states' rights.

dan·i·o /ˈdanēˌō/ ▸*n.* (*pl.* **-os**) a small, typically brightly colored freshwater fish native to the Indian subcontinent and Southeast Asia. • Genera *Danio* and *Brachydanio*, family Cyprinidae: several species. ▷modern Latin (genus name).

Dan·ish /ˈdāniSH/ ▸*adj.* of or relating to Denmark or its people or language.

▸*n.* **1** the North Germanic language of Denmark, which is also the official language of Greenland and the Faeroes. **2** [as *plural n.*] (**the Danish**) the people of Denmark. **3** *informal* short for DANISH PASTRY. ▷Old English *Denisc*, of Germanic origin; superseded in Middle English by forms influenced by Old French *daneis* and medieval Latin *Danensis* (from late Latin *Dani* 'Danes').

Dan·ish blue ▸*n.* a soft, salty, strong-flavored white cheese with blue veins.

Dan·ish pas·try ▸*n.* a pastry made of sweetened yeast dough with toppings or fillings such as fruit, nuts, or cheese.

dank /daNGk/ ▸*adj.* disagreeably damp, musty, and typically cold. ▷Middle English: probably of Scandinavian origin and related to Swedish *dank* 'marshy spot.' **—dank·ly** *adv.* **—dank·ness** *n.*

Dan·mark /ˈdänˌmärk/ Danish name for DENMARK.

Dan·ne·brog /ˈdanəˌbräg/ ▸*n.* the Danish national flag. ▷early 18th cent.: Danish, literally 'Danish cloth.'

Da·no-Nor·we·gian /ˈdānō nôrˈwējən/ ▸*n.* another term for BOKMÅL.

Dan Riv·er /dan/ a river that flows for 180 miles (290 km) from southwestern Virginia into North Carolina to the Roanoke River.

danse ma·ca·bre /ˈdäns məˈkäbrə/ ▸*n.* another term for DANCE OF DEATH. ▷French, recorded from late Middle English in anglicized forms such as *dance of Machabray, dance of Macaber* (see also MACABRE).

dan·seur /dänˈsər/ ▸*n.* a male ballet dancer. ▷French, from *danser* 'to dance.'

dan·seuse /dänˈso͞oz; -ˈsœz/ ▸*n.* a female ballet dancer. ▷early 19th cent.: French, literally 'female dancer.'

Dan·te /ˈdänˌtā; ˈdanˌtā; ˈdantē/ (1265–1321), Italian poet; full name *Dante Alighieri.* He wrote *The Divine Comedy* (*c.*1309–20), an epic poem that describes his spiritual journey through Hell and Purgatory and finally to Paradise. His love for Beatrice Portinari is described in *Vita nuova* (*c.*1290–94).

Dan·te·an /ˈdäntēən; ˈdan-/ ▸*adj.* of or reminiscent of the poetry of Dante, esp. in invoking his vision of hell in *The Divine Comedy*.

▸*n.* an admirer or student of Dante or his writing.

Dan·tesque /dänˈtesk/ (also **Dan·te-esque** /ˌdäntāˈesk/) ▸*adj.* another term for DANTEAN.

Dan·ton /dänˈtôN/, Georges (Jacques) (1759–94), French revolutionary. Initially an ally of Robespierre, he later revolted against the severity of the Revolutionary Tribunal and was executed on Robespierre's orders.

Dan·ube /ˈdanyo͞ob/ a river that rises in the Black Forest in southwestern Germany and flows for about 1,770 miles (2,850 km) into the Black Sea. It is the second longest river in Europe (after the Volga); the cities of Vienna, Budapest, and Belgrade are situated on its banks. German name DONAU. **—Dan·u·bi·an** /danˈyo͞obēən/ *adj.*

Dan·ube School a group of landscape painters working in the Danube region in the early 16th century. Its members included Altdorfer and Cranach the Elder.

Dan·vers /ˈdanvərz/ a town in northeastern Massachusetts, northeast of Boston; pop. 24,174.

Dan·ville /ˈdanˌvil/ **1** a city in north central California, northeast of Oakland; pop. 31,306. **2** a city in east central Illinois; pop. 33,828. **3** a city in southern Virginia, on the Dan River; pop. 48,411.

Dan·zig /ˈdäntsig; ˈdant-/ German name for GDAŃSK.

dap /dap/ ▸*v.* (**dapped, dap·ping**) [*intrans.*] fish by letting the fly bob lightly on the water without letting the line touch the water. ▷mid 17th cent. (as a verb): symbolic of a flicking movement, similar to DAB.

Daph·ne /ˈdafnē/ *Greek Mythology* a nymph who was turned into a laurel bush to save her from the amorous pursuit of Apollo.

daph·ne /ˈdafnē/ ▸*n.* a small Eurasian shrub with sweet-scented flowers and, typically, evergreen leaves. • Genus *Daphne*, family Thymelaeaceae: several species, including mezereon and spurge laurel. ▷late Middle English (denoting the laurel or bay tree): from Greek *daphnē*, from the name of the nymph DAPHNE.

daph·ni·a /ˈdafnēə/ ▸*n.* (*pl.* same) a tiny and semitransparent freshwater crustacean with long antennae and prominent eyes, often used as food for aquarium fish. Also called WATER FLEA. • Genus *Daphnia*, order Cladocera. ▷modern Latin, from Greek *Daphnē*, from the name of the nymph DAPHNE.

Daph·nis /ˈdafnis/ *Greek Mythology* a Sicilian shepherd who, according to one version of the legend, was struck with blindness for his infidelity to the nymph Echenaïs. He consoled himself with pastoral poetry, of which he was the inventor.

dap·per /ˈdapər/ ▸*adj.* (typically of a man) neat and trim in dress, appearance, or bearing. ▷late Middle English: probably from a Middle Low German or Middle Dutch word meaning 'strong, stout.' **—dap·per·ly** *adv.* **—dap·per·ness** *n.*

dap·ple /ˈdapəl/ ▸*v.* [*trans.*] (usu. **be dappled**) mark with spots or rounded patches: *the floor was dappled with pale moonlight* | [as *adj.*] (**dappled**) *dappled sunlight lay upon her straight brown hair.*

▸*n.* a patch or spot of color or light. ■ an animal whose coat is marked with patches or spots. ▷late 16th cent. (earlier as an adjective): perhaps related to Old Norse *depill* 'spot.'

dap·ple gray ▸*adj.* (of a horse) gray or white with darker ringlike markings.
▸*n.* a horse of this type.

Dap·sang /däp'säNG/ another name for **K2**.

dap·sone /'dap,sōn/ ▸*n. Medicine* a sulfur compound with bacteriostatic action, used chiefly in the treatment of leprosy. • Alternative name: **bis(4-aminophenyl)sulfone**; chem. formula: $(H_2NC_6H_4)_2SO_2$. ▷1950s: from elements of its alternative systematic name *dipara-aminophenyl sulfone*.

Da·qing /'dä'CHING/ (also **Ta·ching**) a major industrial city in northeastern China, in Heilongjiang province; pop. 996,800.

DAR ▸*abbr.* Daughters of the American Revolution.

Dard /därd/ ▸*n.* **1** a member of a group of peoples inhabiting eastern Afghanistan, northern Pakistan, and Kashmir. **2** a group of languages, including Kashmiri, usually classified as Indic but showing strong Iranian influence.
▸*adj.* of or relating to the Dards or their languages. ▷the name in Dard. **—Dard·ic** /'därdik/ *n.* & *adj.*

Dar·da·nelles /,därdn'elz/ a narrow strait between Europe and Asiatic Turkey (called the Hellespont in classical times) that links the Sea of Marmara with the Aegean Sea. It is 38 miles (60 km) long. In 1915, it was the scene of an unsuccessful attack on Turkey by Allied troops (see **GALLIPOLI**).

Dare /de(ə)r/, Virginia (1587–?), first English child born in North America. Born on Roanoke Island, Virginia, to Ananias Dare and Elinor White, she disappeared with the other 117 Roanoke colonists, as was discovered in 1591.

dare /de(ə)r/ ▸*v.* (*3rd sing. present* usu. **dare** before an expressed or implied infinitive without **to**) **1** [usu. with *infinitive* with or without **to**] [often with *negative*] have the courage to do something: *a story he dare not write down* | *she leaned forward as far as she dared.* **2** [*trans.*] defy or challenge (someone) to do something: *she was daring him to disagree* | [*trans.*] *swap with me, I dare you.* **3** [*trans.*] *poetic/literary* take the risk of; brave: *few dared his wrath.*
▸*n.* a challenge, esp. to prove courage: *athletes who eat ground glass* ***on a dare.*** ▷Old English *durran*, of Germanic origin; related to Gothic *gadaursan*, from an Indo-European root shared by Greek *tharsein* and Sanskrit *dhṛṣ-* 'be bold.' **—dar·er** *n.*
▸*PHRASES* □ **don't you dare** used to order someone threateningly not to do something: *don't you dare touch me!* □ **how dare you** used to express indignation: *how dare you talk to me like that!* □ **I dare say** (or **daresay**) used to indicate that one believes something is probable: *I dare say you've heard about her.*

dare·dev·il /'de(ə)r,devəl/ ▸*n.* a reckless person who enjoys doing dangerous things.
▸*adj.* [*attrib.*] reckless and daring. **—dare·dev·il·ry** /-rē/ *n.*

Dar es Sa·laam /,där ,es sə'läm/ the chief port and former capital of Tanzania; pop. 1,360,850. Its Arabic name means "haven of peace."

Da·ri /'därē/ ▸*n.* the form of Persian spoken in Afghanistan.

Dar·i·en /där'yen; ,de(ə)rē'en/ a sparsely populated province in eastern Panama. The name was formerly applied to the whole of the Isthmus of Panama.

Dar·i·en, Gulf of part of the Caribbean Sea between Panama and Colombia.

dar·ing /'de(ə)riNG/ ▸*adj.* (of a person or action) adventurous or audaciously bold: *a daring crime.* ■ boldly unconventional: *a pretty girl in daring clothes.*
▸*n.* adventurous courage: *the zeal and daring of climbers.* **—dar·ing·ly** *adv.*

dar·i·ole /'darē,ōl/ (also **dariole mold**) ▸*n.* (in French cooking) a small, round metal mold in which an individual sweet or savory dish is cooked and served. ▷late Middle English: from Old French.

Da·ri·us I /'de(ə)rēəs; də'rīəs/ (*c.*550–486 BC), king of Persia 521–486 BC; known as **Darius the Great.** After a revolt by the Greek cities in Ionia (499–494 BC), he invaded Greece but was defeated at Marathon (490 BC).

Dar·jee·ling /där'jēliNG/ ▸*n.* a high-quality tea grown in the mountainous regions of northern India.

dark /därk/ ▸*adj.* **1** with little or no light: *it's too dark to see much.* ■ hidden from knowledge; mysterious: *a dark secret.* ■ *archaic* ignorant; unenlightened: *he is dark on certain points of scripture.* ■ (of a theater) closed; not in use: *on Tuesdays he'd wait tables because the theater was dark.* **2** (of a color or object) not reflecting much light; approaching black in shade: *dark green.* ■ (of someone's skin, hair, or eyes) brown or black in color. ■ (of a person) having such skin, hair, or eyes: *both my father and I are very dark.* ■ *figurative* (of a sound or taste) having richness or depth: *a distinctive dark, sweet flavor.* ■ served or drunk with only a little or no milk or cream. **3** (of a period of time or situation) characterized by tragedy, unhappiness, or unpleasantness: *the dark days of the war.* ■ gloomily pessimistic: *a dark vision of the future.* ■ (of an expression) angry; threatening: *Matthew flashed a dark look at her.* ■ suggestive of or arising from evil characteristics or forces; sinister: *so many dark deeds had been committed.* **4** *Phonetics* denoting a velarized form of the sound of the letter *l* (as in *pull*).
▸*n.* **1** (**the dark**) the absence of light in a place: *Carolyn was sitting in the dark* | *he's scared of the dark.* ■ nightfall: *I'll be home before dark.* **2** a dark color or shade, esp. in a painting. ▷Old English *deorc*, of Germanic origin, probably distantly related to German *tarnen* 'conceal.' **—dark·ish** *adj.* **—dark·some** /-səm/ *adj.* (*poetic/literary*).
▸*PHRASES* □ **the darkest hour is just before the dawn** *proverb* when things seem to be at their worst, they are about to start improving. □ **in the dark** in a state of ignorance about something: *we're clearly being* ***kept in the dark*** *about what's happening.* □ **keep something dark** keep something secret from other people: *I asked Ann to keep my identity dark.* □ **a shot** (or **stab**) **in the dark** an act whose outcome cannot be foreseen; a mere guess.

dark ad·ap·ta·tion ▸*n.* the adjustment of the eye to low light intensities, involving reflex dilation of the pupil and activation of the rod cells in preference to the cone cells. **—dark-a·dapt·ed** *adj.*

Dark Ag·es **1** the period in western Europe between the fall of the Roman Empire and the high Middle Ages, *c.*AD 500–1100, during which Germanic tribes swept through Europe and North Africa, often attacking and destroying towns and settlements. ■ a period of supposed unenlightenment: ***the dark ages of*** *racism.* ■ (**the dark ages**) *humorous* or *derogatory* an obscure or little-regarded period in the past, esp. as characterizing an outdated attitude or practice: *the judge is living in the dark ages.* **2** *Archaeology* a period in Greece and the Aegean from the end of the Bronze Age until the beginning of the archaic period. There was no building of palaces and fortresses, and the art of writing was apparently lost.

Dark and Blood·y Ground a nickname for the state of **KENTUCKY**.

dark choc·o·late ▸*n.* slightly bitter chocolate, of a deep brown color, without added milk.

Dark Con·ti·nent *historical* a name given to Africa at a time when it was little known to Europeans.

dark cur·rent ▸*n.* the residual electric current flowing in a photoelectric device when there is no incident illumination.

dark·en /'därkən/ ▸*v.* **1** make or become dark or darker: [*intrans.*] *the sky was darkening rapidly* | [*trans.*] *darken the eyebrows with black powder* | [as *adj.*] (**darkened**) *a darkened room.* ■ [*trans.*] *figurative* (of an unpleasant event or state of affairs) cast a shadow over something; spoil: *the abuse darkened the rest of their lives.* **2** make or become gloomy, angry, or unhappy: [*intrans.*] *his mood darkened.* ■ [*intrans.*] (of someone's eyes or expression) show anger or another strong negative emotion: *his face darkened and he lunged away.* ■ [*trans.*] (of such an emotion) show in (someone's eyes or expression): *misery darkened her gaze.* **—dark·en·er** *n.*
▸*PHRASE* □ **darken someone's door** visit someone's home: *never darken my door again!*

dark en·er·gy ▸*n. Physics* a theoretical repulsive force that counteracts gravity and causes the universe to expand at an accelerating rate: *Einstein's theories allow for the possible existence of dark energy.*

dark-field mi·cros·co·py ▸*n.* a type of light microscopy that produces brightly illuminated objects on a dark background.

dark glass·es ▸*plural n.* glasses with tinted lenses, worn to protect or conceal a person's eyes.

dark horse ▸*n.* **1** a person about whom little is known, esp. someone whose abilities and potential for success are concealed: [as *adj.*] *a dark-horse candidate.* **2** a competitor or candidate who has little chance of winning, or who wins against expectations: *a preseason dark horse as the nation's top collegiate football team.* ▷early 19th cent.: originally racing slang.

dark·ie /'därkē/ ▸*n.* variant spelling of **DARKY**.

dark lan·tern ▸*n.* a lantern with a movable panel that can be used to hide the light.

dark line ▸*n. Physics* a line in an absorption spectrum, appearing as a black line at visible wavelengths.

dark·ling /'därkliNG/ ▸*adj. poetic/literary* of or relating to growing darkness: *the darkling sky.* ▷Middle English: from **DARK** + *-ling*, a suffix denoting condition or situation. The verb *darkle* is a back-formation dating from the 15th century.

dark·ling bee·tle ▸*n.* a dark-colored nocturnal beetle, typically with reduced or absent wings. • Family Tenebrionidae: numerous genera and species.

dark·ly /'därklē/ ▸*adv.* **1** in a threatening, mysterious, or ominous way: *"You can't trust him," said Jacob darkly.* ■ in a depressing or pessimistic way: *I wondered darkly if I was wasting my time.* **2** with a dark color: *a figure silhouetted darkly against the trees.*

dark mat·ter ▸*n. Astronomy* (in some cosmological theories) nonluminous material that is postulated to exist in space and that could take any of several forms including weakly interacting particles (**cold dark matter**) or high-energy randomly moving particles created soon after the big bang (**hot dark matter**).

dark neb·u·la ▸*n. Astronomy* a nonluminous nebula of dust and gas that is observable because it obscures light from other sources.

dark·ness /'därknis/ ▸*n.* **1** the partial or total absence of light: *the office was in darkness.* ■ night: *they began to make camp before darkness fell.* ■ the quality of being dark in color: *the darkness of his jacket.* **2** wickedness or evil: *the forces of darkness.* ■ unhappiness, distress, or gloom: *moments of darkness were rare.* ■ secrecy or mystery: *they drew a veil of darkness across the proceedings.* ■ lack of spiritual or intellectual enlightenment; ignorance: *his accomplishments shone in a world of darkness.*

dark night of the soul (also **dark night**) ▸*n. Christian Theology* a period of spiritual aridity suffered by a mystic in which all sense of consolation is removed. ▷mid 19th cent.: translating Spanish *noche oscura* (St. John of the Cross).

dark re·ac·tion ▸*n. Biochemistry* the cycle of reactions (the Calvin cycle) that occurs in the second phase of photosynthesis and does not require the presence of light. It involves the fixation of carbon dioxide and its reduction to carbohydrate and the dissociation of water, using chemical energy stored in ATP.

dark·room /'därk,ro͞om; -,ro͝om/ ▸*n.* a room from which normal light is excluded, used for developing photographs.

dark star ▸*n. Astronomy* a starlike object that emits little or no visible light. Its existence is inferred from other evidence, such as the eclipsing of other stars.

dark·y /'därkē/ (also **dark·ie**) ▸*n.* (*pl.* **dark·ies**) *informal, offensive* a person with black or dark skin.

dar·ling /'därliNG/ ▸*n.* used as an affectionate form of address to a beloved person: *good night, my darling.* ■ a lovable or endearing person: *he's such a darling.* ■ a person who is particularly popular with a certain group: *she is* ***the darling of*** *the media.*
▸*adj.* [*attrib.*] beloved: *his darling wife.* ■ (esp. in affected use) pretty; charming: *a darling little pillbox hat.* ▷Old English *dēorling* (see **DEAR**, **-LING**). **—dar·ling·ness** *n.*
▸*PHRASE* □ **be a darling** used as a friendly or encouraging preface to a request: *be a darling and don't mention I'm here.*

Dar·ling Riv·er /'därliNG/ a river in southeastern Australia that flows southwest for 1,712 miles (2,757 km) to join the Murray River.

Darm·stadt /'därm,stat; -,SHtät/ an industrial town in western Germany, in the state of Hesse; pop. 140,040.

darm·stadt·i·um /därm'statēəm; -'SHtät-/ ▸*n.* the synthetic chemical element of atomic number 110. It is a superheavy metal that decays in thousandths of a second. ▷early 21st cent.: after a laboratory in *Darmstadt*, Germany, where the element was first created.

darn[1] /därn/ ▸*v.* [*trans.*] mend (knitted material or a hole in this) by weaving yarn across the hole with a needle: *I don't expect you to darn my socks.* ■ embroider (material) with a large running stitch.
▸*n.* a place in a garment that has been mended in such a way. ▷early 17th cent.: perhaps from dialect *dern* 'to hide,' which is from Old English *diernan*;

compare with Middle Dutch *dernen* 'stop holes in (a dike).'

darn2 (also **durn**) ▸*v., adj. & exclam. informal* euphemism for DAMN: [as *v.*] *darn it all, Poppa* | [as *adj.*] *the darn things were expensive.*

darned /därnd/ (also **durned** /dərnd/) ▸*adj. informal* euphemism for DAMNED: *you have to work a darned sight harder* | [as *submodifier*] *they're darned good songwriters.* —**darned·est** *adj.*

dar·nel /ˈdärnl/ ▸*n.* a Eurasian ryegrass. • Genus *Lolium*, family Gramineae: several species, in particular the widespread *L. temulentum.* ▹Middle English: of unknown origin; apparently related to French (Walloon dialect) *darnelle.*

darn·er /ˈdärnər/ ▸*n.* **1** a darning needle. **2** a large slender-bodied dragonfly. Also called DARNING NEEDLE, DEVIL'S DARNING NEEDLE. [said to be so named because of the popular belief that the dragonfly sews up the lips and eyelids of people sleeping.] • Family Aeshnidae: several genera.

darn·ing /ˈdärniNG/ ▸*n.* the skill or activity of one who darns: *long hours of tedious darning.* ■ articles being darned or needing to be darned: *Aunt Edie bent her head to her darning.*

darn·ing egg ▸*n.* an egg-shaped piece of wood or other smooth hard material used to stretch and support material being darned.

darn·ing nee·dle ▸*n.* a long sewing needle with a large eye, used in darning. ■ another term for DARNER (sense 2).

Darn·ley /ˈdärnlē/, Henry Stewart (or Stuart), Lord (1545–67), Scottish nobleman; second husband of Mary, Queen of Scots; father of James I of England.

DARPA /ˈdärpə/ ▸*abbr.* Defense Advanced Research Projects Agency, the central research and development organization for the U.S. Department of Defense.

Dar·row /ˈdarō/, Clarence Seward (1857–1938), U.S. lawyer. He served as defense counsel in several well-publicized trials, including that of John T. Scopes, a teacher in Dayton, Tennessee, who was charged with violating state law for teaching evolution in a public school in 1925.

dar·shan /ˈdär,SHän; -SHən/ ▸*n. Hinduism* an opportunity or occasion of seeing a holy person or the image of a deity. ▹via Hindi from Sanskrit *darśana* 'sight or seeing.'

Dart /därt/, Raymond Arthur (1893–1988), South African anthropologist and anatomist; born in Australia. In 1925, he found the first specimen of the hominid species *A. africanus*, for which he coined the genus name *Australopithecus.*

dart /därt/ ▸*n.* **1** a small pointed missile that can be thrown or fired. ■ a small pointed missile with a feather or plastic tail, used in the game of darts. ■ an act of running somewhere suddenly and rapidly: *the cat made a dart for the door.* ■ *figurative* a sudden, intense pang of a particular emotion: *a dart of panic.* ■ *Zoology* a dartlike calcareous organ of a snail forming part of the reproductive system, exchanged during copulation. **2** a tapered tuck stitched into a garment in order to shape it.

▸*v.* [*intrans.*] move or run somewhere suddenly or rapidly: *she darted across the street.* ■ [*trans.*] cast (a look or one's eyes) suddenly and rapidly in a particular direction: *she darted a glance across the table.* ■ [*trans.*] *archaic* throw (a missile). ■ [*trans.*] shoot (an animal) with a dart, typically in order to administer a drug. ▹Middle English: from Old French, accusative of *darz, dars*, from a West Germanic word meaning 'spear, lance.'

dart·board /ˈdärt,bôrd/ ▸*n.* a circular board marked with numbered segments, used as a target in the game of darts.

dart·er /ˈdärtər/ ▸*n.* **1** another term for ANHINGA. **2** a small North American freshwater fish, the male of which may develop bright coloration during the breeding season. • Genera *Etheostoma* and *Percina*, family Percidae: numerous species.

darts /därts/ ▸*plural n.* [usu. treated as *sing.*] an indoor game in which small pointed missiles with feather or plastic flights are thrown at a circular target marked with numbers in order to score points.

Dar·win /ˈdärwin/, Charles (Robert) (1809–82), English natural historian and geologist; a proponent of the theory of evolution by natural selection. While the naturalist on HMS *Beagle* for her voyage around the Southern Hemisphere 1831–36, he collected the material that became the basis for his ideas on natural selection. Notable works: *On the Origin of Species* (1859) and *The Descent of Man* (1871).

Dar·win·i·an /därˈwinēən/ ▸*adj.* of or relating to Darwinism.

▸*n.* an adherent of Darwinism.

Dar·win·ism /ˈdärwə,nizəm/ ▸*n.* the theory of the evolution of species by natural selection advanced by Charles Darwin.

> Darwin argued that since offspring tend to vary slightly from their parents, mutations that make an organism better adapted to its environment will be encouraged and developed by the pressures of natural selection, leading to the evolution of new species differing widely from one another and from their common ancestors. Darwinism was later developed by the findings of Mendelian genetics (see NEO-DARWINIAN).

—**Dar·win·ist** *n. & adj.*

Dar·win's finch·es ▸*plural n.* a group of songbirds related to the buntings and found on the Galapagos Islands, discovered by Charles Darwin and used by him to illustrate his theory of natural selection. They are believed to have evolved from a common ancestor and have developed a variety of bills to suit various modes of life. • Family Emberizidae (subfamily Emberizinae): four to six genera, esp. *Geospiza* (the **ground finches**) and *Camarhynchus* (the **tree finches**).

Da·sein /ˈdä,zīn/ ▸*n. Philosophy* (in Hegelianism) existence or determinate being; (in existentialism) human existence. ▹mid 19th cent.: German, from *dasein* 'exist,' from *da* 'there' + *sein* 'be.'

dash /daSH/ ▸*v.* **1** [*intrans.*] run or travel somewhere in a great hurry: *I dashed into the garden* | *I must dash, I'm late.* ■ (often **dash about/around**) move about in a great hurry, esp. in the attempt to do several things in a short period of time: *I dash about for four days in a manic fit to straighten things up.* **2** [*trans.*] strike or fling (something) somewhere with great force, esp. so as to have a destructive effect; hurl: *the ship was dashed upon the rocks.* ■ [*intrans.*] strike forcefully against something: *a gust of rain dashed against the bricks.* ■ [*trans.*] destroy or frustrate (a person's hopes or expectations): *the budget dashed hopes of an increase in funding.* ■ [*trans.*] cause (someone) to lose confidence; dispirit: *I won't tell Stuart—I think he'd be dashed.*

▸*phrasal v.* □ **dash something off** write something hurriedly and without much premeditation.

▸*exclam. Brit., informal, dated* used to express mild annoyance: *"Dash it all, I am in charge."*

▸*n.* **1** [in *sing.*] an act of running somewhere suddenly and hastily: *she* **made a dash for** *the door.* ■ a journey or period of time characterized by urgency or eager haste: *a 20-mile dash to the airport.* ■ a short fast race run in one heat; a sprint: *the 100-yard dash.* **2** a small quantity of a substance, esp. a liquid, added to something else: *whiskey with* **a dash of** *soda.* ■ *figurative* a small amount of a particular quality adding piquancy or distinctiveness to something else: *a casual atmosphere with a dash of sophistication.* **3** a horizontal stroke in writing or printing to mark a pause or break in sense, or to represent omitted letters or words. ■ the longer signal of the two used in Morse code. Compare with DOT1. ■ *Music* a short vertical mark placed above or beneath a note to indicate that it is to be performed in a very staccato manner. **4** impetuous or flamboyant vigor and confidence; panache: *he has youthful energy, dash, and charisma.* **5** short for DASHBOARD. ▹Middle English (in the sense 'strike forcibly against'): probably symbolic of forceful movement and related to Swedish *daska* and Danish *daske.*

dash·board /ˈdaSH,bôrd/ ▸*n.* the panel facing the driver of a vehicle or the pilot of an aircraft, containing instruments and controls. ■ *historical* a board of wood or leather in front of a carriage, to keep out mud.

dashed /daSHt/ ▸*adj.* [*attrib.*] **1** *Brit., informal, dated* used for emphasis: *it's a dashed shame* | [as *submodifier*] *she was dashed rude.* **2** (of a line on a piece of paper) composed of dashes.

da·sheen /daˈSHēn/ ▸*n.* another term for TARO. ▹late 19th cent. (originally West Indian): of unknown origin.

dash·er /ˈdaSHər/ ▸*n.* **1** *informal* a person who dresses or acts flamboyantly or stylishly. **2** a plunger for agitating cream in a churn. **3** *Hockey* the ledge along the top of the boards of a rink.

da·shi /ˈdäSHē/ ▸*n.* stock made from fish and kelp, used in Japanese cooking.

da·shi·ki /dəˈSHēkē/ ▸*n.* (*pl.* **-kis**) a loose, brightly colored shirt or tunic, originally from West Africa. ▹from Yoruba or Hausa.

dash·ing /ˈdaSHiNG/ ▸*adj.* (of a man) attractive in a romantic, adventurous way: *a dashing pirate on the high seas.* ■ stylish or fashionable: *a dashing S-type Jaguar.* —**dash·ing·ly** *adv.*

dash·pot /ˈdaSH,pät/ ▸*n.* a device for damping shock or vibration.

das·sie /ˈdasē/ ▸*n.* (*pl.* **-sies**) a hyrax, esp. the rock hyrax of southern Africa. • Family Procaviidae, in particular *Procavia capensis.* ▹late 18th cent.: from Afrikaans, from South African Dutch *dasje*, diminutive of Dutch *das* 'badger.'

das·tard /ˈdastərd/ ▸*n. dated, humorous* a dishonorable or despicable person. ▹late Middle English (in the sense 'stupid person'): probably from *dazed*, influenced by *dotard* and *bastard.*

das·tard·ly /ˈdastərdlē/ ▸*adj. dated, humorous* wicked and cruel: *pirates and their dastardly deeds.* ▹mid 16th cent. (in the sense 'dull or stupid'): from DASTARD in the obsolete sense 'base coward.' —**das·tard·li·ness** *n.*

das·y·ure /ˈdasē,yo͝or/ ▸*n.* another term for QUOLL. ▹mid 19th cent.: from French, from modern Latin *dasyurus*, from Greek *dasus* 'rough, hairy' + *oura* 'tail.'

DAT /dat/ ▸*abbr.* digital audiotape.

da·ta /ˈdatə; ˈdātə/ ▸*n.* [treated as *sing.* or *pl.*] facts and statistics collected together for reference or analysis. See also DATUM. ■ *Computing* the quantities, characters, or symbols on which operations are performed by a computer, being stored and transmitted in the form of electrical signals and recorded on magnetic, optical, or mechanical recording media. ■ *Philosophy* things known or assumed as facts, making the basis of reasoning or calculation. ▹mid 17th cent. (as a term in philosophy): from Latin, plural of DATUM.

> ***USAGE*** Data was originally the plural of the Latin word *datum*, 'something (e.g., a piece of information) given.' **Data** is now used as a singular where it means 'information': *this data was prepared for the conference.* It is used as a plural in technical contexts and when the collection of bits of information is stressed: *all recent data on hurricanes are being compared.* Avoid *datas* and *datae*, which are false plurals, neither English nor Latin.

da·ta bank (also **da·ta·bank**) ▸*n. Computing* a large repository of data on a particular topic, sometimes formed from more than one database, and accessible by many users.

da·ta·base /ˈdatə,bās; ˈdā-/ ▸*n.* a structured set of data held in a computer, esp. one that is accessible in various ways.

da·ta·base man·age·ment sys·tem (abbr.: **DBMS**) ▸*n. Computing* software that handles the storage, retrieval, and updating of data in a computer system.

dat·a·ble /ˈdātəbəl/ (also **date·a·ble**) ▸*adj.* able to be dated to a particular time.

da·ta com·mu·ni·ca·tions ▸*n.* the electronic transmission of encoded information to, from, or between computers.

da·ta dic·tion·ar·y ▸*n. Computing* a set of information describing the contents, format, and structure of a database and the relationship between its elements, used to control access to and manipulation of the database.

da·ta·glove /ˈdatə,gləv; ˈdā-/ ▸*n. Computing* a device, worn like a glove, that allows the manual manipulation of images in virtual reality.

da·ta·link /ˈdatə,liNGk; ˈdātə-/ ▸*n.* an electronic connection for the exchange of information: *a datalink system that would allow aircraft controllers and pilots to exchange electronic messages.*

da·ta min·ing ▸*n. Computing* the practice of examining large databases in order to generate new information.

da·ta·point /ˈdatə,point; ˈdātə-/ ▸*n.* an identifiable element in a data set: *software that can quickly process tens of thousands of datapoints.*

da·ta proc·ess·ing ▸*n.* a series of operations on data, esp. by a computer, to retrieve, transform, or classify information. —**da·ta proc·es·sor** *n.*

da·ta set ▸*n. Computing* a collection of related sets of information that is composed of separate elements but can be manipulated as a unit by a computer.

da·ta smog ▸*n. informal* an overwhelming excess of information, especially from the Internet: *nowadays, people need help getting their intellectual bearings because cable has become a torrent of ideology, dueling experts and data smog.*

da·ta ter·mi·nal ▸*n. Computing* a terminal at which a person can enter data into a computer-based system or receive data from one.

da·ta type ▸*n. Computing* a particular kind of data item, as defined by the values it can take, the programming language used, or the operations that can be performed on it.

da·ta·veil·lance /ˌdatəˈvāləns; ˌdātə-/ ▸*n.* the extraction of private information about a people or groups from algorithmic study of the residue of their various electronic and digital transactions and activities. ▷1980s: blend of *data* and *surveillance.*

da·ta ware·house ▸*n. Computing* a large store of data accumulated from a wide range of sources within a company and used to guide management decisions. **—da·ta ware·hous·ing** *n.*

date[1] /dāt/ ▸*n.* **1** the day of the month or year as specified by a number: *what's the date today?* | *please give your name, address, and* ***date of birth.*** ■ a particular day or year when a given event occurred or will occur: *significant dates like 1776 and 1789* | *they've set a date for the wedding.* ■ **(dates)** the years of a person's birth and death or of the beginning and end of a period or event: *giving the dates of kings and queens.* ■ the period of time to which an artifact or structure belongs: *the church is the largest of its date.* ■ a written, printed, or stamped statement on an item giving the day, month, and year of writing, publication, or manufacture: *these Roman coins bear an explicit date.* **2** *informal* a social or romantic appointment or engagement: *a college student* ***on a date*** *with someone he met in class.* ■ a person with whom one has such an engagement: *my date isn't going to show, it seems.* ■ an appointment: *he has a date with a specialist next week.* ■ a musical or theatrical engagement or performance, esp. as part of a tour: *possible live dates in the near future.*
▸*v.* [*trans.*] **1** establish or ascertain the date of (an object or event): *they* ***date*** *the paintings* ***to*** *1460–70.* ■ mark with a date: *sign and date the document* | [as *adj.*] **(dated)** *a signed and dated painting.* ■ [*intrans.*] have its origin at a particular time; have existed since: *the controversy* ***dates back to*** *1986.* **2** indicate or expose as being old-fashioned: *disco—that word alone dates me.* ■ [*intrans.*] seem old-fashioned: [as *adj.*] **(dated)** *his style would sound dated nowadays.* **3** *informal* go out with (someone in whom one is romantically or sexually interested): *my sister's pretty judgmental about the girls I date* | [*intrans.*] *they have been dating for more than a year.* ▷Middle English: via Old French from medieval Latin *data,* feminine past participle of *dare* 'give'; from the Latin formula used in dating letters, *data (epistola)* '(letter) given or delivered,' to record a particular time or place. **—dat·er** *n.*
▸*PHRASE* □ **to date** until now: *their finest work to date.*

date[2] ▸*n.* **1** a sweet, dark brown, oval fruit containing a hard stone, often eaten dried. **2** (also **date palm**) the tall palm tree that bears clusters of this fruit, native to western Asia and North Africa. • *Phoenix dactylifera,* family Palmae. ▷Middle English: from Old French, via Latin from Greek *daktulos* 'finger' (because of the fingerlike shape of its leaves).

date·a·ble ▸*adj.* variant spelling of DATABLE.

date·book /ˈdātˌbo͝ok/ ▸*n.* a book with spaces for each day of the year in which one notes appointments or important information for each day.

date·less /ˈdātlis/ ▸*adj.* **1** not clearly belonging to any particular period, therefore not likely to go out of date: *dateless dresses.* ■ (of a document or stamp) having no date mark. **2** not having, or incapable of having, social or romantic appointments or engagements: *dateless men reduce women to sex objects and dateless women become space-age scanners.*

date·line /ˈdātˌlīn/ ▸*n.* a line at the head of a dispatch or special article in a newspaper showing the date and place of writing.
▸*v.* furnish (a dispatch or article) with a dateline.

Date Line (also **International Date Line**) an imaginary north–south line through the Pacific Ocean, adopted in 1884, to the east of which the date is a day earlier than it is to the west. It lies chiefly along the meridian furthest from Greenwich, England (i.e., longitude 180°), with diversions to pass around some island groups.

date palm ▸*n.* see DATE[2].

date rape ▸*n.* rape committed by the victim's escort.

date-rape drug ▸*n.* a drug that causes temporary loss of memory or inhibition, surreptitiously given to a girl or a woman so that her date may sexually abuse or rape her.

date stamp ▸*n.* a stamped mark indicating a date, typically used on food packaging or mailed envelopes. ■ an adjustable stamp used to make such a mark.
▸*v.* **(date-stamp)** [*trans.*] mark (something) with a date stamp.

dat·ing serv·ice ▸*n.* an agency that arranges introductions for people seeking romantic partners or friends with similar interests.

da·tive /ˈdātiv/ *Grammar* ▸*adj.* (in Latin, Greek, German, and other languages) denoting a case of nouns and pronouns, and words in grammatical agreement with them, indicating an indirect object or recipient.
▸*n.* a noun or other word of this type. ■ **(the dative)** the dative case. ▷late Middle English: from Latin *(casus) dativus* '(case) of giving,' from *dat-* 'given,' from the verb *dare.*

Da·tong /ˈdäˈto͝ong/ a city in northern China, in Shanxi province; pop. 1,090,000.

da·tum /ˈdātəm; ˈdatəm/ ▸*n.* (*pl.* **da·ta** /ˈdātə; ˈdatə/) **1** See also DATA. a piece of information. ■ an assumption or premise from which inferences may be drawn. See SENSE DATUM. **2** a fixed starting point of a scale or operation. ▷mid 18th cent.: from Latin, literally 'something given,' neuter past participle of *dare* 'give.'

da·tum line (also **datum level**) ▸*n.* a standard of comparison or point of reference. ■ *Surveying* an assumed surface used as a reference for the measurement of heights and depths. ■ a line to which dimensions are referred on engineering drawings, and from which measurements are calculated.

da·tu·ra /dəˈt(y)o͝orə/ ▸*n.* a shrubby annual plant with large trumpet-shaped flowers, native to southern North America. Daturas contain toxic or narcotic alkaloids and are used as hallucinogens by some American Indian peoples. See also ANGEL'S TRUMPET. • Genus *Datura,* family Solanaceae: several species, including the jimson weed. ▷modern Latin, from Hindi *dhatūrā.*

daub /dôb/ ▸*v.* [*trans.*] coat or smear (a surface) with a thick or sticky substance in a carelessly rough or liberal way: *she* ***daubed*** *her face* ***with*** *night cream.* ■ spread (a thick or sticky substance) on a surface in such a way: *a canvas with paint* ***daubed on*** *it.* ■ paint (words or drawings) on a surface in such a way: *they* ***daubed*** *graffiti* ***on*** *the walls.*
▸*n.* **1** plaster, clay, or another substance used for coating a surface, esp. when mixed with straw and applied to laths or wattles to form a wall: *square huts, mostly daub and wattle.* ■ a patch or smear of a thick or sticky substance: *a daub of paint.* **2** a painting executed without much skill. ▷late Middle English: from Old French *dauber,* from Latin *dealbare* 'whiten, whitewash,' based on *albus* 'white.'

daube /dōb/ ▸*n.* a stew of meat, typically beef, braised slowly in wine. ▷French; compare with Italian *addobbo* 'seasoning.'
▸*PHRASE* □ **en daube** (of meat) cooked in this way.

daub·er /ˈdôbər/ ▸*n.* a crude or inartistic painter. ■ an implement used for daubing.

Dau·bi·gny /ˌdôbēˈnyē/, Charles François (1817–78), French landscape painter. A member of the Barbizon School, he is often regarded as a linking figure between this group and the Impressionists.

daugh·ter /ˈdôtər; ˈdä-/ ▸*n.* a girl or woman in relation to her parents. ■ a female offspring of an animal. ■ a female descendant: *we are the sons and daughters of Adam.* ■ a woman considered as the product of a particular person, influence, or environment: *a daughter of the dry savannas of Africa.* ■ *archaic* used as a term of affectionate address to a woman or girl, typically by an older person. ■ *poetic/literary* a thing personified as a daughter in relation to its origin or source: *Italian, the eldest daughter of ancient Latin.* ■ *Physics* a nuclide formed by the radioactive decay of another.
▸*adj. Biology* originating through division or replication: *daughter cells.* ▷Old English *dohtor,* of Germanic origin; related to Dutch *dochter* and German *Tochter,* from an Indo-European root shared by Greek *thugatēr.* **—daugh·ter·hood** /-ˌho͝od/ *n.* **—daugh·ter·ly** *adj.*

daugh·ter·board /ˈdôtərˌbôrd; ˈdä-/ ▸*n. Electronics* an expansion circuit card affixed to a motherboard that accesses memory and the CPU directly rather than through a bus. Also called DAUGHTERCARD.

daugh·ter-in-law ▸*n.* (*pl.* **daugh·ters-in-law**) the wife of one's son.

Daugh·ters of the A·mer·i·can Rev·o·lu·tion (abbr.: **DAR**) a patriotic society whose aims include encouraging education and the study of U.S. history and that tends to be politically conservative. Membership is limited to female descendants of those who aided the cause of independence.

Dau·mier /dōˈmyā/, Honoré (1808–78), French painter and lithographer. Working as a cartoonist, he produced lithographs satirizing French society and politics.

daunt /dônt; dänt/ ▸*v.* [*trans.*] (usu. **be daunted**) make (someone) feel intimidated or apprehensive: *some people are daunted by technology.* ▷Middle English: from Old French *danter,* from Latin *domitare,* frequentative of *domare* 'to tame.'
▸*PHRASE* □ **nothing daunted** without having been made fearful or apprehensive: *nothing daunted, the committee set to work.*

daunt·ing /ˈdôntiNG; ˈdänt-/ ▸*adj.* seeming difficult to deal with in anticipation; intimidating: *a daunting task.* **—daunt·ing·ly** *adv.*

daunt·less /ˈdôntlis; ˈdänt-/ ▸*adj.* showing fearlessness and determination: *dauntless bravery.* **—daunt·less·ly** *adv.* **—daunt·less·ness** *n.*

dau·phin /ˈdôfin/ ▸*n. historical* the eldest son of the king of France. ▷French, from the family name of the lords of the Dauphiné (first used in this way in the 14th cent.), ultimately a nickname meaning 'dolphin.'

D

dau·phi·nois /ˌdôfinˈwä/ (also **dau·phi·noise** /-ˈwäz/) ▸*adj.* (of potatoes or other vegetables) sliced and cooked in milk, typically with a topping of cheese. ▷French, 'from the province of Dauphiné.'

Da·vao /ˈdäˌvou; däˈvou/ a seaport in the southern Philippines, on the island of Mindanao; pop. 850,000.

da·ven /ˈdävən/ ▸*v.* (**da·vened, da·ven·ing**) [*intrans.*] (in Judaism) recite the prescribed liturgical prayers. ▷Yiddish.

Dav·en·port /ˈdavənˌpôrt/ an industrial city in southeastern Iowa, on the Mississippi River, one of the Quad Cities; pop. 98,359.

dav·en·port /ˈdavənˌpôrt/ ▸*n.* **1** a large upholstered sofa, typically able to be converted into a bed. [perhaps from a manufacturer's name.] **2** *Brit.* an ornamental writing desk with drawers and a sloping surface for writing. [probably named after Captain *Davenport,* for whom early examples of this type of desk were made in the late 18th cent.]

Da·vid[1] /ˈdāvid/ (died *c.*962 BC), king of Judah and Israel *c.*1000–*c.*962 BC. In the biblical account, he killed the Philistine Goliath and, on Saul's death, became king, making Jerusalem his capital. He is traditionally regarded as the author of the Psalms, although this has been disputed.

Da·vid[2] the name of two kings of Scotland: ■ **David I** (*c.*1084–1153), sixth son of Malcolm III; reigned 1124–53. In 1136, he invaded England in support of his niece Matilda's claim to the throne, but he was defeated at the Battle of the Standard in 1138. ■ **David II** (1324–71), son of Robert the Bruce; reigned 1329–71.

Da·vid[3] /däˈvēd/, Jacques-Louis (1748–1825), French painter. He is noted for neoclassical paintings such as *The Oath of the Horatii* (1784) and *The Intervention of the Sabine Women* (1799).

Da·vid, St. /ˈdāvid/ (6th century), Welsh monk; Welsh name **De·wi** /ˈde-wē/. Since the 12th century he has been regarded as the patron saint of Wales. Feast day, March 1.

da Vin·ci /də ˈvinCHē/ Leonardo, see **LEONARDO DA VINCI.**

Da·vis /ˈdāvis/ an academic and agricultural city in north central California, west of Sacramento; pop. 46,209.

Da·vis[1] /ˈdāvis/, Angela Yvonne (1944–), U.S. civil rights leader and writer. She wrote *Women, Race and Class* (1980).

Da·vis[2], Benjamin Oliver (1877–1970), U.S. military leader. In 1940, he became the first African-American general in the U.S. Army. His son, **Benjamin O. Davis, Jr.** (1912–2002), an aviator, became the first African-American Air Force general in 1953.

Da·vis[3], Bette (1908–89), U.S. actress; born *Ruth Elizabeth Davis.* She established her Hollywood career playing a number of strong, independent female characters in such movies as *Dangerous* (1935) and *Jezebel* (1938). Her flair for suggesting the macabre

Pronunciation Key ə *ago;* ər *over;* ˈə *or* ˌə *up;* ˈər *or* ˌər *fur;* a *hat;* ā *rate;* ä *car;* CH *chew;* e *let;* ē *see;* e(ə)r *air;* i *fit;* ī *by;* i(ə)r *ear;* NG *sing;* ō *go;* ô *for;* oi *boy;* o͝o *good;* o͞o *goo;* ou *out;* SH *she;* TH *thin;* T͟H *then;* (h)w *why;* ZH *vision*

and menacing emerged in later movies, such as *Whatever Happened to Baby Jane?* (1962).

Bette Davis

Da·vis[4], David (1815–86), U.S. Supreme Court associate justice 1862–77 and a U.S. senator from Illinois 1877–83.

Da·vis[5], Jefferson (1808–89), U.S. politician and president of the Confederate States of America (CSA). As a U.S. senator from Mississippi 1847–51 and a defender of slavery, he withdrew from the Senate when Mississippi seceded from the Union and was elected president of CSA in 1862. He wrote *The Rise and Fall of the Confederate Government* (1881).

Jefferson Davis

Da·vis[6], Miles (Dewey) (1926–91), U.S. jazz trumpeter, composer, and bandleader. In the 1950s, he played and recorded arrangements in a new style that became known as "cool" jazz, heard on albums such as *Kind of Blue* (1959). In the 1960s, he pioneered the fusion of jazz and rock.

Da·vis[7], Sammy, Jr. (1925–90), U.S. actor, singer, and dancer. Most notably, he appeared in *Ocean's Eleven* (1960) along with Frank Sinatra and other members of the "Rat Pack." His recording of "Candy Man" (1972) became his theme song.

Da·vis Cup an annual tennis championship for men, first held in 1900, between teams from different countries. ▷named after Dwight F. *Davis* (1879–1945), the U.S. doubles champion who donated the trophy.

Da·vis Moun·tains a range in southwestern Texas, site of the Mount Locke observatory and several resorts.

Da·vis·son /ˈdāvəsən/, Clinton Joseph (1881–1958), U.S. physicist. With **L. H. Germer** (1896–1971), he discovered electron diffraction, thus confirming de Broglie's theory of the wave nature of electrons. Nobel Prize for Physics (1937, shared with George P. Thomson 1892–1975).

Da·vis Strait a sea passage 400 miles (645 km) long that separates Greenland from Baffin Island and connects Baffin Bay with the Atlantic Ocean. ▷named after John *Davis* (*c.*1550–1605), the English explorer who sailed through it in 1587.

da·vit /ˈdavit; ˈdā-/ ▸*n.* a small crane on board a ship, esp. one of a pair for suspending or lowering a lifeboat. ▷late 15th cent.: from Old French *daviot*, diminutive of *david*, denoting a kind of carpenter's tool.

Da·vy /ˈdāvē/, Sir Humphry (1778–1829), English chemist; a pioneer of electrochemistry. He discovered nitrous oxide (laughing gas) and the elements sodium, potassium, magnesium, calcium, strontium, and barium. He also identified and named the element chlorine, determined the properties of iodine, and demonstrated that diamond was a form of carbon.

Da·vy Jones's lock·er /ˌdāvē ˈjōnz(əz)/ ▸*n. informal* the bottom of the sea, esp. regarded as the grave of those drowned at sea. ▷extension of early 18th-cent. nautical slang *Davy Jones*, denoting the evil spirit of the sea.

Da·vy lamp ▸*n. historical* a miner's portable safety lamp with the flame enclosed by wire gauze to reduce the risk of an explosion of gas.

daw /dô/ ▸*n.* another term for **JACKDAW**. ▷late Middle English: of Germanic origin; related to German *Dohle*.

daw·dle /ˈdôdl/ ▸*v.* [*intrans.*] waste time; be slow: *I couldn't dawdle over my coffee any longer.* ■ [with *adverbial of direction*] move slowly and idly: *Ruth dawdled back through the woods.* See note at **LOITER**. ▷mid 17th cent.: related to dialect *daddle*, *doddle* 'dally.' **—daw·dler** /ˈdôd(ə)lər/ *n.*

Dawes[1] /dôz/, Charles Gates (1865–1951), U.S. politician, lawyer, and financier. He was vice president of the U.S. 1925–29 and was instrumental in formulating the 1923 plan for restructuring post-World War I Germany's economy. Nobel Peace Prize (1925, shared with Sir Austen Chamberlain).

Dawes[2], William (1745–99), U.S. patriot. With Paul Revere he rode from Lexington to Concord, Massachusetts, to warn of approaching British soldiers on April 18, 1775.

dawn /dôn; dän/ ▸*n.* the first appearance of light in the sky before sunrise: *the rose-pink light of dawn.* ■ *figurative* the beginning of a phenomenon or period of time, esp. one considered favorable: *the dawn of civilization.*

▸*v.* [*intrans.*] **1** (of a day) begin: [with *complement*] *Thursday dawned bright and sunny.* ■ *figurative* come into existence: *a new era of land-use policy was dawning.* **2** become evident to the mind; be perceived or understood: *the awful truth was beginning to* ***dawn on*** *him* | [as *adj.*] (**dawning**) *he smiled with dawning recognition.* ▷late 15th cent. (as a verb): back-formation from Middle English **DAWNING**.

▸*PHRASE* □ **from dawn to dusk** all day; ceaselessly: *day after day from dawn to dusk, they drove those loaded canoes.*

dawn cho·rus ▸*n.* [in *sing.*] the singing of a large number of birds before dawn each day, particularly during the breeding season.

dawn·ing /ˈdôniNG; ˈdän-/ ▸*n. poetic/literary* dawn. ■ the beginning or first appearance of something: *the dawning of civilization.* ▷Middle English: alteration of earlier *dawing*, from Old English *dagian* 'to dawn,' of Germanic origin; related to Dutch *dagen* and German *tagen*, also to **DAY**.

dawn red·wood ▸*n.* a coniferous tree with deciduous needles, known only as a fossil until it was found growing in southwestern China in 1941. Also called **METASEQUOIA**. • *Metasequoia glyptostroboides*, family Taxodiaceae.

Daw·son /ˈdôsən/ a town in the west central Yukon Territory, on the Klondike and Yukon rivers, center of a gold rush after 1896.

DAX ▸*abbr.* Deutsche Aktienindex, the German stock exchange.

Day[1] /dā/, Doris (1924–), U.S. actress and singer; born *Doris Kappelhoff*. She became a movie star in the 1950s with roles in lighthearted musicals, comedies, and romances, such as *Calamity Jane* (1953) and *Pillow Talk* (1959).

Day[2], Dorothy (1897–1980), U.S. journalist and reformer. She founded the *Catholic Worker* newspaper with social activist Peter Maurin (1877–1949) in 1933.

Day[3], William Rufus (1849–1923), U.S. Supreme Court associate justice 1903–22. He was appointed to the Court by President Theodore Roosevelt.

day /dā/ ▸*n.* **1** a period of twenty-four hours as a unit of time, reckoned from one midnight to the next, corresponding to a rotation of the earth on its axis. ■ the part of this period when it is light; the time between sunrise and sunset: *she sleeps all day and goes out at night* | *the animals hunt* ***by day***. ■ the time spent working during such a period: *he works an eight-hour day.* ■ *Astronomy* a single rotation of a planet in relation to its primary. ■ *Astronomy* the period on a planet when its primary star is above the horizon. ■ *archaic* daylight: *by the time they had all gone it was broad day.* **2** (usu. **days**) a particular period of the past; an era: *the laws were very strict in those days.* ■ (**the day**) the present time: *the political issues of the day.* ■ [with *adj.*] a day associated with a particular event or purpose: *graduation day* | *Christmas Day.* ■ a day's endeavor, or the period of an endeavor, esp. as bringing success: *speed and surprise would win the day.* ■ [usu. with *adj.*] (**days**) a particular period in a person's life or career: *my student days.* ■ (**one's day**) the successful, fortunate, or influential period of a person's life or career: *he had been a matinée idol in his day.* ■ (**one's days**) the span of someone's life: *she cared for him for* ***the rest of his days***.

▸*adj.* [*attrib.*] carried out during the day as opposed to the evening or at night: *my day job.* ■ (of a person) working during the day as opposed to at night: *a day nurse.* ▷Old English *dæg*, of Germanic origin; related to Dutch *dag* and German *Tag*.

▸*PHRASES* □ **all in a** (or **the**) **day's work** (of something unusual or difficult) accepted as part of someone's normal routine or as a matter of course: *dodging sharks is all in a day's work for these scientists.* □ **any day** *informal* at any time: *you can take me dancing* ***any day of the week***. ■ (used to express one's strong preference for something) under any circumstances: *I'd rather live in a shack in the woods than a penthouse in the city, any day.* ■ very soon: *she's expected to give birth any day.* □ **at the end of the day** see **END**. □ **by the day** gradually and steadily: *the campaign is growing by the day.* □ **call it a day** end a period of activity, esp. resting content that enough has been done: *we were prepared to do another long march before calling it a day.* □ **day after day** on each successive day, esp. over a long period: *the rain poured down day after day.* □ **day and night** all the time: *they kept working, day and night.* □ **day by day** gradually and steadily: *day by day I grew worse.* □ **day in, day out** continuously or repeatedly over a long period of time. □ **day of reckoning** the time when past mistakes or misdeeds must be punished or paid for; a testing time when the degree of one's success or failure will be revealed. [with allusion to Judgment Day, on which (in some beliefs) the judgment of humankind is expected to take place.] □ **from day one** from the very beginning: *children need a firm hand from day one.* □ **have had one's** (or **its**) **day** be no longer popular, successful, or influential: *power dressing has had its day.* □ **if someone is a day** at least (added to a statement about a person's age): *he must be seventy if he's a day.* □ **in this day and age** at the present time; in the modern era: *it simplifies housekeeping, which is essential in this day and age.* □ **not someone's day** used to convey that someone has had a bad day. □ **—— of the day** a thing currently considered to be particularly interesting or important: *the big news story of the day.* □ **one day** (or **one of these days**) at some time in the future: *our wishes will come true one of these days.* □ **one of those days** a day when several things go wrong. □ **that will** (or **that'll**) **be the day** *informal* that will never happen. □ **these days** at present: *he was drinking far too much these days.* □ **those were the days** used to assert that a particular past time was better than the present. □ **to the day** exactly: *it's four years to the day since we won the lottery.* □ **to this day** up to the present time; still: *the tradition continues to this day.*

Day·ak /ˈdīˌak/ (also **Dy·ak**) ▸*n.* (*pl.* same or **-aks**) **1** a member of a group of indigenous peoples inhabiting parts of Borneo. **2** the group of Austronesian languages spoken by these peoples.

▸*adj.* of or relating to these peoples or their languages. ▷mid 19th cent.: Malay, literally 'up-country.'

Da·yan /däˈyän/, Moshe (1915–81), Israeli statesman and general. As minister of defense he oversaw Israel's victory in the Six Day War, and as foreign minister he played a prominent role in negotiations that led to the Camp David agreements of 1979.

day·bed /ˈdāˌbed/ ▸*n.* a couch that can be made up into a bed. ■ a bed for daytime rest.

day·book /ˈdāˌbo͝ok/ ▸*n.* an account book in which a day's transactions are entered for later transfer to a ledger. ■ a diary.

day·break /ˈdāˌbrāk/ ▸*n.* the time in the morning when daylight first appears; dawn: *she set off* ***at daybreak***.

day care ▸*n.* daytime care for the needs of people who cannot be fully independent, such as children or the elderly: *family issues such as day care* | [as *adj.*] *a* ***day-care center*** *for employees' children.*

day·dream /ˈdāˌdrēm/ ▸*n.* a series of pleasant thoughts that distract one's attention from the present.

▸*v.* [*intrans.*] indulge in such a series of thoughts: *stop daydreaming and pay attention.* **—day·dream·er** *n.* **—day·dream·y** *adj.*

day·flow·er /ˈdāˌflou(-ə)r/ ▸*n.* a plant related to the spiderwort, with short-lived flowers that are typically blue. • Genus *Commelina*, family Commelinaceae.

Day-Glo /ˈdā ˌglō/ ▸*n. trademark* a fluorescent paint or other coloring.
▸*adj.* (also **day-glo**) of or denoting very bright or fluorescent coloring: *wearing Day-Glo pink T-shirts.* ▷1950s: blend of DAY and GLOW.

day job ▸*n.* a person's regular job and main source of income, usually performed during the normal business day, and either allowing them to practice an avocation or contrasting to a vocation they would rather pursue.

day la·bor ▸*n.* unskilled labor paid by the day. —**day la·bor·er** *n.*

Day Lew·is [1] /dā ˈlo͞oəs/, C. (1904–72), English poet, novelist, and critic; full name *Cecil Day Lewis.* He served as Britain's poet laureate 1968–72 and also wrote detective novels under the name **Nicholas Blake.**

Day-Lew·is [2] /dā ˈlo͞oəs/ ▸, Daniel 1957–, English actor; full name *Daniel Michael Blake Day-Lewis.* His films include *The Unbearable Lightness of Being* (1988), *My Left Foot* (Academy Award, 1989), *The Age of Innocence* (1993), and *Gangs of New York* (2002).

day·light /ˈdāˌlīt/ ▸*n.* **1** the natural light of the day: *there were two hours of daylight left* | [as *adj.*] *the daylight hours.* ■ the first appearance of light in the morning; dawn: *I returned at daylight.* ■ *figurative* visible distance between one person or thing and another: *the growing daylight between himself and the leading jockey.* **2** (**daylights**) used to emphasize the severity or thoroughness of an action: *my father beat* ***the living daylights*** *out of them.* [from *daylights* meaning 'eyes,' hence 'any vital organ.']
▸*PHRASE* □ **see daylight** begin to understand what was previously puzzling or unclear.

day·light·ing /ˈdāˌlītiNG/ ▸*n.* the illumination of buildings by natural light: *daylighting is achieved by using properly designed windows and skylights.*

day·light sav·ing time (also **day·light sav·ings time**) ▸*n.* time as adjusted to achieve longer evening daylight, esp. in summer, by setting the clocks an hour ahead of the standard time.

day·lil·y /ˈdāˌlilē/ (also **day lil·y**) ▸*n.* a lily that bears large yellow, red, or orange flowers, each flower lasting only one day. • Genus *Hemerocallis*, family Liliaceae.

day·long /ˈdāˈlôNG/ ▸*adj.* of a day's duration; lasting all day: *a daylong deluge.*

day·mare /ˈdāˌme(ə)r/ ▸*n.* a frightening or oppressive trance or hallucinatory condition experienced while awake. ▷mid 17th cent.: from DAY, on the pattern of *nightmare.*

day nurs·er·y ▸*n.* a place where young children are cared for during the working day.

Day of A·tone·ment another term for YOM KIPPUR.

day off ▸*n.* (*pl.* **days off**) a day's vacation from work or school on what would normally be a working day.

Day of Judg·ment another term for JUDGMENT DAY.

day·pack /ˈdāˌpak/ ▸*n.* a small backpack, used for day hikes or for carrying books, etc.

day room (also **day·room**) ▸*n.* a room used for daytime recreation, esp. a communal room in an institution.

day·sail /ˈdāˌsāl/ ▸*v.* [*intrans.*] sail a yacht for a single day: [as *n.*] (**daysailing**) *an outstanding boat for daysailing.*

day·sail·er /ˈdāˌsālər/ ▸*n.* a sailboat without a cabin, designed for day trips.

day school ▸*n.* a nonresidential school, typically a private one.

day shift ▸*n.* a period of time worked during the daylight hours in a hospital, factory, etc., as opposed to the night shift. ■ [treated as *sing.* or *pl.*] the employees who work during this period.

day·side /ˈdāˌsīd/ ▸*n. Astronomy* the side of a planet that is facing its primary star.

Days of Awe *plural n.* another term for HIGH HOLIDAYS.

day·spring /ˈdāˌspriNG/ ▸*n. poetic/literary* dawn.

day stu·dent ▸*n.* a student who attends classes at a boarding school or college but who does not live at the school.

day·time /ˈdāˌtīm/ ▸*n.* the time of the day between sunrise and sunset: *she was alone* ***in the daytime*** | [as *adj.*] *a daytime telephone number.*

day-to-day ▸*adj.* [*attrib.*] happening regularly every day: *the day-to-day management of the classroom.* ■ ordinary; everyday: *our day-to-day domestic life.* ■ short-term; without consideration for the future: *the struggle for day-to-day survival.* ■ *Sports* (of an injured player) not playing owing to a minor injury that is being treated and evaluated on a daily basis: *their shortstop has an ankle sprain and is listed as day-to-day*
▸*n.* [in *sing.*] an ordinary, everyday routine: *they have come to escape the day-to-day.*
▸*adv.* on a daily basis: *the information to be traded is determined day-to-day.*

Day·ton /ˈdātn/ a city in western Ohio; pop. 166,179. It was the home of aviation pioneers Wilbur and Orville Wright and is still a center of aerospace research.

Day·to·na Beach /dāˈtōnə/ a resort city in northeastern Florida, on the Atlantic coast; pop. 61,921.

day trad·ing ▸*n.* the buying and selling of securities on the same day, often online, on the basis of small, short-term price fluctuations. —**day-trade** *v.* —**day trad·er** *n.*

day trip ▸*n.* a journey or excursion completed in one day. —**day-trip·per** (or **day trip·per**) *n.*

day·wear /ˈdāˌwe(ə)r/ ▸*n.* articles of casual clothing suitable for informal or everyday occasions.

day·work /ˈdāˌwərk/ ▸*n.* casual work paid for on a daily basis. —**day·work·er** *n.* .

daze /dāz/ ▸*v.* [*trans.*] (usu. **be dazed**) make (someone) unable to think or react properly; stupefy; bewilder: *she was dazed by his revelations* | [as *adj.*] (**dazed**) *he staggered home dazed and confused.*
▸*n.* [in *sing.*] a state of stunned confusion or bewilderment: *he was walking around* ***in a daze.*** ▷Middle English: back-formation from *dazed* (adjective), from Old Norse *dasathr* 'weary'; compare with Swedish *dasa* 'lie idle.' —**daz·ed·ly** /ˈdāzidlē/ *adv.*

da·zi·bao /ˌdädzēˈbou/ ▸*n.* (*pl.* same) (in the People's Republic of China) a wall poster written in large characters. ▷Chinese, from *dà* 'big' + *zi* 'character' + *bào* 'newspaper or poster.'

daz·zle /ˈdazəl/ ▸*v.* [*trans.*] (of a bright light) blind (a person) temporarily: *she was dazzled by the headlights.* ■ *figurative* amaze or overwhelm (someone) with a particular impressive quality: *I was dazzled by the beauty and breadth of the exhibition.* ■ [*intrans.*] *archaic* (of the eyes) be affected by a bright light: *my eyes dazzled and I could not move.*
▸*n.* brightness that confuses someone's vision temporarily: [in *sing.*] *a dazzle of green and red spotlights.* ▷late 15th cent. (in the sense 'be dazzled'): frequentative of the verb DAZE. —**daz·zle·ment** *n.*

daz·zler /ˈdaz(ə)lər/ ▸*n.* a person or thing that dazzles, in particular a person who is overwhelmingly impressive or skillful.

daz·zling /ˈdaz(ə)liNG/ ▸*adj.* extremely bright, esp. so as to blind the eyes temporarily: *the sunlight was dazzling* | *figurative a dazzling smile.* ■ *figurative* extremely impressive, beautiful, or skillful: *a dazzling display of football.* —**daz·zling·ly** *adv.*

Db ▸*symbol* the chemical element dubnium.

dB ▸*abbr.* decibel(s).

dba (also **d/b/a**) ▸*abbr.* ■ doing business as.

DBMS ▸*abbr.* database management system.

DBS ▸*abbr.* ■ direct broadcasting by satellite. ■ direct-broadcast satellite.

dbx ▸*n. trademark* electronic circuitry designed to increase the dynamic range of reproduced sound and reduce noise in the system. ▷1970s: from DB 'decibel' + *x* (representing *expander*).

DC ▸*abbr.* ■ *Music* da capo. ■ direct current. ■ District of Columbia: *Washington, DC.* ■ Doctor of Chiropractic.

DCC ▸*abbr.* ■ digital compact cassette.

DCL ▸*abbr.* Doctor of Civil Law.

DCM ▸*abbr.* (in the UK) Distinguished Conduct Medal, awarded for bravery.

DD ▸*abbr.* ■ Department of Defense (on forms and documents): *a DD 214.* ■ *Military* dishonorable discharge. ■ Doctor of Divinity.

D-Day ▸*n.* the day (June 6, 1944) in World War II on which Allied forces invaded northern France by means of beach landings in Normandy. ■ the day on which an important operation is to begin or a change to take effect: *it's D-day at the Websters', as Sally gives Kevin an ultimatum.* ▷from *D* for *day* + DAY. Compare with H-HOUR.

DDC (also **ddC**) ▸*abbr.* dideoxycytidine.

DDE ▸*n. Computing* a standard allowing data to be shared between different programs. ▷1980s: abbreviation of *Dynamic Data Exchange.*

DDI (also **ddI**) ▸*abbr.* ■ dideoxyinosine.

DDoS (also **DDOS**) ▸*abbr.* distributed denial of service, the intentional paralyzing of a computer network by flooding it with data sent simultaneously from many individual computers: [as *modifier*] *so-called zombies which are used to stage DDOS attacks.*

DDR ▸*abbr.* German Democratic Republic. ▷abbreviation of German *Deutsche Demokratische Republik.*

D.D.S. ▸*abbr.* ■ Doctor of Dental Science. ■ Doctor of Dental Surgery.

DDT ▸*abbr.* dichlorodiphenyltrichloroethane, a synthetic organic compound introduced in the 1940s and used as an insecticide. Like other chlorinated aromatic hydrocarbons, DDT tends to persist in the environment and become concentrated in animals at the head of the food chain. Its use is now banned in many countries. • Chem. formula: $CCl_3CH(C_6H_4Cl)_2$.

DE ▸*abbr.* ■ *Football* defensive end. ■ Delaware (in official postal use).

de- ▸*prefix* **1** (forming verbs and their derivatives) down; away: *descend* | *deduct.* ■ completely: *denude* | *derelict.* **2** (added to verbs and their derivatives) denoting removal or reversal: *deaerate* | *de-ice.* **3** denoting formation from: *deverbal.* ▷from Latin *de* 'off, from'; sense 2 via Old French *des-* from Latin *dis-*.

D

de·ac·ces·sion /ˌdēakˈseSHən/ ▸*v.* [*trans.*] officially remove (an item) from the listed holdings of a library, museum, or art gallery, typically in order to sell it to raise funds.
▸*n.* the disposal of books, works of art, or other items in this way.

dea·con /ˈdēkən/ ▸*n.* (in Catholic, Anglican, and Orthodox churches) an ordained minister of an order ranking below that of priest. ■ (in some Protestant churches) a lay officer appointed to assist a minister, esp. in secular affairs. ■ *historical* (in the early church) an appointed minister of charity.
▸*v.* [*trans.*] appoint or ordain as a deacon. ▷Old English *diacon*, via ecclesiastical Latin from Greek *diakonos* 'servant' (in ecclesiastical Greek 'Christian minister'). —**dea·con·ship** /-ˌSHip/ *n.*

dea·con·ess /ˈdēkənis/ ▸*n.* (in the early church and some modern churches) a woman with duties similar to those of a deacon.

de·ac·ti·vate /dēˈaktəvāt/ ▸*v.* **1** [*trans.*] make (something, typically technical equipment or a virus) inactive by disconnecting or destroying it: *the switch deactivates the alarm.* **2** [*trans.*] *Military* remove from active duty. —**de·ac·ti·va·tion** /dēˌaktəˈvāSHən/ *n.* —**de·ac·ti·va·tor** /-vātər/ *n.*

dead /ded/ ▸*adj.* **1** no longer alive: *a dead body* | [as *complement*] *he was shot dead by terrorists.* ■ (of a part of the body) having lost sensation; numb. ■ having or displaying no emotion, sympathy, or sensitivity: *a cold, dead voice.* ■ no longer current, relevant, or important: *pollution had become a dead issue.* ■ devoid of living things: *a dead planet.* ■ resembling death: *a dead faint.* ■ (of a place or time) characterized by a lack of activity or excitement: *Brussels isn't dead after dark, if you know where to look.* ■ (of money) not financially productive. ■ (of sound) without resonance; dull. ■ (of a color) not glossy or bright. ■ (of a piece of equipment) no longer functioning, esp. because of a fault: *the phone had gone dead.* ■ (of an electric circuit or conductor) carrying or transmitting no current: *the batteries are dead.* ■ no longer burning: *the fire had been dead for some days.* ■ (of air or water) not circulating; stagnant. ■ (of a glass or bottle) empty or no longer being used. ■ (of the ball in a game) out of play. See also DEAD BALL. ■ (of a playing field, ball, or other surface) lacking springiness or bounce. **2** [*attrib.*] complete; absolute: *we sat in dead silence.*
▸*adv.* [often as *submodifier*] absolutely; completely: *you're dead right* | *he was dead against the idea.* ■ exactly: *they arrived dead on time.* ■ straight; directly: *red flares were seen dead ahead.* ■ *Brit., informal* very: *omelets are dead easy to prepare.*
▸*n.* [as *plural n.*] (**the dead**) those who have died. ▷Old English *dēad*, of Germanic origin: related to Dutch *dood* and German *tot*, also to DIE[1]. —**dead·ness** *n.*
▸*PHRASES* □ **dead and buried** over; finished: *the incident is dead and buried.* □ **(as) dead as a** (or **the**) **dodo** see DODO. □ **(as) dead as a doornail** see DOORNAIL. □ **dead from the neck up** *informal* stupid. □ **dead in the water** (of a ship) unable to move. ■ *figurative* unable to function effectively: *the economy is dead in the water.* □ **dead meat** *informal* in serious trouble: *if anyone finds out, you're dead meat.* □ **the dead of night** the quietest, darkest part of the night.

□ **the dead of winter** the coldest part of winter. □ **dead on** exactly right: *her judgment was dead on.* □ **dead on arrival** used to describe a person who is declared dead immediately upon arrival at a hospital. ■ *figurative* (of an idea, etc.) declared ineffective without ever having been put into effect: *why are people pronouncing the plan dead on arrival in the legislature?* □ **dead on one's feet** *informal* extremely tired. □ **dead set against** *informal* strongly opposed to: *they were dead set against seeing any more open spaces divided up.* □ **dead to rights** *informal* in the act of doing something wrong; red-handed: *he had me dead to rights, so I meekly suffered the rebuke.* □ **dead to the world** *informal* fast asleep. □ **from the dead** from a state of death: *Christ rose from the dead.* ■ *figurative* from a period of obscurity or inactivity: *the cartoon brought animation back from the dead.* □ **make a dead set at** see SET². □ **over my dead body** see BODY. □ **wouldn't be seen** (or **caught**) **dead** *informal* used to express strong dislike for a particular thing: *James Bond wouldn't be caught dead wearing a paper napkin bib.*

dead air ▸*n.* an unintended interruption of the video or audio signal during a television or radio broadcast.

dead ball ▸*n. Sports* a ball that has gone out of play or is declared to be out of play.

dead-ball line ▸*n. Soccer* the part of the goal line to either side of the goal.

dead·beat /ˈdedˌbēt/ ▸*n. informal* a person who tries to evade paying debts. ■ (also **deadbeat dad**) a man who avoids paying child support. ■ an idle, feckless, or disreputable person.
▸*adj.* (of a clock escapement or other mechanism) without recoil.

dead·bolt /ˈdedˌbōlt/ ▸*n.* a bolt engaged by turning a knob or key, rather than by spring action.

dead cat bounce ▸*n. Stock Market* a temporary recovery in share prices after a substantial fall, caused by speculators buying in order to cover their positions.

dead cen·ter ▸*n.* the position of a crank when it is in line with the connecting rod and not exerting torque.

dead duck ▸*n. informal* **1** an unsuccessful or useless person or thing: *totalitarianism is a dead duck, he says.* **2** a person who is beyond help; one who is doomed: *if they put their finger on Billy, he's a dead duck.* ▷from the old saying "never waste powder on a dead duck."

dead·en /ˈdedn/ ▸*v.* [*trans.*] make (a noise or sensation) less intense: *ether was used to deaden the pain.* ■ deprive of the power of sensation: *diabetes can deaden the nerve endings.* ■ deprive of force or vitality; stultify: *the syllabus has deadened the teaching process* | [as *adj.*] (**deadening**) *a deadening routine.* ■ make (someone) insensitive to something: *laughter might deaden us to the moral issue.* —**dead·en·er** *n.*

dead end ▸*n.* an end of a road or passage from which no exit is possible; a cul-de-sac: *the path* ***came to a dead end.*** ■ a road or passage having such an end. ■ a situation offering no prospects of progress or development: [as *adj.*] *a dead-end job.*
▸*v.* [*intrans.*] (**dead-end**) (of a road or passage) come to a dead end: *he kept walking, until the corridor dead-ended.*

dead·eye /ˈdedˌī/ ▸*n.* **1** *Sailing* a circular wooden block with a groove around the circumference to take a lanyard, used singly or in pairs to tighten a shroud. **2** *informal* an expert marksman.

dead·fall /ˈdedˌfôl/ ▸*n.* **1** a trap consisting of a heavy weight positioned to fall on an animal. **2** a tangled mass of fallen trees and brush. ■ a fallen tree.

dead hand ▸*n.* an undesirable persisting influence: *the dead hand of government control.* ■ *Law* see MORTMAIN.

dead·head /ˈdedˌhed/ (also **dead-head**) ▸*n.* **1** (**Deadhead**) a fan and follower of the rock group The Grateful Dead: [as *adj.*] *the Deadhead hard core shadows the band, selling tie-dyes and beads.* **2** *informal* a commercial carrier with no paying passengers or freight on a trip. ■ a passenger or member of an audience with a free ticket. ■ *informal* a boring or unenterprising person. **3** a sunken or partially submerged log.
▸*v.* **1** [*intrans.*] *informal* (of a commercial driver, etc.) complete a trip without paying passengers or freight: *trucks deadheading into California to pick up outbound loads.* ■ ride (in a plane or other vehicle) without paying for a ticket: *he calls his airline and gets a seat on the red-eye to deadhead to Boston.* **2** [*trans.*] remove dead flowerheads from (a plant) to encourage further blooming.

dead heat ▸*n.* a situation in or result of a race in which two or more competitors are exactly even.
▸*v.* [*intrans.*] (**dead-heat**) run or finish a race exactly even.

dead lan·guage ▸*n.* a language no longer in everyday spoken use, such as Latin.

dead let·ter ▸*n.* **1** a law or treaty that has not been repealed but is ineffectual or defunct in practice. ■ *figurative* a thing that is impractical or obsolete: *theoretical reasoning is a dead letter to a child.* **2** a letter that is undeliverable and unreturnable, typically one with an incorrect address.

dead lift ▸*n. Weightlifting* a lift made from a standing position, without the use of a bench or other equipment.

dead·light /ˈdedˌlīt/ ▸*n.* **1** a protective cover or shutter fitted over a porthole or window on a ship. **2** a skylight designed not to be opened.

dead·line /ˈdedˌlīn/ ▸*n.* **1** the latest time or date by which something should be completed: *the deadline for submissions is February 5th.* **2** *historical* a line drawn around a prison beyond which prisoners were liable to be shot.

dead load ▸*n.* the intrinsic weight of a structure or vehicle, excluding the weight of passengers or goods. Often contrasted with LIVE LOAD.

dead·lock /ˈdedˌläk/ ▸*n.* **1** [in *sing.*] a situation, typically one involving opposing parties, in which no progress can be made: *an attempt to* ***break the deadlock.*** **2** British term for DEADBOLT.
▸*v.* [*trans.*] **1** [*intrans.*] (usu. **be deadlocked**) cause (a situation or opposing parties) to come to a point where no progress can be made because of fundamental disagreement: *the jurors were deadlocked on six charges.* ■ cause (a contest or game) to be in a tie: *with the score still deadlocked at three-three.* **2** *Brit.* secure (a door) with a deadlock.

dead loss ▸*n.* a venture or situation that produces no profit whatsoever. ■ *informal, chiefly Brit.* a person or thing that is completely useless.

dead·ly /ˈdedlē/ ▸*adj.* (**-li·er**, **-li·est**) causing or able to cause death: *a deadly weapon.* ■ filled with hate: *his voice was cold and deadly.* ■ (typically in the context of shooting or sports) extremely accurate, effective, or skillful: *his aim is deadly.* ■ *informal* extremely boring: *he's well meaning, but so utterly deadly.* ■ [*attrib.*] complete; total: *she was in deadly earnest.*
▸*adv.* [as *submodifier*] in a way resembling or suggesting death; as if dead: *her skin was deadly pale.* ■ extremely: *a deadly serious remark.* ▷Old English *dēadlīc* 'mortal, in danger of death' (see DEAD, -LY¹). —**dead·li·ness** *n.*

dead·ly night·shade ▸*n.* a poisonous bushy Eurasian plant with drooping purple flowers and black cherrylike fruit. Also called BELLADONNA. • *Atropa belladonna*, family Solanaceae.

dead·ly sin ▸*n.* (in Christian tradition) a sin regarded as leading to damnation, esp. one of a traditional list of seven. See SEVEN DEADLY SINS.

dead·man /ˈdedˌman/ ▸*n.* an object buried in or secured to the ground for the purpose of providing anchorage or leverage.

dead man's fin·gers (also **dead-man's-fin·gers**) ▸*plural n.* **1** a soft coral that has spongy lobes stiffened by calcareous spines. When found washed up on the beach it is said to resemble the fingers of a corpse. • *Alcyonium digitatum*, order Alcyonacea. **2** a fungus that produces clumps of dull black, irregular, fingerlike fruiting bodies at the bases of dead tree stumps in both Eurasia and North America. • *Xylaria polymorpha*, family Xylariaceae, phylum Ascomycota. **3** *informal* the fingerlike divisions of a lobster's or crab's gills.

dead-man's float ▸*n.* a floating position, often used by beginning swimmers, in which a person lies face down in the water with arms outstretched or extended forward and legs extended backward.

dead man's han·dle (also **dead man's pedal**) ▸*n.* (esp. in a diesel or electric train) a lever that acts as a safety device by shutting off power when not held in place by the driver.

dead march ▸*n.* a slow, solemn piece of music suitable to accompany a funeral procession.

dead-net·tle ▸*n.* an Old World plant of the mint family, with leaves that resemble those of a nettle but lack stinging hairs. • *Lamium* and related genera, family Labiatae: several species, including the common **white dead-nettle** (*L. album*).

dead·pan /ˈdedˌpan/ ▸*adj.* deliberately impassive or expressionless: *answers his phone in a deadpan tone* | *deadpan humor.*
▸*adv.* in a deadpan manner.
▸*v.* (**-panned**, **-pan·ning**) [with *direct speech*] say something amusing while affecting a serious manner: *"I'm an undercover dentist," he deadpanned.*

dead reck·on·ing ▸*n.* the process of calculating one's position, esp. at sea, by estimating the direction and distance traveled rather than by using landmarks, astronomical observations, or electronic navigation methods.

dead ring·er ▸*n.* a person or thing that seems exactly like someone or something else: *he is* ***a dead ringer for*** *his late papa.*

dead·rise /ˈdedˌrīz/ ▸*n.* the vertical distance between a line horizontal to the keel of a vessel and its chine.

Dead Sea a salt lake or inland sea in the Jordan valley, on the Israel–Jordan border. Its surface is 1,300 feet (400 m) below sea level.

Dead Sea scrolls a collection of Hebrew and Aramaic manuscripts discovered in pottery storage jars in caves near Qumran between 1947 and 1956. Thought to have been hidden by the Essenes or a similar Jewish sect shortly before the revolt against Roman rule AD 66–70, the scrolls include texts of many books of the Bible; they are some 1,000 years older than previously known versions.

dead set ▸*n.* see SET² (sense 2).

dead·stick land·ing /ˈdedˌstik/ ▸*n.* an unpowered landing of an aircraft.

dead time ▸*n.* time in which someone or something is inactive or unable to act productively. ■ *Physics* the period after the recording of a particle or pulse when a detector is unable to record another.

dead weight (also **dead·weight**) ▸*n.* the weight of an inert person or thing: *the net was a dead weight on his shoulders.* ■ a heavy or oppressive burden: *the past was just so much dead weight, excess baggage.* ■ the total weight of cargo, stores, etc., that a ship carries or can carry at a particular draft. ■ another term for DEAD LOAD. ■ *Farming* animals sold by the estimated weight of salable meat that they will yield. ■ [usu. as *adj.*] *Economics* losses incurred because of the inefficient allocation of resources, esp. through taxation or restriction: ***a dead-weight burden.***

dead white Eu·ro·pe·an male (also **dead white male**) ▸*n. informal* a writer, philosopher, or other significant figure whose importance and talents may have been exaggerated by virtue of his belonging to a historically dominant gender and ethnic group.

Dead·wood /ˈdedˌwo͝od/ a city in western South Dakota, in the Black Hills, known for its 1870s gold rush and Boot Hill cemetery; pop. 1,830.

dead·wood /ˈdedˌwo͝od/ ▸*n.* a branch or part of a tree that is dead. ■ *figurative* people or things that are no longer useful or productive.

dead zone ▸*n.* an area of the ocean that is depleted of oxygen, frequently due to pollution.

de·aer·ate /dēˈe(ə)rāt/ ▸*v.* [*trans.*] (usu. **be deaerated**) partially or completely remove dissolved air from (something): *the electrolyte was deaerated by purging it with argon.* —**de·aer·a·tion** /ˌdē-erˈāsʜən/ *n.*

deaf /def/ ▸*adj.* lacking the power of hearing or having impaired hearing: [as *plural n.*] (**the deaf**) *subtitles for the deaf.* ■ unwilling or unable to hear or pay attention to something: *she is* ***deaf to*** *all advice.* ▷Old English *dēaf*, of Germanic origin; related to Dutch *doof* and German *taub*, from an Indo-European root shared by Greek *tuphlos* 'blind.' —**deaf·ness** *n.*
▸***PHRASES*** □ (**as**) **deaf as a post** completely or extremely deaf. □ **fall on deaf ears** (of a statement or request) be ignored. □ **turn a deaf ear** refuse to listen or respond to a statement or request.

deaf aid ▸*n. Brit.* a hearing aid.

deaf-blind ▸*adj.* having a severe impairment of both hearing and vision.

deaf·en /ˈdefən/ ▸*v.* [*trans.*] (usu. **be deafened**) cause (someone) to lose the power of hearing permanently or temporarily: *we were deafened by the explosion.* ■ (of a loud noise) overwhelm (someone) with sound: *the roar of the water deafened them.* ■ (**deafen someone to**) (of a sound) cause someone to be unaware of (other sounds): *the noise deafened him to Ron's approach.*

deaf·en·ing /ˈdefənɪɴɢ/ ▸*adj.* (of a noise) so loud as to make it impossible to hear anything else: *the music reached a deafening crescendo.* —**deaf·en·ing·ly** *adv.*

de·af·fer·en·ta·tion /dēˌafərenˈtāsʜən/ ▸*n. Biology* the interruption or destruction of the afferent connections of nerve cells, performed esp. in animal experiments to demonstrate the spontaneity of locomotor movement. —**de·af·fer·ent·ed** /dēˈafəˌrentid/ *adj.*

deaf-mute ▸*n. chiefly offensive* a person who is both deaf and unable to speak.

▸*adj. chiefly offensive* (of a person) both deaf and unable to speak. ■ of or relating to such people.

USAGE In modern use, **deaf-mute** has acquired offensive connotations (implying, wrongly, that such people are without the capacity for communication). It should be avoided in favor of other terms such as *profoundly deaf*.
See also **usage** at MUTE.

deal[1] /dēl/ ▸*v.* (*past* and *past part.* **dealt** /delt/) **1** [*trans.*] distribute (cards) in an orderly rotation to the players for a game or round: *the cards were dealt for the last hand* | [with *two objs.*] | *figurative fate dealt her a different hand.* ■ (**deal someone in**) include a new player in a card game by giving them cards. ■ distribute or mete out (something) to a person or group: *the funds raised were* **dealt out to** *the needy.* **2** [*intrans.*] take part in commercial trading of a particular commodity: *directors were prohibited from* **dealing in** *the company's shares.* ■ *figurative* be concerned with: *a movie that* **deals in** *ideas and issues.* ■ *informal* buy and sell illegal drugs: [*trans.*] *Frankie started dealing cocaine.* **3** [*intrans.*] (**deal with**) take measures concerning (someone or something), esp. with the intention of putting something right: *the government had been unable to deal with the economic crisis.* ■ cope with (a difficult person or situation): *you'll have to find a way of dealing with those feelings.* ■ [with *adverbial*] treat (someone) in a particular way: *life had dealt harshly with her.* ■ have relations with (a person or organization), esp. in a commercial context: *the bank deals directly with the private sector.* ■ take or have as a subject; discuss: *the novel deals with several different topics.* **4** [with *two objs.*] inflict (a blow) on (someone or something): *hopes of an economic recovery were dealt another blow.*
▸*n.* **1** an agreement entered into by two or more parties for their mutual benefit, esp. in a business or political context: *the band signed a major recording deal.* ■ an attractive price on a commodity for a purchaser; a bargain: *we've got great deals on the latest camcorders.* ■ [with *adj.*] a particular form of treatment given or received: *working mothers get a bad deal.* **2** a significant but unspecified amount of something: *he lost* **a great deal of** *blood.* **3** [in *sing.*] the process of distributing the cards to players in a card game. ■ a player's turn to distribute cards. ■ the round of play following this. ■ the set of hands dealt to the players. ▷Old English *dǣlan* 'divide,' 'participate,' of Germanic origin; related to Dutch *deel* and German *Teil* 'part' (noun), also to DOLE[1]. The sense 'divide' gave rise to 'distribute,' hence senses 1 and 4 of the *verb*; the sense 'participate' gave rise to 'have dealings with,' hence senses 2 and 3 of the verb.
▸*PHRASES* □ **a big deal** *informal* [usu. with *negative*] a thing considered important: *they don't make a big deal out of minor irritations.* ■ an important person: *Sam Kinison became a big deal.* ■ (**big deal**) used to express one's contempt for something regarded as impressive or important by another person. □ **a raw** (or **rough**) **deal** *informal* a situation in which someone receives unfair or harsh treatment. □ **a good** (or **great**) **deal** a large amount: *I don't know a great deal about politics.* ■ to a considerable extent: *she had gotten to know him a good deal better.* □ **cut a deal** *informal* make an agreement: *he had gone to the board of directors with his new robot design and cut a deal.* □ **it's a deal** *informal* used to express one's assent to an agreement.

deal[2] ▸*n.* fir or pine wood, esp. when sawn into planks of a standard size. ■ a plank of such wood. ▷Middle English: from Middle Low German and Middle Dutch *dele* 'plank.'

de-al·co·hol·ize /dē'alkəhô,līz/ ▸*v.* [*trans.*] [usu. as *adj.*] (**de-alcoholized**) remove the alcohol from (a normally alcoholic drink): *de-alcoholized beer.*

deal·er /'dēlər/ ▸*n.* **1** a person or business that buys and sells goods: *a car dealer.* ■ a person who buys and sells shares, securities, or other financial assets as a principal (rather than as a broker or agent). See also BROKER-DEALER. ■ *informal* a person who buys and sells drugs: *posed as a dealer willing to buy heroin.* **2** the player who distributes the cards at the start of a game or hand. **—deal·er·ship** /-,SHip/ *n.* (in sense 1).

deal·fish /'dēl,fiSH/ ▸*n.* (*pl.* same or **-fish·es**) a slender silvery fish with a dorsal fin running the length of the body, living in the northeastern Atlantic. • *Trachipterus arcticus*, family Trachipteridae. ▷mid 19th cent.: from DEAL[2] in the sense 'board' (with reference to its shape) + FISH[1].

de·a·lign /,dēə'līn/ ▸*v.* [*intrans.*] (of a voter) withdraw allegiance to a political party. **—de·a·lign·ment** *n.*

deal·ing /'dēliNG/ ▸*n.* **1** (usu. **dealings**) a business relation or transaction: *they had dealings with an insurance company.* ■ a personal connection or association with someone: *my dealings with David consisted of giving him his late-night formula.* ■ the activity of buying and selling a particular commodity: *car dealing* | *drug dealing.* **2** the particular way in which someone behaves toward others: *fair dealing came naturally to him.*

de·al·lo·cate /dē'alə,kāt/ ▸*v.* [*trans.*] *Computing* return (allocated memory) to the store of available RAM. **—de·al·lo·ca·tion** /dē,alə'kāSHən/ *n.*

dealt /delt/ ▸ past participle of DEAL[1].

de·am·i·na·tion /dē,ami'nāSHən/ ▸*n. Biochemistry* the removal of an amino group from an amino acid or other compound. **—de·am·i·nat·ed** /dē'amə,nātid/ *adj.*

Dean[1] /dēn/, Dizzy (1911–74), U.S. baseball player and broadcaster; born *Jay Hanna Dean.* He pitched for the St. Louis Cardinals 1932–37 and the Chicago Cubs 1938–41. Baseball Hall of Fame (1953).

Dean[2], Howard (1948–), U.S. politician and physician. After serving as governor of Vermont 1881–2003, he became a candidate for the Democratic presidential nomination, running a campaign that energized young people, especially because of his opposition to the war in Iraq, and raised a record amount of money over the Internet.

Dean[3], James (Byron) (1931–55), U.S. actor. Although he starred in only three movies before dying in a car accident, he became a cult figure closely identified with the title role of *Rebel Without a Cause* (1955), symbolizing for many the disaffected youth of the postwar era. Other movies: *East of Eden* (1955) and *Giant* (1956).

James Dean

Dean[4], John (Wesley III) (1938–), U.S. political adviser. After serving as presidential counsel to Richard Nixon, he became the chief witness in the Watergate hearings 1973–74, was convicted of conspiracy, and served four months in prison. He wrote *Blind Ambition* (1976).

dean[1] /dēn/ ▸*n.* **1** the head of a college or university faculty or department: *the dean of the law school.* ■ a college or university official, esp. one with disciplinary and advisory functions: *the dean of students.* ■ the leader or senior member of a group: *the dean of California winemakers.* **2** the head of the chapter of a cathedral or collegiate church. ▷Middle English: from Old French *deien*, from late Latin *decanus* 'chief of a group of ten,' from *decem* 'ten.' Compare with DOYEN.

dean[2] ▸*n.* variant spelling of DENE[1].

dean·er·y /'dēnərē/ ▸*n.* (*pl.* **-er·ies**) **1** *Brit.* the group of parishes presided over by a rural dean. **2** the official residence of a dean. ■ the position or office of a dean.

dean's list ▸*n.* a list of students recognized for academic achievement during a semester by the dean of the college they attend.

dear /di(ə)r/ ▸*adj.* **1** regarded with deep affection; cherished by someone: *a dear friend* | *he is very* **dear to** *me.* ■ used in speech as a way of addressing a person in a polite way: *Martin, my dear fellow.* ■ used as part of the polite introduction to a letter, esp. in a formula denoting the degree of formality involved: *Dear Sir or Madam.* ■ endearing; sweet: *a* **dear little** *puppy.* **2** expensive. ■ (of money) available as a loan only at a high rate of interest.
▸*n.* used as an affectionate or friendly form of address: *don't you worry, dear.* ■ a sweet or endearing person.
▸*adv.* at a high cost: *they buy property cheaply and sell dear.*
▸*exclam.* used in expressions of surprise, dismay, or sympathy: *oh dear, I've upset you.* ▷Old English *dēore*, of Germanic origin; related to Dutch *dier* 'beloved,' also to Dutch *duur* and German *teuer* 'expensive.' **—dear·ness** *n.*
▸*PHRASE* □ **for dear life** see LIFE.

Dear·born /'di(ə)r,bôrn; -bərn/ a city in southeastern Michigan, southwest of Detroit, home to the Ford Motor Company and to the Henry Ford Museum and Greenfield Village; pop. 97,775.

dear·est /'di(ə)rist/ ▸*adj.* **1** most loved or cherished: *one of my dearest friends.* **2** most expensive: *beer is dearest in Germany.*
▸*n.* used as an affectionate form of address to a much-loved person: *you make me so happy, dearest.* ■ a much-loved person: *I was going to miss my dearest.*

dear·ie /'di(ə)rē/ ▸*n.* (*pl.* **-ies**) *informal, chiefly Brit.* used as a friendly or condescending form of address.

Dear John let·ter (also **Dear John**) ▸*n. informal* a letter from a woman to a man, esp. a serviceman, terminating a personal relationship: *a young officer gets his Dear John letter.*

dear·ly /'di(ə)rlē/ ▸*adv.* **1** very much: *he loved his parents dearly.* **2** with much loss or suffering; at great cost: *freedom to worship our religion has been bought dearly.*

dearth /dərTH/ ▸*n.* [in *sing.*] a scarcity or lack of something: *there is* **a dearth of** *evidence.* See note at LACK. ▷Middle English *derthe* (originally in the sense 'shortage and dearness of food') (see DEAR, -TH[2]).

death /deTH/ ▸*n.* the action or fact of dying or being killed; the end of the life of a person or organism: *I don't believe in life after death* | [as *adj.*] *a death sentence.* ■ an instance of a person or an animal dying: *there's been a death in his family.* ■ the state of being dead: *even in death, she was beautiful.* ■ the permanent ending of vital processes in a cell or tissue. ■ (**Death**) [in *sing.*] the personification of the power that destroys life, often represented in art and literature as a skeleton or an old man holding a scythe. ■ [in *sing.*] *figurative* the destruction or permanent end of something: *the death of her hopes.* ■ *figurative, informal* a damaging or destructive state of affairs: *to be driven to a dance by one's father would be social death.* ▷Old English *dēath*, of Germanic origin; related to Dutch *dood* and German *Tod*, also to DIE[1]. **—death·like** /-,līk/ *adj.*
▸*PHRASES* □ **at death's door** (esp. in hyperbolic use) so ill that one might die. □ **be the death of** (often used hyperbolically or humorously) cause someone's death: *you'll be the death of me with all your questions.* □ **be in at the death** be present when a hunted animal is caught and killed. ■ be present when something fails or comes to an end. □ **catch one's death (of cold)** *informal* catch a severe cold or chill. □ **do someone to death** kill someone. □ **do something to death** perform or repeat something so frequently that it becomes tediously familiar: *a subject that has been done to death by generations of painters.* □ **a fate worse than death** a terrible experience, esp. that of seduction or rape. □ **like death warmed over** (or **up**) *informal* extremely tired or ill. □ **a matter of life and death** see LIFE. □ **put someone to death** kill someone, esp. with official sanction. □ **till** (or **until**) **death us do part** for as long as both persons in a couple live. [from the marriage service in the *Book of Common Prayer.*] □ **to death** used of a particular action or process that results in someone's death: *he was stabbed to death.* ■ used to emphasize the extreme nature of a specific action, feeling, or state of mind: *I'm sick to death of you.* □ **to the death** until dead: *a fight to the death.*

death ad·der ▸*n.* a venomous Australian snake that has a thin wormlike tail, which it uses to lure birds and other prey. • Genus *Acanthophis*, family Elapidae: three species, in particular *A. antarcticus.*

death·bed /'deTH,bed/ ▸*n.* the bed where someone is dying or has died. ■ used in reference to the time when someone is dying: *she visited him on his deathbed* | [as *adj.*] *a deathbed confession.*

death ben·e·fit ▸*n.* the amount paid to a beneficiary upon the death of an insured person. Also called FACE AMOUNT.

death blow ▸*n.* an impact or stroke that causes death. ■ *figurative* an event, circumstance, or action that ends something abruptly: *it was Galileo Galilei who* **dealt the death blow to** *the geocentric theory.*

death camp ▸*n.* a prison camp, esp. one for political prisoners or prisoners of war, in which many die from poor conditions and treatment or from mass execution.

death cer·tif·i·cate ▸*n.* an official statement, signed by a physician, of the cause, date, and place of a person's death.

death-deal·ing ▸*adj.* capable of causing death: *death-dealing drugs.*

death house ▸*n. informal* the building in which prisoners are kept in preparation for execution.

death in·stinct ▸*n. Psychoanalysis* an innate desire for self-annihilation, thought to be manifest in the conservative and regressive tendency of the psyche to reduce tension. Compare with LIFE INSTINCT.

death knell ▸*n.* [in *sing.*] the tolling of a bell to mark someone's death. ■ *figurative* an event that heralds the end or destruction of something: *the chaos may sound the death knell for the peace plan.*

death·less /ˈdeTHlis/ ▸*adj. chiefly poetic/literary, humorous* immortal: *deathless beauty | he died before his song could be recorded, but his compositions are deathless.* **—death·less·ness** *n.*

death·ly /ˈdeTHlē/ ▸*adj.* (**-li·er, -li·est**) resembling or suggestive of death: *a deathly hush fell over the breakfast table* | [as *submodifier*] *she felt deathly cold.* ■ *archaic, poetic/literary* of, relating to, or causing death: *an eagle carrying a snake in its deathly grasp.*

death mask ▸*n.* a plaster cast taken of a dead person's face, used to make a mask or model.

death met·al ▸*n.* a form of heavy metal music using lyrics preoccupied with death, suffering, and destruction.

death pen·al·ty ▸*n.* the punishment of execution, administered to someone legally convicted of a capital crime.

death rate ▸*n.* the ratio of deaths to the population of a particular area during a particular period of time, usually calculated as the number of deaths per one thousand people per year.

death rat·tle ▸*n.* a gurgling sound heard in a dying person's throat.

death row /ˈrō/ ▸*n.* a prison block or section for prisoners sentenced to death: *a convicted killer* ***on death row.***

death sen·tence ▸*n. Law* a sentence to be put to death for a capital crime. ■ *figurative* a disastrous result or outcome: *the market crash was a death sentence for many dot-coms.*

death's head ▸*n.* a human skull as a symbol of mortality.

death's-head hawk moth ▸*n.* a large dark European hawk moth with a skull-like marking on the thorax and a very large caterpillar. • *Acherontia atropos*, family Sphingidae.

death song ▸*n.* a song sung before or after someone's death or to commemorate the dead.

death squad ▸*n.* an armed paramilitary group formed to kill particular people, esp. political opponents.

death tax ▸*n.* another term for ESTATE TAX, INHERITANCE TAX.

death toll ▸*n.* the number of deaths resulting from a particular cause, esp. an accident, battle, or natural disaster.

death trap ▸*n.* a place, structure, or vehicle that is potentially dangerous: *the theaters were often death traps.*

Death Val·ley a deep arid desert basin below sea level in southeastern California and southwestern Nevada, the hottest and driest part of North America. It contains the lowest point in the U.S. at Badwater, which is 282 feet (86 m) below sea level.

death war·rant ▸*n.* an official order for the execution of a condemned person: *figurative in making his announcement he has signed his political death warrant.*

death·watch /ˈdeTH,wäCH/ ▸*n.* **1** a vigil kept beside a dead or dying individual. ■ a guard set over a person due for execution. **2** (also **deathwatch beetle**) a small beetle with larvae that bore into dead wood and structural timbers, causing considerable damage. The adult makes a sound like a watch ticking that was formerly believed to portend death. • *Xestobium rufovillosum*, family Anobiidae.

death wish ▸*n.* a desire for someone's death, esp. an unconscious desire for one's own death. Compare with DEATH INSTINCT.

de·at·tri·bute /dē-əˈtri,byoo͞t/ ▸*v.* [*trans.*] cease to attribute (a work of art) to a particular artist. **—de·at·tri·bu·tion** /dē,atrəˈbyoo͞SHən/ *n.*

deb /deb/ ▸*n. informal* short for DEBUTANTE.

de·ba·cle /diˈbakəl; -ˈbäkəl/ ▸*n.* a sudden and ignominious failure; a fiasco: *the economic debacle that became known as the Great Depression.* ▷early 19th cent.: from French *débâcle*, from *débâcler* 'unleash,' from *dé-* 'un-' + *bâcler* 'to bar' (from Latin *baculum* 'staff').

de·bag /dēˈbag/ ▸*v.* (**-bagged, -bag·ging**) [*trans.*] *Brit., informal* remove the pants of (someone) as a joke or punishment.

de·bal·last /dēˈbaləst/ ▸*v.* [*trans.*] remove ballast from (a ship) in order to increase its buoyancy.

de·bar /dēˈbär/ ▸*v.* (**-barred, -bar·ring**) [*trans.*] (usu. **be debarred**) exclude or prohibit (someone) officially from doing something: *people declaring that they were HIV-positive could be debarred entry.* ▷late Middle English: from French *débarrer*, from Old French *desbarrer* 'unbar,' from *des-* (expressing reversal) + *barrer* 'to bar.' **—de·bar·ment** *n.* /-mənt/

de·bark[1] /dēˈbärk/ ▸*v.* [*intrans.*] leave a ship or aircraft. ■ [*trans.*] unload (cargo or troops) from a ship or aircraft. ▷mid 17th cent.: from French *débarquer*. **—de·bar·ka·tion** /,dēbärˈkāSHən/ *n.*

de·bark[2] ▸*v.* [*trans.*] remove (the bark) from a tree.

de·base /diˈbās/ ▸*v.* [*trans.*] reduce (something) in quality or value; degrade: *the love episodes debase the dignity of the drama* | [as *adj.*] (**debased**) *the debased traditions of sportsmanship.* ■ lower the moral character of (someone): *war debases people.* See note at HUMBLE. ■ *historical* lower the value of (coinage) by reducing the content of precious metal. ▷mid 16th cent. (in the sense 'humiliate, belittle'): from DE- 'down' + the obsolete verb *base* (compare with ABASE), expressing the notion 'bring down completely.' **—de·base·ment** *n.* **—de·bas·er** *n.*

de·bat·a·ble /diˈbātəbəl/ ▸*adj.* open to discussion or argument: *it is debatable whether the country is coming out of recession.* ■ *historical* (of land) on the border between two countries and claimed by each. **—de·bat·a·bly** /-blē/ *adv.*

de·bate /diˈbāt/ ▸*n.* a formal discussion on a particular topic in a public meeting or legislative assembly, in which opposing arguments are put forward. ■ an argument about a particular subject, esp. one in which many people are involved: *the national* ***debate on*** *abortion | there has been much debate about prices.*
▸*v.* [*trans.*] argue about (a subject), esp. in a formal manner: *the board debated his proposal | the date when people first entered America is hotly debated.* ■ [with *clause*] consider a possible course of action in one's mind before reaching a decision: *he debated whether he should leave the matter alone or speak to her.* ▷Middle English: via Old French from Latin *dis-* (expressing reversal) + *battere* 'to fight.' **—de·bat·er** *n.*
▸*PHRASES* □ **be open to debate** be unproven; require further discussion. □ **under debate** being discussed or disputed.

de·bat·ing point ▸*n.* an extraneous proposition or inessential piece of information used to gain advantage in a debate.

de·bauch /diˈbôCH/ ▸*v.* [*trans.*] destroy or debase the moral purity of; corrupt. ■ *dated* seduce (a woman): *he debauched sixteen schoolgirls.*
▸*n.* a bout of excessive indulgence in sensual pleasures, esp. eating and drinking. ■ the habit or practice of such indulgence; debauchery: *his life had been spent in debauch.* ▷late 16th cent.: from French *débaucher* (verb) 'turn away from one's duty,' from Old French *desbaucher*, of uncertain ultimate origin. **—de·bauch·er** *n.*

de·bauched /diˈbôCHt/ ▸*adj.* indulging in or characterized by sensual pleasures to a degree perceived to be morally harmful; dissolute: *a debauched lifestyle.*

deb·au·chee /di,bôˈCHē/ ▸*n.* a person given to excessive indulgence in sensual pleasures. ▷mid 17th cent.: from French *débauché* 'turned away from duty,' past participle of *débaucher* (see DEBAUCH).

de·bauch·er·y /diˈbôCHərē/ ▸*n.* excessive indulgence in sensual pleasures.

de·beak /dēˈbēk/ ▸*v.* [*trans.*] remove the upper part of the beak of (a bird) to prevent it from injuring other birds: [as *n.*] (**debeaking**) *debeaking is thought to cause chickens chronic pain.*

de Beau·voir /də bōˈvwär; də ˈbō,vwär/, Simone (1908–86), French existentialist philosopher, novelist, and feminist. Her best-known work is *The Second Sex* (1949), a central book of the "second wave" of feminism. She was closely associated with Jean-Paul Sartre.

de·ben·ture /diˈbenCHər/ ▸*n.* (also **debenture bond**) an unsecured loan certificate issued by a company, backed by general credit rather than by specified assets. ■ *Brit.* a long-term security yielding a fixed rate of interest, issued by a company and secured against assets. ▷late Middle English (denoting a voucher issued by a royal household, giving the right to claim payment for goods or services): from Latin *debentur* 'are owing' (from *debere* 'owe'), used as the first word of a certificate recording a debt. The current sense dates from the mid 19th cent.

de·bil·i·tate /diˈbili,tāt; dē-/ ▸*v.* [*trans.*] [often as *adj.*] (**debilitating**) make (someone) weak and infirm: *a debilitating disease* | [as *adj.*] (**debilitated**) *a woman who had felt chronically debilitated and unwell for years.* ■ hinder, delay, or weaken: *the debilitating effects of underinvestment.* ▷mid 16th cent.: from Latin *debilitat-* 'weakened,' from the verb *debilitare*, from *debilitas* (see DEBILITY). **—de·bil·i·tat·ing·ly** *adv.* **—de·bil·i·ta·tion** /di,biliˈtāSHən/ *n.* **—de·bil·i·ta·tive** /diˈbili,tātiv/ *adj.*

de·bil·i·ty /diˈbilitē/ ▸*n.* physical weakness, esp. as a result of illness. ▷late Middle English: from Old French *debilite*, from Latin *debilitas*, from *debilis* 'weak.'

deb·it /ˈdebit/ ▸*n.* an entry recording an amount owed, listed on the left-hand side or column of an account. The opposite of CREDIT. ■ a payment made or owed.
▸*v.* (**deb·it·ed, deb·it·ing**) [*trans.*] (usu. **be debited**) (of a bank or other financial organization) remove (an amount of money) from a customer's account, typically as payment for services or goods: *$10,000 was debited from their account.* ■ remove an amount of money from (a bank account): *the tag on the rear window automatically activates the pump and debits any major credit card.* ▷late Middle English (in the sense 'debt'): from French *débit*, from Latin *debitum* 'something owed' (see DEBT). The verb sense dates from the 17th cent.; the current noun sense from the late 18th cent.
▸*PHRASE* □ **on the debit side** as an unsatisfactory aspect of the situation: *on the debit side, they predict a rise in book prices.*

deb·it card ▸*n.* a card issued by a bank allowing the holder to transfer money electronically to another bank account when making a purchase.

deb·o·nair /,debəˈne(ə)r/ ▸*adj.* (of a man) confident, stylish, and charming. ▷Middle English (in the sense 'meek or courteous'): from Old French *debonaire*, from *de bon aire* 'of good disposition.' **—deb·o·nair·ly** *adv.*

de·bone /dēˈbōn/ ▸*v.* remove the bones from (meat, poultry, or fish), esp. before cooking.

Deb·o·rah /ˈdeb(ə)rə/ a biblical prophet and leader who inspired the Israelite army to defeat the Canaanites (Judges 4–5). The "Song of Deborah," a song of victory attributed to her, is thought to be one of the oldest sections of the Bible.

de·bouch /diˈbouCH; -ˈboo͞SH/ ▸*v.* [*intrans.*] emerge from a narrow or confined space into a wide, open area: *the soldiers debouched from their jeeps and dispersed among the trees | the stream finally debouches into a silent pool.* ▷mid 18th cent.: from French *déboucher*, from *dé-* (expressing removal) + *bouche* 'mouth' (from Latin *bucca* 'cheek'). **—de·bouch·ment** *n.*

De·bre·cen /ˈdebrət,sen/ an industrial and commercial city in eastern Hungary; pop. 217,290.

de·bride·ment /diˈbrēdmənt/ ▸*n. Medicine* the removal of damaged tissue or foreign objects from a wound. ▷mid 19th cent.: from French, from *débrider*, literally 'unbridle,' based on *bride* 'bridle' (of Germanic origin).

de·brief /dēˈbrēf/ ▸*v.* [*trans.*] question (someone, typically a soldier or spy) about a completed mission or undertaking: *together they debriefed their two colleagues* | [as *n.*] (**debriefing**) *during his debriefing, he exposed two Russian spies.*
▸*n.* a series of questions about a completed mission or undertaking. **—de·brief·er** *n.*

de·bris /dəˈbrē; ,dā-/ ▸*n.* scattered fragments, typically of something wrecked or destroyed: *the bomb hits it, showering debris from all sides.* ■ loose natural material consisting esp. of broken pieces of rock: *a stable arrangement of planets, comets, and debris orbiting the sun.* ■ dirt or refuse: *clean away any collected dust or debris.* ▷early 18th cent.: from French *débris*, from obsolete *débriser* 'break down.'

de Bro·glie /də ˈbrôyə; də ˈbroi/, Louis-Victor, Prince (1892–1987), French physicist. He was the first to suggest that subatomic particles can also have the properties of waves, and his name is now applied to such a wave. Nobel Prize for Physics (1929).

debt /det/ ▸*n.* something, typically money, that is owed or due: *I paid off my debts | a way to reduce Third World debt.* ■ the state of owing money: *the firm is heavily* ***in debt.*** ■ [usu. in *sing.*] a feeling of gratitude for a service or favor: *we owe them a debt of thanks.* ▷Middle English *dette*: from Old French, based on Latin *debitum* 'something owed,' past participle of *debere* 'owe.' The spelling change in French and English was by association with the Latin word.

▸PHRASE □ **be in someone's debt** owe gratitude to someone for a service or favor.

debt coun·se·lor ▸*n.* a person who offers professional advice on methods of debt repayment.

debt of hon·or ▸*n.* a debt that is not legally recoverable, esp. one incurred in gambling.

debt·or /ˈdetər/ ▸*n.* a person or institution that owes a sum of money.

debt se·cu·ri·ty ▸*n.* a negotiable or tradable liability or loan.

debt swap (also **debt-for-na·ture swap**) ▸*n.* a transaction in which a foreign exchange debt owed by a developing country is transferred to another organization on the condition that the country use local currency for a designated purpose, usually environmental protection.

de·bug /dēˈbəg/ ▸*v.* (**-bugged**, **-bug·ging**) [*trans.*] **1** identify and remove errors from (computer hardware or software): *games are the worst to debug* | [as *n.*] (**debugging**) *software debugging.* **2** detect and remove concealed microphones from (an area). **3** remove insects from (something), esp. with a pesticide.

▸*n.* the process of identifying and removing errors from computer hardware or software.

de·bug·ger /dēˈbəgər/ ▸*n.* a computer program that assists in the detection and correction of errors in computer programs.

de·bunk /diˈbəNGk/ ▸*v.* [*trans.*] expose the falseness or hollowness of (a myth, idea, or belief): *the magazine that debunks claims of the paranormal.* ■ reduce the inflated reputation of (someone), esp. by ridicule: *comedy takes delight in debunking heroes.* —**de·bunk·er** *n.* —**de·bunk·er·y** *n.*

de·burr /dēˈbər/ (also **de·bur**) ▸*v.* (**-burred**, **-bur·ring**) [*trans.*] neaten and smooth the rough edges or ridges of (an object, typically one made of metal): *hand tools for deburring holes in metal.*

De·bus·sy /ˌdebyo͝oˈsē; ˌdā-/, (Achille) Claude (1862–1918), French composer and critic. Debussy incorporated the ideas of impressionist art and symbolist poetry into music, using melodies based on the whole-tone scale and delicate harmonies that exploit overtones.

de·but /dāˈbyo͞o/ ▸*n.* a person's first appearance or performance in a particular capacity or role: *the film marked his debut as a director.* ■ the first public appearance of a new product or presentation of a theatrical show: *the car makes its world debut.* ■ [as *adj.*] denoting the first recording or publication of a group, singer, or writer: *a debut album.* ■ *dated* the first appearance of a debutante in society.

▸*v.* [*intrans.*] perform in public for the first time: *the Rolling Stones debuted at the Marquee.* ■ (of a new product) be launched: *the model is expected to debut at $19,000.* ■ [*trans.*] (of a company) launch (a new product): *the company is to debut new software.* ▷mid 18th cent.: from French *début*, from *débuter* 'lead off.'

deb·u·tant /ˈdebyo͝oˌtänt; ˈdebyə-/ ▸*n.* a person making a first appearance in a career or in fashionable society. ▷early 19th cent.: from French *débutant* 'leading off,' from the verb *débuter*.

deb·u·tante /ˈdebyo͝oˌtänt; ˈdebyə-/ ▸*n.* an upper-class young woman making her first appearance in fashionable society. ▷early 19th cent.: from French *débutante* (feminine) 'leading off,' from the verb *débuter*.

De·bye /dəˈbī/, Peter Joseph William (1884–1966), U.S. chemical physicist; born in the Netherlands. He is noted for establishing the existence of permanent electric dipole moments in many molecules, for demonstrating the use of these to determine molecular size and shape, and for modifying Einstein's theory of specific heats as applied to solids. Nobel Prize for Chemistry (1936).

de·bye /diˈbī/ (also **debye unit**) ▸*n.* *Chemistry* a unit used to express electric dipole moments of molecules. One debye is equal to 3.336×10^{-30} coulomb meter. ▷early 20th cent.: named after P. J. DEBYE.

Dec. ▸*abbr.* December.

dec. ▸*abbr.* deceased.

deca- (also **dec-** before a vowel) ▸*comb. form* (used commonly in units of measurement) ten; having ten: *decahedron* | *decane.* ▷from Greek *deka* 'ten.'

dec·ade /ˈdekād/ ▸*n.* **1** a period of ten years: *he taught at the university for nearly a decade.* ■ a period of ten years beginning with a year ending in 0: *the fourth decade of the nineteenth century.* **2** a set, series, or group of ten, in particular: ■ /ˈdekid/ each of the five divisions of each chapter of the rosary. ▷late Middle English (denoting each of ten parts of a literary work): via Old French and late Latin from Greek *deka* 'ten.' Sense 1 dates from the early 17th cent. —**dec·a·dal** /ˈdekədl/ *adj.*

USAGE 1 The U.S. (and primary British) pronunciation of **decade** puts the stress on *dec-*. An alternative pronunciation used in Britain sounds like the word *decayed*. This latter pronunciation is disapproved of by some traditionalists, but it is regarded by many as a standard, acceptable alternative.
2 Note that when **decade** means 'a division of the rosary,' the pronunciation is distinct: the stress is on *dec-*, but the second syllable sounds like *id*, not *ade*.

dec·a·dence /ˈdekədəns/ ▸*n.* moral or cultural decline, esp. after a peak or culmination of achievement: *he denounced Western decadence.* ■ behavior reflecting such a decline: *the rituals of joy and grief had become so ornate as to verge on decadence.* ■ luxurious self-indulgence: *"French" connotes richness and decadence, and that's the idea of this ice cream.* ▷mid 16th cent.: from French *décadence*, from medieval Latin *decadentia*; related to DECAY.

dec·a·dent /ˈdekədənt/ ▸*adj.* characterized by or reflecting a state of moral or cultural decline. ■ luxuriously self-indulgent: *a decadent soak in a scented bath.*

▸*n.* a person who is luxuriously self-indulgent. ■ (often **Decadent**) a member of a group of late 19th-cent. French and English poets associated with the Aesthetic Movement. ▷mid 19th cent.: from French *décadent*, from medieval Latin *decadentia* (see DECADENCE). —**dec·a·dent·ly** *adv.*

de·caf /ˈdēˌkaf/ ▸*n.* *informal* decaffeinated coffee. ▷1960s: abbreviation.

de·caf·fein·ate /dēˈkafəˌnāt/ ▸*v.* [*trans.*] [usu. as *adj.*] (**decaffeinated**) remove most or all of the caffeine from (coffee or tea): *decaffeinated coffee.* —**de·caf·fein·a·tion** /dēˌkafəˈnāSHən/ *n.*

dec·a·gon /ˈdekəˌgän/ ▸*n.* a plane figure with ten straight sides and angles. ▷mid 17th cent.: via medieval Latin from Greek *dekagōnon*, neuter (used as a noun) of *dekagōnos* 'ten-angled.' —**de·cag·o·nal** /dəˈkagənl/ *adj.*

dec·a·gram /ˈdekəˌgram/ ▸(also **dek·a·gram**) *n.* a metric unit of mass or weight, equal to 10 grams.

dec·a·he·dron /ˌdekəˈhēdrən/ ▸*n.* (*pl.* **-drons** or **-dra** /-drə/) a solid figure with ten plane faces. ▷early 19th cent.: from DECA- 'ten' + -HEDRON, on the pattern of words such as *polyhedron*. —**dec·a·he·dral** /-drəl/ *adj.*

de·cal /ˈdēkal/ ▸*n.* a design prepared on special paper for transfer onto another surface such as glass, porcelain, or metal. ▷1950s: abbreviation of DECALCOMANIA.

de·cal·ci·fied /dēˈkalsəˌfīd/ ▸*adj.* (of rock or bone) containing a reduced quantity of calcium salts: *decalcified chalk.* —**de·cal·ci·fi·ca·tion** /dēˌkalsəfiˈkāSHən/ *n.* —**de·cal·ci·fi·er** /-ˌfīər/ *n.*

de·cal·co·ma·ni·a /dēˌkalkəˈmānēə/ ▸*n.* the process of transferring designs from prepared paper on to glass or porcelain. ■ a technique used by some surrealist artists that involves pressing paint between sheets of paper. ▷mid 19th cent.: from French *décalcomanie*, from *décalquer* 'transfer a tracing' + *-manie* '-mania' (with reference to the enthusiasm for the process in the 1860s).

dec·a·li·ter /ˈdekəˌlētər/ (also **dek·a·li·ter**) (abbr.: **dal** or **dkl**) ▸*n.* a metric unit of capacity, equal to 10 liters.

Dec·a·logue /ˈdekəˌlôg; -ˌläg/ ▸*n.* (usu. **the Decalogue**) the Ten Commandments. ▷late Middle English: via French and ecclesiastical Latin from Greek *dekalogos (biblos)* '(book of) the Ten Commandments,' from *hoi deka logoi* 'the Ten Commandments' (literally 'the ten sayings').

De·cam·er·on /diˈkamərən; -ˌrän/ a work by Boccaccio, written between 1348 and 1358, containing a hundred tales supposedly told in ten days by a party of ten young people who had fled from the Black Death in Florence. The work was influential on later writers such as Chaucer and Shakespeare.

dec·a·me·ter /ˈdekəˌmētər/ (also **dek·a·me·ter**) (abbr.: **dam** or **dkm**) ▸*n.* a metric unit of length, equal to 10 meters. —**dec·a·met·ric** /ˌdekəˈmetrik/ *adj.* .

de·camp /diˈkamp/ ▸*v.* [*intrans.*] depart suddenly, esp. to relocate one's business or household in another area: *now he has* ***decamped to*** *Hollywood.* ■ abscond hurriedly to avoid prosecution or detection: *the copyists sold the originals and decamped with the proceeds.* ■ *archaic* break up or leave a military camp: *the armies of both chiefs had decamped.* ▷late 17th cent.: from French *décamper*, from *dé-* (expressing removal) + *camp* 'camp.' —**de·camp·ment** *n.*

dec·an /ˈdekən/ ▸*n.* *Astrology* each of three equal ten-degree divisions of a sign of the zodiac. ▷late 16th cent.: from late Latin *decanus* 'chief of a group of ten' (see DEAN[1]).

dec·a·nal /ˈdekənl; diˈkānl/ ▸*adj.* of or relating to a dean or deanery. ■ relating to or denoting the south side of the choir of a church, the side on which the dean sits. The opposite of CANTORIAL. ▷early 18th cent.: from medieval Latin *decanalis*, from late Latin *decanus* (see DEAN[1]).

dec·ane /ˈdekān/ ▸*n.* *Chemistry* a colorless liquid hydrocarbon of the alkane series, present in petroleum products such as kerosene. • Chem. formula: $C_{10}H_{22}$; many isomers, esp. the straight-chain isomer (***n*-decane**), which is used as a solvent and in jet fuel research.

de·cant /diˈkant/ ▸*v.* [*trans.*] gradually pour (liquid, typically wine or a solution) from one container into another, esp. without disturbing the sediment: *the wine was decanted about 40 minutes before being served.* ■ *figurative* empty out; move as if by pouring: *she had learned to decant her seizures of feeling into theatrical performances.* ▷mid 17th cent.: from medieval Latin *decanthare*, from Latin *de-* 'away from' + *canthus* 'edge, rim' (used to denote the angular lip of a beaker), from Greek *kanthos* 'corner of the eye.'

de·cant·er /diˈkantər/ ▸*n.* a stoppered glass container into which wine is decanted.

de·cap·i·tate /diˈkapiˌtāt/ ▸*v.* [*trans.*] cut off the head of (a person or animal): *how to decapitate a snapping turtle* | [as *adj.*] (**decapitated**) *a decapitated body.* ■ cut the end or top from (something). ■ *figurative* attempt to undermine (a group or organization) by removing its leaders: *Italy's organized-crime network was decapitated when the godfather of the Sicilian Mafia was arrested.* ▷early 17th cent.: from late Latin *decapitat-* 'decapitated,' from the verb *decapitare*, from *de-* (expressing removal) + *caput, capit-* 'head.' —**de·cap·i·ta·tion** /diˌkapiˈtāSHən/ *n.* —**de·cap·i·ta·tor** /-ˌtātər/ *n.*

de·cap·i·ta·tion strike ▸*n.* a debilitating military attack, esp. one aimed at the enemy's leadership.

De·cap·o·da /diˈkapədə/ *Zoology* **1** an order of crustaceans that includes shrimps, crabs, and lobsters. They have five pairs of walking legs and are typically marine. **2** a former order of cephalopod mollusks that includes squids and cuttlefishes, having eight arms and two long tentacles. Compare with OCTOPODA. ▷modern Latin (plural), from DECA- 'ten' + Greek *pous, pod-* 'foot.' —**dec·a·pod** /ˈdekəˌpäd/ *n.* & *adj.*

de·cap·su·late /dēˈkapso͞oˌlāt/ ▸*v.* [*trans.*] *Surgery* remove the capsule or covering from (a kidney or other encapsulated organ). —**de·cap·su·la·tion** /dēˌkapso͞oˈlāSHən/ *n.*

de·car·bon·ize /dēˈkärbəˌnīz/ ▸*v.* [*trans.*] remove carbon or carbonaceous deposits from (an engine or other metal object). —**de·car·bon·i·za·tion** /dēˌkärbənəˈzāSHən/ *n.* —**de·car·bon·iz·er** *n.*

de·car·box·yl·ase /ˌdēkärˈbäksəˌlās; -ˌlāz/ ▸*n.* *Biochemistry* an enzyme that catalyzes the decarboxylation of a particular organic molecule.

de·car·box·yl·ate /ˌdēkärˈbäksəˌlāt/ ▸*v.* [*trans.*] *Chemistry* eliminate a carboxylic acid group from (an organic compound). ■ [*intrans.*] undergo this process. —**de·car·box·yl·a·tion** /ˌdēkärˌbäksəˈlāSHən/ *n.*

de·car·bu·rize /dēˈkärb(y)əˌrīz/ ▸*v.* [*trans.*] *Metallurgy* remove carbon from (iron or steel); decarbonize. ▷mid 19th cent.: from DE- (expressing removal) + CARBURIZE, on the pattern of French *décarburer*. —**de·car·bu·ri·za·tion** /dēˌkärb(y)ərəˈzāSHən/ *n.*

dec·a·syl·lab·ic /ˌdekəsiˈlabik/ *Prosody* ▸*adj.* (of a metrical line) consisting of ten syllables.

▸*n.* a metrical line of ten syllables.

de·cath·lon /diˈkaTH(ə)ˌlän/ ▸*n.* an athletic event taking place over two days, in which each competitor takes part in the same prescribed ten events (100-meter dash, long jump, shot put, high jump, 400-meter dash, 110-meter hurdles, discus, pole vault, javelin, and 1,500-meter run). ▷early 20th cent.: from DECA- 'ten' + Greek *athlon* 'contest.' —**de·cath·lete** /-ˈkaTH(ə)ˌlēt/ *n.*

De·ca·tur[1] /diˈkātər/ **1** an industrial city in northern Alabama, on the Tennessee River; pop. 53,929. **2** an industrial and commercial city in central Illinois; pop. 81,860.

De·ca·tur[2], Stephen (1779–1820), U.S. naval officer. He was a daring commander in the Tripolitan War and the War of 1812. He is noted for his well-known toast, "Our country! In her intercourse with foreign nations may she always be in the right; but our country, right or wrong!"

de·cay /di'kā/ ▸*v.* [*intrans.*] (of organic matter) rot or decompose through the action of bacteria and fungi: [as *adj.*] (**decayed**) *a decayed cabbage leaf* | [as *adj.*] (**decaying**) *the odor of decaying fish.* ■ [*trans.*] cause to rot or decompose: *the fungus will decay soft timber.* ■ (of a building or area) fall into disrepair; deteriorate: *urban neighborhoods decay when elevated freeways replace surface roads.* ■ decline in quality, power, or vigor: *the moral authority of the party was decaying.* ■ *Physics* (of a radioactive substance, particle, etc.) undergo change to a different form by emitting radiation: *the trapped radiocarbon begins to decay at a known rate.* ■ *technical* (of a physical quantity) undergo a gradual decrease: *the time taken for the current to* ***decay to*** *zero.*

▸*n.* the state or process of rotting or decomposition: *hardwood is more resistant to decay than softwood* | *tooth decay.* ■ structural or physical deterioration: *the old barn rapidly* ***fell into decay.*** ■ rotten matter or tissue: *fluoride heals small spots of decay.* ■ the process of declining in quality, power, or vigor: *preachers warning of moral decay.* ■ *Physics* the change of a radioactive substance, particle, etc., into another by the emission of radiation: *the gas radon is produced by the decay of uranium in rocks and soil.* ■ *technical* gradual decrease in the magnitude of a physical quantity: *the decay of electrical fields in the electromagnets.* ▷late Middle English: from Old French *decair,* based on Latin *decidere* 'fall down or off,' from *de-* 'from' + *cadere* 'fall.'

Dec·can /'dekən; 'dek,an/ a triangular plateau in southern India, bounded by the Malabar Coast in the west, the Coromandel Coast in the east, and the Vindhaya mountains in the north.

de·cease /di'sēs/ ▸*n.* [in *sing.*] *formal* or *Law* death: *a doctor's sudden decease.*

▸*v.* [*intrans.*] *archaic* die. ▷Middle English: from Old French *deces,* from Latin *decessus* 'death,' past participle (used as a noun) of *decedere* 'to die.'

de·ceased /di'sēst/ *formal Law* ▸*n.* (**the deceased**) a person who has died: *in memory of the deceased.*

▸*adj.* dead; no longer living: *the cremation of a deceased person.*

de·ce·dent /di'sēdnt/ ▸*n. Law* a person who has died: *to make sure the decedent's property passes to his children.* ▷late 16th cent.: from Latin *decedent-* 'dying,' from the verb *decedere* (see **DECEASE**).

de·ceit /di'sēt/ ▸*n.* the action or practice of deceiving someone by concealing or misrepresenting the truth: *a web of deceit.* ■ a dishonest act or statement. ■ deceitful disposition or character: *I can't stand your treachery and deceit.* ▷Middle English: from Old French, past participle (used as a noun) of *deceveir* 'deceive.'

de·ceit·ful /di'sētfəl/ ▸*adj.* (of a person) deceiving or misleading others, typically on a habitual basis. ■ intended to deceive or mislead: *such an act would have been deceitful and irresponsible.* **—de·ceit·ful·ly** *adv.* **—de·ceit·ful·ness** *n.*

de·ceive /di'sēv/ ▸*v.* [*trans.*] (of a person) cause (someone) to believe something that is not true, typically in order to gain some personal advantage: *I didn't intend to* ***deceive*** *people* ***into*** *thinking it was French champagne.* ■ (often **be deceived**) (of a thing) give a mistaken impression: *the area may seem to offer nothing of interest, but don't be deceived* | [*intrans.*] *everything about him was intended to deceive.* ■ (**deceive oneself**) fail to admit to oneself that something is true: *enabling the rulers to deceive themselves about the nature of their own rule.* ■ be sexually unfaithful to (one's regular partner). ▷Middle English: from Old French *deceivre,* from Latin *decipere* 'catch, ensnare, cheat.' **—de·ceiv·a·ble** *adj.* **—de·ceiv·er** *n.*

de·cel·er·ate /dē'selə,rāt/ ▸*v.* [*intrans.*] (of a vehicle, machine, or process) reduce speed; slow down: *international growth rates decelerated in the early 1970s.* ■ [*trans.*] cause to move more slowly: *gravity decelerates the cosmic expansion.* ▷late 19th cent.: from **DE-** (expressing removal) + a shortened form of **ACCELERATE**. **—de·cel·er·a·tion** /-,selə'rāsʜən/ *n.* **—de·cel·er·a·tor** /-,rātər/ *n.* **—de·cel·er·om·e·ter** /-,selə'rämitər/ *n.*

De·cem·ber /di'sembər/ ▸*n.* the twelfth month of the year, in the northern hemisphere usually considered the first month of winter: *the fuel shortage worsened during December* | [as *adj.*] *a December day.* ▷Middle English: from Latin, from *decem* 'ten' (being originally the tenth month of the Roman year).

De·cem·brist /di'sembrist/ ▸*n.* a member of a group of Russian revolutionaries who in December 1825 led an unsuccessful revolt against Tsar Nicholas I. The leaders were executed and later came to be regarded as martyrs by the Left.

de·cen·cy /'dēsənsē/ ▸*n.* (*pl.* **-cies**) behavior that conforms to accepted standards of morality or respectability: *she* ***had the decency to*** *come and confess.* ■ modesty and propriety: *a loose dress, rather too low-cut for decency.* ■ (**decencies**) the requirements of accepted or respectable behavior: *an appeal to common decencies.* ■ (**decencies**) things required for a reasonable standard of life: *I can't afford any of the decencies of life.*

de·cen·ni·al /di'senēəl/ ▸*adj.* recurring every ten years: *the decennial census.* ■ lasting for or relating to a period of ten years: *decennial insurance.* ▷mid 17th cent.: from Latin *decennium* 'a decade,' from *decennis* 'of ten years' (from *decem* 'ten' + *annus* 'year'), + **-AL**. **—de·cen·ni·al·ly** *adv.*

de·cen·ni·um /di'senēəm/ ▸*n.* (*pl.* **-cen·ni·a** /-'senēə/ or **-cen·ni·ums**) a decade. ▷late 17th cent.: from Latin, from *decem* 'ten' + *annus* 'year.'

de·cent /'dēsənt/ ▸*adj.* **1** conforming with generally accepted standards of respectable or moral behavior: *the good name of such a decent and innocent person.* ■ appropriate; fitting: *they would meet again after a decent interval.* ■ not likely to shock or embarrass others: *a decent high-necked dress.* ■ *informal* sufficiently clothed to see visitors: *make yourself decent.* **2** [*attrib.*] of an acceptable standard; satisfactory: *find me a decent cup of coffee* | *people need decent homes.* ■ good: *the deer are small: a 14-inch spread is a pretty decent buck.* ■ kind, obliging, or generous: *that was pretty awfully decent of him.* ▷mid 16th cent. (in the sense 'suitable, appropriate'): from Latin *decent-* 'being fitting,' from the verb *decere.* **—de·cent·ly** *adv.*

▸*PHRASE* □ **do the decent thing** take the most honorable or appropriate course of action, even if is not necessarily in one's own interests: *after his defeat, he should do the decent thing and step down.*

de·cen·ter /dē'sentər/ (*Brit.* **de·cen·tre**) ▸*v.* [*trans.*] displace from the center or from a central position. ■ remove or displace (the individual human subject, such as the author of a text) from a primary place or central role: [as *n.*] (**decentering**) *the egocentric infant develops by a progressive decentering.*

de·cen·tral·ize /dē'sentrə,līz/ ▸*v.* [*trans.*] [often as *adj.*] (**decentralized**) transfer (authority) from central to local government: *Canada has one of the most decentralized governments in the world* | [*intrans.*] *European countries were trying to decentralize.* ■ move departments of (a large organization) away from a single administrative center to other locations, usually granting them some degree of autonomy. **—de·cen·tral·ist** /-list/ *n.* & *adj.* **—de·cen·tral·i·za·tion** /dē,sentrəli'zāsʜən/ *n.*

de·cep·tion /di'sepsʜən/ ▸*n.* the action of deceiving someone: *obtaining property by deception.* ■ a thing that deceives: *a range of elaborate deceptions.* See note at **FICTION**. ▷late Middle English: from late Latin *deceptio(n-),* from *decipere* 'deceive.'

de·cep·tive /di'septiv/ ▸*adj.* giving an appearance or impression different from the true one; misleading: *he put the question with deceptive casualness.* **—de·cep·tive·ness** *n.*

de·cep·tive·ly /di'septivlē/ ▸*adv.* [usu. as *submodifier*] in a way or to an extent that gives a misleading impression. ■ to a lesser extent than appears the case: *the idea was deceptively simple.* ■ to a greater extent than appears the case: *the airy and deceptively spacious lounge.*

> *USAGE* **Deceptively** belongs to a very small set of words whose meaning is genuinely ambiguous in that it can be used in similar contexts to mean both one thing and also its complete opposite. A ***deceptively smooth*** *surface* is one that appears smooth but in fact is not smooth at all, while a ***deceptively spacious*** *room* is one that does not look spacious but is in fact *more* spacious than it appears. But what is a ***deceptively steep*** *gradient*? Or a person who is described as ***deceptively strong***? To avoid confusion, use with caution (or not at all) unless the context makes clear in what way the thing modified is not what it first appears to be.

de·cer·e·brate /dē'serə,brāt/ ▸*v.* [*trans.*] [usu. as *adj.*] (**decerebrated**) *Biology* remove the cerebrum from (a laboratory animal). **—de·cer·e·bra·tion** /-,serə'brāsʜən/ *n.*

de·cer·ti·fy /dē'sərtə,fī/ ▸*v.* (**-fies**, **-fied**) [*trans.*] remove a certificate or certification from (someone or something), typically for failure to comply with a regulating authority's rules or standards. **—de·cer·ti·fi·ca·tion** /-,sərtəfi'kāsʜən/ *n.*

de·chris·tian·i·za·tion /dē,krisсʜənə'zāsʜən/ ▸*n.* the action or process or removing Christian influences or characteristics from something: *the dechristianization of modern society.* **—de·chris·tian·ize** /-'krisсʜə,nīz/ *v.*

deci- ▸*comb. form* (used commonly in units of measurement) one tenth: *deciliter.* ▷from Latin *decimus* 'tenth.'

dec·i·bel /'desə,bel; -bəl/ (abbr.: **dB**) ▸*n.* a unit used to measure the intensity of a sound or the power level of an electrical signal by comparing it with a given level on a logarithmic scale. ■ (in general use) a degree of loudness: *his voice went up several decibels.* ▷early 20th cent.: from **DECI-** 'ten' + **BEL** (the unit being one tenth of a bel).

de·cide /di'sīd/ ▸*v.* [*intrans.*] come to a resolution in the mind as a result of consideration: [with *infinitive*] *they decided to appoint someone else* | [with *clause*] *you've decided that a hedge is what you want.* ■ [*trans.*] cause to come to such a resolution: *this business about the letter decided me.* ■ make a choice from a number of alternatives: *she had* ***decided on*** *her plan of action* | *I've* ***decided against*** *having children.* ■ give a judgment concerning a matter or legal case: *the courts decided in favor of the New York claimants* | [*trans.*] *the judge will decide the case.* ■ [*trans.*] come to a decision about (something): *we must decide the fates of the people who headed the coup.* ■ [*trans.*] resolve or settle (a question or contest): *an exciting game was decided in a sudden-death overtime.* ▷late Middle English (in the sense 'bring to a settlement'): from French *décider,* from Latin *decidere* 'determine,' from *de-* 'off' + *caedere* 'cut.' **—de·cid·a·ble** *adj.* **—de·cid·er** *n.*

de·cid·ed /di'sīdid/ ▸*adj.* [*attrib.*] (of a quality) definite; unquestionable: *the sunshine is a decided improvement.* ■ (of a person) having clear opinions; resolute. ■ [*attrib.*] (of a legal case) that has been resolved. **—de·cid·ed·ness** *n.*

de·cid·ed·ly /di'sīdidlē/ ▸*adv.* **1** [usu. as *submodifier*] undoubtedly; undeniably: *he looked decidedly uncomfortable.* **2** in a decisive and confident way: *"No," Donna said decidedly.* **—de·cid·ed·ness** *n.*

de·cid·u·a /di'sijo͞oə/ ▸*n. Physiology* the thick layer of modified mucous membrane that lines the uterus during pregnancy and is shed with the afterbirth. ▷late 18th cent.: from modern Latin *decidua (membrana),* literally 'falling off (membrane).' **—de·cid·u·al** /-jo͞oəl/ *adj.*

de·cid·u·ous /di'sijo͞oəs/ ▸*adj.* (of a tree or shrub) shedding its leaves annually. Often contrasted with **EVERGREEN**. ■ *informal* (of a tree or shrub) broad-leaved. ■ denoting the milk teeth of a mammal, which are shed after a time. ▷late 17th cent.: from Latin *deciduus* (from *decidere* 'fall down or off') + **-OUS**. **—de·cid·u·ous·ly** *adv.* **—de·cid·u·ous·ness** *n.*

dec·ile /'des,īl; -əl/ ▸*n. Statistics* each of ten equal groups into which a population can be divided according to the distribution of values of a particular variable: *the lowest income decile of the population.* ■ each of the nine values of the random variable that divide a population into ten such groups. ▷late 17th cent.: from French *décile,* from a medieval Latin derivative of Latin *decem* 'ten.'

dec·i·li·ter /'desə,lētər/ (*Brit.* **dec·i·li·tre**) (abbr.: **dl**) ▸*n.* a metric unit of capacity, equal to one tenth of a liter.

dec·i·mal /'des(ə)məl/ ▸*adj.* relating to or denoting a system of numbers and arithmetic based on the number ten, tenth parts, and powers of ten: *decimal arithmetic.* ■ relating to or denoting a system of currency, weights and measures, or other units in which the smaller units are related to the principal units as powers of ten: *decimal coinage.*

▸*n.* (also **decimal fraction**) a fraction whose denominator is a power of ten and whose numerator is expressed by figures placed to the right of a decimal point. ■ the system of decimal numerical notation. ▷early 17th cent.: from modern Latin *decimalis* (adjective), from Latin *decimus* 'tenth.' **—dec·i·mal·ly** *adv.*

dec·i·mal·ize /'desəmə,līz/ ▸*v.* [*trans.*] convert (a system of coinage or weights and measures) to a decimal system. **—dec·i·mal·i·za·tion** /,des(ə)mələ'zāsʜən/ *n.*

dec·i·mal place ▸*n.* the position of a digit to the right of a decimal point.

dec·i·mal point ▸*n.* a dot placed after the figure representing units in a decimal fraction.

dec·i·mate /ˈdesəˌmāt/ ▸*v.* [*trans.*] (often **be decimated**) **1** kill, destroy, or remove a large percentage or part of: *the project would decimate the fragile wetland wilderness | the American chestnut, a species decimated by blight.* ■ drastically reduce the strength or effectiveness of (something): *plant viruses that can decimate yields.* **2** *historical* kill one in every ten of (a group of soldiers or others) as a punishment for the whole group. ▷late Middle English: from Latin *decimat-* 'taken as a tenth,' from the verb *decimare,* from *decimus* 'tenth.' In Middle English the term *decimation* denoted the levying of a tithe, and later the tax imposed in England by Cromwell on the Royalists (1655). The verb *decimate* originally alluded to the Roman punishment of executing one man in ten of a mutinous legion. **—dec·i·ma·tion** /ˌdesəˈmāSHən/ *n.* **—dec·i·ma·tor** /-ˌmātər/ *n.*

USAGE Historically, the meaning of the word **decimate** is 'kill one in every ten of (a group of people).' This sense has been superseded by the later, more general sense 'kill or destroy a large percentage or part of,' as in *the virus has* **decimated** *the population.* Some traditionalists argue that this and other later senses are incorrect, but it is clear that these extended senses are now part of standard English. It is sometimes also argued that **decimate** should refer to people and not to things or animals such as weeds or insects. It is generally agreed that **decimate** should not be used to mean 'defeat utterly.'

dec·i·me·ter /ˈdesəˌmētər/ (*Brit.* **dec·i·me·tre**) (abbr.: **dm**) ▸*n.* a metric unit of length, equal to one tenth of a meter. **—dec·i·met·ric** /ˌdesəˈmetrik/ *adj.* .

de·ci·pher /diˈsīfər/ ▸*v.* [*trans.*] convert (a text written in code, or a coded signal) into normal language: *enable the government to decipher coded computer transmissions.* ■ succeed in understanding, interpreting, or identifying (something): *an expression she could not decipher came and went upon his face.* ▷early 16th cent.: from **DE-** (expressing reversal) + **CIPHER**, on the pattern of French *déchiffrer.* **—de·ci·pher·a·ble** *adj.* **—de·ci·pher·ment** *n.*

de·ci·sion /diˈsiZHən/ ▸*n.* a conclusion or resolution reached after consideration: *I'll make the decision on my own | the editor's decision is final.* ■ the action or process of deciding something or of resolving a question: *the information was used as the basis for decision.* ■ a formal judgment: *last year's Supreme Court decision.* ■ the ability or tendency to make decisions quickly; decisiveness: *she was a woman* ***of decision.*** ■ *Boxing* the awarding of a fight, in the absence of a knockout or technical knockout, to the boxer with the most rounds won or with the most points. ■ *Baseball* a win or a loss assigned to a pitcher. ▷late Middle English: from Latin *decisio(n-),* from *decidere* 'determine' (see **DECIDE**).

de·ci·sion prob·lem ▸*n. Logic* the problem of finding a way to decide whether a formula or class of formulas is true or provable within a given system of axioms. ▷1930s: translating German *Entscheidungsproblem.*

de·ci·sion sup·port sys·tem (abbr.: **DSS**) ▸*n. Computing* a set of related computer programs and the data required to assist with analysis and decision-making within an organization.

de·ci·sion the·o·ry ▸*n.* the mathematical study of strategies for optimal decision-making between options involving different risks or expectations of gain or loss depending on the outcome. Compare with **GAME THEORY**.

de·ci·sive /diˈsīsiv/ ▸*adj.* settling an issue; producing a definite result: *the Supreme Court voided the statute by a decisive 7–2 vote | decisive evidence.* ■ (of a person) having or showing the ability to make decisions quickly and effectively. See note at **RESOLUTE**. ▷early 17th cent.: from French *décisif, -ive,* from medieval Latin *decisivus,* from *decis-* 'determined,' from the verb *decidere* (see **DECIDE**). **—de·ci·sive·ly** *adv.* **—de·ci·sive·ness** *n.*

De·cius /ˈdēSH(ē)əs/, Gaius Messius Quintus Trajanus (*c.*201–251), Roman emperor 249–251. He was the first Roman emperor to promote systematic persecution of the Christians.

deck /dek/ ▸*n.* **1** a structure of planks or plates, approximately horizontal, extending across a ship or boat at any of various levels, esp. one of those at the highest level and open to the weather: *he stood on the deck of his flagship.* ■ the accommodations on a particular deck of a ship: *the first-class deck.* ■ a floor or platform resembling or compared to a ship's deck, esp. the floor of a pier or a platform for sunbathing. ■ a platformlike structure, typically made of lumber and unroofed, attached to a house or other building: *they cooked hamburgers on the deck adjoining the living room.* ■ a level of a large, open building, esp. a sports stadium: *Jeter hit an enormous home run into the upper deck.* ■ (**the deck**) *informal* the ground or floor: *there was a big thud when I* ***hit the deck.*** ■ the flat part of a skateboard or snowboard. **2** a component or unit in sound-reproduction equipment that incorporates a playing or recording mechanism for discs or tapes: *the car has cruise control and a tape deck.* **3** a pack of cards: *shuffle the deck.* ■ *informal* a packet of narcotics.
▸*v.* [*trans.*] **1** (usu. **be decked**) decorate or adorn brightly or festively: *Ingrid was* ***decked out in*** *her Sunday best.* **2** *informal* knock (someone) to the ground with a punch. ▷late Middle English: from Middle Dutch *dec* 'covering, roof, cloak,' *dekken* 'to cover.' Originally denoting canvas used to make a covering (esp. on a ship), the term came to mean the covering itself, later denoting a solid surface serving as roof and floor. **—decked** *adj.* [in *combination*] *a three-decked vessel.*
▸*PHRASES* □ **below decks** see **BELOW DECKS**. □ **clear the decks** see **CLEAR**. □ **not playing with a full deck** *informal* mentally deficient. □ **on deck** on or onto a ship's main deck: *she stood on deck for hours.* ■ *figurative* ready for action or work. ■ *Baseball* next to hit in the batting order.

deck chair ▸*n.* a folding chair of wood and canvas, typically used near the sea or on the deck of passenger ships.

-decker ▸*comb. form* having a specified number of decks or layers: *double-decker.*

deck·hand /ˈdekˌhand/ ▸*n.* a member of a ship's crew whose duties include maintenance of hull, decks, and superstructure, mooring, and cargo handling.

deck·house /ˈdekˌhous/ ▸*n.* a superstructure on the deck of a ship or boat, used primarily to house equipment or for storage, or (formerly) for accommodations.

deck·ing /ˈdekiNG/ ▸*n.* **1** the material of the deck of a ship, a floor, or a platform. **2** the action of ornamenting something.

deck·le /ˈdekəl/ ▸*n.* (also **deckle strap**) a device in a papermaking machine for limiting the size of the sheet, consisting of a continuous belt on either side of the wire. ■ a frame on the mold used to shape the pulp when making paper by hand. ▷mid 18th cent.: from German *Deckel,* diminutive of *Decke* 'covering.'

deck·le edge ▸*n.* the rough uncut edge of a sheet of paper, formed by a deckle. **—deck·le-edged** *adj.*

deck of·fi·cer ▸*n.* an officer in charge of the above-deck workings and maneuvers at sea of a ship or boat.

deck pas·sen·ger ▸*n.* a passenger on a ship who does not have a cabin.

deck shoe ▸ another term for **BOAT SHOE**.

de·claim /diˈklām/ ▸*v.* [*reporting verb*] utter or deliver words or a speech in a rhetorical or impassioned way, as if to an audience: [*trans.*] *she declaimed her views* | [*intrans.*] *a preacher declaiming from the pulpit.* ■ [*intrans.*] (**declaim against**) forcefully protest against or criticize (something). ▷late Middle English: from French *déclamer* or Latin *declamare,* from *de-* (expressing thoroughness) + *clamare* 'to shout.' **—de·claim·er** *n.* **—de·clam·a·to·ry** /-ˈklaməˌtôrē/ *adj.*

dec·la·ma·tion /ˌdekləˈmāSHən/ ▸*n.* the action or art of declaiming: *Shakespearean declamation | declamations of patriotism.* ■ a rhetorical exercise or set speech. ■ forthright or distinct projection of words set to music: *a soprano soloist with wonderfully clear declamation.* ▷late Middle English (in the sense 'a set speech'): from Latin *declamatio(n-),* from the verb *declamare* (see **DECLAIM**).

de·clar·ant /diˈkle(ə)rənt/ *chiefly Law* ▸*n.* **1** a person or party who makes a formal declaration. ■ an alien who has signed a declaration of intent to become a U.S. citizen. **2** a person who makes a statement, even an informal one.
▸*adj.* making or having made a formal declaration. ▷late 17th cent.: from French *déclarant,* present participle of *déclarer,* from Latin *declarare* 'make quite clear' (see **DECLARE**).

dec·la·ra·tion /ˌdekləˈrāSHən/ ▸*n.* a formal or explicit statement or announcement: *they issued a declaration at the close of the talks | declarations of love.* ■ the formal announcement of the beginning of a state or condition: *the declaration of war | a declaration of independence.* ■ a listing of goods, property, income, etc., subject to duty or tax. ■ a statement asserting or protecting a legal right. ■ a written public announcement of intentions or of the terms of an agreement. ■ *Law* a plaintiff's statement of claims in proceedings. ■ *Law* an affirmation made instead of taking an oath. ■ the naming of trump in bridge, whist, or a similar card game. ▷late Middle English: from Latin *declaratio(n-),* from *declarare* 'make quite clear' (see **DECLARE**).

Dec·la·ra·tion of In·de·pen·dence a document declaring the U.S. to be independent of the British Crown, signed on July 4, 1776, by the congressional representatives of the Thirteen Colonies, including Thomas Jefferson, Benjamin Franklin, and John Adams.

de·clar·a·tive /diˈkle(ə)rətiv; -ˈklar-/ ▸*adj.* **1** of the nature of or making a declaration: *declarative statements.* ■ *Grammar* (of a sentence or phrase) taking the form of a simple statement. **2** *Computing* denoting high-level programming languages that can be used to solve problems without requiring the programmer to specify an exact procedure to be followed.
▸*n.* a statement in the form of a declaration. ■ *Grammar* a declarative sentence or phrase. **—de·clar·a·tive·ly** *adv.*

de·clare /diˈkle(ə)r/ ▸*v.* **1** [*reporting verb*] say something in a solemn and emphatic manner: [with *clause*] *Mao declared that his forces were henceforth to be known as the People's Liberation Army* | [with *direct speech*] *"I was under too much pressure," he declared.* See note at **ANNOUNCE**. ■ [*trans.*] formally announce the beginning of (a state or condition): *Spain* ***declared war on*** *Britain in 1796.* ■ [*trans.*] pronounce or assert (a person or thing) to be something specified: *the mansion was declared a fire hazard.* ■ [*intrans.*] (**declare for/against**) openly align oneself for or against (a party or position) in a dispute: *Mr. Roosevelt had declared for "a new deal."* ■ [*intrans.*] announce oneself as a candidate for an election: *he declared last April.* ■ (**declare oneself**) reveal one's intentions or identity. ■ (**declare oneself**) *archaic* express feelings of love to someone: *she waited in vain for him to declare himself.* **2** [*trans.*] acknowledge possession of (taxable income or dutiable goods). **3** [*trans.*] announce that one holds (certain combinations of cards) in a card game. ▷Middle English: from Latin *declarare,* from *de-* 'thoroughly' + *clarare* 'make clear' (from *clarus* 'clear'). **—de·clar·a·ble** *adj.* **—de·clar·a·to·ry** /-ˈkle(ə)rəˌtôrē/ *adj.* **—de·clar·ed·ly** /-ˈkle(ə)ridlē/ *adv.*
▸*PHRASE* □ **well, I declare** (or **I do declare**) an exclamation of incredulity, surprise, or vexation.

de·clar·er /diˈkle(ə)rər/ ▸*n. Bridge* the player whose bid establishes the suit of the contract and who must therefore play both their own hand and the exposed hand of the dummy.

de·class /dēˈklas/ ▸*v.* [*trans.*] (usu. **be declassed**) demote (someone) from their original social class to a lower one.

dé·clas·sé /ˌdākläˈsā/ (also **dé·clas·sée**) ▸*adj.* having fallen in social status: *his parents were poor and déclassé.* ▷late 19th cent.: French, 'removed from one's class, degraded,' past participle of *déclasser.*

de·clas·si·fy /dēˈklasəˌfī/ ▸*v.* (**-fies, -fied**) [*trans.*] (often **be declassified**) officially declare (information or documents) to be no longer secret: *government documents were declassified.* **—de·clas·si·fi·ca·tion** /dēˌklasəfiˈkāSHən/ *n.*

de·claw /dēˈklô/ ▸*v.* [*trans.*] remove the claws from. ■ make harmless or less threatening: *the Grimms' fairy tales were declawed beyond recognition.*

de·clen·sion /diˈklenSHən/ ▸*n.* **1** (in the grammar of Latin, Greek, and other languages) the variation of the form of a noun, pronoun, or adjective, by which its grammatical case, number, and gender are identified. ■ the class to which a noun or adjective is assigned according to the manner of this variation. **2** *poetic/literary* a condition of decline or moral deterioration: *the declension of the new generation.* ▷late Middle English *declinson,* from Old French *declinaison,* from *decliner* 'to decline.' The change in the ending was probably due to association with words such as *ascension.* **—de·clen·sion·al** /-SHənl/ *adj.*

de Cle·ram·bault's syn·drome /də ˌklerəmˈbōz ˌsindrōm/ ▸*n. Psychiatry* another term for **EROTOMANIA**. ▷from the name of French psychiatrist Gatin *de Clérambault* (1872–1934), who first described it.

D

dec·li·na·tion /ˌdekləˈnāSHən/ ▸*n.* **1** *Astronomy* the angular distance of a point north or south of the celestial equator. Compare with **RIGHT ASCENSION** and **CELESTIAL LATITUDE.** ■ the angular deviation of a compass needle from true north (because the magnetic north pole and the geographic north pole do not coincide). **2** formal refusal: *in the face of this declination of the proposition.* ▷late Middle English: from Latin *declinatio(n-)*, from the verb *declinare* (see **DECLINE**). **—dec·li·na·tion·al** /-SHənl/ *adj.*

dec·li·na·tion ax·is ▸*n. Astronomy* the axis of an equatorially mounted telescope that is at right angles to the polar axis, about which the telescope is turned in order to view points at different declinations but at a constant right ascension.

de·cline /diˈklīn/ ▸*v.* **1** [*intrans.*] become smaller, fewer, or less; decrease: *the birth rate continued to decline.* ■ diminish in strength or quality; deteriorate: *her health began to decline* | [as *adj.*] (**declining**) *the victims of declining educational standards.* **2** [*trans.*] politely refuse (an invitation or offer): *Caroline declined the coffee.* ■ [with *infinitive*] politely refuse to do something: *the company declined to comment.* **3** [*intrans.*] (esp. of the sun) move downward. ■ *archaic* bend down; droop. **4** [*trans.*] (in the grammar of Latin, Greek, and certain other languages) state the forms of (a noun, pronoun, or adjective) corresponding to cases, number, and gender.
▸*n.* [in *sing.*] a gradual and continuous loss of strength, numbers, or quality: *a serious* **decline in** *bird numbers* | *a civilization* **in decline.** ■ a fall in value or price: *able to halt the stock's decline.* ■ *archaic* the gradual setting of the sun. ■ *archaic* any disease in which bodily strength gradually fails, esp. tuberculosis. ▷late Middle English: from Old French *decliner*, from Latin *declinare* 'bend down, turn aside,' from *de-* 'down' + *clinare* 'to bend.' **—de·clin·a·ble** *adj.* **—de·clin·er** *n.*

de·clin·ing years ▸*plural n.* a person's old age, esp. when regarded as the time when health, vigor, and mental faculties deteriorate. ■ *figurative* the period leading up to the demise of something, often characterized by a loss of effectiveness: *the council's declining years.*

de·cliv·i·ty /diˈklivitē/ ▸*n.* (*pl.* **-ties**) a downward slope: *a thickly wooded declivity.* ▷early 17th cent.: from Latin *declivitas*, from *declivis* 'sloping down,' from *de-* 'down' + *clivus* 'a slope.' **—de·cliv·i·tous** /-təs/ *adj.*

dec·o /ˈdekō/ ▸*n.* **1** short for **ART DECO. 2** (in scuba diving) short for **DECOMPRESSION.**

de·coct /diˈkäkt/ ▸*v.* [*trans.*] *archaic* extract the essence from (something) by heating or boiling it. ▷late Middle English (in the sense 'cook, heat up'): from Latin *decoct-* 'boiled down,' from the verb *decoquere*, from *de-* 'down' + *coquere* 'cook.'

de·coc·tion /diˈkäkSHən/ ▸*n.* the liquor resulting from concentrating the essence of a substance by heating or boiling, esp. a medicinal preparation made from a plant: *a* **decoction of** *a root.* ■ the action or process of extracting the essence of something. ▷late Middle English: from late Latin *decoctio(n-)*, from *decoquere* 'boil down' (see **DECOCT**).

de·code /diˈkōd/ ▸*v.* [*trans.*] convert (a coded message) into intelligible language. ■ analyze and interpret (a verbal or nonverbal communication or image): *a handbook to help parents decode street language.* ■ convert (audio or video signals) into another form, e.g., to analog from digital in sound reproduction: *processors used to decode CD-quality digital audio signals.*
▸*n. informal* a translation of a coded message. **—de·cod·a·ble** *adj.*

de·cod·er /diˈkōdər/ ▸*n.* a person or thing that analyzes and interprets something, in particular: ■ an electronic device for analyzing the information components of an audio or visual signal and feeding them to separate amplifier channels. ■ an electronic device that converts a coded signal into one that can be used by other equipment, esp. a device to decode satellite television signals.

de·col·late[1] /diˈkäˌlāt/ ▸*v.* [*trans.*] *archaic* behead (someone). ▷late Middle English: from Latin *decollat-* 'beheaded,' from the verb *decollare*, from *de-* (expressing removal) + *collum* 'neck.' **—de·col·la·tion** /ˌdekəˈlāSHən/ *n.*

de·col·late[2] /ˈdekəˌlāt; ˈdēkə-/ ▸*v.* [*intrans.*] separate sheets of paper, such as multi-ply computer paper, into different piles. ▷1960s: from **DE-** 'away from' + **COLLATE. —de·col·la·tion** /ˌdekəˈlāSHən; ˌdēkə-/ *n.* **—de·col·la·tor** /-ˌlātər/ *n.*

dé·colle·tage /dāˌkäləˈtäZH ˌdekələ-/ ▸*n.* a low neckline on a woman's dress or top. ▷late 19th cent.: French, from *décolleter* 'expose the neck,' from *dé-* (expressing removal) + *collet* 'collar of a dress.'

dé·colle·té /dāˌkäləˈtā ˌdekələ-/ ▸*adj.* (also **dé·colle·tée**) (of a woman's dress or top) having a low neckline.
▸*n.* a low neckline on a woman's dress or top. ▷mid 19th cent.: French, past participle of *décolleter* 'expose the neck.'

de·col·o·nize /dēˈkäləˌnīz/ ▸*v.* [*trans.*] (of a country) withdraw from (a colony), leaving it independent: *they must decolonize French Polynesia.* **—de·col·o·ni·za·tion** /-ˌkälənəˈzāSHən/ *n.*

de·col·or·ize /dēˈkələˌrīz/ ▸*v.* [*trans.*] remove the color from: *ethane decolorizes bromine water.* **—de·col·or·i·za·tion** /-ˌkələrəˈzāSHən/ *n.*

de·com·mis·sion /ˌdēkəˈmiSHən/ ▸*v.* [*trans.*] withdraw (someone or something) from service, in particular: ■ make (a nuclear reactor or weapon) inoperative, and dismantle and decontaminate it to make it safe. ■ take (a ship) out of service.

de·com·mu·nize /dēˈkämyəˌnīz/ ▸*v.* [*trans.*] remove the features or influence of communism from. **—de·com·mu·ni·za·tion** /-ˌkämyənəˈzāSHən/ *n.*

de·com·pen·sa·tion /dēˌkämpənˈsāSHən/ ▸*n. Medicine* the failure of an organ (esp. the liver or heart) to compensate for the functional overload resulting from disease. ■ *Psychiatry* the failure to generate effective psychological coping mechanisms in response to stress, resulting in personality disturbance or disintegration, esp. that which causes relapse in schizophrenia. **—de·com·pen·sat·ed** /-ˈkämpənˌsātid/ *adj.*

de·com·pile /ˌdēkəmˈpīl/ ▸*v.* [*trans.*] *Computing* produce source code from (compiled code). **—de·com·pi·la·tion** /dēˌkämpəˈlāSHən; ˌdēkäm-/ *n.* **—de·com·pil·er** *n.*

de·com·pose /ˌdēkəmˈpōz/ ▸*v.* [*intrans.*] (of a dead body or other organic matter) decay; become rotten: *leaves stuffed in plastic bags do not decompose* | [as *adj.*] (**decomposed**) *the body was badly decomposed.* ■ [*trans.*] cause (something) to decay or rot: *dead plant matter can be completely decomposed by microorganisms.* ■ (of a chemical compound) break down into component elements or simpler constituents: *many chemicals decompose rapidly under high temperature.* ■ [*trans.*] break down (a chemical compound) into its component elements or simpler constituents: *to decompose the compound by means of an acid.* ▷mid 18th cent. (in the sense 'separate into simpler constituents'): from French *décomposer*, from *de-* (expressing reversal) + *composer*. **—de·com·pos·a·ble** *adj.* **—de·com·po·si·tion** /dēˌkämpəˈziSHən/ *n.*

de·com·pos·er /ˌdēkəmˈpōzər/ ▸*n.* an organism, esp. a soil bacterium, fungus, or invertebrate, that decomposes organic material. ■ a device or installation that is used to break down a chemical substance.

de·com·press /ˌdēkəmˈpres/ ▸*v.* [*trans.*] relieve of compressing forces, in particular: ■ expand (compressed computer data) to its normal size so that it can be read and processed by a computer. ■ subject (a diver) to decompression. ■ [*intrans.*] *informal* calm down and relax: *Michael sits for a minute to decompress before walking home.*

de·com·pres·sion /ˌdēkəmˈpreSHən/ ▸*n.* a release of compressing forces, in particular: ■ reduction in air pressure: *decompression of the aircraft cabin.* ■ a gradual reduction of air pressure on a person who has been experiencing high pressure while diving in order to prevent decompression sickness. ■ the process of expanding computer data to its normal size so that it can be read by a computer. ■ a surgical procedure that relieves excessive pressure on an internal part of the body such as the cranium or spinal cord.

de·com·pres·sion cham·ber ▸*n.* a small room in which the air pressure can be varied, used chiefly to allow deep-sea divers to adjust gradually to normal air pressure.

de·com·pres·sion sick·ness ▸*n.* a condition that results when sudden decompression causes nitrogen bubbles to form in the tissues of the body. It is suffered particularly by divers (who often call it **the bends**), and can cause pain in the muscles and joints, cramps, numbness, nausea, and paralysis. Also called **CAISSON DISEASE.**

de·com·pres·sor /ˌdēkəmˈpresər/ ▸*n.* an instrument or device for decompressing something. ■ a computer program that decompresses data by digitally expanding it to its original size and form.

de·con·di·tion /ˌdēkənˈdiSHən/ ▸*v.* [*trans.*] **1** [usu. as *adj.*] (**deconditioned**) cause to lose fitness or muscle tone, esp. through lack of exercise: *deconditioned muscles.* **2** [usu. as *n.*] (**deconditioning**) *Psychiatry* reform or reverse (previously conditioned behavior), esp. in the treatment of phobia and other anxiety disorders in which the fear response to certain stimuli is brought under control. Compare with **COUNTERCONDITIONING.** ■ *informal* persuade (someone) to abandon a habitual mode of thinking.

de·con·flict /ˌdēkənˈflikt/ ▸*v.* resolve the conflicts or contradictions in (something): [trans.] *the spreadsheet is used to show approved events and to deconflict unit participation* [intrans.] *why the U.S. should deconflict.* **—de·con·flic·tion** *n.*

de·con·gest /ˌdēkənˈjest/ ▸*v.* [*trans.*] relieve the congestion of (something). **—de·con·ges·tion** /-ˈjesCHən/ *n.*

de·con·ges·tant /ˌdēkənˈjestənt/ ▸*adj.* (chiefly of a medicine) used to relieve nasal congestion.
▸*n.* a decongestant medicine.

de·con·se·crate /dēˈkänsiˌkrāt/ ▸*v.* [*trans.*] (usu. **be deconsecrated**) transfer (a building) from sacred to secular use: *the church was deconsecrated in the early nineteenth century.* **—de·con·se·cra·tion** /-ˌkänsiˈkrāSHən/ *n.*

de·con·struct /ˌdēkənˈstrəkt/ ▸*v.* [*trans.*] analyze (a text or a linguistic or conceptual system) by deconstruction, typically in order to expose its hidden internal assumptions and contradictions and subvert its apparent significance or unity. ■ (in general use) dismantle: *do we need to deconstruct all the institutions that we've created in order to improve them?* ▷late 19th cent.: back-formation from **DECONSTRUCTION. —de·con·struc·tive** /-tiv/ *adj.*

de·con·struc·tion /ˌdēkənˈstrəkSHən/ ▸*n.* a method of critical analysis of philosophical and literary language that emphasizes the internal workings of language and conceptual systems, the relational quality of meaning, and the assumptions implicit in forms of expression.

Deconstruction focuses on a text as such rather than as an expression of the author's intention, stressing the limitlessness (or impossibility) of interpretation and rejecting the Western philosophical tradition of seeking certainty through reasoning by privileging certain types of interpretation and repressing others. It was effectively named and popularized by the French philosopher Jacques Derrida from the late 1960s and taken up particularly by U.S. literary critics.

▷late 19th cent. (originally in the general sense 'taking to pieces'): from **DE-** (expressing reversal) + **CONSTRUCTION. —de·con·struc·tion·ism** /-ˌnizəm/ *n.* **—de·con·struc·tion·ist** /-ist/ *adj.* & *n.*

de·con·tam·i·nate /ˌdēkənˈtaməˌnāt/ ▸*v.* [*trans.*] neutralize or remove dangerous substances, radioactivity, or germs from (an area, object, or person): *they tried to decontaminate nearby villages.* **—de·con·tam·i·na·tion** /-ˌtaməˈnāSHən/ *n.*

de·con·tex·tu·al·ized /ˌdēkənˈteksCHōōəˌlīzd/ ▸*adj.* considered in isolation from its context: *coffee-table photo books with their beautiful but decontextualized photographs.* **—de·con·tex·tu·al·i·za·tion** /-ˌteksCHōōələˈzāSHən/ *n.* **—de·con·tex·tu·al·ize** *v.*

de·con·trol /ˌdēkənˈtrōl/ ▸*v.* (**-trolled, -trol·ling**) [*trans.*] release (a commodity, market, etc.) from controls or restrictions: *whether gas prices should be totally decontrolled.*
▸*n.* the action of decontrolling something.

de·con·vo·lu·tion /dēˌkänvəˈlōōSHən/ ▸*n.* a process of resolving something into its constituent elements or removing complication in order to clarify it: *the editor helped in the deconvolution of phrase and thought.* ■ *Mathematics* the resolution of a convolution function into the functions from which it was formed in order to separate their effects. ■ (also **deconvolution analysis**) the improvement of resolution of images or other data by a mathematical algorithm designed to separate the information from artifacts that result from the method of collecting it.

de·cor /dāˈkôr; di-/ ▸*n.* the furnishing and decoration of a room. ■ the decoration and scenery of a stage. ▷late 19th cent.: from French *décor*, from the verb *décorer*, from Latin *decorare* 'embellish' (see **DECORATE**).

dec·o·rate /ˈdekəˌrāt/ ▸*v.* [*trans.*] **1** make (something) look more attractive by adding ornament to it. ■ provide (a room or building) with a color scheme, paint, wallpaper, etc.: *the five bedrooms are individually decorated.* **2** confer an award or medal on (a member of the armed forces): *he was decorated for outstanding bravery.* ▷mid 16th cent. (in the sense 'to grace or honor'): from Latin *decoratus* 'embellished' (past participle of *decorare*), from *decus, decor-* 'beauty, honor, or embellishment.'

Dec·o·rat·ed /ˈdekəˌrātid/ ▶*adj.* denoting a stage of English Gothic church architecture typical of the 14th century (between Early English and Perpendicular), with increasing use of decoration and geometric, curvilinear, and reticulated tracery.

dec·o·ra·tion /ˌdekəˈrāSHən/ ▶*n.* **1** the process or art of decorating or adorning something: *the lavish decoration of cloth with gilt.* ■ ornamentation: *pearwood inlaid with floral decoration of stained woods.* ■ a thing that serves as an ornament: *Christmas tree decorations.* ■ the application of paint or wallpaper in a room or building. ■ the paint or wallpaper applied: *an authority on English furniture and decoration.* **2** a medal or award conferred as an honor.

Dec·o·ra·tion Day ▶*n.* another term for **MEMORIAL DAY**.

dec·o·ra·tive /ˈdek(ə)rətiv; ˈdekəˌrātiv/ ▶*adj.* serving to make something look more attractive; ornamental: *the outside of the building is functional rather than decorative.* ■ relating to decoration: *a decorative artist.* **—dec·o·ra·tive·ly** *adv.* **—dec·o·ra·tive·ness** *n.*

dec·o·ra·tive arts ▶*plural n.* the arts concerned with the production of high-quality objects that are both useful and beautiful.

dec·o·ra·tor /ˈdekəˌrātər/ ▶*n.* a person who decorates, in particular: ■ a person whose job is to design the interior of someone's home, by choosing colors, carpets, materials, and furnishings. ■ *chiefly Brit.* a person whose job is to decorate the interior of buildings by painting the walls and hanging wallpaper: *she became a painter and decorator.*

dec·o·rous /ˈdekərəs; diˈkôrəs/ ▶*adj.* in keeping with good taste and propriety; polite and restrained: *dancing with decorous space between partners.* ▷mid 17th cent. (in the sense 'appropriate, seemly'): from Latin *decorus* 'seemly' + **-OUS**. **—dec·o·rous·ly** *adv.* **—dec·o·rous·ness** *n.*

de·cor·ti·cate /dēˈkôrtiˌkāt/ ▶*v.* [*trans.*] **1** [often as *adj.*] (**decorticated**) *technical* remove the bark, rind, or husk from: *decorticated peanuts.* **2** subject to surgical decortication.
▶*adj.* *Biology & Psychology* of or relating to an animal that has had the cortex of the brain removed or separated. ▷early 17th cent.: from Latin *decorticat-* 'stripped of its bark,' from the verb *decorticare*, from *de-* (expressing removal) + *cortex, cortic-* 'bark.'

de·cor·ti·ca·tion /dēˌkôrtiˈkāSHən/ ▶*n.* the removal of the outer layer or cortex from a structure, esp. the lung, brain, or other organ. ■ *Medicine* the operation of removing fibrous scar tissue that prevents expansion of the lung. ▷early 17th cent.: from Latin *decorticatio(n-)*, from *decorticare* 'strip of bark' (see **DECORTICATE**).

de·co·rum /diˈkôrəm/ ▶*n.* behavior in keeping with good taste and propriety: *you exhibit remarkable modesty and decorum.* ■ etiquette: *he had no idea of funeral decorum.* ■ (usu. **decorums**) *archaic* a particular requirement of good taste and propriety. ■ *archaic* suitability to the requirements of a person, rank, or occasion. ▷mid 16th cent. (as a literary term, denoting suitability of style): from Latin, neuter of the adjective *decorus* 'seemly.'

de·cou·page /ˌdākōōˈpäZH/ ▶*n.* the decoration of the surface of an object with paper cut-outs, which is then usu. varnished or lacquered. ▷1960s: French, from *découper* 'cut out.'

de·cou·ple /dēˈkəpəl/ ▶*v.* [*trans.*] separate, disengage, or dissociate (something) from something else: *the mountings effectively* **decouple** *movements of the engine* **from** *those of the wheels.* ■ make the interaction between (electrical components) so weak that there is little transfer of energy between them, esp. to remove unwanted AC distortion or oscillations in circuits with a common power supply. ■ muffle the sound or shock of (a nuclear explosion) by causing it to take place in an underground cavity.

de·coy ▶*n.* /ˈdēˌkoi/ **1** a bird or mammal, or an imitation of one, used by hunters to attract other birds or mammals: [as *adj.*] *a decoy duck.* ■ a person or thing used to lure an animal or person into a trap. ■ a fake or nonworking article, esp. a weapon, used to mislead or misdirect. **2** a pond from which narrow netted channels lead, into which wild ducks may be enticed for capture.
▶*v.* /diˈkoi/ [*trans.*] lure or entice (a person or animal) away from an intended course, typically into a trap: *they would try to decoy the enemy toward the hidden group.* ▷mid 16th cent. (earlier as *coy*): from Dutch *de kooi* 'the decoy,' from Middle Dutch *de kouw* 'the cage,' from Latin *cavea* 'cage.' Sense 2 is from the practice of using tamed ducks to lead wild ones along channels into captivity.

de·crease ▶*v.* /diˈkrēs/ [*intrans.*] become smaller or less in size, amount, intensity, or degree: *the population of the area has decreased radically.* ■ [*trans.*] make smaller or less in size, amount, intensity, or degree: *in some cases vitamin E has decreased cholesterol levels.*
▶*n.* /ˈdēˌkrēs; diˈkrēs/ an instance or example of becoming smaller or less: *a* **decrease in** *births.* ■ the action or process of becoming smaller or fewer: *the rate of decrease became greater.* ▷late Middle English: from Old French *decreis* (noun), *decreistre* (verb), based on Latin *decrescere*, from *de-* 'down' + *crescere* 'grow.' **—de·creas·ing·ly** /diˈkrēsiNGlē/ *adv.* [as *submodifier*] *voters have proved decreasingly willing to support the party.*
▶PHRASE □ **on the decrease** becoming less common or widespread; decreasing.

de·cree /diˈkrē/ ▶*n.* an official order issued by a legal authority. ■ the issuing of such an order: *the king* **ruled by decree.** ■ a judgment or decision of certain law courts.
▶*v.* (**-crees, -creed, -cree·ing**) [*trans.*] order (something) by decree: *the government decreed a ban on any contact with the guerrillas* | [with *clause*] *the president decreed that the military was to be streamlined.* ▷Middle English (denoting an edict issued by an ecclesiastical council to settle a point of doctrine or discipline): from Old French *decre, decret*, from Latin *decretum* 'something decided,' from *decernere* 'decide.'

dec·re·ment /ˈdekrəmənt/ ▶*n.* a reduction or diminution: *relaxation produces a decrement in sympathetic nervous activity.* ■ an amount by which something is reduced or diminished: *the dose was reduced by 10 mg weekly decrements.* ■ *Physics* the ratio of the amplitudes in successive cycles of a damped oscillation.
▶*v.* [*trans.*] *chiefly Computing* cause a discrete reduction in (a numerical quantity): *the instruction decrements the accumulator by one.* ▷early 17th cent. (as a noun): from Latin *decrementum* 'diminution,' from the stem of *decrescere* 'to decrease.'

de·cre·o·lize /dēˈkrēəˌlīz/ ▶*v.* [*trans.*] [usu. as *adj.*] (**decreolized**) modify (a Creole language) toward the local standard language. **—de·cre·o·li·za·tion** /-ˌkrēələˈzāSHən/ *n.*

de·crep·it /diˈkrepit/ ▶*adj.* (of a person) elderly and infirm: *a decrepit old drunk.* See note at **WEAK**. ■ worn out or ruined because of age or neglect: *centuries-old buildings, now decrepit and black with soot.* ▷late Middle English: from Latin *decrepitus*, from *de-* 'down' + *crepitus*, past participle of *crepare* 'rattle, creak.' **—de·crep·i·tude** /-ˌt(y)ōōd/ *n.*

de·crep·i·tate /diˈkrəpiˌtāt/ ▶*v.* [*intrans.*] *technical* (of a crystal or an inclusion of something within a crystal) disintegrate audibly when heated. ▷mid 17th cent.: from **DE-** 'away' + Latin *crepitat-* 'crackled,' from the verb *crepitare*, frequentative of *crepare* 'rattle' (see **DECREPIT**). **—de·crep·i·ta·tion** /-ˌkrepiˈtāSHən/ *n.*

de·cre·scen·do /ˌdēkrəˈSHendō/ ▶*n.* (*pl.* **-dos**), *adv.*, *adj.*, & *v.* (**-dos, -doed**) another term for **DIMINUENDO**: [as *n.*] *faded like the decrescendo of distant thunder* | [as *adj.*] *a decrescendo heart murmur* | [as *v.*] *he decrescendos down to a whisper.* ▷early 19th cent.: Italian, literally 'decreasing.'

de·cres·cent /diˈkresənt/ ▶*adj.* [*attrib.*] (of the moon) waning. ▷early 17th cent.: from Latin *decrescent-* 'growing less,' from the verb *decrescere* (see **DECREASE**).

de·cre·tal /diˈkrētl/ ▶*n.* a papal decree concerning a point of canon law.
▶*adj.* of the nature of a decree. ▷Middle English: from late Latin *decretale*, neuter of *decretalis* (adjective), from Latin *decret-* 'decided,' from the verb *decernere*.

De·cre·tum /diˈkrētəm/ ▶*n.* a collection of decisions and judgments in canon law. ▷Latin, literally 'something decreed.'

de·crim·i·nal·ize /dēˈkriminlˌīz/ ▶*v.* [*trans.*] cease by legislation to treat (something) as illegal: *a battle to decriminalize drugs.* **—de·crim·i·nal·i·za·tion** /-ˌkriminl-iˈzāSHən/ *n.*

de·cry /diˈkrī/ ▶*v.* (**-cries, -cried**) [*trans.*] publicly denounce: *they decried human rights abuses.* ▷early 17th cent. (in the sense 'decrease the value of coins by royal proclamation'): from **DE-** 'down' + **CRY**, on the pattern of French *décrier* 'cry down.' **—de·cri·er** *n.*

de·crypt /diˈkript/ ▶*v.* [*trans.*] make (a coded or unclear message) intelligible: *the computer can be used to encrypt and decrypt sensitive transmissions.*
▶*n.* a text that has been decoded. ▷1930s: from **DE-** (expressing reversal) + *crypt* as in *encrypt*. **—de·cryp·tion** /-ˈkripSHən/ *n.*

de·cub·i·tus /diˈkyōōbitəs/ ▶*n.* *chiefly Medicine* the posture adopted by a person who is lying down: [as *adj.*] *lumbar puncture with the patient in the lateral decubitus position.* ▷late 19th cent.: modern Latin, from Latin *decumbere* 'lie down,' on the pattern of words such as *accubitus* 'reclining at table.'

de·cub·i·tus ul·cer ▶*n.* technical term for **BEDSORE**.

de·cum·bent /diˈkəmbənt/ ▶*adj.* *Botany* (of a plant or part of a plant) lying along the ground or along a surface, with the extremity curving upward. ▷late 18th cent.: from Latin *decumbent-* 'lying down,' from the verb *decumbere*, based on *de-* 'down' + a verb related to *cubare* 'to lie.'

de·cur·rent /diˈkərənt; -ˈkə-rənt/ ▶*adj.* *Botany* (of a fungus gill, leaf, etc.) extending down the stem below the point of attachment. ■ (of a shrub or the crown of a tree) having several roughly equal branches. ▷mid 18th cent.: from Latin *decurrent-* 'running down,' from the verb *decurrere*.

de·curved /dēˈkərvd/ ▶*adj.* *Biology* (esp. of a bird's bill) curved downward.

de·cus·sate /ˈdekəˌsāt; diˈkəsāt/ *technical* ▶*v.* [*reciprocal*] (of two or more things) cross or intersect each other to form an X: *the fibers decussate in the collar.*
▶*adj.* shaped like an X. ■ *Botany* (of leaves) arranged in opposite pairs, each pair being at right angles to the pair below. ▷mid 17th cent. (as a verb): from Latin *decussatus*, past participle of *decussare* 'divide crosswise,' from *decussis* (describing the figure X, i.e., the Roman numeral for the number 10), from *decem* 'ten.' **—de·cus·sa·tion** /ˌdekəˈsāSHən/ *n.*

de·dans /dəˈdän/ ▶*n.* (in court tennis) an open gallery for spectators at the service side of a court. ▷early 18th cent.: French, literally 'inside.'

de·den·dum /diˈdendəm/ ▶*n.* *Engineering* the radial distance from the pitch circle of a cogwheel or worm wheel to the bottom of the tooth space or groove. Compare with **ADDENDUM**. ▷early 20th cent.: from Latin, 'to be given up, surrendered'.

Ded·ham /ˈdedəm/ a town in eastern Massachusetts, southwest of Boston; pop. 23,782.

ded·i·cate /ˈdediˌkāt/ ▶*v.* [*trans.*] devote (time, effort, or oneself) to a particular task or purpose: *Joan has* **dedicated** *her life* **to** *animals.* ■ devote (something) to a particular subject or purpose: *you should dedicate a telephone line to each modem you plan to install.* ■ (usu. **be dedicated**) cite (a book or other artistic work) as being issued or performed in someone's honor: *the novel is* **dedicated to** *the memory of my mother.* ■ open (a building or other facility) formally for public use: *the ex-president came to dedicate a $2.6 million recreation center.* ■ (usu. **be dedicated**) ceremonially assign (a church or other building) to a deity or saint: *the parish church is* **dedicated to** *St. Paul.* ▷late Middle English (in the sense 'devote to sacred use by solemn rites'): from Latin *dedicat-* 'devoted, consecrated,' from the verb *dedicare*. **—ded·i·ca·tee** /ˌdedikāˈtē/ *n.* **—ded·i·ca·tor** /-ˌkātər/ *n.* **—ded·i·ca·to·ry** /-kəˌtôrē/ *adj.*

ded·i·cat·ed /ˈdediˌkātid/ ▶*adj.* (of a person) devoted to a task or purpose; having single-minded loyalty or integrity: *a team of dedicated doctors.* ■ (of a thing) exclusively allocated to or intended for a particular service or purpose: *investing in dedicated bike lanes will encourage more bicycle commuters.* **—ded·i·cat·ed·ly** *adv.*

ded·i·ca·tion /ˌdediˈkāSHən/ ▶*n.* **1** the quality of being dedicated or committed to a task or purpose: *his* **dedication to** *his duties.* **2** the words with which a book or other artistic work is dedicated: *the hardback edition contained a warm* **dedication to** *his wife.* ■ the action of formally opening a building or other facility for public use: *the dedication and unveiling was attended by some 5,000 people.* ■ the action of dedicating a church or other building to a deity or saint. ■ an inscription dedicating a church or other building in this way. ▷late Middle English: from Latin *dedicatio(n-)*, from *dedicare* 'devote, consecrate' (see **DEDICATE**).

de dic·to /dā ˈdiktō/ ▶*adj.* *Philosophy* relating to the form of an assertion or expression itself, rather than any property of a thing it refers to. Compare with **DE RE**. ▷Latin, 'from what is said.'

de·dif·fer·en·ti·ate /dēˌdifəˈrenSHēˌāt/ ▶*v.* [*intrans.*] *Biology* (of a cell or tissue) undergo a reversal of differentiation and lose specialized characteristics. **—de·dif·fer·en·ti·a·tion** /-ˌrenSHēˈāSHən/ *n.*

de·duce /di'd(y)o͞os/ ▸*v.* [*trans.*] arrive at (a fact or a conclusion) by reasoning; draw as a logical conclusion: *little can be safely* ***deduced from*** *these figures* | [with *clause*] *they* ***deduced that*** *the fish died because of water pollution.* ■ *archaic* trace the course or derivation of: *he cannot deduce his descent wholly by heirs male.* ▷late Middle English (in the sense 'lead or convey'): from Latin *deducere*, from *de-* 'down' + *ducere* 'lead.' **—de·duc·i·ble** /-səbəl/ *adj.*

de·duct /di'dəkt/ ▸*v.* [*trans.*] subtract or take away (an amount or part) from a total: *tax has been* ***deducted from*** *the payments.* ▷late Middle English: from Latin *deduct-* 'taken or led away,' from the verb *deducere*. *Deduct* and *deduce* were not distinguished in sense until the mid 17th cent.

de·duct·i·ble /di'dəktəbəl/ ▸*adj.* able to be deducted, esp. from taxable income or tax to be paid: *child-care vouchers will be deductible expenses for employers.* See also TAX-DEDUCTIBLE.
▸*n.* (in an insurance policy) a specified amount of money that the insured must pay before an insurance company will pay a claim: *a traditional insurance policy with a low deductible.* **—de·duct·i·bil·i·ty** /-ˌdəktə'bilitē/ *n.*

de·duc·tion /di'dəkSHən/ ▸*n.* **1** the action of deducting or subtracting something: *the dividend will be paid without deduction of tax.* ■ an amount that is or may be deducted from something, esp. from taxable income or tax to be paid: *tax deductions.* **2** the inference of particular instances by reference to a general law or principle: *the detective must uncover the murderer by deduction from facts.* Often contrasted with INDUCTION. ■ a conclusion that has been deduced. ▷late Middle English: from Latin *deductio(n-)*, from the verb *deducere* (see DEDUCE).

de·duc·tive /di'dəktiv/ ▸*adj.* characterized by the inference of particular instances from a general law: *deductive reasoning.* ■ based on reason and logical analysis of available facts: *I used my deductive powers.* ▷mid 17th cent.: from medieval Latin *deductivus*, from *deduct-* 'deduced,' from the verb *deducere* (see DEDUCE). **—de·duc·tive·ly** *adv.*

de Du·ve /də 'do͞ov; də 'dyv/, Christian René (1917–), Belgian biochemist; born in Britain. He was a pioneer in the study of cell biology. Nobel Prize for Physiology or Medicine (1974, shared with Albert Claude 1899–1983 and George Palade 1912–).

Dee /dē/ **1** a river in northeastern Scotland that rises in the Grampian Mountains and flows east to the North Sea at Aberdeen. **2** a river that rises in North Wales and flows past Chester and on into the Irish Sea.

deed /dēd/ ▸*n.* **1** an action that is performed intentionally or consciously: *doing good deeds.* ■ a brave or noble act: *their deeds will live on in song.* ■ action or performance: *she had erred in both deed and manner.* **2** a legal document that is signed and delivered, esp. one regarding the ownership of property or legal rights. See also TITLE DEED.
▸*v.* [*trans.*] convey or transfer (property or rights) by legal deed: *they* ***deeded*** *their property* ***to*** *their children.* ▷Old English *dēd*, *dǣd*, of Germanic origin; related to Dutch *daad* and German *Tat*, from an Indo-European root shared by DO[1].

dee·jay /'dēˌjā/ *informal* ▸*n.* a disc jockey.
▸*v.* (**-jays, -jayed, -jay·ing**) [*intrans.*] act as, or hold a job as, a disc jockey. ▷1950s: representing the pronunciation of *DJ*.

deem /dēm/ ▸*v.* [*trans.*] regard or consider in a specified way: *the event was deemed a great success* | [*trans.*] *the strike was deemed to be illegal.* ▷Old English *dēman* (also in the sense 'act as judge'), of Germanic origin; related to Dutch *doeman*, also to DOOM.

de-em·pha·size /dē'emfəˌsīz/ ▸*v.* [*trans.*] reduce the importance or prominence given to (something): *the reform de-emphasized central planning and placed more power in the association of socialized industries.* **—de-em·pha·sis** /-fəˌsis/ *n.*

de-en·er·gize /dē'enərˌjīz/ ▸*v.* [*trans.*] disconnect (an electric circuit) from a power supply. ■ [*intrans.*] undergo loss of electrical power: *the starter relay automatically de-energizes.*

deep /dēp/ ▸*adj.* **1** extending far down from the top or surface: *a deep gorge* | *the lake was deep and cold.* ■ extending or situated far in or down from the outer edge or surface: *a deep alcove* | ***deep in*** *the woods.* ■ [*predic.*] (after a measurement and in questions) extending a specified distance from the top, surface, or outer edge: *the well was 200 feet deep.* ■ [*in combination*] as far up or down as a specified point: *standing waist-deep in the river.* ■ [*predic.*] in a specified number of ranks one behind another: [in *combination*] *they were standing three-deep at the bar.* ■ taking in or giving out a lot of air: *she took a deep breath.* ■ *Baseball* far back in the outfield: *his first pitch was hit into deep left field.* **2** very intense or extreme: *she was in deep trouble* | *a deep sleep* | *a deep economic recession.* ■ (of an emotion or feeling) intensely felt: *deep disappointment.* ■ profound or penetrating in awareness or understanding: *a deep analysis.* ■ difficult to understand: *this is all getting too deep for me.* ■ [*predic.*] (**deep in**) fully absorbed or involved in (a state or activity): *they were deep in their own thoughts.* ■ (of a person) unpredictable and secretive: *that Thomas is a deep one.* **3** (of sound) low in pitch and full in tone; not shrill: *a deep, resonant voice.* **4** (of color) dark and intense: *a deep pink.*
▸*n.* (**the deep**) *poetic/literary* the sea: *denizens of the deep.* ■ (usu. **deeps**) a deep part of the sea: *the dark and menacing deeps.* ■ (usu. **deeps**) *figurative* a remote and mysterious region: *the deeps of her imagination.*
▸*adv.* far down or in; deeply: *traveling deep into the countryside* | *figurative his passion runs deep.* ■ (in sports) distant from the start of a play or the forward line of one's team: *the defense played deep.* ▷Old English *dēop* (adjective), *dīope*, *dēope* (adverb), of Germanic origin; related to Dutch *diep* and German *tief*, also to DIP. **—deep·ness** *n.*
▸*PHRASES* □ **the deep end** the end of a swimming pool where the water is deepest. □ **go off** (or **go in off**) **the deep end** *informal* give way immediately to an emotional outburst, esp. of anger. ■ go mad; behave extremely strangely: *they looked at me as if I had gone off the deep end.* □ **in deep** *informal* inextricably involved in or committed to a situation: *he knew that he was in deep when his things began to proliferate in her apartment.* □ **in deep water** (or **waters**) *informal* in trouble or difficulty: *he landed in deep water when he began the affair.* □ **jump** (or **be thrown**) **in at the deep end** *informal* face a difficult problem or undertaking with little experience of it.

deep brain stim·u·la·tion ▸*n.* a nonsurgical treatment to reduce tremor and to block involuntary movements in patients with motion disorders. Small electric shocks are delivered to the thalamus (esp. in the treatment of multiple sclerosis) or the globus pallidus (esp. in the treatment of Parkinson's disease), rendering these parts of the brain inactive without surgically destroying them.

deep breath·ing ▸*n.* breathing with long breaths, esp. as exercise or a method of relaxation.

deep-cy·cle ▸*adj.* denoting a type of electric battery that can be totally discharged and recharged several times.

deep-dis·count ▸*adj.* denoting financial securities carrying a low rate of interest relative to prevailing market rates and issued at a discount to their redemption value, thus mainly providing capital gain rather than income. ■ heavily discounted; greatly reduced in price: *deep-discount pricing has kept airfares affordable.*

deep-dish ▸*adj.* **1** (of a pie) baked in a deep dish to allow for a large filling: *deep-dish apple pie.* ■ (of a pizza) baked in a deep dish and having a thick dough base. **2** *informal* extreme or thoroughgoing: *a deep-dish Catholic.*

deep-dyed ▸*adj. informal* thoroughgoing; complete: *a deep-dyed Beatles fan.*

deep e·col·o·gy ▸*n.* an environmental movement and philosophy that regards human life as just one of many equal components of a global ecosystem.

deep·en /'dēpən/ ▸*v.* make or become deep or deeper: [*intrans.*] *the crisis deepened* ■ (of a weather system) decrease in barometric pressure. Compare with FILL. [as *adj.*] (**deepening**) *a deepening depression.*

deep freeze ▸*n.* (also **deep freez·er**) a refrigerated cabinet or room in which food can be quickly frozen and kept for long periods at a low temperature: *plenty of garden space to keep our deep freezes supplied with fruit and vegetables.* ■ *figurative* a place or situation in which progress or activity is suspended: *the nation is now beginning to resume its history after twenty years in the deep freeze.*
▸*v.* (**deep-freeze**) [*trans.*] [often as *adj.*] (**deep-frozen**) store (something) in a deep freeze.

deep-fry ▸*v.* [*trans.*] [as *adj.*] (**deep-fried**) fry (food) in an amount of fat or oil sufficient to cover it completely: *deep-fried onion rings.*

deep kiss ▸*n. dated* a kiss involving insertion of the tongue into the partner's mouth.

deep-laid ▸*adj.* (of a scheme) secret and elaborate: *a deep-laid plot.*

deep·ly /'dēplē/ ▸*adv.* far down or in: *he breathed deeply* | *fragments of rock were deeply embedded within the wood.* ■ intensely: [as *submodifier*] *she was deeply hurt.*

deep mourn·ing ▸*n.* a state of mourning, conventionally expressed by wearing only black clothing. ■ the black clothing worn by someone in deep mourning.

deep pock·ets ▸*n.* abundant financial resources: *these companies have deep pockets and don't mind spending to get their projects off the ground.*

deep-root·ed ▸*adj.* (of a plant) deeply implanted. ■ firmly embedded in thought, behavior, or culture, and so having a persistent influence: *deep-rooted concern about declining values.* **—deep-root·ed·ness** *n.*

deep sea ▸*n.* [usu. as *adj.*] the deeper parts of the ocean, esp. those beyond the edge of the continental shelf: *deep-sea diving.*

deep-seat·ed ▸*adj.* firmly established at a deep or profound level: *deep-seated anxiety.*

deep-set ▸*adj.* (of a person's eyes) positioned deeply in the head: *his deep-set black eyes are powerful, still, and unrelenting.* ■ embedded firmly: *the bees found only a few deep-set plants.* ■ long-established, ingrained, or profound: *a deep-set enmity.*

deep-six ▸*v.* [*trans.*] *informal* destroy or dispose of (something) irretrievably: *someone had deliberately deep-sixed evidence.* ▷1920s (as *the deep six* 'the grave'): perhaps from the custom of burial at sea at a depth of six fathoms.

Deep South (**the Deep South**) the southeastern region of the U.S. that is regarded as embodying traditional Southern culture and traditions.

deep space ▸*n.* another term for OUTER SPACE.

deep struc·ture ▸*n.* (in generative grammar) the abstract representation of the syntactic structure of a sentence. Contrasted with SURFACE STRUCTURE.

deep throat ▸*n. informal* a concealed informant, esp. one who is hated by those persons informed upon. ▷1970s: from the pseudonym used by a Watergate informant, the name having been taken from the title of a pornographic movie (1972).

deep time ▸*n. Geology* the multimillion year time frame within which scientists believe the earth has existed, and which is supported by the observation of natural, mostly geological, phenomena.

deep-vein throm·bo·sis ▸*n.* thrombosis in a vein lying deep below the skin, especially in the legs. It is a particular hazard of long-haul flying.

deer /di(ə)r/ ▸*n.* (*pl.* same) a hoofed grazing or browsing animal, with branched bony antlers that are shed annually and typically borne only by the male. See also MOUSE DEER, MUSK DEER. • Family Cervidae: several genera and many species. ▷Old English *dēor*, also originally denoting any quadruped, used in the (now archaic) phrase *small deer* meaning 'small creatures collectively'; of Germanic origin; related to Dutch *dier*, German *Tier*.

Deere /di(ə)r/, John (1804–86), U.S. manufacturer. He founded John Deere & Co. in 1868, originally manufacturing steel plows.

Deer·field /'di(ə)rˌfēld/ a historic town in northwestern Massachusetts, on the Connecticut River; pop. 5,018. It suffered major Indian attacks in 1675 and 1704.

Deer·field Beach a resort city in southeastern Florida, north of Fort Lauderdale; pop. 46,325.

deer·fly /'di(ə)rˌflī/ ▸*n.* **1** a bloodsucking horsefly that attacks humans and other large mammals. It can transmit various diseases, including tularemia. • Genus *Chrysops*, family Tabanidae: several species, including *C. callidus*, widespread throughout North America. **2** a bloodsucking louse fly that is a parasite of deer. It loses its wings on finding a host, and the female gives birth to fully grown larvae. • *Lipoptena cervi*, family Hippoboscidae.

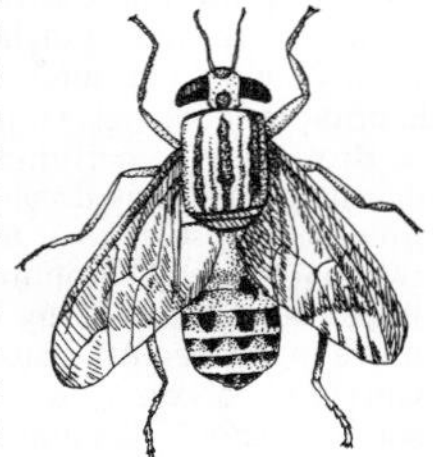

deerfly 1

deer hair ▸*n.* hair from a deer, particularly as used in making artificial fishing flies.

deer·hound /'di(ə)rˌhound/ ▸*n.* a large dog of a rough-haired breed resembling the greyhound.

deer lick ▸*n.* a place where deer come to lick salt, either from a block of salt placed there or from a natural source.

deer mouse ▸*n.* a mainly nocturnal mouse found in

a wide range of habitats in North and Central America. • Genus *Peromyscus*, family Muridae: numerous species, in particular *P. maniculatus*.

deer·skin /ˈdi(ə)rˌskin/ ▸*n.* leather made from a deer's skin.

deer·stalk·er /ˈdi(ə)rˌstôkər/ ▸*n.* **1** a soft cloth cap, originally worn for hunting, with bills in front and behind, and ear flaps that can be tied together over the top. **2** a person who stalks deer.

deerstalker 1

de-es·ca·late /dēˈeskəˌlāt/ ▸*v.* [*trans.*] reduce the intensity of (a conflict or potentially violent situation). —**de-es·ca·la·tion** /-ˌeskəˈlāshən/ *n.*

Deet /dēt/ ▸*n. trademark* a brand of diethyltoluamide, a colorless oily liquid with a mild odor, used as an insect repellent.

def /def/ ▸*adj. informal* excellent: *a truly def tattoo.* ▷1980s: probably an alteration of DEATH (used in Jamaican English as an intensifier), or shortened from DEFINITIVE or DEFINITE.

de·face /diˈfās/ ▸*v.* [*trans.*] spoil the surface or appearance of (something), e.g., by drawing or writing on it: *he defaced library books.* ■ mar; disfigure: *the canyon's spectacular limestone walls have been defaced by the reservoir.* ▷Middle English: from Old French *desfacier*, from *des-* (expressing removal) + *face* 'face.' —**de·face·ment** *n.* —**de·fac·er** *n.*

de fac·to /di ˈfaktō; dā/ ▸*adv.* in fact, whether by right or not: *the island has been de facto divided into two countries.* Often contrasted with DE JURE.
▸*adj.* [*attrib.*] denoting someone or something that is such in fact: *a de facto one-party system.* ▷early 17th cent.: Latin, literally 'of fact.'

de·fal·cate /diˈfalkāt; -ˈfôl-/ ▸*v.* [*trans.*] *formal* embezzle (funds with which one has been entrusted): *the officials were charged with defalcating government money.* ▷mid 16th cent. (in the sense 'deduct, subtract'): from medieval Latin *defalcat-* 'lopped,' from the verb *defalcare*, from *de-* 'away from, off' + Latin *falx, falc-* 'sickle.' —**de·fal·ca·tion** /ˌdēfalˈkāshən; -fôl-/ *n.* —**de·fal·ca·tor** /-kātər/ *n.*

de·fame /diˈfām/ ▸*v.* [*trans.*] damage the good reputation of (someone); slander or libel: *he claimed that the article defamed his family.* See note at MALIGN. ▷Middle English: from Old French *diffamer*, from Latin *diffamare* 'spread evil report,' from *dis-* (expressing removal) + *fama* 'report.' —**def·a·ma·tion** /ˌdefəˈmāshən/ *n.* —**de·fam·a·to·ry** /-ˈfaməˌtôrē/ *adj.* —**de·fam·er** *n.*

de·fa·mil·iar·ize /ˌdēfəˈmilyərīz/ ▸*v.* [*trans.*] render unfamiliar or strange (used esp. in the context of art and literature): *art serves to defamiliarize our experience of our own present.*

de·fang /dēˈfaNG/ ▸*v.* [*trans.*] [often as *adj.*] (**defanged**) render harmless or ineffectual: *the military, demoralized and defanged, gave up their campaign.*

de·fat /dēˈfat/ ▸*v.* (**-fat·ted, -fat·ting**) [*trans.*] [usu. as *adj.*] (**defatted**) remove fat from (food): *soup made with defatted chicken stock.*

de·fault /diˈfôlt/ ▸*n.* **1** failure to fulfill an obligation, esp. to repay a loan or appear in a court of law: *it will have to restructure its debts to avoid default.* **2** a preselected option adopted by a computer program or other mechanism when no alternative is specified by the user or programmer: *the default is fifty lines* | [as *adj.*] *default settings.*
▸*v.* [*intrans.*] **1** fail to fulfill an obligation, esp. to repay a loan or to appear in a court of law: *some had* **defaulted on** *student loans.* ■ [*trans.*] declare (a party) in default and give judgment against that party: *the possibility that cases would be defaulted and defendants released.* **2** (**default to**) (of a computer program or other mechanism) revert automatically to (a preselected option): *when you start a fresh letter, the system will default to its own style.* ▷Middle English: from Old French *defaut*, from *defaillir* 'to fail,' based on Latin *fallere* 'disappoint, deceive.'
▸**PHRASES** □ **by default** because of a lack of opposition: *they won the last election by default.* ■ through lack of positive action rather than conscious choice: *legislation dies by default if the governor fails to act on it.* □ **in default** guilty of failing to repay a loan or appear in a court of law: *the company is already* **in default on** *its loans.* □ **in default of** in the absence of: *in default of agreement, the rent was to be determined by a surveyor.*

de·fault·er /diˈfôltər/ ▸*n.* a person who fails to fulfill a duty, obligation, or undertaking, esp. to pay a debt. ■ a person who fails to complete a course of medical treatment.

de·fea·sance /diˈfēzəns/ ▸*n. Law* the action or process of rendering something null and void. ■ a clause or condition which, if fulfilled, renders a deed or contract null and void. ▷late Middle English (as a legal term): from Old French *defesance*, from *defaire, desfaire* 'undo' (see DEFEAT).

de·fea·si·ble /diˈfēzəbəl/ ▸*adj. chiefly Law Philosophy* open in principle to revision, valid objection, forfeiture, or annulment. ▷Middle English: via Anglo-Norman French from the stem of Old French *desfesant* 'undoing' (see also DEFEASANCE). —**de·fea·si·bil·i·ty** /-ˌfēzəˈbilitē/ *n.* —**de·fea·si·bly** /-blē/ *adv.*

de·feat /diˈfēt/ ▸*v.* [*trans.*] win a victory over (someone) in a battle or other contest; overcome or beat: *Arab armies defeated the Byzantine garrison.* ■ prevent (someone) from achieving an aim: *she was defeated by the last steep hill.* ■ prevent (an aim) from being achieved: *don't cheat by allowing your body to droop—this defeats the object of the exercise.* ■ reject or block (a motion or proposal): *the amendment was defeated.* ■ be impossible for (someone) to understand: *this line of reasoning defeats me, I must confess.* ■ *Law* render null and void; annul.
▸*n.* an instance of defeating or being defeated: *the defeat of Nazi Germany in 1945* | *she had still not quite admitted defeat.* ▷late Middle English (in the sense 'undo, destroy, annul'): from Old French *desfait* 'undone,' past participle of *desfaire*, from medieval Latin *disfacere* 'undo.'

de·feat·ed /diˈfētid/ ▸*adj.* having been beaten in a battle or other contest: *the defeated army.* ■ demoralized and overcome by adversity. —**de·feat·ed·ly** *adv.*

de·feat·ist /diˈfētist/ ▸*n.* a person who expects or is excessively ready to accept failure.
▸*adj.* demonstrating expectation or acceptance of failure: *we have a duty not to be so defeatist.* ▷early 20th cent.: from French *défaitiste*, from *défaite* 'defeat.' —**de·feat·ism** /-tizəm/ *n.*

def·e·cate /ˈdefiˌkāt/ ▸*v.* [*intrans.*] discharge feces from the body. ▷late Middle English (in the sense 'clear of dregs, purify'): from Latin *defaecat-* 'cleared of dregs,' from the verb *defaecare*, from *de-* (expressing removal) + *faex, faec-* 'dregs.' The current sense dates from the mid 19th cent. —**def·e·ca·tion** /ˌdefiˈkāshən/ *n.* —**def·e·ca·tor** /-ˌkātər/ *n.* —**def·e·ca·to·ry** /-kəˌtôrē/ *adj.*

de·fect[1] /ˈdēˌfekt/ ▸*n.* a shortcoming, imperfection, or lack: *genetic defects* | *the property is free from defect.* ▷late Middle English (as a noun, influenced by Old French *defect* 'deficiency'): from Latin *defectus*, past participle of *deficere* 'desert or fail,' from *de-* (expressing reversal) + *facere* 'do.'

de·fect[2] /diˈfekt/ ▸*v.* [*intrans.*] abandon one's country or cause in favor of an opposing one: *he* **defected to** *the Soviet Union after the war.* ▷late 16th cent.: from Latin *defect-* 'failed,' from the verb *deficere* (see DEFECT[1]). —**de·fec·tion** /diˈfekshən/ *n.* —**de·fec·tor** /-tər/ *n.*

de·fec·tive /diˈfektiv/ ▸*adj.* imperfect or faulty: *complaints over defective goods.* ■ *archaic* or *offensive* mentally handicapped. ■ lacking or deficient: *dystrophin is commonly* **defective in** *muscle tissue.* ■ *Grammar* (of a word) not having all the inflections normal for the part of speech.
▸*n. archaic* or *offensive* a mentally handicapped person. —**de·fec·tive·ly** *adv.* —**de·fec·tive·ness** *n.*

de·fem·i·nize /dēˈfeməˌnīz/ ▸*v.* [*trans.*] deprive of feminine characteristics.

de·fence ▸*n.* British spelling of DEFENSE.

de·fend /diˈfend/ ▸*v.* [*trans.*] resist an attack made on (someone or something); protect from harm or danger: *we shall defend our country, whatever the cost.* ■ speak or write in favor of (an action or person); attempt to justify: *he defended his policy of imposing high taxes.* ■ conduct the case for (the party being accused or sued) in a lawsuit: *the lawyer had defended anticommunist dissidents.* ■ compete to retain (a title or seat) in a contest or election: *he successfully defended his Congressional seat in new elections* | [as *adj.*] (**defending**) *the defending champion.* ■ [*intrans.*] (in sports) protect one's goal rather than attempt to score against one's opponents. ▷Middle English: from Old French *defendre*, from Latin *defendere*, from *de-* 'off' + *-fendere* 'to strike.' Compare with OFFEND. —**de·fend·a·ble** *adj.*

de·fend·ant /diˈfendənt/ ▸*n.* an individual, company, or institution sued or accused in a court of law. Compare with PLAINTIFF. ▷Middle English (as an adjective in the sense 'defending'): from Old French, 'warding off,' present participle of *defendre* (see DEFEND).

de·fend·er /diˈfendər/ ▸*n.* a person who defends someone or something: *a defender of family values.* ■ (in soccer, hockey, and other games) a player whose task it is to protect the team's goal. ■ *Bridge* either member of the partnership that did not win the auction. Compare with DECLARER. ▷Middle English: from Old French *defendeor.*

De·fend·er of the Faith ▸*n.* a title conferred on Henry VIII by Pope Leo X in 1521. It was recognized by Parliament as an official title of the English monarch in 1544 and has been borne by all subsequent sovereigns. ▷translation of Latin *Fidei Defensor.*

de·fen·es·tra·tion /dēˌfenəˈstrāshən/ ▸*n. formal or humorous* the action of throwing someone or something out of a window. ▷early 17th cent.: from modern Latin *defenestratio(n-)*, from *de-* 'down from' + Latin *fenestra* 'window.' —**de·fen·es·trate** /-ˈfenəˌstrāt/ *v.*

de·fense /diˈfens; ˈdēˌfens/ (*Brit.* **de·fence**) ▸*n.* **1** the action of defending from or resisting attack: *they relied on missiles for the country's defense* | *she came* **to the defense of** *the eccentric professor.* ■ attempted justification or vindication of something: *he spoke* **in defense of** *a disciplined approach.* ■ an instance of defending a title or seat in a contest or election: *his first title defense against Jones.* ■ military measures or resources for protecting a country: *the minister of defense* | [as *adj.*] *defense policy.* ■ a means of protecting something from attack: *education is the best defense against tyranny.* ■ (**defenses**) fortifications or barriers against attack: *coastal defenses.* ■ (in sports) the action or role of defending one's goal against the opposition: *we played solid defense.* ■ (**the defense**) the players in a team who perform this role. **2** the case presented by or on behalf of the party being accused or sued in a lawsuit. **3** one or more defendants in a trial. ■ (usu. **the defense**) [treated as *sing.* or *pl.*] the counsel for the defendant in a lawsuit: *the defense requested more time to prepare their case.* ▷Middle English: from Old French *defens*, from late Latin *defensum* (neuter), *defensa* (feminine), past participles of *defendere* 'defend.'
▸**PHRASE** □ **defense in depth** the practice of arranging defensive lines or fortifications so that they can defend each other, esp. in case of an enemy incursion.

de·fense·less /diˈfenslis/ ▸*adj.* without defense or protection; totally vulnerable: *attacks on defenseless civilians.* —**de·fense·less·ness** *n.*

de·fense·man /diˈfensmən/ ▸*n.* (*pl.* **-men**) (in ice hockey and lacrosse) a player in a defensive position.

de·fense mech·an·ism ▸*n.* an automatic reaction of the body against disease-causing organisms. ■ a mental process (e.g., repression or projection) initiated, typically unconsciously, to avoid conscious conflict or anxiety.

de·fen·si·ble /diˈfensəbəl/ ▸*adj.* **1** justifiable by argument: *a morally defensible penal system.* **2** able to be protected: *a fort with a defensible yard at its feet.* ▷Middle English (used as a weapon, a fortified place, etc., in the sense 'capable of giving protective defense'): from late Latin *defensibilis*, from Latin *defendere* (see DEFEND). —**de·fen·si·bil·i·ty** /diˌfensəˈbilitē/ *n.* —**de·fen·si·bly** /-blē/ *adv.*

de·fen·sive /diˈfensiv/ ▸*adj.* **1** used or intended to defend or protect: *troops in defensive positions.* ■ [*attrib.*] (in sports) relating to or intended as defense. **2** very anxious to challenge or avoid criticism: *he was very defensive about that side of his life.* ▷late Middle English: from Old French *défensif, -ive*, from medieval Latin *defensivus*, from Latin *defens-* 'warded off,' from the verb *defendere* (see DEFEND). —**de·fen·sive·ness** *n.*
▸**PHRASE** □ **on the defensive** expecting or resisting criticism or attack: *the forces have remained on the defensive.*

de·fen·sive end ▸*n. Football* either of the two defensive players positioned at the end of the players who are linemen.

de·fen·sive·ly /diˈfensivlē/ ▸*adv.* in a defensive manner: *"No, I didn't," he replied defensively.* ■ (in sports) in terms of defense: *we must tighten up defensively.*

de·fer[1] /diˈfər/ ▸*v.* (**-ferred, -fer·ring**) [*trans.*] put off (an action or event) to a later time; postpone: *they deferred the decision until February.* See note at POSTPONE.

▪ *historical* postpone the conscription of (someone): *he was no longer* ***deferred from*** *the draft.* ▷late Middle English (also in the sense 'put on one side'): from Old French *differer* 'defer or differ,' from Latin *differre,* from *dis-* 'apart' + *ferre* 'bring, carry.' Compare with DEFER[2] and DIFFER. —**de·fer·ment** *n.* —**de·fer·ra·ble** *adj.* —**de·fer·ral** /-ˈfərəl/ *n.*

de·fer[2] ▸*v.* (**-ferred, -fer·ring**) [*intrans.*] (**defer to**) submit humbly to (a person or a person's wishes or qualities): *he deferred to Tim's superior knowledge.* ▷late Middle English: from Old French *deferer,* from Latin *deferre* 'carry away, refer (a matter),' from *de-* 'away from' + *ferre* 'bring, carry.' Compare with DEFER[1]. —**de·fer·rer** *n.*

def·er·ence /ˈdefərəns/ ▸*n.* humble submission and respect: *he addressed her with the deference due to age.* See note at HONOR. ▷mid 17th cent.: from French *déférence,* from *déférer* 'refer' (see DEFER[2]).

▸*PHRASE* □ **in deference to** out of respect for; in consideration of.

def·er·ent[1] /ˈdefərənt/ ▸*adj.* another term for DEFERENTIAL. ▷early 19th cent.: from DEFER[2] and DEFERENCE.

def·er·ent[2] ▸*n.* (in the Ptolemaic system of astronomy) the large circular orbit followed by the center of the small epicycle in which a planet was thought to move. ▷late Middle English: from medieval Latin *deferent-* 'carrying away,' from the verb *deferre.*

def·er·en·tial /ˌdefəˈrenCHəl/ ▸*adj.* showing deference; respectful: *people were always* ***deferential to*** *him.* ▷early 19th cent.: from DEFERENCE, on the pattern of pairs such as *prudence, prudential.* —**def·er·en·tial·ly** *adv.*

de·ferred an·nu·i·ty ▸*n.* an annuity that commences only after a lapse of some specified time after the final purchase premium has been paid.

de·fer·ves·cence /ˌdēfərˈvesəns; ˌdefər-/ ▸*n. Medicine* the abatement of a fever as indicated by a decrease in bodily temperature. ▷early 18th cent.: from Latin *defervescent-* 'ceasing to boil,' from the verb *defervescere.* —**de·fer·vesce** /-ˈves/ *v.*

de·fi·ance /diˈfīəns/ ▸*n.* open resistance; bold disobedience: *the demonstration was held* ***in defiance of*** *official warnings.* ▷Middle English (denoting the renunciation of an allegiance or friendship): from Old French, from *defier* 'defy.'

de·fi·ant /diˈfīənt/ ▸*adj.* showing defiance: *she was in a defiant mood.* ▷late 16th cent.: from French *défiant* or directly from DEFIANCE. —**de·fi·ant·ly** *adv.*

de·fib·ril·la·tion /dēˌfibrəˈlāSHən/ ▸*n. Medicine* the stopping of fibrillation of the heart by administering a controlled electric shock in order to allow restoration of the normal rhythm. —**de·fib·ril·late** /dēˈfibrəˌlāt/ *v.*

de·fib·ril·la·tor /dēˈfibrəˌlātər/ ▸*n. Medicine* an apparatus used to control heart fibrillation by application of an electric current to the chest wall or heart.

de·fi·cien·cy /diˈfiSHənsē/ ▸*n.* (*pl.* **-cies**) a lack or shortage: *vitamin A deficiency in children.* ▪ a failing or shortcoming: *they did not like having the deficiencies of their city pointed out to them.*

de·fi·cien·cy dis·ease ▸*n.* a disease caused by the lack of some essential or important element in the diet, usually a particular vitamin or mineral. See also IMMUNODEFICIENCY.

de·fi·cien·cy pay·ment ▸*n.* a payment made, typically by a government body, to cover a financial deficit incurred in the course of an activity such as farming or education.

de·fi·cient /diˈfiSHənt/ ▸*adj.* [*predic.*] not having enough of a specified quality or ingredient: *this diet is* ***deficient in*** *vitamin B.* ▪ insufficient or inadequate: *they trashed the legislation as deficient.* ▪ (also **mentally deficient**) *offensive* having a mental handicap. ▷late 16th cent. (originally in the theological phrase *deficient cause,* denoting a failure or deficiency that has a particular consequence): from Latin *deficient-* 'failing,' from the verb *deficere* (see DEFECT[1]).

def·i·cit /ˈdefəsit/ ▸*n.* the amount by which something, esp. a sum of money, is too small. ▪ an excess of expenditure or liabilities over income or assets in a given period: *an annual operating deficit | the budget will remain* ***in deficit.*** ▪ (in sports) the amount or score by which a team or individual is losing: *came back from a 3–0 deficit.* ▪ *technical* a deficiency or failing, esp. in a neurological or psychological function: ***deficits in*** *speech comprehension.* ▷late 18th cent.: via French from Latin *deficit* 'it is lacking,' from the verb *deficere* (see DEFECT[1]).

def·i·cit fi·nanc·ing ▸*n.* government funding of spending by borrowing.

def·i·cit spend·ing ▸*n.* government spending, in excess of revenue, of funds raised by borrowing rather than from taxation.

def·i·lade /ˈdefəˌlād; ˌdefəˈlād/ *Military* ▸*n.* the protection of a position, vehicle, or troops against enemy observation or gunfire.

▸*v.* [*trans.*] protect (a position, vehicle, or troops) against enemy observation or gunfire: [as *adj.*] (**defiladed**) *a defiladed tank.* ▷early 19th cent.: from French *défiler* 'protect from the enemy' + -ADE[1].

de·file[1] /diˈfīl/ ▸*v.* [*trans.*] sully, mar, or spoil: *the land was defiled by a previous owner.* See note at POLLUTE. ▪ desecrate or profane (something sacred): *the tomb had been defiled and looted.* ▪ *archaic* violate the chastity of (a woman). ▷late Middle English: alteration of obsolete *defoul,* from Old French *defouler* 'trample down,' influenced by obsolete *befile* 'befoul, defile.' —**de·file·ment** *n.* —**de·fil·er** *n.*

de·file[2] /diˈfīl; ˈdēˌfīl/ ▸*n.* a steep-sided, narrow gorge or passage (originally one requiring troops to march in single file).

▸*v.* [*intrans.*] *archaic* (of troops) march in single file: *we emerged after defiling through the mountainsides.* ▷late 17th cent.: from French *défilé* (noun), *défiler* (verb), from *dé* 'away from' + *file* 'column, file.'

de·fine /diˈfīn/ ▸*v.* [*trans.*] **1** state or describe exactly the nature, scope, or meaning of: *the contract will seek to define the client's obligations.* ▪ give the meaning of (a word or phrase), esp. in a dictionary. ▪ make up or establish the character of: *for some, the football team defines their identity.* **2** mark out the boundary or limits of: [as *adj.*] (**defined**) *clearly defined boundaries.* ▪ make clear the outline of; delineate: *she defined her eyes by applying eyeshadow.* ▷late Middle English (also in the sense 'bring to an end'): from Old French *definer,* from a variant of Latin *definire,* from *de-* (expressing completion) + *finire* 'finish' (from *finis* 'end'). —**de·fin·a·ble** *adj.* —**de·fin·er** *n.*

de·fin·i·en·dum /diˌfinēˈendəm/ ▸*n.* (*pl.* **-da** /-də/) a word, phrase, or symbol that is the subject of a definition, esp. in a dictionary entry, or that is introduced into a logical system by being defined. Contrasted with DEFINIENS. ▷late 19th cent.: from Latin, 'that which is to be defined,' from the verb *definire* (see DEFINE).

de·fin·i·ens /diˈfinēənz/ ▸*n.* (*pl.* **de·fin·i·en·ti·a** /diˌfinēˈensH(ē)ə/) a word, phrase, or symbolic expression used to define something, esp. in a dictionary entry, or introducing a word or symbol into a logical system by providing a statement of its meaning. Contrasted with DEFINIENDUM. ▷late 19th cent.: from medieval Latin, 'defining,' present participle of *definire* (see DEFINE).

de·fin·ing mo·ment ▸*n.* an event that typifies or determines all subsequent related occurrences.

def·i·nite /ˈdefənit/ ▸*adj.* clearly stated or decided; not vague or doubtful: *we had no definite plans.* ▪ clearly true or real; unambiguous: *no definite proof has emerged.* ▪ [*predic.*] (of a person) certain or sure about something: *you're very definite about that!* ▪ clear or undeniable (used for emphasis): *video is a definite asset in the classroom.* ▪ having exact and discernible physical limits or form. ▷mid 16th cent.: from Latin *definitus* 'defined, set within limits,' past participle of *definire* (see DEFINE). —**def·i·nite·ness** *n.*

USAGE For an explanation of the difference between **definite** and **definitive**, see **usage** at DEFINITIVE.

def·i·nite ar·ti·cle ▸*n. Grammar* a determiner (*the* in English) that introduces a noun phrase and implies that the thing mentioned has already been mentioned, or is common knowledge, or is about to be defined (as in *the book on the table; the art of government; the famous poet and short story writer*). Compare with INDEFINITE ARTICLE.

def·i·nite de·scrip·tion ▸*n. chiefly Philosophy* a noun phrase introduced by the definite article or its equivalent, and purporting to denote a particular entity or phenomenon.

def·i·nite in·te·gral ▸*n. Mathematics* an integral expressed as the difference between the values of the integral at specified upper and lower limits of the independent variable.

def·i·nite·ly /ˈdefənitlē/ ▸*adv.* without doubt (used for emphasis): *I will definitely be at the airport to meet you.* | ▪ in a definite manner; clearly: *we couldn't plan to go elsewhere until we had heard from you more definitely.*

def·i·ni·tion /ˌdefəˈniSHən/ ▸*n.* **1** a statement of the exact meaning of a word, esp. in a dictionary. ▪ an exact statement or description of the nature, scope, or meaning of something: *our definition of what constitutes poetry.* ▪ the action or process of defining something. **2** the degree of distinctness in outline of an object, image, or sound, esp. of an image in a photograph or on a screen. ▪ the capacity of an instrument or device for making images distinct in outline: [in *combination*] *high-definition television.* ▷late Middle English: from Latin *definitio(n-),* from the verb *definire* 'set bounds to' (see DEFINE). —**def·i·ni·tion·al** /-SHənl/ *adj.* —**def·i·ni·tion·al·ly** /-SHənl-ē/ *adv.*

▸*PHRASE* □ **by definition** by its very nature; intrinsically: *underachievement, by definition, is not due to lack of talent.*

de·fin·i·tive /diˈfinitiv/ ▸*adj.* **1** (of a conclusion or agreement) done or reached decisively and with authority: *a definitive diagnosis.* ▪ (of a book or other text) the most authoritative of its kind: *the definitive biography of Harry Truman.* **2** (of a postage stamp) for general use and typically of standard design, not special or commemorative.

▸*n.* a definitive postage stamp. ▷late Middle English: from Old French *definitif, -ive,* from Latin *definitivus,* from *definit-* 'set within limits,' from the verb *definire* (see DEFINE). —**de·fin·i·tive·ly** *adv.*

USAGE **Definitive** in the sense 'decisive, unconditional, final' is sometimes confused with **definite. Definite** means 'clearly defined, precise, having fixed limits,' but **definitive** goes further, meaning 'most complete, satisfying all criteria, most authoritative': *although some critics found a few* ***definite*** *weak spots in the author's interpretations, his book was nonetheless widely regarded as the* ***definitive*** *history of the war.* A **definite** decision is simply one that has been made clearly and is without doubt, whereas a **definitive** decision is one that is not only conclusive but also carries the stamp of authority or is a benchmark for the future, as in a Supreme Court ruling. It is a common error to use **definitive** as though it were a more elegant way of saying **definite.**

de·fin·i·tive host ▸*n. Biology* an organism that supports the adult or sexually reproductive form of a parasite. Compare with INTERMEDIATE HOST.

def·la·grate /ˈdefləˌgrāt/ ▸*v. dated Chemistry* burn away or cause (a substance) to burn away with a sudden flame and rapid, sharp combustion: [*trans.*] *the current will deflagrate some of the particles.* ▷early 18th cent.: from Latin *deflagrat-* 'burned up,' from the verb *deflagrare,* from *de-* 'away, thoroughly' + *flagrare* 'to burn.' —**def·la·gra·tor** /-tər/ *n.*

def·la·gra·tion /ˌdefləˈgrāSHən/ ▸*n.* the action of heating a substance until it burns away rapidly. ▪ *technical* combustion that propagates through a gas or across the surface of an explosive at subsonic speeds, driven by the transfer of heat. Compare with DETONATION. ▷early 17th cent.: from Latin *deflagratio(n-),* from the verb *deflagrare* (see DEFLAGRATE).

de·flate /diˈflāt/ ▸*v.* **1** [*trans.*] let air or gas out of (a tire, balloon, or similar object): *he deflated one of the tires.* ▪ [*intrans.*] be emptied of air or gas: *the balloon deflated.* **2** cause (someone) to suddenly lose confidence or feel less important: [as *adj.*] (**deflated**) *the news left him feeling utterly deflated.* ▪ reduce the level of (an emotion or feeling): *her anger was deflated.* **3** *Economics* bring about a general reduction of price levels in (an economy). ▷late 19th cent.: from DE- (expressing reversal) + *-flate* (as in *inflate*). —**de·fla·tor** /-tər/ *n.*

de·fla·tion /diˈflāSHən/ ▸*n.* **1** the action or process of deflating or being deflated: *deflation of the illusion that the 1960s were a perpetual party.* **2** *Economics* reduction of the general level of prices in an economy. **3** *Geology* the removal of particles of rock, sand, etc., by the wind. ▷late 19th cent. (in the sense 'release of air from something inflated'): from DEFLATE; sense 3 via German from Latin *deflat-* 'blown away,' from the verb *deflare.* —**de·fla·tion·ist** /-ist/ *n.* & *adj.*

de·fla·tion·ar·y /diˈflāSHəˌnerē/ ▸*adj.* of, characterized by, or tending to cause economic deflation.

de·flect /diˈflekt/ ▸*v.* [*trans.*] cause (something) to change direction by interposing something; turn aside from a straight course: *the bullet was deflected harmlessly into the ceiling | figurative he attempted to deflect attention away from his private life.* ▪ [*intrans.*] (of an object) change direction after hitting something: *the ball* ***deflected off*** *his body.* ▪ cause (someone) to deviate from an intended purpose: *she refused to be* ***deflected from*** *anything she had set her mind on.* ▪ cause (something) to change orientation: *the compass needle is* ***deflected from*** *magnetic north by metal in the aircraft.*

▷mid 16th cent.: from Latin *deflectere*, from *de-* 'away from' + *flectere* 'to bend.'

de·flec·tion /di'flekSHən/ (also **de·flex·ion**) ▶*n.* the action or process of deflecting or being deflected: *the deflection of the light beam.* ■ the amount by which something is deflected: *an 11-mile deflection of the river.* ▷early 17th cent.: from late Latin *deflexio(n-)*, from *deflectere* 'bend away' (see DEFLECT).

de·flec·tor /di'flektər/ ▶*n.* a device that deflects something, in particular: ■ a plate or other attachment for deflecting a flow of air, water, heat, etc. ■ an electrode in a cathode-ray tube whose magnetic field is used to deflect a beam of electrons onto a phosphor screen to form an image.

de·flexed /di'flekst/ ▶*adj. technical* (typically of plant or animal structures) bent or curving downward or backward: *a deflexed beak.* ▷early 19th cent. (earlier as *deflex*): from Latin *deflexus* 'bent away' (past participle of *deflectere*) + -ED[1].

de·floc·cu·late /dē'fläkyə,lāt/ ▶*v.* [*trans.*] *Chemistry* break up the floccules (of a substance suspended in a liquid) into fine particles, producing a dispersion. —**de·floc·cu·la·tion** /dē,fläkyə'lāSHən/ *n.*

def·lo·ra·tion /,deflə'rāSHən/ ▶*n. poetic/literary* the taking of a woman's virginity. ▷late Middle English: from late Latin *defloratio(n-)*, from the verb *deflorare* (see DEFLOWER).

de·flow·er /dē'flou(-ə)r/ ▶*v.* [*trans.*] **1** *dated or poetic/literary* deprive (a woman) of her virginity. **2** [usu. as *adj.*] (**deflowered**) strip (a plant or garden) of flowers: *deflowered rose bushes.* ▷late Middle English: from Old French *desflourer*, from a variant of late Latin *deflorare*, from *de-* (expressing removal) + Latin *flos, flor-* 'a flower.'

de·fo·cus /dē'fōkəs/ ▶*v.* (**-fo·cused**, **-fo·cus·ing** or **-fo·cussed**, **-fo·cus·sing**) [*trans.*] cause (an image, lens, or beam) to go out of focus: *the filter lets you defocus all or part of an image.* ■ [*intrans.*] go out of focus: *the view defocused, then resolved.* ■ take the focus of interest or activity away from (something): *defocusing the traditional contract approach in business.*

De·foe /də'fō/, Daniel (1660–1731), English novelist and journalist. His novel, *Robinson Crusoe* (1719), is loosely based on the true story of shipwrecked sailor Alexander Selkirk and has a claim to being the first British novel. Other notable works: *Moll Flanders* (1722) and *A Journal of the Plague Year* (1722).

de·fog·ger /dē'fôgər; -'fä-/ ▶*n.* a device on a vehicle that removes condensation from the windshield by directing a jet of air onto it. —**de·fog** *v.*

de·fo·li·ant /dē'fōlēənt/ ▶*n.* a chemical that removes the leaves from trees and plants and is often used in warfare.

de·fo·li·ate /dē'fōlē,āt/ ▶*v.* [*trans.*] remove leaves from (a tree, plant, or area of land), for agricultural purposes or as a military tactic: *the area was defoliated and napalmed many times.* ▷late 18th cent.: from late Latin *defoliat-* 'stripped of leaves,' from the verb *defoliare*, from *de-* (expressing removal) + *folium* 'leaf.' —**de·fo·li·a·tion** /dē,fōlē'āSHən/ *n.*

de·fo·li·a·tor /dē'fōlē,ātər/ ▶*n.* an adult or larval insect that strips all the leaves from a tree or shrub. ■ a machine that removes the leaves from a root crop.

de·force /di'fôrs/ ▶*v.* [*trans.*] *Law* withhold (land or other property) wrongfully or forcibly from the rightful owner. ■ deprive (someone) wrongfully or forcibly of rightful property. ▷late Middle English: from Anglo-Norman French *deforcer*, from *de-* (expressing removal) + *forcer* 'to force.'

de·for·est /dē'fôrist; -'fär-/ ▶*v.* [*trans.*] (often **be deforested**) clear (an area) of forests or trees. —**de·for·est·a·tion** /dē,fôrə'stāSHən; -,fär-/ *n.*

De For·est /də 'fôrəst; 'fär-/, Lee (1873–1961), U.S. physicist and electrical engineer. He designed a triode valve that was crucial to the development of radio communication, television, and computers. De Forest successfully transmitted a live broadcast in 1910.

de·form /di'fôrm/ ▶*v.* [*trans.*] distort the shape or form of; make misshapen: [as *adj.*] (**deformed**) *deformed hands.* ■ [*intrans.*] become distorted or misshapen; undergo deformation: *the suspension deforms slightly on corners.* ▷late Middle English: from Old French *desformer*, via medieval Latin from Latin *deformare*, from *de-* (expressing reversal) + *forma* 'a shape.' —**de·form·a·ble** *adj.*

de·for·ma·tion /,dēfôr'māSHən; ,defər-/ ▶*n.* the action or process of changing in shape or distorting, esp. through the application of pressure: *solid rock undergoing slow deformation.* ■ the result of such a process: *the deformation will be temporary.* ■ an altered form of a word, esp. one used to avoid overt profanity (e.g., *dang* for *damn*). —**de·for·ma·tion·al** /-SHənl/ *adj.*

de·form·i·ty /di'fôrmitē/ ▶*n.* (*pl.* **-ties**) a deformed part, esp. of the body; a malformation: *children born with deformities.* ■ the state of being deformed or misshapen: *respiratory problems caused by spinal deformity.* ▷late Middle English: from Old French *desformite*, from Latin *deformitas*, from *deformis* 'misshapen.'

de·frag /dē'frag/ ▶*v.* (**-fragged**, **-frag·ging**) [*trans.*] *Computing* short for DEFRAGMENT.
▶*n.* an instance of defragging a disk, or the utility that does this.

de·frag·ment /,dēfrag'ment/ ▶*v.* [*trans.*] *Computing* (of software) reduce the fragmentation of (a file) by concatenating parts stored in separate locations on a disk: *the safe way to defragment your files.* —**de·frag·men·ta·tion** /dē,fragmən'tāSHən; -,men-/ *n.* —**de·frag·ment·er** *n.*

de·fraud /di'frôd/ ▶*v.* [*trans.*] illegally obtain money from (someone) by deception: *he used a false identity to* ***defraud** the bank **of** thousands of dollars* | [*intrans.*] *conspiracy to defraud.* ▷late Middle English: from Old French *defrauder* or Latin *defraudare*, from *de-* 'from' + *fraudare* 'to cheat' (from *fraus, fraud-* 'fraud'). —**de·fraud·er** *n.*

de·fray /di'frā/ ▶*v.* [*trans.*] provide money to pay (a cost or expense): *the proceeds from the raffle help to defray the expenses of the evening.* ▷late Middle English (in the general sense 'spend money'): from French *défrayer*, from *dé-* (expressing removal) + obsolete *frai* 'cost, expenses' (from medieval Latin *fredum* 'a fine for breach of the peace'). —**de·fray·a·ble** *adj.* —**de·fray·al** /-'frāəl/ *n.* —**de·fray·ment** *n.*

de·frock /dē'fräk/ ▶*v.* [*trans.*] deprive (a person in holy orders) of ecclesiastical status. ■ [usu. as *adj.*] (**defrocked**) deprive (someone) of professional status or membership in a prestigious group: *a defrocked psychiatrist.* ▷early 17th cent.: from French *défroquer*, from *dé-* (expressing removal) + *froc* 'frock.'

de·frost /di'frôst/ ▶*v.* [*trans.*] remove frost or ice from (the windshield of a motor vehicle). ■ thaw (frozen food) before cooking it: *defrost the turkey slowly.* ■ [*intrans.*] (of frozen food) thaw before being cooked: *make sure that it has thoroughly defrosted.* ■ free (the interior of a refrigerator) of accumulated ice, usually by turning it off for a period. ■ [*intrans.*] (of a refrigerator) become free of accumulated ice in this way: *she opened the door to let the fridge defrost.* —**de·frost·er** *n.*

deft /deft/ ▶*adj.* neatly skillful and quick in one's movements: *a deft piece of footwork.* ■ demonstrating skill and cleverness: *the script was both deft and literate.* ▷Middle English: variant of DAFT, in the obsolete sense 'meek.' —**deft·ly** *adv.* —**deft·ness** *n.*

de·funct /di'fəNGkt/ ▶*adj.* no longer existing or functioning: *the now defunct communist common market.* ▷mid 16th cent. (in the sense 'deceased'): from Latin *defunctus* 'dead,' past participle of *defungi* 'carry out, finish,' from *de-* (expressing reversal) + *fungi* 'perform.'

de·fund /dē'fənd/ ▶*v.* [*trans.*] prevent from continuing to receive funds: *the California legislature has defunded the Industrial Welfare Commission.*

de·fuse /di'fyo͞oz/ ▶*v.* [*trans.*] remove the fuse from (an explosive device) in order to prevent it from exploding: *explosives specialists tried to defuse the grenade.* ■ *figurative* reduce the danger or tension in (a difficult situation): *he had the ability to defuse tense moments with humor.*

> ***USAGE*** On the difference between **defuse** and **diffuse**, see **usage** at DIFFUSE.

de·fy /di'fī/ ▶*v.* (**-fies**, **-fied**) [*trans.*] openly resist or refuse to obey: *a woman who defies convention.* ■ (of a thing) make (an action or quality) almost impossible: *his actions defy belief.* ■ [*trans.*] appear to be challenging (someone) to do or prove something: *he glowered at her, defying her to mock him.* ■ *archaic* challenge to combat: *go now, defy him to the combat.* ▷Middle English (in the senses 'renounce an allegiance' and 'challenge to combat'): from Old French *desfier*, based on Latin *dis-* (expressing reversal) + *fidus* 'faithful.' —**de·fi·er** *n.*

deg. ▶*abbr.* degree(s).

dé·ga·gé /,dāgä'ZHā/ ▶*adj.* unconcerned or unconstrained; relaxed.
▶*n.* (*pl.* same) *Ballet* pointing of the foot to an open position with an arched instep slightly off the floor. ▷late 17th cent.: French, past participle of *dégager* 'set free.'

De·gas /dā'gä/, Edgar (1834–1917), French painter and sculptor. Full name *Hilaire Germain Edgar Degas*.An Impressionist painter, he is known for his paintings of ballet dancers, such as *Dancer Lacing Her Shoe* (*c.*1878).

de·gas /dē'gas/ ▶*v.* (**-gassed**, **-gas·sing**) make or become free of unwanted or excess gas: [*trans.*] *the column has not been degassed* | [*intrans.*] *the summit craters were degassing freely.*

de Gaulle /də 'gôl/, Charles (André Joseph Marie) (1890–1970), French general and statesman; head of government 1944–46; president 1959–69. A wartime organizer of the Free French movement, he is remembered particularly for his assertive foreign policy and for quelling the student uprisings and strikes of May 1968.

de·gauss /dē'gous/ ▶*v.* [*trans.*] [often as *n.*] (**degaussing**) *Electronics* remove unwanted magnetism from (a television or monitor) in order to correct color disturbance. ■ *historical* neutralize the magnetic field of (a ship) by encircling it with a conductor carrying electric currents. —**de·gauss·er** *n.*

de·gen·er·a·cy /di'jenərəsē/ ▶*n.* the state or property of being degenerate: *the ills of society, from sexual degeneracy to political corruption.*

de·gen·er·ate ▶*adj.* /di'jenərit/ **1** having lost the physical, mental, or moral qualities considered normal and desirable; showing evidence of decline: *a degenerate form of a higher civilization.* See note at DEPRAVED. **2** *technical* lacking some property, order, or distinctness of structure previously or usually present, in particular: ■ *Mathematics* relating to or denoting an example of a particular type of equation, curve, or other entity that is equivalent to a simpler type, often occurring when a variable or parameter is set to zero. ■ *Physics* relating to or denoting an energy level that corresponds to more than one quantum state. ■ *Physics* relating to or denoting matter at densities so high that gravitational contraction is counteracted either by the Pauli exclusion principle or by an analogous quantum effect between closely packed neutrons. ■ *Biology* having reverted to a simpler form as a result of losing a complex or adaptive structure present in the ancestral form.
▶*n.* /di'jenərit/ an immoral or corrupt person.
▶*v.* /di'jenə,rāt/ [*intrans.*] decline or deteriorate physically, mentally, or morally: *the quality of life had degenerated* | *the debate* ***degenerated into** a brawl.* ▷late 15th cent.: from Latin *degeneratus* 'no longer of its kind,' from the verb *degenerare*, from *degener* 'debased,' from *de-* 'away from' + *genus, gener-* 'race, kind.' —**de·gen·er·a·cy** /-rəsē/ *n.* —**de·gen·er·ate·ly** /-ritlē/ *adv.*

de·gen·er·a·tion /di,jenə'rāSHən/ ▶*n.* the state or process of being or becoming degenerate; decline or deterioration: *overgrazing has caused serious degeneration of grassland.* ■ *Medicine* deterioration and loss of function in the cells of a tissue or organ: *degeneration of the muscle fibers.*

de·gen·er·a·tive /di'jenərətiv; -ə,rātiv/ ▶*adj.* (of a disease or symptom) characterized by progressive, often irreversible deterioration, and loss of function in the organs or tissues: *degenerative diseases.* ■ of or tending to decline and deterioration: *the young generation had fallen into a degenerative backslide.*

de·gen·er·a·tive joint dis·ease ▶*n.* another term for OSTEOARTHRITIS.

de·gen·er·es·cence /di,jenə'resəns/ ▶*n.* another term for DEGENERATION. ▷mid 19th cent.: from French *dégénérescence*, from *dégénérer* 'to degenerate.'

de·gla·ci·a·tion /dē,glāSHē'āSHən; -,glāsē-/ ▶*n. Geology* the disappearance of ice from a previously glaciated region. ■ a period of geological time during which this takes place: *the last deglaciation.*

de·glam·or·ize /dē'glamə,rīz/ ▶*v.* [*trans.*] make (someone or something) less glamorous or attractive. —**de·glam·or·i·za·tion** /dē,glamərə'zāSHən/ *n.*

de·glaze /dē'glāz/ ▶*v.* [*trans.*] dilute meat sediments in (a pan) in order to make a gravy or sauce, typically using wine: *deglaze the pan with the white wine.* ▷late 19th cent.: from French *déglacer*.

de·glu·ti·tion /,dēglo͞o'tiSHən/ ▶*n. technical* the action or process of swallowing. ▷mid 17th cent.: from French *déglutition* or modern Latin *deglutitio(n-)*, from *deglutire* 'swallow down.' —**de·glu·ti·tive** /dē'glo͞otətiv/ *adj.*

deg·ra·da·tion /,degrə'dāSHən/ ▶*n.* the condition or process of degrading or being degraded: *a trail of human misery and degradation.* ■ *Geology* the wearing

Pronunciation Key ə *ago*; ər *over*; 'ə or ,ə *up*; 'ər or ,ər *fur*; a *hat*; ā *rate*; ä *car*; CH *chew*; e *let*; ē *see*; e(ə)r *air*; i *fit*; ī *by*; i(ə)r *ear*; NG *sing*; ō *go*; ô *for*; oi *boy*; o͝o *good*; o͞o *goo*; ou *out*; SH *she*; TH *thin*; TH *then*; (h)w *why*; ZH *vision*

down of rock by disintegration. ▷mid 16th cent. (in the sense 'deposition from an office or rank as a punishment'): from Old French, or from ecclesiastical Latin *degradatio(n-)*, from the verb *degradare* (see DEGRADE).

de·grade /di'grād/ ▶*v.* **1** [*trans.*] treat or regard (someone) with contempt or disrespect: *she thought that many supposedly erotic pictures degraded women.* See note at HUMBLE. ■ lower the character or quality of: *repeaters clean up and amplify the degraded signal.* ■ *archaic* reduce (someone) to a lower rank, esp. as a punishment: *he was degraded from his high estate.* **2** break down or deteriorate chemically: [*intrans.*] *when exposed to light, the materials will degrade* | [*trans.*] *the bacteria will degrade hydrocarbons.* ■ [*trans.*] *Physics* reduce (energy) to a less readily convertible form. ■ [*trans.*] *Geology* wear down (rock) and cause it to disintegrate. ▷late Middle English: from Old French *degrader*, from ecclesiastical Latin *degradare*, from *de-* 'down, away from' + Latin *gradus* 'step or grade.' **—de·grad·a·bil·i·ty** /di,grādə'bilitē/ *n.* **—de·grad·a·ble** *adj.* **—deg·ra·da·tive** /'degrə,dātiv/ *adj.* **—de·grad·er** *n.*

de·grad·ing /di'grādiNG/ ▶*adj.* causing a loss of self-respect; humiliating: *cruel or degrading treatment.* **—de·grad·ing·ly** *adv.*

de·gran·u·late /dē'granyə,lāt/ ▶*v.* [*intrans.*] *Physiology* (of a cell) lose or release granules of a substance, typically as part of an immune reaction: *the eosinophils degranulate, releasing the toxic contents of the granules.* **—de·gran·u·la·tion** /dē,granyə'lāSHən/ *n.*

de·grease /dē'grēs/ ▶*v.* [*trans.*] [often as *n.*] (**degreasing**) remove excess grease or fat from (something). **—de·greas·ant** /-sənt/ *n.* **—de·greas·er** *n.*

de·gree /di'grē/ ▶*n.* **1** [in *sing.*] the amount, level, or extent to which something happens or is present: *a degree of caution is probably wise* | *a question of degree.* **2** a unit of measurement of angles, one three-hundred-and-sixtieth of the circumference of a circle: *set at an angle of 45 degrees.* (Symbol: °) **3** a stage in a scale or series, in particular: ■ a unit in any of various scales of temperature, intensity, or hardness: *water boils at 100 degrees Celsius.* (Symbol: °) ■ [in *combination*] each of a set of grades (usually three) used to classify burns according to their severity. See FIRST-DEGREE, SECOND-DEGREE, THIRD-DEGREE. ■ [in *combination*] a legal grade of crime or offense, esp. murder: *second-degree murder.* ■ [often in *combination*] a step in direct genealogical descent: *second-degree relatives.* ■ *Music* a position in a musical scale, counting upward from the tonic or fundamental note: *the lowered third degree of the scale.* ■ *Mathematics* the class into which an equation falls according to the highest power of unknowns or variables present: *an equation of the second degree.* ■ *Grammar* any of the three steps on the scale of comparison of gradable adjectives and adverbs, namely positive, comparative, and superlative. ■ *archaic* a thing placed like a step in a series; a tier or row. **4** an academic rank conferred by a college or university after examination or after completion of a course of study, or conferred as an honor on a distinguished person: *a degree in zoology.* ■ *archaic* social or official rank: *persons of unequal degree.* ■ a rank in an order of Freemasonry. ▷Middle English (in the senses 'step,' 'tier,' 'rank,' or 'relative state'): from Old French, based on Latin *de-* 'down' + *gradus* 'step or grade.'

▶*PHRASES* □ **by degrees** a little at a time; gradually: *rivalries and prejudice were by degrees fading out.* □ **to a degree** to some extent: *to a degree, it is possible to educate oneself.* ■ *dated* to a considerable extent: *the pressure you were put under must have been frustrating to a degree.*

de·gree day ▶*n.* a unit used to determine the heating requirements of buildings, representing a fall of one degree below a specified average outdoor temperature (usually 18°C or 65°F) for one day.

de·gree of free·dom ▶*n.* each of a number of independently variable factors affecting the range of states in which a system may exist, in particular: ■ *Physics* a direction in which independent motion can occur. ■ *Chemistry* each of a number of independent factors required to specify a system at equilibrium. ■ *Statistics* the number of independent values or quantities which can be assigned to a statistical distribution.

de·gres·sive /di'gresiv/ ▶*adj.* reducing by gradual amounts. ■ (of taxation) at successively lower rates on lower amounts. ▷early 20th cent.: from Latin *degress-* 'descended' (from the verb *degredi*, from *de-* 'down' + *gradi* 'walk') + -IVE.

de·gu /'dāgo͞o/ ▶*n.* a ratlike rodent with a long silky coat, found in southern South America. • Genus *Octodon*, family Octodontidae: three species. ▷mid 19th cent.: from American Spanish, from South American Indian *deuñ*.

de·gust /di'gəst/ ▶*v.* [*trans.*] *rare* taste (something) carefully, so as to appreciate it fully. ▷early 17th cent.: from Latin *degustare*, from *de-* 'completely' + *gustare* 'to taste.' **—de·gus·ta·tion** /,dēgə'stāSHən/ *n.*

de haut en bas /də ,ōt än 'bä; də ,ō täN 'bä/ ▶*adv.* & *adj.* in a condescending or superior manner: [as *adv.*] *he never addressed his students de haut en bas* | [as *adj.*] *he has a certain de haut en bas style.* ▷late 17th cent.: French, literally 'from above to below.'

de Hav·il·land[1] /də 'havələnd/, Sir Geoffrey (1882–1965), English aircraft designer and manufacturer. He designed and built many aircraft, including the Mosquito used in World War II.

de Hav·il·land[2], Olivia (1916–), U.S. actress; born in Japan; sister of Joan Fontaine. She is noted for her role as Melanie Hamilton in *Gone with the Wind* (1939). Other significant movies in which she appeared included *Hold Back the Dawn* (1941), *To Each His Own* (Academy Award, 1946), and *The Heiress* (Academy Award, 1949).

de·hisce /di'his/ ▶*v.* [*intrans.*] *technical* (of a pod or seed vessel, or of a cut or wound) gape or burst open: *after the anther lobes dehisce, the pollen is set free.* ▷mid 17th cent.: from Latin *dehiscere*, from *de-* 'away' + *hiscere* 'begin to gape' (from *hiare* 'gape'). **—de·his·cence** /-'hisəns/ *n.* **—de·his·cent** /-'hisənt/ *adj.*

de Hooch /də 'hōKH/ (also **de Hoogh**), Pieter (*c.*1629–*c.*1684), Dutch genre painter. He is noted for his depictions of domestic interior and courtyard scenes.

de·horn /dē'hôrn/ ▶*v.* [*trans.*] remove the horns from (an animal).

de·hors /də'(h)ôr/ ▶*prep. Law* other than, not including, or outside the scope of: *the plea shows that no request, dehors the letter, existed.* ▷early 18th cent.: from an Old French usage as a preposition (in modern French functioning as an adverb and noun).

Deh·ra Dun /'dārə 'do͞on/ a city in northern India, in a valley at the foot of the Himalaya Mountains in Uttar Pradesh state; pop. 270,000.

de·hu·man·ize /dē'(h)yo͞omə,nīz/ ▶*v.* [*trans.*] deprive of positive human qualities: [as *adj.*] (**dehumanizing**) *the dehumanizing effects of war.* **—de·hu·man·i·za·tion** /dē,(h)yo͞omənі'zāSHən/ *n.*

de·hu·mid·i·fi·er /,dē(h)yo͞o'midə,fīər/ ▶*n.* a device that removes excess moisture from the air.

de·hu·mid·i·fy /,dē(h)yo͞o'midə,fī/ ▶*v.* (**-fies**, **-fied**) [*trans.*] remove moisture from (the air or a gas). **—de·hu·mid·i·fi·ca·tion** /-midəfi'kāSHən/ *n.*

de·hy·drate /dē'hīdrāt/ ▶*v.* [*trans.*] [often as *adj.*] (**dehydrated**) cause (a person or a person's body) to lose a large amount of water: *his body temperature was high, and he had become dehydrated.* ■ [*intrans.*] lose a large amount of water from the body. ■ remove water from (food) in order to preserve and store it: *dehydrated mashed potatoes.* ▷late 19th cent.: from DE- (expressing removal) + Greek *hudōr, hudr-* 'water.' **—de·hy·dra·tion** /,dēhī'drāSHən/ *n.* **—de·hy·dra·tor** /-tər/ *n.*

de·hy·dro·cho·les·ter·ol /dē,hīdrōkə'lestə,rôl/ ▶*n. Biochemistry* a derivative of cholesterol present in the skin. It can be converted to cholecalciferol (vitamin D_3) by the action of ultraviolet radiation. • Chem. formula: $C_{27}H_{44}O$. The particular isomer involved in vitamin D_3 formation is **7-dehydrocholesterol**. ▷1930s: from *dehydro-* 'that has lost hydrogen' + CHOLESTEROL.

de·hy·dro·ep·i·an·dro·ste·rone (abbr.: **DHEA**) ▶*n.* a naturally occurring weak androgenic steroid hormone produced by the adrenal glands with benefits such as the prevention of aging, the improvement of sexual function, the enhancement of athletic performance, and the treatment of osteoporosis.

de·hy·dro·gen·ase /,dē'hīdrəjə,nās; -,nāz/ ▶*n. Biochemistry* an enzyme that catalyzes the removal of hydrogen atoms from a particular molecule, particularly in the electron transport chain reactions of cell respiration in conjunction with the coenzymes NAD and FAD: [with *adj.*] *glucose-6-phosphate dehydrogenase.* ▷early 20th cent.: from DE- (expressing removal) + HYDROGEN + -ASE.

de·hy·dro·gen·ate /dē'hīdrəjə,nāt/ ▶*v.* [*trans.*] *Chemistry* remove a hydrogen atom or atoms from (a compound). ▷mid 19th cent.: from DE- (expressing removal) + HYDROGEN + -ATE[3]. **—de·hy·dro·gen·a·tion** /dē,hīdrəjə'nāSHən/ *n.*

De·ia·ni·ra /,dēyə'nīrə/ *Greek Mythology* the wife of Hercules, who was tricked into smearing poison on a garment that caused his death.

de·ice /dē'īs/ ▶*v.* [*trans.*] remove ice from: *airplanes are de-iced before takeoff.* **—de·ic·er** *n.*

de·i·cide /'dēə,sīd/ ▶*n.* the killer of a god. ■ the killing of a god. ▷early 17th cent.: from ecclesiastical Latin *deicida* 'killer of a god,' or directly from Latin *deus* 'god' + -CIDE. **—de·i·cid·al** /,dēə'sīdl/ *adj.*

deic·tic /'dīktik/ *Linguistics* ▶*adj.* of, relating to, or denoting a word or expression whose meaning is dependent on the context in which it is used, e.g., *here, you, me, that one there,* or *next Tuesday.* Also called INDEXICAL.

▶*n.* a deictic word or expression. ▷early 19th cent.: from Greek *deiktikos, deiktos* 'demonstrative' **—deic·ti·cal·ly** /-ik(ə)lē/ *adv.* .

de·i·fy /'dēə,fī/ ▶*v.* (**-fies**, **-fied**) [*trans.*] (usu. **be deified**) worship, regard, or treat (someone or something) as a god: *she was deified by the early Romans as a fertility goddess.* ▷Middle English (in the sense 'make godlike in character'): from Old French *deifier*, from ecclesiastical Latin *deificare*, from *deus* 'god.' **—de·i·fi·ca·tion** /,dēəfi'kāSHən/ *n.*

Deigh·ton /'dātn/, Len (1929–), English writer; full name *Leonard Cyril Deighton.* Several of his spy thrillers have been adapted as movies and for television. Notable works: *The Ipcress File* (1962) and the trilogy *Berlin Game, Mexico Set,* and *London Match* (1983–85).

deign /dān/ ▶*v.* [*intrans.*] do something that one considers to be beneath one's dignity: *she did not deign to answer the maid's question.* ■ [*trans.*] *archaic* condescend to give (something): *he had deigned an apology.* ▷Middle English: from Old French *degnier*, from Latin *dignare, dignari* 'deem worthy,' from *dignus* 'worthy.'

De·i gra·ti·a /'dēē 'grätsēə/ ▶*adv.* by the grace of God. ▷early 17th cent.: Latin.

deil /dēl/ ▶*n.* Scottish form of DEVIL.

Dei·mos /'dīməs/ *Astronomy* the outer, and smaller, of the two satellites of Mars, discovered in 1877. It is football-shaped and 10 miles (16 km) long. Compare with PHOBOS. ▷named after one of the sons of Ares in Greek mythology, the name means literally 'fear, terror'.

de·in·dex /dē'in,deks/ ▶*v.* [*trans.*] end the indexation to inflation of (pensions or other benefits).

de·in·dus·tri·al·i·za·tion /,dē-in,dəstrēəli'zāSHən/ ▶*n.* a change from industry to other forms of activity. ■ decline in industrial activity in a region or economy: *severe deindustrialization with substantial job losses.* **—de·in·dus·tri·al·ize** /-'dəstrēə,līz/ *v.*

de-ink /dē-'iNGk/ ▶*v.* [*trans.*] remove ink from (paper being recycled).

dei·non·y·chus /dī'nänikəs/ ▶*n.* a dromaeosaurid dinosaur of the mid Cretaceous period, growing up to 11 feet (3.3 m) in length. • Genus *Deinonychus*, family Dromaeosauridae, suborder Theropoda. ▷modern Latin, from Greek *deinos* 'terrible' + *onux, onukh-* 'claw.'

dei·no·the·ri·um /,dīnə'THi(ə)rēəm/ (also **dei·no·there** /'dīnə,THi(ə)r/) ▶*n.* (*pl.* **-the·ri·a** /-THi(ə)rēə/ or **-the·ri·ums**) an elephantlike fossil mammal found mainly in the Pliocene epoch, the lower jaw having tusks that curve downward and backward. • Genus *Deinotherium*, suborder Deinotherioidea, order Proboscidea. ▷modern Latin, from Greek *deinos* 'terrible' + *thērion* 'wild beast.'

de·in·stall /,dē-in'stôl/ (*Brit.* also **de·in·stal**) ▶*v.* [*trans.*] uninstall.■ *humorous* dismiss from employment: *the company lost funding and I was deinstalled.* **—de·in·stal·la·tion** /,dē-instə'lāSHən/ *n.* **—de·in·stall·er** *n.*

de·in·sti·tu·tion·al·ize /dē,instə't(y)o͞oSHənl,īz/ ▶*v.* [*trans.*] discharge (a long-term inmate) from an institution such as a mental hospital or prison: *the changes aim to deinstitutionalize mentally ill people.* **—de·in·sti·tu·tion·al·i·za·tion** /-,t(y)o͞oSHənl-ə'zāSHən/ *n.*

de·i·on·ize /dē'īə,nīz/ ▶*v.* [*trans.*] [usu. as *adj.*] (**deionized**) remove the ions or ionic constituents from (a substance, esp. water). **—de·i·on·i·za·tion** /dē,īənə'zāSHən/ *n.* **—de·i·on·iz·er** *n.*

Deir·dre /'di(ə)rdrə/ *Irish Mythology* a tragic heroine of whom it was prophesied that her beauty would bring banishment and death to heroes. King Conchobar of Ulster wanted to marry her, but she fell in love with Naoise, son of Usnach, who with his brothers carried her off to Scotland. They were lured back by Conchobar and treacherously slain, and Deirdre took her own life.

de·ism /'dēizəm/ ▶*n.* belief in the existence of a supreme being, specifically of a creator who does not intervene in the universe. The term is used chiefly of an intellectual movement of the 17th and

18th centuries that accepted the existence of a creator on the basis of reason but rejected belief in a supernatural deity who interacts with humankind. Compare with **THEISM.** ▷late 17th cent.: from Latin *deus* 'god' + **-ISM.** **—de·ist** *n.* **—de·is·tic** /dē'istik/ *adj.* **—de·is·ti·cal** /dē'istikəl/ *adj.*

de·i·ty /'dēitē/ ▸*n.* (*pl.* **-ties**) a god or goddess (in a polytheistic religion): *a deity of ancient Greece.* ■ divine status, quality, or nature: *a ruler driven by delusions of deity.* ■ (usu. **the Deity**) the creator and supreme being (in a monotheistic religion such as Christianity). ■ a representation of a god or goddess, such as a statue or carving. ▷Middle English (denoting the divine nature of God): from Old French *deite,* from ecclesiastical Latin *deitas* (translating Greek *theotēs*), from *deus* 'god.'

deix·is /'dīksis/ ▸*n.* *Linguistics* the function or use of deictic words, forms, or expressions. ▷1940s: from Greek, literally 'demonstrative force, reference'.

dé·jà vu /,dāZHä 'vōō/ ▸*n.* a feeling of having already experienced the present situation. ■ tedious familiarity: *to list the opponents of his policies is to invite boredom and a sense of déjà vu.* ▷early 20th cent.: French, literally 'already seen.'

de·ject /di'jekt/ ▸*v.* [*trans.*] *archaic* make sad or dispirited; depress: *nothing dejects a trader like the interruption of his profits.* ▷late Middle English (also in the sense 'overthrow, abase, degrade'): from Latin *deject-* 'thrown down,' from the verb *deicere,* from *de-* 'down' + *jacere* 'to throw.'

de·ject·ed /di'jektəd/ ▸*adj.* sad and depressed; dispirited: *he stood in the street looking dejected.* **—de·ject·ed·ly** *adv.*

de·jec·tion /di'jekSHən/ ▸*n.* a sad and depressed state; low spirits: *he was slumped in deep dejection.* ▷late Middle English: from Latin *dejectio(n-),* from *deicere* 'throw down' (see **DEJECT**).

de·junk /dē'jəNGk/ ▸*v.* [*trans.*] *informal* clear (a room or other space) by disposing of clutter and unwanted possessions: *dejunk the house before you move* | *figurative how to dejunk your life.*

de ju·re /di 'jŏŏrē; dā 'jŏŏrā/ ▸*adv.* according to rightful entitlement or claim; by right. Often contrasted with **DE FACTO.**
▸*adj.* denoting something or someone that is rightfully such: *he had been de jure king since his father's death.* ▷mid 16th cent.: Latin, literally 'of law.'

dek·a·gram ▸*n.* variant spelling of **DECAGRAM.**

De Kalb /di'kalb/ an industrial city in north central Illinois; pop. 34,925.

dek·a·li·ter ▸*n.* variant spelling of **DECALITER.**

dek·a·me·ter ▸*n.* variant spelling of **DECAMETER.**

deke /dēk/ *Ice Hockey* ▸*n.* a deceptive movement or feint that induces an opponent to move out of position.
▸*v.* [*trans.*] draw (a player) out of position by such a movement. ▷1960s: shortened form of **DECOY.**

dek·ko /'dekō/ ▸*n.* [in *sing.*] *Brit., informal* a quick look or glance: *come and have a dekko at this.* ▷late 19th cent. (originally used by the British army in India): from Hindi *dekho* 'look!,' imperative of *dekhnā.*

de Klerk /də 'klerk/, F. W. (1936–), South African statesman; state president 1989–94; full name *Frederik Willem de Klerk.* As state president, he freed Nelson Mandela in 1990, lifted the ban on membership in the African National Congress (ANC), and opened the negotiations that led to the first democratic elections in 1994. Nobel Peace Prize (1993, shared with Nelson Mandela).

de Koo·ning /də 'kōōniNG/, Willem (1904–97), U.S. painter; born in the Netherlands; a leading exponent of abstract expressionism. He usually retained figurative elements in his work, either represented or merely hinted at, as in *Painting* (1948). The female form became a central theme in his later work, notably in the *Women* series (1950–53).

del /del/ ▸*n.* *Mathematics* an operator used in vector analysis. (Symbol: ∇) • del is defined as $\mathbf{i}\,\partial/\partial x + \mathbf{j}\,\partial/\partial y + \mathbf{k}\,\partial/\partial z$, where **i**, **j**, and **k** are vectors directed respectively along the Cartesian axes *x*, *y*, and *z*. ▷early 20th cent.: abbreviation of **DELTA**[1], from the representation of the operator as an inverted capital delta.

Del. ▸*abbr.* Delaware.

De·la·croix /,delə'krwä/, (Ferdinand Victor) Eugène (1798–1863), French painter. The chief painter of the French romantic school, he is known for his use of vivid color, free drawing, and sometimes violent subject matter.

de la Mare /,del ə 'me(ə)r/, Walter (John) (1873–1956), English poet. He is known for his children's poetry.

de·lam·i·nate /dē'lamə,nāt/ ▸*v.* divide or become divided into layers: [*trans.*] *delaminating the horn into thin sheets* | [*intrans.*] *the plywood was starting to delaminate.* ▷late 19th cent.: from **DE-** 'away' + Latin *lamina* 'thin plate' + **-ATE**[3].

De·la·no /də'lānō/ an agricultural city in south central California; pop. 22,762.

de·late /di'lāt/ ▸*v.* [*trans.*] *archaic* report (an offense or crime): *they may delate my slackness to my patron.* ■ inform against or denounce (someone): *they deliberated together on delating her as a witch.* ▷late 15th cent.: from Latin *delat-* 'referred, carried away,' from the verb *deferre* (see **DEFER**[2]). **—de·la·tion** /-'lāSHən/ *n.* **—de·la·tor** /-'lātər/ *n.*

De·lau·nay /dəlō'nā/, Robert (1885–1941), French painter. He painted some of the first purely abstract pictures and was one of the founding members of Orphism, together with his wife Sonia Delaunay-Terk.

De·lau·nay-Terk /dəlô'nā 'terk/, Sonia (1885–1979), French painter and textile designer; born in Russia; wife of Robert Delaunay. She created abstract paintings based on harmonies of form and color.

Del·a·ware[1] /'delə,we(ə)r/ **1** a river in the northeastern U.S. that rises in the Catskill Mountains in New York and flows south for about 280 miles (450 km) to northern Delaware, where it meets the Atlantic Ocean at Delaware Bay. For much of its length it forms the eastern border of Pennsylvania. **2** a state in the eastern U.S., on the Atlantic coast;; pop. 683,600; capital, Dover; statehood, Dec. 7, 1787 (1). One of the original thirteen states, it was the first to ratify the U.S. Constitution.

Del·a·ware[2] ▸*n.* (*pl.* same or **-wares**) **1** a member of an American Indian people formerly inhabiting the Delaware River valley of New Jersey and eastern Pennsylvania. **2** either of two Algonquian languages (Munsi and Unami) spoken by this people.
▸*adj.* of or relating to the Delaware or their languages. ▷named after the *Delaware* River (see **DELAWARE**[1]).

de·lay /di'lā/ ▸*v.* [*trans.*] make (someone or something) late or slow: *the train was delayed.* ■ [*intrans.*] be late or slow; loiter: *time being of the essence, they delayed no longer.* ■ postpone or defer (an action): *he may decide to delay the next cut in interest rates.* See note at **POSTPONE.**
▸*n.* a period of time by which something is late or postponed: *a two-hour delay* | *long* **delays in** *obtaining passports.* ■ the action of delaying or being delayed: *I set off without delay.* ■ *Electronics* the time interval between the propagation of an electrical signal and its reception. ■ an electronic device that introduces such an interval, esp. in an audio signal. ▷Middle English: from Old French *delayer* (verb). **—de·lay·er** *n.*

de·layed-ac·tion ▸*adj.* [*attrib.*] operating or effective after a predetermined length of time: *delayed-action bombs.*
▸*n.* (**de·layed ac·tion**) the operation of something after a predetermined length of time.

de·lay·ing ac·tion ▸*n.* action taken to gain time, esp. a military engagement that delays the advance of an enemy.

de·lay·ing tac·tics ▸*plural n.* tactics designed to defer or postpone something in order to gain an advantage for oneself.

de·lay line ▸*n.* a device producing a specific desired delay in the transmission of a signal. ■ a set of mirrors controlling the path lengths between outlying telescopes and a central receiver.

de·le /'dēlē/ ▸*v.* (**de·led, de·le·ing**) [*trans.*] delete or mark (a part of a text) for deletion.
▸*n.* a proofreader's sign indicating matter to be deleted. ▷early 18th cent.: Latin, 'blot out! efface!,' imperative of *delere.*

de·lec·ta·ble /di'lektəbəl/ ▸*adj.* (of food or drink) delicious: *delectable handmade chocolates.* ■ *chiefly humorous* extremely beautiful or attractive: *the delectable Ms. Davis.* ▷late Middle English: via Old French from Latin *delectabilis,* from *delectare* 'to charm' (see **DELIGHT**). **—de·lec·ta·bil·i·ty** /-,lektə'bilitē/ *n.* **—de·lec·ta·bly** /-blē/ *adv.*

de·lec·ta·tion /,dēlek'tāSHən/ ▸*n.* *formal, chiefly humorous* pleasure and delight: *a box of chocolates* **for their delectation.** ▷late Middle English: via Old French from Latin *delectatio(n-),* from *delectare* 'to charm' (see **DELIGHT**).

del·e·ga·cy /'deligəsē/ ▸*n.* (*pl.* **-cies**) [treated as *sing.* or *pl.*] a body of delegates; a committee or delegation. ■ an appointment as a delegate. ▷late Middle English: from **DELEGATE**, on the pattern of the pair *prelate, prelacy.*

del·e·gate ▸*n.* /'deligit/ a person sent or authorized to represent others, in particular an elected representative sent to a conference. ■ a member of a committee.
▸*v.* /'delə,gāt/ [*trans.*] entrust (a task or responsibility) to another person, typically one who is less senior than oneself: *he delegates routine tasks* | *the power* **delegated to** *him must never be misused.* ■ [*trans.*] send or authorize (someone) to do something as a representative: *Edward was delegated to meet new arrivals.* ▷late Middle English: from Latin *delegatus* 'sent on a commission,' from the verb *delegare,* from *de-* 'down' + *legare* 'depute.' **—del·e·ga·ble** /-gəbəl/ *adj.* **—del·e·ga·tor** /-,gātər/ *n.*

del·e·ga·tion /,deli'gāSHən/ ▸*n.* [treated as *sing.* or *pl.*] a body of delegates or representatives; a deputation: *a delegation of teachers.* ■ the act or process of delegating or being delegated: *prioritizing tasks for delegation.* ▷early 17th cent. (denoting the act or process of delegating; also in the sense 'delegated power'): from Latin *delegatio(n-),* from *delegare* 'send on a commission' (see **DELEGATE**).

de·le·git·i·mate /,dēli'jitə,māt/ ▸*v.* another term for **DELEGITIMIZE.**

de·le·git·i·ma·tize /,dēli'jitəmə,tīz/ ▸*v.* another term for **DELEGITIMIZE.**

de·le·git·i·mize /,dēli'jitə,mīz/ ▸*v.* [*trans.*] withdraw legitimate status or authority from (someone or something): *political efforts to delegitimize nuclear weapons.* **—de·le·git·i·mi·za·tion** /-,jitəmə'zāSHən/ *n.*

de·lete /di'lēt/ ▸*v.* [*trans.*] remove or obliterate (written or printed matter), esp. by drawing a line through it or marking it with a delete sign: *the passage was deleted.* ■ (usu. **be deleted**) remove (data) from a computer's memory. ■ (**be deleted**) *Genetics* (of a section of genetic code, or its product) be lost or excised from a nucleic acid or protein sequence: *if one important gene is deleted from an animal's DNA, other genes can stand in.* ■ remove (a product, esp. a recording) from the catalog of those available for purchase: *their EMI release has already been deleted.*
▸*n.* a command or key on a computer that erases text. ▷late Middle English (in the sense 'destroy'): from Latin *delet-* 'blotted out, effaced,' from the verb *delere.*

del·e·te·ri·ous /,deli'ti(ə)rēəs/ ▸*adj.* causing harm or damage: *divorce is assumed to have deleterious effects on children.* ▷mid 17th cent.: via medieval Latin from Greek *dēlētērios* 'noxious' + **-OUS.** **—del·e·te·ri·ous·ly** *adv.*

de·le·tion /di'lēSHən/ ▸*n.* **1** the action or process of deleting something: *deletion of a file.* **2** *Genetics* the loss or absence of a section from a nucleic acid molecule or chromosome.

de·lex·i·cal /dē'leksikəl/ ▸*adj.* *Linguistics* (of a verb) having little or no meaning in its own right, for example *take* in *take a photograph.*

Delft /delft/ a town in the Netherlands, in the province of South Holland; pop. 89,400. The home of painters Pieter de Hooch and Jan Vermeer, it also is noted for its pottery. ▷originally *Delf,* from Dutch *delf* 'ditch,' still the name of the town's main canal.

delft /delft/ ▸*n.* English or Dutch tin-glazed earthenware, typically decorated by hand in blue on a white background. ▷late 17th cent. (originally *Delf ware*): see **DELFT**, where the pottery originated. **—delft·ware** /-,we(ə)r/ *n.*

Del·hi /'delē/ a union territory in northern central India that contains the cities of Old and New Delhi; pop. 7,175,000. **Old Delhi**, a walled city on the Jumna River, was made the capital of the Mogul empire in 1638 by Shah Jahan (1592–1666). **New Delhi**, the capital of India, was built 1912–29 to replace Calcutta as the capital of British India.

del·i /'delē/ ▸*n.* (*pl.* **del·is**) *informal* short for **DELICATESSEN.**

De·li·an /'dēlēən/ ▸*adj.* of or relating to Delos.
▸*n.* a native or inhabitant of Delos.

De·li·an League an alliance of ancient Greek city-states, dominated by Athens, that joined in 478–447 BC against the Persians. The league was disbanded on the defeat of Athens in the Peloponnesian War (404 BC), but again united under Athens' leadership against Spartan aggression in 377–338 BC. Also called the **ATHENIAN EMPIRE.**

de·lib·er·ate ▸*adj.* /di'libərit/ done consciously and intentionally: *a deliberate attempt to provoke conflict.* ■ fully considered; not impulsive: *a deliberate decision.* ■ done or acting in a careful and unhurried way: *a careful and deliberate worker.*
▸*v.* /-ˌrāt/ [*intrans.*] engage in long and careful consideration: *she* ***deliberated over*** *the menu.* ■ [*trans.*] consider (a question) carefully: *jurors deliberated the fate of those charged* | [with *clause*] *deliberating what she should do.* ▷late Middle English (as an adjective): from Latin *deliberatus,* 'considered carefully,' past participle of *deliberare,* from *de-* 'down' + *librare* 'weigh' (from *libra* 'scales'). **—de·lib·er·ate·ly** /-ritlē/ *adv.* **—de·lib·er·ate·ness** /-ritnis/ *n.* **—de·lib·er·a·tor** /-ˌrātər/ *n.*

de·lib·er·a·tion /diˌlibə'rāsʜən/ ▸*n.* **1** long and careful consideration or discussion: *after much deliberation, we arrived at a compromise* | *the commission's deliberations.* **2** slow and careful movement or thought: *he replaced the glass on the table with deliberation.* ▷late Middle English: via Old French from Latin *deliberatio(n-),* from *deliberare* 'consider carefully' (see DELIBERATE).

de·lib·er·a·tive /di'libərətiv; -əˌrātiv/ ▸*adj.* relating to or intended for consideration or discussion: *a deliberative assembly.* **—de·lib·er·a·tive·ly** *adv.*

del·i·ca·cy /'delikəsē/ ▸*n.* (*pl.* **-cies**) **1** the quality of being delicate, in particular: ■ fineness or intricacy of texture or structure: *miniature pearls of exquisite delicacy.* ■ susceptibility to illness or adverse conditions; fragility. ■ the quality of requiring discretion or sensitivity: *the delicacy of the situation.* ■ tact and consideration: *I have to treat this matter with the utmost delicacy.* ■ accuracy of perception; sensitiveness. **2** a choice or expensive food: *a Chinese delicacy.* ▷late Middle English (in the senses 'voluptuousness' and 'luxuriousness'): from DELICATE + -ACY.

del·i·cate /'delikit/ ▸*adj.* **1** very fine in texture or structure; of intricate workmanship or quality: *a spider's web, strong yet delicate.* ■ (of a color or a scent) subtle and subdued: *delicate pastel shades* | *a delicate fragrance.* ■ (of food or drink) subtly and pleasantly flavored: *a delicate cream sauce.* **2** easily broken or damaged; fragile: *delicate china.* ■ (of a person, animal, or plant) susceptible to illness or adverse conditions: *his delicate health.* ■ (of a state or condition) easily upset or damaged: *owls have a delicate balance with their habitat.* **3** requiring sensitive or careful handling: *delicate negotiations.* ■ (of a person or an action) tactful and considerate: *the most delicate tact was called for.* ■ skillful and finely judged; deft: *his delicate ball-playing skills.* ■ (of an instrument) highly sensitive.
▸*n. informal* a delicate fabric or garment made of such fabric. ▷late Middle English (in the sense 'delightful, charming'): from French *délicat* or Latin *delicatus,* of unknown origin. Senses also expressed in Middle English (now obsolete) include 'voluptuous,' 'self-indulgent,' 'fastidious,' and 'effeminate.' **—del·i·cate·ly** *adv.* **—del·i·cate·ness** *n.*
▸*PHRASE* □ **in a delicate condition** *archaic* pregnant.

del·i·ca·tes·sen /ˌdelikə'tesən/ ▸*n.* a store selling cold cuts, cheeses, and a variety of salads, as well as a selection of unusual or foreign prepared foods. ■ a counter or section within a supermarket or grocery store at which a range of such foods is available. ■ foods of this type collectively. ▷late 19th cent. (originally denoting prepared foods for sale): from German *Delikatessen* or Dutch *delicatessen,* from French *délicatesse* 'delicateness,' from *délicat* (see DELICATE).

de·li·cense /dē'līsəns/ ▸*v.* [*trans.*] deprive of a license or authority to operate: *physicians are being threatened, impoverished, delicensed, and imprisoned for prescribing in good faith with the intention of relieving pain.*

De·li·cious /di'lisʜəs/ ▸*n.* a red or yellow variety of eating apple with a sweet flavor and a slightly elongated shape, originally cultivated in the U.S.

de·li·cious /di'lisʜəs/ ▸*adj.* highly pleasant to the taste: *delicious home-baked brown bread.* ■ delightful: *a delicious irony.* ▷Middle English (also in the sense 'characterized by sensuous indulgence'): via Old French from late Latin *deliciosus,* from Latin *deliciae* (plural) 'delight, pleasure.' **—de·li·cious·ly** *adv.* **—de·li·cious·ness** *n.*

de·lict /di'likt/ ▸*n. Law* a violation of the law; a tort: *an international delict.* ▷late Middle English: from Latin *delictum* 'something showing fault,' neuter past participle of *delinquere* (see DELINQUENT).

de·light /di'līt/ ▸*v.* [*trans.*] please (someone) greatly: *an experience guaranteed to delight both young and old.* ■ [*intrans.*] (**delight in**) take great pleasure in: *they delight in playing tricks.*
▸*n.* great pleasure: *she* ***took great delight*** *in telling your story.* ■ a cause or source of great pleasure: *the trees here are a delight.* ▷Middle English: from Old French *delitier* (verb), *delit* (noun), from Latin *delectare* 'to charm,' frequentative of *delicere.* The *-gh-* was added in the 16th cent. by association with LIGHT[1].

de·light·ed /di'lītid/ ▸*adj.* feeling or showing great pleasure: *a delighted smile* | [with *infinitive*] *we were delighted to see her.* **—de·light·ed·ly** *adv.*

de·light·ful /di'lītfəl/ ▸*adj.* causing delight; charming: *a delightful secluded garden.* **—de·light·ful·ly** *adv.* **—de·light·ful·ness** *n.*

De·li·lah /di'līlə/ (in the Bible) a woman who betrayed Samson to the Philistines (Judges 16) by revealing to them that the secret of his strength lay in his long hair. ■ [as *n.*] (**a Delilah**) a seductive and wily temptress.

de·lim·it /di'limit/ ▸*v.* (**-lim·it·ed, -lim·it·ing**) [*trans.*] determine the limits or boundaries of: *agreements delimiting fishing zones.* ▷mid 19th cent.: from French *délimiter,* from Latin *delimitare,* from *de-* 'down, completely' + *limitare* (from *limes, limit-* 'boundary, limit'). **—de·lim·i·ta·tion** /-ˌlimi'tāsʜən/ *n.* **—de·lim·it·er** *n.*

de·lin·e·ate /di'linēˌāt/ ▸*v.* [*trans.*] describe or portray (something) precisely: *the law should delineate and prohibit behavior that is socially abhorrent.* ■ indicate the exact position of (a border or boundary). ▷mid 16th cent. (in the sense 'trace the outline of something'): from Latin *delineat-* 'outlined,' from the verb *delineare,* from *de-* 'out, completely' + *lineare* (from *linea* 'line'). **—de·lin·e·a·tion** /-ˌlinē'āsʜən/ *n.* **—de·lin·e·a·tor** /-ˌātər/ *n.*

de·link /dē'lingk/ ▸*v.* (**delinking**) break the connection between (something) and something else: *if an invasion of Iraq is* ***delinked from*** *Middle East peace, then all America will gain is more terror cells in the Muslim world.*

de·lin·quen·cy /di'lingkwənsē/ ▸*n.* (*pl.* **-cies**) minor crime, esp. that committed by young people: *social causes of crime and delinquency.* ■ *formal* neglect of one's duty: *he relayed this in such a manner as to imply grave delinquency on the host's part.* ■ a failure to pay an outstanding debt. ▷mid 17th cent.: from ecclesiastical Latin *delinquentia,* from Latin *delinquent-* 'offending' (see DELINQUENT).

de·lin·quent /di'lingkwənt/ ▸*adj.* (typically of a young person or that person's behavior) showing or characterized by a tendency to commit crime, particularly minor crime: *delinquent children.* ■ in arrears: *delinquent accounts.* ■ *formal* failing in one's duty.
▸*n.* a delinquent person: *young delinquents.* ▷late 15th cent.: from Latin *delinquent-* 'offending,' from the verb *delinquere,* from *de-* 'away' + *linquere* 'to leave.' **—de·lin·quent·ly** *adv.*

del·i·quesce /ˌdeli'kwes/ ▸*v.* [*intrans.*] (of organic matter) become liquid, typically during decomposition. ■ *Chemistry* (of a solid) become liquid by absorbing moisture from the air. ▷mid 18th cent.: from Latin *deliquescere* 'dissolve,' from *de-* 'down' + *liquescere* 'become liquid' (from *liquere* 'be liquid').

del·i·ques·cent /deli'kwesənt/ ▸*adj.* becoming liquid or having a tendency to become liquid. ■ *Chemistry* (of a solid) tending to absorb moisture from the air and dissolve in it. ▷late 18th cent.: from Latin *deliquescent-* 'dissolving,' from the verb *deliquescere* (see DELIQUESCE). **—del·i·ques·cence** *n.*

de·lir·i·ous /di'li(ə)rēəs/ ▸*adj.* in an acutely disturbed state of mind resulting from illness or intoxication and characterized by restlessness, illusions, and incoherence of thought and speech. ■ in a state of wild excitement or ecstasy: *there was a great roar from the delirious crowd.* **—de·lir·i·ant** /-ənt/ *adj.* **—de·lir·i·ous·ly** *adv.*

de·lir·i·um /di'li(ə)rēəm/ ▸*n.* an acutely disturbed state of mind that occurs in fever, intoxication, and other disorders and is characterized by restlessness, illusions, and incoherence of thought and speech. ■ wild excitement or ecstasy. ▷mid 16th cent.: from Latin, from *delirare* 'deviate, be deranged' (literally 'deviate from the furrow'), from *de-* 'away' + *lira* 'ridge between furrows.'

de·lir·i·um tre·mens /di'li(ə)rēəm 'trēmənz/ ▸*n.* a psychotic condition typical of withdrawal in chronic alcoholics, involving tremors, hallucinations, anxiety, and disorientation. ▷early 19th cent.: from Latin, 'trembling delirium.'

de·lish /di'lisʜ/ ▸*adj. informal* delicious.

de·list /dē'list/ ▸*v.* [*trans.*] remove (something) from a list, in particular: ■ remove (a security) from the official register of a stock exchange: *the stock collapsed and was delisted.* ■ remove (a product) from the list of those sold by a particular retailer.

de·liv·er /di'livər/ ▸*v.* [*trans.*] **1** bring and hand over (a letter, parcel, or ordered goods) to the proper recipient or address: *the products should be delivered on time* | [*intrans.*] *we'll deliver direct to your door.* ■ formally hand over (someone): *they would have* ***delivered*** *him* ***to*** *the Germans for vengeance.* ■ obtain (a vote) in favor of a candidate or cause: *he had been able to deliver votes in huge numbers.* ■ launch or aim (a blow, a ball, or an attack): *the pitcher winds up to deliver the ball.* ■ provide (something promised or expected): *the struggle to deliver election commitments* | *she's waiting for him to* ***deliver on*** *his promise.* ■ (**deliver someone/something from**) save, rescue, or set free from: *deliver us from misery.* ■ (**deliver someone/something up**) surrender someone or something: *to deliver up to justice a member of his own family.* ■ *Law* acknowledge that one intends to be bound by (a deed), either explicitly by declaration or implicitly by formal handover. **2** state in a formal manner: *the President will deliver a speech* | *he* ***delivered himself of*** *a sermon.* ■ (of a judge or court) give (a judgment or verdict): *the judge delivered his verdict.* **3** assist in the birth of: *the village midwife delivered the baby.* ■ give birth to: *she will deliver a child.* ■ (**be delivered of**) give birth to: *she has never been delivered of a foal that lived.* ■ assist (a woman) in giving birth. ▷Middle English: from Old French *delivrer,* based on Latin *de-* 'away' + *liberare* 'set free.' **—de·liv·er·ee** /-ˌliv(ə)'rē/ *n.* **—de·liv·er·er** *n.*
▸*PHRASE* □ **deliver the goods** *informal* provide what is promised or expected.

de·liv·er·a·ble /di'livərəbəl/ ▸*adj.* able to be delivered: *goods in a deliverable state.*
▸*n.* (usu. **deliverables**) a thing able to be provided, esp. as a product of a development process.

de·liv·er·ance /di'livərəns/ ▸*n.* **1** the action of being rescued or set free: *prayers for deliverance.* **2** a formal or authoritative utterance. ▷Middle English: from Old French *delivrance,* from the verb *delivrer* (see DELIVER).

de·liv·er·y /di'livərē/ ▸*n.* (*pl.* **-er·ies**) **1** the action of delivering letters, packages, or ordered goods: *allow up to 28 days for delivery.* ■ a regular or scheduled occasion for this: *there will be around 15 deliveries a week.* ■ an item or items delivered on a particular occasion: *they are getting smaller deliveries.* ■ *Law* the formal or symbolic handing over of property, esp. a sealed deed, to a grantee or third party. **2** the process of giving birth: *injuries sustained during delivery* | *practically all deliveries take place in a hospital* | [as *adj.*] *the delivery room.* **3** an act of throwing or bowling a ball or striking a blow: *a quick, compact delivery that sent the ball zinging.* ■ the style or manner of such an action: *hints to speed up his delivery.* **4** the manner or style of giving a speech: *her delivery was stilted.* **5** the supply or provision of something: *delivery of electricity at a specified price.* ▷late Middle English: from Anglo-Norman French *delivree,* feminine past participle of *delivrer* (see DELIVER).
▸*PHRASE* □ **take delivery of** receive (something purchased): *we took delivery of the software in February.*

dell /del/ ▸*n. poetic/literary* a small valley, usually among trees: *lush green valleys and wooded dells.* ▷Old English, of Germanic origin; related to Dutch *del* and German dialect *Telle,* also to DALE.

Del·la Crus·can /ˌdelə 'krəskən/ ▸*adj.* of or relating to the Academy della Crusca in Florence, an institution established in 1582, with the purity of the Italian language as its chief interest. ■ of or relating to a late 18th-century school of English poets with an artificial style modeled on that of purist Italian writers.
▸*n.* a member of the Academy della Crusca. ■ a Della Cruscan poet. ▷from Italian *(Accademia) della Crusca* '(Academy) of the bran' (with reference to "sifting" of the language).

del·la Quer·cia /ˌdelə 'kwercʜə/, Jacopo (*c.*1374–1438), Italian sculptor. He is noted for the biblical reliefs on the portal of San Petronio in Bologna (1425–35).

del·la Rob·bia /ˌdelə 'rōbēə; 'räb-/, Luca (1400–82), Italian sculptor and ceramicist. He is best known for his relief panels in Florence Cathedral and his color-glazed terra-cotta figures.

Del·mar·va /del'märvə/ (also **Delmarva Peninsula**) a peninsular region 180 miles (290 km) long in the eastern U.S. that includes Delaware, the Eastern Shore of Maryland, and a small strip of Virginia that separates Chesapeake Bay from the Atlantic Ocean. ▷acronym from *Delaware, Maryland,* and *Virginia.*

Del·mon·i·co steak /del'mäniˌkō/ ▸*n.* a small steak cut from the front section of the short loin of beef. Also called CLUB STEAK. ▷named for Lorenzo Delmonico (1813–81), Swiss-born U.S. restaurateur.

de·lo·cal·ize /dē'lōkəˌlīz/ ▸*v.* [*trans.*] detach or remove (something) from a particular place or location: [as *adj.*] (**delocalized**) *delocalized cortical activity.* ■ not limit to a particular location: [as *n.*] (**delocalizing**) *delocalizing of finance capital.* ■ (**be delocalized**) *Chemistry* (of electrons) be shared among more than two atoms in a molecule: *the pi electrons are delocalized and energetically stable.* —**de·lo·cal·i·za·tion** /-ˌlōkələˈzāsHən/ *n.*

De·lors /dəˈlôr/, Jacques (Lucien Jean) (1925–), French socialist politician; president of the European Commission 1985–94. During his presidency, he pressed for closer European union and oversaw the introduction of a single market within the European Community, which came into effect on January 1, 1993.

De·los /ˈdēläs; ˈdelōs/ a small Greek island in the Aegean Sea, regarded as the center of the Cyclades. Although it is now virtually uninhabited, it was considered to be sacred to Apollo in classical times and, according to legend, was the birthplace of Apollo and Artemis.

de·louse /dēˈlous/ ▸*v.* [*trans.*] rid (a person or animal) of lice and other parasitic insects.

Del·phi /ˈdelˌfī/ one of the most important religious sanctuaries of the ancient Greek world, dedicated to Apollo, situated on the lower southern slopes of Mount Parnassus above the Gulf of Corinth. Thought of as the navel of the earth, it was the seat of the Delphic Oracle, whose riddling responses to a wide range of questions were delivered by the Pythia. Greek name **Dhelfoí**.

Del·phic /ˈdelfik/ (also **Del·phi·an** /-fēən/) ▸*adj.* of or relating to the ancient Greek oracle at Delphi. ■ (typically of a pronouncement) deliberately obscure or ambiguous.

del·phin·i·um /delˈfinēəm/ ▸*n.* (*pl.* **-ums**) a popular garden plant of the buttercup family that bears tall spikes of blue flowers. • Genus *Delphinium*, family Ranunculaceae. ▷modern Latin, from Greek *delphinion* 'larkspur,' from *delphin* 'dolphin' (because of the shape of the spur, thought to resemble a dolphin's back).

Del·phi·nus /delˈfīnəs/ *Astronomy* a small constellation (the Dolphin), just north of the celestial equator near Cygnus. ■ [as *genitive*] (**Delphini**) used with a preceding letter or numeral to designate a star in this constellation: *the star Alpha Delphini.* ▷Latin.

Del·phi tech·nique ▸*n.* a method of group decision-making and forecasting that involves successively collating the judgments of experts. ▷in allusion to the ancient Greek oracle at *Delphi.*

Del·ray Beach /ˈdelˌrā/ a resort city in southeastern Florida, north of Fort Lauderdale; pop. 47,181.

Del Ri·o /del ˈrēō/ a city in southwestern Texas, on the Rio Grande; pop. 30,705.

del Sar·to /del ˈsärtō/, Andrea, see **Sarto**.

Del·ta (**the Delta**) a region in northern Mississippi that lies between the Yazoo and Mississippi rivers and is known for its cotton and for blues music. Also called the **Yazoo Delta** or **Mississippi Delta**.

del·ta[1] /ˈdeltə/ ▸*n.* **1** the fourth letter of the Greek alphabet (Δ, δ), transliterated as "d." ■ [as *adj.*] the fourth in a series of items, categories, etc.: *delta hepatitis.* ■ (**Delta**) [followed by Latin genitive] *Astronomy* the fourth (usually fourth-brightest) star in a constellation: *Delta Cephei.* **2** a code word representing the letter D, used in radio communication.
▸*symbol* ■ (δ) *Mathematics* variation of a variable or function. ■ (Δ) *Mathematics* a finite increment. ■ (δ) *Astronomy* declination.

del·ta[2] ▸*n.* a triangular tract of sediment deposited at the mouth of a river, typically where it diverges into several outlets. ▷mid 16th cent.: originally specifically as *the Delta* (of the Nile River), from the shape of the Greek letter (see **delta**[1]). —**del·ta·ic** /delˈtāik/ *adj.*

del·ta con·nec·tion ▸*n.* a triangular arrangement of electrical three-phase windings in series, each of the three wires of the circuit being connected to a junction of two windings.

Del·ta Force an elite U.S. Army unit whose main responsibilities are rescue operations and special forces work.

del·ta rays ▸*plural n.* *Physics* rays of low penetrative power consisting of slow electrons or other particles ejected from atoms by the impact of ionizing radiation.

del·ta rhythm ▸*n.* electrical activity of the brain at a frequency of around 1–8 Hz, typical of sleep. The resulting oscillations, detected using an electroencephalograph, are called **delta waves**.

del·ta-v (also **del·ta-vee**) ▸*n.* *informal* acceleration: *four hundred knots of delta-v.* ▷late 20th cent.: from **delta**[1] (as a mathematical symbol denoting variation) + *v* for *velocity*.

del·ta wing ▸*n.* the single triangular swept-back wing on some aircraft, typically on military aircraft. —**del·ta-winged** *adj.*

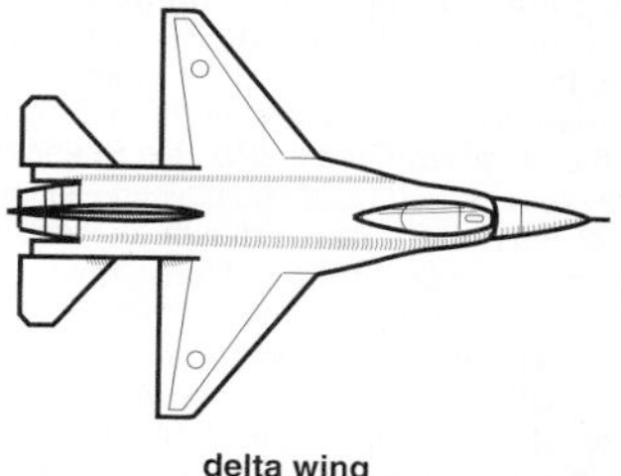

delta wing

del·ti·ol·o·gist /ˌdeltēˈäləjist/ ▸*n.* a person who collects postcards as a hobby. ▷1940s: from Greek *deltion* (diminutive of *deltos* 'writing tablet') + **-logist**. —**del·ti·ol·o·gy** /-jē/ *n.*

del·toid /ˈdeltoid/ ▸*adj.* *technical* triangular: *a tree with large deltoid leaves.* ■ denoting a thick triangular muscle covering the shoulder joint and used for raising the arm away from the body.
▸*n.* a deltoid muscle. ■ each of the three parts of a deltoid muscle, attached at the front, side, and rear of the shoulder: *the anterior deltoid.* ▷mid 18th cent.: from French *deltoïde*, or via modern Latin from Greek *deltoeidēs*.

de·lude /diˈlo͞od/ ▸*v.* [*trans.*] impose a misleading belief upon (someone); deceive; fool: *too many theorists have deluded the public* | [as *adj.*] (**deluded**) *the poor deluded creature.* ▷late Middle English: from Latin *deludere* 'to mock,' from *de-* (with pejorative force) + *ludere* 'to play.' —**de·lud·ed·ly** *adv.* —**de·lud·er** *n.*

del·uge /ˈdel(y)o͞oj/ ▸*n.* a severe flood. ■ (**the Deluge**) the biblical Flood (recorded in Genesis 6–8). ■ a heavy fall of rain: *a deluge of rain hit the plains.* ■ *figurative* a great quantity of something arriving at the same time: *a deluge of complaints.*
▸*v.* [*trans.*] (usu. **be deluged**) inundate with a great quantity of something: *he has been* **deluged with** *offers of work.* ■ flood: *the country was deluged with rain.* ▷late Middle English: from Old French, variant of *diluve*, from Latin *diluvium*, from *diluere* 'wash away.'

de·lu·sion /diˈlo͞ozHən/ ▸*n.* an idiosyncratic belief or impression that is firmly maintained despite being contradicted by what is generally accepted as reality or rational argument, typically a symptom of mental disorder: *the delusion of being watched.* ■ the action of deluding someone or the state of being deluded: *what a capacity television has for delusion.* ▷late Middle English (in the sense 'act of deluding or of being deluded'): from late Latin *delusio(n-)*, from the verb *deludere* (see **delude**). —**de·lu·sion·al** /-zHənl/ *adj.*
▸*PHRASE* □ **delusions of grandeur** a false impression of one's own importance.

de·lu·sive /diˈlo͞osiv/ ▸*adj.* giving a false or misleading impression: *the delusive light of Venice.* —**de·lu·sive·ly** *adv.* —**de·lu·sive·ness** *n.*

de·lu·so·ry /diˈlo͞osərē; -zərē/ ▸*adj.* another term for **delusive**. ▷late 15th cent.: from late Latin *delusorius*, from *delus-* 'mocked,' from the verb *deludere* (see **delude**).

de·lust·er /dēˈləstər/ (*Brit.* **de·lus·tre**) ▸*v.* [*trans.*] remove the luster from (a textile), typically by chemical treatment.

de·luxe /diˈləks/ ▸*adj.* luxurious or sumptuous; of a superior kind: *a deluxe hotel.* ▷early 19th cent.: from French *de luxe*, literally 'of luxury.'

delve /delv/ ▸*v.* [*intrans.*] reach inside a receptacle and search for something: *she* **delved in** *her pocket.* ■ research or make painstaking inquiries into something: *a machine designed to* **delve** *further* **into** *the atom's secrets.* ■ [*trans.*] *poetic/literary* dig; excavate: [as *adj.*] (**delved**) *the approach from the surface above had awed her, so hugely delved were the tunnels.* ▷Old English *delfan* 'dig'; related to Dutch *delven*. —**delv·er** *n.*

Dem. ▸*abbr.* Democrat.

de·mag·net·ize /dēˈmagniˌtīz/ ▸*v.* [*trans.*] remove magnetic properties from. —**de·mag·net·i·za·tion** /-ˌmagnitəˈzāsHən/ *n.* —**de·mag·net·iz·er** *n.*

dem·a·gogue /ˈdeməˌgäg/ ▸*n.* a political leader who seeks support by appealing to popular desires and prejudices rather than by using rational argument. ■ (in ancient Greece and Rome) a leader or orator who espoused the cause of the common people. ▷mid 17th cent.: from Greek *dēmagōgos*, from *dēmos* 'the people' + *agōgos* 'leading' (from *agein* 'to lead'). —**dem·a·gog·ic** /ˌdeməˈgäjik; -ˈgägik; -ˈgōjik/ *adj.* —**dem·a·gogu·er·y** /ˈdeməˌgägərē/ *n.* —**dem·a·go·gy** /ˈdeməˌgäjē; -ˌgōjē/ *n.*

de Main·te·non /də mantˈnôn/ see **Maintenon**.

de·mand /diˈmand/ ▸*n.* an insistent and peremptory request, made as if by right: *a series of* **demands for** *far-reaching reforms.* ■ (**demands**) pressing requirements: *he's got enough* **demands on** *his time already.* ■ *Economics* the desire of purchasers, consumers, clients, employers, etc., for a particular commodity, service, or other item: *a recent slump in demand* | *a demand for specialists.*
▸*v.* [*reporting verb*] ask authoritatively or brusquely: [with *direct speech*] *"Where is she?" he demanded* | [with *clause*] *the police demanded that he give them the names.* ■ [*trans.*] insist on having: *an outraged public demanded retribution* | *too much was being* **demanded of** *the top players.* ■ require; need: *a complex activity demanding detailed knowledge.* ■ *Law* call into court; summon. ▷Middle English (as a noun): from Old French *demande* (noun), *demander* (verb), from Latin *demandare* 'hand over, entrust' (in medieval Latin 'demand'), from *de-* 'formally' + *mandare* 'to order.' —**de·mand·er** *n.*
▸*PHRASES* □ **in demand** sought after: *all these skills are much in demand.* □ **on demand** as soon as or whenever required: *he promised us endless coffee on demand.*

de·mand curve ▸*n.* a graph showing how the demand for a commodity or service varies with changes in its price.

de·mand de·pos·it ▸*n.* a deposit of money that can be withdrawn without prior notice.

de·mand draft ▸*n.* a financial draft payable on demand.

de·mand feed·ing ▸*n.* the practice of feeding a baby when it cries to be fed rather than at set times.

de·mand·ing /diˈmandiNG/ ▸*adj.* (of a task) requiring much skill or effort: *she has a busy and demanding job.* ■ (of a person) making others work hard or meet high standards. —**de·mand·ing·ly** *adv.*

de·mand-led (also **de·mand-driv·en**) ▸*adj.* *Economics* caused or determined by demand from consumers or clients.

de·mand note ▸*n.* a formal request for payment. ■ another term for **demand draft**.

de·mand pull ▸*adj.* relating to or denoting inflation caused by an excess of demand over supply.

de·man·toid /diˈmantoid/ ▸*n.* a lustrous green variety of andradite (garnet). ▷late 19th cent.: from German, from *Demant* 'diamond.'

de·mar·cate /diˈmärˌkāt; ˈdēmärˌkāt/ (also **de·mar·kate**) ▸*v.* [*trans.*] set the boundaries or limits of: *plots of land demarcated by barbed wire.* ■ separate or distinguish from: *art was being demarcated from the more objective science.* ▷early 19th cent.: back-formation from **demarcation**.

de·mar·ca·tion /ˌdēmärˈkāsHən/ ▸*n.* the action of fixing the boundary or limits of something: *the demarcation of the maritime border.* ■ a dividing line: *a horizontal band that produces a distinct demarcation two inches from the top.* ▷early 18th cent.: from Spanish *demarcación*, from *demarcar* 'mark the bounds of,' ultimately of Germanic origin and related to **mark**[1]. Originally used in the phrase *line of demarcation* (Spanish *linea de demarcación*, Portuguese *linha de marcação*), the word denoted a line dividing the New World between the Spanish and Portuguese, laid down by the pope in 1493. —**de·mar·ca·tor** /diˈmärˌkātər/ *n.*

dé·marche /dāˈmärsH/ ▸*n.* a political step or initiative: *foreign policy démarches.* ▷mid 17th cent.: French, from *démarcher* 'take steps.'

de·mas·si·fy /dēˈmasiˌfī/ ▸*v.* (**-fies**, **-fied**) [*trans.*] divide or break up (a social or political unit) into its component parts. —**de·mas·si·fi·ca·tion** /-ˌmasifiˈkāsHən/ *n.*

de·ma·te·ri·al·ize /ˌdēməˈti(ə)rēəˌlīz/ ▸*v.* [*intrans.*] become free of physical substance, in particular: ■ (in science fiction) disappear or cease to be physically present through some imagined technological process: *he watched the time machine dematerialize.* ■ become spiritual rather than physical: *the kiss dematerializes into a kind of spiritual rebirth.* ■ [*trans.*] [usu. as *adj.*] (**dematerialized**) replace (physical records or certificates) with a paperless computerized system: *a dematerialized stock lending service.* —**de·ma·te·ri·al·i·za·tion** /-ˌti(ə)rēələˈzāsHən/ *n.*

Pronunciation Key ə *ago*; ər *over*; ˈə or ˌə *up*; ˈər or ˌər *fur*; a *hat*; ā *rate*; ä *car*; CH *chew*; e *let*; ē *see*; e(ə)r *air*; i *fit*; ī *by*; i(ə)r *ear*; NG *sing*; ō *go*; ô *for*; oi *boy*; o͝o *good*; o͞o *goo*; ou *out*; SH *she*; TH *thin*; T͟H *then*; (h)w *why*; ZH *vision*

de Mau·pas·sant /də ˌmōpəˈsänt; də mōpaˈsän/, Guy, see **MAUPASSANT.**

deme /dēm/ ▶*n.* **1** a political division of Attica in ancient Greece. ■ an administrative division in modern Greece. **2** *Biology* a subdivision of a population consisting of closely related plants, animals, or people, typically breeding mainly within the group. ▷from Greek *dēmos* 'people'; sense 2 is an extended use dating from the 1930s.

de·mean1 /diˈmēn/ ▶*v.* [*trans.*] [often as *adj.*] (**demeaning**) cause a severe loss in the dignity of and respect for (someone or something): *the poster was not demeaning to women | I had demeaned the profession.* See note at **HUMBLE.** ■ (**demean oneself**) do something that is beneath one's dignity. ▷early 17th cent.: from **DE-** 'away, down' + the adjective **MEAN**2, on the pattern of *debase.*

de·mean2 ▶*v.* (**demean oneself**) *archaic* conduct oneself in a particular way: *no man demeaned himself so honorably.* ▷Middle English (also in the sense 'manage, control'): from Old French *demener* 'to lead,' based on Latin *de-* 'away' + *minare* 'drive (animals), drive on with threats' (from *minari* 'threaten').

de·mean·or /diˈmēnər/ (*Brit.* **de·mean·our**) ▶*n.* outward behavior or bearing: *a quiet, somber demeanor.* ▷late 15th cent.: from **DEMEAN**2, probably influenced by obsolete *havour* 'behavior.'

de' Med·i·ci1, Catherine, see **CATHERINE DE' MEDICI.**

de' Med·i·ci2, Cosimo, see **COSIMO DE' MEDICI.**

de' Med·i·ci3, Giovanni, the name of Pope Leo X (see **LEO**1).

de' Med·i·ci4, Lorenzo, see **LORENZO DE' MEDICI.**

de Méd·i·cis, Marie, see **MARIE DE MÉDICIS.**

de·ment /diˈment/ ▶*n. archaic* a person suffering from dementia. ▷late 15th cent. (as an adjective in the sense 'demented'): from French *dément* or Latin *demens, dement-* 'insane.' The noun use dates from the late 19th cent.

de·ment·ed /diˈmentid/ ▶*adj.* suffering from dementia. ■ *informal* driven to behave irrationally due to anger, distress, or excitement: *a demented, dangerous, and sadistic Mafioso.* ▷mid 17th cent.: past participle of earlier *dement* 'drive mad,' from Old French *dementer* or late Latin *dementare,* from *demens* 'out of one's mind.' —**de·ment·ed·ly** *adv.* —**de·ment·ed·ness** *n.*

dé·men·ti /ˌdāmänˈtē/ ▶*n.* an official denial of a published statement. ▷French, from *démentir* 'contradict or accuse of lying.'

de·men·tia /diˈmensHə/ ▶*n. Medicine* a chronic or persistent disorder of the mental processes caused by brain disease or injury and marked by memory disorders, personality changes, and impaired reasoning. ▷late 18th cent.: from Latin, from *demens, dement-* 'out of one's mind.'

de·men·tia prae·cox /diˈmensHə ˈprēˌkäks/ ▶*n.* dated term for **SCHIZOPHRENIA.** ▷late 18th cent. Latin, literally 'early insanity.'

Dem·e·ra·ra /ˌdeməˈre(ə)rə; -ˈrärə/ a river in northern Guyana. Rising in the Guiana Highlands, it flows north for about 200 miles (320 km) to the Atlantic Ocean.

dem·e·ra·ra /ˌdeməˈre(ə)rə; -ˈrärə/ ▶*n.* **1** (also **demerara sugar**) light brown cane sugar coming originally and chiefly from Guyana. **2** (also **demerara rum**) a dark rum fermented from molasses, made in Guyana. ▷mid 19th cent.: named after the region of **DEMERARA.**

de·mer·it /diˈmerit/ ▶*n.* **1** a feature or fact deserving censure: *the merits and demerits of these proposals.* **2** a mark awarded against someone for a fault or offense. ▷late Middle English (also in the sense 'merit'): from Old French *desmerite* or Latin *demeritum* 'something deserved,' neuter past participle of *demereri,* from *de-* 'thoroughly' (also understood in medieval Latin as denoting reversal) + *mereri* 'to merit.' —**de·mer·i·to·ri·ous** /-ˌmeriˈtôrēəs/ *adj.*

Dem·e·rol /ˈdeməˌrôl; -ˌräl/ ▶*n.* trademark for **MEPERIDINE.** ▷1940s: of unknown origin.

de·mer·sal /diˈmərsəl/ ▶*adj.* (typically of fish) living close to the floor of the sea or a lake. Often contrasted with **PELAGIC.** ▷late 19th cent.: from Latin *demersus* (past participle of *demergere* 'submerge, sink,' from *de-* 'down' + *mergere* 'plunge') + **-AL.**

de·mesne /diˈmān/ ▶*n. historical* **1** land attached to a manor and retained for the owner's own use. ■ the lands of an estate. ■ *archaic* a region or domain: *she may one day queen it over that fair demesne.* **2** *historical Law* possession of real property in one's own right. ▷Middle English: from Old French *demeine* (later Anglo-Norman French *demesne*) 'belonging to a lord,' from Latin *dominicus,* from *dominus* 'lord, master.' Compare with **DOMAIN.**

▶*PHRASE* □ **held in demesne** (of an estate) occupied by the owner, not by tenants.

De·me·ter /diˈmētər/ *Greek Mythology* the goddess of cereal grains, daughter of Cronus and Rhea and mother of Persephone. She is associated with Cybele; her symbol is typically an ear of wheat. The Eleusinian mysteries were held in honor of her. Roman equivalent **CERES.** See also **PERSEPHONE.**

demi- ▶*prefix* **1** half; half-size: *demisemiquaver | demitasse.* **2** partially; in an inferior degree: *demigod | demimonde.* ▷via French from medieval Latin *dimedius* 'half,' from earlier *dimidius.*

de·mi-ca·rac·tère /ˌdemē ˌkarəkˈte(ə)r/ ▶*n.* (*pl.* same) a style of ballet having elements of character dance but executed with steps based on the classical technique. ■ a dancer specializing in this type of dance. ▷late 18th cent.: French, literally 'half character.'

de·mi-glace /ˈdemē ˌglas/ (also **de·mi-glaze** /ˌglāz/) ▶*n.* a rich, glossy brown sauce from which the liquid has been partly evaporated, typically flavored with wine and served with meat. ▷early 20th cent.: French, literally 'half glaze.'

dem·i·god /ˈdemēˌgäd/ ▶*n.* (*fem.* **dem·i·god·dess** /ˈdemēˌgädis/) a being with partial or lesser divine status, such as a minor deity, the offspring of a god and a mortal, or a mortal raised to divine rank. ■ *figurative* a person who is greatly admired or feared. ▷mid 16th cent.: translating Latin *semideus.*

dem·i·john /ˈdemēˌjän/ ▶*n.* a bulbous, narrow-necked bottle holding from 3 to 10 gallons of liquid, typically enclosed in a wicker cover. ▷mid 18th cent.: probably an alteration of French *dame-jeanne* 'Lady Jane,' by association with **DEMI-** 'half-sized' and the given name *John.*

de·mil·i·ta·rize /dēˈmilitəˌrīz/ ▶*v.* [*trans.*] [usu. as *adj.*] (**demilitarized**) remove all military forces from (an area): *a demilitarized zone.* —**de·mil·i·ta·ri·za·tion** /-ˌmilitərəˈzāsHən/ *n.*

De Mille /də ˈmil/, Cecil B. (1881–1959), U.S. movie producer and director, noted for his spectacular epics; full name *Cecil Blount De Mille.* He founded the Jesse L. Lasky Feature Play Company (later Paramount) with Samuel Goldwyn in 1913 and chose the then little-known Los Angeles suburb of Hollywood as a location for their first movie, *The Squaw Man* (1914). Other notable movies: *The Ten Commandments* (1923; remade 1956) and *Samson and Delilah* (1949).

de Mille /də ˈmil/, Agnes George (1905–93), U.S. dancer and choreographer; the niece of movie director Cecil B. De Mille. Her style of dancing mixed classical ballet with folk dance. She choreographed the ballet *Rodeo* (1942) and the Broadway musicals *Oklahoma!* (1943), *Brigadoon* (1947), *Gentlemen Prefer Blondes* (1949), and *Paint Your Wagon* (1951), among others.

dem·i·mon·daine /ˌdemēmänˈdān/ (also **dem·i-mon·daine**) ▶*n.* a woman considered to belong to the demimonde. ▷late 19th cent.: from French *demi-mondaine,* literally 'woman of the demimonde.'

dem·i·monde /ˈdemēˌmänd/ (also **dem·i-monde**) ▶*n.* (in 19th-century France) the class of women considered to be of doubtful morality and social standing. ■ a group of people considered to be on the fringes of respectable society: *the demimonde of arms deals.* ▷mid 19th cent.: from French *demi-monde,* literally 'half-world.'

de·mine /dēˈmīn/ ▶*v.* [*trans.*] remove explosive mines from: *the money will be used to demine a field in Afghanistan.* —**de·min·er** *n.*

de·min·er·al·ize /dēˈminərəˌlīz/ ▶*v.* [*trans.*] [often as *adj.*] (**demineralized**) remove salts from (water). ■ deprive (teeth or bones) of minerals, causing loss of tooth enamel or softening of the skeleton. —**de·min·er·al·i·za·tion** /-ˌminərələˈzāsHən/ *n.*

de·mi-pen·sion /ˌdemēpänˈsyôn/ ▶*n.* hotel accommodations with bed, breakfast, and one main meal per day. ▷mid 20th cent.: French, literally 'half board.'

dem·i·rep /ˈdemēˌrep/ ▶*n. archaic* a woman whose chastity is considered doubtful. ▷mid 18th cent.: abbreviation of *demi-reputable.*

de·mise /diˈmīz/ ▶*n.* [in *sing.*] **1** a person's death: *Mr. Grisenthwaite's tragic demise.* ■ the end or failure of an enterprise or institution: *the demise of industry.* **2** *Law* conveyance or transfer of property or a title by demising.

▶*v.* [*trans.*] *Law* convey or grant (an estate) by will or lease. ■ transmit (a sovereign's title) by death or abdication. ▷late Middle English (as a legal term): from Anglo-Norman French, past participle (used as a noun) of Old French *desmettre* 'dismiss,' (in reflexive) 'abdicate,' based on Latin *dimittere* (see **DISMISS**).

dem·i-sec /ˈdemēˌsek/ ▶*adj.* (of wine) medium dry. ▷mid 20th cent.: French, literally 'half-dry.'

dem·i·sem·i·qua·ver /ˌdemēˈsemīˌkwāvər/ ▶*n. Music, chiefly Brit.* a thirty-second note.

de·mit /diˈmit/ ▶*v.* (**-mit·ted, -mit·ting**) [*trans.*] *archaic* resign from (an office or position): *arguments within his congregation led to his demitting his post.* ▷early 16th cent. (in the sense 'dismiss'): from French *démettre,* from *dé-* 'away from' + *mettre* 'put.' —**de·mis·sion** /-ˈmisHən/ *n.*

dem·i·tasse /ˈdemēˌtäs; -ˌtas/ ▶*n.* a small coffee cup. ▷mid 19th cent.: from French, literally 'half-cup.'

dem·i·urge /ˈdemēˌərj/ ▶*n.* a being responsible for the creation of the universe, in particular: ■ (in Platonic philosophy) the Maker or Creator of the world. ■ (in Gnosticism and other theological systems) a heavenly being, subordinate to the Supreme Being, that is considered to be the controller of the material world and antagonistic to all that is purely spiritual. ▷early 17th cent. (denoting a magistrate in certain ancient Greek states): via ecclesiastical Latin from Greek *dēmiourgos* 'craftsman,' from *dēmios* 'public' (from *dēmos* 'people') + *-ergos* 'working.' —**dem·i·ur·gic** /ˌdemēˈərjik/ *adj.* —**dem·i·ur·gi·cal** /ˌdemēˈərjikəl/ *adj.*

dem·o /ˈdemō/ *informal* ▶*n.* (*pl.* **-os**) a demonstration of the capabilities of something, typically computer software or a musical group: [as *adj.*] *a demo tape.*

▶*v.* (**-os, -oed**) [*trans.*] demonstrate the capabilities of (software or equipment). ■ record (a song) for demonstration purposes: *they've already demoed twelve new songs.*

de·mob /dēˈmäb/ *Brit., informal* ▶*v.* (**-mobbed, -mobbing**) [*trans.*] (usu. **be demobbed**) demobilize.

▶*n.* demobilization: *we were waiting for our demob.* ▷1920s (following World War I): abbreviation.

de·mo·bi·lize /dēˈmōbəˌlīz/ ▶*v.* [*trans.*] (usu. **be demobilized**) take (troops) out of active service, typically at the end of a war: *he was demobilized in February 1946.* ■ [*intrans.*] cease military operations: *Germany demanded that they demobilize within twelve hours.* ▷late 19th cent.: from French *démobiliser,* from *dé-* (expressing reversal) + *mobiliser* 'mobilize.' —**de·mo·bi·li·za·tion** /-ˌmōbəliˈzāsHən/ *n.*

de·moc·ra·cy /diˈmäkrəsē/ ▶*n.* (*pl.* **-cies**) a system of government by the whole population or all the eligible members of a state, typically through elected representatives: *capitalism and democracy are ascendant in the third world.* ■ a state governed in such a way: *a multiparty democracy.* ■ control of an organization or group by the majority of its members: *the intended extension of industrial democracy.* ■ the practice or principles of social equality: *demands for greater democracy.* ▷late 16th cent.: from French *démocratie,* via late Latin from Greek *dēmokratia,* from *dēmos* 'the people' + *-kratia* 'power, rule.'

dem·o·crat /ˈdeməˌkrat/ ▶*n.* **1** an advocate or supporter of democracy. **2** (**Democrat**) a member of the Democratic Party. ▷late 18th cent. (originally denoting an opponent of the aristocrats in the French Revolution of 1790): from French *démocrate,* on the pattern of *aristocrate* 'aristocrat.'

dem·o·crat·ic /ˌdeməˈkratik/ ▶*adj.* **1** of, relating to, or supporting democracy or its principles: *democratic reforms | democratic government.* ■ favoring or characterized by social equality; egalitarian: *cycling is a democratic activity that can be enjoyed by anyone.* **2** (**Democratic**) of or relating to the Democratic Party. ▷early 17th cent.: from French *démocratique,* via medieval Latin from Greek *dēmokratikos,* from *dēmokratia* (see **DEMOCRACY**). —**dem·o·crat·i·cal·ly** /-ik(ə)lē/ *adv.*

dem·o·crat·ic cen·tral·ism ▶*n.* the Leninist organizational system in which policy is decided centrally and is binding on all members.

Dem·o·crat·ic Par·ty one of the two main U.S. political parties (the other being the Republican Party), which follows a liberal program, tending to promote a strong central government and expansive social programs.

Dem·o·crat·ic Re·pub·li·can Par·ty a U.S. political party that was founded in 1792 by Thomas Jefferson and was a forerunner of the modern Democratic Party.

de·moc·ra·tize /diˈmäkrəˌtīz/ ▶*v.* [*trans.*] (often **be democratized**) introduce a democratic system or democratic principles to: *public institutions need to be democratized.* ■ make (something) accessible to everyone: *mass production has not democratized fashion.*

▷late 18th cent.: from French *démocratiser*. —**de·moc·ra·ti·za·tion** /-ˌmäkrətəˈzāSHən/ *n.*

De·moc·ri·tus /dəˈmäkritəs; dē-/ (*c.*460–*c.*370 BC), Greek philosopher. He developed the atomic theory originated by his teacher Leucippus that explained natural phenomena in terms of the arrangement and rearrangement of atoms moving in a void.

dé·mo·dé /ˌdāmōˈdā/ ▶*adj.* out of fashion. ▷French, past participle of *démoder* 'go out of fashion.'

de·mo·dec·tic mange /ˌdēməˈdektik ˈmānj/ ▶*n.* a form of mange caused by follicle mites and tending to affect chiefly the head and foreparts. Compare with SARCOPTIC MANGE. ▷late 19th cent.: *demodectic* from modern Latin *Demodex* (from Greek *dēmos* 'fat' + *dēx* 'woodworm') + -IC.

de·mod·u·late /dēˈmäjəˌlāt/ ▶*v.* [*trans.*] *Electronics* extract (a modulating signal) from its carrier. ■ separate a modulating signal from (its carrier). —**de·mod·u·la·tion** /-ˌmäjəˈlāSHən/ *n.* —**de·mod·u·la·tor** /-ˌlātər/ *n.*

dem·o·graph·ic /ˌdeməˈgrafik/ ▶*adj.* relating to the structure of populations: *the demographic trend is toward an older population.* —**dem·o·graph·i·cal** *adj.* —**dem·o·graph·i·cal·ly** /-ik(ə)lē/ *adv.*

dem·o·graph·ics /ˌdeməˈgrafiks/ ▶*plural n.* statistical data relating to the population and particular groups within it: *the demographics of book buyers.*

de·mog·ra·phy /diˈmägrəfē/ ▶*n.* the study of statistics such as births, deaths, income, or the incidence of disease, which illustrate the changing structure of human populations. ■ the composition of a particular human population: *Europe's demography is changing.* ▷late 19th cent.: from Greek *dēmos* 'the people' + -GRAPHY. —**de·mog·ra·pher** /-fər/ *n.*

de·moi /ˈdēmoi/ ▶ plural form of DEMOS.

dem·oi·selle /ˌdem(w)əˈzel/ ▶*n.* **1** (also **demoiselle crane**) a small, graceful Old World crane with a black head and breast and white ear tufts, breeding in southeastern Europe and central Asia. • *Anthropoides virgo*, family Gruidae. **2** a damselfly, esp. of the genus *Agrion*. **3** a damselfish. **4** *archaic or poetic/literary* a young woman. ▷early 16th cent. (sense 4): from French, from Old French *dameisele* 'damsel.'

de Moi·vre's the·o·rem /də ˈmwäv(rə)z/ *Mathematics* a theorem that states that $(\cos\vartheta + i\sin\vartheta)^n = \cos n\vartheta + i\sin n\vartheta$, where i is the square root of -1. ▷early 18th cent.: named after Abraham *de Moivre* (1667–1754) French-born English mathematician, fellow of the Royal Society.

de·mol·ish /diˈmäliSH/ ▶*v.* [*trans.*] pull or knock down (a building). See note at DESTROY. ■ comprehensively refute (an argument or its proponent): *I looked forward keenly to demolishing my opponent.* ■ *informal* overwhelmingly defeat (a player or team): *they demolished the Denver Broncos, 55-10.* ■ *humorous* eat up (food) quickly: *we demolished the potato pancakes.* ▷mid 16th cent.: from French *démoliss-*, lengthened stem of *démolir*, from Latin *demoliri*, from *de-* (expressing reversal) + *moliri* 'construct' (from *moles* 'mass'). —**de·mol·ish·er** *n.*

dem·o·li·tion /ˌdeməˈliSHən/ ▶*n.* the action or process of demolishing or being demolished: *the monument was saved from demolition.* ■ *informal* an overwhelming defeat. ▷mid 16th cent.: via French from Latin *demolitio(n-)*, from the verb *demoliri* (see DEMOLISH).

dem·o·li·tion der·by ▶*n.* a competition in which typically older cars are driven into each other until only one is left running.

de·mon[1] /ˈdēmən/ ▶*n.* **1** an evil spirit or devil, esp. one thought to possess a person or act as a tormentor in hell. ■ a cruel, evil, or destructive person or thing: *I was a little demon, I can tell you.* ■ [often as *adj.*] a forceful, fierce, or skillful performer of a specified activity: *a friend of mine is a demon cook | **a demon for** work.* ■ reckless mischief; devilry: *his eyes are bursting with pure demon.* **2** another term for DAEMON[1] (sense 1). ▷Middle English: from medieval Latin, from Latin *daemon*, from Greek *daimōn* 'deity, genius'; in sense 1 also from Latin *daemonium* 'lesser or evil spirit,' from Greek *daemonion*, diminutive of *daimōn*.
▶*PHRASE* □ **like a demon** in a very forceful, fierce, or skillful way: *he worked like a demon.*

de·mon[2] ▶*n.* variant spelling of DAEMON[2].

de·mon·e·tize /dēˈmäniˌtīz/ ▶*v.* [*trans.*] (usu. **be demonetized**) deprive (a coin or precious metal) of its status as money. ▷mid 19th cent.: from French *démonétiser*, from *dé-* (expressing reversal) + Latin *moneta* 'money.' —**de·mon·e·ti·za·tion** /-ˌmänitəˈzāSHən/ *n.*

de·mo·ni·ac /diˈmōnēˌak/ ▶*adj.* of, like, or characteristic of a demon or demons: *a goddess with both divine and demoniac qualities | demoniac rage.*
▶*n.* a person believed to be possessed by an evil spirit. ▷late Middle English: from Old French *demoniaque*, from ecclesiastical Latin *daemoniacus*, from *daemonium* 'lesser or evil spirit' (see DEMON[1]). —**de·mo·ni·a·cal** /ˌdēməˈnīəkəl/ *adj.* —**de·mo·ni·a·cal·ly** /ˌdēməˈnīək(ə)lē/ *adv.*

de·mon·ic /diˈmänik/ ▶*adj.* of, resembling, or characteristic of demons or evil spirits: *demonic possession | her laughter was demonic.* ■ fiercely energetic or frenzied: *in a demonic hurry.* ▷mid 17th cent.: via late Latin from Greek *daimonikos*, from *daimōn* (see DEMON[1]). —**de·mon·i·cal·ly** /-ik(ə)lē/ *adv.*

de·mon·ism /ˈdēməˌnizəm/ ▶*n.* **1** belief in the power of demons. **2** action or behavior that seems too cruel or wicked to be human: *the demonism of warfare.*

de·mon·ize /ˈdēməˌnīz/ ▶*v.* [*trans.*] portray as wicked and threatening: *seeking to demonize one side in the conflict.* —**de·mon·i·za·tion** /ˌdēməniˈzāSHən/ *n.*

demono- ▶*comb. form* of or relating to demons: *demonolatry.* ▷from Greek *daimōn* 'demon.'

de·mon·ol·a·try /ˌdēməˈnälətrē/ ▶*n.* the worship of demons.

de·mon·ol·o·gy /ˌdēməˈnäləjē/ ▶*n.* the study of demons or of demonic belief. —**de·mon·o·log·i·cal** /-nəˈläjikəl/ *adj.* —**de·mon·ol·o·gist** /-jist/ *n.*

de·mo·nop·o·lize /ˌdēməˈnäpəˌlīz/ ▶*v.* [*trans.*] introduce competition into (a market or economy) by privatizing previously nationalized assets. —**de·mo·nop·o·li·za·tion** /-ˌnäpələˈzāSHən/ *n.*

de·mon·stra·ble /diˈmänstrəbəl/ ▶*adj.* clearly apparent or capable of being logically proved: *the demonstrable injustices of racism.* ▷late Middle English: from Latin *demonstrabilis*, from *demonstrare* 'point out.' —**de·mon·stra·bil·i·ty** /-ˌmänstrəˈbilitē/ *n.*

de·mon·stra·bly /diˈmänstrəblē/ ▶*adv.* clearly and undeniably: *the situation is demonstrably unfair.*

dem·on·strate /ˈdemənˌstrāt/ ▶*v.* **1** [*trans.*] clearly show the existence or truth of (something) by giving proof or evidence: *their shameful silence demonstrates their ineptitude.* ■ give a practical exhibition and explanation of (how a machine, skill, or craft works or is performed): *computerized design methods will be demonstrated* | [with *clause*] *he **demonstrated how** to make his favorite hotdog.* ■ show or express (a feeling or quality) by one's actions: *she began to demonstrate a new-found confidence.* **2** [*intrans.*] take part in a public demonstration: *thousands demonstrated in favor of the government.* ▷mid 16th cent. (in the sense 'point out'): from Latin *demonstrat-* 'pointed out,' from the verb *demonstrare*.

dem·on·stra·tion /ˌdemənˈstrāSHən/ ▶*n.* **1** the action or process of showing the existence or truth of something by giving proof or evidence: *it is not capable of mathematical demonstration | Lind's **demonstration that** citrus fruits cure scurvy.* ■ something that proves or makes evident: *the letter was a demonstration of good faith.* ■ the outward showing of feeling: *physical demonstrations of affection.* ■ a practical exhibition and explanation of how something works or is performed: *a microwave cooking demonstration.* ■ a show of military force: *the flight demonstration squadron.* **2** a public meeting or march protesting against something or expressing views on a political issue. ▷late Middle English (also in the senses 'proof provided by logic' and 'sign, indication'): from Latin *demonstratio(n-)*, from *demonstrare* 'point out' (see DEMONSTRATE). Sense 2 dates from the mid 19th cent.

de·mon·stra·tive /diˈmänstrətiv/ ▶*adj.* **1** (of a person) tending to show feelings, esp. of affection, openly. **2** serving as conclusive evidence of something; giving proof: *demonstrative evidence.* ■ involving demonstration, esp. by scientific means: *the possibility of a demonstrative science of ethics.* **3** *Grammar* (of a determiner or pronoun) indicating the person or thing referred to (e.g., *this, that, those*).
▶*n. Grammar* a demonstrative determiner or pronoun. ▷late Middle English (in the senses 'serving as conclusive evidence of' and 'making manifest'): from Old French *demonstratif, -ive*, from Latin *demonstrativus*, from *demonstrare* 'point out' (see DEMONSTRATE). —**de·mon·stra·tive·ly** *adv.* —**de·mon·stra·tive·ness** *n.*

de·mon·stra·tive leg·a·cy ▶*n. Law* a legacy that is directed to be paid from a specified fund or pool.

dem·on·stra·tor /ˈdemənˌstrātər/ ▶*n.* **1** a person who takes part in a public protest meeting or march. **2** a person who shows how a particular piece of equipment works or how a skill or craft is performed. ■ a person who teaches in this way, esp. in a laboratory. ■ a piece of merchandise that can be tested by potential buyers.

de Mon·tes·pan /də ˌmôntəˈspäN/, Marquise de, see MONTESPAN.

de Mont·fort /də ˈmäntfərt; -ˌfôrt/, Simon, see MONTFORT[1].

de·mor·al·ize /diˈmôrəˌlīz/ ▶*v.* [*trans.*] **1** [usu. as *adj.*] (**demoralized**) cause (someone) to lose confidence or hope; dispirit: *the army was demoralized and scattered.* **2** *archaic* corrupt the morals of (someone). ▷late 18th cent.: from French *démoraliser* (a word of the French Revolution), from *dé-* (expressing reversal) + *moral* 'moral,' from Latin *moralis*. —**de·mor·al·i·za·tion** /-ˌmôrələˈzāSHən/ *n.* —**de·mor·al·iz·ing** *adj.* —**de·mor·al·iz·ing·ly** *adv.*

de Mor·gan's laws /di ˈmôrgənz/ *Mathematics* two laws in Boolean algebra and set theory that state that AND and OR, or union and intersection, are dual. They are used to simplify the design of electronic circuits. • The laws can be expressed in Boolean logic as: NOT (*a* AND *b*) = NOT *a* OR NOT *b*; NOT (*a* OR *b*) = NOT *a* AND NOT *b*. ▷early 20th cent.: named after Augustus *de Morgan* (1806–71), English mathematician, but already known (by logicians) as principles in the Middle Ages.

de·mos /ˈdēmäs/ ▶*n.* (*pl.* **-moi** /-moi/) the common people of an ancient Greek state. ■ the populace as a political unit, esp. in a democracy. ▷from Greek *dēmos*.

De·mos·the·nes /dəˈmäsTHəˌnēz/ (384–322 BC), Athenian orator and statesman. He is known for his political speeches on the need to resist the aggressive tendencies of Philip II of Macedon (the *Philippics*).

de·mote /diˈmōt/ ▶*v.* [*trans.*] (often **be demoted**) give (someone) a lower rank or less senior position, usually as a punishment: *the head of the army was demoted to deputy defense secretary.* ▷late 19th cent.: from DE- 'down' + a shortened form of PROMOTE.

de·mot·ic /diˈmätik/ ▶*adj.* denoting or relating to the kind of language used by ordinary people; popular or colloquial: *a demotic idiom.* ■ relating to or denoting the form of modern Greek used in everyday speech and writing. Compare with KATHAREVOUSA. ■ relating to or denoting a simplified, cursive form of ancient Egyptian script, dating from *c.*650 BC and replaced by Greek in the Ptolemaic period. Compare with HIERATIC.
▶*n.* ordinary colloquial speech. ■ demotic Greek. ■ demotic Egyptian script. ▷early 19th cent. (in the sense 'relating to the Egyptian demotic'): from Greek *dēmotikos* 'popular,' from *dēmotēs* 'one of the people,' from *dēmos* 'the people.'

de·mo·tion /diˈmōSHən/ ▶*n.* reduction in rank or status: *too many demotions would weaken morale.* ▷early 20th cent.: from DEMOTE, on the pattern of *promotion*.

de·mo·ti·vate ▶*v.* [*trans.*] make (someone) less eager to work or study: *some children disrupt classes and demotivate pupils.* —**de·mo·tiv·a·tion** *n.*

de·mount·a·ble /dēˈmountəbəl/ ▶*adj.* able to be dismantled or removed from its setting and readily reassembled or repositioned. —**de·mount** *v.*

Demp·sey /ˈdem(p)sē/, Jack (1895–1983), U.S. boxer; full name *William Harrison Dempsey*. He was world heavyweight champion 1919–26.

de·mul·cent /diˈməlsənt/ *Medicine* ▶*adj.* (of a substance) relieving inflammation or irritation.
▶*n.* a substance that relieves irritation of the mucous membranes in the mouth by forming a protective film. ▷mid 18th cent.: from Latin *demulcent-* 'stroking caressingly,' from the verb *demulcere*, from *de-* 'away' + *mulcere* 'soothe.'

de·mur /diˈmər/ ▶*v.* (**-murred**, **-mur·ring**) [*intrans.*] raise doubts or objections or show reluctance: *normally she would have accepted the challenge, but she demurred.* ■ *dated Law* put forward a demurrer.
▶*n.* [usu. with *negative*] the action or process of objecting to or hesitating over something: *they accepted this ruling **without demur**.* See note at QUALM. ▷Middle English (in the sense 'linger, delay'): from Old French *demourer* (verb), *demeure* (noun), based on Latin *de-* 'away, completely' + *morari* 'delay.'

de·mure /diˈmyo͝or/ ▶*adj.* (**-mur·er**, **-mur·est**) (of a woman or her behavior) reserved, modest, and shy: *a demure little wife who sits at home minding the house.* ■ (of clothing) lending such an appearance. ▷late Middle English (in the sense 'sober, serious, reserved'): perhaps from Old French *demoure*, past participle of *demourer* 'remain, stay' (see DEMUR); influenced by Old French *mur* 'grave,' from Latin *maturus* 'ripe or mature.' The sense 'reserved, shy' dates from the late 17th cent. **—de·mure·ly** *adv.* **—de·mure·ness** *n.*

de·mur·ra·ble /di'mərəbəl; -'mə-rə-/ ▸*adj. dated, chiefly Law* open to demurrer.

de·mur·rage /di'mərij; -'mə-rij/ ▸*n. Law* a charge payable to the owner of a chartered ship in respect of failure to load or discharge the ship within the time agreed. ▷mid 17th cent. (also in the general sense 'procrastination, delay'): from Old French *demourage*, from the verb *demourer* (see **DEMUR**).

de·mur·ral /di'mərəl; -'mə-rəl/ ▸*n.* the action of demurring: *words of demurral.*

de·mur·rer /di'mərər; -'mə-rər/ ▸*n.* an objection. ▪ *dated Law* an objection that an opponent's point is irrelevant or invalid, while granting the factual basis of the point: ***on demurrer** it was held that the plaintiff's claim succeeded.* ▷early 16th cent.: from Anglo-Norman French (infinitive used as a noun), from Old French *demourer* 'remain, stay' (see **DEMUR**).

de·mu·tu·al·ize /dē'myoōchoōwə,līz/ ▸*v.* [*trans.*] change (a mutual organization such as a savings and loan association) to one of a different kind. **—de·mu·tu·al·i·za·tion** /-,myoōchoōwəli'zāshən/ *n.*

de·my /di'mī/ (in full **metric demy**) ▸*n.* a paper size, now standardized at 564 × 444 mm. ▪ (in full **demy octavo**) a book size, now standardized at 216 × 138 mm. ▪ (in full **demy quarto**) a book size, now standardized at 276 × 219 mm. ▷late Middle English (as an adjective in the sense 'half-sized'): from **DEMI-**, or from its source, French *demi* 'half.'

de·my·e·li·nate /dē'mīələ,nāt/ ▸*v.* [*trans.*] [usu. as *adj.*] (**demyelinating**) *Medicine* cause the loss or destruction of myelin in (nerve tissue): *a chronic demyelinating disease.* **—de·my·e·li·na·tion** /-,mīəli'nāshən/ *n.*

de·mys·ti·fy /dē'mistə,fī/ ▸*v.* (**-fies, -fied**) [*trans.*] make (a difficult or esoteric subject) clearer and easier to understand: *this book attempts to demystify technology.* **—de·mys·ti·fi·ca·tion** /-,mistəfi'kāshən/ *n.*

de·my·thol·o·gize /,dēmi'thälə,jīz/ ▸*v.* [*trans.*] reinterpret (a subject or text) so that it is free of mythical or heroic elements: *he undertakes to demythologize the man who has been for many the modern counterpart of St. Augustine.* ▪ reinterpret what are considered to be mythological elements of (the Bible).

den /den/ ▸*n.* a wild animal's lair or habitation. ▪ *informal* a small, comfortable room in a house where a person can pursue an activity in private. ▪ a place where people meet in secret, typically to engage in some illicit activity: *an opium den | a den of iniquity.* ▪ a small subdivision of a Cub Scout pack.

▸*v.* (**denned, den·ning**) [*intrans.*] (of a wild animal) live in or retreat to a den: *the cubs denned in the late autumn.* ▷Old English *denn*, of Germanic origin; related to German *Tenne* 'threshing floor,' also to **DENE**[1].

De·na·li /də'nälē/ another name for Mount McKinley (see **McKINLEY, MOUNT**).

de·nar /di'när/ ▸*n.* the basic monetary unit of the former Yugoslav Republic of Macedonia. ▷based on Latin *denarius*; compare with **DINAR**.

de·nar·i·us /di'ne(ə)rēəs/ ▸*n.* (*pl.* **-nar·i·i** /-'ne(ə)rē,ī/) an ancient Roman silver coin, originally worth ten asses. ▪ a unit of weight equal to that of a silver denarius. ▪ an ancient Roman gold coin worth 25 silver denarii. ▷late Middle English: Latin, literally 'containing ten,' from the phrase *denarius nummus* 'coin worth ten asses' (see **AS**[2]), from *deni* 'in tens,' from *decem* 'ten.'

den·a·ry /'denərē; 'dē-/ ▸*adj.* relating to or based on the number ten; less common term for **DECIMAL**: *denary numbers.* ▷mid 19th cent.: from Latin *denarius* 'containing ten' (see **DENARIUS**).

de·na·tion·al·ize /dē'nashənl,īz/ ▸*v.* [*trans.*] **1** transfer (a nationalized industry or institution) from public to private ownership. **2** deprive (a country or person) of nationality or national characteristics. ▷early 19th cent. (sense 2): from French *dénationaliser* (a word of the French Revolution), from *dé-* (expressing reversal) + *nationaliser* 'nationalize.' **—de·na·tion·al·i·za·tion** /-,nashənlə'zāshən/ *n.*

de·nat·u·ral·ize /dē'nachərə,līz/ ▸*v.* [*trans.*] **1** make (something) unnatural. **2** deprive (someone) of citizenship of a country. **—de·nat·u·ral·i·za·tion** /-,nachərələ'zāshən/ *n.*

de·na·tur·ant /dē'nāchərənt/ ▸*n.* a substance added to alcohol to make it unfit for drinking. ▪ *Biochemistry* a substance that causes denaturation of proteins or other biological compounds.

de·na·ture /dē'nāchər/ ▸*v.* [*trans.*] [often as *adj.*] (**denatured**) take away or alter the natural qualities of: *empty verbalisms and denatured ceremonies.* ▪ make (alcohol) unfit for drinking by the addition of toxic or foul-tasting substances. ▪ *Biochemistry* destroy the characteristic properties of (a protein or other biological macromolecule) by heat, acidity, or other effects that disrupt its molecular conformation. ▪ [*intrans.*] (of a substance) undergo this process. ▷late 17th cent. (in the sense 'make unnatural'): from French *dénaturer*, from *dé-* (expressing reversal) + *nature* 'nature.' **—de·na·tur·a·tion** /dē,nāchə'rāshən/ *n.*

de·na·zi·fi·ca·tion /dē,nätsəfi'kāshən/ ▸*n.* the process of bringing the leaders of the National Socialist regime in Germany to justice and of purging all elements of Nazism from public life, carried out esp. between 1945 and 1948.

de·na·zi·fy /dē'nätsə,fī/ ▸*v.* (**-fies, -fied**) [*trans.*] remove the Nazi (or figuratively, the fascist or repressive) influence from.

Dench /dench/, Dame Judi (1934–), English actress; full name *Judith Olivia Dench.* She appeared in numerous theatrical, movie, and television productions. Her movies include *A Handful of Dust* (1987), *Mrs. Brown,* (1997), *Shakespeare in Love* (Academy Award, 1998), and *Iris* (2001).

den·dri·form /'dendrə,fôrm/ ▸*adj.* having the shape or form of a tree.

den·dri·mer /'dendrəmər/ ▸*n.* a synthetic polymer with a branching, treelike structure. ▷1990s: from Greek *dendron* 'tree' + *-i-* + *-mer.*

den·drite /'dendrīt/ ▸*n.* **1** *Physiology* a short branched extension of a nerve cell, along which impulses received from other cells at synapses are transmitted to the cell body. Compare with **AXON**. **2** a crystal or crystalline mass with a branching, treelike structure. ▪ a natural treelike or mosslike marking on a piece of rock or mineral. ▷early 18th cent.: from French, from Greek *dendritēs* 'treelike,' from *dendron* 'tree.'

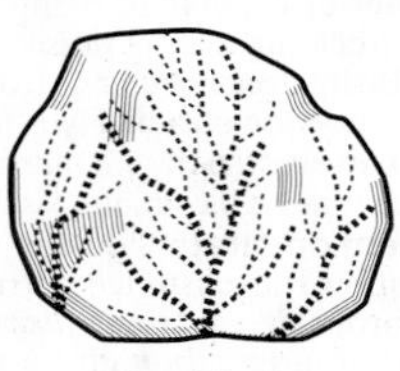

dendrite 2

den·drit·ic /den'dritik/ ▸*adj. technical* having a branched form resembling a tree. ▪ *Physiology* of or relating to a dendrite or dendrites. ▪ (of a solid) consisting of crystalline dendrites: *dendritic salt.* **—den·drit·i·cal·ly** /-ik(ə)lē/ *adv.*

dendro- ▸*comb. form* of or relating to a tree or trees: *dendrology.* ▷from Greek *dendron* 'tree.'

den·dro·chro·nol·o·gy /,dendrōkrə'näləjē/ ▸*n.* the science or technique of dating events, environmental change, and archaeological artifacts by using the characteristic patterns of annual growth rings in timber and tree trunks. **—den·dro·chron·o·log·i·cal** /-,kränl'äjikəl/ *adj.* **—den·dro·chro·nol·o·gist** /-jist/ *n.*

den·dro·gram /'dendrə,gram/ ▸*n.* a tree diagram, esp. one showing taxonomic relationships.

den·droid /'dendroid/ ▸*adj. Biology* (of a plant, marine invertebrate, or structure) tree-shaped; arborescent; branching. ▪ *Paleontology* denoting graptolites of a type that formed many-branched colonies, found chiefly in the Ordovician and Silurian periods.

▸*n. Paleontology* a graptolite of this type. • Order Dendroidea, class Graptolithina. ▷mid 19th cent.: from **DENDRO-** 'tree' + **-OID**.

den·drol·o·gy /den'dräləjē/ ▸*n.* the scientific study of trees. **—den·dro·log·i·cal** /,dendrə'läjikəl/ *adj.* **—den·drol·o·gist** /-jist/ *n.*

den·dron /'dendrän/ ▸*n.* another term for **DENDRITE** (sense 1). ▷late 19th cent.: from **DENDRITE**, on the pattern of words such as *axon.*

De·ne /di'nā/ ▸*n.* (*pl.* same) **1** a member of a group of American Indian peoples of the Canadian Northwest and Alaska, traditionally speaking Athabaskan languages, and having collective representation in Canadian political life. **2** any of the languages of these peoples.

▸*adj.* of or relating to these peoples or their languages. ▷from French *Déné*, from an Athabaskan word meaning 'people.'

dene[1] /dēn/ (also **dean**) ▸*n.* [usu. in *place names*] *Brit.* a vale, esp. the deep, narrow, wooded valley of a small river: *Rottingdean | Deepdene.* ▷Old English *denu*, of Germanic origin; related to **DEN**.

dene[2] ▸*n. dialect* a bare, sandy tract or low dune by the sea. ▷Middle English: perhaps of Germanic origin and related to **DUNE**.

Den·eb /'den,eb/ *Astronomy* the brightest star in the constellation Cygnus, a yellow supergiant. ▷from Arabic, literally 'tail' (i.e., of the "swan").

De·neb·o·la /də'nebələ/ *Astronomy* the second brightest star in the constellation Leo. ▷from Arabic *dhanab al(-asad)* '(lion's) tail.'

de·ner·vate /dē'nərvāt/ ▸*v.* [*trans.*] *Medicine* remove or cut off the nerve supply from (an organ or other body part): [as *adj.*] (**denervated**) *the denervated muscle fibers.* **—de·ner·va·tion** /,dēnər'vāshən/ *n.*

De·neuve /də'noōv; də'nœv/, Catherine (1943–), French actress; born *Catherine Dorléac.* Notable movies: *Repulsion* (1965), *Belle de jour* (1967), and *Indochine* (1992).

den·gue /'denggē; -gā/ (also **dengue fever**) ▸*n.* a debilitating viral disease of the tropics, transmitted by mosquitoes, and causing sudden fever and acute pains in the joints. ▷early 19th cent.: from West Indian Spanish, from Kiswahili *dinga* (in full *kidingapopo*), influenced by Spanish *dengue* 'fastidiousness' (with reference to the dislike of movement by affected patients).

Deng Xiao·ping /'dəng 'shou'ping/ (also **Teng Hsiao-p'ing**) (1904–97), Chinese communist statesman; vice-premier 1973–76 and 1977–80; vice-chairman of the Central Committee of the Chinese Communist Party 1977–80. Discredited during the Cultural Revolution, he was reinstated in 1977 and became the leader of China. In 1989, his orders led to the massacre of some 2,000 pro-democracy demonstrators in Beijing's Tiananmen Square.

Den Haag /den 'häg/ Dutch name for The Hague (see **HAGUE**).

de·ni·a·ble /di'nīəbəl/ ▸*adj.* able to be denied: *the government did agree to play a limited and deniable role in the rebellion.* **—de·ni·a·bil·i·ty** /-,nīə'bilitē/ *n.* **—de·ni·a·bly** /-blē/ *adv.*

de·ni·al /di'nīəl/ ▸*n.* the action of declaring something to be untrue: *she shook her head **in denial.*** ▪ the refusal of something requested or desired: *the denial of insurance to people with certain medical conditions.* ▪ a statement that something is not true: *official denials | his **denial that** he was having an affair.* ▪ *Psychology* failure to acknowledge an unacceptable truth or emotion or to admit it into consciousness, used as a defense mechanism: *you're living **in denial.*** ▪ short for **SELF-DENIAL**. ▪ disavowal of a person as one's leader.

de·ni·al of ser·vice ▸*n.* (abbr.: **DoS**) *Computing* an interruption in an authorized user's access to a computer network, typically one caused with malicious intent.

de·ni·er ▸*n.* **1** /də'ni(ə)r; 'denyər/ a unit of weight by which the fineness of silk, rayon, or nylon yarn is measured, equal to the weight in grams of 9000 meters of the yarn and often used to describe the thickness of hosiery: *840 denier nylon.* **2** /də'ni(ə)r; dən'yā/ *historical* a French coin, equal to one twelfth of a sou, which was withdrawn from use in the 19th century. ▷late Middle English: via Old French from Latin *denarius* (see **DENARIUS**). Sense 1 dates from the mid 19th cent.

den·i·grate /'deni,grāt/ ▸*v.* [*trans.*] criticize unfairly; disparage: *there is a tendency to denigrate the poor.* ▷late Middle English (in the sense 'blacken, make dark'): from Latin *denigrat-* 'blackened,' from the verb *denigrare*, from *de-* 'away, completely' + *nigrare* (from *niger* 'black'). **—den·i·gra·tion** /,deni'grāshən/ *n.* **—den·i·gra·tor** /-,grātər/ *n.* **—den·i·gra·to·ry** /-grə-,tôrē/ *adj.*

den·im /'denəm/ ▸*n.* a sturdy cotton twill fabric, typically blue, used for jeans, overalls, and other clothing. ▪ (**denims**) clothing made of such fabric: *a pair of denims.* ▷late 17th cent. (as *serge denim*): from French *serge de Nimes*, denoting a kind of serge from the manufacturing town of **NÎMES**.

De Ni·ro /də 'ni(ə)rō/, Robert (1943–), U.S. actor. The star of many movies, he often played tough

Robert De Niro

characters and frequently worked with director Martin Scorsese. He won Academy Awards for *The Godfather Part II* (1974) and *Raging Bull* (1980) and made his debut as a director with *A Bronx Tale* (1994), in which he also acted.

Den·is, St. /'denis; də'nē/ (also **Den·ys**) (died *c.*250), French bishop; born in Italy; patron saint of France; Roman name *Dionysius*. According to tradition, he was one of a group of seven missionaries sent from Rome to convert Gaul; he became bishop of Paris and was martyred in the reign of the emperor Valerian. Feast day, October 9.

Den·i·son /'denəsən/ a city in northern Texas, on the Red River; pop. 21,505.

de·ni·tri·fy /dē'nītrə,fī/ ▸*v.* (**-fies, -fied**) [*trans.*] (chiefly of bacteria) remove the nitrates or nitrites from (soil, air, or water) by chemical reduction. —**de·ni·tri·fi·ca·tion** /-,nītrəfi'kāsʜən/ *n.*

den·i·zen /'denəzən/ ▸*n. formal* or *humorous* an inhabitant or occupant of a particular place: *denizens of field and forest.* ■ *Brit., historical* a foreigner allowed certain rights in the adopted country. ▷late Middle English *deynseyn*, via Anglo-Norman French from Old French *deinz* 'within' (from Latin *de* 'from' + *intus* 'within') + *-ein* (from Latin *-aneus* '-aneous'). The change in the form of the word was due to association with CITIZEN. —**den·i·zen·ship** /-,sʜip/ *n.*

De·niz·li /,deniz'lē/ a commercial city in southwestern Turkey, the site of ancient ruins; pop. 203,000.

Den·mark /'den,märk/ a country in northwestern Europe, on the Jutland peninsula, between the North and the Baltic seas; pop. 5,400,000; capital, Copenhagen; official language, Danish. Danish name **DANMARK.**

Denmark emerged as a separate country during the Viking period of the 10th and 11th centuries. In the 14th century Denmark and Norway were united under a Danish king; the union was joined between the late 1300s and 1523 by Sweden, and Norway was ceded to Sweden in 1814. Although neutral, Denmark was occupied by Germany for much of World War II. It joined the EC (now the EU) in 1973.

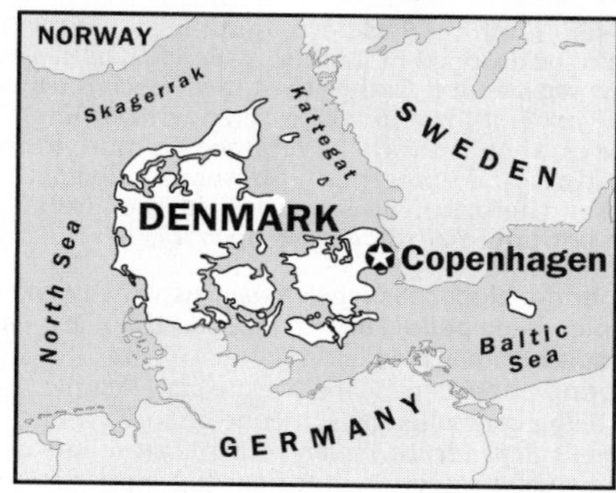

den moth·er ▸*n.* the female leader of a den of Cub Scouts.

de·nom·i·nal /dē'nämənl/ ▸*adj.* [*attrib.*] (of a word) derived from a noun.
▸*n.* a verb or other word that is derived from a noun. ▷1930s: from DE- + NOMINAL.

de·nom·i·nate /di'nämə,nāt/ ▸*v.* **1** (**be denominated**) (of sums of money) be expressed in a specified monetary unit: *the borrowings were* **denominated in** *U.S. dollars.* **2** [*trans.*] *formal* call; name: *the whole train was denominated a "bull-outfit."* ▷late Middle English (in the sense 'give a name to'): from Latin *denominat-* 'named,' from the verb *denominare*, from *de-* 'away, formally' + *nominare* 'to name' (from *nomen, nomin-* 'name'). Sense 1 dates from the mid 20th cent.

de·nom·i·na·tion /di,nämə'nāsʜən/ ▸*n.* **1** a recognized autonomous branch of the Christian Church. ■ a group or branch of any religion: *Jewish clergy of all denominations.* **2** the face value of a banknote, a coin, or a postage stamp: *a hundred dollars or so, in small denominations.* ■ the rank of a playing card within a suit, or of a suit relative to others: *two cards of the same denomination.* **3** *formal* a name or designation, esp. one serving to classify a set of things. ■ the action of naming or classifying something: *denomination of oneself as a fat woman.* ▷late Middle English (sense 3): from Latin *denominatio(n-)*, from the verb *denominare* (see DENOMINATE). Sense 1 dates from the mid 17th cent.

de·nom·i·na·tion·al /di',nämə'nāsʜənl/ ▸*adj.* relating to or according to the principles of a particular religious denomination: *denominational relief agencies.* —**de·nom·i·na·tion·al·ism** /-,izəm/ *n.*

de·nom·i·na·tive /di'nämə,nātiv; -nətiv/ ▸*adj.* old-fashioned term for DENOMINAL. ▷late 16th cent. (as a noun in the grammatical sense): from late Latin *denominativus*, from *denominat-* 'named,' from the verb *denominare* (see DENOMINATE).

de·nom·i·na·tor /di'nämə,nātər/ ▸*n. Mathematics* the number below the line in a common fraction; a divisor. ■ a figure representing the total population in terms of which statistical values are expressed. ▷mid 16th cent.: from French *dénominateur* or medieval Latin *denominator*, from *denominare* 'to name' (see DENOMINATE).

de·no·ta·tion /,dēnō'tāsʜən/ ▸*n.* the literal or primary meaning of a word, in contrast to the feelings or ideas that the word suggests: *beyond their immediate denotation, the words have a connotative power.* ■ the action or process of indicating or referring to something by means of a word, symbol, etc. ■ *Philosophy* the object or concept to which a term refers, or the set of objects of which a predicate is true. Often contrasted with CONNOTATION. —**de·no·ta·tion·al** /-sʜənl/ *adj.*

de·note /di'nōt/ ▸*v.* [*trans.*] be a sign of; indicate: *this mark denotes purity and quality.* ■ (often **be denoted**) stand as a name or symbol for: *the level of output per firm, denoted by X.* ▷late 16th cent. (in the sense 'be a sign of, mark out'): from French *dénoter* or Latin *denotare*, from *de-* 'away, thoroughly' + *notare* 'observe, note' (from *nota* 'a mark'). —**de·no·ta·tive** /'dēnō,tātiv; di'nōtətiv/ *adj.*

USAGE For an explanation of the difference between **denote** and **connote**, see **usage** at CONNOTE.

de·noue·ment /,dānōō'mäɴ/ ▸*n.* the final part of a play, movie, or narrative in which the strands of the plot are drawn together and matters are explained or resolved. ■ the climax of a chain of events, usually when something is decided or made clear: *I waited by the eighteenth green to see the denouement.* ▷mid 18th cent.: French *dénouement*, from *dénouer* 'unknot.'

de·nounce /di'nouns/ ▸*v.* [*trans.*] publicly declare to be wrong or evil: *the Assembly denounced the use of violence | he was widely* **denounced as** *a traitor.* ■ inform against: *some of his own priests* **denounced** *him* **to** *the King for heresy.* ▷Middle English (originally in the sense 'proclaim, announce,' also 'proclaim someone to be wicked, cursed, a rebel, etc.'): from Old French *denoncier*, from Latin *denuntiare* 'give official information,' based on *nuntius* 'messenger.' —**de·nounce·ment** *n.* —**de·nounc·er** *n.*

de nou·veau /,də nōō'vō/ ▸*adv. archaic* starting again from the beginning; anew. ▷late 18th cent.: French, literally 'from new.'

de no·vo /dā 'nōvō; di/ ▸*adv. & adj.* starting from the beginning; anew: [as *adv.*] *in a pure meritocracy, everyone must begin de novo* | [as *adj.*] *a general strategy for de novo protein design.* ▷early 17th cent.: Latin, literally 'from new.'

Den·pa·sar /den'pä,sär/ the chief city of the island of Bali in Indonesia, a seaport on the southern coast; pop. 261,200.

dense /dens/ ▸*adj.* closely compacted in substance: *dense volcanic rock | swirling, dense smoke.* ■ having the constituent parts crowded closely together: *an estuary* **dense with** *marine life.* ■ *figurative* (of a text) hard to understand because of complexity of ideas. ■ *informal* (of a person) stupid. See note at STUPID. ▷late Middle English: from Latin *densus*. —**dense·ly** *adv.* —**dense·ness** *n.*

den·si·fy /'densə,fī/ ▸*v.* (**-fies, -fied**) [*trans.*] [often as *adj.*] (**densified**) make (something) more dense: *densified hardboard.* —**den·si·fi·ca·tion** /,densəfi'kāsʜən/ *n.*

den·sim·e·ter /den'simitər/ ▸*n.* an instrument for measuring density, esp. of liquids. ▷mid 19th cent.: from Latin *densus* 'dense' + -METER.

den·si·tom·e·ter /,densi'tämitər/ ▸*n.* **1** an instrument for measuring the photographic density of an image on a film or photographic print. **2** a device for measuring the optical density of a material by measuring the amount of light it reflects or transmits. —**den·si·to·met·ric** /-sitə'metrik/ *adj.* —**den·si·to·met·ri·cal·ly** /-sitə'metrik(ə)lē/ *adv.* —**den·si·tom·e·try** /-'tämətrē/ *n.*.

den·si·ty /'densitē/ ▸*n.* (*pl.* **-ties**) the degree of compactness of a substance: *a reduction in bone density.* ■ *Computing* a measure of the amount of information on a storage medium (tape or disk). For magnetic tape it is the amount of information recorded per unit length of tape (bits per inch or millimeter); for a disk, a fixed number of bits per sector, sectors per track, and tracks per disk: *chip density doubles every eighteen months* | [as *modifier*, in *combination*] *a* **low-density** *5.25-inch floppy disk | a drive capable of handling* **high-density** *1.44 megabyte disks.* ■ *Physics* degree of consistency measured by the quantity of mass per unit volume. ■ the opacity of a photographic image. ■ the quantity of people or things in a given area or space: *areas of low population density | a density of 10,000 per square mile.* ▷early 17th cent.: from French *densité* or Latin *densitas*, from *densus* 'dense.'

den·si·ty func·tion ▸*n.* short for PROBABILITY DENSITY FUNCTION.

dent /dent/ ▸*n.* a slight hollow in a hard, even surface made by a blow or by the exertion of pressure. ■ a diminishing effect; a reduction: *a dent in profits.*
▸*v.* [*trans.*] mark with a dent: *the moose dropped a hind foot and dented the hood of the car.* ■ have an adverse effect on; diminish: *this neither deterred him nor dented his enthusiasm.* ▷Middle English (as a noun designating a blow with a weapon): variant of DINT.

dent. ▸*abbr.* ■ dental. ■ dentist. ■ dentistry.

den·tal /'dentl/ ▸*adj.* **1** [*attrib.*] of or relating to the teeth: *dental health.* ■ (abbr.: **dent.**) of or relating to dentistry: *dental councils.* **2** *Phonetics* (of a consonant) pronounced with the tip of the tongue against the upper front teeth (as *th*) or the alveolar ridge (as *n, d, t*).
▸*n. Phonetics* a dental consonant. ▷late 16th cent.: from late Latin *dentalis*, from Latin *dens, dent-* 'tooth.' —**den·tal·ize** /'dentl,īz/ *v.* (*Phonetics*) —**den·tal·ly** *adv.*

den·tal dam ▸*n.* a thin sheet of latex used by dentists to isolate a tooth being worked on. ■ a thin sheet of latex used as a prophylactic device during cunnilingus and anilingus.

den·tal floss ▸*n.* a soft thread of floss silk or similar material used to clean between the teeth.

den·tal for·mu·la ▸*n. Zoology* a formula expressing the number and kinds of teeth possessed by a mammal. A dental formula is usually written in the form of four "fractions," one for each type of tooth, with the upper and lower lines describing the upper and lower jaws respectively.

den·tal hy·gien·ist ▸*n.* an ancillary dental worker specializing in scaling and polishing teeth and in giving advice on cleaning the teeth. —**den·tal hy·giene** *n.*

den·ta·li·um /den'tālēəm/ ▸*n.* tooth shells used as ornaments or as a form of currency: *a white mare purchased with dentalium.* ▷modern Latin, from late Latin *dentalis* (see DENTAL).

den·tal nurse ▸*n.* a nurse who assists a dentist.

den·tal sur·geon ▸*n.* a dentist.

den·tal tech·ni·cian ▸*n.* a person who makes and repairs artificial teeth.

den·ta·ry /'dentərē/ ▸*n.* (*pl.* **-ries**) *Zoology* the anterior bone of the lower jaw, which bears the teeth. In mammals it forms the whole of the lower jaw (or mandible). ▷mid 19th cent.: from late Latin *dentarius*, from Latin *dens, dent-* 'tooth.'

den·tate /'den,tāt/ ▸*adj. Botany & Zoology* having a toothlike or serrated edge. ▷late Middle English: from Latin *dentatus*, from *dens, dent-* 'tooth.'

den·telle /den'tel/ ▸*n.* (*pl.* or *pronunc.* same) ornamental tooling used in bookbinding, resembling lace edging. ▷mid 19th cent.: from French, 'lace,' from *dent* 'tooth' + the diminutive suffix *-elle*.

den·tex /'den,teks/ ▸*n.* (*pl.* same or **-tex·es**) any of various sea breams of the genus *Dentex*, especially *D. dentex* of the Mediterranean and the North African Atlantic coast. Many are important food fishes. ▷modern Latin (genus name), from Latin.

den·ti·cle /'dentikəl/ ▸*n. Zoology* a small tooth or toothlike projection. ▷late Middle English (denoting a pointer on an astrolabe): from Latin *denticulus*, diminutive of *dens, dent-* 'tooth.'

den·tic·u·late /den'tikyəlit/ ▸*adj.* having small teeth or toothlike projections; finely toothed. ▷mid 17th cent.: from Latin *denticulatus*, from *denticulus* 'small tooth' (see DENTICLE). —**den·tic·u·lat·ed** /-,lātid/ *adj.*

den·ti·frice /'dentəfris/ ▸*n.* a paste or powder for cleaning the teeth. ▷late Middle English: from French, from Latin *dentifricium*, from *dens, dent-* 'tooth' + *fricare* 'to rub.'

den·til /'dentl; -til/ ▸*n.* [often as *adj.*] (in classical architecture) one of a number of small, rectangular blocks resembling teeth and used as a decoration under the soffit of a cornice: *a dentil frieze.* ▷late 16th cent.: from Italian *dentello* or obsolete French *dentille*, diminutive of *dent* 'tooth,' from Latin *dens, dent-*.

den·ti·lin·gual /ˌdentəˈlinggwəl/ ▶*adj. Phonetics* (of a consonant) pronounced with the teeth and the tongue; dental. ▷late 19th cent.: from Latin *dens, dent-* 'tooth' + LINGUAL.

den·tin /ˈdentn; -tin/ (also **den·tine** /ˈdenˌtēn/) ▶*n.* hard, dense, bony tissue forming the bulk of a tooth beneath the enamel. ▷mid 19th cent.: from Latin *dens, dent-* 'tooth' + -IN[1]. —**den·tin·al** /ˈdentn-əl/ *adj.*

den·tist /ˈdentist/ (abbr.: **dent.**) ▶*n.* a person qualified to treat the diseases and conditions that affect the teeth and gums, esp. the repair and extraction of teeth and the insertion of artificial ones. ▷mid 18th cent.: from French *dentiste*, from *dent* 'tooth,' from Latin *dens, dent-*. —**den·tist·ry** /-strē/ *n.*

den·ti·tion /denˈtishən/ ▶*n.* the arrangement or condition of the teeth in a particular species or individual. ▷late 16th cent. (denoting the process of developing of teeth): from Latin *dentitio(n-)*, from *dentire* 'teethe,' from *dens, dent-* 'tooth.'

Den·ton /ˈdentn/ a commercial city in northeastern Texas; pop. 66,270.

den·ture /ˈdenchər/ ▶*n.* (usu. **dentures**) a removable plate or frame holding one or more artificial teeth. ▷late 19th cent.: from French, from *dent* 'tooth,' from Latin *dens, dent-*.

den·tur·ist /ˈdenchərist/ ▶*n.* a person who makes dentures.

de·nu·cle·ar·ize /dēˈn(y)o͞oklēəˌrīz/ ▶*v.* [*trans.*] remove nuclear weapons from. —**de·nu·cle·ar·i·za·tion** /-ˌn(y)o͞oklēərəˈzāshən/ *n.*

de·nude /diˈn(y)o͞od/ ▶*v.* [*trans.*] (often **be denuded**) strip (something) of its covering, possessions, or assets; make bare: *almost overnight the Arctic was* **denuded** *of animals.* ▷late Middle English: from Latin *denudare*, from *de-* 'completely' + *nudare* 'to bare' (from *nudus* 'naked'). —**den·u·da·tion** /ˌden(y)o͞oˈdāshən/ *n.*

de·nu·mer·a·ble /dēˈn(y)o͞omərəbəl/ ▶*adj. Mathematics* able to be counted by a one-to-one correspondence with the infinite set of integers. ▷early 20th cent.: from late Latin *denumerare* 'count out' + -ABLE. —**de·nu·mer·a·bil·i·ty** /-ˌn(y)o͞oməraˈbilitē/ *n.* —**de·nu·mer·a·bly** /-blē/ *adv.*

de·nun·ci·a·tion /diˌnənsēˈāshən/ ▶*n.* public condemnation of someone or something. ■ the action of informing against someone. ▷late Middle English: from Latin *denuntiatio(n-)*, from the verb *denuntiare* (see DENOUNCE). The original sense was 'public announcement,' also 'formal accusation or charge'; the main sense dates from the mid 19th cent. —**de·nun·ci·a·tor** /-ˈnənsēˌātər/ *n.* —**de·nun·ci·a·to·ry** /-ˈnənsēəˌtôrē/ *adj.*

Den·ver[1] /ˈdenvər/ the capital of Colorado, in the central part of the state, on the South Platte River; pop. 554,636. It is situated at an altitude of 5,280 feet (1,608 m) on the eastern side of the Rocky Mountains.

Den·ver[2], John (1943–97), U.S. country and pop singer and songwriter and actor; born *Henry John Deutschendorf.* He celebrated the simple life and his love of Colorado in his songs such as "Take Me Home, Country Roads" (1971), "Rocky Mountain High" (1972), and "Sunshine on My Shoulders" (1974). He also acted in movies, most notably *Oh, God!* (1977).

Den·ver boot ▶*n.* see BOOT[1] (sense 1). ▷mid 20th cent.: named after *Denver*, Colorado, where the boot was introduced in 1949.

de·ny /diˈnī/ ▶*v.* (**-nies, -nied**) [*trans.*] refuse to admit the truth or existence of (something): *they deny any responsibility for the tragedy.* ■ [with *two objs.*] refuse to give (something requested or desired) to (someone): *the inquiry was denied access to intelligence sources.* ■ refuse to accept or agree to: *judges would retain the discretion to grant or deny the requests.* ■ refuse to acknowledge or recognize; disown: *Peter repeatedly denied Jesus.* ■ (**deny oneself**) refrain from satisfying oneself: *he had denied himself sexually for years.* ■ *archaic* refuse access to (someone): *the servants are ordered to deny him.* ▷Middle English: from Old French *deni-*, stressed stem of *deneier*, from Latin *denegare*, from *de-* 'formally' + *negare* 'say no.'

Den·ys, St. see DENIS, ST.

de·o·dar /ˈdēəˌdär/ ▶*n.* a tall, broadly conical cedar that is native to the Himalayas and has drooping branches and large barrel-shaped cones. • *Cedrus deodara*, family Pinaceae. ▷early 19th cent.: from Hindi *deodār*, from Sanskrit *devadāru* 'divine tree.'

de·o·dor·ant /dēˈōdərənt/ ▶*n.* a substance that removes or conceals unpleasant smells, esp. bodily odors. ▷mid 19th cent.: from DE- (expressing removal) + Latin *odor* 'smell' + -ANT.

de·o·dor·ize /dēˈōdəˌrīz/ ▶*v.* [*trans.*] remove or conceal an unpleasant smell in: *people used dried flowers to deodorize their homes.* ▷mid 19th cent.: from DE- (expressing removal) + Latin *odor* 'smell' + -IZE. —**de·o·dor·i·za·tion** /-ˌōdərəˈzāshən/ *n.* —**de·o·dor·iz·er** *n.*

De·o gra·ti·as /ˈdāō ˈgrätsēəs/ ▶*exclam.* thanks be to God. ▷late 16th cent.: Latin.

de·on·tic /dēˈäntik/ ▶*adj.* [*attrib.*] *Philosophy* of or relating to duty and obligation as ethical concepts. ■ *Linguistics* expressing duty or obligation. ▷mid 20th cent.: from Greek *deont-* 'being right' (from *dei* 'it is right') + -IC.

de·on·tol·o·gy /ˌdēänˈtäləjē/ ▶*n. Philosophy* the study of the nature of duty and obligation. ▷early 19th cent.: from Greek *deont-* 'being necessary' (from *dei* 'it is necessary') + -LOGY. —**de·on·to·log·i·cal** /dēˌänt ˈäjikəl/ *adj.* —**de·on·tol·o·gist** /-jist/ *n.*

De·o vo·len·te /ˈdāō vəˈlentē/ ▶*adv.* God willing; if nothing prevents it. ▷mid 18th cent.: Latin.

de·ox·i·dize /dēˈäksiˌdīz/ ▶*v.* [*trans.*] remove combined oxygen from (a substance, usually a metal). —**de·ox·i·da·tion** /-ˌäksiˈdāshən/ *n.* —**de·ox·i·diz·er** *n.*

de·ox·y·cor·ti·cos·ter·one /dēˌäksēˌkôrtiˈkästəˌrōn/ ▶*n. Biochemistry* a corticosteroid hormone involved in regulating the salt and water balance in the human body.

de·ox·y·gen·ate /dēˈäksijəˌnāt/ ▶*v.* [*trans.*] [usu. as *adj.*] (**deoxygenated**) remove oxygen from: *deoxygenated air.* —**de·ox·y·gen·a·tion** /-ˌäksijəˈnāshən/ *n.*

de·ox·y·ri·bo·nu·cle·ase /dēˌäksēˌrībōˈn(y)o͞oklēˌās; -ˌāz/ ▶*n. Biochemistry* another term for DNASE.

de·ox·y·ri·bo·nu·cle·ic ac·id /dēˌäksēˌrībōn(y)o͞oˈklēik/ ▶*n.* see DNA. ▷1930s: *deoxyribonucleic* from a blend of DEOXYRIBOSE and NUCLEIC ACID.

de·ox·y·ri·bose /dēˌäksēˈrībōs; -bōz/ ▶*n. Biochemistry* a sugar derived from ribose by replacing a hydroxyl group with hydrogen. • Chem. formula; $C_5H_{10}O_4$. There are several isomers; the isomer **2-deoxyribose** is a constituent of DNA. ▷1930s: from DE- (expressing reduction) + OXY-[2] + RIBOSE.

dep. ▶*abbr.* ■ departs. ■ deputy.

Dé·par·dieu /ˌdāpärˈd(y)o͞o; -ˈdyœ/ ▶, Gérard 1948–, French actor. His films include *Jean de Florette* (1986) and *Tous les matins du monde* (1991).

de·part /diˈpärt/ ▶*v.* [*intrans.*] leave, typically in order to start a journey: *they* **departed for** *Germany* | *a contingent was* **departing from** *Cairo.* ■ (**depart from**) deviate from (an accepted, prescribed, or traditional course of action): *he departed from the precedent set by many.* ▷Middle English: from Old French *departir*, based on Latin *dispertire* 'to divide.' The original sense was 'separate,' also 'take leave of each other,' hence 'go away.'

▶*PHRASE* □ **depart this life** *archaic* die.

de·part·ed /diˈpärtid/ ▶*adj.* deceased: *a dear departed relative.*

▶*n.* (**the departed**) a particular dead person or dead people: *the prayer for the departed.*

de·part·ment /diˈpärtmənt/ ▶*n.* a division of a large organization such as a government, university, business, or shop, dealing with a specific subject, commodity, or area of activity: *the English department.* ■ an administrative district in France and other countries. ■ (**one's department**) *informal* an area of special expertise or responsibility: *that's not my department.* ■ [with *adj.*] *informal* the specified subject under discussion: *I never thought of myself as above average in the looks department.* ▷late Middle English: from Old French *departement*, from *departir* (see DEPART). The original sense was 'division or distribution,' later 'separation,' hence 'a separate part' (core sense, mid 18th cent.).

de·part·men·tal /diˌpärtˈmentl; ˌdēpärt-/ ▶*adj.* concerned with or belonging to a department of an organization: *a departmental meeting.* —**de·part·men·tal·ly** *adv.*

de·part·men·tal·ism /dipärtˈmentlˌizəm; ˌdēpärt-/ ▶*n.* adherence to departmental methods or structure.

de·part·men·tal·ize /dipärtˈmentlˌīz; ˌdēpärt-/ ▶*v.* [*trans.*] (usu. **be departmentalized**) divide (an organization or its work) into departments. —**de·part·men·tal·i·za·tion** /-ˌmentl-əˈzāshən/ *n.*

De·part·ment of Ag·ri·cul·ture ▶*n.* the department of the U.S. government that administers federal programs related to food production and rural life. The department's principal duty is to aid farmers, but it also serves consumers through its food-assistance and food-inspection programs.

de·part·ment store ▶*n.* a large store stocking many varieties of goods in different departments.

de·par·ture /diˈpärchər/ ▶*n.* the action of leaving, typically to start a journey: *the day of departure* | *she made a hasty departure.* ■ a deviation from an accepted, prescribed, or traditional course of action or thought: *a* **departure from** *their usual style.* ■ *Nautical* the east–west distance between two points, esp. as traveled by a ship or aircraft and expressed in miles. ▷late Middle English: from Old French *departeure*, from the verb *departir* (see DEPART).

de·pau·per·ate /diˈpôpərit/ ▶*adj. Biology* (of a flora, fauna, or ecosystem) lacking in numbers or variety of species: *oceanic islands are generally depauperate in mayflies.* ■ (of a plant or animal) imperfectly developed. ▷late Middle English (in the sense 'impoverished'): from medieval Latin *depauperatus*, past participle of *depauperare*, from *de-* 'completely' + *pauperare* 'make poor' (from *pauper* 'poor').

dé·pay·sé /ˌdāpāˈzā/ (also **dé·pay·sée**) ▶*adj.* removed from one's habitual surroundings. ▷early 20th cent.: French, literally '(removed) from one's own country.'

de·pend /diˈpend/ ▶*v.* [*intrans.*] **1** (**depend on/upon**) be controlled or determined by: *differences in earnings depended on a wide variety of factors.* **2** (**depend on/upon**) rely on: *the kind of person you could depend on.* ■ need or require for financial or other support: *a town that had depended heavily upon the wool industry.* ■ be grammatically dependent on. **3** *archaic* or *poetic/literary* hang down: *his tongue* **depended from** *open jaws.* ▷late Middle English (sense 3; also in the sense 'wait or be in suspense'): from Old French *dependre*, from Latin *dependere*, from *de-* 'down' + *pendere* 'hang.'

▶*PHRASES* □ **depending on** being conditioned by; contingent on: *makes 8–10 burgers (depending on size)* | [with *clause*] *the article sneered or just condescended,* **depending on how** *you read it.* □ **it** (or **that**) (**all**) **depends** used to express uncertainty or qualification in answering a question: *How many people use each screen? It all depends.*

USAGE In informal use, it is quite common for the **on** to be dropped in sentences such as *it all depends how you look at it* (rather than *it all depends on how you look at it*), but in well-formed written English, the **on** should always be retained. In more formal writing, and sometimes for sound, rhythm, or other rhetorical effect, **upon** is the preferred preposition: *You may depend upon it.*

de·pend·a·ble /diˈpendəbəl/ ▶*adj.* trustworthy and reliable. —**de·pend·a·bil·i·ty** /-ˌpendəˈbilitē/ *n.* —**de·pend·a·bly** /-blē/ *adv.*

de·pend·ence /diˈpendəns/ ▶*n.* the state of relying on or being controlled by someone or something else: *Japan's* **dependence on** *imported oil.* ■ reliance on someone or something for financial support: *the* **dependence** *of our medical schools* **on** *grant funds.* ■ addiction to drink or drugs: *alcohol dependence.* ▷late Middle English (in the sense 'hanging down or something that hangs down'): from Old French *dependance*, from the verb *dependre* (see DEPEND).

de·pend·en·cy /diˈpendənsē/ ▶*n.* (*pl.* **-cies**) **1** a dependent or subordinate thing, esp. a country or province controlled by another. **2** dependence: *the country's* **dependency on** *the oil industry.*

de·pend·ent /diˈpendənt/ ▶*adj.* **1** [*predic.*] (**dependent on/upon**) contingent on or determined by: *the various benefits will be dependent on length of service.* **2** requiring someone or something for financial, emotional, or other support: *an economy heavily* **dependent on** *oil exports* | *households with dependent children.* ■ unable to do without: *people* **dependent on** *drugs* | [in *combination*] *welfare-dependent families.* ■ *Grammar* (of a clause, phrase, or word) subordinate to another clause, phrase, or word.

▶*n.* (*Brit.* also **de·pend·ant**) a person who relies on another, esp. a family member, for financial support: *a single man with no dependents.* ▷late Middle English *dependant* 'hanging down,' from Old French, present participle of *dependre* (see DEPEND). The spelling change in the 16th cent. was due to association with the Latin participial stem *dependent-*. —**de·pend·ent·ly** *adv.*

de·pend·ent var·i·a·ble ▶*n. Mathematics* a variable (often denoted by *y*) whose value depends on that of another.

de·per·son·al·i·za·tion /dēˌpərsənələˈzāshən/ ▶*n.* the action of divesting someone or something of human characteristics or individuality. ■ *Psychiatry* a state in which one's thoughts and feelings seem unreal or not to belong to oneself, or in which one loses all sense of identity.

de·per·son·al·ize /dē'pərsənə,līz/ ▶*v.* [*trans.*] divest of human characteristics or individuality: *medical technology depersonalizes treatment.*

de·phlo·gis·ti·cat·ed /,dēflə'jisti,kātid/ ▶*adj. historical Chemistry* deprived of "phlogiston." Oxygen was originally called **dephlogisticated air** by Joseph Priestley.

de·pict /di'pikt/ ▶*v.* [*trans.*] show or represent by a drawing, painting, or other art form. ■ portray in words; describe: *youth is depicted as a time of vitality and good health.* ▷late Middle English: from Latin *depict-* 'portrayed,' from the verb *depingere*, from *de-* 'completely' + *pingere* 'to paint.' **—de·pict·er** *n.* **—de·pic·tion** /-'pikshən/ *n.*

de·pig·ment /dē'pigmənt/ ▶*v.* [*trans.*] [usu. as *adj.*] (**depigmented**) reduce or remove the pigmentation of (the skin). **—de·pig·men·ta·tion** /-,pigmən'tāshən/ *n.*

dep·i·late /'depə,lāt/ ▶*v.* [*trans.*] remove the hair from: *they scrubbed and depilated her* | [as *adj.*] (**depilated**) *his permanently depilated and tattooed skull.* ▷mid 16th cent.: from Latin *depilat-* 'stripped of hair,' from the verb *depilare*, from *de-* (expressing removal) + *pilare* (from *pilus* 'hair'). **—dep·i·la·tion** /,depə'lāshən/ *n.*

dep·i·la·tor /'depə,lātər/ ▶*n.* an instrument that removes unwanted bodily hair, typically by plucking it from the root.

de·pil·a·to·ry /di'pilə,tôrē/ ▶*adj.* used to remove unwanted hair.

▶*n.* (*pl.* **-ries**) a cream or lotion for removing unwanted hair. ▷early 17th cent.: from Latin *depilatorius*, from *depilat-* 'stripped of hair,' from the verb *depilare* (see **DEPILATE**).

de·plane /dē'plān/ ▶*v.* [*intrans.*] disembark from an aircraft: *we landed and deplaned.*

de·plete /di'plēt/ ▶*v.* [often as *adj.*] (**depleted**) use up the supply of; exhaust the abundance of: *fish stocks are severely depleted.* ■ [*intrans.*] diminish in number or quantity: *supplies are depleting fast.* ■ exhaust: *avoid getting depleted and depressed.* ▷early 19th cent.: from Latin *deplet-* 'emptied out,' from the verb *deplere*, from *de-* (expressing reversal) + *plere* 'fill' (from *plenus* 'full'). **—de·ple·tion** /-'plēshən/ *n.*

de·plet·ed u·ra·ni·um (abbr.: **DU**) ▶*n.* uranium from which most of the fissile isotope uranium-235 has been removed.

de·ple·tion al·low·ance /di'plēshən/ ▶*n.* a tax concession allowable to a company whose normal business activities (in particular oil extraction) reduce the value of its own assets.

de·plor·a·ble /di'plôrəbəl/ ▶*adj.* deserving strong condemnation: *the deplorable conditions in which most prisoners are held.* ■ shockingly bad in quality: *her spelling was deplorable.* ▷early 17th cent.: from French *déplorable* or late Latin *deplorabilis*, from the verb *deplorare* (see **DEPLORE**). **—de·plor·a·bly** /-blē/ *adv.*

de·plore /di'plôr/ ▶*v.* [*trans.*] feel or express strong disapproval of (something): *we deplore this act of violence.* ▷mid 16th cent. (in the sense 'weep for, regret deeply'): from French *déplorer* or Italian *deplorare*, from Latin *deplorare*, from *de-* 'away, thoroughly' + *plorare* 'bewail.' **—de·plor·ing·ly** *adv.*

de·ploy /di'ploi/ ▶*v.* [*trans.*] move (troops) into position for military action: *forces were deployed at strategic locations.* ■ [*intrans.*] (of troops) move into position for such action: *the air force began to deploy forward.* ■ bring into effective action; utilize: *they are not always able to deploy this skill.* ▷late 18th cent.: from French *déployer*, from Latin *displicare* and late Latin *deplicare* 'unfold or explain,' from *dis-*, *de-* 'un-' + *plicare* 'to fold.' Compare with **DISPLAY**. **—de·ploy·ment** *n.*

de·plume /dē'plo͞om/ ▶*v.* [*trans.*] deprive (a bird) of feathers. ■ *archaic, figurative* strip or deprive of honor, status, or wealth. ▷late Middle English: from Old French *desplumer* or medieval Latin *deplumare*, from *des-*, *de-* (expressing reversal) + Latin *pluma* 'feather.'

de·po·lar·ize /dē'pōlə,rīz/ ▶*v.* [*trans.*] *Physics* reduce or remove the polarization of: *the threshold necessary to depolarize the membrane.* **—de·po·lar·i·za·tion** /-,pōlərə'zāshən/ *n.*

de·po·lit·i·cize /,dēpə'liti,sīz/ ▶*v.* [*trans.*] remove from political activity or influence: *we have to depoliticize sex education.* **—de·po·lit·i·ci·za·tion** /-,litisə'zāshən/ *n.*

de·po·lym·er·ize /dē'pälәmə,rīz/ ▶*v.* [*trans.*] *Chemistry* break (a polymer) down into monomers or other smaller units. ■ [*intrans.*] undergo this process: *the ideal disposable polymer would depolymerize naturally.* **—de·po·lym·er·i·za·tion** /-,pälәmərә'zāshən/ *n.*

de·po·nent /di'pōnənt/ ▶*adj. Grammar* (of a verb, esp. in Latin or Greek) passive or middle in form but active in meaning.

▶*n.* **1** *Grammar* a deponent verb. **2** *Law* a person who makes a deposition or affidavit under oath. ▷late Middle English: from Latin *deponent-* 'laying aside, putting down' (in medieval Latin 'testifying'), from the verb *deponere*, from *de-* 'down' + *ponere* 'place.' The use in grammar arose from the notion that the verb had "laid aside" the passive sense (although in fact these verbs were originally reflexive).

de·pop·u·late /dē'päpyə,lāt/ ▶*v.* [*trans.*] substantially reduce the population of (an area): *the disease could depopulate a city the size of New Haven.* ▷mid 16th cent. (in the sense 'ravage, lay waste'): from Latin *depopulat-* 'ravaged,' from the verb *depopulari*, from *de-* 'completely' + *populari* 'lay waste' (from *populus* 'people'). **—de·pop·u·la·tion** /-,päpyə'lāshən/ *n.*

de·port /di'pôrt/ ▶*v.* **1** [*trans.*] expel (a foreigner) from a country, typically on the grounds of illegal status or for having committed a crime: *he was deported for violation of immigration laws.* ■ exile (a native) to another country. **2** (**deport oneself**) *archaic* conduct oneself in a specified manner: *he has deported himself with great dignity.* ▷late 16th cent. (sense 2): from French *déporter*, from Latin *deportare*, from *de-* 'away' + *portare* 'carry.' **—de·port·a·ble** *adj.* **—de·por·ta·tion** /,dēpôr'tāshən/ *n.*

de·por·tee /,dēpôr'tē/ ▶*n.* a person who has been or is being expelled from a country.

de·port·ment /di'pôrtmənt/ ▶*n.* a person's behavior or manners: *there are team rules governing deportment on and off the field.* ▷early 17th cent.: from French *déportement*, from the verb *déporter* (see **DEPORT**).

de·pose /di'pōz/ ▶*v.* [*trans.*] **1** remove from office suddenly and forcefully: *he had been deposed by a military coup.* **2** *Law* testify to or give (evidence) on oath, typically in a written statement: *every affidavit shall state which of the facts* **deposed to** *are within the deponent's knowledge.* **3** *Law* to question (a witness) in deposition. ▷Middle English: from Old French *deposer*, from Latin *deponere* (see **DEPONENT**), but influenced by Latin *depositus* and Old French *poser* 'to place.'

de·pos·it /di'päzit/ ▶*n.* **1** a sum of money placed or kept in a bank account, usually to gain interest. ■ an act of placing money in a bank account: *I'd like to* **make a deposit**. **2** a sum payable as a first installment on the purchase of something or as a pledge for a contract, the balance being payable later: *we've saved enough for a* **deposit on** *a house.* ■ a returnable sum payable on the rental of something, to cover any possible loss or damage. **3** a layer or body of accumulated matter: *the deposits of salt on the chrome.* ■ a natural layer of sand, rock, coal, or other material.

▶*v.* (**-it·ed**, **-it·ing**) **1** [*trans.*] put or set down (something or someone) in a specific place, typically unceremoniously: *he deposited a pile of schoolbooks on the kitchen table.* ■ (usu. **be deposited**) (of water, the wind, or other natural agency) lay down (matter) gradually as a layer or covering: *beds where salt is deposited by the tide.* ■ lay (an egg): *the female deposits a line of eggs.* **2** [*trans.*] store or entrust with someone for safekeeping. ■ pay (a sum of money) into a bank account: *the money is deposited with a bank.* ■ pay (a sum) as a first installment or as a pledge for a contract: *I had to deposit 10% of the price of the house.* ▷late 16th cent. (esp. in the phrases *in deposit* or *on deposit*): from Latin *depositum* (noun), medieval Latin *depositare* (verb), both from Latin *deposit-* 'laid aside,' from the verb *deponere*.

de·pos·i·tar·y /di'päzi,terē/ (also **de·pos·i·tor·y**) ▶*n.* (*pl.* **-tar·ies**) a person to whom something is lodged in trust.

▶*adj.* (of a share or receipt) representing a share in a foreign company. The depositary share or receipt is traded on the stock exchange of the investor's country rather than the actual share, which is deposited in a foreign bank. ▷early 17th cent.: from late Latin *depositarius*, from the verb *deponere* (see **DEPOSIT**).

dep·o·si·tion /,depə'zishən/ ▶*n.* **1** the action of deposing someone, esp. a monarch: *Edward V's deposition.* **2** *Law* the process of giving sworn evidence: *the deposition of four expert witnesses.* **3** *Law* the written record of a witness's out-of-court testimony. ■ a formal, usually written, statement to be used as evidence outside court. **4** the action of depositing something: *pebbles formed by the deposition of calcium in solution.* **5** (**the Deposition**) the taking down of the body of Jesus Christ from the Cross. ▷late Middle English: from Latin *depositio(n-)*, from the verb *deponere* (see **DEPOSIT**).

de·pos·i·tor /di'päzitər/ ▶*n.* a person who keeps money in a bank account.

de·pos·i·to·ry /di'päzi,tôrē/ ▶*n.* (*pl.* **-ries**) **1** a place where things are stored. **2** variant spelling of **DEPOSITARY**. ▷mid 17th cent. (denoting a depositary): from late Latin *depositorium*, from *deposit-* 'laid aside,' from the verb *deponere* (see **DEPOSIT**).

de·pot /'dēpō; 'de-/ ▶*n.* a place for the storage of large quantities of equipment, food, or some other commodity: *an arms depot.* ■ a railroad or bus station. ■ a place where buses, trains, or other vehicles are housed and maintained and from which they are dispatched for service. ■ the headquarters of a regiment; a place where recruits or other troops are assembled. ▷late 18th cent. (in the sense 'act of depositing'): from French *dépôt*, from Latin *depositum* 'something deposited' (see **DEPOSIT**).

de·prave /di'prāv/ ▶*v.* [*trans.*] make (someone) immoral or wicked: *this book would deprave and corrupt young children.* ▷late Middle English (in the sense 'pervert the meaning or intention of something'): from Old French *depraver* or Latin *depravare*, from *de-* 'down, thoroughly' + *pravus* 'crooked, perverse.' **—dep·ra·va·tion** /,deprə'vāshən/ *n.*

de·praved /di'prāvd/ ▶*adj.* morally corrupt: *a depraved indifference to human life.*

THE RIGHT WORD **corrupt, debased, degenerate, depraved, perverted, vile**

There are many terms to describe the dark side of human nature.

Someone who preys on young children would be considered **depraved**, a term that means totally immoral and implies a warped character or a twisted mind (*a depraved man who stole money from his own mother and eventually murdered her*).

While *depraved* suggests an absolute condition, **degenerate** is a relative term that implies deterioration from a mental, moral, or physical standard (*her degenerate habits eventually led to her arrest for possession of drugs*).

Corrupt also suggests a deterioration or loss of soundness, particularly through a destructive or contaminating influence. But unlike *depraved*, which usually applies to the lower end of the human spectrum, people in high positions are often referred to as *corrupt* (*a corrupt politician from a prominent family*).

To say that someone or something is **debased** suggests a lowering in quality, value, dignity, or character (*debased by having to spend time in prison*).

Perverted and **vile** are the strongest of these words describing lack of moral character.

Perverted suggests a distortion of someone or something from what is right, natural, or true; in a moral sense, it means to use one's appetites or natural desires for other ends than those which are considered normal or natural (*a perverted individual who never should have been left alone with young children*).

Most people find criminals who prey on either very old or very young victims to be **vile**, a more general term for whatever is loathsome, repulsive, or utterly despicable (*a vile killer who deserved the maximum sentence*).

de·prav·i·ty /di'pravitē/ ▶*n.* (*pl.* **-ties**) moral corruption: *a tale of wickedness and depravity.* ■ a wicked or morally corrupt act. ■ *Christian Theology* the innate corruptness of human nature, due to original sin. ▷mid 17th cent.: alteration (influenced by **DEPRAVE**) of obsolete *pravity*, from Latin *pravitas*, from *pravus* 'crooked, perverse.'

dep·re·cate /'depri,kāt/ ▶*v.* [*trans.*] **1** express disapproval of: [as *adj.*] (**deprecating**) *he sniffed in a deprecating way.* **2** another term for **DEPRECIATE** (sense 2): *he deprecates the value of children's television.* ▷early 17th cent. (in the sense 'pray against'): from Latin *deprecat-* 'prayed against (as being evil),' from the verb *deprecari*, from *de-* (expressing reversal) + *precari* 'pray.' **—dep·re·cat·ing·ly** *adv.* **—dep·re·ca·tion** /,deprə'kāshən/ *n.* **—dep·re·ca·tive** /-,kātiv/ *adj.* **—dep·re·ca·tor** /-,kātər/ *n.*

USAGE See usage at **SELF-DEPRECATING**.

dep·re·ca·to·ry /'deprikə,tôrē/ ▶*adj.* expressing disapproval; disapproving. ■ apologetic or appeasing: *a deprecatory smile.*

D

de·pre·ci·ate /di'prēSHē,āt/ ▸*v.* **1** [*intrans.*] diminish in value over a period of time: *the pound is expected to* ***depreciate against*** *the dollar.* ■ reduce the recorded value in a company's books of (an asset) each year over a predetermined period: *the computers would be depreciated at 50 percent per annum.* **2** [*trans.*] disparage or belittle (something): *she was already depreciating her own aesthetic taste.* ▷late Middle English (sense 2): from late Latin *depreciat-* 'lowered in price, undervalued,' from the verb *depreciare*, from Latin *de-* 'down' + *pretium* 'price.' **—de·pre·ci·a·to·ry** /-SHēə-,tôrē/ *adj.*

USAGE See usage at SELF-DEPRECATING.

de·pre·ci·a·tion /di,prēSHē'āSHən/ ▸*n.* a reduction in the value of an asset with the passage of time, due in particular to wear and tear. ■ decrease in the value of a currency relative to other currencies: *depreciation leads to losses for nondollar-based investors | a currency depreciation.*

dep·re·da·tion /,deprə'dāSHən/ ▸*n.* (usu. **depredations**) an act of attacking or plundering: *protecting grain from the depredations of rats and mice.* ▷late 15th cent. (in the sense 'plundering, robbery,' (plural) 'ravages'): from French *déprédation*, from late Latin *depraedatio(n-)*, from *depraedari* 'plunder.'

dep·re·da·tor /'deprə,dātər/ ▸*n. archaic* a person or thing that makes depredations, esp. a predatory animal. **—dep·re·da·to·ry** /di'predə,tôrē/ *adj.*

de·press /di'pres/ ▸*v.* [*trans.*] **1** make (someone) feel utterly dispirited or dejected: *that first day at school depressed me.* ■ reduce the level or strength of activity in (something, esp. an economic or biological system): *fear of inflation in America depressed bond markets | alcohol depresses the nervous system.* **2** push or pull (something) down into a lower position: *depress the lever.* ▷late Middle English: from Old French *depresser*, from late Latin *depressare*, frequentative of *deprimere* 'press down.' **—de·press·i·ble** *adj.*

de·pres·sant /di'presənt/ ▸*adj.* (chiefly of a drug) reducing functional or nervous activity.
▸*n.* a depressant drug. ■ an influence that depresses economic or other activity: *higher taxation is a depressant.*

de·pressed /di'prest/ ▸*adj.* (of a person) in a state of general unhappiness or despondency. ■ (of a person) suffering from clinical depression. ■ (of a place or economic activity) suffering the damaging effects of a lack of demand or employment: *depressed urban areas.* ■ (of an object or part of an object) in a physically lower position, having been pushed or forced down: *a depressed fracture of the skull.*

de·press·ing /di'presiNG/ ▸*adj.* causing or resulting in a feeling of miserable dejection: *that thought is too depressing for words.* ■ causing a damaging reduction in economic activity: *the mortgage rate increase will have a depressing effect on the housing market.* **—de·press·ing·ly** *adv.*

de·pres·sion /di'preSHən/ ▸*n.* **1** severe despondency and dejection, typically felt over a period of time and accompanied by feelings of hopelessness and inadequacy. ■ *Medicine* a condition of mental disturbance characterized by such feelings to a greater degree than seems warranted by the external circumstances, typically with lack of energy and difficulty in maintaining concentration or interest in life: *clinical depression.* ■ a long and severe recession in an economy or market: *the depression in the housing market.* ■ (**the Depression** or **the Great Depression**) the financial and industrial slump of 1929 and subsequent years. **2** the lowering or reducing of something: *the depression of prices.* ■ the action of pressing down on something: *depression of the plunger delivers two units of insulin.* ■ a sunken place or hollow on a surface: *the original shallow depressions were slowly converted to creeks.* ■ *Astronomy & Geography* the angular distance of an object below the horizon or a horizontal plane. ■ *Meteorology* a region of lower atmospheric pressure, esp. a cyclonic weather system. ▷late Middle English: from Latin *depressio(n-)*, from *deprimere* 'press down' (see DEPRESS).

De·pres·sion glass ▸*n.* machine-pressed, tinted glassware that was mass-produced in the U.S. from the late 1920s to the 1940s and often used as giveaways to persuade customers to purchase goods.

de·pres·sive /di'presiv/ ▸*adj.* causing feelings of hopelessness, despondency, and dejection. ■ *Medicine* relating to or tending to suffer from clinical depression: *a depressive illness.* ■ causing a reduction in strength, effectiveness, or value: *steroids have a depressive effect on the immune system.*
▸*n. Medicine* a person suffering from or with a tendency to suffer from depression.

de·pres·sor /di'presər/ ▸*n.* **1** *Anatomy* (also **depressor muscle**) a muscle whose contraction pulls down the part of the body to which it is attached. ■ any of several specific muscles in the face: [followed by Latin genitive] *depressor anguli oris.* **2** *Physiology* a nerve whose stimulation results in a lowering of blood pressure. **3** an instrument for pressing something down. ▷early 17th cent. (in the general sense 'someone or something that depresses'): from Latin, from *depress-* 'pressed down,' from the verb *deprimere* (see DEPRESS).

de·pres·sur·ize /dē'preSHə,rīz/ ▸*v.* [*trans.*] release the pressure of the gas inside (a pressurized vehicle or container). ■ [*intrans.*] (of a pressurized vehicle or container) lose pressure. **—de·pres·sur·i·za·tion** /-,preSHərə'zāSHən/ *n.*

dep·ri·va·tion /,deprə'vāSHən/ ▸*n.* the damaging lack of material benefits considered to be basic necessities in a society: *low wages mean that 3.75 million people suffer serious deprivation.* ■ the lack or denial of something considered to be a necessity: *sleep deprivation.* ■ *archaic* the action of depriving someone of office, esp. an ecclesiastical office. ▷late Middle English (in the sense 'removal from office'): from medieval Latin *deprivatio(n-)*, from the verb *deprivare* (see DEPRIVE).

de·prive /di'prīv/ ▸*v.* [*trans.*] deny (a person or place) the possession or use of something: *the city was* ***deprived of*** *its water supplies.* ■ *archaic* depose (someone, esp. a clergyman) from office: *Archbishop Bancroft deprived a considerable number of puritan clergymen.* ▷Middle English (in the sense 'depose from office'): from Old French *depriver*, from medieval Latin *deprivare*, from *de-* 'away, completely' + *privare* (see PRIVATE). **—de·priv·al** /-vəl/ *n.*

de·prived /di'prīvd/ ▸*adj.* suffering a severe and damaging lack of basic material and cultural benefits: *the charity cares for destitute and deprived children.* ■ (of a person) suffering a lack of a specified benefit that is considered important: *the men felt sexually deprived.*

de pro·fun·dis /,dā prə'fo͝ondis/ ▸*n.* a heartfelt cry of appeal expressing one's deepest feelings of sorrow or anguish. ▷late Middle English: Latin, literally 'from the depths,' the opening words of Psalm 130.

de·pro·gram /dē'prō,gram; -grəm/ ▸*v.* (**-grammed**, **-gram·ming** or **-gramed**, **-gram·ing**) [*trans.*] release (someone) from apparent brainwashing, typically that of a religious cult, by the systematic reindoctrination of conventional values.

de·pro·tein·ize /dē'prōtē(ə),nīz/ ▸*v.* [*trans.*] remove the protein from (a substance), usually as a stage in chemical purification. **—de·pro·tein·i·za·tion** /-,prōtē(ə)nə'zāSHən/ *n.*

Dept. ▸*abbr.* Department.

depth /depTH/ ▸*n.* **1** the distance from the top or surface of something to its bottom: *shallow water of no more than 12 feet* ***in depth.*** ■ distance from the nearest to the farthest point of something or from the front to the back: *the depth of the wardrobe.* ■ used to specify the distance below the top or surface of something to which someone or something percolates or at which something happens: [in *sing.*] *loosen the soil to* ***a depth of*** *8 inches.* ■ the apparent existence of three dimensions in a picture, photograph, or other two-dimensional representation; perspective: *texture in a picture gives it depth.* ■ lowness of pitch: *my voice had not yet acquired husky depths.* **2** complexity and profundity of thought: *the book has unexpected depth.* ■ extensive and detailed study or knowledge: *third-year courses typically go into more depth.* ■ intensity of emotion, usually considered as a laudable quality: *a man of compassion and depth of feeling.* ■ intensity of color: *the wine shows good depth of color.* **3** (**the depths**) a point far below the surface: *he lifted the manhole cover and peered into the depths beneath.* ■ (also **the depth**) the worst or lowest part or state: *4 a.m. in* ***the depths of winter*** *| the putrid depths to which morality has sunk.* ■ a time when one's negative feelings are at their most intense: *she was in* ***the depths of despair.*** ■ a place that is remote and inaccessible: *a remote little village somewhere in the depths of Russia.* **4** *Sports* the strength of a team in its reserve of substitute players: *they have so much depth that they could afford the luxury of breaking in their players slowly.* ▷late Middle English: from DEEP + -TH², on the pattern of pairs such as *long, length.*
▸***PHRASES*** □ **hidden depths** usually admirable but previously unnoticed qualities of a person: *hidden depths and insights within children.* ■ obscure or secretive aspects of a situation: *the hidden depths of marital life.* □ **in depth** in great detail; comprehensively and thoroughly: *research students pursue a specific aspect of a subject in depth.* See also IN-DEPTH. □ **out of one's depth** in water too deep to stand in. ■ *figurative* beyond one's knowledge or ability to cope: *the Governor is out of his depth, politically adrift.*

depth charge ▸*n.* an explosive charge designed to be dropped from a ship or aircraft and to explode under water at a preset depth, used for attacking submarines.

depth find·er ▸*n.* an echo sounder or other device for measuring water depth, esp. for navigation and fishing.

depth gauge ▸*n.* a device fitted to a drill bit to ensure that the hole drilled does not exceed the required depth.

depth·less /'depTHlis/ ▸*adj.* unfathomably deep: *a depthless gorge.* ■ *figurative* shallow and superficial. **—depth·less·ly** *adv.*

depth of field ▸*n.* the distance between the nearest and the furthest objects that give an image judged to be in focus in a camera.

depth of fo·cus ▸*n.* the distance between the two extreme axial points behind a lens at which an image is judged to be in focus.

depth per·cep·tion ▸*n.* the ability to perceive the relative distance of objects in one's visual field.

depth psy·chol·o·gy ▸*n.* the study of unconscious mental processes and motives, esp. in psychoanalytic theory and practice.

depth sound·er ▸*n.* another term for ECHO SOUNDER.

de·pub·li·ca·tion /dē,pəbli'kāSHən/ ▸*n.* the act of depublishing: *the League of California cities had requested depublication of the Div. Seven ruling.*

de·pub·lish /dē'pəbliSH/ ▸*v.* [*trans.*] *chiefly Law* remove from an official record or publication: *the Supreme Court may also elect to depublish a case on its own motion.*

dep·u·rate /'depyə,rāt/ ▸*v.* [*trans.*] *rare* free (something) of impurities. ▷early 17th cent.: from medieval Latin *depurat-* 'purified,' from the verb *depurare*, from *de-* 'completely' + *purare* 'purify' (from *purus* 'pure'). **—dep·u·ra·tion** /,depyə'rāSHən/ *n.* **—dep·u·ra·tive** /-,rātiv/ *adj.* & *n.* **—dep·u·ra·tor** /-,rātər/ *n.*

dep·u·ta·tion /,depyə'tāSHən/ ▸*n.* a group of people appointed to undertake a mission or take part in a formal process on behalf of a larger group: *he had been a member of a deputation to Napoleon III.* ▷late Middle English (in the sense 'appointment to an office or function'): from late Latin *deputatio(n-)*, from the verb *deputare* (see DEPUTE).

de·pute /di'pyo͞ot/ ▸*v.* [*trans.*] appoint or instruct (someone) to perform a task for which one is responsible: *she had been deputed to look after him while Clarissa was away.* ■ delegate (authority or a task). ▷late Middle English: via Old French from Latin *deputare* 'consider to be, assign,' from *de-* 'away'+ *putare* 'think over, consider.'

dep·u·tize /'depyə,tīz/ ▸*v.* [*trans.*] make (someone) a deputy: *some officers will be deputized as federal marshals.* ■ [*intrans.*] temporarily act or speak as a deputy.

dep·u·ty /'depyətē/ ▸*n.* (*pl.* **-ties**) a person whose immediate superior is a senior figure within an organization and who is empowered to act as a substitute for this superior. ■ a parliamentary representative in certain countries. ▷late Middle English: from Old French *depute*, from late Latin *deputatus*, past participle of *deputare* (see DEPUTE). **—dep·u·ty·ship** /-,SHip/ *n.*
▸***PHRASE*** □ **by deputy** *historical* instructing another person to act in one's stead; by proxy: *the wardens of the forests performed important duties by deputy.*

de·queue /dē'kyo͞o/ ▸*v.* (**-queued**, **-queu·ing** or **-queue·ing**) [*trans.*] *Computing* remove (an item) from a queue.

De Quin·cey /də 'kwinsē/, Thomas (1785–1859), English essayist and critic. He was known for his *Confessions of an English Opium Eater* (1822), a study of his addiction to opium and its psychological effects.

de·rac·in·ate /di'rasə,nāt/ ▸*v.* [*trans.*] *poetic/literary* tear (something) up by the roots. ▷late 16th cent.: from French *déraciner*, from *dé-* (expressing removal) + *racine* 'root' (based on Latin *radix*). **—de·rac·i·na·tion** /-,rasə'nāSHən/ *n.*

de·rac·i·nat·ed /di'rasə,nātid/ ▸*adj.* another term for DÉRACINÉ.

dé·ra·ci·né /dā,räsi'nā/ ▸*adj.* uprooted or displaced from one's geographical or social environment: *the self-consciousness of déraciné Americans.*
▸*n.* a person who has been or feels displaced. ▷early 20th cent.: French, literally 'uprooted.'

de·rail /dē'rāl/ ▶*v.* [*trans.*] (usu. **be derailed**) cause (a train or trolley car) to leave its tracks accidentally: *a train was derailed after it collided with a herd of cattle.* ■ [*intrans.*] (of a train or trolley car) accidentally leave the tracks: *the trolley cars had a tendency to derail on sharp corners.* ■ [*trans.*] *figurative* obstruct (a process) by diverting it from its intended course: *the plot is seen by some as an attempt to derail the negotiations.* ▷mid 19th cent.: from French *dérailler,* from *dé-* (expressing removal) + *rail* 'rail.' —**de·rail·ment** *n.*

de·rail·leur /di'rālər/ ▶*n.* a bicycle mechanism that moves the chain out and up, allowing it to shift to different cogs. ▷1930s: from French, from *dérailler* 'derail.'

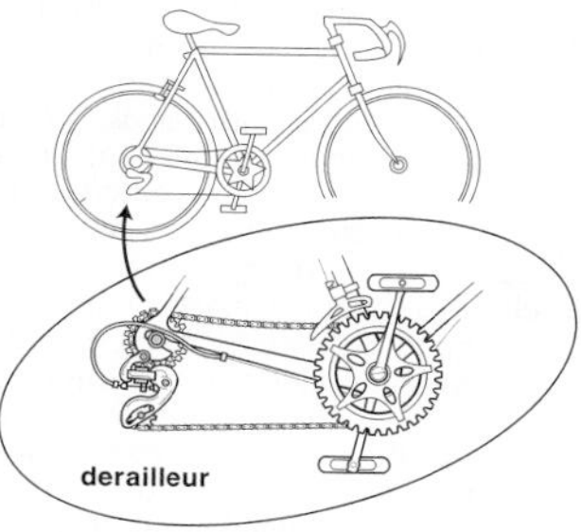

derailleur

De·rain /də'ran/, André (1880–1954), French painter; an exponent of fauvism.

de·range /di'rānj/ ▶*v.* [*trans.*] [usu. as *adj.*] (**deranged**) cause (someone) to become insane: *a deranged man.* ■ throw (something) into confusion; cause to act irregularly: *stress deranges the immune system.* ■ *archaic* intrude on; interrupt: *I am sorry to have deranged you for so small a matter.* ▷late 18th cent.: from French *déranger,* from Old French *desrengier,* literally 'move from orderly rows.' —**de·range·ment** *n.*

de·rate /dē'rāt/ ▶*v.* [*trans.*] reduce the power rating of (a component or device): *the engines were derated to 90 horse power.*

Der·by[1] /'därbē/ a city in north central England, on the Derwent River; pop. 214,000.

Der·by[2] /'därbē/ Edward George Geoffrey Smith Stanley, 14th Earl of (1799–1869), British statesman; prime minister 1852, 1858–59, and 1866–68.

Der·by[3] /'dərbē/ ▶*n.* (*pl.* **-bies**) **1** an annual horse race for three-year-olds, founded in 1780 by the 12th Earl of Derby. The race is run on Epsom Downs in England in late May or early June. ■ a similar race elsewhere: *the Kentucky Derby.* ■ (**derby**) a sporting contest open to the general public: *sign up for the fishing derby.* **2** (**derby**, also **derby hat**) a bowler hat. [said to be from American demand for a hat of the type worn at the Epsom Derby.] **3** a boot or shoe having the eyelet tabs stitched on top of the vamp. [so named because originally a sports boot.]

Derby[3]

Der·by[4] /'dərbē/ ▶*n.* a hard pressed cheese made from skimmed milk, chiefly in Derbyshire.

Der·by Day ▶*n.* the day on which the Epsom Derby is run.

Der·by·shire /'därbēshər; -,shi(ə)r/ a county in north central England; county town, Matlock.

Der·by·shire neck ▶*n. historical* goiter, formerly endemic in parts of Derbyshire.

de re /dā 'rā/ ▶*adj. Philosophy* relating to the properties of things mentioned in an assertion or expression, rather than to the assertion or expression itself. Compare with **DE DICTO**. ▷Latin, literally 'about the thing.'

de·re·al·i·za·tion /dē,rē(ə)lə'zāshən/ ▶*n.* a feeling that one's surroundings are not real, esp. as a symptom of mental disturbance. —**de·re·al·ized** /dē'rē(ə),līzd/ *adj.*

de·re·cho /dā'rā,chō/ ▶*n.* a line of intense, widespread, and fast-moving windstorms and sometimes thunderstorms that moves across a great distance and is characterized by damaging straight-line winds. ▷Spanish, literally 'straight.'

de·ref·er·ence /dē'refərəns/ ▶*v.* [*trans.*] *Computing* obtain the address of a data item held in another location from (a pointer).

de·reg·u·late /dē'regyə,lāt/ ▶*v.* [*trans.*] remove regulations or restrictions from: *a law that would deregulate cable TV prices.* —**de·reg·u·la·tion** /-,regyə'lāshən/ *n.* —**de·reg·u·la·to·ry** /-lə,tôrē/ *adj.*

der·e·lict /'derə,likt/ ▶*adj.* in a very poor condition as a result of disuse and neglect: *the cities were derelict and dying.* ■ (of a person) shamefully negligent in not having done what one should have done: *he was **derelict in** his duty to his country.*
▶*n.* a person without a home, job, or property: *derelicts who could fit all their possessions in a paper bag.* ■ a piece of property, esp. a ship, abandoned by the owner and in poor condition. ▷mid 17th cent.: from Latin *derelictus* 'abandoned,' past participle of *derelinquere,* from *de-* 'completely' + *relinquere* 'forsake.'

der·e·lic·tion /,derə'likshən/ ▶*n.* the state of having been abandoned and become dilapidated: *every year valuable gardens start the slow slide to dereliction.* ■ (usu. **dereliction of duty**) the shameful failure to fulfill one's obligations. ▷late 16th cent.: from Latin *derelictio(n-),* from the verb *derelinquere* (see **DERELICT**).

de·re·press /,dēri'pres/ ▶*v.* [*trans.*] *Biochemistry & Genetics* activate (enzymes, genes, etc.) from an inoperative or latent state. —**de·re·pres·sion** /-'preshən/ *n.*

de·req·ui·si·tion /dē,rekwə'zishən/ ▶*v.* [*trans.*] *dated* return (requisitioned property) to its former owner.

de·re·strict /,dēri'strikt/ ▶*v.* [*trans.*] remove restrictions from. —**de·re·stric·tion** /-'strikshən/ *n.*

de·ride /di'rīd/ ▶*v.* [*trans.*] express contempt for; ridicule: *critics derided the proposals as clumsy attempts to find a solution.* ▷mid 16th cent.: from Latin *deridere* 'scoff at.' —**de·rid·er** *n.*

de ri·gueur /də ri'gər; rē'gœr/ ▶*adj.* required by etiquette or current fashion: *it was de rigueur for bands to grow their hair long.* ▷mid 19th cent.: French, literally 'in strictness.'

de·ri·sion /di'rizhən/ ▶*n.* contemptuous ridicule or mockery: *my stories were greeted with derision and disbelief.* ▷late Middle English: via Old French from late Latin *derisio(n-),* from *deridere* 'scoff at.' —**de·ris·i·ble** /-'rizəbəl/ *adj.*
▶*PHRASE* □ **hold** (or **have**) **in derision** *archaic* regard with mockery.

de·ri·sive /di'rīsiv/ ▶*adj.* expressing contempt or ridicule: *a harsh, derisive laugh.* ▷mid 17th cent.: from **DERISION**, on the pattern of the pair *decision, decisive.* —**de·ri·sive·ly** *adv.* —**de·ri·sive·ness** *n.*

USAGE On the difference between **derisive** and **derisory**, see **usage** at **DERISORY**.

de·ri·so·ry /di'rīsərē; -'rī-/ ▶*adj.* **1** ridiculously small or inadequate: *they were given a derisory pay rise.* **2** another term for **DERISIVE**: *his derisory gaze swept over her.* ▷early 17th cent. (in the sense 'derisive'): from late Latin *derisorius,* from *deris-* 'scoffed at,' from the verb *deridere* (see **DERISION**).

USAGE Although the words **derisory** and **derisive** share similar roots, they have different core meanings. **Derisory** usually means 'ridiculously small or inadequate,' as in *a **derisory** pay offer* or *the security arrangements were **derisory.*** **Derisive**, on the other hand, is used to mean 'showing contempt,' as in *he gave a **derisive** laugh.*

der·i·vate /'derəvit/ ▶*n.* something derived, esp. a product obtained chemically from a raw material. ▷late Middle English: from Latin *derivat-* 'derived,' from the verb *derivare* (see **DERIVE**).

der·i·va·tion /,derə'vāshən/ ▶*n.* **1** the obtaining or developing of something from a source or origin: *the **derivation** of scientific laws **from** observation.* ■ the formation of a word from another word or from a root in the same or another language. ■ *Linguistics* in generative grammar the set of stages that link the abstract underlying structure of an expression to its surface form. ■ *Mathematics* a sequence of statements showing that a formula, theorem, etc., is a consequence of previously accepted statements. ■ *Mathematics* the process of deducing a new formula, theorem, etc., from previously accepted statements. **2** origin; extraction: *music of primarily Turkish derivation.* ■ something derived; a derivative: *the derivation "sheepish" has six definitions.* ▷late Middle English (denoting the drawing of a fluid, specifically the drawing of pus or blood; also in the sense 'formation of a word from another word'): from Latin *derivatio(n-),* from the verb *derivare* (see **DERIVE**). —**der·i·va·tion·al** /-shənl/ *adj.*

de·riv·a·tive /di'rivətiv/ ▶*adj.* (typically of an artist or work of art) imitative of the work of another person, and usually disapproved of for that reason: *an artist who is not in the slightest bit derivative.* ■ originating from, based on, or influenced by: *Darwin's work is **derivative of** the moral philosophers.* ■ [*attrib.*] (of a financial product) having a value deriving from an underlying variable asset: *equity-based derivative products.*
▶*n.* something that is based on another source: *a derivative of the system was chosen for the Marine Corps' V-22 tilt rotor aircraft.* ■ (often **derivatives**) an arrangement or instrument (such as a future, option, or warrant) whose value derives from and is dependent on the value of an underlying asset: [as *adj.*] *the derivatives market.* ■ a word derived from another or from a root in the same or another language. ■ a substance that is derived chemically from a specified compound: *crack is a highly addictive cocaine derivative.* ■ *Mathematics* an expression representing the rate of change of a function with respect to an independent variable. ▷late Middle English (in the adjective sense 'having the power to draw off,' and in the noun sense 'a word derived from another'): from French *dérivatif, -ive,* from Latin *derivativus,* from *derivare* (see **DERIVE**). —**de·riv·a·tive·ly** *adv.*

de·rive /di'rīv/ ▶*v.* [*trans.*] (**derive something from**) obtain something from (a specified source): *they derived great comfort from this assurance.* ■ (**derive something from**) base a concept on a logical extension or modification of (another concept): *Marx derived his philosophy of history from Hegel.* ■ [*intrans.*] (**derive from**) (of a word) have (a specified word, usually of another language) as a root or origin: *the word "punch" derives from the Hindustani "pancha"* | (**be derived from**) *the word "man" is derived from the Sanskrit "manas."* ■ [*intrans.*] (**derive from**) arise from or originate in (a specified source): *words whose spelling derives from Dr. Johnson's incorrect etymology.* ■ (**be derived from**) *Linguistics* (of an expression in a natural language) be linked by a set of stages to (its underlying abstract form). ■ (**be derived from**) (of a substance) be formed or prepared by (a chemical or physical process affecting another substance): *strong acids are derived from the combustion of fossil fuels.* ■ *Mathematics* obtain (a function or equation) from another by a sequence of logical steps, for example by differentiation. ▷late Middle English (in the sense 'draw a fluid through or into a channel'): from Old French *deriver* or Latin *derivare,* from *de-* 'down, away' + *rivus* 'brook, stream.' —**de·riv·a·ble** *adj.*

de·rived de·mand ▶*n. Economics* a demand for a commodity, service, etc., that is a consequence of the demand for something else.

de·rived fos·sil ▶*n.* a fossil redeposited in a sediment that is younger than the one in which it first occurred.

derm /dərm/ ▶*n.* another term for **DERMIS**.

der·ma[1] /'dərmə/ ▶*n.* another term for **DERMIS**. ▷early 18th cent.: modern Latin, from Greek 'skin.'

der·ma[2] ▶*n.* beef or chicken intestine, stuffed and cooked in dishes such as kishke. ▷from Yiddish *derme,* plural of *darm* 'intestine'; related to Old English *tharm* 'intestine.'

der·ma- (also **dermo-**) ▶*comb. form* skin: *dermabrasion.* ▷from Greek, *derma* 'skin.'

derm·a·bra·sion /,dərmə'brāzhən/ ▶*n.* the removal of superficial layers of skin with a rapidly revolving abrasive tool, as a technique in cosmetic surgery. ▷1950s: from Greek *derma* 'skin' + **ABRASION**.

Der·map·te·ra /dər'maptərə/ *Entomology* an order of insects that comprises the earwigs. ▷modern Latin (plural), from Greek *derma* 'skin' + *pteron* 'wing.' —**der·map·ter·an** *n.* & *adj.* —**der·map·ter·ous** /-rəs/ *adj.*

der·ma·ti·tis /,dərmə'tītis/ ▶*n.* a condition of the skin in which it becomes red, swollen, and sore, sometimes with small blisters, resulting from direct irritation of the skin by an external agent or an allergic reaction to it. Compare with **ECZEMA**. ▷late 19th cent.: from Greek *derma, dermat-* 'skin' + **-ITIS**.

dermato- ▶*comb. form* of or relating to the skin: *dermatomycosis.* ▷from Greek *derma, dermat-* 'skin, hide.'

der·mat·o·glyph·ics /,dərmətə'glifiks; dər,matə-/ ▶*plural n.* [treated as *sing.*] the study of skin markings or patterns on fingers, hands, and feet, and its application, esp. in criminology. ▷1920s: from **DERMATO-** 'skin' + Greek *gluphikos* 'carved' (from *gluphē* 'carving'). —**der·mat·o·glyph** /dər'matə,glif/ *n.* —**der·mat·o·glyph·ic** *adj.* —**der·mat·o·glyph·i·cal·ly** /-ik(ə)lē/ *adv.*

Pronunciation Key ə *ago;* ər *over;* 'ə or ,ə *up;* 'ər or ,ər *fur;* a *hat;* ā *rate;* ä *car;* ch *chew;* e *let;* ē *see;* e(ə)r *air;* i *fit;* ī *by;* i(ə)r *ear;* ng *sing;* ō *go;* ô *for;* oi *boy;* o͝o *good;* o͞o *goo;* ou *out;* sh *she;* th *thin;* th *then;* (h)w *why;* zh *vision*

D

der·ma·tol·o·gy /ˌdərməˈtäləjē/ ▸*n.* the branch of medicine concerned with the diagnosis and treatment of skin disorders. —**der·ma·to·log·i·cal** /-mətlˈäjikəl/ *adj.* —**der·ma·to·log·i·cal·ly** /-mətlˈäjik(ə)lē/ *adv.* —**der·ma·tol·o·gist** /-jist/ *n.*

der·ma·tome /ˈdərməˌtōm/ ▸*n. Embryology* the lateral wall of each somite in a vertebrate embryo, giving rise to the connective tissue of the skin. Compare with MYOTOME, SCLEROTOME. ■ *Physiology* an area of the skin supplied by nerves from a single spinal root.

der·mat·o·my·co·sis /dərˌmatəmīˈkōsis; ˈdərmətō-/ ▸*n.* (*pl.* **-ses** /-ˌsēz/) a fungal infection of the skin, esp. by a dermatophyte.

der·mat·o·my·o·si·tis /dərˌmatəmīəˈsītis; ˈdərmətō-/ ▸*n. Medicine* inflammation of the skin and underlying muscle tissue, involving degeneration of collagen, discoloration, and swelling, typically occurring as an autoimmune condition or associated with internal cancer.

der·mat·o·phyte /dərˈmatəˌfīt; ˈdərmətə-/ ▸*n.* a pathogenic fungus that grows on skin, mucous membranes, hair, nails, feathers, and other body surfaces, causing ringworm and related diseases. • *Trichophyton* and other genera, subdivision Deuteromycotina. —**der·mat·o·phyt·ic** /dərˌmatəˈfitik; ˌdərmətə-/ *adj.*

der·mat·o·phy·to·sis /dərˌmatəfīˈtōsis/ ▸*n.* (*pl.* **-ses** /-sēz/) another term for DERMATOMYCOSIS.

der·ma·to·sis /ˌdərməˈtōsis/ ▸*n.* (*pl.* **-ses** /-sēz/) a disease of the skin, esp. one that does not cause inflammation.

der·mes·tid /dərˈmestid/ ▸*n. Entomology* a small beetle of a family (Dermestidae) that includes many kinds that are destructive (esp. as larvae) to hides, skin, fur, wool, and other animal substances. ▷late 19th cent.: from modern Latin *Dermestidae* (plural), from the genus name *Dermestes*, formed irregularly from Greek *derma* 'skin' + *esthiein* 'eat.'

der·mis /ˈdərmis/ ▸*n. technical* the skin. ■ *Anatomy* the thick layer of living tissue below the epidermis that forms the true skin, containing blood capillaries, nerve endings, sweat glands, hair follicles, and other structures. ▷mid 19th cent.: modern Latin, suggested by *epidermis*. —**der·mal** /-məl/ *adj.* —**der·mic** /-mik/ *adj.* (*rare*).

der·moid /ˈdərˌmoid/ ▸*n.* short for DERMOID CYST.

der·moid cyst ▸*n. Medicine* an abnormal growth (teratoma) containing epidermis, hair follicles, and sebaceous glands, derived from residual embryonic cells.

Der·mop·ter·a /dərˈmäptərə/ *Zoology* a small order of mammals that comprises the flying lemurs or colugos. ▷modern Latin (plural), from Greek *derma* 'skin' + *pteron* 'wing.'

der·nier cri /ˈdernyā ˈkrē/ ▸*n.* (**the/le dernier cri**) the very latest fashion: *as soon as he was passé on the European scene, he became the dernier cri here.* ▷late 19th cent.: French, literally 'last cry.'

der·o·gate /ˈderəˌgāt/ ▸*v. formal* **1** [*trans.*] disparage (someone or something): *it is typical of Pirandello to derogate the powers of reason.* **2** [*intrans.*] (**derogate from**) detract from: *this does not derogate from his duty to act honestly and faithfully.* **3** [*intrans.*] (**derogate from**) deviate from (a set of rules or agreed form of behavior): *one country has derogated from the Rome Convention.* ▷late Middle English: from Latin *derogat-* 'abrogated,' from the verb *derogare*, from *de-* 'aside, away' + *rogare* 'ask.' —**de·rog·a·tive** /diˈrägətiv/ *adj.*

der·o·ga·tion /ˌderəˈgāsʜən/ ▸*n.* **1** an exemption from or relaxation of a rule or law: *the massive derogation of human rights.* **2** the perception or treatment of someone as being of little worth: *the derogation of women.* ▷late Middle English (in the sense 'impairment of the force of'): from Latin *derogatio(n-)*, from the verb *derogare* (see DEROGATE).

de·rog·a·to·ry /diˈrägəˌtôrē/ ▸*adj.* showing a critical or disrespectful attitude: *she tells me I'm fat and is always making derogatory remarks.* ▷early 16th cent. (in the sense 'impairing in force or effect'): from late Latin *derogatorius*, from *derogat-* 'abrogated,' from the verb *derogare* (see DEROGATE). —**de·rog·a·to·ri·ly** /-ˌtôrəlē/ *adv.*

der·rick /ˈderik/ ▸*n.* **1** a kind of crane with a movable pivoted arm for moving or lifting heavy weights, esp. on a ship. **2** the framework over an oil well or similar boring that holds the drilling machinery. ▷early 17th cent. (denoting a hangman, also the gallows): from *Derrick*, the surname of a hangman in London, England.

Der·ri·da /dəriˈdä; ˌderi-/, Jacques (1930–2004), French philosopher and literary critic. He was an important figure in the theory of deconstructionism.

der·ri·ère /ˌderēˈe(ə)r/ ▸*n. informal* euphemistic term for a person's buttocks. ▷late 18th cent.: French, literally 'behind.'

der·ring-do /ˈderiɴɢ ˈdo͞o/ ▸*n. dated, humorous* action displaying heroic courage: *tales of derring-do.* ▷late 16th cent.: from late Middle English *dorryng do* 'daring to do,' used by Chaucer, and, in a passage by Lydgate based on Chaucer's work, misprinted in 16th-cent. editions as *derrynge do*; this was misinterpreted by Spenser to mean 'manhood, chivalry,' and subsequently taken up and popularized by Sir Walter Scott.

der·rin·ger /ˈderinjər/ ▸*n.* a small pistol that has a large bore and is very effective at close range. ▷mid 19th cent.: named after Henry *Deringer* (1786–1868), the American gunsmith who invented it.

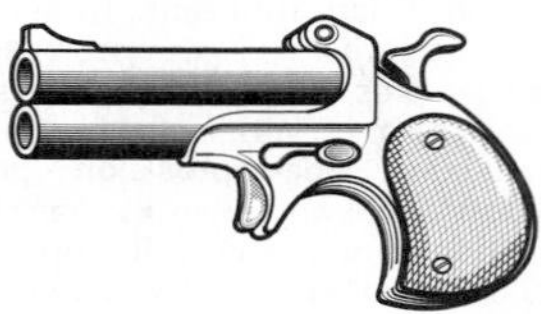

derringer

der·ris /ˈderis/ ▸*n.* **1** an insecticide made from the powdered roots of certain tropical plants containing rotenone. [late 19th cent.: originally used in Malaya to stupefy fish.] **2** a woody, climbing plant of the pea family that bears leathery pods and has tuberous roots from which this insecticide is obtained. [modern Latin, from Greek, 'leather covering' (referring to its pod).] • Genus *Derris*, family Leguminosae.

Der·ry /ˈderē/ **1** see LONDONDERRY. **2** a town in southeastern New Hampshire, southeast of Manchester; pop. 34,021.

der·vish /ˈdərvisʜ/ ▸*n.* a Muslim (specifically Sufi) religious man who has taken vows of poverty and austerity. Dervishes first appeared in the 12th century; they were noted for their wild or ecstatic rituals and were known as **dancing**, **whirling**, or **howling dervishes** according to the practice of their order. ▷from Turkish *derviş*, from Persian *darvīš* 'poor,' (as a noun) 'religious mendicant.'

DES ▸*abbr.* ■ diethylstilbestrol. ■ *Computing* data encryption standard.

de·sa·cral·ize /dēˈsākrəˌlīz/ ▸*v.* [*trans.*] remove the religious or sacred status or significance from: *we have chosen to desacralize the world through modern science.* —**de·sa·cral·i·za·tion** /-ˌsākrələˈzāsʜən/ *n.*

de Sade /də ˈsäd/, Marquis, see SADE.

de·sal·i·nate /dēˈsaləˌnāt/ ▸*v.* [*trans.*] [usu. as *adj.*] (**desalinated**) remove salt from (seawater). —**de·sal·i·na·tion** /-ˌsaləˈnāsʜən/ *n.* —**de·sal·i·na·tor** /-ˌnātər/ *n.*

de·sal·in·ize /dēˈsaləˌnīz/ ▸*v.* another term for DESALINATE. —**de·sal·in·i·za·tion** /-ˌsalənəˈzāsʜən/ *n.*

de·salt /dēˈsôlt/ ▸*v.* another term for DESALINATE.

de·sa·pa·re·ci·do /ˌdesəˌpärəˈsēdō/ ▸*n.* (*pl.* **-dos**) (esp. in South America), a person who has disappeared, presumed killed by members of the armed services or the police. ▷late 20th cent.: Spanish, literally 'disappeared.'

de·sat·u·rate /dēˈsacʜəˌrāt/ ▸*v.* [*trans.*] make less saturated; cause to become unsaturated. —**de·sat·u·ra·tion** /-ˌsacʜəˈrāsʜən/ *n.*

des·ca·mi·sa·do /ˌdeskaməˈsädō/ ▸*n.* (*pl.* **-dos**) (in Latin America) a very poor person. ▷mid 19th cent.: Spanish, literally 'shirtless.'

des·cant ▸*n.* /ˈdesˌkant/ *Music* an independent treble melody usually sung or played above a basic melody. ■ *archaic or poetic/literary* a melodious song. ■ a discourse on a theme or subject: *his descant of deprivation.*

▸*v.* /desˈkant/ [*intrans.*] talk tediously or at length: *I have* **descanted on** *this subject before.* ▷late Middle English: from Old French *deschant*, from medieval Latin *discantus* 'part-song, refrain.'

des·cant re·cord·er ▸*n.* British term for SOPRANO RECORDER.

Des·cartes /dāˈkärt/, René (1596–1650), French philosopher, mathematician, and man of science. He concluded that everything was open to doubt except conscious experience and existence as a necessary condition of this: *"Cogito, ergo sum"* (I think, therefore I am). In mathematics, he developed the use of coordinates to locate a point in two or three dimensions.

de·scend /diˈsend/ ▸*v.* [*intrans.*] **1** move or fall downward: *the aircraft began to descend.* ■ [*trans.*] move down (a slope or stairs): *the vehicle descended a ramp.* ■ (of stairs, a road or path, or a piece of land) be on a slope or incline and extend downward: *a side road descended into the forest* | [*trans.*] *a narrow flight of stairs descended a steep slope.* ■ come or go down a scale, esp. from the superior to the inferior: [as *adj.*] (**descending**) *the categories are listed in descending order of usefulness.* ■ *Music* (of sound) become lower in pitch: [as *adj.*] (**descending**) *a passage of descending chords.* ■ (**descend to**) act in a specified shameful way that is far below one's usual standards: *she descended to self-pity.* ■ (**descend into**) (of a situation or group of people) reach (a state considered undesirable or shameful): *the army had descended into chaos.* **2** (**descend on/upon**) make a sudden attack on: *the militia descended on Rye.* ■ make an unexpected and typically unwelcome visit to: *treasure-seekers descended upon the site.* ■ (of a feeling or atmosphere) develop suddenly and be felt throughout a place or by a person or group of people: *an air of gloom descended on the Democratic Party headquarters.* ■ (of night or darkness) begin to occur: *as the winter darkness descended, the fighting ceased.* **3** (**be descended from**) be a blood relative of (a specified, typically illustrious ancestor): *Jews believe they* **are descended from** *Abraham.* ■ (of an asset) pass by inheritance, typically from parent to child: *his lands* **descended to** *his eldest son.* ▷Middle English: from Old French *descendre*, from Latin *descendere*, from *de-* 'down' + *scandere* 'to climb.' —**de·scend·ent** /-dənt/ *adj.*

de·scend·ant /diˈsendənt/ ▸*n.* a person, plant, or animal that is descended from a particular ancestor: *Shakespeare's last direct descendant.* ■ a machine, artifact, system, etc., that has developed from an earlier, more rudimentary version. ▷late Middle English (as an adjective in the sense 'descending'): from French, present participle of *descendre* 'to descend' (see DESCEND). The noun dates from the early 17th cent.

de·scend·er /diˈsendər/ ▸*n.* a part of a letter that extends below the level of the base of a letter such as *x* (as in g and *p*). ■ a letter having such a part.

de·scen·deur /diˈsendər/ ▸*n. Climbing* a piece of metal around which a rope is passed and which makes use of friction to slow descent during rappelling. ▷late 20th cent.: French, literally 'descender.'

de·scend·i·ble /diˈsendəbəl/ ▸*adj. Law* (of property) able to be inherited by a descendant.

de·scend·ing co·lon ▸*n. Anatomy* the part of the large intestine that passes downward on the left side of the abdomen toward the rectum.

de·scent /diˈsent/ ▸*n.* **1** [usu. in *sing.*] an action of moving downward, dropping, or falling: *the plane had gone into a steep descent.* ■ a downward slope, esp. a path or track: *a steep, badly eroded descent.* ■ a moral, social, or psychological decline into a specified undesirable state: *the ancient empire's slow* **descent into** *barbarism.* **2** the origin or background of a person in terms of family or nationality: *American families* **of** *Hungarian* **descent**. ■ the transmission of qualities, property, or privileges by inheritance. **3** (**descent on**) a sudden, violent attack: *a descent on the enemy airstrip.* ▷Middle English: from Old French *descente*, from *descendre* 'to descend' (see DESCEND).

de·scram·ble /dēˈskrambəl/ ▸*v.* [*trans.*] convert or restore (a signal) to intelligible form. —**de·scram·bler** /-b(ə)lər/ *n.*

de·scribe /diˈskrīb/ ▸*v.* [*trans.*] **1** give an account in words of (someone or something), including all the relevant characteristics, qualities, or events: *the police said the man was* **described as** *white, 6 ft. tall, with mousy, cropped hair.* ■ indicate; denote: *"Jim Crow" describes a policy of segregation.* **2** mark out or draw (a geometric figure): *on the diameter of a circle an equilateral triangle is described.* ▷late Middle English: from Latin *describere*, from *de-* 'down' + *scribere* 'write.' —**de·scrib·a·ble** *adj.* —**de·scrib·er** *n.*

de·scrip·tion /diˈskripsʜən/ ▸*n.* **1** a spoken or written representation or account of a person, object, or event: *people who had seen him were able to give a description.* ■ the action of giving such a representation or account: *teaching by demonstration and description.* **2** a sort, kind, or class of people or things: *ships* **of every description**. ▷late Middle English: via Old French from Latin *descriptio(n-)*, from *describere* 'write down.'

▸*PHRASES* □ **beyond description** to a great and astonishing extent: *his face was swollen beyond* *description.* □ **defy description** be so unusual or remarkable as to be impossible to describe: *the sheer scale of the Requiem defies description.* □ **answers** (or **fits**) **the description** has the qualities specified.

de·scrip·tive /di'skriptiv/ ▸*adj.* **1** serving or seeking to describe. ■ *Grammar* (of an adjective) assigning a quality rather than restricting the application of the expression modified, e.g., *blue* as distinct from *few.* **2** describing or classifying without expressing feelings or judging. ■ *Linguistics* denoting or relating to an approach to language analysis that describes accents, forms, structures, and usage without making value judgments. Often contrasted with PRESCRIPTIVE. ▷mid 18th cent.: from late Latin *descriptivus,* from *descript-* 'written down,' from the verb *describere* (see DESCRIBE). **—de·scrip·tive·ly** *adv.* **—de·scrip·tive·ness** *n.*

de·scrip·tiv·ism /di'skriptə,vizəm/ ▸*n. Philosophy* the doctrine that the meanings of ethical or aesthetic terms and statements are purely descriptive rather than prescriptive, evaluative, or emotive. **—de·scrip·tiv·ist** *n. & adj.*

de·scrip·tor /di'skriptər/ ▸*n.* an element or term that has the function of describing, identifying, or indexing, in particular: ■ *Linguistics* a word or expression used to describe or identify something. ■ *Computing* a piece of stored data that indicates how other data is stored.

de·scry /di'skrī/ ▸*v.* (**-scries, -scried**) [*trans.*] *poetic/literary* catch sight of: *she descried two figures.* See note at DISTINGUISH. ▷Middle English: perhaps confused with obsolete *descry* 'describe,' variant of obsolete *descrive* (via Old French from Latin *describere* 'write down'), which also had the meaning 'perceive.'

des·e·crate /'desi,krāt/ ▸*v.* [*trans.*] (often **be desecrated**) treat (a sacred place or thing) with violent disrespect; violate: *more than 300 graves were desecrated.* ▷late 17th cent.: from DE- (expressing reversal) + a shortened form of CONSECRATE. **—des·e·cra·tion** /,desi'krāsHən/ *n.* **—des·e·cra·tor** /-,krātər/ *n.*

de·seed /dē'sēd/ ▸*v.* [*trans.*] [usu. as *adj.*] (**deseeded**) remove the seeds from (a plant, vegetable, or fruit). **—de·seed·er** *n.*

de·seg·re·gate /dē'segri,gāt/ ▸*v.* [*trans.*] end a policy of racial segregation in: *actions to desegregate schools.* **—de·seg·re·ga·tion** /dē,segri'gāsHən/ *n.*

de·se·lect /,dēsə'lekt/ ▸*v.* [*trans.*] turn off (a selected feature) on a list of options on a computer menu. **—de·se·lec·tion** /-'leksHən/ *n.*

de·sen·si·tize /dē'sensi,tīz/ ▸*v.* [*trans.*] make less sensitive: *creams to desensitize the skin at the site of the injection.* ■ make (someone) less likely to feel shock or distress at scenes of cruelty, violence, or suffering by overexposure to such images: [as *adj.*] (**desensitized**) *people who view such movies become* ***desensitized to*** *violence.* ■ free (someone) from a phobia or neurosis by gradually exposing the person to the thing that is feared. See SYSTEMATIC DESENSITIZATION. **—de·sen·si·ti·za·tion** /dē,sensitə'zāsHən/ *n.* **—de·sen·si·tiz·er** *n.*

Des·er·et /,dezə'ret/ the name proposed in the 1840s by Mormon settlers for what became Utah.

de·sert[1] /də'zərt/ ▸*v.* [*trans.*] abandon (a person, cause, or organization) in a way considered disloyal or treacherous: *he deserted his wife and daughter and went back to England.* ■ [usu. as *adj.*] (**deserted**) (of a number of people) leave (a place), causing it to appear empty: *the lobby of the hotel was virtually deserted.* ■ (of a quality or ability) fail (someone), esp. at a crucial moment when most needed: *her luck deserted her.* ■ [*intrans.*] *Military* (of a soldier) illegally run away from military service. ▷late Middle English: from Old French *deserter,* from late Latin *desertare,* from Latin *desertus* 'left waste' (see DESERT[2]). **—de·ser·tion** /-'zərsHən/ *n.*

des·ert[2] /'dezərt/ ▸*n.* a dry, barren area of land, esp. one covered with sand, that is characteristically desolate, waterless, and without vegetation. ■ a lifeless and unpleasant place, esp. one consisting of or covered with a specified substance: *the interior of Iceland is an ice desert.* ■ a situation or area considered dull and uninteresting: *a cultural desert.*

▸*adj.* [*attrib.*] like a desert: *overgrazing has created desert conditions.* ■ uninhabited and desolate: *desert wastes.* ▷Middle English: via Old French from late Latin *desertum* 'something left waste,' neuter past participle of *deserere* 'leave, forsake.' **—de·ser·tic** *adj.*

de·sert[3] /di'zərt/ ▸*n.* (usu. **deserts**) a person's worthiness or entitlement to reward or punishment: *the penal system fails to punish offenders in accordance with their deserts.* ▷Middle English: via Old French from *deservir* 'serve well' (see DESERVE).

▸*PHRASE* □ **get** (or **receive**) **one's just deserts** receive the appropriate reward or (more usually) punishment for one's actions: *those who caused great torment to others rarely got their just deserts.*

des·ert boot /'dezərt/ ▸*n.* a lightweight boot with the upper made from suede.

de·sert·er /də'zərtər/ ▸*n.* a member of the armed forces who deserts: *deserters from the army.* ▷mid 17th cent.: from DESERT[1], on the pattern of French *déserteur.*

de·sert·i·fi·ca·tion /di,zərtəfi'kāsHən/ ▸*n.* the process by which fertile land becomes desert, typically as a result of drought, deforestation, or inappropriate agriculture.

des·ert is·land /'dezərt/ ▸*n.* a remote tropical island, typically uninhabited.

des·ert pave·ment /'dezərt/ ▸*n. Geology* a surface layer of closely packed or cemented pebbles, rock fragments, etc., from which fine material has been removed by the wind in arid regions.

des·ert rat /'dezərt/ ▸*n. informal* a soldier of the 7th British armored division (with the jerboa as a badge) in the North African desert campaign of 1941–42.

des·ert rose /'dezərt/ ▸*n.* **1** a flowerlike aggregate of crystals of a mineral occurring in arid areas. **2** a succulent plant with pink, tubular flowers and a swollen, woody stem containing toxic, milky sap that is sometimes used for arrow poison. It is native to East Africa and Arabia. • *Adenium obesum,* family Apocynaceae. **3** (also **Sturt's desert rose**) a dense shrub with pinkish-lilac flowers and black spotted leaves and fruit. Native to arid regions of Australia, it is the floral emblem of the Northern Territory of Australia. • *Gossypium sturtianum,* family Malvaceae.

des·ert var·nish /'dezərt/ ▸*n. Geology* a dark, hard film of oxides formed on exposed rock surfaces in arid regions.

de·serve /də'zərv/ ▸*v.* [*trans.*] do something or have or show qualities worthy of (reward or punishment): *the referee deserves a pat on the back for his bravery* | [with *infinitive*] *people who park like that deserve to be towed away.* ▷Middle English: from Old French *deservir,* from Latin *deservire* 'serve well or zealously.' **—de·serv·ed·ly** /-vidlē/ *adv.*

de·serv·ing /də'zərviNG/ ▸*adj.* worthy of being treated in a particular way, typically of being given assistance: *the deserving poor.* **—de·serv·ing·ly** *adv.* **—de·serv·ing·ness** *n.*

de·sex /dē'seks/ ▸*v.* [*trans.*] [usu. as *adj.*] (**desexed**) **1** deprive (someone) of sexual qualities or attraction: *Lawrence portrays feminists as shrill, humorless, and desexed.* **2** castrate or spay (an animal).

de·sex·u·al·ize /dē'seksHōōə,līz/ ▸*v.* [*trans.*] deprive of sexual character or the distinctive qualities of a sex. **—de·sex·u·al·i·za·tion** /-,seksHōōələ'zāsHən/ *n.*

des·ha·bille /,dezə'bēl; -'bē/ ▸*n.* variant spelling of DISHABILLE.

De Si·ca /də 'sēkə/, Vittorio (1901–74), Italian movie director and actor; a key figure in Italian neorealist cinema. His movies include *Bicycle Thieves* (1948) and *Two Women* (1960), both of which won Academy Awards.

des·ic·cant /'desikənt/ ▸*n.* a hygroscopic substance used as a drying agent. ▷late 17th cent.: from Latin *desiccant-* 'making thoroughly dry,' from the verb *desiccare.*

des·ic·cate /'desi,kāt/ ▸*v.* [*trans.*] [usu. as *adj.*] (**desiccated**) remove the moisture from (something, esp. food), typically in order to preserve it: *desiccated coconut.* ■ [as *adj.*] (**desiccated**) *figurative* lacking interest, passion, or energy: *a desiccated history of ideas.* ▷late 16th cent.: from Latin *desiccat-* 'made thoroughly dry,' from the verb *desiccare.* **—des·ic·ca·tion** /-'kāsHən/ *n.* **—des·ic·ca·tive** /-,kātiv/ *adj.*

des·ic·ca·tor /'desi,kātər/ ▸*n.* a glass container or other apparatus holding a drying agent for removing moisture from specimens and protecting them from water vapor in the air.

de·sid·er·ate /di'sidə,rāt/ ▸*v.* [*trans.*] *archaic* feel a keen desire for (something lacking or absent): *I desiderate the resources of a family.* ▷mid 17th cent.: from Latin *desiderat-* 'desired,' from the verb *desiderare,* perhaps from *de-* 'down' + *sidus, sider-* 'star.' Compare with CONSIDER.

de·sid·er·a·tive /di'sidərətiv; -,rātiv/ ▸*adj. Grammar* (in Latin and other inflected languages) denoting a verb formed from another and expressing a desire to do the act denoted by the root verb (such as Latin *esurire* 'want to eat,' from *edere* 'eat'). ■ having, expressing, or relating to desire.

▸*n. Grammar* a desiderative verb. ▷mid 16th cent.: from late Latin *desiderativus,* from Latin *desiderat-* 'desired,' from the verb *desiderare* (see DESIDERATE).

de·sid·er·a·tum /di,sidə'rätəm; -'rātəm; -,zidə-/ ▸*n.* (*pl.* **-ta** /-tə/) something that is needed or wanted: *integrity was a desideratum.* ▷mid 17th cent.: from Latin, 'something desired,' neuter past participle of *desiderare* (see DESIDERATE).

de·sign /də'zīn/ ▸*n.* **1** a plan or drawing produced to show the look and function or workings of a building, garment, or other object before it is built or made: *he has just unveiled his design for the new museum.* ■ the art or action of conceiving of and producing such a plan or drawing: *good design can help the reader understand complicated information* | *the cloister is of late twelfth century design.* ■ an arrangement of lines or shapes created to form a pattern or decoration: *pottery with a lovely blue and white design.* **2** purpose, planning, or intention that exists or is thought to exist behind an action, fact, or material object: *the appearance of design in the universe.*

▸*v.* [*trans.*] decide upon the look and functioning of (a building, garment, or other object), typically by making a detailed drawing of it: *a number of architectural students were designing a factory* | [as *adj.* with *submodifier*] (**designed**) *specially designed buildings.* ■ (often **be designed**) do or plan (something) with a specific purpose or intention in mind: [*trans.*] *the tax changes were designed to stimulate economic growth.* See note at INTEND. ▷late Middle English (as a verb in the sense 'to designate'): from Latin *designare* 'to designate,' reinforced by French *désigner.* The noun is via French from Italian.

▸*PHRASES* □ **by design** as a result of a plan; intentionally: *I became a presenter by default rather than by design.* □ **have designs on** aim to obtain (something desired), typically in a secret and dishonest way: *he suspected her of having designs on the family fortune.*

des·ig·nate ▸*v.* /'dezig,nāt/ [*trans.*] (often **be designated**) appoint (someone) to a specified position: *he was* ***designated as*** *prime minister.* ■ officially assign a specified status or ascribe a specified name or quality to: [*trans.*] *certain schools are designated "science schools"* | *a personality disorder that Adler designates the Ruling Type.* ■ signify; indicate: *the term "brainstem" designates the medulla, pons, and mesencephalon.*

▸*adj.* /-nit; -,nāt/ [*postpositive*] appointed to an office or position but not yet installed: *the Director designate.* ▷mid 17th cent. (as an adjective): from Latin *designatus* 'designated,' past participle of *designare,* based on *signum* 'a mark.' The verb dates from the late 18th cent. **—des·ig·na·tor** /-,nātər/ *n.*

des·ig·nat·ed driv·er ▸*n.* a member of a group who abstains from alcohol in order to drive the others safely.

des·ig·nat·ed hit·ter ▸*n. Baseball* a nonfielding player named before the start of a game to be in the batting order, typically in place of the pitcher.

des·ig·na·tion /,dezig'nāsHən/ ▸*n.* the choosing and naming of someone to be the holder of an official position: *a leader's designation of his own successor.* ■ the action of choosing a place for a special purpose or giving it a special status: *the designation of parts of Santa Ana as an enterprise zone.* ■ a name, description, or title, typically one that is officially bestowed: *a group of tribes banded together under the designation "Sheepeaters."* ▷late Middle English (in the sense 'the action of marking'): from Latin *designatio(n-),* from the verb *designare* (see DESIGNATE).

de·sign·ed·ly /də'zīnidlē/ ▸*adv.* deliberately in order to produce a specific effect: [as *submodifier*] *let me propose a designedly vague criterion.*

des·ig·nee /,dezig'nē/ ▸*n.* a person who has been designated.

de·sign·er /də'zīnər/ ▸*n.* a person who plans the form, look, or workings of something before its being made or built, typically by drawing it in detail: *he's one of the world's leading car designers.* ■ [as *adj.*] made by or having the expensive sophistication of a famous and prestigious fashion designer: *a designer label.* ■ [as *adj.*] upscale and fashionable: *designer food.*

de·sign·er drug ▸*n.* a synthetic analog of an illegal drug, esp. one devised to circumvent drug laws. ■ a fashionable artificial drug.

de·sign·er stub·ble ▸*n.* beard stubble that is deliberately groomed to look fashionable or trendy.

de·sign·ing /də'zīniNG/ ▸*adj.* [*attrib.*] acting in a calculating, deceitful way: *she was a designing little minx.*

D

de·sir·a·ble /də'zī(ə)rəbəl/ ▸*adj.* wanted or wished for as being an attractive, useful, or necessary course of action: [with *infinitive*] *it is desirable to exercise some social control over technology.* ■ (of a person) arousing sexual desire: *she had never looked more desirable.*
▸*n.* a desirable person, thing, or quality. ▷late Middle English: from Old French, suggested by Latin *desiderabilis*, from *desiderare* 'to desire' (see DESIDERATE). **—de·sir·a·bil·i·ty** /-,zī(ə)rə'bilitē/ *n.* **—de·sir·a·ble·ness** *n.* **—de·sir·a·bly** /-blē/ *adv.*

de·sire /də'zī(ə)r/ ▸*n.* a strong feeling of wanting to have something or wishing for something to happen: [with *infinitive*] *a desire to work in the dirt with your bare hands.* ■ strong sexual feeling or appetite: *they were clinging together in fierce mutual desire.*
▸*v.* [*trans.*] strongly wish for or want (something): *he never achieved the status he so desired* | [as *adj.*] (**desired**) *it failed to create the desired effect.* ■ want (someone) sexually: *there had been a time, years ago, when he had desired her.* ■ *archaic* express a wish to (someone); request or entreat. ▷Middle English: from Old French *desir* (noun), *desirer* (verb), from Latin *desiderare* (see DESIDERATE).

De·si·ree /'dezə,rā/ ▸*n.* a potato of a pink-skinned variety with yellow, waxy flesh.

de·sir·ous /di'zīrəs/ ▸*adj.* [*predic.*] having or characterized by desire: *the pope was* ***desirous of*** *peace in Europe.* ▷Middle English: from Old French *desireus*, based on Latin *desiderare* 'to desire' (see DESIDERATE).

de·sist /di'sist/ ▸*v.* [*intrans.*] cease; abstain: *each pledged to* ***desist from*** *acts of sabotage.* ▷late Middle English: from Old French *desister*, from Latin *desistere*, from *de-* 'down from' + *sistere* 'to stop' (reduplication of *stare* 'to stand').

desk /desk/ ▸*n.* a piece of furniture with a flat or sloped surface and typically with drawers, at which one can read, write, or do other work. ■ *Music* a position in an orchestra at which two players share a music stand: *an extra desk of first and second violins.* ■ a counter in a hotel, bank, or airport at which a customer may check in or obtain information: *the reception desk.* ■ [with *adj.*] a specified section of a news organization, esp. a newspaper: *he landed a job on the sports desk.* ▷late Middle English: from medieval Latin *desca*, probably based on Provençal *desca* 'basket' or Italian *desco* 'table, butcher's block,' both based on Latin *discus* (see DISCUS).

desk-bound ▸*adj.* restricted to working in an office, rather than in an active, physical capacity: *he is no desk-bound theoretician.*

desk dic·tion·ar·y ▸*n.* a one-volume dictionary of medium size.

de·skill /dē'skil/ ▸*v.* [*trans.*] reduce the level of skill required to carry out (a job): *advances in technology had deskilled numerous working-class jobs.* ■ make the skills of (a worker) obsolete.

desk job ▸*n.* a job based at a desk, esp. as opposed to one in active military or police service.

desk jock·ey ▸*n. informal, humorous* the holder of a desk job, especially an unimportant one. ▷on the pattern of *disc jockey*.

desk ser·geant ▸*n.* a sergeant in administrative charge of a police station.

desk·top /'desk,täp/ ▸*n.* the working surface of a desk. ■ [as *adj.*] denoting a piece of equipment such as a microcomputer that is suitable for use at an ordinary desk: *a desktop machine.* ■ a desktop computer. ■ the working area of a computer screen regarded as a representation of a notional desktop and containing icons representing items such as files and a wastebasket.

desk·top pub·lish·ing (abbr.: **DTP**) ▸*n.* the production of printed matter by means of a printer linked to a desktop computer, with special software. The system enables reports, advertising matter, company magazines, etc., to be produced cheaply with a layout and print quality similar to that of typeset books, for xerographic or other reproduction.

des·man /'desmən/ ▸*n.* a small, semiaquatic European mammal related to the mole, with a long, tubular muzzle and webbed toes. • Family Talpidae: the **Russian desman** (*Desmana moschata*) and the **Pyrenean desman** (*Galemys pyrenaicus*). ▷late 18th cent.: via French and German from Swedish *desman-råtta* 'muskrat,' from *desman* 'musk.'

des·mid /'dezmid/ ▸*n. Biology* a single-celled, freshwater alga that appears to be composed of two rigid cells with a shared nucleus. The presence of desmids is usually an indicator of unpolluted water. • Family Desmidiaceae, division Chlorophyta (or phylum Gamophyta, kingdom Protista). ▷mid 19th cent.: from modern Latin *Desmidium* (genus name), from Greek *desmos* 'band, chain' (because the algae are often found united in chains or masses).

des·moid /'dezmoid/ ▸*adj. Medicine* denoting a type of fibrous tumor of muscle and connective tissue, typically in the abdomen. ▷mid 19th cent.: from Greek *desmos* 'bond' or *desmē* 'bundle' + -OID.

Des Moines /di 'moin/ the capital of and the largest city in Iowa, in the southern central part of the state; pop. 198,682.

des·mo·some /'dezmə,sōm/ ▸*n. Biology* a structure by which two adjacent cells are attached, formed from protein plaques in the cell membranes linked by filaments. ▷1930s: from Greek *desmos* 'bond, chain' + -SOME[3]. **—des·mo·so·mal** /,dezmə'sōməl/ *adj.*

Des·na Riv·er /dyis'nä; də'snä/ a river in western Russia and Ukraine that rises east of Smolensk and flows for 550 miles (885 km) to enter the Dnieper River near Kiev.

des·o·late ▸*adj.* /'desəlit/ (of a place) deserted of people and in a state of bleak and dismal emptiness: *a desolate moor.* ■ feeling or showing misery, unhappiness, or loneliness: *I suddenly felt desolate and bereft.*
▸*v.* /'desə,lāt/ [*trans.*] make (a place) bleakly and depressingly empty or bare: *the droughts that desolated the dry plains.* ■ (usu. **be desolated**) make (someone) feel utterly wretched and unhappy: *he was desolated by the deaths of his treasured friends.* ▷late Middle English: from Latin *desolatus* 'abandoned,' past participle of *desolare*, from *de-* 'thoroughly' + *solus* 'alone.' **—des·o·late·ly** *adv.* **—des·o·late·ness** /-litnis/ *n.* **—des·o·la·tor** /-,lātər/ *n.*

des·o·la·tion /,desə'lāsHən/ ▸*n.* a state of complete emptiness or destruction: *the stony desolation of the desert.* See note at SOLITUDE. ■ anguished misery or loneliness: *in choked desolation, she watched him leave.* ▷late Middle English: from late Latin *desolatio(n-)*, from Latin *desolare* 'to abandon' (see DESOLATE).

de·sol·der /dē'sädər/ ▸*v.* [*trans.*] remove the solder from (electrical components), usually to effect separation: *cut the pins one by one on the component side, desolder the halves, then throw the chip out.*

de·sorb /dē'sôrb; -'zôrb/ ▸*v.* [*trans.*] *Chemistry* cause the release of (an adsorbed substance) from a surface. ■ [*intrans.*] (of an adsorbed substance) become released. ▷1920s: originally as *desorption* (from *de-* 'away' + *adsorption*), from which *desorb* is a back-formation. **—de·sorb·ent** /-bənt/ *adj.* & *n.* **—de·sorb·er** *n.* **—de·sorp·tion** /-'zôrpsHən; -'sôrp-/ *n.*

De So·to /də 'sōtō/ a city in northeastern Texas, south of Dallas; pop. 30,544.

de So·to /də 'sōtō/, Hernando (c.1496–1542), Spanish soldier and explorer. After serving as military commander of Nicaragua and of Peru, he landed in Florida in 1539 and explored much of what is now the southeastern U.S., as far west as Oklahoma. He died of a fever on the banks of the Mississippi River.

de·spair /di'spe(ə)r/ ▸*n.* the complete loss or absence of hope: ***driven to despair,*** *he throws himself under a train* | ***in despair,*** *I hit the bottle.*
▸*v.* [*intrans.*] lose or be without hope: *we should not despair* | *he was beginning to* ***despair of*** *ever knowing* | [as *adj.*] (**despairing**) *he gave a despairing little shrug.* ▷Middle English: the noun via Anglo-Norman French from Old French *desespeir*; the verb from Old French *desperer*, from Latin *desperare*, from *de-* 'down from' + *sperare* 'to hope.' **—des·pair·ing·ly** *adv.*
▸*PHRASE* □ **be the despair of** be the cause of a feeling of hopelessness in (someone else): *my handwriting was the despair of my teachers.*

des·patch ▸*v.* & *n.* variant spelling of DISPATCH.

des·per·a·do /,despə'rädō/ ▸*n.* (*pl.* **-does** or **-dos**) a desperate or reckless person, esp. a criminal. ▷early 17th cent.: pseudo-Spanish alteration of the obsolete noun *desperate*. Both *desperate* and *desperado* originally denoted a person in despair or in a desperate situation, hence someone made reckless by despair. **—des·per·a·do·ism** /-,izəm/ *n.*

des·per·ate /'desp(ə)rit/ ▸*adj.* feeling, showing, or involving a hopeless sense that a situation is so bad as to be impossible to deal with: *a desperate sadness enveloped Ruth.* ■ (of an act or attempt) tried in despair or when everything else has failed; having little hope of success: *drugs used in a desperate attempt to save his life.* ■ (of a situation) extremely bad, serious, or dangerous: *there is a desperate shortage of teachers.* ■ [*predic.*] (of a person) having a great need or desire for something: *I am* ***desperate for*** *a cigarette* | [with *infinitive*] *the government is desperate to clean up Rio's streets.* ■ (of a person or fight) violent or dangerous: *a desperate criminal* | *a desperate struggle.* ▷late Middle English (in the sense 'in despair'): from Latin *desperatus* 'deprived of hope,' past participle of *desperare* (see DESPAIR). **—des·per·ate·ness** *n.*
▸*PHRASE* □ **desperate diseases must have desperate remedies** *proverb* extreme measures are justified as a response to a difficult or dangerous situation.

des·per·ate·ly /'despəritlē/ ▸*adv.* in a way that shows despair: *he looked around desperately.* ■ used to emphasize the extreme degree of something: *he desperately needed a drink* | [as *submodifier*] *I am desperately disappointed.*

des·per·a·tion /,despə'rāsHən/ ▸*n.* a state of despair, typically one that results in rash or extreme behavior: *she wrote to him* ***in desperation.*** ▷late Middle English: from Old French, from Latin *desperatio(n-)*, from the verb *desperare* (see DESPAIR).

des·pi·ca·ble /di'spikəbəl/ ▸*adj.* deserving hatred and contempt: *a despicable crime.* ▷mid 16th cent.: from late Latin *despicabilis*, from *despicari* 'look down on.' **—des·pi·ca·bly** /-blē/ *adv.*

de Spi·no·za /də spi'nōzə/, Baruch, see SPINOZA.

de·spise /di'spīz/ ▸*v.* [*trans.*] feel contempt or a deep repugnance for: *he* ***despised*** *himself* ***for*** *being selfish.* ▷Middle English: from Old French *despire*, from Latin *despicere*, from *de-* 'down' + *specere* 'look at.' **—de·spis·er** *n.*

> ***THE RIGHT WORD*** **abhor, contemn, despise, detest, disdain, loathe, scorn**
>
> It's one thing to dislike someone; it's quite another to **despise** or **detest** the person. Both are strong words, used to describe extreme dislike or hatred.
>
> *Detest* is probably the purest expression of hatred (*she detested the woman who had raised her, and longed to find her own mother*), while *despise* suggests looking down with great contempt and regarding the person as mean, petty, weak, or worthless (*he despised men whose only concern was their own safety*).
>
> **Disdain** carries even stronger connotations of superiority, often combined with self-righteousness (*to disdain anyone lacking a college education*).
>
> **Scorn** is a stronger word for *disdain*, and it implies an attitude of not only contempt but of haughty rejection or refusal (*to scorn the woman he'd once loved*).
>
> To **loathe** something is to feel utter disgust toward it (*he grew to loathe peanut butter and jelly sandwiches*) and to **abhor** it is to feel a profound, shuddering, repugnance (*she abhorred the very idea of asking her husband for the money*).
>
> **Contemn** is a more literary word meaning to treat with disdain, scorn, or contempt.

de·spite /di'spīt/ ▸*prep.* without being affected by; in spite of: *he remains a great leader despite age and infirmity.*
▸*n. archaic or poetic/literary* **1** outrage; injury: *the despite done by him to the holy relics.* **2** contempt; disdain: *the theater only earns my despite.* ▷Middle English (originally used as a noun meaning 'contempt, scorn' in the phrase *in despite of*): from Old French *despit*, from Latin *despectus* 'looking down on,' past participle (used as a noun) of *despicere* (see DESPISE). **—de·spite·ful** /-fəl/ *adj.* (*archaic* or *poetic/literary*).
▸*PHRASES* □ **despite** (or **in despite**) **of** *archaic* in spite of. □ **despite oneself** used to indicate that one did not intend or expect to do the thing mentioned: *despite herself Fran felt a ripple of appreciation for his beauty.*

Des Plaines /des 'plānz/ a city in northeastern Illinois, northwest of Chicago; pop. 53,223.

de·spoil /di'spoil/ ▸*v.* [*trans.*] (often **be despoiled**) steal or violently remove valuable or attractive possessions from; plunder: *the church was* ***despoiled of*** *its marble wall covering.* See note at RAVAGE. ▷Middle English: from Old French *despoillier*, from Latin *despoliare* 'rob, plunder' (from *spolia* 'spoil'). **—de·spoil·er** *n.* **—de·spoil·ment** *n.* **—de·spo·li·a·tion** /-,spōlē'āsHən/ *n.*

de·spond /di'spänd/ ▸*v.* [*intrans.*] *archaic* become dejected and lose confidence.
▸*n.* a state of unhappiness and low spirits. ▷mid 17th cent.: from Latin *despondere* 'give up, abandon,' from *de-* 'away' + *spondere* 'to promise.' The word was originally used as a noun in SLOUGH OF DESPOND.

de·spond·en·cy /di'spändənsē/ ▸*n.* a state of low spirits caused by loss of hope or courage: *he hinted at his own deep despondency.* **—de·spond·ence** /-dəns/ *n.*

de·spond·ent /di'spändənt/ ▸*adj.* in low spirits from loss of hope or courage. **—de·spond·ent·ly** *adv.*

des·pot /'despət/ ▸*n.* a ruler or other person who holds absolute power, typically one who exercises it in a cruel or oppressive way. ▷mid 16th cent.: from French *despote*, via medieval Latin from Greek *despotēs* 'master, absolute ruler.' Originally (after the Turkish conquest of Constantinople) the term denoted a petty Christian ruler under the Turkish empire. The current sense dates from the late 18th cent. **—des·pot·ic** /di'spätik/ *adj.* **—des·pot·i·cal·ly** /di'spätik(ə)lē/ *adv.*

des·pot·ism /'despə,tizəm/ ▸*n.* the exercise of absolute power, esp. in a cruel and oppressive way: *the King's arbitrary despotism.* ■ a country or political system where the ruler holds absolute power. ▷early 18th cent.: from French *despotisme*, from *despote* (see DESPOT).

des·qua·mate /'deskwə,māt/ ▸*v.* [*intrans.*] (of a layer of cells, e.g., of the skin) come off in scales or flakes: [as *adj.*] (**desquamated**) *desquamated cells.* ▷early 18th cent. (in the sense 'remove the scales from'): from Latin *desquamat-* 'scaled,' from the verb *desquamare*, from *de-* 'away from' + *squama* 'a scale.' **—des·qua·ma·tion** /,deskwə'māsʜən/ *n.* **—des·qua·ma·tive** /-,mātiv/ *adj.*

des·sert /di'zərt/ ▸*n.* the sweet course eaten at the end of a meal: *a dessert of chocolate mousse.* ▷mid 16th cent.: from French, past participle of *desservir* 'clear the table,' from *des-* (expressing removal) + *servir* 'to serve.'

des·sert·spoon /di'zərt,spo͞on/ ▸*n.* a spoon used for dessert, smaller than a tablespoon and larger than a teaspoon. ■ the amount held by such a spoon. **—des·sert·spoon·ful** /-fo͝ol/ *n.* (*pl.* **-fuls**) .

des·sert wine ▸*n.* a sweet wine drunk with or following dessert.

de·sta·bi·lize /dē'stābə,līz/ ▸*v.* [*trans.*] upset the stability of; cause unrest in: *the discovery of an affair can destabilize a relationship.* **—de·sta·bi·li·za·tion** /-,stābələ'zāsʜən/ *n.*

de Staël /də 'stäl/, Madame (1766–1817), French novelist and critic; a precursor of the French romantics; born *Anne Louise Germaine Necker*. Her critical work, *De l'Allemagne* (1810), introduced late 18th-century German writers and thinkers to France.

de·stain /dē'stān/ ▸*v.* [*trans.*] *Biology* selectively remove stain from (a specimen for microscopy, a chromatography gel, etc.) after it has previously been stained.

de-Sta·lin·i·za·tion /dē ,stälənə'zāsʜən/ ▸*n.* (in communist countries) the policy of eradicating the memory or influence of Joseph Stalin and Stalinism, esp. after 1956.

De Stijl /də 'stīl/ a 20th-century Dutch art movement founded in 1917 by Theo van Doesburg (1883–1931) and Piet Mondrian. The movement favored an abstract, economical style. It was influential on the Bauhaus and constructivist movements. ▷Dutch, literally 'the style,' originally the name of the movement's periodical.

des·ti·na·tion /,destə'nāsʜən/ ▸*n.* the place to which someone or something is going or being sent: *a popular destination for golfers.*
▸*adj.* being a place that people will make a special trip to visit: *a destination restaurant.* ▷late Middle English: from Latin *destinatio(n-)*, from *destinare* 'make firm, establish.' The original sense was 'the action of intending someone or something for a particular purpose,' later 'being destined for a particular place,' hence (from the early 19th cent.) the place itself.

des·ti·na·tion charge ▸*n.* a fee added to the price of a new car to cover the cost of shipping the vehicle from the manufacturer to the dealer.

des·tine /'destin/ ▸*v.* [*trans.*] intend or choose (someone or something) for a particular purpose or end. ▷Middle English (in the sense 'predetermine, decree'): from Old French *destiner*, from Latin *destinare* 'make firm, establish.'

des·tined /'destind/ ▸*adj.* [*predic.*] (of a person's future) developing as though according to a plan: *she could see that he was **destined for** great things* | [with *infinitive*] *they were destined to become diplomats.* ■ (**destined to**) certain to meet (a particular fate): *she was destined to become a life-long friend.* ■ (**destined for**) intended for or traveling toward (a particular place): *a shipment of steel tubes destined for Iraq.* ■ [*attrib.*] preordained: *your heroine will be united with her destined mate.*

des·ti·ny /'destinē/ ▸*n.* (*pl.* **-nies**) the events that will necessarily happen to a particular person or thing in the future: *she was unable to control her own destiny.* ■ the hidden power believed to control what will happen in the future; fate: *he believes in destiny.* ▷Middle English: from Old French *destinee*, from Latin *destinata*, feminine past participle of *destinare* 'make firm, establish.'

des·ti·tute /'desti,t(y)o͞ot/ ▸*adj.* without the basic necessities of life: *the charity cares for destitute children.* ■ [*predic.*] (**destitute of**) not having: *towns destitute of commerce.* ▷late Middle English (in the sense 'deserted, abandoned, empty'): from Latin *destitutus*, past participle of *destituere* 'forsake,' from *de-* 'away from' + *statuere* 'to place.' **—des·ti·tu·tion** /,desti't(y)o͞osʜən/ *n.*

de-stress /dē'stres/ ▸*v.* [*intrans.*] relax after a period of work or tension.

des·tri·er /'destrēər/ ▸*n.* a medieval knight's warhorse. ▷Middle English: from Old French, based on Latin *dextera* 'the right hand,' from *dexter* 'on the right' (because the squire led the knight's horse with his right hand).

de·stroy /di'stroi/ ▸*v.* [*trans.*] put an end to the existence of (something) by damaging or attacking it: *the room had been destroyed by fire.* ■ completely ruin or spoil (something): *she had destroyed his dreams.* ■ ruin (someone) emotionally or spiritually: *he has been determined to destroy her.* ■ defeat (someone) utterly: *the Tigers destroyed the Padres in five games.* ■ (usu. **be destroyed**) kill (a sick, savage, or unwanted animal) by humane means: *their terrier was destroyed after the attack.* ▷Middle English: from Old French *destruire*, based on Latin *destruere*, from *de-* (expressing reversal) + *struere* 'build.'

THE RIGHT WORD **annihilate, demolish, destroy, eradicate, exterminate, extirpate, raze**

If you're interested in getting rid of something, you've got a number of options at your disposal.

Destroy is a general term covering any force that wrecks, ruins, kills, etc. (*to destroy an ant hill by pouring boiling water on it*).

If it's a building, you'll want to **demolish** or **raze** it, two words that are generally applied only to very large things.

Raze is used almost exclusively with structures; it means to bring something down to the level of the ground (*they razed the apartment building to make way for the new hospital*).

Demolish implies pulling or smashing something to pieces; when used with regard to buildings, it conjures up a vision of complete wreckage and often a heap of rubble (*their new house was demolished by the first hurricane of the season*). But unlike *raze*, *demolish* can also be applied to nonmaterial things (*to demolish the theory with a few simple experiments*).

If you **eradicate** something, you eliminate it completely, literally or figuratively, pull it out by the roots (*to eradicate smallpox with a vaccine*) and prevent its reappearance.

Extirpate, like *eradicate*, implies the utter destruction of something (*the species was extirpated from the park by the flooding*).

If you're dealing with cockroaches, you'll probably want to **exterminate** them, which means to wipe out or kill in great numbers.

Or better yet, you'll want to **annihilate** them, which is the most extreme word in this group and literally means to reduce to nothingness.

de·stroy·er /di'stroiər/ ▸*n.* a small, fast warship, esp. one equipped for a defensive role against submarines and aircraft. ■ someone or something that destroys: *the greatest destroyer of love and peace.*

de·stroy·ing an·gel ▸*n.* a deadly poisonous white toadstool that grows in woodlands and is native to both Eurasia and North America. • *Amanita virosa*, family Amanitaceae, class Hymenomycetes.

de·struct /di'strəkt/ ▸*v.* [*trans.*] cause deliberate, irreparable damage to (something, typically a rocket or missile).
▸*n.* [in *sing.*] [usu. as *adj.*] the deliberate causing of terminal damage: *he had ordered him to go for the destruct button.* ▷1950s: back-formation from DESTRUCTION.

de·struct·i·ble /di'strəktəbəl/ ▸*adj.* able to be destroyed. ▷mid 18th cent. (earlier in *indestructible*): from French, from late Latin *destructibilis*, from Latin *destruct-* 'destroyed,' from the verb *destruere* (see DESTROY). **—de·struct·i·bil·i·ty** /-,strəktə'bilitē/ *n.*

de·struc·tion /di'strəksʜən/ ▸*n.* the action or process of causing so much damage to something that it no longer exists or cannot be repaired: *the destruction of the library in Alexandria* | *the avalanche left a trail of destruction.* ■ the action or process of killing or being killed: *weapons of mass destruction.* ■ the ruination or ending of a system or state of affairs: *the destruction of a traditional way of life.* ■ [in *sing.*] a cause of someone's ruin: *gambling was his destruction.* ▷Middle English: from Latin *destructio(n-)*, from the verb *destruere* (see DESTROY).

de·struc·tive /di'strəktiv/ ▸*adj.* causing great and irreparable harm or damage: *the destructive power of weapons.* ■ tending to refute or disparage; negative and unhelpful: *destructive criticism.* **—de·struc·tive·ly** *adv.* **—de·struc·tive·ness** *n.*

de·struc·tive dis·til·la·tion ▸*n.* *Chemistry* decomposition of a solid by heating it in a closed container and collecting the volatile constituents given off.

des·ue·tude /'deswi,t(y)o͞od/ ▸*n.* *formal* a state of disuse: *the docks **fell into desuetude**.* ▷early 17th cent. (in the sense 'cessation'): from French, from Latin *desuetudo*, from *desuet-* 'made unaccustomed,' from the verb *desuescere*, from *de-* (expressing reversal) + *suescere* 'be accustomed.'

de·sul·fu·rize /dē'səlf(y)ə,rīz/ (also **de·sul·phu·rize**) ▸*v.* [*trans.*] remove sulfur or sulfur compounds from (a substance). **—de·sul·fu·ri·za·tion** *n.* **—de·sul·fu·riz·er** *n.*

des·ul·to·ry /'desəl,tôrē/ ▸*adj.* lacking a plan, purpose, or enthusiasm: *a few people were left, dancing in a desultory fashion.* ■ (of conversation or speech) going constantly from one subject to another in a half-hearted way; unfocused: *the desultory conversation faded.* ■ occurring randomly or occasionally: *desultory passengers were appearing.* ▷late 16th cent. (also in the literal sense 'skipping around'): from Latin *desultorius* 'superficial' (literally 'relating to a vaulter'), from *desultor* 'vaulter,' from the verb *desilire*. **—des·ul·to·ri·ly** /-,tôrəlē/ *adv.* **—des·ul·to·ri·ness** *n.*

de·su·per·heat·er /dē'so͞opər,hētər/ ▸*n.* a container for reducing the temperature of steam to make it less superheated.

de·syn·chro·nize /dē'sɪɴgkrə,nīz/ ▸*v.* [*trans.*] disturb the synchronization of; put out of step or phase. **—de·syn·chro·ni·za·tion** /-,sɪɴgkrənə'zāsʜən/ *n.*

de·tach /di'tacʜ/ ▸*v.* [*trans.*] **1** disengage (something or part of something) and remove it: *he **detached** the front lamp **from** its bracket* | *figurative federal strings need to be detached to restore parental authority.* ■ [*intrans.*] be easily removable: *the screen **detaches from** the keyboard.* ■ (**detach oneself from**) leave or separate oneself from (a group or place): *a figure in brown detached itself from the shadows.* ■ (**detach oneself from**) avoid or put an end to any connection or association with: *the newspaper detached itself from the political parties.* **2** (usu. **be detached**) *Military* send (a group of soldiers or ships) on a separate mission: *our crew was detached to Puerto Rico for the exercise.* ▷late 16th cent. (in the sense 'discharge a gun'): from French *détacher*, earlier *destacher*, from *des-* (expressing reversal) + *attacher* 'attach.' **—de·tach·a·bil·i·ty** /-,tacʜə'bilitē/ *n.* **—de·tach·a·ble** *adj.*

de·tached /di'tacʜt/ ▸*adj.* separate or disconnected, in particular: ■ (of a house or other building) not joined to another on either side: *a four-bedroom detached house.* ■ aloof and objective: *he managed to remain **detached from** petty politics.* **—de·tach·ed·ly** /-cʜidlē/ *adv.*

de·tached ret·i·na ▸*n.* a retina that has become separated from the underlying choroid tissue at the back of the eye, causing loss of vision in the affected area.

de·tach·ment /di'tacʜmənt/ ▸*n.* **1** the state of being objective or aloof: *he felt a sense of detachment from what was going on.* **2** *Military* a group of troops, aircraft, or ships sent away on a separate mission: *a detachment of Marines* | *the battallion went **on detachment** to Florida.* ■ a party of people similarly separated from a larger group: *a truck containing a detachment of villagers.* **3** the action or process of detaching; separation: *structural problems resulted in cracking and detachment of the wall.* ▷mid 17th cent.: from French *détachement*, from *détacher* 'to detach' (see DETACH).

de·tail /di'tāl; 'dētāl/ ▸*n.* **1** an individual feature, fact, or item: *we shall consider every detail of the bill* | *her meticulous **attention to detail**.* ■ a minor or less significant item or feature: *he didn't want them to get sidetracked on a detail of policy.* ■ a minor decorative feature of a building or work of art: *a detail on Charlemagne's tomb.* ■ the style or treatment of such features: *the classical French detail of the building's facade.* ■ a small part of a picture or other work of art reproduced separately for close study: *detail of right eye showing marks on the lids.* ■ (**details**) *Brit.* itemized facts or information about someone; personal particulars: *the official asked for my father's details.* **2** a small detachment of troops or police officers given a special duty: *the candidate's security detail.* ■ [often with *adj.*] a special duty assigned to such a detachment.

Pronunciation Key ə *ago*; ər *over*; 'ə or ,ə *up*; 'ər or ,ər *fur*; a *hat*; ā *rate*; ä *car*; cʜ *chew*; e *let*; ē *see*; e(ə)r *air*; i *fit*; ī *by*; i(ə)r *ear*; ɴɢ *sing*; ō *go*; ô *for*; oi *boy*; o͝o *good*; o͞o *goo*; ou *out*; sʜ *she*; ᴛʜ *thin*; T͟H *then*; (h)w *why*; ᴢʜ *vision*

D

▸*v.* [*trans.*] **1** describe item by item; give the full particulars of: *the report details the environmental and health costs of the car.* **2** [*trans.*] assign (someone) to undertake a particular task: *the ships were detailed to keep watch.* **3** clean (a motor vehicle) intensively and minutely: *the Buick dealer gave him a job washing and detailing cars.* ▷early 17th cent. (in the sense 'minor items or events regarded collectively'): from French *détail* (noun), *détailler* (verb), from *dé-* (expressing separation) + *tailler* 'to cut' (based on Latin *talea* 'twig, cutting'). **—de·tail·er** *n.* (in sense 3 of the *verb*).
▸*PHRASES* □ **go into detail** give a full account of something. □ **in detail** as regards every feature or aspect; fully: *we will have to examine the proposals in detail.*

de·tailed /di'tāld; 'dē,tāld/ ▸*adj.* having many details or facts; showing attention to detail: *more detailed information was needed.* ■ (of a work of art) executed with many minor decorative features: *an exquisitely detailed carving.*

de·tail·ing /'dētāliNG/ ▸*n.* small, decorative features on a building, garment, or work of art.

de·tain /di'tān/ ▸*v.* [*trans.*] keep (someone) in official custody, typically for questioning about a crime or in politically sensitive situations: *she was detained without trial for two years.* ■ keep (someone) from proceeding; hold back: *she made to open the door, but he detained her.* ▷late Middle English (in the sense 'be afflicted with sickness or infirmity'): from Old French *detenir*, from a variant of Latin *detinere*, from *de-* 'away, aside' + *tenere* 'to hold.' **—de·tain·ment** *n.*

de·tain·ee /di,tā'nē; ,dētā'nē/ ▸*n.* a person held in custody, esp. for political reasons.

de·tain·er /di'tānər; dē-/ ▸*n.* **1** *Law* the action of detaining or withholding property. ■ the detention of a person in custody. ■ an order authorizing the continued detention of a person in custody. **2** *chiefly Law* a person who detains someone or something. ▷early 17th cent.: from Anglo-Norman French *detener* 'detain' (used as a noun), variant of Old French *detenir* (see **DETAIN**).

de·tan·gle /dē'taNGgəl/ ▸*v.* [*trans.*] remove tangles from (hair).

de·tect /di'tekt/ ▸*v.* [*trans.*] discover or identify the presence or existence of: *cancer may soon be detected in its earliest stages.* ■ discover or investigate (a crime or its perpetrators): *the public can help the police to detect crime.* ■ discern (something intangible or barely perceptible): *Paul detected a faint note of weariness in his father's voice.* ▷late Middle English: from Latin *detect-* 'uncovered,' from the verb *detegere*, from *de-* (expressing reversal) + *tegere* 'to cover.' The original senses were 'uncover, expose' and 'give someone away,' later 'expose the real or hidden nature of something or someone'; hence the current senses (partly influenced by **DETECTIVE**). **—de·tect·a·ble** *adj.* **—de·tect·a·bly** /-əblē/ *adv.*

de·tec·tion /di'tekSHən/ ▸*n.* the action or process of identifying the presence of something concealed: *the early detection of fetal abnormalities.* ■ the work of a detective in investigating a crime: [as *adj.*] *the detection rate for murder is over 90 percent* ■ another term for **DEMODULATION** (see **DEMODULATE**). ▷late 15th cent. (in the sense 'revelation of what is concealed'): from late Latin *detectio(n-)*, from Latin *detegere* 'uncover' (see **DETECT**).

de·tec·tive /di'tektiv/ ▸*n.* a person, esp. a police officer, whose occupation is to investigate and solve crimes. ■ [as *adj.*] denoting a particular rank of police officer: *Detective Sergeant Fox.* ■ [as *adj.*] concerning crime and its investigation: *detective work.* ▷mid 19th cent.: from **DETECT**, on the pattern of pairs such as *elect, elective*. The noun was originally short for *detective policeman*, from an adjectival use of the word in the sense 'serving to detect.'

de·tec·tive sto·ry (also **detective novel**) ▸*n.* a story whose plot revolves around the investigation and solving of a crime.

de·tec·tor /di'tektər/ ▸*n.* [often with *adj.*] a device or instrument designed to detect the presence of a particular object or substance and to emit a signal in response: *methane detectors.* ■ another term for **DEMODULATOR** (see **DEMODULATE**).

de·tent /di'tent/ ▸*n.* a catch in a machine that prevents motion until released. ■ (in a clock) a catch that regulates striking. ▷late 17th cent. (denoting a catch in clocks and watches): from French *détente*, from Old French *destente*, from *destendre* 'slacken,' from *des-* (expressing reversal) + Latin *tendere* 'to stretch.'

dé·tente /dā'tänt/ (also **de·tente**) ▸*n.* the easing of hostility or strained relations, esp. between countries: *a serious effort at détente with the eastern bloc.* ▷early 20th cent.: French, literally 'loosening, relaxation.'

de·ten·tion /di'tenSHən/ ▸*n.* the action of detaining someone or the state of being detained in official custody, esp. as a political prisoner: *he committed suicide while in police detention.* ■ the punishment of being kept in school after hours: *he has made students fear after-school detention | arbitrary after-school detentions.* ▷late Middle English (in the sense 'withholding of what is claimed or due'): from late Latin *detentio(n-)*, from Latin *detinere* 'hold back' (see **DETAIN**).

de·ten·tion cen·ter ▸*n.* an institution where people are held in detention for short periods, in particular illegal immigrants, refugees, people awaiting trial or sentence, or youthful offenders.

de·ter /di'tər/ ▸*v.* (**-terred, -ter·ring**) [*trans.*] discourage (someone) from doing something, typically by instilling doubt or fear of the consequences: *only a health problem would* **deter** *him* **from** *seeking reelection.* ■ prevent the occurrence of: *strategists think not only about how to deter war, but about how war might occur.* ▷mid 16th cent.: from Latin *deterrere*, from *de-* 'away from' + *terrere* 'frighten.'

de·terge /di'tərj/ ▸*v.* [*trans.*] *rare* cleanse thoroughly. ▷early 17th cent.: from French *déterger* or Latin *detergere* 'wipe away.'

de·ter·gent /di'tərjənt/ ▸*n.* a water-soluble cleansing agent that combines with impurities and dirt to make them more soluble and differs from soap in not forming a scum with the salts in hard water. ■ any additive with a similar action, e.g., an oil-soluble substance that holds dirt in suspension in lubricating oil.
▸*adj.* of or relating to such compounds or their action: *staining that resists detergent action.* ▷early 17th cent. (as an adjective): from Latin *detergent-* 'wiping away,' from the verb *detergere*, from *de-* 'away from' + *tergere* 'to wipe.' **—de·ter·gence** *n.* **—de·ter·gen·cy** *n.*

de·te·ri·o·rate /di'ti(ə)rēə,rāt/ ▸*v.* [*intrans.*] become progressively worse: *relations between the countries had deteriorated sharply* | [as *adj.*] (**deteriorating**) *deteriorating economic conditions.* ▷late 16th cent. (used transitively in the sense 'make worse'): from late Latin *deteriorat-* 'worsened,' from the verb *deteriorare*, from Latin *deterior* 'worse.' **—de·te·ri·o·ra·tion** /-,ti(ə)rēə'rāSHən/ *n.* **—de·te·ri·o·ra·tive** /-,rātiv/ *adj.*

de·ter·mi·na·ble /di'tərminəbəl/ ▸*adj.* **1** able to be firmly decided or definitely ascertained: *a readily determinable market value.* **2** *Law* capable of being brought to an end under given conditions; terminable. ▷late Middle English: via Old French from late Latin *determinabilis* 'finite,' from the verb *determinare* (see **DETERMINE**).

de·ter·mi·nant /di'tərminənt/ ▸*n.* **1** a factor that decisively affects the nature or outcome of something: *pure force of will was the main determinant of his success.* ■ *Biology* a gene or other factor that determines the character and development of a cell or group of cells in an organism, a set of which forms an individual's idiotype. **2** *Mathematics* a quantity obtained by the addition of products of the elements of a square matrix according to a given rule.
▸*adj.* serving to determine or decide something. ▷early 17th cent.: from Latin *determinant-* 'determining,' from the verb *determinare* (see **DETERMINE**).

de·ter·mi·nate /də'tərmənit/ ▸*adj.* having exact and discernible limits or form: *the phrase has lost any determinate meaning.* ■ *Botany* (of a flowering shoot) having the main axis ending in a flower bud and therefore no longer extending in length, as in a cyme. ▷late Middle English: from Latin *determinatus* 'limited, determined,' past participle of *determinare* (see **DETERMINE**). **—de·ter·mi·na·cy** /-minəsē/ *n.* **—de·ter·mi·nate·ly** *adv.* **—de·ter·mi·nate·ness** *n.*

de·ter·mi·na·tion /di,tərmə'nāSHən/ ▸*n.* **1** firmness of purpose; resoluteness: *he advanced with an unflinching determination.* **2** the process of establishing something exactly, typically by calculation or research: *determination of molecular structures.* ■ *Law* the settlement of a dispute by the authoritative decision of a judge or arbitrator. ■ *Law* a judicial decision or sentence. **3** the controlling or deciding of something's nature or outcome: *genetic sex determination.* **4** *Law* the cessation of an estate or interest. **5** *archaic* a tendency to move in a fixed direction. ▷late Middle English (in the senses 'settlement of a controversy by a judge or by reasoning' and 'authoritative opinion'): via Old French from Latin *determinatio(n-)*, from the verb *determinare* (see **DETERMINE**).

de·ter·mi·na·tive /də'tərmə,nātiv; -nətiv/ ▸*adj.* [*predic.*] *chiefly Law* serving to define, qualify, or direct: *the employer's view is not determinative of the issue.*
▸*n.* *Grammar* another term for **DETERMINER**.

de·ter·mine /di'tərmin/ ▸*v.* [*trans.*] **1** cause (something) to occur in a particular way; be the decisive factor in: *it will be her mental attitude that determines her future.* ■ firmly decide: [with *infinitive*] *she determined to tackle Stephen the next day* | [*intrans.*] *he* **determined on** *a withdrawal of his forces.* **2** ascertain or establish exactly, typically as a result of research or calculation: *our aim is to determine the electric field* | [with *clause*] *the point of our study was to* **determine what** *is true, not what is practicable.* ■ *Mathematics* specify the value, position, or form of (a mathematical or geometric object) uniquely. **3** *archaic Law* bring or come to an end. ▷late Middle English: from Old French *determiner*, from Latin *determinare* 'limit, fix,' from *de-* 'completely' + *terminare* 'terminate.'

de·ter·mined /di'tərmind/ ▸*adj.* having made a firm decision and being resolved not to change it: [with *infinitive*] *Alice was determined to be heard.* ■ processing or displaying resolve: *Helen was a determined little girl | a determined effort to reduce inflation.* See note at **RESOLUTE**. **—de·ter·mined·ly** *adv.* **—de·ter·mined·ness** *n.*

de·ter·min·er /di'tərminər/ ▸*n.* **1** a person or thing that determines or decides something. **2** *Grammar* a modifying word that determines the kind of reference a noun or noun group has, for example *a, the, every*. See also **DEFINITE ARTICLE, INDEFINITE ARTICLE**.

de·ter·min·ism /di'tərmə,nizəm/ ▸*n.* *Philosophy* the doctrine that all events, including human action, are ultimately determined by causes external to the will. Some philosophers have taken determinism to imply that individual human beings have no free will and cannot be held morally responsible for their actions. **—de·ter·min·ist** *n.* & *adj.* **—de·ter·min·is·tic** /-,tərmə'nistik/ *adj.* **—de·ter·min·is·ti·cal·ly** /-,tərmə'nistik(ə)lē/ *adv.*

de·ter·rent /di'tərənt/ ▸*n.* a thing that discourages or is intended to discourage someone from doing something. ■ a nuclear weapon or weapons system regarded as deterring an enemy from attack.
▸*adj.* able or intended to deter: *the deterrent effect of heavy prison sentences.* ▷early 19th cent.: from Latin *deterrent-* 'deterring,' from the verb *deterrere* (see **DETER**). **—de·ter·rence** *n.*

de·ter·ri·to·ri·al·i·za·tion /dē,teri,tôrēələ'zāSHən/ ▸*n.* the severance of social, political, or cultural practices from their native places and populations. **—de·ter·ri·to·ri·al·ize** *v.*

de·test /di'test/ ▸*v.* [*trans.*] dislike intensely: *democratic socialism was feared and detested by doctrinaire Marxists.* See note at **DESPISE**. ▷late 15th cent.: from Latin *detestari*, from *de-* 'down' + *testari* 'witness, call upon to witness' (from *testis* 'a witness'). **—de·test·er** *n.*

de·test·a·ble /di'testəbəl/ ▸*adj.* deserving intense dislike: *I found the film's violence detestable.* See note at **OFFENSIVE**. ▷late Middle English: from Old French, or from Latin *detestabilis*, from the verb *detestari* (see **DETEST**). **—de·test·a·bly** /-blē/ *adv.*

de·tes·ta·tion /,dēte'stāSHən/ ▸*n.* intense dislike: *Wordsworth's detestation of aristocracy.* ■ *archaic* a detested person or thing: *he is the detestation of the neighborhood.* ▷late Middle English: via Old French from Latin *detestatio(n-)*, from the verb *detestari* (see **DETEST**).

de·throne /dē'THrōn/ ▸*v.* [*trans.*] remove (a ruler, esp. a monarch) from power. ■ *figurative* remove from a position of authority or dominance: *he dethroned the defending title-holder.* **—de·throne·ment** *n.*

det·i·nue /'detn,(y)o͞o/ ▸*n.* *Law* a legal claim to recover wrongfully detained goods or possessions. ■ legal action against this. ▷late Middle English: from Old French *detenue*, past participle (used as a noun) of *detenir* 'detain.'

det·o·nate /'detn,āt/ ▸*v.* explode or cause to explode: [*intrans.*] *two other bombs failed to detonate* | [*trans.*] *a trigger that can detonate nuclear weapons.* ▷early 18th cent.: from Latin *detonat-* 'thundered down or forth,' from the verb *detonare*, from *de-* 'down' + *tonare* 'to thunder.' **—det·o·na·tive** /-,ātiv/ *adj.*

det·o·na·tion /,detn'āSHən/ ▸*n.* the action of causing a bomb or explosive device to explode. ■ a loud explosion: *a series of deafening detonations was heard.* ■ *technical* combustion of a substance that is initiated suddenly and propagates extremely rapidly, giving rise to a shock wave. Compare with **DEFLAGRATION**. ■ the premature combustion of fuel in an internal combustion engine, causing knocking. ▷late 17th cent.: from French *détonation*, from the verb *détoner*, from Latin *detonare* 'thunder down' (see **DETONATE**).

det·o·na·tor /'detn,ātər/ ▸*n.* a device or a small, sensitive charge used to detonate an explosive. ■ another term for **TORPEDO** (sense 1).

de·tor·sion /di'tôrsHən/ ▸*n. Zoology* (in gastropod mollusks) the evolutionary reversion of a group to a primitive linear body plan. Compare with **TORSION.**

de·tour /'dē,to͝or/ ▸*n.* a long or roundabout route taken to avoid something or to visit somewhere along the way: *he had **made a detour to** a cafe.* ■ an alternative route for use by traffic when the usual road is temporarily closed.
▸*v.* [*intrans.*] take a long or roundabout route: *he detoured around the walls.* ■ [*trans.*] avoid or bypass (something) by taking such a route: *I would detour the endless stream of motor homes.* ▷mid 18th cent. (as a noun): from French *détour* 'change of direction,' from *détourner* 'turn away.'

de·tox /'dētäks/ *informal* ▸*n.* short for **DETOXIFICATION**: *he ended up **in detox** for three months.*
▸*v.* short for **DETOXIFY.**

de·tox·i·cate /dē'täksi,kāt/ ▸*v.* another term for **DETOXIFY.** ▷mid 19th cent.: from **DE-** (expressing removal) + Latin *toxicum* 'poison,' on the pattern of *intoxicate.* **—de·tox·i·ca·tion** /-,täksi'kāsHən/ *n.*

de·tox·i·fi·ca·tion /dē,täksəfi'kāsHən/ ▸*n.* the process of removing toxic substances or qualities. ■ medical treatment of an alcoholic or drug addict involving abstention from drink or drugs until the bloodstream is free of toxins.

de·tox·i·fy /dē'täksə,fī/ ▸*v.* (**-fies, -fied**) [*trans.*] remove toxic substances or qualities from: *the process uses chemical reagents to detoxify the oil.* ■ (usu. **be detoxified**) treat (an alcoholic or drug addict) to remove the effects of drink or drugs in order to help them overcome addiction: *he was twice detoxified from heroin.* ■ [*intrans.*] abstain from drink and drugs until the bloodstream is free of toxins in order to overcome alcoholism or drug addiction. ■ [*intrans.*] become free of poisonous substances or qualities: *you can help your body detoxify by cutting down on coffee.* ▷early 20th cent.: from **DE-** (expressing removal) + Latin *toxicum* 'poison' + **-FY.** **—de·tox·i·fi·er** *n.*

de·tract /di'trakt/ ▸*v.* **1** [*intrans.*] (**detract from**) reduce or take away the worth or value of: *these quibbles in no way detract from her achievement.* ■ [*trans.*] deny or take away (a quality or achievement) so as to make its subject seem less impressive: *it detracts not one iota from the credit due to them.* **2** [*trans.*] (**detract someone/something from**) divert or distract (someone or something) away from: *the complaint was timed to detract attention from the ethics issue.* ▷late Middle English: from Latin *detract-* 'drawn away,' from the verb *detrahere,* from *de-* 'away from' + *trahere* 'draw.' **—de·trac·tion** /-'traksHən/ *n.* **—de·trac·tive** /-'traktiv/ *adj.*

de·trac·tor /di'traktər/ ▸*n.* a person who disparages someone or something.

de·train /dē'trān/ ▸*v.* [*intrans.*] leave a train. ■ [*trans.*] cause or assist to leave a train: *passengers were detrained because the train was on fire.* **—de·train·ment** *n.*

de·trib·al·ize /dē'trībə,līz/ ▸*v.* [*trans.*] [usu. as *adj.*] (**detribalized**) remove (someone) from a traditional tribal social structure: *the 250,000 Australian Aboriginals include many detribalized urban people.* ■ remove a traditional tribal social structure from (a culture). **—de·trib·al·i·za·tion** /-,trībələ'zāsHən/ *n.*

det·ri·ment /'detrəmənt/ ▸*n.* the state of being harmed or damaged: *he is engrossed in his work **to the detriment of** his married life.* ■ a cause of harm or damage: *such tests are **a detriment to** good education.* ▷late Middle English in the sense 'loss sustained by damage': from Old French, from Latin *detrimentum,* from *detri-,* stem of *deterere* 'wear away.'

det·ri·men·tal /,detrə'mentl/ ▸*adj.* tending to cause harm: *releasing the documents would be **detrimental to** national security* | *moving her could have a **detrimental effect on** her health.* **—det·ri·men·tal·ly** *adv.*

de·tri·tion /di'trisHən/ ▸*n. rare* the action of wearing away by friction. ▷late 17th cent.: from medieval Latin *detritio(n-),* from *detri-,* stem of *deterere* 'wear away.'

de·tri·ti·vore /di'tritə,vôr/ ▸*n. Zoology* an animal that feeds on dead organic material, esp. plant detritus. ▷1960s: from **DETRITUS** + *-vore* 'eating' (see **-VOROUS**). **—det·ri·tiv·or·ous** /,detrə'tivərəs/ *adj.*

de·tri·tus /di'trītəs/ ▸*n.* waste or debris of any kind: *streets filled with rubble and detritus.* ■ gravel, sand, silt, or other material produced by erosion. ■ organic matter produced by the decomposition of organisms. ▷late 18th cent. (in the sense 'detrition'): from French *détritus,* from Latin *detritus,* from *deterere* 'wear away.' **—de·tri·tal** /-təl/ *adj.*

De·troit /di'troit; 'dē,troit/ a major industrial city and Great Lakes shipping center in northeastern Michigan; pop. 951,270. It is the center of the U.S. automobile industry. In the 1960s, it was also an important center for rock and soul music.

de trop /də 'trō/ ▸*adj.* not wanted; unwelcome: *she had no grasp of the conversation and felt herself de trop.* ▷mid 18th cent.: French, literally 'excessive.'

de Troyes /də 'trwä/, Chrétien, see **CHRÉTIEN DE TROYES.**

de·tru·sor /di'tro͞ozər/ (also **detrusor muscle**) ▸*n. Anatomy* a muscle that forms a layer of the wall of the bladder. ▷mid 18th cent.: modern Latin, from Latin *detrus-* 'thrust down,' from the verb *detrudere.*

de·tu·mes·cence /,dēt(y)o͞o'mesəns/ ▸*n.* the process of subsiding from a state of tension, swelling, or (esp.) sexual arousal. ▷late 17th cent.: from Latin *detumescere,* from *de-* 'down, away'+ *tumescere* 'to swell.' **—de·tu·mesce** /-'mes/ *v.* **—de·tu·mes·cent** *adj.*

de·tune /dē't(y)o͞on/ ▸*v.* [*trans.*] cause (a musical instrument) to become out of tune. ■ [usu. as *adj.*] (**detuned**) reduce the performance or efficiency of (a motor vehicle or engine) by adjustment. ■ alter the wavelength of the light emitted by (a laser).

Deu·ca·li·on /d(y)o͞o'kālēən/ *Greek Mythology* the son of Prometheus.With his wife Pyrrha he survived a flood sent by Zeus to punish human wickedness; they were then instructed to throw stones over their shoulders, and these turned into humans to repopulate the world.

deuce[1] /d(y)o͞os/ ▸*n.* **1** a thing representing, or represented by, the number two, in particular: ■ the two on dice or playing cards. ■ a throw of two at dice. ■ *informal, dated* a two-dollar bill. **2** *Tennis* the tie score of 40-all in a game, at which a player needs two consecutive points to win the game. ▷late 15th cent.: from Old French *deus* 'two,' from Latin *duos.*

deuce[2] ▸*n.* (**the deuce**) *informal* used as a euphemism for "devil" in expressions of annoyance, impatience, or surprise or for emphasis: ***how the deuce** are we to make a profit?* | ***what the deuce** are you trying to do?* ▷mid 17th cent.: from Low German *duus,* probably of the same origin as **DEUCE**[1] (two aces at dice being the worst throw).
▸*PHRASE* □ **a** (or **the**) **deuce of a ——** used to emphasize how bad, difficult, or serious something is.

deuc·ed /'d(y)o͞osid/ *informal, dated* ▸*adj.* [*attrib.*] used for emphasis, esp. to express disapproval or frustration: *I know it's deuced awkward for you* | [as *submodifier*] *I'm so deuced fond of you.* **—deuc·ed·ly** *adv.* [as *submodifier*] *they're deucedly hard to find.*

de·us ex ma·chi·na /'dāəs eks 'mäkənə; -'mak-/ ▸*n.* an unexpected power or event saving a seemingly hopeless situation, esp. as a contrived plot device in a play or novel. ▷late 17th cent.: modern Latin, translation of Greek *theos ek mēkhanēs,* 'god from the machinery.' In Greek theater, actors representing gods were suspended above the stage, the denouement of the play being brought about by their intervention.

Deut. ▸*abbr. Bible* Deuteronomy.

deu·ter·ag·o·nist /,d(y)o͞otə'ragənist/ ▸*n.* the person second in importance to the protagonist in a drama. ▷mid 19th cent.: from Greek *deuteragōnistēs,* from *deuteros* 'second' + *agōnistēs* 'actor.'

deu·ter·a·nope /'d(y)o͞otərə,nōp/ ▸*n.* a person suffering from deuteranopia.

deu·ter·a·no·pi·a /,d(y)o͞otərə'nōpēə/ ▸*n.* color-blindness resulting from insensitivity to green light, causing confusion of greens, reds, and yellows. Compare with **PROTANOPIA.** ▷early 20th cent.: from **DEUTERO-** 'second' (the color green being regarded as the second component of color vision) + **AN-**[1] + **-OPIA.**

deu·ter·at·ed /'d(y)o͞otə,rātid/ (also **deu·te·ri·at·ed** /d(y)o͞o'ti(ə)rē,ātid/) ▸*adj. Chemistry* (of a compound) in which the ordinary isotope of hydrogen has been replaced with deuterium. **—deu·ter·a·tion** /,d(y)o͞otə'rāsHən/ *n.*

deu·ter·ic /d(y)o͞o'terik/ ▸*n. Geology* relating to or denoting alteration of the minerals of an igneous rock during the later stages of consolidation. ▷early 20th cent.: from **DEUTERO-** 'secondary' + **-IC.**

deu·te·ri·um /d(y)o͞o'ti(ə)rēəm/ ▸*n. Chemistry* a stable isotope of hydrogen with a mass approximately twice that of the usual isotope. (Symbol: **D**)

> Deuterium atoms have a neutron as well as a proton in the nucleus, and the isotope is present to about 1 part in 6,000 in naturally occurring hydrogen. It is used as a fuel in thermonuclear bombs, and heavy water (D_2O) is used as a moderator in nuclear reactors.

▷1930s: modern Latin, from Greek *deuteros* 'second.'

deutero- ▸*comb. form* second: *Deutero-Isaiah.* ■ secondary: *deuterocanonical.* ▷from Greek *deuteros* 'second.'

deu·ter·o·ca·non·i·cal /,d(y)o͞otə,rōkə'nänikəl/ ▸*adj.* (of sacred books or literary works) forming a secondary canon.

Deu·ter·o-I·sa·iah /,d(y)o͞otə,rō ,ī'zāə/ the supposed later author of Isaiah 40–55.

deu·ter·on /'d(y)o͞otə,rän/ ▸*n.* the nucleus of a deuterium atom, consisting of a proton and a neutron. ▷1930s: from Greek *deuteros* 'second,' on the pattern of *proton.*

Deu·ter·on·o·my /,d(y)o͞otə'ränəmē/ the fifth book of the Bible, containing a recapitulation of the Ten Commandments and much of the Mosaic law.

Deutsch·land /'doicH,länt/ German name for **GERMANY.**

Deutsch·mark /'doicH,märk/ (also **Deutsch·e Mark** /'doicHə/) ▸*n.* the basic monetary unit of Germany (until the introduction of the euro), equal to 100 pfennigs. ▷mid 20th cent.: from German *deutsche Mark* 'German mark.'

deut·zi·a /'d(y)o͞otsēə/ ▸*n.* an ornamental shrub with white or pinkish flowers native to Asia and Central America. • Genus *Deutzia,* family Hydrangeaceae. ▷modern Latin, named after Johann van der *Deutz,* 18th-cent. Dutch patron of botany.

de·va /'dāvə/ ▸*n.* a member of a class of divine beings in the Vedic period, which in Indian religion are benevolent and in Zoroastrianism are evil. Compare with **ASURA.** ■ *Indian* (in general use) a god. ▷early 19th cent.: Sanskrit, literally 'shining one,' later 'god.'

de·va·da·si /,dāvə'däsē/ ▸*n.* (*pl.* **-sis** /-sēz/) a hereditary female dancer and courtesan in a Hindu temple. ▷from Sanskrit *devadāsī,* literally 'female servant of a god.'

de Va·le·ra /,devə'lerə; ,dā-/, Eamon (1882–1975), Irish statesman; born in the U.S., taoiseach (prime minister) 1937–48, 1951–54, and 1957–59 and president of the Republic of Ireland 1959–73. He was the leader of Sinn Fein 1917–26 and the founder of the Fianna Fáil Party in 1926. As president of the Irish Free State from 1932, de Valera was largely responsible for the new constitution of 1937 that created the state of Eire.

de·val·or·ize /dē'valə,rīz/ ▸*v.* [*trans.*] *rare* devalue. ▷early 20th cent.: from French *dévaloriser.* **—de·val·or·i·za·tion** /-,valərə'zāsHən/ *n.*

de·val·ue /dē'valyo͞o/ ▸*v.* (**-val·ues, -val·ued, -val·u·ing**) [*trans.*] reduce or underestimate the worth or importance of: *I resent the way people seem to devalue my achievement.* ■ (often **be devalued**) *Economics* reduce the official value of (a currency) in relation to other currencies: *the dinar was devalued by 20 percent.* **—de·val·u·a·tion** /,dēvalyo͞o'āsHən/ *n.*

De·va·na·ga·ri /,dävə'nägərē/ ▸*n.* the alphabet used for Sanskrit, Hindi, and other Indian languages. ▷late 18th cent.: Sanskrit, literally 'divine town script,' from *deva* 'god' + *nāgarī* (from *nagara* 'town'), an earlier name of the script.

dev·as·tate /'devə,stāt/ ▸*v.* [*trans.*] destroy or ruin (something): *the city was devastated by a huge earthquake* | *bad weather has devastated the tourist industry.* See note at **RAVAGE.** ■ cause (someone) severe and overwhelming shock or grief: *she was devastated by the loss of Damian.* ▷mid 17th cent.: from Latin *devastat-* 'laid waste,' from the verb *devastare,* from *de-* 'thoroughly' + *vastare* 'lay waste.' **—dev·as·ta·tion** /,devə'stāsHən/ *n.* **—dev·as·ta·tor** /-,stātər/ *n.*

dev·as·tat·ing /'devə,stātiNG/ ▸*adj.* highly destructive or damaging: *a devastating cyclone struck Bangladesh.* ■ causing severe shock, distress, or grief: *the news came as a devastating blow.* ■ *informal* extremely impressive, effective, or attractive: *she had a devastating wit.* **—dev·as·tat·ing·ly** *adv.* [as *submodifier*] *a devastatingly attractive man.*

de·vein /dē'vān/ ▸*v.* [*trans.*] remove the main central vein from (a shrimp or prawn).

de·vel·op /di'veləp/ ▸*v.* (**-vel·oped, -vel·op·ing**) **1** grow or cause to grow and become more mature, advanced, or elaborate: See note at **MATURE.** [*intrans.*] *motion pictures **developed into** mass entertainment* | [as *adj.*] (**developing**) *this is a rapidly developing field* | [*trans.*] *entrepreneurs develop their skills through trial and error.* ■ [*intrans.*] [often as *adj.*] (**developing**) (of a poor agricultural country) become more economically

Pronunciation Key ə *ago;* ər *over;* 'ə *or* ,ə *up;* 'ər *or* ,ər *fur;* a *hat;* ā *rate;* ä *car;* CH *chew;* e *let;* ē *see;* e(ə)r *air;* i *fit;* ī *by;* i(ə)r *ear;* NG *sing;* ō *go;* ô *for;* oi *boy;* o͝o *good;* o͞o *goo;* ou *out;* SH *she;* TH *thin;* TH *then;* (h)w *why;* ZH *vision*

and socially advanced: *the developing world.* ■ [*trans.*] convert (land) to a new purpose by constructing buildings or making other use of its resources. ■ construct or convert (a building) so as to improve existing resources. ■ [*trans.*] elaborate (a musical theme) by modification of the melody, harmony, or rhythm. ■ [*trans.*] *Chess* bring (a piece) into play from its initial position on a player's back rank. ■ *Geometry* [*trans.*] convert (a curved surface) conceptually into a plane figure as if by unrolling. ■ [*trans.*] *Mathematics* expand (a function, etc.) in the form of a series. **2** start to exist, experience, or possess: [*intrans.*] *a strange closeness developed* | [*trans.*] *I developed an interest in law* | [*trans.*] *AIDS patients often develop a rare type of cancer.* **3** [*trans.*] treat (a photographic film) with chemicals to make a visible image. ▷mid 17th cent. (in the sense 'unfold, unfurl'): from French *développer*, based on Latin *dis-* 'un-' + a second element of unknown origin found also in ENVELOP.

de·vel·op·a·ble /di'veləpəbəl/ ▸*adj.* able to be developed, in particular: ■ (of land or property) able to be adapted or improved so as to become productive or profitable. ■ *Geometry* (of a curved surface) capable of being flattened into a plane without overlap or separation, as with a cylinder. ■ *Mathematics* (of a function or expression) capable of being expanded as a series.

de·vel·oped /di'veləpt/ ▸*adj.* advanced or elaborated to a specified degree: *a fully developed system of public law.* ■ (of a person or part of the body) having specified physical proportions: *a strongman with well-developed muscles.* ■ (of a country or region) advanced economically and socially: *economic assistance to the less-developed countries* | *the developed world.*

de·vel·op·er /di'veləpər/ ▸*n.* a person or thing that develops something: *a property developer* | *software developers.* ■ [with *adj.*] a person who grows or matures at a specified time or rate: *I was a slow developer.* ■ a chemical agent used for treating photographic film to make a visible image.

de·vel·op·ing coun·try ▸*n.* a poor agricultural country that is seeking to become more advanced economically and socially.

de·vel·op·ment /di'veləpmənt/ ▸*n.* **1** the process of developing or being developed: *she traces the development of the novel* | *the development of less invasive treatment.* ■ a specified state of growth or advancement: *the wings attain their full development several hours after birth.* ■ a new and refined product or idea: *the latest developments in information technology.* ■ an event constituting a new stage in a changing situation: *I don't think there have been any new developments since yesterday.* ■ the process of converting land to a new purpose by constructing buildings or making use of its resources: *land suitable for development.* ■ an area of land with new buildings on it: *a major housing development in Chicago.* ■ *Chess* the process of bringing one's pieces into play in the opening phase of a game. **2** the process of starting to experience or suffer from an ailment or feeling: *the development of brittle bones.* **3** the process of treating photographic film with chemicals to make a visible image.

de·vel·op·men·tal /di,veləp'mentl/ ▸*adj.* concerned with the development of someone or something: *developmental problems* | *developmental psychology.* ■ concerned with the evolution of animals and plants: *developmental biology.* **—de·vel·op·men·tal·ly** *adv.*

de·vel·op·men·tal de·lay ▸*n.* the condition of a child being less developed mentally or physically than is normal for its age: *mercury contributes to many known health problems, including neurological injury, developmental delay, and cerebral palsy.*

de·vel·op·ment sys·tem ▸*n.* *Computing* a system of software and hardware designed to assist in the development of new software or products.

dé·vel·op·pé /də,velə'pā/ ▸*n.* (*pl.* **-pés** *pronunc.* same) *Ballet* a movement in which one leg is raised to the knee of the supporting leg, then unfolded and kept in a fully extended position.

de·verb·al /dē'vərbəl/ ▸*adj.* (of a noun or adjective) derived from a verb.
▸*n.* a deverbal noun or adjective.

De·vi /'dāvē/ *Hinduism* the supreme goddess, often identified with Parvati and Shakti. ■ (**devi**) *Indian* (in general use) a goddess. ■ *Indian* used after the first name of a Hindu woman as a form of respect: *Deval Devi.*

de·vi·ance /'dēvēəns/ ▸*n.* the fact or state of departing from usual or accepted standards, esp. in social or sexual behavior. **—de·vi·an·cy** /-ənsē/ *n.*

de·vi·ant /'dēvēənt/ ▸*adj.* departing from usual or accepted standards, esp. in social or sexual behavior: *deviant behavior* | *a deviant ideology.* ■ *chiefly offensive* homosexual.
▸*n.* a deviant person or thing. ▷late Middle English: from late Latin *deviant-* 'turning out of the way,' from the verb *deviare* (see DEVIATE).

de·vi·ate ▸*v.* /'dēvē,āt/ [*intrans.*] depart from an established course: *you must not* ***deviate from*** *the agreed route.* ■ depart from usual or accepted standards: *those who* ***deviate from*** *society's values.*
▸*n.* & *adj.* /'dēvē,it/ old-fashioned term for DEVIANT. ▷mid 16th cent. (as an adjective in the sense 'remote'): from late Latin *deviat-* 'turned out of the way,' from the verb *deviare*, from *de-* 'away from' + *via* 'way.' The verb dates from the mid 17th cent. **—de·vi·a·tor** /-,ātər/ *n.*

de·vi·a·tion /,dēvē'āsнən/ ▸*n.* **1** the action of departing from an established course or accepted standard: ***deviation from*** *a norm* | *sexual deviation* | ***deviations from*** *standard English.* **2** *Statistics* the amount by which a single measurement differs from a fixed value such as the mean. **3** the deflection of a vessel's compass needle caused by iron in the vessel, which varies with the vessel's heading. ▷late Middle English: via French from medieval Latin *deviatio(n-)*, from Latin *deviare* (see DEVIATE). **—de·vi·a·tion·ism** /-,izəm/ *n.* **—de·vi·a·tion·ist** /-ist/ *n.*

de·vice /di'vīs/ ▸*n.* **1** a thing made or adapted for a particular purpose, esp. a mechanical or electronic contrivance: *a measuring device.* ■ an explosive contrivance; a bomb: *an incendiary device.* ■ *archaic* the design or look of something: *works of strange device.* **2** a plan, scheme, or trick with a particular aim: *writing a public letter is a traditional device for signaling dissent.* ■ a turn of phrase intended to produce a particular effect in speech or a literary work: *a rhetorical device.* **3** a drawing or design: *the decorative device on the invitations.* ■ an emblematic or heraldic design: *their shields bear the device of the Blazing Sun.* ▷Middle English: from Old French *devis*, based on Latin *divis-* 'divided,' from the verb *dividere*. The original sense was 'desire or intention,' found now only in *leave a person to his or her own devices* (which has become associated with sense 2).
▸PHRASE □ **leave someone to their own devices** leave someone to do as they wish without supervision.

dev·il /'devəl/ ▸*n.* **1** (usu. **the Devil**) (in Christian and Jewish belief) the chief evil spirit; Satan. ■ an evil spirit; a demon. ■ a very wicked or cruel person: *they prefer voting for devils than for decent men.* ■ a mischievously clever or self-willed person: *the cunning old devil is up to something.* ■ [with *adj.*] *informal* a person with specified characteristics: *the poor devil* | *a lucky devil.* ■ (**the devil**) fighting spirit; wildness: *he was dangerous when the devil was in him.* ■ (**the devil**) a thing that is very difficult or awkward to do or deal with: *it's going to be* ***the very devil*** *to disentangle.* **2** (**the devil**) expressing surprise or annoyance in various questions or exclamations: *"Where the devil is he?"* **3** an instrument or machine, esp. one fitted with sharp teeth or spikes, used for tearing or other destructive work. **4** *informal, dated* a junior assistant of a lawyer or other professional. See also PRINTER'S DEVIL.
▸*v.* (**dev·iled**, **dev·il·ing**; *Brit.* **dev·illed**, **dev·il·ling**) **1** [*intrans.*] *informal, dated* act as a junior assistant for a lawyer or other professional. **2** [*trans.*] harass or worry (someone): *he was deviled by a new-found fear.* ▷Old English *dēofol* (related to Dutch *duivel* and German *Teufel*), via late Latin from Greek *diabolos* 'accuser, slanderer' (used in the Septuagint to translate Hebrew *śāṭān* 'Satan'), from *diaballein* 'to slander,' from *dia* 'across' + *ballein* 'to throw.'
▸PHRASES □ **between the devil and the deep (blue) sea** caught in a dilemma. [alluding to two equally dangerous alternatives.] □ **devil a ——** *archaic* not even one or any: *the devil a man of you stirred himself over it.* □ **the devil can quote scripture for his purpose** *proverb* people may conceal unworthy motives by reciting words that sound morally authoritative. [with allusion to Jesus' Temptation in Matt. 4.] □ **the devil finds work for idle hands to do** *proverb* someone who doesn't have enough work to do is liable to cause or get into trouble. □ **the devil looks after his own** *proverb* success or good fortune often seem to come to those who least deserve it. □ **devil-may-care** cheerful and reckless: *lighthearted, devil-may-care young pilots.* □ **a devil of a ——** *informal* used to emphasize great size or degree: *we are in a devil of a mess here.* □ **the devil is in the details** the details of a matter are its most problematic aspect. □ **the devil to pay** serious trouble to be dealt with: *there was the devil to pay when we got home.* □ **the devil's own ——** *informal* used to emphasize the difficulty or seriousness of something: *he was in the devil's own hurry.* □ **(the) devil take the hindmost** *proverb* everyone should (or does) look after their own interests rather than considering those of others: *full speed ahead and the devil take the hindmost.* [with allusion to a chase by the Devil, in which the slowest will be caught.] □ **give the devil his due** *proverb* acknowledge the good qualities of even a bad or undeserving person. □ **go to the devil 1** said in angry rejection or condemnation of someone. **2** fall into moral depravity: *he must go to the devil in his own way.* □ **like the devil** with great speed or energy: *he drove like the devil.* □ **play the devil with** have a damaging or disruptive effect on: *this brandy plays the devil with one's emotions!* □ **speak** (or **talk**) **of the devil** said when a person appears just after being mentioned. [from the superstition that the devil will appear if his name is spoken.]

dev·iled /'devəld/ ▸*adj.* (of food) cooked with hot seasoning: *deviled eggs.*

dev·il·fish /'devəl,fisн/ ▸*n.* (*pl.* same or **-fish·es**) any of a number of marine creatures that are perceived as having a sinister appearance, in particular a devil ray, a stonefish, or an octopus or squid.

dev·il·ish /'devəlisн/ ▸*adj.* of, like, or appropriate to a devil in evil and cruelty: *devilish tortures.* ■ mischievous and rakish: *a wide, devilish grin.* ■ very difficult to deal with or use: *it turned out to be a devilish job.*
▸*adv.* [as *submodifier*] *informal, dated* very; extremely: *a devilish clever chap.* **—dev·il·ish·ness** *n.*

dev·il·ish·ly /'devəlisнlē/ ▸*adv.* in a devilish manner. ■ [as *submodifier*] *informal* very; extremely: *their music is devilishly difficult.*

dev·il·ment /'devəlmənt/ ▸*n.* reckless mischief; wild spirits: *his eyes were blazing with devilment.*

dev·il ray ▸*n.* a large, long-tailed ray that has a fleshy, hornlike projection on each side of the mouth. It occurs on or near the surface of warm seas and feeds on plankton. • Family Mobulidae: two genera and several species, including the manta.

dev·il·ry /'devəlrē/ ▸*n.* wicked activity: *some devilry was afoot.* ■ reckless mischief: *a perverse sense of devilry urged her to lead him on.* ■ black magic; dealings with the devil.

dev·il's ad·vo·cate ▸*n.* a person who expresses a contentious opinion in order to provoke debate or test the strength of the opposing arguments: *the interviewer will need to* ***play devil's advocate*** *to put the other side's case forward.* ■ *historical* the popular title of the person appointed by the Roman Catholic Church to challenge a proposed beatification or canonization, or the verification of a miracle.

dev·il's bit ▸*n.* a North American plant of the lily family bearing tightly packed spikes of white flowers. • *Chamaelirium luteum*, family Liliaceae).

dev·il's claw ▸*n.* a plant whose seedpods bear clawlike hooks that can harm livestock. • Two genera in the family Pedaliaceae: genus *Proboscidea* of warm regions of America, used in basketry or grown for their fruit, and *Harpagophytum procumbens* of southern Africa and Madagascar, used in herbal medicine.

dev·il's club ▸*n.* a very spiny, straggling shrub of western North America. • *Oplopanax horridus*, family Araliaceae.

dev·il's darn·ing nee·dle ▸*n.* another term for DARNER (sense 2).

dev·il's food cake ▸*n.* a rich chocolate cake.

dev·il's grip ▸*n.* informal term for BORNHOLM DISEASE.

Dev·il's Is·land a rocky island off the coast of French Guiana that has been used from 1852 as a penal settlement, esp. for political prisoners.The last prisoner was released in 1953.

dev·il's paint·brush ▸*n.* a deep orange European hawkweed, which has become naturalized in North America. • *Hieracium aurantiacum*, family Compositae.

Dev·il's Tower /'devəlz/ a rock column that is 865 feet (264 m) high in northeastern Wyoming, a national monument on the Belle Fourche River.

dev·il's walk·ing stick ▸*n.* See HERCULES-CLUB.

dev·il·try /'devəltrē/ ▸*n.* archaic variant of DEVILRY.

de·vi·ous /'dēvēəs/ ▸*adj.* **1** showing a skillful use of underhanded tactics to achieve goals: *he's as devious as a politician needs to be* | *they have devious ways of making money.* **2** (of a route or journey) longer and less direct than the most straightforward way: *they* *arrived at the town by a devious route.* ▷late 16th cent.: from Latin *devius* (from *de-* 'away from' + *via* 'way') + **-OUS**. The original sense was 'remote or sequestered'; the later sense 'departing from the direct route' gave rise to the figurative sense 'deviating from the straight way' and hence 'skilled in underhanded tactics.' **—de·vi·ous·ly** *adv.* **—de·vi·ous·ness** *n.*

de·vise /di'vīz/ ▸*v.* [*trans.*] **1** plan or invent (a complex procedure, system, or mechanism) by careful thought: *a training program should be devised | a complicated game **of his own devising**.* **2** *Law* leave (real estate) to someone by the terms of a will.
▸*n.* *Law* a clause in a will leaving real estate to someone. ▷Middle English: the verb from Old French *deviser*, from Latin *divis-* 'divided,' from the verb *dividere* (this sense being reflected in the original English sense of the verb); the noun is a variant of **DEVICE** (in the early sense 'will, desire'). **—de·vis·a·ble** *adj.* **—de·vi·see** /di,vī'zē/ *n.* (in sense 2). **—de·vis·er** *n.* **—de·vi·sor** /-'vīzər/ *n.* (in sense 2).

de·vi·tal·ize /dē'vītl,īz/ ▸*v.* [*trans.*] [usu. as *adj.*] (**devitalized**) deprive of strength and vigor: *an effective product to treat devitalized skin.* **—de·vi·tal·i·za·tion** /dē,vītl-ə'zāsʜən/ *n.*

de·vit·ri·fy /dē'vitrə,fī/ ▸*v.* (**-fies, -fied**) [*intrans.*] (of glass or vitreous rock) become hard, opaque, and crystalline. ■ [*trans.*] make hard, opaque, and crystalline. **—de·vit·ri·fi·ca·tion** /-,vitrəfi'kāsʜən/ *n.*

de·voice /dē'vois/ ▸*v.* [*trans.*] *Phonetics* make (a vowel or voiced consonant) voiceless.

de·void /di'void/ ▸*adj.* [*predic.*] (**devoid of**) entirely lacking or free from: *Lisa kept her voice devoid of emotion.* ▷late Middle English: past participle of obsolete *devoid* 'cast out,' from Old French *devoidier*.

de·voir /dəv'wär/ ▸*n.* *archaic* a person's duty: *you have **done your devoir** right well.* ■ (**pay one's devoirs**) pay one's respects formally. ▷Middle English: from Old French *deveir*, from Latin *debere* 'owe.' The spelling, and subsequently the pronunciation, was changed under the influence of modern French *devoir*.

dev·o·lu·tion /,devə'lo͞osʜən/ ▸*n.* the transfer or delegation of power to a lower level, esp. by central government to local or regional administration. ■ *formal* descent or degeneration to a lower or worse state: *the **devolution** of the gentlemanly ideal **into** a glorification of drunkenness.* ■ *Law* the legal transfer of property from one owner to another. ■ *Biology* evolutionary degeneration. ▷late 15th cent. (in the sense 'transference by default'): from late Latin *devolutio(n-)*, from Latin *devolvere* 'roll down' (see **DEVOLVE**). **—dev·o·lu·tion·ar·y** /-,nerē/ *adj.* **—dev·o·lu·tion·ist** /-ist/ *n.*

de·volve /di'välv/ ▸*v.* [*trans.*] transfer or delegate (power) to a lower level, esp. from central government to local or regional administration: *measures to **devolve** power **to** the provinces* | [as *adj.*] (**devolved**) *devolved and decentralized government.* ■ [*intrans.*] (**devolve on/upon/to**) (of duties or responsibility) pass to (a body or person at a lower level): *his duties devolved on a comrade.* ■ [*intrans.*] (**devolve into**) *formal* degenerate or be split into: *the Empire devolved into separate warring states.* ▷late Middle English (in the sense 'roll down'): from Latin *devolvere*, from *de-* 'down' + *volvere* 'to roll.' **—de·volve·ment** *n.*

Dev·on[1] /'devən/ (also **Dev·on·shire** /-sʜər; -,sʜi(ə)r/) a county in southwestern England; county town, Exeter.

Dev·on[2] ▸*n.* an animal of a breed of red beef cattle. ▷mid 19th cent.: named after the county of *Devon* (see **DEVON**[1]).

De·vo·ni·an /di'vōnēən/ ▸*adj.* **1** of or relating to Devon. **2** *Geology* of, relating to, or denoting the fourth period of the Paleozoic era, between the Silurian and Carboniferous periods.

The Devonian period lasted from about 409 million to 363 million years ago. During this period fish became abundant; the first amphibians evolved, and the first forests appeared.

▸*n.* **1** a native or inhabitant of Devon. **2** (**the Devonian**) *Geology* the Devonian period or the system of rocks deposited during it.

Dev·on·shire cream /'devənsʜər; -,sʜi(ə)r/ ▸*n.* clotted cream.

de·vo·ré /də'vôrā/ (also **de·vo·re**) ▸*n.* a velvet fabric with a pattern formed by burning the pile away with acid: [as *modifier*] *a devoré top.* ▷1990s: from French *dévoré*, lit. 'devoured,' past part. of *dévorer*.

de·vote /di'vōt/ ▸*v.* [*trans.*] **1** (**devote something to**) give all or a large part of one's time or resources to (a person, activity, or cause): *I wanted to devote more time to my family | she **devoted herself to** fund-raising.* **2** *archaic* invoke or pronounce a curse upon. ▷late 16th cent. (in the sense 'dedicate formally, consecrate'): from Latin *devot-* 'consecrated,' from the verb *devovere*, from *de-* 'formally' + *vovere* 'to vow.'

de·vot·ed /di'vōtid/ ▸*adj.* **1** very loving or loyal: *he was a devoted husband | Leo was **devoted to** his job.* **2** [*predic.*] (**devoted to**) given over to the display, study, or discussion of: *there is a museum devoted to her work.* **—de·vot·ed·ly** *adv.* (sense 1) **—de·vot·ed·ness** *n.* (sense 1).

dev·o·tee /,devə'tē; -'tā/ ▸*n.* a person who is very interested in and enthusiastic about someone or something: *a devotee of Chinese calligraphy.* ■ a strong believer in a particular religion or god: *devotees of Krishna | devotees thronged the temple.*

de·vo·tion /di'vōsʜən/ ▸*n.* love, loyalty, or enthusiasm for a person, activity, or cause: *Eleanor's **devotion** to her husband | his courage and **devotion to duty** never wavered.* ■ religious worship or observance: *the order's aim was to live a life of devotion.* ■ (**devotions**) prayers or religious observances. ▷Middle English: from Latin *devotio(n-)*, from *devovere* 'consecrate' (see **DEVOTE**).

de·vo·tion·al /di'vōsʜənl/ ▸*adj.* of or used in religious worship: *devotional books.*

de·vour /di'vou(ə)r/ ▸*v.* [*trans.*] eat (food or prey) hungrily or quickly: *he devoured half of his burger in one bite.* ■ (of fire, disease, or other forces) consume (someone or something) destructively: *the hungry flames devoured the old house.* ■ read (something) quickly and eagerly: *she spent her evenings devouring the classics.* ■ (**be devoured**) (of a person) be totally absorbed by an unpleasant feeling: *she was devoured by need.* ▷Middle English: from Old French *devorer*, from Latin *devorare*, from *de-* 'down' + *vorare* 'to swallow.' **—de·vour·er** *n.* **—de·vour·ing·ly** *adv.*

de·vout /di'vout/ ▸*adj.* having or showing deep religious feeling or commitment: *she was a devout Catholic | a rabbi's devout prayers.* ■ totally committed to a cause or belief: *the most devout environmentalist.* ▷Middle English: from Old French *devot*, from Latin *devotus* 'devoted,' past participle of *devovere* (see **DEVOTE**). **—de·vout·ly** *adv.* **—de·vout·ness** *n.*

de Vries /də 'vrēz/, Hugo (1848–1935), Dutch plant physiologist and geneticist. He did much work on osmosis and water relations in plants, coining the term *plasmolysis*. His subsequent work on heredity contributed substantially to the chromosome theory of heredity.

DEW ▸*abbr.* ■ distant early warning.

dew /d(y)o͞o/ ▸*n.* tiny drops of water that form on cool surfaces at night, when atmospheric vapor condenses: *the grass was wet with dew* | [in *sing.*] *a cold, heavy dew dripped from the leaves.* ■ [in *sing.*] a beaded or glistening liquid resembling such drops: *her body had broken out in a fine dew of perspiration.*
▸*v.* [*trans.*] wet (a part of someone's body) with a beaded or glistening liquid: *sweat dewed her lashes.* ▷Old English *dēaw*, of Germanic origin; related to Dutch *dauw* and German *Tau* (noun), *tauen* (verb).

de·wan ▸*n.* variant spelling of **DIWAN**.

Dew·ar /'d(y)o͞oər/, Sir James (1842–1923), Scottish chemist and physicist. He devised the vacuum flask, achieved temperatures close to absolute zero, and was the first to produce liquid oxygen and hydrogen in quantity.

dew·ar /'d(y)o͞oər/ ▸*n.* a double-walled flask of metal or silvered glass with a vacuum between the walls, used to hold liquids at well below ambient temperature. ▷late 19th cent.: named after Sir James **DEWAR**.

de·wa·ter /dē'wätər; -'wô-/ ▸*v.* [*trans.*] drain (a waterlogged or flooded area). ■ remove water from (sediment or waste materials).

dew·ber·ry /'d(y)o͞o,berē/ ▸*n.* (*pl.* **-ries**) a trailing European bramble with soft prickles and edible, blackberrylike fruit, which has a dewy white bloom on the skin. • *Rubus caesius*, family Rosaceae. ■ any of a number of trailing brambles. ■ the blue-black fruit of any of these plants.

dew·claw /'d(y)o͞o,klô/ ▸*n.* a rudimentary inner toe present in some dogs. ■ a false hoof on an animal such as a deer, which is formed by its rudimentary side toes. ▷late 16th cent.: apparently from the nouns **DEW** and **CLAW**.

dewclaw

dew·drop /'d(y)o͞o,dräp/ ▸*n.* a drop of dew.

Dew·ey[1] /'d(y)o͞o-ē/, George (1837–1917), U.S. naval officer. Appointed commodore of the navy in 1896, he was the hero of the battle of Manila Bay in the Philippines in 1898 during the Spanish-American War.

Dew·ey[2], John (1859–1952), U.S. philosopher and educational theorist. He defined knowledge as successful practice and espoused the educational theory that children learn best by doing.

Dew·ey[3], Melvil (1851–1931), U.S. librarian. He devised a decimal system of classifying books that used ten main subject categories.

Dew·ey[4], Thomas Edmund (1902–71), U.S. lawyer and politician. He served as governor of New York 1943–55 and was the Republican presidential candidate in 1944 and 1948.

Dew·ey dec·i·mal clas·si·fi·ca·tion (also **Dewey system**) ▸*n.* an internationally applied decimal system of library classification that uses a three-figure code from 000 to 999 to represent the major branches of knowledge, and allows finer classification to be made by the addition of further figures after a decimal point. ▷late 19th cent.: named after M. *Dewey*.

dew·fall /'d(y)o͞o,fôl/ ▸*n.* *poetic/literary* the formation of dew, or the time of the evening when dew begins to form. ■ the film of dew covering an area.

De·wi /'dāwē/ Welsh name for St. David (see **DAVID, ST.**).

dew·lap /'d(y)o͞o,lap/ ▸*n.* a fold of loose skin hanging from the neck or throat of an animal or bird, esp. that present in many cattle. ▷Middle English: from **DEW** and **LAP**[1], perhaps influenced by a Scandinavian word (compare with Danish *doglæp*).

dewlap

de·worm /dē'wərm/ ▸*v.* [*trans.*] treat (an animal) to free it of worms. **—de·worm·er** *n.*

dew point ▸*n.* the atmospheric temperature (varying according to pressure and humidity) below which water droplets begin to condense and dew can form.

dew worm ▸*n.* an earthworm, in particular one used as fishing bait. ▷Old English *deaw-wyrm* 'ringworm'; compare with East Frisian *dauworm*, denoting both ringworm and the earthworm.

dew·y /'d(y)o͞oē/ ▸*adj.* (**dew·i·er, dew·i·est**) wet with dew. ■ (of a person's skin) appearing soft and lustrous: *your skin will begin to feel revitalized and dewy.* ■ youthful and fresh: *the girls have yet to lose their dewy charm.* ▷Old English *dēawig* (see **DEW, -Y**[1]). **—dew·i·ly** /'d(y)o͞oəlē/ *adv.* **—dew·i·ness** *n.*

dew·y-eyed ▸*adj.* having eyes that are moist with tears (used typically to indicate that a person is nostalgic, naive, or sentimental: *she gets slightly dewy-eyed as she talks about her family.*

dex /deks/ ▸*n.* *informal* short for **DEXEDRINE**.

dex·a·meth·a·sone /,deksə'meтʜə,zōn/ ▸*n.* *Medicine* a synthetic drug of the corticosteroid type, used esp. as an anti-inflammatory agent. ▷1950s: from *dexa-* (blend of **DECA-** and **HEXA-**) + *meth(yl)* + *-a-* + *(cortis)one*.

Dex·e·drine /'deksə,drən; -,drin/ ▸*n.* trademark for **AMPHETAMINE SULFATE** (see **AMPHETAMINE**). ▷1940s: probably from **DEXTRO-**, on the pattern of *Benzedrine*.

dex·ter[1] /'dekstər/ ▸*adj.* [*attrib.*] *archaic* & *Heraldry* of, on, or toward the right-hand side (in a coat of arms, from the bearer's point of view, i.e., the left as it is depicted). The opposite of **SINISTER**. ▷mid 16th cent.: from Latin, 'on the right.'

dex·ter[2] ▸*n.* an animal of a small, hardy breed of Irish

Pronunciation Key ə *ago*; ər *over*; 'ə or ,ə *up*; 'ər or ,ər *fur*; a *hat*; ā *rate*; ä *car*; cʜ *chew*; e *let*; ē *see*; e(ə)r *air*; i *fit*; ī *by*; i(ə)r *ear*; ɴɢ *sing*; ō *go*; ô *for*; oi *boy*; o͝o *good*; o͞o *goo*; ou *out*; sʜ *she*; тʜ *thin*; тʜ *then*; (h)w *why*; ᴢʜ *vision*

cattle. ▷late 19th cent.: said to have been named after the breeder.

dex·ter·i·ty /dek'steritē/ ▶*n.* skill in performing tasks, esp. with the hands: *her dexterity with chopsticks | his record testifies to a certain dexterity in politics.* ▷early 16th cent. (in the sense 'mental adroitness'): from French *dextérité*, from Latin *dexteritas*, from *dexter* 'on the right.'

dex·ter·ous /'dekst(ə)rəs/ (also **dex·trous**) ▶*adj.* demonstrating neat skill, esp. with the hands: *dexterous accordion playing.* ■ mentally adroit; clever: *power users are dexterous at using software, rather than creating it.* ▷early 17th cent. (in the sense 'mentally adroit, clever'): from Latin *dexter* 'on the right' + **-ous**. **—dex·ter·ous·ly** *adv.* **—dex·ter·ous·ness** *n.*

dex·tral /'dekstrəl/ ▶*adj.* of or on the right side or the right hand (the opposite of **SINISTRAL**), in particular: ■ right-handed. ■ *Geology* relating to or denoting a strike-slip fault in which the motion of the block on the further side of the fault from an observer is toward the right. ■ *Zoology* (of a spiral mollusk shell) with whorls rising to the right and coiling in a counterclockwise direction.
▶*n.* a right-handed person. ▷mid 17th cent.: from medieval Latin *dextralis*, from Latin *dextra* 'the right hand,' from *dexter* 'on the right.' **—dex·tral·i·ty** /dek'stralitē/ *n.* **—dex·tral·ly** *adv.*

D

dex·tran /'dek,stran; -strən/ ▶*n.* *Chemistry* a carbohydrate gum formed by the fermentation of sugars and consisting of polymers of glucose. ■ *Medicine* a solution containing a hydrolyzed form of this, used as a substitute for blood plasma. ▷late 19th cent.: from **DEXTRO-** + **-AN**.

dex·trin /'dekstrin/ ▶*n.* a soluble gummy substance obtained by hydrolysis of starch, used as a thickening agent and in adhesives and dietary supplements. ▷mid 19th cent.: from **DEXTRO-** + **-IN**[1].

dextro- ▶*comb. form* on or to the right: *dextrorotatory.* ▷from Latin *dexter, dextr-* 'right.'

dex·tro·ro·ta·to·ry /,dekstrə'rōtə,tôrē/ ▶*adj.* *Chemistry* (of a compound) having the property of rotating the plane of a polarized light ray to the right, i.e., clockwise facing the oncoming radiation. The opposite of **LEVOROTATORY**. **—dex·tro·ro·ta·tion** /-,rō'tāshən/ *n.*

dex·trose /'dekstrōs/ ▶*n.* *Chemistry* the dextrorotatory form of glucose (and the predominant naturally occurring form). ▷mid 19th cent.: from Latin *dexter, dextr-* 'on the right' + **-OSE**[2].

dex·trous ▶*adj.* variant spelling of **DEXTEROUS**.

dex·y /'deksē/ ▶*n.* (*pl.* **dex·ies**) *informal* Dexedrine. ■ a tablet of Dexedrine. ▷1950s: abbreviation.

de·zinc·i·fi·ca·tion /dē,ziNGkifi'kāshən/ ▶*n.* a form of corrosion and weakening of brass objects in which zinc is dissolved out of the brass alloy.

DF ▶*abbr.* ■ Defender of the Faith. [from Latin *Defensor Fidei*.] ■ direction finder.

DFC ▶*abbr.* Distinguished Flying Cross.

Dfl ▶*abbr.* Dutch florins.

DFM ▶*abbr.* (in the UK) Distinguished Flying Medal, a decoration awarded to RAF personnel for acts of courage or devotion to duty when not in action against an enemy, instituted in 1918.

DG ▶*abbr.* ■ Dei gratia, by the grace of God. ■ Deo gratias, thanks be to God. ■ (in the UK) director general.

DH ▶*abbr.* ■ Doctor of Humanities. ■ *Baseball* designated hitter.
▶*v.* (**DH's, DH'd, DHing**) [*intrans.*] act as a designated hitter. ■ [*trans.*] use (a player) as a designated hitter.

Dhah·ran /dä'rän; ,dähə'rän/ an oil town in eastern Saudi Arabia that was an Allied forces port and military base during the Persian Gulf War; pop. 74,000.

Dha·ka /'däkə; 'dakə/ (also **Dac·ca**) the capital of Bangladesh, in the central part of the country, on the Ganges delta; pop. 3,637,890. **—Dha·kai** /'däk,ī; 'dak,ī/ *adj.*

dhal /däl/ (also **dal** or **dahl**) ▶*n.* lentils, a common foodstuff in India. ■ a dish made with these. ▷from Hindi *dāl*.

dham·ma /'dämə/ ▶*n.* another term for **DHARMA**, esp. among Theravada Buddhists. ▷Pali, from Sanskrit *dharma* 'decree or custom.'

Dhan·bad /'dän,bäd/ a city in northeastern India, in Bihar; pop. 818,000.

dhan·sak /'dən,säk/ ▶*n.* an Indian dish of meat or vegetables cooked with lentils and coriander: *chicken dhansak.* ▷Gujarati.

dhar·ma /'därmə/ ▶*n.* **1** *Hinduism* the principle of cosmic order. ■ virtue, righteousness, and duty, esp. social and caste duty in accord with the cosmic order. **2** *Buddhism* the teaching or religion of the Buddha. ■ one of the fundamental elements of which the world is composed. ▷late 18th cent.: Sanskrit, literally 'decree or custom.'

dhar·ma·sha·la /,därmə'sHälə/ (also **dhar·ma·sa·la** /-'sälə/) ▶*n.* (in the Indian subcontinent) a building devoted to religious or charitable purposes, esp. a rest house for travelers. ▷from Sanskrit *dharmaśālā*, from *dharma* 'virtue' + *śālā* 'house.'

dhar·na /'därnə/ ▶*n.* *Indian* a mode of compelling payment or compliance, by sitting at the debtor's or offender's door without eating until the demand is complied with. ■ a peaceful demonstration. ▷from Hindi *dharnā* 'sitting in restraint, placing.'

Dha·ruk /'də,ro͝ok/ ▶*n.* an Aboriginal language of the area around Sydney, Australia, now extinct.

Dhar·war /där'wär/ a city in southern India, twinned with Hubli, in Karnataka state, noted for manufacturing textiles; pop. 648,000.

Dhau·la·gi·ri /,doulə'gi(ə)rē/ a mountain massif in Nepal, in the Himalayas, that has six peaks and rises to 26,810 feet (8,172 m) at its highest point.

DHEA ▶*abbr.* dihydroepiandrosterone.

dhikr /'THikər/ (also **zikr** /'zēkər/) ▶*n.* *Islam* a form of devotion, associated chiefly with Sufism, in which the worshiper is absorbed in the rhythmic repetition of the name of God or his attributes. ■ a Sufi ceremony in which this is practiced.

dho·bi /'dōbē/ ▶*n.* (*pl.* **-bis**) (in the Indian subcontinent) a washerman or washerwoman. ▷from Hindi *dhobī*, from *dhob* 'washing.'

dho·bi itch ▶*n.* *informal* itching inflammation of the skin, esp. in the groin region, suffered particularly in the tropics and typically caused by certain types of ringworm infection or by allergic dermatitis.

Dho·far /dō'fär/ the fertile southern province of Oman.

dhol /dōl/ ▶*n.* a large, barrel-shaped or cylindrical wooden drum, typically two-headed, used in the Indian subcontinent. ▷from Hindi *ḍhol*.

dho·lak /'dōlək/ ▶*n.* a dhol, esp. a relatively small one. ▷Hindi, from *ḍhol* (see **DHOL**) + the diminutive suffix *-ak*.

dhole /dōl/ ▶*n.* an Asian wild dog that has a sandy coat and a black, bushy tail and lives in packs. • *Cuon alpinus*, family Canidae. ▷early 19th cent.: of unknown origin.

dho·ti /'dōtē/ ▶*n.* (*pl.* **dho·tis**) a loincloth worn by male Hindus. ▷from Hindi *dhotī*.

dhow /dou/ ▶*n.* a lateen-rigged ship with one or two masts, used in the Indian Ocean. ▷late 18th cent.: from Arabic *dāwa*, probably related to Marathi *dāw*.

dhow

DHT ▶*abbr.* dihydrotestosterone.

DHTML ▶*abbr.* *Computing* dynamic HTML, a collection of Web browser enhancements that enable dynamic and interactive features on Web pages.

dhur·rie /'do͝orē/ (also **dur·rie**) ▶*n.* (*pl.* **-ries**) a heavy cotton rug of Indian origin. ▷from Hindi *darī*.

dhya·na /di'yänə/ ▶*n.* (in Hindu and Buddhist practice) profound meditation that is the penultimate stage of yoga. ▷from Sanskrit *dhyāna*.

DI ▶*abbr.* drill instructor.

di-[1] ▶*comb. form* twice; two-; double: *dichromatic.* ■ *Chemistry* containing two atoms, molecules, or groups of a specified kind: *dioxide.* ▷from Greek *dis* 'twice.'

di-[2] ▶*prefix* variant spelling of **DIS-** before *l, m, n, r, s* (followed by a consonant), and *v*; also often before *g*, and sometimes before *j*. ▷from Latin.

di-[3] ▶*prefix* variant spelling of **DIA-** before a vowel (as in *dielectric*).

dia. ▶*abbr.* diameter.

dia- (also **di-** before a vowel) ▶*prefix* **1** through; across: *diameter | diaphanous | diuretic.* **2** apart: *diakinesis.* ▷from Greek *dia* 'through.'

di·a·base /'dīə,bās/ ▶*n.* *Geology* another term for **DOLERITE**. ▷mid 19th cent. (originally denoting diorite): from French, formed irregularly as if from *di-* 'two' + *base* 'base' (thus 'rock with two bases,' referring to the base minerals of diorite), but associated later perhaps with Greek *diabasis* 'transition.'

di·a·be·tes /,dīə'bētēz; -tis/ ▶*n.* a disorder of the metabolism causing excessive thirst and the production of large amounts of urine. ▷mid 16th cent.: via Latin from Greek, literally 'siphon,' from *diabainein* 'go through.'

di·a·be·tes in·sip·i·dus /in'sipidəs/ ▶*n.* a rare form of diabetes caused by a deficiency of the pituitary hormone vasopressin, which regulates kidney function. ▷late 19th cent.: from **DIABETES** + Latin *insipidus* 'insipid.'

di·a·be·tes mel·li·tus /mə'lītəs; 'meli-/ ▶*n.* the commonest form of diabetes, caused by a deficiency of the pancreatic hormone insulin, which results in a failure to metabolize sugars and starch. Sugars accumulate in the blood and urine, and the byproducts of alternative fat metabolism disturb the acid–base balance of the blood, causing a risk of convulsions and coma. ▷late 19th cent.: from **DIABETES** + Latin *mellitus* 'sweet.'

di·a·bet·ic /,dīə'betik/ ▶*adj.* having diabetes. ■ relating to or designed to relieve diabetes: *a diabetic clinic | a diabetic diet.*
▶*n.* a person suffering from diabetes.

di·a·ble·rie /dē'äblərē/ ▶*n.* reckless mischief; charismatic wildness: *the beauty and diablerie of the great actor.* ■ *archaic* sorcery supposedly assisted by the devil. ▷mid 18th cent.: from French, from *diable*, from ecclesiastical Latin *diabolus* 'devil.'

di·a·bol·i·cal /,dīə'bälikəl/ (also **di·a·bol·ic**) ▶*adj.* belonging to or so evil as to recall the Devil: *his diabolical cunning.* **—di·a·bol·i·cal·ly** /-ik(ə)lē/ *adv.* [as *submodifier*] *I am going to get diabolically drunk.*

di·ab·o·lism /dī'abə,lizəm/ ▶*n.* worship of the Devil. ■ devilish or atrociously wicked conduct. ▷early 17th cent.: from ecclesiastical Latin *diabolus* or Greek *diabolos* 'devil' + **-ISM**. **—di·ab·o·list** *n.*

di·ab·o·lize /dī'abə,līz/ ▶*v.* [*trans.*] *archaic* represent as diabolical.

di·ab·o·lo /dē'abə,lō/ ▶*n.* (*pl.* **-los**) a game in which a two-headed top is thrown up and caught with a string stretched between two sticks. ■ the wooden top used in this game. ▷early 20th cent.: from Italian, from ecclesiastical Latin *diabolus* 'devil'; the game was formerly called *devil on two sticks*.

di·a·bu·lim·i·a /,dīəbo͞o'limēə; -'lē-/ ▶*n.* the manipulation by diabetic patients of insulin treatments in order to lose weight. ▷from **DIABETES** + **BULIMIA**.

di·a·ce·tyl·mor·phine /,dīə,sētl'môrfēn/ ▶*n.* technical term for **HEROIN**.

di·a·chron·ic /,dīə'kränik/ ▶*adj.* concerned with the way in which something, esp. language, has developed and evolved through time. Often contrasted with **SYNCHRONIC**. ▷mid 19th cent.: from **DIA-** 'through' + Greek *khronos* 'time' + **-IC**. **—di·a·chro·ne·i·ty** /-krə'nāitē/ *n.* **—di·a·chron·i·cal·ly** /-ik(ə)lē/ *adv.* **—di·a·chron·is·tic** /-,krə'nistik/ *adj.* **—di·ach·ro·ny** /dī'akrənē/ *n.*

di·a·chron·ism /dī'akrə,nizəm/ ▶*n.* *Geology* the occurrence of a feature or phenomenon in different geological periods. **—di·ach·ro·nous** /-nəs/ *adj.* **—di·ach·ro·nous·ly** /-nəslē/ *adv.*

di·ac·o·nal /dī'akənl/ ▶*adj.* relating to a deacon, or to the role of a deacon. ▷early 17th cent.: from ecclesiastical Latin *diaconalis*, from *diaconus* (see **DEACON**).

di·ac·o·nate /dī'akənit; -,nāt/ ▶*n.* the office of deacon, or a person's tenure of it. ■ a body of deacons collectively. ▷early 18th cent.: from ecclesiastical Latin *diaconatus*, from *diaconus* (see **DEACON**).

di·a·crit·ic /,dīə'kritik/ ▶*n.* a sign, such as an accent or cedilla, which when written above or below a letter indicates a difference in pronunciation from the same letter when unmarked or differently marked.
▶*adj.* (of a mark or sign) indicating a difference in pronunciation. ▷late 17th cent.: from Greek *diakritikos*, from *diakrinein* 'distinguish,' from *dia-* 'through' + *krinein* 'to separate.'

di·a·crit·i·cal /,dīə'kritikəl/ ▶*adj.* (of a mark or sign) serving to indicate different pronunciations of a letter above or below which it is written. **—di·a·crit·i·cal·ly** /-ik(ə)lē/ *adv.*

di·a·del·phous /,dīə'delfəs/ ▶*adj.* *Botany* (of stamens) united by their filaments so as to form two groups. ▷early 19th cent.: from **DI-**[1] 'two' + Greek *adelphos* 'brother' + **-OUS**.

di·a·dem /'dīə,dem/ ▶*n.* a jeweled crown or headband worn as a symbol of sovereignty. ■ (**the diadem**) *archaic* the authority or dignity symbolized by a diadem: *the princely diadem.* ▷Middle English: from Old French *diademe,* via Latin from Greek *diadēma* 'the regal headband of the Persian kings,' from *diadein* 'bind around.' **—di·a·demed** *adj.*

di·aer·e·sis ▸*n.* variant spelling of DIERESIS.

diag. ▸*abbr.* ■ diagonal. ■ diagram.

di·a·gen·e·sis /ˌdīəˈjenəsis/ ▸*n. Geology* the physical and chemical changes occurring during the conversion of sediment to sedimentary rock. **—di·a·ge·net·ic** /-jəˈnetik/ *adj.* **—di·a·ge·net·i·cal·ly** /-jəˈnetik(ə)lē/ *adv.* .

Dia·ghi·lev /dēˈägəˌlef/, Sergei (Pavlovich) (1872–1929), Russian ballet impresario. In 1909, he formed the Ballets Russes, which he directed until his death.

di·ag·nose /ˌdīəgˈnōs/ ▸*v.* [*trans.*] identify the nature of (an illness or other problem) by examination of the symptoms: *doctors diagnosed a rare and fatal liver disease.* ■ (usu. **be diagnosed**) identify the nature of the medical condition of (someone): *she was finally* ***diagnosed as*** *having epilepsy* | *20,000 men are* ***diagnosed with*** *skin cancer every year.* ▷mid 19th cent.: back-formation from DIAGNOSIS. **—di·ag·nos·a·ble** *adj.*

di·ag·no·sis /ˌdīəgˈnōsis/ ▸*n.* (*pl.* **-ses** /-ˌsēz/) **1** the identification of the nature of an illness or other problem by examination of the symptoms: *early diagnosis and treatment are essential* | *a diagnosis of Crohn's disease was made.* **2** the distinctive characterization in precise terms of a genus, species, or phenomenon. ▷late 17th cent.: modern Latin, from Greek, from *diagignōskein* 'distinguish, discern,' from *dia* 'apart' + *gignōskein* 'recognize, know.'

di·ag·nos·tic /ˌdīəgˈnästik/ ▸*adj.* **1** concerned with the diagnosis of illness or other problems: *a diagnostic tool.* ■ (of a symptom) distinctive, and so indicating the nature of an illness: *there are fifteen infections that are* ***diagnostic of*** *AIDS.* **2** characteristic of a particular species, genus, or phenomenon: *the diagnostic character of having not one but two pairs of antennae.*
▸*n.* **1** a distinctive symptom or characteristic. ■ *Computing* a program or routine that helps a user to identify errors. **2** (**diagnostics**) the practice or techniques of diagnosis: *advanced medical diagnostics.* ▷early 17th cent.: from Greek *diagnōstikos* 'able to distinguish,' from *diagignōskein* 'distinguish'; the noun from *hē diagnōstikē tekhnē* 'the art of distinguishing (disease).' **—di·ag·nos·ti·cal·ly** /-ik(ə)lē/ *adv.* **—di·ag·nos·ti·cian** /-ˌnäsˈtisʜən/ *n.*

di·ag·o·nal /dīˈagənl/ (abbr.: **diag.**) ▸*adj.* (of a straight line) joining two opposite corners of a square, rectangle, or other straight-sided shape. ■ (of a line) straight and at an angle; slanting: *a tie with diagonal stripes.*
▸*n.* a straight line joining two opposite corners of a square, rectangle, or other straight-sided shape. ■ *Mathematics* the set of elements of a matrix that lie on a line joining two opposite corners. ■ a slanting straight pattern or line: *the bars of light made diagonals across the entrance* | *tiles can be laid* ***on the diagonal.*** ■ *Chess* a slanting row of squares whose color is the same. ▷mid 16th cent.: from Latin *diagonalis,* from Greek *diagōnios* 'from angle to angle,' from *dia* 'through' + *gōnia* 'angle.' **—di·ag·o·nal·ly** *adv.*

di·ag·o·nal ma·trix ▸*n. Mathematics* a matrix having nonzero elements only in the diagonal running from the upper left to the lower right.

di·a·gram /ˈdīəˌgram/ ▸*n.* (abbr.: **diag.**) a simplified drawing showing the appearance, structure, or workings of something; a schematic representation: *a diagram of the living room.* ■ *Geometry* a figure composed of lines that is used to illustrate a definition or statement or to aid in the proof of a proposition.
▸*v.* (**-gramed, -gram·ing;** also **-grammed, -gram·ming**) [*trans.*] represent (something) in graphic form: *the experiment is diagramed on page fourteen.* ▷early 17th cent.: from Latin *diagramma,* from Greek, from *diagraphein* 'mark out by lines,' from *dia* 'through' + *graphein* 'write.' **—di·a·gram·mat·ic** /ˌdīəgrəˈmatik/ *adj.* **—di·a·gram·mat·i·cal·ly** /ˌdīəgrəˈmatik(ə)lē/ *adv.*

di·a·ki·ne·sis /ˌdīəkəˈnēsis/ ▸*n.* (*pl.* **-ses** /-sēz/) *Biology* the fifth and last stage of the prophase of meiosis, following diplotene, when the separation of homologous chromosomes is complete and crossing over has occurred. ▷early 20th cent.: from DIA- 'through, across' + Greek *kinēsis* 'motion.'

di·al /ˈdī(ə)l/ ▸*n.* a face of a clock, watch, or sundial that is marked to show units of time. ■ a similar face or flat plate with a scale and pointer for showing measurements of weight, volume, pressure, compass direction, etc. ■ a disk with numbered holes on a telephone, enabling someone to make a call by inserting a finger in each of the holes corresponding to the number to be called and turning the disk. ■ a plate or disk on a radio, stove, washing machine, or other piece of equipment that is tuned to select a wavelength or setting.
▸*v.* (**di·aled, di·al·ing;** *Brit.* **di·alled, di·al·ling**) [*trans.*] call (a telephone number) by turning a disk with numbered holes or pressing a set of buttons: *he dialed room service* | [*intrans.*] *company employees* ***dial out from*** *their office.* ■ (**dial something up**) gain access to a service using a telephone line: *plans to enable customers to dial up videos from their living room.* ■ indicate or regulate by means of a dial: *you're expected to* ***dial in*** *volume and tone settings.* ▷Middle English (denoting a mariner's compass): from medieval Latin *diale* 'clock dial,' based on Latin *dies* 'day.'

dial-a- ▸*comb. form* denoting a service available for booking by telephone: *dial-a-ride.*

di·al-a·round ▸*adj.* used to describe a telephone service that requires callers to dial a special access code that enables them to bypass (or 'dial around') their chosen long-distance carrier in order to obtain a better rate.

di·a·lect /ˈdīəˌlekt/ ▸*n.* a particular form of a language that is peculiar to a specific region or social group: *this novel is written in the dialect of Trinidad.* ■ *Computing* a particular version of a programming language. ▷mid 16th cent. (denoting the art of investigating the truth of opinions): from French *dialecte,* or via Latin from Greek *dialektos* 'discourse, way of speaking,' from *dialegesthai* 'converse with' (see DIALOGUE). **—di·a·lec·tal** /ˌdīəˈlektəl/ *adj.*

> ***THE RIGHT WORD*** **argot, cant, dialect, jargon, lingo, slang, vernacular**
>
> When a New York City cab driver calls out the window, "Hey, wassa madda wichoo?" he is using the **vernacular**, which is the authentic, natural pattern of speech among those belonging to a certain community.
>
> In some areas of London, on the other hand, one might hear the Cockney **dialect**, which is a form or variety of a language that is confined to a specific group or locality; it has its own pronunciation, usage, and vocabulary, and may persist for generations or even centuries (*he spoke in the dialect of the Appalachian backwoodsman*).
>
> A teenager who tells his parents to "Chill out" is using **slang**, which is a very informal language that includes "substitute" vocabulary ("wheels" for *car*, "rug" for *toupee*), grammatical distortions, and other departures from formal or polite usage.
>
> **Argot** refers to the slang of a group that feels threatened by the hostility of society as a whole; it traditionally refers to the slang used by criminals and thieves, although it may refer to any peculiar language that a clique or other closely knit group uses to communicate with each other.
>
> At one time **cant** was a synonym for *argot*, but now it usually refers to pompous, inflated language or the hackneyed use of words and phrases by members of a particular class or profession (*the cant of the fashion industry*).
>
> In contrast to *cant*, which can at least be understood, **jargon** is nearly impossible for the average person to decipher. This term refers to the technical or highly specialized language used by members of an occupational or professional group (*medical jargon; the jargon of the theater*).
>
> If you are frustrated because you can't understand the language used by a particular class or group, you're apt to refer to their way of talking as **lingo**, which is a term for any language that is not readily understood (*she tried to reason with the cab driver, but she couldn't understand his lingo*).

di·a·lec·tic /ˌdīəˈlektik/ *Philosophy* ▸*n.* (also **di·a·lec·tics**) [usu. treated as *sing.*] **1** the art of investigating or discussing the truth of opinions. **2** inquiry into metaphysical contradictions and their solutions. ■ the existence or action of opposing social forces, concepts, etc.

> The ancient Greeks used the term dialectic to refer to various methods of reasoning and discussion in order to discover the truth. More recently, Kant applied the term to the criticism of the contradictions that arise from supposing knowledge of objects beyond the limits of experience, e.g., the soul. Hegel applied the term to the process of thought by which apparent contradictions (which he termed thesis and antithesis) are seen to be part of a higher truth (synthesis).

▸*adj.* of or relating to dialectic or dialectics; dialectical. ▷late Middle English: from Old French *dialectique* or Latin *dialectica,* from Greek *dialektikē (tekhnē)* '(art) of debate,' from *dialegesthai* 'converse with' (see DIALOGUE).

di·a·lec·ti·cal /ˌdīəˈlektikəl/ ▸*adj.* **1** relating to the logical discussion of ideas and opinions: *dialectical ingenuity.* **2** concerned with or acting through opposing forces: *a dialectical opposition between social convention and individual libertarianism.* **—di·a·lec·ti·cal·ly** /-ik(ə)lē/ *adv.*

di·a·lec·ti·cal ma·te·ri·al·ism ▸*n.* the Marxist theory (adopted as the official philosophy of the Soviet communists) that political and historical events result from the conflict of social forces and are interpretable as a series of contradictions and their solutions. The conflict is believed to be caused by material needs. **—di·a·lec·ti·cal ma·te·ri·al·ist** *n.* & *adj.*

di·a·lec·ti·cian /ˌdīəlekˈtisʜən/ ▸*n.* a person skilled in philosophical debate. ▷mid 16th cent.: from French *dialecticien,* from Latin *dialecticus,* based on Greek *dialegesthai* 'converse with.'

di·a·lec·tics /ˌdīəˈlektiks/ ▸*plural n.* & *adj.* see DIALECTIC.

di·a·lec·tol·o·gy /ˌdīəlekˈtäləjē/ ▸*n.* the branch of linguistics concerned with the study of dialects. **—di·a·lec·to·log·i·cal** /-təˈläjikəl/ *adj.* **—di·a·lec·tol·o·gist** /-jist/ *n.*

di·al·er /ˈdī(ə)lər/ ▸*n.* a device or piece of software for calling telephone numbers automatically: *hackers can break in with speed dialers.*

di·al-in ▸*adj.* another term for DIAL-UP.

di·a·log box /ˈdīəˌläg; -ˌlôg/ ▸*n. Computing* a small area on screen, in which the user is prompted to provide information or select commands.

di·a·log·ic /ˌdīəˈläjik/ ▸*adj.* relating to or in the form of dialogue. ▷mid 19th cent.: via late Latin from Greek *dialogikos,* from *dialogos* (see DIALOGUE). **—di·a·log·i·cal** *adj.*

di·al·o·gism /dīˈaləˌjizəm/ ▸*n.* the use in a text of different tones or viewpoints, whose interaction or contradiction is important to the text's interpretation. ▷mid 16th cent.: from late Latin *dialogismos,* from Greek *dialogizesthai* 'to converse,' from *dialogos* 'discourse' (see DIALOGUE).

di·a·logue /ˈdīəˌläg; -ˌlôg/ (also **di·a·log**) ▸*n.* conversation between two or more people as a feature of a book, play, or movie: *the book consisted of a series of dialogues* | *passages of dialogue.* See note at CONVERSATION. ■ a discussion between two or more people or groups, esp. one directed toward exploration of a particular subject or resolution of a problem: *the U.S. would enter into a direct* ***dialogue with*** *Vietnam* | *interfaith dialogue.*
▸*v.* [*intrans.*] take part in a conversation or discussion to resolve a problem: *he stated that he wasn't going to* ***dialogue with*** *the guerrillas.* ■ [*trans.*] provide (a movie or play) with a dialogue. ▷Middle English: from Old French *dialoge,* via Latin from Greek *dialogos,* from *dialegesthai* 'converse with,' from *dia* 'through' + *legein* 'speak.'
▸*PHRASE* □ **dialogue of the deaf** a discussion in which each party is unresponsive to what the others say.

di·al tone ▸*n.* a sound that a telephone produces indicating that a caller may start to dial.

di·al-up ▸*adj.* (of a computer system or service) used remotely via a telephone line.

di·al·y·sis /dīˈaləsis/ ▸*n.* (*pl.* **-ses** /-sēz/) *Chemistry* the separation of particles in a liquid on the basis of differences in their ability to pass through a membrane. ■ *Medicine* the clinical purification of blood by this technique, as a substitute for the normal function of the kidney. ▷mid 19th cent.: via Latin from Greek *dialusis,* from *dialuein* 'split, separate,' from *dia* 'apart' + *luein* 'set free.' **—di·a·lyt·ic** /ˌdīəˈlitik/ *adj.*

di·al·y·zate /dīˈaləˌzāt/ (also **di·al·y·sate**) ▸*n.* the part of a mixture that passes through the membrane in dialysis. ■ the solution this forms with the fluid on the other side of the membrane. ■ the fluid used on the other side of the membrane during dialysis to remove impurities. ▷late 19th cent.: from DIALYSIS + -ATE[1]; the term originally denoted the part of the mixture that does *not* pass through the membrane.

di·a·lyze /ˈdīəˌlīz/ (*Brit.* **di·a·lyse**) ▸*v.* [*trans.*] purify (a mixture) by means of dialysis. ■ treat (a patient) by means of dialysis. ▷mid 19th cent.: from DIALYSIS, on the pattern of *analyze.*

diam. ▸*abbr.* ■ diameter.

Pronunciation Key ə *ago;* ər *over;* ˈə or ˌə *up;* ˈər or ˌər *fur;* a *hat;* ā *rate;* ä *car;* ch *chew;* e *let;* ē *see;* e(ə)r *air;* i *fit;* ī *by;* i(ə)r *ear;* ng *sing;* ō *go;* ô *for;* oi *boy;* o͝o *good;* o͞o *goo;* ou *out;* sh *she;* th *thin;* t͟h *then;* (h)w *why;* zh *vision*

di·a·mag·net·ic /ˌdīəmagˈnetik/ ▸*adj. Physics* (of a substance or body) tending to become magnetized in a direction at 180° to the applied magnetic field. ▹1846: coined by Faraday, from Greek *dia* 'through, across' + MAGNETIC. —**di·a·mag·net** /ˈdīəˌmagnit/ *n.* —**di·a·mag·net·i·cal·ly** /-ik(ə)lē/ *adv.* —**di·a·mag·net·ism** /-ˈmagnəˌtizəm/ *n.*

di·a·man·té /ˌdēəmänˈtā/ ▸*adj.* decorated with artificial jewels: *a diamanté brooch.*
▸*n.* artificial jewels. ■ fabric or costume jewelry decorated with artificial jewels. ▹early 20th cent.: French, literally 'set with diamonds,' past participle of *diamanter*, from *diamant* 'diamond.'

di·a·man·tif·er·ous /ˌdīəmənˈtifərəs/ ▸*adj.* (of a rock formation, region, etc.) producing or yielding diamonds. ▹late 19th cent.: from French *diamantifère*, from *diamant* 'diamond' + *-fère* 'producing.'

di·a·man·tine /ˌdīəˈmanˌtīn; ˈdīəˌman-; -ˌtēn/ ▸*adj.* made from or reminiscent of diamonds. ▹mid 16th cent. (in the sense 'hard as diamond'): from French *diamantin*, from *diamant* 'diamond.'

di·am·e·ter /dīˈamitər/ (abbr.: **diam.**) ▸*n.* **1** a straight line passing from side to side through the center of a body or figure, esp. a circle or sphere. ■ the length of this line. ■ a transverse measurement of something; width or thickness. **2** a unit of linear measurement of magnifying power. ▹late Middle English: from Old French *diametre*, via Latin from Greek *diametros (grammē)* '(line) measuring across,' from *dia* 'across' + *metron* 'measure.' —**di·am·e·tral** /-trəl/ *adj.*

di·a·met·ri·cal /ˌdīəˈmetrikəl/ ▸*adj.* **1** used to emphasize how completely different two or more things are: *he's the diametrical opposite of Gabriel.* **2** of or along a diameter. ▹mid 16th cent. (sense 2): from Greek *diametrikos* (from *diametros* 'measuring across': see DIAMETER) + -AL. —**di·a·met·ric** *adj.* —**di·a·met·ri·cal·ly** /-ik(ə)lē/ *adv.*

di·am·ine /ˈdīəˌmēn; dīˈamin/ ▸*n. Chemistry* a compound whose molecule contains two amino groups, esp. when not part of amide groups.

Dia·mond /ˈdī(ə)mənd/, Neil (1941–), U.S. pop songwriter and singer. Among his many hits are "Cherry, Cherry" (1966), "Sweet Caroline" (1969) "You Don't Bring Me Flowers" (1978, a duet with Barbra Streisand), and "Hello Again" (1980).

dia·mond /ˈdī(ə)mənd/ ▸*n.* **1** a precious stone consisting of a clear and typically colorless crystalline form of pure carbon, the hardest naturally occurring substance. ■ a tool with a small stone of such a kind for cutting glass. ■ in extended and metaphorical use with reference to the brilliance, form, or hardness of diamonds: *the air glitters like diamonds.*

Diamonds occur in some igneous rock formations (kimberlite) and alluvial deposits. They are typically octahedral in shape but can be cut in many ways to enhance the internal reflection and refraction of light, producing jewels of sparkling brilliance. Diamonds are also used in cutting tools and abrasives.

2 [often as *adj.*] a figure with four straight sides of equal length forming two opposite acute angles and two opposite obtuse angles; a rhombus: *decorative diamond shapes.* ■ (**diamonds**) one of the four suits in a conventional pack of playing cards, denoted by a red figure of such a shape. ■ a card of this suit: *she led a losing diamond.* ■ the area delimited by the four bases of a baseball field, forming a square shape. ■ a baseball field. ▹Middle English: from Old French *diamant*, from medieval Latin *diamas, diamant-*, variant of Latin *adamans* (see ADAMANT). —**dia·mond·if·er·ous** /ˌdī(ə)mənˈdifərəs/ *adj.*
▸*PHRASE* □ **diamond in the rough** a person who is generally of good character but lacks manners, education, or style.

dia·mond·back /ˈdī(ə)məndˌbak/ ▸*n.* **1** (also **diamondback rattlesnake**) a large, common North American rattlesnake with diamond-shaped markings. Also called DIAMOND RATTLESNAKE. • Genus *Crotalus*, family Viperidae: two species. **2** another term for TERRAPIN (sense 1).

dia·mond·back moth ▸*n.* a small, grayish moth that displays a pattern of diamonds along its back when the wings are folded. The caterpillar can be a pest of brassicas and other cultivated vegetables. • *Plutella xylostella*, family Yponomeutidae.

dia·mond-cut ▸*adj.* **1** cut with facets like a diamond. **2** cut into the shape of a diamond.

Dia·mond Head a volcanic crater that overlooks the port of Honolulu on the Hawaiian island of Oahu.

dia·mond ju·bi·lee ▸*n.* the sixtieth anniversary of a notable event, esp. a sovereign's accession or the foundation of an organization.

dia·mond plate ▸*n.* a diamond-shaped design that is stamped into metal to give it industrial strength.

dia·mond py·thon ▸*n.* a carpet python of a race occurring in the coastal areas of New South Wales. • *Morelia spilota spilota*, family Pythonidae.

dia·mond rat·tle·snake ▸*n.* another term for DIAMONDBACK (sense 1).

Dia·mond State a nickname for the state of DELAWARE[1].

dia·mond wed·ding (also **diamond wedding anniversary**) ▸*n.* the sixtieth (or seventy-fifth) anniversary of a wedding.

dia·mond wil·low ▸*n.* a willow with diamond-shaped depressions on the trunk as a result of fungal attack, resulting in timber with a diamond-shaped pattern of pale sapwood and darker heartwood. • Several species in the genus *Salix* are affected, in particular *S. bebbiana.*

di·a·mor·phine /ˌdīəˈmôrfēn/ ▸*n.* short for DIACETYLMORPHINE (heroin).

Di·an·a /dīˈanə/ *Roman Mythology* an early Italian goddess associated with hunting, virginity, and, in later literature, with the moon. Greek equivalent ARTEMIS.

di·an·a /dīˈanə/ ▸*n.* a North American fritillary (butterfly), the male of which is orange and black and the female blue and black. • *Speyeria diana*, subfamily Argynninae, family Nymphalidae. ▹modern Latin; associated with the goddess of the moon, because of the silvery crescents on the wings.

Di·an·a mon·key ▸*n.* a West African monkey that has a black face with a white crescent on the forehead. • *Cercopithecus diana*, family Cercopithecidae. ▹early 19th cent.: named after the Roman moon goddess DIANA.

Di·an·a, Princess of Wales (1961–97), former wife of Prince Charles; title before marriage *Lady Diana Frances Spencer*. The daughter of the 8th Earl Spencer, she married Prince Charles in 1981; the couple were divorced in 1996. She became a popular figure through her charity work and glamorous media appearances, and her death in an automobile accident in Paris gave rise to intense international mourning.

Di·a·net·ics /ˌdīəˈnetiks/ ▸*plural n.* [treated as *sing.*] a system developed by the founder of the Church of Scientology, L. Ron Hubbard, that aims to relieve psychosomatic disorder by cleansing the mind of harmful mental images. ▹1950s: from Greek *dianoētikos* 'relating to thought' + -ICS.

di·an·thus /dīˈanTHəs/ ▸*n.* (*pl.* **-thus·es**) a flowering plant of a genus that includes the pinks and carnations. • Genus *Dianthus*, family Caryophyllaceae. ▹from Greek *Dios* 'of Zeus' + *anthos* 'a flower.'

di·a·pa·son /ˌdīəˈpāzən; -sən/ ▸*n.* (also **open diapason** or **stopped diapason**) an organ stop sounding a main register of flue pipes, typically of eight-foot pitch. ■ *poetic/literary* the entire compass, range, or scope of something. ■ *figurative* a grand swelling burst of harmony. ▹late Middle English (denoting the interval of an octave): via Latin from Greek *dia pasōn (khordōn)* 'through all (notes).'

di·a·pause /ˈdīəˌpôz/ *Zoology* ▸*n.* a period of suspended development in an insect, other invertebrate, or mammal embryo, esp. during unfavorable environmental conditions.
▸*v.* [*intrans.*] [usu. as *adj.*] (**diapausing**) (of an insect or other animal) undergo such a period of suspended development. ▹late 19th cent.: from DIA- 'through' + the noun PAUSE.

di·a·pe·de·sis /ˌdīəpəˈdēsis/ ▸*n. Medicine* the passage of blood cells through the intact walls of the capillaries, typically accompanying inflammation. ▹early 17th cent.: modern Latin, based on Greek *dia* 'through' + *pēdan* 'throb or leap.'

dia·per /ˈdī(ə)pər/ ▸*n.* **1** a piece of absorbent material wrapped around a baby's bottom and between its legs to absorb and retain urine and feces. **2** a linen or cotton fabric woven in a repeating pattern of small diamonds. ■ a repeating geometric or floral pattern used to decorate a surface.
▸*v.* [*trans.*] **1** put a diaper on (a baby). **2** decorate (a surface) with a repeating geometric or floral pattern. ▹Middle English: from Old French *diapre*, from medieval Latin *diasprum*, from medieval Greek *diaspros* (adjective), from *dia* 'across' + *aspros* 'white.' The term seems originally to have denoted a costly fabric, but after the 15th cent. it was used as in noun sense 2; babies' diapers were originally made from pieces of this fabric, hence sense 1 (late 16th cent.).

dia·per rash ▸*n.* inflammation of a baby's skin caused by prolonged contact with a damp diaper.

di·aph·a·nous /dīˈafənəs/ ▸*adj.* (esp. of fabric) light, delicate, and translucent: *a diaphanous dress of pale gold.* ▹early 17th cent.: from medieval Latin *diaphanus*, from Greek *diaphanēs*, from *dia* 'through' + *phainein* 'to show.'

di·a·phone /ˈdīəˌfōn/ ▸*n.* a low-pitched fog signal operated by compressed air, characterized by the "grunt" that ends each note. ▹early 20th cent.: from Greek *dia* 'through' + *phōnē* 'sound.'

di·aph·o·rase /dīˈafəˌrās; -ˌrāz/ ▸*n. Biochemistry* an enzyme of the flavoprotein type, able to oxidize a reduced form of the coenzyme NAD. ▹1930s: from Greek *diaphoros* 'different' + -ASE.

di·a·pho·re·sis /ˌdīəfəˈrēsis/ ▸*n. technical* sweating, esp. to an unusual degree as a symptom of disease or a side effect of a drug. ▹late 17th cent.: via late Latin from Greek, from *diaphorein* 'carry off, sweat out,' from *dia* 'through' + *phorein* 'carry.'

di·a·pho·ret·ic /ˌdīəfəˈretik/ ▸*adj. Medicine* (chiefly of a drug) inducing perspiration. ■ (of a person) sweating heavily. ▹late Middle English: via late Latin from Greek *diaphorētikos*, from *diaphorein* 'sweat out.'

di·a·phragm /ˈdīəˌfram/ ▸*n.* **1** a dome-shaped, muscular partition separating the thorax from the abdomen in mammals. It plays a major role in breathing, as its contraction increases the volume of the thorax and so inflates the lungs. **2** a thin sheet of material forming a partition. ■ a taut, flexible membrane in mechanical or acoustic systems. ■ a thin contraceptive cap fitting over the cervix. **3** a device for varying the effective aperture of the lens in a camera or other optical system. ▹late Middle English: from late Latin *diaphragma*, from Greek, from *dia* 'through, apart' + *phragma* 'a fence.' —**di·a·phrag·mat·ic** /ˌdīəfragˈmatik/ *adj.*

di·a·phragm pump ▸*n.* a pump using a flexible diaphragm in place of a piston.

di·aph·y·sis /dīˈafəsis/ ▸*n.* (*pl.* **-ses** /-ˌsēz/) *Anatomy* the shaft or central part of a long bone. Compare with EPIPHYSIS. ▹mid 19th cent.: from Greek *diaphusis* 'growing through,' from *dia* 'through' + *phusis* 'growth.'

di·a·pir /ˈdīəˌpir/ ▸*n. Geology* a domed rock formation in which a core of rock has moved upward to pierce the overlying strata. ▹early 20th cent.: from Greek *diapeirainein* 'pierce through,' from *dia* 'through' + *peirainein* (from *peran* 'pierce'). —**di·a·pir·ic** /ˌdīəˈpirik/ *adj.* —**di·a·pir·ism** /-ˌizəm/ *n.*

di·a·pos·i·tive /ˌdīəˈpäzitiv/ ▸*n.* a positive photographic slide or transparency.

di·ap·sid /dīˈapsid/ ▸*n. Zoology* a reptile of a large group characterized by the presence of two temporal openings in the skull, including the lizards, snakes, crocodiles, dinosaurs, and pterosaurs. • Subclass Anapsida. ▹early 20th cent.: from modern Latin *Diapsida*, from DI-[1] 'two' + Greek *apsis, apsid-* 'arch.'

di·ar·chy /ˈdīˌärkē/ (also **dy·ar·chy**) ▸*n.* (*pl.* **-chies**) government by two independent authorities (esp. in India 1919–35). ▹late 19th cent.: from DI-[1] 'two' + Greek *arkhia* 'rule,' on the pattern of *monarchy.* —**di·ar·chal** /dīˈärkəl/ *adj.* —**di·ar·chic** /dīˈärkik/ *adj.*

di·a·rist /ˈdīərist/ ▸*n.* a person who writes a diary. —**di·a·ris·tic** /ˌdīəˈristik/ *adj.*

di·a·rize /ˈdīəˌrīz/ ▸*v.* [*intrans.*] *archaic* keep a record of events in a diary.

di·ar·rhe·a /ˌdīəˈrēə/ (*Brit.* **di·ar·rhoe·a**) ▸*n.* a condition in which feces are discharged from the bowels frequently and in a liquid form. ▹late Middle English: via late Latin *diarrhoea* from Greek *diarrhoia*, from *diarrhein* 'flow through,' from *dia* 'through' + *rhein* 'to flow.' —**di·ar·rhe·al** *adj.* —**di·ar·rhe·ic** /-ˈrēik/ *adj.*

di·a·ry /ˈdīərē/ ▸*n.* (*pl.* **-ries**) a book in which one keeps a daily record of events and experiences: *I resolved to **keep a diary** of events during the war.* ■ a datebook. ▹late 16th cent.: from Latin *diarium*, from *dies* 'day.'

Di·as /ˈdēəs; ˈdēˌäsH/ (also **Di·az** /ˈdēəsH/), Bartolomeu (*c.*1450–1500), Portuguese navigator and explorer. He was the first European to sail around the Cape of Good Hope 1488, thereby establishing a sea route from the Atlantic Ocean to Asia.

di·as·po·ra /dīˈaspərə/ ▸*n.* (often **the Diaspora**) Jews living outside Israel. ■ the dispersion of the Jews beyond Israel. ■ the dispersion of any people from their original homeland: *the diaspora of boat people from Asia.* ■ the people so dispersed: *the Ukrainian diaspora flocked back to Kiev.*

The main diaspora began in the 8th–6th centuries BC, and even before the sack of Jerusalem in AD 70, the number of Jews dispersed by the diaspora was greater than that living in Israel. Thereafter Jews were dispersed even more widely throughout the Roman world and beyond.

▷Greek, from *diaspeirein* 'disperse,' from *dia* 'across'+ *speirein* 'scatter.' The term originated in the Septuagint (Deuteronomy 28:25) in the phrase *esē diaspora en pasais basileiais tēs gēs* 'thou shalt be a dispersion in all kingdoms of the earth.'

di·a·spore /ˈdīəˌspôr/ ▶*n. Botany* a spore, seed, or other structure that functions in plant dispersal; a propagule.

di·a·stase /ˈdīəˌstās; -ˌstāz/ ▶*n. Biochemistry* another term for **AMYLASE**. ▷mid 19th cent.: from Greek *diastasis* 'separation,' from *dia* 'apart' + *stasis* 'placing.'

di·a·ste·ma /ˌdīəˈstēmə/ ▶*n.* (*pl.* **-ma·ta** /-mətə/) a gap between the teeth, in particular: ■ *Zoology* a space separating teeth of different functions, esp. that between the biting teeth (incisors and canines) and grinding teeth (premolars and molars) in rodents and ungulates. ■ a gap between a person's two upper front teeth. ▷mid 19th cent.: via late Latin from Greek *diastēma* 'space between.'

di·a·ste·re·o·i·so·mer /ˌdīəˌsterēōˈīsəmər/ ▶*n. Chemistry* each of a pair of stereoisomeric compounds that are not mirror images of one another. **—di·a·ste·re·o·i·so·mer·ic** /-ˌīsəˈmerik/ *adj.*

di·as·to·le /dīˈastl-ē/ ▶*n. Physiology* the phase of the heartbeat when the heart muscle relaxes and allows the chambers to fill with blood. Often contrasted with **SYSTOLE**. ▷late 16th cent.: via late Latin from Greek, 'separation, expansion,' from *diastellein*, from *dia* 'apart' + *stellein* 'to place.' **—di·as·tol·ic** /ˌdīəˈstälik/ *adj.*

di·a·tes·sa·ron /ˌdīəˈtesərən/ ▶*n.* the four Gospels combined into a single narrative.

di·a·ther·my /ˈdīəˌᴛʜərmē/ ▶*n.* a medical and surgical technique involving the production of heat in a part of the body by high-frequency electric currents, to stimulate the circulation, relieve pain, destroy unhealthy tissue, or cause bleeding vessels to clot. ▷early 20th cent.: from **DIA-** 'through' + *thermon* 'heat.'

di·ath·e·sis /dīˈaᴛʜəsis/ ▶*n.* **1** [usu. with *adj.*] *Medicine* a tendency to suffer from a particular medical condition: *a bleeding diathesis.* **2** *Linguistics* another term for **VOICE**(sense 4). ▷mid 17th cent.: modern Latin, from Greek, 'disposition,' from *diatithenai* 'arrange.' Sense 2 dates from the mid 20th cent.

di·a·tom /ˈdīəˌtäm/ ▶*n. Biology* a single-celled alga that has a cell wall of silica. Many kinds are planktonic, and extensive fossil deposits have been found. • Class Bacillariophyceae, division Chromophycota or Heterokontophyta (or phylum Bacillariophyta, kingdom Protista). ▷mid 19th cent.: from modern Latin *Diatoma* (genus name), from Greek *diatomos* 'cut in two,' from *diatemnein* 'to cut through.' **—di·a·to·ma·ceous** /ˌdīətəˈmāsʜəs/ *adj.*

di·a·to·ma·ceous earth ▶*n.* a soft, crumbly, porous sedimentary deposit formed from the fossil remains of diatoms.

di·a·tom·ic /ˌdīəˈtämik/ ▶*adj. Chemistry* consisting of two atoms.

di·at·o·mite /dīˈatəˌmīt/ ▶*n. Geology* a fine-grained sedimentary rock formed from consolidated diatomaceous earth. ▷late 19th cent.: from **DIATOM** + **-ITE**[1].

di·a·ton·ic /ˌdīəˈtänik/ ▶*adj. Music* (of a scale, interval, etc.) involving only notes proper to the prevailing key without chromatic alteration. ■ (of a melody or harmony) constructed from such a scale. ▷early 17th cent. (denoting a tetrachord divided into two tones and a lower semitone, or ancient Greek music based on this): from French *diatonique*, or via late Latin from Greek *diatonikos* 'at intervals of a tone,' from *dia* 'through' + *tonos* 'tone.'

di·a·treme /ˈdīəˌtrēm/ ▶*n. Geology* a long, vertical pipe or plug formed when gas-filled magma forced its way up through overlying strata. ▷early 20th cent.: from **DIA-** 'through' + Greek *trēma* 'perforation.'

di·a·tribe /ˈdīəˌtrīb/ ▶*n.* a forceful and bitter verbal attack against someone or something: *a diatribe against the Roman Catholic Church.* ▷late 16th cent. (denoting a disquisition): from French, via Latin from Greek *diatribē* 'spending of time, discourse,' from *dia* 'through' + *tribein* 'rub.'

Di·az /ˈdēəsʜ/ variant spelling of **DIAS**.

Dí·az /ˈdē-äs/, Porfirio (1830–1915), Mexican general and statesman; president 1877–80 and 1884–1911.

di·az·e·pam /dīˈazəˌpam/ ▶*n.* a tranquilizing muscle-relaxant drug used chiefly to relieve anxiety. Also called **VALIUM** (*trademark*). • A member of the benzodiazepine group; chem. formula: $C_{16}H_{13}N_2OCl$. ▷1960s: blend of **BENZODIAZEPINE** and **AMIDE**.

di·az·i·non /dīˈazəˌnän/ ▶*n.* an organophosphorus insecticide derived from pyrimidine. ▷mid 20th cent.: from *diazine* (see **DI-**[1], **AZINE**) + *-on* (suffix of unknown origin).

di·az·o /dīˈazō/ (also **di·az·o·type**) ▶*n.* a copying or coloring process using a diazo compound decomposed by ultraviolet light: [as *adj.*] *diazo printers.*

di·az·o com·pound ▶*n. Chemistry* an organic compound containing two nitrogen atoms bonded together, esp. a diazonium compound. ▷late 19th cent.: *diazo* from **DIAZONIUM**.

di·az·o·meth·ane /dīˌazōˈmeᴛʜān/ ▶*n. Chemistry* a poisonous, reactive yellow gas used as a methylating agent in chemical synthesis. • Chem. formula: CH_2N_2. ▷late 19th cent.: from *diazo-* (indicating the presence of two nitrogen atoms) + **METHANE**.

di·a·zo·ni·um /dīəˈzōnēəm/ ▶*n.* [as *adj.*] *Chemistry* an organic cation containing the group $-N_2^+$ bonded to an organic group. Aromatic diazonium compounds are typically intensely colored and include many synthetic dyes. ▷late 19th cent.: coined in German from *diazo-* (indicating the presence of two nitrogen atoms) + the suffix *-onium* (from **AMMONIUM**).

dib /dib/ ▶*v.* (**dibbed, dib·bing**) *Fishing* another term for **DAP**. ▷late 17th cent.: related to **DAB**[1].

di·ba·sic /dīˈbāsik/ ▶*adj. Chemistry* (of an acid) having two replaceable hydrogen atoms. ▷mid 19th cent.: from **DI-**[1] 'two' + **BASIC**.

dib·ble /ˈdibəl/ ▶*n.* a pointed hand tool for making holes in the ground for seeds or young plants.
▶*v.* [*trans.*] make (a hole) in soil with a dibble. ■ sow (a seed or plant) with a dibble. ▷late Middle English: apparently related to **DIB** (also used in this sense in dialect).

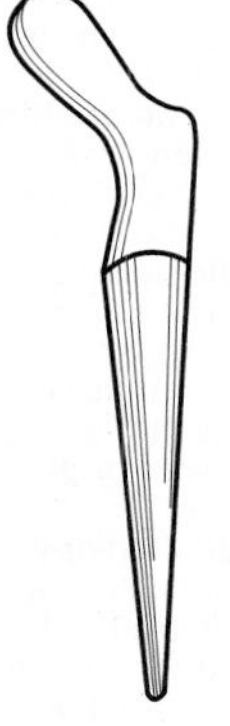

dibble

di·bo·rane /dīˈbôrˌān/ ▶*n. Chemistry* a poisonous, reactive gas made by the action of acids on some borides. It is the simplest of the boranes and is an example of electron-deficient bonding. • Chem. formula: B_2H_6.

dibs /dibz/ ▶*plural n. informal* money. ▷mid 18th cent. (denoting pebbles used in a children's game): from earlier *dib-stones*, perhaps from **DIB**.
▶*PHRASE* □ **have first dibs on** have the first right to or choice of: *they never got first dibs on great prospects.*

dice /dīs/ ▶*n.* (*pl.* same) a small cube with each side having a different number of spots on it, ranging from one to six, thrown and used in gambling and other games involving chance. See also **DIE**[2]. ■ a game played with dice. ■ small cubes of food.
▶*v.* **1** [*intrans.*] play or gamble with dice: [as *n.*] (**dicing**) *prohibitions on all dancing and dicing.* **2** [*trans.*] cut (food or other matter) into small cubes: *dice the peppers* | [as *adj.*] (**diced**) *add the diced onions.* ▷Middle English: from Old French *des*, plural of *de* (see **DIE**[2]). **—dic·er** *n.*
▶*PHRASES* □ **dice with death** take serious risks. □ **no dice** *informal* used to refuse a request or indicate no chance of success. □ **roll** (or **throw**) **of the dice** a risky attempt to do or achieve something: *the merger was their last roll of the dice, and it failed miserably.*

USAGE Historically, **dice** is the plural of **die**, but in modern standard English, **dice** is both the singular and the plural: *throw the dice* could mean a reference to two or more dice, or to just one. In fact, the singular **die** (rather than **dice**) is increasingly uncommon.

di·cen·tra /dīˈsentrə/ ▶*n.* a plant of the genus *Dicentra* (family Fumariaceae), esp. (in gardening) a bleeding heart. ▷modern Latin, from Greek *dikentros*, from *di-* 'two' + *kentron* 'spur, sharp point.'

di·cen·tric /dīˈsentrik/ *Genetics* ▶*adj.* (of a chromosome) having two centromeres.
▶*n.* a chromosome of this type.

dic·ey /ˈdīsē/ ▶*adj.* (**dic·i·er, dic·i·est**) *informal* unpredictable and potentially dangerous: *the lot of a wanderer is always dicey.*

di·cha·si·um /dīˈkāzʜ(ē)əm; -zēəm/ ▶*n.* (*pl.* **-si·a** /-zʜēə; -zēə/) *Botany* a cyme in which each flowering branch gives rise to two or more branches symmetrically placed. ▷late 19th cent.: modern Latin, from **DI-**[1] 'two' + Greek *khasis* 'separation.'

di·chlor·vos /dīˈklôrvəs/ ▶*n. Chemistry* a pale yellow liquid used as an insecticide and veterinary anthelmintic. • An organophosphorus compound; alternative name: 2,2-dichlorovinyl dimethyl phosphate; chem. formula: $(CH_3O)_2PO_2CHCCl_2$. ▷mid 20th cent.: from elements of the systematic name (see above).

di·chog·a·my /dīˈkägəmē/ ▶*n. Botany* the ripening of the stamens and pistils of a flower at different times, so that self-fertilization is prevented. Compare with **HOMOGAMY** (sense 3). ▷mid 19th cent.: from Greek *dikho-* 'apart, in two' + *gamos* 'marriage.' **—di·chog·a·mous** /-məs/ *adj.*

di·chot·ic /dīˈkätik/ ▶*adj.* involving or relating to the simultaneous stimulation of the right and left ear by different sounds. ▷mid 20th cent.: from Greek *dikho-* 'apart' + *ous, ōt-* 'ear' + **-IC**.

di·chot·o·mize /dīˈkätəˌmīz/ ▶*v.* [*trans.*] regard or represent as divided or opposed: *these rules dichotomize love and sex.*

di·chot·o·mous /dīˈkätəməs/ ▶*adj.* exhibiting or characterized by dichotomy: *a dichotomous view of the world.* ■ *Botany* (of branching) in which the axis is divided into two branches. ▷late 17th cent.: via late Latin from Greek *dikhotomos* (from *dikho-* 'in two' + *temnein* 'to cut') + **-OUS**. **—di·chot·o·mous·ly** *adv.*

di·chot·o·my /dīˈkätəmē/ ▶*n.* (*pl.* **-mies**) [usu. in *sing.*] a division or contrast between two things that are or are represented as being opposed or entirely different: *a rigid* **dichotomy between** *science and mysticism.* ■ *Botany* repeated branching into two equal parts. ▷late 16th cent.: via modern Latin from Greek *dikhotomia*, from *dikho-* 'in two, apart' + *-tomia* (see **-TOMY**).

di·chro·ic /dīˈkrō-ik/ ▶*adj.* (of a crystal) showing different colors when viewed from different directions, or (more generally) having different absorption coefficients for light polarized in different directions. ▷mid 19th cent.: from Greek *dikhroos* (from *di-* 'twice' + *khrōs* 'color') + **-IC**. **—di·chro·ism** /ˈdīkrōˌizəm/ *n.*

di·chro·mate /dīˈkrōmāt/ ▶*n. Chemistry* a salt, typically red or orange, containing the anion $Cr_2O_7^{2-}$. ▷mid 19th cent.: from **DI-**[1] 'two' + **CHROMATE**.

di·chro·ma·tism /dīˈkrōməˌtizəm/ ▶*n.* **1** (typically in an animal species) the occurrence of two different kinds of coloring. **2** color-blindness in which only two of the three primary colors can be discerned. **—di·chro·mat·ic** /ˌdīkrōˈmatik/ *adj.*

dick[1] /dik/ ▶*n.* **1** *vulgar slang* a penis. **2** [with *negative*] *vulgar slang* anything at all: *you don't know dick about this—you haven't a clue!*
▶*v.* **1** [*intrans.*] *vulgar slang* handle something inexpertly; meddle: *he started* **dicking around** *with the controls.* **2** [*trans.*] *vulgar slang* (of a man) have sexual intercourse with (someone). ▷mid 16th cent. (in the general sense 'fellow'): nickname for the given name *Richard*. Sense 1 of the *noun* dates from the late 18th cent.

dick[2] ▶*n. dated, informal* a detective. ▷early 20th cent.: perhaps an arbitrary shortening of **DETECTIVE**, or from obsolete slang *dick* 'look,' from Romany.

dick·cis·sel /dikˈsisəl; ˈdikˌsisəl/ ▶*n.* a sparrowlike North American songbird related to the cardinals, with a black-and-white throat and bright yellow breast. • *Spiza americana*, family Emberizidae (subfamily Cardinalinae). ▷late 19th cent.: imitative of its call.

Dick·ens /ˈdikənz/, Charles (John Huffam) (1812–70), English novelist. His novels are notable for their satirical humor and treatment of contemporary social problems, including the plight of the urban poor and the corruption and inefficiency of the legal system. Some of his most well-known novels include *Oliver Twist* (1837–38), *A Christmas Carol* (1843), *David Copperfield* (1850), and *Great Expectations* (1860–61).

dick·ens /ˈdikinz/ ▶*n.* [in *sing.*] *informal, dated* used for emphasis, euphemistically invoking the Devil: *they work* **like the dickens** | *she was* **in a dickens of a** *rush.* ■ (**the dickens**) used when asking questions to express annoyance or surprise: ***what the dickens*** *is going on?* ▷late 16th cent.: probably a use of the surname *Dickens*.

Dick·en·si·an /diˈkenzēən/ ▶*adj.* of or reminiscent of the novels of Charles Dickens, esp. in suggesting the poor social conditions or comically repulsive

Pronunciation Key ə *ago*; ər *over*; ˈə *or* ˌə *up*; ˈər *or* ˌər *fur*; a *hat*; ā *rate*; ä *car*; ᴄʜ *chew*; e *let*; ē *see*; e(ə)r *air*; i *fit*; ī *by*; i(ə)r *ear*; ɴɢ *sing*; ō *go*; ô *for*; oi *boy*; o͝o *good*; o͞o *goo*; ou *out*; sʜ *she*; ᴛʜ *thin*; T͟H *then*; (h)w *why*; zʜ *vision*

characters that they portray: *the back streets of Dickensian London.*

dick·er /ˈdikər/ ▸*v.* [*intrans.*] **1** engage in petty argument or bargaining: *she advised him not to dicker over the extra fee.* **2** treat something casually or irresponsibly; toy with something: [as *n.*] (**dickering**) *there was no dickering with the lyrics.* ▷early 19th cent.: perhaps from obsolete *dicker* 'set of ten (hides),' used as a unit of trade, based on Latin *decem* 'ten.' **—dick·er·er** *n.*

Dick·er·son /ˈdikərsən/, Eric (1960–), U.S. football player. He set the National Football League's single-season rushing record of 2,105 yards in 1984. He played for the Los Angeles Rams 1982–87, the Indianapolis Colts 1987–91, the Los Angeles Raiders 1992, and the Atlanta Falcons 1993.

Dick·ey /ˈdikē/, James (Lafayette) (1923–97), U.S. poet and writer. His works include the poetry in *Buckdancer's Choice* (1965) and the novel *Deliverance* (1970).

dick·ey /ˈdikē/ (also **dick·y**) ▸*n.* (*pl.* **dick·eys** or **dick·ies**) *informal* **1** a false shirtfront. **2** *dated, chiefly Brit.* a folding outside seat at the back of a vehicle; a rumble seat. ■ *historical, chiefly Brit.* a driver's seat in a carriage. ▷mid 18th cent. (denoting a petticoat): each sense probably having different origins; perhaps partly from *Dicky*, nickname for the given name *Richard.*

dick·ey bird ▸*n.* *informal* used by children to refer to a little bird. [late 18th cent.: probably from *Dicky*, nickname for the given name *Richard.*]

dick·head /ˈdik,hed/ ▸*n.* *vulgar slang* a stupid, irritating, or ridiculous person, particularly a man. ▷1960s: from DICK[1] + HEAD.

Dick·in·son /ˈdikənsən/, Emily (Elizabeth) (1830–86), U.S. poet. Her poems use an elliptical language and emphasize assonance and alliteration rather than rhyme. They reflect the struggles of her reclusive life. Although she wrote nearly 2,000 poems, only 7 were published during her lifetime.

Emily Dickinson

dick·wad /ˈdik,wäd/ ▸*n.* *vulgar slang* a contemptible person. ▷1980s: from *dick* in the sense 'penis' + *wad.*

dick·y /ˈdikē/ ▸*adj.* (**dick·i·er**, **dick·i·est**) *Brit., informal* (of a part of the body, a structure, or a device) not strong, healthy, or functioning reliably: *a man with a dicky leg.* ▷late 18th cent. (in the sense 'almost over'): perhaps from the given name *Dick*, in the old saying *as queer as Dick's hatband.*

di·cot /ˈdīkät/ ▸*n.* short for DICOTYLEDON.

di·cot·y·le·don /dī,kätlˈēdn/ ▸*n.* *Botany* a flowering plant with an embryo that bears two cotyledons (seed leaves). Dicotyledons constitute the larger of the two great divisions of flowering plants, and typically have broad, stalked leaves with netlike veins (e.g., daisies, hawthorns, oaks). Compare with MONOCOTYLEDON. • Class Dicotyledoneae (or -donae, -dones; sometimes Magnoliopsida), subdivision Angiospermae. ▷early 18th cent.: from modern Latin *dicotyledones* (plural), from *di-* 'two' + *cotyledon* (see COTYLEDON). **—di·cot·y·le·don·ous** /-əs/ *adj.*

di·crot·ic /dīˈkrätik/ ▸*adj.* *Medicine* denoting a pulse in which a double beat is detectable for each beat of the heart. ▷early 19th cent.: from Greek *dikrotos* 'beating twice' + -IC.

dict. ▸*abbr.* ■ dictation. ■ dictionary.

dic·ta /ˈdiktə/ ▸ plural form of DICTUM.

dic·tam·nus /dikˈtamnəs/ ▸*n.* **1** another term for DITTANY OF CRETE (see DITTANY). **2** another term for GAS PLANT. ▷mid 16th cent.: from Latin.

Dic·ta·phone /ˈdiktə,fōn/ (also **dic·ta·phone**) ▸*n.* *trademark* a small cassette recorder used to record speech for transcription at a later time. ▷early 20th cent.: from DICTATE or DICTATION + -PHONE.

dic·tate /ˈdik,tāt/ [*trans.*] ▸*v.* **1** lay down authoritatively; prescribe: *the tsar's attempts to dictate policy* | [*intrans.*] *that doesn't give you the right to* **dictate to** *me.* ■ control or decisively affect; determine: *choice is often dictated by availability* | [*intrans.*] *a review process can be changed* **as circumstances dictate.** **2** say or read aloud (words to be typed, written down, or recorded on tape): *I have four letters to dictate.*
▸*n.* (usu. **dictates**) an order or principle that must be obeyed: *the dictates of fashion.* ▷late 16th cent. (sense 2): from Latin *dictat-* 'dictated,' from the verb *dictare.*

dic·ta·tion /dikˈtāSHən/ ▸*n.* **1** (abbr.: **dict.**) the action of saying words aloud to be typed, written down, or recorded on tape: *the dictation of letters.* ■ the activity of taking down a passage that is read aloud by a teacher as a test of spelling, writing, or language skills: *passages for dictation.* ■ an utterance that is typed, written down, or recorded: *the person who writes the dictation down is his agent.* **2** the action of giving orders authoritatively or categorically. ▷mid 17th cent. (sense 2): from late Latin *dictatio(n-)*, from the verb *dictare* (see DICTATE).

dic·ta·tor /ˈdik,tātər/ ▸*n.* **1** a ruler with total power over a country, typically one who has obtained power by force. ■ a person who tells people what to do in an autocratic way or who determines behavior in a particular sphere: *the prewar era was a period whose apple-cheeked dictator was Doris Day.* ■ (in ancient Rome) a chief magistrate with absolute power, appointed in an emergency. **2** a machine that records words spoken into it, used for personal or administrative purposes. ▷late Middle English: from Latin, from *dictat-* 'dictated,' from the verb *dictare* (see DICTATE).

dic·ta·to·ri·al /,diktəˈtôrēəl/ ▸*adj.* of or typical of a ruler with total power: *a dictatorial regime.* ■ having or showing a tendency to tell people what to do in an autocratic way: *his dictatorial manner.* **—dic·ta·to·ri·al·ly** *adv.*

dic·ta·tor·ship /dikˈtātər,SHip; ˈdiktātər-/ ▸*n.* government by a dictator: *forty years of dictatorship.* ■ a country governed by a dictator. ■ absolute authority in any sphere.

dic·tion /ˈdikSHən/ ▸*n.* **1** the choice and use of words and phrases in speech or writing: *Wordsworth campaigned against exaggerated poetic diction.* **2** the style of enunciation in speaking or singing: *she began imitating his careful diction.* ▷mid 16th cent. (denoting a word or phrase): from Latin *dictio(n-)*, from *dicere* 'to say.'

dic·tion·ar·y /ˈdikSHə,nerē/ (abbr.: **dict.**) ▸*n.* (*pl.* **-ar·ies**) a book that lists the words of a language in alphabetical order and gives their meaning, or that gives the equivalent words in a different language. ■ a reference book on any subject, the items of which are arranged in alphabetical order: *a dictionary of quotations.* ▷early 16th cent.: from medieval Latin *dictionarium (manuale)* or *dictionarius (liber)* 'manual or book of words,' from Latin *dictio* (see DICTION).
▸*PHRASE* □ **have swallowed a dictionary** *informal* (of a person) use long and obscure words when speaking.

dic·tion·ar·y at·tack ▸*n.* an attempted illegal entry to a computer system that uses a dictionary headword list to generate possible passwords.

dic·tum /ˈdiktəm/ ▸*n.* (*pl.* **-ta** /-tə/ or **-tums**) a formal pronouncement from an authoritative source: *the Politburo's dictum that the party will become a "left-wing parliamentary party."* ■ a short statement that expresses a general truth or principle: *the old dictum "might makes right."* ■ *Law* short for OBITER DICTUM. ▷late 16th cent.: from Latin, literally 'something said,' neuter past participle of *dicere.*

dic·ty /ˈdiktē/ ▸*adj.* *black slang* ostentatiously stylish; pretentious: *up there in their dicty Detroit suburb living the so-called good life.* ▷early 20th cent.: of unknown origin.

Dic·ty·op·ter·a /,diktēˈäptərə/ *Entomology* an order of insects that comprises the cockroaches and mantises. They have a somewhat flattened form, two pairs of wings, and long spiky legs. ▷modern Latin (plural), from Greek *diktuon* 'net' + *pteron* 'wing.' **—dic·ty·op·ter·an** *n.* & *adj.*

di·cyn·o·dont /dīˈsinə,dänt/ ▸*n.* a herbivorous, mammallike fossil reptile of the late Permian and Triassic periods, with beaked jaws and no teeth apart from two tusks in the upper jaw of the male. • *Dicynodon* and other genera, infra-order Dicynodontia, order Therapsida. ▷mid 19th cent.: from modern Latin *Dicynodontia* (plural), from Greek *di-* 'two' + *kuōn* 'dog' + *odous, odont-* 'tooth.'

did /did/ ▸ past of DO[1].

di·dac·tic /dīˈdaktik/ ▸*adj.* intended to teach, particularly in having moral instruction as an ulterior motive: *a didactic novel that set out to expose social injustice.* ■ in the manner of a teacher, particularly so as to treat someone in a patronizing way: *slow-paced, didactic lecturing.* ▷mid 17th cent.: from Greek *didaktikos*, from *didaskein* 'teach.' **—di·dac·ti·cal·ly** /-ik(ə)lē/ *adv.* **—di·dac·ti·cism** /-tə,sizəm/ *n.*

di·dan·o·sine /dīˈdanə,sēn/ ▸*n.* *Medicine* another term for DIDEOXYINOSINE.

did·di·coy ▸*n.* variant spelling of DIDICOI.

did·dle /ˈdidl/ ▸*v.* *informal* **1** [*trans.*] (usu. **be diddled**) cheat or swindle (someone) so as to deprive them of something: *he thought he'd been* **diddled out of** *his change.* ■ deliberately falsify (something): *he diddled his income tax returns.* **2** [*intrans.*] *informal* pass time aimlessly or unproductively: *why* **diddle around** *with slow costly tests?* ■ (**diddle with**) play or mess with: *he diddled with the graphics on his computer.* **3** [*trans.*] *vulgar slang* have sexual intercourse with (someone). [originally in Scots dialect use in the sense 'jerk from side to side,' apparently corresponding to dialect *didder* 'tremble.'] ▷early 19th cent.: probably from the name of Jeremy *Diddler*, a character in the farce *Raising the Wind* (1803) by the Irish dramatist James Kenney (1780–1849). Diddler constantly borrowed and failed to repay small sums of money: the name may have been based on an earlier verb *diddle* 'walk unsteadily, swerve.' **—did·dler** *n.*

did·dly-squat /ˈdidlē ,skwät/ (also **did·dly**, **did·dley**, or **dood·ly-squat**) ▸*pron.* [usu. with *negative*] *informal* anything: *she didn't care diddly-squat about what Darryl thought* | *they don't know diddly about softball.* ▷late 20th cent.: probably from slang *doodle* 'excrement' + SQUAT in the sense 'defecate.'

di·de·ox·y·cyt·i·dine /,dīdē,äksīˈsitə,dēn/ (abbr.: **DDC** or **ddC**) ▸*n.* *Medicine* a drug that inhibits the replication of HIV and is used in the treatment of AIDS, esp. in combination with zidovudine. It is a synthetic analog of a pyrimidine nucleoside.

di·de·ox·y·in·o·sine /,dīdē,äksēˈinə,sēn/ (abbr.: **DDI** or **ddI**) ▸*n.* *Medicine* a drug that inhibits the replication of HIV and is used in the treatment of AIDS, esp. in combination with zidovudine. It is a synthetic analog of a purine nucleoside. ▷1970s: from DI-[1] 'two' + *deoxy-* (in the sense 'that has lost oxygen'') + INOSINE.

Di·de·rot /ˈdēdə,rō/, Denis (1713–84), French philosopher, writer, and critic. A leading figure of the Enlightenment in France, he was principal editor of the *Encyclopédie* (1751–76). Other notable works: *Le Rêve de D'Alembert* (1782) and *Le Neveu de Rameau* (1805).

didg·er·i·doo /,dijərēˈdo͞o/ (also **didj·er·i·doo** or **didj·er·i·du**) ▸*n.* an Australian Aboriginal wind instrument in the form of a long wooden tube, traditionally made from a hollow branch, which is blown to produce a deep, resonant sound, varied by rhythmic accents of timbre and volume. ▷1920s: imitative; from an Aboriginal language of Arnhem Land, Northern Territory.

did·i·coi /ˈdidi,koi/ (also **did·di·coy**) ▸*n.* (*pl.* **-cois**) *dialect* a gypsy; an itinerant tinker. ▷mid 19th cent.: perhaps an alteration of Romany *dik akei* 'look here.'

did·n't /ˈdidnt/ ▸*contraction of* did not.

Di·do /ˈdīdō/ (in the *Aeneid*) the queen and founder of Carthage, who fell in love with the shipwrecked Aeneas and killed herself when he deserted her.

di·do /ˈdī,dō/ ▸*n.* (*pl.* **-does** or **-dos**) (in phrase **cut/cut up didoes**) *informal* perform mischievous tricks or deeds. ▷early 19th cent.: of unknown origin.

Did·rik·son, Babe, see **ZAHARIAS**.

didst /didst/ ▸ archaic second person singular past of DO[1].

Did·y·ma /ˈdidimə/ an ancient sanctuary of Apollo, site of one of the most famous oracles of the Aegean region, close to the west coast of Asia Minor.

di·dym·i·um /dīˈdimēəm/ ▸*n.* *Chemistry* a mixture containing the rare earth elements praseodymium and neodymium, used to color glass for optical filters. It was originally regarded as a single element. ▷mid 19th cent.: from Greek *didumos* 'twin' (because it was closely associated with lanthanum) + *-ium* (used as a suffix for new metals).

die[1] /dī/ ▸*v.* (**dy·ing** /ˈdīiNG/) [*intrans.*] **1** (of a person, animal, or plant) stop living: *she* **died of** *cancer* | *the sheep* **died from** *the heat* | [*trans.*] *the king died a violent death.* ■ (**die for**) be killed for (a cause): *they were prepared to die for their country.* ■ [with *complement*] have a specified status at the time of one's death: *the inventor died a pauper.* ■ (**die out**) become extinct: *many species died out.* ■ be forgotten: *her genius has assured her name will* *never die.* ■ [with *adverbial*] become less loud or strong: *after a while, the noise* **died down** | *at last the storm* **died away**. ■ (**die back**) (of a plant) decay from the tip toward the root: *rhubarb dies back to a crown of buds each winter.* ■ (**die off**) die one after another until few or none are left: *the original founders died off or retired.* ■ be no longer under the influence of something: *we* **died to** *our former selves.* ■ (of a fire or light) stop burning or gleaming. ■ *informal* (of a machine) stop functioning: *three toasters have* **died on** *me.* ■ *poetic/literary* have an orgasm. **2** *informal* used to emphasize that one wants to do or have something very much: *they must be* **dying for** *a drink* | [with *infinitive*] *he's dying to meet you.* ■ *informal* used to emphasize how keenly one feels something: *I'm simply* **dying of** *thirst.* **3** *informal* used to emphasize feelings of shock, embarrassment, amusement, or misery: *I* **nearly died** *when I saw them* | *we nearly died laughing when he told us.* ▷Middle English: from Old Norse *deyja*, of Germanic origin; related to **DEAD**.

▸*PHRASES* □ **die hard** disappear or change very slowly: *old habits die hard.* □ **die on the vine** be unsuccessful at an early stage. □ **never say die** used to encourage someone in a difficult situation. □ **to die for** *informal* extremely good or desirable: *the ice cream is to die for.*

die[2] ▸*n.* **1** singular form of **DICE**. ■ *Architecture* the cubical part of a pedestal between the base and the cornice; a dado or plinth. **2** (*pl.* **dies**) a device for cutting or molding metal into a particular shape. ■ an engraved device for stamping a design on coins or medals. ▷Middle English: from Old French *de*, from Latin *datum* 'something given or played,' neuter past participle of *dare*.

▸*PHRASES* □ **the die is cast** an event has happened or a decision has been made that cannot be changed. □ (**as**) **straight as a die** absolutely straight.

USAGE See usage at **DICE**.

die·back /ˈdīˌbak/ ▸*n.* a condition in which a tree or shrub begins to die from the tip of its leaves or roots backward, owing to disease or an unfavorable environment.

die-cast ▸*adj.* (of a metal object) formed by pouring molten metal into a reusable mold: *a die-cast aluminum loudspeaker chassis.*

▸*v.* [*trans.*] [usu. as *n.*] (**die-casting**) make (a metal object) in this way.

dief·fen·bach·i·a /ˌdēfənˈbäkēə/ ▸*n.* a plant of a genus that includes dumb cane and its relatives. • Genus *Dieffenbachia*, family Araceae. ▷modern Latin, named after Ernst *Dieffenbach* (1811–55), German horticulturalist.

di·e·ge·sis /ˌdīəˈjēsis/ ▸*n.* (*pl.* **-ses** /-sēz/) a narrative or plot, typically in a movie. ▷early 19th cent.: from Greek *diēgēsis* 'narrative.' —**di·e·get·ic** /-ˈjetik/ *adj.*

die·hard /ˈdīˌhärd/ ▸*n.* [often as *adj.*] a person who strongly opposes change or who continues to support something in spite of opposition: *several hundred diehard communists shouted slogans* | *she was a diehard Yankees fan.* ▷mid 19th cent.: from *die hard* (see **DIE**[1]).

die-in ▸*n.* *informal* a demonstration in which people lie down as if dead: *should it be a mass die-in on the campus main lawn?*

di·el /ˈdī(ə)l; ˈdē(ə)l/ ▸*adj.* *Biology* denoting or involving a period of 24 hours: *tidal and diel cycles.* ▷1930s: from Latin *dies* 'day' + *-(a)l* (see **-AL**).

diel·drin /ˈdēldrin/ ▸*n.* a toxic insecticide produced by the oxidation of aldrin, now largely banned because of its persistence in the environment. • A chlorinated epoxide; chem. formula: $C_{12}H_8Cl_6O$. ▷1940s: blend of the name *Diels* (see **DIELS–ALDER REACTION**) + **ALDRIN**.

di·e·lec·tric /ˌdīəˈlektrik/ *Physics* ▸*adj.* having the property of transmitting electric force without conduction; insulating.

▸*n.* a medium or substance with such a property; an insulator. ▷mid 19th cent.: from **DI-**[3] + **ELECTRIC**, literally 'across which electricity is transmitted (without conduction).' —**di·e·lec·tri·cal·ly** /-ik(ə)lē/ *adv.*

di·e·lec·tric con·stant ▸*n.* *Physics* a quantity measuring the ability of a substance to store electrical energy in an electric field.

di·e·lec·tro·pho·re·sis /ˌdīəˌlektrəfəˈrēsis/ ▸*n.* *Physics* the migration of uncharged particles toward the position of maximum field strength in a nonuniform electric field. ▷mid 20th cent.: blend of **DIELECTRIC** and **ELECTROPHORESIS**.

die link ▸*n.* an established connection between coins struck from the same die.

▸*v.* [*trans.*] (**die-link**) establish a connection between (coins).

Diels-Al·der re·ac·tion /ˈdēlz ˈôldər/ ▸*n.* *Chemistry* an addition reaction in which a conjugated diene reacts with a compound with a double or triple bond so as to form a six-membered ring. ▷1940s: named after Otto *Diels* (1876–1954), and Kurt Alder (1902–58), German chemists.

Dien Bien Phu /ˌdyen ˌbyen ˈfo͞o/ a village in northwestern Vietnam. It was the site of a French military post that was captured by the Vietminh after a 55-day siege in 1954.

di·en·ceph·a·lon /ˌdīenˈsefəˌlän/ ▸*n.* *Anatomy* the caudal (posterior) part of the forebrain, containing the epithalamus, thalamus, hypothalamus, and ventral thalamus and the third ventricle. Compare with **TELENCEPHALON**. ▷late 19th cent.: from **DI-**[3] 'across' + Greek *enkephalos* 'brain.' —**di·en·ce·phal·ic** /-səˈfalik/ *adj.*

di·ene /ˈdīˌēn/ ▸*n.* *Chemistry* an unsaturated hydrocarbon containing two double bonds between carbon atoms. ▷early 20th cent.: from **DI-**[1] 'two' + **-ENE**.

die-off ▸*n.* a period in which a significant proportion of a population dies naturally, usually within a short time. ■ a process causing this. ■ (mass noun) the death of a significant proportion of a population in this way.

di·er·e·sis /dīˈerəsis/ (also **di·aer·e·sis**) ▸*n.* (*pl.* **-ses** /-ˌsēz/) **1** a mark ([die]) placed over a vowel to indicate that it is sounded in a separate syllable, as in *naïve, Brontë.* ■ the division of a sound into two syllables, esp. by sounding a diphthong as two vowels. **2** *Prosody* a natural rhythmic break in a line of verse where the end of a metrical foot coincides with the end of a word. ▷late 16th cent. (denoting the division of one syllable into two): via Latin from Greek *diairesis* 'separation,' from *diairein* 'take apart,' from *dia* 'apart' + *hairein* 'take.'

Die·sel /ˈdēzəl/, Rudolf (Christian Karl) (1858–1913), German engineer; born in France. He invented the diesel engine in the late 19th century.

die·sel /ˈdēzəl; -səl/ ▸*n.* (also **diesel engine**) an internal combustion engine in which heat produced by the compression of air in the cylinder is used to ignite the fuel: [as *adj.*] *a diesel locomotive.* ■ a heavy petroleum fraction used as fuel in diesel engines: *eleven liters of diesel.* ▷late 19th cent.: named after R. **DIESEL**. —**die·sel·ize** /-ˌlīz/ *v.*

die·sel-e·lec·tric ▸*adj.* denoting or relating to a locomotive driven by the electric current produced by a diesel-engined generator.

▸*n.* a locomotive of this type.

die·sel-hy·drau·lic ▸*adj.* denoting or relating to a locomotive driven by a hydraulic transmission system powered by a diesel engine.

▸*n.* a locomotive of this type.

die-sink·er ▸*n.* a person who engraves dies used to stamp designs on coins or medals.

Di·es I·rae /ˈdēās ˈi(ə)rā/ ▸*n.* a Latin hymn formerly sung in a Mass for the dead. ▷Latin, literally 'day of wrath' (the opening words of the hymn).

di·es non /ˌdēāz ˈnän/ ▸*n.* (*pl.* same) a day on which no legal business can be done, or which does not count for legal or other purposes. ▷Latin, short for *dies non juridicus* 'nonjudicial day.'

die-stamp·ing ▸*n.* a method of embossing paper or another surface using a die. ■ a method of printing using an inked die to produce raised print.

die·stock /ˈdīˌstäk/ ▸*n.* a hand tool used in the cutting of external screw threads, consisting of a holder for the die that is turned using long handles.

di·es·trus /dīˈestrəs/ ▸*n.* *Zoology* (in most female mammals) a period of sexual inactivity between recurrent periods of estrus.

di·et[1] /ˈdī-it/ ▸*n.* the kinds of food that a person, animal, or community habitually eats: *a vegetarian diet* | *a specialist in diet.* ■ a special course of food to which one restricts oneself, either to lose weight or for medical reasons: *I'm* **going on a diet**. ■ [as *adj.*] (of food or drink) with reduced fat or sugar content: *diet soft drinks.* ■ *figurative* a regular occupation or series of activities in which one participates: *a healthy diet of classical music.*

▸*v.* (**di·et·ed**, **di·et·ing**) [*intrans.*] restrict oneself to small amounts or special kinds of food in order to lose weight: *it's difficult to diet.* ▷Middle English: from Old French *diete* (noun), *dieter* (verb), via Latin from Greek *diaita* 'a way of life.' —**di·et·er** *n.*

di·et[2] ▸*n.* a legislative assembly in certain countries. ■ *historical* a regular meeting of the states of a confederation. ■ *Scots Law* a meeting or session of a court. ▷late Middle English: from medieval Latin *dieta* 'day's work, wages, etc.,' also 'meeting of councilors.'

di·e·tar·y /ˈdī-iˌterē/ ▸*adj.* of or relating to diets or dieting: *dietary advice for healthy skin and hair.* ■ provided by one's diet: *the average dietary calcium intake was 140 milligrams per day.*

▸*n.* (*pl.* **-tar·ies**) *dated* a regulated or restricted diet. ▷late Middle English (as a noun): from medieval Latin *dietarium*, from Latin *diaeta* (see **DIET**[1]).

di·e·tet·ic /ˌdī-iˈtetik/ ▸*adj.* concerned with diet and nutrition: *experienced dietetic advice.* ▷mid 16th cent. (as a noun in the sense 'dietetics'): via Latin from Greek *diaitētikos*, from *diaita* 'a way of life.' —**di·e·tet·i·cal·ly** /-ik(ə)lē/ *adv.*

di·e·tet·ics /ˌdī-iˈtetiks/ ▸*plural n.* [treated as *sing.*] the branch of knowledge concerned with the diet and its effects on health, esp. with the practical application of a scientific understanding of nutrition.

di·eth·yl·ene gly·col /dīˈethəˌlēn ˈglīkôl/ ▸*n.* *Chemistry* a colorless, soluble liquid used as a solvent and antifreeze. • Chem. formula: $(C_2H_4OH)_2O$.

di·eth·yl e·ther /dīˈethəl ˈēthər/ ▸*n.* see **ETHER** (sense 1).

di·eth·yl·stil·bes·trol /dīˌethəlstilˈbestrôl/ ▸*n.* another term for **STILBESTROL**.

di·e·ti·tian /ˌdī-iˈtishən/ (also **di·e·ti·cian**) ▸*n.* an expert on diet and nutrition.

Di·et of Worms a meeting of the Holy Roman Emperor Charles V's imperial diet at Worms in 1521, at which Martin Luther was summoned to appear. Luther committed himself there to the cause of Protestant reform, and his teaching was formally condemned in the Edict of Worms.

Die·trich /ˈdētrik/, Marlene (1901–92), U.S. actress and singer; born in Germany; born *Maria Magdelene von Losch*. She became known for her part as Lola in *The Blue Angel* (1930), one of many movies that she made with Josef von Sternberg. From the 1950s, she was also successful as a cabaret performer.

Marlene Dietrich

Dieu et mon droit /ˈdyo͞o ā môN ˈdwä/ ▸*n.* God and my right (the motto of the British monarch). ▷French.

dif- ▸*prefix* **1** variant spelling of **DIS-**. **2** assimilated before *f* (as in *diffraction, diffuse.*). ▷from Latin, variant of **DIS-**.

diff /dif/ ▸*n.* *informal* short for **DIFFERENCE**.

▸*v.* [*trans.*] *Computing* compare (files) in order to determine how or whether they differ.

dif·fer /ˈdifər/ ▸*v.* [*intrans.*] be unlike or dissimilar: *the second set of data* **differed from** *the first* | *tastes differ* | [as *adj.*] (**differing**) *widely differing circumstances.* ■ disagree: *he* **differed from** *his contemporaries in ethical matters.* ▷late Middle English (also in the sense 'put off, defer'): from Old French *differer* 'differ, defer,' from Latin *differre*, from *dis-* 'from, away' + *ferre* 'bring, carry.' Compare with **DEFER**[1].

▸*PHRASES* □ **agree to differ** cease to argue about something because neither party will compromise or be persuaded. □ **beg to differ** politely disagree: *that's your opinion—I beg to differ.*

dif·fer·ence /ˈdif(ə)rəns/ ▸*n.* a point or way in which people or things are not the same: *the* **differences between** *men and women.* ■ the state or condition of being dissimilar or unlike: *their* **difference from** *one another.* ■ a disagreement, quarrel, or dispute: *the couple are patching up their differences.* ■ a quantity by which amounts differ; the remainder left after subtraction of one value from another: *the gross margin is the difference between the total cost of the goods and the final selling price.* ■ *Heraldry* an alteration in a coat of arms to distinguish members or branches of a family.

▸*v.* [*trans.*] *Heraldry* alter (a coat of arms) to distinguish members or branches of a family. ▷Middle English: via Old French from Latin *differentia* (see DIFFERENTIA).

▸*PHRASES* □ **make a** (or **no**) **difference** have a significant effect (or no effect) on a person or situation: *the law will* ***make no difference to*** *my business.* □ **with a difference** having a new or unusual feature or treatment: *a fashion show with a difference.*

dif·fer·ence thresh·old ▸*n.* the smallest amount by which two sensory stimuli can differ in order for an individual to perceive them as different.

dif·fer·ent /ˈdif(ə)rənt/ ▸*adj.* **1** not the same as another or each other; unlike in nature, form, or quality: *you can play this game in different ways.* | (**different from/than**) *the car is different from anything else on the market.* ■ *informal* novel and unusual: *try something deliciously different.* **2** distinct; separate: *on two different occasions.* ▷late Middle English: via Old French from Latin *different-* 'carrying away, differing,' from the verb *differre* (see DIFFER). —**dif·fer·ent·ly** *adv.* —**dif·fer·ent·ness** *n.*

▸*PHRASE* □ **different strokes for different folks** *proverb* different things appeal to different people.

USAGE In general, **different from** is the construction most often used in the U.S. and Britain, although **different than** (used almost exclusively in North America) is also used, esp. in speech. **Different from** can sometimes lead to wordy constructions, whereas **different than** implies a comparison that **from** usually does not. (*Different* is an adjective of contrast, but is not a comparative adjective such as *sooner* or *faster.*) If neither construction sounds right, recast the sentence. **Different to** is common in Britain, but sounds strange to American ears. **Than** is more often acceptable when following the adverb **differently**, but still implies a comparison.

dif·fer·en·ti·a /ˌdifəˈrenSH(ē)ə/ ▸*n.* (*pl.* **-ti·ae** /-SHēˌē/) a distinguishing mark or characteristic. ■ *chiefly Philosophy* an attribute that distinguishes a species of thing from other species of the same genus. ▷late 17th cent.: from Latin, literally 'difference,' from *different-* 'carrying away' (see DIFFERENT).

dif·fer·en·ti·a·ble /ˌdifəˈrenSHəbəl/ ▸*adj.* able to be differentiated. ▷mid 19th cent.: from DIFFERENTIATE, on the pattern of pairs such as *depreciate, depreciable.* —**dif·fer·en·ti·a·bil·i·ty** /-ˌrenSHəˈbilitē/ *n.*

dif·fer·en·tial /ˌdifəˈrenSHəl/ *chiefly technical* ▸*adj.* [*attrib.*] of, showing, or depending on a difference; differing or varying according to circumstances or relevant factors: *the differential achievements of boys and girls.* ■ constituting a specific difference; distinctive: *the differential features between benign and malignant tumors.* ■ *Mathematics* relating to infinitesimal differences or to the derivatives of functions. ■ of or relating to a difference in a physical quantity: *a differential amplifier.*

▸*n.* a difference between amounts of things: *the* ***differential between*** *gasoline and diesel prices.* ■ *Mathematics* an infinitesimal difference between successive values of a variable. ■ (also **differential gear**) a set of gears allowing a vehicle's driven wheels to revolve at different speeds when going around corners. ▷mid 17th cent.: from medieval Latin *differentialis*, from Latin *differentia* 'difference' (see DIFFERENTIA). —**dif·fer·en·tial·ly** *adv.*

dif·fer·en·tial cal·cu·lus ▸*n.* a branch of mathematics concerned with the determination, properties, and application of derivatives and differentials. Compare with INTEGRAL CALCULUS.

dif·fer·en·tial co·ef·fi·cient ▸*n. Mathematics* another term for DERIVATIVE.

dif·fer·en·tial di·ag·no·sis ▸*n. Medicine* the process of differentiating between two or more conditions that share similar signs or symptoms.

dif·fer·en·tial e·qua·tion ▸*n.* an equation involving derivatives of a function or functions.

dif·fer·en·tial lock ▸*n.* a device that disables the differential of a motor vehicle in slippery conditions to improve grip.

dif·fer·en·tial op·er·a·tor ▸*n. Mathematics* another term for DEL.

dif·fer·en·tial wind·lass ▸*n.* a hoisting device consisting of two drums of different diameters on the same axis and turning at the same rate, so that a line wound on the larger drum and unwound from the smaller drum provides a mechanical advantage in lifting. Also called **Chinese windlass.**

dif·fer·en·ti·ate /ˌdifəˈrenSHēˌāt/ ▸*v.* [*trans.*] **1** recognize or ascertain what makes (someone or something) different: *children can* ***differentiate*** *the past* ***from*** *the present.* See note at DISTINGUISH. ■ [*intrans.*] (**differentiate between**) identify differences between (two or more things or people): *he is unable to differentiate between fantasy and reality.* ■ make (someone or something) appear different or distinct: *Twain was careful to* ***differentiate*** *Huck's speech* ***from*** *that of other white people.* **2** *technical* make or become different in the process of growth or development: [*trans.*] *the receptors are developed and differentiated into sense organs* | [*intrans.*] *the cells differentiate into a wide variety of cell types.* **3** *Mathematics* transform (a function) into its derivative. ▷early 19th cent.: from medieval Latin *differentiat-* 'carried away from,' from the verb *differentiare*, from *differentia* (see DIFFERENTIA). —**dif·fer·en·ti·a·tion** /-ˌrenSHēˈāSHən/ *n.* —**dif·fer·en·ti·a·tor** /-ˌātər/ *n.*

dif·fer·ent·ly a·bled ▸*adj.* disabled.

USAGE **Differently abled** was first proposed (in the 1980s) as an alternative to **disabled**, **handicapped**, etc., on the grounds that it gave a more positive message and so avoided discrimination toward people with disabilities. The term has gained little currency, however, because of its being overeuphemistic and condescending. The accepted term in general use is still **disabled**.

dif·fi·cult /ˈdifikəlt/ ▸*adj.* needing much effort or skill to accomplish, deal with, or understand: *she had a difficult decision to make* | *the questions are too* ***difficult for*** *the children.* See note at HARD. ■ characterized by or causing hardships or problems: *a difficult economic climate.* ■ (of a person) not easy to please or satisfy: *Lily could be difficult.* ▷late Middle English: back-formation from DIFFICULTY. —**dif·fi·cult·ly** *adv.* (*rare*) —**dif·fi·cult·ness** *n.*

dif·fi·cul·ty /ˈdifikəltē/ ▸*n.* (*pl.* **-ties**) the state or condition of being difficult: *Guy had no* ***difficulty in*** *making friends* | *she walks* ***with difficulty.*** ■ a thing that is hard to accomplish, deal with, or understand: *there is a practical difficulty* | *a club with financial difficulties.* ■ (often **difficulties**) a situation that is difficult or dangerous: *they went for a swim but* ***got into difficulties.*** ▷late Middle English (in the senses 'requiring effort or skill' and 'something difficult'): from Latin *difficultas*, from *dis-* (expressing reversal) + *facultas* 'ability, opportunity.'

dif·fi·dent /ˈdifidənt/ ▸*adj.* modest or shy because of a lack of self-confidence: *a diffident youth.* ▷late Middle English (in the sense 'lacking confidence or trust in someone or something'): from Latin *diffident-* 'failing in trust,' from the verb *diffidere*, from *dis-* (expressing reversal) + *fidere* 'to trust.' —**dif·fi·dence** *n.* —**dif·fi·dent·ly** *adv.*

dif·fract /diˈfrakt/ ▸*v.* [*trans.*] *Physics* cause to undergo diffraction. ▷early 19th cent.: from Latin *diffract-* 'broken in pieces,' from the verb *diffringere*, from *dis-* 'away, from' + *frangere* 'to break.' —**dif·frac·tive** /-tiv/ *adj.* —**dif·frac·tive·ly** /-tivlē/ *adv.*

dif·frac·tion /diˈfrakSHən/ ▸*n.* the process by which a beam of light or other system of waves is spread out as a result of passing through a narrow aperture or across an edge, typically accompanied by interference between the wave forms produced.

dif·frac·tion grat·ing ▸*n.* a plate of glass or metal ruled with very close parallel lines, producing a spectrum by diffraction and interference of light.

dif·frac·tom·e·ter /ˌdifrakˈtämitər/ ▸*n.* an instrument for measuring diffraction, chiefly used to determine the structure of a crystal by analysis of the diffraction of X-rays.

dif·fuse ▸*v.* /diˈfyo͞oz/ spread or cause to spread over a wide area or among a large number of people: [*intrans.*] *technologies diffuse rapidly* | [*trans.*] *the problem is how to diffuse power without creating anarchy.* See note at SCATTER. ■ become or cause (a fluid, gas, individual atom, etc.) to become intermingled with a substance by movement, typically in a specified direction or at specified speed: [*intrans.*] *oxygen molecules* ***diffuse across*** *the membrane* | [*trans.*] *gas is* ***diffused into*** *the bladder.* ■ [*trans.*] cause (light) to glow faintly by dispersing it in many directions.

▸*adj.* /diˈfyo͞os/ spread out over a large area; not concentrated: *the diffuse community centered on the church* | *the light is more diffuse.* ■ (of disease) not localized in the body: *diffuse hyperplasia.* ■ lacking clarity or conciseness: *the second argument is more diffuse.* ▷late Middle English: from Latin *diffus-* 'poured out,' from the verb *diffundere*, from *dis-* 'away' + *fundere* 'pour'; the adjective via French *diffus* or Latin *diffusus* 'extensive,' from *diffundere*. —**dif·fuse·ly** /-ˈfyo͞oslē/ *adv.* —**dif·fuse·ness** /-ˈfyo͞osnis/ *n.*

USAGE The verbs **diffuse** and **defuse** sound similar but have different meanings. **Diffuse** means, broadly, 'disperse'; **defuse** means 'remove the fuse from (a bomb), reduce the danger or tension in.' Thus *Cooper successfully* ***diffused*** *the situation* is incorrect, and *Cooper successfully* ***defused*** *the situation* is correct.

dif·fus·er /diˈfyo͞ozər/ (also **dif·fu·sor**) ▸*n.* a thing that diffuses something, in particular: ■ an attachment or duct for broadening an airflow and reducing its speed. ■ *Photography* a device that spreads the light from a light source evenly and reduces harsh shadows.

dif·fus·i·ble /diˈfyo͞ozəbəl/ ▸*adj.* able to intermingle by diffusion: *diffusible factors in the cytoplasm.*

dif·fu·sion /diˈfyo͞oZHən/ ▸*n.* the spreading of something more widely: *the diffusion of Marxist ideas.* ■ the action of spreading the light from a light source evenly so as to reduce glare and harsh shadows. ■ *Chemistry* the intermingling of substances by the natural movement of their particles: *the rate of diffusion of a gas.* ■ *Anthropology* the dissemination of elements of culture to another region or people. ▷late Middle English (in the sense 'pouring out, effusion'): from Latin *diffusion-*, from *diffundere* 'pour out.' —**dif·fu·sive** /-siv/ *adj.* (*Chemistry*).

dif·fu·sion·ist /diˈfyo͞oZHənist/ *Anthropology* ▸*adj.* advocating the theory of the dissemination of elements of culture to another region or people: *the rural sociological literature of the diffusionist school.*

▸*n.* an advocate of such a theory. —**dif·fu·sion·ism** /-ˌnizəm/ *n.*

dif·fu·siv·i·ty /ˌdifyo͞oˈsivitē/ ▸*n.* (*pl.* **-ties**) *Physics* a measure of the capability of a substance or energy to be diffused or to allow something to pass by diffusion.

dig /dig/ ▸*v.* (**dig·ging**; *past* **dug** /dəg/) **1** [*intrans.*] break up and move earth with a tool or machine, or with hands, paws, snout, etc.: *the boar had been* ***digging for*** *roots* | [*trans.*] *she had to dig the garden* | *authorities cause chaos by* ***digging up*** *roads.* ■ [*trans.*] make (a hole, grave, etc.) by breaking up and moving earth in such a way: *he took a spade and dug a hole* | [as *adj.*] (**dug**) *the newly dug grave.* ■ [*trans.*] extract from the ground by breaking up and moving earth: *they* ***dug up*** *fossils of an animal about the size of a turkey.* ■ (**dig in**) (of a soldier) protect oneself by making a trench or similar ground defense. ■ [in *imperative*] (**dig in**) *informal* used to encourage someone to start eating with gusto and have as much as they want: *put the sausage on top of the polenta; then dig in.* ■ [*trans.*] (**dig something in/into**) push or poke something in or into: *he dug his hands into his pockets.* ■ [*trans.*] excavate (an archaeological site): *apart from digging a site, recording evidence is important.* ■ [*trans.*] (**dig something out**) bring out something that is hidden or has been stored for a long time: *they dug out last year's notes.* ■ (**dig into**) *informal* find money from (somewhere): *members have to dig deep into their pockets.* ■ [*intrans.*] search or rummage in a specified place: *Catherine dug into her handbag and produced her card.* ■ engage in research; conduct an investigation: *a professional* ***digging for*** *information* | *he had no compunction about* ***digging into*** *her private affairs.* ■ [*trans.*] (**dig something up/out**) discover information after a search or investigation: *have you* ***dug up*** *any information on the captain?* **2** [*trans.*] *informal, dated* like, appreciate, or understand: *I really dig heavy rock.*

▸*n.* **1** [in *sing.*] an act or spell of digging: *a thorough dig of the whole plot.* ■ an archaeological excavation. **2** a push or poke with one's elbow, finger, etc.: *Ginnie* ***gave*** *her sister* ***a dig in the ribs.*** ■ *informal* a remark intended to mock or criticize: *this was a cruel* ***dig at*** *Jenny.* ▷Middle English: perhaps from Old English *dīc* 'ditch.'

▸*PHRASES* □ **dig up dirt** *informal* discover and reveal damaging information about someone. □ **dig oneself into a hole** (or **dig a hole for oneself**) get oneself into an awkward or restrictive situation. □ **dig in one's heels** resist stubbornly; refuse to give in: *he has dug in his heels and refuses to leave.* □ **dig's one's own grave** see GRAVE[1].

Di·gam·ba·ra /diˈgəmbərə/ ▸*n.* a member of one of two principal sects of Jainism, which was formed as a result of doctrinal schism in about AD 80 and continues today in parts of southern India. The sect's adherents reject property ownership and usually do not wear clothes. See also SVETAMBARA. ▷from Sanskrit *Digāmbara*, literally 'sky-clad.'

di·gam·ma /dīˈgamə/ ▸*n.* the sixth letter of the early Greek alphabet ([Digamma], [digamma]), pronounced as "w." It became obsolete in many Greek dialects before the Classical period. ▷late 17th cent.: via Latin from Greek, from *di-* 'twice' + GAMMA (because of the shape of the letter, resembling gamma (Γ) with an extra stroke).

di·gas·tric /dīˈgastrik/ (also **digastric muscle**) ▸*n. Anatomy* each of a pair of muscles that run under the jaw and act to open it. ▷late 17th cent.: from modern Latin *digastricus*, from *di-* 'twice' + Greek *gastēr* 'belly' (because the muscle has two fleshy parts or "bellies" at an angle, connected by a tendon).

di·ge·ne·an /dīˈjēnēən/ *Zoology* ▸*adj.* of or relating to a group of flukes that are internal parasites needing two to four hosts to complete their life cycle. Compare with MONOGENEAN.
▸*n.* a digenean fluke; a trematode. • Subclass Digenea, class Trematoda. ▷1960s: from modern Latin *Digenea* (from Greek *di-* 'twice' + *genea* 'generation, race') + -AN.

di·ge·ra·ti /dijəˈrätē/ ▸*plural n.* people with expertise or professional involvement in information technology. ▷1990s: blend of DIGITAL and LITERATI.

di·gest ▸*v.* /diˈjest; dī-/ [*trans.*] break down (food) in the stomach and intestines into substances that can be used by the body. ■ understand or assimilate (new information or the significance of something) by a period of reflection. ■ arrange (something) in a systematic or convenient order, esp. by reduction: *the computer* ***digested*** *your labors* ***into*** *a form understandable by a program.* ■ *Chemistry* treat (a substance) with heat, enzymes, or a solvent in order to decompose it or extract essential components.
▸*n.* /ˈdī,jest/ **1** a compilation or summary of material or information: *a digest of their findings.* ■ a periodical consisting of condensed versions of pieces of writing or news published elsewhere. ■ a methodical summary of a body of laws. ■ (**the Digest**) the compendium of Roman law compiled in the reign of Justinian. **2** *Chemistry* a substance or mixture obtained by digestion: *a digest of cloned DNA.* ▷late Middle English: from Latin *digest-* 'distributed, dissolved, digested,' from the verb *digerere*, from *di-* 'apart' + *gerere* 'carry'; the noun from Latin *digesta* 'matters methodically arranged,' from *digestus* 'divided,' from *digerere*.

di·gest·er /diˈjestər; dī-/ ▸*n. Chemistry* a container in which substances are treated with heat, enzymes, or a solvent in order to promote decomposition or extract essential components.

di·gest·i·ble /diˈjestəbəl; dī-/ ▸*adj.* (of food) able to be digested. ■ (of information) easy to understand or follow: *her books convey philosophical issues in digestible form.* ▷late Middle English: via Old French from Latin *digestibilis*, from *digest-* 'digested,' from the verb *digerere* (see DIGEST). —**di·gest·i·bil·i·ty** /-,jestəˈbilitē/ *n.*

di·ges·tif /,dējesˈtēf/ ▸*n.* a drink or portion of food drunk or eaten in order to aid the digestion. ▷early 20th cent.: French, literally 'digestive.'

di·ges·tion /diˈjesCHən; dī-/ ▸*n.* the process of breaking down food by mechanical and enzymatic action in the stomach and intestines into substances that can be used by the body. ■ a person's capacity to break down food in such a way: *bouts of dysentery impaired his digestion.* ■ *Chemistry* the process of treating a substance by means of heat, enzymes, or a solvent to promote decomposition or extract essential components. ▷late Middle English: via Old French from Latin *digestio(n-)*, from the verb *digerere* (see DIGEST).

di·ges·tive /diˈjestiv; dī-/ ▸*adj.* of or relating to the process of digesting food: *stomach ulcers and other digestive disorders.* ■ (of food or medicine) aiding or promoting the process of digestion: *digestive mints.*
▸*n.* a food or medicine that aids or promotes the digestion of food. ■ (also **digestive biscuit**) *Brit.* a round, semisweet cookie made of whole-wheat flour. ▷late Middle English: from Old French *digestif, -ive* or Latin *digestivus*, from *digest-* 'digested,' from the verb *digerere* (see DIGEST). —**di·ges·tive·ly** *adv.*

di·ges·tive gland ▸*n. Zoology* a glandular organ of digestion present in crustaceans, mollusks, and certain other invertebrates.

dig·ger /ˈdigər/ ▸*n.* **1** a person, animal, or large machine that digs earth: [*in combination*] *a grave-digger.* ■ (**Digger**, in full **Digger Indian**) *offensive* a North American Indian of any of several tribes that subsisted on roots dug from the ground. **2** *Austral./NZ, informal* a man, esp. a private soldier (often used as a friendly form of address): *how are you, Digger?* [early 20th cent.: from *digger* 'miner,' reinforced by association with the digging of trenches on the battlefields.]

dig·ger wasp ▸*n.* a solitary wasp that typically excavates a burrow in sandy soil, filling it with one or more paralyzed insects or spiders for its larvae to feed on. • Families Sphecidae (which includes sand wasps) and Pompilidae (which includes spider-hunting wasps).

dig·gings /ˈdigiNGz/ ▸*plural n.* **1** a site such as a mine or goldfield that has been excavated: *hills scarred with peat diggings.* ■ material that has been dug from the ground. **2** *Brit., informal, dated* lodgings.

dig·ging stick ▸*n.* a primitive digging implement consisting of a pointed stick, sometimes weighted with a stone.

dight /dīt/ ▸*adj. archaic* clothed or equipped.
▸*v.* [*trans.*] *poetic/literary* make ready for a use or purpose; prepare: *let the meal be dighted.* ▷Middle English: past participle of archaic *dight* 'order, deal with,' based on Latin *dictare* 'compose (in language), order.' The wide and varied use of the word in Middle English is reflected dialectally.

dig·i·cam /ˈdiji,kam/ ▸*n.* a digital camera. ▷blend.

dig·i·pet /ˈdiji,pet/ ▸*n.* another term for CYBERPET. ▷blend of *digital* and *pet*.

dig·it /ˈdijit/ ▸*n.* **1** any of the numerals from 0 to 9, esp. when forming part of a number. **2** a finger (including the thumb) or toe. ■ *Zoology* an equivalent structure at the end of the limbs of many higher vertebrates. ▷late Middle English: from Latin *digitus* 'finger, toe'; sense 1 arose from the practice of counting on the fingers.

dig·it·al /ˈdijitl/ ▸*adj.* **1** relating to or using signals or information represented by discrete values (digits) of a physical quantity, such as voltage or magnetic polarization, to represent arithmetic numbers or approximations to numbers from a continuum or logical expressions and variables: *digital TV.* Often contrasted with ANALOG. ■ (of a clock or watch) showing the time by means of displayed digits rather than hands or a pointer. **2** of or relating to a finger or fingers. ▷late 15th cent.: from Latin *digitalis*, from *digitus* 'finger, toe.' —**dig·it·al·ly** *adv.*

dig·it·al au·di·o·tape (abbr.: **DAT**) ▸*n.* magnetic tape used to make digital sound recordings of very high quality.

dig·it·al cam·er·a ▸*n.* a camera that records and stores digital images.

dig·it·al cash (also **digital money**) ▸*n.* money that may be transferred electronically from one party to another during a transaction.

dig·it·al com·pact cas·sette (abbr.: **DCC**) ▸*n.* a format for tape cassettes similar to ordinary audiocassettes but with digital rather than analog recording.

dig·it·al com·press·ion ▸*n.* a method of reducing the number of bits (zeros and ones) in a digital signal by using mathematical algorithms to eliminate redundant information.

dig·it·al di·vide ▸*n.* the gulf between those who have ready access to computers and the Internet, and those who do not: *a worrying "digital divide" based on race, gender, educational attainment, and income.*

dig·i·tal·in /,dijiˈtalin/ ▸*n.* a drug containing the active constituents of digitalis. ▷mid 19th cent.: from DIGITALIS + -IN[1].

dig·i·tal·is /,dijiˈtalis/ ▸*n.* a drug prepared from the dried leaves of foxglove and containing substances (notably digoxin and digitoxin) that stimulate the heart muscle. ▷late 18th cent.: from the modern Latin genus name of the foxglove, from *digitalis (herba)* '(plant) relating to the finger,' from *digitus* 'finger, toe'; suggested by German *Fingerhut* 'thimble or foxglove.'

dig·i·tal·ize[1] /ˈdijitl,īz/ ▸*v.* another term for DIGITIZE. —**dig·i·tal·i·za·tion** /,dijitl-əˈzāSHən/ *n.*

dig·i·tal·ize[2] ▸*v.* [*trans.*] *Medicine* administer digitalis or digoxin to (a patient with a heart complaint). —**dig·i·tal·i·za·tion** /,dijitl-əˈzāSHən/ *n.*

dig·it·al lock·er ▸*n. Computing* an Internet service that allows registered users to access music, movies, videos, photographs, videogames, and other multimedia files.

Dig·it·al Mil·len·ni·um Cop·y·right Act (abbr.: **DMCA**) ▸a 1998 U.S. law intended to update copyright law for electronic commerce and electronic content providers. It criminalizes the circumvention of electronic and digital copyright protection systems.

dig·it·al ob·ject i·den·ti·fi·er ▸*n.* (abbr.: **DOI**) *Computing* a unique identifying number allocated to a Web site.

dig·i·tal sig·na·ture ▸*n. Computing* a digital code (generated and authenticated by public key encryption) that is attached to an electronically transmitted document to verify its contents and the sender's identity.

dig·i·tal sub·scrib·er line ▸*n. Computing* see **DSL**

dig·it·al tel·e·vi·sion (abbr.: **DTV**) ▸*n.* television broadcasting in which the pictures are transmitted as digital signals that are decoded by a device in or attached to the receiving television set.

dig·i·tal-to-an·a·log con·vert·er ▸*n.* an electronic device for converting digital signals to analog form.

dig·i·tal ver·sa·tile disc ▸*n. Computing* see **DVD**.

dig·i·tal vid·e·o re·cord·er ▸*n.* (abbr. **DVR**) a programmable electronic device that writes audio and video input, typically from a television signal, to a rewritable hard disk.

dig·i·tate /ˈdiji,tāt/ ▸*adj. technical* shaped like a spread hand: *digitate leaves | a digitate delta.* ▷mid 17th cent.: from Latin *digitatus*, from *digitus* 'finger, toe.'

dig·i·ta·tion /,dijiˈtāSHən/ ▸*n.* **1** *Zoology & Botany* a fingerlike protuberance or division. **2** *Computing* the process of converting data to digital form.

dig·i·ti·grade /ˈdijiti,grād/ ▸*adj. Zoology* (of a mammal) walking on its toes and not touching the ground with its heels, as a dog, cat, or rodent. Compare with PLANTIGRADE. ▷mid 19th cent.: from Latin *digitus* 'finger, toe' + *-gradus* '-walking.'

dig·i·tize /ˈdiji,tīz/ ▸*v.* [*trans.*] [usu. as *adj.*] (**digitized**) convert (pictures or sound) into a digital form that can be processed by a computer. —**dig·i·ti·za·tion** /,dijitəˈzāSHən/ *n.* —**dig·i·tiz·er** *n.*

dig·i·tox·in /,dijiˈtäksin/ ▸*n. Chemistry* a compound with similar properties to digoxin and found with it in the foxglove and similar plants.

di·glos·si·a /dīˈglôsēə; -ˈglä-/ ▸*n. Linguistics* a situation in which two languages (or two varieties of the same language) are used under different conditions within a community, often by the same speakers. The term is usually applied to languages with distinct "high" and "low" (colloquial) varieties, such as Arabic. ▷1950s: from Greek *diglōssos* 'bilingual,' on the pattern of French *diglossie*. —**di·glos·sic** /-sik/ *adj.*

dig·ni·fied /ˈdigni,fīd/ ▸*adj.* having or showing a composed or serious manner that is worthy of respect: *she maintained a dignified silence | a dignified old lady.* —**dig·ni·fied·ly** /-,fī(ə)dlē/ *adv.*

dig·ni·fy /ˈdignə,fī/ ▸*v.* (**-fies, -fied**) [*trans.*] make (something) seem worthy and impressive: *the Americans had dignified their departure with a ceremony.* ■ (often **be dignified**) give an impressive name to (someone or something that one considers worthless): *dumps are increasingly* ***dignified as*** *landfills.* ▷late Middle English: from Old French *dignefier*, from late Latin *dignificare*, from Latin *dignus* 'worthy.'

dig·ni·tar·y /ˈdigni,terē/ ▸*n.* (*pl.* **-tar·ies**) a person considered to be important because of high rank or office. ▷late 17th cent.: from DIGNITY, on the pattern of the pairs *propriety, proprietary*.

dig·ni·ty /ˈdignitē/ ▸*n.* (*pl.* **-ties**) the state or quality of being worthy of honor or respect: *a man of dignity and unbending principle | the dignity of labor.* ■ a composed or serious manner or style: *he bowed with great dignity.* ■ a sense of pride in oneself; self-respect: *it was* ***beneath his dignity*** *to shout.* ■ a high or honorable rank or position: *he promised dignities to the nobles in return for his rival's murder.* ▷Middle English: from Old French *dignete*, from Latin *dignitas*, from *dignus* 'worthy.'
▸*PHRASE* □ **stand on one's dignity** insist on being treated with due respect.

dig·ox·in /dijˈäksin/ ▸*n. Chemistry* a poisonous compound present in the foxglove and other plants. It is a steroid glycoside and is used in small doses as a cardiac stimulant. ▷1930s: contraction of DIGITOXIN.

di·graph /ˈdī,graf/ ▸*n.* a combination of two letters representing one sound, as in *ph* and *ey*. ■ *Printing* a character consisting of two joined letters; a ligature. —**di·graph·ic** /dīˈgrafik/ *adj.*

di·gress /dīˈgres/ ▸*v.* [*intrans.*] leave the main subject temporarily in speech or writing: *I have* ***digressed*** *a little* ***from*** *my original plan.* ▷early 16th cent.: from Latin *digress-* 'stepped away,' from the verb *digredi*, from *di-* 'aside' + *gradi* 'to walk.' —**di·gress·er** *n.*

D

—**di·gres·sion** /-ˈgreshən/ *n.* —**di·gres·sive** /-ˈgresiv/ *adj.* —**di·gres·sive·ly** /-ˈgresivlē/ *adv.* —**di·gres·sive·ness** /-ˈgresivnis/ *n.*

digs ▸*plural n. informal* living quarters: *settled into new digs in Los Angeles.* ▷late 19th cent.: short for *diggings*, used in the same sense, probably referring to the land where a farmer digs, i.e., works and, by extension, lives.

di·he·dral /dīˈhēdrəl/ ▸*adj.* having or contained by two plane faces: *a dihedral angle.*
▸*n.* an angle formed by two plane faces. ■ *Aeronautics* inclination of an aircraft's wing from the horizontal, esp. upward away from the fuselage. Compare with ANHEDRAL. ■ *Climbing* a place where two planes of rock meet at an angle of between 60° and 120°. ▷late 18th cent.: from DI-[1] 'two' + *-hedral* (see -HEDRON).

di·hy·brid /dīˈhībrid/ ▸*n. Genetics* a hybrid that is heterozygous for alleles of two different genes: [as *adj.*] *a dihybrid cross.*

di·hy·dric /dīˈhīdrik/ ▸*adj. Chemistry* (of an alcohol) containing two hydroxyl groups. ▷late 19th cent.: from DI-[1] 'two' + HYDROGEN + -IC.

di·hy·dro·tes·tos·ter·one /dī,hīdrōtesˈtästə,rōn/ ▸*n. Biochemistry* a male sex hormone that is the active form of testosterone, formed from testosterone in bodily tissue. ▷1950s: from *dihydro-* (in the sense 'containing two hydrogen atoms in the molecule') + TESTOSTERONE.

di·hy·drox·y·ac·e·tone /,dīhī,dräksēˈasi,tōn/ ▸*n. Chemistry* a synthetic compound with strong reducing properties, used in lotions for coloring the skin in sunlight. • Chem. formula: $(CH_2OH)CO$. ▷late 19th cent.: from *dihydroxy-* (in the sense 'containing two hydroxyl groups in the molecule') + ACETONE.

Di·jon /dēˈzhôn; dēˈzhän/ an industrial city in eastern central France, the former capital of Burgundy; pop. 151,640.

Di·jon mus·tard ▸*n.* a medium-hot mustard, typically prepared with white wine and originally made in Dijon, France.

dik-dik /ˈdik ,dik/ ▸*n.* a dwarf antelope found on the dry savanna of Africa, the female of which is larger than the male. • Genus *Madoqua*, family Bovidae: several species. ▷late 19th cent.: a local word in East Africa, imitative of its call.

dike[1] /dīk/ (also **dyke**) ▸*n.* **1** a long wall or embankment built to prevent flooding from the sea. ■ [often in *place names*] a low wall or earthwork serving as a boundary or defense: *Offa's Dike.* ■ a causeway. ■ *Geology* an intrusion of igneous rock cutting across existing strata. Compare with SILL. **2** a ditch or watercourse.
▸*v.* [*trans.*] [often as *adj.*] (**diked**) provide (land) with a wall or embankment to prevent flooding. ▷Middle English (denoting a trench or ditch): from Old Norse *dík*, related to DITCH. Sense 1 has been influenced by Middle Low German *dīk* 'dam' and Middle Dutch *dijc* 'ditch, dam.'
▸*PHRASE* □ **put one's finger in the dike** attempt to stem the advance of something undesirable. [from a story of a small Dutch boy who saved his community from a flood by placing his finger in a hole in a dike.]

dike[2] ▸*n.* variant spelling of DYKE[2].

dik·tat /dikˈtät/ ▸*n.* an order or decree imposed by someone in power without popular consent: *a diktat from the Bundestag | he can disband the legislature and rule by diktat.* ▷1930s: from German, from Latin *dictatum* 'something dictated,' neuter past participle of *dictare*.

DIL *Electronics* ▸*abbr.* dual in-line (package). See **DIP**.

Di·lan·tin /dīˈlantin/ ▸*n. Medicine* trademark for PHENYTOIN. ▷1930s: from DI-[1] 'two' + *-l-* + *(hyd)ant(o)in*.

di·lap·i·date /diˈlapi,dāt/ ▸*v.* [*trans.*] *archaic* cause (something) to fall into disrepair or ruin. ▷early 16th cent. (in the sense 'waste, squander'): from Latin *dilapidat-* 'demolished, squandered,' from the verb *dilapidare*, literally 'scatter as if throwing stones,' from *di-* 'apart, abroad'+ *lapis, lapid-* 'stone.' —**di·lap·i·da·tion** /di,lapiˈdāshən/ *n.*

di·lap·i·dat·ed /diˈlapi,dātid/ ▸*adj.* (of a building or object) in a state of disrepair or ruin as a result of age or neglect.

di·lat·an·cy /dīˈlātnsē/ ▸*n. Chemistry* the phenomenon exhibited by some fluids, sols, and gels in which they become more viscous or solid under pressure.

dil·a·ta·tion /,diləˈtāshən; ,dī-/ ▸*n. chiefly Medicine Physiology* the process of becoming dilated. ■ the action of dilating a vessel or opening. ■ a dilated part of a hollow organ or vessel. ▷late Middle English: via Old French from late Latin *dilatatio(n-)*, from the verb *dilatare* (see DILATE).

dil·a·ta·tion and cu·ret·tage (also **di·la·tion and cu·ret·tage**) (abbr.: **D and C**) ▸*n. Medicine* a surgical procedure involving dilatation of the cervix and curettage of the uterus, performed after a miscarriage or for the removal of cysts or tumors.

di·late /ˈdī,lāt; dīˈlāt/ ▸*v.* **1** make or become wider, larger, or more open: [*intrans.*] *her eyes dilated with horror* | [*trans.*] *the woman dilated her nostrils.* **2** [*intrans.*] (**dilate on**) speak or write at length on (a subject). ▷late Middle English: from Old French *dilater*, from Latin *dilatare* 'spread out,' from *di-* 'apart' + *latus* 'wide.' —**di·lat·a·ble** *adj.* —**di·la·tion** /dīˈlāshən/ *n.*

di·la·tor /ˈdī,lātər; dīˈlātər/ ▸*n.* a thing that dilates something, in particular: ■ (also **dilator muscle**) *Anatomy* a muscle whose contraction dilates an organ or aperture, such as the pupil of the eye. ■ a surgical instrument for dilating a tube or cavity in the body. ■ a vasodilatory drug.

dil·a·to·ry /ˈdilə,tôrē/ ▸*adj.* slow to act: *he had been dilatory in appointing a solicitor.* ■ intended to cause delay: *they resorted to dilatory procedural tactics, forcing a postponement of peace talks.* ▷late Middle English: from late Latin *dilatorius* 'delaying,' from Latin *dilator* 'delayer,' from *dilat-* 'deferred,' from the verb *differre*. —**dil·a·to·ri·ly** /,diləˈtôrəlē/ *adv.* —**dil·a·to·ri·ness** *n.*

dil·do /ˈdildō/ ▸*n.* (*pl.* **-dos**) an object shaped like an erect penis used for sexual stimulation. ■ *vulgar slang* a stupid or ridiculous person. ▷late 16th cent.: of unknown origin.

di·lem·ma /diˈlemə/ ▸*n.* a situation in which a difficult choice has to be made between two or more alternatives, esp. equally undesirable ones: *the people often face the dilemma of feeding themselves or their cattle.* ■ *informal* a difficult situation or problem: *the insoluble dilemma of adolescence.* ■ *Logic* an argument forcing an opponent to choose either of two unfavorable alternatives. ▷early 16th cent. (denoting a form of argument involving a choice between equally unfavorable alternatives): via Latin from Greek *dilēmma*, from *di-* 'twice' + *lēmma* 'premise.'

> ***USAGE*** **Dilemma** should be reserved for reference to a predicament in which a difficult choice must be made between undesirable alternatives: *You see his dilemma? If he moves to London, he may never see his parents again. But if he stays in Seattle, he may be giving up the best job offer of his life.* The weakened use of **dilemma** to mean simply 'a difficult situation or problem' (*the **dilemma** of a teacher shortage*) is recorded as early as the first part of the 17th century, but many regard this use as unacceptable and it should be avoided in written English.

dil·et·tante /,diliˈtänt/ ▸*n.* (*pl.* **-tan·ti** /-ˈtäntē/ or **-tantes**) a person who cultivates an area of interest, such as the arts, without real commitment or knowledge: [as *adj.*] *a dilettante approach to science.* ■ *archaic* a person with an amateur interest in the arts. ▷mid 18th cent.: from Italian, 'person loving the arts,' from *dilettare* 'to delight,' from Latin *delectare*. —**dil·et·tan·tish** *adj.* —**dil·et·tant·ism** /-,tizəm/ *n.*

Di·li /ˈdilē/ (also **Di·lí, Dil·li, Dil·ly**) the capital and chief port of East Timor, on the northern coast of the island; pop. 51,700.

dil·i·gence[1] /ˈdiləjəns/ ▸*n.* careful and persistent work or effort. ▷Middle English (in the sense 'close attention, caution'): via Old French from Latin *diligentia*, from *diligent-* 'assiduous' (see DILIGENT).

dil·i·gence[2] ▸*n. historical* a public stagecoach. ▷late 17th cent.: from French, shortened from *carrosse de diligence* 'coach of speed.'

dil·i·gent /ˈdiləjənt/ ▸*adj.* having or showing care and conscientiousness in one's work or duties: *many caves are located only after a diligent search.* See note at BUSY. ▷Middle English: via Old French from Latin *diligens, diligent-* 'assiduous,' from *diligere* 'love, take delight in.' —**dil·i·gent·ly** *adv.*

dill /dil/ ▸*n.* an aromatic annual herb of the parsley family, with fine blue-green leaves and yellow flowers. The leaves and seeds of dill are used for flavoring and for medicinal purposes. • *Anethum graveolens*, family Umbelliferae. ■ (also **dill·weed** or **dill weed**) the fresh or dried leaves of this plant used to flavor food. ▷Old English *dile, dyle*; related to Dutch *dille* and German *Dill*; of unknown ultimate origin.

Dil·lin·ger /ˈdilinjər/, John (1903–34), U.S. criminal. He was a bank robber who made daring escapes from jail and was named "Public Enemy Number 1" by the Federal Bureau of Investigation (FBI). He was eventually betrayed by the "lady in red" in an ambush set up by the FBI.

dill pick·le ▸*n.* pickled cucumber flavored with dill.

dill wa·ter ▸*n.* an extract distilled from dill, used to relieve flatulence.

dil·ly /ˈdilē/ ▸*n.* (*pl.* **-lies**) [usu. in *sing.*] *informal* an excellent example of a particular type of person or thing: *that's a dilly of a breakfast recipe.* ▷late 19th cent. (as an adjective in the sense 'delightful'): alteration of the first syllable of DELIGHTFUL or DELICIOUS.

dil·ly-dal·ly ▸*v.* (**-lies, -lied**) [*intrans.*] *informal* waste time through aimless wandering or indecision: *don't dilly-dally for too long.* ▷early 17th cent.: reduplication of DALLY.

di·loph·o·saur /dī,läfəˈsôr/ (also **di·loph·o·sau·rus** /dī-,läfəˈsôrəs/) ▸*n.* one of the earliest of the large bipedal dinosaurs, which had two long crests on the head and occurred in the early Jurassic period. • Genus *Dilophosaurus*, infraorder Carnosauria, suborder Theropoda. ▷modern Latin, from Greek *dilophos* 'two-crested' + *sauros* 'lizard.' —**di·loph·o·sau·ri·an** *adj.*

dil·u·ent /ˈdilyooənt/ *technical* ▸*n.* a substance used to dilute something.
▸*adj.* acting to cause dilution. ▷early 18th cent. (denoting a medicine used to increase the proportion of water in the blood): from Latin *diluent-* 'dissolving,' from the verb *diluere*.

di·lute /dīˈloot; dī-/ ▸*v.* [*trans.*] (often **be diluted**) make (a liquid) thinner or weaker by adding water or another solvent to it: *bleach can be diluted with cold water.* ■ make (something) weaker in force, content, or value by modifying it or adding other elements to it: *the reforms have been diluted.* ■ reduce the value of (a shareholding) by issuing more shares in a company without increasing the values of its assets.
▸*adj.* (of a liquid) made thinner or weaker by having had water or another solvent added to it. ■ *Chemistry* (of a solution) having a relatively low concentration of solute: *a dilute solution of potassium permanganate.* ■ (of color or light) weak or low in concentration: *a short measure of dilute sun.* ▷mid 16th cent.: from Latin *dilut-* 'washed away, dissolved,' from the verb *diluere*. —**di·lut·er** *n.*

di·lu·tion /diˈlooshən; dī-/ ▸*n.* the action of making a liquid more dilute. ■ the action of making something weaker in force, content, or value: *he is resisting any dilution of dogma.* ■ a liquid that has been diluted. ■ the degree to which a solution has been diluted: *the antibody was applied **at a dilution of** 1:50.* ■ a reduction in the value of a shareholding due to the issue of additional shares in a company without an increase in assets. —**di·lu·tive** /-ˈlootiv/ *adj.* (*chiefly Finance*).

di·lu·vi·al /diˈloovēəl/ ▸*adj.* of or relating to a flood or floods, esp. the biblical Flood. ▷mid 17th cent.: from late Latin *diluvialis*, from *diluvium* 'deluge,' from *diluere* 'wash away.'

di·lu·vi·an /diˈloovēən/ ▸*adj.* another term for DILUVIAL.

dim /dim/ ▸*adj.* (**dim·mer, dim·mest**) **1** (of a light, color, or illuminated object) not shining brightly or clearly: *her face was softened by the dim light.* ■ (of an object or shape) made difficult to see by darkness, shade, or distance: *a dim figure in the dark kitchen.* ■ (of a room or space) made difficult to see in by darkness: *long dim corridors.* ■ (of the eyes) not able to see clearly: *his eyes became dim.* ■ (of a sound) indistinct or muffled: *the dim drone of their voices.* ■ (of prospects) not giving cause for hope or optimism: *their prospects for the future looked pretty dim.* **2** not clearly recalled or formulated in the mind: *she had dim memories of that time | the matter was in the dim and distant past.* ■ *informal* stupid or slow to understand: *you're just incredibly dim.*
▸*v.* (**dimmed, dim·ming**) make or become less bright: [*trans.*] *a smoky inferno that dimmed the sun* | [*intrans.*] *the lights dimmed and the curtains parted.* ■ [*trans.*] lower (a vehicle's headlights) from high to low beam: [as *adj.*] (**dimmed**) *the car moved slowly, its headlights dimmed.* ■ make or become less intense or favorable: [*trans.*] *the difficulty in sleeping couldn't dim her happiness* | [*intrans.*] *the company's prospects have dimmed.* ■ make or become less able to see clearly: [*trans.*] *your sight is dimmed* | [*intrans.*] *his eyes dimmed.* ■ make or become less clear in the mind: [*trans.*] *his win dimmed the memory of the booing he'd received.* ▷Old English *dim, dimm*, of Germanic origin; related to German dialect *timmer*. —**dim·ly** *adv.* —**dim·mish** *adj.* —**dim·ness** *n.*
▸*PHRASE* □ **take a dim view of** regard with disapproval.

dim. ▸*abbr.* ■ dimension. ■ diminuendo. ■ diminutive.

Di·Mag·gi·o /də'majē,ō/, Joe (1914–99), U.S. baseball player; full name *Joseph Paul DiMaggio*; called **Joltin' Joe** and the **Yankee Clipper**. Star of the New York Yankees 1936–51, he was renowned for his outstanding batting ability and for his outfield play. In 1941, he achieved a 56-game hitting streak, a record that has not been challenged. He was briefly married to Marilyn Monroe in 1954. Baseball Hall of Fame (1955).

Joe DiMaggio

dime /dīm/ ▸*n.* a ten-cent coin. ■ *informal* a small amount of money: *he didn't have a dime.* ■ *informal* used to refer to something small in size, area, or degree: *there's not a dime's worth of difference between you and him.* ■ *informal* short for DIME BAG., ▷late Middle English: from Old French *disme*, from Latin *decima pars* 'tenth part.' The word originally denoted a tithe or tenth part; the modern sense 'ten-cent coin' dates from the late 18th cent.

▸*PHRASES* □ **a dime a dozen** *informal* very common and of no particular value: *experts in this field are a dime a dozen.* □ **drop a** (or **the**) **dime on someone** *informal* inform on someone. □ **get off the dime** *informal* be decisive and show initiative: *at some point you have to get off the dime and do something.* □ **on a dime** *informal* used to refer to a maneuver that can be performed by a moving vehicle or person within a small area or short distance: *boats that can* **turn on a dime**.

dime bag ▸*n. informal* a specified amount of an illegal drug, packaged and sold for a fixed price.

dime nov·el ▸*n. historical* a cheap, popular novel, typically a melodramatic romance or adventure story.

di·men·sion /di'menCHən/ ▸*n.* **1** an aspect or feature of a situation, problem, or thing: *sun-dried tomatoes add a new dimension to this sauce.* **2** (usu. **dimensions**) a measurable extent of some kind, such as length, breadth, depth, or height: *the final dimensions of the pond were 14 ft. x 8 ft.* | *the drawing must be precise* **in dimension**. ■ a mode of linear extension of which there are three in space and two on a flat surface, which corresponds to one of a set of coordinates specifying the position of a point. ■ *Physics* an expression for a derived physical quantity in terms of fundamental quantities such as mass, length, or time, raised to the appropriate power (acceleration, for example, having the dimension of *length* × *time*$^{-2}$).

▸*v.* [*trans.*] (often **be dimensioned**) cut or shape (something) to particular measurements. ■ mark (a diagram) with measurements: [as *adj.*] (**dimensioned**) *draw a dimensioned front elevation.* ▷late Middle English (sense 2): via Old French from Latin *dimensio(n-)*, from *dimetiri* 'measure out.' Sense 1 dates from the 1920s. **—di·men·sion·al** /-CHənl/ *adj.* [in *combination*] *multidimensional scaling.* **—di·men·sion·al·i·ty** /di-,menCHə'nalətē/ *n.* **—di·men·sion·al·ly** /-CHənl-ē/ *adj.* **—di·men·sion·less** *adj.*

di·men·sion·al a·nal·y·sis /də'menCHənl/ ▸*n. Mathematics* analysis using the fact that physical quantities added to or equated with each other must be expressed in terms of the same fundamental quantities (such as mass, length, or time) for inferences to be made about the relations between them.

di·mer /'dīmər/ ▸*n. Chemistry* a molecule or molecular complex consisting of two identical molecules linked together. ▷1930s: from DI-[1] 'two,' on the pattern of *polymer*. **—di·mer·ic** /dī'merik/ *adj.*

di·mer·cap·rol /,dīmər'kaprôl/ ▸*n. Chemistry* a colorless, oily liquid with an unpleasant smell, used as an antidote for poisoning by mercury, arsenic, lead, and other heavy metals. • Alternative name: **2,3,-dimercapto-1-propanol**; chem. formula: $CH_2(SH)CH(SH)CH_2OH$. ▷1940s: from elements of the systematic name (see above).

di·mer·ize /'dīmə,rīz/ ▸*v.* [*intrans.*] *Chemistry* combine with a similar molecule to form a dimer: *ClO dimerizes to form* Cl_2O_2. **—di·mer·i·za·tion** /,dīmərə-'zāSHən/ *n.*

dim·er·ous /'dimərəs/ ▸*adj. Botany & Zoology* having parts arranged in groups of two. ■ consisting of two joints or parts. ▷early 19th cent.: from modern Latin *dimerus* (from Greek *dimerēs* 'bipartite') + -OUS.

dime store ▸*n.* a shop selling cheap merchandise (originally one where the maximum price was a dime). ■ [as *adj.*] cheap and inferior: *plastic dime-store toys.*

dim·e·ter /'dimitər/ ▸*n. Prosody* a line of verse consisting of two metrical feet. ▷late 16th cent.: via late Latin from Greek *dimetros* 'of two measures,' from *di-* 'twice' + *metron* 'a measure.'

di·meth·o·ate /dī'meTHō,āt/ ▸*n.* a crystalline, synthetic, organophosphorus compound used in solution as an insecticide. ▷1960s: from DI-[1] 'two' + METHYL + THIO- + -ATE[1].

di·meth·yl sulf·ox·ide /dī'meTHəl səl'fäk,sīd/ (*chiefly Brit.* **di·meth·yl sulph·ox·ide**) (abbr.: **DMSO**) ▸*n. Chemistry* a colorless liquid used as a solvent and synthetic reagent. It is readily able to penetrate the skin and is used in medicinal preparations for skin application. • Chem. formula: $(CH_3)_2SO$.

di·met·ric /dī'metrik/ ▸*adj.* (in technical drawing) denoting or incorporating a method of showing projection or perspective using a set of three geometric axes, of which two are of the same scale or dimension but the third is of another. ▷mid 19th cent.: from DI-[1] 'two' + Greek *metron* 'measure' + -IC.

di·met·ro·don /dī'metrə,dän/ ▸*n.* a large, carnivorous, synapsid fossil reptile of the Permian period, with long spines on its back supporting a sail-like crest. • Genus *Dimetrodon*, order Pelycosauria, subclass Synapsida. ▷modern Latin, from *di-* 'twice' + Greek *metron* 'measure' + *odous, odont-* 'tooth' (taken in the sense 'two long teeth').

di·mid·i·ate /di'midē,āt/ ▸*v.* [*trans.*] *Heraldry* (of a coat of arms or charge) adjoin (another) so that only half of each is visible. ■ [as *adj.*] (**dimidiated**) (of a charge) having only one half depicted. ▷late 16th cent.: from Latin *dimidiat-* 'halved,' from the verb *dimidiare*, from *dimidium* 'half.'

di·mid·i·a·tion /di,midē'āSHən/ ▸*n. Heraldry* the combination of two coats of arms by juxtaposing the dexter half of one and the sinister half of the other on a single shield (a practice largely superseded by impalement).

di·min·ish /di'miniSH/ ▸*v.* make or become less: [*trans.*] *a tax whose purpose is to diminish spending* | [*intrans.*] *the pain will gradually diminish.* ■ [*trans.*] make (someone or something) seem less impressive or valuable: *the trial has aged and diminished him.* ▷late Middle English: blend of archaic *minish* 'diminish' (based on Latin *minutia* 'smallness') and obsolete *diminue* 'speak disparagingly' (based on Latin *deminuere* 'lessen' (in late Latin *diminuere*), from *minuere* 'make small'). **—di·min·ish·a·ble** *adj.*

▸*PHRASE* □ (**the law of**) **diminishing returns** used to refer to a point at which the level of profits or benefits gained is less than the amount of money or energy invested.

di·min·ished /di'miniSHt/ ▸*adj.* **1** made smaller or less: *a diminished role for local government.* ■ [*predic.*] made to seem less impressive or valuable: *she felt diminished by the report.* **2** [*attrib.*] *Music* denoting or containing an interval that is one semitone less than the corresponding minor or perfect interval: *a diminished fifth.*

di·min·ished ca·pac·i·ty ▸*n. Law* an unbalanced mental state that is considered to make a person less answerable for a crime and is recognized as grounds to reduce the charge.

di·min·ished sev·enth ▸*n. Music* **1** the interval that is a semitone less than a minor seventh, e.g., from A to G flat (which in equal tuning sounds the same as a major sixth). **2** (also **diminished seventh chord**) a chord formed by a note together with those above it at intervals of a minor third, a diminished fifth, and a diminished seventh. The resulting chord consists entirely of superimposed minor thirds, and is much used in modern music in modulating between keys.

di·min·u·en·do /di,minyoo'endō/ *Music* ▸*n.* (*pl.* **-dos** or **-di** /-dē/) a decrease in loudness: *the sudden diminuendos are brilliantly effective.* ■ a passage to be performed with such a decrease.

▸*adv.* & *adj.* (esp. as a direction) with a decrease in loudness: [as *adj.*] *the diminuendo chorus before the final tumult.*

▸*v.* (**-dos, -doed**) [*intrans.*] decrease in loudness or intensity: *the singers left and the buzz diminuendoed.* ▷Italian, literally 'diminishing,' from *diminuire*, from Latin *deminuere* 'lessen' (see DIMINISH).

dim·i·nu·tion /,dimə'n(y)ooSHən/ ▸*n.* a reduction in the size, extent, or importance of something: *a permanent diminution in value* | *the disease shows no signs of diminution.* ■ *Music* the shortening of the time values of notes in a melodic part. ▷Middle English: via Old French from Latin *deminutio(n-)*, from the verb *deminuere* (see DIMINISH).

di·min·u·tive /di'minyətiv/ ▸*adj.* extremely or unusually small: *a diminutive figure dressed in black.* See note at SMALL. ■ (of a word, name, or suffix) implying smallness, either actual or imputed in token of affection, scorn, etc., (e.g., *teeny, -let, -kins*).

▸*n.* a smaller or shorter thing, in particular: ■ a diminutive word or suffix. ■ a shortened form of a name, typically used informally: *"Nick" is a diminutive of "Nicholas."* ■ *Heraldry* a charge of the same form as an ordinary but of lesser size or width. ▷late Middle English (as a grammatical term): from Old French *diminutif, -ive*, from late Latin *diminutivus*, from Latin *deminut-* 'diminished,' from the verb *deminuere* (see DIMINISH). **—di·min·u·tive·ly** *adv.* **—di·min·u·tive·ness** *n.*

dim·i·ty /'dimitē/ ▸*n.* a hard-wearing, sheer cotton fabric woven with raised stripes or checks. ▷late Middle English: from Italian *dimito* or medieval Latin *dimitum*, from Greek *dimitos*, from *di-* 'twice' + *mitos* 'warp thread'; the origin of the final *-y* is unknown.

dim·mer /'dimər/ ▸*n.* **1** (also **dimmer switch**) a device for varying the brightness of an electric light. **2** a headlight with a low beam. ■ (**dimmers**) small parking lights on a motor vehicle.

di·mor·phic /dī'môrfik/ ▸*adj. chiefly Biology* occurring in or representing two distinct forms: *in this sexually dimorphic species only the males have wings.* ▷mid 19th cent.: from Greek *dimorphos* (from *di-* 'twice' + *morphē* 'form') + -IC. **—di·mor·phism** /-fizəm/ *n.*

dim·ple /'dimpəl/ ▸*n.* a small depression in the flesh, either one that exists permanently or one that forms in the cheeks when one smiles. ■ [often as *adj.*] a slight depression in the surface of something: *a sheet of dimple foam.*

▸*v.* [*trans.*] produce a dimple or dimples in the surface of (something): *a sucking swirl dimpled the water.* ■ [*intrans.*] form or show a dimple or dimples: *the water ruffled and dimpled* | [as *adj.*] (**dimpled**) *a dimpled smile.* ▷Middle English: of Germanic origin; related to German *Tümpel* 'pond.' **—dim·ply** /'dimp(ə)lē/ *adj.*

dim sum /'dim 'səm/ ▸*n.* a Chinese dish of small steamed or fried savory dumplings containing various fillings, served as a snack or main course. ▷from Chinese (Cantonese dialect) *tim sam*, from *tim* 'dot' and *sam* 'heart.'

dim·wit /'dim,wit/ ▸*n. informal* a stupid or silly person. **—dim·wit·ted** *adj.* **—dim·wit·ted·ly** *adv.* **—dim·wit·ted·ness** *n.* .

DIN /din/ ▸*n.* any of a series of technical standards originating in Germany and used internationally, esp. to designate electrical connections, film speeds, and paper sizes: [as *adj.*] *a DIN socket.* ▷early 20th cent.: acronym from *Deutsche Industrie-Norm* 'German Industrial Standard' (as laid down by the *Deutsches Institut für Normung* 'German Institute for Standards').

din /din/ ▸*n.* [in *sing.*] a loud, unpleasant, and prolonged noise: *the fans made an awful din.*

▸*v.* (**dinned, din·ning**) **1** [*trans.*] (**be dinned into**) (of a fact) be instilled in (someone) by constant repetition: *the doctrine that has been dinned into all our heads.* **2** [*intrans.*] make a loud, unpleasant, and prolonged noise: *the sound dinning in my ears was the telephone ringing.* ▷Old English *dyne, dynn* (noun), *dynian* (verb), of Germanic origin; related to Old High German *tuni* (noun) and Old Norse *dynr* (noun), *dynja* 'come rumbling down.'

di·nar /di'när/ ▸*n.* **1** the basic monetary unit of the states of Yugoslavia, equal to 100 paras. **2** the basic monetary unit of certain countries of the Middle East and North Africa, equal to 1000 fils in Jordan, Bahrain, and Iraq, 1000 dirhams in Libya, 100 centimes in Algeria, and 10 pounds in the Sudan. **3** a monetary unit of Iran, equal to one hundredth of a rial. ▷from Arabic and Persian *dīnār*, Turkish and

Serbo-Croat *dinar*, via late Greek from Latin *denarius* (see DENARIUS).

Di·nar·ic Alps /di'narik/ a mountain range in the Balkans that runs parallel to the Adriatic coast from Slovenia in the northwest, through Croatia, Bosnia, and Montenegro, to Albania in the southeast.

din-din /'din ˌdin/ ▸*n.* a child's word for dinner.

dine /dīn/ ▸*v.* [*intrans.*] eat dinner: *we dined at a restaurant* | [as *n.*] (**dining**) *a dining area.* ■ (**dine out**) eat dinner in a restaurant or the home of friends. ■ (**dine on**) eat (something) for dinner. ■ (**dine out on**) regularly entertain friends with (a humorous story or interesting piece of information): *it should have been one of those stories one dines out on afterward.* ■ [*trans.*] take (someone) to dinner: *I'll dine you soon.* ▷Middle English: from Old French *disner*, probably from *desjëuner* 'to break fast,' from *des-* (expressing reversal) + *jëun* 'fasting' (from Latin *jejunus*).

▸*PHRASE* □ **wine and dine** see WINE.

din·er /'dīnər/ ▸*n.* **1** a person who is eating, typically a customer in a restaurant. **2** a dining car on a train. ■ a small roadside restaurant with a long counter and booths, originally one designed to resemble a dining car on a train.

D

di·ne·ro /di'ne(ə)rō/ ▸*n. informal* money: *their pockets full of dinero.* ▷mid 19th cent.: Spanish, 'coin, money.'

Din·e·sen /'dinəsən/, Isak, see BLIXEN.

di·nette /dī'net/ ▸*n.* a small room or part of a room used for eating meals. ■ a set of table and chairs for such an area. ▷1930s: formed irregularly from DINE + -ETTE.

ding[1] /diNG/ ▸*v.* [*intrans.*] make a ringing sound: *cash registers were dinging softly.*

▸*exclam.* used to imitate a metallic ringing sound resembling a bell. ▷early 17th cent.: imitative.

ding[2] ▸*n. informal* a deliberate or accidental blow, esp. a mark or dent on the bodywork of a car, boat, or other vehicle.

▸*v.* [*trans.*] *informal* dent (something). ■ hit (someone), esp. on the head: *I dinged him one.* ▷Middle English: probably of Scandinavian origin; compare with Danish *dænge* 'beat, bang.'

ding-a-ling /'diNG ə ˌliNG/ ▸*n.* **1** [in *sing.*] the ringing sound of a bell. **2** *informal* an eccentric or stupid person. ▷late 19th cent.: imitative.

Ding an sich /ˌdiNG än 'sisH/ ▸*n.* (in Kant's philosophy) a thing as it is in itself, not mediated through perception by the senses or conceptualization, and therefore unknowable. ▷mid 19th cent.: German, literally 'thing in itself.'

ding·bat /'diNGˌbat/ *informal* ▸*n.* **1** a stupid or eccentric person. **2** a typographical device other than a letter or numeral (such as an asterisk), used to signal divisions in text or to replace letters in a euphemistically presented vulgar word. ▷mid 19th cent. (in early use applied to various vaguely specified objects): origin uncertain; perhaps based on obsolete *ding* 'to beat, deal heavy blows.' Sense 1 dates from the early 20th cent.

ding-dong /'diNG ˌdôNG/ ▸*n. informal* a silly or foolish person.

▸*adv.* & *adj.* **1** with the simple alternate chimes of or as of a bell: [as *adv.*] *the church bells go ding-dong* | [as *adj.*] *he heard the ding-dong tones.* **2** [as *adj.*] *Brit., informal* (of a contest) evenly matched and intensely waged: *the game was an exciting ding-dong battle.* ▷mid 16th cent.: imitative.

ding·er /'diNGər/ ▸*n. informal* a thing outstanding of its kind: *by God, ain't that a dinger!* ■ *Baseball* a home run: *he beat the Braves twice with extra-inning dingers.* ▷late 19th cent.: shortening of HUMDINGER.

din·ghy /'diNGē/ ▸*n.* (*pl.* **-ghies**) a small boat for recreation or racing, esp. an open boat with a mast and sails. ■ a small, inflatable rubber boat. ■ the smallest of a ship's boats. ▷early 19th cent. (denoting a rowboat used on rivers in India): from Hindi *diṅgī*.

din·gle /'diNGgəl/ ▸*n. poetic/literary or dialect* a deep wooded valley or dell. ▷Middle English (denoting a deep abyss): of unknown origin. The current sense dates from the mid 17th cent.

din·gle·ber·ry /'diNGəlˌberē/ ▸*n.* (*pl.* **-ries**) **1** *vulgar slang* a particle of fecal matter attached to the anal hair of an animal. **2** *vulgar slang* a foolish or inept person. ▷mid 20th cent.: from *dingle* of unknown origin + BERRY.

din·go /'diNGgō/ ▸*n.* (*pl.* **-goes** or **-gos**) a wild or half-domesticated dog with a sandy-colored coat, found in Australia. It is believed to have been introduced by early Aboriginal immigrants. • *Canis dingo*, family Canidae. ▷late 18th cent.: from Dharuk *din-gu* 'domesticated dingo.'

ding·us /'diNGgəs/ ▸*n.* (*pl.* **ding·us·es**) *informal* used to refer to something whose name the speaker cannot remember, is unsure of, or is humorously or euphemistically omitting: *here's a doohickey—and there's the dingus.* ▷late 19th cent.: via Afrikaans from Dutch *ding* 'thing.'

din·gy /'dinjē/ ▸*adj.* (**-gi·er**, **-gi·est**) gloomy and drab: *a dingy room.* ▷mid 18th cent.: perhaps based on Old English *dynge* 'dung.' **—din·gi·ly** /-jəlē/ *adv.* **—din·gi·ness** *n.*

din·ing car ▸*n.* a railroad car equipped as a restaurant.

din·ing hall ▸*n.* a large room, typically in a school or other institution, in which people eat meals together.

din·ing room ▸*n.* a room in a house or hotel in which meals are eaten.

din·ing ta·ble ▸*n.* a table on which meals are served in a dining room.

di·ni·tro·gen te·trox·ide /dī'nītrəjən te'träkˌsīd/ ▸*n.* see NITROGEN DIOXIDE.

dink[1] /diNGk/ ▸*n. informal* a partner in a well-off working couple with no children. ▷1980s: acronym from *double income, no kids.*

dink[2] *chiefly Tennis* ▸*n.* a drop shot.

▸*v.* [*trans.*] hit (the ball) with a drop shot. ▷1930s: symbolic of the light action.

Din·ka /'diNGkə/ ▸*n.* (*pl.* same or **-kas**) **1** a member of a Sudanese people of the Nile basin. **2** the Nilotic language of this people, with about 1.4 million speakers.

▸*adj.* of or relating to this people or their language. ▷from the local word *Jieng* 'people.'

din·kum /'diNGkəm/ ▸*adj. Austral./NZ, informal* (of an article or person) genuine: *Andy's dinkum hat from Australia.* ▷late 19th cent.: of unknown origin.

▸*PHRASE* □ **fair dinkum** used to emphasize that or query whether something is genuine or true: *it's a fair dinkum Aussie wedding* ■ used to emphasize that behavior complies with accepted standards: *they were asking a lot for the car, but fair dinkum considering its list price.*

dink·y /'diNGkē/ ▸*adj.* (**dink·i·er**, **dink·i·est**) *informal* small; insignificant: *I can't believe the dinky salaries they pay here.* ▷late 18th cent.: from Scots and northern English dialect *dink* 'neat, trim,' of unknown origin.

din·ner /'dinər/ ▸*n.* the main meal of the day, taken either around midday or in the evening. ■ a formal evening meal, typically one in honor of a person or event. ▷Middle English: from Old French *disner* (infinitive used as a noun: see DINE).

din·ner dance ▸*n.* a formal social event in which guests have dinner, followed by dancing.

din·ner jack·et ▸*n.* a man's short jacket without tails, typically a black one, worn with a bow tie for formal occasions in the evening.

din·ner pail ▸*n. dated* a pail in which a laborer's or schoolchild's dinner is carried and kept warm.

▸*PHRASE* □ **hand in one's dinner pail** *informal* die.

din·ner par·ty ▸*n.* a social occasion at which guests eat dinner together.

din·ner ring ▸*n.* a woman's dress ring, usually with a large stone or an ornate setting, often worn on special occasions.

din·ner serv·ice (also **dinner set**) ▸*n.* a set of matching dishes for serving a meal.

din·ner the·a·ter ▸*n.* a theater in which a meal is included in the price of a ticket.

din·ner·ware /'dinərˌwe(ə)r/ ▸*n.* tableware, including plates, glassware, and cutlery. ▷late 19th cent.

din·o·flag·el·late /ˌdīnō'flajəlit; -ˌlāt/ ▸*n. Biology* a single-celled organism with two flagella, occurring in large numbers in marine plankton and also found in fresh water. Some produce toxins that can accumulate in shellfish, resulting in poisoning when eaten. • Division Dinophyta or class Dinophyceae, division Chromophycota (or phylum Dinophyta, kingdom Protista). ▷late 19th cent. (as an adjective): from modern Latin *Dinoflagellata* (plural), from Greek *dinos* 'whirling' + Latin *flagellum* 'small whip' (see FLAGELLUM).

di·no·saur /'dīnəˌsôr/ ▸*n.* **1** a fossil reptile of the Mesozoic era, often reaching an enormous size.

The dinosaurs are placed, according to their hip structure, in two distantly related orders (see ORNITHISCHIAN and SAURISCHIAN). Some of them may have been warm-blooded, and their closest living relatives are the birds. Dinosaurs were all extinct by the end of the Cretaceous period (65 million years ago), a popular theory being that the extinctions were the result of the impact of a large meteorite.

2 a person or thing that is outdated or has become obsolete because of failure to adapt to changing circumstances. ▷mid 19th cent.: from modern Latin *dinosaurus*, from Greek *deinos* 'terrible' + *sauros* 'lizard.' **—di·no·sau·ri·an** /ˌdīnə'sôrēən/ *adj.* & *n.*

dint /dint/ ▸*n.* **1** an impression or hollow in a surface: *the soft dints at the top of a coconut.* **2** *archaic* a blow or stroke, typically one made with a weapon in fighting. ■ force of attack; impact: *I perceive you feel the dint of pity.*

▸*v.* [*trans.*] mark (a surface) with impressions or hollows: [as *adj.*] (**dinted**) *the metal was dull and dinted.* ▷Old English *dynt* 'stroke with a weapon,' reinforced in Middle English by the related Old Norse word *dyntr*; of unknown ultimate origin. Compare with DENT.

▸*PHRASE* □ **by dint of** by means of: *he had gotten to where he was today by dint of sheer hard work.*

di·oc·e·san /dī'äsisən/ ▸*adj.* of or concerning a diocese.

▸*n.* the bishop of a diocese. ▷late Middle English: from French *diocésain*, from medieval Latin *diocesanus*, from Latin *dioecesis* (see DIOCESE).

di·o·cese /'dīəsis; -ˌsēz; -ˌsēs/ ▸*n.* (*pl.* **-ces·es**) a district under the pastoral care of a bishop in the Christian Church. ▷Middle English: from Old French *diocise*, from late Latin *diocesis*, from Latin *dioecesis* 'governor's jurisdiction, diocese,' from Greek *dioikēsis* 'administration, diocese,' from *dioikein* 'keep house, administer.'

Di·o·cle·tian /ˌdīə'klēsHən/ (245–313), Roman emperor 284–305; full name *Gaius Aurelius Valerius Diocletianus.* Faced with mounting military problems, in 286 he divided the empire between himself in the east and Maximian in the west. He launched the final persecution of the Christians 303.

di·ode /'dīˌōd/ ▸*n. Electronics* a semiconductor device with two terminals, typically allowing the flow of current in one direction only. ■ a thermionic tube having two electrodes (an anode and a cathode). ▷early 20th cent.: from DI-[1] 'two' + a shortened form of ELECTRODE.

di·oe·cious /dī'ēsHəs/ ▸*adj. Biology* (of a plant or invertebrate animal) having the male and female reproductive organs in separate individuals. Compare with MONOECIOUS. ▷mid 18th cent.: from modern Latin *Dioecia* (a class in Linnaeus's sexual system), from DI-[1] 'two' + Greek *-oikos* 'house.' **—di·oe·cy** /'dī ˌēsē/ *n.*

Di·og·e·nes /dī'äjəˌnēz/ (*c.*400–*c.*325 BC), Greek philosopher. The most noted of the Cynics, he emphasized self-sufficiency and the need for natural, uninhibited behavior, regardless of social conventions.

di·og·e·nite /dī'äjəˌnīt/ ▸*n.* a stony meteorite of a kind consisting largely of pyroxenes and plagioclase. ▷late 19th cent.: from Greek *Diogenēs* 'descended from Zeus' + -ITE[1].

di·ol /'dīôl/ ▸*n. Chemistry* an alcohol containing two hydroxyl groups in its molecule. ▷1920s: from DI-[1] 'two' + -OL.

Di·o·mede Is·lands /'dīəˌmēd/ two islands in the Bering Strait, separated by the International Date Line. Big Diomede belongs to Russia, and Little Diomede belongs to the U.S.

Di·o·ne /dī'ōnē/ *Astronomy* a satellite of Saturn, the twelfth closest to the planet, discovered by Cassini in 1684. Icy with a partly cratered and partly smooth surface, it has a diameter of 696 miles (1,120 km). ▷named after a Titan, the mother of Aphrodite, in Greek mythology.

Di·o·ny·sian /ˌdīə'nisHən; -'nisēən; -'nīsēən/ (also **Di·o·ny·si·ac** /-'nisēˌak; -'nīsē-/) ▸*adj.* **1** *Greek Mythology* of or relating to the god Dionysus. **2** of or relating to the sensual, spontaneous, and emotional aspects of human nature: *dark, grand Dionysian music.* Compare with APOLLONIAN.

Di·o·ny·si·us /ˌdīə'nisēəs; -'nisHəs/ the name of two rulers of Syracuse: ■ **Dionysius I** (*c.*430–367 BC), ruled 405–367; known as **Dionysius the Elder**. A tyrannical ruler, he waged three wars against the Carthaginians for control of Sicily, the third of which resulted in his defeat at Cronium in 375. ■ **Dionysius II** (*c.*397–*c.*344 BC), son of Dionysius I; ruled 367–357 and 346–344; known as **Dionysius the Younger**. He lacked his father's military ambitions and signed a peace treaty with Carthage in 367.

Di·o·ny·si·us Ex·ig·u·us /eg'zigyo͞oəs/ (died *c.*556), Scythian-born monk and scholar. He is noted for developing in 505 the system of dates BC and AD that is still in use today. His calculation of Jesus Christ's incarnation being 753 years after the founding of Rome has since been shown to be mistaken by several years. He is said to have taken the nickname *Exiguus* ("little") as a sign of humility.

Di·o·ny·si·us of Hal·i·car·nas·sus /ˌhalikärˈnasəs/ (1st century BC), Greek historian, literary critic, and rhetorician. He lived in Rome from 30 BC and is best known for his detailed history of the city, written in Greek.

Di·o·ny·si·us the Ar·e·op·a·gite /ˌarēˈäpəˌgīt; -ˌjīt/ (1st century AD), Greek churchman. His conversion by St. Paul is recorded in Acts 17:34, and according to tradition he went on to become the first bishop of Athens.

Di·o·ny·sus /ˌdīəˈnisəs/ *Greek Mythology* a Greek god, son of Zeus and Semele. He was originally a god of the fertility of nature, associated with wild and ecstatic religious rites; in later traditions he is a god of wine who loosens inhibitions and inspires creativity in music and poetry. Also called **BACCHUS**.

Di·o·phan·tine e·qua·tion /ˌdīəˈfanˌtin; -tīn/ ▸*Mathematics* a polynomial equation with integral coefficients for which integral solutions are required. ▷early 18th cent.: named after **DIOPHANTUS**.

Di·o·phan·tus /ˌdīəˈfantəs/ (*fl.c.*AD 250), Greek mathematician. He was the first to attempt an algebraical notation, showing in *Arithmetica* how to solve simple and quadratic equations.

di·op·side /dīˈäpˌsīd/ ▸*n.* a mineral occurring as white to pale green crystals in metamorphic and basic igneous rocks. It consists of a calcium and magnesium silicate of the pyroxene group, often also containing iron and chromium. ▷early 19th cent.: from French, formed irregularly from **DI-**[3] 'through' + Greek *opsis* 'aspect,' later interpreted as derived from Greek *diopsis* 'a view through.'

di·op·tase /dīˈäptās; -tāz/ ▸*n.* a rare mineral occurring as emerald green or blue-green crystals. It consists of a hydrated silicate of copper. ▷early 19th cent.: from French, formed irregularly from Greek *dioptos* 'transparent.'

di·op·ter /dīˈäptər/ ▸*n.* a unit of refractive power that is equal to the reciprocal of the focal length (in meters) of a given lens. ▷late 16th cent. (originally denoting an alidade): from French, from Latin *dioptra*, from Greek, from *di-* 'through' + *optos* 'visible.' The term was used in the early 17th cent. to denote an ancient form of theodolite; the current sense dates from the late 19th cent.

dinosaurs

di·op·tric /dīˈäptrik/ ▸*adj.* of or relating to the refraction of light, esp. in the organs of sight or in devices that aid or improve the vision. ▷mid 17th cent.: from Greek *dioptrikos*, from *dioptra*, a kind of theodolite (see **DIOPTER**).

di·op·trics /dīˈäptriks/ ▸*plural n.* [treated as *sing.*] the branch of optics that deals with refraction.

Di·or /dēˈôr/, Christian (1905–57), French couturier. His first collection 1947 featured the narrow-waisted New Look, with tightly fitted bodices and full pleated skirts. He later created the A-line style.

di·o·ram·a /ˌdīəˈramə; -ˈrä-/ ▸*n.* a model representing a scene with three-dimensional figures, either in miniature or as a large-scale museum exhibit. ■ *chiefly historical* a scenic painting, viewed through a peephole, in which changes in color and direction of illumination simulate changes in the weather, time of day, etc. ■ a miniature movie set used for special effects or animation. ▷early 19th cent.: coined in French from **DIA-** 'through,' on the pattern of *panorama*.

di·o·rite /ˈdīəˌrīt/ ▸*n. Geology* a speckled, coarse-grained igneous rock consisting essentially of plagioclase, feldspar, and hornblende or other mafic minerals. ▷early 19th cent.: coined in French, formed irregularly from Greek *diorizein* 'distinguish' + **-ITE**[1]. —**di·o·rit·ic** /ˌdīəˈritik/ *adj.*

Di·os·cu·ri /ˌdīəˈskyoorē/ *Greek & Roman Mythology* the twins Castor and Pollux, born to Leda after her seduction by Zeus. Castor was mortal, but Pollux was immortal; at Pollux's request they shared his immortality between them, spending half their time below the earth in Hades and the other half on Olympus. They are often identified with the constellation Gemini. ▷from Greek *Dioskouroi* 'sons of Zeus.'

di·os·gen·in /ˌdī-äzˈjenin; dīˈäzjənin/ ▸*n. Chemistry* a steroid compound obtained from Mexican yams and used in the synthesis of steroid hormones. ▷1930s: from *dios-* (from the modern Latin genus name *Dioscorea*) + *genin*, denoting steroids that occur as the nonsugar part of certain glycosides.

di·ox·ane /dīˈäkˌsān/ (also **di·ox·an** /-ˈäksän; -sən/) ▸*n. Chemistry* a colorless, toxic liquid used as an organic solvent. • A heterocyclic compound with a ring of four carbon and two oxygen atoms; chem. formula: $C_4H_8O_2$. ▷early 20th cent.: from **DI-**[1] 'two' + **OX-** 'oxygen' + **-AN** (or **-ANE**[2]).

di·ox·ide /dīˈäkˌsīd/ ▸*n. Chemistry* an oxide containing two atoms of oxygen in its molecule or empirical formula.

di·ox·in /dīˈäksin/ ▸*n.* a highly toxic compound produced as a byproduct in some manufacturing processes, notably herbicide production and paper bleaching. It is a serious and persistent environmental pollutant. • A heterocyclic organochlorine compound; alternative name: 2,3,7,8-tetrachlorodibenzoparadioxin (abbr.: **TCDD**); chem. formula: $C_{12}H_4O_2Cl_4$. ■ any of the class of compounds to which this belongs. ▷early 20th cent.: from **DI-**[1] 'two' + **OX-** 'oxygen' + **-IN**[1].

DIP /dip/ ▸*abbr.* ■ *Computing* document image processing, a system for the digital storage and retrieval of documents as scanned images. ■ *Electronics* dual in-line package, a package for an integrated circuit consisting of a rectangular sealed unit with two parallel rows of downward-pointing pins.

dip /dip/ ▸*v.* (**dipped**, **dip·ping**) **1** [*trans.*] (**dip something in/into**) put or let something down quickly or briefly in or into (liquid): *he dipped a brush in the paint.* ■ [*intrans.*] (**dip into**) put a hand or tool into (a bag or container) in order to take something out: *Ian dipped into his briefcase and pulled out a photograph.* ■ [*intrans.*] (**dip into**) spend from or make use of (one's financial resources): *you won't have to dip into your savings.* ■ [*intrans.*] (**dip into**) read only parts of (a book) in a desultory manner. ■ take (snuff). ■ immerse (sheep) in a chemical solution that kills parasites. ■ make (a candle) by immersing a wick repeatedly in hot wax: [as *adj.*] (**dipped**) *dipped candles are made using simple equipment.* ■ *informal, dated* baptize (someone) by immersion in water. **2** [*intrans.*] sink or drop downward: *swallows dipped and soared | the sun had dipped below the horizon.* ■ (of a level or amount) become lower or smaller, typically temporarily: *the president's popularity has dipped | audiences dipped below 600,000 for the series.* ■ (of a road, path, or area of land) slope downward: *the path rose and dipped.* ■ [*trans.*] lower or move (something) downward: *the plane dipped its wings.*

▸*n.* **1** a brief swim: *she went for a dip in a pool.* ■ a brief immersion in liquid: *a dip in hot water is prescribed to destroy fruit flies.* ■ short for **SHEEP DIP**. ■ a cursory read of part of a book: *a quick dip into this publication.* **2** a thick sauce in which pieces of food are dunked before eating: *tasty garlic dip.* ■ a quantity that has been scooped up from a mass: *ice cream sold by the dip.* **3** a brief downward slope followed by an upward one: *the road's precipitous dips and turns.* ■ an act of sinking or dropping briefly before rising again: *a dip in the share price.* **4** *technical* the extent to which something is angled downward from the horizontal, in particular: ■ (also **magnetic dip**) the angle made with the horizontal at any point by the earth's magnetic field, or by a magnetic needle in response to this. ■ *Geology* the angle a stratum makes with the horizontal: *the cliff profile tends to be dominated by the dip of the beds.* ■ *Astronomy & Surveying* the apparent depression of the horizon from the line of observation, due to the curvature of the earth. **5** *informal, dated* a pickpocket. **6** *informal* a stupid or foolish person. **7** *archaic* a candle made by immersing a wick repeatedly in hot wax. ▷Old English *dyppan*, of Germanic origin; related to **DEEP**.

▸***PHRASE*** □ **dip one's toe into** (or **in**) put one's toe briefly in (water), typically to check the temperature. ■ begin to do or test (something) cautiously: *the company has already dipped its toe into the market.*

Dip. ▸*abbr.* diploma.

dip-dye ▸*v.* [*trans.*] immerse (a yarn or fabric) in a special solution in order to color it.

di·pep·tide /dī'pep,tīd/ ▸*n. Biochemistry* a peptide composed of two amino-acid residues.

di·phen·hy·dra·mine /,dīfen'hīdrə,mēn/ ▸*n. Medicine* an antihistamine compound used for the symptomatic relief of allergies. • A synthetic amine, usually used as a hydrochloride salt; chem. formula: $C_{17}H_{21}NO$. ▷1940s: from *diphen-* (denoting the presence of two phenyl groups) + **HYDR-** + **AMINE**.

di·phen·yl·a·mine /dī'fenl-ə,mēn; -'fē-/ ▸*n. Chemistry* a synthetic crystalline compound with basic properties, used in making azo dyes and as an insecticide and larvicide. • Chem. formula: $(C_6H_5)_2NH$.

diph·the·ri·a /dif'THi(ə)rēə; dip-/ ▸*n.* an acute, highly contagious bacterial disease causing inflammation of the mucous membranes, formation of a false membrane in the throat that hinders breathing and swallowing, and potentially fatal heart and nerve damage by a bacterial toxin in the blood. It is now rare in developed countries because of immunization. • The disease is caused by *Corynebacterium diphtheriae.* ▷mid 19th cent.: modern Latin, from French *diphthérie* (earlier *diphthérite*), from Greek *diphthera* 'skin, hide.' —**diph·the·ri·al** *adj.* —**diph·the·rit·ic** /,difTHə'ritik; ,dip-/ *adj.*

USAGE In the past, **diphtheria** was correctly pronounced with an **f** sound representing the two letters **ph** (as in *telephone, phantom,* and other **ph** words derived from Greek). In recent years, the pronunciation has shifted and today the more common pronunciation, no longer incorrect in standard English, is with a **p** sound. Nevertheless, the **f** sound remains the primary pronunciation.

diph·the·roid /'difTHə,roid; 'dip-/ ▸*n. Microbiology* any bacterium of a genus that includes the diphtheria bacillus, esp. one that does not cause disease. See **CORYNEBACTERIUM**.

▸*adj.* [*attrib.*] *Medicine* similar to diphtheria.

diph·thong /'dif,THäNG; 'dip-; -,THôNG/ ▸*n.* a sound formed by the combination of two vowels in a single syllable, in which the sound begins as one vowel and moves toward another (as in *coin, loud,* and *side*). Often contrasted with **MONOPHTHONG, TRIPHTHONG**. ■ a digraph representing the sound of a diphthong or single vowel (as in *feat*). ■ a compound vowel character; a ligature (such as *æ*). ▷late Middle English: from French *diphtongue*, via late Latin from Greek *diphthongos*, from *di-* 'twice' + *phthongos* 'voice, sound.' —**diph·thon·gal** /dif'THäNGgəl; dip-; -'THôNG-/ *adj.*

diph·thong·ize /'difTHäNG,gīz; dip-; -THôNG-/ ▸*v.* [*trans.*] change (a vowel) into a diphthong. —**diph·thong·i·za·tion** /,difTHäNGgə'zāSHən; ,dip-; -THôNG-/ *n.*

diph·y·cer·cal /difi'sərkəl/ ▸*adj. Zoology* (of a fish's tail) approximately symmetrical and with the vertebral column continuing to the tip, as in lampreys. Contrasted with **HETEROCERCAL, HOMOCERCAL**. ▷mid 19th cent.: from Greek *diphu-* 'of double form' + *kerkos* 'tail' + **-AL**.

di·ple·gia /dī'plēj(ē)ə/ ▸*n. Medicine* paralysis of corresponding parts on both sides of the body, typically affecting the legs more severely than the arms. ▷late 19th cent.: from **DI-**[1] 'two,' on the pattern of *hemiplegia* and *paraplegia*.

diplo- ▸*comb. form* **1** double: *diplococcus.* **2** diploid: *diplohaplontic.* ▷from Greek *diplous* 'double.'

dip·lo·blas·tic /diplō'blastik/ ▸*adj. Zoology* having a body derived from only two embryonic cell layers (ectoderm and endoderm, but no mesoderm), as in sponges and coelenterates.

dip·lo·coc·cus /,diplō'käkəs/ ▸*n.* (*pl.* **-coc·ci** /-'käk(s)ī; -(s)ē/) a bacterium that occurs as pairs of cocci, e.g., pneumococcus.

di·plod·o·cus /di'plädəkəs/ ▸*n.* a huge, herbivorous dinosaur of the late Jurassic period, with a long, slender neck and tail. • Genus *Diplodocus*, infraorder Sauropoda, order Saurischia. ▷modern Latin, from **DIPLO-** 'double' + Greek *dokos* 'wooden beam.'

dip·lo·hap·lon·tic /,diplōhap'läntik/ ▸*adj. Genetics* (of an alga or other lower plant) having a life cycle in which full-grown haploid and diploid forms alternate. Compare with **DIPLONTIC** and **HAPLONTIC**.

dip·loid /'dip,loid/ *Genetics* ▸*adj.* (of a cell or nucleus) containing two complete sets of chromosomes, one from each parent. Compare with **HAPLOID**. ■ (of an organism or part) composed of diploid cells.

▸*n.* a diploid cell, organism, or species. ▷late 19th cent.: from Greek *diplous* 'double' + **-OID**. —**dip·loi·dy** /-,loidē/ *n.*

dip·loid num·ber ▸*n. Genetics* the number of chromosomes present in the body cells of a diploid organism.

di·plo·ma /di'plōmə/ ▸*n.* a certificate awarded by an educational establishment to show that someone has successfully completed a course of study. ■ an official document or charter. ▷mid 17th cent. (in the sense 'state paper'): via Latin from Greek *diplōma* 'folded paper,' from *diploun* 'to fold,' from *diplous* 'double.'

di·plo·ma·cy /di'plōməsē/ ▸*n.* the profession, activity, or skill of managing international relations, typically by a country's representatives abroad: *an extensive round of diplomacy in the Middle East.* ■ the art of dealing with people in a sensitive and effective way: *his genius for tact and diplomacy.* ▷late 18th cent.: from French *diplomatie*, from *diplomatique* 'diplomatic,' on the pattern of *aristocratie* 'aristocracy.'

dip·lo·mat /'diplə,mat/ ▸*n.* an official representing a country abroad. ■ a person who can deal with people in a sensitive and effective way. ▷early 19th cent.: from French *diplomate*, back-formation from *diplomatique* 'diplomatic,' from Latin *diploma* (see **DIPLOMA**).

dip·lo·mate /'diplə,māt/ ▸*n.* a person who holds a diploma, esp. a doctor certified as a specialist by a board of examiners.

dip·lo·mat·ic /,diplə'matik/ ▸*adj.* **1** of or concerning the profession, activity, or skill of managing international relations: *diplomatic relations between the U.S. and Iran.* ■ having or showing an ability to deal with people in a sensitive and effective way: *that was a very diplomatic way of putting it.* **2** (of an edition or copy) exactly reproducing an original version: *a diplomatic transcription.* ▷early 18th cent. (in the sense 'relating to official documents'): from modern Latin *diplomaticus* and French *diplomatique*, from Latin *diploma* (see **DIPLOMA**). Sense 1 (late 18th cent.) is probably due to the publication of the *Codex Juris Gentium Diplomaticus* (1695), a collection of public documents, many of which dealt with international affairs. —**dip·lo·mat·i·cal·ly** /-ik(ə)lē/ *adv.*

dip·lo·mat·ic corps ▸*n.* the body of diplomats residing in a particular country.

dip·lo·mat·ic im·mu·ni·ty ▸*n.* the privilege of exemption from certain laws and taxes granted to diplomats by the country in which they are working.

dip·lo·mat·ic pouch ▸*n.* a container in which official mail is sent to or from an embassy without being subject to customs inspection.

dip·lo·mat·ic serv·ice ▸*n.* another term for **FOREIGN SERVICE**.

di·plo·ma·tist /di'plōmətist/ ▸*n.* old-fashioned term for **DIPLOMAT**.

dip·lont·ic /dip'läntik/ ▸*n. Genetics* (of an alga or other lower plant) having a life cycle in which the main form, except for the gametes, is diploid. Compare with **HAPLONTIC** and **DIPLOHAPLONTIC**. ▷1920s: from **DIPLO-** 'double' + Greek *ōn, ont-* 'being' (from *einai* 'be, exist') + **-IC**. —**dip·lont** /'dip,länt/ *n.*

di·plo·pi·a /di'plōpēə/ ▸*n.* technical term for **DOUBLE VISION**.

Di·plop·o·da /diplə'pōdə/ *Zoology* a class of myriapod arthropods that comprises the millipedes. ▷modern Latin (plural), from Greek *diploos* 'double' + *pous, pod-* 'foot.' —**dip·lo·pod** /'diplə,päd/ *n.*

dip·lo·tene /'diplə,tēn/ ▸*n. Biology* the fourth stage of the prophase of meiosis, following pachytene, during which the paired chromosomes begin to separate into two pairs of chromatids. ▷1920s: from **DIPLO-** 'double' + Greek *tainia* 'band.'

Di·plu·ra /di'plo͝orə/ *Entomology* an order of small, primitive, wingless insects that resemble the true bristletails but have two bristles at the end of the abdomen. • Order Diplura, subclass Apterygota, class Insecta (or Hexapoda). ▷modern Latin (plural), from **DI-**[1] 'two' + Greek *pleura* 'side of the body.' —**di·plu·ran** *n. & adj.*

dip net ▸*n.* a small fishing net with a long handle.

▸*v.* (**dip-net**) [*trans.*] catch (fish) using such a net.

di·pole /'dī,pōl/ ▸*n. Physics* a pair of equal and oppositely charged or magnetized poles separated by a distance. ■ an antenna consisting of a horizontal metal rod with a connecting wire at its center. ■ *Chemistry* a molecule in which a concentration of positive electric charge is separated from a concentration of negative charge. —**di·po·lar** /dī'pōlər/ *adj.*

di·pole mo·ment ▸*n. Physics & Chemistry* the mathematical product of the separation of the ends of a dipole and the magnitude of the charges.

dip·per /'dipər/ ▸*n.* **1** a short-tailed songbird related to the wrens, frequenting fast-flowing streams and able to swim, dive, and walk under water to feed. • Family Cinclidae and genus *Cinclus*: five species, in particular the Eurasian (**white-throated**) **dipper** (*C. cinclus*). **2** a ladle or scoop. **3** a person who immerses something in liquid. ■ *archaic* an informal term for a Baptist or Anabaptist.

dip·py /'dipē/ ▸*adj.* (**dip·pi·er, dip·pi·est**) *informal* stupid; foolish. ▷early 20th cent.: of unknown origin.

dip·shit /'dip,SHit/ ▸*n. vulgar slang* a contemptible or inept person. ▷1970s: perhaps a blend of **DIPPY** and **SHIT**.

dip·so /'dipsō/ ▸*n.* (*pl.* **-sos**) *informal* a person suffering from dipsomania; an alcoholic.

dip·so·ma·ni·a /,dipsə'mānēə/ ▸*n.* alcoholism, specifically in a form characterized by intermittent bouts of craving for alcohol. ▷mid 19th cent.: from Greek *dipso-* (from *dipsa* 'thirst') + **-MANIA**. —**dip·so·ma·ni·ac** /-nē,ak/ *n.* —**dip·so·ma·ni·a·cal** /-mə'nīəkəl/ *adj.*

dip·stick /'dip,stik/ ▸*n.* **1** a graduated rod for measuring the depth of a liquid, esp. oil in a vehicle's engine. **2** *informal* a stupid or inept person.

DIP switch ▸*n. Computing* an arrangement of switches in a dual in-line package used to select the operating mode of a device such as a printer.

dip·sy-doo·dle /'dipsē 'do͞odl/ ▸*n. informal* a quick, dipping or sliding motion, such as that made by football players to avoid a tackle. ■ an act or movement designed to evade, confuse, or distract an opponent or competitor.

▸*v.* [*intrans.*] follow a zigzag course.

Dip·ter·a /'diptərə/ *Entomology* a large order of insects that comprises the two-winged or true flies, which have the hind wings reduced to form balancing organs (halteres). It includes many biting forms, such as mosquitoes and tsetse flies, that are vectors of disease. ■ [as *plural n.*] (**diptera**) insects of this order; flies. ▷modern Latin (plural), from Greek *diptera*, neuter plural of *dipteros* 'two-winged,' from *di-* 'two' + *pteron* 'wing.' —**dip·ter·an** *n. & adj.*

dip·ter·al /'diptərəl/ ▸*adj. Architecture* having a double peristyle. ▷early 19th cent.: from Latin *dipteros* (from Greek, from *di-* 'twice' + *pteron* 'wing') + **-AL**.

dip·ter·ist /'diptərist/ ▸*n.* a person who studies or collects flies. ▷late 19th cent.: from **DIPTERA** + **-IST**.

dip·ter·o·carp /'diptərə,kärp/ ▸*n.* a tall forest tree from which are obtained resins and timber for the export trade, occurring mainly in Southeast Asia. • Family Dipterocarpaceae: numerous species. ▷late 19th cent.: from modern Latin *Dipterocarpus*, from Greek *dipteros* 'two-winged' + *karpos* 'fruit.'

dip·ter·ous /'diptərəs/ ▸*adj.* **1** *Entomology* of or relating to flies of the order Diptera. **2** *Botany* having two winglike appendages. ▷late 18th cent.: from modern Latin *dipterus* (from Greek *dipteros* 'two-winged') + **-ous**.

dip·tych /ˈdiptik/ ▸*n.* **1** a painting, esp. an altarpiece, on two hinged wooden panels that may be closed like a book. **2** an ancient writing tablet consisting of two hinged leaves with waxed inner sides. ▷early 17th cent.: via late Latin from late Greek *diptukha* 'pair of writing tablets,' neuter plural of Greek *diptukhos* 'folded in two,' from *di-* 'twice' + *ptukhē* 'a fold.'

di·pyr·id·a·mole /dīˈpiridəˌmōl/ ▸*n. Medicine* a synthetic drug used as a coronary vasodilator to treat angina and to reduce platelet aggregation and hence the chance of thrombosis. ▷mid 20th cent.: from **DI-**[1] 'two' + *pyr(imidine)* + *(piper)id(ine)* + *am(ino-)* + **-OL**.

di·quat /ˈdīˌkwät/ ▸*n.* a synthetic compound used in controlling plant growth, often as a nonpersistent contact herbicide. • A bromide of a quaternary amine; chem. formula: $(C_5H_4NCH_2)_2Br_2$. ▷1960s: from **DI-**[1] 'two' + **QUATERNARY**.

dir. ▸*abbr.* ■ director.

Di·rac /dəˈräk/, Paul Adrian Maurice (1902–84), English theoretical physicist. He described the behavior of the electron, including its spin, and predicted the existence of the positron by applying Albert Einstein's theory of relativity to quantum mechanics. Nobel Prize for Physics (1933, shared with Schrödinger).

dire /dīr/ ▸*adj.* (of a situation or event) extremely serious or urgent: *dire consequences.* ■ (of a warning or threat) presaging disaster: *dire warnings about breathing the fumes.* ▷mid 16th cent.: from Latin *dirus* 'fearful, threatening.' —**dire·ly** *adv.* —**dire·ness** *n.*

di·rect /diˈrekt; dī-/ ▸*adj.* extending or moving from one place to another by the shortest way without changing direction or stopping: *there was no direct flight that day.* ■ without intervening factors or intermediaries: *the complications are a direct result of bacteria spreading.* ■ (of a person or their behavior) going straight to the point; frank. ■ (of evidence or proof) bearing immediately and unambiguously upon the facts at issue: *there is no direct evidence that officials accepted bribes.* ■ (of light or heat) proceeding from a source without being reflected or blocked: *ferns like a bright position out of direct sunlight.* ■ (of genealogy) proceeding in continuous succession from parent to child. ■ [*attrib.*] (of a quotation) taken from someone's words without being changed. ■ complete (used for emphasis): *nonviolence is the direct opposite of compulsion.* ■ perpendicular to a surface; not oblique: *a direct butt joint between surfaces of steel.* ■ *Astronomy & Astrology* (of apparent planetary motion) proceeding from west to east in accord with actual motion.
▸*adv.* with no one or nothing in between: *buy direct and save.* ■ by a straight route or without breaking a journey: *Austrian Airlines is flying direct to Innsbruck again.*
▸*v.* [*trans.*] **1** control the operations of; manage or govern: *an economic elite directed the nation's affairs.* ■ supervise and control (a movie, play, or other production, or the actors in it). ■ (usu. **be directed**) train and conduct (a group of musicians). **2** [*trans.*] aim (something) in a particular direction or at a particular person: *heating ducts to direct warm air to rear-seat passengers* | *his smile was directed at Laura.* ■ tell or show (someone) how to get somewhere: *can you direct me to the railroad station, please?* ■ address or give instructions for the delivery of (a letter or parcel). ■ focus or concentrate (one's attention, efforts, or feelings) on: *we* **direct** *our anger and frustration* **at** *family.* ■ (**direct something at/to**) address a comment to or aim a criticism at: *he directed his criticism at media coverage of the Catholic Church* | *I suggest that he direct his remarks to the council.* ■ (**direct something at**) target a product specifically at (someone): *the book is directed at the younger reader.* ■ *archaic* guide or advise (someone or their judgment) in a course or decision: *the conscience of the credulous prince was directed by saints and bishops.* **3** [*trans.*] give (someone) an official order or authoritative instruction: *the judge directed him to perform community service* | [with *clause*] *he* **directed that** *no picture from his collection could be sold.* ▷late Middle English: from Latin *directus*, past participle of *dirigere*, from *di-* 'distinctly' or *de-* 'down' + *regere* 'put straight.' —**di·rect·ness** *n.*

di·rect ac·cess ▸*n.* the facility of retrieving data immediately from any part of a computer file, without having to read the file from the beginning. Compare with **RANDOM ACCESS** and **SEQUENTIAL ACCESS**.

di·rect ac·tion ▸*n.* the use of strikes, demonstrations, or other public forms of protest rather than negotiation to achieve one's demands.

di·rect cur·rent (abbr.: **DC**) ▸*n.* an electric current flowing in one direction only. Compare with **ALTERNATING CURRENT**.

di·rect deb·it ▸*n.* a payment system whereby creditors are authorized to debit a customer's bank account directly at regular intervals.

di·rect de·pos·it ▸*n.* the electronic transfer of a payment directly from the account of the payer to the recipient's account.

di·rect di·al·ing ▸*n.* the facility of making a telephone call without connection by the operator. —**di·rect di·al** *adj.*

di·rect dis·course ▸*n.* another term for **DIRECT SPEECH**.

di·rect-drive ▸*adj.* [*attrib.*] denoting or relating to mechanical parts driven directly by a motor, without a belt or other device to transmit power.

di·rect ex·am·i·na·tion ▸*n. Law* the questioning of a witness by the party that has called that witness to give evidence, in order to support the case that is being made. Also called **EXAMINATION-IN-CHIEF**. Compare with **CROSS-EXAMINE**.

di·rect in·jec·tion ▸*n.* (in diesel engines) the use of a pump to spray fuel into the cylinder at high pressure, without the use of compressed air.

di·rec·tion /diˈreksHən; dī-/ ▸*n.* **1** a course along which someone or something moves: *she set off in the opposite direction* | *the storm was expected to take a more northwesterly direction.* ■ the course that must be taken in order to reach a destination: *he had a terrible sense of direction.* ■ a point to or from which a person or thing moves or faces: *a house with views in all directions* | *figurative support came from an unexpected direction.* ■ a general way in which someone or something is developing: *new directions in painting and architecture* | *any dialogue between them is* **a step in the right direction** | *it is time to change direction and find a new job.* ■ general aim or purpose: *the campaign's lack of direction.* **2** the management or guidance of someone or something: *under his direction, the college has developed an international reputation.* ■ the work of supervising and controlling the actors and other staff in a movie, play, or other production. ■ (**directions**) instructions on how to reach a destination or about how to do something: *Preston gave him directions to a restaurant* | *directions for making puff pastry.* ■ an authoritative order or command: *to suggest that members of Congress would* **take direction** *on how to vote is an affront.* ▷late Middle English (sense 2): from Latin *directio(n-)*, from the verb *dirigere* (see **DIRECT**).

di·rec·tion·al /diˈreksHənl/ ▸*adj.* **1** relating to or indicating the direction in which someone or something is situated, moving, or developing: *directional signs wherever two paths joined.* **2** having a particular direction of motion, progression, or orientation: *coiling the wire permits directional flow of the magnetic flux.* ■ relating to, denoting, or designed for the projection, transmission, or reception of light, radio, or sound waves in or from a particular direction or directions: *a directional microphone.* —**di·rec·tion·al·i·ty** /diˌreksHəˈnalitē/ *n.* —**di·rec·tion·al·ly** *adv.*

di·rec·tion find·er ▸*n.* a special radio receiver with a system of antennas for locating the source of radio signals, used as an aid to navigation.

di·rec·tion·less /diˈreksHənlis/ ▸*adj.* lacking in general aim or purpose: *I feel directionless and miserable.*

di·rec·tive /diˈrektiv/ ▸*n.* an official or authoritative instruction: *moral and ethical directives.*
▸*adj.* involving the management or guidance of operations: *he is seeking a directive role in energy policy.* ▷late Middle English (as an adjective): from medieval Latin *directivus*, from *direct-* 'guided, put straight,' from the verb *dirigere* (see **DIRECT**).

di·rect la·bor ▸*n.* **1** labor involved in production rather than administration, maintenance, and other support services. **2** labor employed by the authority commissioning the work, not by a contractor.

di·rect·ly /diˈrektlē/ ▸*adv.* **1** without changing direction or stopping: *they went directly to the restaurant.* ■ at once; immediately: *I went directly after breakfast.* ■ *dated* in a little while; soon: *I'll be back directly.* **2** with nothing or no one in between: *the decisions directly affect people's health* | *the security forces were directly responsible for the massacre.* ■ exactly in a specified position: *the ceiling directly above the door the houses directly opposite.* **3** in a frank way: *she spoke simply and directly.*
▸*conj. Brit.* as soon as: *she fell asleep directly she got into bed.*

di·rect mail ▸*n.* unsolicited advertising sent to prospective customers through the mail. —**di·rect mail·ing** *n.*

di·rect mar·ket·ing ▸*n.* the business of selling products or services directly to the public, e.g., by mail order or telephone selling, rather than through retailers.

di·rect ob·ject ▸*n.* a noun phrase denoting a person or thing that is the recipient of the action of a transitive verb, for example *the dog* in *Jimmy fed the dog.* Compare with **INDIRECT OBJECT**.

Di·rec·toire /ˌdirekˈtwär/ ▸*adj.* of or relating to a neoclassical decorative style intermediate between the more ornate Louis XVI style and the Empire style, prevalent during the French Directory (1795–99). ▷late 18th cent.: French, from Late Latin *directorius*, from *director* 'one who directs, director.'

Di·rec·toire draw·ers (also **Directoire knickers**) ▸*plural n. Brit., historical* underpants that are straight, full, and knee-length.

di·rec·tor /diˈrektər/ (abbr.: **dir.**) ▸*n.* a person who is in charge of an activity, department, or organization: *he has been appointed finance director.* ■ a member of the board of people that manages or oversees the affairs of a business. ■ a person who supervises the actors, camera crew, and other staff for a movie, play, television program, or similar production. ■ short for **MUSICAL DIRECTOR**. ▷late Middle English: from Anglo-Norman French *directour*, from late Latin *director* 'governor,' from *dirigere* 'to guide.' —**di·rec·to·ri·al** /diˌrekˈtôrēəl; ˌdīrek-/ *adj.* —**di·rec·tor·ship** /-ˌsHip/ *n.*

di·rec·to·rate /diˈrektərit/ ▸*n.* [treated as *sing.* or *pl.*] the board of directors of a company. ■ a section of a government department in charge of a particular activity: *the Directorate of Intelligence.*

di·rec·tor gen·er·al ▸*n.* (also **di·rec·tor-gen·er·al**) (*pl.* **di·rec·tors gen·er·al**) *chiefly Brit.* the chief executive of a large organization.

di·rec·tor's chair ▸*n.* a folding armchair with crossed legs and a canvas seat and back piece.

director's chair

di·rec·to·ry /diˈrektərē/ ▸*n.* (*pl.* **-ries**) **1** a book listing individuals or organizations alphabetically or thematically with details such as names, addresses, and telephone numbers. ■ *Computing* a file that consists solely of a set of other files (which may themselves be directories). **2** *chiefly historical* a book of directions for the conduct of Christian worship, esp. in Presbyterian and Roman Catholic Churches. **3** (**the Directory**) the French revolutionary government in France 1795–99, comprising two councils and a five-member executive. It maintained an aggressive foreign policy but could not control events at home and was overthrown by Napoleon Bonaparte. ▷late Middle English (in the general sense 'something that directs'): from late Latin *directorium*, from *director* 'governor,' from *dirigere* 'to guide.'

di·rec·to·ry as·sis·tance ▸*plural n.* a telephone service used to find out someone's telephone number.

di·rect pro·por·tion (also **di·rect ra·ti·o**) ▸*n.* the relation between quantities whose ratio is constant: *sensors emit an electronic signal* **in direct proportion to** *the amount of light detected.*

di·rec·tress /diˈrektris/ (also **di·rec·trice**) ▸*n.* a female director. ▷early 17th cent.: from **DIRECTOR** + **-ESS**[1]; the variant *directrice* is an adopted French form.

di·rec·trix /diˈrektriks/ ▸*n.* (*pl.* **-tri·ces** /-trəˌsēz/) *Geometry* a fixed line used in describing a curve or surface. ▷early 18th cent.: from medieval Latin, literally 'directress,' based on Latin *dirigere* 'to guide.'

di·rect rule ▸*n.* a system of government in which a province is controlled by a central government.

di·rect speech ▸*n.* the reporting of speech by repeating the actual words of a speaker, for example *"I'm going," she said.* Contrasted with **REPORTED SPEECH**.

di·rect tax ▸*n.* a tax, such as income tax, that is levied on the income or profits of the person who pays it, rather than on goods or services.

dire·ful /ˈdīrfəl/ ▸*adj. archaic or poetic/literary* extremely bad; dreadful. ▷late 16th cent.: from **DIRE** + **-FUL**. —**dire·ful·ly** *adv.*

dire wolf ▸*n.* a large extinct wolf of the Pleistocene epoch that preyed on large mammals. • *Canis dirus*, family Canidae. ▷*dire* in the sense 'threatening,' translating the modern Latin taxonomic name.

dirge /dərj/ ▸*n.* a lament for the dead, esp. one forming part of a funeral rite. ■ a mournful song, piece of music, or poem: *singers chanted dirges figurative the wind howled dirges around the chimney.* ▷Middle English (denoting the Office for the Dead): from Latin *dirige!* (imperative) 'direct!,' the first word of an antiphon (Ps. 5:8) used in the Latin Office for the Dead. **—dirge·ful** /-fəl/ *adj.*

dir·ham /də'ram/ ▸*n.* **1** the basic monetary unit of Morocco and the United Arab Emirates, equal to 100 centimes in Morocco and 100 fils in the United Arab Emirates. **2** a monetary unit of Libya and Qatar, equal to one thousandth of a dinar in Libya and one hundredth of a riyal in Qatar. ▷from Arabic, from Greek *drakhmē*, denoting an Attic weight or coin. Compare with DRACHMA.

dir·i·gi·ble /'dirijəbəl; də'rijə-/ ▸*adj.* capable of being steered, guided, or directed: *a dirigible spotlight.*
▸*n.* a dirigible airship, esp. one with a rigid structure. ▷late 16th cent.: from Latin *dirigere* 'to direct' + -IBLE.

di·ri·gisme /'diri,zhizəm; ,diri'zhizəm; ,dērē'zhēsm(ə)/ ▸*n.* state control of economic and social matters. ▷1950s: from French, from the verb *diriger*, from Latin *dirigere* 'to direct.' **—di·ri·giste** /,diri'zhēst; ,dirē-/ *adj.*

dir·i·ment im·ped·i·ment /'dirəmənt / ▸*n.* (in ecclesiastical law) a factor that invalidates a marriage, such as the existence of a prior marriage. ▷mid 19th cent.: *diriment* from Latin *diriment-* 'interrupting,' from the verb *dirimere*.

dirk /dərk/ ▸*n.* a short dagger of a kind formerly carried by Scottish Highlanders. ▷mid 16th cent.: of unknown origin.

Dirk·sen /'dərksən/, Everett McKinley (1896–1969), U.S. politician. An Illinois Republican, he was a member of the U.S. House of Representatives 1933–48 and a U.S. senator 1950–69.

dirn·dl /'dərndl/ ▸*n.* **1** (also **dirndl skirt**) a full, wide skirt with a tight waistband. **2** a woman's dress in the style of Alpine peasant costume, with such a skirt and a close-fitting bodice. ▷1930s: from south German dialect, diminutive of *Dirne* 'girl.'

dirndl 2

dirt /dərt/ ▸*n.* a substance, such as mud or dust, that soils someone or something: *his face was covered in dirt.* ■ loose soil or earth; the ground: *the soldier sagged to the dirt.* ■ [usu. as *adj.*] earth used to make a surface for a road, floor, or other area of ground: *a dirt road.* ■ short for DIRT TRACK. ■ *informal* excrement: *a lawn covered in dog dirt.* ■ a state or quality of uncleanliness: *Pittsburgh used to be renowned for the sweat and dirt of industry.* ■ *informal* gossip, esp. information about someone's activities or private life that could prove damaging if revealed: *is there any* **dirt on** *Desmond?* ■ obscene or sordid material: *we object to the dirt that television projects into homes.* ■ *informal* a worthless or contemptible person or thing: *she treats him like dirt.* ▷Middle English: from Old Norse *drit* 'excrement,' an early sense in English.
▸*PHRASES* □ **do someone dirt** *informal* harm someone's reputation maliciously. □ **drag the name of someone** (or **something**) **through the dirt** *informal* give someone or something a bad reputation through bad behavior or damaging revelations: *he condemned players for dragging the name of football through the dirt.* □ **eat dirt** *informal* suffer insults or humiliation: *the film bombed at the box office and the critics made it eat dirt.*

dirt·bag /'dərt,bag/ ▸*n. informal* a very unkempt or unpleasant person.

dirt bike ▸*n.* a motorcycle designed for use on rough terrain, such as unsurfaced roads or tracks, and used esp. in scrambling.

dirt·board /'dərt,bôrd/ ▸*n.* a long skateboard with larger-than-average wheels, designed for off-road use. **—dirt·board·ing** *n.*

dirt cheap ▸*adv.* & *adj. informal* extremely cheap: [as *adv.*] *the auctioneers let us have the stuff dirt cheap* | [as *adj.*] *a dirt-cheap price.*

dirt farm·er ▸*n.* a farmer who ekes out a living from a farm or poor land, typically without the help of hired labor. **—dirt farm** *n.*

dirt poor ▸*adv.* & *adj.* extremely poor: [as *adv.*] *making people dirt poor* | [as *adj.*] *dirt-poor villages.*

dirt track ▸*n.* a course made of rolled cinders for motorcycle racing or of earth for flat racing. **—dirt track·er** *n.*

dirt·y /'dərtē/ ▸*adj.* (**dirt·i·er**, **dirt·i·est**) covered or marked with an unclean substance: *a tray of dirty cups and saucers* | *her boots were dirty.* ■ causing a person or environment to become unclean: *farming is a hard, dirty job.* ■ (of a nuclear weapon) producing considerable radioactive fallout. ■ (of a color) not bright, clear, or pure: *the sea was a waste of dirty gray.* ■ concerned with sex in an unpleasant or obscene way: *he told a stream of dirty jokes.* ■ [*attrib.*] *informal* used to emphasize one's disgust for someone or something: *you dirty rat!* ■ (of an activity) dishonest; dishonorable: *he had a reputation for dirty dealing.* ■ (of weather) rough, stormy, and unpleasant: *the yacht was ready for dirty weather.* ■ (of popular music) having a distorted or rasping tone: *Nirvana's dirty guitar sound.*
▸*v.* (**dirt·ies**, **dirt·ied**) [*trans.*] cover or mark with an unclean substance: *she didn't like him dirtying her nice clean towels.* ■ cause to feel or appear morally tainted: *the criminals have dirtied the city.* **—dirt·i·ly** /'dərtəlē/ *adv.* **—dirt·i·ness** *n.*
▸*PHRASES* □ **the dirty end of the stick** *informal* the difficult or unpleasant part of a task or situation. □ **get one's hands dirty** do manual, menial, or other hard work: *unlike most chairmen, he gets his hands dirty working alongside the other managers.* ■ *informal* become involved in dishonest or dishonorable activity: *they can make a lot of money, but fat cats don't get their hands dirty.* □ **play dirty** *informal* act in a dishonest or unfair way. □ **talk dirty** *informal* speak about sex in a coarse or obscene way. □ **wash one's dirty laundry in public** see WASH.

dirt·y bomb ▸*n.* an improvised nuclear weapon from radioactive nuclear waste material and conventional explosives.

dirt·y look ▸*n. informal* a facial expression of disapproval, disgust, or anger: *they were giving me dirty looks for taking up so much room at the bar.*

dirt·y mon·ey ▸*n.* money obtained unlawfully or immorally: *the bank was found to have been laundering dirty money.*

dirt·y old man ▸*n. informal* an older man who is sexually interested in younger women or girls.

dirt·y pool ▸*n. informal* dishonest, unfair, or unsportsmanlike conduct.

dirt·y rice ▸*n.* a Cajun dish consisting of white rice cooked with onions, peppers, chicken livers, and herbs.

dirt·y trick ▸*n.* a dishonest or unkind act. ■ (**dirty tricks**) underhanded political or commercial activity designed to discredit an opponent.

dirt·y word ▸*n.* an offensive or indecent word. ■ *figurative* a thing regarded with dislike or disapproval: *people can talk about profit without it being a dirty word.*

dirt·y work ▸*n.* activities or tasks that are unpleasant or dishonest and given to someone else to undertake.

dis /dis/ *informal* ▸*v.* (also **diss**) (**dissed**, **diss·ing**) [*trans.*] act or speak in a disrespectful way toward: *he was expelled for dissing the gym teacher.*
▸*n.* disrespectful talk: *the airwaves bristle with the sexual dis of shock jocks.* ▷1980s: abbreviation of DISRESPECT.

dis- ▸*prefix* **1** expressing negation: *dislike* | *disquiet.* **2** denoting reversal or absence of an action or state: *dishonor* | *disintegrate.* ■ denoting separation: *discharge* | *disengage* ■ denoting expulsion: *disbar* | *disinherit.* **3** denoting removal of the thing specified: *disbud* | *dismember.* **4** expressing completeness or intensification of an unpleasant or unattractive action: *discombobulate* | *disgruntled.* ▷from Latin, sometimes via Old French *des-*.

dis·a·bil·i·ty /,disə'bilitē/ ▸*n.* (*pl.* **-ties**) a physical or mental condition that limits a person's movements, senses, or activities: *children with severe physical disabilities.* ■ a disadvantage or handicap, esp. one imposed or recognized by the law: *he had to quit his job and go* **on disability**.

dis·a·ble /dis'ābəl/ ▸*v.* [*trans.*] (of a disease, injury, or accident) limit (someone) in their movements, senses, or activities: *it's an injury that could disable somebody for life* | [as *adj.*] (**disabling**) *a progressively disabling disease* | [*intrans.*] *anxiety can disrupt and disable.* ■ put out of action: *the raiders tried to disable the alarm system.* **—dis·a·ble·ment** *n.*

dis·a·bled /dis'ābəld/ ▸*adj.* (of a person) having a physical or mental condition that limits their movements, senses, or activities: *facilities for disabled people* | [as *plural n.*] (**the disabled**) *the needs of the disabled.* ■ (of an activity, organization, or facility) specifically designed for or relating to people with such a physical or mental condition.

USAGE See usage at HANDICAPPED and LEARNING DISABILITY.

dis·a·bled list (abbr.: **DL**) ▸*Sports* a list of players who are not available for play, owing to injury.

dis·a·buse /,disə'byōōz/ ▸*v.* [*trans.*] persuade (someone) that an idea or belief is mistaken: *he quickly* **disabused** *me* **of** *my fanciful notions.*

di·sac·cha·ride /dī'sakə,rīd/ ▸*n. Chemistry* any of a class of sugars whose molecules contain two monosaccharide residues.

dis·ac·cord /,disə'kôrd/ ▸*n. rare* lack of agreement or harmony: *the disaccord remains in effect.*
▸*v.* [*intrans.*] *archaic* disagree; be at variance: *this disaccords with the precise date.*

dis·ad·van·tage /,disəd'vantij/ ▸*n.* an unfavorable circumstance or condition that reduces the chances of success or effectiveness: *a major disadvantage is the limited nature of the data* | *the impact of poverty and disadvantage on children.*
▸*v.* [*trans.*] place in an unfavorable position in relation to someone or something else: *we are disadvantaging the next generation.* ▷late Middle English: from Old French *desavantage*, from *des-* (expressing reversal) + *avantage* 'advantage.'
▸*PHRASES* □ **at a disadvantage** in an unfavorable position relative to someone or someone else: *stringent regulations have* **put** *farmers* **at a disadvantage**. □ **to one's disadvantage** so as to cause harm to one's interests or standing: *his poor record inevitably worked to his disadvantage.*

dis·ad·van·taged /,disəd'vantijd/ ▸*adj.* (of a person or area) in unfavorable circumstances, esp. with regard to financial or social opportunities: *disadvantaged groups such as the elderly and unemployed* | [as *plural n.*] (**the disadvantaged**) *we began to help the disadvantaged.*

dis·ad·van·ta·geous /dis,advən'tājəs/ ▸*adj.* involving or creating unfavorable circumstances that reduce the chances of success or effectiveness: *the system was* **disadvantageous to** *the Connecticut merchants* | *the disadvantageous position in which some people are placed.* **—dis·ad·van·ta·geous·ly** *adv.*

dis·af·fect·ed /,disə'fektid/ ▸*adj.* dissatisfied with the people in authority and no longer willing to support them: *a military plot by disaffected elements in the army.* ▷mid 17th cent.: past participle of *disaffect*, originally in the sense 'dislike or disorder,' from DIS- (expressing reversal) + AFFECT[2]. **—dis·af·fect·ed·ly** *adv.*

dis·af·fec·tion /,disə'fekshən/ ▸*n.* a state or feeling of being dissatisfied with the people in authority and no longer willing to support them: *there is growing* **disaffection with** *large corporations.* See note at .

dis·af·fil·i·ate /,disə'filē,āt/ ▸*v.* [*trans.*] (of a group or organization) end its official connection with (a subsidiary group): *the party disaffiliated the Socialist League.* ■ [*intrans.*] (of a subsidiary group) end such a connection: *a region may elect to* **disaffiliate from** *a dominant state.* **—dis·af·fil·i·a·tion** /,disə,filē'āshən/ *n.*

dis·af·firm /,disə'fərm/ ▸*v.* [*trans.*] *Law* repudiate; declare void: *to disaffirm a contract is to say it never existed.* **—dis·af·fir·ma·tion** /dis,afər'māshən/ *n.*

dis·ag·gre·gate /dis'agrigāt/ ▸*v.* [*trans.*] separate (something) into its component parts: *a method for disaggregating cells.* **—dis·ag·gre·ga·tion** /-,agri'gāshən/ *n.*

dis·a·gree /,disə'grē/ ▸*v.* (**-a·grees**, **-a·greed**, **-a·gree·ing**) [*intrans.*] **1** have or express a different opinion: *no one was willing to* **disagree with** *him* | *historians often disagree.* ■ (**disagree with**) disapprove of: *she disagreed with the system of apartheid.* **2** (of statements or accounts) be inconsistent or fail to correspond: *results that disagree with the findings reported so far.* ■ (**disagree with**) (of food, climate, or an experience) have an adverse effect on (someone): *the North Sea crossing seemed to have disagreed with her.* ▷late 15th cent. (sense 2, also in the sense 'refuse to agree to'): from Old French *desagreer*.

dis·a·gree·a·ble /,disə'grēəbəl/ ▸*adj.* unpleasant or unenjoyable: *another disagreeable thought came to him* | *some aspects of his work are* **disagreeable to** *him.* ■ unfriendly and bad-tempered: *Henry was always a very* *disagreeable boy.* ▷late Middle English (in the sense 'discordant, incongruous'): from Old French *desagreable*, based on *agreer* 'agree.' **—dis·a·gree·a·ble·ness** *n.* **—dis·a·gree·a·bly** /-blē/ *adv.*

dis·a·gree·ment /ˌdisəˈgrēmənt/ ▸*n.* lack of consensus or approval: *there was some disagreement about the details | the meeting ended* ***in disagreement*** *| disagreements between parents and adolescents.* ■ lack of consistency or correspondence: *disagreement between the results of the two assessments.*

dis·al·low /ˌdisəˈlou/ ▸*v.* [*trans.*] (usu. **be disallowed**) refuse to declare valid: *the judge disallowed his evidence.* See note at **PROHIBIT**. ▷late Middle English (in the sense 'disown, refuse to accept'): from Old French *desalouer*. **—dis·al·low·ance** /ˌdisəˈlouəns/ *n.*

dis·am·big·u·ate /ˌdisamˈbigyo͞oˌāt/ ▸*v.* [*trans.*] remove uncertainty of meaning from (an ambiguous sentence, phrase, or other linguistic unit). **—dis·am·big·u·a·tion** /-ˌbigyo͞oˈāsʜən/ *n.*

dis·ap·pear /ˌdisəˈpi(ə)r/ ▸*v.* **1** [intrans.] cease to be visible: *he* ***disappeared into*** *the trees | the sun had disappeared.* ■ cease to exist or be in use: *the tension had completely disappeared.* ■ (of a thing) be lost or impossible to find: *my wallet seems to have disappeared.* ■ (of a person) go missing or (in coded political language) be killed: *the family disappeared after being taken into custody.* **2** [trans.] cause to disappear, as by consumption: *statistics show that the community disappears about 200 pounds of cabbage a year.* ▷late Middle English: from **DIS-** (expressing reversal) + **APPEAR**, on the pattern of French *disparaître*.

dis·ap·pear·ance /ˌdisəˈpi(ə)rəns/ ▸*n.* [usu. in *sing.*] an instance or fact of someone or something ceasing to be visible. ■ an instance or fact of someone going missing or (in coded political language) being killed: *the police were investigating her disappearance.* ■ an instance or fact of something being lost or stolen: *an investigation is being carried out into the disappearance of the money.* ■ the process or fact of something ceasing to exist or be in use: *the disappearance of grammar schools.*

dis·ap·point /ˌdisəˈpoint/ ▸*v.* [*trans.*] fail to fulfill the hopes or expectations of (someone): *I have no wish to disappoint everyone by postponing the visit.* ■ prevent (hopes or expectations) from being realized: *public ownership had sadly disappointed socialist hopes.* ▷late Middle English (in the sense 'deprive of an office or position'): from Old French *desappointer*.

dis·ap·point·ed /ˌdisəˈpointid/ ▸*adj.* (of a person) sad or displeased because someone or something has failed to fulfill one's hopes or expectations: *I'm* ***disappointed in*** *you, Mary | thousands of disappointed customers were kept waiting.* ■ (of hopes or expectations) prevented from being realized. **—dis·ap·point·ed·ly** *adv.*

dis·ap·point·ing /ˌdisəˈpointiɴɢ/ ▸*adj.* failing to fulfill someone's hopes or expectations: *the team made a disappointing start |* [with *clause*] *it's* ***disappointing that*** *the market hasn't gone higher.* **—dis·ap·point·ing·ly** *adv.* [as *submodifier*] *there was disappointingly little change |* [*sentence adverb*] *disappointingly, my German failed to improve.*

dis·ap·point·ment /ˌdisəˈpointmənt/ ▸*n.* the feeling of sadness or displeasure caused by the nonfulfillment of one's hopes or expectations: ***to her disappointment****, there was no chance to talk privately with Luke.* ■ a person, event, or thing that causes such a feeling: *the job proved a disappointment | I was a big* ***disappointment to*** *her.*

dis·ap·pro·ba·tion /disˌaprəˈbāsʜən/ ▸*n.* strong disapproval, typically on moral grounds: *she braved her mother's disapprobation and slipped out to enjoy herself.*

dis·ap·prov·al /ˌdisəˈpro͞ovəl/ ▸*n.* possession or expression of an unfavorable opinion: *Jill replied with a hint of disapproval in her voice.*

dis·ap·prove /ˌdisəˈpro͞ov/ ▸*v.* [*intrans.*] have or express an unfavorable opinion about something: *Bob strongly* ***disapproved of*** *drinking and driving |* [as *adj.*] (**disapproving**) *he shot a disapproving glance at her.* ■ [*trans.*] officially refuse to agree to: *a company may take power to disapprove the transfer of shares.* **—dis·ap·prov·er** *n.* **—dis·ap·prov·ing·ly** *adv.*

dis·arm /disˈärm/ ▸*v.* [*trans.*] **1** take a weapon or weapons away from (a person, force, or country): *guerrillas had completely disarmed and demobilized their forces.* ■ [*intrans.*] (of a country or force) give up or reduce its armed forces or weapons: *the other militias had disarmed by the agreed deadline.* ■ remove the fuse from (a bomb), making it safe. ■ deprive (a ship, etc.) of its means of defense. **2** allay the hostility or suspicions of: *his tact and political skills will disarm critics.* ■ deprive of the power to injure or hurt: *camp humor acts to provoke rather than disarm moral indignation.* ▷late Middle English: from Old French *desarmer*.

dis·ar·ma·ment /disˈärməmənt/ ▸*n.* the reduction or withdrawal of military forces and weapons.

dis·ar·mer ▸*n.* a person who advocates or campaigns for the withdrawal of nuclear weapons.

dis·arm·ing /disˈärmiɴɢ/ ▸*adj.* (of manner or behavior) having the effect of allaying suspicion or hostility, esp. through charm: *he gave her a disarming smile.* **—dis·arm·ing·ly** *adv.*

dis·ar·range /ˌdisəˈrānj/ ▸*v.* [*trans.*] (often **be disarranged**) make (something) untidy or disordered: *her hair was disarranged all around her face.* **—dis·ar·range·ment** *n.*

dis·ar·ray /ˌdisəˈrā/ ▸*n.* a state of disorganization or untidiness: *her gray hair was* ***in disarray*** *| his plans have been* ***thrown into disarray****.* See note at **JUMBLE**.
▸*v.* [*trans.*] **1** throw (someone or something) into a state of disorganization or untidiness: *the inspection disarrayed the usual schedule.* **2** *poetic/literary* strip (someone) of clothing: *attendant damsels to help to disarray her.* ▷late Middle English: from Anglo-Norman French *dissairay*.

dis·ar·tic·u·late /ˌdisärˈtikyəˌlāt/ ▸*v.* [*trans.*] separate (bones) at the joints: *the African egg-eating snake can disarticulate its lower jaw from its upper.* ■ break up and disrupt the logic of (an argument or opinion): *novels disarticulate theories.* **—dis·ar·tic·u·la·tion** /-ˌtikyəˈlāsʜən/ *n.*

dis·as·sem·ble /ˌdisəˈsembəl/ ▸*v.* [*trans.*] (often **be disassembled**) take (something) to pieces: *the piston can be disassembled for transport.* ■ *Computing* translate (a program) from machine code into a symbolic language. **—dis·as·sem·bly** /-blē/ *n.*

dis·as·sem·bler /ˌdisəˈsemb(ə)lər/ ▸*n.* *Computing* a program for converting machine code into a low-level symbolic language.

dis·as·so·ci·ate /ˌdisəˈsōsʜēˌāt; -ˈsōsē-/ ▸*v.* another term for **DISSOCIATE**. **—dis·as·so·ci·a·tion** /ˌdisəˌsōsʜēˈāsʜən; -ˌsōsē-/ *n.*

dis·as·ter /diˈzastər/ ▸*n.* a sudden event, such as an accident or a natural catastrophe, that causes great damage or loss of life: *159 people died in the disaster | disaster struck within minutes of takeoff.* ■ [as *adj.*] denoting a genre of films that use natural or accidental catastrophe as the mainspring of plot and setting: *a disaster movie.* ■ an event or fact that has unfortunate consequences: *a string of personal disasters | reduced legal aid could spell financial disaster.* ■ *informal* a person, act, or thing that is a failure: *my perm is a total disaster.* ▷late 16th cent.: from Italian *disastro* 'ill-starred event,' from *dis-* (expressing negation) + *astro* 'star' (from Latin *astrum*).
▸*PHRASE* □ **be a recipe for disaster** be extremely likely to have unfortunate consequences: *sky-high interest rates are a recipe for disaster.*

dis·as·ter ar·e·a ▸*n.* an area in which a major disaster has recently occurred: *the vicinity of the explosion was declared a disaster area.* ■ [in *sing.*] *informal* a place, situation, person, or activity regarded as chaotic, ineffectual, or failing in some fundamental respect: *the room was a disaster area, stuff piled everywhere | she was a disaster area in fake leopard skin and stacked heels.*

dis·as·trous /diˈzastrəs/ ▸*adj.* causing great damage: *a disastrous fire swept through the museum.* ■ *informal* highly unsuccessful: *the team made a disastrous start to the season.* ▷late 16th cent. (in the sense 'ill-fated'): from French *désastreux*, from Italian *disastroso*, from *disastro* 'disaster.' **—dis·as·trous·ly** *adv.*

dis·a·vow /ˌdisəˈvou/ ▸*v.* [*trans.*] deny any responsibility or support for: *does her apology mean she disavows her communist sympathies?* ▷late Middle English: from Old French *desavouer*. **—dis·a·vow·al** /-ˈvouəl/ *n.*

dis·band /disˈband/ ▸*v.* [*trans.*] (usu. **be disbanded**) cause (an organized group) to break up. ■ [*intrans.*] (of an organized group) break up and stop functioning as an organization. ▷late 16th cent.: from obsolete French *desbander*. **—dis·band·ment** *n.*

dis·bar /disˈbär/ ▸*v.* (**-barred, -bar·ring**) [*trans.*] **1** (usu. **be disbarred**) expel (a lawyer) from the Bar, so that they no longer have the right to practice law. **2** exclude (someone) from something: *competitors wearing rings will be* ***disbarred from*** *competition.* ▷mid 16th cent. (sense 2): from **DIS-** 'away' + **BAR**[1]. **—dis·bar·ment** /-mənt/ *n.*

dis·be·lief /ˌdisbəˈlēf/ ▸*n.* inability or refusal to accept that something is true or real: *Laura shook her head in disbelief.* ■ lack of faith in something: *I'll burn in hell for disbelief.*

dis·be·lieve /ˌdisbəˈlēv/ ▸*v.* [*trans.*] be unable to believe (someone or something): *he seemed to disbelieve her |* [as *adj.*] (**disbelieving**) *the disbelieving look in her eyes.* ■ [*intrans.*] have no faith in God, spiritual beings, or a religious system: *to disbelieve is as much an act of faith as belief.* **—dis·be·liev·er** *n.* **—dis·be·liev·ing·ly** *adv.*

dis·bound /disˈbound/ ▸*adj.* (of a portion of a book) removed from a bound volume.

dis·bud /disˈbəd/ ▸*v.* (**-bud·ded, -bud·ding**) [*trans.*] remove superfluous or unwanted buds from (a plant). ■ *Farming* remove the horn buds from (a young animal).

dis·bur·den /disˈbərdn/ ▸*v.* [*trans.*] relieve (someone or something) of a burden or responsibility: *I decided to disburden myself of the task.* ■ *archaic* relieve (someone's mind) of worries and anxieties.

dis·burse /disˈbərs/ ▸*v.* [*trans.*] (often **be disbursed**) pay out (money from a fund): *$67 million of the pledged aid had already been disbursed.* ▷mid 16th cent.: from Old French *desbourser*, from *des-* (expressing removal) + *bourse* 'purse.' **—dis·bur·sal** /-səl/ *n.* **—dis·burse·ment** *n.* **—dis·burs·er** *n.*

disc ▸*n.* variant spelling of **DISK**.

dis·calced /disˈkalst/ ▸*adj.* denoting or belonging to one of several strict orders of Catholic friars or nuns who go barefoot or wear only sandals. ▷mid 17th cent.: variant, influenced by French *déchaux*, of earlier *discalceated*, from Latin *discalceatus*, from *dis-* (expressing removal) + *calceatus* (from *calceus* 'shoe').

dis·card ▸*v.* /disˈkärd/ [*trans.*] get rid of (someone or something) as no longer useful or desirable: *Hilary bundled up the clothes she had discarded.* ■ (in bridge, whist, and similar card games) play (a card that is neither of the suit led nor a trump), when one is unable to follow suit.
▸*n.* /ˈdisˌkärd/ a person or thing rejected as no longer useful or desirable. ■ (in bridge, whist, and similar card games) a card played which is neither of the suit led nor a trump, when one is unable to follow suit. ▷late 16th cent. (originally in the sense 'reject (a playing card)'): from **DIS-** (expressing removal) + the noun **CARD**[1]. **—dis·card·a·ble** /disˈkärdəbəl/ *adj.*

dis·car·nate /disˈkärnit; -ˌnāt/ ▸*adj.* (of a person or being) not having a physical body. ▷late 19th cent.: from **DIS-** 'without' + Latin *caro, carn-* 'flesh' or late Latin *carnatus* 'fleshy.'

disc brake ▸*n.* a type of vehicle brake employing the friction of pads against a disc that is attached to the wheel.

disc cam·er·a ▸*n.* a camera in which the frames of film are formed on a disc, rather than on a long strip.

disc drive ▸*n.* British spelling of **DISK DRIVE**.

disc·ec·to·my /disˈkektəmē/ ▸*n.* surgical removal of the whole or a part of an intervertebral disc.

dis·cern /diˈsərn/ ▸*v.* [*trans.*] perceive or recognize (something): *I can discern no difference between the two policies |* [with *clause*] *students quickly discern what is acceptable to the teacher.* ■ distinguish (someone or something) with difficulty by sight or with the other senses: *she could faintly discern the shape of a skull.* See note at **DISTINGUISH**. ▷late Middle English: via Old French from Latin *discernere*, from *dis-* 'apart' + *cernere* 'to separate.' **—dis·cern·er** *n.* **—dis·cern·i·ble** *adj.* **—dis·cern·i·bly** /-əblē/ *adv.*

dis·cern·ing /diˈsərniɴɢ/ ▸*adj.* having or showing good judgment: *the restaurant attracts discerning customers.* **—dis·cern·ing·ly** *adv.*

dis·cern·ment /diˈsərnmənt/ ▸*n.* **1** the ability to judge well: *an astonishing lack of discernment.* **2** (in Christian contexts) perception in the absence of judgment with a view to obtaining spiritual direction and understanding: *without providing for a time of healing and discernment, there will be no hope of living through this present moment without a shattering of our common life.*

dis·cerp·tion /diˈsərpsʜən/ ▸*n.* *archaic* the action of pulling something apart. ■ a piece severed from something. ▷mid 17th cent.: from late Latin *discerptio(n-)*, from Latin *discerpere* 'pluck to pieces.' **—dis·cerp·ti·bil·i·ty** /-ˌsərptəˈbilitē/ *n.* **—dis·cerp·ti·ble** /-təbəl/ *adj.*

dis·charge ▸*v.* /disˈcʜärj/ [*trans.*] **1** (often **be discharged**) tell (someone) officially that they can or must leave, in particular: ■ send (a patient) out of the hospital because they are judged fit to go home. ■ dismiss or release (someone) from a job, esp. from service in the armed forces or police. ■ release

Pronunciation Key ə *ago*; ər *over*; ˈə or ˌə *up*; ˈər or ˌər *fur*; a *hat*; ā *rate*; ä *car*; cʜ *chew*; e *let*; ē *see*; e(ə)r *air*; i *fit*; ī *by*; i(ə)r *ear*; ɴɢ *sing*; ō *go*; ô *for*; oi *boy*; o͝o *good*; o͞o *goo*; ou *out*; sʜ *she*; ᴛʜ *thin*; <u>ᴛʜ</u> *then*; (h)w *why*; ᴢʜ *vision*

(someone) from the custody or restraint of the law: *he ordered that 1,671 prisoners of war be* ***discharged from*** *prison.* ■ relieve (a juror or jury) from serving in a case. ■ *Law* relieve (a bankrupt) of liability. ■ release (a party) from a contract or obligation: *the insurer is discharged from liability from the day of breach.* **2** allow (a liquid, gas, or other substance) to flow out from where it has been confined: *industrial plants* ***discharge*** *highly toxic materials* ***into*** *rivers* | [*intrans.*] *the overflow should discharge in an obvious place.* ■ (of an orifice or diseased tissue) emit (pus, mucus, or other liquid): *the swelling will eventually break down and discharge pus* | [*intrans.*] *the eyes and nose began to discharge.* ■ (often **be discharged**) *Physics* release or neutralize the electric charge of (an electric field, battery, or other object): *the electrostatic field that builds up on a monitor screen can be discharged* | [*intrans.*] *batteries have a tendency to discharge slowly.* ■ (of a person) fire (a gun or missile): *when you shoot you can discharge as many barrels as you wish.* ■ [*intrans.*] (of a firearm) be fired: *there was a dull thud as the gun discharged.* ■ (of a person) allow (an emotion) to be released: *he discharged his resentment in the harmless form of memoirs.* ■ unload (cargo or passengers) from a ship: *the ferry was discharging passengers* | [*intrans.*] *ninety ships were waiting to discharge.* **3** do all that is required to fulfill (a responsibility) or perform (a duty). ■ pay off (a debt or other financial claim). **4** *Law* (of a judge or court) cancel (an order of a court). ■ cancel (a contract) because of completion or breach: *an existing mortgage to be discharged on completion.*

▸*n.* /ˈdisˌCHärj/ **1** the action of discharging someone from a hospital or from a job: *his discharge from the hospital* | *offending policemen receive a dishonorable discharge.* ■ *Brit.* an act of releasing someone from the custody or restraint of the law: *four days in jail and one year conditional discharge.* ■ *Law* the action of relieving a bankrupt from residual liability. **2** the action of allowing a liquid, gas, or other substance to flow out from where it is confined. ■ the quantity of material allowed to flow out in such a way: *large volumes of sewage discharge* | *environmental damage from toxic chemical discharges.* ■ the emission of pus, mucus, or other liquid from an orifice or from diseased tissue: *those germs might lead to vaginal discharge* | *a yellow nasal discharge.* ■ *Physics* the release of electricity from a charged object: *slow discharge of a condenser is fundamental to oscillatory circuits.* ■ a flow of electricity through air or other gas, esp. when accompanied by emission of light: *a sizzling discharge between sky and turret.* ■ the action of firing a gun or missile: *a police permit for discharge of an air gun* | *sounds like discharges of artillery.* ■ the action of unloading a ship of its cargo or passengers. **3** the action of doing all that is required to fulfill a responsibility or perform a duty: *directors must use skill in the discharge of their duties.* ■ the payment of a debt or other financial claim: *money paid* ***in discharge of*** *a claim.* **4** *Law* the action of canceling an order of a court. ▷Middle English (in the sense 'relieve of (an obligation)'): from Old French *descharger*, from late Latin *discarricare* 'unload,' from *dis-* (expressing reversal) + *carricare* 'to load' (see CHARGE). —**dis·charge·a·ble** /disˈCHärjəbəl/ *adj.* —**dis·charg·er** /disˈCHärjər/ *n.*

dis·charge lamp /ˈdis CHärj/ ▸*n.* a lamp in which the light is produced by a discharge tube.

dis·charge tube /ˈdis CHärj/ ▸*n.* a tube containing charged electrodes and filled with a gas in which ionization is induced by an electric field. The gas molecules emit light as they return to the ground state.

dis·ci·ple /diˈsīpəl/ ▸*n.* a personal follower of Jesus during his life, esp. one of the twelve Apostles. ■ a follower or student of a teacher, leader, or philosophy: *a disciple of Rousseau.*

▸*v.* [*trans.*] guide (someone) in becoming a follower of Jesus or another leader: *the new believer was discipled by a missionary.* ▷Old English, from Latin *discipulus* 'learner,' from *discere* 'learn'; reinforced by Old French *deciple.* —**dis·ci·ple·ship** /-ˌSHip/ *n.* —**dis·cip·u·lar** /-ˈsipyələr/ *adj.*

dis·ci·ple·ship /diˈsīpəlˌSHip/ ▸*n.* the state of attempting to follow the example of Jesus or another teacher: *Jesus taught that discipleship was a journey.*

Dis·ci·ples of Christ a Protestant denomination, originating among American Presbyterians in the early 19th century and found chiefly in the U.S., which rejects creeds and regards the Bible as the only basis of faith.

dis·ci·pli·nar·i·an /ˌdisəpləˈnerēən/ ▸*n.* a person who believes in or practices firm discipline.

dis·ci·pli·nar·y /ˈdisəpləˌnerē/ ▸*adj.* concerning or enforcing discipline: *a soldier will face disciplinary action after going absent without leave.* ▷late 15th cent. (originally with reference to ecclesiastical order): from medieval Latin *disciplinarius*, from Latin *disciplina*, from *discipulus* 'learner' (see DISCIPLE).

dis·ci·pline /ˈdisəplin/ ▸*n.* **1** the practice of training people to obey rules or a code of behavior, using punishment to correct disobedience: *a lack of proper parental and school discipline.* ■ the controlled behavior resulting from such training: *he was able to maintain discipline among his men.* ■ activity or experience that provides mental or physical training: *the tariqa offered spiritual discipline* | *Kung fu is a discipline open to old and young.* ■ a system of rules of conduct: *he doesn't have to submit to normal disciplines.* **2** a branch of knowledge, typically one studied in higher education: *sociology is a fairly new discipline.*

▸*v.* [*trans.*] train (someone) to obey rules or a code of behavior, using punishment to correct disobedience: *many parents have been afraid to discipline their children.* ■ (often **be disciplined**) punish or rebuke (someone) formally for an offense: *a member of the staff was to be disciplined by management.* ■ (**discipline oneself to do something**) train oneself to do something in a controlled and habitual way: *every month discipline yourself to go through the file.* ▷Middle English (in the sense 'mortification by scourging oneself'): via Old French from Latin *disciplina* 'instruction, knowledge,' from *discipulus* (see DISCIPLE). —**dis·ci·plin·a·ble** *adj.* —**dis·ci·pli·nal** /-nəl/ *adj.*

dis·ci·plined /ˈdisəplind/ ▸*adj.* showing a controlled form of behavior or way of working: *a disciplined approach to management.*

disc jock·ey (also **disk jock·ey**) ▸*n.* a person who introduces and plays recorded popular music, esp. on radio or at a disco.

dis·claim /disˈklām/ ▸*v.* [*trans.*] refuse to acknowledge; deny: *the school disclaimed any responsibility for his death.* ■ *Law* renounce a legal claim to (a property or title). ▷late Middle English (in legal contexts): from Anglo-Norman French *desclamer*, from *des-* (expressing reversal) + *clamer* 'to claim' (see CLAIM).

dis·claim·er /disˈklāmər/ ▸*n.* a statement that denies something, esp. responsibility: *the novel carries the usual disclaimer about the characters bearing no relation to living persons.* ■ *Law* an act of repudiating another's claim or renouncing one's own. ▷late Middle English (as a legal term): from Anglo-Norman French *desclamer* (infinitive used as noun: see DISCLAIM).

dis·close /disˈklōz/ ▸*v.* [*trans.*] make (secret or new information) known: *they* ***disclosed*** *her name* ***to*** *the press* | [with *clause*] *the magazine disclosed that he had served a prison sentence for fraud.* ■ allow (something) to be seen, esp. by uncovering it: *he cleared away the grass and disclosed a narrow opening descending into the darkness.* ▷late Middle English: from Old French *desclos-*, stem of *desclore*, based on Latin *claudere* 'to close.' —**dis·clos·er** *n.*

dis·clo·sure /disˈklōZHər/ ▸*n.* the action of making new or secret information known: *a judge ordered the disclosure of the government documents.* ■ a fact, esp. a secret, that is made known: *the government's disclosures about missile programs.* ▷late 16th cent.: from DISCLOSE, on the pattern of *closure.*

dis·co /ˈdiskō/ *informal* ▸*n.* (*pl.* **-cos**) **1** (also **di·sco·theque** /ˈdiskōˌtek/) a club or party at which people dance to pop music. **2** pop music intended mainly for dancing to at discos, typically soul-influenced and melodic with a regular bass beat and popular particularly in the late 1970s.

▸*v.* (**-coes, -coed**) [*intrans.*] attend or dance at such a club or party: *for the next three hours he discoed nonstop.* ▷1960s (originally U.S.): abbreviation.

dis·cog·ra·phy /disˈkägrəfē/ ▸*n.* (*pl.* **-phies**) a descriptive catalog of musical recordings, particularly those of a particular performer or composer. ■ all of a performer's or composer's recordings considered as a body of work: *his discography is overwhelmingly classical.* ■ the study of musical recordings and compilation of descriptive catalogs. ▷1930s: from DISC + -GRAPHY, on the pattern of *biography.* —**dis·cog·ra·pher** /-fər/ *n.*

dis·coid /ˈdisˌkoid/ ▸*adj.* *technical* shaped like a disc.

▸*n.* a thing that is shaped like a disc, particularly a type of ancient stone tool. ▷late 18th cent.: from Greek *diskoeidēs*, from *diskos* (see DISCUS). —**dis·coi·dal** /disˈkoidl/ *adj.*

dis·col·or /disˈkələr/ ▸*v.* [*intrans.*] become a different, less attractive color: *do not overknead the dough while adding the fruit or it will discolor.* ■ [*trans.*] change or spoil the color of: *too much aluminum can discolor water* | [as *adj.*] (**discolored**) *her beauty was marred by discolored teeth.* ▷late Middle English: from Old French *descolorer* or medieval Latin *discolorare*, from *des-*, *dis-* (expressing reversal) + Latin *colorare* 'to color.' —**dis·col·or·a·tion** /-ˌkələˈrāSHən/ *n.*

dis·com·bob·u·late /ˌdiskəmˈbäbyəˌlāt/ ▸*v.* [*trans.*] *humorous* disconcert or confuse (someone): *this attitude totally discombobulated Bruce* | [as *adj.*] (**discombobulated**) *he is looking a little pained and discombobulated.* ▷mid 19th cent.: probably based on DISCOMPOSE or DISCOMFIT.

dis·com·fit /disˈkəmfit/ ▸*v.* (**-fit·ed, -fit·ing**) [*trans.*] (usu. **be discomfited**) make (someone) feel uneasy or embarrassed: *he was not noticeably discomfited by her tone.* ▷Middle English (in the sense 'defeat in battle'): from Old French *desconfit*, past participle of *desconfire*, based on Latin *dis-* (expressing reversal) + *conficere* 'put together' (see CONFECTION). —**dis·com·fi·ture** /disˈkəmfiˌCHo͝or/ *n.*

USAGE The words **discomfit** and **discomfort** are etymologically unrelated. Further, **discomfit** is a verb and **discomfort** is primarily a noun. But in modern use their principal meanings as a verb have collapsed into one: 'make (someone) feel uneasy.'

dis·com·fort /disˈkəmfərt/ ▸*n.* lack of physical comfort: *the discomforts of too much sun in summer.* ■ slight pain: *the patient complained of discomfort in the left calf.* ■ a state of mental unease; worry or embarrassment: *his remarks caused her discomfort.*

▸*v.* [*trans.*] make (someone) feel uneasy, anxious, or embarrassed: *she liked to discomfort my mother by her remarks.* ■ [often as *adj.*] (**discomforting**) cause (someone) slight pain: *the patient's condition has discomforting symptoms.* ▷Middle English (as a verb in the sense 'dishearten, distress'): from Old French *desconforter* (verb), *desconfort* (noun), from *des-* (expressing reversal) + *conforter* 'to comfort' (see COMFORT).

USAGE On the difference between **discomfort** and **discomfit**, see **usage** at DISCOMFIT.

dis·com·mode /ˌdiskəˈmōd/ ▸*v.* [*trans.*] *formal* cause (someone) trouble or inconvenience: *I am sorry to have discommoded you.* ▷early 18th cent.: from obsolete French *discommoder*, variant of *incommoder* (see INCOMMODE). —**dis·com·mo·di·ous** /-ˈmōdēəs/ *adj.* —**dis·com·mod·i·ty** /-ˈmäditē/ *n.*

dis·com·pose /ˌdiskəmˈpōz/ ▸*v.* [*trans.*] [often as *adj.*] (**discomposed**) disturb or agitate (someone): *she looked a little discomposed as she spoke.* —**dis·com·po·sure** /-ˈpōZHər/ *n.*

dis·con·cert /ˌdiskənˈsərt/ ▸*v.* [*trans.*] disturb the composure of; unsettle: *the abrupt change of subject disconcerted her* | [as *adj.*] (**disconcerted**) *she was amused to see a disconcerted expression on his face.* ▷late 17th cent. (in the sense 'upset the progress of'): from obsolete French *desconcerter*, from *des-* (expressing reversal) + *concerter* 'bring together.' —**dis·con·cert·ed·ly** *adv.* —**dis·con·cer·tion** /-ˈsərSHən/ *n.* —**dis·con·cert·ment** *n.* (*rare*).

dis·con·cert·ing /ˌdiskənˈsərtiNG/ ▸*adj.* causing one to feel unsettled: *he had a disconcerting habit of offering jobs to people he met at dinner parties.* —**dis·con·cert·ing·ly** *adv.*

dis·con·firm /ˌdiskənˈfərm/ ▸*v.* [*trans.*] show that (a belief or hypothesis) is not or may not be true. —**dis·con·fir·ma·tion** /disˌkänfərˈmāSHən/ *n.* —**dis·con·fir·ma·to·ry** /-məˌtôrē/ *adj.*

dis·con·form·i·ty /ˌdiskənˈfôrmitē/ ▸*n.* (*pl.* **-ties**) **1** lack of conformity. **2** *Geology* a break in a sedimentary sequence that does not involve a difference of inclination between the strata on each side of the break. Compare with UNCONFORMITY.

dis·con·nect /ˌdiskəˈnekt/ ▸*v.* [*trans.*] break the connection of or between: *take all violence out of television drama and you* ***disconnect*** *it* ***from*** *reality.* ■ take (an electrical device) out of action by detaching it from a power supply. ■ interrupt or terminate (a telephone conversation) by breaking the connection: *that might explain why her call got disconnected mid-expletive.* ■ (usu. **be disconnected**) terminate the connection of (a household) to water, electricity, gas, or telephone, typically because of nonpayment of bills.

▸*n.* *Computing* a discrepancy or lack of connection: *there can be a disconnect between boardrooms and IT departments when it comes to technology.* —**dis·con·nec·tion** /-ˈnekSHən/ *n.*

dis·con·nect·ed /ˌdiskəˈnektid/ ▸*adj.* having a connection broken: *he expected the disconnected phone to start ringing.* ■ [*predic.*] (of a person) lacking contact with reality: *I drove away, feeling* ***disconnected from*** *the real world.* ■ (of speech, writing, or thought) lacking a logical sequence; incoherent: *a disconnected narrative.* **—dis·con·nect·ed·ly** *adv.* **—dis·con·nect·ed·ness** *n.*

dis·con·so·late /dis'känsəlit/ ▸*adj.* without consolation or comfort; unhappy: *he'd met the man's disconsolate widow.* ▪ (of a place or thing) causing or showing a complete lack of comfort; cheerless: *solitary, disconsolate clumps of cattails.* ▷late Middle English: from medieval Latin *disconsolatus,* from *dis-* (expressing reversal) + Latin *consolatus* (past participle of *consolari* 'to console'). **—dis·con·so·late·ly** *adv.* **—dis·con·so·late·ness** *n.* **—dis·con·so·la·tion** /-ˌkänsə'lāSHən/ *n.*

dis·con·tent /ˌdiskən'tent/ ▸*n.* lack of contentment; dissatisfaction with one's circumstances: *popular* ***discontent with*** *the system had been general for several years | the discontents and anxieties of the working class.* ▪ a person who is dissatisfied, typically with the prevailing social or political situation: *the cause attracted a motley crew of discontents and zealots.* **—dis·con·tent·ment** *n.*

dis·con·tent·ed /ˌdiskən'tentid/ ▸*adj.* dissatisfied, esp. with one's circumstances: *I am so* ***discontented with*** *my work | a discontented housewife* | [as *plural n.*] (**the discontented**) *the ranks of the discontented were swelled by returning soldiers.* **—dis·con·tent·ed·ly** *adv.* **—dis·con·tent·ed·ness** *n.*

dis·con·tin·ue /ˌdiskən'tinyo͞o/ ▸*v.* (**-tin·ues, -tin·ued, -tin·u·ing**) [*trans.*] cease doing or providing (something), typically something provided on a regular basis: *he discontinued his visits | the ferry service was discontinued by the proprietors.* ▪ (usu. **be discontinued**) stop making (a particular product): *their current top-of-the-range running shoe is being discontinued* | [as *adj.*] (**discontinued**) *discontinued fabrics.* ▪ cease taking (medication or a medical treatment): *many women wish to discontinue antidepressants during pregnancy.* ▪ cease taking (a newspaper or periodical) or paying (a subscription). ▷late Middle English (in the sense 'interrupt, disrupt'): via Old French from medieval Latin *discontinuare,* from Latin *dis-* 'not' + *continuare* (see CONTINUE). **—dis·con·tin·u·ance** /-yo͞oəns/ *n.* **—dis·con·tin·u·a·tion** /-ˌtinyo͞o'āSHən/ *n.*

dis·con·ti·nu·i·ty /ˌdiskäntn'(y)o͞oitē/ ▸*n.* (*pl.* **-ties**) a distinct break in physical continuity or sequence in time: *there is no significant discontinuity between modern and primitive societies.* ▪ a sharp difference of characteristics between parts of something: *changes in government have resulted in discontinuities in policy.* ▪ *Mathematics* a point at which a function is discontinuous or undefined. ▷late 16th cent.: from medieval Latin *discontinuitas,* from *discontinuus* (see DISCONTINUOUS).

dis·con·tin·u·ous /ˌdiskən'tinyo͞oəs/ ▸*adj.* having intervals or gaps: *a person with a discontinuous employment record.* ▪ *Mathematics* (of a function) having at least one discontinuity, and whose differential coefficient may become infinite. ▷mid 17th cent. (in the sense 'producing discontinuity'): from medieval Latin *discontinuus,* from *dis-* 'not' + *continuus* (see CONTINUOUS). **—dis·con·tin·u·ous·ly** *adv.*

dis·cord /'diskôrd/ ▸*n.* **1** disagreement between people: *a prosperous family who showed no signs of discord.* ▪ lack of agreement or harmony between things: *the discord between indigenous and Western cultures.* **2** *Music* lack of harmony between notes sounding together: *the music faded in discord.* ▪ a chord that (in conventional harmonic terms) is regarded as unpleasing or requiring resolution by another. ▪ any interval except a unison, an octave, a perfect fifth or fourth, a major or minor third and sixth, or their octaves. ▪ a single note dissonant with another.
▸*v.* [*intrans.*] *archaic* (of people) disagree: *we discorded commonly on two points.* ▪ (of things) be different or in disharmony: *the party's views were apt to* ***discord with*** *those of the leading members of the administration.* ▷Middle English: from Old French *descord* (noun), *descorder* (verb), from Latin *discordare,* from *discors* 'discordant,' from *dis-* (expressing negation, reversal) + *cor, cord-* 'heart.'

dis·cord·ant /dis'kôrdnt/ ▸*adj.* **1** disagreeing or incongruous: *the principle of meritocracy is discordant with claims of inherited worth.* ▪ characterized by quarreling and conflict: *a study of children in discordant homes.* **2** (of sounds) harsh and jarring because of a lack of harmony: *bombs, guns, and engines mingled in discordant sound.* ▷late Middle English: from Old French *descordant,* present participle of *descorder* (see DISCORD). **—dis·cord·ance** *n.* **—dis·cor·dan·cy** /-dnsē/ *n.* **—dis·cord·ant·ly** *adv.*
▸*PHRASE* ▫ **strike a discordant note** appear strange and out of place: *the chair's modernity struck a discordant note in a room full of eighteenth-century furniture.*

dis·co·theque /'diskəˌtek/ ▸*n.* another term for DISCO (sense 1). ▷1950s: from French *discothèque,* originally 'record library,' on the pattern of *bibliothèque* 'library.'

dis·count ▸*n.* /'diskount/ a deduction from the usual cost of something, typically given for prompt or advance payment or to a special category of buyers: *many stores will offer a discount on bulk purchases.* ▪ *Finance* a percentage deducted from the face value of a bill of exchange or promissory note when it changes hands before the due date.
▸*v.* /'diskount; dis'kount/ [*trans.*] **1** deduct an amount from (the usual price of something): [as *adj.*] (**discounted**) *current users qualify for a discounted price.* ▪ reduce (a product or service) in price: *merchandise that was deeply discounted—up to 50 percent* | [as *adj.*] (**discounted**) *discounted books.* ▪ buy or sell (a bill of exchange) before its due date at less than its maturity value. **2** regard (a possibility, fact, or person) as being unworthy of consideration because it lacks credibility: *I'd heard rumors, but discounted them.*
▸*adj.* /'diskount/ (of a store or business) offering goods for sale at discounted prices: *a discount drugstore chain.* ▪ at a price lower than the usual one: *a discount flight.* ▷early 17th cent. (denoting a reduction in the amount or value of something): from obsolete French *descompte* (noun), *descompter* (verb), or (in commercial contexts) from Italian *(di)scontare,* both from medieval Latin *discomputare,* from Latin *dis-* (expressing reversal) + *computare* (see COMPUTE). **—dis·count·a·ble** /dis'kountəbəl/ *adj.* **—dis·count·er** *n.*
▸*PHRASE* ▫ **at a discount** below the nominal or usual price: *a plan that allows tenants to buy their homes at a discount.* Compare with AT A PREMIUM (see PREMIUM).

dis·count·ed cash flow ▸*n.* *Finance* a method of assessing investments taking into account the expected accumulation of interest.

dis·coun·te·nance /dis'kountn-əns/ ▸*v.* [*trans.*] (usu. **be discountenanced**) **1** refuse to approve of (something): *the best solution to alcohol abuse is a healthy family life where alcohol consumption is discountenanced.* **2** disturb the composure of: *Amanda was not discountenanced by the accusation.*

dis·count house ▸*n.* **1** another term for DISCOUNT STORE. **2** *Brit.* a company that buys and sells bills of exchange.

dis·count rate ▸*n.* *Finance* **1** the minimum interest rate set by the Federal Reserve for lending to other banks. **2** a rate used for discounting bills of exchange.

dis·count store ▸*n.* a store that sells goods at less than the normal retail price.

dis·cour·age /dis'kərij; -'kə-rij/ ▸*v.* [*trans.*] cause (someone) to lose confidence or enthusiasm: *I don't want to discourage you, but I don't think it's such a good idea* | [as *adj.*] (**discouraging**) *the discouraging effect of poor employment prospects.* ▪ prevent or seek to prevent (something) by showing disapproval or creating difficulties: *the plan is designed to discourage the use of private cars.* ▪ persuade (someone) against an action: *we want to* ***discourage*** *children* ***from*** *smoking.* ▷late Middle English: from Old French *descouragier,* from *des-* (expressing reversal) + *corage* 'courage.' **—dis·cour·age·ment** *n.* **—dis·cour·ag·er** *n.* **—dis·cour·ag·ing·ly** *adv.*

dis·course ▸*n.* /'disˌkôrs/ written or spoken communication or debate: *the language of political discourse | an imagined discourse between two people traveling in France.* ▪ a formal discussion of a topic in speech or writing: *a discourse on critical theory.* ▪ *Linguistics* a connected series of utterances; a text or conversation.
▸*v.* /dis'kôrs/ [*intrans.*] speak or write authoritatively about a topic: *she could* ***discourse*** *at great length* ***on*** *the history of Europe.* ▪ engage in conversation: *he spent an hour* ***discoursing with*** *his supporters in the courtroom.* ▷late Middle English (denoting the process of reasoning, also in the phrase *discourse of reason*): from Old French *discours,* from Latin *discursus* 'running to and fro' (in medieval Latin 'argument'), from the verb *discurrere,* from *dis-* 'away' + *currere* 'to run'; the verb influenced by French *discourir.*

dis·course mark·er /'disˌkôrs/ ▸*n.* *Grammar* a word or phrase whose function is to organize discourse into segments, for example *well* or *I mean.*

dis·cour·te·ous /dis'kərtēəs/ ▸*adj.* showing rudeness and a lack of consideration for other people: *it would be unkind and discourteous to decline a visit.* **—dis·cour·te·ous·ly** *adv.* **—dis·cour·te·ous·ness** *n.*

dis·cour·te·sy /dis'kərtəsē/ ▸*n.* (*pl.* **-sies**) rude and inconsiderate behavior: *he was able to discourage visitors without obvious discourtesy.* ▪ an impolite act or remark: *the fact that senators were not kept informed was an extraordinary discourtesy.*

dis·cov·er /dis'kəvər/ ▸*v.* [*trans.*] **1** find (something or someone) unexpectedly or in the course of a search: *firemen discovered a body in the debris | she discovered her lover in the arms of another woman.* ▪ become aware of (a fact or situation): *the courage to discover the truth and possibly be disappointed* | [with *clause*] *it was a relief to discover that he wasn't in.* ▪ be the first to find or observe (a place, substance, or scientific phenomenon): *Fleming discovered penicillin early in the twentieth century.* ▪ perceive the attractions of (an activity or subject) for the first time: *a teenager who has recently discovered fashion.* ▪ be the first to recognize the potential of (an actor, singer, or musician): *I discovered the band back in the mid 70s.* **2** *archaic* divulge (a secret): *they contain some secrets which Time will discover.* ▪ disclose the identity of (someone): *she at last discovered herself to me.* ▪ display (a quality or feeling): *with what agility did these military men discover their skill in feats of war.* ▷Middle English (in the sense 'make known'): from Old French *descovrir,* from late Latin *discooperire,* from Latin *dis-* (expressing reversal) + *cooperire* 'cover completely' (see COVER). **—dis·cov·er·a·ble** *adj.* **—dis·cov·er·er** *n.*

dis·cov·ered check ▸*n.* *Chess* a check that results when a player moves a piece or pawn so as to put the opponent's king in check from another piece.

dis·cov·er·y /dis'kəvərē/ ▸*n.* (*pl.* **-ver·ies**) **1** the action or process of discovering or being discovered: *the discovery of the body | he made some startling discoveries.* ▪ a person or thing discovered: *the drug is not a new discovery.* **2** *Law* the compulsory disclosure, by a party to an action, of relevant documents referred to by the other party. ▷mid 16th cent.: from DISCOVER, on the pattern of the pair *recover, recovery.*

dis·cov·er·y well ▸*n.* the first successful oil well in a new field.

dis·cred·it /dis'kredit/ ▸*v.* (**-cred·it·ed, -cred·it·ing**) [*trans.*] harm the good reputation of (someone or something): *his remarks were taken out of context in an effort to discredit him* | [as *adj.*] (**discredited**) *a discredited former governor.* ▪ cause (an idea or piece of evidence) to seem false or unreliable: *recent attempts to discredit evolution.*
▸*n.* loss or lack of reputation or respect: *they committed crimes that brought discredit upon the administration.* ▪ a person or thing that is a source of disgrace: *the ships were a* ***discredit to*** *the country.* ▷mid 16th cent.: from DIS- (expressing reversal) + CREDIT, on the pattern of Italian *(di)scredito* (noun), *(di)screditare* (verb), and French *discrédit* (noun), *discréditer* (verb).

dis·cred·it·a·ble /dis'kreditəbəl/ ▸*adj.* tending to bring harm to a reputation: *allegations of discreditable conduct.* **—dis·cred·it·a·bly** /-blē/ *adv.*

dis·creet /dis'krēt/ ▸*adj.* (**-creet·er, -creet·est**) careful and circumspect in one's speech or actions, esp. in order to avoid causing offense or to gain an advantage: *we made some discreet inquiries.* ▪ intentionally unobtrusive: *a discreet cough.* ▷Middle English: from Old French *discret,* from Latin *discretus* 'separate,' past participle of *discernere* 'discern,' the sense arising from late Latin *discretio* (see DISCRETION). Compare with DISCRETE. **—dis·creet·ly** *adv.* **—dis·creet·ness** *n.*

USAGE The words **discrete** and **discreet** are pronounced in the same way and share the same origin but they do not mean the same thing. **Discrete** means 'separate, distinct' (*a finite number of* ***discrete*** *categories*), while **discreet** means 'careful, judicious, circumspect' (*you can rely on him to be* ***discreet***).

dis·crep·an·cy /dis'krepənsē/ ▸*n.* (*pl.* **-cies**) a lack of compatibility or similarity between two or more facts: *there's a* ***discrepancy between*** *your account and his.* ▷early 17th cent.: from Latin *discrepantia,* from *discrepare* 'be discordant,' from *dis-* 'apart, away' + *crepare* 'to creak.' **—dis·crep·ant** /-pənt/ *adj.*

dis·crete /dis'krēt/ ▸*adj.* individually separate and distinct: *speech sounds are produced as a continuous sound signal rather than discrete units.* ▷late Middle English: from Latin *discretus* 'separate'; compare with DISCREET. **—dis·crete·ly** *adv.* **—dis·crete·ness** *n.*

USAGE On the difference between **discrete** and **discreet**, see **usage** at DISCREET.

dis·cre·tion /dis'kreSHən/ ▸*n.* **1** the quality of behaving or speaking in such a way as to avoid causing offense or revealing private information: *she knew she could rely on his discretion.* **2** the freedom to decide what should be done in a particular situation: *it is up to local authorities to* ***use their discretion*** *in setting the charges* | *a pass-fail grading system may be used* ***at the discretion of*** *the department.* ▷Middle English (in the sense 'discernment'): via Old French from Latin *discretio(n-)* 'separation' (in late Latin 'discernment'), from *discernere* (see DISCERN).

▸*PHRASE* □ **discretion is the better part of valor** *proverb* it is better to avoid a dangerous situation than to confront it.

dis·cre·tion·ar·y /dis'kreSHə,nerē/ ▸*adj.* available for use at the discretion of the user: *rules are inevitably less flexible than a discretionary policy.* ■ denoting or relating to investment funds placed with a broker or manager who has discretion to invest them on the client's behalf: *discretionary portfolios.*

dis·cre·tion·ar·y in·come ▸*n.* income remaining after deduction of taxes, other mandatory charges, and expenditure on necessary items. Compare with DISPOSABLE INCOME.

dis·cret·ize /dis'krē,tīz/ ▸*v.* [*trans.*] *Mathematics* represent or approximate (a quantity or series) using a discrete quantity or quantities. —**dis·cret·i·za·tion** /dis,krētə'zāSHən/ *n.*

dis·crim·i·na·ble /dis'krimənəbəl/ ▸*adj.* able to be discriminated; distinguishable: *the target contours will not be discriminable from their background.* ▷mid 18th cent.: from DISCRIMINATE, on the pattern of the pair *separate, separable.* —**dis·crim·i·na·bil·i·ty** /dis,krimənə'bilitē/ *n.* —**dis·crim·i·na·bly** /-blē/ *adv.*

dis·crim·i·nant /dis'krimənənt/ ▸*n.* an agent or characteristic that enables things, people, or classes to be distinguished from one another: *anemia is commonly present in patients with both conditions, and is therefore not a helpful discriminant.* ■ *Mathematics* a function of the coefficients of a polynomial equation whose value gives information about the roots of the polynomial. See also DISCRIMINANT FUNCTION. ▷mid 19th cent. (in the sense 'showing discernment'): from Latin *discriminant-* 'distinguishing between,' from the verb *discriminare* (see DISCRIMINATE).

dis·crim·i·nant a·nal·y·sis ▸*n.* statistical analysis using a discriminant function to assign data to one of two or more groups.

dis·crim·i·nant func·tion ▸*n.* *Statistics* a function of several variates used to assign items into one of two or more groups. The function for a particular set of items is obtained from measurements of the variates of items that belong to a known group.

dis·crim·i·nate /dis'krimə,nāt/ ▸*v.* [*intrans.*] **1** recognize a distinction; differentiate: *babies can* ***discriminate between*** *different facial expressions of emotion.* See note at DISTINGUISH. ■ [*trans.*] perceive or constitute the difference in or between: *bats can discriminate a difference in echo delay of between 69 and 98 millionths of a second* | *features that* ***discriminate*** *this species* ***from*** *other gastropods.* **2** make an unjust or prejudicial distinction in the treatment of different categories of people or things, esp. on the grounds of race, sex, or age: *existing employment policies* ***discriminate against*** *women.* ▷early 17th cent.: from Latin *discriminat-* 'distinguished between,' from the verb *discriminare*, from *discrimen* 'distinction,' from the verb *discernere* (see DISCERN). —**dis·crim·i·nate·ly** /-nitlē/ *adv.* —**dis·crim·i·na·tive** /-,nātiv/ *adj.*

dis·crim·i·nat·ing /dis'krimə,nātiNG/ ▸*adj.* (of a person) having or showing refined taste or good judgment: *he became a discriminating collector and patron of the arts.* —**dis·crim·i·nat·ing·ly** *adv.*

dis·crim·i·na·tion /dis,krimə'nāSHən/ ▸*n.* **1** the unjust or prejudicial treatment of different categories of people or things, esp. on the grounds of race, age, or sex: *victims of racial discrimination* | ***discrimination against*** *homosexuals.* **2** recognition and understanding of the difference between one thing and another: *discrimination between right and wrong* | *young children have difficulties in making fine discriminations.* ■ the ability to discern what is of high quality; good judgment or taste: *those who could afford to buy showed little taste or discrimination.* ■ *Psychology* the ability to distinguish between different stimuli: [as *adj.*] *discrimination learning.* **3** *Electronics* the selection of a signal having a required characteristic, such as frequency or amplitude, by means of a discriminator that rejects all unwanted signals.

dis·crim·i·na·tor /dis'krimə,nātər/ ▸*n.* **1** a characteristic that enables things, people, or classes to be distinguished from one another: *age should not be used as a primary discriminator in recruitment.* **2** *Electronics* a circuit or device that only produces an output when the input exceeds a fixed value. ■ a circuit that converts a frequency-modulated signal into an amplitude-modulated one.

dis·crim·i·na·to·ry /dis'krimənə,tôrē/ ▸*adj.* making or showing an unfair or prejudicial distinction between different categories of people or things, esp. on the grounds of race, age, or sex: *discriminatory employment practices.*

dis·cur·sive /dis'kərsiv/ ▸*adj.* **1** digressing from subject to subject: *students often write dull, secondhand, discursive prose.* ■ (of a style of speech or writing) fluent and expansive rather than formulaic or abbreviated: *the short story is concentrated, whereas the novel is discursive.* **2** of or relating to discourse or modes of discourse: *the attempt to transform utterances from one discursive context to another.* **3** *archaic Philosophy* proceeding by argument or reasoning rather than by intuition. ▷late 16th cent.: from medieval Latin *discursivus*, from Latin *discurs-*, literally 'gone hastily to and fro,' from the verb *discurrere* (see DISCOURSE). —**dis·cur·sive·ly** *adv.* —**dis·cur·sive·ness** *n.*

dis·cus /'diskəs/ ▸*n.* (*pl.* **-cus·es**) a heavy thick-centered disk thrown by an athlete, in ancient Greek games or in modern field events. ■ the athletic event or sport of throwing the discus: *she had placed first in the discus.* ▷via Latin from Greek *diskos.*

discus thrower

dis·cuss /dis'kəs/ ▸*v.* [*trans.*] talk about (something) with another person or group of people: *I* ***discussed*** *the matter* ***with*** *my wife* | [with *clause*] *they were discussing where to go for a drink.* ■ talk or write about (a topic) in detail, taking into account different ideas and opinions: *in Chapter Six I discuss problems that arise in applying Darwin's ideas.* ▷late Middle English (in the sense 'dispel, disperse,' also 'examine by argument'): from Latin *discuss-* 'dashed to pieces,' later 'investigated,' from the verb *discutere*, from *dis-* 'apart' + *quatere* 'shake.' —**dis·cuss·a·ble** *adj.* —**dis·cuss·er** *n.*

dis·cus·sant /dis'kəsənt/ ▸*n.* a person who takes part in a discussion, esp. an arranged one.

dis·cus·sion /dis'kəSHən/ ▸*n.* the action or process of talking about something, typically in order to reach a decision or to exchange ideas: *the proposals are not a blueprint but ideas for discussion* | *the specific content of the legislation was* ***under discussion.*** ■ a conversation or debate about a certain topic: *discussions about environmental improvement programs.* ■ a detailed treatment of a particular topic in speech or writing. ▷Middle English (denoting judicial examination): via Old French from late Latin *discussio(n-)*, from *discutere* 'investigate' (see DISCUSS).

dis·cus·sion board ▸*n.* *Computing* another term for MESSAGE BOARD.

dis·dain /dis'dān/ ▸*n.* the feeling that someone or something is unworthy of one's consideration or respect; contempt: *her upper lip curled in disdain* | *an aristocratic* ***disdain for*** *manual labor.*

▸*v.* [*trans.*] consider to be unworthy of one's consideration: *gamblers disdain four-horse races.* See note at DESPISE. ■ refuse or reject (something) out of feelings of pride or superiority: *she remained standing, pointedly disdaining his invitation to sit down* | [with *infinitive*] *he disdained to discuss the matter further.* ▷Middle English: from Old French *desdeign* (noun), *desdeignier* (verb), based on Latin *dedignari*, from *de-* (expressing reversal) + *dignari* 'consider worthy' (from *dignus* 'worthy').

dis·dain·ful /dis'dānfəl/ ▸*adj.* showing contempt or lack of respect: *with a last disdainful look, she turned toward the door.* —**dis·dain·ful·ly** *adv.* —**dis·dain·ful·ness** *n.*

dis·ease /di'zēz/ ▸*n.* a disorder of structure or function in a human, animal, or plant, esp. one that produces specific signs or symptoms or that affects a specific location and is not simply a direct result of physical injury: *bacterial meningitis is a rare disease* | *a possible cause of heart disease.* ■ *figurative* a particular quality, habit, or disposition regarded as adversely affecting a person or group of people: *departmental administration has often led to the dread disease of departmentalitis.* ▷Middle English (in the sense 'lack of ease; inconvenience'): from Old French *desaise* 'lack of ease,' from *des-* (expressing reversal) + *aise* 'ease.'

dis·eased /di'zēzd/ ▸*adj.* suffering from disease: *all the diseased cattle have been removed.* ■ *figurative* abnormal and corrupt: *I cannot bear your diseased view of mankind.*

di·sease man·age·ment ▸*n.* a system that seeks to manage the chronic conditions of high-risk, high-cost patients as a group.

dis·e·con·o·my /,disi'känəmē/ ▸*n.* (*pl.* **-mies**) an economic disadvantage such as an increase in cost arising from an increase in the size of an organization: *in an ideal world, these* ***diseconomies of scale*** *would be minimized.*

dis·em·bark /,disem'bärk/ ▸*v.* [*intrans.*] leave a ship, aircraft, or other vehicle: *the passengers began to disembark.* ▷late 16th cent.: from French *désembarquer*, Spanish *desembarcar*, or Italian *disimbarcare*, based on Latin *barca* 'ship's boat.' —**dis·em·bar·ka·tion** /dis-,embär'kāSHən/ *n.*

dis·em·bar·rass /,disem'barəs/ ▸*v.* (**disembarrass oneself of/from**) free oneself of (a burden or nuisance): *he would do well to disembarrass himself of his too officious advisers.* ■ [*trans.*] *rare* make (someone or something) free from embarrassment. —**dis·em·bar·rass·ment** *n.*

dis·em·bod·ied /,disem'bädēd/ ▸*adj.* separated from or existing without the body: *a disembodied ghost.* ■ (of a sound) lacking any obvious physical source: *a disembodied voice at the end of the phone.*

dis·em·bod·y /,disem'bädē/ ▸*v.* (**-bod·ies**, **-bod·ied**) [*trans.*] separate or free (something) from its concrete form. —**dis·em·bod·i·ment** *n.*

dis·em·bogue /,disem'bōg/ ▸*v.* (**-bogues**, **-bogued**, **-bogu·ing**) [*intrans.*] *poetic/literary* (of a river or stream) emerge or be discharged in quantity; pour out. ▷late 16th cent.: from Spanish *desembocar*, from *des-* (expressing reversal) + *embocar* 'run into a creek or strait' (based on *boca* 'mouth').

dis·em·bow·el /,disem'bouəl/ ▸*v.* (**-bow·eled**, **-bow·el·ing**; *Brit.* **-bow·elled**, **-bow·el·ling**) [*trans.*] cut open and remove the internal organs of. —**dis·em·bow·el·ment** *n.*

dis·em·broil /,disem'broil/ ▸*v.* [*trans.*] *archaic* free (someone or something) from confusion: *to disembroil a subject that seems to have perplexed even Antiquity.*

dis·em·pow·er /,disem'pouər/ ▸*v.* [*trans.*] make (a person or group) less powerful or confident: *leaving the decision in a government agent's hands disempowers and disrespects women.* —**dis·em·pow·er·ment** *n.*

dis·en·chant /,disen'CHant/ ▸*v.* [*trans.*] (usu. **be disenchanted**) free (someone) from illusion; disappoint: *he may have been disenchanted by the loss of his huge following* | [as *adj.*] (**disenchanted**) *he became* ***disenchanted with*** *his erstwhile ally.* ▷late 16th cent.: from French *désenchanter*, from *dés-* (expressing reversal) + *enchanter* (see ENCHANT). —**dis·en·chant·ing·ly** *adv.* —**dis·en·chant·ment** *n.*

dis·en·cum·ber /,disen'kəmbər/ ▸*v.* [*trans.*] free from or relieve of an encumbrance: *it would disencumber the world of a plague.*

dis·en·dow /,disen'dou/ ▸*v.* [*trans.*] deprive (someone or something) of an endowment. —**dis·en·dow·ment** *n.*

dis·en·fran·chise /,disen'franCHīz/ (also **dis·fran·chise** /dis'franCHīz/) ▸*v.* [*trans.*] deprive (someone) of the right to vote: *the law disenfranchised some 3,000 voters on the basis of a residence qualification.* ■ [as *adj.*] (**disenfranchised**) deprived of power; marginalized: *a hard core of kids who are disenfranchised and don't feel connected to the school.* ■ deprive (someone) of a right or privilege: *the move would disenfranchise the disabled from using the town center.* ■ *archaic* deprive (someone) of the rights and privileges of a free inhabitant of a borough, city, or country. —**dis·en·fran·chise·ment** *n.*

dis·en·gage /,disen'gāj/ ▸*v.* **1** [*trans.*] detach, free, loosen, or separate (something): *I* ***disengaged*** *his hand* ***from*** *mine.* ■ detach oneself; get loose: *they clung together for a moment, then she* ***disengaged herself.*** ■ [*intrans.*] become released: *the clutch will not disengage.* ■ remove (troops) from an area of conflict: *the ceasefire gave the commanders a chance to disengage their forces* | [*intrans.*] *it seemed the only means by which the Americans could* ***disengage from*** *Korea.* **2** [*intrans.*] *Fencing* pass the point of one's sword over or under the opponent's sword to change the line of attack.

dis·en·gaged /,disen'gājd/ ▸*adj.* emotionally detached: *the students were oddly disengaged, as if they didn't believe they could control their lives.*

dis·en·gage·ment /,disen'gājmənt/ ▸*n.* **1** the action or process of withdrawing from involvement in a particular activity, situation, or group: *their steady* ***disengagement from*** *politics and politicians.* ■ the withdrawal of military forces or the renunciation of military or political influence in a particular area. ■ the process of separating or releasing something or of becoming separated or released: *the mechanism prevents accidental disengagement.* ■ *archaic* the breaking off of an engagement to be married. **2** emotional detachment; objectivity: *contemporary criticism can afford neutral disengagement.*

dis·en·tail·ment /ˌdisenˈtālmənt/ ▸*n. Law* the action of freeing property from entail: *the disentailment of the church's landed property.* **—dis·en·tail** *v.*

dis·en·tan·gle /ˌdisenˈtaNGgəl/ ▸*v.* [*trans.*] free (something or someone) from an entanglement; extricate: *"I must go," she said,* ***disentangling*** *her fingers* ***from*** *Gabriel's* | *figurative it was often difficult to* ***disentangle*** *fact* ***from*** *fiction.* ■ remove knots or tangles from (wool, rope, or hair): *Allen was on his knees disentangling a coil of rope.* **—dis·en·tan·gle·ment** *n.*

dis·en·thrall /ˌdisenˈTHrôl/ (*Brit.* **dis·en·thral**) ▸*v.* [*trans.*] *poetic/literary* set free: *I disenthrall my mind from theories.* **—dis·en·thrall·ment** *n.*

dis·en·ti·tle /ˌdisenˈtītl/ ▸*v.* [*trans.*] (often **be disentitled**) deprive (someone) of a right: *he was* ***disentitled to*** *gain damages for the injuries.* **—dis·en·ti·tle·ment** *n.*

dis·en·tomb /ˌdisenˈto͞om/ ▸*v.* [*trans.*] remove (something) from a tomb: *a mummy that we saw disentombed.* **—dis·en·tomb·ment** *n.*

dis·e·qui·lib·ri·um /disˌēkwəˈlibrēəm/ ▸*n.* a loss or lack of balance or stability: *I was in a state of emotional disequilibrium.* ■ a loss or lack of equilibrium in relation to supply, demand, and prices.

dis·es·tab·lish /ˌdisiˈstabliSH/ ▸*v.* [*trans.*] (usu. **be disestablished**) deprive (an organization, esp. a country's national church) of its official status. **—dis·es·tab·lish·ment** *n.*

dis·es·teem /ˌdisiˈstēm/ *dated* ▸*n.* low esteem or regard: *language is not insulting unless it is intended to show contempt or disesteem.*

▸*v.* [*trans.*] have a low opinion of.

di·seuse /dēˈzo͞oz/ ▸*n.* a female entertainer who performs monologues. ▷late 19th cent.: French, literally 'talker,' feminine of *diseur*, from *dire* 'to say.'

dis·fa·vor /disˈfāvər/ (*Brit.* **dis·fa·vour**) ▸*n.* disapproval or dislike: *the headmaster regarded her with disfavor.* ■ the state of being disliked: *raises could be taken away if an employee* ***fell into disfavor.***

▸*v.* [*trans.*] regard or treat (someone or something) with disfavor: *the hypothesis was favored and disfavored by approximately equal numbers of scientists.*

dis·fel·low·ship /disˈfelōˌSHip/ ▸*n.* exclusion from fellowship, esp. as a form of discipline in some Protestant and Mormon churches.

▸*v.* (**-shiped**, **-ship·ing**; *Brit.* **-shipped**, **-ship·ping**.) [*trans.*] exclude (someone) from fellowship.

dis·fig·ure /disˈfigyər/ ▸*v.* [*trans.*] spoil the attractiveness of: *litter disfigures the countryside* | [as *adj.*] (**disfiguring**) *a disfiguring birthmark.* ▷late Middle English: from Old French *desfigurer*, based on Latin *figura* 'figure.' **—dis·fig·u·ra·tion** /-ˌfigyəˈrāSHən/ *n.* **—dis·fig·ure·ment** *n.*

dis·fran·chise /disˈfranCHīz/ ▸*v.* another term for DISENFRANCHISE.

dis·gorge /disˈgôrj/ ▸*v.* [*trans.*] **1** cause to pour out: *the combine disgorged a steady stream of grain.* ■ (of a building or vehicle) discharge (the occupants): *an aircraft disgorging paratroopers.* ■ yield or give up (funds, esp. funds that have been dishonestly acquired): *they were made to disgorge all the profits made from the record.* ■ eject (food) from the throat or mouth. ■ [*intrans.*] (of a river) empty into a sea: *the Nile disgorges into the sea at Rashid.* **2** (usu. **be disgorged**) remove the sediment from (a sparkling wine) after fermentation: *the wine is aged in the bottle before it is disgorged.* ▷late 15th cent.: from Old French *desgorger*, from *des-* (expressing removal) + *gorge* 'throat.' **—dis·gorge·ment** *n.*

dis·gorg·er /disˈgôrjər/ ▸*n. Fishing* a device for extracting a hook from a fish's throat.

dis·grace /disˈgrās/ ▸*n.* loss of reputation or respect, esp. as the result of a dishonorable action: *he left the army* ***in disgrace*** | *if he'd gone back, it would have brought disgrace on the family.* ■ [in *sing.*] a person or thing regarded as shameful and unacceptable: *he's* ***a disgrace to*** *the legal profession.*

▸*v.* [*trans.*] bring shame or discredit on (someone or something): *you have disgraced the family name* | *John stiffened his jaw so he wouldn't* ***disgrace himself*** *by crying.* ■ (**be disgraced**) fall from favor or lose a position of power or honor: *he has been publicly disgraced for offenses of which he was not guilty* | [as *adj.*] (**disgraced**) *an officer's sword was broken in half over the head of the disgraced soldier.* ▷mid 16th cent. (as a verb): via French from Italian *disgrazia* (noun), *disgraziare* (verb), from *dis-* (expressing reversal) + Latin *gratia* 'grace.'

dis·grace·ful /disˈgrāsfəl/ ▸*adj.* shockingly unacceptable: *a disgraceful waste of money* | [with *clause*] *it is disgraceful that they should be denied unemployment benefits.* **—dis·grace·ful·ly** *adv.*

dis·grun·tled /disˈgrəntld/ ▸*adj.* angry or dissatisfied: *judges receive letters from disgruntled members of the public.* ▷mid 17th cent.: from DIS- (as an intensifier) + dialect *gruntle* 'utter little grunts,' from GRUNT. **—dis·grun·tle·ment** *n.*

dis·guise /disˈgīz/ ▸*v.* [*trans.*] give (someone or oneself) a different appearance in order to conceal one's identity: *he* ***disguised himself as*** *a girl* | *Brian was disguised as a priest.* ■ make (something) unrecognizable by altering its appearance, sound, taste, or smell: *does holding a handkerchief over the mouthpiece really disguise your voice?* ■ conceal the nature or existence of (a feeling or situation): *he made no effort to disguise his contempt.*

▸*n.* a means of altering one's appearance or concealing one's identity: *his bizarre disguise drew stares from fellow shoppers.* ■ the state of having altered one's appearance in order to conceal one's identity: *I told them you were a policewoman* ***in disguise.*** ■ the concealing of one's true intentions or feelings: *rows of small children looked at her without disguise.* ▷Middle English (meaning 'change one's usual style of dress,' with no implication of concealing one's identity): from Old French *desguisier*. **—dis·guise·ment** *n.* (*archaic*).

dis·gust /disˈgəst/ ▸*n.* a feeling of revulsion or profound disapproval aroused by something unpleasant or offensive: *the sight filled her with disgust* | *some of the audience walked out* ***in disgust.***

▸*v.* [*trans.*] (often **be disgusted**) cause (someone) to feel revulsion or profound disapproval: *I was disgusted with myself for causing so much misery* | [as *adj.*] (**disgusted**) *a disgusted look.* ▷late 16th cent.: from early modern French *desgoust* or Italian *disgusto*, from Latin *dis-* (expressing reversal) + *gustus* 'taste.' **—dis·gust·ed·ly** *adv.*

dis·gust·ful /disˈgəstfəl/ ▸*adj.* old-fashioned term for DISGUSTING.

dis·gust·ing /disˈgəstiNG/ ▸*adj.* arousing revulsion or strong indignation: *he had the most disgusting rotten teeth* | *I think the decision is disgusting.* **—dis·gust·ing·ly** *adv.* **—dis·gust·ing·ness** *n.*

dish /diSH/ ▸*n.* **1** a shallow, typically flat-bottomed container for cooking or serving food: *an ovenproof dish.* ■ the food contained or served in such a container: ***a dish of*** *oysters.* ■ a particular variety or preparation of food served as part of a meal: *fresh fish dishes* | *pasta was served as a* ***main dish.*** ■ (**the dishes**) all the items that have been used in the preparation, serving, and eating of a meal: *it was our turn to wash the dishes.* ■ [usu. with *adj.*] a shallow, concave receptacle, esp. one intended to hold a particular substance: *a soap dish.* ■ (also **dish aerial**) a bowl-shaped radio antenna. See also SATELLITE DISH. **2** *informal* a sexually attractive person: *I gather she's quite a dish.* ■ (**one's dish**) *dated* a thing that one particularly enjoys or does well: *as a public relations man this was my dish and the campaign was right up my street.* **3** (**the dish**) *informal* information that is not generally known or available: *if he has the real dish I wish he'd tell us.* **4** concavity of a spoked wheel resulting from a difference in spoke tension on each side and consequent sideways displacement of the rim in relation to the hub.

▸*v.* [*trans.*] **1** (**dish something out/up**) put (food) onto a plate or plates before a meal: *Steve was dishing up vegetables* | *figurative pop stars who dish up remixes of their old hits.* ■ (**dish something out**) dispense something in a casual or indiscriminate way: *the banks dished out loans to all and sundry.* ■ (**dish it out**) *informal* subject others to criticism or punishment: *you can dish it out but you can't take it.* ■ [*intrans.*] *informal* gossip or share information, esp. information of an intimate or scandalous nature: *groups gather to brag about babies and dish about romances.* **2** *informal, chiefly Brit.* utterly destroy, confound, or defeat (someone or something). **3** give concavity to (a wheel) by tensioning the spokes (see sense 4 of the *noun*).

▸*phrasal v.* □ **dish something off** pass to a teammate, esp. in basketball. ▷Old English *disc* 'plate, bowl' (related to Dutch *dis*, German *Tisch* 'table'), based on Latin *discus* (see DISCUS). **—dish·ful** /-ˌfo͝ol/ *n.* (*pl.* **-fuls**).

▸PHRASE □ **dish the dirt** *informal* reveal or spread scandalous information or gossip.

dis·ha·bille /ˌdisəˈbēl/ (also **des·ha·bille**) ▸*n.* the state of being only partly or scantily clothed: *the paintings of Venus all shared the same state of dishabille.* ▷late 17th cent.: from French *déshabillé*, 'undressed.'

dish an·ten·na ▸*n.* a receiver or transmitter of electromagnetic energy, esp. microwaves or radiowaves, that consists of a reflector shaped like a shallow dish.

dis·har·mo·ny /disˈhärmənē/ ▸*n.* lack of harmony or agreement. **—dis·har·mo·ni·ous** /-ˌhärˈmōnēəs/ *adj.* **—dis·har·mo·ni·ous·ly** /-ˌhärˈmōnēəslē/ *adv.*

dish·cloth /ˈdiSHˌklôTH/ ▸*n.* a cloth for washing or drying dishes.

dish·cloth gourd ▸*n.* another term for LOOFAH.

dis·heart·en /disˈhärtn/ ▸*v.* [*trans.*] (often **be disheartened**) cause (someone) to lose determination or confidence: *the farmer was disheartened by the damage to his crops.* **—dis·heart·en·ing·ly** *adv.* **—dis·heart·en·ment** *n.*

dished /diSHt/ ▸*adj.* having the shape of a dish; concave: *overloaded timber floors are likely to sag, producing a dished or sloping floor surface.*

di·shev·eled /diˈSHevəld/ (*Brit.* **di·shev·elled**) ▸*adj.* (of a person's hair, clothes, or appearance) untidy; disordered: *a man with long, disheveled hair.* ▷late Middle English: from obsolete *dishevely*, from Old French *deschevele*, past participle of *descheveler* (based on *chevel* 'hair,' from Latin *capillus*). The original sense was 'having the hair uncovered'; later, referring to the hair itself, 'hanging loose,' hence 'disordered, untidy.' Compare with UNKEMPT. **—di·shev·el** /-ˈSHevəl/ *v.* **—di·shev·el·ment** *n.*

dis·hon·est /disˈänist/ ▸*adj.* behaving or prone to behave in an untrustworthy or fraudulent way: *he was a dishonest hypocrite prepared to exploit his family.* ■ intended to mislead or cheat: *he gave the editor a dishonest account of events.* ▷late Middle English (in the sense 'dishonorable, unchaste'): from Old French *deshoneste*, Latin *dehonestus*. **—dis·hon·est·ly** *adv.*

dis·hon·es·ty /disˈänəstē/ ▸*n.* (*pl.* **-ties**) deceitfulness shown in someone's character or behavior: *the dismissal of thirty civil servants for dishonesty and misconduct.* ■ a fraudulent or deceitful act. ▷late Middle English (in the sense 'dishonor, sexual misconduct'): from Old French *deshoneste* 'indecency' (see DISHONEST).

dis·hon·or /disˈänər/ (*Brit.* **dis·hon·our**) ▸*n.* a state of shame or disgrace: *the incident brought dishonor upon the police.*

▸*v.* [*trans.*] **1** bring shame or disgrace on: *the mayor dishonors his good battle by resorting to sniping.* ■ *archaic* violate the chastity of (a woman); rape. **2** fail to observe or respect (an agreement or principle): *the community has its own principles it can itself honor or dishonor.* ■ refuse to accept or pay (a check or a promissory note). ▷Middle English: from Old French *deshonor* (noun), *deshonorer* (verb), based on Latin *honor* 'honor.'

dis·hon·or·a·ble /disˈänərəbəl/ (*Brit.* **dis·hon·our·a·ble**) ▸*adj.* bringing shame or disgrace on someone or something: *his crimes are petty and dishonorable.* **—dis·hon·or·a·ble·ness** *n.* **—dis·hon·or·a·bly** /-blē/ *adv.*

dis·hon·or·a·ble dis·charge ▸*n.* the dismissal of someone from the armed forces as a result of criminal or morally unacceptable actions.

dish·pan /ˈdiSHˌpan/ ▸*n.* a large basin in which dishes are washed.

dish·pan hands ▸*plural n.* red, rough, or chapped hands caused by sensitivity to or excessive use of household detergents or other cleaning agents.

dish·rag /ˈdiSHˌrag/ ▸*n.* a dishcloth.

dish tow·el ▸*n.* a cloth for drying washed dishes, utensils, and glasses.

dish·wash·er /ˈdiSHˌwôSHər; -ˌwäSH-/ ▸*n.* **1** a machine for washing dishes automatically. **2** a person employed to wash dishes.

dish·wa·ter /ˈdiSHˌwôtər; -ˌwätər/ ▸*n.* dirty water in which dishes have been washed: *figurative I sipped the barely brown dishwater he passed off as coffee.*

▸PHRASE □ **dull as dishwater** see DULL.

dish·y /ˈdiSHē/ ▸*adj.* (**dish·i·er**, **dish·i·est**) *informal* sexually attractive. ■ scandalous or gossipy: *she's the perfect candidate for a dishy biography.*

dis·il·lu·sion /ˌdisəˈlo͞ozHən/ ▸*n.* disappointment resulting from the discovery that something is not as good as one believed it to be: *enthusiasm for the government evaporated into a more cynical disillusion.*

▸*v.* [*trans.*] cause (someone) to realize that a belief or an ideal is false: *if they think we have a magic formula to solve the problem, don't disillusion them.*

dis·il·lu·sioned /ˌdisəˈlo͞ozhənd/ ▸*adj.* disappointed in someone or something that one discovers to be less good than one had believed: *the minority groups were completely* ***disillusioned with*** *the party.*

dis·il·lu·sion·ment /ˌdisəˈlo͞ozhənmənt/ ▸*n.* a feeling of disappointment resulting from the discovery that something is not as good as one believed it to be: *the high abstention rate at the election reflected the voters' growing* ***disillusionment with*** *politics.*

dis·in·car·nate /ˌdisinˈkärnit; -ˌnāt/ ▸*adj.* another term for DISCARNATE.

dis·in·cen·tive /ˌdisinˈsentiv/ ▸*n.* a factor, esp. a financial disadvantage, that tends to discourage people from doing something: *spiraling house prices are beginning to act as a disincentive to development.*

dis·in·cli·na·tion /disˌinkləˈnāshən; disˌiNGklə-/ ▸*n.* [in *sing.*] a reluctance or lack of enthusiasm: *Lucy felt a strong* ***disinclination to*** *talk about her engagement.*

dis·in·clined /ˌdisinˈklīnd/ ▸*adj.* [*predic.*, with *infinitive*] unwilling; reluctant: *the rural community was disinclined to abandon the old ways.*

dis·in·cor·po·rate /ˌdisinˈkôrpəˌrāt/ ▸*v.* [*trans.*] dissolve (a corporate body).

dis·in·fect /ˌdisinˈfekt/ ▸*v.* [*trans.*] clean (something) with a disinfectant in order to destroy bacteria: *he disinfected and dressed the cut on his forehead.* ▷late 16th cent. (in the sense 'rid of infection'): from French *désinfecter*, from *dés-* (expressing reversal) + *infecter* 'to infect.' **—dis·in·fec·tion** /-ˈfekshən/ *n.*

dis·in·fect·ant /ˌdisinˈfektənt/ ▸*n.* a chemical liquid that destroys bacteria.
▸*adj.* causing the destruction of bacteria: *cleansing and disinfectant products.*

dis·in·fest /ˌdisinˈfest/ ▸*v.* [*trans.*] rid (someone or something) of infesting vermin. **—dis·in·fes·ta·tion** /-ˌinfeˈstāshən/ *n.*

dis·in·fla·tion /ˌdisinˈflāshən/ ▸*n.* reduction in the rate of inflation. **—dis·in·fla·tion·ar·y** /-ˌnerē/ *adj.*

dis·in·for·ma·tion /disˌinfərˈmāshən/ ▸*n.* false information that is intended to mislead, esp. propaganda issued by a government organization to a rival power or the media. ▷1950s: formed on the pattern of Russian *dezinformatsiya.*

dis·in·gen·u·ous /ˌdisinˈjenyo͞oəs/ ▸*adj.* not candid or sincere, typically by pretending that one knows less about something than one really does. **—dis·in·gen·u·ous·ly** *adv.* **—dis·in·gen·u·ous·ness** *n.*

dis·in·her·it /ˌdisinˈherit/ ▸*v.* (**-her·it·ed**, **-her·it·ing**) [*trans.*] change one's will or take other steps to prevent (someone) from inheriting one's property. ▷late Middle English (superseding earlier *disherit*): from DIS- (expressing removal) + *inherit* in the obsolete sense 'make someone an heir.' **—dis·in·her·i·tance** /-ˈheritəns/ *n.*

dis·in·hib·it /ˌdisinˈhibit/ ▸*v.* (**-hib·it·ed**, **-hib·it·ing**) [*trans.*] make (someone or something) less inhibited: *as well as disinhibiting me, he educated me.* **—dis·in·hi·bi·tion** /disˌinhiˈbishən/ *n.*

dis·in·te·grate /disˈintəˌgrāt/ ▸*v.* [*intrans.*] break up into small parts, typically as the result of impact or decay: *when the missile struck, the car disintegrated in a sheet of searing flame.* ■ (of a society, family, or other social group) weaken or break apart: *the marriage disintegrated amid allegations that she was having an affair.* ■ *informal* deteriorate mentally or physically: *I thought that when I finished working on the book I'd disintegrate.* ■ *Physics* undergo or cause to undergo disintegration at a subatomic level: [*intrans.*] *a meson can spontaneously disintegrate* | [*trans.*] *it has become a relatively easy matter to disintegrate almost any atom.* **—dis·in·te·gra·tive** /-ˌgrātiv/ *adj.* **—dis·in·te·gra·tor** /-ˌgrātər/ *n.*

dis·in·te·gra·tion /disˌintəˈgrāshən/ ▸*n.* the process of losing cohesion: *the twin problems of economic failure and social disintegration.* ■ the process of coming to pieces: *the disintegration of infected cells.* ■ breakdown of the personality: *loss of self-esteem leads to the disintegration of a proud man.* ■ *Physics* a process in which a nucleus or other subatomic particle emits a smaller particle or divides into smaller particles.

dis·in·ter /ˌdisinˈtər/ ▸*v.* (**-terred**, **-ter·ring**) [*trans.*] dig up (something that has been buried, esp. a corpse). ■ discover (something that is well hidden): *he has disinterred and translated an important collection of writings.* ▷early 17th cent.: from French *désenterrer*, from *dis-* (expressing reversal) + *enterrer* 'to inter.' **—dis·in·ter·ment** *n.*

dis·in·ter·est /disˈint(ə)rist/ ▸*n.* **1** the state of not being influenced by personal involvement in something; impartiality: *I do not claim any scholarly disinterest with this book.* **2** lack of interest in something: *he chided Dennis for his* ***disinterest in*** *anything that is not his own idea.*

dis·in·ter·est·ed /disˈintəˌrestid; -tristid/ ▸*adj.* **1** not influenced by considerations of personal advantage: *a banker is under an obligation to give disinterested advice.* **2** having or feeling no interest in something: *her father was so disinterested in her progress that he only visited the school once.* ▷early 17th cent.: past participle of the rare verb *disinterest* 'rid of interest or concern,' from DIS- (expressing removal) + the verb INTEREST. **—dis·in·ter·est·ed·ly** *adv.* **—dis·in·ter·est·ed·ness** *n.*

> *USAGE* A common source of confusion is the difference between **disinterested** and **uninterested**. **Disinterested** means 'not having a personal interest, impartial': *a juror must be* ***disinterested*** *in the case being tried.* **Uninterested** means 'not interested, indifferent': *on the other hand, a juror must not be* ***uninterested.***

dis·in·ter·me·di·a·tion /ˌdisintərˌmēdēˈāshən/ ▸*n.* reduction in the use of banks and savings institutions as intermediaries in the borrowing and investment of money, in favor of direct involvement in the securities market.

dis·in·vent /ˌdisinˈvent/ ▸*v.* [*trans.*] undo the invention of (something): *you can't disinvent nuclear power.*

dis·in·vest /ˌdisinˈvest/ ▸*v.* [*intrans.*] withdraw or reduce an investment: *the oil industry began to disinvest, and oil share prices have fallen* | [*trans.*] *they opposed the move to disinvest shares.* **—dis·in·vest·ment** *n.*

dis·in·vite /ˌdisinˈvīt/ ▸*v.* [*trans.*] withdraw or cancel an invitation to (someone): *the White House called to disinvite him from the president's party.*

di·sin·vol·tu·ra /disˌinvälˈtyo͝orə; -vôl-/ ▸*n.* self-assurance; lack of constraint. ▷mid 19th cent.: from Italian, from *disinvolto* 'unembarrassed,' from *disinvolgere* 'unwind.'

dis·jec·ta mem·bra /disˈjektə ˈmembrə/ ▸*plural n.* scattered fragments, esp. of written work. ▷Latin, alteration of *disjecti membra poetae* (used by Horace) 'limbs of a dismembered poet.'

dis·join /disˈjoin/ ▸*v.* separate; take or come apart: [*intrans.*] *the paired chromosomes fail to separate or disjoin during cell division.* ▷late Middle English: from Old French *desjoindre*, from Latin *disjungere*, from *dis-* (expressing reversal) + *jungere* 'to join.'

dis·joint /disˈjoint/ ▸*v.* [*trans.*] disturb the cohesion or organization of: *the loss of the area disjointed military plans.* ■ *dated* take apart at the joints: *disjoint a four-pound chicken, put in a pot, and simmer until tender.*
▸*adj. Mathematics* (of two or more sets) having no elements in common. ▷late Middle English (as an adjective in the sense 'disjointed'): from Old French *desjoint* 'separated,' from the verb *desjoindre* (see DISJOIN).

dis·joint·ed /disˈjointid/ ▸*adj.* lacking a coherent sequence or connection: *piecing together disjointed fragments of information.* **—dis·joint·ed·ly** *adv.* **—dis·joint·ed·ness** *n.*

dis·junct ▸*adj.* /disˈjəNGkt/ disjoined and distinct from one another: *these items of evidence are just phrases and clauses, often wildly disjunct.* ■ of or relating to the movement of a melody from one note to another by a leap.
▸*n.* /ˈdisˌjəNGkt/ **1** *Logic* each of the terms of a disjunctive proposition. **2** *Grammar* another term for SENTENCE ADVERB. ▷late Middle English: from Latin *disjunctus* 'disjoined, separated,' from the verb *disjungere.*

dis·junc·tion /disˈjəNGkshən/ ▸*n.* **1** the process or an act of disjoining; separation: *the Indians emphasized the disjunction between themselves and the invaders.* ■ a lack of correspondence or consistency: *there is a* ***disjunction between*** *the skills taught in education and those demanded in the labor market.* **2** *Logic* the relationship between two distinct alternatives. ■ a statement expressing this relationship (esp. one using the word "or"). ▷late Middle English: from Latin *disjunctio(n-)*, from *disjungere* 'disjoin' (see DISJUNCT).

dis·junc·tive /disˈjəNGktiv/ ▸*adj.* **1** lacking connection: *the novel's disjunctive detail.* **2** *Grammar* (of a conjunction) expressing a choice between two mutually exclusive possibilities, for example *or* in *she asked if he was going or staying.* Compare with COPULATIVE. ■ *Logic* (of a proposition) expressing alternatives.
▸*n. Grammar* a disjunctive conjunction or other word. ■ *Logic* a disjunctive proposition. ▷late Middle English (sense 2): from Latin *disjunctivus*, from *disjunct-* 'disjoined' (see DISJUNCT). **—dis·junc·tive·ly** *adv.*

dis·junc·ture /disˈjəNGkCHər/ ▸*n.* a separation or disconnection: *the monstrous disjuncture between his private and his public life.* ▷late Middle English: from medieval Latin *disjunctura*, from Latin *disjunct-* 'disjoined' (see DISJUNCT).

disk /disk/ (also **disc**) ▸*n.* **1** a flat, thin, round object: *heavy metal disks the size of hockey pucks* | *onion soup ladled over a disk of cheese.* ■ an information storage device for a computer in the shape of a round flat plate that can be rotated to give access to all parts of the surface. The data may be stored either magnetically (in a **magnetic disk**) or optically (in an **optical disk** such as a CD-ROM). ■ (**disc**) short for COMPACT DISC. ■ (**disc**) *dated* a phonograph record. ■ (**discs**) one of the suits in some tarot packs, corresponding to coins in others. **2** a shape or surface that is round and flat in appearance: *the smudged yellow disk of the moon.* **3** a roundish, flattened part in an animal or plant, in particular: ■ (**disc** or **in·ter·ver·te·bral disc**) a layer of cartilage separating adjacent vertebrae in the spine: *he suffered a prolapsed disc.* ■ *Botany* (in a composite flowerhead of the daisy family) a close-packed cluster of disk florets in the center, forming the yellow part of the flowerhead.
▸v. [trans.] cultivate (a field) with a disk harrow. ▷mid 17th cent. (originally referring to the seemingly flat round form of the sun or moon): from French *disque* or Latin *discus* (see DISCUS). **—disk·less** *adj.*

> *USAGE* Generally speaking, the U.S. spelling is **disk** and the British spelling is **disc**, although there is much overlap and variation between the two. In particular the spelling for senses relating to computers is nearly always **disk**, as in **floppy disk**, **disk drive**, etc., but **compact disc**, **disc brakes**, **disc camera**.

disk drive ▸*n.* a device that allows a computer to read from and write to computer disks.

disk·ette /disˈket/ ▸*n.* another term for FLOPPY DISK.

disk flo·ret ▸*n. Botany* (in a composite flowerhead of the daisy family) any of a number of small, tubular, and usually fertile florets that form the disk. In rayless plants such as the tansy, the flowerhead is composed entirely of disk florets. Compare with RAY FLORET.

disk har·row ▸*n.* a harrow with cutting edges consisting of a row of concave disks set at an oblique angle.

disk jock·ey ▸*n.* variant spelling of DISC JOCKEY.

Dis·ko /ˈdiskō/ an island with extensive coal deposits on the western coast of Greenland. Its chief settlement is Godhavn.

disk op·er·at·ing sys·tem ▸*n.* see **DOS**.

disk wheel ▸*n.* a wheel, esp. a bicycle wheel, with a central disk in place of spokes.

dis·like /disˈlīk/ ▸*v.* [*trans.*] feel distaste for or hostility toward: *he was not distressed by the death of a man he had always disliked.*
▸*n.* a feeling of distaste or hostility: *despite her dislike of publicity, she was quite a celebrated figure* | *they had* ***taken a dislike to*** *each other.* ■ a thing to which one feels aversion: *I know all his likes and dislikes.* **—dis·lik·a·ble** (also **dis·like·a·ble**) *adj.*

dis·lo·cate /disˈlōkāt; ˈdislōˌkāt/ ▸*v.* [*trans.*] disturb the normal arrangement or position of (something, typically a joint in the body): *he dislocated his shoulder in training.* ■ (often **be dislocated**) disturb the organization of; disrupt: *trade was dislocated by a famine.* ■ (often **be dislocated**) move from its proper place or position: *the symbol is dislocated from its political context.* ▷late 16th cent.: probably a back-formation from DISLOCATION, but perhaps from medieval Latin *dislocatus* 'moved from a former position,' from the verb *dislocare.*

dis·lo·ca·tion /ˌdislōˈkāshən/ ▸*n.* disturbance from a proper, original, or usual place or state: *he fell prey to loneliness and a wrenching sense of dislocation* | *the social dislocations caused by government policies.* ■ injury or disability caused when the normal position of a joint or other part of the body is disturbed: *congenital dislocation of the hip* | *dealing with fractures and dislocations.* ■ *Crystallography* a displacement of part of a crystal lattice structure. ▷late Middle English: from Old French, or from medieval Latin *dislocatio(n-)*, from the verb *dislocare* (see DISLOCATE), based on Latin *locare* 'to place.'

dis·lodge /disˈläj/ ▸*v.* [*trans.*] remove from an established or fixed position: *the hoofs of their horses dislodged loose stones* | *figurative this gripping race still offers the opportunity to dislodge the leader.* ▷late Middle English: from Old French *deslogier*, from *des-* (expressing reversal) + *logier* 'encamp,' from *loge* (see LODGE).

—**dis·lodge·a·ble** *adj.* —**dis·lodg·ment** (also **dis·lodge·ment**) *n.*

dis·loy·al /dis'loiəl/ ▸*adj.* failing to be loyal to a person, country, or body to which one has obligations: *she felt that inquiring into her father's past would be* **disloyal to** *her mother.* ■ (of an action, speech, or thought) demonstrating a lack of loyalty: *disloyal mutterings about his leadership.* ▷late 15th cent.: from Old French *desloial*, from *des-* (expressing negation) + *loial* 'loyal.' —**dis·loy·al·ly** *adv.* —**dis·loy·al·ty** /-tē/ *n.*

dis·mal /'dizməl/ ▸*adj.* depressing; dreary: *the dismal weather made the late afternoon seem like evening.* ■ (of a person or a mood) gloomy: *his dismal mood was not dispelled by finding the house empty.* ■ *informal* pitifully or disgracefully bad: *he shuddered as he watched his team's dismal performance.* ▷late Middle English: from earlier *dismal* (noun), denoting the two days in each month that in medieval times were believed to be unlucky, from Anglo-Norman French *dis mal*, from medieval Latin *dies mali* 'evil days.' —**dis·mal·ly** *adv.* —**dis·mal·ness** *n.*

dis·mal sci·ence ▸*n.* [in *sing.*] (usu. **the dismal science**) *humorous* economics.

Dis·mal Swamp another name for GREAT DISMAL SWAMP.

dis·man·tle /dis'mantl/ ▸*v.* [*trans.*] (often **be dismantled**) take to pieces: *the engines were dismantled and the bits piled into a heap figurative the old regime was dismantled.* ▷late 16th cent. (in the sense 'destroy the defensive capability of (a fortification)'): from Old French *desmanteler*, from *des-* (expressing reversal) + *manteler* 'fortify' (from Latin *mantellum* 'cloak'). —**dis·man·tle·ment** *n.* —**dis·man·tler** /-t(ə)lər/ *n.*

dis·mast /dis'mast/ ▸*v.* [*trans.*] break or topple the mast or masts of (a ship): [as *adj.*] (**dismasted**) *a dismasted ship wallowing in stormy seas.*

dis·may /dis'mā/ ▸*v.* [*trans.*] (usu. **be dismayed**) cause (someone) to feel consternation and distress: *they were dismayed by the U-turn in policy.*
▸*n.* consternation and distress, typically that caused by something unexpected: ***to his dismay****, she left him.* ▷Middle English: from Old French, based on Latin *dis-* (expressing negation) + the Germanic base of MAY[1].

dis·mem·ber /dis'membər/ ▸*v.* [*trans.*] cut off the limbs of (a person or animal): *I can picture you in a white jacket dismembering rats* | [as *adj.*] (**dismembered**) *he buried their dismembered bodies in the back yard.* ■ partition or divide up (a territory or organization): *Russia intended to dismember the Ottoman Empire.* ▷Middle English: from Old French *desmembrer*, based on Latin *dis-* 'apart' + *membrum* 'limb.' —**dis·mem·ber·ment** *n.*

dis·miss /dis'mis/ ▸*v.* [*trans.*] order or allow to leave; send away: *she dismissed the taxi at the corner of the road.* ■ discharge from employment or office: *CBS Records dismissed another 120 people.* See note at EJECT. ■ treat as unworthy of serious consideration: *it would be easy to* **dismiss** *him* **as** *all brawn and no brain.* ■ deliberately cease to think about: *he suspected a double meaning in her words, but dismissed the thought.* ■ [*intrans.*] (of a group assembled under someone's authority) disperse: *he told his company to dismiss.* ■ *Law* refuse further hearing to (a case): *the judge dismissed the case for lack of evidence.* ■ (in sports) defeat or end an opponent's turn. ▷late Middle English: from medieval Latin *dismiss-*, variant of Latin *dimiss-* 'sent away,' from the verb *dimittere.* —**dis·miss·al** /-əl/ *n.* —**dis·miss·i·ble** *adj.*

dis·mis·sive /dis'misiv/ ▸*adj.* feeling or showing that something is unworthy of consideration: *he is too dismissive of the importance of the industrialists.* —**dis·mis·sive·ly** *adv.* —**dis·mis·sive·ness** *n.*

dis·mount /dis'mount/ ▸*v.* **1** [*intrans.*] alight from a horse, bicycle, or other thing that one is riding. ■ [*trans.*] cause to fall or alight. **2** [*trans.*] remove (something) from its support: *we have to dismount the pump.* ■ *Computing* make (a disk or disk drive) unavailable for use.
▸*n.* *Gymnastics* a move in which a gymnast jumps off an apparatus or completes a floor exercise: *on the uneven bars the women go for ever more complex dismounts.* ▷mid 16th cent.: from DIS- + MOUNT[1], probably on the pattern of Old French *desmonter*, medieval Latin *dismontare.*

Dis·ney /'diznē/, Walt (1901–66), U.S. animator and movie and television producer; full name *Walter Elias Disney*. He became known for his cartoon characters that included Mickey Mouse (who first appeared in 1928), Donald Duck, Goofy, and Pluto. *Snow White and the Seven Dwarfs* (1937) was the first full-length cartoon with sound and color. Other notable animated movies: *Pinocchio* (1940), *Dumbo* (1941), *Bambi* (1942), *Cinderella* (1950), and *Peter Pan* (1953).

Dis·ney·land ▸*n.* a theme park in Anaheim, California, that opened in 1955. [from Walt *Disney*] ■ a large, bustling place filled with colorful attractions. ■ a place of fantasy or make-believe: *their own think tank, their own Disneyland of future ideas* [as *adj.*] *Disneyland conceptions of defense which have no genuine relevance.*

Dis·ney World an amusement park in Lake Buena Vista, southwest of Orlando, Florida, that opened in 1971. Formally **Walt Disney World.**

dis·o·be·di·ence /ˌdisə'bēdēəns/ ▸*n.* failure or refusal to obey rules or someone in authority: *he made no allowances for neglect or disobedience of orders.*

dis·o·be·di·ent /ˌdisə'bēdēənt/ ▸*adj.* refusing to obey rules or someone in authority: *Larry was stern with disobedient employees.* ▷late Middle English: from Old French *desobedient*, based on Latin *oboedient-* 'obeying' (see OBEDIENT). —**dis·o·be·di·ent·ly** *adv.*

dis·o·bey /ˌdisə'bā/ ▸*v.* [*trans.*] fail to obey (rules, a command, or someone in authority): *around 1,000 soldiers had disobeyed orders and surrendered.* ▷late Middle English: from Old French *desobeir*, based on Latin *oboedire* 'obey' (see OBEY). —**dis·o·bey·er** *n.*

dis·o·blige /ˌdisə'blīj/ ▸*v.* [*trans.*] offend (someone) by not acting in accordance with their wishes: *one didn't disoblige them if one could help it.* ▷late 16th cent. (in the sense 'release from an obligation'): from French *désobliger*, based on Latin *obligare* 'oblige.'

dis·o·blig·ing /ˌdisə'blījiNG/ ▸*adj.* deliberately unhelpful; uncooperative.

di·so·my /dī'sōmē/ ▸*n.* *Genetics* the condition of having a chromosome represented twice in a chromosomal complement. ▷late 20th cent.: from DI-[1] 'two' + -SOME[3] + -Y[3]. —**di·so·mic** /-mik/ *adj.*

dis·or·der /dis'ôrdər/ ▸*n.* a state of confusion: *tiresome days of mess and disorder.* ■ the disruption of peaceful and law-abiding behavior: *recurrent food crises led to periodic outbreaks of disorder.* ■ *Medicine* a disruption of normal physical or mental functions; a disease or abnormal condition: *eating disorders* | *an improved understanding of mental disorder.*
▸*v.* [*trans.*] [usu. as *adj.*] (**disordered**) disrupt the systematic functioning or neat arrangement of: *she went to comb her disordered hair* | *his sleep is disordered.* ■ *Medicine* disrupt the healthy or normal functioning of: *a patient who is mentally disordered.* ▷late 15th cent. (as a verb in the sense 'upset the order of'): alteration, influenced by ORDER, of earlier *disordain*, from Old French *desordener*, ultimately based on Latin *ordinare* 'ordain.'

dis·or·der·ly /dis'ôrdərlē/ ▸*adj.* lacking organization; untidy: *his life was as disorderly as ever* | *a disorderly pile of books.* ■ involving or contributing to a breakdown of peaceful and law-abiding behavior: *they had no intention of staging a disorderly protest.* —**dis·or·der·li·ness** *n.*

dis·or·der·ly con·duct ▸*n.* *Law* unruly behavior constituting a minor offense.

dis·or·der·ly house ▸*n.* *archaic Law* a brothel.

dis·or·gan·ize /dis'ôrgəˌnīz/ ▸*v.* [*trans.*] disrupt the systematic order or functioning of: *attacks on leading government figures might disorganize the regime.* ▷late 18th cent. (dating from the French Revolution): from French *désorganiser.* —**dis·or·gan·i·za·tion** /-ˌôrgənə'zāSHən/ *n.*

dis·or·gan·ized /dis'ôrgəˌnīzd/ ▸*adj.* not properly planned and controlled: *the campaign was hopelessly disorganized.* ■ (of a person) unable to plan one's activities efficiently: *my boss decided that I was unproductive and disorganized.*

dis·o·ri·ent /dis'ôrēˌent/ ▸*v.* [*trans.*] [often as *adj.*] (**disoriented**) make (someone) lose their sense of direction: *she was so disoriented that Joe had to walk her to her room.* ■ make (someone) feel confused: *jet lag leaves you irritable, disoriented, and tired.* ▷mid 17th cent.: from French *désorienter* 'turn from the east.'

dis·o·ri·en·tate /dis'ôrēənˌtāt/ ▸*v.* another term for DISORIENT. —**dis·o·ri·en·ta·tion** /-ˌôrēən'tāSHən/ *n.*

dis·own /dis'ōn/ ▸*v.* [*trans.*] refuse to acknowledge or maintain any connection with: *Howard's rich family had disowned him because of his marriage.* —**dis·own·er** *n.* —**dis·own·ment** *n.*

dis·par·age /dis'parij/ ▸*v.* [*trans.*] regard or represent as being of little worth: *he never missed an opportunity to disparage his competitors* | [as *adj.*] (**disparaging**) *disparaging remarks.* ▷late Middle English (in the sense 'marry someone of unequal rank,' also 'bring discredit on'): from Old French *desparagier* 'marry someone of unequal rank,' based on Latin *par* 'equal.' —**dis·par·age·ment** *n.* —**dis·par·ag·ing·ly** *adv.*

dis·pa·rate /'dispərit; di'sparit/ ▸*adj.* essentially different in kind; not allowing comparison: *they inhabit disparate worlds of thought.* ■ containing elements very different from one another: *a culturally disparate country.*
▸*n.* (**disparates**) *archaic* things so unlike that there is no basis for comparison. ▷late Middle English: from Latin *disparatus* 'separated,' from the verb *disparare*, from *dis-* 'apart' + *parare* 'to prepare'; influenced in sense by Latin *dispar* 'unequal.' —**dis·pa·rate·ly** *adv.* —**dis·pa·rate·ness** *n.*

dis·par·i·ty /di'sparitē/ ▸*n.* (*pl.* **-ties**) a great difference: *economic* **disparities between** *different regions of the country* | *the great disparity of weight between the sun and the planets.* ▷mid 16th cent.: from French *disparité*, from late Latin *disparitas*, based on Latin *paritas* 'parity.'

dis·pas·sion·ate /dis'paSHənit/ ▸*adj.* not influenced by strong emotion, and so able to be rational and impartial: *she dealt with life's disasters in a calm, dispassionate way.* —**dis·pas·sion** /-SHən/ *n.* —**dis·pas·sion·ate·ly** *adv.* —**dis·pas·sion·ate·ness** *n.*

dis·patch /dis'paCH/ (also **des·patch**) ▸*v.* [*trans.*] **1** send off to a destination or for a purpose: *he dispatched messages back to base* | [*trans.*] *the mayor dispatched 150 police officers to restore order.* **2** deal with (a task, problem, or opponent) quickly and efficiently: *they dispatched the opposition.* ■ kill: *he dispatched the animal with one blow.* See note at KILL.
▸*n.* **1** the sending of someone or something to a destination or for a purpose: *a resolution authorizing the dispatch of a peacekeeping force.* ■ speed in action: *the situation might change, so he should proceed* ***with dispatch.*** **2** an official report on state or military affairs: *in his battle dispatch he described the gunner's bravery.* ■ a report sent in by a newspaper's correspondent from a faraway place. **3** the killing of someone or something: *the legendary dispatch of villains by a hero.* ▷early 16th cent.: from Italian *dispacciare* or Spanish *despachar* 'expedite,' from *dis-*, *des-* (expressing reversal) + the base of Italian *impacciare*, Spanish *empachar* 'hinder.' —**dis·patch·er** *n.*

dis·patch box ▸*n.* (also **dispatch case**) a container for dispatches, esp. official state or military documents.

dis·patch rid·er ▸*n.* *chiefly Brit.* a messenger who delivers urgent business documents or military dispatches by motorcycle or (formerly) on horseback.

dis·pel /dis'pel/ ▸*v.* (**-pelled, -pel·ling**) [*trans.*] make (a doubt, feeling, or belief) disappear: *the brightness of the day did nothing to dispel Elaine's dejection.* ■ drive (something) away; scatter: *sprinkle catnip tea to dispel beetles from garden plants.* See note at SCATTER. ▷late Middle English: from Latin *dispellere*, from *dis-* 'apart' + *pellere* 'to drive.' —**dis·pel·ler** *n.*

dis·pen·sa·ble /dis'pensəbəl/ ▸*adj.* able to be replaced or done without; superfluous: *tiny battlefield robots will be cheap and dispensable.* ■ (of a law or other rule) able to be relaxed in special cases. ▷early 16th cent. (in the sense 'permissible in special circumstances'): from medieval Latin *dispensabilis*, from Latin *dispensare* (see DISPENSE). —**dis·pen·sa·bil·i·ty** /-ˌpensə'bilitē/ *n.*

dis·pen·sa·ry /dis'pensərē/ ▸*n.* (*pl.* **-ries**) **1** a room where medicines are prepared and provided. **2** a clinic provided by public or charitable funds. ▷late 17th cent.: from medieval Latin *dispensarium*, neuter (used as a noun) of *dispensarius*, from Latin *dispensare* (see DISPENSE).

dis·pen·sa·tion /ˌdispən'sāSHən; -pen-/ ▸*n.* **1** exemption from a rule or usual requirement: *although she was too young, she was given special dispensation to play two matches* | *they were given a dispensation to take most of the first week off.* ■ permission to be exempted from the laws or observances of a church: *he received papal dispensation to hold a number of benefices.* **2** a system of order, government, or organization of a nation, community, etc., esp. as existing at a particular time: *scholarship is conveyed to a wider audience than under the old dispensation.* ■ (in Christian theology) a divinely ordained order prevailing at a particular period of history: *the Mosaic dispensation.* ■ *archaic* an act of divine providence: *the laws to which the creator in all his dispensations conforms.* **3** the action of distributing or supplying something: *regulations controlling dispensation of medications.* ▷late Middle English:

from Latin *dispensatio(n-)*, from the verb *dispensare* (see DISPENSE). —**dis·pen·sa·tion·al** /-SHənl/ *adj.*

dis·pen·sa·tion·al·ism /ˌdispən'sāSHənlˌizəm; -pen-/ ▸*n. Christian Theology* belief in a system of historical progression, as revealed in the Bible, consisting of a series of stages in God's self-revelation and plan of salvation. —**dis·pen·sa·tion·al·ist** *n.*

dis·pense /dis'pens/ ▸*v.* **1** [*trans.*] distribute or provide (a service or information) to a number of people: *he dispensed a gentle pat on Claude's back.* ■ (of a machine) supply (a product or cash): *the machines dispense a range of drinks and snacks.* ■ (of a pharmacist) make up and give out (medicine) according to a doctor's prescription. **2** [*intrans.*] (**dispense with**) manage without; get rid of: *let's dispense with the formalities, shall we?* ■ give special exemption from (a law or rule): *the Secretary of State was empowered to dispense with the nationality requirement in individual cases.* ■ [*trans.*] grant (someone) an exemption from a religious obligation: *the pope personally nominated him as bishop, **dispensing** him **from** his impediment.* ▷late Middle English: via Old French from Latin *dispensare* 'continue to weigh out or disburse,' from the verb *dispendere*, based on *pendere* 'weigh.'

▸*PHRASE* □ **dispense with someone's services** dismiss someone from a job.

dis·pens·er /dis'pensər/ ▸*n.* a person or thing that dispenses something: *his role as protector of the weak and dispenser of justice.* ■ [often with *adj.*] an automatic machine or container that is designed to release a specific amount of something: *a paper towel dispenser.*

dis·per·sal /dis'pərsəl/ ▸*n.* the action or process of distributing things or people over a wide area: *the dispersal of people to increasingly distant suburbs.* ■ the splitting up of a group or gathering of people, causing them to leave in different directions: *the dispersal of the crowd by mounted police.* ■ the splitting up and selling off of a collection of artifacts or books: *the dispersal of the John Willett Collection.*

dis·per·sant /dis'pərsənt/ ▸*n.* a liquid or gas used to disperse small particles in a medium.

dis·perse /dis'pərs/ ▸*v.* [*trans.*] distribute or spread over a wide area: *storms can disperse seeds via high altitudes | camping sites could be **dispersed among** trees so as to be out of sight.* See note at SCATTER. ■ go or cause to go in different directions or to different destinations: [*intrans.*] *the crowd dispersed* | [*trans.*] *the police used tear gas to disperse the protesters.* ■ cause (gas, smoke, mist, or cloud) to thin out and eventually disappear: *winds dispersed the bomb's radioactive cloud high in the atmosphere.* ■ [*intrans.*] thin out and disappear: *the earlier mist had dispersed.* ■ *Physics* divide (light) into constituents of different wavelengths. ■ *Chemistry* distribute (small particles) uniformly in a medium.

▸*adj.* [*attrib.*] *Chemistry* denoting a phase dispersed in another phase, as in a colloid: *emulsions should be examined after storage for droplet size of the disperse phase.* ▷late Middle English: from Latin *dispers-* 'scattered,' from the verb *dispergere*, from *dis-* 'widely' + *spargere* 'scatter, strew.' —**dis·pers·er** *n.* —**dis·pers·i·ble** *adj.* —**dis·per·sive** /-siv/ *adj.*

dis·per·sion /dis'pərZHən; -SHən/ ▸*n.* the action or process of distributing things or people over a wide area: *some seeds rely on birds for dispersion.* ■ the state of being dispersed over a wide area: *the general dispersion of Hellenistic culture.* ■ *Ecology* the pattern of distribution of individuals within a habitat. ■ (also **the Dispersion**) another term for DIASPORA. ■ a mixture of one substance dispersed in another medium. ■ *Physics* the separation of white light into colors, or the separation of any radiation according to wavelength. ■ *Statistics* the extent to which values of a variable differ from a fixed value such as the mean. ▷late Middle English: from late Latin *dispersio(n-)*, from Latin *dispergere* (see DISPERSE).

dis·pir·it /di'spirit/ ▸*v.* [*trans.*] (often **be dispirited**) cause (someone) to lose enthusiasm or hope: *the army was dispirited by the uncomfortable winter conditions* | [as *adj.*] (**dispiriting**) *it was a dispiriting occasion.* —**dis·pir·it·ed·ly** *adv.* —**dis·pir·it·ed·ness** *n.* —**dis·pir·it·ing·ly** *adv.*

dis·place /dis'plās/ ▸*v.* [*trans.*] take over the place, position, or role of (someone or something): *in the northern states of India, Hindi has largely displaced English.* See note at REPLACE. ■ cause (something) to move from its proper or usual place: *he seems to have displaced some vertebrae.* ■ (usu. **be displaced**) force (someone) to leave their home, typically because of war, persecution, or natural disaster: *thousands of people have been displaced by the civil war.* ■ remove (someone) from a job or position of authority against their will: *his aides were discredited and displaced.* ▷mid 16th cent.: from Old French *desplacer*.

dis·placed per·son ▸*n.* a person who is forced to leave their home country because of war, persecution, or natural disaster; a refugee.

dis·place·ment /dis'plāsmənt/ ▸*n.* **1** the moving of something from its place or position: *vertical displacement of the shoreline | a displacement of the vertebra at the bottom of the spine.* ■ the removal of someone or something by someone or something else that takes their place: *males may be able to resist displacement by other males.* ■ the enforced departure of people from their homes, typically because of war, persecution, or natural disaster: *the displacement of farmers by guerrilla activity.* ■ the amount by which a thing is moved from its normal position: *a displacement of 6.8 meters along the San Andreas fault.* **2** the occupation by a submerged body or part of a body of a volume that would otherwise be occupied by a fluid. ■ the amount or weight of fluid that would fill such a volume in the case of a floating ship, used as a measure of the ship's size: *the submarine has a surface displacement of 2,185 tons.* ■ *technical* the volume swept by a reciprocating system, as in a pump or engine. **3** *Psychoanalysis* the unconscious transfer of an intense emotion from its original object to another one: *this phobia was linked with the displacement of fear of his father.* **4** *Physics* the component of an electric field due to free separated charges, regardless of any polarizing effects. ■ the vector representing such a component. ■ the flux density of such an electric field.

dis·place·ment ac·tiv·i·ty ▸*n. Psychology* an animal or human activity that seems inappropriate to the context, such as head-scratching when one is confused, considered to arise unconsciously when a conflict between antagonistic urges cannot be resolved.

dis·place·ment pump ▸*n.* a pump in which liquid is moved out of the pump chamber by a moving surface or by the introduction of compressed air or gas.

dis·place·ment ton ▸*n.* see TON[1] (sense 1).

dis·play /dis'plā/ ▸*v.* [*trans.*] make a prominent exhibition of (something) in a place where it can be easily seen: *the palace used to display a series of Flemish tapestries | a handwritten notice was displayed in the ticket office.* ■ (of a computer or other device) show (information) on a screen. ■ give a conspicuous demonstration of (a quality, emotion, or skill): *the aggressive kind of baseball he displayed as a player.* ■ [*intrans.*] (of a male bird, reptile, or fish) engage in a specialized pattern of behavior that is intended to attract a mate: *she photographed the peacock, which chose that moment to display.*

▸*n.* **1** a performance, show, or event intended for public entertainment: *a display of fireworks.* ■ a collection of objects arranged for public viewing: *the museum houses an informative display of rocks | work by lesser-known artists is also **on display*** | [as *adj.*] *a display case.* ■ a notable or conspicuous demonstration of a particular type of behavior, emotion, or skill: *a display of great virtuosity.* ■ conspicuous or flashy exhibition; ostentation: *a flagrant display of wealth.* ■ a specialized pattern of behavior by the males of some species of birds, reptiles, and fish that is intended to attract a mate: *the teal were indulging in delightful courtship displays.* ■ *Printing* the arrangement and choice of type in a style intended to attract attention. **2** an electronic device for the visual presentation of data: *a 17-inch color display* | [as *adj.*] *a visual display screen.* ■ the process or facility of presenting data on a computer screen or other device: *the processing and display of high volumes of information.* ■ the data shown on a computer screen or other device. ▷Middle English (in the sense 'unfurl, unfold'): from Old French *despleier*, from Latin *displicare* 'scatter, disperse' (in medieval Latin 'unfold'). Compare with DEPLOY. —**dis·play·er** *n.*

dis·play ad ▸*n.* a large advertisement, esp. in a newspaper or magazine, that features eye-catching type or illustrations.

dis·played /dis'plād/ ▸*adj.* **1** (of information) shown on a computer screen or other device: *a utility designed to allow you to cut up pieces of displayed graphics.* **2** *Heraldry* (of a bird of prey) depicted with the wings extended. ■ (of the wings of a bird of prey) extended.

dis·play type ▸*n.* large or eye-catching type used for headings or advertisements.

dis·please /dis'plēz/ ▸*v.* [*trans.*] make (someone) feel annoyed or dissatisfied: *the tone of the letter displeased him* | [as *adj.*] (**displeasing**) *it was not entirely displeasing to be the center of such a drama.* ▷late Middle English: from Old French *desplaisir*, from *des-* (expressing reversal) + *plaisir* 'to please,' from Latin *placere*. —**dis·pleas·ing·ly** *adv.*

dis·pleas·ure /dis'pleZHər/ ▸*n.* a feeling of annoyance or disapproval: *his grin turns into thin-lipped displeasure.*

▸*v.* [*trans.*] *archaic* annoy; displease: *not for worlds would I do aught that might displeasure thee.* ▷late Middle English: from Old French *desplaisir* (see DISPLEASE), influenced by PLEASURE.

dis·port /dis'pôrt/ ▸*v.* [*intrans.*] *archaic or humorous* enjoy oneself unrestrainedly; frolic: *a painting of lords and ladies **disporting themselves** by a lake.*

▸*n.* diversion from work or serious matters; recreation or amusement: *the King and all his Court were met for solace and disport.* ■ *archaic* a pastime, game, or sport. ▷late Middle English: from Old French *desporter*, from *des-* 'away' + *porter* 'carry' (from Latin *portare*).

dis·pos·a·ble /dis'pōzəbəl/ ▸*adj.* **1** (of an article) intended to be used once and then thrown away: *disposable diapers | a disposable razor.* ■ (of a person or idea) able to be dispensed with; easily dismissed: *the poor performer is motivated by the fear that he or she is highly disposable.* **2** (chiefly of financial assets) readily available for the owner's use as required: *he made a mental inventory of his disposable assets.*

▸*n.* an article designed to be thrown away after use: *don't buy disposables, such as razors, cups, and plates.* —**dis·pos·a·bil·i·ty** /-ˌpōzə'bilitē/ *n.*

dis·pos·a·ble in·come ▸*n.* income remaining after deduction of taxes and other mandatory charges, available to be spent or saved as one wishes. Compare with DISCRETIONARY INCOME.

dis·pos·al /dis'pōzəl/ ▸*n.* **1** the action or process of throwing away or getting rid of something: *the disposal of radioactive waste.* ■ (also **dis·pos·er**) *informal* an electrically operated device fitted to the waste pipe of a kitchen sink for grinding up food waste: *garbage disposals that never worked.* **2** the sale of shares, property, or other assets: *the disposal of his shares in the company.* **3** the arrangement or positioning of something: *she brushed her hair carefully, as if her success lay in the sleek disposal of each gleaming black thread.*

▸*PHRASE* □ **at one's disposal** available for one to use whenever or however one wishes: *a helicopter was put at their disposal.*

dis·pose /dis'pōz/ ▸*v.* **1** [*intrans.*] (**dispose of**) get rid of by throwing away or giving or selling to someone else: *whose responsibility is it to dispose of scrap materials? | people now have substantial assets to dispose of after their death.* ■ *informal* kill; destroy: *her lover came up with hundreds of schemes for disposing of her husband.* ■ overcome (a rival or threat): *team members were buoyant after they disposed of the champions.* ■ *informal* consume (food or drink) quickly or enthusiastically: *she watched him dispose of a large slice of cheese.* **2** [*trans.*] arrange in a particular position: *the chief disposed his attendants in a circle.* ■ bring (someone) into a particular frame of mind: *prolactin is released, **disposing** you **toward** sleep* | [*trans.*] *fundamentalism disposes you to believe in miracles.* ■ [*intrans.*] *poetic/literary* determine the course of events: *the city proposed, but the unions disposed.* [from the proverb 'Man proposes, (but) God disposes,' translating Latin *Homo proponit, sed Deus disponit* (Thomas à Kempis's *De Imitatione Christ* I. xix).] ▷late Middle English: from Old French *disposer*, from Latin *disponere* 'arrange,' influenced by *dispositus* 'arranged' and Old French *poser* 'to place.' —**dis·pos·er** *n. a waste disposer | a disposer of grants and subsidies.*

dis·posed /dis'pōzd/ ▸*adj.* [*predic.*, usu. with *infinitive*] inclined or willing: *James didn't seem disposed to take the hint.* ■ [with *submodifier*] having a specified attitude to or toward: *it is expected that he will be favorably **disposed toward** the proposals.*

dis·po·si·tion /ˌdispə'ziSHən/ ▸*n.* **1** a person's inherent qualities of mind and character: *a sweet-natured girl of a placid disposition.* ■ [often with *infinitive*] an inclination or tendency: *the cattle showed a decided disposition to run | the judge's **disposition to** clemency.* **2** the way in which something is placed or arranged, esp. in relation to other things: *the plan need not be accurate so long as it shows the disposition of the rooms.* ■ the action of arranging or ordering people or things in a particular way: *the prerogative gives the state widespread powers regarding the disposition and control of the armed forces* ■ (**dispositions**) military preparations, in particular the stationing of troops ready for attack or defense: *the new strategic dispositions of our forces.* **3** *Law* the action of distributing or transferring property or money to someone, in particular by bequest: *this is a tax that affects the disposition of assets on death.* **4** the power to deal with something as one pleases: *if Napoleon had had railroads* ***at his disposition****, he would have been invincible.* ■ *archaic* the determination of events, esp. by divine power. ▷late Middle English: via Old French from Latin *dispositio(n-)*, from *disponere* 'arrange' (see DISPOSE).

dis·pos·i·tive /dis'päzitiv/ ▸*adj.* relating to or bringing about the settlement of an issue or the disposition of property: *such litigation will rarely be dispositive of any question.* ■ *Law* dealing with the disposition of property by deed or will: *the testator had to make his signature after making the dispositive provisions.* ■ dealing with the settling of international conflicts by an agreed disposition of disputed territories: *a peace settlement in the nature of a dispositive treaty.* ▷late Middle English (in the sense 'contributory, conducive'): from Old French, or from medieval Latin *dispositivus*, from Latin *disposit-* 'arranged, disposed,' from the verb *disponere* (see DISPOSE).

dis·pos·sess /,dispə'zes/ ▸*v.* [*trans.*] (often **be dispossessed**) deprive (someone) of something that they own, typically land or property: *they were* ***dispossessed of*** *lands and properties at the time of the Reformation* | [as *plural n.*] (**the dispossessed**) *a champion of the poor and the dispossessed.* ■ oust (a person) from a dwelling or position: *he used to ride out and dispossess his tenants as the spirit moved him.* ▷late 15th cent.: from Old French *despossesser*, from *des-* (expressing reversal) + *possesser* 'possess.' —**dis·pos·ses·sion** /-'zeshən/ *n.*

dis·praise /dis'prāz/ ▸*n. rare* censure; criticism: *this engraving has on occasion elicited dispraise for Raphael.* ▸*v.* [*trans.*] *archaic* express censure or criticism of (someone): *men cannot praise Dryden without dispraising Coleridge.* ▷Middle English: from Old French *despreisier*, based on late Latin *depreciare* (see DEPRECIATE).

dis·proof /dis'pro͞of/ ▸*n.* a set of facts that prove that something is untrue: *the theory also provides a disproof of the principle of closure.* ■ the action of proving that something is untrue: *considerations that are subject to scientific verification or disproof.*

dis·pro·por·tion /,disprə'pôrshən/ ▸*n.* an instance of being out of proportion with something else: *there is a disproportion between the scale of expenditure and any benefit that could possibly result.* ▷mid 16th cent.: from DIS- (expressing absence) + PROPORTION, on the pattern of French *disproportion*. —**dis·pro·por·tion·al** /-shənl/ *adj.* —**dis·pro·por·tion·al·i·ty** /-,pôrshə'nalitē/ *n.* —**dis·pro·por·tion·al·ly** /-shənl-ē/ *adv.*

dis·pro·por·tion·ate[1] /,disprə'pôrshənit/ ▸*adj.* too large or too small in comparison with something else: *people on lower incomes spend a disproportionate amount of their income on fuel* | *their sentences were disproportionate to the offenses they had committed.* ▷mid 16th cent.: from DIS- (expressing absence) + PROPORTIONATE, on the pattern of French *disproportionné*. —**dis·pro·por·tion·ate·ly** *adv.* —**dis·pro·por·tion·ate·ness** *n.*

dis·pro·por·tion·ate[2] /,disprə'pôrshə,nāt/ ▸*v.* [*intrans.*] *Chemistry* undergo disproportionation: *water disproportionates to oxygen and hydrogen.*

dis·pro·por·tion·a·tion /,disprə,pôrshə'nāshən/ ▸*n.* *Chemistry* a reaction in which a substance is simultaneously oxidized and reduced, giving two different products.

dis·prove /dis'pro͞ov/ ▸*v.* [*trans.*] prove that (something) is false: *he has given the Department of Transportation two months to disprove the allegation.* ▷late Middle English: from Old French *desprover*. —**dis·prov·a·ble** *adj.*

dis·put·a·ble /dis'pyo͞otəbəl/ ▸*adj.* not established as fact, and so open to question or debate: *whether it can be described as art criticism may be disputable.* ▷late 15th cent.: from Latin *disputabilis*, from the verb *disputare* 'to estimate,' later 'to dispute' (see DISPUTE). —**dis·put·a·bly** /-blē/ *adv.*

dis·pu·ta·tion /,dispyo͞o'tāshən/ ▸*n.* debate or argument: *promoting consensus rather than disputation* | *a lengthy disputation about the rights and wrongs of a particular request.* ■ formal academic debate: *the founding father of logical disputation* | *scholastic disputations.* ▷late Middle English: from Latin *disputatio(n-)*, from the verb *disputare* (see DISPUTE). —**dis·put·a·tive** /-'pyo͞otətiv/ *adj.*

dis·pu·ta·tious /,dispyo͞o'tāshəs/ ▸*adj.* (of a person) fond of having heated arguments: *a congenial hangout for disputatious academics.* ■ (of an argument or situation) motivated by or causing strong opinions: *disputatious council meetings.* —**dis·pu·ta·tious·ly** *adv.* —**dis·pu·ta·tious·ness** *n.*

dis·pute /dis'pyo͞ot/ ▸*n.* a disagreement, argument, or debate: *a territorial dispute between the two countries* | *the question* ***in dispute*** *is altogether insignificant.* See note at QUARREL. ■ a disagreement between management and employees that leads to an action of protest by the employees: *if this dispute cannot be resolved quickly, a formal strike is inevitable.* ▸*v.* [*trans.*] argue about (something); discuss heatedly: *I disputed the charge on the bill* | [*intrans.*] *he taught and* ***disputed with*** *local poets.* ■ question whether (a statement or alleged fact) is true or valid: *the accusations are not disputed* | [with *clause*] *the estate disputes that it is responsible for the embankment.* ■ compete for; strive to win: *the two drivers crashed while disputing the lead.* ■ *archaic* resist (a landing or advance): *the Sudanese chose Teb as the ground upon which to dispute the advance.* ▷Middle English: via Old French from Latin *disputare* 'to estimate' (in late Latin 'to dispute'), from *dis-* 'apart' + *putare* 'reckon.' —**dis·pu·tant** /-'pyo͞otnt/ *n.* —**dis·put·er** *n.*

▸PHRASES □ **beyond dispute** certain or certainly; without doubt: *the main part of his argument was beyond dispute.* □ **open to dispute** not definitely decided: *such estimates are always open to dispute.*

dis·qual·i·fi·ca·tion /dis,kwäləfi'kāshən/ ▸*n.* the action of disqualifying or the state of being disqualified. ■ a fact or condition that disqualifies someone from a position or activity: *such an offense is no longer a disqualification for office.*

dis·qual·i·fy /dis'kwälə,fī/ ▸*v.* (**-fies, -fied**) [*trans.*] (often **be disqualified**) pronounce (someone) ineligible for an office or activity because of an offense or infringement: *he was* ***disqualified from*** *driving for six months.* ■ eliminate (someone) from a competition because of an infringement of the rules: *he was disqualified after failing a drug test.* ■ (of a feature or characteristic) make (someone) unsuitable for an office or activity: *a heart murmur disqualified him for military service.*

dis·qui·et /dis'kwī-it/ ▸*n.* a feeling of anxiety or worry: *public disquiet about animal testing.* ▸*v.* [*trans.*] [usu. as *adj.*] (**disquieted**) make (someone) worried or anxious: *she felt disquieted at the lack of interest the girl had shown.*

dis·qui·et·ing /dis'kwī-iting/ ▸*adj.* inducing feelings of anxiety or worry: *he found Jean's gaze disquieting.* —**dis·qui·et·ing·ly** *adv.*

dis·qui·e·tude /dis'kwī-i,t(y)o͞od/ ▸*n.* a state of uneasiness or anxiety.

dis·qui·si·tion /,diskwə'zishən/ ▸*n.* a long or elaborate essay or discussion on a particular subject: *nothing can kill a radio show quicker than a disquisition on intertextual analysis.* ▷late 15th cent.: via French from Latin *disquisitio(n-)* 'investigation,' based on *quaerere* 'seek.' The original sense was 'topic for investigation,' whence 'discourse in which a subject is investigated' (mid 17th cent.). —**dis·qui·si·tion·al** /-shənl/ *adj.* (*archaic*).

Dis·rae·li /diz'rālē/, Benjamin, 1st Earl of Beaconsfield (1804–81), British statesman; prime minister 1868 and 1874–80. He was largely responsible for the introduction of the second Reform Act (1867). He also ensured that Britain bought a controlling interest in the Suez Canal (1875) and made Queen Victoria empress of India.

dis·rate /dis'rāt/ ▸*v.* [*trans.*] (usu. **be disrated**) reduce (a sailor) to a lower rank.

dis·re·gard /,disri'gärd/ ▸*v.* [*trans.*] pay no attention to; ignore: *the body of evidence is too substantial to disregard.* See note at NEGLECT. ▸*n.* the action or state of disregarding or ignoring something: *blatant* ***disregard for*** *the law.*

dis·rel·ish /dis'relish/ *archaic* ▸*n.* a feeling of dislike or distaste: *disrelish for any pursuit is ample reason for abandoning it.* ▸*v.* [*trans.*] regard (something) with dislike or distaste: *I am not surprised that some members should disrelish your report.*

dis·re·mem·ber /,disri'membər/ ▸*v.* [*trans.*] *dialect* fail to remember: *they had a word for it, but I disremember it now.*

dis·re·pair /,disri'pe(ə)r/ ▸*n.* poor condition of a building or structure due to neglect: *the station gradually* ***fell into disrepair.***

dis·rep·u·ta·ble /dis'repyətəbəl/ ▸*adj.* not considered to be respectable in character or appearance: *think twice before buying cheap fireworks from disreputable sources* | *he was heavy, grubby, and vaguely disreputable.* —**dis·rep·u·ta·ble·ness** *n.* —**dis·rep·u·ta·bly** /-blē/ *adv.*

dis·re·pute /,disrə'pyo͞ot/ ▸*n.* the state of being held in low esteem by the public: *one of the top clubs in the country is close to bringing the game* ***into disrepute.***

dis·re·spect /,disri'spekt/ ▸*n.* lack of respect or courtesy: *growing disrespect for the rule of law.* ▸*v.* [*trans.*] *informal* show a lack of respect for; insult: *a young brave who disrespects his elders.* —**dis·re·spect·ful** /-fəl/ *adj.* —**dis·re·spect·ful·ly** /-fəlē/ *adv.*

dis·robe /dis'rōb/ ▸*v.* [*intrans.*] take off one's clothes: *the girl disrobed slowly and climbed into the high bed.* ■ take off the clothes worn for an official ceremony: *they walked to the vestry to disrobe.* ■ [*trans.*] undress (someone): *Kate remembers being disrobed.* ▷late Middle English: from DIS- (expressing reversal) + ROBE, perhaps on the pattern of French *desrober*.

dis·rupt /dis'rəpt/ ▸*v.* [*trans.*] interrupt (an event, activity, or process) by causing a disturbance or problem: *a rail strike that could disrupt both passenger and freight service.* ■ drastically alter or destroy the structure of (something): *alcohol can disrupt the chromosomes of an unfertilized egg.* ▷late Middle English: from Latin *disrupt-* 'broken apart,' from the verb *disrumpere*. —**dis·rupt·er** (also **dis·rup·tor** /-tər/) *n.* —**dis·rup·tion** /-'rəpshən/ *n.*

dis·rup·tive /dis'rəptiv/ ▸*adj.* causing or tending to cause disruption: *disruptive and delinquent children* | *the hours of work are* ***disruptive to*** *home life.* —**dis·rup·tive·ly** *adv.* —**dis·rup·tive·ness** *n.*

diss ▸*v.* variant spelling of DIS.

dis·sat·is·fac·tion /dis,satis'fakshən/ ▸*n.* lack of satisfaction: *widespread public* ***dissatisfaction with*** *incumbent politicians.*

dis·sat·is·fied /dis'satis,fīd/ ▸*adj.* not content or happy with something: *small investors* ***dissatisfied with*** *rates on certificates of deposit* | *dissatisfied customers.* —**dis·sat·is·fied·ly** *adv.*

dis·sat·is·fy /dis'satis,fī/ ▸*v.* (**-fies, -fied**) [*trans.*] fail to satisfy (someone).

dis·sav·ing /dis'sāving/ ▸*n.* the action of spending more than one has earned in a given period. ■ (**dissavings**) the excess amount spent. —**dis·sav·er** /-vər/ *n.*

dis·sect /di'sekt; dī-/ ▸*v.* [*trans.*] (often **be dissected**) methodically cut up (a body, part, or plant) in order to study its internal parts. ■ analyze (something) in minute detail: *novels that dissect our obsession with cities and urban angst.* ▷late 16th cent.: from Latin *dissect-* 'cut up,' from the verb *dissecare*, from *dis-* 'apart' + *secare* 'to cut.' —**dis·sec·tion** /-'sekshən/ *n.* —**dis·sec·tor** /-tər/ *n.*

dis·sect·ed /di'sektid; dī-/ ▸*adj.* **1** having been cut up for anatomical study. **2** having a divided form or structure, in particular: ■ *Botany* (of a leaf) divided into many deep lobes. ■ *Geology* (of a plateau or upland) divided by a number of deep valleys.

dis·sem·ble /di'sembəl/ ▸*v.* [*intrans.*] conceal one's true motives, feelings, or beliefs: *an honest, sincere person with no need to dissemble.* ■ [*trans.*] disguise or conceal (a feeling or intention): *she smiled, dissembling her true emotion.* ▷late Middle English: alteration (suggested by SEMBLANCE) of obsolete *dissimule*, via Old French from Latin *dissimulare* 'disguise, conceal.' —**dis·sem·blance** /-bləns/ *n.* —**dis·sem·bler** /-b(ə)lər/ *n.*

dis·sem·i·nate /di'semə,nāt/ ▸*v.* [*trans.*] spread or disperse (something, esp. information) widely: *health authorities should foster good practice by disseminating information.* See note at SCATTER. ■ [usu. as *adj.*] (**disseminated**) spread throughout an organ or the body: *disseminated colonic cancer.* ▷late Middle English: from Latin *disseminat-* 'scattered,' from the verb *disseminare*, from *dis-* 'abroad' + *semen, semin-* 'seed.' —**dis·sem·i·na·tion** /-,semə'nāshən/ *n.* —**dis·sem·i·na·tor** /-,nātər/ *n.*

dis·sem·i·nule /di'semə,nyo͞ol/ ▸*n.* *Botany* a part of a plant that serves to propagate it, such as a seed or a fruit. ▷early 20th cent.: formed irregularly from *dissemination* (see DISSEMINATE) + -ULE.

dis·sen·sion /di'senshən/ ▸*n.* disagreement that leads to discord: *this maneuver caused dissension within feminist ranks.* ▷Middle English: via Old French from Latin *dissensio(n-)*, from the verb *dissentire* (see DISSENT).

dis·sen·sus /di'sensəs/ ▸*n.* widespread dissent: *analysis reveals notable dissensus in evaluations of occupational roles.* ▷1960s: from DIS- (expressing reversal) + a shortened form of CONSENSUS, or from Latin *dissensus* 'disagreement.'

dis·sent /di'sent/ ▶*v.* [*intrans.*] hold or express opinions that are at variance with those previously, commonly, or officially expressed: *two members* ***dissented from*** *the majority* | [as *adj.*] (**dissenting**) *there were only a couple of dissenting voices.* ■ separate from an established or orthodox church because of doctrinal disagreement.
▶*n.* the expression or holding of opinions at variance with those previously, commonly, or officially held: *there was no* ***dissent from*** *this view.* ■ (also **Dissent**) refusal to accept the doctrines of an established or orthodox church; nonconformity. ▷late Middle English: from Latin *dissentire* 'differ in sentiment.'

dis·sent·er /di'sentər/ ▶*n.* a person who dissents. ■ (**Dissenter**) *Brit., historical* a member of a nonestablished church; a Nonconformist.

dis·sen·tient /di'sensHənt/ ▶*adj.* in opposition to a majority or official opinion: *dissentient voices were castigated as "hopeless bureaucrats."*
▶*n.* a person who opposes a majority or official opinion. ▷early 17th cent.: from Latin *dissentient-* 'differing in opinion,' from the verb *dissentire.*

D

dis·sep·i·ment /di'sepəmənt/ ▶*n. Botany & Zoology* a partition in a part or organ; a septum. ▷early 18th cent.: from Latin *dissaepimentum,* from *dissaepire* 'make separate,' from *dis-* (expressing separation) + *saepire* 'divide by a hedge.'

dis·ser·ta·tion /ˌdisər'tāsHən/ ▶*n.* a long essay on a particular subject, esp. one written as a requirement for the Doctor of Philosophy degree: *Joe wrote his doctoral dissertation on Thucydides* | *figurative she went on then into a dissertation on her family's love of Ireland.* ▷early 17th cent. (in the sense 'discussion, debate'): from Latin *dissertatio(n-),* from *dissertare* 'continue to discuss,' from *disserere* 'examine, discuss.' **—dis·ser·ta·tion·al** /-sHənl/ *adj.*

dis·serv·ice /dis'sərvis/ ▶*n.* [usu. in *sing.*] a harmful action: *you have* ***done a disservice to*** *the African people by ignoring this fact.*

dis·sev·er /di'sevər/ ▶*v.* [*trans.*] *rare* divide or sever (something). ▷Middle English (in the sense 'separate'): from Old French *dessevrer,* from late Latin *disseparare,* from *dis-* (expressing intensive force) + Latin *separare* 'to separate.' **—dis·sev·er·ance** /-'sev(ə)rəns/ *n.* **—dis·sev·er·ment** *n.*

dis·si·dence /'disidəns/ ▶*n.* protest against official policy; dissent. ▷mid 17th cent.: from Latin *dissidentia,* from *dissident-* 'sitting apart' (see DISSIDENT).

dis·si·dent /'disidənt/ ▶*n.* a person who opposes official policy, esp. that of an authoritarian state: *a dissident who had been jailed by a military regime.*
▶*adj.* in opposition to official policy: *a group of dissident workers set up communist China's first free trade union.* ▷mid 16th cent. (in the sense 'differing in opinion or character'): from Latin *dissident-* 'sitting apart, disagreeing,' from *dis-* 'apart' + *sedere* 'sit.'

dis·sim·i·lar /dis'similər/ ▶*adj.* not alike; different: *a collection of dissimilar nations lacking overall homogeneity* | *the pleasures of the romance novel are* ***not dissimilar from*** *those of the chocolate bar.* ▷late 16th cent.: from DIS- (expressing reversal) + SIMILAR, on the pattern of Latin *dissimilis,* French *dissimilaire.* **—dis·sim·i·lar·i·ty** /-ˌsimə'laritē/ *n.* **—dis·sim·i·lar·ly** *adv.*

dis·sim·i·late /di'siməˌlāt/ ▶*v.* [*trans.*] *Linguistics* change (a sound in a word) in order to be unlike the sounds near it: *in "pilgrim," from Latin "peregrinus," the first "r" is dissimilated to "l."* ■ [*intrans.*] (of a sound) undergo such a change: *the first "r" dissimilates to "l."* ▷mid 19th cent.: from DIS- (expressing reversal) + Latin *similis* 'like, similar,' on the pattern of *assimilate.* **—dis·sim·i·la·tion** /-ˌsimə'lāsHən/ *n.* **—dis·sim·i·la·to·ry** /-ləˌtôrē/ *adj.*

dis·si·mil·i·tude /ˌdis-si'miliˌt(y)o͞od/ ▶*n. formal* dissimilarity or diversity. ▷late Middle English: from Latin *dissimilitudo,* from *dissimilis* 'unlike,' from *dis-* (expressing reversal) + *similis* 'like, similar.'

dis·sim·u·late /di'simyəˌlāt/ ▶*v.* [*trans.*] conceal or disguise (one's thoughts, feelings, or character): *a country gentleman who dissimulates his wealth beneath ragged pullovers* | [*intrans.*] *now that they have power, they no longer need to dissimulate.* ▷late Middle English: from Latin *dissimulat-* 'hidden, concealed,' from the verb *dissimulare.* **—dis·sim·u·la·tion** /-ˌsimyə'lāsHən/ *n.* **—dis·sim·u·la·tor** /-ˌlātər/ *n.*

dis·si·pate /'disəˌpāt/ ▶*v.* **1** [*intrans.*] disperse or scatter: *the cloud of smoke dissipated.* See note at SCATTER. ■ (of a feeling or other intangible thing) disappear or be dispelled: *the concern she'd felt for him had wholly dissipated.* ■ [*trans.*] cause (a feeling or other intangible thing) to disappear or disperse: *he wanted to dissipate his anger.* **2** [*trans.*] squander or fritter away (money, energy, or resources): *he had dissipated his entire fortune.* ■ (usu. **be dissipated**) *Physics* cause (energy) to be lost, typically by converting it to heat. ▷late Middle English: from Latin *dissipat-* 'scattered,' from the verb *dissipare,* from *dis-* 'apart, widely' + *supare* 'to throw.' **—dis·si·pa·tive** /-ˌpātiv/ *adj.* **—dis·si·pa·tor** /-ˌpātər/ (also **dis·si·pat·er**) *n.*

dis·si·pat·ed /'disəˌpātid/ ▶*adj.* (of a person or way of life) overindulging in sensual pleasures: *dissipated behavior.*

dis·si·pa·tion /ˌdisə'pāsHən/ ▶*n.* **1** dissipated living: *a descent into drunkenness and sexual dissipation.* **2** squandering of money, energy, or resources: *the dissipation of the country's mineral wealth.* ■ *Physics* loss of energy, esp. by its conversion into heat. ■ scattering or dispersion: *the complete dissipation of paint fumes.* ▷late Middle English (in the sense 'complete disintegration'): from Latin *dissipatio(n-),* from the verb *dissipare* (see DISSIPATE).

dis·so·ci·a·ble /di'sōsHəbəl/ ▶*adj.* able to be dissociated; separable: *language and cognition are not dissociable.* ▷mid 19th cent.: from French, from Latin *dissociabilis,* from *dissociare* 'to separate.'

dis·so·ci·ate /di'sōsHēˌāt; -'sōsē-/ ▶*v.* [*trans.*] **1** disconnect or separate (used esp. in abstract contexts) : *voices should not be* ***dissociated from*** *their social context.* ■ (**dissociate oneself from**) declare that one is not connected with or a supporter of (someone or something): *he took pains to dissociate himself from the religious radicals.* ■ [*intrans.*] become separated or disconnected: *the area would* ***dissociate from*** *the country.* ■ (usu. **be dissociated**) *Psychiatry* split off (a component of mental activity) to act as an independent part of mental life. **2** (usu. **be dissociated**) *Chemistry* cause (a molecule) to split into separate smaller atoms, ions, or molecules, esp. reversibly: *these compounds are dissociated by solar radiation to yield atoms of chlorine.* ■ [*intrans.*] (of a molecule) undergo this process. ▷mid 16th cent.: from Latin *dissociat-* 'separated,' from the verb *dissociare,* from *dis-* (expressing reversal) + *sociare* 'join together' (from *socius* 'companion'). **—dis·so·ci·a·tive** /-ˌātiv; -sHətiv/ *adj.*

dis·so·ci·at·ed per·son·al·i·ty ▶*n.* another term for MULTIPLE PERSONALITY.

dis·so·ci·a·tion /diˌsōsē'āsHən/ ▶*n.* the disconnection or separation of something from something else or the state of being disconnected: *the dissociation between the executive and the judiciary is the legacy of the Act of Settlement.* ■ *Chemistry* the splitting of a molecule into smaller molecules, atoms, or ions, esp. by a reversible process. ■ *Psychiatry* separation of normally related mental processes, resulting in one group functioning independently from the rest, leading in extreme cases to disorders such as multiple personality.

dis·so·ci·a·tion con·stant ▶*n. Chemistry* a quantity expressing the extent to which a particular substance in solution is dissociated into ions, equal to the product of the concentrations of the respective ions divided by the concentration of the undissociated molecule.

dis·sol·u·ble /di'sälyəbəl/ ▶*adj.* able to be dissolved, loosened, or disconnected: *permitting divorce would render every marriage dissoluble.* ▷mid 16th cent.: from Latin *dissolubilis,* from the verb *dissolvere* (see DISSOLVE). **—dis·sol·u·bil·i·ty** /-ˌsälyə'bilitē/ *n.*

dis·so·lute /'disəˌlo͞ot/ ▶*adj.* lax in morals; licentious: *a dissolute, drunken, disreputable rogue.* ▷late Middle English: from Latin *dissolutus* 'disconnected, loose,' from the verb *dissolvere* (see DISSOLVE). **—dis·so·lute·ly** *adv.* **—dis·so·lute·ness** *n.*

dis·so·lu·tion /ˌdisə'lo͞osHən/ ▶*n.* **1** the closing down or dismissal of an assembly, partnership, or official body: *the dissolution of their marriage* | *Henry VIII declared the abbey's dissolution in 1540.* ■ *technical* the action or process of dissolving or being dissolved: *minerals susceptible to dissolution.* ■ disintegration; decomposition: *the dissolution of the flesh.* ■ *formal* death. **2** debauched living; dissipation: *an advanced state of dissolution.* ▷late Middle English: from Latin *dissolutio(n-),* from the verb *dissolvere* (see DISSOLVE).

dis·solve /di'zälv/ ▶*v.* **1** [*intrans.*] (of a solid) become incorporated into a liquid so as to form a solution: *glucose dissolves easily in water.* ■ [*trans.*] cause (a solid) to become incorporated into a liquid in this way: *dissolve a bouillon cube in a pint of hot water.* ■ (of something abstract, esp. a feeling) disappear: *my courage dissolved.* ■ deteriorate or degenerate: *the community policy could* ***dissolve into*** *chaos.* ■ subside uncontrollably into (an expression of strong feelings): *she suddenly* ***dissolved into*** *floods of tears.* ■ (in a movie) change gradually to (a different scene or picture): ***dissolve to*** *side view, looking down the street.* **2** [*trans.*] close down or dismiss (an assembly or official body): *the country's president can dissolve parliament under certain circumstances.* ■ annul or put an end to (a partnership or marriage): *it only takes 28 days to dissolve a domestic partnership.*
▶*n.* (in a film) an act or instance of moving gradually from one picture to another. ▷late Middle English (also in the sense 'break down into component parts'): from Latin *dissolvere,* from *dis-* 'apart' + *solvere* 'loosen or solve.' **—dis·solv·a·ble** *adj.* **—dis·solv·er** *n.*

dis·sol·vent /di'zälvənt/ ▶*n.* a substance that dissolves something else. ▷mid 17th cent.: from Latin *dissolvent-* 'dissolving,' from the verb *dissolvere* (see DISSOLVE).

dis·so·nance /'disənəns/ ▶*n. Music* lack of harmony among musical notes: *an unusual degree of dissonance for such choral styles* | *the harsh dissonances give a sound which is quite untypical of the Renaissance.* ■ a tension or clash resulting from the combination of two disharmonious or unsuitable elements: *dissonance between campaign rhetoric and personal behavior.* ▷late Middle English: from Old French, from late Latin *dissonantia,* from Latin *dissonant-* 'not agreeing in sound,' from the verb *dissonare.*

dis·so·nant /'disənənt/ ▶*adj. Music* lacking harmony: *irregular, dissonant chords.* ■ unsuitable or unusual in combination; clashing: *Jackson employs both harmonious and dissonant color choices.* ▷late Middle English (in the sense 'clashing'): from Old French, or from Latin *dissonant-* 'being discordant or inharmonious,' from the verb *dissonare,* from *dis-* 'apart' + *sonare* 'to sound.' **—dis·so·nant·ly** *adv.*

dis·suade /di'swād/ ▶*v.* [*trans.*] persuade (someone) not to take a particular course of action: *his friends tried to* ***dissuade*** *him* ***from*** *flying.* ▷late 15th cent. (in the sense 'advise against'): from Latin *dissuadere,* from *dis-* (expressing reversal) + *suadere* 'advise, persuade.' **—dis·suad·er** *n.* **—dis·sua·sion** /-'swāzHən/ *n.* **—dis·sua·sive** /-'swāsiv/ *adj.*

dis·syl·la·ble /dī'siləbəl/ ▶*n.* variant spelling of DISYLLABLE. **—dis·syl·lab·ic** /ˌdīsi'labik/ *adj.*

dis·sym·me·try /dis'simitrē/ ▶*n.* (*pl.* **-tries**) lack of symmetry. ■ *technical* the symmetrical relation of mirror images, the left and right hands, or crystals with two corresponding forms. **—dis·sym·met·ric** /ˌdis-si'metrik/ *adj.* **—dis·sym·met·ri·cal** /ˌdis-si'metrikəl/ *adj.*

dis·taff /'distaf/ ▶*n.* a stick or spindle onto which wool or flax is wound for spinning. ■ [as *adj.*] of or concerning women. ▷Old English *distæf*: the first element is apparently related to Middle Low German *dise, disene* 'distaff, bunch of flax'; the second is STAFF[1]. The extended sense arose because spinning was traditionally done by women.

dis·taff side ▶*n.* the female side of a family: *the family title could be passed down through the distaff side.* The opposite of SPEAR SIDE. ■ the female members of a group: *this fascination was not limited to the distaff side of society.* ▷late 19th cent.: because spinning (see DISTAFF) was traditionally done by women while men did the weaving.

dis·tal /'distl/ ▶*adj. Anatomy* situated away from the center of the body or from the point of attachment: *the distal end of the tibia* | *axons* ***distal to*** *the injury will degenerate.* The opposite of PROXIMAL. ■ *Geology* relating to or denoting the outer part of an area affected by geological activity: *the distal zone.* Often contrasted with PROXIMAL. ▷early 19th cent.: from DISTANT, on the pattern of words such as *dorsal.* **—dis·tal·ly** *adv.*

dis·tance /'distəns/ ▶*n.* **1** an amount of space between two things or people: *I bicycled the short distance home* | *the* ***distance between*** *front and rear wheels.* ■ the condition of being far off; remoteness: *distance makes things look small* | *figurative a significant distance between German and Allied understandings of the war.* ■ a far-off point or place: *watching them* ***from a distance.*** ■ (**the distance**) the more remote part of what is visible or discernible: *I heard police sirens* ***in the distance*** | *they sped off* ***into the distance.*** ■ an interval of time: *a distance of more than twenty years.* ■ *figurative* the avoidance of familiarity; aloofness or reserve: *a mix of warmth and distance makes a good neighbor.* **2** the full length of a race: *he claimed the 10,000 meter title in only his second race over the distance.* ■ (**the distance**) *Boxing* the scheduled length of a fight: *he has won his first five fights* ***inside the distance.*** ■ the distance from the winning post that a horse must have reached when the winner finishes in order to qualify for a subsequent heat.

▶*v.* [*trans.*] make (someone or something) far off or remote in position or nature: *her mother wished to* **distance** *her* **from** *the rough village children.* ■ (**distance oneself from**) declare that one is not connected with or a supporter of (someone or something): *he sought to distance himself from the proposals.* ■ *Horse Racing* beat (a horse) by a distance. ▷Middle English (in the sense 'discord, debate'): from Old French or from Latin *distantia*, from *distant-* 'standing apart,' from the verb *distare* (see DISTANT).

▶*PHRASES* □ **go the distance** *Boxing* complete a fight without being knocked out: *he went the distance after being floored in the first round.* ■ (of a boxing match) last the scheduled length: *six of his fights went the distance.* ■ *Baseball* pitch for the entire length of a game. ■ last for a long time: *this amplifier system should go the distance.* □ **keep one's distance** stay far away: *keep your distance from birds feeding their young.* ■ maintain one's reserve: *you had to say nothing and keep your distance.* □ **within —— distance** near enough to reach by the means specified: *the parking lot is within easy walking distance* | *he wanted to be* **within** *driving* **distance of** *his grandparents.* □ **within spitting distance** within a very short distance. □ **within striking distance** near enough to hit or achieve something: *the aircraft carrier is dispatched to deep waters within striking distance of Moscow.*

dis·tance learn·ing ▶*n.* a method of studying in which lectures are broadcast or classes are conducted by correspondence or over the Internet, without the student's needing to attend a school or college. Also called **distance education**.

dis·tance post ▶*n.* a post placed at a specified distance before the finishing post on a racecourse, which a horse must have passed when the winner finishes in order to qualify for a subsequent heat.

dis·tance run·ner ▶*n.* an athlete who competes in long- or middle-distance races.

dis·tant /'distənt/ ▶*adj.* **1** far away in space or time: *distant parts of the world* | *I remember that distant afternoon.* ■ [*predic.*] (after a measurement) at a specified distance: *the star is 30,000 light years* **distant from** *earth* | *the town lay half a mile distant.* ■ (of a sound) faint or vague because far away: *the distant bark of some farm dog.* ■ *figurative* remote or far apart in resemblance or relationship: *a distant acquaintance.* ■ [*attrib.*] (of a person) not closely related: *a distant cousin.* **2** (of a person) not intimate; cool or reserved: *his children found him strangely distant* | *she and my father were* **distant with** *each other.* ■ remote; abstracted: *a distant look in his eyes.* ▷late Middle English: from Latin *distant-* 'standing apart,' from the verb *distare*, from *dis-* 'apart' + *stare* 'stand.'

dis·tant ear·ly warn·ing (abbr.: **DEW**) ▶*n.* a radar system in North America for the early detection of a missile attack.

dis·tant·ly /'distəntlē/ ▶*adv.* far away: *distantly he heard shouts.* ■ not closely: *they are distantly related to the elephants.* ■ coolly or remotely: *she smiled distantly.*

dis·taste /dis'tāst/ ▶*n.* [in *sing.*] mild dislike or aversion: *Harry nurtured a* **distaste for** *all things athletic* | *his mouth twisted with distaste.* ▷late 16th cent.: from DIS- (expressing reversal) + TASTE, on the pattern of early modern French *desgout*, Italian *disgusto*. Compare with DISGUST.

dis·taste·ful /dis'tāstˌfəl/ ▶*adj.* causing dislike or disgust; offensive; unpleasant: *customers complained about the distasteful odor.* ▷early 17th cent. —**dis·taste·ful·ly** *adv.* —**dis·taste·ful·ness** *n.*

dist. atty. ▶*abbr.* ■ district attorney.

dis·tem·per[1] /dis'tempər/ ▶*n.* **1** a viral disease of some animals, esp. dogs, causing fever, coughing, and catarrh. **2** *archaic* political disorder: *an attempt to illuminate the moral roots of the modern world's distemper.* ▷mid 16th cent. (originally in the sense 'bad temper,' later 'illness'): from Middle English *distemper* 'upset, derange,' from late Latin *distemperare* 'soak, mix in the wrong proportions,' from *dis-* 'thoroughly' + *temperare* 'mingle.' Compare with TEMPER. Sense 1 dates from the mid 18th cent.

dis·tem·per[2] ▶*n.* a kind of paint using glue or size instead of an oil base, for use on walls or for scene-painting. ■ a method of mural and poster painting using this.

▶*v.* [*trans.*] [often as *adj.*] (**distempered**) paint (something) with distemper: *the distempered roof timbers.* ▷late Middle English (originally as a verb in the senses 'dilute' and 'steep'): from Old French *destremper* or late Latin *distemperare* 'soak.'

dis·tend /dis'tend/ ▶*v.* [*trans.*] cause (something) to swell by stretching it from inside: *air is introduced into the stomach to distend it* | [as *adj.*] (**distended**) *a distended belly.* ■ [*intrans.*] swell out because of pressure from inside: *the abdomen distended rapidly.* ▷late Middle English: from Latin *distendere*, from *dis-* 'apart' + *tendere* 'to stretch.' —**dis·ten·si·bil·i·ty** /-ˌtensə'bilitē/ *n.* —**dis·ten·si·ble** /-'tensəbəl/ *adj.* —**dis·ten·sion** /-'tenSHən/ *n.*

dis·tich /'distik/ ▶*n. Prosody* a pair of verse lines; a couplet. ▷early 16th cent.: via Latin from Greek *distikhon (metron)* '(measure) of two lines,' neuter of *distikhos*, from *di-* 'twice' + *stikhos* 'line.'

dis·ti·chous /'distikəs/ ▶*adj. Botany* (of parts) arranged alternately in two opposite vertical rows. ▷mid 18th cent.: via Latin from Greek *distikhos* (see DISTICH) + -OUS. —**dis·ti·chous·ly** *adv.*

dis·till /dis'til/ (*Brit.* **distil**) ▶*v.* [*trans.*] purify (a liquid) by vaporizing it, then condensing it by cooling the vapor, and collecting the resulting liquid: *they managed to distill a small quantity of water* | [as *adj.*] (**distilled**) *dip the slide in distilled water.* ■ (usu. **be distilled**) make (something, esp. liquor or an essence) in this way: *whiskey is* **distilled from** *a mash of grains* | [as *n.*] (**distilling**) *the distilling industry.* ■ extract the essence of (something) by heating it with a solvent. ■ remove (a volatile constituent) of a mixture by using heat: *coal tar is made by* **distilling out** *the volatile products in coal.* ■ (often **be distilled**) *figurative* extract the essential meaning or most important aspects of: *my travel notes were* **distilled into** *a book* | [as *adj.*] (**distilled**) *the employee report is a distilled version of the main accounts.* ■ [*intrans.*] *poetic/literary* emanate as a vapor or in minute drops: *she drew back from the dank breath that distilled out of the earth.* ▷late Middle English: from Latin *distillare*, variant of *destillare*, from *de-* 'down, away' + *stillare* (from *stilla* 'a drop'). —**dis·til·la·tion** /ˌdistə'lāSHən/ *n.* —**dis·til·la·to·ry** /-əˌtôrē/ *adj.*

dis·til·late /'distilit; -ˌlāt/ ▶*n.* something formed by distilling: *petroleum distillates* | *natural gas mixed with distillate.* ▷mid 19th cent.: from Latin *distillatus* 'fallen in drops,' from the verb *distillare* (see DISTILL).

dis·till·er /dis'tilər/ ▶*n.* a person or company that manufactures liquor: *barrels that the master distiller deems to be of superior quality.*

dis·till·er·y /dis'tilərē/ ▶*n.* (*pl.* **-er·ies**) a place where liquor is manufactured: *the world's oldest whiskey distillery.*

dis·tinct /dis'tiNGkt/ ▶*adj.* **1** recognizably different in nature from something else of a similar type: *the patterns of spoken language are* **distinct from** *those of writing* | *there are two distinct types of sickle cell disease.* ■ physically separate: *the gallery is divided into five distinct spaces.* **2** readily distinguishable by the senses: *a distinct smell of nicotine.* ■ [*attrib.*] (used for emphasis) so clearly apparent as to be unmistakable; definite: *he got the distinct impression that Melissa wasn't pleased.* ▷late Middle English (in the sense 'differentiated'): from Latin *distinctus* 'separated, distinguished,' from the verb *distinguere* (see DISTINGUISH). —**dis·tinct·ly** *adv.* —**dis·tinct·ness** *n.*

dis·tinc·tion /dis'tiNGkSHən/ ▶*n.* **1** a difference or contrast between similar things or people: *there is a sharp* **distinction between** *domestic politics and international politics* | *I was completely unaware of class distinctions.* ■ the separation of things or people into different groups according to their attributes or characteristics: *these procedures were to be applied to all births, without distinction.* **2** excellence that sets someone or something apart from others: *a novelist of distinction.* ■ a decoration or honor awarded to someone in recognition of outstanding achievement: *he gained the highest distinction awarded for excellence in photography.* ■ recognition of outstanding achievement, such as on an examination: *I made a distinction in Greek.* Compare with MERIT. ▷Middle English (in the sense 'subdivision, category'): via Old French from Latin *distinctio(n-)*, from the verb *distinguere* (see DISTINGUISH).

▶*PHRASES* □ **distinction without a difference** an artificially created distinction where no real difference exists. □ **have the distinction of** be different from others of a similar type by virtue of a notable characteristic or achievement: *pinto beans have the distinction of being one of the quickest beans to cook.*

dis·tinc·tive /dis'tiNGktiv/ ▶*adj.* characteristic of one person or thing, and so serving to distinguish it from others: *juniper berries give gin its distinctive flavor.* ▷late Middle English (in the sense 'serving to differentiate'): from late Latin *distinctivus*, from Latin *distinct-* 'distinguished' (see DISTINCT). —**dis·tinc·tive·ly** *adv.* —**dis·tinc·tive·ness** *n.*

dis·tin·gué /ˌdistaNG'gā/ ▶*adj.* (*fem.* **dis·tin·guée** *pronunc.* same) having a distinguished manner or appearance: *he was lean and distingué, with a small goatee.* ▷early 19th cent.: French, literally 'distinguished.'

dis·tin·guish /dis'tiNGgwiSH/ ▶*v.* [*trans.*] recognize or treat (someone or something) as different: *the child is perfectly capable of* **distinguishing** *reality* **from** *fantasy.* ■ [*intrans.*] perceive or point out a difference: *bees are unable to* **distinguish between** *red, black, and various grays.* ■ manage to discern (something barely perceptible): *it was too dark to distinguish anything more than their vague shapes.* ■ be an identifying or characteristic mark or property of: *what* **distinguishes** *sports* **from** *games?* | [as *adj.*] (**distinguishing**) *a yellow brick house with no distinguishing features.* ■ (**distinguish oneself**) make oneself prominent and worthy of respect through one's behavior or achievements: *many distinguished themselves in the fight against Hitler.* ▷late 16th cent.: formed irregularly from French *distinguer* or Latin *distinguere*, from *dis-* 'apart' + *stinguere* 'put out' (from a base meaning 'prick'). —**dis·tin·guish·a·ble** *adj.*

THE RIGHT WORD **descry, differentiate, discern, discriminate, distinguish**

What we **discern** we see apart from all other objects (*to discern the lighthouse beaming on the far shore*).

Descry puts even more emphasis on the distant or unclear nature of what we're seeing (*the lookout was barely able to descry a man approaching in the dusk*).

To **discriminate** is to perceive the differences between or among things that are very similar; it may suggest that some aesthetic evaluation is involved (*to discriminate between two painters' styles*).

Distinguish requires making even finer distinctions among things that resemble each other even more closely (*unable to distinguish the shadowy figures moving through the forest*). *Distinguish* can also mean recognizing by some special mark or outward sign (*the sheriff could be distinguished by his silver badge*).

Differentiate, on the other hand, suggests the ability to perceive differences between things that are easily confused. In contrast to *distinguish*, *differentiate* suggests subtle differences that must be compared in some detail (*the color of her dress was difficult to differentiate from the color of the chair in which she was seated; it took a sharp eye to distinguish where her skirt ended and the upholstery began*).

If you have trouble *differentiating* among these closely related verbs, you're not alone.

dis·tin·guished /dis'tiNGgwiSHt/ ▶*adj.* successful, authoritative, and commanding great respect: *a distinguished American educationist.* ■ showing dignity or authority in one's appearance or manner: *that hairstyle makes you look quite distinguished.*

Dis·tin·guished Fly·ing Cross (abbr.: **DFC**) ▶*n.* a U.S. or British military decoration for heroism or distinguished achievement while on aerial duty.

dis·tort /dis'tôrt/ ▶*v.* [*trans.*] pull or twist out of shape: *a grimace distorted her fine mouth* | [as *adj.*] (**distorted**) *his face was* **distorted with** *rage.* ■ [*intrans.*] become twisted out of shape: *the pipe will distort as you bend it.* ■ *figurative* give a misleading or false account or impression of: *many factors can distort the results* | [as *adj.*] (**distorted**) *his report gives a distorted view of the meeting.* ■ change the form of (an electrical signal or sound wave) during transmission, amplification, or other processing: *you're distorting the sound by overdriving the amp.* ▷late 15th cent. (in the sense 'twist to one side'): from Latin *distort-* 'twisted apart,' from the verb *distorquere*, from *dis-* 'apart' + *torquere* 'to twist.' —**dis·tort·ed·ly** *adv.* —**dis·tort·ed·ness** *n.* —**dis·tor·tion** /-'tôrSHən/ *n.* —**dis·tor·tion·al** /-'tôrSHənl/ *adj.* —**dis·tor·tion·less** /-'tôrSHənləs/ *adj.*

distr. ▶*abbr.* ■ distribution. ■ distributor. ■ district.

dis·tract /dis'trakt/ ▶*v.* [*trans.*] prevent (someone) from giving full attention to something: *don't allow noise to* **distract** *you* **from** *your work* | [as *adj.*] (**distracting**) *she found his nearness distracting.* ■ divert (attention) from something: *it was another attempt to* **distract** *attention* **from** *the truth.* ■ (**distract oneself**) divert one's attention from something worrying or unpleasant by doing something different or more pleasurable: *I tried to distract myself by concentrating on Jane.* ■ *archaic* perplex and bewilder: *horror and doubt distract His troubl'd thoughts.* ▷late Middle English (also in the sense 'pull in different directions'): from Latin *distract-* 'drawn apart,' from the verb *distrahere*, from *dis-* 'apart' + *trahere* 'to draw, drag.'

dis·tract·ed /dis'traktəd/ ▸*adj.* unable to concentrate because one's mind is preoccupied: *Charlotte seemed too distracted to give him much attention | she ran her fingers through her hair in a distracted fashion.* ■ troubled or distraught: *distracted with grief.* **—dis·tract·ed·ly** *adv.*

dis·trac·tion /dis'trakSHən/ ▸*n.* **1** a thing that prevents someone from giving full attention to something else: *the company found passenger travel a* ***distraction from*** *the main business of moving freight.* ■ a diversion or recreation: *there are plenty of distractions such as sailing.* **2** extreme agitation of the mind or emotions: *he knew she was nervous by her uncharacteristic air of distraction.* ▷late Middle English: from Latin *distractio(n-)*, from the verb *distrahere* (see DISTRACT).
▸*PHRASES* □ **drive someone to distraction** annoy someone intensely: *he was* ***driven to distraction*** *by the pain in his shoulder.* □ **to distraction** (in hyperbolic use) intensely: *she loved him to distraction.*

dis·trac·tor /dis'traktər/ ▸*n.* a person or thing that distracts. ■ an incorrect option in a multiple-choice question: *four pictures, three of which are distractors.*

dis·train /dis'trān/ ▸*v.* [*trans.*] *Law* seize (someone's property) to obtain payment of rent or other money owed: *legislation has restricted the right to distrain goods found on the premises.* ■ seize the property of (someone) for this purpose: *the government applied political pressure by distraining debtors.* ▷Middle English: from Old French *destreindre*, from Latin *distringere* 'stretch apart,' from *dis-* 'apart' + *stringere* 'tighten.' **—dis·train·er** *n.* **—dis·train·ment** *n.*

dis·traint /dis'trānt/ ▸*n. Law* the seizure of someone's property in order to obtain payment of money owed, esp. rent: *many faced heavy fines and the distraint of goods.* ▷mid 18th cent.: from DISTRAIN, on the pattern of *constraint.*

dis·trait /dis'trā/ ▸*adj.* (*fem.* **dis·traite** /dis'trāt/) [*predic.*] distracted or absentminded: *he seemed oddly distrait.* ▷mid 18th cent.: French, from Old French *destrait*, past participle of *destraire* 'distract,' from Latin *distrahere* 'pull apart' (see DISTRACT).

dis·traught /dis'trôt/ ▸*adj.* deeply upset and agitated: *a distraught woman sobbed and screamed for help | he appeared on television, grief-ravaged and distraught.* ▷late Middle English: alteration of the obsolete adjective *distract* (from Latin *distractus* 'pulled apart'), influenced by *straught*, archaic past participle of STRETCH.

dis·tress /dis'tres/ ▸*n.* **1** extreme anxiety, sorrow, or pain: *to his distress he saw that she was trembling.* ■ the state of a ship or aircraft when in danger or difficulty and needing help: *vessels* ***in distress*** *on or near the coast.* ■ suffering caused by lack of money or the basic necessities of life: *the poor were helped in their distress.* ■ *Medicine* a state of physical strain, exhaustion, or, in particular, breathing difficulty: *they said the baby was in distress.* **2** *Law* another term for DISTRAINT.
▸*v.* [*trans.*] cause (someone) anxiety, sorrow, or pain: *I didn't mean to distress you | [trans.] he was distressed to find that Anna would not talk to him |* [as *adj.*] (**distressing**) *some very distressing news.* ■ give (furniture, leather, or clothing) simulated marks of age and wear: *the manner in which leather jackets are industrially distressed.* ▷Middle English: from Old French *destresce* (noun), *destrecier* (verb), based on Latin *distringere* 'stretch apart.' **—dis·tress·ful** /-fəl/ *adj.* **—dis·tress·ing·ly** *adv.*

dis·tressed /dis'trest/ ▸*adj.* suffering from anxiety, sorrow, or pain: *I was distressed at the news of his death.* ■ *dated* impoverished: *women in distressed circumstances.* ■ (of furniture, leather, or clothing) having simulated marks of age and wear: *a distressed leather jacket.* ■ (of property) for sale, esp. below market value, due to mortgage foreclosure or because it is part of an insolvent estate. ■ (of goods) for sale at unusually low prices or at a loss because of damage or previous use.

dis·tress sale ▸*n.* a sale of goods or assets at reduced prices to raise much-needed funds.

dis·tress sig·nal ▸*n.* a signal from a ship or aircraft in danger.

dis·trib·u·tar·y /dis'tribyo͞o,terē/ ▸*n.* (*pl.* **-tar·ies**) a branch of a river that does not return to the main stream after leaving it (as in a delta).

dis·trib·ute /dis'tribyo͞ot/ ▸*v.* [*trans.*] **1** give shares of (something); deal out: *information leaflets are being distributed to hotels and guest houses.* ■ supply (goods) to stores and other businesses that sell to consumers: *the journal is distributed worldwide.* ■ (**be distributed**) occur throughout an area: *the birds are mainly distributed in marshes and river valleys.* ■ *Printing* separate (metal type that has been set up) and return the characters to their separate compartments in a type case. **2** *Logic* use (a term) to include every individual of the class to which it refers: *the middle term must be distributed, at least once, in the premises.* ▷late Middle English: from Latin *distribut-* 'divided up,' from the verb *distribuere*, from *dis-* 'apart' + *tribuere* 'assign.' **—dis·trib·ut·a·ble** *adj.*

dis·trib·ut·ed sys·tem ▸*n.* a number of independent computers linked by a network.

dis·tri·bu·tion /,distrə'byo͞oSHən/ (abbr.: **distr.**) ▸*n.* the action of sharing something out among a number of recipients: *the government donated 4,000 pounds of coffee for distribution among refugees.* ■ the way in which something is shared out among a group or spread over an area: *changes undergone by the area have affected the distribution of its wildlife.* ■ the action or process of supplying goods to stores and other businesses that sell to consumers: *a manager has the choice of four types of distribution |* [as *adj.*] *an established* ***distribution channel.*** ■ *Bridge* the different number of cards of each suit in a player's hand: *strength has two ingredients, high cards and distribution.* ▷late Middle English: from Latin *distributio(n-)*, from the verb *distribuere* (see DISTRIBUTE). **—dis·tri·bu·tion·al** /-SHənl/ *adj.*

dis·tri·bu·tion func·tion ▸*n.* short for CUMULATIVE DISTRIBUTION FUNCTION.

dis·tri·bu·tive /dis'tribyətiv/ ▸*adj.* **1** concerned with the supply of goods to stores and other businesses that sell to consumers: *transportation and distributive industries.* ■ concerned with the way in which things are shared between people: *the distributive effects of public expenditure | distributive justice.* **2** *Grammar* (of a determiner or pronoun) referring to each individual of a class, not to the class collectively, e.g., *each, either.* **3** *Mathematics* (of an operation) fulfilling the condition that, when it is performed on two or more quantities already combined by another operation, the result is the same as when it is performed on each quantity individually and the products then combined.
▸*n. Grammar* a distributive word. ▷late Middle English: from Old French *distributif, -ive* or late Latin *distributivus*, from Latin *distribut-* 'divided up,' from the verb *distribuere* (see DISTRIBUTE). **—dis·trib·u·tive·ly** *adv.*

dis·trib·u·tor /dis'tribyətər/ (abbr.: **distr.**) ▸*n.* **1** an agent who supplies goods to stores and other businesses that sell to consumers: *a wholesale liquor distributor | the movie's distributor booked the film into theaters.* **2** a device in a gasoline engine for passing electric current to each spark plug in turn.

dis·trib·ut·or cap ▸*n.* an insulated cap that fits over the distributor in a gasoline engine and that distributes voltage to the spark plugs.

dis·trict /'distrikt/ ▸*n.* (abbr.: **distr.**) an area of a country or city, esp. one regarded as a distinct unit because of a particular characteristic: *an elegant shopping district.* ■ a region defined for an administrative purpose: *the city school district.* ■ (**the District**) the District of Columbia; Washington, DC.
▸*v.* [*trans.*] divide into districts. ▷early 17th cent. (denoting the territory under the jurisdiction of a feudal lord): from French, from medieval Latin *districtus* '(territory of) jurisdiction,' from Latin *distringere* 'draw apart.'

dis·trict at·tor·ney (abbr.: **DA**) ▸*n.* a public official who acts as prosecutor for the state or the federal government in court in a particular district.

dis·trict court ▸*n.* a state of federal trial court.

Dis·trict of Co·lum·bi·a (abbr.: **DC**) a federal district of the U.S., coextensive with the city of Washington, on the Potomac River with boundaries on the states of Virginia and Maryland.

dis·tro /'distrō/ ▸*n. Computing* a distribution, especially of Linux software or of webzines: *I've been working on this project for a little while and decided to post this here in case anyone who runs a distro is interested.* ■ a particular distributable or distributed version of Linux software: *I was excited enough about this distro that I forked over the cash to buy it.* ▷by shortening and alteration.

dis·trust /dis'trəst/ ▸*n.* the feeling that someone or something cannot be relied on: *distrust of Soviet intentions soon followed.*
▸*v.* [*trans.*] doubt the honesty or reliability of; regard with suspicion: *like a skillful gambler, Dave distrusted a sure thing.* **—dis·trust·er** *n.* **—dis·trust·ful** /-fəl/ *adj.* **—dis·trust·ful·ly** /-fəlē/ *adv.*

dis·turb /dis'tərb/ ▸*v.* [*trans.*] interfere with the normal arrangement or functioning of: *being sent to jail had apparently not disturbed his cheerfulness | the site surface had been disturbed by bulldozer activity.* ■ destroy the sleep or relaxation of: *he crept in so as not to disturb his sleeping parents.* ■ (often **be disturbed**) cause to feel anxious: *I am disturbed by the document I have just read |* [as *adj.*] (**disturbing**) *disturbing unemployment figures.* ■ (often **be disturbed**) interrupt or intrude on (someone) when they want privacy or secrecy: *I'll see my patient now and we are not to be disturbed.* ▷Middle English: from Old French *destourber*, from Latin *disturbare*, from *dis-* 'utterly' + *turbare* 'disturb' (from *turba* 'tumult'). **—dis·turb·er** *n.* **—dis·turb·ing·ly** *adv.*

dis·tur·bance /dis'tərbəns/ ▸*n.* the interruption of a settled and peaceful condition: *a helicopter landing can cause disturbance to residents.* ■ a breakdown of peaceful and law-abiding behavior; a riot: *the disturbances were precipitated when four men were refused bail.* ■ the disruption of healthy functioning: *her severe mental disturbance was diagnosed as schizophrenia.* ■ *Meteorology* a local variation from normal or average wind conditions, usually a small tornado or cyclone. ■ *Law* interference with rights or property; molestation. ▷Middle English: from Old French *destourbance*, from *destourber* (see DISTURB).

dis·turbed /dis'tərbd/ ▸*adj.* having had its normal pattern or function disrupted: *disturbed sleep.* ■ suffering or resulting from emotional and mental problems: *the treatment of disturbed children | disturbed behavior.*

di·sub·sti·tut·ed /dī'səbsti,t(y)o͞otid/ ▸*adj. Chemistry* (of a molecule) having two substituent groups.

di·sul·fide /dī'səl,fīd/ (*Brit.* **di·sul·phide**) ▸*n. Chemistry* a sulfide containing two atoms of sulfur in its molecule or empirical formula. ■ an organic compound containing the group −S−S− bonded to other groups.

di·sul·fir·am /dī'səlfə,ram/ ▸*n. Medicine* a synthetic compound used in the treatment of alcoholics to make drinking alcohol produce unpleasant aftereffects. Also called ANTABUSE (*trademark*). • Alternative name: **tetraethylthiuram disulfide**; chem. formula: $(C_2H_5)_2NCSSCN(C_2H_5)_2$. ▷1940s: blend of *disulfide* (see DISULFIDE) and THIURAM.

dis·un·ion /dis'yo͞onyən/ ▸*n.* the breaking up of something such as a federation: *his rejection of disunion was consistent with his nationalism.*

dis·u·nit·ed /,disyo͞o'nītid/ ▸*adj.* lacking unity: *a disunited nation.*

dis·u·ni·ty /dis'yo͞onitē/ ▸*n.* disagreement and conflict within a group: *the disunity among opposition parties.*

dis·use /dis'yo͞os/ ▸*n.* the state of not being used: *the machines* ***fell into disuse*** *with the advent of computers.*
▸*PHRASE* □ **fall into disuse** cease to be used: *the old tracks fell into disuse and neglect.*

dis·used /dis'yo͞ozd/ ▸*adj.* no longer being used: *they held an exhibition in a disused warehouse.*

dis·u·til·i·ty /,disyo͞o'tilitē/ ▸*n. Economics* the adverse or harmful effects associated with a particular activity or process, esp. when carried out over a long period.

dis·val·ue /dis'valyo͞o/ ▸*v.* (**-val·ues**, **-val·ued**, **-val·u·ing**) [*trans.*] undervalue (something or someone): *I'm not going to disvalue the way they feel.*
▸*n.* a negative value or worth. **—dis·val·u·a·tion** /-,valyo͞o'āSHən/ *n.*

di·syl·lab·ic /,dīsi'labik; di-/ (also **dis·syl·lab·ic**) ▸*adj.* (of a word or metrical foot) consisting of two syllables. ■ (of a bird's call) consisting of two distinct sounds, such as the call of the cuckoo. ▷mid 17th cent.: from French *dissyllabique*, via Latin from Greek *disullabos* 'of two syllables.'

di·syl·la·ble /dī'siləbəl; di-/ (also **dis·syl·la·ble**) ▸*n. Prosody* a word or metrical foot consisting of two syllables. ▷late 16th cent.: alteration (influenced by SYLLABLE) of French *disyllabe*, via Latin from Greek *disullabos* 'of two syllables,' from *di-* 'two' + *sullabē* 'syllable.'

dit /dit/ ▸*n.* (in Morse code) another term for DOT[1]. ▷World War II: imitative.

ditch /diCH/ ▸*n.* a narrow channel dug in the ground, typically used for drainage alongside a road or the edge of a field.
▸*v.* [*trans.*] **1** provide with ditches: *he was praised for ditching the coastal areas.* ■ [*intrans.*] make or repair ditches: [as *n.*] (**ditching**) *they would have to pay for hedging and ditching.* **2** *informal* get rid of; give up: *it crossed her mind to ditch her shoes and run | plans for the road were ditched following a public inquiry.* ■ *informal* end a relationship with (someone) peremptorily; abandon: *she ditched her husband to marry the window cleaner.* ■ *informal* be truant from (school or another obligation): *maybe she could ditch school and run away.* **3** *informal* bring (an aircraft) down on water in an

emergency: *he was picked up by a frigate after ditching his plane in the Mediterranean.* ■ [*intrans.*] (of an aircraft) make a forced landing on water: *the aircraft was obliged to ditch in the sea off the North African coast.* ■ derail (a train). ▷Old English *dīc*, of Germanic origin; related to Dutch *dijk* 'ditch, dike' and German *Teich* 'pond, pool,' also to DIKE[1]. —**ditch·er** *n.*

ditch·wa·ter /ˈdicH,wôtər; -ˌwä-/ ▸*n.* stagnant water in a ditch.

▸*PHRASE* □ **dull as ditchwater** see DULL.

di·the·ism /ˈdīTHēˌizəm; dīˈTHē-/ ▸*n.* a belief in two gods, esp. as independent and opposed principles of good and evil. —**di·the·ist** *n.*

dith·er /ˈdiT͟Hər/ ▸*v.* [*intrans.*] **1** be indecisive: *he was dithering about the election date.* **2** [*trans.*] *Computing* display or print (an image) without sharp edges so that there appear to be more colors in it than are really available: [as *adj.*] (**dithered**) *dithered bit maps.* ▸*n.* **1** *informal* indecisive behavior: *after months of dither they had still not agreed.* **2** [in *sing.*] a state of agitation: *buses are jammed and dirty and everyone is* ***in a dither*** *over taxis.* ▷mid 17th cent. (in the dialect sense 'tremble, quiver'): variant of dialect *didder*; related to DODDER[1]. —**dith·er·er** *n.* —**dith·er·y** *adj.*

di·thi·o·nite /dīˈTHīəˌnīt/ ▸*n. Chemistry* a salt containing the anion $S_2O_4{}^{2-}$. ▷mid 20th cent.: from DI-[1] 'two' + Greek *theion* 'sulfur' + -ITE[1].

di·thi·zone /dīˈTHīˌzōn/ ▸*n. Chemistry* a synthetic compound used as a reagent for the analysis and separation of lead and other metals. • Alternative name: **diphenylthiocarbazone**; chem. formula: $C_{13}H_{12}N_4S$. ▷1920s: from elements of the systematic name (see above).

dith·y·ramb /ˈdiTHəˌram/ ▸*n.* a wild choral hymn of ancient Greece, esp. one dedicated to Dionysus. ■ a passionate or inflated speech, poem, or other writing. ▷early 17th cent.: via Latin from Greek *dithurambos*, of unknown ultimate origin. —**dith·y·ram·bic** /ˌdiTHəˈrambik/ *adj.*

di·tran·si·tive /dīˈtranzətiv/ ▸*adj. Grammar* (of a verb) taking two objects, for example *give* as in *I gave her the book.*

dit·sy ▸*adj.* variant spelling of DITZY.

dit·ta·ny /ˈditn-ē/ ▸*n.* any of a number of aromatic herbaceous or shrubby plants: • (also **dittany of Crete**) a dwarf shrub with white woolly leaves and pink flowers, native to Crete and Greece (*Origanum dictamnus*, family Labiatae). • (also **American dittany**) an American herb used in cooking and herbal medicine (genus *Cunila*, family Labiatae). • another term for GAS PLANT. ▷late Middle English: from Old French *ditain* or medieval Latin *ditaneum*, from Latin *dictamnus, dictamnum*, from Greek *diktamnon*, perhaps from *Diktē*, the name of a mountain in Crete.

dit·to /ˈditō/ ▸ **1** used in accounts and lists to indicate that an item is repeated (often indicated by ditto marks under the word or figure to be repeated). ■ *informal* used to indicate that something already said is applicable a second time: *if one folds his arms, so does the other; if one crosses his legs, ditto.* **2** a similar thing; a duplicate. ▷early 17th cent. (in the sense 'in the aforesaid month'): from Tuscan dialect, variant of Italian *detto* 'said,' from Latin *dictus* 'said.'

dit·tog·ra·phy /diˈtägrəfē/ ▸*n.* (*pl.* **-phies**) a mistaken repetition of a letter, word, or phrase by a copyist. ▷late 19th cent.: from Greek *dittos* 'double' + -GRAPHY. —**dit·to·graph·ic** /ˌditəˈgrafik/ *adj.*

dit·to marks ▸*plural n.* two apostrophes (") representing "ditto."

dit·ty /ˈditē/ ▸*n.* (*pl.* **-ties**) a short simple song: *a lovely little music-hall ditty.* ▷Middle English: from Old French *dite* 'composition,' from Latin *dictatum* (neuter) 'something dictated,' from *dictare* 'to dictate.'

dit·ty bag (also **ditty box**) ▸*n.* a receptacle for odds and ends, esp. one used by sailors or fishermen. ▷mid 19th cent.: of unknown origin.

ditz /dits/ ▸*n. informal* a scatterbrained person. ▷1970s: back-formation from DITZY.

dit·zy /ˈditsē/ (also **dit·sy**) ▸*adj. informal* silly or scatterbrained: *don't tell me my ditzy secretary didn't send you an invitation!* ▷1970s: of unknown origin. —**dit·zi·ness** *n.*

di·u·re·sis /ˌdīyəˈrēsis/ ▸*n. Medicine* increased or excessive production of urine. Compare with POLYURIA. ▷late 17th cent.: modern Latin, from DI-[3] 'through' + Greek *ourēsis* 'urination.'

di·u·ret·ic /ˌdīyəˈretik/ *Medicine* ▸*adj.* (chiefly of drugs) causing increased passing of urine. ▸*n.* a diuretic drug. ▷late Middle English: from Old French *diuretique*, or via late Latin from Greek *diourētikos*, from *diourein* 'urinate,' from *dia* 'through' + *ouron* 'urine.'

di·ur·nal /dīˈərnl/ ▸*adj.* **1** of or during the day. ■ *Zoology* (of animals) active in the daytime. ■ *Botany* (of flowers) open only during the day. **2** daily; of each day: *diurnal rhythms.* ■ *Astronomy* of or resulting from the daily rotation of the earth. ▷late Middle English (as a term in astronomy): from late Latin *diurnalis*, from Latin *diurnus* 'daily,' from *dies* 'day.' —**di·ur·nal·ly** *adv.*

div ▸*abbr.* divergence (in mathematical equations).

Div. ▸*abbr.* ■ Division. ■ divorced.

di·va /ˈdēvə/ ▸*n.* a famous female opera singer: *your average opera isn't over till the diva trills her high notes.* ■ a female singer who has enjoyed great popular success: *a chance to create a full-blown pop diva.* ■ an admired, glamorous, or distinguished woman: *the former director of the association is still a downtown diva.* ■ a haughty, spoiled woman: *she's such a diva that she won't enter a restaurant until they change the pictures on the walls to her liking.* ▷late 19th cent.: via Italian from Latin, literally 'goddess.'

di·va·gate /ˈdīvəˌgāt/ ▸*v. poetic/literary* [*intrans.*] stray; digress: *Yeats divagated into Virgil's territory only once.* ▷late 16th cent.: from Latin *divagat-* 'wandered around,' from the verb *divagari*, from *di-* 'widely' + *vagari* 'wander.' —**di·va·ga·tion** /ˌdīvəˈgāSHən/ *n.*

di·va·lent /dīˈvālənt/ ▸*adj. Chemistry* having a valence of two.

Di·va·li ▸*n.* variant spelling of DIWALI.

di·van ▸*n.* **1** /diˈvan; ˈdīˌvan/ a long low sofa without a back or arms, typically placed against a wall. **2** /diˈvan; -ˈvän/ *historical* a legislative body, council chamber, or court of justice in the Ottoman Empire or elsewhere in the Middle East. ▷late 16th cent. (sense 2): via French or Italian from Turkish *dīvān*, from Persian *dīwān* 'anthology, register, court, or bench'; compare with DIWAN. As a piece of furniture, a *divan* was originally (early 18th cent.) a low bench or raised section of floor used as a long seat against the wall of a room, common in Middle Eastern countries; European imitation of this led to the sense 'low flat sofa or bed' (late 19th cent.).

di·var·i·cate ▸*v.* [*intrans.*] /dīˈvariˌkāt; di-/ *technical* or *poetic/literary* stretch or spread apart; diverge widely: *her crow's feet are divaricating like deltas.* ▸*adj.* /-kit; -ˌkāt/ *Botany* (of a branch) coming off the stem almost at a right angle. ▷early 17th cent.: from Latin *divaricat-* 'stretched apart,' from the verb *divaricare*, from *di-* (expressing intensive force) + *varicare* 'stretch the legs apart' (from *varicus* 'straddling'). —**di·var·i·ca·tion** /-ˌvariˈkāSHən/ *n.*

dive /dīv/ ▸*v.* (*past* **dived** or **dove** /dōv/; *past part.* **dived**) [*intrans.*] **1** [with *adverbial of direction*] plunge head first into water: *she walked to the deep end, then she dived in | he dived off the bridge for a bet.* ■ move quickly or suddenly in a specified direction: *a bullet passed close to his head, and he dived for cover* | [as *adj.*] (**diving**) *he attempted a diving catch.* ■ (of an aircraft or bird) plunge steeply downward through the air: *the aircraft dove for the ground to avoid the attack.* ■ (**dive into**) occupy oneself suddenly and enthusiastically with (a meal or an engrossing subject or activity): *dive into a barbecued beef burrito.* ■ *figurative* (of prices or profits) drop suddenly: *profits before tax dived by 61 percent.* ■ *informal* put one's hand quickly into something, esp. a pocket or purse, in order to find something: *she* ***dived into*** *her bag and extracted a card.* ■ *Soccer, Ice Hockey* (of a player) deliberately fall when challenged in order to deceive the referee into awarding a foul. **2** swim under water using breathing equipment: *he had been diving in the area to test equipment.* ■ (of a fish, a submarine, or a vessel used for underwater exploration) go to a deeper level in water: *the fish dive down to about 1,400 feet and then swim southwest.* ▸*n.* **1** an act of diving, in particular: ■ a plunge head first into water, esp. from a diving board in a way prescribed for competition: *he hit the sea in a shallow dive | a high dive.* ■ an instance of swimming or exploring under water with breathing equipment: *divers should have a good intake of fluid before each dive.* ■ an act of going deeper under water by a fish, submarine, or diving vessel: *pilot whales can go to 600 meters in a dive lasting 18 minutes.* ■ a steep descent by an aircraft or bird: *the jumbo jet went into a dive.* See also NOSEDIVE. ■ a sudden movement in a specified direction: *she* ***made a dive for*** *the fridge to quench her raging thirst.* ■ *figurative* a sudden and significant fall in prices or profits: *an 11 percent dive in profits.* ■ *Soccer, Ice Hockey* a deliberate fall by a player, intended to deceive the referee into awarding a foul. **2** *informal* a disreputable nightclub or bar: *he got into a fight in some dive.* ▷Old English *dūfan* 'dive, sink' and *dȳfan* 'immerse,' of Germanic origin; related to DEEP and DIP.

▸*PHRASES* □ **dive in** help oneself to food. □ **take a dive** *Boxing* pretend to be knocked out. ■ (of prices, hopes, fortunes, etc.) fall suddenly: *profits could take a dive as easily as they could soar | her reputation took a dive from which it has not recovered.*

dive-bomb ▸*v.* [*trans.*] bomb (a target) while diving steeply downward in an aircraft: *news that kamikazes had dive-bombed a U.S. destroyer.* ■ (of a bird or flying insect) attack (something) by swooping down on it: *the crow folded its wings and dive-bombed the vulture.* —**dive-bomb·er** *n.*

div·er /ˈdīvər/ ▸*n.* **1** a person or animal that dives, in particular: ■ a person who dives as a sport: *an Olympic diver.* ■ a person who wears a diving suit to work under water: *a diver at the oil terminal | a police diver.* **2** British term for LOON[1].

di·verge /diˈvərj; dī-/ ▸*v.* [*intrans.*] **1** (of a road, route, or line) separate from another route, esp. a main one, and go in a different direction. ■ develop in a different direction: *howler and spider monkeys* ***diverged from*** *a common ancestor.* ■ (of an opinion, theory, approach, etc.) differ markedly: *the coverage by the columnists* ***diverged from*** *that in the main news stories* | [as *adj.*] (**diverging**) *studies from different viewpoints yield diverging conclusions.* ■ deviate from a set course or standard: *suddenly he* ***diverged from*** *his text.* **2** *Mathematics* (of a series) increase indefinitely as more terms are added. ▷mid 17th cent.: from medieval Latin *divergere*, from Latin *dis-* 'in two ways' + *vergere* 'to turn or incline.'

di·ver·gence /diˈvərjəns; dī-/ ▸*n.* **1** the process or state of diverging: *the divergence between primates and other groups.* ■ a difference or conflict in opinions, interests, wishes, etc.: *a fundamental divergence of attitude.* ■ a place where airflows or ocean currents diverge, typically marked by downwelling (of air) or upwelling (of water). **2** *Mathematics* the inner product of the operator del and a given vector, which gives a measure of the quantity of flux emanating from any point of the vector field or the rate of loss of mass, heat, etc., from it.

di·ver·gent /diˈvərjənt; dī-/ ▸*adj.* **1** tending to be different or develop in different directions: *divergent interpretations | varieties of English can remain astonishingly* ***divergent from*** *one another.* ■ *Psychology* (of thought) using a variety of premises, esp. unfamiliar premises, as bases for inference, and avoiding common limiting assumptions in making deductions. **2** *Mathematics* (of a series) increasing indefinitely as more of its terms are added. —**di·ver·gen·cy** *n.* —**di·ver·gent·ly** *adv.*

di·vers /ˈdīvərz/ ▸*adj.* [*attrib.*] *archaic or poetic/literary* of varying types; several: *in divers places.* ▷Middle English: via Old French from Latin *diversus* 'diverse,' from *divertere* 'turn in separate ways' (see DIVERT).

di·verse /diˈvərs; dī-/ ▸*adj.* showing a great deal of variety: *a culturally diverse population.* ■ (of two or more things) markedly different from one another: *subjects as diverse as architecture, language teaching, and the physical sciences.* ▷Middle English: variant of DIVERS. —**di·verse·ly** *adv.*

di·ver·si·fy /diˈvərsiˌfī; dī-/ ▸*v.* (**-fies**, **-fied**) make or become more diverse or varied: [*intrans.*] *the trilobites* ***diversified into*** *a great number of species* | [*trans.*] *they seek to diversify their approach to teaching* | [as *adj.*] (**diversified**) *a diversified economy.* ■ [*intrans.*] (of a company) enlarge or vary its range of products or field of operation: *the company expanded rapidly and* ***diversified into*** *computers.* ■ [*trans.*] [often as *adj.*] (**diversified**) enlarge or vary the range of products or the field of operation of (a company): *the rise of the diversified corporation.* ■ [*trans.*] spread (investment) over several enterprises or products in order to reduce the risk of loss: *a prudent investor should diversify his or her holdings* | [as *adj.*] (**diversified**) *a diversified portfolio of assets.* ▷late Middle English (in the sense 'show diversity'): via Old French from medieval Latin *diversificare* 'make dissimilar,' from Latin *diversus*, past participle of *divertere* (see DIVERT). —**di·ver·si·fi·ca·tion** /-ˌvərsifiˈkāSHən/ *n.*

di·ver·sion /diˈvərZHən; dī-/ ▸*n.* **1** an instance of turning something aside from its course: *a diversion of resources from defense to civil research.* ■ *Brit.* an alternative route for use by traffic when the usual road is temporarily closed; a detour: *the road was closed and diversions put into operation.* **2** an activity that diverts the mind from tedious or serious concerns; a recreation or pastime: *our chief diversion was reading.* ■ something intended to distract someone's attention from something more important: *a subsidiary raid was carried out on the airfield to create a diversion.* ▷late Middle English: from late Latin *diversio(n-)*, from Latin *divertere* 'turn aside' (see DIVERT). —**di·ver·sion·ar·y** /-ˌnerē/ *adj.*

di·ver·si·ty /diˈvərsitē; dī-/ ▸*n.* (*pl.* **-ties**) the state of being diverse; variety: *there was considerable diversity in the style of the reports.* ■ [usu. in *sing.*] a range of different things: *newspapers were obliged to allow a diversity of views to be printed.* ▷Middle English: from Old French *diversite*, from Latin *diversitas*, from *diversus* 'diverse,' past participle of *divertere* 'turn aside' (see DIVERT).

di·vert /diˈvərt; dī-/ ▸*v.* [*trans.*] **1** cause (someone or something) to change course or turn from one direction to another: *a scheme to **divert** water **from** the river to irrigate agricultural land.* ■ [*intrans.*] (of a vehicle or person) change course: *an aircraft has diverted and will be with you shortly.* ■ reallocate (something, esp. money or resources) to a different purpose: *more of their advertising budget was **diverted into** promotions.* **2** distract (someone or their attention) from something: *public relations policies are sometimes intended to divert attention away from criticism.* ■ [usu. as *adj.*] (**diverting**) draw the attention of (someone) away from tedious or serious concerns; entertain or amuse: *a diverting book | nursery rhymes can calm and divert all but the most fractious child.* ▷late Middle English: via French from Latin *divertere*, from *di-* 'aside' + *vertere* 'to turn.' —**di·vert·er** *n.* —**di·vert·ing·ly** *adv.*

di·ver·tic·u·la /ˌdīvərˈtikyələ/ ▸ plural form of DIVERTICULUM.

di·ver·tic·u·lar /ˌdīvərˈtikyələr/ ▸*adj.* [*attrib.*] *Medicine* of or relating to diverticula.

di·ver·tic·u·lar dis·ease ▸*n.* a condition in which muscle spasm in the colon (lower intestine) in the presence of diverticula causes abdominal pain and disturbance of bowel function without inflammation.

di·ver·tic·u·li·tis /ˌdīvərˌtikyəˈlītis/ ▸*n. Medicine* inflammation of a diverticulum, esp. in the colon, causing pain and disturbance of bowel function. Compare with DIVERTICULOSIS.

di·ver·tic·u·lo·sis /ˌdīvərˌtikyəˈlōsis/ ▸*n. Medicine* a condition in which diverticula are present in the intestine without signs of inflammation. Compare with DIVERTICULITIS.

di·ver·tic·u·lum /ˌdīvərˈtikyələm/ ▸*n.* (*pl.* **-la** /-lə/) *Anatomy & Zoology* a blind tube leading from a cavity or passage. ■ *Medicine* an abnormal sac or pouch formed at a weak point in the wall of the alimentary tract. ▷early 19th cent.: from medieval Latin, variant of Latin *deverticulum* 'byway,' from *devertere* 'turn down or aside.'

di·ver·ti·men·to /diˌvərtəˈmentō/ ▸*n.* (*pl.* **-men·ti** /-ˈmentē/ or **-men·tos**) *Music* a light and entertaining composition, typically one in the form of a suite for chamber orchestra. ▷mid 18th cent. (denoting a diversion or amusement): Italian, literally 'diversion.'

di·ver·tisse·ment /diˈvərtismənt/ ▸*n.* a minor entertainment or diversion: *as a Sunday divertissement Wittgenstein would play Schubert quartets.* ■ *Ballet* a short dance within a ballet that displays a dancer's technical skill without advancing the plot or character development. ▷early 18th cent. (specifically denoting a short ballet): French, from *divertiss-*, stem of *divertir*, from Latin *divertere* 'turn in separate ways.'

Di·ves /ˈdīˌvēz/ ▸*n. poetic/literary* used to refer to a typical or hypothetical rich man: *there must be rich and poor, Dives says, smacking his claret.* ▷late Middle English: from late Latin, used in the Vulgate translation of the Bible (Luke 16).

di·vest /diˈvest; dī-/ ▸*v.* [*trans.*] deprive (someone) of power, rights, or possessions: *men are unlikely to be **divested of** power without a struggle.* ■ deprive (something) of a particular quality: *he has **divested** the original play **of** its charm.* ■ [*intrans.*] rid oneself of something that one no longer wants or requires, such as a business interest or investment: *it appears easier to carry on in the business than to divest | the government's policy of **divesting itself of** state holdings.* ■ *dated* or *humorous* relieve (someone) of something being worn or carried: *she divested him of his coat.* ▷early 17th cent.: alteration of *devest*, from Old French *desvestir*, from *des-* (expressing removal) + Latin *vestire* (from *vestis* 'garment').

di·vest·i·ture /diˈvestiˌCHər; -ˌCHo͝or; dī-/ (also **di·ves·ture** /-ˈvesCHər; -CHo͝or/) ▸*n.* the action or process of selling off subsidiary business interests or investments: *the divestiture of state-owned assets.* ▷early 17th cent.: from medieval Latin *divestit-* 'divested' (from the verb *divestire*) + -URE.

di·vest·ment /diˈvestmənt; dī-/ ▸*n.* another term for DIVESTITURE.

div·i ▸*n.* (*pl.* **div·is**) variant spelling of DIVVY.

di·vide /diˈvīd/ ▸*v.* **1** separate or be separated into parts: [*trans.*] *consumer magazines can be **divided into** a number of different categories* | [*intrans.*] *the cell clusters began to divide rapidly.* ■ [*trans.*] separate (something) into portions and distribute a share to each of a number of people: *Jack **divided up** the rest of the cash | the property was **divided among** his heirs.* ■ [*trans.*] allocate (different parts of one's time, attention, or efforts) to different activities or places: *the last years of her life were **divided between** Bermuda and Paris.* ■ [*trans.*] form a boundary between (two people or things): *the artificial barrier that has **divided** an academic education **from** a vocational one.* ■ (of a legislative assembly) separate or be separated into two groups for voting: [*intrans.*] *the House divided: 287 for, 196 against.* **2** disagree or cause to disagree: [*trans.*] *the question had divided Frenchmen since the Revolution* | [as *adj.*] (**divided**) *a divided party leadership* | [*intrans.*] *cities where politicians frequently divide along racial lines.* **3** [*trans.*] *Mathematics* find how many times (a number) contains another: *36 **divided by** 2 equals 18* | [*intrans.*] *the program helps children to multiply and divide quickly and accurately.* ■ [*intrans.*] (of a number) be susceptible to division without a remainder: *30 does not divide by 8.* ■ find how many times (a number) is contained in another: ***divide** 4 **into** 20.* ■ [*intrans.*] (of a number) be contained in a number without a remainder: *3 divides into 15.*
▸*n.* a wide divergence between two groups, typically producing tension or hostility: *there was still a profound cultural **divide between** the parties.* ■ a boundary between two things: *symbolically, the difference of sex is a divide.* ■ a ridge or line of high ground forming the division between two valleys or river systems. ▷Middle English (as a verb): from Latin *dividere* 'force apart, remove.' The noun dates from the mid 17th cent.
▸*PHRASES* □ **divide and conquer** (or **rule**) the policy of maintaining control over one's subordinates or subjects by encouraging dissent between them. □ **divided against itself** (of a group that should be coherent) split by factional interests: *the regime is profoundly divided against itself.*

di·vid·ed high·way ▸*n.* a road with a median strip between the traffic in opposite directions and typically two or more lanes in each direction.

di·vid·ed skirt ▸*n. dated* culottes.

div·i·dend /ˈdiviˌdend/ ▸*n.* **1** a sum of money paid regularly (typically quarterly) by a company to its shareholders out of its profits (or reserves). ■ a payment divided among a number of people, e.g., members of a cooperative or creditors of an insolvent estate. ■ an individual's share of a dividend. ■ (**dividends**) a benefit from an action or policy: *persistence **pays dividends**.* See also PEACE DIVIDEND. **2** *Mathematics* a number to be divided by another number. ▷late 15th cent. (in the general sense 'portion, share'): from Anglo-Norman French *dividende*, from Latin *dividendum* 'something to be divided,' from the verb *dividere* (see DIVIDE).

div·i·dend cov·er·age ▸*n.* the ratio of a company's dividends to its net income.

div·i·dend yield ▸*n.* a dividend expressed as a percentage of a current share price.

di·vid·er /diˈvīdər/ ▸*n.* **1** a person or thing that divides a whole into parts. ■ an issue on which opinions are divided: *the big divider was still nuclear weapons.* ■ (also **room divider**) a screen or piece of furniture that divides a room into two parts. **2** (**dividers**) a measuring compass, esp. one with a screw for making fine adjustments.

di·vid·ing line ▸*n.* the boundary between two areas: ***the dividing line between** eastern and western zones.* ■ a distinction or set of distinctions marking the difference between two related things: ***the dividing line between** drama and reality.*

div·i-div·i /ˈdivē ˈdivē/ ▸*n.* (*pl.* **div·i-div·is**) a tropical American tree of the pea family, bearing curled pods. • *Caesalpinia coriaria*, family Leguminosae. ■ these pods, used as a source of tannin. ▷mid 19th cent.: via American Spanish from Carib.

div·i·na·tion /ˌdivəˈnāSHən/ ▸*n.* the practice of seeking knowledge of the future or the unknown by supernatural means. ▷late Middle English: from Latin *divinatio(n-)*, from *divinare* 'predict' (see DIVINE²). —**di·vin·a·to·ry** /diˈvinəˌtôrē/ *adj.*

di·vine¹ /diˈvīn/ ▸*adj.* (**-vin·er**, **-vin·est**) **1** of, from, or like God or a god: *heroes with divine powers | paintings of shipwrecks being prevented by divine intervention.* ■ devoted to God; sacred: *divine liturgy.* **2** *informal, dated* excellent; delightful: *that succulent clementine tasted divine | he had the most divine smile.*
▸*n.* **1** *dated* a cleric or theologian. **2** (**the Divine**) providence or God. ▷late Middle English: via Old French from Latin *divinus*, from *divus* 'godlike' (related to *deus* 'god'). —**di·vine·ly** *adv.* —**di·vine·ness** *n.*

THE RIGHT WORD **consecrated, divine, hallowed, holy, sacred**

Holy is the only one of these words associated with religion and worship that may be applied directly to the Supreme Being.

Something that is *holy* is regarded with the highest reverence because of its connection with God or a god (*Christmas is a holy day in the Christian calendar*). Something that is **sacred**, on the other hand, is set apart as holy or is dedicated to some exalted purpose (*sacred music*) but may derive its holiness from a human source rather than from God (*a sacred oath between brothers*).

In its strictest sense, **divine** means associated with or derived from God (*the divine right of kings*), but it has also been used to describe anything that is admirable or treasured (*her wedding dress was divine*).

Hallowed and **consecrated** refer to what has been made sacred or holy, with *hallowed* connotating intrinsic holiness (*they walked on hallowed ground*) and *consecrated* meaning blessed by a formal rite or formally dedicated to some religious use (*the old building had been consecrated as a church*).

di·vine² ▸*v.* [*trans.*] discover (something) by guesswork or intuition: *his brother usually divined his ulterior motives* | [with *clause*] *they had divined that he was a fake.* See note at PREDICT. ■ have supernatural or magical insight into (future events): *frauds who claimed to divine the future in chicken's entrails.* ■ discover (water) by dowsing. ▷late Middle English: from Old French *deviner* 'predict,' from Latin *divinare*, from *divinus* (see DIVINE¹). —**di·vin·er** *n.*

Di·vine Of·fice ▸*n.* see OFFICE (sense 4).

Di·vine One, the, see VAUGHAN².

di·vine right of kings ▸*n.* the doctrine that kings derive their authority from God, not from their subjects, from which it follows that rebellion is the worst of political crimes. It was claimed in Britain by the earlier Stuarts and is also associated with the absolutism of Louis XIV of France.

di·vine serv·ice ▸*n.* public Christian worship.

div·ing /ˈdīviNG/ ▸*n.* **1** the sport or activity of swimming or exploring under water. **2** the sport or activity of diving into water from a diving board.

div·ing bee·tle ▸*n.* a predatory water beetle that has fringed back legs for swimming and stores air under its wing cases while diving. • Family Dytiscidae: numerous genera and species, including the **great diving beetle** (*Dytiscus marginalis*).

div·ing bell ▸*n.* an open-bottomed chamber supplied with compressed air, in which a person can be let down under water.

div·ing board ▸*n.* an elevated board projecting over a swimming pool or other body of water, from which people dive or jump in.

div·ing duck ▸*n.* a duck of a type that dives under water for food, such as the pochard, scaup, tufted duck, and goldeneye. Compare with DABBLING DUCK. • Tribes Aythyini and Mergini, family Anatidae: several genera, in particular *Aythya* and *Bucephala*.

div·ing pet·rel ▸*n.* a stocky auklike seabird of southern oceans, having black upper parts and white underparts. • Family Pelecanoididae and genus *Pelecanoides*: four species, in particular the **common** (or **northern**) **diving petrel** (*P. urinatrix*).

div·ing suit ▸*n.* a watertight suit, typically with a helmet and an air supply, worn for working or exploring deep under water.

di·vin·ing rod ▸*n.* a stick or rod used for dowsing.

di·vin·i·ty /diˈvinitē/ ▸*n.* **1** (*pl.* **-ies**) the state or quality of being divine: *Christ's divinity.* ■ the study of religion; theology: *a doctor of divinity.* ■ a divine being; a god or goddess: *busts of various Roman divinities.* ■ (**the Divinity**) God. **2** a fluffy, creamy candy made with stiffly beaten egg whites. ▷Middle English: from

Old French *divinite*, from Latin *divinitas*, from *divinus* 'belonging to a deity' (see DIVINE[1]).

di·vi·nize /ˈdivəˌnīz/ ▶*v.* [*trans.*] make (someone) divine; deify: *this brush with death seems to have divinized her.* ▷mid 17th cent.: from French *diviniser*, from *divin* 'divine.'

di·vi·si /diˈvēzē/ ▶*adj.* a musical direction indicating that a section of players should be divided into two or more groups, each playing a different part: [*postpositive*] *violas divisi* | *divisi passages.*
▶*n.* (*pl.* same) a passage written or played in this manner. ▷Italian, literally 'divided' (plural), from *dividere* 'to divide.'

di·vis·i·ble /diˈvizəbəl/ ▶*adj.* capable of being divided: *the marine environment is divisible into a number of areas.* ■ *Mathematics* (of a number) capable of being divided by another number without a remainder: *24 **is divisible by** 4.* ▷late Middle English: from late Latin *divisibilis*, from *divis-* 'divided,' from the verb *dividere* (see DIVIDE). —**di·vis·i·bil·i·ty** /-ˌvizəˈbilitē/ *n.*

di·vi·sion /diˈvizHən/ ▶*n.* **1** the action of separating something into parts, or the process of being separated: *the division of the land into small fields* | *a gene that helps regulate cell division.* ■ the distribution of something separated into parts: *the **division** of his estates **between** the two branches of his family.* ■ an instance of members of a legislative body separating into two groups to vote for or against a bill: *the new clause was agreed without a division.* ■ the action of splitting the roots of a perennial plant into parts to be replanted separately, as a means of propagation: *the plant can also be easily increased by division in autumn.* ■ *Logic* the action of dividing a wider class into two or more subclasses. **2** disagreement between two or more groups, typically producing tension or hostility: *a growing sense of **division between** north and south* | *a country with ethnic and cultural divisions.* **3** the process or skill of dividing one number by another. See also LONG DIVISION, SHORT DIVISION. ■ *Mathematics* the process of dividing a matrix, vector, or other quantity by another under specific rules to obtain a quotient. **4** each of the parts into which something is divided: *the main divisions of the book.* ■ a major unit or section of an organization, typically one handling a particular kind of work: *a retail division.* ■ a group of army brigades or regiments: *an infantry division.* ■ a number of teams or competitors grouped together in a sport for competitive purposes according to such characteristics as ability, size, or geographic location: *the team will finish in fifth place in Division One.* ■ a part of a county, country, or city defined for administrative or political purposes: *a licensing division of a district.* ■ *Brit.* a part of a county or borough forming a parliamentary constituency: *he was MP for the Lancaster division of North Lancashire.* ■ *Botany* a principal taxonomic category that ranks above class and below kingdom, equivalent to the phylum in zoology. ■ *Zoology* any subsidiary category between major levels of classification. **5** a partition that divides two groups or things: *the villagers lived in a communal building and there were no solid divisions between neighbors.* ▷late Middle English: from Old French *devisiun*, from Latin *divisio(n-)*, from the verb *dividere* (see DIVIDE).
▶*PHRASE* □ **division of labor** the assignment of different parts of a manufacturing process or task to different people in order to improve efficiency.

di·vi·sion·al /diˈvizHənl/ ▶*adj.* of or relating to an organizational or administrative division: *a divisional manager.* ■ forming a partition: *divisional walls.* —**di·vi·sion·al·ly** *adv.*

di·vi·sion·al·ize /diˈvizHənlˌīz/ ▶*v.* [*trans.*] [usu. as *adj.*] (**divisionalized**) subdivide (a company or other organization) into a number of separate divisions: *a large divisionalized Western corporation.* ■ [*intrans.*] undergo this process. —**di·vi·sion·al·i·za·tion** /diˌvizHənələˈzāsHən/ *n.*

di·vi·sion·ism /diˈvizHəˌnizəm/ ▶*n.* another term for POINTILLISM.

di·vi·sion sign ▶*n.* the sign ÷, placed between two numbers showing that the first is to be divided by the second, as in *6 ÷ 3 = 2.*

di·vi·sive /diˈvisiv/ ▶*adj.* tending to cause disagreement or hostility between people: *the highly divisive issue of abortion.* ▷mid 16th cent. (as a noun denoting something that divides or separates): from late Latin *divisivus*, from Latin *dividere* (see DIVIDE). —**di·vi·sive·ly** *adv.* —**di·vi·sive·ness** *n.*

di·vi·sor /diˈvīzər/ ▶*n.* *Mathematics* a number by which another number is to be divided. ■ a number that divides into another without a remainder: *the greatest common divisor.* ▷late Middle English: from French *diviseur* or Latin *divisor*, from *dividere* (see DIVIDE).

di·vorce /diˈvôrs/ ▶*n.* the legal dissolution of a marriage by a court or other competent body: *her **divorce from** her first husband* | *one in three marriages ends in divorce* | [as *adj.*] *divorce proceedings.* ■ a legal decree dissolving a marriage. ■ [in *sing.*] a separation between things that were or ought to be connected: *the bitter divorce between the company and its largest shareholder.*
▶*v.* [*trans.*] legally dissolve one's marriage with (someone): *he divorced his first wife after 10 months* | [as *adj.*] (**divorced**) *a divorced couple* | [*intrans.*] *they divorced eight years later.* ■ separate or dissociate (something) from something else: *we knew how to **divorce** an issue **from** an individual.* ■ (**divorce oneself from**) distance or dissociate oneself from (something): *he wanted to divorce himself from all contact with the syndicate.* ▷late Middle English: the noun from Old French *divorce*, from Latin *divortium*, based on *divertere* (see DIVERT); the verb from Old French *divorcer*, from late Latin *divortiare*, from *divortium*. —**di·vorce·ment** *n.*

di·vor·cée /divôrˈsā -ˈsē/ (also **di·vor·cee**) ▶*n.* a divorced woman. ▷early 19th cent.: from French *divorcée* 'divorced woman.'

div·ot /ˈdivət/ ▶*n.* a piece of turf cut out of the ground by a golf club in making a stroke. ■ *chiefly Scottish* a piece of turf, as formerly used for roofing cottages. ▷early 16th cent.: of unknown origin.

di·vulge /diˈvəlj; dī-/ ▶*v.* [*trans.*] make known (private or sensitive information): *I am too much of a gentleman to divulge her age.* ▷late Middle English (in the sense 'announce publicly'): from Latin *divulgare*, from *di-* 'widely' + *vulgare* 'publish' (from *vulgus* 'common people'). —**div·ul·ga·tion** /ˌdivəlˈgāsHən/ *n.* —**di·vul·gence** /-jəns/ *n.*

div·vy /ˈdivē/ *informal* ▶*v.* (**div·vies, div·vied**) [*trans.*] divide up and share: *they **divvied up** the proceeds.*
▶*n.* **1** (also **div·i**) (*pl.* **div·ies**) *Brit.* a dividend or share, esp. of profits earned by a cooperative. **2** a distribution. ■ a portion or share. ▷late 19th cent.: abbreviation of DIVIDEND.

Di·wa·li /diˈwälē/ (also **Di·va·li** /diˈvälē/) ▶*n.* a Hindu festival of lights, held in the period October to November, to celebrate the new season at the end of the monsoon. It is particularly associated with Lakshmi, the goddess of prosperity, and marks the beginning of the fiscal year in India. ▷from Hindi *dīvālī*, from Sanskrit *dīpāvali* 'row of lights,' from *dīpā* 'lamp' + *vali* 'row.'

di·wan /diˈwän/ (also **de·wan**) ▶*n.* **1** (in Islamic societies) a central finance department, chief administrative office, or regional governing body. **2** a chief treasury official, finance minister, or prime minister in some Indian states. ▷Urdu, from Persian *dīwān* 'fiscal register'; compare with DIVAN.

Dix /diks/, Dorothea Lynde (1802–87), U.S. social reformer. She was a pioneer in U.S. prison reform, a creator of almshouses and insane asylums, and superintendent of women army nurses during the Civil War.

Dix·ie (also **Dix·ie·land**) an informal name for the southern U.S. states. It was used in the song "Dixie" (1859), a marching song popular with Confederate soldiers in the Civil War.
▶*PHRASE* □ **whistle Dixie** engage in unrealistic fantasies; waste one's time: *until you nail down the facts, you're just whistling Dixie.*

Dix·ie·crat /ˈdiksēˌkrat/ ▶*n.* *informal* any of the Southern Democrats who seceded from the party in 1948 in opposition to its policy of extending civil rights.

Dix·ie Cup ▶*n.* *trademark* a brand of disposable paper cup.

Dix·ie·land /ˈdiksēˌland/ ▶*n.* a kind of jazz with a strong two-beat rhythm and collective improvisation that originated in New Orleans in the early 20th century.

DIY ▶*abbr.* do-it-yourself.

Di·yar·ba·kir /diˈyärˌbəkər/ a city in southeastern Turkey; pop. 381,100.

di·zy·got·ic /ˌdīzīˈgätik/ (also **di·zy·gous** /dīˈzīgəs/) ▶*adj.* (of twins) derived from two separate ova, and so not identical.

diz·zy /ˈdizē/ ▶*adj.* (**-zi·er, -zi·est**) having or involving a sensation of spinning around and losing one's balance: *Jonathan had begun to suffer dizzy spells* | *figurative he looked around, dizzy with happiness.* ■ causing such a sensation: *a sheer, dizzy drop figurative a dizzy range of hues.* ■ *informal* (of a woman) silly but attractive: *he only married me because he wanted a dizzy blonde.*
▶*v.* (**-zies, -zied**) [*trans.*] [usu. as *adj.*] (**dizzying**) make (someone) feel unsteady, confused, or amazed: *the dizzying rate of change* | *her nearness dizzied him.* ▷Old English *dysig* 'foolish'; related to Low German *dusig*, *dösig* 'giddy' and Old High German *tusic* 'foolish, weak.' —**diz·zi·ly** /ˈdizəlē/ *adv.* —**diz·zi·ness** *n.*

DJ ▶*n.* a disc jockey. ■ a person who uses samples of recorded music to make techno, rap, or dance music.

Dja·kar·ta variant spelling of JAKARTA.

djeb·el ▶*n.* variant spelling of JEBEL.

djel·la·ba /jəˈläbə/ (also **djel·la·bah** or **jel·la·ba**) ▶*n.* a loose hooded cloak, typically woolen, of a kind traditionally worn by Arabs. ▷early 19th cent.: from Moroccan Arabic *jellāba, jellābiyya*.

djem·be /ˈjembə; -bā/, ▶*n.* *Music* a kind of goblet-shaped hand drum originating in West Africa. ▷French *djembé*, from Mande *jembe*.

DJIA ▶*abbr.* Dow Jones Industrial Average.

djib·ba /ˈjibə/ (also **djib·bah**) ▶*n.* variant spelling of JIBBA.

Dji·bou·ti /jəˈbo͞otē/ (also **Ji·bu·ti**) a country on the northeastern coast of Africa; pop. 466,900; capital, Djibouti; languages, Arabic and French (official), Somali and other Cushitic languages. ■ the capital of Djibouti, a port at the western end of the Gulf of Aden; pop. 290,000. —**Dji·bou·ti·an** /-tēən/ *adj.* & *n.*

The territory became a French protectorate under the name of French Somaliland in 1897. It was renamed the French Territory of the Afars and Issas in 1946 because the Afars and the Issas are the country's two main ethnic groups. In 1977, the country achieved independence as the Republic of Djibouti.

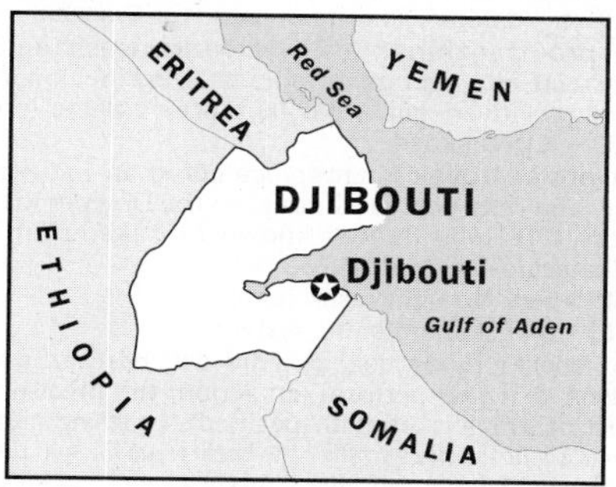

djinn /jin/ ▶*n.* variant spelling of JINN.

dkl ▶*abbr.* dekaliter(s).

dkm ▶*abbr.* dekameter(s).

DL ▶*abbr.* ■ *Football* defensive lineman. ■ disabled list.

dl ▶*abbr.* deciliter(s).

D lay·er ▶*n.* the lowest layer of the ionosphere, able to reflect low-frequency radio waves. ▷1930s: from an arbitrary use of the letter *D*.

DLitt (also **DLit**) ▶*abbr.* ■ Doctor of Letters. ■ Doctor of Literature. ▷from Latin *Doctor Litterarum*.

DLL *Computing* ▶*abbr.* dynamic link library, a collection of subroutines stored on disk, which can be loaded into memory and executed when accessed by a running program.

DM (also **D-mark**) ▶*abbr.* Deutschmark.

dm ▶*abbr.* decimeter(s).

DMA ▶*abbr.* ■ Doctor of Musical Arts. ■ direct memory access, a method allowing a peripheral device to transfer data to or from the memory of a computer system using operations not under the control of the central processor.

DMAE ▶*abbr.* dimethylaminoethanol, a naturally occurring metabolite with cholinergic properties that is used therapeutically in attention and motion disorders, and topically as an antiwrinkle treatment.

D-mark ▶*n.* short for DEUTSCHMARK.

DMCA ▶*abbr.* Digital Millennium Copyright Act.

DMD ▶*abbr.* ■ Doctor of Dental Medicine. [from Latin *Dentariae Medicinae Doctor* or *Doctor Medicinae Dentalis*] ■ Duchenne muscular dystrophy.

DMSO *Chemistry* ▶*abbr.* dimethyl sulfoxide.

DMus ▶*abbr.* Doctor of Music.

DMV ▶*abbr.* Department of Motor Vehicles.

DMZ ▶*abbr.* demilitarized zone, an area from which warring parties agree to remove their military forces.

DNA ▶*n.* *Biochemistry* deoxyribonucleic acid, a self-replicating material present in nearly all living

Pronunciation Key ə *ago;* ər *over;* ˈə *or* ˌə *up;* ˈər *or* ˌər *fur;* a *hat;* ā *rate;* ä *car;* CH *chew;* e *let;* ē *see;* e(ə)r *air;* i *fit;* ī *by;* i(ə)r *ear;* NG *sing;* ō *go;* ô *for;* oi *boy;* o͝o *good;* o͞o *goo;* ou *out;* SH *she;* TH *thin;* T͟H *then;* (h)w *why;* ZH *vision*

D

organisms as the main constituent of chromosomes. It is the carrier of genetic information.

Each molecule of DNA consists of two strands coiled around each other to form a double helix, a structure like a spiral ladder. Each rung of the ladder consists of a pair of chemical groups called bases (of which there are four types), which combine in specific pairs so that the sequence on one strand of the double helix is complementary to that on the other. It is the specific sequence of bases that constitutes the genetic information.

DNA fin·ger·print·ing (**DNA profiling**) ▸*n.* the analysis of DNA from samples of body tissues or fluids in order to identify individuals.

DNase /ˌdēˈenās; -āz/ ▸*n.* *Biochemistry* an enzyme that catalyzes the hydrolysis of DNA into oligonucleotides and smaller molecules. Also called DEOXYRIBONUCLEASE. ▷1940s: from **DNA** + **-ASE**.

DNA vi·rus ▸*n.* a virus in which the genetic information is stored in the form of DNA (as opposed to RNA).

Dnie·per /ˈnēpər; dəˈnēpər/ a river in eastern Europe that rises in Russia west of Moscow and flows south for about 1,370 miles (2,200 km) through Ukraine to the Black Sea. Ukrainian name DNIPRO .

Dnies·ter /ˈnēstər; dəˈnēstər/ a river in eastern Europe that rises in the Carpathian Mountains in western Ukraine and flows 876 miles (1,410 km) to the Black Sea near Odessa. Russian name DNESTR, Ukrainian name DNISTER.

Dnipro /ˈ(d)nēprō/ Ukrainian name for DNIEPER.

Dni·pro·dzer·zhinsk /dəˌnyēprōdzirˈzHēnsk/ an industrial city and river port in Ukraine, on the Dnieper River; pop. 283,600. Former name (until 1936) KAMENSKOYE.

Dni·pro·pe·trovsk /dəˌnyēprōpəˈtrôfsk/ an industrial city and river port in Ukraine, on the Dnieper River; pop. 1,187,000. It was known as Yekaterinoslav (Ekaterinoslav) until 1926.

DNR ▸*abbr.* ■ do not resuscitate.

DNS ▸*abbr.* domain name system.

do[1] /do͞o/ ▸*v.* (**does** /dəz/; *past* **did** /did/; *past part.* **done** /dən/) **1** [*trans.*] perform (an action, the precise nature of which is often unspecified): *something must be done about the city's traffic* | *she knew what she was doing* | *what can I do for you?* | *Brian was making eyes at the girl, and had been* **doing so** *for most of the hearing.* ■ perform (a particular task): *Dad always did the cooking on Sundays.* ■ work on (something) to bring it to completion or to a required state: *it takes them longer to do their hair than me* | *she's the secretary and does the publicity.* ■ make or have available and provide: *he's doing bistro food* | *many hotels don't do single rooms at all* | [with *two objs.*] *he decided to do her a favor.* ■ solve; work out: *Joe was doing sums aloud.* ■ cook (food) to completion or to a specified degree: *if a knife inserted into the center comes out clean, then your pie is done.* ■ (often in questions) work at for a living: *what does she do?* ■ produce or give a performance of (a particular play, opera, etc.): *the Royal Shakespeare Company is doing* Macbeth *next month.* ■ perform (a particular role, song, etc.) or imitate (a particular person) in order to entertain people: *he not only does Schwarzenegger and Groucho, he becomes them.* ■ *informal* take (a narcotic drug): *he doesn't smoke, drink, or do drugs.* ■ attend to (someone): *the barber said he'd do me next.* ■ *vulgar slang* have sexual intercourse with. ■ (**do it**) *informal* have sexual intercourse. ■ (**do it**) *informal* urinate; defecate. **2** [*trans.*] achieve or complete, in particular: ■ travel (a specified distance): *one car I looked at had done 112,000 miles.* ■ travel at (a specified speed): *I was speeding, doing seventy-five.* ■ make (a particular journey): *last time I did New York–Philadelphia round trip by train it was over 80 bucks.* ■ achieve (a specified sales figure): *our best-selling album did about a million worldwide.* ■ [*trans.*] *informal* visit as a tourist, esp. in a superficial or hurried way: *the tourists are allotted only a day to "do" Verona.* ■ spend (a specified period of time), typically in prison or in a particular occupation: *he did five years for manslaughter.* ■ [*intrans.*] *informal* finish: *you must sit there and wait till I'm done* | [with *present participle*] *we're done arguing.* ■ (**be done**) be over: *the special formula continues to beautify your tan when the day is done.* ■ (**be/have done with**) give up concern for: have finished with: *I would sell the place and* **have done with it** | *Steve was not done with her.* **3** [*intrans.*] act or behave in a specified way: *they are free to do as they please* | *you did well to bring her back.* ■ make progress or perform in a specified way; get on: *when a team is doing badly, it's not easy for a new player to settle in* | *Mrs. Walters, how're you doing?* ■ [*trans.*] have a specified effect on: *the walk will do me good.* ■ [*trans.*] result in: *the years of stagnation did a lot of harm to the younger generation.* **4** [*intrans.*] be suitable or acceptable: *if he's anything like you, he'll do* | [*trans.*] *a couple of bucks'll do me.* **5** [*trans.*] *informal* beat up; kill: *he was the guy who did Maranzano.* ■ (usu. **be done**) ruin: *once you falter, you're done.* ■ rob (a place): *this would be an easy place to do, and there was plenty of money lying around.* ■ *Brit.* swindle: *in business you had to do your competitors before they did you.* **6** [*trans.*] (usu. **be/get done for**) *Brit., informal* prosecute; convict: *we got done for conspiracy to commit murder.*

▸*auxiliary v.* **1** used before a verb (except *be, can, may, ought, shall, will*) in questions and negative statements: *do you have any pets?* | *did he see me?* | *I don't smoke* | *it does not matter.* ■ used to make tag questions: *you write poetry, don't you?* | *I never seem to say the right thing, do I?* ■ used in negative commands: *don't be silly* | *do not forget.* **2** used to refer to a verb already mentioned: *he looks better than he did before* | *you wanted to enjoy yourself, and you did* | *as the cops get smarter, so do the crooks.* **3** used to give emphasis to a positive verb: *I do want to act on this* | *he did look tired.* ■ used in positive commands to give polite encouragement: *do tell me!* | *do sit down.* **4** used with inversion of a subject and verb when an adverbial phrase begins a clause for emphasis: *only rarely did they succumb* | *not only did the play close, the theater closed.*

▸*phrasal v.* □ **do away with** *informal* put an end to; remove: *the desire to do away with racism.* ■ kill: *he didn't have the courage to do away with her.* □ **do by** *dated* treat or deal with in a specified way: *do as you would be done by* | *she did well by them.* □ **do someone/something down** *Brit., informal* get the better of someone, typically in an underhanded way. ■ criticize someone or something: *they're always moaning and doing British industry down.* □ **do for 1** *informal* defeat, ruin, or kill: *without that contract we're done for.* **2** *Brit., informal* do the cleaning for (a person or private household): *Florrie usually did for the Shermans in the mornings.* **3** suffice for: *the old version will do for now.* □ **do something** (or **nothing**) **for** *informal* enhance (or detract from) the appearance or quality of: *that scarf does nothing for you.* □ **do someone in** *informal* kill someone. ■ (usu. **be done in**) *informal* tire someone out: *after hiking in the hills all day, I was utterly done in.* □ **do someone out of** *informal* deprive someone of (something) in an underhanded or unfair way. □ **do something out** *Brit., informal* decorate or furnish a room or building in a particular style, color, or material: *the basement* **is done out in** *limed oak.* □ **do someone over** *Brit., informal* beat someone up. □ **do something over 1** *informal* repeat something: *to absorb the lesson, I had to do it over and over.* **2** *informal* decorate or furnish a room or building. □ **do someone up** (usu. **be done up**) dress someone up, esp. in an elaborate or impressive way: *Agnes was all done up in a slinky black number.* □ **do something up** (usu. **be done up**) arrange one's hair in a particular way, esp. so as to be pulled back from one's face or shoulders: *her dark hair was done up in a pony tail.* ■ wrap something up: *unwieldy packages all done up with twine.* □ **do with** [with *modal*] would find useful or would like to have or do: *I could do with a cup of coffee.* ■ (**can't/won't be doing with**) *Brit.* be unwilling to tolerate or be bothered with: *she couldn't be doing with meals for one.* □ **do without** (usu. **can do without**) manage without: *she could do without cigarettes for a day.* ■ *informal* would prefer not to have: *I can do without your complaints first thing in the morning.*

▸*n.* (*pl.* **dos** or **do's**) **1** (also **'do**) *informal* short for HAIRDO. **2** *informal, chiefly Brit.* a party or other social event: *the soccer club Christmas do.* **3** *Brit., archaic or informal* a swindle or hoax. ▷Old English *dōn*, of Germanic origin; related to Dutch *doen* and German *tun*, from an Indo-European root shared by Greek *tithēmi* 'I place' and Latin *facere* 'make, do.'

▸PHRASES □ **be to do with** be concerned or connected with: *the problems are usually to do with family tension.* □ **do a ——** *informal* behave in a manner characteristic of (a specified person): *he did a Garbo after his flop in the play.* □ **do battle** enter into a conflict. □ **do one's head** (or **nut**) **in** (or **do one's head**) *Brit., informal* be extremely angry, worried, or agitated. □ **do the honors** see HONOR. □ **do someone/something justice** see JUSTICE. □ **don't —— me** *informal* do not use the word —— to me: *"Don't morning me. Where the hell've you been all night?"* □ **do or die** persist, even if death is the result. ■ used to describe a critical situation where one's actions may result in victory or defeat: *the 72nd hole was do or die.* □ **dos and don'ts** rules of behavior: *I have no knowledge of the political dos and don'ts.* □ **do well for oneself** become successful or wealthy. □ **have** (**got**) **—— to do with** be connected with (someone or something) to the extent specified: *half the country believed rock 'n' roll had something to do with national decline* | *John's got a lot to do with that bribery scandal.* □ **have nothing to do with** have no contact or dealings with: *Billy and his father have had nothing to do with each other for nearly twenty years.* ■ be no business or concern of: *it's my decision—it has nothing to do with you.* ■ be unconnected with: *he says his departure has nothing to do with the calls for his resignation.* □ **it isn't done** *Brit.* used to express the speaker's opinion that something contravenes custom, opinion, or propriety: *in such a society it is not done to admit to taking religion seriously.* □ **it won't do** used to express the speaker's opinion that someone's behavior is unsatisfactory and cannot be allowed to continue: *Don't talk like that—I've told you before, it won't do.* □ **no you don't** *informal* used to indicate that one intends to prevent someone from doing what they were about to do: *Sharon went to get in the taxi. "Oh no you don't," said Steve.* □ **that does it!** *informal* used to indicate that one will not tolerate something any longer: *That does it! Let's go!* □ **that's done it!** *Brit., informal* used to express dismay or anger when something has gone wrong.

do[2] /dō/ ▸*n.* *Music* (in solmization) the first and eighth note of a major scale. ■ the note C in the fixed-do system. ▷mid 18th cent.: from Italian *do*, an arbitrarily chosen syllable replacing *ut*, taken from a Latin hymn (see SOLMIZATION).

do. *dated* ▸*abbr.* ditto.

DOA ▸*abbr.* dead on arrival, used to describe a person who is declared dead immediately upon arrival at a hospital.

do·a·ble /ˈdo͞oəbəl/ ▸*adj.* *informal* within one's powers; feasible: *none of the jobs were fun, but they were doable.*

dob·bin /ˈdäbin/ ▸*n.* *dated* a pet name for a draft horse or a farm horse. ▷late 16th cent.: nickname for the given name *Robert*.

dob·by /ˈdäbē/ ▸*n.* (*pl.* **-bies**) a mechanism attached to a loom for weaving small patterns similar to but simpler than those produced by a Jacquard loom. ▷late 19th cent.: perhaps an application of the given name *Dobbie*, from *Dob* (alteration of the given name *Rob*). The usage is probably an extension of the earlier sense 'benevolent elf' (who performed household tasks secretly).

dob·by weave ▸*n.* a style of patterned weave consisting of small geometric devices repeated frequently.

do·be /ˈdōbē/ ▸*n.* *informal* adobe. ▷mid 19th cent.: abbreviation.

Do·ber·man /ˈdōbərmən/ (also **Do·ber·man pin·scher** /ˈpincHər/) ▸*n.* a large dog of a German breed with powerful jaws and a smooth coat, typically black with tan markings. ▷early 20th cent.: from the name of Ludwig *Dobermann*, 19th-cent. German dog breeder (+ German *Pinscher* 'terrier').

Doberman pinscher

Do·bos To·rte /ˈdôbəs ˈtôrtə; ˌtôrt/ ▸*n.* a rich cake made of alternate layers of sponge and chocolate or mocha cream, with a crisp caramel topping. ▷from German *Dobostorte*, named after József C. *Dobos* (1847–1924), Hungarian pastry cook.

do·bra /ˈdōbrə/ ▸*n.* the basic monetary unit of São Tomé and Principe, equal to 100 centavos. ▷from Portuguese *dóbra* 'doubloon.'

Do·brich /ˈdôbrēcH/ a city in northeastern Bulgaria, the center of an agricultural region; pop. 115,800. It was called Tolbukhin 1949–91 after Soviet marshal Fyodor Ivanovich Tolbukhin.

do·bro /ˈdōbrō/ ▸*n.* (*pl.* **-bros**) *trademark* a type of acoustic guitar with steel resonating disks inside the body under the bridge. ▷1950s: from *Do(pěra) Bro(thers)*, the Czech-American inventors of the instrument.

dobro

Do·bru·ja /ˈdôbro͞oˌjä/ a district in eastern Romania and northeastern Bulgaria on the Black Sea coast, bounded on the north and west by the Danube River.

dob·son·fly /ˈdäbsənˌflī/ ▸*n.* (*pl.* **-flies**) a large gray North American winged insect related to the alderflies. Its predatory aquatic larva (the hellgrammite) is often used as fishing bait. • Family Corydalidae, order Neuroptera: several genera and species, in particular *Corydalus cornutus*. ▷early 20th cent.: of unknown origin.

Dob·so·ni·an /däbˈsōnēən/ ▸*adj.* relating to or denoting a low-cost Newtonian reflecting telescope with large aperture and short focal length, or the simple altazimuth mount used for it. ▷late 20th cent.: from the name of John *Dobson*, American amateur astronomer, + **-IAN**.

Dob·son u·nit /ˈdäbsən/ (abbr.: **DU**) ▸*n.* a unit of measurement for the total amount of ozone in the atmosphere above a point on the earth's surface, one Dobson unit being equivalent to a layer of pure ozone 0.01 mm thick at standard temperature and pressure. ▷1980s: from the name of G. M. B. *Dobson* (1889–1976), British meteorologist.

doc /däk/ *informal* ▸*abbr.* ■ doctor. ■ *Computing* document.

do·cent /ˈdōsənt/ ▸*n.* **1** a person who acts as a guide, typically on a voluntary basis, in a museum, art gallery, or zoo. **2** (in certain universities and colleges) a member of the teaching staff immediately below professorial rank. ▷late 19th cent.: via German from Latin *docent-* 'teaching,' from *docere* 'teach.'

Do·ce·tism /dōˈsēˌtizəm; ˈdōsi-/ ▸*n.* the doctrine, important in Gnosticism, that Christ's body was not human but either a phantasm or of real but celestial substance, and that therefore his sufferings were only apparent. ▷mid 19th cent.: from medieval Latin *Docetae* (the name, based on Greek *dokein* 'seem,' given to a group of 2nd-cent. Christian heretics) + **-ISM**. **—Do·ce·tist** *n.*

doc·ile /ˈdäsəl/ ▸*adj.* ready to accept control or instruction; submissive: *a cheap and docile workforce.* See note at **OBEDIENT**. ▷late 15th cent. (in the sense 'apt or willing to learn'): from Latin *docilis*, from *docere* 'teach.' **—doc·ile·ly** *adv.* **—do·cil·i·ty** /däˈsilitē/ *n.*

dock[1] /däk/ ▸*n.* a structure extending alongshore or out from the shore into a body of water, to which boats may be moored: *the gangplank was lowered to the dock.* ■ an enclosed area of water in a port for the loading, unloading, and repair of ships. ■ (**docks**) a group of such enclosed areas of water along with the wharves and buildings near them. ■ short for **DRY DOCK**. ■ (also **loading dock**) a platform for loading or unloading trucks or freight trains.
▸*v.* [*intrans.*] (of a ship) tie up at a dock, esp. in order to load or unload passengers or cargo: *the ship docked at San Francisco.* ■ [*trans.*] bring (a ship or boat) into such a place: *the riverbank where the fur traders docked their boats.* ■ (of a spacecraft) join with a space station or another spacecraft in space. ■ attach (a piece of equipment) to another: *the user wants to dock a portable into a desktop computer.* ▷late Middle English: from Middle Dutch, Middle Low German *docke*, of unknown origin.

dock[2] ▸*v.* [*trans.*] (usu. **be docked**) deduct (something, esp. an amount of money): *their wages are docked for public displays of affection* | [with *two objs.*] *he will be docked an hour's pay.* ■ cut short (an animal's tail): *fifteen of the dogs had had their tails docked.* ■ cut short the tail of (an animal): *the dog had been docked.*
▸*n.* the solid bony or fleshy part of an animal's tail, excluding the hair. ■ the stump left after a tail has been docked. ▷late Middle English: perhaps related to Frisian *dok* 'bunch, ball (of string, etc.)' and German *Docke* 'doll.' The original noun sense was 'the solid part of an animal's tail,' whence the verb sense 'cut short (an animal's tail),' later generalized to 'reduce, deduct.'

dock[3] ▸*n.* (usu. **the dock**) the enclosure in a criminal court where a defendant is placed. ▷late 16th cent.: probably originally slang and related to Flemish *dok* 'chicken coop, rabbit hutch,' of unknown origin.
▸*PHRASE* □ **in the dock** (of a defendant) on trial in court.

dock[4] ▸*n.* a coarse weed of temperate regions, with inconspicuous greenish or reddish flowers. The leaves are popularly used to relieve nettle stings. • Genus *Rumex*, family Polygonaceae. ▷Old English *docce*, of Germanic origin; related to Dutch dialect *dokke*.

dock·age /ˈdäkij/ ▸*n.* accommodation or berthing of ships at docks. ■ the charge made for using docks.

dock·er /ˈdäkər/ ▸*n.* another term for **LONGSHOREMAN**.

dock·et /ˈdäkit/ ▸*n.* **1** a calendar or list of cases for trial or people having cases pending. ■ an agenda or list of things to be done. **2** a document or label listing the contents of a package or delivery.
▸*v.* (**dock·et·ed, dock·et·ing**) [*trans.*] (usu. **be docketed**) **1** enter (a case or suit) onto a list of those due to be heard: *the case will go to the Supreme Court, and may be docketed for the fall term.* **2** mark (goods or a package) with a document or label listing the contents. ■ annotate (a letter or document) with a brief summary of its contents. ▷late 15th cent.: perhaps from **DOCK**[2]. The word originally denoted a short summary or abstract; hence, in the early 18th cent., 'a document giving particulars of a consignment.'

dock·hand /ˈdäkˌhand/ ▸*n.* a longshoreman.

dock·ing sta·tion ▸*n.* a device to which a portable computer is connected so that it can be used like a desktop computer, with an external power supply, monitor, data transfer capability, etc.

dock·land /ˈdäkˌland/ ▸*n. chiefly Brit.* (also **docklands**) the area containing a city's docks: *plans to redevelop London's docklands.*

dock·o·min·i·um /ˌdäkəˈminēəm/ ▸*n.* (*pl.* **-ums**) a waterfront condominium with a private mooring. ■ a privately owned dock at a marina. ▷1980s: from **DOCK**[1], on the pattern of *condominium*.

dock·side /ˈdäkˌsīd/ ▸*n.* [in *sing.*] the area immediately adjacent to a dock.

dock·work·er /ˈdäkˌwərkər/ ▸*n.* a longshoreman.

dock·yard /ˈdäkˌyärd/ ▸*n.* an area or establishment with docks and equipment for repairing and maintaining ships.

Doc Mar·tens /ˌdäk ˈmärtnz/ (also **Dr. Mar·tens** *trademark (in the UK)*) ▸*plural n. trademark* a type of heavy lace-up boot or shoe with an air-cushioned sole. ▷1970s: named after Klaus *Maertens*, German inventor of the sole.

doc·tor /ˈdäktər/ ▸*n.* **1** a qualified practitioner of medicine; a physician. ■ a qualified dentist or veterinary surgeon. ■ [with *adj.*] *informal* a person who gives advice or makes improvements: *the script doctor rewrote the original.* **2** (**Doctor**) a person who holds a doctorate: *he was made a Doctor of Divinity.* ■ short for **DOCTOR OF THE CHURCH**. ■ *archaic* a teacher or learned person: *the wisest doctor is graveled by the inquisitiveness of a child.* **3** an artificial fishing fly.
▸*v.* [*trans.*] **1** change the content or appearance of (a document or picture) in order to deceive; falsify: *the reports could have been doctored.* ■ alter the content of (a drink, food, or substance) by adding strong or harmful ingredients: *he denied doctoring Stephen's drinks.* ■ *Baseball* tamper with (a ball) so as to affect its movement when pitched. **2** [usu. as *n.*] (**doctoring**) *informal* treat (someone) medically: *he contemplated giving up doctoring.* ■ (often **be doctored**) *Brit.* remove the sexual organs of (an animal) so that it cannot reproduce. ■ (usu. **be doctored**) repair (a machine). ▷Middle English (in the senses 'learned person' and 'Doctor of the Church'): via Old French from Latin *doctor* 'teacher' (from *docere* 'teach'). **—doc·tor·ly** *adj.*
▸*PHRASE* □ **be** (**just**) **what the doctor ordered** *informal* be very beneficial or desirable under the circumstances: *a 2-0 victory is just what the doctor ordered.*

doc·tor·al /ˈdäktərəl/ ▸*adj.* [*attrib.*] relating to or designed to achieve a doctorate: *a doctoral dissertation.*

doc·tor·ate /ˈdäktərit/ ▸*n.* the highest degree awarded by a graduate school or other approved educational organization: *a doctorate in Classics.* ▷mid 17th cent.: from medieval Latin *doctoratus* 'made a doctor.'

Doc·tor of Phi·los·o·phy (abbr.: **Ph.D.**) ▸*n.* a doctorate in any discipline except a few such as law, medicine, or sometimes theology. ■ a person holding such a degree.

Doc·tor of the Church ▸*n.* one of the early Christian theologians regarded as esp. authoritative in the Western Church (particularly St. Augustine of Hippo, St. Jerome, St. Ambrose, and St. Gregory the Great) or later so designated by the pope (e.g., St. Thomas Aquinas, St. Teresa of Ávila). Compare with **FATHERS OF THE CHURCH** (see **FATHER** sense 3).

Doc·tor·ow /ˈdäktəˌrō/, E(dgar) L(awrence) (1931–), U.S. writer. His novels include *Ragtime* (1975), *Billy Bathgate* (1989), *The Waterworks* (1994), and *City of God* (2000).

doc·tri·naire /ˌdäktrəˈner/ ▸*adj.* seeking to impose a doctrine in all circumstances without regard to practical considerations: *a doctrinaire socialist.*
▸*n.* a person who seeks to impose a theory in such a way. ▷early 19th cent.: from French, from *doctrine* (see **DOCTRINE**). **—doc·tri·nair·ism** /-ˌizəm/ *n.*

doc·tri·nal /ˈdäktrənl/ ▸*adj.* concerned with a doctrine or doctrines: *doctrinal disputes.* ▷late Middle English: from late Latin *doctrinalis*, from *doctrina* 'teaching, learning' (see **DOCTRINE**). **—doc·tri·nal·ly** *adv.*

doc·trine /ˈdäktrin/ ▸*n.* a belief or set of beliefs held and taught by a church, political party, or other group: *the doctrine of predestination.* ■ a stated principle of government policy, mainly in foreign or military affairs: *the Monroe Doctrine.* ▷late Middle English: from Old French, from Latin *doctrina* 'teaching, learning,' from *doctor* 'teacher,' from *docere* 'teach.'

D

doc·u·dra·ma /ˈdäkyəˌdrämə/ ▸*n.* a dramatized television movie based on real events. ▷1960s: blend of **DOCUMENTARY** and **DRAMA**.

doc·u·ment ▸*n.* /ˈdäkyəmənt/ a piece of written, printed, or electronic matter that provides information or evidence or that serves as an official record.
▸*v.* /ˈdäkyəˌment/ [*trans.*] record (something) in written, photographic, or other form: *the photographer spent years documenting the lives of miners.* ■ support or accompany with documentation. ▷late Middle English: from Old French, from Latin *documentum* 'lesson, proof' (in medieval Latin 'written instruction, official paper'), from *docere* 'teach.' **—doc·u·ment·a·ble** /ˌdäkyəˈmentəbəl/ *adj.* **—doc·u·ment·al** /ˌdäkyəˈmentl/ *adj.* **—doc·u·ment·er** /-ˌmentər/ *n.*

doc·u·men·tar·i·an /ˌdäkyəmenˈte(ə)rēən/ ▸*n.* **1** a photographer specializing in producing a factual record. ■ a director or producer of documentaries. **2** an expert analyst of historical documents.

doc·u·men·ta·rist /ˌdäkyəˈmentərist/ ▸*n.* another term for **DOCUMENTARIAN** (sense 1).

doc·u·men·ta·ry /ˌdäkyəˈmentərē/ ▸*adj.* consisting of official pieces of written, printed, or other matter: *his book is based on documentary sources.* ■ (of a movie, a television or radio program, or photography) using pictures or interviews with people involved in real events to provide a factual record or report: *he has directed documentary shorts and feature films.*
▸*n.* (*pl.* **-ries**) a movie or a television or radio program that provides a factual record or report.

doc·u·men·ta·tion /ˌdäkyəmenˈtāsʜən/ ▸*n.* **1** material that provides official information or evidence or that serves as a record: *you will have to complete the relevant documentation.* ■ the written specification and instructions accompanying a computer program or hardware. **2** the process of classifying and annotating texts, photographs, etc.: *she arranged the collection and documentation of photographs.*

doc·u·ment case ▸*n.* a lightweight, typically flexible case for carrying papers.

doc·u·ment type def·i·ni·tion (abbr. **DTD**) ▸*n. Computing* a template that sets out the format and tag structure of an SGML-compliant document.

doc·u·soap /ˈdäkyəˌsōp/ ▸*n.* a documentary, usually produced for television and having elements of soap opera, following people in a particular occupation or location over a period of time. ▷1990s: blend of *documentary* and *soap (opera)*.

doc·u·tain·ment /ˌdäkyəˈtānmənt/ ▸*n.* entertainment provided by movies or other presentations that include documentary materials, intended both to inform and to entertain. ■ a movie or other presentation of this kind. ▷1970s: blend of **DOCUMENTARY** and **ENTERTAINMENT**.

DOD ▸*abbr.* Department of Defense.

dod·der[1] /ˈdädər/ ▸*v.* [*intrans.*] tremble or totter, typically because of old age: *spent and nerve-weary, I doddered into the foyer of a third-rate hotel* [as *adj.*] (**doddering**) *that doddering old fool.* ▷early 17th cent.: variant of obsolete dialect *dadder*; related to **DITHER**. **—dod·der·er** *n.* **—dod·der·y** *adj.*

dod·der[2] ▸*n.* a widely distributed parasitic climbing plant of the morning glory family, with leafless threadlike stems that are attached to the host plant by means of suckers. • Genus *Cuscuta*, family Convolvulaceae. ▷Middle English: related to Middle Low German *doder, dodder*, Middle High German *toter*.

dod·dle /ˈdädl/ ▸*n.* [in *sing.*] *Brit., informal* a very easy task: *this printer is a doddle to set up and use.* ▷1930s: perhaps from dialect *doddle* 'toddle,' of unknown origin.

dodeca- ▸*comb. form* (used chiefly in scientific and musical terms) twelve; having twelve: *dodecahedron* | *dodecaphonic.* ▷from Greek.

do·dec·a·gon /dōˈdekəˌgän/ ▸*n.* a plane figure with twelve sides. ▷late 17th cent.: from Greek *dōdekagōnon*, neuter (used as a noun) of *dōdekagōnos* 'twelve-angled.'

do·dec·a·he·dron /dōˌdekəˈhēdrən/ ▸*n.* (*pl.* **-drons** or **-dra** /-drə/) a three-dimensional shape having twelve plane faces, in particular a regular solid figure with twelve equal pentagonal faces. ▷late 16th cent.: from Greek *dōdekaedron*, neuter (used as a noun) of *dōdekaedros* 'twelve-faced.' **—do·dec·a·he·dral** /-drəl/ *adj.*

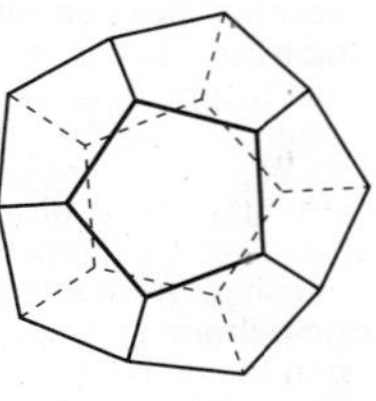

dodecahedron

Do·dec·a·nese /dōˌdekəˈnēz; -ˈnēs; ˌdōdekə-/ a group of twelve islands in the southeastern Aegean Sea, of which the largest is Rhodes.

do·dec·a·phon·ic /dōˌdekəˈfänik/ ▸*adj. Music* another term for **twelve-tone**.

dodge /däj/ ▸*v.* [*trans.*] **1** avoid (someone or something) by a sudden quick movement: *we ducked inside our doorway to dodge shrapnel that was raining down.* ■ [*intrans.*] move quickly to one side or out of the way: *Adam dodged between the cars.* ■ avoid (something) in a cunning or dishonest way: *he went after people who had either dodged the war or invented a record in it.* **2** [often as *n.*] (**dodging**) *Photography* expose (one area of a print) less than the rest during processing or enlarging.
▸*n.* a sudden quick movement to avoid someone or something. ■ a cunning trick or dishonest act, in particular one intended to avoid something unpleasant: *bartering can be seen as a tax dodge.* ▷mid 16th cent. (in the senses 'dither' and 'haggle'): of unknown origin.

dodge·ball /ˈdäjˌbôl/ ▸*n.* a game in which players in a circle try to hit opponents inside the circle, thus eliminating them, with an inflated ball.

Dodge Cit·y /däj/ a city in southwestern Kansas; pop. 21,129. Established in 1872 as a shipping station on the Santa Fe Trail, it rapidly gained a reputation as a rowdy frontier town.

dodg·em /ˈdäjəm/ (also **dodgem car**) ▸*n.* another term for **bumper car**. ▷1920s: U.S. proprietary name (as *Dodg'em*), from the phrase *dodge them.*

dodg·er /ˈdäjər/ ▸*n.* **1** [often with *adj.*] a person who engages in cunning tricks or dishonest practices to avoid something unpleasant: *tax dodgers.* **2** *Nautical* a canvas screen on a ship giving protection from spray. **3** a small handbill or leaflet. **4** see **corn dodger**.

Dodg·son /ˈdäjsən/, Charles Lutwidge, see **Carroll**.

dodg·y /ˈdäjē/ ▸*adj.* (**dodg·i·er, dodg·i·est**) *Brit., informal* dishonest or unreliable: *a dodgy secondhand car salesman.* ■ potentially dangerous: *activities like these could be dodgy for your heart.* ■ of low quality.

do·do /ˈdōdō/ ▸*n.* (*pl.* **-dos** or **-does**) an extinct flightless bird with a stout body, stumpy wings, a large head, and a heavy hooked bill. It was found on Mauritius until the end of the 17th century. • *Raphus cucullatus*, family Raphidae. See also **solitaire** (sense 3). ■ *informal* an old-fashioned and ineffective person or thing. ▷early 17th cent.: from Portuguese *doudo* 'simpleton' (because the bird had no fear of man and was easily killed). Compare with **dotterel**.
▸*PHRASE* □ (**as**) **dead as a** (or **the**) **dodo** *informal* dead (used for emphasis). ■ no longer effective, valid, or interesting: *the campaign was as dead as a dodo.*

Do·do·ma /ˈdōdəmə; -ˌmä/ the capital of Tanzania, in the center of the country; pop. 203,830.

DOE ▸*abbr.* Department of Energy.

doe /dō/ ▸*n.* a female deer. ■ a female of certain other animal species, such as hare, rabbit, rat, ferret, or kangaroo. ▷Old English *dā*, of unknown origin.

doe-eyed ▸*adj.* having large, gentle, dark eyes: *portraits of doe-eyed young girls.*

do·er /ˈdōōər/ ▸*n.* the person who does something: *the doer of the action.* ■ a person who acts rather than merely talking or thinking: *I'm a doer, not a moaner.*

does /dəz/ ▸ third person singular present of **do**[1].

doe·skin /ˈdōˌskin/ ▸*n.* leather made from the skin of a female fallow deer. ■ a fine satin-weave woolen cloth resembling such leather.

does·n't /ˈdəzənt/ ▸*contraction of* does not.

do·est /ˈdōōist/ ▸ *archaic* second person singular present of **do**[1].

do·eth /ˈdōōith/ ▸ *archaic* third person singular present of **do**[1].

doff /däf; dôf/ ▸*v.* [*trans.*] *dated* remove (an item of clothing): *he had doffed tie and jacket and rolled up his shirtsleeves.* ■ tip (one's hat) as a greeting or token of respect: *the manager doffed his hat to her.* ▷late Middle English: contraction of *do off.* Compare with **don**[2].

dog /dôg/ ▸*n.* **1** a domesticated carnivorous mammal that typically has a long snout, an acute sense of smell, and a barking, howling, or whining voice. It is widely kept as a pet or for work or field sports. • *Canis familiaris*, family Canidae (the **dog family**); probably domesticated from the wolf in the Mesolithic period. The dog family also includes the wolves, coyotes, jackals, and foxes. ■ a wild animal of the dog family. ■ the male of an animal of the dog family, or of some other mammals such as the otter: [as *adj.*] *a dog fox.* ■ (in extended and metaphorical use) referring to behavior considered to be savage, dangerous, or wildly energetic: *he bit into the chop voraciously, like a dog.* **2** [often with *adj.*] *informal* a person regarded as unpleasant, contemptible, or wicked (used as a term of abuse): *come out, Michael, you dog!* ■ [with *adj.*] *dated* used to refer to a person of a specified kind in a tone of playful reproof, commiseration, or congratulation: *you lucky dog!* ■ used in various phrases to refer to someone who is abject or miserable, esp. because they have been treated harshly: *I make him* **work like a dog** | *Rob* **was treated like a dog.** ■ *informal, derogatory* a woman regarded as unattractive. ■ *informal* a thing of poor quality; a failure: ***a dog of a** movie.* **3** short for **firedog**. **4** a mechanical device for gripping. **5** (**dogs**) *informal* feet: *if only I could sit down and rest my tired dogs.*
▸*v.* (**dogged, dog·ging**) [*trans.*] **1** follow (someone or their movements) closely and persistently: *photographers seemed to dog her every step.* ■ (of a problem) cause continual trouble for: *their finance committee has been dogged by controversy.* **2** (**dog it**) *informal* act lazily; fail to try one's hardest. **3** grip (something) with a mechanical device: [*trans.*] *she has* ***dogged** the door* ***shut.*** ▷Old English *docga*, of unknown origin. **—dog·like** /-ˌlīk/ *adj.*
▸*PHRASES* □ **dog eat dog** used to refer to a situation of fierce competition in which people are willing to harm each other in order to succeed: *in this business, it's always dog eat dog* | *popular music is a dog-eat-dog industry.* □ **a dog's age** *informal* a very long time: *the best I've seen in a dog's age.* □ **a dog's life** an unhappy existence, full of problems or unfair treatment. □ **the dogs of war** *poetic/literary* the havoc accompanying military conflict. [from Shakespeare's *Julius Caesar* (III. 1. 274).] □ **every dog has its day** *proverb* everyone will have good luck or success at some point in their lives. □ **go to the dogs** *informal* deteriorate shockingly: *the country is going to the dogs.* □ **hair of the dog** see **hair**. □ **let sleeping dogs lie** see **sleep**. □ **not a dog's chance** no chance at all. □ **put on the dog** *informal* behave in a pretentious or ostentatious way: *we have to put on the dog for Anne Marie.* □ **rain cats and dogs** see **rain**. □ (**as**) **sick as a dog** see **sick**[1]. □ **throw someone to the dogs** discard someone as worthless: *the weak and oppressed must not* ***be thrown to the dogs.*** □ **you can't teach an old dog new tricks** *proverb* you cannot make people change their established patterns of opinion and behavior.

dog and pon·y show ▸*n.* an elaborate display or presentation, esp. as part of a promotional campaign.

dog·bane /ˈdôgˌbān/ ▸*n.* a shrubby North American plant, typically having bell-shaped flowers and reputed to be poisonous to dogs. • Genus *Apocynum*, family Apocynaceae: several species, including the common **spreading dogbane** (*A. androsaemifolium*).

dog·ber·ry /ˈdôgˌberē/ ▸*n.* (*pl.* **-ries**) *informal* the fruit of the dogwood. ■ (also **dogberry tree**) the dogwood. ■ a fruit of poor eating quality from any of a number of other shrubs or small trees, e.g., the American rowan.

dog bis·cuit ▸*n.* a hard thick biscuit for feeding to dogs.

dog·cart /ˈdôgˌkärt/ ▸*n.* a two-wheeled horse-drawn cart, with cross seats back to back, originally incorporating a box under the seat for sportsmen's dogs.

dog·catch·er /ˈdôgˌkachər; -ˌkech-/ ▸*n.* an official or employee who rounds up and impounds stray dogs in a community. Also called **dog warden**. ■ *figurative* a low-level political official.

dog clutch ▸*n.* a device for coupling two shafts in order to transmit motion, one part having teeth that engage with slots in another.

dog cock·le ▸*n.* a burrowing bivalve mollusk that has a highly convex, almost spherical, shell. • Family Glycimeridae: many species, including the European *Glycymeris glycymeris.*

dog col·lar ▸*n.* a collar for a dog. ■ informal term for **clerical collar**.

dog days ▸*plural n.* the hottest period of the year (reckoned in antiquity from the heliacal rising of Sirius, the Dog Star). ■ a period of inactivity or sluggishness: *in August the baseball races are in the dog days.*

dog·dom /ˈdôgdəm/ ▸*n.* the world of dogs and dog enthusiasts: *he knows 200 commands and 70 hand signals, a vocabulary record in dogdom.*

doge /dōj/ ▸*n. historical* the chief magistrate of Venice or Genoa. ▷mid 16th cent.: from French, from Venetian Italian *doze*, based on Latin *dux, duc-* 'leader.'

dog-ear ▸*v.* [*trans.*] fold down the corner of (a book or magazine), typically to mark a place.
▸*adj.* (**dog-eared**) (of an object made from paper) with the corners worn or battered with use.

dog-end ▸*n. Brit., informal* a cigarette butt. ■ the last and least pleasing part of something: *the dog-end of a hard day.*

dog·face /ˈdôgˌfās/ ▸*n. informal, dated* a U.S. soldier, esp. an infantryman.

dog-fall ▸*n.* a fall in which wrestlers touch the ground together.

dog·fight /ˈdôgˌfīt/ ▸*n.* a close combat between military aircraft. ■ a ferocious struggle for supremacy between interested parties: *the meeting deteriorated into a dogfight.* ■ a fight between dogs, esp. one organized illegally for public entertainment.
▸*v.* engage in a dogfight: [*intrans.*] *resplendent model airplanes dogfighting in the updrafts.* **—dog·fight·er** *n.*

dog·fish /ˈdôgˌfish/ ▸*n.* (*pl.* same or **-fish·es**) **1** a small sand-colored bottom-dwelling shark with a long tail, common on European coasts. • *Scyliorhinus canicula*, family Scyliorhinidae. **2** [with *adj.*] a small shark that resembles or is related to the dogfish, sometimes caught for food. • Several genera in the families Scyliorhinidae, Squalidae, and Triakidae.

dog·ged /ˈdôgid/ ▸*adj.* having or showing tenacity and grim persistence: *success required dogged determination.* See note at **stubborn**. **—dog·ged·ly** *adv.* **—dog·ged·ness** *n.*

dog·ger[1] /ˈdôgər/ ▸*n. historical* a two-masted, bluff-bowed Dutch sailboat, used for fishing. ▷Middle English: from Middle Dutch.

dog·ger[2] ▸*n. Geology* a large spherical concretion occurring in sedimentary rock. ▷late 17th cent. (originally a dialect word denoting a kind of ironstone): perhaps from **dog**.

dog·ger·el /ˈdôgərəl; ˈdäg-/ ▸*n.* comic verse composed in irregular rhythm. ■ verse or words that are badly written or expressed: *the last stanza deteriorates into doggerel.* ▷late Middle English (as an adjective describing such verse): apparently from **dog** (used contemptuously, as in **dog Latin**) + **-rel**.

dog·gie ▸*n.* variant spelling of **doggy**.

dog·gie bag ▸*n.* a bag used by a restaurant customer or party guest to take home leftover food, supposedly for their dog.

dog·gish /ˈdôgish/ ▸*adj.* of or like a dog. ■ *archaic* (of a person) having the bad qualities of a dog, esp. by being bad-tempered or snappish.

dog·go /ˈdôgō/ ▸*adv.* (in phrase **lie doggo**) *informal* remain motionless and quiet to escape detection: *a dozen officers had been lying doggo for hours.* ▷late 19th cent.: of obscure origin; apparently from **dog** + **-o**.

dog·gone /ˈdôgˈgôn/ *informal* ▸*adj.* [*attrib.*] used to express feelings of annoyance, surprise, or pleasure: *now just a doggone minute* | [as *submodifier*] *it's doggone good to be home.*
▸*v.* [*trans.*] used to express surprise, irritation, or anger: *from that moment,* ***doggone it** if I didn't see a motivation in Joey!* | ***I'll be doggoned if** every fourth kid is affected.* ▷early 19th cent.: probably from *dog on it*, euphemism for *God damn it.*

dog·gy /ˈdôgē/ ▸*adj.* of or like a dog: *his doggy brown eyes.* ■ fond of dogs: *it was a doggy household.*
▸*n.* (also **dog·gie**) (*pl.* **-gies**) a child's word for a dog. **—dog·gi·ness** *n.*

dog·gy style (also **doggy fashion**) ▸*n. and adv. vulgar slang* (in) a position for human sexual intercourse inspired by that of dogs.

dog·house /ˈdôgˌhous/ ▸*n.* a dog's kennel. ■ *Sailing* a raised area at the after end of a yacht's coachroof, providing standing room.
▸*PHRASE* □ **(be) in the doghouse** *informal, often humorous* (be) in mild or temporary disfavor.

do·gie /ˈdōgē/ ▸*n.* (*pl.* **-gies**) a motherless or neglected calf. ▷late 19th cent.: of unknown origin.

dog in the man·ger ▸*n.* a person who is inclined to prevent others from having things that they do not need themselves: *what a dog in the manger you must be!* | [as *adj.*] *she can be so dog in the manger about updating things in the office.* ▷alluding to the fable of the dog that lay in a manger to prevent the ox and horse from eating the hay.

dog Lat·in ▸*n.* a debased form of Latin.

dog·leg /ˈdôgˌleg/ ▸*n.* a thing that bends sharply, in particular a sharp bend in a road or route. ■ *Golf* a hole at which the player cannot aim directly at the green from the tee.
▸*adj.* (also **dog-legged**) bent like a dog's hind leg: *the surf splashes over the dogleg concrete jetty.*
▸*v.* (**-legged, -leg·ging**) [*intrans.*] follow a sharply bending route: *Highway 60 now doglegs northwest toward Frankfort.*

dog·ma /ˈdôgmə/ ▸*n.* a principle or set of principles laid down by an authority as incontrovertibly true: *the Christian dogma of the Trinity* | *the rejection of political dogma.* ▷mid 16th cent.: via late Latin from Greek *dogma* 'opinion,' from *dokein* 'seem good, think.'

dog·mat·ic /dôgˈmatik/ ▸*adj.* inclined to lay down principles as incontrovertibly true: *he gives his opinion without trying to be dogmatic.* ▷early 17th cent. (as a noun denoting a philosopher or physician of a school based on a priori assumptions): via late Latin from Greek *dogmatikos,* from *dogma, dogmat-* (see **DOGMA**). **—dog·mat·i·cal·ly** /-ik(ə)lē/ *adv.*

dog·mat·ics /dôgˈmatiks/ ▸*plural n.* [treated as *sing.*] a system of principles laid down by an authority, esp. the Roman Catholic Church, as incontrovertibly true: *it is a work of analysis, not of dogmatics.*

dog·ma·tism /ˈdôgməˌtizəm/ ▸*n.* the tendency to lay down principles as incontrovertibly true, without consideration of evidence or the opinions of others: *a culture of dogmatism and fanaticism.* ▷early 17th cent.: via French from medieval Latin *dogmatismus,* from Latin *dogma* (see **DOGMA**). **—dog·ma·tist** *n.*

dog·ma·tize /ˈdôgməˌtīz/ ▸*v.* [*trans.*] represent as an incontrovertible truth: *I find views dogmatized to the point of absurdity.* ▷early 17th cent.: via French and late Latin from Greek *dogmatizein* 'lay down one's opinion,' from *dogma* (see **DOGMA**).

dog·nap /ˈdôgˌnap/ ▸*v.* (**-napped, -nap·ping** or **-naped, -nap·ing**) [*trans.*] *informal* steal (a dog), esp. in order to sell it. **—dog·nap·per** *n.*

do-good·er /ˈdo͞o ˌgo͝odər/ ▸*n.* a well-meaning but unrealistic or interfering philanthropist or reformer. **—do-good** *adj.* & *n.* **—do-good·er·y** /-ərē/ *n.* **—do-good·ism** /-go͝odˌizəm/ *n.*

dog pad·dle ▸*n.* an elementary swimming stroke like that of a swimming dog.
▸*v.* (**dog-paddle**) [*intrans.*] swim using this stroke.

dog rac·ing ▸*n.* another term for **GREYHOUND RACING.**

Dog·rib /ˈdôgˌrib/ ▸*n.* **1** a member of a Dene people of northwestern Canada. **2** the Athabaskan language of this people.
▸*adj.* of or relating to this people or their language. ▷translation of Cree *atimospikay*; from the legend that the people's common ancestor was a dog.

dog rose ▸*n.* a delicately scented Eurasian wild rose with pink or white flowers. • Genus *Rosa,* family Rosaceae: several closely related species, in particular *R. canina.*

dogs·bod·y /ˈdôgzˌbädē/ ▸*n.* (*pl.* **-bod·ies**) *informal, chiefly Brit.* a person who is given boring, menial tasks to do: *I got myself a job as typist and general dogsbody on a small magazine.* **—dogs·bod·y·ing** *n.*

dog·skin /ˈdôgˌskin/ ▸*n.* leather made of or imitating dog's skin, esp. as used for gloves.

dog·sled /ˈdôgˌsled/ (also **dog sled**) ▸*n.* a sled designed to be pulled by dogs.
▸*v.* [*intrans.*] [usu. as *n.*] (**dogsledding**) travel by dogsled: *winter activities include cross-country skiing and dogsledding.*

dog's mer·cu·ry ▸*n.* a Eurasian plant of the spurge family, with hairy stems and small green flowers, widely found as a dominant plant of old woodland. • *Mercurialis perennis,* family Euphorbiaceae. ▷late 16th cent.: translating modern Latin *Mercurialis canina* (former taxonomic name); the plant is poisonous and is contrasted with *Mercurialis annua* 'annual mercury,' useful in medicine.

dogs·tail /ˈdôgzˌtāl/ (also **dog's-tail**) ▸*n.* an Old World fodder grass with spiky flowerheads. • Genus *Cynosurus,* family Gramineae: several species, in particular **crested dogstail** (*C. cristatus*), a common pasture grass.

Dog Star the star Sirius. ▷translating Greek *kuon* or Latin *canicula* 'small dog,' both names of the star; so named as it appears to follow at the heels of Orion (the hunter).

dog tag ▸*n.* a metal tag attached to a dog's collar, typically giving its name and owner's address. ■ *informal* a soldier's metal identity tag, worn on a chain around the neck.

dog-tired ▸*adj.* extremely tired; worn out: *he'd gone to bed dog-tired.*

dog·tooth /ˈdôgˌto͞oTH/ ▸*n. Architecture* a small pointed ornament repeated along a molding consisting of four petals radiating from a raised center, used esp. in the Early English style.

dog·tooth vi·o·let ▸*n.* a plant of the lily family that has backward-curving pointed petals. • Genus *Erythronium,* family Liliaceae: several species, in particular the trout lily of North America and the Eurasian *E. dens-canis,* with speckled leaves and pinkish-purple flowers.

dog-trot ▸*n.* **1** [in *sing.*] a gentle easy trot. **2** a breezeway connecting two cabins.
▸*v.* [*intrans.*] move at such a pace.

dog vi·o·let ▸*n.* a scentless wild violet, typically having purple or lilac flowers. • Genus *Viola,* family Violaceae: several species, in particular *V. conspersa* of eastern North America.

dog war·den ▸*n.* another term for **DOGCATCHER.**

dog·watch /ˈdôgˌwäCH/ ▸*n.* either of two short watches on a ship (4–6 or 6–8 p.m.).

dog-wea·ry ▸*adj.* another term for **DOG-TIRED.**

dog whelk ▸*n.* a predatory marine mollusk that typically occurs on the shore or in shallow waters. • Family Nassaridae, class Gastropoda: *Nucella* and other genera.

dog·wood /ˈdôgˌwo͝od/ ▸*n.* a shrub or small tree of north temperate regions that yields hard timber and is grown for its decorative foliage, red stems, and colorful berries. • Genus *Cornus,* family Cornaceae: many species, including the **flowering dogwood** (*C. florida*), common to the eastern U.S. ■ used in names of trees that resemble the dogwood or yield similar hard timber. ▷so named because the wood was formerly used to make "dogs" (i.e., skewers).

flowering dogwood

Do·ha /ˈdōhə/ the capital of Qatar, in the eastern part of the country; pop 300,000.

DOHC ▸*abbr.* double overhead camshaft.

DOI ▸*abbr. Computing* digital object identifier.

doi·ly /ˈdoilē/ ▸*n.* (*pl.* **-lies**) an ornamental mat, typically made of lace and placed under decorative objects. ■ a small ornamental napkin, typically placed under a cake or other sweet foods. ▷late 17th cent.: from *Doiley* or *Doyley,* the name of a 17th-cent. London draper. The word originally denoted a woolen material used for summer wear, said to have been introduced by this draper. The current sense (originally *doily napkin*) dates from the early 18th cent.

do·ing /ˈdo͞oiNG/ ▸*n.* **1** (usu. **doings**) the activities in which a particular person engages: *the latest doings of television stars.* ■ deeds; accomplishments: *he didn't want to trumpet his doings on an open line.* ■ social events: *informal Cajun doings with some fiddling goodtimers.* **2** effort; activity: *it would* **take some doing** *to calm him down.* **3** *informal, chiefly Brit.* a beating or scolding: *someone had* **given** *her* **a doing.**
▸*PHRASE* □ **be someone's doing** be the creation or fault of the person named: *he looked at Lisa as though it was all her doing.*

doit /doit/ ▸*n.* [in *sing.*] *archaic* a very small amount of money. ▷late 16th cent.: from Middle Low German *doyt,* Middle Dutch *duit,* of unknown origin.

do-it-your·self (abbr. **DIY**) ▸*adj.* (of work, esp. building, painting, or decorating) done or to be done by an amateur at home: *easy-to-use materials and do-it-yourself kits for plumbing fittings.* **—do-it-your·self·er** *n.*

do·jo /ˈdōˌjō/ ▸*n.* (*pl.* **-jos**) a room or hall in which judo and other martial arts are practiced. ▷Japanese, from *dō* 'way, pursuit' + *jō* 'a place.'

dol. ▸*abbr.* dollar(s).

Dol·by /ˈdōlbē; ˈdôl-/ ▸*n. trademark* an electronic noise-reduction system used in tape recording to reduce hiss. ■ an electronic system used to provide stereophonic sound for movie theaters and television sets. ▷1960s: named after Ray M. *Dolby* (born 1933), the American engineer who devised it.

dol·ce /ˈdōlCHā/ ▸*adv.* & *adj. Music* (esp. as a direction) sweetly and softly. ▷Italian, literally 'sweet.'

dol·ce far nien·te /ˈdōlCHā fär nēˈentā/ ▸*n.* pleasant idleness. ▷Italian, 'sweet doing nothing.'

dol·ce vi·ta /ˌdōlCHā ˈvētə/ ▸*n.* [in *sing.*] (usu. **la dolce vita**) a life of heedless pleasure and luxury. ▷Italian, literally 'sweet life.'

dol·drums /ˈdōldrəmz; ˈdäl-; ˈdôl-/ ▸*plural n.* (**the doldrums**) low spirits; a feeling of boredom or depression: *color catalogs will rid you of February doldrums.* ■ a period of inactivity or a state of stagnation: *the mortgage market has been* **in the doldrums** *for three years.* ■ an equatorial region of the Atlantic Ocean with calms, sudden storms, and light unpredictable winds. ▷late 18th cent. (as *doldrum* 'dull, sluggish person'): perhaps from **DULL**, on the pattern of *tantrums.*

Dole[1] /dōl/, Bob (1923–), U.S. politician; full name *Robert Joseph Dole.* A U.S. senator 1968–96, he became leader of the Republican Party in 1992. He was defeated by Bill Clinton in the presidential election of 1996.

Dole[2], Elizabeth Hanford (1936–), U.S. politician. She served as U.S. secretary of transportation 1983–87 and U.S. secretary of labor 1989–90 before heading the American Red Cross 1990–99. In 1999, she made an unsuccessful bid for the 2000 Republican presidential nomination. She is married to Bob Dole.

dole[1] /dōl/ ▸*n.* **1** (usu. **the dole**) *chiefly Brit., informal* benefit paid by the government to the unemployed: *she is drawing on the dole.* ■ *dated* a charitable gift of food, clothes, or money. **2** *poetic/literary* a person's lot or destiny.
▸*v.* [*trans.*] (**dole something out**) distribute shares of something: *the scanty portions of food* **doled out** *to them.* ▷Old English *dāl* 'division, portion, or share,' of Germanic origin; related to **DEAL**[1]. The sense 'distribution of charitable gifts' dates from Middle English; the sense 'unemployment benefit' dates from the early 20th cent.
▸*PHRASE* □ **on the dole** *informal* registered as unemployed and receiving benefit from the government.

dole[2] ▸*n. archaic* or *poetic/literary* sorrow; mourning. ▷Middle English: from Old French *doel* 'mourning,' from popular Latin *dolus,* from Latin *dolere* 'grieve.'

dole·ful /ˈdōlfəl/ ▸*adj.* expressing sorrow; mournful: *a doleful look.* See note at **GLUM.** ■ causing grief or misfortune: *doleful consequences.* **—dole·ful·ly** *adv.* **—dole·ful·ness** *n.*

dol·er·ite /ˈdäləˌrīt/ ▸*n. Geology* a dark, medium-grained igneous rock, typically with ophitic texture, containing plagioclase, pyroxene, and olivine. It typically occurs in dikes and sills. Also called **DIABASE.** ▷mid 19th cent.: from French *dolérite,* from Greek *doleros* 'deceptive' (because it is difficult to distinguish from diorite).

dol·i·cho·ce·phal·ic /ˌdälikōsəˈfalik/ ▸*adj. Anatomy* having a relatively long skull (typically with the breadth less than 80 [or 75] percent of the length). Often contrasted with **BRACHYCEPHALIC.** ▷mid 19th cent.: from Greek *dolikhos* 'long' + **-CEPHALIC.** **—dol·i·cho·ceph·a·ly** /-ˈsefəlē/ *n.*

doll /däl/ ▸*n.* a small model of a human figure, often one of a baby or girl, used as a child's toy. ■ *informal* an attractive young woman, often with connotations of unintelligence and frivolity. ■ *informal* an attractive young man. ■ a generous or considerate person: *would you be a doll and set the table?* ■ *informal* used as an affectionate, sometimes offensive, form of address: *hey, doll, wanna dance?*
▸*v.* [*trans.*] (**doll someone up**) *informal* dress someone or oneself smartly and attractively: *I* **got** *all* **dolled up** *for a party.* ■ (**doll something up**) *informal* decorate or dress up something: *you can doll up a plain ham with spiced apples and kale.* ▷mid 16th cent. (denoting a

Pronunciation Key ə *ago*; ər *over*; ˈə or ˌə *up*; ˈər or ˌər *fur*; a *hat*; ā *rate*; ä *car*; CH *chew*; e *let*; ē *see*; e(ə)r *air*; i *fit*; ī *by*; i(ə)r *ear*; NG *sing*; ō *go*; ô *for*; oi *boy*; o͝o *good*; o͞o *goo*; ou *out*; SH *she*; TH *thin*; T͟H *then*; (h)w *why*; ZH *vision*

mistress): nickname for the given name *Dorothy*. The sense 'small model of a human figure' dates from the late 17th cent.

dol·lar /ˈdälər/ ▸*n.* the basic monetary unit of the U.S., Canada, Australia, and certain countries in the Pacific, Caribbean, Southeast Asia, Africa, and South America. ▷from early Flemish or Low German *daler*, from German *T(h)aler*, short for *Joachimsthaler*, a coin from the silver mine of *Joachimsthal* ('Joachim's valley'), now *Jáchymov* in the Czech Republic. The term was later applied to a coin used in the Spanish-American colonies, which was also widely used in the British North American colonies at the time of the American Revolution, hence adopted as the name of the U.S. monetary unit in the late 18th cent.

▸*PHRASE* □ **dollars to doughnuts** *informal* used to emphasize one's certainty: *I'd* ***bet dollars to doughnuts*** *he's a medical student.*

dol·lar ar·e·a ▸*n.* the area of the world in which currency is linked to the U.S. dollar.

dol·lar di·plo·ma·cy ▸*n.* the use of a country's financial power to extend its international influence.

dol·lar gap ▸*n.* the amount by which a country's import trade with the dollar area exceeds the corresponding export trade.

dol·lar·i·za·tion /ˌdäləriˈzāsʜən/ (also **dol·lar·i·sa·tion**) ▸*n.* the process of aligning a country's currency with the U.S. dollar. ■ the dominating effect of the U.S. on the economy of a country.

dol·lar sign (also **dollar mark**) ▸*n.* the sign $, representing a dollar.

doll·house /ˈdälˌhous/ (also *chiefly Brit.* **doll's house**) ▸*n.* a miniature toy house used for playing with dolls.

dol·lop /ˈdäləp/ ▸*n. informal* a shapeless mass or blob of something, esp. soft food: *great* ***dollops of*** *cream* | *figurative a* ***dollop of*** *romance here and there.*

▸*v.* (**-loped, -lop·ing**) [*trans.*] add (a shapeless mass or blob of something) casually and without measuring: *Chekov stopped him from dolloping sugar into his coffee.* ▷late 16th cent. (denoting a clump of grass or weeds in a field): perhaps of Scandinavian origin and related to Norwegian dialect *dolp* 'lump.'

dol·ly /ˈdälē/ ▸*n.* (*pl.* **-lies**) **1** a child's word for a doll. ■ *informal, dated* an attractive and stylish young woman, usually with connotations of unintelligence. **2** a small platform on wheels used for holding heavy objects, typically film or television cameras. **3** *historical* a short wooden pole for stirring clothes in a washtub.

▸*v.* (**-lies, -lied**) [*intrans.*] (of a film or television camera) be moved on a mobile platform in a specified direction: *the camera dollies back to reveal hundreds of people.*

dol·ly bird (also **dol·ly-bird**) ▸*n. chiefly Brit., informal, dated* an attractive and stylish young woman, considered with reference only to her appearance.

dol·ly tub ▸*n. historical* a washtub. ▷late 19th cent.: from dialect *dolly* (used as a term for various contrivances thought to resemble a doll in some way) and **TUB**.

Dol·ly Var·den /ˌdälē ˈvärdn/ ▸*n.* **1** (also **Dolly Varden hat**) a large hat with one side drooping and with a floral trimming, formerly worn by women. **2** a brightly spotted edible char (fish) occurring in fresh water on both sides of the North Pacific. • *Salvelinus malma*, family Salmonidae. ▷late 19th cent.: from the name of a character in Dickens's *Barnaby Rudge*, who wore a similar hat.

dol·ma /ˈdôlmə/ ▸*n.* (*pl.* **dol·mas** or **dol·ma·des** /dôlˈmä*ᴛʜ*ēs/) a Greek and Turkish delicacy in which ingredients such as rice, meat, and spices are wrapped in vine or cabbage leaves. ▷from modern Greek *ntolmas* or its source, Turkish *dolma*, from *dolmak* 'fill, be filled.'

dol·man /ˈdōlmən/ ▸*n.* a long Turkish robe open in front. ■ a woman's loose cloak with capelike sleeves. ▷late 16th cent.: based on Turkish *dolama*, *dolaman*.

dol·man sleeve ▸*n.* a loose sleeve cut in one piece with the body of a garment.

dol·men /ˈdōlmən; ˈdäl-/ ▸*n.* a megalithic tomb with a large flat stone laid on upright ones, found chiefly in Britain and France. ▷mid 19th cent.: from French, perhaps via Breton from Cornish *tolmen* 'hole of a stone.'

do·lo·mite /ˈdäləˌmīt; ˈdō-/ ▸*n.* a translucent mineral consisting of a carbonate of calcium and magnesium. ■ a sedimentary rock formed chiefly of this mineral. ▷late 18th cent.: from French, from the name of *Dolomieu* (1750–1801), the French geologist who discovered it, + **-ITE**[1]. —**dol·o·mit·ic** /ˌdäləˈmitik/ *adj.*

Do·lo·mite Moun·tains /ˈdōləˌmīt; ˈdäl-/ (also **the Do·lo·mites**) a mountain range in northern Italy, part of the Alps, so named because the characteristic rock of the region is dolomitic limestone.

do·lor /ˈdōlər/ (*Brit.* **do·lour**) ▸*n. poetic/literary* a state of great sorrow or distress: *they squatted, hunched in their habitual dolor.* ▷Middle English, as *dolor*, (denoting both physical and mental pain or distress), via Old French from Latin *dolor* 'pain, grief.'

do·lo·rim·e·ter /ˌdōləˈrimitər/ ▸*n.* an instrument for measuring sensitivity to, or levels of, pain. —**do·lo·rim·e·try** /-itrē/ *n.*

dol·or·ous /ˈdōlərəs/ ▸*adj. poetic/literary* feeling or expressing great sorrow or distress. ▷late Middle English: from Old French *doleros*, from late Latin *dolorosus*, from Latin *dolor* 'pain, grief.' —**dol·or·ous·ly** *adv.*

do·lo·stone /ˈdäləˌstōn; ˈdō-/ ▸*n. Geology* rock consisting of dolomite. ▷mid 20th cent.: from **DOLOMITE** + **STONE**.

dol·phin /ˈdälfin; ˈdôl-/ ▸*n.* **1** a small gregarious toothed whale that typically has a beaklike snout and a curved fin on the back. Dolphins have become well known for their sociable nature and high intelligence. • Families Delphinidae (marine) and Platanistidae (the **river dolphins**): several genera and many species. ■ a dolphinlike creature depicted in heraldry or art, typically with an arched body and fins like a fish. **2** (also **dol·phin·fish**) another term for **MAHIMAHI**. **3** a bollard, pile, or buoy for mooring. **4** a structure for protecting the pier of a bridge or other structure from collision with ships. ▷late Middle English: from Old French *dauphin*, from Provençal *dalfin*, from Latin *delphinus*, from Greek *delphin*.

dol·phi·nar·i·um /ˌdälfiˈne(ə)rēəm; ˌdôl-/ ▸*n.* (*pl.* **-nar·i·ums** or **-nar·i·a** /-ˈne(ə)rēə/) an aquarium in which dolphins are kept and trained for public entertainment. ▷1960s: from **DOLPHIN**, on the pattern of *oceanarium*.

dol·phin-safe ▸*adj.* (on canned tuna labels) indicating that the tuna has been harvested using fishing methods that are not harmful to dolphins.

dolt /dōlt/ ▸*n.* a stupid person. ▷mid 16th cent.: perhaps a variant of *dulled*, past participle of **DULL**. —**dolt·ish** *adj.* —**dolt·ish·ly** *adv.* —**dolt·ish·ness** *n.*

Dom /däm/ ▸*n.* **1** a title prefixed to the names of some Roman Catholic dignitaries and Benedictine and Carthusian monks: *Dom Bede Griffiths.* **2** Portuguese form of **DON**[1] (sense 2). ▷from Latin *dominus* 'master.'

-dom ▸*suffix* forming nouns: **1** denoting a state or condition: *freedom.* **2** denoting rank or status: *earldom.* **3** denoting a domain: *fiefdom.* **4** denoting a class of people or the attitudes associated with them, regarded collectively: *officialdom.* ▷Old English *-dōm*, originally meaning 'decree, judgment.'

do·main /dōˈmān/ ▸*n.* an area of territory owned or controlled by a ruler or government: *the southwestern French domains of the Plantagenets.* ■ an estate or territory held in legal possession by a person or persons. ■ a specified sphere of activity or knowledge: *the expanding domain of psychology* | *figurative visual communication* ***is the domain of*** *the graphic designer.* ■ *Physics* a discrete region of magnetism in ferromagnetic material. ■ *Computing* a distinct subset of the Internet with addresses sharing a common suffix, such as the part in a particular country or used by a particular group of users. ■ *Mathematics* the set of possible values of the independent variable or variables of a function. ▷late Middle English (denoting heritable or landed property): from French *domaine*, alteration (by association with Latin *dominus* 'lord') of Old French *demeine* 'belonging to a lord' (see **DEMESNE**). —**do·ma·ni·al** /-nēəl/ *adj.*

do·maine /dəˈmān/ ▸*n.* a vineyard. ▷1960s: from French, literally 'estate' (see **DOMAIN**).

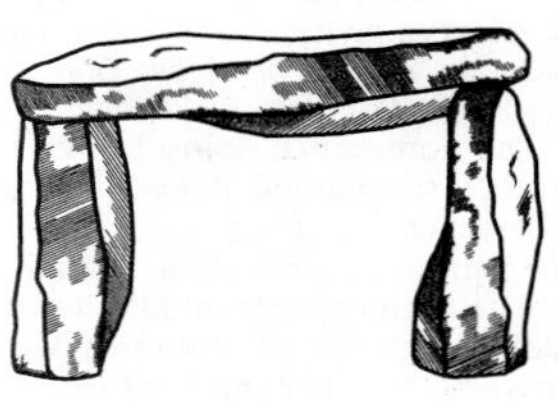

dolmen

do·main name ▸*n.* a series of alphanumeric strings separated by periods, such as *www.oup-usa.org*, serving as an address for a computer network connection and identifying the owner of the address. The last three letters in a domain name indicate what type of organization owns the address: for instance, .com stands for commercial, .edu for educational, and .org for nonprofit.

do·main name sys·tem (abbr.: **DNS**) ▸*n. Computing* the system by which Internet domain names and addresses are tracked and regulated.

dome /dōm/ ▸*n.* **1** a rounded vault forming the roof of a building or structure, typically with a circular base: *the dome of St. Paul's Cathedral.* ■ the revolving openable hemispherical roof of an observatory. ■ [in *names*] a sports stadium with a domed roof. **2** a thing shaped like such a roof, in particular: ■ the rounded summit of a hill or mountain: *the great dome of Mont Blanc.* ■ a natural vault or canopy, such as that of the sky or trees: *the dome of the sky.* ■ *Geology* a rounded uplifted landform or underground structure. ■ *informal* the top of the head: *a content face topped by a shaved dome.* **3** *poetic/literary* a stately building.

▸*v.* [*trans.*] [usu. as *adj.*] (**domed**) cover with or shape as a dome: *a domed stadium.* ■ [*intrans.*] [often as *n.*] (**doming**) (of stratified rock or a surface) become rounded in formation; swell. ▷early 16th cent. (sense 3): from French *dôme*, from Italian *duomo* 'cathedral, dome,' from Latin *domus* 'house.' Sense 3 derives directly from Latin *domus*. —**dome·like** /-ˌlīk/ *adj.*

Dome of the Rock an Islamic shrine in Jerusalem, for Muslims the third most holy place after Mecca and Medina. It surrounds the sacred rock on which, according to tradition, Abraham prepared to sacrifice his son Isaac and from which the prophet Muhammad made his miraculous night ascent into heaven (the Night Journey).

Dome of the Rock

Domes·day /ˈdo͞omzˌdā/ ▸*n.* **1** (also **Domesday Book, Doomsday Book**) a comprehensive record of the extent, value, ownership, and liabilities of land in England, made in 1086 by order of William I. **2** (also **domesday**) archaic spelling of **DOOMSDAY**. ▷Middle English: sense 1 was apparently a popular name applied during the 12th cent. because the book was regarded as a final authority (with allusion to *doomsday* 'the Day of Judgment').

do·mes·tic /dəˈmestik/ ▸*adj.* **1** of or relating to the running of a home or to family relations: *domestic chores* | *domestic violence.* ■ *chiefly Brit.* of or for use in the home rather than in an industrial or office environment: *domestic appliances.* ■ (of a person) fond of family life and running a home: *she was not at all domestic.* ■ (of an animal) tame and kept by humans: *domestic cattle.* **2** existing or occurring inside a particular country; not foreign or international: *Korea's domestic affairs.*

▸*n.* **1** (also **domestic worker** or **domestic help**) a person who is paid to help with menial tasks such as cleaning. **2** a product not made abroad. ▷late Middle English: from French *domestique*, from Latin *domesticus*, from *domus* 'house.' —**do·mes·ti·cal·ly** /-ik(ə)lē/ *adv.*

do·mes·ti·cate /dəˈmestiˌkāt/ ▸*v.* [*trans.*] (usu. **be domesticated**) tame (an animal) and keep it as a pet or for farm produce: *mammals were first domesticated for their milk.* ■ cultivate (a plant) for food. ■ *humorous* make (someone) fond of and good at home life and the tasks that it involves: *you've quite domesticated him* | [as *adj.*] (**domesticated**) *he is thoroughly domesticated.* ▷mid 17th cent.: from medieval Latin *domesticat-* 'domesticated,' from the verb *domesticare*, from Latin *domesticus* 'belonging to the house' (see **DOMESTIC**). —**do·mes·ti·ca·ble** /-kəbəl/ *adj.* —**do·mes·ti·ca·tion** /-ˌmestiˈkāsʜən/ *n.*

do·mes·tic·i·ty /ˌdōmeˈstisitē/ ▸*n.* home or family life: *the atmosphere is one of happy domesticity.*

do·mes·tic part·ner ▸*n.* a person who shares a

residence with a sexual partner, esp. without a legally recognized union. —**do·mes·tic part·ner·ship** *n.*

do·mes·tic pi·geon ▸*n.* see PIGEON[1] (sense 1).

do·mes·tic sci·ence ▸*n. dated* the study of household skills such as cooking or sewing, esp. as taught at school; home economics.

dom·i·cal /ˈdōmikəl; ˈdäm-/ ▸*adj.* domed: *an octagonal, domical vault.*

dom·i·cile /ˈdäməˌsīl; ˈdō-; ˈdäməsəl/ (also **dom·i·cil** /ˈdäməsəl/) ▸*n. formal* or *Law* the country that a person treats as their permanent home, or lives in and has a substantial connection with: *his wife has a* ***domicile of origin*** *in Germany.* ■ a person's residence or home: *the builder I've hired to renovate my new domicile.* ■ the place at which a company or other body is registered, esp. for tax purposes.

▸*v.* [with *adverbial of place*] (**be domiciled**) *formal* or *Law* treat a specified country as a permanent home: *the tenant is domiciled in the U.S.* ■ reside; be based: *he was domiciled in a frame house on the outskirts of town.* ▹late Middle English: via Old French from Latin *domicilium* 'dwelling,' from *domus* 'home.'

dom·i·cil·i·ar·y /ˌdäməˈsilēˌerē; ˌdō-/ ▸*adj.* concerned with or occurring in someone's home: *a study compared domiciliary care with hospital care.* ▹late 19th cent.: from French *domiciliaire*, from medieval Latin *domiciliarius*, from Latin *domicilium* 'dwelling' (see DOMICILE).

dom·i·nance /ˈdämənəns/ ▸*n.* power and influence over others: *the worldwide dominance of Hollywood.* ■ *Genetics* the phenomenon whereby, in an individual containing two allelic forms of a gene, one is expressed to the exclusion of the other. ■ *Ecology* the predominance of one or more species in a plant (or animal) community. —**dom·i·nan·cy** /-sē/ *n.*

dom·i·nant /ˈdämənənt/ ▸*adj.* most important, powerful, or influential: *they are now in an even more dominant position in the market.* ■ (of a high place or object) overlooking others. ■ *Genetics* relating to or denoting heritable characteristics that are controlled by genes that are expressed in offspring even when inherited from only one parent. Often contrasted with RECESSIVE. ■ *Ecology* denoting the predominant species in a plant (or animal) community. ■ in decision theory, (of a choice) at least as good as the alternatives in all circumstances, and better in some: *holding back is here a dominant strategy.*

▸*n.* a dominant thing, in particular: ■ *Genetics* a dominant trait or gene. ■ *Ecology* a dominant species in a plant (or animal) community. ■ *Music* the fifth note of the diatonic scale of any key, or the key based on this, considered in relation to the key of the tonic. ▹late Middle English: via Old French from Latin *dominant-* 'ruling, governing,' from the verb *dominari* (see DOMINATE). —**dom·i·nant·ly** *adv.*

dom·i·nant sev·enth ▸*n. Music* the common chord of the dominant note in a key, plus the minor seventh from that note (e.g., in the key of C, a chord of G-B-D-F). It is important in conventional harmony, as it naturally resolves to the tonic or subdominant.

dom·i·nate /ˈdäməˌnāt/ ▸*v.* [*trans.*] (often **be dominated**) have a commanding influence on; exercise control over: *the company dominates the market for operating system software.* ■ be the most important or conspicuous person or thing in: *the race was dominated by the 1992 champion.* ■ (of something tall or high) have a commanding position over; overlook: *a picturesque city dominated by the cathedral tower.* ▹early 17th cent.: from Latin *dominat-* 'ruled, governed,' from the verb *dominari*, from *dominus* 'lord, master.' —**dom·i·na·tor** /-ˌnātər/ *n.*

dom·i·na·tion /ˌdäməˈnāSHən/ ▸*n.* **1** the exercise of control or influence over someone or something, or the state of being so controlled: *the Soviet domination of Eastern Europe.* **2** (**dominations**) (in traditional Christian angelology) the fourth highest order of the ninefold celestial hierarchy. ▹late Middle English: via Old French from Latin *dominatio(n-)*, from the verb *dominari* (see DOMINATE).

dom·i·na·trix /ˌdäməˈnātriks/ ▸*n.* (*pl.* **-tri·ces** /-trəˌsēz/ or **-trix·es**) a dominating woman, esp. one who takes the sadistic role in sadomasochistic sexual activities. ▹mid 16th cent. (rare before the late 20th cent.): from Latin, feminine of *dominator*, from *dominat-* 'ruled,' from the verb *dominari* (see DOMINATE).

dom·i·neer /ˌdäməˈni(ə)r/ ▸*v.* [*intrans.*] [usu. as *adj.*] (**domineering**) assert one's will over another in an arrogant way: *Cathy had been a martyr to her gruff, domineering husband.* ▹late 16th cent.: from Dutch *dominieren*, from French *dominer*, from Latin *dominari* (see DOMINATE). —**dom·i·neer·ing·ly** *adv.*

Do·min·go /dəˈmiNGgō/, Placido (1941–), Spanish opera singer. He moved to Mexico in 1950 and made his debut as an operatic tenor in 1957. His performances in operas by Verdi and Puccini have met with particular acclaim.

Dom·i·nic, St. /ˈdämənik/ (*c.*1170–1221), Spanish priest and friar; Spanish name *Domingo de Guzmán.* In 1216, he founded the Order of Friars Preachers at Toulouse in France; its members became known as Dominicans or Black Friars. Feast day, August 8.

Dom·i·ni·ca /ˌdäməˈnēkə; dəˈminikə/ a country in the western West Indies, a mountainous island, the most northern of the Windward Islands, in the Caribbean Sea; pop. 71,790; capital, Roseau; languages, English (official) and Creole. ▹named by Columbus, who discovered it on a Sunday (Latin *dies dominica* 'the Lord's day') in 1493.

The island came into British possession at the end of the 18th century and became an independent republic within the Commonwealth of Nations in 1978.

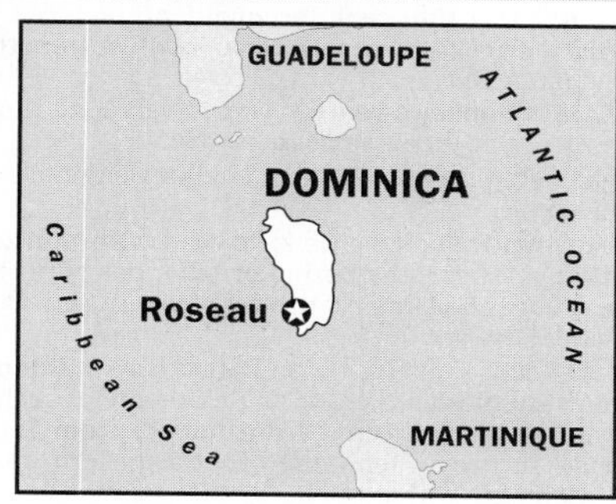

do·min·i·cal /dəˈminikəl/ ▸*adj.* **1** of Sunday as the Lord's day. **2** of Jesus Christ as the lord. ▹Middle English: from late Latin *dominicalis*, from Latin *dominicus*, from *dominus* 'lord, master.'

do·min·i·cal let·ter ▸*n.* any of the seven letters A–G used in church calendars to indicate the date (January 1–7) on which the first Sunday in the year falls, and hence in dating movable feasts.

Do·min·i·can[1] /dəˈminikən/ ▸*n.* a member of the Roman Catholic order of preaching friars founded by St. Dominic, or of a religious order for women founded on similar principles.

▸*adj.* of or relating to St. Dominic or the Dominicans. ▹late 16th cent.: from medieval Latin *Dominicanus*, from *Dominicus*, the Latin name of *Domingo de Guzmán* (see DOMINIC, ST.).

Do·min·i·can[2] ▸*adj.* of or relating to the Dominican Republic or its people.

▸*n.* a native or national of the Dominican Republic. ▹from Spanish *Dominicana*, influenced by SANTO DOMINGO.

Do·min·i·can[3] ▸*adj.* of or relating to the island of Dominica or its people.

▸*n.* a native or national of the island of Dominica.

Do·min·i·can Re·pub·lic /dəˈminəkən/ a country in the Caribbean Sea that occupies the eastern part of the island of Hispaniola; pop. 8,830,000; capital, Santo Domingo; official language, Spanish.

The **Dominican Republic** is the former Spanish colony of Santo Domingo, the part of Hispaniola that Spain retained when it ceded the western portion (now Haiti) to France in 1697. It was proclaimed a republic in 1844.

dom·i·nie /ˈdämənē; ˈdō-/ ▸*n.* (*pl.* **-nies**) **1** *Scottish* a schoolmaster. **2** a pastor or clergyman. ▹late 17th cent.: alteration of Latin *domine!* (vocative) 'master!, sir!,' from *dominus* 'lord' (formerly used as a polite form of address to a clergyman or member of one of the professions).

do·min·ion /dəˈminyən/ ▸*n.* **1** sovereignty; control: *man's attempt to establish* ***dominion over*** *nature.* See note at JURISDICTION. **2** (usu. **dominions**) the territory of a sovereign or government: *the Angevin dominions.* ■ (**Dominion**) *historical* each of the self-governing territories of the British Commonwealth. **3** (**dominions**) another term for DOMINATION (sense 2). ▹Middle English: via Old French from medieval Latin *dominio(n-)*, from Latin *dominium*, from *dominus* 'lord, master.'

Do·min·ion Day ▸former name for July 1, a national holiday observed in Canada to commemorate the formation of the Dominion in 1867. Since 1982, it has been known as **Canada Day**.

do·min·i·um /dəˈminēəm/ ▸*n. Law* absolute ownership and control of property. ▹mid 18th cent.: from Latin.

Dom·i·no /ˈdäməˌnō/, Fats (1928–), U.S. pianist, singer, and songwriter; born *Antoine Domino.* His music represents part of the transition from rhythm and blues to rock and roll and shows the influence of jazz, boogie-woogie, and gospel music. Notable songs: "Ain't That a Shame" (1955) and "Blueberry Hill" (1956).

dom·i·no /ˈdäməˌnō/ ▸*n.* (*pl.* **-noes** or **-nos**) **1** any of 28 small oblong pieces marked with 0–6 dots (pips) in each half. ■ (**dominoes**) [treated as *sing.*] the game played with such pieces, in which they are laid down to form a line, each player in turn trying to find and lay down a domino with a value matched by that of a piece at either end of the line already formed.

domino 1

2 *historical* a loose cloak, worn with a mask for the upper part of the face at masquerades. ▹late 17th cent.: from French, denoting a hood worn by priests in winter, probably based on Latin *dominus* 'lord, master.'

dom·i·no ef·fect ▸*n.* the effect of the domino theory.

dom·i·no the·o·ry ▸*n.* the theory that a political event in one country will cause similar events in neighboring countries, like a falling domino causing an entire row of upended dominoes to fall.

Do·mi·tian /dəˈmiSHən/ (AD 51–96), son of Vespasian; Roman emperor 81–96; full name *Titus Flavius Domitianus.*

Don /dän/ **1** a river in Russia that rises near Tula, southeast of Moscow, and flows for 1,224 miles (1,958 km) to the Sea of Azov. **2** a river in Scotland that rises in the Grampian Mountains and flows east for 82 miles (131 km) to the North Sea at Aberdeen. **3** a river in northern England that rises in the Pennine Hills and flows east for 70 miles (112 km) to join the Ouse River shortly before it, in turn, joins the Humber River.

don[1] /dän/ ▸*n.* **1** (**Don**) a Spanish title prefixed to a male forename. ■ a Spanish gentleman; a Spaniard. ■ *informal* a high-ranking member of the Mafia. **2** a university teacher, esp. a senior member of a college at Oxford or Cambridge. [transferred colloquial use of the Spanish title (see above).] ▹early 16th cent. : from Spanish, from Latin *dominus* 'lord, master.' Compare with DONNA. —**don·ship** /-ˌSHip/ *n.*

don[2] ▸*v.* (**donned, don·ning**) [*trans.*] put on (an item of clothing): *in the locker room the players donned their football jerseys.* ▹late Middle English: contraction of *do on.* Compare with DOFF.

Don·a·hue /ˈdänəˌhyoo/, Phil (1935–), U.S. talk show host; full name *Phillip John Donahue.* He began the award-winning "Phil Donahue Show" in 1967 and retired in 1996.

do·nate /ˈdōnāt; dōˈnāt/ ▸*v.* [*trans.*] give (money or goods) for a good cause, for example to a charity: *the proceeds will be donated to an AIDS awareness charity.* See note at GIVE. ■ allow the removal of (blood or an organ) from one's body for transplantation, transfusion, or other use. ▹late 18th cent.: back-formation from DONATION. —**do·na·tor** /ˈdōnātər/ *n.*

Don·a·tel·lo /ˌdänəˈtelō/ (1386–1466), Italian sculptor; born *Donato di Betto Bardi.* He was one of the pioneers of scientific perspective and is especially known for his lifelike sculptures, including the bronze *David* (c.1430–60).

do·na·tion /dō'nāSHən/ ▶*n.* something that is given to a charity, esp. a sum of money: *a tax-deductible donation of $200.* See note at PRESENT. ■ the action of donating something. ▷late Middle English: via Old French from Latin *donatio(n-)*, from the verb *donare*, based on *donum* 'gift.'

Don·a·tist /'dänətist; 'dō-/ ▶*n.* a member of a schismatic Christian group in North Africa, formed in 311, who held that only those living a blameless life belonged in the Church. They survived until the 7th century. ▷from *Donatus* (died c.355), a Christian prelate in Carthage and the group's leader, + -IST. **—Don·a·tism** /-,tizəm/ *n.*

don·a·tive /'dōnətiv; 'dän-/ *rare* ▶*n.* a donation, esp. one given formally or officially as a largesse.
▶*adj.* given as a donation. ■ *historical* (of a benefice) given directly, not presentative. ▷late Middle English: from Latin *donativum* 'gift, largesse,' from *donat-* 'given,' from the verb *donare* (see DONATION).

Do·na·tus /də'nātəs/, Aelius (4th century), Roman grammarian. The *Ars Grammatica*, which contained his treatises on Latin grammar, was the sole textbook used in schools in the Middle Ages.

D

Do·nau /'dō,nou/ German name for **DANUBE**.

Don·bas /dən'bäs; 'dän,bas/ Ukrainian name for **DONETS BASIN**.

Don·cas·ter /'däNGkəstər/ an industrial town in northern England; pop. 284,300.

done /dən/ ▶ past participle of DO[1].
▶*v. informal* used as a nonstandard past tense of DO[1]: *I done a lot of rodeoin'.* ■ *informal* used with a standard past tense verb to indicate absoluteness or completion: *I done told you to zipper your lips.*
▶*adj.* **1** carried out, completed, or treated in a particular way: *the path needed replacing and she wanted it done in asphalt.* ■ (of food) cooked thoroughly: *the turkey will be done soon.* ■ no longer happening or existing: *her hunting days were done.* **2** *informal* socially acceptable: *therapy was* **not the done thing** *then.*
▶*exclam.* used to indicate that the speaker accepts the terms of an offer: *"I'll give ten to one he misses by a mile!" called Reilly. "Done," said the conductor.*
▶*PHRASES* □ **a done deal** a plan or project that has been finalized. □ **done for** *informal* in a situation so bad that it is impossible to get out: *if he gets them, we'll all be done for.* □ **done in** *informal* extremely tired: *you look done in.* □ **over and done with** see OVER.

do·nee /dō'nē/ ▶*n.* a person who receives a gift. ■ *Law* a person who is given a power of appointment. ▷early 16th cent.: from DONOR + -EE.

Don·e·gal /,däni'gôl; ,dən-/ a county in extreme northwestern Republic of Ireland, part of the old province of Ulster; capital, Lifford.

don·e·gal /'dänigəl; -,gôl/ (also **Donegal tweed**) ▶*n.* a tweed characterized by bright flecks randomly distributed on a background usually of light gray, originally woven in County Donegal, northwestern Ireland.

Do·nets /də'n(y)ets/ a river in eastern Europe that rises near Belgorod in southern Russia and flows southeast for about 630 miles (1,000 km) through Ukraine before reentering Russia and joining the Don River near Rostov.

Do·nets Ba·sin a coal-mining and industrial region in southeastern Ukraine that stretches between the valleys of the Donets and lower Dnieper rivers. Ukrainian name **DONBAS**.

Do·netsk /də'n(y)etsk/ a city in the Donets Basin in Ukraine; pop. 1,117,000. The city was called Yuzovka 1872–1924, and Stalin or Stalino 1924–61.

dong[1] /dôNG; däNG/ ▶*v.* [*intrans.*] (of a bell) make a deep resonant sound.
▶*n.* **1** the deep resonant sound of a large bell. **2** *vulgar slang* a penis. ▷late 16th cent.: imitative.

dong[2] ▶*n.* the basic monetary unit of Vietnam, equal to 100 xu. ▷from Vietnamese *dông* 'coin.'

don·gle /'däNGgəl; 'dôNG-/ ▶*n. Computing* an electronic device that must be attached to a computer in order to use protected computer software. ▷1980s: an arbitrary formation.

Dong·nai Riv·er /'dôNG 'nī/ (also (also **Don·nai** /'dôn-'nī/)) a river in Vietnam that flows for 300 miles (483 km) from south central Vietnam to join the Saigon River below Ho Chi Minh City.

dong quai /'do͝oNG 'kwā; 'kwī/ ▶*n.* an aromatic herb of the parsley family, native to China and Japan, the root of which is used to treat premenstrual syndrome, menstrual cramps, menopausal symptoms, and other gynecological complaints. • *Angelica sinensis*, family Umbelliferae.

Dong·ying /'do͝oNG 'yiNG/ a city in Hebei province, in eastern China, near the mouth of the Yellow River, in an area rich in oil; pop. 540,000.

Don·i·zet·ti /,dänə'zetē/, Gaetano (1797–1848), Italian composer. His operas include tragedies such as *Lucia di Lammermoor* (1835) and comedies such as *Don Pasquale* (1843).

don·jon /'dänjən; 'dən-/ ▶*n.* the great tower or innermost keep of a castle. ▷Middle English: variant of DUNGEON.

Don Juan /,dän '(h)wän/ a legendary Spanish nobleman known for his dissolute life and for seducing women. ■ [as *n.*] (**a Don Juan**) a seducer of women; a libertine.

don·key /'dôNGkē; 'däNG-/ ▶*n.* (*pl.* **-keys**) **1** a domesticated hoofed mammal of the horse family with long ears and a braying call, used as a beast of burden; an ass. • *Equus asinus*, family Equidae, descended from the wild ass of Africa. **2** *informal* a stupid or foolish person. ▷late 18th cent. (originally pronounced to rhyme with *monkey*): perhaps from DUN[1], or from the given name *Duncan*.
▶*PHRASE* □ **donkey's years** *informal* a very long time: *we've been close friends for donkey's years.*

don·key en·gine ▶*n.* a small or auxiliary engine, esp. on a ship.

don·key·work /'dôNGkē,wərk; 'däNG-/ (also **don·key work**) ▶*n. informal* the boring or laborious part of a job; drudgery: *supervisors who get a research student to do the donkeywork.*

don·na /'dänə; 'dôn-nä/ ▶*n.* an Italian lady. ■ (**Donna**) a courtesy title prefixed to the forename of such a lady. ▷early 17th cent.: from Italian, from Latin *domina* 'mistress,' feminine of *dominus* 'lord, master.' Compare with DON[1].

Don·nan e·qui·lib·ri·um /'dänən/ ▶*n. Chemistry* the equilibrium reached between two ionic solutions separated by a semipermeable membrane when one or more of the kinds of ion present cannot pass through the membrane. The result is a difference in osmotic pressure and electrical potential between the solutions. ▷early 20th cent.: named after Frederick G. *Donnan* (1870–1956), British physical chemist.

Donne /dən/, John (1572–1631), English poet and clergyman. A metaphysical poet, he is noted for his *Satires* (c.1590–99), *Elegies* (c.1590–99), and love poems, which appeared in the collection *Songs and Sonnets*. As dean of St. Paul's Cathedral, he was one of the most celebrated preachers of his age.

don·née /dä'nā/ (also **don·né**) ▶*n.* **1** a subject or theme of a narrative. **2** a basic fact or assumption. ▷late 19th cent.: French, literally 'given.'

Don·ner Pass /'dänər/ a site in the Sierra Nevada in northeastern California where some members of an 1844 emigrant party survived a blizzard partly by eating the dead.

don·nish /'däniSH/ ▶*adj.* thought to resemble or suit a college don, particularly because of a pedantic, scholarly manner. **—don·nish·ly** *adv.* **—don·nish·ness** *n.*

don·ny·brook /'dänē,bro͝ok/ ▶*n.* a scene of uproar and disorder; a heated argument: *raucous ideological donnybrooks.* ▷mid 19th cent.: from the name of a suburb of Dublin, Ireland, formerly famous for its annual fair.

do·nor /'dōnər/ ▶*n.* a person who donates something, esp. money to a fund or charity: *an anonymous donor has given $25* | [as *adj.*] *loans from rich donor countries.* ■ a person who provides blood for transfusion, semen for insemination, or an organ or tissue for transplantation. ■ *Chemistry* an atom or molecule that provides electrons in forming a coordinate bond. ■ *Physics* an impurity atom in a semiconductor that contributes a conducting electron to the material. ▷Middle English: from Old French *doneur*, from Latin *donator*, from *donare* 'give.'

do·nor fa·tigue ▶*n.* a lessening of public willingness to respond generously to charitable appeals, resulting from the frequency of such appeals.

do-noth·ing ▶*n.* a person who is idle or lacks ambition.
▶*adj.* idle or lacking ambition.

Don Quix·o·te /,dän kē'hōtē; -tā/ the hero of a romance (1605–15) by Cervantes, a satirical account of chivalric beliefs and conduct. The character of Don Quixote is typified by a romantic vision and naive, unworldly idealism.

don't /dōnt/ ▶*contraction of* do not. ■ *informal* does not: *she don't drink tea.*
▶*PHRASE* □ **dos and don'ts** see DO[1].

do·nut /'dō,nət/ ▶*n.* variant spelling of **DOUGHNUT**.

doo·dad /'do͞o,dad/ ▶*n.* a fancy article or trivial ornament: *there were crystal doodads all over the place.* ■ a gadget, esp. one whose name the speaker does not know or cannot recall: *the latest electronic doodads.* ▷early 20th cent.: of unknown origin.

doo·dle /'do͞odl/ ▶*v.* [*intrans.*] scribble absentmindedly: *he was only doodling in the margin.* ■ engage in idle activity; dawdle: *they could plan another attack while we're just* **doodling around**.
▶*n.* a rough drawing made absentmindedly. ▷early 17th cent. (originally as a noun denoting a fool, later as a verb in the sense 'make a fool of, cheat'): from Low German *dudeltopf, dudeldopp* 'simpleton.' Current senses date from the 1930s. **—doo·dler** /-d(ə)lər/ *n.*

doo·dle·bug /'do͞odl,bəg/ ▶*n. informal* **1** the larva of an ant lion. **2** an unscientific device for locating oil or minerals; a divining rod. **3** *Brit.* informal term for **V-1**. ▷mid 19th cent. (sense 1): from 17th-cent. *doodle* 'ninny' + BUG.

doo·dly-squat /'do͞odl-ē ,skwät/ ▶*n.* another term for **DIDDLY-SQUAT**.

doo-doo /'do͞o ,do͞o/ ▶*n.* a child's word for excrement, used euphemistically in other contexts: *when our fax machine isn't working, we're* **in deep doo-doo**.

doo·fus /'do͞ofəs/ (also **du·fus**) ▶*n.* (*pl.* **doo·fuses**) *informal* a stupid person. ▷1960s: perhaps an alteration of GOOFUS, or from Scots *doof* 'dolt.'

doo·hick·ey /'do͞o,hikē/ ▶*n.* (*pl.* **-eys**) *informal* a small object or gadget, esp. one whose name the speaker does not know or cannot recall: *a garage filled with electronic parts and other valuable doohickeys.* ▷early 20th cent. (originally servicemen's slang): blend of DOODAD and HICKEY.

doo·lal·ly /'do͞o,lälē/ ▶*adj. Brit., informal* temporarily deranged or feebleminded: *Uncle Orville's gone doolally again.* ▷early 20th cent.: originally *doolally tap*, Indian army slang, from *Deolali* (the name of a town near Bombay) + Urdu *tap* 'fever.'

Doo·ley /'do͞olē/, Thomas Anthony (1927–61), U.S. physician and writer. He established medical missions in Laos in 1956 as well as hospitals in Cambodia, Laos, and Vietnam. In 1957, he established Medico, an international medical aid mission. He wrote about his experiences in *Deliver Us from Evil* (1956), *The Edge of Tomorrow* (1958), and *The Night They Burned the Mountain*(1960).

doo·lie /'do͞olē/ ▶*n.* (*pl.* **-lies**) *informal* a freshman at the U.S. Air Force Academy. ▷from Hindi *ḍolī*, diminutive of *ḍolā* 'cradle or litter.'

Doo·lit·tle /'do͞o,litl/, Hilda (1886–1961), U.S. poet; pseudonym **H.D.** From 1911, she lived in London. Her work shows the influence of Ezra Pound and other imagist poets; it also shows the influence of classical mythology.

doom /do͞om/ ▶*n.* death, destruction, or some other terrible fate: *the aircraft was sent crashing* **to its doom** *in the water.* ■ [in *sing.*] *archaic* (in Christian belief) the Last Judgment.
▶*v.* [*trans.*] (usu. **be doomed**) condemn to certain destruction or death: *fuel was spilling out of the damaged wing and the aircraft was doomed.* ■ cause to have an unfortunate and inescapable outcome: *her plan was* **doomed to** *failure* | [as *adj.*] (**doomed**) *the moving story of their doomed love affair.* ▷Old English *dōm* 'statute, judgment,' of Germanic origin, from a base meaning 'to put in place'; related to DO[1].
▶*PHRASE* □ **doom and gloom** (also **gloom and doom**) a general feeling of pessimism or despondency: *the national feeling of doom and gloom.*

doom·lad·en ▶*adj.* conveying a sense of tragedy: *a doom-laden speech.*

doom·say·er /'do͞om,sāər/ ▶*n.* a person who predicts disaster, esp. in politics or economics. **—doom·say·ing** /-,sāiNG/ *n.*

dooms·day /'do͞omz,dā/ (also **domes·day**) ▶*n.* [in *sing.*] the last day of the world's existence. ■ (in Christian belief) the day of the Last Judgment. ■ *figurative* a time or event of crisis or great danger: [as *adj.*] *in all the concern over greenhouse warming, one* **doomsday scenario** *stands out.* ▷Old English *dōmes dæg* (see DOOM, DAY).
▶*PHRASE* □ **till doomsday** *informal* forever: *we'll be here till doomsday if you don't hurry up.*

Dooms·day Book ▶*n.* see **DOMESDAY**.

doom·y /'do͞omē/ ▶*adj.* (**doom·i·er**, **doom·i·est**) suggesting or predicting disaster; ominous: *doomy forecasts.* —**doom·i·ly** /-məlē/ *adv.*

door /dôr/ ▸*n.* a hinged, sliding, or revolving barrier at the entrance to a building, room, or vehicle, or in the framework of a cupboard. ■ a doorway: *she walked through the door.* ■ used to refer to the distance from one building in a row to another: *they lived within three doors of each other.* ■ *figurative* a means of access, admission, or exit; a means to a specified end: *that audition was the door to all my future successes | a democratic educational system requires multiple doors.* ▷Old English *duru, dor*, of Germanic origin; related to Dutch *deur* 'door' and German *Tür* 'door,' *Tor* 'gate'; from an Indo-European root shared by Latin *foris* 'gate' and Greek *thura* 'door.' —**doored** *adj.* [in *combination*] *a glass-doored desk.*

▸*PHRASES* □ **at the door** on admission to an event rather than in advance: *tickets will be available at the door.* □ **close** (or **shut**) **the door on** (or **to**) exclude the opportunity for: *she had closed the door on ever finding out what he was feeling.* □ **(from) door to door 1** from start to finish of a journey: *the trip from door to door could take more than four hours.* **2** visiting all the houses in an area to sell or publicize something: *he went from door to door selling insurance policies* | [as *adj.*] *a door-to-door-salesman.* □ **lay something at someone's door** regard someone as responsible for something: *the failure is laid at the door of the government.* □ **leave the door open** ensure that there is still an opportunity for something: *he is leaving the door open for future change.* □ **open the door to** create an opportunity for: *her research has opened the door to a deeper understanding of the subject.* □ **out of doors** in or into the open air: *food tastes even better out of doors.* □ **show someone the door** see SHOW.

door·bell /ˈdôr,bel/ ▸*n.* a bell in a building that can be rung by visitors outside to signal their arrival.

door·bust·er /ˈdôr,bəstər/ ▸*n. informal* **1** (in retailing) a special discount price available for a limited period, typically during special early-opening hours. **2** a firearm with special attachments for forcing entry through a door.

do-or-die /ˈdo͞o ər ˈdī/ ▸*adj.* [*attrib.*] (of a person's attitude or a situation) showing or requiring a determination not to compromise or be deterred: *the mercenaries fought with a do-or-die resolution.*

door·frame /ˈdôr,frām/ (also **door frame**) ▸*n.* the frame in a doorway into which a door is fitted.

door·jamb /ˈdôr,jam/ ▸*n.* each of the two upright parts of a doorframe, on one of which the door is hung.

door·keep·er /ˈdôr,kēpər/ ▸*n.* a person on duty at the entrance to a building.

door·knob /ˈdôr,näb/ ▸*n.* a handle on a door that is turned to release the latch.

door knock·er ▸*n.* a metal or wooden instrument hinged to a door and rapped by visitors to attract attention and gain entry.

door·man /ˈdôr,man; -mən/ ▸*n.* (*pl.* **-men**) a man such as a porter, bouncer, or janitor who is on duty at the entrance to a large building.

door·mat /ˈdôr,mat/ ▸*n.* a mat placed in a doorway, on which people can wipe their shoes on entering a building. ■ *figurative* a submissive person who allows others to dominate them: *to put up with such treatment you must be either a saint or a doormat.*

door·nail /ˈdôr,nāl/ ▸*n.* a stud set in a door for strength or as an ornament.

▸*PHRASE* □ **(as) dead as a doornail** quite dead.

Door Pen·in·su·la a resort region in northeastern Wisconsin that lies between Green Bay and Lake Michigan.

door·plate /ˈdôr,plāt/ ▸*n.* a plate on the door of a house or room that gives information about the occupant.

door·post /ˈdôr,pōst/ ▸*n.* another term for DOORJAMB.

door prize ▸*n.* a prize awarded by lottery to the holder of a ticket purchased or distributed at a dance, party, or other function.

door·sill /ˈdôr,sil/ ▸*n.* the sill or threshold of a doorway.

door·step /ˈdôr,step/ ▸*n.* a step leading up to the outer door of a house.

▸*PHRASE* □ **on one's** (or **the**) **doorstep** situated very close by: *the airport is on my doorstep, so flying is easy.*

door·stop /ˈdôr,stäp/ (also **door·stop·per**) ▸*n.* a fixed or heavy object that keeps a door open or stops it from banging against a wall. ■ *figurative* a heavy or bulky object (used esp. in reference to a thick book): *his sixth novel is a thumping 400-page doorstop.*

door·way /ˈdôr,wā/ ▸*n.* an entrance to a room or building through a door: *Beth stood there in the doorway figurative the doorway to success.*

door·yard /ˈdôr,yärd/ ▸*n.* a yard or garden by the door of a house.

doo-wop /ˈdo͞o ,wäp/ ▸*n.* a style of pop music marked by the use of close harmony vocals using nonsense phrases, originating in the U.S. in the 1950s. ▷imitative. —**doo-wop·per** *n.*

doo·zy /ˈdo͞ozē/ (also **doo·zie**) ▸*n.* (*pl.* **-zies**) *informal* something outstanding or unique of its kind: *it's gonna be a doozy of a black eye.* ▷early 20th cent.: of unknown origin.

do·pa /ˈdōpə/ ▸*n. Biochemistry* a compound that is present in nervous tissue as a precursor of dopamine, used in the treatment of Parkinson's disease. See also L-DOPA. • An amino acid; alternative name: dihydroxyphenylalanine; chem. formula: $C_9H_{11}NO_4$. ▷early 20th cent.: from German, acronym from the systematic name.

do·pa·mine /ˈdōpə,mēn/ ▸*n. Biochemistry* a compound present in the body as a neurotransmitter and a precursor of other substances including epinephrine. • Alternative name: **3,4-dihydroxyphenylethylamine**; chem. formula: $C_8H_{11}NO_2$. ▷1950s: blend of DOPA and AMINE.

do·pa·min·er·gic /,dōpəmiˈnərjik/ ▸*adj. Biochemistry* releasing or involving dopamine as a neurotransmitter. Drugs with this effect are used in the treatment of Parkinson's disease and some psychiatric disorders; some are subject to abuse. ▷1960s: from *dopamine* + Greek *ergon* 'work' + *-ic*.

dop·ant /ˈdōpənt/ ▸*n. Electronics* a substance used to produce a desired electrical characteristic in a semiconductor. ▷1960s: from the verb DOPE + -ANT.

dope /dōp/ ▸*n.* **1** *informal* a drug taken illegally for recreational purposes, esp. marijuana or heroin. ■ a drug given to a racehorse or greyhound to inhibit or enhance its performance. ■ a drug taken by an athlete to improve performance: [as *adj.*] *he failed a dope test.* **2** *informal* a stupid person: *though he wasn't an intellectual giant, he was no dope, either.* **3** *informal* information about a subject, esp. if not generally known: *our reviewer will give you* **the dope on** *hot spots around the town.* **4** a varnish applied to the fabric surface of model aircraft to strengthen them and keep them airtight. ■ a thick liquid used as a lubricant.

▸*v.* [*trans.*] **1** administer drugs to (a racehorse, greyhound, or athlete) in order to inhibit or enhance sporting performance: *the horse was doped before the race.* ■ (**be doped up**) *informal* be heavily under the influence of drugs, typically illegal ones: *he was so doped up that he can't remember a thing.* ■ treat (food or drink) with drugs: *maybe they had doped her Perrier.* ■ [*intrans.*] *informal, dated* regularly take illegal drugs. **2** smear or cover with varnish or other thick liquid: *she doped the surface with photographic emulsion.* **3** *Electronics* add an impurity to (a semiconductor) to produce a desired electrical characteristic.

▸*phrasal v.* □ **dope something out** *informal, dated* work out something: *they met to dope out plans for covering the event.*

▸*adj. black slang* very good: *that suit is dope!* ▷early 19th cent. (in the sense 'thick liquid'): from Dutch *doop* 'sauce,' from *doopen* 'to dip, mix.' —**dop·er** *n.*

dope·ster /ˈdōpstər/ ▸*n. informal* a person who collects and supplies information, typically on sporting events or elections: *they are* **inside dopesters** *with special access to the racing world.*

dope·y /ˈdōpē/ (also **dop·y**) ▸*adj.* (**dop·i·er**, **dop·i·est**) *informal* stupefied by sleep or a drug: *she was under sedation and a bit dopey.* ■ idiotic: *did you ever hear such dopey names?* —**dop·i·ly** /ˈdōpəlē/ *adv.* —**dop·i·ness** *n.*

dop·pel·gäng·er /ˈdäpəl,gaNGər/ ▸*n.* an apparition or double of a living person. ▷mid 19th cent.: from German, literally 'double-goer.'

Dop·pler /ˈdäplər/, Johann Christian (1803–53), Austrian physicist. In 1842, he discovered what is now known as the Doppler effect.

Dop·pler broad·en·ing ▸*n. Physics* the broadening of spectral lines as a result of the different velocities of the emitting atoms giving rise to different Doppler shifts.

Dop·pler ef·fect ▸*n. Physics* an increase (or decrease) in the frequency of sound, light, or other waves as the source and observer move toward (or away from) each other. The effect causes the sudden change in pitch noticeable in a passing siren, as well as the redshift seen by astronomers.

Dop·pler ra·dar ▸*n. Meteorology* a radar tracking system using the Doppler effect to determine the location and velocity of a storm, clouds, precipitation, etc.

Dop·pler shift ▸*n. Physics* a change in frequency due to the Doppler effect.

dop·y /ˈdōpē/ ▸*adj.* variant spelling of DOPEY.

dor /dôr/ (also **dor beetle**) ▸*n.* a large black dung beetle that makes a droning sound in flight and excavates burrows in which its young develop. • Family Geotrupidae: several genera and species. ▷Old English (denoting a bee or buzzing fly), probably imitative.

Do·ra·do /dəˈrädō/ *Astronomy* a southern constellation (the Goldfish), containing most of the Large Magellanic Cloud. ■ [as *genitive*] (**Doradus** /-dəs/) used with a preceding letter or numeral to designate a star in this constellation: *the star R Doradus.* ▷Spanish (see DORADO).

do·ra·do /dəˈrädō/ ▸*n.* (*pl.* **-dos**) **1** a South American freshwater fish with a golden body and red fins, popular as a game fish. • *Salminus maxillosus*, family Characidae. **2** another term for MAHIMAHI. ▷early 17th cent.: from Spanish, literally 'gilded,' from late Latin *deauratus*, from *deaurare* 'to gild over' (see also DORY[1]).

do-rag ▸*n. informal* a scarf or cloth worn to protect one's hairstyle: *13-year-old kids in big pants, "wife beater" T-shirts, and do-rags dancing to the sound of 50 Cent and calling each other "G."* ▷1990s: from *hairdo* and *rag*.

Do·ra·ti /ˈdôräti; dôˈrätē/, Antal (1906–88), U.S. composer and conductor; born in Hungary. As musical director of symphonies in Dallas 1945–49; Minneapolis 1949–60; Stockholm 1966–70; Washington, DC 1970–77; and Detroit 1977–81, he made over 500 recordings.

Dor·ches·ter /ˈdôrCHəstər; -,CHestər/ a residential section of Boston in Massachusetts, south of downtown.

Dor·dogne /dôrˈdōnyə/ a river in western France that rises in the Auvergne region and flows west for 297 miles (472 km) to meet the Garonne River and form the Gironde estuary. ■ a department in southwestern France. It contains caves that have yielded remains of early humans and their artifacts and art, such as at Lascaux.

Dor·drecht /ˈdôr,dreKHt/ an industrial city and river port in the Netherlands, near the mouth of the Rhine (there called the Waal) River, 12 miles (19 km) southeast of Rotterdam; pop. 110,500. Also called DORT.

Do·ri·an /ˈdôrēən/ ▸*n.* a member of a Hellenic people speaking the Doric dialect of Greek, thought to have entered Greece from the north *c.*1100 BC. They settled in Peloponnesus and later colonized Sicily and southern Italy.

▸*adj.* of or relating to this people or to Doris in central Greece. ▷via Latin from Greek *Dōrios* 'of Doris' + -IAN.

Do·ri·an mode ▸*n. Music* the mode represented by the natural diatonic scale D–D (containing a minor 3rd and minor 7th).

Dor·ic /ˈdôrik; ˈdär-/ ▸*adj.* **1** relating to or denoting a classical order of architecture characterized by a plain, sturdy column and a thick square abacus resting on a rounded molding. **2** relating to or denoting the ancient Greek dialect of the Dorians. ■ *archaic* (of a dialect) broad; rustic.

▸*n.* **1** the Doric order of architecture. **2** the ancient Greek dialect of the Dorians. ■ a broad or rustic dialect, esp. the dialect spoken in northeastern Scotland. [by association with the ancient Greek dialect, perceived as rustic.] ▷via Latin from Greek *Dōrikos*, from *Dōrios* (see DORIAN).

dork /dôrk/ ▸*n. informal* a dull, slow-witted, or socially inept person. ■ *vulgar slang* the penis. ▷1960s (originally U.S., in the sense 'penis'): perhaps a variant of DIRK, influenced by DICK[1]. —**dork·y** *adj.*

dorm /dôrm/ ▸*n. informal* a dormitory. ▷early 20th cent.: abbreviation.

dor·mant /ˈdôrmənt/ ▸*adj.* (of an animal) having normal physical functions suspended or slowed down for a period of time; in or as if in a deep sleep: *dormant butterflies figurative the event evoked memories that she would rather had* **lain dormant**. ■ (of a plant or bud) alive but not actively growing. See note at LATENT. ■ (of a volcano) temporarily inactive. ■ (of a disease) causing no symptoms but not cured and liable to recur. ■ [usu. *postpositive*] *Heraldry* (of an animal) depicted lying with its head on its paws. ▷late Middle English (in the senses 'fixed in position' and 'latent'): from Old French, 'sleeping,' present participle of *dormir*, from Latin *dormire* 'to sleep.' **—dor·man·cy** *n.*

dor·mer /ˈdôrmər/ (also **dormer window**) ▶*n.* a window that projects vertically from a sloping roof. ■ the projecting structure that houses such a window: *the windowed dormer above the sink.* ▷late 16th cent. (denoting the window of a dormitory or bedroom): from Old French *dormeor* 'dormitory,' from *dormir* 'to sleep.'

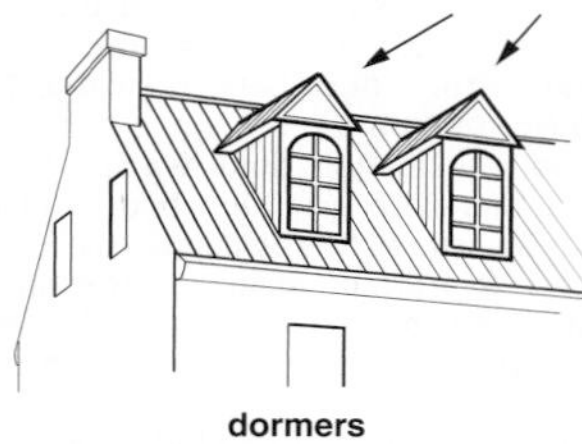

dormers

Dor·mi·tion /dôrˈmisʜən/ ▶*n.* (in the Orthodox Church) the passing of the Virgin Mary from earthly life. ■ the feast held in honor of this on August 15, corresponding to the Assumption in the Western Church. ▷late 15th cent.: from French, from Latin *dormitio(n-)* 'falling asleep,' from *dormire* 'to sleep.'

dor·mi·to·ry /ˈdôrmi,tôrē/ ▶*n.* (*pl.* **-ries**) a large bedroom for a number of people in a school or institution. ■ a university or college hall of residence or hostel. ■ [as *adj.*] *chiefly Brit.* denoting a small town or suburb providing a residential area for those who work in a nearby city. ▷late Middle English: from Latin *dormitorium*, neuter (used as a noun) of *dormitorius*, from *dormire* 'to sleep.'

dor·mouse /ˈdôr,mous/ ▶*n.* (*pl.* **-mice** /-,mīs/) an agile mouselike rodent with a hairy or bushy tail, found in Africa and Eurasia. Some kinds are noted for spending long periods in hibernation. • Family Gliridae: several genera and species, including the **common** (or **hazel**) **dormouse** (*Muscardinus avellanarius*) and the **fat dormouse**. ▷late Middle English: of unknown origin, but associated with French *dormir* or Latin *dormire* 'to sleep' and MOUSE.

do·ron·i·cum /dəˈränəkəm/ ▶*n.* (*pl.* **-cums**) a plant of the genus *Doronicum* in the daisy family, esp. (in gardening) leopard's bane. ▷modern Latin (Linnaeus), from modern Greek *dōronikon*, from Persian *darūnak*.

dorp /dôrp/ ▶*n.* *chiefly S. African* a small rural town or village: *dreary little dorps.* ▷late 15th cent.: Dutch, literally 'village' (see THORP).

dor·sal /ˈdôrsəl/ ▶*adj.* *Anatomy, Zoology, & Botany* of, on, or relating to the upper side or back of an animal, plant, or organ: *a dorsal view of the body | the dorsal aorta.* Compare with VENTRAL. ▷late Middle English: from late Latin *dorsalis*, from Latin *dorsum* 'back.' **—dor·sal·ly** *adv.*

dor·sal fin ▶*n.* *Zoology* an unpaired fin on the back of a fish or whale, e.g., the tall triangular fin of a shark or killer whale.

Dor·set /ˈdôrsit/ a county of southwestern England; county town, Dorchester.

dorsi- ▶*comb. form* **1** of, to, or on the back: *dorsiventral.* **2** another term for DORSO-. ▷from Latin *dorsum* 'back.'

dor·si·flex /ˈdôrsə,fleks/ ▶*v.* [*trans.*] *Physiology* bend (something, typically the hand or foot) dorsally or toward its upper surface: *the subject dorsiflexed his ankle.* **—dor·si·flex·ion** /,dôrsəˈfleksʜən/ *n.*

dor·si·flex·or /ˈdôrsə,fleksər/ ▶*n.* *Anatomy* a muscle whose contraction dorsiflexes the hand or foot.

dor·si·ven·tral /,dôrsəˈventrəl/ ▶*adj.* *chiefly Botany* (of a leaf or other part of a plant) having dissimilar dorsal and ventral surfaces. ■ another term for DORSOVENTRAL. **—dor·si·ven·tral·i·ty** /-venˈtralitē/ *n.* **—dor·si·ven·tral·ly** *adv.*

dorso- ▶*comb. form* **1** of, to, or on the back and (what is denoted by the second element): *dorsoventral.* **2** another term for DORSI-. ▷from Latin *dorsum* 'back.'

dor·so·lat·er·al /,dôrsōˈlatərəl/ ▶*adj.* *Anatomy & Biology* of, relating to, or involving the dorsal and lateral surfaces. **—dor·so·lat·er·al·ly** *adv.*

dor·so·ven·tral /,dôrsōˈventrəl/ ▶*adj.* *Anatomy & Biology* extending along or denoting an axis joining the dorsal and ventral surfaces. ■ of, relating to, or involving these surfaces. **—dor·so·ven·tral·ly** *adv.*

dor·sum /ˈdôrsəm/ ▶*n.* (*pl.* **dor·sa**) *Anatomy & Zoology* the dorsal part of an organism or structure. ▷late 18th cent. (denoting a long hill or ridge): from Latin, 'back.'

Dort /dôrt/ another name for DORDRECHT.

Dort·mund /ˈdôrtmənd/ an industrial city in northwestern Germany, in North Rhine-Westphalia; pop. 601,000.

do·ry[1] /ˈdôrē/ ▶*n.* (*pl.* **-ries**) a narrow deep-bodied fish with a mouth that can be opened very wide. • Several genera and species in the families Zeidae and Oreosomatidae. See also JOHN DORY. ▷late Middle English: from French *dorée*, feminine past participle of *dorer* 'gild,' from late Latin *deaurare* 'gild over,' based on Latin *aurum* 'gold.' Compare with DORADO.

do·ry[2] ▶*n.* (*pl.* **-ries**) a small flat-bottomed rowboat with a high bow and stern, of a kind originally used for fishing in New England. ▷early 18th cent.: perhaps from Miskito *dóri* 'dugout.'

do·ry·phore /ˈdôri,fôr/ ▶*n.* *rare* a pedantic and annoyingly persistent critic. ▷1950s (introduced by Sir Harold Nicolson): from French, literally 'Colorado beetle,' from Greek *doruphoros* 'spearcarrier.'

DOS /dôs/ *Computing* ▶*abbr.* disk operating system, an operating system originally developed for IBM personal computers.

DoS ▶*abbr.* *Computing* denial of service.

dos-à-dos /,dōz ə ˈdō/ ▶*adj.* (of two books) bound together with a shared central board and facing in opposite directions.
▶*n.* (*pl.* same) **1** a seat or carriage in which the occupants sit back to back. **2** variant spelling of DO-SI-DO.
▶*v.* variant spelling of DO-SI-DO. ▷mid 19th cent.: French, literally 'back to back.'

dos·age /ˈdōsij/ ▶*n.* the size or frequency of a dose of a medicine or drug: *a dosage of 450 milligrams a day | there are recommendations about dosage for elderly patients.* ■ a level of exposure to or absorption of ionizing radiation.

dose /dōs/ ▶*n.* a quantity of a medicine or drug taken or recommended to be taken at a particular time: *he took **a dose of** cough medicine.* ■ an amount of ionizing radiation received or absorbed at one time or over a specified period: ***a dose of** radiation exceeding safety limits.* ■ *informal* a venereal infection. ■ *informal* a quantity of something regarded as analogous to medicine in being necessary but unpleasant: *I wanted to give you **a dose of** the hell you put me through.*
▶*v.* [*trans.*] administer a dose to (a person or animal): *he **dosed** himself **with** vitamins.* ■ adulterate or blend (a substance) with another substance: *the champagne was **dosed with** sugar.* ▷late Middle English: from French, via late Latin from Greek *dosis* 'gift,' from *didonai* 'give.'
▶*PHRASE* □ **in small doses** *informal* when experienced or engaged in a little at a time: *computer games are great in small doses.*

dose e·quiv·a·lent ▶*n.* an estimate of the biological effect of a dose of ionizing radiation, calculated by multiplying the dose received by a factor depending on the type of radiation. It is measured in sieverts.

do-si-do /ˈdō sē ˈdō/ (also **dos-à-dos**) ▶*n.* (*pl.* **-dos**) (in square dancing, and other country dancing) a figure in which two dancers pass around each other back to back and return to their original positions.
▶*v.* [*intrans.*] dance a do-si-do. ▷1920s: alteration of DOS-À-DOS.

do·sim·e·ter /dōˈsimitər/ ▶*n.* a device used to measure an absorbed dose of ionizing radiation. **—do·si·met·ric** /,dōsəˈmetrik/ *adj.* **—do·sim·e·try** /-ˈsimitrē/ *n.*

Dos Pas·sos /däs ˈpasəs/, John (Roderigo) (1896–1970), U.S. novelist. He is known for his portrayal of life in the U.S. in such novels as *Manhattan Transfer* (1925) and *U.S.A.* (1938).

doss /däs/ *Brit., informal* ▶*v.* [*intrans.*] sleep (in rough or inexpensive accommodations): *he **dossed down** on a friend's floor.*
▶*n.* an instance of sleeping in such accommodations. ■ *archaic* a bed in a cheap lodging house. ▷late 18th cent.: perhaps based on Latin *dorsum* 'back.'

dos·sal /ˈdäsəl/ ▶*n.* an ornamental cloth hung behind an altar in a church or at the sides of a chancel. ▷mid 17th cent. (denoting an ornamental cloth to cover the back of a seat): from medieval Latin *dossale*, from late Latin *dorsalis* 'on the back' (see DORSAL).

doss·house /ˈdäs,hous/ ▶*n.* *Brit., informal* a cheap lodging house, esp. for homeless people and tramps.

dos·si·er /ˈdôsē,ā; ˈdäs-/ ▶*n.* a collection of documents about a particular person, event, or subject: *we have a **dossier on** him | **a dossier of** complaints.* ▷late 19th cent.: from French, denoting a bundle of papers with a label on the back, from *dos* 'back,' based on Latin *dorsum.*

dost /dəst/ ▶ archaic second person singular present of DO[1].

Do·sto·ev·sky /,dästəˈyefskē/ (also **Do·stoy·ev·sky**), Fyodor (Mikhailovich) (1821–81), Russian novelist. His novels reveal his psychological insight, savage humor, and concern with the religious, political, and moral problems posed by human suffering. Notable works: *Crime and Punishment* (1866), *The Idiot* (1868), and *The Brothers Karamazov* (1880).

DOT ▶*abbr.* Department of Transportation.

dot[1] /dät/ ▶*n.* a small round mark or spot: *a symbol depicted in colored dots.* ■ such a mark written or printed as part of an *i* or *j*, as a diacritical mark, as one of a series of marks to signify omission, or as a period. ■ *Music* such a mark used to denote the lengthening of a note or rest by half, or to indicate staccato. ■ the shorter signal of the two used in Morse code. Compare with DASH (sense 3). ■ used to refer to an object that appears tiny because it is far away: *the desert shrank figures to mere dots.* ■ used in speech to indicate the punctuation separating parts of an electronic mail or Web site address.
▶*v.* (**dot·ted, dot·ting**) [*trans.*] mark with a small spot or spots: *wet spots of rain began to dot his shirt.* ■ (of a number of items) be scattered over (an area): *churches dot the countryside.* ■ place a dot over (a letter): *you need to dot the i.* ■ *Music* mark (a note or rest) to show that the time value is increased by half: [as *adj.*] (**dotted**) *a dotted quarter note.* ▷Old English *dott* 'head of a boil.' The word is recorded only once in Old English, then not until the late 16th cent., when it is found in the sense 'a small lump or clot,' perhaps influenced by Dutch *dot* 'a knot.' The sense 'small mark or spot' dates from the mid 17th cent. **—dot·ter** *n.*
▶*PHRASES* □ **dot the i's and cross the t's** *informal* ensure that all details are correct. □ **on the dot** *informal* exactly on time: *he arrived on the dot at nine o'clock.*

dot[2] ▶*n.* *archaic* a dowry, particularly one from which only the interest or annual income was available to the husband. ▷from French, from Latin *dos, dot-* 'dowry' (see DOWER).

dot·age /ˈdōtij/ ▶*n.* [in *sing.*] the period of life in which a person is old and weak: *you could live here and look after me **in my dotage**.* ■ the state of having the intellect impaired, esp. through old age; senility. ▷late Middle English: from DOTE + -AGE.

do·tard /ˈdōtərd/ ▶*n.* an old person, esp. one who has become weak or senile. ▷late Middle English: from DOTE + -ARD.

dot-bomb (also **dot bomb** or **dot.bomb**) ▶*n.* *informal* an unsuccessful dot-com: *many promising Internet start-ups ended up as dot-bombs.* ▷on the pattern of *dot-com.* **—dot-bomb** *v.* [*intrans.*]

dot-com (also **dot.com**) ▶*n.* a company that relies largely or exclusively on Internet commerce.
▶*adj.* of or relating to business conducted on the Internet.

dot-com·mer /ˈdät ˈkämər/ (also **dot.com·mer**) ▶*n.* someone who works for or owns an Internet-based company.

dote /dōt/ ▶*v.* [*intrans.*] **1** (**dote on/upon**) be extremely and uncritically fond of: *she doted on her two young children* | [as *adj.*] (**doting**) *she was spoiled outrageously by her doting father.* **2** *archaic* be silly or feebleminded, esp. as a result of old age: *the parson is now old and dotes.* ▷Middle English (in the sense 'act or talk foolishly'): of uncertain origin; related to Middle Dutch *doten* 'be silly.' **—dot·er** *n.* **—dot·ing·ly** *adv.*

doth /dəᴛʜ/ ▶ *archaic* third person singular present of DO[1].

Do·than /ˈdōᴛʜən/ a city in southeastern Alabama, near the Florida border; pop. 57,737.

dot ma·trix ▶*n.* [usu. as *adj.*] a grid of dots that are filled selectively to produce an image on a screen or paper: *a dot matrix display board.*

dot ma·trix print·er ▶*n.* a printer that forms images of letters, numbers, etc., from a number of tiny dots.

dot prod·uct ▶*n.* another term for INNER PRODUCT.

dot·ted line ▶*n.* a line made up of dots or dashes (often used in reference to the space left for a signature on a contract): *Adam **signed on the dotted line**.*

dot·ted rhythm ▶*n.* *Music* rhythm in which the beat is unequally subdivided into a long dotted note and a short note.

dot·ter·el /ˈdätərəl/ ▶*n.* a small plover with a brown streaked back and a chestnut or buff belly with black below. Dotterels breed in mountainous areas and in the tundra. • Genus *Eudromias*, family Charadriidae: two species, esp. the Eurasian *E. morinellus*, which is noted for its tameness. ▷Middle English: from DOTE (so named because it is easily caught) + -REL. Compare with DODO.

dot·tle /ˈdätl/ ▸*n.* a remnant of tobacco left in a pipe after smoking. ▷late Middle English (denoting a plug for a barrel or other container): from DOT[1] + -LE[1].

dot·ty /ˈdätē/ ▸*adj.* (**dot·ti·er**, **dot·ti·est**) *informal* (of a person, action, or idea) somewhat mad or eccentric: *he was slightly dotty by the end of his second term.* ▷late 19th cent.: perhaps from obsolete *dote* 'simpleton, fool,' apparently from Dutch *dote* 'folly.' —**dot·ti·ly** /ˈdätəlē/ *adv.* —**dot·ti·ness** *n.*

Dou·a·la /do͞oˈälə/ the chief port of and largest city in Cameroon; pop. 1,200,000.

douane /dwän/ ▸*n. archaic* a custom house in France or other Mediterranean countries. ▷mid 17th cent.: from French, from Italian *do(g)ana*, from Arabic *dīwān* 'office,' from Persian *dīwān* (see DIVAN). Compare with DIWAN.

Dou·ay Bi·ble /ˈdo͞o-ā/ (also **Douay version**) ▸*n.* an English translation of the Bible formerly used in the Roman Catholic Church, completed at Douai in France early in the 17th century.

dou·ble /ˈdəbəl/ ▸*adj.* **1** consisting of two equal, identical, or similar parts or things: *the double doors.* ■ having twice the usual size, quantity, or strength: *she sipped a double brandy.* ■ designed to be used by two people: *a double bed.* ■ having two different roles or interpretations, esp. in order to deceive or confuse: *the furtive* **double life** *of a terrorist.* **2** having some essential part or feature twice, in particular: ■ (of a flower variety) having more than one circle of petals: *large double blooms.* ■ (of a domino) having the same number of dots on each half. ■ used to indicate that a letter or number occurs twice in succession: *"otter" is spelled with a double t.* **3** *Music* lower in pitch by an octave.
▸*predeterminer* twice as much or as many: *the jail now houses almost double the number of prisoners it was designed for | I'll pay double what I paid last time.*
▸*adv.* at or to twice the amount or extent: *you have to be careful, and this counts double for older people.* ■ as two instead of the more usual one: *she thought she was seeing double.*
▸*n.* **1** a thing that is twice as large as usual or is made up of two standard units or things: *join the two sleeping bags together to make a double.* ■ a double measure of liquor. ■ a thing designed to be used by two people, esp. a bed or a hotel room: *we'll use the bunk beds, you take the double | our rates are $200 per night for a double.* ■ *Baseball* a hit that allows the batter to reach second base safely: *Sabo came home on a double by O'Neill.* ■ a system of betting in which the winnings and stake from the first bet are transferred to a second. ■ *Bridge* a call that will increase the points won if the declarer is successful, or increase the penalty points won by the defenders if the declarer fails to make the contract. ■ *Darts* a hit on the narrow ring enclosed by the two outer circles of a dartboard, scoring double. **2** a person who looks exactly like another: *you could pass yourself off as his double.* ■ a person who stands in for an actor in a film. ■ an apparition of a living person: *she had seen her husband's double.* **3** (**doubles**) (esp. in tennis and badminton) a game or competition involving sides made up of two players: *the semifinals of the doubles.*
▸*pron.* a number or amount that is twice as large as a contrasting or usual number or amount: *he paid double and had a room all to himself.*
▸*v.* **1** [*intrans.*] become twice as much or as many: *profits doubled in one year.* ■ [*trans.*] make twice as much or as many of (something): *Clare doubled her income overnight.* ■ [*trans.*] *archaic* amount to twice as much as: *thy fifty yet doth double five and twenty.* ■ (**double up**) use the winnings from a bet as stake for another bet. ■ (of a member of the armed forces) move at twice the usual speed; run: *I doubled across the deck to join the others.* ■ (**double up**) share a room: *"Where's Jimmy going to sleep?" "He can* **double up with** *Bert."* ■ *Baseball* (of a batter) get a two-base hit: *Strawberry doubled with two outs.* ■ *Bridge* make a call increasing the value of the penalty points to be scored on an opponent's bid if it wins the auction and is not fulfilled. ■ *informal* go out on a double date: *they* **doubled with** *his sister and her oafish boyfriend.* **2** [*trans.*] fold or bend (paper, cloth, or other material) over on itself: *the muslin is doubled and then laid in a sieve over the bowl.* ■ [*intrans.*] (**double up**) bend over or curl up, typically because one is overcome with pain or mirth: *Billy started to double up with laughter.* ■ clench (a fist): *he had one arm around her and the other fist doubled.* ■ [*intrans.*] (usu. **double back**) go back in the direction one has come: *he had to double back to pick them up.* ■ *Nautical* sail around (a headland): *we struck out seaward to double the headland of the cape.* **3** [*intrans.*] (of a person or thing) be used in or play another, different role: *a laser printer* **doubles as** *a photocopier.* ■ [*trans.*] (of an actor) play (two parts) in the same piece. ■ *Music* play two or more musical instruments. ■ [*trans.*] *Music* add the same note in a higher or lower octave to (a note). ▷Middle English: via Old French from Latin *duplus* (see DUPLE). The verb is from Old French *dobler*, from late Latin *duplare*, from *duplus*. —**dou·bler** *n.* —**dou·bly** *adv.*
▸PHRASES □ **on the double** at running speed; very fast: *he disappeared on the double.* ■ without hesitation; immediately *he summoned his officers on the double.* □ **double or nothing** a gamble to decide whether a loss or debt should be doubled or canceled.

dou·ble a·cros·tic ▸*n.* an acrostic in which the first and last letters of each line form a hidden word or words.

dou·ble-act·ing ▸*adj.* denoting a device or product that combines two different functions: *double-acting hydraulic shock absorbers | double-acting baking powder.* ■ (of an engine) having pistons pushed from both sides alternately.

dou·ble-ac·tion ▸*adj.* another term for DOUBLE-ACTING: *double-action moss killer.* ■ (of a gun) needing to be cocked and fired as two separate actions.

dou·ble a·gent ▸*n.* an agent who pretends to act as a spy for one country or organization while in fact acting on behalf of an enemy.

dou·ble bar ▸*n.* a pair of closely spaced bar lines marking the end of a piece or section of music.

dou·ble-bar·reled ▸*adj.* (of a gun) having two barrels. ■ having two parts or aspects.

dou·ble bass /bās/ ▸*n.* the largest and lowest-pitched instrument of the violin family, providing the bass line of the orchestral string section and also much used in jazz.

dou·ble bas·soon ▸*n.* another term for CONTRABASSOON.

dou·ble bill ▸*n.* a program of entertainment with two main items or personalities: *a double bill of pianist Donegan and alto sax star Woods.*
▸*v.* [*trans.*] (**dou·ble-bill**) charge (different accounts) for the same expenses: *her two restaurants were double-billed for the one refrigerator | [intrans.] the previous accounting program had a tendency to double-bill.* —**dou·ble bill·ing** (also **dou·ble-bill·ing**) *n.*

dou·ble bind ▸*n.* a situation in which a person is confronted with two irreconcilable demands or a choice between two undesirable courses of action.

dou·ble-bit·ted ax ▸*n.* an ax with two blades.

dou·ble-blind ▸*adj.* [*attrib.*] denoting a test or trial, esp. of a drug, in which any information that may influence the behavior of the tester or the subject is withheld until after the test. Compare with SINGLE BLIND.

dou·ble bluff ▸*n.* an action or statement that is intended to appear as a bluff but is in fact genuine.

dou·ble bo·gey *Golf* ▸*n.* a score of two strokes over par for a hole.
▸*v.* (**dou·ble-bo·gey**) [*trans.*] complete (a hole) in two strokes over par.

dou·ble boil·er ▸*n.* a saucepan with a detachable upper compartment heated by boiling water in the lower one.

dou·ble bond ▸*n.* a chemical bond in which two pairs of electrons are shared between two atoms.

dou·ble-book ▸*v.* [*trans.*] (usu. **be double-booked**) inadvertently reserve (something, esp. a seat or a hotel room) for two different customers or parties at the same time: *the hotel was double-booked.* ■ book (someone) into a seat or room that is already reserved for another.

dou·ble-breast·ed ▸*adj.* (of a jacket or coat) having a substantial overlap of material at the front and showing two rows of buttons when fastened.

dou·ble bri·dle ▸*n.* a bridle that has both a curb and a snaffle bit, each with its own set of reins.

dou·ble-check ▸*v.* [*trans.*] go over (something) for a second time to ensure that it is accurate or safe: *he double-checked our credentials | [with clause] double-check that all windows are firmly locked.*

dou·ble chin ▸*n.* a roll of fatty flesh below a person's chin. —**dou·ble-chinned** *adj.*

dou·ble-click ▸*v.* [*intrans.*] *Computing* press a mouse button twice in quick succession to select a file, program, or function: *to run a window just* **double-click on** *the icon.* ■ [*trans.*] select (a file) in this way.

dou·ble-clutch ▸*v.* [*intrans.*] release and reengage the clutch of a vehicle twice when changing gear.

dou·ble con·cer·to ▸*n.* a concerto for two solo instruments.

dou·ble cream ▸*n.* British term for HEAVY CREAM.

dou·ble-cross ▸*v.* [*trans.*] deceive or betray (a person with whom one is supposedly cooperating): *he was blackmailed into double-crossing his own government.*
▸*n.* a betrayal of someone with whom one is supposedly cooperating. —**dou·ble-cross·er** *n.*

dou·ble-cut ▸*adj.* (of a file) having two sets of grooves crossing each other diagonally.

dou·ble dag·ger ▸*n.* a symbol (‡) used in printed text to introduce an annotation.

dou·ble date ▸*n.* a social outing in which two couples participate.
▸*v.* [*intrans.*] (**double-date**) take part in a double date. ■ [*trans.*] accompany (someone) on a double date.

Dou·ble·day /ˈdəbəlˌdā/, Abner (1819–93), U.S. army officer. A Union general in the Civil War, he is credited with creating the modern game of baseball, although this claim has been disproved.

dou·ble-deal·ing ▸*n.* the practice of working to people's disadvantage behind their backs.
▸*adj.* working deceitfully to injure others: *she is a backstabbing, double-dealing twister.* —**dou·ble-deal·er** *n.*

dou·ble-deck·er ▸*n.* something, esp. a bus, that has two floors or levels: [*as adj.*] *a double-decker bus | double-decker sandwiches.*

dou·ble de·com·po·si·tion ▸*n. Chemistry* another term for METATHESIS (sense 2).

dou·ble-den·si·ty ▸*adj. Computing* (of a disk) able to store twice as much information as other, older disks of the same physical size.

dou·ble-dig·it ▸*adj.* [*attrib.*] (of a number, variable, or percentage) between 10 and 99: *double-digit inflation.*
▸*n.* (**double digits**) another term for DOUBLE FIGURES.

dou·ble-dip ▸*v.* [*intrans.*] *informal* obtain an income from two different sources, typically in an illicit way. —**dou·ble-dip·per** *n.* —**dou·ble-dip·ping** *n.*

dou·ble dot ▸*n.* (in musical composition or transcription) two dots placed side by side after a note to indicate that it is to be lengthened by three quarters of its value.
▸*v.* (**dou·ble-dot**) [*trans.*] write or perform (music) with a rhythm of alternating long and short notes in a ratio of approximately seven to one, producing a more marked effect than ordinary dotted rhythm.

dou·ble drib·ble ▸*n. Basketball* an illegal dribble that occurs when a player dribbles with both hands simultaneously or interrupts a dribble by holding the ball briefly in one or both hands.
▸*v.* (**dou·ble-drib·ble**) commit or be charged with a double dribble.

dou·ble dum·my ▸*n. Bridge* a way of playing with two hands exposed, allowing every card to be located, for instructional purposes.

dou·ble Dutch (also **dou·ble dutch**) ▸*n.* a jump-rope game played with two long jump ropes swung in opposite directions so that they cross rhythmically: [*as adv.*] *three girls jumped double Dutch, the white cords whirring like an electric fan.*

dou·ble-dyed ▸*adj.* (of an item of clothing) dyed twice in order to give a very deep color. ■ *figurative* (of a person) thoroughly imbued with a particular quality: *a double-dyed liberal.*

dou·ble ea·gle ▸*n.* **1** a gold coin worth twenty dollars. **2** *Golf* a score of three strokes under par at a hole.

dou·ble-edged ▸*adj.* (of a knife or sword) having two cutting edges. ■ having two contradictory aspects or possible outcomes: *the consequences can be double-edged.*
▸PHRASE □ **a double-edged sword** a situation or course of action having both positive and negative effects.

dou·ble ef·fect ▸*n.* (in ethics) the good and bad effect of an action, compared according to a principle that seeks to justify the action if the bad effect, though foreseen, is outweighed by the good effect.

dou·ble-end·er ▸*n.* a boat in which stern and bow are similarly tapered.

dou·ble en·ten·dre /änˈtändrə/ ▸*n.* (*pl.* **dou·ble**

en·ten·dres *pronunc.* same) a word or phrase open to two interpretations, one of which is usually risqué or indecent. ■ humor using such words or phrases. ▷late 17th cent.: from obsolete French (now *double entente*), 'double understanding.'

dou·ble-en·try ▸*adj.* [*attrib.*] denoting a system of bookkeeping in which each transaction is entered as a debit in one account and a credit in another.

dou·ble ex·po·sure ▸*n.* the repeated exposure of a photographic plate or film to light, often producing ghost images. ■ the photograph that results from such exposure.

dou·ble-faced ▸*adj.* having two faces: *a double-faced clock.* ■ tending to say one thing and do another; deceitful. ■ (of a fabric or material) finished on both sides so that either may be used as the right side.

dou·ble fault ▸*n. Tennis* an instance of two consecutive faults in serving, counting as a point against the server.
▸*v.* (**dou·ble-fault**) [*intrans.*] serve a double fault.

double fea·ture ▸*n.* a movie program with two full-length films.

dou·ble fig·ures ▸*plural n.* a number or amount, esp. a percentage, between 10 and 99: *inflation was* **in double figures**.

dou·ble flat ▸*n.* a sign (♭♭) placed before a musical note to indicate that it is to be lowered two semitones. ■ a note so marked or lowered.

dou·ble fugue ▸*n. Music* a fugue with two subjects, each similarly treated.

dou·ble glaz·ing ▸*n.* windows that have two layers of glass with a space between them, designed to reduce loss of heat and exclude noise. —**dou·ble-glaze** *v.*

dou·ble-hand·ed ▸*adj.* made to be lifted or held with two hands: *a long sword with a double-handed hilt.* ■ using both hands: *a double-handed backhand.*

dou·ble-head·ed ▸*adj.* having a double head or two heads: *a double-headed monster* | *double-headed nails.* ■ (of a train) pulled by two locomotives. ■ (of a weapon) having two cutting implements, typically one at each end of the shaft: *a double-headed ax.*

dou·ble·head·er /ˌdəbəlˈhedər/ (also **dou·ble-head·er**) ▸*n.* **1** a sporting event in which two games or contests are played in succession at the same venue, typically between the same teams or players. **2** a train pulled by two locomotives coupled together.

dou·ble he·lix ▸*n.* a pair of parallel helices intertwined about a common axis, esp. that in the structure of the DNA molecule.

dou·ble-hung ▸*adj.* (of a window) consisting of two sliding vertical sashes.

dou·ble in·dem·ni·ty ▸*n.* provision for payment of double the face amount of an insurance policy under certain conditions, e.g., when death occurs as a result of an accident.

dou·ble jeop·ard·y ▸*n. Law* the prosecution of a person twice for the same offense. ■ risk or disadvantage incurred from two sources simultaneously: *he is* **in double jeopardy**, *unable to speak either language adequately.*

dou·ble-joint·ed ▸*adj.* (of a person) having unusually flexible joints, typically those of the fingers, arms, or legs.

dou·ble-knit ▸*adj.* (of fabric) knit of two joined layers for extra thickness: *a green double-knit suit.* ▷mid 19th cent.: *double* with reference to the "doubling" of the yarn to four-ply.

dou·ble-lock ▸*v.* [*trans.*] lock (a door) with two complete turns of the key so as to engage a second bolt.
▸*n.* (**double lock**) a type of lock that may be secured in this way.

dou·ble neg·a·tive ▸*n. Grammar* a negative statement containing two negative elements (for example *didn't say nothing*). ■ a positive statement in which two negative elements are used to produce the positive force, usu. for some particular rhetorical effect (for example *there is not nothing to worry about!*).

USAGE According to standard English grammar, a **double negative** used to express a single negative, such as *I don't know nothing* (rather than *I don't know anything*), is incorrect. The rules dictate that the two negative elements cancel each other out to give an affirmative statement, so that, logically, *I don't know nothing* means *I know something.*

In practice, this sort of double negative is widespread in dialect and nonstandard usage and rarely causes confusion about the intended meaning. Double negatives are standard in other languages such as Spanish and Polish, and they have not always been unacceptable in English. It was normal in Old English and Middle English and did not come to be frowned upon until some time after the 16th century.

The double negative can be used in speech or in written dialogue for emphasis or other rhetorical effects. Such constructions as 'has not gone unnoticed' or 'not wholly unpersuasive' may be useful for making a point through understatement, but the double negative should be used judiciously because it may cause confusion or annoy the reader.

007 /ˈdəbəlˌōˈsevən; ˈōˌōˈsevən/ ▸*n.* the fictional British secret agent James Bond, or someone based on, inspired by, or reminiscent of him.
▸*adj.* reminiscent of or inspired by features of the James Bond films: *This is not 007 territory; it can be achieved with the tools that are available already.*

dou·ble-park ▸*v.* [*trans.*] (usu. **be double-parked**) park (a vehicle) alongside one that is already parked at the side of the road.

dou·ble play ▸*n. Baseball* a defensive play in which two players are put out.

dou·ble pneu·mo·nia ▸*n.* pneumonia affecting both lungs.

dou·ble pre·ci·sion ▸*n. Computing* the use of twice the usual number of bits to represent a number, giving greater arithmetic accuracy.

dou·ble-quick ▸*adj.* & *adv. informal* very quick or quickly: [as *adj.*] *I got changed* **in double-quick time** | [as *adv.*] *you get upstairs double-quick!*

dou·ble reed ▸*n. Music* a reed with two slightly separated blades, used for playing a wind instrument such as an oboe or bassoon.

dou·ble re·frac·tion ▸*n. Physics* division of a single incident light ray or other electromagnetic wave into two separate rays in an anisotropic medium.

dou·ble rhyme ▸*n.* a feminine rhyme involving one stressed and one unstressed syllable in each rhyming line.

dou·ble salt ▸*n. Chemistry* a crystalline salt having the composition of a mixture of two simple salts but with a different crystal structure from either.

dou·ble sharp ▸*n.* a sign (𝄪) placed before a musical note to indicate that it is to be raised two semitones. ■ a note so marked or raised.

dou·ble-sid·ed ▸*adj.* using or able to be used on both sides: *double-sided adhesive tape.* —**dou·ble-sid·ed·ness** *n.*

dou·ble-space ▸*v.* type or format with a full space between lines.

dou·ble·speak /ˈdəbəlˌspēk/ ▸*n.* deliberately euphemistic, ambiguous, or obscure language: *the art of political doublespeak.*

dou·ble stand·ard ▸*n.* a rule or principle that is unfairly applied in different ways to different people or groups: *the smaller pay received by black soldiers demonstrated a double standard.*

dou·ble star ▸*n.* two stars physically very close together, as a binary star, or apparently so, as an optical double.

dou·ble steal ▸*n. Baseball* a play in which two base runners each steal a base.

dou·ble stop ▸*n.* the sound of two strings at once on a violin or similar bowed instrument. —**dou·ble-stop** *v.* —**dou·ble-stop·ping** *n.*

dou·blet /ˈdəblət/ ▸*n.* **1** either of a pair of similar things, in particular: ■ either of two words of the same historical source, but with two different stages of entry into the language and different resultant meanings, for example *fashion* and *faction*, *cloak* and *clock*. ■ (**doublets**) the same number on two dice thrown at once. ■ *Physics & Chemistry* a pair of associated lines close together in a spectrum or electrophoretic gel. ■ a combination of two simple lenses. **2** a man's short close-fitting padded jacket, commonly worn from the 14th to the 17th century. ▷Middle English: from Old French, 'something folded,' also denoting a fur-lined coat, from *double* 'double.'

dou·ble take ▸*n.* a delayed reaction to something unexpected, immediately after one's first reaction: *Tony glanced at her, then* **did a double take**.

dou·ble-talk ▸*n.* deliberately unintelligible speech combining nonsense syllables and actual words. ■ another term for **DOUBLESPEAK**.

dou·ble-team ▸*v.* [*trans.*] (in ball games, esp. basketball) block (an opponent) with two players.
▸*n.* an act of double-teaming.

dou·ble·think /ˈdəbəlˌTHiNGk/ ▸*n.* the acceptance of or mental capacity to accept contrary opinions or beliefs at the same time, esp. as a result of political indoctrination. ▷1949: coined by George Orwell in his novel *Nineteen Eighty-Four.*

dou·ble time ▸*n.* **1** a rate of pay equal to double the standard rate, sometimes paid for working on holidays or outside normal working hours. **2** *Military* a regulation running pace. **3** *Music* a rhythm that is twice as fast as an earlier one.

dou·ble·ton /ˈdəbəltən/ ▸*n.* (in card games, esp. bridge) a pair of cards that are the only cards of their suit in a hand. ■ [as *adj.*] denoting a card that is one of a doubleton: *a doubleton ace.* ■ a pair of people or things. ▷early 20th cent.: from **DOUBLE**, on the pattern of *singleton.*

dou·ble tongu·ing ▸*n. Music* the use of two alternating movements of the tongue (usually as in sounding *t* and *k*) in playing rapid passages on a wind instrument. —**dou·ble-tongue** *v.*

dou·ble·tree /ˈdəbəlˌtrē/ ▸*n.* a crossbar in front of a wagon with a swingletree at each end, enabling two horses to be harnessed. ▷mid 19th cent.: from **DOUBLE**, on the pattern of *singletree.*

dou·ble vi·sion ▸*n.* the simultaneous perception of two images, usually overlapping, of a single scene or object.

dou·ble wham·my ▸*n. informal* a twofold blow or setback: *a double whammy of taxation and price increases.* ▷1950s: originally with reference to the comic strip *Li'l Abner* (see **WHAMMY**).

dou·ble-wide ▸*adj.* (of a semipermanent mobile home) consisting of two separate units connected on site.
▸*n.* such a mobile home: *she left the double-wide empty.*

dou·bloon /dəˈblo͞on/ ▸*n. historical* a Spanish gold coin. ▷from French *doublon* or its source, Spanish *doblón*, from *doble* 'double' (so named because the coin was worth double the value of a pistole).

doubt /dout/ ▸*n.* a feeling of uncertainty or lack of conviction: *some* **doubt** *has been* **cast** *upon the authenticity of this account* | *they had doubts that they would ever win.* See note at **UNCERTAINTY**.
▸*v.* **1** [*trans.*] feel uncertain about: *I doubt my ability to do the job.* ■ question the truth or fact of (something): *who can doubt the value of these services?* | [with *clause*] *I doubt if anyone slept that night.* ■ disbelieve (a person or their word): *I have no reason to doubt him.* ■ [*intrans.*] feel uncertain, esp. about one's religious beliefs. **2** [with *clause*] *archaic* fear; be afraid of: *I doubt not your contradictions.* ▷Middle English: from Old French *doute* (noun), *douter* (verb), from Latin *dubitare* 'hesitate,' from *dubius* 'doubtful' (see **DUBIOUS**). —**doubt·a·ble** *adj.* —**doubt·er** *n.* —**doubt·ing·ly** *adv.*
▸***PHRASES*** □ **beyond** (**a** or **a shadow of a**) **doubt** allowing no uncertainty: *you've proved it beyond doubt* | *they knew beyond a shadow of a doubt what made them happy.* □ **in doubt** open to question: *the outcome is no longer in doubt.* ■ feeling uncertain about something: *by the age of 14 he was in no doubt about his career aims.* □ **no doubt** used to indicate the speaker's firm belief that something is true even if evidence is not given or available: *those who left were attracted, no doubt, by higher pay.* ■ used to introduce a concession that is subsequently dismissed as unimportant or irrelevant: *they no doubt did what they could to help her, but their best proved insufficient.* □ **without** (**a**) **doubt** indisputably: *he was without doubt the very worst kind of reporter.*

doubt·ful /ˈdoutfəl/ ▸*adj.* **1** feeling uncertain about something: *he looked doubtful, but gave a nod* | *I was* **doubtful of** *my judgment.* **2** not known with certainty: *the fire was of doubtful origin.* ■ improbable: [with *clause*] *it is doubtful whether these programs have any lasting effect.* ■ not established as genuine or acceptable: *of doubtful legality.* —**doubt·ful·ly** *adv.* —**doubt·ful·ness** *n.*

THE RIGHT WORD **ambiguous, doubtful, dubious, enigmatic, equivocal, problematic, questionable**

If you are **doubtful** about the outcome of a situation, you might be understandably **dubious** about getting involved in it.

While all of these adjectives express suspicion, indecision, or a lack of clarity, *doubtful* carries such strong connotations of uncertainty that the thing being described is as good as worthless, unsound, invalid, unlikely, or doomed to fail (*it was doubtful that the plane could land safely*).

Dubious is not quite as strong, suggesting suspicion, mistrust, or hesitation (*a dubious reputation*). It can also mean inclined to doubt or full of hesitation.

If you're *doubtful* about the outcome of a particular situation, it means that you are fairly certain it will not turn out well. If you're *dubious*, on the other hand, it means that you're wavering or hesitating in your opinion.

Questionable may merely imply the existence of doubt (*a questionable excuse*), but like *dubious*, it also has connotations of dishonesty and immorality (*a place where questionable activities were going on*).

Problematic, in contrast to both *dubious* and *questionable*, is free from any suggestion of moral judgment or suspicion. It is applied to things that are genuinely uncertain, and to outcomes that are as likely to be positive as negative (*getting everyone in the family to agree could be problematic*).

Ambiguous and **equivocal** refer to lack of clarity. But while *ambiguous* can refer to either an intentional or unintentional lack of clarity (*her ambiguous replies to our questions*), *equivocal* suggests an intentional wish to remain unclear (*his equivocal responses indicated that he wasn't keen to cooperate*). It can also mean capable of different interpretations (*an equivocal statement that could be taken to mean opposite things*).

Something that is **enigmatic** is likely to be intentionally unclear as well (*an enigmatic statement designed to provoke controversy*), although *enigmatic* can also mean perplexing or mysterious.

doubt·ing Thom·as ▸*n.* a person who is skeptical and refuses to believe something without proof. ▷early 17th cent.: with biblical allusion to the apostle Thomas (John 20: 24–29).

doubt·less /ˈdoutlis/ ▸*adv.* [*sentence adverb*] used to indicate the speaker's belief that a statement is certain to be true given what is known about the situation: *the company would doubtless find the reduced competition to their liking.* ■ used to refer to a desirable outcome as though it were certain: *doubtless you'll solve the problem.* **—doubt·less·ly** *adv.*

douce /do͞os/ ▸*adj. chiefly Scottish* sober, gentle, and sedate: *stories which would have outraged their douce minds.* ▷Middle English (in the sense 'pleasant, sweet'): from Old French *dous, douce*, from Latin *dulcis* 'sweet.'

dou·ceur /do͞oˈsər/ ▸*n.* a financial inducement; a bribe: *Pericles gave a handsome douceur to the Spartan commanders to withdraw without fighting.* ■ a gratuity or tip. ▷mid 18th cent.: French, literally 'sweetness.'

dou·ceur de vi·vre /do͞oˈsər də ˈvēvrə/ ▸*n.* a way of living that is pleasant and free from worries. ▷mid 20th cent.: French, literally 'sweetness of living (or life).'

douche /do͞osh/ ▸*n.* a shower of water: *a daily douche.* ■ a jet of liquid applied to part of the body for cleansing or medicinal purposes. ■ a device for washing out the vagina as a contraceptive measure. ▸*v.* [*trans.*] spray or shower with water. ■ [*intrans.*] use a douche as a method of contraception. ▷mid 18th cent. (as a noun): via French from Italian *doccia* 'conduit pipe,' from *docciare* 'pour by drops,' based on Latin *ductus* 'leading' (see **DUCT**).

douche bag ▸*n.* a small syringe for douching the vagina, esp. as a contraceptive measure. ■ *informal* a loathsome or contemptible person (used as a term of abuse).

dough /dō/ ▸*n.* **1** a thick, malleable mixture of flour and liquid, used for baking into bread or pastry. **2** *informal* money: *lots of dough.* ▷Old English *dāg*, of Germanic origin; related to Dutch *deeg* and German *Teig*, from an Indo-European root meaning 'smear, knead.' **—dough·i·ness** *n.* **—dough·y** *adj.* (**dough·i·er, dough·i·est**).

dough·boy /ˈdōˌboi/ ▸*n.* **1** a boiled or deep-fried dumpling. **2** *informal* a U.S. infantryman, esp. one in World War I. [said to have been a term applied in the Civil War to the large globular brass buttons on the infantry uniform; also said to derive from the use of pipe clay 'dough' to clean the white belts worn by infantrymen.]

dough-faced ▸*adj. informal* pasty-faced: *his dough-faced niece.*

dough·nut /ˈdōˌnət/ (also **do·nut**) ▸*n.* a small fried cake of sweetened dough, typically in the shape of a ball or ring. ■ a ring-shaped object, in particular a vacuum chamber in some types of particle accelerator.

dough·ty /ˈdoutē/ ▸*adj.* (**-ti·er, -ti·est**) *archaic, humorous* brave and persistent: *his doughty spirit kept him going.* ▷late Old English *dohtig*, variant of *dyhtig*, of Germanic origin; related to Dutch *duchtig* and German *tüchtig*. **—dough·ti·ly** /ˈdoutl-ē/ *adv.* **—dough·ti·ness** *n.*

Doug·las[1] /ˈdəgləs/, Kirk (1916–), U.S. actor; born *Issur Danielovitch Demsky.* Notable films include *Lust for Life* (1957), *Spartacus* (1960), which he also produced, and *Seven Days in May* (1964). He received an honorary Academy Award in 1995. He is the father of Michael Douglas.

Doug·las[2], Michael(1944–), U.S. actor; and producer. His films include *The China Syndrome* (1979), which he also produced, *Fatal Attraction* (1987), *Wall Street* (Academy Award, 1987), and *Basic Instinct* (1992). He is the son of Kirk Douglas.

Doug·las[3], Stephen Arnold (1813–61), U.S. lawyer and politician; know as the **Little Giant**. An Illinois Democrat, he was a member of the U.S. House of Representatives 1843–47 and U.S. Senate 1847–61. He is best remembered for the Lincoln-Douglas debates, a series of seven senatorial-campaign debates in 1858 with Republican candidate Abraham Lincoln. He won the Senate seat in 1858, but lost his 1860 bid for the presidency to Lincoln.

Stephen A. Douglas

Doug·las[4], William Orville (1898–1980), U.S. Supreme Court associate justice 1939–75. Appointed to the Court by President Franklin D. Roosevelt, he worked to uphold the New Deal programs and was a strong advocate of free speech. He also was noted for defending the environment.

Doug·las fir ▸*n.* a tall, slender conifer with soft foliage and, in mature trees, deeply fissured bark. It is widely planted as a timber tree. • Genus *Pseudotsuga*, family Pinaceae: several species, in particular the **common Douglas fir** (*P. menziesii*) of British Columbia and the western U.S. ▷mid 19th cent.: named after David *Douglas* (1798–1834), the Scottish botanist and explorer who introduced it to Europe from North America.

Doug·las-Home /ˈdəgləs ˈhyo͞om/, Sir Alec (1903–95), British statesman; prime minister 1963–64; born *Alexander Frederick Douglas-Home.*

Doug·lass /ˈdəgləs/, Frederick (1817–95), U.S. abolitionist and writer; born *Frederick Augustus Washington Bailey.* He escaped from slavery in 1838 and became an antislavery lecturer. He established an antislavery newspaper *North Star* (1847–64) and published his autobiography, *Narrative of the Life of Frederick Douglass* (1845, revised 1892).

Frederick Douglass

dou·la /ˈdo͞olə/ ▸*n.* a person, usually a woman, who is professionally trained to assist a woman during childbirth and who may provide support to the family after the baby is born.

Doul·ton /ˈdōltən; ˈdôltən/ (also **Royal Doulton**) ▸*n. trademark* fine, decorative pottery or porcelain made at the factories of John Doulton (1793–1873) or his successors.

doum palm /do͞om/ ▸*n.* a palm tree with a forked trunk, producing edible fruit and a vegetable ivory substitute. It is native to the Nile region of Upper Egypt. • *Hyphaene thebaica*, family Palmae. ▷early 18th cent.: *doum* from Arabic *dawm, dūm.*

dour /do͝or; dou(ə)r/ ▸*adj.* relentlessly severe, stern, or gloomy in manner or appearance: *a hard, dour, humorless fanatic.* See note at **GLUM**. ▷late Middle English (originally Scots): probably from Scottish Gaelic *dúr* 'dull, obstinate, stupid,' perhaps from Latin *durus* 'hard.' **—dour·ly** *adv.* **—dour·ness** *n.*

Dou·ro /ˈdōˌro͞o/ a river on the Iberian peninsula that rises in central Spain and flows west for 556 miles (900 km) through Portugal to the Atlantic Ocean near Oporto. Spanish name **DUERO**.

dou·rou·cou·li /ˌdo͞orəˈko͞olē/ ▸*n.* (*pl.* **-lis**) a large-eyed chiefly nocturnal monkey found in South America. Also called **NIGHT MONKEY, OWL MONKEY**. • Genus *Aotus*, family Cebidae: two or more species. ▷mid 19th cent.: probably a South American Indian name.

douse /dous/ (also **dowse**) ▸*v.* [*trans.*] pour a liquid over; drench: *he doused the car with gasoline and set it on fire.* ■ extinguish (a fire or light): *stewards appeared and the fire was doused | figurative nothing could douse her sudden euphoria.* ■ *Sailing* lower (a sail) quickly. ▷early 17th cent.: perhaps imitative, influenced by **SOUSE**, or perhaps from dialect *douse* 'strike, beat,' from Middle Dutch and Low German *dossen.*

Dove /dōv/, Rita (1952–), U.S. poet and novelist. The youngest poet and the first African-American woman to hold the post of poet laureate of the U.S. 1993–94, her work includes the Pulitzer Prize–winning poem "Thomas and Beulah" (1987) and the novel *Through the Ivory Gate* (1992).

dove[1] /dəv/ ▸*n.* **1** a stocky seed- or fruit-eating bird with a small head, short legs, and a cooing voice. Doves are generally smaller and more delicate than pigeons, but many kinds have been given both names. • Family Columbidae: numerous genera and species; white doves are a variety of the domestic pigeon. **2** a person who advocates peaceful or conciliatory policies, esp. in foreign affairs. Compare with **HAWK**[1] (sense 2). **3** (**Dove**) (in Christian art and poetry) the Holy Spirit (as represented in John 1:32). ▷Middle English: from Old Norse *dúfa.* **—dove·like** /-ˌlīk/ *adj.* **—dov·ish** *adj.* (in sense 2).

dove[2] /dōv/ ▸ past of **DIVE**.

dove·cote /ˈdəvˌkōt/ (also **dove·cot**) ▸*n.* a shelter with nest holes for domesticated pigeons.

dove gray /dəv/ ▸*n.* a light gray.

dove·kie /ˈdəvkē/ ▸*n.* a small, stubby short-billed auk with black plumage and white underparts, breeding in the Arctic. • *Alle alle*, family Alcidae. ▷early 19th cent. (originally denoting the black guillemot, *Cepphus grylle*, also formerly called the *Greenland dove*): from a Scots diminutive of **DOVE**[1].

Do·ver /ˈdōvər/ **1** a ferry port in Kent, on the coast of the English Channel; pop. 34,300. It is mainland Britain's nearest point to the Continent, being only 22 miles (35 km) from Calais, France. **2** the capital of Delaware, in the central part of the state; pop. 32,135. **3** an industrial city in southeastern New Hampshire; pop. 26,884. **4** a township in southeastern New Jersey, on Barnegat Bay; pop. 89,706.

Do·ver, Strait of a sea passage between England and France that connects the English Channel with the North Sea.

Do·ver sole ▸*n.* either of two flatfishes that are highly valued as food: • a true sole that is common in European waters (*Solea solea*, family Soleidae). • a relative of the lemon sole found in the eastern Pacific (*Microstomus pacificus*, family Pleuronectidae).

dove·tail /ˈdəvˌtāl/ ▸*n.* (also **dovetail joint**) a joint formed by one or more tapered projections (tenons) on one piece that interlock with corresponding notches or recesses (mortises) in another. ■ a tenon used in such a joint, typically wider at its extremity. ▸*v.* [*trans.*] join together by

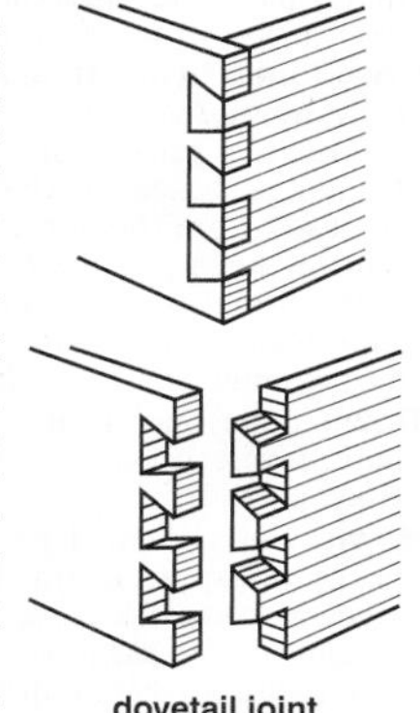

dovetail joint

Pronunciation Key ə *ago*; ər *over*; ˈə or ˌə *up*; ˈər or ˌər *fur*; a *hat*; ā *rate*; ä *car*; ch *chew*; e *let*; ē *see*; e(ə)r *air*; i *fit*; ī *by*; i(ə)r *ear*; ng *sing*; ō *go*; ô *for*; oi *boy*; o͝o *good*; o͞o *goo*; ou *out*; sh *she*; th *thin*; t͟h *then*; (h)w *why*; zh *vision*

means of a dovetail. ■ fit or cause to fit together easily and conveniently: [*trans.*] *plan to enable parents to dovetail their career and family commitments* [*intrans.*] *flights that* **dovetail with** *the working day.*

dove tree ▸*n.* a slender deciduous Chinese tree with flowers that bear large white bracts said to resemble doves' wings, grown as an ornamental. • *Davidia involucrata*, family Nyssaceae.

Dow /dou/ short for **Dow Jones Industrial Average**: *the Dow fell sharply that summer.*

dow·a·ger /ˈdouəjər/ ▸*n.* a widow with a title or property derived from her late husband: [as *adj.*] *the dowager duchess* | [*postpositive*] *the queen dowager.* ■ *informal* a dignified elderly woman. ▷mid 16th cent.: from Old French *douagiere*, from *douage* 'dower,' from *douer* 'endow,' from Latin *dotare* 'endow' (see **dower**).

dow·a·ger's hump ▸*n.* forward curvature of the spine resulting in a stoop, typically in women with osteoporosis, caused by collapse of the front edges of the thoracic vertebrae.

dow·dy /ˈdoudē/ ▸*adj.* (**dow·di·er**, **dow·di·est**) (of a person, typically a woman, or their clothes) unfashionable and without style in appearance: *she could achieve the kind of casual chic that made every other woman around her look dowdy.*
▸*n.* (*pl.* **-dies**) a woman who is unfashionably and unattractively dressed. ▷late 16th cent.: from *dowd* 'person of unfashionable appearance' (of unknown origin) + **-y**[1] **—dow·di·ly** /ˈdoudəlē/ *adv.* **—dow·di·ness** *n.*

dow·el /ˈdouəl/ ▸*n.* a peg of wood, metal, or plastic without a distinct head, used for holding together components of a structure.
▸*v.* (**dow·eled**, **dow·el·ing**; *Brit.* **dow·elled**, **dow·el·ling**) [*trans.*] fasten with a dowel or dowels. ▷Middle English: perhaps from Middle Low German *dovel.*

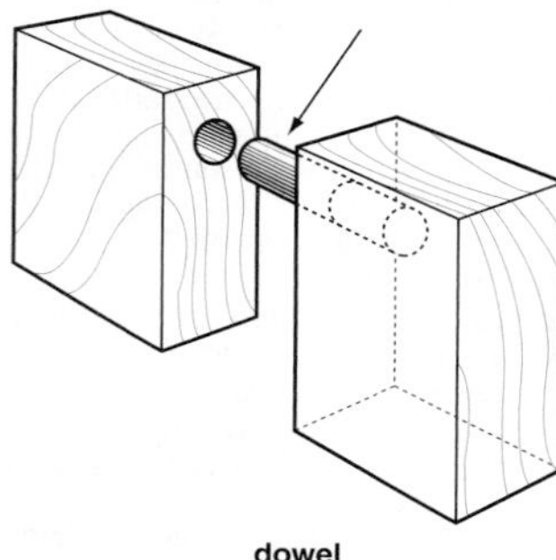

dowel

dow·el·ing /ˈdouəliNG/ (*Brit.* **dow·el·ling**) ▸*n.* cylindrical rods for cutting into dowels.

dow·er /ˈdou(-ə)r/ ▸*n.* a widow's share for life of her husband's estate. ■ *archaic* a dowry.
▸*v.* [*trans.*] *archaic* give a dowry to. ▷late Middle English: from Old French *douaire*, from medieval Latin *dotarium*, from Latin *dotare* 'endow,' from *dos, dot-* 'dowry'; related to *dare* 'give.'

dow·itch·er /ˈdouiCHər/ ▸*n.* a wading bird of the sandpiper family, with a long straight bill, breeding in arctic and subarctic North America and eastern Asia. • Genus *Limnodromus*, family Scolopacidae: three species, in particular the **short-billed dowitcher** (*L. griseus*) and the **long-billed dowitcher** (*L. scolopaceus*). ▷mid 19th cent.: from Iroquoian.

Dow Jones In·dus·tri·al Av·er·age /ˈdou ˈjōnz/ (also **Dow Jones Average**) an index of figures indicating the relative price of shares on the New York Stock Exchange, based on the average price of selected stocks. ▷from the name of *Dow Jones & Co, Inc.*, a financial news agency founded by Charles H. Dow (1851–1902) and Edward D. Jones (*c.*1855–1920), American economists whose company compiled the first average of U.S. stock prices in 1884.

Down /doun/ one of the six counties of Northern Ireland, formerly an administrative area; chief town, Downpatrick.

down[1] /doun/ ▸*adv.* **1** toward or in a lower place or position, esp. to or on the ground or another surface: *she looked down* | *the sun started to go down* | *he put his glass down* | *she flicked the switch up and down* | *he swung the ax to chop down the tree.* ■ at or to a specified distance below: *you can plainly see the bottom 35 feet down.* ■ downstairs: *I went down to put the kettle on.* ■ expressing movement or position away from the north: *they're living down south.* ■ to or at a place perceived as lower (often expressing casualness or lack of hurry): *I'd rather be down at the villa* | *I'm going down to the arcade.* ■ *Brit.* away from the capital or major city: *there are eight trains a day, four up and four down.* ■ *Brit.* away from a university, esp. Oxford or Cambridge. ■ (with reference to food or drink swallowed) in or into the stomach: *she couldn't keep anything down.* ■ so as to lie or be fixed flush or flat: *she stuck down a Christmas label.* ■ [as *exclam.*] used as a command to a person or animal to sit or lie down: *down, boy!* ■ a crossword answer that reads vertically: *how many letters in fifteen down?* **2** to or at a lower level of intensity, volume, or activity: *keep the noise down* | *the panic was dying down* | *at night it would cool down.* ■ to or at a lower price, value, or rank: *output was down by 20 percent* | *soup is down from 59 cents to 49 cents.* ■ to a finer consistency, a smaller amount or size, or a simpler or more basic state: *I must slim down a bit* | *a formal statement that can't be edited down* | *thin down an oil-based paint with spirits.* ■ from an earlier to a later point in time or order: *everyone, from the president* **down to** *the guy selling hot dogs, is outraged.* **3** in or into a weaker or worse position, mood, or condition: *the scandal brought down the government* | *he was* **down with** *the flu.* ■ losing or at a disadvantage by a specified amount: *the Braves, down 7–6, rallied for two runs in the sixth inning.* ■ used to express progress through a series of tasks or items: *one down and only six more to go.* ■ (of a computer system) out of action or unavailable for use (esp. temporarily): *the system went down yesterday.* ■ (**down with** ——) shouted to express strong dislike of a specified person or thing: *crowds chanted "Down with bureaucracy!"* **4** in or into writing: *I just* **write down** *whatever comes into my head* | *taking down notes.* ■ on or on to a list, schedule, or record: *I'll put you* **down for** *the evening shift.* **5** (with reference to partial payment of a sum of money) made initially or on the spot: *pay $500 down and the rest at the end of the month.* **6** (of sailing) with the current or the wind. ■ (of a ship's helm) moved around to leeward so that the rudder is to windward and the vessel swings toward the wind. **7** *Football* (of the ball or a player in possession) not in play, typically because forward progress has been stopped.
▸*prep.* **1** from a higher to a lower point of (something): *up and down the stairs* | *tears streaming down her face.* ■ at or to a lower part of (a river or stream); nearer the sea: *a dozen miles or so down the Mississippi.* ■ at a point further along the course of (something): *he lived down the street.* ■ along the course or extent of: *I wandered down the road* | *an incision down the middle.* ■ *informal* at or to (a place): *tired of going down the pub every night.* **2** throughout (a period of time): *astrologers down the ages.*
▸*adj.* **1** [*attrib.*] directed or moving toward a lower place or position: *the down escalator* | *click on the down arrow.* ■ *Physics* denoting a flavor of quark having a charge of $-1/3$. Protons and neutrons are thought to be composed of combinations of up and down quarks. **2** [*predic.*] (of a person) unhappy; depressed: *he's been so down lately.* ■ [*attrib.*] *informal* (of a period of time) causing or characterized by unhappiness or depression: *of course, there were up days and down days.* **3** [*predic.*] (of a computer system) temporarily out of action or unavailable: *sorry, but the computer's down.* **4** [*predic.*] *chiefly slang* supporting or going along with someone or something: *"You going to the movies?" "Yo, I'm down."* ■ aware of and following the latest fashion: *a seriously down, hip-hop homie.*
▸*v.* [*trans.*] *informal* **1** knock or bring to the ground: *175 enemy aircraft had been downed* | *he struck Slater on the face, downing him.* **2** consume (something, typically a drink): *he downed five pints of cider.* ■ (of a golfer) sink (a putt).
▸*n.* **1** *Football* a chance for a team to advance the ball, ending when the ball carrier is tackled or the ball becomes out of play. A team must advance at least ten yards in a series of four downs in order to keep possession. **2** (**downs**) *informal* unwelcome experiences or events: *there had been more downs than ups during his years at the company.* **3** *informal* a feeling or period of unhappiness or depression: *everyone gets their downs, their depressive periods.* ■ *informal* short for **downer** (sense 1). ▷Old English *dūn, dūne*, shortened from *adūne* 'downward,' from the phrase *of dūne* 'off the hill' (see **down**[3]).
▸**PHRASES** □ **be down on** *informal* disapprove of; feel hostile or antagonistic toward. □ **be down to 1** be attributable to (a particular factor or circumstance): *he claimed his problems were down to the media.* ■ be the responsibility of (a particular person): *it's down to you to make sure the boiler receives regular servicing.* **2** be left with only (the specified amount): *I'm down to my last few dollars.* □ **down in the mouth** *informal* (of a person or their expression) unhappy; dejected. □ **down on one's luck** *informal* experiencing a period of bad luck. □ **down pat** (or **cold**) memorized or mastered perfectly: *she had the baby's medical routine down pat* | *a guy who has his art history down cold.* □ **have** (or **put**) **someone/something down as** judge someone or something to be (a particular type): *I never had Jake down as a ladies' man.* □ **down to the ground** *informal* completely:

down[2] ▸*n.* soft fine fluffy feathers that form the first covering of a young bird or an insulating layer below the contour feathers of an adult bird. ■ such feathers taken from ducks or their nests and used for stuffing cushions, quilts, etc.; eiderdown. ■ fine soft hair on the face or body of a person: *the little girl had a covering of golden down on her head.* ■ short soft hairs on some leaves, fruit, or seeds. ▷Middle English: from Old Norse *dúnn.*

down[3] ▸*n.* (usu. **downs**) a gently rolling hill: *the gentle green contours of the downs.* ■ (**the Downs**) ridges of undulating chalk and limestone hills in southern England, with few trees and used mainly for pasture. ▷Old English *dūn* 'hill' (related to Dutch *duin* 'dune'), perhaps ultimately of Celtic origin and related to Old Irish *dún* and obsolete Welsh *din* 'fort,' which are from an Indo-European root shared by **town**.

down-and-dirt·y ▸*adj. informal* **1** highly competitive or unprincipled: *backstabbing slander and electronic harassment are freely employed in down-and-dirty hacker feuds.* **2** earthy, direct, and explicit: *the down-and-dirty realities about these diseases.* ■ unvarnished; in a raw or prototypical form: *they serve up some down-and-dirty Texas blues.*

down-and-out ▸*adj.* (of a person) without money, a job, or a place to live; destitute: *a down-and-out homeless vagrant.*
▸*n.* (also **down-and-out·er**) a person without money, a job, or a place to live.

down-at-the-heels (also **down-at-the-heel** or **down-at-heel**) ▸*adj.* (of a person, thing, or place) showing signs of neglect and deterioration; shabby: *a down-at-the-heels house.*

down·beat /ˈdoun,bēt/ ▸*adj.* pessimistic; gloomy: *the assessment of current economic prospects is downbeat.*
▸*n. Music* an accented beat, usually the first of the bar.

down-bow /,bō/ ▸*n. Music* (on a stringed instrument) a stroke in which the bow, from handle to tip, is slid across the strings in a motion of the hand moving away from the strings.

down·burst /ˈdoun,bərst/ ▸*n.* a strong downward current of air from a cumulonimbus cloud, usually associated with intense rain or a thunderstorm.

down·cast /ˈdoun,kast/ ▸*adj.* **1** (of a person's eyes) looking downward: *her modestly downcast eyes.* **2** (of a person) feeling despondent.
▸*n.* a shaft dug in a mine for extra ventilation.

down·code /ˈdoun,kōd/ ▸*v.* [*trans* .] **1** designate (a medical procedure or insurance claim) with a lower value: *an insurer who systematically downcodes professional charge submissions for critical care services* | [*intrans.*] *we cannot turn to Medicaid to pay if Medicare downcodes.* **2** *Computing* rewrite or convert (programs or software) into a lower level language: *some of the libraries written into C were downcoded into assembly.* **—down·cod·ing** *n.*

down·com·er /ˈdoun,kəmər/ ▸*n.* a pipe for the downward transport of water or gas from the top of a furnace or boiler.

down·con·vert·er /ˈdounkən,vərtər/ ▸*n. Electronics* a device that converts a signal to a lower frequency, esp. in television reception. **—down·con·ver·sion** /-,vərZHən/ *n.*

down·coun·try /ˈdounˈkəntrē/ ▸*adj.* & *adv.* in, into, or relating to the low-lying and generally more densely settled part of a country as opposed to hilly regions: [as *adj.*] *even the downcountry conservatives support this reform.* | [as *adv.*] *distant summer storms a hundred miles downcountry.*

down·court /ˈdounˈkôrt/ ▸*adv.* & *adj. Sports* to or into the opposite end of the court, esp. in basketball.

down-curved ▸*adj.* [*attrib.*] curved downward: *the slightly down-curved bill of a starling.*

down·cut /ˈdoun,kət/ ▸*v.* (**-cut·ting** *past* and *past part.* **-cut**) [*intrans.*] *Geology* (of a river) erode downward through its bed.

down·draft /ˈdoun,draft/ (*Brit.* **down·draught**) ▸*n.* a downward current or draft of air, esp. one down a chimney into a room.

Down East a name for northeastern New England and for the Maritime Provinces that is derived from an old term for sailing downwind, to the east.

down·er /ˈdounər/ ▸*n. informal* **1** (usu. **downers**) a depressant or tranquilizing drug, esp. a barbiturate. **2** a dispiriting or depressing experience or factor: *the thought of the danger his son was in put something of a downer on the situation.* ■ a period of consistent failure: *the Red Sox enter the season* ***on a downer.*** **3** a cow or other animal that is sick or injured and cannot get to its feet unaided.

Dow·ners Grove /ˈdounərz/ a village in northeastern Illinois, west of Chicago; pop. 46,858.

Dow·ney /ˈdounē/ a city in southwestern California, southeast of Los Angeles; pop. 91,444.

down·fall /ˈdoun,fôl/ ▸*n.* a loss of power, prosperity, or status: *the crisis led to the downfall of the government.* ■ the cause of such a loss: *his intractability will prove to be his downfall.*

down·field /ˈdounˈfēld/ ▸*adv. adj. Football* in or to a position nearer to the opponents' end of a field.

down·force /ˈdoun,fôrs/ ▸*n.* a force acting on a moving vehicle having the effect of pressing it down toward the ground, giving it increased stability. Downforce is produced by a combination of air resistance and gravity.

down·grade /ˈdoun,grād/ ▸*v.* [*trans.*] (usu. **be downgraded**) reduce to a lower grade, rank, or level of importance: *some jobs had gradually been downgraded from skilled to semiskilled.*

▸*n.* **1** an instance of reducing someone or something's rank, status, or level of importance. **2** a downward gradient, typically on a railroad track or road.

▸*PHRASE* □ **on the downgrade** in decline: *profits are on the downgrade.*

down·haul /ˈdoun,hôl/ ▸*n. Nautical* a rope used for hauling down a sail, spar, etc., esp. in order to control a sail's shape.

down·heart·ed /ˈdounˈhärtid/ ▸*adj.* discouraged; in low spirits: *fans must not be downhearted even though we lost.* —**down·heart·ed·ly** *adv.* —**down·heart·ed·ness** *n.*

down·hill /ˈdounˈhil/ ▸*adv.* toward the bottom of a slope: *he ran downhill | follow the road downhill.* ■ *figurative* into a steadily worsening situation: *his marriage continued to slide downhill.* ■ [*predic.*] *figurative* used to describe easy or quick progress toward an objective after initial difficulties have been overcome: *up by six runs in the eighth inning—it should have been* ***downhill all the way.***

▸*adj.* leading down toward the bottom of a slope: *the route is downhill for part of the way.* ■ *figurative* leading to a steadily worsening situation: *the downhill road to delinquency.* ■ *figurative* without difficulty or challenge: *we can take the easy road, the downhill road, or we can put America on the path to greatness again.* ■ of or relating to the sport of skiing or cycling downhill: *the world downhill champion.*

▸*n.* **1** a downward slope. **2** *Skiing* a downhill race. ■ the activity of downhill skiing.

▸*PHRASE* □ **go downhill** become worse; deteriorate: *the business is going downhill fast.*

down·hill·er /ˈdounˈhilər/ ▸*n.* a skier or cyclist who takes part in downhill races.

down·hole (also **down-hole**) ▸*adj.* & *adv.* (in the oil industry) used, occurring, or performed in a well or borehole.

down-home ▸*adj.* connected with an unpretentious way of life, esp. that of rural peoples or areas: *some good down-home cooking.*

Down·ing Street /ˈdouniNG/ a street in Westminster, London, between Whitehall and St. James's Park. No. 10 is the official residence of the Prime Minister; No. 11 is the official home of the Chancellor of the Exchequer. ■ used allusively for the British government or the Prime Minister. ▹named after the original developer of the site, Sir George *Downing* (*c.*1624–84), a diplomat under both Oliver Cromwell and Charles II.

down·lev·el /ˈdoun,levəl/ ▸*adj.* using an earlier version of software, hardware, or an operating system: *there are still 600 million computers, many of them downlevel, that wouldn't have all of these vulnerabilities fixed.*

down·light /ˈdoun,līt/ (also **down·light·er**) ▸*n.* a light placed or designed so as to throw illumination downward. —**down·light·ing** *n.*

down·link /ˈdoun,liNGk/ ▸*n.* a telecommunications link for signals coming to the earth from a satellite, spacecraft, or aircraft.

▸*v.* [*trans.*] relay to the earth (a telecommunications signal or the information it conveys): *any TV station can downlink just about any game.*

down·load /ˈdoun,lōd/ *Computing* ▸*v.* [*trans.*] copy (data) from one computer system to another or to a disk. Compare with **UPLOAD.**

▸*n.* the act or process of copying data in such a way: [as *adj.*] *a download and upload routine.* ■ a computer file transferred in such a way: *a popular download from bulletin boards.* —**down·load·a·ble** *adj.*

down·mar·ket /ˈdoun,märkit/ (also **down-mar·ket**) ▸*adj.* & *adv.* toward or relating to the cheaper or less prestigious sector of the market: [as *adj.*] *an interview for the downmarket tabloids* | [as *adv.*] *competition threatens to drive broadcasters further downmarket.*

down pay·ment ▸*n.* an initial payment made when something is bought on credit.

down·play /ˈdoun,plā/ ▸*v.* [*trans.*] make (something) appear less important than it really is: *this report downplays the seriousness of global warming.*

down·pour /ˈdoun,pôr/ ▸*n.* a heavy rainfall: *a sudden downpour had filled the gutters and drains.*

down·range /ˈdoun,rānj/ ▸*adv.* & *adj.* (of a missile, space launch, etc.) traveling in a specified direction away from the launch site and toward the target: *rounds streaked downrange at more than a mile a second.*

down·rate /ˈdoun,rāt/ ▸*v.* [*trans.*] make (someone or something) lower in value, standard, or importance.

down·right /ˈdoun,rīt/ ▸*adj.* **1** [*attrib.*] (of something bad or unpleasant) utter; complete (used for emphasis): *it's a downright disgrace.* **2** (of a person's manner or behavior) straightforward; so direct as to be blunt: *her common sense and downright attitude to life surprised him.*

▸*adv.* [as *submodifier*] to an extreme degree; thoroughly: *he was downright rude.* —**down·right·ness** *n.*

down·riv·er /ˈdounˈrivər/ ▸*adv.* & *adj.* toward or situated at a point nearer the mouth of a river: [as *adv.*] *the cabin cruiser started to drift downriver* | [as *adj.*] *the downriver side of the bridge.*

down·scale /ˈdoun,skāl/ ▸*v.* [*trans.*] reduce in size, scale, or extent: *he was unable to downscale his strongly unionized workforce.*

▸*adj.* at the lower end of a scale, esp. a social scale; downmarket: *these brands appeal to downscale shoppers who are looking for a low price.*

down·shift /ˈdoun,SHift/ ▸*v.* [*intrans.*] change to a lower gear in a motor vehicle or bicycle. ■ slow down; slacken off: *well before the country slipped into recession, business was downshifting.* ■ change a financially rewarding but stressful career or lifestyle for a less pressured and less highly paid but more fulfilling one: *they want to downshift from full-time work.*

▸*n.* a change to a lower gear in a motor vehicle or bicycle. ■ a change in quality or quantity to a lesser or lower degree: *the downshift of human position from the center of the cosmos.* ■ an instance of changing a financially rewarding but stressful career or lifestyle for a less pressured and less highly paid but more fulfilling one.

down·side /ˈdoun,sīd/ ▸*n.* **1** the negative aspect of something, esp. something regarded as in general good or desirable: *a magazine feature on the downside of fashion modeling.* **2** [often as *adj.*] a downward movement of share prices: *each fund aims to reduce the downside risk by using futures and options.*

down·size /ˈdoun,sīz/ ▸*v.* [*trans.*] make (something) smaller: *I downsized the rear wheel to 26 inches.* ■ make (a company or organization) smaller by eliminating staff positions. ■ [*intrans.*] (of a company) eliminate staff positions: *recession forced many companies to downsize.*

down·slope /ˈdoun,slōp/ ▸*n.* a downward slope.

▸*adv.* & *adj.* at or toward a lower point on a slope.

down·spout /ˈdoun,spout/ ▸*n.* a pipe to carry rainwater from a roof to a drain or to ground level.

down·stage /ˈdounˈstāj/ ▸*adj.* & *adv.* at or toward the front of a stage: [as *adv.*] *all four run for their lives downstage* | [as *adj.*] *a crowd of dancers occupies the downstage area.*

down·stairs /ˈdounˈste(ə)rz/ ▸*adv.* down a flight of stairs: *I tripped over the cat and fell downstairs.* ■ on or to a lower floor: *we were waiting for you downstairs | she called him downstairs.*

▸*adj.* [*attrib.*] situated downstairs: *the downstairs bathroom.*

▸*n.* the ground floor or lower floors of a building: *the downstairs was hardly damaged at all.*

down·state /ˈdounˈstāt/ ▸*adj.* & *adv.* of, in, or to the southern part of a state.

▸*n.* such an area. —**down·stat·er** *n.*

down·stream /ˈdounˈstrēm/ ▸*adv.* & *adj.* situated or moving in the direction in which a stream or river flows: [as *adv.*] *the bridge spanned the river just* ***downstream of*** *the rail line* | [as *adj.*] *deforestation could have disastrous consequences for downstream regions.* ■ *Biology* situated in or toward the part of a sequence of genetic material where transcription takes place later than at a given point: *a termination signal was found downstream from the coding region.* ■ at a stage in the process of gas or oil extraction and production after the raw material is ready for refining.

down·stroke /ˈdoun,strōk/ ▸*n.* a stroke made downward: *he writes the figure seven with a line through the downstroke | the blade angles back on the downstroke.*

down·swing /ˈdoun,swiNG/ ▸*n.* **1** another term for **DOWNTURN.** **2** *Golf* the downward movement of a club when the player is about to hit the ball.

Down syn·drome /ˈdoun ˈsindrōm/ (also **Down's syn·drome**) ▸*n. Medicine* a congenital disorder arising from a chromosome defect, causing intellectual impairment and physical abnormalities including short stature and a broad facial profile. It arises from a defect involving chromosome 21, usually an extra copy (trisomy-21). ▹1960s: named after John L. H. *Down* (1828–96), the English physician who first described it.

USAGE Of relatively recent coinage, **Down syndrome** is the accepted term in modern use, and former terms such as **mongol**, **Mongoloid**, and **mongolism**, which are likely to cause offense, should be avoided. See also **usage** at **MONGOLOID.**

down·tem·po /ˈdoun,tempō/ ▸*adj.* (of music) having a relatively slower beat.

▸*n.* a genre of electronic dance music with influences from jazz, bossa nova, and dub reggae.

down-the-line ▸*adj. informal* thorough and uncompromising: *the party avoids down-the-line support of unions.*

down·throw /ˈdoun,THrō/ *Geology* ▸*v.* (*past* **-threw**; *past part.* **-thrown**) [*trans.*] displace (a rock formation) downward.

▸*n.* a downward displacement of rock strata.

down tim·ber ▸*n.* fallen trees brought down by wind, storm, or other natural agency.

down·time /ˈdoun,tīm/ (also **down time**) ▸*n.* time during which a machine, esp. a computer, is out of action or unavailable for use. ■ *figurative* a time of reduced activity or inactivity: *everyone needs downtime to unwind | downtimes for real estate and construction.*

down-to-earth ▸*adj.* with no illusions or pretensions; practical and realistic: *a down-to-earth view of marriage.* —**down-to-earth·ness** *n.*

down·town /ˈdounˈtoun/ ▸*adj.* of, in, or characteristic of the central area or main business and commercial area of a town or city: *downtown Chicago | a downtown bar.*

▸*adv.* in or into such an area: *I drove downtown.*

▸*n.* such an area of a town or city: *the heart of Pittsburgh's downtown.* —**down·town·er** *n.*

down·trend /ˈdoun,trend/ ▸*n.* a downward trend, tendency, or movement: *there is not yet a confirmed downtrend in interest rates.*

down·trod·den /ˈdoun,trädn/ ▸*adj.* oppressed or treated badly by people in power: *a downtrodden proletarian struggling for social justice.*

down·turn /ˈdoun,tərn/ ▸*n.* a decline in economic, business, or other activity: *a downturn in the housing market.*

▸*v.* [*trans.*] [usu. as *adj.*] (**downturned**) turn (something) downward: *his downturned mouth.*

Down Un·der (also **down un·der**) *informal* ▸*adv.* in or to Australia or New Zealand: *selling wines under the name of the grape variety, just as they do Down Under.*

▸*n.* Australia and New Zealand: *thousands of men from Down Under.* ▹late 19th cent.: with reference to the position of these countries on a globe.

down·ward /ˈdounwərd/ ▸*adv.* (also **down·wards**) toward a lower place, point, or level: *he was lying face downward.* ■ used to indicate that something applies to everyone in a certain hierarchy or set: *new rules on sick leave affect employees of all grades, from managers downward.*

▸*adj.* moving or leading toward a lower place or level: *the downward curve of the stairs | a downward trend in inflation.* ▹Middle English: shortening of Old English *adūnweard.* —**down·ward·ly** *adv.*

down·ward·ly mo·bile ▸*adj.* moving to a lower social class; losing wealth and status. —**down·ward mo·bil·i·ty** *n.*

Pronunciation Key ə *ago*; ər *over*; ˈə or ˌə *up*; ˈər or ˌər *fur*; a *hat*; ā *rate*; ä *car*; CH *chew*; e *let*; ē *see*; e(ə)r *air*; i *fit*; ī *by*; i(ə)r *ear*; NG *sing*; ō *go*; ô *for*; oi *boy*; o͝o *good*; o͞o *goo*; ou *out*; SH *she*; TH *thin*; T͟H *then*; (h)w *why*; ZH *vision*

D

down·warp /ˈdounˌwôrp/ *Geology* ▶*n.* a broad depression of the earth's surface.
▶*v.* [*trans.*] displace (a rock formation) downward so as to form such a depression.

down·wash /ˈdounˌwäsh; -ˌwôsh/ ▶*n.* the downward deflection of an airstream by an aircraft wing or helicopter rotor blade.

down·well·ing /ˈdounˌweliNG/ ▶*n.* the downward movement of fluid, esp. in the sea, the atmosphere, or deep in the earth.
▶*adj.* characterized by or undergoing such movement: *downwelling mantle.*

down·wind /ˈdounˈwind/ ▶*adv. & adj.* in the direction in which the wind is blowing: [as *adv.*] *warnings were issued to people living downwind of the fire* | [as *adj.*] *downwind landings.*

down·wind·er /ˈdounˈwindər/ ▶*n.* a person living downwind of a nuclear test site or reactor, where the risk from fallout or radiation leaks is greatest.

down·y /ˈdounē/ ▶*adj.* (**down·i·er, down·i·est**) covered with fine soft hair or feathers: *the baby's downy cheek.* ■ filled with soft feathers: *a downy pillow.* ■ soft and fluffy: *pale downy hair.* —**down·i·ly** /-nəlē/ *adv.* —**down·i·ness** *n.*

D

down·y mil·dew ▶*n.* mildew on a plant that is marked by a whitish down composed of spore-forming hyphae, penetrating more deeply into the plant than powdery mildew. • Family Peronosporaceae, subdivision Mastigomycotina.

down·y wood·peck·er ▶*n.* a widespread small North American woodpecker with a short bill, black and white plumage, and (on the male) a red patch on the back of the head. • *Picoides pubescens*, family Picidae.

downy woodpecker

down·zone /ˈdounˌzōn/ ▶*v.* [*trans.*] assign (land or property) to a zoning grade under which the permitted density of housing and development is reduced.

dow·ry /ˈdou(ə)rē/ ▶*n.* (*pl.* **-ries**) property or money brought by a bride to her husband on their marriage. ▷Middle English (denoting a widow's life interest in her husband's estate): from Anglo-Norman French *dowarie*, from medieval Latin *dotarium* (see **DOWER**).

dow·ry death ▶*n.* (in the Indian subcontinent) the murder or suicide of a married woman caused by a dispute over her dowry.

dowse[1] /douz/ ▶*v.* [*intrans.*] practice dowsing: *water is easy to dowse for.* ■ [*trans.*] search for or discover by dowsing: *he dowsed a spiral of energy on the stone.* ▷late 17th cent.: of unknown origin. —**dows·er** *n.*

dowse[2] ▶*v.* variant spelling of **DOUSE**.

dows·ing /ˈdouziNG/ ▶*n.* a technique for searching for underground water, minerals, or anything invisible, by observing the motion of a pointer (traditionally a forked stick, now often paired bent wires) or the changes in direction of a pendulum, supposedly in response to unseen influences: [as *adj.*] *a dowsing rod.*

dox·ol·o·gy /däkˈsäləjē/ ▶*n.* (*pl.* **-gies**) a liturgical formula of praise to God. ▷mid 17th cent.: via medieval Latin from Greek *doxologia*, from *doxa* 'appearance, glory' (from *dokein* 'seem') + *-logia* (see **-LOGY**). —**dox·o·log·i·cal** /ˌdäksəˈläjikəl/ *adj.*

dox·o·ru·bi·cin /ˌdäksəˈroōbəsin/ ▶*n. Medicine* a bacterial antibiotic that is widely used to treat leukemia and various other forms of cancer. • This is produced by the streptomycete bacterium *Streptomyces peucetius caesius.* ▷1970s: from *deoxy-* (in the sense 'that has lost oxygen') + Latin *rubus* 'red' + **-MYCIN**.

dox·y /ˈdäksē/ ▶*n.* (*pl.* **dox·ies**) *archaic* a lover or mistress. ■ a prostitute. ▷mid 16th cent. (originally slang): of unknown origin.

dox·y·cy·cline /ˌdäksēˈsīklēn/ ▶*n. Medicine* a broad-spectrum antibiotic of the tetracycline group, which has a long half-life in the body. ▷1960s: from *d(e)oxy-* + **TETRACYCLINE**.

doy·en /doiˈen; ˈdoi-en/ ▶*n.* the most respected or prominent person in a particular field: *the doyen of Canadian poetry.* ▷late 17th cent.: via French from Old French *deien* (see **DEAN**[1]).

doy·enne /doiˈen/ ▶*n.* a woman who is the most respected or prominent person in a particular field: *she's the doyenne of daytime TV.* ▷mid 19th cent.: from French, feminine of *doyen* (see **DOYEN**).

Doy·enne du Co·mice /doiˈen ˌdyoō kəˈmēs/ ▶*n.* see **COMICE**.

Doyle /doil/, Sir Arthur Conan (1859–1930), Scottish novelist and short-story writer. He is known for his creation of private detective Sherlock Holmes, who first appeared (with his friend Dr. Watson, the narrator of the stories) in *A Study in Scarlet* (1887). Other notable works: *The Adventures of Sherlock Holmes* (1892) and *The Hound of the Baskervilles* (1902).

doy·ley ▶*n. dated* variant spelling of **DOILY**.

D'Oy·ly Carte /ˈdoilē ˈkärt/, Richard (1844–1901), English impresario and producer. He brought together the librettist Sir W. S. Gilbert and the composer Sir Arthur Sullivan, producing many of their operettas in London's Savoy Theatre, which he had established in 1881.

doz. ▶*abbr.* dozen.

doze /dōz/ ▶*v.* [*intrans.*] sleep lightly: *he found his mother dozing by the fire.* ■ (**doze off**) fall lightly asleep: *I dozed off for a few seconds.*
▶*n.* [in *sing.*] a short light sleep. ▷mid 17th cent. (in the sense 'stupefy, bewilder, or make drowsy'): perhaps related to Danish *døse* 'make drowsy.'

doz·en /ˈdəzən/ (abbr.: **dz.**) ▶*n.* **1** (*pl.* same) a group or set of twelve: *a dozen bottles of sherry.* ■ (**dozens**) *informal* a lot: *she has dozens of admirers.* **2** (**the dozens**) an exchange of insults engaged in as a game or ritual among black Americans. ▷Middle English: from Old French *dozeine*, based on Latin *duodecim* 'twelve.' —**doz·enth** /ˈdəzənTH/ *adj.*
▶*PHRASES* □ **by the dozen** in large quantities. □ **talk nineteen to the dozen** *Brit.* talk incessantly.

doz·er /ˈdōzər/ ▶*n. informal* short for **BULLDOZER**.

do·zy /ˈdōzē/ ▶*adj.* (**do·zi·er, do·zi·est**) drowsy and lazy: *he grew dozy at the end of a long day.* —**do·zi·ly** /-zəlē/ *adv.* —**do·zi·ness** *n.*

DP ▶*abbr.* ■ data processing. ■ dew point. ■ displaced person. ■ *Baseball* double play.

DPhil ▶*abbr.* Doctor of Philosophy.

dpi ▶*abbr. Computing* dots per inch, a measure of the resolution of printers, scanners, etc.

DPT (also **DTP**) ▶*abbr.* diphtheria, pertussis (whooping cough), and tetanus, a combined vaccine given to small children.

Dr. ▶*abbr.* ■ (as a title) Doctor: *Dr. Michael Russell.* ■ (in street names) Drive.

dr. ▶*abbr.* ■ debit. [formerly representing *debtor.*] ■ drachma(s). ■ dram(s).

drab[1] /drab/ ▶*adj.* (**drab·ber, drab·best**) **1** lacking brightness or interest; drearily dull: *the landscape was drab and gray* | *her drab suburban existence.* **2** of a dull light brown color: *drab camouflage uniforms.*
▶*n.* fabric of a dull brownish color. ▷mid 16th cent. (as a noun denoting undyed cloth): probably from Old French *drap* 'cloth' (see **DRAPE**). —**drab·ly** *adv.* —**drab·ness** *n.*

drab[2] ▶*n. archaic* **1** a slovenly woman. **2** a prostitute. ▷early 16th cent.: perhaps related to Low German *drabbe* 'mire' and Dutch *drab* 'dregs.'

Drab·ble /ˈdrabəl/, Margaret (1939–), English novelist. Notable works: *The Millstone* (1966), *The Radiant Way* (1987), *The Peppered Moth* (2001), and *The Red Queen* (2004). She is the younger sister of A. S. Byatt.

dra·cae·na /drəˈsēnə/ ▶*n.* a tropical palmlike shrub or tree with ornamental foliage, popular as a greenhouse or indoor plant. • Genera *Dracaena* and *Cordyline*, family Agavaceae. See also **DRAGON TREE**. ▷modern Latin, from Greek *drakaina*, feminine of *drakōn* 'serpent, dragon' (the genus *Dracaena* includes *Dracaena draco*, the dragon tree).

drachm /dram/ (abbr.: **dr.**) ▶*n.* **1** a unit of weight formerly used by apothecaries, equivalent to 60 grains or one eighth of an ounce. ■ (also **fluid drachm**) a liquid measure formerly used by apothecaries, equivalent to 60 minims or one eighth of a fluid ounce. **2** (in numismatics) an ancient silver coin based on the Attic or Hellenistic drachma. See also **DRACHMA**. ▷late Middle English (denoting the ancient Greek drachma): from Old French *dragme* or late Latin *dragma*, via Latin from Greek *drakhmē* (see **DRACHMA**).

drach·ma /ˈdräkmə/ ▶*n.* (*pl.* **-mas** or **-mae** /-mē/) the basic monetary unit of Greece (until the introduction of the euro), notionally equal to 100 lepta. ■ a silver coin of ancient Greece. ▷via Latin from Greek *drakhmē*, an Attic weight and coin. Compare with **DIRHAM** and **DRACHM**.

Dra·co[1] /ˈdrākō/ *Astronomy* a large northern constellation (the Dragon), stretching around the north celestial pole and said to represent the dragon killed by Hercules. It has no bright stars. ■ [as *genitive*] (**Draconis** /drāˈkōnis/) used with a preceding letter or numeral to designate a star in this constellation: *the star Gamma Draconis.* ▷Latin.

Dra·co[2] (7th century BC), Athenian legislator. His codification of Athenian law was notorious for its severity; for instance, the death penalty was imposed even for trivial crimes, which gave rise to the adjective *draconian* in English.

dra·co·ni·an /drəˈkōnēən; drā-/ ▶*adj.* (of laws or their application) excessively harsh and severe. ▷late 19th cent.: from the Greek name *Drakōn* (see **DRACO**[2]) + **-IAN**. —**dra·con·ic** /-ˈkänik/ *adj.*

Drac·u·la /ˈdrakyələ/ the Transylvanian vampire in Bram Stoker's novel *Dracula* (1897). ▷variant of *Drakula, Dragwlya*, names given to Vlad Țepeș (Vlad the Impaler), a 15th-cent. prince of Wallachia renowned for his cruelty.

draff /draf/ ▶*n. poetic/literary* dregs or refuse. ▷Middle English: perhaps from an unrecorded Old English word related to German *Treber, Träber* 'husks, grains,' and perhaps also to **DRIVEL**.

draft /draft/ ▶*n.* **1** a preliminary version of a piece of writing: *the first draft of the party's manifesto* | [as *adj.*] *a draft document.* ■ a plan, sketch, or rough drawing. ■ (in full **draft mode**) *Computing* a mode of operation of a printer in which text is produced rapidly but with relatively low definition. **2** (**the draft**) compulsory recruitment for military service: *25 million men were subject to the draft* | [as *adj.*] *draft cards.* ■ a procedure whereby new or existing sports players are made available for selection or reselection by the teams in a league, usually with the earlier choices being given to the weaker teams. ■ *rare* a group or individual selected from a larger group for a special duty, e.g., for military service. **3** (*Brit.* **draught**) a current of cool air in a room or other confined space: *heavy curtains at the windows cut out drafts.* **4** (*Brit.* **draught**) the action or act of pulling something along, esp. a vehicle or farm implement. **5** a written order to pay a specified sum; a check. **6** (*Brit.* **draught**) a single act of drinking or inhaling: *she downed the remaining beer in one draft.* ■ the amount swallowed or inhaled in one such act: *he took deep drafts of oxygen into his lungs.* **7** (*Brit.* **draught**) the depth of water needed to float a ship: *the shallow draft enabled her to get close to shore.* **8** (*Brit.* **draught**) the drawing in of a fishing net. ■ the fish taken at one drawing; a catch.
▶*v.* (*Brit.* **draught**) [*trans.*] **1** prepare a preliminary version of (a text): *I drafted a letter of resignation.* **2** select (a person or group of people) for a certain purpose: *he was drafted to make a film about the Iraqi president's life.* ■ conscript (someone) for military service. ■ select (a player) for a sports team through the draft. **3** pull or draw. **4** [*intrans.*] *Auto Racing* benefit from reduced wind resistance by driving very closely behind another vehicle.
▶*adj.* (*Brit.* **draught**) [*attrib.*] **1** denoting beer or other drink that is kept in and served from a barrel or tank rather than from a bottle or can: *draft beer.* **2** denoting an animal used for pulling heavy loads: *draft oxen.* ▷mid 16th cent.: phonetic spelling of **DRAUGHT**. —**draft·er** *n.*
▶*PHRASE* □ **on draft** (of beer or other drink) on tap; ready to be drawn from a barrel or tank; not bottled or canned.

draft board ▶*n.* a board of civilians that is responsible for registering, classifying, and selecting people for compulsory military service.

draft dodg·er ▶*n. derogatory* a person who has avoided compulsory military service. —**draft dodg·ing** *n.*

draft·ee /drafˈtē/ ▶*n.* a person conscripted for military service.

draft horse (*Brit.* **draught horse**) ▶*n.* a large horse used for pulling heavy loads, esp. a cart or plow.

draft pick ▶*n.* the right of a sports team to select a player during the annual selection process. ■ a player selected during the draft.

drafts·man /ˈdraftsmən/ (*Brit.* **draughts·man**) ▶*n.* (*pl.* **-men**) **1** a person, esp. a man, who makes detailed technical plans or drawings. ■ an artist skilled in drawing. **2** a person who drafts legal documents. —**drafts·man·ship** /-ˌSHip/ *n.*

drafts·per·son /ˈdraftsˌpərsən/ ▶*n.* (*pl.* **-peo·ple**) a draftsman or draftswoman (used as a neutral alternative).

drafts·wom·an /ˈdraftsˌwoŏmən/ ▶*n.* (*pl.* **-wom·en**) a woman who makes detailed technical plans or drawings.

draft·y /ˈdraftē/ (*Brit.* **draught·y**) ▶*adj.* (**draft·i·er,**

draft·i·est) (of an enclosed space) cold and uncomfortable because of currents of cool air: *anyone would get pneumonia living in the drafty old house.* ■ (of a door or window) ill-fitting, and so allowing currents of cool air in. —**draft·i·ly** /-təlē/ *adv.* —**draft·i·ness** *n.*

drag /drag/ ▸*v.* (**dragged, drag·ging**) **1** [*trans.*] pull (someone or something) along forcefully, roughly, or with difficulty: *we dragged the boat up the beach* | *figurative I dragged my eyes away.* ■ take (someone) to or from a place or event, despite their reluctance: *my girlfriend is dragging me off to Atlantic City for a week.* ■ (**drag oneself**) go somewhere wearily, reluctantly, or with difficulty: *I have to drag myself out of bed each day.* ■ move (an icon or other image) across a computer screen using a tool such as a mouse. ■ [*intrans.*] (of a person's clothes or an animal's tail) trail along the ground: *the nuns walked in meditation, their habits dragging on the grass.* ■ [*intrans.*] (**drag at**) catch hold of and pull (something): *desperately, Jinny dragged at his arm.* ■ [*intrans.*] engage in a drag race: *they were caught dragging on Francis Lewis Blvd.* ■ [*trans.*] (of a ship) trail (an anchor) along the seabed, causing the ship to drift. ■ [*intrans.*] (of an anchor) fail to hold, causing a ship or boat to drift. ■ [*trans.*] search the bottom of (a river, lake, or the sea) with grapnels or nets: *frogmen had dragged the local river.* **2** [*trans.*] (**drag something up**) *informal* deliberately mention an unwelcome or unpleasant fact: *pieces of evidence about his early life were dragged up.* ■ (**drag someone/something into**) involve someone or something in (a situation or matter), typically when such involvement is inappropriate or unnecessary: *he had no right to drag you into this sort of thing.* ■ (**drag something in/into**) introduce an irrelevant or inappropriate subject: *politics were never dragged into the conversation.* ■ (**drag someone/something down**) bring someone or something to a lower level or standard: *the economy will be dragged down by inefficient firms.* **3** [*intrans.*] (of time, events, or activities) pass slowly and tediously: *the day dragged—eventually it was time for bed.* ■ (of a process or situation) continue at tedious and unnecessary length: *the dispute between the two families **dragged on** for years.* ■ [*trans.*] (**drag something out**) protract something unnecessarily: *he dragged out the process of serving them.* **4** [*intrans.*] (**drag on**) *informal* (of a person) inhale the smoke from (a cigarette).
▸*phrasal v.* □ **drag something out** extract information from someone against their will: *the truth was being **dragged out of** us.*
▸*n.* **1** the action of pulling something forcefully or with difficulty: *the drag of the current.* ■ the longitudinal retarding force exerted by air or other fluid surrounding a moving object. ■ [in *sing.*] a person or thing that impedes progress or development: *Larry was turning out to be **a drag on** her career.* ■ *Fishing* unnatural motion of a fishing fly caused by the pull of the line. ■ *archaic* an iron shoe that can be applied as a brake to the wheel of a cart or wagon. **2** [in *sing.*] *informal* a boring or tiresome person or thing: *working nine to five can be a drag.* **3** *informal* an act of inhaling smoke from a cigarette: *he **took a** long **drag on** his cigarette.* **4** clothing more conventionally worn by the opposite sex, esp. women's clothes worn by a man: *a fashion show, complete with men **in drag*** | [as *adj.*] *a live drag show.* **5** short for DRAG RACE. ■ *informal* a street or road: *the main drag.* ■ *historical* a private vehicle like a stagecoach, drawn by four horses. **6** a thing that is pulled along the ground or through water, in particular: ■ *historical* a harrow used for breaking up the surface of land. ■ an apparatus for dredging a river or for recovering the bodies of drowned people from a river, a lake, or the sea. ■ another term for DRAGNET. **7** *informal* influence over other people: *they had the education but they didn't have the drag.* **8** a strong-smelling lure drawn before hounds as a substitute for a fox or other hunted animal. ■ a hunt using such a lure. **9** *Music* one of the basic patterns (rudiments) of drumming, consisting of a stroke preceded by two grace notes, which are usually played with the other stick. See also RUFF[4]. ▷Middle English: from Old English *dragan* or Old Norse *draga* 'to draw'; the noun partly from Middle Low German *dragge* 'grapnel.'
▸*PHRASES* □ **drag one's feet** walk slowly and wearily or with difficulty. ■ (also **drag one's heels**) *figurative* (of a person or organization) be deliberately slow or reluctant to act: *the government has dragged its heels over permanent legislation.* □ **drag someone/something through the mud** make damaging allegations about someone or something: *he felt enough loyalty to his old school not to drag its name through the mud.* □ **in drag** wearing the clothing of the opposite sex.

drag-and-drop *Computing* ▸*v.* [*trans.*] move (an icon or other image) to another part of the screen using a mouse or similar device, typically in order to perform some operation on a file or document.
▸*adj.* of, relating to, or permitting the movement of images in this way: *drag-and-drop transfer of messages.*

drag bunt ▸*n. Baseball* a bunt, usually by a left-handed batter, that is hit down the first baseline.

dra·gée /drä'ZHā/ ▸*n.* a candy consisting of a center covered with a coating, such as a sugared almond or a chocolate. ■ a small silver ball for decorating cookies or a cake. ▷late 17th cent. (also denoting a mixture of spices): French, from Old French *dragie* (see DREDGE[2]).

drag·ger /'dragər/ ▸*n.* a trawler.

drag·gle /'dragəl/ ▸*v.* [*trans.*] make (something) dirty or wet, typically by trailing it through mud or water: [as *adj.*] (**draggled**) *she wore a draggled skirt.* ■ [*intrans.*] hang untidily: *red hairs draggled from under her cap.* ■ [*intrans.*] *archaic* trail behind others; lag behind: *they draggled at the heels of his troop.* ▷early 16th cent.: diminutive and frequentative of DRAG.

drag·gle-tailed ▸*adj. archaic* having untidily trailing skirts: *a draggle-tailed wench.*

drag·gy /'dragē/ ▸*adj.* (**drag·gi·er, drag·gi·est**) *informal* dreary and lacking liveliness: *a long, draggy, boring Friday afternoon.*

drag·line /'drag,līn/ ▸*n.* **1** a large excavator with a bucket pulled in by a wire cable. **2** a rope used for dragging or hauling something. ■ a rope that drags from something, e.g., a mooring line of a hot-air balloon. ■ a line of silk produced by a spider and acting as a safety line or (in newly hatched spiderlings) a parachute.

drag·net /'drag,net/ ▸*n.* a net drawn through a river or across ground to trap fish or game. ■ *figurative* a systematic search for someone or something, esp. criminals or criminal activity.

drag·o·man /'dragəmən/ ▸*n.* (*pl.* **-mans** or **-men**) an interpreter or guide, esp. in countries speaking Arabic, Turkish, or Persian. ▷late Middle English: from obsolete French, from Italian *dragomanno,* from medieval Greek *dragoumanos,* from Arabic *tarjumān* 'interpreter.'

drag·on /'dragən/ ▸*n.* **1** a mythical monster like a giant reptile. In European tradition the dragon is typically fire-breathing and tends to symbolize chaos or evil, whereas in the Far East it is usually a beneficent symbol of fertility, associated with water and the heavens. ■ *derogatory* a fierce and intimidating person, esp. a woman. **2** another term for FLYING DRAGON. ■ see KOMODO DRAGON. **3** *historical* (in the 16th and 17th centuries) a short musket carried on the belt of a soldier, esp. a mounted infantryman. ■ a soldier armed with such a musket. Compare with DRAGOON. ▷Middle English (also denoting a large serpent): from Old French, via Latin from Greek *drakōn* 'serpent.'

drag·on ar·um ▸*n.* any of a number of plants of the arum family, in particular the North American green dragon.

drag·on boat ▸*n.* a boat of a traditional Chinese design, typically decorated to resemble a dragon, propelled with paddles by a large crew and used for racing.

drag·on·et /,dragə'net; 'dragənit/ ▸*n.* a marine fish that often lies partly buried in the seabed. The male is brightly colored. • Two genera in the family Callionymidae: several species, in particular the European *Callionymus lyra.* ▷Middle English (denoting a small dragon): from Old French, diminutive of *dragon* 'dragon.'

drag·on·fish /'dragən,fiSH/ ▸*n.* (*pl.* same or **-fish·es**) a deep-sea fish with a long slender body: • a fish with fanglike teeth, a barbel on the chin, and luminous organs on the body (families Stomiatidae and Idiacanthidae). • (**Antarctic dragonfish**) a fish of southern polar seas with a flattened head (family Bathydraconidae).

drag·on·fly /'dragən,flī/ ▸*n.* (*pl.* **-flies**) a fast-flying long-bodied predatory insect with two pairs of large transparent wings that are spread out sideways at rest. The voracious aquatic larvae take up to five years to reach adulthood. Compare with DAMSELFLY. • Suborder Anisoptera, order Odonata: several families. Dragonflies include darners and skimmers.

drag·on·nade /,dragə'nād/ ▸*n.* one of a series of persecutions directed by Louis XIV against French Protestants, in which troops were quartered upon them. ▷early 18th cent.: from French, from *dragon* 'dragon' (see DRAGOON).

drag·on's blood ▸*n.* a red gum or powder that is derived from the fruit of certain palm trees and from the stem of the dragon tree and related plants. It is used as an acid shield in photoengraving and to color varnishes.

drag·on's mouth ▸*n.* another term for ARETHUSA.

drag·on tree ▸*n.* a slow-growing palmlike tree of the agave family, which is native to the Canary Islands and yields dragon's blood. • *Dracaena draco,* family Agavaceae.

dra·goon /drə'go͞on/ ▸*n.* a member of any of several cavalry regiments in the household troops of the British army. ■ *historical* a mounted infantryman armed with a short rifle or musket.
▸*v.* [*trans.*] coerce (someone) into doing something: *she had been **dragooned into** helping with the housework.* ▷early 17th cent. (denoting a kind of carbine or musket, thought of as breathing fire): from French *dragon* 'dragon.'

drag queen ▸*n.* a man who dresses up in women's clothes, typically for the purposes of entertainment. ■ a male homosexual transvestite.

drag race ▸*n.* a race between two or more cars over a short distance, usually a quarter of a mile, as a test of acceleration. —**drag rac·er** *n.* —**drag rac·ing** *n.*

drag·ster /'dragstər/ ▸*n.* a car built or modified to take part in drag races.

drag strip ▸*n.* a straight, paved track or section of road used for drag racing.

drail /'drāl/ ▸*n. Fishing* a fishhook and line weighted with lead for dragging below the surface of the water. ▷late 16th cent. (denoting part of a plow): from the obsolete verb *drail,* an alteration of TRAIL.

drain /drān/ ▸*v.* [*trans.*] **1** cause the water or other liquid in (something) to run out, leaving it empty, dry, or drier: *we drained the swimming pool.* ■ cause or allow (liquid) to run off or out of something: *fry the pork and **drain off** any excess fat.* ■ make (land) drier by providing channels for water to flow away in: *the land was drained and the boggy ground reclaimed.* ■ (of a river) carry off the superfluous water from (a district): *the stream drains a wide moorland above the waterfall.* ■ [*intrans.*] (of water or another liquid) flow away from, out of, or into something: *the river drains into the Pacific* | *figurative Polly felt the blood drain from her face.* ■ [*intrans.*] become dry or drier as liquid runs off or away: *dishes left to drain* | *the plant should be watered well and allowed to drain.* ■ (of a person) drink the entire contents of (a glass or other container): *he seized the Scotch set before him and drained it.* ■ [*intrans.*] *figurative* (of a feeling or emotion) become progressively less strongly felt: *gradually the tension and stress **drained away.*** **2** deprive of strength or vitality: *his limbs were **drained of** all energy* | *Ruth slumped down in her seat, drained by all that had happened.* ■ cause (money, energy, or another valuable resource) to be lost, wasted, or used up: *my mother's hospital bills are draining my income.* ■ [*intrans.*] (of such a resource) be lost, wasted, or used up: *votes and campaign funds drained away from the Republican candidate.* **3** *informal Golf* (of a player) hole (a putt).
▸*n.* **1** a channel or pipe carrying off surplus liquid, esp. rainwater or liquid waste. ■ a tube for drawing off accumulating fluid from a body cavity or an abscess. ■ *Electronics* the part of a field-effect transistor to which the charge carriers flow after passing the gate. **2** [in *sing.*] a thing that uses up a particular resource: *nuclear power is **a** serious **drain on** the public purse.* ■ the continuous loss or expenditure of a particular resource: *the drain of our heritage.* ▷Old English *drēahnian, drēhnian* 'strain (liquid),' of Germanic origin; related to DRY.
▸*PHRASE* □ **go down the drain** *informal* be totally wasted: *the government must stop public money from going down the drain.*

drain·age /'drānij/ ▸*n.* the action or process of draining something: *the pot must have holes in the base for good drainage* | *the drainage of wetlands.* ■ the means of removing surplus water or liquid waste; a system of drains.

drain·board /'drān,bôrd/ ▸*n.* a sloping grooved board or surface, on which washed dishes are left to drain, typically into a sink.

drain·er /'drānər/ ▸*n.* a device used to drain things, in particular a rack placed on a drainboard to hold washed dishes while they drain. ■ a drainboard. ■ a person or device that drains a flooded area.

drain·pipe /ˈdrān,pīp/ ▸*n.* a pipe for carrying off rainwater or liquid refuse from a building.

Draize test /drāz/ ▸*n.* a pharmacological test in which a substance is introduced into the eye or applied to the skin of a laboratory animal in order to ascertain the likely effect of that substance on the corresponding human tissue. ▷1970s: named after John H. *Draize* (1900–92), the American pharmacologist who helped to develop this type of test.

Drake /drāk/, Sir Francis (*c.*1540–96), English sailor and explorer. In his ship the *Golden Hind* he was the first Englishman to circumnavigate the globe (1577–80). He also played an important part in the defeat of the Spanish Armada.

drake[1] /drāk/ ▸*n.* a male duck: *ducks and drakes* | [as *adj.*] *a drake mallard.* ▷Middle English: related to Low German *drake* and German *Enterich.*

drake[2] ▸*n.* (in fishing) a natural or artificial mayfly, esp. a subadult or gravid female. ▷Old English *draca,* from Latin *draco* 'dragon.'

Drake e·qua·tion *Astronomy* a speculative equation that gives an estimate of the likelihood of discovering intelligent extraterrestrial life in the galaxy, expressed as the product of a series of factors such as the number of stars, the fraction of stars with planets, the fraction of planets on which life evolves, the average lifetime of a civilization, etc. It was formulated by the U.S. astronomer Frank Drake in 1961.

Dra·kens·berg Moun·tains /ˈdrākənz,bərg/ a mountain range in southern Africa that stretches northeast–southwest for a distance of 700 miles (1,126 km) through Lesotho and parts of South Africa. The highest peak is Thabana Ntlenyana (11,425 feet; 3,482 m).

Drake Pas·sage an area of ocean, noted for its violent storms, that connects the South Atlantic Ocean with the South Pacific Ocean and separates the southern tip of South America (Cape Horn) from the Antarctic Peninsula. ▷named after Sir Francis DRAKE.

Drakes Bay /drāks/ an inlet of the Pacific Ocean, northwest of San Francisco in California, visited by Francis Drake in 1579.

DRAM /ˈdē,ram/ ▸*n. Electronics* a memory chip that depends upon an applied voltage to keep the stored data. ▷acronym from *dynamic random-access memory.*

dram[1] /dram/ ▸*n.* **1** a small drink of whiskey or other spirits (often used in humorous imitation of Scottish speech): *a wee dram to ward off the winter chill.* **2** another term for DRACHM (sense 1). ▷late Middle English (in sense 2): from Old French *drame* or medieval Latin *drama,* variants of *dragme* and *dragma* (see DRACHM).

dram[2] ▸*n.* the basic monetary unit of Armenia, equal to 100 luma.

dra·ma /ˈdrämə/ ▸*n.* **1** a play for theater, radio, or television: *a gritty urban drama about growing up in Harlem.* ■ such works as a genre or style of literature: *Renaissance drama.* **2** an exciting, emotional, or unexpected series of events or set of circumstances: *a hostage drama* | *an afternoon of high drama at Fenway Park.* ▷early 16th cent.: via late Latin from Greek *drama,* from *dran* 'do, act.'

Dram·a·mine /ˈdramə,mēn/ ▸*n. trademark* an antihistamine compound used to counter nausea (esp. travel sickness). ▷1940s: from *dram-* (of unknown origin) + AMINE.

dra·mat·ic /drəˈmatik/ ▸*adj.* **1** [*attrib.*] of or relating to drama or the performance or study of drama: *the dramatic arts* | *a dramatic society.* **2** (of an event or circumstance) sudden and striking: *a dramatic increase in recorded crime.* ■ exciting or impressive: *he recalled his dramatic escape from the building* | *dramatic mountain peaks.* ■ (of a person or their behavior) intending or intended to create an effect; theatrical: *with a dramatic gesture, she put a hand to her brow.* ▷late 16th cent.: via late Latin from Greek *dramatikos,* from *drama, dramat-* (see DRAMA). **—dra·mat·i·cal·ly** /-ik(ə)lē/ *adv.*

dra·mat·ic i·ro·ny ▸*n.* see IRONY[1].

dra·mat·ic mon·o·logue ▸*n.* a poem in the form of a speech or narrative by an imagined person, in which the speaker inadvertently reveals aspects of their character while describing a particular situation or series of events.

dra·mat·ics /drəˈmatiks/ ▸*plural n.* **1** [often treated as *sing.*] the study or practice of acting in and producing plays: *amateur dramatics.* **2** theatrically exaggerated or overemotional behavior: *cut out the dramatics.*

dram·a·tis per·so·nae /ˈdrämətis pərˈsōnē/ ▸*plural n.* the characters of a play, novel, or narrative. ■ the participants in a series of events. ▷mid 18th cent.: Latin, literally 'persons of the drama.'

dram·a·tist /ˈdrämə,tist/ ▸*n.* a person who writes plays.

dram·a·tize /ˈdrämə,tīz/ ▸*v.* [*trans.*] adapt (a novel) or present (a particular incident) as a play or movie: *Miss Akins intends to dramatize my book.* ■ present in a vivid or striking way: *he used scare tactics to dramatize the deficit.* ■ exaggerate the seriousness or importance of (an incident or situation): *they have a tendency to dramatize things.* **—dram·a·ti·za·tion** /,drämətiˈzāsHən/ *n.*

dram·a·turge /ˈdrämə,tərj/ (also **dram·a·turg**) ▸*n.* **1** a dramatist. **2** a literary editor on the staff of a theater who consults with authors and edits texts. ▷mid 19th cent.: via French and German from Greek *dramatourgos,* from *drama, dramat-* 'drama' + *-ergos* 'worker.'

dram·a·tur·gy /ˈdrämə,tərjē/ ▸*n.* the theory and practice of dramatic composition: *studies of Shakespeare's dramaturgy.* **—dram·a·tur·gic** /-jik/ *adj.* **—dram·a·tur·gi·cal** /,drämәˈtərjikəl/ *adj.* **—dram·a·tur·gi·cal·ly** /,drämәˈtərjik(ə)lē/ *adv.*

Dram·bu·ie /dramˈbo͞oē/ ▸*n. trademark* a sweet Scotch whiskey liqueur. ▷from Scottish Gaelic *dram buidheach* 'satisfying drink.'

Drang nach O·sten /ˈdräNG näk ˈästən/ ▸*n.* the former German policy of eastward expansion, esp. that espoused under Nazi rule. ▷early 20th cent.: German, literally 'pressure toward the east.'

drank /draNGk/ ▸ past of DRINK.

drape /drāp/ ▸*v.* [*trans.*] arrange (cloth or clothing) loosely or casually on or around something: *she draped a shawl around her shoulders.* ■ (usu. **be draped**) adorn, cover, or wrap (someone or something) loosely with folds of cloth: *the body was draped in a blanket.* ■ let (oneself or a part of one's body) rest somewhere in a casual or relaxed way: *he draped an arm around her shoulders.* ■ [*intrans.*] (of fabric) hang or be able to hang in loose, graceful folds: *velvet drapes beautifully.*
▸*n.* **1** (**drapes**) long curtains: *Katherine pulled back the heavy velvet drapes.* ■ *informal* a man's suit consisting of a long jacket and narrow trousers, as worn by a Teddy boy: *teds dressed in Edwardian-style drapes and suede shoes.* ■ a cloth for covering parts of a patient's body other than that part on which a surgical operation is being performed. **2** [in *sing.*] the way in which a garment or fabric hangs: *by fixing the band lower down you obtain a fuller drape in the fabric.* ▷mid 19th cent.: back-formation from DRAPERY, influenced by French *draper* 'to drape.' The noun senses date from the early 20th cent.

drap·er /ˈdrāpər/ ▸*n. Brit., dated* a person who sells cloth and dry goods. ▷late Middle English (denoting a maker of woolen cloth): from Old French *drapier,* from *drap* 'cloth,' from late Latin *drappus.*

dra·per·y /ˈdrāpərē/ ▸*n.* (*pl.* **-per·ies**) cloth coverings hanging in loose folds: *the hall of the school was hung with green drapery.* ■ (**draperies**) long curtains of heavy fabric. ■ the artistic arrangement of clothing in sculpture or painting: *the effigy is notable for its flowing drapery.* ▷Middle English (in the sense 'cloth, fabrics'): from Old French *draperie,* from *drap* 'cloth' (see DRAPER).

dras·tic /ˈdrastik/ ▸*adj.* likely to have a strong or far-reaching effect; radical and extreme: *a drastic reduction of staffing levels.* ▷late 17th cent. (originally applied to the effect of medicine): from Greek *drastikos,* from *dran* 'do.' **—dras·ti·cal·ly** /-ik(ə)lē/ *adv.*

drat /drat/ ▸*exclam.* (often **drat someone/something**) a mild expression of anger or annoyance: *"Drat!" said Mitchell, kicking the fence* | *"Drat you!"* ▷early 19th cent.: shortening of *od rat,* euphemism for *God rot.* **—drat·ted** *adj.*

draught ▸*n.* British spelling of DRAFT (senses 3, 4, 6, 7, and 8).
▸*v.* & *adj.* British spelling of DRAFT. ▷Middle English (in the sense 'drawing, pulling'; also 'something drawn, a load'): from Old Norse *dráttr,* of Germanic origin; related to German *Tracht,* also to DRAW. Compare with DRAFT.

draught horse ▸*n.* British spelling of DRAFT HORSE.

draughts /ˈdraf(t)s/ ▸*n. Brit.* checkers. See CHECKER[2] (sense 2). ▷late Middle English: from DRAUGHT; related to obsolete *draught* in the sense 'move' (in chess or any similar game); compare with French *trait,* from Latin *tractus* 'a dragging.'

draughts·man ▸*n.* British spelling of DRAFTSMAN.

draught·y ▸*adj.* British spelling of DRAFTY.

Dra·va Riv·er /ˈdrävə/ (also **Dra·ve**) a river that rises in northern Italy and flows for 456 miles (725 km) through southern Austria, Slovenia, and Croatia to join the Danube River near Osijek. It forms part of the border between Hungary and Croatia.

Dra·vid·i·an /drəˈvidēən/ ▸*adj.* of, relating to, or denoting a family of languages spoken in southern India and Sri Lanka, or the peoples who speak them.
▸*n.* **1** this family of languages. **2** a member of any of the peoples speaking a Dravidian language.

> **Dravidian** languages were once spoken throughout the Indian subcontinent but were restricted to the south following the arrival of speakers of Indic languages *c.*1000 BC. Those still used, by over 160 million people, include Tamil, Kannada, Malayalam, and Telugu.

▷from Sanskrit *drāviḍa* 'relating to the Tamils' (from *Dravida* 'Tamil') + -IAN.

draw /drô/ ▸*v.* (*past* **drew** /dro͞o/; *past part.* **drawn** /drôn/) [*trans.*] **1** produce (a picture or diagram) by making lines and marks, esp. with a pen or pencil, on paper: *he drew a map.* ■ produce an image of (someone or something) in such a way: *I asked her to draw me* | [*intrans.*] *she draws really well.* ■ trace or produce (a line or mark) on a surface: *she drew a wavering line down the board* | *figurative where will we draw the outer boundaries of this Europe?* **2** pull or drag (something such as a vehicle) so as to make it follow behind: *a cart drawn by two horses.* ■ [*trans.*] pull or move (something) in a specified direction: *I drew back the blanket and uncovered the body.* ■ [*trans.*] gently pull or guide (someone) in a specified direction: *"David," she whispered, **drawing him aside.*** ■ [*intrans.*] move in a slow steady way: *the driver slowed as he drew even with me* | *the train drew into the station.* ■ [*intrans.*] come to or arrive at a point in time or a specified point in a process: *the campaign **drew to a close*** | *the time for the parade itself is **drawing near.*** ■ pull (curtains, blinds, or other such coverings) shut or open: *do you want me to draw the drapes?* | *she **drew back** the curtains and looked out.* ■ make (wire) by pulling a piece of metal through successively smaller holes. **3** extract (an object or liquid) from a container or receptacle: *he drew his gun and peered into the gloomy apartment* | *the children went down to the pond to draw water* | *the syringe **drew off** most of the fluid* | [as *adj.*] (**drawn**) *he met them with a drawn sword.* ■ run (a bath): *she drew him a hot bath.* ■ (**draw something from**) obtain something from (a particular source): *an independent panel of judges drawn from members of the public* | *he draws inspiration from ordinary scenes and simple places.* ■ (**draw on**) use (one's experience, talents, or skills) as a resource: *Sue has a lot of past experience to draw on.* ■ obtain or withdraw (money) from a bank or other source: *this check **draws against** my personal account.* ■ *Hunting* search (cover) for game. ■ *Bridge* (of player) force the opponents to play (cards in a particular suit) by leading cards in that suit: *before establishing his diamonds, declarer must draw trumps.* ■ [*intrans.*] suck smoke from (a cigarette or pipe). ■ [*intrans.*] (of a chimney, flue, or fire) allow air to flow in and upward freely, so that a fire can burn: *failure of a fire to draw properly can have a number of causes.* ■ take in (a breath): *Mrs. Feather drew a long breath and let it out.* ■ [*intrans.*] (of tea) be left standing so that the flavor is extracted from the leaves: *a pot of tea is allowed to draw.* ■ disembowel: *after a mockery of a trial he was **hanged, drawn, and quartered.*** **4** be the cause of (a specified response): *he drew criticism for his lavish spending.* ■ attract (someone) to come to a place or an event: *you really drew the crowds with your playing* | *customers drawn in by the reductions.* ■ (usu. **be drawn**) induce (someone) to reveal or do something: *I would rather not be **drawn into** your argument.* ■ direct or attract (someone's attention) to something: *it was an outrage and we had to draw people's attention to it.* ■ reach (a conclusion) by deduction or inference from a set of circumstances: *the moral to be drawn is that spending wins votes.* ■ formulate or perceive (a comparison or distinction): *the law drew a clear distinction between innocent and fraudulent misrepresentation.* **5** *Golf* hit (the ball) so that it travels slightly to the left (for a left-handed player, the right), usually as a result of spin given to the ball: *he had to learn to draw the ball—not least for the tee shots at Augusta.* Compare with FADE (sense 3). ■ *Billiards* impart backspin to (the cue ball), making it move backwards after hitting an object ball. **6** (of a ship) require (a specified depth of water) to float in; have (a certain draft): *boats that draw only a few inches of water.* **7** [*intrans.*] (of a sail) be filled with wind. **8** *Brit.* finish (a contest or game) with an even score; tie: [*trans.*] *Brazil had drawn a stormy match 1–1.*
▸*phrasal v.* □ **draw back** choose not to do something

that one was expected to do: *the government has* **drawn back from** *attempting reform.* □ **draw on** (of a period of time) pass by and approach its end: *he remembered sitting in silence with his grandmother as evening drew on.* □ **draw something on** put an item of clothing on: *she drew on her gloves.* □ **draw someone out** gently or subtly persuade someone to talk or become more expansive: *she drew me out and flattered me.* □ **draw something out** make something last longer: *the transition was long drawn out.* □ **draw up** come to a halt: *drivers drew up at the lights.* □ **draw something up** prepare a plan, proposal, agreement, or other document in detail: *they instructed an attorney to draw up a sales agreement.* □ **draw oneself up** make oneself stand in a stiffly upright manner: *Sarah drew herself up, full of indignation that he should presume to judge her.*

▸*n.* **1** an act of selecting names randomly, typically by extracting them from a bag or other container, to match competitors in a game or tournament: *the draw has been made for this year's tournament.* **2** a game that ends with the score even; a tie. **3** a person or thing that is very attractive or interesting: *the big city was a powerful draw to youngsters.* **4** an act of inhaling smoke from a cigar: *superb cigars offering tons of peppery smoke on each draw.* **5** an act of removing a gun from its holster in order to shoot. **6** *Golf* a shot causing the ball to deviate to the left (or, for a left-handed golfer, the right). ■ *Billiards* backspin imparted to a cue ball, causing it to move backwards after hitting an object ball. ▷Old English *dragan*, of Germanic origin; related to Dutch *dragen* and German *tragen*, also to DRAFT.

▸*PHRASES* □ **draw a bead on** see BEAD. □ **draw a blank** see BLANK. □ **draw blood** cause someone to bleed, esp. in the course of a fight: *the blow drew blood from the corner of his mouth* | *figurative she knew she'd drawn blood when the smile faded from his face.* □ **draw fire** attract hostile criticism, usually away from a more important target: *the vaccination campaign continued to draw fire.* □ **draw the line at** set a limit of what one is willing to do or accept, beyond which one will not go: *she drew the line at prostitution.* □ **draw lots** see LOT. □ **draw the short straw** see STRAW. □ **quick on the draw** very fast in taking one's gun from its holster. ■ *figurative* very fast in acting or reacting.

draw·back /'drô,bak/ ▸*n.* **1** a feature that renders something less acceptable; a disadvantage or problem: *the main drawback of fitting catalytic converters is the cost.* **2** an amount of excise or import duty remitted on imported goods that the importer reexports rather than sells domestically.

draw·bar /'drô,bär/ ▸*n.* **1** a bar on a vehicle to which something can be attached to pull it or be pulled. ■ a coupler on a railroad car. **2** one of a number of bars that may be pulled out to control harmonics on an electric organ.

draw·bridge /'drô,brij/ ▸*n. historical* a bridge, esp. one over a castle's moat, that is hinged at one end so that it may be raised to prevent people's crossing or to allow vessels to pass under it.

drawbridge

draw·cord /'drô,kôrd/ ▸*n. Brit.* another term for DRAWSTRING.

draw·down /'drô,doun/ ▸*n.* a reduction in the size or presence of a military force: *the unit is the first to leave Germany as part of the drawdown.* ■ a reduction in the volume of water in a lake or reservoir. ■ a withdrawal of oil or other commodity from stocks.

draw·ee /drô'ē/ ▸*n.* the person or organization, typically a bank, who must pay a draft or bill.

draw·er /'drô(ə)r/ ▸*n.* **1** a boxlike storage compartment without a lid, made to slide horizontally in and out of a desk, chest, or other piece of furniture. **2** (**drawers**) *dated or humorous* underpants. **3** a person who draws something, in particular: ■ a person who writes a check. ■ a person who produces a drawing or design. ■ *archaic* another term for TAPSTER. **—draw·er·ful** /-,fo͝ol/ *n.* (*pl.* **-fuls**) .

draw·ing /'drô-iNG/ ▸*n.* **1** a picture or diagram made with a pencil, pen, or crayon rather than paint, esp. one drawn in monochrome: *a series of charcoal drawings on white paper.* ■ the art or skill or making such pictures or diagrams: *she took lessons in drawing.* **2** the selection of a winner or winners in a lottery or raffle: *entrants need not be present at the drawing.*

draw·ing board ▸*n.* a large flat board on which paper may be spread for artists or designers to work on.

▸*PHRASES* □ **back to the drawing board** used to indicate that an idea, scheme, or proposal has been unsuccessful and that a new one must be devised: *the government must go back to the drawing board and review the whole issue of youth training.* □ **on the drawing board** (of an idea, scheme, or proposal) under consideration and not yet ready to put into practice: *there are plans to enlarge the runway, but at present all this remains on the drawing board.*

draw·ing card /'drô-iNG/ (*Brit.* **draw·card** /'drô,kärd/) ▸*n. informal* a quality or feature that evokes interest or liking; an attraction: *rookie fireball flingers are the prime drawing cards of spring baseball.*

draw·ing pin ▸*n.* British term for THUMBTACK.

draw·ing room ▸*n.* a room in a large private house in which guests can be received and entertained. ■ a private compartment in a train, typically one that accommodates two or three people.

▸*adj.* [*attrib.*] consciously refined, lighthearted, and elegant: *drawing-room small talk.* ■ (of a song or play) characterized by a polite observance of social proprieties: *a stock figure of Thirties drawing-room comedy.* ▷mid 17th cent. (denoting a private room attached to a more public one): abbreviation of 16th-cent. *withdrawing-room* 'a room to withdraw to.'

draw·knife /'drô,nīf/ ▸*n.* (*pl.* **-knives** /-,nīvz/) a knife consisting of a blade with a handle at each end at right angles to it, which is drawn over a surface, toward the user, with a paring effect.

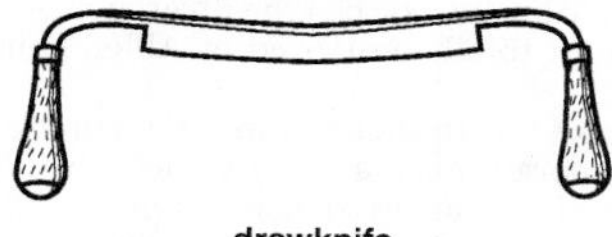

drawknife

drawl /drôl/ ▸*v.* [*intrans.*] speak in a slow, lazy way with prolonged vowel sounds: [with *direct speech*] *"Suits me fine," he drawled.*

▸*n.* [in *sing.*] a slow, lazy way of speaking or an accent with unusually prolonged vowel sounds: *a Texas drawl.* ▷late 16th cent.: probably originally slang, from Low German or Dutch *dralen* 'delay, linger.' **—drawl·er** *n.* **—drawl·y** *adj.*

drawn /drôn/ ▸ past participle of DRAW.

▸*adj.* (of a person or a person's face) looking strained from illness, exhaustion, anxiety, or pain: *Cathy was pale and drawn and she looked tired out.*

drawn but·ter ▸*n.* melted butter.

drawn-out ▸*adj.* (often **long-drawn-out**) lasting or seeming to last longer than is necessary: *a long-drawn-out courtship.*

drawn·work /'drôn,wərk/ (also **drawn threadwork**) ▸*n.* ornamental work on linen or other fabric, done by drawing out threads and usually with additional needlework.

draw pok·er ▸*n.* a variety of poker in which each player is dealt five cards and, after the first round of betting, may discard some (usually up to three) of these cards and draw replacements from the dealer.

draw reins ▸*n.* a pair of reins that are attached to a horse's saddle or girth and pass through the bit rings to the rider's hands.

draw·sheet /'drô,sHēt/ (also **draw sheet**) ▸*n.* a sheet that is placed in such a way that it can be taken from under a patient or invalid without disturbing the bedclothes.

draw·string /'drô,striNG/ ▸*n.* a string in the seam of the material of a garment or a bag, which can be pulled to tighten or close it.

dray /drā/ ▸*n.* a truck or cart for delivering beer barrels or other heavy loads, esp. a low one without sides. ▷late Middle English (denoting a sledge): perhaps from Old English *dræge* 'dragnet,' related to *dragan* 'to pull' (see DRAW).

dray horse ▸*n.* a large, powerful horse used to pull heavy loads.

dray·man /'drāmən/ ▸*n.* (*pl.* **-men**) a person who delivers beer for a brewery.

dread /dred/ ▸*v.* [*trans.*] anticipate with great apprehension or fear: *Jane was dreading the party* | [with *infinitive*] *I* **dread to think** *what Russell will say.* ■ *archaic* regard with great awe or reverence.

▸*n.* **1** great fear or apprehension: *the thought of returning to New Jersey filled her with dread* | [in *sing.*] *I used to have a dread of Sunday afternoons.* **2** *informal* a person with dreadlocks. ■ (**dreads**) dreadlocks.

▸*adj.* [*attrib.*] greatly feared; dreadful: *he was stricken with the dread disease and died.* ■ *archaic* regarded with awe; greatly revered: *that dread being we dare oppose.* ▷Old English *ādrǣdan, ondrǣdan*; related to Old High German *intrātan*.

dread·ed /'dredid/ ▸*adj.* [*attrib.*] regarded with great fear or apprehension: *the dreaded news came that Joe had been wounded* | *humorous the dreaded fax machine.*

dread·ful /'dredfəl/ ▸*adj.* causing or involving great suffering, fear, or unhappiness; extremely bad or serious: *there's been a dreadful accident.* ■ extremely disagreeable: *the weather was dreadful.* ■ [*attrib.*] used to emphasize the degree to which something is the case, esp. something regarded with sadness or disapproval: *you're a dreadful flirt.* ■ (of a person or their feelings) troubled: *I feel dreadful—I hate myself.* ■ (of a person or their appearance) feeling or looking ill: *she looked dreadful and she was struggling for breath.* **—dread·ful·ness** *n.*

dread·ful·ly /'dredfəlē/ ▸*adv.* **1** [often as *submodifier*] extremely: *you're dreadfully thin* | *I'm dreadfully sorry!* ■ very much: *I'll miss you dreadfully.* **2** very badly: *the company has performed dreadfully.*

dread·locks /'dred,läks/ ▸*plural n.* a hairstyle in which the hair is washed but not combed and twisted while wet into tight braids or ringlets hanging down on all sides. **—dread·locked** *adj.*

dread·nought /'dred,nôt/ (also **dread·naught**) ▸*n.* **1** *historical* a type of battleship introduced in the early 20th century, larger and faster than its predecessors and equipped entirely with large-caliber guns. [named after Britain's HMS *Dreadnought*, which was the first to be completed (1906).] **2** *archaic* a heavy overcoat for stormy weather.

dream /drēm/ ▸*n.* a series of thoughts, images, and sensations occurring in a person's mind during sleep: *I had a recurrent dream about falling from great heights.* ■ [in *sing.*] a state of mind in which someone is or seems to be unaware of their immediate surroundings: *he had been walking around* **in a dream** *all day.* ■ a cherished aspiration, ambition, or ideal: *I fulfilled a childhood dream when I became champion* | *the girl* **of my dreams** | [as *adj.*] *they'd found their dream home.* ■ an unrealistic or self-deluding fantasy: *maybe he could get a job and earn some money—but he knew this was just a dream.* ■ a person or thing perceived as wonderful or perfect: *her new man's an absolute dream* | *it was a* **dream of** *a backhand* | *she's a couturier's dream.*

▸*v.* (*past* and *past part.* **dreamed** or **dreamt** /dremt/) [*intrans.*] **1** experience dreams during sleep: *I* **dreamed about** *her last night.* ■ [*trans.*] see, hear, or feel (something) in a dream: *maybe you dreamed it* | [with *clause*] *I dreamed that I was going to be executed.* ■ indulge in daydreams or fantasies, typically about something greatly desired: *she had* **dreamed of** *a trip to Italy.* ■ [*trans.*] (**dream time away**) waste one's time in a lazy, unproductive way. **2** [with *negative*] contemplate the possibility of doing something or that something might be the case: *I wouldn't* **dream of** *foisting myself on you* | [with *clause*] *I never dreamed anyone would take offense.*

▸*phrasal v.* □ **dream on** [in *imperative*] *informal* used, esp. in spoken English, as an ironic comment on the unlikely or impractical nature of a plan or aspiration: *Dean thinks he's going to get the job. Dream on, babe.* □ **dream something up** imagine or invent something: *he's been dreaming up new ways of attracting customers.* ▷Middle English: of Germanic origin, related to Dutch *droom* and German *Traum*, and probably also to Old English *drēam* 'joy, music.' **—dream·ful** /-fəl/ *adj.* (*poetic/literary*) **—dream·less** *adj.* **—dream·like** /-,līk/ *adj.*

▸*PHRASES* □ **beyond one's wildest dreams** bigger or better than could be reasonably expected: *stockbrokers command salaries beyond the wildest dreams of most* *workers.* □ **in your dreams** used in spoken English to assert that something much desired is not likely ever to happen. □ **in one's wildest dreams** [with *negative*] used to emphasize that a situation is beyond the scope of one's imagination: *she could never in her wildest dreams have imagined the summer weather in New York.* □ **like a dream** *informal* very well or successfully: *the car is still running like a dream.*

dream·boat /ˈdrēmˌbōt/ ▸*n. informal* a very attractive person, esp. a man.

dream·catch·er /ˈdrēmˌkaCHər; -ˌkeCH-/ ▸*n.* a small hoop containing a horsehair mesh, or a similar construction of string or yarn, decorated with feathers and beads, believed to give its owner good dreams. Dreamcatchers were originally made by American Indians.

dreamcatcher

dream·er /ˈdrēmər/ ▸*n.* a person who dreams or is dreaming. ■ a person who is unpractical or idealistic: *a rebellious young dreamer.*

dream·land /ˈdrēmˌland/ ▸*n.* sleep regarded as a world of dreams: *she tries to lull herself into dreamland.* ■ an imagined and unrealistically ideal world: *there was always in the Cotton Club a certain dreamland aspect.*

dream·scape /ˈdrēmˌskāp/ ▸*n.* a landscape or scene with the strangeness or mystery characteristic of dreams: *surrealism's popular manifestations were the dreamscapes of Salvador Dali.*

dream team ▸*n.* a team of people perceived as the perfect combination for a particular purpose: *the two have been linked as the dream team that will revitalize New York Democrats.*

dream·time /ˈdrēmˌtīm/ ▸*n.* [in *sing.*] (in the mythology of some Australian Aboriginals) the "golden age" when the first ancestors were created.

dream·work /ˈdrēmˌwərk/ ▸*n. Psychoanalysis* the processes by which the unconscious mind alters the manifest content of dreams in order to conceal their real meaning from the dreamer.

dream·world /ˈdrēmˌwərld/ ▸*n.* a fantastic or idealized view of life: *somebody who can live in a romantic dreamworld.*

dream·y /ˈdrēmē/ ▸*adj.* (**dream·i·er**, **dream·i·est**) reflecting a preoccupation with pleasant thoughts that distract one from one's present surroundings: *a dreamy smile.* ■ (of a person) not practical; given to daydreaming: *a dreamy boy who grew up absorbed in poetry.* ■ having a magical or dreamlike quality; peacefully gentle and relaxing: *a slow dreamy melody.* ■ *informal* delightful; gorgeous: *I bet he was really dreamy.* **—dream·i·ly** /-məlē/ *adv.* **—dream·i·ness** *n.*

drear /dri(ə)r/ ▸*adj.* poetic/literary term for DREARY. ▷early 17th cent.: abbreviation.

drear·y /ˈdri(ə)rē/ ▸*adj.* (**drear·i·er**, **drear·i·est**) dull, bleak, and lifeless; depressing: *the dreary routine of working, eating, and trying to sleep.* ▷Old English *drēorig* 'gory, cruel,' also 'melancholy,' from *drēor* 'gore,' of Germanic origin; related to German *traurig* 'sorrowful,' also to DROWSY, and probably to DRIZZLE. **—drear·i·ly** /ˈdri(ə)rəlē/ *adv.* **—drear·i·ness** *n.*

dreck /drek/ (also **drek**) ▸*n. informal* rubbish; trash: *this so-called art is pure dreck.* ▷early 20th cent.: from Yiddish *drek* 'filth, dregs,' from a Germanic base shared by Old English *threax*; probably related to Greek *skōr* 'dung.' **—dreck·ish** *adj.* **—dreck·y** *adj.*

dredge[1] /drej/ ▸*v.* [*trans.*] clean out the bed of (a harbor, river, or other area of water) by scooping out mud, weeds, and rubbish with a dredge. ■ bring up or clear (something) from a river, harbor, or other area of water with a dredge: *mud was dredged out of the harbor* | [*intrans.*] *they start to* **dredge for** *oysters in November.* ■ (**dredge something up**) *figurative* bring to people's attention an unpleasant or embarrassing fact or incident that had been forgotten: *I don't understand why you had to dredge up this story.*
▸*n.* an apparatus for bringing up objects or mud from a river or seabed by scooping or dragging. ■ a dredger. ▷late 15th cent. (as a noun; originally in *dredge-boat*): perhaps related to Middle Dutch *dreghe* 'grappling hook.'

dredge[2] ▸*v.* [*trans.*] sprinkle (food) with a powdered substance, typically flour or sugar: *dredge the bananas with sugar and cinnamon.* ▷late 16th cent.: from obsolete *dredge* 'sweetmeat, mixture of spices,' from Old French *dragie*, perhaps via Latin from Greek *tragēmata* 'spices.' Compare with DRAGÉE.

dredg·er /ˈdrejər/ ▸*n.* a barge or other vessel designed for dredging harbors or other bodies of water.

dree /drē/ ▸*v.* (**drees**, **dreed**, **dree·ing**) [*trans.*] *Scottish* or *archaic* endure (something burdensome or painful): *he dreed pain and dolor.* ▷Old English *drēogan*, of Germanic origin; related to Old Norse *drýgja* 'practice, perpetrate.'
▸*PHRASE* □ **dree one's weird** submit to one's destiny.

dregs /dregz/ ▸*n.* the remnants of a liquid left in a container, together with any sediment or grounds: *coffee dregs.* ■ *figurative* the most worthless part or parts of something: *the dregs of society.* ▷Middle English: probably of Scandinavian origin and related to Swedish *drägg* (plural). **—dreg·gy** /ˈdregē/ *adj.*

drei·del /ˈdrādl/ ▸*n.* a small four-sided spinning top with a Hebrew letter on each side, used by the Jews. ■ a gambling game played with such a top, esp. at Hanukkah. ▷1930s: from Yiddish *dreydl*; compare with German *drehen* 'to turn.'

Drei·ser /ˈdrīzər/, Theodore (Herman Albert) (1871–1945), U.S. novelist. His first novel, *Sister Carrie* (1900), caused controversy for its frank treatment of the heroine's sexuality and ambition. Other notable works: *An American Tragedy* (1925) and *America Is Worth Saving* (1941).

drek ▸*n.* variant spelling of DRECK.

drench /drenCH/ ▸*v.* [*trans.*] **1** (usu. **be drenched**) wet thoroughly; soak: *I fell in the stream and got drenched* | [as *n.*] (**drenching**) *a severe drenching would kill his uncle.* ■ *figurative* cover (something) liberally or thoroughly: *cool patios drenched in flowers* | [as *adj.*, in *combination*] (**-drenched**) *a sun-drenched clearing.* **2** forcibly administer a drug in liquid form orally to (an animal).
▸*n.* a dose of medicine administered to an animal. ■ *archaic* a draft of a medicinal or poisonous liquid. ▷Old English *drencan* 'force to drink,' *drenc* 'a drink or draft,' of Germanic origin; related to German *tränken* (verb), *Trank* (noun), also to DRINK.

Dres·den[1] /ˈdrezdən/ a city in eastern Germany, the capital of Saxony, on the Elbe River; pop. 485,130. It was almost totally destroyed by Allied bombing in 1945.

Dres·den[2] (also **Dresden china**) ▸*n.* porcelain ware with elaborate decoration and delicate colorings, made originally at Dresden and (since 1710) at nearby Meissen: [as *adj.*] *a fine Dresden china cup.*

dress /dres/ ▸*v.* **1** [*intrans.*] put on one's clothes: *Graham showered and dressed quickly* | *I'll go and* **get dressed.** ■ [with *adverbial*] wear clothes in a particular way or of a particular type: *she's nice-looking and dresses well* | (**be dressed**) *he was dressed in jeans and a thick sweater.* ■ [*trans.*] put clothes on (someone): *they dressed her in a white hospital gown.* ■ put on clothes appropriate for a formal occasion: *we* **dressed for dinner** *every night.* ■ [*trans.*] design or supply clothes for (a celebrity): *for over four decades he dressed the royal family.* ■ [*trans.*] decorate (something) in an artistic or attractive way: *they had dressed the doorframes with sprays of bittersweet.* **2** [*trans.*] treat or prepare (something) in a certain way, in particular: ■ clean, treat, or apply a dressing to (a wound). ■ clean and prepare (food, esp. poultry or shellfish) for cooking or eating: [as *adj.*] (**dressed**) *dressed crab.* ■ add a dressing to (a salad). ■ apply a fertilizing substance to (a field, garden, or plant). ■ complete the preparation or manufacture of (leather or fabric) by treating its surface in some way. ■ smooth the surface of (stone): [as *adj.*] (**dressed**) *a tower built of dressed stone.* ■ arrange or style (one's own or someone else's hair), esp. in an elaborate way. **3** [*trans.*] *Military* draw up (troops) in the proper alignment. ■ [*intrans.*] (of troops) come into such an alignment. **4** [*trans.*] prepare (an artificial fly) for use in fishing: [as *adj.*] (**dressed**) *a dressed wet fly.*
▸*phrasal v.* □ **dress down** dress informally: *Sue dressed down in old jeans and a white blouse.* □ **dress someone down** *informal* reprimand someone. □ **dress ship** decorate a ship with flags, for a special occasion. □ **dress up** dress in smart or formal clothes. ■ dress in a special costume for fun or as part of an entertainment: *he dressed up as a gorilla.* □ **dress something up** present something in such a way that it appears better than it really is: *the company dressed up the figures a little.*
▸*n.* **1** a one-piece garment for a woman or girl that covers the body and extends down over the legs. **2** clothing of a specified kind for men or women: *traditional African dress* | *figurative the underlying theme is recognizable even when it appears in feminist dress.* ■ [as *adj.*] denoting military uniform or other clothing used on formal or ceremonial occasions: *a dress suit.* ▷Middle English (in the sense 'put straight'): from Old French *dresser* 'arrange, prepare,' based on Latin *directus* 'direct, straight.'
▸*PHRASES* □ **dressed to kill** wearing glamorous clothes intended to create a striking impression. □ **dressed to the nines** dressed very elaborately.

dres·sage /drəˈsäZH/ ▸*n.* the art of riding and training a horse in a manner that develops obedience, flexibility, and balance. ▷1930s: from French, literally 'training'.

dress cir·cle ▸*n.* the first level of seats above the ground floor in a theater.

dress coat ▸*n.* another term for TAILCOAT.

dress code ▸*n.* a set of rules, usually written and posted, specifying the required manner of dress at a school, office, club, restaurant, etc.: *while the dress code doesn't require two-tone shoes, you will get turned away if you wear jeans.* ■ the customary style of dress of a specified group: *jeans or shorts, the standard dress code for producer types.*

dress-down ▸*adj.* of or relating to dress that is informal or less formal than would be expected: *his genius for causal, dress-down clothes* | *at his company, 'dress-down day' lasts all week.*

dres·ser[1] /ˈdresər/ ▸*n.* a chest of drawers. ■ a sideboard with shelves above for storing and displaying plates and kitchen utensils. ▷late Middle English (denoting a kitchen sideboard or table on which food was prepared): from Old French *dresseur*, from *dresser* 'prepare' (see DRESS).

dres·ser[2] ▸*n.* **1** [usu. with *adj.*] a person who dresses in a specified way: *a snappy dresser.* ■ a person who habitually dresses in a smart or elegant way: *she's gorgeous—and she's a dresser.* **2** a person whose job is to look after theatrical costumes and help actors to dress. **3** a person who prepares, treats, or finishes a material or piece of equipment.

dress-down Fri·day ▸*n.* another term for CASUAL FRIDAY.

dress·ing /ˈdresiNG/ ▸*n.* **1** (also **salad dressing**) a sauce for salads, typically one consisting of oil and vinegar mixed together with herbs or other flavorings: *vinaigrette dressing.* ■ stuffing: *turkey with apple dressing.* **2** a piece of material placed on a wound to protect it: *an antiseptic dressing.* **3** size or stiffening used in the finishing of fabrics. **4** a fertilizing substance such as compost or manure spread over or plowed into land.

dress·ing-down ▸*n.* [in *sing.*] *informal* a severe reprimand: *the secretary received a public dressing-down.*

dress·ing gown ▸*n.* a long loose robe, typically worn after getting out of bed or bathing.

dress·ing room ▸*n.* a room in which actors change clothes before and after their performance. ■ a small room or cubicle in a clothing store, used by customers to try on clothes.

dress·ing ta·ble ▸*n.* a table with a mirror and drawers for cosmetics, etc., used while dressing or applying makeup.

dress·mak·er /ˈdresˌmākər/ ▸*n.* a person whose job is making women's clothes. **—dress·mak·ing** /-kiNG/ *n.*

dress pa·rade ▸*n.* a military parade in full dress uniform.

dress re·hears·al ▸*n.* the final rehearsal of a live show, in which everything is done as it would be in a real performance.

dress shield ▸*n.* a piece of waterproof material fastened in the armpit of a dress to protect it from perspiration.

dress shirt ▸*n.* a man's white shirt worn with a bow tie and a dinner jacket on formal occasions. ■ a man's long-sleeved shirt, suitable for wearing with a tie.

dress·y /ˈdresē/ ▸*adj.* (**dress·i·er**, **dress·i·est**) (of clothes) suitable for a festive or formal occasion: *wear something dressy, Kate, we're going to a cocktail party.* ■ requiring or given to wearing such clothes: *this isn't a dressy place, but it's clean.* **—dress·i·ly** /ˈdresəlē/ *adv.* **—dress·i·ness** *n.*

drew /dro͞o/ ▸ past of DRAW.

Drex·el /ˈdreksəl/, Anthony Joseph (1826–93), U.S. banker and philanthropist. He joined his father's brokerage firm in 1847 and merged with J. P. Morgan in 1871, making Drexel, Morgan, and Co. the most powerful investment banking house in the U.S. He was the founder 1892 and benefactor of Drexel Institute of Technology.

drey /drā/ ▶*n.* (*pl.* **dreys**) the nest of a squirrel, typically in the form of a mass of twigs in a tree. ▷early 17th cent.: of unknown origin.

Drey·fus /ˈdrāfəs; ˈdrī-/, Alfred (1859–1935), French army officer. In 1894, he was falsely accused of providing military secrets to the Germans; his trial and imprisonment caused a major political crisis in France. He was eventually fully exonerated in 1906.

drib·ble /ˈdribəl/ ▶*v.* **1** [*intrans.*] (of a liquid) fall slowly in drops or a thin stream: *rain dribbled down the window* | *figurative refugees from central Europe dribbled into Britain.* ■ [*trans.*] pour (a liquid) in such a way: *he dribbled cream into his coffee.* ■ [*intrans.*] allow saliva to run from the mouth: *his mouth was open and he was dribbling.* **2** [*trans.*] (chiefly in soccer, field hockey, and basketball) take (the ball) forward past opponents with slight touches of the feet or the stick, or (in basketball) by continuous bouncing: *he attempted to dribble the ball from the goal area* | [*intrans.*] *he dribbled past a swarm of defenders.*
▶*n.* **1** a thin stream of liquid; a trickle: *a dribble of blood.* ■ saliva running from the mouth. **2** *figurative* foolish talk or ideas; nonsense: *don't believe a word of that dribble.* **3** (in soccer, hockey, and basketball) an act or instance of taking the ball forward with repeated slight touches or bounces. ▷mid 16th cent.: frequentative of obsolete *drib*, variant of **DRIP**. The original sense was 'shoot an arrow short or wide of its target,' which was also a sense of *drib*. Sense 2 of the *noun* may have been influenced by **DRIVEL**. —**drib·bler** /-b(ə)lər/ *n.*

drib·let /ˈdriblit/ ▶*n.* a thin stream or small drop of liquid: ***driblets of** spittle run from her mouth.* ■ a small or insignificant amount: *the prisoners were let out **in driblets**.* ▷late 16th cent. (in the sense 'small sum of money'): from obsolete *drib* (see **DRIBBLE**) + **-LET**.

dribs and drabs /ˈdribz and ˈdrabz/ ▶*plural n.* (**in dribs and drabs**) *informal* in small scattered or sporadic amounts: *doing the work in dribs and drabs.* ▷mid 19th cent.: from obsolete *drib* (see **DRIBBLE**) and *drab* (by reduplication).

dried /drīd/ ▶ past and past participle of **DRY**.

dri·er¹ /ˈdrīər/ ▶*adj.* comparative of **DRY**.

dri·er² ▶*n.* variant spelling of **DRYER**.

drift /drift/ ▶*v.* [*intrans.*] **1** be carried slowly by a current of air or water: *the cabin cruiser started to drift downstream* | *figurative excited voices drifted down the hall.* ■ [with *adverbial of direction*] (of a person) walk slowly, aimlessly, or casually: *people began to drift away.* ■ [with *adverbial*] move passively, aimlessly, or involuntarily into a certain situation or condition: *I was drifting off to sleep* | *Lewis and his father drifted apart.* ■ (of a person or their attention) digress or stray to another subject: *I noticed my audience's attention drifting.* **2** (esp. of snow or leaves) be blown into heaps by the wind: *fallen leaves start to drift in the gutters* | [as *adj.*] (**drifting**) *drifting snow.*
▶*n.* **1** [in *sing.*] a continuous slow movement from one place to another: *there was a drift to the towns.* ■ the deviation of a vessel, aircraft, or projectile from its intended or expected course as the result of currents or winds: *the pilot had not noticed any appreciable drift.* ■ a steady movement or development from one thing toward another, esp. one that is perceived as unwelcome: *the drift toward a more repressive style of policing.* ■ a state of inaction or indecision: *after so much drift, any expression of enthusiasm is welcome.* **2** [in *sing.*] the general intention or meaning of an argument or someone's remarks: *he didn't understand much Greek, but he **got her drift**.* **3** a large mass of snow, leaves, or other material piled up or carried along by the wind. ■ *Geology* glacial and fluvioglacial deposits left by retreating ice sheets. ■ a large mass of flowering plants growing together: *a drift of daffodils.* **4** *Mining* a horizontal or inclined passage following a mineral vein or coal seam. ▷Middle English (in the sense 'mass of snow, leaves, etc.'): originally from Old Norse *drift* 'snowdrift, something driven'; in later use from Middle Dutch *drift* 'course, current'; related to **DRIVE**. —**drift·y** *adj.*

drift·er /ˈdriftər/ ▶*n.* **1** a person who is continually moving from place to place, without any fixed home or job. **2** a fishing boat equipped with a drift net.

drift·fish /ˈdrift,fisʜ/ ▶*n.* (*pl.* same or **-fish·es**) a slender-bodied bottom-dwelling fish found in the deeper waters of warm seas. • Family Nomeidae (or Stromateidae): several genera, in particular *Ariomma*.
▶*v.* (also **drift-fish**) [*intrans.*] fish with a drift net: [as *n.*] (**driftfishing**) *open-water driftfishing.*

drift ice ▶*n.* detached pieces of ice drifting with the wind or ocean currents.

drift net (also **drift·net**) ▶*n.* a large net for herring and similar fish, kept upright by weights at the bottom and floats at the top and allowed to drift with the tide. —**drift net·ter** *n.* —**drift net·ting** *n.*

drift pin ▶*n.* a steel pin driven into a hole in a piece of metal to enlarge, shape, or align the hole.

drift·wood /ˈdrift,wo͝od/ ▶*n.* pieces of wood that are floating on the sea or have been washed ashore.

drill¹ /dril/ ▶*n.* **1** a hand tool, power tool, or machine with a rotating cutting tip or reciprocating hammer or chisel, used for making holes. ■ such a tool used by a dentist for cutting away part of a tooth before filling it. **2** instruction or training in military exercises: *parade-ground drill.* ■ intensive instruction or training in something, typically by means of repeated exercises: *tables can be mastered by drill and practice* | *language-learning drills.* ■ a rehearsal of the procedure to be followed in an emergency: *air-raid drills.* ■ (**the drill**) *informal* the correct or recognized procedure or way of doing something: *he didn't know the drill.* **3** a predatory mollusk that bores into the shells of other mollusks in order to feed on the soft tissue. • Family Muricidae, class Gastropoda: several genera and species, in particular the American **oyster drill** (*Urosalpinx cinerea*), which is a serious pest of oyster beds.

drill 1

▶*v.* [*trans.*] **1** produce (a hole) in something by or as if by boring with a drill: *drill holes through the tiles for the masonry pins.* ■ make a hole in (something) by boring with a drill: *a power tool for drilling wood.* ■ [*intrans.*] make a hole in or through something by using a drill: *do not attempt to drill through a joist* | *figurative his eyes drilled into her.* ■ [*intrans.*] sink a borehole in order to obtain a certain substance, typically oil or water: *they are licensed to **drill for** oil in the area* | [as *n.*] (**drilling**) *drilling should begin next year.* ■ (of a dentist) cut away part of (a tooth) before filling it. ■ [*trans.*] *informal* (of a sports player) hit, throw, or kick (a ball or puck) hard and in a straight line: *Rose drilled a ball deep to right center.* **2** subject (someone) to military training exercises: *a sergeant was drilling new recruits.* ■ [*intrans.*] (of a person) take part in such exercises: *the troops were drilling.* ■ instruct (someone) in something by the means of repeated exercises or practice: *I reacted instinctively because I had been drilled to do just that.* ■ (**drill something into**) cause (someone) to learn something by repeating it regularly: *his mother had drilled into him the need to pay for one's sins.* **3** (**drill down**) *Computing* access data that is in a lower level of a hierarchically structured database. ▷early 17th cent.: from Middle Dutch *drillen* 'bore, turn in a circle.' —**drill·er** *n.*

drill² ▶*n.* a machine that makes small furrows, sows seed in them, and then covers the sown seed. ■ a small furrow, esp. one made by such a machine. ■ a ridge with such a furrow on top. ■ a row of plants sown in such a furrow: *drills of lettuces.*
▶*v.* [*trans.*] (of a person or machine) sow (seed) with a drill: *crops drilled in autumn.* ■ plant (the ground) in furrows: [as *n.*] (**drilling**) *accurate ridging and drilling make hoeing much easier.* ▷early 18th cent. (as a noun in the sense 'small furrow'): perhaps from **DRILL**¹.

drill³ ▶*n.* a dark brown baboon with a short tail and a naked blue or purple rump, found in the rain forests of West Africa. Compare with **MANDRILL**. • *Mandrillus leucophaeus*, family Cercopithecidae. ▷mid 17th cent.: probably a local word. Compare with **MANDRILL**.

drill⁴ ▶*n.* a coarse twilled cotton or linen fabric. ▷early 18th cent.: abbreviation of earlier *drilling*, from German *Drillich*, from Latin *trilix* 'triple-twilled,' from *tri-* 'three' + *licium* 'thread.'

drill·ing rig ▶*n.* a large structure with equipment for drilling an oil well.

drill·mas·ter /ˈdril,mastər/ ▶*n.* one who instructs or leads others, esp. recruits, in military drills and marching. ■ a rigorous, exacting, or severe instructor; a martinet.

drill press ▶*n.* a machine tool for drilling holes, set on a fixed stand.

drill ser·geant ▶*n.* a noncommissioned officer who trains soldiers in basic military skills.

drill stem ▶*n.* a rotating rod or cylinder used in drilling.

drill·stock /ˈdril,stäk/ ▶*n.* the part of a drilling tool or machine that holds the bit.

dri·ly ▶*adv.* variant spelling of **DRYLY**.

Dri·na Riv·er /ˈdrēnə/ a river that flows for 285 miles (459 km), partly along the border between Bosnia–Herzegovina and Serbia, into the Sava River west of Belgrade in Serbia.

drink /driNGk/ ▶*v.* (*past* **drank** /draNGk/; *past part.* **drunk** /drəNGk/) [*trans.*] take (a liquid) into the mouth and swallow: *we sat by the fire, drinking our coffee* | [*intrans.*] *he drank thirstily.* ■ [*intrans.*] consume or be in the habit of consuming alcohol, esp. to excess: *she doesn't drink or smoke* | *he **drank himself into** a stupor* | [as *n.*] (**drinking**) *Les was ordered to cut down his drinking.* ■ [*intrans.*] (**drink up**) consume the rest of a drink, esp. in a rapid manner. ■ (**drink something in**) *figurative* watch or listen to something with eager pleasure or interest: *she strolled to the window to drink in the view.* ■ *informal* (of a plant or a porous substance) absorb (moisture). ■ [*intrans.*] (of wine) have a specified flavor or character when drunk: *this wine is really drinking beautifully.*
▶*n.* a liquid that can be swallowed as refreshment or nourishment: *cans of soda and other drinks* | *a table covered with food and drink.* ■ a quantity of liquid swallowed: *he had a drink of water.* ■ alcohol, or the habitual or excessive consumption of alcohol: *the effects of too much drink* | *they both **took to drink**.* ■ a glass of liquid, esp. when alcoholic: *we went for a drink.* ■ (**the drink**) *informal* the sea or another large area of water. ▷Old English *drincan* (verb), *drinc* (noun), of Germanic origin; related to Dutch *drinken* and German *trinken*. —**drink·a·ble** *adj.*
▶*PHRASES* □ **drink and drive** drive a vehicle while under the influence of alcohol. □ **drink deep** take a large draft or drafts of something: *figurative he learned to **drink deep of** the Catholic tradition.* □ **drink someone's health** express one's good wishes for someone by raising one's glass and drinking a small amount. □ **drink (a toast) to** celebrate or wish for the good fortune of someone or something by raising one's glass and drinking a small amount. □ **drink someone under the table** *informal* consume as much alcohol as one's drinking companion without becoming as drunk. □ **I'll drink to that** uttered to express one's agreement with or approval of a statement.

drink-driv·ing ▶*n.* British term for **DRUNK DRIVING**. —**drink-driv·er** *n.*

drink·er /ˈdriNGkər/ ▶*n.* a person who drinks a particular drink: *coffee drinkers.* ■ a person who drinks alcohol, esp. to excess: *a heavy drinker.*

drink·ing foun·tain ▶*n.* a device producing a small jet of water for drinking.

drink·ing song ▶*n.* a hearty song, typically concerning drink and having bawdy lyrics, which is sung while drinking alcohol.

drip /drip/ ▶*v.* (**dripped, drip·ping**) [*intrans.*] let fall or be so wet as to shed small drops of liquid: *the faucet won't stop dripping* | *his hands were **dripping with** blood.* ■ [with *adverbial*] (of liquid) fall in small drops: *water dripped from her clothing.* ■ [*trans.*] cause or allow (a liquid) to fall in such a way: *the candle was dripping wax down one side.* ■ *figurative* display a copious amount or degree of a particular quality or thing: *the women were **dripping with** gold and diamonds* | [*trans.*] *her voice dripped sarcasm.*
▶*n.* **1** a small drop of a liquid: *she put the bucket on top of the dresser to catch the drips.* ■ [in *sing.*] the action or sound of liquid falling steadily in small drops: *the drip, drip, drip of the leak in the roof.* ■ short for **DRIP FEED**. **2** *informal* a weak and ineffectual person. **3** *Architecture* a projection or groove on the underside of a cornice, windowsill, or molding that prevents rain from running down the wall below. Compare with **DRIPSTONE**. ▷Old English *dryppan*, *drȳpen*, of Germanic origin; related to Danish *dryppe*, also to **DROP**.

drip-dry ▶*adj.* (of a fabric or garment) capable of drying without creasing when hung up after washing: *drip-dry shirts.*
▶*v.* [*intrans.*] (of fabric or a garment) become dry without forming creases when hung up after washing. ■ [*trans.*] dry (fabric or a garment) by hanging it up in this way: *it's easy to wash and simple to drip-dry.*

drip feed ▸*n.* a device for introducing fluid drop by drop into a system, e.g., lubricating oil into an engine. ■ *Medicine* a device that passes fluid, nutrients, or drugs drop by drop into a patient's body on a continuous basis, usually intravenously: *he had been **on a drip feed** for several days.*
▸*v.* (**drip-feed**) [*trans.*] introduce (fluid) drop by drop: *the oiler drip-feeds oil on to all drive chains.* ■ supply (a patient) with fluid, nutrients, or drugs through a drip feed.

drip·less /ˈdrip,ləs/ ▸*adj.* designed to prevent dripping: *dripless valve.*

drip·ping /ˈdripiNG/ ▸*n.* (**drippings**) fat that has melted and dripped from roasting meat, used in cooking. ■ wax, fat, or other liquid produced from something by the effect of heat.
▸*adj.* extremely wet: [as *submodifier*] ***dripping wet** hair.*

drip·py /ˈdripē/ ▸*adj.* (**drip·pi·er, drip·pi·est**) **1** *informal* weak, ineffectual, or sloppily sentimental: *a drippy love song.* **2** tending to drip: *drippy food.* —**drip·pi·ly** /ˈdripilē/ *adv.* —**drip·pi·ness** *n.*

drip·stone /ˈdrip,stōn/ ▸*n.* **1** *Architecture* a molding over a door or window that deflects rain and enhances the opening, typically in medieval architecture. **2** *Geology* rock deposited by precipitation from dripping water, such as that which forms stalactites and stalagmites.

D

drive /drīv/ ▸*v.* (*past* **drove** /drōv/; *past part.* **driv·en** /ˈdrivən/) **1** [*intrans.*] operate and control the direction and speed of a motor vehicle: *he got into his car and drove off | they drove back into town.* ■ [*trans.*] own or use (a specified type of motor vehicle): *Sue drives an old Chevy.* ■ [*intrans.*] be licensed or competent to drive a motor vehicle: *I take it you can drive?* ■ [*trans.*] convey (someone) in a vehicle, esp. a private car: *Shelley drove him to the supermarket.* **2** [*trans.*] propel or carry along by force in a specified direction: *the wind will drive you onshore.* ■ [*intrans.*] (of wind, water, or snow) move or fall with great force: *the snow **drove against** him.* ■ [*trans.*] (of a source of power) provide the energy to set and keep (an engine or piece of machinery) in motion: *turbines driven by steam.* ■ *Electronics* (of a device) power or operate (another device): *the interface can be used to drive a printer.* ■ [*trans.*] force (a stake or nail) into place by hitting or pushing it: *nails are driven through the boards.* ■ [*trans.*] bore (a tunnel). ■ (in ball games) hit or kick (the ball) hard with a free swing of the bat, racket, or foot. ■ [*trans.*] *Golf* strike (a ball) from the tee, typically with a driver. **3** [*trans.*] urge or force (animals or people) to move in a specified direction: *they drove a flock of sheep through the center of the city.* ■ [*trans.*] urge forward and direct the course of (an animal drawing a vehicle or plow). ■ [*trans.*] chase or frighten (wild animals) into nets, traps, or into a small area where they can be killed or captured: *they were up on the hill before dawn, ready to drive the deer.* ■ compel to leave: *troops drove out the demonstrators | he wanted to drive me away.* **4** [*trans.*] (usu. **be driven**) (of a fact or feeling) compel (someone) to act in a particular way, esp. one that is considered undesirable or inappropriate: *he was driven by ambition* | [*trans.*] *some people are driven to murder their tormentors* | [as *adj.*] (**driven**) *my husband is a driven man.* ■ [*trans.*] bring (someone) forcibly into a specified negative state: *the thought **drove** him **to** despair* | [*trans.*] *my laziness drives my wife crazy.* ■ [*trans.*] force (someone) to work to an excessive extent: *you're **driving yourself** too hard.*
▸*n.* **1** a trip or journey in a car: *they **went for a drive** in the country.* ■ [in *names*] a street or road: *Hammond Drive.* ■ short for DRIVEWAY. **2** *Psychology* an innate, biologically determined urge to attain a goal or satisfy a need: *her emotional and sexual drives.* ■ the determination and ambition of a person to achieve something: *her drive has sustained her through some shattering personal experiences.* **3** an organized effort by a number of people to achieve a particular purpose, often to raise money: *we're planning a massive membership drive.* ■ *Football* a series of offensive plays that advance the ball for the purpose of a score: *an 80-yard scoring drive.* **4** the transmission of power to machinery or to the wheels of a motor vehicle. ■ (in a car with automatic transmission) the position of the gear selector in which the car will move forward, changing gears automatically as required: *he threw the car into drive.* ■ *Computing* short for DISK DRIVE. **5** (in ball games) a forceful stroke made with a free swing of the bat, racket, or foot against the ball. ■ *Golf* a shot from the tee. **6** an act of driving a group of animals to a particular destination. ▷Old English *drīfan* 'urge (a person or animal) to go forward,' of Germanic origin; related to Dutch *drijven* and German *treiben.* —**driv·a·bil·i·ty** /,drīvəˈbilitē/ (also **drive·a·bil·i·ty**) *n.* —**driv·a·ble** (also **drive·a·ble**) *adj.*
▸*PHRASES* □ **drive something home** see HOME. □ **what someone is driving at** the point that someone is attempting to make: *I don't understand what you're driving at.*

drive bay ▸*n.* *Computing* a space inside a computer in which a floppy disk, hard disk, or disk drive can be accommodated.

drive belt ▸*n.* a belt that transmits drive from a motor, engine, or line shaft to a moving part or machine tool.

drive-by ▸*adj.* [*attrib.*] (of a shooting or other act) carried out from a passing vehicle: *a drive-by shooting.* ■ *informal* superficial or casual: *they practice drive-by journalism rather than trying to elevate the level of discussion.* ■ *informal* (of a medical procedure in a hospital or clinic) involving a brief duration of on-site care for the patient: *she had been shaken by tales of drive-by mastectomies.* ■ *informal* denoting a facility that performs such procedures as a customary practice: *the respondents recommend drive-by clinics.*
▸*n.* a shooting carried out from a passing vehicle.

drive-by-wire ▸*n.* [usu. as *adj.*] a semiautomatic and normally computer-regulated system for controlling the engine, handling, suspension, and other functions of a motor vehicle.

drive chain ▸*n.* an endless chain with links that engage with toothed wheels in order to transmit power from one shaft to another in an engine or machine tool.

drive-in ▸*adj.* [*attrib.*] denoting a facility such as a restaurant that one can visit without leaving one's car: *it looked like the screen from an old drive-in theater.*
▸*n.* a facility of this type.

driv·el /ˈdrivəl/ ▸*n.* silly nonsense: *don't talk such drivel!* See note at NONSENSE.
▸*v.* (**driv·eled, driv·el·ing**; *Brit.* **driv·elled, driv·el·ling**) [*intrans.*] **1** talk nonsense: *he was **driveling on** about the glory days.* **2** *archaic* let saliva or mucus flow from the mouth or nose; dribble. ▷Old English *dreflian* (sense 2), of uncertain origin; perhaps related to DRAFF. —**driv·el·er** (*Brit.* **driv·el·ler**) *n.*

drive·line /ˈdrīv,līn/ ▸*n.* another term for DRIVETRAIN.

driv·en /ˈdrivən/ ▸ past participle of DRIVE.
▸*adj.* **1** [in *combination*] operated, moved, or controlled by a specified person or source of power: *a chauffeur-driven limousine | wind-driven sand.* ■ motivated or determined by a specified factor or feeling: *a market-driven response to customer needs.* **2** (of snow) piled into drifts or made smooth by the wind: *figurative she was as pure as the driven snow.*

driv·er /ˈdrīvər/ ▸*n.* **1** a person who drives a vehicle: *a taxi driver | student drivers.* ■ a person who drives a specified kind of animal: *mule drivers.* **2** a wheel or other part in a mechanism that receives power directly and transmits motion to other parts. ■ *Electronics* a device or part of a circuit that provides power for output. ■ *Computing* a program that controls the operation of a device such as a printer or scanner. **3** a golf club with a flat face and wooden head, used for driving from the tee. —**driv·er·less** *adj.*
▸*PHRASE* □ **in the driver's seat** in control of or dominating a situation: *the tax issue is back in the driver's seat of American politics.*

driv·er ant ▸*n.* another term for ARMY ANT.

driv·er's li·cense ▸*n.* a document permitting a person to drive a motor vehicle.

drive·shaft /ˈdrīv,SHaft/ ▸*n.* a rotating shaft that transmits torque in an engine.

drive sys·tem ▸*n.* the part of an engine, computer, or mechanical device that brings about its dynamic movement.

drive-through (also *informal* **drive-thru**) ▸*adj.* [*attrib.*] denoting a facility through or to which one can drive, esp. to be served without leaving one's car: *a drive-through car wash | drive-through restaurants | the drive-thru window.*
▸*n.* a place or facility of this type.

drive time ▸*n.* (esp. in broadcasting) the parts of the day when many people commute by car: [as *adj.*] *drive-time radio.*

drive·train /ˈdrīv,trān/ ▸*n.* the system in a motor vehicle that connects the transmission to the drive axles.

drive-up ▸*adj.* & *n.* another term for DRIVE-THROUGH.

drive·way /ˈdrīv,wā/ ▸*n.* a short road leading from a public road to a house or garage.

driv·ing /ˈdrīviNG/ ▸*adj.* [*attrib.*] (of rain or snow) falling and being blown by the wind with great force: *driving rain.* ■ having a strong and controlling influence: *Macmillan was the **driving force** behind the plan | a driving ambition.* ■ energetic; dynamic: *driving dance rhythms.*
▸*n.* the control and operation of a motor vehicle: *he was convicted of reckless driving* | [as *adj.*] *a driving course.*

driv·ing li·cence ▸*n.* British term for DRIVER'S LICENSE.

driv·ing range ▸*n.* an area where golfers can practice drives.

driv·ing wheel ▸*n.* **1** any of the large wheels of a locomotive, to which power is applied either directly or via coupling rods. **2** a wheel transmitting motive power in machinery.

driz·zle /ˈdrizəl/ ▸*n.* light rain falling in very fine drops: *Boston will be cloudy with patchy drizzle* | [in *sing.*] *a steady drizzle has been falling since 3 a.m.* ■ [in *sing.*] *Cooking* a thin stream of a liquid ingredient trickled over something.
▸*v.* [*intrans.*] (**it drizzles, it is drizzling**, etc.) rain lightly: *it's started to drizzle* | [as *adj.*] (**drizzling**) *the drizzling rain.* ■ [*trans.*] *Cooking* cause a thin stream of (a liquid ingredient) to trickle over food: *drizzle the clarified butter over the top.* ■ [*trans.*] cause a liquid ingredient to trickle over (food) in this way: *raspberries drizzled with melted chocolate.* ▷mid 16th cent.: probably based on Old English *drēosan* 'to fall,' of Germanic origin; probably related to DREARY. —**driz·zly** /-z(ə)lē/ *adj.*

drogue /drōg/ ▸*n.* a device, typically conical or funnel-shaped with open ends, towed behind a boat, aircraft, or other moving object to reduce speed or improve stability. ■ a similar object used as an aerial target for gunnery practice or as a windsock. ■ (in tanker aircraft) a funnel-shaped part on the end of the hose into which a probe is inserted by an aircraft being refueled in flight. ■ short for DROGUE PARACHUTE. ▷early 18th cent. (originally a whaling term denoting a piece of stout board attached to a harpoon line, used to slow down or mark the position of a harpooned whale): perhaps related to DRAG.

drogue par·a·chute ▸*n.* a small parachute used as a brake or to pull out a larger parachute or other object from an aircraft in flight or a fast-moving vehicle.

droid /droid/ ▸*n.* (in science fiction) a robot. ■ *figurative* a person regarded as lifeless or mechanical: *she will probably leave you for a sales droid.* ■ *Computing* a program that automatically collects information from remote systems. ▷1970s: shortening of ANDROID.

droit /droit/ ▸*n.* *historical Law* a right or due. ▷late Middle English: from Old French, based on Latin *directus* 'straight, right, direct.'

droit de sei·gneur /,drwä də sānˈyər/ ▸*n.* the alleged right of a medieval feudal lord to have sexual intercourse with a vassal's bride on her wedding night. ▷French, literally 'lord's right.'

droll /drōl/ ▸*adj.* curious or unusual in a way that provokes dry amusement: *his unique brand of droll self-mockery.*
▸*n.* *archaic* a jester or entertainer; a buffoon. ▷early 17th cent. (as an adjective): from French *drôle*, perhaps from Middle Dutch *drolle* 'imp, goblin.' —**droll·er·y** /ˈdrōlərē/ *n.* —**droll·ness** *n.* —**drol·ly** *adv.*

dro·mae·o·sau·rid /,drōmēəˈsôrid/ (also **dro·mae·o·saur** /ˈdrōmēə,sôr/) ▸*n.* a carnivorous bipedal dinosaur of a late Cretaceous family that included deinonychus and the velociraptors. They had a large slashing claw on each hind foot. • Family Dromaeosauridae, suborder Theropoda, order Saurischia. ▷1970s: from modern Latin *Dromaeosauridae*, based on Greek *dromaios* 'swift-running' + *sauros* 'lizard.'

-drome ▸*comb. form* **1** denoting a place for running or racing: *velodrome.* **2** denoting something that runs or proceeds in a certain way: *palindrome.* ▷from Greek *dromos* 'course, running' .

drom·e·dar·y /ˈdrämə,derē/ ▸*n.* (*pl.* **-dar·ies**) an Arabian camel, esp. one of a light and swift breed trained for riding or racing. ▷Middle English: from Old French *dromedaire* or late Latin *dromedarius (camelus)* 'swift camel,' based on Greek *dromas, dromad-* 'runner.'

drone /drōn/ ▸*v.* [*intrans.*] make a continuous low humming sound: *in the far distance a machine droned.* ■ speak tediously in a dull monotonous tone: *he reached for another beer while Jim **droned on**.* ■ [with *adverbial of direction*] move with a continuous humming sound: *traffic droned up and down the street.*
▸*n.* **1** a low continuous humming sound: *he nodded off to the drone of the car engine.* ■ *informal* a monotonous

speech: *only twenty minutes of the hour-long drone had passed.* ■ a continuous musical note, typically of low pitch. ■ a musical instrument, or part of one, sounding such a continuous note, in particular (also **drone pipe**) a pipe in a bagpipe or (also **drone string**) a string in an instrument such as a hurdy-gurdy or a sitar. **2** a male bee in a colony of social bees, which does no work but can fertilize a queen. ■ *figurative* a person who does no useful work and lives off others. **3** a remote-controlled pilotless aircraft or missile. ▷Old English *drān*, *drǣn* 'male bee,' from a West Germanic verb meaning 'resound, boom'; related to Dutch *dreunen* 'to drone,' German *dröhnen* 'to roar,' and Swedish *dröna* 'to drowse.'

drone fly ▸*n.* a hoverfly that resembles a honeybee. Its larva is the rat-tailed maggot. • *Eristalis tenax*, family Syrphidae.

droog /dro͞og/ ▸*n. informal* a young man belonging to a street gang. ▷1962: coined by Anthony Burgess in *Clockwork Orange*; alteration of Russian *drug* 'friend.'

drool /dro͞ol/ ▸*v.* [*intrans.*] drop saliva uncontrollably from the mouth: *the baby begins to drool, then to cough.* ■ *informal* make an excessive and obvious show of pleasure or desire: *I could imagine him as a teacher being* ***drooled over*** *by the girls.*
▸*n.* saliva falling from the mouth. ▷early 19th cent.: contraction of DRIVEL.

droop /dro͞op/ ▸*v.* [*intrans.*] bend or hang downward limply: *a long black cloak drooped from his shoulders.* ■ sag down from or as if from weariness or dejection: *his eyelids drooped and he became drowsy* | *figurative the scenes are so lengthy that the reader's spirits droop.* ■ [*trans.*] cause to bend or hang downward: *James hid his face in his hands and drooped his head.*
▸*n.* [in *sing.*] an act or instance of drooping; a limp or weary attitude: *the exhausted droop of her shoulders.* ▷Middle English: from Old Norse *drúpa* 'hang the head'; related to DRIP and DROP.

droop-snoot ▸*n. informal* a downward-sloping nose of an aircraft or motor vehicle, esp. one that is of variable pitch, giving an efficient aerodynamic profile. —**droop-snoot·ed** *adj.*

droop·y /ˈdro͞opē/ ▸*adj.* (**droop·i·er**, **droop·i·est**) hanging down limply; drooping: *a droopy mustache.* ■ lacking strength or spirit: *the girls looked rather droopy* | *figurative a period of droopy sales.* —**droop·i·ly** /-pəlē/ *adv.* —**droop·i·ness** *n.*

drop /dräp/ ▸*v.* (**dropped**, **drop·ping**) [*trans.*] **1** let or make (something) fall vertically: *the fire was caused by someone dropping a lighted cigarette* | *they dropped bombs on London during the raid.* ■ deliver (supplies or troops) by parachute: *the airlift dropped food into the camp.* ■ *Rugby* score (a goal) by a drop kick. ■ (of an animal, esp. a mare, cow, or ewe) give birth to (young). ■ *informal* take (a drug, esp. LSD) orally: *he dropped a lot of acid in the Sixties.* **2** [*intrans.*] fall vertically: *the spoon dropped with a clatter from her hand.* ■ (of a person) allow oneself to fall; let oneself down without jumping: *they escaped by climbing out of the window and dropping to the ground.* ■ (of a person or animal) sink to or toward the ground: *he dropped to his knees in the mud.* ■ *informal* collapse or die from exhaustion: *he looked* ***ready to drop.*** ■ (of ground) slope steeply down: *the cliff drops ninety yards to the valley below.* **3** make or become lower, weaker, or less: [*trans.*] *he dropped his voice as she came into the room* | [*intrans.*] *pretax profits dropped by 37 percent* | *tourism has* ***dropped off*** *in the last few years.* **4** abandon or discontinue (a course of action or study): *the charges against him were dropped last year* | *drop everything and get over here!* ■ discard or exclude (someone or something): *they were dropped from the team in the reshuffle.* ■ *informal* stop associating with: *I was under pressure from family and friends to drop Barbara.* ■ omit (a letter or syllable) in speech: *our English au pair drops her h's.* **5** set down or unload (a passenger or goods), esp. on the way to somewhere else: *he* ***dropped*** *the load* ***off*** *at a dealer's* | *his mom dropped him outside and drove off to work.* ■ [*trans.*] put or leave in a particular place without ceremony or formality: *just drop it in the mail when you've got time.* ■ mention in passing, typically in order to impress: *she dropped a remark about having been included in the selection.* **6** (in sports) fail to win (a point, game, or match). ■ *informal* lose (money), esp. through gambling: *they drifted into a roulette parlor and dropped about fifteen dollars.* **7** *Bridge* be forced to play (a relatively high card) as a loser under an opponent's higher card, because it is the only card in its suit held in the hand. ■ force (an opponent's high card) to be played as a loser in this way: *declarer dropped West's queen on the second round of spades.* ■ [*intrans.*] (of a card) be played in this way: *the queen dropped.*
▸*phrasal v.* □ **drop back/behind** fall back or get left behind: *the colt was struggling to stay with the pace and started to drop back.* □ **drop by/in** call informally and briefly as a visitor: *they would unexpectedly* ***drop in on*** *us.* □ **drop into 1** call casually and informally at (a place): *he'd actually considered dropping into one of the pickup bars.* **2** pass quickly and easily into (a habitual state or manner): *she couldn't help dropping into a Brooklyn accent.* □ **drop off** fall asleep easily, esp. without intending to: *struggle as she might, she kept dropping off.* □ **drop out 1** cease to participate in a race or competition. **2** abandon a course of study: *kids who had* ***dropped out of*** *college.* **3** reject conventional society to pursue an alternative lifestyle: *a child of the sixties who had temporarily dropped out.* **4** *Rugby* restart play with a drop kick. ■ score a drop goal.
▸*n.* **1** a small round or pear-shaped portion of liquid that hangs or falls or adheres to a surface: *the first* ***drops of*** *rain splashed on the ground.* ■ [often with *negative*] a very small amount of liquid: *there was not a drop of water in sight.* ■ [usu. with *negative*] a drink of alcoholic liquor: *he doesn't touch a drop during the week.* ■ (**drops**) liquid medicine to be measured or applied in very small amounts: *eye drops.* **2** [usu. in *sing.*] an instance of falling or dropping: *they left within five minutes of the drop of the curtain.* ■ an act of dropping supplies or troops by parachute: *the planes finally managed to make the drop.* ■ a fall in amount, quality, or rate: *a significant* ***drop in*** *consumer spending.* ■ an abrupt fall or slope: *standing on the lip of a sixty-foot drop.* ■ (**the drop**) *Bridge* the playing of a high card underneath an opponent's higher card, because it is the only card in its suit held in the hand. **3** something that drops or is dropped, in particular: ■ a section of theatrical scenery lowered from the flies; a drop cloth or drop curtain. ■ a trapdoor on a gallows, the opening of which causes the prisoner to fall and thus be hanged. ■ (**the drop**) execution by hanging. **4** something resembling a drop of liquid in shape, in particular: ■ [usu. with *adj.*] a piece of candy or a lozenge: *a lemon drop.* ■ a pendant earring. **5** *informal* a delivery: *I got to the depot and made the drop.* ■ a mailbox. ■ a hiding place for stolen, illicit, or secret things: *the lavatory's toilet tank could be used as a letter drop.* ▷Old English *dropa* (noun), *droppian* (verb), of Germanic origin; related to German *Tropfen* 'a drop,' *tropfen* 'to drip,' also to DRIP and DROOP. —**drop·pa·ble** *adj.*
▸*PHRASES* □ **at the drop of a hat** *informal* without delay or good reason: *he used to be very bashful, blushing at the drop of a hat.* □ **drop the ball** *informal* make a mistake; mishandle things: *I really dropped the ball on this one.* [with allusion to mishandling in baseball.] □ **drop dead** die suddenly and unexpectedly: *she had seen her father drop dead of a heart attack.* ■ [in *imperative*] *informal* used as an expression of intense scorn or dislike. □ **drop a** (or **the**) **dime on** *informal* inform on (someone) to the police. □ **drop like flies** see FLY[2]. □ **drop one's guard** abandon one's habitual defensive or protective stance. □ **drop a hint** (or **drop hints**) let fall a hint or hints, as if casually or unconsciously: *he was dropping hints that in the future he would be taking a back seat in politics.* □ **a drop in the bucket** (or *Brit.* **ocean**) a very small amount compared with what is needed or expected: *the $550 million is likely to be a drop in the bucket.* □ **drop someone a line** send someone a note or letter in a casual manner: *drop me a line at the usual address.* □ **drop names** see NAME-DROPPING. □ **drop one's serve** (in tennis) lose a game in which one is serving. □ **drop a stitch** let a stitch fall off the end of a knitting needle. □ **drop one's trousers** deliberately let one's trousers fall down, esp. in a public place. □ **have the drop on** *informal* have the advantage over: *if your enemy gets the drop on you he can kill you.* □ **a drop too much** *informal* enough alcohol to make one drunk: *you drive, because he has taken a drop too much.*

drop box ▸*n.* **1** (in weaving) a box situated on either side of the race plate of the loom that is designed to hold shuttles and to bring bobbins of colored thread in line as desired. **2** a secured receptacle into which items such as returned books or videotapes, payments, keys, or donated clothing can be deposited.

drop cloth ▸*n.* a large sheet for covering furniture or flooring to protect it from dust or while decorating.

drop cur·tain ▸*n.* a curtain or painted cloth lowered vertically on to a theater stage.

drop-dead ▸*adj. informal* used to emphasize how attractive someone or something is: *her drop-dead good looks* | [as *submodifier*] *a* ***drop-dead gorgeous*** *Hollywood icon.*

drop-down ▸*adj.* [*attrib.*] dropping down or unfolding when required: *an RV with two drop-down beds.* ■ *Computing* (of a menu) appearing below a menu title when it is selected, and remaining until used or dismissed. Compare with PULL-DOWN.

drop-forged ▸*adj.* (of a metal object) made by forcing hot metal into or through a die with a drop hammer. —**drop-forg·ing** *n.*

drop goal ▸*n. Rugby* a goal scored in open play by drop-kicking the ball over the crossbar, scoring three points (rugby union) or one point (rugby league).

drop ham·mer ▸*n.* a large heavy weight raised mechanically and allowed to drop, as used in drop-forging and pile-driving.

drop han·dle·bars ▸*plural n.* bicycle handlebars of which the handles are bent below the rest of the bar, used esp. on racing cycles.

drop-in ▸*adj.* **1** visited on an informal basis without booking or appointments: *a drop-in disco.* **2** (of an object such as a chair seat) designed to drop into position.

drop-in cen·ter ▸*n.* a place run by a welfare agency or charity where people may call casually for advice or assistance.

drop kick ▸*n.* (formerly, in football) a kick for a goal made by dropping the ball and kicking after it touches the ground. ■ (chiefly in martial arts) a flying kick made against an opponent while dropping to the ground.
▸*v.* (**drop-kick**) [*trans.*] kick using a drop kick.

drop leaf ▸*n.* a hinged table leaf: *both drop leaves are badly scratched* | [as *adj.*] *a mahogany drop-leaf table.*

drop·let /ˈdräplit/ ▸*n.* a very small drop of a liquid: *droplets of water.*

drop·light ▸*n.* a light that is suspended from a reel so that it can be raised or lowered, typically over a work area.

drop-off ▸*n.* **1** a decline or decrease: *a sudden* ***drop-off in*** *tourism.* **2** a sheer downward slope; a cliff: *dizzy drop-offs on either side.*
▸*adj.* [*attrib.*] relating to or allowing the delivery or depositing of something: *the mailbags are left at drop-off points.*

drop·out /ˈdräpˌout/ ▸*n.* **1** a person who has abandoned a course of study or who has rejected conventional society to pursue an alternative lifestyle: *a college dropout.* **2** a momentary loss of recorded audio signal or an error in reading data on a magnetic tape or disk, usually due to a flaw in the coating. **3** (usu. **dropouts**) a U-shaped slot at the end of a fork on a bicycle, made to receive the axle and enabling the wheel to be changed rapidly.

drop·per /ˈdräpər/ ▸*n.* **1** a short glass tube with a rubber bulb at one end and a tiny hole at the other, for measuring out drops of medicine or other liquids. **2** (in full **dropper line**) *Fishing* a subsidiary line or loop of filament attached to a main line or leader. ▷mid 17th cent. (in the sense 'a person who lets something drop'); sense 1 is first recorded in the late 19th cent.

drop·pings /ˈdräpiNGz/ ▸*plural n.* the excrement of certain animals, such as rodents, sheep, birds, and insects.

drop scene ▸*n.* a drop curtain used as part of stage scenery, esp. one in front of which a scene is played while the setting is changed behind. ■ the last scene of a play.

drop scone ▸*n.* a small thick pancake made by dropping spoonfuls of batter onto a frying pan or other heated surface.

drop·seed /ˈdräpˌsēd/ ▸*n.* a grass that readily drops its seeds. • Genus *Sporobolus*, family Gramineae: several species, including the widespread North American **sand dropseed** (*S. cryptandrus*), which has a high yield of edible grain.

drop-ship /ˈdräp ˌSHip/ ▸*v.* (**-shipped**, **-ship·ping**) [*trans.*] move (goods) from the manufacturer directly to the retailer without going through the usual distribution channels: *the shopping network has begun drop-shipping orders taken by telephone or over the Internet.* —**drop ship·ment** *n.*

drop ship·ment ▸*n. Commerce* a shipment sent directly by a manufacturer to a customer, but billed through a wholesaler or distributor. —**drop-ship** *v.*

drop shot ▸*n.* (chiefly in tennis or squash) a softly hit shot, usually with backspin, which drops abruptly to the ground.

drop shoul·der (also **dropped shoul·der**) ▸*n.* a style of shoulder on a garment cut so that the seam is positioned on the upper arm rather than the shoulder.

drop·si·cal /ˈdräpsikəl/ ▸*adj.* affected with or characteristic of dropsy; edematous. ▷late 17th cent.: from DROPSY, replacing earlier *hydropic(al)*, via Latin from Greek *hudrōps* 'dropsy.'

drop·side /ˈdräpˌsīd/ ▸*adj.* [*attrib.*] (of a crib or a hospital bed) having a side that drops down to open.
▸*n.* a side that drops down in this way.

drop-stitch ▸*adj.* denoting an openwork pattern in knitted garments made by dropping a made stitch at intervals: *a drop-stitch cardigan.*

drop·sy /ˈdräpsē/ ▸*n.* (*pl.* **-sies**) old-fashioned or less technical term for EDEMA. [Middle English: shortening of *idropesie*, earlier form of obsolete *hydropsy*, via Old French and Latin from Greek *hudrōps* 'dropsy,' from *hudōr* 'water.']

drop tank ▸*n.* an external fuel tank on an aircraft that can be jettisoned when empty.

drop test ▸*n.* a test of the strength of an object, in which it is dropped under standard conditions or a set weight is dropped on it from a given height. **—drop-test·ing** *n.*

drop·top /ˈdräpˌtäp/ ▸*n.* a car having a fabric roof that can be folded down; a convertible.

drop waist (also **dropped waist**) ▸*n.* a style of waistline on a dress cut so that the seam is positioned at the hips rather than the waist.

drop zone ▸*n.* a designated area into which troops or supplies are dropped by parachute or in which skydivers land.

dros·er·a /ˈdräsərə/ ▸*n.* a sundew. • Genus *Drosera*, family Droseraceae. ▷modern Latin, from Greek *droseros* 'dewy' (from the appearance of the glistening hairs on the leaves).

drosh·ky /ˈdräshkē/ ▸*n.* (*pl.* **-kies**) *historical* a low four-wheeled open carriage of a kind formerly used in Russia. ▷early 19th cent.: from Russian *drozhki*, diminutive of *drogi* 'wagon,' from *droga* 'shaft, carriage pole.'

dro·soph·i·la /drəˈsäfələ/ ▸*n.* a small fruit fly, used extensively in genetic research because of its large chromosomes, numerous varieties, and rapid rate of reproduction. • Genus *Drosophila*, family Drosophilidae: in particular *D. melanogaster*. ▷modern Latin, from Greek *drosos* 'dew, moisture' + *philos* 'loving.'

dross /drôs; dräs/ ▸*n.* something regarded as worthless; rubbish: *there are bargains if you have the patience to sift through the dross.* ■ foreign matter, dregs, or mineral waste, in particular scum formed on the surface of molten metal. ▷Old English *drōs* (in the sense 'scum on molten metal'); related to Dutch *droesem* and German *Drusen* 'dregs, lees.' **—dross·y** *adj.*

drought /drout/ ▸*n.* a prolonged period of abnormally low rainfall; a shortage of water resulting from this. ■ [usu. with *adj.*] *figurative* a prolonged absence of something specified: *he ended a five-game hitting drought.* ■ *archaic* thirst. ▷late Old English *drūgath* 'dryness,' of Germanic origin; compare with Dutch *droogte*; related to DRY. **—drought·i·ness** *n.* **—drought·y** *adj.*

drouth /drouth/ ▸*n.* dialect or poetic form of DROUGHT. **—drouth·y** *adj.*

drove[1] /drōv/ ▸ past of DRIVE.

drove[2] ▸*n.* **1** a herd or flock of animals being driven in a body: *a drove of cattle.* ■ a large number of people or things doing or undergoing the same thing: *tourists have stayed away* **in droves** *this summer.* **2** a broad chisel for use by stonemasons. ▷Old English *drāf*, related to *drīfan* 'to drive.' **—dro·ver** *n.*

drown /droun/ ▸*v.* [*intrans.*] die through submersion in and inhalation of water: *she drowned in the pond* | (**be drowned**) *two fishermen were drowned when their motorboat capsized.* ■ [*trans.*] deliberately kill (a person or animal) in this way: *he killed his wife then drowned himself in a fit of despair.* ■ [*trans.*] submerge or flood (an area): *when the ice melted, the valleys were drowned.* ■ [*trans.*] (of a sound) make (another sound) inaudible by being much louder: *his voice was* **drowned out** *by the approaching engine noise.*
▸*phrasal v.* □ **drowned in** be overwhelmed or enveloped by: *a phase of being completely drowned in his work.* ■ (of food) immersed in or covered by: *ham drowned in maple syrup.* ▷Middle English (originally northern): related to Old Norse *drukkna* 'to be drowned,' also to DRINK.
▸*PHRASES* □ **drown one's sorrows** forget one's problems by getting drunk. □ **like a drowned rat** extremely wet and bedraggled: *she arrived at the church looking like a drowned rat.*

drowse /drouz/ ▸*v.* [*intrans.*] be half asleep; doze intermittently: *he was beginning to drowse in his chair.* ■ [*trans.*] *archaic* make sleepy. ■ *archaic* be sluggish or inactive: *let not your prudence drowse.*
▸*n.* [in *sing.*] a light sleep; a condition of being half asleep. ▷late 16th cent.: back-formation from DROWSY.

drow·sy /ˈdrouzē/ ▸*adj.* (**-si·er**, **-si·est**) sleepy and lethargic; half asleep: *the wine had made her drowsy.* ■ causing sleepiness: *the drowsy heat of the meadows.* ■ (esp. of a place) very peaceful and quiet: *a drowsy suburb.* ▷late 15th cent.: probably from the stem of Old English *drūsian* 'be languid or slow,' of Germanic origin; related to DREARY. **—drow·si·ly** /-zəlē/ *adv.* **—drow·si·ness** *n.*

drub /drəb/ ▸*v.* (**drubbed**, **drub·bing**) [*trans.*] hit or beat (someone) repeatedly. ■ *informal* defeat thoroughly in a match or contest: *Cleveland drubbed Baltimore 9–0.* ▷early 17th cent.: probably from Arabic *ḍaraba* 'to beat, bastinado.' The first recorded uses in English are by travelers in the Near East referring specifically to the punishment of bastinado.

drub·bing /ˈdrəbiNG/ ▸*n.* a beating; a thrashing: *I'll give the scoundrels a drubbing if I can!* ■ *informal* a resounding defeat in a match or contest.

drudge /drəj/ ▸*n.* a person made to do hard, menial, or dull work: *she was little more than a drudge around the house.*
▸*v.* [*intrans.*] *archaic* do such work. ▷Middle English (as a noun): of unknown origin; perhaps related to DRAG.

drudg·er·y /ˈdrəjərē/ ▸*n.* hard, menial, or dull work: *domestic drudgery.* See note at LABOR.

drug /drəg/ ▸*n.* a substance that has a physiological effect when ingested or otherwise introduced into the body, in particular: ■ a medicine, esp. a pharmaceutical preparation: *a new drug aimed at sufferers from Parkinson's disease.* ■ a substance taken for its narcotic or stimulant effects, often illegally: [as *adj.*] *a drug addict* | *figurative mass adoration is a highly addictive drug.*
▸*v.* (**drugged**, **drug·ging**) [*trans.*] administer a drug to (someone) in order to induce stupor or insensibility: *they were drugged to keep them quiet.* ■ add a drug to (food or drink): [as *adj.*] (**drugged**) *he offered them drugged wine.* ■ [*intrans.*] [usu. as *n.*] (**drugging**) *informal* take illegally obtained drugs: *fifteen years of drinking and drugging.* ▷Middle English: from Old French *drogue*, possibly from Middle Dutch *droge vate*, literally 'dry vats,' referring to the contents (i.e., dry goods).
▸*PHRASES* □ **do drugs** *informal* take illegal drugs. □ **on drugs** taking medically prescribed drugs: *on drugs for high blood pressure.* ■ under the influence of or habitually taking illegal drugs.

drug a·buse ▸*n.* the habitual taking of addictive or illegal drugs.

drug ba·ron ▸*n.* a person who controls an organization dealing in illegal drugs: *the deportation of a reputed drug baron.*

drug bust ▸*n. informal* a seizure of illegal drugs by the police or other law-enforcement agency.

drug-free ▸*adj.* (of a place or situation) where no illegal drugs are used or available: *we advocate a drug-free high school* | *a drug-free weekend.* ■ (of a medical procedure or treatment) involving no administration of drugs: *drug-free births.* ■ (of a person) not taking drugs, esp. illegal ones. ■ (of a product) containing no drugs: *a drug-free sleep inducer.*

drug·get /ˈdrəgit/ ▸*n.* a floor or table covering made of a coarse woven fabric. ■ the fabric used for such coverings. ▷mid 16th cent.: from French *droguet*, from *drogue* in the sense 'poor-quality article.'

drug·gie /ˈdrəgē/ (also **drug·gy**) ▸*n. informal* a drug addict.

drug·gist /ˈdrəgist/ ▸*n.* a pharmacist or retailer of medicinal drugs. ▷early 17th cent.: from French *droguiste*, from *drogue* 'drug.'

drug·gy /ˈdrəgē/ *informal* ▸*adj.* caused by or involving drugs: *a druggy haze.* ■ given to taking drugs, esp. illegal ones: *the druggy world of rock and roll.*
▸*n.* variant spelling of DRUGGIE. ▷late 16th cent.: from DRUG + -Y[1].

drug mule ▸*n.* a person who transports illegal drugs by swallowing them or concealing them in a body cavity.

drug·store /ˈdrəgˌstôr/ ▸*n.* a pharmacy that also sells toiletries and other articles.

drug·store bee·tle ▸*n.* a small beetle related to the furniture beetle, with larvae that feed on stored foodstuffs such as pasta and seeds. • *Stegobium paniceum*, family Anobiidae.

Dru·id /ˈdrooid/ ▸*n.* a priest, magician, or soothsayer in the ancient Celtic religion. ■ a member of a present-day group claiming to represent or be derived from this religion. ▷from Latin *druidae*, *druides* (plural), from Gaulish; related to Irish *draoidh* 'magician, sorcerer.' **—Dru·id·ic** /drooˈidik/ *adj.* **—Dru·id·i·cal** /drooˈidikəl/ *adj.* **—Dru·id·ism** /-ˌizəm/ *n.*

drum[1] /drəm/ ▸*n.* **1** a percussion instrument sounded by being struck with sticks or the hands, typically cylindrical, barrel-shaped, or bowl-shaped with a taut membrane over one or both ends. ■ (**drums**) a set of drums. ■ (**drums**) the percussion section of a band or orchestra. ■ [in *sing.*] a sound made by or resembling that of a drum: *the drum of their feet.* ■ *historical* a military drummer. **2** something resembling or likened to a drum in shape, in particular: ■ a cylindrical container or receptacle. See also OIL DRUM. ■ a rotating cylindrical part in a washing machine, in which the laundry is placed. ■ a similar cylindrical part in certain other appliances. ■ *Architecture* the circular vertical wall supporting a dome. ■ *Architecture* a stone block forming part of a column. **3** an evening or afternoon tea party of a kind that was popular in the late 18th and early 19th century.
▸*v.* (**drummed**, **drum·ming**) [*intrans.*] play on a drum. ■ make a continuous rhythmic noise: *she felt the blood drumming in her ears* | [as *n.*] (**drumming**) *the drumming of hooves.* ■ [*trans.*] beat (the fingers, feet, etc.) repeatedly on a surface, esp. as a sign of impatience or annoyance: *waiting around an empty table, drumming their fingers.* ■ (of a woodpecker) strike the bill rapidly on a dead trunk or branch, esp. as a sound indicating a territorial claim. ■ (of a snipe) vibrate the outer tail feathers in a diving display flight, making a throbbing sound.
▸*phrasal v.* □ **drum something into** drive a lesson into (someone) by constant repetition: *it had been drummed into them to dress correctly.* □ **drum someone out** expel or dismiss someone with ignominy from a place or institution: *he was* **drummed out of** *the air force.* [with allusion to the formal military drumbeat accompanying dismissal from a regiment.] □ **drum something up** attempt to obtain something by canvassing or soliciting: *the organizers are hoping to drum up support from local businesses.* ▷Middle English: from Middle Dutch or Low German *tromme*, of imitative origin.
▸*PHRASE* □ **beat** (or **bang**) **the drum for** (or **against**) be ostentatiously in support of (or in opposition to): *he limited campaign contributions in order to beat the drum against political action committees* | *feminists bang the drum for 'quality time.'*

drum[2] ▸*n. Scottish & Irish* a long narrow hill, esp. one separating two parallel valleys. ▷early 18th cent.: from Scottish Gaelic and Irish *druim* 'ridge.'

drum[3] (also **drum·fish**) ▸*n.* (*pl.* same or **drums**) a fish that makes a drumming sound by vibrating its swim bladder, found mainly in estuarine and shallow coastal waters. Also called CROAKER. • Family Sciaenidae (the **drum family**): many species, including the **black drum** (*Pogonias cromis*) of the western Atlantic. The drum family also includes the mulloway and a number of marine fishes that resemble salmon (e.g., the weakfish).

drum and bass /bās/ ▸*n.* a type of dance music characterized by bare instrumentation consisting largely of electronic drums and bass, originating in Britain during the early 1990s.

drum·beat /ˈdrəmˌbēt/ ▸*n.* a stroke or pattern of strokes on a drum: *she was aware of a constant, faint drumbeat.*

drum brake ▸*n.* a type of vehicle brake in which brake shoes press against the inside of a drum on the wheel.

drum·fire /ˈdrəmˌfīr/ ▸*n.* heavy continuous rapid artillery fire.

drum·fish /ˈdrəmˌfish/ ▸*n.* (*pl.* same or **-fish·es**) see DRUM[3].

drum·head /ˈdrəmˌhed/ ▸*n.* **1** the membrane or skin of a drum. **2** a winter cabbage of a flat-topped variety. **3** *chiefly historical* the circular top of a ship's capstan, with holes into which bars are placed to turn it.
▸*adj.* [*attrib.*] carried out by or as if by an army in the field; improvised or summary: *a drumhead court-martial.*

drum kit (also **drum set**) ▸*n.* a set of drums, cymbals, and other percussion instruments used with drumsticks in jazz and popular music. The most basic components are a foot-operated bass drum, a snare drum, a suspended cymbal, and one or more tom-toms.

drum·lin /ˈdrəmlin/ ▸*n. Geology* a low oval mound or small hill, typically one of a group, consisting of compacted boulder clay molded by past glacial action. ▷mid 19th cent.: probably from DRUM[2] + *-lin* from -LING.

drum ma·chine ▸*n.* a programmable electronic device able to imitate the sounds of a drum kit.

drum ma·jor ▸*n.* **1** a noncommissioned officer commanding the drummers of a regimental band. **2** the male leader of a marching band, who often twirls a baton. ■ a male member of a baton-twirling parading group.

drum ma·jor·ette ▸*n.* the female leader of a marching band. ■ a girl or woman who twirls a baton, typically with a marching band or drum corps.

drum·mer /ˈdrəmər/ ▸*n.* **1** a person who plays a drum or drums. **2** *informal* a traveling sales representative: *a drummer in electronic software.* [from *drum up* (see DRUM[1]).]

drum pad ▸*n.* an electronic device with one or more flat pads that imitate the sounds of a drum kit when struck.

drum·roll /ˈdrəm,rōl/ (also **drum roll**) ▸*n.* a rapid succession of beats sounded on a drum, often used to introduce an announcement or event.

drum·stick /ˈdrəm,stik/ ▸*n.* a stick, typically with a shaped or padded head, used for beating a drum. ■ the lower joint of the leg of a cooked chicken, turkey, or other fowl.

drunk /drəNGk/ ▸ past participle of DRINK.
▸*adj.* affected by alcohol to the extent of losing control of one's faculties or behavior: *he was so drunk he lurched from wall to wall | **drunk on** vodka.* ■ [*predic.*] (**drunk with**) *figurative* overcome with (a strong emotion): *the crowd was high on euphoria and drunk with patriotism.*
▸*n.* a person who is drunk or who habitually drinks to excess. ■ *informal* a drinking bout; a period of drunkenness: *he used to go on these blind drunks.*
▸*PHRASES* □ **drunk and disorderly** creating a public disturbance under the influence of alcohol. □ (**as**) **drunk as a lord** (or **skunk**) extremely drunk.

THE RIGHT WORD **blotto, drunk, drunken, inebriated, intoxicated, tight, tipsy**

Anyone who is obviously or legally under the influence of alcohol is said to be **drunk**.

Drunken means the same thing, but only *drunk* should be used predicatively—that is, after a linking verb (*she was drunk*)—while *drunken* is more often used to modify a noun (*a drunken sailor*) and, in some cases, to imply habitual drinking to excess. *Drunken* is also used to modify nouns that do not refer to a person (*a drunken celebration*).

To say **intoxicated** or **inebriated** is a more formal and less offensive way of calling someone *drunk*, with *intoxicated* implying that the person is only slightly drunk, and *inebriated* implying drunkenness to the point of excitement or exhilaration (*the streets were filled with inebriated revelers*).

Tight and **tipsy** are two of the more common slang expressions (there are dozens more) meaning *drunk*. Like *intoxicated*, *tipsy* implies that someone is only slightly drunk, while *tight* implies obvious drunkenness but without any loss of muscular coordination. An elderly woman who has had one sherry too many might be described as *tipsy*, but someone who has been drinking all evening and is still able to stand up and give a speech might be described as *tight*.

Either condition is preferable to being **blotto**, a word that means drunk to the point of incomprehensibility or unconsciousness.

drunk·ard /ˈdrəNGkərd/ ▸*n.* a person who is habitually drunk. ▷Middle English: from Middle Low German *drunkert*.

drunk driv·ing (also **drunk·en driv·ing**) ▸*n.* the crime of driving a vehicle with an excess of alcohol in the blood. —**drunk driv·er** *n.*

drunk·en /ˈdrəNGkən/ ▸*adj.* [*attrib.*] drunk or intoxicated: *gangs of drunken youths roamed the streets.* See note at DRUNK. ■ habitually or frequently drunk: *his violent, drunken father.* ■ caused by or showing the effects of drink: *the man's drunken, slurred speech.* ▷Old English, archaic past participle of DRINK. —**drunk·en·ly** *adv.* —**drunk·en·ness** *n.*

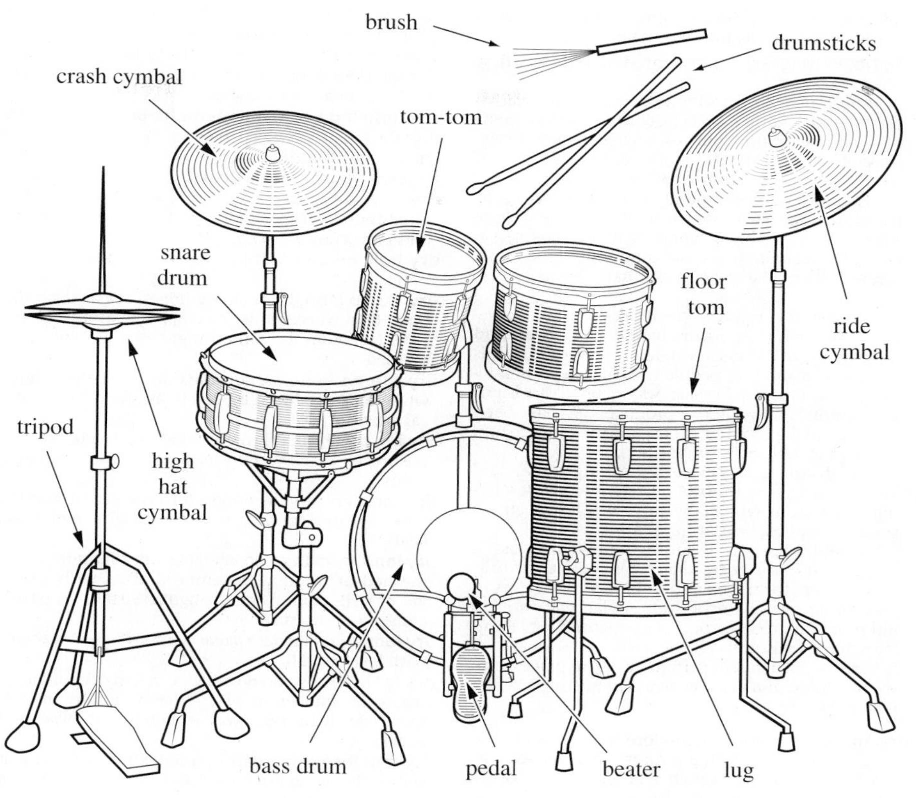

drum kit

drunk tank ▸*n. informal* a large prison cell for the detention of drunks.

drupe /dro͞op/ ▸*n. Botany* a fleshy fruit with thin skin and a central stone containing the seed, e.g., a plum, cherry, almond, or olive. ▷mid 18th cent.: from Latin *drupa* 'overripe olive,' from Greek *druppa* 'olive.' —**dru·pa·ceous** /dro͞oˈpāSHəs/ *adj.*

drupe·let /ˈdro͞oplit/ ▸*n. Botany* any of the small individual drupes forming a fleshy aggregate fruit such as a blackberry or raspberry. ▷mid 19th cent.: from modern Latin *drupella*, diminutive of *drupa* 'overripe olive' (see DRUPE).

Dru·ry Lane /ˈdro͝orē/ the site in London of the Theatre Royal, one of London's most famous theaters.

druse /dro͞oz/ ▸*n.* **1** *Geology* a rock cavity lined with a crust of projecting crystals. ■ the crust of crystals lining such a cavity. **2** *Botany* a rounded cluster of calcium oxalate crystals found in some plant cells. ▷early 19th cent.: via French from German *Druse* 'weathered ore.' —**drus·y** *adj.* (*Geology*).

druth·er /ˈdreT͟Hər/ *informal* ▸*n.* (usu. **one's druthers**) a person's preference in a matter: *if I had my druthers, I would prefer to be a writer.*
▸*adv.* rather; by preference. ▷late 19th cent.: from a U.S. regional pronunciation of *I'd rather*, contraction of *would rather*. Compare with RUTHER.

Druze /dro͞oz/ (also **Druse**) ▸*n.* (*pl.* same, **Druz·es** or **Drus·es** /ˈdro͞oziz/) a member of a political and religious sect of Islamic origin, living chiefly in Lebanon and Syria. The Druze broke away from the Ismaili Muslims in the 11th century; they are regarded as heretical by the Muslim community at large. ▷from French, from Arabic *durūz* (plural), from the name of one of their founders, Muhammad ibn Ismail *al-Darazī* (died 1019).

dry /drī/ ▸*adj.* (**dri·er**, **dri·est**) **1** free from moisture or liquid; not wet or moist: *the jacket kept me warm and dry | he wiped it dry with his shirt.* ■ having lost all wetness or moisture over a period of time: *dry paint.* ■ for use without liquid: *the conversion of dry latrines into flush toilets.* ■ with little or no rainfall or humidity: *the West Coast has had two dry winters in a row.* ■ (of a river, lake, or stream) empty of water as a result of evaporation and lack of rainfall: *the river is always dry at this time of year.* ■ (of a source) not yielding a supply of water or oil: *a dry well.* ■ thirsty or thirst-making: *working in the hot sun is making me dry | dry work.* ■ (of a cow or other domestic animal) having stopped producing milk. ■ without grease or other moisturizer or lubricator: *cream conditioners for dry hair | his throat was dry and sore.* ■ (of bread or toast) without butter or other spreads: *only dry bread and water.* **2** *figurative* bare or lacking adornment: *the dry facts.* ■ unexciting; dull: *by current tastes the text is dry.* ■ unemotional, undemonstrative, or impassive: *Ralph gave me a dry, silent wave.* ■ (of a joke or sense of humor) subtle, expressed in a matter-of-fact way, and having the appearance of being unconscious or unintentional: *he delighted his friends with a dry, covert sense of humor.* **3** prohibiting the sale or consumption of alcoholic drink: *the country is strictly dry, in accordance with Islamic law.* ■ (of a person) no longer addicted to or drinking alcohol: *I heard much talk about how sobriety was more than staying straight or dry.* **4** (of an alcoholic drink) not sweet: *a dry, medium-bodied red wine.*
▸*v.* (**dries, dried**) [*intrans.*] **1** become dry: *waiting for the paint to dry | come in out of the rain and **dry off** | do not let the soil **dry out** | pools are left as the rivers **dry up**.* ■ [*trans.*] cause to become dry: *they had washed and dried their hair.* ■ [*trans.*] wipe tears from (the eyes): *she dried her eyes and blew her nose.* ■ wipe dishes dry with a cloth after they have been washed. ■ [*trans.*] [usu. as *adj.*] (**dried**) preserve by allowing or encouraging evaporation of moisture from: *dried flowers.* **2** *theatrical slang* forget one's lines: *a colleague of mine once dried in the middle of a scene.*
▸*phrasal v.* □ **dry out** *informal* (of an alcoholic) abstain from alcoholic drink, esp. as part of a detoxification program: *he intends to dry out and get his life back together again.* □ **dry up 1** *informal* cease talking: *then he dried up, and Phil couldn't get another word out of him.* **2** (of something perceived as a continuous flow or source) decrease and stop: *his commissions began to dry up.*
▸*n.* (*pl.* **dries** or **drys**) a person in favor of the prohibition of alcohol. ▷Old English *drȳge* (adjective), *drȳgan* (verb), of Germanic origin; related to Middle Low German *dröge*, Dutch *droog*, and German *trocken*. —**dry·ish** *adj.* —**dry·ness** *n.*
▸*PHRASES* □ **come up dry** be unsuccessful: *experiments have so far come up dry.* □ (**as**) **dry as a bone** extremely dry. □ (**as**) **dry as dust** extremely dry. ■ extremely dull; lacking emotion, expression, or interest: *what the students learned was as dry as dust.* □ **there wasn't a dry eye (in the house)** (with

Pronunciation Key ə *ago*; ər *over*; ˈə or ,ə *up*; ˈər or ,ər *fur*; a *hat*; ā *rate*; ä *car*; CH *chew*; e *let*; ē *see*; e(ə)r *air*; i *fit*; ī *by*; i(ə)r *ear*; NG *sing*; ō *go*; ô *for*; oi *boy*; o͝o *good*; o͞o *goo*; ou *out*; SH *she*; TH *thin*; T͟H *then*; (h)w *why*; ZH *vision*

reference to a play, film, or similar event) everyone in the audience was moved to tears.

THE RIGHT WORD **arid, dehydrated, dessicated, dry, parched, sere**

Almost anything lacking in moisture (in relative terms)—whether it's a piece of bread, the basement of a house, or the state of Arizona—may be described as **dry**, a word that also connotes a lack of life or spirit (*a dry lecture on cell division*).

Arid, on the other hand, applies to places or things that have been deprived of moisture and are therefore extremely or abnormally dry (*one side of the island was arid*); it is most commonly used to describe a desertlike region or climate that is lifeless or barren.

Desiccated is used as a technical term for something from which moisture has been removed, and in general use it suggests lifelessness, although it is applied very often to people who have lost their vitality (*a desiccated old woman who never left her house*) or to animal and vegetable products that have been completely deprived of their vital juices (*desiccated oranges hanging limply from the tree*).

Dehydrated is very close in meaning to *desiccated* and is often the preferred adjective when describing foods from which the moisture has been extracted (*they lived on dehydrated fruit*).

Dehydrated may also refer to an unwanted loss of moisture (*the virus had left him seriously dehydrated*), as may the less formal term **parched**, which refers to an undesirable or uncomfortable lack of water in either a human being or a place (*parched with thirst; the parched landscape*).

Sere is associated primarily with places and means *dry* or *arid* (*a harsh, sere land where few inhabitants could survive*).

dry·ad /ˈdrīˌad; -əd/ ▶*n.* (in folklore and Greek mythology) a nymph inhabiting a forest or a tree, esp. an oak tree. ▷via Old French and Latin from Greek *druas, druad-* 'tree nymph,' from *drus* 'tree.'

dry·ad sad·dle ▶*n.* a common polypore growing on tree stumps and logs, having a scaly, yellowish-brown upper surface, found in both North America and Eurasia and edible when young. • *Polyporus squamosus*, family Polyporaceae, class Hymenomycetes.

dry·as /ˈdrīəs/ ▶*n.* **1** a plant of a genus that comprises the mountain avens. • Genus *Dryas*, family Rosaceae. **2** (**Dryas**) *Geology* the first and third climatic stages of the late-glacial period in northern Europe, in which cold tundralike conditions prevailed and plants of the genus *Dryas* were abundant. The **Older Dryas** (about 15,000 to 12,000 years ago) followed the last ice retreat, and the **Younger Dryas** (about 10,800 to 10,000 years ago) followed the Allerød stage. ▷modern Latin, from Greek *druas* (see DRYAD). The plant (sense 1) has leaves that resemble those of the oak (hence the association with dryads, being originally nymphs of the oak).

dry·as·dust /ˈdrīəzˌdəst/ ▶*n.* a boring, pedantic speaker or writer.
▶*adj.* (also **dry-as-dust**) dull and boring. ▷late 19th cent.: from the name of the character Dr. Jonas *Dryasdust*, featured in prefaces to Sir Walter Scott's novels.

dry bat·ter·y ▶*n.* an electric battery consisting of one or more dry cells.

dry bulb ▶*n.* an ordinary exposed thermometer bulb, esp. as used in conjunction with a wet bulb.

dry cell ▶*n.* an electric cell in which the electrolyte is absorbed in a solid to form a paste, preventing spillage. Compare with WET CELL.

dry-clean ▶*v.* [*trans.*] (usu. **be dry-cleaned**) clean (a garment) with an organic solvent, without using water: *I had my winter coat dry-cleaned recently* | [as *n.*] (**dry cleaning**) *premises that offered dry cleaning.* —**dry clean·er** *n.*

dry cough ▶*n.* a cough not accompanied by phlegm production.

dry-cure ▶*v.* another term for DRY-SALT.

Dry·den /ˈdrīdn/, John (1631–1700), English poet, critic, and playwright of the Augustan Age. He is best known for *Marriage à la mode* (1673), *All for Love* (1678), and *Absalom and Achitophel* (1681).

dry dock ▶*n.* a dock that can be drained of water to allow the inspection and repair of a ship's hull.
▶*v.* (**dry-dock**) [*trans.*] place (a ship) in a dry dock.

dry·er /ˈdrīər/ (also **dri·er**) ▶*n.* **1** a machine or device for drying something, esp. the hair or laundry. **2** a substance mixed with oil paint or ink to promote drying. ▷Middle English (in the sense 'person who dries'): from the verb DRY + -ER¹.

dry·er sheet ▶*n.* a fabric softener sheet.

dry-eyed ▶*adj.* (of a person) not crying: *Janet was dry-eyed and stoical under assault.*

dry farm·ing ▶*n.* another term for DRYLAND FARMING.

dry fly ▶*n.* an artificial fishing fly that is made to float lightly on the water.
▶*v.* (**dry-fly**) fish using a dry fly.

dry goods ▶*plural n.* fabric, thread, clothing, and related merchandise, esp. as distinct from hardware and groceries.

dry hole ▶*n.* a well drilled for oil or gas but yielding none.

dry hump (also **dry fuck**) ▶*v.* [*trans.*] *vulgar slang* simulate or unsuccessfully attempt sexual intercourse with (someone or something), usually while fully dressed.

dry ice ▶*n.* solid carbon dioxide. ■ the cold dense white mist produced by this in air, used for theatrical effects.

dry·ing oil ▶*n.* an oil that thickens or hardens on exposure to air, esp. one used by artists in mixing paint.

dry land ▶*n.* land as opposed to the sea or another body of water: *the tide came in and cut off his route to dry land.*

dry·land farm·ing /ˈdrīˌland/ (also **dry farm·ing**) ▶*n.* a method of farming in semiarid areas without the aid of irrigation, using drought-resistant crops and conserving moisture.

dry·lands /ˈdrīˌlandz/ ▶*plural n.* an arid area; a region with low rainfall.

dry·ly /ˈdrīlē/ (also **dri·ly**) ▶*adv.* **1** in a matter-of-fact or ironically humorous way: *"How very observant," he said dryly.* **2** in a dry way or condition: *Evans swallowed dryly.*

dry mat·ter ▶*n.* the part of a foodstuff or other substance that would remain if all its water content was removed.

dry meas·ure ▶*n.* a measure of volume for loose dry commodities such as grain, tea, and sugar.

dry mop ▶*n.* another term for DUST MOP.

dry mount·ing ▶*n.* *Photography* a process in which a print is bonded to a mount using a layer of adhesive in a hot press. —**dry-mount** *v.* —**dry-mount·ed** *adj.*

dry nurse ▶*n.* *archaic* a woman who looks after a baby but does not breastfeed it. —**dry-nurse** *v.*

Dry·o·pith·e·cus /ˌdrīōˈpiTHikəs/ ▶*n.* a fossil anthropoid ape of the middle Miocene to early Pliocene epochs, including the supposed common ancestor of gorillas, chimpanzees, and humans. • Genus *Dryopithecus*, family Pongidae. ▷modern Latin, from Greek *drus* 'tree' + *pithēkos* 'ape.' —**dry·o·pith·e·cine** /-ˈpiTHiˌsēn/ *n.* & *adj.*

dry paint·ing ▶*n.* another term for SAND PAINTING.

dry plate ▶*n.* *Photography* a glass plate coated with a light-sensitive gelatin-based emulsion, used formerly as an improvement on the earlier wet plate.

dry point ▶*n.* a steel needle for engraving on a bare copper plate without acid. ■ an engraving or print so produced. ■ engraving by this means.

dry-roast·ed ▶*adj.* roasted without fat or oil: *dry-roasted peanuts.*

dry rot ▶*n.* **1** fungal timber decay occurring in poorly ventilated conditions in buildings, resulting in cracking and powdering of the wood. **2** (also **dry rot fungus**) the fungus that causes this. • *Serpula lacrymans*, family Corticiaceae, class Hymenomycetes.

dry run ▶*n.* *informal* a rehearsal of a performance or procedure before the real one: *the president went through a dry run of his speech.*

dry-salt ▶*v.* [*trans.*] cure (meat or fish) with salt rather than in liquid.

dry-salt·er ▶*n.* *Brit., historical* a dealer in dyes, gums, and drugs, and sometimes also in pickles and other preserved foodstuffs.

dry sham·poo ▶*n.* a shampoo in powder form, used without the addition of water.

dry-shod ▶*adj.* & *adv.* without wetting one's shoes: [as *adj.*] *dry-shod evacuation involved getting into a lifeboat at deck level.*

dry sink ▶*n.* an antique kitchen cabinet with an inset basin, now generally used as an ornament rather than for practical purposes.

dry-ski ▶*adj.* [*attrib.*] denoting or relating to skiing on an artificial surface: *a dry-ski slope.*

dry slope ▶*n.* an artificial ski slope used for practice and training: [as *adj.*] *dry-slope racers.*

dry·stone /ˈdrīˌstōn/ ▶*adj.* [*attrib.*] (of a stone wall) built without using mortar.

dry·suit /ˈdrīˌso͞ot/ ▶*n.* a waterproof rubber suit worn for water sports and diving, under which warm clothes can be worn.

Dry Tor·tu·gas /tôrˈto͞ogəz/ an island group in southwestern Florida, west of Key West, that is noted for its wildlife. Also **the Tortugas** or **Tortugas Keys**.

dry val·ley ▶*n.* a valley cut by water erosion but containing no permanent surface stream, typically one occurring in an area of porous rock such as limestone.

dry·wall /ˈdrīˌwôl/ ▶*n.* a type of board made from plaster, wood pulp, or other material, used esp. to form the interior walls of houses.

dry wash ▶*n.* the dry bed of an intermittent stream.

dry well ▶*n.* **1** a shaft or chamber constructed in the ground in order to aid drainage, sometimes containing pumping equipment. **2** another term for DRY HOLE.

DS ▶*abbr.* ■ *Music* dal segno. ■ document signed.

DSC ▶*abbr.* Distinguished Service Cross, (in the U.S.) an Army decoration for heroism in combat or (in the UK) a decoration for distinguished active service at sea.

DSc ▶*abbr.* Doctor of Science.

DSL ▶*abbr.* ■ deep scattering layer. ■ digital subscriber line. See also ADSL.

DSM ▶*abbr.* Distinguished Service Medal, (in the U.S.) a military decoration for exceptionally meritorious performance of a duty of great responsibility during wartime or (in the UK) a medal for distinguished service at sea.

DSO ▶*abbr.* Distinguished Service Order, a British military decoration for distinguished service awarded to officers of the army and navy.

DSP ▶*abbr.* ■ (in genealogy) died without issue. [from Latin *decessit sine prole.*] ■ (in computing and sound reproduction) digital signal processor or processing.

DSS ▶*abbr.* ■ decision support system. ■ Department of Social Services. ■ digital satellite system; digital satellite services. ■ digital signature standard.

DST ▶*abbr.* daylight saving time.

DTD ▶*abbr.* *Computing* document type definition.

DTP ▶*abbr.* desktop publishing.

DTs ▶*plural n.* (usu. **the DTs**) *informal* delirium tremens. ▷mid 19th cent.: abbreviation, originally in the singular form *DT* (now rare).

DTV ▶*abbr.* digital television.

DU ▶*abbr.* ■ depleted uranium. ■ Dobson unit(s).

du·al /ˈd(y)o͞oəl/ ▶*adj.* **1** [*attrib.*] consisting of two parts, elements, or aspects: *their dual role at work and home.* ■ *Grammar* (in some languages) denoting an inflection that refers to exactly two people or things (as distinct from singular and plural): *Old English has dual number for first- and second-person pronouns.* ■ (in an aircraft) using dual controls: *a dual flight.* **2** (often **dual to**) *Mathematics* (of a theorem, expression, etc.) related to another by the interchange of particular pairs of terms, such as "point" and "line."
▶*n.* **1** *Grammar* a dual form of a word. ■ the dual number. **2** *Mathematics* a theorem, expression, etc., that is dual to another. ▷late Middle English (as a noun denoting either of the two middle incisor teeth in each jaw): from Latin *dualis*, from *duo* 'two.' —**du·al·ize** /-ˌlīz/ *v.* —**du·al·ly** *adv.*

du·al car·riage·way ▶*n.* British term for DIVIDED HIGHWAY.

du·al cit·i·zen·ship (also *chiefly Brit.* **dual nationality**) ▶*n.* citizenship in two countries concurrently.

du·al con·trol ▶*adj.* (of an aircraft or a vehicle) having two sets of controls, one of which is used by the instructor: *a dual-control pilot trainer.*
▶*n.* (usu. **dual controls**) two such sets of controls in an aircraft or vehicle.

du·al in-line pack·age ▶*n.* *Electronics* see **DIP**.

du·al·ism /ˈd(y)o͞oəˌlizəm/ ▶*n.* **1** the division of something conceptually into two opposed or contrasted aspects, or the state of being so divided: *a dualism between man and nature.* ■ *Philosophy* a theory or system of thought that regards a domain of reality in terms of two independent principles, esp. mind and matter (**Cartesian dualism**). Compare with IDEALISM, MATERIALISM, and MONISM. ■ the religious doctrine that the universe contains opposed powers of good and evil, esp. seen as balanced equals. ■ in Christian theology, the heresy that in the incarnate Christ there were two coexisting persons, human and divine. **2** the quality or condition of being dual; duality. ▷late 18th cent.: from DUAL, on the pattern of French *dualisme*. —**du·al·ist** *n.* & *adj.*

—**du·al·is·tic** /ˌd(y)o͞oəˈlistik/ *adj.* —**du·al·is·ti·cal·ly** /ˌd(y)o͞oəˈlistik(ə)lē/ *adv.*

du·al·i·ty /d(y)o͞oˈalitē/ ▸*n.* (*pl.* **-ties**) **1** the quality or condition of being dual: *the novel's deep duality about human motive.* ■ *Mathematics* the property of two theorems, expressions, etc., being dual to each other. ■ *Physics* the quantum-mechanical property of being regardable as both a wave and a particle. **2** an instance of opposition or contrast between two concepts or two aspects of something; a dualism: *the simple dualities of his youthful Marxism: capitalism against socialism, bourgeois against prole.* ▷late Middle English: from late Latin *dualitas*, from *dualis* (see DUAL).

du·al-pur·pose ▸*adj.* serving two purposes or functions: *a dual-purpose hand and nail cream.*

du·al-use /yo͞os/ ▸*adj.* (of technology or equipment) designed or suitable for both civilian and military purposes.

dub[1] /dəb/ ▸*v.* (**dubbed, dub·bing**) **1** [*trans.*] give an unofficial name or nickname to (someone or something): *the media dubbed anorexia "the slimming disease."* ■ make (someone) a knight by the ritual touching of the shoulder with a sword: *he should be dubbed Sir Hubert.* **2** [*trans.*] dress (an artificial fishing fly) with strands of fur or wool or with other material. ■ incorporate (fur, wool, or other materials) into a fishing fly. **3** [*trans.*] smear (leather) with grease. Compare with DUBBIN. **4** trim or make smooth (wood) with an adze. ▷late Old English (in the sense 'make a knight'): from Old French *adober* 'equip with armor,' of unknown origin. Sense 2 is from the obsolete meaning 'dress or adorn.'

dub[2] ▸*v.* (**dubbed, dub·bing**) [*trans.*] **1** provide (a film) with a soundtrack in a different language from the original: *the film will be* **dubbed into** *French and Flemish.* ■ add (sound effects or music) to a film or a recording: *background sound can be* **dubbed in** *at the editing stage.* **2** make a copy of (a sound or video recording). ■ transfer (a recording) from one medium to another. ■ combine (two or more sound recordings) into one composite soundtrack.

▸*n.* **1** an instance of dubbing sound effects or music: *the level of the dub can be controlled manually.* **2** a style of popular music originating from the remixing of recorded music (esp. reggae), typically with the removal of some vocals and instruments and the exaggeration of bass guitar. ▷1920s: abbreviation of DOUBLE.

dub[3] *informal* ▸*n.* an inexperienced or unskillful person.

▸*v.* (**dubbed, dub·bing**) [*trans.*] *Golf* misplay (a shot). ▷late 19th cent.: perhaps from DUB[1] in the obsolete technical sense 'make blunt.'

Du·bai /do͞oˈbī; də-/ a member state of the United Arab Emirates; pop. 674,100. ■ its capital city, a port on the Persian Gulf; pop. 265,700.

Du Bar·ry /d(y)o͞o ˈbarē/, Marie Jeanne Bécu, Comtesse (1743–93), French courtier and mistress of Louis XV. During the French Revolution she was arrested by the Revolutionary Tribunal and guillotined.

dub·bin /ˈdəbin/ *Brit.* ▸*n.* prepared grease used for softening and waterproofing leather.

▸*v.* (**dub·bined, dub·bin·ing**) [*trans.*] apply such a grease to (leather). ▷early 19th cent.: alteration of *dubbing*, present participle of DUB[1] (sense 3).

dub·bing /ˈdəbiNG/ ▸*n.* material used for the bodies of artificial fishing flies, esp. fur or wool on waxed silk. ▷late 17th cent.: from DUB[1] + -ING[1].

Dub·ček /ˈdo͞obCHek/, Alexander (1921–92), Czech statesman, first secretary of the Czechoslovak Communist Party 1968–69. He was the driving force behind the political reforms of 1968, which prompted the Soviet invasion of Czechoslovakia in 1968 and his removal from office. After the collapse of communism in 1989, he was elected speaker of the federal assembly in the new Czechoslovak parliament.

dub-dub-dub /ˈdəb ˈdəb ˈdəb/ ▸*n. informal Computing* short form used instead of pronouncing the three letters in the abbreviation WWW (World Wide Web).

du·bi·e·ty /d(y)o͞oˈbī-itē/ ▸*n. formal* the state or quality of being doubtful; uncertainty: *his enemies made much of the dubiety of his paternity.* See note at UNCERTAINTY. ▷mid 18th cent.: from late Latin *dubietas*, from Latin *dubium* 'a doubt.'

Du·bin·sky /do͞oˈbinskē/, David (1892–1982), U.S. labor leader and social reformer; born in Russia. He served as president of the International Ladies' Garment Workers Union 1932–66 and was responsible for reforms such as improved housing and health-care.

du·bi·ous /ˈd(y)o͞obēəs/ ▸*adj.* **1** hesitating or doubting: *Alex looked dubious, but complied.* See note at DOUBTFUL. **2** not to be relied upon; suspect: *extremely dubious assumptions.* ■ morally suspect: *timesharing has been brought into disrepute by dubious sales methods.* ■ of questionable value: *she earned the dubious distinction of being the lowest-paid teacher in the nation.* ▷mid 16th cent. (sense 2): from Latin *dubiosus*, from *dubium* 'a doubt,' neuter of *dubius* 'doubtful.' —**du·bi·ous·ly** *adv.* —**du·bi·ous·ness** *n.*

du·bi·ta·ble /ˈd(y)o͞obitəbəl/ ▸*adj. rare* (of a belief, conclusion, etc.) open to doubt. ▷early 17th cent.: from Latin *dubitabilis*, from *dubitare* 'to doubt.' —**du·bi·ta·bil·i·ty** /ˌd(y)o͞obitəˈbilitē/ *n.*

du·bi·ta·tion /ˌd(y)o͞obiˈtāSHən/ ▸*n. formal* doubt; hesitation: *a judgment fenced around with proper scholarly dubitation.* ▷late Middle English: from Latin *dubitatio(n-)*, from *dubitare* 'to doubt.'

du·bi·ta·tive /ˈd(y)o͞obiˌtātiv/ ▸*adj. formal* expressing or inclined to doubt or hesitation. ▷early 18th cent.: from French *dubitatif, -ive* or late Latin *dubitativus*, from *dubitare* 'to doubt.'

Dub·lin /ˈdəblən/ the capital city of the Republic of Ireland, on the Irish Sea at the mouth of the Liffey River; pop. 477,700. Irish name BAILE ÁTHA CLIATH. ■ a county in the Republic of Ireland, in the province of Leinster; county town, Dublin.

dub·ni·um /ˈdəbnēəm/ ▸*n.* the chemical element of atomic number 105, a very unstable element made by high-energy atomic collisions. (Symbol: **Db**) See also HAHNIUM, JOLIOTIUM. ▷1967: modern Latin, from *Dubna* in Russia, site of the Joint Nuclear Institute.

Du Bois /d(y)o͞o ˈbois/, W. E. B. (1868–1963), U.S. writer, sociologist, and political activist; full name *William Edward Burghardt Du Bois.* He was an important figure in the movement for equality for black Americans and co-founded the National Association for the Advancement of Colored People (NAACP) in 1909.

Du·bon·net /ˌd(y)o͞obəˈnā/ ▸*n. trademark* a sweet French red wine. ▷from the name of a family of French wine merchants.

dub reg·gae ▸*n.* a genre of popular dance music made by remixing reggae recordings: *Phase Selector Sound's inventive dub reggae recordings transcend their Music City origins.*

Du·brov·nik /do͞oˈbrôvnik; ˈdo͞oˌbrôvnik/ a port and resort on the Adriatic coast of Croatia; pop. 66,100. Italian name (until 1918) RAGUSA .

Du·buf·fet /ˌd(y)o͞obəˈfā/, Jean (1901–85), French painter. He rejected traditional techniques and incorporated materials such as sand and plaster in his paintings and produced sculptures made from garbage.

Du·buque /dəˈbyo͞ok/ an industrial and commercial city in northeastern Iowa, on the Mississippi River; pop. 57,686.

du·cal /ˈd(y)o͞okəl/ ▸*adj.* [*attrib.*] of, like, or relating to a duke or dukedom: *the ducal palace in Rouen.* ▷late 15th cent.: from Old French, from *duc* 'duke.'

duc·at /ˈdəkət/ ▸*n.* **1** a gold coin formerly current in most European countries. ■ (**ducats**) *informal* money: *their production of* Hamlet *has kept the ducats pouring in.* **2** *informal* a ticket, esp. an admission ticket. ▷from Italian *ducato*, originally referring to a silver coin minted by the Duke of Apulia in 1190: from medieval Latin *ducatus* (see DUCHY). Sense 2 dates from the late 19th cent.

Du·ce /ˈdo͞oCHā/ (**Il Duce** /il/) the title assumed by Benito Mussolini in 1922. ▷Italian, literally 'leader.'

Du·champ /d(y)o͞oˈSHäN/, Marcel (1887–1968), U.S. artist; born in France. A leading figure of the Dada movement and originator of conceptual art, he invented "ready-mades," mass-produced articles selected at random and displayed as works of art.

Du·chenne mus·cu·lar dys·tro·phy /do͞oˈSHen/ (abbr.: **DMD**) ▸*n.* a severe form of muscular dystrophy caused by a genetic defect and usually affecting boys. ▷late 19th cent.: named after G. B. A. *Duchenne* (1806–75), the French neurologist who first described it.

duch·ess /ˈdəCHis/ ▸*n.* the wife or widow of a duke. ■ a woman holding a rank equivalent to duke in her own right. ■ *Brit., informal* (esp. among cockneys) an affectionate form of address used by a man to a girl or woman he knows well. ▷late Middle English: via Old French from medieval Latin *ducissa*, from Latin *dux, duc-* (see DUKE).

duch·esse /d(y)o͞oˈSHes/ ▸*n.* **1** (also **duchesse satin**) a soft, heavy, glossy kind of satin, usually of silk. **2** a chaise longue resembling two armchairs linked by a stool. **3** (also **duchesse dressing table**) a dressing table with a pivoting mirror. ▷late 18th cent. (sense 2): from French, literally 'duchess.'

duch·esse lace ▸*n.* a kind of Brussels pillow lace characterized by bold floral patterns worked with a fine thread.

duch·esse po·ta·toes ▸*plural n.* mashed potatoes mixed with egg yolk, formed into small shapes and baked.

duch·y /ˈdəCHē/ ▸*n.* (*pl.* **duch·ies**) the territory of a duke or duchess; a dukedom. ▷Middle English: from Old French *duche*, from medieval Latin *ducatus*, from Latin *dux, duc-* (see DUKE).

duck[1] /dək/ ▸*n.* (*pl.* same or **ducks**) **1** a waterbird with a broad blunt bill, short legs, webbed feet, and a waddling gait. • Family Anatidae (the **duck family**); domesticated ducks are mainly descended from the mallard. The duck family also includes geese and swans, from which ducks are distinguished by their generally smaller size and shorter necks. ■ such a bird as food: *a duck for tomorrow's dinner.* **2** a pure white thin-shelled bivalve mollusk found off the Atlantic coasts of America. • Genus *Anatina*, family Mactridae. **3** another term for **DUKW**. ▷Old English *duce*, from the Germanic base of DUCK[2] (expressing the notion of 'diving bird').

▸**PHRASES** □ **get** (or **have**) **one's ducks in a row** get (or have) one's facts straight; get (or have) everything organized. □ **take to something like a duck to water** take to something very readily: *he shows every sign of taking to University politics like a duck to water.* □ **water off a duck's back** a potentially hurtful or harmful remark or incident that has no apparent effect on the person mentioned: *it was like water off a duck's back to Nick, but I'm sure it upset Paul.*

duck[2] ▸*v.* **1** [*intrans.*] lower the head or the body quickly to avoid a blow or so as not to be seen: *spectators ducked for cover | she* **ducked into** *the doorway to get out of the line of fire |* [*trans.*] *he ducked his head and entered.* ■ (**duck out**) depart quickly: *I thought I saw you duck out.* ■ [*trans.*] avoid (a blow) by moving down quickly: *he ducked a punch from an angry first baseman.* ■ [*trans.*] *informal* evade or avoid (an unwelcome duty or undertaking): *a responsibility which a less courageous man might well have ducked |* [*intrans.*] *I was engaged twice and* **ducked out** *both times.* **2** [*intrans.*] plunge one's head or body under water briefly: *I had to keep ducking down to get my head cool.* **3** *Bridge* refrain from playing a winning card on a particular trick for tactical reasons.

▸*n.* [in *sing.*] a quick lowering of the head. ▷Middle English: of Germanic origin; related to Dutch *duiken* and German *tauchen* 'dive, dip, plunge,' also to DUCK[1]. —**duck·er** *n.*

duck[3] (also **ducks**) ▸*n. Brit.* dear; darling (used as an informal or affectionate form of address, esp. among cockneys). ▷late 16th cent.: from DUCK[1].

duck[4] ▸*n.* a strong untwilled linen or cotton fabric, used chiefly for casual or work clothes and sails. ■ (**ducks**) pants made of such a fabric. ▷mid 17th cent.: from Middle Dutch *doek* 'linen, linen cloth'; related to German *Tuch* 'cloth.'

duck[5] ▸*n. Cricket* a batsman's score of zero: *out for a duck.* ▷mid 19th cent.: short for *duck's egg*, used for the figure 0 because of its similar outline.

duck·bill /ˈdəkˌbil/ ▸*n.* an animal with jaws resembling a duck's bill, e.g., a platypus or a duck-billed dinosaur.

▸*adj.* [*attrib.*] shaped like a duck's bill: *duckbill pliers.*

duck-billed di·no·saur ▸*n.* another term for HADROSAUR.

duck·bill plat·y·pus (also **duck-billed plat·y·pus**) ▸*n.* see PLATYPUS.

duck·board /ˈdəkˌbôrd/ ▸*n.* (usu. **duckboards**) a board consisting of a number of wooden slats joined together, placed so as to form a path over muddy ground or in a trench.

duck hawk ▸*n. dated* the peregrine falcon.

duck·ing stool ▸*n. historical* a chair fastened to the end of a pole, used formerly to plunge offenders into a pond or river as a punishment.

duck·ling /ˈdəkliNG/ ▸*n.* a young duck. ■ the flesh of a young duck as food.

duck mus·sel ▸*n.* a freshwater bivalve mollusk that is smaller and darker than the related swan mussel, found in rivers with sandy or gravelly bottoms. • *Anodonta anatina*, family Unionidae.

Pronunciation Key ə *ago*; ər *over*; ˈə or ˌə *up*; ˈər or ˌər *fur*; a *hat*; ā *rate*; ä *car*; CH *chew*; e *let*; ē *see*; e(ə)r *air*; i *fit*; ī *by*; i(ə)r *ear*; NG *sing*; ō *go*; ô *for*; oi *boy*; o͝o *good*; o͞o *goo*; ou *out*; SH *she*; TH *thin*; T͟H *then*; (h)w *why*; ZH *vision*

duck·pin /ˈdək,pin/ ▸*n.* a short, squat bowling pin. ■ (**duckpins**) [treated as *sing.*] a game played with such pins.

ducks and drakes ▸*n.* a game of throwing flat stones so that they skim along the surface of water. ▷late 16th cent.: from the movement of the stone over the water.
▸*PHRASE* □ **play ducks and drakes with** trifle with; treat frivolously.

duck's ass ▸*n.* another term for DUCKTAIL.

duck soup ▸*n. informal* an easy task, or someone easy to overcome: *we had some great battles, but against me he was duck soup.*

duck·tail /ˈdək,tāl/ (also **duck's ass**) (abbr.: **DA**) ▸*n. informal* a man's hairstyle, associated esp. with the 1950s, in which the hair is slicked back on both sides and tapered at the nape.

duck·walk /ˈdək,wôk/ ▸*v.* [*intrans.*] walk with the body in a squatting posture.
▸*n.* a walk with the body in this posture.

duck·weed /ˈdək,wēd/ ▸*n.* a tiny aquatic flowering plant that floats in large quantities on still water, often forming an apparently continuous green layer on the surface. • Family Lemnaceae, in particular the genus *Lemna.*

duck·y /ˈdəkē/ *informal* ▸*n.* (*pl.* **duck·ies**) *Brit.* darling; dear (used as a form of address): *come and sit down, ducky.*
▸*adj.* charming; delightful: *everything here is just ducky.* ▷early 19th cent.: from DUCK3.

duct /dəkt/ ▸*n.* a channel or tube for conveying something, in particular: ■ (in a building or a machine) a tube or passageway for air, liquid, cables, etc. ■ (in the body) a vessel for conveying lymph or glandular secretions such as tears or bile. ■ (in a plant) a vessel for conveying water, sap, or air.
▸*v.* [*trans.*] (usu. **be ducted**) convey through a duct: *a ventilation system that must be ducted through the wall* | [as *adj.*] (**ducted**) *a ducted air system* . ▷mid 17th cent. (in the sense 'course' or 'direction'): from Latin *ductus* 'leading, aqueduct,' from *duct-* 'led,' from the verb *ducere.*

duc·tile /ˈdəktl; -,tīl/ ▸*adj.* (of a metal) able to be drawn out into a thin wire. ■ able to be deformed without losing toughness; pliable, not brittle. ■ *figurative* (of a person) docile or gullible. ▷Middle English (in the sense 'malleable'): from Latin *ductilis,* from *duct-* 'led,' from the verb *ducere.* **—duc·til·i·ty** /dəkˈtilitē/ *n.*

duct·ing /ˈdəktiNG/ ▸*n.* a system of ducts. ■ tubing or piping forming such a system.

duct·less /ˈdəktlis/ ▸*adj. Anatomy* denoting a gland that secretes directly into the bloodstream, such as an endocrine gland or a lymph gland.

duct tape ▸*n.* strong, cloth-backed, waterproof adhesive tape. ▷1970s: originally used for repairing leaks in ducted ventilation and heating systems.

duc·tule /ˈdəkt(y)o͞ol/ ▸*n. Anatomy* a minute duct. ▷late 19th cent.: Latin, diminutive of *ductus* 'leading.' **—duc·tu·lar** /-tyələr/ *adj.* .

duc·tus /ˈdəktəs/ ▸*n. Anatomy* a duct. ▷mid 17th cent.: from Latin, literally 'leading.'

duct·work /ˈdəkt,wərk/ ▸*n.* a system or network of ducts.

dud /dəd/ *informal* ▸*n.* **1** a thing that fails to work properly or is otherwise unsatisfactory or worthless: *a high-grade collection, not a dud in the lot* | *all three bombs were duds.* ■ an ineffectual person: *a complete dud, incapable of even hitting the ball.* **2** (**duds**) clothes: *buy yourself some new duds.*
▸*adj.* not working or meeting standards; faulty: *a dud ignition switch.* ■ counterfeit: *charged with issuing dud checks.* ▷Middle English (in the sense 'item of clothing'): of unknown origin.

dude /do͞od/ *informal* ▸*n.* a man; a guy: *if some dude smacked me, I'd smack him back.* ■ a stylish, fastidious man: *cool dudes.* [a slang term that came into vogue in New York *c.*1883, in connection with the 'aesthetic' craze of the period.] ■ a city-dweller, esp. one vacationing on a ranch in the western U.S.
▸*v.* [*intrans.*] (**dude up**) dress up elaborately: [as *adj.*] (**duded**) *my brother was all duded up in silver and burgundy.* ▷late 19th cent.: probably from German dialect *Dude* 'fool.' **—dud·ish** *adj.*

dude ranch ▸*n.* (in the western U.S.) a cattle ranch converted to a vacation resort for tourists.

dudg·eon /ˈdəjən/ ▸*n.* a feeling of offense or deep resentment: *the manager walked out* **in high dudgeon.** ▷late 16th cent.: of unknown origin.

Dud·ley1 /ˈdədlē/ an industrial town in western central England, near Birmingham; pop. 187,000.

Dud·ley2, Robert, Earl of Leicester (*c.*1532–88), English nobleman, military commander, and favorite of Elizabeth I.

due /d(y)o͞o/ ▸*adj.* **1** [*predic.*] expected at or planned for at a certain time: *the baby's due in August* | *he is due back soon* | [with *infinitive*] *talks are due to adjourn tomorrow.* ■ (of a payment) required at a certain time: *the May installment was due.* ■ (of a person) having reached a point where the thing mentioned is required or owed: *she was* **due for** *a raise* | *you're more than due a vacation.* ■ (of a thing) required or owed as a legal or moral obligation: *he was only taking back what was* **due to** *him* | *you must pay any income tax due.* **2** [*attrib.*] of the proper quality or extent; adequate: *driving without due care and attention.*
▸*n.* **1** (**one's due**) a person's right; what is owed to someone: *he attracts more criticism than is his due.* **2** (**dues**) an obligatory payment; a fee: *he had paid trade union dues for years.*
▸*adv.* (with reference to a point of the compass) exactly; directly: *we'll head due south again on the same road.* ▷Middle English (in the sense 'payable'): from Old French *deu* 'owed,' based on Latin *debitus* 'owed,' from *debere* 'owe' .
▸*PHRASES* □ **due to 1** caused by or ascribable to: *unemployment due to automation will grow steadily.* **2** because of; owing to: *he had to withdraw due to a knee injury.* See **usage** below. □ **give someone their due** be fair to someone: *to give him his due, he was a generous employer.* □ **in due course** at the appropriate time: *Reynolds will respond in due course to the letter.* □ **pay one's dues** fulfill one's obligations: *he had paid his dues to society for his previous convictions.* ■ experience difficulties before achieving success: *this drummer has paid his dues with the best.*

USAGE The use of **due to** as a prepositional phrase meaning 'because of,' as in *he had to retire* **due to** *an injury* first appeared in print in 1897, and traditional grammarians have opposed this prepositional usage for more than a century on the grounds that it is a misuse of the adjectival phrase **due to** in the sense of 'attributable to, likely or expected to' (*the train is due to arrive at 11:15*), or 'payable or owed to' (*render unto Caesar what is due to Caesar*). Nevertheless, this prepositional usage is now widespread and common in all types of literature and must be regarded as standard English.
The phrase **due to the fact that** is very common in speech, but it is wordy, and, especially in writing, one should use the simple word 'because.'

due date ▸*n.* the date on which something falls due, esp. the payment of a bill or the expected birth of a baby.

due dil·i·gence ▸*n. Law* reasonable steps taken by a person in order to satisfy a legal requirement, esp. in buying or selling something.

du·el /ˈd(y)o͞oəl/ ▸*n. chiefly historical* a contest with deadly weapons arranged between two people in order to settle a point of honor. ■ (in modern use) a contest or race between two parties: *two eminent critics engaged in a verbal duel.*
▸*v.* (**du·eled, du·el·ing**; *Brit.* **du·elled, du·el·ling**) [*intrans.*] fight a duel or duels: [as *n.*] (**dueling**) *dueling had been forbidden for serving officers.* ▷late 15th cent.: from Latin *duellum,* archaic form of *bellum* 'war,' used in medieval Latin with the meaning 'combat between two persons,' partly influenced by *dualis* 'of two.' The original sense was 'single combat used to decide a judicial dispute'; the sense 'contest to decide a point of honor' dates from the early 17th cent. **—du·el·er** (*Brit.* **du·el·ler**) *n.* **—du·el·ist** /-ist/ (*Brit.* **du·el·list**) *n.*

duen·de /do͞oˈendā/ ▸*n.* a quality of passion and inspiration. ■ a spirit. ▷1920s: from Spanish, contraction of *duen de casa,* from *dueño de casa* 'owner of the house.'

du·en·na /d(y)o͞oˈenə/ ▸*n.* an older woman acting as a governess and companion in charge of girls, esp. in a Spanish family; a chaperone. ▷mid 17th cent.: earlier form of Spanish *dueña,* from Latin *domina* 'lady, mistress.'

due proc·ess (also **due process of law**) ▸*n.* fair treatment through the normal judicial system, esp. as a citizen's entitlement.

Due·ro /ˈdwerō/ Spanish name for DOURO.

du·et /d(y)o͞oˈet/ ▸*n.* a performance by two people, esp. singers, instrumentalists, or dancers. ■ a musical composition for two performers.
▸*v.* (**du·et·ted, du·et·ting**) [*intrans.*] perform a duet. ▷mid 18th cent.: from Italian *duetto,* diminutive of *duo* 'duet,' from Latin *duo* 'two.' **—du·et·tist** *n.*

duff1 /dəf/ ▸*n.* [usu. with *adj.*] a flour pudding boiled or steamed in a cloth bag: *a currant duff.* ▷mid 19th cent.: northern English form of DOUGH.

duff2 ▸*n.* **1** decaying vegetable matter covering the ground under trees. **2** *Mining* coal dust; dross.
▸*adj. Brit., informal* of very poor quality: *duff lyrics.* ■ incorrect or false: *she played a couple of duff notes.* ▷late 18th cent. (denoting something worthless): of unknown origin.

duff3 ▸*v.* [*trans.*] *informal* **1** (**duff someone up**) *Brit.* beat someone up. [1960s: of uncertain origin.] **2** *Golf Brit.* mishit (a shot). [early 19th cent.: back-formation from DUFFER.]

duff4 ▸*n. informal* a person's buttocks: *I did not get where I am today by sitting on my duff.* ▷mid 19th cent.: of unknown origin.

duf·fel /ˈdəfəl/ (also **duf·fle**) ▸*n.* **1** a coarse woolen cloth with a thick nap. ■ short for DUFFEL COAT. **2** sporting or camping equipment. ■ short for DUFFEL BAG. ▷mid 17th cent.: from *Duffel,* the name of a town in Belgium where the cloth was originally made.

duf·fel bag ▸*n.* a cylindrical canvas bag closed by a drawstring and carried over the shoulder. ▷early 20th cent.: from DUFFEL (sense 2), originally denoting a bag for equipment.

duf·fel coat ▸*n.* a coat made of duffel, typically hooded and fastened with toggles.

duf·fer /ˈdəfər/ ▸*n. informal* an incompetent or stupid person, esp. an elderly one: *he's the most worthless old duffer.* ■ a person inexperienced at something, esp. at playing golf. ▷mid 19th cent.: from Scots *dowfart* 'stupid person,' from *douf* 'spiritless.'

Du Fu /ˈdo͞o ˈfo͞o/ variant of **TU FU.**

du·fus ▸*n.* variant spelling of DOOFUS.

Du·fy /d(y)o͞oˈfē/, Raoul (1877–1953), French painter and textile designer. His characteristic style involved calligraphic outlines sketched on brilliant background washes.

dug1 /dəg/ ▸ past and past participle of DIG.

dug2 ▸*n.* (usu. **dugs**) the udder, teat, or nipple of a female animal. ■ *archaic* a woman's breast. ▷mid 16th cent.: possibly of Old Norse origin and related to Swedish *dägga,* Danish *dægge* 'suckle.'

du·gong /ˈdo͞ogäNG; -gôNG/ ▸*n.* (*pl.* same or **-gongs**) an aquatic mammal found on the coasts of the Indian Ocean from eastern Africa to northern Australia. It is distinguished from the manatees by its forked tail. • *Dugong dugon,* family Dugongidae. ▷early 19th cent.: based on Malay *duyong.*

dugong

dug·out /ˈdəg,out/ ▸*n.* **1** a shelter that is dug in the ground and roofed over, esp. one used by troops in warfare. ■ a low shelter at the side of a baseball field, with seating from which a team's coaches and players not taking part can watch the game. **2** (also **dugout canoe**) a canoe made from a hollowed tree trunk.

duh /də; do͞o/ ▸*exclam. informal* used to comment on an action perceived as foolish or stupid: *they got back together—duh!*

DUI ▸*abbr.* driving under the influence (of drugs or alcohol).

dui·ker /ˈdīkər/ ▸*n.* (*pl.* same or **-kers**) a small African antelope that typically has a tuft of hair between the horns, found mainly in the rain forest. • *Cephalophus* and other genera, family Bovidae: several species, including the **common duiker** (*Sylvicapra grimmia*), of southern African savannah and bush, and the very small **blue duiker** (*Philantomba monticola*), prized for its skin. ▷late 18th cent.: from South African Dutch, from Dutch, literally 'diver,' from the animal's habit of plunging through bushes when pursued; related to DUCK2.

Duis·burg /ˈd(y)o͞oz,bərg; ˈd(y)o͞os-; -,bo͝ork/ an industrial city in northwestern Germany, in North Rhine-Westphalia; pop. 537,440.

du jour /də ˈZHo͝or; ,d(y)o͞o/ ▸*adj.* [*postpositive*] (of food in a restaurant) available and being served on this day: *cream of mussel, an occasional soup du jour.* ■ *informal* used to describe something that is enjoying great but probably short-lived popularity or publicity: *attention deficit disorder is the disease du jour.* ▷French, literally 'of the day.'

Du·ka·kis[1] /dōō'kākis/, Michael Stanley (1933–), U.S. politician. He was governor of Massachusetts 1975–79, 1983–91 and a Democratic presidential candidate in 1988. Olympia Dukakis is his cousin.

Du·ka·kis[2], Olympia (1931–), U.S. actress. Her movies include *Moonstruck* (Academy Award, 1987) and *Steel Magnolias* (1989). She is a cousin of Michael Dukakis.

duke /d(y)ōōk/ ▸*n.* **1** a male holding the highest hereditary title in the British and certain other peerages. ■ *chiefly historical* (in some parts of Europe) a male ruler of a small independent state. **2** (**dukes**) *informal* the fists, esp. when raised in a fighting attitude. [from rhyming slang *Duke of Yorks* 'forks' (= fingers).] ▷Old English (denoting the ruler of a duchy), from Old French *duc*, from Latin *dux, duc-* 'leader'; related to *ducere* 'to lead.'

▸*PHRASE* □ **duke it out** *informal* fight it out.

duke cher·ry ▸*n.* a cultivated cherry that is a hybrid between the mazzard and the morello. • *Prunus × gondouinii*, family Rosaceae.

duke·dom /'d(y)ōōkdəm/ ▸*n.* a territory ruled by a duke. ■ the rank of duke.

DUKW ▸*n.* an amphibious transport vehicle, esp. as used by the Allies during World War II. Also called DUCK[1]. ▷an official designation, being a combination of factory-applied letters referring to features of the vehicle.

dul·ca·ma·ra /ˌdəlkə'merə/ ▸*n.* an extract of woody nightshade, used in homeopathy esp. for treating skin diseases and chest complaints. ▷late 16th cent.: from medieval Latin (used as a specific epithet in *Solanum dulcamara*), from Latin *dulcis* 'sweet' + *amara* 'bitter.'

dul·ce /'dəlsā/ ▸*n.* a sweet food or drink, esp. a candy or jam. [Spanish.]

▸*adj.* sweet or mild. [from Latin *dulcis*.]

dul·ce de le·che /'dōōlsā de ˌ'lecHā/ ▸*n.* a traditional Argentinian dessert made by caramelizing sugar in milk.

dul·cet /'dəlsit/ ▸*adj.* (esp. of sound) sweet and soothing (often used ironically): *record the* **dulcet tones** *of your family and friends.* ▷late Middle English *doucet*, from Old French *doucet*, diminutive of *doux*, from Latin *dulcis* 'sweet.' The Latin form influenced the modern spelling.

dul·ci·an /'dəlsēən/ ▸*n.* an early type of bassoon made in one piece. ■ any of various organ stops, typically with 8-foot funnel-shaped flue pipes or 8- or 16-foot reed pipes. ▷mid 19th cent.: from German *Dulzian*, or a variant of DULCIANA.

dul·ci·an·a /ˌdəlsē'anə; -'änə/ ▸*n.* an organ stop, typically with small conical open metal pipes. ▷late 18th cent.: via medieval Latin from Latin *dulcis* 'sweet.'

dul·ci·fy /'dəlsəˌfī/ ▸*v.* (**-fies, -fied**) [*trans.*] *poetic/literary* sweeten: *cider pap dulcified with molasses.* ■ calm or soothe: *his voice dulcified the panic.* ▷late 16th cent. (in the sense 'sweeten'): from Latin *dulcificare* 'sweeten,' from *dulcis* 'sweet.' —**dul·ci·fi·ca·tion** /ˌdəlsəfi'kāsHən/ *n.*

dul·ci·mer /'dəlsəmər/ ▸*n.* (also **hammered dulcimer**) a musical instrument with a sounding board or box, typically trapezoidal in shape, over which strings of graduated length are stretched, played by being struck with hand-held hammers. ■ (**Appalachian dulcimer**) a musical instrument with a long rounded body and a fretted fingerboard, played by bowing, plucking, and strumming. Also called MOUNTAIN DULCIMER. ▷late 15th cent.: from Old French *doulcemer*, probably from Latin *dulce melos* 'sweet melody.'

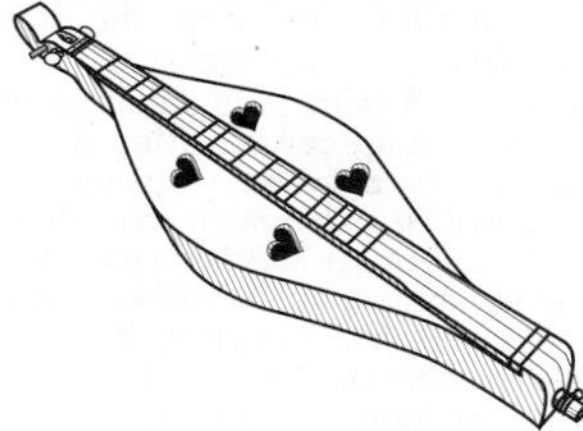

Appalachian dulcimer

dul·ci·tone /'dəlsəˌtōn/ ▸*n.* a musical keyboard instrument in which a series of steel tuning forks is struck by hammers. It was invented in the late 19th century and was superseded by the celesta. ▷late 19th cent.: coined by T. Machell, the instrument's inventor, from Latin *dulcis* 'sweet' + *tonus* 'tone.'

du·li·a /d(y)ōō'līə/ ▸*n.* (in Roman Catholic theology) the reverence accorded to saints and angels. Compare with LATRIA. ▷late Middle English: via medieval Latin from Greek *douleia* 'servitude,' from *doulos* 'slave.'

dull /dəl/ ▸*adj.* **1** lacking interest or excitement: *your diet doesn't have to be dull and boring.* ■ *archaic* (of a person) feeling bored and dispirited: *she said she wouldn't be dull and lonely.* **2** lacking brightness, vividness, or sheen: *his face glowed in the dull lamplight | his black hair looked dull.* ■ (of the weather) overcast; gloomy: *next morning dawned dull.* ■ (of sound) not clear; muffled: *a dull thud of hooves.* ■ (of pain) indistinctly felt; not acute: *there was a dull pain in his lower jaw.* ■ (of an edge or blade) blunt: *a lot more people are cut with dull knives than with sharp ones.* **3** (of a person) slow to understand; stupid: *the voice of a teacher talking to a rather dull child.* See note at STUPID. ■ *archaic* (of a person's senses) not perceiving things distinctly; insensitive. ■ (of activity) sluggish, slow-moving: *gold closed lower in dull trading.*

▸*v.* make or become dull or less intense: [*trans.*] *time dulls the memory* | [*intrans.*] *Albert's eyes dulled a little.* ▷Old English *dol* 'stupid,' of Germanic origin; related to Dutch *dol* 'crazy' and German *toll* 'mad, fantastic, wonderful.' —**dull·ish** *adj.* —**dull·ness** (also **dul·ness**) *n.* —**dul·ly** *adv.*

▸*PHRASES* □ (**as**) **dull as dishwater** extremely dull. □ **dull the edge of** cause to be less keenly felt; reduce the intensity or effectiveness of: *she'd have to find something to dull the edges of the pain.*

dull·ard /'dələrd/ ▸*n.* a slow or stupid person. ▷Middle English: from Middle Dutch *dullaert*, from *dul* 'dull.'

Dul·les /'dələs/, John Foster (1888–1959), U.S. statesman and international lawyer. He was the U.S. adviser at the founding of the UN in 1945. As secretary of state at the height of the Cold War 1953–59, he urged the stockpiling of nuclear arms to deter Soviet aggression.

dulls·ville /'dəlzˌvil/ *informal* ▸*n.* a dull or monotonous place or condition.

▸*adj.* dull or monotonous: *she transforms their dullsville life.*

dull-wit·ted ▸*adj.* slow to understand; stupid.

du·lo·sis /d(y)ōō'lōsis/ ▸*n.* *Entomology* the practice by slave-making ants of capturing the pupae of other ant species and rearing them as workers of their own colony. ▷early 20th cent.: from Greek *doulōsis* 'slavery,' from *doulos* 'slave.' —**du·lot·ic** /-'lätik/ *adj.*

dulse /dəls/ ▸*n.* a dark red edible seaweed with flattened branching fronds. • *Rhodymenia palmata*, division Rhodophyta. ▷early 17th cent.: from Irish and Scottish Gaelic *duileasg*.

Du·luth /də'lōōTH/ a port in northeastern Minnesota, at the western end of Lake Superior; pop. 86,918.

du·ly /'d(y)ōōlē/ ▸*adv.* in accordance with what is required or appropriate; following proper procedure or arrangement: *a document duly signed and authorized by the inspector | the ceremony duly began at midnight.* ■ as might be expected or predicted: *I used the tent and was duly impressed.*

dum /dəm/ ▸*adj.* *Indian* cooked with steam: *dum aloo.* ▷from Hindi *dam.*

Du·ma /'dōōmə/ ▸*n.* a legislative body in the ruling assembly of Russia and of some other republics of the former USSR.

> **Duma** originally denoted pre-19th century advisory municipal councils in Russia. It later referred to any of four elected legislative bodies established due to popular demand in Russia between 1906 and 1917. After the collapse of communism in 1991, a new **Duma** was set up as the lower chamber of the Russian parliament.

Du·mas /d(y)ōō'mä/ the name of two French novelists and playwrights: ■ **Alexandre** (1802–70); known as **Dumas *père*** (father). He wrote the historical adventure novels, *The Three Musketeers* (1844–45) and *The Count of Monte Cristo* (1844–45). ■ **Alexandre** (1824–95), son of Dumas *père*; known as **Dumas *fils*** (son). He wrote the novel (and play) *La Dame aux camélias* (1848), which formed the basis of Verdi's opera *La Traviata* (1853).

Du Mau·ri·er[1] /d(y)ōō 'môrēˌā/, Dame Daphne (1907–89), English novelist; granddaughter of George du Maurier. Notable works: *Jamaica Inn* (1936) and *Rebecca* (1938).

Du Mau·ri·er[2], George (Louis Palmella Busson) (1834–96), French novelist, cartoonist, and illustrator. He wrote *Trilby* (1894), which included the character Svengali.

dumb /dəm/ ▸*adj.* **1** *chiefly offensive* (of a person) unable to speak, most typically because of congenital deafness: *he was born deaf, dumb, and blind.* ■ (of animals) unable to speak as a natural state and thus regarded as helpless or deserving pity. ■ [*predic.*] temporarily unable or unwilling to speak: *she stood dumb while he poured out a stream of abuse.* ■ [*attrib.*] resulting in or expressed by speechlessness: *they stared in dumb amazement.* **2** *informal* stupid: *a dumb question.* See note at STUPID. ■ (of a computer terminal) able only to transmit data to or receive data from a computer; having no independent processing capability. Often contrasted with INTELLIGENT.

▸*v.* [*trans.*] **1** (**dumb something down**) *informal* simplify or reduce the intellectual content of something so as to make it accessible to a larger number of people: *critics have accused publishers of dumbing down books.* ■ [*intrans.*] (**dumb down**) become less intellectually challenging: *the need to dumb down for mass audiences.* **2** *poetic/literary* make dumb or unheard; silence: *a splendor that dazed the mind and dumbed the tongue.* ▷Old English, of Germanic origin; related to Old Norse *dumbr* and Gothic *dumbs* 'mute,' also to Dutch *dom* 'stupid' and German *dumm* 'stupid.' —**dumb·ly** *adv.* —**dumb·ness** *n.*

> *USAGE* Although **dumb** meaning 'not able to speak' is the older sense, it has been overwhelmed by the newer sense (meaning 'stupid') to such an extent that the use of the first sense is now almost certain to cause offense. Alternatives such as **speech-impaired** should be used instead.
> See also **usage** at DEAF-MUTE.

Dum·bar·ton Oaks /'dəmˌbärtn 'ōks/ a historic site in Washington, DC, an estate at which plans for the UN were formulated at a 1944 meeting.

dumb-ass ▸*adj.* [*attrib.*] *informal* stupid; brainless: *dumb-ass politicians.*

dumb·bell /'dəmˌbel/ ▸*n.* **1** a short bar with a weight at each end, used typically in pairs for exercise or muscle-building. ■ [as *adj.*] shaped like a dumbbell: *a dumbbell molecule.* **2** *informal* a stupid person. ▷early 18th cent.: originally denoting an apparatus similar to that used to ring a church bell (but without the bell, so noiseless or "dumb"); sense 2 (dating from the 1920s) is an extended use by association with DUMB 'stupid.'

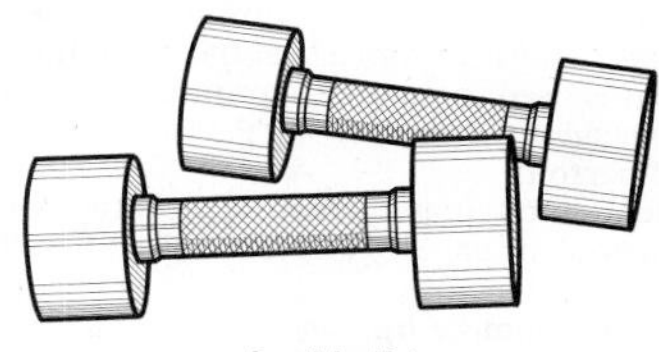

dumbbell 1

dumb blond (also **dumb blonde**) ▸*n.* *informal* a blond-haired woman perceived in a stereotypical way as being attractive but unintelligent.

dumb cane ▸*n.* a thick-stemmed plant with large variegated leaves, native to tropical America and widely grown as a houseplant. • Genus *Dieffenbachia*, family Araceae: several species, in particular the Caribbean *D. seguine*, which has a poisonous sap that swells the tongue and temporarily disables the power of speech.

dumb cluck ▸*n.* *informal* a stupid person.

dumb·found /'dəmˌfound/ (also **dum·found**) ▸*v.* [*trans.*] (usu. **be dumbfounded**) greatly astonish or amaze: *they were dumbfounded at his popularity.* ▷mid 17th cent.: blend of DUMB and CONFOUND.

dumb·head /'dəmˌhed/ ▸*n.* *informal* a stupid person.

dumb i·ron ▸*n.* *historical* a curved side piece of a vehicle chassis, to which the front springs are attached.

dum·bo /'dəmbō/ ▸*n.* (*pl.* **-bos**) *informal* a stupid person. ▷1950s: from DUMB + -O, popularized by the 1941 cartoon film *Dumbo*.

dumb·show /'dəmˌsHō/ (also **dumb show**) ▸*n.* gestures used to convey a meaning or message without speech; mime: *they demonstrated* **in dumbshow** *how the tea should be made.* ■ a piece of dramatic mime: *there were gags, spoofs, and dumbshows.* ■ (esp. in English drama of the 16th and 17th centuries) a part of a play acted in mime to summarize, supplement, or comment on the main action.

dumb·size /ˈdəm,sīz/ ▸*v.* [*intrans.*] (of a company) reduce staff numbers to levels so low that work can no longer be carried out effectively. ▷1990s: humorously, on the pattern of *downsize*.

dumb·struck /ˈdəm,strək/ ▸*adj.* so shocked or surprised as to be unable to speak: *he was dumbstruck with terror.*

dumb wait·er ▸*n.* **1** a small elevator for carrying things, esp. food and dishes, between the floors of a building. **2** *Brit.* a movable table, typically with revolving shelves, used in a dining room.

dum·dum /ˈdəm,dəm/ (also **dumdum bullet**) ▸*n.* a kind of soft-nosed bullet that expands on impact and inflicts laceration. ▷late 19th cent.: from *Dum Dum*, name of a town and arsenal near Calcutta, India, where such bullets were first produced.

dum-dum ▸*n. informal* a stupid person. ▷1970s: reduplication of DUMB.

dum·found ▸*v.* variant spelling of DUMBFOUND.

Dum·fries and Gal·lo·way /dəmˈfrēs and ˈgalə,wā/ an administrative region in southwestern Scotland, formed in 1975; administrative center, Dumfries.

dum·ka /ˈdo͝omkə/ ▸*n.* (*pl.* **-kas** or **-ky** /-kē/) a piece of Slavic music, originating as a folk ballad or lament, typically melancholy with contrasting lively sections. ▷late 19th cent.: via Czech and Polish from Ukrainian.

dumm·kopf /ˈdo͝om,kôf; -,kôpf; ˈdəm-/ ▸*n.* a stupid person; a blockhead. ▷early 19th cent.: from German *dumm* 'dumb' + *Kopf* 'head.'

dum·my /ˈdəmē/ ▸*n.* (*pl.* **-mies**) **1** a model or replica of a human being: *a waxwork dummy.* ■ a figure used for displaying or fitting clothes: *a tailor's dummy.* ■ a ventriloquist's doll. ■ a person taking no real part or present only for appearances; a figurehead. ■ *Bridge* the declarer's partner, whose cards are exposed on the table after the opening lead and played by the declarer. ■ *Bridge* the exposed hand of the declarer's partner. ■ an imaginary fourth player in whist: [as *adj.*] *dummy whist.* **2** an object designed to resemble and serve as a substitute for the real or usual one: *tests using stuffed owls and wooden dummies* | [as *adj.*] *a dummy torpedo.* ■ an enterprise existing mainly on paper, set up to facilitate fraud: [mainly as *adj.*] *an elaborate scheme of dummy invoices, and even a dummy corporation, designed to underprice products.* ■ a prototype or mock-up, esp. of a book or the layout of a page. ■ a blank round of ammunition. ■ [as *adj.*] *Grammar* denoting a word that has no semantic content but is used to maintain grammatical structure: *a dummy subject, as in "it is" or "there are."* **3** *informal* a stupid person.
▸*v.* (**-mies, -mied**) [*trans.*] create a prototype or mock-up of a book or page: *officials **dummied up** a set of photos.*
▸*phrasal v.* □ **dummy up** *informal* keep quiet; give no information. ▷late 16th cent.: from DUMB + -Y[1]. The original sense was 'a person who cannot speak,' then 'an imaginary fourth player in whist' (mid 18th cent.), whence 'a substitute for the real thing' and 'a model of a human being' (mid 19th cent.).

dum·my cord ▸*n.* a cord or strap that secures an object (such as a weapon) to one's person.
▸*v.* [*trans.*] secure an object with such a cord: *he'll show you how to dummy cord your knife.*

dum·my head ▸*n. Electronics* a model of a human head with a microphone in each ear, used in making binaural and other sound-recording techniques.

du·mor·ti·er·ite /d(y)o͞oˈmôrtēə,rīt/ ▸*n.* a rare blue or violet mineral occurring typically as needles and fibrous masses in gneiss and schist. It consists of an aluminum and iron borosilicate. ▷late 19th cent.: from the name of V.-E. *Dumortier* (1802–76), French geologist, + -ITE[1].

dump /dəmp/ ▸*n.* **1** a site for depositing garbage. ■ [usu. with *adj.*] a place where a particular kind of waste, esp. dangerous waste, is left: *a nuclear waste dump.* ■ a heap of garbage left at a dump. ■ *informal* an unpleasant or dreary place: *she says the town has become a dump.* ■ *informal* an act of defecation. **2** *Computing* a copying of stored data to a different location, performed typically as a protection against loss. ■ a printout or list of the contents of a computer's memory, occurring typically after a system failure.
▸*v.* [*trans.*] **1** deposit or dispose of (garbage, waste, or unwanted material), typically in a careless or hurried way: *trucks dumped 1,900 tons of refuse here* | [*intrans.*] *an attempt to prevent people from dumping on vacant lots.* ■ put down or abandon (something) hurriedly in order to make an escape: *the couple dumped the car and fled.* ■ put (something) down firmly or heavily and carelessly: *she dumped her knapsack on the floor.* ■ *informal* abandon or desert (someone): *his girlfriend dumped him for being fat.* ■ send (goods unsalable in the home market) to a foreign market for sale at a low price: *other countries dump steel in the U.S. at below-market prices.* ■ *informal* sell off (assets) rapidly: *investors dumped shares in scores of other consumer-goods firms.* **2** *Computing* copy (stored data) to a different location, esp. so as to protect against loss. ■ print out or list the contents of (a store), esp. after a system failure. **3** *Football* tackle (a quarterback) before he can throw a pass.
▸*phrasal v.* □ **dump on** *informal* criticize or abuse (someone); treat badly: *you get dumped on just because of your name.* ▷Middle English: perhaps from Old Norse; related to Danish *dumpe* and Norwegian *dumpa* 'fall suddenly' (the original sense in English); in later use partly imitative; compare with THUMP.

dump·er /ˈdəmpər/ ▸*n.* a person or thing that dumps something. ■ (**the dumper**) *informal* used in reference to a bad or unwanted state: *his career's **in the dumper**.* ■ (also **dumper truck**) *Brit.* a dump truck.

dump·ing ground ▸*n.* a place where garbage or unwanted material is left.

dump·ing syn·drome ▸*n. Medicine* a group of symptoms, including weakness, abdominal discomfort, and sometimes abnormally rapid bowel evacuation, occurring after meals in some patients who have undergone gastric surgery.

dump·ling /ˈdəmpliNG/ ▸*n.* a small savory ball of dough (usually made with suet) that may be boiled, fried, or baked in a casserole. ■ a pudding consisting of apples or other fruit enclosed in a sweet dough and baked. ■ *humorous* a small, fat person: *he was a 250-pound dumpling.* ▷early 17th cent.: apparently from the rare adjective *dump* 'of the consistency of dough,' although *dumpling* is recorded much earlier.

dumps /dəmps/ ▸*plural n.* (in phrase (**down**) **in the dumps**) *informal* (of a person) depressed or unhappy. ▷early 16th cent. (originally singular in the sense 'a dazed or puzzled state'): probably a figurative use of Middle Dutch *domp* 'haze, mist.'

dump·ster /ˈdəmpstər/ (also **Dump·ster**) ▸*n. trademark* a large trash receptacle designed to be hoisted and emptied into a truck. ▷1930s: originally *Dempster Dumpster*, proprietary name (based on DUMP) given by the American manufacturers, Dempster Brothers of Knoxville, Tennessee.

dump·ster div·ing ▸*n.* the practice of raiding dumpsters to find discarded items that are still useful, can be recycled, and have value.

dump truck ▸*n.* a truck with a body that tilts or opens at the back for unloading.

dump·y /ˈdəmpē/ ▸*adj.* (**dump·i·er, dump·i·est**) **1** (of a person) short and stout: *her plain, dumpy sister.* **2** (of a room or building) ugly, dirty, and run-down: *a dumpy little diner with a closed sign hanging in the window.* ▷mid 18th cent.: from DUMPLING + -Y[1].
—**dump·i·ly** /-pəlē/ *adv.* —**dump·i·ness** *n.*

Dum·yat /do͞omˈyät/ Arabic name for DAMIETTA.

dun[1] /dən/ ▸*adj.* of a dull grayish-brown color: *a dun cow.* ■ *poetic/literary* dark; dusky: *when the dun evening comes.*
▸*n.* **1** a dull grayish-brown color. **2** a thing that is dun in color, in particular: ■ a horse with a sandy or sandy-gray coat, black mane, tail, and lower legs, and a dark dorsal stripe. ■ a sub-adult mayfly, which has drab coloration and opaque wings. ■ an artificial fishing fly imitating this. ▷Old English *dun*, *dunn*, of Germanic origin; probably related to DUSK.

dun[2] ▸*v.* (**dunned, dun·ning**) [*trans.*] make persistent demands on (someone), esp. for payment of a debt: *they would very likely start dunning you for payment of your taxes* | [as *adj.*] (**dunning**) *she received two dunning letters from the bank.*
▸*n. archaic* a debt collector or an insistent creditor. ■ a demand for payment. ▷early 17th cent. (as a noun): from obsolete *Dunkirk privateer*, from the French port of DUNKIRK.

du·nam /ˈdo͞onəm/ ▸*n.* a measure of land area used in parts of the former Turkish empire, including Israel (where it is equal to about 900 square meters). ▷from modern Hebrew *dûnām* or Arabic *dūnum*, from Turkish *dönüm*, from *dönmek* 'go around.'

Dun·can /ˈdəNGkən/, Isadora (1878–1927), U.S. dancer and teacher. A pioneer of modern dance, she was famous for her "free" barefoot dancing. She died by strangulation when her long scarf became entangled in the wheels of a car.

Dun·can I (*c.*1010–40), king of Scotland 1034–40. He was killed in battle by Macbeth.

dunce /dəns/ ▸*n.* a person who is slow at learning; a stupid person. ▷early 16th cent.: originally an epithet for a follower of John DUNS SCOTUS, whose followers were ridiculed by 16th-cent. humanists and reformers as enemies of learning.

dunce cap (*Brit.* also **dunce's cap**) ▸*n.* a paper cone formerly put on the head of a dunce at school as a mark of disgrace.

Dun·dalk /ˈdən,dôk/ a community in north central Maryland, a port just southeast of Baltimore; pop. 65,800.

Dun·dee /dənˈdē/ a city in eastern Scotland, on the northern side of the Firth of Tay; pop. 165,500.

Dun·dee cake ▸*n. chiefly Brit.* a rich fruitcake, typically decorated on top with almonds.

Dun·dee mar·ma·lade ▸*n.* a type of orange marmalade, originally made in Dundee.

dun·der·head /ˈdəndər,hed/ ▸*n. informal* a stupid person. ▷early 17th cent.: compare with obsolete Scots *dunder, dunner* 'resounding noise'; related to DIN.
—**dun·der·head·ed** *adj.*

dune /d(y)o͞on/ ▸*n.* a mound or ridge of sand or other loose sediment formed by the wind, esp. on the sea coast or in a desert: *a sand dune.* ▷late 18th cent.: from French, from Middle Dutch *dūne*; related to Old English *dūn* 'hill' (see DOWN[3]).

dune bug·gy ▸*n.* a low, wide-wheeled motor vehicle for recreational driving on sand.

Dun·e·din /dənˈēdn/ **1** a city and port on South Island in New Zealand, founded in 1848 by Scottish settlers; pop. 113,900. **2** a resort city in western Florida, on the Gulf of Mexico, west of Tampa; pop. 34,012.

dung /dəNG/ ▸*n.* the excrement of animals; manure.
▸*v.* [*trans.*] drop or spread dung on (a piece of ground). ▷Old English, of Germanic origin; related to German *Dung*, Swedish *dynga*, Icelandic *dyngja* 'dung, dunghill, heap,' and Danish *dynge* 'heap.'

dun·ga·rees /,dəNGgəˈrēz/ ▸*plural n.* **1** blue jeans or overalls. **2** [in *sing.*] (**dungaree**) blue denim. ▷late 17th cent. (in the sense 'cotton cloth from India'); from Hindi *duṅgrī*.

dung bee·tle ▸*n.* a beetle whose larvae feed on dung, esp. a scarab. The larger kinds place the dung in a hole before the eggs are laid, and some of them roll it along in a ball. • Superfamily Scarabaeoidea, in particular families Scarabaeidae and Geotrupidae.

Dun·ge·ness crab /ˈdənjə,nes/ ▸*n.* a large crab found off the west coast of North America, where it is popular as food. • *Cancer magister*, family Cancridae. ▷mid 20th cent.: from *Dungeness*, the name of a fishing village on the coast of Washington.

dun·geon /ˈdənjən/ ▸*n.* a strong underground prison cell, esp. in a castle. ■ (in fantasy role-playing games) a labyrinthine subterranean setting. ■ archaic term for DONJON.
▸*v.* [*trans.*] *poetic/literary* imprison (someone) in a dungeon. ▷Middle English (also with the sense 'castle keep'): from Old French (perhaps originally with the sense 'lord's tower' or 'mistress tower'), based on Latin *dominus* 'lord, master.' Compare with DONJON.

Dun·geons and Drag·ons ▸*n. trademark* a fantasy role-playing game set in an imaginary world based loosely on medieval myth.

dung fly ▸*n.* a hairy fly that lays its eggs in fresh dung. • Families Scathophagidae and Sphaeroceridae: several species.

dung·hill /ˈdəNG,hil/ (also **dung·heap**) ▸*n.* a heap of dung or refuse, esp. in a farmyard.

du·nite /ˈdənīt/ ▸*n. Geology* a green to brownish coarse-grained igneous rock consisting largely of olivine. ▷mid 19th cent.: from the name of *Dun* Mountain, New Zealand, + -ITE[1].

dunk /dəNGk/ ▸*v.* **1** [*trans.*] dip (bread or other food) into a drink or soup before eating it: *she dunked a piece of bread into her coffee.* ■ immerse or dip in water: *the bikers dunked themselves in the ocean* | [as *n.*] (**dunking**) *the camera survived a dunking in a stream.* ■ baptize (someone) by immersion: *he's always trying to get me to go and be dunked into the church.* **2** [*intrans.*] *Basketball* score by shooting the ball down through the basket with the hands above the rim.
▸*n. Basketball* a shot downward into the basket with the hands above the rim. ▷early 20th cent.: from Pennsylvania Dutch *dunke* 'dip,' from German *tunken* 'dip or plunge.'
—**dunk·er** *n.*

Dunk·ard /ˈdəNGkərd/ ▸*n.* another term for DUNKER.

Dunk·er /ˈdəNGkər/ ▸*n.* a member of the German Baptist Brethren, a sect of Baptist Christians founded in 1708 but living in the U.S. since the 1720s. ▷early

18th cent.: from Pennsylvania Dutch, from *dunke* (see **DUNK**).

Dun·kirk /ˈdənˌkərk; dənˈkərk/ a port in northern France; pop. 71,070. It was the scene of the evacuation of 335,000 Allied troops in 1940 by warships, requisitioned civilian ships, and a host of small boats while under constant German attack from the air. French name **DUNKERQUE** .

dun·lin /ˈdənlin/ ▸*n.* (*pl.* same or **dun·lins**) a migratory sandpiper with a down-curved bill and (in the breeding season) a reddish-brown back and black belly. It is the commonest small wader of the northern hemisphere. • *Calidris alpina*, family Scolopacidae. ▷mid 16th cent.: probably from **DUN**[1] + **-LING**, from the grayish-brown winter coloring of its upper parts.

Dun·lop /ˈdənläp/, John Boyd (1840–1921), Scottish inventor. He developed the first successful pneumatic bicycle tire in 1888.

dun·nage /ˈdənij/ ▸*n.* pieces of wood, matting, or similar material used to keep a cargo in position in a ship's hold. ■ *informal* a person's belongings, esp. those brought on board ship. ▷Middle English: of unknown origin.

dun·no /dəˈnō/ ▸*contraction of* (I) do not know. ▷mid 19th cent.: representing an informal pronunciation.

Duns Sco·tus /dənz ˈskōtəs/, John (*c.*1265–1308), Scottish theologian and scholar. He was the first major theologian to defend the theory of the immaculate conception and to oppose St. Thomas Aquinas by arguing that faith is a matter of will rather than something dependent on logical proofs.

Dun·stan, St. /ˈdənstən/ (*c.*909–88), Anglo-Saxon prelate. As archbishop of Canterbury, he introduced the strict Benedictine rule in England and succeeded in restoring monastic life. Feast day, May 19.

dunt /dənt/ *chiefly Scottish* ▸*v.* [*trans.*] hit or knock firmly with a dull sound: *she dunted my father in the side with her elbow.*
▸*n.* a firm dull-sounding blow. ▷late Middle English: perhaps a variant of **DINT**.

du·o /ˈd(y)o͞o-ō/ ▸*n.* (*pl.* **du·os**) **1** a pair of people or things, esp. in music or entertainment: *the comedy duo Laurel and Hardy.* **2** *Music* a duet: *he wrote two duos for violin and viola.* ▷late 16th cent. (sense 2): via Italian from Latin *duo* 'two.'

duo- ▸*comb. form* two; having two: *duopoly* | *duotone.* ▷from Latin.

du·o·dec·i·mal /ˌd(y)o͞oəˈdesəməl; ˌd(y)o͞o-ō-/ ▸*adj.* relating to or denoting a system of counting or numerical notation that has twelve as a base.
▸*n.* the system of duodecimal notation. ▷late 17th cent.: from Latin *duodecimus* 'twelfth' (from *duodecim* 'twelve') + **-AL**. **—du·o·dec·i·mal·ly** *adv.*

du·o·dec·i·mo /ˌd(y)o͞oəˈdesəˌmō; ˌd(y)o͞o-ō/ (abbr.: **12mo**) ▸*n.* (*pl.* **-mos**) a size of book page that results from the folding of each printed sheet into 12 leaves (24 pages). Also called **twelvemo**. ■ a book of this size. ▷mid 17th cent.: from Latin *(in) duodecimo* 'in a twelfth,' from *duodecimus* 'twelfth.'

du·o·den·a·ry /ˌd(y)o͞oəˈdenərē; ˌd(y)o͞o-ō-/ ▸*adj. rare* relating to or based on the number twelve. ▷mid 19th cent.: from Latin *duodenarius* 'containing twelve,' based on *duodecim* 'twelve.'

du·o·de·ni·tis /ˌd(y)o͞oədiˈnītis; ˌd(y)o͞o-ō-/ ▸*n. Medicine* inflammation of the duodenum.

duodeno- (also **duoden-** before a vowel) ▸*comb. form Anatomy & Medicine* relating to the duodenum: *duodenitis.*

du·o·de·num /ˌd(y)o͞oəˈdēnəm; d(y)o͞oˈädn-əm/ ▸*n.* (*pl.* **-nums** or **-na** /-nə/) *Anatomy* the first part of the small intestine immediately beyond the stomach, leading to the jejunum. ▷late Middle English: from medieval Latin, from *duodeni* 'in twelves,' its length being equivalent to the breadth of approximately twelve fingers. **—du·o·de·nal** /-ˈdēnl; -ˈädnəl/ *adj.*

du·o·logue /ˈd(y)o͞oəˌläg; -ˌlôg/ ▸*n.* a play or part of a play with speaking roles for only two actors. ▷mid 18th cent.: from **DUO-**, on the pattern of *monologue.*

duo·mo /ˈdwōmō/ ▸*n.* (*pl.* **-mos**) an Italian cathedral. ▷Italian, literally 'dome.'

du·op·o·ly /d(y)o͞oˈäpəlē/ ▸*n.* (*pl.* **-lies**) a situation in which two suppliers dominate the market for a commodity or service. ▷1920s: from **DUO-**, on the pattern of *monopoly.* **—du·op·o·lis·tic** /-ˌäpəˈlistik/ *adj.*

du·o·tone /ˈd(y)o͞oəˌtōn/ ▸*n.* a halftone illustration made from a single original with two different colors at different screen angles. ■ the technique or process of making such illustrations: *the best images that duotone can produce.*

du·pat·ta /dəˈpətə/ ▸*n.* a length of material worn as a scarf or head covering, typically with a salwar, by women from the Indian subcontinent. ▷from Hindi *dupaṭṭā.*

dupe[1] /d(y)o͞op/ ▸*v.* [*trans.*] deceive; trick: *the newspaper was* **duped into** *publishing an untrue story.*
▸*n.* a victim of deception: *knowing accomplices or unknowing dupes.* ▷late 17th cent.: from dialect French *dupe* 'hoopoe,' from the bird's supposedly stupid appearance. **—dup·a·ble** *adj.* **—dup·er** *n.* **—dup·er·y** /-pərē/ *n.*

dupe[2] ▸*v.* & *n.* short for **DUPLICATE**, esp. in photography.

du·pi·on /ˈdo͞opēˌän/ (also **du·pi·o·ni** /ˌdo͞opēˈōnē/ or **silk dupion**) ▸*n.* a rough slubbed silk fabric woven from the threads of double cocoons. ■ an imitation of this with other fibers. ▷early 19th cent. (in the sense 'double cocoon'): from French *doupion*, from Italian *doppione*, from *doppio* 'double.'

du·ple /ˈd(y)o͞opəl/ ▸*adj. Music* (of rhythm) based on two main beats to the bar: *duple time.* ▷mid 16th cent.: from Latin *duplus*, from *duo* 'two.'

du·plet /ˈd(y)o͞oplit/ ▸*n.* a set of two things. ■ *Music* a pair of equal notes to be performed in the time of three. ▷mid 17th cent. (as a dicing term in the sense of *doublets* (see **DOUBLET**)): from Latin *duplus* 'duple,' on the pattern of *doublet.* Current senses date from the 1920s.

du·plex /ˈd(y)o͞opleks/ ▸*n.* something having two parts, in particular: ■ a house divided into two apartments, with a separate entrance for each. ■ an apartment on two floors. ■ *Biochemistry* a double-stranded polynucleotide molecule.
▸*adj.* **1** having two parts, in particular: ■ (of a house) having two apartments. ■ (of an apartment) on two floors. ■ (of paper or board) having two differently colored layers or sides. ■ *Biochemistry* consisting of two polynucleotide strands linked side by side. ■ (of a printer or its software) capable of printing on both sides of the paper. **2** (of a communications system, computer circuit, etc.) allowing the transmission of two signals simultaneously in opposite directions. Compare with **MULTIPLEX, SIMPLEX.** ▷mid 16th cent. (as an adjective): from Latin *duplex, duplic-*, from *duo* 'two' + *plicare* 'to fold.' The noun dates from the 1920s.

du·pli·cate ▸*adj.* /ˈd(y)o͞opləkit/ [*attrib.*] **1** exactly like something else, esp. through having been copied: *a duplicate license is issued to replace a valid license which has been lost.* **2** having two corresponding or identical parts: *a duplicate application form.* ■ twice as large or many; doubled: *duplicate taxes on oil and gas.*
▸*n.* /ˈd(y)o͞opləkit/ **1** one of two or more identical things: *books may be disposed of if they are duplicates.* ■ a copy of an original: *locksmiths can make duplicates of most keys.* **2** short for **DUPLICATE BRIDGE. 3** *archaic* a pawnbroker's ticket.
▸*v.* /ˈd(y)o͞opləˌkāt/ [*trans.*] make or be an exact copy of: *a unique scent, impossible to duplicate or forget* | *figurative they have not been able to duplicate his successes.* ■ (often **be duplicated**) make or supply copies of (a document): *information sheets had to be typed and duplicated* | [as *adj.*] (**duplicating**) *a duplicating machine.* ■ multiply by two; double: *the normal amount of DNA has been duplicated thousands of times.* ■ do (something) again unnecessarily: *most of these proposals duplicated work already done.* ▷late Middle English (in the sense 'having two corresponding parts'): from Latin *duplicat-* 'doubled,' from the verb *duplicare*, from *duplic-* 'twofold' (see **DUPLEX**). **—du·pli·ca·ble** /-plikəbəl/ *adj.* **—du·pli·ca·tive** /-ˌkātiv/ *adj.*
▸*PHRASE* □ **in duplicate** consisting of two exact copies: *forms to complete in duplicate.*

du·pli·cate bridge ▸*n.* a competitive form of bridge in which the same hands are played successively by different partnerships.

du·pli·ca·tion /ˌd(y)o͞opləˈkāshən/ ▸*n.* the action or process of duplicating something. ■ a copy. ■ *Genetics* a DNA segment in a chromosome which is a copy of another segment. ▷late Middle English (used in the mathematical sense 'multiplication by two'): from Old French, or from Latin *duplicatio(n-)*, from *duplicare* 'to double' (see **DUPLICATE**).

du·pli·ca·tor /ˈd(y)o͞opləˌkātər/ ▸*n.* a machine or device for making copies of something, in particular a machine that makes copies of documents by means of fluid ink and a stencil.

du·plic·i·tous /d(y)o͞oˈplisitəs/ ▸*adj.* deceitful: *treacherous, duplicitous behavior.* ■ *Law* (of a charge or plea) containing more than one allegation.

du·plic·i·ty /d(y)o͞oˈplisitē/ ▸*n.* **1** deceitfulness; double-dealing. **2** *archaic* doubleness. ▷late Middle English: from Old French *duplicite* or late Latin *duplicitas*, from Latin *duplic-* 'twofold' (see **DUPLEX**).

du Pont /d(y)o͞o ˈpänt; ˈd(y)o͞o ˌpänt/, E. I. (1771–1834), U.S. industrialist; born in France; full name *Éleuthère Irénée du Pont.* His gunpowder manufacturing plant near Wilmington, Delaware, established in 1802, grew into a corporate giant, due largely to the government contracts that ensured its early success, esp. during the War of 1812.

dup·py /ˈdəpē/ ▸*n.* (*pl.* **-pies**) *W. Indian* a malevolent spirit or ghost. ▷late 18th cent.: probably of West African origin.

du Pré /d(y)o͞o ˈprā/, Jacqueline (1945–87), English cellist. She made her solo debut at 16 and was known for her interpretations of cello concertos. She married Daniel Barenboim in 1967 and was diagnosed with multiple sclerosis in 1973.

Du·puy·tren's con·trac·ture /dəˈpwētrənz / (also **Dupuytren's disease**) ▸*n. Medicine* a condition in which there is fixed forward curvature of one or more fingers, caused by the development of a fibrous connection between the finger tendons and the skin of the palm. ▷late 19th cent.: named after Baron Guillaume *Dupuytren* (1777–1835), the French surgeon who first described the condition.

Du·que de Ca·xi·as /ˈdo͞okē dā käˈshēəs/ a city in southeastern Brazil, a suburb of Rio de Janeiro; pop. 594,380.

du·ra[1] /ˈd(y)o͝orə/ (in full **dura mater**) ▸*n. Anatomy* the tough outermost membrane enveloping the brain and spinal cord. ▷late 19th cent.: from medieval Latin, literally 'hard mother,' translation of Arabic *al-'umm al-jāfiya* 'coarse mother.' **—du·ral** *adj.*

du·ra[2] ▸*n.* variant spelling of **DURRA**.

du·ra·ble /ˈd(y)o͝orəbəl/ ▸*adj.* able to withstand wear, pressure, or damage; hard-wearing: *porcelain enamel is strong and durable* | *figurative a durable peace can be achieved.* ■ *informal* (of a person) having endurance: *the durable Smith lasted the full eight rounds.*
▸*n.* (**durables**) short for **DURABLE GOODS**. ▷Middle English (in the sense 'steadfast'): via Old French from Latin *durabilis*, from *durare* 'to last' (see **DURATION**). **—du·ra·bil·i·ty** /ˌd(y)o͝orəˈbilitē/ *n.* **—du·ra·ble·ness** *n.* **—du·ra·bly** *adv.*

du·ra·ble goods ▸*plural n.* goods not for immediate consumption and able to be kept for a period of time.

du·ral·u·min /d(y)o͝orˈalyəmin/ ▸*n.* a hard, light alloy of aluminum with copper and other elements. ▷early 20th cent.: perhaps from Latin *durus* 'hard' + **ALUMINUM**, but probably influenced by *Düren*, the name of the Rhineland town where such alloys were first produced.

du·ra ma·ter /ˈd(y)o͝orə ˈmātər; ˈmā-/ ▸*n.* see **DURA**[1].

du·ra·men /d(y)o͝orˈāmin/ ▸*n. Botany* the heartwood of a tree. ▷mid 19th cent.: from Latin, literally 'hardness,' from *durare* 'harden.'

dur·ance /ˈd(y)o͝orəns/ ▸*n. archaic* imprisonment or confinement. ▷late Middle English (in the sense 'continuance'): from Old French, from *durer* 'to last,' from Latin *durare.* The sense 'imprisonment' is first recorded in the early 16th cent.

Du·rand /dəˈrand/, Asher Brown (1796–1886), U.S. artist. He was one of the earliest landscape painters of the Hudson River School.

Du·ran·go /d(y)o͞oˈrаnggō/ a state in northern central Mexico. ■ its capital city; pop. 1,352,160. Full name **VICTORIA DE DURANGO.**

Du·ran·te /dəˈrantē/, Jimmy (1893–1980), U.S. entertainer; born *James Francis Durante.* The gravelly-voiced star of Broadway, movies, radio, and television began his career in vaudeville and became known for his trademark song, "Inka Dinka Doo." His movies include *The Man Who Came to Dinner* (1942).

Du·ras /d(y)o͞oˈrä/, Marguerite (1914–96), French novelist, movie director, and playwright; pseudonym of *Marguerite Donnadieu.* Her works include the screenplay for *Hiroshima mon amour* (1959), as well as a semiautobiographical novel *L'Amant* (1984).

du·ra·tion /d(y)o͝orˈāshən/ ▸*n.* the time during which something continues: *the subway stop has been closed for the duration of the convention* | *a flight of over eight hours' duration.* ▷late Middle English: via Old French from medieval Latin *duratio(n-)*, from *durare* 'to last,' from *durus* 'hard.' —**du·ra·tion·al** *adj.*

▸*PHRASE* □ **for the duration** until the end of something, esp. a war: *he was in the navy for the duration plus six.* ■ *informal* for a very long time: *some stains may be there for the duration.*

dur·a·tive /ˈd(y)o͝orətiv/ ▸*adj. Grammar* of or denoting continuing action. Contrasted with **PUNCTUAL**.

Dur·ban /ˈdərbən/ a seaport and resort in South Africa, on the coast of KwaZulu-Natal; pop. 1,137,380. Former name (until 1835) **PORT NATAL**.

dur·bar /ˈdər,bär/ ▸*n. historical* the court of an Indian ruler. ■ a public reception held by an Indian prince or by a British governor or viceroy in India. ▷Urdu, from Persian *darbār* 'court.'

durch·kom·po·niert /,do͝orKH,kômpōˈni(ə)rt/ ▸*adj.* another term for **THROUGH-COMPOSED**. ▷from German, from *durch* 'through' + *komponiert* 'composed' (because the music is different throughout).

Dü·rer /ˈd(y)o͝orər/, Albrecht (1471–1528), German engraver and painter. A leading artist of the Renaissance, he was important for his technically advanced woodcuts and copper engravings and was also noted for his watercolors and drawings.

D

du·ress /d(y)o͝oˈres/ ▸*n.* threats, violence, constraints, or other action brought to bear on someone to do something against their will or better judgment: *confessions extracted* **under duress**. ■ *Law* constraint illegally exercised to force someone to perform an act. ■ *archaic* forcible restraint or imprisonment. ▷Middle English (in the sense 'harshness, severity, cruel treatment'): via Old French from Latin *duritia*, from *durus* 'hard.'

Du·rey /d(y)o͝oˈrā/, Louis (1888–1979), French composer. A member of the Les Six group until 1921, he later wrote music that had mass appeal, in accordance with communist doctrines on art.

Dur·ga /ˈdo͝orgä/ *Hinduism* a fierce goddess, wife of Shiva, often identified with Kali. She is usually depicted riding a tiger or lion and slaying the buffalo demon, and with eight or ten arms.

Dur·ga·pur /ˈdo͝orgə,po͝or/ a city in northeastern India, in the state of West Bengal; pop. 415,990.

Dur·ham[1] /ˈdərəm; ˈdo͝or-/ an industrial and academic city in north central North Carolina, noted for its tobacco industry and as the home of Duke University; pop. 187,035.

Dur·ham[2] a city on the River Wear; pop. 85,800 (1991). It is famous for its 11th-century cathedral, which contains the tomb of the Venerable Bede, and its university.

Dur·ham quilt /ˈdərəm/ ▸*n.* a quilt made by sewing together a piece of fabric, an inner batting, and a lining, the stitches making decorative patterns.

du·ri·an /ˈdo͝orēən; -rē,än/ ▸*n.* **1** an oval spiny tropical fruit containing a creamy pulp. Despite its fetid smell, it is highly esteemed for its flavor. **2** (also **durian tree**) the large tree that bears this fruit, native to Malaysia. • *Durio zibethinus*, family Bombacaceae. ▷late 16th cent.: from Malay *durian*, from *duri* 'thorn.'

dur·i·crust /ˈd(y)o͝ori,krəst/ ▸*n. Geology* a hard mineral crust formed at or near the surface of soil in semiarid regions by the evaporation of groundwater. ▷1920s: from Latin *durus* 'hard' + **CRUST**.

dur·ing /ˈd(y)o͝oriNG/ ▸*prep.* throughout the course or duration of (a period of time): *the restaurant is open during the day.* ■ used to indicate constant development throughout a period: *the period during which he grew to adulthood.* ■ at a particular point in the course of: *the stabbing took place during an argument at a party.* ▷late Middle English: present participle of the obsolete verb *dure* 'last, endure, extend,' via Old French from Latin *durare* 'to last' (see **DURATION**).

Durk·heim /ˈdərk,hīm/, Émile (1858–1917), French sociologist; one of the founders of modern sociology. In 1913, he became the first professor of sociology at the Sorbonne. Notable works: *The Division of Labor in Society* (1893) and *Suicide* (1897).

dur·mast oak /ˈdər,mast/ ▸*n.* a Eurasian oak tree with stalkless, egg-shaped acorns. Also called **SESSILE OAK**. • *Quercus petraea*, family Fagaceae. ▷late 18th cent.: *durmast* perhaps originally an error for *dunmast*, from **DUN**[1] + **MAST**[2].

durn /dərn/ ▸*v., exclam., adj., & adv.* dialect form of **DARN**[2].

durned /dərnd/ ▸*adj. & adv.* dialect form of **DARNED**.

Du·roc /ˈd(y)o͝oräk/ ▸*n.* a pig of a reddish breed developed in North America. ▷early 19th cent.: from the name of a stallion that is said to have been bought by the breeder Isaac Frink on the same day as the pigs from which he developed the breed.

Du·ro·cher /dəˈrōSHər/, Leo (Ernest) (1905–91), U.S. baseball player and manager. After playing the position of shortstop in the major leagues from 1925 to 1945, he managed the Brooklyn Dodgers 1939–46, 1948, New York Giants 1948–55, Chicago Cubs 1966–72, and Houston Astros 1972–73 and was noted for his cantankerous, insolent manner. Baseball Hall of Fame (1994).

dur·ra /ˈdo͝orə/ (also **du·ra**) ▸*n.* grain sorghum of the principal variety grown from northeastern Africa to India. • *Sorghum bicolor* var. *durra*, family Gramineae; **white durra** is var. *cernuum*. ▷late 18th cent.: from Arabic *dura, durra*.

Dur·rell /ˈdərəl/, Lawrence (George) (1912–90), English novelist and poet; brother of Gerald Durrell (1925-95). He spent much of his life abroad, particularly in the Mediterranean. Notable works: *Alexandria Quartet* (1957–60) and *Prospero's Cell* (1945).

dur·rie /ˈdərē/ ▸*n.* (*pl.* **-ries**) variant spelling of **DHURRIE**.

durst /dərst/ ▸ archaic or regional past of **DARE**.

du·rum /ˈd(y)o͝orəm/ (also **durum wheat**) ▸*n.* a kind of hard wheat grown in arid regions, having bearded ears and yielding flour that is used to make pasta. • *Triticum durum*, family Gramineae. ▷early 20th cent.: from Latin, neuter of *durus* 'hard,' used in the species name since 1798.

Du·se /ˈdo͞ozā/, Eleonora (1858–1924), Italian actress. She was known for her tragic roles.

Du·shan·be /d(y)o͞oˈSHämbā; -bə/ the capital of Tajikistan; pop. 602,000. Former name (1929–61) **STALINABAD**.

dusk /dəsk/ ▸*n.* the darker stage of twilight: *dusk was falling rapidly | working the land* **from dawn to dusk**. ■ semidarkness: *in the dusk of an Istanbul nightclub.*

▸*v.* [*intrans.*] *poetic/literary* grow dark: [as *adj.*] (**dusking**) *he saw the lights blaze in the dusking sky.*

▸*adj. poetic/literary* shadowy, dim, or dark. ▷Old English *dox* 'dark, swarthy' and *doxian* 'darken in color,' of Germanic origin; related to Old High German *tusin* 'darkish'; compare with **DUN**[1]. The noun dates from the early 17th cent. The change in form from *-x* to *-sk* occurred in Middle English.

dusk·y /ˈdəskē/ ▸*adj.* (**dusk·i·er, dusk·i·est**) darkish in color: *dusky red | a dusky complexion.* ■ *dated* used in euphemistic or poetic reference to black or other dark-skinned people: *a dusky Moorish maiden.* ■ *poetic/literary* dim: *dusky light came from a small window.* ■ [*attrib.*] used in names of animals with dark coloration, e.g., **dusky dolphin, dusky warbler**. —**dusk·i·ly** /-kəlē/ *adv.* —**dusk·i·ness** *n.*

dusk·y wing ▸*n.* a small, dark-winged butterfly of the skipper family, found in North America. • Genus *Erynnis*, family Hesperiidae; the species are very difficult to tell apart.

Düs·sel·dorf /ˈd(y)o͞osəl,dôrf/ an industrial city in northwestern Germany, on the Rhine River, capital of North Rhine-Westphalia; pop. 577,560.

dust /dəst/ ▸*n.* **1** fine, dry powder consisting of tiny particles of earth or waste matter lying on the ground or on surfaces or carried in the air: *the car sent up clouds of dust | they rolled and fought in the dust.* ■ [with *adj.*] any material in the form of tiny particles: *coal dust.* ■ [in *sing.*] a fine powder: *he ground it into a fine dust.* ■ [in *sing.*] a cloud of dust. ■ *poetic/literary* a dead person's remains: *scatter my dust and ashes.* ■ *poetic/literary* the mortal human body: *the soul, that dwells within your dust.* **2** [in *sing.*] an act of dusting: *a quick dust, to get rid of the cobwebs.*

▸*v.* [*trans.*] **1** remove the dust from the surface of (something) by wiping or brushing it: *I broke the vase I had been dusting | pick yourself up and* **dust** *yourself* **off** | [*intrans.*] *she washed and dusted and tidied.* ■ (**dust something off**) bring something out for use again after a long period of neglect: *a number of aircraft will be dusted off and returned to flight.* ■ *Baseball* (**dust someone off**) deliver a pitch very near a batter so they must fall to the dirt to avoid being hit by it. **2** (usu. **be dusted**) cover lightly with a powdered substance: *roll out on a surface dusted with flour.* ■ sprinkle (a powdered substance) onto something: *orange powder was dusted over the upper body.* **3** *informal* beat up or kill someone: *the officers* **dusted** *him* **up** *a little bit.* ▷Old English *dūst*, of Germanic origin; related to Dutch *duist* 'chaff.' —**dust·less** *adj.*

▸*PHRASES* □ **dust and ashes** used to convey a feeling of great disappointment or disillusion about something: *the party would be dust and ashes if he couldn't come.* □ **the dust settles** things quiet down: *she hoped that the dust would settle quickly and the episode be forgotten.* □ **eat someone's dust** *informal* fall far behind someone in a competitive situation. □ **gather** (or **collect**) **dust** remain unused: *some professors let their computers gather dust.* □ **leave someone/something in the dust** surpass someone or something easily: *today's modems leave their predecessors in the dust.*

dust·ball /ˈdəst,bôl/ ▸*n.* a ball of dust and fluff.

dust·bath /ˈdəst,baTH/ ▸*n.* a bird's rolling in dust to clean its feathers.

dust·bin /ˈdəst,bin/ ▸*n. Brit.* a garbage can.

dust bowl ▸*n.* an area of land where vegetation has been lost and soil reduced to dust and eroded, esp. as a consequence of drought or unsuitable farming practice. ■ (**the Dust Bowl**) an area of Oklahoma, Kansas, and northern Texas affected by severe soil erosion (caused by windstorms) in the early 1930s, which obliged many people to move.

dust bun·ny ▸*n. informal* a ball of dust and fluff.

Dust·bust·er /ˈdəst,bəstər/ ▸*n. trademark* a hand-held vacuum cleaner.

dust cov·er ▸*n.* **1** a dust jacket. **2** a drop cloth.

dust dev·il ▸*n.* a small whirlwind or air vortex over land, visible as a column of dust and debris.

dust·er /ˈdəstər/ ▸*n.* **1** a cloth or brush for dusting furniture. **2** (also **duster coat**) a woman's loose, lightweight, full-length coat without buttons, of a style originally worn in the 1920s when traveling in an open car. ■ a short, light housecoat. **3** *informal* a dust storm.

dust·heap /ˈdəst,hēp/ ▸*n.* a heap of household refuse.

dust·ing pow·der ▸*n.* powder for dusting over something, in particular talcum powder.

dust jack·et ▸*n.* a removable paper cover, generally with a decorative design, used to protect a book from dirt or damage.

dust·man /ˈdəstmən/ ▸*n.* (*pl.* **-men**) *Brit.* a garbage collector.

dust mop ▸*n.* a long-handled mop with a soft, fluffy head, used to collect dust from floors and walls.

dust·pan /ˈdəst,pan/ ▸*n.* a flat hand-held receptacle into which dust and waste can be swept from the floor.

dust ruf·fle ▸*n.* a sheet with a deep pleated or gathered border that is designed to hang down over the mattress and sides of a bed.

dust sheet ▸*n.* British term for **DROP CLOTH**.

dust storm ▸*n.* a strong, turbulent wind that carries clouds of fine dust, soil, and sand over a large area.

dust trap ▸*n.* something on, in, or under which dust readily gathers.

dust-up ▸*n. informal* a fight; a quarrel: *you and Larry had a dust-up over Val?*

dust·y /ˈdəstē/ ▸*adj.* (**dust·i·er, dust·i·est**) covered with, full of, or resembling dust: *dusty old records | a hot, dusty road.* ■ (of a color) dull or muted: *patches of pale gold and dusty pink.* ■ *figurative* staid and uninteresting: *a dusty old bore.* —**dust·i·ly** /ˈdəstəlē/ *adv.* —**dust·i·ness** *n.*

dust·y mill·er ▸*n.* a plant of the daisy family with whitish or grayish foliage. • Several species in the family Compositae, in particular the cultivated *Artemisia stellerana* of North America and *Senecio cineraria* of the Mediterranean. ▷early 19th cent.: named from the fine powder on the flowers and leaves.

Dutch /dəCH/ ▸*adj.* of or relating to the Netherlands or its people or their language.

▸*n.* **1** the West Germanic language of the Netherlands. **2** [as *plural n.*] (**the Dutch**) the people of the Netherlands collectively.

> **Dutch** is most closely related to German and English. It is also the official language of Suriname and the Netherlands Antilles and is spoken in northern Belgium, where it is called Flemish.

▷from Middle Dutch *dutsch* 'Dutch, Netherlandish, German': the English word originally denoted speakers of both High and Low German, but became more specific after the United Provinces adopted the Low German of Holland as the national language on independence in 1579.

▸*PHRASES* □ **go dutch** share the cost of something, esp. a meal, equally. □ **in dutch** *informal, dated* in trouble: *he's been getting in dutch at school.*

Dutch auc·tion ▸*n.* a method of selling in which the price is reduced until a buyer is found.

Dutch cap ▸*n.* a woman's lace cap with triangular flaps on each side, worn as part of Dutch traditional dress.

Dutch cour·age ▸*n.* strength or confidence gained

from drinking alcohol: *I'll have a couple of drinks to give me Dutch courage.*

Dutch door

Dutch door ▸*n.* a door divided into two parts horizontally, allowing one half to be shut and the other left open.

Dutch East In·di·a Com·pa·ny a Dutch trading company founded in 1602 to protect Dutch trading interests in the Indian Ocean. It was dissolved in 1799.

Dutch East In·dies former name (until 1949) of **INDONESIA.**

Dutch elm dis·ease ▸*n.* a fungal disease of elm trees that is spread by elm bark beetles. A virulent strain of the fungus that arose in North America in the early 20th century has destroyed the majority of American elms in many areas. • The disease is caused by the fungus *Ceratocystis ulmi*, phylum Ascomycota.

Dutch·ess Coun·ty /ˈdəCHis/ a county in southeastern New York, east of the Hudson River, traditionally agricultural but increasingly suburban; pop. 280,150. Its seat is Poughkeepsie.

Dutch Gui·an·a former name (until 1948) of **SURINAME.**

Dutch in·te·ri·or ▸*n.* a painting of the interior of a Dutch house in a style characteristic of the work of 17th-century genre painters.

Dutch·man /ˈdəCHmən/ ▸*n.* (*pl.* **-men**) a native or national of the Netherlands, or a person of Dutch descent. ■ a Dutch ship. ■ a wedge or piece used to conceal a flaw in construction. ■ *archaic* a German.

▸*PHRASE* □ **I'm a Dutchman** *Brit.* used to express one's disbelief or as a way of underlining an emphatic assertion: *if she's seventeen, I'm a Dutchman.*

Dutch·man's breech·es ▸*n.* a plant closely related to bleeding heart, but typically having pale yellow or white flowers. • Genus *Dicentra*, family Fumariaceae: several species, in particular *D. cucullaria*. ▹mid 19th cent.: so named because of the shape of the spurred flower.

Dutchman's breeches

Dutch·man's pipe ▸*n.* a vigorous climbing vine with hooked tubular flowers, native to eastern North America. • *Aristolochia durior*, family Aristolochiaceae.

Dutch met·al ▸*n.* an alloy of copper and zinc used in imitation of gold leaf.

Dutch New Guin·ea former name (until 1963) of **IRIAN JAYA.**

Dutch ov·en ▸*n.* a large, heavy cooking pot with a lid. ■ *chiefly historical* a large metal box serving as a simple oven, heated by being placed under or next to hot coals.

Dutch Re·formed Church a branch of the Protestant Church in the Netherlands, formed during the Reformation. It was disestablished in 1798 and replaced in 1816 by the Netherlands Reformed Church. ■ the dominant branch of the Protestant Church among Afrikaners in South Africa.

Dutch tile ▸*n.* a kind of glazed white tile painted with traditional Dutch motifs in blue or brown.
▸*v.* [*trans.*] [usu. as *adj.*] (**Dutch-tiled**) decorate with such tiles: *Dutch-tiled fireplaces.*

Dutch treat ▸*n.* an outing, meal, or other special occasion at which each participant pays for their share of the expenses.

Dutch un·cle ▸*n.* *informal* a person giving firm but benevolent advice.

Dutch West In·di·a Com·pa·ny a Dutch trading company founded in 1621 to develop Dutch trading interests in competition with Spain and Portugal and their colonies in western India, South America, and West Africa. It was dissolved in 1794.

Dutch·wom·an /ˈdəCH,wo͝omən/ ▸*n.* (*pl.* **-wom·en**) a female native or national of the Netherlands, or a woman of Dutch descent.

du·te·ous /ˈd(y)o͞otēəs/ ▸*adj.* *archaic* dutiful: *a duteous vassal.* ▹late 16th cent.: from **DUTY**, on the pattern of words such as *bounteous.* **—du·te·ous·ly** *adv.* **—du·te·ous·ness** *n.*

du·ti·a·ble /ˈd(y)o͞otēəbəl/ ▸*adj.* liable to customs or other duties: *dutiable goods.*

dut·i·ful /ˈd(y)o͞otəfəl/ ▸*adj.* conscientiously or obediently fulfilling one's duty: *a dutiful daughter.* See note at **OBEDIENT.** ■ motivated by duty rather than desire or enthusiasm: *dutiful applause | a dutiful visit.* **—du·ti·ful·ly** *adv.* **—du·ti·ful·ness** *n.*

du·ty /ˈd(y)o͞otē/ ▸*n.* (*pl.* **-ties**) **1** a moral or legal obligation; a responsibility: *it's my duty to uphold the law | she was determined to* **do her duty** *as a citizen | a strong sense of duty.* ■ [as *adj.*] (of a visit or other undertaking) done from a sense of moral obligation rather than for pleasure: *a fifteen-minute duty visit.* **2** (often **duties**) a task or action that someone is required to perform: *the queen's official duties | your duties will include sweeping the switchboard | Juliet reported for duty.* ■ military service: *combat duty in the army.* ■ [as *adj.*] (of a person) engaged in their regular work: *a duty nurse.* ■ (also **duties**) performance of prescribed church services by a priest or minister: *he was willing to take Sunday duties.* **3** a payment due and enforced by law or custom, in particular: ■ a payment levied on the import, export, manufacture, or sale of goods: *a 6 percent* **duty on** *imports | goods subject to excise duty.* **4** *technical* the measure of an engine's effectiveness in units of work done per unit of fuel. ▹late Middle English: from Anglo-Norman French *duete*, from Old French *deu* (see **DUE**).
▸*PHRASES* □ **do duty as** (or **for**) serve or act as a substitute for something else: *her mug was doing duty as a wine glass.* □ **on** (or **off**) **duty** engaged (or not engaged) in one's regular work: *the doorman had* **gone off duty** *and the lobby was unattended.*

du·ty-bound ▸*adj.* [*predic.*, with *infinitive*] morally or legally obliged to do something: *legitimate news stories that the press is duty-bound to report.*

du·ty cy·cle ▸*n.* the cycle of operation of a machine or other device that operates intermittently rather than continuously. ■ the time occupied by this, esp. as a percentage of available time.

du·ty-free ▸*adj.* & *adv.* exempt from payment of duty: [as *adj.*] *the permitted number of duty-free goods* | [as *adv.*] *most EC goods enter almost duty-free.* ■ [as *adj.*] (of a shop or area) selling or trading in goods that are exempt from payment of duty.

du·ty of·fi·cer ▸*n.* an officer, esp. in the police or armed forces, who is on duty at a particular time.

du·um·vir /d(y)o͞oˈəmvər/ ▸*n.* (in ancient Rome) each of two magistrates or officials holding a joint office. ▹Latin, from *duum virum* 'of the two men.'

du·um·vi·rate /d(y)o͞oˈəmvərit/ ▸*n.* a coalition of two people having joint authority or influence. ▹mid 17th cent.: from Latin *duumviratus.*

Du·va·lier /d(y)o͞oˈvälyā/ François (1907–71), Haitian statesman; president 1957–71; known as **Papa Doc.** His regime was noted for its oppressive nature. He was succeeded by his son Jean-Claude (1951–), known as **Baby Doc**, who was overthrown by a mass uprising in 1986.

Du·vall, Gabriel (1752–1844), U.S. Supreme Court associate justice 1811–35. Before being appointed to the Court by President Madison, he was a member of the U.S. House of Representatives 1794–96.

du·vet /,d(y)o͞oˈvā/ ▸*n.* a soft quilt filled with down, feathers, or a synthetic fiber, used instead of an upper sheet and blankets. ▹mid 18th cent.: from French, literally 'down' (see **DOWN**[2]).

dux /dəks/ ▸*n.* (*pl.* **du·ces** /ˈd(y)o͞osēz; ˈdo͞okāz/ or **dux·es**) a Saxon chief or leader. ▹mid 18th cent.: from Latin, 'leader.'

dux·elles /do͝okˈsel/ ▸*n.* a preparation of mushrooms sautéed with onions, shallots, garlic, and parsley and used to make stuffing or sauce: *chilies stuffed with duxelles.* ▹named after the Marquis *d'Uxelles*, a 17th-cent. French nobleman.

DV *formal* ▸*abbr.* ■ Deo volente: *this time next week (DV) I shall be among the mountains.* ■ *Bible* Douay Version.

DVD ▸*n.* a high-density videodisc that stores large amounts of data, esp. high-resolution audio-visual material. ▹abbreviation of *digital videodisc* or *digital versatile disc.*

USAGE The many different DVD formats can be very confusing. A plain-vanilla DVD (sometimes called a DVD-ROM, on the model of CD-ROM) can be played in DVD players and by computers that have a DVD drive, but cannot be written to by the user. A DVD-R can also be played in DVD players and by computer DVD drives, and can be written to, but only once, by a home DVD burner. DVD-Rs come in two sizes; 4.7 GB and 9.4 GB. DVD-RAM discs can be written to many times, but can only be played by a computer's DVD-RAM drive. They cannot be played in other DVD players or drives. DVD-RW discs can be written to as many as a thousand times, but may not play in some older or lower-level DVD players or drives. DVD+R and DVD+RW discs are much like DVD-R discs, but only come in the 4.7 GB size. DVD+RW discs are also unlikely to play back on older or lower-level DVD players.

DVD-R ▸*n.* a blank DVD on which data, including music and movies, can be permanently recorded and read using the DVD-R format. See usage note at **DVD.** ■ a format for recordable DVDs used by some companies. ▹an abbreviation of *DVD recordable.*

DVD+R ▸*n.* a blank DVD on which data, including music and movies, can be permanently recorded and read using the DVD+R format. ■ a format for recordable DVDs used by some companies. See usage note at **DVD.** ▹an abbreviation of *DVD plus recordable.*

DVD-RAM ▸*n.* a blank DVD on which data, including music and movies, can be permanently recorded and read using the DVD-RAM format. A DVD-RAM discs can be recorded over many times, but will only play back in a DVD-RAM drive. ■ a format for recordable DVDs used by some companies. See usage note at **DVD.** ▹an abbreviation of *DVD recordable.*

DVD-ROM ▸*n.* a DVD used as a read-only optical memory device for a computer system. See usage note at **DVD.** ▹1990s: acronym from *DVD read-only memory.*

DVD-RW ▸*n.* a blank DVD that can be recorded, erased, and rerecorded with data many times and read by systems using the DVD-RW format. ■ a format for rewritable DVDs used by some companies. ■ a disc drive that can read and record DVDs. See usage note at **DVD.** ▹an abbreviation of *DVD rewritable.*

DVD+RW ▸*n.* a blank DVD that can be recorded, erased, and rerecorded with data many times and read by systems using the DVD+RW format. ■ a format for rewritable DVDs used by some companies. ■ a disc drive that can read and record DVDs. See usage note at **DVD.** ▹an abbreviation of *DVD plus rewritable.*

Dvi·na Riv·er /d(ə)vēˈnä/ a river that rises in Russia's Valai Hills and flows southwest for 634 miles (1,020 km) across Belarus and Latvia into the Gulf of Riga.

DVM ▸*abbr.* ■ Doctor of Veterinary Medicine.

Dvo·řák /ˈdvôr,ZHäk/, Antonín (1841–1904), Czech composer. He is best known for his ninth symphony "From the New World," (1892–95).

DVR ▸*abbr.* digital video recorder.

dwale /dwāl/ ▸*n.* *archaic* deadly nightshade or belladonna. ■ a soporific drink formerly made from this. ▹Middle English: probably of Scandinavian origin and related to Danish *dvale* 'deep sleep, stupor,' *dvaledrik* 'sleeping draft.'

dwarf /dwôrf/ ▸*n.* (*pl.* **dwarfs** or **dwarves** /dwôrvz/) **1** (in folklore or fantasy literature) a member of a mythical race of short, stocky humanlike creatures who are generally skilled in mining and metalworking. ■ *often offensive* an abnormally small person. ■ [as *adj.*] denoting something, esp. an animal or plant, that is much smaller than the usual size for its type or species: *a dwarf conifer.* **2** (also **dwarf star**) *Astronomy* a star of relatively small size and low luminosity, including the majority of main sequence stars.
▸*v.* [*trans.*] cause to seem small or insignificant in comparison: *the buildings surround and dwarf All Saints Church.* ■ stunt the growth or development of: [as *adj.*] (**dwarfed**) *the dwarfed but solid branch of a tree.* ▹Old English *dweorg, dweorh*, of Germanic origin; related to Dutch *dwerg* and German *Zwerg.* **—dwarf·ish** *adj.*

USAGE In the sense 'an abnormally small person,' **dwarf** is normally considered offensive. However, there are no accepted alternatives in the general language, since terms such as **person of restricted growth** have gained little currency.

Pronunciation Key ə ago; ər over; ˈə or ,ə up; ˈər or ,ər fur; a hat; ā rate; ä car; CH chew; e let; ē see; e(ə)r air; i fit; ī by; i(ə)r ear; NG sing; ō go; ô for; oi boy; o͝o good; o͞o goo; ou out; SH she; TH thin; T͟H then; (h)w why; ZH vision

D

dwarf·ism /ˈd(w)ôrfizəm/ ▸*n.* (in medical or technical contexts) unusually or abnormally low stature or small size.

dwarf le·mur ▸*n.* a small Madagascan primate related to the mouse lemur, feeding primarily on fruit and gums. • Family Cheirogaleidae: three genera and four species.

dweeb /dwēb/ ▸*n. informal* a boring, studious, or socially inept person. ▷1980s: perhaps a blend of DWARF and early 20th-cent. *feeb* 'a feebleminded person' (from FEEBLE). **—dweeb·ish** *adj.* **—dweeb·y** *adj.*

dwell /dwel/ ▸*v.* (*past* and *past part.* **dwelled** or **dwelt** /dwelt/) [*intrans.*] **1** [with *adverbial of place*] *formal* live in or at a specified place: *groups of gypsies still dwell in these caves.* **2** (**dwell on/upon**) think, speak, or write at length about (a particular subject, esp. one that is a source of unhappiness, anxiety, or dissatisfaction): *I've got better things to do than dwell on the past.* ■ (**dwell on/upon**) (of one's eyes or attention) linger on (a particular object or place): *she let her eyes dwell on them for a moment.*
▸*n. technical* a slight regular pause in the motion of a machine. ▷Old English *dwellan* 'lead astray, hinder, delay' (in Middle English 'tarry, remain in a place'), of Germanic origin; related to Middle Dutch *dwellen* 'stun, perplex' and Old Norse *dvelja* 'delay, tarry, stay.' **—dwell·er** *n.* [in *combination*] *city-dwellers.*

dwell·ing /ˈdweliNG/ (also **dwelling place**) ▸*n. formal* a house, apartment, or other place of residence.

dwell·ing house ▸*n. Law* a house used as a residence and not for business purposes.

dwell time ▸*n. technical* time spent in the same position, area, or stage of a process: *dwell time at U.S. airports has reached a new high—almost 70 minutes.*

DWEM ▸*abbr.* dead white European male.

DWI ▸*abbr.* ■ driving while intoxicated.

dwin·dle /ˈdwindl/ ▸*v.* [*intrans.*] diminish gradually in size, amount, or strength: *traffic has dwindled to a trickle* | [as *adj.*] (**dwindling**) *dwindling resources.* ▷late 16th cent.: frequentative of Scots and dialect *dwine* 'fade away,' from Old English *dwīnan*, of Germanic origin; related to Middle Dutch *dwīnen* and Old Norse *dvína.*

DWM ▸*abbr.* ■ (in personal ads) divorced white male. ■ dead white male.

dwt ▸*abbr.* ■ dead-weight tonnage: *a 40,000 dwt slipway.* ■ pennyweight.

Dy ▸*symbol* the chemical element dysprosium.

dy·ad /ˈdīad/ ▸*n. technical* something that consists of two elements or parts: *the mother–child dyad.* ■ *Mathematics* an operator that is a combination of two vectors. ■ *Chemistry* a divalent atom or radical. ▷late 17th cent. (originally denoting the number two or a pair): from late Latin *dyas, dyad-*, from Greek *duas*, from *duo* 'two.' Current senses date from the late 19th cent. **—dy·ad·ic** /dīˈadik/ *adj.*

Dy·ak ▸*n.* & *adj.* variant spelling of **DAYAK**.

dy·ar·chy /ˈdīˌärkē/ ▸*n.* (*pl.* **-chies**) variant spelling of DIARCHY.

dyb·buk /ˈdibək/ ▸*n.* (*pl.* **dyb·buks** or **dyb·bu·kim** /ˌdibŏŏˈkēm/) (in Jewish folklore) a malevolent wandering spirit that enters and possesses the body of a living person until exorcized. ▷from Yiddish *dibek*, from Hebrew *dibbūq*, from *dāḇaq* 'cling.'

dye /dī/ ▸*n.* a natural or synthetic substance used to add a color to or change the color of something.
▸*v.* (**dyed, dye·ing**) [*trans.*] add a color to or change the color of (something) by soaking it in a solution impregnated with a dye: [with *complement*] *I dyed my hair blonde* | [as *adj.*] (**dyed**) *dyed black hair.* ■ [*intrans.*] take color well or badly during such a process: *it's good material—it should dye well.* ▷Old English *dēag* (noun), *dēagian* (verb). The noun is not recorded from Old English to the late 16th cent., when it was re-formed from the verb. **—dye·a·ble** *adj.*
▸*PHRASE* □ **dyed in the wool** unchanging in a particular belief or opinion; inveterate: *she's a dyed-in-the-wool conservative.* [with allusion to the fact that yarn was dyed in the raw state, producing a more even and permanent color.]

dye la·ser ▸*n.* a tunable laser using the fluorescence of an organic dye.

dye·line /ˈdīˌlīn/ ▸*n.* another term for DIAZO.

dy·er /ˈdīər/ ▸*n.* a person whose trade is the dyeing of cloth or other material.

dy·er's green·weed ▸*n.* a bushy, yellow-flowered Eurasian plant of the pea family, which has become naturalized in North America. The flowers were formerly used to make a yellow or green dye. • *Genista tinctoria*, family Leguminosae.

dy·er's oak ▸*n.* another term for VALONIA.

dy·er's rock·et ▸*n.* another term for WELD[2].

dye·stuff /ˈdīˌstəf/ ▸*n.* a substance that yields a dye or that can be used as a dye, esp. when in solution.

dy·ing /ˈdī-iNG/ ▸*adj.* [*attrib.*] on the point of death: *he visited his dying mother.* ■ occurring at or connected with the time that someone dies: *he strained to catch her dying words.* ■ gradually ceasing to exist or function; in decline and about to disappear: *stone-cutting is a dying art* | *the dying embers of the fire.* ▷late 16th cent.: present participle of DIE[1].
▸*PHRASE* □ **to one's dying day** for the rest of one's life: *I shall remember that to my dying day.*

dyke[1] ▸*n.* variant spelling of DIKE[1].

dyke[2] /dīk/ ▸*n. offensive* a lesbian. ▷1940s (earlier as BULLDYKE): of unknown origin. **—dyke·y** *adj.* .

Dyl·an /ˈdilən/, Bob (1941–), U.S. singer and songwriter; born *Robert Allen Zimmerman.* The leader of an urban folk-music revival in the 1960s, he became known for political and protest songs, such as "The Times They Are A-Changin" (1964). Notable albums: *Highway 61 Revisited* (1965) and *Blood on the Tracks* (1975).

dyn ▸*abbr.* dyne.

dy·nam·ic /dīˈnamik/ ▸*adj.* **1** (of a process or system) characterized by constant change, activity, or progress: *a dynamic economy.* ■ (of a person) positive in attitude and full of energy and new ideas: *she's dynamic and determined.* ■ (of a thing) stimulating development or progress: *the dynamic forces of nature.* ■ *Physics* of or relating to forces producing motion. Often contrasted with STATIC. ■ *Linguistics* (of a verb) expressing an action, activity, event, or process. Contrasted with STATIVE. ■ *Electronics* (of a memory device) needing to be refreshed by the periodic application of a voltage. ■ *Electronics* of or relating to the volume of sound produced by a voice, instrument, or sound recording equipment. **2** *Music* relating to the volume of sound produced by an instrument, voice, or recording: *an astounding dynamic range.*
▸*n.* **1** a force that stimulates change or progress within a system or process: *evaluation is part of the basic dynamic of the project.* **2** *Music* another term for DYNAMICS (sense 3). ▷early 19th cent. (as a term in physics): from French *dynamique*, from Greek *dunamikos*, from *dunamis* 'power.' **—dy·nam·i·cal** *adj.* **—dy·nam·i·cal·ly** /-ik(ə)lē/ *adv.*

dy·nam·ic e·qui·lib·ri·um ▸*n.* a state of balance between continuing processes.

dy·nam·ic link li·brar·y ▸*n.* see DLL.

dy·nam·ic met·a·mor·phism ▸*n. Geology* metamorphism produced by mechanical forces.

dy·nam·ic pric·ing ▸*n.* the practice of pricing items at a level determined by a particular customer's perceived ability to pay.

dy·nam·ic range ▸*n.* the range of acceptable or possible volumes of sound occurring in the course of a piece of music or a performance. ■ the ratio of the largest to the smallest intensity of sound that can be reliably transmitted or reproduced by a particular sound system, measured in decibels.

dy·nam·ics /dīˈnamiks/ ▸*plural n.* **1** [treated as *sing.*] the branch of mechanics concerned with the motion of bodies under the action of forces. Compare with STATICS. ■ [usu. with *adj.*] the branch of any science in which forces or changes are considered: *chemical dynamics.* **2** the forces or properties that stimulate growth, development, or change within a system or process: *the dynamics of changing social relations.* **3** *Music* the varying levels of volume of sound in different parts of a musical performance. **—dy·nam·i·cist** /-ˈnaməsist/ *n.* (in sense 1).

dy·nam·ic vis·cos·i·ty ▸*n.* a quantity measuring the force needed to overcome internal friction in a fluid.

dy·na·mism /ˈdīnəˌmizəm/ ▸*n.* **1** the quality of being characterized by vigorous activity and progress: *the dynamism and strength of the economy.* ■ the quality of being dynamic and positive in attitude: *he was known for his dynamism and strong views.* **2** *Philosophy, chiefly historical* the theory that phenomena of matter or mind are due to the action of forces rather than to motion or matter. ▷mid 19th cent.: from Greek *dunamis* 'power' + -ISM. **—dy·na·mist** *n.*

dy·na·mite /ˈdīnəˌmīt/ ▸*n.* a high explosive consisting of nitroglycerine mixed with an absorbent material and typically molded into sticks. ■ *figurative* something that has the potential to generate extreme reactions or to have devastating repercussions: *that policy is political dynamite.* ■ *informal* an extremely impressive or exciting person or thing: *both her albums are dynamite* | [as *adj.*] *a chick with a dynamite figure.* ■ *informal, dated* a narcotic, esp. heroin.
▸*v.* [*trans.*] blow up (something) with dynamite. ▷mid 19th cent.: from Greek *dunamis* 'power' + -ITE[1]. **—dy·na·mit·er** *n.*

dy·na·mo /ˈdīnəˌmō/ ▸*n.* (*pl.* **-mos**) a machine for converting mechanical energy into electrical energy; a generator. ■ *informal* an extremely energetic person: *she was a dynamo in London politics.* ▷late 19th cent.: abbreviation of *dynamo-electric machine*, from Greek *dunamis* 'power.'

dy·na·mom·e·ter /ˌdīnəˈmämitər/ ▸*n.* an instrument that measures the power output of an engine. ▷early 19th cent.: from French *dynamomètre*, from Greek *dunamis* 'power' + French *-mètre* '(instrument) measuring.'

dy·nast /ˈdīˌnast; -nəst/ ▸*n.* a member of a powerful family, esp. a hereditary ruler. ▷mid 17th cent.: via Latin from Greek *dunastēs*, from *dunasthai* 'be able.'

dy·nas·ty /ˈdīnəstē/ ▸*n.* (*pl.* **-ties**) a line of hereditary rulers of a country: *the Tang dynasty.* ■ a succession of people from the same family who play a prominent role in business, politics, or another field: *the Ford dynasty.* ▷late Middle English: from French *dynastie*, or via late Latin from Greek *dunasteia* 'lordship, power,' from *dunastēs* (see DYNAST). **—dy·nas·tic** /dīˈnastik/ *adj.* **—dy·nas·ti·cal·ly** /dīˈnastik(ə)lē/ *adv.*

dyne /dīn/ ▸*n. Physics* a unit of force that, acting on a mass of one gram, increases its velocity by one centimeter per second every second along the direction that it acts. ▷late 19th cent.: from French, from Greek *dunamis* 'force, power.'

dy·no /ˈdīnō/ ▸*n.* (*pl.* **dy·nos**) **1** short for DYNAMOMETER. **2** *Climbing* a rapid move across a rock face in order to reach a hold.
▸*v.* (**dy·nos, dy·no'd** or **dy·noed**) **1** [*trans.*] measure (the output of an engine) with a dynamometer. **2** [*intrans.*] (in mountaineering) climb using dynos.

dys- ▸*comb. form* bad; difficult (used esp. in medical terms): *dyspepsia* | *dysphasia.* ▷from Greek *dus-*; related to German *zer-*, also to Old English *to-*.

dys·ar·thri·a /disˈärTHrēə/ ▸*n. Medicine* difficult or unclear articulation of speech that is otherwise linguistically normal. ▷late 19th cent.: from DYS- 'difficult' + Greek *arthron* 'joint or articulation.'

dys·cal·cu·li·a /ˌdiskalˈkyo͞olēə/ ▸*n. Psychiatry* severe difficulty in making arithmetical calculations, as a result of brain disorder.

dys·cra·sia /disˈkrāZHə/ ▸*n. Medicine* an abnormal or disordered state of the body or of a bodily part. ▷late Middle English (denoting an imbalance of physical qualities): via late Latin from Greek *duskrasia* 'bad combination,' from *dus-* 'bad' + *krasis* 'mixture.' **—dys·cras·ic** /-ˈkrazik/ *adj.*

dys·en·ter·y /ˈdisənˌterē/ ▸*n.* infection of the intestines resulting in severe diarrhea with the presence of blood and mucus in the feces. • **bacterial dysentery** is caused by bacteria of the genus *Shigella* and can also spread by contact (see AMEBIC DYSENTERY, SHIGELLA). ▷late Middle English: from Old French *dissenterie*, or via Latin from Greek *dusenteria*, from *dusenteros* 'afflicted in the bowels,' from *dus-* 'bad' + *entera* 'bowels.' **—dys·en·ter·ic** /ˌdisənˈterik/ *adj.*

dys·func·tion /disˈfəNGkSHən/ ▸*n.* abnormality or impairment in the function of a specified bodily organ or system: *bowel dysfunction.* ■ deviation from the norms of social behavior in a way regarded as bad: *inner-city dysfunction.*

dys·func·tion·al /disˈfəNGkSHənl/ ▸*adj.* not operating normally or properly: *the telephones are dysfunctional.* ■ deviating from the norms of social behavior in a way regarded as bad: *an emotionally dysfunctional businessman* | *dysfunctional families.* **—dys·func·tion·al·ly** *adv.*

dys·gen·ic /disˈjenik/ ▸*adj.* exerting a detrimental effect on later generations through the inheritance of undesirable characteristics: *dysgenic breeding.*

dys·graph·i·a /disˈgrafēə/ ▸*n. Medicine* inability to write coherently, as a symptom of brain disease or damage. ▷1930s: from DYS- 'difficult' + Greek *-graphia* 'writing.' **—dys·graph·ic** /-ˈgrafik/ *adj.*

dys·ki·ne·sia /ˌdiskiˈnēZHə/ ▸*n. Medicine* abnormality or impairment of voluntary movement. **—dys·ki·net·ic** /-ˈnetik/ *adj.*

dys·la·li·a /disˈlālēə/ ▸*n. Medicine* inability to articulate comprehensible speech, esp. when associated with the use of private words or sounds. ▷mid 19th cent.: from DYS- 'difficult' + Greek *lalia* 'speech.'

dys·lex·i·a /disˈleksēə/ ▸*n.* a general term for disorders that involve difficulty in learning to read or interpret words, letters, and other symbols, but that do not affect general intelligence. ▷late 19th cent.: coined in German from **DYS-** 'difficult' + Greek *lexis* 'speech' (apparently by confusion of Greek *legein* 'to speak' and Latin *legere* 'to read'). **—dys·lec·tic** /-'lektik/ *adj.* & *n.* **—dys·lex·ic** /-'leksik/ *adj.* & *n.*

dys·men·or·rhe·a /ˌdismenə'rēə/ (*Brit.* **dys·men·or·rhoe·a**) ▸*n. Medicine* painful menstruation, typically involving abdominal cramps.

dys·mor·phi·a /dis'môrfēə/ ▸*n. Medicine* deformity or abnormality in the shape or size of a specified part of the body: *muscle dysmorphia.* ▷late 19th cent.: from Greek *dusmorphia* 'misshapenness, ugliness,' from *dus- dys-* + *morphē* 'form.' **—dys·mor·phic** *adj.*

dys·pa·reu·ni·a /ˌdispə'ro͞onēə/ ▸*n. Medicine* difficult or painful sexual intercourse. ▷late 19th cent.: from **DYS-** 'difficult' + Greek *pareunos* 'lying with.'

dys·pep·sia /dis'pepsēə; -'pepshə/ ▸*n.* indigestion. ▷early 18th cent.: via Latin from Greek *duspepsia*, from *duspeptos* 'difficult to digest.'

dys·pep·tic /dis'peptik/ ▸*adj.* of or having indigestion or consequent irritability or depression.
▸*n.* a person who suffers from indigestion or irritability.

dys·pha·gia /dis'fāj(ē)ə/ ▸*n. Medicine* difficulty or discomfort in swallowing, as a symptom of disease: *progressive dysphagia.*

dys·pha·sia /dis'fāzhə/ ▸*n. Medicine* language disorder marked by deficiency in the generation of speech, and sometimes also in its comprehension, due to brain disease or damage. ▷late 19th cent.: from Greek *dusphatos* 'hard to utter,' from *dus-* 'difficult' + *phatos* 'spoken.' **—dys·pha·sic** /-'fāzik/ *adj.*

dys·phe·mism /'disfəˌmizəm/ ▸*n.* a derogatory or unpleasant term used instead of a pleasant or neutral one, such as "loony bin" for "mental hospital." The opposite of **EUPHEMISM**.

dys·pho·ni·a /dis'fōnēə/ ▸*n. Medicine* difficulty in speaking due to a physical disorder of the mouth, tongue, throat, or vocal cords.

dys·pho·ri·a /dis'fôrēə/ ▸*n. Psychiatry* a state of unease or generalized dissatisfaction with life. The opposite of **EUPHORIA**. ▷mid 19th cent.: from Greek *dusphoria*, from *dusphoros* 'hard to bear.' **—dys·phor·ic** /-'fôrik/ *adj.* & *n.*

dys·pla·sia /dis'plāzhə/ ▸*n. Medicine* the enlargement of an organ or tissue by the proliferation of cells of an abnormal type, as a developmental disorder or an early stage in the development of cancer. ▷1930s: from **DYS-** 'bad' + Greek *plasis* 'formation.'

dys·plas·tic /dis'plastik/ ▸*adj.* exhibiting dysplasia. ■ (of dogs) having malformed joints resulting from a genetic condition. ■ (of moles) generally larger and with irregular and indistinct borders; often symptomatic of melanoma.

dysp·ne·a /disp'nēə/ (*Brit.* **dysp·noe·a**) ▸*n. Medicine* difficult or labored breathing. ▷mid 17th cent.: via Latin from Greek *duspnoia*, from *dus-* 'difficult' + *pnoē* 'breathing.' **—dysp·ne·ic** /disp'nēik/ *adj.*

dys·prax·i·a /dis'praksēə/ ▸*n.* another term for **APRAXIA**. ▷early 20th cent.: from Greek *dus-* 'bad or difficult' + *praxis* 'action.'

dys·pro·si·um /dis'prōzēəm/ ▸*n.* the chemical element of atomic number 66, a soft, silvery-white metal of the lanthanide series. (Symbol: **Dy**) ▷late 19th cent.: from Greek *dusprositos* 'hard to get at' + **-IUM**.

dys·rhyth·mi·a /dis'ri<u>th</u>mēə/ ▸*n. Medicine* abnormality in a physiological rhythm, esp. in the activity of the brain or heart. **—dys·rhyth·mic** /-mik/ *adj.* **—dys·rhyth·mi·cal** /-mikəl/ *adj.*

dys·thy·mi·a /dis'thīmēə/ ▸*n. Psychiatry* persistent mild depression. ▷mid 19th cent.: from Greek *dusthumia*. **—dys·thy·mic** /-'thīmik/ *adj.* & *n.*

dys·to·ci·a /dis'tōshə/ ▸*n. Medicine & Veterinary Medicine* difficult birth, typically caused by a large or awkwardly positioned fetus, by smallness of the maternal pelvis, or by failure of the uterus and cervix to contract and expand normally. ▷early 18th cent.: from Greek *dustokia*, from *dus-* 'difficult' + *tokos* 'childbirth.'

dys·to·ni·a /dis'tōnēə/ ▸*n. Medicine* a state of abnormal muscle tone resulting in muscular spasm and abnormal posture, typically due to neurological disease or a side effect of drug therapy. **—dys·ton·ic** /-'tänik/ *adj.*

dys·to·pi·a /dis'tōpēə/ ▸*n.* an imagined place or state in which everything is unpleasant or bad, typically a totalitarian or environmentally degraded one. The opposite of **UTOPIA**. ▷late 18th cent.: from **DYS-** 'bad' + **UTOPIA**. **—dys·to·pi·an** *adj.* & *n.*

dys·troph·ic /dis'träfik/ ▸*adj.* **1** *Medicine* affected by or relating to dystrophy, esp. muscular dystrophy. **2** *Ecology* (of a lake) having brown acidic water that is low in oxygen and supports little life, owing to high levels of dissolved humus. Compare with **EUTROPHIC** and **OLIGOTROPHIC**. ▷late 19th cent.: from Greek *dus-* 'bad' + *-trophia* 'nourishment' + **-IC**.

dys·tro·phin /dis'trōfin/ ▸*n. Biochemistry* a protein found in skeletal muscle, which is absent in sufferers from muscular dystrophy.

dys·tro·phy /'distrəfē/ ▸*n.* **1** *Medicine & Veterinary Medicine* a disorder in which an organ or tissue of the body wastes away. See also **MUSCULAR DYSTROPHY**. **2** *Medicine* impaired nourishment of a bodily part. ▷late 19th cent.: from modern Latin *dystrophia*, from Greek *dus-* 'bad' + *-trophia* 'nourishment.'

dys·u·ri·a /dis'yo͝orēə/ ▸*n. Medicine* painful or difficult urination. ▷late Middle English: via late Latin from Greek *dusouria*, from *dus-* 'difficult' + *ouron* 'urine.'

DZ ▸*abbr.* drop zone: *used parachutes were scattered across the DZ.*

dz. ▸*abbr.* ■ dozen.

Dzau·dzhi·kau /dzou'jēˌkou/ former name (1944–54) of **VLADIKAVKAZ**.

Dzer·zhinsk /dzir'zhēnsk/ a city in western central Russia, west of Nizhni Novgorod; pop. 286,000. Former names **CHERNORECHYE** (until 1919) and **RASTYAPINO** (1919–29).

dzo /zō/ ▸*n.* (*pl.* same or **dzos**) a hybrid of a cow and a yak. ▷mid 19th cent.: from Tibetan *mdso*.

Dzong·kha /'zängkə/ ▸*n.* the official language of Bhutan, closely related to Tibetan.

Ee

E[1] /ē/ (also **e**) ▸*n.* (*pl.* **Es** or **E's**) **1** the fifth letter of the alphabet. ■ denoting the fifth in a set of items, categories, sizes, etc. ■ (**e**) *Chess* denoting the fifth file from the left, as viewed from White's side of the board. ■ denoting the lowest-earning socioeconomic category for marketing purposes. **2** (**E**) a shape like that of a capital E: [in *combination*] *an* ***E-shaped*** *stately home.* **3** (usu. **E**) *Music* the third note of the diatonic scale of C major. ■ a key based on a scale with E as its keynote.

E[2] ▸*abbr.* ■ Earth. ■ East or Eastern: *139° E.* ■ Easter. ■ *informal* the drug Ecstasy or a tablet of Ecstasy. ■ engineer or engineering. ■ English. ■ [in *combination*] (also **e**) electronic: *E-commerce.*
▸*symbol Physics* ■ electric field strength. ■ electromotive force. ■ energy: $E = mc^2$.

E[3] ▸*symbol* (Ɛ) euro(s).

e ▸*symbol* ■ (also **e–**) *Chemistry* an electron. ■ (*e*) *Mathematics* the transcendental number that is the base of Napierian or natural logarithms, approximately equal to 2.71828.

e-[1] ▸*prefix* variant spelling of **EX-**[1] (as in *elect, emit*).

e-[2] ▸*prefix* (also **E-**) denoting anything in an electronic state, esp. the use of electronic data transfer in cyberspace for information exchange and financial transactions, esp. through the Internet: *e-business* | *e-cash* | *e-world* | *e-zine.* ▷from **ELECTRONIC**, on the pattern of *e-mail.*

e[3] /ē/ ▸*n.* (*pl.* **e's**) an e-mail system, message, or messages.
▸*v.* (**e'd, e'ing**) [*trans.*] **1** send an e-mail to (someone): *e me to make an offer.* **2** send (a message) by e-mail. ▷shortening.

ea. ▸*abbr.* each (used esp. when giving retail prices): *T-shirts for $9.95 ea.*

each /ēch/ ▸*adj.* & *pron.* used to refer to every one of two or more people or things, regarded and identified separately: [as *adj.*] *each battery is in a separate compartment* | ***each one*** *of us was asked what went on* | [as *pron.*] *Doug had money from* ***each of*** *his five uncles* | *they each have their own personality.*
▸*adv.* to, for, or by every one of a group (used after a noun or an amount): *they cost $35 each* | *Paul and Bill have a glass each.* ▷Old English *ǣlc*; related to Dutch *elk* and German *jeglich*, based on a West Germanic phrase meaning 'ever alike' (see **AYE**[2], **ALIKE**).
▸*PHRASE* □ **each and every** every single (used for emphasis): *taking each and every opportunity.*

each oth·er ▸*pron.* used to refer to each member of a group when each does something to or for other members: *they communicate with each other in French.*

Ead·wig /'edwig/ variant spelling of **EDWY**.

Ea·gan /'ēgən/ a city in southeastern Minnesota, just south of St. Paul; pop. 63,557.

ea·ger /'ēgər/ ▸*adj.* (of a person) wanting to do or have something very much: *the man was eager to please* | *young intellectuals* ***eager for*** *knowledge.* ■ (of a person's expression or tone of voice) characterized by keen expectancy or interest: *small eager faces looked up and listened.* ▷Middle English (also in the sense 'sharp to the senses, pungent, sour'): from Old French *aigre* 'keen,' from Latin *acer, acr-* 'sharp, pungent.' **—ea·ger·ly** *adv.* **—ea·ger·ness** *n.*

USAGE See usage at **ANXIOUS**.

THE RIGHT WORD **ardent, avid, eager, enthusiastic, fervent, keen, zealous**

You've heard of the "eager beaver"? Anyone who has a strong interest or an impatient desire to pursue or become involved in something is called **eager** (*eager to get started; an eager learner*).

Someone who is especially *eager* might be called **avid**, a word that implies greed or insatiable desire (*an avid golfer, he was never at home on weekends*).

Ardent combines eagerness with intense feelings of passion or devotion (*an ardent lover; an ardent theatergoer*), while **fervent** suggests an eagerness that is ready, at least figuratively, to boil over (*their fervent pleas could not be ignored*). Anyone who is deeply interested in something or who shows a spirited readiness to act is called **keen** (*he was keen on bicycling*), while **zealous** implies the kind of eagerness that pushes all other considerations aside (*a zealous environmentalist*).

Enthusiastic may connote participation rather than expectation: One can be *eager* to take a trip to Switzerland, an *ardent* student of Swiss history, and an *avid* outdoorsperson who is *keen* on hiking, but one is usually called *enthusiastic* about a trip to Switzerland when it is under way. *Enthusiastic* also very often applies to someone who outwardly and forcefully expresses eagerness.

ea·ger bea·ver ▸*n. informal* a keen and enthusiastic person who works very hard.

ea·gle /'ēgəl/ ▸*n.* **1** a large bird of prey with a massive hooked bill and long broad wings, renowned for its keen sight and powerful soaring flight. • Family Accipitridae: several genera, in particular *Aquila.* ■ a figure of an eagle, esp. as a symbol of the U.S., or formerly as a Roman or French ensign. ■ one of a pair of insignia in the shape of an eagle worn by a colonel in the U.S. Army, Air Force, or Marine Corps, or by a captain in the U.S. Navy. **2** *Golf* a score of two strokes under par at a hole. [suggested by **BIRDIE**.] **3** in the U.S., a former gold coin worth ten dollars.
▸*v.* [*trans.*] *Golf* play (a hole) in two strokes under par: *he eagled the last to share fourth place.* ▷Middle English: from Old French *aigle*, from Latin *aquila.*

ea·gle eye ▸*n.* a keen or close watch: *she was* ***keeping an eagle eye on*** *Laura.* **—ea·gle-eyed** /',ēgəl 'īd/ *adj.*

ea·gle owl ▸*n.* a very large Old World owl with ear tufts and a deep hoot. • Genus *Bubo*, family Strigidae: several species, in particular the Eurasian *B. bubo.*

Ea·gle Pass a city in southwestern Texas, on the Rio Grande; pop. 20,651.

ea·gle ray ▸*n.* a large marine ray with long pointed pectoral fins, a long tail, and a distinct head. • Family Myliobatidae: genera *Myliobatis* and *Aetobatus*, and several species.

ea·glet /'ēglit/ ▸*n.* a young eagle.

ea·gre /'ēgər/ ▸*n.* dialect term for **BORE**[3]. ▷early 17th cent.: of unknown origin.

Ea·kins /'ākinz/, Thomas (1844–1916), U.S. painter and photographer. He is known for his portraits and genre pictures of life in Philadelphia. *The Gross Clinic* (1875) aroused controversy because of its explicit depiction of surgery.

-ean ▸*suffix* forming adjectives and nouns such as *Antipodean, Joycean,* and *Pythagorean.* Compare with **-AN**. ▷from Latin *-aeus, -eus* or Greek *-aios, -eios,* + **-AN**.

ear[1] /i(ə)r/ ▸*n.* the organ of hearing and balance in humans and other vertebrates, esp. the external part of this. ■ an organ sensitive to sound in other animals. ■ [in *sing.*] an ability to recognize, appreciate, and reproduce sounds, esp. music or language: ***an ear for*** *melody.* ■ used to refer to a person's willingness to listen and pay attention to something: *she offers a sympathetic ear to worried pet owners.* ■ an ear-shaped thing, esp. the handle of a jug.

The ear of a mammal is composed of three parts. The outer or external ear consists of a fleshy external flap and a tube leading to the eardrum or tympanum. The middle ear is an air-filled cavity connected to the throat, containing three small linked bones that transmit vibrations from the eardrum to the inner ear. The inner ear is a complex fluid-filled labyrinth including the spiral cochlea (where vibrations are converted to nerve impulses) and the three semicircular canals (forming the organ of balance). The ears of other vertebrates are broadly similar.

▷Old English *ēare*, of Germanic origin; related to Dutch *oor* and German *Ohr*, from an Indo-European root shared by Latin *auris* and Greek *ous.* **—eared** *adj.* [in *combination*] *long-eared.* **—ear·less** *adj.*
▸*PHRASES* □ **be all ears** *informal* be listening eagerly and attentively. □ **bring something (down) about one's ears** bring something, esp. misfortune, on oneself: *she brought her world crashing about her ears.* □ **one's ears are burning** one is subconsciously aware of being talked about or criticized. □ **grin** (or **smile**) **from ear to ear** smile broadly. □ **have something coming out of one's ears** *informal* have a substantial or excessive amount of something: *that man's got money coming out of his ears.* □ **have someone's ear** have access to and influence with someone: *he claimed to have the prime minister's ear.* □ **have** (or **keep**) **an ear to the ground** be well informed about events and trends. □ **in one ear and out the other** heard but disregarded or quickly forgotten: *whatever he tells me seems to go in one ear and out the other.* □ **listen with half an ear** not give one's full attention. □ **be out on one's ear** *informal* be dismissed or ejected ignominiously. □ **up to one's ears in** *informal* very busy with or deeply involved in: *I'm up to my ears in work here.*

ear[2] ▸*n.* the seed-bearing head or spike of a cereal plant. ■ a head of corn. ▷Old English *ēar*, of Germanic origin; related to Dutch *aar* and German *Ähre.*

ear·ache /'i(ə)r,āk/ ▸*n.* pain inside the ear. Also called **OTALGIA**.

ear can·dy ▸*n.* light popular music that is pleasant and entertaining but intellectually unchallenging: *the album is mostly ear candy—upbeat melodies and catchy choruses that you can't get out of your head.*

ear drops ▸*plural n.* **1** liquid medication to be applied in small amounts to the ear. **2** (**eardrops**) hanging earrings.

ear·drum /'i(ə)r,drəm/ ▸*n.* a membrane of the middle ear that vibrates in response to sound waves; the tympanic membrane.

eared seal ▸*n.* see **SEAL**[2].

ear·flap /'i(ə)r,flap/ ▸*n.* a flap of material on a hat or cap, covering the ear.

ear·ful /'i(ə)r,fo͝ol/ ▸*n.* [in *sing.*] *informal* a loud blast of a noise: *an earful of static.* ■ a prolonged amount of talking, typically an angry reprimand: *he* ***gave*** *his players* ***an earful*** *at halftime.*

Ear·hart /'e(ə)r,härt/, Amelia (Mary) (1898–1937), U.S. aviator. In 1932, she became the first woman to fly an airplane across the Atlantic Ocean by herself. In 1937, her plane disappeared somewhere over the Pacific Ocean during an around-the-world flight.

ear·hole /'i(ə)r,hōl/ ▸*n.* the external opening of the ear: *seals can close their earholes under water.* ■ *informal* a person's ear.

earl /ərl/ ▸*n.* a British nobleman ranking above a viscount and below a marquess. ▷Old English *eorl*, of Germanic origin. The word *earl* originally denoted a man of noble rank, as opposed to a churl; also the word denoted specifically a hereditary nobleman directly above the rank of thane. It was later an equivalent of **JARL** and, under Canute and his successors, applied to the governor of divisions of England such as Wessex and Mercia. In the late Old English period, as the Saxon court came increasingly under Norman influence, the word was applied to any nobleman bearing the continental title of count (see COUNT[2]).

earl·dom /ˈərldəm/ ▶*n.* the rank or title of an earl. ■ *historical* the territory governed by an earl.

ear·less liz·ard /ˈi(ə)rlis/ ▶*n.* a small, long-legged burrowing lizard without visible external ear openings, native to North America. • *Holbrookia texana*, family Iguanidae.

Earl Grey ▶*n.* a kind of China tea flavored with bergamot. ▷probably named after the 2nd *Earl Grey* (1764–1845), said to have been given the recipe by a Chinese mandarin.

ear·lobe /ˈi(ə)rˌlōb/ ▶*n.* the soft, fleshy lower part of the external ear.

ear·lock /ˈi(ə)rˌläk/ ▶*n.* a lock of hair over or above the ear.

earl pal·a·tine ▶*n.* (*pl.* **earls pal·a·tine**) *historical* an earl having royal authority within his country or domain.

Ear·ly /ˈərlē/, Jubal Anderson (1816–94), U.S. Confederate army officer. He nearly reached the capital in his 1864 raid on Washington, but was defeated several months later by Sheridan in the Shenandoah Valley and was relieved of his command.

ear·ly /ˈərlē/ ▶*adj.* (**ear·li·er, ear·li·est**) **1** happening or done before the usual or expected time: *we ate an early lunch.* ■ (of a plant or crop) flowering or ripening before other varieties: *early potatoes.* **2** happening, belonging to, or done near the beginning of a particular time or period: *an early goal secured victory.* ■ denoting or belonging to the beginning or opening stages of a historical period, cultural movement, or sphere of activity: *early Impressionism.* ■ occurring at the beginning of a sequence: *the earlier chapters of the book.*
▶*adv.* **1** before the usual or expected time: *I was planning to finish work early today.* **2** near the beginning of a particular time or period: *we lost a couple of games early in the season.* ■ (**earlier**) before the present time or before the time one is referring to: *you met my husband earlier.* ▷Old English (as an adverb) *ǣrlīce* (see ERE, -LY[2]), influenced by Old Norse *árliga*. The adjective use dates from Middle English. **—ear·li·ness** *n.*
▶*PHRASES* □ **at the earliest** not before the time or date specified: *the table won't be delivered until next week at the earliest.* □ **early bird** *humorous* a person who rises, arrives, or acts before the usual or expected time. □ **an early grave** a premature or untimely death: *he worked himself into an early grave.* □ **the early hours** the time after midnight and before dawn. □ **an early night** an occasion when someone goes to bed before the usual time. □ **early** (or **earlier**) **on** at an early (or earlier) stage in a particular time or period: *they discovered early on that the published data were wrong.*

ear·ly a·dopt·er ▶*n.* a person who starts using a product or technology as soon as it becomes available.

Ear·ly Eng·lish ▶*adj.* denoting the earliest stage of English Gothic church architecture, typical of the late 12th and 13th centuries and marked by the use of pointed arches and simple lancet windows without tracery.

ear·ly mu·sic ▶*n.* medieval, Renaissance, and early baroque music, esp. as revived and played on period instruments.

ear·ly re·tire·ment ▶*n.* the practice of leaving employment before the statutory age, esp. on favorable financial terms.

ear·ly warn·ing sys·tem ▶*n.* a network of radar stations established at the boundary of a defended region to provide advanced warning of an aircraft or missile attack. ■ a condition, system, or series of procedures indicating a potential development or impending problem.

Amelia Earhart

ear·mark /ˈi(ə)rˌmärk/ ▶*n.* a mark on the ear of a domesticated animal indicating ownership or identity. ■ a characteristic or identifying feature: *this car has all the earmarks of a classic.*
▶*v.* [*trans.*] **1** (usu. **be earmarked**) designate (something, typically funds or resources) for a particular purpose: *the new money will be* **earmarked for** *cancer research.* **2** mark the ear of (an animal) as a sign of ownership or identity.

ear·muffs /ˈi(ə)rˌməfs/ ▶*plural n.* a pair of soft fabric coverings, connected by a band across the top of the head, that are worn over the ears to protect them from cold or noise.

earn /ərn/ ▶*v.* [*trans.*] (of a person) obtain (money) in return for labor or services: *they earn $35 per hour | he now* **earns his living** *as a truck driver.* ■ [with *two objs.*] (of an activity or action) cause (someone) to obtain (money): *this latest win earned them $50,000 in prize money.* ■ (of capital invested) gain (money) as interest or profit. ■ gain or incur deservedly in return for one's behavior or achievements: *through the years she has earned affection and esteem.* ▷Old English *earnian*, from a base shared by Old English *esne* 'laborer.'
▶*PHRASE* □ **earn one's keep** work in return for food and accommodations. ■ be worth the time, money, or effort spent on one.

earned in·come /ərnd/ ▶*n.* money derived from paid work. Often contrasted with UNEARNED INCOME.

earned run ▶*n.* *Baseball* a run scored without the aid of errors by the team in the field (i.e., by hits, walks, and outs that advance base runners).

earned run av·er·age ▶*n.* *Baseball* a statistic used to measure a pitcher's effectiveness, obtained by calculating the average number of earned runs scored against the pitcher in every nine innings pitched.

earn·er /ˈərnər/ ▶*n.* [with *adj.*] a person who obtains money in return for labor or services: *higher rates of income tax for high earners | a wage earner.* ■ an activity or product that brings in income of a specified kind or level: *tobacco is a major foreign currency earner.*

ear·nest[1] /ˈərnist/ ▶*adj.* resulting from or showing sincere and intense conviction: *an earnest student | two girls were in earnest conversation.* ▷Old English *eornoste* (adjective), *eornost* (noun), of Germanic origin; related to German *Ernst* (noun). **—ear·nest·ly** *adv.* **—ear·nest·ness** *n.*
▶*PHRASE* □ **in earnest** occurring to a greater extent or more intensely than before: *after Labor Day the campaign begins in earnest.* ■ (of a person) sincere and serious in behavior or convictions.

ear·nest[2] ▶*n.* [in *sing.*] a thing intended or regarded as a sign or promise of what is to come: *the presence of the troops is an earnest of the world's desire not to see the conflict repeated elsewhere.* ▷Middle English *ernes*, literally 'installment paid to confirm a contract,' based on Old French *erres*, from Latin *arra*, shortened form of *arrabo* 'a pledge.' The spelling was influenced by words ending in -NESS; the final *-t* is probably by association with EARNEST[1].

ear·nest mon·ey ▶*n.* money paid to confirm a contract.

Earn·hardt /ˈərnˌhärt/, (Ralph) Dale (1951–2001), U.S. race car driver; nickname **the Intimidator**. He raced professionally and set many records from 1979 until an accident during the Daytona 500 took his life in February 2001.

earn·ings /ˈərniNGz/ ▶*plural n.* money obtained in return for labor or services. ■ income derived from an investment or product: *savers who are attracted by the tax-free earnings.*

Earp /ərp/, Wyatt (Berry Stapp) (1848–1929), U.S. marshal and frontiersman. He is best known for the gunfight at the OK Corral (1881), in which he, his brothers, and his friend Doc Holliday fought the Clanton brothers at Tombstone, Arizona.

ear·phone /ˈi(ə)rˌfōn/ ▶*n.* (usu. **earphones**) an electrical device worn on the ear to receive radio or telephone communications or to listen to a radio or tape recorder without other people hearing.

ear·piece /ˈi(ə)rˌpēs/ ▶*n.* **1** the part of a telephone, radio receiver, or other aural device that is applied to the ear during use. **2** the part of a pair of glasses that fits around the ear.

ear-pierc·ing ▶*adj.* [*attrib.*] loud and shrill: *the alarm emits an ear-piercing screech.*
▶*n.* the practice of making holes in the lobes or edges of the ears to allow the wearing of earrings.

ear·plug /ˈi(ə)rˌpləg/ ▶*n.* (usu. **earplugs**) **1** a piece of wax, rubber, or cotton placed in the ear as protection against noise or water. **2** *historical* an ornament worn in the lobe of the ear.

ear·ring /ˈi(ə)rˌ(r)iNG/ ▶*n.* a piece of jewelry worn on the lobe or edge of the ear.

ear shell ▶*n.* another term for ABALONE.

ear·shot /ˈi(ə)rˌSHät/ ▶*n.* the range or distance over which one can hear or be heard: *she waited until he was* **out of earshot** *before continuing.*

ear-split·ting ▶*adj.* extremely loud: *an ear-splitting crack of thunder.*

earth /ərTH/ ▶*n.* **1** (also **Earth**) the planet on which we live; the world: *the diversity of life* **on earth.** ■ the surface of the world as distinct from the sky or the sea: *it plummeted back to earth at 60 mph.* ■ the present abode of humankind, as distinct from heaven or hell: *God's will be done on earth as it is in heaven.*

> The earth is the third planet from the sun in the solar system, orbiting between Venus and Mars at an average distance of 90 million miles (149.6 million km) from the sun, and has one natural satellite, the moon. It has an equatorial diameter of 7,654 miles (12,756 km), an average density 5.5 times that of water, and is believed to have formed about 4,600 million years ago. The earth, which is three-quarters covered by oceans and has a dense atmosphere of nitrogen and oxygen, is the only planet known to support life.

2 the substance of the land surface; soil: *a layer of earth.* ■ one of the four elements in ancient and medieval philosophy and in astrology (considered essential to certain signs of the zodiac). ■ a stable, dense, nonvolatile inorganic substance found in the ground. ■ *poetic/literary* the substance of the human body. **3** the underground lair or habitation of a badger or fox. **4** *Electrical* British term for GROUND[1] (sense 7).
▶*v.* [*trans.*] **1** (**earth something up**) cover the root and lower stem of a plant with heaped-up earth. **2** *Hunting* drive (a fox) to its underground lair. ■ [*intrans.*] (of a fox) run to its underground lair. **3** *electrical* British term for GROUND[1] (sense 5). ▷Old English *eorthe*, of Germanic origin; related to Dutch *aarde* and German *Erde*.
▶*PHRASES* □ **come** (or **bring**) **back** (**down**) **to earth** return or cause to return to reality after a period of daydreaming or excitement. □ **the earth moved** (or **did the earth move for you?**) *humorous* one had (or did you have?) an orgasm. □ **go to earth** (of a hunted animal) hide in an underground burrow. ■ *figurative* go into hiding: *he'd gone to earth after that meeting.* □ **like nothing on earth** *informal* very strange: *they looked like nothing on earth.* □ **on earth** used for emphasis: *who on earth would venture out in weather like this?*

E

earth al·mond ▶*n.* another term for CHUFA.

earth·bound /ˈərTHˌbound/ ▶*adj.* **1** attached or restricted to the earth: *a flightless earthbound bird.* ■ attached or limited to material existence as distinct from a spiritual or heavenly one: *her earthbound view of the sacrament.* ■ *figurative* lacking in imaginative reach or drive: *an earthbound performance.* **2** (also **earth-bound**) moving toward the earth: *an earthbound spaceship.*

earth clos·et ▶*n.* *Brit.* a basic type of toilet with dry earth used to cover excrement.

earth·en /ˈərTHən/ ▶*adj.* [*attrib.*] (of a floor or structure) made of compressed earth: *the hillside adjacent to the earthen dam.* ■ (of a pot) made of baked or fired clay. ■ *poetic/literary* of, relating to, or characteristic of the earth or material existence.

earth·en·ware /ˈərTHənˌwer/ ▶*n.* [often as *adj.*] pottery made of clay fired to a porous state that can be made impervious to liquids by the use of a glaze: *an earthenware jug.*

earth·light /ˈərTHˌlīt/ ▶*n.* another term for EARTHSHINE.

earth·ling /ˈərTHliNG/ ▶*n.* an inhabitant of the earth (used esp. in science fiction by members of alien species).

earth loop ▶*n.* *Electrical* British term for GROUND LOOP.

earth·ly /ˈərTHlē/ ▶*adj.* **1** of or relating to the earth or human life on the earth: *water is liquid at normal earthly temperatures.* ■ of or relating to humankind's material existence as distinct from a spiritual or heavenly one: *all earthly happiness is but vanity.* **2** [with *negative*] *informal* used for emphasis: *there* *was* ***no earthly reason*** *why she should not come too.* **—earth·li·ness** *n.*

earth moth·er ▸*n.* (in mythology and primitive religion) a goddess symbolizing fertility and the source of life. ■ an archetypically sensual and maternal woman.

earth·mov·er /ˈərth,mo͞ovər/ ▸*n.* a vehicle or machine designed to excavate large quantities of soil. **—earth·mov·ing** *n.* & *adj.*

earth·nut /ˈərTH,nət/ ▸*n.* **1** a Eurasian plant of the parsley family, which has an edible roundish tuber and is typically found in woodland and acid pasture. Also called **PIGNUT**. • *Conopodium majus*, family Umbelliferae. ■ the almond-flavored tuber of this plant. **2** *chiefly Brit.* another term for **PEANUT**.

earth·quake /ˈərTH,kwāk/ ▸*n.* a sudden and violent shaking of the ground, sometimes causing great destruction, as a result of movements within the earth's crust or volcanic action. ■ *figurative* a great convulsion or upheaval: *a political earthquake.*

Major earthquakes are confined to particular active regions of the earth's crust corresponding to the edges of the crustal plates, and most earthquakes are due to the release of strain energy associated with the relative motions of the plates. The intensity of earthquakes is expressed by the Richter scale, destructive earthquakes generally measuring between about 7 and 9.

earth sci·ence ▸*n.* the branch of science dealing with the physical constitution of the earth and its atmosphere. ■ (**earth sciences**) the various branches of this subject, e.g., geology, oceanography, and meteorology.

earth·shak·ing /ˈərTH,SHākiNG/ ▸*adj.* (of music or sound) loud and throbbing: *earthshaking hard-core metal.* ■ another term for **EARTH-SHATTERING**: *this is not of earthshaking importance.*

earth-shat·ter·ing ▸*adj.* (in hyperbolic use) very important, momentous, or traumatic: *tell me this earth-shattering news of yours.* **—earth-shat·ter·ing·ly** *adv.*

earth·shine /ˈərTH,SHīn/ (also **earth·light**) ▸*n. Astronomy* the glow caused by sunlight reflected off the earth, esp. on the darker portion of a crescent moon.

earth·star /ˈərTH,stär/ ▸*n.* a brownish woodland fungus with a spherical spore-containing fruiting body surrounded by a fleshy star-shaped structure, found in both Eurasia and North America. • Family Geastraceae, class Gasteromycetes: *Geastrum* and other genera.

earth sta·tion ▸*n.* a radio station located on the earth and used for relaying signals from satellites.

earth tone ▸*n.* a rich warm color with a brownish hue.

earth trem·or ▸*n.* see **TREMOR**.

earth·ward /ˈərTHwərd/ (also **earth·wards**) ▸*adv.* & *adj.* toward the earth: [as *adv.*] *we can watch the parachute as it drifts earthward* | [as *adj.*] *the bird's earthward plummet.*

earth·work /ˈərTH,wərk/ ▸*n.* **1** a large artificial bank of soil, esp. one made as a defense. **2** the process of excavating soil in civil engineering work. **3** a work of art consisting of modification of a large piece of land.

earth·worm /ˈərTH,wərm/ ▸*n.* a burrowing annelid worm that lives in the soil. Earthworms play an important role in aerating and draining the soil and in burying organic matter. • Family Lumbricidae, class Oligochaeta: *Lumbricus*, *Allolobophora*, and other genera.

earth·y /ˈərTHē/ ▸*adj.* (**earth·i·er**, **earth·i·est**) resembling or suggestive of earth or soil: *an earthy smell.* ■ (of a person) direct and uninhibited; hearty: *the storefront is given over to a young, earthy crowd.* ■ (of humor) somewhat coarse or crude: *their good-natured vulgarity and earthy humor.* **—earth·i·ly** *adv.* **—earth·i·ness** *n.*

ear trum·pet ▸*n.* a trumpet-shaped device formerly used as a hearing aid.

ear tuft ▸*n.* each of a pair of tufts of longer feathers on the top of the head of some owls. They are unconnected with the true ears.

ear·wax /ˈi(ə)r,waks/ ▸*n.* the protective yellow waxy substance secreted in the passage of the outer ear. Also called **CERUMEN**.

ear·wig /ˈi(ə)r,wig/ ▸*n.* a small elongated insect with a pair of terminal appendages that resemble pincers. The females typically care for their eggs and young until they are grown. • Order Dermaptera: several families.

▸*v.* (**-wigged**, **-wig·ging**) [*intrans.*] *informal, chiefly Brit.* eavesdrop on a conversation: *he looked behind him to see if anyone was earwigging.* ■ [*trans.*] *archaic* influence (someone) by secret means. ▷Old English *ēarwicga*, from *ēare* 'ear' + *wicga* 'earwig' (probably related to *wiggle*). The insect is so named because it was once thought to crawl into the human ear.

ear·wit·ness /ˈi(ə)r,witnis; ,i(ə)rˈwit-/ ▸*n.* a witness whose testimony is based on what they personally heard.

ease /ēz/ ▸*n.* absence of difficulty or effort: *he gave up tobacco and alcohol with ease* | *the guitar's versatility and ease of handling.* ■ absence of rigidity or discomfort; poise: *I was always vexed by her self-contained ease.* ■ freedom from worries or problems, esp. about one's material situation: *a life of wealth and ease.*

▸*v.* **1** [*trans.*] make (something unpleasant, painful, or intense) less serious or severe: *a huge road-building program to ease congestion.* ■ alleviate the mental or physical pain of: *unburdening herself was doing nothing to ease her misery.* ■ [*intrans.*] become less serious or severe: *the pain doesn't usually* ***ease off*** *for several hours.* ■ [*intrans.*] (**ease up**) relax one's efforts; do something with more moderation: *I'd* ***ease up on*** *the hard stuff if I were you.* ■ (**ease something away/down/off**) *Nautical* slacken a rope. ■ (**ease something away/down/off**) *Nautical* sail slowly or gently. ■ make (something) happen more easily; facilitate: *Tokyo's dominance of government was deemed to ease efficient contact-making.* ■ [*intrans.*] *Finance* (of share prices, interest rates, etc.) decrease in value or amount: *these shares should be bought and tucked away for when interest rates ease* | [as *n.*] (**easing**) *a slight easing of inflation.* **2** [*intrans.*] move carefully, gradually, or gently: *I eased down the slope with care* | [*trans.*] *the pilot eased the throttle back.* ■ [*trans.*] (**ease someone out**) gradually exclude someone from a post or place, esp. by devious or subtle maneuvers: *after the scandal he was eased out of his job.* ▷Middle English: from Old French *aise*, based on Latin *adjacens* 'lying close by,' present participle of *adjacere*. The verb is originally from Old French *aisier*, from the phrase *a aise* 'at ease'; in later use from the noun. **—eas·er** *n.*

▸*PHRASES* □ **at (one's) ease** free from worry, awkwardness, or problems; relaxed: *she was never quite* ***at ease with*** *Phil.* ■ (**at ease**) *Military* in a relaxed attitude with the feet apart and the hands behind the back (often as a command): *all right,* ***stand at ease!*** □ **ease someone's mind** alleviate someone's anxiety.

ease·ful /ˈēzfəl/ ▸*adj. poetic/literary* providing or offering comfort or peace: *life was easeful at that time.*

ea·sel /ˈēzəl/ ▸*n.* a self-supporting wooden frame for holding an artist's work while it is being painted or drawn. ■ a similar frame for displaying charts, promotional materials, announcements, etc. ▷late 16th cent.: from Dutch *ezel* 'ass.' The word "horse" is used in English in a similar way to denote a supporting frame.

artist's easel

ease·ment /ˈēzmənt/ ▸*n.* **1** *Law* a right to cross or otherwise use someone else's land for a specified purpose. **2** *poetic/literary* the state or feeling of comfort or peace: *time brings easement.* ▷late Middle English: from Old French *aisement*, from *aisier* (see **EASE**).

eas·i·ly /ˈēz(ə)lē/ ▸*adv.* **1** without difficulty or effort: *he climbed the mountain easily* | *the area is easily accessible by road.* ■ in a relaxed manner: *he shrugged easily.* ■ more quickly or frequently than is usual: *they get bored easily.* **2** without doubt; by far: *English is easily the reigning language in the financial world.* ■ very probably: *events that could easily become stodgy and predictable.*

east /ēst/ ▸*n.* (usu. **the east**) **1** the direction toward the point of the horizon where the sun rises at the equinoxes, on the right-hand side of a person facing north, or the point on the horizon itself: *a gale was blowing from the east* | *the Atlantic Ocean is* ***to the east of*** *Florida.* ■ the compass point corresponding to this. **2** the eastern part of the world or of a specified country, region, or town: *a factory in the east of the city.* ■ (usu. **the East**) the regions or countries lying to the east of Europe, esp. China, Japan, and India: *the mysterious East.* ■ (usu. **the East**) the eastern part of the U.S. from the Alleghenies on the west and north of the Mason-Dixon line: *Pittsburgh beat up on the bottom three teams in the East.* ■ (usu. **the East**) short for **EAST COAST**. ■ (usu. **the East**) *historical* the former communist states of eastern Europe. **3** (**East**) [as *name*] *Bridge* the player sitting to the left of North and partnering West.

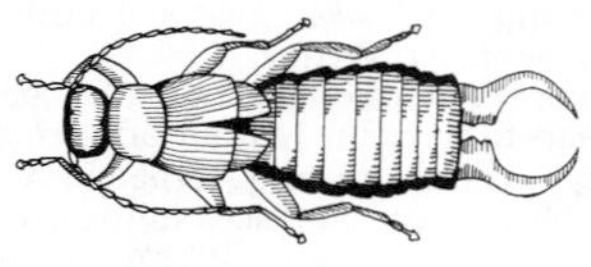

earwig

▸*adj.* [*attrib.*] **1** lying toward, near, or facing the east: *the hospital's east wing.* ■ (of a wind) blowing from the east. ■ situated in the part of a church containing the altar or high altar, usually the actual east. **2** (often **East**) of or denoting the eastern part of a specified area, city, or country or its inhabitants: *East Texas* | *East African.*

▸*adv.* to or toward the east: *traveling east, he met two men* | *the river rises* ***east of*** *the city.* ▷Old English *ēast-*, of Germanic origin; related to Dutch *oost* and German *ost*, from an Indo-European root shared by Latin *aurora*, Greek *auōs* 'dawn.'

East Af·ri·ca the eastern part of the African continent, esp. the countries of Kenya, Uganda, and Tanzania.

East An·gli·a /ˈaNGglēə/ a region in eastern England that consists of the counties of Norfolk and Suffolk, as well as parts of Essex and Cambridgeshire counties.

East Ben·gal the part of the former Indian province of Bengal that was ceded to Pakistan in 1947 and that forms the greater part of the province of East Pakistan. It gained independence as Bangladesh in 1971.

East Ber·lin see **BERLIN**.

east·bound /ˈēs(t),bound/ ▸*adj.* leading or traveling toward the east: *the eastbound lane.*

east by north ▸*n.* a direction or compass point midway between east and east-northeast.

east by south ▸*n.* a direction or compass point midway between east and east-southeast.

East Chi·ca·go an industrial port city in northwestern Indiana, on Lake Michigan, southeast of Chicago in Illinois; pop. 33,892.

East Chi·na Sea see **CHINA SEA**.

East Coast ▸*n.* the eastern seaboard of the U.S., esp. the narrow corridor from Boston to Washington, DC.

East End the part of London, England, north of the Thames and east of the City, including the Docklands. **—East End·er** /,ēst ˈendər/ *n.*

Eas·ter /ˈēstər/ ▸*n.* the most important and oldest festival of the Christian Church, celebrating the resurrection of Jesus Christ and held (in the Western Church) between March 21 and April 25, on the first Sunday after the first full moon following the northern spring equinox. ■ the period in which this occurs, esp. the weekend from Good Friday to Easter Monday. ▷Old English *ēastre*; of Germanic origin and related to German *Ostern* and **EAST**. According to Bede the word is derived from *Ēastre*, the name of a goddess associated with spring.

Eas·ter bun·ny ▸*n.* an imaginary rabbit said to bring gifts to children at Easter.

Eas·ter egg ▸*n.* an egg that is dyed and often decorated as part of the Easter celebration. ■ an artificial egg, typically chocolate, given at Easter, esp. to children.

Eas·ter Is·land an island in the southeastern Pacific Ocean, west of and administered by Chile; pop. 2,000. The island, first settled by Polynesians in about AD 400, is famous for its large monolithic

statues on Easter Island

statues of human heads that are believed to date from 1000–1600.

Eas·ter lil·y ▸*n.* a spring-flowering lily. • Genus *Lilium*, family Liliaceae: several species, in particular the tall, white-flowered Japanese lily *L. longiflorum.*

east·er·ly /ˈēstərlē/ ▸*adj.* & *adv.* in an eastward position or direction: [as *adj.*] *the captain ordered an easterly course.* ■ (of a wind) blowing from the east: [as *adj.*] *the light easterly breeze.*
▸*n.* (often **easterlies**) a wind blowing from the east.

Eas·ter Mon·day ▸*n.* the day after Easter Sunday, a public holiday in some places.

east·ern /ˈēstərn/ ▸*adj.* **1** [*attrib.*] situated in the east, or directed toward or facing the east: *eastern Long Island* | *the eastern slopes of the mountain.* ■ (of a wind) blowing from the east. **2** (usu. **Eastern**) living in or originating from the east, in particular the regions or countries lying to the east of Europe: *an Eastern mystic.* ■ of, relating to, or characteristic of the East or its inhabitants: *Buddhism is no longer seen as an eastern religion.* ▷Old English *ēasterne* (as EAST, -ERN). —**east·ern·most** /ˈēstərn,mōst/ *adj.*

East·ern bloc the countries of eastern and central Europe that were under Soviet domination from the end of World War II until the collapse of the Soviet communist system in 1989–91, usually considered to include Poland, East Germany, Czechoslovakia, Hungary, Romania, Bulgaria, and Yugoslavia.

East·ern Church (also **Eastern Orthodox Church**) another name for ORTHODOX CHURCH. ■ any of the Christian Churches originating in eastern Europe and the Middle East.

East·ern Des·ert another name of the ARABIAN DESERT.

East·ern Em·pire the eastern part of the Roman Empire, after its division in AD 395. See also BYZANTINE EMPIRE.

east·ern e·quine en·ceph·a·li·tis ▸*n.* a rare viral disease that affects horses and humans and is spread by mosquitoes, occurring mainly in eastern U.S. states.

East·ern·er /ˈēstərnər/ (also **east·ern·er**) ▸*n.* a native or inhabitant of the east, esp. of the eastern U.S.

East·ern Eu·rope the portion of the European landmass that lies east of Germany and the Alps and west of the Ural Mountains. It includes the former Eastern bloc countries of Poland, the Czech Republic and Slovakia (formerly as Czechoslovakia), Hungary, Romania, and Bulgaria, as well as the Baltic republics of Estonia, Latvia, and Lithuania, and the former Soviet republics of Belarus and Ukraine, along with Russia west of the Urals.

East·ern Ghats see GHATS.

east·ern hem·i·sphere the half of the earth that contains Europe, Africa, Asia, and Australia.

East·ern Shore region of eastern Maryland on the Delmarva Peninsula, on the east side of Chesapeake Bay.

East·ern time the standard time in a zone including the eastern states of the U.S. and parts of Canada, specifically: • (**Eastern Standard Time**, abbrev.: **EST**), standard time based on the mean solar time at the meridian 75° W, five hours behind GMT. • (**Eastern Daylight Time**, abbrev.: **EDT**) Eastern time during daylight saving time, four hours behind GMT.

East·ern Zhou see ZHOU.

Eas·ter·tide /ˈēstər,tīd/ ▸*n.* the Easter period.

East Flan·ders a province in northern Belgium; capital, Ghent. See also FLANDERS.

East Fri·sian Is·lands see FRISIAN ISLANDS.

East Ger·man·ic ▸*n.* the extinct eastern group of Germanic languages, including Gothic.
▸*adj.* of or relating to this group of languages.

East Ger·many (official name **German Democratic Republic**) the former independent nation created in 1949 from the area of Germany occupied by the Soviet Union after World War II. It was reunited with West Germany after the fall of its communist government in 1990. German name **Deutsche Demokratische Republik**.

East Hamp·ton a resort town in eastern Long Island in New York, noted for its artists' colony; pop. 16,132.

East Har·lem a neighborhood of Harlem in northern Manhattan in New York City. Parts of it have been called Italian Harlem and Spanish Harlem, reflecting local ethnic history.

East Hart·ford an industrial town in central Connecticut, across the Connecticut River from Hartford; pop. 50,452.

East In·di·a another name of EAST INDIES (sense 2).

East In·di·a Com·pa·ny a trading company formed in 1600 to develop commerce in the newly colonized areas of Southeast Asia and India. In the 18th century it took administrative control of Bengal and other areas of India, and held it until the British Crown took over in 1858 in the wake of the Indian Mutiny.

East In·di·a·man /ˈindēəmən/ ▸*n. historical* a trading ship belonging to the East India Company.

East In·dies 1 the islands in Southeast Asia, esp. those of the Malay Archipelago. **2** *archaic* the whole of Southeast Asia to the east of and including India. —**East In·di·an** *adj.*

east·ing /ˈēstiNG/ ▸*n.* distance traveled or measured eastward, esp. at sea. ■ a figure or line representing eastward distance on a map (expressed by convention as the first part of a grid reference, before northing).

East Lan·sing a city in south central Michigan, home to Michigan State University; pop. 50,677.

East Lon·don a port and resort in South Africa, on the southeastern coast; pop. 270,130.

East Los An·ge·les a community in southwestern California, a largely Hispanic suburb east of Los Angeles; pop. 126,379.

East·man[1] /ˈēstmən/, George (1854–1932), U.S. inventor and manufacturer of photographic equipment. He invented flexible roll film that is coated with light-sensitive emulsion and, in 1888, the Kodak camera for use with it.

East·man[2], Linda, see MCCARTNEY[1].

east-north·east ▸*n.* the direction or compass point midway between east and northeast.

Eas·ton /ˈēstən/ an industrial city in eastern Pennsylvania, on the Lehigh and Delaware rivers; pop. 26,276.

East Or·ange a city in northeastern New Jersey, northwest of Newark; pop. 69,824.

East Point a city in northwestern Georgia, south of Atlanta; pop. 39,595.

East·port /ˈēst,pôrt/ a maritime city in eastern Maine, on an island in Passamaquoddy Bay, the easternmost U.S. city; pop. 1,965.

East Prov·i·dence a city in eastern Rhode Island, across the Seekonk River from Providence; pop. 48,688.

East Prus·sia the northeastern part of the former kingdom of Prussia, on the Baltic coast, later part of Germany and divided after World War II between the Soviet Union and Poland.

East Riv·er an arm of the Hudson River in New York City that separates the boroughs of Manhattan and the Bronx from the boroughs of Brooklyn and Queens.

East Si·be·ri·an Sea a part of the Arctic Ocean that lies between the New Siberian Islands and Wrangel Island, to the north of eastern Siberia.

East Side a part of Manhattan in New York City that lies between the East River and Fifth Avenue.

east-south·east ▸*n.* the direction or compass point midway between east and southeast.

East St. Lou·is a city in southwestern Illinois, across the Mississippi River from St. Louis; pop. 40,944.

East Ti·mor a state on the eastern part of the island of Timor in the southern part of the Malay Archipelago; pop. 1,019,252; capital, Dili; languages, Tetum (official), Portuguese (official), Indonesian, English, and indigenous languages. Official name, **Democratic Republic of East Timor.**

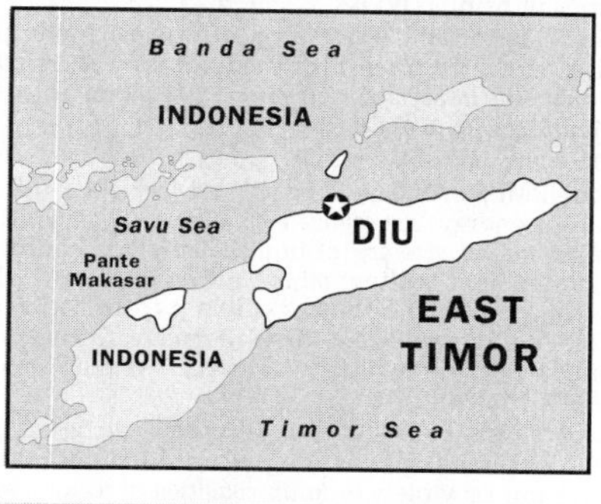

Formerly a Portuguese colony, East Timor declared itself independent in 1975. In 1976 it was invaded by Indonesia, which annexed and claimed it as their 27th state. The region was the scene of bitter fighting and of alleged mass killings by the Indonesian government and military forces. In a UN-supervised referendum in 1999, the people voted for independence from Indonesia. Violence continued, but on May 20, 2002, East Timor achieved international recognition as an independent state.

—**East Ti·mo·rese** *n.* & *adj.*

east·ward /ˈēs(t)wərd/ ▸*adj.* in an easterly direction: *they followed an eastward course.*
▸*adv.* (also **east·wards**) toward the east: *the bus rattled its way eastward.*
▸*n.* (**the eastward**) the direction or region toward the east: *a squall came from the eastward.* —**east·ward·ly** *adv.*

East·wood /ˈēst,wŏŏd/, Clint (1930–), U.S. movie actor and director. He became known after he starred in *A Fistful of Dollars* (1964), the first cult "spaghetti western" (a movie about the Old West filmed in Italy). He portrayed detective Harry Callahan in five movies, beginning with *Dirty Harry* (1971). Movies that he directed as well as starred in include *Bird* (1988), *Unforgiven* (Academy Award for Best Picture, 1992), *The Bridges of Madison County* (1994), and *Mystic River* (2003).

eas·y /ˈēzē/ ▸*adj.* (**eas·i·er**, **eas·i·est**) **1** achieved without great effort; presenting few difficulties: *an easy way of retrieving information.* ■ [*attrib.*] (of an object of attack or criticism) having no defense; vulnerable: *he was vulnerable and an easy target.* ■ *informal, derogatory* (of a woman) open to sexual advances; sexually available: *her reputation at school for being easy.* **2** (of a period of time or way of life) free from worries or problems: *promises of an easy life in the New World.* ■ (of a person) lacking anxiety or awkwardness; relaxed: *his easy and agreeable manner* | *they didn't feel easy about what they were doing.*
▸*adv. informal* without difficulty or effort: *we all scared real easy in those days.*
▸*exclam.* be careful: *easy, girl—you'll knock me over!* ▷Middle English (also in the sense 'comfortable, quiet, tranquil'): from Old French *aisie*, past participle of *aisier* 'put at ease, facilitate' (see EASE). —**eas·i·ness** *n.*
▸*PHRASES* □ **be easier said than done** be more easily talked about than put into practice. □ (**as**) **easy as pie** see PIE[1]. □ **easy come, easy go** used to indicate that a relationship or possession acquired without effort may be abandoned or lost casually and without regret. □ **easy does it** used esp. in spoken English to advise someone to approach a task carefully and slowly. □ **easy on the eye** (or **ear**) *informal* pleasant to look at (or listen to). □ **go** (or **be**) **easy on someone** *informal* refrain from being harsh with or critical of someone. □ **go easy on something** *informal* be sparing or cautious in one's use or consumption of something: *go easy on fatty foods.* □ **have it easy** *informal* be free from difficulties; be fortunate. □ **I'm easy** *informal* said by someone when offered a choice to indicate that they have no particular preference. □ **of easy virtue** *dated* (of a woman) sexually promiscuous. □ **rest** (or **sleep**) **easy** be untroubled by (or go to sleep without) worries: *this insurance policy will let you rest easy.* □ **take the easy way out** extricate oneself from a difficult situation by choosing the simplest or most expedient course rather than the most honorable or ethical one. □ **take it easy** proceed calmly and in a relaxed manner. ■ make little effort; rest.

eas·y-care ▸*adj.* [*attrib.*] (chiefly of man-made fabrics) requiring little effort to wash and dry, and typically no ironing.

eas·y chair ▸*n.* a large, comfortable chair, typically an armchair.

eas·y·go·ing /ˈēzē,gōiNG/ (also **easy-go·ing**) ▸*adj.* relaxed and tolerant in approach or manner: *an outwardly easygoing but fiercely competitive youngster.*

eas·y lis·ten·ing ▸*n.* popular music that is tuneful and undemanding.

eas·y mark ▸*n. informal* a person who is easy prey; a weakling or a sucker: *an easy mark for a grifter.*

eas·y mon·ey ▸*n.* money obtained by dubious means or for little work. ■ money available at relatively low interest.

eas·y street ▸*n. informal* a state of financial comfort or security: *she keeps complaining about her lot, but I think she's* **on easy street.**

eat /ēt/ ▸*v.* (*past* **ate** /āt/; *past part.* **eat·en** /ˈētn/) [*trans.*]

put (food) into the mouth and chew and swallow it: *he was eating a hot dog* | *eat up all your peas* | [*intrans.*] *she watched her son as he ate.* ■ have (a meal): *we ate dinner in a noisy cafe.* ■ [*intrans.*] (**eat out**) have a meal in a restaurant. ■ [*intrans.*] (**eat in**) have a meal at home rather than in a restaurant. ■ [*trans.*] include (a particular food) in one's usual diet: *try to eat more high-fiber foods.* ■ [*intrans.*] follow a diet of a specified kind or quality: *she was very thin, although she was eating properly now.* ■ *informal* bother; annoy: *she knew what was eating him.* ■ *vulgar slang* perform fellatio or cunnilingus on (someone). ■ *vulgar slang* (**eat out**) perform cunnilingus or anilingus on (someone). ■ *informal* absorb (financial loss or cost)

▸*phrasal v.* □ **eat away at something** (or **eat something away**) erode or destroy something gradually: *the sun and wind eat away at the ice* | *prevents bone from being eaten away.* ■ use up (profits, resources, or time), esp. when they are intended for other purposes: *inflation can eat away at the annuity's value over the years.* □ **eat into** another way of saying EAT AWAY AT above. □ **eat someone up** [usu. as *adj.*] (**eaten up**) dominate the thoughts of someone completely: *I'm eaten up with guilt.* □ **eat something up** use resources or time in very large quantities: *an operating system that eats up 200Mb of disk space.* ■ encroach on something: *this is the countryside that villagers fear will be eaten up by concrete.*

▸*n.* (**eats**) *informal* food or snacks: *people would stop for soft drinks or eats.* ▷Old English *etan*, of Germanic origin; related to Dutch *eten* and German *essen*, from an Indo-European root shared by Latin *edere* and Greek *edein*.

▸*PHRASES* □ **eat someone alive** *informal* (of insects) bite someone many times: *we were eaten alive by mosquitoes.* ■ exploit someone's weakness and completely dominate them: *he expects manufacturers to be eaten alive by lawyers in liability suits.* □ **eat crow** see CROW[1]. □ **eat dirt** see DIRT. □ **eat someone's dust** see DUST. □ **eat one's heart out** suffer from excessive longing, esp. for someone or something unattainable. ■ [in *imperative*] *informal* used to encourage feelings of jealousy or regret: *eat your heart out, I'm having a ball!* □ **eat humble pie** see HUMBLE. □ **eat like a bird** (or **a horse**) *informal* eat very little (or a lot). □ **eat someone out of house and home** *informal* eat a lot of someone else's food. □ **eat one's words** retract what one has said, esp. in a humiliated way: *they will eat their words when I win.* □ **have someone eating out of one's hand** have someone completely under one's control. □ **I'll eat my hat** *informal* used to indicate that one thinks the specified thing is extremely unlikely to happen: *if he comes back, I'll eat my hat.*

eat·a·ble /ˈētəbəl/ ▸*adj.* fit to be consumed as food: *eatable fruits.*

▸*n.* (**eatables**) items of food: *parcels of eatables and gifts.*

eat·er /ˈētər/ ▸*n.* [with *adj.*] a person who consumes food in a specified way or of a specified kind: *I'm still a big eater* | *they are meat eaters.*

eat·er·y /ˈētərē/ ▸*n.* (*pl.* **-er·ies**) *informal* a restaurant or other place where people can be served food.

eat-in ▸*adj.* [*attrib.*] (of a kitchen) designed for eating in as well as cooking.

eat·ing ap·ple ▸*n.* an apple that is suitable for eating raw.

eat·ing dis·or·der ▸*n.* any of a range of psychological disorders characterized by abnormal or disturbed eating habits (such as anorexia nervosa).

eat·ing house ▸*n.* a restaurant (usu. used in the names of restaurants): *The Blue Whale Eating House* | *Mrs. Miller's -- a contemporary pub and fine eating house.*

Eau Claire /ō ˈkler/ a city in west central Wisconsin; pop. 61,704.

eau de co·logne /ˌō də kəˈlōn/ ▸*n.* a toilet water with a strong, characteristic scent, originally made in Cologne, Germany. ▷early 19th cent.: French, literally 'water of Cologne.'

eau de Nil /ˌō də ˈnē/ ▸*n.* a pale greenish color. ▷late 19th cent.: from French *eau-de-Nil*, literally 'water of the Nile' (from the supposed resemblance in color).

eau de toi·lette /ˌō də twäˈlet/ ▸*n.* (*pl.* **eaux de toi·lette** *pronunc.* same) a dilute form of perfume; toilet water. ▷early 20th cent.: French, literally 'toilet water.'

eau-de-vie /ˌō də ˈvē/ ▸*n.* (*pl.* **eaux-de-vie** *pronunc.* same) brandy. ▷mid 18th cent.: from French *eau-de-vie*, literally 'water of life.'

eaves /ēvz/ ▸*plural n.* the part of a roof that meets or overhangs the walls of a building. ▷Old English *efes* (singular); of Germanic origin; related to German dialect *Obsen*, also probably to OVER.

eaves·drop /ˈēvzˌdräp/ ▸*v.* (**-dropped**, **-drop·ping**) [*intrans.*] secretly listen to a conversation: *she opened the window just enough to* **eavesdrop on** *the conversation outside.* ▷early 17th cent.: back-formation from *eavesdropper* (late Middle English) 'a person who listens from under the eaves,' from the obsolete noun *eavesdrop* 'the ground on to which water drips from the eaves,' probably from Old Norse *upsardropi*, from *ups* 'eaves' + *dropi* 'a drop.' —**eaves·drop·per** *n.*

ebb /eb/ ▸*n.* (usu. **the ebb**) the movement of the tide out to sea: *I knew the tide would be* **on the ebb** | [as *adj.*] *the ebb tide.*

▸*v.* [*intrans.*] (of tidewater) move away from the land; recede: *the tide began to ebb.* Compare with FLOW. ■ *figurative* (of an emotion or quality) gradually lessen or reduce: *my enthusiasm was* **ebbing away**. ▷Old English *ebba* (noun), *ebbian* (verb); related to Dutch *ebbe* (noun), *ebben* (verb), and ultimately to OF, which had the primary sense 'away from.'

▸*PHRASES* □ **at a low ebb** in a poor state: *the country was at a low ebb due to the recent war.* □ **ebb and flow** a recurrent or rhythmical pattern of coming and going or decline and regrowth.

EBCDIC /ˈebsēˌdik/ ▸*abbr.* Extended Binary Coded Decimal Interchange Code, a standard eight-bit character code used in computing and data transmission.

Eb·la /ˈeblə; ˈēblə/ a city in ancient Syria that was southwest of Aleppo. It became very powerful in the mid-3rd millennium BC, when it dominated a region corresponding to modern Lebanon, northern Syria, and southeastern Turkey.

EbN ▸*abbr.* east by north.

E-boat /ˈē ˌbōt/ ▸*n.* a German torpedo boat used in World War II. ▷from *E-* for *enemy* + BOAT.

Eb·o·la fe·ver /ēˈbōlə/ ▸*n.* an infectious and generally fatal disease marked by fever and severe internal bleeding, spread through contact with infected body fluids by a filovirus (**Ebola virus**), whose normal host species is unknown. ▷1976: named after a river in the Democratic Republic of the Congo (formerly Zaire), near which the disease was first observed.

eb·on /ˈebən/ ▸*n.* *poetic/literary* dark brown or black; ebony: [as *adj.*] *the dark shadows of the mountains gave the river an ebon hue.*

E·bon·ics /ēˈbäniks/ ▸*plural n.* [treated as *sing.*] American black English regarded as a language in its own right rather than as a dialect of standard English. ▷blend of EBONY and PHONICS.

eb·on·ite /ˈebəˌnīt/ ▸*n.* another term for VULCANITE. ▷mid 19th cent.: from EBONY + -ITE[1].

eb·on·ize /ˈebəˌnīz/ ▸*v.* [*trans.*] [usu. as *adj.*] (**ebonized**) make (furniture) look like ebony: *an ebonized casket.*

eb·on·y /ˈebənē/ ▸*n.* **1** heavy blackish or very dark brown timber from a mainly tropical tree. ■ a very dark brown or black color: *his smile flashed against the ebony of his skin* | [as *adj.*] *his ebony hair.* **2** a tree of tropical and warm-temperate regions that produces such timber. • Genera *Diospyros* and *Euclea*, family Ebenaceae: numerous species, in particular *D. ebenum.* ■ used in names of trees of other families that produce similar timber, e.g., **Jamaican** (or **American**) **ebony**. ▷late Middle English: from earlier *ebon* (via Old French and Latin from Greek *ebenos* 'ebony tree'), perhaps on the pattern of *ivory*.

e-book /ˈē ˌbo͝ok/ ▸*n.* an electronic version of a printed book that can be read on a personal computer or hand-held device designed specifically for this purpose.■ a dedicated device for reading electronic versions of printed books.

E·bro /ˈāvrō; ˈäbrō/ a river in northeastern Spain that rises in the mountains of the Cantabria region and flows southeast for 570 miles (910 km) into the Mediterranean Sea.

EbS ▸*abbr.* east by south.

e·bul·lient /iˈbo͝olyənt; iˈbəlyənt/ ▸*adj.* **1** cheerful and full of energy: *she sounded ebullient and happy.* **2** *archaic or poetic/literary* (of liquid or matter) boiling or agitated as if boiling: *misted and ebullient seas.* ▷late 16th cent. (in the sense 'boiling'): from Latin *ebullient-* 'boiling up,' from the verb *ebullire*, from *e-* (variant of *ex-*) 'out' + *bullire* 'to boil.' —**e·bul·lience** *n.* —**e·bul·lient·ly** *adv.*

eb·ul·li·tion /ˌebəˈlisʜən/ ▸*n.* *technical or archaic* the action of bubbling or boiling. ■ a sudden outburst of emotion or violence: *in an ebullition of fervor.* ▷late Middle English (used to describe a state of agitation of the bodily humors): from late Latin *ebullitio(n-)*, from *ebullire* 'boil up' (see EBULLIENT).

e-busi·ness ▸ another term for E-COMMERCE.

EBV ▸*abbr.* Epstein-Barr virus.

EC ▸*abbr.* ■ European Commission. ■ European Community. ■ executive committee.

e·cad /ˈēˌkad; ˈeˌkad/ ▸*n.* *Ecology* an organism that is modified by its environment. ▷early 20th cent.: from Greek *oikos* 'house' + -AD[1].

é·car·té /ˌākärˈtā/ ▸*n.* **1** a card game for two players, played originally in 19th-century France, in which thirty-two cards are used, and certain cards may be discarded in exchange for others. **2** *Ballet* a position in which the dancer, facing diagonally toward the audience, extends one leg to the side with the arm of the same side raised above the head and the other arm extended to the side. ▷early 19th cent.: French, past participle of *écarter* 'discard, throw out,' from *é* 'out' + *carte* 'card.'

e-cash ▸*n.* electronic financial transactions conducted in cyberspace via computer networks.

ec·bol·ic /ekˈbälik/ *Medicine* ▸*adj.* inducing contractions of the uterus leading to expulsion of a fetus: *the ecbolic properties of Indian medicinal plants.*

▸*n.* an agent that induces such contractions. ▷mid 18th cent.: from Greek *ekbolē* 'expulsion' + -IC.

Ec·ce Ho·mo /ˈecʜā ˈhōˌmō; ˈeksē; ˈekā/ ▸*n.* *Art* a painting of Jesus Christ wearing the crown of thorns. ▷early 17th cent.: Latin, literally 'behold the man,' the words of Pontius Pilate to the Jews after Jesus was crowned with thorns (John 19:5).

ec·cen·tric /ikˈsentrik/ ▸*adj.* **1** (of a person or their behavior) unconventional and slightly strange: *my favorite aunt is very eccentric.* **2** *technical* (of a thing) not placed centrally or not having its axis or other part placed centrally. ■ (of a circle) not centered on the same point as another. ■ (of an orbit) not circular.

▸*n.* **1** a person of unconventional and slightly strange views or behavior: *he enjoys a colorful reputation as an engaging eccentric.* **2** a disc or wheel mounted eccentrically on a revolving shaft in order to transform rotation into backward-and-forward motion, e.g., a cam in an internal combustion engine. ▷late Middle English (as a noun denoting a circle or orbit not having the earth precisely at its center): via late Latin from Greek *ekkentros*, from *ek* 'out of' + *kentron* 'center.' —**ec·cen·tri·cal·ly** *adv.*

ec·cen·tric a·nom·a·ly ▸*n.* *Astronomy* the actual anomaly of a planet in an elliptical orbit. Compare with MEAN ANOMALY.

ec·cen·tric·i·ty /ˌeksenˈtrisitē/ ▸*n.* (*pl.* **-ties**) **1** the quality of being eccentric. ■ (usu. **eccentricities**) an eccentric act, habit, or thing: *her eccentricities were amusing rather than irritating.* **2** *technical* deviation of a curve or orbit from circularity. ■ a measure of the extent of such deviation: *Halley's Comet has an eccentricity of about 0.9675.*

ec·chy·mo·sis /ˌekəˈmōsis/ ▸*n.* (*pl.* **-ses** /ˌekəˈmōˌsēz/) *Medicine* a discoloration of the skin resulting from bleeding underneath, typically caused by bruising. ▷mid 16th cent.: modern Latin, from Greek *ekkhumōsis* 'escape of blood,' from *ekkhumonathai* 'force out blood.'

eccl. ▸*abbr.* ■ ecclesiastic. ■ ecclesiastical.

Ec·cles /ˈekəlz/, Sir John Carew (1903–97), Australian physiologist, who demonstrated the way in which nerve impulses are conducted by means of chemical neurotransmitters. Nobel Prize for Physiology or Medicine (1963, shared with A. L. Hodgkin and A. F. Huxley).

Eccles. ▸*abbr.* *Bible* Ecclesiastes.

ec·cle·si·al /iˈklēzēəl/ ▸*adj.* *formal* relating to or constituting a church or denomination: *the modernization of ecclesial buildings.* ▷mid 17th cent. (but rare before the 1960s): via Old French from Greek *ekklēsia* 'assembly, church' (see ECCLESIASTIC).

ec·cle·si·arch /iˈklēzēˌärk/ ▸*n.* *archaic* a ruler of a church. ▷late 18th cent.: from Greek *ekklēsia* 'church' + *arkhos* 'leader.'

Ec·cle·si·as·tes /iˌklēzēˈastēz/ a book of the Bible traditionally attributed to Solomon, consisting largely of reflections on the vanity of human life.

ec·cle·si·as·tic /iˌklēzēˈastik/ *formal* ▸*n.* a priest or clergyman.

▸*adj.* another term for ECCLESIASTICAL. ▷late Middle English: from French *ecclésiastique*, or via late Latin from Greek *ekklēsiastikos*, from *ekklēsiastēs* 'member of an assembly,' from *ekklēsia* 'assembly, church,' based on *ekkalein* 'summon out.'

ec·cle·si·as·ti·cal /iˌklēzēˈastikəl/ ▸*adj.* of or relating to the Christian Church or its clergy: *the ecclesiastical hierarchy.* —**ec·cle·si·as·ti·cal·ly** *adv.*

ec·cle·si·as·ti·cism /iˌklēzēˈastiˌsizəm/ ▸*n.* adherence or overattention to details of church practice: *the ecclesiasticism that so often gets in the way of the gospel.*

Ec·cle·si·as·ti·cus /i,klēzē'astikəs/ a book of the Apocrypha containing moral and practical maxims, probably composed or compiled in the early 2nd century BC.

ec·cle·si·ol·o·gy /i,klēzē'äləjē/ ▶*n.* **1** the study of churches, esp. church building and decoration. **2** theology as applied to the nature and structure of the Christian Church. ▷mid 19th cent.: from Greek *ekklēsia* 'assembly, church' + -LOGY. —**ec·cle·si·o·log·i·cal** /i,klēzēə'läjikəl/ *adj.* —**ec·cle·si·ol·o·gist** /-jist/ *n.*

Ec·clus ▶*abbr. Bible* Ecclesiasticus.

ec·crine /'ekrən; 'ek,rīn; 'ek,rēn/ ▶*adj. Medicine* relating to or denoting multicellular glands that do not lose cytoplasm in their secretions, esp. the sweat glands found widely distributed on the skin. Compare with APOCRINE. ▷1930s: from Greek *ekkrinein* 'secrete,' from *ek-* 'out' + *krinein* 'sift, separate.'

ECCS ▶*abbr. Physics* emergency core cooling system.

ec·dys·i·ast /ek'dēzēəst/ ▶*n. humorous* a striptease performer. ▷1940: coined by H. L. Mencken from Greek *ekdusis* 'shedding,' on the pattern of *enthusiast*.

ec·dy·sis /'ekdəsis/ ▶*n. Zoology* the process of shedding the old skin (in reptiles) or casting off the outer cuticle (in insects and other arthropods). ▷mid 19th cent.: from Greek *ekdusis*, from *ekduein* 'put off,' from *ek-* 'out, off' + *duein* 'put.' —**ec·dys·i·al** /ek-'dizēəl/ *adj.*

ec·dy·sone /'ekdi,sōn/ ▶*n. Biochemistry* a steroid hormone that controls molting in insects and other arthropods. ▷1950s: from Greek *ekdusis* 'shedding' + -ONE.

ECG ▶*abbr.* ■ electrocardiogram. ■ electrocardiograph.

é·chap·pé /,āsнa'pā/ ▶*adj.* [*postpositive*] *Ballet* (of a movement) progressing from a closed position (first, third, or fifth) to an open position (second or fourth) of the feet. ▷French, literally 'escaped.'

ech·e·lon /'esнə,län/ ▶*n.* **1** a level or rank in an organization, a profession, or society: *the upper echelons of the business world.* ■ [often with *adj.*] a part of a military force differentiated by position in battle or by function: *the rear echelon.* **2** *Military* a formation of troops, ships, aircraft, or vehicles in parallel rows with the end of each row projecting further than the one in front.
▶*v.* [*trans.*] *Military* arrange in an echelon formation: [as *n.*] (**echeloning**) *the echeloning of fire teams.* ▷late 18th cent. (sense 2): from French *échelon*, from *échelle* 'ladder,' from Latin *scala*.

ech·e·ver·i·a /,ecнəvə'rēə/ ▶*n.* a succulent plant with rosettes of fleshy colorful leaves, native to warm regions of America and popular as houseplants. • Genus *Echeveria*, family Crassulaceae: numerous species and cultivars. ▷modern Latin, named after Anastasio *Echeveri* or *Echeverría*, 19th-cent. Mexican botanical illustrator.

e·chid·na /ə'kidnə/ ▶*n.* a spiny insectivorous egg-laying mammal with a long snout and claws, native to Australia and New Guinea. Also called SPINY ANTEATER. • Family Tachyglossidae, order Monotremata: two genera and species, in particular *Tachyglossus aculeatus*. ▷mid 19th cent.: modern Latin, from Greek *ekhidna* 'viper,' also the name of a mythical creature that gave birth to the many-headed Hydra; compare with *ekhinos* 'sea urchin, hedgehog.'

ech·i·na·cea /,ekə'nāsнə/ ▶*n.* a North American coneflower. It is used in herbal medicine, largely for its antibiotic and wound-healing properties. • Genus *Echinacea*, family Compositae: several species, in particular the purple coneflower. ▷modern Latin, from Greek *ekhinos* 'hedgehog.'

Echi·no·der·ma·ta /i,kinə'dərmətə; ,ekənə-/ *Zoology* a phylum of marine invertebrates that includes starfishes, sea urchins, brittlestars, crinoids, and sea cucumbers. They have fivefold radial symmetry, a calcareous skeleton, and tube feet operated by fluid pressure. ▷modern Latin (plural), from Greek *ekhinos* 'hedgehog, sea urchin' + *derma* 'skin.' —**echi·no·derm** /i'kīnə,dərm; 'ekənə,dərm/ *n.*

Ech·i·noi·de·a /,ekə'noidēə/ *Zoology* a class of echinoderms that comprises the sea urchins. ▷modern Latin (plural), from ECHINUS. —**echi·noid** /i'kī,noid; 'ekə,noid/ *n.* & *adj.*

e·chi·nus /i'kīnəs/ ▶*n.* (*pl.* **-ni** /-nī/) **1** *Zoology* a sea urchin. • Genus *Echinus*, class Echinoidea: several species, including the common European **edible sea urchin** (*E. esculentus*). **2** *Architecture* a rounded molding below an abacus on a Doric or Ionic capital. ▷late Middle English: via Latin from Greek *ekhinos* 'hedgehog, sea urchin.'

Ech·i·u·ra /,ekē'yŏŏrə/ *Zoology* a small phylum of wormlike marine invertebrates that comprises the spoonworms. ▷modern Latin (earlier *Echiuroidea*), from Greek *ekhis* 'viper' + *oura* 'tail.' —**ech·i·u·ran** *n.* & *adj.* —**ech·i·u·roid** /,ekē'yŏŏ,roid/ *n.* & *adj.*

Ech·o /'ekō/ *Greek Mythology* a nymph deprived of speech by Hera in order to stop her chatter, and left able only to repeat what others had said.

ech·o /'ekō/ ▶*n.* (*pl.* **ech·oes**) **1** a sound or series of sounds caused by the reflection of sound waves from a surface back to the listener: *the walls threw back the echoes of his footsteps.* ■ a reflected radio or radar beam. ■ the deliberate introduction of reverberation into a sound recording. ■ *Linguistics* the repetition in structure and content of one speaker's utterance by another. ■ a close parallel or repetition of an idea, feeling, style, or event: *his love for her* ***found an echo in*** *her own feelings.* ■ (often **echoes**) a detail or characteristic that is suggestive of something else: *the cheese has a sharp rich aftertaste with echoes of salty, earthy pastures.* ■ *archaic* a person who slavishly repeats the words or opinions of another. **2** *Bridge* a play by a defender of a higher card in a suit followed by a lower one in a subsequent trick, used as a signal to request a further lead of that suit by their partner. **3** a code word representing the letter E, used in radio communication.
▶*v.* (**ech·oes, ech·oed**) [*intrans.*] **1** (of a sound) be repeated or reverberate after the original sound has stopped: *their footsteps echoed on the metal catwalks.* ■ (of a place) resound with or reflect back a sound or sounds: *the house* ***echoed with*** *shouts and thundering feet.* ■ *figurative* have a continued significance or influence: *illiteracy echoed through the whole fabric of society.* ■ [*trans.*] (often **be echoed**) repeat (someone's words or opinions), typically to express agreement: *these criticisms are echoed in a number of other studies* | [with *direct speech*] *"A trip?" she echoed.* ■ [*trans.*] (of an object, movement, or event) be reminiscent of or have shared characteristics with: *a blue suit that echoed the color of her eyes.* ■ [*trans.*] *Computing* send a copy of (an input signal or character) back to its source or to a screen for display: *for security reasons, the password will not be echoed to the screen.* **2** *Bridge* (of a defender) play a higher card followed by a lower one in the same suit, as a signal to request one's partner to lead that suit. ▷Middle English: from Old French or Latin, from Greek *ēkhō*, related to *ēkhē* 'a sound.' —**ech·o·er** *n.* —**ech·o·ey** /'ekō-ē/ *adj.* —**ech·o·less** *adj.*

ech·o·car·di·o·gram /,ekō'kärdēə,gram/ ▶*n. Medicine* a test of the action of the heart using ultrasound waves to produce a visual display, used for the diagnosis or monitoring of heart disease.

ech·o·car·di·og·ra·phy /,ekō,kärdē'ägrəfē/ ▶*n. Medicine* the use of ultrasound waves to investigate the action of the heart. —**ech·o·car·di·o·graph** /,ekō-'kärdēə,graf/ *n.* —**ech·o·car·di·o·graph·ic** /-,kärdēə-'grafik/ *adj.*

ech·o cham·ber ▶*n.* an enclosed space for producing reverberation of sound.

ech·o·en·ceph·a·lo·gram /,ekōen'sefələ,gram/ ▶*n. Medicine* a record produced by echoencephalography.

ech·o·en·ceph·a·lo·graph /,ekōen'sefələ,graf/ (abbr.: **EEG**) ▶*n.* an instrument used to examine the skull and brain by means of reflected ultrasonic waves as part of a painless and noninvasive procedure. —**ech·o·en·ceph·a·lo·graph·ic** /-,sefələ'grafik/ *adj.*

ech·o·en·ceph·a·log·ra·phy /,ekōen,sefə'lägrəfē/ ▶*n. Medicine* the use of ultrasound waves to investigate structures within the skull.

ech·o·gram /'ekō,gram/ ▶*n.* a recording of depth or distance under water made by an echo sounder.

ech·o·graph /'ekō,graf/ ▶*n.* an instrument for recording echograms; an automated echo sounder.

e·cho·ic /e'kō-ik/ ▶*adj.* of or like an echo. ■ *Linguistics* representing a sound by imitation; onomatopoeic. —**e·cho·i·cal·ly** *adv.*

ech·o·la·li·a /,ekō'lālēə/ ▶*n. Psychiatry* meaningless repetition of another person's spoken words as a symptom of psychiatric disorder. ■ repetition of speech by a child learning to talk. ▷late 19th cent.: modern Latin, from Greek *ēkhō* 'echo' + *lalia* 'speech.'

ech·o·lo·ca·tion /,ekōlō'kāsнən/ ▶*n.* the location of objects by reflected sound, in particular that used by animals such as dolphins and bats.

ech·o·prax·i·a /,ekō'praksēə/ ▶*n. Psychiatry* meaningless repetition or imitation of the movements of others as a symptom of psychiatric disorder. ▷early 20th cent.: modern Latin, from Greek *ēkhō* 'echo' + *praxis* 'action.'

ech·o sound·er ▶*n.* a device for determining the depth of the seabed or detecting objects in water by measuring the time taken for sound echoes to return to the listener. —**ech·o sound·ing** (also **ech·o-sound·ing**) *n.*

ech·o·vi·rus /'ekō,vīrəs/ (also **ECHO vi·rus**) ▶*n. Medicine* any of a group of enteroviruses that can cause a range of diseases, including respiratory infections and a mild form of meningitis. ▷1950s: from *echo* (acronym from *enteric cytopathogenic human orphan*, because the virus was not originally assignable to any known disease) + VIRUS.

echt /ekt/ ▶*adj.* authentic and typical: *the film's opening was an echt pop snob event.*
▶*adv.* [as *submodifier*] authentically and typically: *echt-American writers as Hawthorne and Cooper and Mark Twain.* ▷early 20th cent.: German, literally 'genuine, real.'

ECL ▶*abbr. Computing* emitter-coupled logic.

é·clair /ā'kler; i'kler/ (also **e·clair**) ▶*n.* a small, soft, log-shaped pastry filled with cream and typically topped with chocolate icing. ▷mid 19th cent.: from French, literally 'lightning.'

é·clair·cisse·ment /ā,klersēs'mäɴ/ ▶*n. archaic or poetic/literary* an enlightening explanation of something, typically someone's conduct, that has been hitherto inexplicable. ▷French, from *éclaircir* 'clear up,' from *é* (expressing a change of state) + *clair* (see CLEAR).

ec·lamp·si·a /i'klam(p)sēə/ ▶*n. Medicine* a condition in which one or more convulsions occur in a pregnant woman suffering from high blood pressure, often followed by coma and posing a threat to the health of mother and baby. See also PREECLAMPSIA. ▷mid 19th cent.: modern Latin, from French *éclampsie*, from Greek *eklampsis* 'sudden development,' from *eklampein* 'shine out.' —**ec·lamp·tic** /i'klam(p)tik/ *adj.*

é·clat /ā'klä/ ▶*n.* brilliant display or effect: *she came into prominence briefly but with éclat.* ■ social distinction or conspicuous success: *such action bestows more éclat upon a warrior than success by other means.* ▷late 17th cent.: from French, from *éclater* 'burst out.'

ec·lec·tic /i'klektik/ ▶*adj.* **1** deriving ideas, style, or taste from a broad and diverse range of sources: *her musical tastes are eclectic.* **2** (**Eclectic**) *Philosophy* of, denoting, or belonging to a class of ancient philosophers who did not belong to or found any recognized school of thought but selected such doctrines as they wished from various schools.
▶*n.* a person who derives ideas, style, or taste from a broad and diverse range of sources. ▷late 17th cent. (as a term in philosophy): from Greek *eklektikos*, from *eklegein* 'pick out,' from *ek* 'out' + *legein* 'choose.' —**ec·lec·ti·cal·ly** *adv.* —**ec·lec·ti·cism** /i'klekti,sizəm/ *n.*

e·clipse /i'klips/ ▶*n.* an obscuring of the light from one celestial body by the passage of another between it and the observer or between it and its source of illumination: *an eclipse of the sun.* ■ *figurative* a loss of significance, power, or prominence in relation to another person or thing: *the election result marked the eclipse of the traditional right and center.* ■ *Ornithology* a phase during which the distinctive markings of a bird (esp. a male duck) are obscured by molting of the breeding plumage: [as *adj.*] *eclipse plumage.*
▶*v.* [*trans.*] (often **be eclipsed**) (of a celestial body) obscure the light from or to (another celestial body): *as the last piece of the sun was eclipsed by the moon.* ■ *poetic/literary* obscure or block out (light): *a sea of blue sky violently eclipsed by showers.* ■ deprive (someone or something) of significance, power, or prominence: *the state of the economy has eclipsed the environment as the main issue.* ▷Middle English: from Old French *e(s)clipse* (noun), *eclipser* (verb), via Latin from Greek *ekleipsis*, from *ekleipein* 'fail to appear, be eclipsed,' from *ek* 'out' + *leipein* 'to leave.'
▶*PHRASE* □ **in eclipse** **1** losing or having lost significance, power, or prominence: *his political power was in eclipse.* **2** *Ornithology* (esp. of a male duck) in its eclipse plumage.

e·clips·ing bi·na·ry ▶*n. Astronomy* a binary star whose brightness varies periodically as the two components pass one in front of the other.

e·clip·tic /i'kliptik/ ▶*n. Astronomy* a great circle on the celestial sphere representing the sun's apparent

path during the year, so called because lunar and solar eclipses can occur only when the moon crosses it.
▸*adj.* of an eclipse or the ecliptic. ▷late Middle English: via Latin from Greek *ekleiptikos*, from *ekleipein* 'fail to appear' (see ECLIPSE).

ec·lo·gite /'eklə,jīt/ ▸*n.* *Geology* a metamorphic rock containing granular minerals, typically garnet and pyroxene. ▷mid 19th cent.: from French, from Greek *eklogē* 'selection' (with reference to the selective content of the rock) + -ITE[1].

ec·logue /'ek,lôg; 'ek,läg/ ▸*n.* a short poem, esp. a pastoral dialogue. ▷late Middle English: via Latin from Greek *eklogē* 'selection,' from *eklegein* 'pick out.'

e·close /i'klōz/ ▸*v.* [*intrans.*] *Entomology* (of an insect) emerge as an adult from the pupa or as a larva from the egg. ▷late 19th cent. (as *eclosion*): from French *éclore* 'to hatch,' based on Latin *ex-* 'out' + *claudere* 'to close.' —**e·clo·sion** /i'klōZHən/ *n.*

ECM ▸*abbr.* electronic countermeasures.

Ec·o /'ekō/, Umberto (1932–), Italian novelist and semiotician. Notable works: *The Name of the Rose* (1981) and *Travels in Hyperreality* (1986).

eco- ▸*comb. form* representing ECOLOGY.

ec·o·cen·trism /,ekō'sen,trizəm; ,ēkō-/ ▸*n.* a point of view that recognizes the ecosphere, rather than the biosphere, as central in importance, and attempts to redress the imbalance created by anthropocentrism. —**ec·o·cen·tric** /-'sentrik/ *adj.*

ec·o·cide /'ekō,sīd; 'ēkō-/ ▸*n.* destruction of the natural environment, esp. when willfully done.

ec·o·cline /'ekō,klīn; 'ēkō-/ ▸*n.* *Ecology* a cline from one ecosystem to another, showing a continuous gradient between the two extremes.

ec·o·con·sum·er /'ekōkən,sōōmər; 'ēkō-/ ▸*n.* a consumer who makes purchasing decisions partly or largely on the basis of ecological issues: *sophisticated ecoconsumers are descending upon some destinations that are not capable of delivering the expected services.*

ec·o·fem·i·nism /,ekō'femə,nizəm; ,ēkō-/ ▸*n.* a philosophical and political movement that combines ecological concerns with feminist ones, regarding both as resulting from male domination of society. —**ec·o·fem·i·nist** *n.*

ec·o·freak /'ekō,frēk; 'ēkō-/ ▸*n.* *informal* a person who is unusually enthusiastic about the protection and preservation of the environment.

ec·o·friend·ly ▸*adj.* not harmful to the environment: *I use only eco-friendly products.*

ecol. ▸*abbr.* ■ ecological. ■ ecology.

ec·o·la·bel·ing ▸*n.* the practice of marking products with a distinctive label to show that their manufacture conforms to recognized environmental standards. —**ec·o·la·bel** *n.*

E. co·li /ē 'kōlī/ ▸*n.* a bacterium commonly found in the intestines of humans and other animals, where it usually causes no harm. Some strains can cause severe food poisoning, esp. in old people and children. • *Escherichia coli*; a motile Gram-negative bacillus.

ec·o·lodge /'ekō,läj; 'ēkō-/ ▸*n.* a type of tourist accommodation designed to have the least possible impact on the natural environment in which it is situated.

ec·o·log·i·cal cas·cade ▸*n.* a shift in the balance of populations in an ecosystem occasioned by marked depletion in one species, usually as a result of human action.

ec·o·log·i·cal foot·print ▸*n.* the sum of an individual's or other entity's impact on the environment, based on consumption and pollution: *the company is working to reduce its ecological footprint by using organic ingredients and supporting a wind farm to offset its CO_2 emissions.*

e·col·o·gy /i'käləjē/ ▸*n.* **1** the branch of biology that deals with the relations of organisms to one another and to their physical surroundings. ■ (also **human ecology**) the study of the interaction of people with their environment. **2** (also **Ecology**) the political movement that seeks to protect the environment, esp. from pollution. ▷late 19th cent. (originally as *oecology*): from Greek *oikos* 'house' + -LOGY. —**ec·o·log·i·cal** /,ekə'läjikəl; ,ēkə-/ *adj.* —**ec·o·log·i·cal·ly** /,ekə',läjik(ə)lē; ,ēkə-/ *adv.* —**e·col·o·gist** /-jist/ *n.*

e-com·merce ▸*n.* commercial transactions conducted electronically on the Internet.

e·con·o·box /i'känə,bäks/ ▸*n.* *informal* a car that is small and economical rather than luxurious or stylish. ▷blend of *economical* and *box*.

e·con·o·met·rics /i,känə'metriks/ ▸*plural n.* [treated as *sing.*] the branch of economics concerned with the use of mathematical methods (esp. statistics) in describing economic systems. ▷1930s: from ECONOMY, on the pattern of words such as *biometrics* and *psychometrics*. —**e·con·o·met·ric** *adj.* —**e·con·o·met·ri·cal** /i,känə'metrikəl; ē,känə-/ *adj.* —**e·con·o·me·tri·cian** /i,känəmə'trisHən/ *n.* —**e·con·o·met·rist** /-'metrist/ *n.*

ec·o·nom·ic /,ekə'nämik; ,ēkə-/ ▸*adj.* of or relating to economics or the economy: *the government's economic policy* | *pest species of great economic importance.* ■ justified in terms of profitability: *many organizations must become larger if they are to remain economic.* ■ requiring fewer resources or costing less money: *solar power may provide a more economic solution.* ■ (of a subject) considered in relation to trade, industry, and the creation of wealth: *economic history.* ▷late Middle English: via Old French and Latin from Greek *oikonomikos*, from *oikonomia* (see ECONOMY). Originally a noun, the word denoted household management or a person skilled in this, hence the early sense of the adjective (late 16th cent.) 'relating to household management.' Modern senses date from the mid 19th cent.

> *USAGE* **Economic** means 'concerning economics': *he's rebuilding a solid* **economic** *base for the country's future.* **Economical** is commonly used to mean 'thrifty, avoiding waste': *small cars should be inexpensive to buy and* **economical** *to run.*

ec·o·nom·i·cal /,ekə'nämikəl; ,ēkə-/ ▸*adj.* giving good value or service in relation to the amount of money, time, or effort spent: *a small, economical car.* ■ (of a person or lifestyle) careful not to waste money or resources. ■ using no more of something than is necessary: *this chassis is economical in metal and therefore light in weight.*
▸*PHRASE* □ **economical with the truth** used euphemistically to describe a person or statement that lies or deliberately withholds information.

> *USAGE* See **usage** at ECONOMIC.

> *THE RIGHT WORD* **economical, frugal, miserly, parsimonious, provident, prudent, sparing, thrifty**
> If you don't like to spend money unnecessarily, you may simply be **economical**, which means that you manage your finances wisely and avoid any unnecessary expenses.
> If you're **thrifty**, you're both industrious and clever in managing your resources (*a thrifty shopper who never leaves home without her coupons*).
> **Frugal**, on the other hand, means that you tend to be sparing with money—sometimes getting a little carried away in your efforts—by avoiding any form of luxury or lavishness (*too frugal to take a taxi, even at night*).
> If you're **sparing**, you exercise such restraint in your spending that you sometimes deprive yourself (*sparing to the point where she allowed herself only one new item of clothing a season*).
> If you're **provident**, however, you're focused on providing for the future (*never one to be provident, she spent her allowance the day she received it*).
> **Miserly** and **parsimonious** are both used to describe frugality in its most extreme form. But while being *frugal* might be considered a virtue, being *parsimonious* is usually considered to be a fault or even a vice (*they could have been generous with their wealth, but they chose to lead a parsimonious life*).
> And no one wants to be called *miserly*, which implies being stingy out of greed rather than need (*so miserly that he reveled in his riches while those around him were starving*).

ec·o·nom·i·cal·ly /,ekə'nämik(ə)lē; ,ēkə-/ ▸*adv.* in a way that relates to economics or finance: [*sentence adverb*] *the region is important economically.* ■ in a way that involves careful use of money or resources: *the new building was erected as economically as possible.* ■ in a way that uses no more of something than is necessary: *a précis aims to express a passage more economically.*

ec·o·nom·ic good ▸*n.* *Economics* a product or service that can command a price when sold: *water is an economic good and should be treated as such.*

ec·o·nom·ic mi·grant ▸*n.* a person who travels from one country or area to another in order to improve their standard of living.

ec·o·nom·ic rent ▸*n.* *Economics* the extra amount earned by a resource (e.g., land, capital, or labor) by virtue of its present use.

ec·o·nom·ics /,ekə'nämiks; ,ēkə-/ ▸*plural n.* [often treated as *sing.*] the branch of knowledge concerned with the production, consumption, and transfer of wealth. ■ the condition of a region or group as regards material prosperity: *he is responsible for the island's modest economics.* ▷late 16th cent. (denoting the science of household management): from ECONOMIC + the plural suffix *-s*, originally on the pattern of Greek *ta oikonomika* (plural), the name of a treatise by Aristotle. Current senses date from the late 18th cent.

e·con·o·mism /i'känə,mizəm/ ▸*n.* belief in the primacy of economic causes or factors. ▷early 20th cent.: from French *économisme*, based on Greek *oikonomia* 'household management' (see ECONOMY).

e·con·o·mist /i'känəmist/ ▸*n.* an expert in economics. ▷late 16th cent. (originally in the Greek sense): from Greek *oikonomos* 'household manager' (see ECONOMY) + -IST. The current sense dates from the early 19th cent.

e·con·o·mize /i'känə,mīz/ ▸*v.* [*intrans.*] spend less; reduce one's expenses: *I have to economize where I can* | *people on low incomes may try to* **economize on** *fuel.* —**e·con·o·mi·za·tion** /i,känəmə'zāsHən/ *n.*

e·con·o·miz·er /i'känə,mīzər/ ▸*n.* **1** a device designed to make a machine or system more energy-efficient. **2** a person who reduces expenditure.

e·con·o·my /i'känəmē/ ▸*n.* (*pl.* **-mies**) **1** the wealth and resources of a country or region, esp. in terms of the production and consumption of goods and services. ■ a particular system or stage of an economy: *a free-market economy* | *the less-developed economies.* **2** careful management of available resources: *even heat distribution and fuel economy.* ■ sparing or careful use of something: *economy of words.* ■ (usu. **economies**) a financial saving: *there were many economies to be made by giving up our offices in Manhattan.* ■ (also **economy class**) the cheapest class of air or rail travel: *we flew economy.*
▸*adj.* [*attrib.*] (of a product) offering the best value for the money: [in *comb.*] *an economy pack.* ■ designed to be economical to use: *an economy car.* ▷late 15th cent. (in the sense 'management of material resources'): from French *économie*, or via Latin from Greek *oikonomia* 'household management,' based on *oikos* 'house' + *nemein* 'manage.' Current senses date from the 17th cent.
▸*PHRASES* □ **economy of scale** a proportionate saving in costs gained by an increased level of production. □ **economy of scope** a proportionate saving gained by producing two or more distinct goods, when the cost of doing so is less than that of producing each separately.

e·con·o·my-class syn·drome ▸*n.* deep-vein thrombosis said to be caused by periods of prolonged immobility on long-haul flights.

e·con·o·my-size (also **e·con·o·my-sized**) ▸*adj.* of a size that offers a large quantity for a proportionally lower cost: *an economy-size container.*

e-con·tent /'ē,käntent/ (also **e-con·tent**) ▸*n.* text and images designed for display on web pages: *Click on this link to license our econtent* [as adj.] *econtent solutions.*

ec·o·phys·i·ol·o·gy /,ekō,fizē'äləjē; ,ēkō-/ ▸*n.* *Biology* the study of the interrelationship between the normal physical function of an organism and its environment.

é·cor·ché /,ākôr'sHā/ ▸*n.* (*pl.* **-chés** *pronunc.* same) a painting or sculpture of a human figure with the skin removed to display the musculature. ▷mid 19th cent.: French, literally 'flayed.'

ec·o·re·gion /'ekō,rējən; 'ēkō-/ ▸*n.* a major ecosystem defined by distinctive geography and receiving uniform solar radiation and moisture: *the Columbia Basin ecoregion.*

ec·o·sphere /'ekō,sfi(ə)r; 'ēkō/ ▸*n.* the biosphere of the earth or another planet, esp. when the interaction between the living and nonliving components is emphasized. ■ *Astronomy* the region of space around a sun or star where conditions are such that planets are theoretically capable of sustaining life.

e·cos·saise /,ākō'sāz/ ▸*n.* (*pl.* **-saises** *pronunc.* same) an energetic country dance in duple time in which couples form lines facing each other. ▷mid 19th cent.: from French, feminine of *écossais* 'Scottish'; the connection with Scotland is unclear.

ec·o·sys·tem /'ekō,sistəm; 'ēkō-/ ▸*n.* *Ecology* a biological community of interacting organisms and their physical environment.

ec·o·tage /'ekə,täzH; ēkə-/ ▸*n.* sabotage carried out for ecological reasons. ▷1970s: blend of *ecological* (see ECOLOGY) and SABOTAGE.

ec·o·ter·ror·ism /,ekō'terə,rizəm; 'ekō-/ (also **ec·o-ter·ror·ism**) ▸*n.* violence carried out to further environmentalist ends. ■ the action of causing deliberate environmental damage in order to further political ends. **—e·co·ter·ror·ist** *n.*

ec·o·tone /ˈekəˌtōn; ˈēkəˌtōn/ ▸*n. Ecology* a region of transition between two biological communities. **—ec·o·ton·al** *adj.*

ec·o·to·pi·a ▸*n.* an ecologically ideal region or form of society, generally viewed as imaginary. ▷1975: from the title of a novel by Ernest Callenbach, originally denoting the Pacific coast of the U.S., from ECO- 'ecological,' on the pattern of *Utopia*. **—ec·o·to·pi·an** *adj.*

ec·o·tour·ism /ˌekōˈto͝orizəm; ˌēkō-/ ▸*n.* tourism directed toward exotic, often threatened, natural environments, esp. to support conservation efforts and observe wildlife. **—ec·o·tour** *n. & v.* **—ec·o·tour·ist** *n.*

ec·o·tox·i·col·o·gy /ˌekōˌtäksiˈkäləjē; ˌēkō-/ ▸*n.* the branch of science that deals with the nature, effects, and interactions of substances that are harmful to the environment. **—ec·o·tox·i·co·log·i·cal** /-kəˈläjikəl/ *adj.* **—ec·o·tox·i·col·o·gist** /-jist/ *n.*

ec·o·type /ˈekōˌtīp; ˈēkō-/ ▸*n. Botany & Zoology* a distinct form or race of a plant or animal species occupying a particular habitat.

ec·o-war·ri·or ▸*n.* a person actively involved in preventing damage to the environment.

ECOWAS ▸*abbr.* Economic Community of West African States.

ec·ru /ˈekro͞o/ ▸*n.* the light beige color of unbleached linen. ▷mid 19th cent.: from French *écru* 'unbleached.'

ec·sta·sy /ˈekstəsē/ ▸*n.* (*pl.* **-sies**) **1** an overwhelming feeling of great happiness or joyful excitement: *there was a look of ecstasy on his face* | *they went into ecstasies over the view.* See note at RAPTURE. **2** *chiefly archaic* an emotional or religious frenzy or trancelike state, originally one involving an experience of mystic self-transcendence. **3** (**Ecstasy**) an illegal amphetamine-based synthetic drug with euphoric and hallucinatory effects, originally promoted as an adjunct to psychotherapy. (abbr.: **MDMA**). ▷late Middle English (sense 2): from Old French *extasie*, via late Latin from Greek *ekstasis* 'standing outside oneself,' based on *ek-* 'out' + *histanai* 'to place.'

ec·stat·ic /ekˈstatik/ ▸*adj.* **1** feeling or expressing overwhelming happiness or joyful excitement: *ecstatic fans filled the stadium.* **2** involving an experience of mystic self-transcendence: *an ecstatic vision of God.*
▸*n.* a person subject to mystical experiences. **—ec·stat·i·cal·ly** *adv.*

ECT ▸*abbr.* electroconvulsive therapy.

ecto- ▸*comb. form* outer; external; on the outside (used commonly in scientific terms): *ectoderm* | *ectoparasite.* ▷from Greek *ektos* 'outside.'

ec·to·derm /ˈektəˌdərm/ ▸*n. Zoology & Embryology* the outermost layer of cells or tissue of an embryo in early development, or the parts derived from this, which include the epidermis, nerve tissue, and nephridia. Compare with ENDODERM and MESODERM. ▷mid 19th cent.: from ECTO- 'outside' + Greek *derma* 'skin.' **—ec·to·der·mal** /ˌektōˈdərməl/ *adj.*

ec·to·gen·e·sis /ˌektəˈjenəsis/ ▸*n.* (chiefly in science fiction) the development of embryos in artificial conditions outside the uterus. **—ec·to·gene** /ˈektəˌjēn/ *n.* **—ec·to·ge·net·ic** /ˌektəjəˈnetik/ *adj.* **—ec·to·ge·net·i·cal·ly** /-ˌjəˈnetik(ə)lē/ *adv.*.

ec·to·morph /ˈektəˌmôrf/ ▸*n. Physiology* a person with a lean and delicate body build. Compare with ENDOMORPH and MESOMORPH. ▷1940s: *ecto-* from *ectodermal* (being the layer of the embryo giving rise to physical characteristics that predominate) + -MORPH. **—ec·to·mor·phic** /ˌektəˈmôrfik/ *adj.* **—ec·to·morph·y** *n.*

-ectomy ▸*comb. form* denoting surgical removal of a specified part of the body: *appendectomy.* ▷from Greek *ektomē* 'excision,' from *ek* 'out' + *temnein* 'to cut.'

ec·to·par·a·site /ˌektəˈparəˌsīt/ ▸*n. Biology* a parasite, such as a flea, that lives on the outside of its host. Compare with ENDOPARASITE. **—ec·to·par·a·sit·ic** /-ˌparəˈsitik/ *adj.*.

ec·top·ic /ekˈtäpik/ ▸*adj. Medicine* in an abnormal place or position.
▸*n.* an ectopic pregnancy. ▷late 19th cent.: from modern Latin *ectopia* 'presence of tissue, cells, etc., in an abnormal place' (from Greek *ektopos* 'out of place') + -IC.

ec·top·ic beat ▸*n.* another term for EXTRASYSTOLE.

ec·top·ic preg·nan·cy ▸*n.* a pregnancy in which the fetus develops outside the uterus, typically in a Fallopian tube.

ec·to·plasm /ˈektəˌplazəm/ ▸*n.* **1** *Biology* the more viscous, clear outer layer of the cytoplasm in ameboid cells. Compare with ENDOPLASM. **2** a supernatural viscous substance that is supposed to exude from the body of a medium during a spiritualistic trance and form the material for the manifestation of spirits. **—ec·to·plas·mic** /ˌektəˈplazmik/ *adj.*

Ec·to·proc·ta /ˌektəˈpräktə/ *Zoology* another term for BRYOZOA. ▷modern Latin (plural), from Greek *ektos* 'outside or external' + *prōktos* 'anus.' **—ec·to·proct** /ˈektəˌpräkt/ *n.*

ec·to·therm /ˈektəˌTHərm/ ▸*n. Zoology* an animal that is dependent on external sources of body heat. Often contrasted with ENDOTHERM. Compare with POIKILOTHERM. **—ec·to·ther·mic** *adj.* **—ec·to·ther·my** *n.*

ec·tro·pi·on /ekˈtrōpēən; -pēˌän/ ▸*n. Medicine* a condition, typically a consequence of advanced age, in which the eyelid is turned outward away from the eyeball. ▷late 17th cent.: from Greek, from *ek-* 'out' + *trepein* 'to turn.'

ECU /āˈk(y)o͞o/ (also **ecu**) ▸*n.* (*pl.* same or **ecus**) the former official monetary unit of the European Union, used to evaluate the exchange rates and reserves of members of the European Monetary System on a common basis and in trading Eurobonds. It was replaced by the euro. ▷acronym from *European currency unit.*

Ec·ua·dor /ˈekwəˌdôr/ a republic in northwestern South America, on the Pacific coast; pop. 13,212,700; capital, Quito; languages, Spanish (official), Quechua. **—Ec·ua·dor·e·an** /ˌekwəˈdôrēən/ *adj. & n.*

Formerly part of the Inca empire, Ecuador was conquered by the Spanish in 1534. It remained part of Spain's American empire until 1822, when independence was gained.

ec·u·men·i·cal /ˌekyəˈmenikəl/ ▸*adj.* representing a number of different Christian churches: See note at UNIVERSAL. ■ promoting or relating to unity among the world's Christian churches: *ecumenical dialogue.* ▷late 16th cent. (in the sense 'belonging to the universal Church'): via late Latin from Greek *oikoumenikos*, from *oikoumenē* 'the (inhabited) earth.' **—ec·u·men·i·cal·ly** *adv.*

Ec·u·men·i·cal Pa·tri·arch ▸*n.* a title of the Orthodox Patriarch of Constantinople.

ec·u·me·nism /ˈekyəməˌnizəm; eˈkyo͞omə-/ ▸*n.* the principle or aim of promoting unity among the world's Christian churches.

ec·ze·ma /ˈegzəmə; ˈeksə-; igˈzēmə/ ▸*n.* a medical condition in which patches of skin become rough and inflamed, with blisters that cause itching and bleeding, sometimes resulting from a reaction to irritation (eczematous dermatitis) but more typically having no obvious external cause. ▷mid 18th cent.: modern Latin, from Greek *ekzema*, from *ekzein* 'boil over, break out,' from *ek-* 'out' + *zein* 'boil.' **—ec·zem·a·tous** /igˈzemətəs; ikˈsem-; igˈzē-/ *adj.*

ED ▸*abbr.* election district.

ed. ▸*abbr.* ■ edited by. ■ edition. ■ editor. ■ education.

-ed[1] ▸*suffix* forming adjectives: **1** (added to nouns) having; possessing; affected by: *talented* | *diseased.* ■ (added to nouns) characteristic of: *ragged.* **2** used in phrases consisting of adjective and noun: *bad-tempered* | *three-sided.* ▷Old English *-ede.*

-ed[2] ▸*suffix* forming: **1** the past tense and past participle of weak verbs: *landed* | *walked.* **2** participial adjectives: *wounded.* ▷Old English *-ed, -ad, -od.*

e·da·cious /iˈdāSHəs/ ▸*adj. rare* of, relating to, or given to eating. ▷early 19th cent.: from Latin *edax, edac-* (from *edere* 'eat') + -IOUS. **—e·dac·i·ty** /iˈdasitē/ *n.*

E·dam /ˈēdəm/ ▸*n.* a round Dutch cheese, typically pale yellow with a red wax coating. ▷early 19th cent.: named after the town of *Edam* in the Netherlands.

ed·a·ma·me /ˌedəˈmämā/ ▸*n.* a dish of green soybeans boiled or steamed in their pods. ▷Japanese, literally 'beans on a branch.'

e·daph·ic /iˈdafik/ ▸*adj. Ecology* of, produced by, or influenced by the soil. ▷late 19th cent.: coined in German from Greek *edaphos* 'floor' + -IC.

ed·a·pho·saur /ˌedəfōˈsôr/ (also **ed·a·pho·sau·rus** /-ˈsôrəs/) ▸*n.* a large herbivorous synapsid reptile of the late Carboniferous and early Permian periods, with long knobbly spines on its back supporting a sail-like crest. • Genus *Edaphosaurus*, order Pelycosuria, subclass Synapsida. ▷modern Latin, from Greek *edaphos* 'floor' + *sauros* 'lizard.' **—ed·a·pho·sau·ri·an** *adj.*

Ed·da /ˈedə/ either of two 13th-century Icelandic books, the **Elder** or **Poetic Edda** (a collection of Old Norse poems on Norse legends) and the **Younger** or **Prose Edda** (a handbook to Icelandic poetry by Snorri Sturluson). The Eddas are the chief source of knowledge of Scandinavian mythology. ▷either from the name of the great-grandmother in the Old Norse poem *Rigsthul*, or from Old Norse *óthr* 'poetry.'

ed·do /ˈedō/ ▸*n.* (*pl.* **-does**) a taro corm or plant, esp. of a West Indian variety with many edible cormlets. • *Colocasia esculenta* var. *antiquorum*, family Araceae. ▷late 17th cent.: of West African origin.

Ed·dy /ˈedē/, Mary Baker (1821–1910), U.S. religious leader; founder of the Christian Science movement. Long a victim of various ailments, she believed herself cured by a faith healer, Phineas Quimby, and later evolved her own system of spiritual healing.

ed·dy /ˈedē/ ▸*n.* (*pl.* **-dies**) a circular movement of water, counter to a main current, causing a small whirlpool. ■ a movement of wind, fog, or smoke resembling this.
▸*v.* (**-dies**, **-died**) [*intrans.*] (of water, air, or smoke) move in a circular way: *the mists from the river eddied around the banks.* ▷late Middle English: probably from the Germanic base of the Old English prefix *ed-* 'again, back.'

ed·dy cur·rent ▸*n.* a localized electric current induced in a conductor by a varying magnetic field.

E·de /ˈādə/ **1** an industrial city in eastern Netherlands; pop. 96,000. **2** an industrial town in southwestern Nigeria, northeast of Ibadan, in a predominantly Yoruba region; pop. 271,000.

Ed·el·man /ˈādlmən/, Marian Wright (1939–), U.S. human rights activist. She was founder 1972 and president of the Children's Defense Fund. She wrote *A Letter to My Children and Yours* (1992).

e·del·weiss /ˈādlˌwīs; -ˌvīs/ ▸*n.* a European mountain plant that has woolly white bracts around its small flowers and downy gray-green leaves. • *Leontopodium alpinum*, family Compositae. ▷mid 19th cent.: from German, from *edel* 'noble' + *weiss* 'white.'

e·de·ma /iˈdēmə/ (*Brit.* also **oe·de·ma**) ▸*n.* a condition characterized by an excess of watery fluid collecting in the cavities or tissues of the body. Also called DROPSY. ▷late Middle English: modern Latin, from Greek *oidēma*, from *oidein* 'to swell.' **—e·dem·a·tous** /iˈdēmətəs/ *adj.*

E·den[1] /ˈēdn/, (Robert) Anthony, 1st Earl of Avon (1897–1977), British statesman; prime minister 1955–57. His premiership was dominated by the Suez crisis of 1956, and widespread opposition to Britain's role in this led to his resignation.

E·den[2] (also **Garden of Eden**) the place where Adam and Eve lived in the biblical account of the Creation, from which they were expelled for disobediently eating the fruit of the tree of the knowledge of good and evil. ■ [as *n.*] (**an Eden**) a place or state of great happiness; an unspoiled paradise: *the lost Eden of his childhood.* ▷from late Latin (Vulgate), Greek *Ēdēn* (Septuagint), and Hebrew *ʿĒḏen*; perhaps related to Akkadian *edinu*, from Sumerian *eden* 'plain, desert' (but believed to be related to Hebrew *ʿēḏen* 'delight').

E·den Prai·rie a city in southeastern Minnesota, southwest of Minneapolis; pop. 54,901.

E·den·ta·ta /ˌēdenˈtātə; -ˈtätə/ *Zoology* another term for XENARTHRA.

e·den·tate /ēˈdenˌtāt/ ▸*n. Zoology* a mammal of an order distinguished by the lack of incisor and canine teeth. The edentates, which include anteaters, sloths, and armadillos, are all native to Central and

Pronunciation Key ə *ago*; ər *over*; ˈə *or* ˌə *up*; ˈər *or* ˌər *fur*; a *hat*; ā *rate*; ä *car*; CH *chew*; e *let*; ē *see*; e(ə)r *air*; i *fit*; ī *by*; i(ə)r *ear*; NG *sing*; ō *go*; ô *for*; oi *boy*; o͝o *good*; o͞o *goo*; ou *out*; SH *she*; TH *thin*; T͟H *then*; (h)w *why*; ZH *vision*

E

South America. • Order Xenarthra (or Edentata). ▷early 19th cent.: from Latin *edentatus*, past participle of *edentare* 'make toothless,' from *e-* (variant of *ex-*) 'out' + *dens, dent-* 'tooth.'

e·den·tu·lous /ē'dencHələs/ ▸*adj. Medicine & Zoology* lacking teeth. ▷early 18th cent.: from Latin *edentulus*, from *e-* (variant of *ex-*) 'out' + *dens, dent-* 'tooth' + -ULOUS.

E·der·le /'edərlē/, Gertrude Caroline (1906–2003), U.S. swimmer. The winner of three Olympic medals in 1924, she became the first woman to swim the English Channel 1926, two hours faster than any man had done.

Ed·gar /'edgər/ (944–75), king of England 959–975; younger brother of Edwy. He became king of Northumbria and Mercia in 957 when these regions renounced their allegiance to Edwy. He succeeded to the throne of England on Edwy's death.

edge /ej/ ▸*n.* **1** the outside limit of an object, area, or surface; a place or part farthest away from the center of something: *a willow tree at the water's edge* | *figurative these measures are merely tinkering at the edges of a wider issue.* See note at BORDER. ■ an area next to a steep drop: *the cliff edge.* ■ [in *sing.*] the point or state immediately before something unpleasant or momentous occurs: *the economy was teetering on* **the edge** *of recession.* **2** the sharpened side of the blade of a cutting implement or weapon: *a knife with a razor-sharp edge.* ■ the line along which two surfaces of a solid meet. ■ [in *sing.*] a sharp, threatening, or bitter tone of voice, usually indicating the speaker's annoyance or tension: *she was still smiling, but there was* **an edge to** *her voice.* ■ [in *sing.*] an intense, sharp, or striking quality: *a flamenco singer brings a primitive edge to the music.* ■ [in *sing.*] a quality or factor that gives superiority over close rivals or competitors: *the veal had the edge on flavor.*

▸*v.* [*trans.*] **1** (often **be edged**) provide with a border or edge: *the pool is edged with paving.* **2** [*intrans.*] move gradually, carefully, or furtively in a particular direction: *she tried to edge away from him* | *Nick* **edged his way** *through the crowd.* ■ [*trans.*] cause to move in such a way: *Hazel quietly edged him away from the others* | *figurative she was edged out of the organization by the director.* ■ [*trans.*] *informal* defeat by a small margin: *Connecticut avoided an upset and edged Yale 49–48.* **3** *figurative* give an intense or sharp quality to: *the bitterness that edged her voice.* **4** [*intrans.*] ski with one's weight on the edges of one's skis. ▷Old English *ecg* 'sharpened side of a blade,' of Germanic origin; related to Dutch *egge* and German *Ecke*, also to Old Norse *eggja* (see EGG2), from an Indo-European root shared by Latin *acies* 'edge' and Greek *akis* 'point.' **—edged** *adj.* [in *combination*] *a black-edged handkerchief.* **—edge·less** *adj.* **—edg·er** *n.*

▸*PHRASES* □ **on edge** tense, nervous, or irritable: *never had she felt so on edge before an interview.* □ **on the edge of one's seat** *informal* very excited and giving one's full attention to something. □ **set someone's teeth on edge** (esp. of an unpleasantly harsh sound) cause someone to feel intense discomfort or irritation: *a grating that set her teeth on edge.* □ **take the edge off** reduce the intensity or effect of (something unpleasant or severe): *the tablets will take the edge off the pain.*

edge cit·y ▸*n.* a relatively large urban area situated on the outskirts of a city, typically beside a major road. ▷1991: coined by J. Garreau in a book of the same name.

edge con·nec·tor ▸*n.* an electrical connector with a row of contacts, fitted to the edge of a printed circuit board to facilitate connection to external circuits.

edge tool ▸*n.* any tool with a sharp cutting edge.

edge·wise /'ej,wīz/ (also **edge·ways** /-,wāz/) ▸*adv.* & *adj.* with the edge uppermost or toward the viewer: [as *adv.*] *could be inserted edgewise between the teeth* | [as *adj.*] *an edgewise view of our own galaxy.*

▸*PHRASE* □ **get a word in edgewise** [usu. with *negative*] contribute to a conversation with difficulty because the other speaker talks almost without pause.

Edge·wood /'ej,wo͝od/ a community in northeastern Maryland that is noted for its U.S. arsenal; pop. 23,903.

edg·ing /'ejiNG/ ▸*n.* a thing forming an edge or border: *the crocheted edging of the cloth.* ■ the process of providing something with an edge or border.

edg·y /'ejē/ ▸*adj.* (**edg·i·er, edg·i·est**) tense, nervous, or irritable: *he became edgy and defensive.* ■ (of a musical performance or a piece of writing) having an intense or sharp quality. **—edg·i·ly** /'ejəlē/ *adv.* **—edg·i·ness** *n.*

edh ▸*n.* variant spelling of ETH.

EDI ▸*abbr.* electronic data interchange (a standard for exchanging information between computer systems).

ed·i·ble /'edəbəl/ ▸*adj.* fit to be eaten (often used to contrast with unpalatable or poisonous examples): *nasturtium seeds are edible.*

▸*n.* (**edibles**) items of food. ▷late 16th cent.: from late Latin *edibilis*, from Latin *edere* 'eat.' **—ed·i·bil·i·ty** /,edə'bilitē/ *n.*

e·dict /'ēdikt/ ▸*n.* an official order or proclamation issued by a person in authority. ▷Middle English: from Latin *edictum* 'something proclaimed,' neuter past participle of *edicere*, from *e-* (variant of *ex-*) 'out' + *dicere* 'say, tell.' **—e·dic·tal** /i'diktl/ *adj.*

E·dict of Nantes see NANTES, EDICT OF.

ed·i·fi·ca·tion /,edəfi'kāsHən/ ▸*n. formal* the instruction or improvement of a person morally or intellectually: *the idea that art's main purpose is to supply moral uplift and edification.* ▷late Middle English: from Latin *aedificatio(n-)*, from *aedificare* 'build' (see EDIFY).

ed·i·fice /'edəfis/ ▸*n. formal* a building, esp. a large, imposing one. ■ *figurative* a complex system of beliefs: *the concepts on which the edifice of capitalism was built.* ▷late Middle English: via Old French from Latin *aedificium*, from *aedis* 'dwelling' + *facere* 'make.'

ed·i·fy /'edə,fī/ ▸*v.* (**-fies, -fied**) [*trans.*] *formal* instruct or improve (someone) morally or intellectually. ▷Middle English: from Old French *edifier*, from Latin *aedificare* 'build,' from *aedis* 'dwelling' + *facere* 'make' (compare with EDIFICE). The word originally meant 'construct a building,' also 'strengthen,' hence to "build up" morally or spiritually.

ed·i·fy·ing /'edə,fī-iNG/ ▸*adj.* providing moral or intellectual instruction: *edifying literature.* **—ed·i·fy·ing·ly** *adv.*

E·di·na /ē'dīnə/ a city in southeastern Minnesota, southwest of Minneapolis; pop. 47,425.

Ed·in·burg /'edn,bərg/ a city in southern Texas, in the Rio Grande valley; pop. 29,885.

Ed·in·burgh /'edn,bərə/ the capital of Scotland, on the southern shore of the Firth of Forth; pop. 421,200. The city grew up around an 11th-century castle built by Malcolm III on a rocky ridge that dominates the landscape.

Ed·in·burgh, Duke of see PHILIP, PRINCE.

Ed·in·burgh Fes·ti·val (also **Edinburgh International Festival**) an international festival of the arts held annually in Edinburgh since 1947. In addition to the main program a flourishing fringe festival has developed.

Ed·i·son1 /'edəsən/ a township in eastern New Jersey, northeast of New Brunswick; pop. 97,687. It is home to Thomas Edison's research laboratory in Menlo Park.

Ed·i·son2, Thomas (Alva) (1847–1931), U.S. inventor. He took out the first of more than 1,000 patents at the age of 21. His inventions include automatic telegraph systems, the carbon microphone for telephones, the phonograph, and the carbon filament lamp.

ed·it /'edit/ ▸*v.* (**ed·it·ed, ed·it·ing**) [*trans.*] (often **be edited**) prepare (written material) for publication by correcting, condensing, or otherwise modifying it: *Volume I was edited by J. Johnson.* ■ choose material for (a movie or a radio or television program) and arrange it to form a coherent whole: *the footage wasn't good enough to be edited into broadcast form* | [as *adj.*] (**edited**) *an edited version drawn from several prerecorded performances.* ■ be editor of (a newspaper or magazine). ■ (**edit something out**) remove unnecessary or inappropriate words, sounds, or scenes from a text, movie, or radio or television program.

▸*n.* a change or correction made as a result of editing. ▷late 18th cent. (as a verb): partly a back-formation from EDITOR, reinforced by French *éditer* 'to edit' (from *édition* 'edition').

edit. ▸*abbr.* ■ edited. ■ edition. ■ editor.

ed·it·a·ble /'editəbəl/ ▸*adj.* (of text or software) in a format that can be edited by the user.

e·di·tion /i'disHən/ ▸*n.* a particular form or version of a published text: *a paperback edition.* ■ a particular version of a text that has been revised or created from a substantially new setting of type: *a first edition.* ■ the total number of copies of a book, newspaper, or other published material issued at one time. ■ a particular version or instance of a regular program or broadcast: *the Monday edition will be repeated on Wednesday afternoons.* ■ [in *sing.*] *figurative* a person or thing that is compared to another as a copy to an original: *the building was a simpler edition of its namesake.* ▷late Middle English: from French *édition*, from Latin *editio(n-)*, from *edere* 'put out,' from *e-* (variant of *ex-*) 'out' + *dare* 'give.'

e·di·ti·o prin·ceps /e'ditēō 'prinkeps; i'disHēō 'prinseps/ ▸*n.* (*pl.* **e·di·ti·o·nes prin·ci·pes** /e,ditē'ōnēs 'priNGkə,pez; i,disHē'ōnēz 'prinsə,pēz/) the first printed edition of a book. ▷Latin, from *editio(n-)* 'edition' and *princeps* 'chief, leader' (from *primus* 'first').

ed·i·tor /'editər/ ▸*n.* a person who is in charge of and determines the final content of a text, particularly a newspaper or magazine: *the editor of* The New York Times | *a sports editor.* ■ a person who works for a publishing company, commissioning or preparing material for publication. ■ a computer program enabling the user to alter or rearrange online text. ▷mid 17th cent.: from Latin, 'producer (of games), publisher,' from *edit-* 'produced, put forth,' from the verb *edere.* **—ed·i·tor·ship** *n.*

ed·i·to·ri·al /,edi'tôrēəl/ ▸*adj.* **1** of or relating to the commissioning or preparing of material for publication: *a pillar of scholarly publishing and editorial excellence.* ■ of or relating to the part of a newspaper or magazine that contains news, information, or comment as opposed to advertising. **2** of or relating to a section in a newspaper, often written by the editor, that expresses an opinion: *buoyed by yesterday's editorial endorsement.*

▸*n.* a newspaper article written by or on behalf of an editor that gives an opinion on a topical issue. ■ the parts of a newspaper or magazine that are not advertising. **—ed·i·to·ri·al·ist** *n.* **—ed·i·to·ri·al·ly** *adv.*

ed·i·to·ri·al·ize /,edi'tôrēə,līz/ ▸*v.* [*intrans.*] (of a newspaper, editor, or broadcasting organization) make comments or express opinions rather than just report the news. ■ offer one's opinion, as if in an editorial.

ed·i·tress /'editris/ ▸*n. chiefly Brit.* another term for EDITRIX.

USAGE See usage at -ESS.

ed·i·trix /'editriks/ ▸*n. dated or humorous* a female editor. ▷early 20th cent.: from EDITOR + -TRIX.

ed·it suite ▸*n.* a room containing equipment for electronically editing video-recorded material.

Ed.M. ▸*abbr.* master of education. ▷from Latin: *Educationis Magister.*

Ed·mond /'edmənd/ a city in central Oklahoma, an oil center north of Oklahoma City; pop. 68,315.

Ed·monds /'edməndz/ a city in west central Washington, on Puget Sound, north of Seattle; pop. 30,744.

Ed·mon·ton /'edməntən/ the capital of the province of Alberta, in western Canada, on the North Saskatchewan River; pop. 703,070.

Ed·mund /'edmənd/ the name of two kings of England: ■ **Edmund I** (921–946), reigned 939–946. After succeeding Athelstan, Edmund spent much of his reign trying to win his northern lands back from Norse control. ■ **Edmund II** (*c.*980–1016), son of Ethelred the Unready; reigned 1016; known as **Edmund Ironside**. Edmund led the resistance to Canute's forces in 1015, but was eventually defeated and forced to divide the kingdom with Canute. On Edmund's death, Canute became king of all England.

Ed·mund, St. (*c.*1175–1240), English churchman and teacher; archbishop of Canterbury 1234–40; born *Edmund Rich.* He was the last primate of all of England. Feast day, November 16.

Ed·mund Cam·pi·on, St. see CAMPION2.

Ed·mund the Mar·tyr, St. (*c.*841–870), king of East Anglia 855–870. After the defeat of his army by the invading Danes in 870, tradition holds that he was captured and shot with arrows for refusing to reject the Christian faith or to share power with his pagan conqueror. Feast day, November 20.

E·do1 /'edō/ former name of TOKYO.

E·do2 ▸*n.* (*pl.* same or **E·dos**) **1** a member of a people inhabiting the district of Benin in Nigeria. **2** the Benue-Congo language of this people.

▸*adj.* of or relating to this people or their language. ▷the name of Benin City in Edo.

E·dom·ite /'ēdə,mīt/ ▸*adj.* of or relating to Edom, an ancient region south of the Dead Sea, or its people.

▸*n.* a member of an ancient people living in Edom in biblical times, traditionally believed to be descended from Esau.

EDP ▸*abbr.* electronic data processing.

EDT ▸*abbr.* Eastern Daylight Time (see EASTERN TIME).

EDTA *Chemistry* ▸*abbr.* ethylenediamine tetra-acetic

acid, a crystalline acid with a strong tendency to form chelates with metal ions. • Chem. formula: $(CH_2COOH)_2NCH_2CH_2N(CH_2COOH)_2$.

educ. ▶*abbr.* ■ educated. ■ education. ■ educational.

ed·u·cate /ˈejəˌkāt/ ▶*v.* [*trans.*] (often **be educated**) give intellectual, moral, and social instruction to (someone, esp. a child), typically at a school or university: *she was educated at a boarding school.* ■ provide or pay for instruction for (one's child), esp. at a school. ■ give (someone) training in or information on a particular field: [*trans.*] *the need to educate people to conserve water a plan to* ***educate*** *the young* ***on*** *the dangers of drug-taking.* ▷late Middle English: from Latin *educat-* 'led out,' from the verb *educare*, related to *educere* 'lead out' (see EDUCE). **—ed·u·ca·bil·i·ty** /ˌejəkəˈbilitē/ *n.* **—ed·u·ca·ble** /-kəbəl/ *adj.* **—ed·u·ca·tive** /-ˌkātiv/ *adj.* **—ed·u·ca·tor** /-ˌkātər/ *n.*

ed·u·cat·ed /ˈejəˌkātid/ ▶*adj.* having been educated: [in *combination*] *a Harvard-educated lawyer.* ■ resulting from or having had a good education: *educated tastes.*

ed·u·cat·ed guess ▶*n.* a guess based on knowledge and experience and therefore likely to be correct.

ed·u·ca·tion /ˌejəˈkāsHən/ ▶*n.* the process of receiving or giving systematic instruction, esp. at a school or university: *a new system of public education.* ■ the theory and practice of teaching: *colleges of education.* ■ a body of knowledge acquired while being educated: *his education is encyclopedic and eclectic.* ■ information about or training in a particular field or subject: *health education.* ■ a particular stage in the process of being educated: *a high-school education.* ■ (**an education**) *figurative* an enlightening experience: *the wares in the shops are an education in quality.* ▷mid 16th cent.: from Latin *educatio(n-)*, from the verb *educare* (see EDUCATE). **—ed·u·ca·tion·ist** *n.*

ed·u·ca·tion·al /ˌejəˈkāsHənl/ ▶*adj.* of or relating to the provision of education: *children with special educational needs.* ■ intended or serving to educate or enlighten. **—ed·u·ca·tion·al·ist** /-ist/ *n.* **—ed·u·ca·tion·al·ly** *adv.*

ed·u·ca·tion·al psy·chol·o·gy ▶*n.* a branch of psychology that studies children in an educational setting and is concerned with teaching and learning methods, cognitive development, and aptitude assessment.

e·duce /iˈd(y)o͞os/ ▶*v.* [*trans.*] *formal* bring out or develop (something latent or potential): *out of love obedience is to be educed.* ■ infer (something) from data: *more information can be educed from these statistics.* ▷late Middle English: from Latin *educere* 'lead out,' from *e-* (variant of *ex-*) 'out' + *ducere* 'to lead.' **—e·duc·i·ble** /ēˈd(y)o͞osəbəl; iˈd(y)o͞os-/ *adj.* **—e·duc·tion** /iˈdəksHən/ *n.*

ed·u·crat /ˈejəˌkrat/ ▶*n. informal, derogatory* an education administrator. ▷blend of *education* and *bureaucrat.*

e·dul·co·rate /iˈdəlkəˌrāt/ ▶*v.* [*trans.*] *rare* make (something) more acceptable or palatable. ▷mid 17th cent.: from medieval Latin *edulcorat-* 'sweetened,' from the verb *edulcorare*, from Latin *e-* (variant of *ex-*) 'out' + *dulcor* 'sweetness.' **—e·dul·co·ra·tion** /iˌdəlkəˈrāsHən/ *n.*

ed·u·tain·ment /ˌejəˈtānmənt/ ▶*n.* entertainment, esp. computer games, with an educational aspect. ▷1980s: blend of EDUCATION and ENTERTAINMENT.

Edw. ▶*abbr.* Edward.

Ed·ward /ˈedwərd/ the name of six kings of England and also one of Great Britain and Ireland and one of the United Kingdom: ■ **Edward I** (1239–1307), son of Henry III; reigned 1272–1307; known as **the Hammer of the Scots**. His campaign against Prince Llewelyn ended with the annexation of Wales in 1284, but he failed to conquer Scotland. ■ **Edward II** (1284–1327), son of Edward I; reigned 1307–27. In 1314, he was defeated by Robert the Bruce at Bannockburn. In 1326, Edward's wife, Isabella of France, and her lover, Roger de Mortimer, invaded England; Edward was deposed in favor of his son and murdered. ■ **Edward III** (1312–77), son of Edward II; reigned 1327–77. In 1330, he took control of his kingdom, banishing Isabella and executing Mortimer. He supported Edward de Baliol, the pretender to the Scottish throne, and started the Hundred Years War. ■ **Edward IV** (1442–83), son of Richard, Duke of York; reigned 1461–83. He became king after defeating the Lancastrian Henry VI. Edward was briefly forced into exile 1470–01 by the Earl of Warwick but regained his position with victory at Tewkesbury in 1471. ■ **Edward V** (1470–*c.*1483), son of Edward IV; reigned 1483 but not crowned. Edward and his brother Richard, known as the Princes in the Tower, were probably murdered and the throne was taken by their uncle, Richard III. ■ **Edward VI** (1537–53), son of Henry VIII; reigned 1547–53. His reign saw the establishment of Protestantism as the state religion. ■ **Edward VII** (1841–1910), son of Queen Victoria; reigned 1901–10. Although he played little part in government on coming to the throne, his popularity helped to revitalize the monarchy. ■ **Edward VIII** (1894–1972), son of George V; reigned 1936 but not crowned. Edward abdicated 11 months after coming to the throne in order to marry U.S. divorcee, Mrs. Wallis Simpson. He was given the title the duke of Windsor by George VI.

Ed·ward, Lake a lake on the border between Uganda and the Democratic Republic of the Congo (formerly Zaire). It is linked to Lake Albert by the Semliki River.

Ed·ward, Prince, Edward Antony Richard Louis (1964–), third son of Elizabeth II. In 1999, he married Sophie Rhys-Jones.

Ed·ward, Prince of Wales see BLACK PRINCE.

Ed·ward·i·an /edˈwôrdēən; -ˈwär-/ ▶*adj.* of, relating to, or characteristic of the reign of King Edward VII: *the Edwardian era | a fine Edwardian house.* ▶*n.* a person who lived during this period.

Ed·ward·i·an·a /edˌwôrdēˈanə; -ˌwär-/ ▶*plural n.* articles, esp. collectors' items, from the reign of Edward VII.

Ed·wards[1] /ˈedwərdz/, Jonathan (1703–58), American cleric and theologian. He was known for the extreme Calvinism of his preaching and writing.

Ed·wards[2], John (1953–), U.S. politician. A liberal Democrat from North Carolina, he was a trial lawyer before running for political office. He served in the U.S. Senate from 1999 and was the Democratic candidate for vice president in 2004.

Ed·ward the Con·fes·sor, St. (*c.*1003–66), son of Ethelred the Unready; king of England 1042–66. He founded Westminster Abbey, where he was eventually buried. Feast day, October 13.

Ed·ward the Eld·er (*c.*870–924), son of Alfred the Great; king of Wessex 899–924. His military successes against the Danes made it possible for his son Athelstan to become the first king of all of England in 925.

Ed·ward the Mar·tyr, St. (*c.*963–978), son of Edgar; king of England 975–978. He was faced with a challenge for the throne by supporters of his half-brother, Ethelred, who eventually had him murdered. Feast day, March 18.

Ed·wy /ˈedwē/ (also **Ead·wig** /ˈedwig/) (died 959), king of England 955–957. He was about 15 years old when he became king. After Mercia and Northumbria renounced him in favor of his brother Edgar, he ruled over only the lands south of the Thames River.

EE ▶*abbr.* ■ electrical engineer. ■ electrical engineering.

-ee ▶*suffix* forming nouns: **1** denoting the person affected directly or indirectly by the action of the formative verb: *employee | lessee.* **2** denoting a person described as or concerned with: *absentee | patentee.* **3** denoting an object of relatively smaller size: *goatee.* ▷from Anglo-Norman French *-é*, from Latin *-atus* (past participial ending). Some forms are anglicized modern French nouns (e.g., *refugee* from *réfugié*).

EEA ▶*abbr.* European Economic Area, a free-trade zone created in 1994, composed of the states of the European Union together with Iceland, Norway, and Liechtenstein: [as *modifier*] *if you are an EEA national you can come and go freely from the country.*

EEC ▶*abbr.* ■ European Economic Community. ■ echoencephalograph.

EEG ▶*abbr.* ■ electroencephalogram. ■ electroencephalograph. ■ electroencephalography.

ee·jit /ˈējit/ ▶*n. informal* Irish and Scottish form of IDIOT.

eek /ēk/ ▶*exclam. informal* used as an expression of alarm, horror, or surprise.

eel /ēl/ ▶*n.* a snakelike fish with a slender elongated body and poorly developed fins, proverbial for its slipperiness: *the man was wanted in a dozen countries but was as slippery as an eel.* • Order Anguilliformes: many families, in particular Anguillidae, which comprises mainly freshwater eels that breed in the sea, including the common *Anguilla anguilla* of Europe and the **American eel** (*A. rostrata*). ■ used in names of unrelated fishes that resemble the true eels, e.g., **electric eel, moray eel.** ▷Old English *ǣl*, of Germanic origin; related to Dutch *aal* and German *Aal.* **—eel·like** /-ˌlīk/ *adj.* **—eel·y** *adj.*

Ee·lam /ˈēləm; ˈēˌlam/ the proposed homeland of the Tamil people of Sri Lanka, for which the Tamil Tigers separatist group has been fighting since the early 1980s.

eel·grass /ˈēlˌgras/ ▶*n.* **1** a marine plant with long ribbonlike leaves that grows in coastal waters and brackish inlets. • *Zostera marina*, family Zosteraceae. **2** another term for TAPE GRASS.

eel·pout /ˈēlˌpout/ ▶*n.* a fish of cool or cold seas, having a broad head with thick lips and an elongated body with the dorsal and anal fins continuous with the tail. • Family Zoarcidae: numerous genera and species, including the widely distributed northern European viviparous blenny (*Zoarces viviparus*). ▷Old English *ǣlepūta* (see EEL, POUT[2]).

eel·worm /ˈēlˌwərm/ ▶*n.* a nematode, esp. a small soil nematode that can become a serious pest of crops and ornamental plants.

Eem·i·an /ˈēmēən/ (also **Eem** /ēm/) ▶*adj. Geology* of, relating to, or denoting the most recent interglacial period of the Pleistocene in northern Europe, preceding the Weichsel glaciation. ■ [as *n.*] (**the Eemian** or **Eem**) the Eemian interglacial or the system of deposits laid down during it. ▷early 20th cent.: from *Eem*, the name of a river in the Netherlands, + -IAN.

e'en /ēn/ *poetic/literary* ▶*contraction of* EVEN[1].

-een ▶*suffix Irish* forming diminutive nouns such as *colleen.* ▷from the Irish diminutive suffix *-ín.*

een·sy /ˈēn(t)sē/ (also **een·sy-ween·sy**) ▶*adj. informal* extremely small; tiny.

EEO ▶*abbr.* equal employment opportunity.

EEPROM /ˌē-ēˈpräm; ˈēˌpräm; ˈdəbəl ē ˈpräm/ ▶*n. Computing* a read-only memory whose contents can be erased and reprogrammed using a pulsed voltage. ▷acronym from *electrically erasable programmable ROM.*

e'er /e(ə)r/ *poetic/literary* ▶*contraction of* ever.

-eer ▶*suffix* **1** (forming nouns) denoting a person concerned with or engaged in an activity: *auctioneer | puppeteer.* **2** (forming verbs) denoting concern or involvement with an activity: *electioneer | profiteer.* ▷from French *-ier*, from Latin *-arius*; verbs (sense 2) are often back-formations (e.g., *electioneer* from *electioneering*).

ee·rie /ˈi(ə)rē/ ▶*adj.* (**ee·ri·er**, **ee·ri·est**) strange and frightening: *an eerie green glow in the sky.* ▷Middle English (originally northern English and Scots in the sense 'fearful'): probably from Old English *earg* 'cowardly,' of Germanic origin; related to German *arg.* **—ee·ri·ly** *adv.* [as *submodifier*] *it was eerily quiet.* **—ee·ri·ness** *n.*

Ee·yor·ish /ˈēyôrisH; ˈēôr-/ (also **Ee·yore·ish**) ▶*adj.* pessimistic or gloomy: *one of the most Eeyorish speeches we have ever heard.* ▷1990s: from *Eeyore*, the name of a donkey in A. A. Milne's *Winnie-the-Pooh* (1926), characterized by his gloomy outlook on life.

ef- ▶*prefix* variant spelling of EX-[1] assimilated before *f* (as in *efface, effloresce*).

USAGE See usage at EX-[1].

EFA ▶*abbr.* essential fatty acid.

eff /ef/ ▶*n.* & *v. chiefly Brit.* used as a euphemism for "fuck." ▷1950s: the letter *F* represented as a word. **—eff·ing** *adj.* & *adv.*

▶***PHRASE*** □ **eff and blind** *informal* use vulgar expletives; swear: *You can eff and blind all you want; the rules still stand.* [*blind* from its use in vulgar imprecations such as *blind me* (see BLIMEY).]

eff. ▶*abbr.* efficiency.

ef·fa·ble /ˈefəbəl/ ▶*adj. rare* able to be described in words. ▷early 17th cent.: from Latin *effabilis*, from *effari* 'utter.'

ef·face /iˈfās/ ▶*v.* [*trans.*] erase (a mark) from a surface: *with time, the words are effaced by the frost and the rain | figurative his anger was effaced when he stepped into the open air.* ■ (**efface oneself**) *figurative* make oneself appear insignificant or inconspicuous. ▷late 15th cent. (in the sense 'pardon or be absolved from (an offense)'): from French *effacer*, from *e-* (from Latin *ex-* 'away from') + *face* 'face.' **—ef·face·ment** *n.*

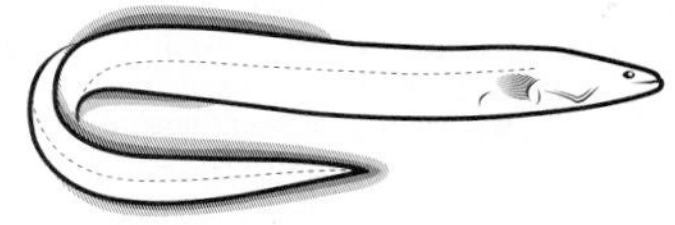

American eel

Pronunciation Key ə *ago*; ər *over*; ˈə or ˌə *up*; ˈər or ˌər *fur*; a *hat*; ā *rate*; ä *car*; CH *chew*; e *let*; ē *see*; e(ə)r *air*; i *fit*; ī *by*; i(ə)r *ear*; NG *sing*; ō *go*; ô *for*; oi *boy*; o͝o *good*; o͞o *goo*; ou *out*; SH *she*; TH *thin*; T͟H *then*; (h)w *why*; ZH *vision*

ef·fect /iˈfekt/ ▶*n.* **1** a change that is a result or consequence of an action or other cause: *the lethal effects of hard drugs | politicians really do have some effect on the lives of ordinary people.* ■ used to refer to the state of being or becoming operative: *they succeeded in* ***putting*** *their strategies* ***into effect*** *| the ban is to* ***take effect*** *in six months.* ■ the extent to which something succeeds or is operative: *wind power can be used to great effect.* ■ [with *adj.*] *Physics* a physical phenomenon, typically named after its discoverer: *the Doppler effect.* ■ an impression produced in the mind of a person: *gentle music can have a soothing effect.* **2** (**effects**) the lighting, sound, or scenery used in a play, movie, or broadcast: *the production relied too much on spectacular effects.* **3** (**effects**) personal belongings: *the insurance covers personal effects.*

▶*v.* [*trans.*] (often **be effected**) cause (something) to happen; bring about: *nature always effected a cure | budget cuts that were quietly effected over four years.* ▷late Middle English: from Old French, or from Latin *effectus*, from *efficere* 'accomplish,' from *ex-* 'out, thoroughly' + *facere* 'do, make.' Sense 3, 'personal belongings,' arose from the obsolete sense 'something acquired on completion of an action.'

▶***PHRASES*** □ **for effect** in order to impress people: *I suspect he's controversial for effect.* □ **in effect** in operation; in force: *a moratorium in effect since 1985 has been lifted.* ■ used to convey that something is the case in practice even if it is not formally acknowledged to be so: *additional payments which are in effect an entrance tax.* □ **to the effect that** used to refer to the general sense of something written or spoken: *some comments to the effect that my essay was a little light on analysis.* □ **to that effect** having that result, purpose, or meaning: *she thought it a foolish rule and put a notice to that effect in a newspaper.*

USAGE For the differences in use between **effect** and **affect**, see **usage** at AFFECT[1].

ef·fec·tive /iˈfektiv/ ▶*adj.* **1** successful in producing a desired or intended result: *effective solutions to environmental problems.* ■ (esp. of a law or policy) operative: *the agreements will be* ***effective from*** *November.* **2** [*attrib.*] fulfilling a specified function in fact, though not formally acknowledged as such: *the companies were under effective Soviet control.* ■ assessed according to actual rather than face value: *an effective price of $176 million.* ■ impressive; striking: *an effective finale.*

▶*n.* a soldier fit and available for service. ▷late Middle English: from Latin *effectivus*, from *efficere* 'work out, accomplish' (see EFFECT). **—ef·fec·tive·ness** *n.* **—ef·fec·tiv·i·ty** /ˌefekˈtivitē; ˌēfek-/ *n.*

THE RIGHT WORD **effective, effectual, efficacious, efficient**

All of these adjectives mean producing or capable of producing a result, but they are not interchangeable.

Use **effective** when you want to describe something that produces a definite effect or result (*an effective speaker who was able to rally the crowd's support*) and **efficacious** when it produces the desired effect or result (*an efficacious remedy that cured her almost immediately*).

If something produces the desired effect or result in a decisive manner, use **effectual** (*an effectual recommendation that got him the job*), an adjective that is often employed when looking back after an event is over (*an effectual strategy that finally turned the tide in their favor*).

Reserve the use of **efficient** for when you want to imply skill and economy of energy in producing the desired result (*so efficient in her management of the company that layoffs were not necessary*).

When applied to people, *efficient* means capable or competent (*an efficient homemaker*) and places less emphasis on the achievement of results and more on the skills involved.

ef·fec·tive de·mand ▶*n.* *Economics* the level of demand that represents a real intention to purchase by people with the means to pay.

ef·fec·tive·ly /iˈfektəvlē/ ▶*adv.* in such a manner as to achieve a desired result: *make sure that resources are used effectively.* ■ [*sentence adverb*] actually but not officially or explicitly: *they were effectively controlled by the people they were supposed to be investigating.* ■ [*sentence adverb*] the real fact or implication is that; in practice: *effectively, this means that companies will be able to avoid regulations.*

ef·fec·tive tem·per·a·ture ▶*n.* *Physics* the temperature of an object calculated from the radiation it emits, assuming black-body behavior.

ef·fec·tor /iˈfektər/ ▶*n.* *Biology* an organ or cell that acts in response to a stimulus: [as *adj.*] *effector cells.*

ef·fec·tu·al /iˈfekCHo͞oəl/ ▶*adj.* (typically of something inanimate or abstract) successful in producing a desired or intended result; effective: *tobacco smoke is the most effectual protection against the mosquito.* See note at EFFECTIVE. ▷late Middle English: from medieval Latin *effectualis*, from Latin *effectus* (see EFFECT). **—ef·fec·tu·al·i·ty** /iˌfekCHo͞oˈalitē/ *n.* **—ef·fec·tu·al·ly** *adv.* **—ef·fec·tu·al·ness** *n.*

ef·fec·tu·ate /iˈfekCHo͞oˌāt/ ▶*v.* [*trans.*] *formal* put into force or operation: *school choice would effectuate a transfer of power from government to individuals.* ▷late 16th cent.: from medieval Latin *effectuat-* 'caused to happen,' from the verb *effectuare*, from Latin *effectus* (see EFFECT). **—ef·fec·tu·a·tion** /iˌfekCHo͞oˈāSHən/ *n.*

ef·fem·i·nate /iˈfemənət/ ▶*adj.* (of a man) having or showing characteristics regarded as typical of a woman; unmanly. ▷late Middle English: from Latin *effeminatus*, past participle of *effeminare* 'make feminine,' from *ex-* (expressing a change of state) + *femina* 'woman.' **—ef·fem·i·na·cy** /iˈfemənəsē/ *n.* **—ef·fem·i·nate·ly** *adv.*

ef·fen·di /iˈfendē/ ▶*n.* (*pl.* **-dis** /-dēz/) a man of high education or social standing in an eastern Mediterranean or Arab country. ■ *historical* a title of respect or courtesy in Turkey. ▷early 17th cent.: from Turkish *efendi*, from modern Greek *aphentēs*, from Greek *authentēs* 'lord, master.'

ef·fer·ent /ˈefərənt/ ▶*adj.* *Physiology* conducted or conducting outward or away from something (for nerves, the central nervous system; for blood vessels, the organ supplied). The opposite of AFFERENT. ▷mid 19th cent.: from Latin *efferent-* 'carrying out,' from the verb *efferre*, from *ex-* 'out' + *ferre* 'carry.'

ef·fer·vesce /ˌefərˈves/ ▶*v.* [*intrans.*] (of a liquid) give off bubbles. ■ *figurative* (of a person) be vivacious and enthusiastic. ▷early 18th cent.: from Latin *effervescere*, from *ex-* 'out, up' + *fervescere* 'begin to boil' (from *fervere* 'be hot, boil').

ef·fer·ves·cent /ˌefərˈvesənt/ ▶*adj.* (of a liquid) giving off bubbles; fizzy. ▷late 17th cent.: from Latin *effervescent-* 'boiling up,' from the verb *effervescere* (see EFFERVESCE). **—ef·fer·ves·cence** *n.*

ef·fete /iˈfēt/ ▶*adj.* (of a person) affected, overrefined, and ineffectual: *effete trendies from art college.* ■ no longer capable of effective action: *the authority of an effete aristocracy began to dwindle.* ▷early 17th cent. (in the sense 'no longer fertile, past bearing young'): from Latin *effetus* 'worn out by bearing young,' from *ex-* 'out' + *fetus* 'breeding'; related to FETUS. **—ef·fete·ness** *n.*

ef·fi·ca·cious /ˌefiˈkāSHəs/ ▶*adj.* *formal* (typically of something inanimate or abstract) successful in producing a desired or intended result; effective: *the vaccine has proved both efficacious and safe.* See note at EFFECTIVE. ▷early 16th cent.: from Latin *efficax*, *efficac-* (from *efficere* 'accomplish': see EFFECT) + -IOUS. **—ef·fi·ca·cious·ly** *adv.* **—ef·fi·ca·cious·ness** *n.*

ef·fi·ca·cy /ˈefikəsē/ ▶*n.* the ability to produce a desired or intended result: *there is little information on the efficacy of this treatment.* ▷early 16th cent.: from Latin *efficacia*, from *efficax*, *efficac-* (see EFFICACIOUS).

ef·fi·cien·cy /iˈfiSHənsē/ ▶*n.* (*pl.* **-cies**) the state or quality of being efficient: *greater energy efficiency.* ■ an action designed to achieve this: *to increase efficiencies and improve earnings.* ■ *technical* the ratio of the useful work performed by a machine or in a process to the total energy expended or heat taken in. ■ short for EFFICIENCY APARTMENT. ▷late 16th cent. (in the sense 'the fact of being an efficient cause'): from Latin *efficientia*, from *efficere* 'accomplish' (see EFFECT).

ef·fi·cien·cy a·part·ment (also **ef·fi·cien·cy**) ▶*n.* an apartment in which one room typically contains the kitchen, living, and sleeping quarters, with a separate bathroom.

ef·fi·cient /iˈfiSHənt/ ▶*adj.* (esp. of a system or machine) achieving maximum productivity with minimum wasted effort or expense: *fluorescent lamps are efficient at converting electricity into light.* See note at EFFECTIVE. ■ (of a person) working in a well-organized and competent way: *an efficient administrator.* ■ [in *combination*] preventing the wasteful use of a particular resource: *an energy-efficient heating system.* ▷late Middle English (in the sense 'making, causing,' usually in EFFICIENT CAUSE): from Latin *efficient-* 'accomplishing,' from the verb *efficere* (see EFFECT). The current sense dates from the late 18th cent. **—ef·fi·cient·ly** *adv.*

ef·fi·cient cause ▶*n.* *Philosophy* an agent that brings a thing into being or initiates a change.

ef·fi·gy /ˈefijē/ ▶*n.* (*pl.* **-gies**) a sculpture or model of a person: *coins bearing the effigy of Maria Theresa of Austria.* ■ a roughly made model of a particular person, made in order to be damaged or destroyed as a protest or expression of anger: *the senator was* ***burned in effigy.*** ▷mid 16th cent.: from Latin *effigies*, from *effingere* 'to fashion (artistically),' from *ex-* 'out' + *fingere* 'to shape.'

ef·fing /ˈefiNG/ ▶*adj.* *informal* a euphemistic substitute for the word FUCKING.

ef·fleu·rage /ˌefləˈräZH/ ▶*n.* a form of massage involving a circular stroking movement made with the palm of the hand.

▶*v.* [*trans.*] massage with such a circular stroking movement: *effleurage the shoulders and press gently.* ▷late 19th cent.: from French, from *effleurer* 'skim the surface, stroke lightly,' literally 'remove the flower or "outer beauty" of (something).'

ef·flo·resce /ˌefləˈres/ ▶*v.* **1** [*intrans.*] (of a substance) lose moisture and turn to a fine powder upon exposure to air. ■ (of salts) come to the surface of brickwork, rock, or other material and crystallize there. ■ (of a surface) become covered with salt particles. **2** reach an optimum stage of development; blossom: *simple concepts that* ***effloresce into*** *testable conclusions.* ▷late 18th cent.: from Latin *efflorescere*, from *e-* (variant of *ex-*) 'out' + *florescere* 'begin to bloom' (from *florere* 'to bloom,' from *flos*, *flor-* 'flower'). **—ef·flo·res·cence** /-ˈresəns/ *n.* **—ef·flo·res·cent** *adj.*

ef·flu·ence /ˈeflo͞oəns/ ▶*n.* a substance that flows out from something. ■ the action of flowing out. ▷late Middle English: from medieval Latin *effluentia*, from Latin *effluere* 'flow out,' from *ex-* 'out' + *fluere* 'to flow.'

ef·flu·ent /ˈeflo͞oənt/ ▶*n.* liquid waste or sewage discharged into a river or the sea: *the bay was contaminated with the effluent from an industrial plant.* ▷late Middle English (in the adjective sense 'flowing out'): from Latin *effluent-* 'flowing out,' from the verb *effluere* (see EFFLUENCE). The noun dates from the mid 19th cent.

ef·flu·vi·um /iˈflo͞ovēəm/ ▶*n.* (*pl.* **-vi·a** /-vēə/) an unpleasant or harmful odor, secretion, or discharge: *the unwholesome effluvia of decaying vegetable matter.* ▷mid 17th cent.: from Latin, from *effluere* 'flow out.'

ef·flux /ˈefləks/ ▶*n.* *technical* the flowing out of a particular substance or particle. ■ material flowing out. ■ another term for EFFLUXION (sense 1). ▷mid 16th cent.: from medieval Latin *effluxus*, from *effluere* 'flow out.'

ef·flux·ion /eˈfləkSHən/ ▶*n.* **1** *Law* (**ef·flux**) the passing of time, in particular when leading to the expiration of an agreement or contract. **2** *archaic* the action of flowing out. ▷early 17th cent.: from French, or from late Latin *effluxio(n-)*, from *effluere* 'flow out.'

ef·fort /ˈefərt/ ▶*n.* a vigorous or determined attempt: *hammer birdhouses to country fenceposts* ***in an effort to*** *bring back the eastern bluebird.* ■ the result of an attempt: *he was a keen gardener, winning many prizes for his efforts.* ■ strenuous physical or mental exertion: *the doctor spared no effort in helping my father.* ■ *technical* a force exerted by a machine or in a process. ■ [with *adj.*] the activities of a group of people with a common purpose: *the war effort.* ▷late 15th cent.: from French, from Old French *esforcier*, based on Latin *ex-* 'out' + *fortis* 'strong.' **—ef·fort·ful** *adj.* **—ef·fort·ful·ly** *adv.*

ef·fort·less /ˈefərtlis/ ▶*adj.* requiring no physical or mental exertion: *went up the steps in two effortless bounds.* ■ achieved with admirable ease: *her effortless sense of style.* **—ef·fort·less·ly** *adv.* **—ef·fort·less·ness** *n.*

ef·fron·ter·y /iˈfrəntərē/ ▶*n.* insolent or impertinent behavior: *one juror* ***had the effrontery to*** *challenge the coroner's decision.* See note at TEMERITY. ▷late 17th cent.: from French *effronterie*, based on late Latin *effrons*, *effront-* 'shameless, barefaced,' from *ex-* 'out' + *frons* 'forehead.'

ef·ful·gent /iˈfo͝oljənt; iˈfəl-/ ▶*adj.* *poetic/literary* shining brightly; radiant. ■ (of a person or their expression) emanating joy or goodness. ▷mid 18th cent.: from Latin *effulgent-* 'shining brightly,' from the verb *effulgere*, from *ex-* 'out' + *fulgere* 'to shine.' **—ef·ful·gence** *n.* **—ef·ful·gent·ly** *adv.*

ef·fuse /iˈfyo͞oz; iˈfyo͞os/ ▶*v.* [*trans.*] give off (a liquid, light, smell, or quality). ■ [*intrans.*] talk in an unrestrained, excited manner: *this was the type of material that they effused about.* ▷late Middle English: from Latin *effusus*, past participle of *effundere* 'pour out,' from *ex-* 'out' + *fundere* 'pour.'

ef·fu·sion /iˈfyo͞oZHən/ ▶*n.* an instance of giving off something such as a liquid, light, or smell: *a massive effusion of poisonous gas.* ■ *Medicine* an escape of fluid into a body cavity. ■ an act of talking or writing in an unrestrained or heartfelt way: *literary effusions.* ▷late Middle English: from Latin *effusio(n-)*, from *effundere* 'pour out' (see **EFFUSE**).

ef·fu·sive /i'fyōōsiv/ ▸*adj.* **1** expressing feelings of gratitude, pleasure, or approval in an unrestrained or heartfelt manner: *an effusive welcome.* See note at **SENTIMENTAL**. **2** *Geology* (of igneous rock) poured out when molten and later solidified. ■ of or relating to the eruption of large volumes of molten rock. **—ef·fu·sive·ly** *adv.* **—ef·fu·sive·ness** *n.*

Ef·ik /'efik/ ▸*n.* (*pl.* same) **1** a member of a people of southern Nigeria. **2** the Benue-Congo language of this people, closely related to Ibibio, and used as a lingua franca.
▸*adj.* of or relating to this people or their language. ▷the name in Efik.

E-fit /'ē ˌfit/ ▸*n.* an electronic picture of a person's face made from composite photographs of facial features, created by a computer program. ▷1980s: from *e-* 'electronic' and *fit*, on the pattern of *Photofit* (trademark method of creating a composite picture of a crime suspect's face).

EFL ▸*abbr.* English as a foreign language.

EFM ▸*abbr.* electronic fetal monitor.

eft /eft/ ▸*n.* a newt. ■ *Zoology* the juvenile stage of a newt. ▷Old English *efeta*, of unknown origin. Compare with **NEWT**.

EFTA /'eftə/ ▸*abbr.* European Free Trade Association.

EFTPOS ▸*abbr.* electronic funds transfer at point of sale.

EFTS ▸*abbr.* electronic funds transfer system.

e.g. ▸*abbr.* for example. ▷from Latin *exempli gratia* 'for the sake of an example.'

e·gad /ē'gad/ (also **e·gads**) ▸*exclam. archaic* expressing surprise, anger, or affirmation. ▷late 17th cent.: representing earlier *A God.*

e·gal·i·tar·i·an /iˌgalə'terēən/ ▸*adj.* of, relating to, or believing in the principle that all people are equal and deserve equal rights and opportunities: *a fairer, more egalitarian society.*
▸*n.* a person who advocates or supports such a principle. ▷late 19th cent.: from French *égalitaire*, from *égal* 'equal,' from Latin *aequalis* (see **EQUAL**). **—e·gal·i·tar·i·an·ism** *n.*

Eg·bert /'egbərt/ (died 839), king of Wessex 802–839. In 825, he won a decisive victory that temporarily brought Mercian supremacy to an end.

EGD ▸*n.* a technology or system that integrates a computer display with a pair of eyeglasses, using a lens or mirror to reflect images into the eyes: *some EGDs are designed to clip right on to your eyeglasses.* ▷abbreviation of 'eyeglass display.'

EGF ▸*abbr.* epidermal growth factor.

egg[1] /eg/ ▸*n.* **1** an oval or round object laid by a female bird, reptile, fish, or invertebrate, usually containing a developing embryo. The eggs of birds are enclosed in a chalky shell, while those of reptiles are in a leathery membrane. ■ an infertile egg, typically of the domestic hen, used for food. ■ *Biology* the female reproductive cell in animals and plants; an ovum. ■ a thing resembling a bird's egg in shape: *chocolate eggs.* ■ *Architecture* a decorative oval molding, used alternately with triangular figures. **2** [with *adj.*] *informal, dated* a person possessing a specified quality: *she was a good egg.* ▷Middle English (superseding earlier *ey*, from Old English *ǣg*): from Old Norse. **—egg·less** *adj.*
▸*PHRASES* □ **don't put all your eggs in one basket** *proverb* don't risk everything on the success of one venture. □ **go suck an egg** [as *imperative*] *informal* used as an expression of anger or scorn. □ **kill the goose that lays the golden egg** destroy a reliable and valuable source of income. [with allusion to one of Aesop's fables.] □ **lay an egg** *informal* be completely unsuccessful; fail badly. □ **with egg on one's face** *informal* appearing foolish or ridiculous: *don't underestimate this team, or you'll be left with egg on your face.*

egg[2] ▸*v.* [*trans.*] (**egg someone on**) urge or encourage someone to do something, esp. something foolish or risky. ▷Middle English: from Old Norse *eggja* 'incite.'

egg and dart ▸*n. Architecture* a motif of alternating eggs and darts, used to enrich an ovolo molding.

egg·ar /'egər/ ▸*n.* a large brownish moth that is often active during the day. The caterpillars typically bear irritant hairs and make an egg-shaped cocoon. • Many species in the family Lasiocampidae. ▷early 18th cent.: probably from **EGG**[1] + **-ER**[1].

egg·beat·er /'egˌbētər/ ▸*n.* a kitchen utensil used for beating ingredients such as eggs or cream. ■ *informal* a helicopter.

egg-bound ▸*adj.* (of a hen) unable through weakness or disease to expel its eggs.

egg cream ▸*n.* a drink consisting of milk and soda water, flavored with syrup.

egg·cup /'egˌkəp/ ▸*n.* a small cup for holding a boiled egg upright while it is being eaten.

egg-eat·ing snake (also **egg-eat·er**) ▸*n.* an Old World snake that swallows birds' eggs. It has weak teeth, and breaks shells with sawlike projections inside the gullet. • Subfamily Dasypeltinae, family Colubridae: genus *Dasypeltis* (of Africa, in particular the widespread *D. scabra*), and *Elachistodon westermanni* (of India).

egg·head /'egˌhed/ ▸*n. informal, often derogatory* a person who is highly academic or studious; an intellectual. ▷by analogy with a bald head. **—egg·head·ed** *adj.*

egg·nog /'egˌnäg; -ˌnôg/ ▸*n.* a drink made from a mixture of eggs, cream, and flavorings, often with alcohol.

egg·plant /'egˌplant/ ▸*n.* **1** the somewhat large egg-shaped fruit of a tropical Old World plant, eaten as a vegetable. Its skin is typically dark purple, but the skin of certain cultivated varieties is white or yellow. ■ a dark purple color like the skin of this fruit. **2** the large plant of the nightshade family that bears this fruit. • *Solanum melongena*, family Solanaceae.

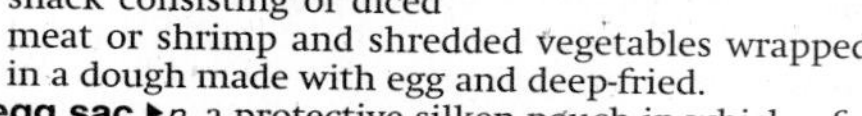

eggplant 1

egg roll ▸*n.* a Chinese-style snack consisting of diced meat or shrimp and shredded vegetables wrapped in a dough made with egg and deep-fried.

egg sac ▸*n.* a protective silken pouch in which a female spider deposits her eggs.

eggs and ba·con (also **egg and ba·con**) ▸*n.* any of a number of plants that have yellow flowers with orange, red, or brown markings, supposedly suggestive of eggs and bacon, in particular: • bird's-foot trefoil. • a shrubby Australian bush plant (*Bossiaea* and other genera, family Leguminosae).

eggs Ben·e·dict ▸*plural n.* a dish consisting of poached eggs and sliced ham on toasted English muffins, covered with hollandaise sauce.

egg·shell /'egˌSHel/ ▸*n.* the thin, hard outer layer of an egg, esp. a hen's egg. ■ used in similes and metaphors to refer to the fragile nature of something: *the truck would crush his car like an eggshell.* ■ (also **eggshell paint**) an oil-based paint that dries with a slight sheen: *the woodwork was painted in eggshell* | [as *adj.*] *an eggshell finish.* ■ [as *adj.*] (of china) of extreme thinness and delicacy: *eggshell porcelains.* ■ a pale yellowish-white color.

egg tem·per·a ▸*n.* an emulsion of pigment and egg yolk, used in tempera painting.

egg tim·er ▸*n.* a device for measuring the time required to cook a boiled egg, traditionally in the form of a miniature hourglass.

egg tooth ▸*n.* a hard white protuberance on the beak or jaw of an embryo bird or reptile that is used for breaking out of the shell and is later lost.

egg white ▸*n.* the clear, viscous substance around the yolk of an egg that turns white when cooked or beaten. Also called **ALBUMEN**.

egg·y /'egē/ ▸*adj.* rich in or covered with egg: *many white wines go passably with eggy dishes.*

eg·lan·tine /'eglənˌtēn; -ˌtīn/ ▸*n.* another term for **SWEETBRIER**. ▷Middle English: from Old French *eglantine*, from Provençale *aiglentina*, based on Latin *acus* 'needle' or *aculeus* 'prickle.'

e·go /'ēgō/ ▸*n.* (*pl.* **e·gos**) a person's sense of self-esteem or self-importance: *a boost to my ego.* ■ *Psychoanalysis* the part of the mind that mediates between the conscious and the unconscious and is responsible for reality testing and a sense of personal identity. Compare with **ID** and **SUPEREGO**. ■ an overly high opinion of oneself: *some major players with really big egos.* ■ *Philosophy* (in metaphysics) a conscious thinking subject. ▷early 19th cent.: from Latin, literally 'I.' **—e·go·less** *adj.*

e·go·cen·tric /ˌēgō'sentrik/ ▸*adj.* thinking only of oneself, without regard for the feelings or desires of others; self-centered: *their egocentric tendency to think of themselves as invulnerable.* ■ centered in or arising from a person's own existence or perspective: *egocentric spatial perception.*
▸*n.* an egocentric person. ▷early 20th cent.: from **EGO**, on the pattern of words such as *geocentric.* **—e·go·cen·tric·al·ly** /-(ə)lē/ *adv.* **—e·go·cen·tric·i·ty** /ˌēgōsen'trisitē/ *n.* **—e·go·cen·trism** /ˌēgō'sentrizəm/ *n.*

e·go i·de·al ▸*n. Psychoanalysis* (in Freudian theory) the part of the mind that imposes on itself concepts of ideal behavior developed from parental and social standards. ■ (in general use) an idealized conception of oneself.

e·go·ism /'ēgōˌizəm/ ▸*n. Ethics* an ethical theory that treats self-interest as the foundation of morality. ■ another term for **EGOTISM**. ▷late 18th cent.: from French *égoïsme* and modern Latin *egoismus*, from Latin *ego* 'I.' **—e·go·ist** *n.* **—e·go·is·tic** /-'istik/ *adj.* **—e·go·is·ti·cal** /-'istikəl/ *adj.* **—e·go·is·ti·cal·ly** /-'istik(ə)lē/ *adv.*

USAGE The words **egoism** and **egotism** are frequently confused, as though interchangeable, but there are distinctions worth noting. Both words derive from Latin *ego* ('I'), the first-person singular pronoun. **Egotism**, the more commonly used term, denotes an excessive sense of self-importance, too-frequent use of the word 'I,' and general arrogance and boastfulness. **Egoism**, a more subtle term, is perhaps best left to ethicists, for whom it denotes a view or theory of moral behavior in which self-interest is the root of moral conduct. An **egoist**, then, might devote considerable attention to introspection, but could be modest about it, whereas an **egotist** would have an exaggerated sense of the importance of his or her self-analysis, and would have to tell everyone.

e·go·ma·ni·a /ˌēgō'mānēə/ ▸*n.* obsessive egotism or self-centeredness. **—e·go·ma·ni·ac** /-nēˌak/ *n.* **—e·go·ma·ni·a·cal** /-mə'nīəkəl/ *adj.*

e·go psy·chol·o·gy ▸*n. Psychology* a system of psychoanalytic developmental psychology concerned esp. with personality. **—e·go psy·chol·o·gist** *n.*

e·go·surf /'ēgōˌsərf/ ▸*v.* [*intrans.*] *informal* search the Internet for instances of one's own name or links to one's own Web site. **—e·go·surf·ing** *n.*

e·go·tism /'ēgəˌtizəm/ ▸*n.* the practice of talking and thinking about oneself excessively because of an undue sense of self-importance: *in his arrogance and egotism, he underestimated Jill.* See note at **PRIDE**. ▷early 18th cent.: from French *égoïste*, from Latin *ego* 'I.' **—e·go·tist** *n.* **—e·go·tis·tic** /ˌēgə'tistik/ *adj.* **—e·go·tis·ti·cal** /ˌēgə'tistikəl/ *adj.* **—e·go·tis·ti·cal·ly** /ˌēgə'tistik(ə)lē/ *adv.* **—e·go·tize** /-ˌtīz/ *v.*

USAGE See usage at **EGOISM**.

THE RIGHT WORD **conceit, egotism, narcissism, solipsism, vanity**

Egotism is a negative term that combines extreme self-preoccupation with a tendency to show off or attract attention.

There is nothing neutral about **conceit**, which carries strong connotations of superiority and a failure to see oneself realistically (*he was so rich and powerful that conceit came easily*).

Vanity, on the other hand, is not based so much on feelings of superiority as it is on a love for oneself and a craving for the admiration of others (*his vanity drove him to cosmetic surgery*).

Narcissism and **solipsism** were once considered technical terms drawn from psychology and philosophy, respectively, but nowadays they are also in the general language.

Narcissism means self-love and preoccupation with one's physical or mental attributes (*the beautiful young actress had a reputation for narcissism*), while *solipsism* refers to someone who is completely wrapped up in his or her own concerns (*the solipsism of the theoretical mathematician*).

e·go trip ▸*n. informal* an activity done in order to increase one's sense of self-importance: *driving that car was the biggest ego trip I'd ever had.*

e·gre·gious /i'grējəs/ ▸*adj.* **1** outstandingly bad; shocking: *egregious abuses of copyright.* **2** *archaic* remarkably good. ▷mid 16th cent. (sense 2): from Latin *egregius* 'illustrious,' literally 'standing out from the flock,' from *ex-* 'out' + *grex, greg-* 'flock.' The

Pronunciation Key ə *ago;* ər *over;* 'ə or ˌə *up;* 'ər or ˌər *fur;* a *hat;* ā *rate;* ä *car;* CH *chew;* e *let;* ē *see;* e(ə)r *air;* i *fit;* ī *by;* i(ə)r *ear;* NG *sing;* ō *go;* ô *for;* oi *boy;* ŏŏ *good;* ōō *goo;* ou *out;* SH *she;* TH *thin;* T͟H *then;* (h)w *why;* ZH *vision*

E

derogatory sense (late 16th cent.) probably arose as an ironical use. **—e·gre·gious·ly** *adv.* **—e·gre·gious·ness** *n.*

e·gress /ˈēˌgres/ ▸*n.* the action of going out of or leaving a place: *direct means of access and egress for passengers.* ■ a way out: *a narrow egress.* ■ *Law* the right or freedom to come out or go out. ■ *Astronomy* another term for EMERSION.
▸*v.* [*trans.*] go out of or leave (a place): *they'd egress the area by heading southwest.* ▷mid 16th cent.: from Latin *egressus* 'gone out,' from the verb *egredi*, from *ex-* 'out' + *gradi* 'to step.'

e·gres·sive /iˈgresiv/ ▸*adj.* *Phonetics* (of a speech sound) produced using the normal outward-flowing airstream. Compare with INGRESSIVE.

e·gret /ˈēgrit; ˈēˌgret; ˈegrit/ ▸*n.* a heron with mainly white plumage, having long plumes in the breeding season. • Genus *Egretta* (and *Bubulcus*), family Ardeidae: several species. ▷Middle English: from Old French *aigrette*, from Provençal *aigreta*, from the Germanic base of HERON.

E·gypt /ˈējəpt/ a country in northeastern Africa, on the Mediterranean Sea; pop. 76,117,000; capital, Cairo; official language, Arabic.

The population of Egypt is concentrated chiefly along the fertile valley of the Nile River because the rest of the country is largely desert. Egypt's history spans 5,000 years: the ancient kingdoms of Upper and Lower Egypt were ruled successively by 31 dynasties, which may be divided into the Old Kingdom, the Middle Kingdom, and the New Kingdom. Egypt was a center of Hellenistic culture and then a Roman province before coming under Islamic rule and then becoming part of the Ottoman Empire. Modern Egypt became independent in 1922. From 1958 to 1961 Egypt was united with Syria as the United Arab Republic, a title it retained until 1971. Wars with Israel were fought in 1967 (the Six Day War) and 1973 (the Yom Kippur or October War); the countries signed a peace treaty in 1979.

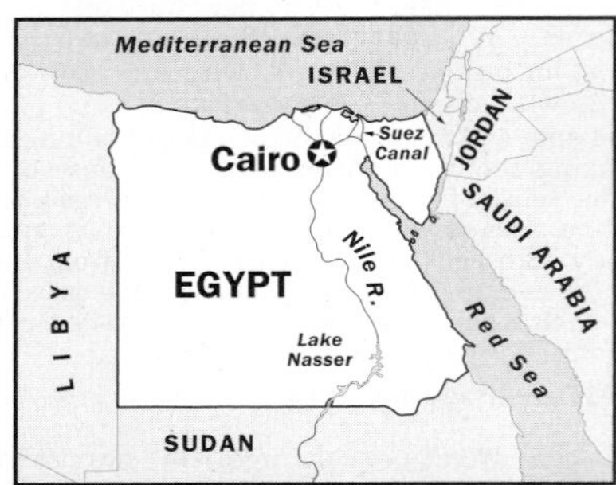

E·gyp·tian /iˈjipSHən/ ▸*adj.* of or relating to Egypt or its people. ■ of or relating to Egyptian antiquities: *a large Egyptian collection was sold at Sotheby's.* ■ of or relating to the language of ancient Egypt.
▸*n.* **1** a native of ancient or modern Egypt, or a person of Egyptian descent. **2** the Afro-Asiatic language used in ancient Egypt, attested from *c.*3000 BC. It is represented in its oldest stages by hieroglyphic inscriptions and in its latest form by Coptic; it has been replaced in modern use by Arabic. **—E·gyp·tian·i·za·tion** /iˌjipSHəniˈzāSHən/ *n.* **—E·gyp·tian·ize** /-ˌnīz/ *v.*

E·gyp·tian black ▸*n.* another term for BASALT (stoneware pottery).

E·gyp·tian clo·ver ▸*n.* another term for BERSEEM CLOVER.

E·gyp·tian co·bra ▸*n.* a large nocturnal African cobra with a thick body and large head. Also called ASP. • *Naja haje*, family Elapidae.

E·gyp·tian goose ▸*n.* a large African goose that has a dark patch around the eye, pink bill and legs, and either reddish-brown or grayish-brown upper parts. • *Alopochen aegyptiacus*, family Anatidae.

E·gyp·tian lo·tus ▸*n.* see LOTUS (sense 1).

E·gyp·tian mon·goose ▸*n.* a mongoose occurring over much of Africa and parts of southwestern Asia and Iberia, noted for its destruction of crocodile eggs. Also called ICHNEUMON. • *Herpestes ichneumon*, family Herpestidae.

E·gyp·tian plov·er ▸*n.* a ploverlike African bird of the courser family, with a striking pattern of black and white over a mainly bluish back and buff-colored underparts. Also called CROCODILE BIRD. • *Pluvianus aegyptius*, family Glareolidae.

E·gyp·tian vul·ture ▸*n.* a small white vulture with black wing tips, common in much of southern Eurasia and Africa. • *Neophron percnopterus*, family Accipitridae.

E·gyp·tol·o·gy /ˌējipˈtäləjē/ ▸*n.* the study of the language, history, and civilization of ancient Egypt. **—E·gyp·to·log·i·cal** /iˌjiptəˈläjikəl/ *adj.* **—E·gyp·tol·o·gist** /ˌējipˈtäləjist/ *n.*

eh /ā; e/ ▸*exclam.* used to represent a sound made in speech in a variety of situations, in particular to ask for something to be repeated or explained or to elicit agreement: *"Eh? What's this?"* | *"Let's hope so, eh?"* ▷natural utterance: first recorded in English in the mid 16th cent.

EHF ▸*abbr.* extremely high frequency.

EHP ▸*abbr.* ■ effective horsepower. ■ electric horsepower.

EHV ▸*abbr.* extra-high voltage.

Eich·mann /ˈīkmən/, (Karl) Adolf (1906–62), German Nazi administrator. He administered the concentration camps during World War II. In 1960, he was traced to Argentina by Israeli agents and executed after trial in Israel.

ei·co·sa·pen·ta·e·no·ic ac·id /ˌīkōsəˌpentəˈnō-ik/ ▸*n.* *Chemistry* a polyunsaturated fatty acid found esp. in fish oils. In humans it is a metabolic precursor of prostaglandins. • Chem. formula: $C_{19}H_{29}COOH$. **—ei·co·sa·pen·ta·e·no·ate** /ˌīkōsəˌpentəˈnō-āt/ *n.* .

Eid /ēd/ (also **Id**) ▸*n.* a Muslim festival, in particular: ■ (in full **Eid ul-Fitr** /ēd o͝ol ˈfētr/) the feast marking the end of the fast of Ramadan. ■ (in full **Eid ul-A·dha** /ēd o͝ol ˈädə/) the festival marking the culmination of the annual pilgrimage to Mecca and commemorating the sacrifice of Abraham. ▷from Arabic *ʿīd* 'feast,' from Aramaic.

EIDE ▸*n.* *Computing* enhanced integrated drive electronics. See **IDE**.

ei·der /ˈīdər/ ▸*n.* (also **ei·der duck**) (*pl.* same or **ei·ders**) a northern sea duck, of which the male has mainly black and white plumage with a colored head, and the brown female has soft down feathers that are used to line the nest. • Genus *Somateria* (and *Polysticta*), family Anatidae: four species, in particular the **common eider** (*S. mollissima*). ■ another term for EIDERDOWN. ▷late 17th cent.: from Icelandic *æthur*, from Old Norse *æthr*.

common eider

ei·der·down /ˈīdərˌdoun/ ▸*n.* small, soft feathers from the breast of the female eider duck. ■ *chiefly Brit.* a quilt filled with down (originally from the eider) or some other soft material.

ei·det·ic /īˈdetik/ ▸*adj.* *Psychology* relating to or denoting mental images having unusual vividness and detail, as if actually visible.
▸*n.* a person able to form or recall eidetic images. ▷1920s: coined in German from Greek *eidētikos*, from *eidos* 'form.' **—ei·det·i·cal·ly** *adv.*

ei·do·lon /īˈdōlən/ ▸*n.* (*pl.* **-lons** or **-la** /-lə/) **1** an idealized person or thing. **2** a specter or phantom. ▷early 19th cent.: from Greek *eidōlon*, from *eidos* 'form.'

ei·dos /ˈīdäs; ˈādäs/ ▸*n.* (*pl.* **ei·de** /ˈīdē; ˈādā/) *Anthropology* the distinctive expression of the cognitive or intellectual character of a culture or social group. ▷1930s: Greek, literally 'form, type, or idea,' partly in contrast to ETHOS.

Eif·fel /ˈīfəl/, Alexandre Gustave (1832–1923), French engineer. He designed and built the Eiffel Tower and was the architect of the inner structure of the Statue of Liberty.

Eif·fel Tow·er a wrought-iron structure erected in Paris for the World Exhibition of 1889. With a height of 984 feet (300 m), it was the tallest man-made structure for many years.

eigen- ▸*comb. form* *Mathematics & Physics* proper; characteristic: *eigenfunction.* ▷from the German adjective *eigen* 'own.'

ei·gen·fre·quen·cy /ˈīgənˌfrēkwənsē/ ▸*n.* (*pl.* **-cies**) *Mathematics & Physics* one of the natural resonant frequencies of a system.

ei·gen·func·tion /ˈīgənˌfəNG(k)SHən/ ▸*n.* *Mathematics & Physics* each of a set of independent functions that are the solutions to a given differential equation.

ei·gen·state /ˈīgənˌstāt/ ▸*n.* *Physics* a quantum-mechanical state corresponding to an eigenvalue of a wave equation.

ei·gen·val·ue /ˈīgənˌvalyo͞o/ ▸*n.* *Mathematics & Physics* **1** each of a set of values of a parameter for which a differential equation has a nonzero solution (an eigenfunction) under given conditions. **2** any number such that a given matrix minus that number times the identity matrix has a zero determinant.

ei·gen·vec·tor /ˈīgənˌvektər/ ▸*n.* *Mathematics & Physics* a vector that when operated on by a given operator gives a scalar multiple of itself.

eight /āt/ ▸*cardinal number* equivalent to the product of two and four; one more than seven, or two less than ten; 8: *a committee of eight members* | *eight were acquitted* | *eight of them were unemployed.* (Roman numeral: **viii** or **VIII.**) ■ a group or unit of eight people or things: *the win placed Canada closer to the final eight.* ■ eight years old: *children as young as eight.* ■ eight o'clock: *in time for dinner at eight.* ■ short for FIGURE EIGHT. ■ a size of garment or other merchandise denoted by eight. ■ an eight-cylinder engine or a motor vehicle with such an engine. ■ a playing card with eight pips. ■ an eight-oared rowboat or its crew. ▷Old English *ehta, eahta*, of Germanic origin; related to Dutch and German *acht*, from an Indo-European root shared by Latin *octo* and Greek *oktō*.

eight ball ▸*n.* **1** *Billiards* the black ball, numbered eight. ■ a game of pool in which one side must pocket all of the striped or solid balls and finally the eight ball to win. **2** (**eightball**) *informal* a portion of an illegal drug weighing an eighth of an ounce (3.54 g).
▸*PHRASE* □ **behind the eight ball** *informal* at a disadvantage.

eight·een /āˈtēn; ˈāˌtēn/ ▸*cardinal number* equivalent to the product of two and nine; one more than seventeen, or eight more than ten; 18: *she wrote eighteen novels* | *out of sixty batches checked, eighteen were incorrect* | *eighteen of the guests were gathered.* (Roman numeral: **xviii** or **XVIII.**) ■ a set or team of eighteen individuals. ■ eighteen years old: *he was barely eighteen.* ■ a size of garment or other merchandise denoted by eighteen. ▷Old English *e(a)htatēne* (see EIGHT, -TEEN). **—eight·eenth** /āˈtēnTH; ˈāˌtēnTH/ *ordinal number* .

eight·een·mo /ˌāˈtēnˌmō/ ▸*n.* (*pl.* **-mos**) another term for OCTODECIMO.

eight·fold /ˈātˌfōld/ ▸*adj.* eight times as great or as numerous: *an eightfold increase in expenditure.* ■ having eight parts or elements: *an eightfold shape.*
▸*adv.* by eight times; to eight times the number or amount: *claims have grown eightfold in ten years.*

eight·fold path *Buddhism* the path to nirvana, comprising eight aspects in which an aspirant must become practiced: right views, intention, speech, action, livelihood, effort, mindfulness, and concentration. See BUDDHISM.

eighth /ā(t)TH/ ▸*ordinal number* constituting number eight in a sequence; 8th: *in the eighth century* | *the eighth of September* | *seven men admitted conspiracy, an eighth admitted assisting an offender.* ■ (**an eighth/one eighth**) each of eight equal parts into which something is or may be divided: *an eighth of an inch.* ■ the eighth finisher or position in a race or competition: *she finished eighth of the eleven runners.* ■ the eighth grade of a school. **—eighth·ly** *adv.*

eighth note (*Brit.* **qua·ver**) ▸*n.* *Music* a note having the time value of an eighth of a whole note or half a quarter note, represented by a large dot with a hooked stem.

eight·pen·ny nail /ˈātˌpenē/ ▸*n.* a nail that is 2.5 inches (64 mm) long.

Eiffel Tower

8vo /äk'tävō/ ▸*abbr.* octavo.

eight·y /'ātē/ ▸*cardinal number* (*pl.* **eight·ies**) equivalent to the product of eight and ten; ten less than ninety; 80: *eighty miles north* | *a buffet for eighty* | *eighty of the nurses fled.* (Roman numeral: **lxxx** or **LXXX**.) ■ (**eighties**) the numbers from 80 to 89, esp. the years of a century or of a person's life: *his grandmother was in her eighties.* ■ eighty years old: *he was over eighty at the time.* ■ eighty miles an hour: *roaring down the highway doing eighty.* ▷Old English *hundeahtatig*, from *hund* (of uncertain origin) + *e(a)hta* 'eight' + *-tig* (see **-TY**[2]); the first element was lost early in the Middle English period. **—eight·i·eth** /'ātēiTH/ *ordinal number* **—eight·y·fold** /'ātē,fōld/ *adj.* & *adv.*

Eijk·man /'īkmən/, Christiaan (1858–1930), Dutch physician. His work resulted in a simple cure for beriberi and led to the discovery of the vitamin thiamine. Nobel Prize for Physiology or Medicine (1929, shared with F. G. Hopkins).

Ei·lat /ā'lät/ (also **E·lat**) the southernmost town in Israel, a port and resort at the head of the Gulf of Aqaba; pop. 36,000. Founded in 1949 near the ruins of biblical Elath, it is Israel's only outlet to the Red Sea.

Eind·ho·ven /'īnt,hōvən; 'ānt-/ a city in southern Netherlands; pop. 193,000.

Ein·fühl·ung /'īnfōō,lōōNG/ ▸*n.* empathy. ▷German, from *ein-* 'into' + *Fühlung* 'feeling.'

ein·korn /'īn,kôrn/ ▸*n.* an old kind of Mediterranean wheat with small bearded ears and spikelets that each contain one slender grain, used as fodder in prehistoric times but now rarely grown. Compare with **EMMER**, **SPELT**[2]. • *Triticum monococcum*, family Gramineae. ▷early 20th cent.: from German, from *ein* 'one' + *Korn* 'seed.'

Ein·stein /'īn,stīn/, Albert (1879–1955), U.S. theoretical physicist; born in Germany; founder of the theory of relativity in 1905. Often regarded as the greatest scientist of the 20th century, he was influential in the decision to build an atomic bomb. After World War II, however, he spoke out against nuclear weapons. ■ [as *n.*] (**an Einstein**) a genius. **—Ein·stein·i·an** /īn'stīnēən/ *adj.*

Albert Einstein

ein·stein·i·um /īn'stīnēəm/ ▸*n.* the chemical element of atomic number 99, a radioactive metal of the actinide series. Einsteinium does not occur naturally and was discovered in 1953 in debris from the first hydrogen bomb explosion. (Symbol: **Es**) ▷1950s: from the name of Albert **EINSTEIN** + **-IUM**.

Eint·ho·ven /'īnt,hōvən/, Willem (1860–1927), Dutch physiologist. He devised the first electrocardiograph, a device that records specific muscular contractions in the heart.

Ei·re /'erə/ the Gaelic name for Ireland; the official name (1937–49) of the Republic of Ireland.

Ei·rene /ī'rēnē/ *Greek Mythology* the goddess of peace. Roman equivalent **PAX**.

ei·ren·ic /ī'renik; -'rē-/ ▸*adj.* variant spelling of **IRENIC**.

Ei·sen·how·er /'īzən,hou-ər/, Dwight David (1890–1969), U.S. general and 34th president of the U.S. 1953–61; nicknamed **Ike**. A Kansas Republican, he was one of the most celebrated U.S. military leaders before entering politics. In World War II, he was Supreme Commander of Allied Expeditionary Forces in western Europe 1943–45. As president, he adopted a hard line toward communism both in his domestic and foreign policy.

Ei·sen·staedt /'īzən,SHtat; -,SHtet; -,stat/, Alfred (1898–1995), U.S. photojournalist; born in Dirschau, Germany (now part of Poland). He was one of the original photographers for *Life* magazine 1932–72.

Ei·sen·stein /'īzən,SHtīn/, Sergei (Mikhailovich) (1898–1948), Russian movie director, born in Latvia. He is noted for *The Battleship Potemkin* (1925), a commemoration of the Russian Revolution of 1905 that is celebrated for its pioneering use of montage.

Eis·ner /'īznər/, Michael Dammann (1942–), U.S. corporate executive. He worked for ABC 1966–76 and Paramount 1976–84 before becoming the CEO of The Walt Disney Company in 1984.

eis·tedd·fod /ī'steTH,väd/ ▸*n.* (*pl.* **-fods** or **-fo·dau** /-'vädī/) a competitive festival of music and poetry in Wales, in particular the annual National Eisteddfod. ▷Welsh, literally 'session,' from *eistedd* 'sit.' **—eis·tedd·fod·ic** /,īsteTH'vädik/ *adj.*

Eis·wein /'īs,vīn/ ▸*n.* (*pl.* **-wei·ne** /-,vīnə/ or **-weins**) wine made from ripe grapes picked while covered with frost. ▷from German, from *Eis* 'ice' + *Wein* 'wine.'

ei·ther /'ēTHər; 'īTHər/ ▸*conj.* & *adv.* **1** used before the first of two (or occasionally more) alternatives that are being specified (the other being introduced by "or"): *either I accompany you to your room, or I wait here* | *available in either black or white.* **2** [*adv.*, with *negative*] used to indicate a similarity or link with a statement just made: *you don't like him, do you? I don't, either* | *it won't do any harm, but won't really help, either.* ■ for that matter; moreover (used to add information): *I was too tired to go. And I couldn't have paid my way, either.*
▸*adj.* & *pron.* one or the other of two people or things: [as *adj.*] *there were no children of either marriage* | [as *pron.*] *they have a mortgage that will be repaid if* **either** *of them dies.* ■ [*adj.*] each of two: *the road was straight with fields of grass on either side.* ▷Old English *ǣgther*, contracted form of *ǣg(e)hwæther*, of Germanic origin; ultimately related to **AYE**[1] and **WHETHER**.
▸*PHRASE* □ **either way** whichever of two given alternatives is the case: *I'm not sure whether he is trying to be clever or controversial, but either way, such writing smacks of racism.*

USAGE In good English writing style, it is important that **either** and **or** are correctly placed so that the structures following each word balance and mirror each other. Thus, sentences such as **either** *I accompany you* **or** *I wait here* and *I'm going to buy* **either** *a new camera* **or** *a new video* are correct, whereas sentences such as **either** *I accompany you* **or** *John* and *I'm* **either** *going to buy a new camera* **or** *a video* are not well-balanced sentences and should not be used in written English.
See also **usage** at **NEITHER**.

ei·ther/or /'ēTHər'ôr; 'īTHər'ôr/ (also **ei·ther-or**) ▸*n.* an unavoidable choice between two alternatives: *you can give him an ultimatum—an either/or.*
▸*adj.* involving such a choice: *falsely posing family and career as an either/or choice for women.*

e·jac·u·late ▸*v.* /i'jakyə,lāt/ **1** [*intrans.*] (of a man or male animal) eject semen from the body at the moment of sexual climax. **2** *dated* utter suddenly (a short prayer). ■ [with *direct speech*] say something quickly and suddenly: *"Indeed?" ejaculated the stranger.*
▸*n.* /-,lit/ semen that has been ejected from the body. ▷late 16th cent.: from Latin *ejaculat-* 'darted out,' from the verb *ejaculari*, from *e-* (variant of *ex-*) 'out' + *jaculari* 'to dart' (from *jaculum* 'dart, javelin,' from *jacere* 'to throw'). **—e·jac·u·la·tion** /i,jakyə'lāSHən/ *n.* **—e·jac·u·la·to·ry** /-lə,tôrē/ *adj.*

e·jac·u·la·tor /i'jakyə,lātər/ ▸*n.* a muscle that causes ejaculation of semen.

Dwight D. Eisenhower

e·ject /i'jekt/ ▸*v.* [*trans.*] (often **be ejected**) force or throw (something) out, typically in a violent or sudden way: *many types of rock are* **ejected from** *volcanoes as solid, fragmentary material.* ■ cause (something) to drop out or be removed, usually mechanically: *he ejected the spent cartridge.* ■ [*intrans.*] (of a pilot) escape from an aircraft by being explosively propelled out of it: *he flew to open sea, put the plane in a nosedive, and ejected.* ■ compel (someone) to leave a place: *angry supporters were forcibly* **ejected from** *the court.* ■ dismiss (someone), esp. from political office: *he was* **ejected from** *office in July.* ■ emit; give off: *plants utilize carbon dioxide in the atmosphere that animals eject* | [as *adj.*] (**ejected**) *ejected electrons.* ■ dispossess (a tenant) by legal process. ▷late Middle English: from Latin *eject-* 'thrown out,' from the verb *eicere*, from *e-* (variant of *ex-*) 'out' + *jacere* 'to throw.' **—e·jec·tion** /i'jekSHən/ *n.*

THE RIGHT WORD **dismiss, eject, evict, expel, oust**
Want to get rid of someone? You can **eject** him or her, which means to throw or cast out (*he was ejected from the meeting room*).
If you hope the person never comes back, use **expel**, a verb that suggests driving someone out of a country, an organization, etc., for all time (*to be expelled from school*); it can also imply the use of voluntary force (*to expel air from the lungs*).
If you exercise force or the power of law to get rid of someone or something, **oust** is the correct verb (*ousted after less than two years in office*).
If as a property owner you are turning someone out of a house or a place of business, you'll want to **evict** the person (*she was evicted for not paying the rent*).
Dismiss is by far the mildest of these terms, suggesting that you are rejecting or refusing to consider someone or something (*to dismiss a legal case*). It is also commonly used of loss of employment (*dismissed from his job for excessive tardiness*).

e·jec·ta /i'jektə/ ▸*plural n.* [often treated as *sing.*] material that is forced or thrown out, esp. as a result of volcanic eruption, meteoritic impact, or stellar explosion. ▷late 19th cent.: from Latin, 'things thrown out,' neuter plural of *ejectus* 'thrown out,' from *eicere* (see **EJECT**).

e·jec·tion seat /i'jekSHən/ ▸*n.* a device that causes the ejection of a pilot from an aircraft, used in an emergency.

e·jec·tive /i'jektiv/ *Phonetics* ▸*adj.* denoting a type of consonant in some languages, e.g., Hausa, produced by sudden release of pressure from the glottis.
▸*n.* an ejective consonant.

e·ject·ment /i'jektmənt/ ▸*n.* *Law* the action or process of evicting a tenant from property: *the landlord shall serve a* **writ in ejectment**. ■ the action or process in which a person evicted from property seeks to recover possession and damages.

e·jec·tor /i'jektər/ ▸*n.* a device that causes something to be removed or to drop out: *a built-in drill ejector.*

e·ji·do /e'hēdō/ ▸*n.* (*pl.* **-dos**) (in Mexico) a piece of land farmed communally under a system supported by the state. ▷Mexican Spanish, from Spanish, denoting common land on the road leading out of the village.

Eka·te·rin·burg /yi,kətyərin'bōōrk; i'katərin,bərg/ (also **Yekaterinburg**) an industrial city in central Russia, in the eastern foothills of the Ural Mountains; pop. 1,372,000. From 1924–91, it was known as **Sverdlovsk**. ▷named in honor of *Ekaterina* (1684–1727), the wife of Peter the Great, who founded the city in 1721.

E·ka·te·ri·no·dar variant spelling of **YEKATERINODAR**.

E·ka·te·ri·no·slav variant spelling of **YEKATERINOSLAV**.

eke[1] /ēk/ ▸*v.* [*trans.*] (**eke something out**) manage to support oneself or make a living with difficulty: *they eked out their livelihoods from the soil.* ■ make an amount or supply of something last longer by using or consuming it frugally: *the remains of yesterday's stew could be eked out to make another meal.* ■ obtain or create, but just barely: *Tennessee eked out a 74–73 overtime victory.* ▷Old English *ēacian*, *ēcan* (in the sense 'increase'), of Germanic origin; related to Old Norse *auka*.

eke[2] ▸*adv.* archaic term for **ALSO**. ▷Old English, of Germanic origin.

EKG ▸*abbr.* ■ electrocardiogram. ■ electrocardiograph. ■ electrocardiography.

el /el/ ▸*n.* (**the El**) an elevated railroad or section of railroad, esp. that in Chicago. ■ a train running on such a railroad.

el. ▸*abbr.* elevation.

-el ▸*suffix* variant spelling of **-LE**2.

El Aa·iún /,el ī'o͞on/ Arabic name of **LA'YOUN**.

e·lab·o·rate ▸*adj.* /i'lab(ə)rit/ involving many carefully arranged parts or details; detailed and complicated in design and planning: *elaborate security precautions | elaborate wrought-iron gates.* ■ (of an action) lengthy and exaggerated: *he made an elaborate pretense of yawning.*

▸*v.* /i'labə,rāt/ **1** [*trans.*] develop or present (a theory, policy, or system) in detail: *the key idea of the book is expressed in the title and elaborated in the text.* ■ [*intrans.*] add more detail concerning what has already been said: *he would not* **elaborate on** *his news.* **2** [*trans.*] *Biology* (of a natural agency) produce (a substance) from its elements or simpler constituents. ▷late 16th cent. (in the sense 'produced by effort of labor,' also in sense 2 of the verb): from Latin *elaborat-* 'worked out,' from the verb *elaborare*, from *e-* (variant of *ex-*) 'out' + *labor* 'work.' **—e·lab·o·rate·ly** *adv.* **—e·lab·o·rate·ness** *n.* **—e·lab·o·ra·tion** /i,labə'rāsнən/ *n.* **—e·lab·o·ra·tive** /-,rātiv/ *adj.* **—e·lab·o·ra·tor** /-tər/ *n.*

El·a·gab·a·lus /,elə'gabələs/ variant spelling of **HELIOGABALUS**.

El A·la·mein, Battle of /el ,älə'mān; ,alə'mān/ a battle of World War II fought in 1942 at El Alamein in Egypt, 60 miles (90 km) west of Alexandria. The German Afrika Korps under Rommel was halted in its advance toward the Nile by the British 8th Army under Montgomery, giving the British a decisive victory.

E

E·lam /'ēləm/ an ancient state in southwestern Iran, established in the 4th millennium BC. Susa was one of its chief cities.

E·lam·ite /'ēlə,mīt/ ▸*n.* **1** a native or inhabitant of ancient Elam. **2** the language of ancient Elam, of unknown affinity and spoken from the 3rd millennium to the 4th century BC.

▸*adj.* of or relating to the ancient Elamites or their language.

é·lan /ā'län; ā'lan/ ▸*n.* energy, style, and enthusiasm: *a rousing march, played with great élan.* ▷mid 19th cent.: from French *élan*, from *élancer* 'to dart,' from *é-* 'out' + *lancer* 'to throw.'

e·land /'ēlənd/ ▸*n.* a spiral-horned African antelope that lives in open woodland and grassland. It is the largest of the antelopes. • Genus *Taurotragus*, family Bovidae: the **giant eland** (*T. derbianus*) and the **common eland** (*T. oryx*). ▷late 18th cent.: via Afrikaans from Dutch, 'elk,' from obsolete German *Elend*, from Lithuanian *élnis*.

e·lapse /i'laps/ ▸*v.* [*intrans.*] (of time) pass or go by: *weeks elapsed before anyone was charged with the attack* | [as *adj.*] (**elapsed**) *a display tells you which track is playing and its elapsed time.* ▷late 16th cent. (in the sense 'slip away'): from Latin *elaps-* 'slipped away,' from the verb *elabi*, from *e-* (variant of *ex-*) 'out, away' + *labi* 'to glide, slip.'

e·las·i·pod /ə'lasə,päd/ ▸*n. Zoology* an aberrant deep-water sea cucumber that lacks a respiratory tree. Most live on the seabed and have leglike appendages, while some swim by means of webbed papillae. • Order Elasipodida, class Holothuroidea. ▷late 19th cent.: from modern Latin *Elasipoda*, from Greek *elasmos* 'beaten metal' + *pous, pod-* 'foot.'

e·las·mo·branch /ə'lazmə,braNGk/ ▸*n. Zoology* a cartilaginous fish of a group that comprises the sharks, rays, and skates. Compare with **SELACHIAN**. • Subclass Elasmobranchii, class Chondrichthyes. ▷late 19th cent.: from modern Latin *Elasmobranchii* (plural), from Greek *elasmos* 'beaten metal' + *brankhia* 'gills.'

e·las·mo·saur /ə'lazmə,sôr/ (also **e·las·mo·sau·rus** /ə,lazmə'sôrəs/) ▸*n.* a Cretaceous plesiosaur with a long neck shaped like that of a swan. • Family Elasmosauridae, infraorder Plesiosauria: several genera, including *Elasmosaurus*. ▷late 19th cent.: from modern Latin *Elasmosaurus*, from Greek *elasmos* 'beaten metal' + *sauros* 'lizard.' **—e·las·mo·sau·ri·an** *adj.*

e·las·tane /ə'lastān/ ▸*n. Brit.* an elastic polyurethane material, used esp. for hosiery, underwear, and other close-fitting clothing. ▷1970s: from **ELASTIC** + **-ANE**2.

e·las·tase /i'lastāz/ ▸*n. Biochemistry* a pancreatic enzyme that digests elastin. ▷1940s: from **ELASTIC** + **-ASE**.

e·las·tic /i'lastik/ ▸*adj.* (of an object or material) able to resume its normal shape spontaneously after contraction, dilatation, or distortion. See note at **FLEXIBLE**. ■ able to encompass variety and change; flexible and adaptable: *the definition of nationality is elastic in this cosmopolitan country.* ■ springy and buoyant: *Annie returned with beaming eyes and elastic step.* ■ *Economics* (of demand or supply) sensitive to changes in price or income: *the labor supply is very elastic.* ■ *Physics* (of a collision) involving no decrease of kinetic energy.

▸*n.* cord, tape, or fabric, typically woven with strips of rubber, that returns to its original length or shape after being stretched. ▷mid 17th cent. (originally describing a gas in the sense 'expanding spontaneously to fill the available space'): from modern Latin *elasticus*, from Greek *elastikos* 'propulsive,' from *elaunein* 'to drive.' **—e·las·ti·cal·ly** /-(ə)lē/ *adv.* **—e·las·tic·i·ty** /i,la'stisitē; ē,la-/ *n.* **—e·las·ti·cize** /i'lastə,sīz/ *v.*

e·las·ti·cat·ed /i'lastə,kātid/ ▸*adj. chiefly Brit.* (of a garment or material) made elastic by the insertion of rubber thread or tape: *ski pants with elasticated waist.*

e·las·tic band ▸*n.* a rubber band.

e·las·tic fi·ber ▸*n. Anatomy* a yellowish fiber composed chiefly of elastin and occurring in networks or sheets that give elasticity to tissues in the body.

e·las·tic lim·it ▸*n. Physics* the maximum extent to which a solid may be stretched without permanent alteration of size or shape.

e·las·tic mod·u·lus ▸*n. Physics* the ratio of the force exerted upon a substance or body to the resultant deformation.

e·las·tin /i'lastin/ ▸*n. Biochemistry* an elastic, fibrous glycoprotein found in connective tissue. ▷late 19th cent.: from **ELASTIC** + **-IN**1.

e·las·to·mer /i'lastəmər/ ▸*n.* a natural or synthetic polymer having elastic properties, e.g., rubber. ▷1930s: from **ELASTIC** + **-MER**. **—e·las·to·mer·ic** /i,lastə'merik/ *adj.*

E·lat variant spelling of **EILAT**.

e·late /i'lāt/ ▸*v.* [*trans.*] [usu. as *adj.*] (**elated**) make (someone) ecstatically happy: *I felt elated at beating Dennis.*

▸*adj. archaic* in high spirits; exultant or proud: *the ladies returned with elate and animated faces.* ▷late Middle English (as an adjective): from Latin *elat-* 'raised,' from the verb *efferre*, from *ex-* 'out, from' + *ferre* 'to bear.' The verb dates from the late 16th cent. **—e·lat·ed·ly** *adv.* **—e·lat·ed·ness** *n.*

e·la·tion /i'lāsнən/ ▸*n.* great happiness and exhilaration: *Richard's* **elation at** *regaining his health was short-lived.* ▷late Middle English: from Old French *elacion*, from Latin *elat-* 'raised,' from the verb *efferre* (see **ELATE**).

E lay·er ▸*n.* a layer of the ionosphere able to reflect medium-frequency radio waves. ▷1930s: arbitrary use of the letter *E*, + **LAYER**.

Ela·zig /,elä'zi/ a commercial city in east central Turkey, east of the upper Euphrates River; pop. 205,000.

El·ba /'elbə/ a small island off the western coast of Italy, known as the place of Napoleon's first exile 1814–15.

El·be /elb(ə)/ a river in central Europe that flows for 720 miles (1,159 km) from the Czech Republic through the German cities of Dresden, Magdeburg, and Hamburg to the North Sea.

El·bert, Mount /'elbərt/ a mountain in Colorado, east of Aspen. Rising to 14,431 feet (4,399 m), it is the highest peak in the Rocky Mountains.

el·bow /'el,bō/ ▸*n.* the joint between the forearm and the upper arm: *she propped herself up on one elbow.* ■ the part of the sleeve of a garment covering the elbow. ■ a thing resembling an elbow, in particular a piece of piping bent through an angle.

▸*v.* [*trans.*] strike (someone) with one's elbow: *one player had elbowed another in the face.* ■ [*intrans.*] move by pushing past people with one's elbows: *people el***bowed past** *each other to the door | furiously, he* **elbowed his way** *through the crowd.* ■ *figurative* get rid of or disregard (a person or idea) in a cursory and dismissive way: *his new TV talk show was elbowed aside in the ratings war.* ▷Old English *elboga, elnboga*, of Germanic origin; related to Dutch *elleboog* and German *Ellenbogen* (see also **ELL**1, **BOW**1).

▸*PHRASES* □ **at one's elbow** close at hand; nearby. □ **elbow-to-elbow** very close together. □ **up to one's elbows in** *informal* with one's hands plunged in (something): *I was up to my elbows in the cheese-potato mixture.* ■ *figurative* deeply involved in (a task or undertaking).

el·bow grease ▸*n. informal* hard physical work, esp. vigorous polishing or cleaning: *you should be able to get the rust off with a wire brush and elbow grease.*

el·bow room ▸*n. informal* adequate space to move or work in: *the car has elbow room for four adults | figurative Quebec wants a little more elbow room within the federation.*

El·brus /el'bro͞os; 'el,bro͞os/ a peak in the Caucasus Mountains, on the border between Russia and Georgia. Rising to 18,481 feet (5,642 m), it is the highest mountain in Europe.

El·burz Moun·tains /el'bo͝orz/ a mountain range in northwestern Iran, close to the southern shore of the Caspian Sea. Damavand is the highest peak, rising to 18,386 feet (5,604 m).

El Ca·jon /,el kə'hōn/ a city in southwestern California, east of San Diego; pop. 88,693.

El Cap·i·tan /el ,kapi'tan/ a peak in Yosemite National Park in California, known for its sheer walls that rise over 3,000 feet (1,000 m) above its base.

El Cen·tro /el 'sentrō/ a city in southern California, the commercial center of the Imperial Valley; pop. 31,384.

El·che /'elcнā/ a town in southeastern Spain, in the province of Alicante; pop. 181,200 .

el cheap·o /el 'cнēpō/ ▸*adj.* & *n.* another way of saying **CHEAPO**. ▷1960s: from **CHEAP**, on the pattern of Spanish phrases such as *El Dorado* and *El Greco*.

El Cid /el 'sid/, see **CID, EL**.

eld /eld/ ▸*n. poetic/literary* old age. ■ former times; the past. ▷Old English *ieldu, eldu*, of Germanic origin; related to **ELDER**1 and **OLD**.

eld·er1 /'eldər/ ▸*adj.* (of one or more out of a group of related or otherwise associated people) of a greater age: *my elder daughter | the elder of the two sons.* ■ (**the Elder**) used to distinguish between related famous people with the same name: *Pliny the Elder.*

▸*n.* (usu. **elders**) a person of greater age than someone specified: *schoolchildren were no less fascinated than their elders | take a bit of advice from your* **elders and betters**. ■ a person of advanced age. ■ (often **elders**) a leader or senior figure in a tribe or other group: *a council of village elders.* ■ an official in the early Christian Church, or of various Protestant Churches and sects. ▷Old English *ieldra, eldra*, of Germanic origin; related to German *älter*, also to **ELD** and **OLD**. **—el·der·ship** /-,sнip/ *n.*

eld·er2 ▸*n.* (also **el·der·ber·ry**) a small tree or shrub with pithy stems, typically having white flowers and bluish-black or red berries. • Genus *Sambucus*, family Caprifoliaceae: numerous species, in particular the common North American *S. canadensis* and the Eurasian *S. nigra*. ▷Old English *ellærn*; related to Middle Low German *ellern, elderne*.

el·der·ber·ry /'eldər,berē/ ▸*n.* the bluish-black or red berry of the elder, used esp. for making jelly or wine. ■ an elder tree or shrub.

el·der·care /'eldər,ke(ə)r/ ▸*n.* care of the elderly or infirm, provided by residential institutions, by paid daily help in the home, or by family members.

el·der·flow·er /'eldər,flou(-ə)r/ ▸*n.* the flower of the elder, used to make wines, cordials, and other drinks.

eld·er hand ▸*n.* (in card games for two players, e.g., piquet) the player who is the first to receive a complete hand, i.e., the player dealt to.

eld·er·ly /'eldərlē/ ▸*adj.* (of a person) old or aging: *she was elderly and silver-haired* [as *plural n.*] (**the elderly**) *teams of volunteers to carry out home repairs for the elderly.* ■ (of a machine or similar object) showing signs of age: *a couple of elderly cars.* **—eld·er·li·ness** /-lēnis/ *n.*

eld·er states·man ▸*n.* a person who is experienced and well-respected, esp. a politician.

eld·est /'eldəst/ ▸*adj.* (of one out of a group of related or otherwise associated people) of the greatest age; oldest: *Swift left the company to his eldest son, Charles | he was the eldest of the three.* ▷Old English *ieldest, eldest*, of Germanic origin; related to German *ältest*, also to **ELD** and **OLD**.

eld·est hand ▸*n.* (in card games for three or more players) the player who is the first to receive a complete hand, usually the player immediately to the left of the dealer.

El Do·ra·do /,el də'rädō/ the name of a fictitious country or city abounding in gold, formerly believed to exist somewhere in the region of the Orinoco and Amazon rivers. ■ [as *n.*] (**an El Dorado** or **eldorado**) (*pl.* **-dos**) a place of great abundance. ▷Spanish, literally 'the gilded one.'

el·dritch /'eldricн/ ▸*adj.* weird and sinister or ghostly: *an eldritch screech.* ▷early 16th cent. (originally Scots): perhaps related to **ELF**.

El·ea·nor of Aq·ui·taine /ˈelənər əv ˈakwəˌtān/ (*c.*1122–1204), daughter of the duke of Aquitaine; queen of France 1137–52 and of England 1154–89. She was married to Louis VII of France from 1137; their marriage was annulled in 1152, and she married the future Henry II of England in 1154. She was the mother of Richard I and John I.

El·e·at·ic /ˌelēˈatik/ ▶*adj.* of or relating to Elea, an ancient Greek city in southwestern Italy, or the school of philosophers which flourished there in about the 5th century BC, including Xenophanes, Parmenides, and Zeno.
▶*n.* an Eleatic philosopher. ▷late 17th cent.: from Latin *Eleaticus,* from *Elea.*

elec. ▶*abbr.* ■ electric, electrical. ■ electrician. ■ electricity.

el·e·cam·pane /ˌelikamˈpān/ ▶*n.* a plant that has yellow daisylike flowers with long slender petals and bitter aromatic roots that are used in herbal medicine, native to central Asia. • *Inula helenium,* family Compositae. ▷late Middle English: from medieval Latin *enula* (from Greek *helenion* 'elecampane') + *campana* probably meaning 'of the fields' (from *campus* 'field').

e·lect /iˈlekt/ ▶*v.* [*trans.*] (often **be elected**) choose (someone) to hold public office or some other position by voting: *the members who were* **elected to** *the committee* | [*trans.*] *they elected him leader.* ■ opt for or choose to do something: *freshman year you could elect Industrial Arts* | [*intrans.*] *more people elected to work at home.* ■ *Christian Theology* (of God) choose (someone) in preference to others for salvation.
▶*adj.* [usu. as *plural n.*] (**the elect**) (of a person) chosen or singled out: *one of the century's elect.* ■ [*postpositive in combination*] elected to or chosen for a position but not yet in office: *the president-elect.* ■ *Christian Theology* chosen by God for salvation. ▷late Middle English: from Latin *elect-* 'picked out,' from the verb *eligere,* from *e-* (variant of *ex-*) 'out' + *legere* 'to pick.' **—e·lect·a·ble** *adj.* **—e·lect·a·bil·i·ty** *n.*

e·lec·tion /iˈleksHən/ ▶*n.* **1** a formal and organized process of electing or being elected, esp. of members of a political body: *the 1860 presidential election* | [as *adj.*] *an election year* | *the first of his family to* **run for election.** ■ the act or an instance of electing: *his election to the House of Representatives.* **2** (in Calvinist theology) predestined salvation. ▷Middle English: via Old French from Latin *electio(n-),* from *eligere* 'pick out' (see **ELECT**).

e·lec·tion·eer /iˌleksHəˈni(ə)r/ ▶*v.* [*intrans.*] [usu. as *n.*] (**electioneering**) (of a politician or political campaigner) take part actively and energetically in the activities of an election campaign: *the election will not be lost or won as the result of a few weeks of electioneering.*
▶*n.* a campaigning politician during an election.

e·lec·tive /iˈlektiv/ ▶*adj.* **1** related to or working by means of election: *an elective democracy.* ■ (of a person or office) appointed or filled by election: *he had never held elective office* | *the National Assembly, with 125 elective members.* ■ (of a body or position) possessing or giving the power to elect. **2** (of a course of study) chosen by the student rather than compulsory. ■ (of surgical or medical treatment) chosen by the patient rather than urgently necessary.
▶*n.* an optional course of study: *up to half the credits in many public high schools are electives.* ▷late Middle English: from Old French *electif, -ive,* from late Latin *electivus,* from *elect-* 'picked out,' from the verb *eligere* (see **ELECT**). **—e·lec·tive·ly** *adv.*

e·lec·tive mut·ism ▶*n.* see **MUTISM.**

e·lec·tor /iˈlektər; -ˌtôr/ ▶*n.* **1** a person who has the right to vote in an election. ■ (in the U.S.) a member of the electoral college. **2** [usu. as *title*] *historical* a German prince entitled to take part in the election of the Holy Roman Emperor: *the Elector of Brandenburg.* **—e·lec·tor·ship** /-ˌsHip/ *n.*

e·lec·tor·al /iˈlektərəl/ ▶*adj.* of or relating to elections or electors: *electoral reform.* **—e·lec·tor·al·ly** *adv.*

e·lec·tor·al col·lege ▶*n.* (also **E·lec·tor·al Col·lege**) (in the U.S.) a body of people representing the states of the U.S., who formally cast votes for the election of the president and vice president. ■ a body of electors chosen or appointed by a larger group.

e·lec·tor·ate /iˈlektərət/ ▶*n.* **1** [treated as *sing.* or *pl.*] all the people in a country or area who are entitled to vote in an election. **2** *historical* the office or territories of a German elector.

E·lec·tra /iˈlektrə/ *Greek Mythology* the daughter of Agamemnon and Clytemnestra. She persuaded her brother Orestes to kill Clytemnestra and Aegisthus (their mother's lover) in revenge for the murder of Agamemnon.

E·lec·tra com·plex ▶*n. Psychoanalysis* old-fashioned term for the Oedipus complex as manifested in young girls. ▷early 20th cent.: named after **ELECTRA.**

e·lec·tress /iˈlektris/ ▶*n.* [usu. as *title*] *historical* the wife of a German elector.

e·lec·tret /iˈlektrit/ ▶*n. Physics* a permanently polarized piece of dielectric material, analogous to a permanent magnet. ▷late 19th cent.: blend of **ELECTRICITY** and **MAGNET.**

e·lec·tric /iˈlektrik/ ▶*adj.* of, worked by, charged with, or producing electricity: *an electric stove* | *an electric current.* ■ *figurative* having or producing a sudden sense of thrilling excitement: *the atmosphere was electric.* ■ (of a musical instrument) amplified through a loudspeaker: *electric bass guitar.* ■ (of a color) brilliant and vivid: *images shot through with jagged streaks of electric blue*
▶*n.* an electric train or other vehicle. ▷mid 17th cent.: from modern Latin *electricus,* from Latin *electrum* 'amber,' from Greek *ēlektron* (because rubbing amber causes electrostatic phenomena).

e·lec·tri·cal /iˈlektrikəl/ ▶*adj.* operating by or producing electricity: *an electrical appliance.* ■ concerned with electricity: *an electrical engineer.* **—e·lec·tri·cal·ly** /-(ə)lē/ *adv.*

e·lec·tri·cal storm ▶*n.* a thunderstorm or other violent disturbance of the electrical condition of the atmosphere.

e·lec·tric arc ▶*n.* see **ARC.**

e·lec·tric-arc fur·nace ▶*n.* another term for **ARC FURNACE.**

e·lec·tric blan·ket ▶*n.* a blanket that can be heated electrically by an internal element.

e·lec·tric chair ▶*n.* a chair in which criminals sentenced to death are executed by electrocution.

e·lec·tric eel ▶*n.* an eellike freshwater fish of South America, using pulses of electricity to kill prey, to assist in navigation, and for defense. • *Electrophorus electricus,* the only member of the family Electrophoridae.

e·lec·tric eye ▶*n. informal* a photoelectric cell operating a relay when the beam of light illuminating it is obscured.

e·lec·tric fence ▶*n.* a fence through which an electric current can be passed, giving an electric shock to any person or animal touching it.

e·lec·tric field ▶*n. Physics* a region around a charged particle or object within which a force would be exerted on other charged particles or objects.

e·lec·tric gui·tar ▶*n.* a guitar with a built-in pickup or pickups that convert sound vibrations into electrical signals for amplification.

e·lec·tri·cian /ilekˈtrisHən; ˌēlek-/ ▶*n.* a person who installs and maintains electrical equipment.

e·lec·tric in·ten·si·ty ▶*n.* the strength of an electric field at any point, equal to the force per unit charge experienced by a small charge placed at that point.

e·lec·tric·i·ty /ilekˈtrisitē; ˌēlek-/ ▶*n.* a form of energy resulting from the existence of charged particles (such as electrons or protons), either statically as an accumulation of charge or dynamically as a current. ■ the supply of electric current to a house or other building for heating, lighting, or powering appliances: *the electricity was back on.* ■ *figurative* a state or feeling of thrilling excitement: *the atmosphere was charged with a dangerous sexual electricity.*

e·lec·tric mo·ment ▶*n. Physics* the product of the distance separating the charges of a dipole and the magnitude of either charge.

e·lec·tric or·gan ▶*n.* **1** *Music* an organ in which the sound is made electrically rather than by pipes. **2** *Zoology* an organ in certain fishes that is used to produce an electrical discharge for stunning prey, for sensing the surroundings, or as a defense.

e·lec·tric ray ▶*n.* a sluggish bottom-dwelling marine ray that typically lives in shallow water and can produce an electric shock for the capture of prey and for defense. Also called **TORPEDO RAY** (see **TORPEDO**). • Family Torpedinidae: several genera, in particular *Torpedo,* and many species.

e·lec·tric shav·er (also **electric razor**) ▶*n.* an electrical device for shaving, with oscillating or rotating blades behind a metal guard.

e·lec·tric shock ▶*n.* a sudden discharge of electricity through a part of the body.

e·lec·tri·fy /iˈlektrəˌfi/ ▶*v.* (**-fies, -fied**) [*trans.*] charge with electricity; pass an electric current through: [as *adj.*] (**electrified**) *an electrified fence.* ■ (often **be electrified**) convert (a machine or system, esp. a railroad line) to the use of electrical power. ■ *figurative* impress greatly; thrill: *he electrified the most sophisticated of audiences.* ▷mid 18th cent.: from **ELECTRIC** + **-FY.** **—e·lec·tri·fi·ca·tion** /iˌlektrəfiˈkāsHən/ *n.* **—e·lec·tri·fi·er** /-ˌfi(ə)r/ *n.*

e·lec·tro /iˈlektrō/ ▶*n.* (*pl.* **-tros**) **1** short for **ELECTROTYPE** or **ELECTROPLATE. 2** a style of dance music with a fast beat and synthesized backing track.

electro- ▶*comb. form* of, relating to, or caused by electricity; involving electricity and . . . : *electromagnetic.*

e·lec·tro·a·cous·tic /iˌlektrōəˈkōōstik/ ▶*adj.* involving the direct conversion of electrical into acoustic energy or vice versa. ■ (of a guitar) having both a pickup and a reverberating hollow body.
▶*n.* an electroacoustic guitar.

e·lec·tro·ac·u·punc·ture (also **e·lec·tro·ac·u·punc·ture**) ▶*n.* acupuncture in which the needles used carry a mild electric current.

e·lec·tro·car·di·o·gram /iˌlektrōˈkärdēəˌgram/ (abbr.: **ECG** or **EKG**) ▶*n. Medicine* a record or display of a person's heartbeat produced by electrocardiography.

e·lec·tro·car·di·o·graph /iˌlektrōˈkärdiəˌgraf/ (abbr.: **ECG** or **EKG**) ▶*n.* a machine used for electrocardiography.

e·lec·tro·car·di·og·ra·phy /iˌlektrōˌkärdēˈägrəfē/ (abbr.: **ECG** or **EKG**) ▶*n.* the measurement of electrical activity in the heart and the recording of such activity as a visual trace (on paper or on an oscilloscope screen), using electrodes placed on the skin of the limbs and chest. **—e·lec·tro·car·di·o·graph·ic** /-ˌkärdiəˈgrafik/ *adj.*

e·lec·tro·cau·ter·y /iˌlektrōˈkôtərē/ ▶*n.* cautery using a needle or other instrument that is electrically heated.

e·lec·tro·chem·is·try /iˌlektrōˈkemistrē/ ▶*n.* the branch of chemistry that deals with the relations between electrical and chemical phenomena. **—e·lec·tro·chem·i·cal** /-ˈkemikəl/ *adj.* **—e·lec·tro·chem·i·cal·ly** /-ˈkemik(ə)lē/ *adv.* **—e·lec·tro·chem·ist** *n.*

e·lec·tro·chrom·ism /iˌlektrōˈkrōˌmizəm/ ▶*n. Chemistry* the property of certain dyes of changing color when placed in an electric field. **—e·lec·tro·chro·mic** /-ˈkrōmik/ *adj.*

e·lec·tro·co·ag·u·la·tion /iˈlektrōkōˌagyəˈlāsHən/ ▶*n.* the coagulation of blood or other tissues by the local application of an electric current to produce concentrated heat.

e·lec·tro·con·vul·sive /iˌlektrōkənˈvəlsiv/ ▶*adj.* of or relating to the treatment of mental illness by the application of electric shocks to the brain.

e·lec·tro·cor·ti·co·gram /iˌlektrōˈkôrtikōˌgram/ ▶*n. Physiology* a chart or record of the electrical activity of the brain made using electrodes in direct contact with it.

e·lec·tro·cute /iˈlektrəˌkyōōt/ ▶*v.* [*trans.*] (often **be electrocuted**) injure or kill someone by electric shock: *a man was electrocuted when he switched on the Christmas tree lights.* ■ execute (a convicted criminal) by means of the electric chair. ▷late 19th cent.: from **ELECTRO-**, on the pattern of *execute.* **—e·lec·tro·cu·tion** /iˌlektrəˈkyōōsHən/ *n.*

e·lec·tro·cyte /iˈlektrəˌsīt/ ▶*n. Zoology* a modified muscle or nerve cell that generates electricity in the electric organ of certain fishes.

e·lec·trode /iˈlektrōd/ ▶*n.* a conductor through which electricity enters or leaves an object, substance, or region. ▷mid 19th cent.: from **ELECTRIC** + Greek *hodos* 'way,' on the pattern of *anode* and *cathode.*

e·lec·tro·der·mal /iˌlektrōˈdərməl/ ▶*adj.* of or relating to measurement of the electrical conductivity of the skin, esp. as an indicator of someone's emotional responses.

e·lec·tro·di·al·y·sis /iˌlektrōdīˈaləsis/ ▶*n. Chemistry* dialysis in which the movement of ions is aided by an electric field applied across the semipermeable membrane.

e·lec·tro·dy·nam·ics /iˌlektrōdīˈnamiks/ ▶*plural n.* [usu. treated as *sing.*] the branch of mechanics concerned with the interaction of electric currents with magnetic fields or with other electric currents. **—e·lec·tro·dy·nam·ic** *adj.*

e·lec·tro·dy·na·mom·e·ter /iˌlektrōˌdīnəˈmämitər/ ▶*n.* an instrument that measures electric current by indicating the strength of repulsion or attraction between the magnetic fields of two sets of coils, one fixed and one movable.

e·lec·tro·en·ceph·a·lo·gram /i,lektrōən'sefələ,gram/ (abbr.: **EEG**) ▸*n.* a test or record of brain activity produced by electroencephalography.

e·lec·tro·en·ceph·a·lo·graph /i,lektrōən'sefələ,graf/ (abbr.: **EEG**) ▸*n.* a machine used for electroencephalography.

e·lec·tro·en·ceph·a·log·ra·phy /i,lektrōən,sefə'lägrəfē/ (abbr.: **EEG**) ▸*n.* the measurement of electrical activity in different parts of the brain and the recording of such activity as a visual trace (on paper or on an oscilloscope screen).

e·lec·tro·fish /i'lektrə,fisH/ ▸*v.* [*trans.*] fish (a stretch of water) using electrocution or a weak electric field.

e·lec·tro·fu·sion /i,lektrō'fyōōzHən/ ▸*n.* fusion (in cells or other materials) that is induced by the application of electric current: *the shell and center are joined by electrofusion, with the reconstructed embryo retaining most of the mother's DNA.*

e·lec·tro·gen·ic /i,lektrō'jenik/ ▸*adj. Physiology* producing a change in the electrical potential of a cell.

e·lec·tro·jet /i'lektrə,jet/ ▸*n.* an intense electric current that occurs in a narrow belt in the lower ionosphere, esp. in the region of strong auroral displays.

e·lec·tro·ki·net·ic /i,lektrōkə'netik/ ▸*adj.* of or relating to the flow of electricity.

e·lec·tro·less /i'lektrōlis/ ▸*adj.* relating to or denoting nickel plating using chemical means, as opposed to electroplating.

e·lec·tro·lier /i,lektrə'lir/ ▸*n.* a chandelier in which the lights are electrical. ▹late 19th cent.: from ELECTRO-, on the pattern of *chandelier.*

e·lec·trol·o·gist /ilek'träləjist/ ▸*n.* a person trained to remove unwanted hair on the body or face or small blemishes on the skin by a method that involves the application of heat using an electric current.

e·lec·tro·lu·mi·nes·cence /i,lektrō,lōōmə'nesəns/ ▸*n. Chemistry* luminescence produced electrically, esp. in a phosphor by the application of a voltage. **—e·lec·tro·lu·mi·nes·cent** *adj.*

e·lec·trol·y·sis /ilek'träləsis; ,ēlek-/ ▸*n.* **1** *Chemistry* chemical decomposition produced by passing an electric current through a liquid or solution containing ions. **2** the removal of hair roots or small blemishes on the skin by the application of heat using an electric current. **—e·lec·tro·lyt·ic** /i,lektrə'litik/ *adj.* **—e·lec·tro·lyt·i·cal** /i,lektrə'litikəl/ *adj.* **—e·lec·tro·lyt·i·cal·ly** /i,lektrə'litik(ə)lē/ *adv.*

e·lec·tro·lyte /i'lektrə,līt/ ▸*n.* a liquid or gel that contains ions and can be decomposed by electrolysis, e.g., that present in a battery. ▪ (usu. **electrolytes**) *Physiology* the ionized or ionizable constituents of a living cell, blood, or other organic matter. ▹mid 19th cent.: from ELECTRO- + Greek *lutos* 'released' (from *luein* 'loosen').

e·lec·tro·lyt·ic cell /i,lektə'litik/ ▸*n.* **1** a cell in which electrolysis occurs, consisting of an electrolyte through which current from an external source is passed, by a system of electrodes, in order to produce an electrochemical reaction. **2** a cell consisting of an electrolyte, its container, and two electrodes, in which the electrochemical reaction between the electrodes and the electrolyte produces an electric current.

e·lec·tro·lyze /i'lektrə,līz/ ▸*v.* [*trans.*] subject to or treat by electrolysis: *when you electrolyze water, it splits into hydrogen and oxygen.* ▹mid 19th cent.: from ELECTROLYSIS, on the pattern of *analyze.* **—e·lec·tro·lyz·er** *n.*

e·lec·tro·mag·net /i,lektrō'magnit/ ▸*n. Physics* a soft metal core made into a magnet by the passage of electric current through a coil surrounding it.

e·lec·tro·mag·net·ic /i,lektrōmag'netik/ ▸*adj.* of or relating to the interrelation of electric currents or fields and magnetic fields. **—e·lec·tro·mag·net·i·cal·ly** /-(ə)lē/ *adv.*

e·lec·tro·mag·net·ic field ▸*n. Physics* a field of force that consists of both electric and magnetic components, resulting from the motion of an electric charge and containing a definite amount of electromagnetic energy.

e·lec·tro·mag·net·ic pulse ▸*n.* an intense pulse of electromagnetic radiation, esp. one generated by a nuclear explosion and occurring high above the earth's surface.

e·lec·tro·mag·net·ic ra·di·a·tion ▸*n. Physics* a kind of radiation including visible light, radio waves, gamma rays, and X-rays, in which electric and magnetic fields vary simultaneously.

e·lec·tro·mag·net·ic spec·trum ▸*n. Physics* the range of wavelengths or frequencies over which electromagnetic radiation extends.

e·lec·tro·mag·net·ic u·nits ▸*plural n. Physics* a largely obsolete system of electrical units derived primarily from the magnetic properties of electric currents.

e·lec·tro·mag·net·ism /i,lektrō'magnə,tizəm/ ▸*n.* the interaction of electric currents or fields and magnetic fields. ▪ the branch of physics concerned with this.

e·lec·tro·me·chan·i·cal /i,lektrōmə'kanikəl/ ▸*adj.* of, relating to, or denoting a mechanical device that is electrically operated.

e·lec·trom·e·ter /ilek'trämitər; ,ēlek-/ ▸*n. Physics* an instrument for measuring electrical potential without drawing any current from the circuit. **—e·lec·tro·met·ric** /i,lektrə'metrik/ *adj.* **—e·lec·trom·e·try** /-'trämitrē/ *n.*

e·lec·tro·mo·tive /i,lektrə'mōtiv/ ▸*adj. Physics* producing or tending to produce an electric current.

e·lec·tro·mo·tive force (abbr.: **emf**) ▸*n. Physics* a difference in potential that tends to give rise to an electric current.

e·lec·tro·my·o·gram /i,lektrō'mīə,gram/ ▸*n. Medicine* a record or display produced by electromyography.

e·lec·tro·my·og·ra·phy /i,lektrōmī'ägrəfē/ ▸*n.* the recording of the electrical activity of muscle tissue, or its representation as a visual display or audible signal, using electrodes attached to the skin or inserted into the muscle. **—e·lec·tro·my·o·graph** /-'mīə,graf/ *n.* **—e·lec·tro·my·o·graph·ic** /-,mīə'grafik/ *adj.* **—e·lec·tro·my·o·graph·i·cal·ly** /-,mīə'grafik(ə)lē/ *adv.*

e·lec·tron /i'lek,trän/ ▸*n. Physics* a stable subatomic particle with a charge of negative electricity, found in all atoms and acting as the primary carrier of electricity in solids.

> The electron's mass is about 9×10^{-28}g, 1,836 times less than that of the proton. Electrons orbit the positively charged nuclei of atoms and are responsible for binding atoms together in molecules and for the electrical, thermal, optical, and magnetic properties of solids. Electric currents in metals and in semiconductors consist of a flow of electrons, and light, radio waves, X-rays, and much heat radiation are all produced by accelerating and decelerating electrons.

▹late 19th cent.: from ELECTRIC + -ON.

e·lec·tron beam ▸*n. Physics* a stream of electrons in a gas or vacuum.

e·lec·tron-dense ▸*adj.* (of biological specimens) allowing the passage of few electrons, and so appearing dark in electron micrographs.

e·lec·tron dif·frac·tion ▸*n. Physics* the diffraction of a beam of electrons by atoms or molecules, used esp. for determining crystal structures.

e·lec·tro·neg·a·tive /i,lektrə'negətiv/ ▸*adj.* **1** *Physics* electrically negative. **2** *Chemistry* (of an element) tending to acquire electrons and form negative ions in chemical reactions. **—e·lec·tro·neg·a·tiv·i·ty** /i,lektrō,negə'tivitē; ē',lektrō,negə'tivədē/ *n.* (sense 2).

e·lec·tron gun ▸*n. Physics* a device for producing a narrow stream of electrons from a heated cathode.

e·lec·tron·ic /ilek'tränik; ,ēlek-/ ▸*adj.* **1** (of a device) having or operating with the aid of many small components, esp. microchips and transistors, that control and direct an electric current: *an electronic calculator.* ▪ (of music) produced by electronic instruments. ▪ of or relating to electronics: *a degree in electronic engineering.* **2** of or relating to electrons. **3** relating to or carried out using a computer or other electronic device, esp. over a network: *electronic banking.* ▹early 20th cent.: from ELECTRON + -IC. **—e·lec·tron·i·cal·ly** /-(ə)lē/ *adv.*

e·lec·tron·ic flash ▸*n. Photography* a flash from a gas-discharge tube, used in high-speed photography.

e·lec·tron·ic mail ▸*n.* another term for E-MAIL.

e·lec·tron·ic mu·sic ▸*n.* music performed using synthesizers and other electronic instruments.

e·lec·tron·ic or·gan·iz·er ▸*n.* a pocket-sized computer used for storing and retrieving information such as addresses and appointments.

e·lec·tron·ic pub·lish·ing ▸*n.* the issuing of books and other material in machine-readable form rather than on paper.

e·lec·tron·ics /ilek'träniks; ,ēlek-/ ▸*plural n.* [usu. treated as *sing.*] the branch of physics and technology concerned with the design of circuits using transistors and microchips, and with the behavior and movement of electrons in a semiconductor, conductor, vacuum, or gas: *electronics is seen as a growth industry* | [as *adj.*] *electronics engineers.* ▪ [treated as *pl.*] circuits or devices using transistors, microchips, and other components.

e·lec·tron·ic tag·ging ▸*n.* the attaching of electronic markers to people or goods for monitoring purposes, e.g., to track offenders under house arrest or to deter shoplifters.

e·lec·tron lens ▸*n. Physics* a device for focusing a stream of electrons by means of electric or magnetic fields.

e·lec·tron mi·cro·scope ▸*n. Physics* a microscope with high magnification and resolution, employing electron beams in place of light and using electron lenses.

e·lec·tron op·tics ▸*plural n.* [treated as *sing.*] the branch of physics that deals with the behavior of electrons and electron beams in magnetic and electric fields.

e·lec·tron pair ▸*n.* **1** *Chemistry* two electrons occupying the same orbital in an atom or molecule. **2** *Physics* an electron and a positron produced in a high-energy reaction.

e·lec·tron spin res·o·nance (abbr.: **ESR**) ▸*n. Physics* a spectroscopic method of locating electrons within the molecules of a paramagnetic substance.

e·lec·tron tube ▸*n. Physics* an evacuated or gas-filled tube in which a current of electrons flows between electrodes.

e·lec·tron volt (abbr.: **eV**) ▸*n. Physics* a unit of energy equal to the work done on an electron in accelerating it through a potential difference of one volt.

e·lec·tro·oc·u·lo·gram /i,lektrō'äkyələ,gram/ ▸*n.* a record produced by electrooculography.

e·lec·tro·oc·u·log·ra·phy /i,lektrō,äkyə'lägrəfē/ ▸*n.* the measurement of the electrical potential between electrodes placed at points close to the eye, used to investigate eye movements esp. in physiological research. **—e·lec·tro·oc·u·lo·graph·ic** /-lə'grafik/ *adj.*

e·lec·tro·op·tics /i,lektrō'äptiks/ ▸*plural n.* [treated as *sing.*] the branch of science that deals with the effect of electric fields on light and on the optical properties of substances. **—e·lec·tro·op·tic** *adj.* **—e·lec·tro·op·ti·cal** /-'äptikəl/ *adj.*

e·lec·tro·os·mo·sis /i,lektrō-äz'mōsis; -äs-/ ▸*n.* osmosis under the influence of an electric field. **—e·lec·tro·os·mot·ic** /-'mätik/ *adj.*

e·lec·tro·phil·ic /i,lektrə'filik/ ▸*adj. Chemistry* (of a molecule or group) having a tendency to attract or acquire electrons. Often contrasted with NUCLEOPHILIC. **—e·lec·tro·phile** /i'lektrə,fīl/ *n.*

e·lec·tro·pho·re·sis /i,lektrəfə'rēsis/ ▸*n. Physics & Chemistry* the movement of charged particles in a fluid or gel under the influence of an electric field. ▹early 20th cent.: from ELECTRO- + Greek *phorēsis* 'being carried.' **—e·lec·tro·pho·rese** /-'rēs/ *v.* **—e·lec·tro·pho·ret·ic** /-'retik/ *adj.* **—e·lec·tro·pho·ret·i·cal·ly** /-'retik(ə)lē/ *adv.*

e·lec·troph·o·rus /i,lek'träfərəs/ ▸*n. Physics* a device for repeatedly generating static electricity by induction. ▹late 18th cent.: from ELECTRO- + Greek *-phoros* 'bearing.'

e·lec·tro·phys·i·ol·o·gy /i,lektrō,fizē'äləjē/ ▸*n.* the branch of physiology that deals with the electrical phenomena associated with nervous and other bodily activity. **—e·lec·tro·phys·i·o·log·i·cal** /-,fizēə'läjikəl/ *adj.* **—e·lec·tro·phys·i·o·log·i·cal·ly** /-,fizēə'läjik(ə)lē/ *adv.* **—e·lec·tro·phys·i·ol·o·gist** /-jist/ *n.*

e·lec·tro·plate /i'lektrə,plāt/ ▸*v.* [*trans.*] [usu. as *n.*] (**electroplating**) coat (a metal object) by electrolytic deposition with chromium, silver, or another metal. ▸*n.* electroplated articles. **—e·lec·tro·plat·er** *n.*

e·lec·tro·plax /i'lektrō,plaks/ (also **e·lec·tro·plaque** /-,plak/) ▸*n. Zoology* each of a number of flattened plates of protoplasm that make up the electric organ of certain fishes, e.g., the electric eel.

e·lec·tro·pol·ish /i'lektrō,pälisH/ ▸*v.* [*trans.*] [often as *n.*] (**electropolishing**) give a shiny surface to (metal) using electrolysis.

e·lec·tro·po·ra·tion /i,lektrōpə'rāsHən/ ▸*n. Biology* the action or process of introducing DNA or chromosomes into bacteria or other cells using a pulse of electricity to briefly open the pores in the cell membranes. **—e·lec·tro·po·rate** /-'pôr,āt/ *v.*

e·lec·tro·pos·i·tive /i,lektrə'päzitiv/ ▸*adj.* **1** *Physics* electrically positive. **2** *Chemistry* (of an element) tending to lose electrons and form positive ions in chemical reactions.

e·lec·tro·re·cep·tion /i,lektrōri'sepsHən/ ▸*n.* the detection by an aquatic animal of electric fields or currents. **—e·lec·tro·re·cep·tor** /-'septər/ *n.*

e·lec·tro·ret·i·no·gram /i,lektrō'retn-ō,gram/ ▸*n.* a record of the electrical activity of the retina, used in medical diagnosis and research.

e·lec·tro·scope /i'lektrə,skōp/ ▶*n. Physics* an instrument for detecting and measuring electricity, esp. as an indication of the ionization of air by radioactivity. —**e·lec·tro·scop·ic** /i,lektrə'skäpik/ *adj.*

e·lec·tro·shock /i'lektrə,SHäk/ ▶*adj.* [*attrib.*] of or relating to medical treatment by means of electric shocks: *electroshock therapy.*

e·lec·tro·so·mat·ic /i,lektrōsə'matik/ ▶*adj.* **1** pertaining to electronic devices implanted in an organism. **2** pertaining to electrical fields within an organism.

e·lec·tro·stat·ic /i,lektrə'statik/ ▶*adj. Physics* of or relating to stationary electric charges or fields as opposed to electric currents. ▷mid 19th cent.: from ELECTRO- + STATIC, on the pattern of *hydrostatic.*

e·lec·tro·stat·ic gen·er·a·tor ▶*n.* any of various devices used to build up an electric charge to an extreme potential in order to generate electricity, esp. the Van de Graaf generator.

e·lec·tro·stat·ic pre·cip·i·ta·tor ▶*n.* a device that removes suspended dust particles from a gas or exhaust by applying a high-voltage electrostatic charge and collecting the particles on charged plates.

e·lec·tro·stat·ics /i,lektrə'statiks/ ▶*plural n.* [treated as *sing.*] *Physics* the study of stationary electric charges or fields as opposed to electric currents.

e·lec·tro·stat·ic u·nits ▶*plural n.* a system of units based primarily on the forces between electric charges.

e·lec·tro·sur·ger·y /i,lektrō'sərjərē/ ▶*n.* surgery using a high-frequency electric current to heat and so cut tissue with great precision. —**e·lec·tro·sur·gi·cal** /-'sərjikəl/ *adj.*

e·lec·tro·tech·nol·o·gy /i,lektrōtek'näləjē/ (also **e·lec·tro·tech·nics** /-'tekniks/) ▶*n.* the science of the application of electricity in technology. —**e·lec·tro·tech·nic** /-'teknik/ *adj.* —**e·lec·tro·tech·ni·cal** /-'teknikəl/ *adj.*

e·lec·tro·ther·a·py /i,lektrō'THerəpē/ ▶*n.* the use of electric currents passed through the body to stimulate nerves and muscles, chiefly in the treatment of various forms of paralysis. —**e·lec·tro·ther·a·peu·tic** /-,THerə'pyōōtik/ *adj.* —**e·lec·tro·ther·a·peu·ti·cal** /-,THerə'pyōōtikəl/ *adj.* —**e·lec·tro·ther·a·pist** /-pist/ *n.*

e·lec·tro·ther·mal /i,lektrə'THərməl/ ▶*adj. Physics* of or relating to heat derived from electricity.

e·lec·tro·type /i'lektrə,tīp/ ▶*v.* [*trans.*] [often as *n.*] (**electrotyping**) make a copy of (something) by the electrolytic deposition of copper on a mold.
▶*n.* a copy made in such a way. —**e·lec·tro·typ·er** *n.*

e·lec·tro·va·lent /i,lektrə'vālənt/ ▶*adj. Chemistry* (of bonding) resulting from electrostatic attraction between positive and negative ions; ionic. ▷1920s: from ELECTRO- + *-valent,* on the pattern of *trivalent.* —**e·lec·tro·va·lence** *n.* —**e·lec·tro·va·len·cy** *n.*

e·lec·tro·weak /i'lektrō,wēk/ ▶*adj. Physics* relating to or denoting electromagnetic and weak interactions regarded as manifestations of the same interaction.

e·lec·trum /i'lektrəm/ ▶*n.* a natural or artificial alloy of gold with at least 20 percent silver, used for jewelry, esp. in ancient times. ▷late Middle English: via Latin from Greek *ēlektron* 'amber, electrum.'

e·lec·tu·ar·y /i'lekCHōō,erē/ ▶*n.* (*pl.* **-ar·ies**) *archaic* a medicinal substance mixed with honey or another sweet substance. ▷late Middle English: from late Latin *electuarium,* probably from Greek *ekleikton,* from *ekleikhein* 'lick up.'

el·ee·mos·y·nar·y /,elə'mäsə,nerē; ,elēə-/ ▶*adj.* of, relating to, or dependent on charity; charitable. ▷late 16th cent. (as a noun denoting a place where alms were distributed): from medieval Latin *eleemosynarius,* from late Latin *eleemosyna* 'alms,' from Greek *eleēmosunē* 'compassion'(see ALMS).

el·e·gan·cy /'eligənsē/ ▶*n.* **1** graceful and stylish appearance or manner; elegance. **2** something that is elegant: *I do hope you will study a little of the proprieties and elegancies of life.*

el·e·gant /'eləgənt/ ▶*adj.* pleasingly graceful and stylish in appearance or manner: *she will look elegant in black | an elegant, comfortable house.* ■ (of a scientific theory or solution to a problem) pleasingly ingenious and simple: *the grand unified theory is compact and elegant in mathematical terms.* ▷late 15th cent. (describing a person dressing tastefully): from French, or from Latin *elegans, elegant-,* related to *eligere* 'choose, select' (see ELECT). —**el·e·gance** *n.* —**el·e·gant·ly** *adv.*

el·e·gant var·i·a·tion ▶*n.* the stylistic fault of studiedly finding different ways to denote the same thing in a piece of writing, merely to avoid repetition.

el·e·gi·ac /,elə'jīək; e'lējē,ak/ ▶*adj.* (esp. of a work of art) having a mournful quality: *the movie score is a somber effort, elegiac in its approach.* ■ (of a poetic meter) used for elegies.
▶*plural n.* (**elegiacs**) verses in an elegiac meter. ▷late 16th cent.: from French *élégiaque,* or via late Latin, from Greek *elegeiakos,* from *elegeia* (see ELEGY). —**el·e·gi·a·cal·ly** /,elə'jīək(ə)lē/ *adv.*

el·e·gi·ac cou·plet ▶*n.* a pair of lines consisting of a dactylic hexameter and a pentameter, esp. in Greek and Latin verse.

el·e·gi·ac stan·za ▶*n.* a quatrain in iambic pentameter rhymed *abab.* Compare with HEROIC STANZA.

el·e·gize /'elə,jīz/ ▶*v.* [*intrans.*] write in a wistfully mournful way about someone or something. —**el·e·gist** /-jist/ *n.*

el·e·gy /'eləjē/ ▶*n.* (*pl.* **-gies**) **1** a poem of serious reflection, typically a lament for the dead. ■ a piece of music in a mournful style. **2** (in Greek and Roman poetry) a poem written in elegiac couplets, as notably by Catullus and Propertius. ▷early 16th cent.: from French *élégie,* or via Latin, from Greek *elegeia,* from *elegos* 'mournful poem.'

elem. ▶*abbr.* elementary.

el·e·ment /'eləmənt/ ▶*n.* **1** a part or aspect of something abstract, esp. one that is essential or characteristic: *the death had* **all the elements of** *a great tabloid story | there are four elements to the proposal.* ■ a small but significant presence of a feeling or abstract quality: *it was the element of danger he loved in flying.* ■ (**elements**) the rudiments of a branch of knowledge: *legal training may include the elements of economics and political science.* ■ [usu. with *adj.*] (often **elements**) a group of people of a particular kind within a larger group or organization: *extreme right-wing elements in the army.* ■ *Mathematics & Logic* an entity that is a single member of a set. **2** (also **chemical element**) each of more than one hundred substances that cannot be chemically interconverted or broken down into simpler substances and are primary constituents of matter. Each element is distinguished by its atomic number, i.e., the number of protons in the nuclei of its atoms. ■ any of the four substances (earth, water, air, and fire) regarded as the fundamental constituents of the world in ancient and medieval philosophy. ■ one of these substances considered as a person's or animal's natural environment: *for the islanders, the sea is their kingdom, water their element | figurative she* **was in her element** *with doctors and hospitals.* ■ (**the elements**) the weather, esp. strong winds, heavy rain, and other kinds of bad weather: *there was no barrier against the elements.* ■ (**elements**) (in church use) the bread and wine of the Eucharist. **3** a part in an electric teapot, heater, or stove that contains a wire through which an electric current is passed to provide heat. ■ on some electric typewriters, a ball with raised letters that print when the keys are pressed. ▷Middle English (denoting fundamental constituents of the world or celestial objects): via Old French from Latin *elementum* 'principle, rudiment,' translating Greek *stoikheion* 'step, component part.'

el·e·men·tal /,elə'mentl/ ▶*adj.* **1** primary or basic: *elemental features from which all other structures are compounded.* ■ concerned with chemical elements or other basic components: *elemental analysis.* ■ consisting of a single chemical element. **2** related to or embodying the powers of nature: *a thunderstorm is the inevitable outcome of battling elemental forces.* ■ *figurative* (of a human emotion or action) having the primitive and inescapable character of a force of nature: *the urge for revenge was too elemental to be ignored.*
▶*n.* a supernatural entity or force thought to be physically manifested by occult means. ▷late 15th cent.: from medieval Latin *elementalis,* from *elementum* 'principle, rudiment' (see ELEMENT). —**el·e·men·tal·ism** /-,izəm/ *n.*

el·e·men·ta·ry /,elə'ment(ə)rē/ ▶*adj.* of or relating to the most rudimentary aspects of a subject: *the six stages take students from elementary to advanced level.* ■ easily dealt with; straightforward and uncomplicated: *it's interesting work, although a lot of it is elementary.* ■ not decomposable into elements or other primary constituents. ▷late Middle English (in the sense 'composed of the four elements, earth, air, fire, and water'): from Latin *elementarius,* from *elementum* 'principle, rudiment' (see ELEMENT). Current senses dates from the mid 16th cent. —**el·e·men·tar·i·ly** /-rəlē/ *adv.* —**el·e·men·ta·ri·ness** *n.*

el·e·men·ta·ry par·ti·cle ▶*n.* any of various fundamental subatomic particles, including those that are the smallest and most basic constituents of matter (leptons and quarks) or are combinations of these (hadrons, which consist of quarks), and those that transmit one of the four fundamental interactions in nature (gravitational, electromagnetic, strong, and weak). Compare with SUBATOMIC PARTICLE, and see BARYON, BOSON, GLUON, GRAVITON, MESON, PHOTON, W PARTICLE, Z PARTICLE.

el·e·men·ta·ry school ▶*n.* a school for the first four to six grades, and usually including kindergarten.

el·e·mi /'eləmē/ ▶*n.* an oleoresin obtained from a tropical tree and used in varnishes, ointments, and aromatherapy. • This resin is obtained from several trees in the family Burseraceae, in particular *Bursera simaruba* (producing **American elemi**) and *Canarium luzanicum* (producing **Manila elemi**). ▷mid 16th cent.: perhaps from Arabic *al-lāmī.*

e·len·chus /i'leNGkəs/ ▶*n.* (*pl.* **-chi** /-kī; -kē/) *Logic* a logical refutation. See also IGNORATIO ELENCHI. ■ (also **Socratic elenchus**) the Socratic method of eliciting truth by question and answer, esp. as used to refute an argument. ▷mid 17th cent. (superseding late Middle English *elench*): via Latin from Greek *elenkhos.*

el·e·phant /'eləfənt/ ▶*n.* (*pl.* same or **-phants**) **1** a heavy plant-eating mammal with a prehensile trunk, long curved ivory tusks, and large ears, native to Africa and southern Asia. It is the largest living land animal. • Family Elephantidae, order Proboscidea: two species. See AFRICAN ELEPHANT, INDIAN ELEPHANT. **2** *chiefly Brit.* a size of paper, now standardized at 28 × 23 inches (approximately 711 × 584 mm). ▷Middle English: from Old French *elefant,* via Latin from Greek *elephas, elephant-* 'ivory, elephant.' —**el·e·phan·toid** /,elə'fantoid; 'eləfən,toid/ *adj.*

African elephant Indian elephant

elephants

el·e·phant bird ▶*n.* a heavily built, giant flightless bird, found in Madagascar until it was exterminated in about AD 1000. The eggs, which are still found occasionally, are the largest known. Also called AEPYORNIS. • Family Aepyornithidae, genera *Aepyornis* and *Mullerornis*: several species, including *A. maximus.*

el·e·phant ear ▶*n.* any of a number of plants with large heart-shaped leaves.

el·e·phant grass ▶*n.* a tall robust tropical African grass that is used for fodder and paper. Also called NAPIER GRASS. • *Pennisetum purpureum,* family Gramineae.

el·e·phan·ti·a·sis /,eləfən'tīəsis/ ▶*n. Medicine* a condition in which a limb or other part of the body becomes grossly enlarged due to obstruction of the lymphatic vessels, typically by the nematode parasites that cause filariasis. ▷mid 16th cent.: via Latin from Greek, from *elephas, elephant-* 'elephant' + -IASIS.

el·e·phan·tine /,elə'fantēn; -,tīn; 'eləfən,tēn; -,tīn/ ▶*adj.* of, resembling, or characteristic of an elephant or elephants, esp. in being large, clumsy, or awkward: *there was an elephantine thud from the bathroom.* ▷early 17th cent.: via Latin from Greek *elephantinos,* from *elephas, elephant-* 'elephant.'

el·e·phant seal ▶*n.* a large seal that breeds on the west coast of North America and the islands around Antarctica. The male is much larger than the female and has a very thick neck and an inflatable snout. • Genus *Mirounga,* family Phocidae: two species.

El·eu·sin·i·an mys·ter·ies /,elyōō'sinēən/ ▶*plural n.* the annual rites performed by the ancient Greeks at the village of Eleusis near Athens in honor of Demeter and Persephone.

E·leu·ther·a /i'lōōTHərə/ an island in the central Bahamas, over 100 miles (160 km) long; pop. 9,000. It was settled by the British in the 1640s.

elev. ▶*abbr.* elevation.

el·e·vate /'elə,vāt/ ▶*v.* [*trans.*] raise or lift (something) up to a higher position: *the exercise will naturally elevate your chest and head.* ■ raise to a more important or impressive level: *in the 1920s he was* **elevated to**

secretary of state | exotic toppings elevate a pizza from fast food to fine food. ■ (of a priest) hold up (a consecrated host or chalice) for adoration. ■ increase the level or amount of (something, esp. the level of a component of a person's blood): *high amounts of the drug can elevate blood pressure.* ■ raise the axis of (a piece of artillery) to increase its range. ▷late Middle English: from Latin *elevat-* 'raised,' from the verb *elevare*, from *e-* (variant of *ex-*) 'out, away' + *levare* 'lighten' (from *levis* 'light'). **—el·e·va·to·ry** /-və,tôrē/ *adj.*

el·e·vat·ed /'elə,vātid/ ▸*adj.* situated or placed higher than the surrounding area: *this hotel has an elevated position above the village.* ■ (of a road or railroad) raised on supports above the surrounding area: *the elevated section of the freeway.* ■ (of a level or amount) higher or greater than what is considered normal: *an elevated temperature.* ■ of a high intellectual or moral standard or level: *the elevated canon of great literary texts.* ■ having a high rank or social standing: *a suitably elevated occupation.*
▸*n.* an elevated railroad.

el·e·va·tion /,elə'vāsʜən/ ▸*n.* **1** the action or fact of elevating or being elevated: *her sudden elevation to the cabinet.* ■ augmentation of or increase in the amount or level of something: ■ (in a Christian Mass) the raising of the consecrated elements for adoration. **2** height above a given level, esp. sea level: *a network of microclimates created by sharp differences in elevation | a total elevation gain of 3,995 feet.* ■ a high place or position: *most early plantation development was at the higher elevations.* ■ the angle of something with the horizontal, esp. of a gun or of the direction of a celestial object. ■ *Ballet* the ability of a dancer to attain height in jumps. **3** a particular side of a building: *a burglar alarm was prominently displayed on the front elevation.* ■ a drawing of the front, side, or back of a house or other building: *a set of plans and elevations.* ■ a drawing or diagram, esp. of a building, made by projection on a vertical plane. Compare with **PLAN** (sense 3). ▷late Middle English: from Latin *elevatio(n-)*, from *elevare* 'raise' (see **ELEVATE**). **—el·e·va·tion·al** /-sʜənl; -sʜnəl/ *adj.*

el·e·va·tor /'elə,vātər/ ▸*n.* **1** a platform or compartment housed in a shaft for raising and lowering people or things to different floors or levels: *in the elevator she pressed the button for the lobby.* ■ a machine consisting of an endless belt with scoops attached, used typically for raising grain to be stored in an upper story: *a grain elevator.* ■ a tall building used for storing large quantities of grain. **2** a hinged flap on the horizontal stabilizer of an aircraft, typically one of a pair, used to control the motion of the aircraft about its lateral axis. **3** a muscle whose contraction raises a part of the body: *elevators of the upper lip.* **4** (also **elevator shoe**) a shoe with a raised insole designed to make the wearer appear taller. ▷mid 17th cent. (denoting a levator muscle): modern Latin, from Latin *elevare* 'raise'; in later use directly from **ELEVATE**.

e·lev·en /i'levən/ ▸*cardinal number* equivalent to the sum of six and five; one more than ten; 11: *the room was about eleven feet wide | eighteen schools were founded, eleven of them in Los Angeles.* (Roman numeral: **xi** or **XI**.) ■ eleven years old: *the eldest is only eleven.* ■ eleven o'clock: *she often worked until eleven at night.* ■ a size of garment or other merchandise denoted by eleven. ■ a group or unit of eleven people or things. ■ a sports team of eleven players. ▷Old English *endleofon*, from the base of **ONE** + a second element (probably expressing the sense 'left over') occurring also in **TWELVE**; of Germanic origin and related to Dutch and German *elf*. **—e·lev·en·fold** /-,fōld/ *adj.* & *adv.*

e·lev·ens·es /i'levənziz/ ▸*plural n. Brit., informal* a short break for light refreshments, usually with tea or coffee, taken about eleven o'clock in the morning.

e·lev·enth /i'levənтн/ ▸*ordinal number* constituting number eleven in a sequence; 11th: *the eleventh century | February the eleventh | the eleventh fairway of a tiny golf course.* ■ (**an eleventh/one eleventh**) each of eleven equal parts into which something is or may be divided. ■ the eleventh grade of a school. ■ *Music* an interval or chord spanning an octave plus a fourth in the diatonic scale, or a note separated from another by this interval.
▸*PHRASE* □ **the eleventh hour** the latest possible moment: *he refused to take a public stand until the eleventh hour of the campaign.*

el·e·von /'elə,vän/ ▸*n. Aeronautics* the movable part of the trailing edge of a delta wing. ▷1940s: blend of **ELEVATOR** and **AILERON** (because the elevon combines the functions of both).

ELF ▸*abbr.* extremely low frequency.

elf /elf/ ▸*n.* (*pl.* **elves** /elvz/) a supernatural creature of folk tales, typically represented as a small, elusive figure in human form with pointed ears, magical powers, and a capricious nature. ▷Old English, of Germanic origin; related to German *Alp* 'nightmare.' **—elf·ish** *adj.* **—elv·en** /'elvən/ *adj.* (*poetic/literary*) **—elv·ish** /'elvisʜ/ *adj.*

El Fai·yum /,el fä'(y)o͞om; fī-/ (also **Fayum** or **Al Fayyum**) a historic oasis town in northern Egypt, southwest of Cairo; pop. 244,000.

elf·in /'elfən/ ▸*adj.* small and delicate, typically with an attractively mischievous or strange charm: *she looked up at him with an elfin grin.*
▸*n.* **1** *archaic* an elf. **2** a small North American butterfly that is typically brownish with markings on the wing margins that give the impression of scalloped edges. • Genus *Incisalia*, family Lycaenidae. ▷late 16th cent.: from **ELF**, probably suggested by Middle English *elvene* 'of elves,' and by *Elphin*, the name of a character in Arthurian romance.

elf·locks /'elf,läks/ ▸*plural n.* a tangled mass of hair.

elf owl ▸*n.* a tiny owl that nests in cacti and trees in the arid country of the southern U.S. and Mexico. • *Micrathene whitneyi*, family Strigidae.

El·gar /'el,gär; -gər/, Sir Edward (William) (1857–1934), British composer. He is known for the five *Pomp and Circumstance* marches (1901–30).

El·gin /'eljin/ an industrial city in northeastern Illinois, west of Chicago, formerly noted for its watch manufacturing; pop. 94,487.

El·gin Mar·bles /'elgin 'märbəlz; -jin/ a collection of classical Greek marble sculptures and architectural fragments, chiefly from the Parthenon in Athens, brought to England by the diplomat and art connoisseur Thomas Bruce (1766–1841), the 7th Earl of Elgin.

Executed by Phidias in the 5th century BC, the sculptures were brought from Greece between 1803 and 1812, when the country was under Turkish control. They are currently housed in the British Museum, but are the subject of a repatriation request from the Greek government, which does not accept the legality of the Turkish sale.

El Gi·za /el 'gēzə/ another name for **GIZA**.

El Gre·co /el 'grekō/ (1541–1614), Spanish painter; born on Crete; born *Domenikos Theotokopoulos.* His portraits and religious works are characterized by distorted perspective, elongated figures, and strident use of color. In Spanish, his name means "the Greek."

el·hi /'el'hī/ ▸*adj. informal* of, relating to, or intended for use in grades 1 to 12.

E·li /'ēlī/ (in the Bible) a priest who acted as a teacher to the prophet Samuel (1 Sam. 1–3).

E·li·a /'ēlēə/ the pseudonym adopted by Charles Lamb in his *Essays of Elia* (1823) and *Last Essays of Elia* (1833).

e·lic·it /i'lisit/ ▸*v.* (**-it·ed, -it·ing**) [*trans.*] evoke or draw out (a response, answer, or fact) from someone in reaction to one's own actions or questions: *they invariably elicit exclamations of approval from guests.* ■ *archaic* draw forth (something that is latent or potential) into existence: *a corrupt heart elicits in an hour all that is bad in us.* ▷mid 17th cent.: from Latin *elicit-* 'drawn out by trickery or magic,' from the verb *elicere*, from *e-* (variant of *ex-*) 'out' + *lacere* 'entice, deceive.' **—e·lic·i·ta·tion** /i,lisi'tāsʜən/ *n.* **—e·lic·i·tor** /-tər/ *n.*

e·lide /i'līd/ ▸*v.* [*trans.*] omit (a sound or syllable) when speaking: [as *adj.*] (**elided**) *the indication of elided consonants or vowels.* ■ join together; merge: *whole periods of time are* ***elided into*** *a few seconds of screen time* | [*intrans.*] *the two things elided in his mind.* ▷mid 16th cent. (in the sense 'annul, do away with,' chiefly as a Scots legal term): from Latin *elidere* 'crush out,' from *e-* (variant of *ex-*) 'out' + *laedere* 'to dash.'

USAGE The standard meaning of the verb **elide** is 'omit,' most frequently used as a term to describe the way that some sounds or syllables are dropped in speech, e.g., in contractions such as **I'll** or **he's**. The result of such omission (or **elision**) is that the two surrounding syllables are merged; this fact has given rise to a new sense, with the meaning 'join together, merge,' as in *the two things* ***elided*** *in his mind.* This new sense is now common in general use.

el·i·gi·ble /'eləjəbəl/ ▸*adj.* having the right to do or obtain something; satisfying the appropriate conditions: *customers who are* ***eligible for*** *discounts* | [with *infinitive*] *a foreign student is eligible to attend the school.* ■ (of a person) desirable or suitable as a partner in marriage: *the world's most eligible bachelor.* ▷late Middle English: via French from late Latin *eligibilis*, from Latin *eligere* 'choose, select' (see **ELECT**). **—el·i·gi·bil·i·ty** /,eləjə'bilitē/ *n.* **—el·i·gi·bly** /-blē/ *adv.*

E·li·jah /i'lījə/ (9th century BC), a Hebrew prophet in the time of Jezebel who maintained the worship of Jehovah against that of Baal and other pagan gods.

e·lim·i·nate /i'limə,nāt/ ▸*v.* [*trans.*] completely remove or get rid of (something): *a policy that would eliminate inflation.* ■ exclude (someone or something) from consideration: *the police have* ***eliminated*** *Larry* ***from*** *their inquiries.* ■ murder (a rival or political opponent). ■ (usu. **be eliminated**) exclude (a person or team) from further participation in a sporting competition following defeat or inadequate results: *the Bears were* ***eliminated from*** *the playoffs in the first round.* ■ *Mathematics* remove (a variable) from an equation, typically by substituting another that is shown by another equation to be equivalent. ■ *Chemistry* generate or remove (a simple substance) as a product in the course of a reaction involving larger molecules. ■ *Physiology* expel (waste matter) from the body. ▷mid 16th cent. (in the sense 'drive out, expel'): from Latin *eliminat-* 'turned out of doors,' from the verb *eliminare*, from *e-* (variant of *ex-*) 'out' + *limen, limin-* 'threshold.' **—e·lim·i·na·ble** /-nəbəl/ *adj.* **—e·lim·i·na·tion** /i,limə'nāsʜən/ *n.* **—e·lim·i·na·tor** /-,nātər/ *n.* **—e·lim·i·na·to·ry** /-nə,tôrē/ *adj.*

e·lim·i·na·tion di·et ▸*n.* a diet that eliminates foods that are suspected of causing disease symptoms in an individual.

ELINT /'elint/ ▸*n.* covert intelligence-gathering by electronic means. ▷1960s: blend of **ELECTRONIC** and **INTELLIGENCE**.

El·i·ot1, A. D., see **JEWETT**.

El·i·ot2, Alice, see **JEWETT**.

El·i·ot3 /'elēət/, George (1819–80), English novelist; pseudonym of *Mary Ann Evans.* Her novels of provincial life are characterized by their exploration of moral problems and their development of the psychological analysis that marks the modern novel. Notable works: *Adam Bede* (1859), *The Mill on the Floss* (1860), and *Middlemarch* (1871–72).

El·i·ot4, T. S. (1888–1965), British poet, critic, and playwright; born in the U.S.; full name *Thomas Stearns Eliot.* Associated with the rise of literary modernism, he was established as the voice of a disillusioned generation by *The Waste Land* (1922). *Four Quartets* (1943) revealed his increasing involvement with Christianity. Nobel Prize for Literature (1948).

ELISA /i'līzə; i'līsə/ ▸*n. Biochemistry* enzyme-linked immunosorbent assay, an immunological assay technique making use of an enzyme bonded to a particular antibody or antigen.

E·lis·a·beth·ville /ə'lizəbəтн,vil/ former name (until 1966) of **LUBUMBASHI**.

E·li·sha /i'līsʜə/ (9th century BC), a Hebrew prophet, disciple, and successor of Elijah.

e·li·sion /i'lizʜən/ ▸*n.* the omission of a sound or syllable when speaking (as in *I'm, let's, e'en*). ■ an omission of a passage in a book, speech, or film: *the movie's elisions and distortions have been carefully thought out.* ■ the process of joining together or merging things, esp. abstract ideas: *unease at the elision of so many vital questions.* ▷late 16th cent.: from late Latin *elision-*, from Latin *elidere* 'crush out' (see **ELIDE**).

USAGE See usage at **ELIDE**.

e·lite /ə'lēt; ā'lēt/ ▸*n.* **1** a group of people considered to be the best in a particular society or category, esp. because of their power, talent, or wealth: *China's educated elite* | [as *adj.*] *an elite combat force.* **2** a size of letter in typewriting, with 12 characters to the inch (about 4.7 to the centimeter). ▷late 18th cent.: from French *élite* 'selection, choice,' from *élire* 'to elect,' from a variant of Latin *eligere* (see **ELECT**). Sense 2 dates from the early 20th cent.

e·lit·ism /ə'lē,tizəm; ā'lē-/ ▸*n.* the advocacy or existence of an elite as a dominating element in a system or society. ■ the attitude or behavior of a person or group who regard themselves as belonging to an elite: *he accused her of racism and white elitism.*

e·lit·ist /ə'lētist; ā'lētist/ ▸*n.* a person who believes that a system or society should be ruled or dominated by an elite. ■ a person who believes that they belong to an elite: *designers are a bunch of elitists who don't live in the real world.*
▸*adj.* favoring, advocating, or restricted to an elite: *the old, elitist image of the string quartet.*

e·lix·ir /i'liksər/ ▸*n.* a magical or medicinal potion: *an elixir guaranteed to induce love.* ■ a preparation that was supposedly able to change metals into gold, sought by alchemists. ■ (also **elixir of life**) a preparation supposedly able to prolong life indefinitely. ■ a medicinal solution of a specified type: *a natural herbal cough elixir.* ▷late Middle English: via medieval Latin from Arabic *al-'iksīr*, from *al* 'the' + *'iksīr* from Greek *xērion* 'powder for drying wounds' (from *xēros* 'dry').

E·liz·a·beth /i'lizəbəTH/ an industrial port city in northeastern New Jersey, on Newark Bay; pop. 120,568.

E·liz·a·beth I /ə'lizəbəTH/ (1533–1603), daughter of Henry VIII and Anne Boleyn; queen of England and Ireland 1558–1603. Succeeding her Catholic sister Mary I, Elizabeth reestablished Protestantism as the state religion. Her reign was dominated by the threat of a Catholic restoration and by war with Spain, culminating in the defeat of the Spanish Armada in 1588. Although frequently courted, she never married.

Elizabeth I

E·liz·a·beth II (1926–), daughter of George VI; queen of the United Kingdom since 1952; born *Princess Elizabeth Alexandra Mary*. She married Prince Philip in 1947; they have four children: Prince Charles, Princess Anne, Prince Andrew, and Prince Edward.

Elizabeth II

E·liz·a·beth, the Queen Mother (1900–2002), wife of George VI; born *Lady Elizabeth Angela Marguerite Bowes-Lyon*. She married George VI in 1923 when he was the Duke of York; they had two daughters, Elizabeth II and Princess Margaret.

E·liz·a·be·than /i,lizə'bēTHən/ ▸*adj.* of, relating to, or characteristic of the reign of Queen Elizabeth I: *a lady in Elizabethan dress.*
▸*n.* a person, esp. a writer, of the time of Queen Elizabeth I.

E·liz·a·be·than son·net ▸*n.* a type of sonnet much used by Shakespeare, written in iambic pentameter and consisting of three quatrains and a final couplet with the rhyme scheme abab cdcd efef gg.

elk /elk/ ▸*n.* **1** (*pl.* same or **elks**) a red deer of a large race native to North America. Also called WAPITI. • *Cervus canadensis*, family Cervidae. ■ British term for MOOSE. **2** (**Elk**) (*pl.* **Elks**) a member of a charitable fraternal organization, the Benevolent and Protective Order of Elks. ▷late 15th cent.: probably from Old English *elh, eolh*, with substitution of *k* for *h*. Other words that have undergone this change are dialect *selk* (Old English *seolh* 'seal') and *fark* (Old English *færh* 'farrow').

Elk·hart /'el,kärt; 'elk,härt/ an industrial city in northern Indiana, a rail center that is also noted for the manufacture of musical instruments; pop. 51,847.

Elk Hills a range in south central California, near Bakersfield, the site of an oil reserve that was involved in the 1920s Teapot Dome scandal.

elk·hound /'elk,hound/ (in full **Norwegian elkhound**) ▸*n.* a large hunting dog of a Scandinavian breed with a shaggy gray coat.

ell[1] /el/ ▸*n.* a former measure of length (equivalent to six hand breadths) used mainly for textiles, locally variable but typically about 45 inches. ▷Old English *eln*, of Germanic origin; from an Indo-European root shared by Latin *ulna* (see ULNA). Compare with ELBOW and also with CUBIT (the measure was originally linked to the length of the human arm or forearm).

ell[2] ▸*n.* something that is L-shaped or that creates an L shape, in particular: ■ an extension of a building or room that is at right angles to the main part. ■ a bend or joint for connecting two pipes at right angles.

el·lag·ic ac·id /ə'lajik/ ▸*n. Chemistry* a compound extracted from oak galls and various fruits and nuts. It has some ability to inhibit blood flow and retard the growth of cancer cells. • A tetracyclic phenol; chem. formula: $C_{14}H_6O_8$. ▷early 19th cent.: *ellagic* from French *ellagique* (an anagram of *galle* 'gallnut' + *-ique*), thus avoiding the form *gallique*, already in use.

Elles·mere Is·land /'elz,mi(ə)r/ the most northern of the islands in the Canadian Arctic.

El·let /'elit/, Charles (1810–62), U.S. engineer. In 1841–42, he built the wire suspension bridge that crosses the Schuylkill River in Philadelphia, the first of its kind in the U.S.

El·lice Is·lands /'eləs/ former name of **TUVALU**.

El·li·cott Cit·y /'elikət/ a historic community in north central Maryland, west of Baltimore; pop. 41,396.

El·ling·ton /'eliNGtən/, Duke (1899–1974), U.S. jazz pianist, composer, and bandleader; born *Edward Kennedy Ellington*. Coming to fame in the early 1930s, he wrote over 900 compositions, including *Mood Indigo* (1930), and was one of the first popular musicians to write extended pieces.

el·lipse /i'lips/ ▸*n.* a regular oval shape, traced by a point moving in a plane so that the sum of its distances from two other points (the foci) is constant, or resulting when a cone is cut by an oblique plane that does not intersect the base. ▷late 17th cent.: via French from Latin *ellipsis* (see ELLIPSIS).

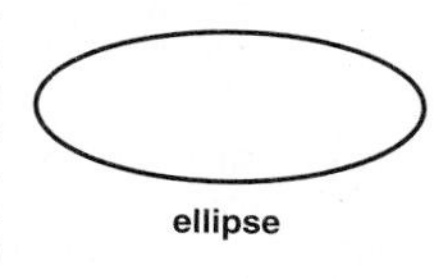

ellipse

el·lip·sis /i'lipsis/ ▸*n.* (*pl.* **-ses** /-sēz/) the omission from speech or writing of a word or words that are superfluous or able to be understood from contextual clues. ■ a set of dots indicating such an omission. ▷mid 16th cent.: via Latin from Greek *elleipsis*, from *elleipein* 'leave out.'

el·lip·soid /i'lipsoid/ ▸*n.* a three-dimensional figure symmetrical around each of three perpendicular axes, whose plane sections normal to one axis are circles and all the other plane sections are ellipses. **—el·lip·soi·dal** /ilip'soidl; ,elip-/ *adj.*

el·lip·tic /i'liptik/ ▸*adj.* **1** of, relating to, or having the form of an ellipse. **2** (of speech or writing) lacking a word or words, esp. when the sense can be understood from contextual clues. ▷early 18th cent.: from Greek *elleiptikos* 'defective,' from *elleipein* 'leave out, fall short.' **—el·lip·ti·cal** *adj.* **—el·lip·ti·cal·ly** /-(ə)lē/ *adv.*

el·lip·tic·i·ty /i,lip'tisitē; ,elip-/ ▸*n.* the condition of being elliptic. ■ the degree of deviation from circularity (or sphericity).

El·lis Is·land /'eləs/ an island in the bay of New York that served as an entry point for immigrants to the U.S. 1892–1943 and as a detention center for people awaiting deportation until 1954. It is now part of a national monument and houses an immigration museum.

El·li·son /'eləsən/, Ralph (Waldo) (1914–94), U.S. writer. He is most noted for his novel *Invisible Man* (1952), but he also published two collections of essays, *Shadow and Act* (1964) and *Going to the Country* (1986), many of which explore blues and African-American folklore.

Ells·berg, Daniel, (1931–) U.S. political analyst, economist, and activist. A former adviser to President Nixon on policy in Southeast Asia, he became an avid opponent of the Vietnam War. Indicted for leaking classified Vietnam-related papers (the "Pentagon Papers") to the press in 1971, he was freed of charges when it was disclosed that Nixon had authorized the theft of Ellsberg's psychiatric records in order to discredit him.

Ells·worth[1] /'elzwərTH/, Lincoln (1880–1951), U.S. explorer. He participated in a number of polar expeditions and was the first person to fly over both the North (1926) and South (1935) poles.

Ells·worth[2], Oliver (1745–1807), U.S. chief justice 1796–1800. As a member of the Continental Congress from 1777 until 1784, he authored the Connecticut Compromise. As a U.S. senator from Connecticut 1789–96, he drafted the Judiciary Act of 1789.

Ells·worth Land a plateau region in Antarctica between the Walgreen Coast and Palmer Land. It rises at the Vinson Massif to 16,863 feet (5,140 m), the highest point in Antarctica, .

elm /elm/ (also **elm tree**) ▸*n.* a tall deciduous tree that typically has rough serrated leaves and propagates from root suckers. • Genus *Ulmus*, family Ulmaceae: several species, including the **English elm** (*U. procera*) and the **American elm** (*U. americana*), now largely lost to Dutch Elm disease. ■ (also **elmwood**) the wood of this tree. ▷Old English, of Germanic origin; related to German dialect *Ilm*, and Swedish and Norwegian *alm*.

El Ma·hal·la el Ku·bra /,el mə'halə 'el 'ko͝obrə/ an industrial city in northern Egypt, in the Nile Delta, west of the Damietta branch; pop. 400,000.

El Man·su·ra /,el män'so͝orə/ (also **Al Mansurah**) an industrial city in northeastern Egypt, in the Nile Delta, on the Damietta branch, a cotton trade center; pop. 362,000.

El·mi·ra /el'mīrə/ an industrial city in south central New York, near the Pennsylvania border; pop. 33,724.

El Mon·te /el 'mäntē/ a city in southwestern California, east of Los Angeles; pop. 106,209.

El Ni·ño /el 'nēnyō/ ▸*n.* (*pl.* **-ños**) an irregularly occurring and complex series of climatic changes affecting the equatorial Pacific region and beyond every few years, characterized by the appearance of unusually warm, nutrient-poor water off northern Peru and Ecuador, typically in late December. ▷late 19th cent.: Spanish, literally 'the (Christ) child,' because of the occurrence near Christmas.

el·o·cu·tion /,elə'kyo͞oSHən/ ▸*n.* the skill of clear and expressive speech, esp. of distinct pronunciation and articulation. ■ a particular style of speaking. ▷late Middle English (denoting oratorical or literary style): from Latin *elocutio(n-)*, from *eloqui* 'speak out' (see ELOQUENCE). **—el·o·cu·tion·ar·y** /-,nerē/ *adj.* **—el·o·cu·tion·ist** /-ist/ *n.*

e·lo·de·a /i'lōdēə/ ▸*n.* an aquatic plant of a genus that includes the ornamental waterweeds. • Genus *Elodea*, family Hydrocharitaceae. ▷modern Latin, from Greek *helōdēs* 'marshy.'

E·lo·him /e'lōhim; ,elō'hēm; ,elō'him/ ▸*n.* a name for God used frequently in the Hebrew Bible. ▷from Hebrew *'ĕlōhīm* (plural).

E·lo·hist /e'lōhist; 'elō,hist/ the postulated author or authors of parts of the Hexateuch in which God is regularly named Elohim. Compare with **YAHWIST**. ▷from Hebrew *'ĕlōhīm* (see **ELOHIM**) + **-IST**.

e·lon·gate /i'lôNG,gāt; i'läNG-/ ▸*v.* [*trans.*] make (something) longer, esp. unusually so in relation to its width. ■ prolong (a sound): *she can sing—notes are elongated and given fullness without a quiver.* ■ [*intrans.*] *chiefly Biology* grow longer.
▸*adj. chiefly Biology* long in relation to width; elongated: *elongate, fishlike creatures.* ▷late Middle English (in the sense 'move away, place at a distance'): from late Latin *elongat-* 'placed at a distance,' from the verb *elongare*, from Latin *e-* (variant of *ex-*) 'away' + *longe* 'far off,' *longus* 'long.'

e·lon·gat·ed /i'lôNG,gātid; i'läNG-/ ▸*adj.* unusually long in relation to its width: *the creature had two sets of arms and an elongated face.* ■ having grown or been made longer.

e·lon·ga·tion /i,lôNG'gāSHən; ē,lôNG-; i,läNG-; ē,läNG-/ ▸*n.* the lengthening of something. ■ a part of a line formed by lengthening; a continuation. ■ the amount of extension of an object under stress, usually expressed as a percentage of the original length. ■ *Astronomy* the angular separation of a planet from the sun or of a satellite from a planet, as seen by an observer. ▷late Middle English: from late Latin elongatio(n-), from elongare 'place at a distance'(see ELONGATE).

e·lope /iˈlōp/ ▸v. [intrans.] run away secretly in order to get married, esp. without parental consent: *later he* ***eloped with*** *one of the maids.* ■ run away with a lover. ▷late 16th cent. (in the general sense 'abscond, run away'): from Anglo-Norman French *aloper*, perhaps related to LEAP. **—e·lope·ment** *n.* **—e·lop·er** *n.*

el·o·quence /ˈeləkwəns/ ▸n. fluent or persuasive speaking or writing: *a preacher of great power and eloquence.* ■ the art or manner of such speech or writing. ▷late Middle English: via Old French from Latin *eloquentia*, from *eloqui* 'speak out,' from *e-* (variant of *ex-*) 'out' + *loqui* 'speak.'

el·o·quent /ˈeləkwənt/ ▸adj. fluent or persuasive in speaking or writing: *an eloquent speech.* ■ clearly expressing or indicating something: *the touches of fatherliness are* ***eloquent of*** *the real man.* ▷late Middle English: via Old French from Latin *eloquent-* 'speaking out,' from the verb *eloqui* (see ELOQUENCE). **—el·o·quent·ly** *adv.*

El Pas·o /el ˈpasō/ a city in western Texas, on the Rio Grande, opposite Ciudad Juárez in Mexico; pop. 563,662.

El Qa·hi·ra /el käˈhērə/ variant spelling of **AL QAHIRA**.

El Sal·va·dor /el ˈsalvəˌdôr; ˌsälvädôr/ a country in western Central America, on the Pacific coast; pop. 6,587,000; capital, San Salvador; official language, Spanish.

The territory was conquered by the Spanish in 1524 and gained its independence in 1821. Between 1979 and 1992 El Salvador was devastated by a civil war that was marked by the activities of right-wing death squads and resistance by left-wing guerrillas. A UN-brokered peace accord was agreed upon in 1992.

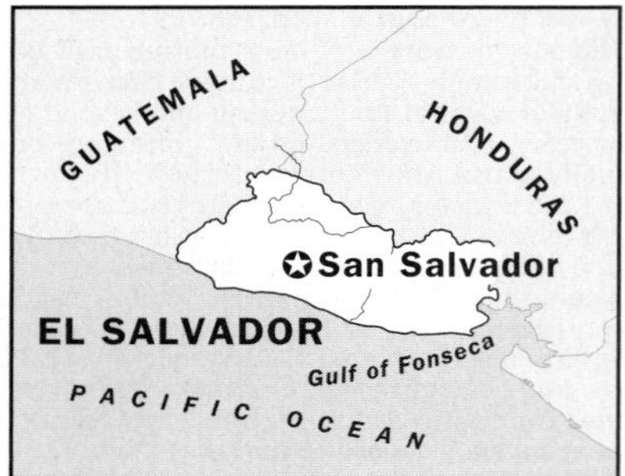

else /els/ ▸adv. **1** [with indefinite *pron.* or *adv.*] in addition; besides: ***anything else*** *you need to know?* | *I just brought basics—I wasn't sure* ***what else*** *you'd want* | *they will offer low prices but* ***little else.*** **2** [with indefinite *pron.* or *adv.*] different; instead: *isn't there* ***anyone else*** *you could ask?*| *it's fate, destiny, or* ***whatever else*** *you like to call it.* **3** short for OR ELSE below. ▷Old English *elles*, of Germanic origin; related to Middle Dutch *els* and Swedish *eljest*.

▸*PHRASE* □ **or else** used to introduce the second of two alternatives: *she felt tempted either to shout at him or else to let his tantrums slide by.* ■ in circumstances different from those mentioned; if it were not the case: *they can't want it, or else they'd request it.* ■ used to warn what will happen if something is not carried out: *you go along with this or else you're going to jail.* ■ used after a demand as a threat: *she'd better shape up, or else.*

else·where /ˈelsˌ(h)wer/ ▸adv. in, at, or to some other place or other places: *he is seeking employment elsewhere.*

▸pron. some other place: *all Hawaiian plants originally came from elsewhere.* ▷Old English *elles hwǣr* (see ELSE, WHERE).

El·si·nore /ˈelsəˌnôr/ a port on the northeastern coast of the island of Zealand in Denmark; pop. 56,750. It is the site of the 16th-century Kronborg Castle, which is the setting for Shakespeare's *Hamlet*. Danish name **HELSINGØR**.

ELSS ▸abbr. extravehicular life support system.

El·ster /ˈelstər/ ▸n. [usu. as *adj.*] *Geology* a Pleistocene glaciation in northern Europe, corresponding to the Anglian of Britain (and possibly the Mindel of the Alps). ■ the system of deposits laid down at this time. ▷1930s: the name of a tributary of the Elbe River in Germany. **—El·ste·ri·an** /elˈsti(ə)rēən/ *adj.* & *n.*

el·u·ant /ˈelyo͞oənt/ ▸n. *Chemistry* a fluid used to elute a substance. ▷1940s: from Latin *eluent-* 'washing out,' from the verb *eluere* (see ELUTE).

el·u·ate /ˈelyo͞oit; -ˌāt/ ▸n. *Chemistry* a solution obtained by elution. ▷1930s: from Latin *eluere* 'wash out' + -ATE[1].

e·lu·ci·date /iˈlo͞osiˌdāt/ ▸v. [trans.] make (something) clear; explain: *work such as theirs will help to elucidate this matter* See note at CLARIFY. | [with *clause*] *in what follows I shall try to elucidate what I believe the problems to be* | [intrans.] *they would not elucidate further.* ▷mid 16th cent.: from late Latin *elucidat-* 'made clear,' from the verb *elucidare*, from *e-* (variant of *ex-*) 'out' + *lucidus* 'lucid.' **—e·lu·ci·da·tion** /iˌlo͞osiˈdāsHən/ *n.* **—e·lu·ci·da·tive** /-ˌdātiv/ *adj.* **—e·lu·ci·da·tor** /-ˌdātər/ *n.* **—e·lu·ci·da·to·ry** /-dəˌtôrē/ *adj.*

e·lude /iˈlo͞od/ ▸v. [trans.] evade or escape from (a danger, enemy, or pursuer), typically in a skillful or cunning way: *he managed to elude his pursuers by escaping into an alley.* ■ (of an idea or fact) fail to be grasped or remembered by (someone): *the logic of this eluded most people.* ■ (of an achievement, or something desired or pursued) fail to be attained by (someone): *sleep still eluded her.* ■ avoid compliance with or subjection to (a law, demand, or penalty). ▷mid 16th cent. (in the sense 'delude, baffle'): from Latin *eludere*, from *e-* (variant of *ex-*) 'out, away from' + *ludere* 'to play.' **—e·lu·sion** /iˈlo͞ozHən/ *n.*

el·u·ent /ˈelyo͞oənt/ ▸n. variant spelling of ELUANT.

E·lul /ˈeləl; eˈlo͞ol/ ▸n. (in the Jewish calendar) the twelfth month of the civil and sixth of the religious year, usually coinciding with parts of August and September. ▷from Hebrew *'ělūl*.

El Uq·sur /el ˈo͝okˌso͝or/ (also **Al Uq·sur** /äl/) Arabic name for LUXOR.

e·lu·sive /iˈlo͞osiv/ (also *rare* **e·lu·so·ry** /-sərē; -zə-/) ▸adj. difficult to find, catch, or achieve: *success will become ever more elusive.* ■ difficult to remember or recall: *the elusive thought he had had moments before.* ▷early 18th cent.: from Latin *elus-* 'eluded' (from the verb *eludere*) + -IVE. **—e·lu·sive·ly** *adv.* **—e·lu·sive·ness** *n.*

e·lute /iˈlo͞ot/ ▸v. [trans.] *Chemistry* remove (an adsorbed substance) by washing with a solvent, esp. in chromatography. ▷1920s: from Latin *elut-* 'washed out,' from the verb *eluere*, suggested by German *eluieren*. **—e·lu·tion** /iˈlo͞osHən/ *n.*

e·lu·tri·ate /iˈlo͞otrēˌāt/ ▸v. [trans.] *Chemistry* separate (lighter and heavier particles in a mixture) by suspension in an upward flow of liquid or gas. ■ purify by straining. ▷mid 18th cent.: from Latin *elutriat-* 'washed out,' from the verb *elutriare*, from *e-* (variant of *ex-*) 'out' + *lutriare* 'to wash.' **—e·lu·tri·a·tion** /iˌlo͞otrēˈāsHən/ *n.*

el·van /ˈelvən/ ▸n. *Geology* hard intrusive igneous rock found in Cornwall, typically quartz porphyry. ▷early 18th cent.: perhaps via Cornish from Welsh *elfen* 'element.'

el·ver /ˈelvər/ ▸n. a young eel, esp. when undergoing mass migration upriver from the sea. ▷mid 17th cent.: variant of dialect *eel-fare* 'the passage of young eels up a river,' also 'a brood of young eels,' from EEL + FARE in its original sense 'a journey.'

elves /elvz/ ▸ plural form of ELF.

E·lyr·i·a /iˈli(ə)rēə/ an industrial city in northern Ohio, west of Cleveland; pop. 55,953.

E·ly·sée Pal·ace /ˌeləˈzā/ a building in Paris that has been the official residence of the French president since 1870. It was built in 1718 and was occupied by Madame de Pompadour, Napoleon I, and Napoleon III.

E·ly·sian /iˈlizHən; iˈlē-/ ▸adj. of, relating to, or characteristic of heaven or paradise: *Elysian visions.*

▸*PHRASE* □ **the Elysian Fields** another name for ELYSIUM.

E·ly·si·um /iˈlizHēəm; iˈlizēəm; iˈlē-/ *Greek Mythology* the place at the ends of the earth to which certain favored heroes were conveyed by the gods after death. ■ [as *n.*] (**an Elysium**) a place or state of perfect happiness. ▷via Latin from Greek *Elusion (pedion)* '(plain) of the blessed.'

el·y·tron /ˈeləˌträn/ ▸n. (*pl.* **-tra** /-trə/) *Entomology* each of the two wing cases of a beetle. ▷mid 18th cent. (denoting a sheath or covering, specifically that of the spinal cord): from Greek *elutron* 'sheath.' **—el·y·trous** /-trəs/ *adj.*

El·ze·vir /ˈelzəˌvi(ə)r/ a family of Dutch printers. Fifteen members were active 1581–1712; **Bonaventure** (1583–1652) and **Abraham** (1592–1652) managed the firm in its prime.

EM ▸abbr. ■ electromagnetic. ■ Engineer of Mines. ■ enlisted man (men).

em /em/ ▸n. *Printing* a unit for measuring the width of printed matter, equal to the height of the type size being used. ■ a unit of measurement equal to twelve points. ▷late 18th cent.: the letter *M* represented as a word, since it is approximately this width.

'em /əm/ ▸pron. short for THEM, esp. in informal use: *let 'em know who's boss.* ▷Middle English: originally a form of *hem*, dative and accusative third person plural pronoun in Middle English; now regarded as an abbreviation of THEM.

em- ▸*prefix* variant spelling of EN-[1], EN-[2] assimilated before *b*, *p* (as in *emblazon*, *emplacement*).

e·ma·ci·ate /iˈmāsHēˌāt/ ▸v. [trans.] [usu. as *adj.*] (**emaciated**) make abnormally thin or weak, esp. because of illness or a lack of food: *she was so emaciated she could hardly stand.* ▷early 17th cent.: from Latin *emaciat-* 'made thin,' from the verb *emaciare*, from *e-* (variant of *ex-*, expressing a change of state) + *macies* 'leanness.' **—e·ma·ci·a·tion** /iˌmāsHēˈāsHən/ *n.*

e-mail /ˈē ˌmāl/ (also **e·mail**) ▸n. messages distributed by electronic means from one computer user to one or more recipients via a network: *reading e-mail has become the first task of the morning* | [as *adj.*] *e-mail messages.* ■ the system of sending messages by such electronic means: *a contract communicated by e-mail.* ■ (**an e-mail**) a message sent by e-mail: *I got three e-mails from my mother today.*

▸v. [trans.] send an e-mail to (someone): *you can e-mail me at my normal address.* ■ send (a message) by e-mail: *employees can e-mail the results back.* ▷late 20th cent.: abbreviation of ELECTRONIC MAIL. **—e-mail·er** *n.*

em·a·lan·gen·i /ˌeməläNGˈgenē/ ▸ plural form of LILANGENI.

em·a·nate /ˈeməˌnāt/ ▸v. [intrans.] (**emanate from**) (of something abstract but perceptible) issue or spread out from (a source): *warmth emanated from the fireplace* | *she felt an undeniable charm emanating from him.* ■ originate from; be produced by: *the proposals emanated from a committee.* ■ [trans.] give out or emit (something abstract but perceptible): *he emanated a powerful brooding air.* ▷mid 18th cent.: from Latin *emanat-* 'flowed out,' from the verb *emanare*, from *e-* (variant of *ex-*) 'out' + *manare* 'to flow.' **—em·a·na·tive** /-ˌnātiv/ *adj.* **—em·a·na·tor** /-ˌnātər/ *n.*

em·a·na·tion /ˌeməˈnāsHən/ ▸n. an abstract but perceptible thing that issues or originates from a source: *she saw the insults as emanations of his own tortured personality.* ■ the action or process of issuing from a source: *the risk of radon gas emanation.* ■ a tenuous substance or form of radiation given off by something: *vaporous emanations surround the mill's foundations.* ■ *archaic Chemistry* a radioactive gas formed by radioactive decay of a solid. ■ a body or organization that has its source or takes its authority from another: *the commission is an emanation of the state.* ■ (in various mystical traditions) a being or force that is a manifestation of God.

e·man·ci·pate /iˈmansəˌpāt/ ▸v. [trans.] set free, esp. from legal, social, or political restrictions: *the citizen must be* ***emancipated from*** *the obsessive secrecy of government* | [as *adj.*] (**emancipated**) *emancipated young women.* ■ *Law* set (a child) free from the authority of its father or parents. ■ free from slavery: *it is estimated that he emancipated 8,000 slaves.* ▷early 17th cent.: from Latin *emancipat-* 'transferred as property,' from the verb *emancipare*, from *e-* (variant of *ex-*) 'out' + *mancipium* 'slave.' **—e·man·ci·pa·tion** /iˌmansəˈpāsHən/ *n.* **—e·man·ci·pa·tor** /-ˌpātər/ *n.* **—e·man·ci·pa·to·ry** /-pəˌtôrē/ *adj.*

E·man·ci·pa·tion Proc·la·ma·tion /iˌmansəˈpāsHən/ the announcement made by President Lincoln during the Civil War on September 22, 1862, emancipating all black slaves in states still engaged in rebellion against the Union. Although implementation was strictly beyond Lincoln's powers, the declaration turned the war into a crusade against slavery. It was signed on January 1, 1863.

e·mas·cu·late /iˈmaskyəˌlāt/ ▸v. [trans.] make (a person, idea, or piece of legislation) weaker or less effective: *our winner-take-all elections emasculate fringe parties like neo-Nazis.* ■ [usu. as *adj.*] (**emasculated**) deprive (a man) of his male role or identity: *he feels emasculated because he cannot control his sons' behavior.* ■ *archaic* castrate (a man or male animal). ■ *Botany* remove the anthers from a flower. ▷early 17th cent.: from Latin *emasculat-* 'castrated,' from the verb *emasculare*, from *e-* (variant of *ex-*, expressing a change of state) + *masculus* 'male.' **—e·mas·cu·la·tion** /iˌmaskyəˈlāsHən/ *n.* **—e·mas·cu·la·tor** /-ˌlātər/ *n.* **—e·mas·cu·la·to·ry** /-ləˌtôrē/ *adj.*

em·balm /emˈbä(l)m/ ▸v. [trans.] **1** [often as *n.*] (**embalming**) preserve (a corpse) from decay, originally with spices and now usually by arterial injection of a preservative: *the Egyptian method of embalming.* ■ *figurative* preserve (someone or something) in an unaltered state: *the band was all about revitalizing pop greats and embalming their legacy.* **2** *archaic* give a pleasant fragrance to: *the sweetness of the linden trees embalmed all the air.* ▷Middle English: from Old French *embaumer*, from *em-* 'in' + *baume* 'balm,' variant of *basme* (see **BALM**). **—em·balm·er** *n.* **—em·balm·ment** *n.*

em·bank /em'bangk/ ▶*v.* [*trans.*] construct a wall or bank of earth or stone in order to confine (a river) within certain limits. ■ construct a bank of earth or stone to carry (a road or railroad) over an area of low ground.

em·bank·ment /em'bangkmənt/ ▶*n.* a wall or bank of earth or stone built to prevent a river flooding an area. ■ a bank of earth or stone built to carry a road or railroad over an area of low ground.

em·bar·go /em'bärgō/ ▶*n.* (*pl.* **-goes**) an official ban on trade or other commercial activity with a particular country: *an* **embargo on** *grain sales | the oil embargo of 1973.* ■ an official prohibition on any activity. ■ *historical* an order of a state forbidding foreign ships to enter, or any ships to leave, its ports. ■ *archaic* a stoppage, prohibition, or impediment.

▶*v.* (**-goes, -goed**) [*trans.*] **1** (usu. **be embargoed**) impose an official ban on (trade or a country or commodity): *the country has been virtually embargoed by most of the noncommunist world.* ■ officially ban the publication of: *documents of national security importance are routinely embargoed.* **2** *archaic* seize (a ship or goods) for state service. ▷early 17th cent.: from Spanish, from *embargar* 'arrest,' based on Latin *in-* 'in, within' + *barra* 'a bar.'

em·bark /em'bärk/ ▶*v.* [*intrans.*] go on board a ship, aircraft, or other vehicle: *he* **embarked for** *India in 1817.* ■ [*trans.*] put or take on board a ship or aircraft: *its passengers were ready to be embarked.* ■ (**embark on/upon**) begin (a course of action, esp. one that is important or demanding): *he embarked on a new career.* ▷mid 16th cent.: from French *embarquer*, from *em-* 'in' + *barque* 'bark, ship.' **—em·bar·ka·tion** /,embär'kāshən/ *n.* **—em·bark·ment** *n.*

em·bar·ras de ri·chesses /änbä'rä də rē'shes/ (also **em·bar·ras de choix** /shwä/) ▶*n.* more options or resources than one knows what to do with: *he had presented us with an embarras de richesses of history and culture.* ▷mid 18th cent.: French, literally 'embarrassment of riches (or choice).'

em·bar·rass /em'barəs/ ▶*v.* [*trans.*] cause (someone) to feel awkward, self-conscious, or ashamed: *she wouldn't embarrass either of them by making a scene.* ■ (**be embarrassed**) be caused financial difficulties: *he would be embarrassed by an inheritance tax.* ■ *archaic* hamper or impede (a person, movement, or action): *the state of the rivers will embarrass the enemy in a considerable degree.* ■ *archaic* make difficult or intricate; complicate. ■ create difficulties for (someone, esp. a public figure or political party) by drawing attention to their failures or shortcomings: ▷early 17th cent. (in the sense 'hamper, impede'): from French *embarrasser*, from Spanish *embarazar*, probably from Portuguese *embaraçar* (from *baraço* 'halter').

em·bar·rassed /em'barəst/ ▶*adj.* feeling or showing embarrassment: *he became embarrassed at his own effusiveness | an embarrassed silence.* ■ having or showing financial difficulties. **—em·bar·rassed·ly** /-əstlē; -əsidlē/ *adv.*

em·bar·rass·ing /em'barəsing/ ▶*adj.* causing embarrassment: *an embarrassing muddle.* ■ creating difficulties, esp. for a political party or public figure: *there may be one or two embarrassing questions at the shareholders' meeting.* **—em·bar·rass·ing·ly** *adv.*

em·bar·rass·ment /-mənt/ ▶*n.* a feeling of self-consciousness, shame, or awkwardness: *I turned red with embarrassment.* ■ a person or thing causing such feelings: *he was an embarrassment who was safely left ignored | her extreme views might be an* **embarrassment to** *the movement.* ■ financial difficulty: *his temporary financial embarrassment.*

▶*PHRASE* □ **embarrassment of riches** see **EMBARRAS DE RICHESSES.**

em·bas·sage /'embəsij/ ▶*n.* *archaic* the business or message of an envoy. ■ a body of people sent as a deputation to or on behalf of a head of state. ■ archaic term for **EMBASSY**. ▷late 15th cent. (denoting the action of sending an envoy): from Old French *ambasse* 'message or embassy' + **-AGE**.

em·bas·sy /'embəsē/ ▶*n.* (*pl.* **-sies**) **1** the official residence or offices of an ambassador: *the Chilean embassy in Moscow.* ■ the staff working in such a building: *the embassy denied any involvement in the murder.* ■ the position or function of an ambassador. **2** *chiefly historical* a deputation or mission sent by one ruler or state to another. ▷late 16th cent. (originally also as *ambassy* denoting the position of ambassador): from Old French *ambasse*, based on Latin *ambactus* 'servant.' Compare with **AMBASSADOR**.

em·bat·tle /em'batl/ ▶*v.* [*trans.*] *archaic* set (an army) in battle array: *it was three o'clock before the king's army was embattled.* ■ fortify (a building or place) against attack. ▷Middle English: from Old French *embataillier*.

em·bat·tled /em'batld/ ▶*adj.* **1** (of a place or people) involved in or prepared for war, esp. because surrounded by enemy forces: *the embattled Yugoslavian republics.* ■ (of a person) beset by problems or difficulties: *the worst may not be over for the embattled senator.* **2** [*postpositive*] *Heraldry* divided or edged by a line of square notches like battlements in outline.

em·bay /em'bā/ ▶*v.* [*trans.*] (usu. **be embayed**) (chiefly of the wind) confine (a sailing vessel) to a bay: *ships were embayed between two headlands.* ■ [as *adj.*] (**embayed**) formed into bays; hollowed out by or as if by the sea: *the embayed island.* ■ *chiefly Geology* enclose (something) in a recess or hollow.

em·bay·ment /em'bāmənt/ ▶*n.* a recess in a coastline forming a bay.

em·bed /em'bed/ (also **im·bed** /im-/) ▶*v.* (**-bed·ded, -bed·ding**) [*trans.*] (often **be embedded**) fix (an object) firmly and deeply in a surrounding mass: *he had an operation to remove a nail* **embedded in** *his chest.* ■ *figurative* implant (an idea or feeling) within something else so it becomes an ingrained or essential characteristic of it: *the Victorian values* **embedded in** *Tennyson's poetry.* ■ *Linguistics* place (a phrase or clause) within another clause or sentence. ■ *Computing* incorporate (a text or code) within the body of a file or document. ■ [often as *adj.*] (**embedded**) design and build (a microprocessor) as an integral part of a system or device. ■ permit a journalist to travel with a military unit: embedded with the 24th Marine Expeditionary Unit.

▶*n.* /'em,bed/ an embedded journalist: *most of the embeds found themselves covering construction and civil works projects.* **—em·bed·ment** *n.*

em·bel·lish /em'belish/ ▶*v.* [*trans.*] make (something) more attractive by the addition of decorative details or features: *blue silk embellished with golden embroidery.* ■ make (a statement or story) more interesting or entertaining by adding extra details, esp. ones that are not true: *she had real difficulty telling the truth because she liked to embellish things.* ▷late Middle English: from Old French *embelliss-*, lengthened stem of *embellir*, based on *bel* 'handsome,' from Latin *bellus*. **—em·bel·lish·er** *n.*

em·bel·lish·ment /em'belishmənt/ ▶*n.* a decorative detail or feature added to something to make it more attractive: *architectural embellishments.* ■ a detail, esp. one that is not true, added to a statement or story to make it more interesting or entertaining. ■ the action of adding such details or features.

em·ber /'embər/ ▶*n.* (usu. **embers**) a small piece of burning or glowing coal or wood in a dying fire: *the dying embers in the fireplace | figurative the flickering embers of nationalism.* ▷Old English *ǣmyrge*, of Germanic origin; related to Old High German *eimuria* 'pyre,' Danish *emmer*, Swedish *mörja* 'embers.' The *b* was added in English for ease of pronunciation when the vowel of the second syllable (*y*) disappeared.

Em·ber day ▶*n.* any of a number of days reserved for fasting and prayer in the Western Christian Church. Ember days traditionally comprise the Wednesday, Friday, and Saturday following St. Lucy's Day (December 13), the first Sunday in Lent, Pentecost (Whitsun), and Holy Cross Day (September 14), though other days are observed locally. ▷Old English *ymbren*, perhaps an alteration of *ymbryne* 'period,' from *ymb* 'around' + *ryne* 'course,' perhaps influenced in part by ecclesiastical Latin *quatuor tempora* 'four periods' (on which the equivalent German *Quatember* is based).

em·bez·zle /em'bezəl/ ▶*v.* [*trans.*] steal or misappropriate (money placed in one's trust or belonging to the organization for which one works): *she had embezzled $5,600,000 in company funds.* ▷late Middle English (in the sense 'steal'): from Anglo-Norman French *embesiler*, from *besiler* in the same sense (compare with Old French *besillier* 'maltreat, ravage'), of unknown ultimate origin. The current sense dates from the late 16th cent. **—em·bez·zle·ment** *n.* **—em·bez·zler** /em'bezlər/ *n.*

Em·bi·op·ter·a /,embē'äptərə; ,embī-/ *Entomology* a small order of insects that comprises the web-spinners. ▷modern Latin (plural), from *Embia* (genus name) + Greek *pteron* 'wing.' **—em·bi·op·ter·an** *n.* & *adj.*

em·bit·ter /em'bitər/ ▶*v.* [*trans.*] [usu. as *adj.*] (**embittered**) cause (someone) to feel bitter or resentful: *he died an embittered man.* ■ *poetic/literary* give a sharp or pungent taste or smell to: *the smell of orange zest and smoke embittered the air.* **—em·bit·ter·ment** *n.*

em·bla·zon /em'blāzn/ ▶*v.* [*trans.*] (often **be emblazoned**) conspicuously inscribe or display (a design) on something: *T-shirts* **emblazoned with** *the names of baseball teams.* ■ depict (a heraldic device): *the Cardinal's coat of arms is emblazoned on the door panel.* ■ *archaic* celebrate or extol publicly: *their success was emblazoned.* **—em·bla·zon·ment** *n.*

em·blem /'embləm/ ▶*n.* a heraldic device or symbolic object as a distinctive badge of a nation, organization, or family: *America's national emblem, the bald eagle.* ■ (**emblem of**) a thing serving as a symbolic representation of a particular quality or concept: *our child would be a dazzling emblem of our love.* ▷late 16th cent. (as a verb): from Latin *emblema* 'inlaid work, raised ornament,' from Greek *emblēma* 'insertion,' from *emballein* 'throw in, insert,' from *em-* 'in' + *ballein* 'to throw.' **—em·blem·at·ic** /,emblə'matik/ *adj.* **—em·blem·at·i·cal** /,emblə'matikəl/ *adj.* **—em·blem·at·i·cal·ly** /,emblə'matik(ə)lē/ *adv.*

THE RIGHT WORD **attribute, emblem, image, sign, symbol, token, type**

When it comes to representing or embodying the invisible or intangible, you can't beat a **symbol**. It applies to anything that serves as an outward sign of something immaterial or spiritual (*the cross as a symbol of salvation; the crown as a symbol of monarchy*), although the association between the symbol and what it represents does not have to be based on tradition or convention and may, in fact, be quite arbitrary (*the annual gathering at the cemetery became a symbol of the family's long and tragic history*).

An **emblem** is a visual symbol or pictorial device that represents the character or history of a family, a nation, or an office (*the eagle is an emblem of the U.S.*).

It is very close in meaning to **attribute**, which is an object that is conventionally associated with a person, a group, or an abstraction (*the spiked wheel as an attribute of St. Catherine; the scales as an attribute of Justice*).

An **image** is also a visual representation or embodiment, but in a much broader sense (*veins popping, he was the image of the angry father*).

Sign is often used in place of *symbol* to refer to a simple representation of an agreed-upon meaning (*the upraised fist as a sign of victory; the white flag as a sign of surrender*), but a *symbol* usually embodies a wider range of meanings, while a *sign* can be any object, event, or gesture from which information can be deduced (*her faltering voice was a sign of her nervousness*).

A **token**, on the other hand, is something offered as a symbol or reminder (*he gave her his class ring as a token of his devotion*) and a **type**, particularly in a religious context, is a symbol or representation of something not present (*Jerusalem as the type of heaven; the paschal lamb as the type of Christ*).

em·blem·a·tist /em'blemətist/ ▶*n.* a creator or user of emblems, esp. in allegorical pictures.

em·blem·a·tize /em'blemə,tīz/ ▶*v.* [*trans.*] *formal* serve as a symbolic representation of (a quality or concept).

em·ble·ments /'embləmənts/ ▶*plural n.* *Law* the profit from growing crops that have been sown, regarded as personal property. ▷late 15th cent.: from Old French *emblaement*, from *emblaier* 'sow with corn' (based on *blé* 'corn').

em·bod·i·ment /em'bädēmənt; im-/ ▶*n.* a tangible or visible form of an idea, quality, or feeling: *she seemed to be a living embodiment of vitality.* ■ the representation or expression of something in such a form: *it was in Germany alone that his hope seemed capable of embodiment.*

em·bod·y /em'bädē/ ▶*v.* (**-bod·ies, -bod·ied**) [*trans.*] **1** be an expression of or give a tangible or visible form to (an idea, quality, or feeling): *a team that embodies competitive spirit and skill.* ■ provide (a spirit) with a physical form. **2** include or contain (something) as a constituent part: *the changes in law* **embodied in** *the Freedom of Information Act.* **3** *archaic* form (people) into a body, esp. for military purposes. ▷mid 16th cent.: from **EM-** + **BODY**, on the pattern of Latin *incorporare*. **—em·bod·i·er** /-'bädēər/ *n.*

em·bold·en /em'bōldən/ ▸*v.* [*trans.*] **1** (often **be emboldened**) give (someone) the courage or confidence to do something or to behave in a certain way: *emboldened* ***by*** *robust passenger traffic, the airlines put through major fare increases.* See note at **ENCOURAGE**. **2** cause (a piece of text) to appear in a bold typeface: *center, embolden, and underline the heading.*

em·bo·lec·to·my /,embə'lektəmē/ ▸*n.* (*pl.* **-mies**) surgical removal of an embolus.

em·bo·lism /'embə,lizəm/ ▸*n.* **1** *Medicine* obstruction of an artery, typically by a clot of blood or an air bubble. **2** the periodic intercalation of days or a month to correct the accumulating discrepancy between the calendar year and the solar year, as in a leap year. ▷mid 19th cent.: via late Latin from Greek *embolismos*, from *emballein* 'insert.'

em·bo·li·za·tion /,embəli'zāsHən/ ▸*n.* *Medicine* the artificial or natural formation or development of an embolus.

em·bo·lus /'embələs/ ▸*n.* (*pl.* **-li** /-,lī; -,lē/) a blood clot, air bubble, piece of fatty deposit, or other object that has been carried in the bloodstream to lodge in a vessel and cause an embolism. ▷mid 17th cent. (denoting something inserted or moving within another, specifically the plunger of a syringe): from Latin, literally 'piston,' from Greek *embolos* 'peg, stopper.' The current sense dates from the mid 19th cent. **—em·bol·ic** /em'bälik/ *adj.*

em·bon·point /,änbôn'pwan/ ▸*n. archaic* the plump or fleshy part of a person's body, in particular a woman's bosom. ▷late 17th cent.: from French *en bon point* 'in good condition.'

em·bos·om /em'bŏŏzəm/ ▸*v.* [*trans.*] (usu. **be embosomed**) *poetic/literary* take or press to one's bosom; embrace. ■ enclose or surround (something) protectively.

em·boss /em'bôs; -'bäs/ ▸*v.* [*trans.*] [usu. as *adj.*] (**embossed**) carve or mold a design on (a surface) so that it stands out in relief: *an embossed brass dish.* ■ decorate (a surface) with a raised design. ▷late Middle English: from the Old French base of obsolete French *embosser*, from *em-* 'into' + *boce* 'protuberance.' **—em·boss·er** *n.* **—em·boss·ment** *n.*

em·bou·chure /,ämbŏŏ'sHŏŏr/ ▸*n.* **1** *Music* the way in which a player applies the mouth to the mouthpiece of a brass or wind instrument. ■ the mouthpiece of a flute or a similar instrument. **2** *archaic* the mouth of a river or valley. ▷mid 18th cent.: French, from *s'emboucher* 'discharge itself by the mouth,' from *emboucher* 'put in or to the mouth,' from *em-* 'into' + *bouche* 'mouth.'

em·bour·geoise·ment /em'bŏŏrzHwäzmənt; -,mänt/ ▸*n.* the proliferation in a society of values perceived as characteristic of the middle class, esp. of materialism. ▷1930s: French, from *embourgeoiser* 'become or make bourgeois.'

em·bowed /em'bōd/ ▸*adj.* *poetic/literary* bent, arched, or vaulted. ■ [*postpositive*] *Heraldry* (of an arm) bent at the elbow; (of a dolphin) with the body curved.

em·bow·el /em'bouəl/ ▸*v.* (**-bow·eled**, **-bow·el·ing**; *Brit.* **-bow·elled**, **-bow·el·ling**) archaic term for **DISEMBOWEL**. ▷early 16th cent.: from Old French *emboweler*, alteration of *esboueler*, from *es-* 'out' + *bouel* 'bowel.'

em·bow·er /em'bou(-ə)r/ ▸*v.* [*trans.*] (usu. **be embowered**) *poetic/literary* surround or shelter (a place or a person), esp. with trees or climbing plants: *the house stood remote,* ***embowered in*** *trees.*

em·brace /em'brās/ ▸*v.* [*trans.*] hold (someone) closely in one's arms, esp. as a sign of affection: *Aunt Sophie embraced her warmly* | [*intrans.*] *the two embraced, holding each other tightly.* ■ accept or support (a belief, theory, or change) willingly and enthusiastically: *much of the population quickly embraced Islam.* ■ include or contain (something) as a constituent part: *his career embraces a number of activities—composing, playing, and acting.*
▸*n.* an act of holding someone closely in one's arms: *they were locked in an embrace.* ■ *figurative* used to refer to something that is regarded as surrounding or holding someone securely, esp. in a restrictive or comforting way: *the first of the former Soviet republics to free itself from the embrace of Moscow.* ■ [in *sing.*] an act of accepting or supporting something willingly or enthusiastically: *their eager embrace of foreign influences.* ▷Middle English (in the sense 'encircle, surround, enclose'; formerly also as *imbrace*): from Old French *embracer*, based on Latin *in-* 'in' + *bracchium* 'arm.' **—em·brace·a·ble** *adj.* **—em·brace·ment** *n.* **—em·brac·er** *n.*

em·bra·sure /em'brāzHər/ ▸*n.* the beveling or splaying of a wall at the sides of a door or window. ■ a small opening in a parapet of a fortified building, splayed on the inside. ▷early 18th cent.: from French, from obsolete *embraser* (earlier form of *ébraser*) 'widen a door or window opening,' of unknown ultimate origin. **—em·bra·sured** *adj.*

em·brit·tle /em'britl/ ▸*v.* make or become brittle. **—em·brit·tle·ment** *n.*

em·bro·ca·tion /,embrə'kāsHən/ ▸*n.* a liquid used for rubbing on the body to relieve pain from sprains and strains. ▷late Middle English: from medieval Latin *embrocatio(n-)*, from the verb *embrocare*, based on Greek *embrokhē* 'lotion.'

em·broi·der /em'broidər/ ▸*v.* [*trans.*] decorate (cloth) by sewing patterns on it with thread: *she had already embroidered a dozen little nighties for the babies* | [as *adj.*] (**embroidered**) *an embroidered handkerchief* | [*intrans.*] *she was teaching one of the girls how to embroider.* ■ produce (a design) on cloth in this way: [as *adj.*] (**embroidered**) *a chunky knit sweater with embroidered flowers.* ■ *figurative* add fictitious or exaggerated details to (an account) to make it more interesting: *she embroidered her stories with colorful detail.* ▷late Middle English: from Anglo-Norman French *enbrouder*, from *en-* 'in, on' + Old French *brouder*, *broisder* 'decorate with embroidery,' of Germanic origin. **—em·broi·der·er** *n.*

em·broi·der·y /em'broid(ə)rē/ ▸*n.* (*pl.* **-der·ies**) the art or pastime of embroidering cloth. ■ cloth decorated in this way. ■ *figurative* embellishment or exaggeration in the description or reporting of an event: *fanciful embroidery of the facts.* ▷late Middle English: from Anglo-Norman French *enbrouderie*, from *enbrouder* 'embroider.'

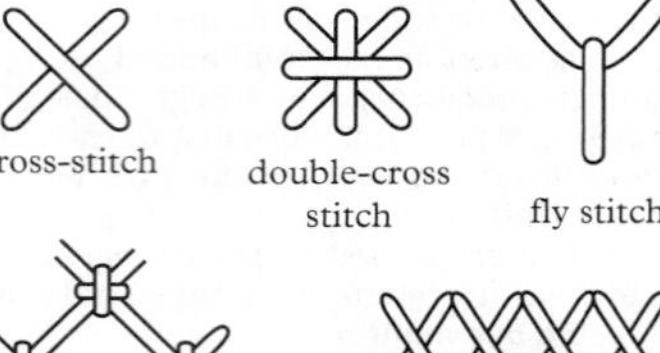

cross-stitch double-cross stitch fly stitch

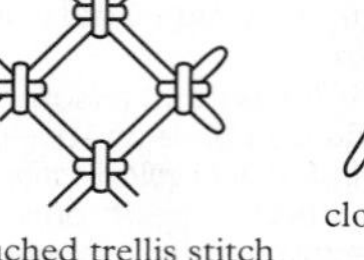

couched trellis stitch

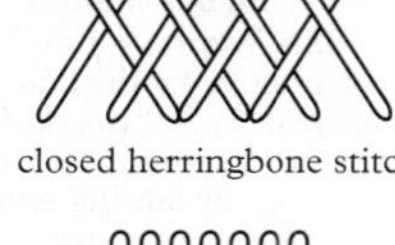

closed herringbone stitch

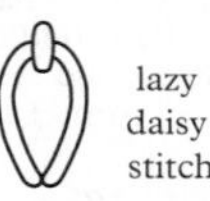

lazy daisy stitch

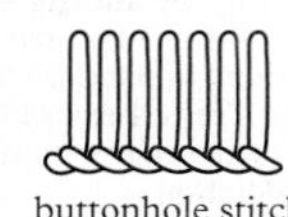

buttonhole stitch

embroidery stitches

em·broil /em'broil/ ▸*v.* [*trans.*] [often as *adj.*] (**embroiled**) involve (someone) deeply in an argument, conflict, or difficult situation: *she became* ***embroiled in*** *a dispute between two women she hardly knew* | *the movie's about a journalist who becomes* ***embroiled with*** *a nightclub owner.* ■ bring into a state of confusion or disorder. ▷early 17th cent.: from French *embrouiller* 'to muddle.' **—em·broil·ment** *n.*

em·bry·ec·to·my /,embrē'ektəmē/ ▸*n.* (*pl.* **-mies**) the surgical removal of an embryo, esp. one implanted outside the uterus in an ectopic pregnancy.

em·bry·o /'embrē,ō/ ▸*n.* (*pl.* **-os**) an unborn or unhatched offspring in the process of development. ■ an unborn human baby, esp. in the first eight weeks from conception, after implantation but before all the organs are developed. Compare with **FETUS**. ■ *Botany* the part of a seed that develops into a plant, consisting (in the mature embryo of a higher plant) of a plumule, a radicle, and one or two cotyledons. ■ *figurative* a thing at a rudimentary stage that shows potential for development: *a simple commodity economy is merely the embryo of a capitalist economy.* ▷late Middle English: via late Latin from Greek *embruon* 'fetus,' from *em-* 'into' + *bruein* 'swell, grow.'
▸*PHRASE* □ **in embryo** at a rudimentary stage with the potential for further development.

embryo- ▸*comb. form* representing **EMBRYO**.

em·bry·o·gen·e·sis /,embrē-ō'jenəsis/ ▸*n.* *Biology* the formation and development of an embryo. **—em·bry·o·ge·net·ic** /-jə'netik/ *adj.* **—em·bry·o·gen·ic** /-'jenik/ *adj.* **—em·bry·og·e·ny** /,embrē'äjənē/ *n.* .

em·bry·ol·o·gy /,embrē'äləjē/ ▸*n.* the branch of biology and medicine concerned with the study of embryos and their development. **—em·bry·o·log·ic** /,embrēə'läjik/ *adj.* **—em·bry·o·log·i·cal** /,embrēə'läjikəl/ *adj.* **—em·bry·o·log·i·cal·ly** /,embrēə'läjik(ə)lē/ *adv.* **—em·bry·ol·o·gist** /-jist/ *n.*

em·bry·o·nate /'embrēə,nāt/ ▸*adj.* (of an egg) containing an embryo.
▸*v.* [*intrans.*] [usu. as *adj.*] (**embryonated**) (of an egg) develop into an embryo: *embryonated duck eggs* | *the eggs were allowed two weeks to embryonate.*

em·bry·on·ic /,embrē'änik/ ▸*adj.* (also **em·bry·o·nal** /'embrēənəl/) of or relating to an embryo. ■ *figurative* (of a system, idea, or organization) in a rudimentary stage with potential for further development: *the plan is still in its embryonic stages.* ▷mid 19th cent.: from late Latin *embryo*, *embryon-* 'embryo' + **-IC**. **—em·bry·on·i·cal·ly** /-(ə)lē/ *adv.*

em·bry·op·a·thy /,embrē'äpəTHē/ ▸*n.* (*pl.* **-thies**) a developmental defect in an embryo or fetus.

em·bry·o sac ▸*n.* a cell inside the ovule of a flowering plant where fertilization occurs and which becomes the female gametophyte, containing the endosperm nucleus and the fertilized ovum that develops into the embryo.

em·cee /,em'sē/ *informal* ▸*n.* a master of ceremonies.
▸*v.* (**em·cees**, **em·ceed**, **em·cee·ing**) [*trans.*] perform the role of a master of ceremonies at (a public entertainment or a large social occasion). ▷1930s: representing the pronunciation of **MC**.

em dash ▸*n.* a long dash used in punctuation.

-eme ▸*suffix Linguistics* forming nouns denoting linguistic units that are in systemic contrast with one other: *grapheme* | *phoneme.* ▷abstracted from **PHONEME**.

e·mend /i'mend/ ▸*v.* [*trans.*] make corrections and improvements to (a text). ■ alter (something) in such a way as to correct it: *the year of his death might need to be emended to 652* | [with *clause*] *he hesitated and quickly emended what he had said.* ▷late Middle English: from Latin *emendare*, from *e-* (variant of *ex-*) 'out of' + *menda* 'a fault.' Compare with **AMEND**. **—e·mend·a·ble** *adj.* **—e·men·da·tion** /,ēmən'dāsHən; ,emən-/ *n.* **—e·mend·er** *n.*

emer. ▸*abbr.* emerita or emeritus.

em·er·ald /'em(ə)rəld/ ▸*n.* **1** a bright green precious stone consisting of a chromium-rich variety of beryl. **2** a bright green color like that of an emerald: [as *adj.*] *the leaves are* ***emerald green.*** **3** a small hummingbird with bright metallic green plumage and darker wings and tail, found mainly in the area of the Caribbean and Central America. • Three genera, in particular *Chlorostilbon* and *Amazilia*, family Trochilidae: numerous species.
▸*adj.* bright green in color: *beyond the airport lay emerald hills.* ▷Middle English: from Old French *e(s)meraud*, ultimately via Latin from Greek *(s)maragdos*, via Prakrit from Semitic (compare with Hebrew *bāreqet*, from *bāraq* 'flash, sparkle').

em·er·ald-cut ▸*adj.* (of a gem) cut in a rectangular shape with stepped facets.

Em·er·ald Isle a name for Ireland.

e·merge /i'mərj/ ▸*v.* [*intrans.*] move out of or away from something and come into view: *black ravens emerged from the fog.* ■ become apparent, important, or prominent: *Philadelphia has* ***emerged as*** *the clear favorite* | [as *adj.*] (**emerging**) *a world of emerging economic giants.* ■ (of facts or circumstances) become known: *reports of a deadlock emerged during preliminary discussions* | [with *clause*] *during the trial* ***it emerged that*** *she had been suffering from a rare personality disorder.* ■ recover from or survive a difficult or demanding situation: *the economy has started to* ***emerge from*** *recession.* ■ (of an insect or other invertebrate) break out from an egg, cocoon, or pupal case. ▷late 16th cent. (in the sense 'become known, come to light'): from Latin *emergere*, from *e-* (variant of *ex-*) 'out, forth' + *mergere* 'to dip.'

e·mer·gence /i'mərjəns/ ▸*n.* the process of coming into being, or of becoming important or prominent: *the emergence of the environmental movement* | *Japan's emergence as a modern state.* ■ the process of coming into view or becoming exposed after being concealed: *I misjudged the timing of my emergence.* ■ the escape of an insect or other invertebrate from an egg, cocoon, pupal case, etc.: *the parasite's eggs hatch synchronously with the emergence of the wasp larvae.* ■ an outgrowth from a stem or leaf composed of epidermal and subepidermal tissue, as the prickles on a thistle plant. ▷mid 17th cent. (in the sense 'unforeseen occurrence'): from medieval Latin *emergentia*, from Latin *emergere* 'bring to light' (see **EMERGE**).

e·mer·gen·cy /i'mərjənsē/ ▸*n.* (*pl.* **-cies**) a serious, unexpected, and often dangerous situation requiring immediate action: *your quick response in an emergency could be a lifesaver* | *times of emergency.* ■ [as *adj.*] arising from or needed or used in an emergency: *an emergency exit.* ■ a person with a medical condition requiring immediate treatment. ■ short for **EMERGENCY ROOM**: *he was rushed into emergency.* ▷mid 17th cent.: from medieval Latin *emergentia*, from Latin *emergere* 'arise, bring to light' (see **EMERGE**).

e·mer·gen·cy med·i·cal tech·ni·cian (abbr.:**EMT**) ▸*n.* a person who is specially trained and certified to administer basic emergency services to victims of trauma or acute illness before and during transportation to a hospital or other healthcare facility.

e·mer·gen·cy room ▸*n.* the department of a hospital that provides immediate treatment for acute illnesses and trauma.

e·mer·gen·cy serv·ic·es ▸*plural n.* the public organizations that respond to and deal with emergencies when they occur, esp. those that provide police, ambulance, and firefighting services.

e·mer·gent /i'mərjənt/ ▸*adj.* **1** in the process of coming into being or becoming prominent: *the emergent democracies of eastern Europe.* ■ *Philosophy* (of a property) arising as an effect of complex causes and not analyzable simply as the sum of their effects. ■ *Botany* of or denoting a plant that is taller than the surrounding vegetation, esp. a tall tree in a forest. ■ *Botany* of or denoting a water plant with leaves and flowers that appear above the water surface. **2** arising and existing only as a phenomenon of independent parts working together, and not predictable on the basis of their properties: *one such emergent property is the ability, already described, of an established ecosystem to repel an invading species.*
▸*n. Philosophy* an emergent property. ■ *Botany* an emergent tree or other plant. ▷late Middle English (in the sense 'occurring unexpectedly'): from Latin *emergent-* 'arising from,' from the verb *emergere* (see **EMERGE**).

e·mer·i·ta /i'meritə/ ▸*adj.* [*postpositive*] (of a woman who is the former holder of an office, esp. a female college professor) having retired but allowed to retain her title as an honor: *a professor emerita* | *the librarian emerita of Wellesley College.*

e·mer·i·tus /i'merətəs/ ▸*adj.* (of the former holder of an office, esp. a college professor) having retired but allowed to retain their title as an honor: *emeritus professor of microbiology* | [*postpositive*] *the gallery's director emeritus.* ▷mid 18th cent.: from Latin, past participle of *emereri* 'earn one's discharge by service,' from *e-* (variant of *ex-*) 'out of, from' + *mereri* 'earn.'

e·mersed /i'mərst/ ▸*adj. Botany* denoting or characteristic of an aquatic plant reaching above the surface of the water. Contrasted with **SUBMERSED** (see **SUBMERSE**). ▷late 17th cent.: from Latin *emersus* 'arisen,' past participle of *emergere* (see **EMERGE**).

e·mer·sion /i'mərzʜən/ ▸*n.* the process or state of emerging from or being out of water after being submerged. ■ *Astronomy* the reappearance of a celestial body after its eclipse or occultation. ▷mid 17th cent.: from late Latin *emersio(n-)*, from Latin *emergere* (see **EMERGE**).

Em·er·son /'emərsən/, Ralph Waldo (1803–82), U.S. philosopher and poet. In 1832, while visiting Britain, he became associated with German idealism. On his return to the U.S., he evolved the concept of transcendentalism, which found expression in his essay *Nature* (1836).

em·er·y /'em(ə)rē/ ▸*n.* a grayish-black mixture of corundum and magnetite, used in powdered form as an abrasive. ■ [*as adj.*] denoting materials coated with emery for polishing, smoothing, or grinding: *emery paper.* ▷late 15th cent.: from French *émeri*, from Old French *esmeri*, from Italian *smeriglio*, based on Greek *smuris, smiris* 'polishing powder.'

em·er·y board ▸*n.* a strip of thin wood or card coated with emery or another abrasive and used as a nail file.

em·e·sis /'eməsis/ ▸*n. technical* the action or process of vomiting. ▷late 19th cent.: from Greek, from *emein* 'to vomit.'

e·met·ic /i'metik/ ▸*adj.* (of a substance) causing vomiting. ■ *informal* nauseating or revolting: *that emetic music in department stores.*
▸*n.* a medicine or other substance that causes vomiting. ▷mid 17th cent.: from Greek *emetikos*, from *emein* 'to vomit.'

em·e·tine /'emi,tēn/ ▸*n.* an alkaloid present in ipecac and formerly used in the treatment of amebic infections and as an emetic in aversion therapy. ▷early 19th cent.: from Greek *emetos* 'vomiting' + **-INE**[4].

EMF ▸*abbr.* ■ electromagnetic field(s). ■ **(emf)** electromotive force. ■ European Monetary Fund.

EMG ▸*abbr.* ■ electromyogram. ■ electromyography.

-emia (also **-hemia**, *Brit.* **-aemia** or **-haemia**) ▸*comb. form* in nouns denoting that a substance is present in the blood, esp. in excess: *septicemia* | *leukemia.* ▷from modern Latin *-aemia*, from Greek *-aimia*, from *haima* 'blood.'

e·mic /'ēmik/ *Anthropology* ▸*adj.* relating to or denoting an approach to the study or description of a particular language or culture in terms of its internal elements and their functioning rather than in terms of any existing external scheme. Often contrasted with **ETIC**.
▸*plural n.* (**emics**) [treated as *sing.*] study adopting this approach. ▷1950s: abstracted from such words as *phonemic* (see **PHONEME**) and **SYSTEMIC**.

em·i·grant /'emigrənt/ ▸*n.* a person who leaves their own country in order to settle permanently in another: *the first emigrants to America* | [as *adj.*] *emigrant workers.*
▸*adj.* used by emigrants: *an emigrant ship.* ▷mid 18th cent.: from Latin *emigrant-* 'migrating from,' from the verb *emigrare* (see **EMIGRATE**).

em·i·grate /'emi,grāt/ ▸*v.* [*intrans.*] leave one's own country in order to settle permanently in another: *Rosa's parents* ***emigrated from*** *Argentina.* ▷late 18th cent.: from Latin *emigrat-* 'emigrated,' from the verb *emigrare*, from *e-* (variant of *ex-*) 'out of' + *migrare* 'migrate.' —**em·i·gra·tion** /,emi'grāsʜən/ *n.*

USAGE To **emigrate** is to leave a country, esp. one's own, intending to remain away. To **immigrate** is to enter a country, intending to remain there: *my aunt* ***emigrated from*** *Poland and* ***immigrated to*** *Canada.*

é·mi·gré /'emə,grā/ (also **e·mi·gre**) ▸*n.* a person who has left their own country in order to settle in another, usually for political reasons. ▷late 18th cent. (originally denoting a person escaping the French Revolution): French, past participle of *émigrer* 'emigrate.'

em·i·nence /'emənəns/ ▸*n.* **1** fame or recognized superiority, esp. within a particular sphere or profession: *her eminence in cinematography.* ■ [*count noun*] an important, influential, or distinguished person: *the Lord Chancellor canvassed the views of various legal eminences.* ■ **(His/Your Eminence)** a title given to a Roman Catholic cardinal, or used in addressing him: *His Eminence, Cardinal Thomas Wolsey.* **2** *formal or poetic/literary* a piece of rising ground: *an eminence commanding the River Emme.* ■ *Anatomy* a slight projection from the surface of a part of the body. ▷Middle English: from Latin *eminentia*, from *eminere* 'jut, project.'

é·mi·nence grise /āmēnäns 'grēz/ ▸*n.* (*pl.* **é·mi·nences grises** *pronunc.* same) a person who exercises power or influence in a certain sphere without holding an official position. ▷1930s: French, literally 'gray eminence.' The term was originally applied to Cardinal Richelieu's gray-cloaked private secretary, Père Joseph (1577–1638).

em·i·nent /'emənənt/ ▸*adj.* (of a person) famous and respected within a particular sphere or profession: *one of the world's most eminent statisticians.* ■ [*attrib.*] used to emphasize the presence of a positive quality: *the guitar's eminent suitability for recording studio work.* ▷late Middle English: from Latin *eminent-* 'jutting, projecting,' from the verb *eminere*. —**em·i·nent·ly** *adv.* [as *submodifier*] *an eminently readable textbook.*

USAGE A trio of frequently confused words is **eminent, imminent,** and **immanent. Eminent** means 'outstanding, famous': *the book was written by an eminent authority on folk art.* **Imminent** means 'about to happen': *people brushed aside the possibility that war was* ***imminent.*** **Immanent,** often used in religious or philosophical contexts, means 'inherent': *he believed in the* ***immanent*** *unity of nature taught by the Hindus.*

em·i·nent do·main ▸*n. Law* the right of a government or its agent to expropriate private property for public use, with payment of compensation.

e·mir /ə'mi(ə)r/ (also **a·mir**) ▸*n.* a title of various Muslim (mainly Arab) rulers: *the emir of Kuwait.* ■ *historical* a Muslim (usually Arab) military commander or local chief. ▷late 16th cent. (denoting a male descendant of Muhammad): from French *émir*, from Arabic *'amīr* (see **AMIR**).

e·mir·ate /ə'mi(ə)r,āt; ə'mi(ə)rit; 'emərit/ ▸*n.* the rank, lands, or reign of an emir.

em·is·sar·y /'emə,serē/ ▸*n.* (*pl.* **-sar·ies**) a person sent on a special mission, usually as a diplomatic representative. ▷early 17th cent.: from Latin *emissarius* 'scout, spy,' from *emittere* 'send out' (see **EMIT**).

e·mis·sion /i'misʜən/ ▸*n.* the production and discharge of something, esp. gas or radiation: *the effects of lead emission on health* | *cuts in carbon dioxide emissions.* ■ a thing emitted: *choking on the noxious emission.* ■ an ejaculation of semen. ■ the action of giving off radiation or particles; a flow of electrons from a cathode-ray tube or other source. ▷late Middle English (in the sense 'emanation'): from Latin *emissio(n-)*, from *emiss-* 'sent out,' from the verb *emittere* (see **EMIT**).

e·mis·sion neb·u·la ▸*n. Astronomy* a nebula that shines with its own light.

e·mis·sion spec·trum ▸*n.* a spectrum of the electromagnetic radiation emitted by a source. Compare with **ABSORPTION SPECTRUM**.

e·mis·sive /i'misiv/ ▸*adj. technical* having the power to radiate something, esp. light, heat, or radiation. ▷mid 17th cent. (in the sense 'that is emitted'): from Latin *emiss-* 'emitted, sent out' (from the verb *emittere*) + **-IVE**. —**e·mis·siv·i·ty** /,emə'sivitē; ,ēmə-/ *n.*

e·mit /i'mit/ ▸*v.* (**e·mit·ted, e·mit·ting**) [*trans.*] produce and discharge (something, esp. gas or radiation): *coal-fired power stations continue to emit large quantities of sulfur dioxide.* ■ make (a sound): *she emitted a sound like laughter.* ■ issue formally and with authority; put into circulation, esp. currency. ▷early 17th cent.: from Latin *emittere*, from *e-* (variant of *ex-*) 'out of' + *mittere* 'send.'

e·mit·ter /i'mitər/ ▸*n.* a thing that emits something. ■ *Electronics* a region in a bipolar transistor producing carriers of current.

Em·man·u·el /i'manyōōəl/ (also **Im·man·u·el**) the name given to Christ as the deliverer of Judah prophesied by Isaiah (Isa. 7:14, 8:8; Matt. 1:23).

em·men·a·gogue /ə'menə,gôg; -,gäg; -'mēnə-/ ▸*n. Medicine* a substance that stimulates or increases menstrual flow. ▷early 18th cent.: from Greek *emmēna* 'menses' + *agōgos* 'eliciting.'

Em·men·tal /'emən,täl/ (also **Em·men·thal**) ▸*n.* a kind of hard Swiss cheese with many holes in it, similar to Gruyère. ▷from German *Emmentaler*, from *Emmental*, the name of a valley in Switzerland where the cheese was originally made.

em·mer /'emər/ ▸*n.* an old kind of Eurasian wheat with bearded ears and spikelets that each contain two grains, now grown mainly for fodder and breakfast cereals. Compare with **EINKORN, SPELT**[2]. • *Triticum dicoccum*, family Gramineae. ▷early 20th cent.: from German, from Old High German *amer* 'spelt.'

em·met /'emit/ ▸*n. archaic* an ant. ▷Old English *ǣmete* (see **ANT**).

Em·my /'emē/ ▸*n.* (*pl.* **Em·mys**) a statuette awarded annually to an outstanding television program or performer. ▷1940s: said to be from *Immy*, short for *image orthicon tube* (a kind of television camera tube).

e·mol·lient /i'mälyənt/ ▸*adj.* having the quality of softening or soothing the skin: *an emollient cream.* ■ attempting to avoid confrontation or anger; soothing or calming: *the president's emollient approach to differences.*
▸*n.* a preparation that softens the skin: *formulated with rich emollients.* ▷mid 17th cent.: from Latin *emollient-* 'making soft,' from the verb *emollire*, from *e-* (variant of *ex-*) 'out' + *mollis* 'soft.' —**e·mol·lience** *n.*

e·mol·u·ment /i'mälyəmənt/ ▸*n.* (usu. **emoluments**) *formal* a salary, fee, or profit from employment or office: *the directors' emoluments.* ▷late Middle English: from Latin *emolumentum*, originally probably 'payment to a miller for grinding grain,' from *emolere* 'grind up,' from *e-* (variant of *ex-*) 'out, thoroughly' + *molere* 'grind.'

E·mo·na /i'mōnə/ Roman name of **LJUBLJANA**.

e·mote /i'mōt/ ▸*v.* [*intrans.*] (esp. of an actor) portray emotion in a theatrical manner. ▷early 20th cent. (originally U.S.): back-formation from **EMOTION**. —**e·mot·er** *n.*

e·mo·ti·con /i'mōtə,kän/ ▸*n.* a representation of a facial expression such as :-) (representing a smile), formed by various combinations of keyboard characters and used in electronic communications to convey the writer's feelings or intended tone. ▷1990s: blend of **EMOTION** and **ICON**.

e·mo·tion /i'mōsʜən/ ▸*n.* a natural instinctive state of mind deriving from one's circumstances, mood, or relationships with others: *she was attempting to control her emotions* | *his voice was low and shaky with emotion.* ■ any of the particular feelings that characterize such a state of mind, such as joy, anger, love, hate, horror, etc.: *fear had become his dominant emotion.* ■ instinctive or intuitive feeling as distinguished from reasoning or knowledge: *responses have to be based on historical insight, not simply on emotion.* ▷mid 16th cent. (denoting a public disturbance or commotion): from French *émotion*, from *émouvoir* 'excite,' based on Latin *emovere*, from *e-* (variant of *ex-*) 'out' + *movere* 'move.' The sense 'mental agitation' dates from the mid 17th cent., the current general sense from the early 19th cent. **—e·mo·tion·less** *adj.*

THE RIGHT WORD **affect, emotion, feeling, passion, sentiment**

A **feeling** can be almost any subjective reaction or state—pleasant or unpleasant, strong or mild, positive or negative—that is characterized by an emotional response (*a feeling of insecurity; a feeling of pleasure*).

An **emotion** is a very intense feeling, which often involves a physical as well as a mental response and implies outward expression or agitation (*to be overcome with emotion*).

Passion suggests a powerful or overwhelming emotion, with connotations of sexual love (*their passion remained undiminished after 30 years of marriage*) or intense anger (*a passion for revenge*).

There is more intellect and less feeling in **sentiment**, which is often applied to an emotion inspired by an idea (*political sentiments; antiwar sentiments*). *Sentiment* also suggests a refined or slightly artificial feeling (*a speech marked by sentiment rather than passion*).

Affect is a formal psychological term that refers to an observed emotional state (*heavily sedated, he spoke without affect*).

E

e·mo·tion·al /iˈmōSHənəl/ ▶*adj.* of or relating to a person's emotions: *children with emotional difficulties.* ■ arousing or characterized by intense feeling: *an emotional speech.* ■ (of a person) having feelings that are easily excited and openly displayed: *he was a strongly emotional young man.* ■ based on emotion rather than reason: *sound reason, not an emotional knee-jerk response, is the best recipe for making decisions.* **—e·mo·tion·al·ism** /-ˌizəm/ *n.* **—e·mo·tion·al·ist** /-ist/ *n.* & *adj.* **—e·mo·tion·al·i·ty** /iˌmōSHəˈnalitē/ *n.* **—e·mo·tion·al·ize** /-ˌlīz/ *v.* **—e·mo·tion·al·ly** *adv.*

USAGE See **usage** at **EMOTIVE**.

e·mo·tive /iˈmōtiv/ ▶*adj.* arousing or able to arouse intense feeling: *animal experimentation is an emotive subject | the issue has proved highly emotive.* ■ expressing a person's feelings rather than being neutrally or objectively descriptive: *the comparisons are emotive rather than analytic.* ▷mid 18th cent.: from Latin *emot-* 'moved,' from the verb *emovere* (see **EMOTION**). **—e·mo·tive·ly** *adv.* **—e·mo·tive·ness** *n.* **—e·mo·tiv·i·ty** /ˌēmōˈtivitē/ *n.*

USAGE The words **emotive** and **emotional** share similarities but are not interchangeable. **Emotive** is used to mean 'arousing intense feeling,' while **emotional** tends to mean 'characterized by intense feeling.' Thus an ***emotive** issue* is one likely to arouse people's passions, while an ***emotional** response* is one that is itself full of passion. In sentences such as *we took our **emotive** farewells*, **emotive** has been used where **emotional** is appropriate.

e·mo·tiv·ism /iˈmotiˌvizəm/ ▶*n. Philosophy* an ethical theory that regards ethical and value judgments as expressions of feeling or attitude and prescriptions of action, rather than assertions or reports of anything. **—e·mo·tiv·ist** *n.*

EMP ▶*abbr.* electromagnetic pulse.

emp. ▶*abbr.* ■ emperor. ■ empire. ■ empress.

em·pa·na·da /empəˈnädə/ ▶*n.* a Spanish or Latin American pastry turnover filled with a variety of savory ingredients and baked or fried. ▷Spanish, feminine past participle (used as a noun) of *empanar* 'roll in pastry,' based on Latin *panis* 'bread.'

em·pan·el /emˈpanl/ ▶*v.* variant spelling of **IMPANEL**. **—em·pan·el·ment** *n.*

em·path /ˈempaTH/ ▶*n.* (chiefly in science fiction) a person with the paranormal ability to apprehend the mental or emotional state of another individual.

em·pa·thize /ˈempəˌTHīz/ ▶*v.* [*intrans.*] understand and share the feelings of another: *counselors need to be able to **empathize with** people.*

em·pa·thy /ˈempəTHē/ ▶*n.* the ability to understand and share the feelings of another. ▷early 20th cent.: from Greek *empatheia* (from *em-* 'in' + *pathos* 'feeling') translating German *Einfühlung*. **—em·pa·thet·ic** /ˌempəˈTHetik/ *adj.* **—em·pa·thet·i·cal·ly** /ˌempəˈTHetik(ə)lē/ *adv.* **—em·path·ic** /emˈpaTHik/ *adj.* **—em·path·i·cal·ly** /emˈpaTHik(ə)lē/ *adv.*

Em·ped·o·cles /emˈpedəˌklēz/ (*c.*493–*c.*433 BC), Greek philosopher, born in Sicily. He taught that the universe is composed of fire, air, water, and earth, which mingle and separate under the influence of the opposing principles of Love and Strife.

em·pen·nage /ˌämpəˈnäZH; ˈempənij/ ▶*n. Aeronautics* an arrangement of stabilizing surfaces at the tail of an aircraft. ▷early 20th cent.: from French, from *empenner* 'to feather an arrow,' from *em-* 'in' + *penne* 'a feather' (from Latin *penna*).

em·per·or /ˈemp(ə)rər/ ▶*n.* **1** a sovereign ruler of great power and rank, esp. one ruling an empire. **2** (also **emperor butterfly**) an orange and brown North American butterfly with a swift dodging flight, breeding chiefly on hackberries. • Genus *Asterocampa*, subfamily Apaturinae, family Nymphalidae: several species, in particular the **tawny emperor** (*A. clyton*). ▷Middle English (esp. representing the title given to the head of the Roman Empire): from Old French *emperere*, from Latin *imperator* 'military commander,' from *imperare* 'to command,' from *in-* 'toward' + *parare* 'prepare, contrive.' **—em·per·or·ship** /-ˌSHip/ *n.*

em·per·or moth ▶*n.* a large moth of the silkworm moth family with eyespots on all four wings. • *Saturnia* and other genera, family Saturniidae: several species, in particular the common European *S. pavonia*.

em·per·or pen·guin ▶*n.* the largest species of penguin. It has a yellow patch on each side of the head and rears its young during the Antarctic winter. • *Aptenodytes forsteri*, family Spheniscidae.

em·pha·sis /ˈemfəsis/ ▶*n.* (*pl.* **-ses** /-ˌsēz/) special importance, value, or prominence given to something: *they placed great emphasis on the individual's freedom | different emphases and viewpoints.* ■ stress laid on a word or words to indicate special meaning or particular importance. ■ vigor or intensity of expression: *he spoke with emphasis and with complete conviction.* ▷late 16th cent.: via Latin from Greek, originally 'appearance, show,' later denoting a figure of speech in which more is implied than is said (the original sense in English), from *emphainein* 'exhibit,' from *em-* 'in, within' + *phainein* 'to show.'

em·pha·size /ˈemfəˌsīz/ ▶*v.* [*trans.*] give special importance or prominence to (something) in speaking or writing: *he jabbed a finger into the tabletop to emphasize his point* | [with *clause*] *he **emphasized that** the drug works in only 30 percent of cases.* ■ lay stress on (a word or phrase) when speaking. ■ make (something) more clearly defined: *a one-piece bathing suit that emphasized her build.*

em·phat·ic /emˈfatik/ ▶*adj.* showing or giving emphasis; expressing something forcibly and clearly: *the children were **emphatic that** they would like to repeat the experience | an emphatic movement of his hand* ■ (of an action or event or its result) definite and clear: *he walked stiffly, with an emphatic limp.* ■ (of word or syllable) bearing the stress. ■ *Linguistics* denoting certain Arabic consonants that are pronounced with both dental articulation and constriction of the pharynx. ▶*n. Linguistics* an emphatic consonant. ▷early 18th cent.: via late Latin from Greek *emphatikos*, from *emphasis* (see **EMPHASIS**).

em·phat·i·cal·ly /emˈfatik(ə)lē/ ▶*adv.* in a forceful way. ■ [as *submodifier*] without doubt; clearly: *Jane, though born in California, feels emphatically Canadian.* ■ [*sentence adverb*] used to give emphasis to a statement: *Greg is emphatically not a slacker.*

em·phy·se·ma /ˌemfəˈsēmə; -ˈzēmə/ ▶*n. Medicine* **1** (also **pulmonary emphysema**) a condition in which the air sacs of the lungs are damaged and enlarged, causing breathlessness. **2** a condition in which air is abnormally present within the body tissues. ▷mid 17th cent. (sense 2): via late Latin from Greek *emphusēma*, from *emphusan* 'puff up.' **—em·phy·sem·a·tous** /ˌemfəˈsemətəs; -ˈsēmə-; -ˈzemə-; -ˈzēmə-/ *adj.* **—em·phy·se·mic** *adj.*

em·pire /ˈemˌpī(ə)r/ ▶*n.* **1** an extensive group of states or countries under a single supreme authority, formerly esp. an emperor or empress: [in *names*] *the Roman Empire.* ■ a government in which the head of state is an emperor or empress. ■ a large commercial organization owned or controlled by one person or group: *her business empire grew.* ■ an extensive operation or sphere of activity controlled by one person or group: *the kitchen had once been the ladies' empire.* ■ supreme political power over several countries when exercised by a single authority: *he encouraged the Greeks in their dream of empire in Asia Minor.* ■ *archaic* absolute control over a person or group. **2** a variety of apple. ▶*adj.* also /ämˈpi(ə)r/ (usu. **Empire**) [*attrib.*] denoting a style of furniture, decoration, or dress fashionable during the First or (less commonly) the Second Empire in France. The decorative style was neoclassical but marked by an interest in Egyptian and other ancient motifs probably inspired by Napoleon's Egyptian campaigns. ■ (of a dress) having a high waist and a low neckline. ▷Middle English: via Old French from Latin *imperium*, related to *imperare* 'to command' (see **EMPEROR**).

empire (adj.)

em·pire build·er ▶*n.* a person who adds to or strengthens an empire. ■ a person who seeks more power, responsibility, or staff within an organization for the purposes of self-aggrandizement. **—em·pire-build·ing** *n.*

Em·pire State a nickname for the state of **NEW YORK**.

Em·pire State Build·ing a skyscraper on Fifth Avenue, New York City, which was for several years the tallest building in the world. When first erected, in 1930–31, it measured 1,250 feet (381 m); the addition of a television mast in 1951 brought its height to 1,472 feet (449 m).

Empire State Building

Em·pire State of the South a nickname for the state of **GEORGIA**.

em·pir·ic /emˈpirik/ ▶*adj.* another term for **EMPIRICAL**. ▶*n. archaic* a person who, in medicine or other branches of science, relies solely on observation and experiment. ■ a quack doctor. ▷late Middle English: via Latin from Greek *empeirikos*, from *empeiria* 'experience,' from *empeiros* 'skilled' (based on *peira* 'trial, experiment').

em·pir·i·cal /emˈpirikəl/ ▶*adj.* based on, concerned with, or verifiable by observation or experience rather than theory or pure logic: *they provided considerable empirical evidence to support their argument.* **—em·pir·i·cal·ly** *adv.*

em·pir·i·cal for·mu·la ▶*n. Chemistry* a formula giving the proportions of the elements present in a compound but not the actual numbers or arrangement of atoms. Compare with **MOLECULAR FORMULA**, **STRUCTURAL FORMULA**.

em·pir·i·cism /emˈpirəˌsizəm/ ▶*n. Philosophy* the theory that all knowledge is derived from sense-experience. Stimulated by the rise of experimental science, it developed in the 17th and 18th centuries, expounded in particular by John Locke, George Berkeley, and David Hume. Compare with **PHENOMENALISM**. ■ practice based on experiment and observation. ■ *dated* ignorant or unscientific practice; quackery. **—em·pir·i·cist** *n.* & *adj.*

em·place·ment /emˈplāsmənt/ ▶*n.* **1** a structure on or in which something is firmly placed. ■ a platform or defended position where a gun is placed for firing. **2** *chiefly Geology* the process or state of setting something in place or being set in place. ▷early 19th cent.: from French, from *em-* 'in' + *place* 'a place.'

em·plane /emˈplān/ ▶*v.* variant spelling of **ENPLANE**.

em·ploy /em'ploi/ ▶*v.* [*trans.*] **1** give work to (someone) and pay them for it: *the firm employs 150 people* | [*trans.*] *temps can be employed to do much of the work.* ■ keep occupied: *most of the newcomers are* ***employed in*** *developing the technology into a product.* **2** make use of: *the methods they have employed to collect the data.*
▶*n.* [in *sing.*] the state or fact of being employed for wages or a salary: *I started work* ***in the employ of*** *a grocer and wine merchant.* ■ *archaic* employment: *her place of employ.* ▷late Middle English (formerly also as *imploy*): from Old French *employer*, based on Latin *implicari* 'be involved in or attached to,' passive form of *implicare* (see IMPLY). In the 16th and 17th cent. the word also had the senses 'enfold, entangle' and 'imply,' derived directly from Latin; compare with IMPLICATE. **—em·ploy·a·bil·i·ty** /em,ploi-ə'bilitē/ *n.* **—em·ploy·a·ble** *adj.*

em·ploy·ee /em'ploi-ē; ,emploi'ē/ ▶*n.* a person employed for wages or salary, esp. at nonexecutive level.

em·ploy·er /em'ploi-ər/ ▶*n.* a person or organization that employs people.

em·ploy·ment /em'ploimənt/ ▶*n.* the condition of having paid work: *a fall in the numbers* ***in full-time employment.*** ■ a person's trade or profession. ■ the action of giving work to someone: *the employment of a full-time tutor.*

em·ploy·ment a·gen·cy ▶*n.* an agency that finds employers or employees for those seeking them.

Em·po·ria /em'pôrēə/ a commercial city in east central Kansas, associated with William Allen White and his Emporia *Gazette*, which he published from 1895 until 1944; pop. 26,760.

em·po·ri·um /em'pôrēəm/ ▶*n.* (*pl.* **-por·i·ums** or **-por·i·a** /-'pôrēə/) a large retail store selling a wide variety of goods. ■ a business establishment that specializes in products or services on a large scale (often used for humorously formal effect): *a Chinese food emporium* | *you know those half-automated carwash emporia that advertise an "all-cloth wash?"* ■ *archaic* a principal center of commerce; a market. ▷late 16th cent.: from Latin, from Greek *emporion*, from *emporos* 'merchant,' based on a stem meaning 'to journey.'

em·pow·er /em'pou(-ə)r/ ▶*v.* [*trans.*] give (someone) the authority or power to do something: *nobody was empowered to sign checks on her behalf.* ■ enable (someone) to do (something): *cryptography will empower individuals to control their information.* ■ [*trans.*] make (someone) stronger and more confident, esp. in controlling their life and claiming their rights: *movements to empower the poor.* **—em·pow·er·ment** *n.*

em·press /'empris/ ▶*n.* a female emperor. ■ the wife or widow of an emperor. ▷Middle English: from Old French *emperesse*, feminine of *emperere* (see EMPEROR).

em·presse·ment /,änpres'män/ ▶*n. archaic* animated eagerness or friendliness; effusion. ▷from French, from *empresser* 'rush eagerly.'

em·press tree ▶*n.* a fast-growing Paulownia widely grown as an ornamental in the U.S. and lately considered an ecological threat, in light of its prolific growth and reproductive capacity. • *paulownia tomentosa*, family Scrophulariaceae.

emp·ty /'em(p)tē/ ▶*adj.* (**-ti·er**, **-ti·est**) containing nothing; not filled or occupied: *he took his empty coffee cup back to the counter* | *the room was* ***empty of*** *furniture.* ■ *figurative* (of words or a gesture) having no meaning or likelihood of fulfillment; insincere: *his answer sounded a little empty* | *empty threats.* ■ *figurative* having no value or purpose: *her life felt empty and meaningless.* ■ *informal* hungry. ■ *Mathematics* (of a set) containing no members or elements. ■ emotionally exhausted: *at the funeral he stood feeling drained and empty.*
▶*v.* (**-ties**, **-tied**) [*trans.*] remove all the contents of (a container): *we empty the cash register each night at closing time* | *pockets were* ***emptied of*** *loose change.* ■ remove (the contents) from a container: *he* ***emptied out*** *the contents of his briefcase.* ■ [*intrans.*] (of a place) be vacated by people in it: *the bar suddenly seemed to empty.* ■ [*intrans.*] (**empty into**) (of a river) discharge itself into (the sea or a lake).
▶*n.* (*pl.* **-ties**) (usu. **empties**) *informal* a container (esp. a bottle or glass) left empty of its contents. ▷Old English *ǣmtig*, *ǣmetig* 'at leisure, unoccupied, empty,' from *ǣmetta* 'leisure,' perhaps from *ā* 'no, not' + *mōt* 'meeting' (see MOOT). **—emp·ti·ly** /-təlē/ *adv.* **—emp·ti·ness** /-tēnis/ *n.*
▶*PHRASES* □ **running on empty** exhausted of all one's resources or sustenance. □ **empty vessels make the most noise** (or **sound**) *proverb* those with least wisdom or knowledge are always the most talkative. □ **on an empty stomach** see STOMACH.

emp·ty cal·o·ries ▶*plural n.* calories derived from food containing no nutrients.

emp·ty-hand·ed ▶*adj.* [*predic.*] having failed to obtain or achieve what one wanted: *the burglars fled empty-handed.*

emp·ty-head·ed ▶*adj.* unintelligent and foolish: *why did they promote that empty-headed man?*

emp·ty nest·er ▶*n. informal* a parent whose children have grown up and left home.

Emp·ty Quar·ter another name for RUB' AL KHALI.

emp·ty word ▶*n. Grammar* a word that has only a grammatical function, and no meaning in itself (for example, the infinitive marker *to* in English).

em·pur·ple /em'pərpəl/ ▶*v.* make or become purple: [*intrans.*] *his face empurpled with fury.*

em·py·e·ma /,empī'ēmə/ ▶*n. Medicine* the collection of pus in a cavity in the body, esp. in the pleural cavity. ▷late Middle English: via late Latin from Greek *empuēma*, from *empuein* 'suppurate,' from *em-* 'in' + *puon* 'pus.'

em·py·re·an /em'pirēən; ,empə'rēən/ (also **em·py·re·al** /-əl/) ▶*adj.* belonging to or deriving from heaven.
▶*n.* (**the empyrean**) heaven, in particular the highest part of heaven. ■ *poetic/literary* the visible heavens; the sky. ▷late Middle English (as an adjective): via medieval Latin from Greek *empurios*, from *en-* 'in' + *pur* 'fire.' The noun dates from the mid 17th cent.

EMS ▶*abbr.* ■ emergency medical service. ■ European Monetary System. ■ expanded memory system, a system for increasing the amount of memory available to a personal computer, now largely superseded by XMS.

EMT ▶*abbr.* emergency medical technician.

EMU ▶*abbr.* European Monetary Union.

e·mu /'ēm(y)o͞o/ ▶*n.* a large flightless fast-running Australian bird resembling the ostrich, with shaggy gray or brown plumage, bare blue skin on the head and neck, and three-toed feet. • *Dromaius novaehollandiae*, the only member of the family Dromaiidae. ▷early 17th cent.: from Portuguese *ema*. The word originally denoted the cassowary, later the greater rhea; current usage dates from the early 19th cent.

em·u·late /'emyə,lāt/ ▶*v.* [*trans.*] match or surpass (a person or achievement), typically by imitation: *lesser men trying to emulate his greatness.* ■ imitate: *hers is not a hairstyle I wish to emulate.* ■ *Computing* reproduce the function or action of (a different computer or software system). ▷late 16th cent.: from Latin *aemulat-* 'rivaled, equaled,' from the verb *aemulari*, from *aemulus* 'rival.' **—em·u·la·tion** /,emyə'lāsʜən/ *n.* **—em·u·la·tive** /-,lātiv/ *adj.* **—em·u·la·tor** /-,lātər/ *n.*

em·u·lous /'emyələs/ ▶*adj.* (often **emulous of**) *formal* seeking to emulate or imitate someone or something. ■ motivated by a spirit of rivalry: *emulous young writers.* ▷late Middle English (in the sense 'resembling, imitating'): from Latin *aemulus* 'rival.' Current senses date from the mid 16th cent. **—em·u·lous·ly** *adv.* **—em·u·lous·ness** *n.*

e·mul·si·fi·er /i'məlsə,fi(ə)r/ ▶*n.* a substance that stabilizes an emulsion, in particular a food additive used to stabilize processed foods. ■ an apparatus used for making an emulsion by stirring or shaking a substance.

e·mul·si·fy /i'məlsə,fi/ ▶*v.* (**-fies**, **-fied**) make into or become an emulsion: [*trans.*] *mustard helps to emulsify a vinaigrette.* **—e·mul·si·fi·a·ble** /-,fiəbəl/ *adj.* **—e·mul·si·fi·ca·tion** /i,məlsəfi'kāsʜən/ *n.*

e·mul·sion /i'məlsʜən/ ▶*n.* a fine dispersion of minute droplets of one liquid in another in which it is not soluble or miscible. ▷early 17th cent. (denoting a milky liquid made by crushing almonds in water): from modern Latin *emulsio(n-)*, from the verb *emulgere* 'milk out,' from *e-* (variant of *ex-*) 'out' + *mulgere* 'to milk.'

en /en/ ▶*n. Printing* a unit of measurement equal to half an em and approximately the average width of typeset characters, used esp. for estimating the total amount of space a text will require. ▷late 18th cent.: the letter *N* represented as a word, since it is approximately this width.

en-[1] (also **em-**) ▶*prefix* **1** forming verbs (added to nouns) expressing entry into the specified state or location: *engulf* | *embed.* **2** forming verbs (added to nouns and adjectives) expressing conversion into the specified state (as in *encrust*, *ennoble*). ■ often forming verbs having the suffix *-en* (as in *embolden*, *enliven*). **3** (added to verbs) in; into; on: *ensnare.* ■ as an intensifier: *entangle.* ▷from French, from Latin *in-*. See also IN-2, a commonly found by-form.

en-[2] (also **em-**) ▶*prefix* within; inside: *encyst* | *endemic* | *embolism* | *empyema.* ▷from Greek.

-en[1] ▶*suffix* forming verbs: **1** (from adjectives) denoting the development, creation, or intensification of a state: *widen* | *deepen* | *loosen.* **2** from nouns (such as *strengthen* from *strength*). ▷Old English *-nian*, of Germanic origin.

-en[2] ▶*suffix* (also **-n**) forming adjectives from nouns: **1** made or consisting of: *earthen* | *woolen.* **2** resembling: *golden* | *silvern.* ▷Old English, of Germanic origin.

-en[3] (also **-n**) ▶*suffix* forming past participles of strong verbs: **1** as a regular inflection: *spoken.* **2** as an adjective: *mistaken* | *torn.* ■ often with a restricted adjectival sense: *drunken* | *sunken.* ▷Old English, of Germanic origin.

-en[4] ▶*suffix* forming the plural of a few nouns such as *children*, *oxen.* ▷Middle English reduction of the earlier suffix *-an.*

-en[5] ▶*suffix* forming diminutives of nouns (such as *chicken*, *maiden*). ▷Old English, of Germanic origin.

-en[6] ▶*suffix* **1** forming feminine nouns such as *vixen.* **2** forming abstract nouns such as *burden.* ▷Old English, of Germanic origin.

en·a·ble /en'ābəl/ ▶*v.* [*trans.*] give (someone or something) the authority or means to do something: *the evidence would enable us to arrive at firm conclusions.* ■ [*trans.*] make possible: *a number of courses are available to enable an understanding of a broad range of issues.* ■ [*trans.*] *chiefly Computing* make (a device or system) operational; activate. ▷late Middle English (formerly also as *inable*): from EN-1, IN-2, + ABLE. **—en·a·ble·ment** *n.* **—en·a·bler** *n.*

en·a·bling act ▶*n.* a statute empowering a person or body to take certain action, esp. to make regulations, rules, or orders.

en·act /en'akt/ ▶*v.* [*trans.*] **1** (often **be enacted**) make (a bill or other proposal) law: *legislation was enacted in 1987 to attract international companies.* ■ put into practice (a belief, idea, or suggestion). **2** act out (a role or play) on stage. ▷late Middle English (formerly also as *inact*): from EN-1, IN-2, + ACT, suggested by medieval Latin *inactare*, *inactitare.* **—en·act·a·ble** *adj.* **—en·ac·tion** /en'aksʜən/ *n.* **—en·ac·tor** /-tər/ *n.*

en·act·ment /en'aktmənt/ ▶*n.* **1** the process of passing legislation. ■ a law that is passed. **2** a process of acting something out: *the story becomes an enactment of his fantasies.* **—en·ac·tive** /-tiv/ *adj.*

e·nam·el /i'naməl/ ▶*n.* an opaque or semitransparent glassy substance applied to metallic or other hard surfaces for ornament or as a protective coating. ■ a work of art executed in such a substance. ■ the hard glossy substance that covers the crown of a tooth. ■ (also **enamel paint**) a paint that dries to give a smooth, hard coat. ■ *dated* nail polish.
▶*v.* (**-eled**, **-el·ing**; *Brit.* **-elled**, **-el·ling**) [*trans.*] [often as *adj.*] (**enameled**) coat or decorate (a metallic or hard object) with enamel: *an enameled roasting pan.* ■ *dated* apply nail polish to (fingernails or toenails). ▷late Middle English (originally as a verb; formerly also as *inamel*): from Anglo-Norman French *enamailler*, from *en-* 'in, on' + *amail* 'enamel,' ultimately of Germanic origin. **—e·nam·el·er** *n.* **—e·nam·el·ist** /-ist/ *n.*

e·nam·el·ware /i'naməl,wer/ ▶*n.* enameled kitchenware.

e·nam·el·work /i'naməl,wərk/ ▶*n.* the craft of inlaying or decorating metal objects with enamel.

en·am·or /i'namər/ (*chiefly Brit.* **en·am·our**) ▶*v.* (**be enamored of/with/by**) be filled with a feeling of love for: *it is not difficult to see why Edward is enamored of her.* ■ have a liking or admiration for: *she was truly enamored of New York.* ▷Middle English (formerly also as *inamour*): from Old French *enamourer*, from *en-* 'in' + *amour* 'love.'

en·an·the·ma /,enan'tʜēmə/ ▶*n. Medicine* an ulcer or eruption occurring on a mucus-secreting surface such as the inside of the mouth. ▷mid 19th cent.: from EN-2 'within' + a shortened form of EXANTHEMA.

en·an·ti·o·dro·mi·a /i,nantēə'drōmēə/ ▶*n. rare* the tendency of things to change into their opposites, esp. as a supposed governing principle of natural cycles and of psychological development. ▷early 20th cent.: from Greek, literally 'running in opposite ways.'

en·an·ti·o·mer /i'nantēəmər/ ▶*n. Chemistry* each of a pair of molecules that are mirror images of each other. ▷1930s: from Greek *enantios* 'opposite' + -MER. **—en·an·ti·o·mer·ic** /i,nantēə'merik/ *adj.* **—en·an·ti·o·mer·i·cal·ly** /-ik(ə)lē/ *adv.*

Pronunciation Key ə ago; ər over; 'ə or ,ə up; 'ər or ,ər fur; a hat; ā rate; ä car; ᴄʜ chew; e let; ē see; e(ə)r air; i fit; ī by; i(ə)r ear; ɴɢ sing; ō go; ô for; oi boy; o͝o good; o͞o goo; ou out; sʜ she; ᴛʜ thin; T͟H then; (h)w why; ᴢʜ vision

E

en·an·ti·o·morph /i'nantēə,môrf/ ▸*n.* each of two crystalline or other geometric forms that are mirror images of each other. ▷late 19th cent.: from Greek *enantios* 'opposite' + -MORPH. —**en·an·ti·o·mor·phic** /i,nantēə'môrfik/ *adj.* —**en·an·ti·o·mor·phism** /i,nantēə'môrfizəm/ *n.* —**en·an·ti·o·mor·phous** /i,nantēə'môrfəs/ *adj.*

en·ar·gite /en'ärjit; 'enər,jit/ ▸*n.* a dark gray mineral consisting of a sulfide of copper and arsenic. ▷mid 19th cent.: from Greek *enargēs* 'clear, distinct' (referring to evident cleavage) + -ITE[1].

en·ar·thro·sis /,enär'THrōsis/ ▸*n.* (*pl.* **-ses** /-sēz/) *Anatomy* a ball-and-socket joint. ▷late 16th cent.: from Greek *enarthrōsis*, from *enarthros* 'jointed,' from *en-* 'inside' + *arthron* 'joint.'

e·na·tion /ē'nāSHən/ ▸*n.* *Botany* an outgrowth from the surface of a leaf or other part of a plant. ▷mid 19th cent.: from Latin *enatio(n-)*, from *enasci* 'issue forth.'

en bloc /äN 'bläk/ ▸*adv.* all together or all at the same time: *various private museums offered to purchase the trove en bloc.* ▷mid 19th cent.: French.

en bro·chette /äN brō'SHet/ ▸*adj.* *Cooking* (of a dish) cooked on a skewer. ▷French *en brochette* 'on a skewer.'

en brosse /äN 'brôs/ ▸*adj.* [*postpositive*] (of a person's hair) cut in a short and bristly style. ▷early 20th cent.: French, literally 'in the form of a brush.'

enc. ▸*abbr.* ■ enclosed. ■ enclosure.

en·cage /en'kāj/ ▸*v.* [*trans.*] *poetic/literary* confine in or as in a cage.

en·camp /en'kamp/ ▸*v.* [*intrans.*] settle in or establish a camp, esp. a military one: *we encamped for the night by the side of a river.*

en·camp·ment /en'kampmənt/ ▸*n.* a place with temporary accommodations consisting of huts or tents, typically for troops or nomads. ■ the process of setting up a camp.

en·cap·si·date /en'kapsi,dāt/ ▸*v.* [*trans.*] *Biochemistry* enclose (a gene or virus particle) in a protein shell. —**en·cap·si·da·tion** /en,kapsi'dāSHən/ *n.*

en·cap·su·late /en'kaps(y)ə,lāt/ ▸*v.* [*trans.*] enclose (something) in or as if in a capsule. ■ express the essential features of (someone or something) succinctly: *the conclusion is encapsulated in one sentence.* ■ *Computing* enclose (a message or signal) in a set of codes that allow use by or transfer through different computer systems or networks. ■ *Computing* provide an interface for (a piece of software or hardware) to allow or simplify access for the user. ■ [as *adj.*] (**encapsulated**) enclosed by a protective coating or membrane. ▷late 19th cent. (also as *incapsulate*): from EN-[1], IN-[2] 'into' + Latin *capsula* (see CAPSULE). —**en·cap·su·la·tion** /en,kaps(y)ə'lāSHən/ *n.*

en·case /en'kās/ (also *dated* **in·case**) ▸*v.* [*trans.*] (often **be encased**) enclose or cover in a case or close-fitting surround. —**en·case·ment** *n.*

en·caus·tic /en'kôstik/ ▸*adj.* (esp. in painting and ceramics) using pigments mixed with hot wax that are burned in as an inlay. ■ (of bricks and tiles) decorated with differently colored clays, which are inlaid into the surface and burned in.
▸*n.* the art or process of encaustic painting. ▷late 16th cent.: via Latin from Greek *enkaustikos*, from *enkaiein* 'burn in,' from *en-* 'in' + *kaiein* 'to burn.'

-ence /əns; ns/ ▸*suffix* forming nouns: **1** denoting a quality or an instance of it: *impertinence.* **2** denoting an action or its result: *reference* | *reminiscence.* ▷from French *-ence*, from Latin *-entia*, *-antia* (from present participial stems *-ent-*, *-ant-*). Since the 16th cent. many inconsistencies have occurred in the use of *-ence* and *-ance*.

en·ceinte[1] /en'sānt; än'sant/ ▸*n.* *archaic* an enclosure or the enclosing wall of a fortified place. ▷early 18th cent.: from French, from Latin *incincta*, feminine past participle of *incingere* 'gird in,' from *in-* 'in' + *cingere* 'to gird.'

en·ceinte[2] ▸*adj.* *archaic* pregnant. ▷early 17th cent.: from French.

En·cel·a·dus /en'selədəs/ *Astronomy* a satellite of Saturn, the eighth closest to the planet, discovered by W. Herschel in 1789. Probably composed mainly of ice, it has a diameter of 311 miles (500 km). ▷named after a Greek mythological giant killed by Athena.

en·ce·phal·ic /,ensə'falik/ ▸*adj.* *Anatomy* relating to, affecting, or situated in the brain. ▷mid 19th cent.: from Greek *enkephalos* 'brain' (from *en-* 'in' + *kephalē* 'head') + -IC.

en·ceph·a·li·tis /en,sefə'lītis/ ▸*n.* inflammation of the brain, caused by infection or an allergic reaction. —**en·ceph·a·lit·ic** /-'litik/ *adj.*

en·ceph·a·li·tis le·thar·gi·ca /li'THärjikə/ ▸*n.* a form of encephalitis caused by a virus and characterized by headache and drowsiness leading to coma. Also called SLEEPING SICKNESS.

en·ceph·a·li·za·tion /en,sefəli'zāSHən/ ▸*n.* *Zoology* an evolutionary increase in the complexity or relative size of the brain, involving a shift of function from noncortical parts of the brain to the cortex.

encephalo- ▸*comb. form* of or relating to the brain: *encephalopathy.* ▷from Greek *enkephalos*.

en·ceph·a·lo·gram /en'sefələ,gram/ ▸*n.* *Medicine* an image, trace, or other record of the structure or electrical activity of the brain.

en·ceph·a·log·ra·phy /en,sefə'lägrəfē/ ▸*n.* *Medicine* any of various techniques for recording the structure or electrical activity of the brain. —**en·ceph·a·lo·graph** /en'sefələ,graf/ *n.* —**en·ceph·a·lo·graph·ic** /-lə'grafik/ *adj.*

en·ceph·a·lo·my·e·li·tis /en,sefələ,mīə'lītis/ ▸*n.* *Medicine* inflammation of the brain and spinal cord, typically due to acute viral infection.

en·ceph·a·lon /en'sefə,län; -lən/ ▸*n.* *Anatomy* the brain. ▷mid 18th cent.: from Greek *enkephalon* 'what is inside the head,' from *en-* 'inside' + *kephalē* 'head.'

en·ceph·a·lop·a·thy /en,sefə'läpəTHē/ ▸*n.* (*pl.* **-thies**) *Medicine* a disease in which the functioning of the brain is affected by some agent or condition (such as viral infection or toxins in the blood).

en·chain /en'CHān/ ▸*v.* [*trans.*] *poetic/literary* bind with or as with chains. ▷late Middle English: from Old French *enchainer*, based on Latin *catena* 'chain.' —**en·chain·ment** *n.*

en·chaîne·ment /,äNSHen'mäN/ ▸*n.* (*pl.* **-ments** *pronunc.* same) *Ballet* a linked sequence of steps or movements constituting a phrase. ▷mid 19th cent.: French, 'chaining together.'

en·chant /en'CHant/ ▸*v.* [*trans.*] (often **be enchanted**) fill (someone) with great delight; charm: *Isabel was* **enchanted with** *the idea.* ■ put (someone or something) under a spell: [as *adj.*] (**enchanted**) *an enchanted garden.* ▷late Middle English (in the senses 'put under a spell' and 'delude'; formerly also as *inchant*): from French *enchanter*, from Latin *incantare*, from *in-* 'in' + *cantare* 'sing.' —**en·chant·ed·ly** *adv.* —**en·chant·ment** *n.*

en·chant·er /en'CHantər/ ▸*n.* a person who uses magic or sorcery, esp. to put someone or something under a spell.

en·chant·er's night·shade ▸*n.* a woodland plant with small white flowers and fruit with hooked bristles, native to Eurasia and North America. • Genus *Circaea*, family Onagraceae: several species, including *C. quadrisulcata* and the smaller *C. alpina.* ▷late 16th cent.: believed by early botanists to be the herb used by Circe to charm Odysseus' companions.

en·chant·ing /en'CHanting/ ▸*adj.* delightfully charming or attractive: *Dinah looked enchanting.* —**en·chant·ing·ly** *adv.*

en·chant·ress /en'CHantris/ ▸*n.* a woman who uses magic or sorcery, esp. to put someone or something under a spell. ■ a very attractive and beguiling woman. ▷late Middle English: from Old French *enchanteresse*, from *enchanter* (see ENCHANT).

en·chase /en'CHās/ ▸*v.* [*trans.*] decorate (a piece of jewelry or work of art) by inlaying, engraving, or carving. ■ place (a jewel) in a setting. ▷late Middle English (in the sense 'decorate with figures in relief'): from Old French *enchasser* 'set gems, encase,' from *en-* 'in' + *chasse* 'a case.'

en·chi·la·da /,enCHə'lädə/ ▸*n.* a rolled tortilla with a filling typically of meat and served with a chili sauce. ▷Latin American Spanish, feminine past participle of *enchilar* 'season with chili.'
▸*PHRASES* □ **the big enchilada** *informal* a person or thing of great importance. □ **the whole enchilada** *informal* the whole situation; everything.

en·chi·rid·i·on /,eNGkə'ridēən; ,enkī-/ ▸*n.* (*pl.* **-rid·i·ons** or **-rid·i·a** /-'ridēə/) *formal* a book containing essential information on a subject. ▷late Middle English: via late Latin from Greek *enkheiridion*, from *en-* 'within' + *kheir* 'hand' + the diminutive suffix *-idion*.

En·ci·ni·tas /,ensi'nētəs/ a city in southwestern California, northwest of San Diego; pop. 55,386.

en·ci·pher /en'sīfər/ ▸*v.* [*trans.*] convert (a message or piece of text) into a coded form; encrypt. —**en·ci·pher·ment** *n.*

en·cir·cle /en'sərkəl/ ▸*v.* [*trans.*] form a circle around; surround: *the town is encircled by fortified walls.* See note at CIRCUMSCRIBE. —**en·cir·cle·ment** *n.*

encl. (also **enc.**) ▸*abbr.* ■ enclosed. ■ enclosure.

en clair /äN 'kler/ ▸*adj.* & *adv.* (esp. of a telegram or official message) in ordinary language, rather than in code or cipher. ▷French, literally 'in clear.'

en·clasp /en'klasp/ ▸*v.* [*trans.*] *formal* hold tightly in one's arms.

en·clave /'en,klāv; 'äNG-/ ▸*n.* a portion of territory within or surrounded by a larger territory whose inhabitants are culturally or ethnically distinct. ■ a secured area within another secured area: *the cost of a security service is going to be proportional to the size of the enclave that you must secure.* ■ *figurative* a place or group that is different in character from those surrounding it: *the engineering department is traditionally a male enclave.*
▸*v.* [*trans.*] *rare* surround and isolate; make an enclave of. ▷mid 19th cent.: from French, from Old French *enclaver* 'enclose, dovetail,' based on Latin *clavis* 'key.'

en·clit·ic /en'klitik/ *Linguistics* ▸*n.* a word pronounced with so little emphasis that it is shortened and forms part of the preceding word, e.g., *n't* in *can't*. Compare with PROCLITIC.
▸*adj.* denoting or relating to such a word. ▷mid 17th cent.: via late Latin from Greek *enklitikos*, from *enklinein* 'lean on,' from *en-* 'in, on' + *klinein* 'to lean.' —**en·clit·i·cal·ly** /-(ə)lē/ *adv.*

en·close /en'klōz/ (also *dated* **in·close**) ▸*v.* [*trans.*] **1** (often **be enclosed**) surround or close off on all sides: *the entire estate was* **enclosed with** *walls* | [as *adj.*] (**enclosed**) *a dark enclosed space.* See note at CIRCUMSCRIBE. ■ *historical* fence in (common land) so as to make it private property. ■ [usu. as *adj.*] (**enclosed**) seclude (a religious order or other community) from the outside world. ■ *chiefly Mathematics* bound on all sides; contain. **2** place (something) in an envelope together with a letter: *I enclose a copy of the job description.* ▷Middle English (in the sense 'shut in, imprison'): from Old French *enclos*, past participle of *enclore*, based on Latin *includere* 'shut in.'

en·clo·sure /en'klōZHər/ (also *dated* **in·clo·sure**) ▸*n.* **1** an area that is sealed off with an artificial or natural barrier. ■ an artificial or natural barrier that seals off an area. **2** the state of being enclosed, esp. in a religious community: *the nuns kept strict enclosure.* ■ *historical* the process or policy of fencing in waste or common land so as to make it private property, as pursued in much of Britain in the 18th and early 19th centuries: *one of the chief effects of enclosure was to increase the number of landless workers.* **3** a document or object placed in an envelope together with a letter. ▷late Middle English: from legal Anglo-Norman French and Old French, from *enclos* 'closed in' (see ENCLOSE).

en·code /en'kōd/ ▸*v.* [*trans.*] convert into a coded form. ■ *Computing* convert (information or an instruction) into a digital form. ■ *Biochemistry* (of a gene) be responsible for producing (a substance or behavior). —**en·cod·a·ble** *adj.* —**en·cod·er** *n.* —**en·code·ment** *n.*

en·co·mi·ast /en'kōmē,ast/ ▸*n.* *formal* a person who publicly praises or flatters someone else. ▷early 17th cent.: from Greek *enkōmiastēs*, from *enkōmiazein* 'to praise,' from *enkōmion* (see ENCOMIUM). —**en·co·mi·as·tic** /en,kōmē'astik/ *adj.* —**en·co·mi·as·ti·cal·ly** /en,kōmē'astik(ə)lē/ *adv.*

en·co·mi·en·da /en,kōmē'endə; -,kämē-/ ▸*n.* *historical* a grant by the Spanish Crown to a colonist in America conferring the right to demand tribute and forced labor from the Indian inhabitants of an area. ▷early 19th cent.: Spanish, literally 'commission, charge.'

en·co·mi·um /en'kōmēəm/ ▸*n.* (*pl.* **-mi·ums** or **-mi·a** /-mēə/) *formal* a speech or piece of writing that praises someone or something highly. ▷mid 16th cent.: Latin, from Greek *enkōmion* 'eulogy,' from *en-* 'within' + *komos* 'revel.'

en·com·pass /en'kəmpəs/ ▸*v.* **1** [*trans.*] surround and have or hold within: *a vast halo encompassing the Milky Way galaxy.* See note at CIRCUMSCRIBE. ■ include comprehensively: *no studies encompass all aspects of medical care.* **2** *archaic* cause (something) to take place: *an act designed to encompass the death of the king.* —**en·com·pass·ment** *n.*

en·co·pre·sis /,enkə'prēsis/ ▸*n.* *Medicine* involuntary defecation, esp. associated with emotional disturbance or psychiatric disorder.

en·core /'än,kôr/ ▸*n.* a repeated or additional performance of an item at the end of a concert, as called for by an audience.
▸*exclam.* called out by an audience at the end of a concert to request such a performance.
▸*v.* [*trans.*] (often **be encored**) give or call for a repeated or additional performance of (an item) at the end

of a concert. ▷early 18th cent.: French, literally 'still, again.'

en·coun·ter /en'koun(t)ər/ ▸*v.* [*trans.*] unexpectedly experience or be faced with (something difficult or hostile): *we have encountered one small problem.* ■ meet unexpectedly and confront (an adversary): *the soldiers encountered a large crowd of demonstrators.* ■ meet (someone) unexpectedly.
▸*n.* an unexpected or casual meeting with someone or something. ■ a confrontation or unpleasant struggle: *his **close encounter with** death.* ▷Middle English (in the senses 'meet as an adversary' and 'a meeting of adversaries'; formerly also as *incounter*): from Old French *encontrer* (verb), *encontre* (noun), based on Latin *in-* 'in' + *contra* 'against.'

en·coun·ter group ▸*n.* a group of people who meet to gain psychological benefit through close contact with one another.

en·cour·age /en'kərij; -'kə-rij/ ▸*v.* [*trans.*] give support, confidence, or hope to (someone): *we were encouraged by the success of this venture* | [as *adj.*] (**encouraging**) *the results are very encouraging* | [as *adj.*] (**encouraged**) *I feel much encouraged.* ■ give support and advice to (someone) so that they will do or continue to do something: [*trans.*] *pupils are encouraged to be creative.* ■ help or stimulate (an activity, state, or view) to develop: *the intention is to encourage new writing talent.* ▷Middle English (formerly also as *incourage*): from French *encourager*, from *en-* 'in' + *corage* 'courage.' **—en·cour·age·ment** *n.* **—en·cour·ag·er** *n.* **—en·cour·ag·ing·ly** *adv.* [*sentence adverb*] *encouragingly, there is more research being done today* | [as *submodifier*] *the level of activity continues to be encouragingly high.*

THE RIGHT WORD **embolden, encourage, foster, hearten, inspire, instigate, stimulate**

To **encourage** is to give active help or to raise confidence to the point where one dares to do what is difficult (*encouraged by her teacher, she set her sights on attending Harvard*).

Embolden also entails giving confidence or boldness, but it implies overcoming reluctance or shyness (*success as a public speaker emboldened her to enter politics*).

To **hearten** is to put one's heart into or to renew someone's spirit (*heartened by the news of his recovery*), and to **inspire** is to infuse with confidence, resolution, or enthusiasm (*inspired by her mother's example, she started exercising regularly*).

To **foster** is to encourage by nurturing or extending aid (*to foster the growth of small businesses by offering low-interest loans*); in some contexts, *foster* suggests an unwise or controversial kind of help (*to foster rebellion among local farmers*).

Instigate also implies that what is being encouraged is not necessarily desirable (*to instigate a fight*), while **stimulate** is a more neutral term meaning to rouse to action or effort (*to stimulate the growth of crops*; | *to stimulate an interest in literature*).

en·croach /en'krōCH/ ▸*v.* [*intrans.*] (**encroach on/upon**) intrude on (a person's territory or a thing considered to be a right): *rather than encroach on his privacy, she might have kept to her room.* ■ advance gradually and in a way that causes damage: *the sea has encroached all around the coast.* ▷late Middle English (in the sense 'obtain unlawfully, seize'; formerly also as *incroach*): from Old French *encrochier* 'seize, fasten upon,' from *en-* 'in, on' + *crochier* (from *croc* 'hook,' from Old Norse *krókr*). **—en·croach·er** *n.*

en·croach·ment /en'krōCHmənt/ ▸*n. Football* a penalty in which a defensive player is positioned in the neutral zone at the start of a play.

en croute /än 'kro͞ot/ ▸*adj.* & *adv.* in a pastry crust: [as *postpositive adj.*] *salmon en croute* | [as *adv.*] *goat's cheese is particularly tasty baked en croute.* ▷French *en croûte.*

en·crust /en'krəst/ (also **in·crust**) ▸*v.* [*trans.*] cover (something) with a hard surface layer: *the mussels encrust navigation buoys* | [as *adj.*] (**encrusted**) *the dried and encrusted blood.* ■ overlay (something) with an ornamental crust of gems or other precious material: *a crown **encrusted with** rubies.* ■ [*intrans.*] form a crust. ▷early 17th cent. (in the sense 'cause to form a crust'): from French *incruster* or *encroûter*, both from Latin *incrustare*, from *in-* 'into' + *crusta* 'a crust.'

en·crus·ta·tion /ˌenkrəs'tāSHən/ (also **in·crus·ta·tion**) ▸*n.* the action of encrusting or state of being encrusted. ■ a crust or hard coating on the surface of something: *the sides are white with encrustations of salt.* ■ an outer layer or crust of ornamentation. ■ *Architecture* a facing of marble on a building. ▷early 17th cent. (originally as *incrustation*): from late Latin *incrustatio(n-)*, from the verb *incrustare* (see **ENCRUST**).

en·crypt /en'kript/ ▸*v.* [*trans.*] convert (information or data) into a cipher or code, esp. to prevent unauthorized access. ■ (**encrypt something in**) conceal information or data in something by this means. ▷1950s (originally U.S.): from **EN-**[1] 'in' + Greek *kruptos* 'hidden.' **—en·cryp·tion** /-'kripSHən/ *n.*

en·cul·tu·ra·tion /enˌkəlCHə'rāSHən/ (also **in·cul·tu·ra·tion**) ▸*n.* the gradual acquisition of the characteristics and norms of a culture or group by a person, another culture, etc. ■ the adaptation of Christian liturgy to a non-Christian cultural background.

en·cum·ber /en'kəmbər/ ▸*v.* [*trans.*] (often **be encumbered**) restrict or burden (someone or something) in such a way that free action or movement is difficult: *she was **encumbered by** her heavy skirts* | *they had arrived **encumbered with** families.* See note at **HINDER**. ■ saddle (a person or estate) with a debt or mortgage: *an estate heavily **encumbered with** debt.* ■ fill or block up (a place): *we tripped over sticks and stones, which encumber most of the trail.* ▷Middle English (in the sense 'cause trouble to, entangle'; formerly also as *incumber*): from Old French *encombrer* 'block up,' from *en-* 'in' + *combre* 'river barrage.'

en·cum·brance /en'kəmbrəns/ ▸*n.* a burden or impediment. ■ *Law* a mortgage or other charge on property or assets. ■ *archaic* a person, esp. a child, who is dependent on someone else for support. ▷Middle English (denoting an encumbered state; formerly also as *incumbrance*): from Old French *encombrance*, from *encombrer* 'block up' (see **ENCUMBER**).

ency. ▸*abbr.* encyclopedia.

-ency /ənsē; n-sē/ ▸*suffix* forming nouns: **1** denoting a quality: *efficiency.* **2** denoting a state: *presidency.* ▷from Latin *-entia* (compare with **-ENCE**).

encyc. ▸*abbr.* encyclopedia.

encycl. ▸*abbr.* encyclopedia.

en·cyc·li·cal /en'siklikəl/ ▸*n.* a papal letter sent to all bishops of the Roman Catholic Church.
▸*adj.* of or relating to such a letter. ▷mid 17th cent. (as an adjective): via late Latin from Greek *enkuklios* 'circular, general,' from *en-* 'in' + *kuklos* 'a circle.'

en·cy·clo·pe·di·a /enˌsīklə'pēdēə/ (also *chiefly Brit.* **en·cy·clo·pae·di·a**) ▸*n.* a book or set of books giving information on many subjects or on many aspects of one subject and typically arranged alphabetically. ▷mid 16th cent.: modern Latin, from pseudo-Greek *enkuklopaideia* for *enkuklios paideia* 'all-around education.'

en·cy·clo·pe·dic /enˌsīklə'pēdik/ (also *chiefly Brit.* **en·cy·clo·pae·dic**) ▸*adj.* comprehensive in terms of information: *he has an almost encyclopedic knowledge of food.* ■ relating to or containing names of famous people and places and information about words that is not simply linguistic: *a dictionary with encyclopedic material.* **—en·cy·clo·pe·di·cal·ly** /-(ə)lē/ *adv.*

en·cy·clo·pe·dism /enˌsīklə'pēˌdizəm/ (also *chiefly Brit.* **en·cy·clo·pae·dism**) ▸*n.* comprehensive learning or knowledge.

en·cy·clo·pe·dist /enˌsīklə'pēdist/ (also *chiefly Brit.* **en·cy·clo·pae·dist**) ▸*n.* a person who writes, edits, or contributes to an encyclopedia.

en·cyst /en'sist/ ▸*v. Zoology* enclose or become enclosed in a cyst. **—en·cys·ta·tion** /ˌensi'stāSHən/ *n.* **—en·cyst·ment** *n.*

end /end/ ▸*n.* **1** a final part of something, esp. a period of time, an activity, or a story: *the end of the year* | *Mario led the race **from beginning to end.*** ■ a termination of a state or situation: *the party called for **an end to** violence* | *one notice will be effective to **bring** the tenancy **to an end.*** ■ used to emphasize that something, typically a subject of discussion, is considered finished: *you will go to church and **that's the end of it.*** ■ death or ruin: *if she's caught stealing again, it will **be the end of** her career.* ■ *archaic* (in biblical use) an ultimate state or condition: *the end of that man is peace.* **2** the furthest or most extreme part or point of something: *a length of wire with a hook at the end* | [as *adj.*] *the end house.* ■ a small piece that is left after something has been used: *a box of candle ends.* ■ a specified extreme point on a scale: *homebuyers at the lower end of the market.* ■ the part or share of an activity with which someone is concerned: *you're going to honor your end of the deal.* ■ a place that is linked to another by a telephone call, letter, or journey: *"Hello," said a voice at the other end.* ■ the part of an athletic field or court defended by one team or player. **3** a goal or result that one seeks to achieve: *each would use the other to **further his own ends*** | ***to this end**, schools were set up for peasant women.* **4** *Lawn Bowling & Curling* a session of play in one particular direction across the playing area. **5** *Football* an offensive or defensive lineman positioned nearest to the sideline.
▸*v.* come or bring to a final point; finish: [*intrans.*] *when the war ended, policy changed* | *the chapter **ends with** a case study* | [*trans.*] *she wanted to end the relationship.* ■ [*intrans.*] reach a point and go no further: *the boundary where agnosticism ends and atheism begins.* ■ [*intrans.*] perform a final act: *the man **ended by** attacking a police officer.* ■ [*intrans.*] (**end in**) have as its final part, point, or result: *one in three marriages is now likely to end in divorce.* ■ [*intrans.*] (**end up**) eventually reach or come to a specified place, state, or course of action: *I **ended up in** Connecticut* | *you could **end up with** a higher income.* ▷Old English *ende* (noun), *endian* (verb), of Germanic origin; related to Dutch *einde* (noun), *einden* (verb) and German *Ende* (noun), *enden* (verb).
▸***PHRASES*** □ **at the end of the day** *informal* when everything is taken into consideration: *at the end of the day, I'm responsible for what happens in the school.* □ **be at** (or **have come to**) **an end** be finished or completed. ■ (of a supply of something) become exhausted: *our patience has come to an end.* □ **be at the end of** be close to having no more of (something): *he was at the end of his ability to cope.* □ **be the end** *informal* be the limit of what one can tolerate: *you really are the end!* □ **come to** (or **meet**) **a bad end** be led by one's own actions to ruin or an unpleasant death. □ **end one's days** (or **life**) spend the final part of one's existence in a specified place or state: *the last passenger pigeon ended her days in the Cincinnati Zoo.* □ **an end in itself** a goal that is pursued in its own right to the exclusion of others. □ **end in tears** have an unhappy or painful outcome (often as a warning): *this treaty will end in tears.* □ **end it all** commit suicide. □ **the end of the road** (or **line**) the point beyond which progress or survival cannot continue: *if the lawsuit is not dropped it could **be the end of the road for** the publisher.* □ **the end of one's rope** (or **tether**) having no patience or energy left to cope with something: *after enduring four years of mice in the house, we were **at the end of our rope*** | *they have **reached the end of their tether.*** □ **the end of the world** the termination of life on the earth. ■ *informal* a complete disaster: ***it's not the end of the world** if you're not great at sports.* □ **end on** with the furthest point of an object facing toward one: *seen end on, their sharp, rocky summits point like arrows.* ■ with the furthest point of an object touching that of another: *slim stone tiles had been layered end on with incredible skill.* □ **end to end** in a row with the furthest point of one object touching that of another object. □ **in the end** eventually or on reflection: *in the end, I saw that she was right.* □ **keep** (or **hold**) **one's end up** *informal* perform well in a difficult or competitive situation. □ **make an end of** cause (someone or something) to stop existing. □ **make** (**both**) **ends meet** earn enough money to live without getting into debt. □ **never** (or **not**) **hear the end of** be continually reminded of (an unpleasant topic or cause of annoyance). □ **no end** *informal* to a great extent; very much: *this cheered me up no end.* □ **no end of** *informal* a vast number or amount of (something): *we shared no end of good times.* □ **on end** **1** continuing without stopping for a specified period of time: *sometimes they'll be gone for days on end.* **2** in an upright position: *he brushed his hair, leaving a tuft standing on end.* □ **put an end to** cause someone or something to stop existing: *injury put an end to his career.* □ **a —— to end all ——s** *informal* used to emphasize how impressive or successful something is of its kind: *it was a party to end all parties.* □ **without end** without a limit or boundary: *a war without end.*

-end ▸*suffix* denoting a person or thing to be treated in a specified way: *dividend* | *reverend.* ▷from Latin *-endus*, gerundive ending.

end-all ▸*n.* (**the end-all**) the thing that is final or definitive.

en·dan·ger /en'dānjər/ ▸*v.* [*trans.*] put (someone or something) at risk or in danger: *he was driving in a manner likely to endanger life.* **—en·dan·ger·ment** *n.*

en·dan·gered /en'dānjərd/ ▸*adj.* (of a species) seriously at risk of extinction.

end-a·round ▸*n. Football* a play in which an end carries the ball around the opposing side of the line of scrimmage.
▸*adj. Computing* involving the transfer of a digit from one end of a register to the other.

end·ar·ter·ec·to·my /ˌendärtə'rektəmē/ ▸*n.* (*pl.* **-mies**) surgical removal of part of the inner lining of an

E

artery, together with any obstructive deposits, most often carried out on the carotid artery or on vessels supplying the legs.

end·ar·te·ri·tis /ˌendärtəˈrītis/ ▶*n. Medicine* inflammation of the inner lining of an artery.

en dash ▶*n.* a short dash, the width of an en, used in punctuation.

en·dear /enˈdi(ə)r/ ▶*v.* [*trans.*] cause to be loved or liked: *Flora's spirit and character* ***endeared*** *her* ***to*** *everyone who met her.*

en·dear·ing /enˈdi(ə)riNG/ ▶*adj.* inspiring love or affection: *an endearing little grin.* **—en·dear·ing·ly** *adv.*

en·dear·ment /enˈdi(ə)rmənt/ ▶*n.* a word or phrase expressing love or affection. ■ love or affection: *a term of endearment.*

en·deav·or /enˈdevər/ (*Brit.* **en·deav·our**) ▶*v.* [*intrans.*] try hard to do or achieve something: *he is endeavoring to help the Third World.*
▶*n.* an attempt to achieve a goal: [with *infinitive*] *an endeavor to reduce serious injury.* ■ earnest and industrious effort, esp. when sustained over a period of time: *enthusiasm is a vital ingredient in all human endeavor.* ■ an enterprise or undertaking: *a political endeavor.* ▷late Middle English (in the sense 'exert oneself'): from the phrase *put oneself in devoir* 'do one's utmost' (see **DEVOIR**).

en·dem·ic /enˈdemik/ ▶*adj.* **1** (of a disease or condition) regularly found among particular people or in a certain area: *areas where malaria is endemic* | *complacency is* ***endemic in*** *industry today.* See note at **EPIDEMIC**. ■ [*attrib.*] denoting an area in which a particular disease is regularly found. **2** (of a plant or animal) native or restricted to a certain country or area: *a marsupial* ***endemic to*** *northeastern Australia.*
▶*n.* an endemic plant or animal. ■ an endemic disease. ▷mid 17th cent. (as a noun): from French *endémique* or modern Latin *endemicus*, from Greek *endēmios* 'native' (based on *dēmos* 'people'). **—en·dem·i·cal·ly** /-(ə)lē/ *adv.* **—en·de·mic·i·ty** /ˌendəˈmisitē/ *n.* **—en·de·mism** /ˈendəˌmizəm/ *n.* (in sense 2 of the *adjective*).

USAGE On the difference between **endemic**, **epidemic**, and **pandemic**, see **usage** at **EPIDEMIC**.

En·der·by Land /ˈendərbē länd; länt/ a part of Antarctica that is claimed by Australia.

end·er·gon·ic /ˌendərˈgänik/ ▶*adj. Biochemistry* (of a metabolic or chemical process) accompanied by or requiring the absorption of energy, the products being of greater free energy than the reactants. The opposite of **EXERGONIC**. ▷mid 20th cent.: from **ENDO-** 'within' + Greek *ergon* 'work' + **-IC**.

En·ders /ˈendərz/, John Franklin (1897–1985), U.S. virologist. With **Frederick C. Robbins** (1916–92) and **Thomas H. Weller** (1915–92) he devised a method of growing viruses in tissue cultures, which led to the development of vaccines against mumps, polio, and measles. Nobel Prize for Physiology or Medicine (1954, shared with Robbins and Weller).

end·game /ˈen(d)ˌgām/ (also **end game**) ▶*n.* the final stage of a game such as chess or bridge, when few pieces or cards remain: *the knight was trapped in the endgame* | *figurative the retaliatory endgame of nuclear warfare.*

end·gate /ˈen(d)ˌgāt/ ▶*n.* another term for **TAILGATE**.

end grain ▶*n.* the grain of wood seen when it is cut across the growth rings.

end·i·an /ˈendēən/ ▶*adj. Computing* denoting or relating to a system of ordering data in a computer's memory whereby the most significant (**big endian**) or least significant (**little endian**) byte is put first. ▷1980s: a reference to Swift's *Gulliver's Travels*, in which the Lilliputians were divided into two camps, those who ate their eggs by opening the 'big' end and those who ate them by opening the 'little' end.

end·ing /ˈendiNG/ ▶*n.* an end or final part of something, esp. a period of time, an activity, or a book or movie: *the ending of the Cold War.* ■ the furthest part or point of something: *a nerve ending.* ■ the final part of a word, constituting a grammatical inflection or formative element. ▷Old English *endung* 'termination, completion' (see **END**, **-ING**[1]).

en·dive /ˈenˌdīv; ˈänˌdēv/ ▶*n.* **1** an edible Mediterranean plant whose bitter leaves may be blanched and used in salads. • *Cichorium endivia*, family Compositae (including both curly-leaved and smooth-leaved varieties). **2** (also **Belgian endive**) a young, typically blanched chicory plant, eaten as a cooked vegetable or in salads. ▷late Middle English (also denoting the sow thistle): via Old French from medieval Latin *endivia*, based on Greek *entubon*.

end·less /ˈen(d)ləs/ ▶*adj.* having or seeming to have no end or limit: *endless ocean wastes* | *the list is endless.* See note at **ETERNAL**. ■ countless; innumerable: *we smoked endless cigarettes.* ■ (of a belt, chain, or tape) having the ends joined to form a loop allowing continuous action. ▷Old English *endelēas* (see **END**, **-LESS**). **—end·less·ly** *adv.* **—end·less·ness** *n.*

end·less screw ▶*n.* the threaded cylinder in a worm gear.

end line ▶*n. Football* the line that marks the back of the end zone.

end·long /ˈendˌlôNG; -ˌläNG/ ▶*adv. archaic* from end to end; lengthwise.

end man ▶*n.* **1** a man at the end of a row, line, or series. **2** *historical* a man at the end of a line of performers in a minstrel show who engaged in comic repartee with the interlocutor.

end·most /ˈen(d)ˌmōst/ ▶*adj.* nearest to the end.

end·note /ˈen(d)ˌnōt/ ▶*n.* a note printed at the end of a book or section of a book.

endo- ▶*comb. form* internal; within: *endoderm* | *endogenous.* ▷from Greek *endon* 'within.'

en·do·car·di·al /ˌendōˈkärdēəl/ ▶*adj. Anatomy & Medicine* **1** of or relating to the endocardium. **2** situated inside the heart.

en·do·car·di·tis /ˌendōˌkärˈdītis/ ▶*n. Medicine* inflammation of the endocardium. **—en·do·car·dit·ic** /-ˈditik/ *adj.*

en·do·car·di·um /-ˈkärdēəm/ ▶*n.* the thin, smooth membrane that lines the inside of the chambers of the heart and forms the surface of the valves. ▷late 19th cent.: modern Latin, from **ENDO-** 'within' + Greek *kardia* 'heart.'

en·do·carp /ˈendəˌkärp/ ▶*n. Botany* the innermost layer of the pericarp that surrounds a seed in a fruit. It may be membranous (as in apples) or woody (as in the stone of a peach or cherry). ▷early 19th cent.: from **ENDO-** 'within' + a shortened form of **PERICARP**. **—en·do·car·pic** /ˌendōˈkärpik/ *adj.*

en·do·cen·tric /ˌendōˈsentrik/ ▶*adj. Linguistics* denoting or being a construction in which the whole has the same syntactic function as the head, for example *big black dogs.* Contrasted with **EXOCENTRIC**.

en·do·crine /ˈendəkrin/ ▶*adj. Physiology* of, relating to, or denoting glands that secrete hormones or other products directly into the blood: *the endocrine system.*
▶*n.* an endocrine gland: *the pituitary gland is sometimes called the "master gland" of the endocrines.* ▷early 20th cent.: from **ENDO-** 'within' + Greek *krinein* 'sift.'

en·do·cri·nol·o·gy /ˌendəkrəˈnäləjē/ ▶*n.* the branch of physiology and medicine concerned with endocrine glands and hormones. **—en·do·crin·o·log·i·cal** /-ˌkrinəˈläjikəl/ *adj.* **—en·do·cri·nol·o·gist** /-jist/ *n.*

en·do·cy·to·sis /ˌendōsīˈtōsis/ ▶*n. Biology* the taking in of matter by a living cell by invagination of its membrane to form a vacuole. **—en·do·cy·tose** /ˌendōsīˈtōs; -ˈtōz/ *v.* **—en·do·cy·tot·ic** /-ˈtätik/ *adj.*

en·do·derm /ˈendəˌdərm/ (also **en·to·derm**) ▶*n. Zoology & Embryology* the innermost layer of cells or tissue of an embryo in early development, or the parts derived from this, which include the lining of the gut and associated structures. Compare with **ECTODERM** and **MESODERM**. ▷mid 19th cent.: from **ENDO-** 'within' + Greek *derma* 'skin.' **—en·do·der·mal** /ˌendəˈdərməl; ˌendō-/ *adj.* **—en·do·der·mic** /ˌendəˈdərmik; ˌendō-/ *adj.*

en·do·der·mis /ˌendōˈdərməs/ ▶*n. Botany* an inner layer of cells in the cortex of a root and of some stems, surrounding a vascular bundle. ▷early 20th cent.: from **ENDO-** 'within' + modern Latin *dermis* 'skin.'

en·dog·a·my /enˈdägəmē/ ▶*n. Anthropology* the custom of marrying only within the limits of a local community, clan, or tribe. Compare with **EXOGAMY**. ■ *Biology* the fusion of reproductive cells from related individuals; inbreeding; self-pollination. ▷mid 19th cent.: from **ENDO-** 'within' + Greek *gamos* 'marriage,' on the pattern of *polygamy.* **—en·do·gam·ic** /ˌendōˈgamik/ *adj.* **—en·dog·a·mous** /-gəməs/ *adj.*

en·do·ge·net·ic /ˌendōjəˈnetik/ ▶*adj.* another term for **ENDOGENIC**.

en·do·gen·ic /ˌendōˈjenik/ ▶*adj. Geology* formed or occurring beneath the surface of the earth. Often contrasted with **EXOGENIC**.

en·dog·e·nous /enˈdäjənəs/ ▶*adj.* having an internal cause or origin: *the expected rate of infection is endogenous to the system.* Often contrasted with **EXOGENOUS**. ■ *Biology* growing or originating from within an organism: *endogenous gene sequences.* ■ *chiefly Psychiatry* (of a disease or symptom) not attributable to any external or environmental factor: *endogenous depression.* ■ confined within a group or society. **—en·dog·e·nous·ly** *adv.*

en·do·lith·ic /ˌendōˈliTHik/ ▶*adj. Biology* living in or penetrating into stone: *endolithic algae.*

en·do·lymph /ˈendəˌlimf/ ▶*n. Anatomy* the fluid in the membranous labyrinth of the ear.

en·do·me·tri·o·sis /ˌendōˌmētrēˈōsis/ ▶*n. Medicine* a condition resulting from the appearance of endometrial tissue outside the uterus and causing pelvic pain.

en·do·me·tri·tis /ˌendōmiˈtrītis/ ▶*n. Medicine* inflammation of the endometrium.

en·do·me·tri·um /ˌendōˈmētrēəm/ ▶*n. Anatomy* the mucous membrane lining the uterus, which thickens during the menstrual cycle in preparation for possible implantation of an embryo. ▷late 19th cent.: modern Latin, from **ENDO-** 'within' + Greek *mētra* 'womb.' **—en·do·me·tri·al** /-trēəl/ *adj.*

en·do·morph /ˈendəˌmôrf/ ▶*n.* **1** *Physiology* a person with a soft round body build and a high proportion of fat tissue. Compare with **ECTOMORPH** and **MESOMORPH**. **2** *Mineralogy* a mineral or crystal enclosed within another. ▷1940s: *endo-* from *endodermal* (being the layer of the embryo giving rise to the physical characteristics that predominate) + **-MORPH**. **—en·do·mor·phic** /ˌendəˈmôrfik/ *adj.* **—en·do·mor·phy** /-ˌmôrfē/ *n.*

en·do·nu·cle·ase /ˌendōˈn(y)o͞oklēˌās; -ˌāz/ ▶*n. Biochemistry* an enzyme that cleaves a polynucleotide chain by separating nucleotides other than the two end ones.

en·do·par·a·site /ˌendōˈparəˌsīt/ ▶*n. Biology* a parasite, such as a tapeworm, that lives inside its host. Compare with **ECTOPARASITE**. **—en·do·par·a·sit·ic** /-ˌparəˈsitik/ *adj.* .

en·do·pep·ti·dase /ˌendōˈseptiˌdās/ ▶*n. Biochemistry* an enzyme that breaks peptide bonds other than terminal ones in a peptide chain.

en·doph·o·ra /enˈdäfərə/ ▶*n. Linguistics* the set of relationships among words having the same reference within a text, contributing to textual cohesion; anaphora and cataphora. Compare with **EXOPHORA**. ▷late 20th cent.: from **ENDO-** 'within,' on the pattern of *anaphora.* **—en·do·phor·ic** /ˌendəˈfôrik; -fär-/ *adj.*

en·do·phyte /ˈendəˌfīt/ ▶*n. Botany* a plant, esp. a fungus, that lives inside another plant. **—en·do·phyt·ic** /ˌendəˈfitik/ *adj.* **—en·do·phyt·i·cal·ly** /ˌendəˈfitik(ə)lē/ *adv.*

en·do·plasm /ˈendōˌplazəm/ ▶*n. dated Biology* the more fluid, granular inner layer of the cytoplasm in ameboid cells. Compare with **ECTOPLASM** (sense 1).

en·do·plas·mic re·tic·u·lum /ˌendōˈplazmik riˈtikyələm/ ▶*n. Biology* a network of membranous tubules within the cytoplasm of a eukaryotic cell, continuous with the nuclear membrane. It usually has ribosomes attached and is involved in protein and lipid synthesis.

en·dop·o·dite /enˈdäpəˌdīt/ (also **en·do·pod** /ˈendəˌpäd/) ▶*n. Zoology* the inner branch of the biramous limb or appendage of a crustacean. Compare with **EXOPODITE**, **PROTOPODITE**. ▷late 19th cent.: from **ENDO-** 'within' + Greek *pous*, *pod-* 'foot' + **-ITE**[1].

end or·gan ▶*n.* **1** *Anatomy* a specialized, encapsulated ending of a peripheral sensory nerve, which acts as a receptor for a stimulus. **2** another term for **TARGET ORGAN**.

en·dor·phin /enˈdôrfin/ ▶*n. Biochemistry* any of a group of hormones secreted within the brain and nervous system and having a number of physiological functions. They are peptides that activate the body's opiate receptors, causing an analgesic effect. ▷1970s: blend of **ENDOGENOUS** and **MORPHINE**.

en·dorse /enˈdôrs/ (also *dated* **in·dorse**) ▶*v.* [*trans.*] **1** declare one's public approval or support of: *the report was endorsed by the college.* See note at **APPROVE**. ■ recommend (a product) in an advertisement. **2** sign (a check or bill of exchange) on the back to make it payable to someone other than the stated payee or to accept responsibility for paying it. ■ (usu. **be endorsed on**) write (a comment) on the front or back of a document. ▷late 15th cent. (in the sense 'write on the back of'; formerly also as *indorse*): from medieval Latin *indorsare*, from Latin *in-* 'in, on' + *dorsum* 'back.' **—en·dors·a·ble** *adj.* **—en·dors·er** *n.*

en·dor·see /ˌendôrˈsē/ ▶*n.* a person to whom a check or bill of exchange is made payable instead of the stated payee.

en·dorse·ment /enˈdôrsmənt/ (also *dated* **in·dorse·ment**) ▶*n.* **1** an act of giving one's public approval or support to someone or something. ■ a recommendation of a product in an advertisement. **2** a clause in an insurance policy detailing an exemption from or change in coverage. **3** the action of endorsing a check or bill of exchange.

en·do·scope /ˈendəˌskōp/ ▸*n. Medicine* an instrument that can be introduced into the body to give a view of its internal parts. —**en·do·scop·ic** /ˌendəˈskäpik/ *adj.* —**en·do·scop·i·cal·ly** /ˌendəˈskäpik(ə)lē/ *adv.* —**en·dos·co·pist** /enˈdäskəpist/ *n.* —**en·dos·co·py** /enˈdäskəpē/ *n.*

en·do·skel·e·ton /ˌendōˈskelitn/ ▸*n. Zoology* an internal skeleton, such as the bony or cartilaginous skeleton of vertebrates. Compare with EXOSKELETON. —**en·do·skel·e·tal** /-ˈskelitl/ *adj.*

en·do·sperm /ˈendəˌspərm/ ▸*n. Botany* the part of a seed that acts as a food store for the developing plant embryo, usually containing starch with protein and other nutrients.

en·do·spore /ˈendəˌspôr/ ▸*n. Biology* a resistant asexual spore that develops inside some bacteria cells. ▪ the inner layer of the membrane or wall of some spores and pollen grains. —**en·dos·por·ous** /enˈdäspərəs; ˌendəˈspôrəs/ *adj.*

en·do·sym·bi·o·sis /ˌendōˌsimbēˈōsis; -ˌsimbī-/ ▸*n. Biology* symbiosis in which one of the symbiotic organisms lives inside the other. —**en·do·sym·bi·ont** /-ˈsimbēˌänt; -ˈsimbī-/ *n.* —**en·do·sym·bi·ot·ic** /-ˈätik/ *adj.*

en·do·the·li·um /ˌendəˈTHēlēəm/ (*pl.* **-li·a** /-lēə/) ▸*n.* the tissue that forms a single layer of cells lining various organs and cavities of the body, esp. the blood vessels, heart, and lymphatic vessels. It is formed from the embryonic mesoderm. Compare with EPITHELIUM. ▷late 19th cent.: modern Latin, from ENDO- 'within' + Greek *thēlē* 'nipple.' —**en·do·the·li·al** /-lēəl/ *adj.*

en·do·therm /ˈendəˌTHərm/ ▸*n. Zoology* an animal that is dependent on or capable of the internal generation of heat; a warm-blooded animal. Often contrasted with ECTOTHERM. Compare with HOMEOTHERM. ▷1940s: from ENDO- 'within,' on the pattern of *homoiotherm*. —**en·do·ther·my** *n.*

en·do·ther·mic /ˌendəˈTHərmik/ ▸*adj.* **1** (also **en·do·ther·mal**) *Chemistry* (of a reaction or process) accompanied by or requiring the absorption of heat. The opposite of EXOTHERMIC. ▪ (of a compound) requiring a net input of heat for its formation from its constituent elements. **2** *Zoology* (of an animal) dependent on or capable of the internal generation of heat. —**en·do·ther·mi·cal·ly** /-(ə)lē/ *adv.*

en·do·tox·in /ˈendəˌtäksin/ ▸*n. Microbiology* a toxin that is present inside a bacterial cell and is released when the cell disintegrates. It is sometimes responsible for the characteristic symptoms of a disease, e.g., in botulism. Compare with EXOTOXIN. —**en·do·tox·ic** /ˌendōˈtäksik/ *adj.*

en·do·tra·che·al /ˌendōˈtrākēəl/ ▸*adj.* situated or occurring within or performed by way of the trachea: *endotracheal tube.* —**en·do·tra·che·al·ly** *adv.*

en·dow /enˈdou/ ▸*v.* [*trans.*] give or bequeath an income or property to (a person or institution): *he endowed the church with lands.* ▪ establish (a college post, annual prize, or project) by donating the funds needed to maintain it. ▪ (usu. **be endowed with**) provide with a quality, ability, or asset: *he was endowed with tremendous physical strength.* ▷late Middle English (also in the sense 'provide a dower or dowry'; formerly also as *indow*): from legal Anglo-Norman French *endouer*, from *en-* 'in, toward' + Old French *douer* 'give as a gift' (from Latin *dotare*: see DOWER). —**en·dow·er** *n.*

en·dow·ment /enˈdoumənt/ ▸*n.* the action of endowing something or someone: *he tried to promote the endowment of a Chair of Psychiatry.* ▪ an income or form of property given or bequeathed to someone. ▪ (usu. **endowments**) a quality or ability possessed or inherited by someone. ▪ [usu. as *adj.*] a form of life insurance involving payment of a fixed sum to the insured person on a specified date, or to their estate should they die before this date: *an endowment policy.*

end·pa·per /ˈen(d)ˌpāpər/ (also **end pa·per**) ▸*n.* a blank or decorated leaf of paper at the beginning or end of a book, esp. one fixed to the inside of the cover.

end plate ▸*n.* a flattened piece at or forming the end of something such as a motor or generator. ▪ *Anatomy* each of the discoid expansions of a motor nerve where its branches terminate on a muscle fiber.

end·play /ˈen(d)ˌplā/ *Bridge* ▸*n.* a way of playing the last few tricks that forces an opponent to make a disadvantageous lead.
▸*v.* [*trans.*] force (an opponent) to make such a lead.

end·point /ˈen(d)ˌpoint/ (also **end point**) ▸*n.* the final stage of a period or process. ▪ *Chemistry* the point in a titration at which a reaction is complete, often marked by a color change. ▪ *Mathematics* a point or value that marks the end of a ray or one of the ends of a line segment or interval.

end prod·uct ▸*n.* that which is produced as the final result of an activity or process, esp. the finished article in a manufacturing process.

end re·sult ▸*n.* the final result or outcome of an activity or process.

en·drin /ˈendrin/ ▸*n.* a toxic insecticide that is a stereoisomer of dieldrin. ▷mid 20th cent.: from ENDO- 'within' + a shortened form of DIELDRIN.

end run ▸*n. Football* an attempt by the ballcarrier to run around the end of the defensive line. ▪ an evasive tactic or maneuver.
▸*v.* (**end-run**) [*trans.*] evade; circumvent: *an attempt to end-run regulations for fire protection.*

end-stopped ▸*adj.* (of verse) having a pause at the end of each line.

en·due /enˈd(y)o͞o/ ▸*v.* (**-dues, -dued, -du·ing**) [*trans.*] *poetic/literary* endow or provide with a quality or ability: *our sight would be endued with a far greater sharpness.* ▷late Middle English (also in the sense 'induct into an ecclesiastical living'): from Old French *enduire*, partly from Latin *inducere* 'lead in' (see INDUCE), reinforced by the sense of Latin *induere* 'put on clothes.'

en·dur·ance /enˈd(y)o͝orəns/ ▸*n.* the fact or power of enduring an unpleasant or difficult process or situation without giving way: *she was close to the limit of her endurance.* ▪ the capacity of something to last or to withstand wear and tear. ▷late 15th cent. (in the sense 'continued existence, ability to last'; formerly also as *indurance*): from Old French, from *endurer* 'make hard' (see ENDURE).

en·dure /enˈd(y)o͝or/ ▸*v.* **1** [*trans.*] suffer (something painful or difficult) patiently: *it seemed impossible that anyone could endure such pain.* ▪ tolerate (someone or something): *I was a fool to endure him for so long.* **2** [*intrans.*] remain in existence; last: *these cities have endured through time.* ▷Middle English: from Old French *endurer*, from Latin *indurare* 'harden,' from *in-* 'in' + *durus* 'hard.' —**en·dur·a·ble** *adj.* —**en·dur·er** *n.*

en·dur·ing /enˈd(y)o͝oriNG/ ▸*adj.* continuing or long-lasting: *he formed a number of enduring relationships with women | an enduring problem.* —**en·dur·ing·ly** *adv.*

en·dur·o /enˈd(y)o͝orō/ ▸*n.* (*pl.* **-os**) a long-distance race, esp. for motor vehicles, motorcycles, or bicycles, typically over rough terrain, designed to test endurance. ▷1950s: from ENDURANCE + the informal suffix **-o**.

end use ▸*n.* the application or function for which something is designed or for which it is ultimately used.

end us·er (also **end-us·er**) ▸*n.* the person who actually uses a particular product.

end·ways /ˈen(d)ˌwāz/ (also **end·wise** /-ˌwīz/) ▸*adv.* with its end facing upward, forward, or toward the viewer: *a little town looking endways on to the river.* ▪ in a row with the end of one object touching that of another: *strips of rubber cemented endways.*

En·dym·i·on /enˈdimēən/ *Greek Mythology* a remarkably beautiful young man, loved by the Moon (Selene). According to one story, he was put in an eternal sleep by Zeus for having fallen in love with Hera, and was then visited every night by Selene.

end zone ▸*n.* **1** *Football* the rectangular area at each end of the field into which the ball must be carried or passed and caught to score a touchdown. **2** *Hockey* the area at either end of the rink, extending from the blue line to the boards behind the goal.

ENE ▸*abbr.* east-northeast.

-ene ▸*suffix* **1** denoting an inhabitant: *Nazarene.* **2** *Chemistry* forming names of unsaturated hydrocarbons containing a double bond: *benzene | ethylene.* ▷from Greek *-ēnos*.

en éch·e·lon /än ˈesHəˌlän/ ▸*adj.* & *adv. chiefly Geology* in approximately parallel formation at an oblique angle to a particular direction. ▷early 19th cent.: French, literally 'in rung formation.'

en·e·ma /ˈenəmə/ ▸*n.* (*pl.* **en·e·mas** or *rare* **en·em·a·ta** /əˈnemətə/) a procedure in which liquid or gas is injected into the rectum, typically to expel its contents, but also to introduce drugs or permit X-ray imaging. ▪ a quantity of fluid or a syringe used in such a procedure. ▷late Middle English: via late Latin from Greek, from *enienai* 'send or put in,' from *en-* 'in' + *hienai* 'send.'

en·e·my /ˈenəmē/ ▸*n.* (*pl.* **-mies**) a person who is actively opposed or hostile to someone or something. ▪ (**the enemy**) [treated as *sing.* or *pl.*] a hostile nation or its armed forces or citizens, esp. in time of war: *the enemy shot down four helicopters* | [as *adj.*] *enemy aircraft.* ▪ a thing that harms or weakens something else: *routine is the enemy of art.* ▷Middle English: from Old French *enemi*, from Latin *inimicus*, from *in-* 'not' + *amicus* 'friend.'
▸*PHRASE* □ **be one's own worst enemy** act in a way contrary to one's own interests.

en·er·get·ic /ˌenərˈjetik/ ▸*adj.* showing or involving great activity or vitality: *energetic exercise.* ▪ powerfully operative; forceful. ▪ *Physics* characterized by a high level of energy (in the technical sense): *energetic X-rays.* ▪ of or relating to energy (in the technical sense). ▷mid 17th cent. (in the sense 'powerfully effective'): from Greek *energētikos*, from *energein* 'operate, work in or upon' (based on *ergon* 'work'). —**en·er·get·i·cal·ly** /-(ə)lē/ *adv.*

en·er·get·ics /ˌenərˈjetiks/ ▸*plural n.* **1** the properties of something in terms of energy. **2** [treated as *sing.*] the branch of science dealing with the properties of energy and the way in which it is redistributed in physical, chemical, or biological processes. —**en·er·get·i·cist** /-ˈjetisist/ *n.*

en·er·gize /ˈenərˌjīz/ ▸*v.* [*trans.*] give vitality and enthusiasm to: *people were energized by his ideas.* ▪ supply energy, typically kinetic or electrical energy, to (something). —**en·er·giz·er** *n.*

en·er·gu·men /ˌenərˈgyo͞omən/ ▸*n. archaic* a person believed to be possessed by the devil or a spirit. ▷early 18th cent. (also denoting an enthusiast or fanatic): via late Latin from Greek *energoumenos*, passive participle of *energein* 'work in or upon.'

en·er·gy /ˈenərjē/ ▸*n.* (*pl.* **-gies**) **1** the strength and vitality required for sustained physical or mental activity: *changes in the levels of vitamins can affect energy and well-being.* ▪ a feeling of possessing such strength and vitality. ▪ force or vigor of expression. ▪ (**energies**) a person's physical and mental powers, typically as applied to a particular task or activity. **2** power derived from the utilization of physical or chemical resources, esp. to provide light and heat or to work machines. **3** *Physics* the property of matter and radiation that is manifest as a capacity to perform work (such as causing motion or the interaction of molecules): *a collision in which no energy is transferred.* ▪ a degree or level of this capacity possessed by something or required by a process. ▷mid 16th cent. (denoting force or vigor of expression): from French *énergie*, or via late Latin from Greek *energeia*, from *en-* 'in, within' + *ergon* 'work.'

en·er·gy au·dit ▸*n.* an assessment of the energy needs and efficiency of a building or buildings.

en·er·gy ef·fi·cient ra·ti·o (abbr.: **EER**) ▸*n.* the ratio of a heating or cooling system's output, per hour, in British thermal units to the input in watts, used to measure the system's efficiency.

en·er·gy lev·el ▸*n. Physics* the fixed amount of energy that a system described by quantum mechanics, such as a molecule, atom, electron, or nucleus, can have.

en·er·vate ▸*v.* /ˈenərˌvāt/ [*trans.*] cause (someone) to feel drained of energy or vitality; weaken.
▸*adj.* /ˈenərvit/ *poetic/literary* lacking in energy or vitality: *the enervate slightness of his frail form.* ▷early 17th cent.: from Latin *enervat-* 'weakened (by extraction of the sinews),' from the verb *enervare*, from *e-* (variant of *ex-*) 'out of' + *nervus* 'sinew.' —**en·er·va·tion** /ˌenərˈvāSHən/ *n.* —**en·er·va·tor** /-ˌvātər/ *n.*

en·er·vat·ing /ˈenərˌvātiNG/ ▸*adj.* causing one to feel drained of energy or vitality: *the enervating humidity of the coast.*

En·e·we·tak variant spelling of ENIWETOK.

en face /äN ˈfäs/ ▸*adv.* & *adj.* facing forward. ▷mid 18th cent.: French.

en fa·mille /ˌäN fäˈmē/ ▸*adv.* with one's family: *when they went out en famille, Steven always drove.* ▪ as or like a member or members of a family. ▷early 18th cent.: French, literally 'in family.'

en·fant ter·ri·ble /äNˌfäN teˈrēbl(ə)/ ▸*n.* (*pl.* **en·fants ter·ri·bles** *pronunc.* same) a person whose unconventional or controversial behavior or ideas shock, embarrass, or annoy others. ▷mid 19th cent.: French, literally 'terrible child.'

en·fee·ble /enˈfēbəl/ ▸*v.* [*trans.*] make weak or feeble:

[as *adj.*] (**enfeebled**) *trade unions are in an enfeebled state.* ▷Middle English: from Old French *enfeblir,* from *en-* (expressing a change of state) + *feble* 'feeble.' —**en·fee·ble·ment** *n.* —**en·fee·bler** /-'fēblər/ *n.*

en·feoff /en'fēf/ ▸*v.* [*trans.*] *historical* (under the feudal system) give (someone) freehold property or land in exchange for their pledged service. ■ give (property or land) in this way: *the lands were enfeoffed to the baron.* ▷late Middle English: from Anglo-Norman French *enfeoffer,* from Old French *en-* 'in' + *fief* 'fief.' Compare with **FEOFFMENT.** —**en·feoff·ment** *n.*

en·fet·ter /en'fetər/ ▸*v.* [*trans.*] *poetic/literary* restrain (someone) with shackles.

en·fe·vered /en'fēvərd/ ▸*adj. poetic/literary* having or showing the signs of fever.

en·fi·lade /'enfə,lād; -,läd/ ▸*n.* **1** a volley of gunfire directed along a line from end to end. **2** a suite of rooms with doorways in line with each other.
▸*v.* [*trans.*] direct a volley of gunfire along the length of (a target). ▷early 18th cent. (denoting the position of a military post commanding the length of a line): from French, from *enfiler* 'thread on a string, pierce from end to end,' from *en-* 'in, on' + *fil* 'thread.'

en·flesh /en'flesh/ ▸*v.* [*trans.*] *poetic/literary* give bodily form to; make real or concrete. —**en·flesh·ment** *n.*

en·fleu·rage /,änflə'räzh/ ▸*n.* the extraction of essential oils and perfumes from flowers using odorless animal or vegetable fats. ▷mid 19th cent.: French, from *enfleurer* 'saturate with the perfume from flowers.'

en·flu·rane /en'floo,rān/ ▸*n. Medicine* a volatile organic liquid used as a general anesthetic. • A halogenated ether; chem. formula: CHF_2OCF_2CHFCl. ▷1970s: from *en-* (of unknown origin) + **FLUORO-** + **-ANE**[2].

en·fold /en'fōld/ (also *dated* **in·fold**) ▸*v.* [*trans.*] **1** surround; envelop: *he shut off the engine and silence enfolded them.* ■ hold or clasp (someone) lovingly in one's arms. **2** fold or shape into folds. ▷late Middle English (in the sense 'involve, entail, imply'; formerly also as *infold*): from **EN-**[1], **IN-**[2] 'within' + **FOLD**[1]. —**en·fold·ment** *n.*

en·force /en'fôrs/ ▸*v.* [*trans.*] compel observance of or compliance with (a law, rule, or obligation). ■ cause (something) to happen by necessity or force: *there is no outside agency to enforce cooperation between the players* | [as *adj.*] (**enforced**) *a period of enforced idleness.* ▷Middle English (in the senses 'strive' and 'impel by force'; formerly also as *inforce*): from Old French *enforcir, enforcier,* based on Latin *in-* 'in' + *fortis* 'strong.' —**en·force·a·bil·i·ty** /-,fôrsə'bilitē/ *n.* —**en·force·a·ble** /-əbəl/ *adj.* —**en·forc·ed·ly** /-sidlē/ *adv.* —**en·force·ment** *n.* —**en·forc·er** *n.*

en·fran·chise /en'fran,chīz/ ▸*v.* [*trans.*] give the right to vote to: *a proposal that foreigners should be enfranchised for local elections.* ■ *historical* free (a slave). ▷late Middle English (formerly also as *infranchise*): from Old French *enfranchiss-,* lengthened stem of *enfranchir,* from *en-* (expressing a change of state) + *franc, franche* 'free.' —**en·fran·chise·ment** *n.*

ENG ▸*abbr.* electronic news gathering.

eng. ▸*abbr.* ■ engine. ■ engineer. ■ engineering. ■ engraved. ■ engraver. ■ engraving.

en·gage /en'gāj/ ▸*v.* **1** [*trans.*] occupy, attract, or involve (someone's interest or attention): *he plowed on, trying to outline his plans and engage Sutton's attention.* ■ (**engage someone in**) cause someone to become involved in (a conversation or discussion). ■ arrange to employ or hire (someone): *he was engaged as a trainee copywriter.* ■ [with *infinitive*] pledge or enter into a contract to do something: *he engaged to pay them $10,000 against a bond.* ■ *dated* reserve (accommodations, a place, etc.) in advance: *he had engaged a small sailboat.* **2** [*intrans.*] (**engage in**) participate or become involved in: *organizations engage in a variety of activities* | (**be engaged in**) *some are actively engaged in crime.* ■ (**engage with**) establish a meaningful contact or connection with: *the teams needed to engage with local communities.* ■ (of a part of a machine or engine) move into position so as to come into operation: *the clutch will not engage.* ■ [*trans.*] cause (a part of a machine or engine) to do this. ■ [*trans.*] (of fencers or swordsmen) bring (weapons) together preparatory to fighting. ■ [*trans.*] enter into conflict or combat with (an adversary). ▷late Middle English (formerly also as *ingage*): from French *engager,* ultimately from the base of **GAGE**[1]. The word originally meant 'to pawn or pledge something,' later 'pledge oneself (to do something),' hence 'enter into a contract' (mid 16th cent.), 'involve oneself in an activity,' 'enter into combat' (mid 17th cent.), giving rise to the notion 'involve someone or something else.'

en·ga·gé /,änggä'zhā/ ▸*adj.* (of a writer, artist, or their works) morally committed to a particular aim or cause. ▷French, past participle of *engager* (see **ENGAGE**).

en·gaged /en'gājd/ ▸*adj.* **1** [*predic.*] busy; occupied: *I told him I was otherwise engaged.* See note at **BUSY.** ■ *Brit.* (of a telephone line) unavailable because already in use. ■ (of a toilet) already in use. **2** having formally agreed to marry. **3** *Architecture* (of a column) attached to or partly let into a wall.

en·gage·ment /en'gājmənt/ ▸*n.* **1** a formal agreement to get married. ■ the duration of such an agreement: *a good long engagement to give you time to be sure.* **2** an arrangement to do something or go somewhere at a fixed time: *a dinner engagement.* ■ a period of paid employment. **3** the action of engaging or being engaged: *Britain's continued* **engagement in** *open trading* | *the engagement of the gears.* **4** a fight or battle between armed forces. ▷early 17th cent. (in the general sense 'a legal or moral obligation'): French, from *engager* 'to pledge' (see **ENGAGE**).

en·gage·ment ring ▸*n.* a ring given by a man to a woman when they agree to marry.

en·gag·ing /en'gājing/ ▸*adj.* charming and attractive: *Sophie had a sunny personality that was very engaging.* —**en·gag·ing·ly** *adv.* —**en·gag·ing·ness** *n.*

en garde /än 'gärd; än/ ▸*interj. Fencing* a direction to be ready to fence, taking the opening position for action. ▷French *en garde* '(be) on guard.'

En·gel·mann spruce /'enggəlmən/ (also **En·gel·mann's spruce**) ▸*n.* a tall spruce found in the mountains of western North America and Mexico. • *Picea engelmannii,* family Pinaceae. ▷mid 19th cent.: named after George *Engelmann* (1809–84), American botanist.

En·gels /'enggəlz/, Friedrich (1820–95), German socialist and political philosopher. He collaborated with Karl Marx in the writing of the *Communist Manifesto* (1848) and translated and edited Marx's later work.

en·gen·der /en'jendər/ ▸*v.* [*trans.*] cause or give rise to (a feeling, situation, or condition): *the issue engendered continuing controversy.* ■ *archaic* (of a father) beget (offspring). ■ [*intrans.*] come into being; arise. ▷Middle English (formerly also as *ingender*): from Old French *engendrer,* from Latin *ingenerare,* from *in-* 'in' + *generare* 'beget' (see **GENERATE**).

en·gine /'enjən/ ▸*n.* **1** a machine with moving parts that converts power into motion. ■ a thing that is the agent or instrument of a particular process: *exports used to be the engine of growth.* **2** a railroad locomotive. ■ short for **FIRE ENGINE.** ■ *historical* a mechanical device or instrument, esp. one used in warfare: *a siege engine.* ▷Middle English (formerly also as *ingine*): from Old French *engin,* from Latin *ingenium* 'talent, device,' from *in-* 'in' + *gignere* 'beget'; compare with **INGENIOUS.** The original sense was 'ingenuity, cunning' (surviving in Scots as *ingine*), hence 'the product of ingenuity, a plot or snare,' also 'tool, weapon,' later specifically denoting a large mechanical weapon; whence a machine (mid 17th cent.), used commonly later in combinations such as *steam engine, internal combustion engine.* —**en·gined** *adj.* [in *combination*] *a twin-engined helicopter.* —**en·gine·less** *adj.*

en·gine block ▸*n.* see **BLOCK** (sense 1).

en·gine driv·er ▸*n. Brit.* a driver of a locomotive; an engineer.

en·gi·neer /,enjə'ni(ə)r/ ▸*n.* a person who designs, builds, or maintains engines, machines, or public works. ■ a person qualified in a branch of engineering, esp. as a professional: *aeronautical engineer.* ■ the operator or supervisor of an engine, esp. a railroad locomotive or the engine on an aircraft or ship. ■ a skillful contriver or originator of something: *the prime engineer of the approach.*
▸*v.* [*trans.*] design and build (a machine or structure): *the men who engineered the tunnel.* ■ skillfully or artfully arrange for (an event or situation) to occur: *she engineered another meeting with him.* ■ modify (an organism) by manipulating its genetic material: [as *adj.,* with *submodifier*] (**engineered**) *genetically engineered plants.* ▷Middle English (denoting a designer and constructor of fortifications and weapons; formerly also as *ingineer*): in early use from Old French *engigneor,* from medieval Latin *ingeniator,* from *ingeniare* 'contrive, devise,' from Latin *ingenium* (see **ENGINE**); in later use from French *ingénieur* or Italian *ingegnere,* also based on Latin *ingenium,* with the ending influenced by **-EER.**

en·gi·neer·ing /,enjə'ni(ə)ring/ ▸*n.* the branch of science and technology concerned with the design, building, and use of engines, machines, and structures. ■ the work done by, or the occupation of, an engineer. ■ the action of working artfully to bring something about: *if not for Keegan's shrewd engineering, the election would have been lost.*

en·gi·neer·ing sci·ence (also **en·gi·neer·ing sci·enc·es**) ▸*n.* the parts of science concerned with the physical and mathematical basis of engineering and machine technology.

en·gine room ▸*n.* the room containing the engines, esp. in a ship.

en·gine·ry /'enjənrē/ ▸*n. archaic* engines collectively; machinery.

en·gine turn·ing ▸*n.* the decoration of metal or ceramic objects with regular engraved patterns using a lathe. —**en·gine-turned** *adj.*

en·gir·dle /en'gərdl/ (also **en·gird**) ▸*v.* [*trans.*] *poetic/literary* surround; encircle: *railroads engirdled this tract of country.*

en·gla·cial /en'glāshəl/ ▸*adj.* situated, occurring, or formed inside a glacier. —**en·gla·cial·ly** *adv.*

Eng·land /'ing(g)lənd/ a European country that forms the largest and most southern part of Great Britain and of the United Kingdom, surrounded on three sides by water (Irish Sea on west, English Channel on south, North Sea on east); pop. 46,170,300; capital, London; language, English.

England was conquered by the Romans in the first century AD, when it was inhabited by Celtic peoples. It was a Roman province until the early 5th century. During the 3rd–7th centuries Germanic-speaking tribes, traditionally known as Angles, Saxons, and Jutes, established a number of independent kingdoms here. England emerged as a distinct political entity in the 9th century before being conquered by William, Duke of Normandy, in 1066.

Eng·lish /'ing(g)lish/ ▸*adj.* of or relating to England or its people or language.
▸*n.* **1** the West Germanic language of England, now widely used in many varieties throughout the world. **2** [as *plural n.*] (**the English**) the people of England. **3** spin given to a ball, esp. in pool or billiards.

English is the principal language of Great Britain, the U.S., Ireland, Canada, Australia, New Zealand, and many other countries. There are some 400 million native speakers, and it is the medium of communication for many millions more; it is the most widely used second language in the world. It belongs to the West Germanic group of Indo-European languages though its vocabulary has been much influenced by Old Norse, Norman French, and Latin.

▷Old English *Englisc* (see **ANGLE, -ISH**[1]). The word originally denoted the early Germanic settlers of Britain (Angles, Saxons, and Jutes), or their language (now called **OLD ENGLISH**). —**Eng·lish·man** *n.* (*pl.* **-men**) —**Eng·lish·ness** *n.* —**Eng·lish·wom·an** *n.* (*pl.* **-wom·en**)

Eng·lish bond ▸*n. Building* a bond used in brickwork consisting of alternate courses of stretchers and headers.

Eng·lish break·fast ▸*n.* a substantial breakfast including hot cooked food such as bacon and eggs.

Eng·lish Ca·na·di·an ▸*n.* a Canadian whose principal language is English.
▸*adj.* of or relating to English-speaking Canadians.

Eng·lish Chan·nel a sea channel that separates southern England from northern France. It is 22 miles (35 km) wide at its narrowest point. A railroad tunnel (the Channel Tunnel) underneath the channel opened in 1994.

Eng·lish Civ·il War the war between Charles I and his Parliamentary opponents, 1642–49.

Civil war broke out after Charles refused to accede to a series of demands made by Parliament. The king's forces (the Royalists or Cavaliers) were decisively defeated by the Parliamentary forces (or Roundheads) at the Battle of Naseby (1645), and an attempt by Charles to regain power in alliance with the Scots was defeated in 1648. Charles himself was tried and executed by Parliament in 1649.

Eng·lish horn ▸*n. Music* an alto woodwind instrument of the oboe family, having a bulbous bell and sounding a fifth lower than the oboe.

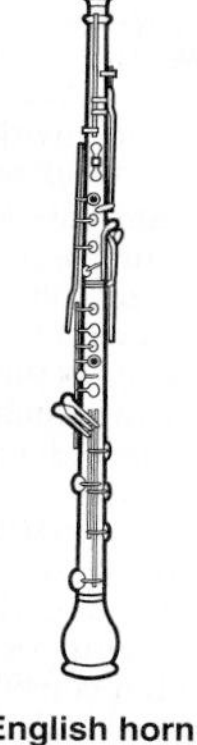
English horn

Eng·lish i·vy ▸*n.* see IVY.

Eng·lish muf·fin ▸*n.* a flat circular spongy bread roll made from yeast dough and eaten split, toasted, and buttered.

Eng·lish mus·tard ▸*n.* a kind of mustard made from mustard seeds milled to a powder, having a very hot taste and typically bright yellow in color.

Eng·lish Pale (also **the Pale**) that part of Ireland over which England exercised jurisdiction before the whole country was conquered. Centered in Dublin, it varied in extent at different times from the reign of Henry II until the full conquest under Elizabeth I. ▷*Pale* from PALE[2].

Eng·lish set·ter ▸*n.* a setter of a breed of dog with a long white or partly white coat.

Eng·lish son·net ▸*n.* another term for ELIZABETHAN SONNET.

Eng·lish spar·row ▸*n.* another term for HOUSE SPARROW.

Eng·lish spring·er ▸*n.* (usu. **English springer spaniel**) see SPRINGER (sense 1).

en·globe /en'glōb/ ▸*v.* [*trans.*] *poetic/literary* enclose in or shape into a globe.

en·gorge /en'gôrj/ ▸*v.* **1** [*trans.*] cause to swell with blood, water, or another fluid: *the river was engorged by a day-long deluge.* ■ [*intrans.*] become swollen in this way. **2** (**engorge oneself**) *archaic* eat to excess. ▷late 15th cent. (in the sense 'gorge; eat or fill to excess'): from Old French *engorgier* 'feed to excess,' from *en-* 'into' + *gorge* 'throat.' —**en·gorge·ment** *n.*

engr. ▸*abbr.* ■ engineer. ■ engraved. ■ engraver. ■ engraving.

en·graft /en'graft/ (also **in·graft**) ▸*v.* another term for GRAFT[1]. —**en·graft·ment** *n.*

en·grailed /en'grāld/ ▸*adj. chiefly Heraldry* having semicircular indentations along the edge. Compare with INVECTED.

en·grain /en'grān/ ▸*v.* variant spelling of INGRAIN.

en·grained /en'grānd/ ▸*adj.* variant spelling of INGRAINED.

en·gram /'engram/ ▸*n.* a hypothetical permanent change in the brain accounting for the existence of memory; a memory trace. ▷early 20th cent.: coined in German from Greek *en-* 'within' + *gramma* 'letter of the alphabet.' —**en·gram·mat·ic** /,engrə'matik/ *adj.*

en·grave /en'grāv/ ▸*v.* [*trans.*] (usu. **be engraved**) cut or carve (a text or design) on the surface of a hard object: *my name was engraved on the ring.* ■ cut or carve a text or design on (such an object). ■ cut (a design) as lines on a metal plate for printing. ■ (**be engraved on** or **in**) be permanently fixed in (one's memory or mind): *the image would be forever engraved in his memory.* ▷late 15th cent. (formerly also as *ingrave*): from EN-[1], IN-[2] 'in, on' + GRAVE[3], influenced by obsolete French *engraver.* —**en·grav·er** *n.*
▸*PHRASE* □ **be engraved in stone** see STONE.

en·grav·ing /en'grāviNG/ ▸*n.* a print made from an engraved plate, block, or other surface. ■ the process or art of cutting or carving a design on a hard surface, esp. so as to make a print.

en·gross /en'grōs/ ▸*v.* [*trans.*] **1** absorb all the attention or interest of: *the notes totally engrossed him.* ■ *archaic* gain or keep exclusive possession of (something): *the country had made the best of its position to engross trade.* [from Old French *en gros,* from medieval Latin *in grosso* 'wholesale.'] **2** *Law* produce (a legal document) in its final or definitive form. ▷late Middle English (formerly also as *ingross*): based on EN-[1], IN-[2] 'in' + late Latin *grossus* 'large.' —**en·gross·ment** *n.*

en·grossed /en'grōst/ ▸*adj.* [*predic.*] having all one's attention or interest absorbed by someone or something: *they seemed to be* **engrossed in** *conversation.*

en·gross·ing /en'grōsiNG/ ▸*adj.* absorbing all one's attention or interest: *the most engrossing parts of the book.* —**en·gross·ing·ly** *adv.*

en·gulf /en'gəlf/ ▸*v.* [*trans.*] (often **be engulfed**) (of a natural force) sweep over (something) so as to surround or cover it completely: *the cafe was* **engulfed in** *flames* | *figurative Europe might be engulfed by war.* ■ eat or swallow (something) whole. —**en·gulf·ment** *n.*

en·hance /en'hans/ ▸*v.* [*trans.*] intensify, increase, or further improve the quality, value, or extent of: *his refusal does nothing to enhance his reputation* | *computer techniques that enhance images.* ▷Middle English (formerly also as *inhance*): from Anglo-Norman French *enhauncer,* based on Latin *in-* (expressing intensive force) + *altus* 'high.' The word originally meant 'elevate' (literally and figuratively), later 'exaggerate, make appear greater,' also 'raise the value or price of something.' Current senses date from the early 16th cent. —**en·hance·ment** *n.* —**en·hanc·er** *n.*

en·har·mon·ic /,enhär'mänik/ ▸*adj. Music* of or relating to notes that are the same in pitch (in modern tuning) though bearing different names (e.g., F sharp and G flat or B and C flat). ■ of or having intervals smaller than a semitone (e.g., between notes such as F sharp and G flat, in systems of tuning that distinguish them). ▷early 17th cent. (designating ancient Greek music based on a tetrachord divided into two quartertones and a major third): via late Latin from Greek *enarmonikos,* from *en-* 'in' + *harmonia* 'harmony.' —**en·har·mon·i·cal·ly** *adv.*

E·nid /'ēnid/ a city in north central Oklahoma; pop. 47,045.

e·nig·ma /i'nigmə/ ▸*n.* (*pl.* **-mas** or **-ma·ta** /-mətə/) a person or thing that is mysterious, puzzling, or difficult to understand. ■ a riddle or paradox. See note at RIDDLE. ▷mid 16th cent.: via Latin from Greek *ainigma,* from *ainissesthai* 'speak allusively,' from *ainos* 'fable.'

en·ig·mat·ic /,enig'matik/ (also **en·ig·mat·i·cal**) ▸*adj.* difficult to interpret or understand; mysterious: *he took the money with an enigmatic smile.* See note at DOUBTFUL. ▷early 17th cent.: from French *énigmatique* or late Latin *aenigmaticus,* based on Greek *ainigma* 'riddle' (see ENIGMA). —**en·ig·mat·i·cal·ly** /-(ə)lē/ *adv.*

en·isle /en'īl/ ▸*v.* [*trans.*] *poetic/literary* isolate on or as if on an island: *in the sea of life enisled, we mortal millions live alone.*

En·i·we·tok /,enə'wē,täk; ə'nēwi-/ (also **En·e·we·tak**) an uninhabited island in the North Pacific Ocean, one of the Marshall Islands. After its population was evacuated, it was used by the U.S. as a testing ground for atom bombs 1948–54.

en·jambed /en'jamd/ ▸*adj.* (of a line, couplet, or stanza of verse) ending partway through a sentence or clause that continues in the next. ▷late 19th cent.: from French *enjamber* 'stride over' + -ED[2].

en·jamb·ment /en'jam(b)mənt/ (also **en·jambe·ment**) ▸*n.* (in verse) the continuation of a sentence without a pause beyond the end of a line, couplet, or stanza. ▷mid 19th cent.: from French *enjambement,* from *enjamber* 'stride over, go beyond,' from *en-* 'in' + *jambe* 'leg.'

en·join /en'join/ ▸*v.* [*trans.*] instruct or urge (someone) to do something: *the code enjoined members to trade fairly.* ■ [*trans.*] prescribe (an action or attitude) to be performed or adopted: *the charitable deeds* **enjoined on** *him by religion.* ■ [*trans.*] (**enjoin someone from**) *Law* prohibit someone from performing (a particular action) by issuing an injunction. See note at PROHIBIT. ▷Middle English (formerly also as *injoin*): from Old French *enjoindre,* from Latin *injungere* 'join, attach, impose,' from *in-* 'in, toward' + *jungere* 'to join.' —**en·join·er** *n.* —**en·join·ment** *n.*

en·join·der /en'joindər/ ▸*n. Law* a prohibition ordered by an injunction.

en·joy /en'joi/ ▸*v.* [*trans.*] **1** take delight or pleasure in (an activity or occasion): *Joe enjoys reading Icelandic family sagas.* ■ (**enjoy oneself**) have a pleasant time: *I could never enjoy myself, knowing you were in your room alone.* ■ [*intrans.*] *informal* used to urge someone to take pleasure in what is about happen or be done: *your love life and love for life get stronger after the 28th—enjoy!* **2** possess and benefit from: *the security forces enjoy legal immunity from prosecution.* ▷late Middle English: from Old French *enjoier* 'give joy to' or *enjoïr* 'enjoy,' both based on Latin *gaudere* 'rejoice.' —**en·joy·er** *n.* —**en·joy·ment** *n.*

en·joy·a·ble /en'joi-əbəl/ ▸*adj.* (of an activity or occasion) giving delight or pleasure: *the decision is aimed at making shopping more enjoyable.* See note at PLEASANT. —**en·joy·a·bil·i·ty** /en,joi-ə'bilitē/ *n.* —**en·joy·a·ble·ness** *n.* —**en·joy·a·bly** /-əblē/ *adv.*

en·keph·al·in /en'kefəlin/ ▸*n. Biochemistry* either of two compounds that occur naturally in the brain. They are peptides related to the endorphins, with similar physiological effects. ▷1970s: from Greek *enkephalos* 'brain' (from *en-* 'in' + *kephalē* 'head') + -IN[1].

en·kin·dle /en'kindl/ ▸*v.* [*trans.*] *poetic/literary* set on fire. ■ arouse or inspire (an emotion): *fresh remembrance of vexation must still enkindle rage.* ■ inflame with passion: *he confidently believed it would enkindle Clara's cold temperament.*

enl. ▸*abbr.* ■ enlarge. ■ enlarged. ■ enlisted.

en·lace /en'lās/ ▸*v.* [*trans.*] *poetic/literary* entwine or entangle: *a web of green enlaced the thorn trees.* ■ encircle tightly; embrace. ▷Middle English: from Old French *enlacier,* based on Latin *laqueus* 'noose.'

en·large /en'lärj/ ▸*v.* make or become bigger or more extensive: [*trans.*] *recently my son enlarged our garden pond* | [*intrans.*] *lymph nodes enlarge and become hard* | [as *adj.*] (**enlarged**) *an enlarged spleen.* ■ [*trans.*] (often **be enlarged**) develop a bigger print of (a photograph).
▸*phrasal v.* □ **enlarge on/upon** speak or write about (something) in greater detail: *I would like to enlarge on this theme.* ▷Middle English (formerly also as *inlarge*): from Old French *enlarger,* from *en-* (expressing a change of state) + *large* 'large.'

en·large·ment /en'lärjmənt/ ▸*n.* the action or state of enlarging or being enlarged. ■ a photograph that is larger than the negative from which it is produced or than a print that has already been made from it.

en·larg·er /en'lärjər/ ▸*n. Photography* an apparatus for enlarging or reducing negatives or positives.

en·light·en /en'lītn/ ▸*v.* [*trans.*] give (someone) greater knowledge and understanding about a subject or situation: *Christopher had not enlightened Frances as to their relationship.* ■ give (someone) spiritual knowledge or insight. ■ *figurative* illuminate or make clearer (a problem or area of study): *this will enlighten the studies of origins of myths and symbols.* ■ *archaic* shed light on (an object). ▷Middle English (in the sense 'make luminous'; formerly also as *inlighten*): in early use from Old English *inlīhtan* 'to shine'; later from EN-[1], IN-[2] (as an intensifier) + LIGHTEN[2] or the noun LIGHT[1]. —**en·light·en·er** *n.*

en·light·ened /en'lītnd/ ▸*adj.* having or showing a rational, modern, and well-informed outlook: *the more enlightened employers offer better terms.* ■ spiritually aware.

en·light·en·ment /en'lītnmənt/ ▸*n.* **1** the action of enlightening or the state of being enlightened: *Robbie looked to me for enlightenment.* ■ the action or state of attaining or having attained spiritual knowledge or insight, in particular (in Buddhism) that awareness which frees a person from the cycle of rebirth. **2** (**the Enlightenment**) a European intellectual movement of the late 17th and 18th centuries emphasizing reason and individualism rather than tradition. It was heavily influenced by 17th-century philosophers such as Descartes, Locke, and Newton, and its prominent exponents include Kant, Goethe, Voltaire, Rousseau, and Adam Smith.

en·list /en'list/ ▸*v.* enroll or be enrolled in the armed services: [*intrans.*] *he* **enlisted in** *the army* | [*trans.*] *hundreds of thousands of recruits had been enlisted.* ■ [*trans.*] engage (a person or their help or support): *the company enlisted the help of independent consultants.* ▷mid 16th cent. (formerly also as *inlist*): from EN-[1], IN-[2] 'in, on' + LIST[1], perhaps suggested by Dutch *inlijsten* 'put on a list.' —**en·list·er** *n.* —**en·list·ment** *n.*

en·list·ed man ▸*n.* a member of the armed forces below the rank of NCO.

en·liv·en /en'līvən/ ▸*v.* [*trans.*] make (something) more entertaining, interesting, or appealing: *the wartime routine was enlivened by a series of concerts.* ■ make (someone) more cheerful or animated: *the visit had clearly enlivened my mother.* See note at QUICKEN. ▷mid 17th cent. (in the sense 'restore to life, give life to'; formerly also as *inliven*): from 16th-cent. *enlive, inlive*

Pronunciation Key ə ago; ər over; 'ə or ,ə up; 'ər or ,ər fur; a hat; ā rate; ä car; CH chew; e let; ē see; e(ə)r air; i fit; ī by; i(ə)r ear; NG sing; ō go; ô for; oi boy; o͝o good; o͞o goo; ou out; SH she; TH thin; T͟H then; (h)w why; ZH vision (in the same sense), from EN-1, IN-2 (as an intensifier) + LIFE. —**en·liv·en·er** *n.* —**en·liv·en·ment** *n.*

en masse /än 'mas/ ▸*adv.* in a group; all together: *the board of directors resigned en masse.* ▷late 18th cent.: French, literally 'in a mass.'

en·mesh /en'mesн/ ▸*v.* [*trans.*] (usu. **be enmeshed in**) cause to become entangled in something: *whales enmeshed in drift nets* | *figurative she is enmeshed in an adulterous affair.* —**en·mesh·ment** *n.*

en·mi·ty /'enmitē/ ▸*n.* (*pl.* **-ties**) the state or feeling of being actively opposed or hostile to someone or something: *enmity between Protestants and Catholics* | *family feuds and enmities.* ▷Middle English: from Old French *enemi(s)tie,* based on Latin *inimicus* (see ENEMY).

en·ne·ad /'enē,ad/ ▸*n. rare* a group or set of nine. ▷mid 16th cent.: from Greek *enneas, ennead-,* from *ennea* 'nine.'

en·ne·a·gram /'enēə,gram/ ▸*n.* a nine-sided figure used in a particular system of analysis to represent the spectrum of possible personality types. ▷from Greek *ennea* 'nine' + -GRAM1.

En·ni·us /'enēəs/, Quintus (239–169 BC), Roman epic poet and playwright. He was largely responsible for the creation of a native Roman literature based on Greek models.

en·no·ble /en'nōbəl/ ▸*v.* [*trans.*] give (someone) a noble rank or title. ■ lend greater dignity or nobility of character to: *the theater is a moral instrument to ennoble the mind.* ▷late 15th cent. (formerly also as *innoble*): from French *ennoblir,* from *en-* (expressing a change of state) + *noble* 'noble.' —**en·no·ble·ment** *n.*

en·nui /än'wē/ ▸*n.* a feeling of listlessness and dissatisfaction arising from a lack of occupation or excitement. ▷mid 18th cent.: French, from Latin *mihi in odio est* 'it is hateful to me.' Compare with ANNOY.

E·noch /'ēnək; 'ē,näk/ **1** (in the Bible) the eldest son of Cain. ■ the first city, built by Cain (Gen. 4:17). **2** a Hebrew patriarch, father of Methuselah.

e·no·ki /i'nōkē/ (also **enoki mushroom**) ▸*n.* an edible Japanese mushroom, growing in clusters, with slender stems and small caps. ▷1980s: from Japanese *enoki-take,* from *enoki* 'nettle-tree' + *take* 'mushroom.'

e·nol·o·gy /ē'näləjē/ (also **oe·nol·o·gy**) ▸*n.* the study of wines. ▷early 19th cent.: from Greek *oinos* 'wine' + -LOGY. —**e·no·log·i·cal** /,ēnə'läjikəl/ *adj.* —**e·nol·o·gist** /-jist/ *n.*

e·nor·mi·ty /i'nôrmitē/ ▸*n.* (*pl.* **-ties**) **1** (**the enormity of**) the great or extreme scale, seriousness, or extent of something perceived as bad or morally wrong: *a thorough search disclosed the full enormity of the crime.* ■ (in neutral use) the large size or scale of something: *the enormity of his intellect.* See **usage** below. **2** a grave crime or sin: *the enormities of the Hitler regime.* ▷late Middle English: via Old French from Latin *enormitas,* from *enormis,* from *e-* (variant of *ex-*) 'out of' + *norma* 'pattern, standard.' The word originally meant 'deviation from legal or moral rectitude' and 'transgression.' Current senses have been influenced by ENORMOUS.

USAGE This word is imprecisely used to mean 'great size,' as in *it is difficult to comprehend the* **enormity** *of the continent,* but the original and preferred meaning is 'extreme wickedness,' as in *the* **enormity** *of the mass murders.* To indicate enormous size, the words *enormousness, immensity, vastness, hugeness,* etc., are preferable.

e·nor·mous /i'nôrməs/ ▸*adj.* very large in size, quantity, or extent: *her enormous blue eyes* | *the possibilities are enormous.* ▷mid 16th cent.: from Latin *enormis* 'unusual, huge' (see ENORMITY) + -OUS. —**e·nor·mous·ly** *adv.* [as *submodifier*] *she has been enormously successful.* —**e·nor·mous·ness** *n.*

e·no·sis /i'nōsis; ē'nō-; 'enōsēs/ ▸*n.* the political union of Cyprus and Greece, as an aim or ideal of certain Greeks and Cypriots. ▷1920s: from modern Greek *henōsis,* from *hena* 'one.'

e·nough /i'nəf/ ▸*adj.* & *pron.* as much or as many as required: [as *adj.*] *too much work and not* **enough** *people to do it* | *there was just* **enough** *room* **for** *two cars* | [as *pron.*] *they ordered* **more than enough** *for five people* | *getting* **enough of** *the right things to eat* | [as *postpositive adj.*] *there will be time enough to tell you when we meet.* ■ used to indicate that one is unwilling to tolerate any more of something undesirable: [as *adj.*] *we've got enough problems without that* | [as *pron.*] *I've* **had enough** *of this arguing* | **that's enough,** *pack it in.*
▸*adv.* **1** to the required degree or extent (used after an adjective, adverb, or verb); adequately: *before he was old* **enough to** *shave* | *you're not big* **enough for** *basketball.* **2** to a moderate degree; fairly: *he can get there easily enough* | *he seems nice enough.* **3** [with *sentence adverb*] used for emphasis: *curiously enough, there is no mention of him.*
▸*exclam.* used to express an impatient desire for the cessation of undesirable behavior or speech: *Enough! After six years of your arguing, I've had it!* ▷Old English *genōg,* of Germanic origin; related to Dutch *genoeg* and German *genug.*
▸*PHRASES* □ **enough is enough** no more will be tolerated. □ **enough said** there is no need to say more; all is understood.

en pa·pil·lote /äɴ ,papē'yōt/ ▸*adj.* & *adv.* (of food) cooked and served in a paper wrapper: [as *postpositive adj.*] *fish en papillote .*

en pas·sant /,än pä'sänt; äɴ pä'säɴ/ ▸*adv.* by the way; incidentally: *the group's disbandment was announced, almost en passant, by the president.* ■ *Chess* by the en passant rule. ▷early 17th cent.: French, literally 'in passing.'
▸*PHRASE* □ **en passant rule** (or **law**) *Chess* the rule that a pawn making a first move of two squares instead of one may nevertheless be immediately captured by an opposing pawn on the fifth rank.

en·plane /en'plān/ (also **em·plane**) ▸*v.* go or put on board an aircraft.

en pointe /äɴ 'pwaɴt/ ▸*adj.* & *adv.* see ON POINTE at POINTE. ▷French.

en poste /äɴ 'pôst/ ▸*adv.* in an official diplomatic position at a particular place.

en pri·meur /äɴ prē'mœr/ ▸*adj.* & *adv.* (of wine) newly produced and made available. ▷late 20th cent.: French, literally 'as being new.'

en prise /äɴ 'prēz/ ▸*adj.* [*predic.*] *Chess* (of a piece or pawn) in a position to be taken. ▷early 19th cent.: French.

en·queue /en'kyoō/ ▸*v.* (**-queued, -queu·ing** or **-queue·ing**) [*trans.*] *Computing* add (an item of data) to a queue: *your message has been enqueued and undeliverable for 1 day.*

en·quire /en'kwīr/ ▸*v. chiefly Brit.* another term for INQUIRE. ▷Middle English *enquere,* from Old French *enquerre,* based on Latin *inquirere* (based on *quaerere* 'seek'). —**en·quir·er** *n.*

en·quir·ing /en'kwī(ə)riɴɢ/ ▸*adj. chiefly Brit.* another term for INQUIRING.

en·quir·y /en'kwī(ə)rē; 'enkwərē/ ▸*n.* (*pl.* **-quir·ies**) *chiefly Brit.* another term for INQUIRY.

en·rage /en'rāj/ ▸*v.* [*trans.*] (usu. **be enraged**) make very angry: *the students were enraged at these new rules* | [as *adj.*] (**enraged**) *an enraged mob screamed abuse.* ▷late 15th cent. (formerly also as *inrage*): from French *enrager,* from *en-* 'into' + *rage* 'rage, anger.'

en rap·port /,än ra'pôr/ ▸*adv.* having a close and harmonious relationship: *his improvisation indicates that he is* **en rapport with** *the rhythm of the band.* ▷French (see RAPPORT).

en·rapt /en'rapt/ ▸*adj.* fascinated; enthralled: *the enrapt audience.*

en·rap·ture /en'rapcнər/ ▸*v.* [*trans.*] (usu. **be enraptured**) give intense pleasure or joy to: *Ruth was enraptured by the child who was sleeping in her arms so peacefully.*

en·rich / en'ricн/ ▸*v.* [*trans.*] **1** improve or enhance the quality or value of: *her exposure to museums enriched her life in France.* ■ (often **be enriched**) add to the nutritive value of (food) by adding vitamins or nutrients: *cereal enriched with extra oat bran.* ■ add to the cultural, intellectual, or spiritual wealth of: *the collection was enriched by a bequest of graphic works.* ■ [usu. as *adj.*] (**enriched**) increase the proportion of a particular isotope in (an element), esp. that of the fissile isotope U-235 in uranium so as to make it more powerful or explosive. ■ *Architecture* embellish a molding by carving or otherwise forming a sculpted, ornamental pattern, such as egg and dart: *one may enrich the echinus of a Doric capital with the egg and dart motif.* **2** make (someone) wealthy or wealthier: *top party members had* **enriched themselves.** ▷late Middle English (in the sense 'make wealthy'): from Old French *enrichir,* from *en-* 'in' + *riche* 'rich.' —**en·rich·ment** *n.*

en·robe /en'rōb/ ▸*v.* [*trans.*] *formal* dress in a robe or vestment.

en·roll /en'rōl/ (*Brit.* **en·rol**) ▸*v.* (**-rolled, -rol·ling**) [*intrans.*] officially register as a member of an institution or a student on a course: *he* **enrolled in** *drama school.* ■ [*trans.*] register (someone) as a member or student: *the school enrolls approximately 1,000 students.* ■ [*trans.*] recruit (someone) to perform a service: *a campaign to enroll more foster carers.* ■ [*trans.*] *historical Law* enter (a deed or other document) among the rolls of a court of justice. ■ *archaic* write the name of (someone) on a list or register. ▷late Middle English (formerly also as *inroll*): from Old French *enroller,* from *en-* 'in' + *rolle* 'a roll' (names being originally written on a roll of parchment). —**en·roll·ee** /,enrō'lē/ *n.*

en·roll·ment /en'rōlmənt/ (*Brit.* **en·rol·ment**) ▸*n.* the action of enrolling or being enrolled: *the amount due must be paid on enrollment in October* | *enrollments for teacher training have dropped off sharply.* ■ the number of people enrolled, typically at a school or college.

en route /än 'roōt; en; äɴ/ ▸*adv.* during the course of a journey; on the way: *he stopped in Turkey en route to Geneva.* ▷late 18th cent.: French (see ROUTE).

ENS ▸*abbr.* ensign.

En·sche·de /'enskə,dā/ a city in eastern Netherlands; pop. 146,500.

en·sconce /en'skäns/ ▸*v.* [*trans.*] establish or settle (someone) in a comfortable, safe, or secret place: *Agnes* **ensconced herself** *in their bedroom* | *spectators who were once comfortably ensconced in the old stadium's box seats.* ▷late 16th cent. (in the senses 'fortify' and 'shelter within or behind a fortification'; formerly also as *insconce*): from EN-1, IN-2 'in' + SCONCE2.

en·sem·ble /än'sämbəl/ ▸*n.* **1** a group of musicians, actors, or dancers who perform together: *a Bulgarian folk ensemble.* ■ a scene or passage written for performance by a whole cast, choir, or group of instruments. ■ the coordination between performers executing such a passage: *a high level of tuning and ensemble is guaranteed.* **2** a group of items viewed as a whole rather than individually: *the buildings in the square present a charming provincial ensemble.* ■ [usu. in *sing.*] a set of clothes chosen to harmonize when worn together. ■ *chiefly Physics* a group of similar systems, or different states of the same system, often considered statistically. ▷late Middle English (as an adverb (long rare) meaning 'at the same time'): from French, based on Latin *insimul,* from *in-* 'in' + *simul* 'at the same time.' The noun dates from the mid 18th cent.

En·se·na·da /,ensə'nädə/ a city in northwestern Mexico, in Baja California state, on the Pacific Ocean; pop. 260,000.

en·sheathe /en'sнēтн/ (also **en·sheath**) ▸*v.* [*trans.*] *chiefly Biology* enclose (an organism, tissue, structure, etc.) in or as in a sheath. —**en·sheath·ment** *n.*

en·shrine /en'sнrīn/ ▸*v.* [*trans.*] (usu. **be enshrined**) place (a revered or precious object) in an appropriate receptacle: *relics are enshrined under altars.* ■ preserve (a right, tradition, or idea) in a form that ensures it will be protected and respected: *the right of all workers to strike was* **enshrined in** *the new constitution.* —**en·shrine·ment** *n.*

en·shroud /en'sнroud/ ▸*v.* [*trans.*] *poetic/literary* envelop completely and hide from view: *heavy gray clouds enshrouded the city.*

en·si·form /'ensə,fôrm/ ▸*adj. chiefly Botany* shaped like a sword blade; long and narrow with sharp edges and a pointed tip. ▷mid 16th cent.: from Latin *ensis* 'sword' + -FORM.

en·si·form car·ti·lage ▸*n.* another term for XIPHOID PROCESS.

en·sign ▸*n.* **1** /'ensən; 'en,sīn/ a flag or standard, esp. a military or naval one indicating nationality. ■ *archaic* a sign or emblem of a particular thing: *all the ensigns of our greatness.* **2** /'ensən/ a commissioned officer of the lowest rank in the U.S. Navy and Coast Guard, ranking above chief warrant officer and below lieutenant. ■ *historical* the lowest rank of commissioned infantry officer in the British army. ■ *historical* a standard-bearer. ▷late Middle English: from Old French *enseigne,* from Latin *insignia* 'signs of office' (see INSIGNIA). Compare with ANCIENT2.

en·si·lage /'ensəlij/ ▸*n.* another term for SILAGE.
▸*v.* another term for ENSILE. ▷late 19th cent.: from French, from *ensiler* (see ENSILE).

en·sile /en'sīl/ ▸*v.* [*trans.*] put (grass or another crop) into a silo or silage clamp in order to preserve it as silage. ▷late 19th cent.: from French *ensiler,* from Spanish *ensilar,* from *en-* 'in' + *silo* 'silo.'

en·slave /en'slāv/ ▸*v.* [*trans.*] make (someone) a slave. ■ cause (someone) to lose their freedom of choice or action: *they were enslaved by their need to take drugs.* ▷early 17th cent. (in the sense 'make (a person) subject to a superstition, passion, etc.'; formerly also as *inslave*): from EN-1, IN-2 (as an intensifier) + SLAVE. —**en·slave·ment** *n.* —**en·slav·er** *n.*

en·snare /en'sner/ ▸*v.* [*trans.*] catch in or as in a trap: *they were ensnared in downtown traffic.* —**en·snare·ment** *n.*

en·snarl /en'snärl/ ▸*v.* [*trans.*] cause to become caught up in complex difficulties or problems.

En·sor /'ensôr/, James (Sydney), Baron (1860–1949), Belgian painter and engraver. Noted for macabre subjects, his work is significant both for symbolism and for the development of 20th-century expressionism.

en·sor·cell /en'sôrsəl/ (also **en·sor·cel**) ▸*v.* (**-celled, -cel·ling**; also **-celed, -cel·ing**) [*trans.*] *poetic/literary* enchant; fascinate. ▷mid 16th cent.: from Old French *ensorceler*, alteration of *ensorcerer*, from *sorcier* 'sorcerer.' **—en·sor·cell·ment** (also **en·sor·cel·ment**) *n.*

en·soul /en'sōl/ ▸*v.* [*trans.*] endow with a soul. **—en·soul·ment** *n.*

en·sta·tite /'enstəˌtīt/ ▸*n.* a translucent crystalline mineral of varying colors that occurs in some igneous rocks and stony meteorites. It consists of magnesium silicate and is a member of the pyroxene group. ▷mid 19th cent.: from Greek *enstatēs* 'adversary' (because of its refractory nature) + **-ITE**[1]. **—en·sta·tit·ic** /ˌenstə'titik/ *adj.*

en·sue /en'so͞o/ ▸*v.* (**en·sues, en·sued, en·su·ing**) [*intrans.*] happen or occur afterward or as a result: *the difficulties that* **ensued from** *their commitment to Cuba* | [as *adj.*] (**ensuing**) *there were repeated clashes in the ensuing days.* ▷late Middle English (formerly also as *insue*): from Old French *ensivre*, from Latin *insequi*, based on *sequi* 'follow.'

en suite /än 'swēt/ ▸*adj.* & *adv.* (of a bathroom) immediately adjoining a bedroom and forming part of the same set of rooms. ■ [as *adj.*] (of a bedroom) having such a bathroom. ▷late 18th cent. (in the sense 'in agreement or harmony'): from French, literally 'in sequence.'

en·sure /en'sHo͝or/ ▸*v.* [*trans.*] make certain that (something) shall occur or be the case: [with *clause*] *the client must ensure that accurate records be kept.* ■ make certain of obtaining or providing (something): [with *two objs.*] *she would ensure him a place in society.* ■ [*intrans.*] (**ensure against**) make sure that (a problem) shall not occur. ▷late Middle English (in the senses 'convince' and 'make safe'): from Anglo-Norman French *enseurer*, alteration of Old French *aseurer*, earlier form of *assurer* (see **ASSURE**). Compare with **INSURE**.

USAGE On the difference between **ensure** and **insure**, see **usage** at **INSURE**.

en·swathe /en'swä*TH*; en'swā*TH*/ ▸*v.* [*trans.*] *poetic/literary* envelop or wrap in a garment or piece of fabric.

ENT ▸*abbr.* ear, nose, and throat (as a department in a hospital).

-ent /ənt; nt/ ▸*suffix* **1** (forming adjectives) denoting an occurrence of action: *refluent.* ■ denoting a state: *convenient.* **2** (forming nouns) denoting an agent: *coefficient.* ▷from French, or from the Latin present participial verb stem *-ent-* (see also **-ANT**).

en·tab·la·ture /en'tablәCHәr; -ˌCHo͝or/ ▸*n. Architecture* a horizontal, continuous lintel on a classical building supported by columns or a wall, comprising the architrave, frieze, and cornice. ▷early 17th cent. (formerly also as *intablature*): from Italian *intavolatura* 'boarding' (partly via French *entablement* 'entablement'), from *intavolare* 'board up' (based on *tavola* 'table').

en·ta·ble·ment /en'tābəlmənt/ ▸*n. Architecture* a platform supporting a statue, above the dado and base. ▷mid 17th cent. (in the sense 'entablature'): from French, based on *table* 'table.'

en·tail ▸*v.* /en'tāl/ [*trans.*] **1** involve (something) as a necessary or inevitable part or consequence: *a situation that entails considerable risks.* ■ *Logic* have as a logically necessary consequence. **2** *Law* settle the inheritance of (property) over a number of generations so that ownership remains within a particular group, usually one family: *her father's estate was* **entailed on** *a cousin.* ■ *archaic* cause to experience or possess in a way perceived as permanent or inescapable: *I cannot get rid of the disgrace that you have* **entailed upon** *us.*

▸*n.* /'enˌtāl/ *Law* a settlement of the inheritance of property over a number of generations so that it remains within a family or other group. ■ a property that is bequeathed under such conditions. ▷late Middle English (referring to settlement of property; formerly also as *intail*): from **EN-**[1], **IN-**[2] 'into' + Old French *taille* 'notch, tax' (see **TAIL**[2]). **—en·tail·ment** *n.*

ent·a·me·ba /ˌentə'mēbə/ (also **ent·a·moe·ba**) ▸*n.* (*pl.* **-me·bae** /-'mēbē/ or **-me·bas**) an ameba that typically lives harmlessly in the gut, though one kind can cause amebic dysentery. • Genus *Entamoeba*, phylum Rhizopoda, kingdom Protista. ▷modern Latin, from Greek *entos* 'within' + **AMEBA**.

en·tan·gle /en'taNGgəl/ ▸*v.* [*trans.*] (usu. **be entangled**) cause to become twisted together with or caught in: *fish attempt to swim through the mesh and become entangled.* ■ involve (someone) in difficulties or complicated circumstances from which it is difficult to escape: *the case of murder in which she had found herself so painfully entangled.*

en·tan·gle·ment /en'taNGgəlmənt/ ▸*n.* the action or fact of entangling or being entangled: *many dolphins die from entanglement in fishing nets.* ■ a complicated or compromising relationship or situation: *romantic entanglements.* ■ an extensive barrier, typically made of interlaced barbed wire and stakes, erected to impede enemy soldiers or vehicles: *the attackers were caught up on wire entanglements.*

en·ta·sis /'entəsis/ ▸*n.* (*pl.* **-ses** /-sēz/) *Architecture* a slight convex curve in the shaft of a column, introduced to correct the visual illusion of concavity produced by a straight shaft. ▷mid 17th cent.: modern Latin, from Greek, from *enteinein* 'to stretch or strain.'

en·tel·e·chy /en'teləkē/ ▸*n.* (*pl.* **-chies**) *Philosophy* the realization of potential. ■ the supposed vital principle that guides the development and functioning of an organism or other system or organization. ■ *Philosophy* the soul. ▷late Middle English: via late Latin from Greek *entelekheia* (used by Aristotle), from *en-* 'within' + *telos* 'end, perfection' + *ekhein* 'be in a certain state.'

en·tel·lus /en'teləs/ (also **entellus monkey**) ▸*n.* another term for **HANUMAN**. ▷mid 19th cent.: from the name of an aged Trojan in Virgil's *Aeneid*.

en·tente /än'tänt/ ▸*n.* (also **en·tente cor·diale** /kôr 'dyäl/) a friendly understanding or informal alliance between states or factions: *the growing entente between former opponents.* ■ a group of states in such an alliance. ■ (**the Entente Cordiale**) the understanding between Britain and France reached in 1904, forming the basis of Anglo-French cooperation in World War I. ▷mid 19th cent.: French *entente (cordiale)* '(friendly) understanding.'

en·ter /'entər/ ▸*v.* **1** come or go into (a place): [*trans.*] *she entered the kitchen* | [*intrans.*] *the door opened and Karl entered* | *figurative reading the Bible, we* **enter into** *an amazing new world of thoughts.* ■ [*intrans.*] used as a stage direction to indicate when a character comes on stage: *enter Hamlet.* ■ [*trans.*] penetrate (something): *the bullet entered his stomach.* ■ [*trans.*] (of a man) insert the penis into the vagina of (a woman). ■ [*trans.*] come or be introduced into: *the thought never entered my head.* **2** [*trans.*] begin to be involved in: *in 1941 America entered the war.* ■ become a member of or start working in (an institution or profession): *that autumn, he entered college.* ■ register as a competitor or participant in (a tournament, race, or examination). ■ register (a person, animal, or thing) to compete or participate in a tournament, race, or examination. ■ start or reach (a stage or period of time) in an activity or situation: *the election campaign entered its final phase.* ■ [*intrans.*] (of a particular performer in an ensemble) start or resume playing or singing. **3** write or key (information) in a book, computer, etc., so as to record it: *children can* **enter** *the data* **into** *the computer.* ■ *Law* submit (a statement) in an official capacity, usually in a court of law: *an attorney entered a plea of guilty on her behalf.*

▸*phrasal v.* □ **enter into** become involved in (an activity, situation, or matter): *they have entered into a relationship.* ■ undertake to bind oneself by (an agreement or other commitment): *the council entered into an agreement with a private firm.* ■ form part of or be a factor in: *medical ethics also enter into the question.* □ **enter on/upon 1** *formal* begin (an activity or job); start to pursue (a particular course in life): *he entered upon a turbulent political career.* **2** *Law* (as a legal entitlement) go freely into property as or as if the owner.

▸*n.* (also **enter key**) a key on a computer keyboard that is used to perform various functions, such as executing a command or selecting options on a menu. ▷Middle English: from Old French *entrer*, from Latin *intrare*, from *intra* 'within.'

en·ter·al /'entərəl/ ▸*adj. Medicine* (chiefly of nutrition) involving or passing through the intestine, either naturally via the mouth and esophagus, or through an artificial opening. Often contrasted with **PARENTERAL**. ▷early 20th cent.: from Greek *enteron* 'intestine' + **-AL**, partly as a back-formation from **PARENTERAL**. **—en·ter·al·ly** *adv.*

en·ter·ic /en'terik/ ▸*adj.* of, relating to, or occurring in the intestines. ▷early 19th cent.: from Greek *enterikos*, from *enteron* 'intestine.'

en·ter·ic fe·ver ▸*n.* another term for **TYPHOID** or **PARATYPHOID**.

en·ter·i·tis /ˌentə'rītis/ ▸*n. Medicine* inflammation of the intestine, esp. the small intestine, usually accompanied by diarrhea.

entero- ▸*comb. form* of or relating to the intestine: *enterovirus.* ▷from Greek *enteron*.

en·ter·o·coc·cus /'entərōˌkäkəs/ ▸*n.* (*pl.* **-coc·ci** /-ˌkäk(s)ī; -ˌkäk(s)ē/) a streptococcus of a group that occurs naturally in the intestine but causes inflammation and blood infection if introduced elsewhere in the body (e.g., by injury or surgery). • Genus *Streptococcus* (or *Enterococcus*); Gram-positive cocci. **—en·ter·o·coc·cal** /ˌentərō'käkəl/ *adj.*

en·ter·o·coele /'entərōˌsēl/ (also **en·ter·o·coel**) ▸*n. Zoology* a coelom or coelomic cavity developed from the wall of the archenteron in some invertebrates. **—en·ter·o·coe·lic** /ˌentərō'sēlik/ *adj.* **—en·ter·o·coe·ly** /-ˌsēlē/ *n.*

en·ter·o·co·li·tis /ˌentərōkə'lītis/ ▸*n. Medicine* inflammation of both the small intestine and the colon.

en·ter·o·cyte /'entərōˌsīt/ ▸*n. Physiology* a cell of the intestinal lining.

en·ter·o·hep·a·tic /ˌentərōhi'patik/ ▸*adj. Physiology* relating to or denoting the circulation of bile salts and other secretions from the liver to the intestine, where they are reabsorbed into the blood and returned to the liver.

en·ter·op·a·thy /ˌentə'räpəTHē/ ▸*n.* (*pl.* **-thies**) *Medicine* a disease of the intestine, esp. the small intestine.

en·ter·os·to·my /ˌentə'rästəmē/ ▸*n.* (*pl.* **-mies**) an ileostomy or similar surgical operation in which the small intestine is diverted to an artificial opening in the abdominal wall or in another part of the intestine. ■ an opening in the abdominal wall formed in this way.

en·ter·ot·o·my /ˌentə'rätəmē/ ▸*n.* the surgical cutting open of the intestine.

en·ter·o·tox·e·mi·a /ˌentərōˌtäk'sēmēə/ (*Brit.* **en·ter·o·tox·ae·mi·a**) ▸*n. chiefly Veterinary Medicine* blood poisoning caused by an enterotoxin.

en·ter·o·tox·i·gen·ic /'entərōˌtäksi'jenik/ ▸*adj. Medicine* (of bacteria) producing an enterotoxin.

en·ter·o·tox·in /ˌentərō'täksin/ ▸*n. Medicine* a toxin produced in or affecting the intestines, such as those causing food poisoning or cholera.

en·ter·o·vi·rus /ˌentərō'vīrəs/ ▸*n. Medicine* any of a group of RNA viruses (including those causing polio and hepatitis A) that typically occur in the gastrointestinal tract, sometimes spreading to the central nervous system or other parts of the body.

en·ter·prise /'entərˌprīz/ ▸*n.* **1** a project or undertaking, typically one that is difficult or requires effort: *a joint enterprise between French and Japanese companies.* ■ initiative and resourcefulness: *success came quickly, thanks to a mixture of talent, enterprise, and luck.* **2** a business or company: *a state-owned enterprise.* ■ entrepreneurial economic activity. ▷late Middle English: from Old French, 'something undertaken,' feminine past participle (used as a noun) of *entreprendre*, based on Latin *prendere*, *prehendere* 'to take.' **—en·ter·pris·er** *n.*

en·ter·prise zone ▸*n.* an impoverished area in which incentives such as tax concessions are offered to encourage business investment and provide jobs for the residents.

en·ter·pris·ing /'entərˌprīziNG/ ▸*adj.* having or showing initiative and resourcefulness: *some enterprising teachers have started their own recycling programs.* **—en·ter·pris·ing·ly** *adv.*

en·ter·tain /ˌentər'tān/ ▸*v.* [*trans.*] **1** provide (someone) with amusement or enjoyment: *a tremendous game that thoroughly entertained the crowd.* ■ receive (someone) as a guest and provide them with food and drink: *a private dining room where members could entertain groups of friends.* **2** give attention or consideration to (an idea, suggestion, or feeling): *Washington entertained little hope of an early improvement in relations.* ▷late Middle English: from French *entretenir*, based on Latin *inter* 'among' + *tenere* 'to hold.' The word originally meant 'maintain, continue,' later 'maintain in a certain condition, treat in a certain way,' also 'show hospitality' (late 15th cent.).

en·ter·tain·er /ˌentər'tānər/ ▸*n.* a person, such as a

singer, dancer, or comedian, whose job is to entertain others.

en·ter·tain·ing /ˌentərˈtāniNG/ ▸*adj.* providing amusement or enjoyment: *the magazine is both entertaining and informative.* —**en·ter·tain·ing·ly** *adv.*

en·ter·tain·ment /ˌentərˈtānmənt/ ▸*n.* the action of providing or being provided with amusement or enjoyment: *everyone just sits in front of the TV for entertainment.* ■ an event, performance, or activity designed to entertain others: *a theatrical entertainment.* ■ the action of receiving a guest or guests and providing them with food and drink.

en·thal·py /ˈenˌTHalpē; enˈTHalpē/ ▸*n. Physics* a thermodynamic quantity equivalent to the total heat content of a system. It is equal to the internal energy of the system plus the product of pressure and volume. (Symbol: **H**) ■ the change in this quantity associated with a particular chemical process. ▷1920s: from Greek *enthalpein* 'warm in,' from *en-* 'within' + *thalpein* 'to heat.'

en·the·o·gen /enˈthēəˌjen; -jən/ ▸*n.* a chemical substance, typically of plant origin, that is ingested to produce a nonordinary state of consciousness for religious or spiritual purposes. ▷1970s: from Greek, literally 'becoming divine within'; coined by an informal committee studying the inebriants of shamans. —**en·the·o·gen·ic** /enˌthēəˈjenik/ *adj.*

en·thrall /enˈTHrôl/ (*Brit.* also **en·thral**) ▸*v.* (**-thralled, -thrall·ing**) [*trans.*] (often **be enthralled**) capture the fascinated attention of: *she had been so enthralled by the adventure that she had hardly noticed the cold* | [as *adj.*] (**enthralling**) *an enthralling best seller.* ■ (also **in·thrall**) *archaic* enslave. ▷late Middle English (in the sense 'enslave'; formerly also as *inthrall*): from **EN-**[1], **IN-**[2] (as an intensifier) + **THRALL**. —**en·thrall·ment** (*Brit* also **en·thral·ment**) *n.*

en·throne /enˈTHrōn/ ▸*v.* [*trans.*] (usu. **be enthroned**) install (a monarch) on a throne, esp. during a ceremony to mark the beginning of their rule. ■ *figurative* give or ascribe a position of authority to: *he was enthroned as the guru of the avant-garde.* —**en·throne·ment** *n.*

en·thuse /enˈTHo͞oz/ ▸*v.* [*reporting verb*] say something that expresses one's eager enjoyment, interest, or approval: [*intrans.*] *they both* **enthused over** *my new look* | [with *direct speech*] *"This place is superb!" she enthused.* ■ [*trans.*] make (someone) interested and eagerly appreciative: *public art is a tonic that can enthuse alienated youth.*

USAGE The verb **enthuse** is formed as a back-formation from the noun **enthusiasm** and, like many verbs formed from nouns in this way, it is regarded by traditionalists as unacceptable. It is difficult to see why: it is a perfectly established means for creating new words in the language (verbs like **classify**, **commentate**, and **edit** were also formed as back-formations from nouns, for example).**Enthuse** itself has been in the language for more than 150 years.

en·thu·si·asm /enˈTHo͞ozēˌazəm/ ▸*n.* **1** intense and eager enjoyment, interest, or approval: *her energy and* **enthusiasm for** *life* | *few expressed enthusiasm about the current leaders.* ■ a thing that arouses such feelings: *the three enthusiasms of his life were politics, religion, and books.* **2** *archaic, derogatory* religious fervor supposedly resulting directly from divine inspiration, typically involving speaking in tongues and wild, uncoordinated movements of the body. ▷early 17th cent. (in sense 2): from French *enthousiasme*, or via late Latin from Greek *enthousiasmos*, from *enthous* 'possessed by a god, inspired' (based on *theos* 'god').

en·thu·si·ast /enˈTHo͞ozēˌast/ ▸*n.* a person who is highly interested in a particular activity or subject: *a sports car enthusiast.* See note at **ZEALOT**. ■ *archaic, derogatory* a person of intense and visionary Christian views. ▷early 17th cent. (denoting a person believing that he or she is divinely inspired): from French *enthousiaste* or ecclesiastical Latin *enthusiastes* 'member of a heretical sect,' from Greek *enthousiastēs* 'person inspired by a god,' from the adjective *enthous* (see **ENTHUSIASM**).

en·thu·si·as·tic /enˌTHo͞ozēˈastik/ ▸*adj.* having or showing intense and eager enjoyment, interest, or approval: *the promoter was enthusiastic about the concert venue.* See note at **EAGER**. ▷early 17th cent.: from Greek *enthousiastikos*, from *enthous* 'possessed by a god' (see **ENTHUSIASM**). —**en·thu·si·as·ti·cal·ly** *adv.*

en·thy·meme /ˈenTHəˌmēm/ ▸*n. Logic* an argument in which one premise is not explicitly stated. ▷mid 16th cent.: via Latin from Greek *enthumēma*, from *enthumeisthai* 'consider,' from *en-* 'within' + *thumos* 'mind.'

en·tice /enˈtīs/ ▸*v.* [*trans.*] attract or tempt by offering pleasure or advantage: *a show that should* **entice** *a new audience* **into** *the theater* | [*trans.*] *the whole purpose of bribes is to entice governments to act against the public interest* | [as *adj.*] (**enticing**) *the idea of giving up sounds enticing but would be a mistake.* See note at **TEMPT**. ▷Middle English (also in the sense 'incite, provoke'; formerly also as *intice*): from Old French *enticier*, probably from a base meaning 'set on fire,' based on an alteration of Latin *titio* 'firebrand.' —**en·tice·ment** *n.* —**en·tic·er** *n.* —**en·tic·ing·ly** *adv.*

en·tire /enˈtīr/ ▸*adj.* [*attrib.*] with no part left out; whole: *my plans are to travel the entire world.* ■ not broken or decayed. ■ without qualification or reservations; absolute: *an ideological system with which he is in entire agreement.* ■ (of a male horse) not castrated. ■ *Botany* (of a leaf) without indentations or division into leaflets.
▸*n.* an uncastrated male horse. ▷late Middle English (formerly also as *intire*): from Old French *entier*, based on Latin *integer* 'untouched, whole,' from *in-* 'not' + *tangere* 'to touch.'

en·tire·ly /enˈtīrlē/ ▸*adv.* completely (often used for emphasis): *the juries were made up entirely of men* | [as *submodifier*] *we have an entirely different outlook.* ■ solely: *eight coaches entirely for passenger transport.*

en·tire·ty /enˈtī(ə)rtē; -ˈtīritē/ ▸*n.* the whole of something: *she would have to stay in her room over* **the entirety of** *the weekend.* ▷Middle English: from Old French *entierete*, from Latin *integritas*, from *integer* 'untouched, whole' (see **ENTIRE**). Compare with **INTEGRITY**.
▸***PHRASE*** □ **in its entirety** as a whole; completely: *the poem is too long to quote in its entirety here.*

en·ti·sol /ˈentiˌsäl; -sôl/ ▸*n. Soil Science* a soil of an order comprising mineral soils that have not yet differentiated into distinct horizons. ▷mid 20th cent.: from **ENTIRE** + **-SOL**.

en·ti·tle /enˈtītl/ ▸*v.* [*trans.*] (usu. **be entitled**) **1** give (someone) a legal right or a just claim to receive or do something: *employees are normally* **entitled to** *severance pay* | [*trans.*] *the landlord is entitled to require references.* **2** give (something, esp. a text or work of art) a particular title: *an article entitled "The Harried Society."* ■ [*trans.*] *archaic* give (someone) a specified title expressing their rank, office, or character: *they entitled him Sultan.* ▷late Middle English (formerly also as *intitle*): via Old French from late Latin *intitulare*, from *in-* 'in' + Latin *titulus* 'title.'

en·ti·tle·ment /enˈtītlmənt/ ▸*n.* the fact of having a right to something: *full* **entitlement to** *fees and maintenance should be offered* | *you should be fully aware of your legal entitlements.* ■ the amount to which a person has a right: *annual leave entitlement.*

en·ti·tle·ment pro·gram ▸*n.* a government program that guarantees certain benefits to a particular group or segment of the population.

en·ti·ty /ˈentitē/ ▸*n.* (*pl.* **-ties**) a thing with distinct and independent existence: *church and empire were fused in a single entity.* ■ existence; being: *entity and nonentity.* ▷late 15th cent. (denoting a thing's existence): from French *entité* or medieval Latin *entitas*, from late Latin *ens*, *ent-* 'being' (from *esse* 'be'). —**en·ti·ta·tive** /-ˌtātiv/ *adj.* (*chiefly Philosophy*)

entom. ▸*abbr.* entomology.

en·tomb /enˈto͞om/ ▸*v.* [*trans.*] (usu. **be entombed**) place (a dead body) in a tomb. ■ bury or trap in or under something: *many people died, most entombed in collapsed buildings.* ▷late Middle English (formerly also as *intomb*): from Old French *entomber*, from *en-* 'in' + *tombe* 'tomb.' —**en·tomb·ment** *n.*

entomo- ▸*comb. form* of an insect; of or relating to insects: *entomophagous.* ▷from Greek *entomon*, neuter (denoting an insect) of *entomos* 'cut up, segmented.'

en·to·mol·o·gy /ˌentəˈmäləjē/ ▸*n.* the branch of zoology concerned with the study of insects. ▷mid 18th cent.: from French *entomologie* or modern Latin *entomologia*, from Greek *entomon* (denoting an insect) + *-logia* (see **-LOGY**). —**en·to·mo·log·i·cal** /-məˈläjikəl/ *adj.* —**en·to·mol·o·gist** /-jist/ *n.*

en·to·moph·a·gy /ˌentəˈmäfəjē/ ▸*n.* the practice of eating insects, esp. by people. —**en·to·moph·a·gist** /-jist/ *n.* —**en·to·moph·a·gous** /-ˈmäfəgəs/ *adj.*

en·to·moph·i·lous /ˌentəˈmäfələs/ ▸*adj. Botany* (of a plant or flower) pollinated by insects. —**en·to·moph·i·ly** /-ˈmäfəlē/ *n.*

en·to·par·a·site /ˌentōˈparəˌsīt/ ▸*n. Biology* another term for **ENDOPARASITE**. ▷late 19th cent.: from Greek *entos* 'within' + **PARASITE**.

En·to·proc·ta /ˌentəˈpräktə/ *Zoology* a small phylum of sedentary aquatic invertebrates that resemble moss animals. They have a rounded body on a long stalk, bearing a ring of tentacles for filtering food from the water. ▷modern Latin (plural), from Greek *entos* 'within' + *prōktos* 'anus,' the anus being within the ring of tentacles. —**en·to·proct** /ˈentəˌpräkt/ *n.*

ent·op·tic /enˈtäptik/ ▸*adj.* (of visual images) occurring or originating inside the eye. ▷late 19th cent.: from Greek *entos* 'within' + **OPTIC**.

en·tou·rage /ˌäntōōˈräzH/ ▸*n.* a group of people attending or surrounding an important person: *an entourage of bodyguards.* ▷mid 19th cent.: French, from *entourer* 'to surround.'

en·tr'acte /ˈänˌtrakt; änˈtrakt/ ▸*n.* an interval between two acts of a play or opera. ■ a piece of music or a dance performed during such an interval. ▷mid 19th cent.: French (earlier form of *entracte,*) from *entre* 'between' + *acte* 'act.'

en·trails /ˈentrālz; ˈentrəlz/ ▸*plural n.* a person or animal's intestines or internal organs, esp. when removed or exposed. ■ *figurative* the innermost parts of something: *digging copper out of the entrails of the earth.* ▷Middle English: from Old French *entrailles*, from medieval Latin *intralia*, alteration of Latin *interanea* 'internal things,' based on *inter* 'among.'

en·train[1] /enˈtrān/ ▸*v.* [*intrans.*] board a train. ■ [*trans.*] put or allow (someone or something) on board a train.

en·train[2] ▸*v.* [*trans.*] **1** (of a current or fluid) incorporate and sweep along in its flow. ■ cause or bring about as a consequence: *the triumph of a revolution was measured in terms of the social revision it entrained.* **2** *Biology* (of a rhythm or something that varies rhythmically) cause (another) gradually to fall into synchronism with it. ■ [*intrans.*] (**entrain to**) fall into synchronism with (something) in such a way. ▷mid 16th cent. (in the sense 'bring on as a consequence'): from French *entraîner*, from *en-* 'in' + *traîner* 'to drag.' —**en·train·ment** *n.*

en·trance[1] /ˈentrəns/ ▸*n.* an opening, such as a door, passage, or gate, that allows access to a place. ■ [usu. in *sing.*] an act or instance of going or coming in: *at their abrupt entrance he rose to his feet.* ■ [usu. in *sing.*] the coming of an actor or performer onto a stage: *her final entrance is as a triumphant princess.* ■ [usu. in *sing.*] an act of becoming involved in something: *their entrance into the political arena.* ■ the right, means, or opportunity to enter somewhere or be a member of an institution, society, or other body: *about fifty people attempted to gain entrance* | [as *adj.*] *an entrance examination.* ■ *Music* another term for **ENTRY**. ▷late 15th cent. (in the sense 'right or opportunity of admission'): from Old French, from *entrer* 'enter.'
▸***PHRASE*** □ **make an** (or **one's**) **entrance** (of an actor or performer) come on stage. ■ enter somewhere in a conspicuous or impressive way: *she slowly counted to ten before making her entrance.*

en·trance[2] /enˈtrans/ ▸*v.* [*trans.*] (often **be entranced**) fill (someone) with wonder and delight, holding their entire attention: *I was entranced by a cluster of trees that were lit up by fireflies* | [as *adj.*] (**entrancing**) *he had never seen a more entrancing woman.* ■ cast a spell on: *Orpheus entranced the wild beasts.* —**en·trance·ment** *n.* —**en·tranc·ing·ly** *adv.*

en·trance·way /ˈentrənsˌwā/ ▸*n.* a way into a place or thing, esp. a doorway or corridor at the entrance to a building.

en·trant /ˈentrənt/ ▸*n.* a person or group that enters, joins, or takes part in something. ▷early 17th cent. (denoting a person taking legal possession of land or property): from French, literally 'entering,' present participle of *entrer* (see **ENTER**).

en·trap /enˈtrap/ ▸*v.* (**-trapped, -trap·ping**) [*trans.*] catch (someone or something) in or as in a trap: *she was entrapped by family expectations.* ■ trick or deceive (someone), esp. by inducing them to commit a crime in order to secure their prosecution. ▷mid 16th cent.: from Old French *entraper*, from *en-* 'in' + *trappe* 'a trap.' —**en·trap·ment** *n.* —**en·trap·per** *n.*

en tra·ves·ti /än ˌtraveˈstē/ ▸*adv.* & *adj.* dressed as a member of the opposite sex, esp. for a theatrical role. ▷mid 20th cent.: from French, literally '(dressed) in disguise, cross-dressed.'

en·treat /enˈtrēt/ ▸*v.* **1** [*reporting verb*] ask someone earnestly or anxiously to do something: [*trans.*] *his friends entreated him not to go.* See note at **BEG**. ■ [*trans.*] ask earnestly or anxiously for (something): *a message had been sent, entreating aid for the Navajos.* **2** [*trans.*] *archaic* treat (someone) in a specified manner: *the King, I fear, hath ill entreated her.* ▷late Middle English (in the sense 'treat, act toward (someone)';

formerly also as *intreat*): from Old French *entraitier*, based on *traitier* 'to treat,' from Latin *tractare* 'to handle.' —**en·treat·ing·ly** *adv.* —**en·treat·ment** *n.*

en·treat·y /en'trētē/ ▸*n.* (*pl.* **-treat·ies**) an earnest or humble request: *the king turned a deaf ear to his entreaties.* ▷late Middle English (in the sense 'treatment, management'; formerly also as *intreaty*): from ENTREAT, on the pattern of *treaty*.

en·tre·chat /ˌäntrə'SHä/ ▸*n. Ballet* a vertical jump during which the dancer repeatedly crosses the feet and beats them together. ▷French, from Italian *(capriola) intrecciata* 'complicated (caper).'

en·tre·côte /'äntrəˌkōt/ ▸*n.* a boned steak cut off the sirloin. ▷French, from *entre* 'between' + *côte* 'rib.'

en·trée /'änˌtrā; ˌän'trā/ (also **en·tree**) ▸*n.* the main course of a meal. ■ *Brit.* a dish served between the fish and meat courses at a formal dinner. ▷early 18th cent. (denoting a piece of instrumental music forming the first part of a suite): French, feminine past participle of *entrer* 'enter' (see ENTRY).

en·tre·mets /ˌäntrə'mā/ ▸*n.* a light dish served between two courses of a formal meal. ▷French, from *entre* 'between' + *mets* 'dish.'

en·trench /en'trenCH/ (also *dated* **in·trench**) ▸*v.* **1** [*trans.*] (often **be entrenched**) establish (an attitude, habit, or belief) so firmly that change is very difficult or unlikely: *ageism is* ***entrenched in*** *our society.* ■ establish (a person or their authority) in a position of great strength or security: *by 1947 de Gaulle's political opponents were firmly* ***entrenched in*** *power.* ■ apply extra legal safeguards to (a right, esp. a constitutional right, guaranteed by legislation). ■ establish (a military force, camp, etc.) in trenches or other fortified positions. **2** [*intrans.*] (**entrench on/upon**) *archaic* encroach or trespass upon. ▷mid 16th cent. (in the sense 'place within a trench'): from EN-[1], IN-[2] 'into' + TRENCH. —**en·trench·ment** *n.*

en·tre nous /ˌäntrə 'no͞o/ ▸*adv.* between ourselves; privately: *entre nous, the old man's a bit of a problem.* ▷late 17th cent.: French.

en·tre·pôt /'äntrəˌpō/ ▸*n.* (*pl.* **-pôts** *pronunc.* same or /-ˌpōz/) a port, city, or other center to which goods are brought for import and export, and for collection and distribution. ▷early 18th cent.: French, from *entreposer* 'to store,' from *entre* 'among' + *poser* 'to place.'

en·tre·pre·neur /ˌäntrəprə'no͝or; -'nər/ ▸*n.* a person who organizes and operates a business or businesses, taking on greater than normal financial risks in order to do so. ■ a promoter in the entertainment industry. ▷early 19th cent. (denoting the director of a musical institution): from French, from *entreprendre* 'undertake' (see ENTERPRISE). —**en·tre·pre·neur·i·al** *adj.* —**en·tre·pre·neur·i·al·ism** *n.* —**en·tre·pre·neur·i·al·ly** *adv.* —**en·tre·pre·neur·ism** *n.* —**en·tre·pre·neur·ship** *n.*

en·tre·sol /'entərˌsäl; 'äntrəˌsäl; -sôl/ ▸*n.* a low story between the first floor and the second floor of a building; a mezzanine floor. ▷early 18th cent.: French, from Spanish *entresuelo*, from *entre* 'between' + *suelo* 'story.'

en·tro·pi·on /en'trōpēˌän; -pēən/ ▸*n. Medicine* a condition in which the eyelid is rolled inward against the eyeball, typically caused by muscle spasm or by inflammation or scarring of the conjunctiva (as in diseases such as trachoma), and resulting in irritation of the eye by the lashes (trichiasis). ▷late 19th cent.: from EN-[2] 'inside,' on the pattern of *ectropion*.

en·tro·py /'entrəpē/ ▸*n. Physics* a thermodynamic quantity representing the unavailability of a system's thermal energy for conversion into mechanical work, often interpreted as the degree of disorder or randomness in the system. (Symbol: **S**) ■ *figurative* lack of order or predictability; gradual decline into disorder: *a marketplace where entropy reigns supreme.* ■ (in information theory) a logarithmic measure of the rate of transfer of information in a particular message or language. ▷mid 19th cent.: from EN-[2] 'inside' + Greek *tropē* 'transformation.' —**en·tro·pic** /en'träpik/ *adj.* —**en·tro·pi·cal·ly** /en'träpik(ə)lē/ *adv.*

en·trust /en'trəst/ ▸*v.* [*trans.*] assign the responsibility for doing something to (someone): *I've been* ***entrusted with*** *the task of getting him safely back.* ■ put (something) into someone's care or protection: *you persuade people to* ***entrust*** *their savings* ***to*** *you.* —**en·trust·ment** *n.*

en·try /'entrē/ ▸*n.* (*pl.* **-tries**) **1** an act of going or coming in: *the door was locked, but he forced an entry.* ■ a place of entrance, such as a door or lobby. ■ the right, means, or opportunity to enter a place or be a member of something: *the flood of refugees seeking entry to western Europe.* ■ the action of undertaking something or becoming a member of something: *more young people are postponing their entry into full-time work.* ■ *Bridge* a card providing an opportunity to transfer the lead to a particular hand. ■ *Law* the action of taking up the legal right to property. ■ *Music* the point in a piece of music at which a particular performer in an ensemble starts or resumes playing or singing. ■ *dialect* a passage between buildings. **2** an item written or printed in a diary, list, ledger, or reference book. ■ the action of recording such an item: *sophisticated features to help ensure accurate data entry.* **3** a person or thing competing in a race or competition: *from the hundreds of entries we received, twelve winners were finally chosen.* ■ [in *sing.*] the number of competitors in a particular race or competition. ■ the action of participating in a race or competition. **4** the forward part of a ship's hull below the waterline, considered in terms of breadth or narrowness. ▷Middle English: from Old French *entree*, based on Latin *intrata*, feminine past participle of *intrare* (see ENTER).

en·try form ▸*n.* an application form for a competition.

en·try in·hib·i·tor ▸*n.* a class of anti-HIV drugs that work by blocking the entry of the virus into a host cell.

en·try-lev·el ▸*adj.* at the lowest level in an employment hierarchy: *he was hired as an entry-level research assistant.* ■ (of a product) suitable for a beginner or first-time user; basic: *entry-level computers.*

en·try·way /'entrēˌwā/ ▸*n.* a way in to somewhere or something; an entrance.

en·try word ▸*n.* a word, phrase, or name that is the subject of and heading for an entry in a dictionary, glossary, or encyclopedia, and is usu. set in boldface or another distinctive type; a headword or lemma.

en·try wound /wo͞ond/ ▸*n.* a wound made by a bullet or other missile at the point where it entered the body.

en·twine /en'twīn/ ▸*v.* [*trans.*] (often **be entwined**) wind or twist together; interweave: *they lay entwined in each other's arms* | *figurative the nations' histories were closely entwined.* —**en·twine·ment** *n.*

e·nu·cle·ate /i'n(y)o͞oklēˌāt/ ▸*v.* [*trans.*] **1** *Biology* remove the nucleus from (a cell). **2** surgically remove (a tumor or gland, or the eyeball) intact from its surrounding capsule.
▸*adj. Biology* (of a cell) lacking a nucleus. ▷mid 16th cent. (in the sense 'clarify, explain'): from Latin *enucleat-* 'extracted, made clear,' from the verb *enucleare*, from *e-* (variant of *ex-*) 'out of' + *nucleus* 'kernel' (see NUCLEUS). —**e·nu·cle·a·tion** /iˌn(y)o͞oklē'āSHən/ *n.*

E·nu·gu /ā'no͞ogo͞o/ an industrial city in southeastern Nigeria, capital of the state of Enugu; pop. 293,000. It was the capital of BIAFRA.

e·nu·mer·a·ble /i'n(y)o͞omərəbəl/ ▸*adj. Mathematics* able to be counted by one-to-one correspondence with the set of all positive integers.

e·nu·mer·ate /i'n(y)o͞oməˌrāt/ ▸*v.* [*trans.*] mention (a number of things) one by one: *there is not space to enumerate all his works.* ■ *formal* establish the number of: *the 2000 census enumerated 10,493 households living in the county.* ▷early 17th cent.: from Latin *enumerat-* 'counted out,' from the verb *enumerare*, from *e-* (variant of *ex-*) 'out' + *numerus* 'number.' —**e·nu·mer·a·tion** /iˌn(y)o͞omə'rāSHən/ *n.* —**e·nu·mer·a·tive** /-rətiv; -ˌrātiv/ *adj.*

e·nu·mer·a·tor /i'n(y)o͞oməˌrātər/ ▸*n.* a person employed in taking a census of the population.

e·nun·ci·ate /i'nənsēˌāt/ ▸*v.* [*trans.*] say or pronounce clearly: *she enunciated each word slowly.* ■ express (a proposition or theory) in clear or definite terms: *a written document enunciating this policy.* ■ proclaim: *a prophet enunciating the Lord's wisdom.* ▷mid 16th cent. (as *enunciation*): from Latin *enuntiat-* 'announced clearly,' from the verb *enuntiare*, from *e-* (variant of *ex-*) 'out' + *nuntiare* 'announce' (from *nuntius* 'messenger'). —**e·nun·ci·a·tion** /iˌnənsē'āSHən/ *n.* —**e·nun·ci·a·tive** /i'nənsēətiv; -ˌātiv/ *adj.* —**e·nun·ci·a·tor** /-ˌātər/ *n.*

en·ure /i'n(y)o͝or/ ▸*v.* variant spelling of INURE.

en·u·re·sis /ˌenyə'rēsis/ ▸*n. Medicine* involuntary urination, esp. by children at night. ▷early 19th cent.: modern Latin, from Greek *enourein* 'urinate in,' from *en-* 'in' + *ouron* 'urine.' —**en·u·ret·ic** /-'retik/ *adj.* & *n.*

en·urn /in'ərn/ ▸*v.* variant spelling of INURN. —**en·urn·ment** *n.*

en·vel·op /en'veləp/ ▸*v.* (**-vel·oped, -vel·op·ing**) [*trans.*] wrap up, cover, or surround completely: *a figure enveloped in a black cloak* See note at CIRCUMSCRIBE. | *figurative a feeling of despair enveloped him.* ■ make obscure; conceal. ■ (of troops) surround (an enemy force). ▷late Middle English (formerly also as *invelop(e)*): from Old French *envoluper*, from *en-* 'in' + a second element (also found in DEVELOP) of unknown origin. —**en·vel·op·ment** *n.*

en·vel·ope /'envəˌlōp; 'änvə-/ ▸*n.* **1** a flat paper container with a sealable flap, used to enclose a letter or document. **2** a covering or containing structure or layer: *the external envelope of the swimming pool.* ■ the outer metal or glass housing of a vacuum tube, electric light, etc. ■ the structure within a balloon or nonrigid airship containing the gas. ■ *Microbiology* a membrane forming the outer layer of certain viruses. ■ *Electronics* a curve joining the successive peaks of a modulated wave. ■ *Mathematics* a curve or surface tangent to each of a family of curves or surfaces. ■ *Astronomy* the nebulous covering of the head of a comet; coma. ▷mid 16th cent. (in the sense 'wrapper, enveloping layer'): from French *enveloppe*, from *envelopper* 'envelop.' The sense 'covering of a letter' dates from the early 18th cent.
▸**PHRASE** □ **push the envelope** *informal* approach or extend the limits of what is possible: *these are extremely witty and clever stories that consistently push the envelope of TV comedy.* [originally aviation slang, relating to graphs of aerodynamic performance.]

en·ven·om /en'venəm/ ▸*v.* [*trans.*] *archaic* put poison on or into; make poisonous. ■ *figurative* infuse with hostility or bitterness: *tribal rivalries envenom the bitter civil war.* ▷Middle English (formerly also as *invenom*): from Old French *envenimer*, from *en-* 'in' + *venim* 'venom.'

en·ven·o·mate /en'venəˌmāt/ ▸*v.* [*trans.*] *Zoology & Medicine* (of a snake, scorpion, spider, or insect) poison by biting or stinging. —**en·ven·o·ma·tion** /enˌvenə'māSHən/ *n.*

En·ver Pa·sha /en'ver pə'SHä/ (1881–1922), Turkish political and military leader. A leader of the Young Turks in 1908, he was part of a ruling triumvirate that followed a coup d'état in 1913.

en·vi·a·ble /'envēəbəl/ ▸*adj.* arousing or likely to arouse envy: *an enviable reputation for academic achievement.* —**en·vi·a·bly** /-əblē/ *adv.*

en·vi·ous /'envēəs/ ▸*adj.* feeling or showing envy: *I'm* ***envious of*** *their happiness* | *an envious glance.* See note at JEALOUS. ▷Middle English: from Old French *envieus*, from *envie* 'envy,' on the pattern of Latin *invidiosus* 'invidious.' —**en·vi·ous·ly** *adv.*

en·vi·ro /en'vīrō/ ▸*n.* (*pl.* **-ros**) *informal* an environmentalist: *command-and-control solutions demanded by the more radical enviros.*
▸*adj.* environmental: *an enviro group that combats the committee's advocates for Western ranching, mining, and energy interests.* ▷shortening.

en·vi·ron /en'vīrən; -'vī(ə)rn/ ▸*v.* [*trans.*] *formal* surround; enclose: *the stone circle was environed by an expanse of peat soil.* ▷Middle English (formerly also as *inviron*): from Old French *environer*, from *environ* 'surroundings,' from *en* 'in' + *viron* 'circuit' (from *virer* 'to turn, veer').

en·vi·ron·ment /en'vīrənmənt; -'vī(ə)rn-/ ▸*n.* **1** the surroundings or conditions in which a person, animal, or plant lives or operates. ■ [usu. with *adj.*] the setting or conditions in which a particular activity is carried on: *a good learning environment.* ■ [with *adj.*] *Computing* the overall structure within which a user, computer, or program operates: *a desktop development environment.* **2** (**the environment**) the natural world, as a whole or in a particular geographical area, esp. as affected by human activity.

en·vi·ron·men·tal /enˌvīrən'men(t)l; -ˌvī(ə)rn-/ ▸*adj.* **1** relating to the natural world and the impact of human activity on its condition: *acid rain may have caused major environmental damage.* ■ aiming or designed to promote the protection of the natural world: *environmental tourism.* **2** relating to or arising from a person's surroundings: *environmental noise.* —**en·vi·ron·men·tal·ly** *adv.*

en·vi·ron·men·tal art ▸*n.* **1** the production of artistic works intended to enhance or become part of an urban or other outdoor environment. ■ the production of works of art by manipulation of the natural landscape. **2** the production of works of art in the form of large installations or assemblages that surround the observer.

E

en·vi·ron·men·tal au·dit ▸*n.* an assessment of the extent to which an organization is observing practices that seek to minimize harm to the environment.

en·vi·ron·men·tal·ist /en,vīrən'men(t)l-ist; -,vī(ə)rn-/ ▸*n.* **1** a person who is concerned with or advocates the protection of the environment. **2** a person who considers that environment, as opposed to heredity, has the primary influence on the development of a person or group. **—en·vi·ron·men·tal·ism** *n.*

en·vi·ron·men·tal med·i·cine ▸*n.* a branch of medicine that studies environmental inputs and the individual's physical, mental, and emotional responses to them

en·vi·ron·ment-friend·ly ▸*adj.* another term for **ECO-FRIENDLY.**

en·vi·rons /en'vīrənz; -'vī(ə)rnz/ ▸*plural n.* the surrounding area or district: *the picturesque environs of the lake.* ▷mid 17th cent.: from French, plural of *environ* (see **ENVIRON**).

en·vis·age /en'vizij/ ▸*v.* [*trans.*] contemplate or conceive of as a possibility or a desirable future event: *the Rome Treaty envisaged free movement across frontiers.* ■ form a mental picture of (something not yet existing or known): *he knew what he liked but had difficulty envisaging it.* ▷early 19th cent.: from French *envisager*, from *en-* 'in' + *visage* 'face.'

en·vi·sion /en'vizHən/ ▸*v.* [*trans.*] imagine as a future possibility; visualize: *she envisioned the admiring glances of guests seeing her home.*

en·voi /'en,voi; 'än,voi/ (also **en·voy**) ▸*n.* **1** a short stanza concluding a ballade. **2** *archaic* an author's concluding words. ▷late Middle English: from Old French *envoi*, from *envoyer* 'send' (see **ENVOY**[1]).

en·voy /'en,voi; 'än,voi/ ▸*n.* **1** a messenger or representative, esp. one on a diplomatic mission. **2** short for **ENVOY EXTRAORDINARY** ▷mid 17th cent.: from French *envoyé*, past participle of *envoyer* 'send,' from *en voie* 'on the way,' based on Latin *via* 'way.'

en·voy ex·traor·di·nar·y ▸*n.* (*pl.* **en·voys ex·traor·di·nar·y**) a minister plenipotentiary, ranking below an ambassador and above a chargé d'affaires.

en·vy /'envē/ ▸*n.* (*pl.* **-vies**) a feeling of discontented or resentful longing aroused by someone else's possessions, qualities, or luck: *she felt a twinge of envy for the people on board.* ■ (**the envy of**) a person or thing that inspires such a feeling: *their national health service is the envy of many in Europe.*
▸*v.* (**-vies, -vied**) [*trans.*] desire to have a quality, possession, or other desirable attribute belonging to (someone else): *he envied people who did not have to work on weekends* | [with *two objs.*] *I envy Jane her happiness.* ■ desire for oneself (something possessed or enjoyed by another): *a lifestyle that most of us would envy.* ▷Middle English (also in the sense 'hostility, enmity'): from Old French *envie* (noun), *envier* (verb), from Latin *invidia*, from *invidere* 'regard maliciously, grudge,' from *in-* 'into' + *videre* 'to see.' **—en·vi·er** /'envēər/ *n.*

en·wrap /en'rap/ ▸*v.* (**-wrapped, -wrap·ping**) [*trans.*] wrap; envelop: *the book jacket enwraps a plain blue paper binding.* ■ (usu. **be enwrapped**) engross or absorb (someone): *they were* **enwrapped in** *conversation.*

en·wreathe /en'rēTH/ ▸*v.* [*trans.*] (usu. **be enwreathed**) *poetic/literary* surround or envelop (something): *the lofty battlements, thickly enwreathed with ivy.*

en·zo·ot·ic /,enzō'ätik/ ▸*adj.* of, relating to, or denoting a disease that regularly affects animals in a particular district or at a particular season. Compare with **EPIZOOTIC, ENDEMIC** (sense 1). ▷late 19th cent.: from **EN-**[2] 'within' + Greek *zōion* 'animal' + **-IC**.

en·zyme /'enzīm/ ▸*n.* *Biochemistry* a substance produced by a living organism that acts as a catalyst to bring about a specific biochemical reaction.

Most enzymes are proteins with large complex molecules whose action depends on their particular molecular shape. Some enzymes control reactions within cells and some, such as the enzymes involved in digestion, outside them.

▷late 19th cent.: coined in German from modern Greek *enzumos* 'leavened,' from *en-* 'within' + Greek *zumē* 'leaven.' **—en·zy·mat·ic** /,enzə'matik/ *adj.* **—en·zy·mat·i·cal·ly** /,enzə'matik(ə)lē/ *adv.* **—en·zy·mic** /en'zīmik; -'zimik/ *adj.* **—en·zy·mi·cal·ly** /en'zīmik(ə)lē; -zim-/ *adv.*

en·zy·mol·o·gy /,enzə'mäləjē/ ▸*n.* the branch of biochemistry concerned with enzymes. **—en·zy·mo·log·i·cal** /-mə'läjikəl/ *adj.* **—en·zy·mol·o·gist** /-jist/ *n.*

EO ▸*abbr.* executive order.

e.o. ▸*abbr.* ex officio.

eo- ▸*comb. form.* early, primeval: *eohippus.* ▷from Greek, *ēōs*, 'dawn.'

E·o·cene /'ēə,sēn/ ▸*adj.* *Geology* of, relating to, or denoting the second epoch of the Tertiary period, between the Paleocene and Oligocene epochs. ■ [as *n.*] (**the Eocene**) the Eocene epoch or the system of rocks deposited during it.

The Eocene epoch lasted from 56.5 million to 35.4 million years ago. It was a time of rising temperatures, and there was an abundance of mammals, including the first horses, bats, and whales.

▷mid 19th cent.: from Greek *ēōs* 'dawn' + *kainos* 'new.'

e·o·hip·pus /,ē-ō'hipəs/ ▸*n.* (*pl.* **-pus·es**) another term for **HYRACOTHERIUM.** ▷late 19th cent.: from Greek *ēōs* 'dawn' + *hippos* 'horse.'

e·o ip·so /'ē-ō 'ipsō; 'ā-ō/ ▸*adv.* *formal* by that very act or quality; thereby: *such a grand theory would* eo ipso *give an account of how we communicate using language.* ▷Latin, ablative of *id ipsum* 'the thing itself.'

e·o·li·an /ē'ōlēən/ ▸*adj.* (also **ae·o·li·an**) *chiefly Geology* relating to or arising from the action of the wind: *fluvial and eolian sediments.*

e·o·lith /'ēə,liTH/ ▸*n.* *Archaeology* a roughly chipped flint found in Tertiary strata, originally thought to be an early artifact but probably of natural origin. ▷late 19th cent.: from Greek *ēōs* 'dawn' + *lithos* 'stone.'

E·o·lith·ic /,ēə'liTHik/ ▸*adj.* *dated Archaeology* of, relating to, or denoting a period at the beginning of the Stone Age, preceding the Paleolithic and characterized by the earliest crude stone tools. ■ [as *n.*] (**the Eolithic**) the Eolithic period. ▷late 19th cent.: from French *éolithique*, from Greek *ēōs* 'dawn'+ *lithikos* (from *lithos* 'stone').

e.o.m. ▸*abbr.* end of the month.

e·on /'ēən; 'ē,än/ (*chiefly Brit.* also **ae·on**) ▸*n.* (often **eons**) an indefinite and very long period of time, often a period exaggerated for humorous or rhetorical effect: *he reached the crag eons before I arrived* | *his eyes searched her face for what seemed like eons.* ■ *Astronomy & Geology* a unit of time equal to a billion years. ■ *Geology* a major division of geological time, subdivided into eras: *the Precambrian eon.* ■ *Philosophy* (in Neoplatonism, Platonism, and Gnosticism) a power existing from eternity; an emanation or phase of the supreme deity. ▷mid 17th cent.: via ecclesiastical Latin from Greek *aiōn* 'age.'

E·os /'ē,äs/ *Greek Mythology* the Greek goddess of the dawn. Roman equivalent **AURORA**.

e·o·sin /'ēəsin/ ▸*n.* a red fluorescent dye that is a bromine derivative of fluorescein, or one of its salts or other derivatives. ▷late 19th cent.: from Greek *ēōs* 'dawn' + **-IN**[1].

e·o·sin·o·phil /,ēə'sinə,fil/ ▸*n.* *Physiology* a white blood cell containing granules that are readily stained by eosin.

e·o·sin·o·phil·i·a /,ēə,sinə'filēə/ ▸*n.* *Medicine* an increase in the number of eosinophils in the blood, occurring in response to some allergens, drugs, and parasites, and in some types of leukemia.

e·o·sin·o·phil·ic /,ēə,sinə'filik/ ▸*adj.* **1** *Physiology* (of a cell or its contents) readily stained by eosin. **2** *Medicine* relating to or marked by eosinophilia.

EOT ▸*abbr.* ■ *Computing* end of tape. ■ *Telecommunications* end of transmission.

-eous ▸*suffix* (forming adjectives) resembling; displaying the nature of: *aqueous* | *erroneous.* ▷from the Latin suffix *-eus* + **-OUS**.

EP ▸*abbr.* ■ electroplate. ■ European Parliament. ■ European plan. ■ extended-play (of a record or compact disc): *an EP of remixes.* ■ extreme pressure (used in grading lubricants).

Ep. ▸*abbr.* Epistle.

e.p. *Chess* ▸*abbr.* en passant.

ep- ▸*prefix* variant spelling of **EPI-** before a vowel or *h* (as in *eparch, ephemeral*).

EPA ▸*abbr.* Environmental Protection Agency.

e·pact /'ē,pakt/ ▸*n.* [in *sing.*] the number of days by which the solar year differs from the lunar year. ■ the number of days into the moon's phase cycle at the beginning of the solar (calendar) year. ▷mid 16th cent. (denoting the age of the moon in days at the beginning of the calendar year): from French *épacte*, via late Latin from Greek *epaktai* (*hēmerai*) 'intercalated (days),' from *epagein* 'bring in,' from *epi* 'in addition' + *agein* 'bring.'

ep·arch /'ep,ärk/ ▸*n.* the chief bishop of an eparchy. ▷mid 17th cent. (denoting the governor of an administrative division of Greece): from Greek *eparkhos*, from *epi* 'above' + *arkhos* 'ruler.'

ep·ar·chy /'ep,ärkē/ ▸*n.* (*pl.* **-chies**) a province of the Orthodox Church. ▷late 18th cent.: from Greek *eparkhia*, from *eparkhos* (see **EPARCH**).

épa·ter /ā'pätā/ ▸*v.* (in phrase **épater les bourgeois**) shock people who are conventional or complacent. ▷early 20th cent.: French, literally 'startle, shock.'

ep·au·let /'epə,let; ,epə-'let/ (also **ep·au·lette**) ▸*n.* an ornamental shoulder piece on an item of clothing, typically on the coat or jacket of a military uniform. ▷late 18th cent.: from French *épaulette*, diminutive of *épaule* 'shoulder,' from Latin *spatula* in the late Latin sense 'shoulder blade.'

epaulet

ep·ax·i·al /e'paksēəl/ ▸*adj.* *Anatomy & Zoology* situated on the dorsal side of an axis: *epaxial muscles.*

e·pa·zo·te /,epə'zōtā/ ▸*n.* a pungent herb used in Latin-American cooking and for tea.

é·pée /,e'pā/ ▸*n.* a sharp-pointed dueling sword, designed for thrusting and used, with the end blunted, in fencing. ■ the sport of fencing with an épée. ▷late 19th cent.: French, 'sword,' from Old French *espee* (see **SPAY**). **—é·pée·ist** /-ist/ *n.*

ep·ei·rog·e·ny /,epī'räjənē/ ▸*n.* *Geology* the regional uplift of an extensive area of the earth's crust. ▷late 19th cent.: from Greek *ēpeiros* 'mainland' + **-GENY**. **—e·pei·ro·gen·e·sis** /i,pīrō'jenəsis/ *n.* **—e·pei·ro·gen·ic** /i,pīrō'jenik/ *adj.*

ep·en·dy·ma /ə'pendəmə/ ▸*n.* *Anatomy* the thin membrane of glial cells lining the ventricles of the brain and the central canal of the spinal cord. ▷late 19th cent.: from Greek *ependuma*, from *ependuein* 'put on over.' **—ep·en·dy·mal** *adj.*

ep·en·the·sis /i'penTHəsis/ ▸*n.* (*pl.* **-ses** /-,sēz/) the insertion of a sound or an unetymological letter within a word, e.g., the *b* in *thimble.* ▷mid 16th cent.: via late Latin from Greek, from *epentithenai* 'insert,' from *epi* 'in addition' + *en-* 'within' + *tithenai* 'to place.' **—ep·en·thet·ic** /,epen'THetik/ *adj.*

e·pergne /i'pərn; ā'pərn/ ▸*n.* an ornamental centerpiece for a dining table, typically used for holding fruit or flowers. ▷early 18th cent.: perhaps an altered form of French *épargne* 'saving, economy.'

ep·ex·e·ge·sis /e,peksə'jēsis/ ▸*n.* (*pl.* **-ses** /-sēz/) the addition of words to clarify meaning. ■ words added for such a purpose. ▷late 16th cent.: from Greek *epexēgēsis*, from *epi* 'in addition' + *exēgēsis* 'explanation' (see **EXEGESIS**). **—ep·ex·e·get·ic** /-'jetik/ *adj.* **—ep·ex·e·get·i·cal** /-'jetikəl/ *adj.* **—ep·ex·e·get·i·cal·ly** /-'jetik(ə)lē/ *adv.*

Eph. ▸*abbr.* *Bible* Ephesians.

e·phah /'ēfə; 'ēfä/ ▸*n.* an ancient Hebrew dry measure equivalent to a bushel (35 l). ▷from Hebrew *'ēpāh*, probably from Egyptian.

e·phebe /'efēb; i'fēb/ ▸*n.* (in ancient Greece) a young man of 18–20 years undergoing military training. ▷via Latin from Greek *ephēbos*, from *epi* 'near to' + *hēbē* 'early manhood.' **—e·phe·bic** /i'fēbik; e'fēbik/ *adj.*

e·phed·ra /ə'fedrə; 'efidrə/ ▸*n.* an evergreen shrub of warm, arid regions that has trailing or climbing stems and tiny, scalelike leaves. Some kinds are a source of ephedrine and are used medicinally. • Family Ephedraceae and genus *Ephedra.* ▷modern Latin, from Latin, 'equisetum,' literally 'horse tail' (which it resembles), from Greek *ephedra*, equivalent to *hippouris*,'horse tail.'

e·phed·rine /ə'fedrin; 'efə,drēn/ ▸*n.* *Medicine* a crystalline alkaloid drug obtained from some ephedras. It causes constriction of the blood vessels and widening of the bronchial passages and is used to relieve asthma and hay fever. • Alternative name: **1-phenyl-2-methylaminopropanol**; chem. formula: $C_{10}H_{15}NO$. ▷late 19th cent.: from **EPHEDRA** + **-INE**[4].

e·phem·er·a /ə'fem(ə)rə/ ▸*plural n.* things that exist or are used or enjoyed for only a short time. ■ items of collectible memorabilia, typically written or printed ones, that were originally expected to have only short-term usefulness or popularity: *Mickey Mouse ephemera.* ▷late 16th cent.: plural of **EPHEMERON**. Current use has been influenced by plurals such as *trivia* and *memorabilia*.

e·phem·er·al /ə'fem(ə)rəl/ ▸*adj.* lasting for a very short time: *fashions are ephemeral.* See note at **TEMPORARY**. ■ (chiefly of plants) having a very short life cycle.
▸*n.* an ephemeral plant. ▷late 16th cent.: from Greek *ephēmeros* (see **EPHEMERA**) + **-AL**. **—e·phem·er·al·i·ty**

E

/ə,femə'ralitē/ *n.* **—e·phem·er·al·ly** *adv.* **—e·phem·er·al·ness** *n.*

e·phem·er·is /i'fem(ə)ris/ ▶*n.* (*pl.* **-er·i·des** /-ərədēz/) *Astronomy & Astrology* a table or data file giving the calculated positions of a celestial object at regular intervals throughout a period. ■ a book or set of such tables or files. ▷early 16th cent.: from Latin, from Greek *ephēmeros* 'lasting only a day.'

e·phem·er·is time ▶*n.* time on a scale defined by the orbital period rather than the axial rotation of the earth.

e·phem·er·on /i'femə,rän/ ▶*n.* (*pl.* **-ons**) an insect that lives only for a day or a few days. ▷from Greek, neuter of *ephēmeros* 'lasting only a day.'

E·phem·er·op·ter·a /ə,femə'räptərə/ *Entomology* an order of insects that comprises the mayflies. ■ [as *plural n.*] (**ephemeroptera**) insects of this order; mayflies. ▷modern Latin (plural), from *Ephemera* (genus name) + *pteron* 'wing.' **—e·phem·er·op·ter·an** /-tərən/ *n. & adj.*

E·phe·sians /i'fēzHənz/ a book of the New Testament ascribed to St. Paul, consisting of an epistle to the Church at Ephesus.

Eph·e·sus /'efəsəs/ an ancient Greek city on the western coast of Asia Minor, in modern Turkey, site of the temple of Diana. An important center of early Christianity, St. Paul preached here and St. John is said to have lived here.

eph·od /'efäd; 'ēfäd/ ▶*n.* (in ancient Israel) a sleeveless garment worn by Jewish priests. ▷late Middle English: from Hebrew *'ēpōḏ*.

eph·or /'efôr; 'efər/ ▶*n.* (in ancient Greece) one of five senior Spartan magistrates. ▷from Greek *ephoros* 'overseer,' from *epi* 'above' + the base of *horan* 'see.' **—eph·or·ate** /'efə,rāt; 'eførit/ *n.*

eph·y·ra /'efərə/ ▶*n.* (*pl.* **-rae** /-,rē/) *Zoology* a larval jellyfish, after it has separated from the scyphistoma. ▷mid 19th cent.: modern Latin, from Greek *Ephura*, denoting a Nereid and an Oceanid.

epi- (also **ep-**) ▶*prefix* **1** on; upon: *epicycle* | *epigraph*. **2** above: *epicotyl* | *epicontinental*. **3** in addition: *epigenesis* | *epiphenomenon*. ▷from Greek *epi* 'upon, near to, in addition.'

ep·i·ben·thos /,epə'ben,THäs/ ▶*n.* *Ecology* the flora and fauna living on the surface of the bottom of a sea or lake. ▷early 20th cent.: from Greek *epi* 'upon' + *benthos* 'depth of the sea.' **—ep·i·ben·thic** /-'ben-THik/ *adj.*

ep·i·blast /'epə,blast/ ▶*n.* *Embryology* the outermost layer of an embryo before it differentiates into ectoderm and mesoderm.

ep·ic /'epik/ ▶*n.* a long poem, typically one derived from ancient oral tradition, narrating the deeds and adventures of heroic or legendary figures or the history of a nation. ■ the genre of such poems: *the romances display gentler emotions not found in Greek epic.* ■ a long film, book, or other work portraying heroic deeds and adventures or covering an extended period of time: *a Hollywood biblical epic.*
▶*adj.* of, relating to, or characteristic of an epic or epics: *England's national epic poem* Beowulf. ■ heroic or grand in scale or character: *his epic journey around the world* | *a tragedy of epic proportions.* ▷late 16th cent. (as an adjective): via Latin from Greek *epikos*, from *epos* 'word, song,' related to *eipein* 'say.' **—ep·i·cal** *adj.* **—ep·i·cal·ly** /-(ə)lē/ *adv.*

ep·i·can·thic /,epi'kanTHik/ ▶*adj.* denoting a fold of skin from the upper eyelid covering the inner angle of the eye, typical in many peoples of eastern Asia and found as a congenital abnormality elsewhere.

ep·i·car·di·um /,epi'kärdēəm/ ▶*n.* *Anatomy* a serous membrane that forms the innermost layer of the pericardium and the outer surface of the heart. ▷mid 19th cent.: from **EPI-** 'above' + Greek *kardia* 'heart,' on the pattern of *pericardium*. **—ep·i·car·di·al** /-dēəl/ *adj.*

ep·i·ce·di·um /,epi'sēdēəm/ ▶*n.* (*pl.* **-di·a** /-dēə/) *formal* a funeral ode. ▷mid 16th cent. (originally in the anglicized form *epicede* and the Greek form *epicedeon*): from Latin, from Greek *epikēdeion*, neuter of *epokēdeios* 'of a funeral' (based on *kēdos* 'care, grief'). **—ep·i·ce·di·an** /-dēən/ *adj.*

ep·i·cene /'epi,sēn/ ▶*adj.* having characteristics of both sexes or no characteristics of either sex; of indeterminate sex: *the sort of epicene beauty peculiar to boys of a certain age.* ■ effeminate; effete: *the actor infused the role with an epicene languor.* ■ *Grammar* (of a noun or pronoun) denoting either sex without change of gender.
▶*n.* an epicene person. ▷late Middle English (as a grammatical term): via late Latin from Greek *epikoinos* (based on *koinos* 'common').

ep·i·cen·ter /'epi,sentər/ (*Brit.* **ep·i·cen·tre**) ▶*n.* the point on the earth's surface vertically above the focus of an earthquake. ■ *figurative* the central point of something, typically a difficult or unpleasant situation: *the patient was at the epicenter of concern.* ▷late 19th cent.: from Greek *epikentros* 'situated on a center,' from *epi* 'upon' + *kentron* 'center.' **—ep·i·cen·tral** /,epi'sentrəl/ *adj.*

ep·i·con·dyle /,epi'kän,dīl; -'kändl/ ▶*n.* *Anatomy* a protuberance above or on the condyle of a long bone, esp. either of the two at the elbow end of the humerus. ▷mid 19th cent.: from French *épicondyle*, modern Latin *epicondylus* (see **EPI-**, **CONDYLE**). **—ep·i·con·dyl·ar** /-'kändl-ər/ *adj.*

ep·i·con·dy·li·tis /,epi,kändī'lītis; -,kändl'ītis/ ▶*n.* *Medicine* a painful inflammation of tendons surrounding an epicondyle.

ep·i·con·ti·nen·tal /,epi,käntə'nen(t)l/ ▶*adj.* denoting those areas of sea or ocean overlying the continental shelf.

ep·i·cor·mic /,epi'kôrmik/ ▶*adj.* *Botany* (of a shoot or branch) growing from a previously dormant bud on the trunk or a limb of a tree. ▷early 20th cent.: from **EPI-** 'upon' + Greek *kormos* 'tree trunk.'

ep·i·cot·yl /,epi'kätl/ ▶*n.* *Botany* the region of an embryo or seedling stem above the cotyledon.

ep·i·crit·ic /,epi'kritik/ ▶*adj.* *Physiology* relating to or denoting those sensory nerve fibers of the skin that are capable of fine discrimination of touch or temperature stimuli. Often contrasted with **PROTOPATHIC**. ▷early 20th cent.: from Greek *epikritikos* 'giving judgment over,' from *epi* 'upon or over' + *krinein* ' to judge.'

Ep·ic·te·tus /,epik'tētəs/ (*c.*AD 55–*c.*135), Greek philosopher. He preached the common brotherhood of man and advocated a Stoic philosophy.

ep·i·cure /'epi,kyŏŏr/ ▶*n.* a person who takes particular pleasure in fine food and drink. ▷late Middle English (denoting a disciple of **EPICURUS**): via medieval Latin from Greek *Epikouros* 'Epicurus.' **—ep·i·cur·ism** /-,rizəm; ,epi'kyŏŏ-/ *n.*

Ep·i·cu·re·an /,epikyə'rēən; ,epi'kyŏŏrēən/ ▶*n.* a disciple or student of the Greek philosopher Epicurus. ■ (**epicurean**) a person devoted to sensual enjoyment, esp. that derived from fine food and drink.
▶*adj.* of or concerning Epicurus or his ideas: *Epicurean philosophers.* ■ (**epicurean**) relating to or suitable for an epicure: *epicurean feasts.* See note at **SENSUOUS**.

Ep·i·cu·re·an·ism /,epəkyə'rēə,nizəm; -'kyŏŏrēə-/ ▶*n.* an ancient school of philosophy founded in Athens by Epicurus. The school rejected determinism and advocated hedonism (pleasure as the highest good), but of a restrained kind: mental pleasure was regarded more highly than physical, and the ultimate pleasure was held to be freedom from anxiety and mental pain, esp. that arising from needless fear of death and of the gods.

Ep·i·cu·rus /,epə'kyŏŏrəs/ (341–270 BC), Greek philosopher, founder of Epicureanism. His physics is based on Democritus' theory of a materialist universe composed of indestructible atoms moving in a void, unregulated by divine providence.

ep·i·cu·ti·cle /,epi'kyŏŏtikəl/ ▶*n.* *Botany & Zoology* the thin, waxy, protective outer layer covering the surfaces of some plants, fungi, insects, and other arthropods. **—ep·i·cu·tic·u·lar** /-kyŏŏ'tikyələr/ *adj.*

ep·i·cy·cle /'epi,sīkəl/ ▶*n.* *Geometry* a small circle whose center moves around the circumference of a larger one. ■ *historical* a circle of this type used to describe planetary orbits in the Ptolemaic system. ▷late Middle English: from Old French, or via late Latin from Greek *epikuklos*, from *epi* 'upon' + *kuklos* 'circle.' **—ep·i·cy·clic** /,epi'sīklik; 'epi-/ *adj.*

ep·i·cy·cloid /,epi'sī,kloid/ ▶*n.* *Mathematics* a curve traced by a point on the circumference of a circle rolling on the exterior of another circle. **—ep·i·cy·cloi·dal** /-sī'kloidl/ *adj.*

ep·i·deic·tic /,epi'dīktik/ ▶*adj.* *formal* characterized by or designed to display rhetorical or oratorical skill. ▷late 18th cent.: from Greek *epideiktikos* (based on *deiknunai* 'to show').

ep·i·dem·ic /,epi'demik/ ▶*n.* a widespread occurrence of an infectious disease in a community at a particular time: *a flu epidemic.* ■ a disease occurring in such a way. ■ a sudden, widespread occurrence of a particular undesirable phenomenon: *an epidemic of violent crime.*
▶*adj.* of, relating to, or of the nature of an epidemic: *shoplifting has reached epidemic proportions.* Compare with **ENDEMIC**, **PANDEMIC**, **EPIZOOTIC**. ▷early 17th cent. (as an adjective): from French *épidémique*, from *épidémie*, via late Latin from Greek *epidēmia* 'prevalence of disease,' from *epidēmios* 'prevalent,' from *epi* 'upon' + *dēmos* 'the people.'

USAGE A disease that quickly and severely affects a large number of people and then subsides is an **epidemic**: *throughout the Middle Ages, successive epidemics of the plague killed millions.* **Epidemic** is also used as an adjective: *she studied the causes of epidemic cholera.*
A disease that is continually present in an area and affects a relatively small number of people is **endemic**: *malaria is* **endemic in** (or **to**) *hot, moist climates.*
A **pandemic** is a widespread epidemic that may affect entire continents or even the world: *the pandemic of 1918 ushered in a period of frequent epidemics of gradually diminishing severity.* Thus, from an epidemiologist's point of view, the Black Death in Europe and AIDS in sub-Saharan Africa are pandemics rather than epidemics.

ep·i·de·mi·ol·o·gy /,epi,dēmē'äləjē/ ▶*n.* the branch of medicine that deals with the incidence, distribution, and possible control of diseases and other factors relating to health. ▷late 19th cent.: from Greek *epidēmia* 'prevalence of disease' + **-LOGY**. **—ep·i·de·mi·o·log·i·cal** /-ə'läjikəl/ *adj.* **—ep·i·de·mi·ol·o·gist** /-jist/ *n.*

ep·i·der·mal growth fac·tor (abbr.: **EGF**) ▶*n.* a mitogenic protein thought to be involved in such physical processes as normal cell growth, wound healing, and the formation of tumors. ▷First observed in 1959.

ep·i·der·mis /,epi'dərmis/ ▶*n.* *Biology* the outer layer of cells covering an organism, in particular: ■ *Zoology & Anatomy* the surface epithelium of the skin of an animal, overlying the dermis. ■ *Botany* the outer layer of tissue in a plant, except where it is replaced by periderm. ▷early 17th cent.: via late Latin from Greek, from *epi* 'upon' + *derma* 'skin.' **—ep·i·der·mal** /-'dərməl/ *adj.* **—ep·i·der·mic** /-'dərmik/ *adj.* **—ep·i·der·moid** /-'dər,moid/ *adj.*

ep·i·der·mol·y·sis /,epidər'mäləsis/ (also **ep·i·der·mol·y·sis bul·lo·sa** /bə'lōsə/) ▶*n.* *Medicine* loosening of the epidermis, with extensive blistering of the skin and mucous membranes, occurring either after injury, or as a spontaneous and potentially dangerous condition, particularly in children.

ep·i·di·a·scope /,epi'dīə,skōp/ ▶*n.* an optical projector capable of giving images of both opaque and transparent objects. ▷early 20th cent.: from **EPI-** + **DIA-** + **-SCOPE**.

ep·i·did·y·mis /,epi'didəməs/ ▶*n.* (*pl.* **-did·y·mi·des** /-'didəmi,dēz; -di'dimi,dēz/) *Anatomy* a highly convoluted duct behind the testis, along which sperm passes to the vas deferens. ▷early 17th cent.: from Greek *epididumis*, from *epi* 'upon' + *didumos* 'testicle' (from *duo* 'two'). **—ep·i·did·y·mal** /-məl/ *adj.*

ep·i·dote /'epi,dōt/ ▶*n.* a lustrous yellow-green crystalline mineral, common in metamorphic rocks. It consists of a hydroxyl silicate of calcium, aluminum, and iron. ▷early 19th cent.: from French *épidote*, from Greek *epididonai* 'give additionally' (because of the length of the crystals).

ep·i·du·ral /,epi'd(y)ŏŏrəl/ ▶*adj.* *Anatomy & Medicine* on or around the dura mater, in particular, (of an anesthetic) introduced into the space around the dura mater of the spinal cord.
▶*n.* an epidural anesthetic, used esp. in childbirth to produce loss of sensation below the waist. ▷late 19th cent.: from **EPI-** 'upon' + **DURA**[1] + **-AL**.

ep·i·fau·na /,epə'fônə/ ▶*n.* *Ecology* animals living on the surface of the seabed or a riverbed, or attached to submerged objects or aquatic animals or plants. Compare with **INFAUNA**. ▷early 20th cent.: from **EPI-** 'upon' + **FAUNA**. **—ep·i·fau·nal** /-'fônl/ *adj.*

ep·i·fluo·res·cence /,epəflŏŏ'resəns/ ▶*n.* *Optics* the fluorescence of an object in an optical microscope when irradiated from the viewing side.

ep·i·gas·tri·um /,epi'gastrēəm/ ▶*n.* (*pl.* **-tri·a** /-trēə/) *Anatomy* the part of the upper abdomen immediately over the stomach. ▷late 17th cent.: via late Latin from Greek *epigastrion*, neuter of *epigastrios* 'over the belly,' from *epi* 'upon' + *gastēr* 'belly.' **—ep·i·gas·tric** /-trik/ *adj.*

ep·i·ge·al /,epi'jēəl/ ▶*adj.* *Botany* growing on or close to the ground. Compare with **HYPOGEAL**. ■ (of seed germination) with one or more seed leaves appearing above the ground. ▷mid 19th cent.: from Greek *epigeios* (from *epi* 'upon' + *gē* 'earth') + -AL.

ep·i·gene /ˈepi,jēn/ ▸*adj.* *Geology* taking place or produced on the surface of the earth. ▷early 19th cent.: from French *épigène*, from Greek *epigenēs*, from *epi* 'upon' + *genēs* (see -GEN).

ep·i·gen·e·sis /,epiˈjenəsis/ ▸*n.* *Biology* the theory, now generally held, that an embryo develops progressively from an undifferentiated egg cell. Often contrasted with PREFORMATION. ▷mid 17th cent.: from EPI- 'in addition' + GENESIS. **—ep·i·gen·e·sist** /-sist/ *n.* & *adj.*

ep·i·ge·net·ic /,epijəˈnetik/ ▸*adj.* *Biology* resulting from external rather than genetic influences: *epigenetic carcinogens.* ■ *Biology* of, relating to, or of the nature of epigenesis. ■ *Geology* formed later than the surrounding or underlying rock formation. **—ep·i·ge·net·i·cal·ly** /-(ə)lē/ *adv.* **—ep·i·ge·net·i·cist** /-ˈnetisist/ *n.*

ep·i·glot·tis /,epiˈglätəs/ ▸*n.* a flap of cartilage at the root of the tongue, which is depressed during swallowing to cover the opening of the windpipe. ▷late Middle English: from Greek *epiglōttis*, from *epi* 'upon, near to' + *glōtta* 'tongue.' **—ep·i·glot·tal** /-ˈglätl/ *adj.* **—ep·i·glot·tic** /-ˈglätik/ *adj.*

ep·i·gone /ˈepi,gōn/ ▸*n.* (*pl.* **ep·i·gones** /ˈepi,gōnz/ or **e·pig·o·ni** /iˈpigə,nī/) a less distinguished follower or imitator of someone, esp. an artist or philosopher: *the epigone's habit of exaggerating his master's voice.* ▷mid 18th cent.: plurals from French *épigones* and Latin *epigoni*, from Greek *epigonoi* 'those born afterward' (based on *gignesthai* 'be born').

ep·i·gram /ˈepi,gram/ ▸*n.* a pithy saying or remark expressing an idea in a clever and amusing way. See note at SAYING. ■ a short poem, esp. a satirical one, having a witty or ingenious ending. ▷late Middle English: from French *épigramme*, or Latin *epigramma*, from Greek, from *epi* 'upon, in addition' + *gramma* (see -GRAM[1]). **—ep·i·gram·ma·tist** /,epiˈgramətist/ *n.* **—ep·i·gram·ma·tize** /,epiˈgramə,tīz/ *v.*

ep·i·gram·mat·ic /,epigrəˈmatik/ ▸*adj.* of the nature or in the style of an epigram; concise, clever, and amusing: *an epigrammatic style.* ▷early 17th cent.: from late Latin *epigrammaticus*, from Latin *epigramma* (see EPIGRAM). **—ep·i·gram·mat·i·cal·ly** /-(ə)lē/ *adv.*

ep·i·graph /ˈepi,graf/ ▸*n.* an inscription on a building, statue, or coin. ■ a short quotation or saying at the beginning of a book or chapter, intended to suggest its theme. ▷late 16th cent. (denoting the heading of a document or letter): from Greek *epigraphē*, from *epigraphein* 'write on.'

e·pig·ra·phy /iˈpigrəfē/ ▸*n.* the study and interpretation of ancient inscriptions. ■ epigraphs collectively. **—e·pig·ra·pher** *n.* **—ep·i·graph·ic** /,epiˈgrafik/ *adj.* **—ep·i·graph·i·cal** /,epiˈgrafikəl/ *adj.* **—ep·i·graph·i·cal·ly** /,epiˈgrafik(ə)lē/ *adv.* **—e·pig·ra·phist** /-fist/ *n.*

e·pig·y·nous /iˈpijənəs/ ▸*adj.* *Botany* (of a plant or flower) having the ovary enclosed in the receptacle, with the stamens and other floral parts situated above. Compare with HYPOGYNOUS, PERIGYNOUS. ▷mid 19th cent.: from modern Latin *epigynus*, from EPI- 'upon, above' + Greek *gunē* 'woman' + -OUS. **—e·pig·y·ny** /iˈpijənē/ *n.*

ep·i·la·tion /,epəˈlāsʜən/ ▸*n.* the removal of hair by the roots. ▷late 19th cent.: from French *épiler*, from *é-* (expressing removal) + Latin *pilus* 'strand of hair,' on the pattern of *depilation*. **—ep·i·late** /ˈepə,lāt/ *v.* **—ep·i·la·tor** /ˈepə,lātər/ *n.*

ep·i·lep·sy /ˈepə,lepsē/ ▸*n.* a neurological disorder marked by sudden recurrent episodes of sensory disturbance, loss of consciousness, or convulsions, associated with abnormal electrical activity in the brain. ▷mid 16th cent.: from French *épilepsie*, or via late Latin from Greek *epilēpsia*, from *epilambanein* 'seize, attack,' from *epi* 'upon' + *lambanein* 'take hold of.'

ep·i·lep·tic /,epəˈleptik/ ▸*adj.* of, relating to, or having epilepsy: *he had an epileptic fit.*
▸*n.* a person who has epilepsy. ▷early 17th cent.: from French *épileptique*, via late Latin from Greek *epilēptikos*, from *epilēpsia* (see EPILEPSY).

ep·i·lep·to·gen·ic /,epə,leptəˈjenik/ ▸*adj.* *Medicine* capable of causing an epileptic attack.

ep·i·lim·ni·on /,epəˈlimnē,än; -nēən/ ▸*n.* (*pl.* **-ni·a** /-nēə/) the upper layer of water in a stratified lake. ▷early 20th cent.: from EPI- 'above' + Greek *limnion* (diminutive of *limnē* 'lake').

ep·i·lith·ic /,epəˈliтʜik/ ▸*adj.* *Botany* (of a plant) growing on the surface of rock. ▷early 20th cent.: from EPI- 'upon' + Greek *lithos* 'stone' + -IC.

ep·i·logue /ˈepə,lôg; -,läg/ (also **ep·i·log**) ▸*n.* a section or speech at the end of a book or play that serves as a comment on or a conclusion to what has happened. ▷late Middle English: from French *épilogue*, via Latin from Greek *epilogos*, from *epi* 'in addition' + *logos* 'speech.'

ep·i·mer /ˈepəmər/ ▸*n.* *Chemistry* each of two isomers with different configurations of atoms around one of several asymmetric carbon atoms present. **—ep·i·mer·ic** /,epəˈmerik/ *adj.* **—ep·i·mer·ism** /-,rizəm/ *n.*

ep·i·mer·ize /ˈepəmə,rīz/ ▸*v.* [*trans.*] *Chemistry* convert from one epimeric form into the other.

ep·i·me·ron /,epəˈmi(ə)r,än; iˈpimə,rän/ ▸*n.* (*pl.* **-me·rons** or **-me·ra** /-ˈmi(ə)rə/) *Entomology* (in insects) the posterior part of the sidewall of a thoracic segment. ▷mid 19th cent.: from EPI- 'near' + Greek *mēros* 'thigh.'

ep·i·my·si·um /,epəˈmizēəm; -ˈmizʜēəm/ ▸*n.* *Anatomy* a sheath of fibrous elastic tissue surrounding a muscle. ▷modern Latin, from EPI- 'upon' + Greek *mus* 'muscle.'

ep·i·neph·rine /,epiˈnefrin/ ▸*n.* *Biochemistry* a hormone secreted by the adrenal glands, esp. in conditions of stress, increasing rates of blood circulation, breathing, and carbohydrate metabolism and preparing muscles for exertion. Also called ADRENALINE. ▷late 19th cent.: from EPI- 'above' + Greek *nephros* 'kidney' + -INE[4].

e·piph·a·ny /iˈpifənē/ ▸*n.* (*pl.* **-nies**) (also **E·piph·a·ny**) the manifestation of Christ to the Gentiles as represented by the Magi (Matthew 2:1–12). ■ the festival commemorating this on January 6. ■ a manifestation of a divine or supernatural being. ■ a moment of sudden revelation or insight. ▷Middle English: from Greek *epiphainein* 'reveal.' The sense relating to the Christian festival is via Old French *epiphanie* and ecclesiastical Latin *epiphania*. **—ep·i·phan·ic** /,epəˈfanik/ *adj.*

ep·i·phe·nom·e·non /,epəfəˈnämə,nän; -ˈnämənən/ ▸*n.* (*pl.* **-nom·e·na** /-ˈnämənə/) a secondary effect or byproduct that arises from but does not causally influence a process, in particular: ■ *Medicine* a secondary symptom, occurring simultaneously with a disease or condition but not directly related to it. ■ a mental state regarded as a byproduct of brain activity. **—ep·i·phe·nom·e·nal** /-ˈnämənl/ *adj.*

e·piph·o·ra /əˈpifərə/ ▸*n.* **1** *Medicine* excessive watering of the eye. **2** *Rhetoric* another term for EPISTROPHE. ▷late 16th cent. (sense 2): via Latin from Greek *epi* 'upon' + *pherein* 'to bear or carry.' Sense 1 dates from the mid 17th cent.

ep·i·phyl·lum /,epəˈfiləm/ ▸*n.* (*pl.* **-lums**) a cactus with flattened stems and large, fragrant red or yellow flowers. • Genus *Epiphyllum*, family Cactaceae: several species, in particular the night-flowering cactus (*E. hookeri*). ▷modern Latin, from EPI- 'upon' + Greek *phullon* 'leaf.'

e·piph·y·sis /əˈpifəsis/ ▸*n.* (*pl.* **-ses** /-sēz/) **1** the end part of a long bone, initially growing separately from the shaft. Compare with DIAPHYSIS. **2** another term for PINEAL. ▷mid 17th cent.: modern Latin, from Greek *epiphusis*, from *epi* 'upon, in addition' + *phusis* 'growth.'

ep·i·phyte /ˈepə,fīt/ ▸*n.* *Botany* a plant that grows on another plant but is not parasitic, such as the numerous ferns, bromeliads, air plants, and orchids growing on tree trunks in tropical rain forests. ▷mid 19th cent.: from EPI- 'in addition' + Greek *phuton* 'plant.' **—ep·i·phyt·al** /,epəˈfītl/ *adj.* **—ep·i·phyt·ic** /,epəˈfitik/ *adj.*

EPIRB ▸*abbr.* emergency position-indicating radio beacon.

E·pi·rus /iˈpīrəs/ a coastal region in northwestern Greece; capital, Ioánnina. Greek name **IPIROS**. ■ an ancient country that included the modern region of Epirus and extended north to Illyria and east to Macedonia and Thessaly.

Epis. ▸*abbr.* ■ Episcopal. ■ Episcopalian. ■ Epistle.

Episc. ▸*abbr.* ■ Episcopal. ■ Episcopalian.

e·pis·co·pa·cy /iˈpiskəpəsē/ ▸*n.* (*pl.* **-cies**) government of a church by bishops. ■ (**the episcopacy**) the bishops of a region or church collectively. ■ another term for EPISCOPATE. ▷mid 17th cent.: from ecclesiastical Latin *episcopatus* 'episcopate,' on the pattern of *prelacy*.

e·pis·co·pal /iˈpiskəpəl/ ▸*adj.* of a bishop or bishops: *episcopal power.* ■ (of a church) governed by or having bishops. ▷late Middle English: from French *épiscopal* or ecclesiastical Latin *episcopalis*, from *episcopus* 'bishop,' from Greek *episkopos* 'overseer' (see BISHOP). **—e·pis·co·pal·ism** /-,lizəm/ *n.* **—e·pis·co·pal·ly** *adv.*

E·pis·co·pal Church the Anglican Church in the U.S. and Scotland.

e·pis·co·pa·lian /i,piskəˈpālēən/ ▸*adj.* of or advocating government of a church by bishops. ■ of or belonging to an episcopal church. ■ (**Episcopalian**) of or belonging to the Episcopal Church.
▸*n.* an adherent of episcopacy. ■ (**Episcopalian**) a member of the Episcopal Church. **—e·pis·co·pa·lian·ism** /-,nizəm/ *n.*

e·pis·co·pate /iˈpiskəpət; -,pāt/ ▸*n.* the office or term of office of a bishop. ■ (**the episcopate**) the bishops of a church or region collectively. ▷mid 17th cent.: from ecclesiastical Latin *episcopatus* 'made a bishop,' from *episcopus* 'bishop,' from Greek *episkopos* 'overseer' (see BISHOP).

ep·i·scope /ˈepə,skōp/ ▸*n.* an optical projector that gives images of opaque objects.

ep·i·se·mat·ic /,epəsəˈmatik/ ▸*adj.* *Zoology* (of coloration or markings) serving to help animals recognize other individuals of the same species. ▷late 19th cent.: from EPI- 'upon' + Greek *sēma* 'sign' + -ATIC.

e·pi·si·ot·o·my /i,pēzēˈätəmē/ ▸*n.* (*pl.* **-mies**) a surgical cut made at the opening of the vagina during childbirth, to aid a difficult delivery and prevent rupture of tissues. ▷late 19th cent.: from Greek *epision* 'pubic region' + -TOMY.

ep·i·sode /ˈepi,sōd/ ▸*n.* an event or a group of events occurring as part of a larger sequence; an incident or period considered in isolation: *the latest episode in the feud.* ■ each of the separate installments into which a serialized story or radio or television program is divided. ■ a finite period in which someone is affected by a specified illness: *acute psychotic episodes.* ■ *Music* a passage containing distinct material or introducing a new subject. ■ a section between two choric songs in Greek tragedy. ▷late 17th cent. (denoting a section between two choric songs in Greek tragedy): from Greek *epeisodion*, neuter of *epeisodios* 'coming in besides,' from *epi* 'in addition' + *eisodos* 'entry' (from *eis* 'into' + *hodos* 'way').

ep·i·sod·ic /,epəˈsädik/ ▸*adj.* containing or consisting of a series of loosely connected parts or events: *an episodic narrative.* ■ occurring occasionally and at irregular intervals: *volcanic activity is highly episodic in nature.* ■ (of a television or radio program or magazine story) broadcast or published as a series of installments. **—ep·i·sod·i·cal·ly** /-(ə)lē/ *adv.*

ep·i·some /ˈepi,sōm/ ▸*n.* *Microbiology* a genetic element inside some bacterial cells, esp. the DNA of some bacteriophages, that can replicate independently of the host and also in association with a chromosome with which it becomes integrated. Compare with PLASMID.

Epist. ▸*abbr.* Epistle.

e·pis·ta·sis /əˈpistəsis/ ▸*n.* *Genetics* the interaction of genes that are not alleles, in particular the suppression of the effect of one such gene by another. ▷early 19th cent.: from Greek, literally 'stoppage,' from *ephistanai* 'to stop.' **—ep·i·stat·ic** /,epiˈstatik/ *adj.*

ep·i·stax·is /,epəˈstaksis/ ▸*n.* *Medicine* bleeding from the nose. ▷late 18th cent.: modern Latin, from Greek, from *epistazein* 'bleed from the nose,' from *epi* 'upon, in addition' + *stazein* 'to drip.'

ep·i·ste·mic /,epəˈstemik; -ˈstē-/ ▸*adj.* of or relating to knowledge or to the degree of its validation. ▷1920s: from Greek *epistēmē* 'knowledge' (see EPISTEMOLOGY) + -IC. **—ep·i·ste·mi·cal·ly** /-(ə)lē/ *adv.*

e·pis·te·mol·o·gy /i,pistəˈmäləjē/ ▸*n.* *Philosophy* the theory of knowledge, esp. with regard to its methods, validity, and scope. Epistemology is the investigation of what distinguishes justified belief from opinion. ▷mid 19th cent.: from Greek *epistēmē* 'knowledge,' from *epistasthai* 'know, know how to do.' **—e·pis·te·mo·log·i·cal** /-məˈläjikəl/ *adj.* **—e·pis·te·mo·log·i·cal·ly** /-məˈläjik(ə)lē/ *adv.* **—e·pis·te·mol·o·gist** /-jist/ *n.*

ep·i·ster·num /,epiˈstərnəm/ ▸*n.* (*pl.* **-nums** or **-na** /-nə/) *Zoology* a bone between the clavicles, esp. (in mammals) the upper part of the sternum. ■ *Entomology* (in insects) the anterior part of the sidewall of a thoracic segment.

e·pis·tle /iˈpisəl/ ▸*n.* *formal* a letter. ■ a poem or other literary work in the form of a letter or series of letters. ■ (also **Epistle**) a book of the New Testament in the form of a letter from an Apostle: *St. Paul's epistle to the Romans.* ■ an extract from an Epistle (or another New Testament book not a Gospel) that is read in a church service. ▷Old English, via Latin from Greek *epistolē*, from *epistellein* 'send news,' from *epi* 'upon, in addition' + *stellein* 'send.' The word was reintroduced in Middle English from Old French.

e·pis·to·lar·y /i'pistə,lerē/ ▸*adj.* relating to or denoting the writing of letters or literary works in the form of letters: *an epistolary novel.* ▷mid 17th cent.: from French *épistolaire* or Latin *epistolaris*, from *epistola* (see EPISTLE).

e·pis·tro·phe /ə'pistrəfē/ ▸*n.* *Rhetoric* the repetition of a word at the end of successive clauses or sentences. ▷late 16th cent.: from Greek *epistrophē*, from *epistrephein* 'to turn around,' from *epi* 'in addition' + *strephein* 'to turn.'

ep·i·style /'epi,stīl/ ▸*n.* *Architecture* an architrave. ▷mid 16th cent. (in the Latin form *epistylium*): from French *épistyle* or via Latin, from Greek *epistulion*, from *epi* 'upon' + *stulos* 'pillar.'

ep·i·taph /'epi,taf/ ▸*n.* a phrase or statement written in memory of a person who has died, esp. as an inscription on a tombstone. ▷late Middle English: from Old French *epitaphe*, via Latin from Greek *epitaphion* 'funeral oration,' neuter of *ephitaphios* 'over or at a tomb,' from *epi* 'upon' + *taphos* 'tomb.'

ep·i·tax·y /'epi,taksē/ ▸*n.* *Crystallography* the natural or artificial growth of crystals on a crystalline substrate determining their orientation. ▷1930s: from French *épitaxie*, from Greek *epi* 'upon' + *taxis* 'arrangement.' —**ep·i·tax·i·al** /,epi'taksēəl/ *adj.*

ep·i·tha·la·mi·um /,epəTHə'lāmēəm/ (also **ep·i·tha·la·mi·on** /-mēən/) ▸*n.* (*pl.* **-mi·ums** or **-mi·a** /-mēə/ also **-mi·ons**) a song or poem celebrating a marriage. ▷late 16th cent.: via Latin from Greek *epithalamion*, from *epi* 'upon' + *thalamos* 'bridal chamber.' —**ep·i·tha·lam·ic** /-'lamik/ *adj.*

ep·i·thal·a·mus /,epə'THaləməs/ ▸*n.* (*pl.* **-mi** /-,mī/) *Anatomy* a part of the dorsal forebrain including the pineal gland and a region in the roof of the third ventricle of the brain.

ep·i·the·li·al·ize /,epə'THēlēə,līz/ ▸*v.* [*trans.* & *intrans.*] cover or become covered with epithelial tissue, e.g. during the healing of a wound. —**ep·i·the·li·al·i·za·tion** /,epə,THēlēəli'zāSHən/ *n.*

ep·i·the·li·um /,epə'THēlēəm/ ▸*n.* (*pl.* **-li·a** /-lēə/) *Anatomy* the thin tissue forming the outer layer of a body's surface and lining the alimentary canal and other hollow structures. ■ more specifically, the part of this derived from embryonic ectoderm and endoderm, as distinct from endothelium and mesothelium. ▷mid 18th cent.: modern Latin, from EPI- 'above' + Greek *thēlē* 'teat.' —**ep·i·the·li·al** /-lēəl/ *adj.*

ep·i·thet /'epə,THet/ ▸*n.* an adjective or descriptive phrase expressing a quality characteristic of the person or thing mentioned: *old men are often unfairly awarded the epithet "dirty."* ■ such a word or phrase as a term of abuse: *he felt an urge to hurl epithets in his face.* ■ a descriptive title: *the epithet "Father of Waters," poetically used for the Mississippi River.* ▷late 16th cent.: from French *épithète*, or via Latin from Greek *epitheton*, neuter of *epithetos* 'attributed,' from *epitithenai* 'add,' from *epi* 'upon' + *tithenai* 'to place.' —**ep·i·thet·ic** /epə'THetik/ *adj.* —**ep·i·thet·i·cal** /epə'THetikəl/ *adj.* —**ep·i·thet·i·cal·ly** /epə'THetik(ə)lē/ *adv.*

e·pit·o·me /i'pitəmē/ ▸*n.* **1** (**the epitome of**) a person or thing that is a perfect example of a particular quality or type: *she looked the epitome of elegance and good taste.* **2** a summary of a written work; an abstract. ■ *archaic* a thing representing something else in miniature. ▷early 16th cent.: via Latin from Greek *epitomē*, from *epitemnein* 'abridge,' from *epi* 'in addition' + *temnein* 'to cut.' —**e·pit·o·mist** /-mist/ *n.*

e·pit·o·mize /i'pitə,mīz/ ▸*v.* [*trans.*] **1** be a perfect example of: *Hearst's newspapers epitomized bare-knuckle yellow journalism.* **2** *archaic* give a summary of (a written work). —**e·pit·o·mi·za·tion** /i,pitəmi'zāSHən/ *n.*

ep·i·tope /'epi,tōp/ ▸*n.* *Biochemistry* the part of an antigen molecule to which an antibody attaches itself. Also called ANTIGENIC DETERMINANT. ▷1960s: from EPI- 'upon' + Greek *topos* 'place.'

ep·i·zo·ic /,epi'zō-ik/ ▸*adj.* *Biology* (of a plant or animal) growing or living nonparasitically on the exterior of a living animal. ▷mid 19th cent.: from EPI- 'upon' + Greek *zōion* 'animal' + -IC. —**ep·i·zo·ite** /,epi'zō-īt/ *n.*

ep·i·zo·on /,epi'zō,än/ ▸*n.* (*pl.* **-zo·a** /-'zōə/) *Zoology* an animal that lives on the body of another animal, esp. as a parasite. ▷mid 19th cent.: from EPI- 'upon' + Greek *zōion* 'animal.'

ep·i·zo·ot·ic /,epizō'ätik/ ▸*adj.* of, relating to, or denoting a disease that is temporarily prevalent and widespread in an animal population. Compare with ENZOOTIC, EPIDEMIC.
▸*n.* an outbreak of such a disease. ▷late 18th cent. (as an adjective): from French *épizootique*, from *épizootie*, from Greek *epi* 'upon' + *zōion* 'animal.'

e plu·ri·bus u·num /'ē 'ploorəbəs '(y)oonəm/ ▸*n.* out of many, one (the motto of the U.S.).

EPNS ▸*abbr.* electroplated nickel silver.

EPO ▸*abbr.* erythropoietin, esp. when isolated as a drug for medical use or for illegal use by athletes.

ep·och /'epək/ ▸*n.* a period of time in history or a person's life, typically one marked by notable events or particular characteristics: *the Victorian epoch.* ■ the beginning of a distinctive period in the history of someone or something: *Jewish reimmigration to Palestine marked an epoch in the history of Jewry.* ■ *Geology* a division of time that is a subdivision of a period and is itself subdivided into ages, corresponding to a series in chronostratigraphy: *the Pliocene epoch.* ■ *Astronomy* an arbitrarily fixed date relative to which planetary or stellar measurements are expressed. ▷early 17th cent. (in the Latin form *epocha*; originally in the general sense of a date from which succeeding years are numbered): from modern Latin *epocha*, from Greek *epokhē* 'stoppage, fixed point of time,' from *epekhein* 'stop, take up a position,' from *epi* 'upon, near to' + *ekhein* 'stay, be in a certain state.'

ep·och·al /'epəkəl/ ▸*adj.* forming or characterizing an epoch; epoch-making.

ep·och-mak·ing ▸*adj.* of major importance; likely to have a significant effect on a particular period of time.

ep·ode /'epōd/ ▸*n.* **1** a form of lyric poem written in couplets, in which a long line is followed by a shorter one. **2** the third section of an ancient Greek choral ode, or of one division of such an ode. Compare with STROPHE and ANTISTROPHE. ▷early 17th cent.: from French *épode*, or via Latin *epodos*, from Greek *epōidos*, from *epi* 'upon' + *ōidē* (see ODE).

ep·o·nym /'epə,nim/ ▸*n.* a person after whom a discovery, invention, place, etc., is named or thought to be named. ■ a name or noun formed in such a way. ▷mid 19th cent.: from Greek *epōnumos* 'given as a name, giving one's name to someone or something,' from *epi* 'upon' + *onoma* 'name.' —**e·pon·y·my** /ə'pänəmē/ *n.*

e·pon·y·mous /ə'pänəməs/ ▸*adj.* (of a person) giving their name to something: *the eponymous hero of the novel.* ■ (of a thing) named after a particular person: *Roseanne's eponymous hit TV series.*

EPOS ▸*abbr.* electronic point of sale (used to describe retail outlets that record information electronically).

ep·ox·ide /e'päk,sīd/ ▸*n.* *Chemistry* an organic compound whose molecule contains a three-membered ring involving an oxygen atom and two carbon atoms. ▷1930s: from EPI- 'in addition' + OXIDE.

ep·ox·y /i'päksē/ ▸*n.* (*pl.* **-ox·ies**) (also **ep·ox·y res·in**) an adhesive, plastic, paint, or other material made from a class of synthetic thermosetting polymers containing epoxide groups.
▸*adj.* [*attrib.*] consisting of or denoting such a material: *epoxy cement.*
▸*v.* (**-ox·ies**, **-ox·ied**) [*trans.*] glue (something) using epoxy resin. ▷early 20th cent.: from EPI- 'in addition' + OXY-[2].

EPROM /'ē,präm/ ▸*n.* *Electronics* a read-only memory whose contents can be erased by ultraviolet light or other means and reprogrammed using a pulsed voltage. ▷1970s: acronym from *erasable programmable ROM.*

eps ▸*abbr.* earnings per share.

ep·si·lon /'epsi,län/ ▸*n.* the fifth letter of the Greek alphabet (**Ε, ε**), transliterated as 'e.' ■ [*as adj.*] denoting the fifth in a series of items, categories, etc. ■ (**Epsilon**) [followed by Latin genitive] *Astronomy* the fifth star in a constellation: *Epsilon Carinae.*
▸*symbol* (ε) permittivity. ▷early 18th cent.: Greek, 'plain or simple E,' from *psilos* 'plain,' referring to the need to distinguish epsilon from the diphthong *ai*: in late Greek the two had the same pronunciation.

Ep·som /'epsəm/ a town in southeastern England; pop. 68,500. Its natural mineral waters were used in the production of Epsom salts. The annual Derby and Oaks horse races are held at its racecourse on Epsom Downs.

Ep·som salts ▸*plural n.* crystals of hydrated magnesium sulfate used as a purgative or for other medicinal use. • Chem. formula: $MgSO_4.7H_2O$. ▷mid 18th cent.: named after the town of EPSOM, where it was first found occurring naturally.

Ep·stein /'ep,stīn/, Sir Jacob (1880–1959), British sculptor; born in the U.S. A founder of the vorticist group, he later had great success with his modeled portraits of the famous, in particular *Einstein* (1933).

Ep·stein–Barr vi·rus /'epstīn 'bär/ (abbr.: **EBV**) ▸*n.* *Medicine* a herpesvirus causing infectious mononucleosis and associated with certain cancers, for example Burkitt's lymphoma. ▷1960s: named after Michael A. *Epstein* (born 1921), British virologist, and Y. M. *Barr* (born 1932), Irish-born virologist.

e·pyl·li·on /ə'pilēən; -,än/ ▸*n.* (*pl.* **e·pyl·li·a** /ə'pilēə/) a narrative poem that resembles an epic poem in style but is notably shorter. ▷late 19th cent.: from Greek *epullion*, diminutive of *epos* 'word, song,' from *eipein* 'say.'

EQ ▸*abbr.* ■ educational quotient ■ emotional quotient. [after IQ, 'intelligence quotient.'] ■ equalizer, specifically a graphic equalizer.

eq. ▸*abbr.* ■ equal. ■ equation. ■ equivalent.

eq·ua·ble /'ekwəbəl/ ▸*adj.* (of a person) not easily disturbed or angered; calm and even-tempered. ■ not varying or fluctuating greatly: *an equable climate.* ▷mid 17th cent. (in the sense 'fair, equitable'): from Latin *aequabilis*, from *aequare* 'make equal' (see EQUATE). —**eq·ua·bil·i·ty** /,ekwə'bilitē/ *n.* —**eq·ua·bly** /-blē/ *adv.*

e·qual /'ēkwəl/ ▸*adj.* **1** being the same in quantity, size, degree, or value: *add equal amounts of water and flour* | *1 liter is roughly* **equal to** *1 quart.* See note at SAME. ■ (of people) having the same status, rights, or opportunities. ■ uniform in application or effect; without discrimination on any grounds: *a dedicated campaigner for equal rights.* ■ evenly or fairly balanced: *it was hardly an equal contest.* **2** [*predic.*] (**equal to**) having the ability or resources to meet (a challenge): *the players proved equal to the task.*
▸*n.* a person or thing considered to be the same as another in status or quality: *we all treat each other as equals* | *it was a day* **without equal** *in market history.*
▸*v.* (**e·qualed**, **e·qual·ing**; also *chiefly Brit.* **e·qualled**, **e·qual·ling**) [*trans.*] be the same as in number or amount: *four plus six divided by two equals five* | *the total debits should equal the total credits.* ■ match or rival in performance or extent: *he equaled the world record of 9.93 seconds.* ■ be equivalent to: *his work is concerned with why private property equals exploitation.* ▷late Middle English: from Latin *aequalis*, from *aequus* 'even, level, equal.'
▸*PHRASES* □ (**the**) **first among equals** the person or thing having the highest status in a group. □ **other** (or **all**) **things being equal** provided that other factors or circumstances remain the same: *it follows that, other things being equal, the price level will rise.*

USAGE It is widely held that adjectives such as **equal** and **unique** have absolute meanings and therefore can have no degrees of comparison. Hence they should not be modified, and it is incorrect to say **more equal** or **very unique** on the grounds that these are adjectives that refer to a logical or mathematical absolute.
For more discussion of this question, see **usage** at UNIQUE.

e·qual·i·tar·i·an /i,kwäli'terēən/ ▸*n.* another term for EGALITARIAN. —**e·qual·i·tar·i·an·ism** /-,nizəm/ *n.*

e·qual·i·ty /i'kwälitē/ ▸*n.* the state of being equal, esp. in status, rights, and opportunities: *an organization aiming to promote racial equality.* ■ *Mathematics* the condition of being equal in number or amount. ■ *Mathematics* a symbolic expression of the fact that two quantities are equal; an equation. ▷late Middle English: via Old French from Latin *aequalitas*, from *aequalis* (see EQUAL).

E·qual·i·ty State a nickname for the state of WYOMING.

e·qual·ize /'ēkwə,līz/ ▸*v.* [*trans.*] make the same in quantity, size, or degree throughout a place or group: *incentives to equalize funding for school districts.* ■ [*intrans.*] become equal to a specified or standard level: *equal volumes tend to equalize in temperature.* ■ [*trans.*] make uniform in application or effect: *the act was structured to equalize the status of a defendant.* ■ [*trans.*] *Electronics* correct or modify (a signal, etc.) with an equalizer ■ [*trans.*] *Electronics* compensate for by means of an equalizer. ▷late 16th cent. (in the sense 'be equal to'): from EQUAL + -IZE, partly suggested by French *égaliser*. —**e·qual·i·za·tion** /,ēkwəli'zāSHən/ *n.*

e·qual·iz·er /'ēkwə,līzər/ ▸*n.* a thing that has an equalizing effect: *education is the* **great equalizer.** ■ *informal* a weapon, esp. a gun. ■ *Electronics* a passive network designed to modify a frequency response, esp. to compensate for distortion.

e·qual·ly /ˈēkwəlē/ ▸*adv.* **1** in the same manner: *all children should be treated equally.* ■ in amounts or parts that are the same in size: *the money can be divided equally between you.* **2** to the same extent or degree: [as *submodifier*] *follow-up discussion is equally important.* ■ [*sentence adverb*] in addition and having the same importance (used to introduce a further comment on a topic): *not all who live in inner cities are poor; equally, many poor people live outside inner cities.*

USAGE The construction **equally as**—as in *follow-up discussion is* **equally as** *important*—is relatively common but is sometimes criticized on the grounds of redundancy. **Equally** used alone is adequate: *follow-up discussion is* **equally** *important.*

e·qual op·por·tu·ni·ty ▸*n.* the policy of treating employees and others without discrimination, esp. on the basis of their sex, race, or age: [as *adj.*] *an equal opportunity employer.*

E·qual Rights A·mend·ment (abbr.:**ERA**) ▸*n.* a proposed amendment to the U.S. Constitution stating that civil rights may not be denied on the basis of one's sex.

e·quals sign (also **e·qual sign**) ▸*n.* the symbol =.

e·qual tem·per·a·ment ▸*n. Music* see TEMPERAMENT (sense 2).

e·qual time ▸*n.* (in broadcasting) a principle of allowing equal air time to opposing points of view, esp. to political candidates for two or more parties.

e·qua·nim·i·ty /ˌēkwəˈnimitē; ˌekwə-/ ▸*n.* mental calmness, composure, and evenness of temper, esp. in a difficult situation: *she accepted both the good and the bad* ***with equanimity.*** ▷early 17th cent. (also in the sense 'fairness, impartiality'): from Latin *aequanimitas*, from *aequus* 'equal' + *animus* 'mind.' **—e·quan·i·mous** /iˈkwänəməs/ *adj.*

e·quant /ˈēkwənt/ ▸*adj. Geology* (of a crystal or particle) having its different diameters approximately equal, so as to be roughly cubic or spherical in shape. ▷mid 16th cent.: from Latin *aequant-* 'making equal,' from the verb *aequare.*

e·quate /iˈkwāt/ ▸*v.* [*trans.*] consider (one thing) to be the same as or equivalent to another: *customers* ***equate*** *their name* ***with*** *quality.* ■ [*intrans.*] (**equate to/with**) (of one thing) be the same as or equivalent to (another): *that sum equates to half a million pounds today.* ■ cause (two or more things) to be the same in quantity or value: *the level of prices will move to equate supply and demand.* ▷Middle English (in the sense 'make equal, balance'): from Latin *aequat-* 'made level or equal,' from the verb *aequare*, from *aequus* (see EQUAL). Current senses date from the mid 19th cent. **—e·quat·a·ble** /-təbəl/ *adj.*

e·qua·tion /iˈkwāzhən/ ▸*n.* **1** *Mathematics* a statement that the values of two mathematical expressions are equal (indicated by the sign =). **2** the process of equating one thing with another: *the* ***equation*** *of science* ***with*** *objectivity.* ■ (**the equation**) a situation or problem in which several factors must be taken into account: *money also came into the equation.* **3** *Chemistry* a symbolic representation of the changes that occur in a chemical reaction, expressed in terms of the formulae of the molecules or other species involved. ▷late Middle English: from Latin *aequatio(n-)*, from *aequare* 'make equal' (see EQUATE).

▸*PHRASE* □ **equation of the first order, second order,** etc. *Mathematics* an equation involving only the first derivative, second derivative, etc.

e·qua·tion·al /iˈkwāzhənəl/ ▸*adj.* another term for EQUATIVE.

e·qua·tion of state ▸*n. Chemistry* an equation showing the relationship between the values of the pressure, volume, and temperature of a quantity of a particular substance.

e·qua·tion of time ▸*n.* the difference between mean solar time (as shown by clocks) and apparent solar time (indicated by sundials), which varies with the time of year.

eq·ua·tive /iˈkwātiv/ ▸*adj. Grammar* denoting a sentence or other structure in which one term is identified with another, as in *the winner is Jill.* ■ denoting a use of the verb *to be* that equates one term with another. **—eq·ua·tive·ly** *adv.*

e·qua·tor /iˈkwātər/ ▸*n.* an imaginary line drawn around the earth equally distant from both poles, dividing the earth into northern and southern hemispheres and constituting the parallel of latitude 0°. ■ a corresponding line on a planet or other body. ■ *Astronomy* short for CELESTIAL EQUATOR. ▷late Middle English: from medieval Latin *aequator*, in the phrase *circulus aequator diei et noctis* 'circle equalizing day and night,' from Latin *aequare* 'make equal' (see EQUATE).

e·qua·to·ri·al /ˌekwəˈtôrēəl/ ▸*adj.* of, at, or near the equator: *equatorial regions.* **—e·qua·to·ri·al·ly** /ˌekwəˈtôrēəlē/ *adv.*

E·qua·to·ri·al Guin·ea a small country in West Africa, on the Gulf of Guinea, comprised of several offshore islands and a coastal settlement between Cameroon and Gabon; pop. 523,000; capital, Malabo (on the island of Bioko); languages, Spanish (official), local Niger–Congo languages, pidgin. **—E·qua·to·ri·al Guin·e·an** *adj.* & *n.*

Formerly a Spanish colony, the country became fully independent in 1968. It is the only independent Spanish-speaking state on the continent of Africa. Since 1991 it has been nominally a constitutional democracy.

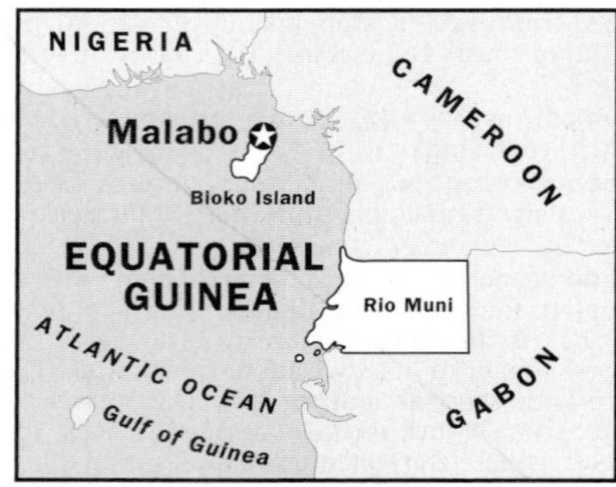

e·qua·to·ri·al mount (also **equatorial mounting**) ▸*n. Astronomy* a telescope mounting with one axis aligned to the celestial pole, which allows the movement of celestial objects to be followed by motion about this axis alone. Compare with ALTAZIMUTH (sense 1).

e·qua·to·ri·al tel·e·scope ▸*n.* an astronomical telescope on an equatorial mount.

eq·uer·ry /ˈekwərē; əˈkwerē/ ▸*n.* (*pl.* **-ries**) an officer of the British royal household who attends or assists members of the royal family. ■ *historical* an officer of the household of a prince or noble who had charge over the stables. ▷early 16th cent. (formerly also as *esquiry*): from Old French *esquierie* 'company of squires, prince's stables,' from Old French *esquier* 'esquire,' perhaps associated with Latin *equus* 'horse.' The historical sense is apparently based on Old French *esquier d'esquierie* 'squire of stables.'

e·ques /ˈekwes/ ▸ singular form of EQUITES.

e·ques·tri·an /iˈkwestrēən/ ▸*adj.* of or relating to horse riding: *his amazing equestrian skills.* ■ depicting or representing a person on horseback: *an equestrian statue.*

▸*n.* (*fem.* **e·ques·tri·enne** /iˌkwestrēˈen/) a rider or performer on horseback. ▷mid 17th cent. (as an adjective): from Latin *equester* 'belonging to a horseman' (from *eques* 'horseman, knight,' from *equus* 'horse') + -IAN.

e·ques·tri·an·ism /iˈkwestrēəˌnizəm/ ▸*n.* the skill or sport of horse riding. As an Olympic sport it is divided into three disciplines: show jumping, dressage, and the three-day event (combining show jumping, dressage, and cross-country riding).

equi- ▸*comb. form* equal; equally: *equiangular | equidistant.* ▷from Latin *aequi-*, from *aequus* 'equal.'

e·qui·an·gu·lar /ˌēkwēˈaNGgyələr; ˌekwē-/ ▸*adj.* having equal angles.

e·qui·an·gu·lar spi·ral ▸*n.* another term for LOGARITHMIC SPIRAL.

eq·uid /ˈēkwid; ˈekwid/ ▸*n. Zoology* a mammal of the horse family (Equidae). ▷late 19th cent.: from modern Latin *Equidae* (plural), from Latin *equus* 'horse.'

e·qui·dis·tant /ˌēkwiˈdistənt; ˌekwi-/ ▸*adj.* at equal distances: *he wants to be* ***equidistant from*** *both political parties.* **—e·qui·dis·tance** *n.* **—e·qui·dis·tant·ly** *adv.*

e·qui·fi·nal /ˌēkwəˈfīnəl; ˌekwə-/ ▸*adj. technical* having the same end or result. **—e·qui·fi·nal·i·ty** /ˌēkwəfīˈnalitē; ˌekwə-/ *n.* **—e·qui·fi·nal·ly** *adv.*

e·qui·lat·er·al /ˌēkwəˈlatərəl; ˌekwə-/ ▸*adj.* having all its sides of the same length: *an equilateral triangle.* ▷late 16th cent.: from French *équilatéral* or late Latin *aequilateralis*, from *aequilaterus* 'equal-sided' (based on Latin *latus, later-* 'side').

e·quil·i·brate /iˈkwiləˌbrāt/ ▸*v.* [*trans.*] *technical* bring into or keep in equilibrium. ■ [*intrans.*] approach or attain a state of equilibrium. ▷mid 17th cent.: from late Latin *aequilibrat-* 'made to balance,' from the verb *aequilibrare*, from *aequi-* 'equally' + *libra* 'balance.' **—e·quil·i·bra·tion** /iˌkwiləˈbrāshən/ *n.*

e·quil·i·brist /iˈkwiləbrist/ ▸*n. chiefly archaic* an acrobat who performs balancing feats, esp. a tightrope walker. ▷mid 18th cent.: from EQUILIBRIUM + -IST.

e·qui·lib·ri·um /ˌēkwəˈlibrēəm; ˌekwə-/ ▸*n.* (*pl.* **-lib·ri·a** /-ˈlibrēə/) a state in which opposing forces or influences are balanced: *the maintenance of social equilibrium.* ■ a state of physical balance: *I stumbled over a rock and recovered my equilibrium.* ■ a calm state of mind: *his intensity could unsettle his equilibrium.* ■ *Chemistry* a state in which a process and its reverse are occurring at equal rates so that no overall change is taking place: *ice is in* ***equilibrium with*** *water.* ■ *Economics* a situation in which supply and demand are matched and prices stable. ▷early 17th cent. (in the sense 'well-balanced state of mind'): from Latin *aequilibrium*, from *aequi-* 'equal'+ *libra* 'balance.' **—e·qui·lib·ri·al** /-ˈlibrēəl/ *adj.*

e·quine /ˈekwīn; ˈēˌkwīn/ ▸*adj.* of, relating to, or affecting horses or other members of the horse family: *equine infectious anemia.* ■ resembling a horse: *her somewhat equine features.*

▸*n.* a horse or other member of the horse family. ▷late 18th cent.: from Latin *equinus*, from *equus* 'horse.'

e·quine en·ceph·a·li·tis ▸*n.* a category of viral diseases that affects horses and, in some cases, humans. See also EASTERN EQUINE ENCEPHALITIS.

e·qui·noc·tial /ˌēkwəˈnäkshəl; ˌekwə-/ ▸*adj.* happening at or near the time of an equinox. ■ of or relating to equal day and night. ■ at or near the equator.

▸*n.* (also **equinoctial line** or **equinoctial circle**) another term for CELESTIAL EQUATOR. ▷late Middle English (in the sense 'relating to equal periods of day and night'): via Old French from Latin *aequinoctialis*, from *aequinoctium* (see EQUINOX).

e·qui·noc·tial point ▸*n.* either of two points at which the ecliptic cuts the celestial equator.

e·qui·noc·tial year ▸*n.* see YEAR (sense 1).

e·qui·nox /ˈekwəˌnäks; ˈēkwə-/ ▸*n.* the time or date (twice each year) at which the sun crosses the celestial equator, when day and night are of equal length (about September 22 and March 20). ■ another term for EQUINOCTIAL POINT. ▷late Middle English: from Old French *equinoxe* or Latin *aequinoctium*, from *aequi-* 'equal' + *nox, noct-* 'night.'

e·quip /iˈkwip/ ▸*v.* (**e·quipped, e·quip·ping**) [*trans.*] supply with the necessary items for a particular purpose: *all bedrooms are* ***equipped with*** *a color TV | they* ***equipped*** *themselves* ***for*** *the campaign.* ■ prepare (someone) mentally for a particular situation or task: *I don't think he's equipped for the modern age.* ▷early 16th cent.: from French *équiper*, probably from Old Norse *skipa* 'to man (a ship),' from *skip* 'ship.' **—e·quip·per** *n.*

equip. ▸*abbr.* equipment.

eq·ui·page /ˈekwəpij/ ▸*n.* **1** *archaic* the equipment for a particular purpose. **2** *historical* a carriage and horses with attendants. ▷mid 16th cent. (denoting the crew of a ship): from French *équipage*, from *équiper* 'equip.'

e·qui·par·ti·tion /ˌēkwəpärˈtishən; ˌekwə-/ (also **equipartition of energy**) ▸*n. Physics* the equal distribution of the kinetic energy of a system among its various degrees of freedom. ■ the principle that this exists for a system in thermal equilibrium. **—e·qui·par·ti·tioned** *adj.*

e·quip·ment /iˈkwipmənt/ ▸*n.* the necessary items for a particular purpose: *office equipment.* ■ the process of supplying someone or something with such necessary items: *the construction and equipment of new harbor facilities.* ■ mental resources: *they lacked the intellectual equipment to recognize the jokes.* ■ *informal* used euphemistically to refer to a man's penis and testicles. ▷early 18th cent.: from French *équipement*, from *équiper* 'equip.'

e·qui·poise /ˈekwəˌpoiz/ ▸*n.* balance of forces or interests: *this temporary equipoise of power.* ■ a counterbalance or balancing force: *capital flows act as an* ***equipoise to*** *international imbalances in savings.*

▸*v.* [*trans.*] balance or counterbalance (something). ▷mid 17th cent.: from EQUI- 'equal' + the noun POISE[1], replacing the phrase *equal poise.*

e·qui·pol·lent /ˌēkwəˈpälənt; ˌekwə-/ *archaic* ▸*adj.* equal or equivalent in power, effect, or significance.

▸*n.* a thing that has equal or equivalent power, effect, or significance. ▷late Middle English: from Old French *equipolent*, from Latin *aequipollent-* 'of equal value,' from *aequi-* 'equally' + *pollere* 'be strong.' **—e·qui·pol·lence** *n.* **—e·qui·pol·len·cy** *n.*

e·qui·po·tent /ˌēkwəˈpōtnt; ˌekwə-/ ▸*adj. technical* (chiefly of chemicals and medicines) equally powerful; having equal potencies.

e·qui·po·ten·tial /ˌēkwəpəˈtenCHəl; ˌekwə-/ ▸*adj.* [*attrib.*] *Physics* (of a surface or line) composed of points all at the same potential.
▸*n.* an equipotential line or surface.

e·qui·prob·a·ble /ˌēkwəˈpräbəbəl; ˌekwə-/ ▸*adj. Mathematics & Logic* (of two or more things) equally likely to occur; having equal probability. **—e·qui·prob·a·bil·i·ty** /-ˌpräbəˈbilitē/ *n.*

eq·ui·se·tum /ˌekwiˈsētəm/ ▸*n.* (*pl.* **-se·ta** /-ˈsētə/ or **-se·tums**) *Botany* a plant of a genus that comprises the horsetails. • Genus *Equisetum*, family Equisetaceae. ▷modern Latin, from Latin *equus* 'horse' + *saeta* 'bristle.'

eq·ui·ta·ble /ˈekwitəbəl/ ▸*adj.* **1** fair and impartial: *an equitable balance of power.* **2** *Law* valid in equity as distinct from law: *the beneficiaries have an equitable interest in the property.* ▷mid 16th cent.: from French *équitable*, from *équité* (see **EQUITY**). **—eq·ui·ta·bil·i·ty** /ˌekwitəˈbilitē/ *n.* **—eq·ui·ta·ble·ness** *n.* **—eq·ui·ta·bly** /-əblē/ *adv.*

eq·ui·tant /ˈekwitənt/ ▸*adj. Botany* (of a leaf) having its base folded and partly enclosing the leaf next above it, as in an iris. ▷late 18th cent.: from Latin *equitant-* 'riding on horseback,' from the verb *equitare*.

eq·ui·ta·tion /ˌekwiˈtāSHən/ ▸*n. formal* the art and practice of horsemanship and horse riding. ▷mid 16th cent.: from French *équitation* or Latin *equitatio(n-)*, from *equitare* 'ride a horse,' from *eques, equit-* 'horseman' (from *equus* 'horse').

eq·ui·tes /ˈekwəˌtās; -ˌtēz/ ▸*plural n.* (*sing.* **eq·ues** /ˈekwes; -wēz/) (in ancient Rome) a class of citizens who originally formed the cavalry of the Roman army and at a later period were a wealthy class of great political importance. ▷Latin, plural of *eques* 'horseman.'

eq·ui·ty /ˈekwitē/ ▸*n.* (*pl.* **-ties**) **1** the quality of being fair and impartial: *equity of treatment.* ■ *Law* a branch of law that developed alongside common law in order to remedy some of its defects in fairness and justice, formerly administered in special courts. ■ (**Equity**) (in the U.S., UK, and several other countries) a trade union to which most professional actors belong. **2** the value of the shares issued by a company: *he owns 62% of the group's equity.* ■ (**equities**) stocks and shares that carry no fixed interest. **3** the value of a mortgaged property after deduction of charges against it. ▷Middle English: from Old French *equité*, from Latin *aequitas*, from *aequus* 'equal.'

eq·ui·ty of re·demp·tion ▸*n. Law* the right of a mortgagor over the mortgaged property, esp. the right to redeem the property on payment of the principal, interest, and costs.

eq·ui·ty stock ▸*n.* capital stock, either common stock or preferred stock.

equiv. ▸*abbr.* equivalent.

e·quiv·a·lence class /iˈkwivələns/ ▸*n. Mathematics & Logic* the class of all members of a set that are in a given equivalence relation.

e·quiv·a·lence prin·ci·ple ▸*n. Physics* a basic postulate of general relativity, stating that at any point of space-time the effects of a gravitational field cannot be experimentally distinguished from those due to an accelerated frame of reference.

e·quiv·a·lence re·la·tion ▸*n. Mathematics & Logic* a relation between elements of a set that is reflexive, symmetric, and transitive. It thus defines exclusive classes whose members bear the relation to each other and not to those in other classes (e.g., "having the same value of a measured property").

e·quiv·a·len·cy /iˈkwivələnsē/ ▸*n.* (*pl.* **-cies**) another term for **EQUIVALENCE** (see **EQUIVALENT**). ■ short for **GENERAL EQUIVALENCY DEGREE/DIPLOMA**.

e·quiv·a·lent /iˈkwivələnt/ ▸*adj.* equal in value, amount, function, meaning, etc.: *one unit is* ***equivalent to*** *one glass of wine.* See note at **SAME**. ■ [*predic.*] (**equivalent to**) having the same or a similar effect as: *some regulations are equivalent to censorship.* ■ *Mathematics* belonging to the same equivalence class.
▸*n.* a person or thing that is equal to or corresponds with another in value, amount, function, meaning, etc.: *the French equivalent of the FBI.* ■ (also **equivalent weight**) *Chemistry* the mass of a particular substance that can combine with or displace one gram of hydrogen or eight grams of oxygen, used in expressing combining powers, esp. of elements. ▷late Middle English (describing persons who were equal in power or rank): via Old French from late Latin *aequivalent-* 'being of equal worth,' from the verb *aequivalere*, from *aequi-* 'equally' + *valere* 'be worth.' **—e·quiv·a·lence** *n.* **—e·quiv·a·lent·ly** *adv.*

e·quiv·o·cal /iˈkwivəkəl/ ▸*adj.* open to more than one interpretation; ambiguous: *the equivocal nature of her remarks.* ■ uncertain or questionable in nature: *the results of the investigation were equivocal.* See note at **DOUBTFUL**. ▷mid 16th cent.: from late Latin *aequivocus*, from Latin *aequus* 'equally' + *vocare* 'to call.' **—e·quiv·o·cal·i·ty** /iˌkwivəˈkalitē/ *n.* **—e·quiv·o·cal·ly** *adv.* **—e·quiv·o·cal·ness** *n.*

e·quiv·o·cate /iˈkwivəˌkāt/ ▸*v.* [*intrans.*] use ambiguous language so as to conceal the truth or avoid committing oneself: [with *direct speech*] *"Not that we are aware of," she equivocated.* See note at **LIE**. ▷late Middle English (in the sense 'use a word in more than one sense'): from late Latin *aequivocat-* 'called by the same name,' from the verb *aequivocare*, from *aequivocus* (see **EQUIVOCAL**). **—e·quiv·o·ca·tion** /iˌkwivəˈkāSHən/ *n.* **—e·quiv·o·ca·tor** /-ˌkātər/ *n.* **—e·quiv·o·ca·to·ry** /-kəˌtôrē/ *adj.*

eq·ui·voque /ˈekwəˌvōk; ˈēkwə-/ (also **eq·ui·voke**) ▸*n.* an expression capable of having more than one meaning; a pun. ■ the fact of having more than one meaning or possible interpretation; ambiguity. ▷late Middle English (as an adjective in the sense 'equivocal'): from Old French *equivoque* or late Latin *aequivocus* (see **EQUIVOCAL**).

E·quu·le·us /ēˈkwo͝olēəs/ *Astronomy* a small northern constellation (the Foal or Little Horse), perhaps representing the brother of Pegasus. It has no bright stars. ■ [as *genitive*] (**Equulei** /-lēˌī/) used with a preceding letter or numeral to designate a star in this constellation: *the star Delta Equulei.* ▷Latin.

ER ▸*abbr.* ■ emergency room. ■ Queen Elizabeth. [from Latin *Elizabetha Regina*.]

Er ▸*symbol* the chemical element erbium.

er /ə; ər/ ▸*exclam.* expressing hesitation: *"Would you like some tea?" "Er . . . yes . . . thank you."* ▷natural utterance: first recorded in English in the mid 19th cent.

-er[1] /ər/ ▸*suffix* **1** denoting a person, animal, or thing that performs a specified action or activity: *farmer* | *sprinkler.* **2** denoting a person or thing that has a specified attribute or form: *foreigner* | *two-wheeler.* **3** denoting a person concerned with a specified thing or subject: *milliner* | *philosopher.* **4** denoting a person belonging to a specified place or group: *city-dweller* | *New Yorker.* ▷Old English *-ere*, of Germanic origin.

-er[2] ▸*suffix* forming the comparative of adjectives (as in *bigger*) and adverbs (as in *faster*). ▷Old English suffix *-ra* (adjectival), *-or* (adverbial), of Germanic origin.

-er[3] ▸*suffix* forming frequentative verbs such as *glimmer, patter.* ▷Old English *-erian, -rian*, of Germanic origin.

-er[4] ▸*suffix* forming nouns: **1** such as *sampler*. Compare with **-AR**[1]. [ending corresponding to Latin *-aris*.] ■ such as *butler, danger.* [ending corresponding to Latin *-arius, -arium*.] ■ such as *border.* [ending corresponding (via Old French *-eure*) to Latin *-atura*.] ■ such as *laver*. See **LAVER**[2]. [ending corresponding (via Old French *-eor*) to Latin *-atorium*.] **2** equivalent to **-OR**[1]. ▷via Old French or Anglo-Norman French (see above).

-er[5] ▸*suffix chiefly Law* (forming nouns) denoting verbal action or a document effecting such action: *disclaimer* | *misnomer.* ▷from Anglo-Norman French (infinitive ending).

ERA ▸*abbr.* ■ *Baseball* earned run average. ■ Equal Rights Amendment.

e·ra /ˈi(ə)rə; ˈerə/ ▸*n.* a long and distinct period of history with a particular feature or characteristic: *his death marked the end of an era* | *the era of glasnost.* ■ a system of chronology dating from a particular noteworthy event: *the dawn of the Christian era.* ■ *Geology* a major division of time that is a subdivision of an eon and is itself subdivided into periods: *the Mesozoic era.* ■ *archaic* a date or event marking the beginning of a new and distinct period of time. ▷mid 17th cent.: from late Latin *aera*, denoting a number used as a basis of reckoning, an epoch from which time is reckoned, plural of *aes, aer-* 'money, counter.'

e·rad·i·cate /iˈradiˌkāt/ ▸*v.* [*trans.*] destroy completely; put an end to: *this disease has been eradicated from the world.* See note at **DESTROY**. ▷late Middle English (in the sense 'pull up by the roots'): from Latin *eradicat-* 'torn up by the roots,' from the verb *eradicare*, from *e-* (variant of *ex-*) 'out' + *radix, radic-* 'root.' **—e·rad·i·ca·ble** /-kəbəl/ *adj.* **—e·rad·i·cant** /-kənt/ *n.* **—e·rad·i·ca·tion** /iˌradiˈkāSHən/ *n.* **—e·rad·i·ca·tor** /-ˌkātər/ *n.*

e·rad·i·cat·ed /iˈradəˌkātid/ ▸*adj.* [*postpositive*] *Heraldry* (of a tree or plant) depicted with the roots exposed.

e·rase /iˈrās/ ▸*v.* [*trans.*] rub out or remove (writing or marks): *graffiti had been erased from the wall.* ■ remove all traces of (a thought, feeling, or memory): *the magic of the landscape erased all else from her mind.* ■ destroy or obliterate (someone or something) so as to leave no trace: *over twenty years, the last vestiges of a rural economy were erased.* ■ remove recorded material from (a magnetic tape or medium); delete (data) from a computer's memory. ▷late 16th cent. (originally as a heraldic term meaning 'represent the head or limb of an animal with a jagged edge'): from Latin *eras-* 'scraped away,' from the verb *eradere*, from *e-* (variant of *ex-*) 'out' + *radere* 'scrape.' **—e·ras·a·ble** /-əbəl/ *adj.* **—e·ra·sure** /iˈrāSHər/ *n.*

e·rased /iˈrāst/ ▸*adj.* [*postpositive*] *Heraldry* (of a head or limb) depicted as cut off in a jagged line.

e·ras·er /iˈrāsər/ ▸*n.* an object, typically a piece of soft rubber or plastic, used to rub out something written.

E·ras·mus /iˈrazməs/, Desiderius (*c.*1469–1536), Dutch humanist and scholar; Dutch name *Gerhard Gerhards*. He was the foremost Renaissance scholar of northern Europe, and paved the way for the Reformation with his satires on the Catholic Church.

E·ras·tian·ism /iˈrastēəˌnizəm; iˈrasCHə-/ ▸*n.* the doctrine that the state should have supremacy over the Church in ecclesiastical matters (wrongly attributed to Erastus). **—E·ras·tian** /iˈrastēən; iˈrasCHən/ *n.* & *adj.*

E·ras·tus /iˈrastəs/ (1524–83), Swiss theologian and physician; Swiss name *Thomas Lieber*, also *Liebler* or *Lüber*. Professor of medicine at Heidelberg from 1558, he opposed the imposition of a Calvinistic system of church government in the city.

Er·a·to /ˈerəˌtō/ *Greek & Roman Mythology* the Muse of lyric poetry and hymns. ▷Greek, literally 'lovely.'

Er·a·tos·the·nes /ˌerəˈtäsTHəˌnēz/ (*c.*275–194 BC), Greek scholar, geographer, and astronomer. The first systematic geographer of antiquity, he accurately calculated the circumference of the earth.

er·bi·um /ˈərbēəm/ ▸*n.* the chemical element of atomic number 68, a soft, silvery-white metal of the lanthanide series. (Symbol: **Er**) ▷mid 19th cent.: modern Latin, from *(Ytt)erb(y)*, in Sweden, where it was first found. Compare with **YTTERBIUM**.

Er·drich /ˈərdrik/, Louise (1954–), U.S. writer. A Native American (Ojibwa), she wrote *Love Medicine* (1984), *The Bingo Palace* (1994), *Tales of Burning Love* (1996), and *The Antelope Wife* (1998).

ere /e(ə)r/ ▸*prep.* & *conj. poetic/literary or archaic* before (in time): [as *prep.*] *we hope you will return ere long* | [as *conj.*] *I was driven for some half mile ere we stopped.* ▷Old English *ǣr*, of Germanic origin; related to Dutch *eer* and German *eher*.

Er·e·bus /ˈerəbəs/ *Greek Mythology* the primeval god of darkness, son of Chaos.

Er·e·bus, Mount a volcanic peak on Ross Island, Antarctica. Rising to 12,452 feet (3,794 m), it is the world's most southern active volcano. ▷named after the *Erebus*, the ship of Sir James Ross's expedition to the Antarctic.

E·rech /ˈerˌek; ˈēˌrek/ biblical name for **URUK**.

E·rech·the·um /iˈrikTHēəm; ˌerikˈTHēəm/ a marble temple of the Ionic order built on the Acropolis in Athens *c.*421–406 BC, with shrines to Athena, Poseidon, and Erechtheus, a legendary king of Athens. It is most famous for its southern portico, in which the entablature is supported by six caryatids.

e·rect /iˈrekt/ ▸*adj.* rigidly upright or straight: *she stood erect with her arms by her sides.* ■ (of the penis, clitoris, or nipples) enlarged and rigid, esp. in sexual excitement. ■ (of hair) standing up from the skin; bristling.
▸*v.* [*trans.*] construct (a building, wall, or other upright structure): *the guest house was erected in the eighteenth century.* ■ put into position and set upright (a barrier, statue, or other object): *the police had erected roadblocks.* ■ create or establish (a theory or system): *the party that erected the welfare state.* ▷late Middle English: from Latin *erect-* 'set up,' from the verb *erigere*, from *e-* (variant of *ex-*) 'out' + *regere* 'to direct.' **—e·rect·a·ble** *adj.* **—e·rect·ly** *adv.* **—e·rect·ness** *n.*

e·rec·tile /iˈrektl; -ˌtīl/ ▸*adj.* able to become erect: *erectile spines.* ■ denoting tissues that are capable of becoming of temporarily engorged with blood, particularly those of the penis or other sexual organs. ■ relating to this process: *men with erectile dysfunction.* ▷mid 19th cent.: from French *érectile*, from Latin *erigere* 'set up' (see ERECT).

e·rec·tile dys·func·tion ▸*n.* inability of a man to maintain an erection sufficient for satisfying sexual activity: *a treatment proven safe for erectile dysfunction.*

e·rec·tion /iˈrekSHən/ ▸*n.* **1** the action of erecting a structure or object: *fees will be levied for the erection of monuments.* ■ a building or other upright structure. **2** an enlarged and rigid state of the penis, typically in sexual excitement.

e·rec·tor /iˈrektər/ ▸*n.* a person or thing that erects something. ■ a muscle that maintains an erect state of a part of the body or an erect posture of the body.

ere·long /e(ə)rˈlôNG; -ˈläNG/ ▸*adv. archaic* before long; soon.

er·e·mite /ˈerəˌmīt/ ▸*n.* a Christian hermit or recluse. ▷Middle English: from Old French *eremite*, from late Latin *eremita* (see HERMIT). **—er·e·mit·ic** /ˌerəˈmitik/ *adj.* **—er·e·mit·i·cal** /ˌerəˈmitikəl/ *adj.*

er·e·thism /ˈerəˌTHizəm/ ▸*n.* **1** excessive sensitivity or rapid reaction to stimulation of a part of the body, esp. the sexual organs. **2** a state of abnormal mental excitement or irritation. ▷early 19th cent.: from French *éréthisme*, from Greek *erethismos*, from *erethizein* 'irritate.'

E·re·van /ˌyeriˈvän/ ▸ another name for YEREVAN.

ere·while /er'(h)wīl/ ▸*adv. archaic* a while before; some time ago. ▷Middle English: from ERE + WHILE.

Er·furt /ˈerˌfŏŏrt/ an industrial city in central Germany; pop. 205,000.

erg[1] /ərg/ ▸*n. Physics* a unit of work or energy, equal to the work done by a force of one dyne when its point of application moves one centimeter in the direction of action of the force. ▷late 19th cent.: from Greek *ergon* 'work.'

erg[2] /ərg/ ▸*n.* an area of shifting sand dunes in the Sahara. ▷late 19th cent.: from French, from Arabic *'irq, 'erg*.

er·ga·tive /ˈərgətiv/ *Grammar* ▸*adj.* relating to or denoting a case of nouns (in some languages, e.g., Basque and Eskimo) that identifies the subject of a transitive verb and is different from the case that identifies the subject of an intransitive verb. ■ (of a language) possessing this case. ■ (in English) denoting verbs that can be used both transitively and intransitively to describe the same action, with the object in the former case being the subject in the latter, as in *I boiled the kettle* and *the kettle boiled*. Compare with INCHOATIVE.
▸*n.* an ergative word. ■ (**the ergative**) the ergative case. ▷1950s: from Greek *ergatēs* 'worker' (from *ergon* 'work') + -IVE. **—er·ga·tiv·i·ty** /ˌərgəˈtivitē/ *n.*

er·go /ˈərgō; ˈergō/ ▸*adv.* [*sentence adverb*] therefore: *she was the sole beneficiary of the will, ergo the prime suspect.* ▷late Middle English: Latin.

er·go·cal·cif·er·ol /ˌərgəkalˈsiferäl; -rôl/ ▸*n. Biochemistry* another term for CALCIFEROL, VITAMIN D_2. ▷1950s: blend of ERGOT and CALCIFEROL.

er·god·ic /ərˈgädik/ ▸*adj. Mathematics* relating to or denoting systems or processes with the property that, given sufficient time, they include or impinge on all points in a given space and can be represented statistically by a reasonably large selection of points. ▷early 20th cent.: from German *ergoden*, from Greek *ergon* 'work' + *hodos* 'way' + -IC. **—er·go·dic·i·ty** /ˌərgəˈdisitē/ *n.*

er·go·gen·ic /ˌərgəˈjenik/ ▸*adj.* (not in technical use) intended to enhance physical performance, stamina, or recovery: *ergogenic supplements.*

er·go·graph /ˈərgəˌgraf/ ▸*n.* an instrument for measuring and recording the work done by a particular muscle group.

er·gom·e·ter /ərˈgämitər/ ▸*n.* an apparatus that measures work or energy expended during a period of physical exercise.

er·go·met·rine /ˌərgəˈmetrēn/ ▸*n. Chemistry* an alkaloid present in ergot. An amide of lysergic acid, it has oxytocic activity and is given to control bleeding after childbirth. ▷1930s: from ERGOT + Greek *mētra* 'womb' + -INE[4].

er·go·nom·ic /ərgəˈnämik/ ▸*adj.* (esp. of workplace design) intended to provide optimum comfort and to avoid stress or injury.

er·go·nom·ics /ˌərgəˈnämiks/ ▸*plural n.* [treated as *sing.*] the study of people's efficiency in their working environment. ▷1950s: from Greek *ergon* 'work,' on the pattern of *economics*. **—er·gon·o·mist** /ərˈgänəmist/ *n.*

er·go·sphere /ˈərgōˌsfir/ ▸*n. Astronomy* a postulated region around a black hole, from which energy could escape.

er·gos·ter·ol /ərˈgästəˌrôl; -ˌräl/ ▸*n. Biochemistry* a compound present in ergot and many other fungi. A steroid alcohol, it is converted to vitamin D_2 when irradiated with ultraviolet light. ▷early 20th cent.: from ERGOT, on the pattern of *cholesterol*.

er·got /ˈərgət; -ˌgät/ ▸*n.* **1** a fungal disease of rye and other cereals in which black, elongated, fruiting bodies grow in the ears of the cereal. Eating contaminated food can result in ergotism. • The fungus is *Claviceps purpurea*, subdivision Ascomycotina. ■ a fruiting body of this fungus. ■ these fruiting bodies used as a source of certain medicinal alkaloids, esp. for inducing uterine contractions or controlling post-partum bleeding. **2** a small, horny protuberance on the back of each of a horse's fetlocks. ▷late 17th cent.: from French, from Old French *argot* 'cock's spur' (because of the appearance produced by the disease).

er·got·a·mine /ərˈgätəˌmēn; -min/ ▸*n. Medicine* a compound present in some kinds of ergot. An alkaloid, it causes constriction of blood vessels and is used in the treatment of migraine.

er·got·ism /ˈərgəˌtizəm/ ▸*n.* poisoning produced by eating food affected by ergot, typically resulting in headache, vomiting, diarrhea, and gangrene of the fingers and toes.

er·hu /ərˈhoo/ (also **erh hu**) ▸*n.* a Chinese two-stringed musical instrument held in the lap and played with a bow. ▷early 20th cent.: from Chinese *èr* 'two' + *hú* 'bowed instrument.'

er·i·ca /ˈerikə/ ▸*n.* a plant of the genus *Erica* (family Ericaceae), esp. (in gardening) heather. ▷modern Latin, from Greek *ereikē*.

er·i·ca·ceous /ˌeriˈkāSHəs/ ▸*adj. Botany* of, relating to, or denoting plants of the heath family (Ericaceae). ▷mid 19th cent.: from modern Latin *Ericaceae* (plural), from the genus name *Erica* (see ERICA).

Er·ics·son[1] /ˈeriksən/, John (1803–89), Swedish engineer whose inventions included the marine screw propeller (1836) and a steam railroad locomotive that rivaled George Stephenson's *Rocket*.

Er·ics·son[2] (also **Er·ic·son** or **Er·iks·son**), Leif, Norse explorer; son of Eric the Red. He sailed west from Greenland (*c.*1000) and reputedly discovered land (variously identified as Labrador, Newfoundland, or New England), which he named Vinland because of the vines he claimed to have found growing there.

Er·ic the Red /ˈerik/ (*c.*940–*c.*1010), Norse explorer. He left Iceland in 982 in search of land to the west and explored Greenland, establishing a Norse settlement there in 986.

E·rid·a·nus /əˈridn-əs/ *Astronomy* a long, straggling southern constellation (the River), said to represent the river into which Phaethon fell when struck by Zeus' thunderbolt. ■ [as *genitive*] (**Eridani** /əˈridnˌī/) used with a preceding letter or numeral to designate a star in this constellation: *the star Phi Eridani.* ▷Latin.

E·rie /ˈi(ə)rē/ an industrial port city in northwestern Pennsylvania, on Lake Erie; pop. 103,717.

E·rie, Lake /ˈi(ə)rē/ one of the five Great Lakes in North America, on the border between Canada and the U.S. It is linked to Lake Huron by the Detroit River and to Lake Ontario by the Welland Ship Canal and the Niagara River, which is its only natural outlet.

E·rie Ca·nal a historic canal that connects the Hudson River at Albany in eastern New York with the Niagara River and the Great Lakes. Opened in 1825, it spurred the growth of New York City. Today it is chiefly recreational.

e·rig·er·on /əˈrijərən; -ˌrän/ ▸*n.* a widely distributed herbaceous plant of the daisy family, which is sometimes cultivated as an ornamental. • Genus *Erigeron*, family Compositae. ▷early 17th cent.: modern Latin, from Latin, 'groundsel' (the original sense in English), from Greek *ērigerōn*, from *ēri* 'early' + *gerōn* 'old man' (because the plant flowers early in the year, and some species bear gray down).

Er·iks·son variant spelling of ERICSSON[2].

Er·in /ˈerən/ ▸*n.* archaic or poetic/literary name for Ireland.

E·rin·ys /iˈrinəs/ ▸*n.* (*pl.* **E·rin·y·es** /iˈrinē-ēz/) (in Greek mythology) a Fury.

er·is·tic /iˈristik/ *formal* ▸*adj.* of or characterized by debate or argument. ■ (of an argument or arguer) aiming at winning rather than at reaching the truth.
▸*n.* a person given to debate or argument. ■ the art or practice or debate or argument. ▷mid 17th cent.: from Greek *eristikos*, from *erizein* 'to wrangle,' from *eris* 'strife.' **—er·is·ti·cal·ly** /-(ə)lē/ *adv.*

Er·i·tre·a /ˌerəˈtrēə; -ˈtrāə/ an independent state in northeastern Africa, on the Red Sea; pop. 4,447,000; capital, Asmara; languages, Tigre and Cushitic. ▷from Italian, from Latin *Mare Erythraeum* the Red Sea. **—Er·i·tre·an** *adj.* & *n.*

Eritrea was an Italian colony from 1890 to 1952, when it became part of Ethiopia. After a long guerrilla war, it became internally self-governing in 1991 and fully independent in 1993. A border dispute with Ethiopia from 1998 to 2000 required the continuing presence of UN peacekeepers.

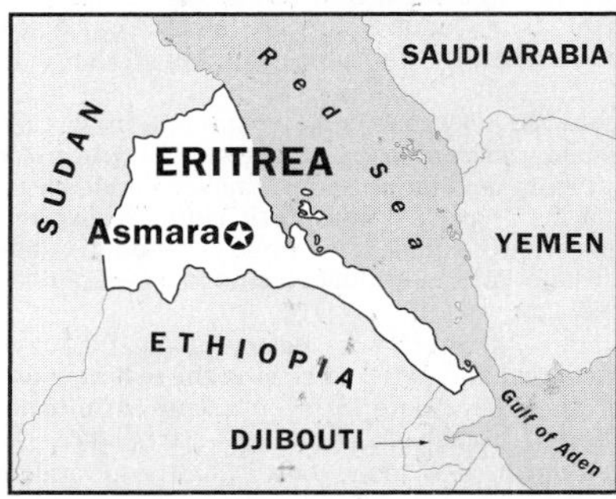

Er·lan·gen /ˈerˌläNGən/ an industrial city in southern Germany, on the Regnitz River; pop. 102,000.

Er·lan·ger /ˈərˌlaNGər/, Joseph (1874–1965), U.S. physiologist. Collaborating with Herbert Gasser, he showed that the velocity of a nerve impulse is proportional to the diameter of the fiber. Nobel Prize for Physiology or Medicine (1944, shared with Gasser).

Er·len·mey·er flask /ˈərlənˌmīər; ˈerlən-/ ▸*n.* a conical, flat-bottomed laboratory flask with a narrow neck. ▷late 19th cent.: named after Emil *Erlenmeyer* (1825–1909), German chemist.

erl-king /ˈərl ˌkiNG/ ▸*n.* (in Germanic mythology) a bearded giant or goblin who lures little children to the land of death. ▷late 18th cent.: from German *Erlkönig* 'alder king,' a mistranslation of Danish *ellerkonge* 'king of the elves.'

ERM ▸*abbr.* Exchange Rate Mechanism.

er·mine /ˈərmən/ ▸*n.* (*pl.* same or **er·mines**) **1** a stoat, esp. when in its white winter coat. ■ the white fur of the stoat, used for trimming garments, esp. the ceremonial robes of judges or peers. ■ *Heraldry* fur represented as black spots on a white ground, as a heraldic tincture. **2** (also **ermine moth**) a stout-bodied moth that has cream or white wings with black spots, and a very hairy caterpillar. • Family Arctiidae: several genera and species. ▷Middle English: from Old French *hermine*, probably from medieval Latin *(mus) Armenius* 'Armenian (mouse).' **—er·mined** *adj.*

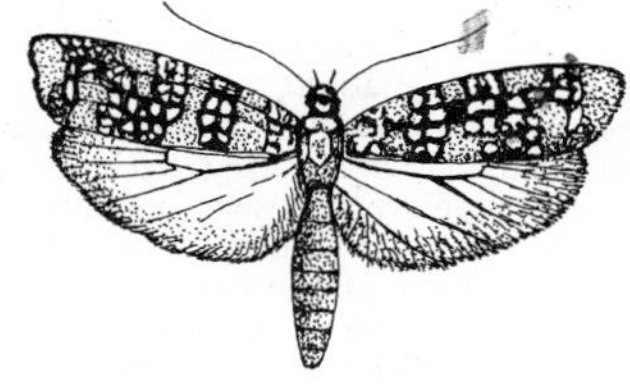
ermine moth

er·mines /ˈərmənz/ ▸*n. Heraldry* fur resembling ermine but with white spots on a black ground. ▷mid 16th cent.: perhaps from Old French *hermines*, plural of *herminet*, diminutive of *hermine* 'ermine.'

er·mi·nois /ˌərməˈnoiz/ ▸*n. Heraldry* fur resembling ermine but with black spots on a gold ground. ▷mid 16th cent.: from Old French, from *hermine* 'ermine.'

-ern ▸*suffix* forming adjectives such as *northern*. ▷Old English *-erne*, of Germanic origin.

erne /ərn/ ▸*n. poetic/literary* the sea eagle. ▷Old English *earn* 'eagle,' of Germanic origin; related to Dutch *arend*.

Ernst /ərnst/, Max (1891–1976), German artist. A leader of the Dada movement, he developed the techniques of collage, photomontage, and frottage.

e·rode /iˈrōd/ ▸*v.* [*trans.*] (often **be eroded**) (of wind, water, or other natural agents) gradually wear away (soil, rock, or land): *the cliffs have been eroded by the* *sea.* ■ [*intrans.*] (of soil, rock, or land) be gradually worn away by such natural agents. ■ *figurative* gradually destroy or be gradually destroyed: [*trans.*] *this humiliation has eroded what confidence Jean has* | [*intrans.*] *profit margins are eroding.* ■ *Medicine* (of a disease) gradually destroy (bodily tissue). ▷early 17th cent.: from French *éroder* or Latin *erodere,* from *e-* (variant of *ex-*) 'out, away' + *rodere* 'gnaw.' **—e·rod·i·ble** /iˈrōdəbəl/ *adj.*

e·rog·e·nous /iˈräjənəs/ ▶*adj.* (of a part of the body) sensitive to sexual stimulation: *erogenous zones.* ▷late 19th cent.: from **Eros** + **-genous**.

E·ros /ˈeräs; ˈi(ə)räs/ **1** *Greek Mythology* the god of love, son of Aphrodite. Roman equivalent **Cupid**. ■ sexual love or desire. ■ (in Freudian theory) the life instinct. Often contrasted with **Thanatos**. ■ (in Jungian psychology) the principle of personal relatedness in human activities, associated with the anima. Often contrasted with **Logos**. **2** *Astronomy* asteroid 433, discovered in 1898, which comes at times nearer to the earth than any celestial body except the moon. ▷Latin, from Greek, literally 'sexual love.'

e·ro·sion /iˈrōzʜən/ ▶*n.* the process of eroding or being eroded by wind, water, or other natural agents: *the problem of soil erosion.* ■ *figurative* the gradual destruction or diminution of something: *the erosion of support for the party.* ■ *Medicine* the gradual destruction of tissue or tooth enamel by physical or chemical action. ■ *Medicine* a place where surface tissue has been gradually destroyed: *patients with gastric erosions.* ▷mid 16th cent.: via French from Latin *erosio(n-),* from *erodere* 'wear or gnaw away' (see **erode**). **—e·ro·sion·al** *adj.* **—e·ro·sive** /iˈrōsiv/ *adj.*

e·rot·ic /iˈrätik/ ▶*adj.* of, relating to, or tending to arouse sexual desire or excitement. ▷mid 17th cent.: from French *érotique,* from Greek *erōtikos,* from *erōs, erōt-* 'sexual love.' **—e·rot·i·cal·ly** /-ik(ə)lē/ *adv.*

e·rot·i·ca /iˈrätikə/ ▶*n.* literature or art intended to arouse sexual desire. ▷mid 19th cent.: from Greek *erōtika,* neuter plural of *erōtikos* (see **erotic**).

e·rot·i·cism /iˈrätiˌsizəm/ ▶*n.* the quality or character of being erotic: *a disturbing blend of violence and eroticism.* ■ sexual desire or excitement.

e·rot·i·cize /iˈrätəˌsīz/ ▶*v.* [*trans.*] give (something or someone) erotic qualities: *certain symbols and body shapes are eroticized.* **—e·rot·i·ci·za·tion** /iˌrätəsəˈzāsʜən/ *n.*

er·o·tism /ˈerəˌtizəm/ ▶*n.* sexual desire or excitement; eroticism. ▷mid 19th cent.: from Greek *erōs, erōt-* 'sexual love' + **-ism**.

eroto- ▶*comb. form* relating to eroticism: *erotomania.* ▷from Greek *erōs, erōt-* 'sexual love.'

e·ro·to·gen·ic /iˌrätəˈjenik; -rōtə-/ (also **e·ro·tog·e·nous** /erəˈtäjənəs/) ▶*adj.* another term for **erogenous**.

er·o·tol·o·gy /ˌerəˈtäləjē/ ▶*n.* the study of sexual love and behavior.

e·ro·to·ma·ni·a /iˌrätəˈmānēə; -ˌrōtə-/ ▶*n.* *Psychiatry* a delusion in which a person (typically a woman) believes that another person (typically of higher social status) is in love with them. Also called **de Clerambault's syndrome**. ■ excessive sexual desire. **—e·ro·to·ma·ni·ac** /-ˈmānēˌak/ *n.*

err /ər; er/ ▶*v.* [*intrans.*] *formal* be mistaken or incorrect; make a mistake: *the judge had* ***erred in*** *ruling that the evidence was inadmissible.* ■ [often as *adj.*] (**erring**) sin; do wrong: *the erring brother who had wrecked his life.* ▷Middle English (in the sense 'wander, go astray'): from Old French *errer,* from Latin *errare* 'to stray.'

▶*PHRASES* □ **err on the right side** act so that the least harmful of possible mistakes or errors in is the most likely to occur. □ **err on the side of** display more rather than less of (a specified quality) in one's actions: *it is better to err on the side of caution.* □ **to err is human, to forgive divine** *proverb* it is human nature to make mistakes oneself while finding it hard to forgive others.

USAGE Traditionally, this word rhymes with *her,* although the pronunciation that rhymes with *hair* is now common.

er·rand /ˈerənd/ ▶*n.* a short journey undertaken in order to deliver or collect something, often on someone else's behalf: *she asked Tim to* ***run an errand*** *for her.* ■ *archaic* the purpose or object of such a journey: *she knew that if she stated her errand, she would not be able to see him.* ▷Old English *ǣrende* 'message, mission,' of Germanic origin; related to Old High German *ārunti,* and obscurely to Swedish *ärende* and Danish *ærinde.*

▶*PHRASE* □ **errand of mercy** a mission carried out to help someone in difficulty.

er·rand boy ▶*n. dated* a boy employed in a shop or office to make deliveries and run other errands. ■ *figurative* a man who is in the lowest rank of an organization: *Louis was Harry's errand boy, a gofer.*

er·rant /ˈerənt/ ▶*adj.* **1** [*attrib.*] erring or straying from the proper course or standards: *he could never forgive his daughter's errant ways.* ■ *Zoology* (of a polychaete worm) of a predatory kind that moves about actively and is not confined to a tube or burrow. **2** [often *postpositive*] *archaic or poetic/literary* traveling in search of adventure: *that same lady errant.* See also **knight-errant**. ▷Middle English (sense 2): sense 1 from Latin *errant-* 'erring,' from the verb *errare;* sense 2 from Old French *errant* 'traveling,' present participle of *errer,* from late Latin *iterare* 'go on a journey,' from *iter* 'journey.' Compare with **arrant**. **—er·ran·cy** /ˈerənsē/ *n.* (in sense 1) **—er·rant·ry** /-trē/ *n.* (in sense 2).

er·rat·ic /iˈratik/ ▶*adj.* not even or regular in pattern or movement; unpredictable: *her breathing was erratic.* ■ deviating from the normal or conventional in behavior or opinions: *neighbors were alarmed by increasingly erratic behavior.*

▶*n.* (also **erratic block** or **boulder**) *Geology* a rock or boulder that differs from the surrounding rock and is believed to have been brought from a distance by glacial action. ▷late Middle English: from Old French *erratique,* from Latin *erraticus,* from *errare* 'to stray, err.' **—er·rat·i·cal·ly** /-(ə)lē/ *adv.* **—er·rat·i·cism** /iˈratiˌsizəm/ *n.*

er·ra·tum /iˈrätəm; -ˈrā-; -ˈrat-/ ▶*n.* (*pl.* **-ta** /-tə/) an error in printing or writing. ■ (**errata**) a list of corrected errors appended to a book or published in a subsequent issue of a journal. ▷mid 16th cent.: from Latin, 'error,' neuter past participle of *errare* 'err.'

Er Rif /ər rif/ another name for **Rif Mountains**.

er·ro·ne·ous /iˈrōnēəs/ ▶*adj.* wrong; incorrect: *employers sometimes make erroneous assumptions.* ▷late Middle English: from Latin *erroneus* (from *erro(n-)* 'vagabond,' from *errare* 'to stray, err') + **-ous**. **—er·ro·ne·ous·ly** *adv.* **—er·ro·ne·ous·ness** *n.*

er·ror /ˈerər/ ▶*n.* a mistake: *spelling errors* | *an error of judgment.* See note at **mistake**. ■ the state or condition of being wrong in conduct or judgment: *the money had been paid* ***in error*** | *the crash was caused by* ***human error.*** ■ *Baseball* a misplay by a fielder that allows a batter to reach base or a runner to advance. ■ *technical* a measure of the estimated difference between the observed or calculated value of a quantity and its true value. ■ *Law* a mistake of fact or of law in a court's opinion, judgment or order. ■ *Philately* a postage stamp or item of postal stationery showing a major printing or perforation mistake. ▷Middle English: via Old French from Latin *error,* from *errare* 'to stray, err.' **—er·ror·less** *adj.*

▶*PHRASE* □ **see the error of one's ways** realize or acknowledge one's wrongdoing.

er·ror bar ▶*n.* *Mathematics* a line through a point on a graph, parallel to one of the axes, which represents the uncertainty or error of the corresponding coordinate of the point.

er·ror cor·rec·tion ▶*n.* *Computing* the automatic correction of errors that arise from the incorrect transmission of digital data.

er·ror mes·sage ▶*n.* *Computing* a message displayed on a monitor screen or printout, indicating that an incorrect instruction has been given, or that there is an error resulting from faulty software or hardware.

er·satz /ˈerˌsäts; -ˌzäts; erˈzäts/ ▶*adj.* (of a product) made or used as a substitute, typically an inferior one, for something else: *ersatz coffee.* ■ not real or genuine: *ersatz emotion.* See note at **spurious**. ▷late 19th cent.: from German, literally 'replacement.'

Erse /ərs/ ▶*n.* the Scottish or Irish Gaelic language. ▷early Scots form of **Irish**.

erst /ərst/ ▶*adv. archaic* long ago; formerly: *the friends whom erst you knew.* ▷Old English *ǣrest,* superlative of *ǣr* (see **ere**).

erst·while /ˈərstˌ(h)wīl/ ▶*adj.* [*attrib.*] former: *his erstwhile rivals.*

▶*adv. archaic* formerly: *Mary Anderson, erstwhile the queen of America's stage.*

e·ru·cic ac·id /iˈrōōsik/ ▶*n.* *Chemistry* a solid compound present in mustard and rape seeds. • An unsaturated fatty acid: chem. formula: $C_{21}H_{41}COOH$. ▷mid 19th cent.: *erucic* from Latin *eruca* 'rocket' (denoting the plant) + **-ic**.

e·ruct /iˈrəkt/ ▶*v.* [*intrans.*] *technical* emit stomach gas noisily through the mouth; belch.

e·ruc·ta·tion /iˌrəkˈtāsʜən/ ▶*n.* *formal* a belch. ▷late Middle English: from Latin *eructatio(n-),* from the verb *eructare,* from *e-* (variant of *ex-*) 'out' + *ructare* 'belch.'

er·u·dite /ˈer(y)əˌdīt/ ▶*adj.* having or showing great knowledge or learning. ▷late Middle English: from Latin *eruditus,* past participle of *erudire* 'instruct, train' (based on *rudis* 'rude, untrained'). **—er·u·dite·ly** *adv.* **—er·u·di·tion** /ˈer(y)ōōˌdisʜən/ *n.*

e·rum·pent /iˈrəmpənt/ ▶*adj. Biology* bursting forth or through a surface: *perithecia separately or collectively erumpent* | *figurative a spectacle of erumpent patriotism.*

e·rupt /iˈrəpt/ ▶*v.* [*intrans.*] (of a volcano) become active and eject lava, ash, and gases: *Mount Pinatubo began erupting in June.* ■ be ejected from an active volcano: *hot lava erupted from the crust.* ■ (of an object) explode with fire and noise resembling an active volcano: *smoke bombs erupted everywhere.* ■ break out or burst forth suddenly and dramatically: *fierce fighting erupted between the army and guerrillas* | *cheers erupted from the crowd.* ■ give vent to anger, enthusiasm, amusement, or other feelings in a sudden and noisy way: *the soldiers erupted in fits of laughter.* ■ (of a pimple, rash, or other prominent mark) suddenly appear on the skin. ■ (of the skin) suddenly develop such a pimple, rash, or mark. ■ (of a tooth) break through the gums during normal development. ▷mid 17th cent.: from Latin *erupt-* 'broken out,' from the verb *erumpere,* from *e-* (variant of *ex-*) 'out' + *rumpere* 'burst out, break.'

e·rup·tion /iˈrəpsʜən/ ▶*n.* an act or instance of erupting: *the eruption of Vesuvius* | *magma is stored in crustal reservoirs before eruption.* ■ a sudden outpouring of a particular substance from somewhere: *successive eruptions of lava from volcanic cones.* ■ a sudden outbreak of something, typically something unwelcome or noisy: *a sudden eruption of street violence.* ■ a spot, rash, or other prominent and reddish mark appearing suddenly on the skin. ▷late Middle English: from Old French, or from Latin *eruptio(n-),* from the verb *erumpere* (see **erupt**).

e·rup·tive /iˈrəptiv/ ▶*adj.* of, relating to, or formed by volcanic activity: *a history of the eruptive activity in an area.* ■ producing or characterized by eruptions: *an acute eruptive disease.*

er·uv /ˈerōōv/ ▶*n.* (*pl.* usu. **er·u·vim** /ˌerōōˈvēm/) *Judaism* an urban area enclosed by a wire boundary that symbolically extends the private domain of Jewish households into public areas, permitting activities within it that are normally forbidden in public on the Sabbath. ▷from Hebrew *ʿērūḇ,* from a base meaning 'mixture.'

Er·ving /ˈərvinɢ/, Julius Winfield (1950–), U.S. basketball player; known as **Dr. J.** He played for the Philadelphia 76ers 1977–87. Basketball Hall of Fame (1993).

-ery (also **-ry**) ▶*suffix* forming nouns: **1** denoting a class or kind: *confectionery* | *greenery.* **2** denoting an occupation, a state, a condition, or behavior: *archery* | *bravery* | *slavery.* ■ with depreciatory reference: *knavery* | *tomfoolery.* **3** denoting a place set aside for an activity or a grouping of things, animals, etc.: *orangery* | *rookery.* ▷from French *-erie,* based on Latin *-arius* and *-ator.*

e·ryn·gi·um /iˈrinjēəm/ ▶*n.* (*pl.* **-ums**) a plant of the genus *Eryngium* in the parsley family, esp. (in gardening) sea holly. ▷late 16th cent.: modern Latin, from Latin *eryngion,* from a diminutive of Greek *ērungos* 'sea holly.'

e·ryn·go /əˈrinɢgō/ ▶*n.* (*pl.* **-gos** or **-goes**) another term for **sea holly** or **eryngium**. ▷late 16th cent.: from Italian and Spanish *eringio,* from Latin *eryngion* (see **eryngium**).

er·y·sip·e·las /ˌerəˈsipələs/ ▶*n.* *Medicine* an acute, sometimes recurrent disease caused by a bacterial infection. It is characterized by large, raised red patches on the skin, esp. that of the face and legs, with fever and severe general illness. • This is caused by *Streptococcus pyogenes,* a Gram-positive coccus. ▷late Middle English: via Latin from Greek *erusipelas;* perhaps related to *eruthros* 'red' and *pella* 'skin.'

er·y·sip·e·loid /ˌerəˈsipəˌloid/ ▶*n.* *Medicine* dermatitis of the hands due to bacterial infection, occurring mainly among handlers of meat and fish products. • This is caused by *Erysipelothrix rhusiopathiae,* a Gram-positive bacterium occurring either as slightly curved rods or as filaments.

er·y·the·ma /ˌerəˈTHēmə/ ▸*n. Medicine* superficial reddening of the skin, usually in patches, as a result of injury or irritation causing dilatation of the blood capillaries. ▷late 18th cent.: from Greek *eruthēma*, from *eruthainein* 'be red,' from *eruthros* 'red.' —**er·y·the·mal** /-məl/ *adj.* —**er·y·them·a·tous** /-ˈTHemətəs; -ˈTHēmətəs/ *adj.*

e·ryth·rism /ˈerəˌTHrizəm; iˈriTH-/ ▸*n. Zoology* a congenital condition of abnormal redness in an animal's fur, plumage, or skin. ▷late 19th cent.: from Greek *eruthros* 'red' + **-ISM**.

e·ryth·ri·tol /əˈriTHrəˌtôl; -ˌtäl/ ▸*n. Chemistry* a sweet substance extracted from certain lichens and algae. It is used medicinally as a vasodilator. • A tetrahydric alcohol; chem. formula: $C_4H_{10}O_4$. ▷late 19th cent.: from *erythrite* (earlier name for *erythritol*) + **-OL**.

erythro- ▸*comb. form* (used commonly in zoological and medical terms) red: *erythrocyte*. ▷from Greek *eruthros* 'red.'

e·ryth·ro·blast /iˈriTHrōˌblast/ ▸*n. Physiology* an immature erythrocyte containing a nucleus. —**e·ryth·ro·blas·tic** /iˌriTHrōˈblastik/ *adj.*

e·ryth·ro·blas·to·sis /iˌriTHrōblaˈstōsis/ ▸*n. Medicine* the abnormal presence of erythroblasts in the blood. ■ (also **erythroblastosis fetalis**) another term for **HEMOLYTIC DISEASE OF THE NEWBORN**.

e·ryth·ro·cyte /iˈriTHrəˌsīt/ ▸*n.* a red blood cell that (in humans) is typically a biconcave disc without a nucleus. Erythrocytes contain the pigment hemoglobin, which imparts the red color to blood, and transport oxygen and carbon dioxide to and from the tissues. —**e·ryth·ro·cyt·ic** /iˌriTHrəˈsitik/ *adj.*

e·ryth·ro·gen·ic /iˌriTHrəˈjenik/ ▸*adj. Medicine* (of a bacterial toxin) causing inflammation and reddening of the skin.

er·y·throid /ˈriTHˌroid/ ▸*adj. Physiology* of or relating to erythrocytes.

e·ryth·ro·leu·ke·mi·a /iˌriTHrōlo͞oˈkēmēə/ ▸*n. Medicine* a rare acute form of leukemia in which there is proliferation of immature red and white blood cells.

e·ryth·ro·my·cin /iˌriTHrəˈmīsin/ ▸*n. Medicine* an antibiotic used in the treatment of infections caused by Gram-positive bacteria. It is similar in its effects to penicillin. • This is obtained from the streptomycete bacterium *Streptomyces erythreus*. ▷1950s: from elements of the modern Latin taxonomic name (see above) + **-IN**[1].

er·y·thro·ni·um /ˌeriˈTHrōnēəm/ ▸*n.* (*pl.* **-ni·ums** or **-ni·a** /-nēə/) a plant of a genus that includes dogtooth violet. • Genus *Erythronium*, family Liliaceae. ▷modern Latin, from Greek *(saturion) eruthronion* 'red-flowered (orchid).'

e·ryth·ro·poi·e·sis /iˌriTHrōpoiˈēsis/ ▸*n. Physiology* the production of red blood cells. —**e·ryth·ro·poi·et·ic** /-ˈetik/ *adj.*

e·ryth·ro·poi·e·tin /iˌriTHrōˈpoi-itn/ ▸*n. Biochemistry* a hormone secreted by the kidneys that increases the rate of production of red blood cells in response to falling levels of oxygen in the tissues.

Erz·ge·bir·ge /ˈertsgəˌbirgə/ a mountain range on the border between Germany and the Czech Republic. Also called the **ORE MOUNTAINS**.

Er·zu·rum /ˌerzo͝orˈo͞om/ a city in northeastern Turkey, capital of a mountainous province of the same name; pop. 242,400.

Es ▸*symbol* the chemical element einsteinium.

-es[1] ▸*suffix* **1** forming plurals of nouns ending in sibilant sounds: *boxes* | *kisses*. **2** forming plurals of certain nouns ending in *-o*: *potatoes* | *heroes*. ▷variant of **-S**[1].

-es[2] ▸*suffix* forming the third person singular of the present tense: **1** in verbs ending in sibilant sounds: *pushes*. **2** in verbs ending in *-o* (but not *-oo*): *goes*. ▷variant of **-S**[2].

ESA ▸*abbr.* European Space Agency.

E·sa·ki /eˈsäkē/, Leo (1925–), Japanese physicist. He investigated and pioneered the development of quantum-mechanical tunneling of electrons in semiconductor devices. He designed the tunnel diode (also called Esaki diode). Nobel Prize for Physics (1973, shared with Ivar Giaever 1929– and Brian D. Josephson 1940–).

E·sau /ˈēsô/ (in the Bible) the elder of the twin sons of Isaac and Rebecca, who sold his birthright to his brother Jacob and was tricked out of his father's blessing by his brother (Gen. 25, 27).

es·ca·be·che /ˌeskəˈbeCHā/ ▸*n.* a Spanish dish consisting of fried fish that is marinated and served cold. ▷Spanish.

es·ca·drille /ˈeskəˌdril; ˌeskəˈdril/ ▸*n.* a French squadron of aircraft. ▷early 20th cent.: French, literally 'flotilla, flight.'

es·ca·lade /ˌeskəˈläd; ˈeskəˌläd/ ▸*n. historical* the scaling of fortified walls using ladders, as a form of military attack. ▷late 16th cent.: from French, or from Spanish *escalada, escalado*, from medieval Latin *scalare* 'to scale, climb,' from Latin *scala* 'ladder.'

es·ca·late /ˈeskəˌlāt/ ▸*v.* [*intrans.*] increase rapidly: *the price of tickets escalated* | [as *adj.*] (**escalating**) *the escalating cost of health care*. ■ become or cause to become more intense or serious: [*intrans.*] *the disturbance* ***escalated into*** *a full-scale riot* | [*trans.*] *we do not want to escalate the war*. ▷1920s (in the sense 'travel on an escalator'): back-formation from **ESCALATOR**. —**es·ca·la·tion** /ˌeskəˈlāSHən/ *n.*

es·ca·la·tor /ˈeskəˌlātər/ ▸*n.* a moving staircase consisting of an endlessly circulating belt of steps driven by a motor, conveying people between the floors of a public building. ▷early 20th cent. (originally as a trade name): from *escalade* 'climb a wall by ladder' (from the noun **ESCALADE**), on the pattern of *elevator*.

es·ca·la·tor clause ▸*n.* a clause in a contract that allows for an increase or a decrease in wages or prices under certain conditions.

es·cal·lop /iˈskäləp; iˈskal-/ ▸*n.* **1** variant spelling of **ESCALOPE**. **2** another term for **SCALLOP** (sense 2). **3** *Heraldry* a scallop shell as a charge.
▸*v.* (**-loped, -lop·ing**) another term for **SCALLOP** (sense 3). ▷late 15th cent. (sense 2): from Old French *escalope* 'shell.' Compare with **ESCALOPE** and **SCALLOP**.

es·ca·lope /ˌeskəˈlōp; iˈskäləp; -ˈskal-/ ▸*n.* a thin slice of meat without any bone, typically a special cut of veal from the leg that is coated, fried, and served in a sauce. Also called **SCALLOP**. ▷French; compare with **ESCALLOP** and **SCALLOP**.

es·ca·pade /ˈeskəˌpād/ ▸*n.* an act or incident involving excitement, daring, or adventure. ▷mid 17th cent. (in the sense 'an escape'): from French, from Provençal or Spanish, from *escapar* 'to escape,' based on medieval Latin *ex-* 'out of' + *cappa* 'cloak.' Compare with **ESCAPE**.

es·cape /iˈskāp/ ▸*v.* [*intrans.*] break free from confinement or control: *two burglars have just escaped from prison* | [as *adj.*] (**escaped**) *escaped convicts*. ■ [*trans.*] elude or get free from (someone): *he drove along I-84 to escape the police*. ■ succeed in avoiding or eluding something dangerous, unpleasant, or undesirable: *the driver* ***escaped with*** *a broken knee* | [*trans.*] *a baby boy narrowly escaped death*. ■ [*trans.*] fail to be noticed or remembered by (someone): *the name escaped him* | *it may have escaped your notice, but this is not a hotel*. ■ (of a gas, liquid, or heat) leak from a container. ■ [*trans.*] (of words or sounds) issue involuntarily or inadvertently from (someone or their lips): *a sob escaped her lips*.
▸*n.* an act of breaking free from confinement or control: *the story of his escape from a POW camp* | *he could think of no way of escape, short of rudeness*. ■ an act of successfully avoiding something dangerous, unpleasant, or unwelcome: *the couple had a* ***narrow escape*** *from serious injury*. ■ a means of escaping from somewhere: [as *adj.*] *he had planned his escape route*. ■ a form of temporary distraction from reality or routine: *romantic novels should present an escape from the dreary realities of life*. ■ a leakage of gas, liquid, or heat from a container. ■ (also **escape key**) *Computing* a key on a computer keyboard that either interrupts the current operation or converts subsequent characters to a control sequence. ■ a garden plant or pet animal that has gone wild and (esp. in plants) become naturalized. ▷Middle English: from Old French *eschaper*, based on medieval Latin *ex-* 'out' + *cappa* 'cloak.' Compare with **ESCAPADE**. —**es·cap·a·ble** *adj.* —**es·cap·er** *n.*

es·cape clause ▸*n.* a clause in a contract that specifies the conditions under which one party can be freed from an obligation.

es·cap·ee /iˌskāˈpē; ˌeskāˈpē/ ▸*n.* a person who has escaped from somewhere, esp. prison.

es·cape hatch ▸*n.* a hatch for use as an emergency exit, esp. from a submarine, ship, or aircraft.

es·cape mech·an·ism ▸*n. Psychology* a mental process such as daydreaming that enables a person to avoid acknowledging unpleasant or threatening aspects of reality.

es·cape·ment /iˈskāpmənt/ ▸*n.* a mechanism in a clock or watch that alternately checks and releases the train by a fixed amount and transmits a periodic impulse from the spring or weight to the balance wheel or pendulum. ■ a mechanism in a typewriter that shifts the carriage a small fixed amount to the left after a key is pressed and released. ■ the part of the mechanism in a piano that enables the hammer to fall back as soon as it has struck the string. ▷late 18th cent.: from French *échappement*, from *échapper* 'to escape.'

es·cape ve·loc·i·ty ▸*n.* the lowest velocity that a body must have in order to escape the gravitational attraction of a particular planet or other object.

es·cape wheel ▸*n.* a toothed wheel in the escapement of a watch or clock.

es·cap·ism /iˈskāpˌizəm/ ▸*n.* the tendency to seek distraction and relief from unpleasant realities, esp. by seeking entertainment or engaging in fantasy. —**es·cap·ist** *n.* & *adj.*

es·cap·ol·o·gist /iˌskāˈpäləjist; ˌeskā-/ ▸*n.* an entertainer specializing in escaping from the confinement of such things as ropes, handcuffs, and chains. —**es·cap·ol·o·gy** /-ˈpäləjē/ *n.*

es·car·got /ˌeskärˈgō/ ▸*n.* a snail, esp. as an item on a menu. ▷French, from Old French *escargol*, from Provençal *escaragol*.

es·ca·role /ˈeskəˌrōl/ ▸*n.* an endive of a variety with broad undivided leaves and a slightly bitter flavor, used in salads. ▷early 20th cent.: from French, from Italian *scar(i)ola*, based on Latin *esca* 'food.'

es·carp·ment /iˈskärpmənt/ ▸*n.* a long, steep slope, esp. one at the edge of a plateau or separating areas of land at different heights. ▷early 19th cent.: from French *escarpement*, *escarpe* 'scarp,' from Italian *scarpa* 'slope.' Compare with **SCARP**.

Es·caut /esˈkō/ French name for **SCHELDT**.

-esce ▸*suffix* forming verbs, often denoting the initiation of action: *coalesce* | *effervesce*. ▷from or suggested by Latin verbs ending in *-escere*.

-escence ▸*suffix* forming nouns corresponding to adjectives ending in *-escent*, (such as *fluorescence* corresponding to *fluorescent*). ▷see **-ESCENT**.

-escent ▸*suffix* forming adjectives denoting a developing state or action: *coalescent* | *fluorescent*. ▷from French, or from Latin *-escent-* (present participial stem of verbs ending in *-escere*).

es·char /ˈesˌkär/ ▸*n. Medicine* a dry, dark scab or falling away of dead skin, typically caused by a burn, or by the bite of a mite, or as a result of anthrax infection. ▷late Middle English: from French *eschare* or late Latin *eschara* 'scar or scab,' from Greek (see also **SCAR**).

es·cha·tol·o·gy /ˌeskəˈtäləjē/ ▸*n.* the part of theology concerned with death, judgment, and the final destiny of the soul and of humankind. ▷mid 19th cent.: from Greek *eskhatos* 'last' + **-LOGY**. —**es·cha·to·log·i·cal** /eˌskatlˈäjikəl; ˌeskətl-/ *adj.* —**es·cha·tol·o·gist** /-jist/ *n.*

es·cha·ton /ˈeskəˌtän/ ▸*n.* (**the eschaton**) *Theology* the final event in the divine plan; the end of the world. ▷1930s: from Greek *eskhaton*, neuter of *eskhatos* 'last.'

es·cheat /esˈCHēt/ *chiefly historical* ▸*n.* the reversion of property to the state, or (in feudal law) to a lord, on the owner's dying without legal heirs. ■ an item of property affected by this.
▸*v.* [*intrans.*] (of land) revert to a lord or the state by escheat. ■ [*trans.*] [usu. as *adj.*] (**escheated**) hand over (land) as an escheat. ▷Middle English: from Old French *eschete*, based on Latin *excidere* 'fall away,' from *ex-* 'out of, from' + *cadere* 'to fall.'

Esch·er /ˈesHər/, M. C. (1898–1972), Dutch graphic artist; full name *Maurits Corneille Escher*. His prints are characterized by their sophisticated use of visual illusion.

es·chew /esˈCHo͞o/ ▸*v.* [*trans.*] deliberately avoid using; abstain from: *he appealed to the crowd to eschew violence*. ▷late Middle English: from Old French *eschiver*, ultimately of Germanic origin and related to German *scheuen* 'shun,' also to **SHY**[1]. —**es·chew·al** *n.*

Es·cof·fier /ˌeskäfˈyā/, Georges-Auguste (1846–1935), French chef. He gained an international reputation while working in London at the Savoy Hotel 1890–99 and later at the Carlton 1899–1919.

es·co·lar /ˌeskəˈlär/ ▸*n.* a large, elongated predatory fish occurring in tropical and temperate oceans throughout the world. Also called **SNAKE MACKEREL**. • Family Gempylidae: several genera and species. ▷mid 19th cent.: from Spanish, literally 'scholar,' so named because the ringed markings around the eyes resemble spectacles.

Es·con·di·do /ˌeskənˈdēdō/ a commercial city in southwestern California, north of San Diego; pop. 108,635.

Es·co·ri·al /eˈskôrēəl; ˌeskôrˈyäl/ a monastery and palace in central Spain, near Madrid, built in the late 16th century by Philip II.

es·cort ▸*n.* /ˈesˌkôrt/ a person, vehicle, ship, or aircraft, or a group of these, accompanying another for protection, security, or as a mark of rank: *a police escort | he was driven away under armed escort.* ■ a man who accompanies a woman to a particular social event. ■ a person, typically a woman, who may be hired to accompany someone socially: [as *adj.*] *an escort agency.*
▸*v.* /iˈskôrt/ [*trans.*] accompany (someone or something) somewhere, esp. for protection or security, or as a mark of rank: *Shiona escorted Janice to the door | the shipment was escorted by armed patrol boats.* ▷late 16th cent. (originally denoting a body of armed men escorting travelers): from French *escorte* (noun), *escorter* (verb), from Italian *scorta,* feminine past participle of *scorgere* 'to conduct, guide,' based on Latin *ex-* 'out of' + *corrigere* 'set right' (see CORRECT).

es·cri·toire /ˌeskriˈtwär/ ▸*n.* a small writing desk with drawers and compartments. ▷late 16th cent.: from French, from medieval Latin *scriptorium* 'writing room' (see SCRIPTORIUM).

es·crow /ˈeskrō/ *Law* ▸*n.* a bond, deed, or other document kept in the custody of a third party, taking effect only when a specified condition has been fulfilled. ■ [usu. as *adj.*] a deposit or fund held in trust or as a security: *an escrow account.* ■ the state of being kept in custody or trust in this way: *the board holds funds in escrow.*
▸*v.* [*trans.*] place in custody or trust in this way. ▷late 16th cent.: from Old French *escroe* 'scrap, scroll,' from medieval Latin *scroda,* of Germanic origin; related to SHRED.

es·cu·do /iˈsko͞odō/ ▸*n.* (*pl.* **-dos**) the basic monetary unit of Portugal (until the introduction of the euro) and Cape Verde, equal to 100 centavos. ▷Spanish and Portuguese, from Latin *scutum* 'shield.'

es·cu·lent /ˈeskyələnt/ *formal* ▸*adj.* fit to be eaten; edible.
▸*n.* a thing, esp. a vegetable, fit to be eaten. ▷early 17th cent.: from Latin *esculentus,* from *esca* 'food,' from *esse* 'eat.'

es·cutch·eon /iˈskəCHən/ ▸*n.* **1** a shield or emblem bearing a coat of arms. **2** (also **escutcheon plate**) a flat piece of metal for protection and often ornamentation, around a keyhole, door handle, or light switch. ▷late 15th cent.: from Anglo-Norman French *escuchon,* based on Latin *scutum* 'shield.' —**es·cutch·eoned** *adj.*
▸**PHRASES** □ **a blot on one's escutcheon** a stain on one's reputation or character. □ **escutcheon of pretense** a small shield within a coat of arms, bearing another coat or device to which the bearer has a claim, esp. one to which a man's wife is heiress.

Esd. ▸*abbr.* Esdras, either in the Apocrypha or the Vulgate (in biblical references).

Es·dras /ˈezdrəs/ **1** either of two books of the Apocrypha. The first is mainly a compilation from Chronicles, Nehemiah, and Ezra; the second is a record of angelic revelation. **2** (in the Vulgate) the books of Ezra and Nehemiah.

ESE ▸*abbr.* east-southeast.

-ese ▸*suffix* forming adjectives and nouns: **1** denoting an inhabitant or language of a country or city: *Taiwanese | Viennese.* **2** *often derogatory* (esp. with reference to language) denoting character or style: *journalese | officialese.* ▷from Old French *-eis,* based on Latin *-ensis.*

es·em·plas·tic /ˌesemˈplastik/ ▸*adj. rare* molding into one; unifying. ▷early 19th cent.: from Greek *es* 'into' + *hen* (neuter of *heis* 'one') + PLASTIC; formed irregularly by Coleridge, probably suggested by German *Ineinsbildung,* in the same sense. —**es·em·plas·ti·cal·ly** /-(ə)lē/ *adv.*

es·er·ine /ˈesəˌrēn; ˈesərin/ ▸*n. Chemistry* another term for PHYSOSTIGMINE. ▷mid 19th cent.: from French *ésérine,* from Efik *esere.*

Es·fa·han /ˌesfəˈhän/ variant spelling of ISFAHAN.

Esk. ▸*abbr.* Eskimo.

es·ker /ˈeskər/ ▸*n. Geology* a long ridge of gravel and other sediment, typically having a winding course, deposited by meltwater from a retreating glacier or ice sheet. ▷mid 19th cent.: from Irish *eiscir.*

Es·ki·mo /ˈeskəˌmō/ ▸*n.* (*pl.* same or **-mos**) **1** *often offensive* a member of an indigenous people inhabiting northern Canada, Alaska, Greenland, and eastern Siberia, traditionally living by hunting (esp. of seals) and by fishing. **2** either of the two main languages of this people (Inuit and Yupik), forming a major division of the Eskimo-Aleut family.
▸*adj.* of or relating to the Eskimos or their languages. ▷via French *Esquimaux,* possibly from Spanish *esquimao, esquimal,* from Montagnais *ayas̆kimew* 'netter of snowshoes,' probably applied first to the Micmac and later to the Eskimo (see HUSKY²).

USAGE 1 In recent years, **Eskimo** has come to be regarded as offensive because of one of its possible etymologies (Abnaki *askimo* 'eater of raw meat'), but this descriptive name is accurate since Eskimos traditionally derived their vitamins from eating raw meat. This dictionary gives another possible etymology above, but the etymological problem is still unresolved.
2 The peoples inhabiting the regions from northwestern Canada to western Greenland call themselves **Inuit** (see **usage** at INUIT). Since there are no Inuit living in the U.S., **Eskimo** is the only term that can be properly applied to all of the peoples as a whole, and it is still widely used in anthropological and archaeological contexts. The broader term **Native American** is sometimes used to refer to Eskimo and Aleut peoples.
See **usage** at NATIVE AMERICAN.

Es·ki·mo-Al·eut ▸*n.* the family of languages comprising Inuit, Yupik, and Aleut.
▸*adj.* of or relating to this family of languages.

Es·ki·mo cur·lew ▸*n.* a small New World curlew with a striped head, formerly common in the arctic tundra but now close to extinction. • *Numenius borealis,* family Scolopacidae.

Es·ki·mo pie ▸*n. trademark* a bar of chocolate-coated ice cream.

Es·ki·mo roll ▸*n.* a complete rollover in kayaking, from upright to capsized to upright.

Es·ki·se·hir /ˌeskisHəˈhi(ə)r/ an industrial and spa city in west central Turkey, the capital of Eskisehir province; pop. 413,000.

ESL ▸*abbr.* English as a second language.

ESN ▸*abbr.* electronic serial number, a unique identifying number programmed into a mobile phone.

ESOL /ˈēˌsäl/ ▸*abbr.* English for speakers of other languages.

ESOP ▸*abbr.* employee stock ownership plan; a plan by which a company's capital stock is bought by its employees or workers.

e·soph·a·gi·tis /iˌsäfəˈjītis/ ▸*n. Medicine* inflammation of the esophagus.

e·soph·a·go·scope /iˈsäfəgəˌskōp/ ▸*n.* an instrument for the inspection or treatment of the esophagus.

e·soph·a·gus /iˈsäfəgəs/ (*Brit.* **oe·soph·a·gus**) ▸*n.* (*pl.* **-gi** /-ˌgī; -ˌjī/ or **-gus·es**) the part of the alimentary canal that connects the throat to the stomach; the gullet. In humans and other vertebrates it is a muscular tube lined with mucous membrane. ▷late Middle English: modern Latin, from Greek *oisophagos.* —**e·soph·a·ge·al** /iˌsäfəˈjēəl/ *adj.*

es·o·ter·ic /ˌesəˈterik/ ▸*adj.* intended for or likely to be understood by only a small number of people with a specialized knowledge or interest: *esoteric philosophical debates.* ▷mid 17th cent.: from Greek *esōterikos,* from *esōterō,* comparative of *esō* 'within,' from *es, eis* 'into.' Compare with EXOTERIC. —**es·o·ter·i·cal·ly** /-(ə)lē/ *adv.* —**es·o·ter·i·cism** /-ˈterəˌsizəm/ *n.* —**es·o·ter·i·cist** /-ˈterəsist/ *n.*

es·o·ter·i·ca /ˌesəˈterikə/ ▸*n.* esoteric or highly specialized subjects or publications. ▷early 20th cent.: from Greek *esōterika,* neuter plural of *esōterikos* 'esoteric.'

ESP ▸*abbr.* ■ electrostatic precipitator. ■ extrasensory perception.

esp. ▸*abbr.* especially.

es·pa·drille /ˈespəˌdril/ ▸*n.* a light canvas shoe with a plaited fiber sole. ▷late 19th cent.: from French, from Provençal *espardi(l)hos,* from *espart* 'esparto,' from Latin *spartum* (see ESPARTO).

espadrille

es·pal·ier /iˈspalyər; -ˌyā/ ▸*n.* a fruit tree or ornamental shrub whose branches are trained to grow flat against a wall, supported on a lattice or a framework of stakes. ■ a lattice or framework of this type.
▸*v.* [*trans.*] train (a tree or shrub) in such a way. ▷mid 17th cent.: from French, from Italian *spalliera,* from *spalla* 'shoulder,' from Latin *spatula* (see SPATULA), in late Latin 'shoulder blade.'

Es·pa·ña /esˈpänyə/ Spanish name for SPAIN.

es·par·to /iˈspärtō/ (also **esparto grass**) ▸*n.* (*pl.* **-tos**) a coarse grass with tough narrow leaves, native to Spain and North Africa. It is used to make ropes, wickerwork, and high-quality paper. • *Stipa tenacissima,* family Gramineae. ▷mid 19th cent.: from Spanish, via Latin from Greek *sparton* 'rope.'

es·pe·cial /iˈspesHəl/ ▸*adj.* [*attrib.*] better or greater than usual; special: *these traditions are of especial interest to feminists.* ■ for or belonging chiefly to one person or thing: *her outburst was for my especial benefit.* ▷late Middle English: via Old French from Latin *specialis* 'special,' from *species* (see SPECIES).

es·pe·cial·ly /iˈspesHəlē/ ▸*adv.* **1** used to single out one person, thing, or situation over all others: *he despised them all, especially Sylvester | a new song, written especially for Jonathan.* **2** to a great extent; very much: *he didn't especially like dancing* | [as *submodifier*] *sleep is especially important for growing children.*

USAGE There is some overlap in the uses of **especially** and **specially**. In the broadest terms, both words mean 'particularly' and the preference for one word over the other is linked with particular conventions of use rather than with any deep difference in meaning. For example, there is little to choose between *written* **especially** *for Jonathan* and *written* **specially** *for Jonathan,* and neither is more correct than the other. On the other hand, in sentences such as *he despised them all,* **especially** *Sylvester,* substitution of **specially** is found in informal uses but should not be used in written English, while in *the car was* **specially** *made for the occasion,* substitution of **especially** is somewhat unusual. Overall, **especially** is by far the more common of the two.

Es·pe·ran·to /ˌespəˈräntō/ ▸*n.* an artificial language devised in 1887 as an international medium of communication, based on roots from the chief European languages. ▷from the name *Dr. Esperanto,* used as a pen name by the inventor of the language, Ludwik L. Zamenhof (1858–1917), Polish physician; the literal sense is 'one who hopes' (based on Latin *sperare* 'to hope'). —**Es·pe·ran·tist** /-tist/ *n.*

es·pi·al /iˈspī(ə)l/ ▸*n. archaic* the action of watching or catching sight of something or someone or the fact of being seen: *he withdrew from his point of espial.* ▷late Middle English (in the sense 'spying'): from Old French *espiaille,* from *espier* 'espy.'

es·pi·o·nage /ˈespēəˌnäzH; -ˌnäj/ ▸*n.* the practice of spying or of using spies, typically by governments to obtain political and military information. ▷late 18th cent.: from French *espionnage,* from *espionner* 'to spy,' from *espion* 'a spy.'

Es·pi·ri·tu San·to /eˈspiritо͞o ˈsäntо͞o/ a volcanic island in northwestern Vanuatu, the largest in the country. Largely agricultural, it was the site of U.S. bases during World War II.

es·pla·nade /ˈespləˌnäd; -ˌnād/ ▸*n.* a long, open, level area, typically beside the sea, along which people may walk for pleasure. ■ an open, level space separating a fortress from a town. ▷late 16th cent. (denoting an area of flat ground on top of a rampart): from French, from Italian *spianata,* from Latin *explanatus* 'flattened, leveled,' from *explanare* (see EXPLAIN).

Es·poo /ˈespō/ the second-largest city in Finland, in the southern part of the country, a western suburb of Helsinki; pop. 173,000.

Es·po·si·to /ˌespəˈzētō/, Phil (1942–), Canadian ice hockey player. He played for the Chicago Blackhawks 1964–67, the Boston Bruins 1967–75, and the New York Rangers 1975–81. Hockey Hall of Fame (1984).

es·pous·al /iˈspouzəl; -səl/ ▸*n.* **1** [in *sing.*] an act of adopting or supporting a cause, belief, or way of life: *his espousal of the leftist cause.* **2** *archaic* a marriage or

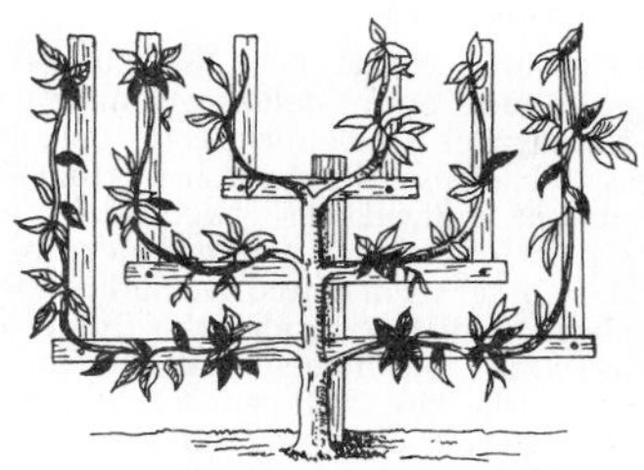
espalier

Pronunciation Key ə ago; ər over; ˈə or ˌə up; ˈər or ˌər fur; a hat; ā rate; ä car; CH chew; e let; ē see; e(ə)r air; i fit; ī by; i(ə)r ear; NG sing; ō go; ô for; oi boy; o͝o good; o͞o goo; ou out; SH she; TH thin; TH then; (h)w why; ZH vision

engagement. ▷late Middle English: from Old French *espousaille*, from Latin *sponsalia* 'betrothal,' neuter plural of *sponsalis* (adjective), from *sponsare* 'espouse, betroth.'

es·pouse /i'spouz/ ▸*v.* [*trans.*] **1** adopt or support (a cause, belief, or way of life): *she espoused communism.* **2** *archaic* marry: *Edward had espoused the Lady Grey.* ■ (**be espoused to**) (of a woman) be engaged to (a particular man). ▷late Middle English (in the sense 'take as a spouse'): from Old French *espouser*, from Latin *sponsare*, from *sponsus* 'betrothed,' past participle of *spondere*. —**es·pous·er** *n.*

es·pres·si·vo /ˌespre'sēvō/ ▸*adv.* & *adj. Music* (esp. as a direction) with expression of feeling. ▷Italian, from Latin *expressus* 'distinctly presented.'

es·pres·so /e'spresō/ ▸*n.* (*pl.* **-sos**) strong black coffee made by forcing steam through ground coffee beans. ▷1940s: from Italian (*caffè*) *espresso*, literally 'pressed out (coffee).'

USAGE The often-occurring variant spelling **expresso**—and its pronunciation /ik'spresō/ —is incorrect and was probably formed by analogy with **express**.

es·prit / e'sprē/ ▸*n.* the quality of being lively, vivacious, or witty. ▷French, from Latin *spiritus* 'spirit.'

es·prit de corps /eˌsprē də 'kôr/ ▸*n.* a feeling of pride, fellowship, and common loyalty shared by the members of a particular group. ▷late 18th cent.: French, literally 'spirit of the body.'

es·prit de l'es·ca·lier /eˌsprē də ˌleskal'yā/ ▸*n.* used to refer to the fact that a witty remark or retort often comes to mind after the opportunity to make it has passed. ▷early 20th cent.: French, literally 'wit of the staircase.'

es·py /i'spī/ ▸*v.* (**-pies, -pied**) [*trans.*] *poetic/literary* catch sight of: *she espied her daughter rounding the corner.* ▷Middle English: from Old French *espier*, ultimately of Germanic origin and related to Dutch *spieden* and German *spähan*. Compare with **SPY**.

Esq. ▸*abbr.* Esquire.

-esque ▸*suffix* (forming adjectives) in the style of; resembling: *carnivalesque | Reaganesque | Houdini-esque.* ▷from French, via Italian *-esco* from medieval Latin *-iscus*.

es·quire /'eskwīr; i'skwīr/ ▸*n.* **1** (**Esquire**) (abbr.: **Esq.**) a title appended to a lawyer's surname. ■ *Brit.* a polite title appended to a man's name when no other title is used, typically in the address of a letter or other documents: *Robert A. Pearson Esquire.* **2** *historical* a young nobleman who, in training for knighthood, acted as an attendant to a knight. ■ an officer in the service of a king or nobleman. ■ [as *title*] a landed proprietor or country squire. ▷late Middle English: from Old French *esquier*, from Latin *scutarius* 'shield-bearer,' from *scutum* 'shield'; compare with **SQUIRE**. Sense 2 was the original denotation, sense 1 being at first a courtesy title given to such a person.

es·qui·va·li·ence /eskwə'vālēəns/ ▸*n.* the willful avoidance of one's official responsibilities; the shirking of duties: *after three subordinates attested to his esquivalience, Lieutenant Claiborne was dismissed.* ■ an unwillingness to work, esp. as part of a group effort: *Bovich was chided by teammates for her esquivalience.* ■ lack of interest or motivation: *a teenager's esquivalience is not necessarily symptomatic of depression.* ▷late 19th cent.: perhaps from French *esquiver* 'dodge, slink away.' —**es·qui·va·li·ent** *adj.* —**es·qui·va·li·ent·ly** *adv.*

ESR *Physics* ▸*abbr.* electron spin resonance.

ess /es/ ▸*n.* a thing shaped like the letter S. ▷mid 16th cent.: the letter *S* represented as a word.

-ess[1] ▸*suffix* forming nouns denoting female gender: *abbess | adulteress | tigress.* ▷from French *-esse*, via late Latin from Greek *-issa*.

USAGE The suffix **-ess** has been used since the Middle Ages to form nouns denoting female persons, using a neutral or a male form as the base (such as **hostess** and **actress** from **host** and **actor**). Despite the apparent equivalence between the male and female pairs of forms, however, they are rarely equivalent in terms of actual use and connotation in modern English (consider the differences in meaning and use between **manager** and **manageress**). In the late 20th century, as the role of women in society changed, some of these feminine forms became problematic and are now regarded as old-fashioned, sexist, and patronizing (e.g., **poetess, authoress, editress**). The 'male' form is increasingly being used as the 'neutral' form, where the gender of the person concerned is simply unspecified.

-ess[2] ▸*suffix* forming abstract nouns from adjectives, such as *largess.* ▷Middle English via French *-esse* from Latin *-itia*.

es·say ▸*n.* /'esā/ **1** a short piece of writing on a particular subject. **2** *formal* an attempt or effort: *a misjudged essay.* ■ a trial design of a postage stamp yet to be accepted.

▸*v.* /e'sā/ [*trans.*] *formal* attempt or try: *essay a smile.* ▷late 15th cent. (as a verb in the sense 'test the quality of'): alteration of **ASSAY**, by association with Old French *essayer*, based on late Latin *exagium* 'weighing,' from the base of *exigere* 'ascertain, weigh'; the noun (late 16th cent.) is from Old French *essai* 'trial.'

es·say·ist /'esā-ist/ ▸*n.* a person who writes essays, esp. as a literary genre.

es·say·is·tic /ˌesā'istik/ ▸*adj.* characteristic of or used in essays; discursive; informal.

es·se /'esē; 'ese/ ▸*n. Philosophy* essential nature or essence. See also **IN ESSE**. ▷mid 16th cent.: Latin, literally 'to be' (used as a noun).

Es·sen /'esən/ an industrial city in the Ruhr valley, in northwestern Germany; pop. 627,000.

es·sence /'esəns/ ▸*n.* the intrinsic nature or indispensable quality of something, esp. something abstract, that determines its character: *conflict is the essence of drama.* ■ *Philosophy* a property or group of properties of something without which it would not exist or be what it is. ■ something that exists; in particular, a spiritual entity: *the position that names express essences.* ■ an extract or concentrate obtained from a particular plant or other matter and used for flavoring or scent. ▷late Middle English: via Old French from Latin *essentia*, from *esse* 'be.'

▸*PHRASES* □ **in essence** basically and without regard for peripheral details; fundamentally: *in detail the class system is complex but in essence it is simple.* □ **of the essence** critically important: *time will be of the essence.*

Es·sene /i'sēn; 'esēn/ ▸*n.* a member of an ancient Jewish ascetic sect of the 2nd century BC–2nd century AD in Palestine, who lived in highly organized groups and held property in common. The Essenes are widely regarded as the authors of the Dead Sea Scrolls. ▷from Latin *Esseni* (plural), from Greek *Essēnoi*, perhaps from Aramaic.

es·sen·tial /i'senSHəl/ ▸*adj.* **1** absolutely necessary; extremely important: [with *infinitive*] *it is essential to keep up-to-date records | fiber is an essential ingredient.* See notes at **INHERENT, NECESSARY**. ■ [*attrib.*] fundamental or central to the nature of something or someone: *the essential weakness of the plaintiff's case.* ■ *Biochemistry* (of an amino acid or fatty acid) required for normal growth but not synthesized in the body and therefore necessary in the diet. **2** *Medicine* (of a disease) with no known external stimulus or cause; idiopathic: *essential hypertension.*

▸*n.* (usu. **essentials**) a thing that is absolutely necessary: *we had only the bare essentials in the way of gear.* ■ (**essentials**) the fundamental elements or characteristics of something: *he was quick to grasp the essentials of an opponent's argument.* ▷Middle English (in the sense 'in the highest degree'): from late Latin *essentialis*, from Latin *essentia*. —**es·sen·ti·al·i·ty** /iˌsenSHē'alitē/ *n.* —**es·sen·tial·ness** *n.*

es·sen·tial·ism /i'senSHəˌlizəm/ ▸*n. Philosophy* a belief that things have a set of characteristics that make them what they are, and that the task of science and philosophy is their discovery and expression; the doctrine that essence is prior to existence. Compare with **EXISTENTIALISM**. ■ the view that all children should be taught on traditional lines the ideas and methods regarded as essential to the prevalent culture. ■ the view that categories of people, such as women and men, or heterosexuals and homosexuals, or members of ethnic groups, have intrinsically different and characteristic natures or dispositions. —**es·sen·tial·ist** *n.* & *adj.*

es·sen·tial·ly /i'senSHəlē/ ▸*adv.* used to emphasize the basic, fundamental, or intrinsic nature of a person, thing, or situation: [*sentence adverb*] *essentially, they are amateurs.*

es·sen·tial oil ▸*n.* a natural oil typically obtained by distillation and having the characteristic fragrance of the plant or other source from which it is extracted.

Es·se·qui·bo /ˌesə'kwēbō;-'kēbō/ a river in Guyana that rises in the Guiana Highlands and flows north for about 600 miles (965 km) to the Atlantic Ocean.

Es·sex /'esiks/ **1** a county in eastern England; county town, Chelmsford. **2** a town in northwestern Vermont that includes the village of Essex Junction; pop. 18,626.

EST ▸*abbr.* Eastern Standard Time (see **EASTERN TIME**).

est /est/ ▸*n.* a system for self-improvement aimed at developing a person's potential through intensive group awareness and training sessions. ▷1970s: acronym from *Erhard Seminars Training*, from the name of Werner *Erhard* (born 1935), the American businessman who devised the technique.

est. ▸*abbr.* ■ established. ■ estimated.

-est[1] /əst; ist/ ▸*suffix* forming the superlative of adjectives (such as *shortest*, *widest*), and of adverbs (such as *soonest*). ▷Old English *-ost-*, *-ust-*, *-ast-*.

-est[2] /əst; ist/ (also **-st** /st/) ▸*suffix archaic* forming the second person singular of verbs: *canst | goest.* ▷Old English *-est*, *-ast*, *-st*.

es·tab·lish /i'stablisH/ ▸*v.* [*trans.*] **1** set up (an organization, system, or set of rules) on a firm or permanent basis: *the British established a rich trade with Portugal.* ■ initiate or bring about (contact or communication): *the two countries established diplomatic relations.* **2** achieve permanent acceptance for (a custom, belief, practice, or institution): *the principle of the supremacy of national parliaments needs to be firmly established.* ■ achieve recognition or acceptance for (someone) in a particular capacity: *he had* ***established himself as*** *a film star.* ■ [*intrans.*] (of a plant) take root and grow. ■ introduce (a character, set, or location) into a film or play and allow its identification: *establish the location with a wide shot.* **3** show (something) to be true or certain by determining the facts: [with *clause*] *the police established that the two passports were forgeries.* **4** *Bridge* ensure that one's remaining cards in (a suit) will be winners (if not trumped) by playing off the high cards in that suit. ▷late Middle English (recorded earlier as *stablish*): from Old French *establiss-*, lengthened stem of *establir*, from Latin *stabilire* 'make firm,' from *stabilis* (adjective) 'stable.' —**es·tab·lish·er** *n.*

es·tab·lished /i'stablisHt/ ▸*adj.* **1** (of a custom, belief, practice, or institution) having been in existence for a long time and therefore recognized and generally accepted: *the ceremony was an established event in the annual calendar.* ■ (of a person) recognized and accepted in a particular capacity: *an established artist.* ■ (of a plant) having taken root; growing well. **2** (of a church or religion) recognized by the government as the national church or religion.

▸*PHRASE* □ **the Established Church** the Church of England or of Scotland.

es·tab·lish·ment /i'stablisHmənt/ ▸*n.* **1** the action of establishing something or being established: *the establishment of a Palestinian state.* ■ the recognition by the state of a national church or religion: *Congress shall make no law respecting an establishment of religion.* ■ *archaic* a marriage. **2** a business organization, public institution, or household: *hotels or catering establishments.* ■ [usu. in *sing.*] the premises or staff of such an organization: *she entered this establishment as our housemaid.* **3** (usu. **the Establishment**) a group in a society exercising power and influence over matters of policy or taste, and seen as resisting change. ■ [with *adj.*] an influential group within a specified profession or area of activity: *rumblings of discontent among the medical establishment.* **4** (**the Establishment** or **the Church Establishment**) the ecclesiastical system organized by law. ■ the Church of England or of Scotland.

es·tab·lish·men·tar·i·an /iˌstablisHmən'terēən/ ▸*adj.* adhering to, advocating, or relating to the principle of an established church.

▸*n.* a person adhering to or advocating this. —**es·tab·lish·men·tar·i·an·ism** /-izəm/ *n.*

Es·tab·lish·ment Clause ▸*n. Law* the clause in the First Amendment of the U.S. Constitution that prohibits the establishment of religion by Congress.

es·ta·mi·net /esˌtamē'nā/ ▸*n.* a small cafe in France that sells alcoholic drinks. ▷French, from Walloon *staminé* 'cowshed,' from *stamo* 'a pole for tethering a cow,' probably from German *Stamm* 'stem.'

es·tan·cia /e'stänsēə/ ▸*n.* a cattle ranch in Latin America or the southwestern U.S. ▷mid 17th cent.: from Spanish, literally 'station,' from medieval Latin *stantia*, based on Latin *stare* 'to stand.'

es·tate /i'stāt/ ▸*n.* **1** an area or amount of land or property, in particular: ■ an extensive area of land in the country, usually with a large house, owned by one person or organization. ■ all the money and property owned by a particular person, esp. at death: *in his will, he divided his estate between his wife and daughter.* ■ a property where coffee, rubber, grapes, or other crops are cultivated. ■ *Brit.* a housing or commercial development. **2** (also **estate of the realm**) a class or order regarded as forming part of the body politic, in particular (in Britain), one of the three groups constituting Parliament, now the Lords Spiritual (the heads of the Church), the Lords Temporal (the peerage), and the Commons. They are also known as **the three estates.** ■ *dated* a particular class or category of people in society: *the spiritual welfare of all estates of men.* **3** *archaic or poetic/literary* a particular state, period, or condition in life: *programs for the improvement of man's estate* | *the holy estate of matrimony.* ■ grandeur, pomp, or state: *a chamber without a chair of estate.* ▷Middle English (in the sense 'state or condition'): from Old French *estat*, from Latin *status* 'state, condition,' from *stare* 'to stand.'

es·tate a·gent ▸*n. Brit.* a real estate agent. **—es·tate a·gen·cy** *n.*

es·tate car ▸*n. Brit.* a station wagon.

es·tate of the realm ▸*n.* see ESTATE (sense 2).

Es·tates Gen·er·al /iˈstāts/ another term for STATES-GENERAL.

es·tate tax ▸*n.* a tax levied on the net value of the estate of a deceased person before distribution to the heirs. Also called DEATH TAX.

es·teem /iˈstēm/ ▸*n.* respect and admiration, typically for a person: *he was held in high esteem by colleagues.* ▸*v.* [*trans.*] (usu. **be esteemed**) respect and admire: *many of these qualities are esteemed by managers* | [as *adj.*, with *submodifier*] (**esteemed**) *a highly esteemed scholar.* ■ *formal* consider; deem: [with *two objs.*] *I should esteem it a favor if you could speak to them.* ▷Middle English (as a noun in the sense 'worth, reputation'): from Old French *estime* (noun), *estimer* (verb), from Latin *aestimare* 'to estimate.' The verb was originally in the Latin sense, also 'appraise' (compare with ESTIMATE), used figuratively to mean 'assess the merit of.' Current senses date from the 16th cent.

THE RIGHT WORD **admire, appreciate, esteem, prize, regard, respect**

If you're a classical music aficionado, you might **appreciate** a good symphony orchestra, **admire** someone who plays the oboe, and **esteem** the works of Beethoven above all other classical composers.

All three of these verbs are concerned with recognizing the worth of something, but in order to *appreciate* it, you have to understand it well enough to judge it critically.

If you *admire* something, you appreciate its superiority (*to admire a pianist's performance*), while *esteem* goes one step further, implying that your admiration is of the highest degree (*a musician esteemed throughout the music world*).

You **prize** what you value highly or cherish, especially if it is a possession (*she prized her Stradivarius violin*), while **regard** is a more neutral term meaning to look at or to have a certain mental view of something, either favorable or unfavorable (*to regard him as a great musician;* | *to regard her as a ruthless competitor*).

To **respect** is to have a deferential regard for someone or something because of its worth or value (*to respect the conductor's interpretation of the music*).

Es·te·fan /eˈstefän; -ən/, Gloria (1957–), U.S. singer; born in Cuba; born *Gloria Fajardo.* She sings with and writes songs for the disco-pop and salsa band Miami Sound Machine.

es·ter /ˈestər/ ▸*n. Chemistry* an organic compound made by replacing the hydrogen of an acid by an alkyl or other organic group. Many naturally occurring fats and essential oils are esters of fatty acids. ▷mid 19th cent.: from German, probably from a blend of *Essig* 'vinegar' and *Äther* 'ether.' **—es·ter·i·fy** /iˈsterəˌfī/ *v.* (**-fies, -fied**).

es·ter·ase /ˈestərās; -rāz/ ▸*n. Biochemistry* an enzyme that hydrolyzes particular esters into acids and alcohols or phenols.

es·ter·i·fi·ca·tion /esˌterəfiˈkāsHən/ ▸*n. Chemistry* a reaction of an alcohol with an acid to produce an ester and water.

Esth. ▸*abbr. Bible* Esther.

Es·ther /ˈestər/ (in the Bible) a woman chosen on account of her beauty by the Persian king Ahasuerus (generally supposed to be Xerxes I) to be his queen. She used her influence with him to save the Israelites in captivity from persecution. ■ a book of the Bible containing an account of these events; a part survives only in Greek and is included in the Apocrypha.

es·thete ▸*n.* variant spelling of AESTHETE.

es·thet·ic, etc. ▸*adj.* AESTHETIC, etc.

es·ti·ma·ble /ˈestəməbəl/ ▸*adj.* worthy of great respect. ▷late 15th cent. (in the sense 'able to be estimated or appraised'; earlier in *inestimable*): via Old French from Latin *aestimabilis*, from *aestimare* 'to estimate.' **—es·ti·ma·bly** /-blē/ *adv.*

es·ti·mate ▸*v.* /ˈestəˌmāt/ [*trans.*] roughly calculate or judge the value, number, quantity, or extent of: *the aim is to estimate the effects of macroeconomic policy on the economy* | [with *clause*] *it is estimated that smoking causes 100,000 premature deaths every year* | [as *adj.*] (**estimated**) *an estimated cost of $140,000,000.*
▸*n.* /ˈestəmit/ an approximate calculation or judgment of the value, number, quantity, or extent of something: *at a rough estimate, our staff is recycling a quarter of the paper used.* ■ a written statement indicating the likely price that will be charged for specified work or repairs: *compare costs by getting estimates from at least two firms.* ■ a judgment of the worth or character of someone or something: *his high estimate of the poem.* ▷late Middle English: from Latin *aestimat-* 'determined, appraised,' from the verb *aestimare*. The noun originally meant 'intellectual ability, comprehension' (only in late Middle English), later 'valuing, a valuation' (compare with ESTIMATION). The verb originally meant 'to think well or badly of someone or something' (late 15th cent.), later 'regard as being, consider to be' (compare with ESTEEM). **—es·ti·ma·tive** /ˈestəˌmātiv/ *adj.*

es·ti·ma·tion /ˌestəˈmāsHən/ ▸*n.* a rough calculation of the value, number, quantity, or extent of something: *estimations of protein concentrations.* ■ [usu. in *sing.*] a judgment of the worth or character of someone or something: *the pop star rose in my estimation.* ▷late Middle English (originally in the sense 'comprehension, intuition,' also 'valuing, a valuation'): from Latin *aestimatio(n-)*, from *aestimare* 'determine, appraise' (see ESTIMATE).

es·ti·ma·tor /ˈestəˌmātər/ ▸*n.* **1** *Statistics* a rule, method, or criterion for arriving at an estimate of the value of a parameter. ■ a quantity used or evaluated as such an estimate. **2** a person who estimates the price, value, number, quantity, or extent of something.

es·ti·val /ˈestəvəl; eˈstī-/ (also **aes·ti·val**) ▸*adj. technical* belonging to or appearing in summer. ▷late Middle English: from Latin *aestivalis*, from *aestivus*, from *aestus* 'heat.'

es·ti·vate /ˈestəˌvāt/ (also **aes·ti·vate**) ▸*v.* [*intrans.*] *Zoology* (of an animal, particularly an insect, fish, or amphibian) spend a hot or dry period in a prolonged state of torpor or dormancy. ▷early 17th cent. (in the sense 'pass the summer'): from Latin *aestivat-*, from *aestivare* 'spend the summer,' from *aestus* 'heat.'

es·ti·va·tion /ˌestəˈvāsHən/ (also **aes·ti·va·tion**) ▸*n.* **1** *Zoology* prolonged torpor or dormancy of an animal during a hot or dry period. **2** *Botany* the arrangement of petals and sepals in a flower bud before it opens. Compare with VERNATION.

es·toile /eˈstoil/ ▸*n. Heraldry* a star with (usually six) wavy points or rays. ▷late 16th cent.: via Old French from Latin *stella* 'star.'

Es·to·ni·a /eˈstōnēə/ a Baltic country on the southern coast of the Gulf of Finland; pop. 1,341,000; capital, Tallinn; languages, Estonian (official) and Russian.

Previously ruled by the Teutonic Knights and then by Sweden, Estonia was ceded to Russia in 1721. It was proclaimed an independent republic in 1918 but was annexed by the Soviet Union in 1940 as a constituent republic, the Estonian SSR. With the breakup of the Soviet Union, Estonia regained its independence in 1991. In 2004 it joined both NATO and the EU.

Es·to·ni·an /eˈstōnēən/ ▸*adj.* of or relating to Estonia or its people or their language.
▸*n.* **1** a native or national of Estonia, or a person of Estonian descent. **2** the Finno-Ugric language of Estonia, closely related to Finnish.

es·top /eˈstäp/ ▸*v.* (**es·topped, es·top·ping**) [*trans.*] (usu. **be estopped from**) *Law* bar or preclude by estoppel. ▷late Middle English (in the sense 'stop up, dam, plug'): from Old French *estopper* 'stop up, impede,' from late Latin *stuppare*, from Latin *stuppa* 'tow, oakum.' Compare with STOP and STUFF.

es·top·pel /eˈstäpəl/ ▸*n. Law* the principle that precludes a person from asserting something contrary to what is implied by a previous action or statement of that person or by a previous pertinent judicial determination. ▷mid 16th cent.: from Old French *estouppail* 'bung,' from *estopper* (see ESTOP).

es·tra·di·ol /ˌestrəˈdīôl; -ˌäl/ (*Brit.* **oes·tra·di·ol**) ▸*n. Biochemistry* a major estrogen produced in the ovaries. ▷1930s: from ESTRUS + DI-[1] + -OL.

es·trange /iˈstrānj/ ▸*v.* [*trans.*] cause (someone) to be no longer close or affectionate to someone; alienate: *are you deliberately seeking to estrange your readers?* ▷late 15th cent.: from Old French *estranger*, from Latin *extraneare* 'treat as a stranger,' from *extraneus* 'not belonging to the family,' used as a noun to mean 'stranger.' Compare with STRANGE. **—es·trange·ment** *n.*

es·tranged /iˈstrānjd/ ▸*adj.* (of a person) no longer close or affectionate to someone; alienated: *Harriet felt more* **estranged from** *her daughter than ever* | *her estranged father.* ■ (of a wife or husband) no longer living with their spouse.

es·treat /iˈstrēt/ *Law, chiefly historical* ▸*v.* [*trans.*] enforce the forfeit of (a surety for bail or other recognizance).
▸*n.* a copy of a court record for use in the enforcement of a fine or forfeiture of a recognizance. ▷Middle English: from Old French *estraite*, feminine past participle of *estraire*, from Latin *extrahere* 'draw out' (see EXTRACT). **—es·treat·ment** *n.*

es·tri·ol /ˈestrīˌôl; -ˌäl; eˈstrīôl; eˈstrīäl/ (also **oes·tri·ol**) ▸*n. Biochemistry* an estrogen that is one of the metabolic products of estradiol. ▷1930s: from *estrane* (the parent molecule of most estrogens) + TRI- + -OL.

es·tro·gen /ˈestrəjən/ (*Brit.* **oes·tro·gen**) ▸*n.* any of a group of steroid hormones that promote the development and maintenance of female characteristics of the body. Such hormones are also produced artificially for use in oral contraceptives or to treat menopausal and menstrual disorders. ▷1920s: from ESTRUS + -GEN. **—es·tro·gen·ic** /ˌestrəˈjenik/ *adj.*

es·trone /ˈestrōn/ (*Brit.* **oes·trone**) ▸*n. Biochemistry* an estrogen similar to but less potent than estradiol. ▷1930s: from *estrane* (parent molecule of most estrogens) + -ONE.

es·trous cy·cle /ˈestrəs/ ▸*n.* the recurring reproductive cycle in many female mammals, including estrus, ovulation, and changes in the uterine lining.

es·trus /ˈestrəs/ (also **es·trum** or *chiefly Brit.* **oes·trus**) ▸*n.* a recurring period of sexual receptivity and fertility in many female mammals; heat: *a mare* **in estrus.** ▷late 17th cent.: from Greek *oistros* 'gadfly or frenzy.' **—es·trous** /ˈestrəs/ *adj.*

es·tu·ar·y /ˈesCHōōˌerē/ ▸*n.* (*pl.* **-ar·ies**) the tidal mouth of a large river, where the tide meets the stream. ▷mid 16th cent. (denoting a tidal inlet of any size): from Latin *aestuarium* 'tidal part of a shore,' from *aestus* 'tide.' **—es·tu·ar·i·al** /ˌesCHōōˈe(ə)rēəl/ *adj.* **—es·tu·a·rine** /ˈesCHōōəˌrīn; -əˌrēn/ *adj.*

Es·tu·ar·y Eng·lish ▸*n.* (in the UK) a type of accent identified as spreading outward from London and containing features of both received pronunciation and London speech.

es·tu·fa /eˈstōōfə/ ▸*n.* **1** a heated chamber in which Madeira wine is stored and matured. **2** an underground chamber in which a fire is kept permanently alight, used as a place of assembly by Pueblo Indians. ▷mid 19th cent.: from Spanish, probably based on Greek *tuphos* 'steam or smoke.'

esu ▸*abbr.* electrostatic unit(s).

e·su·ri·ent /iˈsōōrēənt/ ▸*adj. archaic* hungry or greedy. ▷late 17th cent.: from Latin *esurient-* 'being hungry,' from the verb *esurire*, from *esse* 'eat.' **—e·su·ri·ent·ly** *adv.*

ESV ▸*abbr.* earth satellite vehicle.

ET ▸*abbr.* ■ Eastern time. ■ extraterrestrial.

-et[1] ▸*suffix* forming nouns which were originally diminutives: *baronet* | *hatchet* | *tablet.* ▷from Old French *-et, -ete.*

Pronunciation Key ə *ago;* ər *over;* ˈə or ˌə *up;* ˈər or ˌər *fur;* a *hat;* ā *rate;* ä *car;* CH *chew;* e *let;* ē *see;* e(ə)r *air;* i *fit;* ī *by;* i(ə)r *ear;* NG *sing;* ō *go;* ô *for;* oi *boy;* ŏŏ *good;* ōō *goo;* ou *out;* SH *she;* TH *thin;* TH *then;* (h)w *why;* ZH *vision*

-et[2] (also **-ete**) ▶*suffix* forming nouns such as *comet*, and often denoting people: *athlete* | *poet*. ▷from Greek *-ētēs*.

ETA[1] ▶*abbr.* estimated time of arrival, in particular the time at which an aircraft or ship is expected to arrive at its destination.

ETA[2] /ˈetə/ a Basque separatist movement in Spain, founded in 1959 for an independent Basque state. ▷Basque acronym, from *Euzkadi ta Azkatasuna* 'Basque homeland and liberty.'

e·ta /ˈātə; ˈētə/ ▶*n.* the seventh letter of the Greek alphabet (H, η), transliterated as 'e' or 'ē.' ■ (**Eta**) [followed by Latin genitive] *Astronomy* the seventh star in a constellation: *Eta Carinae.*

é·ta·gère /ˌātäˈZHer/ (also **e·ta·gere**) ▶*n.* (*pl.* **étagères** /ˌātäˈZHer(z)/) a piece of furniture with a number of open shelves for displaying ornaments. ▷French *étagère*, from *étage* 'shelf.'

e-tail·er /ˈē ˌtālər/ ▶*n.* a retailer selling goods via electronic transactions on the Internet. ▷1990s: blend of *e-* 'electronic' and *retailer*.

et al. /ˌet ˈal; ˌet ˈäl/ ▶*abbr.* and others (used esp. in referring to academic books or articles that have more than one author): *the conclusions of Gardner et al.* ▷from Latin *et alii*.

USAGE See usage at **ET CETERA**.

e·ta·lon /ˈātlˌän/ ▶*n. Physics* a device consisting of two reflecting plates for producing interfering light beams. ▷early 20th cent.: from French *étalon*, literally 'standard of measurement.'

etc. ▶*abbr.* et cetera.

et cet·er·a /et ˈsetərə; ˈsetrə/ (also **et·cet·er·a**) ▶*adv.* used at the end of a list to indicate that further, similar items are included: *we're trying to resolve problems of obtaining equipment, drugs, et cetera.* ■ indicating that a list is too tedious or clichéd to give in full: *we've all got to do our duty, pull our weight, et cetera, et cetera.* ▷Latin, from *et* 'and' and *cetera* 'the rest' (neuter plural of *ceterus* 'left over').

USAGE Et cetera (a Latin phrase meaning 'and the other things, the rest') is sometimes mispronounced '*ex cetera*,' and its abbreviation, properly etc., is often misspelled 'ect.' The phrase 'and et cetera' is redundant, for *et* means 'and' in Latin. This abbreviation should be used for things, not for people.
Et al. (an abbreviation of *et alii*, 'and other people, and others') is properly used for others (people) too numerous to mention, as in a list of multiple authors: *Bancroft, Fordwick, et al.* In general, both terms (and their abbreviations) are common enough that it is not necessary to italicize or underline them.

et·cet·er·as /etˈsetərəz; etˈsetrəz/ ▶*plural n. dated* unspecified or typical extra items: *she began to pack her compact, comb, and other etceteras.*

etch /eCH/ ▶*v.* [*trans.*] **1** engrave (metal, glass, or stone) by coating it with a protective layer, drawing on it with a needle, and then covering it with acid to attack the parts the needle has exposed, esp. in order to produce prints from it: [as *adj.*] (**etched**) *etched glass windows.* ■ use such a process to produce (a print or design). ■ (of an acid or other solvent) corrode or eat away the surface of (something). ■ selectively dissolve the surface of (a semiconductor or printed circuit) with a solvent, laser, or stream of electrons. **2** (usu. **be etched**) cut or carve (a text or design) on a surface: *her initials were* **etched on** *the table* | *figurative his name is* **etched in** *baseball history.* ■ mark (a surface) with a carved text or design: *a Pictish stone* **etched with** *mysterious designs.* ■ cause to stand out or be clearly defined or visible: *Jo watched the outline of the town* **etched against** *the sky* | *her face was* **etched with** *tiredness* | [as *adj.*] (**etched**) *her finely etched profile* | *figurative the incident was* **etched** *indelibly* **in** *her mind.*
▶*n.* the action or process of etching something. ▷mid 17th cent.: from Dutch *etsen*, from German *ätzen*, from a base meaning 'cause to eat'; related to **EAT**. —**etch·er** *n.*

etch·ant /ˈeCHənt/ ▶*n.* an acid or corrosive chemical used in etching; a mordant.

etch·ing /ˈeCHiNG/ ▶*n.* a print produced by the process of etching: *etchings of animals and wildflowers.* ■ the art or process of producing etched plates or objects.

ETD ▶*abbr.* estimated time of departure.

-ete ▶*suffix* variant spelling of **-ET**[2] (as in *athlete*).

e·ter·nal /iˈtərnl/ ▶*adj.* lasting or existing forever; without end or beginning: *the secret of eternal youth* | *fear of eternal damnation.* ■ (of truths, values, or questions) valid for all time; essentially unchanging: *eternal truths of art and life.* ■ *informal* seeming to last or persist forever, esp. on account of being tedious or annoying: *eternal nagging demands* | *she is an eternal optimist.* ■ used to emphasize expressions of admiration, gratitude, or other feelings: *to his eternal credit, he maintained his dignity throughout.* ■ (**the Eternal**) used to refer to an everlasting or universal spirit, as represented by God. ▷late Middle English: via Old French from late Latin *aeternalis*, from Latin *aeternus*, from *aevum* 'age.' —**e·ter·nal·i·ty** /ˌētərˈnalitē/ *n.* —**e·ter·nal·ize** /iˈtərnlˌīz/ *v.* —**e·ter·nal·ly** *adv.* —**e·ter·nal·ness** *n.*
▶*PHRASES* □ **the Eternal City** a name for the city of Rome. □ **eternal triangle** a relationship between three people, typically a couple and the lover of one of them, involving sexual rivalry.

THE RIGHT WORD **endless, eternal, everlasting, interminable, never-ending, unending**
There are some things in life that seem to exist beyond the boundaries of time. **Endless** is the most informal and has the broadest scope of all these adjectives. It can mean without end in time (*an endless argument*) or space (*the endless universe*), and it implies never stopping, or going on continuously as if in a circle (*to consult an endless succession of doctors*).
Unending is a less formal word used to describe something that endures or has no end, and it can be used either in an approving sense (*unending devotion*) or a disapproving one (*unending conflict*).
Never-ending is a more emphatic term than *unending*; it, too, can be used in either a positive or a negative sense (*a never-ending delight; a never-ending source of embarrassment*).
In contrast, **interminable** is almost always used in a disapproving or negative sense for something that lasts a long time (*interminable delays in construction*).
Everlasting refers to something that will continue to exist once it is created, while **eternal** implies that it has always existed and will continue to exist in the future. In Christian theology, for example, believers in the *eternal* God look forward to *everlasting* life.

e·ter·ni·ty /iˈtərnitē/ ▶*n.* (*pl.* **-ties**) infinite or unending time: *their love was sealed for eternity* | *this state of affairs has lasted* **for all eternity**. ■ a state to which time has no application; timelessness. ■ *Theology* endless life after death: *immortal souls destined for eternity.* ■ used euphemistically to refer to death: *he could have crashed the car and taken them both to eternity.* ■ (**an eternity**) *informal* a period of time that seems very long, esp. on account of being tedious or annoying: *a silence that lasted an eternity.* ▷late Middle English: from Old French *eternite*, from Latin *aeternitas*, from *aeternus* 'without beginning or end' (see **ETERNAL**).

e·ter·nize /iˈtərˌnīz/ ▶*v.* [*trans.*] *poetic/literary* make eternal; cause to live or last forever.

e·te·sian wind /iˈtēZHən wind/ (also **E·te·sian wind**) ▶*n.* another term for **MELTEMI**. ▷early 17th cent.: *etesian* from Latin *etesius* 'annual' (from Greek *etēsios*, from *etos* 'year') + **-AN**.

eth /eT͟H/ (also **edh**) ▶*n.* an Old English letter, ð or đ, representing the dental fricatives /T͟H/ and /TH/ . It was superseded by the digraph *th*, but is now used as a phonetic symbol for the voiced dental fricative /T͟H/ in the International Phonetic Alphabet (IPA) system. Compare with **THORN** (sense 3). ▷from Danish *edh*, perhaps representing the sound of the letter.

Eth. ▶*abbr.* Ethiopia.

-eth[1] ▶*suffix* variant spelling of **-TH**[1] (as in *fiftieth*).

-eth[2] (also **-th**) ▶*suffix archaic* forming the third person singular of the present tense of verbs: *doeth* | *saith.* ▷Old English *-eth, -ath, -th*.

eth·a·cryn·ic ac·id /ˌeT͟Həˈkrinik/ ▶*n. Medicine* a powerful diuretic drug used in the treatment of fluid retention, esp. that associated with heart, liver, and kidney disorders. • Alternative name: **2,3-dichloro-4-(2-ethylacryloyl) phenoxy acetic acid**; chem. formula: $C_{13}H_{12}Cl_2O_4$. ▷1960s: *ethacrynic* from elements of the systematic name (see above).

eth·am·bu·tol /eˈTHambyəˌtôl; -ˌtäl/ ▶*n. Medicine* a synthetic compound with bacteriostatic properties, used in combination with other drugs in the treatment of tuberculosis. • A derivative of ethylenediamine; chem. formula: $C_{10}H_{24}N_2O_2$. ▷1960s: from *eth(yl)* + *am(ine)* + *but(an)ol*.

eth·a·nal /ˈeTHəˌnäl/ ▶*n.* systematic chemical name for **ACETALDEHYDE**. ▷late 19th cent.: blend of **ETHANE** and **ALDEHYDE**.

eth·an·a·mide /eˈTHanəˌmīd/ ▶*n.* systematic chemical name for **ACETAMIDE**.

eth·ane /ˈeTHˌān/ ▶*n. Chemistry* a colorless, odorless, flammable gas that is a constituent of petroleum and natural gas. It is the second member of the alkane series. • Chem. formula: C_2H_6. ▷late 19th cent.: from **ETHER** + **-ANE**[2].

eth·ane·di·ol /ˌeTHˌānˈdīˌôl/ ▶*n.* systematic chemical name for **ETHYLENE GLYCOL**.

eth·a·no·ic ac·id /ˌeTHəˈnō-ik/ ▶*n.* systematic chemical name for **ACETIC ACID**. —**eth·a·no·ate** /-ˈnōˌāt/ *n.*

eth·a·nol /ˈeTHəˌnôl; -ˌnäl/ ▶*n.* systematic chemical name for **ETHYL ALCOHOL** (see **ALCOHOL**). ▷early 20th cent.: blend of **ETHANE** and **ALCOHOL**.

eth·chlor·vy·nol /ˌeTHklôrˈvīnl/ ▶*n.* another name for **PLACIDYL**.

Eth·el·red /ˈeTHəlˌred/ the name of two English kings: ■ **Ethelred I** (died 871), king of Wessex and Kent 865–871; elder brother of Alfred. His reign was marked by the continuing struggle against the invading Danes. ■ **Ethelred II** (*c.*969–1016), king of England 978–1016; known as **Ethelred the Unready**. His inability to confront the Danes after he succeeded his murdered half-brother St. Edward the Martyr led to his payment of tribute to prevent their attacks. [*Unready*, later form of obsolete *unredy* 'badly advised.']

eth·ene /ˈeTHēn/ ▶*n.* systematic chemical name for **ETHYLENE**. ▷mid 19th cent.: from **ETHER** + **-ENE**.

e·ther /ˈēTHər/ ▶*n.* **1** *Chemistry* a pleasant-smelling, colorless, volatile liquid that is highly flammable. It is used as an anesthetic and as a solvent or intermediate in industrial processes. • Alternative names: **diethyl ether**, ethoxyethane; chem. formula: $C_2H_5OC_2H_5$. ■ any organic compound with a similar structure to this, having an oxygen atom linking two alkyl or other organic groups: *methyl t-butyl ether.* **2** (also **ae·ther**) *chiefly poetic/literary* the clear sky; the upper regions of air beyond the clouds: *nasty gases and smoke disperse into the ether.* **3** (also **ae·ther**) *archaic Physics* a very rarefied and highly elastic substance formerly believed to permeate all space, including the interstices between the particles of matter, and to be the medium whose vibrations constituted light and other electromagnetic radiation. ■ (**the ether**) *informal* air regarded as a medium for radio: *choral evensong still wafts across the ether.* ▷late Middle English: from Old French, or via Latin from Greek *aithēr* 'upper air,' from the base of *aithein* 'burn, shine.' Originally the word denoted a substance believed to occupy space beyond the sphere of the moon. Sense 3 arose in the mid 17th cent. and sense 1 in the mid 18th cent. —**e·ther·ic** /iˈTHerik; iˈTHī(ə)rik/ *adj.*

e·the·re·al /iˈTHi(ə)rēəl/ ▶*adj.* **1** extremely delicate and light in a way that seems too perfect for this world: *her ethereal beauty* | *a singer who has a weirdly ethereal voice.* ■ heavenly or spiritual: *ethereal, otherworldly visions.* **2** *Chemistry* (of a solution) having diethyl ether as a solvent. ▷early 16th cent.: via Latin from Greek *aitherios* (from *aithēr* 'ether') + **-AL**. —**e·the·re·al·i·ty** /iˌTHi(ə)rēˈalitē/ *n.* —**e·the·re·al·ize** /-ˌlīz/ *v.* —**e·the·re·al·ly** *adv.*

e·ther·ize /ˈēTHəˌrīz/ ▶*v.* [*trans.*] *chiefly historical* anesthetize (a person or animal) with ether. —**e·ther·i·za·tion** /ˌēTHəriˈzāSHən/ *n.*

E·ther·net /ˈēTHərˌnet/ ▶*n. Computing trademark* a system for connecting a number of computer systems to form a local area network, with protocols to control the passing of information and to avoid simultaneous transmission by two or more systems. ■ a network using this. ▷1970s: blend of **ETHER** and **NETWORK**.

eth·ic /ˈeTHik/ ▶*n.* [in *sing.*] a set of moral principles, esp. ones relating to or affirming a specified group, field, or form of conduct: *the puritan ethic was being replaced by the hedonist ethic.*
▶*adj. rare* of or relating to moral principles or the branch of knowledge dealing with these. ▷late Middle English (denoting ethics or moral philosophy; also used attributively): from Old French *éthique*, from Latin *ethice*, from Greek *(hē) ēthikē (tekhnē)* '(the science of) morals,' based on *ēthos* (see **ETHOS**).

eth·i·cal /ˈeTHikəl/ ▶*adj.* of or relating to moral principles or the branch of knowledge dealing with these: *ethical issues in nursing* | *ethical churchgoing men.* See note at **MORAL**. ■ morally correct: *can a profitable business be ethical?* ■ [*attrib.*] (of a medicine) legally available only on a doctor's prescription and usually not advertised to the general public. —**eth·i·cal·i·ty** /ˌeTHəˈkalitē/ *n.* —**eth·i·cal·ly** /-ik(ə)lē/ *adv.* [*sentence adverb*] *is capitalism ethically justifiable?*

eth·ics /ˈeTHiks/ ▶*plural n.* **1** [usu. treated as *pl.*] moral principles that govern a person's or group's behavior: *Judeo-Christian ethics.* ■ the moral correctness of specified conduct: *the ethics of euthanasia.* **2** [usu. treated as *sing.*] the branch of knowledge that deals with moral principles.

Schools of ethics in Western philosophy can be divided, very roughly, into three sorts. The first, drawing on the work of Aristotle, holds that the virtues (such as justice, charity, and generosity) are dispositions to act in ways that benefit both the person possessing them and that person's society. The second, defended particularly by Kant, makes the concept of duty central to morality: humans are bound, from a knowledge of their duty as rational beings, to obey the categorical imperative to respect other rational beings. Thirdly, utilitarianism asserts that the guiding principle of conduct should be the greatest happiness or benefit of the greatest number.

—eth·i·cist /ˈeTHisist/ *n.*

E·thi·o·pi·a /ˌēTHēˈōpēə/ a country in northeastern Africa, on the Red Sea; pop. 67,251,000; capital, Addis Ababa; languages, Amharic (official) and several other Afro-Asiatic languages. Former name **ABYSSINIA.** ▷via Latin from Greek *Aethiops*, from *aithein* 'to burn' + *ōps* 'the face.'

Ethiopia is the oldest independent country in Africa, having a recorded civilization that dates from the 2nd millennium BC. Little known to Europeans until the late 19th century, it was invaded and conquered by Italy in 1935. The emperor Haile Selassie was restored by the British in 1941 and ruled until he was overthrown in a Marxist coup in 1974. The subsequent period was marked by civil war, fighting against separatist guerrillas in Eritrea and Tigray, and by repeated famines; after the fall of the government in 1991, a multiparty system was adopted, and elections were held in 1995.

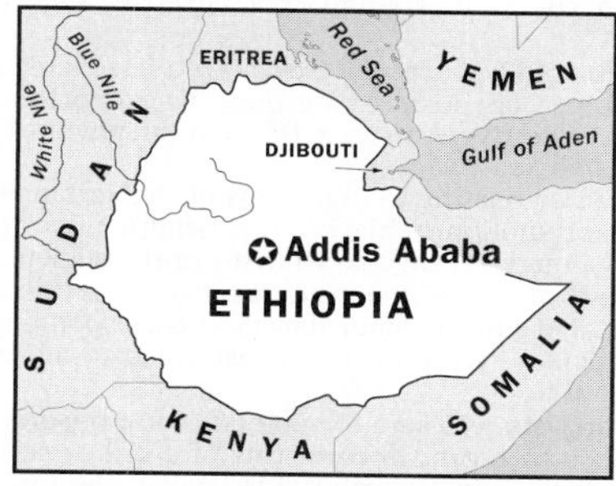

E·thi·o·pi·an /ˌēTHēˈōpēən/ ▶*n.* a native or national of Ethiopia, or a person of Ethiopian descent. ■ *archaic* a black person.
▶*adj.* **1** of or relating to Ethiopia or its people. **2** *Zoology* of, relating to, or denoting a zoogeographical region comprising Africa south of the Sahara, together with the tropical part of the Arabian peninsula and (usually) Madagascar. Distinctive animals include the giraffes, hippopotamuses, aardvark, elephant shrews, tenrecs, and lemurs. Also called **Afrotropical**.

E·thi·op·ic /ˌēTHēˈäpik; -ˈōpik/ ▶*n.* another term for **GE'EZ**.
▶*adj.* of, in, or relating to Ge'ez. ▷mid 17th cent. (as an adjective): via Latin from Greek *aithiopikos*, from *Aethiops* (see **ETHIOPIA**).

eth·moid /ˈeTHˌmoid/ (also **ethmoid bone**) ▶*n. Anatomy* a square bone at the root of the nose, forming part of the cranium, and having many perforations through which the olfactory nerves pass to the nose. ▷mid 18th cent.: from Greek *ēthmoeidēs*, from *ēthmos* 'a sieve.' **—eth·moi·dal** /ˌeTHˈmoidl/ *adj.*

eth·nic /ˈeTHnik/ ▶*adj.* of or relating to a population subgroup (within a larger or dominant national or cultural group) with a common national or cultural tradition: *leaders of ethnic communities.* ■ of or relating to national and cultural origins: *we recruit our employees regardless of ethnic origin.* ■ denoting origin by birth or descent rather than by present nationality: *ethnic Albanians in Kosovo.* ■ characteristic of or belonging to a non-Western cultural tradition: *cheap ethnic dresses | folk and ethnic music.* ■ *archaic* neither Christian nor Jewish; pagan or heathen.
▶*n.* a member of an ethnic minority. ▷late Middle English (denoting a person not of the Christian or Jewish faith): via ecclesiastical Latin from Greek *ethnikos* 'heathen,' from *ethnos* 'nation.' Current senses date from the 19th cent. **—eth·ni·cal·ly** /-(ə)lē/ *adv.* [*sentence adverb*] *Denmark is ethnically Scandinavian.*

eth·nic cleans·ing ▶*n.* the mass expulsion or killing of members of an unwanted ethnic or religious group in a society.

eth·nic·i·ty /eTHˈnisitē/ ▶*n.* (*pl.* **-ties**) the fact or state of belonging to a social group that has a common national or cultural tradition: *the interrelationship between gender, ethnicity, and class | the diverse experience of women of different ethnicities.*

eth·nic mi·nor·i·ty ▶*n.* a group that has different national or cultural traditions from the main population.

ethno- ▶*comb. form* ethnic; ethnological: *ethnocentric | ethnology.* ▷from Greek *ethnos* 'nation.'

eth·no·bot·a·ny /ˌeTHnōˈbätn-ē/ ▶*n.* the scientific study of the traditional knowledge and customs of a people concerning plants and their medical, religious, and other uses. **—eth·no·bo·tan·ic** /-bəˈtanik/ *adj.* **—eth·no·bo·tan·i·cal** /-bəˈtanikəl/ *adj.* **—eth·no·bot·a·nist** /-ˈbätn-ist/ *n.*

eth·no·cen·tric /ˌeTHnōˈsentrik/ ▶*adj.* evaluating other peoples and cultures according to the standards of one's own culture. **—eth·no·cen·tri·cal·ly** /-(ə)lē/ *adv.* **—eth·no·cen·tric·i·ty** /-ˌsenˈtrisitē/ *n.* **—eth·no·cen·trism** /-ˌtrizəm/ *n.*

eth·no·cide /ˈeTHnəˌsīd/ ▶*n.* the deliberate and systematic destruction of the culture of an ethnic group.

eth·no·cul·tur·al /ˌeTHnōˈkəlCHərəl/ ▶*adj.* relating to or denoting a particular ethnic group.

eth·nog·ra·phy /eTHˈnägrəfē/ ▶*n.* the scientific description of the customs of individual peoples and cultures. **—eth·nog·ra·pher** /-fər/ *n.* **—eth·no·graph·ic** /ˌeTHnəˈgrafik/ *adj.* **—eth·no·graph·i·cal** /ˌeTHnəˈgrafikəl/ *adj.* **—eth·no·graph·i·cal·ly** /ˌeTHnəˈgrafik(ə)lē/ *adv.*

eth·no·his·to·ry /ˌeTHnōˈhist(ə)rē/ ▶*n.* the branch of anthropology concerned with the history of peoples and cultures, esp. non-Western ones. **—eth·no·his·to·ri·an** /-hiˈstôrēən; -stär-/ *n.* **—eth·no·his·tor·ic** /-hiˈstôrik; -ˈstär-/ *adj.* **—eth·no·his·tor·i·cal** /-hiˈstôrikəl; -stär-/ *adj.* **—eth·no·his·tor·i·cal·ly** *adv.*

eth·no·lin·guis·tics /ˌeTHnōliNGˈgwistiks/ ▶*plural n.* [treated as *sing.*] the branch of linguistics concerned with the relations between linguistic and cultural behavior. **—eth·no·lin·guist** /-ˈliNGgwist/ *n.* **—eth·no·lin·guis·tic** *adj.*

eth·nol·o·gy /eTHˈnäləjē/ ▶*n.* the study of the characteristics of various peoples and the differences and relationships between them. **—eth·no·log·ic** /ˌeTHnəˈläjik/ *adj.* **—eth·no·log·i·cal** /ˌeTHnəˈläjikəl/ *adj.* **—eth·no·log·i·cal·ly** /ˌeTHnəˈläjik(ə)lē/ *adv.* **—eth·nol·o·gist** /-jist/ *n.*

eth·no·meth·od·ol·o·gy /ˌeTHnōˌmeTHəˈdäləjē/ ▶*n.* a method of sociological analysis that examines how individuals use everyday conversation and gestures to construct a common-sense view of the world. **—eth·no·meth·od·o·log·i·cal** /-dəˈläjikəl/ *adj.* **—eth·no·meth·od·ol·o·gist** /-jist/ *n.*

eth·no·mu·si·col·o·gy /ˌeTHnōˌmyo͞oziˈkäləjē/ ▶*n.* the study of the music of different cultures, esp. non-Western ones. **—eth·no·mu·si·co·log·ic** /-kəˈläjik/ *adj.* **—eth·no·mu·si·co·log·i·cal** /-kəˈläjikəl/ *adj.* **—eth·no·mu·si·col·o·gist** /-jist/ *n.*

eth·no·sci·ence /ˌeTHnōˈsīəns/ ▶*n.* the study of the different ways the world is perceived and categorized in different cultures.

e·tho·gram /ˈēTHəˌgram/ ▶*n. Zoology* a catalog or table of all the different kinds of behavior or activity observed in an animal. ▷1930s: from Greek *ēthos* 'nature, disposition' + **-GRAM**[1].

e·thol·o·gy /ēˈTHäləjē/ ▶*n.* the science of animal behavior. ■ the study of human behavior and social organization from a biological perspective. ▷late 19th cent.: via Latin from Greek *ēthologia*, from *ēthos* (see **ETHOS**). **—e·tho·log·i·cal** /ˌēTHəˈläjikəl/ *adj.* **—e·thol·o·gist** /-jist/ *n.*

e·thos /ˈēTHäs/ ▶*n.* the characteristic spirit of a culture, era, or community as manifested in its beliefs and aspirations: *a challenge to the ethos of the 1960s.* ▷mid 19th cent.: from modern Latin, from Greek *ēthos* 'nature, disposition,' (plural) 'customs.'

eth·ox·y·eth·ane /əˌTHäksēˈeTHˌān/ ▶*n.* systematic chemical name for **DIETHYL ETHER** (see **ETHER** (sense 1)).

eth·yl /ˈeTHəl/ ▶*n.* [usu. as *adj.*] *Chemistry* of or denoting the hydrocarbon radical $-C_2H_5$, derived from ethane and present in many organic compounds: *ethyl acetate | an ethyl group.* ▷mid 19th cent.: from German, from *Äther* 'ether' + **-YL**.

eth·yl ac·e·tate ▶*n. Chemistry* a colorless, volatile liquid with a fruity smell, used as a plastics solvent and in flavorings and perfumes. • Chem. formula: $CH_3COOC_2H_5$.

eth·yl al·co·hol ▶*n.* see **ALCOHOL**.

eth·yl·ben·zene /ˌeTHəlˈbenˌzēn; ˌeTHəlbenˈzēn/ ▶*n. Chemistry* a colorless, flammable liquid hydrocarbon, used in the manufacture of styrene. • Chem. formula: $C_6H_5C_2H_5$.

eth·yl·ene /ˈeTHəˌlēn/ ▶*n. Chemistry* a flammable hydrocarbon gas of the alkene series, occurring in natural gas, coal gas, and crude oil and given off by ripening fruit. It is used in chemical synthesis, esp. in the manufacture of polyethylene. • Alternative name: **ethene**; chem. formula: C_2H_4.

eth·yl·ene·di·a·mine /ˌeTHəlēnˈdīəˌmēn/ ▶*n. Chemistry* a viscous liquid used in making detergents and emulsifying agents. • Chem. formula: $NH_2CH_2CH_2NH_2$.

eth·yl·ene gly·col ▶*n. Chemistry* a colorless viscous hygroscopic liquid used as an antifreeze, in the manufacture of polyesters, and in the preservation of ancient waterlogged timbers. • Alternative name: **ethanediol**; chem. formula: $CH_2(OH)CH_2OH$.

eth·yl·ene ox·ide ▶*n. Chemistry* a flammable toxic gas used as an intermediate and fumigant. • An epoxide; chem. formula: $(CH_2)_2O$.

eth·yne /ˈeTHīn; eˈTHīn/ ▶*n.* systematic chemical name for **ACETYLENE**.

et·ic /ˈetik/ *Anthropology* ▶*adj.* relating to or denoting an approach to the study or description of a particular language or culture that is general, nonstructural, and objective in its perspective. Often contrasted with **EMIC**.
▶*plural n.* (**etics**) [treated as *sing.*] study adopting this approach. ▷1950s: abstracted from **PHONETIC**.

-etic ▶*suffix* forming adjectives and nouns such as *pathetic, peripatetic.* ▷from Greek *-ētikos* or *-ētikos*.

e·ti·o·lat·ed /ˈētēəˌlātid/ ▶*adj.* (of a plant) pale and drawn out due to a lack of light. ■ having lost vigor or substance; feeble: *a tone of etiolated nostalgia.* ▷late 18th cent.: from the verb *etiolate* (from French *étioler*, from Norman French *étieuler* 'grow into haulm') + **-ED**[2]. **—e·ti·o·la·tion** /ˌētēəˈlāSHən/ *n.*

e·ti·ol·o·gy /ˌētēˈäləjē/ (*Brit.* **ae·ti·ol·o·gy**) ▶*n.* (*pl.* **-gies**) **1** *Medicine* the cause, set of causes, or manner of causation of a disease or condition: *a disease of unknown etiology | a group of distinct diseases with different etiologies.* ■ the causation of diseases and disorders as a subject of investigation. **2** the investigation or attribution of the cause or reason for something, often expressed in terms of historical or mythical explanation. ▷mid 16th cent.: via medieval Latin from Greek *aitiologia*, from *aitia* 'a cause' + *-logia* (see **-LOGY**). **—e·ti·o·log·ic** /ˌētēəˈläjik/ *adj.* **—e·ti·o·log·i·cal** /ˌētēəˈläjikəl/ *adj.* **—e·ti·o·log·i·cal·ly** /ˌētēəˈläjik(ə)lē/ *adv.*

et·i·quette /ˈetikit; -ˌket/ ▶*n.* the customary code of polite behavior in society or among members of a particular profession or group. ▷mid 18th cent.: from French *étiquette* 'list of ceremonial observances of a court,' also 'label, etiquette,' from Old French *estiquette* (see **TICKET**).

Et·na, Mount /ˈetnə/ a volcano in eastern Sicily that rises to 10,902 feet (3,323 m). It is the highest and most active volcano in Europe.

ETO ▶*abbr.* (in World War II) European Theater of Operations.

E·ton col·lar /ˈētn/ ▶*n.* a broad, stiff white collar worn outside the coat collar, esp. with an Eton jacket.

E·ton Col·lege a boys' preparatory school in southern England, on the Thames River opposite Windsor, founded in 1440 by Henry VI to prepare scholars for King's College, Cambridge.

E·to·ni·an /ēˈtōnēən/ ▶*n.* a past or present member of Eton College: *an Old Etonian.*
▶*adj.* relating to or typical of Eton College.

E·ton jack·et ▶*n.* a short jacket reaching only to the waist, typically black and having a point at the back, formerly worn by students at Eton College.

E·to·sha Pan /ēˈtōSHə ˈpan/ a depression in the plateau in northern Namibia that is filled with salt water and has no outlets. It covers an area of 1,854 square miles (4,800 sq km).

é·touf·fée /āˌto͞oˈfā/ ▶*n.* a spicy Cajun stew made with vegetables and seafood.

e·tri·er /ˈātrēˌā; ˌātrēˈā/ ▶*n. Climbing* a short rope

ladder with a few rungs of wood or metal. ▷1950s: from French *étrier* 'stirrup.'

E·tru·ri·a /i'troōrēə/ an ancient region in western Italy, between the Arno and Tiber rivers, corresponding approximately to modern Tuscany and parts of Umbria. It was the center of the Etruscan civilization. **—E·tru·ri·an** *n.* & *adj.*

E·trus·can /i'trəskən/ ▶*adj.* of or relating to ancient Etruria, its people, or their language. The Etruscan civilization was at its height *c.*500 BC and was an important influence on the Romans, who subdued the Etruscans by the end of the 3rd century BC.
▶*n.* **1** a native of ancient Etruria. **2** the language of ancient Etruria, of unknown affinity, written in an alphabet derived from Greek. ▷from Latin *Etruscus* + **-AN**.

et seq. (also **et seqq.**) ▶*adv.* and what follows (used in page references): *see volume 35, p. 329 et seq.* ▷from Latin *et sequens* 'and the following,' or from *et sequentes, et sequentia* 'and the following things.'

-ette ▶*suffix* forming nouns: **1** denoting relatively small size: *kitchenette.* **2** denoting an imitation or substitute: *flannelette.* **3** denoting female gender: *suffragette.* ▷from Old French *-ette*, feminine of **-ET**[1].

USAGE The use of **-ette** as a feminine suffix for forming new words is relatively recent: it was first recorded in the word **suffragette** at the beginning of the 20th century and has since been used to form only a handful of well-established words, including **usherette** and **drum majorette**. In the modern context, where the tendency is to use gender-neutral words, the suffix **-ette** is not very productive and new words formed using it tend to be restricted to the deliberately flippant or humorous, as, for example, **bimbette** and **punkette**.

E

é·tude /ā't(y)ood/ ▶*n.* a short musical composition, typically for one instrument, designed as an exercise to improve the technique or demonstrate the skill of the player. ▷mid 19th cent.: from French, literally 'study.'

e·tui /ā'twē/ ▶*n.* (*pl.* **e·tuis**) *dated* a small ornamental case for holding needles, cosmetics, and other articles. ▷early 17th cent.: from French *étui*, from Old French *estui* 'prison,' from *estuier* 'shut up, keep.' Compare with **TWEEZERS**.

-etum ▶*suffix* (forming nouns) denoting a collection or plantation of trees or other plants: *arboretum* | *pinetum.* ▷from Latin.

et ux. ▶*abbr. Latin* et uxor (and wife).

ETV ▶*abbr.* educational television.

etym. ▶*abbr.* ■ etymological. ■ etymology.

et·y·mol·o·gize /,etə'mälə,jīz/ ▶*v.* [*trans.*] (usu. **be etymologized**) give or trace the etymology of (a word). ▷mid 16th cent.: from medieval Latin *etymologizare*, from Latin *etymologia* (see **ETYMOLOGY**).

et·y·mol·o·gy /,etə'mäləjē/ ▶*n.* (*pl.* **-gies**) the study of the origin of words and the way in which their meanings have changed throughout history. ■ the origin of a word and the historical development of its meaning. ▷late Middle English: from Old French *ethimologie*, via Latin from Greek *etumologia*, from *etumologos* 'student of etymology,' from *etumon*, neuter singular of *etumos* 'true.' **—et·y·mo·log·i·cal** /-mə'läjikəl/ *adj.* **—et·y·mo·log·i·cal·ly** /-mə'läjik(ə)lē/ *adv.* **—et·y·mol·o·gist** /-jist/ *n.*

et·y·mon /'etə,män/ ▶*n.* (*pl.* **-mons** or **-ma** /-mə/) a word or morpheme from which a later word is derived. ▷late 16th cent. (denoting the original form of a word): via Latin from Greek *etumon* 'true thing' (see **ETYMOLOGY**).

EU ▶*abbr.* European Union.

Eu ▶*symbol* the chemical element europium.

eu- ▶*comb. form* good; well; easily; normal: *eupeptic* | *euphony.* ▷from Greek *eu* 'well,' from *eus* 'good.'

eu·bac·te·ri·um /,yoobak'ti(ə)rēəm/ ▶*n.* (*pl.* **-ter·i·a** /-'ti(ə)rēə/) **1** a bacterium of a large group typically having simple cells with rigid cell walls and often flagella for movement. The group comprises the "true" bacteria and cyanobacteria, as distinct from archaebacteria. • Kingdom Eubacteria; this group is sometimes taken to exclude nonrigid forms such as spirochetes and mycoplasmas. **2** a bacterium found mainly in the intestines of vertebrates and in the soil. • Genus *Eubacterium*; Gram-positive, anaerobic, rod-shaped bacteria. **—eu·bac·te·ri·al** /-ti(ə)rēəl/ *adj.*

Eu·boe·a /yoo'bēə/ an island in Greece in the western Aegean Sea that is separated from the mainland by a narrow channel at Chalcis, which is its capital. Greek name **ÉVVOIA**.

eu·ca·lyp·tus /,yookə'liptəs/ (also **eu·ca·lypt** /'yookə,lipt/) ▶*n.* (*pl.* **-tus·es** or **-ti** /-tī/) a fast-growing evergreen Australasian tree that has been widely introduced elsewhere. It is valued for its timber, oil, gum, and resin, and as an ornamental tree. Also called **GUM**[1], **GUM TREE**. • Genus *Eucalyptus*, family Myrtaceae: numerous species. ■ (also **eucalyptus oil**) the oil from eucalyptus leaves, chiefly used for its medicinal properties. ▷modern Latin, from Greek *eu* 'well' + *kaluptos* 'covered' (from *kaluptein* 'to cover'), because the unopened flower is protected by a cap.

eu·car·y·ote /yoo'kerē,ōt/ ▶*n.* variant spelling of **EUKARYOTE**.

eu·ca·tas·tro·phe /,yookə'tastrəfē/ ▶*n. rare* a sudden and favorable resolution of events in a story; a happy ending. ▷mid 20th cent.: said to have been coined by J. R. R. Tolkien.

Eu·cha·rist /'yookərist/ ▶*n.* the Christian ceremony commemorating the Last Supper, in which bread and wine are consecrated and consumed. ■ the consecrated elements, esp. the bread.

The bread and wine are referred to as the body and blood of Christ, though much theological controversy has focused on how substantially or symbolically this is to be interpreted. The service of worship is also called **Holy Communion** or (chiefly in the Protestant tradition) **the Lord's Supper** or (chiefly in the Catholic tradition) **the Mass**.
See also **CONSUBSTANTIATION, TRANSUBSTANTIATION**.

▷late Middle English: from Old French *eucariste*, based on ecclesiastical Greek *eukharistia* 'thanksgiving,' from Greek *eukharistos* 'grateful,' from *eu* 'well' + *kharizesthai* 'offer graciously' (from *kharis* 'grace'). **—Eu·cha·ris·tic** /,yookə'ristik/ *adj.* **—Eu·cha·ris·ti·cal** /,yookə'ristikəl/ *adj.*

eu·chre /'yookər/ ▶*n.* a card game for two to four players, usually played with the thirty-two highest cards, the aim being to win at least three of the five tricks played.
▶*v.* [*trans.*] (in such a card game) gain the advantage over (another player) by preventing them from taking three tricks. ■ *informal* deceive, outwit, or cheat (someone): *the merchant can be* **euchred out of** *his caftan by hard bargaining.* ▷early 19th cent.: from German dialect *Jucker(spiel).*

eu·chro·ma·tin /yoo'krōmətin/ ▶*n. Genetics* chromosome material that does not stain strongly except during cell division. It represents the major genes and is involved in transcription. Compare with **HETEROCHROMATIN**. **—eu·chro·mat·ic** /,yookrə'matik/ *adj.*

Eu·clid[1] /'yooklid/ a city in northeastern Ohio, northeast of Cleveland; pop. 54,875.

Eu·clid[2] (*c.*300 BC), Greek mathematician. His *Elements of Geometry*, which covered plane geometry, the theory of numbers, irrationals, and solid geometry, was the standard work until other kinds of geometry were discovered in the 19th century.

Eu·clid·e·an /yoo'klidēən/ ▶*adj.* of or relating to Euclid, in particular: ■ of or denoting the system of geometry based on the work of Euclid and corresponding to the geometry of ordinary experience. ■ of such a nature that the postulates of this system of geometry are valid. Compare with **NON-EUCLIDEAN**.

eu·crite /'yookrīt/ ▶*n. Geology* a highly basic form of gabbro containing anorthite or bytownite with augite. ■ a stony meteorite that contains no chondrules and consists mainly of anorthite and augite. ▷mid 19th cent.: from Greek *eukritos* 'easily discerned,' from *eu-* 'well' + *kritos* 'separated' (from *krinein* 'to separate').

eu·cryph·i·a /yoo'krifēə/ ▶*n.* a shrub or small tree with glossy dark green leaves and large white flowers, native to Australia and South America. • Genus *Eucryphia*, family Eucryphiaceae. ▷modern Latin, from Greek *eu* 'well' + *-kruphos* 'hidden' (with reference to its joined sepals).

eu·dae·mon·ic /,yoodə'mänik/ (also **eu·de·mon·ic**) ▶*adj. formal* conducive to happiness. ▷mid 19th cent.: from Greek *eudaimonikos*, from *eudaimōn* 'happy' (see **EUDAEMONISM**). **—eu·dae·mo·ni·a** /-'mōnēə/ *n.*

eu·dae·mon·ism /yoo'dēmə,nizəm/ (also **eu·de·mon·ism**) ▶*n.* a system of ethics that bases moral value on the likelihood that good actions will produce happiness. ▷early 19th cent.: from Greek *eudaimonismos* 'system of happiness,' from *eudaimōn* 'happy,' from *eu* 'well' + *daimōn* 'guardian spirit.' **—eu·dae·mon·ist** *n.* **—eu·dae·mon·is·tic** /-,dēmə'nistik/ *adj.*

eu·di·om·e·ter /,yoodē'ämitər/ ▶*n. Chemistry* a graduated glass tube in which mixtures of gases can be made to react by an electric spark, used to measure changes in volume of gases during chemical reactions. ▷late 18th cent. (denoting an instrument used to measure amounts of oxygen, thought to be greater in fine weather): from Greek *eudios* 'clear, fine' (weather), from *eu* 'well' + *dios* 'heavenly.' **—eu·di·o·met·ric** /,yoodēə'metrik/ *adj.* **—eu·di·o·met·ri·cal** /,yoodēə'metrikəl/ *adj.* **—eu·di·om·e·try** /-trē/ *n.*

Eu·gene /yoo'jēn/ a city in west central Oregon, on the Willamette River, home to the University of Oregon; pop. 137,893.

eu·gen·ics /yoo'jeniks/ ▶*plural n.* [treated as *sing.*] the science of improving a human population by controlled breeding to increase the occurrence of desirable heritable characteristics. Developed largely by Francis Galton as a method of improving the human race, it fell into disfavor only after the perversion of its doctrines by the Nazis. **—eu·gen·ic** *adj.* **—eu·gen·i·cal·ly** /-ik(ə)lē/ *adv.* **—eu·gen·i·cist** /-'jenisist/ *n.* & *adj.* **—eu·gen·ist** /-'jenist/ *n.* & *adj.*

Eu·gé·nie /yoozhā'nē/ (1826–1920), Spanish empress of France 1853–70 and wife of Napoleon III; born *Eugénia María de Montijo de Guzmán*. She was an important influence on her husband's foreign policy.

eu·ge·nol /'yoojə,nôl; -,näl/ ▶*n. Chemistry* a colorless or pale yellow liquid compound present in oil of cloves and other essential oils and used in perfumery. • Alternative name: **4-allyl-2-methoxyphenol**; chem. formula: $C_{10}H_{12}O_2$. ▷late 19th cent.: from *Eugenia* (genus name of the tree from which oil of cloves is obtained, named in honor of Prince *Eugene* of Savoy (1663–1736)) + **-OL**.

eu·gle·na /yoo'glēnə/ ▶*n. Biology* a green, single-celled, freshwater organism with a flagellum, sometimes forming a green scum on stagnant water. • Genus *Euglena*, division Euglenophyta (or phylum Euglenophyta, kingdom Protista). ▷modern Latin, from **EU-** 'well' + Greek *glēnē* 'eyeball, socket of joint.'

eu·gle·noid /yoo'glēnoid/ *Biology* ▶*n.* a flagellated single-celled organism of a group that comprises euglena and its relatives. • Division (or phylum) Euglenophyta.
▶*adj.* of or relating to organisms of this group. ■ (of cell locomotion) achieved by peristaltic waves that pass along the cell, characteristic of the euglenoids.

eu·he·dral /yoo'hēdrəl/ ▶*adj. Geology* (of a mineral crystal in a rock) bounded by faces corresponding to its regular crystal form unconstrained by adjacent minerals.

eu·kar·y·ote /yoo'karē,ōt; -ēət/ (also **eu·car·y·ote**) ▶*n. Biology* an organism consisting of a cell or cells in which the genetic material is DNA in the form of chromosomes contained within a distinct nucleus. Eukaryotes include all living organisms other than the eubacteria and archaebacteria. Compare with **PROKARYOTE**. ▷1960s: from **EU-** 'easily (formed)' + **KARYO-** 'kernel' + *-ote* as in *zygote*. **—eu·kar·y·ot·ic** /-,karē'ätik/ *adj.*

EULA /'yoolə/ ▶*abbr.* end user license agreement.

eu·la·chon /'yoolə,kän/ ▶*n.* (*pl.* same) another term for **CANDLEFISH**. ▷mid 19th cent.: from Lower Chinook *ulâkân*.

Eu·ler[1] /'oilər/, Leonhard (1707–83), Swiss mathematician. He attempted to elucidate the nature of functions, and his study of infinite series led his successors, notably Neils Abel and Augustin Cauchy, to introduce ideas of convergence and rigorous argument into mathematics.

Eu·ler[2], Ulf Svante von (1905–83), Swedish physiologist; son of Hans Euler-Chelpin. He was the first to discover a prostaglandin, which he isolated from semen. Euler also identified norepinephrine as the principal chemical neurotransmitter of the sympathetic nervous system. Nobel Prize for Physiology or Medicine (1970, shared with Bernard Katz 1911– and Julius Axelrod 1912–).

Eu·ler-Chel·pin /'kelpin/, Hans Karl August Simon von (1873–1964), Swedish biochemist; born in Germany. He worked mainly on enzymes and vitamins and explained the role of enzymes in the alcoholic fermentation of sugar. Nobel Prize for Chemistry (1929, shared with Arthur Harden 1865–1940).

Eu·ler's con·stant *Mathematics* a constant used in numerical analysis, approximately equal to 0.577216. It represents the limit of the series $1 + 1/2 + 1/3 + 1/4 + \ldots 1/n$ – (natural logarithm of n), as n tends to infinity. It is not known whether this is a rational number or not. ▷mid 19th cent.: named after L. Euler (see **EULER**[1]).

Eu·ler's for·mu·la the geometric formula $V - E + F = 2$, where V, E, and F are the numbers of vertices, edges, and faces of any simple convex polyhedron or of an equivalent topological graph.

eu·lo·gi·um /yo͞o'lōjēəm/ ▸*n.* (*pl.* **-gi·a** /-jēə/ or **-gi·ums**) another term for EULOGY. ▷early 17th cent.: from medieval Latin, 'praise.'

eu·lo·gize /'yo͞olə,jīz/ ▸*v.* [*trans.*] praise highly in speech or writing: *Cotton Mather eulogized him as the embodiment of Christian altruism | a plaque that eulogizes the workers.* See note at PRAISE. **—eu·lo·gist** /-jist/ *n.* **—eu·lo·gis·tic** /,yo͞olə'jistik/ *adj.* **—eu·lo·gis·ti·cal·ly** /'yo͞olə'jistik(ə)lē/ *adv.*

eu·lo·gy /'yo͞oləjē/ ▸*n.* (*pl.* **-gies**) a speech or piece of writing that praises someone or something highly, typically someone who has just died: *his good friend delivered a brief eulogy.* ▷late Middle English (in the sense 'high praise'): from medieval Latin *eulogium, eulogia* (from Greek *eulogia* 'praise'), apparently influenced by Latin *elogium* 'inscription on a tomb' (from Greek *elegia* 'elegy'). The current sense dates from the late 16th cent.

Eu·men·i·des /yo͞o'meni,dēz/ *Greek Mythology* a name given to the Furies. The Eumenides probably originated as well-disposed deities of fertility, whose name was given to the Furies either by confusion or euphemistically. ▷via Latin from Greek, from *eumenēs* 'well disposed,' from *eu* 'well' + *menos* 'spirit.'

eu·nuch /'yo͞onək/ ▸*n.* a man who has been castrated, esp. (in the past) one employed to guard the women's living areas at an oriental court. ■ an ineffectual person: *a nation of political eunuchs.* ▷Old English, via Latin from Greek *eunoukhos*, literally 'bedroom guard,' from *eunē* 'bed' + a second element related to *ekhein* 'to hold.'

eu·nuch·oid /'yo͞onə,koid/ ▸*adj.* *chiefly Medicine* resembling a eunuch, typically in having reduced or indeterminate sexual characteristics. **—eu·nuch·oid·ism** /-izəm/ *n.*

eu·on·y·mus /yo͞o'änəməs/ ▸*n.* a shrub or small tree that is widely cultivated for its autumn colors and bright fruit. • Genus *Euonymus*, family Celastraceae: numerous species, including the spindle tree. ▷modern Latin (named by Linnaeus), from Latin *euonymos*, from Greek *euōnumos* 'having an auspicious or honored name,' from *eus* 'good' + *onoma* 'name.'

eu·pep·tic /yo͞o'peptik/ ▸*adj.* of or having good digestion or a consequent air of healthy good spirits. ▷late 17th cent. (in the sense 'helping digestion'): from Greek *eupeptos*, from *eu* 'well, easily' + *peptein* 'to digest.'

eu·phau·si·id /yo͞o'fôzēid/ ▸*n.* *Zoology* a shrimplike, planktonic marine crustacean of an order that includes krill. Many kinds are luminescent. • Order Euphausiaceae, subclass Malacostraca. ▷late 19th cent.: from modern Latin *Euphausia* (genus name from Greek *eu* 'well' + *phainein* 'to show' + *ousia* 'substance') + -ID[2].

eu·phe·mism /'yo͞ofə,mizəm/ ▸*n.* a mild or indirect word or expression substituted for one considered to be too harsh or blunt when referring to something unpleasant or embarrassing: *"downsizing" as a* ***euphemism for*** *cuts.* The opposite of DYSPHEMISM. ▷late 16th cent.: from Greek *euphēmismos*, from *euphēmizein* 'use auspicious words,' from *eu* 'well' + *phēmē* 'speaking.'

eu·phe·mis·tic /,yo͞ofə'mistik/ ▸*adj.* using or of the nature of a euphemism: *the euphemistic terms she uses to describe her relationships.* **—eu·phe·mis·ti·cal·ly** /-(ə)lē/ *adv.*

eu·phe·mize /'yo͞ofə,mīz/ ▸*v.* [*trans.*] refer to (something unpleasant or embarrassing) by means of a euphemism. ▷mid 19th cent.: from Greek *euphēmizein* 'use auspicious words' (see EUPHEMISM).

eu·pho·ni·ous /yo͞o'fōnēəs/ ▸*adj.* (of sound, esp. speech) pleasing to the ear: *this successful candidate delivers a stream of fine, euphonious phrases.* **—eu·pho·ni·ous·ly** *adv.*

eu·pho·ni·um /yo͞o'fōnēəm/ ▸*n.* a valved brass musical instrument resembling a small tuba of tenor pitch, played mainly in military and brass bands. ▷mid 19th cent.: from Greek *euphōnos* 'having a pleasing sound' + -IUM.

eu·pho·ny /'yo͞ofənē/ ▸*n.* (*pl.* **-nies**) the quality of being pleasing to the ear, esp. through a harmonious combination of words. ■ the tendency to make phonetic change for ease of pronunciation. ▷late Middle English: from French *euphonie*, via late Latin from Greek *euphōnia*, from *euphōnos* 'well sounding' (based on *phōnē* 'sound'). **—eu·phon·ic** /yo͞o'fänik/ *adj.* **—eu·pho·nize** /-,nīz/ *v.*

eu·phor·bi·a /yo͞o'fôrbēə/ ▸*n.* a plant of a genus that comprises the spurges. • Genus *Euphorbia*, family Euphorbiaceae. ▷late Middle English: from Latin *euphorbea*, named after *Euphorbus*, Greek physician to the reputed discoverer of the plant, Juba II of Mauretania (1st cent. BC).

eu·pho·ri·a /yo͞o'fôrēə/ ▸*n.* a feeling or state of intense excitement and happiness: *the euphoria of success will fuel your desire to continue training.* See note at RAPTURE. ▷late 17th cent. (denoting well-being produced in a sick person by the use of drugs): modern Latin, from Greek, from *euphoros* 'borne well, healthy,' from *eu* 'well' + *pherein* 'to bear.'

eu·pho·ri·ant /yo͞o'fôrēənt/ ▸*adj.* (chiefly of a drug) producing a feeling of euphoria.
▸*n.* a euphoriant drug.

eu·phor·ic /yo͞o'fôrik; -'fär-/ ▸*adj.* characterized by or feeling intense excitement and happiness: *a euphoric sense of freedom.* **—eu·phor·i·cal·ly** /yo͞o'fôrik(ə)lē; -'fär-/ *adv.*

eu·phra·sia /yo͞o'frāzʜə/ ▸*n.* a plant of the genus *Euphrasia* in the figwort family, esp. eyebright. ■ a preparation of eyebright used in herbal medicine and homeopathy, esp. for treating eye problems. ▷early 18th cent.: via medieval Latin from Greek, literally 'cheerfulness'.

Eu·phra·tes /yo͞o'frātēz/ a river of southwestern Asia that rises in the mountains of eastern Turkey and flows for 1,700 miles (2,736 km) through Syria and Iraq to join the Tigris River to form the Shatt al-Arab waterway.

eu·phu·ism /'yo͞ofyə,wizəm/ ▸*n.* *formal* an artificial, highly elaborate way of writing or speaking. ▷late 16th cent.: from *Euphues*, the name of a character in John Lyly's prose romance of the same name (1578–80), from Greek *euphuēs* 'well endowed by nature,' from *eu* 'well' + the base of *phuē* 'growth.' **—eu·phu·ist** *n.* **—eu·phu·is·tic** /,yo͞ofyə'wistik/ *adj.* **—eu·phu·is·ti·cal·ly** /,yo͞ofyə'wistik(ə)lē/ *adv.*

eu·ploid /'yo͞oploid/ ▸*adj.* *Biology* (of a nucleus, cell, or organism) having an exact multiple of the haploid number of chromosomes. ▷from EU- + -PLOID.

Eur·a·sia /yo͞o'rāzʜə/ a term used to describe the combined continental landmass of Europe and Asia.

Eur·a·sian /yo͞or'āzʜən/ ▸*adj.* **1** of mixed European (or European-American) and Asian parentage. **2** of or relating to Eurasia.
▸*n.* a person of mixed European (or European-American) and Asian parentage.

> ***USAGE*** In the 19th century, the word **Eurasian** was normally used to refer to a person of mixed British and Indian parentage. In its modern uses, however, the **-asian** part of the term more often implies Southeast Asian, and **Eurasian** is often used as a synonym for **Amerasian**.

Eu·re·ka /yo͞o'rēkə; yə-/ a port city in northwestern California, on Humboldt Bay off the Pacific Ocean, a noted lumbering center; pop. 27,025.

eu·re·ka /yo͞o'rēkə; yə-/ ▸*exclam.* a cry of joy or satisfaction when one finds or discovers something. ▷early 17th cent.: from Greek *heurēka* 'I have found it' (from *heuriskein* 'find'), said to have been uttered by Archimedes when he hit upon a method of determining the purity of gold. The noun dates from the early 20th cent.

eu·rhyth·mics ▸*plural n.* variant spelling of EURYTHMICS.

eu·rhyth·my ▸*n.* variant spelling of EURYTHMY.

Eu·rip·i·des /yo͞o'ripə,dēz/ (480–*c.*406 BC), Greek playwright. His 19 surviving plays show important innovations in the handling of traditional myths, such as the introduction of realism, an interest in feminine psychology, and the portrayal of abnormal and irrational states of mind. Notable works: *Medea, Hippolytus, Electra, Trojan Women*, and *Bacchae*.

eu·ro[1] /'yərō; 'yo͞orō/ ▸*n.* (*pl.* **eu·ros** or **eu·ro**) (also **Euro**) the single European currency adopted in 1999 by eleven countries in the European Union (Belgium, Austria, Finland, Spain, Ireland, Portugal, Germany, France, Netherlands, Italy, Luxembourg) as an alternative currency in noncash transactions. In 2002 it replaced the national currencies of twelve member countries (the original eleven, plus Greece). (Symbol: €)
▸*adj.* (usu. **Euro**) [*attrib.*] *informal* European, esp. concerned with the European Union: *he voted with the government in the Euro debate.* ▷independent usage of EURO-.

eu·ro[2] ▸*n.* (*pl.* **-ros**) the common wallaroo (see WALLAROO). ▷mid 19th cent.: from Adnyamadhanha *yuru*.

Euro- ▸*comb. form* European; European and ... : *Euro-American.* ■ relating to Europe or the European Union: *Eurocommunism | a Euro-MP.*

Eu·ro·bond /'yərə,bänd; 'yo͞orō-/ ▸*n.* an international bond issued in Europe or elsewhere outside the country in whose currency its value is stated (usually the U.S. or Japan).

Eu·ro·cen·tric /,yərō'sentrik; ,yo͞orō-/ ▸*adj.* focusing on European culture or history to the exclusion of a wider view of the world; implicitly regarding European culture as preeminent. **—Eu·ro·cen·tric·i·ty** /-,sen'trisitē/ *n.* **—Eu·ro·cen·trism** /-'sen,trizəm/ *n.*

Eu·ro·cheque /'yərō,cʜek; 'yərə-; 'yo͞orō-; 'yo͞orə-/ ▸*n.* a check issued under an arrangement between European banks that enables account-holders from one country to use their checks in another.

Eu·ro·com·mu·nism /,yərō'kämyə,nizəm; ,yo͞orō-/ ▸*n.* a political system advocated by some communist parties in western European countries, stressing independence from the former Soviet Communist Party and preservation of many elements of Western liberal democracy. **—Eu·ro·com·mu·nist** *adj.* & *n.*

Eu·ro·crat /'yərə,krat; 'yo͞orə-/ ▸*n.* *informal, chiefly derogatory* a bureaucrat in the administration of the European Union.

eu·ro·creep /'yərō,krēp; 'yo͞orō-/ (also **Eu·ro·creep**) ▸*n.* *informal* the gradual acceptance of the euro in European Union countries that have not yet officially adopted it as their national currency.

Eu·ro·cur·ren·cy /'yərō,kərənsē; 'yo͞orō-/ ▸*n.* **1** a form of money held or traded outside the country in whose currency its value is stated (originally U.S. dollars held in Europe). **2** [in *sing.*] a single currency for use by the member states of the European Union.

Eu·ro·dol·lar /'yərō,dälər; 'yo͞orō-/ ▸*n.* a U.S. dollar deposit held in Europe or elsewhere outside the U.S.

Eu·ro·land /'yərō,land; 'yo͞orō-/ popular term for the group of European nations whose national currency is the euro. See also EURO.

Eu·ro·mar·ket /'yərō,märkit; 'yo͞orō-/ ▸*n.* **1** a financial market that deals with Eurocurrencies. **2** the European Union regarded as a single commercial or financial market.

Eu·ro·pa /yo͞o'rōpə/ **1** *Greek Mythology* a princess of Tyre who was courted by Zeus in the form of a bull. She was carried off by him to Crete, where she bore him three sons (Minos, Rhadamanthus, and Sarpedon). **2** *Astronomy* one of the Galilean moons of Jupiter, the sixth closest satellite to the planet, having a network of dark lines on a bright icy surface and a diameter of 1,951 miles (3,140 km).

Eu·rope /'yo͞orəp/ a continent in the northern hemisphere, separated from Africa on the south by the Mediterranean Sea and from Asia on the east roughly by the Bosporus, the Caucasus Mountains, and the Ural Mountains. Europe contains approximately 10 percent of the world's population. It consists of the western part of the landmass of which Asia forms the eastern (and greater) part and includes the British Isles, Iceland, and most of the Mediterranean islands. Its recent history has been dominated by the decline of European states from their former colonial and economic preeminence, the emergence of the European Union among the wealthy democracies of western Europe, and the collapse of the Soviet Union with consequent changes of power in central and eastern Europe. *See page 582.*

Eu·rope, Council of an association of European states founded in 1949 to safeguard the political and cultural heritage of Europe and promote economic and social cooperation. One of the Council's principal achievements is the European Convention on Human Rights.

Eu·ro·pe·an /,yərə'pēən; ,yo͞orə-/ ▸*adj.* of, relating to, or characteristic of Europe or its inhabitants. ■ of or relating to the European Union: *a single European currency.*
▸*n.* a native or inhabitant of Europe. ■ a national of a state belonging to the European Union. ■ a person who is committed to the European Union: *they claimed to be the party of good Europeans.* ■ a person who is white or of European parentage, esp. in a country with a large nonwhite population. ▷from French *européen*, from Latin *europaeus*, based on Greek *Eurōpē* 'Europe.' **—Eu·ro·pe·an·ism** /-,nizəm/ *n.*

Eu·ro·pe·an Com·mis·sion a group, appointed by agreement among the governments of the

Pronunciation Key ə *ago*; ər *over*; 'ə or ,ə *up*; 'ər or ,ər *fur*; a *hat*; ā *rate*; ä *car*; cʜ *chew*; e *let*; ē *see*; e(ə)r *air*; i *fit*; ī *by*; i(ə)r *ear*; ɴɢ *sing*; ō *go*; ô *for*; oi *boy*; o͝o *good*; o͞o *goo*; ou *out*; sʜ *she*; tʜ *thin*; t̲h̲ *then*; (h)w *why*; zʜ *vision*

European Union, which initiates Union action and safeguards its treaties. It meets in Brussels.

Eu·ro·pe·an Com·mis·sion for Hu·man Rights an institution of the Council of Europe, set up to examine complaints of alleged breaches of the Convention. It is based in Strasbourg.

Eu·ro·pe·an Com·mu·ni·ty (abbr.: **EC**) an economic and political association of certain European countries, incorporated since 1993 in the European Union.

The European Community was formed in 1967 and includes the European Commission, the European Parliament, and the European Court of Justice. Until 1987 it was still commonly known as the EEC. The name "European Communities" is still used in legal contexts where the three distinct organizations are recognized.
See also EUROPEAN UNION.

Eu·ro·pe·an Court of Jus·tice an institution of the European Union, with thirteen judges appointed by its member governments, meeting in Luxembourg. Established in 1958, it exists to safeguard the law in the interpretation and application of Community treaties.

Eu·ro·pe·an cur·ren·cy u·nit ▸*n.* see ECU.

Eu·ro·pe·an Ec·o·nom·ic Com·mu·ni·ty (abbr.: **EEC**) an institution of the European Union, an economic association of western European countries set up by the Treaty of Rome (1957). The original members were France, West Germany, Italy, Belgium, the Netherlands, and Luxembourg. See also EUROPEAN COMMUNITY and EUROPEAN UNION.

Eu·ro·pe·an Free Trade As·so·ci·a·tion (abbr.: **EFTA**) a customs union of western European countries, established in 1960 as a trade grouping without the political implications of the European Economic Community. The original members were Austria, Denmark, Norway, Portugal, Sweden, Switzerland, and the UK.

Eu·ro·pe·an In·vest·ment Bank a bank set up in 1958 by the Treaty of Rome to finance capital investment projects promoting the balanced development of members of the European Community. It is based in Luxembourg.

Eu·ro·pe·an·ize /ˌyərəˈpēəˌnīz; ˌyo͝orə-/ ▸*v.* [*trans.*] [often as *adj.*] (**Europeanized**) give (someone or something) a European character or scope: *the name marked him as a Europeanized Turk.* ■ transfer to the control or responsibility of the European Union. —**Eu·ro·pe·an·i·za·tion** /ˌyərəˌpēəniˈzāsHən; ˌyo͝orə-/ *n.*

Eu·ro·pe·an kitch·en ▸*n.* a compact kitchen with fitted cabinets and appliances, usually white.

Eu·ro·pe·an Mon·e·tar·y Sys·tem (abbr.: **EMS**) a monetary system inaugurated by the European Community in 1979 to coordinate and stabilize the exchange rates of the currencies of member countries, as a prelude to monetary union. It is based on the use of the Exchange Rate Mechanism.

Eu·ro·pe·an Mon·e·tar·y Un·ion (abbr.: **EMU**) a European Union program intended to work toward full economic unity in Europe based on the phased introduction of a common currency (originally, the ECU). The program was announced in 1989; the second stage came into effect on January 1, 1994 under the terms of the Maastricht Treaty, and in 2002 the euro replaced the currencies of twelve European Union countires.

Eu·ro·pe·an Par·lia·ment the Parliament of the European Community, originally established in 1952. From 1958 to 1979 it was composed of representatives drawn from the parliaments of member countries, but since 1979 direct elections have taken place every five years. Through the Single European Act (1987) it assumed a degree of sovereignty over national parliaments. The European Parliament meets in Strasbourg, and its committee is in Brussels.

Eu·ro·pe·an plan ▸*n.* a system of charging for a hotel room only, without meals. Often contrasted with AMERICAN PLAN.

Eu·ro·pe·an Re·cov·er·y Pro·gram official name for the MARSHALL PLAN.

Eu·ro·pe·an Space A·gen·cy (abbr.: **ESA**) an organization set up in 1975 to coordinate the national space programs of the collaborating countries. It is based in Paris.

Eu·ro·pe·an Un·ion (abbr.: **EU**) an economic and political association of European countries as a unit with internal free trade and common external tariffs.

The European Union was created on November 1, 1993. Its fifteen member countries are Austria, Belgium, Denmark, Finland, France, Germany, Greece, Ireland, Italy, Luxembourg, the Netherlands, Portugal, Spain, Sweden, and the UK.
See also EUROPEAN COMMUNITY and EUROPEAN ECONOMIC COMMUNITY.

eu·ro·pi·um /yəˈrōpēəm/ ▸*n.* the chemical element of atomic number 63, a soft silvery-white metal of the lanthanide series. Europium oxide is used with yttrium oxide as a red phosphor in color television screens. (Symbol: **Eu**) ▹early 20th cent.: modern Latin, based on EUROPE.

Eu·ro·poort /ˈyo͝orōˌpôrt/ a major European port in the Netherlands, near Rotterdam.

Eu·ro·skep·tic (also **Eu·ro·scep·tic**) ▸*n.* a person who is opposed to increasing the powers of the European Union. —**Eu·ro·skep·ti·cism** *n.*

Eu·ro·trash /ˈyərōˌtrasH; ˈyo͝orō-/ ▸*n. informal* rich European socialites, esp. those living or working in the U.S.

Eur·o·zone /ˈyərəˌzōn; ˈyo͝orə-/ (also **eur·o·zone**) ▸*n.* another term for EUROLAND.

eury- ▸*comb. form* denoting a wide variety or range of something specified: *eurytopic.* ▹from Greek *eurus* 'wide.'

eu·ry·ap·sid /ˌyo͝orēˈapsid/ ▸*n.* a Mesozoic marine reptile of a group characterized by a single upper temporal opening in the skull, including the nothosaurs, plesiosaurs, and ichthyosaurs. • Sometimes placed in a subclass Euryapsida, though this taxon is no longer widely recognized. ▷from Greek *eurus* 'wide' + *apsis, apsid-* 'arch.'

Eu·ryd·i·ce /yəˈridəsē/ *Greek Mythology* the wife of Orpheus. After she was killed by a snake, Orpheus secured her release from the underworld on the condition that he not look back at her on their way back to the world of the living. But Orpheus did look back, whereupon Eurydice disappeared.

eu·ry·ha·line /ˌyərəˈhālīn; -ˈhal-/ ▸*adj. Ecology* (of an aquatic organism) able to tolerate a wide range of salinity. Often contrasted with **STENOHALINE.** ▷late 19th cent.: from Greek *eurus* 'wide' + *halinos* 'of salt.'

eu·ryp·ter·id /yəˈriptərid/ ▸*n.* an extinct marine arthropod of a group occurring in the Paleozoic era. They are related to horseshoe crabs and resemble large scorpions with a terminal pair of paddle-shaped swimming appendages. • Subclass Eurypterida, class Merostomata, subphylum Chelicerata. ▷late 19th cent.: from modern Latin *Eurypterus* (genus name), from **EURY-** + Greek *pteron* 'wing' + **-ID**[2].

eu·ry·ther·mal /ˌyo͝orəˈTHərməl/ (also **eu·ry·ther·mic** /-ˈTHərmik/) ▸*adj. Ecology* (of an organism) able to tolerate a wide range of temperatures. Often contrasted with **STENOTHERMAL.**

eu·ryth·mic /yəˈri<u>TH</u>mik; yo͞o-/ ▸*adj. rare* (esp. of architecture or art) in or relating to harmonious proportion. ▷mid 19th cent.: based on Greek *eurüthmia* 'proportion' + **-IC.**

eu·ryth·mics /yəˈri<u>TH</u>miks; yo͞o-/ ▸*plural n.* [treated as *sing.*] a system of rhythmical physical movements to music used to teach musical understanding (esp. in Steiner schools) or for therapeutic purposes, created by Émile Jaques-Dalcroze. ▷early 20th cent.: from **EU-** 'well' + **RHYTHM** + **-ICS.**

eu·ryth·my /yo͞oˈri<u>TH</u>mē/ ▸*n.* another term for **EURYTHMICS.** ▷early 17th cent. (also as *eurythmia* in early use): via Latin from Greek *eurüthmia*, from *eu-* 'well' + *rhuthmos* 'proportion, rhythm.'

eu·ry·top·ic /ˌyərəˈtäpik; yo͝orə-/ ▸*adj. Ecology* (of an organism) able to tolerate a wide range of habitats or ecological conditions. Often contrasted with **STENOTOPIC.**

Eu·se·bi·us /yo͞oˈsēbēəs/ (*c.*AD 264–*c.*340), bishop and church historian; known as **Eusebius of Caesaria.** His *Ecclesiastical History* is the principal source for the history of Christianity (esp. in the Eastern Church) from the age of the Apostles until 324.

eu·so·cial /yo͞oˈsōSHəl/ ▸*adj. Zoology* (of an animal species, esp. an insect) showing an advanced level of social organization, in which a single female or caste produces the offspring and nonreproductive individuals cooperate in caring for the young. —**eu·so·ci·al·i·ty** /-ˌsōSHēˈalitē/ *n.*

Eu·sta·chian tube /yo͞oˈstāSH(ē)ən; -kēən/ ▸*n. Anatomy* a narrow passage leading from the pharynx to the cavity of the middle ear, permitting the equalization of pressure on each side of the eardrum. ▷mid 18th cent.: named after Bartolomeo *Eustachio* (died 1574), the Italian anatomist who identified and described it.

eu·sta·sy /ˈyo͞ostəsē/ ▸*n.* a change of sea level throughout the world, caused typically by movements of parts of the earth's crust or melting of glaciers. ▷1940s: back-formation from *eustatic*, coined in German from Greek *eu* 'well' + *statikos* 'static.' —**eu·sta·tic** /yo͞oˈstatik/ *adj.*

Eus·ton Road /ˈyo͞ostn/ ▸*n.* [as *adj.*] relating to or denoting a group of English post-Impressionist realistic painters of the 1930s. ▷from the name of a road in London, England, site of a former School of Drawing and Painting (1938–39).

eu·stress /yo͞oˈstres/ ▸*n.* moderate or normal psychological stress interpreted as being beneficial for the experiencer ▷late 20th cent.: **EU-+ STRESS,** on the pattern of *distress.*

eu·tec·tic /yo͞oˈtektik/ *Chemistry* ▸*adj.* relating to or denoting a mixture of substances (in fixed proportions) that melts and solidifies at a single temperature that is lower than the melting points of the separate constituents or of any other mixture of them.
▸*n.* a eutectic mixture. ■ short for **EUTECTIC POINT.** ▷late 19th cent.: from Greek *eutēktos* 'easily melting,' from *eu* 'well, easily' + *tēkein* 'melt.'

eu·tec·tic point (also **eutectic temperature**) ▸*n. Chemistry* the temperature at which a particular eutectic mixture freezes or melts.

eu·tec·toid /yo͞oˈtektoid/ *Metallurgy* ▸*adj.* relating to or denoting an alloy that has a minimum transformation temperature between a solid solution and a simple mixture of metals.
▸*n.* a eutectoid mixture or alloy.

Eu·ter·pe /yo͞oˈtərpē/ *Greek & Roman Mythology* the Muse of flute playing and lyric poetry. ▷Greek, literally 'well-pleasing.'

eu·tha·na·sia /ˌyo͞oTHəˈnāZHə/ ▸*n.* the painless killing of a patient suffering from an incurable and painful disease or in an irreversible coma. The practice is illegal in most countries. ▷early 17th cent. (in the sense 'easy death'): from Greek, from *eu* 'well' + *thanatos* 'death.'

eu·tha·nize /ˈyo͞oTHəˌnīz/ ▸*v.* [*trans.*] (usu. **be euthanized**) put (a living being, esp. a dog or cat) to death humanely. ▷1970s: formed irregularly from **EUTHANASIA + -IZE.**

Eu·the·ri·a /yo͞oˈTHi(ə)rēə/ *Zoology* a major group of mammals that comprises the placentals. Compare with **METATHERIA.** • Infraclass Eutheria, subclass Theria. ▷modern Latin (plural), from **EU-** 'well, prospering' + Greek *thērion* 'wild beast.' —**eu·the·ri·an** *n.* & *adj.*

eu·thy·roid /yo͞oˈTHīˌroid/ ▸*adj. Medicine* having a normally functioning thyroid gland.

eu·troph·ic /yo͞oˈträfik; -trō-/ ▸*adj. Ecology* (of a lake or other body of water) rich in nutrients and so supporting a dense plant population, the decomposition of which kills animal life by depriving it of oxygen. Compare with **DYSTROPHIC** and **OLIGOTROPHIC.** ▷early 18th cent. (denoting a medicine promoting good nutrition): from Greek *eutrophia*, from *eu* 'well' + *trephein* 'nourish.' The current sense dates from the 1930s.

eu·troph·i·ca·tion /yo͞oˌträfiˈkāSHən/ ▸*n.* excessive richness of nutrients in a lake or other body of water, frequently due to runoff from the land, which causes a dense growth of plant life and death of animal life from lack of oxygen. —**eu·troph·i·cate** /yo͞oˈträfiˌkāt/ *v.*

eV ▸*abbr.* electron-volt(s).

EVA ▸*abbr.* ■ ethyl vinyl acetate, a material used as cushioning in running shoes, consisting of a rubbery copolymer of ethylene and vinyl acetate. ■ (in space) extravehicular activity.

e·vac·u·ant /iˈvakyo͞oənt/ ▸*n.* a medicine that induces some kind of bodily discharge, such as an emetic, a sudorific, or esp. a laxative.
▸*adj.* (of a medicine or treatment) acting to induce some kind of bodily discharge. ▷mid 18th cent.: from Latin *evacuant-* 'emptying (the bowels),' from the verb *evacuare*, later in the more general sense 'remove (contents).'

e·vac·u·ate /iˈvakyəˌwāt/ ▸*v.* [*trans.*] **1** remove (someone) from a place of danger to a safe place: *several families were evacuated from their homes.* ■ leave or cause the occupants to leave (a place of danger): *fire alarms forced staff to evacuate the building* | [*intrans.*] *nearly five million had to evacuate because of air terror.* ■ (of troops) withdraw from (a place): *the last American troops evacuated the Canal Zone.* **2** *technical* remove air, water, or other contents from (a container): *when it springs a leak, evacuate the pond* | [as *adj.*] (**evacuated**) *an evacuated bulb.* ■ empty (the bowels or another bodily organ). ■ discharge (feces or other matter) from the body. ■ *figurative* deprive (something) of contents, value, or force: *he* ***evacuated*** *time and history of significance.* ▷late Middle English (in the sense 'clear the contents of'): from Latin *evacuat-* '(of the bowels) emptied,' from the verb *evacuare*, from *e-* (variant of *ex-*) 'out of' + *vacuus* 'empty.'

e·vac·u·a·tion /iˌvakyo͞oˈāSHən/ ▸*n.* **1** the action of evacuating a person or a place: *there were waves of evacuation during the blitz* | *a full-scale evacuation of the city center.* **2** the action of emptying the bowels or another bodily organ. ■ a quantity of matter discharged from the bowels or another bodily organ. ■ *technical* the action of emptying a container of air, water, or other contents.

e·vac·u·a·tive /iˈvakyəˌwātiv/ ▸*adj.* & *n.* another term for **EVACUANT.**

e·vac·u·ee /iˌvakyo͞oˈē/ ▸*n.* a person evacuated from a place of danger to somewhere safe. ▷early 20th cent. (originally in the French form): from French *évacué*, past participle of *évacuer*, from Latin *evacuare* (see **EVACUATE**).

e·vade /iˈvād/ ▸*v.* escape or avoid, esp. by cleverness or trickery: *friends helped him to evade capture for a time* | *he tried to kiss her, but she evaded him.* ■ (of an abstract thing) elude (someone): *sleep still evaded her.* ■ avoid giving a direct answer to (a question): *he denied evading the question.* ■ avoid dealing with or accepting; contrive not to do (something morally or legally required): *difficulties to be faced and not evaded.* ■ escape paying (tax or duty), esp. by illegitimate presentation of one's finances. ■ defeat the intention of (a law or rule), esp. while complying with its letter. ▷late 15th cent.: from French *évader*, from Latin *evadere*, from *e-* (variant of *ex-*) 'out of' + *vadere* 'go.' —**e·vad·a·ble** *adj.* —**e·vad·er** *n.*

e·vag·i·nate /iˈvajəˌnāt/ ▸*v.* [*trans.*] *Biology & Physiology* turn (a tubular or pouch-shaped organ or structure) inside out. ■ [*intrans.*] (of such a structure or organ) turn inside out. ▷mid 17th cent.: from Latin *evaginat-* 'unsheathed,' from the verb *evaginare*, from *e-* (variant of *ex-*) 'out of' + *vagina* 'sheath.' —**e·vag·i·na·tion** /iˌvajəˈnāSHən/ *n.*

e·val·u·ate /iˈvalyo͞oˌāt/ ▸*v.* [*trans.*] form an idea of the amount, number, or value of; assess: *when you evaluate any hammer, look for precision machining* | [with *clause*] *computer simulations evaluated how the aircraft would perform.* ■ *Mathematics* find a numerical expression or equivalent for (an equation, formula, or function). ▷mid 19th cent.: back-formation from *evaluation*, from French *évaluer*, from *es-* (from Latin *ex-*) 'out, from' + Old French *value* 'value.' —**e·val·u·a·tion** /iˌvalyo͞oˈāSHən/ *n.* —**e·val·u·a·tive** /-yo͞oˌātiv; -ətiv/ *adj.* —**e·val·u·a·tor** /-yo͞oˌātər/ *n.*

evan. ▸*abbr.* ■ evangelical. ■ evangelist.

ev·a·nesce /ˌevəˈnes/ ▸*v.* [*intrans.*] *poetic/literary* pass out of sight, memory, or existence. ▷mid 19th cent.: from Latin *evanescere*, from *e-* (variant of *ex-*) 'out of' + *vanus* 'empty.'

ev·a·nes·cent /ˌevəˈnesənt/ ▸*adj. chiefly poetic/literary* soon passing out of sight, memory, or existence; quickly fading or disappearing: *a shimmering evanescent bubble.* See note at **TEMPORARY.** ■ *Physics* denoting a field or wave that extends into a region where it cannot propagate and whose amplitude therefore decreases with distance. ▷early 18th cent. (in the sense 'almost imperceptible'): from Latin *evanescent-* 'disappearing,' from the verb *evanescere* (see **EVANESCE**). —**ev·a·nes·cence** *n.* —**ev·a·nes·cent·ly** *adv.*

evang. (or **Evang.**) ▸*abbr.* ■ evangelical. ■ evangelist.

e·van·gel /iˈvanjəl/ ▸*n.* **1** *archaic* the Christian gospel. ■ any of the four Gospels. **2** another term for **EVANGELIST.** ▷Middle English (in the sense 'gospel'): from Old French *evangile*, via ecclesiastical Latin from Greek *euangelion* 'good news,' from *euangelos* 'bringing good news,' from *eu-* 'well' + *angelein* 'announce.'

e·van·gel·i·cal /ˌivanˈjelikəl/ ▸*adj.* of or according to the teaching of the gospel or the Christian religion. ■ of or denoting a tradition within Protestant Christianity emphasizing the authority of the Bible, personal conversion, and the doctrine of salvation by faith in the Atonement. ■ zealous in advocating something.
▸*n.* a member of the evangelical tradition in the Christian Church. ▷mid 16th cent.: via ecclesiastical Latin from ecclesiastical Greek *euangelikos*, from *euangelos* (see **EVANGEL**). —**e·van·gel·ic** /-ˈjelik/ *adj.* —**e·van·gel·i·cal·ism** /-izəm/ *n.* —**e·van·gel·i·cal·ly** *adv.*

e·van·ge·lism /iˈvanjəˌlizəm/ ▸*n.* the spreading of the Christian gospel by public preaching or personal witness. ■ zealous advocacy of a cause.

e·van·ge·list /iˈvanjəlist/ ▸*n.* **1** a person who seeks to convert others to the Christian faith, esp. by public preaching. ■ a layperson engaged in Christian missionary work. ■ a zealous advocate of something: *he is an evangelist of junk bonds.* **2** the writer of one of the four Gospels (Matthew, Mark, Luke, or John): *St. John the Evangelist.* ▷Middle English (sense 2): from Old French *évangéliste*, via ecclesiastical Latin from ecclesiastical Greek *euangelistēs*, from *euangelizesthai* 'evangelize.' —**e·van·ge·lis·tic** /iˌvanjəˈlistik/ *adj.*

e·van·ge·lize /iˈvanjəˌlīz/ ▸*v.* [*trans.*] convert or seek to convert (someone) to Christianity. ■ [*intrans.*] preach the Christian gospel: *the Church's mission to evangelize and declare the faith.* ▷late Middle English: from ecclesiastical Latin *evangelizare*, from Greek *euangelizesthai*, from *euangelos* (see **EVANGEL**). —**e·van·ge·li·za·tion** /iˌvanjəliˈzāSHən/ *n.* —**e·van·ge·liz·er** *n.*

Ev·ans[1] /ˈevənz/, Sir Arthur (John) (1851–1941), English archaeologist. His excavations at Knossos (1899–1935) resulted in the discovery of the Bronze Age civilization of Crete, which he named Minoan after the legendary Cretan king Minos.

Pronunciation Key ə *ago*; ər *over*; ˈə or ˌə *up*; ˈər or ˌər *fur*; a *hat*; ā *rate*; ä *car*; CH *chew*; e *let*; ē *see*; e(ə)r *air*; i *fit*; ī *by*; i(ə)r *ear*; NG *sing*; ō *go*; ô *for*; oi *boy*; o͝o *good*; o͞o *goo*; ou *out*; SH *she*; TH *thin*; <u>TH</u> *then*; (h)w *why*; ZH *vision*

Ev·ans[2], Dame Edith (Mary) (1888–1976), English actress. She is particularly remembered as Lady Bracknell in Oscar Wilde's *The Importance of Being Earnest.*

Ev·ans[3], Ernest, see CHECKER.

Ev·ans[4], Mary Ann, see ELIOT[3].

Ev·ans·ton /ˈevənstən/ **1** a city in northeastern Illinois, just north of Chicago, home to Northwestern University; pop. 74,239. **2** a city in southwestern Wyoming, next to the Utah border, southwest of Green River; pop. 11,507.

Ev·ans·ville /ˈevənz,vil/ an industrial port city in southwestern Indiana, on the Ohio River; pop. 121,582.

evap. ▸*abbr.* evaporate.

e·vap·o·rate /iˈvapə,rāt/ ▸*v.* turn from liquid into vapor: [*intrans.*] *cook until most of the liquid has evaporated* | [*trans.*] *this gets the oil hot enough to evaporate any moisture.* ■ lose or cause to lose moisture or solvent as vapor: [*trans.*] *the solution was evaporated to dryness.* ■ [*intrans.*] (of something abstract) cease to exist: *the militancy of earlier years had evaporated in the wake of defeat.* ▷late Middle English: from Latin *evaporat-* 'changed into vapor,' from the verb *evaporare,* from *e-* (variant of *ex-*) 'out of' + *vapor* 'steam, vapor.' **—e·vap·o·ra·ble** /-rəbəl/ *adj.* **—e·vap·o·ra·tion** /i,vapəˈrāsʜən/ *n.* **—e·vap·o·ra·tor** /-,rātər/ *n.*

e·vap·o·rat·ed milk ▸*n.* thick, sweetened milk that has had some of the liquid removed by evaporation.

e·vap·o·rat·ing dish /iˈvapə,rātiɴɢ/ ▸*n. Chemistry* a small ceramic dish in which liquids are heated over a flame so that they evaporate, leaving a solid residue.

e·vap·o·ra·tive /iˈvapə,rātiv/ ▸*adj.* relating to or involving evaporation: *evaporative water loss.* ▷late Middle English: from late Latin *evaporativus,* from *evaporare* 'change into vapor' (see EVAPORATE).

e·vap·o·ra·tive cool·ing ▸*n.* reduction in temperature resulting from the evaporation of a liquid, which removes latent heat from the surface from which evaporation takes place. This process is employed in industrial and domestic cooling systems, and is also the physical basis of sweating.

e·vap·o·rite /iˈvapə,rīt/ ▸*n. Geology* a natural salt or mineral deposit left after the evaporation of a body of water. ▷1920s: alteration of EVAPORATE (see also -ITE[1]).

e·vap·o·tran·spi·ra·tion /i,vapō,transpəˈrāsʜən/ ▸*n.* the process by which water is transferred from the land to the atmosphere by evaporation from the soil and other surfaces and by transpiration from plants.

e·va·sion /iˈvāzʜən/ ▸*n.* the action of evading something: *their adroit evasion of almost all questions.* ■ an indirect answer; a prevaricating excuse: *the protestations and evasions of a witness.* ▷late Middle English (in the sense 'prevaricating excuse'): via Old French from Latin *evasio(n-),* from *evadere* (see EVADE).

e·va·sive /iˈvāsiv/ ▸*adj.* tending to avoid commitment or self-revelation, esp. by responding only indirectly: *she was evasive about her phone number.* ■ directed toward avoidance or escape: *they decided to* ***take evasive action.*** ▷early 18th cent.: from Latin *evas-* 'evaded' (from the verb *evadere*) + -IVE. **—e·va·sive·ly** *adv.* **—e·va·sive·ness** *n.*

Eve /ēv/ (in the Bible) the first woman, wife of Adam and mother of Cain and Abel.

eve /ēv/ ▸*n.* the day or period of time immediately before an event or occasion: ***on the eve of*** *her departure he gave her a little parcel.* ■ the evening or day before a religious festival: *the service for Passover eve.* ■ *chiefly poetic/literary* evening: *a bitter winter's eve.* ▷late Middle English (in the sense 'close of day'): short form of EVEN[2].

e·vec·tion /iˈveksʜən/ ▸*n. Astronomy* regular variation in the eccentricity of the moon's orbit around the earth, caused mainly by the sun's attraction. ▷mid 17th cent. (in the sense 'elevation, exaltation'): from Latin *evectio(n-),* from *evehere* 'carry out or up,' from *e-* (variant of *ex-*) 'out' + *vehere* 'carry.'

Eve hy·poth·e·sis ▸*n.* the hypothesis (based on study of mitochondrial DNA) that modern humans have a common female ancestor who lived in Africa around 200,000 years ago. Also called AFRICAN EVE HYPOTHESIS.

E·ven /ˈāwən; ˈevən/ ▸*n.* (*pl.* same) **1** a member of an indigenous people of eastern Siberia. **2** the language of this people, a Tungusic language with about 6,000 speakers, closely related to Evenki.
▸*adj.* of or relating to this people or their language.

e·ven[1] /ˈēvən/ ▸*adj.* (**e·ven·er, e·ven·est**) **1** flat and smooth: *prepare the site, then lay an even bed of mortar.* ■ in the same plane or line; level: *run a file along the saw to make all of the teeth* ***even with*** *each other.* ■ having little variation in quality; regular: *they traveled at an even and leisurely pace.* ■ equal in number, amount, or value: *an even gender balance among staff and students.* ■ equally balanced: *it's not an even fight.* ■ exactly equal to a round number; not having any fractions: *the Dow Jones ended at an even 10,000.* ■ (of a person's temper or disposition) equable; calm: *a man of good humor and even temper.* **2** (of a number, such as 2, 6, or 108) divisible by two without a remainder. ■ bearing such a number: *headers can be placed on odd or even pages or both.*
▸*v.* make or become even: [*trans.*] *she cut the hair again to* ***even up*** *the ends.*
▸*adv.* used to emphasize something surprising or extreme: *they have never even heard of the U.S.* | *they wore fur hats, even in summer.* ■ used in comparisons for emphasis: *he knows even less about it than I do.* ▷Old English *efen* (adjective), *efne* (adverb), of Germanic origin; related to Dutch *even, effen* and German *eben.* **—e·ven·ly** *adv.* **—e·ven·ness** *n.*
▸*PHRASES* □ **even as** at the very same time as: *even as he spoke, their baggage was being unloaded.* □ **an even break** *informal* a fair chance: *suckers never get an even break.* □ **even if** despite the possibility that; no matter whether: *always try everything even if it turns out to be a dud.* ■ despite the fact that: *he is a great President, even if he has many enemies.* □ **even now** (or **then**) **1** now (or then) as well as before: *even now, after all these years, it upsets me.* **2** in spite of what has (or had) happened: *even then he never raised his voice to me.* **3** at this (or that) very moment: *very likely you are even now picking up the telephone to call.* □ **even so** in spite of that; nevertheless: *not the most exciting of places, but even so I was having a good time.* □ **even though** despite the fact that: *even though he was bigger, he never looked down on me.* □ **get** (or **be**) **even** *informal* inflict trouble or harm on someone similar to that which they have inflicted on oneself: *I'll* ***get even with*** *you for this.* □ **of even date** *Law* or *formal* of the same date. □ **on an even keel** (of a ship or aircraft) having the same draft forward and aft. ■ *figurative* (of a person or situation) functioning normally after a period of difficulty: *getting her life back on to an even keel after their breakup had been difficult.*

e·ven[2] ▸*n. archaic* or *poetic/literary* the end of the day; evening: *bring it to my house this even.* ▷Old English *ǣfen,* of Germanic origin; related to Dutch *avont* and German *Abend.*

e·ven-aged ▸*adj. Forestry* (of woodland) composed of trees of approximately the same age. ■ (of trees) of approximately the same age.

e·ven-hand·ed /ˈēvənˈhandid/ ▸*adj.* fair and impartial in treatment or judgment: *an even-handed approach.* **—e·ven-hand·ed·ly** *adv.* **—e·ven-hand·ed·ness** *n.*

eve·ning /ˈēvniɴɢ/ ▸*n.* the period of time at the end of the day, usually from about 6 p.m. to bedtime: *it was seven o'clock* ***in the evening*** | [as *adj.*] *the evening meal.* ■ this time characterized by a specified type of activity or particular weather conditions: *they could have a relaxing evening.* ■ [as *adj.*] prescribed by fashion as suitable for relatively formal social events held in the evening: *a couple in evening dress.*
▸*adv.* (**evenings**) *informal* in the evening; every evening: *Saturday evenings he invariably fell asleep.*
▸*exclam. informal* short for GOOD EVENING. ▷Old English *ǣfnung* 'dusk falling, the time around sunset,' from *ǣfnian* 'approach evening,' from *ǣfen* (see EVEN[2]).

eve·ning gown ▸*n.* a long, elegant dress suitable for wearing on formal occasions.

eve·ning gros·beak ▸*n.* a grosbeak native to North America, with yellow coloring. • *Coccothraustes vespertinus.*

eve·ning prayer ▸*n.* a prayer said in the evening. ■ (usu. **evening prayers**) a formal act of worship held in the evening. ■ [in *sing.*] (in the Anglican Church) the service of evensong.

eve·ning prim·rose ▸*n.* a plant with yellow flowers that open in the evening and yield seeds from which a medicinal oil is extracted. • Genus *Oenothera,* family Onagraceae: numerous species, in particular the **common evening primrose** (*O. biennis*).

common evening primrose

eve·ning star ▸*n.* (**the evening star**) the planet Venus, seen shining in the western sky after sunset.

eve·ning wear ▸*n.* clothing, esp. for women, that is suitable for formal social occasions: *the fifth floor is beginning to fill with men in dark suits and women in evening wear.*

E·ven·ki /iˈweɴɢkē; iˈveɴɢkē/ ▸*n.* (*pl.* same or **-kis**) **1** a member of a native people of northern Siberia. Also called TUNGUS. **2** the Tungusic language of this people.
▸*adj.* of or relating to this people or their language.

e·ven mon·ey ▸*n.* (in betting) odds offering an equal chance of winning or losing, with the amount won being the same as the stake: *players bet on each throw for even money* | [as *adj.*] *Romany King swept past the even-money favorite Paco's Boy.* ■ [as *adj.*] (of a chance) equally likely to happen or not; fifty-fifty: *above those engines there was an even-money chance of being heard.*

e·ven·song /ˈēvən,sôɴɢ; ˈevən,säɴɢ/ (also **E·ven·song**) ▸*n.* (in the Christian Church) a service of evening prayers, psalms, and canticles, conducted according to a set form, esp. that of the Anglican Church: *choral evensong.* ▷Old English *ǣfensang,* originally applied to the pre-Reformation service of vespers (see EVEN[2], SONG).

e·ven-ste·ven /ˈēvən ˈstēvən/ ▸*adj.* & *adv. informal* used in reference to fair and equal competition or distribution of resources: [as *adj.*] *the race was an even-steven affair* | [as *adv.*] *I split the money with my wife even-steven.* ▷mid 19th cent.: rhyming phrase, used as an intensive.

e·vent /iˈvent/ ▸*n.* a thing that happens, esp. one of importance: *the media's focus on events in the Middle East.* ■ a planned public or social occasion: *events to raise money for charity.* ■ each of several particular contests making up a sports competition: *a star sprinter in the 100- and 200-meter events.* ■ *Physics* a single occurrence of a process, e.g., the ionization of one atom. ▷late 16th cent.: from Latin *eventus,* from *evenire* 'result, happen,' from *e-* (variant of *ex-*) 'out of' + *venire* 'come.' **—e·vent·less** *adj.* **—e·vent·less·ness** *n.*
▸*PHRASES* □ **in any event** (or **at all events**) whatever happens or may have happened: *in any event, there was one promise the trickster did keep.* □ **in the event** *chiefly Brit.* as it turns (or turned) out: *he was sent on this important and, in the event, quite fruitless mission.* □ **in the event of —— if ——** happens: *this will reduce the chance of serious injury in the event of an accident.* □ **in the event that** if; should it happen that: *in the event that an attack is launched, the defenders will have been significantly weakened by air attacks.* □ **in that event** if that happens: *in that event, the US would incline toward a lifting of the arms embargo.*

e·vent cre·a·tion ▸*n.* **1** the activity of planning, organizing, and staging public events. **2** (in computer programming) the activity of or facility for creating an event that will unfold in real time when conditions for it have been met.

e·ven-tem·pered ▸*adj.* not easily annoyed or angered: *a gentle and even-tempered man.*

e·vent·er /iˈventər/ ▸*n. Brit.* a horse or rider that takes part in eventing. ▷1970s: from EVENT, in *three-day event* (see EVENTING).

e·vent·ful /iˈventfəl/ ▸*adj.* marked by interesting or exciting events: *his long and eventful life.* **—e·vent·ful·ly** *adv.* **—e·vent·ful·ness** *n.*

e·vent ho·ri·zon ▸*n. Astronomy* a theoretical boundary around a black hole beyond which no light or other radiation can escape. ■ an area or time frame within which something is considered to have inevitable implications: *they judge a new SARS outbreak to be beyond the event horizon at this point.*

e·ven·tide /ˈēvən,tīd/ ▸*n. archaic* or *poetic/literary* the end of the day; evening: *the moon flower opens its white, trumpetlike flowers* ***at eventide.*** ▷Old English *ǣfentīd* (see EVEN[2], TIDE).

e·vent·ing /iˈventiɴɢ/ ▸*n.* an equestrian sport in which competitors must take part in each of several contests, usually cross-country, dressage, and show jumping. ▷1960s: from EVENT, in *three-day event,* horse trials held on three consecutive days. Compare with EVENTER.

e·vent·ive /iˈventiv/ ▸*adj. Linguistics* (of the subject or object of a sentence) denoting an event.

e·ven-toed un·gu·late ▸*n.* a hoofed mammal of an

order that includes the ruminants, camels, pigs, and hippopotamuses. Mammals of this group have either two or four toes on each foot. Compare with ODD-TOED UNGULATE. • Order Artiodactyla: three suborders. See also RUMINANT, TYLOPOD.

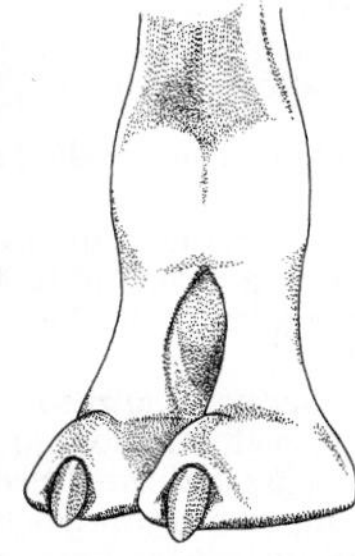
even-toed ungulate

e·ven·tu·al /iˈvenCHo͞oəl/ ▸*adj.* [*attrib.*] occurring at the end of or as a result of a series of events; final; ultimate: *it's impossible to predict the eventual outcome of the competition.* ▷early 17th cent. (in the sense 'relating to an event or events'): from Latin *eventus* (see EVENT), on the pattern of *actual.*

e·ven·tu·al·i·ty /iˌvenCHo͞oˈalitē/ ▸*n.* (*pl.* **-ties**) a possible event or outcome: *you must be prepared for all eventualities.*

e·ven·tu·al·ly /iˈvenCHo͞oəlē/ ▸*adv.* [*sentence adverb*] in the end, esp. after a long delay, dispute, or series of problems: *eventually, after midnight, I arrived at the hotel.*

e·ven·tu·ate /iˈvenCHo͞oˌāt/ ▸*v.* [*intrans.*] *formal* occur as a result: *you never know what might eventuate.* ■ (**eventuate in**) lead to as a result: *circumstances that eventuate in crime.* ▷late 18th cent.: from EVENT, on the pattern of *actuate.* —**e·ven·tu·a·tion** /iˌvenCHo͞oˈāSHən/ *n.*

ev·er /ˈevər/ ▸*adv.* **1** [usu. with *negative* or in *questions*] at any time: *nothing ever seemed to ruffle her | don't you ever regret giving up all that money?* ■ used in comparisons for emphasis: *they felt better than ever before | our biggest ever range.* **2** at all times; always: *ever the man of action, he was impatient with intellectuals | it remains* **as popular as ever** *| they lived* **happily ever after** | [in *combination*] *he toyed with his ever-present cigar.* **3** [with *comparative*] increasingly; constantly: *having to borrow ever larger sums.* **4** used for emphasis in questions expressing astonishment or outrage: *who ever heard of a grown man being frightened of the dark? | don't you ever forget it.* ▷Old English *ǣfre*, of unknown origin.

▸*PHRASES* □ **ever and anon** *archaic* occasionally: *ever and anon the stillness is rent by the scream of a gibbon.* [from Shakespeare's *Love's Labour's Lost* (v. ii. 101).] □ **ever since** throughout the period since: *she had lived alone ever since her husband died.* □ **ever so** very: *I am ever so grateful.* □ **ever such** *Brit., informal* very much: *ever such a pretty little cat.* □ **for ever** see FOREVER. □ **yours ever** (also **ever yours**) *Brit.* a formula used to end an informal letter, before the signature.

ev·er·bloom·ing /ˈevərˈblo͞omiNG/ ▸*adj.* (of a plant) in bloom throughout most or all of the growing season: *others prefer an everblooming variety like the rugosa roses.*

Ev·er·est, Mount /ˈev(ə)rəst/ a mountain in the Himalayas, on the border between Nepal and Tibet. Rising to 29,028 feet (8,848 m), it is the highest mountain in the world; it was first climbed in 1953 by Sir Edmund Hillary and Tenzing Norgay. ▷named after Sir George *Everest* (1790–1866), a supervisor for the British government in India.

Ev·er·ett /ˈev(ə)rit/ **1** an industrial city in northeastern Massachusetts, just north of Boston; pop. 35,701. **2** an industrial port city in northwestern Washington, north of Seattle, noted for its huge Boeing aircraft-assembly plant; pop. 91,488.

ev·er·glade /ˈevərˌglād/ ▸*n.* a marshy tract of land that is mostly under water and covered with tall grass.

Ev·er·glades /ˈevərˌglādz/ a vast area of marshland and coastal mangrove in southern Florida, part of which is protected as a national park.

ev·er·green /ˈevərˌgrēn/ ▸*adj.* of or denoting a plant that retains green leaves throughout the year: *the glossy laurel is hardy and evergreen | evergreen shrubs.* Often contrasted with DECIDUOUS.

▸*n.* a plant that retains green leaves throughout the year: *evergreens planted to cut off the east wind.*

ev·er·green oak ▸*n.* another term for HOLM OAK.

Ev·er·green State a nickname for the state of WASHINGTON[1].

ev·er·last·ing /ˌevərˈlastiNG/ ▸*adj.* lasting forever or for a very long time: *the damned would suffer everlasting torment | it would be an everlasting reminder of this evening.* See note at ETERNAL.

▸*n.* **1** *poetic/literary* eternity. **2** (also **everlasting flower**) a flower of the daisy family with a papery texture, retaining its shape and color after being dried, esp. a helichrysum. Also called IMMORTELLE. —**ev·er·last·ing·ly** *adv.* —**ev·er·last·ing·ness** *n.*

ev·er·more /ˌevərˈmôr/ ▸*adv.* (chiefly used for rhetorical effect or in ecclesiastical contexts) always: *we pray that we may evermore dwell in him and he in us.*

Ev·ers /ˈevərz/, Medgar Wiley (1925–63), U.S. civil rights leader. He was Mississippi field secretary of the NAACP from 1954; his assassination was a factor in President Kennedy's call for new, comprehensive civil rights legislation.

E·vert /ˈevərt/, Chris (1954–), U.S. tennis player; full name *Christine Marie Evert.* Between 1974 and 1986, she won the women's singles championship at the French Open seven times, the U.S. Open six times, Wimbledon three times, and the Australian Open two times.

e·vert /iˈvərt/ ▸*v.* [*trans.*] *Biology & Physiology* turn (a structure or organ) outward or inside out: [as *adj.*] (**everted**) *the characteristic facial appearance of full, often everted lips.* ▷mid 16th cent. (in the sense 'upset, overthrow'): from Latin *evertere*, from *e-* (variant of *ex-*) 'out' + *vertere* 'to turn.' The current sense dates from the late 18th cent. —**e·ver·si·ble** /iˈvərsəbəl/ *adj.* —**e·ver·sion** /iˈvərZHən; -SHən/ *n.*

ev·er·where /ˈevərˌ(h)we(ə)r/ ▸*adv. dialect* **1** everywhere. **2** wherever.

ev·er·which /ˈevərˌ(h)wiCH/ ▸*adj. dialect* whichever.

eve·ry /ˈevrē/ ▸*adj.* (preceding a singular noun) used to refer to all the individual members of a set without exception: *the hotel assures every guest of personal attention* | [with *possessive adj.*] *the children hung on his every word.* ■ used before an amount to indicate something happening at specified intervals: *tours are every thirty minutes | they had every third week off.* ■ (used for emphasis) all possible; the utmost: *you have every reason to be disappointed.* ▷Old English *ǣfre ǣlc* (see EVER, EACH).

▸*PHRASES* □ **every bit as** (in comparisons) equally as: *the planning should be every bit as enjoyable as the event itself.* □ **every inch** see INCH[1]. □ **every last** (or **every single**) used to emphasize that every member of a group is included: *unbelievers, every last one of them | they insist you weigh every single thing.* □ **every man has his price** *proverb* everyone is open to bribery if the inducement offered is large enough. □ **every now and then** (or **now and again**) from time to time; occasionally: *I used to see him every now and then.* □ **every other** each second in a series; each alternate: *I train with weights every other day.* □ **every so often** from time to time; occasionally: *every so often I need a laugh to stay sane.* □ **every time** without exception: *it brews a perfect blend of coffee every time.* □ **every which way** *informal* in all directions: *you can see cracks moving every which way.* ■ by all available means: *since then he has tried every which way to avoid contact with his ex.*

eve·ry·bod·y /ˈevrēˌbädē; -ˌbədē/ ▸*pron.* every person: *everybody agrees with his views | it's not everybody's cup of tea.*

USAGE **Everybody**, along with **everyone**, traditionally used a singular pronoun of reference: *everybody must sign* **his** *own name.* Because the use of *his* in this context is now perceived as sexist by some, a second option became popular: *everybody must sign* **his or her** *own name.* But *his or her* is often awkward, and many feel that the plural simply makes more sense: *everybody must sign* **their** *own name.* Although this violates what many consider standard, it is in fact standard in British English and increasingly so in U.S. English. In some sentences, only *they* makes grammatical sense: *everybody agreed to convict the defendant, and* **they** *voted unanimously.*

eve·ry·day /ˈevrēˌdā/ ▸*adj.* [*attrib.*] happening or used every day; daily: *everyday chores like shopping and housework.* ■ commonplace: *everyday drugs like aspirin.*

USAGE The adjective **everyday**, 'pertaining to every day, ordinary,' is correctly spelled as one word (*carrying out their everyday activities*), but the adverbial phrase **every day**, meaning 'each day,' is always spelled as two words (*it rained every day*).

Eve·ry·man /ˈevrēˌman/ ▸*n.* [in *sing.*] an ordinary or typical human being: *it is Everyman's dream car.* ▷early 20th cent.: the name of the principal character in a 15th-cent. morality play.

eve·ry·one /ˈevrēˌwən/ ▸*pron.* every person: *everyone needs time to unwind | he knew everyone in the business.*

USAGE See **usage** at EVERYBODY.

eve·ry one ▸*pron.* each one.

USAGE The pronoun **everyone**, meaning 'every person,' is correctly spelled as one word: *everyone had a great time at the party.*
The pronoun **every one**, meaning 'each one,' is spelled as two words: *every one of the employees got a bonus at the end of the year.*
The word **everybody** is substitutable in the first example but not in the second example.
See also **usage** at EVERYDAY.

eve·ry·place /ˈevrēˌplās/ ▸*adv.* informal term for EVERYWHERE.

eve·ry·thing /ˈevrēˌTHiNG/ ▸*pron.* **1** all things; all the things of a group or class: *he taught me everything I know | herbal cures for* **everything from** *leprosy* **to** *rheumatism.* ■ all things of importance; a great deal: *I lost everything in the crash | he owed everything to his years in Munich.* ■ the most important thing or aspect: *money isn't everything.* **2** the current situation; life in general: *how's everything? | everything is going okay.*

▸*PHRASES* □ **and everything** *informal* used to refer vaguely to other things associated with what has been mentioned: *you'll still get paid and everything.* □ **have everything** *informal* possess every attraction or advantage: *she was articulate, she was fun—it seemed to me she had everything.*

eve·ry·where /ˈevrēˌ(h)wer/ ▸*adv.* in or to all places: *I've looked everywhere | everywhere she went she was fêted.* ■ in many places; common or widely distributed: *sandwich bars are everywhere.*

▸*n.* all places or directions: *everywhere was in darkness.* ▷Middle English: formerly also as two words.

▸*PHRASE* □ **everywhere else** in all other places: *they are the same machines used everywhere else in the world.*

eve·ry·wom·an /ˈevrēˌwo͝omən/ (also **Eve·ry·wom·an**) ▸*n.* the ordinary or typical woman: *the book is a compilation of memorably silly moments in the life of a hapless Everywoman.*

evg. ▸*abbr.* evening.

e·vict /iˈvikt/ ▸*v.* [*trans.*] expel (someone) from a property, esp. with the support of the law: *he had court orders to* **evict** *the trespassers* **from** *three camps.* See note at EJECT. ▷late Middle English (in the sense 'recover property, or the title to property, by legal process'): from Latin *evict-* 'overcome, defeated,' from the verb *evincere*, from *e-* (variant of *ex-*) 'out' + *vincere* 'conquer.' —**e·vic·tion** /iˈvikSHən/ *n.* —**e·vic·tor** /-tər/ *n.*

ev·i·dence /ˈevədəns/ ▸*n.* the available body of facts or information indicating whether a belief or proposition is true or valid: *the study finds little evidence of overt discrimination.* ■ *Law* information given personally, drawn from a document, or in the form of material objects, tending or used to establish facts in a legal investigation or admissible as testimony in a law court: *without evidence, they can't bring a charge.* ■ signs; indications: *there was no obvious evidence of a break-in.*

▸*v.* [*trans.*] (usu. **be evidenced**) be or show evidence of: *that it has been populated from prehistoric times is evidenced by the remains of Neolithic buildings.* ▷Middle English: via Old French from Latin *evidentia*, from *evident-* 'obvious to the eye or mind' (see EVIDENT).

▸*PHRASES* □ **give evidence** *Law* give information and answer questions formally and in person in a law court or at an inquiry. □ **in evidence** noticeable; conspicuous: *his dramatic flair is still very much in evidence.* □ **turn state's** (or *Brit.* **King's** or **Queen's**) **evidence** *Law* (of a criminal) give information in court against one's partners in order to receive a less severe punishment oneself.

ev·i·dence-based ▸*adj. Medicine* denoting disciplines of health care that proceed empirically with regard to the patient and reject more traditional protocols.

ev·i·dent /ˈevədənt/ ▸*adj.* plain or obvious; clearly seen or understood: *she ate the cookies with evident enjoyment.* ▷late Middle English: from Old French, or from Latin *evidens, evident-* 'obvious to the eye or mind,' from *e-* (variant of *ex-*) 'out' + *videre* 'to see.'

ev·i·den·tial /ˌeviˈdenCHəl/ ▸*adj. formal* of or providing evidence: *the evidential value of the record.* ▷early 17th cent.: from medieval Latin *evidentialis*, from Latin *evidentia* (see EVIDENCE). —**ev·i·den·ti·al·i·ty** /ˌeviˌdenCHēˈalitē/ *n.* —**ev·i·den·tial·ly** *adv.*

ev·i·den·tia·ry /ˌeviˈdenSHərē/ ▸*adj. chiefly Law* another term for EVIDENTIAL.

ev·i·dent·ly /ˈevidəntlē; ˈeviˌdentlē; ˌevəˈdentlē/ ▸*adv.* **1** plainly or obviously; in a way that is clearly seen or understood: *a work so evidently laden with significance.* **2** [*sentence adverb*] it is plain that; it would seem that: *evidently Mrs. Smith thought differently.* ■ used as an affirmative response or reply: *"Were they old pals or something?" "Evidently."*

e·vil /ˈēvəl/ ▶*adj.* profoundly immoral and malevolent: *his evil deeds | no man is so evil as to be beyond redemption.* ■ (of a force or spirit) embodying or associated with the forces of the devil: *we have been driven out of the house by this evil spirit.* ■ harmful or tending to harm: *the evil effects of high taxes.* ■ (of something seen or smelled) extremely unpleasant: *a bathroom with an evil smell.*
▶*n.* profound immorality, wickedness, and depravity, esp. when regarded as a supernatural force: *the world is stalked by relentless evil | good and evil in eternal opposition.* ■ a manifestation of this, esp. in people's actions: *the evil that took place last Thursday.* ■ something that is harmful or undesirable: *sexism, racism, and all other unpleasant social evils.* ▷Old English *yfel*, of Germanic origin; related to Dutch *euvel* and German *Übel*. **—e·vil·ly** /ˈēvəl(l)ē/ *adv.* **—e·vil·ness** *n.*
▶*PHRASES* □ **the evil eye** a gaze or stare superstitiously believed to cause material harm: *he gave me **the evil eye** as I walked down the corridor.* □ **the Evil One** *archaic* the Devil. □ **put off the evil day** (or **hour**) postpone something unpleasant for as long as possible. □ **speak evil of** slander: *it is a sin to speak evil of the king.*

e·vil·do·er /ˈēvəlˌdo͞oər/ ▶*n.* a person who commits profoundly immoral and malevolent deeds. **—e·vil·do·ing** /ˈēvəlˌdo͞oiNG/ *n.*

e·vil-mind·ed ▶*adj.* having wicked thoughts, ideas, or intentions.

e·vince /iˈvins/ ▶*v.* [*trans.*] *formal* reveal the presence of (a quality or feeling): *his letters evince the excitement he felt at undertaking this journey.* ■ be evidence of; indicate: *man's inhumanity to man **as evinced in** the use of torture.* ▷late 16th cent. (in the sense 'prove by argument or evidence'): from Latin *evincere* 'overcome, defeat' (see **EVICT**).

e·vis·cer·ate /iˈvisəˌrāt/ ▶*v.* [*trans.*] *formal* disembowel (a person or animal): *the goat had been skinned and neatly eviscerated.* ■ *figurative* deprive (something) of its essential content: *myriad little concessions that would eviscerate the project.* ■ *Surgery* remove the contents of (a body organ). ▷late 16th cent.: from Latin *eviscerat-* 'disemboweled,' from the verb *eviscerare*, from *e-* (variant of *ex-*) 'out' + *viscera* 'internal organs.' **—e·vis·cer·a·tion** /iˌvisəˈrāSHən/ *n.*

ev·i·ter·ni·ty /ˌeviˈtərnitē/ ▶*n. archaic or poetic/literary* eternal existence; everlasting duration. ▷late 16th cent.: from Latin *aeviternus* 'eternal' + **-ITY**. **—ev·i·ter·nal** /-ˈtərnl/ *adj.*

e·voc·a·tive /iˈväkətiv/ ▶*adj.* bringing strong images, memories, or feelings to mind: *powerfully evocative lyrics | the building's cramped interiors are highly **evocative of** past centuries.* ▷mid 17th cent.: from Latin *evocativus*, from *evocat-* 'called forth,' from the verb *evocare* (see **EVOKE**). **—e·voc·a·tive·ly** *adv.* **—e·voc·a·tive·ness** *n.*

e·voke /iˈvōk/ ▶*v.* [*trans.*] **1** bring or recall to the conscious mind: *the sight of American asters evokes pleasant memories of childhood.* ■ elicit (a response): *the awkward kid who evoked giggles from his sisters.* **2** invoke (a spirit or deity). ▷early 17th cent. (sense 2): from Latin *evocare*, from *e-* (variant of *ex-*) 'out of, from' + *vocare* 'to call.' **—ev·o·ca·tion** /ˌēvōˈkāSHən; ˌevə-/ *n.* **—e·vok·er** *n.*

ev·o·lute /ˈevəˌlo͞ot/ (also **evolute curve**) ▶*n. Mathematics* a curve that is the locus of the centers of curvature of another curve (its involute). ▷mid 18th cent.: from Latin *evolutus*, past participle of *evolvere* 'roll out' (see **EVOLVE**).

ev·o·lu·tion /ˌevəˈlo͞oSHən/ ▶*n.* **1** the process by which different kinds of living organisms are thought to have developed and diversified from earlier forms during the history of the earth.

> The idea of organic evolution was proposed by some ancient Greek thinkers but was long rejected in Europe as contrary to the literal interpretation of the Bible. Lamarck proposed a theory that organisms became transformed by their efforts to respond to the demands of their environment, but he was unable to explain a mechanism for this. Lyell demonstrated that geological deposits were the cumulative product of slow processes over vast ages. This helped Darwin toward a theory of gradual evolution over a long period by the natural selection of those varieties of an organism slightly better adapted to the environment and hence more likely to produce descendants. Combined with the later discoveries of the cellular and molecular basis of genetics, Darwin's theory of evolution has, with some modification, become the dominant unifying concept of modern biology.

2 the gradual development of something, esp. from a simple to a more complex form: *the forms of written languages undergo constant evolution.* **3** *Chemistry* the giving off of a gaseous product, or of heat. **4** a pattern of movements or maneuvers: *silk ribbons waving in fanciful evolutions.* **5** *dated Mathematics* the extraction of a root from a given quantity. ▷early 17th cent.: from Latin *evolutio(n-)* 'unrolling,' from the verb *evolvere* (see **EVOLVE**). Early senses related to physical movement, first recorded in describing a tactical "wheeling" maneuver in the realignment of troops or ships. Current senses stem from a notion of "opening out" and "unfolding," giving rise to a general sense of 'development.' **—ev·o·lu·tion·al** /-SHənl/ *adj.* **—ev·o·lu·tion·al·ly** /-(ə)lē/ *adv.* **—ev·o·lu·tion·ar·i·ly** /ˌevəˌlo͞oSHəˈne(ə)rəlē/ *adv.* **—ev·o·lu·tion·ar·y** /-ˌnerē/ *adj.* **—ev·o·lu·tive** /-ˈlo͞otiv/ *adj.*

ev·o·lu·tion·ist /ˌevəˈlo͞oSHənist/ ▶*n.* a person who believes in the theories of evolution and natural selection.
▶*adj.* of or relating to the theories of evolution and natural selection: *an evolutionist model.* **—ev·o·lu·tion·ism** /-ˌnizəm/ *n.*

e·volve /iˈvälv/ ▶*v.* **1** develop gradually, esp. from a simple to a more complex form: [*intrans.*] *the company has **evolved into** a major chemical manufacturer | the Gothic style **evolved** steadily and naturally **from** the Romanesque* | [*trans.*] *each school must evolve its own way of working.* ■ (with reference to an organism or biological feature) develop over successive generations, esp. as a result of natural selection: [*intrans.*] *the populations are cut off from each other and evolve independently.* **2** [*trans.*] *Chemistry* give off (gas or heat). ▷early 17th cent. (in the general sense 'make more complex, develop'): from Latin *evolvere*, from *e-* (variant of *ex-*) 'out of' + *volvere* 'to roll.' **—e·volv·a·ble** *adj.* **—e·volve·ment** *n.*

Év·ros /ˈevˌrôs/ Greek name for the **MARITSA**.

e·vul·sion /iˈvəlSHən/ ▶*n.* the action of plucking something out by force; violent or forcible extraction.

Év·voi·a /ˈevyä; ˈevēä/ Greek name for **EUBOEA**.

ev·zone /ˈevˌzōn/ ▶*n.* a kilted soldier belonging to a select Greek infantry regiment. ▷late 19th cent.: from modern Greek *euzōnos*, from Greek, 'dressed for exercise' (from *eu-* 'fine' + *zōnē* 'belt'), because of their distinctive uniform, which includes a fustanella.

EW ▶*abbr.* enlisted woman (women).

Ewe /ˈāwā; ˈāvā/ ▶*n.* (*pl.* same) **1** a member of a people of Ghana, Togo, and Benin. **2** the Kwa language of this people.
▶*adj.* of or relating to this people or their language. ▷the name in Ewe.

ewe /yo͞o/ ▶*n.* a female sheep. ▷Old English *eowu*, of Germanic origin; related to Dutch *ooi* and German *Aue*.

ewe neck ▶*n.* a horse's neck of which the upper outline curves downward instead of upward. **—ewe-necked** *adj.*

ew·er /ˈyo͞oər/ ▶*n.* a large jug with a wide mouth, formerly used for carrying water for someone to wash in. ▷late Middle English: from Anglo-Norman French *ewer*, variant of Old French *aiguiere*, based on Latin *aquarius* 'of water,' from *aqua* 'water.'

Ew·ing /ˈyo͞o-iNG/, Patrick (1962–), U.S. basketball player. A center for the New York Knicks 1985–2000, he led the U.S. Olympic team to gold medals in 1984 and 1992. He played for the Seattle SuperSonics 2000–2001 and the Orlando Magic 2001–2002 before announcing his retirement.

ex[1] /eks/ ▶*prep.* **1** (of goods) sold direct from: *carpet tiles offered at a special price, ex stock.* **2** without; excluding: *the discount and market price are ex dividend.* ▷mid 19th cent. (sense 2): from Latin, 'out of.'

ex[2] ▶*n. informal* a former husband, wife, or partner in a relationship: *I don't want my ex to spoil what I have now.* ▷early 19th cent.: independent usage of **EX-**[1].

Ex. ▶*abbr. Bible* Exodus.

ex-[1] (also **e-**) ▶*prefix* **1** out; outside of: *expand | express.* **2** up and away; upward: *excel | extol.* **3** thoroughly: *exacerbate | excruciate.* **4** removal or release: *excommunicate | exculpate | expel.* **5** forming verbs expressing inducement of a state: *exasperate | excite.* **6** forming nouns (from titles of office, status, etc.) expressing a former state: *ex-husband | ex-convict.* ▷from Latin *ex* 'out of.'

> *USAGE* Ex- is assimilated as **ef-** before **f** (as in *effeminate*). *Exfiltrate* and *exfoliate* and their derivatives are exceptions.

ex-[2] ▶*prefix* out: *exodus | exorcism.* ▷from Greek *ex* 'out of.'

exa- ▶*comb. form* (used in units of measurement) denoting a factor of 10^{18}: *exajoule.* ▷from *(h)exa-* (see **HEXA-**), based on the supposed analogy of *tera-* and *tetra-*.

ex·ac·er·bate /igˈzasərˌbāt/ ▶*v.* [*trans.*] make (a problem, bad situation, or negative feeling) worse: *the forest fire was exacerbated by the lack of rain.* ▷mid 17th cent.: from Latin *exacerbat-* 'made harsh,' from the verb *exacerbare*, from *ex-* (expressing inducement of a state) + *acerbus* 'harsh, bitter.' The noun *exacerbation* (late Middle English) originally meant 'provocation to anger.' **—ex·ac·er·ba·tion** /igˌzasərˈbāSHən/ *n.*

> *USAGE* On the difference between **exacerbate** and **exasperate**, see usage at **EXASPERATE**.

ex·act /igˈzakt/ ▶*adj.* not approximated in any way; precise: *the exact details were still being worked out.* ■ accurate or correct in all details: *an exact replica, two feet tall, was constructed.* ■ (of a person) tending to be accurate and careful about minor details: *she was an exact, clever manager.* ■ (of a subject of study) permitting precise or absolute measurements as a basis for rigorously testable theories: *psychomedicine isn't an exact science yet.*
▶*v.* [*trans.*] demand and obtain (something, esp. a payment) from someone: *tributes exacted from the Slavic peoples | William's advisers exacted an oath of obedience from the clergy.* ■ inflict (revenge) on someone: *a frustrated woman bent on exacting a cruel revenge for his rejection.* ▷late Middle English (as a verb): from Latin *exact-* 'completed, ascertained, enforced,' from the verb *exigere*, from *ex-* 'thoroughly' + *agere* 'perform.' The adjective dates from the mid 16th cent. and reflects the Latin *exactus* 'precise.' **—ex·act·a·ble** *adj.* **—ex·ac·ti·tude** /-təˌt(y)o͞od/ *n.* **—ex·act·ness** *n.* **—ex·ac·tor** /-tər/ *n.*

ex·act·a /igˈzaktə/ ▶*n.* a bet in which the first two places in a race must be predicted in the correct order. Compare with **QUINELLA**. ▷1960s: from American Spanish (*quiniela*) *exacta* 'exact (quinella).'

ex·act·ing /igˈzaktiNG/ ▶*adj.* making great demands on one's skill, attention, or other resources: *living up to such exacting standards.* **—ex·act·ing·ly** *adv.* **—ex·act·ing·ness** *n.*

ex·ac·tion /igˈzakSHən/ ▶*n. formal* the action of demanding and obtaining something from someone, esp. a payment or service: *he supervised the exaction of tolls at various ports.* ■ a sum of money demanded in such a way. ■ an act of demanding unfair and exorbitant payment; an act of extortion. ▷late Middle English: from Latin *exactio(n-)*, from *exigere* 'ascertain, perfect, enforce' (see **EXACT**).

ex·act·ly /igˈzak(t)lē/ ▶*adv.* **1** without discrepancy (used to emphasize the accuracy of a figure or description): *they met in 1989 and got married exactly two years later | fold the second strip of paper in exactly the same way.* **2** in exact terms; without vagueness: *what exactly are you looking for?* **3** used as a reply to confirm or agree with what has just been said: *"You mean that you're going to tell me the truth?" "Exactly."*
▶*PHRASE* □ **not exactly** *informal* **1** not at all: *that was not exactly convincing.* **2** not quite but close to being: *not exactly agitated, but disturbed.*

ex·ag·ger·ate /igˈzajəˌrāt/ ▶*v.* [*trans.*] represent (something) as being larger, greater, better, or worse than it really is: *they were apt to exaggerate any aches and pains* | [*intrans.*] *I couldn't sleep for three days—I'm not exaggerating.* ■ [*as adj.*] (**exaggerated**) enlarged or altered beyond normal or due proportions: *her plump thighs, exaggerated hips, and minuscule waist.* ▷mid 16th cent.: from Latin *exaggerat-* 'heaped up,' from the verb *exaggerare*, from *ex-* 'thoroughly' + *aggerare* 'heap up' (from *agger* 'heap'). The word originally meant 'pile up, accumulate,' later 'intensify praise or blame,' 'dwell on a virtue or fault,' giving rise to current senses. **—ex·ag·ger·at·ed·ly** *adv.* **—ex·ag·ger·a·tion** /igˌzajəˈrāSHən/ *n.* **—ex·ag·ger·a·tive** /-ˌrātiv/ *adj.* **—ex·ag·ger·a·tor** /-ˌrātər/ *n.*

ex·alt /igˈzôlt/ ▶*v.* [*trans.*] hold (someone or something) in very high regard; think or speak very highly of: *the party will continue to exalt its hero.* ■ raise to a higher rank or a position of greater power: *this naturally exalts the peasant above his brethren in the same rank of society.* ■ make noble in character; dignify: *romanticism liberated the imagination and exalted the emotions.* ▷late

Middle English: from Latin *exaltare*, from *ex-* 'out, upward' + *altus* 'high.'

ex·al·ta·tion /ˌegzôlˈtāsʜən; ˌeksôl-/ ▶*n.* **1** a feeling or state of extreme happiness: *she beams with exaltation.* **2** the action of elevating someone in rank, power, or character: *the exaltation of Jesus to the Father's right hand.* ■ the action of praising someone or something highly: *the exaltation of the army as a place for brotherhood.* ▷late Middle English (in the sense 'the action of raising high'): from late Latin *exaltatio(n-)*, from Latin *exaltare* 'raise aloft' (see **EXALT**).

ex·alt·ed /igˈzôltid; eg-/ ▶*adj.* **1** (of a person or their rank or status) placed at a high or powerful level; held in high regard: *it had taken her years of hard infighting to reach her present exalted rank.* ■ (of an idea) noble; lofty: *his exalted hopes of human progress.* **2** in a state of extreme happiness: *I felt exalted and newly alive.* —**ex·alt·ed·ly** *adv.* —**ex·alt·ed·ness** *n.*

ex·am /igˈzam/ ▶*n.* **1** short for **EXAMINATION** (sense 2): *he was likely to fail his exams again* | [as *adj.*] *exam results.* **2** [with *adj.*] a medical test of a specified kind: *routine eye exams.*

ex·a·men /igˈzāmən/ ▶*n.* a formal examination of the soul or conscience, made usually daily by Jesuits and some other Roman Catholics. ▷mid 17th cent.: from Latin, in the figurative sense 'examination' (literally 'tongue of a balance'), from *exigere* 'weigh accurately.'

ex·am·i·na·tion /igˌzaməˈnāsʜən/ ▶*n.* **1** a detailed inspection or investigation: *an examination of marketing behavior* | *a medical examination is conducted without delay.* ■ the action or process of conducting such an inspection or investigation: *the treaty is under examination by the Senate Foreign Relations Committee.* **2** a formal test of a person's knowledge or proficiency in a particular subject or skill: *he scraped through the examinations at the end of his first year.* **3** *Law* the formal questioning of a defendant or witness in court. ▷late Middle English (also in the sense 'testing (one's conscience) by a standard'): via Old French from Latin *examinatio(n-)*, from *examinare* 'weigh, test' (see **EXAMINE**).

ex·am·i·na·tion-in-chief ▶*n.* another term for **DIRECT EXAMINATION.**

ex·am·ine /igˈzamən/ ▶*v.* [*trans.*] **1** inspect (someone or something) in detail to determine their nature or condition; investigate thoroughly: *a doctor examined me and said I might need a caesarean* | *this forced us to examine every facet of our business.* **2** test the knowledge or proficiency of (someone) by requiring them to answer questions or perform tasks: *the colleges set standards by examining candidates.* ■ *Law* formally question (a defendant or witness) in court. Compare with **CROSS-EXAMINE.** ▷Middle English: from Old French *examiner*, from Latin *examinare* 'weigh, test,' from *examen* (see **EXAMEN**). —**ex·am·in·a·ble** *adj.* —**ex·am·i·nee** /igˌzaməˈnē/ *n.* —**ex·am·in·er** *n.*

ex·am·ple /igˈzampəl/ ▶*n.* **1** a thing characteristic of its kind or illustrating a general rule: *it's a good example of how European action can produce results* | *some of these carpets are among the finest examples of the period.* See note at **MODEL.** ■ a printed or written problem or exercise designed to illustrate a rule. **2** a person or thing regarded in terms of their fitness to be imitated or the likelihood of their being imitated: *it is vitally important that parents should* **set an example** | *she* **followed** *her brother's* **example** *and deserted her family.*
▶*v.* (**be exampled**) be illustrated or exemplified: *the extent of Allied naval support is exampled by the navigational specialists provided.* ▷late Middle English: from Old French, from Latin *exemplum*, from *eximere* 'take out,' from *ex-* 'out' + *emere* 'take.' Compare with **SAMPLE.**
▶*PHRASES* □ **for example** used to introduce something chosen as a typical case: *many, like Helen, for example, come from very poor backgrounds.* □ **make an example of** punish as a warning to others.

ex an·te /ˈeks ˈantē/ ▶*adj.* & *adv.* based on forecasts rather than actual results: [as *adj.*] *this is an ex ante estimate of the variance.* ▷modern Latin, from Latin *ex* 'from, out of' + *ante* 'before.'

ex·an·the·ma /ˌegzanˈᴛʜēmə/ ▶*n.* (*pl.* **-them·a·ta** /-ˈᴛʜemətə/) *Medicine* a skin rash accompanying a disease or fever. ▷mid 17th cent.: via late Latin from Greek *exanthēma* 'eruption,' from *ex-* 'out' + *antheein* 'to blossom' (from *anthos* 'flower'). —**ex·an·the·mat·ic** /egˌzanᴛʜəˈmatik/ *adj.* —**ex·an·them·a·tous** /-ˈᴛʜemətəs/ *adj.*

ex·arch /ˈekˌsärk/ ▶*n.* **1** (in the Orthodox Church) a bishop lower in rank than a patriarch and having jurisdiction wider than the metropolitan of a diocese. **2** *historical* a governor of a distant province under the Byzantine emperors. ▷late 16th cent.: via ecclesiastical Latin from Greek *exarkhos*, from *ex-* 'out of' + *arkhos* 'ruler.'

ex·ar·chate /ˈeksärˌkāt/ ▶*n. historical* a distant province governed by an exarch under the Byzantine emperors. ▷mid 16th cent.: from medieval Latin *exarchatus*, from ecclesiastical Latin *exarchus*, from Greek (see **EXARCH**).

ex·as·per·ate /igˈzaspəˌrāt/ ▶*v.* [*trans.*] irritate intensely; infuriate: *this futile process exasperates prison officials* | [as *adj.*] (**exasperated**) *she grew exasperated with his inability to notice anything* | [as *adj.*] (**exasperating**) *they suffered a number of exasperating setbacks.* ▷mid 16th cent.: from Latin *exasperat-* 'irritated to anger,' from the verb *exasperare* (based on *asper* 'rough'). —**ex·as·per·at·ed·ly** *adv.* —**ex·as·per·at·ing·ly** *adv.* —**ex·as·per·a·tion** /igˌzaspəˈrāsʜən/ *n.*

USAGE The verbs **exasperate** and **exacerbate** are sometimes confused. **Exasperate**, the more common of the two, means 'irritate or annoy to an extreme degree' (*He calls me three times a day asking for money. It's exasperating!*).
Exacerbate means 'increase the bitterness or severity of' (*the star shortstop's loud self-congratulations only exacerbated his teammates' resentment*).

Exc. ▶*abbr.* Excellency.

exc. ▶*abbr.* ■ except. ■ exception. ■ excursion.

Ex·cal·i·bur /ekˈskaləbər/ (in Arthurian legend) King Arthur's magic sword.

ex ca·the·dra /ˌeks kəˈᴛʜēdrə/ ▶*adv.* & *adj.* with the full authority of office (esp. of the pope's infallibility as defined in Roman Catholic doctrine): [as *adv.*] *for an encyclical to be infallible the pope must speak ex cathedra.* ▷early 19th cent.: Latin, 'from the (teacher's) chair,' from *ex* 'from' and *cathedra* 'seat' (from Greek *kathedra*).

ex·ca·vate /ˈekskəˌvāt/ ▶*v.* [*trans.*] **1** make (a hole or channel) by digging: *the cheapest way of doing this was to excavate a long trench.* ■ dig out material from (the ground): *the ground was largely excavated by hand.* ■ extract (material) from the ground by digging: *a very large amount of gravel would be excavated to form the channel.* **2** remove earth carefully and systematically from (an area) in order to find buried remains. ■ reveal or extract (buried remains) in this way: *clothing and weapons were excavated from the burial site.* ▷late 16th cent.: from Latin *excavat-* 'hollowed out,' from the verb *excavare*, from *ex-* 'out' + *cavare* 'make or become hollow' (from *cavus* 'hollow').

ex·ca·va·tion /ˌekskəˈvāsʜən/ ▶*n.* the action of excavating something, esp. an archaeological site: *the methods of excavation have to be extremely rigorous* | *students often participate in excavations.* ■ a site that is being or has been excavated.

ex·ca·va·tor /ˈekskəˌvātər/ ▶*n.* a person who removes earth carefully and systematically from an archaeological site in order to find buried remains. ■ a large machine for removing soil from the ground, esp. on a building site.

ex·ceed /ikˈsēd/ ▶*v.* [*trans.*] be greater in number or size than (a quantity, number, or other measurable thing): *production costs have exceeded $60,000.* ■ go beyond what is allowed or stipulated by (a set limit, esp. of one's authority): *the Tribunal's decision clearly exceeds its powers under the statute.* ■ be better than; surpass: *catalog sales have exceeded expectations.* ▷late Middle English (in the sense 'go over (a boundary or specified point)'): from Old French *exceder*, from Latin *excedere*, from *ex-* 'out' + *cedere* 'go.'

ex·ceed·ing /ikˈsēdiɴɢ/ *archaic or poetic/literary* ▶*adj.* very great: *she spoke warmly of his exceeding kindness.*
▶*adv.* [as *submodifier*] extremely; exceedingly: *an ale of exceeding poor quality.*

ex·ceed·ing·ly /ikˈsēdiɴɢlē/ ▶*adv.* **1** [as *submodifier*] extremely: *the team played exceedingly well.* **2** *archaic* to a great extent: *the supply multiplied exceedingly.*

ex·cel /ikˈsel/ ▶*v.* (**ex·celled**, **ex·cel·ling**) [*intrans.*] be exceptionally good at or proficient in an activity or subject: *a sturdy youth who excelled at football.* ▷late Middle English: from Latin *excellere*, from *ex-* 'out, beyond' + *celsus* 'lofty.'

ex·cel·lence /ˈeksələns/ ▶*n.* the quality of being outstanding or extremely good: *the award for excellence in engineering* | *a center of academic excellence.* ■ *archaic* an outstanding feature or quality. ▷late Middle English: from Latin *excellentia*, from the verb *excellere* 'surpass' (see **EXCEL**).

ex·cel·len·cy /ˈeksələnsē/ ▶*n.* (*pl.* **-cies**) **1** (**His**, **Your**, etc., **Excellency**) a title given to certain high officials of state, esp. ambassadors, or of the Roman Catholic Church, or used in addressing them: *His Excellency the Indian Consul General.* **2** *archaic* an outstanding feature or quality. ▷Middle English (in the sense 'excellence'): from Latin *excellentia*, from *excellere* 'surpass' (see **EXCEL**). The use of the word as a title dates from the mid 16th cent.

ex·cel·lent /ˈeksələnt/ ▶*adj.* extremely good; outstanding: *a 3-bedroom house in excellent condition* | *their results are excellent.*
▶*exclam.* used to indicate approval or pleasure: *"What a lovely idea! Excellent!"* ▷late Middle English (in the general sense 'excelling, outstanding,' referring to either a good or bad quality): from Old French, from Latin *excellent-* 'being preeminent,' from *excellere* (see **EXCEL**). The current appreciatory sense dates from the early 17th cent. —**ex·cel·lent·ly** *adv.*

ex·cel·si·or /ikˈselsēər/ ▶*n.* used in the names of hotels, newspapers, and other products used to indicate superior quality: *they stayed at the* **Excelsior.** ■ softwood shavings used for packing fragile goods or stuffing furniture. ▷late 18th cent. (as an exclamation): from Latin, comparative of *excelsus*, from *ex-* 'out, beyond' + *celsus* 'lofty.'

Ex·cel·si·or State a nickname for the state of **NEW YORK.**

ex·cen·tric /ikˈsentrik/ ▶*adj. chiefly Biology* not centrally placed or not having its axis or other part placed centrally: *a distinct excentric nucleus.* —**ex·cen·tri·cal·ly** /-(ə)lē/ *adv.*

ex·cept /ikˈsept/ ▶*prep.* not including; other than: *naked* **except for** *my socks* | *they work every day except Sunday.*
▶*conj.* used before a statement that forms an exception to one just made: *I didn't tell him anything,* **except that** *I needed the money* | *our berets were the same except mine had a leather band inside.* ■ *archaic* unless: *she never offered advice, except it were asked of her.*
▶*v.* [*trans.*] *formal* specify as not included in a category or group; exclude: *he excepted from his criticism a handful of distinguished writers.* ▷late Middle English: from Latin *except-* 'taken out,' from the verb *excipere*, from *ex-* 'out of' + *capere* 'take.'

USAGE See **usage** at **ACCEPT.**

ex·cept·ed /ikˈseptid/ ▶*adj.* [*postpositive*] not included in the category or group specified: *most museums (the Getty excepted) have small acquisitions budgets.*

ex·cept·ing /ikˈseptiɴɢ/ ▶*prep. formal* except for; apart from: *excepting some of the dialogue, the book is in every way superior to the movie.*

ex·cep·tion /ikˈsepsʜən/ ▶*n.* a person or thing that is excluded from a general statement or does not follow a rule: *the drives between towns are a delight, and the journey to Graz is* **no exception** | *while he normally shies away from introducing resolutions, he* **made an exception** *in this case.* ▷late Middle English: via Old French from Latin *exceptio(n-)*, from *excipere* 'take out' (see **EXCEPT**).
▶*PHRASES* □ **the exception proves the rule** *proverb* the fact that some cases do not follow a rule proves that the rule applies in all other cases. [from Latin *exceptio probat regulam in casibus non exceptis* 'The exception confirms the rule in the cases not excepted.' The exception here is 'the action of excepting' not 'that being excepted.' By specifically excluding cases where the rule doesn't apply, you make the rule stronger for the cases still governed by it.] □ **take exception to** object strongly to; be offended by: *they took exception to his bohemian demeanor.* □ **with the exception of** except; not including. □ **without exception** with no one or nothing excluded.

ex·cep·tion·a·ble /ikˈsepsʜənəbəl/ ▶*adj. formal* open to objection; causing disapproval or offense: *his drawings are almost the only exceptionable part of his work.*

USAGE **Exceptionable** means 'open to objection' and is usually found in negative contexts: *there was nothing exceptionable in the evidence.* It is sometimes confused with the much more common **exceptional**, meaning 'unusual, outstanding.' Their opposites, **unexceptionable** ('unobjectionable, beyond criticism') and **unexceptional** ('ordinary'), are also sometimes confused. See also **usage** at **UNEXCEPTIONABLE.**

ex·cep·tion·al /ikˈsepsʜənəl/ ▶*adj.* unusual; not typical: *crimes of exceptional callousness and cruelty.* ■ unusually good; outstanding: *a pepper offering exceptional flavor and juiciness.* ■ (of a child) mentally or

E

Pronunciation Key ə *ago*; ər *over*; ˈə or ˌə *up*; ˈər or ˌər *fur*; a *hat*; ā *rate*; ä *car*; ᴄʜ *chew*; e *let*; ē *see*; e(ə)r *air*; i *fit*; ī *by*; i(ə)r *ear*; ɴɢ *sing*; ō *go*; ô *for*; oi *boy*; o͝o *good*; o͞o *goo*; ou *out*; sʜ *she*; ᴛʜ *thin*; T̲H̲ *then*; (h)w *why*; ᴢʜ *vision*

physically disabled so as to require special schooling: *helping parents of exceptional children.* **—ex·cep·tion·al·i·ty** /ik,sepSHə'nalitē/ *n.* **—ex·cep·tion·al·ly** *adv.*

USAGE See usage at **EXCEPTIONABLE.**

ex·cerpt ▸*n.* /'ek,sərpt/ a short extract from a film, broadcast, or piece of music or writing.
▸*v.* /ik'sərpt/ [*trans.*] take (a short extract) from a text: *the notes are excerpted from his forthcoming biography.* ■ take an excerpt or excerpts from (a text). ▷mid 16th cent. (as a verb): from Latin *excerpt-* 'plucked out,' from the verb *excerpere,* from *ex-* 'out of' + *carpere* 'to pluck.' **—ex·cerpt·i·ble** /ek'sərptəbəl; ik-/ *adj.* **—ex·cerp·tion** /ek'sərpSHən; ik-/ *n.*

ex·cess /ik'ses; 'ekses/ ▸*n.* **1** an amount of something that is more than necessary, permitted, or desirable: *are you suffering from* **an excess of** *stress in your life?* ■ the amount by which one quantity or number exceeds another: *the excess of imports over exports rose $1.4 billion.* **2** lack of moderation in an activity, esp. eating or drinking: *bouts of alcoholic excess.* ■ (**excesses**) outrageous or immoderate behavior: *the worst excesses of the French Revolution.* **3** the action of exceeding a permitted limit: *there is no issue as to excess of jurisdiction.*
▸*adj.* [*attrib.*] exceeding a prescribed or desirable amount: *trim any excess fat off the meat.* ▷late Middle English: via Old French from Latin *excessus,* from *excedere* 'go out, surpass' (see **EXCEED**).
▸*PHRASES* □ **in** (or **to**) **excess** exceeding the proper amount or degree: *she insisted that he did not drink to excess.* □ **in excess of** more than; exceeding: *a top speed in excess of 20 knots.*

ex·cess bag·gage ▸*n.* luggage weighing more than the limit allowed on an aircraft and liable to an extra charge. ■ *figurative* a thing that is surplus to requirements.

ex·ces·sive /ik'sesiv/ ▸*adj.* more than is necessary, normal, or desirable; immoderate: *he was drinking excessive amounts of brandy.* ▷late Middle English: from Old French *excessif, -ive,* from medieval Latin *excessivus,* from Latin *excedere* 'surpass' (see **EXCEED**). **—ex·ces·sive·ly** *adv.* [as *submodifier*] *excessively high taxes.* **—ex·ces·sive·ness** *n.*

exch. ▸*abbr.* ■ exchange. ■ exchequer.

ex·change /iks'CHānj/ ▸*n.* an act of giving one thing and receiving another (esp. of the same type or value) in return: *negotiations should eventually lead to an* **exchange of** *land* **for** *peace | an exchange of prisoners of war | opportunities for the exchange of information.* ■ a visit or visits in which two people or groups from different countries stay with each other or do each other's jobs: [as *adj.*] *nine colleagues were away on an exchange visit to Germany.* ■ a short conversation; an argument: *there was a heated exchange.* ■ the giving of money for its equivalent in the money of another country. ■ the fee or percentage charged for converting the currency of one country into that of another. ■ a system or market in which commercial transactions involving currency, shares, commodities, etc., can be carried out within or between countries. See also **FOREIGN EXCHANGE.** ■ a central office or station of operations providing telephone service: *private branch exchanges to automate internal telephone networks.* ■ *Chess* a move or short sequence of moves in which both players capture material of comparable value, or particularly (**the exchange**) in which one captures a rook in return for a knight or bishop (and is said to *win the exchange*). ■ a building or institution used for the trading of a particular commodity or commodities: *the New York Stock Exchange.*
▸*v.* [*trans.*] give something and receive something of the same kind in return: *we exchanged addresses | he* **exchanged** *a concerned glance* **with** *Stephen.* ■ give or receive one thing in place of another: *we regret that tickets cannot be exchanged | she* **exchanged** *her suburban housewife look* **for** *leathers and tattoos.* ▷late Middle English: from Old French *eschange* (noun), *eschangier* (verb), based on *changer* (see **CHANGE**). The spelling was influenced by Latin *ex-* 'out, utterly' (see **EX-**[1]). **—ex·change·a·bil·i·ty** /iks,CHānjə'bilitē/ *n.* **—ex·change·a·ble** *adj.* **—ex·chang·er** *n.*
▸*PHRASE* □ **in exchange** as a thing exchanged: *at 8, he was carrying bags of groceries* **in exchange for** *a nickel.*

ex·change con·trol ▸*n.* a governmental restriction on the movement of currency between countries.

ex·change rate ▸*n.* (also **rate of exchange**) the value of one currency for the purpose of conversion to another.

ex·change rate mech·an·ism (abbr.: **ERM**) an arrangement within the European Monetary System that allows the value of participating currencies to fluctuate to a defined degree in relation to each other so as to control exchange rates. Each currency is given a rate of exchange with the euro, from which it is allowed to fluctuate by no more than a specified amount; if it moves beyond this the government in question must alter its economic policies or reset the currency's rate with the euro.

ex·change trans·fu·sion ▸*n. Medicine* the simultaneous removal of a patient's blood and replacement by donated blood, used in treating serious conditions such as hemolytic disease of the newborn.

ex·cheq·uer /eks'CHekər; iks-/ ▸*n.* a royal or national treasury. ■ (**Exchequer**) *Brit.* the bank account into which tax receipts and other public monies are paid; the funds of the British government. ■ (**Exchequer**) *Brit., historical* the former government office responsible for collecting revenue and making payments on behalf of the sovereign, auditing official accounts, and trying legal cases relating to revenue. ▷Middle English: from Old French *eschequier,* from medieval Latin *scaccarium* 'chessboard,' from *scaccus* (see **CHECK**[1]). The original sense was 'chessboard.' Current senses derive from the department of state established by the Norman kings of England to deal with the royal revenues, named *Exchequer* from the checkered tablecloth on which accounts were kept by means of counters. The spelling was influenced by Latin *ex-* 'out' (see **EX**[1]). Compare with **CHEQUER.**

ex·ci·mer /'eksəmər/ ▸*n. Chemistry* an unstable molecule that is formed in an excited state by the combination of two smaller molecules or atoms and rapidly dissociates with emission of radiation. Such species are utilized in some kinds of lasers. ▷1960s: blend of **EXCITED** and **DIMER.**

ex·cip·i·ent /ik'sipēənt/ ▸*n.* an inactive substance that serves as the vehicle or medium for a drug or other active substance. ▷early 18th cent. (as an adjective in the sense 'that takes exception'): from Latin *excipient-* 'taking out,' from the verb *excipere.*

ex·cise[1] ▸*n.* /'ek,sīz/ [usu. as *adj.*] a tax levied on certain goods and commodities produced or sold within a country and on licenses granted for certain activities: *excise taxes on cigarettes.*
▸*v.* /ik'sīz; ek-/ [*trans.*] [usu. as *adj.*] (**excised**) charge excise on (goods): *excised goods.* ▷late 15th cent. (in the general sense 'a tax or toll'): from Middle Dutch *excijs, accijs,* perhaps based on Latin *accensare* 'to tax,' from *ad-* 'to' + *census* 'tax' (see **CENSUS**).

ex·cise[2] /ik'sīz/ ▸*v.* [*trans.*] cut out surgically: *the precision with which surgeons can excise brain tumors* | [as *adj.*] (**excised**) *excised tissue.* ■ remove (a section) from a text or piece of music: *the clauses were* **excised from** *the treaty.* ▷late 16th cent. (in the sense 'notch or hollow out'): from Latin *excis-* 'cut out,' from the verb *excidere,* from *ex-* 'out of' + *caedere* 'to cut.' **—ex·ci·sion** /-'siZHən/ *n.*

ex·cise·man /'ek,sīzmən; -man/ ▸*n.* (*pl.* **-men**) *Brit., historical* an official responsible for collecting excise tax and preventing infringement of the excise laws (esp. by smuggling).

ex·cit·a·ble /ik'sītəbəl/ ▸*adj.* responding rather too readily to something new or stimulating; too easily excited: *Chip could be a bit wayward and excitable.* ■ (of tissue or a cell) responsive to stimulation. **—ex·cit·a·bil·i·ty** /ik,sītə'bilitē/ *n.* **—ex·cit·a·bly** /-əblē/ *adv.*

ex·cit·ant /ik'sītnt/ ▸*n. Biology* a substance that elicits an active physiological or behavioral response. ▷early 17th cent.: perhaps suggested by French *excitant.*

ex·ci·ta·tion /ek,sī'tāSHən/ ▸*n.* **1** *technical* the application of energy to a particle, object, or physical system, in particular: ■ *Physics* the process in which an atom or other particle adopts a higher energy state when energy is supplied: *thermal excitation.* ■ *Physiology* the state of enhanced activity or potential activity of a cell, organism, or tissue that results from its stimulation. ■ *Physics* the process of applying current to the winding of an electromagnet to produce a magnetic field. ■ *Electronics* the process of applying a signal voltage to the control electrode of an electron tube or the base of a transistor. **2** the action or state of exciting or being excited; excitement: *a state of sexual excitation.* ▷late Middle English: from Old French, from late Latin *excitatio(n-),* from *excitare* 'rouse, call forth' (see **EXCITE**).

ex·cit·a·tive /ik'sītətiv/ ▸*adj. rare* causing excitation.

ex·cit·a·to·ry /ik'sītə,tôrē/ ▸*adj. chiefly Physiology* characterized by, causing, or constituting excitation: *the excitatory action of these impulses.*

ex·cite /ik'sīt/ ▸*v.* [*trans.*] **1** cause strong feelings of enthusiasm and eagerness in (someone): *flying still excites me | Gould was excited by these discoveries.* ■ arouse (someone) sexually: *his kiss thrilled and excited her.* **2** bring out or give rise to (a feeling or reaction): *the ability to excite interest in others.* **3** produce a state of increased energy or activity in (a physical or biological system): *the energy of an electron is sufficient to excite the atom.* ▷Middle English (in the sense 'stir someone up, incite someone to do something'): from Old French *exciter* or Latin *excitare,* frequentative of *exciere* 'call out or forth.' Sense 1 dates from the mid 19th cent.

ex·cit·ed /ik'sītid/ ▸*adj.* **1** very enthusiastic and eager: *they were excited about the prospect | the excited children.* ■ sexually aroused. **2** *Physics* of or in an energy state higher than the normal or ground state. **—ex·cit·ed·ly** *adv.*

ex·cite·ment /ik'sītmənt/ ▸*n.* a feeling of great enthusiasm and eagerness: *her cheeks were flushed with excitement | the excitement of seeing a live leopard.* ■ something that arouses such a feeling; an exciting incident: *the excitements of the previous night.* ■ sexual arousal.

ex·cit·er /ik'sītər/ ▸*n.* a thing that produces excitation, in particular a device that provides a magnetizing current for the electromagnets in a motor or generator.

ex·cit·ing /ik'sītiNG/ ▸*adj.* causing great enthusiasm and eagerness: *an exciting breakthrough.* ■ sexually arousing. **—ex·cit·ing·ly** *adv.* **—ex·cit·ing·ness** *n.*

ex·ci·ton /'eksi,tän; ik'sītän/ ▸*n. Physics* a mobile concentration of energy in a crystal formed by an excited electron and an associated hole. ▷1930s: from **EXCITATION** + **-ON.**

excl. ▸*abbr.* ■ exclamation. ■ excluding. ■ exclusive.

ex·claim /ik'sklām/ ▸*v.* [*intrans.*] [often with *direct speech*] cry out suddenly, esp. in surprise, anger, or pain: *"Well, I never," she exclaimed | she looked in the mirror, exclaiming in dismay at her appearance.* ▷late 16th cent.: from French *exclamer* or Latin *exclamare,* from *ex-* 'out' + *clamare* 'to shout.'

ex·cla·ma·tion /,eksklə'māSHən/ ▸*n.* a sudden cry or remark, esp. expressing surprise, anger, or pain: *Meg gave an involuntary exclamation | an exclamation of amazement.* ▷late Middle English: from Latin *exclamatio(n-),* from *exclamare* 'shout out' (see **EXCLAIM**).

ex·cla·ma·tion point (*Brit.* **exclamation mark**) ▸*n.* a punctuation mark (!) indicating an exclamation.

ex·clam·a·to·ry /ik'sklamə,tôrē/ ▸*adj.* of or relating to a sudden cry or remark, esp. one expressing surprise, anger, or pain.

ex·clave /'ek,sklāv/ ▸*n.* a portion of territory of one state completely surrounded by territory of another or others, as viewed by the home territory. Compare with **ENCLAVE.** ▷late 19th cent.: from **EX-**[1] 'out' + a shortened form of **ENCLAVE.**

ex·clo·sure /ik'sklōZHər/ ▸*n. Forestry* an area from which unwanted animals are excluded. ▷1920s: from **EX-**[1] 'out' + **CLOSURE,** on the pattern of *enclosure.*

ex·clude /ik'sklood/ ▸*v.* [*trans.*] deny (someone) access to or bar (someone) from a place, group, or privilege: *women had been* **excluded from** *many scientific societies.* ■ keep (something) out of a place: *apply flux to exclude oxygen.* ■ (often **be excluded**) remove from consideration; rule out: *computer software is excluded from the mandatory 15-year write-off.* ■ prevent the occurrence of; preclude: *clauses seeking to exclude liability for loss or damage.* ▷late Middle English: from Latin *excludere,* from *ex-* 'out' + *claudere* 'to shut.' **—ex·clud·a·ble** *adj.* **—ex·clud·er** *n.*
▸*PHRASE* □ **law** (or **principle**) **of the excluded middle** *Logic* the principle that one (and one only) of two contradictory propositions must be true.

ex·clud·ing /ik'sklooding/ ▸*prep.* not taking someone or something into account; apart from; except: *you have eight more days, excluding Sundays.*

ex·clu·sion /ik'skloozHən/ ▸*n.* the process or state of excluding or being excluded: *drug users are subject to exclusion from the military.* ■ an item or risk specifically not covered by an insurance policy or other contract: *exclusions can be added to your policy.* ▷late Middle English: from Latin *exclusio(n-),* from *excludere* 'shut out' (see **EXCLUDE**). **—ex·clu·sion·ar·y** /-,nerē/ *adj.*
▸*PHRASE* □ **to the exclusion of** so as to exclude something specified: *don't revise a few topics to the exclusion of all others.*

ex·clu·sion·ar·y rule /ik'skloozHə,nerē/ ▸*n.* a law that prohibits the use of illegally obtained evidence in a criminal trial.

ex·clu·sion clause ▸*n.* (in a contract) a clause disclaiming liability for a particular risk.

ex·clu·sion·ist /ik'skloozHənist/ ▸*adj.* acting to shut

out or bar someone from a place, group, or privilege: *an exclusionist foreign policy.*
▶*n.* a person favoring the exclusion of someone from a place, group, or privilege.

ex·clu·sion prin·ci·ple (in full **Pauli exclusion principle**) ▶*n.* see PAULI.

ex·clu·sion zone ▶*n.* an area into which entry is forbidden, esp. by ships or aircraft of particular nationalities.

ex·clu·sive /ik'sklo͞osiv/ ▶*adj.* **1** excluding or not admitting other things: *my exclusive focus is on San Antonio issues.* ■ unable to exist or be true if something else exists or is true: *these approaches are not exclusive; many students will combine them | **mutually exclusive** political views.* ■ (of terms) excluding all but what is specified. **2** restricted or limited to the person, group, or area concerned: *the couple had exclusive possession of the condo | the jaguar and puma are **exclusive to** the New World.* ■ (of an item or story) not published or broadcast elsewhere: *an exclusive interview.* ■ (of a commodity) not obtainable elsewhere: *exclusive designer jewelry.* **3** catering or available to only a few, select persons; high class and expensive: *an exclusive Georgetown neighborhood.* **4** [*predic.*] (**exclusive of**) not including; excepting: *prices are exclusive of tax and delivery.*
▶*n.* an item or story published or broadcast by only one source. ▷late 15th cent. (as a noun denoting something that excludes or causes exclusion): from medieval Latin *exclusivus,* from Latin *excludere* 'shut out' (see EXCLUDE). —**ex·clu·sive·ness** *n.* —**ex·clu·siv·i·ty** /ˌekskloo'sivitē/ *n.*

Ex·clu·sive Breth·ren ▶*plural n.* the more rigorous of two principal divisions of the Plymouth Brethren (the other being the Open Brethren). The Exclusive Brethren restrict their contact with outsiders and with modern technology.

ex·clu·sive ec·o·nom·ic zone ▶*n.* an area of coastal water and seabed within a certain distance of a country's coastline, to which the country claims exclusive rights for fishing, drilling, and other economic activities.

ex·clu·sive·ly /ik'sklo͞osəvlē/ ▶*adv.* to the exclusion of others; only; solely: *paints produced exclusively for independent retailers |* [as *submodifier*] *exclusively female concerns.*

ex·clu·sive OR ▶*n.* *Electronics* a Boolean operator working on two variables that has the value of one if one but not both of the variables has a value of one. Also called **XOR**. ■ (also **exclusive OR gate**) a circuit that produces an output signal when a signal is received through one and only one of its two inputs.

ex·clu·siv·ism /ik'sklo͞osəˌvizəm/ ▶*n.* the action or policy of excluding a person or group from a place, group, or privilege. —**ex·clu·siv·ist** *adj.* & *n.*

ex·cog·i·tate /ek'skäjiˌtāt/ ▶*v.* [*trans.*] *formal* think out, plan, or devise: *scholars straining to excogitate upon subjects of which they know little.* ▷early 16th cent.: from Latin *excogitat-* 'found by process of thought,' from the verb *excogitare,* from *ex-* 'out' + *cogitare* 'think.' —**ex·cog·i·ta·tion** /ekˌskäji'tāsʜən/ *n.*

ex·com·mu·ni·cate ▶*v.* /ˌekskə'myo͞oniˌkāt/ [*trans.*] officially exclude (someone) from participation in the sacraments and services of the Christian Church.
▶*adj.* /ˌekskə'myo͞oniˌkit/ excommunicated: *all violators were to be pronounced excommunicate.*
▶*n.* /ˌekskə'myo͞oniˌkit/ an excommunicated person. ▷late Middle English: from ecclesiastical Latin *excommunicat-* 'excluded from communication with the faithful,' from the verb *excommunicare,* from *ex-* 'out' + Latin *communis* 'common to all,' on the pattern of Latin *communicare* (see COMMUNICATE). —**ex·com·mu·ni·ca·tion** /ˌekskəˌmyo͞oni'kāsʜən/ *n.* —**ex·com·mu·ni·ca·tive** /-ˌkātiv/ *adj.* —**ex·com·mu·ni·ca·tor** /-ˌkātər/ *n.* —**ex·com·mu·ni·ca·to·ry** /-kəˌtôrē/ *adj.*

ex·con ▶*n.* *informal* an ex-convict; a former inmate of a prison. ▷early 20th cent.: abbreviation.

ex·co·ri·ate /ik'skôrēˌāt/ ▶*v.* [*trans.*] **1** *formal* censure or criticize severely: *the papers that had been excoriating him were now lauding him.* **2** *chiefly Medicine* damage or remove part of the surface of (the skin). ▷late Middle English: from Latin *excoriat-* 'skinned,' from the verb *excoriare,* from *ex-* 'out, from' + *corium* 'skin, hide.' —**ex·co·ri·a·tion** /ikˌskôrē'āsʜən/ *n.*

ex·cre·ment /'ekskrəmənt/ ▶*n.* waste matter discharged from the bowels; feces. ▷mid 16th cent.: from French *excrément* or Latin *excrementum,* from *excernere* 'to sift out' (see EXCRETE). —**ex·cre·men·tal** /ˌekskrə'men(t)l/ *adj.*

ex·cres·cence /ik'skresəns/ ▶*n.* a distinct outgrowth on a human or animal body or on a plant, esp. one that is the result of disease or abnormality. ■ an unattractive or superfluous addition or feature: *removing the excrescences of later interpretation.* ▷late Middle English: from Latin *excrescentia,* from *excrescere* 'grow out,' from *ex-* 'out' + *crescere* 'grow.'

ex·cres·cent /ik'skresənt/ ▶*adj.* **1** forming or constituting an excrescence. **2** (of a speech sound) added without etymological justification (e.g., the *-t* at the end of the surname *Bryant*).

ex·cre·ta /ik'skrētə/ ▶*n.* [treated as *sing.* or *pl.*] waste matter discharged from the body, esp. feces and urine. ▷mid 19th cent.: from Latin, 'things sifted out,' neuter plural of *excretus,* past participle of *excernere* (see EXCRETE).

ex·crete /ik'skrēt/ ▶*v.* [*trans.*] (of a living organism or cell) separate and expel as waste (a substance, esp. a product of metabolism): *excess bicarbonate is excreted by the kidney |* [*intrans.*] *the butterfly pupa neither feeds nor excretes.* ▷early 17th cent. (in the sense 'cause to excrete'): from Latin *excret-* 'sifted out,' from the verb *excernere,* from *ex-* 'out' + *cernere* 'sift.' —**ex·cret·er** *n.* —**ex·cre·tive** /'ekskritiv; ik'skrētiv/ *adj.*

ex·cre·tion /ik'skrēsʜən/ ▶*n.* (in living organisms and cells) the process of eliminating or expelling waste matter. ■ a product of this process: *bodily excretions.* ▷early 17th cent.: from French *excrétion* or Latin *excretio(n-),* from *excernere* 'sift out' (see EXCRETE).

ex·cre·to·ry /'ekskriˌtôrē/ ▶*adj.* of, relating to, or concerned with excretion: *the excretory organs.*

ex·cru·ci·ate /ik'skro͞osʜēˌāt/ ▶*v.* [*trans.*] *rare* torment (someone) physically or mentally: *I stand back, excruciated by the possibility.* ▷late 16th cent.: from Latin *excruciat-* 'tormented,' from the verb *excruciare* (based on *crux, cruc-* 'a cross'). —**ex·cru·ci·a·tion** /ikˌskro͞osʜē'āsʜən/ *n.*

ex·cru·ci·at·ing /ik'skro͞osʜēˌātiɴɢ/ ▶*adj.* intensely painful: *excruciating back pain.* ■ mentally agonizing; very embarrassing, awkward, or tedious: *excruciating boredom.* —**ex·cru·ci·at·ing·ly** *adv.* [as *submodifier*] *the sting can prove excruciatingly painful.*

ex·cul·pate /'ekskəlˌpāt/ ▶*v.* [*trans.*] *formal* show or declare that (someone) is not guilty of wrongdoing: *the article exculpated the mayor.* ▷mid 17th cent.: from medieval Latin *exculpat-* 'freed from blame,' from the verb *exculpare,* from *ex-* 'out, from' + Latin *culpa* 'blame.' —**ex·cul·pa·tion** /ˌekskəl'pāsʜən/ *n.* —**ex·cul·pa·to·ry** /ˌeks'kəlpəˌtôrē/ *adj.*

ex·cur·rent /ek'skərənt/ ▶*adj.* *chiefly Zoology* (of a vessel or opening) conveying fluid outward. The opposite of INCURRENT. ▷early 17th cent.: from Latin *excurrent-* 'running out,' from the verb *excurrere.*

ex·cur·sion /ik'skərzʜən/ ▶*n.* **1** a short journey or trip, esp. one engaged in as a leisure activity: *an excursion to Mount Etna | figurative **an excursion into** theology.* See note at JOURNEY. ■ [usu. as *adj.*] a trip at reduced rates: *a popular excursion fare for travel during the next two weeks.* **2** *technical* an instance of the movement of something along a path or through an angle. ■ a deviation from a regular pattern, path, or level of operation. **3** *archaic* a digression. **4** *archaic* a military sortie (see ALARUM). ▷late 16th cent. (in the sense 'act of running out,' also meaning 'sortie' in the phrase *alarums and excursions* (see ALARUM)): from Latin *excursio(n-),* from the verb *excurrere* 'run out,' from *ex-* 'out' + *currere* 'to run.' —**ex·cur·sion·ist** /-ist/ *n.*

ex·cur·sive /ik'skərsiv/ ▶*adj.* *formal* of the nature of an excursion; ranging widely; digressive. ▷late 17th cent.: from Latin *excurs-* 'digressed, run out' (from the verb *excurrere*) + -IVE, perhaps influenced by *discursive.* —**ex·cur·sive·ly** *adv.* —**ex·cur·sive·ness** *n.*

ex·cur·sus /ek'skərsəs/ ▶*n.* (*pl.* same or **-sus·es**) a detailed discussion of a particular point in a book, usually in an appendix. ■ a digression in a written text. ▷early 19th cent.: from Latin, 'excursion,' from *excurrere* 'run out.'

ex·cus·al /ik'skyo͞ozəl/ ▶*n.* (typically in legal contexts) the action or fact of excusing or being excused: *he harbored views that would prevent or substantially impair the performance of his duties so as to support his excusal for cause.* ▷late 16th cent.: from *excuse* (verb) + *-al.*

ex·cuse ▶*v.* /ik'skyo͞oz/ [*trans.*] **1** attempt to lessen the blame attaching to (a fault or offense); seek to defend or justify: *he did nothing to hide or excuse Jacob's cruelty.* ■ forgive (someone) for a fault or offense: *you must excuse my sister | he **could be excused for** feeling that he was born at the wrong time.* ■ overlook or forgive (a fault or offense): *sit down—excuse the mess.* ■ (of a fact or circumstance) serve in mitigation of (a person or act): *his ability excuses most of his faults.* **2** release (someone) from a duty or requirement: *it will not be possible to **excuse** you **from** jury duty.* ■ (used in polite formulas) allow (someone) to leave a room or gathering: *now, if you'll excuse us, we have to be getting along.* ■ (**excuse oneself**) say politely that one is leaving. ■ (**be excused**) (used esp. by school pupils) be allowed to leave the room, esp. to go to the bathroom: *please, can I be excused?*
▶*n.* /ik'skyo͞os/ **1** a reason or explanation put forward to defend or justify a fault or offense: *there can be no possible **excuse for** any further delay | Hong Kong does have **the excuse that** it is the gateway to China.* ■ a reason put forward to conceal the real reason for an action; a pretext: *they use their hunting as an excuse to get away from the womenfolk.* **2** (**an excuse for**) *informal* a poor or inadequate example of: *that pathetic excuse for a man!* ▷Middle English: from Old French *escuser* (verb), from Latin *excusare* 'to free from blame,' from *ex-* 'out' + *causa* 'accusation, cause.' —**ex·cus·a·ble** /-zəbəl/ *adj.* —**ex·cus·a·bly** /-zəblē/ *adv.* —**ex·cus·a·to·ry** /-zəˌtôrē/ *adj.*
▶*PHRASES* □ **excuse me** said politely in various contexts, for example when attempting to get someone's attention, asking someone to move so that one may pass, or interrupting or disagreeing with a speaker. ■ said when asking someone to repeat what they have just said. □ **make one's excuses** say politely that one is leaving or cannot be present.

ex div. ▶*abbr.* ex dividend.

ex div·i·dend ▶*adj.* & *adv.* (of stocks or shares) not including the next dividend.

ex·ec /eg'zek/ ▶*n.* *informal* an executive: *top execs.* ▷late 19th cent.: abbreviation.

ex·e·cra·ble /'eksikrəbəl/ ▶*adj.* extremely bad or unpleasant: *execrable cheap wine.* ▷late Middle English (in the sense 'expressing or involving a curse'): via Old French from Latin *execrabilis,* from *exsecrari* 'to curse' (see EXECRATE). —**ex·e·cra·bly** /-blē/ *adv.*

ex·e·crate /'eksiˌkrāt/ ▶*v.* [*trans.*] feel or express great loathing for: *they were execrated as dangerous and corrupt.* ■ [*intrans.*] *archaic* curse; swear. ▷mid 16th cent.: from Latin *exsecrat-* 'cursed,' from the verb *exsecrari,* based on *sacrare* 'dedicate' (from *sacer* 'sacred'). —**ex·e·cra·tion** /ˌeksi'krāsʜən/ *n.* —**ex·e·cra·tive** /-ˌkrātiv/ *adj.* —**ex·e·cra·to·ry** /-krəˌtôrē/ *adj.*

ex·e·cut·a·ble /'eksiˌkyo͞otəbəl/ *Computing* ▶*adj.* (of a file or program) able to be run by a computer.
▶*n.* an executable file or program.

ex·ec·u·tant /ig'zekyətənt/ *formal* ▶*n.* a person who carries something into effect: *executants of the publisher's will.* ■ a person who performs music or makes a work of art or craft.
▶*adj.* of or relating to the performance of music or the making of works of art or craft: *music is both an art and an executant skill.* ▷mid 19th cent.: from French *exécutant* 'carrying out,' present participle of *exécuter* (see EXECUTE).

ex·e·cute /'eksiˌkyo͞ot/ ▶*v.* [*trans.*] **1** carry out or put into effect (a plan, order, or course of action): *the corporation executed a series of financial deals.* ■ produce (a work of art): *not only does she execute embroideries, she designs them, too.* ■ perform (an activity or maneuver requiring care or skill): *they had to execute their dance steps with the greatest precision.* ■ *Law* make (a legal instrument) valid by signing or sealing it. ■ *Law* carry out (a judicial sentence, the terms of a will, or other order): *police executed a search warrant.* ■ *Computing* carry out an instruction or a program. **2** (often **be executed**) carry out a sentence of death on (a legally condemned person): *he was convicted of treason and executed.* ■ kill (someone) as a political act. See note at KILL. ▷late Middle English: from Old French *executer,* from medieval Latin *executare,* from Latin *exsequi* 'follow up, carry out, punish,' from *ex-* 'out' + *sequi* 'follow.'

ex·e·cu·tion /ˌeksi'kyo͞osʜən/ ▶*n.* **1** the carrying out or putting into effect of a plan, order, or course of action: *he was fascinated by the entire operation and its execution.* ■ the technique or style with which an artistic work is produced or carried out: *the opera's creative execution.* ■ *Law* the putting into effect of a legal instrument or order. ■ *Law* seizure of the property or person of a debtor in default of payment. ■ *Law* short for WRIT OF EXECUTION. ■ *Computing* the performance of an instruction or a program. **2** the carrying out of a sentence of death on a condemned person: *the place of execution | executions of convicted murderers.* ■ the killing of someone as a political act.

ex·e·cu·tion·er /ˌeksi'kyo͞osʜ(ə)nər/ ▶*n.* an official who carries out a sentence of death on a legally condemned person.

ex·ec·u·tive /ig'zekyətiv; eg-/ ▸*adj.* [*attrib.*] having the power to put plans, actions, or laws into effect: *an executive chairman | executive authority.* ■ relating to managing an organization or political administration and putting into effect plans, policies, or laws: *the executive branch of government | the state has various executive functions.* Often contrasted with **LEGISLATIVE**.
▸*n.* **1** a person with senior managerial responsibility in a business organization. ■ [as *adj.*] suitable or appropriate for a senior business executive: *the executive suite | an executive jet.* ■ an executive committee or other body within an organization: *the union executive.* **2** (**the executive**) the person or branch of a government responsible for putting policies or laws into effect. ▷late Middle English (as an adjective): from medieval Latin *executivus*, from *exsequi* 'carry out' (see **EXECUTE**). —**ex·ec·u·tive·ly** *adv.*

ex·ec·u·tive a·gree·ment ▸*n.* an international agreement, usu. regarding routine administrative matters not warranting a formal treaty, made by the executive branch of the U.S. government without ratification by the Senate.

ex·ec·u·tive of·fi·cer ▸*n.* an officer with executive power. ■ (in naval vessels and some other military contexts) the officer who is second in command to the captain or commanding officer.

ex·ec·u·tive or·der ▸*n.* a rule or order issued by the president to an executive branch of the government and having the force of law.

ex·ec·u·tive priv·i·lege ▸*n.* the privilege, claimed by the president for the executive branch of the U.S. government, of withholding information in the public interest.

ex·ec·u·tive sec·re·tar·y ▸*n.* a secretary with administrative responsibilities, esp. one managing the business affairs and activities of an executive or an organization.

ex·ec·u·tive ses·sion ▸*n.* a meeting, esp. a private one, of a legislative body for executive business.

ex·ec·u·tor ▸*n.* **1** /ig'zekyətər/ *Law* a person or institution appointed by a testator to carry out the terms of their will. **2** /'eksə,kyo͞otər/ a person who produces something or puts something into effect: *the makers and executors of policy.* ▷Middle English: via Anglo-Norman French from Latin *execut-* 'carried out,' from *exsequi* (see **EXECUTE**). —**ex·ec·u·to·ri·al** /ig-,zekyə'tôrēəl/ *adj.* (*rare*) —**ex·ec·u·tor·ship** /-,SHip/ *n.* —**ex·ec·u·to·ry** /-,tôrē/ *adj.*

ex·ec·u·trix /ig'zekyə,triks/ ▸*n.* (*pl.* **-tri·ces** /-,trisēz/ or **-trix·es** /-,triksiz/) *Law* a female executor of a will. ▷late Middle English: from late Latin, from Latin *executor* (see **EXECUTOR**).

ex·e·dra /'eksidrə; ik'sēdrə/ ▸*n.* (*pl.* **-drae** /-drē/) *Architecture* a room, portico, or arcade with a bench or seats where people may converse, esp. in ancient Roman and Greek houses and gymnasia, typically semicircular in plan. ■ an outdoor recess containing a seat. ▷Latin, from Greek *ex-* 'out of' + *hedra* 'seat.'

ex·e·ge·sis /,eksi'jēsis/ ▸*n.* (*pl.* **-ses** /-sēz/) critical explanation or interpretation of a text, esp. of scripture: *the task of biblical exegesis | an exegesis of Marx.* ▷early 17th cent.: from Greek *exēgēsis*, from *exēgeisthai* 'interpret,' from *ex-* 'out of' + *hēgeisthai* 'to guide, lead.' —**ex·e·get·ic** /-'jetik/ *adj.* —**ex·e·get·i·cal** /-'jetikəl/ *adj.*

ex·e·gete /'eksə,jēt/ ▸*n.* an expounder or textual interpreter, esp. of scripture.
▸*v.* [*trans.*] expound or interpret (a text, esp. scripture): *I am able to exegete the scriptures in ways that make sense.* ▷mid 18th cent.: from Greek *exēgētēs*, from *exēgeisthai* 'interpret.'

ex·em·plar /ig'zemplər; -,plär/ ▸*n.* a person or thing serving as a typical example or excellent model: *he became the leading exemplar of conservative philosophy.* ▷late Middle English: from Old French *exemplaire*, from late Latin *exemplarium*, from Latin *exemplum* 'sample, imitation' (see **EXAMPLE**).

ex·em·pla·ry /ig'zemplərē/ ▸*adj.* **1** serving as a desirable model; representing the best of its kind: *an award for exemplary community service.* ■ characteristic of its kind or illustrating a general rule: *her works are exemplary of certain feminist arguments.* **2** (of a punishment) serving as a warning or deterrent: *exemplary sentencing may discourage the ultraviolent minority.* ■ *Law* (of damages) exceeding the amount needed for simple compensation. ▷late 16th cent.: from late Latin *exemplaris*, from Latin *exemplum* 'sample, imitation' (see **EXAMPLE**). —**ex·em·pla·ri·ly** /-ələ̄/ *adv.* —**ex·em·pla·ri·ness** *n.* —**ex·em·plar·i·ty** /,egzem'plaritē/ *n.*

ex·em·pli·fy /ig'zemplə,fī/ ▸*v.* (**-fies**, **-fied**) [*trans.*] be a typical example of: *rock bands that best exemplify the spirit of the age.* ■ give an example of; illustrate by giving an example. ■ *Law* make an attested copy of (a document) under an official seal. ▷late Middle English (in the sense 'illustrate by examples'): from medieval Latin *exemplificare*, from Latin *exemplum* 'sample' (see **EXAMPLE**). —**ex·em·pli·fi·ca·tion** /ig,zempləfi'kāSHən/ *n.*

ex·em·plum /ig'zempləm/ ▸*n.* (*pl.* **-pla** /-plə/) an example or model, esp. a moralizing or illustrative story. ▷late 19th cent.: Latin, literally 'example.'

ex·empt /ig'zem(p)t/ ▸*adj.* free from an obligation or liability imposed on others: *these patients are* ***exempt from*** *all charges | they are not* ***exempt from*** *criticism.* See note at **ABSOLVE**.
▸*v.* [*trans.*] free (a person or organization) from an obligation or liability imposed on others: *they were* ***exempted from*** *paying the tax.*
▸*n.* a person who is exempt from something, esp. the payment of tax. ▷late Middle English: from Latin *exemptus* 'taken out, freed,' past participle of *eximere*.

ex·emp·tion /ig'zem(p)SHən/ ▸*n.* the process of freeing or state of being free from an obligation or liability imposed on others: ***exemption from*** *prescription charges | regulatory exemptions.* ■ (also **personal exemption**) the process of exempting a person from paying taxes on a specified amount of income for themselves and their dependents. ■ a dependent exempted in this way. ▷late Middle English: from Old French, or from Latin *exemptio(n-)*, from *eximere* 'take out, free.'

ex·en·ter·a·tion /ig,zentə'rāSHən/ ▸*n.* complete surgical removal of a body organ, esp. the eyeball and other contents of the eye socket, usually in cases of malignant cancer. ▷mid 17th cent. (originally in the sense 'disembowelment'): from Latin *exenterat-* 'removed,' from the verb *exenterare* (suggested by Greek *exenterizein*), from *ex-* 'out of' + *enteron* 'intestine.'

ex·e·qua·tur /,eksə'kwātər/ ▸*n.* an official recognition by a government of a consul, agent, or other representative of a foreign state, authorizing them to exercise the duties of office. ▷early 17th cent.: Latin, literally 'let him or her perform.'

ex·e·quy /'eksikwē/ ▸*n.* (**exequies**) *formal* funeral rites; obsequies: *he attended the exequies for the dead pope.* ▷late Middle English: via Old French from Latin *exsequias*, accusative of *exsequiae* 'funeral ceremonies,' from *exsequi* 'follow after.'

ex·er·cise /'eksər,sīz/ ▸*n.* **1** activity requiring physical effort, carried out esp. to sustain or improve health and fitness: *exercise improves your heart and lung power | loosening-up exercises.* ■ a task or activity done to practice or test a skill: *there are exercises at the end of each chapter to check comprehension.* ■ a process or activity carried out for a specific purpose, esp. one concerned with a specified area or skill: *an* ***exercise in*** *public relations.* ■ (often **exercises**) a military drill or training maneuver. ■ (**exercises**) ceremonies: *graduation exercises.* **2** the use or application of a faculty, right, or process: *the free exercise of religion.*
▸*v.* [*trans.*] **1** use or apply (a faculty, right, or process): *control is exercised by the Board | anyone receiving a suspect package should exercise extreme caution.* **2** [*intrans.*] engage in physical activity to sustain or improve health and fitness; take exercise: *she still exercised every day.* ■ exert (part of the body) to promote or improve muscular strength: *raise your knee to exercise the upper leg and hip muscles.* ■ cause (an animal) to engage in exercise: *she exercised her dogs before breakfast.* **3** occupy the thoughts of; worry or perplex: *the knowledge that a larger margin was possible still exercised him.* ▷Middle English (in the sense 'application of a faculty, right, or process'): via Old French from Latin *exercitium*, from *exercere* 'keep busy, practice,' from *ex-* 'thoroughly' + *arcere* 'keep in or away.' —**ex·er·cis·a·ble** /-əbəl/ *adj.*

ex·er·cise bike (also **exercise bicycle**) ▸*n.* a piece of exercise equipment having handlebars, pedals, and a saddle like a bicycle, on which the user replicates the movements of bicycling.

ex·er·cise book ▸*n.* a book containing printed exercises for the use of students.

ex·er·cise price ▸*n.* *Stock Market* the price per share at which the owner of a traded option is entitled to buy or sell the underlying security.

ex·er·cis·er /'eksər,sīzər/ ▸*n.* a person who exercises. ■ an apparatus used to exercise.

ex·er·cise yard ▸*n.* an enclosed outdoor area used for physical exercise in a prison.

Ex·er·cy·cle /'eksər,sīkəl/ ▸*n.* *trademark* an exercise bike. ▷1930s: blend of **EXERCISE** and **BICYCLE**.

ex·er·gon·ic /,eksər'gänik/ ▸*adj.* *Biochemistry* (of a metabolic or chemical process) accompanied by the release of energy. The opposite of **ENDERGONIC**. ▷mid 20th cent.: from **EX-**[2] 'out of' + Greek *ergon* 'work' + **-IC**.

ex·ergue /ig'zərg; 'eksərg; 'egzərg/ ▸*n.* a small space or inscription below the principal emblem on a coin or medal, usually on the reverse side. ▷late 17th cent.: from French, from medieval Latin *exergum*, from *ex-* 'out' + Greek *ergon* 'work' (probably as a rendering of French *hors d'oeuvre* 'something lying outside the work').

ex·ert /ig'zərt/ ▸*v.* [*trans.*] **1** apply or bring to bear (a force, influence, or quality): *the moon* ***exerts*** *a force* ***on*** *the Earth |* ***exerting*** *influence* ***over*** *the next generation.* **2** (**exert oneself**) make a physical or mental effort: *he needs to exert himself to try to find an answer.* ▷mid 17th cent. (in the sense 'perform, practice'): from Latin *exserere* 'put forth,' from *ex-* 'out' + *serere* 'bind.'

ex·er·tion /ig'zərSHən/ ▸*n.* **1** physical or mental effort: *she was panting with the exertion | a well-earned rest after their mental exertions.* **2** the application of a force, influence, or quality: *the exertion of authority.*

Ex·e·ter[1] /'eksətər; 'egzətər/ the county town of Devon, in southwestern England, on the Exe River; pop. 101,000. Exeter was founded by the Romans, who called it Isca.

Ex·e·ter[2] /'eksitər; 'egzitər/ a historic town in southeastern New Hampshire, home to Phillips (Exeter) Academy; pop. 12,481.

ex·e·unt /'eksēənt; 'eksē,o͝ont/ ▸*v.* used as a stage direction in a printed play to indicate that a group of characters leave the stage: *exeunt Hamlet and Polonius.* See also **EXIT**. ▷late 15th cent.: Latin, literally 'they go out.'
▸*PHRASE* □ **exeunt omnes** used in this way to indicate that all the actors leave the stage.

ex·fil·trate /eks'filtrāt/ ▸*v.* [*trans.*] withdraw (troops or spies) surreptitiously, esp. from a dangerous position. ▷late 20th cent.: back-formation from *exfiltration*, perhaps suggested by the pair *infiltration*, *infiltrate*. —**ex·fil·tra·tion** /,eksfil'trāSHən/ *n.*

ex·fo·li·ant /eks'fōlēənt/ ▸*n.* a cosmetic product designed to remove dead cells from the surface of the skin. ▷1980s: from **EXFOLIATE** + **-ANT**.

ex·fo·li·ate /eks'fōlē,āt/ ▸*v.* [*intrans.*] (of a material) come apart or be shed from a surface in scales or layers: *the bark exfoliates in papery flakes.* ■ [*trans.*] cause to do this: *salt solutions exfoliate rocks on evaporating.* ■ [*trans.*] wash or rub (a part of the body) with a granular substance to remove dead cells from the surface of the skin: *exfoliate your legs to get rid of dead skin.* ■ [*trans.*] (often **be exfoliated**) shed (material) in scales or layers. ▷mid 17th cent.: from late Latin *exfoliat-* 'stripped of leaves,' from the verb *exfoliare*, from *ex-* 'out, from' + *folium* 'leaf.' —**ex·fo·li·a·tion** /eks,fōlē'āSHən/ *n.* —**ex·fo·li·a·tive** /-,ātiv/ *adj.* —**ex·fo·li·a·tor** /-,ātər/ *n.*

ex gra·ti·a /eks 'grāSHēə/ ▸*adv.* & *adj.* (esp. with reference to the paying of money) done from a sense of moral obligation rather than because of any legal requirement: [as *adj.*] *an ex gratia payment.* ▷mid 18th cent.: Latin, literally 'from favor,' from *ex* 'from' and *gratia* (see **GRACE**).

ex·ha·la·tion /,eks(h)ə'lāSHən/ ▸*n.* the process or action of exhaling. ■ an expiration of air from the lungs: *he let his breath out in a long exhalation of relief.* ■ an amount of vapor or fumes given off.

ex·hale /eks'hāl; 'eks,hāl/ ▸*v.* breathe out in a deliberate manner: [*intrans.*] *she sat back and exhaled deeply* | [*trans.*] *he exhaled the smoke toward the ceiling.* ■ [*trans.*] give off (vapor or fumes): *the jungle exhaled mists of early morning.* ▷late Middle English (in the sense 'be given off as vapor'): from Old French *exhaler*, from Latin *exhalare*, from *ex-* 'out' + *halare* 'breathe.' —**ex·hal·a·ble** *adj.*

ex·haust /ig'zôst/ ▸*v.* [*trans.*] **1** drain (someone) of their physical or mental resources; tire out: *her day trip had exhausted her* | [as *adj.*] (**exhausting**) *it had been a long and exhausting day.* **2** use up (resources or reserves) completely: *the country has exhausted its treasury reserves.* ■ expound on, write about, or explore (a subject or options) so fully that there is nothing further to be said or discovered: *she seemed to have exhausted all permissible topics of conversation.* **3** expel (gas or steam) from or into a particular place.
▸*n.* waste gases or air expelled from an engine, turbine, or other machine in the course of its operation: *buses spewing out black clouds of exhaust* | [as *adj.*] *exhaust fumes.* ■ the system through which such gases are expelled: [as *adj.*] *an exhaust pipe.* ▷mid 16th cent. (in the general sense 'draw off or out'): from Latin *exhaust-* 'drained out,' from the verb

exhaurire, from *ex-* 'out'+ *haurire* 'draw (water), drain.' —**ex·haust·er** *n.* —**ex·haust·i·bil·i·ty** /ig,zôstə'bilitē/ *n.* —**ex·haust·i·ble** *adj.* —**ex·haust·ing·ly** *adv.*

ex·haust·ed /ig'zôstid/ ▸*adj.* **1** drained of one's physical or mental resources; very tired: *I was cold and exhausted | she returned home, **exhausted from** her day in the city.* See note at TIRED. **2** (of resources or reserves) completely used up: *Karl spat, his patience suddenly exhausted.* —**ex·haust·ed·ly** *adv.*

ex·haus·tion /ig'zôsCHən/ ▸*n.* **1** a state of extreme physical or mental fatigue: *he was pale with exhaustion.* **2** the action or state of using something up or of being used up completely: *the rapid exhaustion of fossil fuel reserves.* ■ the action of exploring a subject or options so fully that there is nothing further to be said or discovered: *the total exhaustion of viable systematic alternatives.* ■ *Logic* the process of establishing a conclusion by eliminating all the alternatives. ▷early 17th cent.: from late Latin *exhaustio(n-)*, from Latin *exhaurire* 'drain out' (see EXHAUST).

ex·haus·tive /ig'zôstiv/ ▸*adj.* examining, including, or considering all elements or aspects; fully comprehensive: *she has undergone exhaustive tests since becoming ill.* —**ex·haus·tive·ly** *adv.* —**ex·haus·tive·ness** *n.*

ex·haust trail ▸*n.* another term for CONTRAIL.

ex·hib·it /ig'zibit/ ▸*v.* [*trans.*] **1** publicly display (a work of art or item of interest) in an art gallery or museum or at a trade fair: *only one sculpture was exhibited in the artist's lifetime.* ■ [*intrans.*] (of an artist) display one's work to the public in an art gallery or museum: *she was invited to exhibit at several French museums.* ■ (usu. **be exhibited**) publicly display the work of (an artist) in an art gallery or museum: *no foreign painters were exhibited.* **2** manifest or deliberately display (a quality or a type of behavior): *he could exhibit a saintlike submissiveness.* ■ show as a sign or symptom: *patients with alcoholic liver disease exhibit many biochemical abnormalities.*

▸*n.* an object or collection of objects on public display in an art gallery or museum or at a trade fair: *the museum is rich in exhibits.* ■ an exhibition: *people flocked to the exhibit in record-breaking numbers.* ■ *Law* a document or other object produced in a court as evidence. ▷late Middle English (in the sense 'submit for consideration,' also specifically 'present a document as evidence in court'): from Latin *exhibit-* 'held out,' from the verb *exhibere*, from *ex-* 'out' + *habere* 'hold.'

ex·hi·bi·tion /,eksə'bisHən/ ▸*n.* **1** a public display of works of art or other items of interest, held in an art gallery or museum or at a trade fair: *an exhibition of French sculpture | he never lent his treasures out for exhibition.* **2** a display or demonstration of a particular skill: *fields that have been plowed with a supreme exhibition of the farm worker's skills* | [as *adj.*] *exhibition games.* ■ [in *sing.*] an ostentatious or insincere display of a particular quality or emotion: *a false but convincing exhibition of concern for smaller nations.* **3** *Brit.* a scholarship awarded to a student at a school or college, usually after a competitive examination. ▷late Middle English (in the sense 'maintenance, support'; hence sense 3, mid 17th cent.): via Old French from late Latin *exhibitio(n-)*, from Latin *exhibere* 'hold out' (see EXHIBIT).

▸*PHRASE* □ **make an exhibition of oneself** behave in a conspicuously foolish way in public.

ex·hi·bi·tion·er /,eksə'bisHənər/ ▸*n. Brit.* a student who has been awarded an exhibition (scholarship).

ex·hi·bi·tion·ism /,eksə'bisHə,nizəm/ ▸*n.* extravagant behavior that is intended to attract attention to oneself. ■ *Psychiatry* a mental condition characterized by the compulsion to display one's genitals in public. —**ex·hi·bi·tion·ist** *n.* —**ex·hi·bi·tion·is·tic** /-,bisHə'nistik/ *adj.* —**ex·hi·bi·tion·is·ti·cal·ly** /-,bisHə'nistik(ə)lē/ *adv.*

ex·hib·i·tor /ig'zibitər/ ▸*n.* a person who displays works of art or other items of interest at an exhibition.

ex·hil·a·rate /ig'zilə,rāt/ ▸*v.* (usu. **be exhilarated**) make (someone) feel very happy, animated, or elated: *the children were exhilarated by a sense of purpose* | [as *adj.*] (**exhilarated**) *all this hustle and bustle makes me feel exhilarated* | [as *adj.*] (**exhilarating**) *riding was one of the most exhilarating experiences he knew.* ▷mid 16th cent.: from Latin *exhilarat-* 'made cheerful,' from the verb *exhilarare*, from *ex-* (expressing inducement of a state) + *hilaris* 'cheerful.' —**ex·hil·a·rat·ing·ly** *adv.* —**ex·hil·a·ra·tion** /ig,zilə'rāsHən/ *n.*

ex·hort /ig'zôrt/ ▸*v.* [*trans.*] strongly encourage or urge (someone) to do something: *the media have been exhorting people to turn out for the demonstration* | [with *direct speech*] *"Come on, you guys," exhorted Linda.* See note at INCITE. ▷late Middle English: from Old French *exhorter* or Latin *exhortari*, from *ex-* 'thoroughly' + *hortari* 'encourage.' —**ex·hort·a·tive** /-tətiv/ *adj.* —**ex·hort·a·to·ry** /-tə,tôrē/ *adj.* —**ex·hort·er** *n.*

ex·hor·ta·tion /,egzôr'tāsHən; ,eksôr-/ ▸*n.* an address or communication emphatically urging someone to do something: *exhortations to eat well | no amount of exhortation had any effect.*

ex·hume /ig'z(y)o͞om; ek's(y)o͞om/ ▸*v.* [*trans.*] dig out (something buried, esp. a corpse) from the ground. ■ (usu. **be exhumed**) *Geology* expose (a land surface) that was formerly buried. ▷late Middle English: from medieval Latin *exhumare*, from *ex-* 'out of' + *humus* 'ground.' —**ex·hu·ma·tion** /,egz(y)o͞o'māsHən; ,eks(h)yo͞o-/ *n.*

ex hy·poth·e·si /,eks hī'päTHə,sī/ ▸*adv.* according to the hypothesis proposed. ▷modern Latin, from *ex* 'from' and *hypothesi*, ablative of late Latin *hypothesis* (see HYPOTHESIS).

ex·i·gence /'eksijəns/ ▸*n.* another term for EXIGENCY.

ex·i·gen·cy /'eksijənsē; ig'zijənsē/ ▸*n.* (*pl.* **-cies**) an urgent need or demand: *women worked long hours when the exigencies of the family economy demanded it | he put financial exigency before personal sentiment.* ▷late 16th cent.: from late Latin *exigentia*, from Latin *exigere* 'enforce' (see EXACT).

ex·i·gent /'eksijənt/ ▸*adj. formal* pressing; demanding: *the exigent demands of the music took a toll on her voice.* ▷early 17th cent.: from Latin *exigent-* 'completing, ascertaining,' from the verb *exigere* (see EXACT).

ex·i·gi·ble /'eksijəbəl/ ▸*adj.* (of a tax, duty, or other payment) able to be charged or levied. ▷early 17th cent.: from French, from *exiger* 'demand, exact,' from Latin *exigere* (see EXACT).

ex·ig·u·ous /ig'zigyo͞oəs; ik'sig-/ ▸*adj. formal* very small in size or amount: *my exiguous musical resources.* ▷mid 17th cent.: from Latin *exiguus* 'scanty' (from *exigere* 'weigh exactly') + -OUS. —**ex·i·gu·i·ty** /,eksi'gyo͞oitē/ *n.* —**ex·ig·u·ous·ly** *adv.* —**ex·ig·u·ous·ness** *n.*

ex·ile /'eg,zīl; 'ek,sīl/ ▸*n.* the state of being barred from one's native country, typically for political or punitive reasons: *he knew now that he would die in exile.* ■ a person who lives away from their native country, either from choice or compulsion: *the return of political exiles.* ■ (**the Exile**) another term for BABYLONIAN CAPTIVITY.

▸*v.* [*trans.*] (usu. **be exiled**) expel and bar (someone) from their native country, typically for political or punitive reasons: *a corrupt dictator who had been **exiled from** his country | he was **exiled to** Tasmania in 1849* | [as *adj.*] (**exiled**) *supporters of the exiled king.* ▷Middle English: the noun partly from Old French *exil* 'banishment' and partly from Old French *exile* 'banished person'; the verb from Old French *exiler*; all based on Latin *exilium* 'banishment,' from *exul* 'banished person.'

ex·il·ic /eg'zilik; ek'silik/ ▸*adj.* of or relating to a period of exile, esp. that of the Jews in Babylon in the 6th century BC.

ex·ine /'ek,sēn; -,sīn/ ▸*n. Botany* the decay-resistant outer coating of a pollen grain or spore. It typically bears a highly characteristic surface pattern that is used in palynology. ▷late 19th cent.: perhaps from EX-[2] 'out' + Greek *is, in-* 'fiber.'

ex·ist /ig'zist/ ▸*v.* [*intrans.*] **1** have objective reality or being: *remains of these baths still exist on the south side of the Pantheon | there existed no organization to cope with espionage.* ■ be found, esp. in a particular place or situation: *two conflicting stereotypes of housework exist in popular thinking today.* **2** live, esp. under adverse conditions: *how am I going to exist without you? | only a minority of people **exist on** unemployment benefits alone.* ▷early 17th cent.: probably a back-formation from EXISTENCE.

ex·ist·ence /ig'zistəns/ ▸*n.* the fact or state of living or having objective reality: *the plane was the oldest Boeing remaining **in existence** | the need to acknowledge the existence of a problem.* ■ continued survival: *she helped to keep the company alive when its very existence was threatened.* ■ a way of living: *living in a city was more expensive than a rural existence.* ■ any of a person's supposed current, future, or past lives on this earth: *reaping the consequences of evil deeds sown in previous existences.* ■ *archaic* a being or entity. ■ all that exists. ▷late Middle English: from Old French, or from late Latin *existentia*, from Latin *exsistere* 'come into being,' from *ex-* 'out' + *sistere* 'take a stand.'

ex·ist·ent /ig'zistənt/ ▸*adj. formal* having reality or existence: *the technique has been existent for some years.* ▷mid 16th cent.: from Latin *exsistent-* 'coming into being, emerging,' from the verb *exsistere* (see EXISTENCE).

ex·is·ten·tial /,egzi'stencHəl/ ▸*adj.* of or relating to existence. ■ *Philosophy* concerned with existence, esp. human existence as viewed in the theories of existentialism. ■ *Logic* (of a proposition) affirming or implying the existence of a thing. ▷late 17th cent.: from late Latin *existentialis*, from *existentia* (see EXISTENCE). —**ex·is·ten·tial·ly** *adv.*

ex·is·ten·tial·ism /,egzi'stencHə,lizəm/ ▸*n.* a philosophical theory or approach that emphasizes the existence of the individual person as a free and responsible agent determining their own development through acts of the will.

> Generally taken to originate with Kierkegaard and Nietzsche, existentialism tends to be atheistic (although there is a strand of Christian existentialism deriving from the work of Kierkegaard), to disparage scientific knowledge, and to deny the existence of objective values, stressing instead the reality and significance of human freedom and experience. The approach was developed chiefly in 20th-century Europe, notably by Martin Heidegger, Jean-Paul Sartre, Albert Camus, and Simone de Beauvoir.

▷translating Danish *existents-forhold* 'condition of existence' (frequently used by Kierkegaard), from EXISTENTIAL. —**ex·is·ten·tial·ist** *n.* & *adj.*

ex·is·ten·tial quan·ti·fi·er ▸*n. Logic* a formal expression used in asserting that something exists of which a stated general proposition can be said to be true.

ex·ist·ing /ig'zistiNG/ ▸*adj.* [*attrib.*] in existence or operation at the time under consideration; current: *opponents of the existing political system.*

ex·it /'egzit; 'eksit/ ▸*n.* **1** a way out, esp. of a public building, room, or passenger vehicle: *she slipped out by the rear exit | a fire exit.* ■ a ramp where traffic can leave a highway, major road, or traffic circle: *he pulled off at an exit and stopped his Mercedes-Benz.* **2** an act of going out of or leaving a place: *he made a hasty **exit from** the room.* ■ a departure of an actor from the stage: *the brief soliloquy following Clarence's exit.* ■ a departure from a particular situation: *Australia's early **exit from** the World Cup.*

▸*v.* (**ex·it·ed**, **ex·it·ing**) [*intrans.*] go out of or leave a place: *they **exited from** the aircraft | the bullet entered her back and exited through her chest* | [*trans.*] *elephants enter and exit the forest on narrow paths.* ■ (of an actor) leave the stage. ■ (**exit**) used as a stage direction in a printed play to indicate that a character leaves the stage: *exit Pamela.* See also EXEUNT. ■ leave a particular situation: *organizations which do not have freedom to exit from unprofitable markets.* ■ *Computing* terminate a process or program, usually returning to an earlier or more general level of interaction: *this key enables you to temporarily exit from a LIFESPAN option.* ■ *Bridge* relinquish the lead. ▷mid 16th cent. (as a stage direction): from Latin *exit* 'he or she goes out,' third person singular present tense of *exire*, from *ex-* 'out' + *ire* 'go.' The noun use (late 16th cent.) is from Latin *exitus* 'going out,' from the verb *exire*, and the other verb uses (early 17th cent.) are from the noun.

ex·it line ▸*n.* a line spoken by an actor immediately before leaving the stage. ■ a parting remark.

ex·it poll ▸*n.* a poll of people leaving a polling place, asking how they voted.

ex·it vi·sa (also **exit permit**) ▸*n.* a document giving authorization to leave a particular country.

ex·it wound /wo͞ond/ ▸*n.* a wound made by a bullet or other missile passing out of the body.

ex li·bris /eks 'lēbris; 'lībris/ ▸*adv.* used as an inscription on a bookplate to show the name of the book's owner: *ex libris Edith Wharton.*

▸*n.* (*pl.* same) a bookplate inscribed in such a way, esp. a decorative one. ▷late 19th cent.: Latin, literally 'out of the books or library (of someone).'

ex ni·hi·lo /'eks 'nē(h)əlō; 'nī(h)əlō/ ▸*adv. formal* out of nothing: *the fashioning of life ex nihilo by God.* ▷late 16th cent.: Latin.

exo- ▸*prefix* external; from outside: *exodermis.* ▷from Greek *exō* 'outside.'

ex·o·at·mos·pher·ic /'eksō,atmə'sfi(ə)rik; -'sferik/ ▸*adj.* operating or taking place outside the atmosphere.

ex·o·bi·ol·o·gy /,eksōbī'äləjē/ ▸*n.* the branch of science that deals with the possibility and likely nature of life on other planets or in space. —**ex·o·bi·o·log·i·cal** /-,bīə'läjikəl/ *adj.* —**ex·o·bi·ol·o·gist** /-jist/ *n.*

ex·o·carp /ˈeksōˌkärp/ ▸*n. Botany* the outer layer of the pericarp of a fruit.

ex·o·cen·tric /ˌeksōˈsentrik/ ▸*adj. Linguistics* denoting or being a construction that has no explicit head, for example *John slept.* Contrasted with ENDOCENTRIC.

Ex·o·cet /ˈeksōˌset/ ▸*n. trademark* a French-made guided anti-ship missile. ▷1970s: from French, literally 'flying fish,' via Latin from Greek *ekōkoitos* 'fish that comes up on the beach' (literally 'out of bed').

ex·o·crine /ˈeksəˌkrin; ˈeksəˌkrēn/ ▸*adj. Physiology* relating to or denoting glands that secrete their products through ducts opening onto an epithelium rather than directly into the bloodstream. Often contrasted with ENDOCRINE. ▷early 20th cent.: from EXO- 'outside' + Greek *krinein* 'sift.'

ex·o·cy·to·sis /ˈeksōsīˈtōsis/ ▸*n. Biology* a process by which the contents of a cell vacuole are released to the exterior through fusion of the vacuole membrane with the cell membrane. **—ex·o·cy·tot·ic** /-ˈtätik/ *adj.*

ex·o·der·mis /ˌeksōˈdərməs/ ▸*n. Botany* a specialized layer in a root beneath the epidermis or velamen. ▷early 20th cent.: from EXO- 'outside,' on the pattern of *endodermis, epidermis.*

Ex·o·dus /ˈeksədəs/ the second book of the Bible, which recounts the departure of the Israelites from slavery in Egypt, their journey across the Red Sea and through the wilderness led by Moses, and the giving of the Ten Commandments. The events have been variously dated by scholars between about 1580 and 1200 BC. ▷Old English, via ecclesiastical Latin from Greek *exodos,* from *ex-* 'out of' + *hodos* 'way.'

ex·o·dus /ˈeksədəs/ ▸*n.* a mass departure of people, esp. emigrants. ■ (**the Exodus**) the departure of the Israelites from Egypt. ▷early 17th cent.: from Greek (see EXODUS).

ex·o·en·zyme /ˌeksōˈenˌzīm/ ▸*n. Biochemistry* an enzyme that acts outside the cell that produces it.

ex of·fi·ci·o /ˈeks əˈfishēō/ ▸*adv. & adj.* by virtue of one's position or status: [as *adj.*] *an ex officio member of the committee.* ▷Latin, from *ex* 'out of, from' + *officium* 'duty.'

ex·og·a·my /ekˈsägəmē/ ▸*n. Anthropology* the custom of marrying outside a community, clan, or tribe. Compare with ENDOGAMY. ■ *Biology* the fusion of reproductive cells from distantly related or unrelated individuals; outbreeding; cross-pollination. **—ex·og·a·mous** /-məs/ *adj.*

ex·o·gen·ic /ˌeksəˈjenik/ ▸*adj. Geology* formed or occurring on the surface of the earth. Often contrasted with ENDOGENIC.

ex·og·e·nous /ekˈsäjənəs/ ▸*adj.* of, relating to, or developing from external factors. Often contrasted with ENDOGENOUS. ■ *Biology* growing or originating from outside an organism: *an exogenous hormone.* ■ *chiefly Psychiatry* (of a disease, symptom, etc.) caused by an agent or organism outside the body: *exogenous depression.* ■ relating to an external group or society: *exogenous marriage.* ▷mid 19th cent.: from modern Latin *exogena* (denoting an exogenous plant, suggested by classical Latin *indigena* 'native') + -OUS. **—ex·og·e·nous·ly** *adv.*

ex·on /ˈeksän/ ▸*n. Biochemistry* a segment of a DNA or RNA molecule containing information coding for a protein or peptide sequence. Compare with INTRON. ▷late 20th cent.: from *expressed* (see EXPRESS[1]) + -ON. **—ex·on·ic** *adj.*

ex·on·er·ate /igˈzänəˌrāt/ ▸*v.* [*trans.*] **1** (esp. of an official body) absolve (someone) from blame for a fault or wrongdoing, esp. after due consideration of the case: *the court-martial exonerated me | they should* ***exonerate*** *these men* ***from*** *this crime.* See note at ABSOLVE. **2** (**exonerate someone from**) release someone from (a duty or obligation). ▷late Middle English: from Latin *exonerat-* 'freed from a burden,' from the verb *exonerare,* from *ex-* 'from' + *onus, oner-* 'a burden.' **—ex·on·er·a·tion** /igˌzänəˈrāshən/ *n.* **—ex·on·er·a·tive** /-ˌrātiv/ *adj.*

ex·o·nu·cle·ase /ˌeksōˈn(y)o͞oklēˌās/ ▸*n. Biochemistry* an enzyme that removes successive nucleotides from the end of a polynucleotide molecule.

ex·o·pep·ti·dase /ˌeksōˈpeptiˌdās/ ▸*n. Biochemistry* an enzyme that breaks the terminal peptide bond in a peptide chain.

ex·oph·o·ra /ekˈsäfərə/ ▸*n. Linguistics* reference in a text or utterance to something external to it, which is only fully intelligible in terms of information about the extralinguistic situation. Compare with ENDOPHORA. **—ex·o·phor·ic** /ˌeksōˈfôrik; -ˈfär-/ *adj.*

ex·oph·thal·mic /ˌeksäfˈthalmik/ ▸*adj. Medicine* having or characterized by protruding eyes.

ex·oph·thal·mic goi·ter ▸*n.* another term for GRAVES' DISEASE.

ex·oph·thal·mos /ˌeksäfˈthalməs/ (also **ex·oph·thal·mus** or **ex·oph·thal·mi·a** /-mēə/) ▸*n. Medicine* abnormal protrusion of the eyeball or eyeballs. ▷early 17th cent.: from modern Latin *exophthalmus,* from Greek *exophthalmos* 'having prominent eyes,' from *ex-* 'out' + *ophthalmos* 'eye.'

ex·o·plan·et /ˈeksōˌplanit/ ▸*n.* a planet that orbits a star outside the solar system: *most of the 100 known exoplanets are comparable in mass to Jupiter.*

ex·op·o·dite /ekˈsäpəˌdīt/ (also **ex·o·pod** /ˈeksəˌpäd/) ▸*n. Zoology* the outer branch of the biramous limb or appendage of a crustacean. Compare with ENDOPODITE, PROTOPODITE. ▷late 19th cent.: from EXO- 'outside' + Greek *pous, pod-* 'foot' + -ITE[1].

exor. ▸*abbr.* an executor (of a will).

ex·or·bi·tant /igˈzôrbitənt/ ▸*adj.* (of a price or amount charged) unreasonably high: *the exorbitant price of tickets.* ▷late Middle English (originally as a legal term describing a case that is outside the scope of a law): from late Latin *exorbitant-* 'going off the track,' from *exorbitare,* from *ex-* 'out from' + *orbita* 'course, track.' **—ex·or·bi·tance** /egˈzôrbətns/ *n.* **—ex·or·bi·tant·ly** *adv.*

ex·or·cise /ˈeksôrˌsīz; ˈeksər-/ (also **ex·or·cize**) ▸*v.* [*trans.*] drive out or attempt to drive out (an evil spirit) from a person or place: *an attempt to exorcise an unquiet spirit | figurative inflation has been exorcised.* ■ (often **be exorcised**) rid (a person or place) of an evil spirit: *infants were exorcised prior to baptism.* ▷late Middle English: from French *exorciser* or ecclesiastical Latin *exorcizare,* from Greek *exorkizein,* from *ex-* 'out' + *horkos* 'oath.' The word originally meant 'conjure up or command (an evil spirit)'; the specific sense of driving out an evil spirit dates from the mid 16th cent.

ex·or·cism /ˈeksôrˌsizəm; ˈeksər-/ ▸*n.* the expulsion or attempted expulsion of an evil spirit from a person or place. ▷late Middle English: via ecclesiastical Latin from ecclesiastical Greek *exorkismos,* from *exorkizein* 'exorcize.' **—ex·or·cist** *n.*

ex·or·di·um /igˈzôrdēəm; ikˈsôr-/ ▸*n.* (*pl.* **-di·ums** or **-di·a** /-dēə/) *formal* the beginning or introductory part, esp. of a discourse or treatise. ▷late 16th cent.: from Latin, from *exordiri* 'begin,' from *ex-* 'out, from' + *ordiri* 'begin.' **—ex·or·di·al** /-dēəl/ *adj.*

ex·o·skel·e·ton /ˌeksōˈskelitn/ ▸*n. Zoology* a rigid external covering for the body in some invertebrate animals, esp. arthropods, providing both support and protection. Compare with ENDOSKELETON. **—ex·o·skel·e·tal** /ˌeksōˈskelətl/ *adj.*

ex·o·sphere /ˈeksōˌsfi(ə)r/ ▸*n. Astronomy* the outermost region of a planet's atmosphere. **—ex·o·spher·ic** /ˌeksōˈsfi(ə)rik; -ˈsferik/ *adj.* .

ex·o·spore /ˈeksōˌspôr/ ▸*n.* **1** the outer layer of the membrane in some spores. **2** a spore formed by separation and release from a sporophore, the spore-bearing structure of a fungus. **—ex·o·spor·al** /ˌeksəˈspôrəl/ *adj.*

ex·o·spor·i·um /ˌeksōˈspôrēəm/ ▸*n.* (*pl,* **-spor·i·a**) *Botany* another term for EXINE. **—ex·o·spor·ial** /-ˈspôrēəl/ *adj.*

ex·os·to·sis /ˌeksäˈstōsis/ ▸*n.* (*pl.* **-ses** /-sēz/) *Medicine* a benign outgrowth of cartilaginous tissue on a bone. ▷late 16th cent.: from Greek, from *ex-* 'out' + *osteon* 'bone.'

ex·o·ter·ic /ˌeksəˈterik/ ▸*adj. formal* (esp. of a doctrine or mode of speech) intended for or likely to be understood by the general public: *an exoteric, literal meaning and an esoteric, inner teaching.* The opposite of ESOTERIC. ■ relating to the outside world; external: *the exoteric and esoteric aspects of life.* ■ current or popular among the general public. ▷mid 17th cent.: via Latin from Greek *exōterikos,* from *exōterō* 'outer,' comparative of *exō* 'outside.'

ex·o·ther·mic /ˌeksəˈthərmik/ ▸*adj. Chemistry* (of a reaction or process) accompanied by the release of heat. The opposite of ENDOTHERMIC (sense 1). ■ (of a compound) formed from its constituent elements with a net release of heat. ▷late 19th cent.: from French *exothermique.* **—ex·o·ther·mi·cal·ly** /-(ə)lē/ *adv.*

ex·ot·ic /igˈzätik/ ▸*adj.* originating in or characteristic of a distant foreign country: *exotic birds | they loved to visit exotic places.* ■ attractive or striking because colorful or out of the ordinary: *an exotic outfit* | [as *n.*] (**the exotic**) *there was a touch of the exotic in her appearance.* ■ of a kind not used for ordinary purposes or not ordinarily encountered: *exotic elementary particles as yet unknown to science.*
▸*n.* an exotic plant or animal: *he planted exotics in the sheltered garden.* ■ a thing that is imported or unusual: *the market in exotics has gone crazy with speculators.* ▷late 16th cent.: via Latin from Greek *exōtikos* 'foreign,' from *exō* 'outside.' **—ex·ot·i·cal·ly** /-(ə)lē/ *adv.* **—ex·ot·i·cism** /igˈzätəˌsizəm/ *n.*

ex·ot·i·ca /igˈzätikə/ ▸*plural n.* objects considered strange or interesting because they are out of the ordinary, esp. because they originated in a distant foreign country. ▷late 19th cent.: from Latin, neuter plural of *exoticus* 'foreign' (see EXOTIC).

ex·ot·ic danc·er ▸*n.* a striptease dancer.

ex·o·tox·in /ˈeksōˌtäksin/ ▸*n. Microbiology* a toxin released by a living bacterial cell into its surroundings. Compare with ENDOTOXIN.

exp. ▸*abbr.* ■ expenses. ■ experience (usually in the context of job advertisements): *previous exp. an advantage.* ■ (**Exp.**) experimental (in titles of periodicals): *J. Exp. Biol.* ■ expiration: *exp. date.* ■ *Mathematics* the exponential function raising *e* to the power of the given quantity: *it is reduced by exp. (–U).* ■ exposures (in the context of photography): *$4.45 for 24 exp.* ■ express.

ex·pand /ikˈspand/ ▸*v.* become or make larger or more extensive: [*intrans.*] *their business* ***expanded into*** *other hotels and properties* | [*trans.*] *baby birds cannot expand and contract their lungs.* ■ [*intrans.*] *Physics* (of the universe) undergo a continuous change whereby, according to theory based on observed redshifts, all the galaxies recede from one another. ■ [*intrans.*] (**expand on**) give a fuller version or account of: *Anne expanded on the theory.* ▷late Middle English: from Latin *expandere* 'to spread out,' from *ex-* 'out' + *pandere* 'to spread.' **—ex·pand·a·ble** *adj.* **—ex·pand·er** *n.* **—ex·pan·si·bil·i·ty** /ikˌspansəˈbilitē/ *n.* **—ex·pan·si·ble** /-ˈspansəbəl/ *adj.*

ex·pand·ed /ikˈspandid/ ▸*n.* being or having been enlarged, extended, or broadened, in particular: ■ denoting materials which have a light cellular structure: *expanded polystyrene.* ■ denoting sheet metal slit and stretched into a mesh, used to reinforce concrete and other brittle materials. ■ relatively broad in shape: *the expanded fins of the ray.*

ex·panse /ikˈspans/ ▸*n.* an area of something, typically land or sea, presenting a wide continuous surface: *the green expanse of the forest.* ■ the distance to which something expands or can be expanded: *the moth has a wing expanse of 20 to 24 mm.* ▷mid 17th cent.: from modern Latin *expansum* 'something expanded,' neuter past participle of *expandere* (see EXPAND).

ex·pan·sile /ikˈspansəl; -ˌsīl/ ▸*adj. Physics* of, relating to, or capable of expansion.

ex·pan·sion /ikˈspanshən/ ▸*n.* the action of becoming larger or more extensive: *the rapid expansion of suburban Washington | a small expansion of industry.* ■ extension of a state's territory by encroaching on that of other nations, pursued as a political strategy: *German expansion in the 1930s.* ■ a thing formed by the enlargement, broadening, or development of something: *the book is an expansion of a lecture given last year.* ■ the increase in the volume of fuel on combustion in the cylinder of an engine, or the piston stroke in which this occurs. ▷early 17th cent.: from late Latin *expansion-,* from Latin *expandere* (see EXPAND).

ex·pan·sion·ar·y /ikˈspanshəˌnerē/ ▸*adj.* (of a policy or action) intended to result in economic or political expansion: *an expansionary budget.*

ex·pan·sion bolt ▸*n.* a bolt that expands when inserted, no thread being required in the surrounding material.

ex·pan·sion card (also **expansion board**) ▸*n. Computing* a circuit board that can be inserted in a computer to give extra facilities or memory.

ex·pan·sion·ism /ikˈspanshəˌnizəm/ ▸*n.* the policy of territorial or economic expansion: *communist expansionism in Asia.* **—ex·pan·sion·ist** *n. & adj.* **—ex·pan·sion·is·tic** /ikˌspanshəˈnistik/ *adj.*

ex·pan·sion joint ▸*n.* a joint that makes allowance for thermal expansion of the parts joined without distortion.

ex·pan·sion slot ▸*n. Computing* a place in a computer where an expansion card can be inserted.

ex·pan·sion team ▸*n.* a new team added to an established professional sport league.

ex·pan·sive /ikˈspansiv/ ▸*adj.* **1** covering a wide area in terms of space or scope; extensive or wide-ranging: *deep, expansive canyons.* **2** (of a person or their manner) open, demonstrative, and communicative: *she felt expansive and inclined to talk.* **3** tending toward economic or political expansion: *expansive domestic economic policies.* **—ex·pan·sive·ly** *adv.* **—ex·pan·sive·ness** *n.*

ex·pan·siv·i·ty /ˌekspanˈsivitē/ ▸*n.* *Physics* the amount a material expands or contracts per unit length due to a one-degree change in temperature.

ex par·te /eks ˈpärtē/ ▸*adj.* & *adv.* *Law* with respect to or in the interests of one side only or of an interested outside party. ▷late 17th cent.: Latin, literally 'from a side.'

ex·pat /eksˈpat/ ▸*n.* & *adj.* *informal* short for EXPATRIATE.

ex·pa·ti·ate /ikˈspāSHēˌāt/ ▸*v.* [*intrans.*] speak or write at length or in detail: *she* ***expatiated on*** *working-class novelists.* ▷mid 16th cent. (in the sense 'roam freely'): from Latin *exspatiari* 'move beyond one's usual bounds,' from *ex-* 'out, from' + *spatiari* 'to walk' (from *spatium* 'space'). **—ex·pa·ti·a·tion** /ikˌspāSHēˈāSHən/ *n.*

ex·pa·tri·ate ▸*n.* /eksˈpātrēit/ a person who lives outside their native country: *American expatriates in London.* ■ *archaic* a person exiled from their native country.

▸*adj.* /eksˈpātrēit/ [*attrib.*] (of a person) living outside their native country: *expatriate writers and artists.* ■ *archaic* expelled from one's native country.

▸*v.* /eksˈpātrēˌāt/ [*intrans.*] settle oneself abroad: *candidates should be willing to expatriate.* ▷mid 18th cent. (as a verb): from medieval Latin *expatriat-* 'gone out from one's country,' from the verb *expatriare*, from *ex-* 'out' + *patria* 'native country.' **—ex·pa·tri·a·tion** /eksˌpātrēˈāSHən/ *n.*

ex·pect /ikˈspekt/ ▸*v.* [*trans.*] regard (something) as likely to happen: *we expect the best* | [*trans.*] *he expects the stock market to sink further* | [with *clause*] *we expect that farmers will harvest 63 million acres of hay.* ■ regard (someone) as likely to do or be something: [*trans.*] *they were not expecting him to continue.* ■ believe that (someone or something) will arrive soon: *Celia was expecting a visitor.* ■ look for (something) from someone as rightfully due or requisite in the circumstances: *we* ***expect*** *great things* ***of*** *you.* ■ require (someone) to fulfill an obligation: [*trans.*] *we expect employers to pay a reasonable salary.* ■ (**I expect**) *informal* used to indicate that one supposes something to be so, but has no firm evidence or knowledge: *they're just friends of his, I expect* | [with *clause*] *I expect you know them?* ▷mid 16th cent. (in the sense 'defer action, wait'): from Latin *exspectare* 'look out for,' from *ex-* 'out' + *spectare* 'to look' (frequentative of *specere* 'see'). **—ex·pect·a·ble** *adj.*

▸*PHRASES* □ **be expecting** (**a baby**) *informal* be pregnant. □ **to be expected** completely normal: *wild swings in the weather are to be expected.* □ **what can** (or **do**) **you expect?** used to emphasize that there was nothing unexpected about a person or event, however disappointed one might be.

ex·pect·an·cy /ikˈspektənsē/ ▸*n.* (*pl.* **-cies**) the state of thinking or hoping that something, esp. something pleasant, will happen or be the case: *they waited with an* ***air of expectancy.*** ▷early 17th cent.: from Latin *exspectantia*, from *exspectare* 'look out for' (see EXPECT).

ex·pect·ant /ikˈspektənt/ ▸*adj.* having or showing an excited feeling that something is about to happen, esp. something pleasant and interesting: *an expectant conference crowd.* ■ [*attrib.*] (of a woman) pregnant: *an expectant mother.*

▸*n.* *archaic* a person who anticipates receiving something, esp. high office. ▷late Middle English: from Latin *exspectant-* 'expecting,' from the verb *exspectare* (see EXPECT). **—ex·pect·ant·ly** *adv.*

ex·pec·ta·tion /ˌekspekˈtāSHən/ ▸*n.* a strong belief that something will happen or be the case in the future: *reality had not lived up to expectations* | *an* ***expectation that*** *the government will provide the resources* | *he drilled his men in expectation of a Prussian advance.* ■ a belief that someone will or should achieve something: *students had high expectations for their future.* ■ (**expectations**) *archaic* one's prospects of inheritance. ■ *Mathematics* another term for EXPECTED VALUE.

ex·pect·ed u·til·i·ty ▸*n.* *Mathematics & Economics* a predicted utility value for one of several options, calculated as the sum of the utility of every possible outcome each multiplied by the probability of its occurrence.

ex·pect·ed val·ue ▸*n.* *Mathematics* a predicted value of a variable, calculated as the sum of all possible values each multiplied by the probability of its occurrence.

ex·pec·to·rant /ikˈspektərənt/ ▸*n.* a medicine that promotes the secretion of sputum by the air passages, used esp. to treat coughs. ▷mid 18th cent.: from Latin *expectorant-* 'expelling from the chest,' from the verb *expectorare* (see EXPECTORATE).

ex·pec·to·rate /ikˈspektəˌrāt/ ▸*v.* [*intrans.*] cough or spit out phlegm from the throat or lungs. ■ [*trans.*] spit out (phlegm) in this way. ▷early 17th cent. (in the sense 'enable sputum to be coughed up,' referring to medicine): from Latin *expectorat-* 'expelled from the chest,' from the verb *expectorare*, from *ex-* 'out' + *pectus, pector-* 'breast.' **—ex·pec·to·ra·tion** /ikˌspektəˈrāSHən/ *n.*

ex·pe·di·ent /ikˈspēdēənt/ ▸*adj.* (of an action) convenient and practical, although possibly improper or immoral: *either side could break the agreement if it were expedient to do so.* ■ (of an action) suitable or appropriate: *holding a public inquiry into the scheme was not expedient.*

▸*n.* a means of attaining an end, esp. one that is convenient but considered improper or immoral: *the current policy is a political expedient.* ▷late Middle English: from Latin *expedient-* 'extricating, putting in order,' from the verb *expedire* (see EXPEDITE). The original sense was neutral; the depreciatory sense, implying disregard of moral considerations, dates from the late 18th cent. **—ex·pe·di·ence** *n.* **—ex·pe·di·en·cy** *n.* **—ex·pe·di·ent·ly** *adv.*

ex·pe·dite /ˈekspəˌdīt/ ▸*v.* [*trans.*] make (an action or process) happen sooner or be accomplished more quickly: *he promised to expedite economic reforms.* ▷late 15th cent. (in the sense 'perform quickly'): from Latin *expedire* 'extricate (originally by freeing the feet), put in order,' from *ex-* 'out' + *pes, ped-* 'foot.' **—ex·pe·dit·er** (also **ex·pe·di·tor** /-tər/) *n.*

ex·pe·di·tion /ˌekspəˈdiSHən/ ▸*n.* **1** a journey or voyage undertaken by a group of people with a particular purpose, esp. that of exploration, scientific research, or war: *an expedition to the jungles of the Orinoco* | *informal a shopping expedition.* See note at JOURNEY. ■ the people involved in such a journey or voyage: *many of the expedition have passed rigorous courses.* **2** *formal* promptness or speed in doing something: *the landlord shall remedy the defects with all possible expedition.* ▷late Middle English: via Old French from Latin *expeditio(n-)*, from *expedire* 'extricate' (see EXPEDITE). Early senses included 'prompt supply of something' and 'setting out with aggressive intent.' The notions of 'speed' and 'purpose' are retained in current senses. Sense 1 dates from the late 16th cent.

ex·pe·di·tion·ar·y /ˌekspəˈdiSHəˌnerē/ ▸*adj.* [*attrib.*] of or forming an expedition, esp. a military expedition: *an expeditionary force.*

ex·pe·di·tious /ˌekspəˈdiSHəs/ ▸*adj.* done with speed and efficiency: *an expeditious investigation.* ▷late 15th cent.: from EXPEDITION + -OUS. **—ex·pe·di·tious·ly** *adv.* **—ex·pe·di·tious·ness** *n.*

ex·pel /ikˈspel/ ▸*v.* (**ex·pelled**, **ex·pel·ling**) [*trans.*] (often **be expelled**) deprive (someone) of membership of or involvement in a school or other organization: *she* ***was expelled from*** *school.* ■ force (someone) to leave a place, esp. a country. ■ force out or eject (something), esp. from the body: *she expelled a shuddering breath.* See note at EJECT. ▷late Middle English (in the general sense 'eject, force to leave'): from Latin *expellere*, from *ex-* 'out' + *pellere* 'to drive.' **—ex·pel·la·ble** *adj.* **—ex·pel·lee** /ˌekspelˈlē/ *n.* **—ex·pel·ler** *n.*

ex·pend /ikˈspend/ ▸*v.* [*trans.*] spend or use up (a resource such as money, time, or energy): *we do not need to expend energy working on our marriage.* ▷late Middle English: from Latin *expendere*, from *ex-* 'out' + *pendere* 'weigh, pay.' Compare with SPEND.

ex·pend·a·ble /ikˈspendəbəl/ ▸*adj.* (of an object) designed to be used only once and then abandoned or destroyed: *the need for unmanned and expendable launch vehicles.* ■ of little significance when compared to an overall purpose, and therefore able to be abandoned: *the region is expendable in the wider context of national politics.* **—ex·pend·a·bil·i·ty** /ikˌspendəˈbilitē/ *n.* **—ex·pend·a·bly** /-əblē/ *adv.*

ex·pend·i·ture /ikˈspendiCHər/ ▸*n.* the action of spending funds: *the expenditure of taxpayers' money.* ■ an amount of money spent: *cuts in public expenditure.* ▷mid 18th cent.: from EXPEND, suggested by obsolete *expenditor* 'officer in charge of expenditure,' from medieval Latin, from *expenditus*, irregular past participle of Latin *expendere* 'pay out' (see EXPEND).

ex·pense /ikˈspens/ ▸*n.* the cost required for something; the money spent on something: *we had ordered suits* ***at great expense*** | *the committee does not expect members to be* ***put to any expense.*** ■ (**expenses**) the costs incurred in the performance of one's job or a specific task, esp. one undertaken for another person: *his hotel and travel expenses.* ■ a thing on which one is required to spend money: *tolls are a daily expense.*

▸*v.* [*trans.*] (usu. **be expensed**) offset (an item of expenditure) as an expense against taxable income. ▷late Middle English: from Anglo-Norman French, alteration of Old French *espense*, from late Latin *expensa (pecunia)* '(money) spent,' from Latin *expendere* 'pay out' (see EXPEND).

▸*PHRASES* □ **at someone's expense** paid for by someone: *the document was printed at the taxpayer's expense.* ■ with someone as the victim, esp. of a joke: *my friends all had a good laugh at my expense.* □ **at the expense of** so as to cause harm to or neglect of: *the pursuit of profit at the expense of the environment* | *language courses that emphasize communication skills at the expense of literature.*

ex·pense ac·count ▸*n.* an arrangement under which sums of money spent in the course of business by an employee are later reimbursed by their employer.

ex·pen·sive /ikˈspensiv/ ▸*adj.* costing a lot of money: *keeping a horse is expensive* | *an expensive bottle of wine.* ▷early 17th cent. (in the sense 'lavish, extravagant'): from Latin *expens-* 'paid out,' from the verb *expendere* (see EXPEND), + -IVE. **—ex·pen·sive·ly** *adv.* **—ex·pen·sive·ness** *n.*

ex·pe·ri·ence /ikˈspi(ə)rēəns/ ▸*n.* practical contact with and observation of facts or events: *he had already learned his lesson by painful experience* | *he spoke from experience.* ■ the knowledge or skill acquired by such means over a period of time, esp. that gained in a particular profession by someone at work: *older men whose experience could be called upon* | *candidates with the necessary experience.* ■ an event or occurrence that leaves an impression on someone: *for the younger players it has been* ***a learning experience.***

▸*v.* [*trans.*] encounter or undergo (an event or occurrence): *the company is experiencing difficulties.* ■ feel (an emotion): *an opportunity to experience the excitement of New York.* ▷late Middle English: via Old French from Latin *experientia*, from *experiri* 'try.' Compare with EXPERIMENT and EXPERT. **—ex·pe·ri·ence·a·ble** *adj.* **—ex·pe·ri·enc·er** *n.*

ex·pe·ri·enced /ikˈspi(ə)rēənst/ ▸*adj.* having knowledge or skill in a particular field, esp. a profession or job, gained over a period of time: *an experienced social worker* | *she was* ***experienced in*** *marketing.*

ex·pe·ri·en·tial /ekˌspi(ə)rēˈenCHəl/ ▸*adj.* involving or based on experience and observation: *the experiential learning associated with employment.* ▷early 19th cent.: from EXPERIENCE, on the pattern of words such as *inferential.* **—ex·pe·ri·en·tial·ly** *adv.*

ex·per·i·ment ▸*n.* /ikˈsperəmənt/ a scientific procedure undertaken to make a discovery, test a hypothesis, or demonstrate a known fact: *laboratory* ***experiments on*** *guinea pigs* | *I have tested this by experiment.* ■ a course of action tentatively adopted without being sure of the eventual outcome: *the previous* ***experiment in*** *liberal democracy had ended in disaster.*

▸*v.* /-ˌment/ [*intrans.*] perform a scientific procedure, esp. in a laboratory, to determine something: *she* ***experimented on*** *chickens as well as mice.* ■ try out new concepts or ways of doing things: *the designers* ***experimented with*** *new ideas in lighting.* ▷Middle English: from Old French, or from Latin *experimentum*, from *experiri* 'try.' Compare with EXPERIENCE and EXPERT. **—ex·per·i·men·ta·tion** /ikˌsperəmənˈtāSHən/ *n.* **—ex·per·i·ment·er** *n.*

ex·per·i·men·tal /ikˌsperəˈmen(t)l/ ▸*adj.* (of a new invention or product) based on untested ideas or techniques and not yet established or finalized: *an experimental drug.* ■ (of a work of art or an artistic technique) involving a radically new and innovative style: *experimental music.* ■ of or relating to scientific experiments: *experimental results.* ■ *archaic* based on experience as opposed to authority or conjecture: *an experimental knowledge of God.* ▷late 15th cent. (in the sense 'having personal experience,' also 'experienced, observed'): from medieval Latin *experimentalis*, from Latin *experimentum* (see EXPERIMENT). **—ex·per·i·men·tal·ism** /-izəm/ *n.* **—ex·per·i·men·tal·ist** /-ist/ *n.* **—ex·per·i·men·tal·ly** *adv.*

ex·per·i·men·tal psy·chol·o·gy ▸*n.* the branch of psychology concerned with the scientific investigation of basic psychological processes such as learning, memory, and cognition in humans and animals.

ex·per·i·ment·er ef·fect /ik'sperə,mentər/ ▶n. an influence exerted by the experimenter's expectations or other characteristics on the results of an experiment, esp. in psychology.

ex·pert /'ek,spərt/ ▶n. a person who has a comprehensive and authoritative knowledge of or skill in a particular area: *experts in child development | a financial expert.*
▶adj. having or involving such knowledge or skill: *he had received expert academic advice | an expert witness.* ▷Middle English (as an adjective): from French, from Latin *expertus,* past participle of *experiri* 'try.' The noun use dates from the early 19th cent. Compare with EXPERIENCE and EXPERIMENT. —**ex·pert·ly** *adv.* —**ex·pert·ness** *n.*

ex·per·tise /,ekspər'tēz; -'tēs/ ▶n. expert skill or knowledge in a particular field: *technical expertise.* ▷mid 19th cent.: from French, from *expert* (see EXPERT).

ex·pert sys·tem ▶n. *Computing* a piece of software programmed using artificial intelligence techniques. Such systems use databases of expert knowledge to offer advice or make decisions in such areas as medical diagnosis and trading on the stock exchange.

ex·pert wit·ness ▶n. *Law* a person who is permitted to testify at a trial because of their special knowledge or proficiency in a particular field that is relevant to the case: *She was hired as an expert witness because she had assisted in more than 100 similar surgical procedures.*

E

ex·pi·ate /'ekspē,āt/ ▶v. [*trans.*] atone for (guilt or sin): *their sins must be expiated by sacrifice.* ▷late 16th cent. (in the sense 'end (rage, sorrow, etc.) by suffering it to the full'): from Latin *expiat-* 'appeased by sacrifice,' from the verb *expiare,* from *ex-* 'out' + *piare* (from *pius* 'pious'). —**ex·pi·a·ble** /'ekspēəbəl/ *adj.* —**ex·pi·a·tion** /,ekspē'āsʜən/ *n.* —**ex·pi·a·tor** /-,ātər/ *n.* —**ex·pi·a·to·ry** /'ekspēə,tôrē/ *adj.*

ex·pi·ra·tion /,ekspə'rāsʜən/ ▶n. **1** the ending of the fixed period for which a contract is valid: *the expiration of the lease.* ■ the end of a period of time: *the expiration of three years.* **2** *technical* exhalation of breath. ▷late Middle English (denoting a vapor or exhalation): from Latin *exspiratio(n-),* from the verb *exspirare* (see EXPIRE).

ex·pir·a·to·ry /ik'spīrə,tôrē/ ▶adj. of or relating to the exhalation of air from the lungs.

ex·pire /ik'spīr/ ▶v. **1** [*intrans.*] (of a document, authorization, or agreement) cease to be valid, typically after a fixed period of time: *the old contract had expired.* ■ (of a period of time) come to an end: *the three-year period has expired.* ■ (of a person) die. **2** [*trans.*] *technical* exhale (air) from the lung. ▷late Middle English: from Old French *expirer,* from Latin *exspirare* 'breathe out,' from *ex-* 'out' + *spirare* 'breathe.'

ex·pi·ry /ik'spī(ə)rē; ek-/ ▶n. *Brit. & Canadian* the end of the period for which something is valid: *the expiry of the patent | [as adj.] an expiry date.* ■ the end of a fixed period of time: *the expiry of the six-month period.* ■ *archaic* death.

ex·plain /ik'splān/ ▶v. [*reporting verb*] make (an idea, situation, or problem) clear to someone by describing it in more detail or revealing relevant facts or ideas: [with *clause*] *they explained that their lives centered on the religious rituals* | [with *direct speech*] *"my daddy has spells," Ben explained* | [*trans.*] *he explained the situation.* See note at CLARIFY. ■ [*trans.*] account for (an action or event) by giving a reason as excuse or justification: *Callie found it necessary to explain her blackened eye* | [with *clause*] *he makes athletes explain why they made a mistake* | [*intrans.*] *she had tried to* **explain about** *Adam, hadn't she?* ■ (**explain something away**) minimize the significance of an embarrassing fact or action by giving an excuse or justification: *they know stories about me that I can't explain away.* ▷late Middle English: from Latin *explanare,* based on *planus* 'plain.' —**ex·plain·a·ble** *adj.* —**ex·plain·er** *n.*
▶PHRASE □ **explain oneself** expand on what one has said in order to make one's meaning clear. ■ give an account of one's motives or conduct in order to excuse or justify oneself: *he was too panicked to stay and explain himself to the policeman.*

ex·pla·nan·dum /,eksplə'nandəm/ ▶n. (*pl.* **-da** /-də/) *Philosophy* another term for EXPLICANDUM. ▷late 19th cent.: from Latin, '(something) to be explained.'

ex·pla·nans /ek'splā,nans/ ▶n. (*pl.* **ex·pla·nan·ti·a** /,eksplə'nanсʜēə/) *Philosophy* another term for EXPLICANS. ▷1940s: Latin, 'explaining.'

ex·pla·na·tion /,eksplə'nāsʜən/ ▶n. a statement or account that makes something clear: *the birth rate is central to any explanation of population trends.* ■ a reason or justification given for an action or belief: *Freud tried to make sex the explanation for everything | my application was rejected without explanation.* ▷late Middle English: from Latin *explanatio(n-),* from the verb *explanare* (see EXPLAIN).

ex·plan·a·to·ry /ik'splanə,tôrē/ ▶adj. serving to explain something: *explanatory notes.* —**ex·plan·a·to·ri·ly** /ik,splanə'tôrəlē/ *adv.*

ex·plant *Biology* ▶v. /ek'splant/ [*trans.*] [often as *adj.*] (**explanted**) transfer (living cells, tissues, or organs) from animals or plants to a nutrient medium.
▶n. /'eks,plant/ a cell, organ, or piece of tissue that has been transferred in this way. ▷early 20th cent.: from modern Latin *explantare,* from *ex-* 'out' + *plantare* 'to plant.' —**ex·plan·ta·tion** /,eksplan'tāsʜən/ *n.*

ex·ple·tive /'eksplitiv/ ▶n. an oath or swear word. ■ *Grammar* a word or phrase used to fill out a sentence or a line of verse without adding to the sense.
▶adj. *Grammar* (of a word or phrase) serving to fill out a sentence or line of verse. ▷late Middle English (as an adjective): from late Latin *expletivus,* from *explere* 'fill out,' from *ex-* 'out' + *plere* 'fill.' The general noun sense 'word used merely to fill out a sentence' (early 17th cent.) was applied specifically to an oath or swearword in the early 19th cent.

ex·pli·ca·ble /ek'splikəbəl; 'eksplik-/ ▶adj. able to be accounted for or understood: *the English class system is not entirely explicable in terms of money.* ▷mid 16th cent.: from French, or from Latin *explicabilis,* from *explicare* (see EXPLICATE).

ex·pli·can·dum /,ekspli'kandəm/ ▶n. (*pl.* **-da** /-də/) *Philosophy* the fact, thing, or expression that is to be explained or explicated. Compare with EXPLICANS. ▷mid 19th cent.: Latin, 'something to be explained,' neuter gerundive of *explicare.*

ex·pli·cans /'ekspli,kanz/ ▶n. (*pl.* **-can·ti·a** /-,kansʜēə/) *Philosophy* the explanation or explication given for a fact, thing, or expression. Compare with EXPLICANDUM. ▷late 19th cent.: Latin, present participle of *explicare* 'explain.'

ex·pli·cate /'ekspli,kāt/ ▶v. [*trans.*] analyze and develop (an idea or principle) in detail: *attempting to explicate the relationship between crime and economic forces.* See note at CLARIFY. ■ analyze (a literary work) in order to reveal its meaning. ▷mid 16th cent.: from Latin *explicat-* 'unfolded,' from the verb *explicare,* from *ex-* 'out' + *plicare* 'to fold.' —**ex·pli·ca·tion** /,ekspli'kāsʜən/ *n.* —**ex·pli·ca·tive** /-,kātiv/ *adj.* —**ex·pli·ca·tor** /-,kātər/ *n.* —**ex·pli·ca·to·ry** /ik'splikə,tôrē/ *adj.*

ex·plic·it /ik'splisit/ ▶adj. stated clearly and in detail, leaving no room for confusion or doubt: *the speaker's intentions were not* **made explicit**. ■ (of a person) stating something in such a way: *let me be explicit.* ■ describing or representing sexual activity in a graphic fashion: *explicit photos showing poses and acts.*
▶n. the closing words of a text, manuscript, early printed book, or chanted liturgical text. Compare with INCIPIT. [Middle English: late Latin, 'here ends,' or abbreviation of *explicitus est liber* 'the scroll is unrolled.'] ▷early 17th cent. (as an adjective): from French *explicite* or Latin *explicitus,* past participle of *explicare* 'unfold' (see EXPLICATE). —**ex·plic·it·ly** *adv.* —**ex·plic·it·ness** *n.*

ex·plode /ik'splōd/ ▶v. [*intrans.*] **1** burst or shatter violently and noisily as a result of rapid combustion, decomposition, excessive internal pressure, or other process, typically scattering fragments widely: *a large bomb exploded in a park.* ■ [*trans.*] cause (a bomb) to do this: *the USSR had not yet exploded its first nuclear weapon.* ■ *technical* undergo a violent expansion in which much energy is released as a shock wave: *lead ensures that gasoline burns rather than explodes.* ■ (of a person) suddenly give expression to violent and uncontainable emotion, esp. anger: *he can* **explode with** *anger* | [with *direct speech*] *"This is ludicrous!" she exploded.* ■ (of a violent emotion or a situation) arise or develop suddenly: *tension that could* **explode into** *violence at any time.* ■ (**explode into**) suddenly begin to move or start a new activity: *a bird exploded into flight.* ■ increase suddenly or rapidly in size, number, or extent: *the car population of Warsaw has exploded.* ■ [as *adj.*] (**exploded**) (of a diagram or drawing) showing the components of a mechanism as if separated by an explosion but in the normal relative positions: *an exploded diagram of the rifle's parts.* **2** [*trans.*] (often **be exploded**) show (a belief or theory) to be false or unfounded: *the myths that link smoking with glamour need to be exploded.* ▷mid 16th cent. (in the sense 'reject scornfully, discard'): from Latin *explodere* 'drive out by clapping, hiss off the stage,' from *ex-* 'out' + *plaudere* 'to clap.' Sense 2 is derived from the original sense of the word. Sense 1 (late 18th cent.) evolved via an old sense 'expel with violence and sudden noise,' perhaps influenced by obsolete *displode* 'burst with a noise.' —**ex·plod·er** *n.*

ex·ploit ▶v. /ik'sploit/ [*trans.*] make full use of and derive benefit from (a resource): *500 companies sprang up to exploit this new technology.* ■ use (a situation or person) in an unfair or selfish way: *the company was exploiting a legal loophole | accusations that he exploited a wealthy patient.* ■ benefit unfairly from the work of (someone), typically by overworking or underpaying them: *making money does not always mean exploiting others.*
▶n. /'ek,sploit/ a bold or daring feat: *the most heroic and secretive exploits of the war.* ▷Middle English: from Old French *esploit* (noun), based on Latin *explicare* 'unfold' (see EXPLICATE). The early notion of 'success, progress' gave rise to the sense 'attempt to capture,' 'military expedition,' hence the current sense of the noun. Current verb senses (mid 19th cent.) are taken from modern French *exploiter.* —**ex·ploit·a·ble** *adj.* —**ex·ploi·ta·tion** /,eksploi'tāsʜən/ *n.* —**ex·ploit·a·tive** /ik'sploitətiv/ *adj.* —**ex·ploit·er** /ik'sploitər/ *n.* —**ex·ploit·ive** /ik'sploitiv/ *adj.*

ex·plo·ra·tion /,eksplə'rāsʜən/ ▶n. the action of traveling in or through an unfamiliar area in order to learn about it: *voyages of exploration | an exploration of the African interior.* ■ thorough analysis of a subject or theme: *an exploration of the religious dimensions of our lives.* ▷mid 16th cent. (denoting an investigation): from French, or from Latin *exploratio(n-),* from the verb *explorare* (see EXPLORE). The current sense dates from the early 19th cent. —**ex·plo·ra·tion·al** /-'rāsʜənl/ *adj.*

ex·plor·a·to·ri·um /ik,splôrə'tôrēəm/ ▶n. [usu. in *names*] a scientific museum or similar center at which visitors have the opportunity of performing prearranged experiments or demonstrations. ▷1970s: from EXPLORATION + -ORIUM.

ex·plor·a·to·ry /ik'splôrə,tôrē/ ▶adj. relating to or involving exploration or investigation: *surgeons performed an exploratory operation | exploratory talks.* ▷late Middle English: from Latin *exploratorius,* from *explorare* (see EXPLORE).

ex·plore /ik'splôr/ ▶v. [*trans.*] travel in or through (an unfamiliar country or area) in order to learn about or familiarize oneself with it: *the best way to explore Iceland's northwest | figurative explore the world of science and technology.* ■ [*intrans.*] (**explore for**) search for resources such as mineral deposits: *the company explored for oil.* ■ inquire into or discuss (a subject or issue) in detail: *he sets out to explore fundamental questions.* ■ examine or evaluate (an option or possibility): *he met with Israeli leaders to explore new peace proposals.* ■ examine by touch: *her fingers explored his hair.* ■ *Medicine* surgically examine (a wound or body cavity) in detail. ▷mid 16th cent. (in the sense 'investigate (why)'): from French *explorer,* from Latin *explorare* 'search out,' from *ex-* 'out' + *plorare* 'utter a cry.' —**ex·plor·a·tive** /-rətiv/ *adj.*

ex·plo·sion /ik'splōzʜən/ ▶n. a violent and destructive shattering or blowing apart of something, as is caused by a bomb. ■ *technical* a violent expansion in which energy is transmitted outward as a shock wave. ■ a sudden outburst of something such as noise, light, or violent emotion, esp. anger: *an explosion of anger.* ■ a sudden political or social upheaval. ■ a rapid or sudden increase in amount or extent: *an explosion in the adder population.* ■ *Phonetics* another term for PLOSION. ▷early 17th cent.: from Latin *explosio(n-)* 'scornful rejection,' from the verb *explodere* (see EXPLODE).

ex·plo·sive /ik'splōsiv/ ▶adj. able or likely to shatter violently or burst apart, as when a bomb explodes: *an explosive device.* ■ likely to cause an eruption of anger or controversy: *Marco's explosive temper | the idea was politically explosive.* ■ of or relating to a sudden and dramatic increase in amount or extent: *the explosive growth of personal computers in the 1980s.* ■ (of a vocal sound) produced with a sharp release of air. ■ *Phonetics* another term for PLOSIVE.
▶n. (often **explosives**) a substance that can be made to explode, esp. any of those used in bombs or shells. —**ex·plo·sive·ly** *adv.* —**ex·plo·sive·ness** *n.*

ex·plo·sive bolt ▶n. a bolt that can be released by being blown out of position by an integral explosive charge.

ex·po /'ekspō/ ▶n. (*pl.* **-pos**) a large exhibition. ▷1960s (referring to the World Fair held in Montreal in 1967): abbreviation of EXPOSITION.

ex·po·nent /ik'spōnənt; 'ekspōnənt/ ▸*n.* **1** a person who believes in and promotes the truth or benefits of an idea or theory: *an early* ***exponent of*** *the teachings of Thomas Aquinas.* ■ a person who has and demonstrates a particular skill, esp. to a high standard: *he's the world's leading exponent of country rock guitar.* **2** *Mathematics* a quantity representing the power to which a given number or expression is to be raised, usually expressed as a raised symbol beside the number or expression (e.g., 3 in $2^3 = 2 \times 2 \times 2$). **3** *Linguistics* a linguistic unit that realizes another, more abstract unit. ▷late 16th cent. (as an adjective in the sense 'expounding'): from Latin *exponent-* 'putting out,' from the verb *exponere* (see EXPOUND).

ex·po·nen·tial /ˌekspə'nenCHəl/ ▸*adj.* *Mathematics* of or expressed by a mathematical exponent: *an exponential curve.* ■ (of an increase) becoming more and more rapid: *the social security budget was rising at an exponential rate.* ▷early 18th cent.: from French *exponentiel*, from Latin *exponere* 'put out' (see EXPOUND). **—ex·po·nen·tial·ly** *adv.*

ex·po·nen·tial func·tion ▸*n.* *Mathematics* a function whose value is a constant raised to the power of the argument, esp. the function where the constant is *e*.

ex·po·nen·tial growth ▸*n.* growth whose rate becomes ever more rapid in proportion to the growing total number or size.

ex·po·nen·ti·a·tion /ˌekspəˌnenCHē'āSHən/ ▸*n.* *Mathematics* the operation of raising one quantity to the power of another. **—ex·po·nen·ti·ate** /-'nenCHēˌāt/ *v.*

ex·port ▸*v.* /ik'spôrt; 'ekspôrt/ [*trans.*] send (goods or services) to another country for sale: *we exported $16 million worth of mussels to Japan.* ■ spread or introduce (ideas and beliefs) to another country: *the Greeks exported Hellenic culture around the Mediterranean basin.* ■ *Computing* transfer (data) in a format that can be used by other programs.
▸*n.* /'ekˌspôrt/ (usu. **exports**) a commodity, article, or service sold abroad: *wool and mohair were the principal exports.* ■ (**exports**) sales of goods or services to other countries, or the revenue from such sales: *meat exports.* ■ the selling and sending out of goods or services to other countries: *the export of Western technology.* ■ [as *adj.*] of a high standard suitable for export: *high-grade export coal.* ▷late 15th cent. (in the sense 'take away'): from Latin *exportare*, from *ex-* 'out' + *portare* 'carry.' Current senses date from the 17th cent. **—ex·port·a·bil·i·ty** /ikˌspôrtə'bilitē/ *n.* **—ex·port·a·ble** /ik'spôrtəbəl/ *adj.* **—ex·por·ta·tion** /ˌekspôr'tāSHən/ *n.* **—ex·port·er** *n.*

ex·port sur·plus ▸*n.* the amount by which the value of a country's exports exceeds that of its imports.

ex·pose /ik'spōz/ ▸*v.* [*trans.*] (often **be exposed**) make (something) visible, typically by uncovering it: *at low tide the sands are exposed.* ■ [often as *adj.*] (**exposed**) leave (something) uncovered or unprotected, esp. from the weather: *the coast is very exposed to the southwest.* ■ subject (photographic film) to light, esp. when operating a camera. ■ (**expose oneself**) publicly and indecently display one's genitals. ■ [usu. as *adj.*] (**exposed**) leave or put (someone) in an unprotected and vulnerable state: *Miranda felt exposed and lonely.* ■ (**expose someone to**) cause someone to experience or be at risk of: *he exposed himself unnecessarily to gunfire in the war.* ■ make (something embarrassing or damaging) public: *investigations exposed a vast network of illegalities.* ■ reveal the true and typically objectionable nature of (someone or something): *he has been* ***exposed as*** *a liar and a traitor.* ■ (**expose someone to**) introduce (someone) to (a subject or area of knowledge): *students were exposed to probability and statistics in high school.* ■ leave (a child) in the open to die. ▷late Middle English: from Old French *exposer*, from Latin *exponere* (see EXPOUND), but influenced by Latin *expositus* 'put or set out' and Old French *poser* 'to place.' **—ex·pos·er** *n.*

ex·po·sé /ˌekspō'zā/ ▸*n.* a report of the facts about something, esp. a journalistic report that reveals something scandalous: *a shocking exposé of a medical cover-up.* ▷early 19th cent.: from French, 'shown, set out,' past participle of *exposer* (see EXPOSE).

ex·po·si·tion /ˌekspə'ziSHən/ ▸*n.* **1** a comprehensive description and explanation of an idea or theory: *an exposition and defense of Marx's writings.* ■ *Music* the part of a movement, esp. in sonata form, in which the principal themes are first presented. ■ the part of a play or work of fiction in which the background to the main conflict is introduced. **2** a large public exhibition of art or trade goods. ■ *archaic* the action of making public; exposure: *the country squires dreaded the exposition of their rustic conversation.* ▷Middle English: from Latin *expositio(n-)*, from the verb *exponere* 'put out, exhibit, explain.' **—ex·po·si·tion·al** /-ziSHənl/ *adj.*

ex·pos·i·tor /ik'späzitər/ ▸*n.* a person or thing that explains complicated ideas or theories: *a lucid expositor of difficult ideas.* ▷Middle English: via Old French or late Latin, from Latin *exposit-* 'exposed, explained,' from *exponere* (see EXPOUND).

ex·pos·i·to·ry /ik'späziˌtôrē/ ▸*adj.* intended to explain or describe something: *formal expository prose.*

ex post ▸*adj.* & *adv.* based on actual results rather than forecasts: [as *adj.*] *the ex post trade balance* | [as *adv.*] *the real-wage rate had fallen ex post.* ▷modern Latin, from *ex* 'from' and *post* 'after.'

ex post fac·to /ˌeks pōst 'faktō/ ▸*adj.* & *adv.* with retroactive effect or force: [as *adj.*] *ex post facto laws.* ▷erroneous division of Latin *ex postfacto* 'in the light of subsequent events.'

ex·pos·tu·late /ik'späsCHəˌlāt/ ▸*v.* [*intrans.*] express strong disapproval or disagreement: *I* ***expostulated with*** *him in vain.* ▷mid 16th cent. (in the sense 'demand how or why, state a complaint'): from Latin *expostulat-* 'demanded,' from the verb *expostulare*, from *ex-* 'out' + *postulare* 'demand.' **—ex·pos·tu·la·tion** /ikˌspäsCHə'lāSHən/ *n.* **—ex·pos·tu·la·tor** /-lātər/ *n.* **—ex·pos·tu·la·to·ry** /ikˌspäsCHələˌtôrē/ *adj.*

ex·po·sure /ik'spōZHər/ ▸*n.* **1** the state of being exposed to contact with something: *the dangers posed by* ***exposure to*** *asbestos.* ■ an act or instance of being uncovered or unprotected: *thick exposures of ice in the western Arctic islands.* ■ a physical condition resulting from being outside in severe weather conditions without adequate protection: *he died of exposure at 8,000 feet.* ■ experience of something: *his* ***exposure to*** *the banking system.* ■ the action of exposing a photographic film to light or other radiation: *a camera which would give a picture immediately after exposure* | *trial exposures made with a UV filter.* ■ the quantity of light or other radiation reaching a photographic film, as determined by shutter speed and lens aperture. ■ the action of placing oneself at risk of financial losses, e.g., through making loans, granting credit, or underwriting insurance. **2** the revelation of an identity or fact, esp. one that is concealed or likely to arouse disapproval: *she took her life for fear of exposure as a spy.* ■ the publicizing of information or an event: *scientific findings receive regular exposure in the media.* **3** the direction in which a building faces; an outlook: *the exposure is perfect—a gentle slope to the southwest.* ▷early 17th cent.: from EXPOSE, on the pattern of words such as *enclosure*.

ex·po·sure me·ter ▸*n.* another term for LIGHT METER.

ex·pound /ik'spound/ ▸*v.* [*trans.*] present and explain (a theory or idea) systematically and in detail: *he was expounding a powerful argument* | [*intrans.*] *he declined to* ***expound on*** *his decision.* ■ explain the meaning of (a literary or doctrinal work): *the abbess expounded the scriptures to her nuns.* ▷Middle English *expoune* (in the sense 'explain (what is difficult)'): from Old French *espon-*, present tense stem of *espondre*, from Latin *exponere* 'expose, publish, explain,' from *ex-* 'out' + *ponere* 'put.' The origin of the final *-d* (recorded from the Middle English period) is uncertain (compare with COMPOUND[1], PROPOUND). **—ex·pound·er** *n.*

ex·press[1] /ik'spres/ ▸*v.* [*trans.*] **1** convey (a thought or feeling) in words or by gestures and conduct: *he expressed complete satisfaction.* ■ (**express oneself**) say what one thinks or means: *with a diplomatic smile, she expressed herself more subtly.* ■ *chiefly Mathematics* represent (a number, relation, or property) by a figure, symbol, or formula: *constants can be* ***expressed in terms of*** *the Fourier transform.* ■ (usu. **be expressed**) *Genetics* cause (an inherited characteristic or gene) to appear in a phenotype. **2** squeeze out (liquid or air). ▷late Middle English (also in the sense 'press out, obtain by squeezing or wringing,' used figuratively to mean 'extort'): from Old French *expresser*, based on Latin *ex-* 'out' + *pressare* 'to press.' **—ex·press·er** *n.* **—ex·press·i·ble** *adj.*

ex·press[2] ▸*adj.* operating at high speed: *an express airmail service.* ■ (of a train or other vehicle of public transportation) making few intermediate stops and so reaching its destination quickly: *an express train bound for Innsbruck* | *express bus service* | *an express elevator.* Compare with LOCAL. ■ denoting a company undertaking the transportation of letters and packages, esp. one promising overnight or other rapid delivery: *the nation's biggest express package shipper.* ■ *chiefly Brit.* denoting a service in which messages or goods are delivered by a special messenger to ensure speed or security: *an express letter.*
▸*adv.* by express train or delivery service: *I got my wife to send my gloves express to the hotel.*
▸*n.* **1** an express train or other vehicle of public transportation: *we embarked for the south of France on an overnight express.* **2** an overnight or rapid delivery service: *the books arrived* ***by express.*** ■ used in names of delivery services, trains, and newspapers to denote speed of service: *the Orient Express* | *Federal Express.* ■ used in names of airlines to denote nonstop regional service on small planes: *United Express.* **3** an express rifle.
▸*v.* [*trans.*] send by express delivery or messenger: *I expressed my clothes to my destination.* ▷early 18th cent. (in the sense of the verb): extension of EXPRESS[3]; sense 1 from *express train*, so named because it served a particular destination without intermediate stops, reflecting an earlier sense of *express* 'done or made for a special purpose,' later interpreted in the sense 'rapid.' Senses relating to *express delivery* date from the institution of this postal service in Britain in 1891.

ex·press[3] ▸*adj.* definitely stated, not merely implied: *it was his express wish that the celebration continue.* ■ precisely and specifically identified to the exclusion of anything else: *the schools were founded for the express purpose of teaching deaf children.* ■ *archaic* (of a likeness) exact. ▷late Middle English: from Old French *expres*, from Latin *expressus* 'distinctly presented,' past participle of *exprimere* 'press out, express,' from *ex-* 'out' + *primere* 'press.' **—ex·press·ly** *adv.*

ex·pres·sion /ik'spreSHən/ ▸*n.* **1** the process of making known one's thoughts or feelings: *his views* ***found expression*** *in his moral sermons* | *she accepted his expressions of sympathy.* ■ the conveying of opinions publicly without interference by the government: *the right to freedom of expression.* ■ the look on someone's face that conveys a particular emotion: *a sad expression.* ■ the ability to put an emotion into words: *envious beyond expression.* ■ a word or phrase, esp. an idiomatic one, used to convey an idea: *nowhere is the expression "garbage in, garbage out" any truer.* ■ the style or phrasing of written or spoken words: *subtlety of expression.* ■ the conveying of feeling in the face or voice, in a work of art, or in the performance of a piece of music: *eyes empty of expression* | *their instruments have a rich variety of expression.* ■ *Mathematics* a collection of symbols that jointly express a quantity: *the expression for the circumference of a circle is* $2\pi r$. ■ *Genetics* the appearance in a phenotype of a characteristic or effect attributed to a particular gene. ■ (also **gene expression**) *Genetics* the process by which possession of a gene leads to the appearance in the phenotype of the corresponding character. **2** the production of something, esp. by pressing or squeezing it out: *essential oils obtained by distillation or expression.* ▷late Middle English: from Latin *expressio(n-)*, from *exprimere* 'press out, express.' Compare with EXPRESS[1]. **—ex·pres·sion·al** /ek'spreSHənl/ *adj.* **—ex·pres·sion·less** *adj.* **—ex·pres·sion·less·ly** *adv.* **—ex·pres·sion·less·ness** *n.*

ex·pres·sion·ism /ik'spreSHəˌnizəm/ ▸*n.* a style of painting, music, or drama in which the artist or writer seeks to express emotional experience rather than impressions of the external world.

Expressionists characteristically reject traditional ideas of beauty or harmony and use distortion, exaggeration, and other nonnaturalistic devices in order to emphasize and express the inner world of emotion. The paintings of El Greco and Grünewald exemplify expressionism in this broad sense, but the term is also used of a late 19th and 20th century European and specifically German movement tracing its origins to Van Gogh, Edvard Munch, and James Ensor, which insisted on the primacy of the artist's feelings and mood, often incorporating violence and the grotesque.

—ex·pres·sion·ist *n.* & *adj.* **—ex·pres·sion·is·tic** /ikˌspreSHə'nistik/ *adj.* **—ex·pres·sion·is·ti·cal·ly** /ikˌspreSHə'nistik(ə)lē/ *adv.*

ex·pres·sion mark ▸*n.* *Music* a word or phrase on a musical score that indicates the expression required of a performer.

ex·pres·sive /ik'spresiv/ ▸*adj.* effectively conveying thought or feeling. ■ [*predic.*] (**expressive of**) conveying (the specified quality or idea): *the spires are expressive of religious aspiration.* ▷late Middle English (in the sense 'tending to press out'): from French *expressif*, *-ive* or medieval Latin *expressivus*, from *exprimere* 'press out' (see EXPRESS[3]). Compare with EXPRESS[1].

Pronunciation Key ə *ago*; ər *over*; 'ə or ˌə *up*; 'ər or ˌər *fur*; a *hat*; ā *rate*; ä *car*; CH *chew*; e *let*; ē *see*; e(ə)r *air*; i *fit*; ī *by*; i(ə)r *ear*; NG *sing*; ō *go*; ô *for*; oi *boy*; o͝o *good*; o͞o *goo*; ou *out*; SH *she*; TH *thin*; T͟H *then*; (h)w *why*; ZH *vision*

—**ex·pres·sive·ly** *adv.* —**ex·pres·sive·ness** *n.* —**ex·pres·siv·i·ty** /ˌekspreˈsivitē/ *n.*

ex·press lane ▸*n.* (on a highway) a lane for through traffic, having fewer exits. ■ (in a grocery store) a checkout aisle for shoppers buying only a few items.

Ex·press Mail ▸*n. trademark* a special delivery service of the U.S. Postal Service that guarantees overnight delivery.

ex·pres·so /ikˈspresō/ ▸*n.* variant spelling of ESPRESSO.

USAGE See usage at ESPRESSO.

ex·press ri·fle ▸*n.* a rifle that discharges a bullet at high speed and is used in big-game hunting.

ex·press·way /ikˈspresˌwā/ ▸*n.* a highway designed for fast traffic, with controlled entrance and exit, a dividing strip between the traffic in opposite directions, and typically two or more lanes in each direction.

ex·pro·pri·ate /ˌeksˈprōprēˌāt/ ▸*v.* [*trans.*] (esp. of the state) take away (property) from its owner: *government plans to expropriate farmland.* ■ dispossess (someone) of property: *the land reform expropriated the Irish landlords.* ▷late 16th cent.: from medieval Latin *expropriat-* 'taken from the owner,' from the verb *expropriare*, from *ex-* 'out, from' + *proprium* 'property,' neuter singular of *proprius* 'own.' —**ex·pro·pri·a·tion** /ˌeksˌprōprēˈāsHən/ *n.* —**ex·pro·pri·a·tor** /-ˌātər/ *n.*

expt. ▸*abbr.* experiment.

exptl. ▸*abbr.* experimental.

ex·pul·sion /ikˈspəlsHən/ ▸*n.* the action of depriving someone of membership in an organization: ***expulsion from** school.* ■ the process of forcing someone to leave a place, esp. a country: *the expulsion of Jews from Berlin | mass expulsions of Croats during the savage fighting.* ■ the process of forcing something out of the body. ▷late Middle English: from Latin *expulsio(n-)*, from *expellere* 'drive out' (see EXPEL). —**ex·pul·sive** /ikˈspəlsiv/ *adj.*

ex·punge /ikˈspənj/ ▸*v.* [*trans.*] erase or remove completely (something unwanted or unpleasant): *the communists had expunged references to the Hitler-Stalin pact.* ▷early 17th cent.: from Latin *expungere* 'mark for deletion by means of points,' from *ex-* 'out' + *pungere* 'to prick.' —**ex·punc·tion** /ikˈspəNG(k)sHən/ *n.* —**ex·punge·ment** *n.* —**ex·pung·er** *n.*

ex·pur·gate /ˈekspərˌgāt/ ▸*v.* [*trans.*] [often as *adj.*] (**expurgated**) remove matter thought to be objectionable or unsuitable from (a book or account): *the expurgated* Arabian Nights. ▷early 17th cent. (in the sense 'purge of excrement'): from Latin *expurgat-* 'thoroughly cleansed,' from the verb *expurgare*, from *ex-* 'out' + *purgare* 'cleanse.' —**ex·pur·ga·tion** /ˌekspərˈgāsHən/ *n.* —**ex·pur·ga·tor** *n.* —**ex·pur·ga·to·ry** /ikˈspərgəˌtôrē/ *adj.*

ex·quis·ite /ekˈskwizit; ˈekskwizit/ ▸*adj.* extremely beautiful and, typically, delicate: *exquisite, jewellike portraits.* ■ intensely felt: *the most exquisite kind of agony.* ■ highly sensitive or discriminating: *her exquisite taste in painting.*
▸*n.* a man who is affectedly concerned with his clothes and appearance; a dandy. ▷late Middle English (in the sense 'carefully ascertained, precise'): from Latin *exquisit-* 'sought out,' from the verb *exquirere*, from *ex-* 'out' + *quaerere* 'seek.' —**e·quis·ite·ly** *adv.* —**ex·quis·ite·ness** *n.*

exr. ▸*abbr.* executor.

exrx. ▸*abbr.* executrix.

ex·san·gui·na·tion /ekˌsaNGgwəˈnāsHən/ ▸*n. Medicine* the action of draining a person, animal, or organ of blood. ■ severe loss of blood. ▷early 20th cent.: from Latin *exsanguinatus* 'drained of blood' (from *ex-* 'out' + *sanguis, sanguin-* 'blood') + -ION. —**ex·san·gui·nate** /ekˈsaNGgwəˌnāt/ *v.*

ex·san·guine /eksˈsaNGgwin/ ▸*adj. poetic/literary* bloodless; anemic. ▷mid 17th cent.: from EX-[1] 'out' + Latin *sanguis, sanguin-* 'blood.'

ex·sert /ekˈsərt/ ▸*v.* [*trans.*] *Biology* cause to protrude; push out: [as *adj.*] (**exserted**) *an exserted stigma.* ▷mid 17th cent.: from Latin *exsert-* 'put forth,' from the verb *exserere* (see EXERT).

ex-serv·ice·man ▸*n.* (*pl.* **-men**) *chiefly Brit.* a man who was formerly a member of the armed forces.

ex si·len·ti·o /ˌeks səˈlencHē-ō/ ▸*adj.* & *adv.* by the absence of contrary evidence. ▷early 20th cent.: Latin, literally 'from silence.'

ex·solve /eksˈsälv/ ▸*v.* [*intrans.*] *Geology* (of a mineral or other substance) separate out from solution, esp. from solid solution in a rock. ■ [*trans.*] [usu. as *adj.*] (**exsolved**) form (a mineral or other substance) in this way: *coarsely exsolved ilmenites.* —**ex·so·lu·tion** /ˌeksəˈlo͞osHən/ *n.*

ext. ▸*abbr.* ■ extension (in a telephone number). ■ exterior. ■ external. ■ extra.

ex·tant /ˈekstənt; ekˈstant/ ▸*adj.* (esp. of a document) still in existence; surviving: *the original manuscript is no longer extant.* ▷mid 16th cent. (in the sense 'accessible, able to be publicly seen or reached'): from Latin *exstant-* 'being visible or prominent, existing,' from the verb *exstare*, from *ex-* 'out' + *stare* 'to stand.'

ex·tem·po·ra·ne·ous /ikˌstempəˈrānēəs/ ▸*adj.* spoken or done without preparation: *an extemporaneous speech.* —**ex·tem·po·ra·ne·ous·ly** *adv.* —**ex·tem·po·ra·ne·ous·ness** *n.*

ex·tem·po·rar·y /ikˈstempəˌrerē/ ▸*adj.* another term for EXTEMPORANEOUS. ▷late 16th cent.: from EXTEMPORE, on the pattern of *temporary.* —**ex·tem·po·rar·i·ly** /ikˌstempəˈrerəlē/ *adv.* —**ex·tem·po·rar·i·ness** *n.*

ex·tem·po·re /ikˈstempərē/ ▸*adj.* & *adv.* spoken or done without preparation: [as *adj.*] *extempore public speaking* | [as *adv.*] *he recited the poem extempore.* ▷mid 16th cent.: from Latin *ex tempore* 'on the spur of the moment' (literally 'out of the time').

ex·tem·po·rize /ikˈstempəˌrīz/ ▸*v.* [*intrans.*] compose, perform, or produce something such as music or a speech without preparation; improvise: *he extemporized at the piano* | [*trans.*] *she was extemporizing touching melodies.* —**ex·tem·po·ri·za·tion** /ikˌstempəriˈzāsHən/ *n.*

ex·tend /ikˈstend/ ▸*v.* [*trans.*] **1** cause to cover a larger area; make longer or wider: *the Forest Service plans to extend a gravel road nearly a mile.* ■ expand in scope, effect, or meaning: *we have continued to extend our range of specialist services.* ■ cause to last longer: *high schools may consider extending the class day to seven periods.* ■ postpone (a starting or ending time) beyond the original limit: *he extended the deadline to 4 p.m. today.* ■ straighten or spread out (the body or a limb) at full length: *she is unable to extend her thumb.* ■ [*intrans.*] spread from a central point to cover a wider area: *the pipeline currently extends 1,200 miles from Santa Barbara.* ■ [*intrans.*] occupy a specified area or stretch to a specified point: *the mountains **extend over** the western end of the island | a fault that may extend to a depth of 12 miles.* ■ [*intrans.*] (**extend to**) include within one's scope; be applicable to: *her generosity did not extend to all adults.* ■ increase the volume or bulk of (something) by adding a cheaper substance: *recipes that extended stews with more potatoes.* ■ (**extend oneself**) exert or exercise oneself to the utmost: *you have to extend yourself to change rather than keep on doing the same thing.* **2** hold (something) out toward someone: *I nod and extend my hand.* ■ offer: *she extended an invitation to her to stay.* ■ make (a resource) available to someone: *I can't extend credit indefinitely.* ▷late Middle English: from Latin *extendere* 'stretch out,' from *ex-* 'out' + *tendere* 'stretch.' —**ex·tend·a·bil·i·ty** /ikˌstendəˈbilitē/ *n.* —**ex·tend·a·ble** *adj.* —**ex·tend·i·bil·i·ty** /ikˌstendəˈbilitē/ *n.* —**ex·tend·i·ble** /-əbəl/ *adj.* —**ex·ten·si·bil·i·ty** /ikˌstensəˈbilitē/ *n.* —**ex·ten·si·ble** /-ˈstensəbəl/ *adj.*

ex·tend·ed fam·i·ly ▸*n.* a family that extends beyond the nuclear family, including grandparents, aunts, uncles, and other relatives, who all live nearby or in one household.

ex·tend·ed-play ▸*adj.* denoting a record that plays for longer than most singles. ■ denoting an audio- or videotape that is thinner and longer than standard.

ex·tend·er /ikˈstendər/ ▸*n.* a person or thing that extends something. ■ a substance added to a product such as paint, ink, or glue, to dilute its color or increase its bulk. ■ *Photography* another term for EXTENSION TUBE.

ex·ten·sile /ikˈstensəl; -sīl/ ▸*adj.* capable of being stretched out or protruded. ▷mid 18th cent.: from Latin *extens-* 'stretched out' (from the verb *extendere*) + -ILE.

ex·ten·sion /ikˈstensHən/ ▸*n.* **1** a part that is added to something to enlarge or prolong it; a continuation: *the railroad's southern extension.* ■ a room or set of rooms added to an existing building. ■ the action or process of becoming or making something larger: *the extension of the president's powers.* ■ an application of an existing system or activity to a new area: *direct marketing is an extension of telephone selling.* ■ an increase in the length of time given to someone to hold office, complete a project, or fulfill an obligation. ■ *Computing* an optional suffix to a file name, typically consisting of a period followed by several characters, indicating the file's content or function. **2** (also **extension cord**) a length of electric cord that permits the use of an appliance at some distance from a fixed socket. ■ an extra telephone on the same line as the main one. ■ a subsidiary telephone in a set of offices or similar building, on a line leading from the main switchboard but having its own additional number. **3** [usu. as *adj.*] instruction by a university or college for students who do not attend full time: *extension courses.* **4** (**extensions**) lengths of real or artificial hair woven into a person's own hair to create a long hairstyle: *the type of female with with big trunk jewelry and extensions in her hair.* **5** the action of moving a limb from a bent to a straight position: *seizures with sudden rigid extension of the limbs.* ■ the muscle action controlling this: *triceps extension.* ■ *Ballet* the ability of a dancer to raise one leg above the waist, or an instance of this: *she has amazing extension | he could perform 180-degree extensions.* ■ *Medicine* the application of traction to a fractured or dislocated limb or to an injured or diseased spinal column to restore it to its normal position. ■ the lengthening of a horse's stride within a particular gait. **6** *Logic* the range of a term or concept as measured by the objects that it denotes or contains, as opposed to its internal content. Often contrasted with INTENSION. ■ *Physics & Philosophy* the property of occupying space; spatial magnitude: *nature, for Descartes, was pure extension in space.* ▷late Middle English: from late Latin *extensio(n-)*, from *extendere* 'stretch out' (see EXTEND). —**ex·ten·sion·al** /-sHənl/ *adj.*
▸*PHRASE* □ **by extension** taking the same line of argument further: *the disclosures raised serious questions about his credibility and, by extension, the credibility of the company.*

ex·ten·sion lad·der ▸*n.* a ladder that can be extended by means of sliding sections.

ex·ten·sion tube ▸*n. Photography* a tube fitted to a camera between the body and lens to shorten the distance of closest focus of an object so that close-up pictures can be taken.

ex·ten·sive /ikˈstensiv/ ▸*adj.* **1** covering or affecting a large area: *an extensive garden.* ■ large in amount or scale: *an extensive collection of silver.* **2** (of agriculture) obtaining a relatively small crop from a large area with a minimum of attention and expense: *extensive farming techniques.* Often contrasted with INTENSIVE (sense 1). ▷late Middle English: from French *extensif, -ive* or late Latin *extensivus*, from *extens-* 'stretched out,' from the verb *extendere* (see EXTEND). —**ex·ten·sive·ly** *adv.* —**ex·ten·sive·ness** *n.*

ex·ten·som·e·ter /ekstenˈsämitər/ ▸*n.* an instrument for measuring the deformation of a material under stress. ▷late 19th cent.: from Latin *extens-* 'extended' (from the verb *extendere*) + -METER.

ex·ten·sor /ikˈstensər; -sôr/ (also **extensor muscle**) ▸*n. Anatomy* a muscle whose contraction extends or straightens a limb or other part of the body. Often contrasted with FLEXOR. ■ any of a number of specific muscles in the arm, hand, leg, and foot. ▷early 18th cent.: from late Latin, from *extens-* 'stretched out,' from the verb *extendere* (see EXTEND).

ex·tent /ikˈstent/ ▸*n.* [in *sing.*] the area covered by something: *an enclosure ten acres in extent.* ■ the degree to which something has spread; the size or scale of something: *the extent of AIDS infection.* ■ the amount to which something is or is believed to be the case: *everyone will have to compromise to some extent | they altered the document to such an extent that it contained little in the way of new policy.* ■ a large space or area: *considerable extents of land.* ▷Middle English (in the sense 'valuation of property, esp. for taxation purposes'): from Anglo-Norman French *extente*, from medieval Latin *extenta*, feminine past participle of Latin *extendere* 'stretch out' (see EXTEND).

ex·ten·u·ate /ikˈstenyəˌwāt/ ▸*v.* [*trans.*] **1** [usu. as *adj.*] (**extenuating**) make (guilt or an offense) seem less serious or more forgivable: *there were **extenuating circumstances** that caused me to say the things I did.* **2** [usu. as *adj.*] (**extenuated**) *poetic/literary* make (someone) thin: *drawings of extenuated figures.* ▷late Middle English (in the sense 'make thin, emaciate'): from Latin *extenuat-* 'made thin,' from the verb *extenuare* (based on *tenuis* 'thin'). —**ex·ten·u·a·tion** /ikˌstenyəˈwāsHən/ *n.* —**ex·ten·u·a·to·ry** /-wəˌtôrē/ *adj.*

ex·te·ri·or /ikˈsti(ə)rēər/ ▸*adj.* forming, situated on, or relating to the outside of something: *exterior and interior walls.* ■ coming from outside: *exterior noise.* ■ (in filming) outdoor: *exterior locations.*
▸*n.* the outer surface or structure of something: *a jar with floral designs on the exterior.* ■ the outer structure of a building: *the museum has a modern exterior.* ■ a person's behavior and appearance, often contrasted

with their true character: *beneath that assured exterior, she's vulnerable.* ■ (in filming) an outdoor scene. ▷early 16th cent.: from Latin, comparative of *exter* 'outer.' **—ex·te·ri·or·i·ty** /ikˌsti(ə)rēˈôritē; -ˈärite/ *n.* **—ex·te·ri·or·ize** /-ˌrīz/ *v.* **—ex·te·ri·or·ly** *adv.*

ex·te·ri·or an·gle ▶*n. Geometry* the angle between a side of a rectilinear figure and an adjacent side extended outward.

ex·ter·mi·nate /ikˈstərməˌnāt/ ▶*v.* [*trans.*] (often **be exterminated**) destroy completely: *leftist ideals had not been totally exterminated.* See note at **DESTROY**. ■ kill (a pest): *they use poison to exterminate moles.* ▷late Middle English (in the sense 'drive out, banish'): from Latin *exterminat-* 'driven out, banished,' from the verb *exterminare*, from *ex-* 'out' + *terminus* 'boundary.' The sense 'destroy' (mid 16th cent.) comes from the Latin of the Vulgate. **—ex·ter·mi·na·tion** /ikˌstərməˈnāsHən/ *n.* **—ex·ter·mi·na·tor** /-ˌnātər/ *n.* **—ex·ter·mi·na·to·ry** /-nəˌtôrē/ *adj.*

ex·tern /ˈekstərn/ ▶*n.* **1** a person working in but not living in an institution, such as nonresident doctor or other worker in a hospital. **2** (in a strictly enclosed order of nuns) a sister who does not live exclusively within the enclosure and goes on outside errands. ▷mid 16th cent. (as an adjective in the sense 'external'): from French *externe* or Latin *externus*, from *exter* 'outer.' The word was used by Shakespeare to mean 'outward appearance'; current senses date from the early 17th cent. **—ex·tern·ship** /-sHip/ *n.*

ex·ter·nal /ikˈstərnl/ ▶*adj.* **1** belonging to or forming the outer surface or structure of something: *the external walls.* ■ relating to or denoting a medicine or similar substance for use on the outside of the body: *for external application only.* **2** coming or derived from a source outside the subject affected: *for many people the church was a symbol of external authority.* ■ coming from or relating to a foreign country or an outside institution: *responsibility for defense and external affairs.* ■ existing outside the mind: *the child learns to form conceptions of the external world.* ■ *Computing* (of hardware) not contained in the main computer; peripheral. ■ *Computing* (of storage) using a disk or tape drive rather than the main memory.
▶*n.* (**externals**) the outward features of something: *the place has all the appropriate externals, such as chimneys choked with ivy and windows with jasmine.* ■ features which are only superficial; inessentials. ▷late Middle English: from medieval Latin, from Latin *exter* 'outer.' **—ex·ter·nal·ly** *adv.*

ex·ter·nal au·di·to·ry me·a·tus ▶*n.* see **MEATUS**.

ex·ter·nal ear ▶*n.* the parts of the ear outside the eardrum, esp. the pinna.

ex·ter·nal·ism /ikˈstərnəˌlizəm/ ▶*n.* **1** excessive regard for outward form in religion: *religion needs to be questioned for its negative attitudes, hypocrisy, and externalism.* **2** *Philosophy* the view that mental events and acts are essentially dependent on the world external to the mind, in opposition to the Cartesian separation of mental and physical worlds. **—ex·ter·nal·ist** *n. & adj.*

ex·ter·nal·i·ty /ˌekˌstərˈnalitē/ ▶*n.* (*pl.* **-ties**) **1** *Economics* a side effect or consequence of an industrial or commercial activity that affects other parties without this being reflected in the cost of the goods or services involved, such as the pollination of surrounding crops by bees kept for honey. **2** *Philosophy* the fact of existing outside the perceiving subject.

ex·ter·nal·ize /ikˈstərnəˌlīz/ ▶*v.* [*trans.*] (usu. **be externalized**) give external existence or form to: *elements of the internal construction were externalized onto the façade.* ■ express (a thought or feeling) in words or actions: *an urgent need to externalize the experience.* ■ *Psychology* project (a mental image or process) onto a figure outside oneself: *such neuroses are externalized as interpersonal conflicts.* **—ex·ter·nal·i·za·tion** /ikˌstərnəliˈzāsHən/ *n.*

ex·ter·o·cep·tive /ˌekstərōˈseptiv/ ▶*adj. Physiology* relating to stimuli that are external to an organism. Compare with **INTEROCEPTIVE**. ▷early 20th cent.: probably a blend of **EXTERIOR** or **EXTERNAL** and **RECEPTIVE**. **—ex·ter·o·cep·tion** /-ˈsepsHən/ *n.* **—ex·ter·o·cep·tiv·i·ty** /-sepˈtivitē/ *n.*

ex·ter·o·cep·tor /ˌekstərōˈseptər/ ▶*n. Physiology* a sensory receptor that receives external stimuli. Compare with **INTEROCEPTOR**.

ex·tinct /ikˈstiNG(k)t/ ▶*adj.* (of a species, family, or other larger group) having no living members: *trilobites and dinosaurs are extinct.* ■ *often humorous* no longer in existence: *the sort of girls' school that is now extinct.* ■ (of a volcano) not having erupted in recorded history. ■ no longer burning: *his now extinct pipe.* ■ (of a title of nobility) having no qualified claimant. ▷late Middle English (in the sense 'no longer alight'): from Latin *exstinct-* 'extinguished,' from the verb *exstinguere* (see **EXTINGUISH**).

ex·tinc·tion /ikˈstiNG(k)sHən/ ▶*n.* **1** the state or process of a species, family, or larger group being or becoming extinct: *the extinction of the great auk | mass extinctions.* ■ the state or process of ceasing or causing something to cease to exist: *the extinction of liberalism.* ■ the wiping out of a debt. **2** *Physics* reduction in the intensity of light or other radiation as it passes through a medium or object, due to absorption, reflection, and scattering: *ultraviolet extinction.* ▷late Middle English: from Latin *exstinctio(n-)*, from *exstinguere* 'quench' (see **EXTINGUISH**).

ex·tin·guish /ikˈstiNGgwisH/ ▶*v.* [*trans.*] cause (a fire or light) to cease to burn or shine: *firemen were soaking everything to extinguish the blaze.* ■ (often **be extinguished**) put an end to; annihilate: *hope is extinguished little by little.* ■ (often **be extinguished**) cancel (a debt) by full payment: *the debt was absolutely extinguished.* ■ *Law* render (a right or obligation) void: *rights of common pasture were extinguished.* ▷mid 16th cent.: from Latin *exstinguere*, from *ex-* 'out' + *stinguere* 'quench.' Compare with **DISTINGUISH**. **—ex·tin·guish·a·ble** *adj.* **—ex·tin·guish·ment** *n.* (*Law*).

ex·tin·guish·er /ikˈstiNGgwisHər/ ▶*n.* short for **FIRE EXTINGUISHER**.

ex·tir·pate /ˈekstərˌpāt/ ▶*v.* [*trans.*] root out and destroy completely: *those who tried to extirpate Christianity.* See note at **DESTROY**. ▷late Middle English (as *extirpation*): from Latin *exstirpare*, from *ex-* 'out' + *stirps* 'a stem.' **—ex·tir·pa·tion** /ˌekstərˈpāsHən/ *n.* **—ex·tir·pa·tor** /-ˌpātər/ *n.*

ex·tol /ikˈstōl/ ▶*v.* (**ex·tolled, ex·tol·ling**) [*trans.*] praise enthusiastically: *he* **extolled the virtues of** *the Russian peoples.* See note at **PRAISE**. ▷late Middle English: from Latin *extollere*, from *ex-* 'out, upward' + *tollere* 'raise.' **—ex·tol·ler** *n.* **—ex·tol·ment** *n.*

ex·tort /ikˈstôrt/ ▶*v.* obtain (something) by force, threats, or other unfair means: *he was convicted of trying to extort $1 million from a developer.* ▷early 16th cent.: from Latin *extort-* 'wrested,' from the verb *extorquere*, from *ex-* 'out' + *torquere* 'to twist.' **—ex·tort·er** *n.* **—ex·tor·tive** /-tiv/ *adj.*

ex·tor·tion /ikˈstôrsHən/ ▶*n.* the practice of obtaining something, esp. money, through force or threats. ▷Middle English: from late Latin *extortio(n-)*, from Latin *extorquere* 'wrest' (see **EXTORT**). **—ex·tor·tion·er** *n.* **—ex·tor·tion·ist** /-ist/ *n.*

ex·tor·tion·ate /ikˈstôrsHənit/ ▶*adj.* **1** (of a price) much too high; exorbitant: *extortionate ticket prices.* **2** using or given to extortion: *the extortionate power of the unions.* **—ex·tor·tion·ate·ly** *adv.* [as *submodifier*] lobster *is extortionately expensive here.*

ex·tra /ˈekstrə/ ▶*adj.* added to an existing or usual amount or number: *they offered him an extra thirty-five cents an hour.*
▶*adv.* **1** [as *submodifier*] to a greater extent than usual; especially: *he is trying to be extra good.* **2** in addition: *installation will cost about $60 extra.*
▶*n.* an item in addition to what is usual or strictly necessary: *I had an education with all the extras.* ■ an item for which an additional charge is made: *the price you pay includes all major charges—there are no hidden extras.* ■ a person engaged temporarily to fill out a scene in a movie or play, esp. as one of a crowd. ■ *dated* a special issue of a newspaper. ▷mid 17th cent. (as an adjective): probably a shortening of **EXTRAORDINARY**, suggested by similar forms in French and German.

extra- ▶*prefix* outside; beyond: *extracellular | extraterritorial.* ■ beyond the scope of: *extracurricular.* ▷via medieval Latin from Latin *extra* 'outside.'

ex·tra-base hit ▶*n. Baseball* a base hit that allows a batter to safely reach second base, third base, or home without the benefit of a fielding error; a double, triple, or home run.

ex·tra·cel·lu·lar /ˌekstrəˈselyələr/ ▶*adj. Biology* situated or taking place outside a cell or cells: *extracellular space in the cortex.* **—ex·tra·cel·lu·lar·ly** *adv.*

ex·tra·chro·mo·so·mal /ˌekstrəˌkrōməˈsōməl/ ▶*adj. Biology* situated or operating outside the chromosome: *extrachromosomal DNA.*

ex·tra·con·sti·tu·tion·al /ˌekstrəˌkänstəˈt(y)o͞osHənl/ ▶*adj.* not based on or authorized by a political constitution: *security forces sentenced alleged rebels to death in extraconstitutional courts.*

ex·tra·cor·po·re·al /ˈekstrəkôrˈpôrēəl/ ▶*adj. chiefly Surgery* situated or occurring outside the body. ■ denoting a technique of lithotripsy using shock waves generated externally.

ex·tract /ˈekˌstrakt/ ▶*n.* [with *adj.*] a preparation containing the active ingredient of a substance in concentrated form: *vanilla extract.* ▷late Middle English: from Latin *extract-* 'drawn out,' from the verb *extrahere*, from *ex-* 'out' + *trahere* 'draw.'

ex·trac·tion /ikˈstraksHən/ ▶*n.* **1** the action of taking out something, esp. using effort or force: *mineral extraction | a dental extraction.* **2** [with *adj.*] the ethnic origin of someone's family: *a worker of Polish extraction.* ▷late Middle English: via Old French from late Latin *extractio(n-)*, from Latin *extrahere* 'draw out' (see **EXTRACT**).

ex·trac·tive /ikˈstraktiv/ ▶*adj.* of or involving extraction, esp. the extensive extraction of natural resources without provision for their renewal: *extractive industry.*

ex·trac·tor /ikˈstraktər/ ▶*n.* [often with *adj.*] a machine or device used to extract something: *a juice extractor.* ■ [as *adj.*] denoting a device used to ventilate and remove bad smells from an area: *the engine room's* **extractor fans**.

ex·tra·cur·ric·u·lar /ˌekstrəkəˈrikyələr/ ▶*adj.* (of an activity at a school or college) pursued in addition to the normal course of study: *extracurricular activities include sports, drama, music, chess.* ■ *often humorous* outside the normal routine, esp. that provided by a job or marriage: *Harriet's extracurricular sweetheart.* **—ex·tra·cur·ric·u·lar·ly** *adv.*

ex·tra·dit·a·ble /ˈekstrəˌdītəbəl; ˌekstrəˈdītəbəl/ ▶*adj.* (of a crime) making a criminal liable to extradition: *possession of explosives will be an extraditable offense.* ■ (of a criminal) liable to extradition.

ex·tra·dite /ˈekstrəˌdīt/ ▶*v.* [*trans.*] hand over (a person accused or convicted of a crime) to the jurisdiction of the foreign state in which the crime was committed: *Greece refused to* **extradite** *him* **to** *Italy.* ▷mid 19th cent.: back-formation from **EXTRADITION**.

ex·tra·di·tion /ˌekstrəˈdisHən/ ▶*n.* the action of extraditing a person accused or convicted of a crime: *they fought to prevent his extradition to the U.S. | extraditions of drug suspects.* ▷mid 19th cent.: from French, from *ex-* 'out, from' + *tradition* 'delivery.'

ex·tra·dos /ˈekstrəˌdäs/ ▶*n.* (*pl.* same or **-dos·es**) *Architecture* the upper or outer curve of an arch. Often contrasted with **INTRADOS**. ▷late 18th cent.: from French, from Latin *extra* 'outside' + French *dos* 'back' (from Latin *dorsum*).

ex·tra·du·ral /ˌekstrəˈd(y)o͝orəl/ ▶*adj. Medicine* another term for **EPIDURAL**.

ex·tra·flo·ral /ˌekstrəˈflôrəl/ ▶*adj. Botany* (of a nectary) situated outside a flower, esp. on a leaf or stem.

ex·tra·ga·lac·tic /ˌekstrəgəˈlaktik/ ▶*adj. Astronomy* situated, occurring, or originating outside the Milky Way galaxy: *extragalactic radio sources.*

ex·tra in·nings ▶*n. Baseball* the continuation of a tie game beyond the usual nine innings. ■ any continuation beyond the expected or scheduled time.

ex·tra·ju·di·cial /ˌekstrəjo͞oˈdisHəl/ ▶*adj. Law* (of a sentence) not legally authorized: *there have been reports of extrajudicial executions.* ■ (of a settlement, statement, or confession) not made in court; out-of-court. **—ex·tra·ju·di·cial·ly** *adv.*

ex·tra·le·gal /ˌekstrəˈlēgəl/ ▶*adj.* (of an action or situation) beyond the authority of the law; not regulated by the law.

ex·tra·lim·it·al /ˌekstrəˈlimitl/ ▶*adj. chiefly Biology* situated, occurring, or derived from outside a particular area.

ex·tra·lin·guis·tic /ˌekstrəliNGˈgwistik/ ▶*adj.* not involving or beyond the bounds of language: *extralinguistic reality.*

ex·tra·mar·i·tal /ˌekstrəˈmaritl/ ▶*adj.* (esp. of sexual relations) occurring outside marriage: *an extramarital affair.* **—ex·tra·mar·i·tal·ly** *adv.*

ex·tra·mun·dane /ˌekstrəmənˈdān/ ▶*adj. rare* outside or beyond the physical world.

ex·tra·mu·ral /ˌekstrəˈmyo͝orəl/ ▶*adj.* outside the walls or boundaries of a town, college, or institution: *extramural researchers.* ■ additional to one's work or course of study and typically not connected with it: *extramural activities.* ▷mid 19th cent.: from Latin *extra muros* 'outside the walls' + **-AL**. **—ex·tra·mu·ral·ly** *adv.*

ex·tra·mu·si·cal /ˌekstrəˈmyo͞ozikəl/ ▶*adj.* extrinsic to a piece of music or outside the field of music.

ex·tra·ne·ous /ikˈstrānēəs/ ▶*adj.* irrelevant or

Pronunciation Key ə *ago;* ər *over;* ˈə or ˌə *up;* ˈər or ˌər *fur;* a *hat;* ā *rate;* ä *car;* CH *chew;* e *let;* ē *see;* e(ə)r *air;* i *fit;* ī *by;* i(ə)r *ear;* NG *sing;* ō *go;* ô *for;* oi *boy;* o͝o *good;* o͞o *goo;* ou *out;* SH *she;* TH *thin;* T͟H *then;* (h)w *why;* ZH *vision*

unrelated to the subject being dealt with: *one is obliged to wade through many pages of extraneous material.* ■ of external origin: *when the transmitter pack is turned off, no extraneous noise is heard.* ■ separate from the object to which it is attached: *other insects attach extraneous objects or material to themselves.* ▷mid 17th cent.: from Latin *extraneus* + **-OUS**. **—ex·tra·ne·ous·ly** *adv.* **—ex·tra·ne·ous·ness** *n.*

ex·tra·net /ˈekstrəˌnet/ ▶*n.* an intranet that can be partially accessed by authorized outside users, enabling businesses to exchange information over the Internet securely. ▷1990s: from *extra-* 'outside' + *net*, by analogy with *intranet*.

ex·tra·nu·cle·ar /ˌekstrəˈn(y)o͞oklēər/ ▶*adj.* **1** situated in or affecting parts of a cell outside the nucleus. **2** situated or occurring outside the nucleus of an atom.

ex·tra·oc·u·lar mus·cle /ˌekstrəˈäkyələr/ ▶*n.* each of six small voluntary muscles controlling movement of the eyeball within the socket.

ex·tra·or·di·naire /ˌekstrəˌôrdnˈer/ ▶*adj.* [*postpositive*] *informal* outstanding or remarkable in a particular capacity: *memories of a gardener extraordinaire.* ▷1940s: French, 'extraordinary.'

ex·traor·di·nar·y /ikˈstrôrdnˌerē; ˌekstrəˈôrdn-/ ▶*adj.* very unusual or remarkable: *the extraordinary plumage of the male* | [with *clause*] *it is extraordinary that no consultation took place.* ■ unusually great: *young children need extraordinary amounts of attention.* ■ [*attrib.*] (of a meeting) specially convened: *an extraordinary session of the Congress.* ■ [*postpositive*] (of an official) additional; specially employed: *his appointment as Ambassador Extraordinary in London.*
▶*n.* (usu. **extraordinaries**) an item in a company's accounts not arising from its normal activities. Compare with **EXCEPTIONAL**. ▷late Middle English: from Latin *extraordinarius*, from *extra ordinem* 'outside the normal course of events.' **—ex·traor·di·nar·i·ly** /-ˌerəlē/ *adv.* [as *submodifier*] *an extraordinarily beautiful girl* **—ex·traor·di·nar·i·ness** *n.*

ex·traor·di·nar·y ray ▶*n.* *Optics* (in double refraction) the light ray that does not obey the ordinary laws of refraction. Compare with **ORDINARY RAY**.

ex·tra point ▶*n.* *Football* a point awarded for a successful placekick following a touchdown. Also called **POINT AFTER TOUCHDOWN**.

ex·trap·o·late /ikˈstrapəˌlāt/ ▶*v.* [*trans.*] extend the application of (a method or conclusion, esp. one based on statistics) to an unknown situation by assuming that existing trends will continue or similar methods will be applicable: *the results cannot be extrapolated to other patient groups.* | [*intrans.*] *it is always dangerous to* ***extrapolate from*** *a sample.* ■ estimate or conclude (something) in this way: *attempts to extrapolate likely human cancers from laboratory studies.* ■ *Mathematics* extend (a graph, curve, or range of values) by inferring unknown values from trends in the known data: [as *adj.*] (**extrapolated**) *a set of extrapolated values.* ▷late 19th cent.: from **EXTRA-** 'outside' + a shortened form of **INTERPOLATE**. **—ex·trap·o·la·tion** /ikˌstrapəˈlāsʜən/ *n.* **—ex·trap·o·la·tive** /-ˌlātiv/ *adj.* **—ex·trap·o·la·tor** /-ˌlātər/ *n.*

ex·tra·po·si·tion /ˌekstrəpəˈzisʜən/ ▶*n.* *Grammar* the placing of a word or group of words outside or at the end of a clause, while retaining the sense. The subject is often postponed and replaced by *it* at the start, as in *it's no use crying over spilt milk* rather than *crying over spilt milk is no use.*

ex·tra·py·ram·i·dal /ˌekstrəpəˈramidl/ ▶*adj.* *Anatomy & Medicine* relating to or denoting nerves concerned with motor activity that descend from the cortex to the spine and are not part of the pyramidal system: *extrapyramidal symptoms.*

ex·tra·sen·so·ry per·cep·tion /ˌekstrəˈsensərē/ (abbr.: **ESP**) ▶*n.* the faculty of perceiving things by means other than the known senses, e.g., by telepathy or clairvoyance.

ex·tra·so·lar /ˌekstrəˈsōlər/ ▶*adj.* existing or occurring outside the solar system: *extrasolar planets.*

ex·tra·sys·to·le /ˌekstrəˈsistəlē/ ▶*n.* *Medicine* a heartbeat outside the normal rhythm, as often occurs in normal individuals.

ex·tra·ter·res·tri·al /ˌekstrətəˈrestrēəl/ ▶*adj.* of or from outside the earth or its atmosphere: *searches for extraterrestrial intelligence.*
▶*n.* a hypothetical or fictional being from outer space, esp. an intelligent one.

ex·tra·ter·ri·to·ri·al /ˌekstrəˌterəˈtôrēəl/ ▶*adj.* (of a law or decree) valid outside a country's territory. ■ denoting the freedom of an ambassador or other embassy staff from the jurisdiction of the territory of residence: *foreign embassies have extraterritorial rights.* ■ situated outside a country's territory: *extraterritorial industrial zones.* ▷mid 19th cent.: from Latin *extra territorium* 'outside the territory' + **-AL**. **—ex·tra·ter·ri·to·ri·al·i·ty** /-ˌtôrēˈalitē/ *n.*

ex·tra·trop·i·cal /ˌekstrəˈträpikəl/ ▶*adj.* *chiefly Meteorology* situated, existing, or occurring outside the tropics.

ex·tra·u·ter·ine /ˌekstrəˈyo͞otərin; -rīn/ ▶*adj.* *Medicine* existing, formed, or occurring outside the uterus: *the first hour of extrauterine life.*

ex·trav·a·gance /ikˈstravəgəns/ ▶*n.* lack of restraint in spending money or use of resources: *his reckless extravagance with other people's money.* ■ a thing on which too much money has been spent or which has used up too many resources: *salmon trout is an unnecessary extravagance.* ■ excessive elaborateness of style, speech, or action: *the extravagance of the decor.* ▷mid 17th cent.: from French, from medieval Latin *extravagant-* 'diverging greatly,' from the verb *extravagari* (see **EXTRAVAGANT**). **—ex·trav·a·gan·cy** /-gənsē/ *n.*

ex·trav·a·gant /ikˈstravəgənt/ ▶*adj.* lacking restraint in spending money or using resources: *it was rather extravagant to buy both.* See note at **PROFUSE**. ■ costing too much money: *extravagant gifts like computer games.* ■ exceeding what is reasonable or appropriate; absurd: *extravagant claims for its effectiveness.* ■ excessively elaborate in style, speech, or action: *large, beautiful, extravagant paintings.* ▷late Middle English (in the sense 'unusual, abnormal, unsuitable'): from medieval Latin *extravagant-* 'diverging greatly,' from the verb *extravagari*, from Latin *extra-* 'outside' + *vagari* 'wander.' **—ex·trav·a·gant·ly** *adv.*

ex·trav·a·gan·za /ikˌstravəˈganzə/ ▶*n.* an elaborate and spectacular entertainment or production: *an extravaganza of dance in many forms.* ▷mid 18th cent. (in the sense 'extravagance in language or behavior'): from Italian *estravaganza* 'extravagance.' The change was due to association with words beginning with **EXTRA-**.

ex·trav·a·sate /ikˈstravəˌsāt/ ▶*v.* [*trans.*] [usu. as *adj.*] (**extravasated**) *chiefly Medicine* let or force out (a fluid, esp. blood) from the vessel that naturally contains it into the surrounding area. ▷mid 17th cent.: from **EXTRA-** 'outside' + Latin *vas* 'vessel' + **-ATE**³. **—ex·trav·a·sa·tion** /ikˌstravəˈsāsʜən/ *n.*

ex·tra·vas·cu·lar /ˌekstrəˈvaskyələr/ ▶*adj.* *Medicine* situated or occurring outside the vascular system: *extravascular fluid.*

ex·tra·ve·hic·u·lar /ˌekstrəvēˈhikyələr/ ▶*adj.* of or relating to an activity performed in space outside a spacecraft.

ex·tra·vert ▶*n.* variant spelling of **EXTROVERT**.

ex·tra-vir·gin ▶*adj.* denoting a particularly fine grade of olive oil made from the first pressing of the olives and containing a maximum of one percent oleic acid.

ex·tre·ma /ikˈstrēmə/ ▶ plural form of **EXTREMUM**.

ex·treme /ikˈstrēm/ ▶*adj.* **1** reaching a high or the highest degree; very great: *extreme cold.* ■ not usual; exceptional: *in extreme cases the soldier may be discharged.* ■ very severe or serious: *expulsion is an extreme sanction.* ■ (of a person or their opinions) advocating severe or drastic measures; far from moderate, esp. politically: *their more extreme socialist supporters.* ■ denoting or relating to a sport performed in a hazardous environment and involving great physical risk, such as parachuting or white-water rafting. **2** [*attrib.*] furthest from the center or a given point; outermost: *the extreme northwest of Scotland.*
▶*n.* **1** either of two abstract things that are as different from each other as possible: *at one extreme he feared communist adventurism in the Far East, and at the other a resurgence of isolationism among the American public.* ■ the highest or most extreme degree of something: *extremes of temperature.* ■ a very severe or serious act: *he was unwilling to go to the extreme of civil war.* **2** *Logic* the subject or predicate in a proposition, or the major or minor term in a syllogism (as contrasted with the middle term). ▷late Middle English: via Old French from Latin *extremus* 'outermost, utmost,' superlative of *exterus* 'outer.' **—ex·treme·ly** *adv.* [as *submodifier*] *this is an extremely difficult and dangerous thing to do.* **—ex·treme·ness** *n.*
▶***PHRASES*** □ **extremes meet** *proverb* opposite extremes have much in common. □ **go** (or **take something**) **to extremes** take an extreme course of action; do something to an extreme degree: *we may go to extremes to find peace and quiet.* □ **in the extreme** to an extreme degree: *the reasoning was convoluted in the extreme.*

ex·treme unc·tion ▶*n.* (in the Roman Catholic Church) a former name for the sacrament of anointing of the sick, esp. when administered to the dying.

ex·trem·ist /ikˈstrēmist/ ▶*n.* a person who holds extreme or fanatical political or religious views, esp. one who resorts to or advocates extreme action: *political extremists* | [as *adj.*] *an extremist conspiracy.* See note at **ZEALOT**. **—ex·trem·ism** /-ˌmizəm/ *n.*

ex·trem·i·ty /ikˈstremitē/ ▶*n.* (*pl.* **-ties**) **1** the furthest point or limit of something: *the peninsula's western extremity.* ■ (**extremities**) the hands and feet: *tingling and numbness in the extremities.* **2** the extreme degree or nature of something: *the extremity of the violence concerns us.* ■ a condition of extreme adversity or difficulty: *the terror of an animal* ***in extremity.*** ▷late Middle English: from Old French *extremite* or Latin *extremitas*, from *extremus* 'utmost' (see **EXTREME**).

ex·trem·o·phile /ekˈstreməˌfīl/ ▶*n.* *Biology* a microorganism, esp. an archaean, that lives in conditions of extreme temperature, acidity, alkalinity, or chemical concentration.

ex·tre·mum /ikˈstrēməm/ ▶*n.* (*pl.* **-mums** or **-ma** /-mə/) [usu. as *adj.*] *Mathematics* the maximum or minimum value of a function. ▷early 20th cent.: from Latin, neuter of *extremus* 'utmost' (see **EXTREME**).

ex·tri·cate /ˈekstriˌkāt/ ▶*v.* [*trans.*] free (someone or something) from a constraint or difficulty: *he was trying to* ***extricate*** *himself* ***from*** *official duties.* ▷early 17th cent. (in the sense 'unravel, untangle'): from Latin *extricat-* 'unraveled,' from the verb *extricare*, from *ex-* 'out' + *tricae* 'perplexities.' **—ex·tri·ca·ble** /ˈekstrikəbəl; ikˈstrik-/ *adj.* **—ex·tri·ca·tion** /ˌekstriˈkāsʜən/ *n.*

ex·trin·sic /ikˈstrinzik; -sik/ ▶*adj.* not part of the essential nature of someone or something; coming or operating from outside: *extrinsic factors that might affect time budgets* | *the idea that power is* ***extrinsic to*** *production and profits.* ■ (of a muscle, such as any of the eye muscles) having its origin some distance from the part that it moves. ▷mid 16th cent. (in the sense 'outward'): from late Latin *extrinsecus* 'outward,' from Latin *extrinsecus* 'outwardly,' based on *exter* 'outer'; the ending was altered under the influence of **-IC**. **—ex·trin·si·cal·ly** /-(ə)lē/ *adv.*

Ex·tro·py /ˈekstrəpē/ ▶*n.* the pseudoscientific principle that life will expand indefinitely and in an orderly, progressive way throughout the entire universe by the means of human intelligence and technology. ▷1980s: from **EX-**¹ 'out' + a shortened form of **ENTROPY**. **—Ex·tro·pi·an** /ekˈstrōpēən/ *adj.* & *n.*

ex·trorse /ˈekˌstrôrs/ ▶*adj.* *Botany & Zoology* turned outward. The opposite of **INTRORSE**. ■ (of anthers) releasing their pollen on the outside of the flower. ▷mid 19th cent.: from late Latin *extrorsus* 'outward'(adverb). **—ex·trorse·ly** *adv.*

ex·tro·vert /ˈekstrəˌvərt/ (also **extravert**) ▶*n.* an outgoing, overtly expressive person. ■ *Psychology* a person predominantly concerned with external things or objective considerations. Compare with **INTROVERT**.
▶*adj.* of, denoting, or typical of an extrovert: *his extrovert personality made him the ideal host.* ▷early 20th cent.: from *extro-* (variant of **EXTRA-**, on the pattern of *intro-*) + Latin *vertere* 'to turn.' **—ex·tro·ver·sion** /ˌekstrəˈvərzʜən/ *n.* **—ex·tro·vert·ed** *adj.*

USAGE The original spelling **extravert** is now rare in general use but is found in technical use in psychology.

ex·trude /ikˈstro͞od/ ▶*v.* [*trans.*] (usu. **be extruded**) thrust or force out: *lava was being extruded from the volcano.* ■ shape (a material such as metal or plastic) by forcing it through a die. ▷mid 16th cent.: from Latin *extrudere*, from *ex-* 'out' + *trudere* 'to thrust.' **—ex·trud·a·ble** *adj.* **—ex·tru·sile** /ikˈstro͞osəl; -ˌsīl/ *adj.* **—ex·tru·sion** /ikˈstro͞ozʜən/ *n.*

ex·tru·sive /ikˈstro͞osiv/ ▶*adj.* *Geology* relating to or denoting rock that has been extruded at the earth's surface as lava or other volcanic deposits.

ex·u·ber·ant /igˈzo͞obərənt/ ▶*adj.* filled with or characterized by a lively energy and excitement: *giddily exuberant crowds* | *flamboyant and exuberant architectural invention.* ■ growing luxuriantly or profusely: *exuberant foliage.* ▷late Middle English (in the sense 'overflowing, abounding'): from French *exubérant*, from Latin *exuberant-* 'being abundantly fruitful,' from the verb *exuberare* (based on *uber* 'fertile'). **—ex·u·ber·ance** *n.* **—ex·u·ber·ant·ly** *adv.*

ex·u·date /ˈeksyo͞oˌdāt; ˈeksə-/ ▶*n.* an exuded substance, in particular: ■ *Medicine* a mass of cells and fluid that has seeped out of blood vessels or an organ, esp. in inflammation. ■ *Botany & Entomology* a substance secreted by a plant or insect. ▷late 19th cent.: from Latin *exsudat-* 'exuded,' from the verb *exsudare.*

ex·ude /ig'zo͞od/ ▶*v.* [*trans.*] discharge (moisture or a smell) slowly and steadily: *the beetle exudes a caustic liquid.* ■ [*intrans.*] (of moisture or a smell) be discharged by something in such a way: *slime* ***exudes from*** *the fungus.* ■ *figurative* (of a person) display (an emotion or quality) strongly and openly: *Mr. Thomas exuded friendship and goodwill.* ■ [*intrans.*] *figurative* (of an emotion or quality) be displayed by someone in such a way: *sexuality* ***exuded from*** *him.* ■ *figurative* (of a place) have a strong atmosphere of: *the building exudes an air of tranquility.* ▷late 16th cent.: from Latin *exsudare,* from *ex-* 'out' + *sudare* 'to sweat.' **—ex·u·da·tion** /ˌeksyo͞o'dāsʜən; ˌeksə-/ *n.* **—ex·u·da·tive** /ig'zo͞odətiv; 'eksəˌdātiv; 'eksyo͞o-/ *adj.*

ex·ult /ig'zəlt/ ▶*v.* [*intrans.*] show or feel elation or jubilation, esp. as the result of a success: ***exulting in*** *her escape, Annie closed the door behind her.* ▷late 16th cent.: from Latin *exsultare,* frequentative of *exsilire* 'leap up,' from *ex-* 'out, upward' + *salire* 'to leap.' **—ex·ul·ta·tion** /ˌeksəl'tāsʜən; ˌegzəl-/ *n.* **—ex·ult·ing·ly** *adv.*

ex·ult·ant /ig'zəltnt/ ▶*adj.* triumphantly happy: *she felt exultant and powerful.* ▷mid 17th cent.: from Latin *exsultant-* 'exulting,' from the verb *exsultare.* **—ex·ult·an·cy** /-'zəltnsē/ *n.* **—ex·ult·ant·ly** *adv.*

Ex·u·ma Cays /ik'so͞omə 'kēz; ig'zo͞omə/ a group of about 350 small islands in the Bahamas.

ex·urb /'eksərb/ ▶*n.* a district outside a city, esp. a prosperous area beyond the suburbs. ▷1955: coined by A. C. Spectorsky (1919–72), American author and editor, either from Latin *ex* 'out of' + *urbs* 'city,' or as a back-formation from the earlier adjective *exurban.* **—ex·ur·ban** /ek'sərbən/ *adj.* **—ex·ur·ban·ite** /ek'sərbəˌnīt/ *n.* & *adj.*

ex·ur·bi·a /ek'sərbēə/ ▶*n.* the exurbs collectively; the region beyond the suburbs. ▷1955: from EX-[1] 'out of' + *-urbia,* on the pattern of *suburbia.* See EXURB.

ex·u·vi·ae /ig'zo͞ovēˌē/ ▶*plural n.* [also treated as *sing.*] *Zoology* an animal's cast or sloughed skin, esp. that of an insect larva. ▷mid 17th cent.: from Latin, literally 'animal skins, spoils of the enemy,' from *exuere* 'divest oneself of.' **—ex·u·vi·al** /-vēəl/ *adj.*

ex·u·vi·ate /ig'zo͞ovēˌāt/ ▶*v.* [*trans.*] *technical* shed (a skin or shell). ▷mid 19th cent.: from EXUVIAE + -ATE[3]. **—ex·u·vi·a·tion** /igˌzo͞ovē'āsʜən/ *n.*

ex-vo·to /eks 'vōtō/ ▶*n.* (*pl.* **-vo·tos**) a religious offering given in order to fulfill a vow. ▷late 18th cent.: from Latin *ex voto* 'from a vow.'

-ey ▶*suffix* variant spelling of -Y[2] (as in *Charley, Limey*).

ey·as /'īəs/ (also **ey·ass**) ▶*n.* (*pl.* **ey·as·ses**) a young hawk, esp. (in falconry) an unfledged nestling taken from the nest for training. ▷late 15th cent. (originally *nyas*): from French *niais,* based on Latin *nidus* 'nest.' The initial *n* was lost by wrong division of *a nyas*; compare with ADDER[1], APRON, and UMPIRE.

eye /ī/ ▶*n.* **1** each of a pair of globular organs in the head through which people and vertebrate animals see, the visible part typically appearing almond-shaped in animals with eyelids: *my cat is blind in one eye | closing her eyes, she tried to relax.* ■ the corresponding visual or light-detecting organ of many invertebrate animals. ■ the region of the face surrounding the eyes: *her eyes were swollen with crying.* ■ a person's eye as characterized by the color of the iris: *he had piercing blue eyes.* ■ used to refer to someone's power of vision and in descriptions of the manner or direction of someone's gaze: *his sharp eyes had missed nothing | I couldn't take my eyes off him.* ■ used to refer to someone's opinion or attitude toward something: ***in the eyes of*** *his younger colleagues, Mr. Arnett was an eccentric |* ***to*** *European* ***eyes,*** *it may seem that the city is overcrowded.*

The basic components of the vertebrate eye are a transparent cornea, an adjustable iris, a lens for focusing, a sensitive retina lining the back of the eye, and a clear fluid- or jelly-filled center. The most primitive animals only have one or two eyespots, while many other invertebrates have several simple eyes or a pair of compound eyes.

2 a thing resembling an eye in appearance, shape, or relative position, in particular: ■ the small hole in a needle through which the thread is passed. ■ a small metal loop into which a hook is fitted as a fastener on a garment. See also HOOK AND EYE. ■ *Nautical* a loop at the end of a rope, esp. one at the top end of a shroud or stay. ■ a rounded eyelike marking on an animal, such as those on the tail of a peacock; an eyespot. ■ a round, dark spot on a potato from which a new shoot can grow. ■ a center cut of meat: *eye of round.* ■ the center of a flower, esp. when distinctively colored. ■ the calm region at the center of a storm or hurricane. See also THE EYE OF THE STORM below. ■ (**eyes**) *Nautical* the extreme forward part of a ship: *it was hanging in* ***the eyes of*** *the ship.*

▶*v.* (**eye·ing** or **ey·ing**) [*trans.*] look at or watch closely or with interest: *Rose eyed him warily.* ▷Old English *ēage,* of Germanic origin; related to Dutch *oog* and German *Auge.* **—eyed** /īd/ *adj.* [in *combination*] *a brown-eyed girl.* **—eye·less** *adj.*

▶*PHRASES* □ **all eyes** used to convey that a particular person or thing is currently the focus of public interest or attention: ***all eyes are on*** *the hot spots of eastern Europe.* □ **be all eyes** be watching eagerly and attentively. □ **before** (or **under**) **one's** (**very**) **eyes** right in front of one (used for emphasis, esp. in the context of something surprising or unpleasant): *he saw his life's work destroyed before his very eyes.* □ **close** (or **shut**) **one's eyes to** refuse to notice or acknowledge something unwelcome or unpleasant: *he couldn't close his eyes to the truth—he had cancer.* □ **an eye for an eye and a tooth for a tooth** used to refer to the belief that punishment in kind is the appropriate way to deal with an offense or crime. [with biblical allusion to Exod. 21: 24.] □ **the eye of the storm** the calm region at the center of a storm. ■ the most intense part of a tumultuous situation: *he was* ***in the eye of the storm*** *of abstract art.* □ **the eye of the wind** (also **the wind's eye**) the direction from which the wind is blowing. □ **eyes front** (or **left** or **right**) a military command to turn the head in the particular direction stated. □ **a ——'s-eye view** a view from the position or standpoint of a ——: *a satellite's-eye view of global warming.* See also BIRD'S-EYE VIEW, WORM'S-EYE VIEW. □ **give someone the eye** *informal* look at someone in a way that clearly indicates one's sexual interest in them: *this blonde was giving me the eye.* □ **half an eye** used in reference to a slight degree of perception or attention: *he kept* ***half an eye on*** *the house as he worked.* □ **have an eye for** be able to recognize, appreciate, and make good judgments about: *applicants should have an eye for detail.* □ **have** (or **keep**) **one's eye on** keep under careful observation. ■ (**have one's eye on**) hope or plan to acquire: *the county sheriff has his eye on retirement.* □ **have** (or **with**) **an eye to** have (or having) as one's objective: *with an eye to transatlantic business, he made a deal in New York.* ■ consider (or be considering) prudently; look (or be looking) ahead to: *the charity must have an eye to the future.* □ **have** (or **with**) **an eye to** (or **for** or **on**) **the main chance** look or be looking for an opportunity to take advantage of a situation for personal gain, typically a financial one: *a developer with an eye on the main chance.* □ **one's eyes are bigger than one's stomach** one has asked for or taken more food than one can actually eat. □ (**only**) **have eyes for** be (exclusively) interested in or attracted to: *he has eyes for no one but you.* □ **have eyes in the back of one's head** know what is going on around one even when one cannot see it. □ **hit someone between the eyes** (or **in the eye**) *informal* be very obvious or impressive: *he wouldn't notice talent if it hit him right between the eyes.* □ **keep an eye** (or **a sharp eye**) **on** keep under careful observation: *dealers are keeping an eye on the currency markets.* □ **keep an eye out** (or **open**) look out for something with particular attention: ***keep an eye out for*** *his car.* □ **keep one's eyes open** (or **peeled** or *Brit.* **skinned**) be on the alert; watch carefully or vigilantly for something: *visitors should* ***keep their eyes peeled for*** *lions.* □ **lay** (or **set** or **clap**) **eyes on** *informal* see: *Harry has not laid eyes on Alice for twenty years.* □ **make eyes at someone** look at someone in a way that indicates one's sexual interest. □ **my eye** *informal, dated* used esp. in spoken English to indicate surprise or disbelief. [said to be originally nautical slang.] □ **open someone's eyes** enlighten someone about certain realities; cause someone to realize or discover something: *the letter finally* ***opened my eyes to*** *the truth.* □ **see eye to eye** have similar views or attitudes to something; be in full agreement: *Mr. Trumble and I do not always see eye to eye.* □ **a twinkle** (or **gleam**) **in someone's eye** something that is as yet no more than an idea or dream: *not every gleam in a grocer's eye becomes a store.* □ **what the eye doesn't see, the heart doesn't grieve over** *proverb* if you're unaware of an unpleasant fact or situation, you can't be troubled by it. □ **with one's eyes open** fully aware of the possible difficulties or consequences: *I went into this job with my eyes open.* □ **with one's eyes shut** (or **closed**) **1** without having to make much effort; easily: *I could do it with my eyes shut.* **2** without considering the possible difficulties or consequences: *she didn't go to Hollywood with her eyes closed.* □ **with one eye on** giving some but not all one's attention to: *I sat with one eye on the clock, waiting for my turn.*

eye·ball /'īˌbôl/ ▶*n.* the round part of the eye of a vertebrate, within the eyelids and socket. In mammals it is typically a firm, mobile, spherical structure enclosed by the sclera and the cornea.

▶*v.* [*trans.*] *informal* look or stare at closely: *we eyeballed one another.*

▶*PHRASES* □ **eyeball to eyeball** face to face with someone, esp. in an aggressive way: *he wheeled around to confront John eyeball to eyeball.* □ **up to the** (or **one's**) **eyeballs** *informal* used to emphasize the extreme degree of an undesirable situation or condition: *he's* ***up to his eyeballs*** *in debt.*

eye·black /'īˌblak/ ▶*n.* old-fashioned term for MASCARA.

eye·bolt /'īˌbōlt/ ▶*n.* a bolt or bar with an eye at the end for attaching a hook or ring to.

eye·bright /'īˌbrīt/ ▶*n.* a small plant of the figwort family with little snapdragonlike flowers. Found in dry fields and along roadsides, it was formerly used as a remedy for eye problems. • Genus *Euphrasia,* family Scrophulariaceae: several species, in particular the European *E. officinalis* and the North American *E. americana.*

eye·brow /'īˌbrou/ ▶*n.* the strip of hair growing on the ridge above a person's eye socket.

▶*PHRASE* □ **raise one's eyebrows** (or **an eyebrow**) show surprise, disbelief, or mild disapproval.

eye·brow pen·cil ▶*n.* a cosmetic pencil for defining or accentuating the eyebrows.

eye can·dy ▶*n. informal* visual images that are superficially attractive and entertaining but intellectually undemanding: *the film's success rested on a promotional campaign showcasing its relentless eye candy.*

eye-catch·ing ▶*adj.* immediately appealing or noticeable; striking: *an eye-catching poster.* **—eye-catch·er** *n.* **—eye-catch·ing·ly** *adv.*

eye con·tact ▶*n.* the act of looking directly into one another's eyes: ***make eye contact*** *with your interviewers.*

eye·cup /īˌkəp/ ▶*n.* **1** a piece of an optical device such as a microscope, camera, or pair of binoculars that is contoured to provide a comfortable rest against the user's eye. **2** a small container used for applying cleansing solutions to the eye.

eye·ful /'īˌfo͝ol/ ▶*n.* [in *sing.*] *informal* a long, steady look at something: *they wanted to get an eyeful of Lily.* ■ a visually striking person or thing: *she was quite an eyeful.* ■ a quantity or piece of something thrown or blown into the eye: *an* ***eyeful of*** *fluid.*

eye·glass /'īˌglas/ ▶*n.* a single lens for correcting or assisting defective eyesight, esp. a monocle. ■ (**eyeglasses**) another term for GLASSES. ■ another term for EYEPIECE.

eye·hole /'īˌhōl/ ▶*n.* a hole to look through, esp. in a curtain or mask. ■ the eye socket. ■ an eyelet.

eye·lash /'īˌlasʜ/ ▶*n.* each of the short curved hairs growing on the edges of the eyelids, serving to protect the eyes from dust particles.

eye·let /'īlit/ ▶*n.* a small round hole in leather or cloth for threading a lace, string, or rope through. ■ a metal ring used to reinforce such a hole. ■ a small hole ornamented with stitching around its edge, used as a form of decoration in embroidery. ■ a fabric pierced with these holes in an ornamental pattern. ■ a small hole or slit in a wall for looking through.

▶*v.* (**eye·let·ed, eye·let·ing**) [*trans.*] make eyelets in (fabric). ▷late Middle English *oilet,* from Old French *oillet,* diminutive of *oil* 'eye,' from Latin *oculus.* The change in the first syllable in the 17th cent. was due to association with EYE.

eye lev·el ▶*n.* the level of the eyes looking straight ahead: *pictures hung at eye level.*

eye·lid /'īˌlid/ ▶*n.* each of the upper and lower folds of skin that cover the eye when closed.

eye·lin·er /'īˌlīnər/ ▶*n.* a cosmetic applied as a line around the eyes to make them appear larger or more noticeable.

eye-o·pen·er ▶*n. informal* **1** [in *sing.*] an event or situation that proves to be unexpectedly enlightening: *a visit to the docks can be a fascinating eye-opener.* **2** an alcoholic drink taken early in the day. **—eye-o·pen·ing** *adj.*

eye·patch /ˈī,pacн/ ▸*n.* a patch worn to protect an injured eye.

eye pen·cil ▸*n.* a pencil for applying makeup around the eyes.

eye·piece /ˈī,pēs/ ▸*n.* the lens or group of lenses that is closest to the eye in a microscope, telescope, or other optical instrument. Also called **EYEGLASS** or **OCULAR**.

eye-pop·ping ▸*adj. informal* astonishingly large, impressive, or blatant: *the company has doubled its assets to an eye-popping $113 billion.*

eye rhyme ▸*n.* a similarity between words in spelling but not in pronunciation, e.g., *love* and *move*.

eye·shade /ˈī,sнād/ ▸*n.* a translucent visor used to protect the eyes from strong light.

eye·shad·ow /ˈī,sнadō/ ▸*n.* a colored cosmetic, typically in powder form, applied to the eyelids or to the skin around the eyes to accentuate them.

eye·shot /ˈī,sнät/ ▸*n.* the distance for which one can see: *he is* ***within eyeshot.***

eye·sight /ˈī,sīt/ ▸*n.* a person's ability to see: *poor eyesight ended his plans for a naval career.*

eye sock·et ▸*n.* the cavity in the skull that encloses an eyeball with its surrounding muscles. Also called **ORBIT**.

eyes-on·ly ▸*adj.* intended to be seen or read only by the person addressed; confidential, secret: *this information is eyes-only to you | the KGB made clear in its eyes-only reports to the Politburo that the regime was in grave danger.*

eye·sore /ˈī,sôr/ ▸*n.* a thing that is very ugly, esp. a building that disfigures a landscape.

eye splice ▸*n.* a splice made by turning the end of a rope back on itself and interlacing the strands, thereby forming a loop.

eye·spot /ˈī,spät/ ▸*n.* **1** *Zoology* a light-sensitive pigmented spot on the bodies of invertebrate animals such as flatworms, starfishes, and microscopic crustaceans, and also in some unicellular organisms. **2** a rounded eyelike marking on an animal, esp. on the wing of a butterfly or moth. **3** a fungal disease of cereals, sugar cane, and other cultivated grasses, characterized by yellowish oval spots on the leaves and stems. • The fungus is typically *Pseudocercosporella herpotrichoides*, subdivision Deuteromycotina.

eye·stalk /ī,stôk/ ▸*n. Zoology* a movable stalk that bears an eye near its tip, esp. in crabs, shrimps, and related crustaceans, and in some mollusks.

eye strain ▸*n.* fatigue of the eyes, such as that caused by reading or looking at a computer screen for too long.

eye·stripe /ī,strīp/ ▸*n.* a stripe on a bird's head that encloses or appears to run through the eye.

eye·tooth /ˈīˈ,tōōтн/ ▸*n.* a canine tooth, esp. one in the upper jaw.

▸*PHRASE* □ **give one's eyeteeth for** (or **to be**) do anything in order to have or be something: *I'd give my eyeteeth for a lover.*

eye track·ing (also **eye-track·ing**) ▸*n.* a technology that monitors eye movements as a means of detecting abnormalities or of studying how people interact with text or online documents: *a company that uses eye tracking to evaluate visual products.*

eye wall ▸*Meteorology n.* the area immediately outside the eye of a hurricane or cyclone, associated with tall clouds, heavy rainfall, and high winds.

eye·wash /ˈī,wôsн; -,wäsн/ ▸*n.* **1** cleansing solution for a person's eye. **2** *informal* insincere talk; nonsense: *their rhetoric about reducing intrusive federal rules is so much eyewash.*

eye·wear /ī,wer/ ▸*n.* things worn on the eyes, such as spectacles and contact lenses.

eye·wit·ness /ˈīˈwitnəs/ ▸*n.* [often as *adj.*] a person who has personally seen something happen and so can give a first-hand description of it: ***eyewitness accounts*** *of the London blitz.*

eye worm ▸*n.* either of two parasitic nematode worms that affect the eyes of mammals: • a filarial worm of equatorial Africa, infesting humans and other primates, causing loiasis and sometimes passing across the cornea (*Loa loa*, class Phasmida). • a nematode that occurs in the region of the eyelid and tear duct, found chiefly in hoofed mammals (genus *Thelazia*, class Phasmida).

ey·ra /ˈe(ə)rə/ ▸*n.* a reddish-brown form of the jaguarundi. ▹early 17th cent.: from Spanish, from Tupi *eirara, irara*.

Eyre, Lake /e(ə)r/ a lake in northeastern South Australia, in southern Australia, the country's largest salt lake. ▹named after explorer E. J. Eyre (1815–1901).

eyre /e(ə)r/ ▸*n. historical* a circuit court held in medieval England by a judge (a **justice in eyre**) who rode from county to county for that purpose. ▹Middle English: from Old French *eire*, from Latin *iter* 'journey.'

ey·rie /ˈe(ə)rē; ˈi(ə)rē/ ▸*n.* variant spelling of **AERIE**.

ey·rir /ˈāri(ə)r/ ▸*n.* (*pl.* **au·rar** /ˈirär/) a monetary unit of Iceland, equal to one hundredth of a krona.

Ey·senck /ˈīsəngk/, Hans (Jürgen) (1916–97), British psychologist; born in Germany. He was noted for his strong criticism of Freudian psychoanalysis and for his ideas concerning the assessment of intelligence and personality.

E·ze·ki·el /iˈzēkēəl/ a Hebrew prophet of the 6th century BC who prophesied the forthcoming destruction of Jerusalem and the Jewish nation and inspired hope for the future well-being of a restored state. ■ a book of the Bible containing his prophecies.

e-zine /ˈē ,zēn/ ▸*n.* a magazine published only in electronic form on a computer network.

Ez·ra /ˈezrə/ a Jewish priest and scribe who played a central part in the reform of Judaism in the 5th or 4th century BC, continuing the work of Nehemiah and forbidding mixed marriages. ■ a book of the Bible telling of Ezra, the return of the Jews from Babylon, and the rebuilding of the Temple.

E

Ff

F[1] /ef/ (also **f**) ▸*n.* (*pl.* **Fs** or **F's**) **1** the sixth letter of the alphabet. ■ denoting the next after E in a set of items, categories, etc. ■ the sixth highest or lowest class of academic marks (also used to represent "Fail"). ■ (**f**) *Chess* denoting the sixth file from the left, as viewed from White's side of the board. **2** (usu. **F**) *Music* the fourth note of the diatonic scale of C major. ■ a key based on a scale with F as its keynote.

F[2] ▸*abbr.* ■ Fahrenheit: *60°F.* ■ failure. ■ false. ■ farad(s). ■ *Chemistry* faraday(s). ■ (in racing results) favorite. ■ February. ■ Fellow. ■ female. ■ fighter (in designations of U.S. aircraft types): *the F117 Stealth fighter.* ■ forint. ■ (in auto racing) formula: *an F1 driver.* ■ Franc(s). ■ France. ■ French.
▸*symbol* ■ the chemical element fluorine. ■ *Physics* force: *F = ma.*

f ▸*abbr.* ■ farad. ■ farthing. ■ father. ■ fathom. ■ feet. ■ *Grammar* feminine. ■ female. ■ [in *combination*] (in units of measurement) femto- (10^{-15}). ■ filly. ■ fine. ■ (in textual references) folio. ■ following. ■ foot. ■ form. ■ *Music* forte. ■ (in racing results) furlong(s). ■ franc. ■ from. ■ *Chemistry* denoting electrons and orbitals possessing three units of angular momentum: *f-orbitals.* [*f* from *fundamental*, originally applied to lines in atomic spectra.]
▸*symbol* ■ focal length: *apertures of f/5.6 to f/11.* See also **F-NUMBER**. ■ *Mathematics* a function of a specified variable: *the value of f(x).* ■ *Electronics* frequency.

f/ ▸*abbr. Symbol* f-number.

F_1 (also **F1**) *Biology* ▸*abbr.* the first filial generation, i.e., the generation of hybrids arising from a first cross. The second filial generation is designated **F_2** (or **F2**) , and so on.

fa /fä/ ▸*n. Music* (in solmization) the fourth note of a major scale. ■ the note F in the fixed-do system. ▷Middle English: representing (as an arbitrary name for the note) the first syllable of *famuli*, taken from a Latin hymn (see **SOLMIZATION**).

FAA ▸*abbr.* Federal Aviation Administration.

f.a.a. ▸*abbr.* free of all average.

fab[1] /fab/ ▸*adj. informal* fabulous; wonderful. ▷1960s: abbreviation.

fab[2] ▸*n. Electronics* a microchip fabrication plant. ■ a particular fabrication process in such a plant. ▷late 20th cent.: abbreviation of *fabrication* (see **FABRICATE**).

Fa·ber·gé /ˌfabər'zнā/, Peter Carl (1846–1920), Russian goldsmith and jeweler. He is known for the intricate Easter eggs that he made for Tsar Alexander III and other royalty.

Fa·bi·an /'fābēən/ ▸*n.* a member or supporter of the Fabian Society, an organization of socialists aiming at the gradual rather than revolutionary achievement of socialism.
▸*adj.* relating to or characteristic of the Fabians: *the Fabian movement.* ■ employing a cautiously persistent and dilatory strategy to wear out an enemy: *Fabian tactics.* ▷late 18th cent.: from the name of *Quintus Fabius Maximus Verrucosus* (see **FABIUS**), after whom the Fabian Society is also named. **—Fa·bi·an·ism** /-izəm/ *n.* **—Fa·bi·an·ist** /-əst/ *n.*

Fa·bi·us /'fābēəs/ (died 203 BC), Roman general and statesman; full name *Quintus Fabius Maximus Verrucosus*; known as **Fabius Cunctator** (Fabius the Delayer). After Hannibal's defeat of the Roman army at Cannae in 216 BC, Fabius successfully wore down the Carthaginian invaders.

fa·ble /'fābəl/ ▸*n.* a short story, typically with animals as characters, conveying a moral. ■ a story, typically a supernatural one incorporating elements of myth and legend. See note at **FICTION**. ■ myth and legend: *the unnatural monsters of fable.* ■ a false statement or belief.
▸*v.* [*intrans.*] *archaic* tell fictitious tales: *I do not dream nor fable.* ■ [*trans.*] fabricate or invent (an incident, person, or story). ▷Middle English: from Old French *fable* (noun), from Latin *fabula* 'story,' from *fari* 'speak.' **—fa·bler** /'fāb(ə)lər/ *n.*

fa·bled /'fābəld/ ▸*adj.* [*attrib.*] well known for being of great quality or rarity; famous: *a fabled art collection.* ■ mythical; imaginary: *the fabled kingdom.*

fab·less /'fablis/ ▸*adj.* denoting or relating to a company that designs microchips but contracts out their production rather than owning its own factory: *the newcomers' strategy was fabless production.* ▷1980s: from *fab* 'a microchip fabrication plant' + *-less.*

fab·li·au /'fablēˌō/ ▸*n.* (*pl.* **-aux** /-ˌōz/) a metrical tale, typically a bawdily humorous one, of a type found chiefly in early French poetry. ▷from Old French (Picard dialect) *fabliaux*, plural of *fablel* 'short fable,' diminutive of *fable.*

Fa·bri·a·no, Gentile da, see **GENTILE DA FABRIANO**.

fab·ric /'fabrik/ ▸*n.* **1** cloth, typically produced by weaving or knitting textile fibers: *heavy silk fabric* | *waterproof fabrics.* **2** the walls, floor, and roof of a building. ■ the body of a car or aircraft. ■ *figurative* the essential structure of anything, esp. a society or culture: *the fabric of society.* ▷late 15th cent.: from French *fabrique*, from Latin *fabrica* 'something skillfully produced,' from *faber* 'worker in metal, stone, etc.' The word originally denoted a building, later a machine or appliance, the general sense being 'something made,' hence sense 1 (mid 18th cent., originally denoting any manufactured material). Sense 2 dates from the mid 17th cent.

fab·ri·cate /'fabrəˌkāt/ ▸*v.* [*trans.*] invent or concoct (something), typically with deceitful intent: *officers fabricated evidence.* See note at **LIE**. ■ construct or manufacture (something, esp. an industrial product), esp. from prepared components: *you will have to fabricate an exhaust system.* ▷late Middle English: from Latin *fabricat-* 'manufactured,' from the verb *fabricare*, from *fabrica* 'something skillfully produced' (see **FABRIC**). **—fab·ri·ca·tion** /ˌfabrə'kāsнən/ *n.* See note at **FICTION**. **—fab·ri·ca·tor** /-ˌkātər/ *n.*

fab·ric soft·en·er ▸*n.* liquid used to soften clothes when they are being washed, or specially treated squares of cloth used to soften clothes in the dryer.

Fa·bry–Pé·rot in·ter·fe·rom·e·ter /fä'brē pä'rō/ ▸*n.* an interferometer that incorporates an etalon, used chiefly in astronomy. ▷early 20th cent.: named after Charles *Fabry* (1867–1945) and Alfred *Pérot* (1863–1925), French physicists.

fab·u·late /'fabyəˌlāt/ ▸*v.* [*trans.*] relate (an event or events) as a fable or story. ■ [*intrans.*] relate untrue or invented stories. ▷early 17th cent.: from Latin *fabulat-* 'narrated as a fable,' from the verb *fabulari*, from *fabula* (see **FABLE**). **—fab·u·la·tion** /ˌfabyə'lāsнən/ *n.* **—fab·u·la·tor** /-ˌlātər/ *n.*

fab·u·list /'fabyəlist/ ▸*n.* a person who composes or relates fables. ■ a liar, esp. a person who invents elaborate, dishonest stories. ▷late 16th cent.: from French *fabuliste*, from Latin *fabula* (see **FABLE**).

fab·u·lous /'fabyələs/ ▸*adj.* extraordinary, esp. extraordinarily large: *fabulous riches.* ■ *informal* amazingly good; wonderful: *a fabulous two-week vacation.* ■ having no basis in reality; mythical: *fabulous creatures.* ▷late Middle English (in the sense 'known through fable, unhistorical'): from French *fabuleux* or Latin *fabulosus* 'celebrated in fable,' from *fabula* (see **FABLE**). **—fab·u·los·i·ty** /ˌfabyə'läsətē/ *n.* **—fab·u·lous·ly** *adv.* **—fab·u·lous·ness** *n.*

fac. ▸*abbr.* ■ facsimile. ■ faculty.

fa·cade /fə'säd/ (also **fa·çade**) ▸*n.* the face of a building, esp. the principal front that looks onto a street or open space. ■ *figurative* an outward appearance that is maintained to conceal a less pleasant or creditable reality: *her flawless public facade masked private despair.* ▷mid 17th cent.: from French *façade*, from *face* 'face,' on the pattern of Italian *facciata.*

face /fās/ ▸*n.* **1** the front part of a person's head from the forehead to the chin, or the corresponding part in an animal. ■ the face as expressing emotion; an expression shown on the face: *the happy faces of these children.* ■ a manifestation or outward aspect of something: *the unacceptable face of social drinking.* ■ [with *adj.*] a person conveying a particular quality or association: *this season's squad has a lot of old faces in it.* **2** the surface of a thing, esp. one that is presented to the view or has a particular function, in particular: ■ *Geometry* each of the surfaces of a solid: *the faces of a cube.* ■ a vertical or sloping side of a mountain or cliff: *the south face of Broad Peak.* ■ the side of a planet or moon facing the observer. ■ the front of a building. ■ the plate of a clock or watch bearing the digits or hands. ■ the distinctive side of a playing card. ■ short for **TYPEFACE**. ■ the side of a coin showing the head or principal design.
▸*v.* [*trans.*] **1** be positioned with the face or front toward (someone or something): *he turned to face her.* ■ [*intrans.*] have the face or front pointing in a specified direction: *the house faces due east.* ■ [*intrans.*] (of a soldier) turn in a particular direction: *they immediately faced about.* **2** confront and deal with or accept: *honesty forced her to* **face facts** | [*intrans.*] *the candidates choose not to* **face up to** *the pragmatic issues.* ■ (**face someone/something down**) overcome someone or something by a show of determination: *he faced down persistent hecklers at a noontime rally.* ■ have (a difficult event or situation) in prospect: *each defendant faced a maximum sentence of 10 years.* ■ (of a problem or difficult situation) present itself to and require action from (someone): *if you were suddenly* **faced with** *an emergency, would you know how to cope?* **3** (usu. **be faced with**) cover the surface of (a thing) with a layer of a different material: *the external basement walls* **were faced with** *granite slabs.*
▸*phrasal v.* □ **face off** take up an attitude of confrontation, esp. at the start of a fight or game: *close to a million soldiers face off in the desert.* ■ *Ice Hockey* start or restart play with a face-off. ▷Middle English: from Old French, based on Latin *facies* 'form, appearance, face.' **—faced** /fāst/ *adj.* [in *combination*] *red-faced.*
▸*PHRASES* □ **face down** with the face or surface turned toward the ground: *he lay face down on his bed.* □ **face the music** be confronted with the unpleasant consequences of one's actions. □ **the face of the earth** used for emphasis or exaggeration, to refer to the existence or disappearance of someone or something: *he's just disappeared* **off the face of the earth** | *the most grueling training* **on the face of the earth.** □ **face up** with the face or surface turned upward to view: *place the panel face up before cutting.* □ **get out of someone's face** [usu. as *imperative*] *informal* stop harassing or annoying someone: *shut up and get out of my face.* □ **have the face to do something** *dated* have the effrontery to do something. □ **in one's face** directly at or against one; as one approaches: *she slammed the door in my face.* □ **in the face of** when confronted with: *her resolution in the face of the enemy.* ■ in spite of: *reform had been introduced in the face of considerable*

Pronunciation Key ə *ago*; ər *over*; 'ə or ˌə *up*; 'ər or ˌər *fur*; a *hat*; ā *rate*; ä *car*; CH *chew*; e *let*; ē *see*; e(ə)r *air*; i *fit*; ī *by*; i(ə)r *ear*; NG *sing*; ō *go*; ô *for*; oi *boy*; ŏŏ *good*; ōō *goo*; ou *out*; SH *she*; TH *thin*; T͟H *then*; (h)w *why*; ZH *vision*

opposition. □ **in your face** see IN-YOUR-FACE. □ **lose face** suffer a loss of respect; be humiliated: *the code of conduct required that he strike back or lose face.* □ **loss of face** a loss of respect; humiliation: *he could step aside now without loss of face.* □ **make a face** (or **faces**) produce an expression on one's face that shows dislike, disgust, or some other negative emotion, or that is intended to be amusing: *she made a face and tossed her purse at him.* □ **on the face of it** without knowing all of the relevant facts; at first glance: *on the face of it, these improvements look to be insignificant.* □ **put a good** (or **brave** or **bold**) **face on something** act as if something unpleasant or upsetting is not as bad as it really is: *he tried to put a good face on the financial picture.* □ **put one's face on** *informal* apply makeup to one's face. □ **save face** retain respect; avoid humiliation: *an outcome that allows them all to save face.* □ **set one's face against** oppose or resist with determination: *he had set his face against the idea.* □ **throw something back in someone's face** reject something in a brusque or ungracious manner: *she'd given him her trust and he'd thrown it back in her face.* □ **to one's face** openly in one's presence: *you're telling me to my face I'm a liar.*

face a·mount ▶*n.* another term for DEATH BENEFIT.

face card ▶*n.* a playing card that is a king, queen, or jack of a suit.

face-cen·tered ▶*adj.* denoting a crystal structure in which there is an atom at each vertex and at the center of each face of the unit cell. Compare with BODY-CENTERED.

face·cloth /ˈfās,klôTH/ ▶*n.* a washcloth.

face·less /ˈfāsləs/ ▶*adj.* (of a person) remote and impersonal; anonymous: *the faceless bureaucrats who made the rules.* ■ (of a building or place) characterless and dull. —**face·less·ness** *n.*

face-lift (also **face·lift**) ▶*n.* a cosmetic surgical operation to remove unwanted wrinkles by tightening the skin of the face. ■ *figurative* a procedure carried out to improve the appearance of something: *the station has undergone a multimillion-dollar face-lift.*

face mask ▶*n.* a protective mask covering the nose and mouth or nose and eyes.

face-off ▶*n.* a direct confrontation between two people or groups: *a face-off for the championship title.* ■ *Ice Hockey* the start or a restart of play, in which the referee drops the puck between two opposing players.

face paint ▶*n.* bold-colored paint used to decorate the face. —**face paint·er** *n.* —**face paint·ing** *n.*

face·plate /ˈfās,plāt/ ▶*n.* **1** an enlarged end or attachment on the end of the mandrel on a lathe, with slots and holes on which work can be mounted. ■ a plate protecting a piece of machinery, a light switch, or an electrical outlet. ■ the part of a cathode-ray tube that carries the phosphor screen. **2** the transparent window of a diver's or astronaut's helmet.

face pow·der ▶*n.* flesh-tinted cosmetic powder used to improve the appearance of the face by reducing shine and concealing blemishes.

face·print /ˈfās,print/ ▶*n.* a digital scan or photograph of a human face, used for identifying individuals from the unique characteristics of facial structure: *hidden cameras and faceprints are used to single out individuals in a crowd.* ▷on the pattern of *fingerprint.*

face·print·ing /ˈfās,printiNG/ ▶*n.* the process of creating a digital faceprint and using software to compare it with a database of photographs, especially to identify known criminals. ▷on the pattern of *fingerprinting.*

fac·er /ˈfāsər/ ▶*n. informal, chiefly Brit.* a blow to the face. ■ a sudden difficulty or obstacle.

face-sav·ing ▶*adj.* preserving one's reputation, credibility, or dignity: *a face-saving solution for both sides.* —**face-sav·er** *n.*

fac·et /ˈfasət/ ▶*n.* one side of something many-sided, esp. of a cut gem. ■ a particular aspect or feature of something: *participation by the laity in all facets of church life.* ■ *Zoology* any of the individual units (ommatidia) that make up the compound eye of an insect or crustacean. ▷early 17th cent.: from French *facette,* diminutive of *face* 'face, side' (see FACE). —**fac·et·ed** /ˈfasətid/ *adj.* [in *combination*] *multifaceted.*

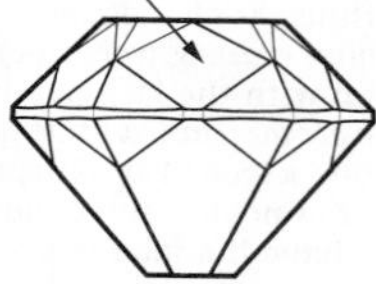

facet of a gem

fa·ce·ti·ae /fəˈsēSHē,ē; -SHē,ī/ ▶*plural n.* **1** *dated* pornographic literature. **2** *archaic* humorous or witty sayings. ▷early 16th cent.: from Latin, plural of *facetia* 'jest,' from *facetus* 'witty.'

face time ▶*n. informal* time spent in face-to-face contact with someone. ■ time spent being filmed or photographed by the media.

fa·ce·tious /fəˈsēSHəs/ ▶*adj.* treating serious issues with deliberately inappropriate humor; flippant. ▷late 16th cent. (in the general sense 'witty, amusing'): from French *facétieux,* from *facétie,* from Latin *facetia* 'jest,' from *facetus* 'witty.' —**fa·ce·tious·ly** *adv.* —**fa·ce·tious·ness** *n.*

face to face ▶*adv.* & *adj.* with the people involved being close together and looking directly at each other: [as *adv.*] *the two men stood face to face.* | [as *adj.*] *a face-to-face conversation.* ■ [as *adv.*] in direct confrontation: *he **came face to face with** a tiger.*

face va·lid·i·ty ▶*n.* the degree to which a procedure, esp. a psychological test or assessment, appears effective in terms of its stated aims.

face val·ue ▶*n.* the value printed or depicted on a coin, banknote, postage stamp, ticket, etc., esp. when less than the actual or intrinsic value. ■ *figurative* the superficial appearance or implication of something: *she felt the lie was unconvincing, but he seemed to **take it at face value.***

fa·cia /ˈfaSH(ē)ə; ˈfā-/ ▶*n. chiefly Brit.* variant spelling of FASCIA (sense 1).

fa·cial /ˈfāSHəl/ ▶*adj.* of or affecting the face: *facial expressions.*
▶*n.* a beauty treatment for the face. ▷early 17th cent. (as a theological term meaning 'face to face, open'): from medieval Latin *facialis,* from *facies* (see FACE). The current sense of the adjective dates from the early 19th cent. —**fa·cial·ly** *adv.*

fa·cial nerve ▶*n. Anatomy* each of the seventh pair of cranial nerves, supplying the facial muscles and the tongue.

fa·cial pro·fil·ing ▶*n.* the recording and analysis of a person's facial characteristics, especially to assist in identifying an individual: *the police have set up a system of facial profiling at major sporting events.*

fa·cial tis·sue ▶*n.* tissue that is used to blow one's nose, contain a sneeze, etc.

-facient ▶*comb. form* producing a specified action or state: *abortifacient.* ▷from Latin *facient-* 'doing, making.'

fa·ci·es /ˈfā,SHēz; ˈfāSHē,ēz/ ▶*n.* (*pl.* same) **1** *Medicine* the appearance or facial expression of an individual that is typical of a particular disease or condition. **2** *Geology* the character of a rock expressed by its formation, composition, and fossil content. **3** *Ecology* the characteristic set of dominant species in a habitat. ▷early 17th cent. (denoting the face): from Latin, 'form, appearance, face.'

fac·ile /ˈfasəl/ ▶*adj.* **1** (esp. of a theory or argument) appearing neat and comprehensive only by ignoring the true complexities of an issue; superficial. ■ (of a person) having a superficial or simplistic knowledge or approach: *a man of facile and shallow intellect.* **2** (of success, esp. in sports) easily achieved; effortless: *a facile victory.* ■ acting or done in a quick, fluent, and easy manner: *he was revealed to be a facile liar.* ▷late 15th cent. (in the sense 'easily accomplished'): from French, or from Latin *facilis* 'easy,' from *facere* 'do, make.' —**fac·ile·ly** /ˈfasəl(l)ē/ *adv.* —**fac·ile·ness** *n.*

fa·cil·i·tate /fəˈsili,tāt/ ▶*v.* [*trans.*] make (an action or process) easy or easier: *schools were located on the same campus to facilitate the sharing of resources.* ▷early 17th cent.: from French *faciliter,* from Italian *facilitare,* from *facile* 'easy,' from Latin *facilis* (see FACILE). —**fa·cil·i·ta·tive** /-,tātiv/ *adj.* —**fa·cil·i·ta·tor** /-,tātər/ *n.* —**fa·cil·i·ta·to·ry** /-tə,tôrē/ *adj.*

fa·cil·i·ta·tion /fə,siləˈtāSHən/ ▶*n.* the action of facilitating something. ■ *Physiology* the enhancement of the response of a neuron to a stimulus following stimulation.

fa·cil·i·ty /fəˈsilətē/ ▶*n.* (*pl.* **-ties**) **1** space or equipment necessary for doing something: *cooking facilities* | *facilities for picnicking, camping, and hiking.* ■ an amenity or resource, esp. one connected with leisure or hygiene: *facilities include two swimming pools.* ■ (**the facilities**) a public toilet. ■ an establishment set up to fulfill a particular function or provide a particular service, typically an industrial or medical one: *a manufacturing facility.* ■ an option or service that gives the opportunity to do or benefit from something: *the program includes a help facility and interactive windows.* **2** [usu. in *sing.*] an ability to do or learn something well and easily; a natural aptitude: *he had **a facility for** languages.* ■ absence of difficulty or effort: *the pianist played with great facility.* ▷early 16th cent. (denoting the means or unimpeded opportunity for doing something): from French *facilité* or Latin *facilitas,* from *facilis* 'easy' (see FACILE).

fac·ing /ˈfāsiNG/ ▶*n.* **1** a layer of material covering part of a garment and providing contrast, decoration, or strength. ■ (**facings**) the cuffs, collar, and lapels of a military jacket, contrasting in color with the rest of the garment. **2** an outer layer covering the surface of a wall.
▶*adj.* [*attrib.*] positioned with the front toward a certain direction; opposite: *a book with Italian and English lyrics printed on facing pages* | [in *combination*] *a south-facing garden.*

FACP ▶*abbr.* Fellow of the American College of Physicians.

FACS ▶*abbr.* Fellow of the American College of Surgeons.

fac·sim·i·le /fakˈsiməlē/ ▶*n.* an exact copy, esp. of written or printed material. ■ another term for FAX.
▶*v.* (**-led, -le·ing**) [*trans.*] make a copy of: *the ride was facsimiled for Disney World.* ▷late 16th cent. (originally as *fac simile,* denoting the making of an exact copy, esp. of writing): modern Latin, from Latin *fac!* (imperative of *facere* 'make') and *simile* (neuter of *similis* 'like').
▶*PHRASE* □ **in facsimile** as an exact copy.

fact /fakt/ ▶*n.* a thing that is indisputably the case: *she lacks political experience—a fact that becomes clear when she appears in public* | *a body of fact.* ■ (**the fact that**) used in discussing the significance of something that is the case: *the real problem facing them is the fact that their funds are being cut.* ■ (usu. **facts**) a piece of information used as evidence or as part of a report or news article. ■ *chiefly Law* the truth about events as opposed to interpretation: *there was a question of fact as to whether they had received the letter.* ▷late 15th cent.: from Latin *factum,* neuter past participle of *facere* 'do.' The original sense was 'an act or feat,' later 'bad deed, a crime,' surviving in the phrase *before (or after) the fact.* The earliest of the current senses ('truth, reality') dates from the late 16th cent.
▶*PHRASES* □ **before** (or **after**) **the fact** before (or after) the committing of a crime: *an accessory before the fact.* □ **a fact of life** something that must be accepted as true and unchanging, even if it is unpleasant: *it is a fact of life that young girls write horrible things about people in their diaries.* □ **facts and figures** precise details. □ **the facts of life** information about sexual functions and practices, esp. as given to children. □ **the fact of the matter** the truth. □ **in** (**point of**) **fact** used to emphasize the truth of an assertion, esp. one contrary to what might be expected or what has been asserted: *Aunt Madeline isn't in fact an aunt but a more distant relative.*

fact-find·ing ▶*adj.* [*attrib.*] (esp. of a committee or its activity) having the purpose of discovering and establishing the facts of an issue: *a fact-finding mission.*
▶*n.* the discovery and establishment of the facts of an issue. —**fact-find·er** *n.*

fac·tic·i·ty /fakˈtisətē/ ▶*n.* the quality or condition of being fact: *the facticity of death.*

fac·tion[1] /ˈfakSHən/ ▶*n.* a small, organized, dissenting group within a larger one, esp. in politics: *the left-wing faction of the party.* ■ a state of conflict within an organization; dissension. ▷late 15th cent. (denoting the action of doing or making something): via French from Latin *factio(n-),* from *facere* 'do, make.'

fac·tion[2] ▶*n.* a literary and cinematic genre in which real events are used as a basis for a fictional narrative or dramatization. ▷1960s: blend of FACT and FICTION.

-faction ▶*comb. form* in nouns of action derived from verbs ending in *-fy* (such as *satisfaction* from *satisfy*). ▷from Latin *factio(n)-,* from *facere* 'do, make.'

fac·tion·al /ˈfakSHənl/ ▶*adj.* relating or belonging to a faction: *factional leaders.* ■ characterized by dissent: *factional conflicts.* —**fac·tion·al·ism** /-,izəm/ *n.* —**fac·tion·al·ly** *adv.*

fac·tion·al·ize /ˈfakSHənl-īz/ ▶*v.* [*intrans.*] (esp. of a political party or other organized group) split or divide into factions: *there was a tendency for students to factionalize.*

fac·tious /ˈfakSHəs/ ▶*adj.* relating or inclined to a state of faction: *a factious country.* ▷mid 16th cent.: from French *factieux* or Latin *factiosus,* from *factio* (see FACTION[1]). —**fac·tious·ly** *adv.* —**fac·tious·ness** *n.*

fac·ti·tious /fakˈtiSHəs/ ▶*adj.* artificially created or developed: *a largely factitious national identity.* ▷mid 17th cent. (in the general sense 'made by human skill or effort'): from Latin *facticius* 'made by art,' from *facere* 'do, make.' —**fac·ti·tious·ly** *adv.* —**fac·ti·tious·ness** *n.*

fac·ti·tive /ˈfaktətiv/ ▸*adj. Linguistics* (of a verb) having a sense of causing a result and taking a complement as well as an object, as in *he appointed me captain.* ▷mid 19th cent.: from modern Latin *factitivus,* formed irregularly from Latin *factitare,* frequentative of *facere* 'do, make.'

fac·tive /ˈfaktiv/ ▸*adj. Linguistics* denoting a verb that assigns the status of an established fact to its object (normally a clausal object), e.g., *know, regret, resent.*

fac·toid /ˈfakˌtoid/ ▸*n.* a brief or trivial item of news or information. ■ an assumption or speculation that is reported and repeated so often that it becomes accepted as fact.

fac·tor /ˈfaktər/ ▸*n.* **1** a circumstance, fact, or influence that contributes to a result or outcome: *his legal problems were not a* ***factor in*** *his decision | she worked fast, conscious of the time factor.* ■ *Biology* a gene that determines a hereditary characteristic: *the Rhesus factor.* **2** a number or quantity that when multiplied with another produces a given number or expression. ■ *Mathematics* a number or algebraic expression by which another is exactly divisible. **3** *Physiology* any of a number of substances in the blood, mostly identified by numerals, which are involved in coagulation. See **FACTOR VIII.** **4** a business agent; a merchant buying and selling on commission. ■ a company that buys a manufacturer's invoices at a discount and takes responsibility for collecting the payments due on them. ■ *archaic* an agent, deputy, or representative.

▸*v.* [*trans.*] **1** *Mathematics* another term for **FACTORIZE.** **2** sell (one's receivable debts) to a factor.

▸*phrasal v.* □ **factor something in** (or **out**) include (or exclude) something as a relevant element when making a calculation or decision: *when the psychological costs are factored in, a different picture will emerge.* ▷late Middle English (meaning 'doer, perpetrator,' also in the Scots sense 'agent'): from French *facteur* or Latin *factor,* from *fact-* 'done,' from the verb *facere.* **—fac·tor·a·ble** *adj.*

▸*PHRASE* □ **the —— factor** used to indicate that something specified will have a powerful, though unpredictable, influence on a result or outcome: *the feel-good factor.*

fac·tor VIII (also **fac·tor eight**) ▸*n. Physiology* a blood protein (a beta globulin) involved in clotting. A deficiency of this causes one of the main forms of hemophilia.

fac·tor·age /ˈfaktərij/ ▸*n.* the commission or charges payable to a factor.

fac·tor a·nal·y·sis ▸*n. Statistics* a process in which the values of observed data are expressed as functions of a number of possible causes in order to find which are the most important.

fac·tor cost ▸*n.* the cost of an item or a service in terms of the various factors that have played a part in its production or availability, and exclusive of tax costs.

fac·to·ri·al /fakˈtôrēəl/ ▸*n. Mathematics* the product of an integer and all the integers below it; e.g., factorial four (*4!*) is equal to 24. (Symbol: !) ■ the product of a series of factors in an arithmetic progression.

▸*adj. chiefly Mathematics* relating to a factor or such a product: *a factorial design.* **—fac·to·ri·al·ly** *adv.*

fac·tor·ize /ˈfaktəˌrīz/ ▸*v.* [*trans.*] *Mathematics* express (a number or expression) as a product of factors. ■ [*intrans.*] (of a number) be capable of resolution into factors: *f factorizes completely into linear factors.* **—fac·tor·i·za·tion** /ˌfaktərəˈzāshən/ *n.*

fac·to·ry /ˈfakt(ə)rē/ ▸*n.* (*pl.* **-ries**) **1** a building or group of buildings where goods are manufactured or assembled chiefly by machine. ■ [with *adj.*] *figurative* a person, group, or institution that produces a great quantity of something on a regular basis or in a short space of time: *a huge factory of lying, slander, and bad English.* **2** *historical* an establishment for traders carrying on business in a foreign country. ▷late 16th cent. (sense 2): from medieval Latin *factoria;* sense 1 from late Latin *factoria,* literally 'oil press.'

fac·to·ry farm·ing ▸*n.* a system of rearing livestock using intensive methods, by which poultry, pigs, or cattle are confined indoors under strictly controlled conditions. **—fac·to·ry farm** *n.*

fac·to·ry floor ▸*n.* the workers in a company or industry, rather than the management: *the unions had almost no influence on the factory floor.*

fac·to·ry out·let ▸*n.* a store in which goods, esp. surplus stock, are sold directly by the manufacturers at a discount.

fac·to·ry ship ▸*n.* a fishing or whaling ship, or a ship accompanying a fishing or whaling fleet, with facilities for immediate processing of the catch.

fac·to·tum /fakˈtōtəm/ ▸*n.* (*pl.* **-tums**) an employee who does all kinds of work: *he was employed as the general factotum.* ▷mid 16th cent. (originally in the phrases *dominum* (or *magister*) *factotum,* translating roughly as 'master of everything,' and *Johannes factotem* 'John do-it-all' or 'Jack of all trades'): from medieval Latin, from Latin *fac!* 'do!' (imperative of *facere*) + *totum* 'the whole thing' (neuter of *totus*).

fact sheet ▸*n.* a sheet of paper giving useful information about a particular issue, esp. one distributed for publicity purposes.

fac·tu·al /ˈfakcho͞oəl/ ▸*adj.* concerned with what is actually the case rather than interpretations of or reactions to it: *a mixture of comment and factual information.* ■ actually occurring: *cases mentioned are factual.* ▷mid 19th cent.: from **FACT,** on the pattern of *actual.* **—fac·tu·al·i·ty** /ˌfakcho͞oˈalitē/ *n.* **—fac·tu·al·ly** *adv.* **—fac·tu·al·ness** *n.*

fac·tum /ˈfaktəm/ ▸*n.* (*pl.* **-tums** /-təmz/ or **-ta** /-tə/) *Law, chiefly Canadian* a statement of the facts of a case. ▷late 18th cent.: from Latin, literally 'something done or made.'

fac·ture /ˈfakchər/ ▸*n.* the quality of the execution of a painting; an artist's characteristic handling of the paint: *Manet's sensuous facture.* ▷late Middle English (in the general sense 'construction, workmanship'): via Old French from Latin *factura* 'formation, manufacture,' from *facere* 'do, make.' The current sense dates from the late 19th cent.

fac·u·la /ˈfakyələ/ ▸*n.* (*pl.* **-lae** /-ˌlē/) *Astronomy* a bright region on the surface of the sun, linked to the subsequent appearance of sunspots in the same area. ■ a bright spot on the surface of a planet. ▷early 18th cent.: from Latin, diminutive of *fax, fac-* 'torch.' **—fac·u·lar** /-lər/ *adj.*

fac·ul·ta·tive /ˈfakəlˌtātiv/ ▸*adj.* occurring optionally in response to circumstances rather than by nature: *prison-style, facultative homosexuality.* ■ *Biology* capable of but not restricted to a particular function or mode of life: *a facultative parasite.* Often contrasted with **OBLIGATE.** ▷early 19th cent.: from French *facultatif, -ive,* from *faculté* (see **FACULTY**). **—fac·ul·ta·tive·ly** *adv.*

fac·ul·ty /ˈfakəltē/ ▸*n.* (*pl.* **-ties**) **1** an inherent mental or physical power: *her critical faculties.* ■ an aptitude or talent for doing something: *the author's faculty for philosophical analysis.* **2** the teaching staff of a university or college, or of one of its departments or divisions, viewed as a body: *there were then no tenured women* ***on the faculty*** *| the English faculty.* ■ a group of university departments concerned with a major division of knowledge: *the Faculty of Arts and Sciences.* ■ *dated* the members of a particular profession, esp. medicine, considered collectively. **3** a license or authorization, esp. from a church authority. ▷late Middle English: from Old French *faculte,* from Latin *facultas,* from *facilis* 'easy,' from *facere* 'make, do.'

FA Cup a major annual competition for soccer clubs in England, first held in 1872. ▷from *Football Association.*

FAD *Biochemistry* ▸*abbr.* flavin adenine dinucleotide, a coenzyme derived from riboflavin and important in various metabolic reactions.

fad /fad/ ▸*n.* an intense and widely shared enthusiasm for something, esp. one that is short-lived and without basis in the object's qualities; a craze: *prairie restoration is the latest gardening fad in the Midwest.* ▷mid 19th cent. (originally dialect): probably the second element of *fidfad,* contraction of **FIDDLE-FADDLE.** **—fad·dish** *adj.* **—fad·dish·ly** *adv.* **—fad·dish·ness** *n.* **—fad·dism** /-ˌizəm/ *n.* **—fad·dist** /-ist/ *n.*

fade /fād/ ▸*v.* [*intrans.*] **1** gradually grow faint and disappear: *the noise* ***faded away*** *| figurative hopes of peace had faded.* ■ lose or cause to lose color or brightness: [*intrans.*] *the fair hair had faded to a dusty gray |* [*trans.*] [usu. as *adj.*] (**faded**) *faded jeans.* ■ (of a flower) lose freshness and wither. ■ gradually become thin and weak, esp. to the point of death. ■ (of a racehorse, runner, etc.) lose strength or drop back, esp. after a promising start: *she faded near the finish.* ■ (of a radio signal) gradually lose intensity: *the signal faded away.* ■ (of a vehicle brake) become temporarily less efficient as a result of frictional heating. **2** [with *adverbial*] (with reference to film and television images) come or cause to come gradually into or out of view, or to merge into another shot: [*intrans.*] *fade into scenes of rooms strewn with festive remains |* [*trans.*] *some shots have to be faded in.* ■ (with reference to recorded sound) increase or decrease in volume or merge into another recording: [*intrans.*] *they let you edit the digital data, making it fade in and out |* [*trans.*] *fade up natural sound.* **3** *Golf* (of the ball) deviate to the right (or, for a left-handed golfer, the left), typically as a result of spin given to the ball. ■ [*trans.*] cause (the ball) to move in such a way: *he had to fade the ball around a light pole.* Compare with **DRAW** sense 5. **4** [*trans.*] *informal* (in craps) match the bet of (another player): *Lovejoy faded him for twenty-five cents.*

▸*phrasal v.* □ **fade back** *Football* move back from the scrimmage line.

▸*n.* **1** the process of becoming less bright: *the sun can cause color-fade.* ■ an act of causing a film or television picture to darken and disappear gradually: *a fade to black would bring the sequence to a close.* Compare with **FADE-OUT.** **2** *Golf* a shot causing the ball to deviate to the right (or, for a left-handed golfer, the left), usually purposely. ▷Middle English (in the sense 'grow weak, waste away'; compare with *fade away*): from Old French *fader,* from *fade* 'dull, insipid,' probably based on a blend of Latin *fatuus* 'silly, insipid' and *vapidus* 'vapid.' **—fade·less** *adj.*

▸*PHRASE* □ **do a fade** *informal* run away.

fade·a·way /ˈfādəˌwā/ ▸*adj. Basketball* another term for **FALLAWAY.**

fade-in ▸*n.* a filmmaking and broadcasting technique whereby an image is made to appear gradually or the volume of sound is gradually increased from zero.

fade-out ▸*n.* a filmmaking and broadcasting technique whereby an image is made to disappear gradually or the sound volume is gradually decreased to zero. ■ a gradual and temporary loss of a broadcast signal: *radio fade-outs.*

fad·er /ˈfādər/ ▸*n.* a device for varying the volume of sound, the intensity of light, or the gain on a video or audio signal.

fade-up ▸*n.* an instance of increasing the brightness of an image or the volume of a sound.

fa·do /ˈfäTHo͞o/ ▸*n.* (*pl.* **-dos**) a type of popular Portuguese song, usually with a melancholy theme and accompanied by mandolins or guitars. ■ the music for such a song. ▷early 20th cent.: Portuguese, literally 'fate.'

fae·ces ▸*n.* British spelling of **FECES.**

fa·er·ie /ˈferē/ (also **fa·er·y**) ▸*n. archaic or poetic/literary* fairyland: *the world of faerie.* ■ a fairy. ■ [as *adj.*] imaginary; mythical: *faerie dragons.* ▷late 16th cent. (introduced by Spenser): pseudoarchaic variant of **FAIRY.**

Faer·oe Is·lands /ˈferō/ (also **Far·oe** or **the Faer·oes**) islands in the North Atlantic Ocean between Iceland and the Shetland Islands that belong to Denmark but are semi-autonomous; pop. 43,000); capital, Tórshavn.

Faer·o·ese /ˌfe(ə)rōˈēz; -ˈēs/ (also **Far·o·ese**) ▸*adj.* of or relating to the Faeroe Islands or their people or language.

▸*n.* (*pl.* same) **1** a native or national of the Faeroes, or a person of Faeroese descent. **2** the official language of the Faeroes, a North Germanic language closely related to Icelandic.

FAF ▸*abbr.* Financial Aid Form.

fag[1] /fag/ ▸*n.* [in *sing.*] *informal chiefly Brit.* a tiring or unwelcome task: *it's too much of a fag to drive all the way there and back again.* ■ *Brit.* a junior pupil at a private preparatory school who works and runs errands for a senior pupil.

▸*v.* (**fagged, fag·ging**) [*intrans.*] *Brit., informal* work hard, esp. at a tedious job or task: *he didn't have to* ***fag away*** *in a lab to get the right answer.* ■ *Brit.* (of a pupil at a private preparatory school) work and run errands for a senior pupil. ▷mid 16th cent. (as a verb in the sense 'grow weary'): of unknown origin. Compare with **FLAG**[1].

fag[2] ▸*n. informal, chiefly offensive* a male homosexual. See **usage** at **QUEER.** ▷1920s: short for **FAGGOT.** **—fag·gy** *adj.*

fag[3] ▸*n. Brit., informal* a cigarette. ▷late 19th cent.: elliptically from **FAG END.**

fag end ▸*n. informal, chiefly Brit.* a cigarette butt. ■ an inferior and useless remnant of something: *the fag ends of rope figurative a culture reaching the fag end of its existence.* ▷early 17th cent. (in the sense 'remnant'): from 15th-cent. *fag* 'a flap,' of unknown origin. The sense 'a cigarette butt' dates from the early 20th cent.

fagged /fagd/ ▸*adj.* [*predic.*] extremely tired; exhausted: *we were all absolutely* ***fagged out.***

fag·got /ˈfagət/ ▸*n.* **1** *informal, chiefly offensive* a male

Pronunciation Key ə *ago;* ər *over;* ˈə or ˌə *up;* ˈər or ˌər *fur;* a *hat;* ā *rate;* ä *car;* CH *chew;* e *let;* ē *see;* e(ə)r *air;* i *fit;* ī *by;* i(ə)r *ear;* NG *sing;* ō *go;* ô *for;* oi *boy;* o͝o *good;* o͞o *goo;* ou *out;* SH *she;* TH *thin;* TH *then;* (h)w *why;* ZH *vision*

homosexual. See **usage** at **QUEER**. **2** British spelling of **FAGOT**. ▷early 20th cent.: perhaps from the obsolete sense of *fagot* 'contemptible woman.' —**fag·got·y** *adj.*

fag hag ▸*n. informal, offensive* a heterosexual woman who spends much of her time with homosexual men.

fag·ot /ˈfagət/ (*Brit.* **faggot**) ▸a bundle of sticks or twigs bound together as fuel. ■ a bundle of iron rods bound together for reheating, welding, and hammering into bars.

fag·ot·ing /ˈfagətiNG/ (*Brit.* **fag·got·ing**) ▸*n.* embroidery in which threads are fastened together in bundles: *a black silk dress with tiers of fagoting.* ■ *archaic* the joining of materials in such a way.

Fahd /fäd/ (1923–), king of Saudi Arabia 1982–; full name *Fahd ibn Abdul-Aziz al Saud.*

fahl·erz /ˈfälərts/ ▸*n.* a gray copper ore, of which tetrahedrite and tennantite are the typical minerals. ▷late 18th cent.: from German, from *fahl* 'ash-colored' + *Erz* 'ore.'

Fahr. ▸*abbr.* Fahrenheit.

Fahr·en·heit /ˈfarənˌhīt/ (abbr.: **F**) ▸*adj.* [*postpositive* when used with a numeral] of or denoting a scale of temperature on which water freezes at 32° and boils at 212° under standard conditions.
▸*n.* (also **Fahrenheit scale**) this scale of temperature. ▷mid 18th cent.: named after Gabriel Daniel *Fahrenheit* (1686–1736), German physicist.

FAIA ▸*abbr.* Fellow of the American Institute of Architects.

fa·ience /fīˈäns; fā-/ ▸*n.* glazed ceramic ware, in particular decorated tin-glazed earthenware of the type that includes delftware and maiolica. ▷late 17th cent. (originally denoting pottery made at Faenza, Italy): from French *faïence*, from *Faïence*, the French name for *Faenza.*

fail /fāl/ ▸*v.* [*intrans.*] **1** be unsuccessful in achieving one's goal: *he* ***failed in*** *his attempt to secure election* | [*with infinitive*] *they failed to be ranked in the top ten.* ■ [*trans.*] be unsuccessful in (an examination, test, or interview): *she failed her finals.* ■ [*trans.*] (of a person or a commodity) be unable to meet the standards set by (a test of quality or eligibility): *the player has failed a drug test.* ■ [*trans.*] judge (someone, esp. in an examination) not to have passed. **2** neglect to do something: [*with infinitive*] *the firm failed to give adequate risk warnings.* ■ [*with infinitive*] behave in a way contrary to hopes or expectations by not doing something: *commuter chaos has again failed to materialize.* ■ (**cannot fail to be/do something**) used to express a strong belief that something must be the case: *you cannot fail to be deeply impressed.* ■ (**never fail to do something**) used to indicate that something invariably happens: *such comments never failed to annoy him.* ■ [*trans.*] desert or let down (someone): *at the last moment her nerve failed her.* **3** break down; cease to work well: *a truck whose brakes had failed.* ■ become weaker or of poorer quality; die away: *the light began to fail* | [*as adj.*] (**failing**) *his failing health.* ■ (esp. of a rain or a crop or supply) be lacking or insufficient when needed or expected. ■ (of a business or a person) be obliged to cease trading because of lack of funds; become bankrupt.
▸*n.* a grade that is not high enough to pass an examination or test. ▷Middle English: from Old French *faillir* (verb), *faille* (noun), based on Latin *fallere* 'deceive.' An earlier sense of the noun was 'failure to do or perform a duty,' surviving in the phrase *without fail.*
▸*PHRASE* □ **without fail** absolutely predictably; with no exception: *he writes every week without fail.*

failed /fāld/ ▸*adj.* [*attrib.*] **1** (of an undertaking or a relationship) not achieving its end or not lasting; unsuccessful: *a failed coup attempt.* ■ (of a person) unsuccessful in a particular activity, esp. not good enough to make a living by it: *a failed writer.* ■ (of a business) unable to continue owing to financial difficulties. **2** (of a mechanism) not functioning properly; broken-down: *an aircraft with a failed engine.*

fail·ing /ˈfāliNG/ ▸*n.* a weakness, esp. in character; a shortcoming: *pride is a terrible failing.*
▸*prep.* in default of; in the absence of: *she longed to be with him and,* ***failing that,*** *to be on her own.*

faille /fīl/ ▸*n.* a soft, light-woven fabric having a ribbed texture and originally made of silk. ▷mid 16th cent. (denoting a kind of hood or veil worn by women): from Old French. The current sense dates from the mid 19th cent.

fail·o·ver /ˈfālˌōvər/ ▸*n. Computing* a method of protecting computer systems from failure, in which standby equipment automatically takes over when the main system fails.

fail-safe ▸*adj.* causing a piece of machinery or other mechanism to revert to a safe condition in the event of a breakdown or malfunction: *a forklift with a fail-safe device.* ■ unlikely or unable to fail: *the computer that runs the place is supposed to be fail-safe.*
▸*n.* [usu. in *sing.*] a system or plan that comes into operation in the event of something going wrong or that is there to prevent such an occurrence: *the secondary safety system is indeed a fail-safe.*

fail·ure /ˈfālyər/ ▸*n.* **1** lack of success: *an economic policy that is doomed to failure* | *the failures of his policies.* ■ an unsuccessful person, enterprise, or thing: *bad weather had resulted in crop failures.* ■ lack of success in passing an examination or test: *exam failure.* ■ a grade that is not high enough to pass an examination or test. **2** the omission of expected or required action: *their failure to comply with the basic rules.* ■ a lack or deficiency of a desirable quality: *a failure of imagination.* **3** the action or state of not functioning: *symptoms of heart failure* | *an engine failure.* ■ a sudden cessation of power. ■ the collapse of a business. ▷mid 17th cent. (originally as *failer*, in the senses 'nonoccurrence' and 'cessation of supply'): from Anglo-Norman French *failer* for Old French *faillir* (see **FAIL**).

fain /fān/ *archaic* ▸*adj.* pleased or willing under the circumstances: *the traveler was* ***fain to*** *proceed.* ■ compelled by the circumstances; obliged: *he was fain to acknowledge that the agreement was sacrosanct.*
▸*adv.* with pleasure; gladly: *I am weary and* ***would fain*** *get a little rest.* ▷Old English *fægen* 'happy, well pleased,' of Germanic origin, from a base meaning 'rejoice'; related to **FAWN**[2].

fai·né·ant /ˈfānēənt/ ▸*adj. archaic* idle or ineffective. ▷early 17th cent.: from French, from *fait* 'does' + *néant* 'nothing.'

faint /fānt/ ▸*adj.* **1** (of a sight, smell, or sound) barely perceptible: *the faint murmur of voices.* ■ (of a hope, chance, or possibility) slight; remote: *there is a faint chance that the enemy may flee.* **2** [*predic.*] weak and dizzy; close to losing consciousness: *the heat made him feel faint.* ■ appearing feeble or lacking in strength: *the faint beat of a butterfly's wing.*
▸*v.* [*intrans.*] lose consciousness for a short time because of a temporarily insufficient supply of oxygen to the brain. ■ *archaic* grow weak or feeble; decline: *the fires were fainting.*
▸*n.* [in *sing.*] a sudden loss of consciousness: *she hit the floor* ***in a dead faint.*** ▷Middle English (sense 2; also in the sense 'cowardly,' surviving in **FAINT HEART**): from Old French *faint*, past participle of *faindre* (see **FEIGN**). Compare with **FEINT**[1]. —**faint·ly** *adv.* [*as submodifier*] *his faintly ridiculous air.* —**faint·ness** *n.*
▸*PHRASE* □ **not have the faintest** *informal* have no idea: *I haven't the faintest what it means.*

faint heart ▸*n.* a person who has a timid or reserved nature.
▸*PHRASE* □ **faint heart never won fair lady** *proverb* timidity will prevent you from achieving your objective.

faint-heart·ed ▸*adj.* lacking courage; timid: *they were feeling faint-hearted at the prospect of war* | [*as plural n.*] (**the faint-hearted**) *litigation is* ***not for the faint-hearted.*** —**faint-heart·ed·ly** *adv.* —**faint-heart·ed·ness** *n.*

fair[1] /fer/ ▸*adj.* **1** in accordance with the rules or standards; legitimate: *the group has achieved fair and equal representation for all its members.* ■ just or appropriate in the circumstances: ***to be fair,*** *this subject poses special problems.* ■ *archaic* (of a means or procedure) gentle; not violent. ■ *Baseball* (of a batted ball) within the field of play marked by the first and third baselines. ■ *Baseball* pertaining to this part of the field: *the ball was hit into fair territory.* **2** (of hair or complexion) light; blond. ■ (of a person) having such a complexion or hair. **3** considerable though not outstanding in size or amount: *he did a fair bit of coaching.* ■ moderately good though not outstandingly so: *he believes he has a fair chance of success.* **4** (of weather) fine and dry. ■ (of the wind) favorable: *they set sail with a fair wind.* **5** *archaic* beautiful: attractive: *the fairest of her daughters.* ■ (of words, a speech, or a promise) false, despite being initially attractive or pleasing; specious. **6** (of handwriting) easy to read.
▸*adv.* **1** without cheating or trying to achieve unjust advantage: *no one could say he played fair.* **2** [*as submodifier*] *dialect* to a high degree: *she'll be fair delighted to see you.*
▸*n. archaic* a beautiful woman.
▸*v.* [*intrans.*] *dialect* (of the weather) become fine: *looks like it's fairing off some.* ▷Old English *fæger* 'pleasing, attractive,' of Germanic origin, related to Norwegian *vakker*, 'beautiful'. —**fair·ish** *adj.* —**fair·ness** *n.*
▸*PHRASES* □ **all's fair in love and war** *proverb* in certain highly charged situations, any method of achieving your objective is justifiable. □ **by fair means or foul** using whatever means are necessary: *they were determined to ensure victory for themselves, by fair means or foul.* □ **fair and square** honestly and straightforwardly: *we won the match fair and square.* □ **a fair deal** equitable treatment. □ **fair dinkum** see **DINKUM**. □ **fair enough** *informal* used to admit that something is reasonable or acceptable: *"I can't come because I'm working late." "Fair enough."* □ **fair-to-middling** slightly above average: *she manages to capitalize on some fair-to-middling material.* □ **fair name** *dated* a good reputation. □ **the fair sex** (also **the fairer sex**) *dated* or *humorous* women. □ **fair's fair** *informal* used to request just treatment or assert that an arrangement is just: *Fair's fair—we were here first.* □ **for fair** *informal dated* completely and finally: *then we'd be rid of him for fair.* □ **in a fair way to do something** *dated* having nearly done something, and likely to achieve it: *he is in a fair way to get well.* □ **it's a fair cop** *Brit.* an admission that the speaker has been caught doing wrong and deserves punishment. □ **no fair** *informal* unfair (often used in or as a petulant protestation): *no fair—we're the only kids in the whole school who don't get to watch TV on school nights.*

fair[2] ▸*n.* a gathering of stalls and amusements for public entertainment. ■ (also **agricultural fair**) a competitive exhibition of livestock, agricultural products, and household skills held annually by a town, county, or state and also featuring entertainment and educational displays. ■ a periodic gathering for the sale of goods. ■ an exhibition to promote particular products: *the Contemporary Art Fair.* ▷Middle English (in the sense 'periodic gathering for the sale of goods'): from Old French *feire*, from late Latin *feria*, singular of Latin *feriae* 'holy days' (on which such fairs were often held).

fair[3] ▸*v.* [*trans.*] [usu. as *adj.*] (**faired**) streamline (a vehicle, boat, or aircraft) by adding fairings. ▷Old English in the senses 'beautify' and 'appear or become clean.' The current sense dates from the mid 19th cent.

Fair·banks[1] /ˈfe(ə)rˌbaNGks/ the second-largest city in Alaska, in the central part of the state, near the junction of the Chena and Tanana rivers; pop. 30,224.

Fair·banks[2] the name of two U.S. actors. **Douglas (Elton)** (1883–1939); born *Julius Ullman*). He cofounded United Artists in 1919 and became known for his swashbuckling movie roles. His son **Douglas** (1909–2000), known as **Douglas Fairbanks Jr.**, played similar roles.

Fair·born /ˈfe(ə)rˌbôrn/ a city in southwestern Ohio, northeast of Dayton; pop. 31,300.

fair catch ▸*n. Football* a catch of a punt in which a player raises a hand and does not advance the ball.

fair cop·y ▸*n.* written or printed matter transcribed or reproduced after final correction.

Fair·fax Coun·ty a county in northeastern Virginia that incorporates many suburbs of Washington, DC; pop. 969,749.

Fair·field /ˈfe(ə)rˌfēld/ **1** a city in north central California, an agricultural processing center; pop. 77,211. **2** a residential town in southwestern Connecticut; pop. 57,340. **3** a city in southwestern Ohio, north of Cincinnati; pop. 39,729.

fair game ▸*n.* a person or thing that is considered a reasonable target for criticism, exploitation, or attack.

fair·ground /ˈferˌground/ (often **fair·grounds**) ▸*n.* an outdoor area where a fair is held.

fair-haired ▸*adj.* **1** having light-colored hair. **2** (of a person) favorite; cherished: *the* ***fair-haired boy*** *of American advertising.*

fair·ies' bon·nets ▸*plural n.* a small toadstool with a grooved, yellowish-brown, thimble-shaped cap, growing in large clusters on rotten wood or in soil. • *Coprinus disseminatus*, family Coprinaceae, class Hymenomycetes.

fair·ing /ˈferiNG/ ▸*n.* an external metal or plastic structure added to increase streamlining and reduce drag, esp. on a high-performance car, motorcycle, boat, or aircraft.

Fair I·saac Cor·po·ra·tion (abbr.: **FICO**) ▸*n. Finance* the largest and best known of several companies that provide software for calculating a person's credit score.

Fair Isle one of the Shetland Islands, about halfway between Orkney and the main Shetland group.

■ [usu. as *adj.*] traditional multicolored geometric designs used in woolen knitwear: *Fair Isle sweaters.*

fair·lead /ˈfer,lēd/ ▶*n.* a ring mounted on a boat or ship to guide a rope, keeping it clear of obstructions and preventing it from being cut or chafed.

fair·ly /ˈferlē/ ▶*adv.* **1** with justice: *he could not fairly be accused of wasting police time.* **2** [usu. as *submodifier*] to quite a high degree: *I was fairly certain she had nothing to do with the affair.* ■ to an acceptable extent: *I get along fairly well with everybody.* ■ actually (used to emphasize something surprising or extreme): *he fairly snarled at her.*

▶*PHRASE* □ **fairly and squarely** another term for FAIR AND SQUARE (see FAIR[1]).

fair-mar·ket val·ue ▶*n.* a selling price for an item to which a buyer and seller can agree.

fair-mind·ed ▶*adj.* impartial in judgment; just: *a fair-minded employer.* —**fair-mind·ed·ly** *adv.* —**fair-mind·ed·ness** *n.*

fair·ness doc·trine ▶*n.* a former federal policy requiring television and radio broadcasters that presented one side of a controversy to provide the opportunity for opposing points of view to be expressed at no charge.

fair play ▶*n.* respect for the rules or equal treatment of all concerned.

fair-spo·ken ▶*adj. archaic* (of a person) courteous and pleasant.

fair trade ▶*n.* **1** trade carried on legally. **2** trade in which fair prices are paid to producers in developing countries.

fair-trade a·gree·ment ▶*n.* an agreement, typically illegal, between a manufacturer of a trademarked item in the U.S. and its retail distributors to sell the item at a price at or above that designated by the manufacturer.

fair use ▶*n.* (in U.S. copyright law) the doctrine that copyright material may be quoted verbatim without need for permission from or payment to the copyright holder, provided that attribution is clearly given and that the material quoted is reasonably brief in extent.

fair·wa·ter /ˈfer,wôtər; -,wätər/ ▶*n.* a structure that improves the streamlining of a ship to assist its smooth passage through water.

fair·way /ˈfer,wā/ ▶*n.* **1** the part of a golf course between a tee and the corresponding green, where the grass is kept short. **2** a navigable channel in a river or harbor. ■ a regular course or track followed by ships.

fair-weath·er friend ▶*n.* a person who stops being a friend in times of difficulty.

fair·y /ˈfe(ə)rē/ ▶*n.* (*pl.* **fair·ies**) **1** a small imaginary being of human form that has magical powers, esp. a female one. **2** *informal, offensive* a male homosexual.

▶*adj.* belonging to, resembling, or associated with fairies: *fairy gold.* ▷Middle English (denoting fairyland, or fairies collectively): from Old French *faerie,* from *fae* 'a fairy,' from Latin *fata* 'the Fates,' plural of *fatum* (see FATE). Compare with FAY. —**fair·y·like** /-līk/ *adj.*

fair·y ar·ma·dil·lo ▶*n.* a very small burrowing armadillo found in southern South America. • Genus *Clamyphorus,* family Dasypodidae: two species.

fair·y blue·bird ▶*n.* a South Asian forest songbird related to the orioles, the male of which has bright blue and black plumage. • Genus *Irena,* family Irenidae (or Oriolidae): two species, in particular the widespread *I. puella.*

fair·y fly ▶*n.* a minute parasitic wasp that lays its eggs in the eggs of other insects. • Family Mymaridae, order Hymenoptera: numerous genera.

fair·y god·moth·er ▶*n.* a female character in some fairy tales who has magical powers and brings unexpected good fortune to the hero or heroine.

fair·y·land /ˈferē,land/ ▶*n.* the imaginary home of fairies. ■ a beautiful or seemingly enchanted place: [as *adj.*] *a fairyland castle.* ■ an imagined ideal place; a utopia.

fair·y ring ▶*n.* a circular area of grass that is darker in color than the surrounding grass due to the growth of certain fungi. They were popularly believed to have been caused by fairies dancing.

fair·y shrimp ▶*n.* a small, transparent crustacean that typically swims on its back, using its legs to filter food particles from the water. • Order Anostraca, class Branchiopoda: many species, including brine shrimps.

fair·y tale (also **fairy story**) ▶*n.* a children's story about magical and imaginary beings and lands. ■ [as *adj.*] denoting something regarded as resembling a fairy story in being magical, idealized, or extremely happy: *a fairy-tale romance.*

fair·y tern ▶*n.* a small white tropical tern that lays its single egg on a narrow ledge or on the bare branch of a tree. When it flies against a bright sky, the wings appear somewhat translucent, allowing the bone structure to be seen. • *Gygis alba,* family Sternidae.

fair·y wren ▶*n.* a small Australian songbird with a long cocked tail, the male of which has partly or mainly blue plumage. • Genus *Malurus,* family Maluridae: several species, in particular the common **superb fairy wren** or blue wren (*M. cyaneus*).

Fai·sal /ˈfīsəl/ the name of two kings of Iraq: ■ **Faisal I** (1885–1933); reigned 1921–33. He was supported by the British and by fervent Arab nationalists. Under his rule, Iraq achieved full independence in 1932. ■ **Faisal II** (1935–58), grandson of Faisal I; reigned 1939–58.He was assassinated in a military coup, after which a republic was established.

Fai·sa·la·bad /,fī,sälə'bäd; -'bad/ an industrial city in Punjab, Pakistan; pop. 1,092,000. Until 1979 it was known as Lyallpur.

fait ac·com·pli /ˈfet əkäm'plē; 'fāt/ ▶*n.* [in *sing.*] a thing that has already happened or been decided before those affected hear about it, leaving them with no option but to accept: *the results were presented to shareholders as a fait accompli.* ▷mid 19th cent.: from French, literally 'accomplished fact.'

faith /fāTH/ ▶*n.* **1** complete trust or confidence in someone or something: *this restores one's faith in politicians.* **2** strong belief in God or in the doctrines of a religion, based on spiritual apprehension rather than proof. ■ a system of religious belief: *the Christian faith.* ■ a strongly held belief or theory: *the faith that life will expand until it fills the universe.* ▷Middle English: from Old French *feid,* from Latin *fides.*

▶*PHRASE* □ **break** (or **keep**) **faith** be disloyal (or loyal): *an attempt to make us* ***break faith with*** *our customers.*

faith-based ▶*adj.* affiliated with or based on religion or a religious group: *a faith-based plan that bilked investors out of millions.*

USAGE The preponderance of usage for this term today connects it with institutions and programs that are affiliated with an organized religion, and with President George W. Bush's *faith-based initiative,* which enables religious institutions doing social work to receive government funding.

faith·ful /ˈfāTHfəl/ ▶*adj.* **1** loyal, constant, and steadfast: *he exhorted them to remain* ***faithful to*** *the principles of Reaganism | employees who had notched up decades of faithful service* | [as *plural n.*] (**the faithful**) *the struggle to please the party faithful.* ■ (of a spouse or partner) never having a sexual relationship with anyone else: *her husband was faithful to her.* ■ (of an object) reliable: *my faithful compass.* See note at RESOLUTE. **2** [usu. as *plural n.*] (**the faithful**) having a strong belief in a particular religion, esp. Islam. **3** true to the facts or the original: *the rugs they make today remain faithful to their ancestors' methods.* —**faith·ful·ness** *n.*

faith·ful·ly /ˈfāTHfəlē/ ▶*adv.* **1** in a loyal manner. **2** in a manner that is true to the facts or the original: *she translated the novel as faithfully as possible.*

▶*PHRASE* □ **yours faithfully** *chiefly Brit.* a formula for ending a formal letter to someone whose name you do not know.

faith heal·ing ▶*n.* healing achieved by religious belief and prayer, rather than by medical treatment. —**faith heal·er** *n.*

faith·less /ˈfāTHlis/ ▶*adj.* **1** disloyal, esp. to a spouse or partner; untrustworthy: *her faithless lover.* **2** without religious faith. —**faith·less·ly** *adv.* —**faith·less·ness** *n.*

fa·ji·ta /fəˈhētə/ ▶*n.* a dish of Mexican origin consisting of strips of spiced beef or chicken, chopped vegetables, and grated cheese, wrapped in a soft tortilla and often served with sour cream. ▷late 20th cent.: Mexican Spanish, literally 'little strip or belt.'

fake[1] /fāk/ ▶*n.* a thing that is not genuine; a forgery or sham: *the painting was a fake.* ■ a person who appears or claims to be something that they are not. See note at QUACK. ■ a pretense or trick: *his excuse for coming was a fake.*

▶*adj.* not genuine; counterfeit: *fake designer clothing | expressing fake emotions.* ■ (of a person) claiming to be something that one is not: *a fake doctor.*

▶*v.* [*trans.*] forge or counterfeit (something): *the woman faked her spouse's signature.* ■ pretend to feel or suffer from (an emotion or illness): *he had begun to fake a bad stomach ache.* ■ make (an event) appear to happen: *he faked his own death.* ■ accomplish (a task) by improvising: *all the experts agree that you can't* ***fake it*** ■ *Music* improvise: *he fakes the melody line of a standard tune.* ▷late 18th cent. (as an adjective; originally slang): origin uncertain; perhaps ultimately related to German *fegen* 'sweep, thrash.' Compare with FIG[2]. —**fak·er** *n.* —**fak·er·y** /ˈfākərē/ *n.*

fake[2] ▶*n.* & *v.* variant spelling of FLAKE[4]. ▷late Middle English (as a verb): of unknown origin.

fake bake (also **fake-bake**) ▶*n. informal* the process of getting a sunless tan, as under sunlamps or by applying a sunless-tanning lotion: *they're advertising reasonable prices for fake bakes.*

▶*v.* [*intrans.*] get a sunless tan: *in the winter months, she likes to fake-bake about once a week.*

fake book ▶*n. Music* a book of music containing the basic chord sequences of jazz or other tunes.

fak·ie /ˈfākē/ ▶*n.* (*pl.* **-ies**) (in skateboarding or snowboarding) a movement in which the board is ridden backward.

▶*adv.* with such a movement: *once you can do it forward, try it fakie.*

fa·kir /fəˈki(ə)r; ˈfākər/ (also **fa·keer, fa·qir, fa·quir**) ▶*n.* a Muslim (or, loosely, a Hindu) religious ascetic who lives solely on alms. ▷early 17th cent.: via French from Arabic *faḳīr* 'needy man.'

Fa·la·bel·la /,faləˈbelə/ ▶*n.* a horse of a miniature breed, the adult of which does not usually exceed 30 inches (75 cm) in height. ▷late 20th cent.: named after Julio *Falabella* (died 1981), an Argentinian breeder.

fa·la·fel /fəˈläfəl/ (also **fe·la·fel**) ▶*n.* a Middle Eastern dish of spiced mashed chickpeas or other pulses formed into balls or fritters and deep-fried, usually eaten with or in pita bread. ▷from colloquial Egyptian Arabic *falāfil,* plural of Arabic *fulful, filfil* 'pepper.'

Fa·lange /fəˈlanj; ˈfā,lanj/ the Spanish Fascist movement that merged with traditional right-wing elements in 1937 to form the ruling party, the Falange Española Tradicionalista, under General Franco. It was formally abolished in 1977. ▷Spanish, from Latin *phalanx, phalang-* (see PHALANX). —**Fa·lan·gism** /-izəm/ *n.* —**Fa·lan·gist** /-jist/ *n.* & *adj.*

Fa·la·sha /fəˈläSHə/ ▶*n.* (*pl.* same or **-shas**) *often offensive* a member of a group of people in Ethiopia who hold the Jewish faith but use Ge'ez rather than Hebrew as a liturgical language. The Falashas were not formally recognized as Jews until 1975, and many of them were airlifted to Israel in 1984–85 and after. ▷early 18th cent.: Amharic, literally 'exile, immigrant.'

fal·cate /ˈfal,kāt; ˈfôl-/ ▶*adj. Botany & Zoology* curved like a sickle; hooked: *the mandibles are falcate.* ▷early 19th cent.: from Latin *falcatus,* from *falx, falc-* 'sickle.'

fal·cat·ed teal ▶*n.* a small duck that is native to China and northeastern Asia. • *Anas falcata,* family Anatidae. ▷early 18th cent.: named from the long sickle-shaped inner secondary feathers of the male.

fal·chion /ˈfôlCHən; -SHən/ ▶*n. historical* a broad, slightly curved sword with the cutting edge on the convex side. ▷Middle English *fauchon,* from Old French, based on Latin *falx, falc-* 'sickle.' The *-l-* was added in the 16th cent. to conform with the Latin spelling.

fal·ci·form /ˈfalsə,fôrm/ ▶*adj. Anatomy & Zoology* curved like a sickle; hooked: *the falciform ligament.* ▷mid 18th cent.: from Latin *falx, falc-* 'sickle' + -IFORM.

fal·cip·a·rum /falˈsipərəm/ (also **falciparum malaria**) ▶*n.* the most severe form of malaria, caused by infection with *Plasmodium falciparum:* [as *adj.*] *the falciparum parasite.* ▷1930s: modern Latin, from Latin *falx, falc-* 'sickle' + *-parum* (from *-parus* 'bearing').

fal·con /ˈfalkən; ˈfôl-/ ▶*n.* a diurnal bird of prey with long pointed wings and a notched beak, typically catching prey by diving on it from above. Compare with HAWK[1] (sense 1). • Family Falconidae, in particular the genus *Falco:* many species, including the peregrine, hobby, merlin, and kestrel. ■ one of these birds kept and trained to hunt small game for sport. ■ *Falconry* the female of such a bird, esp. a peregrine. Compare with TERCEL. ▷Middle English *faucon* (originally denoting any diurnal bird of prey used in falconry): from Old French, from late Latin *falco.* The *-l-* was added in the 15th cent. to conform with the Latin spelling.

fal·con·er /ˈfalkənər; ˈfôl-/ ▶*n.* a person who keeps, trains, or hunts with falcons, hawks, or other birds

F

Pronunciation Key ə *ago;* ər *over;* ˈə or ,ə *up;* ˈər or ,ər *fur;* a *hat;* ā *rate;* ä *car;* CH *chew;* e *let;* ē *see;* e(ə)r *air;* i *fit;* ī *by;* i(ə)r *ear;* NG *sing;* ō *go;* ô *for;* oi *boy;* o͝o *good;* o͞o *goo;* ou *out;* SH *she;* TH *thin;* T͟H *then;* (h)w *why;* ZH *vision*

of prey. ▷late Middle English: from Old French *faucon*ier, from *faucon* (see **FALCON**).

fal·co·net /ˌfalkəˈnet; ˌfôl-/ ▸*n.* **1** *historical* a light cannon. [mid 16th cent.: from Italian *falconetto*, diminutive of *falcone* 'falcon,' from Latin *falco* (see **FALCON**).] **2** a very small South Asian (or South American) falcon, typically having bold black-and-white plumage. [mid 19th cent.: from **FALCON** + **-ET**1.] • Genus *Microhierax* (and *Spiziapteryx*), family Falconidae: six species.

fal·con·ry /ˈfalkənrē; ˈfôl-/ ▸*n.* the sport of hunting with falcons or other birds of prey; the keeping and training of such birds. ▷late 16th cent.: from French *fauconnerie*, from *faucon* (see **FALCON**).

fal·de·ral ▸*n.* variant spelling of **FOLDEROL**.

Fal·do /ˈfôldō/, Nick (1957–), English golfer; full name *Nicholas Alexander Faldo*. He won the British Open championship in 1987 and 1990 and the U.S. Masters in 1989, 1990, and 1996.

fald·stool /ˈfôl(d)ˌsto͞ol/ ▸*n.* **1** a folding chair used by a bishop when not occupying the throne or when officiating in a church other than his own. **2** a small movable folding desk or stool for kneeling at prayer. ▷late Old English *fældestōl*, of Germanic origin, from the base of **FOLD**1 and **STOOL**, influenced by medieval Latin *faldistolium*, from Germanic. Compare with **FAUTEUIL**

Falk·land Is·lands /ˈfôklənd/ (also **the Falk·lands**) a group of more than 100 islands in the South Atlantic Ocean, a British colony, about 300 miles (500 km) east of the Strait of Magellan; pop. 2,121; capital, Stanley (on East Falkland). They were occupied and colonized by Britain in 1832–33, following the expulsion of an Argentine garrison. Argentina has contested British sovereignty and continues to refer to the islands by their old Spanish name, the Malvinas. In 1982, an Argentine invasion led to the Falklands War, which ended in a successful British reoccupation.

Falk·land Is·lands De·pen·den·cies an overseas territory of the UK in the South Atlantic Ocean that consists of the South Sandwich Islands and South Georgia (which is administered from the Falkland Islands).

Falk·lands War an armed conflict between Britain and Argentina in 1982.

On the orders of Argentina's military junta, Argentine forces invaded the Falkland Islands in support of their claim to sovereignty. In response, Britain sent a task force of ships and aircraft, which forced the Argentine forces to surrender.

fall /fôl/ ▸*v.* (*past* **fell** /fel/; *past part.* **fall·en** /ˈfôlən/) [*intrans.*] **1** move downward, typically rapidly and freely without control, from a higher to a lower level: *bombs could be seen* ***falling from*** *the planes* | [as *adj.*] (**falling**) *the power lines had been brought down by falling trees.* ■ (**fall off**) become detached accidentally and drop to the ground: *my sunglasses fell off and broke on the pavement.* ■ hang down: *hair that was allowed to fall to the shoulders.* ■ (of land) slope downward; drop away: *the land* ***fell away*** *in a steep bank.* ■ (**fall into**) (of a river) flow or discharge itself into. ■ [*intrans.*] (of someone's eyes or glance) be directed downward. ■ [*intrans.*] (of someone's face) show dismay or disappointment by appearing to sag or droop: *her face fell as she thought about her life with George.* ■ *figurative* occur, arrive, or become apparent as if by dropping suddenly: *when night fell we managed to crawl back to our lines* | *the information might* ***fall into*** *the wrong hands.* **2** (of a person) lose one's balance and collapse: *she* ***fell down*** *at school today.* ■ throw oneself down, typically in order to worship or implore someone: *they fell on their knees, rendering thanks to God.* ■ (of a tree, building, or other structure) collapse to the ground: *the house looked as if it were going to* ***fall down*** *at any moment.* ■ (of a building or place) be captured or defeated: *their mountain strongholds* ***fell to*** *enemy attack.* ■ die in battle: *an English leader who had fallen at the hands of the Danes.* ■ [*intrans.*] *archaic* commit sin; yield to temptation: *it is their husband's fault if wives do fall.* ■ [*intrans.*] (of a government or leader) lose office. ■ (in sports) lose or be eliminated from play. **3** decrease in number, amount, intensity, or quality: *in 1987 imports into Britain* ***fell by*** *12 percent* | *we're worried that standards are falling.* ■ find a lower level; subside or abate: *the water table in the Rift Valley fell.* ■ (of a measuring instrument) show a lower reading: *the barometer had fallen a further ten points.* **4** pass into a specified state: *many of the buildings* ***fell into*** *disrepair* | [] *she fell pregnant.* ■ (**fall to doing something**) begin to do something: *he fell to musing about how it had happened.* ■ be drawn accidentally into: *you must not* ***fall into*** *this common error.* ■ occur at a specified time: *Mother's birthday fell on Flag Day.* ■ be classified or ordered in the way specified: *canals* ***fall within*** *the Minister's brief.*

▸*phrasal v.* □ **fall apart** (or **to pieces**) break up, come apart, or disintegrate: *their marriage is likely to fall apart.* ■ (of a person) lose one's capacity to cope: *Angie fell to pieces because she had lost everything.* □ **fall back** move or turn back; retreat. □ **fall back on** have recourse to when in difficulty: *they normally fell back on one of three arguments.* □ **fall behind** fail to keep up with one's competitors. ■ fail to meet a commitment to make a regular payment: *borrowers* ***falling behind with*** *their mortgage payments.* □ **fall down** be shown to be inadequate or false; fail: *the deal fell down partly because there were a lot of unanswered questions.* □ **fall for** *informal* **1** be captivated by; fall in love with. **2** be deceived by (something): *he should have known better than to expect Duncan to fall for a cheap trick like that.* □ **fall in 1** take one's place in a military formation: *the soldiers fell in by the side of the road.* **2** (of a structure) collapse inward. □ **fall in with 1** meet by chance and become involved with: *he fell in with thieves.* **2** act in accordance with (someone's ideas or suggestions); agree to: *falling in with other people's views.* □ **fall on** (or **upon**) **1** attack fiercely or unexpectedly: *the army fell on the besiegers.* ■ seize enthusiastically: *she fell on the sandwiches as though she had not eaten in weeks.* **2** (of someone's eyes or gaze) be directed toward: *her gaze fell on the mud-stained coverlet.* **3** (of a burden or duty) be borne or incurred by: *the cost of tuition should not fall on the student.* □ **fall out 1** (of the hair, teeth, etc.) become detached and drop out. **2** have an argument: *he had* ***fallen out with*** *his family.* **3** leave one's place in a military formation, or on parade: *the two policemen at the rear fell out of the formation.* **4** happen; turn out: *matters fell out as Stephen arranged.* □ **fall through** come to nothing; fail: *the project fell through due to lack of money.* □ **fall to** (of a task) become the duty or responsibility of: *it fell to me to write to Shephard.* ■ (of property) revert to the ownership of.

▸*n.* **1** [usu. in *sing.*] an act of falling or collapsing; a sudden uncontrollable descent: *his mother had a fall, hurting her leg as she alighted from a train.* ■ a controlled act of falling, esp. as a stunt or in martial arts. ■ *Wrestling* a move which pins the opponent's shoulders on the ground for a count of three. ■ a state of hanging or drooping downward: ***the fall of*** *her hair.* ■ a downward difference in height between parts of a surface: *at the corner of the massif this fall is interrupted by other heights of considerable stature.* ■ a sudden onset or arrival as if by dropping: *the fall of darkness.* **2** a thing that falls or has fallen: *in October came the first thin fall of snow* | *a rock fall.* ■ (usu. **falls**) a waterfall or cascade. ■ *chiefly poetic/literary* a downward turn in a melody: *that strain again, it had a dying fall.* ■ (**falls**) the parts or petals of a flower that bend downward, esp. the outer perianth segments of an iris. **3** a decrease in size, number, rate, or level; a decline: *a big* ***fall in*** *unemployment.* **4** a loss of office: *the fall of the government.* ■ the loss of a city or fortified place during battle: ***the fall of*** *Jerusalem.* ■ a person's moral descent, typically through succumbing to temptation. ■ (**the Fall** or **the Fall of Man**) the lapse of humankind into a state of sin, ascribed in traditional Jewish and Christian theology to the disobedience of Adam and Eve as described in Genesis. **5** (also **Fall**) autumn. ▷Old English *fallan, feallan*, of Germanic origin; the noun is partly from the verb, partly from Old Norse *fall* 'downfall, sin.'

▸*PHRASES* □ **fall foul** (or **afoul**) **of** come into conflict with and be undermined by: *any commitment of resources is likely to fall foul of government cash limitations.* □ **fall in** (or **into**) **line** conform with others or with accepted behavior. [with reference to military formation.] □ **fall into place** (of a series of events or facts) begin to make sense or cohere: *once he knew what to look for, the theory fell quickly into place.* □ **fall on stony ground** see **STONY**. □ **fall over oneself to do something** *informal* be excessively eager to do something: *critics and audiences fell over themselves to compliment him.* □ **fall prey to** see **PREY**. □ **fall short** (**of**) (of a missile) fail to reach its target. ■ *figurative* be deficient or inadequate; fail to reach a required goal: *the total vote fell short of the required two-thirds majority.* □ **fall to pieces** see **FALL APART** below. □ **fall victim to** see **VICTIM**. □ **take the fall** *informal* receive blame or punishment, typically in the place of another person.

fal·la·cy /ˈfaləsē/ ▸*n.* (*pl.* **-cies**) a mistaken belief, esp. one based on unsound argument: *the notion that the camera never lies is a fallacy.* ■ *Logic* a failure in reasoning that renders an argument invalid. ■ faulty reasoning; misleading or unsound argument: *the potential for fallacy which lies behind the notion of self-esteem.* ▷late 15th cent. (in the sense 'deception, guile'; gradually superseding Middle English *fallace*): from Latin *fallacia*, from *fallax, fallac-* 'deceiving,' from *fallere* 'deceive.' —**fal·la·cious** /fəˈlāshəs/ *adj.* —**fal·la·cious·ly** /fəˈlāshəslē/ *adv.* —**fal·la·cious·ness** /fəˈlāshəsnəs/ *n.*

fal·la·cy of com·po·si·tion ▸*n.* the error of assuming that what is true of a member of a group is true for the group as a whole.

fal·la·way /ˈfôləˌwā/ ▸*n.* [usu. as *adj.*] made or done while moving or falling away, esp. (in basketball) from the basket: *he hit a* ***fallaway jumper*** *with five minutes left in the half.*

fall·back /ˈfôlˌbak/ ▸*n.* **1** an alternative plan that may be used in an emergency: *teaching was a last resort, a fallback.* **2** a reduction or retreat: *the offering will hit the market after a fallback from record highs.*

Fall Clas·sic ▸*n.* *Baseball* a nickname for the World Series.

fall·en /ˈfôlən/ ▸ past participle of **FALL**.
▸*adj.* [*attrib.*] **1** *Theology* subject to sin or depravity: *fallen human nature.* ■ *dated* (of a woman) regarded as having lost her honor through engaging in a sexual relationship outside marriage: *a fallen woman with a checkered past.* **2** (of a soldier) killed in battle: *fallen heroes.* —**fall·en·ness** *n.*

fall·en an·gel ▸*n.* (in Christian, Jewish, and Muslim tradition) an angel who rebelled against God and was cast out of heaven.

fall·er /ˈfôlər/ ▸*n.* a person who fells trees for a living.

fall·fish /ˈfôlˌfish/ ▸*n.* (*pl.* same or **-fish·es**) a North American freshwater fish resembling the chub. Also called **CORPORAL**1. • *Semotilus corporalis*, family Cyprinidae.

fall guy ▸*n.* *informal* a scapegoat: *he contends that he is innocent, that he was set up as a fall guy.*

fal·li·bi·lism /ˈfaləbəˌlizəm/ ▸*n.* *Philosophy* the principle that propositions concerning empirical knowledge can be accepted even though they cannot be proved with certainty. —**fal·li·bi·list** *n.* & *adj.*

fal·li·ble /ˈfaləbəl/ ▸*adj.* capable of making mistakes or being erroneous: *experts can be fallible.* ▷late Middle English: from medieval Latin *fallibilis*, from Latin *fallere* 'deceive.' —**fal·li·bil·i·ty** /ˌfaləˈbilətē/ *n.* —**fal·li·bly** /-blē/ *adv.*

fall·ing-out ▸*n.* [in *sing.*] a quarrel or disagreement: *the two of them had a falling-out.*

fall·ing sick·ness ▸*n.* (**the falling sickness**) archaic term for **EPILEPSY**.

fall·ing star ▸*n.* a meteor or shooting star.

fall line ▸*n.* **1** a narrow zone that marks the geological boundary between an upland region and a plain, distinguished by the occurrence of falls and rapids where rivers and streams cross it. ■ (**the Fall Line**) (in the U.S.) the zone demarcating the Piedmont from the Atlantic coastal plain. **2** (**the fall line**) *Skiing* the route leading straight down any particular part of a slope.

fall-off /ˈfôlˌôf/ ▸*n.* [in *sing.*] a decrease in something: *even top schools have seen a* ***falloff in*** *applications.*

fal·lo·pi·an tube /fəˈlōpēən/ (also **Fal·lo·pi·an**) ▸*n.* *Anatomy* (in a female mammal) either of a pair of tubes along which eggs travel from the ovaries to the uterus. ▷early 18th cent.: from *Fallopius*, Latinized form of the name of Gabriello *Fallopio* (1523–62), the Italian anatomist who first described them.

fall·out /ˈfôlˌout/ ▸*n.* radioactive particles that are carried into the atmosphere after a nuclear explosion or accident and gradually fall back as dust or in precipitation. ■ *figurative* the adverse side effects or results of a situation: *almost as dramatic as the financial scale of the mess is the growing political fallout.* ■ [usu. with *adj.*] airborne substances resulting from an industrial process or accident: *acid fallout from power stations.*

fal·low1 /ˈfalō/ ▸*adj.* (of farmland) plowed and harrowed but left unsown for a period in order to restore its fertility as part of a crop rotation or to avoid surplus production: *incentives for farmers to let the land* ***lie fallow*** *in order to reduce grain surpluses.* ■ *figurative* inactive: *long fallow periods when nothing seems to happen.* ■ (of a sow) not pregnant.
▸*n.* a piece of fallow or uncultivated land.
▸*v.* [*trans.*] leave (land) fallow. ▷Old English *fealgian* 'to break up land for sowing,' of Germanic origin; related to Low German *falgen*. —**fal·low·ness** *n.*

fal·low2 ▸*n.* a pale brown or reddish yellow color. ▹Old English *falu, fealu.*

fal·low deer ▸*n.* a Eurasian deer with branched palmate antlers, typically having a white-spotted reddish-brown coat in summer. • *Cervus dama,* family Cervidae.

Fall Riv·er an industrial city in southeastern Massachusetts, a longtime textile center that is also associated with the Lizzie Borden legend; pop. 91,938.

Fal·mouth /ˈfalməTH/ a commercial town in southeastern Massachusetts, southwest of Cape Cod, home to the Woods Hole ocean science complex; pop. 27,960.

false /fôls/ ▸*adj.* **1** not according with truth or fact; incorrect: *the test can produce false results | the allegations were false.* ■ not according with rules or law: *false imprisonment.* **2** appearing to be the thing denoted; deliberately made or meant to deceive: *check to see if the trunk has a false bottom | a false passport.* ■ artificial: *false eyelashes.* ■ feigned: *a horribly false smile.* **3** illusory; not actually so: *sunscreens give users a false sense of security.* ■ [*attrib.*] used in names of plants, animals, and gems that superficially resemble the thing properly so called, e.g., **false oat, false killer whale. 4** treacherous; unfaithful: *a false lover.* ▹Old English *fals* 'fraud, deceit,' from Latin *falsum* 'fraud,' neuter past participle of *fallere* 'deceive'; reinforced or re-formed in Middle English from Old French *fals, faus* 'false.' **—false·ly** *adv.* **—false·ness** *n.* **—fal·si·ty** /ˈfôlsətē/ *n.*

▸*PHRASES* □ **false position** a situation in which one is compelled to act in a manner inconsistent with one's true nature or principles. □ **play someone false** deceive or cheat someone.

false a·ca·cia ▸*n.* a tree of the same family as the true acacias (Leguminosae), but of a different genus (*Robinia*), in particular the black locust of North America.

false a·larm ▸*n.* a false report of a fire to a fire department. ■ a warning given about something that fails to happen.

false bed·ding ▸*n. Geology* another term for CROSS-BEDDING.

false beech·drops ▸*n.* see PINESAP.

false card *Bridge* ▸*n.* a card played in order to give one's opponents a misleading impression of one's strength in the suit led.

▸*v.* **(false-card)** [*trans.*] play (a card) in such a way.

false col·or ▸*n.* color added during the processing of a photographic or computer image to aid interpretation of the subject.

false cor·al snake ▸*n.* a harmless snake that mimics the bright coloration of the venomous coral snakes. • Several genera in the family Colubridae, in particular *Simophis* and *Pliocercus* of South America.

false cy·press ▸*n.* a conifer of a genus that includes Lawson cypress (see PORT ORFORD CEDAR). • Genus *Chamaecyparis,* family Cupressaceae.

false dawn ▸*n.* a transient light that precedes the rising of the sun by about an hour. ■ *figurative* a promising sign that comes to nothing.

false face ▸*n.* a mask, usually wooden, traditionally worn ceremonially by some North American Indian peoples to cure the sick.

false friend ▸*n.* a word or expression that has a similar form to one in a person's native language, but a different meaning (for example English *magazine* and French *magasin* 'shop'). ▹translating French *faux ami.*

false fruit ▸*n.* a fruit formed from other parts of the plant as well as the ovary, esp. the receptacle, as occurs in the strawberry or fig. Also called PSEUDOCARP.

false gha·ri·al /ˈgerēəl/ ▸*n.* a rare, narrow-snouted crocodile that resembles the gharial, native to Indonesia and Malaysia. • *Tomistoma schlegelii,* family Crocodylidae.

false hel·le·bore /ˈheləˌbôr/ ▸*n.* a herbaceous plant of the lily family, with pleated leaves and a tall spike of densely packed yellow-green flowers, found in damp soils in north temperate regions. Also called INDIAN POKE. • Genus *Veratrum,* family Liliaceae: several species, in particular *V. viride* of North America.

false·hood /ˈfôlsˌho͝od/ ▸*n.* the state of being untrue: *the truth or falsehood of the many legends that surround her.* ■ a lie. See note at FICTION. ■ lying: *the right to sue for malicious falsehood.*

false mem·o·ry ▸*n. Psychology* an apparent recollection of an event that did not actually occur, esp. one of childhood sexual abuse arising from suggestion during psychotherapy: [as *adj.*] *false memory syndrome.*

false move ▸*n.* an unwise or careless action that could have dangerous consequences: *one false move would lead to nuclear war.*

false ox·lip ▸*n.* see OXLIP.

false preg·nan·cy ▸*n. Medicine* an abnormal condition in which signs of pregnancy such as amenorrhea, nausea, and abdominal swelling are present in a woman who is not pregnant.

false pre·tens·es ▸*plural n.* behavior intended to deceive others: *he obtained money by false pretenses.*

false rib ▸*n.* another term for FLOATING RIB.

false scor·pi·on ▸*n.* another term for PSEUDOSCORPION.

false start ▸*n.* an invalid or disallowed start to a race, usually due to a competitor beginning before the official signal has been given. ■ an unsuccessful attempt to begin something.

false step ▸*n.* [usu. in *sing.*] a slip or stumble: *one false step and we would have fallen in the sea.* ■ a careless or unwise act; a mistake.

false sun·bird ▸*n.* a small asity of Madagascar that resembles a sunbird. • Genus *Neodrepanis,* family Philepittidae: two species.

false teeth ▸*plural n.* another term for DENTURES (see DENTURE).

false to·paz ▸*n.* another term for CITRINE.

fal·set·to /fôlˈsetō/ ▸*n.* (*pl.* **-tos**) *Music* a method of voice production used by male singers, esp. tenors, to sing notes higher than their normal range: *he sang in a piercing falsetto | he was singing falsetto in this role.* ■ a singer using this method. ■ a voice or sound that is unusually or unnaturally high. ▹late 18th cent.: from Italian, diminutive of *falso* 'false,' from Latin *falsus* (see FALSE).

false vam·pire ▸*n.* a large carnivorous bat that preys on rodents, reptiles, and other small vertebrates. • an Old World bat (three species in the family Megadermatidae, including the large Australian ghost bat, *Macroderma gigas*). • a tropical New World bat (*Vampyrum spectrum,* family Phyllostomidae).

false·work /ˈfôlsˌwərk/ ▸*n.* temporary framework structures used to support a building during its construction.

fals·ies /ˈfôlsēz/ ▸*plural n. informal* pads of material in women's clothing used to increase the apparent size of the breasts.

fal·si·fy /ˈfôlsəˌfī/ ▸*v.* (**-fies, -fied**) [*trans.*] **1** alter (information or evidence) so as to mislead. ■ forge or alter (a document) fraudulently: [as *adj.*] **(falsified)** *falsified documents.* **2** prove (a statement or theory) to be false: *the hypothesis is falsified by the evidence.* ■ fail to fulfill (a hope, fear, or expectation); remove the justification for: *changes falsify individual expectations.* ▹late Middle English (sense 2): from French *falsifier,* from medieval Latin *falsificare,* from Latin *falsificus* 'making false,' from *falsus* 'false.' **—fal·si·fi·a·bil·i·ty** /ˌfôlsəˌfīəˈbilətē/ *n.* **—fal·si·fi·a·ble** /ˌfôlsəˈfīəbəl/ *adj.* **—fal·si·fi·ca·tion** /ˌfôlsəfəˈkāSHən/ *n.*

Fal·staff·i·an /fôlˈstafēən/ ▸*adj.* of or resembling Shakespeare's character Sir John Falstaff in being fat, jolly, and debauched: *a Falstaffian gusto for life.*

fal·ter /ˈfôltər/ ▸*v.* [*intrans.*] start to lose strength or momentum: *her smile faltered and then faded* | [as *adj.*] **(faltering)** *his faltering career.* ■ speak in a hesitant or unsteady voice: [with *direct speech*] *"I c-c-can't," he faltered.* ■ move unsteadily or in a way that shows lack of confidence: *he faltered and finally stopped in midstride.* ▹late Middle English (in the senses 'stammer' and 'stagger'). **—fal·ter·er** *n.* **—fal·ter·ing·ly** *adv.*

Fa·lun Gong /ˈfälo͞on ˈgo͝oNG; ˈgäNG/ (also **Fa·lun Da·fa** /ˈfälo͞on ˈdäfä/) *n.* a spiritual exercise and meditation regime with similarities to t'ai chi ch'uan, practiced predominantly in China. ■ a Taoist-Buddhist sect practicing Falun Gong. ▹1990s: Chinese, literally 'wheel of law,' from *fǎ* 'law' + *lún* 'wheel' (+ *gōng* 'skill' or *dà fǎ* 'great method').

Fal·well /ˈfôlˌwel/, Jerry L. (1933–), U.S. Baptist clergyman. He was the founder and president of the Moral Majority conservative political action group 1979–89.

FAM ▸*abbr.* the Family Channel.

fam. ▸*abbr.* ■ familiar. ■ family.

fame /fām/ ▸*n.* **1** the condition of being known or talked about by many people, esp. on account of notable achievements: *winning the Olympic title has brought her* ***fame and fortune.*** **2** *archaic* reputation. **3** *archaic* public report; rumor. ▹Middle English (also in the sense 'reputation,' which survives in the phrase *house of ill fame*): via Old French from Latin *fama.*

▸*PHRASES* □ **fifteen minutes of fame** see FIFTEEN. □ **of —— fame** having a particular famous association; famous for having or being ——: *the Cariboo country of gold rush fame.*

famed /fāmd/ ▸*adj.* known about by many people; renowned: *he is* ***famed for*** *his eccentricities.* ■ *archaic* widely reported or rumored. ▹Middle English: past participle of archaic *fame* (verb), from Old French *famer,* from Latin *fama.*

fa·mil·ia /fəˈmilyə; -ˈmilēə/ ▸*n.* (*pl.* **-mil·i·ae** /-ˈmilēˌē; -ēˌī/) *historical* a household or religious community under one head, regarded as a unit. ▹early 18th cent.: Latin, literally 'family, household.'

fa·mil·ial /fəˈmilēəl; -ˈmilyəl/ ▸*adj.* of, relating to, or occurring in a family or its members: *the familial Christmas dinner.* ▹early 20th cent.: from French, from Latin *familia* 'family.'

fa·mil·iar /fəˈmilyər/ ▸*adj.* **1** well known from long or close association: *their faces will be* ***familiar to*** *many of you | a familiar voice.* ■ often encountered or experienced; common: *the situation was all too familiar.* ■ [*predic.*] **(familiar with)** having a good knowledge of: *ensure that you are familiar with the heating controls.* **2** in close friendship; intimate: *she had not realized they were on such familiar terms.* ■ informal to an inappropriate degree.

▸*n.* **1** (also **familiar spirit**) a demon supposedly attending and obeying a witch, often said to assume the form of an animal. **2** (in the Roman Catholic Church) a person rendering certain services in a pope's or bishop's household. **3** a close friend or associate. ▹Middle English (in the sense 'intimate,' 'on a family footing'): from Old French *familier,* from Latin *familiaris,* from *familia* 'household servants, household, family,' from *famulus* 'servant.' **—fa·mil·iar·ly** *adv.*

fa·mil·iar·i·ty /fəˌmilēˈaritē; -milˈyar-/ ▸*n.* (*pl.* **-ties**) close acquaintance with or knowledge of something: *increase customer* ***familiarity with*** *a product.* ■ the quality of being well known; recognizability based on long or close association: *the reassuring familiarity of his parents' home.* ■ relaxed friendliness or intimacy between people: *familiarity allows us to give each other nicknames.* ■ inappropriate and often offensive informality of behavior or language: *the unnecessary familiarity made me dislike him at once.* ▹Middle English (in the senses 'close relationship' and 'sexual intimacy'): via Old French from Latin *familiaritas,* from *familiaris* 'familiar, intimate' (see FAMILIAR).

▸*PHRASE* □ **familiarity breeds contempt** *proverb* extensive knowledge of or close association with someone or something leads to a loss of respect for them or it.

fa·mil·iar·ize /fəˈmilyəˌrīz/ ▸*v.* [*trans.*] give (someone) knowledge or understanding of something: *to* ***familiarize*** *pupils* ***with*** *the microscope and its uses.* ■ make (something) better known or more easily grasped: *exercises which will help to familiarize the terms used.* **—fa·mil·iar·i·za·tion** /fəˌmilyərəˈzāSHən/ *n.*

Fam·i·list /ˈfaməlist/ ▸*n.* a member of the Christian sect of the 16th and 17th centuries called the Family of Love, which asserted the importance of love and the necessity for absolute obedience to any government.

fam·i·list /ˈfaməlist/ ▸*adj.* of, relating to, or advocating a social framework centered on family relationships rather than on the needs of the individual. **—fam·i·lism** /-izəm/ *n.* **—fam·i·lis·tic** /ˌfaməˈlistik/ *adj.*

fa·mille /fäˈmē(ə)/ ▸*n.* Chinese enameled porcelain of particular periods in the 17th and 18th centuries with a predominant color, **famille jaune** (yellow), **famille noire** (black), **famille rose** (red), **famille verte** (green). ▹late 19th cent.: French, literally 'family.'

fam·i·ly /ˈfam(ə)lē/ ▸*n.* (*pl.* **-lies**) **1** [treated as *sing.* or *pl.*] a group consisting of parents and children living together in a household. ■ a group of people related to one another by blood or marriage: *friends and family can provide support.* ■ the children of a person or couple: *she has the sole responsibility for a large family.* ■ a person or people related to one and so to be treated with a special loyalty or intimacy: *I could not turn him away, for he was family.* ■ a group of people united in criminal activity. ■ *Biology* a principal taxonomic category that ranks above genus and below order, usually ending in *-idae* (in zoology) or *-aceae* (in botany). ■ a group of objects united by a significant shared characteristic. ■ *Mathematics* a group of

curves or surfaces obtained by varying the value of a constant in the equation generating them. **2** all the descendants of a common ancestor: *the house has been owned by the same family for 300 years.* ■ a race or group of peoples from a common stock. ■ all the languages ultimately derived from a particular early language, regarded as a group: *the Austronesian language family.*
▸*adj.* [*attrib.*] designed to be suitable for children as well as adults: *a family newspaper.* ▷late Middle English (sense 2; also denoting the servants of a household or the retinue of a nobleman): from Latin *familia* 'household servants, household, family,' from *famulus* 'servant.'
▸*PHRASES* □ **the** (or **one's**) **family jewels** *informal* a man's genitals. □ **in the family way** *informal* pregnant.

fam·i·ly Bi·ble ▸*n.* a Bible designed to be used at family prayers, typically one with space on its flyleaves for recording important family events.

fam·i·ly court ▸*n. Law* a court of law that handles cases involving domestic issues such as divorce, child custody, etc.

fam·i·ly hour ▸*n.* a period in the evening during which many children and their families watch television, esp. 8 to 9 p.m.: *the rise in the amount of sex and profanity, as well as violence, in the family hour does American families a disservice.*

fam·i·ly leave ▸*n.* an excused absence from work for the purpose of dealing with family matters, esp. the birth or adoption of a child or to care for a sick parent or spouse.

fam·i·ly man ▸*n.* a man who lives with his wife and children, esp. one who enjoys home life.

fam·i·ly med·i·cine ▸*n.* the branch of medicine designed to provide basic health care to all the members of a family.

fam·i·ly name ▸*n.* a surname. ■ a first or middle name that is frequently given in a family. ■ a family's good reputation: *he won't disgrace the family name.*

fam·i·ly plan·ning ▸*n.* [often as *adj.*] the practice of controlling the number of children in a family and the intervals between their births, particularly by means of artificial contraception or voluntary sterilization: *family-planning clinics.* ■ artificial contraception.

fam·i·ly style ▸*adj.* **1** designating a style of preparation or serving of food in which diners help themselves from plates of food that have been put on the table: *a family-style Italian restaurant.* **2** suitable for an entire family, including children: *family-style entertainment.*
▸*adv.* with plates of food from which individual diners can serve themselves: *spaghetti served in a huge bowl, family style.*

fam·i·ly tree ▸*n.* a diagram showing the relationships between people in several generations of a family; a genealogical tree. ■ all of the descendants and ancestors in a family: *award winners thanked their entire family tree.*

fam·i·ly val·ues ▸*plural n.* values held to be traditionally learned or reinforced within a family, such as those of high moral standards and discipline.

fam·ine /ˈfamən/ ▸*n.* extreme scarcity of food: *drought could result in famine throughout the region | the famine of 1921–22.* ■ a shortage: *the cotton famine of the 1860s.* ■ *archaic* hunger. ▷late Middle English: from Old French, from *faim* 'hunger,' from Latin *fames.*

fam·ished /ˈfamisʜt/ ▸*adj. informal* extremely hungry. ▷late Middle English: past participle of the verb *famish,* from Middle English *fame* 'starve,' from Old French *afamer,* based on Latin *fames* 'hunger.'

fa·mous /ˈfāməs/ ▸*adj.* known about by many people: *the country is* **famous for** *its natural beauty | a famous star.* ▷late Middle English: from Old French *fameus,* from Latin *famosus* 'famed,' from *fama* (see **FAME**). **—fa·mous·ness** *n.*
▸*PHRASES* □ **famous for being famous** having no recognizable or distinct reason for one's fame other than high media exposure. □ **famous last words** said as an ironic comment on or reply to an overconfident assertion that may well be proved wrong by events: *"I'll be perfectly OK on my own." "Famous last words," she thought to herself.*

fa·mous·ly /ˈfāməslē/ ▸*adv.* **1** *informal* excellently: *he wasn't difficult at all—we* **got on famously.** **2** indicating that the fact asserted is widely known: *they have famously reclusive lifestyles.*

fam·u·lus /ˈfamyələs/ ▸*n.* (*pl.* **-li** /-ˌlē; -ˌlī/) *historical* an assistant or servant, esp. one working for a magician or scholar. ▷mid 19th cent.: from Latin, 'servant.'

Fan /fan; fän/ ▸*n.* & *adj.* variant spelling of **FANG.**

fan[1] /fan/ ▸*n.* **1** an apparatus with rotating blades that creates a current of air for cooling or ventilation. **2** a device, typically folding and shaped like a segment of a circle when spread out, that is held in the hand and waved so as to cool the person holding it by causing the air to move. ■ a thing or shape resembling such a device when open. ■ an alluvial or talus deposit spread out in such a shape at the foot of a slope. ■ a small sail for keeping the head of a windmill toward the wind. **3** a device for winnowing grain.

fan[1] 2

▸*v.* (**fanned, fan·ning**) **1** [*trans.*] cool (esp. a person or a part of the body) by waving something to create a current of air: *he fanned himself with his hat.* ■ (of breath or a breeze) blow gently on: *his breath fanned her skin as he leaned toward her.* ■ [*trans.*] brush or drive away with a waving movement: *a veil of smoke which she* **fanned away** *with a jeweled hand.* ■ [*intrans.*] *Baseball & Ice Hockey* swing at and miss the ball or puck. ■ [*intrans.*] *Baseball* (of a batter) strike out. ■ *Baseball* (of a pitcher) strike out (a batter). **2** [*trans.*] increase the strength of (a fire) by blowing on it or stirring up the air near it: *gusty wind fanned fires in Yellowstone Park.* ■ cause (a belief or emotion) to become stronger or more widespread: *long-range weather forecasts fanned fears of drought damage.* **3** [*intrans.*] disperse or radiate from a central point to cover a wide area: *the arriving passengers began to* **fan out** *through the town in search of lodgings.* ■ spread out or cause to spread out into a semicircular shape: [*intrans.*] *a dress made of tiny pleats that* **fanned out** *as she walked* | [*trans.*] *a wind* **fanned** *her hair* **out** *behind her.* ▷Old English *fann* (as a noun denoting a device for winnowing grain), *fannian* (verb), from Latin *vannus* 'winnowing fan.' Compare with **VANE.** **—fan·like** /-ˌlīk/ *adj.* **—fan·ner** *n.*

fan[2] ▸*n.* a person who has a strong interest in or admiration for a particular sport, art form, or famous person: *football fans | I'm a fan of this author.* ▷late 19th cent. (originally U.S.): abbreviation of **FANATIC.** **—fan·dom** /ˈfandəm/ *n.*

fa·nat·ic /fəˈnatik/ ▸*n.* a person filled with excessive and single-minded zeal, esp. for an extreme religious or political cause. See note at **ZEALOT.** ■ [often with *adj.*] *informal* a person with an obsessive interest in and enthusiasm for something, esp. an activity: *a fitness fanatic.*
▸*adj.* [*attrib.*] filled with or expressing excessive zeal: *his fanatic energy.* ▷mid 16th cent. (as an adjective): from French *fanatique* or Latin *fanaticus* 'of a temple, inspired by a god,' from *fanum* 'temple.' The adjective originally described behavior or speech that might result from possession by a god or demon, hence the earliest sense of the noun 'a religious maniac' (mid 17th cent.). **—fa·nat·i·cism** /fəˈnatəˌsizəm/ *n.* **—fa·nat·i·cize** /fəˈnatəˌsīz/ *v.*

fa·nat·i·cal /fəˈnatikəl/ ▸*adj.* filled with excessive and single-minded zeal: *fanatical revolutionaries.* ■ obsessively concerned with something: *he was* **fanatical about** *security at night.* **—fa·nat·i·cal·ly** /-(ə)lē/ *adv.*

fan base ▸*n.* the fans of a sports team, pop music group, etc., considered as a distinct social grouping.

fan belt ▸*n.* (in a motor-vehicle engine) a belt that transmits motion from the driveshaft to the radiator fan and the generator or alternator.

fan·boy /ˈfanˌboi/ ▸*n. informal, derogatory* an obsessive male fan (usually of movies, comic books, or science fiction).: from **FAN**[2] + **BOY.**

fan·ci·er /ˈfansēər/ ▸*n.* [with *adj.*] a connoisseur or enthusiast of something, esp. someone who has a special interest in or breeds a particular animal: *a pigeon fancier.*

fan·ci·ful /ˈfansəfəl/ ▸*adj.* (of a person or their thoughts and ideas) overimaginative and unrealistic: *a fanciful story about a pot of gold.* ■ existing only in the imagination or fancy: *the Moon Maiden is one of a number of fanciful lunar inhabitants.* ■ designed to be exotically ornamental rather than practical: *fanciful bonnets.* **—fan·ci·ful·ly** /-f(ə)lē/ *adv.* **—fan·ci·ful·ness** *n.*

fan club ▸*n.* an organized group of fans of a famous person.

fan·cy /ˈfansē/ ▸*adj.* (**-ci·er, -ci·est**) **1** elaborate in structure or decoration: *the furniture was very fancy | a fancy computerized system.* ■ designed to impress: *converted fishing boats with fancy new names.* ■ (esp. of foodstuffs) of high quality: *fancy molasses.* ■ (of flowers) of two or more colors. ■ (of an animal) bred to develop particular points of appearance: *fancy goldfish.* **2** *archaic* (of a drawing, painting, or sculpture) created from the imagination rather than from life.
▸*v.* (**-cies, -cied**) [*trans.*] **1** feel a desire or liking for: *do you fancy a drink?* ■ find sexually attractive: *he saw a woman he fancied.* ■ (**fancy oneself**) *informal* have an unduly high opinion of oneself, or of one's ability in a particular area: *he fancied himself an amateur psychologist.* **2** [with *clause*] imagine; think: *he fancied he could smell the perfume of roses.* ■ [in *imperative*] used to express one's surprise at something: *fancy meeting all those television actors!*
▸*n.* (*pl.* **-cies**) **1** a feeling of liking or attraction, typically one that is superficial or transient: *this does not mean that the law should change with every* **passing fancy.** **2** the faculty of imagination: *my research assistant is prone to* **flights of fancy.** ■ a thing that one supposes or imagines, typically an unfounded or tentative belief or idea; notion or whim: *scientific fads and fancies.* **3** (in sixteenth and seventeenth cent. music) a composition for keyboard or strings in free or variation form. ▷late Middle English: contraction of **FANTASY.** **—fan·ci·ly** /ˈfansəlē/ *adv.* **—fan·ci·ness** *n.*
▸*PHRASES* □ **as** (or **when** or **where**) **the fancy takes one** according to one's inclination: *I shall go where the fancy takes me.* □ **take** (or **catch**) **someone's fancy** appeal to someone: *she'll grab any toy that takes her fancy.* □ **take a fancy to** become fond of, esp. without an obvious reason.

fan·cy dress ▸*n.* an unusual or amusing costume worn to make someone look like a famous person, fictional character, or an animal, esp. as part of a theme at a party.

fan·cy-free ▸*adj.* free from emotional involvement or commitment to anyone: *her recent divorce meant that she was* **footloose and fancy-free.**

fan·cy goods ▸*plural n. dated* items for sale that are purely or chiefly ornamental.

fan·cy man ▸*n. dated* a woman's lover. ■ *archaic* a pimp.

fan·cy wom·an ▸*n. dated* a married man's mistress. ■ a prostitute.

fan·cy·work /ˈfansēˌwərk/ (also **fan·cy-work**) ▸*n.* ornamental needlework, crochet, or knitting, as opposed to plain or purely functional stitches.

fan dance ▸*n.* a dance in which the female performer is apparently nude and remains partly concealed throughout by large fans.

fan·dan·go /fanˈdaɴɢgō/ ▸*n.* (*pl.* **-goes** or **-gos**) **1** a lively Spanish dance for two people, typically accompanied by castanets or tambourine. **2** a foolish or useless act or thing: *the Washington inaugural fandango.* ▷mid 18th cent.: Spanish, of unknown origin.

fane /fān/ ▸*n. archaic* a temple or shrine. ▷late Middle English: from Latin *fanum.*

Fan·euil /ˈfanyəl; ˈfanl/, Peter (1700–43), U.S. merchant. He donated the building known as Faneuil Hall to the city of Boston in 1742.

fan·fare /ˈfanˌfer/ ▸*n.* a short ceremonial tune or flourish played on brass instruments, typically to introduce something or someone important. ■ *figurative* an ostentatious or noisy display: *he turned 25 on Saturday with little fanfare.* ▷mid 18th cent.: from French, ultimately of imitative origin.

fan·fa·ron·ade /ˌfanˌfarəˈnād/ ▸*n.* arrogant or boastful talk. ▷mid 17th cent.: from French *fanfaronnade,* from *fanfaron* 'braggart,' from *fanfare* (see **FANFARE**).

fan·fic /ˈfanˌfik/ (also **Fan·Fic**) ▸*n.* another term for **FAN FICTION.** ▷blend.

fan fic·tion ▸*n.* a genre of imaginative amateur writing that uses characters and events from mass entertainment or popular culture: *fan fiction developed within a decade of the debut of* Star Trek.

Fang /faɴɢ; fäɴɢ/ (also **Fan** /fan; fän/) ▸*n.* (*pl.* same or **Fangs**) **1** a member of a people inhabiting parts of Cameroon, Equatorial Guinea, and Gabon. **2** the Bantu language of this people.
▸*adj.* of or relating to this people or their language. ▷French, probably from Fang *Pangwe.*

fang /faNG/ ▸*n.* a large, sharp tooth, esp. a canine tooth of a dog or wolf. ■ the tooth of a venomous snake, by which poison is injected. ■ the biting mouthpart of a spider. ▷late Old English (denoting booty or spoils), from Old Norse *fang* 'capture, grasp'; compare with **VANG**. A sense 'trap, snare' is recorded from the mid 16th cent.; both this and the original sense survive in Scots. The current sense (also mid 16th cent.) reflects the same notion of 'something that catches and holds.' **—fanged** *adj.* [also in *combination*] **—fang·less** *adj.*

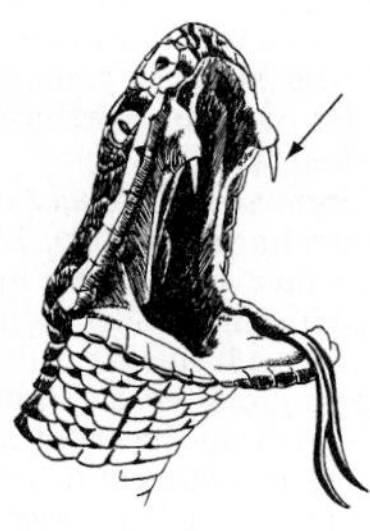
fang

fan·girl /ˈfan,gərl/ ▸*n. informal, derogatory* an obsessive female fan (usually of movies, comic books, or science fiction).: from **FAN**[2] + **GIRL**.

fan·go /ˈfaNGō/ ▸*n.* [usu. as *adj.*] mud from thermal springs in Italy, used in curative treatment at spas and health clubs: *fango therapies.* ▷early 20th cent.: Italian, literally 'mud.'

fan-in ▸*n. Electronics* the number of inputs that can be connected to a circuit.

fan·jet /ˈfan,jet/ ▸*n.* another term for **TURBOFAN**.

fan·light /ˈfan,līt/ ▸*n.* a small semicircular or rectangular window over a door or another window.

fanlight

fan mail ▸*n.* letters from fans to a famous person they admire.

Fan·nie Mae /ˈfanē ˈmā/ ▸*n. informal* the Federal National Mortgage Association, a corporation (now privately owned) that trades in mortgages. ▷1940s: elaboration of the acronym FNMA, suggested by the given names *Fanny* and *Mae*.

fan·ny /ˈfanē/ ▸*n.* (*pl.* **-nies**) **1** *informal* a person's buttocks. **2** *Brit., vulgar slang* a woman's genitals. ▷late 19th cent.: of unknown origin.

fan·ny pack ▸*n.* a small pouch on a belt, for money and small articles, worn around the waist or hips.

fan-out ▸*n. Electronics* the number of inputs that can be connected to a specified output.

fan palm ▸*n.* a palm with large, lobed, fan-shaped leaves. • *Chamaerops* and other genera, family Palmae: many species, including the **dwarf** (or **European**) **fan palm** (*C. humilis*), which is the only palm native to Europe.

fan·tab·u·lous /fanˈtabyələs/ ▸*adj. informal* excellent; wonderful: *a fantabulous prize.* ▷1950s: blend of **FANTASTIC** and **FABULOUS**.

fan·tail /ˈfan,tāl/ ▸*n.* a fan-shaped tail or end. ■ the rounded overhanging part of the stern of a vessel, esp. a warship. ■ (also **fantail pigeon**) a domestic pigeon of a broad-tailed variety. ■ the fan of a windmill. **—fan-tailed** *adj.*

fan-tan ▸*n.* **1** a Chinese gambling game in which players try to guess the remainder after the banker has divided a number of hidden objects into four groups. **2** a card game in which players build on sequences of sevens. ▷late 19th cent.: from Chinese *fān tān*, literally 'repeated divisions.'

fan·ta·sia /fanˈtāzHə; fantəˈzēə/ ▸*n.* a musical composition with a free form and often an improvisatory style. ■ a musical composition that is based on several familiar tunes. ■ a thing that is composed of a mixture of different forms or styles: *the theater is a kind of Moorish and Egyptian fantasia.* ▷early 18th cent.: from Italian, 'fantasy,' from Latin *phantasia* (see **FANTASY**).

fan·ta·size /ˈfantə,sīz/ ▸*v.* [*intrans.*] indulge in daydreaming about something desired: *he sometimes fantasized about emigrating.* ■ [*trans.*] imagine (something that one wants to happen): *they sometimes fantasize the destruction of the world.* **—fan·ta·sist** /-sist/ *n.*

fan·tast /ˈfan,tast/ (also **phan·tast**) ▸*n.* an impractical, impulsive person; a dreamer. ▷late 16th cent.: originally via medieval Latin from Greek *phantastēs* 'boaster,' from *phantazein* or *phantazesthai* (see **FANTASTIC**); in modern use from German *Phantast*.

fan·tas·tic /fanˈtastik/ ▸*adj.* **1** imaginative or fanciful; remote from reality: *novels are capable of mixing fantastic and realistic elements.* ■ of extraordinary size or degree: *the prices were fantastic, far higher than elsewhere.* ■ (of a shape or design) bizarre or exotic; seeming more appropriate to a fairy tale than to reality or practical use: *visions of a fantastic, mazelike building.* **2** *informal* extraordinarily good or attractive: *your support has been fantastic.* ▷late Middle English (in the sense 'existing only in the imagination, unreal'): from Old French *fantastique*, via medieval Latin from Greek *phantastikos*, from *phantazein* 'make visible,' *phantazesthai* 'have visions, imagine,' from *phantos* 'visible'. From the 16th to the 19th centuries the Latinized spelling *phantastic* was also used. **—fan·tas·ti·cal** *adj.* (in sense 1). **—fan·tas·ti·cal·i·ty** /,fan,tastəˈkalitē/ *n.* (in sense 1). **—fan·tas·ti·cal·ly** /-(ə)lē/ *adv.*

fan·tas·ti·cate /fanˈtasti,kāt/ ▸*v.* [*trans.*] *rare* make (something) seem fanciful or fantastic: *I do not think I have fantasticated these accounts.* **—fan·tas·ti·ca·tion** /,fan,tastiˈkāSHən/ *n.*

fan·ta·sy /ˈfantəsē/ ▸*n.* (*pl.* **-sies**) **1** the faculty or activity of imagining things, esp. things that are impossible or improbable: *his research had moved into the realm of fantasy.* ■ the product of this faculty or activity: *the scene is clearly fantasy.* ■ a fanciful mental image, typically one on which a person dwells at length or repeatedly and which reflects their conscious or unconscious wishes: *the notion of being independent is a child's ultimate fantasy.* ■ an idea with no basis in reality: *it is a misleading fantasy to suggest that the bill can be implemented.* ■ a genre of imaginative fiction involving magic and adventure, esp. in a setting other than the real world. **2** a musical composition, free in form, typically involving variation on an existing work or the imaginative representation of a situation or story; a fantasia.
▸*v.* (**-sies, -sied**) [*trans.*] *poetic/literary* imagine the occurrence of; fantasize about. ▷late Middle English: from Old French *fantasie*, from Latin *phantasia*, from Greek, 'imagination, appearance,' later 'phantom,' from *phantazein* 'make visible.' From the 16th to the 19th centuries the Latinized spelling *phantasy* was also used.

fan·ta·sy foot·ball ▸*n.* a competition in which participants select imaginary teams from among the players in a league and score points according to the actual performance of their players.

fan·ta·sy·land /ˈfantəsē,land/ ▸*n.* a fantastic place exciting wonder, esp. one with imaginary creatures: *the 30-story Luxor pyramid is a futuristic fantasyland.*

Fan·te /ˈfäntē; ˈfantē/ (also **Fan·ti**) ▸*n.* (*pl.* same or **-tis** /-tēz/) **1** a member of a people of southern Ghana. **2** the dialect of Akan spoken by this people.
▸*adj.* of or relating to this people or their language. ▷the name in Akan.

fan·tod /ˈfan,täd/ ▸*n. informal* a state or attack of uneasiness or unreasonableness: *the mumbo-jumbo gave me the fantods.* ▷mid 19th cent.: of unknown origin.

fan vault ▸*n. Architecture* a type of vault consisting of a set of concave ribs spreading out from a central point like the ribs of an opened umbrella, used esp. in the English Perpendicular style. **—fan vault·ing** *n.*

fan worm ▸*n.* a tube-dwelling marine bristle worm that bears a fanlike crown of filaments that are typically brightly colored and project from the top of the tube, filtering the water for food particles. • Families Sabellidae and Serpulidae, class Polychaeta: numerous species.

fan·zine /ˈfan,zēn; fanˈzēn/ ▸*n.* a magazine, usually produced by amateurs, for fans of a particular performer, group, or form of entertainment. ▷1940s (originally U.S.): blend of **FAN**[2] and **MAGAZINE**.

FAO ▸*abbr.* Food and Agriculture Organization.

FAQ /fak/ ▸*n. Computing* a text file containing a list of questions and answers relating to a particular subject, esp. one giving basic information for users of an Internet newsgroup. ▷1990s: acronym from *frequently asked questions.*

fa·quir ▸*n.* variant spelling of **FAKIR**.

far /fär/ ▸*adv.* (**far·ther** /ˈfärTHər/, **far·thest** /ˈfärTHəst/ or **fur·ther** /ˈfərTHər/, **fur·thest** /ˈfərTHəst/) **1** [often with *adverbial*] at, to, or by a great distance (used to indicate the extent to which one thing is distant from another): *it was not too* **far away** | *the mountains far in the distance glowed in the sun.* **2** over a large expanse of space or time: *he had not traveled far* | *figurative that's the reason why we have come so far and done as well as we have.* **3** by a great deal: *he is able to function far better than usual* | *the reality has fallen* **far short of** *early expectations.*
▸*adj.* [*attrib.*] situated at a great distance in space or time: *the far reaches of the universe.* ■ more distant than another object of the same kind: *he was standing in the far corner.* ■ distant from a point seen as central; extreme: *she was brought up in the far north of Scotland* | *the largest electoral success for the far right since the war.* ▷Old English *feorr*; from an Indo-European root shared by Sanskrit *para* and Greek *pera* 'further.'

▸*PHRASES* □ **as far as** for as great a distance as: *the river stretched away as far as he could see.* ■ for a great enough distance to reach: *I decided to walk as far as the village.* ■ to the extent that: *as far as I am concerned, it is no big deal.* □ **be a far cry from** be very different from: *the hotel's royal suite is a far cry from the poverty of his home country.* □ **by far** by a great amount: *this was by far the largest city in the area.* □ **far and away** by a great amount: *he is far and away the most accomplished player.* □ **far and near** (also **near and far**) everywhere: *they came from far and near to New York City.* □ **far and wide** over a large area: *the high plains where bison roamed far and wide.* □ **far be it from me to** used to express reluctance, esp. to do something that one thinks may be resented: *far be it from me to speculate on his reasons.* □ **far from** very different from being; tending to the opposite of: *conditions were far from satisfactory.* □ **far gone** in a bad or worsening state, esp. so as to be beyond recovery: *a few frames from the original film were too far gone to salvage.* ■ advanced in time: *the legislative session is too far gone for the lengthy hearings needed to pass the bill.* □ **go far 1** achieve a great deal: *he was the bright one, and everyone was sure he would go far.* **2** contribute greatly: *a book that* **goes far toward** *bridging the gap.* **3** be worth or amount to much: *the money would not go far at this year's prices.* □ **go so far as to do something** do something regarded as extreme: *surely they wouldn't go so far as to break in?* □ **go too far** exceed the limits of what is reasonable or acceptable. □ **how far 1** used to ask how great a distance is: *they wanted to know how far he could travel.* **2** to what extent: *he was not sure how far she was committed.* □ **so far 1** to a certain limited extent: *the commitment to free trade goes only so far.* **2** (of a trend that seems likely to continue) up to this time: *we've only had one honest man so far.* □ (**in**) **so far as** to the extent that: *it was a windless storm so far as blizzards go.* □ **so far, so good** progress has been satisfactory up to now: *"How's the job going?" "So far, so good."*

Far. ▸*abbr.* faraday.

far·ad /ˈfarəd; -,ad/ (abbr.: **F**) ▸*n.* the SI unit of electrical capacitance, equal to the capacitance of a capacitor in which one coulomb of charge causes a potential difference of one volt. ▷mid 19th cent.: shortening of **FARADAY**. The term was originally proposed as a unit of electrical charge.

far·a·da·ic /,farəˈdāik/ ▸*adj.* another term for **FARADIC**. ▷late 19th cent.: from the name of M. **FARADAY** + **-IC**.

Far·a·day /ˈfarə,dā/, Michael (1791–1867), English physicist and chemist. He contributed significantly to the study of electromagnetism and discovered the laws of electrolysis.

far·a·day /ˈfarə,dā/ (abbr.: **F**) ▸*n. Chemistry* a unit of electric charge equal to Faraday's constant. ▷early 20th cent.: coined in German from the name of M. **FARADAY**.

Far·a·day cage ▸*n. Physics* a grounded metal screen surrounding a piece of equipment, used to exclude electrostatic influences.

Far·a·day ef·fect ▸*n. Physics* the rotation of the plane of polarization of electromagnetic waves in certain substances in a magnetic field.

Far·a·day's con·stant *Chemistry* the quantity of electric charge carried by one mole of electrons (equal to 96.49 coulombs). Compare with **FARADAY**.

Far·a·day's law 1 *Physics* a law stating that when the magnetic flux linking a circuit changes, an electromotive force is induced in the circuit proportional to the rate of change of the flux linkage. **2** *Chemistry* a law stating that the amount of any substance deposited or liberated during electrolysis is proportional to the quantity of electric charge passed and to the equivalent weight of the substance.

fa·rad·ic /fəˈradik/ (also **far·a·da·ic** /,fe(ə)rəˈdāik; ,far-/) ▸*adj.* produced by or associated with electrical induction.

Far·al·lon Is·lands /ˈfarə,län/ a small, uninhabited

F

island group in the Pacific Ocean, west of San Francisco in California. Also, the **Farallones.**

far·an·dole /ˌfarən'dōl; 'farənˌdōl/ ▸*n. historical* a lively Provençal dance in which the dancers join hands and wind in and out in a chain. ▹mid 19th cent.: French, from modern Provençal *farandoulo.*

far·a·way /'färəˌwā/ ▸*adj.* distant in space or time: *exotic and faraway locations.* ■ seeming remote from the immediate surroundings; dreamy: *she had a strange faraway look in her eyes.*

farce /färs/ ▸*n.* a comic dramatic work using buffoonery and horseplay and typically including crude characterization and ludicrously improbable situations. ■ the genre of such works. ■ an absurd event: *the debate turned into a drunken farce.* ▹early 16th cent.: from French, literally 'stuffing,' from *farcir* 'to stuff,' from Latin *farcire.* An earlier sense of 'forcemeat stuffing' became used metaphorically for comic interludes "stuffed" into the texts of religious plays, whence current usage.

far·ceur /fär'sər/ ▸*n.* a writer of or performer in farces. ■ a joker or comedian. ▹late 17th cent.: French, from obsolete *farcer* 'act in farces.'

far·ci·cal /'färsikəl/ ▸*adj.* of or resembling a farce, esp. because of absurd or ridiculous aspects: *a farcical tangle of events.* **—far·ci·cal·i·ty** /ˌfärsi'kalitē/ *n.* **—far·ci·cal·ly** *adv.*

far·cy /'färsē/ ▸*n.* glanders in horses (or a similar disease in cattle) in which there is inflammation of the lymph vessels, causing nodules (**farcy buds** or **farcy buttons**). ▹late Middle English: from Old French *farcin,* from late Latin *farciminum,* from *farcire* 'to stuff' (because of the appearance of the swollen nodules).

far·del /'färdl/ ▸*n. archaic* a bundle: *a* **fardel of** *stories, personages, emotions.* ▹Middle English: from Old French, diminutive of *fard,* from Arabic *farda* 'piece, pack'.

F

fare /fer/ ▸*n.* **1** the money a passenger on public transportation has to pay. ■ a passenger paying to travel in a vehicle, esp. a taxicab. **2** a range of food, esp. of a particular type: *delicious Provençal fare.* ■ *figurative* performance or entertainment of a particular style: *conventional Hollywood fare.*
▸*v.* [*intrans.*] **1** [with *adverbial*] perform in a specified way in a particular situation or over a particular period of time: *the party fared badly in the spring elections.* ■ *archaic* happen; turn out: *beware that* **it fare** *not with you as with your predecessor.* **2** *archaic* travel: *a young knight* **fares forth.** ▹Old English *fær, faru* 'traveling, a journey or expedition,' *faran* 'to travel,' also 'get on (well or badly'), of Germanic origin; related to Old Norse *ferja* 'ferryboat,' also to **FORD**. Sense 1 of the *noun* stems from an earlier meaning 'a journey for which a price is paid.' Noun sense 2 was originally used with reference to the quality or quantity of food provided, probably from the idea of faring well or badly.

Far East China, Japan, and other countries in eastern Asia. **—Far East·ern** *adj.*

fare-thee-well (also **fare-you-well**) ▸*n.* (in phrase **to a fare-thee-well**) to perfection; thoroughly: *the inn is touristy to a fare-thee-well.*

fare·well /fer'wel/ ▸*exclam.* used to express good wishes on parting: *farewell, Albert!*
▸*n.* an act of parting or of marking someone's departure: *the dinner had been arranged as a farewell.* ■ parting good wishes: *he had come on the pretext of* **bidding** *her* **farewell** | *I bade him a* **fond farewell.** ▹late Middle English: from the imperative of **FARE** + the adverb **WELL**[1].

far·fal·le /fär'fälā; -'falē/ ▸ *n.* small pieces of pasta shaped like bows or butterflies' wings. ▹Italian, plural of *farfalla* 'butterfly.'

far·fel /'färfəl/ ▸*n.* ground noodle dough that when cooked in boiling water forms small pellets, or the pellets so formed, which are used in soups. ▹Yiddish *farfl.*

far-fetched ▸*adj.* (of an explanation or theory) contrived and unconvincing; unlikely. ■ (of a story or idea) implausible, silly, or exaggerated.

far-flung ▸*adj.* distant or remote: *the far-flung corners of the world.* ■ widely distributed: *newsletters provided an important link to a far-flung membership.*

Far·go[1] /'färgō/ the largest city in North Dakota, in the southeastern part of the state, across the Red River of the North from Moorhead in Minnesota; pop. 90,599.

Far·go[2], William, see **WELLS, FARGO & CO.**

Fa·ri·da·bad /fə'rēdəˌbäd; -ˌbad/ an industrial city in northern India, south of Delhi, in the state of Haryana; pop. 614,000.

fa·ri·na /fə'rēnə/ ▸*n.* flour or meal made of cereal grains, nuts, or starchy roots. ■ *archaic* a powdery substance, or a substance in powdered form. ■ *archaic* starch. ▹late Middle English: from Latin, from *far* 'grain.' **—far·i·na·ceous** /ˌfarə'nāsнəs/ *adj.*

far·kle·ber·ry /'färkəlˌberē/ ▸*n.* a shrub or small tree with thick leathery leaves and inedible black berries, native to the southeastern U.S. • *Vaccinium arboreum,* family Ericaceae. ▹mid 18th cent.: probably an alteration of **WHORTLEBERRY.**

farm /färm/ ▸*n.* an area of land and its buildings used for growing crops and rearing animals, typically under the control of one owner or manager. ■ the main dwelling place on such a site; a farmhouse: *a half-timbered farm.* ■ [with *adj.*] a place for breeding a particular type of animal or producing a specified crop: *a fish farm.* ■ [with *adj.*] an establishment at which something is produced or processed: *an energy farm.*
▸*v.* **1** [*intrans.*] make one's living by growing crops or keeping livestock: *he has farmed organically for five years.* ■ [*trans.*] use (land) for growing crops and rearing animals, esp. commercially. ■ [*trans.*] breed or grow commercially (a type of livestock or crop, esp. one not normally domesticated or cultivated). **2** [*trans.*] (**farm someone/something out**) send out or subcontract work to others: *it saves time and money to farm out some writing work to specialized companies.* ■ arrange for a child or other dependent person to be looked after by someone, usually for payment. ■ send a sports player to a farm team. **3** [*trans.*] *historical* allow someone to collect and keep the revenues from (a tax) on payment of a fee: *the customs had been farmed to the collector for a fixed sum.* ▹Middle English: from Old French *ferme,* from medieval Latin *firma* 'fixed payment,' from Latin *firmare* 'fix, settle' (in medieval Latin 'contract for'), from *firmus* 'constant, firm'; compare with **FIRM**[2]. The noun originally denoted a fixed annual amount payable as rent or tax; this is reflected in sense 3 of the verb, which later gave rise to 'to subcontract' (sense 2). The noun came to denote a lease, and, in the early 16th cent., land leased specifically for farming. The verb sense 'grow crops or keep livestock' dates from the early 19th cent. **—farm·a·ble** /'färməbəl/ *adj.*
▸*PHRASE* ▫ **buy the farm** see **BUY.**

Farm Belt the states of the Midwest that are noted particularly for their agricultural production: Iowa, Kansas, Minnesota, Nebraska, North Dakota, and South Dakota.

Far·mer /'färmər/, Fannie Merritt (1857–1915), U.S. educator and author. She opened Miss Farmer's School of Cookery in 1902; her *Boston Cooking School Cook Book* (1896) was known as "the mother of level measurements."

farm·er /'färmər/ ▸*n.* **1** a person who owns or manages a farm. **2** [with *adj.*] *historical* a person to whom the collection of taxes was contracted for a fee. ▹late Middle English: from Old French *fermier,* from medieval Latin *firmarius,* from *firma* (see **FARM**). Sense 1 originally denoted a bailiff or steward who farmed land on the owner's behalf, or a tenant farmer.

farm·er cheese ▸*n.* an unripened cheese that is mild in flavor, firmer than cottage cheese and somewhat crumbly in texture. Also called **farm cheese.**

far·mer's lung ▸*n.* informal term for **ASPERGILLOSIS.**

farm·ers' mar·ket ▸*n.* a food market, often held in a public place outdoors at regular intervals, at which local farmers sell fruit and vegetables, and often meat, cheese, bakery products, and flowers directly to consumers.

farm·hand /'färmˌhand/ ▸*n.* a worker on a farm.

farm·house /'färmˌhous/ ▸*n.* a house attached to a farm, esp. the main house in which the farmer lives.

farm·ing /'färmiɴɢ/ ▸*n.* the activity or business of growing crops and raising livestock.

Farm·ing·ton /'färmiɴɢtən/ a city in northwestern New Mexico; pop. 37,844.

Farm·ing·ton Hills a city in southeastern Michigan, west of Detroit; pop. 82,111.

farm·land /'färmˌland/ ▸*n.* (also **farmlands**) land used for farming.

farm·stead /'färmˌsted/ ▸*n.* a farm and its buildings.

farm team ▸*n. Baseball* a minor league team that provides players as needed to an affiliated major league team.

farm·yard /'färmˌyärd/ ▸*n.* a yard or enclosure attached to a farmhouse.

Farne Is·lands /färn/ a group of 17 small islands off the coast of Northumberland, England, noted for their wildlife.

Far·ne·se /fär'nāzā/, Alessandro, see **PAUL III.**

Farn·ham /'färnəm/, Eliza Wood (1815–64), U.S. reformer and writer. As matron of the women's department of Sing Sing prison in Ossining, New York 1844–48, she instituted major reforms.

far·o /'ferō/ ▸*n.* a gambling card game in which players bet on the order in which the cards will appear. ▹early 18th cent. (originally as *pharaoh* or *pharo*): from French *pharaon* (see **PHARAOH**), said to have been the name of the king of hearts.

Far·oe Is·lands variant spelling of **FAEROE ISLANDS**

Far·o·ese ▸*adj.* & *n.* variant spelling of **FAEROESE.**

far-off ▸*adj.* remote in time or space: *a far-off country.*

fa·ro·li·to /ˌfarə'lētō; ˌfär-/ ▸ another term for **LUMINARIA.**

fa·rouche /fə'ro͞osн/ ▸*adj.* sullen or shy in company. ▹mid 18th cent.: from French, alteration of Old French *forache,* based on Latin *foras* 'out of doors.'

Fa·rouk /fə'ro͝ok/ (1920–65), king of Egypt; reigned 1936–52. His defeat in the Arab–Israeli conflict of 1948, together with the general corruption of his reign, led to a military coup in 1952. Farouk was forced to abdicate in favor of his infant son, Fuad.

far-out ▸*adj.* unconventional or avant-garde: *far-out politics.* ■ [often as *exclam.*] *informal* excellent: *it's really far-out!*

Far·quhar /'färkwər/, George (1678–1707), Irish playwright. He was a principal figure in Restoration comedy. Notable works: *The Recruiting Officer* (1706) and *The Beaux' Stratagem* (1707).

far·ra·go /fə'rägō; -'rā-/ ▸*n.* (*pl.* **-goes**) a confused mixture: *a farrago of fact and myth about Abraham Lincoln.* See note at **JUMBLE.** ▹mid 17th cent.: from Latin, literally 'mixed fodder,' from *far* 'corn.' **—far·rag·i·nous** /fə'rajənəs/ *adj.*

Far·ra·gut /'farəgət/, David Glasgow (1801–70), U.S. navy admiral; born *James Glasgow Farragut.* The outstanding naval commander of the Civil War, he captured the city of New Orleans in April 1862 and extended Union control of the Mississippi River north to Vicksburg.

David Farragut

Far·ra·khan /'farəˌkan; 'färəˌkän/, Louis (1933–), U.S. Nation of Islam leader since 1978 and African-American nationalist; born *Louis Eugene Walcott.* He is known for advocating black separation and black economic power.

far-reach·ing ▸*adj.* having important and widely applicable effects or implications: *a series of far-reaching political reforms.*

Far·rell[1] /'farəl/, J. T. (1904–79), U.S. novelist; full name *James Thomas Farrell.* He is known for his trilogy about Studs Lonigan, which began with *Young Lonigan* (1932) and was followed by *The Young Manhood of Studs Lonigan* (1934) and *Judgment Day* (1935).

Far·rell[2], Suzanne (1945–), U.S. dancer; born *Roberta Sue Fricker.* She performed with the New York City Ballet 1961–69, where she became principal dancer 1965–69. She is noted for her performance in the movie version of *A Midsummer Night's Dream* (1966).

far·ri·er /'farēər/ ▸*n.* a craftsman who trims and shoes horses' hooves. ▹mid 16th cent.: from Old French *ferrier,* from Latin *ferrarius,* from *ferrum* 'iron, horseshoe.' **—far·ri·er·y** *n.*

Far·row /'farō/, Mia (1945–), U.S. actress; daughter of Maureen O'Sullivan. She starred in *Rosemary's Baby* (1968), *The Great Gatsby* (1973), *Hannah and Her Sisters* (1986), and *Husbands and Wives* (1992).

far·row /ˈfarō/ ▸*n.* a litter of pigs. ■ an act of giving birth to a litter of pigs.
▸*v.* [*trans.*] (of a sow) give birth to (piglets): *the pig is one of a litter of nine farrowed in July.* ▷Old English *fearh, færh* 'young pig,' from an Indo-European root shared by Greek *porkos* and Latin *porcus* 'pig.'

far·ru·ca /fəˈrōōkə/ ▸*n.* a type of flamenco dance. ▷1930s: Spanish, feminine of *farruco* 'Galician or Asturian,' from *Farruco*, pet form of the given name *Francisco*.

far-see·ing ▸*adj.* having shrewd judgment and an ability to predict and plan for future eventualities.

Far·si /ˈfärsē/ ▸*n.* the modern Persian language that is the official language of Iran. ▷from Arabic *fārsī*, from *Fārs*, from Persian *Pārs* 'Persia.' Compare with **PARSEE**.

far·sight·ed /ˈfärˌsītid; -ˈsītid/ ▸*adj.* unable to see things clearly, esp. if they are relatively close to the eyes, owing to the focusing of rays of light by the eye at a point behind the retina; hyperopic. ■ seeing or able to see for a great distance. ■ *figurative* having imagination or foresight: *a farsighted businessman.* **—far·sight·ed·ly** *adv.* **—far·sight·ed·ness** *n.*

fart /färt/ *informal* ▸*v.* [*intrans.*] emit gas from the anus. ■ (**fart about/around**) waste time on silly or trivial things.
▸*n.* an emission of gas from the anus. ■ a boring or contemptible person: *he was such an* ***old fart.*** ▷Old English (recorded in the verbal noun *feorting* 'farting').

far·ther /ˈfärT͟Hər/ ▸ used as comparative of **FAR**.
▸*adv.* (also **fur·ther** /ˈfərT͟Hər/) **1** at, to, or by a greater distance (used to indicate the extent to which one thing or person is or becomes distant from another): *the farther away you are from your home, the better you should behave* | *figurative his action pushes Haiti even farther away from democratic rule.* **2** over a greater expanse of space or time; for a longer way: *the stream fills the passage, and only a cave diver can explore farther* | *figurative people were trying to get their food dollars to go farther.*
▸*adj.* more distant in space than another item of the same kind: *the farther side of the mountain.* ■ more remote from a central point: *the farther stretches of the diocese.*

USAGE Traditionally, **farther** and **farthest** were used in referring to physical distance: *the falls were still two or three miles farther up the path.* **Further** and **furthest** were restricted to figurative or abstract senses: *we decided to consider the matter further.* Although **farther** and **farthest** are still restricted to measurable distances, **further** and **furthest** are now common in both senses: *put those plants the furthest from the window.*

far·ther·most /ˈfärT͟Hərˌmōst/ (also **fur·ther·most** /ˈfər-/) ▸*adj.* (of an edge or extreme) at the greatest distance from a central point or implicit standpoint: *the pitch broke sharply over the farthermost part of the strike zone.*

far·thest /ˈfärT͟Hist/ (also **fur·thest** /ˈfər-/) ▸ used as superlative of **FAR**.
▸*adj.* [*attrib.*] situated at the greatest distance from a specified or understood point: *the farthest door led to a kitchen* | *figurative it was the farthest thing from my mind.* ■ covering the greatest area or distance: *his record for the farthest flight.* ■ extremely remote: *the farthest ends of the earth.*
▸*adv.* **1** at or by the greatest distance (used to indicate how far one thing or person is or becomes distant from another): *the bed farthest from the window* | *figurative the people who are furthest removed from the political process.* **2** over the greatest distance or area: *his group probably had farthest to ride* | *figurative the areas where prices have fallen farthest.* ■ used to indicate the most distant point reached in a specified direction: *it was the farthest north I had ever traveled.* ■ to the most extreme or advanced point: *countries where industrialization had gone furthest* | ***the farthest*** *he'll go is to admit a sort of resentment.* ▷late Middle English: formed as a superlative of **FURTHER**.
▸*PHRASE* □ **at the farthest** at the greatest distance; at most: *the Allied line had been pushed forward, at the farthest, about one mile.*

USAGE On the differences between **farthest** and **furthest**, see **usage** at **FARTHER**.

far·thing /ˈfärT͟HiNG/ ▸*n.* a former monetary unit and coin of the UK, withdrawn in 1961, equal to a quarter of an old penny. ■ [usu. with *negative*] the least possible amount: *she didn't care a farthing for the woman.* ▷Old English *fēorthing*, from *fēortha* 'fourth.'

far·thin·gale /ˈfärT͟HiNGˌgāl/ ▸*n. historical* a hooped petticoat or circular pad of fabric around the hips, formerly worn under women's skirts to extend and shape them. ▷early 16th cent. (formerly also as *vardingale*): from French *verdugale*, alteration of Spanish *verdugado*, from *verdugo* 'rod, stick,' from *verde* 'green.'

farthingale

fart·lek /ˈfärtlik/ ▸*n. Track & Field* a system of training for distance runners in which the terrain and pace are continually varied to eliminate boredom and enhance psychological aspects of conditioning. ▷1940s: from Swedish, from *fart* 'speed' + *lek* 'play.'

Far West the region of North America west of the Great Plains.

FAS ▸*abbr.* ■ fetal alcohol syndrome. ■ Foreign Agricultural Service.

f.a.s. ▸*abbr.* free alongside ship.

fasc. ▸*abbr.* fascicle.

fas·ces /ˈfasˌēz/ ▸*plural n. historical* (in ancient Rome) a bundle of rods with a projecting ax blade, carried by a lictor as a symbol of a magistrate's power. ■ (in Fascist Italy) such items used as emblems of authority. ▷Latin, plural of *fascis* 'bundle.'

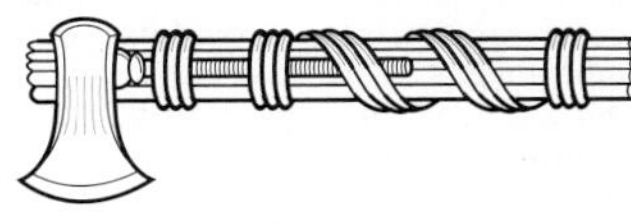

fasces

fas·ci·a /ˈfasH(ē)ə; ˈfā-/ ▸*n.* **1** (*chiefly Brit.* also **fa·ci·a**) a wooden board or other flat piece of material such as that covering the ends of rafters. ■ a covering, typically a detachable one, for the front part of a cellular phone. ■ (in classical architecture) a long flat surface between moldings on an architrave. ■ *chiefly Brit.* the dashboard of a motor vehicle. **2** (*pl.* **fas·ci·ae** /-sHēˌē/) *Anatomy* a thin sheath of fibrous tissue enclosing a muscle or other organ. ▷mid 16th cent.: from Latin, 'band, doorframe,' related to **FASCES**. Compare with **FESS**[1]. **—fas·ci·al** /ˈfasH(ē)əl; fā-/ *adj.* (in sense 2).

fas·ci·at·ed /ˈfasHēˌātəd; ˈfā-/ (also **fas·ci·ate**) ▸*adj.* **1** *Botany* showing abnormal fusion of parts or organs, resulting in a flattened, ribbonlike structure. **2** *Zoology* striped or banded. ▷mid 18th cent. (in the sense 'striped, banded'): from Latin *fasciatus* (past participle of *fasciare* 'swathe,' from *fascia* 'band') + **-ED**[1]. **—fas·ci·a·tion** /ˌfasHēˈāsHən; ˌfā-/ *n.*

fas·ci·cle /ˈfasikəl/ ▸*n.* **1** (also **fas·ci·cule** /-ˌkyōōl/) a separately published installment of a book or other printed work. **2** (also **fas·cic·u·lus** /fəˈsikyələs/) *Anatomy & Biology* a bundle of structures, such as nerve or muscle fibers or conducting vessels in plants. ▷late 15th cent. (sense 2): from Latin *fasciculus*, diminutive of *fascis* 'bundle.' **—fas·ci·cled** *adj.* **—fas·cic·u·lar** /fəˈsikyələr/ *adj.* **—fas·cic·u·late** /fəˈsikyəˌlāt; -yəlit/ *adj.*

fas·cic·u·la·tion /fəˌsikyəˈlāsHən/ ▸*n.* **1** *Medicine* a brief, spontaneous contraction affecting a small number of muscle fibers, often causing a flicker of movement under the skin. It can be a symptom of disease of the motor neurons. **2** *chiefly Biology* arrangement in bundles.

fas·ci·i·tis /ˌfasēˈītəs; ˌfasHē-/ ▸*n. Medicine* inflammation of the fascia of a muscle or organ.

fas·ci·nate /ˈfasəˌnāt/ ▸*v.* [*trans.*] (usu. **be fascinated**) draw irresistibly the attention and interest of (someone): *I've always been fascinated by other cultures* | [*trans.*] *she was fascinated to learn about this strange land.* ■ *archaic* (esp. of a snake) deprive (a person or animal) of the ability to resist or escape by the power of a look or gaze: *the serpent fascinates its prey.* ▷late 16th cent. (in the sense 'bewitch, put under a spell'): from Latin *fascinat-* 'bewitched,' from the verb *fascinare*, from *fascinum* 'spell, witchcraft.' **—fas·ci·na·tion** /ˌfasəˈnāsHən/ *n.* **—fas·ci·na·tor** /-ˌnātər/ *n.*

fas·ci·nat·ing /ˈfasəˌnātiNG/ ▸*adj.* extremely interesting: *fascinating facts.* **—fas·ci·nat·ing·ly** *adv.*

fas·cine /fəˈsēn/ ▸*n.* a bundle of rods, sticks, or plastic pipes bound together, used in construction or military operations for filling in marshy ground or other obstacles and for strengthening the sides of embankments, ditches, or trenches. ▷late 17th cent.: via French from Latin *fascina*, from *fascis* 'bundle.'

fas·ci·o·li·a·sis /fəˌsēəˈlīəsis; fəˌsīə-/ ▸*n. Medicine* infestation of a human or an animal with the liver fluke. ▷late 19th cent.: from modern Latin *Fasciola hepatica*, the name of the liver fluke (from Latin *fasciola* 'small bandage') + **-IASIS**.

fas·cism /ˈfasHˌizəm/ (also **Fas·cism**) ▸*n.* an authoritarian and nationalistic right-wing system of government and social organization. ■ (in general use) extreme right-wing, authoritarian, or intolerant views or practice.

The term Fascism was first used of the totalitarian right-wing nationalist regime of Mussolini in Italy (1922–43), and the regimes of the Nazis in Germany and Franco in Spain were also fascist. Fascism tends to include a belief in the supremacy of one national or ethnic group, a contempt for democracy, an insistence on obedience to a powerful leader, and a strong demagogic approach.

▷from Italian *fascismo*, from *fascio* 'bundle, political group,' from Latin *fascis* (see **FASCES**). **—fas·cist** *n.* & *adj.* **—fa·scis·tic** /faˈsHistik/ *adj.*

fash·ion /ˈfasHən/ ▸*n.* **1** a popular trend, esp. in styles of dress and ornament or manners of behavior: *his hair is cut in the latest fashion.* ■ the production and marketing of new styles of goods, esp. clothing and cosmetics: [as *adj.*] *a fashion magazine.* **2** a manner of doing something: *the work is done in a rather casual fashion.*
▸*v.* [*trans.*] (often **be fashioned**) make into a particular or the required form: *the bottles were* ***fashioned from*** *green glass.* ■ (**fashion something into**) use materials to make into: *the skins were fashioned into boots and shoes.* ▷Middle English (in the sense 'make, shape, appearance,' also 'a particular make or style'): from Old French *façon*, from Latin *factio(n-)*, from *facere* 'do, make.' **—fash·ion·er** *n.*
▸*PHRASES* □ **after a fashion** to a certain extent but imperfectly or unsatisfactorily: *he could read after a fashion.* □ **after** (or **in**) **the fashion of** in a manner similar to: *she took servants for granted after the fashion of wealthy and pampered girls.* □ **in** (or **out of**) **fashion** popular (or unpopular) and considered (or not considered) to be attractive at the time in question.

-fashion ▸*comb. form* in the manner of something specified: *dog-fashion* | *castanet-fashion.* ■ in the style associated with a specified place or people: *American-fashion* | *Bristol-fashion.*

fash·ion·a·ble /ˈfasH(ə)nəbəl/ ▸*adj.* characteristic of, influenced by, or representing a current popular trend or style: *fashionable clothes.* ■ (of a person) dressing or behaving according to the current trend. **—fash·ion·a·bil·i·ty** /ˌfasH(ə)nəˈbilətē/ *n.* **—fash·ion·a·ble·ness** *n.* **—fash·ion·a·bly** /-əblē/ *adv.*

fash·ion·is·ta /ˌfasHəˈnēstə/ ▸*n. informal* **1** a designer of haute couture. **2** a devoted follower of fashion: *sleek designs that press all the fashionistas' buttons.* ▷1990s: from *fashion* + Spanish suffix *-ista*, as in *Sandinista, turista.*

fash·ion plate ▸*n.* a picture showing a fashion, esp. in dress. ■ *figurative* a person who dresses very fashionably.

fash·ion vic·tim ▸*n.* a person who follows popular trends in dress and behavior slavishly.

Fast /fast/, Howard Melvin (1914–2003), U.S. writer. He is best known for his historical novels and as a member of the Communist party 1943–56 who was imprisoned in 1950 for refusing to cooperate with the House Committee on Un-American Activities. His works include *Spartacus* (1951), *The Naked God* (1957), *The Immigrants* (1977), and *The Immigrant's Daughter* (1985).

fast[1] /fast/ ▸*adj.* **1** moving or capable of moving at high speed: *a fast and powerful car.* ■ performed or taking place at high speed; taking only a short time: *the journey was fast and enjoyable.* ■ [*attrib.*] allowing people or things to move at high speed: *a wide, fast road.* ■ performing or able to perform a particular type of action quickly: *a fast reader.* ■ *Sports* (of a playing field) likely to make the ball bounce or run quickly or to allow competitors to reach a high speed. ■ (of a person or lifestyle) engaging in or involving exciting or shocking activities: *the fast life she led in London.* **2** [*predic.* or as *complement*] (of a clock or watch) showing a time ahead of the correct time: *I keep my watch fifteen minutes fast.* **3** firmly fixed or attached: *he* ***made*** *a rope* ***fast*** *to each corner.* ■ (of friends) close and loyal. ■ (of a dye) not fading in light or when washed. **4** *Photography* (of a film) needing only a short exposure. ■ (of a lens) having a large aperture and therefore allowing short exposure times.

▸*adv.* **1** at high speed: *he was driving too fast.* ■ within a short time: *they think they're going to get rich fast.* **2** so as to be hard to move; firmly or securely: *the ship was held fast by the anchor chain.* ■ (of someone or something sleeping) so as to be hard to wake: *they were too fast asleep to reply.* ▷Old English *fæst* 'firmly fixed, steadfast' and *fæste* 'firmly, securely.' In Middle English the adverb developed the senses 'strongly, vigorously' (compare with *run hard*), and 'close, immediate' (just surviving in the archaic and poetic *fast by*; compare with *hard by*), hence 'closely, immediately' and 'quickly'; the idea of rapid movement was then reflected in adjectival use.

▸*PHRASE* □ **pull a fast one** *informal* try to gain an unfair advantage: *Joey* ***pulled a fast one on*** *us.*

fast[2] ▸*v.* [*intrans.*] abstain from all or some kinds of food or drink, esp. as a religious observance.

▸*n.* an act or period of fasting: *a five-day fast.* ▷Old English *fæstan* (verb); related to Old Norse *fasta*, the source of the noun.

fast and fu·ri·ous ▸*adv.* **1** very rapidly: *my heart was beating fast and furious.* **2** eagerly; uproariously.

▸*adj.* full of rapid action; lively and exciting: *the game was fast and furious.*

fast·back /ˈfas(t),bak/ ▸*n.* a car with a roofline that slopes continuously down at the back.

fast·ball /ˈfas(t),bôl/ ▸*n.* a baseball pitch thrown at or near a pitcher's maximum speed. ■ another term for **FAST-PITCH SOFTBALL**.

fast break ▸*n.* a swift attack from a defensive position in basketball, soccer, and other ball games: *a defense that shut off our fast break altogether* [as *adj.*] *there are no fast-break baskets.*

▸*v.* (**fast-break**) [*intrans.*] make such an attack: *fast-breaking relentlessly is harder than playing a control game.*

fast breed·er (also **fast breeder reactor**) ▸*n.* a breeder reactor in which the neutrons causing fission are not slowed by any moderator.

fast buck ▸*n.* see **BUCK**[2].

fas·ten /ˈfasən/ ▸*v.* [*trans.*] close or join securely: *fasten your seat belts.* ■ [*intrans.*] be closed or done up in a particular place or part or in a particular way: *a blue nightie that fastens down the back.* ■ [*trans.*] fix or hold in place: *she fastened her locket around her neck.* ■ (**fasten something on/upon**) direct one's eyes, thoughts, feelings, etc., intently at: *Maggie fastened her eyes on him* | [*intrans.*] *speculation fastened on three candidates.* ■ (**fasten something on/upon**) ascribe responsibility to: *blame hadn't been fastened on anyone.* ■ [*intrans.*] (**fasten on/upon**) single out (someone or something) and concentrate on them or it obsessively: *the critics fastened on two sections of the report.* ▷Old English *fæstnian* 'make sure, confirm,' also 'immobilize'; related to **FAST**[1]. **—fas·ten·er** *n.*

fast·en·ing /ˈfasəniNG/ ▸*n.* a device that closes or secures something: *a front-zip fastening.*

fast food ▸*n.* food that can be prepared quickly and easily and is sold in restaurants and snack bars as a quick meal or to be taken out: [as *adj.*] *a fast-food restaurant.*

fast for·ward ▸*n.* a control on a tape or video player for advancing the tape rapidly: [as *adj.*] *the fast-forward button.* ■ a facility for cueing audio equipment by allowing the tape to be played at high speed and stopped when the desired place is reached.

▸*v.* (**fast-for·ward**) [*trans.*] advance (a tape) rapidly, sometimes while simultaneously playing it at high speed. ■ [*intrans.*] *figurative* move speedily forward in time when considering or dealing with something over a period: *the text fast-forwards to 1990.*

fast ice ▸*n.* ice that extends out from the shore and is attached to it.

fas·tid·i·ous /fasˈtidēəs/ ▸*adj.* very attentive to and concerned about accuracy and detail: *he chooses his words with fastidious care.* ■ very concerned about matters of cleanliness: *the child seemed fastidious about getting her fingers sticky or dirty.* ▷late Middle English: from Latin *fastidiosus*, from *fastidium* 'loathing.' The word originally meant 'disagreeable, distasteful,' later 'disgusted.' Current senses date from the 17th cent. **—fas·tid·i·ous·ly** *adv.* **—fas·tid·i·ous·ness** *n.*

fas·tig·i·ate /fəˈstijēət/ ▸*adj. Botany* (of a tree or shrub) having the branches sloping upward more or less parallel to the main stem. ▷mid 17th cent.: from Latin *fastigium* 'tapering point, gable' + **-ATE**[2].

fast lane ▸*n.* [usu. in *sing.*] a lane of a highway for use by traffic that is moving faster than the rest. ■ a hectic or highly pressured lifestyle: *his face showed the strain of a life lived* ***in the fast lane.***

fast·ness /ˈfas(t)nəs/ ▸*n.* **1** a secure refuge, esp. a place well protected by natural features: *a remote Himalayan mountain fastness.* **2** the ability of a material or dye to maintain its color without fading or washing away: *the dyes differ in their fastness to light.* ▷Old English *fæstnes* (see **FAST**[1], **-NESS**).

fast neu·tron ▸*n.* a neutron with high kinetic energy, esp. one released by nuclear fission and not slowed by any moderator.

fast-pitch soft·ball (also **fast-pitch**) ▸*n.* a variety of the game of softball featuring fast underhand pitching.

fast re·ac·tor ▸*n.* a nuclear reactor in which fission is caused mainly by fast neutrons.

fast-talk ▸*v.* [*trans.*] *informal* pressure (someone) into doing something using rapid or misleading speech: *heroin dealers tried to* ***fast-talk*** *him* ***into*** *a quick sale* | [as *adj.*] (**fast-talking**) *a fast-talking confidence trickster.*

fast track ▸*n.* [in *sing.*] a route, course, or method that provides for more rapid results than usual: *a career in the fast track of the civil service.*

▸*v.* (**fast-track**) [*trans.*] accelerate the development or progress of (a person or project); compare with **SLOW TRACK**: *the old boys' network fast-tracks men to the top of the corporate ladder.*

fast-twitch ▸*adj.* [*attrib.*] *Physiology* (of a muscle fiber) contracting rapidly, thus providing power rather than endurance.

fat /fat/ ▸*n.* a natural oily or greasy substance occurring in animal bodies, esp. when deposited as a layer under the skin or around certain organs. ■ a substance of this type, or a similar one made from plant products, used in cooking. ■ the presence of an excessive amount of such a substance in a person or animal, causing them to appear corpulent: *he was a tall man,* ***running to fat.*** ■ *Chemistry* any of a group of natural esters of glycerol and various fatty acids, which are solid at room temperature and are the main constituents of animal and vegetable fat. Compare with **OIL**. ■ something excessive or unnecessary: *fat in the state budget.*

▸*adj.* (**fat·ter, fat·test**) (of a person or animal) having a large amount of excess flesh: *the driver was a fat, wheezing man.* ■ (of an animal bred for food) made plump for slaughter. ■ containing much fat: *fat bacon.* ■ large in bulk or circumference: *a fat cigarette.* ■ *informal* (of an asset or opportunity) financially substantial or desirable: *a fat profit* | *fat motion picture deals.* ■ *informal* used ironically to express the belief that there is none or very little of something: ***fat chance*** *she had of influencing him* | ***a fat lot*** *of good that'll do him.* ■ (of coal) containing a high proportion of volatile oils. ■ (of wood) containing a high proportion of resin: *fat pine.*

▸*v.* (**fat·ted, fat·ting**) *archaic* make or become fat: [*trans.*] *numbers of black cattle are fatted here* | [*intrans.*] *the hogs have been fatting* | [as *adj.*] (**fatted**) *a fatted duck.* ▷Old English *fætt* 'well fed, plump,' also 'fatty, oily.' **—fat·less** *adj.* **—fat·ly** *adv.* **—fat·ness** *n.* **—fat·tish** *adj.*

▸*PHRASES* □ **the fat is in the fire** something has happened that will surely lead to an unpleasant result or angry reaction. □ **kill the fatted calf** produce one's best food to celebrate, esp. at a prodigal's return. [with biblical allusion to Luke 15.] □ **live off** (or **on**) **the fat of the land** have the best of everything.

Fa·tah, Al /,äl fəˈtä; äl ˈfätə/ a Palestinian political and military organization founded in 1958 by Yasser Arafat and others to bring about the establishment of a Palestinian state. It has dominated the Palestine Liberation Organization since the 1960s, despite challenges from more extreme groups. ▷Arabic, literally 'victory.'

fa·tal /ˈfātl/ ▸*adj.* causing death: *a fatal accident.* ■ leading to failure or disaster: *there were three fatal flaws in the strategy.* ▷late Middle English (in the senses 'destined by fate' and 'ominous'): from Old French, from Latin *fatalis*, from *fatum* (see **FATE**). **—fa·tal·ly** *adv.*

fa·tal·ism /ˈfātl,izəm/ ▸*n.* the belief that all events are predetermined and therefore inevitable. ■ a submissive attitude to events, resulting from such a belief. **—fa·tal·ist** *n.* **—fa·tal·is·tic** /,fātlˈistik/ *adj.* **—fa·tal·is·ti·cal·ly** /,fātlˈistik(ə)lē/ *adv.*

fa·tal·i·ty /fāˈtalətē; fə-/ ▸*n.* (*pl.* **-ties**) **1** an occurrence of death by accident, in war, or from disease: *shooting was heard and there were fatalities.* ■ a person killed in this way. **2** helplessness in the face of fate: *the plot needs a darker sense of fatality to cover its absurdities.* ▷late 15th cent. (denoting the quality of causing death or disaster): from French *fatalité*, from late Latin *fatalitas*, from Latin *fatalis* 'decreed by fate,' from *fatum* (see **FATE**). Sense 1 dates from the mid 19th cent.

Fa·ta Mor·ga·na /ˈfätə môrˈgänə/ ▸*n.* a mirage. ▷Italian, literally 'fairy Morgan'; originally referring to a mirage seen in the Strait of Messina between Italy and Sicily and attributed to **MORGAN LE FAY**, whose legend and reputation were carried to Sicily by Norman settlers.

fat·back /ˈfat,bak/ ▸*n.* **1** fat from the upper part of a side of pork, esp. when dried and salted in strips. **2** informal term for **MENHADEN**.

fat bod·y ▸*n. Zoology* each of a number of small white structures in the body of an animal, esp. an insect, that act as a store of fats and glycogen.

fat burn·er ▸*n.* an over-the-counter drug that claims to burn calories by increasing the rate of the body's metabolism.

fat cat ▸*n. derogatory* a wealthy and powerful person, esp. a businessman or politician: [as *adj.*] *a fat-cat developer.*

fat cit·y ▸*n.* (often **Fat City**) *informal* **1** a condition of great prosperity or good fortune: *when school was out, we were in fat city, man!* **2** the condition of being overweight.

fate /fāt/ ▸*n.* **1** the development of events beyond a person's control, regarded as determined by a supernatural power: *fate decided his course for him* | *his injury is a cruel* ***twist of fate.*** ■ the course of someone's life, or the outcome of a particular situation for someone or something, seen as beyond their control: *he suffered the same* ***fate*** *as his companion.* ■ [in *sing.*] the inescapable death of a person: *the guards led her to her fate.* **2** (**the Fates**) *Greek & Roman Mythology* the three goddesses who preside over the birth and life of humans. Each person's destiny was thought of as a thread spun, measured, and cut by the three Fates, Clotho, Lachesis, and Atropos. Also called the **MOIRAI** and the **PARCAE**. ■ (**Fates**) another term for **NORNS**.

▸*v.* (**be fated**) be destined to happen, turn out, or act in a particular way: [with *infinitive*] *the regime was fated to end badly.* ▷late Middle English: from Italian *fato* or Old French *fator* (later) from their source, Latin *fatum* 'that which has been spoken,' from *fari* 'speak.'

▸*PHRASES* □ **a fate worse than death** see **DEATH**. □ **seal someone's fate** make it inevitable that something unpleasant will happen to someone.

fate·ful /ˈfātfəl/ ▸*adj.* having far-reaching and typically disastrous consequences or implications: *a fateful oversight.* See note at **OMINOUS**. **—fate·ful·ly** *adv.* **—fate·ful·ness** *n.*

fat farm ▸*n. informal* a residential establishment where overweight people seek improved health by dieting, exercise, and treatment.

fat-free ▸*adj.* (of a food) not containing animal or vegetable fats: *virtually fat-free yogurt.*

fat·head /ˈfat,hed/ ▸*n. informal* a stupid person. **—fat·head·ed** *adj.* **—fat·head·ed·ness** *n.*

fat hen ▸*n.* another name for **LAMB'S-QUARTERS**.

fa·ther /ˈfäT͟Hər/ ▸*n.* **1** a man in relation to his natural child or children. ■ a man who has continuous care of a child, esp. by adoption; an adoptive father, stepfather, or foster father. ■ a father-in-law. ■ a male animal in relation to its offspring. ■ (usu. **fathers**) *poetic/literary* an ancestor. ■ (also **founding father**) an important figure in the origin and early history of something: *Dorsey should be remembered as* ***the father of*** *gospel music.* ■ a man who gives care and protection to someone or something: *the prince is widely regarded as* ***the father of*** *the nation.* ■ the oldest or most respected member of a society or other body. ■ (**the Father**) (in Christian belief) the first person of the Trinity; God. ■ (**Father**) *poetic/literary* used in proper names, esp. when personifying time or a river, to suggest an old and venerable character: *Father Thames.* **2** (also **Father**) (often as a title or form of address) a priest: *pray for me, Father.* **3** (**the Fathers** or **the Church Fathers**) early Christian theologians (in particular of the first five centuries) whose writings are regarded as especially authoritative.

▸*v.* [*trans.*] be the father of: *he fathered three children.* ■ [usu. as *n.*] (**fathering**) treat with the protective care usually associated with a father: *the two males share the fathering of the cubs.* ■ be the source or originator of: *a culture which has fathered half the popular music in the world.* ■ (**father someone on**) make a woman pregnant: *he fathered a child on a one-night* *stand.* ■ assign the paternity of a child or responsibility for a book, idea, or action to: *a collection of Irish stories was fathered on him.* ■ *archaic* appear as or admit that one is the father or originator of: *a singular letter from a lady, requesting I would father a novel of hers.* ▷Old English *fæder*; from an Indo-European root shared by Latin *pater* and Greek *patēr*. —**fa·ther·hood** /-,ho͝od/ *n.* —**fa·ther·less** *adj.* —**fa·ther·less·ness** *n.* —**fa·ther·like** /-,līk/ *adj.* & *adv.*

▸*PHRASE* □ **like father, like son** *proverb* a son's character or behavior can be expected to resemble that of his father.

Fa·ther Christ·mas *Brit.* another name for **SANTA CLAUS.**

fa·ther con·fes·sor ▸*n.* a priest or minister who hears confessions. ■ *figurative* someone with whom one seeks comfort by trusting with one's confidences: *he was growing tired of acting as the father confessor to every student.*

fa·ther fig·ure ▸*n.* an older man who is respected for his paternal qualities and may be an emotional substitute for a father.

fa·ther-in-law ▸*n.* (*pl.* **fa·thers-in-law**) the father of one's spouse.

fa·ther·land /ˈfäT͟Hər,land/ ▸*n.* (often **the Fatherland**) a person's native country, esp. when referred to in patriotic terms. ■ *chiefly historical* Germany, esp. during the period of Hitler's control.

fa·ther·ly /ˈfäT͟Hərlē/ ▸*adj.* of, resembling, or characteristic of a father, esp. in being protective and affectionate: *he gave me such a kind and fatherly look.* —**fa·ther·li·ness** *n.*

Fa·ther's Day ▸*n.* a day of the year on which fathers are particularly honored by their children, esp. with gifts and greetings cards. It was first observed in the state of Washington in 1910 and is now usually observed on the third Sunday in June.

Fa·ther Time ▸*n.* see **TIME** (sense 1).

fath·om /ˈfaT͟Həm/ ▸*n.* a unit of length equal to six feet (approximately 1.8 m), chiefly used in reference to the depth of water: *sonar says that we're* **in** *eighteen* **fathoms.**

▸*v.* [*trans.*] **1** [usu. with *negative*] understand (a difficult problem or an enigmatic person) after much thought: *he could scarcely fathom the idea that people actually lived in Las Vegas* | [with *clause*] *he couldn't fathom why she was being so anxious.* **2** measure the depth of (water): *an attempt to fathom the ocean.* ▷Old English *fæthm*. The original sense was 'something that embraces,' (plural) 'the outstretched arms'; hence, a unit of measurement based on the span of the outstretched arms, later standardized to six feet. —**fath·om·a·ble** *adj.* —**fath·om·less** *adj.*

Fa·thom·e·ter /faT͟Hˈämətər; ˈfaT͟Hə(m),mētər/ ▸*n.* *trademark* a type of echo sounder.

fa·tigue /fəˈtēg/ ▸*n.* **1** extreme tiredness, typically resulting from mental or physical exertion or illness: *he was nearly dead with fatigue.* ■ a reduction in the efficiency of a muscle or organ after prolonged activity. ■ weakness in materials, esp. metal, caused by repeated variations of stress: *metal fatigue.* ■ [with *adj.*] a lessening in one's response to or enthusiasm for something, typically as a result of overexposure to it: *museum fatigue.* **2** (also **fa·tigue de·tail**) a group of soldiers ordered to perform menial, nonmilitary tasks, sometimes as a punishment. ■ (**fatigues**) loose-fitting clothing, typically khaki, olive drab, or camouflaged, of a sort worn by soldiers when performing such menial tasks or while on active duty: *battle fatigues.*

▸*v.* (**-tigues, -tigued, -ti·guing**) [*trans.*] (often **be fatigued**) cause (someone) to feel tired or exhausted: *they were fatigued by their journey.* ■ reduce the efficiency of (a muscle or organ) by prolonged activity. ■ weaken (a material, esp. metal) by repeated variations of stress. ▷mid 17th cent. (in the sense 'task or duty that causes weariness'): from French *fatigue* (noun), *fatiguer* (verb), from Latin *fatigare* 'tire out,' from *ad fatim*, *affatim* 'to satiety or surfeit, to bursting.' —**fa·tigu·a·bil·i·ty** /fə,tēgəˈbilitē/ *n.* —**fa·tigu·a·ble** (also **fat·i·ga·ble**) *adj.*

Fa·ti·ha /ˈfätē,hä/ (also **Fa·ti·hah**) ▸*n.* the short first sura of the Koran, used by Muslims as an essential element of ritual prayer. ▷from Arabic *al-Fātiḥah* 'the opening (sura),' from *fātiḥa* 'opening,' from *fataḥa* 'to open.'

Fat·i·ma /ˈfatəmə/ (*c.* AD 606–632), youngest daughter of the prophet Muhammad; wife of the fourth caliph, Ali. The descendants of Muhammad trace their lineage through her; she is revered, especially by Shiite Muslims, as the mother of the imams Hasan and Husayn.

Fá·ti·ma /ˈfatəmə; ˈfätēmə/ a village in western central Portugal, northeast of Lisbon; pop. 5,000. It became a center of Roman Catholic pilgrimage after the reported sighting there of the Virgin Mary in 1917.

Fat·i·mid /ˈfatəməd; -,mid/ ▸*n.* a member of a dynasty that ruled in parts of northern Africa, Egypt, and Syria from 909 to 1171, and founded Cairo as its capital in 969.

▸*adj.* of or relating to the Fatimids. ▷from Arabic *Fāṭima* (see **FATIMA**, from whom the dynasty is said to descend) + **-ID**3. —**Fat·i·mite** /-,mīt/ *n.* & *adj.*

fat·ling /ˈfatliNG/ ▸*n.* a young animal that has been fattened in readiness for slaughter.

fa·toush /faˈto͞osH/ ▸*n.* a Middle Eastern salad consisting of tomatoes, cucumber, and other vegetables together with croutons made from toasted pita bread. ▷Arabic.

fat·so /ˈfatsō/ ▸*n.* (*pl.* **-sos**) *informal, derogatory* a fat person.

fat·ten /ˈfatn/ ▸*v.* [*trans.*] make (a person or animal) fat or fatter: *he could do with some good food to* **fatten** *him* **up** | *figurative this may fatten their profits.* ■ [*intrans.*] become fat or fatter.

fat·ten·ing /ˈfatn-iNG/ ▸*adj.* (of a food) causing an increase in the weight of someone who eats it.

fat·ty /ˈfatē/ ▸*adj.* (**-ti·er, -ti·est**) containing a large amount of fat: *go easy on fatty foods* | *fatty tissue.* ■ *Medicine* (of a disease or lesion) marked by abnormal deposition of fat in cells: *fatty degeneration of the liver.*

▸*n.* (*pl.* **-ties**) *informal* a fat person (esp. as a nickname). —**fat·ti·ness** *n.*

fat·ty ac·id ▸*n.* *Chemistry* a carboxylic acid consisting of a hydrocarbon chain and a terminal carboxyl group, esp. any of those occurring as esters in fats and oils.

fat·ty oil ▸*n.* another term for **FIXED OIL.**

fat·u·ous /ˈfacHo͞oəs/ ▸*adj.* silly and pointless: *a fatuous comment.* ▷early 17th cent.: from Latin *fatuus* 'foolish' + **-OUS.** —**fa·tu·i·ty** /fəˈt(y)o͞oitē/ *n.* (*pl.* **-ties**) —**fat·u·ous·ly** *adv.* —**fat·u·ous·ness** *n.*

fat·wa /ˈfätwä/ ▸*n.* a ruling on a point of Islamic law given by a recognized authority. ▷early 17th cent.: from Arabic *fatwā*, from *aftā'aā* 'decide a point of law.' Compare with **MUFTI**1.

fau·bourg / fōˈbo͝or; -bərg/ ▸*n.* [usu. in *place names*] a suburb, esp. one in Paris: *the Faubourg Saint-Germain.* ▷French (earlier *faux-bourg* 'false borough'), perhaps an alteration of *forsborc*, literally 'outside the town,' but perhaps based on Middle High German *phâlburgere* 'burgers of the pale,' i.e., people living outside the city wall but still inside the palisade.

fau·ces /ˈfō,sēz/ ▸*plural n.* *Anatomy* the arched opening at the back of the mouth leading to the pharynx. ▷late Middle English: from Latin, 'throat.' —**fau·cial** /ˈfôsHəl/ *adj.*

fau·cet /ˈfôsit; ˈfäs-/ ▸*n.* a device by which a flow of liquid or gas from a pipe or container can be controlled; a tap. ▷late Middle English (denoting a bung for the vent-hole of a cask, or a tap for drawing liquor from a container): from Old French *fausset*, from Provençal *falset*, from *falsar* 'to bore.' The current sense dates from the mid 19th cent.

faugh /fô/ ▸*exclam.* *dated* expressing disgust: *"Faugh! This place stinks!"* ▷natural exclamation: first recorded in English in the mid 16th cent.

Faulk·ner /ˈfôknər/, William (1897–1962), U.S. novelist. His works deal with the history and legends of the U.S. South and have a strong sense of a society in decline. Notable works: *The Sound and the Fury* (1929), *As I Lay Dying* (1930), and *Absalom! Absalom!* (1936). Nobel Prize for Literature (1949).

fault /fôlt/ ▸*n.* **1** an unattractive or unsatisfactory feature, esp. in a piece of work or in a person's character: *my worst fault is impatience.* See note at **SIN.** ■ a break or other defect in an electrical circuit or piece of machinery: *a fire caused by an electrical fault.* ■ a misguided or dangerous action or habit: *it has been the great fault of our politicians that they have all wanted to do something.* ■ (in tennis and similar games) a service of the ball not in accordance with the rules. ■ (usu. **faults**) (in show jumping) a penalty point imposed for an error. **2** responsibility for an accident or misfortune: *an ordinary man thrust into peril* **through no fault of his own** | *it was his fault she had died.* **3** *Geology* an extended break in a body of rock, marked by the relative displacement and discontinuity of strata on either side of a particular surface.

▸*v.* [*trans.*] **1** criticize for inadequacy or mistakes: *her colleagues and superiors could not fault her dedication to the job* | *you cannot* **fault him for** *the professionalism of his approach.* ■ [*intrans.*] *archaic* do wrong: *the people of Caesarea faulted greatly when they called King Herod a god.* **2** (**be faulted**) *Geology* (of a rock formation) be broken by a fault or faults: *rift valleys where the crust has been stretched and faulted* | [as *n.*] (**faulting**) *a complex pattern of faulting.* ▷Middle English *faut(e)* 'lack, failing,' from Old French, based on Latin *fallere* 'deceive.' The *-l-* was added (in French and English) in the 15th cent. to conform with the Latin word, but did not become standard in English until the 17th cent., remaining silent in pronunciation until well into the 18th.

▸*PHRASES* □ **at fault** **1** responsible for an undesirable situation or event; in the wrong: *we recover compensation from the person at fault.* **2** mistaken or defective: *he suspected that his calculator was at fault.* □ **find fault** make an adverse criticism or objection, sometimes unfairly or destructively: *he* **finds fault with** *everything I do.* □ **— to a fault** (of someone who displays a particular commendable quality) to an extent verging on excess: *you're kind, caring and generous to a fault.*

THE RIGHT WORD **blemish, defect, failing, fault, flaw, foible, shortcoming**

No one is perfect. But when it comes to cataloging your own imperfections, it's best to start with your **foibles**—the slight weaknesses or eccentricities for which you will be most quickly forgiven.

You also have a good chance of being forgiven for your **shortcomings**, which are not necessarily damaging to others (*his ardent devotion to his dog was a shortcoming that was readily overlooked*).

Failing suggests a more severe shortcoming, usually with more serious consequences (*chronic tardiness was one of her failings*), but a *failing* can also be a weakness of character that you're not responsible for and perhaps not even aware of (*pride is a common failing among those who have met with great success early in life*).

Fault also implies failure—but not necessarily a serious failure—to reach moral perfection (*his major fault was his outspokenness*).

While *fault* usually indicates something inherent in your nature rather than external to it, a **flaw** can be either superficial (*a flaw in his otherwise immaculate appearance*) or profound (*a personality flaw that made her impossible to work with*), and it can refer to things as well as people (*a flaw in the table's finish*).

A **blemish** is usually a physical flaw (*a facial blemish*), although it can be anything that disfigures or mars the perfection of someone or something (*a blemish on her otherwise spotless academic record*).

You can get rid of a blemish and even overcome your shortcomings, but a **defect** is a flaw so serious that you may never be able to get rid of it (*a defect in his hearing*).

fault-find·ing ▸*n.* **1** continual criticism, typically concerning trivial things. **2** the investigation of the cause of malfunction in machinery, esp. electronic equipment. —**fault-find·er** *n.*

fault·less /ˈfôltləs/ ▸*adj.* free from defect or error: *your logic is faultless.* —**fault·less·ly** *adv.* —**fault·less·ness** *n.*

fault·y /ˈfôltē/ ▸*adj.* (**fault·i·er, fault·i·est**) working badly or unreliably because of imperfections: *a car with faulty brakes.* ■ (of reasoning and other mental processes) mistaken or misleading because of flaws: *faulty logic.* ■ having or displaying weaknesses: *her character was faulty.* —**fault·i·ly** /ˈfôltəlē/ *adv.* —**fault·i·ness** *n.*

faun /fôn/ ▸*n.* *Roman Mythology* one of a class of lustful rural gods, represented as a man with a goat's horns, ears, legs, and tail. ▷late Middle English: from the name of the pastoral god **FAUNUS.**

fau·na /ˈfônə; ˈfänə/ ▸*n.* (*pl.* **-nas** /-nəz/ or **-nae** /-nē/) the animals of a particular region, habitat, or geological period: *the* **flora and fauna** *of Siberia* | *islands that support one of the richest of all marine faunas.* Compare with **FLORA.** ■ a book or other work describing or listing the animal life of a region. ▷late 18th cent.: modern Latin application of *Fauna*, the name of a rural goddess, sister of **FAUNUS.** —**fau·nal** /ˈfônl; ˈfänl/ *adj.* —**fau·nis·tic** /fôˈnistik; fä-/ *adj.*

fau·nal re·gion /ˈfônl; ˈfänl/ ▸*n.* another term for **ZOOGEOGRAPHICAL REGION.**

Faun·tle·roy /ˈfôntlə,roi/ (also **Little Lord Fauntleroy**) ▸*n.* an excessively well-mannered or elaborately dressed young boy. ▷from the name of the boy hero of Frances Hodgson Burnett's novel *Little Lord Fauntleroy* (1886).

Fau·nus /ˈfônəs; ˈfänəs/ *Roman Mythology* an ancient Italian pastoral god, grandson of Saturn, associated with wooded places.

Faust /foust/ (also **Faus·tus** /ˈfoustəs; ˈfô-/) (died *c.*1540), German astronomer and necromancer. Reputed to have sold his soul to the Devil, he became the subject of dramas by Marlowe and Goethe, an opera by Gounod, and a novel by Thomas Mann. **—Faus·ti·an** /ˈfoustēən/ *adj.*

faute de mieux /ˌfōt də ˈmyœ/ ▸*adv.* for want of a better alternative: *the show is, faute de mieux, the most eagerly anticipated musical of the season to come.* ▷mid 18th cent.: French, literally 'for want of (something) better.'

fau·teuil /ˈfōtil; fōˈtœyə/ ▸*n.* a wooden seat in the form of an armchair with open sides and upholstered arms. ▷French, from Old French *faudestuel,* from medieval Latin *faldistolium* (see **FALDSTOOL**).

Fauve /fōv/ (also **fauve**) ▸*n.* a member of a group of French painters who favored Fauvism: [as *adj.*] *a Fauve canvas by Matisse.*

Fauv·ism /ˈfōˌvizəm/ (also **fauv·ism**) ▸*n.* a style of painting with vivid expressionistic and nonnaturalistic use of color that flourished in Paris from 1905 and, although short-lived, had an important influence on subsequent artists, esp. the German expressionists. Matisse was regarded as the movement's leading figure. ▷from French *fauvisme,* from *fauve* 'wild beast.' The name originated from a remark of the French art critic Louis Vauxcelles at the Salon of 1905; coming across a quattrocento-style statue in the midst of works by Matisse and his associates, he is reputed to have said, "Donatello au milieu des fauves!" ('Donatello among the wild beasts'). **—fauv·ist** *n.* & *adj.*

faux /fō/ ▸*adj.* [*attrib.*] artificial or imitation; false: *a string of faux pearls.* ▷late 20th cent.: French, literally 'false.'

faux-na·ïf /ˌfō näˈēf/ ▸*adj.* (of a work of art or a person) artificially or affectedly simple or naive: *faux-naïf pastoralism.*

▸*n.* (**faux naïf**) a person who pretends to be ingenuous: *the old device of a faux naïf observing his own country as a foreigner.* ▷mid 20th cent.: from French *faux* 'false' + *naïf* 'naive.'

faux pas /fō ˈpä; ˈfō ˌpä/ ▸*n.* (*pl.* same) an embarrassing or tactless act or remark in a social situation. ▷late 17th cent.: French, literally 'false step.'

fa·va bean /ˈfävə ˌbēn/ ▸*n.* another term for **BROAD BEAN**. ▷Italian *fava,* from Latin *faba* 'bean.'

fave /fāv/ ▸*n.* & *adj. informal* short for **FAVORITE**.

fa·ve·la /fəˈvelə/ ▸*n.* a Brazilian shack or shanty town; a slum. ▷Portuguese. **—fa·ve·la·do** /ˌfävəˈlädō/ *n.*

fa·vor /ˈfāvər/ (*Brit.* **fa·vour**) ▸*n.* **1** an attitude of approval or liking: *the legislation is viewed with favor.* ■ support or advancement given as a sign of approval: *a struggle between competing aides for presidential favor.* ■ overgenerous preferential treatment: *they accused you of showing favor to one of the players.* ■ a small gift or souvenir: *good party favors include stickers, hair barrettes, or crayons.* ■ *archaic* a thing such as a badge or knot of ribbons that is given or worn as a mark of liking or support. **2** an act of kindness beyond what is due or usual: *I've come to ask you a favor.* ■ (**one's favors**) *dated* used with reference to a woman allowing a man to have sexual intercourse with her: *she had granted her favors to him.*

▸*v.* [*trans.*] **1** feel or show approval or preference for: *slashing public spending is a policy that few politicians favor.* ■ give unfairly preferential treatment to: *critics argued that the policy favored the private sector.* ■ work to the advantage of: *natural selection has favored bats.* **2** (**favor someone with**) (often used in polite requests) give someone (something that they want): *please favor me with an answer.* **3** *informal* resemble (a parent or relative) in facial features: *she's pretty, and she favors you.* **4** treat (an injured limb) gently, not putting one's full weight on it: *he favors his sore leg.* ▷Middle English (in the noun sense 'liking, preference'): via Old French from Latin *favor,* from *favere* 'show kindness to' (related to *fovere* 'cherish'). **—fa·vor·er** *n.*

▸*PHRASES* □ **do someone a favor** do something for someone as an act of kindness. □ **in favor 1** meeting with approval: *they were not in favor with the party.* **2** having or showing approval: *the appeals court ruled 2-1 **in favor of** his extradition.* □ **in one's favor** to one's advantage: *events were moving in his favor.* □ **in favor of 1** to be replaced by: *he stepped down as leader in favor of his rival.* **2** to the advantage of: *the final score was 25-16 in favor of Washington.* □ **out of favor** lacking or having lost approval or popularity: *proper dancing has gone out of favor.*

fa·vor·a·ble /ˈfāv(ə)rəbəl/ (*Brit.* **fa·vour·a·ble**) ▸*adj.* **1** expressing approval: *the book received highly favorable reviews.* ■ giving consent: *their demands rarely received a favorable response.* **2** to the advantage of someone or something: *they made a settlement **favorable to** the unions.* ■ (of a wind) blowing in the direction of travel. ■ (of weather, or a period of time judged in terms of its weather) fine. ■ suggesting a good outcome: *a favorable prognosis.* ▷Middle English: via Old French from Latin *favorabilis,* from *favor* (see **FAVOR**). **—fa·vor·a·ble·ness** *n.* **—fa·vor·a·bly** /-r(ə)blē/ *adv.*

fa·vor·ite /ˈfāv(ə)rət/ (Brit. **fa·vour·ite**) ▸*adj.* [*attrib.*] preferred before all others of the same kind: *their favorite Italian restaurant.*

▸*n.* a person or thing that is especially popular or particularly well liked by someone: *the song is still a favorite after 20 years.* ■ the competitor thought most likely to win a game or contest, esp. by people betting on the outcome: *he was the early favorite to win the South Carolina caucuses.* ▷late 16th cent. (as a noun): from obsolete French *favorit,* from Italian *favorito,* past participle of *favorire* 'to favor,' from Latin *favor* (see **FAVOR**).

▸*PHRASE* □ **favorite son** a famous man who is particularly popular and praised for his achievements in his native area: *Green Bay's favorite son is equal parts laid-back and hot-blooded.* ■ a person supported as a presidential candidate by delegates from the candidate's home state.

fa·vor·it·ism /ˈfāv(ə)rəˌtizəm/ ▸*n.* the practice of giving unfair preferential treatment to one person or group at the expense of another.

fa·vrile glass /fəvˈrēl/ ▸*n.* a richly colored iridescent glass, developed by L. C. Tiffany. ▷late 19th cent.: formed as a trademark from the obsolete adjective *fabrile* 'of a craftsman.'

Fawkes /fôks/, Guy (1570–1606), English conspirator. He was hanged for his part in the Gunpowder Plot of November 5, 1605. The occasion is commemorated annually in Britain on November 5 with fireworks, bonfires, and the burning of an effigy called a *guy.*

fawn[1] /fôn; fän/ ▸*n.* **1** a young deer in its first year. **2** a light yellowish-brown color.

▸*v.* [*intrans.*] (of a deer) produce young. ▷late Middle English: from Old French *faon,* based on Latin *fetus* 'offspring'; compare with **FETUS**.

▸*PHRASE* □ **in fawn** (of a deer) pregnant.

fawn[2] ▸*v.* [*intrans.*] (of a person) give a servile display of exaggerated flattery or affection, typically in order to gain favor or advantage: *congressmen **fawn over** the President.* ■ (of an animal, esp. a dog) show slavish devotion, esp. by crawling and rubbing against someone. ▷Old English *fagnian* 'make or be glad'; related to **FAIN**. **—fawn·ing·ly** *adv.*

fax /faks/ ▸*n.* an image of a document made by electronic scanning and transmitted as data by telecommunication links. ■ the production or transmission of documents in this way: *he received the report by fax.* ■ (also **fax machine**) a machine for transmitting and receiving such documents.

▸*v.* [*trans.*] send (a document) by such means. ■ contact (someone) by such means: *to obtain a brochure, fax the agent* | [*intrans.*] *the best way to order materials was to fax.* ▷1940s.: abbreviation of **FACSIMILE**.

fay /fā/ ▸*n. poetic/literary* a fairy. ▷late Middle English: from Old French *fae, faie,* from Latin *fata* 'the Fates,' plural of *fatum* (see **FATE**). Compare with **FAIRY**.

fay·al·ite /fəˈyälˌīt/ ▸*n.* a black or brown mineral that is an iron-rich form of olivine and occurs in many igneous rocks. ▷mid 19th cent.: from *Fayal* (the name of an island in the Azores) + **-ITE**[1].

Fay·ette·ville /ˈfāətˌvil; -vəl/ **1** a commercial city in northwestern Arkansas, home to the University of Arkansas; pop. 59,047. **2** a commercial city in south central North Carolina; pop. 121,015.

fayre /fer/ ▸*n.* pseudoarchaic spelling of **FAIR**[2].

faze /fāz/ ▸*v.* [*trans.*] [usu. with *negative*] (often **be fazed**) *informal* disturb or disconcert (someone): *she was not fazed by his show of anger.* ▷mid 19th cent.: variant of dialect *feeze* 'drive or frighten off,' from Old English *fēsian.*

fa·zen·da /fəˈzendə/ ▸*n.* an estate or large farm in Portugal, Brazil, and other Portuguese-speaking countries. ▷Portuguese (see **HACIENDA**).

fa·zen·dei·ro /ˌfazənˈdāˌrō/ ▸*n.* (*pl.* **-ros**) a person who owns or occupies a fazenda. ▷Portuguese.

FB ▸*abbr.* ■ foreign body. ■ freight bill.

fb (also **f.b.**) ▸*abbr. Sports* fullback.

FBI ▸*abbr.* Federal Bureau of Investigation.

f.c. ▸*abbr.* ■ fielder's choice. ■ follow copy.

FCA ▸*abbr.* Farm Credit Association.

fcap. ▸*abbr.* foolscap.

FCC ▸*abbr.* Federal Communications Commission.

FCS ▸*abbr.* Fellow of the Chemical Society.

fcy. ▸*abbr.* fancy.

FD ▸*abbr.* ■ Defender of the Faith. [from Latin *Fidei Defensor.*] ■ Fire Department.

FDA ▸*abbr.* Food and Drug Administration.

FDC ▸*abbr.* first day cover.

FDDI ▸*abbr.* fiber-distributed data interface, a communications, cabling, and hardware standard for high-speed optical-fiber networks.

FDIC ▸*abbr.* Federal Deposit Insurance Corporation, a body that underwrites most private bank deposits.

FDR the nickname of President Franklin Delano Roosevelt (see **ROOSEVELT**[2]).

Fe ▸*symbol* the chemical element iron. ▷from Latin *ferrum.*

fe·al·ty /ˈfēltē/ ▸*n. historical* a feudal tenant's or vassal's sworn loyalty to a lord: *they owed **fealty to** the Earl rather than the King.* ■ formal acknowledgment of this: *a property for which she **did fealty**.* ▷Middle English: from Old French *feau(l)te, fealte,* from Latin *fidelitas* (see **FIDELITY**).

fear /fi(ə)r/ ▸*n.* an unpleasant emotion caused by the belief that someone or something is dangerous, likely to cause pain, or a threat: *drivers are threatening to quit their jobs in fear after a cabby's murder* | *fear of increasing unemployment* | *he is prey to irrational fears.* ■ *archaic* a mixed feeling of dread and reverence: *the love and fear of God.* ■ (**fear for**) a feeling of anxiety concerning the outcome of something or the safety and well-being of someone: *police launched a search for the family amid fears for their safety.* ■ the likelihood of something unwelcome happening: *she could observe the other guests without too much fear of attracting attention.*

▸*v.* [*trans.*] be afraid of (someone or something) as likely to be dangerous, painful, or threatening: *he said he didn't care about life so why should he fear death?* | [with *clause*] *farmers fear that they will lose business.* ■ [*intrans.*] (**fear for**) feel anxiety or apprehension on behalf of: *I fear for the city with this madman let loose in it.* ■ [with *infinitive*] avoid or put off doing something because one is afraid: *they aim to make war so horrific that potential aggressors will fear to resort to it.* ■ used to express regret or apology: *I'll buy her book, though not, I fear, the hardback version.* ■ *archaic* regard (God) with reverence and awe. ▷Old English *fǣr* 'calamity, danger,' *fǣran* 'frighten,' also 'revere.'

▸*PHRASES* □ **for fear of** (or **that**) to avoid the risk of (or that): *no one dared refuse the order for fear of losing their job.* □ **never fear** used to reassure someone: *we shall meet again, never fear.* □ **put the fear of God in** (or **into**) **someone** cause someone to be very frightened. □ **without fear or favor** impartially: *make all your decisions without fear or favor.*

fear·ful /ˈfi(ə)rfəl/ ▸*adj.* **1** feeling afraid; showing fear or anxiety: *bond traders have remained fearful of inflation* | [with *clause*] *the mothers were fearful that their daughters would marry and move abroad.* ■ causing or likely to cause people to be afraid; horrifying: *a fearful accident.* **2** *informal* very great: *he could cause a fearful commotion.* **—fear·ful·ly** *adv.* **—fear·ful·ness** *n.*

fear·less /ˈfi(ə)rlis/ ▸*adj.* lacking fear: *a fearless defender of freedom.* **—fear·less·ly** *adv.* **—fear·less·ness** *n.*

fear·some /ˈfi(ə)rsəm/ ▸*adj.* frightening, esp. in appearance: *the cat mewed, displaying a fearsome set of teeth.* **—fear·some·ly** *adv.* **—fear·some·ness** *n.*

fea·si·bil·i·ty /ˌfēzəˈbilətē/ ▸*n.* the state or degree of being easily or conveniently done: *the feasibility of a manned flight to Mars.*

fea·si·bil·i·ty stud·y ▸*n.* an assessment of the practicality of a proposed plan or method.

fea·si·ble /ˈfēzəbəl/ ▸*adj.* possible to do easily or conveniently: *it is not feasible to put most finds from excavations on public display.* ■ *informal* likely; probable: *the most feasible explanation.* ▷late Middle English: from Old French *faisible,* from *fais-,* stem of *faire* 'do, make,' from Latin *facere.* **—fea·si·bly** /-zəblē/ *adv.*

USAGE The primary meaning of **feasible** is 'capable of being done or effected.' There is rarely a need to use **feasible** to mean 'likely' or 'probable' when those words can do the job. There are cases, however, in which a careful writer finds that the sense of likelihood or probability (as with an explanation or theory) is more naturally or idiomatically expressed with **feasible** than with *possible* or *probable.*

feast /fēst/ ▸*n.* a large meal, typically one in celebration of something: *a wedding feast.* ■ a plentiful supply of something enjoyable, esp. for the mind or senses: *the concert season offers a feast of classical music.* ■ an annual religious celebration. ■ a day dedicated to a particular saint: *the feast of St. Joseph.*
▸*v.* [*intrans.*] eat and drink sumptuously: *the men would congregate and feast after hunting.* ■ (**feast on**) eat large quantities of: *we sat feasting on barbecued chicken and beer.* ■ [*trans.*] give (someone) a plentiful and delicious meal: *he was feasted and invited to all the parties.* ▷Middle English: from Old French *feste* (noun), *fester* (verb), from Latin *festa*, neuter plural of *festus* 'joyous.' Compare with **FÊTE** and **FIESTA**. **—feast·er** *n.*
▸*PHRASES* □ **skeleton at the feast** a person or thing that brings gloom or sadness to an otherwise pleasant or celebratory occasion. □ **feast one's eyes on** gaze at with pleasure. □ **feast or famine** either too much of something or too little.

feast day ▸*n.* a day on which a celebration, esp. an annual Christian one, is held.

Feast of Ded·i·ca·tion ▸*n.* another name for **HANUKKAH**.

Feast of Tab·er·nac·les ▸*n.* another name for **SUCCOTH**.

Feast of Weeks ▸*n.* another name for **SHAVUOTH**.

feat /fēt/ ▸*n.* an achievement that requires great courage, skill, or strength: *the new printing presses were considerable feats of engineering.* ▷late Middle English (in the general sense 'action or deed'): from Old French *fait*, from Latin *factum* (see **FACT**).

feath·er /ˈfe*TH*ər/ ▸*n.* any of the flat appendages growing from a bird's skin and forming its plumage, consisting of a partly hollow horny shaft fringed with vanes of barbs. ■ (often **feathers**) one of these appendages as decoration. ■ one of the feathers or featherlike vanes fastened to the shaft of an arrow or a dart. ■ (**feathers**) a fringe of long hair on the legs of a dog, horse, or other animal. ■ a small side branch on a tree.
▸*v.* **1** [*trans.*] rotate the blades of (a propeller) about their own axes in such a way as to lessen the air or water resistance. ■ vary the angle of attack of (rotor blades). ■ *Rowing* turn (an oar) so that it passes through the air edgewise: *he turned, feathering one oar slowly.* **2** [*intrans.*] float, move, or wave like a feather: *the green fronds feathered against a blue sky.* ■ [*trans.*] touch (someone or something) very lightly. **3** [*trans.*] shorten or taper the hair by cutting or trimming: *my sister had her hair feathered.* ▷Old English *fether*, from an Indo-European root shared by Latin *penna* 'feather' and Greek *pteron* 'wing.' **—feath·er·i·ness** *n.* **—feath·er·less** *adj.* **—feath·er·y** *adj.*
▸*PHRASES* □ **a feather in one's cap** an achievement to be proud of. □ **feather one's (own) nest** make money illicitly and at someone else's expense. □ **(as) light as a feather** extremely light and insubstantial.

feath·er·back /ˈfe*TH*ərˌbak/ ▸*n.* a tropical freshwater fish native to South Asia and Africa, with a strongly humped back, a small, featherlike dorsal fin, and a long anal fin that runs from the belly to the tail. • Family Notopteridae: four genera and several species, in particular the large edible *Notopterus chitala* of Asia.

feath·er·bed /ˈfe*TH*ərˌbed/ ▸*n.* (also **feath·er bed**) a bed that has a mattress stuffed with feathers.
▸*v.* (also **feath·er-bed**) [*trans.*] provide (someone) with advantageous economic or working conditions: *apart from the fees he earns, a practicing lawyer is not featherbedded in any way.* ■ [usu. as *n.*] (**featherbedding**) deliberately limit production or retain excess staff in (a business) in order to create jobs or prevent unemployment, typically as a result of a union contract.

feath·er·brain /ˈfe*TH*ərˌbrān/ (also **feath·er-brain** or **feath·er·head**) ▸*n.* a silly or absentminded person. **—feath·er·brained** (also **feath·er-brained** or **feath·er·head·ed**) *adj.*

feath·er dust·er ▸*n.* a long-handled brush with a head made of feathers, used for dusting. ■ (also **feather duster worm**) another term for **FAN WORM**.

feath·ered /ˈfe*TH*ərd/ ▸*adj.* (of a bird) covered with feathers: [in *combination*] *black-feathered ostriches.* ■ decorated with feathers: *a feathered hat.*

feath·ered friend ▸*n.* (usu. **feathered friends**) *informal, humorous* a bird.

feath·er edge ▸*n.* a fine edge produced by tapering a board or other object.

feath·er·ing /ˈfe*TH*əriNG/ ▸*n.* **1** the plumage of a bird or part of a bird. ■ featherlike markings or structure: *traditional finishes such as marbling and feathering.* ■ the feathers of an arrow. ■ fringes of hairs on the appendages or body of a dog. ■ *Architecture* cusping in tracery. **2** the action of varying the angle of propellers, rotor blades, or oars so as to reduce air or water resistance.

feath·er·light /ˈfe*TH*ərˌlīt/ (also **feath·er-light**) ▸*adj.* extremely light: *a featherlight touch.*

feath·er star ▸*n.* an echinoderm with a small disklike body, long feathery arms for feeding and movement, and short appendages for grasping the surface. • Order Comatulida, class Crinoidea.

feath·er·stitch /ˈfe*TH*ərˌstiCH/ ▸*n.* ornamental zigzag sewing.
▸*v.* [*trans.*] [usu. as *n.*] (**feath·er·stitch·ing**) sew (something) with such a stitch.

feath·er·tail glid·er /ˈfe*TH*ərˌtāl/ ▸*n.* an Australian pygmy possum with a flap of skin between the fore- and hind limbs for gliding, and a feathery tail. • *Acrobates pygmaeus*, family Burramyidae. Alternative name: **flying mouse**.

feath·er·weight /ˈfe*TH*ərˌwāt/ ▸*n.* a weight in boxing and other sports intermediate between bantamweight and lightweight. It ranges from 118 to 126 pounds (54 to 57 kg). ■ a boxer or other competitor of this weight. ■ a very light person or thing. ■ a person or thing not worth serious consideration: *he is an intellectual featherweight.*

fea·ture /ˈfēCHər/ ▸*n.* **1** a distinctive attribute or aspect of something: *safety features like dual air bags.* ■ (usu. **features**) a part of the face, such as the mouth or eyes, making a significant contribution to its overall appearance. ■ *Linguistics* a distinctive characteristic of a linguistic unit, esp. a speech sound or vocabulary item, that serves to distinguish it from others of the same type. **2** a newspaper or magazine article or a broadcast program devoted to the treatment of a particular topic, typically at length: *a feature on Detroit's downtown fishery.* ■ (also **feature film**) a full-length film intended as the main item in a movie theater program.
▸*v.* [*trans.*] have as a prominent attribute or aspect: *the hotel features a large lounge, a sauna, and a coin-operated solarium.* ■ have as an important actor or participant: *the film featured Glenn Miller and his Orchestra.* ■ [*intrans.*] (often **be featured**) be a significant characteristic of or take an important part in: *this famous photograph is prominently featured in art collections.* ■ [*intrans.*] be apparent: *women rarely feature in writing on land settlement.* ▷late Middle English (originally denoting the form or proportions of the body, or a physical feature): from Old French *faiture* 'form,' from Latin *factura* (see **FACTURE**). **—fea·tured** *adj.* [in *combination*] *fine-featured women.* **—fea·ture·less** *adj.*

fea·ture-length ▸*adj.* of the length of a typical feature film or program: *a feature-length documentary.*

Feb. ▸*abbr.* February.

feb·ri·fuge /ˈfebrəˌfyo͞oj/ ▸*n.* a medicine used to reduce fever. ▷late 17th cent.: from French *fébrifuge*, from Latin *febris* 'fever' + *fugare* 'drive away.' Compare with **FEVERFEW**. **—fe·brif·u·gal** /ˌfebrəˈf(y)o͞ogəl/ *adj.*

fe·brile /ˈfebˌrīl; ˈfēˌbrīl/ ▸*adj.* having or showing the symptoms of a fever: *a febrile illness.* ■ having or showing a great deal of nervous excitement or energy: *a febrile imagination.* ▷mid 17th cent.: from French *fébrile* or medieval Latin *febrilis*, from Latin *febris* 'fever.' **—fe·bril·i·ty** /fēˈbrilətē/ *n.*

Feb·ru·ar·y /ˈfeb(y)o͞oˌerē; ˈfebro͞o-/ ▸*n.* (*pl.* **-ar·ies**) the second month of the year, in the northern hemisphere usually considered the last month of winter: *even in February the place is busy* | [as *adj.*] *a freezing February morning.* ▷Middle English *feverer*, from Old French *feverier*, based on Latin *februarius*, from *februa*, the name of a purification feast held in this month. The spelling change in the 15th cent. was due to association with the Latin word.

USAGE To pronounce **February** in the way traditionally regarded as correct is not easy. It requires the explicit pronunciation of both the **r** following the **Feb-** and the **r** in **-ary**, with an unstressed vowel in between. In popular pronunciation, the **rə** following **Feb-** has been replaced by a **yoo** sound: **Feb-yoo-** rather than **Feb-roo-**. This change is due to two processes: *dissimilation*, in which one sound identical with or similar to an adjacent sound is replaced by a different sound, and *analogy*, in which a member of a series, in this case *January*, affects the sound of another member (**February**) of the series. **Feb-yoo-** is now the norm, esp. in spontaneous speech, and is fast becoming a standard pronunciation.

Feb·ru·ar·y Rev·o·lu·tion see **RUSSIAN REVOLUTION**.

fec. ▸*abbr.* he or she made it. ▷from Latin *fecit.*

fe·ces /ˈfēsēz/ (*Brit.* **fae·ces**) ▸*plural n.* waste matter discharged from the bowels after food has been digested; excrement. ▷late Middle English: from Latin, plural of *faex* 'dregs.' **—fe·cal** /ˈfēkəl/ *adj.*

feck·less /ˈfekləs/ ▸*adj.* (of a person) lacking in efficiency or vitality: *a feckless mama's boy.* ■ unthinking and irresponsible: *the feckless exploitation of the world's natural resources.* ▷late 16th cent.: from Scots and northern English dialect *feck* (from *effeck*, variant of **EFFECT**) + **-LESS**. **—feck·less·ly** *adv.* **—feck·less·ness** *n.*

fec·u·lent /ˈfekyələnt/ ▸*adj.* of or containing dirt, sediment, or waste matter: *their feet were forever slipping on feculent bog.* ▷late 15th cent.: from French *féculent* or Latin *faeculentus*, from *faex, faec-* 'dregs.' **—fec·u·lence** *n.*

fe·cund /ˈfekənd; ˈfē-/ ▸*adj.* producing or capable of producing an abundance of offspring or new growth; fertile: *a lush and fecund garden* | *figurative her fecund imagination.* See note at **FERTILE**. ■ *technical* (of a woman or women) capable of becoming pregnant and giving birth. ▷late Middle English: from French *fécond* or Latin *fecundus* 'fruitful'. **—fe·cun·di·ty** /fəˈkəndətē; fiˈkən-/ *n.*

fe·cun·date /ˈfekənˌdāt/ ▸*v.* [*trans.*] fertilize: *there were no insects to fecundate flowering plants.* ■ *poetic/literary* make fruitful: *he actuates and fecundates our souls.* ▷mid 17th cent.: from Latin *fecundat-* 'made fruitful,' from the verb *fecundare*, from *fecundus* 'fruitful.' **—fe·cun·da·tion** /ˌfēkənˈdāSHən/ *n.*

Fed /fed/ ▸*n. informal* **1** a federal agent or official, esp. a member of the FBI: *I don't think he has any friends since he ratted to the Feds.* **2** (usu. **the Fed**) short for **FEDERAL RESERVE**. ▷early 20th cent.: abbreviation of **FEDERAL**. The abbreviation *fed* had previously been used in the late 18th cent. to denote a member of the Federalist party, who advocated a union of American colonies after the American Revolution.

fed /fed/ ▸ past and past participle of **FEED**.

fed. ▸*abbr.* ■ federal. ■ federated. ■ federation.

fe·da·yeen /ˌfedāˈēn; -dīˈēn/ ▸*plural n.* Arab guerrillas operating esp. in Israel and Palestine against the Israeli government, and in Iraq against the occupying coalition forces during and after the Second Gulf War. ▷1950s: from colloquial Arabic *fidā'iyīn*, plural of classical Arabic *fidā'ī* 'one who gives his life for another or for a cause,' from *fadā* 'to ransom someone.' The singular *fedai* (from Arabic and Persian *fidā'ī*) had previously been used (late 19th cent.) to denote an Ismaili Muslim assassin.

fed·er·al /ˈfed(ə)rəl/ ▸*adj.* having or relating to a system of government in which several states form a unity but remain independent in internal affairs: *Russia's federation treaty shares powers among Russia's federal and local governments.* ■ of, relating to, or denoting the central government as distinguished from the separate units constituting a federation: *the federal agency that provides legal services to the poor.* ■ of, relating to, or denoting the central government of the U.S. ■ (**Federal**) *historical* of the Northern States in the Civil War: *a loud Federal cheer was heard, proving Stonewall to be hard pressed.* ▷mid 17th cent.: from Latin *foedus, foeder-* 'league, covenant' + **-AL**. **—fed·er·al·i·za·tion** /ˌfed(ə)rəliˈzāSHən/ *n.* **—fed·er·al·ize** /-ˌlīz/ *v.* **—fed·er·al·ly** *adv.*

Fed·er·al Bu·reau of In·ves·ti·ga·tion (abbr.: **FBI**) an agency of the U.S. federal government that deals principally with internal security and counterintelligence and that also conducts investigations in federal law enforcement. It was established in 1908 as a branch of the Department of Justice, but was substantially reorganized under the controversial directorship (1924–72) of J. Edgar Hoover.

fed·er·al case ▸*n. Law* a criminal case that falls under the jurisdiction of a federal court. ■ *figurative* a matter of great concern or with dire consequences: *I'm not trying to* ***make a federal case out of this****, Christine, but you've got to do something.*

fed·er·al·ism /ˈfed(ə)rəˌlizəm/ ▸*n.* **1** the federal principle or system of government: *the politics of federalism, that great migraine of Canada* | *Tito's highly decentralized federalism came under Serbian attack as a 'parcelization' of power.* ■ (**Federalism**) the principles of the Federalist Party. **2** advocacy of a federal system of government. ■ in Canada, support of confederation in opposition to Quebec separatism.

fed·er·al·ist /ˈfed(ə)rəlist/ ▸*n.* **1** an advocate or supporter of federalism: *dark designs to advance the schemes of world federalists and Communist internationalists.* **2** (**Federalist**) a member or supporter of the Federalist Party: *captured both the legislative and the executive branches of the federal government from the Federalists.*
▸*adj.* **1** of, pertaining to, or favoring federalism or federalists: *the Quebec Liberal Party and the federalist cause would be greatly strengthened by his candidacy | Britain can achieve what it wants, more power to the federalist European Parliament | even the moderates here sounded more Reaganite than Ronald Reagan ever did in his federalist riffs.* **2** (**Federalist**) designating or pertaining to the Federalist Party: *it was not a weapon that could reach John Marshall and the other Federalist judges.*

Fed·er·al·ist Pa·pers (also **The Federalist**) a collection of essays written under the pseudonym "Publius" by Alexander Hamilton, John Jay, and James Madison, addressed to "The People of the State of New York," first published in New York City newspapers between October 1787 and August 1788. The purpose of *The Federalist* was to persuade New Yorkers to ratify the Constitution adopted in Philadelphia in September 1787.

Fed·er·al·ist Par·ty an early political party in the U.S., joined by George Washington during his presidency (1789–97) and in power until 1801. The party's emphasis on strong central government was extremely important in the early years after independence, but by the 1820s it had been superseded by the Democratic Republican Party.

Fed·er·al O·pen Mar·ket Com·mit·tee ▸*n.* a committee of the Federal Reserve Board that meets regularly to set monetary policy, including the interest rates that are charged to banks.

Fed·er·al Reg·is·ter ▸*n.* a daily publication of the U.S. federal government that issues proposed and final administrative regulations of federal agencies.

Fed·er·al Re·pub·lic of Ger·ma·ny former name of **West Germany** (see **GERMANY**).

Fed·er·al Re·serve the federal banking authority in the U.S. that performs the functions of a central bank and is used to implement the country's monetary policy, providing a national system of reserve cash available to banks. Created in 1913, the Federal Reserve System consists of twelve Federal Reserve Districts, each having a Federal Reserve Bank. These are controlled from Washington, DC, by the Federal Reserve Board consisting of governors appointed by the U.S. president with Senate approval.

Fed·er·al Trade Com·mis·sion ▸*n. Finance* a federal agency, established in 1914, that administers antitrust and consumer protection legislation in pursuit of free and fair competition in the marketplace.

Fed·er·al Un·ion see **UNION** (sense 3).

Fed·er·al Way a city in west central Washington that lies between Seattle and Tacoma; pop. 83,259.

fed·er·ate ▸*v.* /ˈfedəˌrāt/ [*intrans.*] (of a number of states or organizations) form a single centralized unit, within which each keeps some internal autonomy. ■ [*trans.*] [usu. as *adj.*] (**federated**) form (states or organizations) into such a centralized unit: *the establishment of 20 federated states in Mindanao.*
▸*adj.* /ˈfedərit/ of or relating to such an arrangement: *federate armies.* ▷early 18th cent. (as an adjective): from late Latin *foederatus*, based on *foedus, foeder-* 'league, covenant.' **—fed·er·a·tive** /-ˌrātiv; -rətiv/ *adj.*

Fed·er·at·ed States of Mi·cro·ne·sia full name for **MICRONESIA** (sense 2).

fed·er·a·tion /ˌfedəˈrāsʜən/ ▸*n.* a group of states with a central government but independence in internal affairs: [in *names*] *should the world be governed by a Pax Americana or by a democratic UN federation?* ■ an organization or group within which smaller divisions have some degree of internal autonomy: [in *names*] *the best tag team in the World Wrestling Federation.* ■ the action of forming states or organizations into a single group with centralized control: *a first step in the federation of Europe.* ▷early 18th cent.: from French *fédération*, from late Latin *foederatio(n-)*, from the verb *foederare* 'to ally,' from *foedus* 'league.' **—fed·er·a·tion·ist** /-ist/ *n.*

fedora

fe·do·ra /fəˈdôrə/ ▸*n.* a low, soft felt hat with a curled brim and the crown creased lengthwise. ▷late 19th cent. (originally U.S.): from *Fédora*, the title of a drama (1882) written by the French dramatist Victorien Sardou (1831–1908).

fed up ▸*adj.* [*predic.*] annoyed or upset at a situation or treatment: *he was* **fed up with** *doing all the work.*

fee /fē/ ▸*n.* **1** a payment made to a professional person or to a professional or public body in exchange for advice or services. ■ money paid as part of a special transaction, e.g., for a privilege or for admission to something: *the gallery charges an admission fee.* ■ (usu. **fees**) money regularly paid (esp. to a school or similar institution) for continuing services: *high tuition fees required by the schools.* **2** *historical Law* an estate of land, esp. one held on condition of feudal service.
▸*v.* (**fees, fee'd** or **feed, fee·ing**) [*trans.*] *rare* make a payment to (someone) in return for services. ▷Middle English: from an Anglo-Norman French variant of Old French *feu, fief*, from medieval Latin *feodum, feudum*, ultimately of Germanic origin. Compare with **FEU** and **FIEF**.
▸*PHRASE* □ **hold something in fee** *Law, historical* hold an estate in return for feudal service to a superior.

feeb /fēb/ *informal* ▸*n.* **1** a feebleminded person. **2** an FBI agent.

fee·bate /ˈfēˌbāt/ ▸*n.* a system of charges and rebates whereby energy-efficient or environmentally friendly practices are rewarded while failure to adhere to such practices is penalized. ▷1990s: blend of *fee* and *rebate*.

fee·ble /ˈfēbəl/ ▸*adj.* (**-bler, -blest**) lacking physical strength, esp. as a result of age or illness: *my legs are very feeble after the flu.* See note at **WEAK**. ■ (of a sound) faint: *his voice sounded feeble and far away.* ■ lacking strength of character: *she overreacted in such a feeble, juvenile way.* ■ failing to convince or impress: *a feeble excuse.* ▷Middle English: from Old French *fieble*, earlier *fleible*, from Latin *flebilis* 'lamentable,' from *flere* 'weep.' **—fee·ble·ness** *n.* **—fee·bly** /ˈfēb(ə)lē/ *adv.*

fee·ble·mind·ed /ˈfēbəlˌmīndəd/ (also **fee·ble-mind·ed**) ▸*adj.* (of a person) unable to make intelligent decisions or judgments. ■ (of an idea or proposal) lacking in sense or clear direction: *a feeble-minded policy.* ■ *dated* (of a person) having less than average intelligence. **—fee·ble·mind·ed·ly** (also **fee·ble-mind·ed·ly**) *adv.* **—fee·ble·mind·ed·ness** (also **fee·ble-mind·ed·ness**) *n.*

feed /fēd/ ▸*v.* (*past* **fed** /fed/) [*trans.*] **1** give food to: *the raiders fed the guard dog to keep it quiet* | [with *two objs.*] *he fed her brownies he had just baked.* ■ [*intrans.*] (esp. of an animal or baby) take food; eat something: *morays emerge at night to feed.* ■ provide an adequate supply of food for: *the island's simple agriculture could hardly feed its inhabitants.* ■ [*intrans.*] (**feed on/off**) derive regular nourishment from (a particular substance): *the bird feeds on cliff-top vegetation | figurative his powerful mind fed off political discussion.* ■ encourage the growth of: *I could feed my melancholy by reading Romantic poetry.* ■ give fertilizer to (a plant). ■ put fuel on (a fire). **2** supply (a machine) with material, power, or other things necessary for its operation: *the programs are* **fed into** *the computer.* ■ [with *two objs.*] supply (someone) with (information, ideas, etc.): *I think he is feeding his old employer commercial secrets.* ■ supply water to (a body of water): *the pond is fed by a small stream* | [*intrans.*] *water* **feeds into** *the lower pool.* ■ insert further coins into (a meter) to extend the time for which it operates. ■ [with *two objs.*] prompt (an actor) with (a line): *you were still in the wings feeding Micky his lines.* ■ (in ball games) pass (the ball) to a player: *he took the ball and fed Salley.* ■ distribute (a broadcast) to local television or radio stations via satellite or network: *programs that the national networks feed to local stations.* **3** [*trans.*] cause to move gradually and steadily, typically through a confined space: *make holes through which to feed the cables.*
▸*phrasal v.* □ **feed back 1** (of a response) influence the development of the thing that has given rise to it: *what the audience tells me feeds back into my work.* **2** (of an electrical or other system) produce feedback.
▸*n.* **1** an act of giving food, esp. to animals or a baby, or of having food given to one: *I've just given the horse her feed.* ■ *informal* a meal: *how 'bout I fix up a nice hot feed?* ■ food for domestic animals: *cow feed.* **2** a device or conduit for supplying material to a machine: *the plotter has a continuous paper feed.* ■ the supply of raw material to a machine or device: [as *adj.*] *a feed pipe.* ■ a broadcast distributed by satellite or network from a central source to a large number of radio or television stations: *a satellite feed from Washington.* **3** a line or prompt given to an actor on stage. ■ an actor who provides such a line or prompt. ▷Old English *fēdan* (verb); related to **FOOD**.
▸*PHRASE* □ **off one's feed** *informal* having no appetite.

feed·back /ˈfēdˌbak/ ▸*n.* **1** information about reactions to a product, a person's performance of a task, etc., used as a basis for improvement. **2** the modification or control of a process or system by its results or effects, e.g., in a biochemical pathway or behavioral response. See also **NEGATIVE FEEDBACK, POSITIVE FEEDBACK**. ■ the return of a fraction of the output signal from an amplifier, microphone, or other device to the input of the same device; sound distortion produced by this.

feed dog ▸*n.* the mechanism in a sewing machine that feeds the material under the needle.

feed·er /ˈfēdər/ ▸*n.* **1** a person or animal that eats a particular food or in a particular manner: *a plankton feeder.* **2** a container filled with food for birds or mammals. **3** a person or thing that supplies something, in particular: ■ a device supplying material to a machine: *the automatic sheet feeder holds up to 10 sheets of paper.* ■ a tributary stream. ■ [usu. as *adj.*] a branch road or railroad line linking outlying districts with a main communication system. ■ a transmission line carrying electricity to a distribution point. ■ [usu. as *adj.*] a school, sports team, etc., from which members move on to one more advanced: *a feeder school for Florida State University.*

feed·for·ward /ˈfēdˌfôrwərd/ ▸*n.* the modification or control of a process using its anticipated results or effects.

feed·ing bot·tle ▸*n. Brit.* a baby-bottle.

feed·ing fren·zy ▸*n.* an aggressive and competitive group-attack on prey by a number of sharks or piranhas. ■ *figurative* an episode of frantic competition or rivalry for something: *his casual remark caused a media feeding-frenzy.*

feed·lot /ˈfēdˌlät/ ▸*n.* an area or building where livestock are fed and fattened up.

feed·stock /ˈfēdˌstäk/ ▸*n.* raw material to supply or fuel a machine or industrial process.

feed·stuff /ˈfēdˌstəf/ ▸*n.* (usu. **feedstuffs**) a food provided for cattle and other livestock.

feed·through /ˈfēdˌᴛʜro͞o/ ▸*n.* an electrical connector used to join two parts of a circuit on opposite sides of something, such as a circuit board or a grounding screen.

feel /fēl/ ▸*v.* (*past* **felt** /felt/) [*trans.*] **1** be aware of (a person or object) through touching or being touched: *she felt someone touch her shoulder.* ■ be aware of (something happening) through physical sensation: *she felt the ground give way beneath her.* ■ examine or search by touch: *he touched her head and felt her hair* | [*intrans.*] *he* **felt around** *for the matches.* ■ [*intrans.*] be capable of sensation: *the dead cannot feel.* ■ [*intrans.*] give a sensation of a particular physical quality when touched: *the wool feels soft.* ■ (**feel one's way**) find one's way by touch rather than sight: *she plunged into the darkness of the tunnel, feeling her way along the walls.* ■ (**feel one's way**) *figurative* act cautiously, esp. in an area with which one is unfamiliar: *she was new in the job, still feeling her way.* ■ (**feel something out**) *informal* investigate something cautiously: *they want to feel out the situation.* ■ (**feel someone up**) *informal* fondle someone for one's own sexual stimulation. **2** experience (an emotion or sensation): *I felt a sense of excitement* | [*intrans.*] *I felt angry and humiliated.* ■ [*intrans.*] consider oneself to be in a particular state or exhibiting particular qualities: *he doesn't feel obliged to visit every weekend.* ■ (**feel up to**) have the strength and energy to do or deal with: *after the accident she didn't feel up to driving.* ■ [usu. with *negative*] (**feel oneself**) be healthy and well: *Ruth was not quite feeling herself.* ■ be emotionally affected by: *he didn't feel the loss of his mother so keenly.* ■ [*intrans.*] have a specified reaction or attitude, esp. an emotional one, toward something: *we* **feel** *very strongly* **about** *freedom of expression.* ■ (**feel for**) have compassion for: *poor woman—I feel for her.* **3** [with *clause*] have a belief or impression, esp. without an identifiable reason: *she felt that the woman positively disliked her.* ■ hold an opinion: *I felt I could make a useful contribution.*
▸*n.* [usu. in *sing.*] **1** an act of touching something to examine it. ■ the sense of touch: *he worked by feel rather than using his eyes.* **2** a sensation given by an object or material when touched: *nylon cloth with a cotton feel.* ■ the impression given by something: *the restaurant has a modern bistro feel.* ▷Old English *fēlan*.
▸*PHRASES* □ **feel one's age** become aware that one is growing older and less energetic. □ **feel free (to do something)** have no hesitation or shyness (often used as an invitation or for reassurance): *feel free to*

say what you like. □ **feel like (doing) something** be inclined to have or do: *I feel like celebrating.* □ **feel one's oats** see OAT. □ **feel the pinch** see PINCH. □ **feel the pulse of** see PULSE[1]. □ **feel small** see SMALL. □ **feel strange** see STRANGE. □ **get a** (or **the**) **feel for** (or **of**) familiarize oneself with: *you can explore to get a feel of the place.* □ **have a feel for** have a sensitive appreciation or an intuitive understanding of: *you have to have a feel for animals.* □ **make oneself** (or **one's presence**) **felt** make people keenly aware of one; have a noticeable effect: *the economic crisis began to make itself felt.*

feel·er /ˈfēlər/ ▸*n.* an animal organ such as an antenna or palp that is used for testing things by touch or for searching for food. ■ *figurative* a tentative proposal intended to ascertain someone's attitude or opinion: *he **put out feelers** about seeking the party nomination.*

feel·er gauge ▸*n.* a gauge consisting of a number of thin blades of calibrated thickness used for measuring narrow gaps or clearances.

feel-good ▸*adj.* [*attrib.*] causing a feeling of happiness and well-being: *a feel-good movie.* **—feel-good·ism** /-ˌgŏŏdˌizəm/ *n.*

feel·ing /ˈfēliNG/ ▸*n.* **1** an emotional state or reaction: *a feeling of joy.* ■ (**feelings**) the emotional side of someone's character; emotional responses or tendencies to respond: *I don't want to hurt her feelings.* ■ strong emotion: *"God bless you!" she said with feeling.* See note at EMOTION. **2** a belief, esp. a vague or irrational one: [with *clause*] *he had the feeling that he was being watched.* ■ an opinion, typically one shared by several people: *a feeling grew that justice had not been done.* **3** the capacity to experience the sense of touch: *a loss of feeling in the hands.* ■ the sensation of touching or being touched by a particular thing: *the feeling of water against your skin.* **4** (**feeling for**) a sensitivity to or intuitive understanding of: *he seems to have little feeling for art.*
▸*adj.* showing emotion or sensitivity: *he had a warm and feeling heart.* **—feel·ing·less** *adj.*

feel·ing·ly /ˈfēliNGlē/ ▸*adv.* (of the expression of an emotion or opinion) in a heartfelt way: *"Thank goodness," she said feelingly.*

fee sim·ple ▸*n.* (*pl.* **fees sim·ple**) *Law* a permanent and absolute tenure of an estate in land with freedom to dispose of it at will, esp. (in full **fee simple absolute**) a freehold tenure, which is the main type of land ownership.

feet /fēt/ ▸ plural form of FOOT.

fee tail ▸*n.* (*pl.* **fees tail**) *historical Law* a former type of tenure of an estate in land with restrictions or entailment regarding the line of heirs to whom it may be willed. ▷late Middle English: from Anglo-Norman French *fee tailé* (see FEE, TAIL[2]).

feet first ▸*adv.* **1** after death; as a corpse: *everyone told me that they were going to carry me out feet first.* **2** without hesitation or preparation: *the show begins in a way that compels the audience to jump in feet first.*

feh /fe/ ▸*exclam.* conveying disapproval, displeasure, or disgust: *The greatest writer in the English language? Feh!* ▷Yiddish.

Feh·ling's so·lu·tion /ˈfāliNGz/ (also **Fehling's reagent**) ▸*n.* an alkaline solution of copper(II) sulfate and a tartrate, used in a laboratory test for sugars.

Feif·fer, Jules (1929–), U.S. cartoonist and writer. He is best known for his satirical cartoons, which appeared in *The Village Voice* and the *New Yorker.*

feign /fān/ ▸*v.* [*trans.*] pretend to be affected by (a feeling, state, or injury): *she feigned nervousness.* ■ *archaic* invent (a story or excuse). ■ [*intrans.*] *archaic* indulge in pretense. ▷Middle English: from Old French *feign-*, stem of *feindre*, from Latin *fingere* 'mold, contrive.' Senses in Middle English (taken from Latin) included 'make something,' 'invent a story, excuse, or allegation,' hence 'make a pretense of a feeling or response.' Compare with FICTION and FIGMENT.

fei·jo·a /fāˈyōə; -ˈhōə/ ▸*n.* an evergreen shrub or small tree that bears edible green fruit resembling guavas. It is native to tropical South America and cultivated in New Zealand for its fruit. • Genus *Feijoa*, family Myrtaceae: two species. ■ the fruit of this plant. ▷late 19th cent.: modern Latin, named after J. da Silva *Feijó* (1760–1824), Brazilian naturalist.

fei·jo·a·da /ˌfāzhŏŏˈädə; fāˈjwädə/ ▸*n.* a Brazilian or Portuguese stew of black beans with pork or other meat and vegetables, served with rice. ▷Portuguese, from *feijão*, from Latin *phaseolus* 'bean.'

Fein·stein /ˈfīnˌstīn/, Dianne (1933–), U.S. politician. She served as mayor of San Francisco, California 1978–88 before she became a U.S. senator 1992– .

feint[1] /fānt/ ▸*n.* a deceptive or pretended blow, thrust, or other movement, esp. in boxing or fencing: *a brief feint at the opponent's face.* ■ a mock attack or movement in warfare, made in order to distract or deceive an enemy.
▸*v.* [*intrans.*] make a deceptive or distracting movement, typically during a fight: *he feinted left, drawing a punch and slipping it.* ■ [*trans.*] pretend to throw a (punch or blow) in order to deceive or distract an opponent: *Feinting a left, I bobbed to the right.* ▷late 17th cent.: from French *feinte*, past participle (used as a noun) of *feindre* 'feign.'

feint[2] ▸*adj.* denoting paper printed with faint lines as a guide for handwriting; denoting the lines so printed. ▷mid 19th cent.: variant of FAINT.

feist·y /ˈfīstē/ ▸*adj.* (**feist·i·er, feist·i·est**) *informal* having or showing exuberance and strong determination: *a feisty, outspoken, streetwise teenager.* ■ touchy and aggressive: *he got a bit feisty and tried to hit me.* ▷late 19th cent.: from earlier *feist, fist* 'small dog,' from *fisting cur* or *hound*, a derogatory term for a lapdog, from Middle English *fist* 'break wind.' Compare with FIZZLE. **—feist·i·ly** /ˈfīstəlē/ *adv.* **—feist·i·ness** /ˈfīstēnis/ *n.*

fe·la·fel ▸*n.* variant spelling of FALAFEL.

Fel·den·krais meth·od /ˈfeldənˌkrīs/ ▸*n.* a system designed to promote bodily and mental well-being by conscious analysis of neuromuscular activity via exercises that improve flexibility and coordination and increase ease and range of motion. ▷1930s: named after Moshe *Feldenkrais* (1904-84), Russian-born physicist and mechanical engineer.

feld·spar /ˈfel(d)ˌspär/ ▸*n.* an abundant rock-forming mineral typically occurring as colorless or pale-colored crystals and consisting of aluminosilicates of potassium, sodium, and calcium. ▷mid 18th cent.: alteration of German *Feldspat, Feldspath*, from *Feld* 'field' + *Spat, Spath* 'spar' (see SPAR[3]). The form *felspar* is by mistaken association with German *Fels* 'rock.'

feld·spath·ic /fel(d)ˈspaTHik/ ▸*adj. Geology* (of a mineral or rock) of the nature of or containing feldspar.

feld·spath·oid /fel(d)ˈspaTHˌoid/ ▸*n. Geology* any of a group of minerals chemically similar to feldspar but containing less silica, such as nepheline and leucite. **—feld·spath·oid·al** /ˌfel(d)spaTHˈoidl/ *adj.*

fe·li·cif·ic /ˌfēləˈsifik/ ▸*adj. Ethics* relating to or promoting increased happiness: *the institution of a rule against murder is in general felicific.* ▷mid 19th cent.: from Latin *felicificus*, from *felix, felic-* 'happy.'

fe·lic·i·tate /fəˈlisəˌtāt/ ▸*v.* [*trans.*] congratulate: *the award winner was felicitated by the cultural association.* ▷early 17th cent. (in the sense 'regard as or pronounce happy or fortunate'): from late Latin *felicitat-* 'made happy,' from the verb *felicitare*, from Latin *felix, felic-* 'happy.'

fe·lic·i·ta·tion /fəˌlisəˈtāSHən/ *n.* (**felicitations**) words expressing praise for an achievement or good wishes on a special occasion.

fe·lic·i·tous /fəˈlisətəs/ ▸*adj.* well chosen or suited to the circumstances: *a felicitous phrase.* ■ pleasing and fortunate: *the view was the room's only felicitous feature.* **—fe·lic·i·tous·ly** *adv.* **—fe·lic·i·tous·ness** *n.*

fe·lic·i·ty /fəˈlisətē/ ▸*n.* (*pl.* **-ties**) **1** intense happiness: *domestic felicity.* **2** the ability to find appropriate expression for one's thoughts: *speech that pleased by its accuracy, felicity, and fluency.* ■ a particularly effective feature of a work of literature or art: *the King James version, thanks to its felicities of language, ruled supreme.* ▷late Middle English: from Old French *felicite*, from Latin *felicitas*, from *felix, felic-* 'happy.'

fe·lid /ˈfēlid/ ▸*n. Zoology* a mammal of the cat family (Felidae); a wild cat. ▷late 19th cent.: from modern Latin *Felidae* (plural), from Latin *feles* 'cat.'

fe·line /ˈfēˌlīn/ ▸*adj.* of, relating to, or affecting cats or other members of the cat family: *feline leukemia.* ■ catlike, esp. in beauty or slyness: *her face was feline in shape.*
▸*n.* a cat or other member of the cat family. ▷late 17th cent.: from Latin *felinus*, from *feles* 'cat.' **—fe·lin·i·ty** /fēˈlinətē/ *n.*

fe·lix cul·pa /ˈfāliks ˈkŏŏlpə; ˈfēliks/ ▸*n. Christian Theology* the sin of Adam viewed as fortunate, because it brought about the blessedness of the Redemption. ■ an apparent error or disaster with happy consequences: *he presents the revolt of the Noldor as a felix culpa.* ▷mid 20th cent.: Latin, literally 'happy fault.'

fell[1] /fel/ ▸ past of FALL.

fell[2] ▸*v.* [*trans.*] **1** (usu. **be felled**) cut down (a tree). ■ knock down: *strong winds felled power lines* | *figurative corruption that felled the financial system in Thailand.* **2** (also **flat-fell**) stitch down (the edge of a seam) to lie flat: [as *adj.*] (**flat-felled**) *a flat-felled seam.*
▸*n.* an amount of timber cut. ▷Old English *fellan*, of Germanic origin; related to FALL.

fell[3] ▸*n.* a hill or stretch of high moorland, esp. in northern England: [in *place names*] *Cross Fell* | *an area of fell and moor.* ▷Middle English: from Old Norse *fjall, fell* 'hill'.

fell[4] ▸*adj. poetic/literary* of terrible evil or ferocity; deadly: *sorcerers use spells to achieve their fell ends.* ▷Middle English: from Old French *fel*, nominative of *felon* 'wicked (person)' (see FELON[1]).
▸*PHRASE* □ **in** (or **at**) **one fell swoop** all at one time: *nothing can topple the government in one fell swoop.* [from Shakespeare's *Macbeth* (IV. iii. 219).]

fell[5] ▸*n. archaic* an animal's hide or skin with its hair. ▷Old English *fel, fell*, of Germanic origin; from an Indo-European root shared by Latin *pellis* and Greek *pella* 'skin.'

fel·la /ˈfelə/ (also **fel·lah**) ▸*n.* nonstandard spelling of FELLOW, used in representing speech in various dialects: *goodbye, young fella.*

fel·lah /ˈfelə; felˈä/ ▸*n.* (*pl.* **fel·la·hin** /ˌfeləˈhēn, fəˌlä-/) an Egyptian peasant. ▷from Arabic *fallāḥ* 'tiller of the soil,' from *falaḥa* 'till the soil.'

fel·late /ˈfelˌāt/ ▸*v.* [*trans.*] perform fellatio on (a man). ▷late 19th cent.: from Latin *fellat-* 'sucked,' from the verb *fellare.*

fel·la·ti·o /fəˈlāSH(ē)ˌō/ ▸*n.* oral stimulation of a man's penis. ▷late 19th cent.: modern Latin, from Latin *fellare* 'to suck.' **—fel·la·tor** /ˈfelˌātər/ *n.*

Fel·ler /ˈfelər/, Bob (1918–), U.S. baseball player; full name *Robert William Andrew Feller.* He pitched for the Cleveland Indians 1936–56 (with the exception of 1942–44 when he served in the U.S. Navy) and led American League pitchers in strikeouts seven times. Baseball Hall of Fame (1962).

fell·er[1] /ˈfelər/ ▸*n.* nonstandard spelling of FELLOW, used in representing speech in various dialects.

fell·er[2] ▸*n.* a person who cuts down trees.

fellies /ˈfelēz/ ▸*plural n.* another term for FELLOES.

Fel·li·ni /fəˈlēnē/, Federico (1920–93), Italian movie director. He is known for *La Strada* (1954), which won an Academy Award for best foreign movie. Other notable movies: *La Dolce Vita* (1960) and *8½* (1963).

fel·loes /ˈfelōz/ (also **fel·lies** /ˈfelēz/) ▸*plural n.* the outer rim of a wheel, to which the spokes are fixed. ▷Old English *felg* (singular).

fel·low /ˈfelō/ ▸*n.* **1** *informal* a man or boy: *he was an extremely obliging fellow.* ■ a boyfriend or lover: *has she got a fellow?* **2** (usu. **fellows**) a person in the same position, involved in the same activity, or otherwise associated with another: *he was learning with a rapidity unique among his fellows.* ■ a thing of the same kind as or otherwise associated with another: *the page has been torn away from its fellows.* **3** a member of a learned society: *he was elected a fellow of the Geological Society.* ■ (also **research fellow**) a student or graduate receiving a fellowship for a period of research. ■ *Brit.* an incorporated senior member of a college: *a tutorial fellow.* ■ a member of the governing body in some universities.
▸*adj.* [*attrib.*] sharing a particular activity, quality, or condition with someone or something: *they urged the troops not to fire on their fellow citizens.* ▷late Old English *fēolaga* 'a partner or colleague' (literally 'one who lays down money in a joint enterprise'), from Old Norse *félagi*, from *félag* 'partnership' from *fé* 'cattle, property, money' + *lag* 'a laying down', from the Germanic base of LAY[1].

fel·low feel·ing ▸*n.* sympathy and fellowship existing between people based on shared experiences or feelings.

fel·low·ship /ˈfelōˌSHip/ ▸*n.* **1** friendly association, esp. with people who share one's interests: *they valued fun and good fellowship as the cement of the community.* ■ a group of people meeting to pursue a shared interest or aim. ■ a guild or corporation. **2** an endowment established or a sum of money awarded to support a scholar or student engaged in advanced research in a particular field: *a four-year postdoctoral fellowship.* ■ the status of a fellow of a college or society: *she held the Faulkner fellowship.*

fel·low trav·el·er ▸*n.* a person who travels with another. ■ a person who is not a member of a particular group or political party (esp. the Communist

Pronunciation Key ə *ago;* ər *over;* ˈə or ˌə *up;* ˈər or ˌər *fur;* a *hat;* ā *rate;* ä *car;* CH *chew;* e *let;* ē *see;* e(ə)r *air;* i *fit;* ī *by;* i(ə)r *ear;* NG *sing;* ō *go;* ô *for;* oi *boy;* ŏŏ *good;* o͞o *goo;* ou *out;* SH *she;* TH *thin;* T͟H *then;* (h)w *why;* ZH *vision*

F

Party), but who sympathizes with the group's aims and policies. **—fel·low trav·el·ing** *adj.*

fe·lo-de-se /ˌfelō də ˈsā/ ▸*n.* (*pl.* **fe·los-de-se** /ˌfelōz də ˈsā/) suicide. ▷from Anglo-Latin, literally 'felon of himself'; formerly a criminal act in the UK.

fel·on[1] /ˈfelən/ ▸*n.* a person who has been convicted of a felony.
▸*adj.* [*attrib.*] *archaic* cruel; wicked: *the felon undermining hand of dark corruption.* ▷Middle English: from Old French, literally 'wicked, a wicked person' (oblique case of *fel* 'evil'), from medieval Latin *fello, fellon-*. Compare with FELON[2].

fel·on[2] ▸*n.* archaic term for WHITLOW. ▷Middle English: perhaps a specific use of FELON[1]; medieval Latin *fello, fellon-* had the same sense.

fe·lo·ni·ous /fəˈlōnēəs/ ▸*adj.* of, relating to, or involved in crime: *they turned their felonious talents to the smuggling trade.* ■ *Law* relating to or of the nature of felony: *his conduct was felonious.* **—fe·lo·ni·ous·ly** *adv.*

fel·o·ny /ˈfelənē/ ▸*n.* (*pl.* **-nies**) a crime, typically one involving violence, regarded as more serious than a misdemeanor, and usually punishable by imprisonment for more than one year or by death: *he pleaded guilty to six felonies | an accusation of felony.*

The distinction between felonies and misdemeanors usually depends on the penalties or consequences attaching to the crime. In English common law, felony originally comprised those offenses (murder, wounding, arson, rape, and robbery) for which the penalty included forfeiture of land and goods.

▷Middle English: from Old French *felonie*, from *felon* (see FELON[1]).

fel·sic /ˈfelsik/ ▸*adj. Geology* of, relating to, or denoting a group of light-colored minerals including feldspar, feldspathoids, quartz, and muscovite. Often contrasted with MAFIC. ▷early 20th cent.: from FELDSPAR + a contraction of SILICA.

fel·spar /ˈfelˌspär/ ▸*n. Brit.* variant spelling of FELDSPAR.

felt[1] /felt/ ▸*n.* a kind of cloth made by rolling and pressing wool or another suitable textile accompanied by the application of moisture or heat, which causes the constituent fibers to mat together to create a smooth surface.
▸*v.* [*trans.*] make into felt; mat together: *the wood fibers are shredded and felted together.* ■ cover with felt: [as *adj.*] (**felted**) *a felted roof.* ■ [*intrans.*] become matted: *care must be taken in washing, or the wool will shrink and felt.* ▷Old English; related to FILTER. **—felt·y** *adj.*

felt[2] ▸ past and past participle of FEEL.

felt-tip pen (also **felt-tipped pen** or **felt tip**) ▸*n.* a pen with a writing point made of felt or other tightly packed fibers, typically containing a brightly colored ink.

fe·luc·ca /fəˈlo͝okə; -ˈləkə/ ▸*n.* a small vessel propelled by oars or lateen sails or both, used on the Nile and formerly more widely in the Mediterranean region. ▷early 17th cent.: from Italian *feluc(c)a*, probably from obsolete Spanish *faluca*, from Arabic *fulk* 'ship', probably from Greek *epholkion* '(towed) boat'.

fem /fem/ ▸*n.* variant spelling of FEMME.

fem. ▸*abbr.* ■ female. ■ feminine.

FEMA /ˈfēmə/ ▸*abbr.* Federal Emergency Management Agency.

fe·male /ˈfēˌmāl/ ▸*adj.* of or denoting the sex that can bear offspring or produce eggs, distinguished biologically by the production of gametes (ova) that can be fertilized by male gametes: *a herd of female deer.* ■ relating to or characteristic of women or female animals: *a female audience | a female name.* ■ (of a plant or flower) having a pistil but no stamens. ■ (of parts of machinery, fittings, etc.) manufactured hollow so that a corresponding male part can be inserted.
▸*n.* a female person, animal, or plant. ▷Middle English: from Old French *femelle*, from Latin *femella*, diminutive of *femina* 'a woman.' The change in the ending was due to association with MALE, but the words *male* and *female* are not otherwise linked etymologically. **—fe·male·ness** *n.*

fe·male cir·cum·ci·sion ▸*n.* (among some peoples) the action or traditional practice of cutting off the clitoris and sometimes the labia of girls or young women.

fe·male con·dom ▸*n.* a contraceptive device made of thin rubber, inserted into a woman's vagina before sexual intercourse.

feme cov·ert /ˈfem ˈkəvərt; ˈfēm/ ▸*n. historical Law* a married woman. ▷early 16th cent.: from Anglo-Norman French, literally 'a woman covered (i.e., protected by marriage).'

feme sole /ˈfem ˈsōl; ˈfēm/ ▸*n. historical Law* a woman without a husband, esp. one who is divorced. ▷early 16th cent.: from Anglo-Norman French *feme soule* 'a woman alone.'

fem·i·nal /ˈfemənl/ ▸*adj. archaic* of or relating to a woman. ▷late Middle English: from medieval Latin *feminalis*, from Latin *femina* 'woman.' **—fem·i·nal·i·ty** /ˌfeməˈnalətē/ *n.*

fem·i·ne·i·ty /ˌfeməˈnēətē; -ˈnāətē/ ▸*n. archaic* the quality of being feminine. ▷early 19th cent.: from Latin *femineus* 'womanish' (from *femina* 'woman') + -ITY.

fem·i·nine /ˈfemənin/ ▸*adj.* **1** having qualities or appearance traditionally associated with women, esp. delicacy and prettiness: *a feminine frilled blouse.* ■ of or relating to women; female: *he enjoys feminine company.* **2** *Grammar* of or denoting a gender of nouns and adjectives, conventionally regarded as female. **3** *Music* (of a cadence) occurring on a metrically weak beat.
▸*n.* (**the feminine**) the female sex or gender: *the association of the arts with the feminine.* ■ *Grammar* a feminine word or form. ▷late Middle English: from Latin *femininus*, from *femina* 'woman.' **—fem·i·nine·ly** *adv.* **—fem·i·nine·ness** *n.* **—fem·i·nin·i·ty** /ˌfeməˈninətē/ *n.*

fem·i·nine rhyme ▸*n. Prosody* a rhyme between stressed syllables followed by one or more unstressed syllables (e.g., *stocking/shocking, glamorous/amorous.*) Compare with MASCULINE RHYME.

fem·i·nism /ˈfeməˌnizəm/ ▸*n.* the advocacy of women's rights on the grounds of political, social, and economic equality to men.

The issue of rights for women first became prominent during the French and American revolutions in the late 18th century. In Britain it was not until the emergence of the suffragette movement in the late 19th century that there was significant political change. A 'second wave' of feminism arose in the 1960s, with an emphasis on unity and sisterhood.

▷late 19th cent.: from French *féminisme*.

fem·i·nist /ˈfemənist/ ▸*n.* a person who supports feminism.
▸*adj.* of, relating to, or supporting feminism: *feminist literature.* ▷late 19th cent.: from French *féministe*, from Latin *femina* 'woman.'

fem·i·nize /ˈfeməˌnīz/ ▸*v.* [*trans.*] make (something) more characteristic of or associated with women: *as office roles changed, clerical work was increasingly feminized.* ■ induce female sexual characteristics in (a male). **—fem·i·ni·za·tion** /ˌfemənəˈzāshən/ *n.*

femme /fem/ (also **fem**) ▸*n. informal* a lesbian or an effeminate male homosexual who takes a traditionally feminine sexual role. ▷1960s: French, 'woman.'

femme fa·tale /ˌfem fəˈtal; fəˈtäl/ ▸*n.* (*pl.* **femmes fa·tales** *pronunc.* same) an attractive and seductive woman, esp. one who will ultimately bring disaster to a man who becomes involved with her. ▷early 20th cent.: French, literally 'disastrous woman.'

femto- ▸*comb. form* (used in units of measurement) denoting a factor of 10^{-15}: *femtosecond.* ▷from Danish or Norwegian *femten* 'fifteen.'

fe·mur /ˈfēmər/ ▸*n.* (*pl.* **fe·murs** or **fem·o·ra** /ˈfemərə/) *Anatomy* the bone of the thigh or upper hind limb, articulating at the hip and the knee. ■ *Zoology* the third segment of the leg in insects and some other arthropods, typically the longest and thickest segment. ▷late 15th cent.: from Latin *femur, femor-* 'thigh.' **—fem·o·ral** /ˈfemərəl/ *adj.*

fen[1] /fen/ ▸*n.* a low and marshy or frequently flooded area of land: *a flooded fen | 55 acres of fen.* ■ (**the Fens**) flat low-lying areas of eastern England, formerly marshland but largely drained for agriculture since the 17th century. ■ *Ecology* wetland with alkaline, neutral, or only slightly acid peaty soil. Compare with BOG. ▷Old English *fen(n)*. **—fen·ny** *adj.*

fen[2] ▸*n.* (*pl.* same) a monetary unit of China, equal to one hundredth of a yuan. ▷from Chinese *fēn* 'a hundredth part.'

fence /fens/ ▸*n.* **1** a barrier, railing, or other upright structure, typically of wood or wire, enclosing an area of ground to mark a boundary, control access, or prevent escape. ■ a large upright obstacle used in equestrian jumping events. ■ a guard or guide on a plane, saw, or other tool. **2** *informal* a person who deals in stolen goods.
▸*v.* **1** [*trans.*] (often **be fenced**) surround or protect with a fence: *our garden was not fully fenced.* ■ (**fence something in/off**) enclose or separate with a fence for protection or to prevent escape: *everything is fenced in to keep out the wolves.* ■ (**fence someone/something out**) use a barrier to exclude someone or something: *Idaho law requires people to fence out cows.* **2** [*trans.*] *informal* deal in (stolen goods): *after stealing your ring, he didn't even know how to fence it.* **3** [*intrans.*] fight with swords, esp. as a sport. See also FENCING. ■ *figurative* conduct a discussion or argument in such a way as to avoid the direct mention of something: *we were fencing, not talking about the subject we'd come to talk about.* ▷Middle English (in the sense 'defending, defence'): shortening of DEFENCE. Compare with FEND. **—fence·less** *adj.* **—fenc·er** *n.*
▸*PHRASES* □ **mend (one's) fences** see MEND. □ **side of the fence** either of the opposing positions involved in a conflict: *whatever side of the fence you are on, the issue is here to stay.* □ **sit on the fence** avoid making a decision or choice.

fence liz·ard ▸*n.* a small gray-brown North American spiny lizard that typically has bright markings and often basks on rail fences, logs, and tree stumps.
• *Sceloporus undulatus*, family Iguanidae.

fence post ▸*n.* a wooden or metal post set in the ground as a supporting part of a fence.

fence·row /ˈfensˌrō/ ▸*n.* an uncultivated strip of land on each side of and below a fence.

fenc·ing /ˈfensiNG/ ▸*n.* **1** the sport of fighting with swords, esp. foils, épées, or sabers, according to a set of rules, in order to score points against an opponent: [as *adj.*] *a fencing foil.* ■ *figurative* the action of conducting a discussion or argument so as to avoid the direct mention of something. **2** a series of fences: *security fencing.* ■ material used for the construction of fences: *chestnut is still in demand for fencing.* ■ the erection of fences.

fend /fend/ ▸*v.* **1** [*intrans.*] (**fend for oneself**) look after and provide for oneself, without any help from others: *you're old enough to fend for yourself.* **2** [*trans.*] (**fend someone/something off**) defend oneself from a blow, attack, or attacker. ■ evade someone or something in order to protect oneself: *he fended off the awkward questions.* ▷Middle English (in the sense 'defend'): shortening of DEFEND. Compare with FENCE.

Fend·er /ˈfendər/, Leo (1907–91), U.S. guitar-maker. He pioneered the design and production of electric guitars and founded the company named after him.

fend·er /ˈfendər/ ▸*n.* **1** a thing used to keep something off or prevent a collision, in particular: ■ the mudguard or area around the wheel well of a vehicle. ■ a plastic cylinder, tire, etc., hung over a ship's side to protect it against impact. ■ a metal frame at the front of a locomotive or streetcar for pushing aside obstacles on the line; a cowcatcher. **2** a low frame bordering a fireplace to contain burning materials.

fend·er bend·er ▸*n. informal* a minor collision between motor vehicles.

fe·nes·tra /fəˈnestrə/ ▸*n.* (*pl.* **-trae** /-trē; -trī/) **1** *Anatomy & Zoology* a small natural hole or opening, esp. in a bone. The mammalian middle ear is linked by the **fenestra ovalis** to the vestibule of the inner ear, and by the **fenestra rotunda** to the cochlea. **2** *Medicine* an artificial opening. ■ an opening in a bandage or cast. ■ a perforation in a forceps blade. ■ a hole made by surgical fenestration. ▷early 19th cent. (as a botanical term denoting a small scar left by the separation of the seed from the ovary): from Latin, literally 'window.'

fe·nes·trate /ˈfenəˌstrāt/ ▸*adj. Botany & Zoology* having small windowlike perforations or transparent areas. ▷mid 19th cent.: from Latin *fenestratus* 'provided with openings,' from the verb *fenestrare*.

fe·nes·trat·ed /ˈfenəˌstrātid/ ▸*adj.* provided with a window or windows: *the fenestrated heights of nearby buildings.* ■ *chiefly Anatomy* having perforations, apertures, or transparent areas: *the capillaries have a fenestrated epithelium.* ▷early 19th cent.: from Latin *fenestrare* (see FENESTRATE) + -ED[1].

fen·es·tra·tion /ˌfenəˈstrāshən/ ▸*n. Architecture* the arrangement of windows and doors on the elevations of a building. ■ *Botany & Zoology* the condition of being fenestrate. ■ *Medicine* a surgical operation in which a new opening is formed, esp. in the bony labyrinth of the inner ear to treat certain types of deafness.

fen·flu·ra·mine /fenˈflo͝orəˌmēn/ ▸*n. Medicine* an SSRI appetite-suppressant drug once prescribed for obesity, but withdrawn from the U.S. market in 1997 because of safety concerns. It was one component of FEN-PHEN.

feng shui /ˈfəNG ˈSHwē; -SHwā/ ▸*n.* (in Chinese

thought) a system of laws considered to govern spatial arrangement and orientation in relation to the flow of energy (qi), and whose favorable or unfavorable effects are taken into account when siting and designing buildings. ▷Chinese, from *fēng* 'wind' and *shuǐ* 'water.'

Fe·ni·an /ˈfēnēən/ ▸*n.* a member of a 19th-century revolutionary nationalist organization among the Irish in the U.S. and Ireland. The Fenians staged an unsuccessful revolt in Ireland in 1867 and were responsible for isolated revolutionary acts against the British until the early 20th century, when they were gradually eclipsed by the IRA. ■ *informal, offensive* (chiefly in Northern Ireland) a Protestant name for a Catholic. ▷from Old Irish *féne*, the name of an ancient Irish people, confused with *fiann, fianna* (see **FIANNA FÁIL**). **—Fe·ni·an·ism** /-izəm/ *n.*

fen·land /ˈfenlənd/ ▸*n.* (also **fenlands**) land consisting of fens: *thousands of acres of fenland.* ■ (usu. **the Fenland**) the Fens of eastern England.

fen·nec /ˈfenik/ (also **fennec fox**) ▸*n.* a small pale fox with large pointed ears, native to the deserts of North Africa and Arabia. • *Vulpes zerda*, family Canidae. ▷late 18th cent.: via Arabic from Persian *fanak, fanaj*.

fen·nel /ˈfenl/ ▸*n.* an aromatic yellow-flowered European plant of the parsley family, with feathery leaves. • *Foeniculum vulgare*, family Umbelliferae: two subspecies, a hardy perennial (subsp. *dulce*), the seeds and leaves of which are used as culinary herbs, and the annual **Florence** (or **sweet**) **fennel** (subsp. *azoricum*), with swollen leaf bases that are eaten as a vegetable. ▷Old English *finule, fenol*, from Latin *faeniculum*, diminutive of *faenum* 'hay.'

fen-phen /ˈfen ˌfen/ ▸*n.* a combination of the appetite-suppressant drugs fenfluramine and phentermine not used since the withdrawal of fenfluramine from the U.S. market in 1997.

fen·ta·nyl /ˈfentənil; ˈfentn-il/ ▸*n.* a fast-acting narcotic analgesic and sedative that is sometimes abused for its heroinlike effect.

fen·u·greek /ˈfenyəˌgrēk/ ▸*n.* a white-flowered herbaceous plant of the pea family, with aromatic seeds that are used for flavoring, esp. ground and used in curry powder. • *Trigonella foenum-graecum*, family Leguminosae. ▷Old English *fenogrecum* (superseded in Middle English by forms from Old French *fenugrec*), from Latin *faenugraecum*, from *faenum graecum* 'Greek hay' (the Romans used the dried plant as fodder).

Fen·way /ˈfenˌwā/ (**the Fenway**) a park system that incorporates the wetlands in Boston, Massachusetts. Nearby is Fenway Park, the baseball stadium of the Boston Red Sox.

feoff·ee /fefˈē; fēˈfē/ ▸*n.* a trustee invested with a freehold estate to hold in possession for a purpose. ■ *historical* (in feudal law) a person to whom a grant of freehold property is made. ▷late Middle English: from Anglo-Norman French *feoffe* 'enfeoffed,' past participle of *feoffer*, variant of Old French *fieffer* (see **FEOFFMENT**).

feoff·ment /ˈfēfmənt/ ▸*n. historical* (in feudal law) a grant of ownership of freehold property to someone. ▷Middle English: from an Anglo-Norman French variant of Old French *fieffer* 'put in legal possession,' from *fief* (see **FEE** and **FIEF**). **—feof·for** /ˈfēfər/ *n.*

FEP ▸*abbr. Computing* front-end processor.

FEPC ▸*abbr.* Fair Employment Practices Commission.

FERA ▸*abbr.* Federal Emergency Relief Administration.

fe·ral /ˈfi(ə)rəl; ˈferəl/ ▸*adj.* (esp. of an animal) in a wild state, esp. after escape from captivity or domestication: *a feral cat.* ■ resembling a wild animal: *a feral snarl.* ▷early 17th cent.: from Latin *fera* 'wild animal' (from *ferus* 'wild') + **-AL**.

Fer·ber /ˈfərbər/, Edna (1887–1968), U.S. writer. She wrote the novels *So Big* (1924) and *Giant* (1952), as well as stage plays that included *Dinner at Eight* (1932, with George S. Kaufman).

fer·ber·ite /ˈfərbəˌrit/ ▸*n.* a black mineral consisting of ferrous tungstate, typically occurring as elongated prisms. ▷early 19th cent.: named after Rudolph *Ferber* (1743–90), Swedish mineralogist, + **-ITE**[1].

fer de lance /ˌfer dlˈans; -ˈäns/ ▸*n.* (*pl.* **fers de lance** *pronunc.* same or /ˌferz-/; or **fer de lances**) a large and dangerous pit viper native to Central and South America. • Genus *Bothrops*, family Viperidae: several species, in particular *B. atrox*. ▷late 19th cent.: from French, literally 'iron (head) of a lance.'

Fer·di·nand /ˈfərdnˌand/ of Aragon (1452–1516), king of Castile 1474–1516 and of Aragon 1479–1516; known as **Ferdinand the Catholic**. He and his wife Isabella instituted the Spanish Inquisition in 1478 and supported the expedition of Chistopher Columbus in 1492. Their capture of Granada from the Moors in the same year effectively united Spain as one country.

fe·ri·a /ˈfi(ə)rēə; ˈfer-/ ▸*n.* (in Spanish-speaking regions) a local fair or festival, usually in honor of a patron saint. ▷mid 19th cent.: Spanish, from Latin, literally 'holiday.'

fe·ri·al /ˈfi(ə)rēəl; ˈfer-/ ▸*adj. Christian Church* denoting an ordinary weekday, as opposed to one appointed for a festival or fast. ▷late Middle English: from medieval Latin *ferialis*, from Latin *feria* 'holiday.' In late Latin *feria* was used with a prefixed ordinal number to mean 'day of the week' (e.g., *secunda feria* 'second day, Monday'), but Sunday (Dominicus) and Saturday (Sabbatum) were usually referred to by their names; hence *feria* came to mean 'ordinary weekday.'

fe·rin·ghee /fəˈriNGgē/ (also **fe·rin·ghi**) ▸*n.* **1** *chiefly derogatory* (in India and parts of the Middle and Far East) a foreigner, esp. one with white skin. **2** *archaic* a person of Indian–Portuguese parentage. ▷via Urdu from Persian *firangī*, from the base of **FRANK**[2].

Fer·lin·ghet·ti /ˌfərliNGˈgetē/, Lawrence (Monsanto) (1919–), U.S. poet and publisher; born *Lawrence Ferling*. Identified with San Francisco's beat movement, he founded a publishing house called City Lights. Notable works: *A Coney Island of the Mind* (1958) and *Her* (1960).

Ferm. *abbr.* Fermanagh.

Fer·man·agh /fərˈmanə/ one of the six counties of Northern Ireland, formerly an administrative area; chief town, Enniskillen.

Fer·mat /ferˈmä/, Pierre de (1601–65), French mathematician. His work on curves led directly to the general methods of calculus introduced by Isaac Newton and Gottfried Leibniz. He is also recognized as the founder of the modern theory of numbers.

fer·ma·ta /ferˈmätə; fər-/ ▸*n. Music* a pause of unspecified length on a note or rest. ■ a mark (𝄐) over a note or rest that is to be lengthened by an unspecified amount. ▷Italian, from *fermare* 'to stop.'

Fer·mat's last the·o·rem /ferˈmäz/ *Mathematics* a conjecture by Fermat that if *n* is an integer greater than 2, the equation $x^n + y^n = z^n$ has no positive integral solutions. Fermat noted that he had "a truly wonderful proof" of the conjecture, but never wrote it down. In 1995 a general proof was published by the Princeton-based British mathematician Andrew Wiles.

fer·ment ▸*v.* /fərˈment/ **1** [*intrans.*] (of a substance) undergo fermentation: *the drink had fermented, turning some of the juice into alcohol.* ■ [*trans.*] cause the fermentation of (a substance). **2** [*trans.*] incite or stir up (trouble or disorder): *the politicians and warlords who are fermenting this chaos.* ■ [*intrans.*] (of a negative feeling or memory) fester and develop into something worse: *it had been fermenting in my subconscious for a while.*

▸*n.* **1** agitation and excitement among a group of people, typically concerning major change and leading to trouble or violence: *Germany at this time was in a state of religious ferment.* **2** *archaic* a fermenting agent or enzyme. ▷late Middle English: from Old French *ferment* (noun), *fermenter* (verb), based on Latin *fermentum* 'yeast,' from *fervere* 'to boil.' **—fer·ment·a·ble** /ˈferment/ *adj.*

fer·men·ta·tion /ˌfərmənˈtāSHən/ ▸*n.* the chemical breakdown of a substance by bacteria, yeasts, or other microorganisms, typically involving effervescence and the giving off of heat. ■ the process of this kind involved in the making of beer, wine, and liquor, in which sugars are converted to ethyl alcohol. ■ *archaic* agitation; excitement: *I had found Paris in high fermentation.* ▷late Middle English: from late Latin *fermentatio(n-)*, from Latin *fermentare* 'to ferment' (see **FERMENT**). **—fer·ment·a·tive** /fərˈmen(t)ətiv/ *adj.*

fer·ment·er /fərˈmentər/ ▸*n.* a container in which fermentation takes place. ■ an organism that causes fermentation.

Fer·mi /ˈfermē/, Enrico (1901–54), U.S. atomic physicist; born in Italy. He directed the first controlled nuclear chain reaction in 1942 and joined the Manhattan Project to work on the atom bomb. Nobel Prize for Physics (1938).

fer·mi /ˈfermē; ˈfər-/ ▸*n.* (*pl.* same) a unit of length equal to 10^{-15} meter (one femtometer), used in nuclear physics. It is similar to the diameter of a proton. ▷early 20th cent.: named after E. **FERMI**.

Fer·mi-Di·rac sta·tis·tics /ˈfermē dəˈrak/ *plural n.* [treated as *sing.*] *Physics* a type of quantum statistics used to describe systems of fermions. ▷1920s: named after E. **FERMI** and P. A. M. **DIRAC**.

fer·mi·on /ˈfermēˌän; ˈfər-/ ▸*n. Physics* a subatomic particle, such as a nucleon, that has half-integral spin and follows the statistical description given by Fermi and Dirac. ▷1940s: from the name of E. **FERMI** + **-ON**.

fer·mi·um /ˈfermēəm; ˈfər-/ ▸*n.* the chemical element of atomic number 100, a radioactive metal of the actinide series. Fermium does not occur naturally and was discovered in 1953 in the debris of the first hydrogen bomb explosion. (Symbol: **Fm**) ▷1950s: from the name of E. **FERMI** + **-IUM**.

fern /fərn/ ▸*n.* (*pl.* same or **ferns**) a flowerless plant that has feathery or leafy fronds and reproduces by spores released from the undersides of the fronds. Ferns have a vascular system for the transport of water and nutrients. • Class Filicopsida, division Pteridophyta. ▷Old English *fearn*. **—fern·er·y** /ˈfərnərē/ *n.* (*pl.* **-er·ies**) **—fern·y** *adj.*

Fer·nan·do Pó·o /fərˈnandō ˈpō/ former name (until 1973) for **BIOKO**.

fern bar ▸*n. informal* a barroom in a contemporary design that includes ferns and other plants.

fern·brake /ˈfərnˌbrāk/ ▸*n.* a bed or thicket of ferns. ▷early 17th cent.: from **FERN** + **BRAKE**[4].

fe·ro·cious /fəˈrōSHəs/ ▸*adj.* savagely fierce, cruel, or violent: *the wolverine is nature's most ferocious and violent animal.* ■ (of a conflict) characterized by or involving aggression, bitterness, and determination: *a ferocious argument.* ■ extreme and unpleasant: *a ferocious headache.* ▷mid 17th cent.: from Latin *ferox, feroc-* 'fierce' + **-IOUS**. **—fe·ro·cious·ly** *adv.* **—fe·ro·cious·ness** *n.*

fe·roc·i·ty /fəˈräsətē/ ▸*n.* (*pl.* **-ties**) the state or quality of being ferocious: *the ferocity of the storm caught them by surprise.* ▷mid 16th cent.: from French, or from Latin *ferocitas*, from *ferox, feroc-* 'fierce.'

-ferous (usu. **-iferous**) ▸*suffix* having, bearing, or containing (a specified thing): *Carboniferous* | *pestiferous.* ▷from French *-fère* or Latin *-fer* 'producing,' from *ferre* 'to bear.'

-ferously ▸*comb. form* in adverbs corresponding to adjectives ending in *-ferous* (such as *pestiferously* corresponding to *pestiferous*).

-ferousness ▸*comb. form* in nouns corresponding to adjectives ending in *-ferous* (such as *pestiferousness* corresponding to *pestiferous*).

Fer·ra·ra /fəˈrärə/ a city in northern Italy, capital of a province of the same name; pop. 141,000.

Fer·ra·ri /fəˈrärē/, Enzo (1898–1988), Italian car designer and manufacturer. In 1929, he founded the company named after him.

Fer·ra·ro /fəˈrärō/, Geraldine Anne (1935–), U.S. politician. The first woman from a major political party to be nominated, she ran unsuccessfully for vice president of the U.S. with Democratic candidate Walter Mondale in 1984. She had previously served in the U.S. House of Representatives 1979–85.

fer·rate /ˈferˌāt/ ▸*n. Chemistry* a salt in which the anion contains both iron (typically ferric iron) and oxygen. ▷mid 19th cent.: from Latin *ferrum* 'iron' + **-ATE**[1].

Fer·rel's law /ˈferəlz/ *Meteorology* a law stating that Coriolis forces deflect winds and freely moving objects to the right in the northern hemisphere and to the left in the southern hemisphere. ▷early 20th cent.: named after William Ferrel (1817–91), American meteorologist.

fer·ret /ˈferət/ ▸*n.* a domesticated polecat kept as a pet or used, esp. in Europe, for catching rabbits. It is typically albino or brown. • *Mustela putorius furo*, family Mustelidae; descended mainly from the European polecat. ■ (**black-footed ferret**) a rare weasellike animal (*Mustela nigripes*), found in grassland in the U.S.

ferret

▸*v.* (**-ret·ed**, **-ret·ing**) [*intrans.*] (of a person) hunt with ferrets, typically for rabbits. ■ clear (a hole or area of ground) of rabbits with ferrets. ■ [with *adverbial of place*] look around in a place or container in search of something: *he went to the desk and ferreted around.* ■ [*trans.*] (**ferret something out**) search tenaciously for and find something: *she had the ability to ferret out the facts.* ▷late Middle English: from Old French *fuiret*, alteration of *fuiron*, based on late Latin *furo* 'thief, ferret,' from Latin *fur* 'thief.' —**fer·ret·er** *n.* —**fer·ret·y** *adj.*

ferri- ▸*comb. form Chemistry* of iron with a valence of three; ferric. Compare with **FERRO-**. ▷from Latin *ferrum* 'iron.'

fer·ri·age /ˈferē-ij/ ▸*n. archaic* the action of transporting someone or something by ferry. ■ the fare paid for ferry transportation.

fer·ric /ˈferik/ ▸*adj.* of or relating to iron. ■ *Chemistry* of iron with a valence of three; of iron(III). Compare with **FERROUS**. ▷late 18th cent.: from Latin *ferrum* 'iron' + **-IC**.

fer·ri·cy·a·nide /ˌferiˈsīəˌnīd/ ▸*n. Chemistry* a salt containing the anion $Fe(CN)_6{}^{3-}$.

fer·ri·mag·net·ic /ˌferiˌmagˈnetik/ ▸*adj. Physics* (of a substance) displaying a weak form of ferromagnetism associated with parallel but opposite alignment of neighboring atoms. In contrast with antiferromagnetic materials, these alignments do not cancel out and there is a net magnetic moment. —**fer·ri·mag·ne·tism** /ˌferiˈmagnəˌtizəm/ *n.*

Fer·ris wheel /ˈferis/ ▸*n.* an amusement-park or fairground ride consisting of a giant vertical revolving wheel with passenger cars suspended on its outer edge. ▷late 19th cent.: named after George W. G. Ferris (1859–96), the American engineer who invented it.

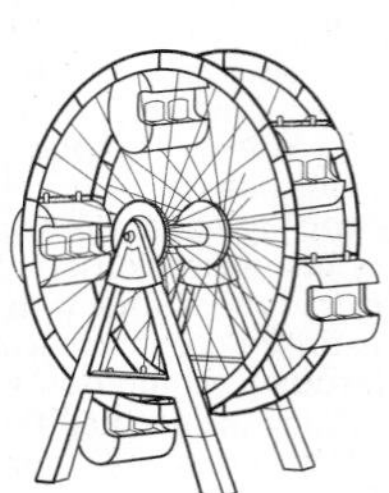
Ferris wheel

fer·rite /ˈferīt/ ▸*n.* **1** a ceramic compound consisting of a mixed oxide of iron and one or more other metals. Ferrite has ferrimagnetic properties and is used in high-frequency electrical components such as antennas. **2** *Metallurgy* a form of pure iron with a body-centered cubic crystal structure, occurring in low-carbon steel. ▷mid 19th cent.: from Latin *ferrum* 'iron' + **-ITE**[1]. —**fer·rit·ic** /fəˈritik/ *adj.* (in sense 2).

fer·ri·tin /ˈferətn/ ▸*n. Biochemistry* a protein produced in mammalian metabolism that serves to store iron in the tissues. ▷1930s: from **FERRI-** + *-t-* (for ease of pronunciation) + **-IN**[1].

ferro- ▸*comb. form* containing iron: *ferroconcrete.* ■ *Chemistry* of iron with a valence of two; ferrous. Compare with **FERRI-**. ▷from Latin *ferrum* 'iron.'

fer·ro·al·loy /ˌferōˈaloi; -əˈloi/ ▸*n.* an alloy of iron with one or more other metals, used in the production of steel.

fer·ro·cene /ˈferəˌsēn/ ▸*n. Chemistry* an orange crystalline compound whose molecule has a sandwich structure in which two planar cyclopentadiene ligands enclose an iron atom. • Chem. formula: $Fe(C_5H_5)_2$. ▷1950s: from **FERRO-** 'containing iron' + *-cene* from *c(yclopentadi)ene.*

fer·ro·con·crete /ˌferōˈkänˌkrēt/ ▸*n.* another term for **REINFORCED CONCRETE**.

fer·ro·cy·a·nide /ˌferōˈsīəˌnīd/ ▸*n. Chemistry* a salt containing the anion $Fe(CN)_6{}^{4-}$.

fer·ro·e·lec·tric /ˌferō-iˈlektrik/ *Physics* ▸*adj.* (of a substance) exhibiting permanent electric polarization that varies in strength with the applied electric field.
▸*n.* a ferroelectric substance. —**fer·ro·e·lec·tric·i·ty** /ˌferō-iˌlekˈtrisətē/ *n.*

fer·ro·flu·id /ˈferōˌflo͞oid/ ▸*n.* [often as *adj.*] a fluid containing a magnetic suspension: *ferrofluid cooling.*

fer·ro·mag·ne·sian /ˌferōˌmagˈnēzʜən; -zēən/ ▸*adj. Geology* (of a rock or mineral) containing iron and magnesium as major components.

fer·ro·mag·net·ic /ˌferōˌmagˈnetik/ ▸*adj. Physics* (of a body or substance) having a high susceptibility to magnetization, the strength of which depends on that of the applied magnetizing field, and that may persist after removal of the applied field. This is the kind of magnetism displayed by iron and is associated with parallel magnetic alignment of neighboring atoms. —**fer·ro·mag·ne·tism** /ˌferōˈmagnəˌtizəm/ *n.*

fer·ro·man·ga·nese /ˌferōˈmanɢgəˌnēz; -ˌnēs/ ▸*n.* an alloy of iron and manganese used in the production of steel.

fer·ro·sil·i·con /ˌferōˈsilikən; -ˌkän/ ▸*n.* an alloy of iron and silicon used in the production of steel and some types of iron.

fer·rous /ˈferəs/ ▸*adj.* (chiefly of metals) containing or consisting of iron. ■ *Chemistry* of iron with a valence of two; of iron(II). Compare with **FERRIC**. ▷mid 19th cent.: from Latin *ferrum* 'iron' + **-OUS**.

fer·rous ox·ide ▸*n.* a black powder, FeO, used in making steel and glass.

fer·rous sul·fate ▸*n.* a pale green iron salt used in inks, tanning, water purification, and treatment of anemia. • Alternative name: **iron(II) sulfate**; chem. formula (crystals): $FeSO_47H_2O$.

fer·ru·gi·nous /fəˈro͞ojənəs/ ▸*adj.* containing iron oxides or rust: *a band of ferruginous limestone.* ■ reddish brown; rust-colored: *the ferruginous earth of southern Brazil.* ▷mid 17th cent.: from Latin *ferrugo, ferrugin-* 'rust, dark red' (from *ferrum* 'iron') + **-OUS**.

fer·rule /ˈferəl/ ▸*n.* a ring or cap, typically a metal one, that strengthens the end of a handle, stick, or tube and prevents it from splitting or wearing. ■ a metal band strengthening or forming a joint. ▷early 17th cent.: alteration (probably by association with Latin *ferrum* 'iron') of obsolete *verrel*, from Old French *virelle*, from Latin *viriola*, diminutive of *viriae* 'bracelets.'

fer·ry /ˈferē/ ▸*n.* (*pl.* **-ries**) (also **fer·ry·boat**) a boat or ship for conveying passengers and goods, esp. over a relatively short distance and as a regular service. ■ a service for conveying passengers or goods in this way. ■ the place from which such a service operates. ■ a similar service using another mode of transportation, esp. aircraft.
▸*v.* (**-ries**, **-ried**) [*trans.*] convey in a boat, esp. across a short stretch of water: *riverboats ferried weekend picnickers to the park.* ■ transport (someone or something) from one place to another: *helicopters ferried 4,000 men into the desert.* ▷Middle English: from Old Norse *ferja* 'ferryboat,' of Germanic origin and related to **FARE**. —**fer·ry·man** /ˈferēmən/ (*pl.* **-men**) *n.*

fer·tile /ˈfərtl/ ▸*adj.* (of soil or land) producing or capable of producing abundant vegetation or crops: *fields along the fertile flood plains of the river* | *figurative Germany in the 1920s and 30s was* **fertile ground** *for such ideas.* ■ (of a seed or egg) capable of becoming a new individual. ■ (of a person, animal, or plant) able to conceive young or produce seed: *Barbara carefully calculated the period when she was most fertile.* ■ (of a person's mind or imagination) producing many new and inventive ideas with ease. ■ (of a situation or subject) fruitful and productive in generating new ideas: *a series of fertile debates within the social sciences.* ■ *Physics* (of nuclear material) able to become fissile by the capture of neutrons. ▷late Middle English: via French from Latin *fertilis*, from *ferre* 'to bear.' —**fer·til·i·ty** /fərˈtilitē/ *n.*

THE RIGHT WORD **fecund, fertile, fruitful, prolific**

A **fertile** woman is one who has the power to produce offspring, just as *fertile* soil produces crops and a *fertile* imagination produces ideas. This adjective pertains to anything in which seeds (or thoughts) can take root and grow.

A woman with ten children might be described as **fecund**, which means that she is not only capable of producing many offspring but has actually done it. A woman can be *fertile*, in other words, without necessarily being *fecund*.

Fruitful, whose meaning is very close to that of *fecund* when used to describe plants and may replace *fertile* in reference to soil or land, pertains specifically to something that promotes fertility or fecundity (*a fruitful downpour*). It can also apply in a broader sense to anything that bears or promotes results (*a fruitful idea; a fruitful discussion*).

While it's one thing to call a woman with a large family *fecund*, **prolific** is more usually applied to animals or plants in the literal sense of fertility, and suggests reproducing in great quantity or with rapidity. Figuratively, *prolific* is often used of highly productive creative efforts (*a prolific author with 40 titles published*).

Fer·tile Cres·cent a crescent-shaped area of fertile land in the Middle East that extends from the eastern Mediterranean coast through the valley of the Tigris and Euphrates rivers to the Persian Gulf. It was the center of the Neolithic development of agriculture (from 7000 BC), and the cradle of the Assyrian, Sumerian, and Babylonian civilizations.

fer·til·i·ty cult /fərˈtilitē/ ▸*n.* a pagan religious system of some agricultural societies in which seasonal rites are performed with the aim of ensuring good harvests and the future well-being of the community.

fer·til·i·za·tion /ˌfərtl-iˈzāsʜən/ ▸*n. Biology* the action or process of fertilizing an egg, female animal, or plant, involving the fusion of male and female gametes to form a zygote. ■ the action or process of applying a fertilizer to soil or land.

fer·ti·lize /ˈfərtlˌīz/ ▸*v.* [*trans.*] cause (an egg, female animal, or plant) to develop a new individual by introducing male reproductive material. ■ make (soil or land) more fertile or productive by adding suitable substances to it. —**fer·ti·liz·a·ble** *adj.*

fer·ti·liz·er /ˈfərtlˌīzər/ ▸*n.* a chemical or natural substance added to soil or land to increase its fertility: *a nitrogenous fertilizer* | *these varieties need pesticides and more fertilizer.*

fer·u·la /ˈfer(y)ələ/ ▸*n.* **1** a tall large-leaved Eurasian plant of a genus that includes asafetida and its relatives. • Genus *Ferula*, family Umbelliferae. **2** rare term for **FERULE**. ▷late Middle English: from Latin, 'giant fennel, rod.'

fer·ule /ˈferəl/ ▸*n. historical* a flat ruler with a widened end, formerly used for punishing children. ▷late Middle English (denoting the giant fennel): from Latin *ferula* (see **FERULA**).

fer·vent /ˈfərvənt/ ▸*adj.* having or displaying a passionate intensity: *a fervent disciple of tax reform.* See note at **EAGER**. ■ *archaic* hot, burning, or glowing. ▷Middle English: via Old French from Latin *fervent-* 'boiling,' from the verb *fervere*. Compare with **FERVID** and **FERVOR**. —**fer·ven·cy** /-vənsē/ *n.* —**fer·vent·ly** *adv.*

fer·vid /ˈfərvid/ ▸*adj.* intensely enthusiastic or passionate, esp. to an excessive degree: *a letter of fervid thanks.* ■ *poetic/literary* burning, hot, or glowing. ▷late 16th cent. (in the sense 'glowing, hot'): from Latin *fervidus*, from *fervere* 'to boil.' Compare with **FERVENT** and **FERVOR**. —**fer·vid·ly** *adv.*

fer·vor /ˈfərvər/ (*Brit.* **fer·vour**) ▸*n.* intense and passionate feeling: *he talked with all the fervor of a new convert.* ■ *archaic* intense heat. ▷Middle English: via Old French from Latin *fervor*, from *fervere* 'to boil.' Compare with **FERVENT** and **FERVID**.

Fès /fes/ variant spelling of **FEZ**.

fes·cue /ˈfeskyo͞o/ ▸*n.* any of a number of narrow-leaved grasses: • a perennial grass that is a valuable lawn, pasture, and fodder species (genus *Festuca*, family Gramineae). • an annual grass that typically occurs on drier soils such as on dunes and wasteland (genus *Vulpia*, family Gramineae). ▷Middle English *festu, festue* 'straw, twig,' from Old French *festu*, based on Latin *festuca* 'stalk, straw.' The change of *-t-* to *-c-* occurred in the 16th cent.; the current sense dates from the mid 18th cent.

fess[1] /fes/ (also **fesse**) ▸*n. Heraldry* an ordinary in the form of a broad horizontal stripe across the middle of the shield. ▷late 15th cent.: from Old French *fesse*, alteration of *faisse*, from Latin *fascia* 'band.' Compare with **FASCIA**.
▸***PHRASE*** □ **in fess** across the middle third of the field.

fess[2] ▸*v.* [*intrans.*] (**fess up**) *informal* confess; own up: *"Fess up," she demanded. "What were you doing in Peter's private office?"* ▷early 19th cent.: shortening of **CONFESS**.

Fes·sen·den /ˈfesəndən/, Reginald Aubrey (1866–1932), U.S. pioneer of radiotelephony, born in Canada. He invented the heterodyne receiver.

fess point ▸*n. Heraldry* a point at the center of a shield.

-fest ▸*comb. form* in nouns denoting a festival or large gathering of a specified kind: *gabfest* | *slugfest.* ▷from German *Fest* 'festival.'

fes·ta /ˈfestə/ ▸*n.* (in Italy and other Mediterranean countries) a religious or other festival. ▷early 19th cent.: from Italian, 'festival,' from Latin.

fes·tal /ˈfestəl/ ▸*adj.* of, like, or relating to a celebration or festival: *he appeared in festal array.* ▷late 15th cent.: via Old French from late Latin *festalis*, from Latin *festum*, (plural) *festa* 'feast.' —**fes·tal·ly** *adv.*

fes·ter /ˈfestər/ ▸*v.* [*intrans.*] (of a wound or sore) become septic; suppurate: *I developed a tropical sore that festered badly* | [as *adj.*] (**festering**) *a festering abscess.* ■ (of food or garbage) become rotten and offensive to the senses: *a gully full of garbage that festered in the shade* ■ (of a negative feeling or a problem) become worse or more intense, esp. through long-term neglect or indifference: *anger which festers and grows in his heart.* ■ (of a person) undergo physical and mental deterioration in isolated inactivity: *I might be* *festering in jail now.* ▷late Middle English: from the rare word *fester* 'fistula,' later 'festering sore,' or Old French *festrir* (verb), both from Old French *festre* (noun), from Latin *fistula* 'pipe, reed, fistula.'

fes·ti·val /ˈfestəvəl/ ▸*n.* a day or period of celebration, typically a religious commemoration: *a tabulation of saints' days and other festivals* | [as *adj.*] *a festival atmosphere.* ■ an annual celebration or anniversary: *highlights of this year's pumpkin festival.* ■ an organized series of concerts, plays, or movies, typically one held annually in the same place: *numbers that are still heard at traditional jazz festivals.* ▷Middle English (as an adjective): via Old French from medieval Latin *festivalis,* from Latin *festivus,* from *festum,* (plural) *festa* 'feast.'

fes·ti·val of lights ▸*n.* **1** another term for **HANUKKAH.** **2** another term for **DIWALI.**

Fes·ti·val of the Dead ▸*n.* another term for **BON.**

fes·tive /ˈfestiv/ ▸*adj.* of or relating to a festival: *parties are held and festive food is served.* ■ cheerful and jovially celebratory: *the somber atmosphere has given way to a festive mood.* ▷mid 17th cent.: from Latin *festivus,* from *festum,* (plural) *festa* 'feast.' **—fes·tive·ly** *adv.* **—fes·tive·ness** *n.*

fes·tiv·i·ty /feˈstivətē/ ▸*n.* (*pl.* **-ties**) the celebration of something in a joyful and exuberant way: *the season of festivity and goodwill.* ■ a festive celebration: *she had caught Susan taking a bunch of bouquets at the conclusion of an earlier festivity.* ■ (**festivities**) activities or events celebrating a special occasion: *the Chinese New Year is celebrated with a multitude of festivities.* ▷late Middle English: from Old French *festivite* or Latin *festivitas,* from *festivus* 'festive,' from *festum,* (plural) *festa* 'feast.'

fes·toon /fesˈto͞on/ ▸*n.* a chain or garland of flowers, leaves, or ribbons, hung in a curve as a decoration. ■ a carved or molded ornament representing such a garland.
▸*v.* [*trans.*] (often **be festooned with**) adorn (a place) with chains, garlands, or other decorations: *the room was festooned with balloons and streamers.* ▷mid 17th cent.: from French *feston,* from Italian *festone* 'festal ornament,' from *festum* 'feast.'

Fest·schrift /ˈfes(t),SHrift/ (also **fest·schrift**) ▸*n.* (*pl.* **-schrift·en** /-,SHriftən/ or **-schrifts**) a collection of writings published in honor of a scholar. ▷late 19th cent.: from German, from *Fest* 'celebration' + *Schrift* 'writing.'

FET ▸*abbr.* field-effect transistor.

fet·a /ˈfetə/ (also **fet·a cheese**) ▸*n.* a white salty Greek cheese made from the milk of ewes or goats. ▷from modern Greek *pheta.*

fe·tal /ˈfētl/ ▸*adj.* of or relating to a fetus: *nutrients essential for normal fetal growth.* ■ denoting a posture characteristic of a fetus, with the back curved forward and the limbs folded in front of the body: *he retired to his bed, curled in the* ***fetal position.***

fe·tal al·co·hol syn·drome (abbr.: **FAS**) ▸*n. Medicine* a congenital syndrome caused by excessive consumption of alcohol by the mother during pregnancy, characterized by retardation of mental development and of physical growth, particularly of the skull and face of the infant.

fetch[1] /feCH/ ▸*v.* [*trans.*] **1** go for and then bring back (someone or something): *he ran to fetch help.* ■ *archaic* bring forth (blood or tears): *kind offers fetched tears from me.* ■ *archaic* draw or take a (breath); heave (a sigh). **2** achieve (a particular price) when sold: *handwoven blankets and rugs that can fetch as much as $45,000.* **3** [with *two objs.*] *informal* inflict (a blow or slap) on (someone): *he always used to slam the gate and try and fetch her shins a wallop.* **4** *informal, dated* cause great interest or delight in (someone): *Nadine thought his deductions were good, but she was not as fetched by them as Larry was.*
▸*phrasal v.* □ **fetch up** *informal* arrive or come to rest somewhere, typically by accident or unintentionally.
▸*n.* **1** [in *sing.*] an act of going for something and then bringing it back: *he thought the best part of the fetch was wrestling over the stick.* **2** the distance traveled by wind or waves across open water. ■ the distance a vessel must sail to reach open water. **3** *archaic* a contrivance, dodge, or trick: *it is no ingenious fetches of argument that we want.* ▷Old English *fecc(e)an,* variant of *fetian,* probably related to *fatian* 'grasp.' **—fetch·er** *n.*
▸PHRASE □ **fetch and carry** run backward and forward bringing things to someone in a servile fashion: *neither is anyone going to fetch and carry for you when you are in bed with influenza.*

fetch[2] ▸*n. chiefly archaic* the apparition or double of a living person, formerly believed to be a warning of that person's impending death. ▷late 17th cent.: of unknown origin.

fetch·ing /ˈfeCHiNG/ ▸*adj.* attractive: *a fetching little garment of pink satin.* **—fetch·ing·ly** *adv.*

fête /fāt; fet/ (also **fete**) ▸*n.* a celebration or festival.
▸*v.* [*trans.*] (usu. **be fêted**) honor or entertain (someone) lavishly: *she was an instant celebrity, fêted by the media.* ▷late Middle English (in the sense 'festival, fair'): from French, from Old French *feste* (see **FEAST**).

fête cham·pê·tre /ˈfāt SHänˈpetr(ə); ˈfet/ ▸*n.* (*pl.* **fêtes cham·pê·tres** *pronunc.* same) an outdoor entertainment; a rural festival. ▷late 18th cent.: French, literally 'rural festival.'

fête ga·lante /ˈfāt gəˈlänt; ˈfet/ ▸*n.* (*pl.* **fêtes ga·lantes** *pronunc.* same or /ˈ,fāts gəˈlänts/) an outdoor entertainment or rural festival, esp. as depicted in 18th-century French painting. ■ a painting in this genre. ▷early 20th cent.: French, literally 'elegant festival.'

fet·ich ▸*n.* archaic spelling of **FETISH.**

fe·ti·cide /ˈfētə,sīd/ ▸*n.* destruction or abortion of a fetus.

fet·id /ˈfetid/ (*Brit.* also **foet·id**) ▸*adj.* smelling extremely unpleasant: *the fetid water of the marsh.* ▷late Middle English: from Latin *fetidus* (often erroneously spelled *foetidus*), from *fetere* 'to stink.' Compare with **FETOR.** **—fet·id·ly** *adv.* **—fet·id·ness** *n.*

fet·ish /ˈfetiSH/ ▸*n.* an inanimate object worshiped for its supposed magical powers or because it is considered to be inhabited by a spirit. ■ a course of action to which one has an excessive and irrational commitment: *he* ***had a fetish for*** *writing more opinions each year than any other justice.* ■ a form of sexual desire in which gratification is linked to an abnormal degree to a particular object, item of clothing, part of the body, etc.: *Victorian men developed fetishes focusing on feet, shoes, and boots.* ▷early 17th cent. (originally denoting an object used by the peoples of West Africa as an amulet or charm): from French *fétiche,* from Portuguese *feitiço* 'charm, sorcery' (originally an adjective meaning 'made by art'), from Latin *factitius* (see **FACTITIOUS**). **—fet·ish·ism** /-,izəm/ *n.* **—fet·ish·ist** /-ist/ *n.* **—fet·ish·is·tic** /,fetiˈSHistik/ *adj.*

fet·ish·ize /ˈfeti,SHīz/ ▸*v.* [*trans.*] have an excessive and irrational commitment to or obsession with (something): *an author who fetishizes privacy.* ■ make (something) the object of a sexual fetish: *women's bodies are so intensely fetishized.* **—fet·ish·i·za·tion** /,fetiSHiˈzāSHən/ *n.*

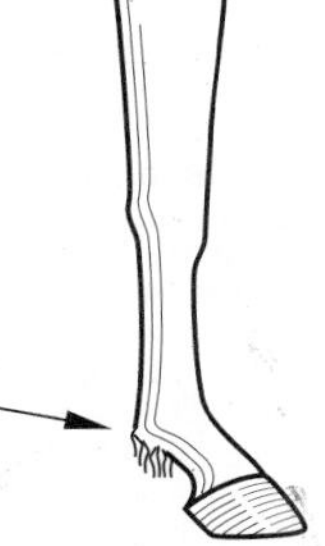
fetlock

fet·lock /ˈfet,läk/ (also **fetlock joint**) ▸*n.* the joint of a horse's or other quadruped's leg between the cannon bone and the pastern. ■ the tuft of hair that grows at this joint. ▷Middle English: ultimately of Germanic origin; related to **FOOT.**

feto- ▸*comb. form* representing **FETUS.**

fe·tor /ˈfētər/ (*Brit.* also **foe·tor**) ▸*n.* a strong, foul smell: *the fetor of decay.* ▷late 15th cent.: from Latin, from *fetere* 'to stink.' Compare with **FETID.**

fet·ter /ˈfetər/ ▸*n.* (usu. **fetters**) a chain or manacle used to restrain a prisoner, typically placed around the ankles: *he lay bound with fetters of iron.* ■ a restraint or check on someone's freedom to do something, typically one considered unfair or overly restrictive: *the fetters of discipline and caution.*
▸*v.* [*trans.*] restrain with chains or manacles, typically around the ankles: [as *adj.*] (**fettered**) *a ragged and fettered prisoner.* ■ (often **be fettered**) restrict or restrain (someone) in an unfair or undesirable fashion: *he was not fettered by tradition.* ▷Old English *feter,* from an Indo-European root shared by **FOOT.**

fet·ter·lock /ˈfetər,läk/ ▸*n.* a D-shaped fetter for tethering a horse by the leg, now only as represented as a heraldic charge.

fet·tle /ˈfetl/ ▸*n.* condition: *the aircraft remains* ***in fine fettle.***
▸*v.* [*trans.*] trim or clean the rough edges of (a metal casting or a piece of pottery) before firing. ■ *N. English* make or repair (something): *the familiar sounds of bikes being prepped and fettled.* ▷late Middle English (as a verb in the general sense 'get ready, prepare,' specifically 'prepare oneself for battle, gird up'): from dialect *fettle* 'strip of material, girdle,' from Old English *fetel.* **—fet·tler** /ˈfetl-ər/ *n.*

fet·tuc·ci·ne /,fetəˈCHēnē/ (also **fet·tu·ci·ni**) ▸ *n.* pasta made in ribbons. ▷from Italian, plural of *fettucina,* diminutive of *fetta* 'slice, ribbon.'

fet·tuc·ci·ne Al·fre·do ▸*n. Cooking* a dish of fettuccine served in a sauce of cream, butter, and grated Parmesan cheese.

fe·tus /ˈfētəs/ (*Brit.* (in nontechnical use) also **foe·tus**) ▸*n.* (*pl.* **-tus·es**) an unborn offspring of a mammal, in particular an unborn human baby more than eight weeks after conception. ▷late Middle English: from Latin, 'pregnancy, childbirth, offspring.'

> ***USAGE*** The spelling **foetus** has no etymological basis but is recorded from the 16th century and until recently was the standard British spelling in both technical and nontechnical use. In technical usage, **fetus** is now the standard spelling throughout the English-speaking world.

feu /fyo͞o/ *Scots Law* ▸*n.* a perpetual lease at a fixed rent. ■ a piece of land held by such a lease.
▸*v.* (**feus, feued, feu·ing**) [*trans.*] grant (land) on such a lease. ▷late 15th cent. (originally denoting a feudal tenure in which an annual payment was made in lieu of military service): from Old French (see **FEE**).

feud /fyo͞od/ ▸*n.* a state of prolonged mutual hostility, typically between two families or communities, characterized by violent assaults in revenge for previous injuries: *the incident rekindled a long-term feud between two ethnic groups.* See note at **QUARREL.** ■ a prolonged and bitter quarrel or dispute: *one of the most volatile feuds that currently rock the scientific community.*
▸*v.* [*intrans.*] take part in such a quarrel or violent conflict: *these two families have been feuding since the Civil War* | *Hoover* ***feuded with*** *the CIA for decades.* ▷Middle English *fede* 'hostility, ill will,' from Old French *feide,* from Middle Dutch, Middle Low German *vēde*; related to **FOE.**

feud. ▸*abbr.* ■ feudal. ■ feudalism.

feu·dal /ˈfyo͞odl/ ▸*adj.* according to, resembling, or denoting the system of feudalism: *feudal barons.* ■ absurdly outdated or old-fashioned: *his view of patriotism was more than old-fashioned—it was positively feudal.* ▷early 17th cent.: from medieval Latin *feudalis,* from *feudum* (see **FEE**). **—feu·dal·i·za·tion** /,fyo͞odl-iˈzāSHən/ *n.* **—feu·dal·ize** /-,īz/ *v.* **—feu·dal·ly** /ˈfyo͞odl-ē/ *adv.*

feu·dal·ism /ˈfyo͞odl,izəm/ ▸*n. historical* the dominant social system in medieval Europe, in which the nobility held lands from the Crown in exchange for military service, and vassals were in turn tenants of the nobles, while the peasants (villeins or serfs) were obliged to live on their lord's land and give him homage, labor, and a share of the produce, notionally in exchange for military protection. **—feu·dal·ist** *n.* **—feu·dal·is·tic** /,fyo͞odlˈistik/ *adj.*

feu·dal·i·ty /fyo͞oˈdalətē/ ▸*n. archaic* the principles and practice of the feudal system. ▷late 18th cent.: from French *féodalité,* from *féodal,* from medieval Latin *feudalis* 'feudal,' from *feudum* (see **FEE**).

feu·da·to·ry /ˈfyo͞odə,tôrē/ *historical* ▸*adj.* owing feudal allegiance to: *they had for a long period been* ***feudatory to*** *the Norwegian Crown.*
▸*n.* (*pl.* **-ries**) a person who holds land under the conditions of the feudal system. ▷late 16th cent.: from medieval Latin *feudatorius,* from *feudare* 'enfeoff,' from *feudum* (see **FEE**).

feu de joie /,fœ də ˈZHwä/ ▸*n.* (*pl.* **feux de joie** *pronunc.* same or /,fœz/) a rifle salute fired by soldiers on a ceremonial occasion, each soldier firing in succession along the ranks to make a continuous sound. ▷early 18th cent.: French, literally 'fire of joy.'

feud·ist /ˈfyo͞odist/ ▸*n.* a person taking part in a feud.

feuil·le·ton /ˈfoi-itn; ,fœyəˈtôN/ ▸*n.* a part of a newspaper or magazine devoted to fiction, criticism, or light literature. ■ an article printed in such a part. ▷mid 19th cent.: French, from *feuillet,* diminutive of *feuille* 'leaf.'

fe·ver /ˈfēvər/ ▸*n.* an abnormally high body temperature, usually accompanied by shivering, headache, and in severe instances, delirium: *I would take aspirin to help me with the pain and reduce the fever* | *African equine fever.* ■ a state of nervous excitement or agitation: *I was mystified, and in a fever of expectation.* ■ [with *adj.*] the excitement felt by a group of people about a particular public event: *election fever reaches its climax tomorrow.*
▸*v.* [*trans.*] *archaic* bring about a high body temperature or a state of nervous excitement in (someone): *a heart which sin has fevered.* ▷Old English *fēfor,* from

Latin *febris*; reinforced in Middle English by Old French *fievre*, also from *febris*.

fe·vered /ˈfēvərd/ ▸*adj.* having or showing the symptoms associated with a dangerously high temperature: *her fevered eyes.* ■ feeling or displaying an excessive degree of nervous excitement, agitation, or energy: *my fevered adolescent imagination.*

fe·ver·few /ˈfēvərˌfyo͞o/ ▸*n.* a bushy aromatic Eurasian plant of the daisy family, with feathery leaves and daisylike flowers. It is used in herbal medicine to treat headaches. • *Tanacetum* (or **Chrysanthemum**) *parthenium*, family Compositae. ▷Old English *feferfuge*, from Latin *febrifuga*, from *febris* 'fever' + *fugare* 'drive away.' Compare with **FEBRIFUGE.**

feverfew

fe·ver grass ▸*n.* West Indian term for **LEMONGRASS.**

fe·ver·ish /ˈfēv(ə)risʜ/ ▸*adj.* having or showing the symptoms of a fever: *he suffered from feverish colds.* ■ displaying a frenetic excitement or energy: *the next couple of weeks were spent in a whirl of feverish activity.* —**fe·ver·ish·ly** *adv.* —**fe·ver·ish·ness** *n.*

fe·ver·ous /ˈfēv(ə)rəs/ ▸*adj. archaic* apt to cause fever. ■ feverish.

fe·ver pitch ▸*n.* a state of extreme excitement: *the football crowd was* **at fever pitch.**

fe·ver tree ▸*n.* any of a number of trees that are believed either to cause or to cure fever, in particular: • a North American tree used in the treatment of malaria during the Civil War (*Pinckneya pubens*, family Rubiaceae). • a southern African tree that was formerly believed to cause malaria (*Acacia xanthophloea*, family Leguminosae).

few /fyo͞o/ ▸*adj.* & *pron.* **1** **(a few)** a small number of: [as *adj.*] *may I ask a few questions?* | [as *pron.*] *I will recount* ***a few of*** *the stories told me* | *many believe it but only a few are prepared to say.* **2** used to emphasize how small a number of people or things is: [as *adj.*] *he had few friends* | [as *pron.*] *few thought to challenge these assumptions* | *very* ***few of*** *the titles have any literary merit* | *one of the few who survived* | [*comparative*] *a population of fewer than two million* | [as *adj.*] *sewing was one of her few pleasures.* | [*superlative*] *ask which products have the fewest complaints.*
▸*n.* [as *plural n.*] **(the few)** the minority of people; the elect: *a world that increasingly belongs to the few.* ▷Old English *fēawe, fēawa*; from an Indo-European root shared by Latin *paucus* and Greek *pauros* 'small.'
▸*PHRASES* □ **every few** once in every small group of (typically units of time): *she visits every few weeks.* □ **few and far between** scarce; infrequent: *my inspired moments are few and far between.* □ **a good few** *Brit.* a fairly large number of: *it had been around for a good few years.* □ **have a few** *informal* drink enough alcohol to be slightly drunk: *I tend to keep my mouth shut, unless I've had a few.* □ **no fewer than** used to emphasize a surprisingly large number: *there are no fewer than seventy different brand names.* □ **not a few** a considerable number: *his fiction has caused not a few readers to see red.* □ **quite a few** a fairly large number: *quite a few people can do it.* □ **some few** some but not many: *some few people are born without any sense of time.*

USAGE **Fewer** versus **less**: strictly speaking, the rule is that **fewer**, the comparative form of **few**, is used with words denoting people or countable things (***fewer*** *members;* ***fewer*** *books;* ***fewer*** *than ten contestants*).
Less, on the other hand, is used with mass nouns, denoting things that cannot be counted (***less*** *money;* ***less*** *music*). In addition, **less** is normally used with numbers (***less*** *than 10,000*) and with expressions of measurement or time (***less*** *than two weeks;* ***less*** *than four miles away*). But to use **less** with count nouns, as in ***less*** *people* or ***less*** *words*, is incorrect in standard English.

fey /fā/ ▸*adj.* giving an impression of vague unworldliness: *his mother was a strange, fey woman.* ■ having supernatural powers of clairvoyance. ■ *chiefly Scottish* fated to die or at the point of death: *now he is fey, he sees his own death, and I see it too.* ▷Old English *fǣge* (in the sense 'fated to die soon'). —**fey·ly** *adv.* —**fey·ness** *n.*

Feyn·man /ˈfīnmən/, Richard Phillips (1918–88), U.S. theoretical physicist. He is noted for his work on quantum electrodynamics. Nobel Prize for Physics (1965, shared with Julian Schwinger 1918–94 and Sin-Itiro Tomonaga 1906–97).

Feyn·man di·a·gram ▸*n. Physics* a diagram showing electromagnetic interactions between subatomic particles.

Fez /fez/ (also **Fès** /fes/) a city in northern Morocco, founded in 808; pop. 564,000.

fez /fez/ ▸*n.* (*pl.* **fez·zes**) a flat-topped conical red hat with a black tassel on top, worn by men in some Muslim countries (formerly the Turkish national headdress). ▷early 19th cent.: from Turkish *fes* (perhaps via French *fez*), named after **FEZ**, once the chief place of manufacture. —**fezzed** *adj.*

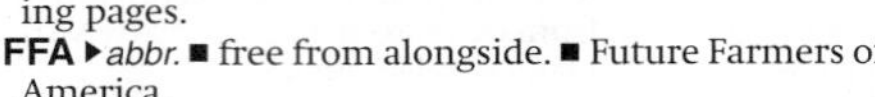

fez

ff *Music* ▸*abbr.* fortissimo.

ff. ▸*abbr.* ■ folios. ■ following pages.

FFA ▸*abbr.* ■ free from alongside. ■ Future Farmers of America.

FFV ▸*abbr.* First Family of Virginia.

FG ▸*abbr.* ■ *Football* & *Basketball* field goal. ■ fine grain.

FHA ▸*abbr.* ■ Federal Housing Administration. ■ Future Homemakers of America.

FHLBB ▸*abbr.* Federal Home Loan Bank Board.

f-hole /ˈef ˌhōl/ ▸*n.* either of a pair of sound holes resembling an *f* and a reversed *f* in shape, cut in the front of musical instruments of the violin family and some other stringed instruments such as semi-acoustic electric guitars and mandolins.

fhp ▸*abbr.* friction horsepower.

fi·a·cre /fēˈäkr(ə)/ ▸*n.* (*pl.* **-cres** /-krə; -krəz/) *historical* a small four-wheeled carriage for public hire. ▷late 17th cent.: from French, named after the Hôtel de St. *Fiacre* in Paris, where such vehicles were first hired out.

fi·an·cé /ˌfēˌänˈsā; fēˈänsā/ ▸*n.* a man who is engaged to be married: *my fiancé and I were childhood sweethearts.* ▷mid 19th cent.: from French, past participle of *fiancer* 'betroth,' from Old French *fiance* 'a promise,' based on Latin *fidere* 'to trust.'

fi·an·cée /ˌfēˌänˈsā; fēˈänsā/ ▸*n.* a woman who is engaged to be married: *he went back to the valley to marry his fiancée.*

fi·an·chet·to /ˌfēənˈcʜetō; -ˈketō/ *Chess* ▸*n.* (*pl.* **-toes**) the development of a bishop by moving it one square to a long diagonal of the board.
▸*v.* **(-toes, -toed)** [*trans.*] develop (a bishop) in such a way. ▷mid 19th cent.: from Italian, diminutive of *fianco* 'flank,' ultimately of Germanic origin. Compare with **FLANK.**

Fi·an·na Fáil /ˈfēənə ˈfoil/ one of the two main political parties of the Republic of Ireland. Larger and traditionally more republican than its rival Fine Gael, it was formed in 1926 in opposition to the Anglo-Irish Treaty of 1921 by Eamon de Valera together with some of the moderate members of Sinn Fein. ▷Irish, from *fianna* 'band of warriors'; compare with **FENIAN**) and *Fáil*, genitive of *Fál*, an ancient name for Ireland. The phrase *Fianna Fáil* was used in 15th-cent. poetry in the neutral sense 'people of Ireland,' but the founders of the political party interpreted it to mean 'soldiers of destiny.'

fi·as·co /fēˈaskō/ ▸*n.* (*pl.* **-cos**) a thing that is a complete failure, esp. in a ludicrous or humiliating way: *his plans turned into a fiasco.* ▷mid 19th cent.: from Italian, literally 'bottle, flask,' in the phrase *far fiasco*, literally 'make a bottle,' figuratively 'fail in a performance': the reason for the figurative sense is unexplained.

fi·at /ˈfēət; ˈfēˌät/ ▸*n.* a formal authorization or proposition; a decree: *adopting a legislative review program, rather than trying to regulate by fiat.* ■ an arbitrary order: *the appraisal dropped the value from $75,000 to $15,000, rendering it worthless by bureaucratic fiat.* ▷late Middle English: from Latin, 'let it be done,' from *fieri* 'be done or made.'

fi·at mon·ey ▸*n.* inconvertible paper money made legal tender by a government decree.

fib /fib/ ▸*n.* a lie, typically an unimportant one: *parents told little white fibs about out-of-wedlock births.* See note at **LIE.**
▸*v.* **(fibbed, fib·bing)** [*intrans.*] tell such a lie. ▷mid 16th cent.: perhaps a shortening of obsolete *fible-fable* 'nonsense,' reduplication of **FABLE.** —**fib·ber** *n.*

fi·ber /ˈfībər/ (*Brit.* **fi·bre**) ▸*n.* **1** a thread or filament from which a vegetable tissue, mineral substance, or textile is formed: *tropical elements like coconut fibers and branches.* ■ a substance formed of such threads or filaments: *ordinary synthetics don't breathe as well as natural fibers* | *high strength carbon fiber.* ■ a threadlike structure forming part of the muscular, nervous, connective, or other tissue in the human or animal body: *there were degenerative changes in muscle fibers* | *figurative she wanted him with every fiber of her being.* ■ *figurative* strength of character: *a weak person with no moral fiber.* **2** dietary material containing substances such as cellulose, lignin, and pectin, which are resistant to the action of digestive enzymes: *cereals high in fiber.* ▷late Middle English (in the sense 'lobe of the liver,' (plural) 'entrails'): via French from Latin *fibra* 'fiber, filament, entrails.' —**fi·bered** *adj.* [in *combination*] *natural-fibered.* —**fi·ber·less** *adj.*

fi·ber·board /ˈfībərˌbôrd/ (*Brit.* **fi·bre·board**) ▸*n.* a building material made of wood or other plant fibers compressed into boards.

fi·ber·fill /ˈfībərˌfil/ ▸*n.* synthetic material used for padding and insulation in garments and soft furnishings such as cushions and duvets.

fi·ber·glass /ˈfībərˌglas/ (*Brit.* **fi·bre·glass**) (also *trademark* **Fi·ber·glas**) ▸*n.* **1** a reinforced plastic material composed of glass fibers embedded in a resin matrix. **2** a woollike mass of glass filaments, used in insulation. **3** a textile fabric made from woven glass filaments.

fi·ber op·tics ▸*plural n.* [treated as *sing.*] the use of thin flexible fibers of glass or other transparent solids to transmit light signals, chiefly for telecommunications or for internal examination of the body. ■ [treated as *pl.*] the fibers and associated devices so used. —**fi·ber-op·tic** *adj.*

fi·ber·scope /ˈfībərˌskōp/ (*Brit.* **fi·bre·scope**) ▸*n.* a fiber-optic device for viewing inaccessible internal structures, esp. in the human body.

Fi·bo·nac·ci /ˌfēbəˈnäcʜē/, Leonardo (*c.*1170–*c.*1250), Italian mathematician; known as **Fibonacci of Pisa.** He made many original contributions in complex calculations, algebra, and geometry and pioneered number theory and indeterminate analysis, discovering the Fibonacci series.

Fi·bo·nac·ci se·ries (also **Fibonacci sequence**) ▸*n. Mathematics* a series of numbers in which each number (**Fibonacci number**) is the sum of the two preceding numbers. The simplest is the series 1, 1, 2, 3, 5, 8, etc.

fi·bre ▸*n.* British spelling of **FIBER.**

fi·bre·board ▸*n.* British spelling of **FIBERBOARD.**

fi·bre·glass ▸*n.* British spelling of **FIBERGLASS.**

fi·bre tip ▸*n.* British term for **FELT-TIP PEN.**

fi·bril /ˈfībrəl; ˈfib-/ ▸*n. technical* a small or slender fiber: *each muscle fiber is subdivided into smaller fibrils.* ▷mid 17th cent.: from modern Latin *fibrilla*, diminutive of Latin *fibra* (see **FIBER**). —**fi·bril·lar** /-lər/ *adj.* —**fi·bril·lar·y** /-ˌlerē/ *adj.*

fi·bril·late /ˈfibrəˌlāt/ ▸*v.* [*intrans.*] **1** (of a muscle, esp. in the heart) make a quivering movement due to uncoordinated contraction of the individual fibrils: *the atria ceased to fibrillate when the temperature was reduced.* **2** (of a fiber) split up into fibrils. ■ [*trans.*] break (a fiber) into fibrils. —**fi·bril·la·tion** /ˌfibrəˈlāsʜən/ *n.*

fi·brin /ˈfībrən/ ▸*n. Biochemistry* an insoluble protein formed from fibrinogen during the clotting of blood. It forms a fibrous mesh that impedes the flow of blood. ▷early 19th cent.: from **FIBER** + **-IN**[1]. —**fi·brin·oid** /ˈfībrəˌnoid; ˈfib-/ *adj.* —**fi·brin·ous** /ˈfībrənəs; ˈfib-/ *adj.*

fi·brin·o·gen /fīˈbrinəjən/ ▸*n. Biochemistry* a soluble protein present in blood plasma, from which fibrin is produced by the action of the enzyme thrombin.

fi·brin·o·gen·ic /ˌfībrənōˈjenik/ ▸*adj.* of or relating to fibrinogen or to the formation of fibrin.

fi·bri·nol·y·sis /ˌfībrəˈnäləsis/ ▸*n. Physiology* the enzymatic breakdown of the fibrin in blood clots. —**fi·bri·no·lyt·ic** /ˈfībrənəˈlitik/ *adj.*

fibro- ▸*comb. form* of, relating to, or characterized by fibers: *fibroblast* | *fibroma.* ▷from Latin *fibra* 'fiber.'

fi·bro·ad·e·no·ma /ˌfībrōˌadnˈōmə/ ▸*n.* (*pl.* **-ad·e·no·mas** or **-ad·e·no·ma·ta** /-adnˈōmətə/) *Medicine* a tumor formed of mixed fibrous and glandular tissue, typically occurring as a benign growth in the breast.

fi·bro·blast /ˈfībrəˌblast; ˈfib-/ ▸*n. Physiology* a cell in connective tissue that produces collagen and other fibers.

fi·bro·car·ti·lage /ˌfībrō'kärtl-ij/ ▸*n.* cartilage that contains fibrous bundles of collagen, such as that of the intervertebral disks in the spinal cord.

fi·bro·cys·tic /ˌfībrə'sistik; ˌfib-/ ▸*adj.* [*attrib.*] *Medicine* (of a disease) characterized by the development of fibrous tissue and cystic spaces, typically in the pancreas or the breast.

fi·broid /'fīˌbroid/ ▸*adj.* of or characterized by fibers or fibrous tissue.

▸*n. Medicine* a benign tumor of muscular and fibrous tissues, typically developing in the wall of the uterus.

fi·bro·in /'fībrō-in; 'fib-/ ▸*n.* a protein that is the chief constituent of silk and spider webs. ▷mid 19th cent.: from FIBRO- + -IN[1].

fi·bro·lite /'fībrəˌlīt/ ▸*n.* another term for SILLIMANITE.

fi·bro·ma /fī'brōmə/ ▸*n.* (*pl.* **-mas** or **-ma·ta** /-mətə/) *Medicine* a benign fibrous tumor of connective tissue. ▷mid 19th cent.: from Latin *fibra* (see FIBER) + -OMA.

fi·bro·my·al·gia /ˌfībrōmī'alj(ē)ə/ ▸*n.* a chronic disorder characterized by widespread musculoskeletal pain, fatigue, and tenderness in localized areas.

fi·bro·sar·co·ma /ˌfībrōˌsär'kōmə/ ▸*n.* (*pl.* **-co·mas** or **-co·ma·ta** /-'kōmətə/) *Medicine* a sarcoma in which the predominant cell type is a malignant fibroblast. **—fi·bro·sar·co·ma·tous** /-'kōmətəs; -'käm-/ *adj.*

fi·bro·sis /fī'brōsəs/ ▸*n. Medicine* the thickening and scarring of connective tissue, usually as a result of injury. ▷late 19th cent.: from Latin *fibra* (see FIBER) + -OSIS. **—fi·brot·ic** /fī'brätik/ *adj.*

fi·bro·si·tis /ˌfībrə'sītis/ ▸*n. Medicine* inflammation of fibrous connective tissue, typically affecting the back and causing stiffness and pain. ▷early 20th cent.: from Latin *fibrosus* 'fibrous' (from *fibra* 'fiber') + -ITIS. **—fi·bro·sit·ic** /-'sitik/ *adj.*

fi·brous /'fībrəs/ ▸*adj.* consisting of or characterized by fibers: *lignin is the fibrous material that gives wood its strength.* **—fi·brous·ly** *adv.* **—fi·brous·ness** *n.*

fib·u·la /'fibyələ/ ▸*n.* (*pl.* **-lae** /-ˌlē; -ˌlī/ or **-las**) **1** *Anatomy* the outer and usually smaller of the two bones between the knee and the ankle in humans (or the equivalent joints in other terrestrial vertebrates), parallel with the tibia. **2** *Archaeology* a brooch or clasp. ▷late 16th cent.: from Latin, 'brooch,' perhaps related to *figere* 'to fix.' The bone is so named because the shape it makes with the tibia resembles a clasp, the fibula being the tongue. **—fib·u·lar** /'fibyələr/ *adj.*

-fic (usu. as **-ific**) ▸*suffix* (forming adjectives) producing; making: *prolific* | *soporific.* ▷from French *-fique* or Latin *-ficus* from *facere* 'do, make.'

FICA ▸*abbr.* Federal Insurance Contributions Act.

-fically (usu. as **-ifically**) ▸*suffix* forming adverbs corresponding to adjectives ending in *-fic,* (such as *prolifically* corresponding to *prolific*). ▷-FICAL + -LY.

-fication (usu. as **-ification**) ▸*suffix* forming nouns of action from verbs ending in *-fy* (such as *simplification* from *simplify*). ▷from French, or from Latin *-fication-* (from verbs ending in *-ficare*).

fi·celle /fē'sel/ ▸*n.* a small, very thin loaf of French bread. ▷French 'twine, string.'

fiche /fēsh/ ▸*n.* short for MICROFICHE.

Fich·te /'fiktə/, Johann Gottlieb (1762–1814), German philosopher. A student of Kant, he postulated that the ego is the basic reality, and the world is posited by the ego in defining and delimiting itself.

fich·u /'fishōō; 'fē-/ ▸*n.* a small triangular shawl, worn around a woman's shoulders and neck. ▷mid 18th cent.: from French, from *ficher* 'to fix, pin', from Latin *figere.* Compare with FIX and MICROFICHE.

fick·le /'fikəl/ ▸*adj.* changing frequently, esp. as regards one's loyalties, interests, or affection: *Web patrons are a notoriously fickle lot, bouncing from one site to another on a whim* | *the weather is forever fickle.* ▷Old English *ficol* 'deceitful'. **—fick·le·ness** *n.* **—fick·ly** /'fik(ə)lē/ *adv.*

FICO score /'fīkō/ ▸*n. Finance* a person's credit score calculated with software from Fair Isaac Corporation (FICO).

The FICO score is a number between 300 and 850, which indicates a person's capacity to repay a loan. The higher the number, the lower the risk that the borrower will default.

fict. ▸*abbr.* ■ fiction. ■ fictitious.

fic·tile /'fiktl; -ˌtīl/ ▸*adj.* made of earth or clay by a potter. ■ of or relating to pottery or its manufacture. ■ capable of being molded; plastic. ▷early 17th cent.: from Latin *fictilis,* from *fict-* 'formed, contrived,' from the verb *fingere.*

fic·tion /'fikshən/ ▸*n.* literature in the form of prose, esp. short stories and novels, that describes imaginary events and people. ■ invention or fabrication as opposed to fact: *he dismissed the allegation as absolute fiction.* ■ [*in sing.*] a belief or statement that is false, but that is often held to be true because it is expedient to do so: *the notion of that country being a democracy is a polite fiction.* ▷late Middle English (in the sense 'invented statement'): via Old French from Latin *fictio(n-),* from *fingere* 'form, contrive.' Compare with FEIGN and FIGMENT. **—fic·tion·ist** /-nist/ *n.*

THE RIGHT WORD deception, fable, fabrication, falsehood, fiction, figment

If a young child tells you there is a dinosaur under his bed, you might assume that his story is a **fiction**, but it is probably a **figment**. A *fiction* is a story that is invented either to entertain or to deceive (*her excuse was ingenious, but it was pure fiction*), while *figment* suggests the operation of fancy or imagination (*a figment of his imagination*).

If a child hides his sandwich under the sofa cushions and tells you that a dinosaur ate it, this would be a **fabrication**, which is a story that is intended to deceive. Unlike a *figment,* which is mostly imagined, a *fabrication* is a false but thoughtfully constructed story in which some truth is often interwoven (*the city's safety record was a fabrication designed to lure tourists downtown*).

A **falsehood** is basically a lie—a statement or story that one knows to be false but tells with intent to deceive (*a deliberate falsehood about where the money had come from*).

A **deception**, on the other hand, is an act that deceives but not always intentionally (*a foolish deception designed to prevent her parents from worrying*).

A **fable** is a fictitious story that deals with events or situations that are clearly fantastic, impossible, or incredible. It often gives animals or inanimate objects the power to speak and conveys a lesson of practical wisdom, as in *Aesop's Fables*.

fic·tion·al /'fikshənl/ ▸*adj.* of or relating to fiction; invented for the purposes of fiction: *fictional texts* | *a fictional character.* **—fic·tion·al·i·ty** /ˌfikshə'nalətē/ *n.* **—fic·tion·al·i·za·tion** /ˌfikshənl-i'zāshən/ *n.* **—fic·tion·al·ize** /-nəˌlīz/ *v.* **—fic·tion·al·ly** *adv.*

fic·ti·tious /fik'tishəs/ ▸*adj.* not real or true, being imaginary or having been fabricated: *she pleaded guilty to stealing thousands in taxpayer dollars by having a fictitious employee on her payroll.* ■ of, relating to, or denoting the imaginary characters and events found in fiction: *the people in this novel are fictitious; the background of public events is not.* ▷early 17th cent.: from Latin *ficticius* (from *fingere* 'contrive, form') + -OUS (see also -ITIOUS[2]). **—fic·ti·tious·ly** *adv.* **—fic·ti·tious·ness** *n.*

fic·tive /'fiktiv/ ▸*adj.* creating or created by imagination: *the novel's fictive universe.* ▷early 17th cent. (but rare before the 19th cent.): from French *fictif, -ive* or medieval Latin *fictivus,* from Latin *fingere* 'contrive, form.' **—fic·tive·ness** *n.*

fi·cus /'fīkəs/ ▸*n.* (*pl.* same) a tree, shrub, or climbing plant of a large genus that includes the figs and the rubber plant. They grow in tropical and warm climates, and several species are of commercial importance. • Genus *Ficus,* family Moraceae. ▷mid 19th cent.: from Latin, 'fig, fig tree.'

fid /fid/ ▸*n. Nautical* a thick peg, wedge, or supporting pin, in particular: ■ a square wooden or iron bar that takes the weight of a topmast stepped to a lower mast by being passed through holes in both masts. ■ a conical pin or spike used in splicing rope. ▷early 17th cent.: of unknown origin.

fid. ▸*abbr.* fiduciary.

fi·da·yeen /ˌfidā'yēn/ ▸*plural n.* variant of FEDAYEEN.

Fid. Def. ▸*abbr.* Fidei Defensor. See DEFENDER OF THE FAITH.

fid·dle /'fidl/ ▸*n.* **1** *informal* a violin, esp. when used to play folk music. **2** *informal, chiefly Brit.* an act of defrauding, cheating, or falsifying: *a major mortgage fiddle.* **3** *Nautical* a contrivance, such as a raised rim, that prevents things from rolling or sliding off a table in bad weather.

▸*v. informal* **1** [*intrans.*] play the fiddle: *he fiddled with the band from 1949 to 1951* | (**fiddling**) *country music with lots of fiddling and banjo playing.* ■ [*trans.*] play (a tune) on the fiddle: *Bill Monroe fiddled his last tune at his annual Beanblossom Bluegrass Festival.* **2** [*intrans.*] touch or fidget with something in a restless or nervous way: *Laura* ***fiddled with*** *her cup.* ■ tinker with something in an attempt to make minor adjustments or improvements: *never* ***fiddle with*** *an electric machine that's plugged in.* ■ (**fiddle around**) pass time aimlessly, without doing or achieving anything of substance. **3** [*trans.*] *chiefly Brit.* falsify (figures, data, or records), typically in order to gain money: *everyone is fiddling their expenses.* ▷Old English *fithele,* denoting a violin or similar instrument (originally not an informal or depreciatory term), based on Latin *vitulari* 'celebrate a festival, be joyful,' perhaps from *Vitula,* the name of a Roman goddess of joy and victory. Compare with VIOL.

▸*PHRASES* □ **fiddle while Rome burns** be concerned with relatively trivial matters while ignoring the serious or disastrous events going on around one. □ (**as**) **fit as a fiddle** in good health. □ **on the fiddle** *chiefly British, informal* engaged in cheating or swindling. □ **play second fiddle to** take a subordinate role to someone or something in a way often considered demeaning: *she had to play second fiddle to the interests of her husband.*

fid·dle·back /'fidlˌbak/ ▸*n.* **1** [usu. as *adj.*] a thing shaped like the back of a violin, with the sides deeply curved inward, in particular: ■ the back of a chair. **2** a rippled effect in the grain of fine wood, often exploited when making the backs of violins: [as *adj.*] *fiddleback mahogany.* **3** (also **fiddleback spider**) another term for BROWN RECLUSE.

fid·dle-de-dee /ˌfidl dē 'dē/ ▸*n.* [often as *exclam.*] *dated* nonsense. ▷late 18th cent.: from FIDDLE + a reduplication.

fid·dle-fad·dle /'fidl ˌfadl/ ▸*n.* trivial matters: nonsense: *he's concerned with petty fiddle-faddle about his personal arrangements.*

▸*v.* [*intrans.*] bother with trifles; fuss: *you haven't time to fiddle-faddle about like that.* ▷late 16th cent.: reduplication of FIDDLE.

fid·dle-foot·ed ▸*adj.* (of a horse) skittish. ■ *figurative* restless or apt to wander: *he was what we might consider a fiddle-footed missionary, moving from place to place.*

fid·dle·head /'fidlˌhed/ ▸*n.* **1** (also **fiddlehead fern**) the young, curled, edible frond of certain ferns. **2** a scroll-like carving at a ship's bow. ▷late 18th cent.: from the resemblance to the head of a violin.

fid·dler /'fidlər; 'fidl-ər/ ▸*n.* **1** *informal* a person who plays the violin, esp. one who plays folk music. **2** *Brit., informal* a person who cheats or swindles, esp. one indulging in petty theft. ▷Old English *fithelere,* from *fithele* (see FIDDLE).

fid·dler crab ▸*n.* a small amphibious crab, the males of which have one greatly enlarged claw that they wave in territorial display and courtship. • Genus *Uca,* family Ocypodidae.

Fid·dler's Green the sailor's Elysium, traditionally a place of wine, women, and song.

fid·dle·stick /'fidlˌstik/ ▸*exclam.* (**fiddlesticks**) nonsense.

▸*n. informal* a violin bow.

fid·dling /'fidliNG; 'fidl-iNG/ ▸*adj.* **1** annoyingly trivial or petty: *fiddling little details.* **2** [*attrib.*] *chiefly Brit., informal* (of a person) involved with a swindle or embezzlement: *a fiddling financier.*

fid·dly /'fidlē/ ▸*adj.* (**-dli·er, -dli·est**) *Brit., informal* complicated or detailed and awkward to do or use: *replacing the battery is fiddly.*

fi·de·ism /'fēdāˌizəm/ ▸*n.* the doctrine that knowledge depends on faith or revelation. ▷late 19th cent.: from Latin *fides* 'faith' + -ISM. **—fi·de·ist** *n.* **—fi·de·is·tic** /ˌfēdāˌistik/ *adj.*

fi·del·i·ty /fə'delətē/ ▸*n.* faithfulness to a person, cause, or belief, demonstrated by continuing loyalty and support: *he sought only the strictest fidelity to justice.* ■ sexual faithfulness to a spouse or partner. ■ the degree of exactness with which something is copied or reproduced: *the 1949 recording provides reasonable fidelity.* ▷late Middle English: from Old French *fidelite* or Latin *fidelitas,* from *fidelis* 'faithful,' from *fides* 'faith.' Compare with FEALTY.

fidg·et /'fijit/ ▸*v.* (**fidg·et·ed, fidg·et·ing**) [*intrans.*] make small movements, esp. of the hands and feet, through nervousness or impatience: *the audience had begun to fidget on their chairs.* ■ [*trans.*] make (someone) uneasy or uncomfortable: *she fidgets me with her never-ending spit and polish.*

▸*n.* a quick, small movement, typically a repeated one, caused by nervousness or impatience: *he disturbed other people with convulsive fidgets.* ■ a person given to such movements, esp. one whom other people find irritating. ■ (usu. **fidgets**) a state of mental or physical restlessness or uneasiness: *a marketing person full of nervous energy and fidgets.* ▷late 17th cent.: from obsolete or dialect *fidge* 'to twitch'; perhaps related to Old Norse *fikja* 'move briskly, be restless or eager.' **—fidg·et·er** *n.* **—fidg·et·i·ness** /ˈfijitēnis/ *n.* **—fidg·et·y** /ˈfijitē/ *adj.*

Fi·do /ˈfīdō/ *historical* a system for dispersing fog using gasoline burners on the ground to enable aircraft to land. It was developed by the Allies during World War I. ▷acronym from *Fog Intensive Dispersal Operation.*

fi·do /ˈfīdō/ *humorous informal* ▸a generic name for a pet dog. ▷from Latin *fidō* 'I trust'.

fi·du·cial /fəˈdo͞oSHəl/ ▸*adj. technical* (esp. of a point or line) assumed as a fixed basis of comparison. ▷late 16th cent.: from late Latin *fiducialis*, from *fiducia* 'trust,' from *fidere* 'to trust.'

fi·du·ci·ar·y /fəˈdo͞oSHēˌerē; -SHərē/ ▸*adj. Law* involving trust, esp. with regard to the relationship between a trustee and a beneficiary: *the company has a fiduciary duty to shareholders.* ■ *archaic* held or given in trust: *fiduciary estates.* ■ *Finance* (of a paper currency) depending for its value on securities (as opposed to gold) or the reputation of the issuer.
▸*n.* (*pl.* **-ar·ies**) a trustee. ▷late 16th cent. (in the sense 'something inspiring trust; credentials'): from Latin *fiduciarius*, from *fiducia* 'trust,' from *fidere* 'to trust.'

fi·dus A·cha·tes /ˈfīdəs əˈkātēz/ ▸*n.* a faithful friend or devoted follower. ▷late 16th cent.: Latin, literally 'faithful Achates' (see **ACHATES**).

fie /fī/ ▸*exclam. archaic or humorous* used to express disgust or outrage: *if people don't answer your first letter, fie on them!* ▷Middle English: via Old French from Latin *fi*, an exclamation of disgust at a stench.

Fied·ler /ˈfēdlər/, Arthur (1894–1979), U.S. conductor. An accomplished violist, he played for the Boston Pops Orchestra 1915–30 and then became its conductor 1930–74.

fief /fēf/ ▸*n.* **1** *historical* an estate of land, esp. one held on condition of feudal service. **2** a person's sphere of operation or control. ▷early 17th cent.: from French (see **FEE**).

fief·dom /ˈfēfdəm/ ▸*n.* a fief.

Field[1] /fēld/, Marshall (1834–1906), U.S. merchant and philanthropist. In 1881, he organized Marshall Field & Co., which became the largest retail store in the world. He made major donations to the University of Chicago, the Art Institute of Chicago, and the Field Museum of Natural History.

Field[2], Sally (1946–), U.S. actress and director; born *Sally Mahoney*. Her many movies include *Sybil* (1977), *Norma Rae* (Academy Award, 1979), *Places in the Heart* (Academy Award, 1984), *Steel Magnolias* (1989), and *Forrest Gump* (1994). She directed *Beautiful* (2000).

Field[3], Stephen Johnson (1816–99), U.S. Supreme Court associate justice 1863–97. Appointed to the Court by President Lincoln, he was a conservative. His brother **David Dudley** (1805–94) was noted for his expertise in law codification; another brother **Cyrus West** (1819–92) was known for his part in the laying of the undersea cable between the U.S. and Europe 1857–66.

field /fēld/ ▸*n.* **1** an area of open land, esp. one planted with crops or pasture, typically bounded by hedges or fences: *a wheat field | a field of corn.* ■ a piece of land used for a particular purpose, esp. an area marked out for a game or sport: *a football field.* ■ *Baseball* defensive play or the defensive positions collectively: *he is fast in the field and on the bases.* ■ a large area of land or water completely covered in a particular substance, esp. snow or ice: *an ice field.* ■ an area rich in a natural product, typically oil or gas: *an oil field.* ■ an area on which a battle is fought: *a field of battle.* ■ an area on a flag with a single background color: *fifty white stars on a blue field.* ■ *archaic* a battle: *many a bloody field was to be fought.* ■ a place where a subject of scientific study or artistic representation can be observed in its natural location or context. **2** a particular branch of study or sphere of activity or interest: *we talked to professionals in various fields.* ■ *Computing* a part of a record, representing an item of data. ■ *Linguistics & Psychology* a general area of meaning within which individual words make particular distinctions. ■ a space or range within which objects are visible from a particular viewpoint or through a piece of apparatus: *the stars drift through this telescope's* ***field of view.*** See also **FIELD OF VISION.** ■ *Heraldry* the surface of an escutcheon or of one of its divisions. **3** (usu. **the field**) all the participants in a contest or sport: *he destroyed the rest of the field with a devastating injection of speed.* **4** *Physics* the region in which a particular condition prevails, esp. one in which a force or influence is effective regardless of the presence or absence of a material medium. ■ the force exerted or potentially exerted in such an area: *the variation in the strength of the field.* ■ *Mathematics* a system subject to two binary operations analogous to those for the multiplication and addition of real numbers, and having similar commutative and distributive laws.
▸*v.* **1** [*intrans.*] *Baseball* play as a fielder. ■ [*trans.*] catch or stop (the ball): *he fielded the ball cleanly, but threw it down the right-field line.* **2** [*trans.*] send out (a team or individual) to play in a game: *a high school that traditionally fielded mediocre teams.* ■ (of a political party) nominate (a candidate) to run in an election: *a radical political party that is beginning to field candidates in local elections.* ■ deploy (an army): *the small gulf sheikhdoms fielded 11,500 troops with the Saudis.* **3** [*trans.*] deal with (a difficult question, telephone call, etc.): *she has fielded five calls from salespeople.*
▸*adj.* [*attrib.*] carried out or working in the natural environment, rather than in a laboratory or office: *field observations.* ■ (of an employee or work) away from the home office; remote: *a field representative.* ■ (of military equipment) light and mobile for use on campaign: *field artillery.* ■ used in names of animals or plants found in the open country, rather than among buildings or as cultivated varieties: *field ant.* ■ denoting a game played outdoors on a marked field. ▷Old English *feld* (also denoting a large tract of open country; compare with **VELD**), of West Germanic origin; related to Dutch *veld* and German *Feld.*
▸PHRASES □ **in the field** on campaign; (while) engaged in combat or maneuvers: *troops in the field.* ■ away from the laboratory or studio; engaged in practical work in a natural environment. ■ (of an employee) away from the home office; working while traveling: *he was a salesman in the field.* □ **keep the field** *archaic* continue a military campaign. □ **lead the field** be the leader in a race. ■ be the best or most popular: *in the executive car group, this model leads the field.* □ **play the field** *informal* indulge in a series of sexual relationships without committing oneself to anyone. □ **take the field** (of a sports team) go onto a field to begin a game. ■ *Baseball* begin one's turn on defense in an inning. ■ start a military campaign.

field book ▸*n.* a book in which a surveyor or other technician or scientist writes down measurements and other technical notes taken in the field.

field boot ▸*n.* a close-fitting, knee-length military boot.

field corn ▸*n.* corn grown to feed livestock.

field·craft /ˈfēld ˌkraft/ ▸*n.* the techniques involved in living, traveling, or making military or scientific observations in the field, esp. while remaining undetected.

field crick·et ▸*n.* a cricket that lives in a burrow in grassland and has a musical birdlike chirp. • Family Gryllidae, numerous species.

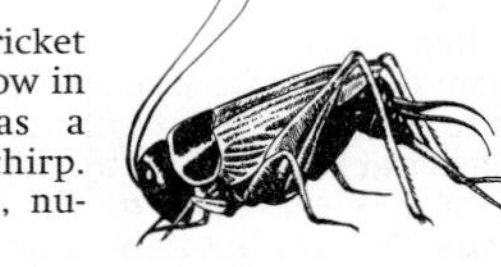
field cricket

field day ▸*n.* **1** *Military* a review or an exercise, esp. in maneuvering. **2** a day devoted to athletic contests or other sporting events, typically at a school. **3** [in *sing.*] an opportunity for action, success, or excitement, esp. at the expense of others: *shoplifters are* ***having a field day*** *in the store.* **4** a day set aside for the display of agricultural machinery and crops, esp. corn and soybeans.

field-ef·fect tran·sis·tor (abbr.: **FET**) ▸*n. Electronics* a transistor in which most current is carried along a channel whose effective resistance can be controlled by a transverse electric field.

field e·mis·sion ▸*n. Physics* the emission of electrons from the surface of a conductor under the influence of a strong electrostatic field, as a result of the tunnel effect.

field·er /ˈfēldər/ ▸*n. Baseball & Cricket* a player who occupies a defensive position in the field while the other side is batting (typically one other than the pitcher or catcher, or bowler).

field·er's choice ▸*n. Baseball* a play in which the fielding team's decision to put out another player allows the batter to reach first base safely.

field e·vents ▸*plural n.* track-and-field contests other than races, such as throwing and jumping events. Compare with **TRACK EVENTS.**

field·fare /ˈfēldˌfer/ ▸*n.* a large migratory thrush with a gray head, breeding in northern Eurasia. • *Turdus pilaris*, subfamily Turdinae, family Muscicapidae. ▷late Old English *feldefare*, perhaps from *feld* 'field' + the base of *faran* 'to travel' (see **FARE**).

field glass·es ▸*plural n.* binoculars for outdoor use.

field goal ▸*n.* **1** *Football* a goal scored by a placekick, scoring three points. **2** *Basketball* a basket scored while the clock is running and the ball is in play.

field-grade of·fi·cer ▸*n. Military* a major, lieutenant colonel, or colonel.

field-grade rank ▸*n.* the rank attained by a military field officer.

field guide ▸*n.* a book for the identification of birds, flowers, minerals, or other things in their natural environment.

field hand ▸*n.* a person employed as a farm laborer.

field hock·ey ▸*n.* a game played between two teams of eleven players who use hooked sticks to drive a small hard ball toward goals at opposite ends of a field.

field hol·ler ▸*n.* see **HOLLER.**

field hos·pi·tal ▸*n.* a temporary hospital set up near a combat zone to provide emergency care for the wounded.

field house ▸*n.* **1** a large building, often part of a college, that provides space for a variety of athletic facilities, such as basketball and squash courts, a running track, a swimming pool, exercise equipment, and often an indoor arena with spectator seating. **2** a building usually adjacent to an athletic field and equipped with changing rooms, lockers, showers, etc., for those using the athletic facility.

Field·ing /ˈfēldiNG/, Henry (1707–54), English novelist. He provoked the introduction of censorship in theaters with his political satire *The Historical Register for 1736.* He then turned to writing picaresque novels, notably *Joseph Andrews* (1742) and *Tom Jones* (1749).

field lens ▸*n.* in a multiple lens optical system, the lens farthest from the eye.

field mark ▸*n.* a visible mark or characteristic that can be used in identifying a bird or other animal in the field.

field mar·shal ▸*n.* an officer of the highest rank in the British and other armies.

field mouse ▸*n.* a dark brown mouse with a long tail and large eyes. **ALSO CALLED WOOD MOUSE.** • Genus *Apodemus*, family Muridae: several species, in particular the widespread *A. sylvaticus.*

field mush·room ▸*n.* another term for **CHAMPIGNON.**

field of·fi·cer ▸*n.* another term for **FIELD-GRADE OFFICER.**

field of hon·or ▸*n.* the place where a duel or battle is fought.

field of vi·sion ▸*n.* the entire area that a person or animal is able to see when their eyes are fixed in one position.

field pea ▸*n.* a pea plant of a variety grown chiefly for fodder or as green manure. ▷early 18th cent.: said to be so named because they were once the only agricultural peas cultivated in the UK.

Fields[1] /ˈfēldz/, Dame Gracie (1898–1979), English singer and comedienne; born *Grace Stansfield.*

Fields[2], W. C. (1880–1946), U.S. comedian; born *William Claude Dukenfield.* Having made his name as a comedy juggler, he became a vaudeville star and appeared in the *Ziegfeld Follies* revues between 1915 and 1921. Notable movies: *The Bank Dick* (1940) and *Never Give a Sucker an Even Break* (1941).

field sports ▸*plural n.* outdoor sports, esp. hunting, shooting, and fishing.

field·stone /ˈfēl(d)ˌstōn/ ▸*n.* [often as *adj.*] stone used in its natural form: *a fieldstone fireplace.*

field test ▸*n.* a test carried out in the environment in which a product or device is to be used.
▸*v.* (**field-test**) [*trans.*] test (something) in the environment in such a way.

field the·o·ry ▸*n. Physics* a theory that explains physical phenomena in terms of a field and the manner in which it interacts with matter or with other fields.

field tri·al ▸*n.* **1** a field test. **2** a competition for hunting dogs to test their levels of skill and training in retrieving or pointing.

field trip ▸*n.* a trip made by students or research workers to study something at first hand: *a field trip to the power plant was organized.*

field·work /ˈfēldˌwərk/ ▸*n.* **1** practical work conducted by a researcher in the natural environment, rather than in a laboratory or office. **2** *rare* a temporary fortification. **—field·work·er** *n.*

fiend /fēnd/ ▸*n.* an evil spirit or demon. ■ (**the fiend**) *archaic* the Devil. ■ a wicked or cruel person: *a fiend thirsty for blood and revenge.* ■ a person causing mischief or annoyance: *you little fiend!* ■ *informal* a person who is excessively fond of or addicted to something: *the restaurant's owner is a wine fiend.* ▷Old English *fēond* 'an enemy, the devil, a demon,' of Germanic origin; related to Dutch *vijand* and German *Feind* 'enemy.' —**fiend·like** /-ˌlīk/ *adj.*

fiend·ish /ˈfēndisн/ ▸*adj.* extremely cruel or unpleasant; devilish: *shrieks of fiendish laughter.* ■ extremely awkward or complex: *a fiendish problem.* —**fiend·ish·ly** *adv.* —**fiend·ish·ness** *n.*

Fiennes[1] /fīnz/, Joseph (1970–), British actor; the brother of Ralph Fiennes. He is best known for his roles in *Shakespeare in Love* (1998) and *Luther* (2003).

Fiennes[2], Ralph (1962–), British actor. Notable films include *Schindler's List* (1993), *Quiz Show* (1994), *The English Patient* (1996) and *The End of the Affair* (1999). He received a Tony Award for his performance in the 1995 Broadway production of *Hamlet.*

fierce /fi(ə)rs/ ▸*adj.* (**fierc·er, fierc·est**) having or displaying an intense or ferocious aggressiveness: *as women, we need to accept that we can be fierce, cunning, and predatory | the fierce air battles that ensued over the Pacific.* ■ (of a feeling, emotion, or action) showing a heartfelt and powerful intensity: *he kissed her with a fierce, demanding passion.* ■ (of the weather or temperature) powerful and destructive in extent or intensity: *fierce storms lashed the country.* ▷Middle English: from Old French *fiers* 'fierce, brave, proud,' from Latin *ferus* 'untamed.' Compare with **FERAL.** —**fierce·ly** *adv.* —**fierce·ness** *n.*

▸*PHRASE* □ **something fierce** *informal* to a great and almost overwhelming extent: *he said he missed me something fierce.*

fi·e·ri fa·ci·as /ˌfīərē ˈfāsн(ē)əs/ ▸*n.* *Law* a writ to a sheriff for executing a judgment. ▷late Middle English Latin, 'you shall make happen.'

fier·y /ˈfī(ə)rē/ ▸*adj.* (**fier·i·er, fier·i·est**) consisting of fire or burning strongly and brightly: *the sun was a fiery ball low on the hills* | [as *submodifier*] *figurative a fiery hot chili sauce.* ■ having the bright color of fire: *the car was painted a fiery red.* ■ (of a person) having a passionate, quick-tempered nature: *a fiery, imaginative Aries.* ■ (of behavior or words) passionately angry and deeply felt: *a fiery speech.* —**fier·i·ly** /ˈfī(ə)rəlē/ *adv.* —**fier·i·ness** *n.*

fier·y cross ▸*n.* a burning wooden cross used as a symbol by the Ku Klux Klan. ■ *historical* a wooden cross, charred and dipped in blood, used among Scottish clans to summon men to battle.

fi·es·ta /fēˈestə/ ▸*n.* (in Spanish-speaking regions) a religious festival: *the yearly fiesta of San Juan.* ■ an event marked by festivities or celebration: *a balloon fiesta.* ▷Spanish, from Latin *festum,* (plural) *festa* (see **FEAST**).

FIFA /ˈfēfə/ the international governing body of soccer, formed in 1904 and based in Zurich, Switzerland. ▷acronym from French *Fédération internationale de football association.*

fi. fa. ▸*abbr.* fieri facias.

fife /fīf/ ▸*n.* a kind of small shrill flute used esp. with the drum in military bands.

▸*v.* [*intrans.*] *archaic* play the fife. ▷mid 16th cent.: from German *Pfeife* 'pipe,' or from French *fifre* from Swiss German *Pfifre* 'piper.' Compare with **PIPE.** —**fif·er** *n.*

fife

fife rail (also **fife-rail**) ▸*n.* *chiefly historical* a rail around the mainmast of a sailing ship, holding belaying pins. ■ the rail on top of the bulwark at the edge of a sailing ship's poop or forecastle. ▷early 18th cent.: of unknown origin.

FIFO /ˈfīˌfō/ ▸*abbr.* first in, first out (chiefly with reference to methods of stock valuation and data storage). Compare with **LIFO.**

fif·teen /fifˈtēn; ˈfifˌtēn/ ▸*cardinal number* equivalent to the product of three and five; one more than fourteen, or five more than ten; 15: *all fifteen species of cranes mate for life | fifteen feet high | fifteen of the passengers made their appearance.* (Roman numeral: **xv** or **XV.**) ■ fifteen years old: *she must be fifteen by now.* ▷Old English *fiftēne, fiftīene* (see **FIVE, -TEEN**).

▸*PHRASE* □ **fifteen minutes of fame** a brief period of fame that a person enjoys before fading back into obscurity. [adapted from Andy Warhol's comment 'in the future everybody will be world famous for fifteen minutes' (1968).]

fif·teenth /fifˈtēnтн; ˈfifˌtēnтн/ ▸*ordinal number* constituting number fifteen in a sequence; 15th: *August the fifteenth | the fifteenth century | on the fifteenth floor.* ■ (**a fifteenth/one fifteenth**) each of fifteen equal parts into which something is or may be divided. ■ an organ stop sounding a register of pipes two octaves (fifteen notes) above the diapason.

fifth /fi(f)тн/ ▸*ordinal number* constituting number five in a sequence; 5th: *the fifth century* BC *| her mother had just given birth to another child, her fifth | the world's fifth-largest oil exporter | the fifth of November.* ■ (**a fifth/one fifth**) each of five equal parts into which something is or may be divided. ■ the fifth finisher or position in a race or competition: *he finished fifth.* ■ (in some vehicles) the fifth (and typically highest) in a sequence of gears: *in my panic I changed from third to fifth.* ■ fifthly (used to introduce a fifth point or reason): *fourth, it can aid the process of life review, and fifth, it is an enjoyable and stimulating experience.* ■ *Music* an interval spanning five consecutive notes in a diatonic scale, in particular (also **perfect fifth**) an interval of three whole steps and a half step (e.g., C to G): *strings tuned a fifth apart.* ■ *Music* the note that is higher by such an interval than the root of a diatonic scale. ■ (**a fifth of**) a fifth of a gallon, as a measure of liquor, or a bottle of this capacity: *a fifth of whiskey.* ■ the fifth grade of a school. —**fifth·ly** *adv.*

▸*PHRASE* □ **take the Fifth** (in the U.S.) exercise the right guaranteed by the Fifth Amendment to the Constitution of refusing to answer questions in order to avoid incriminating oneself.

fifth col·umn ▸*n.* a group within a country at war who are sympathetic to or working for its enemies. ▷The term dates from the Spanish Civil War, when General Mola, leading four columns of troops toward Madrid, declared that he had a fifth column inside the city. —**fifth col·umn·ist** *n.*

fifth-gen·er·a·tion ▸*adj.* denoting a proposed new class of computer or programming language employing artificial intelligence.

Fifth-mon·ar·chy-man ▸*n.* *historical* a member of a 17th-century sect expecting the immediate second coming of Christ and repudiating all other government. ▷from *Fifth Monarchy,* denoting the last of the five great empires prophesied by Daniel (Dan. 2:44).

fifth po·si·tion ▸*n.* **1** *Ballet* a posture in which the feet are placed turned outward, one immediately in front of but touching the other so that the toe of the back foot just protrudes beyond the heel of the front foot. ■ a position of the arms in which they are held curved in front of the body, at hip level, waist level, or above the head, with the palms facing the body. **2** *Music* a position of the left hand on the fingerboard of a stringed instrument nearer to the bridge than the fourth position, enabling a higher set of notes to be played.

Fifth Re·pub·lic the republican regime established in France with de Gaulle's introduction of a new constitution in 1958.

fifth wheel ▸*n.* **1** an extra wheel for a four-wheeled vehicle. ■ *informal* a superfluous person or thing. **2** a coupling between a trailer and a vehicle used for towing. ■ (also **fifth-wheel trailer**) a trailer with accommodations for camping out. ■ *historical* a horizontal turntable over the front axle of a carriage as an extra support to prevent its tipping.

fif·ty /ˈfiftē/ ▸*cardinal number* (*pl.* **-ties**) the number equivalent to the product of five and ten; half of one hundred; 50: *only fifty percent of the aircraft were serviceable | about fifty of us filed in | a fifty-pound salmon.* (Roman numeral: **l** or **L.**) ■ (**fifties**) the numbers from 50 to 59, esp. the years of a century or of a person's life: *Elvis is the icon of the Fifties.* ■ fifty years old: *she looked about fifty.* ■ fifty miles an hour: *doing about fifty.* ■ a fifty-dollar bill. ▷Old English *fiftig* (see **FIVE, -TY**[2]). —**fif·ti·eth** /ˈfiftē-iтн/ *ordinal number* —**fif·ty·fold** /-ˌfōld/ *adj.* & *adv.*

fif·ty-fif·ty ▸*adj.* the same in share or proportion; equal: *fifty-fifty partners.* ■ used to refer to one of two possibilities that are equally likely to happen: *he has a fifty-fifty chance of surviving the operation.*

▸*adv.* equally; half and half: *they divided the spoils fifty-fifty.*

fig[1] /fig/ ▸*n.* **1** a soft pear-shaped fruit with sweet dark flesh and many small seeds, eaten fresh or dried. **2** (also **fig tree**) the deciduous Old World tree or shrub that bears this fruit. • *Ficus carica,* family Moraceae. ■ used in names of other plants of this genus, or in names of nonrelated plants that bear a similar fruit. ▷Middle English: from Old French *figue,* from Provençal *fig(u)a,* based on Latin *ficus.*

▸*PHRASE* □ **not give** (or **care**) **a fig** not have the slightest concern about: *Karla didn't give a fig for Joe's comfort or his state of mind.*

fig[2] *informal* ▸*n.* (in phrase **full fig**) smart clothes, esp. those appropriate to a particular occasion or profession: *a soldier walking up the street* ***in full fig.***

▸*v.* (**figged, fig·ging**) [*trans.*] *archaic* dress up (someone) to look smart: *he was* ***figged out*** *in the latest modes.* ▷late 17th cent. (as a verb): variant of obsolete *feague* 'liven up' (earlier 'whip'); perhaps related to German *fegen* 'sweep, thrash'; compare with **FAKE**[1]. An early sense of the verb was 'fill the head with nonsense'; later (early 19th cent.) 'cause (a horse) to be lively and carry its tail well (by applying ginger to its anus)'; hence 'smarten up.'

fig. ▸*abbr.* figure: *see fig.34.*

fight /fīt/ ▸*v.* (*past* and *past part.* **fought** /fôt/) [*intrans.*] take part in a violent struggle involving the exchange of physical blows or the use of weapons: *the men were fighting | they fight with other children.* ■ [*trans.*] engage in (a war or battle): *there was another war to fight* ■ [*intrans.*] *we fought and died for this country.* ■ quarrel or argue: *she didn't want to fight with her mother all the time | they were* ***fighting over*** *who pays the bill.* ■ [*trans.*] struggle to put out (a fire, esp. a large one): *two fire trucks raced to the scene to fight the blaze.* ■ [*trans.*] endeavor vigorously to win (an election or other contest). ■ campaign determinedly for or against something, esp. to put right what one considers unfair or unjust: *I will* ***fight for*** *more equitable laws.* ■ [*trans.*] struggle or campaign against (something): *the best way to fight fascism abroad and racism at home.* ■ [*trans.*] attempt to repress (a feeling or an expression of a feeling): *she had to* ***fight back*** *tears of frustration.* ■ [*trans.*] take part in a boxing match against (an opponent). ■ (**fight one's way**) move forward with difficulty, esp. by pushing through a crowd or overcoming physical obstacles: *she watched him fight his way across the room.* ■ [*trans.*] *archaic* command, manage, or maneuver (troops, a ship, or military equipment) in battle: *General Hill fights his troops well.*

▸*phrasal v.* □ **fight back** counterattack or retaliate in a fight, struggle, or contest. □ **fight it out** settle a dispute by fighting or competing aggressively: *they fought it out with a tug-of-war.* □ **fight someone/something off** defend oneself against an attack by someone or something: *well-fed people are better able to fight off infectious disease.*

▸*n.* a violent confrontation or struggle: *we'll get into a fight and wind up with bloody noses.* ■ a boxing match. ■ a battle or war: *the country was not eager for a fight with the U.S.* ■ a vigorous struggle or campaign for or against something: *a long fight against cancer.* ■ an argument or quarrel: *she had a fight with her husband.* ■ the inclination or ability to fight or struggle: *Ginny felt the fight trickle out of her.* ▷Old English *feohtan* (verb), *feoht(e), gefeoht* (noun); related to Dutch *vechten, gevecht* and German *fechten, Gefecht.*

▸*PHRASES* □ **fight fire with fire** use the weapons or tactics of one's enemy or opponent, even if one finds them distasteful. □ **fight a losing battle** be fated to fail in one's efforts: *he was fighting a losing battle to stem the tears.* □ **fight shy of** be unwilling to undertake or become involved with: *these musicians fight shy of change.* □ **make a fight of it** put up a spirited show of resistance in a fight or contest: *the Chargers certainly made a fight of it in the second half.* □ **fight or flight** the instinctive physiological response to a threatening situation, which readies one either to resist forcibly or to run away. □ **put up a fight** offer resistance to an attack.

fight·er /ˈfītər/ ▸*n.* **1** a person or animal that fights, esp. as a soldier or a boxer. ■ a person who does not easily admit defeat in spite of difficulties or opposition: *there'll be months of physiotherapy but medical staff say she's a fighter.* **2** a fast military aircraft designed for attacking other aircraft: *designers employ stealth to render a fighter invisible to radar* | [as *adj.*] *fighter pilots.*

fight·er-bomb·er ▸*n.* an aircraft serving as both a fighter and bomber.

fight·ing chair ▸*n.* a fixed chair on a boat used by a person trying to catch large fish.

fight·ing chance ▸*n.* a possibility of success if great effort is made: *they still have a fighting chance of clinching the title.*

F

fight·ing fish (also **Siamese fighting fish**) ▸*n.* a small labyrinth fish native to Thailand, the males of which fight vigorously. It has been bred in a variety of colors for fighting and for aquariums. • *Betta splendens*, family Belontiidae.

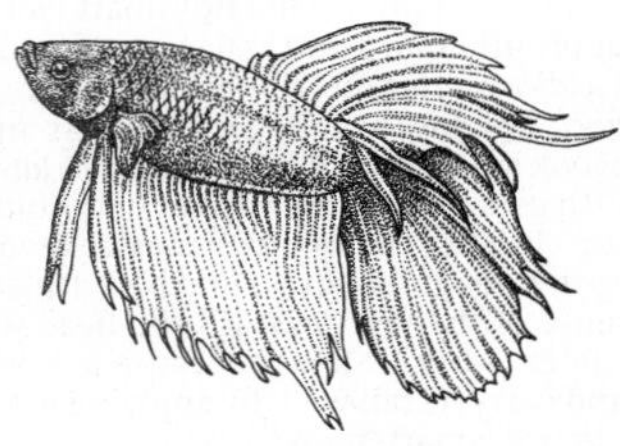

fighting fish

fight·ing words ▸*plural n. informal* words indicating a willingness to fight or challenge someone. ■ words expressing an insult, esp. of an ethnic, racial, or sexist nature.

fig leaf ▸*n.* a leaf of a fig tree, often depicted as concealing the genitals in paintings and sculpture. ■ *figurative* a thing designed to conceal a difficulty or embarrassment: *the amendment was just a fig leaf designed to cover the cracks in the party.* ▷early 16th cent.: with reference to the story of Adam and Eve (Gen. 3:7).

fig·ment /ˈfigmənt/ ▸*n.* a thing that someone believes to be real but that exists only in their imagination: *it really was Ross and not* ***a figment of her*** *overheated* ***imagination***. See note at FICTION. ▷late Middle English (denoting an invented statement or story): from Latin *figmentum*, related to *fingere* 'form, contrive.' Compare with FEIGN and FICTION. The current sense dates from the early 17th cent.

fi·gu·ra /fiˈgyo͝orə/ ▸*n.* (*pl.* **-rae** /-ˌrē/) (in literary theory) a person or thing representing or symbolizing a fact or ideal. ▷mid 20th cent.: Latin, literally 'figure' (representing an early use of *figure* to denote an emblem or type).

fig·ur·al /ˈfigyərəl/ ▸*adj.* **1** another term for FIGURATIVE (sense 1). ■ (in postmodernist writing) relating to or denoting a form of signification that relies on imagery and association rather than on rational and linguistic concepts. **2** *Art* another term for FIGURATIVE (sense 2). ▷late Middle English: from Old French, or from late Latin *figuralis*, from *figura* 'form, shape' (see FIGURE).

fig·u·rant /ˈfigyərənt; ˌfigyəˈränt/ ▸*n.* (*fem.* **fig·u·ran·te** /ˌfigyəˈräntē; -ˈränt/) a supernumerary actor. ▷French, present participle of *figurer* 'to figure.'

fig·u·ra·tion /ˌfigyəˈrāsʜən/ ▸*n.* **1** ornamentation by means of figures or designs. ■ *Music* use of florid counterpoint: *the figuration of the accompaniment comes out too strongly.* **2** allegorical representation: *the figuration of "The Possessed" is much more complex | the opening parable may be read as a figuration of the main idea behind the novel.* ▷Middle English (in the senses 'outline' and 'making of arithmetical figures'): from Latin *figuratio(n-)*, from *figurare* 'to form or fashion,' from *figura* (see FIGURE).

fig·ur·a·tive /ˈfigyərətiv/ ▸*adj.* **1** departing from a literal use of words; metaphorical: *gold, in the figurative language of the people, was "the tears wept by the sun."* **2** (of an artist or work of art) representing forms that are recognizably derived from life. ▷Middle English: from late Latin *figurativus*, from *figurare* 'to form or fashion,' from *figura* (see FIGURE). **—fig·ur·a·tive·ly** *adv.* **—fig·ur·a·tive·ness** *n.*

fig·ure /ˈfigyər/ ▸*n.* **1** a number, esp. one that forms part of official statistics or relates to the financial performance of a company: *official census figures | a figure of 30,000 deaths annually from snakebite.* ■ a numerical symbol, esp. any of the ten in Arabic notation: *the figure 7.* ■ one of a specified number of digits making up a larger number, used to give a rough idea of the order of magnitude: *their market price runs into five figures |* [*in combination*] *a six-figure salary.* ■ an amount of money: *a figure of two thousand dollars.* ■ (**figures**) arithmetical calculations: *she has no* ***head for figures***. **2** a person's bodily shape, esp. that of a woman and when considered to be attractive: *she had always been so proud of her figure.* ■ a person seen indistinctly, esp. at a distance: *a backpacked figure appeared in the distance.* ■ a person of a particular kind, esp. one who is important or distinctive in some way: *Williams became something of a cult figure.* ■ a representation of a human or animal form in drawing or sculpture: *starkly painted figures.* **3** a shape defined by one or more lines in two dimensions (such as a circle or a triangle), or one or more surfaces in three dimensions (such as a sphere or a cuboid), either considered mathematically in geometry or used as a decorative design: *a red ground with white and blue geometric figures.* ■ a diagram or illustrative drawing, esp. in a book or magazine: *figure 1 shows an ignition circuit.* ■ *Figure Skating* a movement or series of movements following a prescribed pattern and often beginning and ending at the same point. ■ a pattern formed by the movements of a group of people, for example in square dancing or synchronized swimming, as part of a longer dance or display. ■ *archaic* the external form or shape of a thing. **4** *Music* a short succession of notes producing a single impression. **5** *Logic* the form of a syllogism, classified according to the position of the middle term.
▸*v.* [*intrans.*] **1** be a significant and noticeable part of something: *the issue of nuclear policy* ***figured*** *prominently* ***in*** *the talks.* ■ (of a person) play a significant role in a situation or event: *he* ***figured*** *largely* ***in*** *opposition to the bill.* ■ (of a fictional character) play a part in a novel, play, or movie: *the four characters who* ***figure in*** *Ridley's play.* **2** [*trans.*] calculate or work out (an amount or value) arithmetically. **3** [with *clause*] *informal* think, consider, or expect to be the case: *I* ***figure that*** *wearing a suit makes you look like a bank clerk |* [*trans.*] *for years, teachers had figured him for a dullard.* ■ (of a recent event or newly discovered fact) be logical and unsurprising: *well, she supposed* ***that figured***. **4** [*trans.*] represent (something) in a diagram or picture: *varieties of this Cape genus are figured from drawings made there.* ■ [usu. as *adj.*] (**figured**) embellish (something) with a pattern: *the floors were covered with figured linoleum.*
▸*phrasal v.* □ **figure on** *informal* count or rely on something happening or being the case in the future: *anyone thinking of salmon fishing should figure on paying $200 a day.* □ **figure something out** *informal* solve or discover the cause of a problem: *he was trying to figure out why the camera wasn't working.* □ **figure someone out** reach an understanding of a person's actions, motives, or personality. ▷Middle English (in the senses 'distinctive shape of a person or thing,' 'representation of something material or immaterial,' and 'numerical symbol,' among others): from Old French *figure* (noun), *figurer* (verb), from Latin *figura* 'shape, figure, form'; related to *fingere* 'form, contrive.' **—fig·ure·less** *adj.*
▸*PHRASES* □ **figure of fun** a person who is considered ridiculous. □ **figure of speech** a word or phrase used in a nonliteral sense to add rhetorical force to a spoken or written passage: *calling her a crab is just a figure of speech.* □ **lose** (or **keep**) **one's figure** lose (or retain) a slim and attractive bodily shape.

fig·ured bass ▸*n. Music* a bass line with the intended harmonies indicated by figures rather than written out as chords, typical of continuo parts in baroque music.

fig·ure eight (*Brit.* **figure of eight**) ▸*n.* an object or movement having the shape of the number eight.

fig·ure-ground ▸*adj.* [*attrib.*] *Psychology & Art* relating to or denoting the perception of images by the distinction of objects from a background from which they appear to stand out, esp. in contexts where this distinction is ambiguous.

fig·ure·head /ˈfigyərˌhed/ ▸*n.* **1** a nominal leader or head without real power. **2** a carving, typically a bust or a full-length figure, set at the prow of an old-fashioned sailing ship.

figurehead 2

fig·ure-hug·ging ▸*adj.* (of a garment) fitting closely to the contours of a woman's body: *a low-cut, figure-hugging dress.*

fig·ure of mer·it ▸*n.* a numerical expression representing the performance or efficiency of a given device, material, or procedure.

fig·ure skat·ing ▸*n.* the competitive sport of ice skating in prescribed patterns (*figures*) and choreographed free skating. **—fig·ure skat·er** *n.*

fig·ur·ine /ˌfigyəˈrēn/ ▸*n.* a statuette, esp. one of a human form. ▷mid 19th cent.: from French, from Italian *figurina*, diminutive of *figura*, from Latin *figura* (see FIGURE).

fig wasp ▸*n.* a tiny Old World wasp that lays its eggs inside the flower of the wild fig. It was introduced into the New World to effect cross-fertilization of the cultivated fig. • *Blastophaga psenes*, family Agaonidae, superfamily Chalcidoidea.

fig·wort /ˈfigˌwərt; -ˌwôrt/ ▸*n.* a widely distributed herbaceous plant with purplish-brown two-lobed flowers. It was formerly considered to be effective in the treatment of scrofula. • Genus *Scrophularia*, family Scrophulariaceae (the **figwort family**): several species. Plants of this family have distinctive two-lobed flowers and include the snapdragons, toadflaxes, foxgloves, mulleins, monkey flowers, and speedwells. ▷mid 16th cent.: from obsolete *fig* 'piles' + WORT. The word originally denoted the pilewort, or lesser celandine, which was used as a treatment for piles; the current sense dates from the late 16th cent.

Fi·ji /ˈfējē/ a republic in the South Pacific consisting of a group of more than 800 islands, of which about a hundred are inhabited; pop. 800,000; capital, Suva; languages, English (official), Fijian, and Hindi.

First visited by Abel Tasman in 1643, the Fiji Islands became a British Crown Colony in 1874 and independent within the Commonwealth of Nations in 1970. In 1987, following a coup, Fiji became a republic and withdrew from the Commonwealth.

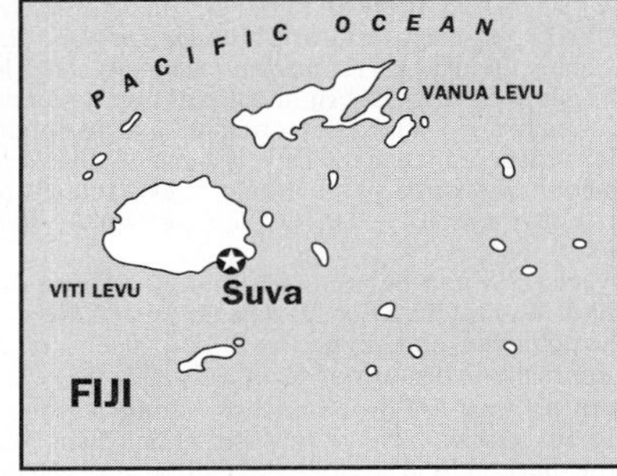

Fi·ji·an /ˌfējēən; fiˈjēən/ ▸*adj.* of or relating to Fiji, its people, or language.
▸*n.* **1** a native or national of Fiji, or a person of Fijian descent. **2** the Austronesian language of the indigenous people of Fiji.

fil·a·beg /ˈfiləˌbeg/ ▸*n.* variant spelling of FILIBEG.

fil·a·gree /ˈfiləˌgrē/ ▸*n.* variant spelling of FILIGREE.

fil·a·ment /ˈfiləmənt/ ▸*n.* a slender threadlike object or fiber, esp. one found in animal or plant structures: *a filament of cellulose.* ■ a conducting wire or thread with a high melting point, forming part of an electric bulb or vacuum tube and heated or made incandescent by an electric current. ■ *Botany* the slender part of a stamen that supports the anther. ■ *Astronomy* a narrow streamer from the sun's chromosphere or in its corona. ■ *Astronomy* a narrow streamer of gas in an interstellar cloud or nebula. ▷late 16th cent.: from French, or from modern Latin *filamentum*, from late Latin *filare* 'to spin,' from Latin *filum* 'thread.' **—fil·a·men·ta·ry** /ˌfiləˈmentərē/ *adj.* **—fil·a·ment·ed** *adj.* **—fil·a·men·tous** /-ˌmentəs/ *adj.*

fi·lar·i·a /fəˈle(ə)rēə/ ▸*n.* (*pl.* **-lar·i·ae** /-ˈle(ə)rēˌē; -ēˌī/) a threadlike parasitic nematode worm transmitted by biting flies and mosquitoes, causing filariasis and related diseases. • Superfamily Filarioidea, class Phasmida. ▷mid 19th cent.: from modern Latin *Filaria* (former genus name), from Latin *filum* 'thread.' **—fi·lar·i·al** /-ˈle(ə)rēəl/ *adj.*

fil·a·ri·a·sis /ˌfiləˈrīəsəs/ ▸*n. Medicine* a tropical disease caused by the presence of filarial worms, esp. in the lymph vessels where heavy infestation can result in elephantiasis.

fil·a·ture /ˈfiləˌcʜər; -cʜo͝or/ ▸*n.* the process of obtaining silk thread from silkworm cocoons. ■ an establishment where such activity takes place. ▷mid 18th cent.: from French, from Italian *filatura*, from *filare* 'to spin.'

fil·bert /ˈfilbərt/ ▸*n.* **1** a cultivated hazel tree that bears edible oval nuts. • Genus *Corylus*, family Betulaceae: several species, in particular the **giant filbert** (*Corylus maxima*). ■ the nut of this tree. **2** (also **filbert brush**) a brush with bristles forming a flattened oval head, used in oil painting. ▷Middle English *fylberd*, from Anglo-Norman French *philbert*, dialect French *noix de filbert* (so named because it is ripe about August 20, the feast day of St. Philibert).

filch /filCH/ ▸*v.* [*trans.*] *informal* pilfer or steal (something, esp. a thing of small value) in a casual way: *I was promptly accused of filching Mr. Muir's idea.* ▷Middle English: of unknown origin. **—filch·er** *n.*

file[1] /fīl/ ▸*n.* a folder or box for holding loose papers that are typically arranged in a particular order for easy reference: *a file of correspondence.* ■ the contents of such a folder or box. ■ *Computing* a collection of data, programs, etc., stored in a computer's memory or on a storage device under a single identifying name: *do you want to save this file?* | [as *adj.*] *a file name.*
▸*v.* [*trans.*] place (a document) in a cabinet, box, or folder in a particular order for preservation and easy reference: *the contract, when signed, is filed* | *figurative he still had the moment* ***filed away*** *in his memory.* ■ submit (a legal document, application, or charge) to be placed on record by the appropriate authority: *criminal charges were* ***filed against*** *the firm* | [*intrans.*] *the company had* ***filed for*** *bankruptcy.* ■ (of a reporter) send (a story) to a newspaper or news organization. ▷late Middle English (as a verb meaning 'string documents on a thread or wire to keep them in order'): from French *filer* 'to string,' *fil* 'a thread,' both from Latin *filum* 'a thread.' Compare with **FILE**[2]. **—fil·er** *n.*
▸PHRASE □ **on file** in a file or filing system.

file[2] ▸*n.* a line of people or things one behind another: *Plains Cree warriors riding* ***in file*** *down the slopes.* ■ *Military* a small detachment of men: *a file of English soldiers had ridden out from Perth.* ■ *Chess* each of the eight rows of eight squares on a chessboard running away from the player toward the opponent. Compare with **RANK**[1] (sense 2).
▸*v.* [*intrans.*] (of a group of people) walk one behind the other, typically in an orderly and solemn manner: *the mourners filed into the church.* ▷late 16th cent.: from French *file*, from *filer* 'to string.'

file[3] ▸*n.* a tool with a roughened surface or surfaces, typically of steel, used for smoothing or shaping a hard material: *it is possible to make the necessary notch with a file.*
▸*v.* [*trans.*] smooth or shape (something) with such a tool: *when I have nothing else to do, I file my nails.* ■ (**file something away/off**) remove something by grinding it off with a file: *the engine numbers were filed away.* ▷Old English *fīl*; related to Dutch *vijl* and German *Feile*. **—fil·er** *n.*

fi·lé /fiˈlā; ˈfēlā/ ▸*n.* pounded or powdered sassafras leaves used to flavor and thicken soup, esp. gumbo. ▷mid 19th cent.: from French, past participle of *filer* 'to twist.'

file cab·i·net ▸*n.* another term for **FILING CABINET**.

file ex·ten·sion ▸*n.* *Computing* a group of letters occurring after a period in a file name, indicating the purpose or contents of the file.

file·fish /ˈfīlˌfiSH/ ▸*n.* (*pl.* same or **-fish·es**) a fish with a dorsal spine and rough scales, related to the triggerfishes and occurring in tropical and sometimes temperate seas. • Numerous genera and species, family Balistidae (or Monacanthidae). ▷late 18th cent.: from **FILE**[3] (because of its rough skin, suggesting the surface of a file).

Fi·lene /fiˈlēn/, Edward Albert (1860–1937), U.S. merchant. As the president of Wm. Filene & Sons, he brought about many innovations, including the bargain basement and charge accounts. In 1921, he helped to establish the Credit Union National Extension Bureau.

file serv·er ▸*n.* *Computing* a device that controls access to separately stored files, as part of a multiuser system.

file-shar·ing ▸*n.* the practice of or ability to transmit files from one computer to another over a network or the Internet: [often as *modifier*] *file-sharing software.*

fi·let /fiˈlā; ˈfilā/ ▸*n.* **1** French spelling of **FILLET**, used esp. in the names of French or French-sounding dishes: *filet de boeuf.* **2** a kind of net or lace with a square mesh. [late 19th cent.: from French, 'net.']

fi·let mi·gnon /fiˌlā mēnˈyōN/ ▸*n.* a small tender piece of beef from the end of the tenderloin. ▷mid 20th cent.: French, literally 'dainty fillet.'

File Trans·fer Pro·to·col ▸ another term for **FTP**.

fil·i·al /ˈfilēəl; ˈfilyəl/ ▸*adj.* of or due from a son or daughter: *a display of filial affection.* ■ *Biology* denoting the generation or generations after the parental generation. See also **F**$_1$. ▷late Middle English: from Old French, or from ecclesiastical Latin *filialis*, from *filius* 'son,' *filia* 'daughter.' **—fil·i·al·ly** *adv.*

fil·i·a·tion /ˌfilēˈāSHən/ ▸*n.* the fact of being or of being designated the child of a particular parent or parents: *relationships based on ties of filiation as opposed to marriage.* ■ the manner in which a thing is related to another from which it is derived or descended in some respect: *the filiation of Old Norse manuscripts.* ■ a branch of a society or language. ▷late Middle English: from French, from ecclesiastical and medieval Latin *filiatio(n-)*, from Latin *filius* 'son,' *filia* 'daughter.'

fil·i·beg /ˈfiləˌbeg/ (also **phil·i·beg**, **fil·a·beg**) ▸*n.* *Scottish, chiefly historical* a kilt. ▷mid 18th cent.: from Scottish Gaelic *feileadh-beag* 'little kilt,' from *feileadh* 'plaid' and *beag* 'little.'

fil·i·bus·ter /ˈfiləˌbəstər/ ▸*n.* **1** an action such as a prolonged speech that obstructs progress in a legislative assembly while not technically contravening the required procedures: *it was defeated by a Senate filibuster in June.* **2** *historical* a person engaging in unauthorized warfare against a foreign country.
▸*v.* [*intrans.*] [often as *n.*] (**filibustering**) act in an obstructive manner in a legislature, esp. by speaking at inordinate length: *several measures were killed by Republican filibustering.* ■ [*trans.*] obstruct (a measure) in such a way. ▷late 18th cent.: from French *flibustier*, first applied to pirates who pillaged the Spanish colonies in the West Indies, ultimately from Dutch *vrijbuiter*; see **FREEBOOTER**. In the mid 19th cent. (via Spanish *filibustero*), the term denoted American adventurers who incited revolution in several Latin American states, whence sense 2. The verb was used to describe tactics intended to sabotage congressional proceedings, whence sense 1.

fil·i·cide /ˈfiləˌsīd/ ▸*n.* the killing of one's son or daughter: *maternal filicide.* ■ a person who kills their son or daughter. ▷mid 17th cent. from Latin *filius* 'son,' *filia* 'daughter' + **-CIDE**.

Fi·li·cop·si·da /ˌfiləˈkäpsədə/ *Botany* a class of pteridophyte plants that comprises the ferns. ▷modern Latin (plural), from Latin *filix*, *filic-* 'fern' + *opsis* 'appearance.'

fil·i·form /ˈfiləˌfôrm/ ▸*adj.* *Biology* threadlike: *the antennae are filiform.* ▷mid 18th cent.: from Latin *filum* 'thread' + **-IFORM**.

fil·i·gree /ˈfiləˌgrē/ (also **fil·a·gree**) ▸*n.* ornamental work of fine (typically gold or silver) wire formed into delicate tracery: [as *adj.*] *delicate silver filigree earrings.* ■ a thing resembling such fine ornamental work: *a wedding cake of gold and white filigree.* ▷late 17th cent. (earlier as *filigreen*, *filigrane*): from French *filigrane*, from Italian *filigrana* (from Latin *filum* 'thread' + *granum* 'seed').

fil·i·greed /ˈfiləˌgrēd/ (also **fil·a·greed**) ▸*adj.* ornamented with or resembling filigree work: *white filigreed stockings.*

fil·ing /ˈfīliNG/ ▸*n.* (usu. **filings**) a small particle rubbed off by a file when smoothing or shaping something: *iron filings.*

fil·ing cab·i·net ▸*n.* a piece of office furniture, typically made of steel, with deep drawers for storing documents.

Fi·li·o·que /ˌfilēˈōkwē; -ˌkwā/ the word inserted in the Western version of the Nicene Creed to assert the doctrine of the procession of the Holy Ghost from the Son as well as from the Father, which is not admitted by the Eastern Church. It was one of the central issues in the Great Schism of 1054. ▷Latin, literally 'and from the Son.'

Fil·i·pi·no /ˌfiləˈpēnō/ (also **Pil·i·pi·no**) ▸*adj.* of or relating to the Philippines, the Filipinos, or their language.
▸*n.* (*pl.* **-nos**) **1** (*fem.* **Fil·i·pi·na** /ˌfiləˈpēnə/) a native or national of the Philippines, or a person of Filipino descent. **2** the national language of the Philippines, a standardized form of Tagalog. ▷Spanish, from *las Islas Filipinas* 'the Philippine Islands.'

Fí·lip·poi /ˈfēlēˌpē/ Greek name for **PHILIPPI**.

fill /fil/ ▸*v.* [*trans.*] put someone or something into (a space or container) so that it is completely or almost completely full: *I* ***filled up*** *the bottle with water* | *the office was* ***filled with*** *reporters.* ■ [*intrans.*] (**fill with**) become full of: *Eleanor's eyes filled with tears.* ■ become an overwhelming presence in: *a pungent smell of garlic filled the air.* ■ cause (someone) to have an intense experience of an emotion or feeling: *his presence* ***filled us with*** *foreboding.* ■ appoint a person to hold (a vacant position): *the number of high-tech jobs and the people who can fill them.* ■ hold and perform the expected duties of (a position or role): *she fills the role of the "good" child.* ■ occupy or take up (a period of time): *the next few days were* ***filled with*** *meetings.* ■ be supplied with the items described in (a prescription or order): *she needed to fill a prescription.* ■ block up (a cavity in a tooth) with cement, amalgam, or gold. ■ [*intrans.*] (of a sail) curve out tautly as the wind blows into it. ■ (of a weather system) increase in barometric pressure. Compare with **DEEPEN**. ■ [*trans.*] (of the wind) blow into (a sail), causing it to curve outward. ■ *Poker* complete (a good hand) by drawing the necessary cards.
▸*phrasal v.* □ **fill in** act as a substitute for someone when they are unable to do their job: *my producer will have to have someone standing by to* ***fill in for*** *me.* □ **fill someone in 1** inform someone more fully of a matter, giving all the details: *the cab driver* ***filled*** *me* ***in on*** *much important economic and sociological data.* **2** *Brit., informal dated* hit or punch someone: *I filled in a chap and took his money.* □ **fill something in** put material into a hole, trench, or space so that it is completely full: *the canal is now disused and partly filled in.* ■ complete a drawing by adding color or shade to the spaces within an outline: *incised letters, filled in with gold.* ■ *chiefly Brit.* add information to complete something, typically a form or other official document: *he filled in all the forms.* □ **fill out** (of a person) put on weight to a noticeable extent. □ **fill something out** add information to complete an official form or document: *he filled out the requisite forms.* ■ give more details to add to someone's understanding of something: *he filled out the background by going into historical questions.* □ **fill up** become completely full: *the dining car filled up.* ■ fill the fuel tank of a car.
▸*n.* (**one's fill**) an amount of something that is as much as one wants or can bear: *we have eaten our fill* | *I've* ***had my fill of*** *surprises for one day.* ■ an amount of something that will occupy all the space in a container. ■ material, loose or compacted, that fills a space, esp. in building or engineering work: *loose polystyrene fill.* ■ the action of filling something, esp. of shading or color in a region of a computer graphics display. ■ (in popular music) a short interjected phrase on a particular instrument. ▷Old English *fyllan* (verb), *fyllu* (noun) of Germanic origin; related to Dutch *vullen* and German *füllen* (verbs), *Fülle* (noun), also to **FULL**[1].
▸PHRASES □ **fill the bill** see **BILL**[1]. □ **fill someone's shoes** *informal* take over someone's function or duties and fulfill them satisfactorily.

fille de joie /ˌfē(yə) də ˈZHwä/ ▸*n.* used euphemistically to refer to a prostitute. ▷early 18th cent.: French, literally 'girl of pleasure.'

filled gold ▸*n.* a relatively inexpensive metal with a layer of gold applied over it.

fill·er[1] /ˈfilər/ ▸*n.* **1** [usu. in *combination*] a thing put in a space or container to fill it: *these plants are attractive gap-fillers or ground cover.* ■ a substance used for filling cracks or holes in a surface, esp. before painting it: *quick-hardening wood filler.* ■ material used to fill a cavity or increase bulk: *foam filler* | *good quality paints should contain little or no filler.* ■ an item serving only to fill space or time, esp. in a newspaper, broadcast, or recording. ■ a word or sound filling a pause in an utterance or conversation (e.g., *er, well, you know*). ■ a linguistic unit that fills a particular slot in syntactic structure. ■ the tobacco blend used in a cigar. **2** [in *combination*] a person or thing that fills a space or container: *supermarket shelf-fillers.*

fill·er[2] ▸*n.* (*pl.* same) a monetary unit of Hungary, equal to one hundredth of a forint. ▷from Hungarian *fillér*.

fil·let ▸*n.* **1** /fiˈlā; ˈfilā/ (also **fi·let**) a fleshy boneless piece of meat from near the loins or the ribs of an animal: *a chicken breast fillet* | *roast* ***fillet of*** *lamb.* ■ (also **fillet steak**) a beef steak cut from the lower part of a sirloin. ■ a boned side of a fish. **2** /ˈfilit/ a band or ribbon worn around the head, esp. for binding the hair. ■ *Architecture* a narrow flat band separating two moldings. ■ *Architecture* a small band between the flutes of a column. ■ a plain or decorated line impressed on the cover of a book. ■ a roller used to impress such a line. **3** /ˈfilit/ a concave strip of material roughly triangular in cross section that rounds off an interior angle between two surfaces: *a splayed mortar fillet at the junction of the roof with the chimney stack* | [as *adj.*] *a fillet weld.*
▸*v.* /fiˈlā; ˈfilā/ (**-leted, -let·ing**) [*trans.*] remove the bones

Pronunciation Key ə *ago*; ər *over*; ˈə or ˌə *up*; ˈər or ˌər *fur*; a *hat*; ā *rate*; ä *car*; CH *chew*; e *let*; ē *see*; e(ə)r *air*; i *fit*; ī *by*; i(ə)r *ear*; NG *sing*; ō *go*; ô *for*; oi *boy*; o͝o *good*; o͞o *goo*; ou *out*; SH *she*; TH *thin*; T͟H *then*; (h)w *why*; ZH *vision*

F

from (a fish). ■ cut (fish or meat) into boneless strips. ▷Middle English (denoting a band worn around the head): from Old French *filet* 'thread,' based on Latin *filum* 'thread.' —**fil·let·er** *n.*

fill·ing /ˈfiliNG/ ▶*n.* a quantity of material that fills or is used to fill something: *a cushion with polyester filling.* ■ a piece of material used to fill a cavity in a tooth: *a gold filling.* ■ an edible substance placed between the layers of a sandwich, cake, or other foodstuff: *a Swiss roll with a chocolate filling.* ■ another term for WEFT.
▶*adj.* (of food) leaving one with a pleasantly satiated feeling: *a filling spicy bean soup.*

fill·ing sta·tion ▶*n.* a service station.

fil·lip /ˈfiləp/ ▶*n.* **1** something that acts as a stimulus or boost to an activity: *the halving of the automobile tax would provide **a fillip to** sales.* **2** *archaic* a movement made by bending the last joint of a finger against the thumb and suddenly releasing it; a flick of the finger: *the Prince, by a fillip, made some of the wine fly in Oglethorpe's face.* ■ a slight smart stroke or tap given in such a way: *she began to give him dainty fillips on the nose with a soft forepaw.*
▶*v.* (**-liped, -lip·ing**) [*trans.*] *archaic* propel (a small object) with a flick of the finger: *our aforesaid merchant filliped a nut sharply against his bullying giant.* ■ strike (someone or something) slightly and smartly: *he filliped him over the nose.* ■ stimulate or urge (someone or something): *pour, that the draught may fillip my remembrance.* ▷late Middle English (in the sense 'make a fillip with the fingers'): symbolic; compare with FLICK, FLIP[1].

fill light ▶*n.* a supplementary light used in photography or filming that does not change the character of the main light and is used chiefly to lighten shadows.

Fill·more /ˈfilmôr/, Millard (1800–74), 13th president of the U.S. 1850–53. A New York Whig, he served in the U.S. House of Representatives 1833–35, 1837–43 and became U.S. vice president in 1849. Seventeen months later, he succeeded to the presidency upon the death of President Zachary Taylor. Fillmore was an advocate of compromise on the slavery issue, but his unpopular enforcement of the 1850 Fugitive Slave Act hastened the end of the Whig Party.

Millard Fillmore

fill-up ▶*n.* an instance of making something completely full, esp. the fuel tank of an automobile: *free coffee with fill-up.*

fil·ly /ˈfilē/ ▶*n.* (*pl.* **-lies**) a young female horse, esp. one less than four years old. ■ *dated* a lively girl or young woman. ▷late Middle English: from Old Norse *fylja,* of Germanic origin; related to FOAL.

film /film/ ▶*n.* **1** a thin flexible strip of plastic or other material coated with light-sensitive emulsion for exposure in a camera, used to produce photographs or motion pictures: *he had already shot a whole roll of film | a new range of films and cameras.* ■ material in the form of a thin flexible sheet: *clear plastic film between the layers of glass.* ■ a thin layer covering a surface: *she quickly wiped away the light film of sweat.* ■ *archaic* a fine thread or filament: *films of silk.* **2** a motion picture; a movie: *a horror film* | [as *adj.*] *a film director.* ■ movies considered as an art or industry: *a critical overview of feminist writing on film.*
▶*v.* **1** [*trans.*] capture on film as part of a series of moving images; make a movie of (a story or event): *she glowered at the television crew who were filming them.* ■ make a movie of (a book). ■ [*intrans.*] (**film well/badly**) be well or badly suited to portrayal in a film: *an adventure story that would film well.* **2** [*intrans.*] become or appear to become covered with a thin layer of something: *his eyes had **filmed over**.* ▷Old English *filmen* 'membrane'; related to FELL[5].

film badge ▶*n.* a device containing photographic film that registers the wearer's exposure to radiation.

film·go·er /ˈfilm,gōər/ ▶*n.* a person who goes to the movies, esp. regularly. —**film·go·ing** /-,gōiNG/ *n.*

film·ic /ˈfilmik/ ▶*adj.* of or relating to movies or cinematography: *he has reconceived the stage production in filmic terms.*

film·mak·er /ˈfilm,mākər/ ▶*n.* a person who directs or produces movies for the theater or television. —**film·mak·ing** *n.*

film noir /,film ˈnwär/ ▶*n.* a style or genre of cinematographic film marked by a mood of pessimism, fatalism, and menace. The term was originally applied (by a group of French critics) to American thriller or detective films made in the period 1944–54 and to the work of directors such as Orson Welles, Fritz Lang, and Billy Wilder. ■ a film of this genre. ▷mid 20th cent.: French, literally 'black film.'

film·og·ra·phy /filˈmägrəfē/ ▶*n.* (*pl.* **-phies**) a list of films by one director or actor, or on one subject. ▷1960s: from FILM + -GRAPHY, on the pattern of *bibliography.*

film·set·ting /ˈfilm,setiNG/ ▶*n.* British term for PHOTOCOMPOSITION. —**film·set** /-,set/ *v.* —**film·set·ter** *n.*

film stock ▶*n.* see STOCK (sense 1).

film·strip /ˈfilm,strip/ ▶*n.* a series of transparencies in a strip for projection, used esp. as a teaching aid.

film·y /ˈfilmē/ ▶*adj.* (**film·i·er, film·i·est**) (esp. of fabric) thin and translucent: *filmy white voile.* ■ covered with or forming a thin layer of something: *her eyes were dull and filmy.* —**film·i·ly** /ˈfilməlē/ *adv.* —**film·i·ness** /ˈfilmēnis/ *n.*

film·y fern ▶*n.* a small fern of damp shady places, with wiry creeping stems and delicate forked fronds that are only one cell thick. They occur chiefly in tropical and subtropical regions. • Family Hymenophyllaceae: *Hymenophyllum* and other genera.

fi·lo /ˈfēlō/ ▶*n.* variant spelling of PHYLLO.

Fi·lo·fax /ˈfīlō,faks; ˈfīlə,-/ ▶*n.* *trademark* a loose-leaf notebook for recording appointments, addresses, and notes. ▷1930s: representing a colloquial pronunciation of *file of facts.*

fil·o·po·di·um /,filəˈpōdēəm; ,fī-/ ▶*n.* (*pl.* **-po·di·a** /-ˈpōdēə/) *Biology* a long, slender, tapering pseudopodium, as found in some protozoans and in embryonic cells. ▷early 20th cent.: from Latin *filium* 'thread' + PODIUM. —**fil·o·po·di·al** /-ˈpōdēəl/ *adj.*

fil·o·selle /ˈfilə,sel/ ▶*n.* floss silk, or silk thread resembling this, used in embroidery. ▷mid 16th cent.: from French, from Italian *filosello* 'raw silk from a cocoon', of uncertain ultimate origin.

fi·lo·vi·rus /ˈfēlō,vīrəs; ˈfī-/ ▶*n.* a filamentous RNA virus of a genus that causes severe hemorrhagic fevers in humans and primates, and that includes the Ebola and Marburg viruses.

fils[1] /fils/ ▶*n.* (*pl.* same) a monetary unit of Iraq, Bahrain, Jordan, Kuwait, and Yemen, equal to one hundredth of a riyal in Yemen and one thousandth of a dinar elsewhere. ▷from a colloquial pronunciation of Arabic *fals,* denoting a small copper coin, from Latin *follis* 'purse, coin'; compare with FOLLIS, FOOL[1].

fils[2] /fēs/ ▶*n.* used after a surname to distinguish a son from a father of the same name: *Alexandre Dumas fils.* Compare with PÈRE. ▷late 19th cent.: French, literally 'son.'

fil·ter /ˈfiltər/ ▶*n.* a porous device for removing impurities or solid particles from a liquid or gas passed through it: *an oil filter.* ■ short for FILTER TIP: [as *adj.*] *a cheap filter cigarette.* ■ a screen, plate, or layer of a substance that absorbs light or other radiation or selectively absorbs some of its components: *filters can be used in photography to reduce haze.* ■ a device for suppressing electrical or sound waves of frequencies not required. ■ *Computing* a piece of software that processes text, for example to remove unwanted spaces or to format it for use in another application. ■ *Brit.* an arrangement whereby vehicles may turn left (or right) while other traffic waiting to go straight ahead or turn right (or left) is stopped by a red light: [as *adj.*] *a filter lane.*
▶*v.* [*trans.*] **1** pass (a liquid, gas, light, or sound) through a device to remove unwanted material: *the patient is hooked up to a dialysis machine twice a week to **filter out** the cholesterol in the blood | figurative you'll be put through to a secretary whose job it is to filter calls.* ■ [*intrans.*, with *adverbial of direction*] move slowly or in small quantities or numbers through something or in a specified direction: *people filtered out of the concert during the last set.* ■ [*intrans.*, with *adverbial*] (of information) gradually become known: *the news began to filter in from the hospital.* **2** *Computing* [*trans.*] process or treat with a filter. ▷late Middle English (denoting a piece of felt): from French *filtre,* from medieval Latin *filtrum* 'felt used as a filter,' related to FELT[1].

fil·ter·a·ble /ˈfiltərəbəl/ (also **fil·tra·ble** /-trəbəl/) ▶*adj.* **1** capable of passing through a filter. **2** capable of being separated out by a filter: *filterable virus | filterable solids.*

fil·ter bed ▶*n.* a tank or pond containing a layer of sand or gravel, used for filtering large quantities of liquid.

fil·ter cake ▶*n.* a deposit of insoluble material left on a filter.

fil·ter feed·ing ▶*n.* *Zoology* (of an aquatic animal) feeding by filtering out plankton or nutrients suspended in the water. —**fil·ter-feed** *v.* —**fil·ter feed·er** *n.*

fil·ter pa·per ▶*n.* a piece of porous paper for filtering liquids, used esp. in chemical processes and coffeemaking.

fil·ter press ▶*n.* a device consisting of a series of cloth filters fixed to frames, used for the large-scale filtration of liquid under pressure.

fil·ter tip ▶*n.* a filter attached to a cigarette for removing some components from the inhaled smoke. ■ a cigarette with such a filter. —**fil·ter-tipped** *adj.*

filth /filTH/ ▶*n.* disgusting dirt: *stagnant pools of filth.* ■ obscene and offensive language or printed material. ■ corrupt behavior; decadence. ■ used as a term of abuse for a person or people one greatly despises: *Nazi filth.* ■ [as *plural n.*] (**the filth**) *Brit., informal, derogatory* the police. ▷Old English *fȳlth* 'rotting matter, rottenness,' also 'corruption, obscenity,' of Germanic origin; related to Dutch *vuilte,* also to FOUL.

filth·y /ˈfilTHē/ ▶*adj.* (**filth·i·er, filth·i·est**) disgustingly dirty: *a filthy hospital with no sanitation.* ■ obscene and offensive: *filthy language.* ■ *informal* used to express one's anger and disgust: *you filthy beast.* ■ (of a mood) bad-tempered and aggressive: *he arrived at the meeting half an hour late in a filthy temper.* ■ *Brit., informal* (of weather) very unpleasant: *it looked like a filthy night.*
▶*adv.* [as *submodifier*] *informal* to an extreme and often disgusting extent: *he has become filthy rich.* —**filth·i·ly** /ˈfilTHəlē/ *adv.* —**filth·i·ness** /ˈfilTHēnəs/ *n.*

filth·y lu·cre ▶*n.* money, esp. when gained in a dishonest or dishonorable way. ▷early 16th cent.: with biblical allusion to Tit. 1:11.

fil·tra·ble /ˈfiltrəbəl/ ▶*adj.* variant spelling of FILTERABLE.

fil·trate /ˈfil,trāt/ ▶*n.* a liquid that has passed through a filter: *filtrates of bacterial cultures | drops of clear filtrate.*
▶*v.* [*trans.*] filter: *the remaining alkali is filtrated.* ▷early 17th cent.: from modern Latin *filtrat-* 'filtered,' from the verb *filtrare,* from medieval Latin *filtrum* (see FILTER).

fil·tra·tion /filˈtrāSHən/ ▶*n.* the action or process of filtering something: *small particles are difficult to remove without filtration.*

fim·bri·a /ˈfimbrēə/ ▶*n.* (*pl.* **-bri·ae** /-brē,ē; -brē,ī/) *chiefly Anatomy* a series of threads or other projections resembling a fringe. ■ [usu. in *pl.*] an individual thread in such a structure, esp. a fingerlike projection at the end of the Fallopian tube near the ovary. ▷mid 18th cent.: from late Latin, literally 'border, fringe.' —**fim·bri·al** /-brēəl/ *adj.*

fim·bri·at·ed /ˈfimbrē,ātid/ (also **fim·bri·ate**) ▶*adj.* **1** *Biology* having a fringe or border of hairlike or fingerlike projections. **2** *Heraldry* having a narrow border, typically of a specified tincture. ▷late 15th cent. (sense 2): from Latin *fimbriatus* (from *fimbria* 'fringe') + -ED[1].

fin /fin/ ▶*n.* a flattened appendage on various parts of the body of many aquatic vertebrates and some invertebrates, including fish and cetaceans, used for propelling, steering, and balancing. ■ an underwater swimmer's flipper. ■ a small flattened projecting surface or attachment on an aircraft, rocket, or automobile, providing aerodynamic stability or serving as a design element. ■ a flattened projection on a device, such as a radiator, used for increasing heat transfer.
▶*v.* (**finned, fin·ning**) [*intrans.*] swim underwater by means of flippers: *I finned madly for the surface.* ▷Old English *finn, fin,* of Germanic origin; related to Dutch *vin* and probably ultimately to Latin *pinna* 'feather, wing.' —**fin·less** *adj.* —**finned** *adj.* [in *combination*] *primitive ray-finned fishes.*

fin. ▶*abbr.* ■ finance. ■ financial. ■ finish.

fi·na·gle /fəˈnāgəl/ ▸*v.* [*trans.*] *informal* obtain (something) by devious or dishonest means: *Ted attended all the football games he could finagle tickets for.* ■ [*intrans.*] act in a devious or dishonest manner: *they wrangled and finagled over the fine points.* ▷1920s (originally U.S.): from dialect *fainaigue* 'cheat'; perhaps from Old French *fornier* 'deny.' —**fi·na·gler** /fəˈnāg(ə)lər/ *n.*

fi·nal /ˈfīnl/ ▸*adj.* coming at the end of a series: *the final version of the report was presented.* ■ reached or designed to be reached as the outcome of a process or a series of events: *the final cost will easily run into six figures.* ■ allowing no further doubt or dispute: *the decision of the judging panel is final.*

▸*n.* **1** the last game in a sports tournament or other competition, which decides the winner of the tournament. ■ (**finals**) a series of games constituting the final stage of a competition: *the World Cup finals.* **2** (**final**) an examination at the end of a term, academic year, or particular class. ■ (**finals**) *Brit.* a series of examinations at the end of a degree course: *she was doing her history finals.* **3** *Music* the principal note in a mode. **4** (**finals**) *Brit.* the final approach of a landing aircraft to a runway: *the plane piloted by Richards was on finals.* ▷Middle English (in the adjectival sense 'conclusive'): from Old French, or from Latin *finalis*, from *finis* 'end.' Compare with FINISH.

▸*PHRASE* □ **the final straw** see STRAW.

fi·nal cause ▸*n. Philosophy* the purpose or aim of an action or the end toward which a thing naturally develops.

fi·nal drive ▸*n.* the last part of the transmission system in a motor vehicle.

fi·na·le /fəˈnalē; -ˈnälē/ ▸*n.* the last part of a piece of music, a performance, or a public event, esp. when particularly dramatic or exciting: *the festival ends with a grand finale.* ▷mid 18th cent.: from Italian, from Latin *finalis* (see FINAL).

Fi·nal Four ▸*n.* the four teams that qualify for the championship round in the annual NCAA men's or women's college basketball tournament.

fi·nal·ist /ˈfīnl-ist/ ▸*n.* a competitor or team in the final or finals of a competition.

fi·nal·i·ty /fīˈnalətē; fi-/ ▸*n.* (*pl.* **-ties**) the fact or impression of being an irreversible ending: *the abrupt finality of death | there's a dreadful finality about cutting down a tree.* ■ a tone or manner that indicates that no further comment or argument is possible: *"No," she said with finality.* ■ the quality of being complete or conclusive: *the desire for justice rather than finality fuels challenges to decisions.* ■ an action or event that ends something irreversibly: *death is the ultimate finality.* ▷mid 19th cent.: from French *finalité*, from late Latin *finalitas*, from Latin *finalis* (see FINAL).

fi·nal·ize /ˈfīnlˌīz/ ▸*v.* [*trans.*] complete (a transaction, esp. in commerce or diplomacy) after discussion of the terms: *the two countries had yet to finalize a peace treaty.* ■ produce or agree on a finished and definitive version of: *efforts intensified to finalize plans for postwar reconstruction.* —**fi·nal·i·za·tion** /ˌfīnl-əˈzāSHən/ *n.*

fi·nal·ly /ˈfīn(ə)lē/ ▸*adv.* after a long time, typically involving difficulty or delay: *he finally arrived to join us.* ■ as the last in a series of related events or objects: *a referendum followed by local, legislative, and, finally, presidential elections.* ■ [*sentence adverb*] used to introduce a final point or reason: *finally, it is common knowledge that travel broadens the horizons.* ■ in such a way as to put an end to doubt and dispute: *to dispel finally the belief that auditors were clients of the company.*

fi·nal so·lu·tion ▸*n.* the Nazi policy of exterminating European Jews. Introduced by Heinrich Himmler and administered by Adolf Eichmann, the policy resulted in the murder of 6 million Jews in concentration camps between 1941 and 1945. ▷translation of German *Endlösung.*

fi·nance /ˈfīnans; fəˈnans/ ▸*n.* the management of large amounts of money, esp. by governments or large companies. ■ monetary support for an enterprise: *housing finance.* ■ (**finances**) the monetary resources and affairs of a country, organization, or person: *the finances of the school were causing serious concern.*

▸*v.* [*trans.*] provide funding for (a person or enterprise): *the city and county originally financed the project.* ▷late Middle English: from Old French, from *finer* 'make an end, settle a debt,' from *fin* 'end' (see FINE[2]). The original sense was 'payment of a debt, compensation, or ransom'; later 'taxation, revenue.' Current senses date from the 18th cent., and reflect sense development in French.

fi·nance com·pa·ny (also *Brit.* **finance house**) ▸*n.* a company concerned primarily with providing money, as for short-term loans.

fi·nan·cial /fəˈnanCHəl; fī-/ ▸*adj.* of or relating to finance: *an independent financial adviser.* —**fi·nan·cial·ly** *adv.*

> *THE RIGHT WORD* **financial, fiscal, monetary, pecuniary**
>
> What's the difference between a **financial** crisis and a **fiscal** one? It all depends on who's having trouble with money and the scale of the difficulties.
>
> *Financial* usually applies to money matters involving large sums or transactions of considerable importance (*the auction was a financial success*).
>
> *Fiscal* refers specifically to the financial affairs of a government, organization, or corporation (*the end of the company's fiscal year*), while **pecuniary** refers to money matters of a more personal or practical nature and is preferred to *financial* when money is being discussed on a smaller scale (*pecuniary motives; pecuniary assistance; pecuniary difficulties*).
>
> Of all these words, **monetary** refers most directly to money as such and is often used when discussing the coinage, distribution, and circulation of money (*the European monetary system; the monetary unit of a country*).

fi·nan·cials /fəˈnanSHəlz/ ▸*plural n.* shares in financial companies. ■ financial data about a company: *take a look at their financials.*

Fi·nan·cial Times in·dex another term for **FTSE INDEX**.

fi·nan·cial year ▸*n.* British term for FISCAL YEAR.

fin·an·cier /ˌfinənˈsi(ə)r; fəˈnanˌsi(ə)r/ ▸*n.* a person concerned with the management of large amounts of money on behalf of governments or other large organizations. ▷early 17th cent.: from French, from *finance* (see FINANCE).

fin·back /ˈfinbak/ (also **finback whale**) ▸*n.* a large rorqual with a small dorsal fin, a dark gray back, and white underparts. Also called FIN WHALE, COMMON RORQUAL (see RORQUAL). • *Balaenoptera physalus*, family Balaenopteridae.

fin·ca /ˈfiNGkə/ ▸*n.* (in Spanish-speaking regions) a country estate; a ranch.

finch /finCH/ ▸*n.* a seed-eating songbird that typically has a stout bill and colorful plumage. • The true finches belong to the family Fringillidae (the **finch family**), which includes chaffinches, canaries, linnets, crossbills, etc. Many other finches belong to the bunting, waxbill, or sparrow families. ▷Old English *finc*; related to Dutch *vink* and German *Fink*.

find /find/ ▸*v.* (*past* **found** /found/) [*trans.*] **1** discover or perceive by chance or unexpectedly: *Lindsey looked up to find Neil watching her | the remains of a headless body had been found.* ■ discover (someone or something) after a deliberate search: *in this climate it could be hard to find a buyer.* ■ (**find oneself**) discover oneself to be in a surprising or unexpected situation: *phobia sufferers often find themselves virtual prisoners in their own home.* ■ succeed in obtaining (something): *she also found the time to raise five children.* ■ summon up (a quality, esp. courage) with an effort: *I found the courage to speak.* ■ recover the use of (an ability or faculty): *the skipper of a Yankee Clipper awkwardly finding his land legs.* ■ [*intrans.*] (of hunters or hounds) discover game, esp. a fox: *she heard the new halloo—they had found.* **2** (often **be found**) recognize or discover (something) to be present: *vitamin B12 is found in dairy products.* ■ become aware of; discover to be the case: [*trans.*] *the majority of staff find the magazine to be informative and useful* | [with *clause*] *she found that none of the local nursery schools had an available slot.* ■ ascertain (something) by study, calculation, or inquiry: *a forum that attempts to find solutions for multimedia publishers.* ■ [*trans.*] perceive or experience (something) to be the case: *both men found it difficult to put ideas into words.* ■ (**find oneself**) discover the fundamental truths about one's own character and identity: *I did psychotherapy for years—I wanted to find myself.* ■ *Law* (of a court) officially declare to be the case: [*trans.*] *he was found guilty of speeding* | [with *clause*] *the court found that a police lab expert had fabricated evidence.* **3** (of a thing) reach or arrive at, either of its own accord or without the human agent being known: *water finds its own level.* ■ (**find one's way**) reach one's destination by one's own efforts, without knowing in advance how to get there: *he* ***found his way to*** *the front door.* ■ (**find one's way**) come to be in a certain situation: *each and every boy* ***found his way into*** *a suitable occupation.* ■ (of a letter) reach (someone). ■ *archaic* reach the understanding or conscience of (someone): *whatever finds me, bears witness for itself that it has proceeded from a Holy Spirit.*

▸*phrasal v.* □ **find against** *Law* (of a court) make a decision against or judge to be guilty. □ **find for** (or **find in favor of**) *Law* (of a court) make a decision in favor of or judge to be innocent: *a jury found for the plaintiff.* □ **find someone out** detect a person's offensive or immoral actions: *she would always find him out if he tried to lie.* □ **find something out** (or **find out about something**) discover a fact: *he hadn't time to find out what was bothering her.*

▸*n.* a discovery of something valuable, typically something of archaeological interest: *he made his most spectacular finds in the Valley of the Kings | this resort is* ***a real find.*** ■ a person who is discovered to be useful or interesting in some way: *Paul had been a real find—he could design the whole hotel complex.* ■ *Hunting* the finding of a fox. ▷Old English *findan*, of Germanic origin; related to Dutch *vinden* and German *finden*. —**find·a·ble** /ˈfindəbəl/ *adj.*

▸*PHRASES* □ **all found** *Brit., dated* (of an employee's wages) with board and lodging provided free: *your wages would be five shillings all found.* □ **find fault** see FAULT. □ **find favor** be liked or prove acceptable: *the ballets did not* ***find favor with*** *the public.* □ **find one's feet** stand up and become able to walk. ■ establish oneself in a particular field: *I think he really started to find his feet with this album.* □ **find God** experience a religious conversion or awakening. □ **find in favor of** see FIND FOR below. □ **find it in one's heart to do something** allow or force oneself to do something: *I ask you to find it in your heart to forgive me.*

find·er /ˈfīndər/ ▸*n.* a person who finds someone or something. ■ (in full **finder-scope**) a small telescope attached to a large one to locate an object for observation. ■ the viewfinder of a camera.

▸*PHRASE* □ **finders keepers** (**losers weepers**) *informal* used, often humorously, to assert that whoever finds something by chance is entitled to keep it.

find·er's fee ▸*n.* a fee paid by a business to a person or organization for bringing to its attention financial investors, potential new employees, or buyers or sellers whose relationship with the business will materially benefit it.

fin de siè·cle /ˌfan də sēˈekl(ə)/ ▸*adj.* relating to or characteristic of the end of a century, esp. the 19th century: *fin-de-siècle art.* ■ decadent: *there was a fin-de-siècle air in the club last night.*

▸*n.* the end of a century, esp. the 19th century. ▷French, 'end of century.'

find·ing /ˈfīndiNG/ ▸*n.* **1** the action of finding someone or something: *a local doctor reported the finding of numerous dead rats.* ■ (often **findings**) a conclusion reached as a result of an inquiry, investigation, or trial: *experimental findings.* **2** (**findings**) small articles or tools used in making garments, shoes, or jewelry.

Find·lay /ˈfin(d)lē/ an industrial city in northwestern Ohio; pop. 35,675.

fine[1] /fīn/ ▸*adj.* **1** of high quality: *this was a fine piece of filmmaking | fine wines.* ■ (of a person) worthy of or eliciting admiration: *what a fine human being he is.* ■ good; satisfactory: *relations in the group were fine.* ■ used to express one's agreement with or acquiescence to something: *anything you want is* ***fine by me,*** *Linda | he said such a solution would be fine.* ■ in good health and feeling well: *"I'm fine, just fine. And you?"* ■ (of the weather) bright and clear: *it was another fine winter day.* ■ of imposing and dignified appearance or size: *a very fine Elizabethan mansion.* ■ (of speech or writing) sounding impressive and grand but ultimately insincere: *fine words seemed to produce few practical benefits.* ■ denoting or displaying a state of good, though not excellent, preservation in stamps, books, coins, etc. ■ (of gold or silver) containing a specified high proportion of pure metal: *the coin is struck in .986 fine gold.* **2** (of a thread, filament, or person's hair) thin: *I have always had fine and dry hair.* ■ (of a point) sharp: *I sharpened the leads to a fine point.* ■ consisting of small particles: *the soils were all fine silt.* ■ having or requiring an intricate delicacy of touch: *exquisitely fine work.* ■ (of something abstract) subtle and therefore perceived only with difficulty and care: *the fine distinctions between the new and old definitions of refugee.* ■ (of feelings) refined; elevated: *you might appeal to their finer feelings.*

▸*n.* (**fines**) very small particles found in mining, milling, etc.

▸*adv. informal* in a satisfactory or pleasing manner; very well: *"And how's the job-hunting going?" "Oh, fine."*

▶v. **1** [trans.] clarify (beer or wine) by causing the precipitation of sediment during production. ■ [intrans.] (of liquid) become clear: *the ale hadn't had quite time to fine down.* **2** make or become thinner: [trans.] *it can be* ***fined*** *right* ***down*** *to the finished shape* | [intrans.] *she'd certainly* ***fined down****—her face was thinner.* ▷Middle English: from Old French *fin,* based on Latin *finire* 'to finish' (see FINISH). **—fine·ly** *adv.* **—fine·ness** *n.*

▶*PHRASES* □ **cut it** (or **things**) **fine** allow a very small margin of something, esp. time: *boys who have cut it rather fine are scuttling into chapel.* □ **do fine** be entirely satisfactory: *an omelet will do fine.* ■ be healthy or well: *the baby's doing fine.* ■ do something in a satisfactory manner: *he was doing fine acquiring all the necessary disciplines in finance.* □ **do someone fine** suit or be enough for someone. □ **fine feathers make fine birds** *proverb* beautiful clothes or an eye-catching appearance make a person appear similarly beautiful or impressive. □ **the finer points of** the more complex or detailed aspects of: *he went on to discuss the finer points of his work.* □ **——'s finest** *informal* the police of a particular city: *Moscow's finest.* □ **one's finest hour** the time of one's greatest success. □ **fine words butter no parsnips** *proverb* nothing is achieved by empty promises or flattery. □ **not to put too fine a point on it** to speak bluntly: *not to put too fine a point on it, your Emily is a liar.* [figuratively, with reference to the sharpening of a weapon, tool, etc.] □ **one fine day** at some unspecified or unknown time: *you want to be the Chancellor one fine day.*

fine² /fīn/ ▶*n.* a sum of money exacted as a penalty by a court of law or other authority: *a parking fine.*

▶v. [trans.] (often **be fined**) punish (someone) by making them pay a sum of money, typically as a penalty for breaking the law: *he was fined $600 and sentenced to one day in jail.* ▷Middle English: from Old French *fin* 'end, payment,' from Latin *finis* 'end' (in medieval Latin denoting a sum paid on settling a lawsuit). The original sense was 'conclusion' (surviving in the phrase IN FINE); also used in the medieval Latin sense, the word came to denote a penalty of any kind, later specifically a monetary penalty. **—fine·a·ble** /'fīnəbəl/ *adj.*

fine³ /fēn/ ▶*n.* French brandy of high quality made from distilled wine rather than from pomace. ■ short for FINE CHAMPAGNE.

fi·ne⁴ /'fēnā/ ▶*n.* (in musical directions) the place where a piece of music finishes (when this is not at the end of the score but at the end of an earlier section that is repeated at the end of the piece). ▷Italian, from Latin *finis* 'end.'

fine art ▶*n.* **1** (also **fine arts**) creative art, esp. visual art, whose products are to be appreciated primarily or solely for their imaginative, aesthetic, or intellectual content: *the convergence of popular culture and fine art.* **2** an activity requiring great skill or accomplishment: *he'll have to learn* ***the fine art of*** *persuasion.*

▶*PHRASE* □ **have** (or **get**) **something down to a fine art** achieve a high level of skill, facility, or accomplishment in some activity through experience: *Mike had gotten the breakfast routine down to a fine art.*

fine cham·pagne ▶*n.* brandy from the Champagne district of the Cognac region of which half or more of the content comes from the central Grande Champagne. ▷mid 19th cent.: French, literally 'fine (brandy from) Champagne.'

fine chem·i·cals ▶*plural n.* chemical substances prepared to a very high degree of purity for use in research and industry.

fine-draw ▶v. [trans.] sew together (two pieces of cloth or edges of a tear) so that the join is imperceptible: *a table cover composed of cloth fine-drawn together.*

Fi·ne Gael /ˌfēnə 'gāl/ one of the two major political parties of the Republic of Ireland (the other being Fianna Fáil). Founded in 1923 as Cumann na nGaedheal, it changed its name in 1933. It has advocated the concept of a united Ireland achieved by peaceful means. ▷Irish, literally 'tribe of Gaels.'

fine-grained ▶*adj.* (chiefly of wood) having a fine or delicate arrangement of fibers. ■ (chiefly of rock) consisting of small particles. ■ involving great attention to detail: *fine-grained analysis.*

fine print ▶*n.* printed matter in small type. ■ inconspicuous details or conditions printed in an agreement or contract, esp. ones that may prove unfavorable: *read the fine print of whatever loan document is shoved under your nose.*

fin·er·y¹ /'fīnərē/ ▶*n.* expensive or ostentatious clothes or decoration: *officers in their blue, gold, and scarlet finery.* ▷late 17th cent.: from FINE¹, on the pattern of *bravery.*

fin·er·y² ▶*n.* (*pl.* **-er·ies**) *historical* a hearth where pig iron was converted into wrought iron. ▷late 16th cent.: from French *finerie,* from Old French *finer* 'refine.'

fines herbes /ˌfēn'(z)erb/ ▶*plural n.* mixed herbs used in cooking, esp. fresh herbs chopped as a flavoring for omelets. ▷mid 19th cent.: French, literally 'fine herbs.'

fine-spun ▶*adj.* (esp. of fabric) fine or delicate in texture. ■ subtle; overly refined.

fi·nesse /fə'nes/ ▶*n.* **1** intricate and refined delicacy: *orchestral playing of great finesse.* ■ artful subtlety, typically that needed for tactful handling of a difficulty: *clients want advice and action that calls for considerable finesse.* ■ subtle or delicate manipulation: *a certain amount of finesse is required to fine-tune the heat output.* **2** (in bridge and whist) an attempt to win a trick with a card that is not a certain winner.

▶v. [trans.] **1** do (something) in a subtle and delicate manner: *his third shot, which he attempted to finesse, failed by a fraction.* ■ slyly attempt to avoid blame or censure when dealing with (a situation or action): *the administration's attempts to finesse its mishaps.* **2** (in bridge and whist) play (a card that is not a certain winner) in the hope of winning a trick with it: *the declarer finesses ♦J.* ▷late Middle English (in the sense 'purity, delicacy': from French, related to FINE¹.

fine struc·ture ▶*n.* the composition of an object, substance, or energy phenomenon as viewed on a small scale and in considerable detail. ■ *Physics* the presence of groups of closely spaced lines in spectra corresponding to slightly different energy levels.

fine-struc·ture con·stant ▶*n.* *Physics* a fundamental and dimensionless physical constant, equal to approximately $^1/_{137}$, that occurs in expressions describing the fine structure of atomic spectra.

fine-tooth comb (also **fine-toothed comb**) ▶*n.* a comb with narrow teeth that are close together. ■ [in *sing.*] used with reference to a very thorough search or analysis of something: *you should check the small print* ***with a fine-tooth comb.***

fine-tune ▶v. [trans.] make small adjustments to (something) in order to achieve the best or a desired performance: *the advanced angler seeking to fine-tune his angling skills.*

fin·ger /'fiNGgər/ ▶*n.* each of the four slender jointed parts attached to either hand (or five, if the thumb is included): *she raked her hair back with her fingers.* ■ a part of a glove intended to cover a finger. ■ a measure of liquor in a glass, based on the breadth of a finger: *he poured three fingers of vodka into a juice glass.* ■ an object that has roughly the long, narrow shape of a finger: *a shortbread finger.*

▶v. [trans.] **1** touch or feel (something) with the fingers: *the thin man fingered his mustache.* ■ play (a musical instrument) with the fingers, esp. in a tentative or casual manner: *a woman fingered a lute.* **2** *informal* inform on (someone) to the police: *you* ***fingered*** *me for those burglaries.* ■ (**finger someone for**) identify or choose someone for (a particular purpose): *a research biologist with impeccable credentials was fingered for team leader.* **3** *Music* play (a passage) with a particular sequence of positions of the fingers. See also FINGERING. ■ mark (music) with signs showing which fingers are to be used. ▷Old English, of Germanic origin; related to Dutch *vinger* and German *Finger.* **—fin·gered** *adj.* [in *combination*] *a two-fingered whistle* **—fin·ger·less** *adj.*

▶*PHRASES* □ **be all fingers and thumbs** *Brit., informal* be clumsy or awkward in one's actions. □ **give someone the finger** *informal* make an obscene gesture with the middle finger raised as a sign of contempt, meaning 'fuck you'. □ **have a finger in every pie** be involved in a large and varied number of activities or enterprises. □ **have** (or **keep**) **one's finger on the pulse** be aware of all the latest news or developments: *he keeps his finger on the pulse of world music.* □ **keep one's fingers crossed** see CROSS. □ **lay a finger on someone** touch someone, esp. with the intention of harming them. □ **lift a finger** see LIFT. □ **put one's finger on something** identify something exactly: *he cannot put his finger on what has gone wrong.* □ **twist** (or **wind** or **wrap**) **someone around one's little finger** see LITTLE FINGER. □ **work one's fingers to the bone** see BONE.

fin·ger·board /'fiNGgərˌbôrd/ ▶*n.* a flat or roughly flat strip on the neck of a stringed instrument, against which the strings are pressed to shorten the vibrating length and produce notes of higher pitches.

fin·ger bowl ▶*n.* a small bowl holding water for rinsing the fingers during or after a meal.

fin·ger-dry ▶v. [trans.] dry and style (hair) by repeatedly running one's fingers through it.

fin·ger food ▶*n.* food served in such a form and style that it can conveniently be eaten with the fingers.

fin·ger·ing /'fiNGgəriNG/ ▶*n.* a manner or technique of using the fingers, esp. to play a musical instrument: *he once studied keyboard fingering* | *the tuning makes some chord fingerings awkward.* ■ an indication of this in a musical score.

Fin·ger Lakes a region in central New York that is named for its series of narrow glacial lakes that lie parallel in a North-South orientation. Canandaigua, Keuka, Seneca, and Cayuga lakes are among the better known.

fin·ger-lick·ing ▶*adj.* tasty; delicious: *a finger-licking meal* | [as *submodifier*] *finger-licking good.*

fin·ger·ling /'fiNGgərliNG/ ▶*n.* **1** a small young fish, esp. a salmon parr. [from FINGER (with reference to its transverse dusky bars) + -LING] **2** a variety of potato having a pink, yellow, blue or light tan skin and flesh.

fin·ger·mark /'fiNGgərˌmärk/ ▶*n.* a mark left on a surface by a dirty or greasy finger.

fin·ger·nail /'fiNGgərˌnāl/ ▶*n.* the flattish horny part on the upper surface of the tip of each finger.

fin·ger of God (also **finger of fate**) ▶*n.* *Astrology* an aspect between three planets where one is quincunx to each of the other two, which are sextile to each other. ▷so named because of the resemblance of the aspect to a pointed finger.

fin·ger paint ▶*n.* thick paint designed to be applied with the fingers, used esp. by young children.

▶v. (**fin·ger-paint**) [intrans.] (esp. of children) apply paint with the fingers. **—fin·ger paint·ing** *n.*

fin·ger·pick /'fiNGgərˌpik/ ▶v. [trans.] play (a guitar or similar instrument) using the fingernails or small plectrums worn on the fingertips to pluck the strings: *black southern guitarists were fingerpicking guitars long before white musicians* | [intrans.] *he fingerpicked with facility.*

▶*n.* a plectrum worn on a fingertip. **—fin·ger·pick·er** *n.*

fin·ger-point·ing ▶*n.* *informal* actions or words that bring attention to a particular person or issue.

fin·ger·post /'fiNGgərˌpōst/ ▶*n.* a post at a road junction from which signs project in the direction of the place or route indicated.

fin·ger·print /'fiNGgərˌprint/ ▶*n.* an impression or mark made on a surface by a person's fingertip, esp. as used for identifying individuals from the unique pattern of whorls and lines: *the police had his fingerprints on file.* ■ *figurative* a distinctive identifying characteristic: *the faint chemical fingerprint of plastic explosives.*

▶v. [trans.] (usu. **be fingerprinted**) record the fingerprints of (someone): *I was booked, fingerprinted, and locked up for the night.*

fin·ger·spell·ing /'fiNGgərˌspeliNG/ ▶*n.* a form of sign language in which individual letters are formed by the fingers to spell out words.

fin·ger·tip /'fiNGgərˌtip/ ▶*n.* the tip of a finger.

▶*adj.* [*attrib.*] using or operated by the fingers: *fingertip electronic controls.* ■ reaching to the fingertips: *the silhouette is close to the waist and flared to fingertip length.*

▶*PHRASES* □ **at one's fingertips** (esp. of information) readily available; accessible: *until we have more facts at our fingertips, there is no use in speculating.* □ **by one's fingertips** only with difficulty; precariously: *the general was clinging to power by his fingertips.* □ **to one's fingertips** completely: *he is a professional to his fingertips.*

fin·ger wave ▶*n.* a wave set in wet hair using the fingers.

fin·i·al /'finēəl/ ▶*n.* a distinctive ornament at the apex of a roof, pinnacle, canopy, or similar structure in a building. ■ an ornament at the top, end, or corner of an object: *ornate curtain poles with decorative finials.* ▷late Middle English: from Old French *fin* or Latin *finis* 'end.'

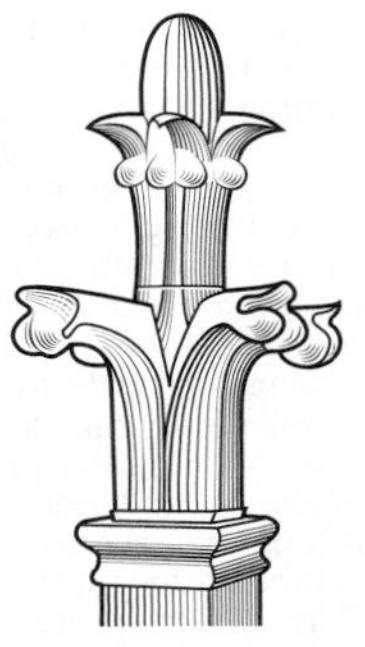

finial

fin·i·cal /'finikəl/ ▶*adj.* another term for FINICKY. ▷late 16th cent. (probably originally college slang): probably from FINE¹ + -ICAL, perhaps suggested by Middle Dutch *fijnkens* 'accurately, neatly, prettily.'

—**fin·i·cal·i·ty** /ˌfiniˈkalitē/ *n.* —**fin·i·cal·ly** /-(ə)lē/ *adv.* —**fin·i·cal·ness** *n.*

fin·ick·ing /ˈfinikiNG/ ▸*adj.* another term for FINICKY. ▷mid 17th cent.: from FINICAL + -ING[2].

fin·ick·y /ˈfinikē/ ▸*adj.* (of a person) fussy about one's needs or requirements: *a finicky eater.* ■ showing or requiring great attention to detail: *a finicky, almost fetishistic collector.* —**fin·ick·i·ness** /-kēnis/ *n.*

fin·ing /ˈfīniNG/ ▸*n.* (usu. **finings**) a substance used for clarifying liquid, esp. beer or wine. ■ the process of clarifying wine or beer: [as *adj.*] *a fining agent.*

fin·is /ˈfinis; fiˈnē/ ▸*n.* the end (printed at the end of a book or shown at the end of a film). ▷late Middle English: from Latin.

fin·ish /ˈfiniSH/ ▸*v.* [*trans.*] **1** bring (a task or activity) to an end; complete: *they were straining to finish the job* | [with *present participle*] *we finished eating our meal* | [*intrans.*] *the musician finished to thunderous applause.* ■ consume or get through the final amount or portion of (something, esp. food or drink): *finish your fajita while it's still hot* | *Jerry* ***finished off*** *a margarita.* ■ [*intrans.*] (of an activity) come to an end: *the war has finished but nothing has changed.* ■ [*intrans.*] (**finish with**) have no more need for or nothing more to do with: *"I've finished with Tom," Gloria said.* ■ reach the end of a race or other sporting competition, typically in a particular position: [with *complement*] *she finished third in the 3-meter springboard diving.* **2** (usu. **be finished**) complete the manufacture or decoration of (a material, object, or place) by giving it an attractive surface appearance: *the interior was finished with V-jointed American oak.* ■ complete the fattening of (livestock) before slaughter. ■ *dated* prepare (a girl) for entry into fashionable society.

▸*phrasal v.* □ **finish someone off** kill, destroy, or comprehensively defeat someone. □ **finish up** complete an action or process: *he hadn't finished up the paperwork on it.* ■ end a period of time or course of action by doing something or being in a particular position: *Tony started out running the back elevator and finished up as bell captain* | *we finished up with a plate of meats.*

▸*n.* **1** [usu. in *sing.*] an end or final part or stage of something: *a bowl of raspberries was the perfect finish to the meal* | *I really enjoyed the film* ***from start to finish.*** ■ a point or place at which a race or competition ends: *he surged into a winning lead 200 meters from the finish.* **2** the manner in which the manufacture of an article is completed in detail: *wide variation in specification and finish.* ■ the surface appearance of a manufactured material or object, or the material used to produce this: *lightweight nylon with a shiny finish.* ■ the final taste impression of a wine or beer: *the wine has a lemony tang on the finish.* ▷Middle English: from Old French *feniss-*, lengthened stem of *fenir*, from Latin *finire*, from *finis* 'end.'

▸PHRASE □ **a fight to the finish** a fight or contest that ends only with the complete defeat of one of the parties involved.

fin·ished /ˈfiniSHt/ ▸*adj.* (of an action, activity, or piece of work) having been completed or ended: *a preparatory drawing for the finished painting.* ■ [*predic.*] (of a person) having completed or ended an action or activity: *they'll be finished here in an hour.* ■ [*predic.*] having lost effectiveness, power, or prestige: *he was told he was finished at the club.* ■ (of an object or room) having been given a particular decorative surface as the final stage in its manufacture or decoration: [in *combination*] *plastic-finished lining paper.* ■ [*attrib.*] (of livestock) having completed fattening before slaughter: *a reduction in prices for finished cattle.*

fin·ish·er /ˈfiniSHər/ ▸*n.* **1** a person or thing that finishes something, in particular: ■ a person who reaches the end of a race or other sporting competition: *a third-place finisher.* ■ (in soccer) a player who scores a goal: *he is one of the best finishers at the club.* ■ a worker or machine performing the last operation in a manufacturing process. **2** an animal that has been fattened ready for slaughter: [as *adj.*] *finisher pigs.*

fin·ish·ing school ▸*n.* a private school where girls are prepared for entry into fashionable society.

fin·ish·ing touch ▸*n.* (usu. **finishing touches**) a final detail or action completing and enhancing a piece of work: *now they're putting the finishing touches to a new album.*

fin·ish line ▸*n.* a line marking the end of a race.

fi·nite /ˈfīnīt/ ▸*adj.* **1** having limits or bounds: *every computer has a finite amount of memory.* ■ not infinitely small: *one's chance of winning may be small, but it is finite.* **2** *Grammar* (of a verb form) having a specific tense, number, and person. Contrasted with NONFINITE. ▷late Middle English: from Latin *finitus* 'finished,' past participle of *finire* (see FINISH). —**fi·nite·ly** *adv.* —**fi·nite·ness** *n.*

fi·nit·ism /ˈfīnəˌtizəm/ ▸*n. Philosophy & Mathematics* rejection of the belief that anything can actually be infinite. —**fi·nit·ist** *n.*

fi·ni·to /fəˈnētō/ ▸*adj.* [*predic.*] *informal* finished: *it's all done—finito.* ▷Italian.

fin·i·tude /ˈfinəˌto͞od; ˈfī-/ ▸*n. formal* the state of having limits or bounds: *one quickly senses the finitude of his patience.*

Fink /fiNGk/, Mike (c.1770–1823), U.S. frontiersman. His exploits as a marksman, Indian scout, trapper, and keelboat man were legendary.

fink /fiNGk/ *informal* ▸*n.* an unpleasant or contemptible person, in particular: ■ a person who informs on people to the authorities: *he was assumed by some to be the management's fink.* ■ *dated* a strikebreaker.

▸*v.* [*intrans.*] **1** (**fink on**) inform on to the authorities: *there was no shortage of people willing to fink on their neighbors.* **2** (**fink out**) fail to do something promised or expected because of a lack of courage or commitment: *administration officials had finked out.* ■ cease to function: *your immune system begins finking out and you get sick.* ▷late 19th cent.: of unknown origin; perhaps from German, literally 'finch,' but also a pejorative term. Students started to refer to nonmembers of fraternities as *finks*, probably by association with the freedom of wild birds as opposed to caged ones. The term was later generalized to denote those not belonging to organizations such as trade unions.

fin keel ▸*n.* a boat's keel shaped like an inverted dorsal fin.

Fin·land /ˈfinlənd/ a country on the Baltic Sea, between Sweden and Russia; pop. 5,214,000; capital, Helsinki; official languages, Finnish and Swedish. Finnish name SUOMI.

The northern third of the country lies within the Arctic Circle. Long an area of Swedish–Russian rivalry, Finland was ceded to Russia in 1809 but became an independent republic after the Russian Revolution of 1917. Wars with the Soviet Union were fought in 1939–40. Finland joined the European Union in 1995.

Fin·land, Gulf of an arm of the Baltic Sea between Finland and Estonia that extends east to St. Petersburg in Russia.

Fin·land·i·za·tion /ˌfinləndiˈzāSHən/ ▸*n. historical* the process or result of being obliged for economic reasons to favor, or at least not oppose, the interests of the former Soviet Union despite not being politically allied to it. ▷1960s: translation of German *Finnlandisierung*, referring to the case of Finland after 1944. —**Fin·land·ize** /ˈfinlənˌdīz/ *v.*

Finn /fin/ ▸*n.* a native or national of Finland or a person of Finnish descent. ▷Old English *Finnas* (plural), originally applied more widely to denote a people of Scandinavia and northeastern Europe speaking a Finno-Ugric language.

fin·nan /ˈfinən/ (also **fin·nan had·die** /ˈhadē/) ▸*n.* haddock cured with the smoke of green wood, turf, or peat. ▷early 18th cent.: alteration of *Findon*, the name of a fishing village near Aberdeen in Scotland, but sometimes confused with the Scottish river and village of *Findhorn*.

finnes·ko /ˈfinəˌskō/ ▸*n.* (*pl.* same) a boot of tanned reindeer skin with the hair on the outside. ▷late 19th cent.: from Norwegian *finnsko*, from *Finn* (see FINN) + *sko* (see SHOE).

Finn·ic /ˈfinik/ ▸*adj.* **1** of, relating to, or denoting the group of Finno-Ugric languages that includes Finnish and Estonian. **2** of, relating to, or denoting the group of peoples that includes the Finns and the Estonians.

Finn·ish /ˈfiniSH/ ▸*adj.* of or relating to the Finns or their language.

▸*n.* the Finno-Ugric language of the Finns, spoken in Finland and in parts of Russia and Sweden.

Fin·no-U·gric /ˈfinō ˈ(y)o͞ogrik/ (also **Fin·no-U·gri·an** /ˈ(y)o͞ogrēən/) ▸*adj.* of or relating to the major group of Uralic languages, whose main branches are Finnic and Ugric.

▸*n.* this group of languages.

fin·ny /ˈfinē/ ▸*adj. poetic/literary* of, relating to, or resembling a fish: *it transfixes its finny prey.*

fi·no /ˈfēnō/ ▸*n.* (*pl.* **-os**) a light-colored dry sherry. ▷mid 19th cent.: Spanish, literally 'fine,' based on Latin *finire* 'to finish' (see FINISH).

fi·noc·chi·o /fəˈnōkēˌō/ ▸*n.* another term for FLORENCE FENNEL (see FENNEL). ▷early 18th cent.: from Italian, from a popular Latin variant of Latin *faeniculum* (see FENNEL).

fin ray ▸*n.* see RAY[1] (sense 2).

fin whale ▸*n.* another term for FINBACK.

fiord ▸*n.* variant spelling of FJORD.

fio·ri·tu·ra /fēˌôriˈto͝orə/ ▸*n.* (*pl.* **-tu·re** /-ˈto͞oˌrā/) *Music* an embellishment of a melody, esp. as improvised by an operatic singer. ▷Italian, literally 'flowering,' from *fiorire* 'to flower.'

fip·ple /ˈfipəl/ ▸*n.* the mouthpiece of a recorder or similar wind instrument that is blown endwise, in which a thin channel cut through a block directs a stream of air against a sharp edge. The term has been applied to various parts of this, including the block and the channel. ▷early 17th cent.

fip·ple flute ▸*n.* a flute, such as a recorder, played by blowing endwise.

fir /fər/ ▸*n.* (also **fir tree**) an evergreen coniferous tree with upright cones and flat needle-shaped leaves, typically arranged in two rows. Firs are an important source of timber and resins. • Genus *Abies*, family Pinaceae: many species. ▷late Middle English: probably from Old Norse *fyri-* (recorded in *fyriskógr* 'fir-woods'). —**fir·ry** *adj.*

fire /fīr/ ▸*n.* **1** combustion or burning, in which substances combine chemically with oxygen from the air and typically give out bright light, heat, and smoke: *his house was destroyed by fire.* ■ one of the four elements in ancient and medieval philosophy and in astrology. ■ a destructive burning of something: *a fire at a hotel.* ■ a collection of fuel, esp. wood or coal, burned in a controlled way to provide heat or a means for cooking: *our small kettle was kept constantly on the fire.* ■ a burning sensation in the body: *the whiskey lit a fire in the back of his throat.* ■ fervent or passionate emotion or enthusiasm: *the fire of their religious conviction.* ■ *poetic/literary* luminosity; glow: *their soft smiles light the air like a star's fire.* **2** the shooting of projectiles from weapons, esp. bullets from guns: *a burst of machine-gun fire.* ■ strong criticism or antagonism: *he directed his fire against policies promoting American capital flight.*

▸*v.* [*trans.*] **1** discharge a gun or other weapon in order to explosively propel (a bullet or projectile): *he fired a shot at the retreating prisoners* | *they* ***fired off*** *a few rounds.* ■ discharge (a gun or other weapon): *another gang fired a pistol* | [*intrans.*] *troops* ***fired on*** *crowds.* ■ [*intrans.*] (of a gun) be discharged. ■ direct (questions or statements, esp. unwelcome ones) toward someone in rapid succession: *they* ***fired*** *questions* ***at*** *me for what seemed like ages.* ■ (**fire something off**) send a message aggressively, esp. as one of a series: *he fired off a letter informing her that he regarded the matter with the utmost seriousness.* **2** *informal* dismiss (an employee) from a job: *having to fire men who've been with me for years* | *you're fired!* **3** supply (a furnace, engine, boiler, or power station) with fuel. ■ [*intrans.*] (of an internal combustion engine, or a cylinder in one) undergo ignition of its fuel when started: *the engine fired and she pushed her foot down on the accelerator.* ■ *archaic* set fire to: *I fired the straw.* **4** stimulate or excite (the imagination or an emotion): *India fired my imagination.* ■ fill (someone) with enthusiasm: *in the locker room they were really **fired up**.* ■ [*intrans.*] (**fire up**) *archaic* show sudden anger: *If I were to hear anyone disparage you, I would fire up in a flash.* **5** bake or dry (pottery, bricks, etc.) in a kiln. **6** start (an engine or other device): *with a flick of his wrist he **fired up** the chainsaw.* ▷Old English *fȳr* (noun), *fȳrian* 'supply with material for a fire'; related to Dutch *vuur* and German *Feuer*. —**fire·less** *adj.* —**fir·er** *n.*

▸*PHRASES* □ **breathe fire** be extremely angry: *I don't want an indignant boyfriend on my doorstep breathing fire.* □ **catch fire** begin to burn. ■ *figurative* become interesting or exciting: *the show never caught fire.* □ **fire and brimstone** the torments of hell: *his father was preaching fire and brimstone sermons.* □ **fire away** *informal* used to give someone permission to begin speaking, typically to ask questions: *"I want to clear up some questions that have been puzzling me." "Fire away."* □ **fire in the** (or **one's**) **belly** a powerful sense of ambition or determination. □ **firing on all** (**four**) **cylinders** working or functioning at a peak level. □ **go through fire** (**and water**) face any peril. □ **light a fire under someone** stimulate someone to work or act more quickly or enthusiastically. □ **on fire** in flames; burning. ■ in a state of excitement: *Wright is now **on fire** with confidence.* □ **open fire** see OPEN. □ **play with fire** see PLAY. □ **set fire to** (or **set something on fire**) cause to burn; ignite. □ **set the world** (or *Brit.* **the Thames**) **on fire** do something remarkable or sensational: *the film hasn't exactly set the world on fire.* □ *Brit.* **take fire** start to burn. □ **under fire** being shot at: *observers sent to look for the men came under heavy fire.* ■ being rigorously criticized: *the president was under fire from all sides.* □ **where's the fire?** *informal* used to ask someone why they are in such a hurry or state of excitement.

fire a·larm ▸*n.* a device making a loud noise that gives warning of a fire.

fire-and-for·get ▸*adj.* [*attrib.*] (of a missile) able to guide itself to its target once fired.

fire ant ▸*n.* a tropical American ant that has a painful and sometimes dangerous sting. • Genus *Solenopsis*, family Formicidae: several species, in particular the South American *S. invicta*, which has become a serious pest in the southeastern U.S.

fire·arm /ˈfī(ə)rˌärm/ ▸*n.* a rifle, pistol, or other portable gun.

fire·back /ˈfīrˌbak/ ▸*n.* the back wall of a fireplace. ■ a metal plate covering such a wall.

fire·ball /ˈfīrˌbôl/ ▸*n.* a ball of flame or fire: *a crashed tanker exploded in a fireball.* ■ an extremely hot, luminous ball of gas generated by a nuclear explosion. ■ a large bright meteor. ■ *historical* a ball filled with combustibles or explosives, fired at an enemy or enemy fortifications. ■ *figurative* a person with a fiery temper or a great deal of energy.

fire·ball·er /ˈfīrˌbôlər/ ▸*n. Baseball* a pitcher who throws a good fastball. —**fire·ball·ing** *adj.*

fire·base /ˈfīrˌbās/ ▸*n.* an area in a war zone in which artillery can be massed to provide heavy firepower in support of other military units.

fire-bel·lied toad ▸*n.* a warty European aquatic toad, the underside of which is vividly marked in red, orange, yellow, black, and white. • Genus *Bombina*, family Discoglossidae: in particular *B. bombina*.

fire·blight /ˈfīrˌblīt/ ▸*n.* a serious bacterial disease of plants of the rose family, esp. fruit trees, giving the leaves a scorched appearance. • The bacterium is *Erwinia amylovora*.

fire·bomb /ˈfīrˌbäm/ ▸*n.* a bomb designed to cause a fire.
▸*v.* [*trans.*] attack or destroy (something) with such a bomb: *he suspects that someone firebombed his business.*

fire·box /ˈfīrˌbäks/ ▸*n.* the chamber of a boiler in which the fuel is burned.

fire·brand /ˈfīrˌbrand/ ▸*n.* **1** a person who is passionate about a particular cause, typically inciting change and taking radical action: *a political firebrand.* **2** a piece of burning wood.

fire·brat /ˈfīrˌbrat/ ▸*n.* a fast-moving brownish insect, a type of bristletail, that frequents warm places indoors. • *Thermobia domestica*, family Lepismatidae, order Thysanura.

fire·break /ˈfīrˌbrāk/ ▸*n.* an obstacle to the spread of fire: *a fire-resistant door designed to be a firebreak | figurative a firebreak against the spread of revolution from Russia.* ■ a strip of open space in a forest or other area of dense vegetation.

fire·brick /ˈfīrˌbrik/ ▸*n.* a brick capable of withstanding intense heat, used esp. to line furnaces and fireplaces.

fire bri·gade ▸*n. chiefly Brit.* an organized body of people trained and employed to extinguish fires.

fire·bug /ˈfīrˌbəg/ ▸*n. informal* an arsonist.

fire·clay /ˈfīrˌklā/ ▸*n.* clay capable of withstanding high temperatures, chiefly used for making firebricks.

fire com·pa·ny ▸*n.* another term for FIRE DEPARTMENT.

fire con·trol ▸*n.* **1** the process of targeting and firing heavy weapons. **2** the prevention and monitoring of forest fires and grass fires. ■ the containment and extinguishing of fires in buildings, ships, etc.

fire cor·al ▸*n.* a colonial corallike hydrozoan, the heavy external skeleton of which forms reefs. The polyps bear nematocysts that can inflict painful stings. • Genus *Millepora*, order Hydroida (or Milleporina), class Hydrozoa.

fire·crack·er /ˈfīrˌkrakər/ ▸*n.* a loud, explosive firework, typically wrapped in paper and lit with a fuse.

fire·crest /ˈfīrˌkrest/ ▸*n.* a small warbler having a red and orange crest and occurring mainly in Europe. • *Regulus ignicapillus*, family Sylviidae.

fire·damp /ˈfīrˌdamp/ ▸*n.* methane, esp. as forming an explosive mixture with air in coal mines.

fire de·part·ment ▸*n.* the department of a local or municipal authority in charge of preventing and fighting fires.

fire·dog /ˈfīrˌdôg/ ▸*n.* another term for ANDIRON.

fire door ▸*n.* a fire-resistant door to prevent the spread of fire. ■ a door to the outside of a building used only as an emergency exit.

fire·drake /ˈfīrˌdrāk/ ▸*n. Germanic Mythology* a fiery dragon. ▷Old English *fȳr-draca*, from *fȳr* (see FIRE) + *draca* 'dragon,' from Latin *draco*.

fire drill ▸*n.* **1** a practice of the emergency procedures to be used in case of fire. **2** a primitive device for kindling fire by frictional heating, consisting of a pointed stick that is twirled in a hole in a flat piece of soft wood.

fire-eat·er ▸*n.* **1** an entertainer who appears to eat fire. **2** *dated* a person prone to quarreling or fighting.

fire en·gine ▸*n.* a vehicle carrying firefighters and equipment for fighting large fires.

fire es·cape ▸*n.* a staircase or other apparatus used for escaping from a building on fire.

fire ex·tin·guish·er ▸*n.* a portable device that discharges a jet of water, foam, gas, or other material to extinguish a fire.

fire·fight /ˈfīrˌfīt/ ▸*n. Military* a battle using guns rather than bombs or other weapons.

fire·fight·er /ˈfīrˌfītər/ ▸*n.* a person whose job is to extinguish fires. —**fire·fight·ing** *n.*

fire·fly /ˈfīrˌflī/ ▸*n.* (*pl.* **-flies**) a soft-bodied beetle related to the glowworm, the winged male and flightless female of which both have luminescent organs. The light is chiefly produced as a signal between the sexes, esp. in flashes. • Family Lampyridae: many species.

firefly

fire·guard /ˈfī(ə)rˌgärd/ ▸*n.* **1** a protective screen or grid placed in front of an open fire. **2** a firebreak in a forest.

fire·hall /ˈfīrˌhôl/ ▸*n.* a fire station.

fire hose ▸*n.* a large-diameter hose used in extinguishing fires.

fire·house /ˈfīrˌhous/ ▸*n.* a fire station.

fire i·rons ▸*plural n.* implements for tending a domestic fire, typically tongs, a poker, and a shovel.

Fire Is·land a barrier island on the southern shore of Long Island in New York, the site of numerous small resort communities.

fire·less cook·er /ˈfīrləs/ ▸*n.* an insulated container capable of maintaining a temperature at which food can be cooked.

fire·light /ˈfīrˌlīt/ ▸*n.* light from a fire in a fireplace. ▷Old English *fȳr-lēoht* (see FIRE, LIGHT[1]).

fire line ▸*n.* a firebreak in a forest.

fire·lock /ˈfīrˌläk/ ▸*n. historical* a firearm in which the priming is ignited by sparks.

fire·man /ˈfīrmən/ ▸*n.* (*pl.* **-men** /-mən/) **1** a firefighter. **2** a person who tends a furnace or the fire of a steam engine or steamship; a stoker. ■ an enlisted person in the U.S. navy who maintains and operates a ship's machinery.

Fi·ren·ze /fēˈrentsā/ Italian name of **FLORENCE**.

fire o·pal ▸*n.* another term for GIRASOL (sense 1).

fire·place /ˈfīrˌplās/ ▸*n.* a place for a domestic fire, esp. a grate or hearth at the base of a chimney. ■ a structure surrounding such a place.

fire·plug /ˈfīrˌpləg/ ▸*n.* a hydrant for a fire hose. ■ *informal* a short, stocky person, esp. an athlete.

fire·pow·er /ˈfīrˌpou(-ə)r/ ▸*n.* the destructive capacity of guns, missiles, or a military force (used with reference to the number and size of weapons available): *the enormous disparity in firepower between the two sides | figurative the well-funded legal firepower of the tobacco companies.*

fire·proof /ˈfīrˌpro͞of/ ▸*adj.* able to withstand fire or great heat: *a fireproof dish.*
▸*v.* [*trans.*] make (something) fireproof: *nearby museum buildings will be fireproofed.*

fire-rais·er ▸*n. Brit.* an arsonist. —**fire-raising** *n.*

fire sal·a·man·der ▸*n.* a robust short-tailed nocturnal salamander that has black skin with bright red, orange, and yellow markings, native to upland forests of Europe, northwestern Africa, and southwestern Asia. • *Salamandra salamandra*, family Salamandridae.

fire sale ▸*n.* a sale of goods remaining after the destruction of commercial premises by fire. ■ a sale of goods or assets at a very low price, typically when the seller is facing bankruptcy.

fire screen ▸*n.* a screen or grid placed in front of an open fire to deflect the direct heat or to protect against sparks. ■ an ornamental screen placed in front of a fireplace when the fire is unlit.

fire serv·ice ▸*n. Brit.* an organization in charge of preventing and fighting fires.

fire·ship /ˈfīrˌSHip/ ▸*n. historical* a ship loaded with burning material and explosives and set adrift to ignite and blow up an enemy's ships.

fire·side /ˈfīrˌsīd/ ▸*n.* the area around a fireplace (used esp. with reference to a person's home or family life): *he preferred the warmth of his own fireside.* ■ one of a series of radio broadcasts made by President Franklin Delano Roosevelt to the nation, beginning in 1933.

fire·side chat ▸*n.* an informal conversation. ■ one of a series of radio broadcasts made by President Franklin Delano Roosevelt to the nation, beginning in 1933.

fire start·er ▸*n.* a piece of flammable material used to help start a fire.

fire sta·tion ▸*n.* a facility where fire engines and other equipment of a fire department are housed.

fire-step ▸*n.* a step or ledge on which soldiers in a trench stand to fire.

Fire·stone /ˈfīrˌstōn/, Harvey Samuel (1868–1938), U.S. industrialist. He organized the Firestone Tire & Rubber Company in 1900 and was its president 1903–32 and chairman 1932–38.

fire·stone /ˈfīrˌstōn/ ▸*n.* stone that can withstand fire and great heat, used esp. for lining furnaces and ovens.

fire·storm /ˈfīrˌstôrm/ ▸*n.* an intense and destructive fire (typically one caused by bombing) in which strong currents of air are drawn into the blaze, making it burn more fiercely: *within the firestorm every building was burned to a shell | figurative the incident ignited a firestorm of controversy.*

fire·thorn /ˈfīrˌTHôrn/ ▸*n.* another term for PYRACANTHA.

fire tow·er ▸*n.* a tower, often at a high elevation, that especially in former years was staffed by a lookout for the detection of fires occurring over a wide area.

fire trail ▸*n.* a track through forest or bush for use in fighting fires.

fire·trap /ˈfīrˌtrap/ ▸*n.* a building without proper provision for escape in case of fire.

fire truck ▸*n.* another term for FIRE ENGINE.

fire-walk·ing ▸*n.* the practice of walking barefoot over something such as hot stones or wood ashes, often as a part of a traditional ceremony. **—fire-walk·er** *n.*

fire·wall /ˈfīrˌwôl/ ▸*n.* a wall or partition designed to inhibit or prevent the spread of fire. ■ any barrier that is intended to thwart the spread of a destructive agent: *a firewall that will prevent further cases of mad cow disease.* ■ *Computing* a part of a computer system or network that is designed to block unauthorized access while permitting outward communication. ■ another term for CHINESE WALL.

fire ward·en ▸*n.* a person employed to prevent or extinguish fires, esp. in a town, camp, or forest.

fire·wa·ter /ˈfīrˌwôtər; -ˌwätər/ ▸*n. informal* strong liquor.

fire·weed /ˈfīrˌwēd/ ▸*n.* **1** a plant that springs up on burned land, esp. the pink-flowered *Epilobium angustifolium*, a widespread willow herb. **2** another term for PILEWORT (sense 1).

FireWire /ˈfī(ə)rˌwī(ə)r/ ▸*n. trademark Computing* a technology that allows high-speed communication and data exchange between a computer and a peripheral or between two computers: *transfer of digital content to DVD over FireWire* | [as *adj.*] *a FireWire port.* Also see **IEEE 1394**.

fire·wood /ˈfīrˌwo͝od/ ▸*n.* wood burned as fuel.

fire·work /ˈfīrˌwərk/ ▸*n.* a device containing gunpowder and other combustible chemicals that causes a spectacular explosion when ignited, used typically for display or in celebrations. ■ **(fireworks)** a display of fireworks: *they were oohing and aahing as if they were watching the fireworks.* ■ **(fireworks)** *figurative* an outburst of anger or other emotion, or a display of brilliance or energy: *when you put these men together, you're bound to get fireworks.*

fir·ing /ˈfīriNG/ ▸*n.* the action of setting fire to something: *the deliberate firing of 600 oil wells.* ■ the discharging of a gun or other weapon: *the prolonged firing caused heavy losses* | *no missile firings were planned.* ■ the dismissal of an employee from a job: *the recent firing of the head of the department.* ■ the baking or drying of pottery or bricks in a kiln.

fir·ing line ▸*n.* the line of positions from which gunfire is directed at targets. ■ the front line of troops in a battle. ■ a position where one is subject to criticism or blame because of one's responsibilities or position: *the referee* **in the firing line** *is an experienced official.*

fir·ing pin ▸*n.* a movable pin in a firearm that strikes the primer of a cartridge to set off the charge.

fir·ing squad ▸*n.* a group of soldiers detailed to shoot a condemned person. ■ a group of soldiers detailed to fire the salute at a military funeral.

fir·kin /ˈfərkən/ ▸*n. chiefly historical* a small cask used chiefly for liquids, butter, or fish. ■ a unit of liquid volume equal to half a kilderkin (about 11 gallons or 41 liters). ▷Middle English *ferdekyn*, probably from the Middle Dutch diminutive of *vierde* 'fourth' (a firkin originally contained a quarter of a barrel).

firm[1] /fərm/ ▸*adj.* **1** having a solid, almost unyielding surface or structure: *the bed should be reasonably firm, but not too hard.* ■ solidly in place and stable: *no building can stand without firm foundations* | *figurative he was unable to establish the store on a firm financial footing.* ■ having steady but not excessive power or strength: *you need a firm grip on the steering.* ■ (of a person, action, or attitude) showing resolute determination and strength of character: *he didn't like being* **firm with** *Larry, but he had to.* **2** strongly felt and unlikely to change: *he retains a firm belief in the efficacy of prayer.* ■ (of a person) steadfast and constant: *we became firm friends.* ■ decided upon and fixed or definite: *she had no firm plans for the next day.* ■ (of a currency, a commodity, or shares) having a steady value or price that is more likely to rise than fall: *the dollar was* **firm against** *the yen.*
▸*v.* [*trans.*] make (something) physically solid or resilient: *an exercise program designed to* **firm up** *muscle tone.* ■ fix (a plant) securely in the soil. ■ [*intrans.*] (of a price) rise slightly to reach a level considered secure: *he believed house prices would firm by the end of the year.* ■ make (an agreement or plan) explicit and definite: *archaeologists have now* **firmed up** *this new view.*
▸*adv.* in a resolute and determined manner: *she will* **stand firm** *against the government's proposal.* ▷Middle English: from Old French *ferme*, from Latin *firmus*. **—firm·ly** *adv.* **—firm·ness** *n.*
▸*PHRASES* □ **be on firm ground** be sure of one's facts or secure in one's position, esp. in a discussion. □ **a firm hand** strict discipline or control.

firm[2] ▸*n.* a business concern, esp. one involving a partnership of two or more people: *a law firm.* ▷late 16th cent.: from Italian *firma*, from medieval Latin, from Latin *firmare* 'fix, settle' (in late Latin 'confirm by signature'), from *firmus* 'firm'; compare with FARM. The word originally denoted one's autograph or signature; later (mid 18th cent.) the name under which the business of a firm was transacted, hence the firm itself (late 18th cent.).

fir·ma·ment /ˈfərməmənt/ ▸*n. poetic/literary* the heavens or the sky, esp. when regarded as a tangible thing. ■ *figurative* a sphere or world viewed as a collection of people: *one of the great* **stars in the** *American golfing* **firmament**. ▷Middle English: via Old French from Latin *firmamentum*, from *firmare* 'fix, settle.' **—fir·ma·men·tal** /ˌfərməˈmentl/ *adj.*

fir·man /ˈfərmən; fərˈmän/ ▸*n.* (*pl.* **-mans**) **1** a Near Eastern sovereign's edict. **2** a grant or permit. ▷early 17th cent.: from Persian *firmān*, Sanskrit *pramāṇa* 'right measure, standard, authority.'

firm·ware /ˈfərmˌwer/ ▸*n. Computing* permanent software programmed into a read-only memory.

firn /fi(ə)rn/ ▸*n.* granular snow, esp. on the upper part of a glacier, where it has not yet been compressed into ice. ▷mid 19th cent.: from German, from Old High German *firni* 'old'; related to Swedish *forn* 'former.'

first /fərst/ ▸*ordinal number* **1** coming before all others in time or order; earliest; 1st: *his first wife* | *the first of five daughters* ■ never previously done or occurring: *her first day at school.* ■ coming next after a specified or implied time or occurrence: *I didn't take the first bus.* ■ met with or encountered before any others: *the first house I came to.* ■ originally: *many valuable drugs have been recognized first as poisons.* ■ before doing something else specified or implied: *do you mind if I take a shower first?* ■ for the first time: *she first picked up a guitar out of sheer boredom.* ■ firstly; in the first place (used to introduce a first point or reason): *first, it is wrong that the victims should have no remedy.* ■ in preference; rather (used when strongly rejecting a suggestion or possibility): *she longed to go abroad, but not at this man's expense—she'd die first!* ■ with a specified part or person in a leading position: *it plunged nose first into the river.* ■ *informal* the first occurrence of something notable: *we traveled by air, a first for both of us.* ■ the first in a sequence of a vehicle's gears: *he stuck the car in first and revved.* ■ *Baseball* first base: *he made it all the way home from first.* ■ the first grade of a school. ■ a first edition of a book. **2** foremost in position, rank, or importance: *the doctor's first duty is to respect this right* | *career women who* **put** *work* **first** | *football must* **come first**. ■ [often with *infinitive*] the most likely, pressing, or suitable: *he is the first to admit he was not the best of patients* | *his first problem is where to live.* ■ the first finisher or position in a race or competition. ■ *Music* performing the highest or chief of two or more parts for the same instrument or voice: *the first violins.* ■ **(firsts)** goods of the best quality: *factory firsts, seconds, and discontinued styles.* ■ *Brit.* a place in the top grade in an examination, esp. that for a degree: *he took a first in Classics.* ■ *Brit.* a person having achieved such a degree. ▷Old English *fyr(e)st*; of Germanic origin, related to Old Norse *fyrstr* and German *Fürst* 'prince,' from an Indo-European root shared by Sanskrit *prathama*, Latin *primus*, and Greek *prōtos*.
▸*PHRASES* □ **at first** at the beginning; in the initial stage or stages: *at first Hugh tried to be patient.* □ **at first glance** see GLANCE[1]. □ **at first hand** see FIRSTHAND. □ **at first instance** see INSTANCE. □ **at first sight** see SIGHT. □ **(the) first among equals** see EQUAL. □ **first blood** see BLOOD. □ **first come, first served** used to indicate that people will be dealt with in the order in which they arrive or apply: *tickets are available on a first come, first served basis.* □ **first and foremost** most importantly; more than anything else: *I'm first and foremost a writer.* □ **first and last** fundamentally; on the whole: *museums are first and last about curatorship.* □ **first of all** before doing anything else; at the beginning: *first of all, let me ask you something.* ■ most importantly: *German unity depends first of all on the German people.* □ **first off** *informal* as a first point; first of all: *first off, I owe you a heck of an apology.* □ **first past the post** (of a contestant, esp. a horse, in a race) winning a race by being the first to reach the finish line. ■ [*attrib.*] *Brit.* denoting an electoral system in which a candidate or party is selected by achievement of a simple majority: *our first-past-the-post electoral system.* □ **first thing** early in the morning; before anything else: *I have to meet Josh first thing tomorrow.* □ **first things first** used to assert that important matters should be dealt with before other things. □ **from the (very) first** from the beginning or the early stages: *he should have realized it from the first.* □ **from first to last** from beginning to end; throughout: *it's a fine performance that commands attention from first to last.* □ **get to first base** see BASE[1]. □ **in the first place** as the first consideration or point: *political reality was not quite that simple—in the first place, divisions existed within the parties.* ■ at the beginning; to begin with (esp. in reference to the time when an action was being planned or discussed): *I should have told you in the first place.* □ **of the first order** (or **magnitude**) used to denote something that is excellent or considerable of its kind: *it is a media event of the first order.* □ **of the first water** see WATER.

USAGE **First, second, third,** etc., are adverbs as well as adjectives: *first, dice three potatoes; second, add the bouillon.* **Firstly, secondly,** etc., are also correct, but make sure not to mix the two groups: *first, second, third;* not *first, secondly, thirdly.*
See also **usage** at FORMER[1].

First A·dar /äˈdär/ see ADAR.

first aid ▸*n.* help given to a sick or injured person until full medical treatment is available: *an expert in emergency first aid* | [as *adj.*] *a first-aid kit.* **—first aid·er** /ˈādər/ *n.*

first·born /ˈfərstˌbôrn/ ▸*adj.* (of a person's child) the first to be born; the eldest: *his new album and his firstborn child are due in the same week.*
▸*n.* a person's first child: *their firstborn arrived.*

First Cause ▸*n. Philosophy* a supposed ultimate cause of all events, which does not itself have a cause, identified with God.

first class ▸*n.* a set of people or things grouped together as the best. ■ the best accommodations in a plane, train, or ship: *a seat in first class.* ■ *Brit.* the highest division in the results of the examinations for a university degree. ■ the highest division in such an examination: *in the college examination he was placed in the first class.*
▸*adj.* & *adv.* of the best quality: [as *adj.*] *a full-scale grand opera needs a first-class orchestra.* ■ of or relating to the best accommodations in a train, ship, or plane: [as *adj.*] *first-class air transportation* | [as *adv.*] *you can travel first class on any train.* ■ of or relating to a class of mail given priority: [as *adj.*] *first-class mail* | [as *adv.*] *send it first class.* ■ [as *adj.*] *Brit.* of or relating to the highest division in a university examination: *a first-class honors degree.*

First Con·sul the title held by Napoleon Bonaparte from 1799 to 1804, when he became Emperor of France.

first cost ▸*n.* another term for PRIME COST.

first cous·in ▸*n.* see COUSIN.

first-day cov·er (also **first day cover**) ▸*n.* an envelope bearing a stamp or stamps postmarked on their day of issue.

first-de·gree ▸*adj.* [*attrib.*] **1** *Medicine* denoting burns that affect only the surface of the skin and cause reddening. **2** *Law* denoting the most serious category of a crime, esp. murder.
▸*PHRASE* □ **first-degree relative** a person's parent, sibling, or child.

first down ▸*n. Football* a gain of ten yards or more in field position during a series of downs, permitting the offensive team to attempt another series of downs.

First Em·pire the period of the reign of Napoleon I as emperor of the French (1804–15).

first fam·i·ly ▸*n.* a family considered to rank first in social prestige or pedigree in a particular place. ■ the family of the president of the U.S. or of the governor of a U.S. state, or of the chief executive of another political unit.

first fin·ger ▸*n.* the finger next to the thumb; the forefinger; the index finger.

first floor ▸*n.* the ground floor of a building. ■ *chiefly Brit.* the floor of a building just above the ground floor.

first-foot ▸*v.* [*trans.*] be the first person to cross the threshold of the house of (someone) in the New Year, in accordance with a Scottish custom.
▸*n.* the first person to cross a threshold in the New Year. **—first-foot·er** /ˈfo͝otər/ *n.*

first fruits ▸*plural n.* the first agricultural produce of a season, esp. when given as an offering to God. ■ the initial results of an enterprise or endeavor: *the* *first fruits of the companies' collaboration.* ▪ *historical* a payment to a superior by the new holder of an office.

first-gen·er·a·tion ▸*adj.* **1** designating the first of a generation to become a citizen in a new country. ▪ designating the first of a generation to be born in a country of parents who had immigrated: *a first-generation Canadian whose parents were born on a farm in Vietnam.* **2** designating the first version of a type made available: *first-generation descrambler technology.*

first·hand /ˈfərstˈhand/ ▸*adj. & adv.* (of information or experience) from the original source or personal experience; direct: [as *adj.*] *neither of them had any first-hand knowledge of Andean culture* | [as *adv.*] *this is something you have to hear firsthand.*

▸*PHRASE* □ **at first hand** directly or from personal experience: *scientists observed the process at first hand.*

first in·ten·tion ▸*n. Medicine* the healing of a wound by natural contact of the parts involved: *healing **by first intention**.* Compare with SECOND INTENTION.

First In·ter·na·tion·al see INTERNATIONAL (sense 2).

first la·dy ▸*n.* (**First La·dy**) the wife of the president of the U.S. or other head of state. ▪ the leading woman in a particular activity or profession: *the first lady of rock.*

first lan·guage ▸*n.* a person's native language.

first lieu·ten·ant ▸*n.* a commissioned officer in the U.S. Army, Air Force, or Marine Corps ranking above second lieutenant and below captain.

first light ▸*n.* the time when light first appears in the morning; dawn: *you are to set off at first light.*

first-line ▸*adj.* of first resort: *first-line drugs for HIV exposure.*

first·ling /ˈfərstliNG/ ▸*n.* (usu. **firstlings**) *archaic* the first agricultural produce or animal offspring of a season.

first·ly /ˈfərstlē/ ▸*adv.* used to introduce a first point or reason: *firstly it is wrong and secondly it is extremely difficult to implement.*

USAGE See usage at FIRST.

first mate ▸*n.* the deck officer second in command to the master of a merchant ship.

first name ▸*n.* a personal name given to someone at birth or baptism and used before a family name.

▸*PHRASE* □ **on a first-name basis** having a friendly and informal relationship: *an amateur ecologist who is on a first-name basis with most reptiles.*

First Na·tion ▸*n.* (in Canada) an indigenous American Indian community officially recognized as an administrative unit by the federal government or functioning as such without official status.

first night ▸*n.* the first public performance of a play or show: [as *adj.*] *first-night nerves.*

first-night·er ▸*n.* a person who attends a first night.

first of·fend·er ▸*n.* a person who is convicted of a criminal offense for the first time.

first of·fi·cer ▸*n.* the first mate on a merchant ship. ▪ the second in command to the captain on an aircraft.

first-or·der ▸*adj.* of or relating to the simplest or most fundamental level of organization, experience, or analysis; primary or immediate: *for a teacher, of course, drama must be a first-order experience.* ▪ *technical* having an order of one, esp. denoting mathematical equations involving only the first power of the independent variable or only the first derivative of a function.

first per·son ▸*n.* see PERSON (sense 2).

first po·si·tion ▸*n.* **1** *Ballet* a posture in which the feet are turned outward with the heels touching. ▪ a position of the arms in which both are held curved in front of the body at waist level, with the palms facing the body. **2** *Music* the lowest position of the hand on the fingerboard of a stringed instrument.

First Pres·i·den·cy ▸*n.* see PRESIDENCY.

first prin·ci·ples ▸*plural n.* the fundamental concepts or assumptions on which a theory, system, or method is based: *I think we have to start again and go right back to first principles.*

first-rate ▸*adj.* of the best class or quality; excellent: *first-rate musicians.* ▪ in good health or condition; very well: *I think you look first-rate.*

first read·ing ▸*n.* **1** the first time that a text is read: *a sentence guaranteed to be parsed incorrectly on first reading.* **2** (in the UK) the first presentation of a bill to Parliament, to permit its introduction.

first re·fus·al ▸*n.* the privilege of deciding whether to accept or reject something before it is offered to others: *tenants have a **right of first refusal** if the landlord proposes to sell the property.*

First Reich see REICH[1].

First Re·pub·lic the republican regime in France from the abolition of the monarchy in 1792 until Napoleon's accession as emperor in 1804.

first re·spond·er ▸*n.* someone designated or trained to respond to an emergency: *the department is expanding its smallpox vaccination program to first responders.*

first ser·geant ▸*n.* (in the U.S. Army or Marine Corps) the highest-ranking noncommissioned officer in a company or equivalent unit.

First State a nickname for the state of DELAWARE[1].

first strike ▸*n.* an attack with nuclear weapons designed to destroy the enemy's nuclear weapons before their use.

first string ▸*n. Sports* the best players on a team, the ones that normally play the most. ▪ *figurative* the best or most talented individuals in any endeavor.

First World ▸*n.* the industrialized capitalist countries of western Europe, North America, Japan, Australia, and New Zealand. Compare with SECOND WORLD and THIRD WORLD.

First World War another term for WORLD WAR I.

Firth /fərTH/, J. R. (1890–1960), English linguist; full name *John Rupert Firth.* Firth was noted for his contributions to linguistic semantics and prosodic phonology.

firth /fərTH/ ▸*n.* a narrow inlet of the sea; an estuary. ▷Middle English (originally Scots), from Old Norse *fjǫrthr* (see FJORD).

fir tree ▸*n.* see FIR.

fisc /fisk/ ▸*n. Roman History* the public treasury of Rome or the emperor's privy purse. ▪ a public treasury or exchequer. ▷late 16th cent.: from French, or from Latin *fiscus* 'rush basket, purse, treasury.'

fis·cal /ˈfiskəl/ ▸*adj.* of or relating to government revenue, esp. taxes: *monetary and fiscal policy.* ▪ of or relating to financial matters: *the domestic fiscal crisis.* See note at FINANCIAL. ▪ used to denote a fiscal year: *the budget deficit for fiscal 1996.*

▸*n. archaic* a legal or treasury official in some countries. ▷mid 16th cent.: from French, or from Latin *fiscalis*, from *fiscus* 'purse, treasury' (see FISC). **—fis·cal·ly** *adv.*

fis·cal year ▸*n.* a year as reckoned for taxing or accounting purposes: *the firm is expected to turn a profit for its fiscal year ending April 30.*

Fisch·er[1] /ˈfisHər/, Bobby (1943–), U.S. chess player; full name *Robert James Fischer.* He defeated Boris Spassky in 1972 to become the world champion, a title he held until 1975.

Fisch·er[2], Emil Hermann (1852–1919), German organic chemist. He studied the structure of sugars, other carbohydrates, and purines and synthesized many of them. He also confirmed that peptides and proteins consist of chains of amino acids. Nobel Prize for Chemistry (1902).

Fisch·er[3], Hans (1881–1945), German organic chemist. He determined the structure of the porphyrin group of many natural pigments. Nobel Prize for Chemistry (1930).

Fish /fisH/, Hamilton (1808–93), U.S. politician. A Republican, he held many political offices, including governor of New York 1849–50, U.S. senator 1851–57, and U.S. secretary of state 1869–77.

fish[1] /fisH/ ▸*n.* (*pl.* same or **fish·es**) a limbless cold-blooded vertebrate animal with gills and fins and living wholly in water: *the sea is thick with fish.* ▪ the flesh of such animals as food: *hot crab appetizers stuffed with fish.* ▪ (**the Fish** or **Fishes**) the zodiacal sign or constellation Pisces. ▪ used in names of invertebrate animals living wholly in water, e.g., **cuttlefish, shellfish, jellyfish.** ▪ [with *adj.*] *informal* a person who is strange in a specified way: *he is generally thought to be a bit of a **cold fish**.* ▪ *informal* a torpedo.

▸*v.* [*intrans.*] catch or try to catch fish, typically by using a net or hook and line: *he was **fishing for** bluefish* | *I've told the girls we've **gone fishing**.* ▪ [*trans.*] catch or try to catch fish in (a particular body of water): *they did fish the mountain streams when game grew scarce.* ▪ search, typically by groping or feeling for something concealed: *he fished for his registration certificate and held it up to the policeman's flashlight.* ▪ try subtly or deviously to elicit a response or some information from someone: *I was not **fishing for compliments**.* ▪ [*trans.*] (**fish something out**) pull or take something out of water or a container: *the body of a woman had been fished out of the river.* ▷Old English *fisc* (as a noun denoting any animal living exclusively in water), *fiscian* (verb), of Germanic origin; related to Dutch *vis*, *vissen* and German *Fisch*, *fischen*. **—fish·like** *adj.*

▸*PHRASES* □ **a big fish** an important or influential person: *he became a big fish in the world of politics.* □ **a big fish in a small** (or **little**) **pond** a person seen as important and influential only within the limited scope of a small organization or group. □ **drink like a fish** drink excessive amounts of alcohol. □ **fish or cut bait** see BAIT. □ **a fish out of water** a person in a completely unsuitable environment or situation. □ **fished out** depleted of fish: *the grayling here have hardly been fished out.* □ **have other** (or **bigger**) **fish to fry** have other (or more important) matters to attend to. □ **like shooting fish in a barrel** extremely easy: *picking cultivated berries is like shooting fish in a barrel.* □ **neither fish nor fowl** (**nor good red herring**) of indefinite character and difficult to identify or classify. □ **there are plenty more fish in the sea** used to console someone whose romantic relationship has ended by pointing out that there are many other people with whom they may have a successful relationship in the future.

USAGE The normal plural of **fish** is **fish** (*a shoal of fish; he caught two huge fish*). The older form **fishes** is still used, but almost exclusively when referring to different kinds of fish (*freshwater **fishes** of the Great Lakes*).

fish[2] /fisH/ ▸*n.* a flat plate of metal, wood, or another material that is fixed on a beam or across a joint in order to give additional strength, esp. on a ship's damaged mast or spar as a temporary repair.

▸*v.* [*trans.*] mend or strengthen (a beam, joint, mast, etc.) with a fish. ▪ join (rails in a railroad track) with a fishplate. ▷early 16th cent.: probably from French *fiche*, from *ficher* 'to fix,' based on Latin *figere*.

fish and chips ▸*n.* a dish of fried fish fillets served with French fries.

fish·bowl /ˈfisH,bōl/ ▸*n.* a round glass bowl for keeping pet fish in. ▪ *figurative* a place open to public view and criticism: *there was no privacy in his office; it was a fishbowl.*

fish cake ▸*n.* a patty of shredded fish and mashed potato, typically coated in batter or breadcrumbs and fried.

fish ea·gle ▸*n.* an eagle that catches and feeds on fish. • Genus *Haliaeetus*, family Accipitridae: two or three species, in particular the white-headed **African fish eagle** (*H. vocifer*).

Fish·er /ˈfisHər/, **St. John** (1469–1535), English cleric. In 1504, he became bishop of Rochester and earned the disfavor of Henry VIII by opposing his divorce from Catherine of Aragon. When he refused to accept the king as supreme head of the English church, he was condemned to death. Feast day, June 22.

fish·er /ˈfisHər/ ▸*n.* **1** a fisherman. **2** a large brown marten valued for its fur, found in North American woodland where it frequently preys on porcupines. Also called PEKAN. • *Martes pennanti*, family Mustelidae. ▷Old English *fiscere* 'fisherman,' of Germanic origin; related to Dutch *visser* and German *Fischer*, also to FISH[1].

fish·er·folk /ˈfisHər,fōk/ ▸*plural n.* people who catch fish for a living.

fish·er·man /ˈfisHərmən/ ▸*n.* (*pl.* **-men**) a person who catches fish for a living or for sport. ▪ a fishing boat.

fish·er·man knit (also **fish·er·man's knit**) ▸*n.* a type of thick ribbed knitting.

fish·er·man's bend ▸*n.* a knot tied by making a full turn around something (typically the ring of an anchor), a half hitch through the turn, and a half hitch around the standing part of the rope.

fish·er·wom·an /ˈfisHər,wo͝omən/ ▸*n.* (*pl.* **-wom·en**) a woman who catches fish, esp. for a living.

fish·er·y /ˈfisHərē/ ▸*n.* (*pl.* **-er·ies**) a place where fish are reared for commercial purposes. ▪ a fishing ground or area where fish are caught. ▪ the occupation or industry of catching or rearing fish.

fish·eye /ˈfisH,ī/ ▸*n.* **1** (also **fisheye lens**) a wide-angle lens with a field of vision covering up to 180°, the scale being reduced toward the edges. **2** *informal* a suspicious or unfriendly look: *Wally gave him the fisheye.*

fish farm ▸*n.* a place where fish are artificially bred or cultivated, e.g., for food, to restock lakes for angling, or to supply aquariums. **—fish farm·er** *n.* **—fish farm·ing** *n.*

fish fin·ger ▸*n.* British term for FISH STICK.

fish hawk ▸*n.* another term for OSPREY.

fish·hook /ˈfisH,ho͝ok/ ▸*n.* see HOOK (sense 1).

fish·ing /ˈfiSHiNG/ ▸*n.* the activity of catching fish, either for food or as a sport.
▸*PHRASE* □ **fishing expedition** a search or investigation undertaken with the hope, though not the stated purpose, of discovering information: *they worried about an FBI fishing expedition.*

fish·ing cat ▸*n.* a small wild cat found in wetland habitats in India and Southeast Asia, having a light brown coat with dark spots, a ringed tail, and slightly webbed paws. • *Felis viverrina*, family Felidae.

fish·ing fly ▸*n.* a natural or artificial flying insect used as bait in fishing.

fish·ing line ▸*n.* a long thread of silk or nylon attached to a baited hook, sometimes with a sinker or float, and used for catching fish.

fish·ing pole ▸*n.* a fishing rod, esp. a simple one with no reel.

fish·ing reel ▸*n.* a device for winding and unwinding fishing line, designed to be attached to a fishing rod.

fish·ing rod ▸*n.* a long, tapering rod to which a fishing line is attached, typically on a reel.

fish knife ▸*n.* a blunt knife with a broad blade for dressing, serving or eating fish.

fish lad·der ▸*n.* a series of pools built like steps to enable fish to bypass a dam or waterfall.

fish louse ▸*n.* an aquatic crustacean that is a parasite of fish, typically attached to the skin or gills: • a free-swimming crustacean with a shieldlike carapace and a pair of suckers (class Branchiura: several genera, in particular *Argulus*). • an elongated crustacean that becomes permanently attached to the host and typically highly modified (class Copepoda: several orders and numerous species).

fish meal (also **fish·meal**) ▸*n.* ground dried fish used as fertilizer or animal feed.

fish·mon·ger /ˈfiSH,məNGgər; -ˌmäNGgər/ ▸*n.* a person or store that sells fish for food.

fish·net /ˈfiSH,net/ ▸*n.* a fabric with an open mesh resembling a fishing net: [as *adj.*] *black fishnet stockings.*

fish·plate /ˈfiSH,plāt/ ▸*n.* a flat piece of metal used to connect adjacent rails in a railroad track. ■ a flat piece of metal with ends like a fish's tail, used to position masonry.

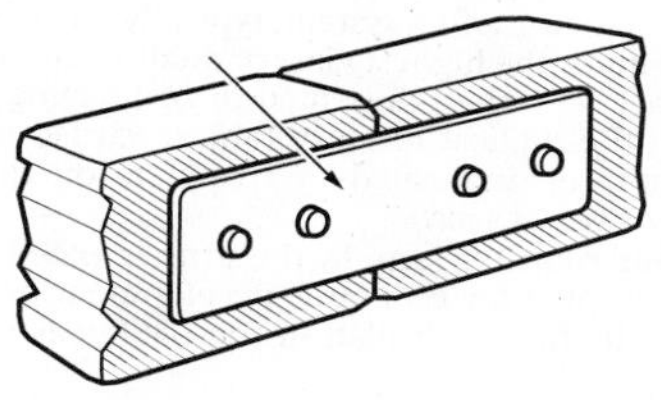

fishplate

fish·pond /ˈfiSH,pänd/ ▸*n.* a pond in which live fish are kept. ■ an attraction at a fair where contestants use a rod and line to attempt to extract a prize, or a token representing a prize, from a pool or other enclosure.

fish sauce ▸*n.* a Thai and Vietnamese sauce used as a flavoring or condiment, prepared from fermented anchovies and salt.

fish stick ▸*n.* a small, oblong piece of fish fillet, usually breaded and fried.

fish sto·ry ▸*n.* an incredible or far-fetched story.

fish·tail /ˈfiSH,tāl/ ▸*n.* [usu. as *adj.*] an object that is forked like a fish's tail: *carved detail including fishtail terminals on the banisters.* ■ an uncontrolled sideways movement of the back of a motor vehicle: *he hit the brakes, sending the car into a fishtail that carried him across the street.*
▸*v.* [*intrans.*] [usu. with *adverbial of direction*] (of a vehicle) make such a movement: *the vehicle fishtailed from one side of the road to the other.* ■ [*trans.*] cause (a vehicle) to make such a movement: *Carson fishtailed the Mercedes out into the road.*

fish·way /ˈfiSH,wā/ ▸*n.* another term for FISH LADDER.

fish·wife /ˈfiSH,wīf/ ▸*n.* (*pl.* **-wives** /-ˌwīvz/) **1** a coarse-mannered woman who is prone to shouting. **2** *archaic* a woman who sells fish.

fish·y /ˈfiSHē/ ▸*adj.* (**fish·i·er, fish·i·est**) **1** of, relating to, or resembling fish or a fish: *a fishy smell.* **2** *informal* arousing feelings of doubt or suspicion: *I'm convinced there is something fishy going on.* —**fish·i·ly** /ˈfiSHəlē/ *adv.* —**fish·i·ness** *n.*

Fisk /fisk/, James (1834–72), U.S. financier. He made his fortune in the stock manipulation that ruined the Erie Railroad, and with Jay Gould he engineered events that involved the U.S. treasury in the Black Friday scandalous attempt to corner the gold market in 1869.

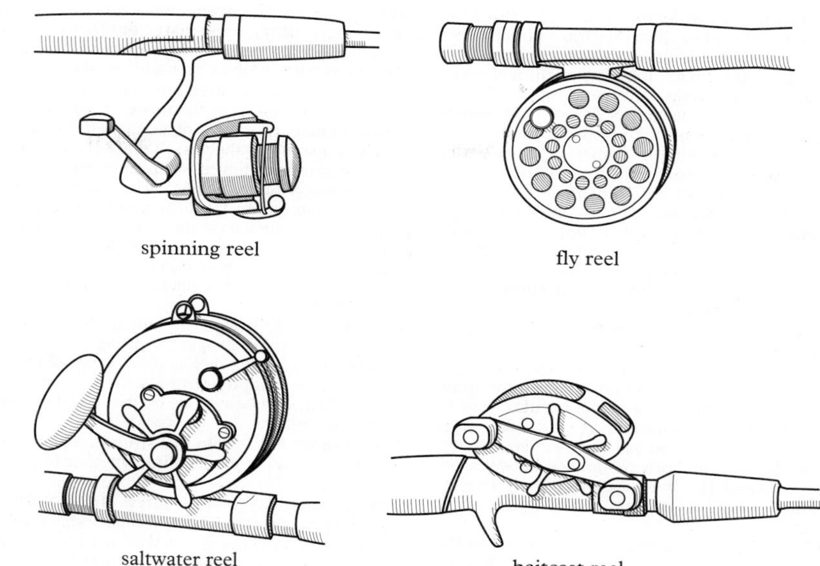

fishing reels

fisk /fisk/ ▸*n. Scottish, archaic* variant spelling of FISC.

fis·sile /ˈfisəl; ˈfis,īl/ ▸*adj.* (of an atom or element) able to undergo nuclear fission: *a fissile isotope.* ■ (chiefly of rock) easily split: *flat-bedded and very highly fissile shale.* ▷mid 17th cent. (in the sense 'easily split'): from Latin *fissilis*, from *fiss-* 'split, cracked,' from the verb *findere.* —**fis·sil·i·ty** /fiˈsilətē/ *n.*

fis·sion /ˈfiSHən; ˈfiZHən/ ▸*n.* the action of dividing or splitting something into two or more parts: *the party dissolved into fission and acrimony.* ■ short for NUCLEAR FISSION. ■ *Biology* reproduction by means of a cell or organism dividing into two or more new cells or organisms: *bacteria divide by transverse* ***binary fission.***
▸*v.* [*intrans.*] (chiefly of atoms) undergo fission: *these heavy nuclei can also fission.* ▷early 17th cent.: from Latin *fissio(n-)*, from *findere* 'to split.'

fis·sion·a·ble /ˈfiSHənəbəl; ˈfiZH-/ ▸*adj.* another term for FISSILE.

fis·sion bomb ▸*n.* another term for ATOM BOMB.

fis·sion-track dat·ing ▸*n. Geology* a technique for establishing the age of a mineral sample from its uranium content. It involves microscopically counting tracks produced by uranium fission fragments and then establishing the existing concentration of uranium by counting again after irradiating the sample with neutrons.

fis·sip·a·rous /fiˈsipərəs/ ▸*adj.* inclined to cause or undergo division into separate parts or groups: *She was unsuccessful in holding a fissiparous membership together.* ■ *Biology* (of an organism) reproducing by fission: *small fissiparous worms.* ▷mid 19th cent.: from Latin *fissus*, past participle of *findere* 'split,' on the pattern of *viviparous.* —**fis·sip·a·rous·ness** *n.*

fis·sure /ˈfiSHər/ ▸*n.* a long, narrow opening or line of breakage made by cracking or splitting, esp. in rock or earth. ■ *chiefly Anatomy* a long narrow opening in the form of a crack or groove, e.g., any of the spaces separating convolutions of the brain. ■ a state of incompatibility or disagreement: *the fissure between private sector business and the newly expanding public sector.*
▸*v.* [*trans.*] [usu. as *adj.*] (**fissured**) split or crack (something) to form a long narrow opening: *the skin becomes dry, fissured, and cracked.* ▷late Middle English: from Old French, or from Latin *fissura*, from *findere* 'to split.'

fis·sure of Syl·vi·us /ˈsilvēəs/ ▸*n.* another term for SYLVIAN FISSURE.

fist /fist/ ▸*n.* a person's hand when the fingers are bent in toward the palm and held there tightly, typically in order to strike a blow or grasp something.
▸*v.* **1** [*trans.*] hit with or as with the fists or a fist: *a fastball he fisted into left field.* **2** (also **fist-fuck**) [*trans.*] *vulgar slang* penetrate (a person's anus or vagina) with one's fist. ▷Old English *fȳst*; related to Dutch *vuist* and German *Faust.* —**fist·ed** *adj.* [in *combination*] *bare-fisted.* —**fist·ful** /-ˌfo͝ol/ *n.*
▸*PHRASE* □ **make a —— fist of** (or **at**) *informal* do something to the specified degree of success: *I think he's made a good fist of it.*

fist·fight /ˈfist,fīt/ ▸*n.* a fight with bare fists.

fist·ic /ˈfistik/ ▸*adj.* of or relating to boxing; pugilistic.

fist·i·cuffs /ˈfisti,kəfs/ ▸*plural n.* fighting with the fists. ▷early 17th cent.: probably from obsolete *fisty* 'relating to the fists or to fistfighting' + CUFF[2].

fis·tu·la /ˈfisCHələ/ ▸*n.* (*pl.* **-las** or **-lae** /-lē/) *Medicine* an abnormal or surgically made passage between a hollow or tubular organ and the body surface, or between two hollow or tubular organs. ▷late Middle English: from Latin, 'pipe, flute, fistula.' Compare with FESTER. —**fis·tu·lar** /-lər/ *adj.* —**fis·tu·lous** /-ləs/ *adj.*

fit[1] /fit/ ▸*adj.* (**fit·ter, fit·test**) **1** [*predic.*] (of a thing) of a suitable quality, standard, or type to meet the required purpose: *the meat is* ***fit for*** *human consumption* | [with *infinitive*] *is the water clean and fit to drink?* ■ (of a person) having the requisite qualities or skills to undertake something competently: *he felt himself quite* ***fit for*** *battle* | [with *infinitive*] *Ted was ghastly pale and fit to do no more than switch channels.* ■ *Biology* possessing or conferring the ability to survive and reproduce in a particular environment: *survival of the fittest.* ■ suitable and correct according to accepted social standards: *a fit subject on which to correspond.* ■ [with *infinitive*] *informal* (of a person or thing) having reached such an extreme condition as to be on the point of doing the thing specified: *he baited even his close companions until they were fit to kill him.* ■ *informal* ready: *well, are you fit?* **2** in good health, esp. because of regular physical exercise: *I swim regularly to keep fit* | *figurative the measures would ensure a leaner, fitter company.* ■ *Brit., informal* sexually attractive; good-looking.
▸*v.* (**fit·ted** or **fit** /fit/, **fit·ting**) [*trans.*] **1** be of the right shape and size for: *those jeans still fit me* | [*intrans.*] *the shoes fit better after being stretched.* ■ (usu. **be fitted for**) try clothing on (someone) in order to make or alter it to the correct size: *she was about to be fitted for her costume.* ■ [*intrans.*] be of the right size, shape, or number to occupy a particular position or place: *Angela says we can all fit in her car.* **2** fix or put (something) into place: *they fitted smoke alarms to their home.* ■ (often **be fitted with**) provide (something) with a particular component or article: *most tools can be fitted with a new handle.* ■ join or cause to join together to form a whole: [*intrans.*] *it took a while to figure out how the confounded things* ***fit together*** | [*trans.*] *many physicists tried to* ***fit together*** *the various pieces of the puzzle.* **3** be in agreement or harmony with; match: *the punishment should fit the crime.* ■ (of an attribute, qualification, or skill) make (someone) suitable to fulfill a particular role or undertake a particular task: *an MS* ***fits*** *the student* ***for*** *a professional career.*
▸*phrasal v.* □ **fit in** (of a person) be socially compatible with other members of a group: *he feels he should*

become tough to ***fit in with*** *his friends.* ■ (of a thing) be in harmony with other things within a larger structure: *produce ideas that* ***fit in with*** *an established approach.* ■ (also **fit into**) (of a person or thing) constitute part of a particular situation or larger structure: *where do your sisters fit in?* □ **fit someone/something in** (or **into**) find room or have sufficient space for someone or something: *can you fit any more books into the box?* ■ succeed in finding time in a busy schedule to see someone or do something: *you're never too busy to fit exercise into your life.* □ **fit someone/something out** (or **up**) provide with the necessary equipment, supplies, clothes, or other items for a particular situation: *the cabin had been fitted out to a high standard.* □ **fit someone up** *Brit., informal* incriminate someone by falsifying evidence against them. □ **fit something on** *Brit.* try on (a garment).

▸*n.* the particular way in which something, esp. a garment or component, fits around or into something: *the dress was a perfect fit.* ■ the particular way in which a thing matches something else: *a close fit between teachers' qualifications and their teaching responsibilities.* ■ *Statistics* the correspondence between observed data and the values expected by theory. ▷late Middle English: of unknown origin. **—fit·ly** /ˈfitlē/ *adv.*

▸*PHRASES* □ (**as**) **fit as a fiddle** see FIDDLE. □ **fit the bill** see BILL[1]. □ **fit like a glove** see GLOVE. □ **fit to be tied** *informal* very angry: *Daddy was fit to be tied when I separated from Hugh.* □ **fit to bust** *informal* with great energy: *they laughed fit to bust.* □ **see** (or **think**) **fit** consider it correct or acceptable to do something: *why did the company see fit to give you the job?*

fit[2] ▸*n.* a sudden uncontrollable outbreak of intense emotion, laughter, coughing, or other action or activity: *in* ***a fit of*** *temper* | *he got coughing fits.* ■ a sudden attack of convulsions and/or loss of consciousness, typical of epilepsy and some other medical conditions: *he thought she was* ***having a fit.*** ▷Old English *fitt* 'conflict,' in Middle English 'position of danger or excitement,' also 'short period'; the sense 'sudden attack of illness' dates from the mid 16th cent.

▸*PHRASES* □ **have** (or **throw**) **a fit** *informal* be very surprised or angry: *my mother would have a fit if she heard that.* □ **in fits** (**of laughter**) *informal* highly amused: *he had us all in fits.* □ **in** (or **by**) **fits and starts** with irregular bursts of activity: *the machine tends to go forward in fits and starts.*

fit[3] (also **fytte**) ▸*n. archaic* a section of a poem. ▷Old English *fitt,* perhaps the same word as FIT[2], or related to German *Fitze* 'skein of yarn,' in the obsolete sense 'thread with which weavers mark off a day's work.'

fitch /fiCH/ ▸*n.* old-fashioned term for POLECAT. ■ (also **fitch fur**) the fur of a polecat. ▷late Middle English (denoting the fur of a polecat): from Middle Dutch *visse* 'polecat.'

Fitch·burg /ˈfiCH,bərg/ a city in north central Massachusetts, northwest of Boston; pop. 41,194.

fitch·é /ˈfiCH,ā/ (also **fitch·y** or **fitched**) ▸*adj. Heraldry* (of a cross) having the foot extended into a point. ▷late 16th cent.: from French *fiché,* past participle of *ficher* 'to fix.'

fit·ful /ˈfitfəl/ ▸*adj.* active or occurring spasmodically or intermittently; not regular or steady: *a few hours' fitful sleep* | *business was fitful.* **—fit·ful·ly** *adv.* **—fit·ful·ness** *n.*

fit·ment /ˈfitmənt/ ▸*n.* (usu. **fitments**) *chiefly Brit.* a fixed item of furniture or piece of equipment, esp. in a house.

fit·ness /ˈfitnis/ ▸*n.* the condition of being physically fit and healthy: *disease and lack of fitness are closely related* | [as *adj.*] *a fitness test.* ■ the quality of being suitable to fulfill a particular role or task: *he had a year in which to establish his* ***fitness for*** *the office.* ■ *Biology* an organism's ability to survive and reproduce in a particular environment: *if sharp teeth increase fitness, then genes causing teeth to be sharp will increase in frequency.*

fit-out ▸*n. chiefly Brit.* an act of providing the necessary equipment for a house or apartment, esp. the final decoration and furniture.

fit·ted /ˈfitid/ ▸*adj.* **1** made or shaped to fill a space or to cover something closely or exactly: *the blouse has a fitted bodice* | *navy blue fitted sheets.* ■ *chiefly Brit.* (of a room) equipped with matching pieces of furniture built to be fixed into a particular space: *a fitted kitchen.* **2** attached to or provided with a particular component or article: *a pistol* ***fitted with*** *a match-grade barrel.* **3** [*predic.*] having the appropriate qualities or skills to do something: *physicists may not be* ***fitted for*** *involvement in industrial processes.*

fit·ter /ˈfitər/ ▸*n.* **1** a person who puts together or installs machinery, engine parts, or other equipment: *a pipe fitter.* **2** a person who supervises the cutting, fitting, or alteration of garments or shoes.

fit·ting /ˈfitiNG/ ▸*n.* **1** (often **fittings**) a small part on or attached to a piece of furniture or equipment: *the wooden fittings were made of walnut.* ■ (**fittings**) items, such as a stove or shelves, that are fixed in a building but can be removed when the owner moves: *little remains of the house's Victorian fittings.* Compare with FIXTURE (sense 1). **2** the action of fitting something, in particular: ■ the installing, assembling, and adjusting of machine parts: *the fitting of new engines by the shipyard.* ■ an occasion when one tries on a garment that is being made or altered: *she's coming tomorrow for a fitting.*

▸*adj.* **1** suitable or appropriate under the circumstances; right or proper: *a fitting reward* | [with *clause*] ***it was fitting that*** *he should reply.* **2** [in *combination*] fitted around or to something or someone in a specified way: *loose-fitting trousers.* **—fit·ting·ly** *adv.* **—fit·ting·ness** *n.*

fit·ting room ▸*n.* a room in a store in which one can try on clothes before deciding whether to purchase them.

Fitz·ger·ald[1] /fitsˈjerəld/, Barry (1888–1961), U.S. actor; born in Ireland; born *William Joseph Shields.* His movies include *Going My Way* (Academy Award, 1944), *Naked City* (1948), and *The Quiet Man* (1952).

Fitz·ger·ald[2], Ella (1917–96), U.S. jazz singer; full name *Ella Jane Fitzgerald.* Known for her distinctive style of scat singing, Fitzgerald joined Norman Granz on his world tours in 1946, appearing with Count Basie and Duke Ellington. From the mid 1950s, she made a series of recordings of songs by George Gershwin and Cole Porter.

Ella Fitzgerald

Fitz·ger·ald[3], F. Scott (1896–1940), U.S. novelist; full name *Francis Scott Key Fitzgerald.* His novels, in particular *The Great Gatsby* (1925), provide a vivid portrait of the U.S. during the jazz era of the 1920s. Fitzgerald later became part of an affluent and fashionable set living on the French Riviera; their lifestyle is reflected in *Tender is the Night* (1934), a semiautobiographical novel.

Fitz·Ger·ald con·trac·tion /fitsˈjerəld/ (also **Fitz·Ger·ald–Lo·rentz con·trac·tion**) ▸*n. Physics* another term for LORENTZ CONTRACTION. ▷named after George. F. FitzGerald (1851–1901), Irish physicist, and H. A. LORENTZ, who independently postulated the theory in 1892.

Fiu·me /ˈfyōōmā/ Italian name of RIJEKA.

five /fīv/ ▸*cardinal number* equivalent to the sum of two and three; one more than four, or half of ten; 5: *a circlet of five petals* | *five of Sweden's top financial experts.* (Roman numeral: **v** or **V.**) ■ a group or unit of five people or things: *the bulbs are planted in threes or fives.* ■ five years old: *he moved with his family to a fish farm when he was five.* ■ five o'clock: *at half past five.* ■ a size of garment or other merchandise denoted by five. ■ a playing card or domino with five spots or pips. ■ a five-dollar bill: *Joe counted his money: six fives and three twenties.* ▷Old English *fīf,* of Germanic origin; related to Dutch *vijf* and German *fünf,* from an Indo-European root shared by Latin *quinque* and Greek *pente.*

five-a·larm ▸*adj.* [*attrib.*] *informal* (of a fire) very large or fierce. ■ (of food, such as chilies) extremely pungent; hot.

five-and-dime (also **five-and-dime store** or **five-and-ten**) ▸*n.* a store selling a wide variety of inexpensive household and personal goods. ■ *historical* a store where all the articles were priced at five or ten cents.

five-fin·ger (also **five·fin·ger**) ▸*n.* any of a number of plants with leaves that are divided into five leaflets or with flowers that have five petals, such as cinquefoil.

five-fin·ger dis·count ▸*n. informal* an act of shoplifting.

five-fin·ger ex·er·cise ▸*n.* an exercise on the piano for all the fingers on both hands.

five·fold /ˈfīv,fōld/ ▸*adj.* five times as great or as numerous: *a fivefold increase in funding.* ■ having five parts or elements: *fivefold rotational symmetry.*
▸*adv.* by five times; to five times the number or amount: *the unemployment rate rose almost fivefold.*

five hun·dred ▸*n.* a form of euchre in which making 500 points wins a game.

five Ks /kāz/ ▸*plural n.* (**the five Ks**) See KHALSA.

Five Na·tions ▸*plural n. historical* the original Iroquois confederacy, comprising the Mohawk, Oneida, Onondaga, Cayuga and Seneca peoples. Compare with SIX NATIONS.

five o'clock shad·ow ▸*n.* a dark appearance on a man's chin and face caused by the slight growth of beard that has occurred since he shaved in the morning.

Five Pil·lars of Is·lam the five duties expected of every Muslim—profession of the faith in a prescribed form, observance of ritual prayer, giving alms to the poor, fasting during the month of Ramadan, and performing a pilgrimage to Mecca.

fiv·er /ˈfīvər/ ▸*n. informal* a five-dollar bill. ■ *Brit.* a five-pound note.

fives /fīvz/ ▸*plural n.* [treated as *sing.*] a game, played esp. in the UK, in which a ball is hit with a gloved hand or a bat against the walls of a court with three walls (**Eton fives**) or four walls (**Rugby fives**). ▷mid 17th cent.: plural of FIVE used as a singular noun; the significance is unknown.

five sens·es ▸*plural n.* (**the five senses**) the faculties of sight, smell, hearing, taste, and touch.

five-spice (also **five-spice powder**) ▸*n.* a blend of five powdered spices, typically fennel seeds, cinnamon, cloves, star anise, and peppercorns, used in Chinese cuisine.

five-star ▸*adj.* (esp. of a hotel or restaurant) given five stars in a grading system, typically one in which this denotes the highest class or quality: *a luxury five-star hotel.* ■ (in the U.S. armed forces) having or denoting the highest military rank (awarded only in wartime), distinguished by five stars on the uniform: *a five-star general.*

five-year plan ▸*n.* (esp. in the former USSR) a government plan for economic development over five years. The first such plan in the USSR was inaugurated in 1928.

fix /fiks/ ▸*v.* [*trans.*] **1** [*trans.*] fasten (something) securely in a particular place or position: *fix the clamp on a rail* | *the upper jaw of an amphibian is firmly fixed to the skull.* ■ *figurative* lodge or implant (an idea, image, or memory) firmly in a person's mind: *he turned back to fix the scene in his mind.* **2** (**fix something on/upon**) direct one's eyes, attention, or mind steadily or unwaveringly toward: *I fixed my attention on the tower.* ■ [*intrans.*] (**fix on/upon**) (of a person's eyes, attention, or mind) be directed steadily or unwaveringly toward: *her gaze fixed on Jess.* ■ attract and hold (a person's attention or gaze): *their taut relationship fixes your attention.* ■ (**fix someone with**) look at someone unwaveringly: *she fixed her nephew with an unwavering stare.* **3** mend; repair: *you should fix that shelf.* ■ (**fix something up**) do the necessary work to improve or adapt something: *we want to fix up the house before we sell it.* ■ make arrangements for (something); organize: *he's sent her on ahead to* ***fix things up*** | *I've* ***fixed it for*** *you to see him on Thursday.* ■ *informal* restore order or tidiness to (something, esp. one's hair, clothes, or makeup): *Laura was fixing her hair.* ■ *informal* prepare or arrange for the provision of (food or drink): [with *two objs.*] *they were fixing him breakfast* | *Ruth* ***fixed herself*** *a cold drink.* ■ (**fix someone up**) *informal* arrange for someone to have something; provide someone with something: *I'll* ***fix you up with*** *a room.* ■ (**fix someone up**) *informal* arrange for someone to meet or go out with someone in order to help them establish a romantic relationship. ■ (**be fixing to do something**) *informal* be intending or planning to do something: *you're fixing to get into trouble.* **4** decide or settle on (a specific price, date, course of action, etc.): *no date has yet been fixed for a hearing* | *the rent will be* ***fixed at*** *$600 a month* | [*intrans.*] *their thinking then seemed* ***fixed on*** *conventional projects.* ■ discover the exact location of (something) by using radar or visual bearings or astronomical observation: *he fixed his* position. ■ settle the form of (a language). ■ assign or determine (a person's liability or responsibility) for legal purposes: *there are no facts that* **fix** *the defendant with liability.* **5** make (something) permanent or static in nature: *the rate of interest is fixed for the life of the loan.* ■ make (a dye, photographic image, or drawing) permanent. ■ *Biology* preserve or stabilize (a specimen) with a chemical substance prior to microscopy or other examination: *specimens were fixed in buffered formalin.* ■ (of a plant or microorganism) assimilate (nitrogen or carbon dioxide) by forming a nongaseous compound: *lupines fix gaseous nitrogen in their root nodules.* **6** *informal* influence the outcome of (something, esp. a race, contest, or election) by illegal or underhanded means: *the foundation denies fixing races.* ■ put (an enemy or rival) out of action, esp. by killing them: *don't you tell nobody, or I'll fix you good!* **7** *informal* [*intrans.*] take an injection of a narcotic drug. **8** castrate or spay (an animal); neuter.

▸*n.* **1** [in *sing.*] *informal* a difficult or awkward situation from which it is hard to extricate oneself; a predicament: *how on earth did you get into such a fix?* **2** *informal* a dose of a narcotic drug to which one is addicted: *he hadn't had his fix.* ■ *figurative* a thing or activity that gives a person a feeling of euphoria or pleasure and that it is difficult to do without: *that rush of adrenaline that is the fix of the professional newsman.* **3** *informal* a solution to a problem, esp. one that is hastily devised or makeshift: *representatives trying to find cheap fixes to meet their obligations.* See also QUICK FIX. **4** a position determined by visual or radio bearings or astronomical observations. **5** [in *sing.*] *informal* a dishonest or underhanded arrangement: *obviously, his appointment was a fix.* ▷late Middle English: partly from Old French *fix* 'fixed,' partly from medieval Latin *fixare* 'to fix,' both from Latin *fixus,* past participle of *figere* 'fix, fasten.' The noun dates from the early 19th cent. **—fix·a·ble** /ˈfiksəbəl/ *adj.*

▸*PHRASE* □ **get a fix on** determine the position of (something) by visual or radio bearings or astronomical observation. ■ *informal* assess or determine the nature or facts of; obtain a clear understanding of: *it is hard to get a fix on their ages.*

fix·ate /ˈfikˌsāt/ ▸*v.* [*trans.*] **1** (usu. **be fixated on/upon**) cause (someone) to acquire an obsessive attachment to someone or something: *she has for some time been fixated on photography.* ■ [*intrans.*] (**fixate on/upon**) acquire such an obsessive attachment to: *it is important not to fixate on animosity.* ■ (in Freudian theory) arrest (a person or their libidinal energy) at an immature stage, causing an obsessive attachment. **2** *technical* direct one's eyes toward: *subjects fixated a central point* | [*intrans.*] *there is tendency to fixate near the beginning of the line of print.* ▷late 19th cent.: from Latin *fixus,* past participle of *figere* (see FIX) + -ATE[3].

fix·a·tion /fikˈsāsʜən/ ▸*n.* **1** an obsessive interest in or feeling about someone or something: *his* **fixation on** *the details of other people's erotic lives* | *our* **fixation with** *diet and fitness.* ■ *Psychoanalysis* the arresting of part of the libido at an immature stage, causing an obsessive attachment: *fixation at the oral phase might result in dependence on others* | *an oral-maternal fixation.* **2** the action of making something firm or stable: *sand dune fixation.* ■ *Biochemistry* the process by which some plants and microorganisms incorporate gaseous nitrogen or carbon dioxide to form nongaseous compounds: *his work on nitrogen fixation in plants.* ■ *Biology* the process of preserving or stabilizing (a specimen) with a chemical substance prior to microscopy or other examination: *biopsy specimens were placed in cassettes before fixation in formalin.* **3** *technical* the action of concentrating the eyes directly on something: *during the period of total blindness there was a complete absence of visual fixation.* ▷late Middle English (originally as an alchemical term denoting the process of reducing a volatile spirit or essence to a permanent bodily form): from medieval Latin *fixatio(n-),* from *fixare* (see FIX).

fix·a·tive /ˈfiksətiv/ ▸*n.* **1** a chemical substance used to preserve or stabilize biological material prior to microscopy or other examination: *an alcoholic fixative* | *ten double drops of fixative.* ■ a substance used to stabilize the volatile components of perfume. ■ a liquid sprayed on to a pastel or charcoal drawing to fix colors or prevent smudging. **2** a substance used to keep things in position or stick them together: *the swift glues these thin twigs to a wall using its own saliva as a fixative.*

▸*adj.* (of a substance) used to fix or stabilize something.

fixed /fikst/ ▸*adj.* **1** fastened securely in position: *a fixed iron ladder down the port side.* ■ remaining in the same place with respect to another object: *a fixed satellite.* ■ (esp. of a price, rate, or time) predetermined and not subject to or able to be changed: *most trusts locked investors in for a fixed period.* ■ (of a person's expression) held for a long time without changing, esp. to conceal other feelings: *a fixed smile.* ■ (of a view or idea) held inflexibly: *the fixed assumptions of the cold war.* **2** [*predic.*] (**fixed for**) *informal* situated with regard to: *how's the club fixed for money now?* **3** (of a sports contest) with the outcome dishonestly predetermined: *the fight's fixed—the ref has your card marked.* **—fix·ed·ly** /ˈfiksidlē/ *adv.* **—fix·ed·ness** /ˈfiksidnis/ *n.*

fixed as·sets ▸*plural n.* assets that are purchased for long-term use and are not likely to be converted quickly into cash, such as land, buildings, and equipment. Compare with CURRENT ASSETS.

fixed cap·i·tal ▸*n.* capital invested in fixed assets.

fixed charge ▸*n.* a liability to a creditor that relates to specific assets of a company.

fixed costs ▸*plural n.* business costs, such as rent, that are constant whatever the quantity of goods or services produced.

fixed-do /ˈfikst ˈdō/ (*Brit.* **fixed-doh**) ▸*adj.* [*attrib.*] *Music* denoting a system of solmization in which C is called "do," D is called "re," etc., irrespective of the key in which they occur. Compare with MOVABLE-DO.

fixed fo·cus ▸*n.* a camera focus that cannot be adjusted, typically used with a small-aperture lens having a large depth of field.

fixed i·de·a ▸*n.* another term for IDÉE FIXE.

fixed in·come ▸*n.* an income from a pension or investment that is set at a particular figure and does not vary (as a dividend) or rise with the rate of inflation.

fixed oil ▸*n.* a nonvolatile oil of animal or plant origin.

fixed point ▸*n.* *Physics* a well-defined reproducible temperature that can be used as a reference point, e.g., one defined by a change of phase.

▸*adj.* (**fixed-point**) *Computing* denoting a mode of representing a number by a single sequence of digits whose values depend on their location relative to a predetermined radix point: *these computers perform arithmetic in fixed-point binary format.* Often contrasted with FLOATING-POINT.

fixed star ▸*n.* see STAR (sense 1).

fixed-wing ▸*adj.* [*attrib.*] denoting aircraft of the conventional type as opposed to those with rotating wings, such as helicopters.

fix·er /ˈfiksər/ ▸*n.* **1** a person who makes arrangements for other people, esp. of an illicit or devious kind. **2** a substance used for fixing a photographic image.

fix·er-up·per ▸*n.* *informal* a house in need of repairs (used chiefly in connection with the purchase of such a house).

fix·ing /ˈfiksiNG/ ▸*n.* **1** the action of fixing something: *artificial price fixing.* **2** (**fixings**) apparatus or equipment for a particular purpose: *picnic fixings.* ■ the ingredients necessary to make a dish or meal: *have all the fixings ready before starting.* ■ *Brit.* screws, bolts, or other items used to fix or assemble building material, furniture, or equipment.

fix·it /ˈfiksit/ ▸*n.* *informal* a person known for repairing things or putting things in order: *he pictured himself as a Mr. Fixit.* ■ [usu. as *adj.*] an act of repairing or putting something right: *a fixit shop.* ▷early 20th cent.: from *Little Miss Fixit,* the title of a musical show.

fix·i·ty /ˈfiksitē/ ▸*n.* the state of being unchanging or permanent: *the fixity of his stare.* ▷mid 17th cent. (denoting the property of a substance of not evaporating or losing weight when heated): partly from obsolete *fix* 'fixed,' partly from French *fixité.*

fix·ture /ˈfiksCHər/ ▸*n.* **1** a piece of equipment or furniture that is fixed in position in a building or vehicle: *a light fixture.* ■ (**fixtures**) articles attached to a house or land and considered legally part of it so that they normally remain in place when an owner moves: *the hotel retains many original* **fixtures and fittings.** Compare with FITTING (sense 1). ■ *informal* a person or thing that is established in a particular place or situation: *palm readers were a fixture in most '40s nightclubs.* **2** *Brit.* a sports event that takes place on a particular date. ▷late 16th cent. (in the sense 'fixing, becoming fixed'): alteration (first found in Shakespeare) of obsolete *fixure* (from late Latin *fixura,* from Latin *figere* 'to fix'), with *t* inserted on the pattern of *mixture.*

fizz /fiz/ ▸*v.* [*intrans.*] (of a liquid) produce bubbles of gas and make a hissing sound: *the mixture fizzed like mad.* ■ make a buzzing or crackling sound: *lightning starts to crackle and fizz.* ■ [with *adverbial*] *figurative* move with or display excitement, exuberance, or liveliness: *anticipation began to fizz through his veins.*

▸*n.* effervescence: *the champagne had lost its fizz.* ■ *informal* an effervescent drink, esp. sparkling wine: *a bottle of grapefruit fizz.* ■ *figurative* exuberance; liveliness: *she saw I had lost some of my fizz.* ■ a buzzing or crackling sound: *the fizz of 300 sparklers.* ▷mid 17th cent.: imitative.

fiz·zle /ˈfizəl/ ▸*v.* [*intrans.*] end or fail in a weak or disappointing way: *their threatened revolt* **fizzled out** *at yesterday's meeting.* ■ make a feeble hissing or spluttering sound: *the strobe lights fizzled and flickered.*

▸*n.* a failure: *in the end the fireworks were a fizzle.* ■ a feeble hissing or spluttering sound: *the electric fizzle of the waves.* ▷late Middle English (in the sense 'break wind quietly'): probably imitative (compare with FIZZ), but perhaps related to Middle English *fist* (see FEISTY). Current senses date from the 19th cent.

fiz·zog /ˈfizˌäg; fizˈäg/ ▸*n.* another term for PHIZ.

fizz·y /ˈfizē/ ▸*adj.* (**fizz·i·er, fizz·i·est**) (of a beverage) containing bubbles of gas; effervescent: *fizzy mineral water.* **—fizz·i·ly** /ˈfizəlē/ *adv.* **—fizz·i·ness** /ˈfizēnis/ *n.*

fjord /fēˈôrd; fyôrd/ (also **fiord**) ▸*n.* a long, narrow, deep inlet of the sea between high cliffs, as in Norway and Iceland, typically formed by submergence of a glaciated valley. ▷late 17th cent.: Norwegian, from Old Norse *fjǫrthr.* Compare with FIRTH.

FL ▸*abbr.* Florida (in official postal use).

fL ▸*abbr.* foot-Lambert.

fl. ▸*abbr.* ■ floor. ■ floruit. ■ fluid.

Fla. ▸*abbr.* Florida.

flab /flab/ ▸*n.* *informal* soft loose flesh on a person's body; fat. ▷1950s: back-formation from FLABBY.

flab·ber·gast /ˈflabərˌgast/ ▸*v.* [*trans.*] [usu. as *adj.*] (**flabbergasted**) *informal* surprise (someone) greatly; astonish: *this news has left me totally flabbergasted.* ▷late 18th cent.: of unknown origin.

flab·by /ˈflabē/ ▸*adj.* (**-bi·er, -bi·est**) (of a part of a person's body) soft, loose, and fleshy: *this exercise helps to flatten a flabby stomach.* ■ (of a person) having soft loose flesh. ■ *figurative* not tightly controlled, powerful, or effective: *the quartet playing was uncommitted and flabby.* ▷late 17th cent.: alteration of earlier *flappy.* **—flab·bi·ly** /ˈflabəlē/ *adv.* **—flab·bi·ness** /ˈflabēnis/ *n.*

fla·bel·lum /fləˈbeləm/ ▸*n.* (*pl.* **-bel·la** /-ˈbelə/) a fan, esp. an elegant, ornamental one used in Christian ritual. ■ *Biology historical* a fan-shaped organ, part, or anatomical structure.

flac·cid /ˈfla(k)səd/ ▸*adj.* (of part of the body) soft and hanging loosely or limply, esp. so as to look or feel unpleasant: *she took his flaccid hand in hers.* ■ (of plant tissue) drooping or inelastic through lack of water. ■ *figurative* lacking force or effectiveness: *the flaccid leadership campaign was causing concern.* ▷early 17th cent.: from French *flaccide* or Latin *flaccidus,* from *flaccus* 'flabby.' **—flac·cid·i·ty** /fla(k)ˈsidətē/ *n.* **—flac·cid·ly** *adv.*

flack[1] /flak/ *informal* ▸*n.* a publicity agent: *a public relations flack.*

▸*v.* [*trans.*] publicize or promote (something or someone): *a crass ambulance-chaser who* **flacks himself** *in TV ads* | [*intrans.*] *the local news media shamelessly* **flack for** *the organizing committee.* ▷1940s: of unknown origin. **—flack·er·y** /-ərē/ *n.*

flack[2] ▸*n.* variant spelling of FLAK.

flac·on /ˈflakən; flaˈkôN/ ▸*n.* (*pl.* **flac·ons** *pronunc.* same or /-kənz/) a small stoppered bottle, esp. one for perfume. ▷early 19th cent.: French, 'flask.'

flag[1] /flag/ ▸*n.* **1** a piece of cloth or similar material, typically oblong or square, attachable by one edge to a pole or rope and used as the symbol or emblem of a country or institution or as a decoration during public festivities: *the American flag.* ■ used in reference to the country to which a person has allegiance: *the private's heroism served as an example for every soldier under the flag.* ■ a ship's country of registry. ■ a small piece of cloth, typically attached at one edge to a pole, used as a marker or signal in various sports: *jumped the starter's flag, did he?* ■ the ensign carried by a flagship as an emblem of an admiral's rank. **2** a device, symbol, or drawing typically resembling a flag, used as a marker: *golf courses are*

F

indicated by a numbered flag on the map. ■ *Computing* a variable used to indicate a particular property of the data in a record. **3** a hook attached to the stem of a musical note, determining the rhythmic value of the note.

▸*v.* (**flagged, flag·ging**) [*trans.*] **1** (often **be flagged**) mark (an item) for attention or treatment in a specified way: *"greatfully" would be flagged as a misspelling of "gratefully."* ■ *Football* charge (a player) with a penalty by dropping a penalty flag: *a play in which he was flagged for being offside.* ■ *figurative* draw attention to: *problems often flag the need for organizational change.* **2** [*trans.*] direct (someone) to go in the specified direction by waving a flag or using hand signals: *have him flagged off the course.* ■ (**flag someone/something down**) signal to a vehicle or driver to stop, esp. by waving one's arm: *she flagged down a patrol car.* ■ [*intrans.*] (of an official in football, soccer, and other sports) raise or throw a flag to indicate a breach of the rules: *the rookie cornerback managed to get flagged for three penalties in one game.* **3** provide or decorate with a flag or flags. ■ register (a vessel) in a specific country, under whose flag it then sails: *the **flagging out** of much of the fleet to flags of convenience.* ▷mid 16th cent.: perhaps from obsolete *flag* 'drooping,' of unknown ultimate origin. **—flag·ger** *n.*

▸*PHRASES* □ **fly the flag** (of a ship) be registered in a particular country and sail under its flag. ■ (also **show** or **carry** or **wave the flag**) represent or demonstrate support for one's country, political party, or organization, esp. when one is abroad: *he will never consider buying an import, because he likes to fly the flag.* □ **show the flag** (of a naval vessel) make an official visit to a foreign port, esp. as a show of strength. □ **wrap oneself in the flag** make an excessive show of one's patriotism, esp. for political ends.

flag[2] ▸*n.* a flat stone slab, typically rectangular or square, used for paving. ▷late Middle English (also in the sense 'turf, sod'): probably of Scandinavian origin and related to Icelandic *flag* 'spot from which a sod has been cut' and Old Norse *flaga* 'slab of stone.' **—flagged** *adj.* [often in *combination*] *stone-flagged steps.*

flag[3] ▸*n.* a plant with sword-shaped leaves that grow from a rhizome: • a plant of the iris family (genus *Iris*, family Iridaceae). See **BLUE FLAG** (sense 1); **YELLOW FLAG** (sense 2). • see **SWEET FLAG**. ■ the long slender leaf of such a plant. ▷late Middle English: related to Middle Dutch *flag* and Danish *flæg*; of unknown ultimate origin.

flag[4] ▸*v.* (**flagged, flag·ging**) [*intrans.*] (of a person) become tired, weaker, or less enthusiastic: *if you begin to flag, there is an excellent café to revive you.* ■ [often as *adj.*] (**flagging**) (esp. of an activity or quality) become weaker or less dynamic: *she should make another similar film to revive her flagging career.* ▷mid 16th cent. (in the sense 'flap about loosely, hang down'): related to obsolete *flag* 'hanging down.'

Flag Day ▸*n.* June 14, the anniversary of the adoption of the Stars and Stripes as the official U.S. flag in 1777.

flag·el·lant /ˈflajələnt; fləˈjelənt/ ▸*n.* a person who subjects themselves or others to flogging, either as a religious discipline or for sexual gratification. ▷late 16th cent.: from Latin *flagellant-* 'whipping,' from the verb *flagellare*, from *flagellum* 'whip' (see **FLAGELLUM**).

flag·el·late[1] /ˈflajəˌlāt/ ▸*v.* [*trans.*] flog (someone), either as a religious discipline or for sexual gratification: *he **flagellated himself** with branches.* ▷early 17th cent.: from Latin *flagellat-* 'whipped,' from *flagellare*. **—flag·el·la·tion** /ˌflajəˈlāsʜən/ *n.* **—flag·el·la·tor** /-ˌlātər/ *n.* **—flag·el·la·to·ry** /fləˈjeləˌtôrē/ *adj.*

flag·el·late[2] /ˈflajələt; -ˌlāt/ *Zoology* ▸*n.* a protozoan that has one or more flagella used for swimming. • Several phyla in the kingdom Protista (formerly subphylum Mastigophora, phylum Protozoa), including forms such as euglena that are sometimes regarded as algae.

▸*adj.* (of a cell or single-celled organism) bearing one or more flagella: *motile flagellate cells.* ▷mid 19th cent.: from **FLAGELLUM** + **-ATE**[2].

fla·gel·lin /fləˈjelən/ ▸*n.* the structural protein of bacterial flagella.

fla·gel·lum /ˌfləˈjeləm/ ▸*n.* (*pl.* **-gel·la** /-ˈjelə/) *Biology* a slender threadlike structure, esp. a microscopic whiplike appendage that enables many protozoa, bacteria, spermatozoa, etc., to swim. ▷early 19th cent. (denoting a whip or scourge): from Latin, diminutive of *flagrum* 'scourge.' **—fla·gel·lar** /fləˈjelər; ˈflajələr/ *adj.*

flag·eo·let[1] /ˌflajəˈlet; -ˈlā/ ▸*n.* a small flutelike instrument resembling a recorder but with four finger holes on top and two thumb holes below. ■ another term for **TIN WHISTLE**. ▷mid 17th cent.: from French, diminutive of Old French *flageol*, from Provençal *flaujol*, of unknown origin.

flag·eo·let[2] ▸*n.* a French kidney bean of a small variety used in cooking. ▷late 19th cent.: from French, based on Latin *phaseolus* 'bean.'

flag·fish /ˈflagˌfisʜ/ ▸*n.* (*pl.* same or **-fish·es**) any of a number of small fish with prominent or boldly marked fins, in particular: • a colorful freshwater fish with spots and iridescent scales, native to Florida (*Jordanella floridae*, family Cyprinodontidae).

flag-fly·ing ▸*n.* the action of making a public display to promote the interests of one's country, or of another organization or group.

flag foot·ball ▸*n.* a modified form of football in which ballcarriers are downed by pulling off a marker, or flag, loosely attached to a belt, rather than by tackling.

Flagg /flag/, James Montgomery (1877–1960), U.S. artist. He created the World War I recruiting poster that features Uncle Sam's pointing finger and the caption "I Want You."

fla·gi·tious /fləˈjisʜəs/ ▸*adj.* (of a person or their actions) criminal; villainous. ▷late Middle English: from Latin *flagitiosus*, from *flagitium* 'importunity, shameful crime,' from *flagitare* 'demand earnestly.' **—fla·gi·tious·ly** *adv.* **—fla·gi·tious·ness** *n.*

Flag·ler /ˈflaglər/, Henry Morrison (1830–1913), U.S. financier. With John D. Rockefeller, he developed the Standard Oil Company. He organized the Florida East Coast railroad in 1886.

flag·man /ˈflagmən/ ▸*n.* (*pl.* **-men**) a person who gives signals with a flag, esp. on railroad lines or during road construction.

flag of con·ven·ience ▸*n.* a flag of a country under which a ship is registered in order to avoid financial charges or restrictive regulations in the owner's country.

flag of·fi·cer ▸*n.* an admiral, vice admiral, or rear admiral. ■ the commodore of a yacht club. ▷mid 17th cent.: *flag*, because the officer had the privilege of carrying a flag that denoted his rank.

flag of truce ▸*n.* a white flag indicating a desire for a truce.

flag·on /ˈflagən/ ▸*n.* a large container in which drink is served, typically with a handle and spout: *there was a flagon of beer in his vast fist.* ■ the amount of liquid held in such a container: *he had at least three **flagons of** wine down him already.* ■ a similar container used to hold the wine for the Eucharist. ■ a large bottle in which wine or cider is sold, typically holding about 2 pints (1.13 liters). ▷late Middle English: from Old French *flacon*, based on late Latin *flasco*, *flascon-*, of unknown origin. Compare with **FLASK**.

flag·pole /ˈflagˌpōl/ ▸*n.* a pole used for flying a flag.

▸*PHRASE* □ **run something up the flagpole (to see who salutes)** test the popularity of a new idea or proposal: *the idea was first run up the flagpole in 1997.*

flag rank ▸*n.* the rank attained by flag officers.

fla·grant /ˈflāgrənt/ ▸*adj.* (of something considered wrong or immoral) conspicuously or obviously offensive: *his flagrant bad taste | a flagrant violation of the law.* ▷late 15th cent. (in the sense 'blazing, resplendent'): from French, or from Latin *flagrant-* 'blazing,' from the verb *flagrare*. **—fla·gran·cy** /-grənsē/ *n.* **—fla·grant·ly** *adv.*

flag·ship /ˈflagˌsʜip/ ▸*n.* the ship in a fleet that carries the commanding admiral. ■ the best or most important thing owned or produced by a particular organization: *this bill is the flagship of the administration's legislative program* | [as *adj.*] *their flagship product.*

Flag·staff /ˈflagˌstaf/ a city in north central Arizona, near the San Francisco Peaks, home to Lowell Observatory and the University of Northern Arizona; pop. 52,894.

flag·staff /ˈflagˌstaf/ ▸*n.* another term for **FLAGPOLE**.

flag sta·tion (also **flag stop**) ▸*n.* *historical* a station at which trains stop only if signaled to do so. ■ a small town or a place of no consequence: *we must go back some years to a little flag station in a pinewood clearing.*

flag·stick /ˈflagˌstik/ ▸*n.* *Golf* another term for **PIN** (sense 2).

flag·stone /ˈflagˌstōn/ ▸*n.* a flat stone slab, typically rectangular or square, used for paving. **—flag·stoned** *adj.*

flag-wav·ing ▸*n.* the expression of patriotism in a populist and emotional way: *what began as jingoistic flag-waving deteriorated into an international crisis.* **—flag-wav·er** *n.*

flail /flāl/ ▸*n.* a threshing tool consisting of a wooden staff with a short heavy stick swinging from it. ■ a similar device used as a weapon or for flogging. ■ a machine for threshing or slashing, with a similar action.

▸*v.* **1** wave or swing or cause to wave or swing wildly: [*intrans.*] *his arms were flailing helplessly* | [*trans.*] *he flailed his arms and drove her away.* ■ [*intrans.*] flounder; struggle uselessly: *I was **flailing about** in the water | he **flailed around** on the snow.* **2** [*trans.*] beat; flog: *he escorted them, flailing their shoulders with his cane.* ▷Middle English, from Old English *fligel*, based on Latin *flagellum* 'whip' (see **FLAGELLUM**); probably influenced in Middle English by Old French *flaiel* or Dutch *vlegel*.

flair /fler/ ▸*n.* **1** [in *sing.*] a special or instinctive aptitude or ability for doing something well: *she had a flair for languages | none of us had much artistic flair.* **2** stylishness and originality: *she dressed with flair.* ▷late 19th cent.: from French, from *flairer* 'to smell,' based on Latin *fragrare* 'smell sweet.' Compare with **FRAGRANT**.

flak /flak/ (also **flack**) ▸*n.* antiaircraft fire. ■ strong criticism: *you must be strong enough to **take the flak** if things go wrong.* ▷1930s: from German, abbreviation of *Fliegerabwehrkanone*, literally 'aircraft-defense gun.'

flake[1] /flāk/ ▸*n.* **1** a small, flat, thin piece of something, typically one that has broken away or been peeled off from a larger piece: *paint peeling off the walls in unsightly flakes | flakes of pastry.* ■ a snowflake. ■ *Archaeology* a piece of hard stone chipped off for use as a tool by prehistoric humans: [as *adj.*] *flake tools.* ■ thin pieces of crushed dried food or bait for fish. **2** *informal* a crazy or eccentric person.

▸*v.* **1** [*intrans.*] come or fall away from a surface in thin pieces: *the paint had been **flaking off** for years.* ■ lose small fragments from the surface: *my nails have started to flake at the ends.* **2** [*trans.*] break or divide (food) into thin pieces: *flake the fish* | [as *adj.*] (**flaked**) *flaked haddock.* ■ [*intrans.*] (of food, esp. when well cooked) come apart in thin pieces. ▷Middle English: the immediate source is unknown, the senses perhaps deriving from different words; probably of Germanic origin and related to **FLAG**[2] and **FLAW**[1].

flake[2] ▸*n.* a rack or shelf for storing or drying food such as fish. ▷Middle English (denoting a wicker framework): perhaps of Scandinavian origin and related to Old Norse *flaki*, *fleki* 'wicker shield' and Danish *flage* 'wicker framework.'

flake[3] ▸*v.* [*intrans.*] (**flake out**) *informal* fall asleep; drop from exhaustion. ▷late 15th cent. (in the senses 'become languid' and (of a garment) 'fall in folds'): variant of obsolete *flack* and the verb **FLAG**[4]. The current sense dates from the 1940s.

flake[4] (also **fake** /fāk/) *Nautical* ▸*n.* a single turn of a coiled rope or hawser.

▸*v.* [*trans.*] lay (a rope) in loose coils in order to prevent it from tangling: *a cable had to be **flaked out**.* ■ lay (a sail) down in folds on either side of the boom. ▷early 17th cent. (as a noun): of unknown origin; compare with German *Flechte* in the same sense.

flake white ▸*n.* a pure white pigment made from flakes of white lead.

flak jack·et (also **flak vest**) ▸*n.* a sleeveless jacket made of heavy fabric reinforced with metal or kevlar, worn as protection against bullets and shrapnel.

flak·y /ˈflākē/ (also **flak·ey**) ▸*adj.* (**flak·i·er**, **flakiest**) **1** breaking or separating easily into small thin pieces: *a tree with flaky bark.* ■ (esp. of skin or paint) tending to crack and come away from a surface in small pieces: *the skin on the shins is often very flaky and dry.* **2** *informal* crazy or eccentric: *flaky ideas about taxes.* ■ *informal* (of a device or software) prone to break down; unreliable. **—flak·i·ness** /-kēnis/ *n.* **—flak·i·ly** /-kəlē/ *adv.*

flak·y pas·try ▸*n.* pastry consisting of thin light layers when baked.

flam /flam/ ▸*n.* *Music* one of the basic patterns (rudiments) of drumming, consisting of a stroke preceded by a grace note. ▷late 18th cent.: probably imitative.

flam·bé /flämˈbā/ ▸*adj.* **1** [*postpositive*] (of food) covered with liquor and set alight briefly: *crêpes flambé.* **2** denoting or characterized by a red copper-based porcelain glaze with purple streaks.

▸*v.* (**-bés, -béed** /-ˈbād/, **-bé·ing**) [*trans.*] cover (food) with liquor and set it alight briefly. ▷late 19th cent.: French, literally 'singed,' past participle of *flamber*, from *flambe* 'a flame.'

flam·beau /ˈflamˌbō/ ▸*n.* (*pl.* **-beaus** or **-beaux** /-ˌbōz/) *historical* a flaming torch, esp. one made of several thick wicks dipped in wax. ■ a large candlestick with several branches. ▷mid 17th cent.: from French, from *flambe* 'a flame.'

flam·boy·ant1 /flamˈboiənt/ ▸*adj.* **1** (of a person or their behavior) tending to attract attention because of their exuberance, confidence, and stylishness: *a flamboyant display of aerobatics | she is outgoing and flamboyant, continuously talking and joking.* ■ (esp. of clothing) noticeable because brightly colored, highly patterned, or unusual in style. **2** *Architecture* of or denoting a style of French Gothic architecture marked by wavy flamelike tracery and ornate decoration. ▷mid 19th cent.: from French, literally 'flaming, blazing,' present participle of *flamboyer*, from *flambe* 'a flame.' **—flam·boy·ance** *n.* **—flam·boy·an·cy** /-ˈboiənsē/ *n.* **—flam·boy·ant·ly** *adv.*

flam·boy·ant2 ▸*n.* another term for ROYAL POINCIANA (see POINCIANA). ▷late 19th cent.: probably a noun use of the French adjective *flamboyant* 'blazing' (see FLAMBOYANT1).

flame /flām/ ▸*n.* **1** a hot glowing body of ignited gas that is generated by something on fire: *the flame of a candle | a sheet of flame blocked my escape.* **2** *figurative* used in similes and metaphors to refer to something resembling a flame in various respects, in particular: ■ a thing resembling a flame in heat, shape, or brilliance: *red and yellow bunting fluttering like flames in the breeze.* ■ a brilliant orange-red color: [in *combination*] *a* ***flame-red*** *trench coat.* ■ a thing compared to a flame's ability to burn fiercely or be extinguished: *the flame of hope burns brightly here.* ■ a very intense emotion: *the sound of his laughter fanned the flame of anger to new heights.* ■ a cause that generates passionate feelings: *her father had been* ***keeper of the*** *formalist* ***flame.*** ■ *Computing* a vitriolic or abusive message sent via electronic mail, typically in quick response to another message: *flames about inexperienced users posting stupid messages.*
▸*v.* [*intrans.*] burn and give off flames: *a great fire flamed in an open fireplace.* ■ [*trans.*] set (something) alight: *warm the whiskey slightly, pour over the lobster, and flame it.* ■ *figurative* shine or glow like a flame: *her thick hair flamed against the light.* ■ *figurative* (of an intense emotion) appear suddenly and fiercely: *hope flamed in her.* ■ (of a person's face) suddenly become red with intense emotion, esp. anger or embarrassment: *Jess's cheeks flamed.* ■ [*trans.*] *Computing* send (someone) abusive or vitriolic electronic mail messages, typically in a quick exchange.
▸*phrasal v.* □ **flame out** (of a jet engine) lose power through the extinction of the flame in the combustion chamber. ■ *informal* fail, esp. conspicuously: *journalists had seared him for flaming out in the second round of the Olympics.* ▷Middle English: from Old French *flame* (noun), *flamer* (verb), from Latin *flamma* 'a flame.' **—flame·less** *adj.* **—flame·like** /-ˌlīk/ *adj.* **—flam·er** *n.* (*Computing*). **—flam·y** /ˈflāmē/ *adj.*
▸PHRASES □ **burst into flame** (or **flames**) suddenly begin to burn fiercely: *the grass looked ready to burst into flame.* □ **go up in flames** be destroyed by fire: *last night two factories went up in flames.* □ **in flames** on fire; burning fiercely: *the plane plunged to the ground in flames.* □ **old flame** *informal* a former lover.

fla·men /ˈflāmən/ ▸*n.* (*pl.* **fla·mens** or **flam·i·nes** /ˈflaməˌnēz/) *Roman History* a priest serving a particular deity. ▷Middle English: Latin, literally 'priest.'

fla·men·co /fləˈmenGkō/ ▸*n.* a style of Spanish music, played esp. on the guitar and accompanied by singing and dancing. ■ a style of spirited, rhythmical dance performed to such music, often with castanets. ▷late 19th cent.: Spanish, 'like a gypsy,' literally 'Fleming,' from Middle Dutch *Vlaminc.*

flame·out /ˈflāˌmout/ ▸*n.* an instance of the flame in the combustion chamber of a jet engine being extinguished, with a resultant loss of power. ■ *informal* a complete or conspicuous failure: *his first-round flameout at the U.S. Open.*

flame·proof /ˈflāmˌpro͞of/ ▸*adj.* (esp. of a fabric) treated so as to be nonflammable. ■ (of cookware) able to be used either in an oven or on a stove: *a flameproof casserole.*
▸*v.* [*trans.*] make (something) flameproof.

flame stitch ▸ another term for BARGELLO.

flame·throw·er /ˈflāmˌTHrōər/ ▸*n.* a weapon that sprays out burning fuel.

flame tree ▸*n.* any of a number of trees with brilliant red flowers, in particular: • an Australian bottle tree (*Brachychiton acerifolius*, family Sterculiaceae). • another term for ROYAL POINCIANA (see POINCIANA).

flam·ing /ˈflāmiNG/ ▸*adj.* [*attrib.*] **1** burning fiercely and emitting flames: *they dragged her away from the flaming car.* ■ very hot: *flaming June.* ■ glowing with a bright orange or red color: *the flaming autumn maples of the St. Lawrence River valley.* ■ (of red or orange) brilliant or intense: *flaming red hair.* ■ (esp. of an argument) passionate: *Gloria's suddenly flaming jealousy.* **2** *informal* used for emphasis to express annoyance: *weeds can become a flaming nuisance.* **—flam·ing·ly** *adv.*

fla·min·go /fləˈmiNGgō/ ▸*n.* (*pl.* **-gos** or **-goes**) a tall wading bird with mainly pink or scarlet plumage and long legs and neck. It has a heavy bent bill that is held upside down in the water in order to filter-feed on small organisms. • Family Phoenicopteridae: three genera and four species, in particular the **greater flamingo** (*Phoenicopterus ruber*). ▷mid 16th cent.: from Spanish *flamengo*, earlier form of *flamenco* (see FLAMENCO); associated, because of its color, with Latin *flamma* 'a flame.'

greater flamingo

flam·ma·ble /ˈflaməbəl/ ▸*adj.* easily set on fire: *the use of highly flammable materials.* ▷early 19th cent.: from Latin *flammare*, from *flamma* 'a flame.' **—flam·ma·bil·i·ty** /ˌflaməˈbilətē/ *n.*

USAGE The words **flammable** and **inflammable** mean the same thing, but **flammable** is preferred to avoid confusion: see **usage** at INFLAMMABLE.

flam·mu·lat·ed owl /ˈflamyəˌlātəd/ ▸*n.* a small reddish-gray migratory American owl that sometimes occurs in loose colonies. • *Otus flammeolus*, family Strigidae.

flan /flan/ ▸*n.* **1** a baked dish consisting of an open-topped pastry case with a savory or sweet filling. ■ a sponge base with a sweet topping. **2** a disk of metal such as one from which a coin is made. ▷mid 19th cent.: from French (originally denoting a round cake) from Old French *flaon*, from medieval Latin *flado, fladon-*, of West Germanic origin; related to Dutch *vlade* 'custard.'

Flan·ders /ˈflandərz/ a region in the southwestern part of the Low Countries, now divided between Belgium, France, and the Netherlands. It was a powerful medieval principality and the scene of prolonged fighting during World War I.

flâ·ne·rie /ˌflän(ə)ˈrē/ ▸*n.* aimless idle behavior. ▷French, from *flâner* 'saunter, lounge.'

flâ·neur /fläˈnər; -ˈnœr/ (also **fla·neur**) ▸*n.* (*pl.* **flâ·neurs** *pronunc.* same) an idler or lounger. ▷French, from *flâner* 'saunter, lounge.'

flange /flanj/ ▸*n.* a projecting flat rim, collar, or rib on an object, serving to strengthen or attach or (on a wheel) to maintain position on a rail: *the flanges that held the tailpipe to the aircraft.* ▷late 17th cent.: perhaps based on Old French *flanchir* 'to bend.' **—flanged** *adj.* **—flange·less** *adj.*

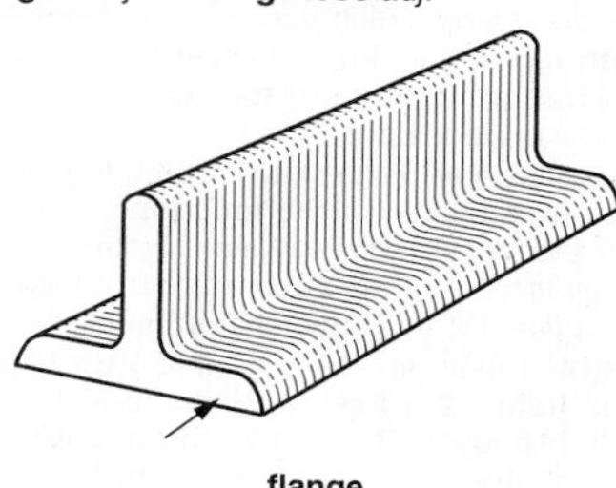

flange

flang·er /ˈflanjər/ ▸*n.* an electronic device that alters a sound signal by introducing a cyclically varying phase shift into one of two identical copies of the signal and recombining them, used esp. in popular music to alter the sound of an instrument.

flang·ing /ˈflanjiNG/ ▸*n.* **1** the provision of a flange or flanges on an object: *the rim displays the same flanging.* **2** the alteration of sound using a flanger.

flank /flaNGk/ ▸*n.* **1** the side of a person's or animal's body between the ribs and the hip: *leaning against his horse's flanks.* ■ a cut of meat from such a part of an animal: *a thick flank of beef on a spit | two pounds of flank.* ■ the side of something large, such as a mountain, building, or ship: *the northern flank of the volcano.* **2** the right or left side of a body of people such as an army, a naval force, or a soccer team: *the left flank of the Russian Third Army.* ■ the right or left side of a game board such as a chessboard.
▸*v.* [*trans.*] (often **be flanked**) be situated on each side of or on one side of (someone or something): *the fireplace is flanked by built-in bookshelves.* ■ [usu. as *adj.*] (**flanking**) guard or strengthen (a military force or position) from the side: *massive walls, defended by four flanking towers.* ■ [usu. as *adj.*] (**flanking**) attack down or from the sides, or rake with gunfire from the sides: *a flanking attack from the northeast.* ▷late Old English, from Old French *flanc*, of Germanic origin.

flank·er /ˈflaNGkər/ ▸*n.* **1** a person or thing situated on the flank of something, in particular: ■ *Football* an offensive back who lines up to the outside of an end. ■ *Military* a fortification guarding or menacing the side of a force or position. **2** *Brit., informal, dated* a trick; a swindle: *he's certainly* ***pulled a flanker on*** *the army.*

flan·nel /ˈflanl/ ▸*n.* **1** a kind of soft-woven fabric, typically made of wool or cotton and slightly milled and raised: [as *adj.*] *my longest, thickest flannel nightgown.* ■ (**flannels**) men's trousers made of such material. ■ short for FLANNELETTE. **2** *Brit.* a washcloth. **3** *Brit., informal* bland fluent talk indulged in to avoid addressing a difficult subject or situation directly: *a simple admittance of ignorance was much to be preferred to any amount of flannel.* ▷Middle English: probably from Welsh *gwlanen* 'woolen article,' from *gwlân* 'wool.'

flan·nel·board /ˈflanlˌbôrd/ ▸*n.* a board covered with flannel to which paper or cloth cutouts will stick, used as a toy or a teaching aid.

flan·nel cake ▸*n.* *dialect* a pancake.

flan·nel·ette /ˌflanlˈet/ ▸*n.* a napped cotton fabric resembling flannel: [as *adj.*] *a flannelette nightdress.*

flan·nel·mouth /ˈflanlˌmouTH/ ▸*n.* *informal* a person who talks too much, esp. in a boastful or deceitful way.

flap /flap/ ▸*v.* (**flapped, flap·ping**) [*trans.*] (of a bird) move (its wings) up and down when flying or preparing to fly: *a pheasant flapped its wings | [intrans.] gulls* ***flapped around*** *uttering their strange cries.* ■ [*intrans.*] (of something attached at one point or loosely fastened) flutter or wave around: *the tent bent with the gale, and the corners flapped furiously.* ■ move (one's arms or hands) up and down or back and forth: *she began flapping her arms to drive away the permeating cold.* ■ [*trans.*] strike or attempt to strike (something) loosely with one's hand, a cloth, or a broad implement, esp. to drive it away: *they flap away the flies with peacock tails.* ■ wave (something, esp. a cloth) around or at something or someone: *she flapped the duster angrily.*
▸*n.* **1** a piece of something thin, such as cloth, paper, or metal, hinged or attached only on one side, that covers an opening or hangs down from something: *the flap of the envelope | he pushed through the tent flap.* ■ a hinged or sliding section of an aircraft wing used to control lift: *flaps are normally moved by the hydraulics | a final approach at sixty knots with 45° of flap.* ■ the part of a dust jacket that folds inside a book's cover, on which a summary of the book or a biographical sketch of the author is typically printed: *I read a book jacket flap that said that the author lived with her husband in Connecticut.* ■ a large broad mushroom. ■ *Phonetics* a type of consonant produced by allowing the tip of the tongue to strike the alveolar ridge very briefly. **2** a movement of a wing or an arm from side to side or up and down: *the surviving bird made a few final despairing flaps.* ■ [in *sing.*] the sound of something making such a movement: *hear the coo of the dove, the flap of its wings.* **3** [in *sing.*] *informal* a state of agitation; a panic: *they're* ***in a flap*** *over who's going to take Henry's lectures.* ▷Middle English: probably imitative. **—flap·py** *adj.*

flap·doo·dle /ˈflapˌdo͞odl/ ▸*n.* *informal* nonsense: *people who are prey to dogmatic flapdoodle.* ■ a fool. ▷mid 19th cent.: an arbitrary formation.

flap·jack /ˈflapˌjak/ ▸*n.* a pancake. ▷from FLAP (in the dialect sense 'toss a pancake') + JACK1.

flap·pa·ble /ˈflapəbəl/ ▸*adj.* excitable and quick to lose one's composure: *he became totally flappable in her presence.*

flap·per /ˈflapər/ ▸*n.* **1** *informal* (in the 1920s) a fashionable young woman intent on enjoying herself and flouting conventional standards of behavior.

F

[late 19th cent.: probably from a dialect sense of the noun *flap*, 'a woman of loose character.'] **2** a thing that flaps, esp. a movable seal inside a toilet tank: *flush the tank to make sure that the flapper is not dropping.*

flap valve (also **flap·per valve**) ▸*n.* a valve opened and closed by a plate hinged at one side.

flare /fler/ ▸*n.* **1** a sudden brief burst of bright flame or light: *the flare of the match lit up his face.* ■ a device producing a bright flame, used esp. as a signal or marker: *a helicopter spotted a flare set off by the crew* | [as *adj.*] *a flare gun.* ■ [in *sing.*] a sudden burst of intense emotion: *she felt a flare of anger within her.* ■ *Astronomy* a sudden explosion in the chromosphere and corona of the sun or another star, resulting in an intense burst of radiation. See also SOLAR FLARE. ■ *Photography* extraneous illumination on film caused by internal reflection in the camera. **2** [in *sing.*] a gradual widening, esp. of a skirt or pants: *as you knit, add a flare or curve a hem.* ■ an upward and outward curve of a vessel's bow, designed to throw the water outward when under way.
▸*v.* [*intrans.*] **1** burn with a sudden intensity: *the blaze across the water flared* | *the bonfire crackled and* ***flared up.*** ■ (of a light or a person's eyes) glow with a sudden intensity: *her eyes flared at the stinging insult.* ■ (of an emotion) suddenly become manifest in a person or their expression: *alarm flared in her eyes* | *tempers flared.* ■ (**flare up**) (of an illness or chronic medical complaint) recur unexpectedly and cause further discomfort: *Tracy's pain has flared up again, this time almost beyond enduring.* ■ (esp. of an argument, conflict, or trouble) suddenly become more violent or intense: *in 1943 the Middle East crisis* ***flared up*** *again.* ■ (**flare up**) (of a person) suddenly become angry: *she flared up, shouting at Jeff.* **2** [often as *adj.*] (**flared**) gradually become wider at one end: *a flared skirt* | *the dress flared out into huge a train.* ■ (of a person's nostrils) dilate: *his head lifted, his nostrils flaring.* ■ [*trans.*] (of a person) cause (the nostrils) to dilate. ▷mid 16th cent. (in the sense 'spread out (one's hair)'): of unknown origin. Current senses date from the 17th cent.

flare star ▸*n.* *Astronomy* a dwarf star that displays spasmodic outbursts of radiation, believed to be due to extremely intense flares.

flare-up ▸*n.* a sudden outburst of something, esp. violence or a medical condition: *a flare-up between the two countries.*

flash /flaSH/ ▸*v.* **1** [*intrans.*] (of a light or something that reflects light) shine in a bright but brief, sudden, or intermittent way: *the lights started flashing* | [as *adj.*] (**flashing**) *a police car with a flashing light.* ■ [*trans.*] cause to shine briefly or suddenly: *the oncoming car flashed its lights.* ■ [*trans.*] shine or show a light to send (a signal): *red lights started to flash a warning.* ■ [*trans.*] give (a swift or sudden look): *Carrie flashed a glance in his direction* | [with *two objs.*] *she flashed him a withering look.* ■ express a sudden burst of emotion, esp. anger, with such a look: *she glared at him, her eyes flashing.* **2** [*trans.*] display (an image, words, or information) suddenly on a television or computer screen or electronic sign, typically briefly or repeatedly: *suddenly the screen flashes a message.* ■ [*intrans.*] (of an image or message) be displayed in such a way: *the election results flashed on the screen.* ■ *informal* hold up or show (something, often proof of one's identity) quickly before replacing it: *she opened her purse and flashed her ID card.* ■ *informal* make a conspicuous display of (something) so as to impress or attract attention: *they all flash their money around.* ■ [*intrans.*] [often as *n.*] (**flashing**) *informal* (esp. of a man) show one's genitals briefly in public. **3** [*intrans.*] move or pass very quickly: *a look of terror flashed across Kirov's face* | *the scenery flashed by.* ■ (of a thought or memory) suddenly come into or pass through the mind: *another stray thought* ***flashed through*** *her mind.* ■ [*trans.*] send (news or information) swiftly by means of telegraphy or telecommunications: *the story was* ***flashed around*** *the world.*
▸*phrasal v.* □ **flash back** (of a person's thoughts or mind) briefly and suddenly recall a previous time or incident: *her thoughts immediately flashed back to last night.* □ **flash over** make an electric circuit by sparking across a gap. ■ (of a fire) spread instantly across a gap because of intense heat.
▸*n.* **1** a sudden brief burst of bright light or a sudden glint from a reflective surface: *the grenade exploded with a yellow flash of light* | *a lightning flash.* ■ a bright patch of color, often one used for decoration or identification: *orange flashes adorn the aircraft.* **2** a thing that occurs suddenly and within a brief period of time, in particular: ■ a sudden instance or manifestation of a quality, understanding, or humor: *she had a* ***flash*** *of inspiration.* ■ a fleeting glimpse of something, esp. something vivid or eye-catching: *the blue flash of a kingfisher.* ■ a news flash. **3** a camera attachment that produces a brief very bright light, used for taking photographs in poor light: *an electronic flash* | *if in any doubt, use flash* | [as *adj.*] *flash photography.* **4** excess plastic or metal forced between facing surfaces as two halves of a mold close up, forming a thin projection on the finished object.
▸*adj. informal, chiefly Brit.* **1** (of a thing) ostentatiously expensive, elaborate, or up to date: *a flash new car.* ■ (of a person) superficially attractive because stylish and full of brash charm: *he was carrying this money around and trying to be flash.* **2** *archaic* of or relating to thieves, prostitutes, or the underworld, esp. their language. **3** *Brit.* counterfeit. ▷Middle English (in the sense 'splash water about'): probably imitative; compare with FLUSH[1] and SPLASH.
▸*PHRASES* □ **flash in the pan** a thing or person whose sudden but brief success is not repeated or repeatable: *our start to the season was just a flash in the pan.* [with allusion to the firing of a flintlock weapon, the ineffective flash that results from the ignition of the priming powder in the gunlock's pan without the desired ignition of the main charge in the gun's chamber.] □ **in** (or **like**) **a flash** very quickly; immediately: *she was out of the back door in a flash.* □ (**as**) **quick as a flash** (esp. of a person's response or reaction) very quickly: *quick as a flash, he was at her side.*

flash·back /ˈflaSH,bak/ ▸*n.* a scene in a movie, novel, etc., set in a time earlier than the main story: *in a series of flashbacks, we follow the pair through their teenage years.* ■ a sudden and disturbing vivid memory of an event in the past, typically as the result of psychological trauma or taking LSD.

flash·board /ˈflaSH,bôrd/ ▸*n.* a board used for increasing the depth of water behind a dam.

flash·bulb /ˈflaSH,bəlb/ ▸*n.* a light bulb that flashes in order to illuminate a photographic subject, of a type that is used only once: *suddenly flashbulbs were popping and whole rolls of film were squeezed off in seconds.*

flash burn ▸*n.* a burn caused by sudden intense heat, as from a nuclear explosion.

flash card ▸*n.* a card containing a small amount of information, held up for students to see, as an aid to learning.

flash·cube /ˈflaSH,kyo͞ob/ ▸*n. chiefly historical* a set of four flashbulbs arranged in a cube and operated in turn.

flash drive ▸*n.* *Computing* a data storage device containing flash memory that has no moving parts and does not need batteries or a power supply. Also see USB FLASH DRIVE.

flash·er /ˈflaSHər/ ▸*n.* **1** an automatic device causing a light to flash on and off rapidly. ■ a signal using such a device, for example a car's turn signal. **2** *informal* a person, esp. a man, who exposes his genitals in public.

flash flood ▸*n.* a sudden local flood, typically due to heavy rain.

flash-freeze ▸*v.* [*trans.*] freeze (food or other material) rapidly so as to prevent the formation of ice crystals: *the steaks were flash-frozen.* —**flash-freez·er** *n.*

flash·gun /ˈflaSH,gən/ ▸*n.* a device that gives a brief flash of intense light, used for taking photographs indoors or in poor light.

flash·ing /ˈflaSHiNG/ ▸*n.* a strip of metal used to stop water from penetrating the junction of a roof with another surface: *flashings around chimneys* | *the lead flashing on the roof.* ▷late 18th cent.: from the earlier synonym *flash* (of unknown origin) + -ING[1].

flash·light /ˈflaSH,līt/ ▸*n.* **1** a battery-operated portable light. **2** a flashing light used for signals and in lighthouses. **3** a light giving an intense flash, used for photographing at night or indoors.

flash mem·o·ry ▸*n.* *Computing* memory that retains data in the absence of a power supply: *the diagnostics are kept in flash memory.*

flash·mob /ˈflaSH,mäb/ ▸*n.* a sudden mass gathering, unanticipated except by participants who communicate electronically: *the flashmob is the idiot child of our instant-communication age.*
▸*v.* (**-mobbed, -mob·bing**) [*intrans.*] hold or subject to a flashmob.

flash·o·ver /ˈflaSH,ōvər/ ▸*n.* **1** a high-voltage electric short circuit made through the air between exposed conductors. **2** an instance of a fire spreading very rapidly across a gap because of intense heat.

flash pho·tol·y·sis ▸*n.* *Chemistry* the use of an intense flash of light to bring about decomposition or dissociation in a heated gas, usually as a means of generating and studying short-lived molecules.

flash point (also **flash·point**) ▸*n.* **1** a place, event, or time at which trouble, such as violence or anger, flares up: *the flash point of the conflagration is just blocks away.* **2** *Chemistry* the temperature at which a particular organic compound gives off sufficient vapor to ignite in air.

flash suit ▸*n.* a set of heatproof protective clothing.

flash tube ▸*n.* a gas discharge tube used, esp. in photography, to provide an electronic flash when a current is suddenly passed through it.

flash weld·ing ▸*n.* a welding process in which the ends of two metal parts are fused by heat generated from their resistance to an electric current and applied pressure.

flash·y /ˈflaSHē/ ▸*adj.* (**flash·i·er, flash·i·est**) ostentatiously attractive or impressive: *he always had a flashy car.* —**flash·i·ly** /ˈflaSHəlē/ *adv.* —**flash·i·ness** /ˈflaSHēnis/ *n.*

flask /flask/ ▸*n.* a container or bottle, in particular: ■ a narrow-necked glass container, typically conical or spherical, used in a laboratory to hold reagents or samples. ■ a metal container for storing a small amount of liquor, typically to be carried in one's pocket: *his silver flask of brandy.* ■ a narrow-necked bulbous glass container, typically with a covering of wickerwork, for storing wine or oil. ■ a small glass bottle for perfume. ■ a vacuum flask. ■ the contents of any of these containers: *a* ***flask of*** *coffee.* ■ *historical* short for POWDER FLASK. ▷Middle English (in the sense 'cask'): from medieval Latin *flasca*. From the mid 16th cent. the word denoted a case of horn, leather, or metal for carrying gunpowder. The sense 'glass container' (late 17th cent.) was influenced by Italian *fiasco*, from medieval Latin *flasco*. Compare with FLAGON.

flat[1] /flat/ ▸*adj.* (**flat·ter, flat·test**) **1** smooth and even; without marked lumps or indentations: *a flat wall* | *trim the surface of the cake to make it completely flat.* ■ (of land) without hills: *thirty-five acres of flat countryside.* ■ (of an expanse of water) calm and without waves. ■ not sloping: *the flat roof of a garage.* ■ having a broad level surface but little height or depth; shallow: *a flat rectangular box* | *a flat cap.* ■ (of shoes) without heels or with very low heels. ■ (of a woman) having small breasts. **2** lacking interest or emotion; dull and lifeless: *"I'm sorry," he said, in a flat voice* | *her drawings were flat and unimaginative.* ■ (of a person) without energy; dispirited: *his sense of intoxication wore off until he felt flat and weary.* ■ (of a market, prices, etc.) showing little activity; sluggish: *cash flow was flat at $214 million* | *flat sales in the drinks industry.* ■ (of a sparkling drink) having lost its effervescence: *flat champagne.* ■ (of something kept inflated, esp. a tire) having lost some or all of its air, typically because of a puncture: *you've got a flat tire.* ■ (of a color) uniform: *the dress was a deadly, flat shade of gray.* ■ (of a photographic print or negative) lacking contrast. **3** [*attrib.*] (of a fee, wage, or price) the same in all cases, not varying with changed conditions or in particular cases: *a $30 flat fare.* See also FLAT RATE. ■ (of a denial, contradiction, or refusal) completely definite and firm; absolute: *his statement was a flat denial that he had misbehaved.* **4** (of musical sound) below true or normal pitch. ■ [*postpositive*, in *combination*] (of a note) a semitone lower than a specified note: *the double basses' opening low E-flat* | *you never have to change key from B-flat major.* ■ (of a key) having a flat or flats in the signature. **5** (**Flat**) of or relating to flat racing: *the Flat season.*
▸*adv.* **1** in or to a horizontal position: *he was lying flat on his back* | *she had been knocked flat by the blast.* ■ lying in close juxtaposition, esp. against another surface: *his black curly hair was blown flat across his skull.* ■ so as to become smooth and even: *I hammered the metal flat.* **2** *informal* completely; absolutely: *I'm turning you down flat* | [as *submodifier*] *she was going to be flat broke in a couple of days.* ■ after a phrase expressing a period of time to emphasize how quickly something can be done or has been done: *you can prepare a healthy meal* ***in ten minutes flat.*** **3** below the true or normal pitch of musical sound: *it wasn't a question of singing flat, but of simply singing the wrong notes.*
▸*n.* **1** [in *sing.*] the flat part of something: *she placed the flat of her hand over her glass.* **2** a flat object, in particular: ■ (often **flats**) an upright section of painted stage scenery mounted on a frame. ■ *informal* a flat tire. ■ a shallow container in which seedlings are grown and sold. ■ (often **flats**) a shoe with a very low heel or no heel. ■ a railroad car with a flat floor and

no sides or roof; a flatcar. **3** (usu. **flats**) an area of low level ground, esp. near water: *the Utah salt flats.* See also MUDFLAT. **4** a musical note lowered a semitone below natural pitch. ■ the sign ( ) indicating this.

▸*v.* (**flat·ted**, **flat·ting**) [*trans.*] **1** [usu. as *adj.*] (**flatted**) *Music* lower (a note) by a semitone: *"blue" harmony emphasizing the flatted third and seventh.* **2** *archaic* make flat; flatten: *flat the loaves down.* ▷Middle English: from Old Norse *flatr*; related to PLANT, PLATY-, PLAZA. —**flat·ness** *n.* —**flat·tish** /ˈflatiSH/ *adj.*

▸*PHRASES* □ **fall flat** fail completely to produce the intended or expected effect: *his jokes fell flat.* □ **fall flat on one's face** fall over forward. ■ *figurative* fail in an embarrassingly obvious way: *the president could fall flat on his face if the economy doesn't start improving soon.* □ (**as**) **flat as a pancake** see PANCAKE. □ **flat out 1** as fast or as hard as possible: *the whole team is working flat out to satisfy demand* | [as *adj.*] (**flat-out**) *the album lacks the flat-out urgency of its predecessor.* **2** *informal* without hesitation or reservation; unequivocally: *in those early days I'd just flat out vote against foreign aid* | [as *adj.*] (**flat-out**) *flat-out perjury.* **3** lying completely stretched out, esp. asleep or exhausted: *she was lying flat out on her pink bath towel.* □ **that's flat** *informal* used to indicate that one has reached a decision and will not be persuaded to change one's mind: *he won't go into a home and that's flat.*

flat[2] ▸*n.* British term for APARTMENT. ▷early 19th cent. (denoting a floor or story): alteration of obsolete *flet* 'floor, dwelling,' of Germanic origin and related to FLAT[1]. —**flat·let** /-lət/ *n.*

flat arch ▸*n.* *Architecture* an arch with a flat lower or inner curve. See also JACK ARCH.

flat·bed /ˈflat,bed/ ▸*n.* a long flat area or structure: *the flatbed of a truck.* ■ a vehicle with a flat load-carrying area: [as *adj.*] *a flatbed truck.* ■ [as *adj.*] denoting a letterpress printing machine in which the form is carried on a horizontal surface: *a flatbed press.* ■ *Computing* a scanner, plotter, or other device that keeps paper flat during use: [as *adj.*] *the flatbed technology lets paper enter and exit the printer directly.*

flat·bed press ▸*n.* a press in which a rotating cylinder equipped with paper makes contact with a horizontal printing surface.

flat·boat /ˈflat,bōt/ ▸*n.* a cargo boat with a flat bottom for use in shallow water.

flat·bread /ˈflat,bred/ ▸*n.* flat, thin, often unleavened bread.

flat·bug /ˈflat,bəg/ ▸*n.* a broad flat bug that typically lives on or under loose bark. • Family Aradidae, suborder Heteroptera: several species.

Flat·bush /ˈflat,bo͝osh/ a residential and commercial section of central Brooklyn in New York City.

flat·car /ˈflat,kär/ ▸*n.* a railroad freight car without a roof or sides.

flat-chest·ed ▸*adj.* (of a woman) having small breasts.

flat-fell ▸*v.* see FELL[2] (sense 2).

flat file ▸*n.* *Computing* a file having no internal hierarchy. ■ [as *adj.*] denoting a system using such files: *a flat-file database.*

flat·fish /ˈflat,fiSH/ ▸*n.* (*pl.* same or **-fish·es**) a flattened marine fish that swims on its side with both eyes on the upper side. They live typically on the seabed and are colored to resemble it. • Order Pleuronectiformes: several families, in particular Bothidae (left-eye flounders), Pleuronectidae (right-eye flounders), and Soleidae (soles).

flat·foot /ˈflat,fo͝ot/ ▸*n.* (also **flat foot**) a condition in which the foot has an arch that is lower than usual. ■ (*pl.* **-foots** or **-feet** /-,fēt/) *informal, dated* a police officer.

flat-foot·ed ▸*adj.* **1** having flat feet: *a flat-footed, overweight cop.* **2** having one's feet flat on the ground: *he landed with a flat-footed thud* | [as *adv.*] *thudding flat-footed through the lane.* ■ *informal* unable to move quickly and smoothly; clumsy: *getting caught in flat-footed ignorance can be uncomfortable.* ■ *informal* not clever or imaginative; uninspired: *he has little space for anecdote, but the text is no flat-footed catalog.* —**flat-foot·ed·ly** *adv.* —**flat-foot·ed·ness** *n.*

▸*PHRASE* □ **catch someone flat-footed** *informal* take someone by surprise: *the rise of regional conflicts has caught military planners flat-footed.*

flat-four ▸*adj.* (of an engine) having four horizontal cylinders, two on each side of the crankshaft.

▸*n.* an engine of this type.

flat·head /ˈflat,hed/ ▸*n.* **1** [often as *adj.*] (**Flathead**) a member of a native people of western Montana.■ the Salishan language spoken by those people. ■ a member of certain other North American Indian peoples, such as the Chinook and Choctaw, who practiced or were thought to practice head-flattening. **2** *informal* a foolish person. **3** an edible tropical marine fish that has a pointed flattened head with the eyes positioned on the top, typically burrowing in the seabed with just the eyes showing. • Family Platycephalidae: several genera and species. **4** (of an engine) having the valves and spark plugs in the cylinder block rather than the cylinder head, which is essentially a flat plate. ■ (of a vehicle) having such an engine. **5** [as *adj.*] (of a screw) countersunk.

Flat·head Range a range of the Rocky Mountains in northwestern Montana. The **Flathead River** flows through the area.

flat·i·ron /ˈflat,īərn/ ▸*n.* *historical* an iron that was heated externally and used for pressing clothes.

flat·land /ˈflat,land/ ▸*n.* **1** (also **flatlands**) land with no hills, valleys, or mountains: *another 100 miles of flatland.* **2** [as *place name*] an imagined land existing in only two dimensions. [from the title of a book, *Flatland,* (1884) by E. A. Abbot.] **3** *Brit.* an urban area in which the majority of dwellings are flats (apartments): *London flatland.* —**flat·land·er** *n.* *she's been enthralling flatlanders with her tales of the mountains.*

flat-leafed pars·ley (also **flat-leaf pars·ley**) ▸*n.* parsley of a variety with large flat leaves. Also called ITALIAN PARSLEY.

flat·line /ˈflat,līn/ ▸*v.* [*intrans.*] *informal* (of a person) die. ▷1980s: from FLAT[1] + LINE[1] (with reference to the continuous straight line displayed on a heart monitor, indicating death). —**flat·lin·er** *n.*

flat·ly /ˈflatlē/ ▸*adv.* **1** showing little interest or emotion: *"You'd better go," she said flatly.* **2** in a firm and unequivocal manner; absolutely: *they flatly refused to play* | [as *submodifier*] *his view seems to me flatly contrary to our evidence.* **3** in a smooth and even way: *I applied the paint flatly.* ■ *Photography* without marked contrast of light and dark: *the photographs were lit very flatly.*

flat·mate /ˈflat,māt/ ▸*n.* *Brit.* a person who shares a flat (apartment) with others: *my flatmate moved out a month ago.*

flat·pack ▸*n.* *Electronics* a package for an integrated circuit consisting of a rectangular sealed unit with a number of horizontal metal pins protruding from its sides.

flat race ▸*n.* a horse race over level ground, as opposed to a steeplechase or hurdles. —**flat rac·ing** *n.*

flat rate ▸*n.* a charge that is the same in all cases, not varying in proportion with something: *a system of charging a flat rate per household* | [as *adj.*] *replacing the fee-for-service system with flat-rate payments.* ■ a rate of taxation that is not progressive, but remains at the same proportion on all amounts.

flat sheet ▸*n.* an ordinary sheet for a bed as distinct from a fitted one.

flat spin ▸*n.* *Aeronautics* a spin in which an aircraft descends in tight circles while remaining almost horizontal.

flat·ten /ˈflatn/ ▸*v.* **1** make or become flat or flatter: [*trans.*] *spoon the mixture into the pan, flatten into cakes, and fry until brown* | [*intrans.*] *the ground* ***flattened out*** *and became marshy* | [as *adj.*] (**flattened**) *they were dancing on the flattened grass.* ■ [*trans.*] press (oneself or one's body) against a surface, typically to get away from something or to let someone pass: *they* ***flattened themselves*** *on the pavement as a bomb came whistling down.* ■ [*trans.*] *Music* lower (a note) in pitch by a half step. **2** [*trans.*] raze (a building or settlement) to the ground: *the hurricane flattened thousands of homes.* ■ *informal* knock someone down with power and vigor: *once I'm in the ring, I know I can flatten him.* ■ *informal* defeat (someone) completely, esp. in a sports contest.

▸*phrasal v.* □ **flatten out 1** (of an increasing quantity or rate) show a less marked rise; slow down. **2** make an aircraft fly horizontally after a dive or climb: *he flattened out and made a fine three-point landing.* —**flat·ten·er** *n.*

flat·ter /ˈflatər/ ▸*v.* [*trans.*] lavish insincere praise and compliments upon (someone), esp. to further one's own interests: *she was flattering him to avoid doing what he wanted.* ■ give an unrealistically favorable impression of: *the portraitist flatters his sitter to the detriment of his art.* ■ (usu. **be flattered**) make (someone) feel honored and pleased: [*trans.*] *I was very flattered to be given the commission* | [*trans.*] *at least I am flattered that you don't find me boring.* ■ (**flatter oneself**) make oneself feel pleased by believing something favorable about oneself, typically something that is unfounded: [with *clause*] *I flatter myself I'm the best dressed man here.* ■ (of a color or a style of clothing) make (someone) appear more attractive or to the best advantage: *the muted fuchsia shade flattered her pale skin.* ■ *archaic* please (the ear or eye): *the beauty of the stone flattered the young clergyman's eyes.* ▷Middle English: perhaps a back-formation from FLATTERY. —**flat·ter·er** *n.*

flat·ter·ing /ˈflatəriNG/ ▸*adj.* (of a person or their remarks) full of praise and compliments: *the article began with some flattering words about us.* ■ pleasing; gratifying: [with *infinitive*] *it was flattering to have a pretty girl like Frances so obviously fond of him.* ■ (esp. of a garment or color) enhancing someone's appearance: *I don't think anything sleeveless is very flattering.* ■ (of a picture or portrait) giving an unrealistically favorable impression of someone or something: *that's a flattering picture of him.* —**flat·ter·ing·ly** *adv.*

flat·ter·y /ˈflatərē/ ▸*n.* (*pl.* **-ter·ies**) excessive and insincere praise, esp. that given to further one's own interests: *his healthy distrust of courtiers' flattery.* ▷Middle English: from Old French *flaterie,* from *flater* 'stroke, flatter,' probably of Germanic origin and related to FLAT[1].

flat·top /ˈflat,täp/ ▸*n.* **1** *informal* an aircraft carrier. **2** a man's hairstyle in which the hair is cropped short so that it bristles up into a flat surface: *a blond flattop and a faint blond mustache.*

flat·u·lent /ˈflaCHələnt/ ▸*adj.* suffering from or marked by an accumulation of gas in the alimentary canal: *treat flatulent cows with caustic soda.* ■ related to or causing this condition: *the flatulent effect of beans.* ■ *figurative* inflated or pretentious in speech or writing: *the days of flatulent oratory are gone.* ▷late 16th cent.: via French from modern Latin *flatulentus,* from Latin *flatus* 'blowing' (see FLATUS). —**flat·u·lence** *n.* —**flat·u·len·cy** *n.* —**flat·u·lent·ly** *adv.*

fla·tus /ˈflātəs/ ▸*n.* *formal* gas in or from the stomach or intestines, produced by swallowing air or by bacterial fermentation. ▷mid 17th cent.: from Latin, literally 'blowing,' from *flare* 'to blow.'

flat·ware /ˈflat,wer/ ▸*n.* eating utensils such as knives, forks, and spoons. ■ relatively flat dishes such as plates and saucers. The opposite of HOLLOWARE.

flat·worm /ˈflat,wərm/ ▸*n.* a worm of a phylum that includes the planarians together with the parasitic flukes and tapeworms. They are distinguished by having a simple flattened body that lacks blood vessels, and a digestive tract that, if present, has a single opening. • Phylum Platyhelminthes: several classes.

flat-wo·ven ▸*adj.* (of a carpet or rug) woven so as not to form a projecting pile. —**flat-weave** *n.*

Flau·bert /flōˈber/, Gustave (1821–80), French novelist and short-story writer. A dominant figure in the French realist school, he is noted for *Madame Bovary* (1857), his first published novel.

flaunt /flônt; flänt/ ▸*v.* [*trans.*] display (something) ostentatiously, esp. in order to provoke envy or admiration or to show defiance: *newly rich consumers eager to flaunt their prosperity.* ■ (**flaunt oneself**) dress or behave in a sexually provocative way. ▷mid 16th cent.: of unknown origin. —**flaunt·er** *n.* —**flaunt·y** *adj.*

▸*PHRASE* □ **if you've got it, flaunt it** *informal* one should make a conspicuous and confident show of one's wealth or attributes rather than be modest about them.

USAGE **Flaunt** and **flout** may sound similar but they have different meanings. **Flaunt** means 'display ostentatiously,' as in *tourists who liked to flaunt their wealth,* while **flout** means 'openly disregard (a rule or convention),' as in *new recruits growing their hair and flouting convention.* It is a common error, since probably around the 1940s, to use **flaunt** when **flout** is intended, as in *the young woman had been* ***flaunting*** *the rules and regulations.*

flau·tist /ˈflôtist; ˈflou-/ ▸*n.* a flutist. ▷mid 19th cent. (superseding 17th-cent. *flutist* in British English use): from Italian *flautista,* from *flauto* 'flute.'

fla·va·none /ˈflāvə,nōn/ ▸*n.* a colorless, crystalline derivative of flavone.

fla·ves·cent /fləˈvesənt/ ▸*adj.* yellowish or turning yellow. ▷mid 19th cent.: from Latin *flavescent-* 'turning yellow,' from the verb *flavescere,* from *flavus* 'yellow.'

Fla·vi·an /ˈflāvēən/ ▸*adj.* of or relating to a dynasty (AD 69–96) of Roman emperors including Vespasian and his sons Titus and Domitian.
▸*n.* a member of this dynasty. ▷from Latin *Flavianus*, from *Flavius*, a given name used by this dynasty.

fla·vin /ˈflāvin/ ▸*n.* *Biochemistry* any of a group of naturally occurring pigments including riboflavin. They have a tricyclic aromatic molecular structure. ▷mid 19th cent.: from Latin *flavus* 'yellow' + **-IN**[1].

fla·vine /ˈflāˌvēn/ ▸*n.* **1** *Medicine* an antiseptic derived from acridine. **2** *Chemistry* another term for **QUERCETIN**. ▷early 20th cent.: from Latin *flavus* 'yellow' + **-INE**[4].

fla·vi·vi·rus /ˈflāvəˌvīrəs/ ▸*n.* a virus whose genome consists of positive RNA, that is capable of reproducing in its arthropod vector, and that causes a number of serious human diseases including yellow fever, dengue, Japanese encephalitis, and West Nile virus. • Family *Flaviviridae*, three genera.

fla·vone /ˈflāˌvōn/ ▸*n.* *Chemistry* a colorless crystalline compound that is the basis of a number of white or yellow plant pigments. • A tricyclic aromatic compound; chem. formula: $C_{15}H_{10}O_2$. ■ any of these pigments. ▷late 19th cent.: from Latin *flavus* 'yellow' + **-ONE**.

fla·vo·noid /ˈflāvəˌnoid/ ▸*n.* *Chemistry* any of a large class of plant pigments having a structure based on or similar to that of flavone.

fla·vo·pro·tein /ˌflāvəˈprōˌtēn; -ˈprōtēən/ ▸*n.* *Biochemistry* any of a class of conjugated proteins that contain flavins and are involved in oxidation reactions in cells. ▷1930s: blend of **FLAVIN** and **PROTEIN**.

fla·vor /ˈflāvər/ (*Brit.* **fla·vour**) ▸*n.* **1** the distinctive quality of a particular food or drink as perceived by the taste buds and the sense of smell: *the chips come in pizza and barbecue flavors.* ■ the general quality of taste in a food: *no other cracker adds so much flavor to cheese or peanut butter.* ■ a substance used to alter or enhance the taste of food or drink; a flavoring: *we use vanilla and almond flavors.* ■ [in sing.] *figurative* an indefinable distinctive quality of something: *this year's seminars have a European flavor.* ■ [in sing.] *figurative* an indication of the essential character of something: *the extracts give* **a flavor of** *the content and tone of the conversation.* **2** *Physics* a quantized property of quarks that differentiates them into at least six varieties (up, down, charmed, strange, top, bottom). Compare with **COLOR**.
▸*v.* [*trans.*] alter or enhance the taste of (food or drink) by adding a particular ingredient: *they use a wide range of spices to flavor their foods* | *chunks of chicken flavored with herbs.* ■ *figurative* give a distinctive quality to: *the faint exasperation that had flavored her tone.* ▷late Middle English (in the sense 'fragrance, aroma'): from Old French *flaor*, perhaps based on a blend of Latin *flatus* 'blowing' and *foetor* 'stench'; the *-v-* appears to have been introduced in Middle English by association with **SAVOR**. Sense 1 dates from the late 17th cent. **—fla·vor·ful** /-fəl/ *adj.* **—fla·vor·less** *adj.* **—fla·vor·some** /-səm/ *adj.*
▸*PHRASE* □ **flavor of the month** a person or thing that enjoys a short period of great popularity: *for many law firms, Hong Kong was a flavor of the month.*

fla·vored /ˈflāvərd/ (*Brit.* **fla·voured**) ▸*adj.* (of food or drink) having a particular type of taste: [in *combination*] *the peanut oil is light but fairly full-flavored.* ■ (of food or drink) having been given a particular taste by the addition of a flavoring: *a flavored drink* | [in *combination*] *chicken breasts prepoached in lemon-flavored stock.* ■ [in *combination*] *figurative* having a particular distinctive quality: *the band knocked out some fine rock 'n' roll-flavored singles.*

fla·vor en·hanc·er ▸*n.* a chemical additive, e.g., monosodium glutamate, used to intensify the flavor of food.

fla·vor·ing /ˈflāvəriNG/ (*Brit.* **flavouring**) ▸*n.* a substance used to give a different, stronger, or more agreeable taste to food or drink: *vanilla flavoring* | *mustard has been used as a flavoring for thousands of years.*

fla·vor·ous /ˈflāvərəs/ ▸*adj.* *dated* having a pleasant or pungent flavor.

flaw[1] /flô/ ▸*n.* a mark, fault, or other imperfection that mars a substance or object: *plates with flaws in them were sold at the outlet store.* See note at **FAULT**. ■ a fault or weakness in a person's character: *he had his flaws, but he was still a great teacher.* ■ a mistake or shortcoming in a plan, theory, or legal document that causes it to fail or reduces its effectiveness: *there were fundamental* **flaws in** *the case for reforming local government.*
▸*v.* [*trans.*] (usu. **be flawed**) (of an imperfection) mar, weaken, or invalidate (something): *the computer game was flawed by poor programming.* ▷Middle English: perhaps from Old Norse *flaga* 'slab'; see **FLAG**[2]. The original sense was 'a flake of snow,' later, 'a fragment or splinter,' hence 'a defect or imperfection'(late 15th cent.).

flaw[2] ▸*n.* *poetic/literary* a squall of wind; a short storm. ▷early 16th cent.

flawed /flôd/ ▸*adj.* (of a substance or object) blemished, damaged, or imperfect in some way: *flawed crystals.* ■ (of something abstract) containing a mistake, weakness, or fault: *a flawed strategy.* ■ (of a person) having a weakness in character: *a flawed hero.*

flaw·less /ˈflôləs/ ▸*adj.* without any blemishes or imperfections; perfect: *her brown flawless skin.* ■ without any mistakes or shortcomings: *he greeted her in almost flawless English.* ■ (of a person) lacking any faults or weaknesses of character. **—flaw·less·ly** *adv.* **—flaw·less·ness** *n.*

flax /flaks/ ▸*n.* a blue-flowered herbaceous plant that is cultivated for its seed (linseed) and for textile fiber made from its stalks. • *Linum usitatissimum*, family Linaceae. ■ textile fiber obtained from this plant: *a mill for the preparation and spinning of flax.* ■ used in names of other plants of the flax family (e.g., **purging flax**) or plants that yield similar fiber (e.g., **false flax**). ▷Old English *flæx*; related to Dutch *vlas* and German *Flachs*, from an Indo-European root shared by Latin *plectere* and Greek *plekein* 'to plait, twist.'

flax·en /ˈflaksən/ ▸*adj.* of flax. ■ (esp. of hair) of the pale yellow color of dressed flax: *her long flaxen hair.*

flax·seed /ˈflak(s)ˌsēd/ ▸*n.* another term for **LINSEED**. ■ a pupa of the Hessian fly, which resembles a seed of flax.

flay /flā/ ▸*v.* [*trans.*] peel the skin off (a corpse or carcass): *one shoulder had been flayed to reveal the muscles.* ■ peel (the skin) off a corpse or carcass: *she flayed the white skin from the flesh.* ■ whip or beat (someone) so harshly as to remove their skin: *Matthew flayed them viciously with a branch.* ■ *figurative* criticize severely and brutally: *he flayed the government for not moving fast enough on economic reform.* ■ *figurative* extort or exact money or belongings from (someone): *plundering cities and temples and flaying the people with requisitions.* ▷Old English *flēan*, of Germanic origin; related to Middle Dutch *vlaen*. **—flay·er** *n.*

F lay·er ▸*n.* the highest and most strongly ionized region of the ionosphere. ▷1920s: arbitrary use of *F* + **LAYER**.

fld. ▸*abbr.* ■ field. ■ fluid.

fl dr ▸*abbr.* fluid dram.

cat flea

flea /flē/ ▸*n.* a small wingless jumping insect that feeds on the blood of mammals and birds. It sometimes transmits diseases through its bite, including plague and myxomatosis. • Order Siphonaptera: several families and many species, including the **human flea** (*Pulex irritans*) and the **cat flea** (*Ctenocephalides felis*). ■ short for **FLEA BEETLE**. ■ a water flea (see **DAPHNIA**). ▷Old English *flēa*, *flēah*, of Germanic origin; related to Dutch *vlo* and German *Floh*.
▸*PHRASE* □ **a flea in one's ear** a sharp reproof: *she expected to be* **sent away with a flea in her ear**.

flea·bag /ˈflēˌbag/ ▸*n.* *informal* a seedy, run-down hotel or lodging house. ■ a shabby and unpleasant person or thing.

flea·bane /ˈflēˌbān/ ▸*n.* a herbaceous plant of the daisy family, reputed to drive away fleas. • *Erigeron*, *Pulicaria*, and other genera, family Compositae: in particular the pink-flowered **common** (or **Philadelphia**) **fleabane** (*E. philadelphicus*) and the white-flowered **daisy fleabane** (*E. annus*).

flea bee·tle ▸*n.* a small jumping leaf beetle that can be a pest of plants such as crucifers. • *Phyllotreta* and other genera, family Chrysomelidae.

flea·bite /ˈflēˌbit/ ▸*n.* a small red mark caused by the bite of a flea. ■ *figurative* a trivial injury or cost: *the proposed energy tax amounted to little more than a fleabite.*

flea-bit·ten ▸*adj.* bitten by or infested with fleas. ■ sordid, shabby, or disreputable: *this flea-bitten gross-out movie seems to believe that it's about something.*

flea cir·cus ▸*n.* a novelty show of performing fleas.

flea col·lar ▸*n.* a collar for a cat or dog that is impregnated with insecticide in order to keep the pet free of fleas.

flea-flick·er ▸*n.* *Football* a designed play in which a pass is thrown to a receiver who then laterals to a teammate.

flea mar·ket ▸*n.* a market, typically outdoors, selling secondhand goods.

flea·pit /ˈflēˌpit/ ▸*n.* *chiefly Brit.* a dingy, dirty place, esp. a run-down movie theater.

flèche /flāsH; flesH/ ▸*n.* a slender spire, typically over the intersection of the nave and the transept of a Gothic church. ▷mid 19th cent.: French, literally 'arrow.'

fle·chette /flāˈsHet; flesHˈet/ (also **flé·chette**) ▸*n.* a type of ammunition resembling a small dart, shot from a gun. ▷early 20th cent.: from French *fléchette*, diminutive of *flèche* 'arrow.'

fleck /flek/ ▸*n.* a very small patch of color or light: *his blue eyes had gray flecks in them* | ***flecks of** sunshine.* ■ a small particle or speck of something: *brushing a few* ***flecks of** dandruff from his suit.*
▸*v.* [*trans.*] (often **be flecked**) mark or dot with small patches of color or particles of something: *the minarets are flecked with gold leaf.* ▷late Middle English (as a verb): perhaps from Old Norse *flekkr* (noun), *flekka* (verb), or from Middle Low German, Middle Dutch *vlecke*.

flec·tion /ˈfleksHən/ ▸*n.* variant spelling of **FLEXION**.

fled /fled/ ▸ past and past participle of **FLEE**.

fledge /flej/ ▸*v.* [*intrans.*] **1** (of a young bird) develop wing feathers that are large enough for flight. ■ [*trans.*] bring up (a young bird) until its wing feathers are developed enough for flight. **2** [*trans.*] provide (an arrow) with feathers. ▷mid 16th cent.: from the obsolete adjective *fledge* 'ready to fly,' from Old English, of Germanic origin; related to Dutch *vlug* 'quick, agile,' also to **FLY**[1].

fledged /flejd/ ▸*adj.* (of a young bird) having wing feathers that are large enough for flight; able to fly. See also **FULL-FLEDGED**. ■ *figurative* (of a person or thing) having just taken on the role specified: *our discipline is so new fledged that the FBI had to take its cases to the Smithsonian for analysis.* ■ *chiefly poetic/literary* (of an arrow) provided with feathers.

fledg·ling /ˈflejliNG/ (also **fledge·ling**) ▸*n.* a young bird that has just fledged. ■ [usu. as *adj.*] a person or organization that is immature, inexperienced, or underdeveloped: *the fledgling democracies of eastern Europe.* ▷mid 19th cent.: from the obsolete adjective *fledge* (see **FLEDGE**), on the pattern of *nestling*.

flee /flē/ ▸*v.* (**flees**, **flee·ing**; *past* and *past part.* **fled** /fled/) [*intrans.*] run away from a place or situation of danger: *a man was shot twice as he* ***fled from** five masked youths.* ■ [*trans.*] run away from (someone or something): *he was forced to* ***flee the country*** | *figurative all remaining doubt that he was a guerilla began to flee my mind.* ▷Old English *flēon*, of Germanic origin; related to Dutch *vlieden* and German *fliehen*.

fleece /flēs/ ▸*n.* **1** the woolly covering of a sheep or goat: *as the sheep came on board, we grabbed their long shaggy fleeces* | *he clutched the ram by two handfuls of thick fleece.* ■ the amount of wool shorn from a sheep in a single piece at one time. **2** a thing resembling a sheep's woolly covering, in particular: ■ a soft warm fabric with a texture similar to sheep's wool, used as a lining material. ■ a jacket or other garment made from such a fabric. ■ *Heraldry* a representation of a fleece suspended from a ring.
▸*v.* [*trans.*] **1** *informal* obtain a great deal of money from (someone), typically by overcharging or swindling them: *money that authorities say he fleeced from well-to-do acquaintances.* **2** *figurative* cover as if with a fleece: *the sky was half blue, half fleeced with white clouds.* ▷Old English *flēos*, *flēs*; related to Dutch *vlies* and German *Vlies*. **—fleeced** *adj.*

fleec·y /ˈflēsē/ ▸*adj.* (**fleec·i·er**, **fleec·i·est**) **1** (esp. of a towel or garment) made of or lined with a soft, warm fabric: *a fleecy sweatshirt.* **2** (esp. of a cloud) white and fluffy. **—fleec·i·ly** /-səlē/ *adv.* **—fleec·i·ness** /-sēnis/ *n.*

fleer /ˈfli(ə)r/ ▸*v.* [*intrans.*] *poetic/literary* laugh impudently or jeeringly: *he fleered at us.*
▸*n.* *archaic* an impudent or jeering look or speech. ▷late Middle English: probably of Scandinavian origin and related to Norwegian and Swedish dialect *flira* 'to grin.'

fleet[1] /flēt/ ▸*n.* the largest group of naval vessels under one commander, organized for specific tactical or other purposes: *an invasion fleet.* ■ (**the fleet**) a country's navy: *the U.S. fleet.* ■ a group of ships sailing together, engaged in the same activity, or under the same ownership: *the small port supports a fishing fleet.* ■ a number of ships, vehicles or aircraft operating together or under the same ownership: ***a fleet of** ambulances took the injured to hospital.* ▷Old English *flēot* 'ship, shipping,' from *flēotan* 'float, swim' (see FLEET[5]).

fleet[2] ▸*adj.* fast and nimble in movement: *a man of advancing years, but **fleet of foot**.* ▹early 16th cent.: probably from Old Norse *fljótr*, of Germanic origin and related to FLEET[5]. **—fleet·ly** *adv.* **—fleet·ness** *n.*

fleet[3] ▸*n. Brit.* a marshland creek, channel, or ditch. ▹Old English *flēot*, of Germanic origin; related to Dutch *vliet*, also to FLEET[5].

fleet[4] ▸*v.* [*intrans.*] *poetic/literary* move or pass quickly: *a variety of expressions fleeted across his face | time may fleet and youth may fade.* ■ [*trans.*] pass (time) rapidly. ■ fade away; be transitory: *the cares of boyhood **fleet away**.* ▹Old English *flēotan* 'float, swim,' of Germanic origin; related to Dutch *vlieten* and German *fliessen*, also to FLIT and FLOAT.

Fleet Ad·mi·ral ▸*n.* an admiral of the highest rank in the U.S. Navy (awarded only in wartime).

fleet-foot·ed ▸*adj.* nimble and fast on one's feet: *the fleet-footed sprinter captured his third gold medal.*

fleet·ing /ˈflētiNG/ ▸*adj.* lasting for a very short time: *hoping to get a fleeting glimpse of a whale underwater.* See note at TEMPORARY. **—fleet·ing·ly** *adv.*

Fleet Street a street in central London in which the offices of national newspapers were located until the mid-1980s (often used to refer to the British press): *the hottest story in Fleet Street.*

Flem. ▸*abbr.* Flemish.

Flem·ing[1] /ˈflemiNG/, Sir Alexander (1881–1955), Scottish bacteriologist. In 1928, Fleming discovered the effect of penicillin on bacteria. Twelve years later Howard Florey and Ernst Chain established its therapeutic use as an antibiotic. Nobel Prize for Physiology or Medicine (1945, shared with Florey and Chain).

Flem·ing[2], Ian (Lancaster) (1908–64), English novelist. He is known for his spy novels whose hero is the secret agent James Bond. Many of these James Bond stories were made into movies.

Flem·ing[3], Peggy (1948–), U.S. figure skater. She was world champion 1966–68 and won an Olympic gold medal in 1968.

Flem·ing[4], Renée (1959–), U.S. opera singer. She made her debut with the Metropolitan Opera in 1991 and is known for her interpretation of the bel canto repertory and for her enthusiasm for contemporary operas.

Flem·ing[5] ▸*n.* **1** a native of Flanders. **2** a member of the Flemish-speaking people inhabiting northern and western Belgium. Compare with WALLOON. ▹late Old English *Flæmingi*, from Old Norse, reinforced by Middle Dutch *Vlāming*, related to *Vlaanderen* 'Flanders.'

Flem·ing's left-hand rule *Physics* a mnemonic concerning the behavior of a current-carrying conductor in a magnetic field, according to which the directions of the magnetic field, the current, and the force exerted on the conductor are indicated respectively by the first finger, second finger, and thumb of the left hand when these are held out perpendicular to each other. ▹1920s: proposed by English engineer John Ambrose Fleming (1849–1945).

Flem·ing's right-hand rule *Physics* a mnemonic concerning the behavior of a conductor moving in a magnetic field, according to which the directions of the magnetic field, the induced current, and the motion of the conductor are indicated respectively by the first finger, second finger, and thumb of the right hand when these are held out perpendicular to each other.

Flem·ish /ˈflemiSH/ ▸*adj.* of or relating to Flanders, its people, or their language.
▸*n.* **1** the Dutch language as spoken in Flanders, one of the two official languages of Belgium. **2** (**the Flemish**) [as *plural n.*] the people of Flanders. ▹Middle English: from Middle Dutch *Vlāmisch*, related to *Vlaanderen* 'Flanders.'

Flem·ish bond ▸*n. Building* a pattern of bricks in a wall in which each course consists of alternate headers and stretchers.

flense /flens/ (also **flench** /flenCH/, **flinch** /flinCH/) ▸*v.* [*trans.*] slice the skin or fat from (a carcass, esp. that of a whale). ■ strip (skin or fat) from a carcass: *the skin had been **flensed off**.* ▹early 19th cent. **—flens·er** *n.*

flesh /fleSH/ ▸*n.* the soft substance consisting of muscle and fat that is found between the skin and bones of an animal or a human: *she grabbed Anna's arm, her fingers sinking into the flesh.* ■ this substance in an animal or fish, regarded as food: *boned lamb flesh* | [in *combination*] *a flesh-eater.* ■ the pulpy substance of a fruit or vegetable, esp. the part that is eaten: *halve the avocados and scrape out the flesh.* ■ fat: *he carries no spare flesh.* ■ the skin or surface of the human body with reference to its color, appearance, or sensual properties: *she gasped as the cold water hit her flesh.* ■ (**the flesh**) the human body and its physical needs and desires, esp. as contrasted with the mind or the soul: *I have never been one to deny the **pleasures of the flesh**.* ■ flesh color.
▸*v.* **1** [*intrans.*] (**flesh out**) put weight on: *he had fleshed out to a solid 220 pounds.* ■ [*trans.*] (**flesh something out**) add more details to something that exists only in a draft or outline form: *the theorists have fleshed out a variety of scenarios.* **2** [*trans.*] *Brit.* give (a hound or hawk) a piece of the flesh of game that has been killed in order to incite it. ■ *poetic/literary* initiate (someone) in bloodshed or warfare: *he fleshed his troops by indulging them with enterprises against the enemy's posts.* **3** [*trans.*] [often as *n.*] (**fleshing**) remove the flesh adhering to (a skin or hide): *after fleshing, the hide is soaked again.* ▹Old English *flæsc*, of Germanic origin; related to Dutch *vlees* and German *Fleisch*. **—fleshed** /flesHt/ *adj.* [usu. in *combination*] *a white-fleshed fish.* **—flesh·less** *adj.*
▸*PHRASES* □ **all flesh** all human and animal life. □ **go the way of all flesh** die or come to an end. □ **in the flesh** in person rather than via a telephone, a movie, the written word, or other means: *they decided that they should meet Alexander in the flesh.* □ **lose flesh** *archaic* become thinner. □ **make someone's flesh creep** (or **crawl**) see MAKE SOMEONE'S SKIN CRAWL at SKIN. □ **one flesh** used to refer to the spiritual and physical union of two people in a relationship, esp. marriage: *my body is his, his is mine: one flesh.* [with biblical allusion to Gen. 2:24.] □ **put flesh on** (**the bones of**) **something** add more details to something that exists only in a draft or outline form: *he has yet to put flesh on his "big idea."* □ **put on flesh** put on weight. □ **sins of the flesh** *archaic & humorous* sins related to physical indulgence, esp. sexual gratification.

flesh and blood ▸*n.* used to emphasize that a person is a physical, living being with human emotions or frailties, often in contrast to something abstract, spiritual, or mechanical: *the customer is flesh and blood, not just a sales statistic* | [as *adj.*] *he seemed more like a creature from a dream than a flesh-and-blood father.*
▸*PHRASE* □ **one's** (**own**) **flesh and blood** a near relative or one's close family: *he felt as much for that girl as if she had been his own flesh and blood.*

flesh col·or ▸*n.* a light brownish pink. **—flesh-col·ored** *adj.*

flesh·er /ˈfleSHər/ ▸*n.* **1** a knife for fleshing hides. **2** a person who fleshes hides.

flesh fly ▸*n.* a fly that breeds in carrion, typically producing live young that are deposited on a carcass. • Family Sarcophagidae: *Sarcophaga* and other genera.

flesh·ings /ˈfleSHiNGz/ ▸*plural n.* flesh-colored tights worn by actors.

flesh·ly /ˈfleSHlē/ ▸*adj.* (**-li·er**, **-li·est**) **1** of or relating to human desire or bodily appetites; sensual: *fleshly pleasures.* **2** having an actual physical presence: *we will shed the lofty metaphysical Cage and incorporate the earlier dynamic and fleshly Cage.* ▹Old English *flæsclic* (see FLESH, -LY[1]).

flesh·pots /ˈflesH,päts/ ▸*plural n.* places providing luxurious or hedonistic living: *he had lived the life of a roué in the fleshpots of London and Paris.* ▹early 16th cent.: with biblical allusion to the *fleshpots of Egypt* (Exod. 16:3).

flesh side ▸*n.* the side of a hide that adjoins the flesh.

flesh wound /wo͞ond/ ▸*n.* a wound that breaks the skin but does not damage bones or vital organs.

flesh·y /ˈfleSHē/ ▸*adj.* (**flesh·i·er**, **flesh·i·est**) **1** (of a person or part of the body) having a substantial amount of flesh; plump: *her torso was full, fleshy, and heavy.* ■ (of plant or fruit tissue) soft and thick: *fleshy, greeny-gray leaves.* ■ (of a wine) full-bodied. **2** resembling flesh in appearance or texture. **—flesh·i·ness** *n.*

fletch /flecH/ ▸*v.* [*trans.*] provide (an arrow) with feathers for flight: *most arrows are fletched with 3- to 5-inch feathers.*
▸*n.* each of the feathered vanes of an arrow: [in *combination*] *a four-fletch arrow.* ▹mid 17th cent.: alteration of FLEDGE, probably influenced by *fletcher*.

Fletch·er /ˈflecHər/, John (1579–1625), English playwright. A writer of Jacobean tragicomedies, he wrote about 15 plays with Francis Beaumont and is also believed to have collaborated with William Shakespeare on such plays as *The Two Noble Kinsmen* and *Henry VIII* (both *c.*1613).

fletch·er /ˈflecHər/ ▸*n. chiefly historical* a person who makes and sells arrows. ▹Middle English: from Old French *flechier*, from *fleche* 'arrow.'

fletch·ing /ˈflecHiNG/ ▸*n.* the feathers of an arrow: *it has good-sized fletching | he repairs damaged fletchings.*

fleur-de-lis /,flər dlˈē; ,flo͝or-/ (also **fleur-de-lys**) ▸*n.* (*pl.* **fleurs-de-lis** *pronunc.* same or /-dlˈēz/) **1** *Art & Heraldry* a stylized lily composed of three petals bound together near their bases. It is especially known from the former royal arms of France, in which it appears in gold on a blue field. **2** a European iris. • Genus *Iris*, family Iridaceae, in particular *I.* × *germanica* 'Florentina' (with bluish-white flowers) or *I. pseudacorus* (the yellow flag). ▹Middle English: from Old French *flour de lys* 'flower of the lily.'

fleur-de-lis 1

fleur de sel /ˈflər də ˈsel; ˈflo͝or/ ▸*n.* French sea salt.

fleu·ron /ˈflər,än; ˈflo͝or-/ ▸*n.* a flower-shaped ornament, used esp. on buildings, coins, books, and pastry. ■ a small pastry puff used for garnishing. ▹late Middle English: from Old French *floron*, from *flour* 'flower.'

fleu·ry /ˈflərē; ˈflo͝orē/ ▸*adj.* variant spelling of FLORY.

flew /flo͞o/ ▸ past of FLY[1].

flews /flo͞oz/ ▸*plural n.* the thick hanging lips of a bloodhound or similar dog. ▹late 16th cent.: of unknown origin.

flex /fleks/ ▸*v.* [*trans.*] bend (a limb or joint): *she saw him flex his ankle and wince.* ■ [*intrans.*] (of a limb or joint) become bent: *prevent the damaged wrist from flexing.* ■ cause (a muscle) to stand out by contracting or tensing it: *bodybuilders flexing their muscles.* ■ [*intrans.*] (of a muscle) contract or be tensed: *a muscle flexed in his jaw.* ■ [*intrans.*] (of a material) be capable of warping or bending and then reverting to shape: *set windows in rubber so they flex during an earthquake.* ■ [usu. as *adj.*] (**flexed**) *Archaeology* place (a corpse) with the legs drawn up under the chin: *a flexed burial.*
▸*n.* the action or state of flexing: *add rigidity and eliminate brake flex.* ▹early 16th cent.: from Latin *flex-* 'bent,' from the verb *flectere*.
▸*PHRASE* □ **flex one's muscles** see MUSCLE.

flex·i·ble /ˈfleksəbəl/ ▸*adj.* capable of bending easily without breaking: *flexible rubber seals.* ■ able to be easily modified to respond to altered circumstances or conditions: *flexible forms of retirement.* ■ (of a person) ready and able to change so as to adapt to different circumstances: *you can save money if you're flexible about where your room is located.* ▹late Middle English: from Old French, or from Latin *flexibilis*, from *flectere* 'to bend.' **—flex·i·bil·i·ty** /,fleksəˈbilətē/ *n.* **—flex·i·bly** /-blē/ *adv.*

THE RIGHT WORD **elastic, flexible, limber, pliable, pliant, resilient, supple**

If you can bend over and touch your toes, you are **flexible**. But a dancer or gymnast is **limber**, an adjective that specifically applies to a body that has been brought into condition through training (*to stay limber, she did yoga every day*).

Flexible applies to whatever can be bent without breaking, whether or not it returns to its original shape (*a flexible plastic hose; a flexible electrical conduit*); it does not necessarily refer, as *limber* does, to the human body.

Unlike *flexible*, **resilient** implies the ability to spring back into shape after being bent or compressed, or to recover one's health or spirits quickly (*so young and resilient that she was back at work in a week*).

Elastic is usually applied to substances or materials that are easy to stretch or expand and that quickly recover their shape or size (*pants with an elastic waist*), while **supple** is applied to whatever is easily bent, twisted, or folded without breaking or cracking (*a soft, supple leather*). When applied to the human body, *supple* suggests the ability to move effortlessly.

Pliant and **pliable** may be used to describe either people or things that are easily bent or manipulated. *Pliant* suggests a tendency to bend without force or pressure from the outside, while *pliable* suggests the use of force or submission to another's will. A *pliant* person is merely adaptable, but a *pliable* person is easy to influence and eager to please.

flex·ile /ˈfleksəl; -ˌsīl/ ▸*adj. archaic* pliant and flexible: *the serpent's flexile body.* ▷mid 17th cent.: from Latin *flexilis,* from *flectere* 'to bend.' **—flex·il·i·ty** /flekˈsilətē/ *n.*

flex·ion /ˈflekSHən/ (also **flec·tion**) ▸*n.* the action of bending or the condition of being bent, esp. the bending of a limb or joint: *flexion of the fingers | these protozoans can move by body flexions.* ▷early 17th cent.: from Latin *flexio(n-),* from *flectere* 'to bend.'

flex·og·ra·phy /flekˈsägrəfē/ ▸*n.* a rotary relief printing method using rubber or plastic plates and fluid inks or dyes for printing on fabrics and impervious materials such as plastics, as well as on paper. ▷1950s: from Latin *flexus* 'a bending' (from the verb *flectere*) + -GRAPHY. **—flex·o·graph·ic** /ˌfleksəˈgrafik/ *adj.*

flex·or /ˈflekˌsər; -ˌsôr/ (also **flexor muscle**) ▸*n. Anatomy* a muscle whose contraction bends a limb or other part of the body. Often contrasted with EXTENSOR. ■ any of a number of specific muscles in the arm, hand, leg, or foot.

flex·time /ˈfleksˌtīm/ (*Brit.* **flex·i·time** /ˈfleksi-/) ▸*n.* a system of working a set number of hours with the starting and finishing times chosen within agreed limits by the employee: *no need for day care—the parents can work flextime.* ▷1970s: blend of FLEXIBLE and TIME.

flex·u·ous /ˈflekSHo͞oəs/ ▸*adj.* full of bends and curves. ▷early 17th cent.: from Latin *flexuosus,* from *flexus* 'a bending,' from the verb *flectere.* **—flex·u·os·i·ty** /ˌflekSHo͞oˈäsitē/ *n.* **—flex·u·ous·ly** *adv.*

flex·ure /ˈflekSHər/ ▸*n. chiefly Anatomy Geology* the action of bending or curving, or the condition of being bent or curved. ■ a bent or curved part: *these lesser hills were flexures of the San Andreas system.* ▷late 16th cent.: from Latin *flexura,* from *flectere* 'to bend.' **—flex·ur·al** /-rəl/ *adj.*

flex·wing /ˈfleksˌwiNG/ ▸*n.* a collapsible fabric delta wing, as used in hang gliders.

flib·ber·ti·gib·bet /ˈflibərtēˌjibit/ ▸*n.* a frivolous, flighty, or excessively talkative person. ▷late Middle English: probably imitative of idle chatter.

flic /flik/ ▸*n. informal* a French policeman. ▷French

flick /flik/ ▸*n.* **1** a sudden sharp movement: *the flick of a switch | a flick of the wrist.* ■ the sudden release of a bent finger or thumb, esp. to propel a small object: *he sent his cigarette spinning away with a flick of his fingers.* ■ a light, sharp, quickly retracted blow, esp. with a whip. **2** *informal* a motion picture: *a Hollywood action flick.* ■ (**the flicks**) *chiefly Brit.* the movies: *fancy a night at the flicks?*

▸*v.* [*trans.*] propel (something) with a sudden sharp movement, esp. of the fingers: *Emily **flicked** some ash **off** her sleeve.* ■ (**flick something on/off**) turn something electrical on or off by means of a switch: *he flicked on the air conditioning.* ■ [*intrans.*] make a sudden sharp movement: *the finch's tail flicks up and down.* ■ [*trans.*] move (a whip) so as to strike.

▸*phrasal v.* □ **flick through** another way of saying FLIP THROUGH (see FLIP). ▷late Middle English: symbolic, *fl-* frequently beginning words denoting sudden movement.

flick·er[1] /ˈflikər/ ▸*v.* [*intrans.*] **1** (of light or a source of light) shine unsteadily; vary rapidly in brightness: *the interior lights flickered and came on.* ■ (of a flame) burn fitfully, alternately flaring up and dying down: *the candle flickered again* | [as *adj.*] (**flickering**) *the flickering flames of the fire.* ■ [with *adverbial of place*] *figurative* (of a feeling or emotion) be experienced or show itself briefly and faintly, esp. in someone's eyes: *amusement flickered briefly in his eyes.* **2** make small, quick movements; flutter rapidly: *her eyelids flickered* | [with *complement*] *the injured killer's eyes flickered open.* ■ [with *adverbial of direction*] (of someone's eyes) move quickly in a particular direction in order to look at something: *her alert hazel eyes flickered around the room.* ■ [with *adverbial*] (of a facial expression) appear briefly: *a look of horror flickered across his face.*

▸*phrasal v.* □ **flicker out** (of a flame or light) die away and go out after a series of flickers. ■ *figurative* (of a feeling) die away and finally disappear: *the swift burst of curiosity and eagerness flickered out.*

▸*n.* **1** an unsteady movement of a flame or light that causes rapid variations in brightness: *the flicker of a candle flame caught our eyes.* ■ fluctuations in the brightness of a movie or television image such as occur when the number of frames per second is too small or the refresh rate too low for persistence of vision. **2** a tiny movement: *then a flicker of movement caught his eye.* ■ a faint indication of a facial expression: *a flicker of a smile passed across her face.* ■ *figurative* a very brief and faint experience of an emotion or feeling: *she felt a small flicker of alarm.* ▷Old English *flicorian, flycerian* 'to flutter,' probably of Germanic origin and related to Low German *flickern* and Dutch *flikkeren.*

flick·er[2] ▸*n.* an American woodpecker that often feeds on ants on the ground. • Genus *Colaptes,* family Picidae: several species, in particular the **common flicker** (*C. auratus*), occurring in two forms that are distinguished by the underside of the tail and wings, which may be yellow (**yellow-shafted flicker**) or salmon red (**red-shafted flicker**). ▷early 19th cent.: imitative of its call.

Flick·er·tail State /ˈflikərˌtāl/ a nickname for the state of NORTH DAKOTA.

flick knife ▸*n.* British term for SWITCHBLADE.

fli·er /ˈflīər/ (also **fly·er**) ▸*n.* **1** a person or thing that flies, esp. in a particular way: *a nervous flier.* ■ a person who flies something, esp. an aircraft. ■ *informal* a fast-moving person or thing. **2** a small handbill advertising an event or product. **3** a speculative investment. **4** a step in a straight flight of stairs.

▸*PHRASE* □ **take a flyer** take a chance.

flight /flīt/ ▸*n.* **1** the action or process of flying through the air: *an eagle in flight | the history of space flight.* ■ an act of flying; a journey made through the air or in space, esp. a scheduled journey made by an airline: *I got the first flight.* ■ the movement or trajectory of a projectile or ball through the air. ■ [as *adj.*] relating to or denoting archery in which the main concern is shooting long distances: *short, light flight arrows.* ■ *poetic/literary* swift passage of time: *the never-ending flight of future days.* **2** a group of creatures or objects flying together, in particular: ■ a flock or large body of birds or insects in the air, esp. when migrating: *flights of Canada geese.* ■ a group of aircraft operating together, esp. an air force unit of about six aircraft: *a refueling mission in which his crew topped off three flights of four F-16A jets.* **3** the action of fleeing or attempting to escape: *refugees on the latest stage of their flight from turmoil.* **4** a series of steps between floors or levels: *she has to come up four flights of stairs to her apartment.* ■ a series of hurdles across a racetrack. ■ a closely spaced sequence of locks in a canal. **5** an extravagant or far-fetched idea or account: *ignoring such ridiculous **flights of fancy**.* **6** the tail of a dart.

▸*v.* [*trans.*] **1** shoot (wildfowl) in flight: [as *n.*] (**flighting**) *duck and geese flighting.* **2** *Brit.* (in soccer, cricket, etc.) deliver (a ball) with well-judged trajectory and pace: *he flighted a free kick into the box.* ▷Old English *flyht* 'action or manner of flying,' of Germanic origin; related to Dutch *vlucht* and FLY[1]. This was probably merged in Middle English with an unrecorded Old English word related to German *Flucht* and to FLEE, which is represented by sense 3 of the *noun.*

▸*PHRASES* □ **in full flight** escaping as fast as possible. ■ having gained momentum in a run or activity: *when this jazz pianist is in full flight he can be mesmerizing.* □ **put someone/something to flight** cause someone or something to flee: *a soldier who held off, and eventually put to flight, waves of attackers.* □ **take flight** **1** (of a bird) take off and fly: *the whole flock took flight | figurative my celebrityhood took flight.* **2** flee: *noise that would prompt a spooked horse to take flight.*

flight at·tend·ant ▸*n.* a steward or stewardess on an aircraft.

flight bag ▸*n.* a small zippered shoulder bag carried by air travelers.

flight cap·i·tal ▸*n.* money transferred abroad to avoid taxes or inflation, achieve better investment returns, or to provide for possible emigration.

flight con·trol ▸*n.* the activity of directing the movement of aircraft: *automatic flight control* | [as *adj.*] *the flight-control computer.* ■ a control surface on an aircraft.

flight crew ▸*n.* [treated as *sing.* or *pl.*] the personnel responsible for the operation of an aircraft during flight.

flight deck ▸*n.* **1** the cockpit of a large aircraft, from which the pilot and crew fly it. **2** the deck of an aircraft carrier, used for takeoff and landing.

flight en·gi·neer ▸*n.* a member of a flight crew responsible for the aircraft's engines and other systems during flight.

flight en·ve·lope ▸*n.* the range of combinations of speed, altitude, angle of attack, etc., within which a flying object is aerodynamically stable.

flight feath·er ▸*n.* any of the large primary or secondary feathers in a bird's wing, supporting it in flight. Also called REMEX.

flight·less /ˈflītlis/ ▸*adj.* (of a bird or an insect) naturally unable to fly. **—flight·less·ness** *n.*

flight line ▸*n.* **1** the part of an airport around the hangars where aircraft can be parked and serviced. **2** a line of flight.

flight path ▸*n.* the actual or planned course of an aircraft or spacecraft.

flight plan ▸*n. Aeronautics* a written account of the details of a particular proposed flight.

flight re·cord·er (also **flight data recorder**) ▸*n.* a device in an aircraft that records technical details during a flight, used in the event of an accident to discover its cause.

flight sim·u·la·tor ▸*n.* a machine designed to resemble the cockpit of an aircraft, with computer-generated images that mimic the pilot's view, typically with mechanisms that move the entire structure in imitation of an aircraft's motion, used for training pilots.

flight suit ▸*n.* a one-piece garment worn by the pilot and crew of a military or light aircraft.

flight sur·geon ▸*n.* a military surgeon specializing in aerospace medicine.

flight test ▸*n.* a flight of an aircraft, rocket, or equipment to see how well it functions.

▸*v.* (**flight-test**) [*trans.*] test (an aircraft or rocket) by flying it: [as *n.*] (**flight-testing**) *it was undergoing cold-weather flight-testing.*

flight·wor·thy /ˈflītˌwər<u>TH</u>ē/ ▸*adj.* (of an aircraft) capable of being flown safely.

flight·y /ˈflītē/ ▸*adj.* (**flight·i·er**, **flight·i·est**) fickle and irresponsible: *you may be seen as too flighty and lightweight for real responsibility.* ▷mid 16th cent.: from FLIGHT + -Y[1]. **—flight·i·ly** /ˈflītl-ē/ *adv.* **—flight·i·ness** /ˈflītēnis/ *n.*

flim·flam /ˈflimˌflam/ *informal* ▸*n.* nonsensical or insincere talk: *I suppose that you suspect me of pseudointellectual flimflam.* ■ a confidence game: *flimflams perpetrated against us by our elected officials.*

▸*v.* (**-flammed, -flam·ming**) [*trans.*] swindle (someone) with a confidence game: *the tribe was flimflammed out of its land.* ▷mid 16th cent.: symbolic reduplication. **—flim·flam·mer** *n.* **—flim·flam·mer·y** /-ˌflamərē/ *n.*

flim·sy /ˈflimzē/ ▸*adj.* (**-si·er**, **-si·est**) comparatively light and insubstantial; easily damaged: *voyagers who crossed the sea in flimsy boats.* ■ (of clothing) light and thin: *I wore flimsy clothes and needed warming.* ■ (of a pretext or account) weak and unconvincing: *a pretty flimsy excuse.*

▸*n.* (*pl.* **-sies**) *Brit.* a document, esp. a copy, made on very thin paper: *credit-card flimsies.* ■ very thin paper: *sheets of yellow flimsy.* ▷early 18th cent.: probably from FLIMFLAM. **—flim·si·ly** /ˈflimzəlē/ *adv.* **—flim·si·ness** /-zēnis/ *n.*

flinch[1] /flinCH/ ▸*v.* [*intrans.*] make a quick, nervous movement of the face or body as an instinctive reaction to surprise, fear or pain: *she **flinched at** the acidity in his voice | he had faced death **without flinching**.* See note at WINCE. ■ (**flinch from**) *figurative* avoid doing or becoming involved in (something) through fear or anxiety: *I rarely flinch from a fight when I'm sure of myself.*

▸*n.* [in *sing.*] an act of flinching: *"Don't call me that," he said with a flinch.* ▷mid 16th cent. (in the sense 'slink or sneak off'): from Old French *flenchir* 'turn aside,' of West Germanic origin and related to German *lenken* 'to guide, steer.' **—flinch·er** *n.* **—flinch·ing·ly** *adv.*

flinch[2] ▸*v.* variant spelling of FLENSE.

Flin·ders /ˈflindərz/, Matthew (1774–1814), English explorer. He circumnavigated Australia (1801–03) for the Royal Navy and charted much of its west coast for the first time.

flin·ders /ˈflindərz/ ▸*plural n.* small fragments or splinters: *the panel has been smashed to flinders.* ▷late Middle English: probably of Scandinavian origin and related to Norwegian *flindra* 'chip, splinter.'

Flin·ders bar ▸*n.* a bar of soft iron placed vertically in or near the housing of a ship's compass to correct deviation caused by the local magnetic field of the ship. ▷late 19th cent.: name after Captain M. FLINDERS.

fling /fliNG/ ▸*v.* (*past* **flung** /fləNG/) [*trans.*] throw or hurl forcefully: *he picked up the debris and flung it away | figurative I was flung into jail.* ■ move or push (something) suddenly or violently: *he flung back the bedclothes* | [*trans.*] *Jennifer flung open a door.* ■ (**fling oneself**) throw oneself headlong: *he flung himself down at her feet with a laugh.* ■ (**fling oneself into**) wholeheartedly engage in or begin on (an enterprise): *the producer flung himself into an ugly battle with the studio.* ■ (**fling something on/off**) put on or take off clothes carelessly or rapidly. ■ utter (words) forcefully: *the words were flung at her like an accusation.*

■ [intrans.] go angrily or violently; rush: *he flung away to his study, slamming the door behind him.*
▸n. **1** a short period of enjoyment or wild behavior: *one final fling before a tranquil retirement.* ■ a short, spontaneous sexual relationship: *I had a fling with someone when I was at college.* **2** short for HIGHLAND FLING. ▷Middle English (in the sense 'go violently'): perhaps related to Old Norse *flengja* 'flog.' Sense 1 is based on an earlier sense 'reckless movement of the body' and dates from the early 19th cent. **—fling·er** *n.*

Flint /flint/ an industrial city in southeastern Michigan, an auto industry center since the Buick Company was established there in 1903; pop. 124,943.

flint /flint/ ▸n. a hard gray rock consisting of nearly pure chert, occurring chiefly as nodules in chalk. ■ a piece of this stone, esp. as flaked or ground in ancient times to form a tool or weapon. ■ a piece of flint used with steel to produce an igniting spark, e.g., in a flintlock gun, or (in modern use) a piece of an alloy used similarly, esp. in a cigarette lighter. ■ used to express how hard and unyielding something or someone is: *mean faces with eyes like flints.* ▷Old English; related to Middle Dutch *vlint* and Old High German *flins.*

flint corn ▸n. corn of a variety that has hard, slightly translucent grains.

flint glass ▸n. a pure lustrous kind of glass originally made with flint.

flint·lock /'flint,läk/ ▸n. **1** an old-fashioned type of gun fired by a spark from a flint. **2** [usu. as adj.] the lock on such a gun: *an antique flintlock pistol.*

flintlock 2

flint·y /'flintē/ ▸adj. (**flint·i·er, flint·i·est**) of, containing, or reminiscent of flint: *flinty soil.* ■ (of a person or their expression) very hard and unyielding: *a flinty stare.* **—flint·i·ly** /'flintl-ē/ *adv.* **—flint·i·ness** /-tēnis/ *n.*

flip[1] /flip/ ▸v. (**flipped, flip·ping**) **1** turn over or cause to turn over with a sudden sharp movement: [trans.] *the yacht was flipped by a huge wave* | [intrans.] *the plane **flipped over** and then exploded.* **2** [trans.] move, push, or throw (something) with a sudden sharp movement: *she flipped off her dark glasses* | *she flipped a few coins on to the bar.* ■ [trans.] turn (an electrical appliance or switch) on or off: *he flipped a switch and the front door opened.* ■ [trans.] toss (a coin) to decide an issue: *given those odds, one may as well flip a coin* | [intrans.] *you want to flip for it?* **3** [trans.] buy and sell (a property) quickly and profitably using a fraudulent evaluation of its worth: *within one week of starting I flipped a property for a quick $3,000 profit.* **4** *Computing* [trans.] access the nonpublic parts of (a Web site): *if you want to learn who the main IT contact at a company is, just flip their Web site.* **5** [intrans.] *informal* suddenly become deranged or very angry: *he had clearly flipped under the pressure.* ■ suddenly become very enthusiastic: *I walked into a store, saw it on the wall, and just flipped.*
▸*phrasal v.* □ **flip through** look or search quickly through (a volume or a collection of papers): *just flip through the phone book and pick a lawyer.*
▸n. **1** a sudden sharp movement: *the fish made little leaps and flips.* ■ (**a flip through**) a quick look or search through a volume or a collection of papers: *a quick flip through my cookbooks.* **2** *Brit., informal* a quick tour or pleasure trip: *I did a flip round the post-show party.* [derived from an earlier sense 'short flight in an aircraft.']
▸adj. glib; flippant: *he couldn't get away with flip, funny conversation.*
▸exclam. used to express mild annoyance. ▷mid 16th cent. (as a verb in the sense 'make a flick with the finger and thumb'): probably a contraction of FILLIP.
▸PHRASE □ **flip one's lid** (or **one's wig**) *informal* suddenly become deranged or lose one's self-control.

flip[2] ▸n. another term for EGGNOG. ▷late 17th cent.: perhaps from FLIP[1] in the sense 'whip up.'

flip chart ▸n. a large pad of paper bound so that each page can be turned over at the top to reveal the next, used on a stand at presentations.

flip-chip ▸n. a computer chip that is installed on a circuit board face-down, with connections formed by solder bumps rather than wires. ▷1990s: from the fact that the chip is rotated 180 degrees from the traditional mode of attachment.

flip-flop ▸n. **1** a light sandal, typically of plastic or rubber, with a thong between the big and second toe. **2** a backward somersault or handspring. **3** *informal* an abrupt reversal of policy: *his **flip-flop on** taxes.* **4** *Electronics* a switching circuit that works by changing from one stable state to another, or through an unstable state back to its stable state, in response to a triggering pulse.
▸v. [intrans.] **1** [with adverbial of direction] move with a flapping sound or motion: *she flip-flopped off the porch in battered sneakers.* **2** perform a backward somersault or handspring: *figurative Julie's stomach flip-flopped.* **3** *informal* make an abrupt reversal of policy: *the candidate **flip-flopped on** a number of issues.* ▷mid 17th cent. (in the general sense 'something that flaps or flops'): imitative reduplication of FLOP.

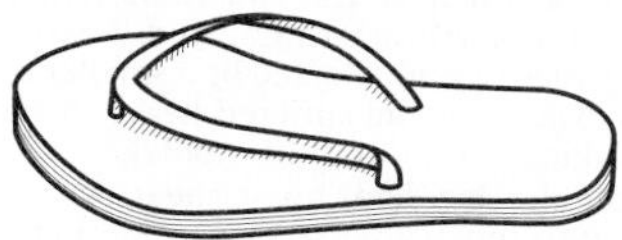

flip-flop 1

flip·pant /'flipənt/ ▸adj. not showing a serious or respectful attitude: *a flippant remark.* ▷early 17th cent.: from FLIP[1] + -ANT, perhaps on the pattern of heraldic terms such as *couchant* and *rampant.* Early senses included 'nimble' and 'talkative,' hence 'playful,' giving rise to the current use 'lacking seriousness.' **—flip·pan·cy** /'flipənsē/ *n.* **—flip·pant·ly** *adv.*

Flip·per /'flipər/, Henry Ossian (1856–1940), U.S. soldier and engineer. The first black graduate of West Point 1877, he was court-martialed on false charges in 1882. The charges were not withdrawn until 1970.

flip·per /'flipər/ ▸n. a broad flat limb without fingers, used for swimming by various sea animals such as seals, whales, and turtles. ■ a flat rubber attachment worn on the foot for underwater swimming. ■ a pivoted arm in a pinball machine, controlled by the player and used for sending the ball back up the table. ■ *informal* a hand.

flip·ping /'flipiNG/ ▸adj. [attrib.] *informal, chiefly Brit.* used for emphasis or to express mild annoyance: *are you out of your flipping mind?* ▷early 20th cent.: from FLIP[1] + -ING[2].

flip side ▸n. *informal* the less important side of a pop single record; the B-side. ■ another aspect or version of something, esp. its reverse or its unwanted concomitant: *virtues are the flip side of vices.*

flip-top ▸adj. [attrib.] denoting or having a lid or cover that can be easily opened by pulling, pushing, or flicking it with the fingers: *an accessory case with a clear flip-top lid.*
▸n. a lid or cover of this kind.

flirt /flərt/ ▸v. **1** [intrans.] behave as though attracted to or trying to attract someone, but for amusement rather than with serious intentions: *it amused him to **flirt with** her.* ■ (**flirt with**) experiment with or show a superficial interest in (an idea, activity, or movement) without committing oneself to it seriously: *a painter who had flirted briefly with Cubism.* ■ (**flirt with**) deliberately expose oneself to (danger or difficulty): *the need of some individuals to flirt with death.* **2** [trans.] (of a bird) wave or open and shut (its wings or tail) with a quick flicking motion. ■ [intrans.] move back and forth with a flicking or fluttering motion: *the lark was flirting around the site.*
▸n. a person who habitually flirts. ▷mid 16th cent.: apparently symbolic, the elements *fl-* and *-irt* both suggesting sudden movement; compare with FLICK and SPURT. The original verb senses were 'give someone a sharp blow' and 'sneer at'; the earliest noun senses were 'joke, gibe' and 'flighty girl' (defined by Dr. Johnson as 'a pert young hussey'), with a notion originally of cheeky behavior, later of playfully amorous behavior. **—flir·ta·tion** /-'tāSHən/ *n.* **—flir·ta·tious** /-'tāSHəs/ *adj.* **—flir·ta·tious·ly** /-'tāSHəslē/ *adv.* **—flir·ta·tious·ness** /-'tāSHəsnəs/ *n.* **—flirt·y** (**flirt·i·er, flirt·i·est**).

flit /flit/ ▸v. (**flit·ted, flit·ting**) [intrans.] move swiftly and lightly: *small birds flitted about in the branches* | *figurative the idea had flitted through his mind.* ■ [intrans.] *Brit.* leave one's home or move, typically secretly so as to escape creditors or obligations.
▸n. *Brit., informal* an act of leaving one's home or moving, typically secretly so as to escape creditors or obligations: ***moonlight flits** from one insalubrious dwelling to another.* ▷Middle English (in the sense 'move house'): from Old Norse *flytja*; related to FLEET[5].

flitch /fliCH/ ▸n. **1** a slab of timber cut from a tree trunk, usually from the outside. **2** (also **flitch plate**) the strengthening plate in a flitch beam. **3** *chiefly dialect* a side of bacon. ▷Old English *flicce*, originally denoting the salted and cured side of any meat, of Germanic origin; related to Middle Low German *vlicke.*

flitch beam ▸n. a compound beam made of a steel plate between two slabs of wood.

flit·ter /'flitər/ ▸v. [intrans.] move quickly in an apparently random or purposeless manner: *if only you would settle down instead of flittering around the countryside.*
▸n. a fluttering movement: *the flash and flitter of colored wings.* ■ (in science fiction) a small personal aircraft. ▷late Middle English: frequentative of FLIT.

flit·ter·mouse /'flitər,mous/ ▸n. (pl. **-mice** /-,mīs/) old-fashioned term for BAT[2] (sense 1). ▷mid 16th cent.: on the pattern of Dutch *vledermuis* or German *Fledermaus.*

fliv·ver /'flivər/ ▸n. *informal, dated* a cheap car or aircraft, esp. one in bad condition. ▷early 20th cent.: of unknown origin.

flix·weed /'fliks,wēd/ ▸n. a Eurasian plant with small yellow flowers and finely divided leaves, formerly thought to cure dysentery. • *Descurainia sophia*, family Brassicaceae. ▷late 16th cent.: from obsolete *flix* (variant of FLUX) + WEED.

FLN ▸abbr. Front de Libération Nationale.

float /flōt/ ▸v. [intrans.] **1** rest or move on or near the surface of a liquid without sinking: *she relaxed, floating gently in the water.* ■ [trans.] cause (a buoyant object) to rest or move in such a way: *trees were felled and floated downstream.* ■ be suspended freely in a liquid or gas: *fragments of chipped cartilage floated in the joint.* **2** [with adverbial of direction] move or hover slowly and lightly in a liquid or the air; drift: *clouds floated across a brilliant blue sky* | *figurative through the open window floated the sound of traffic.* ■ (**float about/around**) (of a rumor, idea, or substance) circulate: *the notion was floating around Capitol Hill.* ■ (of a sight or idea) come before the eyes or mind: *the advice his father had given him **floated into** his mind.* ■ [trans.] (in sports) make (the ball) travel lightly and effortlessly through the air: *he floated the kick into the net.* **3** [trans.] put forward (an idea) as a suggestion or test of reactions. ■ [trans.] offer the shares of (a company) for sale on the stock market for the first time. **4** (of a currency) fluctuate freely in value in accordance with supply and demand in the financial markets: *a policy of letting the pound float.* ■ [trans.] allow (a currency) to fluctuate in such a way.
▸n. **1** a thing that is buoyant in water, in particular: ■ a small object attached to a fishing line to indicate by moving when a fish bites. ■ a cork or buoy supporting the edge of a fishing net. ■ a hollow or inflated organ enabling an organism (such as the Portuguese man-of-war) to float in the water. ■ a hollow structure fixed underneath an aircraft enabling it to take off and land on water. ■ a device floating on the surface of a liquid that forms part of a valve apparatus controlling flow in and out of the enclosing container, e.g., in a toilet tank or a carburetor. **2** a platform mounted on a truck and carrying a display in a parade: *a carnival float.* **3** a hand tool with a rectangular blade used for smoothing plaster or concrete. **4** a soft drink with a scoop of ice cream floating in it: *root-beer floats.* **5** (in critical path analysis) the period of time by which the duration of an activity may be extended without affecting the overall time for the process. ▷Old English *flotian* (verb), of Germanic origin and related to FLEET[5], reinforced in Middle English by Old French *floter*, also from Germanic.
▸PHRASE □ **float someone's boat** *informal* appeal to or excite someone, esp. sexually: *Kevin doesn't exactly float her boat.*

float·a·ble /'flōtəbəl/ ▸adj. capable of floating. ■ (of water) able to support floating objects; deep enough to float in.

Pronunciation Key ə ago; ər over; 'ə or ,ə up; 'ər or ,ər fur; a hat; ā rate; ä car; CH chew; e let; ē see; e(ə)r air; i fit; ī by; i(ə)r ear; NG sing; ō go; ô for; oi boy; o͝o good; o͞o goo; ou out; SH she; TH thin; T͟H then; (h)w why; ZH vision

F

float arm ▸*n.* the hinged arm attached to the ball float in the ball cock of a toilet tank.

float·a·tion /flō'tāsнən/ ▸*n.* variant spelling of **FLOTATION**.

float·el /flō'tel/ (also **flot·el**) ▸*n.* a floating hotel, esp. a boat used as a hotel. ■ a vessel providing housing for workers on an offshore oil rig. ▷1950s: blend of **FLOAT** and **HOTEL**.

float·er /'flōtər/ ▸*n.* **1** a person or thing that floats, in particular: ■ a worker who is required to do a variety of tasks as the need for each arises. ■ *informal* a person who frequently changes occupation or residence. ■ a fishing float. ■ a loose particle within the eyeball that is apparent in one's field of vision. **2** an insurance policy covering loss of articles without specifying a location.

float glass ▸*n.* glass made by allowing it to solidify on molten metal.

float·ing /'flōtiNG/ ▸*adj.* [*attrib.*] **1** buoyant or suspended in water or air: *a massive floating platform.* **2** not settled in a definite place; fluctuating or variable: *the floating population that is migrating to the cities.*

float·ing debt ▸*n.* a debt that is repayable in the short term. Compare with **FUNDED DEBT**.

float·ing dock ▸*n.* a submersible floating structure used as a dry dock.

float·ing kid·ney ▸*n.* a condition in which the kidneys are abnormally movable. ■ such a kidney.

float·ing-point ▸*adj.* *Computing* denoting a mode of representing numbers as two sequences of bits, one representing the digits in the number and the other an exponent that determines the position of the radix point: *speeds of more than one million **floating-point operations** per second.* Often contrasted with **FIXED-POINT**.

float·ing rib ▸*n.* any of the lower ribs that are not attached directly to the breastbone. Also called **FALSE RIB**.

float·plane /'flōt,plān/ ▸*n.* an aircraft equipped with floats for landing on water; a seaplane.

float valve ▸*n.* another term for **BALL VALVE**.

float·y /'flōtē/ ▸*adj.* (of a feeling or experience) feeling as though floating: *she had a floaty feeling that made her unreal to herself.* ■ (esp. of a woman's garment or a fabric) light and flimsy: *elegant floaty dresses.*

floc /fläk/ ▸*n.* *technical* a loosely clumped mass of fine particles. ▷1920s: abbreviation of **FLOCCULUS**.

floc·ci·nau·ci·ni·hil·i·pil·i·fi·ca·tion /,fläksə,nôsə,nī-,hilə,piləfi'kāsнən/ ▸*n.* the action or habit of estimating something as worthless. (The word is used chiefly as a curiosity.) ▷mid 18th cent.: from Latin *flocci, nauci, nihili, pili* (words meaning 'at little value') + **-FICATION**. The Latin elements were listed in a well-known rule of the Latin Grammar used at Eton College, an English public school.

floc·cose /'fläk,ōs/ ▸*adj.* *chiefly Botany* covered with or consisting of woolly tufts. ▷mid 18th cent.: from late Latin *floccosus*, from Latin *floccus* 'flock.'

floc·cu·lant /'fläkyələnt/ ▸*n.* a substance that promotes the clumping of particles, esp. one used in treating waste water.

floc·cu·late /'fläkyə,lāt/ ▸*v.* *technical* form or cause to form into small clumps or masses: [*intrans.*] *it tends to flocculate in high salinities* | [*trans.*] *its ability to flocculate suspended silt.* ▷late 19th cent.: from modern Latin *flocculus* 'floccule' + **-ATE**[3]. —**floc·cu·la·tion** /,fläkyə'lāsнən/ *n.*

floc·cule /'fläk,yo͞ol/ ▸*n.* a small clump of material that resembles a tuft of wool. ▷mid 19th cent.: from modern Latin *flocculus*, diminutive of *floccus* 'flock.'

floc·cu·lent /'fläkyələnt/ ▸*adj.* having or resembling tufts of wool: *the first snows of winter lay thick and flocculent.* ■ having a loosely clumped texture: *a brown flocculent precipitate.* ▷early 19th cent.: from Latin *floccus* 'tuft of wool' + **-ULENT**. —**floc·cu·lence** *n.*

floc·cu·lus /'fläkyələs/ ▸*n.* (*pl.* **-li** /-,lī; -,lē/) **1** *Anatomy* a small egg-shaped lobe on the undersurface of the cerebellum. **2** *Astronomy* a small cloudy wisp on the surface of the sun. **3** a floccule. ▷late 18th cent.: modern Latin, diminutive of Latin *floccus* (see **FLOCCUS**).

floc·cus /'fläkəs/ ▸*n.* (*pl.* **floc·ci** /'fläk,sī; -,sē/) a tuft of wool or similar clump of fibers or filaments. ▷mid 19th cent.: from Latin, 'lock or tuft of wool.' Compare with **FLOCK**[2].

flock[1] /fläk/ ▸*n.* a number of birds of one kind feeding, resting, or traveling together: ***a flock of** gulls.* ■ a number of domestic animals, esp. sheep, goats, or geese, that are kept together: ***a flock of** sheep.* ■ (**flocks**) large crowds of people: ***flocks of** young people hung around at twilight.* ■ a group of children or students in someone's charge. ■ a Christian congregation or body of believers, esp. one under the charge of a particular minister: *Thomas addressed his flock.* [alluding to the metaphor of Christ or a Christian pastor as a shepherd.]
▸*v.* [*intrans.*] congregate or mass in a flock or large group: *students flocked to spring break sites.* ▷Old English *flocc*, of unknown origin. The original sense was 'a band or body of people': this became obsolete, but has been reintroduced as a transferred use of the sense 'a number of animals kept together.'

flock[2] (also **flock·ing**) ▸*n.* [often as *adj.*] a soft material for stuffing cushions, quilts, and other soft furnishings, made of wool refuse or torn-up cloth: *flock mattresses.* ■ powdered wool or cloth, sprinkled on wallpaper, cloth, or metal to make a raised pattern. ■ a lock or tuft of wool or cotton. ▷Middle English: from Old French *floc*, from Latin *floccus* (see **FLOCCUS**). —**flock·y** *adj.*

Flod·den, Battle of /'flädn/ (also **Flodden Field**) a decisive battle of the Anglo-Scottish war of 1513, at Flodden, a hill near the Northumbrian village of Branxton in northeastern England. A Scottish army under James IV was defeated by a smaller but better-led English force and suffered heavy losses, including the king and most of his nobles.

floe /flō/ (also **ice floe**) ▸*n.* a sheet of floating ice. ▷early 19th cent. (superseding **FLAKE**[1] in this sense): probably from Norwegian *flo*, from Old Norse *fló* 'layer.'

flog /fläg/ ▸*v.* (**flogged, flog·ging**) [*trans.*] **1** beat (someone) with a whip or stick as punishment or torture: *the stolen horses will be returned and the thieves flogged* | [as *n.*] (**flogging**) *public floggings.* ■ *informal* promote or talk about (something) repetitively or at excessive length: *rather than **flogging** one idea **to death**, they should be a lighthearted pop group.* **2** *Brit., informal* sell or offer for sale: *he made a fortune flogging beads to hippies.* ▷late 17th cent. (originally slang): perhaps imitative, or from Latin *flagellare* 'to whip,' from *flagellum* 'whip.' —**flog·ger** *n.*

flo·ka·ti /flō'kätē/ (also **flo·ka·ti rug**) ▸*n.* (*pl.* **-tis**) a Greek woven woolen rug with a thick loose pile. ▷mid 20th cent.: from modern Greek *phlokatē* 'peasant's blanket.'

flood /fləd/ ▸*n.* **1** an overflowing of a large amount of water beyond its normal confines, esp. over what is normally dry land: *in a thousand miles the flood destroyed every bridge* | *people uprooted by drought or flood* | [as *adj.*] *a flood barrier.* ■ (**the Flood**) the biblical flood brought by God upon the earth because of the wickedness of the human race (Gen. 6 ff.). ■ the inflow of the tide. ■ *poetic/literary* a river, stream, or sea. **2** an outpouring of tears or emotion: *Rose burst into such a **flood of** tears and sobs as I had never seen.* ■ a very large quantity of people or things that appear or need to be dealt with: *a constant **flood of** callers.* **3** short for **FLOODLIGHT**.
▸*v.* **1** [*trans.*] cover or submerge (a place or area) with water: *the dam burst, flooding a small town* | *watching her father flood their backyard skating rink* | [as *n.*] (**flooding**) *a serious risk of flooding.* ■ [*intrans.*] become covered or submerged in this way: *part of the vessel flooded* | *figurative Sarah's eyes **flooded with** tears.* ■ (usu. **be flooded out**) drive someone out of their home or business with a flood: *most of the families who have been flooded out will receive compensation.* ■ (of a river or sea) become swollen and overflow (its banks): *the river flooded its banks* | [*intrans.*] *the river will flood if it gets much worse.* ■ overfill the carburetor of (an engine) with fuel, causing the engine to fail to start. **2** [*intrans.*] arrive in overwhelming amounts or quantities: *congratulatory messages flooded in* | *his old fears came flooding back.* ■ [*trans.*] overwhelm or swamp with large amounts or quantities: *our switchboard was **flooded with** calls.* ■ [*trans.*] fill or suffuse completely: *she flooded the room with light.* ▷Old English *flōd*, of Germanic origin; related to Dutch *vloed* and German *Flut*, also to **FLOW**.
▸*PHRASE* □ **be in** (**full**) **flood** (of a river) be swollen and overflowing its banks. ■ (**be in full flood**) *figurative* (of a person or action) have gained momentum; be at the height of activity: *discussion was already in full flood and refused to be dammed.*

flood·gate /'fləd,gāt/ ▸*n.* a gate that can be opened or closed to admit or exclude water, esp. the lower gate of a lock. ■ (usu. **the floodgates**) *figurative* a last restraint holding back an outpouring of something powerful or substantial: *his lawsuit could **open the floodgates** for thousands of similar claims.*

flood·light /'fləd,līt/ ▸*n.* a large, powerful light, typically one of several used to illuminate a sports field, a stage, or the exterior of a building. ■ the illumination provided by such a light: *a tennis court where you can play by floodlight.*
▸*v.* (*past* and *past part.* **-lit**) [*trans.*] [usu. as *adj.*] (**floodlit**) illuminate (a building or outdoor area) with such lights: *floodlit football fields.*

flood·plain /'fləd,plān/ ▸*n.* an area of low-lying ground adjacent to a river, formed mainly of river sediments and subject to flooding.

flood tide ▸*n.* an incoming tide. ■ a powerful surge or flow of something: *the trickle of tourists has become a flood tide.*

flood·wa·ter /'fləd,wôtər; -,wätər/ (also **flood·wa·ters**) ▸*n.* water overflowing as the result of a flood: *trying to track the rising floodwaters and coordinate relief efforts.*

floor /flôr/ ▸*n.* **1** the lower surface of a room, on which one may walk: *he dropped the cup and it smashed **on the floor*** | *the kitchen floor.* ■ all the rooms or areas on the same level of a building; a story: *his office was on the twenty-second floor* | [as *adj.*, in *combination*] *a third-floor apartment.* ■ a level area or space used or designed for a particular activity. ■ *figurative* the minimum level of prices or wages: *the dollar's floor against the yen.* ■ *informal* the ground: *the best way to play is to pass the ball on the floor.* ■ the bottom of the sea, a cave, or an area of land: *the ocean floor.* **2** (**the floor**) (in a legislative assembly) the part of the house in which members sit and from which they speak. ■ the right or opportunity to speak next in debate: *other speakers **have the floor**.* ■ (of the stock exchange) the large central hall where trading takes place.
▸*v.* [*trans.*] **1** (often **be floored**) provide (a room or area) with a floor: *a hall floored in gleaming white oak.* | [as *adj.*, in *combination*] (**-floored**) *a stone-floored building.* **2** *informal* knock (someone) to the ground, esp. with a punch. ■ baffle or confound (someone) completely: *that question floored him.* ▷Old English *flōr*, of Germanic origin; related to Dutch *vloer* and German *Flur*.
▸*PHRASES* □ **cross the floor** see **CROSS**. □ **from the floor** (of a speech or question) delivered by an individual member at a meeting, not by a representative on the platform: *questions from the floor will be invited.* □ **take the floor 1** begin to dance on a dance floor. **2** speak in a debate or assembly.

floor·board /'flôr,bôrd/ ▸*n.* a long plank making up part of a wooden floor in a building. ■ the floor of a motor vehicle: *the keys had fallen on the floorboard of her car.*

floor·cloth /'flôr,klôтн/ ▸*n.* a thin canvas rug or similar light floor covering.

floor ex·er·cise ▸*n.* a routine of gymnastic exercises performed without the use any of apparatus.

floor·ing /'flôriNG/ ▸*n.* the boards or other material of which a floor is made.

floor lamp ▸*n.* a tall lamp designed to stand on the floor.

floor lead·er ▸*n.* the leader of a party in a legislative assembly.

floor man·ag·er ▸*n.* **1** the stage manager of a television production. **2** an employee in a large store who supervises other salespeople.

floor·pan /'flôr,pan/ ▸*n.* *chiefly Brit.* the lower part of the body of a motor vehicle, forming the floor of the passenger compartment.

floor plan ▸*n.* a scale diagram of the arrangement of rooms in one story of a building.

floor sam·ple ▸*n.* an article of merchandise that has been displayed in a store and that is offered for sale at a reduced price.

floor show ▸*n.* an entertainment, such as singing or comedy, presented at a nightclub, restaurant, or similar venue.

floor-through a·part·ment ▸*n.* an apartment that occupies an entire floor of a building.

floor·walk·er /'flôr,wôkər/ ▸*n.* a senior employee of a large store who assists customers and supervises salespeople.

floo·zy /'flo͞ozē/ (also **floo·zie, floo·sie**) ▸*n.* (*pl.* **-zies**) *informal* a girl or a woman who has a reputation for promiscuity. ▷early 20th cent.: perhaps related to **FLOSSY** or to dialect *floosy* 'fluffy.'

flop /fläp/ ▸*v.* (**flopped, flop·ping**) **1** [*intrans.*] fall, move, or hang in a heavy, loose, and ungainly way: *black hair flopped across his forehead.* ■ sit or lie down heavily or suddenly in a specified place, esp. when very tired: *Liz flopped down into the armchair.* ■ *informal* rest or sleep in a specified place: *I'm going to flop here for the night.* **2** [*intrans.*] *informal* (of a performer or show) be completely unsuccessful; fail totally:

prime-time dramas that flopped in the U.S. market. **3** [*trans.*] *Photography* invert (a negative) so that the right and left sides of a photograph are reversed: *a cover photograph of downtown Pittsburgh that we inadvertently flopped.*
▸*n.* **1** a heavy, loose, and ungainly movement, or a sound made by it: *they hit the ground with a flop.* ■ *informal* a cheap place to sleep. **2** *informal* a total failure: *the play had been a flop.* ▷early 17th cent.: variant of FLAP.

-flop ▸*comb. form Computing* floating-point operations per second (used as a measure of computing power): *a gigaflop computer.* ▷acronym; originally spelled *-flops* (*s* = second) but shortened to avoid misinterpretation as plural.

flop·house /ˈfläpˌhous/ ▸*n. informal* a cheap hotel or rooming house.

flop·py /ˈfläpē/ ▸*adj.* (**flop·pi·er**, **flop·pi·est**) tending to hang or move in a limp, loose, or ungainly way: *the dog had floppy ears | floppy hats.*
▸*n.* (*pl.* **-pies**) (also **flop·py disk**) *Computing* short for FLOPPY DISK. **—flop·pi·ly** /ˈfläpəlē/ *adv.* **—flop·pi·ness** *n.*

flop·py disk ▸*n. Computing* a flexible removable magnetic disk, typically encased in hard plastic, used for storing data. Also called DISKETTE. Compare with HARD DISK.

flop·ti·cal /ˈfläptikəl/ ▸*adj. trademark Computing* denoting or relating to a type of floppy-disk drive using a laser to position the read-write head.
▸*n.* a floppy-disk drive of this type. ▷1980s: blend of FLOPPY and OPTICAL.

flor /flôr/ ▸*n.* yeast allowed to develop in a whitish film on the surface of dry (fino) sherries and similar wines during fermentation. ▷late 19th cent.: from Spanish, literally 'flower.'

flor. ▸*abbr.* floruit.

Flo·ra /ˈflôrə/ *Roman Mythology* the goddess of flowering plants.

flo·ra /ˈflôrə/ ▸*n.* (*pl.* **flo·ras** or **flo·rae** /ˈflôrē; ˈflôrī/) the plants of a particular region, habitat, or geological period: *the desert flora give way to oak woodlands | the river's **flora and fauna** have been inventoried and protected.* Compare with FAUNA. ■ a treatise on or list of such plant life. ▷late 18th cent.: from Latin *flos, flor-* 'flower.'

flo·ral /ˈflôrəl/ ▸*adj.* of flowers: *celebrations of the season's floral abundance.* ■ decorated with or depicting flowers: *a floral pattern.* ■ *Botany* of flora or floras: *faunal and floral evolution.*
▸*n.* a fabric with a floral design. ▷mid 18th cent.: from Latin *flos, flor-* 'flower' + -AL. **—flo·ral·ly** *adv.*

Flo·ré·al /ˌflôrāˈäl/ ▸*n.* the eighth month of the French Republican calendar (1793–1805), originally running from April 20 to May 19. ▷French, from Latin *floreus* 'flowery,' from *flos, flor-* 'flower.'

Flor·ence /ˈflôrəns; ˈflär-/ **1** a city in western central Italy, the capital of Tuscany, on the Arno River; pop. 408,000. Florence was a leading center of the Italian Renaissance, esp. under the rule of the Medici family during the 15th century. Italian name FIRENZE. **2** an industrial and commercial city in northwestern Alabama, on the Tennessee River, east of Muscle Shoals; pop. 36,264. **3** a city in northern Kentucky, southwest of Covington; pop. 23,551. **4** a commercial city in northeastern South Carolina; pop. 30,248.

Flor·ence fen·nel ▸*n.* see FENNEL.

Flor·en·tine /ˈflôrənˌtēn; -tīn/ ▸*adj.* **1** of or relating to Florence. **2** (**florentine**) [*postpositive*] (of food) served or prepared on a bed of spinach: *eggs florentine.*
▸*n.* **1** a native or citizen of Florence. **2** (**florentine**) a cookie consisting mainly of nuts and preserved fruit, coated on one side with chocolate. ▷Middle English (as a noun): from French *Florentin(e)* or Latin *Florentinus*, from *Florentia* 'Florence.'

Flo·res /ˈflôrəs/ the largest of the Lesser Sunda Islands in Indonesia.

flo·res·cence /flôrˈesəns; fləˈres-/ ▸*n.* the process of flowering: *the Hieracia are erect throughout the process of florescence | figurative a spectacular cultural florescence.* ▷late 18th cent.: from modern Latin *florescentia*, from Latin *florescere* 'begin to flower,' based on *flos, flor-* 'flower.'

flo·ret /ˈflôrət/ ▸*n. Botany* one of the small flowers making up a composite flowerhead. ■ one of the flowering stems making up a head of cauliflower or broccoli. ■ a small flower. ▷late 17th cent.: from Latin *flos, flor-* 'flower' + -ET[1].

Flo·rey /ˈflôrē/, Howard Walter, Baron (1898–1968), Australian pathologist. With Ernst Chain he isolated and purified penicillin. Nobel Prize for Physiology or Medicine (1945, shared with Chain and Fleming).

Flo·ri·a·nó·po·lis /ˌflôrēəˈnôpəlis/ a city in southern Brazil, on the Atlantic coast; pop. 293,000.

flo·ri·at·ed /ˈflôrēˌātid/ ▸*adj.* decorated with floral designs.

flo·ri·bun·da /ˌflôrəˈbəndə/ ▸*n.* a plant, esp. a rose, that bears dense clusters of flowers. ▷late 19th cent.: modern Latin, feminine (used as a noun) of *floribundus* 'freely flowering,' from Latin *flos, flor-* 'flower,' influenced by Latin *abundus* 'copious.'

flo·ri·can /ˈflôrəˌkan/ ▸*n.* a small South Asian bustard, the male of which has mainly black plumage with white wings. • Family Otidae: the **Bengal florican** (*Houbaropsis begalensis*) and the **lesser florican** (*Sypheotides indica*). ▷late 18th cent.: of unknown origin.

flo·ri·cul·ture /ˈflôriˌkəlCHər/ ▸*n.* the cultivation of flowers. ▷early 19th cent.: from Latin *flos, flor-* 'flower' + CULTURE, on the pattern of *horticulture.* **—flo·ri·cul·tur·al** /ˌflôriˈkəlCHərəl/ *adj.* **—flo·ri·cul·tur·ist** /ˌflôriˈkəlCHərist/ *n.*

flor·id /ˈflôrid; ˈflär-/ ▸*adj.* **1** having a red or flushed complexion: *a stout man with a florid face.* **2** elaborately or excessively intricate or complicated: *florid operatic-style music was out.* ■ (of language) using unusual words or complicated rhetorical constructions: *the florid prose of the nineteenth century.* **3** *Medicine* (of a disease or its manifestations) occurring in a fully developed form: *florid symptoms of psychiatric disorder.* ▷mid 17th cent.: from Latin *floridus*, from *flos, flor-* 'flower.' **—flo·rid·i·ty** /fləˈridətē/ *n.* **—flor·id·ly** *adv.* **—flor·id·ness** *n.*

Flor·i·da /ˈflôridə; ˈflär-/ a state in the southeastern U.S., on a peninsula that extends into the Atlantic Ocean and the Gulf of Mexico; pop. 15,982,378; capital, Tallahassee; statehood, Mar. 3, 1845 (27). Explored by Ponce de León in 1513, it was purchased from Spain by the U.S. in 1819. It is a popular resort and retirement area. **—Flo·rid·i·an** /fləˈridēən; flô-; flä-/ *adj.* & *n.*

Flor·i·da Keys a chain of small islands off the tip of the Florida peninsula. Linked to each other and to the mainland by a series of causeways and bridges that form the Overseas Highway, the islands extend southwest over a distance of 100 miles (160 km).

Flor·i·da room ▸*n.* another term for SUNROOM.

Flor·i·da tor·rey·a /ˈtôrēə/ ▸*n.* another term for STINKING CEDAR.

flo·rif·er·ous /flôˈrifərəs/ ▸*adj.* (of a plant) producing many flowers. ▷mid 17th cent.: from Latin *florifer* (from *flos, flor-* 'flower' + *-fer* 'producing') + -OUS.

flo·ri·le·gi·um /ˌflôrəˈlējēəm/ ▸*n.* (*pl.* **-le·gi·a** /-ˈlējēə/ or **-le·gi·ums**) a collection of literary extracts; an anthology. ▷early 17th cent.: modern Latin, literally 'bouquet' (from Latin *flos, flor-* 'flower' + *legere* 'gather'), translation of Greek *anthologion* (see ANTHOLOGY).

flor·in /ˈflôrən; ˈflär-/ ▸*n.* **1** a former British coin and monetary unit worth two shillings. **2** a foreign coin of gold or silver, esp. a Dutch guilder. **3** the basic monetary unit of Aruba, equal to 100 cents. ▷via Old French from Italian *fiorino*, diminutive of *fiore* 'flower,' from Latin *flos, flor-*. The word originally denoted a gold coin issued in Florence, bearing a fleur-de-lis (the city's emblem) on the reverse.

Flor·is·sant /ˈflôrəsənt/ a historic city in east central Missouri, northwest of St. Louis; pop. 50,497.

flo·rist /ˈflôrist/ ▸*n.* a person who sells and arranges plants and cut flowers. ▷early 17th cent.: from Latin *flos, flor-* 'flower,' on the pattern of French *fleuriste* or Italian *florista.* **—flo·rist·ry** /-trē/ *n.*

flo·ris·tic /fləˈristik/ ▸*adj. Botany* relating to the study of the distribution of plants. **—flo·ris·ti·cal·ly** /-(ə)lē/ *adv.*

flo·ris·tics /fləˈristiks/ ▸*plural n.* [treated as *sing.*] *Botany* the branch of phytogeography concerned with the study of plant species present in an area.

flo·ru·it /ˈflôr(y)o͞oit/ (abbr.: **fl.** or **flor.**) ▸*v.* used in conjunction with a specified period or set of dates to indicate when a particular historical figure lived, worked, or was most active.
▸*n.* such a period: *they place Nicander's floruit in the middle of the 2nd century* BC. ▷mid 19th cent.: Latin, literally 'he or she flourished'.

flo·ry /ˈflôrē/ (also **fleu·ry** /ˈflərē; ˈflo͝orē/) ▸*adj.* [*predic.* or *postpositive*] *Heraldry* decorated with fleurs-de-lis. ■ (of a cross) having the end of each limb splayed out into three pointed lobes. ▷late Middle English: from Old French *floure*, from *flour* 'flower.'
▸*PHRASE* □ **flory counter-flory** decorated with fleurs-de-lis set in alternating directions.

floss /flôs; fläs/ ▸*n.* the rough silk enveloping a silkworm's cocoon. ■ (also **floss silk**) untwisted silk fibers used in embroidery. ■ the silky down in corn and other plants: *milkweed floss.* ■ short for DENTAL FLOSS.
▸*v.* [*trans.*] clean between (one's teeth) with dental floss: *I flossed my teeth | [intrans.] you must floss well.* ▷mid 18th cent.: from French *(soie) floche* 'floss (silk),' from Old French *flosche* 'down, nap of velvet,' of unknown origin.

floss·y /ˈflôsē; ˈfläsē/ ▸*adj.* (**floss·i·er**, **floss·i·est**) **1** of or like floss: *short flossy curls.* **2** *informal* excessively showy: *the flossy gleam of a cheap suit | she cultivated flossy friends.*

flo·ta·tion /flōˈtāSHən/ (also **float·a·tion**) ▸*n.* the action of floating in a liquid or gas: *the body form is modified to assist in flotation and propulsion.* ■ the process of offering a company's shares for sale on the stock market for the first time. ■ the process of separating small particles of various materials by treatment with chemicals in water in order to make some particles adhere to air bubbles and rise to the surface for removal while others remain in the water. ■ the capacity to float; buoyancy. ▷early 19th cent.: alteration of *floatation* (from FLOAT) on the pattern of French *flottaison*. The spelling *flot-* was influenced by FLOTILLA.

flo·ta·tion tank ▸*n.* a lightproof, soundproof tank of salt water in which a person floats as a form of deep relaxation.

flo·tel ▸*n.* variant spelling of FLOATEL.

flo·til·la /flōˈtilə/ ▸*n.* a fleet of ships or boats: ***a flotilla** of cargo boats.* ▷early 18th cent.: from Spanish, diminutive of *flota* 'fleet.'

flot·sam /ˈflätsəm/ ▸*n.* the wreckage of a ship or its cargo found floating on or washed up by the sea. Compare with JETSAM. ■ *figurative* people or things that have been rejected and are regarded as worthless: *the room was cleared of boxes and other flotsam.* ▷early 17th cent.: from Anglo-Norman French *floteson*, from *floter* 'to float.'
▸*PHRASE* □ **flotsam and jetsam** useless or discarded objects.

flounce[1] /flouns/ ▸*v.* [*intrans.*] go or move in an exaggeratedly impatient or angry manner: *he stood up in a fury and flounced out.* ■ move with exaggerated motions: *she flounced around, playing the tart and flirting.*
▸*n.* [in *sing.*] an exaggerated action, typically intended to express one's annoyance or impatience: *she left the room with a flounce.* ▷mid 16th cent.: perhaps of Scandinavian origin and related to Norwegian *flunsa* 'hurry,' or perhaps symbolic, like *bounce* or *pounce.*

flounce[2] ▸*n.* a wide ornamental strip of material gathered and sewn to a piece of fabric, typically on a skirt or dress; a frill.
▸*v.* [as *adj.*] (**flounced**) trimmed with a flounce or flounces: *a flounced skirt.* ▷early 18th cent.: from an alteration of obsolete *frounce* 'a fold or pleat,' from Old French *fronce*, of Germanic origin; related to RUCK[2]. **—flounc·y** /ˈflounsē/ *adj.*

floun·der[1] /ˈfloundər/ ▸*v.* [*intrans.*] struggle or stagger helplessly or clumsily in water or mud: *he was **floundering about** in the shallow offshore waters.* ■ *figurative* struggle mentally; show or feel great confusion: *she floundered, not knowing quite what to say.* ■ *figurative* be in serious difficulty: *many firms are floundering.* ▷late 16th cent.: perhaps a blend of FOUNDER[3] and BLUNDER, or perhaps symbolic, *fl-* frequently beginning words connected with swift or sudden movement. **—floun·der·er** *n.*

USAGE See usage at FOUNDER[2].

floun·der[2] ▸*n.* a small flatfish that typically occurs in shallow coastal water. • Families Pleuronectidae and Bothidae: several species, in particular the edible *Platichthys flesus* of European waters. ■ (**flounders**) a collective term for flatfishes other than soles. See FLATFISH. ▷Middle English: from Old French *flondre*, probably of Scandinavian origin and related to Danish *flynder.*

flour /ˈflou(ə)r/ ▸*n.* a powder obtained by grinding grain, typically wheat, and used to make bread, cakes, and pastry. ■ fine soft powder obtained by grinding the seeds or roots of starchy vegetables:

manioc flour. ■ any fine powder: *the resin is mixed with a filler such as wood flour.*

▸v. [*trans.*] sprinkle (something, esp. a work surface or cooking utensil) with a thin layer of flour: *grease and flour two round cake pans.* ■ grind (grain) into flour. ▷Middle English: a specific use of FLOWER in the sense 'the best part,' used originally to mean 'the finest quality of ground wheat.' The spelling *flower* remained in use alongside *flour* until the early 19th cent.

flour bee·tle ▸n. a small brown darkling beetle that is a widespread pest of flour and other cereal products. • Genera *Tribolium, Gnathocerus,* and others, family Tenebrionidae: several species.

flour·ish /ˈflərish/ ▸v. **1** [*intrans.*] (of a person, animal, or other living organism) grow or develop in a healthy or vigorous way, esp. as the result of a particularly favorable environment: *wild plants flourish on the banks of the lake.* ■ develop rapidly and successfully: *the organization has continued to flourish.* ■ [with *adverbial*] (of a person) be working or at the height of one's career during a specified period: *the caricaturist and wit who flourished in the early years of this century.* **2** [*trans.*] (of a person) wave (something) around to attract the attention of others: *"Happy New Year!" he yelled, flourishing a bottle of whiskey.*

▸n. **1** a bold or extravagant gesture or action, made esp. to attract the attention of others: ***with a flourish,*** *she ushered them inside.* ■ an instance of suddenly performing or developing in an impressively successful way: *the Bulldogs produced a late second-half flourish.* ■ an elaborate rhetorical or literary expression. ■ an ornamental flowing curve in handwriting or scrollwork: *spiky gothic letters with an emphatic flourish beneath them.* **2** *Music* a fanfare played by brass instruments: *a flourish of trumpets.* ■ an ornate musical passage. ■ an improvised addition played esp. at the beginning or end of a composition. ▷Middle English: from Old French *floriss-,* lengthened stem of *florir,* based on Latin *florere,* from *flos, flor-* 'a flower.' The noun senses 'ornamental curve' and 'florid expression' come from an obsolete sense of the verb, 'adorn' (originally with flowers). **—flour·ish·er** n.

flour moth (in full **Mediterranean flour moth**) ▸n. a grayish-yellow moth, the caterpillar of which is a pest of flour and cereal products. • *Ephestia kuehniella,* family Pyralidae.

flour·y /ˈflou(ə)rē/ ▸adj. covered with flour: *Maggie wiped her floury hands on her apron.* ■ of or resembling flour: *floury white makeup.* **—flour·i·ness** n.

flout /flout/ ▸v. [*trans.*] openly disregard (a rule, law or convention): *these same companies still flout basic ethical practices.* ■ [*intrans.*] *archaic* mock; scoff: *the women pointed and* ***flouted at*** *her.* ▷mid 16th cent.: perhaps from Dutch *fluiten* 'whistle, play the flute, hiss (in derision)'; German dialect *pfeifen auf,* literally 'pipe at,' has a similar extended meaning.

USAGE **Flout** and **flaunt** do not have the same meaning: see **usage** at FLAUNT.

flow /flō/ ▸v. [*intrans.*] (esp. of a fluid) move along or out steadily and continuously in a current or stream: *from here the river flows north | a cross-current of electricity seemed to flow between them.* ■ (of the sea or a tidal river) move toward the land; rise. Compare with EBB. ■ [with *adverbial of direction*] (of clothing or hair) hang loosely in an easy and graceful manner: *her red hair* ***flowed over*** *her shoulders.* ■ circulate continuously within a particular system: *ventilation channels keep the air flowing | an electric current flows through it.* ■ [with *adverbial of direction*] (of people or things) go from one place to another in a steady stream, typically in large numbers: *the firm is hoping the orders will keep* ***flowing in.*** ■ proceed or be produced smoothly, continuously, and effortlessly: *talk flowed freely around the table.* ■ (**flow from**) result from; be caused by: *there are certain advantages that may flow from that decision.* ■ be available in copious quantities: *their talk and laughter grew louder as the excellent brandy flowed.* ■ (of a solid) undergo a permanent change of shape under stress, without melting.

▸n. [in *sing.*] the action or fact of moving along in a steady, continuous stream: *the flow of water into the pond.* ■ the rate or speed at which such a stream moves: *under the ford the river backs up, giving a deep sluggish flow.* ■ the rise of a tide or a river. Compare with EBB. ■ a steady, continuous stream of something: *she eased the car into* ***the flow of*** *traffic.* ■ menstrual discharge. ■ the gradual permanent deformation of a solid under stress, without melting. ▷Old English *flōwan,* of Germanic origin; related to Dutch *vloeien,* also to FLOOD.

▸*PHRASES* □ **go with the flow** *informal* be relaxed and accept a situation, rather than trying to alter or control it. □ **in full flow** talking fluently and easily and showing no sign of stopping. ■ performing vigorously and enthusiastically: *Richardson was run out when he was in full flow.*

flow chart (also **flow·chart** or **flow diagram**) ▸n. a diagram of the sequence of movements or actions of people or things involved in a complex system or activity. ■ a graphical representation of a computer program in relation to its sequence of functions (as distinct from the data it processes).

flow·er /ˈflou(-ə)r/ ▸n. *Botany* the seed-bearing part of a plant, consisting of reproductive organs (stamens and carpels) that are typically surrounded by a brightly colored corolla (petals) and a green calyx (sepals). ■ a brightly colored and conspicuous example of such a part of a plant together with its stalk, typically used with others as a decoration or gift: *I stopped to buy Bridget some flowers.* ■ the state or period in which a plant's flowers have developed and opened: *the roses were just coming* ***into flower.***

▸v. [*intrans.*] (of a plant) produce flowers; bloom: *these daisies can flower as late as October.* ■ *figurative* be in or reach an optimum stage of development; develop fully and richly: *it is there that the theory of deconstruction has flowered most extravagantly* | [as *n.*] (**flowering**) *the flowering of Viennese intellectual life.* ■ [*trans.*] induce (a plant) to produce flowers. ▷Middle English *flour,* from Old French *flour, flor,* from Latin *flos, flor-.* The original spelling was no longer in use by the late 17th cent. except in its specialized sense 'ground grain' (see FLOUR). **—flow·er·less** *adj.* **—flow·er·like** /-ˌlīk/ *adj.*

▸*PHRASE* □ **the flower of** **1** the finest individuals out of a number of people or things: *the flower of college track athletes.* **2** the period of optimum development: *a young policeman in the flower of his life gunned down.*

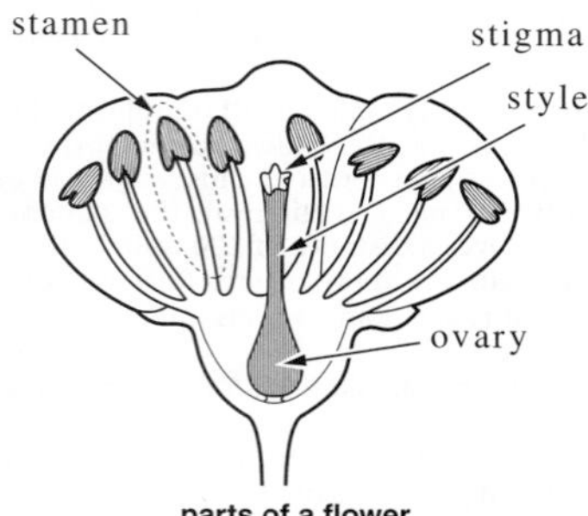

parts of a flower

flow·er·age /ˈflou(-ə)rij/ ▸n. the process of coming into flower: *the flowerage of Romanticism.*

flow·er bed ▸n. a garden plot in which flowers are grown.

flow·er bee·tle ▸n. any of a number of beetles that frequent flowers, in particular: • an elongated beetle with soft wing cases (chiefly of the family Melyridae). • a day-flying chafer (family Scarabaeidae).

flow·er child ▸n. *historical* a hippie who wore flowers as symbols of peace and love.

flow·ered /ˈflou(-ə)rd/ ▸adj. **1** (esp. of fabric or a garment) having a floral design: *flowered curtains.* **2** [in *combination*] (of a plant) bearing flowers of a specified kind or number: *yellow-flowered japonica.*

flow·er·er /ˈflou(-ə)rər/ ▸n. a plant that flowers at a specified time or in a specified manner: *bedding plants and other summer flowerers.*

flow·er es·sence ▸n. a substance prepared from a flowering plant and used therapeutically for its alleged beneficial effects on mood, outlook, etc.

flow·er·et /ˈflou(-ə)rət/ ▸n. a floret, esp. of cauliflower or broccoli.

flow·er girl ▸n. **1** a young girl who carries flowers or scatters them in front of the bride at a wedding; a child bridesmaid. **2** *Brit., dated* a woman or girl who sells flowers, esp. in the street.

flow·er head (also **flow·er·head**) ▸n. a compact mass of flowers at the top of a stem, esp. a capitulum.

flow·er·ing /ˈflou(-ə)ring/ ▸adj. (of a plant) in bloom: *a basket of flowering plants.* ■ capable of producing flowers, esp. in contrast to a similar plant with the flowers inconspicuous or absent: *flowering dogwood.* ■ [in *combination*] producing flowers at a specified time or of a specified type: *winter-flowering heathers.*

flow·er·ing cher·ry ▸n. an ornamental tree grown for its spring blossom, the fruit not being considered edible. • Genus *Prunus,* family Rosaceae: several species, in particular *P. serrulata* and its hybrids.

flow·er·ing cur·rant ▸n. an ornamental shrub grown for its clusters of small pinkish-red flowers. • Genus *Ribes,* family Grossulariaceae: several species, in particular the **red-flowering currant** (*R. sanguineum*).

flow·er·ing plant ▸n. a plant that produces flowers; an angiosperm.

flow·er·ing plum ▸n. another term for PURPLE LEAF PLUM.

flow·er·ing quince ▸n. an Asian shrub of the rose family, with bright red flowers followed by round white, green, or yellow edible fruits. Also called JAPANESE QUINCE, JAPONICA. • Genus *Chaenomeles,* family Rosaceae: several species, in particular *C. speciosa,* which is grown as an ornamental.

flow·er·ing rush ▸n. a tall rushlike plant with long narrow leaves and pinkish flowers, living in shallow slow-moving water. Native to Eurasia, it has become established in North America. • *Butomus umbellatus,* the only member of the family Butomaceae.

flow·er·peck·er /ˈflou(-ə)rˌpekər/ ▸n. a small songbird with a short bill and tail, feeding chiefly on insects in flowers and found in Australasia and Southeast Asia. • Family Dicaeidae (the **flowerpecker family**): two genera, esp. *Dicaeum.* The flowerpecker family also includes the pardalotes and the mistletoe bird.

flow·er·pot /ˈflou(-ə)rˌpät/ ▸n. a small container, typically with sloping sides and made from plastic or earthenware, used for growing a plant in.

flow·er pow·er ▸n. *historical* the ideas of the flower children, esp. the promotion of peace and love as means of changing the world.

flow·ers of sul·fur ▸*plural n.* [treated as *sing.*] *Chemistry* a fine yellow powdered form of sulfur produced by sublimation.

flow·ers of zinc ▸*plural n.* [treated as *sing.*] finely powdered zinc oxide.

flow·er·y /ˈflou(-ə)rē/ ▸adj. full of, resembling, or smelling of flowers: *a flowery meadow | flowery wallpaper.* ■ (of a style of speech or writing) full of elaborate or literary words and phrases: *flowery language.* **—flow·er·i·ness** /-rēnis/ n.

flow·ing /ˈflōiNG/ ▸adj. (esp. of long hair or clothing) hanging or draping loosely and gracefully: *a long flowing gown of lavender silk.* ■ (of a line or contour) smoothly continuous: *the flowing curves of the lawn.* ■ (of language, movement, or style) graceful and fluent: *a flowing prose style.* **—flow·ing·ly** *adv.*

flow·me·ter /ˈflōˌmētər/ ▸n. an instrument for measuring the rate of flow of a fluid, esp. through a pipe.

flown /flōn/ ▸ past participle of FLY[1].

flow·sheet /ˈflōˌSHēt/ ▸n. another term for FLOW CHART.

flow·stone /ˈflōˌstōn/ ▸n. *Geology* rock deposited as a thin sheet by precipitation from flowing water.

fl. oz. ▸*abbr.* fluid ounce.

flu /flo͞o/ ▸n. short for INFLUENZA: *I had a bad case of the flu.* ▷mid 19th cent.: abbreviation. **—flu·like** *adj.*

flub /fləb/ *informal* ▸v. (**flubbed, flub·bing**) [*trans.*] botch or bungle (something): *she glanced at her notes and flubbed her lines* | [*intrans.*] *don't flub again.*

▸n. a thing badly or clumsily done; a blunder: *the textbooks are littered with flubs.* ▷1920s: of unknown origin.

fluc·tu·ant /ˈfləkCHo͞oənt/ ▸adj. *poetic/literary* fluctuating; unstable. ▷mid 16th cent.: from Old French, 'undulating,' from Latin *fluctuare* 'undulate.'

fluc·tu·ate /ˈfləkCHo͞oˌāt/ ▸v. [*intrans.*] rise and fall irregularly in number or amount: *trade with other countries tends to fluctuate from year to year* | [as *adj.*] (**fluctuating**) *a fluctuating level of demand.* ▷mid 17th cent.: from Latin *fluctuat-* 'undulated,' from the verb *fluctuare,* from *fluctus* 'flow, current, wave,' from *fluere* 'to flow.' **—fluc·tu·a·tion** /ˌfləkCHo͞oˈāSHən/ n.

flue /flo͞o/ ▸n. a duct for smoke and waste gases produced by a fire, a gas heater, a power station, or other fuel-burning installation: *no air rises up the chimney, usually because the flue is blocked* | [as *adj.*] *flue gases.* ■ a channel for conveying heat. ▷late Middle English (denoting the mouthpiece of a hunting horn): of unknown origin. Current senses date from the late 16th cent.

flue-cure ▸v. [*trans.*] [often as *adj.*] (**flue-cured**) cure (tobacco) using heat from pipes or flues connected to a furnace; compare with AIR-CURE.

flu·ence /ˈflo͞oəns/ ▸n. *Physics* a stream of particles crossing a unit area, usually expressed as the number of particles per second. ▷early 17th cent. (in the sense 'a flowing, a stream'): from French, from Latin *fluentia*, from *fluere* 'to flow.'

flu·en·cy /'flo͞oənsē/ ▸*n.* the quality or condition of being fluent, in particular: ■ the ability to speak or write a foreign language easily and accurately: *fluency in Spanish is essential.* ■ the ability to express oneself easily and articulately. ■ gracefulness and ease of movement or style: *the horse was jumping with breathtaking fluency.* ▷early 17th cent.: from Latin *fluentia*, from *fluere* 'to flow.'

flu·ent /'flo͞oənt/ ▸*adj.* (of a person) able to express oneself easily and articulately: *a fluent speaker and writer on technical subjects.* ■ (of a person) able to speak or write a particular foreign language easily and accurately: *she became* ***fluent in*** *French and German.* ■ (of a foreign language) spoken accurately and with facility: *he spoke fluent Spanish.* ■ (of speech, language, movement, or style) smoothly graceful and easy: *his style of play was fast and fluent.* ■ able to flow freely; fluid: *a fluent discharge from the nose.* ▷late 16th cent. (also in the literal sense 'flowing freely or abundantly'): from Latin *fluent-* 'flowing,' from the verb *fluere*. **—flu·ent·ly** *adv.*

flue pipe ▸*n.* **1** a pipe acting as a flue. **2** an organ pipe into which the air enters directly without striking a reed.

flue stop ▸*n.* an organ stop for a set of flue pipes.

fluff /fləf/ ▸*n.* **1** soft fibers from fabrics such as wool or cotton that accumulate in small light clumps: *he brushed his sleeve to remove the fluff.* ■ any soft downy substance, esp. the fur or feathers of a young mammal or bird. ■ *figurative* entertainment or writing perceived as trivial or superficial: *the movie is a piece of typical Hollywood fluff.* **2** *informal* a mistake made in speaking or playing music, or by an actor in delivering lines.

▸*v.* [*trans.*] **1** make (something) appear fuller and softer, typically by shaking or brushing it: *I* ***fluffed up*** *the pillows.* **2** *informal* fail to perform or accomplish (something) successfully or well (used esp. in a sporting or acting context): *the extra fluffed his only line.* ▷late 18th cent.: probably a dialect alteration of 16th-cent. *flue* 'down, nap, fluff,' apparently from Flemish *vluwe*.

fluff·y /'fləfē/ ▸*adj.* (**fluff·i·er**, **fluff·i·est**) **1** of, like, or covered with fluff: *fluffy white clouds | a fluffy towel.* ■ (of food) light in texture and containing air: *cream the butter and sugar until pale and fluffy.* **2** *informal* lacking substance, depth, or seriousness: *the commercial wallows in soft, fluffy, feel-good territory.* ■ (of a person, esp. a woman) frivolous, silly, or vague: *fluffy blondes in leopard-skin pedal pushers.* **—fluff·i·ly** /'fləfəlē/ *adv.* **—fluff·i·ness** *n.*

flu·gel·horn /'flo͞ogəl,hôrn/ (also **flü·gel·horn**, **flue·gel·horn**) ▸*n.* a valved brass musical instrument like a cornet but with a mellower tone. ▷mid 19th cent.: from German *Flügelhorn*, from *Flügel* 'wing' + *Horn* 'horn.'

flu·id /'flo͞oid/ ▸*n.* a substance that has no fixed shape and yields easily to external pressure; a gas or (esp.) a liquid: *we all need several glasses of fluid a day | a cleaning fluid.*

▸*adj.* (of a substance) able to flow easily: *the paint is more fluid than tube watercolors | a fluid medium.* ■ not settled or stable; likely or able to change: *our plans are still fluid | the fluid political situation of the 1930s.* ■ smoothly elegant or graceful: *her movements were fluid and beautiful to watch.* ■ (of a clutch or coupling) using a liquid to transmit power. ▷late Middle English (as an adjective): from French *fluide* or Latin *fluidus*, from *fluere* 'to flow.' **—flu·id·ic** /flo͞o'idik/ *adj.* **—flu·id·i·ty** /flo͞o'idətē/ *n.* **—flu·id·ly** *adv.*

flu·id drachm ▸*n.* see **DRACHM**.

flu·id·ics /flo͞o'idiks/ ▸*plural n.* [often treated as *sing.*] the study and technique of using small interacting flows and fluid jets for functions usually performed by electronic devices. **—flu·id·ic** /flo͞o'idik/ *adj.*

flu·id·ize /'flo͞oə,dīz/ ▸*v.* [*trans.*] *technical* cause (a finely divided solid) to acquire the characteristics of a fluid by passing a gas upward through it. **—flu·id·i·za·tion** /,flo͞oədi'zāSHən/ *n.*

flu·id·ized bed ▸*n.* a layer of a fluidized solid, used in chemical processes and in the efficient burning of coal for power generation.

flu·id mech·an·ics ▸*plural n.* [treated as *sing.*] the branch of mechanics dealing with the properties of fluids in various states and with their reaction to forces acting upon them.

flu·id ounce (abbr.: **fl. oz.**) ▸*n.* **1** a unit of capacity equal to one sixteenth of a U.S. pint (approximately 0.03 liter). **2** *Brit.* a unit of capacity equal to one twentieth of a pint (approximately 0.028 liter).

flu·i·dram /,flo͞oi(d)'dram/ ▸*n.* a fluid drachm. See **DRACHM**.

fluke[1] /flo͞ok/ ▸*n.* unlikely chance occurrence, esp. a surprising piece of luck: *their triumph was no fluke.* ▷mid 19th cent. (originally a term in games such as billiards denoting a lucky stroke): perhaps a dialect word.

fluke[2] ▸*n.* **1** a parasitic flatworm that typically has suckers and hooks for attachment to the host. Some species are of veterinary or medical importance. • Classes Trematoda and Monogenea, phylum Platyhelminthes. See **DIGENEAN** and **MONOGENEAN**. **2** a flatfish, esp. a flounder. ▷Old English *flōc* (sense 2), of Germanic origin; related to German *flach* 'flat.'

fluke[3] ▸*n.* a broad triangular plate on the arm of an anchor. ■ either of the lobes of a whale's tail. ▷mid 16th cent.: perhaps from **FLUKE**[2] (because of the shape).

fluk·y /'flo͞okē/ (also **fluk·ey**) ▸*adj.* (**fluk·i·er**, **fluk·i·est**) obtained or achieved more by chance than skill: *a fluky goal.* ■ subject to chance; unpredictable: *sailing conditions are generally good, although winds can be fluky.* **—fluk·i·ly** /-kilē/ *adv.* **—fluk·i·ness** *n.*

flume /flo͞om/ ▸*n.* a deep narrow channel or ravine with a stream running through it. ■ an artificial channel conveying water, typically used for transporting logs or timber. ■ a water-chute ride at an amusement park. ▷Middle English (denoting a river or stream): from Old French *flum*, from Latin *flumen* 'river,' from *fluere* 'to flow.' The sense 'artificial channel' dates from the mid 18th cent.; 'water chute for amusement' is a late 20th-cent. usage.

flum·mer·y /'fləmərē/ ▸*n.* (*pl.* **-mer·ies**) **1** empty compliments; nonsense: *she hated the flummery of public relations.* **2** a sweet dish, typically made with beaten eggs, sugar, and flavorings. ▷early 17th cent. (denoting a dish made with oatmeal or wheatmeal boiled to a jelly): from Welsh *llymru*; perhaps related to *llymrig* 'soft, slippery.'

flum·mox /'fləməks/ ▸*v.* [*trans.*] (usu. **be flummoxed**) *informal* perplex (someone) greatly; bewilder: *he was completely flummoxed by the question.* ▷mid 19th cent.: probably of dialect origin; compare with dialect *flummock* 'to make untidy, confuse.'

flump /fləmp/ ▸*v.* [*intrans.*] fall or sit down heavily: *he went off to flump into a chair.* ■ [*trans.*] set or throw (something) down heavily: *Ellie flumped her hands down on her sewing.*

▸*n.* [in *sing.*] the action or sound of such a heavy fall: *the rocks hit the ground with a flump.* ▷early 17th cent.: imitative; compare with **PLUMP**[2].

flung /fləNG/ ▸ past and past participle of **FLING**.

flunk /fləNGk/ *informal* ▸*v.* [*trans.*] fail to reach the required standard in (an examination, test, or course of study): *I flunked biology in the tenth grade | [intrans.] I didn't flunk but I didn't do too well.* ■ judge (a student or examination candidate) to have failed to reach the required standard: *the teacher flunked thirteen third-graders.* ■ [*intrans.*] (**flunk out**) (of a student) leave or be dismissed from school or college as a result of failing to reach the required standard: *he had* ***flunked out of*** *college.* ▷early 19th cent. (in the general sense 'back down, fail utterly': perhaps related to **FUNK**[1] or to *flink* 'be a coward,' perhaps a variant of **FLINCH**[1].

flun·ky /'fləNGkē/ (also **flun·key**) ▸*n.* (*pl.* **-kies** or **-keys**) *chiefly derogatory* a liveried manservant or footman. ■ a person who performs relatively menial tasks for someone else, esp. obsequiously. ▷mid 18th cent. (originally Scots): perhaps from **FLANK** in the sense 'a person who stands at one's flank.' **—flun·ky·ism** /-,izəm/ *n.*

fluo·resce /flo͝o(ə)'res; flôr'es/ ▸*v.* [*intrans.*] shine or glow brightly due to fluorescence: *the molecules fluoresce when excited by ultraviolet radiation.* ▷late 19th cent.: back-formation from **FLUORESCENCE**.

fluo·res·ce·in /flo͝o(ə)'resēən; flôr'esēən/ ▸*n. Chemistry* an orange dye with a yellowish-green fluorescence, used as an indicator and tracer. • A derivative of resorcinol and phthalic anhydride; chem. formula: $C_{20}H_{12}O_5$. ▷late 19th cent.: from **FLUORESCENCE** + **-IN**[1].

fluo·res·cence /flo͝o(ə)'resəns; flôr'esəns/ ▸*n.* the visible or invisible radiation emitted by certain substances as a result of incident radiation of a shorter wavelength such as X-rays or ultraviolet light. ■ the property of absorbing light of short wavelength and emitting light of longer wavelength. ▷mid 19th cent.: from **FLUORSPAR** (which fluoresces), on the pattern of *opalescence*.

fluo·res·cent /,flo͝o(ə)'resənt; flôr'esənt/ ▸*adj.* (of a substance) having or showing fluorescence: *a fluorescent dye.* ■ containing a fluorescent tube: *fluorescent lighting.* ■ vividly colorful: *a fluorescent T-shirt.*

▸*n.* a fluorescent tube or lamp.

fluo·res·cent screen ▸*n.* a transparent screen coated with fluorescent material to show images from X-rays.

fluo·res·cent tube (also **fluorescent bulb** or **fluorescent lamp**) ▸*n.* a glass tube that radiates light when phosphor on its inside surface is made to fluoresce by ultraviolet radiation from mercury vapor.

fluor·i·date /'flo͝orə,dāt; 'flôr-/ ▸*v.* [*trans.*] add traces of fluorides to (something, esp. a water supply): [as *adj.*] (**fluoridated**) *fluoridated toothpaste.* ▷1940s: back-formation from earlier *fluoridation*. **—fluor·i·da·tion** /,flo͝orə'dāSHən; ,flôr-/ *n.*

fluor·ide /'flo͝or,īd; 'flôr-/ ▸*n. Chemistry* a compound of fluorine with another element or group, esp. a salt of the anion F^- or an organic compound with fluorine bonded to an alkyl group. ■ sodium fluoride or another fluorine-containing salt added to water supplies or toothpaste in order to reduce tooth decay. ▷early 19th cent.: from **FLUORINE** + **-IDE**.

fluor·i·nate /'flo͝orə,nāt; 'flôr-/ ▸*v.* [*trans.*] *Chemistry* introduce fluorine into (a compound). ■ another term for **FLUORIDATE**. **—fluor·i·na·tion** /,flo͝orə'nāSHən; ,flôr-/ *n.*

fluor·ine /'flo͝or,ēn; flôr-/ ▸*n.* the chemical element of atomic number 9, a poisonous pale yellow gas of the halogen series. It is the most reactive of all the elements, causing severe burns on contact with skin. (Symbol: **F**) ▷early 19th cent.: from *fluor* (see **FLUORSPAR**) + **-INE**[4].

fluo·rite /'flo͝or,īt; flôr-/ ▸*n.* a mineral consisting of calcium fluoride that typically occurs as cubic crystals, colorless when pure but often colored by impurities. ▷mid 19th cent.: from *fluor* (see **FLUORSPAR**) + **-ITE**[1].

fluoro- ▸*comb. form* **1** representing **FLUORINE**. **2** representing **FLUORESCENCE**.

fluor·o·car·bon /,flo͝orō'kärbən; ,flôrō-/ ▸*n. Chemistry* a compound formed by replacing one or more of the hydrogen atoms in a hydrocarbon with fluorine atoms.

fluor·o·chrome /'flo͝orə,krōm; 'flôr-/ ▸*n.* a chemical that fluoresces, esp. one used as a label in biological research.

fluo·rog·ra·phy /flo͝or'ägrəfē; flôr-/ ▸*n.* photography in which the image is formed by fluorescence, used chiefly in biomedical research. **—fluo·ro·graph** /'flo͝orə,graf; 'flôr-/ *n.*

fluo·rom·e·ter /flo͝o'rämitər; flô-/ (also **fluo·rim·e·ter** /'rimitər/) ▸*n.* an instrument for measuring the intensity of fluorescence, used chiefly in biochemical analysis. **—fluor·o·met·ric** /,flo͝orə'metrik; ,flôr-/ *adj.* **—fluor·o·met·ri·cal·ly** /,flo͝orə'metrik(ə)lē; ,flôr-/ *adv.* **—fluo·rom·e·try** /flo͝or'ämətrē; flôr-/ *n.*

fluor·o·pol·y·mer /,flo͝orō'päləmər; ,flôr-/ ▸*n.* an organic polymer containing fluorine atoms, such as polytetrafluoroethylene.

fluor·o·quin·o·lone /,flo͝orō'kwinl,ōn; ,flôrō-/ ▸*n.* any of a class of therapeutic antibiotics that are active against a range of bacteria associated with human and animal diseases. Their use in livestock has sparked concerns about the spread of bacteria resistant to them in humans.

fluor·o·scope /'flo͝orə,skōp; 'flôr-/ ▸*n.* an instrument with a fluorescent screen used for viewing X-ray images without taking and developing X-ray photographs. **—fluor·o·scop·ic** /,flo͝orə'skäpik; ,flôr-/ *adj.* **—fluor·o·scop·i·cal·ly** /,flo͝orə'skäpik(ə)lē; ,flôr-/ *adv.* **—fluo·ros·co·py** /flo͝or'äskəpē; flôr-/ *n.*

fluo·ro·sis /flo͝or'ōsəs; flôr-/ ▸*n. Medicine* a chronic condition caused by excessive intake of fluorine compounds, marked by mottling of the teeth and, if severe, calcification of the ligaments.

flu·or·spar /'flo͝or,spär; 'flôr-/ ▸*n.* another term for **FLUORITE**. ▷late 18th cent.: from *fluor* 'a flow, a mineral used as a flux, fluorspar' (from Latin *fluor*, from *fluere* 'to flow') + **SPAR**[3].

flu·ox·e·tine /flo͞o'äksə,tīn/ ▸*n. Medicine* a synthetic compound that inhibits the uptake of serotonin in the brain and is taken to treat depression. Also called **PROZAC** (*trademark*). ▷1970s: from *fluo(rine)* + *ox(y)* + *-etine* (perhaps from *e* + a blend of **TOLUENE** and **AMINE**).

flur·ried /'flərēd; 'flə-rēd/ ▸*adj.* (of a person) agitated,

F

nervous, or anxious: *I sat down, feeling a little flurried and excited.*

flur·ry /ˈflərē; ˈflə-rē/ ▶*n.* (*pl.* **-ries**) a small swirling mass of something, esp. snow or leaves, moved by sudden gusts of wind: *a* ***flurry of*** *snow.* ■ a sudden short period of commotion or excitement: *there was a brief* ***flurry of*** *activity in the hall.* ■ a number of things arriving or happening during the same period: *a* ***flurry of*** *editorials hostile to the administration.*
▶*v.* (**-ries, -ried**) [*intrans.*] (esp. of snow or leaves) be moved in small swirling masses by sudden gusts of wind: *gusts of snow flurried through the door.* ■ (of a person) move quickly in a busy or agitated way: *the waiter flurried between them.* ▷late 17th cent.: from obsolete *flurr* 'fly up, flutter, whir' (imitative), probably influenced by **HURRY**.

flush[1] /fləsн/ ▶*v.* **1** [*intrans.*] (of a person's skin or face) become red and hot, typically as the result of illness or strong emotion: *Mr. Cunningham flushed angrily* | [as *adj.*] (**flushed**) *her flushed cheeks.* ■ [*trans.*] cause (a person's skin or face) to become red and hot: *the chill air flushed the parson's cheeks.* ■ glow or cause to glow with warm color or light: [*intrans.*] *the ash in the center of the fire flushed up* | [*trans.*] *the sky was flushed with the gold of dawn.* ■ (**be flushed with**) *figurative* be excited or elated by: *flushed with success, I was getting into my stride.* **2** [*trans.*] cleanse (something, esp. a toilet) by causing large quantities of water to pass through it: *flush the toilet* | *the nurse* ***flushed out*** *the catheter.* ■ [*intrans.*] (of a toilet) be cleansed in such a way: *Cally heard the toilet flush.* ■ [*trans.*] remove or dispose of (an object or substance) in such a way: *I* ***flushed*** *the pills* ***down*** *the toilet* | *the kidneys require more water to* ***flush out*** *waste products.* ■ [*trans.*] cause (a liquid) to flow through something: *0.3 ml of saline is gently flushed through the tube.* **3** [*trans.*] drive (a bird, esp. a game bird, or an animal) from its cover: *the grouse were flushed from the woods.* ■ *figurative* cause to be revealed; force into the open: *they're trying to* ***flush*** *Tilton* ***out*** *of hiding.* **4** [*intrans.*] (of a plant) send out fresh shoots: *the plant had started to flush by late March.*
▶*n.* **1** a reddening of the face or skin that is typically caused by illness or strong emotion: *a flush of embarrassment rose to her cheeks.* ■ an area of warm color or light: *the bird has a pinkish flush on the breast.* **2** [in *sing.*] a sudden rush of intense emotion: *I was carried away in a* ***flush of*** *enthusiasm.* ■ a sudden abundance or spate of something: *the frogs feast on the great* ***flush of*** *insects.* ■ *figurative* a period when something is new or particularly fresh and vigorous: *he is no longer* ***in the first flush of*** *youth.* ■ a fresh growth of leaves, flowers, or fruit. **3** an act of cleansing something, esp. a toilet, with a sudden flow of water: *an old-fashioned toilet uses six or seven gallons per flush* | *leave the hose running to give the system a good* ***flush out.*** ■ the device used for producing such a flow of water in a toilet: *he pressed the flush absentmindedly.* ■ [as *adj.*] denoting a type of toilet that has such a device: *a flush toilet.* ■ a sudden flow: *the melting snow provides a flush of water.* **4** the action of driving a game bird from its cover: *the dogs retrieve the birds after the flush.* ▷Middle English (in the sense 'move rapidly, spring up,' esp. of a bird 'fly up suddenly'): symbolic, *fl-* frequently beginning words connected with sudden movement; perhaps influenced by **FLASH** and **BLUSH**. **—flush·er** *n.*

flush[2] ▶*adj.* **1** completely level or even with another surface: *the gates are* ***flush with*** *the adjoining fencing.* ■ (of printed text) not indented or protruding: *each line is* ***flush with*** *the left-hand margin.* ■ (of a door) having a smooth surface, without indented or protruding panels or moldings. **2** [*predic.*] *informal* having plenty of something, esp. money: *the banks are flush with funds.* See note at **WEALTHY**. ■ (of money) plentiful: *the years when cash was flush.*
▶*adv.* so as to be level or even: *the screw must fit* ***flush with*** *the surface.* ■ so as to be directly centered; squarely: *Jumbo reached up and hit Bruno flush on the jaw.*
▶*v.* [*trans.*] fill in (a joint) level with a surface. ▷mid 16th cent. (in the sense 'perfect, lacking nothing'): probably related to **FLUSH**[1]. **—flush·ness** *n.*

flush[3] ▶*n.* (in poker) a hand of cards all of the same suit. ▷early 16th cent.: from French *flux* (formerly *flus*), from Latin *fluxus* 'a flow' (see **FLUX**: the use in cards can be compared with English *run*).

flush[4] ▶*n. Ecology* a piece of wet ground over which water flows without being confined to a definite channel. ▷late Middle English (in the sense 'marshy place').

Flush·ing /ˈfləsнiNG/ a commercial and residential section of northern Queens in New York City, noted for its diverse population.

flust·er /ˈfləstər/ ▶*v.* [*trans.*] [often as *adj.*] (**flustered**) make (someone) agitated or confused: *you need to be able to work under pressure and not get flustered.*
▶*n.* [in *sing.*] an agitated or confused state: *the main thing is not to get all in a fluster.* ▷early 17th cent. (in the sense 'make slightly drunk'): perhaps of Scandinavian origin and related to Icelandic *flaustra* 'hurry, bustle.'

flute /flo͞ot/ ▶*n.* **1** a wind instrument made from a tube with holes along it that are stopped by the fingers or keys, held vertically or horizontally so that the player's breath strikes a narrow edge. ■ a modern orchestral instrument of this type, typically of metal, held horizontally, with the mouthpiece near one end, which is closed. ■ an organ stop with wooden or metal flue pipes producing a similar tone. **2** *Architecture* an ornamental vertical groove in a column. ■ a trumpet-shaped frill on a dress or other garment. ■ any similar cylindrical groove, as on pastry. **3** a tall, narrow wine glass: *a flute of champagne.*
▶*v.* **1** [with *direct speech*] speak in a melodious way reminiscent of the sound of a flute: *"What do you do?" she fluted.* ■ [*intrans.*] *poetic/literary* play a flute or pipe: *to him who sat upon the rocks, and fluted to the morning sea* | [*trans.*] *some swan fluting a wild carol.* **2** [*trans.*] [often as *adj.*] (**fluted**) make flutes or grooves in: *fluted columns.* ■ make trumpet-shaped frills on (a garment): *a fluted collar.* ▷Middle English: from Old French *flahute*, probably from Provençal *flaüt*, perhaps a blend of *flaujol* 'flageolet' + *laüt* 'lute.' **—flute·like** /-ˌlīk/ *adj.*

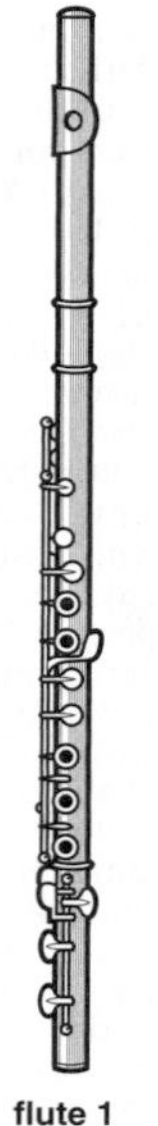
flute 1

flut·ing /ˈflo͞otiNG/ ▶*n.* **1** sound reminiscent of that of a flute: *the silvery fluting of a blackbird.* **2** a groove or set of grooves forming a surface decoration: *a hollow stem with vertical flutings* | *pieces decorated with fluting.*
▶*adj.* reminiscent of the sound of a flute: *the golden, fluting voice filled the room.*

flut·ist /ˈflo͞otist/ (also *chiefly Brit.* **flaut·ist**) ▶*n.* a flute player.

flut·ter /ˈflətər/ ▶*v.* [*intrans.*] (of a bird or other winged creature) fly unsteadily or hover by flapping the wings quickly and lightly: *a couple of butterflies fluttered around the garden.* ■ (with reference to a bird's wings) flap in such a way: *their wings flutter and spread* | [*trans.*] *the lark fluttered its wings, hovering.* ■ [with *adverbial*] move or fall with a light irregular or trembling motion: *the remaining petals fluttered to the ground.* ■ [with *adverbial of direction*] (of a person) move restlessly or uncertainly: *the hostess fluttered forward to greet her guests.* ■ (of a pulse or heartbeat) beat feebly or irregularly.
▶*n.* **1** an act of fluttering: *there was a flutter of wings at the window.* ■ a state or sensation of tremulous excitement: *Sandra felt a flutter in the pit of her stomach* | *her insides were* ***in a flutter.*** ■ *Aeronautics* undesired oscillation in a part of an aircraft under stress. ■ *Medicine* disturbance of the rhythm of the heart that is less severe than fibrillation: *atrial flutter* | *I was diagnosed as having a heart flutter.* ■ *Electronics* rapid variation in the pitch or amplitude of a signal, esp. of recorded sound. Compare with **WOW**[2]. **2** *Brit., informal* a small bet: *a* ***flutter on*** *the horses.* ▷Old English *floterian, flotorian*, a frequentative form related to **FLEET**[5]. **—flut·ter·er** *n.* **—flut·ter·ing·ly** *adv.* **—flut·ter·y** *adj.*
▶**PHRASE** □ **flutter one's eyelashes** open and close one's eyes rapidly in a coyly flirtatious manner.

flut·ter kick ▶*n.* a brisk, alternating, up-and-down movement of the legs when swimming with certain strokes, such as the crawl.

flut·ter-tongu·ing ▶*n.* the action of vibrating the tongue (as if rolling an *r*) in playing a wind instrument to produce a whirring effect.

flut·y /ˈflo͞otē/ (also **flut·ey**) ▶*adj.* (**flut·i·er, flut·i·est**) reminiscent of the sound of a flute: *a drawn-out fluty whistle.*

flu·vi·al /ˈflo͞ovēəl/ ▶*adj. chiefly Geology* of or found in a river. ▷Middle English: from Latin *fluvialis*, from *fluvius* 'river,' from *fluere* 'to flow.'

flu·vi·a·tile /ˈflo͞ovēəˌtīl/ ▶*adj.* of, found in, or produced by a river: *fluviatile sediments.* ▷late 16th cent.: from French, from Latin *fluviatilis*, from *fluviatus* 'wet,' from *fluvius* 'river.'

fluvio- ▶*comb. form* river; relating to rivers: *fluvioglacial.* ▷from Latin *fluvius* 'river.'

flu·vi·o·gla·cial /ˌflo͞ovēōˈglāsнəl/ ▶*adj. Geology* relating to or denoting erosion or deposition caused by flowing meltwater from glaciers or ice sheets.

flu·vox·a·mine /flo͞oˈväksəˌmēn; -min/ ▶*n. Medicine* a synthetic antidepressant drug that acts by prolonging the effect of the neurotransmitter serotonin on the brain.

flux /fləks/ ▶*n.* **1** the action or process of flowing or flowing out: *the flux of men and women moving back and forth* | *a localized flux of calcium into the cell.* ■ *Medicine* an abnormal discharge of blood or other matter from or within the body. ■ (usu. **the flux**) *archaic* diarrhea or dysentery. **2** continuous change: *the whole political system is in a state of flux.* **3** *Physics* the rate of flow of a fluid, radiant energy, or particles across a given area. ■ the amount of radiation or number of particles incident on an area in a given time. ■ the total electric or magnetic field passing through a surface. **4** a substance mixed with a solid to lower its melting point, used esp. in soldering and brazing metals or to promote vitrification in glass or ceramics. ■ a substance added to a furnace during metal smelting or glassmaking that combines with impurities to form slag.
▶*v.* [*trans.*] treat (a metal object) with a flux to promote melting. ▷late Middle English: from Latin *fluxus*, from *fluere* 'to flow.'

flux den·si·ty ▶*n.* the magnitude of a magnetic, electric, or other flux passing through a unit area.

flux·gate /ˈfləksˌgāt/ (also **flux gate**) ▶*n.* a device consisting of one or more soft iron cores each surrounded by primary and secondary windings, used for determining the characteristics of an external magnetic field from the signals produced in the secondary windings.

flux·ion /ˈflәksнәn/ ▶*n.* **1** *dated Mathematics* a function corresponding to the rate of change of a variable quantity; a derivative. **2** another term for **FLUX** (sense 1). ▷late 17th cent.: from French, or from Latin *flux-* 'flowed,' from the verb *fluere*. **—flux·ion·al** /-sнənl/ *adj.*

fly[1] /flī/ ▶*v.* (**flies** /flīz/; *past* **flew** /flo͞o/; *past part.* **flown** /flōn/) [*intrans.*] **1** (of a bird or other winged creature) move through the air under control: *close the door or the moths will fly in* | *the bird can fly enormous distances.* ■ (of an aircraft or its occupants) travel through the air: *I fly back to New York this evening.* ■ [*trans.*] control the flight of (an aircraft); pilot. ■ [*trans.*] transport in an aircraft: *helicopters flew the injured to a hospital.* ■ [*trans.*] accomplish (a purpose) in an aircraft: *pilots trained to fly combat missions.* ■ [*trans.*] release (a bird) to fly, esp. a hawk for hunting or a pigeon for racing. **2** move or be hurled quickly through the air: *balls kept flying over her hedge* | *he was* ***sent flying*** *by the tackle.* ■ [with *adverbial of direction*] (*past* **flied**) *Baseball* hit a ball high into the air: *Gwynn flied to left.* ■ (*past* **flied**) (**fly out**) *Baseball* (of a batter) be put out by hitting a fly ball that is caught. ■ [with *adverbial of direction*] go or move quickly: *she flew along the path.* ■ *informal* depart hastily: *I must fly!* ■ (of time) pass swiftly: *how time flies!* ■ (of a report) be circulated among many people: *rumors were* ***flying around*** *Chicago.* ■ (of accusations or insults) be exchanged swiftly and heatedly: *the accusations flew thick and fast.* **3** [with *adverbial*] (esp. of hair) wave or flutter in the wind: *they were running, hair flying everywhere.* ■ (of a flag) be displayed, esp. on a flagpole: *flags were flying at half-mast.* ■ [*trans.*] display (a flag). **4** *archaic* flee; run away: *those that fly may fight again.* ■ [*trans.*] flee from; escape from in haste: *you must fly the country for a while.*
▶*phrasal v.* □ **fly at** attack (someone) verbally or physically: *Robbie flew at him, fists clenched.* ■ (of a hawk) pursue and attack, or habitually pursue (prey). ■ (**fly a hawk at**) send a hawk to pursue and attack (prey).
▶*n.* (*pl.* **flies**) **1** (*Brit.* often **flies**) an opening at the crotch of a pair of pants, closed with a zipper or buttons and typically covered with a flap. ■ a flap of material covering the opening or fastening of a garment or of a tent: [as *adj.* in *combination*] *a fly-fronted shirt.* **2** (**the flies**) the space over the stage in a theater. **3** *Baseball* short for **FLY BALL**. **4** (*pl.* usu. **flys**) *Brit.* & *historical* a one-horse hackney carriage. ▷Old English *flēogan*, of Germanic origin; related to Dutch *vliegen* and German *fliegen*, also to **FLY**[2]. **—fly·a·ble** *adj.*
▶**PHRASES** □ **fly the coop** *informal* make one's escape. □ **fly the flag** see **FLAG**[1]. □ **fly high** be very successful;

prosper: *that young man is the sort to fly high.* □ **fly in the face of** be openly at variance with (what is usual or expected): *a need to fly in the face of convention.* □ **fly into a rage** (or **temper**) become suddenly or violently angry. □ **fly the nest** (of a young bird) leave its nest on becoming able to fly. ■ *informal* (of a young person) leave their parents' home to set up home elsewhere. □ **fly off the handle** *informal* lose one's temper suddenly and unexpectedly. [figuratively, with reference to the loose head of an ax.] □ **go fly a kite** [in *imperative*] *informal* go away. □ **on the fly** while in motion or progress: *his deep shot was caught on the fly.* ■ *Computing* during the running of a computer program without interrupting the run.

fly[2] ▸*n.* (*pl.* **flies** /flīz/) a flying insect of a large order characterized by a single pair of transparent wings and sucking (and often also piercing) mouthparts. Flies are noted as vectors of disease. See also DIPTERA. • Order Diptera: numerous families. ■ [usu. in *combination*] used in names of flying insects of other orders, e.g., **butterfly**, **dragonfly**, **firefly**. ■ an infestation of flying insects on a plant or animal: *cattle to be treated for warble fly.* ■ a natural or artificial flying insect used as bait in fishing, esp. a mayfly. ▷Old English *flȳge*, *flēoge*, denoting any winged insect; related to Dutch *vlieg* and German *Fliege*, also to FLY[1].

▸*PHRASES* □ **die** (or **drop**) **like flies** die or collapse in large numbers: *people in the area seemed to die like flies in the winter.* □ **a fly in the ointment** a minor irritation that spoils the success or enjoyment of something. □ **fly on the wall** an unnoticed observer of a particular situation. ■ [as *adj.*] denoting a filmmaking technique whereby events are observed realistically with minimum interference rather than acted out under direction: *a fly-on-the-wall documentary.* □ **wouldn't hurt** (or **harm**) **a fly** (of a person or animal) inoffensive and harmless.

fly[3] ▸*adj.* (**fly·er**, **fly·est**) *informal* **1** stylish and fashionable: *they were wearin' fly clothes.* **2** *Brit.* knowing and clever; worldly-wise: *she's fly enough not to get done out of it.* ▷early 19th cent.: of unknown origin. —**fly·ness** *n.*

fly ag·a·ric ▸*n.* a poisonous toadstool that has a red cap with fluffy white spots, growing particularly among birch trees. It contains hallucinogenic alkaloids and has long been used by the native peoples of northeastern Siberia. • *Amanita muscaria*, family Amanitaceae, class Hymenomycetes.

fly ash ▸*n.* ash produced in small dark flecks, typically from a furnace, and carried into the air.

fly·a·way /ˈflīəˌwā/ ▸*adj.* (of a person's hair) fine and difficult to control.

fly·back /ˈflīˌbak/ ▸*n.* the return of the scanning spot in a cathode-ray tube to the starting point.

fly ball ▸*n.* *Baseball* a ball batted high into the air.

fly·blow /ˈflīˌblō/ ▸*n.* flies' eggs contaminating food, esp. meat.

fly·blown /ˈflīˌblōn/ ▸*adj.* dirty or contaminated, esp. through contact with flies and their eggs and larvae: *the room was filthy and flyblown.*

fly·boy /ˈflīˌboi/ ▸*n.* *informal* a pilot, esp. one in the air force.

fly·bridge /ˈflīˌbrij/ (also **fly·ing bridge**) ▸*n.* an open deck above the main bridge of a vessel such as a yacht or cabin cruiser, typically equipped with duplicate controls.

fly·by /ˈflīˌbī/ (also **fly-by**) ▸*n.* (*pl.* **-bys**) a flight past a point, esp. the close approach of a spacecraft to a planet or moon for observation.

fly-by-night ▸*adj.* [*attrib.*] unreliable or untrustworthy, esp. in business or financial matters: *cheap suits made by fly-by-night operators.*

▸*n.* (also **fly-by-nighter**) an unreliable or untrustworthy person.

fly-by-wire ▸*n.* [often as *adj.*] a semiautomatic and typically computer-regulated system for controlling the flight of an aircraft or spacecraft: *sophisticated fly-by-wire technology.*

fly-cast ▸*v.* [*intrans.*] to cast a line with a fly rod in fly-fishing.

fly-cast·ing ▸*n.* another term for FLY-FISHING. —**fly-cast** *v.*

fly·catch·er /ˈflīˌkacHər; -ˌkecHər/ ▸*n.* a bird that catches flying insects, esp. in short flights from a perch. • Typical Old World flycatchers belong to the family Muscicapidae. Many others belong to the Old World family Monarchidae and the New World family Tyrannidae (**tyrant flycatchers**), while some belong to families Eopsaltridae (Australasia), Platysteiridae (Africa), and Bombycillidae (America).

fly-drive ▸*adj.* *chiefly Brit.* denoting a package vacation that includes a flight and car rental at the destination.

▸*n.* a vacation of this type.

fly·er /ˈflīər/ ▸*n.* variant spelling of FLIER.

fly-fish·ing ▸*n.* the sport of fishing using a rod and an artificial fly as bait. —**fly-fish** *v.*

fly gal·ler·y ▸*n.* a raised platform at the side of a stage that contains ropes and equipment for moving props and scenery. Also called **fly floor**.

fly-in ▸*n.* a meeting for pilots who arrive by air: *they are holding a helicopter fly-in.* ■ an act of transporting people or goods by air: *one or two fly-ins to remote lakes.* ■ [as *adj.*] denoting a place or activity that is reached using an aircraft: *fly-in canoe trips.*

fly·ing /ˈflī-iNG/ ▸*adj.* moving or able to move through the air with wings: *a flying ant.* ■ relating to airplanes or aviators: *a flying ace | a flying career.* ■ done while hurling oneself through the air: *he took a flying kick at a policeman.* ■ moving rapidly, esp. through the air: *one passenger was cut by flying glass.* ■ hasty; brief: *a flying visit.* ■ used in names of animals that can glide by using winglike membranes or other structures, e.g., **flying squirrel**.

▸*n.* flight, esp. in an aircraft: *she hates flying.* [as *adj.*]

▸*PHRASE* □ **with flying colors** with distinction: *Sylvia had passed her exams with flying colors.*

fly·ing boat ▸*n.* a large seaplane that lands with its fuselage in the water.

fly·ing bomb ▸*n.* a small pilotless aircraft with an explosive warhead, esp. a V-1. ■ another term for ROBOT BOMB.

fly·ing bridge ▸*n.* another term for FLYBRIDGE.

fly·ing but·tress ▸*n.* *Architecture* a buttress slanting from a separate pier, typically forming an arch with the wall it supports.

fly·ing change ▸*n.* a movement in riding in which the leading leg at the canter is changed without breaking gait while the horse is in the air.

fly·ing drag·on ▸*n.* an arboreal Southeast Asian lizard that has expanding membranes along the sides of the body, used for gliding between trees. Also called DRAGON. • Genus *Draco*, family Agamidae: several species.

Fly·ing Dutch·man a legendary spectral ship supposedly seen in the region of the Cape of Good Hope and presaging disaster. ■ the captain of this ship.

fly·ing fish ▸*n.* a fish of warm seas that leaps out of the water and uses its winglike pectoral fins to glide over the surface for some distance. • Family Exocoetidae: several genera and species, in particular *Exocoetus volitans*.

flying fish

fly·ing fox ▸*n.* a large fruit bat with a foxlike face, found in Madagascar, Southeast Asia, and northern Australia. • *Pteropus* and two other genera, family Pteropodidae: numerous species.

fly·ing frog ▸*n.* a nocturnal arboreal Asian frog that is able to glide between trees using the large webs between its extended toes. • *Polypedates leucomystax*, family Rhacophoridae.

fly·ing gur·nard ▸*n.* a bottom-dwelling marine fish that has bony armor on the skull, spines behind the head, and large brightly colored pectoral fins. It moves through the water with a gliding or flying motion. • Family Dactylopteridae: two genera and several species.

fly·ing le·mur ▸*n.* a tree-dwelling lemurlike mammal with a membrane between the fore- and hind limbs for gliding from tree to tree. It is nocturnal and native to Southeast Asia. Also called COLUGO. • Family Cynocephalidae and genus *Cynocephalus*, order Dermoptera: two species.

fly·ing liz·ard ▸*n.* another term for FLYING DRAGON.

fly·ing ma·chine ▸*n.* an aircraft, esp. an early or unconventional one.

fly·ing mouse ▸*n.* **1** *Computing* a mouse that can be lifted from the desk and used in three dimensions. **2** another term for FEATHERTAIL GLIDER.

fly·ing pha·lan·ger ▸*n.* a small Australasian marsupial with a membrane between the fore- and hind limbs for gliding. • Genera *Petaurus* and *Petauroides*, family Petauridae: five species.

fly·ing sau·cer ▸*n.* a disk-shaped flying craft supposedly piloted by aliens; a UFO.

fly·ing snake ▸*n.* a greenish semiarboreal Southeast Asian snake that can glide down from a tree in a stiff horizontal position, with the belly hollowed to slow its descent. • *Chrysopelea ornata*, family Colubridae.

fly·ing squad ▸*n.* *Brit.* a division of a police force or other organization that is capable of reaching an incident quickly.

fly·ing squir·rel ▸*n.* a small squirrel that has skin joining the fore and hind limbs for gliding from tree to tree. • Subfamily Pteromyinae, family Sciuridae (many species in Southeast Asia, northern Eurasia, and North America) and family Anomaluridae (several species in Africa). The two common North American species are the **northern flying squirrel** (*Glaucomys sabrinus*) and the **southern flying squirrel** (*G. volans*).

southern flying squirrel

fly·ing start ▸*n.* a start of a race or time trial in which the starting point is passed at speed. ■ a good beginning, esp. one giving an advantage over competitors: *the team **got off to a flying start** in last year's rally.*

fly·ing tra·peze ▸*n.* another term for TRAPEZE (sense 1).

fly·ing wedge ▸*n.* a fast-moving group, as of police officers, linked together closely in a V-shaped formation, sometimes used to force a way through a crowd or to protect someone behind them.

fly·ing wing ▸*n.* an aircraft with little or no fuselage and no vertical airfoil.

fly·leaf /ˈflīˌlēf/ ▸*n.* (*pl.* **-leaves** /-ˌlēvz/) a blank page at the beginning or end of a book.

Flynn /flin/, Errol (1909–59), U.S. actor; born in Australia; born *Leslie Thomas Flynn*. His usual role was the swashbuckling hero of romantic costume dramas in movies such as *Captain Blood* (1935) and *The Adventures of Robin Hood* (1938).

fly·o·ver /ˈflīˌōvər/ ▸*n.* **1** a low flight by one or more aircraft over a specific location: *there were artillery platforms in the hills, making a flyover too risky.* ■ a ceremonial flight of an aircraft past a person or a place. **2** *chiefly Brit.* an overpass.

fly·pa·per /ˈflīˌpāpər/ ▸*n.* sticky, poison-treated strips of paper that are hung indoors to catch and kill flies.

Fly Riv·er /flī/ a river in Papua New Guinea—the country's longest—that flows for 750 miles (1,200 km) from the border with Irian Jaya in Indonesia into the Gulf of Papua.

fly rod ▸*n.* a lightweight flexible rod used in fly-fishing.

flysch /flisH/ ▸*n.* *Geology* a sedimentary deposit consisting of thin beds of shale or marl alternating with coarser strata such as sandstone or conglomerate. ▷mid 19th cent.: from Swiss German dialect.

fly·sheet /ˈflīˌsHēt/ ▸*n.* **1** a tract or circular of two or four pages. **2** *Brit.* a fabric cover pitched outside and over a tent to give extra protection against bad weather.; see FLY[1] (sense 1).

fly·speck /ˈflīˌspek/ ▸*n.* a tiny stain made by the excrement of an insect. ■ a thing that is contemptibly small or insignificant: *a sleepy flyspeck of a town.* —**fly·specked** *adj.*

fly spray ▸*n.* a substance sprayed from an aerosol that kills flying insects.

fly strike ▸*n.* infestation of an animal with blowfly maggots.

fly swat·ter (also **fly·swat·ter**) ▸*n.* an implement used for swatting insects, typically a square of plastic mesh attached to a wire handle.

fly-through ▸*n.* a computer-animated simulation of what would be seen by one flying through a particular real or imaginary region.

fly-tip ▸*v.* [*intrans.*] *Brit.* dump waste illegally. **—fly-tip·per** *n.*

fly·trap /ˈflīˌtrap/ ▸*n.* see **VENUS FLYTRAP**.

fly-ty·ing ▸*n.* the making of the artificial flies used in fly-fishing.

fly·way /ˈflīˌwā/ ▸*n.* *Ornithology* a route regularly used by large numbers of migrating birds.

fly·weight /ˈflīˌwāt/ ▸*n.* a weight in boxing and other sports intermediate between light flyweight and bantamweight. In boxing it ranges from 108 to 112 pounds (48 to 51 kg). ■ a boxer or other competitor of this weight.

fly·wheel /ˈflīˌ(h)wēl/ ▸*n.* a heavy revolving wheel in a machine that is used to increase the machine's momentum and thereby provide greater stability or a reserve of available power during interruptions in the delivery of power to the machine.

fly whisk ▸*n.* see **WHISK** (sense 2).

FM ▸*abbr.* frequency modulation: [as *adj.*] *an FM radio station.*

Fm ▸*symbol* the chemical element fermium.

fm. ▸*abbr.* fathom(s).

FMB ▸*abbr.* Federal Maritime Board.

FMCG ▸*abbr.* fast-moving consumer goods: [as *adj.*] *the FMCG sector.*

FMCS ▸*abbr.* Federal Mediation and Conciliation Service.

FMN ▸*abbr.* flavin mononucleotide.

FMV ▸*abbr.* full-motion video.

FN ▸*abbr.* foreign national.

fn. ▸*abbr.* footnote.

FNMA ▸*abbr.* Federal National Mortgage Association; also called **FANNIE MAE**.

f-num·ber ▸*n.* *Photography* the ratio of the focal length of a camera lens to the diameter of the aperture being used for a particular shot (e.g., *f*8, indicating that the focal length is eight times the diameter). ▷early 20th cent.: from *f* (denoting the focal length) and **NUMBER**.

FO ▸*abbr.* ■ field officer. ■ Foreign Office.

Fo /fō/, Dario (1926–), Italian playwright. Notable works: *Accidental Death of an Anarchist* (1970) and *Open Couple* (1983). Nobel Prize for Literature (1997).

fo. ▸*abbr.* folio.

FOAF ▸*abbr.* friend of a friend: *investigations never do succeed in finding the FOAF who started any of these yarns.* ■ a story or urban legend attributed to one of these.

foal /fōl/ ▸*n.* a young horse or related animal.
▸*v.* [*intrans.*] (of a mare) give birth to a foal. ■ (**be foaled**) (of a foal) be born. ▷Old English *fola*, of Germanic origin; related to Dutch *veulen* and German *Fohlen*, also to **FILLY**.
▸*PHRASE* □ **in** (or **with**) **foal** (of a mare) pregnant.

foam /fōm/ ▸*n.* a mass of small bubbles formed on or in liquid, typically by agitation or fermentation: *a beer with a thick head of foam.* ■ a similar mass formed from saliva or sweat. ■ a thick preparation containing many small bubbles: *shaving cream (foam type) does a fine job on my beard.* ■ a lightweight form of rubber or plastic made by solidifying such a liquid. ■ (**the foam**) *poetic/literary* the sea: *Venus rising from the foam.*
▸*v.* [*intrans.*] form or produce a mass of small bubbles; froth: *the sea foamed beneath them.* ■ *figurative, informal* be very angry: *the audience was **foaming at the mouth**, venting their outrage.* ▷Old English *fām* (noun), *fǣman* (verb); related to Old High German *feim* (noun), *feimen* (verb). **—foam·less** *adj.* **—foam·y** *adj.*

foam·flow·er /ˈfōmˌflou(-ə)r/ ▸*n.* see **TIARELLA**.

foam par·ty ▸*n.* a party, especially in a nightclub, at which guests dance and play in foam or soap suds.

foam rub·ber ▸*n.* a spongy material made of rubber or plastic in the form of foam, used for cushioning and in upholstery.

FOB ▸*abbr.* **1** friend of Bill, a friend of Bill Clinton, esp. one of his close circle of advisers and contacts. **2** Forward Operating Base.

fob[1] /fäb/ ▸*n.* (also **fob chain**) a chain attached to a watch for carrying in a waistcoat or waistband pocket. ■ a small ornament attached to a watch chain. ■ (also **fob pocket**) a small pocket for carrying a watch. ■ a tab on a key ring. ▷mid 17th cent. (denoting a fob pocket in a waistband): origin uncertain; probably related to German dialect *Fuppe* 'pocket.'

fob[2] ▸*v.* (**fobbed**, **fob·bing**) [*trans.*] (**fob someone off**) deceitfully attempt to satisfy someone by making excuses or giving them something inferior: *secretaries fob off most unwanted callers by saying their boss is in a meeting.* ■ (**fob something off on**) give (someone) something inferior to or different from what they want: *he fobbed off the chairmanship on Clifford.* ▷late Middle English (in the sense 'cheat out of'): origin uncertain; perhaps related to German *foppen* 'deceive, cheat, banter,' or to **FOP**.

f.o.b. ▸*abbr.* free on board. See **FREE**.

fo·cac·cia /fōˈkäCH(ē)ə/ ▸*n.* a type of flat Italian bread made with yeast and olive oil and flavored with herbs. ▷Italian.

fo·cal /ˈfōkəl/ ▸*adj.* of or relating to the center or main point of interest: *tapestries in which birds or animals provide the focal interest.* ■ *Optics* of or relating to the focus of a lens. ■ (of a disease or medical condition) occurring in one particular site in the body. ▷late 17th cent.: from modern Latin *focalis*, from Latin *focus*, or directly from **FOCUS**. **—fo·cal·ly** *adv.*

fo·cal·ize /ˈfōkəˌlīz/ ▸*v.* [*trans.*] *technical* focus (something), in particular: ■ (in literary theory) provide an internal focus for (a text): *the narrative discourse is focalized around the consciousness of the central protagonist.* ■ *Medicine* confine (a disease or infection) to a particular site in the body. **—fo·cal·i·za·tion** /ˌfōkəliˈzāSHən/ *n.*

fo·cal length ▸*n.* the distance between the center of a lens or curved mirror and its focus. ■ the equivalent distance in a compound lens or telescope.

fo·cal plane ▸*n.* the plane through the focus perpendicular to the axis of a mirror or lens.

fo·cal point ▸*n.* the point at which rays or waves meet after reflection or refraction, or the point from which diverging rays or waves appear to proceed. ■ the center of interest or activity: *almost every sizable city can have a junior college that can act as a focal point for cultural activity.*

Foch /fôsH/, Ferdinand (1851–1929), French general. He supported the use of offensive warfare, which resulted in many of his 20th Corps being killed at the start of World War I in August 1914.

fo'c'sle /ˈfōksəl/ (also **fo'c's'le**) ▸*n.* variant spelling of **FORECASTLE**.

fo·cus /ˈfōkəs/ ▸*n.* (*pl.* **fo·cus·es** or **fo·ci** /ˈfōˌsī; -ˌkī/) **1** the center of interest or activity: *this generation has made the environment a focus of attention.* ■ an act of concentrating interest or activity on something: *our **focus on** the customer's requirements.* ■ *Geology* the point of origin of an earthquake. Compare with **EPICENTER**. ■ *Medicine* the principal site of an infection or other disease. ■ *Linguistics* the part of a sentence given prominence, usually for emphasis or contrast, e.g., *Bob* in *it was Bob who came, not Bill*. Compare with **RHEME**. **2** the state or quality of having or producing clear visual definition: *his face is rather **out of focus**.* ■ another term for **FOCAL POINT**. ■ the point at which an object must be situated with respect to a lens or mirror for an image of it to be well defined. ■ a device on a lens that can be adjusted to produce a clear image. **3** *Geometry* one of the fixed points from which the distances to any point of a given curve, such as an ellipse or parabola, are connected by a linear relation.
▸*v.* (**fo·cused**, **fo·cus·ing** or **fo·cussed**, **fo·cus·sing**) [*intrans.*] **1** (of a person or their eyes) adapt to the prevailing level of light and become able to see clearly: *try to **focus on** a stationary object.* ■ [*trans.*] bring (one's eyes) into such a state: *trying to **focus** his bleary eyes **on** Corbett.* ■ [*trans.*] adjust the focus of (a telescope, camera, or other instrument): *they were **focusing** a telescope **on** a star.* ■ (of rays or waves) meet at a single point. ■ [*trans.*] (of a lens) make (rays or waves) meet at a single point. ■ [*intrans.*] (of light, radio waves, or other energy) become concentrated into a sharp beam of light or energy. ■ [*trans.*] (of a lens) concentrate (light, radio waves, or energy) into a sharp beam. **2** (**focus on**) pay particular attention to: *the study will focus on a number of areas in Wales.* ■ [*trans.*] concentrate: *the course helps to focus and stimulate your thoughts.* ■ [*trans.*] *Linguistics* place the focus on (a part of a sentence). ▷mid 17th cent. (as a term in geometry and physics): from Latin, literally 'domestic hearth.' **—fo·cus·er** *n.*

fo·cus group ▸*n.* a demographically diverse group of people assembled to participate in a guided discussion about a particular product before it is launched, or to provide ongoing feedback on a political campaign, television series, etc.

fo·cus pull·er ▸*n.* an assistant to a film or television cameraman who is responsible for keeping the lens focused during filming.

fod·der /ˈfädər/ ▸*n.* food, esp. dried hay or feed, for cattle and other livestock. ■ a person or thing regarded only as material for a specific use: *young people ending up as factory fodder.* See also **CANNON FODDER**.
▸*v.* [*trans.*] give fodder to (cattle or other livestock). ▷Old English *fōdor*, of Germanic origin; related to Dutch *voeder* and German *Futter*, also to **FOOD**.

fo·dy /ˈfōdē/ ▸*n.* (*pl.* **-dies**) a songbird of the weaver family occurring in Madagascar and islands in the Indian Ocean, the male of which typically has mainly red plumage. • Genus *Foudia*, family Ploceidae: several species. ▷a local word.

FoE ▸*abbr.* Friends of the Earth.

foe /fō/ ▸*n.* an enemy or opponent: *join forces against the common foe.* ▷Old English *fāh* 'hostile' and *gefā* 'enemy'; related to **FEUD**.

foehn /fān; fœn/ (also **föhn**) ▸*n.* (often **the foehn**) a hot southerly wind on the northern slopes of the Alps. ■ (also **foehn wind**) *Meteorology* a warm dry wind of this type developing in the lee of any mountain range. ▷mid 19th cent.: from German *Föhn*, based on Latin *(ventus) Favonius* 'mild west wind,' *Favonius* being the Roman personification of the west or west wind.

foet·id ▸*adj.* variant spelling of **FETID**.

foe·tus ▸*n.* variant spelling of **FETUS** (chiefly in British nontechnical use). **—foe·tal** /ˈfētl/ *adj.* **—foe·ti·cide** /ˈfētəˌsīd/ *n.*

> ***USAGE*** See usage at **FETUS**.

fog[1] /fôg; fäg/ ▸*n.* a thick cloud of tiny water droplets suspended in the atmosphere at or near the earth's surface that obscures or restricts visibility (to a greater extent than mist; strictly, reducing visibility to below 1 km): *the collision occurred in thick fog.* ■ [in *sing.*] an opaque mass of something in the atmosphere: *a whirling **fog of** dust.* ■ [in *sing.*] *figurative* something that obscures and confuses a situation or someone's thought processes: *the origins of local government are lost in a fog of detail.* ■ *Photography* cloudiness that obscures the image on a developed negative or print.
▸*v.* (**fogged**, **fog·ging**) [*trans.*] **1** cause (a glass surface) to become covered with steam: *hot steam drifted about her, **fogging up** the window.* ■ [*intrans.*] (of a glass surface) become covered with steam: *the windshield was starting to **fog up**.* ■ *figurative* bewilder or puzzle (someone): *she stared at him, confusion fogging her brain.* ■ *figurative* make (an idea or situation) difficult to understand: *the government has been fogging the issue.* ■ *Photography* make (a film, negative, or print) obscure or cloudy. **2** treat with something, esp. an insecticide, in the form of a spray: *Winnipeg stopped fogging for mosquitoes three years ago.* ▷mid 16th cent.: perhaps a back-formation from **FOGGY**.
▸*PHRASE* □ **in a fog** in a state of perplexity; unable to think clearly or understand something.

fog[2] ▸*n.* the grass that grows in a field after a crop of hay has been taken. ■ long grass left standing in a pasture and used as winter grazing. ▷late Middle English: origin uncertain; perhaps related to Norwegian *fogg*.

fog bank ▸*n.* a dense mass of fog, esp. at sea.

fog·bound /ˈfôgˌbound; ˈfäg-/ ▸*adj.* unable to travel or function normally because of thick fog. ■ enveloped or obscured by fog: *a fogbound forest.*

fog·bow /ˈfôgˌbō; ˈfäg-/ ▸*n.* a phenomenon similar to a rainbow, produced by sunlight shining on fog.

fo·gey /ˈfōgē/ (also **fo·gy**) ▸*n.* (*pl.* **-geys** or **-gies**) a person, typically an old one, who is considered to be old-fashioned or conservative in attitude or tastes: *a bunch of **old fogeys**.* ▷late 18th cent.: related to earlier slang *fogram*, of unknown origin. **—fo·gey·dom** /-dəm/ *n.* **—fo·gey·ish** *adj.* **—fo·gey·ism** /ˌ-izəm/ *n.*

Fog·gia /ˈfôjə; ˈfōdjä/ a town in southeastern Italy; pop. 160,000.

fog·gy /ˈfôgē; ˈfägē/ ▸*adj.* (**fog·gi·er**, **fog·gi·est**) full of or accompanied by fog: *a dark and foggy night.* ■ unable to think clearly; confused: *she was foggy with sleep.* ■ indistinctly expressed or perceived; obscure: *exactly what the company hopes to achieve is still foggy.* ▷late 15th cent.: perhaps from **FOG**[2]. **—fog·gi·ness** *n.*
▸*PHRASE* □ **not have the foggiest** (**idea** or **notion**) *informal* have no idea at all.

fog·horn /ˈfôg,hôrn; ˈfäg-/ ▸*n.* a device making a loud, deep sound as a warning to ships in fog. ■ *informal* a loud penetrating voice: [as *adj.*] *his foghorn voice.*

fog lamp (also **fog·light**) ▸*n.* a bright light on a motor vehicle, used in foggy conditions to improve road visibility or warn other drivers of one's presence.

fo·gy /ˈfōgē/ ▸*n.* variant spelling of FOGEY.

föhn ▸*n.* variant spelling of FOEHN.

foi·ble /ˈfoibəl/ ▸*n.* **1** a minor weakness or eccentricity in someone's character: *they have to tolerate each other's little foibles.* See note at FAULT. **2** *Fencing* the weaker part of a sword blade, from the middle to the point. Compare with FORTE[1]. ▷late 16th cent. (as an adjective in the sense 'feeble'): from obsolete French, in Old French *fieble* (see FEEBLE). Both noun senses also formerly occurred as senses of the word *feeble* and all date from the 17th cent.

foie gras /fwä ˈgrä/ ▸*n.* short for PÂTÉ DE FOIE GRAS.

foil[1] /foil/ ▸*v.* [*trans.*] prevent (something considered wrong or undesirable) from succeeding: *a brave policewoman foiled the armed robbery.* ■ frustrate the efforts or plans of: *Errol Flynn was a dashing Mountie foiling Nazi agents in Canada.* See note at THWART. ■ *Hunting* (of a hunted animal) run over or cross (ground or a scent or track) in such a way as to confuse the hounds.
▸*n.* **1** *Hunting* the track or scent of a hunted animal. **2** *archaic* a setback in an enterprise; a defeat. ▷Middle English (in the sense 'trample down'): perhaps from Old French *fouler* 'to full cloth, trample,' based on Latin *fullo* 'fuller.' Compare with FULL[2].

foil[2] ▸*n.* **1** metal hammered or rolled into a thin flexible sheet, used chiefly for covering or wrapping food: *aluminum foil.* **2** a person or thing that contrasts with and so emphasizes and enhances the qualities of another: *the earthy taste of grilled vegetables is a perfect foil for the tart bite of creamy goat cheese.* ■ a thin leaf of metal placed under a precious stone to increase its brilliance. **3** *Architecture* a leaf-shaped curve formed by the cusping of an arch or circle, typically occurring in groups of three or more in Gothic tracery. ▷Middle English: via Old French from Latin *folium* 'leaf.'

foil[3] ▸*n.* a light fencing sword without cutting edges but with a button on its point. ■ the sport of fencing with a foil: *for épée and foil, hits must be made with the point.* ▷late 16th cent.: of unknown origin. **—foil·ist** /-ist/ *n.*

foil[4] ▸*n.* each of the winglike structures fitted to a hydrofoil's hull to lift it clear of the water at speed.

foist /foist/ ▸*v.* [*trans.*] (**foist someone/something on**) impose an unwelcome or unnecessary person or thing on: *don't let anyone foist inferior goods on you.* ■ (**foist someone/something into**) introduce someone or something surreptitiously or unwarrantably into: *he attempted to foist a new delegate into the conference.* ▷mid 16th cent. (in the sense 'palm a false die, so as to produce it at the right moment'): from Dutch dialect *vuisten* 'take in the hand,' from *vuist* (see FIST).

Fo·kine /ˈfôkyin; fôˈkēn/, Michel (1880–1942), U.S. dancer and choreographer; born in Russia; born *Mikhail Mikhailovich Fokin.* He reformed classical ballet. He was Sergi Diaghilev's chief choreographer at the Ballets Russes 1909–14.

Fok·ker /ˈfäkər/, Anthony Herman Gerard (1890–1939), U.S. aircraft designer and pilot; born in Java. Having built his first aircraft in 1908, he designed fighters used by the Germans in World War I.

fol. ▸*abbr.* ■ folio. ■ following.

fol·a·cin /ˈfôləsən; ˈfäl-/ ▸*n.* another term for FOLIC ACID.

fold[1] /fōld/ ▸*v.* [*trans.*] **1** bend (something flexible and relatively flat) over on itself so that one part of it covers another: *she folded all her clothes and packed all her bags.* ■ (**fold something in/into**) mix an ingredient gently with (another ingredient), esp. by lifting a mixture with a spoon so as to enclose it without stirring or beating: *fold the egg whites into the chocolate mixture.* ■ [*intrans.*] (of a piece of furniture or equipment) be able to be bent or rearranged into a flatter or more compact shape, typically in order to make it easier to store or carry: [with *complement*] *the deck chair folds flat* | [as *adj.*] (**folding**) *a folding chair.* ■ bend or rearrange (a piece of furniture or equipment) in such a way: *he folded up his tripod.* ■ [*intrans.*] (**fold out**) be able to be opened out; unfold: *the sofa folds out.* ■ (of a bird) collapse (its wings) and lay them flat against its body: *the crow folded its wings to a sharp angle and dive-bombed the vulture.* ■ (often **be folded**) *Geology* cause (rock strata) to undergo bending or curvature: [as *n.*] (**folding**) *a more active period of igneous activity caused intense folding.* **2** [with *adverbial*] cover or wrap something in (a soft or flexible material): *a plastic bag was folded around the book.* ■ hold or clasp (someone) closely in one's arms with passion or deep affection: *Bob folded her in his arms and kissed her.* **3** [*intrans.*] *informal* (of an enterprise or organization) cease operating as a result of financial problems or a lack of support: *the club folded earlier this year.* ■ (esp. of a sports player or team) suddenly stop performing well or effectively: *he folded in the second round.* ■ (of a poker player) drop out of a hand: *an unerring knack for knowing when to fold and when to stay in.*
▸*n.* **1** (usu. **folds**) a form or shape produced by the gentle draping of a loose, full garment or piece of cloth: *the fabric fell in soft folds.* ■ an area of skin that sags or hangs loosely. ■ *chiefly Brit.* an undulation or gentle curve of the ground; a slight hill or hollow: *the house lay in a fold of the hills.* ■ *Geology* a bend or curvature of strata. **2** a line or crease produced in paper or cloth as the result of folding it. ■ a piece of paper or cloth that has been folded: *a fold of paper slipped out of the diary.* ▷Old English *falden, fealden,* of Germanic origin; related to Dutch *vouwen* and German *falten.* **—fold·a·ble** *adj.*
▸*PHRASES* □ **fold one's arms** bring one's arms together and cross them over one's chest. □ **fold one's hands** bring or hold one's hands together.

fold[2] ▸*n.* a pen or enclosure in a field where livestock, esp. sheep, can be kept. ■ (**the fold**) a group or community, esp. when perceived as the locus of a particular set of aims and values: *he's performing a ritual to be accepted into the fold.*
▸*v.* [*trans.*] shut (livestock) in a fold. ▷Old English *fald,* of Germanic origin; related to Dutch *vaalt.*

-fold ▸*suffix* forming adjectives and adverbs from cardinal numbers: **1** in an amount multiplied by: *threefold.* **2** consisting of so many parts or facets: *twofold.* ▷Old English *-fald, -feald*; related to FOLD[1].

fold·a·way /ˈfōldə,wā/ ▸*adj.* [*attrib.*] adapted or designed to be folded up for ease of storage or transport: *a foldaway table.*

fold·er /ˈfōldər/ ▸*n.* a folding cover or holder, typically made of stiff paper or cardboard, for storing loose papers. ■ an icon on a computer screen that can be used to access a directory containing related files or documents. ■ a folded leaflet or a booklet made of folded sheets of paper.

fol·de·rol /ˈfäldə,räl; ˈfôldə,rôl/ (also **fal·de·ral**) ▸*n.* trivial or nonsensical fuss: *all the folderol of the athletic contests and the cheerleaders.* ■ *archaic* used as a meaningless recurring phrase in a song. ■ *dated* a showy but useless item.

fold·ing door ▸*n.* a door with vertical jointed sections that can be folded together to one side to allow access to a room or building.

fold·ing mon·ey ▸*n.* *informal* paper money; banknotes.

fold·out /ˈfōl,dout/ ▸*adj.* [*attrib.*] (of a page in a book or magazine or a piece of furniture) designed to be opened out for use and then folded away: *a fold-out map.*
▸*n.* a page or piece of furniture designed in such a way.

fo·ley /ˈfōlē/ ▸*n.* [as *adj.*] relating to or concerned with the addition of recorded sound effects after the shooting of a film: *the aural details that foley artists duplicate.* ▷named after the inventor of the editing process.

fo·li·a /ˈfōlēə/ ▸ plural form of FOLIUM.

fo·li·a·ceous /,fōlēˈāsнəs/ ▸*adj.* of or resembling a leaf or leaves. ■ *chiefly Geology* consisting of thin sheets or laminae. ▷mid 17th cent.: from Latin *foliaceus* 'leafy' (from *folium* 'leaf') + -OUS.

fo·li·age /ˈfōl(ē)ij/ ▸*n.* plant leaves, collectively: *healthy green foliage.* ▷late Middle English *foilage* (in the sense 'design resembling leaves'): from Old French *feuillage,* from *feuille* 'leaf,' from Latin *folium.* The change in the first syllable was due to association with Latin *folium.*

fo·li·age leaf ▸*n.* *Botany* a normal leaf, as opposed to petals and other modified leaves.

fo·li·ar /ˈfōlēər/ ▸*adj.* [*attrib.*] *technical* of or relating to leaves: *foliar color and shape.* ▷late 19th cent.: from modern Latin *foliaris,* from Latin *folium* 'leaf.'

fo·li·ar feed ▸*n.* nutrients supplied to the leaves of a plant. **—fo·li·ar feed·ing** *n.*

fo·li·ate ▸*adj.* /ˈfōlēət; -,āt/ decorated with leaves or leaflike motifs: *foliate scrolls.*
▸*v.* /ˈfōlē,āt/ [*trans.*] **1** decorate with leaves or leaflike motifs: *the dome is to be foliated.* **2** number the leaves of (a book) rather than the pages. ▷mid 17th cent.: from Latin *foliatus* 'leaved,' from *folium* 'leaf.'

fo·li·at·ed /ˈfōlē,ātid/ ▸*adj.* decorated with leaves or leaflike motifs: *ten columns foliated at the capitals.* ■ *Architecture* decorated with foils or conventionalized leaves. ■ *chiefly Geology* consisting of thin sheets or laminae.

fo·li·a·tion /,fōlēˈāsнən/ ▸*n.* **1** *chiefly Geology* the process of being split into thin sheets or laminae. **2** the process or result of numbering the leaves of a book.

fo·lic ac·id /ˈfōlik; ˈfä-/ ▸*n.* *Biochemistry* a vitamin of the B complex, found esp. in leafy green vegetables, liver, and kidney. A deficiency of folic acid causes megaloblastic anemia. Also called PTEROYLGLUTAMIC ACID, VITAMIN M. ▷1940s: *folic* from Latin *folium* 'leaf' + -IC. **—fo·late** /ˈfō,lāt/ *n.*

fo·lie à deux /fô,lē ä ˈdœ/ ▸*n.* (*pl.* **fo·lies à deux** /fô,lēz/) delusion or mental illness shared by two people in close association. ▷early 20th cent.: French, literally 'shared madness.'

fo·lie de gran·deur /ˈfô,lēdəgränˈdər/ ▸*n.* delusions of grandeur. ▷late 19th cent.: French.

Fo·lies-Ber·gère /fô,lē bərˈzнer; ber-/ a variety theater in Paris, opened in 1869, known for its lavish productions featuring nude and seminude female performers.

fo·li·o /ˈfōlē,ō/ ▸*n.* (*pl.* **-os**) an individual leaf of paper or parchment, numbered on the recto or front side only, occurring either loose as one of a series or forming part of a bound volume. ■ *Printing* the leaf number in a printed book. ■ a sheet of paper folded once to form two leaves (four pages) of a book. ■ a size of book made up of such sheets: *copies **in folio**.* ■ a book or manuscript made up of sheets of paper folded in such a way; a volume of the largest standard size: *old vellum-bound folios* | [as *adj.*] *a folio volume.* ▷late Middle English: from Latin, ablative of *folium* 'leaf,' in medieval Latin used in references to mean 'on leaf so-and-so.' The original sense of *in folio* (from Italian *in foglio*) was 'in the form of a full-sized sheet or leaf folded once' (designating the largest size of book).

fo·li·ose /ˈfōlē,ōs/ ▸*adj.* *Botany* (of a lichen) having a lobed, leaflike shape. ▷early 18th cent.: from Latin *foliosus,* from *folium* 'leaf.'

fo·li·um /ˈfōlēəm/ ▸*n.* (*pl.* **-li·a** /-lēə/) *technical* a thin leaflike structure, e.g., in some rocks or in the cerebellum of the brain. ▷mid 18th cent.: from Latin, literally 'leaf.'

fo·li·vore /ˈfōlə,vôr/ ▸*n.* *Zoology* an animal that feeds on leaves. **—fo·liv·o·rous** /fōˈlivərəs/ *adj.*

folk /fōk/ (also **folks**) ▸*plural n.* **1** *informal* people in general: *some folk will do anything for money* | *an old folks' home.* ■ a specified group of people: *some city folk cringe at the notion of consuming these birds.* ■ (**folks**) used as a friendly form of address to a group of people: *meanwhile, folks, why not relax and enjoy the show?* ■ (**one's folks**) the members of one's family, esp. one's parents: *I get along all right with your folks.* **2** folk music: *a mixture of folk and reggae.*
▸ **1** *adj.* [*attrib.*] of or relating to the traditional art or culture of a community or nation: *a revival of interest in folk customs* | *a folk museum.* ■ relating to or originating from the beliefs and opinions of ordinary people: *a folk hero* | *folk wisdom.* **2** of or relating to folk music: *performing at a folk club in Chicago.* ▷Old English *folc,* of Germanic origin; related to Dutch *volk* and German *Volk.*
▸*PHRASE* □ **just (plain) folks** ordinary, down-to-earth, unpretentious people.

folk dance ▸*n.* a popular dance, considered as part of the tradition or custom of a particular people: *well-known folk dances* | *ballet steps complicated by borrowings from folk dance.* **—folk danc·er** *n.* **—folk danc·ing** *n.*

folk et·y·mol·o·gy ▸*n.* a popular but mistaken account of the origin of a word or phrase. ■ the process by which the form of an unfamiliar or foreign word is adapted to a more familiar form through popular usage.

folk·ie /ˈfōkē/ ▸*n.* *informal* a singer, player, or fan of folk music.

folk·ish /ˈfōkisн/ ▸*adj.* characteristic of ordinary people or traditional culture: *folkish humor.* ■ relating to or like folk music or folk singers: *the most conventionally folkish number on the album.*

F

folk·life /ˈfōkˌlīf/ ▸*n.* the way of life of a rural or traditional community.

folk·lore /ˈfōkˌlôr/ ▸*n.* the traditional beliefs, customs, and stories of a community, passed through the generations by word of mouth. ■ a body of popular myth and beliefs relating to a particular place, activity, or group of people: *Hollywood folklore.* **—folk·lor·ic** /-ˌlôrik/ *adj.* **—folk·lor·ist** /-ist/ *n.* **—folk·lor·is·tic** /ˌfōkləˈristik/ *adj.*

folk mass ▸*n.* a mass in which folk music is used instead of traditional liturgical music.

folk med·i·cine ▸*n.* treatment of disease or injury based on tradition, esp. on oral tradition, rather than on modern scientific practice, and often utilizing indigenous plants as remedies.

folk mem·o·ry ▸*n.* a body of recollections or legends connected with the past that persists among a group of people.

folk mu·sic ▸*n.* music that originates in traditional popular culture or that is written in such a style. Folk music is typically of unknown authorship and is transmitted orally from generation to generation.

folk rock ▸*n.* popular music resembling or derived from folk music but incorporating the stronger beat of rock music and using electric instruments.

folk sing·er (also **folk·sing·er**) ▸*n.* a person who sings folk songs, typically accompanying themselves on a guitar.

folk song ▸*n.* a song that originates in traditional popular culture or that is written in such a style.

folk·sy /ˈfōksē/ ▸*adj.* (**-si·er**, **-si·est**) having the characteristics of traditional culture and customs, esp. in a contrived or artificial way: *the shop's folksy, small-town image.* ■ (of a person) informal and unpretentious: *his tireless energy and folksy oratory were much in demand at constituency lunches.* **—folk·si·ness** /-sēnis/ *n.*

folk tale ▸*n.* a story originating in popular culture, typically passed on by word of mouth.

folk·ways /ˈfōkˌwāz/ ▸*plural n.* the traditional behavior or way of life of a particular community or group of people: *a study of Cherokee folklore and folkways.*

folk·y /ˈfōkē/ ▸*adj.* (**folk·i·er**, **folk·i·est**) another term for FOLKSY or FOLKISH. **—folk·i·ness** /-kēnis/ *n.*

fol·li·cle /ˈfälikəl/ ▸*n.* **1** *Anatomy* a small secretory cavity, sac, or gland, in particular: ■ (also **hair follicle**) the sheath of cells and connective tissue that surrounds the root of a hair. ■ short for GRAAFIAN FOLLICLE. **2** *Botany* a dry fruit that is derived from a single carpel and opens on one side only to release its seeds. ▷late Middle English: from Latin *folliculus* 'little bag,' diminutive of *follis* 'bellows.' **—fol·lic·u·lar** /fəˈlikyələr/ *adj.* **—fol·lic·u·late** /fəˈlikyələt; -ˌlāt/ *adj.* **—fol·lic·u·lat·ed** /fəˈlikyəˌlātid/ *adj.*

fol·li·cle mite ▸*n.* a parasitic mite that burrows into the hair follicles, causing demodectic mange. • Genus *Demodex*, family Demodicidae.

fol·li·cle-stim·u·lat·ing hor·mone (abbr.: **FSH**) ▸*n.* *Biochemistry* a hormone secreted by the anterior pituitary gland that promotes the formation of ova or sperm.

fol·lic·u·li·tis /fəˌlikyəˈlītəs/ ▸*n.* *Medicine* inflammation of the hair follicles.

fol·lis /ˈfälis/ ▸*n.* (*pl.* **fol·les** /ˈfälēz/) a bronze or copper coin of a type introduced by the Roman emperor Diocletian in AD 296 and also used later in Byzantine currency. ▷late 19th cent.: Latin, literally 'bag, purse'; compare with FILS[1], FOOL[1].

fol·low /ˈfälō/ ▸*v.* [*trans.*] **1** go or come after (a person or thing proceeding ahead); move or travel behind: *she went back into the house, and Ben followed her* | [*intrans.*] *he was following behind in his car.* ■ go after (someone) in order to observe or monitor: *the KGB man followed her everywhere.* ■ *archaic* strive after; aim at: *I follow fame.* ■ go along (a route or path). ■ (of a route or path) go in the same direction as or parallel to (another): *the road follows a hidden sweetwater brook.* **2** come after in time or order: *the six years that followed his restoration* | [*intrans.*] *the rates are* **as follows**. ■ happen after (something else) as a consequence: *raucous laughter followed the ribald remark* | [*intrans.*] *retribution soon followed.* ■ [*intrans.*] be a logical consequence: *it thus* **follows from** *this equation that the value must be negative.* ■ [*trans.*] (of a person) do something after (something else): *he* **follows** *his surprise hit movie* **with** *a paranoid thriller.* ■ (often **be followed by**) have (a dish or course) after another or others in a meal: *turkey was followed by dessert.* **3** act according to (an instruction or precept): *he has difficulty in following written instructions.* ■ conform to: *the film faithfully follows Shakespeare's plot.* ■ act according to the lead or example of (someone): *he follows Aristotle in believing this.* ■ treat as a teacher or guide: *those who seek to follow Jesus Christ.* **4** pay close attention to (something): *I've been following this discussion closely.* ■ keep track of; trace the movement or direction of: *she followed his gaze, peering into the gloom.* ■ maintain awareness of the current state or progress of (events in a particular sphere or account): *young Italians follow football.* ■ (of a person or account) be concerned with the development of (something): *the book follows the life and career of Henry Clay.* ■ understand the meaning or tendency of (a speaker or argument): *I still don't follow you.* **5** practice (a trade or profession). ■ undertake or carry out (a course of action or study): *she followed a strict diet.*

▸*phrasal v.* □ **follow through** (in golf, baseball, and other sports) continue one's movement after the ball has been struck or thrown. □ **follow something through** continue an action or task to its conclusion. □ **follow something up** pursue or investigate something further: *I decided to follow up the letters with phone calls.*

▸*n.* *Billiards* topspin imparted to a cue ball, causing it to continue forward after striking the object ball. ▷Old English *folgian*, of Germanic origin; related to Dutch *volgen* and German *folgen*.

▸*PHRASES* □ **follow in someone's footsteps** (or **steps**) do as another person did before, esp. in following a particular career. □ **follow one's nose 1** trust to one's instincts: *you are on the right track so follow your nose.* **2** move along guided by one's sense of smell. **3** go straight ahead. □ **follow suit** (in bridge, whist, and other card games) play a card of the suit led. ■ conform to another's actions: *Spain cut its rates by half a percent but no other country has followed suit.*

fol·low·er /ˈfälō-ər/ ▸*n.* an adherent or devotee of a particular person, cause, or activity: *a freethinker and follower of Voltaire.* ■ a person who moves or travels behind someone or something.

fol·low·ing /ˈfälō-iNG/ ▸*prep.* coming after or as a result of: *police are hunting for two men following a spate of robberies in the area.*

▸*n.* **1** a body of supporters or admirers: *he attracted a worldwide following.* **2** (**the following**) [treated as *sing.* or *pl.*] what follows or comes next: *the following are both grammatically correct sentences.*

▸*adj.* [*attrib.*] **1** next in time: *the following day there was a ceremony in St. Peter's Square.* ■ about to be mentioned: *you are required to provide us with the following information.* **2** (of a wind or sea) blowing or moving in the same direction as the course of a vehicle or vessel.

fol·low-on ▸*n.* the action of occurring as a consequence or result of something: [as *adj.*] *follow-on treatment.* ■ a thing that occurs as a consequence, result, or modification of another: *it will act as the follow-on to the current version of the software.*

fol·low-the-lead·er ▸*n.* a children's game in which the participants copy the actions and words of a person who has been chosen as leader. ■ *figurative* the copying of the actions of others, often without consideration of their suitability for oneself: *consumers play follow-the-leader when it comes to buying fashion* | [as *adj.*] *a follow-the-leader effect in the investments market.*

fol·low-through ▸*n.* the continuing of an action or task to its conclusion: *the company assures follow-through on all aspects of the contract.* ■ a continuation of the movement of an arm, bat, racket, or club after a ball has been thrown or struck: *he has a characteristic swing and follow-through.*

fol·low-up ▸*n.* a continuation or repetition of something that has already been started or done, in particular: ■ an activity carried out as part of a study in order to monitor or further develop earlier work: [as *adj.*] *follow-up interviews.* ■ further observation or treatment of a patient, esp. to monitor earlier treatment: *patients who require proper medical follow-up.* ■ a piece of work that builds on or exploits the success of earlier work: *she is writing* **a follow-up to** *Jane Austen's* Pride and Prejudice.

fol·ly /ˈfälē/ ▸*n.* (*pl.* **-lies**) **1** lack of good sense; foolishness: *an act of sheer folly.* ■ a foolish act, idea, or practice: *the follies of youth.* **2** a costly ornamental building with no practical purpose, esp. a tower or mock-Gothic ruin built in a large garden or park. **3** (**Follies**) a theatrical revue, typically with glamorous female performers: [in *names*] *the Ziegfeld Follies.* ▷Middle English: from Old French *folie* 'madness,' in modern French also 'delight, favorite dwelling' (compare with sense 2), from *fol* 'fool, foolish.'

Fol·som[1] /ˈfōlsəm/ a city in north central California, northeast of Sacramento; pop. 29,802.

Fol·som[2] ▸*n.* [usu. as *adj.*] *Archaeology* a Paleo-Indian culture of Central and North America, dated to about 10,500–8,000 years ago. The culture is distinguished by fluted stone projectile points or spearheads. Compare with CLOVIS[2]. ▷early 20th cent.: from *Folsom*, northeastern New Mexico, the area where remains were first found.

Fo·mal·haut /ˈfōməlˌhôt/ *Astronomy* the brightest star in the constellation Piscis Austrinus. ▷Arabic *fam al-ḥūt* 'mouth of the fish', from *fam* 'mouth' + *al-* 'the' + *ḥūt* 'fish'.

fo·ment /ˈfōˌment; fōˈment/ ▸*v.* [*trans.*] **1** instigate or stir up (an undesirable or violent sentiment or course of action): *they accused him of fomenting political unrest.* See note at INCITE. **2** *archaic* bathe (a part of the body) with warm or medicated lotions. ▷late Middle English (sense 2): from French *fomenter*, from late Latin *fomentare*, from Latin *fomentum* 'poultice, lotion,' from *fovere* 'to heat, cherish.' **—fo·ment·er** *n.*

fo·men·ta·tion /ˌfōmenˈtāSHən; -mən-/ ▸*n.* **1** the action of instigating or stirring up undesirable sentiment or actions. **2** an herbal preparation for external use, typically made by soaking a cloth in an herbal decoction. ■ *archaic* a poultice. ▷late Middle English: from late Latin *fomentatio(n-)*, from the verb *fomentare* (see FOMENT).

fom·i·tes /ˈfōməˌtēz/ ▸*plural n.* *Medicine* objects or materials that are likely to carry infection, such as clothes, utensils, and furniture. ▷early 19th cent.: from Latin, plural of *fomes*, literally 'kindling wood, tinder.'

Fon /fän/ ▸*n.* (*pl.* same or **Fons**) **1** a member of a people inhabiting the southern part of Benin. **2** the Kwa language of this people.

▸*adj.* of or relating to this people or their language. ▷the name in Fon.

fond /fänd/ ▸*adj.* [*predic.*] (**fond of**) having an affection or liking for: *I'm very fond of Mike* | *he was not too fond of dancing.* ■ [*attrib.*] affectionate; loving: *waving a* **fond farewell** *to her parents* | *reading it brought many fond memories of our childhood.* ■ [*attrib.*] (of a hope or belief) foolishly optimistic; naive. ▷late Middle English (in the sense 'infatuated, foolish'): from obsolete *fon* 'a fool, be foolish,' of unknown origin. Compare with FUN. **—fond·ly** *adv.* **—fond·ness** *n.*

Fon·da /ˈfändə/ a family of U.S. actors. **Henry Fonda** (1905–82) was noted for his roles in such movies as *The Grapes of Wrath* (1939) and *Twelve Angry Men* (1957). He won an Academy Award for his role in his final movie, *On Golden Pond* (1981). His daughter **Jane** (1937–) is known for movies including *Klute* (1971), for which she won an Academy Award, and *The China Syndrome* (1979); she also acted alongside her father in *On Golden Pond*. Her brother **Peter** (1939–) and his daughter **Bridget** (1964–) are also actors.

Henry Fonda

fon·dant /ˈfändənt/ ▸*n.* a thick paste made of sugar and water and often flavored or colored, used in the making of candy and the icing and decoration of cakes. ■ a candy made of such a paste. ▷late 19th cent.: from French, literally 'melting,' present participle of *fondre*.

fon·dant po·ta·toes ▸*plural n.* potatoes trimmed in the shape of eggs, fried in butter and then baked.

Fond du Lac /ˈfändlˌak; ˈfänjəˌlak/ an industrial and commercial city in southeastern Wisconsin, on Lake Winnebago; pop. 42,203.

fon·dle /ˈfändl/ ▸*v.* [*trans.*] stroke or caress lovingly or erotically: *the dog came over to have his ears fondled* | *charges that he fondled a patient during an examination.*

▸*n.* an act of fondling. ▷late 17th cent. (in the sense 'pamper'): back-formation from obsolete *fondling* 'much-loved or petted person,' from FOND + -LING. **—fon·dler** /ˈfändlər; ˈfändl-ər/ *n.*

fon·du /fänˈd(y)o͞o/ ▸*adj.* [*postpositive*] *Ballet* (of a position) involving a lowering of the body by bending the knee of the supporting leg: *an arabesque fondu.* ▷mid 19th cent.: French, literally 'melted.'

fon·due /fänˈd(y)o͞o/ ▸*n.* a dish in which small pieces of food are dipped into a hot sauce or a hot cooking medium such as oil or broth: *a Swiss cheese fondue.* ▷French, feminine past participle of *fondre* 'to melt.'

Fon·se·ca, Gulf of /fänˈsākə/ an inlet of the Pacific Ocean in western Central America. El Salvador lies on its north, Honduras on its east, and Nicaragua on its south.

fons et o·ri·go /ˈfänz et ō ˈrīgō; rē-/ ▸*n.* the source and origin of something: *they recognized the sixties as the fons et origo of music as they knew it.* ▷Latin, originally as *fons et origo mali* 'the source and origin of evil.'

font[1] /fänt/ ▸*n.* **1** a receptacle in a church for the water used in baptism, typically a freestanding stone structure. ■ another term for STOUP. ■ a reservoir for oil in an oil lamp. **2** a fount: *they dip down into the font of wisdom.* ▷late Old English: from Latin *fons, font-* 'spring, fountain,' occurring in the ecclesiastical Latin phrase *fons* or *fontes baptismi* 'baptismal water(s).' **—font·al** /ˈfäntl/ *adj.*

font[2] (*Brit.* also **fount** /fount/) ▸*n.* *Printing* a set of type of one particular face and size. ▷late 16th cent. (denoting the action or process of casting or founding): from French *fonte,* from *fondre* 'to melt.'

fonts (typefaces)

SERIF

Bookman
abcdefghijklmnopqrstuvwxyz 1234567890
ABCDEFGHIJKLMNOPQRSTUVWXYZ

Times
abcdefghijklmnopqrstuvwxyz 1234567890
ABCDEFGHIJKLMNOPQRSTUVWXYZ

SANS SERIF

Helvetica
abcdefghijklmnopqrstuvwxyz 1234567890
ABCDEFGHIJKLMNOPQRSTUVWXYZ

Avant Garde
abcdefghijklmnopqrstuvwxyz 1234567890
ABCDEFGHIJKLMNOPQRSTUVWXYZ

SQUARE SERIF

Courier
abcdefghijklmnopqrstuvwxyz 1234567890
ABCDEFGHIJKLMNOPQRSTUVWXYZ

SCRIPT

Boulevard
abcdefghijklmnopqrstuvwxyz 1234567890
ABCDEFGHIJKLMNOPQRSTU-VWXYZ

DISPLAY

ITC Kabel Ultra
abcdefghijklmnopqrstuvwxyz 1234567890
ABCDEFGHIJKLMNOPQRSTUVWXYZ

font[2]

Fon·taine, Joan (de Beauvoir) (1917–), U.S. actress; born in Japan; born *Joan de Havilland;* sister of Olivia de Havilland. Her movies include *Rebecca* (1940), *Suspicion* (Academy Award, 1941), and *The Constant Nymph* (1943).

Fon·taine·bleau /ˌfôNtenˈblō; ˈfäntin,blō/ a town in north central France, southeast of Paris, where King Louis XIV revoked the Edict of Nantes and Napoleon I signed his first abdication; pop. 20,000.

Fon·ta·na /fänˈtanə/ a city in southwestern California, east of Los Angeles; pop. 87,535.

fon·ta·nel /ˌfäntnˈel/ (also **fon·ta·nelle**) ▸*n.* a space between the bones of the skull in an infant or fetus, where ossification is not complete and the sutures not fully formed. The main one is between the frontal and parietal bones. ▷mid 16th cent. (denoting a hollow of the skin between muscles): from French, from modern Latin *fontanella,* from an Old French diminutive of *fontaine* (see FOUNTAIN). The current sense dates from the mid 18th cent.

Fon·tanne /fänˈtan/, Lynn (1887–1983), U.S. actress; born in England. She married actor Alfred Lunt (1892–1977) in 1922 and thereafter they appeared in many plays together, including *The Guardsman* (1924) and *The Visit* (1958).

Fon·teyn /fänˈtān/, Dame Margot (1919–91), English ballet dancer; born *Margaret Hookham.* In 1962, she began a partnership with Rudolf Nureyev, dancing with him in *Giselle* and *Romeo and Juliet.*

fon·ti·na /fänˈtēnə/ ▸*n.* a kind of pale yellow Italian cheese.

Foo·chow /ˈfo͞oˈjō/ variant of FUZHOU.

food /fo͞od/ ▸*n.* any nutritious substance that people or animals eat or drink, or that plants absorb, in order to maintain life and growth: *cans of cat food | baby foods.* ▷late Old English *fōda,* of Germanic origin; related to FODDER.
▸*PHRASE* □ **food for thought** something that warrants serious consideration.

Food and Ag·ri·cul·ture Or·gan·i·za·tion (abbr.: **FAO**) an agency of the United Nations established in 1945 to secure improvements in the production and distribution of food and agricultural products and to raise levels of nutrition. Its headquarters are in Rome.

food bank ▸*n.* a place supplying food to poor or displaced people.

food bod·y ▸*n.* *Botany* a small nutrient-rich structure developed on the leaves, flowers, or petioles of some tropical plants to attract ants.

food chain ▸*n.* a hierarchical series of organisms each dependent on the next as a source of food.

food court ▸*n.* an area, typically in a shopping mall, where fast-food outlets, tables, and chairs are located.

food fish ▸*n.* a species of fish that is used as food by humans or forms a major part of the diet of a particular predator.

Food Guide Pyr·a·mid ▸*n.* a nutritional diagram in the shape of pyramid developed by the U.S. Department of Agriculture, displaying foods and food groups at different levels, with those nearer the apex, such as fatty food, to be eaten less frequently and those at the base, such as bread and cereals, more frequently.

food·ie /ˈfo͞odē/ ▸*n.* *informal* a person with a particular interest in food; a gourmet.

food poi·son·ing ▸*n.* illness caused by bacteria or other toxins in food, typically with vomiting and diarrhea.

food proc·es·sor ▸*n.* an electric kitchen appliance used for chopping, mixing, or puréeing foods.

food pyr·a·mid ▸*n.* **1** a nutritional diagram in the shape of a pyramid, such as the Food Guide Pyramid. **2** *Ecology* a graphic representation of predatory relationships in the food chain, in which various forms of life are shown on different levels, with each level preying on the one below it, so that as the pyramid narrows toward the apex, the number of types decreases as the reliance on predation grows.

food stamp ▸*n.* a voucher issued by the government to those on low income, exchangeable for food.

food·stuff /ˈfo͞od,stəf/ ▸*n.* a substance suitable for consumption as food.

food sup·ple·ment ▸*n.* see SUPPLEMENT.

food vac·u·ole ▸*n.* *Biology* a vacuole with a digestive function in the protoplasm of a protozoan.

food val·ue ▸*n.* the nutritional value of a foodstuff.

food web ▸*n.* *Ecology* a system of interlocking and interdependent food chains.

foo·fa·raw /ˈfo͞ofə,rô/ *informal* ▸*n.* **1** a great deal of fuss or attention given to a minor matter. **2** showy frills added unnecessarily.

foo fight·er /fo͞o/ ▸*n.* an unidentified flying object of a kind reported by U.S. pilots during World War II, usually described as a bright light or ball of fire. ▷1940s: from the comic strip *Smokey Stover* (created in 1935 by Bill Holman (1903–1987)), whose title character used the invented term to mean 'fire-fighter'.

foo-foo /ˈfo͞o ,fo͞o/ ▸*n.* variant spelling of FUFU.

fool[1] /fo͞ol/ ▸*n.* a person who acts unwisely or imprudently; a silly person: *what a fool I was to do this.* ■ *historical* a jester or clown, esp. one retained in a noble household. ■ *informal* a person devoted to a particular activity: *he is a running fool.* ■ *archaic* a person who is duped.
▸*v.* [*trans.*] trick or deceive (someone); dupe: *he* **fooled** *nightclub managers* **into** *believing he was a successful businessman | she had been* **fooling herself** *in thinking she could remain indifferent.* ■ [*intrans.*] act in a joking, frivolous, or teasing way: *I shouted at him impatiently to stop* **fooling around.** ■ [*intrans.*] (**fool around**) engage in casual or extramarital sexual activity.
▸*phrasal v.* □ **fool with** toy with; play idly with: *I like fooling with cameras.* ■ tease (a person): *we've just been fooling with you.*
▸*adj.* [*attrib.*] *informal* foolish or silly: *that damn fool waiter.* ▷Middle English: from Old French *fol* 'fool, foolish,' from Latin *follis* 'bellows, bag,' by extension 'empty-headed person'; compare with FILS[1], FOLLIS.
▸*PHRASES* □ **be no** (or **nobody's**) **fool** be a shrewd or prudent person. □ **a fool and his money are soon parted** *proverb* a foolish person spends money carelessly and will soon be penniless. □ **fools rush in where angels fear to tread** *proverb* people without good sense or judgment will have no hesitation in tackling a situation that even the wisest would avoid. □ **make a fool of** trick or deceive (someone) so that they look foolish. ■ (**make a fool of oneself**) behave in an incompetent or inappropriate way that makes one appear foolish. □ **play** (or **act**) **the fool** behave in a playful or silly way. □ **there's no fool like an old fool** *proverb* the foolish behavior of an older person seems especially foolish as they are expected to think and act more sensibly than a younger one. □ **you could have fooled me!** used to express cynicism or doubt about an assertion: *"Fun, was it? Well, you could have fooled me!"*

fool[2] ▸*n.* [usu. with *adj.*] *chiefly Brit.* a cold dessert made of puréed fruit mixed or served with cream or custard: *raspberry fool with cream.* ▷late 16th cent.: perhaps from FOOL[1].

fool·er·y /ˈfo͞olərē/ ▸*n.* silly or foolish behavior.

fool·har·dy /ˈfo͞ol,härdē/ ▸*adj.* (**-di·er, -di·est**) recklessly bold or rash: *it would be foolhardy to go into the scheme without support.* ▷Middle English: from Old French *folhardi,* from *fol* 'foolish' + *hardi* 'bold' (see HARDY). **—fool·har·di·ly** /-,härdl-ē/ *adv.* **—fool·har·di·ness** *n.*

fool·ish /ˈfo͞olisH/ ▸*adj.* (of a person or action) lacking good sense or judgment; unwise: *it was foolish of you to enter into correspondence.* ■ [as *complement*] silly; ridiculous: *he'd been made to look foolish.* See note at ABSURD. **—fool·ish·ly** *adv.* **—fool·ish·ness** *n.*

fool·proof /ˈfo͞ol,pro͞of/ ▸*adj.* incapable of going wrong or being misused: *a foolproof security system.*

fools·cap /ˈfo͞olz,kap/ ▸*n.* a size of paper, now standardized at about 13 × 8 (or 13 × 15.75) inches (300 × 200 [or 300 × 400] mm). ■ paper of this size: *several sheets of foolscap.* ▷late 17th cent.: said to be named from a former watermark representing a jester's cap.

fool's er·rand ▸*n.* a task or activity that has no hope of success.

fool's gold ▸*n.* a brassy yellow mineral, esp. pyrite, that can be mistaken for gold.

fool's par·a·dise ▸*n.* [in *sing.*] a state of happiness based on a person's not knowing about or denying the existence of potential trouble: *they were living in a fool's paradise, refusing to accept that they were in debt.*

fool's pars·ley ▸*n.* a poisonous white-flowered plant of the parsley family, with fernlike leaves and an unpleasant smell, native to Eurasia and North Africa. • *Aethusa cynapium,* family Umbelliferae.

foos·ball /ˈfo͞os,bôl/ ▸*n.* *trademark* a tabletop version of soccer in which players turn rods fixed on top of a playing box and attached to miniature figures of players, in order to flick the ball and strike it toward the goal. ▷mid 20th cent.: from German *Fussball* 'football.'

foot /fo͝ot/ ▸*n.* (*pl.* **feet** /fēt/) **1** the lower extremity of the leg below the ankle, on which a person stands or walks. ■ a corresponding part of the leg in vertebrate animals. ■ *Zoology* a locomotory or adhesive organ of an invertebrate. ■ the part of a sock or stocking that covers the foot. ■ *poetic/literary* a person's manner or speed of walking or running: *fleet of foot.* ■ [treated as *pl.*] *Brit., historical or formal* infantry; foot soldiers: *a captain of foot.* **2** the lower or lowest part of something standing or perceived as standing vertically; the base or bottom: *the foot of the stairs.* ■ the end of a table that is furthest from where the host sits. ■ the end of a bed, couch, or grave where the occupant's feet normally rest. ■ a device on a sewing machine for holding the material steady as it is sewn. ■ *Botany* the part by which a petal is attached. ■ the lower edge of a sail. **3** a unit of linear measure equal to 12 inches (30.48 cm): *shallow water no more than a foot deep.* ■ [usu. as *adj.*] *Music* a unit used in describing sets of organ pipes or harpsichord strings, in terms of the average or approximate length of the vibrating column of air or the string which produces the sound: *a sixteen-foot stop.* **4** *Prosody* a group of syllables constituting a metrical unit. In English poetry it consists of stressed and

F

unstressed syllables, while in ancient classical poetry it consists of long and short syllables.
▸*v.* [*trans.*] **1** *informal* pay (the bill) for something, esp. when the bill is considered large or unreasonable. **2** (**foot it**) cover a distance, esp. a long one, on foot: *the rider was left to foot it ten or twelve miles back to camp.* ■ *archaic* dance: *the dance of fairies, footing it to the cricket's song.* ▷Old English *fōt*, of Germanic origin; related to Dutch *voet* and German *Fuss*, from an Indo-European root shared by Sanskrit *pad, pāda*, Greek *pous, pod-*, and Latin *pes, ped-* 'foot.' **—foot·ed** /ˈfo͝otəd/ *adj.* [in *combination*] *the black-footed ferret.* **—foot·less** *adj.*
▸*PHRASES* □ **at someone's feet** as someone's disciple or subject: *you would like to sit at my feet and thus acquire my wisdom.* □ **feet of clay** a fundamental flaw or weakness in a person otherwise revered. [with biblical allusion (Dan. 2:33) to the dream of Nebuchadnezzar, in which a magnificent idol has feet "part of iron and part of clay"; Daniel interprets this to signify a future kingdom that will be "partly strong, and partly broken," and will eventually fall.] □ **get one's feet wet** begin to participate in an activity. □ **get** (or **start**) **off on the right** (or **wrong**) **foot** make a good (or bad) start at something, esp. a task or relationship. □ **have something at one's feet** have something in one's power or command: *a perfect couple with the world at their feet.* □ **have** (or **keep**) **one's** (or **both**) **feet on the ground** be (or remain) practical and sensible. □ **have a foot in both camps** have an interest or stake concurrently in two parties or sides: *I can have a foot in both the creative and business camps.* □ **have** (or **get**) **a foot in the door** gain or have a first introduction to a profession or organization. □ **have one foot in the grave** *informal, often humorous* be near death through old age or illness. □ **my foot!** *informal* said to express strong contradiction: *Efficient, my foot!* □ **off one's feet** so as to be no longer standing: *she was blown off her feet by the shock wave from the explosion.* □ **on one's feet** standing: *she's in the shop on her feet all day.* ■ well enough after an illness or injury to walk around: *we'll have you back on your feet in no time.* □ **on** (or **by**) **foot** walking rather than traveling by car or using other transport. □ **put one's best foot forward** embark on an undertaking with as much effort and determination as possible. □ **put one's feet up** *informal* take a rest, esp. when reclining with one's feet raised and supported. □ **put one's foot down** *informal* adopt a firm policy when faced with opposition or disobedience. □ **put one's foot in it** (or **put one's foot in one's mouth**) *informal* say or do something tactless or embarrassing; commit a blunder or indiscretion. □ **set foot on** (or **in**) [often with *negative*] enter; go into: *he hasn't set foot in the place since the war.* □ **set something on foot** *archaic* set an action or process in motion: *a plan had lately been set on foot for their relief.* Compare with **AFOOT** □ **sweep someone off their feet** charm someone quickly and overpoweringly. □ **think on one's feet** react to events decisively, effectively, and without prior thought or planning. □ **to one's feet** to a standing position: *he leaped to his feet.*

foot·age /ˈfo͝otij/ ▸*n.* **1** a length of film made for movies or television: *film footage of the riot.* **2** size or length measured in feet: *the square footage of the room.*

foot-and-mouth dis·ease ▸*n.* a contagious viral disease of cattle and sheep, causing ulceration of the hoofs and around the mouth.

foot·ball /ˈfo͝ot,bôl/ ▸*n.* **1** a form of team game played in North America with an oval ball on a field marked out as a gridiron. ■ play in such a game, esp. when stylish and entertaining: *his team played some impressive football.* ■ British term for **SOCCER**. **2** an oval ball used in such a game, made of leather and filled with compressed air. ■ *figurative* a topical issue or problem that is the subject of continued argument or controversy: *the use of education as a **political football**.* ■ *Brit.* a soccer ball. **—foot·ball·er** *n.* **—foot·ball·ing** *adj.*

foot·ball·ing /ˈfo͝ot,bôliNG/ *Brit.* ▸*adj.* [*attrib.*] of or relating to football (soccer): *footballing ability | his footballing career.*

foot·ball pool ▸*n.* a form of gambling on the results of football games, the winners receiving amounts accumulated from entry money.

foot·bed /ˈfo͝ot,bed/ ▸*n.* an insole in a boot or shoe, used for cushioning or to provide a better fit.

foot·board /ˈfo͝ot,bôrd/ ▸*n.* **1** an upright panel forming the foot of a bed. **2** a board serving as a step up to a vehicle such as a train.

foot·boy /ˈfo͝ot,boi/ ▸*n.* *historical* a boy employed as a servant.

foot·brake /ˈfo͝ot,brāk/ ▸*n.* a brake lever in a motor vehicle, which the driver operates by pressing down with the foot.

foot·bridge /ˈfo͝ot,brij/ ▸*n.* a bridge designed to be used by pedestrians.

foot-can·dle ▸*n.* a unit of illumination (now little used) equal to that given by a source of one candela at a distance of one foot (equivalent to one lumen per square foot or 10.764 lux).

foot-drag·ging ▸*n.* reluctance or deliberate delay concerning a decision or action: *bureaucratic foot-dragging has continued to delay the project.* **—foot-drag·ger** *n.*

foot·er /ˈfo͝otər/ ▸*n.* **1** [in *combination*] a person or thing of a specified number of feet in length or height: *a tall, sturdy six-footer.* **2** a line or block of text appearing at the foot of each page of a book or document. Compare with **HEADER**.

foot·fall /ˈfo͝ot,fôl/ ▸*n.* **1** the sound of a footstep or footsteps: *you will recognize his footfall on the stairs.* **2** *Brit.* the number of people entering a store or shopping area in a given time: *consumer goods shops lost footfall during sunny weekends.*

foot fault ▸*n.* (in tennis, squash, and similar games) an infringement of the rules made by incorrect placement of the feet when serving.
▸*v.* (**foot-fault**) [*intrans.*] (of a player) make a foot fault: *in his anxiety he foot-faulted.* ■ [*trans.*] award a foot fault against (a player): *he was foot-faulted by the umpire.*

foot·gear /ˈfo͝ot,gi(ə)r/ ▸*n.* another term for **FOOTWEAR**.

foot·hill /ˈfo͝ot,hil/ ▸*n.* (usu. **foothills**) a low hill at the base of a mountain or mountain range: *the camp lies in the foothills of the Andes.*

foot·hold /ˈfo͝ot,hōld/ ▸*n.* a place where a person's foot can be lodged to support them securely, esp. while climbing. ■ [usu. in *sing.*] *figurative* a secure position from which further progress may be made: *the company is attempting to gain **a foothold in** the Russian market.*

foot·ing /ˈfo͝otiNG/ ▸*n.* **1** (**one's footing**) a secure grip with one's feet: *he suddenly lost his footing.* ■ the condition of a piece of ground for walking or running: *paths with enough variety to give you practice with uneven footing.* **2** [in *sing.*] the basis on which something is established or operates: *attempts to establish the store on a firm financial footing.* ■ the position or status of a person in relation to others: *the suppliers are **on an equal footing with** the buyers.* **3** (usu. **footings**) the bottommost part of a foundation wall, with a course of concrete wider than the base of the wall.

foo·tle /ˈfo͝otl/ ▸*v.* [*intrans.*] *chiefly Brit.* engage in fruitless activity; mess about: *where's that pesky creature that was footling about outside?* ▷late 19th cent.: perhaps from dialect *footer* 'idle, putter about,' from 16th-cent. *foutre* 'worthless thing,' from Old French, literally 'have sexual intercourse with.'

foot·lights /ˈfo͝ot,līts/ ▸*plural n.* (usu. **the footlights**) a row of spotlights along the front of a stage at the level of the actors' feet.

foot·ling /ˈfo͝otl-iNG/ ▸*adj.* trivial and irritating: *year after year you come with the same footling complaint.*

foot·lock·er /ˈfo͝ot,läkər/ ▸*n.* a small trunk or storage chest, originally stored at the foot of a bed.

foot-log ▸*n.* a log used as a simple footbridge.

foot·long /ˈfo͝ot,lôNG; -,läNG/ ▸*adj.* measuring one foot in length.
▸*n.* a hot dog one foot long.

foot·loose /ˈfo͝ot,lo͞os/ ▸*adj.* able to travel freely and do as one pleases due to a lack of responsibilities or commitments: *I am **footloose and fancy-free**—I can follow my job wherever it takes me.* ■ *chiefly Brit.* (of a commercial, industrial, or financial operation) unrestricted in its location or field of operations and able to respond to fluctuations in the market: *modern factories are largely footloose.*

foot·man /ˈfo͝otmən/ ▸*n.* (*pl.* **-men**) **1** a liveried servant whose duties include admitting visitors and waiting at table. **2** *historical* a soldier in the infantry. **3** *archaic* a trivet to hang on the bars of a grate. **4** a slender moth that is typically of a subdued color, the caterpillar feeding almost exclusively on lichens. • Several genera in the family Arctiidae: many species.

foot·mark /ˈfo͝ot,märk/ ▸*n.* a footprint.

foot·note /ˈfo͝ot,nōt/ ▸*n.* an ancillary piece of information printed at the bottom of a page. ■ *figurative* a thing that is additional or less important: *this incident seemed destined to become a mere footnote in history.*
▸*v.* [*trans.*] add a footnote or footnotes to (a piece of writing).

foot·pace ▸*n.* **1** walking speed. **2** a raised section of a floor.

foot·pad /ˈfo͝ot,pad/ ▸*n.* *historical* a highwayman operating on foot rather than riding a horse.

foot·path /ˈfo͝ot,paTH/ ▸*n.* a path for people to walk along, esp. one in the countryside.

foot·plate /ˈfo͝ot,plāt/ ▸*n.* **1** *Anatomy* the flat oval plate of bone on the stapes that fits into the oval window in the middle ear. **2** *chiefly Brit.* the platform for the crew in the cab of a locomotive. ■ [as *adj.*] denoting railroad staff responsible for operating trains, as opposed to other employees.

foot-pound ▸*n.* a unit of energy equal to the amount required to raise 1 pound a distance of 1 foot.

foot-pound-sec·ond sys·tem ▸*n.* a system of measurement having the foot, pound, and second as basic units.

foot·print /ˈfo͝ot,print/ ▸*n.* **1** the impression left by a foot or shoe on the ground or a surface. **2** the area covered by something, in particular: ■ the area in which a broadcast signal from a particular source can be received. ■ the space taken up on a surface by a piece of computer hardware. ■ the area beneath an aircraft or a land vehicle that is affected by its noise or weight. ■ the area of ground taken up by a building.

foot·rest /ˈfo͝ot,rest/ ▸*n.* a support for the feet or a foot, used when sitting.

foot rope ▸*n.* *Sailing* **1** a rope to which the lower edge of a sail is sewn. **2** a rope below a yard on which a sailor can stand while furling or reefing a sail.

foot rot ▸*n.* a bacterial disease of the feet in hoofed animals, esp. sheep. • The bacteria belong to the genera *Bacteroides* and *Fusobacterium.* ■ any of a number of fungal diseases of plants in which the base of the stem rots.

Foot·sie /ˈfo͝otsē/ ▸*n.* *Brit.* informal term for **FTSE INDEX**. ▷1980s: fanciful elaboration of *FTSE*, influenced by *footsie*.

foot·sie /ˈfo͝otsē/ ▸*n.* (also **foot·sy**) *informal* the action of touching someone's feet lightly with one's own feet, esp. under a table, as a playful expression of romantic interest. ▷1940s: humorous diminutive of **FOOT**.
▸*PHRASE* □ **play footsie** touch someone's feet in such a way. ■ work with someone in a close but covert way: *the FBI reported that the delegate was **playing footsie with** the Soviets.*

foot·slog /ˈfo͝ot,släg/ ▸*v.* (**-slogged**, **-slog·ging**) [*intrans.*] (esp. of a soldier) walk or march for a long distance, typically wearily or with effort: *they footslogged around the two villages.*
▸*n.* a long and exhausting walk or march. **—foot·slog·ger** *n.*

foot sol·dier ▸*n.* a soldier who fights on foot; an infantryman. ■ a person who carries out important work but does not have a role of authority in an organization or field: *programmers are the foot soldiers of the computer revolution.*

foot·sore /ˈfo͝ot,sôr/ ▸*adj.* (of a person or animal) having painful or tender feet from much walking.

foot·stalk /ˈfo͝ot,stôk/ ▸*n.* the short supporting stalk of a leaf or flower, or various stalklike structures in animals.

foot·step /ˈfo͝ot,step/ ▸*n.* a step taken by a person in walking, esp. as heard by another person.

foot·stool /ˈfo͝ot,sto͞ol/ ▸*n.* a low stool for resting the feet on when sitting.

foot·sure /ˈfo͝ot,SHo͝or/ ▸*adj.* another term for **SURE-FOOTED**.

foot-tap·ping ▸*adj.* having or creating a strong rhythmical musical beat: *foot-tapping gospel hymns.*

foot valve ▸*n.* a one-way valve at the inlet of a pipe or the base of a suction pump.

foot·wall /ˈfo͝ot,wôl/ ▸*n.* *Geology* the block of rock that lies on the underside of an inclined fault or of a mineral deposit.

foot·way /ˈfo͝ot,wā/ ▸*n.* *Brit.* a path or track for pedestrians.

foot·wear /ˈfo͝ot,wer/ ▸*n.* outer coverings for the feet, such as shoes, boots, and sandals.

foot·well /ˈfo͝ot,wel/ ▸*n.* a space for the feet in front of a seat in a vehicle or aircraft. ▷1980s: from **FOOT** + **WELL**[2] (in the sense 'a depression in the floor').

foot·work /ˈfo͝ot,wərk/ ▸*n.* the manner in which one moves one's feet in various activities such as sports and dancing: *he speaks with other boxers, stopping to comment on punching angles and footwork.* ■ [usu. with *adj.*] adroit response to sudden danger or new opportunities: *the company had to do a lot of nimble footwork to stay alive.*

foo·ty /ˈfo͝otē/ ▶*n. informal* **1** *Brit.* football (soccer). **2** *Austral./NZ* football (Australian rules). ▷by shortening and alteration.

foo yong /ˈfo͞o ˈyäNG/ ▶*n.* a Chinese dish or sauce made with egg as a main ingredient. ▷from Chinese (Cantonese dialect) *foò yung*, literally 'hibiscus.'

foo·zle /ˈfo͞ozəl/ *informal* ▶*n.* a clumsy or botched attempt at something, esp. a shot in golf.
▶*v.* [*trans.*] botch; bungle: [as *adj.*] (**foozled**) *sliced approach shots and foozled putts.* ▷mid 19th cent.: from German dialect *fuseln* 'work badly'; compare with FUSEL OIL.

fop /fäp/ ▶*n.* a man who is concerned with his clothes and appearance in an affected and excessive way; a dandy. ▷late Middle English (in the sense 'fool'): perhaps related to FOB2. **—fop·per·y** /ˈfäpərē/ *n.* **—fop·pish** *adj.* **—fop·pish·ly** *adv.* **—fop·pish·ness** *n.*

for /fôr; fər/ ▶*prep.* **1** in support of or in favor of (a person or policy): *they voted for independence in a referendum.* **2** affecting, with regard to, or in respect of (someone or something): *she is responsible for the efficient running of their department | the demand for money.* **3** on behalf of or to the benefit of (someone or something): *these parents aren't speaking for everyone.* ■ employed by: *it was a good firm to work for.* **4** having (the thing mentioned) as a purpose or function: *she is searching for enlightenment | the necessary tools for making a picture frame.* **5** having (the thing mentioned) as a reason or cause: *Aileen is proud of her family for their support | I could dance and sing for joy.* **6** having (the place mentioned) as a destination: *they are leaving for Swampscott tomorrow.* **7** representing (the thing mentioned): *the "F" is for Fascinating.* **8** in place of or in exchange for (something): *swap these two bottles for that one.* ■ charged as (a price): *copies are available for only a buck.* **9** in relation to the expected norm of (something): *she was tall for her age | warm weather for this time of year.* **10** indicating the length of (a period of time): *he was in prison for 12 years | I haven't seen him for some time.* **11** indicating the extent of (a distance): *he crawled for 300 yards.* **12** indicating an occasion in a series: *the camcorder failed for the third time.*
▶*conj. poetic/literary* because; since: *he felt guilty, for he knew that he bore a share of responsibility for Fanny's death.* ▷Old English, probably a reduction of a Germanic preposition meaning 'before' (in place or time); related to German *für*, also to FORE.
▶*PHRASES* □ **be for it** *Brit., informal* be in imminent danger of punishment or other trouble. □ **for all —** — see ALL. □ **for ever** see FOREVER. □ **for why** *informal* for what reason: *you're going to and I'll tell you for why.* □ **oh for ——** I long for ——: *oh for a strong black coffee!* □ **there's** (or **that's**) **—— for you** used ironically to indicate a particularly poor example of (a quality mentioned): *there's gratitude for you.*

for. ▶*abbr.* ■ foreign. ■ forest. ■ forester. ■ forestry.

f.o.r. ▶*abbr.* free on rail. See FREE.

for- ▶*prefix* **1** denoting prohibition: *forbid.* **2** denoting abstention, neglect, or renunciation: *forgive | forget | forgo.* **3** denoting extremity of negative state expressed: *forlorn | forsake.* ▷Old English.

fo·ra /ˈfôrə/ ▶ plural form of FORUM (sense 3).

for·age /ˈfôrij; ˈfär-/ ▶*v.* [*intrans.*] (of a person or animal) search widely for food or provisions: *gulls are equipped by nature to* **forage for** *food.* ■ [*trans.*] obtain (food or provisions): *a girl foraging grass for oxen.* ■ [*trans.*] obtain food or provisions from (a place): *a man foraging a dumpster finds some celery.* ■ [*trans.*] *archaic* supply (an animal or person) with food.
▶*n.* **1** bulky food such as grass or hay for horses and cattle; fodder. **2** [in *sing.*] a wide search over an area in order to obtain something, esp. food or provisions: *the nightly forage produces things that can be sold.* ▷Middle English: from Old French *fourrage* (noun), *fourrager* (verb), from *fuerre* 'straw,' of Germanic origin and related to FODDER. **—for·ag·er** *n.*

for·age cap ▶*n.* a billed cap forming part of a soldier's uniform.

for·age fish ▶*n.* a species of fish of interest to humans chiefly as the prey of more valuable game fish.

for·age har·ves·ter ▶*n.* a large agricultural machine for harvesting forage crops.

fo·ra·men /fəˈrāmən/ ▶*n.* (*pl.* **-ram·i·na** /-ˈramənə/) *Anatomy* an opening, hole, or passage, esp. in a bone. ▷late 17th cent.: from Latin, from *forare* 'bore a hole.'

fo·ra·men mag·num ▶*n. Anatomy* the hole in the base of the skull through which the spinal cord passes. ▷late 19th cent.: Latin, 'large opening.'

for·a·min·i·fer /ˌfôrəˈminəfər; ˌfär-/ ▶*n.* (*pl.* **for·a·min·i·fers** or **fo·ram·i·nif·e·ra** /fəˌraməˈnifərə/) *Zoology* a single-celled planktonic animal with a perforated chalky shell through which slender protrusions of protoplasm extend. Most kinds are marine, and when they die, their shells form thick ocean-floor sediments. See also GLOBIGERINA. • Order Foraminiferida, phylum Rhizopoda, kingdom Protista. ▷mid 19th cent.: from Latin *foramen, foramin-* (see FORAMEN) + *-fer* 'bearing' (from *ferre* 'to bear'). **—fo·ram·i·nif·er·al** /fəˌraməˈnifərəl/ *adj.* **—fo·ram·i·nif·er·an** /fəˌraməˈnifərən/ *n. & adj.* **—fo·ram·i·nif·er·ous** /fəˌraməˈnifərəs/ *adj.*

for'ard /ˈfôrərd; ˈfär-/ ▶*adj. & adv.* nonstandard spelling of FORWARD, used to represent a nautical pronunciation.

for·as·much as /ˌfôrəzˈməCH əz/ ▶*conj. archaic* because; since: *forasmuch as the tree returned to life, so too could Arthur be returned to her.* ▷Middle English *for as much*, translating Old French *por tant que* 'for so much as.'

for·as·te·ro /ˌfôrəˈsterō/ (also **forastero tree**) ▶*n.* (*pl.* **-ros**) a cacao tree of a widely grown variety that provides the bulk of the world's cocoa beans. ▷mid 19th cent.: from Spanish, literally 'foreign,' because the tree was imported into Venezuela from the West Indies, as distinct from the CRIOLLO or native variety.

for·ay /ˈfôrˌā; ˈfärˌā/ ▶*n.* a sudden attack or incursion into enemy territory, esp. to obtain something; a raid: *the garrison made a foray against Richard's camp | figurative he made another foray to the bar.* ■ an attempt to become involved in a new activity or sphere: *my first* **foray into** *journalism.*
▶*v.* [*intrans.*] make or go on a foray: *the place into which they were forbidden to foray.* ▷Middle English: backformation from *forayer* 'a person who forays,' from Old French *forrier* 'forager,' from *fuerre* 'straw' (see FORAGE). **—for·ay·er** *n.*

forb /fôrb/ ▶*n. Botany* a herbaceous flowering plant other than a grass. ▷1920s: from Greek *phorbē* 'fodder,' from *phorbein* 'to feed.'

for·bade /fərˈbad; fôr-; -ˈbād/ (also **for·bad**) ▶ past of FORBID.

for·bear1 /fərˈber; fôr-/ ▶*v.* (*past* **-bore**; *past part.* **-borne**) [*intrans.*] *poetic/literary or formal* politely or patiently restrain an impulse to do something; refrain: *the boy* **forbore from** *touching anything* | [with *infinitive*] *he modestly forbears to include his own work.* ■ [*trans.*] refrain from doing or using (something): *Rebecca could not forbear a smile.* ▷Old English *forberan* (see FOR-, BEAR1). The original senses were 'endure, bear with,' hence 'endure the absence of something, do without,' also 'bear up against, control oneself,' hence 'refrain from' (Middle English).

for·bear2 ▶*n.* variant spelling of FOREBEAR.

for·bear·ance /fôrˈberəns; fər-/ ▶*n. formal* patient self-control; restraint and tolerance: **forbearance from** *taking action.* See note at ABSTINENCE. ■ *Law* the action of refraining from exercising a legal right, esp. enforcing the payment of a debt.

for·bear·ing /fôrˈberiNG; fər-/ ▶*adj.* (of a person) patient and restrained. See note at LENIENT.

for·bid /fərˈbid; fôr-/ ▶*v.* (**-bid·ding**; *past* **-bade** /-ˈbad; -ˈbād/ or **forbad** /-ˈbad/; *past part.* **-bid·den**) [*trans.*] refuse to allow (something): *environmental laws forbid alteration of the coast.* See note at PROHIBIT. ■ order (someone) not to do something: *I was* **forbidden from** *leaving Russia* | [*trans.*] *my doctor has forbidden me to eat sugar.* ■ refuse (someone or something) entry to a place or area: *all cars are forbidden.* ■ (of a circumstance or quality) make (something) impossible; prevent: *the cliffs forbid any easy turning movement.* ▷Old English *forbēodan* (see FOR-, BID2).
▶*PHRASE* □ **God** (or **Heaven**) **forbid** used to express a fervent wish that something does not happen: [with *clause*] *God forbid that this should happen to anyone ever again.*

for·bid·den /fərˈbidn; fôr-/ ▶*adj.* not allowed; banned: *a list of forbidden books.* ■ *Physics* denoting or involving a transition between two quantum-mechanical states that does not conform to some selection rule, esp. for electric dipole radiation.
▶*PHRASES* □ **the forbidden degrees** the number of steps of descent from the same ancestor that bar two related people from marrying. □ **forbidden fruit** a thing that is desired all the more because it is not allowed. [with biblical allusion to Gen. 2:17.]

For·bid·den Cit·y **1** an area of Beijing, China, that contains the former imperial palaces, to which entry was forbidden to all except the members of the imperial family and their servants. **2** a name given to Lhasa, Tibet.

for·bid·ding /fərˈbidiNG; fôr-/ ▶*adj.* unfriendly or threatening in appearance: *a grim and forbidding building.* See note at OMINOUS. **—for·bid·ding·ly** *adv.*

for·bore /fərˈbôr; fôr-/ ▶ past of FORBEAR1.

for·borne /fərˈbôrn; fôr-/ ▶ past participle of FORBEAR1.

for·bye /fôrˈbī/ (also **for·by**) ▶*adv. & prep. archaic* or *Scottish* in addition; besides: [as *adv.*] *there's chicken in the fridge, and plenty of soup forbye, if you get hungry again.*

force /fôrs/ ▶*n.* **1** strength or energy as an attribute of physical action or movement: *he was thrown backward by the force of the explosion.* ■ *Physics* an influence tending to change the motion of a body or produce motion or stress in a stationary body. The magnitude of such an influence is often calculated by multiplying the mass of the body by its acceleration. ■ a person or thing regarded as exerting power or influence: *he might still be* **a force for** *peace and unity.* ■ [in *combination*] used with a number as a measure of wind strength on the Beaufort scale: *a force-nine gale.* **2** coercion or compulsion, esp. with the use or threat of violence: *they ruled by law and not* **by force**. **3** mental or moral strength or power: *the force of popular opinion.* ■ the state of being in effect or valid: *the law came into force in January.* ■ the powerful effect of something: *the force of her writing is undiminished.* **4** an organized body of military personnel or police: *a soldier in a UN peacekeeping force.* ■ (**forces**) troops and weaponry: *concealment from enemy forces | figurative a battle between the forces of good and evil.* ■ a group of people brought together and organized for a particular activity: *a sales force.* ■ (**the force**) *informal* a police department. **5** *Baseball* a force out. ■ a situation in which a force out is possible.
▶*v.* [*trans.*] **1** make a way through or into by physical strength; break open by force: *they broke into Fred's house and forced every cupboard door with ax or crowbar.* ■ [*trans.*] drive or push into a specified position or state using physical strength or against resistance: *she forced her feet into flat leather sandals | figurative Fields was forced out as director.* ■ achieve or bring about (something) by coercion or effort: *Sabine forced a smile | she* **forced her way** *up the ladder.* See note at COMPEL. ■ push or strain (something) to the utmost: *she knew if she forced it she would rip it.* ■ artificially hasten the development or maturity of (a plant). **2** (often **be forced**) make (someone) do something against their will: *she was* **forced into** *early retirement* | [*trans.*] *the universities were forced to cut staff.* ■ rape (a woman). ■ *Baseball* put out (a runner), or cause (a runner) to be put out, at the base to which they are advancing when they are forced to run on a batted ball: *I was forced at second base as the first half of a double play.* ■ (in cards) make a play or bid that compels another player to make (a particular response); make a play or bid that compels (another player) to make such a response: *East could force declarer to ruff another spade*
▶*phrasal v.* □ **force something down** **1** manage to swallow food or drink when one does not want to: *I forced down a slice of toast.* **2** compel an aircraft to land: *the plane might have been forced down by fighters.* □ **force oneself on/upon** rape (a woman). □ **force something on/upon** impose or press something on (a person or organization): *economic cutbacks were forced on the government.* ▷Middle English: from Old French *force* (noun), *forcer* (verb), based on Latin *fortis* 'strong.' **—force·a·ble** *adj.* **—forc·er** *n.*
▶*PHRASES* □ **by force of** by means of: *exercising authority by force of arms.* □ **force the bidding** (at an auction) make bids to raise the price rapidly. □ **force**

Forbidden City

someone's hand make someone do something: *the exchange markets may force the Fed's hand.* □ **force the issue** compel the making of an immediate decision. □ **force the pace** adopt a fast pace in a race in order to tire out one's opponents quickly. □ **in force 1** in great strength or numbers: *birdwatchers were out in force.* **2** in effect; valid: *the U.S. has over $8 trillion worth of life insurance in force.*

forced /fôrst/ ▸*adj.* obtained or imposed by coercion or physical power: *the brutal regime of forced labor.* ■ (of a gesture or expression) produced or maintained with effort; affected or unnatural: *a forced smile.* ■ (of a plant) having its development or maturity artificially hastened.
▸*PHRASE* □ **forced march** a fast march by soldiers, typically over a long distance.

forced land·ing ▸*n.* an act of abruptly bringing an aircraft to the ground or the surface of water in an emergency. —**force-land** *v.*

force-feed ▸*v.* [*trans.*] force (a person or animal) to eat. ■ [with *two objs.*] *figurative* impose or force (information or ideology) upon (someone): *no group has the right to force-feed its beliefs on her.*

force feed·back ▸*n.* *Computing* the simulation of physical attributes such as weight in virtual reality, allowing the user to interact directly with virtual objects using touch.

force field ▸*n.* (chiefly in science fiction) an invisible barrier of exerted strength or impetus: *future land combat vehicles will deflect enemy shells with an electromagnetic force field.*

force·ful /ˈfôrsfəl/ ▸*adj.* (esp. of a person or argument) strong and assertive; vigorous and powerful: *she was a forceful personality | forceful, imaginative marketing.* —**force·ful·ly** *adv.* —**force·ful·ness** *n.*

force ma·jeure /ˌfôrs mäˈzнər/ ▸*n.* **1** unforeseeable circumstances that prevent someone from fulfilling a contract. **2** irresistible compulsion or greater force. ▷late 19th cent.: French, literally 'greater force.'

force·meat /ˈfôrsˌmēt/ ▸*n.* a mixture of meat or vegetables chopped and seasoned for use as a stuffing or garnish. ▷late 17th cent.: from obsolete *force* 'to stuff,' alteration (influenced by the verb **FORCE**) of *farce,* from French *farcir* (see **FARCE**).

force out ▸*n.* *Baseball* an out made by holding the ball and touching the base to which a base runner must advance.

force play ▸*n.* *Baseball* an out made at a base to which a player must advance when a ball is hit, when a defensive player with the ball touches the base first.

for·ceps /ˈfôrsəps; -ˌseps/ (also **a pair of forceps**) ▸*plural n.* a pair of pincers or tweezers used in surgery or in a laboratory. ■ a large instrument of such a type with broad blades, used to encircle a baby's head and assist in birth: [as *adj.*] *a forceps delivery.* ■ *Zoology* an organ or structure resembling forceps, esp. the cerci of an earwig. ▷late 16th cent.: from Latin, 'tongs, pincers.'

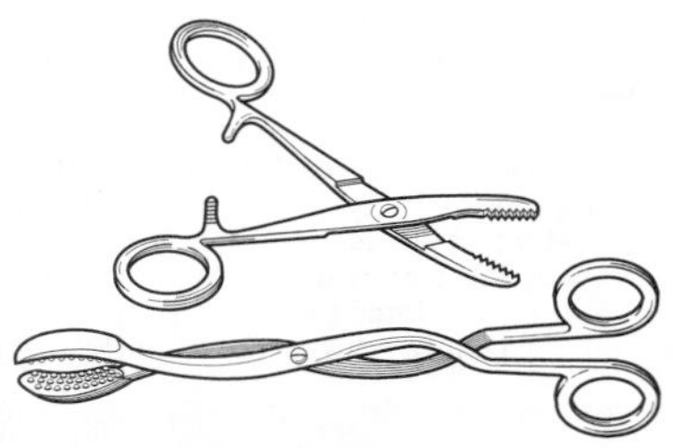

forceps

force pump ▸*n.* a pump used to move water or other liquid under pressure.

for·ci·ble /ˈfôrsəbəl/ ▸*adj.* done by force: *signs of forcible entry.* ■ vigorous and strong; forceful: *they could only be deterred by forcible appeals.* ▷late Middle English: from Old French, from *force* (see **FORCE**). —**for·ci·bly** /-blē/ *adv.*

forc·ing /ˈfôrsiɴɢ/ ▸*adj.* *Bridge* (of a bid) requiring by convention a response from one's partner, no matter how weak their hand may be.

forc·ing house ▸*n.* a place in which the growth or development of something (esp. plants) is artificially hastened.

Ford[1] /fôrd/, Ford Madox (1873–1939), English novelist and editor; born *Ford Hermann Hueffer.* He is known for his novel *The Good Soldier* (1915).

Ford[2], Gerald Rudolph (1913–), 38th president of the U.S. 1974–77; born as *Leslie Lynch King, Jr.* (renamed by his stepfather in 1916). He served in the U.S. House of Representatives 1949–73 and as vice president 1973–74 before succeeding to the presidency upon the resignation of Richard Nixon in the wake of the Watergate affair. Noted for his integrity and candidness, he worked to heal the nation, to curb inflation while stimulating the economy, and to prevent war in the Middle East. He lost the 1976 presidential election to Jimmy Carter.

Gerald Ford

Ford[3], Harrison (1942–), U.S. actor. He first became known for his leading role in the science-fiction movie *Star Wars* (1977) and its two sequels. He also achieved a wide following as a result of his adventure movies *Raiders of the Lost Ark* (1981), *Indiana Jones and the Temple of Doom* (1984), and *Indiana Jones and the Last Crusade* (1989).

Harrison Ford

Ford[4], Henry (1863–1947), U.S. automobile manufacturer. A pioneer of large-scale mass production, he founded the Ford Motor Company, which produced the Model T in 1909. Control of the company passed to his grandson, **Henry Ford II** (1917–1987) in 1945.

Ford[5], John (1895–1973), U.S. movie director; born *Sean Aloysius O'Feeney.* He is chiefly known for his westerns, several of which starred John Wayne, including *Stagecoach* (1939) and *She Wore a Yellow Ribbon* (1949). Other notable movies include *The Grapes of Wrath* (1940), for which he won an Academy Award.

Ford[6], Tennessee Ernie (1919–91), U.S. country singer and songwriter. His notable songs include "Mule Train" (1949) and "Sixteen Tons" (1955). Country Music Hall of Fame (1990).

Ford[7], Whitey (1928–), U.S. baseball player; born *Edward Charles Ford.* His career win percentage (.690) is one of the highest among 20th-century pitchers. Baseball Hall of Fame (1974).

ford /fôrd/ ▸*n.* a shallow place in a river or stream allowing one to walk or drive across.
▸*v.* [*trans.*] (of a person or vehicle) cross (a river or stream) at a shallow place. ▷Old English; related to Dutch *voorde,* also to **FARE**. —**ford·a·ble** *adj.* —**ford·less** *adj.*

Ford·ham /ˈfôrdəm/ a section of the central Bronx in New York City that takes its name from Fordham University.

fore /fôr/ ▸*adj.* [*attrib.*] situated or placed in front: *the fore and hind pairs of wings.*
▸*n.* the front part of something, esp. a ship.
▸*exclam.* called out as a warning to people in the path of a golf ball.
▸*prep.* (also **'fore**) nonstandard form of **BEFORE**: *we'll be harvesting corn 'fore the end of the month.* ▷Old English (as a preposition, also in the sense 'before in time, previously'): of Germanic origin; related to Dutch *voor* and German *vor.* The adjective and noun represent the prefix **FORE-** used independently (late 15th cent.).
▸*PHRASE* □ **to the fore** in or to a conspicuous or leading position: *his persistent effort brought this issue to the fore.*

fore- ▸*comb. form* **1** (added to verbs) in front: *foreshorten.* ■ beforehand; in advance: *forebode | foreshadow.* **2** (added to nouns) situated in front of: *forecourt.* ■ the front part of: *forebrain.* ■ of or near the bow of a ship: *forecastle.* ■ preceding; going before: *forefather.* ▷Old English (see **FORE**).

fore and aft ▸*adv.* at the front and rear (often used with reference to a ship or plane): *we're moored fore and aft.* ■ backward and forward: *a sperm whale cannot see directly fore and aft.*
▸*adj.* [*attrib.*] backward and forward: *the fore-and-aft motion of the handles.* ■ (of a hat, esp. one worn as part of a uniform) having three corners and a brim at the front and back: *we were in full dress, with fore-and-aft hats and swords.* ■ (of a sail or rigging) set lengthwise, not on transverse yards: *a fore-and-aft-rigged yacht.* ▷early 17th cent.: perhaps translating a phrase of Low German origin; compare with Dutch *van voren en van achteren.*

fore·arm[1] /ˈfôrˌärm/ ▸*n.* the part of a person's arm extending from the elbow to the wrist or the fingertips.

fore·arm[2] /fôrˈärm/ ▸*v.* [*trans.*] (usu. **be forearmed**) prepare (someone) in advance for danger, attack, or another undesirable future event.

fore·bear /ˈfôrˌber/ (also **for·bear**) ▸*n.* (usu. **one's forebears**) an ancestor. ▷late 15th cent.: from **FORE** + *bear,* variant of obsolete *beer* 'someone who exists' (from **BE** + **-ER**[1]).

fore·bode /fôrˈbōd/ ▸*v.* [*trans.*] *archaic* or *poetic/literary* (of a situation or occurrence) act as a warning of (something bad): *this lull foreboded some new assault upon him.* ■ have a presentiment of (something bad): *I foreboded mischief the moment I heard.*

fore·bod·ing /fôrˈbōdiɴɢ/ ▸*n.* fearful apprehension; a feeling that something bad will happen: *with a sense of foreboding she read the note.*
▸*adj.* implying or seeming to imply that something bad is going to happen: *when the doctor spoke, his voice was dark and foreboding.* See note at **OMINOUS**. —**fore·bod·ing·ly** *adv.*

fore·brain /ˈfôrˌbrān/ ▸*n.* *Anatomy* the anterior part of the brain, including the cerebral hemispheres, the thalamus, and the hypothalamus. Also called **PROSENCEPHALON**.

fore·cad·die /ˈfôrˌkadē/ ▸*n.* (*pl.* **-dies**) a caddie who goes ahead of golfers to see where the balls fall.

fore·cast /ˈfôrˌkast/ ▸*v.* (*past* **-cast** or **-cast·ed**) [*trans.*] predict or estimate (a future event or trend): *rain is forecast for eastern Ohio | [trans.] coal consumption is forecast to increase.* See note at **PREDICT**.
▸*n.* a prediction or estimate of future events, esp. coming weather or a financial trend. —**fore·cast·er** *n.*

fore·cas·tle /ˈfōksəl; ˈfôrˌkasəl/ (also **fo'c's'le**) ▸*n.* the forward part of a ship below the deck, traditionally used as the crew's living quarters. ■ a raised deck at the bow of a ship.

fore·check /ˈfôrˌcнek/ ▸*v.* [*intrans.*] *Ice Hockey* play an aggressive style of defense, checking opponents in their own defensive zone, before they can organize an attack. —**fore·check·er** *n.*

fore·close /fôrˈklōz/ ▸*v.* **1** [*intrans.*] take possession of a mortgaged property as a result of the mortgagor's failure to keep up their mortgage payments: *the bank was threatening to* **foreclose on** *his mortgage.* ■ [*trans.*] take away someone's power of redeeming (a mortgage) and take possession of the mortgaged property. **2** [*trans.*] rule out or prevent (a course of action): *the decision effectively foreclosed any possibility of his early rehabilitation.* ▷Middle English: from Old French *forclos,* past participle of *forclore,* from *for-* 'out' (from Latin *foras* 'outside') + *clore* 'to close.' The original sense was 'bar from escaping,' in late Middle English 'shut out,' and 'bar from doing something' (sense 2), hence specifically 'bar someone from redeeming a mortgage' (sense 1, early 18th cent.).

fore·clo·sure /fôrˈklōzнər/ ▸*n.* the process of taking possession of a mortgaged property as a result of the mortgagor's failure to keep up mortgage payments.

fore·court /ˈfôrˌkôrt/ ▸*n.* **1** an open area in front of a large building. **2** *Tennis* the part of the court between the service line and the net.

fore·deck /ˈfôrˌdek/ ▸*n.* the deck at the forward part of a ship.

fore·doom /fôrˈdo͞om/ ▸*v.* [*trans.*] (usu. **be foredoomed**) condemn beforehand to certain failure or destruction: *the policy is foredoomed to failure.*

fore·dune /ˈfôrˌdo͞on/ ▸*n. Ecology* a part of a system of sand dunes on the side nearest to the sea.

fore-edge (also **fore edge**) ▸*n. technical* the outer vertical edge of the pages of a book.

fore·fa·ther /ˈfôrˌfäT͟Hər/ ▸*n.* (usu. **one's forefathers**) a member of the past generations of one's family or people; an ancestor. ■ a precursor of a particular movement: *the forefathers of rock 'n' roll.*

fore·fend ▸*v.* variant spelling of **FORFEND** (sense 2).

fore·fin·ger /ˈfôrˌfiNGgər/ ▸*n.* the finger next to the thumb; the first or index finger.

fore·foot /ˈfôrˌfo͝ot/ ▸*n.* (*pl.* **-feet**) each of the front feet of a four-footed animal. ■ the forward end of a vessel's keel where it joins the stern.

fore·front /ˈfôrˌfrənt/ ▸*n.* (**the forefront**) the leading or most important position or place: *we are at the forefront of developments.*

fore·gath·er ▸*v.* variant spelling of **FORGATHER**.

fore·go[1] ▸*v.* variant spelling of **FORGO**.

fore·go[2] /fôrˈgō/ ▸*v.* (**fore·goes**; *past* **fore·went**; *past part.* **fore·gone**) [*trans.*] *archaic* precede in place or time. —**fore·go·er** /fôrˈgōər/ *n.*

fore·go·ing /fôrˈgōiNG/ *formal* ▸*adj.* [*attrib.*] just mentioned or stated; preceding: *the foregoing discussion has juxtaposed management and owner control.*
▸*n.* (**the foregoing**) [treated as *sing.* or *pl.*] the things just mentioned or stated.

fore·gone /ˈfôrˌgôn/ ▸ past participle of **FOREGO**[2].
▸*adj.* [often *postpositive*] *archaic* past: *poets dream of lives foregone in worlds fantastical.*
▸*PHRASE* □ **a foregone conclusion** a result that can be predicted with certainty.

fore·ground /ˈfôrˌground/ ▸*n.* (**the foreground**) the part of a view that is nearest to the observer, esp. in a picture or photograph: *the images show vegetation in the foreground.* ■ the most prominent or important position or situation: *whenever books are chosen for children, meaning should always be in the foreground.*
▸*v.* [*trans.*] make (something) the most prominent or important feature: *sexual relationships are foregrounded and idealized.* ▷late 17th cent.: from **FORE-** + **GROUND**[1], on the pattern of Dutch *voorgrond.*

fore·gut /ˈfôrˌgət/ ▸*n. Anatomy & Zoology* the anterior part of the gut, toward the mouth.

fore·hand /ˈfôrˌhand/ ▸*n.* **1** (in tennis and other racket sports) a stroke played with the palm of the hand facing in the direction of the stroke; compare with **BACKHAND**: [as *adj.*] *a good forehand drive.* **2** the part of a horse in front of the saddle.

fore·hand·ed /ˈfôrˈhandid/ ▸*adj.* **1** another term for **FOREHAND** (as adj.). **2** looking to the future; prudent; thrifty.
▸*adv.* (in tennis and other racket sports) with a forehand stroke.

fore·head /ˈfôrəd; ˈfôrˌhed/ ▸*n.* the part of the face above the eyebrows. ▷Old English *forhēafod* (see **FORE-, HEAD**).

for·eign /ˈfôrən; ˈfär-/ ▸*adj.* **1** of, from, in, or characteristic of a country or language other than one's own: *a foreign language.* ■ dealing with or relating to other countries: *foreign policy.* ■ of or belonging to another district or area. ■ coming or introduced from outside: *the quotation is a foreign element imported into the work.* ■ (of a law or restriction) outside the local jurisdiction. **2** strange and unfamiliar: *I suppose this all feels pretty* **foreign to** *you.* ■ (**foreign to**) not belonging to or characteristic of: *crime and brutality are foreign to our nature and our country.* ▷Middle English *foren, forein*, from Old French *forein, forain*, based on Latin *foras, foris* 'outside,' from *fores* 'door.' The current spelling arose in the 16th cent., by association with **SOVEREIGN**. —**for·eign·ness** *n.*

for·eign aid ▸*n.* money, food, or other resources given or lent by one country to another.

for·eign bill ▸*n.* a bill of exchange payable in another country.

for·eign bod·y ▸*n.* an object or piece of extraneous matter that has entered the body by accident or design.

for·eign·er /ˈfôrənər; ˈfär-/ ▸*n.* a person born in or coming from a country other than one's own. ■ *informal* a person not belonging to a particular place or group; a stranger or outsider.

for·eign ex·change ▸*n.* the currency of other countries. ■ an institution or system for dealing in such currency.

For·eign Le·gion a military unit of the French army founded in the 1830s to fight France's colonial wars. Composed, except for the higher ranks, of non-Frenchmen, the Legion was famed for its audacity and endurance. Its most famous campaigns were in French North Africa in the late 19th and early 20th centuries.

for·eign min·is·ter ▸*n.* (in many countries) a government minister in charge of relations with other countries: *the Tunisian foreign minister will visit Washington.*

for·eign mis·sion ▸*n.* **1** a permanent office established by a nation to represent its interests in a foreign country. **2** a group sent by a church to live in a foreign country for a period of time, esp. to seek converts.

for·eign of·fice in some countries, the department of government in charge of foreign affairs.

for·eign sec·re·tar·y ▸*n.* (in the UK) a foreign minister.

for·eign serv·ice ▸*n.* the government department concerned with the representation of a country abroad. ■ (**Foreign Service**) a division of the U.S. State Department staffed by diplomatic and consular personnel.

fore·know /fôrˈnō/ ▸*v.* (*past* **-knew**; *past part.* **-known**) [*trans.*] *poetic/literary* be aware of (an event) before it happens: *he foreknows his death like a saint.*

fore·knowl·edge /fôrˈnälij/ ▸*n.* awareness of something before it happens or exists.

fore·la·dy /ˈfôrˌlādē/ ▸*n.* (*pl.* **-dies**) another term for **FOREWOMAN**.

fore·land /ˈfôrlənd/ ▸*n.* an area of land bordering on another or lying in front of a particular feature. ■ a cape or promontory. ■ *Geology* a stable unyielding block of the earth's crust, against which compression produces a folded mountain range.

fore·leg /ˈfôrˌleg/ ▸*n.* either of the front legs of a four-footed animal.

fore·limb /ˈfôrˌlim/ ▸*n.* either of the front limbs of an animal.

fore·lock /ˈfôrˌläk/ ▸*n.* a lock of hair growing just above the forehead. ■ the part of the mane (of a horse or similar animal) that grows from the poll and hangs down over the forehead.

Fore·man /ˈfôrmən/, George (1949–), U.S. boxer. Having held the world heavyweight championship 1973–74, he regained the title in 1994–95, becoming the oldest man to do so.

fore·man /ˈfôrmən/ ▸*n.* (*pl.* **-men**) a worker, esp. a man, who supervises and directs other workers. ■ (in a court of law) a person, esp. a man, who presides over a jury and speaks on its behalf. ▷Middle English: perhaps suggested by Dutch *voorman* (compare with German *Vormann*).

fore·mast /ˈfôrˌmast; -məst/ ▸*n.* the mast of a ship nearest the bow.

fore·most /ˈfôrˌmōst/ ▸*adj.* the most prominent in rank, importance, or position: *one of the foremost art collectors of his day.*
▸*adv.* before anything else in rank, importance, or position; in the first place: *O'Keefe's work was, foremost, an expression of the feelings of a woman.* ▷Old English *formest, fyrmest*, from *forma* 'first' (ultimately a superlative formed from the Germanic base of **FORE**) + **-EST**[1]. Compare with **FIRST** and **FORMER**[1]. The current spelling arose by association with **FORE** and **MOST**.
▸*PHRASE* □ **first and foremost** see **FIRST**.

fore·moth·er /ˈfôrˌməT͟Hər/ ▸*n.* (usu. **one's foremothers**) a female ancestor or precursor of something.

fore·name /ˈfôrˌnām/ ▸*n.* another term for **FIRST NAME**.

fore·noon /ˈfôrˌno͞on/ ▸*n.* [in *sing.*] the morning.

fo·ren·sic /fəˈrenzik; -sik/ ▸*adj.* of, relating to, or denoting the application of scientific methods and techniques to the investigation of crime: *forensic evidence.* ■ of or relating to courts of law.
▸*n.* (**forensics**) scientific tests or techniques used in connection with the detection of crime. ■ (also **forensic**) [treated as *sing.* or *pl.*] *informal* a laboratory or department responsible for such tests. ▷mid 17th cent.: from Latin *forensis* 'in open court, public,' from *forum* (see **FORUM**). —**fo·ren·si·cal·ly** /-(ə)lē/ *adv.*

fo·ren·sic med·i·cine ▸*n.* the application of medical knowledge to the investigation of crime, particularly in establishing the causes of injury or death.

fore·or·dain /ˌfôrôrˈdān/ ▸*v.* [*trans.*] (of God or fate) appoint or decree (something) beforehand: *progress is not foreordained.* —**fore·or·di·na·tion** /fôrˌôrdnˈāSHən/ *n.*

fore·paw /ˈfôrˌpô/ ▸*n.* either of the front paws of a quadruped.

fore·peak /ˈfôrˌpēk/ ▸*n.* the forwardmost division of a vessel's hull, often used in ships as a ballast tank.

fore·per·son /ˈfôrˌpərsən/ ▸*n.* a foreman or forewoman (used as a neutral alternative).

fore·play /ˈfôrˌplā/ ▸*n.* sexual activity that precedes intercourse.

fore·quar·ter /ˈfôrˌkwôrtər/ ▸*n.* a front quarter of something, esp. of a carcass (of beef, lamb, etc.). ■ (**forequarters**) the front legs and adjoining parts of a quadruped.

fore·run /fôrˈrən/ ▸*v.* (**-run·ning**; *past* **-ran**; *past part.* **-run**) [*trans.*] *poetic/literary* go before or indicate the coming of: *the vast inquietude that foreruns the storm.*

fore·run·ner /ˈfôrˌrənər/ ▸*n.* a person or thing that precedes the coming or development of someone or something else: *the icebox was a forerunner of today's refrigerator.* ■ a sign or warning of something to come: *overcast mornings are the sure forerunners of steady rain.* ■ *archaic* an advance messenger.

fore·sail /ˈfôrˌsāl; -səl/ ▸*n.* the principal sail on a foremast.

fore·see /fôrˈsē/ ▸*v.* (**-sees, -see·ing**; *past* **-saw**; *past part.* **-seen**) [*trans.*] be aware of beforehand; predict: *we did not foresee any difficulties* | [with *clause*] *it is impossible to foresee how life will work out.* ▷Old English *foresēon* (see **FORE-, SEE**[1]). —**fore·se·er** / -ˈsēər/ *n.*

fore·see·a·ble /fôrˈsēəbəl/ ▸*adj.* able to be foreseen or predicted: *the situation is unlikely to change in the foreseeable future.* —**fore·see·a·bil·i·ty** /fôrˌsēəˈbilətē/ *n.* —**fore·see·a·bly** /-ˈsēəblē/ *adv.*

fore·shad·ow /fôrˈSHadō/ ▸*v.* [*trans.*] be a warning or indication of (a future event): *it foreshadowed my preoccupation with jazz.* See note at **PREDICT**.

fore·sheet /ˈfôrˌSHēt/ ▸*n.* **1** a rope by which the lee corner of a foresail is kept in place. **2** (**foresheets**) the inner part of the bow of a boat.

fore·shock /ˈfôrˌSHäk/ ▸*n.* a mild tremor preceding the violent shaking movement of an earthquake.

fore·shore /ˈfôrˌSHôr/ ▸*n.* the part of a shore between high- and low-water marks, or between the water and cultivated or developed land.

fore·short·en /fôrˈSHôrtn/ ▸*v.* [*trans.*] portray or show (an object or view) as closer than it is or as having less depth or distance, as an effect of perspective or the angle of vision: *seen from the road, the mountain is greatly foreshortened.* ■ prematurely or dramatically shorten or reduce (something) in time or scale: [as *adj.*] (**foreshortened**) *foreshortened reports.*

fore·show /fôrˈSHō/ ▸*v.* (*past part.* **-shown**) [*trans.*] *archaic* give warning or promise of (something); foretell.

fore·sight /ˈfôrˌsīt/ ▸*n.* the ability to predict or the action of predicting what will happen or be needed in the future: *he had the foresight to check that his escape route was clear.* ▷Middle English: from **FORE-** + **SIGHT**, probably suggested by Old Norse *forsjá, forsjó.*

fore·sight·ed /ˈfôrˌsītid/ ▸*adj.* having or using foresight. —**fore·sight·ed·ly** *adv.* —**fore·sight·ed·ness** *n.*

fore·skin /ˈfôrˌskin/ ▸*n.* the retractable roll of skin covering the end of the penis. Also called **PREPUCE**.

for·est /ˈfôrəst; ˈfär-/ ▸*n.* a large area covered chiefly with trees and undergrowth: *a pine forest* | *much of Europe was covered with forest.* ■ a large number or dense mass of vertical or tangled objects: *a* **forest of** *connecting wires.* ■ *historical* (in England) an area, typically owned by the sovereign and partly wooded, kept for hunting and having its own laws.
▸*v.* [*trans.*] [usu. as *adj.*] (**forested**) cover (land) with forest; plant with trees: *a forested area.* ▷Middle English (in the sense 'wooded area kept for hunting,' also denoting any uncultivated land): via Old French from late Latin *forestis (silva)*, literally '(wood) outside,' from Latin *foris* 'outside' (see **FOREIGN**). —**for·est·a·tion** /ˌfôrəˈstāSHən; ˌfär-/ *n.*
▸*PHRASE* □ **cannot see the forest for the trees** fail to grasp the main issue because of overattention to details.

fore·stall /fôrˈstôl/ ▸*v.* [*trans.*] prevent or obstruct (an anticipated event or action) by taking action ahead of time: *vitamins may forestall many diseases of aging.* ■ act in advance of (someone) in order to prevent them from doing something: *she started to rise, but Erica forestalled her and got the telephone.* ■ *historical* buy up (goods) in order to profit by an enhanced price. ▷Old English *foresteall* 'an ambush' (see **FORE-** and

F

STALL). As a verb the earliest sense (Middle English) was 'intercept and buy up (goods) before they reach the market, so as to raise the price' (formerly an offense). —**fore·stall·er** *n.* —**fore·stal·ment** *n.*

fore·stay /ˈfôrˌstā/ ▸*n.* a stay leading forward and down to support a ship's foremast.

fore·stay·sail /ˌfôrˈstāsəl; -ˌsāl/ ▸*n.* a triangular sail set on the forestay.

For·est·er /ˈfôrəstər/, C. S. (1899–1966), English novelist; pseudonym of *Cecil Lewis Troughton Smith.* He is remembered for his seafaring novels set during the Napoleonic Wars and featuring Captain Horatio Hornblower. He also wrote *The African Queen* (1935).

for·est·er /ˈfôrəstər; ˈfär-/ ▸*n.* **1** a person in charge of a forest or skilled in planting, managing, or caring for trees. **2** *chiefly archaic* a person or animal living in a forest. ■ *Austral.* the eastern gray kangaroo. See GRAY KANGAROO. **3** a small black day-flying moth with two white or yellow spots on each wing. • Family Agaristidae: several genera and species, including the **eight-spotted forester** (*Alypia octomaculata*), common throughout the northeastern U.S. ▷Middle English: from Old French *forestier,* from *forest* (see FOREST).

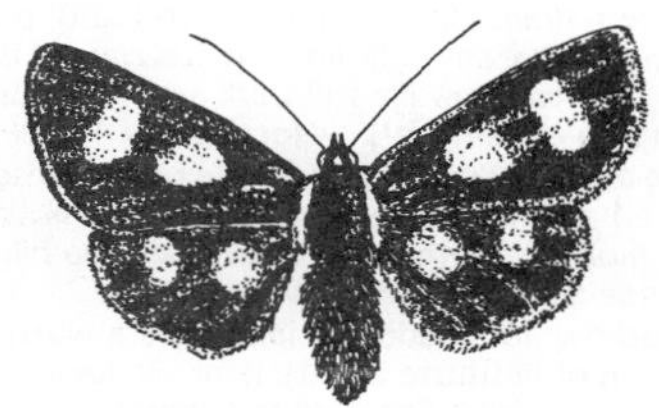

eight-spotted forester

For·est Hills an affluent residential section of central Queens in New York City that is associated with the U.S. Open in tennis, which was played here until 1978.

for·est·land /ˈfôrəstˌland; ˈfär-/ ▸*n.* an area of land covered by forests.

for·est·ry /ˈfôrəstrē; ˈfär-/ ▸*n.* the science or practice of planting, managing, and caring for forests.

fore·taste /ˈfôrˌtāst/ ▸*n.* [in *sing.*] a sample or suggestion of something that lies ahead: *the freezing rain was a foretaste of winter.*

fore·tell /fôrˈtel/ ▸*v.* (*past* and *past part.* **-told**) [*trans.*] predict (the future or a future event): *as he foretold, thousands lost their lives* | [with *clause*] *a seer had foretold that she would assume the throne.* See note at PREDICT. —**fore·tell·er** *n.*

fore·thought /ˈfôrˌTHôt/ ▸*n.* careful consideration of what will be necessary or may happen in the future: *Jim had the forethought to book in advance.*

fore·to·ken ▸*v.* /ˈfôrˌtōkən/ [*trans.*] *poetic/literary* be a sign of (something to come): *a shiver in the night air foretokening December.*
▸*n.* /ˈfôrˌtōkən/ a sign of something to come. ▷Old English *foretācn* (noun: see FORE-, TOKEN).

fore·told /fôrˈtōld/ ▸ past and past participle of FORETELL.

fore·top /ˈfôrˌtäp/ ▸*n.* **1** a platform around the head of the lower section of a sailing ship's foremast. ■ the front seat on top of a horse-drawn vehicle. **2** another term for FORELOCK.

fore-top·gal·lant mast ▸*n.* the third section of a sailing ship's foremast, above the fore-topmast.

fore-top·gal·lant sail ▸*n.* the sail above a sailing ship's fore-topsail.

fore-top·mast ▸*n.* the second section of a sailing ship's foremast.

fore-top·sail ▸*n.* the sail above a sailing ship's foresail.

fore·tri·an·gle /ˈfôrˌtrīˌaNGgəl/ ▸*n.* the triangular space between the deck, foremast, and forestay of a sailing vessel. ■ the area of sail within this area.

for·ev·er /fəˈrevər; fô-/ ▸*adv.* **1** for all future time; for always: *she would love him forever.* ■ a very long time (used hyperbolically): *it took forever to get a passport.* ■ used in slogans of support after the name of something or someone: *Elvis Forever!* **2** continually: *she was forever pushing her hair out of her eyes.*

for·ev·er·more /fəˌrevərˈmôr/ ▸*adv.* forever (used for rhetorical effect): *our military will be invincible forevermore.*

fore·warn /fôrˈwôrn/ ▸*v.* [*trans.*] inform (someone) of a danger or possible problem: *he had been forewarned of a coup plot.* —**fore·warn·er** *n.*
▸*PHRASE* □ **forewarned is forearmed** *proverb* prior knowledge of possible dangers or problems gives one a tactical advantage.

fore·went /fôrˈwent/ ▸ past of FOREGO[1], FOREGO[2].

fore·wing /ˈfôrˌwiNG/ ▸*n.* either of the two front wings of a four-winged insect.

fore·wom·an /ˈfôrˌwo͝omən/ ▸*n.* (*pl.* **-wom·en**) a female worker who supervises and directs other workers. ■ (in a court of law) a woman who presides over a jury and speaks on its behalf.

fore·word /ˈfôrˌwərd/ ▸*n.* a short introduction to a book, typically by a person other than the author. ▷mid 19th cent.: from FORE- + WORD, on the pattern of German *Vorwort.*

forex /ˈfôˌreks/ ▸*abbr.* foreign exchange.

fore·yard /ˈfôrˌyärd/ ▸*n.* the lowest yard on a sailing ship's foremast.

for·feit /ˈfôrfit/ ▸*v.* (**-feit·ed**, **-feit·ing**) [*trans.*] lose or be deprived of (property or a right or privilege) as a penalty for wrongdoing: *those unable to meet their taxes were liable to forfeit their property.* ■ lose or give up (something) as a necessary consequence of something else: *she didn't mind forfeiting an extra hour in bed to get up and clean the stables.*
▸*n.* a fine or penalty for wrongdoing or for a breach of the rules in a club or game. ■ *Law* an item of property or a right or privilege lost as a legal penalty. ■ (**forfeits**) a game in which trivial penalties are exacted. ■ the action of forfeiting something.
▸*adj.* [*predic.*] lost or surrendered as a penalty for wrongdoing or neglect: *the lands which he had acquired were automatically forfeit.* ▷Middle English (originally denoting a crime or transgression, hence a fine or penalty for this): from Old French *forfet, forfait,* past participle of *forfaire* 'transgress,' from *for-* 'out' (from Latin *foris* 'outside') + *faire* 'do' (from Latin *facere*). —**for·feit·a·ble** *adj.* —**for·feit·er** /ˈfôrfitər/ *n.* —**for·fei·ture** /ˈfôrfəCHər/ *n.*

for·fend /fôrˈfend/ ▸*v.* [*trans.*] **1** *archaic* avert, keep away, or prevent (something evil or unpleasant). **2** (also **fore·fend**) protect (something) by precautionary measures.
▸*PHRASE* □ **Heaven** (or **God**) **forfend** *archaic or humorous* used to express dismay or horror at the thought of something happening: *Invite him back? Heaven forfend!* | *God forfend that we should allow the media to tell us how to run our business.*

for·gath·er /fôrˈgaTHər/ (also **fore·gath·er**) ▸*v.* [*intrans.*] *formal* assemble or gather together. ▷late 15th cent. (originally Scots as *forgadder*): from Dutch *vergaderen.*

for·gave /fərˈgāv/ ▸ past of FORGIVE.

forge[1] /fôrj/ ▸*v.* [*trans.*] **1** make or shape (a metal object) by heating it in a fire or furnace and beating or hammering it. ■ *figurative* create (a relationship or new conditions): *the two women forged a close bond* | *the country is forging a bright new future.* **2** produce a copy or imitation of (a document, signature, banknote, or work or art) for the purpose of deception.
▸*n.* a blacksmith's workshop; a smithy. ■ a furnace or hearth for melting or refining metal. ■ a workshop or factory containing such a furnace. ▷Middle English (also in the general sense 'make, construct'): from Old French *forger,* from Latin *fabricare* 'fabricate,' from *fabrica* 'manufactured object, workshop.' The noun is via Old French from Latin *fabrica.* —**forge·a·ble** *adj.* —**forg·er** *n.*

forge[2] ▸*v.* [*intrans.*] move forward gradually or steadily: *he forged through the crowded side streets.*
▸*phrasal v.* □ **forge ahead** move forward or take the lead in a race. ■ continue or make progress with a course or undertaking: *the government is forging ahead with reforms.* ▷mid 18th cent. (originally of a ship): perhaps an aberrant pronunciation of FORCE.

for·ger·y /ˈfôrjərē/ ▸*n.* (*pl.* **-ger·ies**) the action of forging or producing a copy of a document, signature, banknote, or work of art. ■ a forged or copied document, signature, banknote, or work of art.

for·get /fərˈget/ ▸*v.* (**-get·ting**; *past* **-got**; *past part.* **-got·ten** or **-got**) [*trans.*] fail to remember: *he had forgotten his lines* | [with *clause*] *she had completely forgotten how tired and hungry she was.* ■ inadvertently neglect to attend to, do, or mention something: [with *infinitive*] *she forgot to lock her door* | [*intrans.*] *I'm sorry, I just forgot.* ■ inadvertently omit to bring or retrieve: *I forgot my raincoat.* ■ put out of one's mind; cease to think of or consider: *forget all this romantic stuff* | [*intrans.*] *for years she had struggled to **forget about** him.* ■ (**forget it**) said when insisting to someone that there is no need for apology or thanks. ■ (**forget it**) said when telling someone that their idea or aspiration is impracticable. ■ (**forget oneself**) stop thinking about one's own problems or feelings: *he must forget himself in his work.* ■ (**forget oneself**) act improperly or unbecomingly. ▷Old English *forgietan;* related to Dutch *vergeten* and German *vergessen,* and ultimately to FOR- and GET. —**for·get·ter** *n.*
▸*PHRASE* □ **not forgetting** —— (at the end of a list) and also ——: *we depend on them for food and shelter and clothing, not forgetting heat in the wintertime.*

for·get·ful /fərˈgetfəl/ ▸*adj.* apt or likely not to remember: *I'm a bit forgetful these days* | *she was soon **forgetful of** the time.* —**for·get·ful·ly** *adv.* —**for·get·ful·ness** *n.*

for·get-me-not ▸*n.* a low-growing plant of the borage family that typically has blue flowers and is a popular ornamental. • *Myosotis* and other genera, family Boraginaceae: several species, in particular the common **water forget-me-not** (*M. scorpioides*), whose bright blue flowers have a yellow, pink, or white center. ▷mid 16th cent.: translating the Old French name *ne m'oubliez mye;* said to have the virtue of ensuring that the wearer of the flower would never be forgotten by a lover.

for·get·ta·ble /fərˈgetəbəl/ ▸*adj.* easily forgotten, esp. through being uninteresting or mediocre.

for·give /fərˈgiv/ ▸*v.* (*past* **-gave**; *past part.* **-giv·en**) [*trans.*] stop feeling angry or resentful toward (someone) for an offense, flaw, or mistake: *I don't think I'll ever **forgive** David **for** the way he treated her.* See note at ABSOLVE. ■ (usu. **be forgiven**) stop feeling angry or resentful toward someone for (an offense, flaw, or mistake): *they are not going to pat my head and say **all is forgiven*** | [*intrans.*] *he was not a man who found it easy to **forgive and forget**.* ■ used in polite expressions as a request to excuse or regard indulgently one's foibles, ignorance, or impoliteness: *you will have to forgive my suspicious mind.* ■ cancel (a debt): *he proposed that their debts should not be forgiven.* ▷Old English *forgiefan,* of Germanic origin, related to Dutch *vergeven* and German *vergeben,* and ultimately to FOR- and GIVE. —**for·giv·a·ble** *adj.* —**for·giv·a·bly** /-əblē/ *adv.* —**for·giv·er** *n.*
▸*PHRASE* □ **one could** (or **may**) **be forgiven** it would be understandable (if one mistakenly did a particular thing): *the arrangements are so complex that you could be forgiven for feeling confused.*

for·give·ness /fərˈgivnəs/ ▸*n.* the action or process of forgiving or being forgiven: *she is quick to ask forgiveness when she has overstepped the line.* ▷Old English *forgiefenes,* from *forgiefen* (past participle of *forgiefan* 'forgive') + the noun suffix *-nes.*

for·giv·ing /fərˈgiviNG/ ▸*adj.* ready and willing to forgive: *Taylor was in a forgiving mood.* ■ tolerant: *these flooring planks are more durable and forgiving of heavy traffic than real wood.* —**for·giv·ing·ly** *adv.*

for·go /fôrˈgō/ (also **fore·go**) ▸*v.* (**for·goes**; *past* **for·went**; *past part.* **for·gone**) [*trans.*] omit or decline to take (something pleasant or valuable); go without: *she wanted to forgo the dessert and leave while they could.* ■ refrain from: *we forgo any comparison between the two men.* ▷Old English *forgān* (see FOR-, GO[1]).

for·got /fərˈgät/ ▸ past of FORGET.

for·got·ten /fərˈgätn/ ▸ past participle of FORGET.

for·int /ˈfôrˌint/ ▸*n.* the basic monetary unit of Hungary, equal to 100 filler. ▷Hungarian, from Italian *fiorino* (see FLORIN).

for·judge /fôrˈjəj/ ▸*v.* variant spelling of FOREJUDGE.

fork /fôrk/ ▸*n.* **1** an implement with two or more prongs used for lifting food to the mouth or holding it when cutting. ■ a tool of larger but similar form used for digging or lifting in a garden or farm. **2** a device, component, or part with two or more prongs, in particular: ■ a unit consisting of a pair of supports in which a bicycle or motorcycle wheel revolves. ■ a flash of forked lightning. **3** the point where something, esp. a road or river, divides into two parts. ■ either of two such parts. **4** *Chess* a simultaneous attack on two or more pieces by one piece.
▸*v.* **1** [*intrans.*] (esp. of a road or other route) divide into two parts: *the place where the road forks.* ■ [*intrans.*] take or constitute one part or the other at the point where a road or other route divides: *a minor road forked left.* **2** [*trans.*] dig, lift, or manipulate (something) with a fork: *fork in some compost.* **3** [*trans.*] *Chess* attack (two pieces) simultaneously with one piece.
▸*phrasal v.* □ **fork something over/out/up** (or **fork over/out/up**) *informal* pay money for something, esp. reluctantly. ▷Old English *forca, force* (denoting an agricultural implement), based on Latin *furca* 'pitchfork, forked stick'; reinforced in Middle English by Anglo-Norman French *furke* (also from Latin *furca*). —**fork·ful** /-ˌfo͝ol/ *n.* (*pl.* **-fuls**) .

fork·ball /ˈfôrkˌbôl/ ▸*n.* *Baseball* a sinking pitch,

released from between the widely spread index finger and middle finger.

Fork·beard /ˈfôrk,bi(ə)rd/, Sweyn, see **SWEYN I**.

forked /fôrkt/ ▸*adj.* having a divided or pronged end or branches; bifurcated: *a deeply forked tail.*

▸*PHRASE* □ **with forked tongue** *humorous* untruthfully; deceitfully.

forked light·ning ▸*n.* lightning that is visible in the form of a branching line across the sky.

fork·lift /ˈfôrk,lift/ ▸*n.* (also **fork·lift truck**) a vehicle with a pronged device in front for lifting and carrying heavy loads.

▸*v.* [*trans.*] lift and carry (a heavy load) with such a vehicle: *blocks of compacted garbage being* ***forklifted on to*** *a trailer.*

forklift

for·lorn /fərˈlôrn; fôr-/ ▸*adj.* **1** pitifully sad and abandoned or lonely: *forlorn figures at bus stops.* **2** (of an aim or endeavor) unlikely to succeed or be fulfilled; hopeless: *a forlorn attempt to escape.* ▷Old English *forloren* 'depraved, morally abandoned,' past participle of *forlēosan* 'lose,' of Germanic origin; related to Dutch *verliezen* and German *verlieren,* and ultimately to **FOR-** and **LOSE**. Sense 1 dates from the 16th cent. **—for·lorn·ly** *adv.* **—for·lorn·ness** /fərˈlôrn,nəs/ *n.*

▸*PHRASE* □ **forlorn hope** a persistent or desperate hope that is unlikely to be fulfilled. [mid 16th cent.: from Dutch *verloren hoop* 'lost troop,' from *verloren* (past participle of *verliezen* 'lose') and *hoop* 'company' (related to **HEAP**). The phrase originally denoted a band of soldiers picked to begin an attack, many of whom would not survive; the current sense (mid 17th cent.) derives from a misunderstanding of the etymology.]

form /fôrm/ ▸*n.* **1** the visible shape or configuration of something: *the form, color, and texture of the tree.* ■ arrangement of parts; shape: *the entities underlying physical form.* ■ the body or shape of a person or thing: *his eyes scanned her slender form.* ■ arrangement and style in literary or musical composition: *these videos are a triumph of form over content.* ■ *Philosophy* the essential nature of a species or thing, esp. (in Plato's thought) regarded as an abstract ideal that real things imitate or participate in. **2** a mold, frame, or block in or on which something is shaped. ■ a temporary structure for holding fresh concrete in shape while it sets. **3** a particular way in which a thing exists or appears; a manifestation: *her obsession has taken the form of compulsive exercise.* ■ any of the ways in which a word may be spelled, pronounced, or inflected: *an adjectival rather than adverbial form.* ■ the structure of a word, phrase, sentence, or discourse: *every distinction in meaning is associated with a distinction in form.* **4** a type or variety of something: *sponsorship is a form of advertising.* ■ an artistic or literary genre. ■ *Botany* a taxonomic category that ranks below variety, which contains organisms differing from the typical kind in some trivial, frequently impermanent, character, e.g., a color variant. Compare with **SUBSPECIES** and **VARIETY**. **5** the customary or correct method or procedure; what is usually done: *an excessive concern for legal form and precedent.* ■ a set order of words; a formula. ■ a formality or item of mere ceremony: *the outward forms of religion.* **6** a printed document with blank spaces for information to be inserted: *an application form.* **7** *chiefly Brit.* a class or year in a school, usually given a specifying number: *the fifth form.* **8** the state of an athlete or sports team with regard to their current standard of performance: *illness has affected his form | they've been* ***in good form*** *this season.* ■ details of previous performances by a racehorse or greyhound: *an interested bystander studying the form.* **9** *Brit.* a long bench without a back. **10** variant spelling of **FORME**. **11** *chiefly Brit.* a hare's lair.

▸*v.* [*trans.*] **1** bring together parts or combine to create (something): *the company was formed in 1982.* ■ (**form people/things into**) organize people or things into (a group or body): *peasants and miners were formed into a militia.* ■ go to make up or constitute: *the precepts that form the basis of the book.* ■ [*intrans.*] gradually appear or develop: *a thick mist was forming all around.* ■ conceive (an idea or plan) in one's mind. ■ enter into or contract (a relationship): *the women would form supportive friendships.* ■ articulate (a word, speech sound, or other linguistic unit). ■ construct (a new word) by derivation or inflection. **2** make or fashion into a certain shape or form: ***form*** *the dough* ***into*** *balls.* ■ [*intrans.*] (**form into**) be made or fashioned into a certain shape or form: *his strong features formed into a smile of pleasure.* ■ (**be formed**) have a specified shape: *her body was slight and flawlessly formed.* ■ shape or develop by training or discipline. ■ influence or shape (something abstract): *the role of the news media in forming public opinion.* ▷Middle English: from Old French *forme* (noun), *fo(u)rmer* (verb, from Latin *formare* 'to form'), both based on Latin *forma* 'a mold or form.' **—form·a·bil·i·ty** *n.* /,fôrməˈbilətē/ **—form·a·ble** *adj.*

▸*PHRASES* □ **in form** (of an athlete or sports team) playing or performing well. □ **off form** (of an athlete or sports team) not playing or performing well.

-form (usu. as **-iform**) ▸*comb. form* **1** having the form of: *cruciform.* **2** having a particular number of: *multiform.* ▷from French *-forme,* from Latin *-formis,* from *forma* 'form.'

for·mal /ˈfôrməl/ ▸*adj.* **1** done in accordance with rules of convention or etiquette; suitable for or constituting an official or important situation or occasion: *a formal dinner party.* ■ (of a person or their manner) prim or stiff. ■ of or denoting a style of writing or public speaking characterized by more elaborate grammatical structures and more conservative and technical vocabulary. ■ (esp. of a house or garden) arranged in a regular, classical, and symmetrical manner. **2** officially sanctioned or recognized: *a formal complaint.* ■ having a conventionally recognized form, structure, or set of rules: *he had little formal education.* **3** of or concerned with outward form or appearance, esp. as distinct from content or matter: *I don't know enough about art to appreciate the purely formal qualities.* ■ having the form or appearance without the spirit: *his sacrifice will be more formal than real.* ■ of or relating to linguistic or logical form as opposed to function or meaning.

▸*n.* an evening gown. ■ an occasion on which evening dress is worn. ▷late Middle English: from Latin *formalis,* from *forma* 'shape, mold' (see **FORM**).

THE RIGHT WORD **ceremonial, ceremonious, formal, pompous, proper, punctilious**

Formal suggests a suit-and-tie approach to certain situations—reserved, conventional, obeying all the rules (*an engraved invitation to a formal dinner requiring black tie or evening gown*).

Proper, in this regard, implies scrupulously correct behavior that observes rules of etiquette (*the proper way to serve a guest; the proper spoon for dessert*).

Punctilious behavior observes all the proper formalities (a *"punctilio"* is a detail or fine point), but may verge on the annoying (*her punctilious attention to the correct placement of silverware made setting the table an ordeal*).

Someone (usually a man) who likes to show off just how *formal* and *proper* he can be runs the risk of becoming the most dreaded dinner guest of all: the **pompous** ass.

Pompous people may derive more than the normal amount of pleasure from participating in **ceremonial** acts or events, which are those performed according to set rules, but **ceremonious** suggests a less negative and more ritualized approach to formality (*the Japanese woman could not have been more ceremonious than when she was carrying out the ceremonial serving of tea*).

for·mal cause ▸*n.* *Philosophy* (in Aristotelian thought) the pattern that determines the form taken by something.

form·al·de·hyde /fôrˈmaldə,hīd; fər-/ ▸*n.* *Chemistry* a colorless pungent gas in solution made by oxidizing methanol. • Alternative name: **methanal**; chem. formula: CH_2O. ▷late 19th cent.: blend of **FORMIC ACID** and **ALDEHYDE**.

for·ma·lin /ˈfôrməlin/ ▸*n.* a colorless solution of formaldehyde in water, used chiefly as a preservative for biological specimens. ▷late 19th cent.: from **FORMALDEHYDE + -IN**[1].

for·mal·ism /ˈfôrmə,lizəm/ ▸*n.* **1** excessive adherence to prescribed forms: *academic dryness and formalism.* ■ the use of forms of worship without regard to inner significance. ■ the basing of ethics on the form of the moral law without regard to intention or consequences. ■ concern or excessive concern with form and technique rather than content in artistic creation. ■ (in the theater) a symbolic and stylized manner of production. ■ the treatment of mathematics as a manipulation of meaningless symbols. **2** a description of something in formal mathematical or logical terms. **—for·mal·ist** *n.* **—for·mal·is·tic** /,fôrməˈlistik/ *adj.*

for·mal·i·ty /fôrˈmalətē/ ▸*n.* (*pl.* **-ties**) the rigid observance of rules of convention or etiquette: *he retained the formality of his social background.* ■ stiffness of behavior or style: *with disconcerting formality, the brothers shook hands.* ■ (usu. **formalities**) a thing that is done simply to comply with requirements of etiquette, regulations, or custom: *legal formalities.* ■ (**a formality**) something that is done as a matter of course and without question; an inevitability: *her saying no was just a formality, and both of them knew it.* ▷mid 16th cent. (in the sense 'accordance with legal rules or conventions'): from French *formalité* or medieval Latin *formalitas,* from *formalis* (see **FORMAL**).

for·mal·ize /ˈfôrmə,līz/ ▸*v.* [*trans.*] give (something) legal or formal status. ■ give (something) a definite structure or shape: *we became able to formalize our thoughts.* **—for·mal·i·za·tion** /,fôrməliˈzāshən/ *n.*

for·mal log·ic ▸*n.* logic based on argument involving deductively necessary relationships and including the use of syllogisms and mathematical symbols.

for·mal·ly /ˈfôrməlē/ ▸*adv.* **1** in accordance with the rules of convention or etiquette: *he was formally attired.* **2** officially: *the mayor will formally open the new railroad station.* **3** [*sentence adverb*] in outward form or appearance; in theory: *all Javanese are formally Muslims.* ■ in terms of form or structure: *formally complex types of text.*

for·mal·wear /,fôrməl,we(ə)r/ ▸*n.* clothing, such as tuxedos and evening gowns, for formal social occasions.

For·man /ˈfôrmən/, Milos (1932–), U.S. movie director; born in Czechoslovakia. He made *One Flew Over the Cuckoo's Nest* (1975), which won five Academy Awards, and *Amadeus* (1983), which won eight Academy Awards, including that for best director.

for·mant /ˈfôrmənt/ ▸*n.* *Phonetics* any of several prominent bands of frequency that determine the phonetic quality of a vowel. ▷early 20th cent.: coined in German from Latin *formant-* 'forming,' from the verb *formare.*

for·mat /ˈfôr,mat/ ▸*n.* the way in which something is arranged or set out: *the format of the funeral service.* ■ the shape, size, and presentation of a book or periodical. ■ the medium in which a sound recording is made available: *the album is available as a CD as well as on LP and cassette formats.* ■ *Computing* a defined structure for the processing, storage, or display of data: *a data file in binary format.*

▸*v.* (**-mat·ted, -mat·ting**) [*trans.*] (esp. in computing) arrange or put into a format. ■ prepare (a storage medium) to receive data. ▷mid 19th cent.: via French and German from Latin *formatus (liber)* 'shaped (book),' past participle of *formare* 'to form.'

for·mate /ˈfôr,māt/ ▸*n.* a salt or ester of formic acid.

for·ma·tion /fôrˈmāshən/ ▸*n.* **1** the action of forming or process of being formed: *the formation of the Great Rift Valley.* **2** a structure or arrangement of something: *a cloud formation.* ■ a formal arrangement of aircraft in flight or troops: *a battle formation | the helicopters hovered overhead* ***in formation.*** ■ *Geology* an assemblage of rocks or series of strata having some common characteristic. ▷late Middle English: from Latin *formation-,* from *formare* 'to form' (see **FORM**). **—for·ma·tion·al** /-shənl/ *adj.*

for·ma·tive /ˈfôrmətiv/ ▸*adj.* serving to form something, esp. having a profound and lasting influence on a person's development: *his formative years.* ■ of or relating to a person's development: *a formative assessment.* ■ *Linguistics* denoting or relating to any of the smallest meaningful units that are used to form words in a language, typically combining forms and inflections.

▸*n.* *Linguistics* a formative element. ▷late 15th cent.: from Old French *formatif, -ive* or medieval Latin *formativus,* from Latin *formare* 'to form' (see **FORM**). **—for·ma·tive·ly** *adv.*

form class ▸*n.* *Linguistics* a class of linguistic forms with grammatical or syntactic features in common; a part of speech or subset of a part of speech.

form crit·i·cism ▸*n.* analysis of the Bible by tracing the history of its content of parables, psalms, and other literary forms.

form drag ▸*n. Aeronautics* that part of the drag on an airfoil that arises from its shape. It varies according to the angle of attack and can be decreased by streamlining.

forme /fôrm/ ▸*n. Printing* a body of type secured in a chase for printing. ■ a quantity of film arranged for making a plate.

form·er[1] /ˈfôrmər/ ▸*adj.* [*attrib.*] **1** having previously filled a particular role or been a particular thing: *her former boyfriend.* ■ of or occurring in the past or an earlier period: *in former times.* **2** (**the former**) denoting the first or first mentioned of two people or things: *those who take the former view* | [as *n.*] *the powers of the former are more comprehensive than those of the latter.* ▷Middle English: from Old English *forma* (see **FOREMOST**) + **-ER**[2].

USAGE Traditionally, **former** and **latter** are used in relation to pairs of items: either the first of two items (**former**) or the second of two items (**latter**). The reason for this is that **former** and **latter** were formed as comparatives, and comparatives are correctly used with reference to just two things, while a superlative is used where there are more than two things. So, strictly speaking, one should say *the* **longest** *of the* **three** *books* but *the* **longer** *of the* **two** *books.* If there are three items or more, the words **first**, **second**, etc., and **last** should be used even if not all are mentioned: *of winter, spring, and summer, I find the* **last** *most enjoyable.*

form·er[2] ▸*n.* **1** a person or thing that forms something: [in *combination*] *an opinion-former.* ■ a transverse strengthening part in an aircraft wing or fuselage. **2** [in *combination*] *chiefly Brit.* a person in a particular school year: *fifth-formers.*

for·mer·ly /ˈfôrmərlē/ ▸*adv.* in the past; in earlier times: *Bangladesh, formerly East Pakistan* | [*sentence adverb*] *the building formerly housed their accounting offices.*

form fac·tor ▸*n.* a mathematical factor that compensates for irregularity in the shape of an object, usually the ratio between its volume and that of a regular object of the same breadth and height. ■ the physical size and shape of a piece of computer hardware.

form-fit·ting /ˈfôrm,fitiNG/ ▸*adj.* (of clothing) fitting the body snugly, so that its shape is clearly visible: said of clothing: *she wore a formfitting dress.*

form ge·nus ▸*n. Paleontology* a classificatory category used for fossils that are similar in appearance but cannot be reliably assigned to an established animal or plant genus, such as fossil parts of organisms and trace fossils.

For·mi·ca /fôrˈmīkə; fər-/ ▸*n. trademark* a hard durable plastic laminate used for countertops, cupboard doors, and other surfaces. ▷1920s: of unknown origin.

for·mic ac·id /ˈfôrmik/ ▸*n. Chemistry* a colorless irritant volatile acid made catalytically from carbon monoxide and steam. It is present in the fluid emitted by some ants. • Alternative name: **methanoic acid**; chem. formula: HCOOH. ▷late 18th cent.: *formic* from Latin *formica* 'ant.'

for·mi·car·y /ˈfôrmi,kerē/ (also **for·mi·car·i·um** /,fôrmiˈke(ə)rēəm/) ▸*n.* (*pl.* **-car·ies**; **-car·i·a** /-ˈke(ə)rēə/) an ant's nest, esp. one in an artificial container for purposes of study. ▷early 19th cent.: from medieval Latin, from Latin *formica* 'ant.'

for·mi·ca·tion /,fôrmiˈkāsHən/ ▸*n.* a sensation like insects crawling over the skin. ▷early 18th cent.: from Latin *formicatio(n-)*, from *formicare* 'crawl like an ant' (said of the pulse or skin), from *formica* 'ant.'

for·mi·da·ble /ˈfôrmədəbəl; fôrˈmidəbəl; fərˈmid-/ ▸*adj.* inspiring fear or respect through being impressively large, powerful, intense, or capable: *a formidable opponent.* ▷late Middle English: from French, or from Latin *formidabilis*, from *formidare* 'to fear.' **—for·mi·da·ble·ness** *n.* **—for·mi·da·bly** /-əblē/ *adv.*

USAGE The preferred pronunciation of **formidable** is with the stress on **for-**, although the stress is sometimes heard on the second syllable (in Britain more than in the U.S.).

form·less /ˈfôrmləs/ ▸*adj.* without a clear or definite shape or structure: *a dark and formless idea.* **—form·less·ly** *adv.* **—form·less·ness** *n.*

form let·ter ▸*n.* a standardized letter to deal with frequently occurring matters.

For·mo·sa /fôrˈmōsə/ former name of **TAIWAN**. ▷Portuguese, literally 'beautiful.'

for·mu·la /ˈfôrmyələ/ ▸*n.* **1** (*pl.* **-las** or **-lae** /-,lē; -,lī/) a mathematical relationship or rule expressed in symbols. ■ (also **chemical formula**) a set of chemical symbols showing the elements present in a compound and their relative proportions, and in some cases the structure of the compound. See **EMPIRICAL FORMULA, MOLECULAR FORMULA, STRUCTURAL FORMULA.** **2** (*pl.* **-las**) a fixed form of words, esp. one used in particular contexts or as a conventional usage: *a legal formula.* ■ a method, statement, or procedure for achieving something, esp. reconciling different aims or positions: *the forlorn hope of finding a peace formula.* ■ a rule or style unintelligently or slavishly followed: [as *adj.*] *one of those formula tunes.* ■ a statement that formally enunciates a religious doctrine. ■ a stock epithet, phrase, or line repeated for various effects in literary composition, esp. epic poetry. **3** (*pl.* **-las**) a list of ingredients for or constituents of something: *the soft drink company closely guards its secret formula.* ■ a formulation: *an original coal tar formula that helps prevent dandruff.* ■ an infant's liquid food preparation based on cow's milk or soy protein, given as a substitute for breast milk. **4** (usually followed by a number) a classification of race car, esp. by engine capacity. ▷early 17th cent. (in the sense 'fixed form of words (for use on ceremonial or social occasions)'): from Latin, diminutive of *forma* 'shape, mold.'

for·mu·la·ic /,fôrmyəˈlāik/ ▸*adj.* constituting or containing a verbal formula or set form of words: *a formulaic greeting.* ■ produced in accordance with a slavishly followed rule or style; predictable: *much romantic fiction is stylized, formulaic, and unrealistic.* **—for·mu·la·i·cal·ly** /-(ə)lē/ *adv.*

For·mu·la One ▸*n.* an international form of auto racing, whose races are called Grand Prix.

for·mu·lar·ize /ˈfôrmyələ,rīz/ ▸*v.* [*trans.*] make (something) formulaic or predictable: *their stage shows have become a little formularized.*

for·mu·lar·y /ˈfôrmyə,lerē/ ▸*n.* (*pl.* **-lar·ies**) **1** a collection of formulas or set forms, esp. for use in religious ceremonies. **2** an official list giving details of prescribable medicines.
▸*adj.* relating to or using officially prescribed formulas. ▷mid 16th cent.: the noun from French *formulaire* or medieval Latin *formularius (liber)* '(book) of formulae,' from Latin *formula* (see **FORMULA**); the adjective (early 18th cent.) is directly from **FORMULA**.

for·mu·late /ˈfôrmyə,lāt/ ▸*v.* [*trans.*] create or devise methodically (a strategy or a proposal): *economists and statisticians were needed to help formulate economic policy.* ■ express (an idea) in a concise or systematic way: *the argument is sufficiently clear that it can be formulated mathematically.* ▷mid 19th cent.: from **FORMULA** + **-ATE**[3], on the pattern of French *formuler*, from medieval Latin *formulare*. **—for·mu·la·ble** /-ləbəl/ *adj.* **—for·mu·la·tor** /-,lātər/ *n.*

for·mu·la·tion /,fôrmyəˈlāsHən/ ▸*n.* **1** the action of devising or creating something: *the formulation of foreign policy.* ■ a particular expression of an idea, thought, or theory. **2** a material or mixture prepared according to a particular formula.

for·myl /ˈfôr,mil/ ▸*n.* [as *adj.*] *Chemistry* of or denoting the acyl radical −CHO, derived from formic acid: *N-formyl methionine.*

For·nax /ˈfôr,naks/ *Astronomy* an inconspicuous southern constellation (the Furnace), near Eridanus. ■ [as *genitive*] (**Fornacis** /fôrˈnasis; -ˈnā-/) used with a preceding letter or numeral to designate a star in this constellation: *the star Beta Fornacis.* ▷Latin.

for·ni·cate /ˈfôrni,kāt/ ▸*v.* [*intrans.*] *formal humorous* (of two people not married to each other) have sexual intercourse. ▷Middle English (as *fornication*): from ecclesiastical Latin *fornicat-* 'arched,' from *fornicari*, from Latin *fornix, fornic-* 'vaulted chamber,' later 'brothel.' **—for·ni·ca·tion** /,fôrniˈkāsHən/ *n.* **—for·ni·ca·tor** /-,kātər/ *n.*

for·nix /ˈfôrniks/ ▸*n.* (*pl.* **-ni·ces** /-nə,sēz/) *Anatomy* a vaulted or arched structure in the body, in particular: ■ (also **for·nix cer·e·bri** /ˈserə,brī; ˈkerə,brē/) a triangular area of white matter in the mammalian brain between the hippocampus and the hypothalamus. ▷late 17th cent.: from Latin, literally 'arch, vaulted chamber.'

for-prof·it ▸*adj.* [*attrib.*] denoting an organization that operates to make a profit, esp. one (such as a hospital or school) that would more typically be nonprofit.

For·rest /ˈfôrəst; ˈfär-/, Nathan Bedford (1821–77), Confederate cavalry officer. He led a massacre of 300 black Union soldiers at the surrender of Fort Pillow, Tennessee, April 12, 1864.

for·sake /fərˈsāk; fôr-/ ▸*v.* (*past* **-sook** /-ˈsŏŏk/; *past part.* **-sak·en** /-ˈsākən/) [*trans.*] *chiefly poetic/literary* abandon (someone or something): *he would never forsake Tara* | [as *adj.*] (**forsaken**) *figurative a tiny, forsaken island.* ■ renounce or give up (something valued or pleasant): *I won't forsake my vegetarian principles.* ▷Old English *forsacan* 'renounce, refuse'; related to Dutch *verzaken*, and ultimately to **FOR-** and **SAKE**[1]. **—for·sak·en·ness** *n.* **—for·sak·er** *n.*

for·sooth /fərˈsōōTH/ ▸*adv.* [*sentence adverb*] *archaic or humorous* indeed (often used ironically or to express surprise or indignation): *forsooth, there is no one I trust more.* ■ used to give an ironic politeness to questions: *what, forsooth, induced this transformation?* ▷Old English *forsōth* (see **FOR, SOOTH**).

For·ster /ˈfôrstər/, E. M. (1879–1970), English novelist and literary critic; full name *Edward Morgan Forster*. His novels include *A Room with a View* (1908) and *A Passage to India* (1924).

for·ster·ite /ˈfôrstə,rīt/ ▸*n.* a magnesium-rich variety of olivine, occurring as white, yellow, or green crystals. ▷early 19th cent.: from the name of J. R. *Forster* (1729–98), German naturalist, + **-ITE**[1].

for·swear /fôrˈswe(ə)r/ ▸*v.* (*past* **-swore**; *past part.* **-sworn**) [*trans.*] *formal* agree to give up or do without (something): *he would never forswear the religion of his people.* ■ (**forswear oneself/be forsworn**) swear falsely; commit perjury: *I swore that I would lead us safely home and I do not mean to be forsworn.* ▷Old English *forswerian* (see **FOR-, SWEAR**).

For·syth /ˈfôr,sīTH/, Frederick (1938–), English novelist. He is known for political thrillers such as *The Day of the Jackal* (1971), *The Odessa File* (1972), and *The Fourth Protocol* (1984).

for·syth·i·a /fərˈsiTHēə/ ▸*n.* a widely cultivated ornamental Eurasian shrub whose bright yellow flowers appear in early spring before the leaves. • Genus *Forsythia*, family Oleaceae: several species. ▷modern Latin, named after William *Forsyth* (1737–1804), Scottish botanist and horticulturalist, said to have introduced the shrub into Britain from China.

fort /fôrt/ ▸*n.* a fortified building or strategic position. ■ a permanent army post. ■ *historical* a trading post. [so named because such establishments were originally fortified.] ▷late Middle English: from Old French *fort* or Italian *forte*, from Latin *fortis* 'strong.'
▸*PHRASE* □ **hold the fort** see **HOLD**[1].

fort. ▸*abbr.* ■ fortification. ■ fortified.

For·ta·le·za /,fôrtlˈāzə/ a port in northeastern Brazil, on the Atlantic coast; pop. 1,769,000.

for·ta·lice /ˈfôrtl-is/ ▸*n.* a small fort, fortified house, or outwork of fortification. ▷late Middle English: from medieval Latin *fortalitia, -itium*, from Latin *fortis* 'strong.'

For·tas /ˈfôrtəs/, Abe (1910–82), U.S. Supreme Court associate justice 1965–69. Criticized for his financial dealings with a known criminal, he was the first justice ever forced to resign by public criticism.

Fort Col·lins /ˈkälinz/ a commercial and industrial city in north central Colorado, home to Colorado State University; pop. 118,652.

Fort-de-France /,fôr də ˈfräns/ the capital of Martinique; pop. 102,000.

Fort Dodge /däj/ a commercial and mining city in northwestern Iowa; pop. 25,894.

for·te[1] /ˈfôr,tā; fôrt/ ▸*n.* **1** [in *sing.*] a thing at which someone excels: *small talk was not his forte.* **2** *Fencing* the stronger part of a sword blade, from the hilt to the middle. Compare with **FOIBLE**. ▷mid 17th cent. (sense 2; originally as *fort*): from French *fort* (masculine), *forte* (feminine) 'strong,' from Latin *fortis*.

for·te[2] /ˈfôr,tā/ *Music* ▸*adv.* & *adj.* (esp. as a direction) loud or loudly.
▸*n.* a passage performed or marked to be performed loudly. ▷Italian, literally 'strong, loud,' from Latin *fortis*.

Fort·e·an /ˈfôrtēən/ ▸*adj.* of, relating to, or denoting paranormal phenomena. ▷1970s: from the name of Charles H. *Fort* (1874–1932), American student of paranormal phenomena. **—Fort·e·an·a** /,fôrtēˈanə/ *plural n.*

for·te·pi·an·o /,fôrtāpēˈanō; -pēˈänō/ ▸*n.* (*pl.* **-an·os**) *Music* a piano, esp. of the kind made in the 18th and early 19th centuries. ▷mid 18th cent.: from **FORTE**[2] + **PIANO**[2].

for·te-pi·an·o /ˈfôr,tā pēˈanō; pēˈänō/ ▸*adv.* & *adj.* *Music* (esp. as a direction) loud and then immediately soft. ▷Italian.

Forth /fôrTH/ a river in central Scotland that rises on Ben Lomond and flows east into the North Sea.

Forth, Firth of the estuary of the Forth River in

Scotland, spanned by a cantilevered railroad bridge and a highway suspension bridge.

forth /fôrTH/ ▸*adv. chiefly archaic* out from a starting point and forward or into view: *the plants will bush out, putting forth fresh shoots.* ■ onward in time: ***from that day forth*** *he gave me endless friendship.* ▷Old English, of Germanic origin; related to Dutch *voort* and German *fort*, from an Indo-European root shared by FORE-.

▸*PHRASE* □ **and so forth** and so on: *particular services like education, housing, and so forth.*

forth·com·ing /fôrTH'kəmiNG; 'fôrTH,kəmiNG/ ▸*adj.* **1** planned for or about to happen in the near future: *the forthcoming baseball season.* **2** [*predic.*] [often with *negative*] (of something required) ready or made available when wanted or needed: *financial support was not forthcoming.* ■ (of a person) willing to divulge information: *their daughter had never been forthcoming about her time in Europe.* —**forth·com·ing·ness** *n.*

forth·right /'fôrTH,rīt/ ▸*adj.* **1** (of a person or their manner or speech) direct and outspoken; straightforward and honest: *his most forthright attack yet on the reforms.* **2** *archaic* proceeding directly forward.

▸*adv. archaic* directly forward. ■ immediately. ▷Old English *forthriht* 'straightforward, directly' (see FORTH, RIGHT). —**forth·right·ly** *adv.* —**forth·right·ness** *n.*

forth·with /fôrTH'wiTH/ ▸*adv.* (esp. in official use) immediately; without delay: *we undertake to pay forthwith the money required.* ▷Middle English (in the sense 'along with, at the same time'): partly from earlier *forthwithal*, partly representing *forth with* used alone without a following noun.

for·ti·fi·ca·tion /,fôrtəfə'kāSHən/ ▸*n.* (often **fortifications**) a defensive wall or other reinforcement built to strengthen a place against attack. ■ the action of fortifying or process of being fortified: *the fortification of the frontiers.* ▷late Middle English: via French from late Latin *fortificatio(n-)*, from *fortificare* (see FORTIFY).

for·ti·fy /'fôrtə,fī/ ▸*v.* (**-fies, -fied**) [*trans.*] strengthen (a place) with defensive works so as to protect it against attack: *the whole town was heavily fortified* | [as *adj.*] (**fortified**) *a fortified manor house.* ■ strengthen or invigorate (someone) mentally or physically: *I was fortified by the knowledge that I was in a sympathetic house.* ■ [often as *adj.*] (**fortified**) strengthen (a drink) with alcohol: *fortified wine.* ■ increase the nutritive value of (food), esp. with vitamins. ▷late Middle English: from French *fortifier*, from late Latin *fortificare*, from Latin *fortis* 'strong.' —**for·ti·fi·a·ble** *adj.* —**for·ti·fi·er** *n.*

for·tis /'fôrtis/ ▸*adj. Phonetics* (of a consonant, in particular a voiceless consonant) strongly articulated, esp. more so than another consonant articulated in the same place. The opposite of LENIS. ▷mid 20th cent.: from Latin, literally 'strong.'

for·tis·si·mo /fôr'tisə,mō/ *Music* ▸*adv.* & *adj.* (esp. as a direction) very loud or loudly.

▸*n.* (*pl.* **-mos** or **-mi** /-,mē/) a passage marked to be performed very loudly. ▷Italian, from Latin *fortissimus* 'very strong.'

for·ti·tude /'fôrtə,to͞od/ ▸*n.* courage in pain or adversity: *she endured her illness with great fortitude.* See note at COURAGE. ▷Middle English: via French from Latin *fortitudo*, from *fortis* 'strong.'

Fort Knox /näks/ a U.S. military reservation in Kentucky, noted as the site of the depository, which was built in 1936, that holds the bulk of the nation's gold bullion in its vaults.

Fort La·my /,fôr lə'mē/ former name (until 1973) for N'DJAMENA.

Fort Lau·der·dale /'lôdər,dāl/ a resort, commercial, and industrial city in southeastern Florida, north of Miami; pop. 152,397.

Fort Lee /lē/ a commercial and residential borough in northeastern New Jersey, across the Hudson River from New York City; pop. 31,997.

Fort Mc·Hen·ry /mək'henrē/ a historic site in the harbor of Baltimore in Maryland, scene of an 1812 British siege that inspired Francis Scott Key to write "The Star Spangled Banner."

Fort My·ers /'mī-ərz/ a resort and commercial city in southwestern Florida; pop. 45,206.

fort·night /'fôrt,nīt/ ▸*n. chiefly Brit.* a period of two weeks. ■ *informal* used after the name of a day to indicate that something will take place two weeks after that day. ▷Old English *fēowertiene niht* 'fourteen nights.'

fort·night·ly /'fôrt,nītlē/ *chiefly Brit.* ▸*adj.* happening or produced every two weeks: *a fortnightly bulletin.*

▸*adv.* every two weeks: *evening classes will run fortnightly.*

▸*n.* (*pl.* **-lies**) a magazine or similar publication issued every two weeks.

Fort Pierce /pi(ə)rs/ a resort and port city in east central Florida; pop. 36,830.

For·tran /'fôr,tran/ (also **FORTRAN**) ▸*n.* a high-level computer programming language used esp. for scientific computation. ▷1950s: contraction of *formula translation.*

for·tress /'fôrtrəs/ ▸*n.* a military stronghold, esp. a strongly fortified town fit for a large garrison. ■ a heavily protected and impenetrable building. ■ *figurative* a person or thing not susceptible to outside influence or disturbance: *he had proved himself to be a fortress of moral rectitude.* ▷Middle English: from Old French *forteresse* 'strong place,' based on Latin *fortis* 'strong.'

Fort Smith /smiTH/ an industrial city in western Arkansas, on the Arkansas River; pop. 80,268.

Fort Sum·ter /'səmtər/ a historic site in the mouth of the harbor of Charleston in South Carolina. Confederate forces fired on U.S. troops here in April 1861, beginning the Civil War.

for·tu·i·tous /fôr'to͞oətəs/ ▸*adj.* happening by accident or chance rather than design: *the similarity between the paintings may not be simply fortuitous.* See note at ACCIDENTAL. ■ *informal* happening by a lucky chance; fortunate: *from a cash standpoint, the company's timing is fortuitous.* See **usage** below. ▷mid 17th cent.: from Latin *fortuitus*, from *forte* 'by chance,' from *fors* 'chance, luck.' —**for·tu·i·tous·ly** *adv.* —**for·tu·i·tous·ness** *n.*

USAGE The traditional, etymological meaning of **fortuitous** is 'happening by chance': a *fortuitous meeting* is a chance meeting, which might turn out to be either a good thing or a bad thing. In modern uses, however, **fortuitous** tends more often to be used to refer to fortunate outcomes, and the word has become more or less a synonym for 'lucky' or 'fortunate.' This use is frowned upon as being not etymologically correct and is best avoided except in informal contexts.

for·tu·i·ty /fôr'to͞oətē/ ▸*n.* (*pl.* **-ties**) a chance occurrence. ■ the state of being controlled by chance rather than design.

for·tu·nate /'fôrCHənət/ ▸*adj.* favored by or involving good luck or fortune; lucky: [with *infinitive*] *she'd been fortunate to escape more serious injury* ***it was fortunate that*** *the weather was good.* ■ auspicious or favorable: *a most fortunate match for our daughter.* ■ materially well off; prosperous: *less fortunate children still converged on the soup kitchens.* ▷late Middle English: from Latin *fortunatus*, from *fortuna* (see FORTUNE).

for·tu·nate·ly /'fôrCHənətlē/ ▸*adv.* [*sentence adverb*] it is fortunate that: *fortunately, no shots were fired and no one was hurt.*

for·tune /'fôrCHən/ ▸*n.* **1** chance or luck as an external, arbitrary force affecting human affairs: *some malicious act of fortune keeps them separate.* ■ luck, esp. good luck: *this astounding piece of good fortune that has befallen me.* ■ (**fortunes**) the success or failure of a person or enterprise over a period of time or in the course of a particular activity: *he is credited with turning around the company's fortunes.* **2** a large amount of money or assets: *he eventually inherited a substantial fortune.* ■ (**a fortune**) *informal* a surprisingly high price or amount of money: *I spent a fortune on drink and drugs.* ▷Middle English: via Old French from Latin *Fortuna*, the name of a goddess personifying luck or chance.

▸*PHRASES* □ **fortune favors the brave** *proverb* a successful person is often one who is willing to take risks. □ **the fortunes of war** the unpredictable, haphazard events of war. □ **make a** (or **one's**) **fortune** acquire great wealth by one's own efforts. □ **a small fortune** *informal* a large amount of money. □ **tell someone's fortune** make predictions about a person's future by palmistry, using a crystal ball, reading tarot cards, or similar divining methods.

For·tune 500 ▸*n. trademark* an annual list of the five hundred most profitable U.S. industrial corporations.

for·tune cook·ie ▸*n.* a thin folded cookie containing a slip of paper with a prediction or aphorism written on it, served in Chinese restaurants.

for·tune hunt·er ▸*n.* a person who seeks to become rich through marrying someone wealthy.

for·tune-tell·er ▸*n.* a person who tells people's fortunes. —**for·tune-tell·ing** *n.*

Fort Wayne /wān/ an industrial and commercial city in northeastern Indiana; pop. 205,727.

Fort Worth /wərTH/ a city in northern Texas, on the Trinity River, west of Dallas; pop. 534,694.

for·ty /'fôrtē/ ▸*cardinal number* (*pl.* **-ties**) the number equivalent to the product of four and ten; ten less than fifty; 40: *Troy was only forty miles away* | *forty were arrested* | *there were about thirty or forty of them.* (Roman numeral: **xl** or **XL.**) ■ (**forties**) the numbers from forty to forty-nine, esp. the years of a century or of a person's life: *Terry was in his early forties.* ■ forty years old: *a tall woman of about forty.* ■ forty miles an hour: *they were doing about forty.* ▷Old English *fēowertig* (see FOUR, -TY[2]). —**for·ti·eth** /-tēəTH/ *ordinal number* —**for·ty·fold** /-,fōld/ *adj.* & *adv.*

▸*PHRASE* □ **forty winks** *informal* a short sleep or nap, esp. during the day.

for·ty-five ▸*n.* **1** a phonograph record played at 45 rpm; a single. **2** (often **.45**) a 45-caliber revolver.

for·ty-nin·er /,fôrtē 'nīnər/ ▸*n.* a prospector in the California gold rush of 1849.

for·ty-ninth par·al·lel the parallel of latitude 49° north of the equator, esp. referred to as the boundary between Canada and the U.S. west of Lake of the Woods.

fo·rum /'fôrəm/ ▸*n.* (*pl.* **fo·rums**) **1** a place, meeting, or medium where ideas and views on a particular issue can be exchanged: *it will be* ***a forum for*** *consumers to exchange their views on medical research.* **2** a court or tribunal. **3** (*pl.* **fo·ra** /'fôrə/) (in an ancient Roman city) a public square or marketplace used for judicial and other business. ▷late Middle English (sense 3): from Latin, literally 'what is out of doors,' originally denoting an enclosure surrounding a house; related to *fores* '(outside) door.' Sense 1 dates from the mid 18th cent.

for·ward /'fôrwərd/ ▸*adv.* (also **for·wards**) **1** toward the front; in the direction that one is facing or traveling: *he started up the engine and the car moved forward* | *Lori leaned forward over the table.* ■ in, near, or toward the bow or nose of a ship or aircraft. ■ in the normal order or sequence: *the number was the same backward as forward.* **2** onward so as to make progress; toward a successful conclusion: *there's no way forward for the relationship.* ■ into a position of prominence or notice: *he is pushing forward a political ally.* **3** toward the future; ahead in time: *from that day forward, the assembly was at odds with us.* ■ to an earlier time: *the special issue has been moved forward to winter.*

▸*adj.* **1** directed or facing toward the front or the direction that one is facing or traveling: *forward flight* | *the pilot's forward view.* ■ positioned near the enemy lines: *troops moved to the forward areas.* ■ (in sports) moving toward the opponents' goal: *a forward pass.* ■ in, near, or toward the bow or nose of a ship or aircraft. ■ *figurative* moving or tending onwards to a successful conclusion: *the decision is a forward step.* ■ *Electronics* (of a voltage applied to a semiconductor junction) in the direction that allows significant current to flow. **2** [*attrib.*] relating to or concerned with the future: *forward planning.* **3** (of a person) bold or familiar in manner, esp. in a presumptuous way. **4** developing or acting earlier than expected or required; advanced or precocious: *an alarmingly forward yet painfully vulnerable child.* ■ (of a plant or crop) well advanced or early. ■ progressing toward or approaching maturity or completion.

▸*n.* **1** an attacking player in basketball, hockey, or other sports. ■ *Football* an offensive or defensive lineman. **2** (**forwards**) *Finance* short for FORWARD CONTRACT.

▸*v.* [*trans.*] **1** send (a letter) on to a further destination: [as *adj.*] (**forwarding**) *a forwarding address.* ■ hand over or send (an official document): *their final report was forwarded to the Commanding Officer.* ■ dispatch (goods): [as *adj.*] (**forwarding**) *a freight forwarding company.* **2** help to advance (something); promote: *the scientists are forwarding the development of biotechnology.* ▷Old English *forweard* (in the sense 'toward the future,' as in *from this day forward*), variant of *forthweard* (see FORTH, -WARD). —**for·ward·ly** *adv.* —**for·ward·ness** *n.*

for·ward con·tract ▸*n. Finance* an informal agreement traded through a broker-dealer network to buy and sell specified assets, typically currency, at a specified price at a certain future date. Compare with FUTURES CONTRACT.

for·ward·er[1] /'fôrwərdər/ ▸*n.* a person or organization that supervises the dispatch and delivery of goods, esp. by making banking and insurance arrangements and completing required documents.

Pronunciation Key ə *ago*; ər *over*; 'ə or ,ə *up*; 'ər or ,ər *fur*; a *hat*; ā *rate*; ä *car*; CH *chew*; e *let*; ē *see*; e(ə)r *air*; i *fit*; ī *by*; i(ə)r *ear*; NG *sing*; ō *go*; ô *for*; oi *boy*; o͞o *good*; o͞o *goo*; ou *out*; SH *she*; TH *thin*; TH *then*; (h)w *why*; ZH *vision*

F

for·ward·er[2] ▸*adj. & adv. dated or informal* further forward; more advanced: *time was drawing on and we were no forwarder.*

for·ward-look·ing ▸*adj.* favoring innovation and development; progressive.

for·ward pass ▸*n. Football* a pass thrown from behind the line of scrimmage in a forward direction, toward the opponent's goal.

for·wards /ˈfôrwərdz/ ▸*adv.* variant spelling of FORWARD.

for·went /fôrˈwent/ ▸ past of FORGO.

FOS ▸*abbr.* free on steamer.

Fos·bur·y /ˈfäzˌberē/, Richard (1947–), U.S. high jumper. He originated the now standard style of jumping known as the "Fosbury flop," in which the jumper clears the bar head first and backward. In 1968, he won the Olympic gold medal using this technique.

fos·sa[1] /ˈfäsə/ ▸*n.* (*pl.* **fos·sae** /ˈfäsē; -sī/) *Anatomy* a shallow depression or hollow. ▷mid 17th cent.: from Latin, literally 'ditch,' feminine past participle of *fodere* 'to dig.'

fos·sa[2] ▸*n.* a large nocturnal reddish-brown catlike mammal of the civet family, found in the rain forests of Madagascar. • *Cryptoprocta ferox*, family Viverridae. ▷mid 19th cent.: from Malagasy *fosa.*

Fos·se /ˈfôsē; ˈfäsē/, Bob (1927–87), U.S. jazz dancer, choreographer, and director; full name *Robert Louis Fosse.* He directed and choreographed Broadway musicals such as *Pajama Game* (1954), *Redhead* (1958), and *All That Jazz* (1979) and movies such as *Cabaret* (Academy Award, 1972). *Fosse* (1999), a Broadway musical, was dedicated to him.

fosse /fäs/ ▸*n. Archaeology* a long narrow trench or excavation, esp. in a fortification. ▷late Old English, via Old French from Latin *fossa* (see FOSSA[1]).

F

fos·sick /ˈfäsik/ ▸*v.* [*intrans.*] *informal Austral./NZ* rummage; search: *he spent years **fossicking through** documents.* ■ search for gold in abandoned workings. ▷mid 19th cent. (referring to mining): probably from the English dialect sense 'obtain by asking' (i.e., 'ferret out'). —**fos·sick·er** /ˈfäsikər/ *n.*

fos·sil /ˈfäsəl/ ▸*n.* the remains or impression of a prehistoric organism preserved in petrified form or as a mold or cast in rock. ■ *derogatory & humorous* an antiquated or stubbornly unchanging person or thing: *he can be a cantankerous old fossil at times.* ■ a word or phrase that has become obsolete except in set phrases or forms, e.g., *hue* in *hue and cry.* ▷mid 16th cent. (denoting a fossilized fish found, and believed to have lived, underground): from French *fossile*, from Latin *fossilis* 'dug up,' from *fodere* 'dig.'

fos·sil fu·el ▸*n.* a natural fuel such as coal or gas, formed in the geological past from the remains of living organisms.

fos·sil i·vo·ry ▸*n.* ivory from the tusks of a mammoth.

fos·sil·ize /ˈfäsəˌlīz/ ▸*v.* [*trans.*] (usu. **be fossilized**) preserve (an organism) so that it becomes a fossil: *the hard parts of the body are readily fossilized* | [as *adj.*] (**fossilized**) *the fossilized remains of a dinosaur.* ■ [*intrans.*] become a fossil: *flowers do not readily fossilize.* ■ become antiquated, fixed, or incapable of change or development. —**fos·sil·i·za·tion** /ˌfäsəliˈzāsʜən/ *n.*

fos·so·ri·al /fäˈsôrēəl/ ▸*adj. Zoology* (of an animal) burrowing. ■ (of limbs) adapted for use in burrowing. ▷mid 19th cent.: from medieval Latin *fossorius* (from Latin *fossor* 'digger,' from *fodere* 'to dig') + -AL.

Fos·ter[1] /ˈfôstər; ˈfäs-/, Jodie (1962–), U.S. movie actress. She won Academy Award nominations for *Taxi Driver* (1976) and *Nell* (1994) and Academy Awards for her performances in *The Accused* (1988) and *Silence of the Lambs* (1991).

Fos·ter[2], Stephen (Collins) (1826–64), U.S. composer. He wrote more than 200 songs and, although a Northerner, was best known for songs that purported to capture the Southern plantation spirit, such as "Oh! Susannah" (1848), "Camptown Races" (1850), and "Old Folks at Home" (1851).

fos·ter /ˈfôstər; ˈfäs-/ ▸*v.* [*trans.*] **1** encourage or promote the development of (something, typically something regarded as good): *the teacher's task is to foster learning.* See note at ENCOURAGE. ■ develop (a feeling or idea) in oneself: *appropriate praise helps a child foster a sense of self-worth.* **2** bring up (a child that is not one's own by birth).

▸*adj.* denoting someone that has a specified family connection through fostering rather than birth: *foster parent* | *foster child.* ■ involving or concerned with fostering a child: *foster care* | *foster home.* ▷Old English *fōstrian* 'feed, nourish,' from *fōster* 'food, nourishment,' of Germanic origin; related to FOOD. The sense 'bring up another's (originally also one's own) child' dates from Middle English. —**fos·ter·age** /-rij/ *n.* —**fos·ter·er** *n.*

fos·ter·ling /ˈfôstərlɪɴɢ; ˈfäs-/ ▸*n. chiefly archaic* a child who is fostered or adopted. ▷Old English *fōstorling* (see FOSTER, -LING).

Fou·cault[1] /fo͞oˈkō/, Jean Bernard Léon (1819–68), French physicist. He is chiefly remembered for the huge pendulum that he hung from the roof of the Panthéon in Paris in 1851 to demonstrate the rotation of the earth. He also invented the gyroscope.

Fou·cault[2], Michel (Paul) (1926–84), French philosopher. He was concerned with how society defines categories of abnormality, such as insanity, sexuality, and criminality, and the manipulation of social attitudes toward such things by those in power.

fouet·té /fweˈtā/ ▸*n. Ballet* a pirouette performed with a circular whipping movement of the raised leg to the side. ■ a quick shift of direction of the upper body, performed with one leg extended. ▷French, past participle of *fouetter* 'to whip.'

fought /fôt/ ▸ past and past participle of FIGHT.

Fou-hsin variant spelling of FUXIN.

foul /foul/ ▸*adj.* **1** offensive to the senses, esp. through having a disgusting smell or taste or being unpleasantly soiled: *a foul odor* | *his foul breath.* ■ *informal* very disagreeable or unpleasant: *the news had put Michelle in a foul mood.* ■ (of the weather) wet and stormy. ■ *Sailing* (of wind or tide) opposed to one's desired course. **2** wicked or immoral: *murder most foul.* ■ (of language) obscene or profane. ■ done contrary to the rules of a sport: *a foul tackle.* **3** containing or charged with noxious matter; polluted: *foul, swampy water.* ■ [*predic.*] (**foul with**) clogged or choked with: *the land was foul with weeds.* ■ *Nautical* (of a rope or anchor) entangled. ■ (of a ship's bottom) encrusted with algae, barnacles, or other marine growth. ■ *Printing* (of a first copy or proof) defaced by corrections.

▸*n.* **1** (in sports) an unfair or invalid stroke or piece of play, esp. one involving interference with an opponent. ■ a collision or entanglement in riding, rowing, or running. ■ short for FOUL BALL. **2** *informal, dated* a disease in the feet of cattle.

▸*adv.* unfairly; contrary to the rules. ■ (in sports) in foul territory: *if a batter hits a bunt foul with two strikes, he is out.*

▸*v.* [*trans.*] **1** make foul or dirty; pollute: *factories that fouled the atmosphere.* ■ disgrace or dishonor. ■ (of an animal) make (something) dirty with excrement: *make sure that your pet never fouls the sidewalk.* ■ (**foul oneself**) (of a person) defecate involuntarily. **2** (in sports) commit a foul against (an opponent). ■ *Baseball* hit a foul ball: *Carter fouled into the glove of Boggs.* **3** (of a ship) collide with or interfere with the passage of (another). ■ cause (a cable, anchor, or other object) to become entangled or jammed: *watch out for driftwood which might **foul up** the engine.* ■ [*intrans.*] become entangled in this way.

▸*phrasal v.* □ **foul out** *Basketball* be put out of the game for exceeding the permitted number of fouls. ■ *Baseball* (of a batter) be made out by hitting a foul ball that is caught by an opposing player: *Wilson has never fouled out against this young pitcher.* □ **foul something up** (or **foul up**) make a mistake with or spoil something: *leaders should admit when they completely foul things up.* ▷Old English *fūl*, of Germanic origin; related to Old Norse *fúll* 'foul,' Dutch *vuil* 'dirty,' and German *faul* 'rotten, lazy,' from an Indo-European root shared by Latin *pus*, Greek *puos* 'pus,' and Latin *putere* 'to stink.' —**foul·ly** /ˈfou(l)lē/ *adv.* —**foul·ness** *n.*

▸*PHRASES* □ **fall foul of** see FALL. □ **foul one's (own) nest** do something damaging or harmful to oneself or one's own interests.

fou·lard /fo͞oˈlärd/ ▸*n.* a thin, soft material of silk or silk and cotton, typically having a printed pattern. ■ a tie or handkerchief made of such material. ▷mid 19th cent.: from French, of unknown origin.

foul ball ▸*n. Baseball* a ball struck so that it falls or will fall outside the lines extending from home plate past first and third bases. An uncaught foul ball counts as a strike against the batter, unless it would be the third strike. The exception is a bunted foul ball, which can be a third strike. Compare with FOUL TIP.

foul brood ▸*n.* a fatal bacterial disease of larval honeybees. • This disease is caused by the bacteria *Paenibacillus larvae* or *Melissococcus pluton.*

foul line ▸*n. Sports* a line marking the boundary of permissible movement or play, in particular: ■ *Baseball* either of the straight lines extending from home plate past first and third bases into the outfield and marking the limit of the area within which a hit is deemed to be fair. ■ *Basketball* either of the lines 15 feet in front of each backboard, from which free throws are made. Also called FREE-THROW LINE. ■ (in bowling) a line on the alley, perpendicular to the gutters and 60 feet from the head pin.

foul mouth ▸*n.* a tendency to use bad language: *he had a foul mouth and an even fouler disposition.* —**foul-mouthed** /-ˌmoutʜd; -ˌmoutʜt/ *adj.*

foul play ▸*n.* **1** unfair play in a game or sport. **2** unlawful or dishonest behavior, in particular violent crime resulting in another's death.

foul shot ▸*n. Basketball* another term for FREE THROW.

foul tip ▸*n. Baseball* a pitched ball that tips off the bat and travels directly to the catcher's hands. Unlike a foul ball, a foul tip can be a batter's third strike. —**foul-tip** *v.*

foul-up ▸*n.* a mistake resulting in confusion.

found[1] /found/ ▸ past and past participle of FIND.

▸*adj.* **1** having been discovered by chance or unexpectedly, in particular: ■ (of an object or sound) collected in its natural state and presented in a new context as part of a work of art or piece of music: *collages of found photos.* ■ (of art) comprising or making use of such objects. ■ (of poetry) formed by reinterpreting metrically the structure of a nonpoetic text. **2** [with *submodifier*] (of a ship) equipped; supplied: *the ship was two years old, well found and seaworthy.*

found[2] ▸*v.* [*trans.*] **1** establish or originate (an institution or organization), esp. by providing an endowment: *the monastery was founded in 1665* | [as *adj.*] (**founding**) *the three founding partners.* ■ plan and begin the building of (a town or colony). **2** (usu. **be founded on/upon**) construct or base (a principle or other abstract thing) according to a particular principle or grounds: *a society founded on the highest principles of religion and education.* ■ (of a thing) serve as a basis for: *the company's fortunes are founded on its minerals business.* ▷Middle English: from Old French *fonder*, from Latin *fundare*, from *fundus* 'bottom, base.'

found[3] ▸*v.* [*trans.*] melt and mold (metal). ■ fuse (materials) to make glass. ■ make (an article) by melting and molding metal. ▷early 16th cent.: from French *fondre*, from Latin *fundere* 'melt, pour.'

foun·da·tion /founˈdāsʜən/ ▸*n.* **1** (often **foundations**) the lowest load-bearing part of a building, typically below ground level. ■ *figurative* a body or ground on which other parts rest or are overlaid: *he starts playing melody lines on the bass instead of laying the foundation down.* ■ (also **foundation garment**) a woman's supporting undergarment, such as a girdle. ■ a cream or powder used as a base to even out facial skin tone before applying other cosmetics. **2** an underlying basis or principle for something: *specific learning skills as **a foundation for** other subjects.* ■ [often with *negative*] justification or reason: *distorted and misleading accusations with no foundation.* **3** the action of establishing an institution or organization on a permanent basis, esp. with an endowment. ■ an institution established with an endowment, for example a college or a body devoted to financing research or charity. ▷late Middle English: from Old French *fondation*, from Latin *fundatio(n-)*, from *fundare* 'to lay a base for' (see FOUND[2]). —**foun·da·tion·al** /-sʜənl/ *adj.*

foun·da·tion stone ▸*n.* a stone laid with ceremony to celebrate the beginning of construction of a building. ■ *figurative* a basic or essential element of something.

found·er[1] ▸*n.* a person who manufactures articles of cast metal; the owner or operator of a foundry: *an iron founder.* ▷Middle English: probably from Old French *fondeur*, from *fondre* (see FOUND[3]).

found·er[2] ▸*v.* [*intrans.*] (of a ship) fill with water and sink: *six drowned when the yacht foundered off the Florida coast.* ■ *figurative* (of a plan or undertaking) fail or break down, typically as a result of a particular problem or setback: *the talks **foundered on** the issue of reform.* ■ (of a hoofed animal, esp. a horse or pony) succumb to laminitis.

▸*n.* laminitis in horses, ponies, or other hoofed animals. ▷Middle English (in the sense 'knock to the ground'): from Old French *fondrer*, *esfondrer* 'submerge, collapse,' based on Latin *fundus* 'bottom, base.'

USAGE It is easy to confuse the words **founder** and **flounder**, not only because they sound similar but also because the contexts in which they are used overlap. **Founder** means, in its general and extended use, 'fail or come to nothing, sink out of sight' (*the scheme **foundered** because of lack of organizational backing*). **Flounder**, on the other hand, means 'struggle, move clumsily, be in a state of confusion' (*new recruits **floundering** about in their first week*).

found·er ef·fect ▶*n. Biology* the reduced genetic diversity that results when a population is descended from a small number of colonizing ancestors.

found·ing fa·ther ▶*n.* a person who starts or helps to start a movement or institution. ■ (**Founding Father**) a member of the convention that drew up the U.S. Constitution in 1787.

found·ling /'foundliNG/ ▶*n.* an infant that has been abandoned by its parents and is discovered and cared for by others. ▷Middle English: from **FOUND**[1] (past participle) + **-LING**, perhaps on the pattern of Dutch *vondeling*.

found ob·ject ▶*n.* objet trouvé.

found·ress /'foundrəs/ ▶*n. dated, rare* a female founder: *she was the sixth-century foundress of a community of women.*

found·ry /'foundrē/ ▶*n.* (*pl.* **-ries**) a workshop or factory for casting metal. ▷early 17th cent. (earlier as *foundery*): from **FOUND**[3] + **-RY**, perhaps suggested by French *fonderie*.

fount[1] /fänt; fount/ ▶*n.* a source of a desirable quality or commodity: *our courier was a fount of knowledge.* ■ *poetic/literary* a spring or fountain. ▷late 16th cent.: back-formation from **FOUNTAIN**, on the pattern of the pair *mountain, mount*.

fount[2] ▶*n. Brit.* variant spelling of **FONT**[2].

foun·tain /'fountn/ ▶*n.* **1** an ornamental structure in a pool or lake from which one or more jets of water are pumped into the air. ■ short for **DRINKING FOUNTAIN**. ■ *figurative* a thing that spurts or cascades into the air: *little fountains of dust.* **2** *chiefly poetic/literary* a natural spring of water. ■ a source of a desirable quality: *the government always quotes this report as the fountain of truth.*

▶*v.* [*intrans.*] spurt or cascade like a fountain: *an enormous curtain of lava fountained into the sky.* ▷Middle English (sense 2): from Old French *fontaine*, from late Latin *fontana*, feminine of Latin *fontanus*, adjective from *fons, font-* 'a spring.' **—foun·tained** /'fountnd/ *adj.* (*poetic/literary*).

foun·tain·head /'fountn,hed/ ▶*n.* the headwaters or source of a stream. ■ an original source of something: *this president was the fountainhead of patronage.*

foun·tain pen ▶*n.* a pen with a reservoir or cartridge from which ink flows continuously to the nib.

fountain pen

Foun·tain Val·ley a city in southwestern California, southeast of Los Angeles; pop. 53,691.

four /fôr/ ▶*cardinal number* equivalent to the product of two and two; one more than three, or six less than ten; 4: *Francesca's got four brothers | it took four of them to lift it | a four-bedroom house.* (Roman numeral: **iv, IV**, archaic **iiii** or **IIII**.) ■ a group or unit of four people or things: *the girls walked in pairs or fours.* ■ four years old: *I began to teach myself to read at four.* ■ four o'clock: *it's half past four.* ■ a size of garment or other merchandise denoted by four. ■ a playing card or domino with four spots or pips. ▷Old English *fēower*, of Germanic origin; related to Dutch and German *vier*, from an Indo-European root shared by Latin *quattuor* and Greek *tessares*.

four-bag·ger ▶*n. Baseball* a home run.

four-by-four (also **4X4**) ▶*n. informal* a vehicle with four-wheel drive.

Four Can·tons, Lake of the another name for Lake Lucerne (see **LUCERNE, LAKE**).

four·chette /fo͝or'SHet/ ▶*n. Anatomy* a thin fold of skin at the back of the vulva. ▷mid 18th cent.: from French, diminutive of *fourche* 'fork.'

four-col·or ▶*adj.* denoting a color printing process using red, cyan (greenish blue), yellow, and black inks on separate plates that are serially transferred to the same sheet to produce images in full color.

Four Cor·ners the point where Arizona, New Mexico, Colorado, and Utah meet.

four-di·men·sion·al ▶*adj.* having four dimensions, typically the three dimensions of space (length, breadth, and depth) plus time.

Four·drin·i·er ma·chine /,fôrdrə'nir; fôr'drinēər/ ▶*n.* a machine for making paper as a continuous sheet by drainage on a wire mesh belt. ▷mid 19th cent.: named after Henry (died 1854) and Sealy (died 1847) *Fourdrinier*, British papermakers and patentees of such a machine.

four-eyed fish ▶*n.* a small livebearing freshwater fish of tropical America. Each eye is divided into two, allowing the fish to see both above and below the water while swimming at the surface. • Family Anablepidae and genus *Anableps*: several species.

four-eyes ▶*n. derogatory* a person who wears glasses.

four flush ▶*n.* a poker hand of little value, having four cards of the same suit and one of another. Compare with **FLUSH**[3].

▶*v.* (**four-flush**) [*intrans.*] *informal* (in poker) bluff when holding a weak hand, particularly a four flush. ■ keep up a pretense; bluff: *your mother will get wise that you're four-flushing.* **—four-flush·er** *n.*

four·fold /'fôr,fōld/ ▶*adj.* four times as great or as numerous: *there has been a fourfold increase in break-ins.* ■ having four parts or elements: *fourfold symmetry.*

▶*adv.* by four times; to four times the number or amount: *the price of electricity rose fourfold.*

four free·doms (usu. **the four freedoms**) the four essential human freedoms as proclaimed in a speech to Congress by President Franklin D. Roosevelt in 1941: freedom of speech and expression, freedom of worship, freedom from want, and freedom from fear.

Four Hun·dred (usu. **the Four Hun·dred** or **the 400**) ▶*n.* the social elite of a community: *I would like nothing better than to ask the Four Hundred to meet you.* ▷mid 19th cent.: from Ward McAllister's remark "There are only 400 people in New York that one really knows," later popularized in society reports by the New York *Sun*. The notion 'elite' is said to be from the selection of high society guests by the socialite Mrs. William B. Astor Jr., whose ballroom could hold 400.

Fou·rier /'fo͝orē,ā; fo͝or'yā/, Jean Baptiste Joseph (1768–1830), French mathematician. He solved partial differential equations by the method of separation of variables and superposition, which led him to analyze the series and integrals that are now known by his name.

Fou·rier a·nal·y·sis ▶*n. Mathematics* the analysis of a complex waveform expressed as a series of sinusoidal functions, the frequencies of which form a harmonic series.

Fou·ri·er·ism /'fo͝orēə,rizəm/ ▶*n.* a system for the reorganization of society into self-sufficient cooperatives, in accordance with the principles of the French socialist Charles Fourier (died 1837). **—Fou·ri·er·ist** *n.* & *adj.*

Fou·rier se·ries ▶*n. Mathematics* an infinite series of trigonometric functions that represents an expansion or approximation of a periodic function, used in Fourier analysis.

Fou·rier trans·form ▶*n. Mathematics* a function derived from a given function and representing it by a series of sinusoidal functions.

four-in-hand ▶*n.* **1** a vehicle with four horses driven by one person: [as *adj.*] *four-in-hand coaches compete this week for the Devon blue ribbon.* ■ a team of four horses. **2** *historical* a necktie tied in a loose knot with two hanging ends, popular in the late 19th and early 20th centuries. [said to be by association with the sport of driving four-in-hand carriages.]

four-leaf clo·ver (also **four-leafed clo·ver**) ▶*n.* a clover leaf with four leaflets, rather than the typical three, thought to bring good luck.

four-let·ter word ▶*n.* any of several short words referring to sexual or excretory functions, regarded as coarse or offensive.

four no·ble truths (usu. **the Four Noble Truths**) the four central beliefs containing the essence of Buddhist teaching. See **BUDDHISM**.

four-o'clock ▶*n.* a tropical American herbaceous plant with fragrant trumpet-shaped flowers that open late in the afternoon. Also called **MARVEL OF PERU**. • *Mirabilis jalapa*, family Nyctaginaceae.

four-ply ▶*adj.* (of a material) having four strands or layers: *four-ply yarn.*

▶*n.* knitting yarn made of four strands.

four-post·er (also **four-poster bed**) ▶*n.* a bed with a post at each corner, sometimes supporting a canopy.

four·score /'fôr'skôr/ ▶*cardinal number archaic* eighty.

four·some /'fôrsəm/ ▶*n.* a group of four people. ■ a golf match between two pairs of players, with partners playing the same ball.

four-square ▶*adj.* (of a building or structure) having a square shape and solid appearance. ■ (of a person or quality) firm and resolute: *a four-square and formidable hero.*

▶*adv.* squarely and solidly: *a castle **standing four-square** and isolated on a peninsula.* ■ firmly or resolutely, esp. in support of someone or something: *they **stand four-square behind** integration.*

four-star ▶*adj.* (esp. of a hotel or restaurant) given four stars in a grading system, typically one in which this denotes the highest or next to the highest class or quality. ■ (in the U.S. armed forces) having or denoting the second-highest military rank, distinguished by four stars on the uniform.

four-stroke ▶*adj.* denoting an internal combustion engine having a cycle of four strokes (intake, compression, combustion, and exhaust). Compare with **TWO-STROKE**. ■ denoting a vehicle having such an engine.

▶*n.* an engine or vehicle of this type.

four·teen /,fôr'tēn; 'fôr,tēn/ ▶*cardinal number* equivalent to the product of seven and two; one more than thirteen, or six less than twenty; 14: *they had spent fourteen days in solitary confinement | all fourteen of us were seated.* (Roman numeral: **xiv** or **XIV**.) ■ a size of garment or other merchandise denoted by fourteen. ■ fourteen years old: *he left school at fourteen.* ▷Old English *fēowertīene* (see **FOUR, -TEEN**). **—four·teenth** /,fôr'tēnTH; 'fôr,tēnTH/ *ordinal number*.

fourth /fôrTH/ ▶*ordinal number* constituting number four in a sequence; 4th: *the fourth and fifth centuries | there were three bedrooms, with potential for a fourth.* ■ (**a fourth/one fourth**) a quarter: *nearly three fourths of that money is now gone.* ■ the fourth finisher or position in a race or competition: *he could do no better than finish fourth.* ■ the fourth (and often highest) in a sequence of a vehicle's gears: *he took the corner at the end of the road in fourth.* ■ the fourth grade of a school. ■ fourthly (used to introduce a fourth point or reason): *third, visit popular attractions during lunch; fourth, stay late.* ■ *Music* an interval spanning four consecutive notes in a diatonic scale, in particular (also **perfect fourth**) an interval of two tones and a semitone (e.g., C to F). ■ *Music* the note that is higher by this interval than the tonic of a diatonic scale or root of a chord.

fourth-class ▶*adj.* a class of U.S. mail applying to packages weighing more than sixteen ounces and used esp. for sending general merchandise, books, recordings, videotapes, and films.

fourth di·men·sion ▶*n.* **1** a postulated spatial dimension additional to those determining length, area, and volume. **2** time regarded as analogous to linear dimensions.

fourth es·tate ▶*n.* (**the fourth estate**) the press; the profession of journalism: *copy desks are held together by the bad-news contingent of the fourth estate.* ▷originally used humorously in various contexts; its first usage with reference to the press has been attributed to Edmund Burke, but this remains unconfirmed.

Fourth In·ter·na·tion·al see **INTERNATIONAL** (sense 2 of the *noun*).

fourth·ly /'fôrTHlē/ ▶*adv.* in the fourth place (used to introduce a fourth point or reason): *fourthly, and last, there are variations in context that influence the process.*

Fourth of Ju·ly ▶*n.* (in the U.S.) a national holiday celebrating the anniversary of the adoption of the Declaration of Independence in 1776. Also called **INDEPENDENCE DAY**.

fourth po·si·tion ▶*n.* **1** *Ballet* a posture in which the feet are placed turned outward one in front of the other, separated by the distance of one step. ■ a position of the arms in which one is held curved over the head and the other curved in front of the body at waist level. **2** *Music* a position of the left hand on the fingerboard of a stringed instrument nearer to the bridge than the third position, enabling a higher set of notes to be played.

Fourth Re·pub·lic the republican regime in France between the end of World War II (1945) and the introduction of a new constitution by Charles de Gaulle in 1958.

Fourth World ▶*n.* **1** those countries and communities considered to be the poorest and most underdeveloped of the Third World. **2** those communities that form politically and economically

Pronunciation Key ə *ago*; ər *over*; 'ə or ,ə *up*; 'ər or ,ər *fur*; a *hat*; ā *rate*; ä *car*; CH *chew*; e *let*; ē *see*; e(ə)r *air*; i *fit*; ī *by*; i(ə)r *ear*; NG *sing*; ō *go*; ô *for*; oi *boy*; o͝o *good*; o͞o *goo*; ou *out*; SH *she*; TH *thin*; TH *then*; (h)w *why*; ZH *vision*

disadvantaged minorities within societies, owing to factors such as urban deprivation or discrimination against tribal peoples.

4to /ˈkwôrtō/ ▸*abbr.* quarto.

4WD ▸*abbr.* four-wheel drive.

four-wheel drive ▸*n.* a transmission system that provides power directly to all four wheels of a vehicle. ■ a vehicle with such a system, typically designed for off-road driving.

fo·ve·a /ˈfōvēə/ (also **fo·ve·a cen·tra·lis** /senˈtrālis/) ▸*n.* (*pl.* **-ve·ae** /-vē,ē; -vē,ī/) *Anatomy* a small depression in the retina of the eye where visual acuity is highest. The center of the field of vision is focused in this region, where retinal cones are particularly concentrated. ▷late 17th cent.: from Latin, literally 'small pit.' **—fo·ve·al** /-vēəl/ *adj.*

fowl /foul/ ▸*n.* (*pl.* same or **fowls**) (also **domestic fowl**) a gallinaceous bird kept chiefly for its eggs and flesh; a domestic cock or hen. • The domestic fowl is descended from the wild **red junglefowl** of Southeast Asia (see **JUNGLE FOWL**). ■ any other domesticated bird kept for its eggs or flesh, e.g., the turkey, duck, goose, and guineafowl. ■ the flesh of birds, esp. of the domestic cock or hen, as food; poultry. ■ birds collectively, esp. as the quarry of hunters. ■ *archaic* a bird. ▷Old English *fugol,* originally the general term for a bird, of Germanic origin; related to Dutch *vogel* and German *Vogel,* also to **FLY**[1].

Fowl·er /ˈfoulər/, H. W. (1858–1933), English lexicographer and grammarian; full name *Henry Watson Fowler.* He compiled the first edition of the *Concise Oxford Dictionary* (1911) with his brother and wrote a guide to style and idiom, *Modern English Usage,* that was first published in 1926.

Fowles /foulz/, John (Robert) (1926–), English novelist. Notable works: *The Collector* (1963), *The Magus* (1966), and *The French Lieutenant's Woman* (1969).

fowl·ing /ˈfouliNG/ ▸*n.* the hunting, shooting, or trapping of wildfowl. **—fowl·er** /ˈfoulər/ *n.*

fowl pest ▸*n.* either of two similar viral diseases of poultry: ■ Newcastle disease. ■ fowl plague.

fowl plague ▸*n.* an acute and often fatal infectious viral disease of birds, esp. poultry.

fowl·pox /ˈfoul,päks/ ▸*n.* a slow-spreading viral disease of birds that produces wartlike nodules on the skin. Infestations sometimes threaten commercial poultry interests. • *Avipoxvirus,* family Poxviridae.

Fox[1] /fäks/, George (1624–91), English preacher and founder of the Society of Friends (Quakers).

Fox[2] ▸*n.* (*pl.* same) **1** a member of an American Indian people formerly living in southern Wisconsin, and now mainly in Iowa, Nebraska, and Kansas. **2** the Algonquian language of this people.
▸*adj.* of or relating to this people or their language.

fox /fäks/ ▸*n.* **1** a carnivorous mammal of the dog family with a pointed muzzle and bushy tail, proverbial for its cunning. • *Vulpes* and three other genera, family Canidae: several species, including the red fox and the arctic fox. ■ the fur of a fox. **2** *informal* a cunning or sly person: *a wily old fox.* ■ a sexually attractive woman.
▸*v.* **1** [*trans.*] *informal* baffle or deceive (someone): *the bad light and dark shadows foxed him.* ■ [*intrans.*] *dated* behave in a cunning or sly way. **2** [*trans.*] repair (a boot or shoe) by renewing the upper leather. ■ ornament (the upper of a boot or shoe) with a strip of leather. ▷Old English, of Germanic origin; related to Dutch *vos* and German *Fuchs.* **—fox·like** /-,līk/ *adj.*

foxed /fäkst/ ▸*adj.* (of the paper of old books or prints) discolored with brown spots. **—fox·ing** /ˈfäksiNG/ *n.*

fox·fire /ˈfäks,fīr/ ▸*n.* the phosphorescent light emitted by certain fungi on decaying timber.

fox·glove /ˈfäks,gləv/ ▸*n.* a tall Eurasian plant with erect spikes of flowers, typically pinkish-purple or white, shaped like the fingers of gloves. It is a source of the drug digitalis. • Genus *Digitalis,* family Scrophulariaceae: many species, in particular *D. purpurea.*

foxglove

fox grape ▸*n.* a wild grape-bearing vine native to the eastern U.S. Also called **LABRUSCA, ISABELLA.**

fox·hole /ˈfäks,hōl/ ▸*n.* a hole in the ground used by troops as a shelter against enemy fire or as a firing point. ■ a place of refuge or concealment.

fox·hound /ˈfäks,hound/ ▸*n.* a dog of a smooth-haired breed with drooping ears, often trained to hunt foxes in packs over long distances.

fox hunt·ing ▸*n.* the sport of hunting a fox across country with a pack of hounds by a group of people on foot and horseback, a traditional sport of the English landed gentry. **—fox hunt·er** *n.*

Fox Que·sa·da /kāˈsädə/, Vicente (1942–), Mexican statesman. A member of the National Action Party (PAN), he was elected to the presidency in 2000, ending seventy-one years of rule by the Institutional Revolutionary Party (PRI).

Vicente Fox Quesada

fox·tail /ˈfäks,tāl/ ▸*n.* a common meadow grass that has soft brushlike flowering spikes. • Genus *Alopecurus,* family Gramineae: several species, in particular *A. pratensis.*

fox ter·ri·er ▸*n.* a terrier of a short-haired or wire-haired breed originally used for unearthing foxes.

fox·trot /ˈfäks,trät/ ▸*n.* **1** a ballroom dance in 4/4 time, with alternation of two slow and two quick steps. ■ a piece of music written for such a dance. ■ a gait in which a horse walks with its front legs and trots with its hind legs. **2** a code word representing the letter F, used in radio communication.
▸*v.* (**-tro·tted, -tro·tting**) [*intrans.*] perform such a ballroom dance.

Fox·woods /ˈfäks,wo͝odz/ a gambling resort on the Mashantucket Pequot reservation in the town of Ledyard in southeastern Connecticut, north of New London.

fox·y /ˈfäksē/ ▸*adj.* (**fox·i·er, fox·i·est**) resembling or likened to a fox: *a terrier with a foxy expression.* ■ *informal* cunning or sly in character. ■ *informal* (chiefly of a woman) sexually attractive. ■ reddish brown in color. ■ (of wine) having a musky flavor. ■ (of paper or other material) marked with spots; foxed. **—fox·i·ly** /ˈfäksəlē/ *adv.* **—fox·i·ness** *n.*

foy·er /ˈfoiər; ˈfoi,ā/ ▸*n.* an entrance hall or other open area in a building used by the public, esp. a hotel or theater. ■ an entrance hall in a house or apartment. ▷late 18th cent. (denoting the center of attention or activity): from French, 'hearth, home,' based on Latin *focarius* 'kitchen servant,' from *focus* 'domestic hearth.'

Foyt /foit/, A. J. (1935–) U.S. race car driver; full name *Anthony Joseph Foyt, Jr.* He won the Indianapolis 500 four times 1961, 1964, 1967, 1977.

fp ▸*abbr.* ■ (**FP**) Fabricated Plate. ■ fireplace. ■ fortepiano. ■ freezing point.

FPC ▸*abbr.* ■ Federal Power Commission. ■ fish protein concentrate. ■ Friends Peace Committee.

fpl ▸*abbr.* fireplace.

fpm ▸*abbr.* feet per minute.

FPO ▸*abbr.* ■ Field post office. ■ Fleet post office.

fps (also **f.p.s.**) ▸*abbr.* ■ feet per second. ■ foot-pound-second. ■ frames per second.

FPU ▸*abbr. Computing* floating-point unit, a processor that performs arithmetic operations.

Fr. ▸*abbr.* ■ Father (as a courtesy title of priests): *Fr. Buckley.* [from French *frère,* literally 'brother.'] ■ France. ■ French. ■ Friday.
▸*symbol* the chemical element francium.

fr. ▸*abbr.* franc(s).

f.r. ▸*abbr.* folio recto (right-hand page). [Latin]

Fra /frä/ ▸*n.* a prefixed title given to an Italian monk or friar: *Fra Angelico.* ▷Italian, abbreviation of *frate* 'brother,' from Latin *frater.*

frab·jous /ˈfrabjəs/ ▸*adj. humorous* delightful; joyous: *"Oh frabjous day!" she giggled.* ▷1871: coined by Lewis Carroll in *Through the Looking Glass,* apparently to suggest *fair* and *joyous.* **—frab·jous·ly** *adv.*

fra·cas /ˈfrākəs; ˈfrak-/ ▸*n.* (*pl.* **-cas·es**) a noisy disturbance or quarrel. ▷early 18th cent.: French, from *fracasser,* from Italian *fracassare* 'make an uproar.'

frac·tal /ˈfraktəl/ *Mathematics* ▸*n.* a curve or geometric figure, each part of which has the same statistical character as the whole. Fractals are useful in modeling structures (such as eroded coastlines or snowflakes) in which similar patterns recur at progressively smaller scales, and in describing partly random or chaotic phenomena such as crystal growth, fluid turbulence, and galaxy formation.
▸*adj.* relating to or of the nature of a fractal or fractals: *fractal geometry.* ▷1970s: from French, from Latin *fract-* 'broken,' from the verb *frangere.*

frac·tion /ˈfrakSHən/ ▸*n.* **1** a numerical quantity that is not a whole number (e.g., $1/2$, 0.5). ■ a small or tiny part, amount, or proportion of something: *he hesitated for **a fraction of** a second | her eyes widened a fraction.* See note at **FRAGMENT.** ■ a dissenting group within a larger one. ■ each of the portions into which a mixture may be separated by a process in which the individual components behave differently according to their physical properties. **2** (usu. **the Fraction**) (in the Christian Church) the breaking of the Eucharistic bread. ▷late Middle English: via Old French from ecclesiastical Latin *fractio(n-)* 'breaking (bread),' from Latin *frangere* 'to break.'

frac·tion·al /ˈfrakSHənl/ ▸*adj.* of, relating to, or expressed as a numerical value that is not a whole number, esp. a fraction less than one. ■ small or tiny in amount: *there was a fractional hesitation before he said yes.* ■ *Chemistry* relating to or denoting the separation of components of a mixture by making use of their differing physical properties: *fractional crystallization.* **—frac·tion·al·ly** *adv.*

frac·tion·al dis·til·la·tion ▸*n. Chemistry* separation of a liquid mixture into fractions differing in boiling point (and hence chemical composition) by means of distillation, typically using a fractionating column.

frac·tion·al·ize /ˈfrakSHənl,īz/ ▸*v.* [*trans.*] [usu. as *adj.*] (**fractionalized**) divide (someone or something) into separate groups or parts: *fractionalized consumer markets.* **—frac·tion·al·i·za·tion** /,frakSHənl-iˈzāSHən/ *n.*

frac·tion·ate /ˈfrakSHə,nāt/ ▸*v.* [*trans.*] *chiefly technical* divide into fractions or components. ■ separate (a mixture) by fractional distillation. **—frac·tion·a·tion** /,frakSHəˈnāSHən/ *n.*

frac·tion·at·ing col·umn ▸*n. Chemistry* a tall, horizontally subdivided or packed container for fractional distillation in which vapor passes upward and condensing liquid flows downward. The vapor becomes progressively enriched in more volatile components as it ascends, and the less volatile components become concentrated in the descending liquid, which can be drawn off.

frac·tious /ˈfrakSHəs/ ▸*adj.* easily irritated; bad-tempered: *they fight and squabble like fractious children.* ■ (of an organization) difficult to control; unruly: *the fractious coalition of Social Democrats.* ▷late 17th cent.: from **FRACTION,** probably on the pattern of the pair *faction, factious.* **—frac·tious·ly** *adv.* **—frac·tious·ness** *n.*

frac·ture /ˈfrakCHər/ ▸*n.* **1** the cracking or breaking of a hard object or material: *bone density testing can predict the risk for fracture.* ■ a crack or break in a hard object or material, typically a bone or a body of rock: *a fracture of the left leg.* ■ the physical appearance of a freshly broken rock or mineral, esp. as regards the shape of the surface formed. **2** *Phonetics* the replacement of a simple vowel by a diphthong owing to the influence of a following sound, typically a consonant. ■ a diphthong substituted in this way.
▸*v.* break or cause to break: [*intrans.*] *the stone has fractured* | [*trans.*] *ancient magmas fractured by the forces of wind and ice.* ■ [*trans.*] sustain a fracture of (a bone): [as *adj.*] (**fractured**) *she suffered a fractured skull.* ■ *figurative* (with reference to an organization or other abstract thing) split or fragment so as to no longer function or exist: [*intrans.*] *the movement had fractured without his leadership.* ■ [as *adj.*] (**fractured**) (of speech or a language) broken. ▷late Middle English: from

French, or from Latin *fractura*, from *frangere* 'to break.'

frae /frā/ ▸*prep. Scottish* from: *you better collect the tab frae the office.*

frag /frag/ *military slang* ▸*n.* a hand grenade.

▸*v.* (**fragged, frag·ging**) [*trans.*] deliberately kill (an unpopular senior officer), typically with a hand grenade. ▷late 20th cent.: from *fragmentation grenade.*

frag·ile /ˈfrajəl; -ˌjīl/ ▸*adj.* (of an object) easily broken or damaged. ■ flimsy or insubstantial; easily destroyed: *you have a fragile grip on reality.* ■ (of a person) not strong or sturdy; delicate and vulnerable. ▷late 15th cent. (in the sense 'morally weak'): from Latin *fragilis*, from *frangere* 'to break.' The sense 'liable to break' dates from the mid 16th cent. **—frag·ile·ly** /ˈfrajə(l)lē/ *adv.* **—fra·gil·i·ty** /frəˈjilitē/ *n.*

frag·ile X syn·drome ▸*n. Medicine* an inherited condition characterized by an X chromosome that is abnormally susceptible to damage, esp. by folic acid deficiency. Affected individuals tend to be mentally handicapped.

frag·ment ▸*n.* /ˈfragmənt/ a small part broken or separated off something: *small* ***fragments of*** *pottery, glass, and tiles.* ■ an isolated or incomplete part of something: *Nathan remembered fragments of that conversation.*

▸*v.* /ˈfragˌment/ break or cause to break into fragments: [*intrans.*] *his followers* ***fragmented into*** *sects.* ▷late Middle English: from French, or from Latin *fragmentum*, from *frangere* 'to break.' **—frag·men·tal** /fragˈmentl/ *adj.* (*chiefly Geology*).

THE RIGHT WORD **fraction, fragment, part, piece, portion, section, segment**

The whole is equal to the sum of its **parts**—*part* being a general term for any of the components of a whole. But how did the whole come apart?

Fragment suggests that breakage has occurred (*fragments of pottery*) and often refers to a brittle substance such as glass or pottery.

Segment suggests that the whole has been separated along natural or pre-existing lines of division (*a segment of an orange*), and **section** suggests a substantial and clearly separate *part* that fits closely with other parts to form the whole (*a section of a bookcase*).

Fraction usually suggests a less substantial but still clearly delineated *part*(*a fraction of her income*), and a **portion** is a *part* that has been allotted or assigned to someone (*her portion of the program*).

Finally, the frequently used **piece** is any *part* that is separate from the whole.

frag·men·tar·y /ˈfragmənˌterē/ ▸*adj.* consisting of small parts that are disconnected or incomplete: *excavations have revealed fragmentary remains of masonry.* **—frag·men·tar·i·ly** /ˌfragmənˈterəlē/ *adv.*

frag·men·ta·tion /ˌfragmənˈtāsʜən/ ▸*n.* the process or state of breaking or being broken into small or separate parts: *the* ***fragmentation*** *of society* ***into*** *a collection of interest groups.* ■ *Computing* the storing of a file in separate areas of memory scattered throughout a hard disk.

frag·men·ta·tion bomb ▸*n.* a bomb designed to break into small fragments as it explodes.

Fra·go·nard /ˌfragəˈnär/, Jean-Honoré (1732–1806), French painter in the rococo style. He is known for landscapes and for erotic canvases such as *The Progress of Love* (1771).

fra·grance /ˈfrāgrəns/ ▸*n.* a pleasant, sweet smell: *the fragrance of fresh-ground coffee | the bushes fill the air with fragrance.* See note at **SMELL**. ■ a perfume or aftershave. ▷mid 17th cent.: from French, or from Latin *fragrantia*, from *fragrare* 'smell sweet.' **—fra·granced** /ˈfrāgrənst/ *adj.*

fra·gran·cy /ˈfrāgrənsē/ ▸*n.* (*pl.* **-cies**) *dated* fragrance.

fra·grant /ˈfrāgrənt/ ▸*adj.* having a pleasant or sweet smell. ▷late Middle English: from French, or from Latin *fragrant-* 'smelling sweet,' from the verb *fragrare.* **—fra·grant·ly** *adv.*

'fraid /frād/ ▸*v. informal* nonstandard contraction of "afraid" or "I'm afraid," expressing regret: *'fraid not, doll.*

fraid·y cat /ˈfrādē ˌkat/ ▸*n.* a child's term for a timid or fearful person, often used as a taunt when addressed to another child.

frail /frāl/ ▸*adj.* (of a person) weak and delicate: *a frail voice | she looked frail and vulnerable.* See note at **WEAK**. ■ easily damaged or broken; fragile or insubstantial: *the balcony is frail | the frail Russian economy.* ■ weak in character or morals. ▷Middle English: from Old French *fraile*, from Latin *fragilis* (see **FRAGILE**). **—frail·ly** /ˈfrā(l)lē/ *adv.* **—frail·ness** *n.*

frail·ty /ˈfrāltē/ ▸*n.* (*pl.* **-ties**) the condition of being weak and delicate: *the increasing frailty of old age.* ■ weakness in character or morals: *all drama begins with human frailty | you're too self-righteous to see your own frailties.* ▷Middle English (in the sense 'weakness in morals'): from Old French *frailete*, from Latin *fragilitas*, from *fragilis* (see **FRAGILE**).

fraise[1] /frāz/ ▸*n.* (*pl.* same) (in cooking) a strawberry. ▷French, from Latin *fraga* 'wild strawberries.'

fraise[2] ▸*n.* **1** a fortification with sharpened stakes projecting outward. **2** a decorative ruff worn at the neck, esp. in Elizabethan era fashion.

Frak·tur /frākˈto͝or/ ▸*n.* a German style of black-letter type. ▷late 19th cent.: German, from Latin *fractura* 'fracture' (because of its angularity).

fram·be·sia /framˈbēzʜ(ē)ə/ ▸*n.* another term for **YAWS**. ▷early 19th cent.: modern Latin, from French *framboise* 'raspberry,' so named because of the red swellings caused by the disease, likened to raspberries.

fram·boise /fränˈbwäz/ ▸*n.* (in cooking) a raspberry. ▷late 16th cent.: French, 'raspberry,' from a conflation of Latin *fraga ambrosia* 'ambrosial strawberry.'

frame /frām/ ▸*n.* **1** a rigid structure that surrounds or encloses something such as a door or window. ■ (**frames**) a metal or plastic structure holding the lenses of a pair of glasses. ■ a case or border enclosing a mirror or picture. ■ the rigid supporting structure of an object such as a vehicle, building, or piece of furniture. ■ a person's body with reference to its size or build: *a shiver shook her slim frame.* ■ a boxlike structure of glass or plastic in which seeds or young plants are grown. ■ [in *sing.*] *archaic or poetic/literary* the universe, or part of it, regarded as an embracing structure. ■ [in *sing.*] *archaic or poetic/literary* the structure, constitution, or nature of someone or something: *we have in our inward frame various affections.* **2** [usu. in *sing.*] a basic structure that underlies or supports a system, concept, or text: *the establishment of conditions provides a frame for interpretation.* ■ *technical* short for **FRAME OF REFERENCE**: *the Earth's motion relative to the frame of the distant galaxies.* ■ the genre or form of a literary text determining its expected style and content: *my poems look as though they have a classical frame.* ■ [often as *adj.*] an enclosing section of narrative, esp. one which foregrounds or comments on the primary narrative of a text: *a frame narrator reports the narrative spoken by an inner narrator.* **3** *Linguistics* a structural environment within which a class of words or other linguistic units can be correctly used. For example *I —— him* is a frame for a large class of transitive verbs. **4** a single complete picture in a series forming a movie, television, or video film. ■ a single picture in a comic strip. ■ *Computing* a graphic panel in a display window, especially in an Internet browser, that encloses a self-contained section of data and permits multiple independent document viewing. **5** another term for **RACK**[1] (sense 4). ■ a round of play in bowling. ■ *informal* an inning in a baseball game: *he closed out the game by pitching two hitless frames.* **6** short for **FRAME-UP**.

▸*v.* [*trans.*] **1** place (a picture or photograph) in a frame: *he had the photo framed.* ■ surround so as to create a sharp or attractive image: *a short, strong style cut to frame the face.* **2** erect the framework of a building. **3** create or formulate (a concept, plan, or system): *the staff have proved invaluable in framing the proposals.* ■ form or articulate (words): *he walked out before she could frame a reply.* ■ *archaic* make or construct (something) by fitting parts together or in accordance with a plan: *what immortal hand or eye could frame thy fearful symmetry?* **4** *informal* produce false evidence against (an innocent person) so that they appear guilty: *he claims he was framed.* ▷Old English *framian* 'be useful,' of Germanic origin and related to **FROM**. The general sense in Middle English, 'make ready for use,' probably led to sense 2 of the verb; it also gave rise to the specific meaning 'prepare timber for use in building,' later 'make the wooden parts of a building,' essentially the framework, hence the noun sense 'structure' (late Middle English). **—fram·a·ble** /-məbəl/ *adj.* **—frame·less** *adj.* **—fram·er** *n.*

▸***PHRASE*** □ **frame of mind** a particular mood that influences one's attitude or behavior.

framed /frāmd/ ▸*adj.* **1** (of a picture or similar) held in a frame: *a framed photograph of her father.* **2** [in *combination*] (of a building) having a frame of a specified material: *a traditional* ***oak-framed*** *house.*

frame house ▸*n.* a house constructed from a wooden skeleton, typically covered with sheathing.

frame of ref·er·ence ▸*n.* a set of criteria or stated values in relation to which measurements or judgments can be made: *the observer interprets what he sees in terms of his own cultural frame of reference.* ■ (also **reference frame**) a system of geometric axes in relation to which measurements of size, position, or motion can be made.

frame saw ▸*n.* a saw with a thin blade kept rigid by being stretched in a frame.

frame-up ▸*n.* [in *sing.*] *informal* a conspiracy to falsely incriminate someone.

frame·work /ˈfrāmˌwərk/ ▸*n.* an essential supporting structure of a building, vehicle, or object: *a conservatory in a delicate framework of iron.* ■ a basic structure underlying a system, concept, or text: *the theoretical framework of political sociology.*

fram·ing /ˈfrāmiɴɢ/ ▸*n.* the action of framing something. ■ frames collectively. ■ framework. ■ the (usually wooden) skeleton of a building.

Fra·ming·ham /ˈfrāmiɴɢˌham/ an industrial and commercial town in eastern Massachusetts; pop. 66,910.

franc /fraɴɢk/ ▸*n.* the basic monetary unit of Switzerland and several other countries (including France, Belgium, and Luxembourg until the introduction of the euro), equal to 100 centimes. ▷from Old French, from Latin *Francorum Rex* 'king of the Franks,' the legend on gold coins struck in the 14th cent. in the reign of Jean le Bon.

Fran·ca /ˈfräɴɢkə/ an industrial and commercial city in southern Brazil, in São Paulo state; pop. 267,000.

France[1] /frans; fräns/ a country in western Europe, on the Atlantic Ocean; pop. 60,424,000; capital, Paris; official language, French.

France became a major power under the Valois and Bourbon dynasties in the 16th–18th centuries and briefly dominated Europe under Napoleon after the overthrow of the monarchy in the French Revolution 1789. Defeated in the Franco-Prussian War 1870–71, the country also suffered much destruction and loss of life in World War I, and during World War II was occupied by the Germans. France was a founding member of the EEC (now the EU) in 1957.

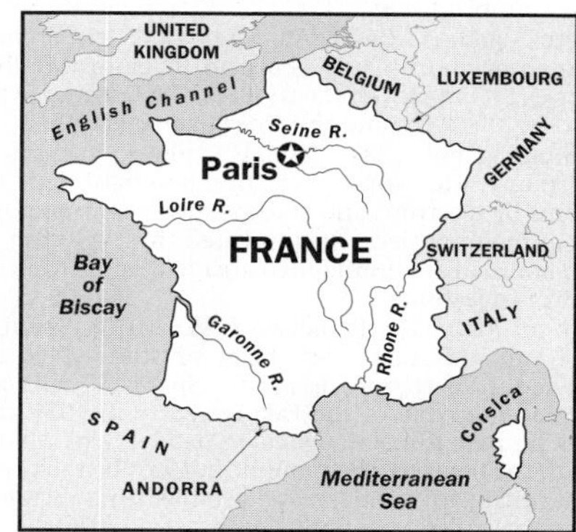

France[2] /frans/, Anatole (1844–1924), French writer; pseudonym of *Jacques-Anatole-François Thibault.* Works include *Le Crime de Sylvestre Bonnard* (1881), *L'Ile des pingouins* (1908), and *Les Dieux ont soif* (1912). Nobel Prize for Literature (1921).

fran·chise /ˈfranˌcʜīz/ ▸*n.* **1** an authorization granted by a government or company to an individual or group enabling them to carry out specified commercial activities, e.g., providing a broadcasting service or acting as an agent for a company's products. ■ a business or service given such authorization to operate. ■ an authorization given by a league to own a sports team. ■ *informal* a professional sports team. ■ (also **franchise player**) *informal* a star player in a team. **2** (usu. **the franchise**) the right to vote. ■ the rights of citizenship.

▸*v.* [*trans.*] grant a franchise to (an individual or group). ■ grant a franchise for the sale of (goods) or the operation of (a service): *all the catering was* ***franchised out.*** ▷Middle English (denoting a grant of legal immunity): from Old French, based on *franc,* *franche* 'free' (see **FRANK**1). Sense 2 dates from the late 18th cent. and sense 1 from the 20th cent. **—fran·chi·see** /ˌfranˌCHī'zē/ *n.* **—fran·chis·er** (also **fran·chi·sor** /ˌfranCHə'zôr/) *n.*

Fran·cis1 /'fransis/, Dick (1920–), English jockey and writer; full name *Richard Stanley Francis.* He was a champion jockey who, after his retirement in 1957, began to write thrillers, mostly set in the world of horse racing.

Fran·cis2, Lydia Marie, see **CHILD**.

Fran·cis I (1494–1547), king of France 1515–47. Much of his reign 1521–44 was spent at war with Charles V of Spain. A supporter of the arts, he commissioned the building of the Louvre.

Fran·cis·can /fran'siskən/ ▸*n.* a friar, sister, or lay member of a Christian religious order founded in 1209 by St. Francis of Assisi or based on its rule, and noted for its preachers and missionaries.

Divergences of practice led to the separation of the Friars Minor of the Observance (the Observants) and the Friars Minor Conventual (the Conventuals) in 1517, and to the foundation of the stricter Friars Minor Capuchin (the Capuchins) in 1529. The order of Franciscan nuns was founded by St. Clare (*c.*1212) under the direction of St. Francis; they are known as 'Poor Clares.'

▸*adj.* of, relating to, or denoting St. Francis or the Franciscans. ▷from French *franciscain,* from modern Latin *Franciscanus,* from *Franciscus* 'Francis.'

Fran·cis of As·si·si, St. (*c.*1181–1226), Italian monk; founder of the Franciscan order 1209; born *Giovanni di Bernardone.* He drew up the original rule, based on complete poverty, of the Franciscan order. He is the patron saint of animals. Feast day, October 4.

Fran·cis of Sales, St. /säl/ (1567–1622), French bishop. A leader of the Counter-Reformation, he was bishop of Geneva 1602–22. The Salesian order (founded in 1859) is named after him. Feast day, January 24.

Fran·cis Xa·vi·er, St., see **XAVIER, ST. FRANCIS**.

fran·ci·um /'fransēəm/ ▸*n.* the chemical element of atomic number 87, a radioactive member of the alkali metal group. Francium occurs naturally as a decay product in uranium and thorium ores. (Symbol: **Fr**) ▷1940s: from **FRANCE**1 (the discoverer's native country) + **-IUM**.

Franck1 /fräNGk/, César (Auguste) (1822–90), French composer and organist; born in Belgium. Notable works: *Symphonic Variations* (1885), the D minor Symphony (1886–88), and the *String Quartet* (1889).

Franck2, James (1882–1964), U.S. physicist; born in Germany. He worked on the bombardment of atoms by electrons and became involved in the U.S. atom bomb project. He advocated the explosion of the bomb in an uninhabited area to demonstrate its power to Japan.

Fran·co /'fraNGkō/, Francisco (1892–1975), Spanish general and statesman; head of state 1939–75. Leader of the Nationalists in the Spanish Civil War, he became head of the Falange Party in 1937 and proclaimed himself *Caudillo* ("leader") of Spain. With the defeat of the republic in 1939, he took control of the government and established a dictatorship that ruled Spain until his death.

Francisco Franco

Franco- (also **franco-**) ▸*comb. form* French; French and . . . : *francophone* | *Franco-German.* ■ relating to France. ▷from medieval Latin *Francus* 'Frank.'

fran·co·lin /'fraNGkəlin/ ▸*n.* a large game bird resembling a partridge, with bare skin on the head or neck, found in Africa and South Asia. • Genus *Francolinus,* family Phasianidae: many species. ▷mid 17th cent.: from French, from Italian *francolino,* of unknown origin.

Fran·co·ni·a /fraNG'kōnēə/ a medieval duchy in southern Germany, inhabited by the Franks.

Fran·co·ni·an /fran'kōnēən/ ▸*adj.* of or relating to Franconia or its inhabitants.

▸*n.* **1** a native or inhabitant of Franconia. **2** a group of medieval West Germanic dialects, combining features of Low and High German. ■ the group of modern German dialects of Franconia.

Fran·co·nia Notch /fraNG'kōnēə/ a valley in the White Mountains of northern New Hampshire, noted for its scenery, including a rock formation called the Old Man of the Mountains.

Fran·co·phile /'fraNGkəˌfīl/ ▸*n.* a person who is fond of or greatly admires France or the French.

fran·co·phone /'fraNGkəˌfōn/ (also **Fran·co·phone**) ▸*adj.* French-speaking: *a summit of francophone countries.*

▸*n.* a person who speaks French. ▷early 20th cent.: from **FRANCO-** 'French' + Greek *phōnē* 'voice.'

Fran·co-Prus·sian War /'fraNGkō/ the war of 1870–71 between France (under Napoleon III) and Prussia, in which Prussian troops advanced into France and decisively defeated the French at Sedan. The defeat marked the end of the French Second Empire. For Prussia, the proclamation of the new German Empire at Versailles was the climax of Bismarck's ambitions to unite Germany.

fran·gi·ble /'franjəbəl/ ▸*adj. formal* fragile; brittle. ▷late Middle English: from Old French, or from medieval Latin *frangibilis,* from Latin *frangere* 'to break.'

fran·gi·pane /'franjəˌpān; ˌfränji'pän/ ▸ **1** *n.* an almond-flavored cream or paste. ■ a pastry filled with this. **2** variant spelling of **FRANGIPANI**. ▷late 17th cent.: from French, named after the Marquis Muzio *Frangipani* (see **FRANGIPANI**). The term originally denoted the frangipani shrub or tree, the perfume of which is said to have been used to flavor the almond cream.

fran·gi·pan·i /ˌfranjə'panē; -'pänē/ (also **fran·gi·pane** /'franjəˌpān/) ▸*n.* (*pl.* same or **-pan·is**) a tropical American tree or shrub with clusters of fragrant white, pink, or yellow flowers. • Genus *Plumeria,* family Apocynaceae: several species, in particular *P. rubra.* ■ perfume obtained from this plant. ▷mid 19th cent.: named after the Marquis Muzio *Frangipani,* a 16th-cent. Italian nobleman who invented a perfume for scenting gloves.

fran·glais /ˌfrän'glā/ (also **Fran·glaise** /-'gläz/) ▸*n.* a form of French using many words and idioms borrowed from English. ▷1960s: coined in French, from a blend of *français* 'French' and *anglais* 'English.'

Frank1 /fraNGk/, Anne (1929–45), German Jewish girl noted for her diary (*The Diary of a Young Girl,* 1953) that records the experiences of her family, who hid from the Nazis for two years in occupied Amsterdam. They were eventually betrayed and sent to concentration camps; Anne died in the concentration camp at Belsen.

Frank2 ▸*n.* a member of a Germanic people that conquered Gaul in the 6th century and controlled much of western Europe for several centuries afterward. ■ (in the eastern Mediterranean region) a person of western European nationality or descent. ▷Old English *Franca,* of Germanic origin; perhaps from the name of a weapon and related to Old English *franca* 'javelin' (compare with **SAXON**); reinforced in Middle English by medieval Latin *Francus* and Old French *Franc,* of the same origin and related to **FRENCH**.

frank1 /fraNGk/ ▸*adj.* open, honest, and direct in speech or writing, esp. when dealing with unpalatable matters: *a long and frank discussion* | *to be perfectly frank, I don't know.* ■ open, sincere, or undisguised in manner or appearance: *Katherine saw her look at Sam with frank admiration.* ■ *Medicine* unmistakable; obvious: *frank ulceration.* ▷Middle English (in the sense 'free'): from Old French *franc,* from medieval Latin *francus* 'free,' from *Francus* (see **FRANK**2 : only Franks had full freedom in Frankish Gaul). Another Middle English sense was 'generous,' which led to the current sense. **—frank·ness** *n.*

frank2 ▸*v.* [*trans.*] (often **be franked**) stamp an official mark on (a letter or parcel), esp. to indicate that postage has been paid or does not need to be paid. ■ *historical* sign (a letter or parcel) to ensure delivery free of charge. ■ *archaic* facilitate or pay the passage of (someone): *English will frank the traveler through most of North America.*

▸*n.* an official mark or signature on a letter or parcel, esp. to indicate that postage has been paid or does not need to be paid. [formerly as a superscribed signature of an eminent person entitled to send letters free of charge.] ▷early 18th cent.: from **FRANK**1, an early sense being 'free of obligation.' **—frank·er** *n.*

frank3 ▸*n.* short for **FRANKFURTER**.

Fran·ken·fish /'fraNGkənˌfiSH/ ▸*n. informal* **1** a genetically modified fish. **2** the northern snakehead, so dubbed for its voracious appetite and ability to survive adverse conditions. ▷from *Franken(stein)* and *fish.*

Frank·en·food /'fraNGkənˌfo͞od/ ▸*n. informal, derogatory* genetically modified food: *a cornucopia of pesticide-laden monocrops and lab-engineered Frankenfoods.* ▷1990s: from *Franken(stein)* + *food.*

Frank·en·stein /'fraNGkənˌstīn/ a character in the novel *Frankenstein, or the Modern Prometheus* (1818) by Mary Shelley. Baron Frankenstein is a scientist who creates and brings to life a manlike monster that eventually turns on him and destroys him; Frankenstein is not the name of the monster itself, as is often assumed. ■ (also **Frankenstein's monster**) [as *n.*] a thing that becomes terrifying or destructive to its maker.

Frank·fort /'fraNGkfərt/ the capital of Kentucky, in the northern part of the state; pop. 25,968.

Frank·furt /'fraNGkfərt; 'fräNGkˌfo͝ort/ a commercial city in western Germany, in the state of Hesse; pop. 654,000. Full name **FRANKFURT AM MAIN**.

Frank·fur·ter /'fraNGkˌfərtər/, Felix (1882–1965), U.S. Supreme Court associate justice 1939–62; born in Austria. He was a founder of the American Civil Liberties Union in 1920 and was awarded the Presidential Medal of Freedom in 1963.

frank·furt·er /'fraNGkfərtər; -ˌfərtər/ ▸*n.* a seasoned smoked sausage typically made of beef and pork. ▷from German *Frankfurter Wurst* 'Frankfurt sausage.'

Frank·furt School a school of philosophy of the 1920s whose adherents were involved in a reappraisal of Marxism, particularly in terms of the cultural and aesthetic dimension of modern industrial society. Principal figures include Theodor Adorno, Max Horkheimer, and Herbert Marcuse.

frank·in·cense /'fraNGkənˌsens/ ▸*n.* an aromatic gum resin obtained from an African tree and burned as incense. Also called **OLIBANUM, GUM OLIBANUM**. • This resin is obtained from the tree *Boswellia sacra,* family Burseraceae, native to Somalia. ▷late Middle English: from Old French *franc encens,* literally 'high-quality incense,' from *franc* (see **FRANK**1) in an obsolete sense 'superior, of high quality' (which also existed in English) + *encens* 'incense.'

frank·ing /'fraNGkiNG/ ▸*n.* the action of franking a letter or parcel: [as *adj.*] *a franking machine.* ■ an official mark or signature on a letter or parcel to indicate that postage has been paid or does not need to be paid.

Frank·ish /'fraNGkiSH/ ▸*adj.* of or relating to the ancient Franks or their language.

▸*n.* the West Germanic language of the ancient Franks.

Frank·lin1 /'fraNGklin/, Aretha (1942–), U.S. soul and gospel singer. She became a hit with the album *I Never Loved a Man (the Way I Love You)* (1967) and went on to record more than 30 albums, including the live gospel set *Amazing Grace* (1972) and *A Rose Is Still a Rose* (1998).

Frank·lin2, Benjamin (1706–90), American statesman, inventor, and scientist. He was the only individual to sign all three principal documents of the new nation: the Declaration of Independence, the treaty with Great Britain that ended the American Revolution, and the U.S. Constitution. His main scientific achievements were the formulation of a

Benjamin Franklin

theory of electricity, which introduced positive and negative electricity, and a demonstration of the electrical nature of lightning, which led to the invention of the lightning conductor.

frank·lin /ˈfraNGklən/ ▸*n.* a landowner of free but not noble birth in the 14th and 15th centuries in England. ▷Middle English: from Anglo-Latin *francalanus*, from *francalis* 'held without dues,' from *francus* 'free' (see FRANK[1]).

Frank·lin stove ▸*n.* a cast-iron stove for heating a room, resembling an open fireplace in shape. ▷late 18th cent.: named after Benjamin *Franklin*.

Franklin stove

frank·ly /ˈfraNGklē/ ▸*adv.* in an open, honest, and direct manner: *she talks very frankly about herself.* ■ [*sentence adverb*] used to emphasize the truth of a statement, however unpalatable or shocking this may be: *frankly, I was pleased to leave.*

USAGE See usage at HOPEFULLY.

fran·tic /ˈfrantik/ ▸*adj.* wild or distraught with fear, anxiety, or other emotion: *she was* ***frantic with*** *worry.* ■ conducted in a hurried, excited, and chaotic way, typically because of the need to act quickly: *frantic attempts to resuscitate the girl.* ▷late Middle English *frentik* 'insane, violently mad,' from Old French *frenetique* (see FRENETIC). **—fran·ti·cal·ly** /-(ə)lē/ *adv.* **—fran·tic·ness** *n.*

Franz Jo·sef /ˌfränz ˈjōzəf; ˌfränts ˈyōzəf/ (1830–1916), emperor of Austria 1848–1916 and king of Hungary 1867–1916. He gave Hungary equal status with Austria in 1867. His annexation of Bosnia–Herzegovina in 1908 contributed to European political tensions, and the assassination in Sarajevo of his heir apparent, Archduke Franz Ferdinand, precipitated World War I.

Franz Jo·sef Land /land; länt/ a group of islands in the Arctic Ocean, discovered in 1873 by an Austrian expedition and annexed by the Soviet Union in 1928.

frap /frap/ ▸*v.* (**frapped, frap·ping**) [*trans.*] *Nautical* bind (something) tightly. ▷Middle English (in the sense 'strike, beat,' now only dialect): from Old French *fraper* 'to bind, strike,' of unknown origin. The current sense dates from the mid 16th cent.

frap·pé[1] /fraˈpā/ ▸*adj.* [*postpositive*] (of a drink) iced or chilled: *a crème de menthe frappé.*
▸*n.* a drink served with ice or frozen to a slushy consistency. ■ (usu. **frappe** /frap/) (chiefly in New England) a milk shake, esp. one made with ice cream. ▷mid 19th cent.: French, literally 'iced.'

frap·pé[2] ▸*adj.* [*postpositive*] *Ballet* (of a position) involving a beating action of the toe of one foot against the ankle of the supporting leg: *a battement frappé.* ▷mid 19th cent.: French, literally 'struck.'

Fras·cat·i /fräsˈkätē/ ▸*n.* a wine, typically white, produced in the region of Frascati, Italy.

Fra·ser /ˈfrāzər; ˈfrāZHər/ a river in British Columbia, Canada. It rises in the Rocky Mountains and flows in a wide curve for 850 miles (1,360 km) into the Strait of Georgia, just south of Vancouver.

Fras·er fir ▸*n.* a North American fir tree, occurring primarily in the mountains of Virginia, Tennessee, and North Carolina. • *Abies fraseri*, family Pinaceae.

frass /fras/ ▸*n.* fine powdery refuse or fragile perforated wood produced by the activity of boring insects. ■ the excrement of insect larvae. ▷mid 19th cent.: from German *Frass*, from *fressen* 'devour.'

frat /frat/ ▸*n.* [usu. as *adj.*] *informal* a students' fraternity: *a frat party.* ▷late 19th cent.: abbreviation.

fra·ter /ˈfrātər/ ▸*n. historical* the dining room or refectory of a monastery. ▷Middle English: from Old French *fraitur*, shortening of *refreitor*, from late Latin *refectorium* 'refectory.'

fra·ter·nal /frəˈtərnl/ ▸*adj.* **1** of or like a brother or brothers: *his lack of fraternal feeling shocked me.* ■ of or denoting an organization or order for people, esp. men, that have common interests or beliefs. **2** (of twins) developed from separate ova and therefore genetically distinct and not necessarily of the same sex or more similar than other siblings. Compare with IDENTICAL (sense 1). ▷late Middle English: from medieval Latin *fraternalis*, from Latin *fraternus*, from *frater* 'brother.' **—fra·ter·nal·ism** /-ˌizəm/ *n.* **—fra·ter·nal·ly** *adv.*

fra·ter·ni·ty /frəˈtərnətē/ ▸*n.* (*pl.* **-ties**) **1** [treated as *sing.* or *pl.*] a group of people sharing a common profession or interests: *members of the hunting fraternity.* ■ a male students' society in a university or college. ■ a religious or masonic society or guild. **2** the state or feeling of friendship and mutual support within a group: *the ideals of liberty, equality, and fraternity.* ▷Middle English: from Old French *fraternite*, from Latin *fraternitas*, from *fraternus* (see FRATERNAL).

frat·er·nize /ˈfratərˌnīz/ ▸*v.* [*intrans.*] associate or form a friendship with someone, esp. when one is not supposed to: *she ignored Elisabeth's warning glare against* ***fraternizing with*** *the enemy.* ▷early 17th cent.: from French *fraterniser*, from medieval Latin *fraternizare*, from Latin *fraternus* 'brotherly' (see FRATERNAL). **—frat·er·ni·za·tion** /ˌfratərniˈzāSHən/ *n.*

frat·ri·cid·al /ˌfratrəˈsīdl/ ▸*adj.* relating to or denoting conflict within a single family or organization: *the fratricidal strife within the party.*

frat·ri·cide /ˈfratrəˌsīd/ ▸*n.* the killing of one's brother or sister. ■ a person who kills their brother or sister. ■ the accidental killing of one's own forces in war. ▷late 15th cent. (denoting a person who kills their brother or sister, derived from Latin *fratricida*): the primary current sense comes via French from late Latin *fratricidium*, from *frater* 'brother' + *-cidium* (see -CIDE).

Frau /frou/ ▸*n.* (*pl.* **Frau·en** /ˈfrou-ən/) a title or form of address for a married or widowed German-speaking woman: *Frau Nordern.* ▷early 19th cent.: German, literally 'wife.'

fraud /frôd/ ▸*n.* wrongful or criminal deception intended to result in financial or personal gain: *he was convicted of fraud | prosecutions for social security frauds.* ■ a person or thing intended to deceive others, typically by unjustifiably claiming or being credited with accomplishments or qualities: *mediums exposed as tricksters and frauds.* ▷Middle English: from Old French *fraude*, from Latin *fraus*, *fraud-* 'deceit, injury.' **—fraud·ster** *n.*

fraud·u·lent /ˈfrôjələnt/ ▸*adj.* obtained, done by, or involving deception, esp. criminal deception: *the fraudulent copying of American software.* ■ unjustifiably claiming or being credited with particular accomplishments or qualities: *he unmasked fraudulent psychics.* ▷late Middle English: from Old French, or from Latin *fraudulentus*, from *fraus*, *fraud-* 'deceit, injury.' **—fraud·u·lence** *n.* **—fraud·u·lent·ly** *adv.*

fraught /frôt/ ▸*adj.* **1** [*predic.*] (**fraught with**) (of a situation or course of action) filled with or destined to result in (something undesirable): *marketing any new product is fraught with danger.* **2** causing or affected by great anxiety or stress: *there was a fraught silence | she sounded a bit fraught.* ▷late Middle English, 'laden, provided, equipped,' past participle of obsolete *fraught* 'load with cargo,' from Middle Dutch *vrachten*, from *vracht* 'ship's cargo.' Compare with FREIGHT.

Fräu·lein /ˈfroiˌlīn/ ▸*n.* a title or form of address for an unmarried German-speaking woman, esp. a young woman: *Fräulein Winkelmann.* ▷German, diminutive of FRAU.

Fraun·ho·fer /ˈfrounˌhōfər/, Joseph von (1787–1826), German optician; a pioneer in spectroscopy. He observed and mapped the dark lines in the solar spectrum (**Fraunhofer lines**) that result from the absorption of particular frequencies of light by elements present in the outer layers of the sun.

frax·i·nel·la /ˌfraksəˈnelə/ ▸*n.* another term for GAS PLANT. ▷mid 17th cent.: modern Latin (former specific epithet), diminutive of Latin *fraxinus* 'ash tree' (because of its leaves, thought to resemble those of the ash).

fray[1] /frā/ ▸*v.* [*intrans.*] (of a fabric, rope, or cord) unravel or become worn at the edge, typically through constant rubbing: *cheap fabric soon frays | [as adj.]* (**frayed**) *the frayed collar of her old coat.* ■ *figurative* (of a person's nerves or temper) show the effects of strain. ■ [*trans.*] (of a male deer) rub (a bush or small tree) with the head in order to remove the velvet from newly formed antlers, or to mark territory during the rut. ▷late Middle English: from Old French *freiier*, from Latin *fricare* 'to rub.'

fray[2] ▸*n.* (**the fray**) a situation of intense activity, typically one incorporating an element of aggression or competition: *nineteen companies intend to bid for the contract, with three more expected to* ***enter the fray.*** ■ a battle or fight. ▷late Middle English: from archaic *fray* 'to quarrel,' from *affray* 'startle,' from Anglo-Norman French *afrayer* (see AFFRAY).

Fra·zier /ˈfrāZHər/, Joe (1944–), U.S. heavyweight boxing champion; full name *Joseph Frazier.* He first won the world title in 1968, lost it to George Foreman in 1973, and subsequently lost to Muhammad Ali twice before retiring in 1976.

fra·zil /ˈfrazəl; frəˈzil/ (also **frazil ice**) ▸*n.* soft or amorphous ice formed by the accumulation of ice crystals in water that is too turbulent to freeze solid. ▷late 19th cent.: from Canadian French *frasil* 'snow floating in the water,' from French *fraisil* 'cinders.'

fraz·zle /ˈfrazəl/ *informal* ▸*v.* [*trans.*] [usu. as *adj.*] (**frazzled**) cause to feel completely exhausted; wear out: *a frazzled parent.* ■ fray: *change the skirt if it gets frazzled | figurative it's enough to frazzle the nerves.*
▸*n.* (**a frazzle**) the state of being completely exhausted or worn out: *I'm tired,* ***worn to a frazzle.*** ▷early 19th cent. (originally dialect): perhaps a blend of FRAY[1] and obsolete *fazle* 'ravel out,' of Germanic origin.

FRB ▸*abbr.* ■ Federal Reserve Bank. ■ Federal Reserve Board.

FRCP ▸*abbr.* Fellow of the Royal College of Physicians.

FRCS ▸*abbr.* Fellow of the Royal College of Surgeons.

freak /frēk/ ▸*n.* **1** a very unusual and unexpected event or situation: *the teacher says the accident was a total freak | [as adj.] a freak storm.* ■ (also **freak of nature**) a person, animal, or plant with an unusual physical abnormality. ■ *informal* a person regarded as strange because of their unusual appearance or behavior. ■ [with *adj.*] *informal* a person who is obsessed with or unusually enthusiastic about a specified interest: *a fitness freak.* ■ [usu. with *adj.*] *informal* a person addicted to a drug of a particular kind: *the twins were cocaine freaks.* **2** *archaic* a sudden arbitrary change of mind; a whim: *follow this way or that, as the freak takes you.*
▸*v.* **1** [*intrans.*] *informal* react or behave in a wild and irrational way, typically because of the effects of extreme emotion, mental illness, or drugs: *I could have* ***freaked out*** *and started smashing the place up.* ■ [*trans.*] cause to act in such a way: *he freaks guest stars out on show day.* **2** [*trans.*] *archaic* fleck or streak randomly: *the white pink and the pansy freaked with jet.*

freak·ing /ˈfrēkən; -kiNG/ ▸*adj. informal* used as a euphemism for "fucking": *I'm going out of my freaking mind!*

freak·ish /ˈfrēkiSH/ ▸*adj.* bizarre or grotesque; abnormal: *freakish and mischievous elves.* ■ capricious or whimsical; unpredictable: *freakish weather.* **—freak·ish·ly** *adv.* **—freak·ish·ness** *n.*

freak-out ▸*n. informal* a wildly irrational reaction or spell of behavior.

freak show ▸*n.* a sideshow at a fair, featuring abnormally developed people or animals. ■ an unusual or grotesque event viewed for pleasure, esp. when in bad taste.

freak·y /ˈfrēkē/ ▸*adj.* (**freak·i·er, freak·i·est**) *informal* very odd, strange, or eccentric. **—freak·i·ly** /-kəlē/ *adv.* **—freak·i·ness** *n.*

freck·le /ˈfrekəl/ ▸*n.* a small patch of light brown color on the skin, often becoming more pronounced through exposure to the sun.
▸*v.* cover or become covered with freckles: [*intrans.*] *skin that freckles easily | [as adj.]* (**freckled**) *a freckled face.* ▷late Middle English: alteration of dialect *frecken*, from Old Norse *freknur* (plural). **—freck·ly** /ˈfrekl-ē; ˈfreklē/ *adj.*

freck·le-faced ▸*adj.* having freckles on the face (often used to suggest innocence or wholesomeness): *a freckle-faced schoolboy who never lost the merriment of his youth.*

Fred·die Mac /ˈfredē ˈmæk/ ▸*n. informal Finance* the Federal Home Loan Mortgage Corporation, a corporation that buys mortgages from lenders such as commercial banks, mortgage bankers, savings institutions, and credit unions.

Fred·er·ick /ˈfred(ə)rik/ a city in northern Maryland; pop. 52,767.

Pronunciation Key ə *ago*; ər *over*; ˈə or ˌə *up*; ˈər or ˌər *fur*; a *hat*; ā *rate*; ä *car*; CH *chew*; e *let*; ē *see*; e(ə)r *air*; i *fit*; ī *by*; i(ə)r *ear*; NG *sing*; ō *go*; ô *for*; oi *boy*; o͝o *good*; o͞o *goo*; ou *out*; SH *she*; TH *thin*; TH *then*; (h)w *why*; ZH *vision*

Fred·er·ick I /ˈfred(ə)rik/ (c.1123–90), king of Germany and Holy Roman Emperor 1152–90; known as **Frederick Barbarossa** ("Redbeard"). He made a sustained effort to subdue Italy and the papacy, but was eventually defeated at the battle of Legnano in 1176.

Fred·er·ick II (1712–86), king of Prussia 1740–86; known as **Frederick the Great**. His campaigns in the War of the Austrian Succession 1740–48 and the Seven Years War 1756–63 succeeded in considerably strengthening Prussia's position; by the end of his reign he had doubled the area of his country.

Fred·er·icks·burg /ˈfred(ə)riks,bərg/ a historic commercial city in northeastern Virginia, on the Rappahannock River; pop. 19,027.

Fred·er·ick Wil·liam (1620–88), elector of Brandenburg 1640–88; known as **the Great Elector**. His program of reconstruction and reorganization following the Thirty Years War brought stability to his country and laid the foundation for the expansion of Prussian power in the 18th century.

Fred·er·ic·ton /ˈfredriktən/ the capital of New Brunswick, Canada; pop. 46,466. The city was founded in 1785 by colonists who left the U.S. after the American Revolution out of loyalty to the British crown. ▷named after *Frederick* Augustus (1763–1827), second son of the British king George III.

free /frē/ ▶*adj.* (**fre·er** /ˈfrēər/, **fre·est** /ˈfrēəst/) **1** not under the control or in the power of another; able to act or be done as one wishes: *I have no ambitions other than to have a happy life and be free | a free choice.* ■ (of a state or its citizens or institutions) subject neither to foreign domination nor to despotic government: *a free press.* ■ [often as *complement*] not or no longer confined or imprisoned: *the researchers set the birds free.* ■ *historical* not a slave. ■ [with *infinitive*] able or permitted to take a specified action: *you are free to leave.* ■ [in *names*] denoting an ethnic or political group actively opposing an occupying or invading force, in particular the groups that continued resisting the Germans in World War II after the fall of their countries. See also FREE FRENCH. **2** [often as *complement*] not physically restrained, obstructed, or fixed; unimpeded: *she lifted the cat free.* ■ *Physics* (of power or energy) disengaged or available. See also FREE ENERGY. ■ *Physics & Chemistry* not bound in an atom, a molecule, or a compound: *the atmosphere of that time contained virtually no free oxygen.* See also FREE RADICAL. ■ *Linguistics* (of a morpheme) able to occur in isolation. ■ *Linguistics* (of syntax) not constrained by word order. **3** not subject to or constrained by engagements or obligations: *she spent her free time shopping.* ■ (of a facility or piece of equipment) not occupied or in use: *the bathroom was free.* **4** [*predic.*] (**free of/from**) not subject to or affected by (a specified thing, typically an undesirable one): *membership is free of charge.* **5** given or available without charge: *free health care.* **6** using or expending something without restraint; lavish: *she was always **free with** her money.* ■ frank or unrestrained in speech, expression, or action: *he was free in his talk of revolution.* ■ *archaic* overfamiliar or forward in manner. **7** (of a literary style) not observing the strict laws of form. ■ (of a translation) conveying only the broad sense; not literal. **8** *Sailing* (of the wind) blowing from a favorable direction to the side or stern of a vessel.
▶*adv.* **1** without cost or payment: *ladies were admitted free.* **2** *Sailing* with the sheets eased.
▶*v.* (**frees, freed, free·ing**) [*trans.*] make free, in particular: ■ from captivity, confinement, or slavery: *they were **freed from** jail.* ■ from physical obstruction, restraint, or entanglement: *I had to tug hard and at last freed him.* ■ from restriction or excessive regulation: *his inheritance **freed** him **from** financial constraints.* ■ from something undesirable: ***free** your mind and body **of** excess tension.* ■ so as to become available for a particular purpose: *this will **free up** funds for development elsewhere.* ▷Old English *frēo* (adjective), *frēon* (verb), of Germanic origin; related to Dutch *vrij* and German *frei*, from an Indo-European root meaning 'to love,' shared by FRIEND. —**free·ness** *n.*
▶PHRASES □ **for free** *informal* without cost or payment: *these professionals were giving their time for free.* □ **free and easy** informal and relaxed. □ **free, gratis, and for nothing** *humorous* without charge. □ **a free hand** freedom to act at one's own discretion. □ **free on board** (abbr.: **f.o.b.**) including or assuming delivery without charge to the buyer's named destination. □ **(a) free rein** see REIN. □ **a free ride** a situation in which someone benefits without having to make a fair contribution: *people have been having a free ride, paying so little rent that there is no money for maintenance.* □ **the free world** the noncommunist countries of the world, as formerly opposed to the Soviet bloc. □ **it's a free country** said when asserting that a course of action is not illegal or forbidden, often in justification of it. □ **make free with** treat without ceremony or proper respect: *he'll have something to say about your making free with his belongings.*

USAGE Free means 'without charge,' and a *gift* is 'something given without charge.' The expression "free gift" is therefore a needless repetition.

-free ▶*comb. form* free of or from: *smoke-free | tax-free.* ▷from FREE.

free a·gent ▶*n.* a person who does not have any commitments that restrict their actions. ■ a sports player who is not bound by a contract and so is eligible to join any team.

free a·long·side ship (abbr.: **FAS**) ▶*adv.* without charge for delivery to the boarding area next to a ship, but with the understanding that the buyer is responsible for the item once it is so delivered.

free as·so·ci·a·tion ▶*n.* **1** *Psychology* the mental process by which one word or image may spontaneously suggest another without any apparent connection. ■ a psychoanalytic technique for investigation of the unconscious mind, in which a relaxed subject reports all passing thoughts without reservation. **2** the forming of a group, political alliance, or other organization without any constraint or external restriction: *it would violate their First Amendment rights of free association and free expression.* —**free-as·so·ci·ate** (usu. in sense1) *v.*

free·base /ˈfrē,bās/ (also **freebase cocaine**) ▶*n.* cocaine that has been converted from its salt to its base form by heating with ether or boiling with sodium bicarbonate, taken by inhaling the fumes or smoking the residue.
▶*v.* [*trans.*] prepare or take (cocaine) in such a way.

free·bie /ˈfrēbē/ (also **free·bee**) ▶*n.* *informal* a thing given free of charge. ▷1940s: an arbitrary formation from FREE.

free·board /ˈfrē,bôrd/ ▶*n.* the height of a ship's side between the waterline and the deck.

free·boot·er /ˈfrē,bo͞otər/ ▶*n.* a pirate or lawless adventurer. ▷late 16th cent.: from Dutch *vrijbuiter*, from *vrij* 'free' + *buit* 'booty,' + the noun suffix *-er*. Compare with FILIBUSTER. —**free·boot** *v.*

free·born /ˈfrē,bôrn/ ▶*adj.* not born in slavery. ■ of or befitting a freeborn person.

Free Church ▶*n.* a Christian Church that has dissented or seceded from an established Church.

free climb·ing ▶*n.* rock climbing without the assistance of devices such as pegs placed in the rock, but occasionally using ropes and belays. Compare with AID CLIMBING. —**free climb** *n.* & *v.*

freed·man /ˈfrēdmən; -,man/ ▶*n.* (*pl.* **-men**) *historical* an emancipated slave.

free·dom /ˈfrēdəm/ ▶*n.* the power or right to act, speak, or think as one wants without hindrance or restraint: *we do have some freedom of choice | he talks of revoking some of the freedoms.* See note at LIBERTY. ■ absence of subjection to foreign domination or despotic government: *he was a champion of Irish freedom.* ■ the state of not being imprisoned or enslaved: *the shark thrashed its way to freedom.* ■ the state of being physically unrestricted and able to move easily: *the shorts have a side split for freedom of movement.* ■ (**freedom from**) the state of not being subject to or affected by (a particular undesirable thing): *government policies to achieve freedom from want.* ■ the power of self-determination attributed to the will; the quality of being independent of fate or necessity. ■ unrestricted use of something: *the dog is happy having the freedom of the house when we are out.* ■ *archaic* familiarity or openness in speech or behavior. ▷Old English *frēodōm* (see FREE, -DOM).

free·dom fight·er ▶*n.* a person who takes part in a violent struggle to achieve a political goal, esp. in order to overthrow their government.

free·dom march ▶*n.* a march organized as a demonstration of protest against a political entity for its oppressive policies, which are often directed at a specific group such as a minority.

free·dom of con·science ▶*n.* the right to follow one's own beliefs in matters of religion and morality.

free·dom of re·li·gion ▶*n.* the right to practice whatever religion one chooses.

free·dom of speech (also **free speech**) ▶*n.* the right to express any opinions without censorship or restraint.

free·dom of the seas ▶*n.* the right of merchant ships to move freely on the seas in peace or war without interference except in territorial zones.

free·dom rid·er ▶*n.* a person who challenged racial laws in the American South in the 1960s, originally by refusing to abide by the laws designating that seating in buses be segregated by race.

Free·dom Trail a walking tour in Boston, Massachusetts, that takes visitors past historic sites relating to the American Revolution.

free en·er·gy ▶*n.* *Physics* a thermodynamic quantity equivalent to the capacity of a system to do work.

free en·ter·prise ▶*n.* an economic system in which private business operates in competition and largely free of state control.

free fall ▶*n.* downward movement under the force of gravity only: *the path of a body in free fall.* ■ the part of a parachute-descent before the parachute opens. ■ the movement of a spacecraft in space without thrust from the engines.
▶*v.* (**free-fall**) [*intrans.*] move under the force of gravity only; fall rapidly.

free fire zone ▶*n.* a military combat zone in which there are no restrictions on the use of fire power. ■ *figurative* an area of activity apparently without rules.

free flight ▶*n.* the flight of a spacecraft, rocket, or missile when the engine is not producing thrust.

free-float·ing ▶*adj.* not attached to anything and able to move freely: *free-floating aquatic plants.* ■ *figurative* not assigned to a fixed or particular position, category, or level: *free-floating exchange rates.* ■ (of a person) not committed to a particular cause or political party. ■ *Psychiatry* (of anxiety) chronic and generalized, without an obvious cause. —**free-float** *v.* —**free-float·er** *n.*

free-for-all ▶*n.* a disorganized or unrestricted situation or event in which everyone may take part, esp. a fight, discussion, or trading market.

free-form ▶*adj.* not conforming to a regular or formal structure or shape: *a free-form jazz improvisation.*

Free French ▶*plural n.* an organization of French troops and volunteers in exile formed under General de Gaulle in 1940. Based in London, the movement organized forces that opposed the Axis powers in French Equatorial Africa, Lebanon, and elsewhere, and cooperated with the French Resistance.

free·hand /ˈfrē,hand/ ▶*adj.* & *adv.* (esp. with reference to drawing) done manually without the aid of instruments such as rulers: [as *adj.*] *a freehand sketch* | [as *adv.*] *the pictures should be drawn freehand.*

free-hand·ed ▶*adj.* generous, esp. with money. —**free-hand·ed·ly** *adv.* —**free-hand·ed·ness** *n.*

free·hold /ˈfrē,hōld/ ▶*n.* permanent and absolute tenure of land or property with freedom to dispose of it at will. Often contrasted with LEASEHOLD. ■ (**the freehold**) the ownership of a piece of land or property by such tenure. ■ a piece of land or property held by such tenure.
▶*adj.* held by or having the status of freehold. —**free·hold·er** *n.*

free jazz ▶*n.* an improvised style of jazz characterized by the absence of set chord patterns or time patterns.

free kick ▶*n.* (in soccer and rugby) an unimpeded kick of the stationary ball awarded to one side as a penalty for a foul or infringement by the other side.

free·lance /ˈfrē,lans/ (also **free-lance**) ▶*adj.* working for different companies at different times rather than being permanently employed by one company: *a freelance journalist.* ■ independent or uncommitted in politics or personal life.
▶*adv.* earning one's living in such a way: *I work freelance from home.*
▶*n.* **1** a person who earns their living in such a way. **2** *historical* (often **free lance**) a medieval mercenary.
▶*v.* [*intrans.*] earn one's living as a freelance. ▷early 19th cent. (denoting a mercenary): originally as two words.

free·lanc·er /ˈfrē,lansər/ ▶*n.* a person who works freelance.

free-liv·ing ▶*adj.* **1** freely indulging in pleasures, esp. that of eating; having an unrestricted or independent lifestyle. **2** *Biology* living freely and independently, not as a parasite or attached to a substrate.

free·load·er /ˈfrē,lōdər/ ▶*n.* *informal* a person who takes advantage of others' generosity without giving anything in return. —**free·load** /ˈfrē,lōd/ *v.*

free love ▶*n.* the idea or practice of having sexual relations according to choice, without being restricted by marriage or other long-term relationships.

free·ly /ˈfrēlē/ ▸adv. not under the control of another; as one wishes: *I roamed freely.* ■ without restriction or interference: *air can freely circulate.* ■ in copious or generous amounts: *she drank freely to keep up her courage.* ■ openly and honestly: *you may speak freely.* ■ willingly and readily; without compulsion: *I freely confess to this failing.*

Freeman ▸, Morgan (1937–), U.S. actor. He received Academy Award nominations for his performances in *Street Smart* (1987), *Driving Miss Daisy* (1989), and *The Shawshank Redemption* (1994).

free·man /ˈfrēmən; -ˌman/ ▸n. (*pl.* **-men**) **1** a person who is entitled to full political and civil rights. **2** *historical* a person who is not a slave or serf.

free mar·ket ▸n. an economic system in which prices are determined by unrestricted competition between privately owned businesses. **—free mar·ket·eer** (also **free-mar·ket·eer**) *n.*

free·mar·tin /ˈfrēˌmärtn/ ▸n. a hermaphrodite or imperfect sterile female calf that is the twin of a male calf whose hormones affected its development. ▷late 17th cent.: of unknown origin.

Free·ma·son /ˈfrēˈmāsən/ ▸n. a member of an international order established for mutual help and fellowship, which holds elaborate secret ceremonies.

The original **freemasons** were itinerant skilled stonemasons of the 14th century, who are said to have recognized fellow craftsmen by secret signs. Modern Freemasonry is usually traced to the formation of the Grand Lodge in London in 1717; members are typically professionals and businessmen.

free·ma·son·ry /ˈfrēˈmāsənrē/ ▸n. **1** (**Freemasonry**) the system and institutions of the Freemasons. **2** instinctive sympathy or fellow feeling between people with something in common: *the unshakable freemasonry of actors in a crisis.*

free pass ▸n. an authorization of free admission or travel.

free path ▸ see MEAN FREE PATH.

Free·port /ˈfrēˌpôrt/ **1** a port city in the northern Bahamas, on Grand Bahama Island; pop. 27,000. **2** a commercial and industrial city in northwestern Illinois; pop. 25,840. **3** a commercial village in the town of Hempstead town on Long Island in New York; pop. 39,894.

free port ▸n. a port open to all traders. ■ a port area where goods in transit are exempt from customs duty.

fre·er /ˈfrēər/ ▸adj. comparative of FREE.
▸n. *rare* a person or agent who frees or sets free someone or something.

free rad·i·cal ▸n. *Chemistry* an uncharged molecule (typically highly reactive and short-lived) having an unpaired valence electron.

free-range ▸adj. (of livestock, esp. poultry) kept in natural conditions, with freedom of movement. ■ (of eggs) produced by birds reared under such conditions.

free safe·ty ▸n. *Football* a defensive back who is usually free from an assignment to cover a particular player on the offensive team.

free·sia /ˈfrēZHə/ ▸n. a small southern African plant of the iris family, with fragrant, colorful, tubular flowers, many varieties of which are cultivated for use by florists. • Genus *Freesia*, family Iridaceae. ▷modern Latin, named after Friedrich H. T. Freese (died 1876), German physician.

free sil·ver ▸adj. denoting a U.S. political movement for the free coinage of silver, esp. that of the last quarter of the nineteenth century.

free skat·ing ▸n. the sport of performing variable skating figures and jumps to music. **—free skate** *n.*

free speech ▸n. another term for FREEDOM OF SPEECH.

free spir·it ▸n. an independent or uninhibited person: *they raised their children to be free spirits.*

free-spo·ken ▸adj. *archaic* speaking candidly and openly.

fre·est /ˈfrēəst/ ▸adj. superlative of FREE.

free·stand·ing /ˈfrēˈstandiNG/ (also **free-stand·ing**) ▸adj. not supported by another structure. ■ not relying on or linked to anything else; independent: *if extracts rather than complete texts are used, they should be freestanding and coherent.*

Free State ▸n. **1** *historical* (before the Civil War) a state of the U.S. in which slavery was illegal. ■ (**the Free State**) a nickname for the state of MARYLAND. **2** a province in central South Africa, situated to the north of the Orange River; capital, Bloemfontein. Formerly called (until 1995) ORANGE FREE STATE.

free·stone /ˈfrēˌstōn/ ▸n. **1** rock that can be cut easily in any direction, in particular a fine-grained sandstone or limestone of uniform texture. [from Old French *franche pere* 'excellent rock'.] **2** a stone fruit in which the pit is easily separated from the flesh when the fruit is ripe: [as *adj.*] *freestone peaches.* Contrasted with CLINGSTONE.

free·style /ˈfrēˌstīl/ ▸adj. denoting a contest or version of a sport in which there are few restrictions on the moves or techniques that competitors employ: *freestyle wrestling.*
▸n. a contest of such a kind, in particular a swimming race in which competitors may use any stroke. **—free·styl·er** *n.*

free-swim·ming ▸adj. *Zoology* (of an aquatic animal) not attached to an object or substrate and able to swim freely.

free-tailed bat (also **free·tail bat**) ▸n. a streamlined fast-flying insectivorous bat with a projecting tail, found in tropical and subtropical countries. • Family Molossidae: several genera and numerous species, including the mastiff bats and hairless bats.

free·think·er /ˈfrēˈTHiNGkər/ ▸n. a person who rejects accepted opinions, esp. those concerning religious belief. **—free·think·ing** *n.* & *adj.*

free throw ▸n. *Basketball* an unimpeded attempt at a basket (worth one point) awarded to a player following a foul or other infringement.

free-throw line (also **free throw line**) ▸n. *Basketball* another term for FOUL LINE.

free-to-air ▸adj. denoting or relating to television programs broadcast on standard public or commercial networks, as opposed to subscription satellite or cable: *free-to-air TV in the highly regulated French market.*

Free·town /ˈfrēˌtoun/ the capital and chief port of Sierra Leone; pop. 505,000.

free trade ▸n. international trade left to its natural course without tariffs, quotas, or other restrictions.

free u·ni·ver·si·ty ▸n. a nontraditional educational program of courses often taught by nonprofessionals as an alternative to traditional academic programs, usually offered without prerequisites at low cost or at no cost.

free verse ▸n. poetry that does not rhyme or have a regular meter. Also called VERS LIBRE.

free·ware /ˈfrēˌwer/ ▸n. software that is available free of charge.

free·way /ˈfrēˌwā/ ▸n. an express highway, esp. one with controlled access. ■ a toll-free highway.

free weight ▸n. a weight used in weightlifting that is not attached to an apparatus.

free·wheel /ˈfrēˌ(h)wēl/ ▸n. a device in a motor vehicle transmission allowing the drive shaft to spin faster than the engine. ■ a device that allows a bicycle wheel to revolve forward while the crank is stationary.
▸v. [*intrans.*] ride a bicycle with the pedals at rest, esp. downhill: *he had come freewheeling down the road.* ■ [usu. as *adj.*] (**freewheeling**) act without concern for rules, conventions, or the consequences of one's actions: *the freewheeling drug scene of the sixties.*

free will ▸n. the power of acting without the constraint of necessity or fate; the ability to act at one's own discretion.
▸adj. [*attrib.*] (esp. of a donation) given readily; voluntary: *free-will offerings.*

freeze /frēz/ ▸v. (*past* **froze** /frōz/; *past part.* **fro·zen** /ˈfrōzən/) **1** [*intrans.*] (of a liquid) be turned into ice or another solid as a result of extreme cold: *in the winter the milk froze.* ■ [*trans.*] turn (a liquid) into ice or another solid in such a way. ■ (of something wet or containing liquid) become blocked, covered, or rigid with ice: *the pipes had frozen.* ■ [*trans.*] cause (something wet or containing liquid) to become blocked, covered, or rigid with ice: [with *complement*] *the ground was **frozen hard**.* ■ be or feel so cold that one is near death (often used hyperbolically): *you'll **freeze to death** standing there.* ■ [*trans.*] (of the weather) cause (someone) to feel so cold that they are near death. ■ (of the weather) be at or below freezing: *at night it froze again.* ■ [*trans.*] deprive (a part of the body) of feeling, esp. by the application of a chilled anesthetic substance. ■ [*trans.*] treat (someone) with a cold manner; stare coldly at (someone): *she would **freeze** him with a look when he tried to talk to her.* **2** [*trans.*] store (something) at a very low temperature in order to preserve it: *the cake can be frozen.* ■ [*intrans.*] (of food) be able to be preserved in such a way: *this soup freezes well.* **3** [*intrans.*] become suddenly motionless or paralyzed with fear or shock: *Mathewson froze on the spot, unable to take the next step.* ■ stop moving when ordered or directed. **4** [*trans.*] hold (something) at a fixed level or in a fixed state for a period of time: *new spending on defense was to be frozen.* ■ prevent (assets) from being used for a period of time: *the charity's bank account has been frozen.* ■ stop (a moving image) at a particular frame when filming or viewing: *the camera will set fast shutter speeds to freeze the action.* ■ [*intrans.*] (of a computer screen) become temporarily locked because of system problems.
▸*phrasal v.* □ **freeze someone out** *informal* behave in a hostile or obstructive way so as to exclude someone from something.
▸n. **1** an act of holding or being held at a fixed level or in a fixed state: *workers faced a pay freeze.* ■ short for FREEZE-FRAME. **2** *informal* a period of frost or very cold weather: *the big freeze surprised the weathermen.* ▷Old English *frēosan* (in the phrase *hit frēoseth* 'it is freezing, it is so cold that water turns to ice'), of Germanic origin; related to Dutch *vriezen* and German *frieren*, from an Indo-European root shared by Latin *pruina* 'hoarfrost' and FROST. **—freez·a·ble** /-zəbəl/ *adj.* **—fro·zen·ly** *adv.*
▸PHRASE □ **freeze one's blood** (or **one's blood freezes**) fill (or be filled) with a sudden feeling of great fear or horror.

freeze-dry ▸v. [*trans.*] [usu. as *adj.*] (**freeze-dried**) preserve (something) by rapidly freezing it and then subjecting it to a high vacuum that removes ice by sublimation: *freeze-dried beef stew.*

freeze-frame ▸n. the facility of stopping a film or videotape in order to view a motionless image. ■ a motionless image obtained with such a facility.
▸v. [*trans.*] use such a facility on (an image or a recording).

freeze-out ▸n. *informal* an exclusion of a person or organization from something, by boycotting or ignoring them.

freez·er /ˈfrēzər/ ▸n. a refrigerated compartment, cabinet, or room for preserving food at very low temperatures. ■ a device for making frozen desserts such as ice cream or sherbet.

freeze-up ▸n. a period of extreme cold. ■ the freezing over of a body of water such as a lake or river: *until freeze-up, the caribou stay near the lake.*

freez·ing /ˈfrēziNG/ ▸adj. below 32°F (0°C): *strong winds and freezing temperatures.* ■ (used hyperbolically) very cold: *he was freezing and miserable* | [as *submodifier*] *it was freezing cold outside.* ■ (of fog or rain) consisting of droplets that freeze rapidly on contact with a surface to form ice.
▸n. the freezing point of water: *the temperature was well above freezing.*

freez·ing point ▸n. the temperature at which a liquid turns into a solid when cooled.

Fre·ge /ˈfrāgə/, Gottlob (1848–1925), German philosopher and mathematician; founder of modern logic.

Frei·burg /ˈfrībərg; -ˌbo͝ork/ an industrial city in southwestern Germany, in the state of Baden-Württemberg, on the edge of the Black Forest; pop. 194,000. Full name FREIBURG IM BREISGAU .

freight /frāt/ ▸n. **1** goods transported by truck, train, ship, or aircraft. ■ the transport of goods by truck, train, ship, or aircraft. ■ a charge for such transport. **2** (in full **freight train**) a train of freight cars: *sugar and molasses moving by freight.* **3** a load or burden.
▸v. [*trans.*] transport (goods) in bulk by truck, train, ship, or aircraft: *the metals had been freighted from the city* | [*intrans.*] *ships freighting to Dublin.* ■ (**be freighted with**) *figurative* be laden or burdened with: *each word was freighted with anger.* ▷late Middle English (in the sense 'rental of a ship for transporting goods'): from Middle Dutch, Middle Low German *vrecht*, variant of *vracht* 'ship's cargo.' Compare with FRAUGHT. **—freight·ing** /frātiNG/ *n.*

freight·age /ˈfrātij/ ▸n. the carrying of goods in bulk. ■ goods carried in bulk; freight.

freight car ▸n. a railroad car for carrying freight.

freight·er /ˈfrātər/ ▸n. a ship or aircraft designed to carry goods in bulk. ■ a person who loads, receives, or forwards goods for transport.

freight ton ▸n. see TON[1] (sense 1).

Fre·li·mo /freˈlēmō/ the nationalist liberation party of Mozambique, founded in 1962. After independence in 1975, Frelimo governed Mozambique as a one-party state until 1990, when a multiparty system

Pronunciation Key ə *ago*; ər *over*; ˈə or ˌə *up*; ˈər or ˌər *fur*; a *hat*; ā *rate*; ä *car*; CH *chew*; e *let*; ē *see*; e(ə)r *air*; i *fit*; ī *by*; i(ə)r *ear*; NG *sing*; ō *go*; ô *for*; oi *boy*; o͝o *good*; o͞o *goo*; ou *out*; SH *she*; TH *thin*; T͟H *then*; (h)w *why*; ZH *vision*

was introduced. ▷Portuguese, contraction of *Frente de Libertação de Moçambique*, the name of the party.

Fre·man·tle /ˈfrēˌmantl/ a city in southwestern Australia, in the state of Western Australia, the port for Perth; pop. 24,000.

Fre·mont /ˈfrēˌmänt/ **1** an industrial and commercial city in north central California, south of Oakland, off San Francisco Bay; pop. 203,413. **2** a city in eastern Nebraska, on the north shore of the Platte River, northwest of Omaha; pop. 25,174.

Fré·mont /ˈfrēˌmänt/, John Charles (1813–90), U.S. explorer and politician. He explored several viable routes to the Pacific Ocean across the Rocky Mountains in the 1840s. During the Mexican War 1846–48, he fought to win California. In 1856, he unsuccessfully opposed James Buchanan for the presidency.

French[1] /frenCH/ ▸*adj.* of or relating to France or its people or language.
▸*n.* **1** the Romance language of France, also used in parts of Belgium, Switzerland, and Canada, in several countries of northern and western Africa and the Caribbean, and elsewhere. **2** *Brit.* short for FRENCH VERMOUTH. **3** [as *plural n.*] (**the French**) the people of France collectively. ▷Old English *Frencisc*, of Germanic origin, from the base of FRANK[2].
—**French·ness** *n.*
▸*PHRASE* □ (**if you'll**) **excuse** (or **pardon**) **my French** *informal* used to apologize for swearing.

French is the first or official language of over 200 million people and is widely used as a second language. It is a Romance language that developed from the Latin spoken in Gaul, the northern dialects becoming dominant after Paris became the capital in the 10th century. French became widely used owing to the cultural influence and colonial expansion of France from the 11th century, and it had a very great influence on English as the language of the Norman ruling class.

French[2] /frenCH/, Daniel Chester (1859–1931), U.S. sculptor. Among his works are the statue of the Minute Man 1873 at Concord, Massachusetts, and the seated figure of Abraham Lincoln 1922 in the Lincoln Memorial in Washington, DC.

French and In·di·an War North American war (1754–63) between France and Great Britain.

France's Canadian colonies and American Indian allies were pitted against Britain and its American colonies. The beginning of these hostilities became the prelude to and major cause of the Seven Years' War and marked the onset of George Washington's rise to prominence. The conflict ended with the Treaty of Paris; Britain won nearly all of French North America.

French braid ▸*n.* a hairstyle in which all the hair is gathered into one large braid down the back of the head, starting from the forehead.
▸*v.* (also **French-braid**) [*trans.*] create such a hairstyle.

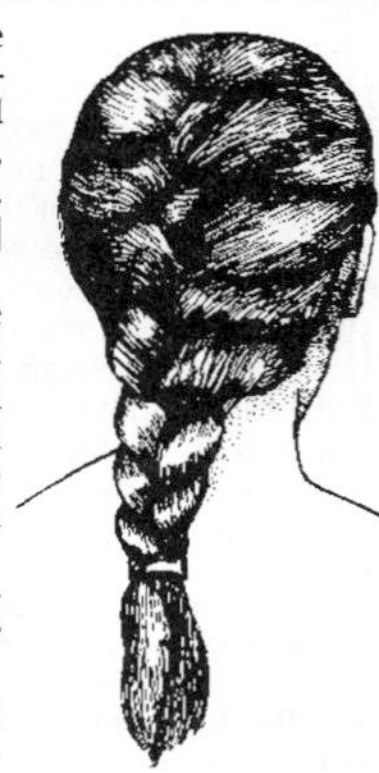
French braid

French bread ▸*n.* white bread in a long, crisp loaf.

French Ca·na·di·an ▸*n.* **1** a Canadian whose principal language is French. **2** the form of French spoken in Canada.
▸*adj.* of or relating to French-speaking Canadians or their language.

French chalk ▸*n.* talc used for marking cloth and removing grease and, in powder form, as a dry lubricant.

French Con·go former name (until 1910) of FRENCH EQUATORIAL AFRICA.

French cuff ▸*n.* a shirt cuff that is folded back before fastening, creating a double-layered cuff.

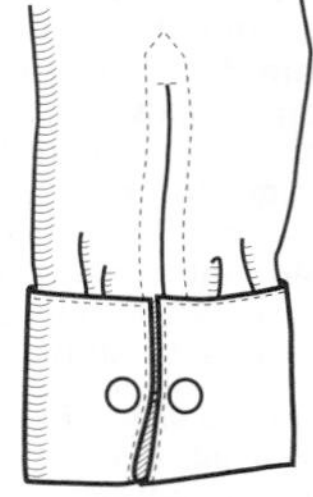
French cuff

French curve ▸*n.* a template used for drawing curved lines.

French-cut ▸*adj.* **1** *Cooking* sliced obliquely: *French-cut green beans.* **2** (of women's panties) cut so as to reveal much of the upper thigh.

French door ▸*n.* a door with glass panes throughout its length. ■ a French window.

French doors

French dress·ing ▸*n.* a salad dressing of vinegar, oil, and seasonings. ■ a sweet, creamy salad dressing commercially prepared from oil, tomato purée, and spices.

French E·qua·to·ri·al Af·ri·ca a former federation of French territories in west central Africa 1910–58. Previously called French Congo, its constituent territories were Chad, Ubanghi Shari (now the Central African Republic), Gabon, and Middle Congo (now Congo).

French fries (also **French fried potatoes**) ▸*plural n.* potatoes cut into strips and deep-fried.

French Gui·an·a /gēˈänə; gīˈanə/ an overseas department of France, in northern South America; pop. 96,000; capital, Cayenne.

french heel ▸*n.* a high, curved heel on a woman's shoe.

French horn ▸*n.* a brass instrument with a coiled tube, valves, and a wide bell, developed from the simple hunting horn in the 17th century. It is played with the right hand in the bell to soften the tone and increase the range of available harmonics.

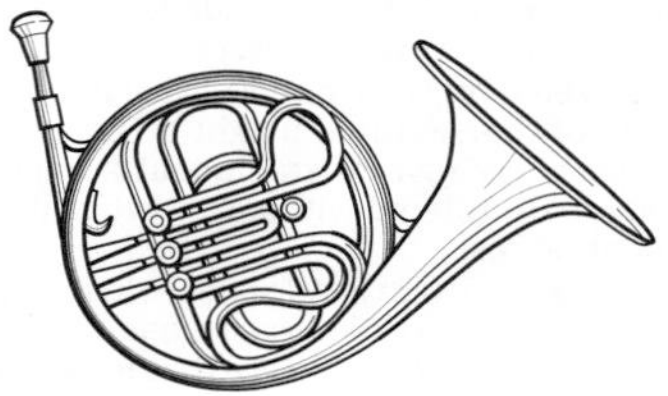
French horn

French·ie /ˈfrenCHē/ ▸*n.* (*pl.* **-ies**) variant spelling of FRENCHY.

French·i·fy /ˈfrenCHiˌfī/ ▸*v.* (**-fies, -fied**) [*trans.*] [usu. as *adj.*] (**Frenchified**) *often derogatory* make French in form, character, or manners: *she pronounced it without the Frenchified accent.*

French kiss ▸*n.* a kiss with contact between tongues. —**French kiss·ing** *n.*

French knot ▸*n.* (in embroidery) a stitch in which the thread is wound around the needle, which is then passed back through the fabric at almost the same point to form a small dot.

French leave ▸*n. informal, dated* an unauthorized or unannounced departure; absence without permission: *he seems to have **taken French leave**.* ▷mid 18th cent.: said to derive from the French custom of leaving a dinner or ball without saying goodbye to the host or hostess. The phrase was first recorded shortly after the Seven Years' War (1756–63); the equivalent French expression is *filer à l'Anglaise*, literally 'to escape in the style of the English.'

French let·ter ▸*n. Brit., informal* a condom.

French·man /ˈfrenCHmən/ ▸*n.* (*pl.* **-men**) a person, esp. a man, who is French by birth or descent.

French pas·try ▸*n.* a rich pastry, often with a filling of fruit or custard.

French pol·ish ▸*n.* shellac polish that produces a high gloss on wood.
▸*v.* [*trans.*] treat (wood) with such a polish.

French Pol·y·ne·sia /ˌpäləˈnēZHə/ an overseas territory of France in the South Pacific; pop. 200,000; capital, Papeete (on the island of Tahiti). French Polynesia includes the Society Islands, the Gambier Islands, the Tuamotu Archipelago, the Tubuai Islands, and the Marquesas. It was granted partial autonomy in 1977.

French curve

French Re·pub·li·can cal·en·dar ▸*n.* a reformed calendar officially introduced by the French Republican government on October 5, 1793.

The calendar was taken to have started on the equinox of September 22, 1792, the day of the proclamation of the Republic. It had twelve months of thirty days each, with five days of festivals at the year's end (six in leap years). The names of the months were Vendémiaire, Brumaire, Frimaire, Nivose, Pluviose, Ventose, Germinal, Floréal, Plairial, Messidor, Thermidor, and Fructidor. The new calendar was abandoned under the Napoleonic regime, and the Gregorian calendar was formally reinstated on January 1, 1806.

French Rev·o·lu·tion the overthrow of the Bourbon monarchy in France (1789–99).

The French Revolution began with the meeting of the legislative assembly (the States General) in May 1789 when the French government was already in crisis; the Bastille was stormed in July of the same year. The revolution became steadily more radical and ruthless with power increasingly in the hands of the Jacobins and Robespierre; Louis XVI's execution in January 1793 was followed by Robespierre's Reign of Terror. The revolution failed to produce a stable form of republican government, and after several different forms of administration, the last, the Directory, was overthrown by Napoleon in 1799.

French roll ▸*n.* **1** a crisp roll of French bread. **2** another term for FRENCH TWIST.

French seam ▸*n.* a seam with the raw edges enclosed.

French So·ma·li·land /səˈmälēˌland/ former name (until 1967) of DJIBOUTI.

French South·ern and Ant·arc·tic Ter·ri·to·ries an overseas territory of France, comprised of Adélie Land in Antarctica, the Kerguelen and Crozet archipelagos, and the islands of Amsterdam and St. Paul in the southern Indian Ocean.

French Su·dan former name of MALI.

French tick·ler ▸*n. informal* a condom with ribbed protrusions.

French toast ▸*n.* bread coated in egg and milk and fried.

French twist ▸*n.* a hairstyle in which the hair is tucked into a vertical roll down the back of the head.

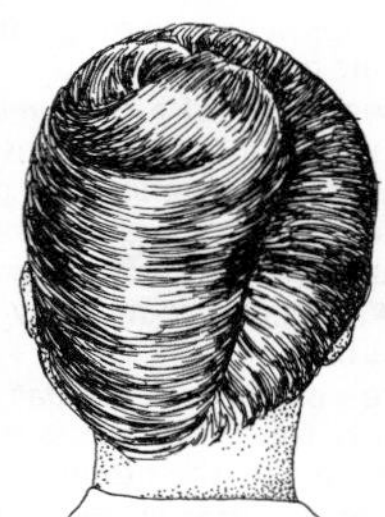
French twist

French ver·mouth ▸*n.* dry vermouth.

French Wars of Re·li·gion a series of religious and political conflicts in France (1562–98) involving the Protestant Huguenots on one side and Catholic groups on the other. The wars were complicated by interventions from Spain, Rome, England, the Netherlands, and elsewhere, and were not brought to an end until the settlement of the Edict of Nantes.

French West Af·ri·ca a former federation of French territories in northwestern Africa 1895–1959. Its constituent territories were Senegal, Mauritania, French Sudan (now Mali), Upper Volta (now Burkina Faso), Niger, French Guinea (now Guinea), the Ivory Coast, and Dahomey (now Benin).

French win·dow ▸*n.* (usu. **French windows**) each of a pair of casement windows extending to the floor in an outside wall, serving as a window and door.

French·wom·an /ˈfrenCHˌwo͝omən/ ▸*n.* (*pl.* **-wom·en**) a female who is French by birth or descent.

French·y /ˈfrenCHē/ (also **French·ie**) ▸*adj. informal, chiefly offensive* perceived as characteristically French: *a perfect example of that kind of progressive Frenchy art.*
▸*n.* (*pl.* **French·ies**) **1** *informal, chiefly offensive* a French person. ■ *Canadian* a French Canadian. **2** *Brit. informal* or *dated* short for FRENCH LETTER.

fre·net·ic /frəˈnetik/ ▸*adj.* fast and energetic in a rather wild and uncontrolled way: *a frenetic pace of activity.*

▷late Middle English (in the sense 'insane'): from Old French *frenetique*, via Latin from Greek *phrenitikos*, from *phrenitis* 'delirium,' from *phrēn* 'mind.' Compare with FRANTIC. —**fre·net·i·cal·ly** /-ik(ə)lē/ *adv.*

fren·u·lum /ˈfrenyələm/ ▶*n.* *Anatomy* a small fold or ridge of tissue that supports or checks the motion of the part to which it is attached, in particular a fold of skin beneath the tongue, or between the lip and the gum. ■ *Entomology* (in some moths and butterflies) a bristle or row of bristles on the edge of the hind wing that keeps it in contact with the forewing. ▷early 18th cent.: modern Latin, diminutive of Latin *frenum* 'bridle.'

fre·num /ˈfrēnəm/ ▶*n.* another term for FRENULUM. ▷mid 18th cent.: from Latin, literally 'bridle.'

fren·zied /ˈfrenzēd/ ▶*adj.* wildly excited or uncontrolled: *a frenzied attack.* —**fren·zied·ly** *adv.*

fren·zy /ˈfrenzē/ ▶*n.* (*pl.* **-zies**) [usu. in *sing.*] a state or period of uncontrolled excitement or wild behavior: *Doreen worked herself into a frenzy of rage.* ▷Middle English: from Old French *frenesie*, from medieval Latin *phrenesia*, from Latin *phrenesis*, from Greek *phrēn* 'mind.'

Fre·on /ˈfrē,än/ (also **fre·on**) ▶*n. trademark* an aerosol propellant, refrigerant, or organic solvent consisting of one or more of a group of chlorofluorocarbons and related compounds. ▷1930s: of unknown origin.

freq. ▶*abbr.* ■ frequency. ■ frequent. ■ *Grammar* frequentative. ■ frequently.

fre·quen·cy /ˈfrēkwənsē/ ▶*n.* (*pl.* **-cies**) **1** the rate at which something occurs or is repeated over a particular period of time or in a given sample: *shops have closed with increasing frequency during the period.* ■ the fact of being frequent or happening often. ■ *Statistics* the ratio of the number of actual to possible occurrences of an event. ■ *Statistics* the (relative) number of times something occurs in a given sample. **2** the rate at which a vibration occurs that constitutes a wave, either in a material (as in sound waves), or in an electromagnetic field (as in radio waves and light), usually measured per second. (Symbol: **f** or *ν*) ■ the particular waveband at which a radio station or other system broadcasts or transmits signals. ▷mid 16th cent. (gradually superseding late Middle English *frequence*; originally denoting a gathering of people): from Latin *frequentia*, from *frequens, frequent-* 'crowded, frequent.'

fre·quen·cy dis·tri·bu·tion ▶*n.* *Statistics* a mathematical function showing the number of instances in which a variable takes each of its possible values.

fre·quen·cy di·vi·sion mul·ti·plex·ing ▶*n.* *Telecommunications* a technique for sending two or more signals over the same telephone line, radio channel, or other medium. Each signal is transmitted as a unique range of frequencies within the bandwidth of the channel as a whole, enabling several signals to be transmitted simultaneously. Compare with TIME DIVISION MULTIPLEXING.

fre·quen·cy mod·u·la·tion (abbr.: **FM**) ▶*n.* the modulation of a radio or other wave by variation of its frequency, esp. to carry an audio signal. Often contrasted with AMPLITUDE MODULATION. ■ the system of radio transmission using such modulation.

fre·quen·cy re·sponse ▶*n.* *Electronics* the dependence on signal frequency of the output–input ratio of an amplifier or other device.

fre·quent ▶*adj.* /ˈfrēkwənt/ occurring or done on many occasions, in many cases, or in quick succession: *frequent changes in policy | the showers will become heavier and more frequent.* ■ [*attrib.*] (of a person) doing something often; habitual: *a frequent visitor to New England.* ■ found at short distances apart: *frequent army roadblocks.* ■ *dated Medicine* (of the pulse) rapid.
▶*v.* /frēˈkwent/ [*trans.*] visit (a place) often or habitually: *bars frequented by soldiers* | [as *adj.*, with *submodifier*] (**frequented**) *one of the most frequented sites.* ▷late Middle English (in the sense 'profuse, ample'): from French, or from Latin *frequens, frequent-* 'crowded, frequent,' of unknown ultimate origin. —**fre·quen·ta·tion** /,frēkwənˈtāsHən; ,frēkwen-/ *n.* —**fre·quent·er** /frēˈkwentər-/ *n.* —**fre·quent·ly** /ˈfrēkwəntlē/ *adv.*

fre·quen·ta·tive /frēˈkwentətiv/ *Grammar* ▶*adj.* (of a verb or verbal form) expressing frequent repetition or intensity of action.
▶*n.* a verb or verbal form of this type, e.g., *chatter* in English. ▷mid 16th cent.: from French *fréquentatif, -ive* or Latin *frequentativus*, from *frequens, frequent-* 'crowded, frequent.'

fre·quent fli·er ▶*n.* a person who regularly travels by air on commercial flights, esp. one who is enrolled in a promotional program for such travelers.

fres·co /ˈfreskō/ ▶*n.* (*pl.* **-coes** or **-cos**) a painting done rapidly in watercolor on wet plaster on a wall or ceiling, so that the colors penetrate the plaster and become fixed as it dries. ■ this method of painting, used in Roman times and by the great masters of the Italian Renaissance including Giotto, Masaccio, and Michelangelo.
▶*v.* [*trans.*] paint in fresco: *four scenes had been frescoed on the wall* | [as *adj.*] *frescoed ceilings.* ▷late 16th cent.: Italian, literally 'cool, fresh.' The word was first recorded in the phrase *in fresco*, representing Italian *affresco, al fresco* 'on the fresh (plaster).'

fres·co sec·co /ˈfreskō ˈsekō/ ▶*n.* see SECCO.

fresh /fresH/ ▶*adj.* **1** not previously known or used; new or different: *the court had heard fresh evidence.* **2** recently created or experienced and not faded or impaired: *the memory was still fresh in their minds.* ■ (of food) recently made or obtained; not canned, frozen, or otherwise preserved. ■ [*predic.*] (of a person) full of energy and vigor: *they are feeling fresh after a good night's sleep.* ■ (of a color or a person's complexion) bright or healthy in appearance. ■ (of a person) attractively youthful and inexperienced. ■ [*predic.*] (**fresh from/out of**) (of a person) having just had (a particular experience) or come from (a particular place): *we were fresh out of art school.* **3** (of water) not salty. ■ pleasantly clean, pure, and cool: *a bit of fresh air does her good.* **4** (of the wind) cool and fairly strong. **5** *informal* presumptuous or impudent toward someone, esp. in a sexual way: *some of the men tried to* **get fresh with** *the girls.* **6** (of a cow) yielding a renewed or increased supply of milk following the birth of a calf.
▶*adv.* [usu. in *combination*] newly; recently: *fresh-baked bread | fresh-cut grass.* ▷Old English *fersc* 'not salt, fit for drinking,' superseded in Middle English by forms from Old French *freis, fresche*; both ultimately of Germanic origin and related to Dutch *vers* and German *frisch.* —**fresh·ness** *n.*
▶*PHRASES* □ **be fresh out of** *informal* have just sold or run out of a supply of (something). □ **(as) fresh as a daisy** see DAISY. □ **fresh blood** see BLOOD.

fresh breeze ▶*n.* a wind of force 5 on the Beaufort scale (17-21 knots or 20–24 mph).

fresh·en /ˈfresHən/ ▶*v.* **1** [*trans.*] make (something) newer, cleaner, or more attractive: *it didn't take long to freshen her makeup.* ■ add more liquid to (a drink); top off. **2** [*intrans.*] (of wind) become stronger and colder. **3** [*intrans.*] (of a cow) give birth and come into milk.
▶*phrasal v.* □ **freshen up** revive oneself by washing oneself or changing into clean clothes: *I freshened up by having a shower.* ■ (**freshen something up**) make something look newer or more attractive.

fresh·er /ˈfresHər/ ▶*n.* *Brit.* informal term for FRESHMAN.

fresh·et /ˈfresHət/ ▶*n.* the flood of a river from heavy rain or melted snow. ■ a rush of fresh water flowing into the sea. ▷late 16th cent.: probably from Old French *freschete*, diminutive of *freis* 'fresh.'

fresh-faced ▶*adj.* having a clear and young-looking complexion.

fresh gale ▶*n.* a wind of force 8 on the Beaufort scale (34-40 knots or 39-46 mph).

fresh·ly /ˈfresHlē/ ▶*adv.* [usu. as *submodifier*] newly; recently: *freshly ground black pepper.*

fresh·man /ˈfresHmən/ ▶*n.* (*pl.* **-men**) a first-year student at a university, college, or high school: *we invited the freshmen* | [as *adj.*] *a freshman second baseman.* ■ a newcomer or novice, esp. someone newly elected to Congress.

fresh·wa·ter /ˈfresH ˈwôtər; -ˈwätər/ ▶*adj.* **1** of or found in fresh water; not of the sea: *freshwater and marine fish.* **2** *informal* (esp. of a school or college) situated in a remote or obscure area; provincial.

fresh·wa·ter flea ▶*n.* another term for DAPHNIA.

fresh·wom·an /ˈfresH,wo͝omən/ ▶*n.* (*pl.* **-wom·en**) a female first-year student at a university, college, or high school.

Fres·nel /fräˈnel/, Augustin Jean (1788–1827), French physicist and civil engineer. He correctly postulated that light moves in a wavelike motion transverse to the direction of propagation.

fres·nel /ˈfreznəl; fräˈnel/ (also **fresnel lens**) ▶*n.* *Photography* a flat lens made of a number of concentric rings, to reduce spherical aberration. ▷mid 19th cent.: named after A. J. FRESNEL.

Fres·no /ˈfreznō/ a city in central California, in the San Joaquin valley; pop. 427,652.

fret[1] /fret/ ▶*v.* (**fret·ted, fret·ting**) **1** [*intrans.*] be constantly or visibly worried or anxious: *she fretted about the cost of groceries* | [with *clause*] *I fretted that my fingers were so skinny.* ■ [*trans.*] cause (someone) worry or distress. **2** [*trans.*] gradually wear away (something) by rubbing or gnawing: *the bay's black waves fret the seafront.* ■ form (a channel or passage) by rubbing or wearing away. ■ [*intrans.*] flow or move in small waves: *soft clay that fretted between his toes.*
▶*n.* [in *sing.*] *chiefly Brit.* a state of anxiety or worry. ▷Old English *fretan* 'devour, consume,' of Germanic origin; related to Dutch *vreten* and German *fressen*, and ultimately to FOR- and EAT.

fret[2] ▶*n.* **1** *Art & Architecture* a repeating ornamental design of interlaced vertical and horizontal lines, such as the Greek key pattern. **2** *Heraldry* a device of narrow diagonal bands interlaced through a diamond.
▶*v.* (**fret·ted, fret·ting**) [*trans.*] [usu. as *adj.*] (**fretted**) decorate with fretwork: *intricately carved and fretted balustrades.* ▷late Middle English: from Old French *frete* 'trelliswork' and *freter* (verb), of unknown origin.

fret[3] ▶*n.* each of a sequence of bars or ridges on the fingerboard of some stringed musical instruments (such as the guitar), used for fixing the positions of the fingers to produce the desired notes.
▶*v.* (**fret·ted, fret·ting**) [*trans.*] [often as *adj.*] (**fretted**) **1** provide (a stringed instrument) with frets. **2** play (a note) while pressing the string down against a fret: *fretted notes.* ▷early 16th cent.: of unknown origin. —**fret·less** *adj.*

fret3

fret·board /ˈfret,bôrd/ ▶*n.* a fretted fingerboard on a guitar or other musical instrument.

fret·ful /ˈfretfəl/ ▶*adj.* feeling or expressing distress or irritation: *the baby was crying with a fretful whimper.* —**fret·ful·ly** *adv.* —**fret·ful·ness** *n.*

fret·saw /ˈfret,sô/ ▶*n.* a saw with a narrow blade stretched vertically on a frame, for cutting thin wood in patterns.

fret·work /ˈfret,wərk/ ▶*n.* ornamental design in wood, typically openwork, done with a fretsaw.

Freud[1] /froid/, Anna (1895–1982), British psychoanalyst; born in Austria; the youngest child of Sigmund Freud. She introduced important innovations in method and theory to her father's work, notably with regard to disturbed children, and set up a child therapy course and clinic in London.

Freud[2], Lucian (1922–), German-born British painter, grandson of Sigmund Freud. His subjects, typically portraits and nudes, are painted in a powerful naturalistic style based on firm draftsmanship and often using striking angles.

Freud[3], Sigmund (1856–1939), Austrian neurologist and psychotherapist. He was the first to emphasize the significance of unconscious processes in normal and neurotic behavior and was the founder of psychoanalysis as both a theory of personality and a therapeutic practice. He proposed the existence of an unconscious element in the mind that influences consciousness and of conflicts in it between various sets of forces. His theory of the sexual origin of neuroses aroused great controversy.

Freud·i·an /ˈfroidēən/ *Psychology* ▶*adj.* relating to or influenced by Sigmund Freud and his methods of psychoanalysis, esp. with reference to the importance of sexuality in human behavior. ■ susceptible to analysis in terms of unconscious desires: *he wasn't sure whether his passion for water power had some deep Freudian significance.*
▶*n.* a follower of Freud or his methods. —**Freud·i·an·ism** /-,nizəm/ *n.*

Freud·i·an slip ▶*n.* an unintentional error regarded as revealing subconscious feelings.

Frey /frā/ (also **Freyr** /frār/) *Scandinavian Mythology* the god of fertility and dispenser of rain and sunshine.

Frey·a /ˈfrāə/ *Scandinavian Mythology* the goddess of love and of the night, sister of Frey. She is often identified with Frigga.

Fri. ▶*abbr.* Friday.

fri·a·ble /ˈfrīəbəl/ ▶*adj.* easily crumbled: *the soil was friable between her fingers.* ▷mid 16th cent.: from French, or from Latin *friabilis*, from *friare* 'to crumble.' —**fri·a·bil·i·ty** /ˌfrīəˈbilətē/ *n.* —**fri·a·ble·ness** *n.*

fri·ar /ˈfrīər/ ▸*n.* a member of any of certain religious orders of men, esp. the four mendicant orders (Augustinians, Carmelites, Dominicans, and Franciscans). ▷Middle English: from Old French *frere*, from Latin *frater* 'brother.'

fri·ar·bird /ˈfrīərˌbərd/ ▸*n.* a large Australasian honeyeater with a dark, partly naked head and a long curved bill. • Genus *Philemon*, family Meliphagidae: many species.

Fri·ar Mi·nor ▸*n.* a Franciscan friar. ▷so named because the Franciscans regarded themselves as of humbler rank than members of other orders.

fri·ar·y /ˈfrīərē/ ▸*n.* (*pl.* **-ar·ies**) a building or community occupied by or consisting of friars.

frib·ble /ˈfribəl/ ▸*n. informal* a frivolous or foolish person. ■ a thing of no great importance.
▸*v.* (**fribble away**) [*trans.*] *dated* part with lightly and wastefully; fritter: *it is no longer respectable to fribble the days away in idle pleasure.* ▷mid 17th cent.: symbolic, from the earlier (now obsolete) verb meaning 'stammer,' also 'act aimlessly or frivolously.'

fric·an·deau /ˈfrikənˌdō/ ▸*n.* (*pl.* **-deaux** *pronunc.* same or /-ˌdōz/) a slice of meat, esp. veal, cut from the leg. ■ a dish made from such meat, usually fried or stewed and served with a sauce. ▷French, probably related to *fricassée* 'stew,' from the verb *fricasser* (see **FRICASSEE**).

fric·as·see /ˈfrikəˌsē; ˌfrikəˈsē/ ▸*n.* a dish of stewed or fried pieces of meat served in a thick white sauce.
▸*v.* (**-sees, -seed, -see·ing**) [*trans.*] make a fricassee of (something). ▷from French *fricassée*, feminine past participle of *fricasser* 'cut up and cook in sauce' (probably a blend of *frire* 'to fry' and *casser* 'to break').

fric·a·tive /ˈfrikətiv/ *Phonetics* ▸*adj.* denoting a type of consonant made by the friction of breath in a narrow opening, producing a turbulent air flow.
▸*n.* a consonant made in this way, e.g., *f* and *th.* ▷mid 19th cent.: from modern Latin *fricativus*, from Latin *fricare* 'to rub.'

Frick /frik/, Henry Clay (1849–1919), U.S. industrialist. He was chairman of the Carnegie Steel Co. 1889–1900; his art collection is housed in his former home, now a museum, in New York City.

Frick·er /ˈfrikər/, Roberta Sue, see **FARRELL**.

fric·tion /ˈfrikSHən/ ▸*n.* the resistance that one surface or object encounters when moving over another: *a lubrication system that reduces friction.* ■ the action of one surface or object rubbing against another: *the friction of braking.* ■ conflict or animosity caused by a clash of wills, temperaments, or opinions: *a considerable amount of* ***friction between*** *father and son.* ▷mid 16th cent. (denoting chafing or rubbing of the body or limbs, formerly much used in medical treatment): via French from Latin *frictio(n-)*, from *fricare* 'to rub.' —**fric·tion·less** *adj.*

fric·tion·al /ˈfrikSHənl/ ▸*adj.* of or produced by the action of one surface or object rubbing against or moving over another: *frictional drag.*

fric·tion·al un·em·ploy·ment ▸*n. Economics* the unemployment which exists in any economy due to people being in the process of moving from one job to another.

fric·tion clutch ▸*n.* a clutch in which friction between two moving surfaces is increased until they move in unison.

fric·tion drive ▸*n.* a transmission system used in motor vehicles that depends upon friction between moving parts in contact to transmit motion.

fric·tion tape ▸*n.* adhesive tape used chiefly to cover exposed electric wires.

fric·tion weld·ing ▸*n.* welding in which the heat is produced by rotating one component against the other under compression.

Fri·day /ˈfrīdā/ ▸*n.* the day of the week before Saturday and following Thursday: *he was arrested* ***on Friday*** | *the cleaning woman came on Fridays* | [as *adj.*] *Friday evening.*
▸*adv.* on Friday: *we'll try again Friday.* ■ (**Fridays**) on Fridays; each Friday: *he goes there Fridays.* ▷Old English *Frīgedæg*, named after the Germanic goddess **FRIGGA**; translation of late Latin *Veneris dies* 'day of the planet Venus'; compare with Dutch *vrijdag* and German *Freitag*.

fridge /frij/ ▸*n. informal* a refrigerator. ▷1920s: abbreviation, probably influenced by the proprietary name *Frigidaire*.

fried /frīd/ ▸ past and past participle of **FRY**[1].
▸*adj.* **1** (of food) cooked in hot fat or oil: *a breakfast of fried eggs and bacon.* **2** [*predic.*] *informal* exhausted or worn out: *I had just come from doing a shoot and I was really fried.* ■ intoxicated with drugs or alcohol.

Frie·dan /friˈdan/, Betty (1921–), U.S. feminist and writer. She wrote *The Feminine Mystique* (1963), which presented femininity as an artificial construct and traced the ways in which U.S. women are socialized to become mothers and housewives. In 1966, she founded the National Organization for Women, serving as its president until 1970. Other works: *The Second Stage* (1981) and *The Fountain of Age* (1993).

Betty Friedan

Fried·man[1] /ˈfrēdmən/, Esther Pauline, see **LANDERS**.

Fried·man[2], Milton (1912–), U.S. economist. As a policy adviser to President Ronald Reagan from 1981 to 1989, he advocated free market forces to produce balanced economic growth. Notable works: *Capitalism and Freedom* (1962) and *Free to Choose* (1980, coauthored with his wife). Nobel Prize for Economics (1976).

Fried·man[3], Pauline Esther, see **VAN BUREN**.

friend /frend/ ▸*n.* a person whom one knows and with whom one has a bond of mutual affection, typically exclusive of sexual or family relations. ■ a person who acts as a supporter of a cause, organization, or country by giving financial or other help: *join the Friends of Guilford Free Library.* ■ a person who is not an enemy or who is on the same side: *she was unsure whether he was* ***friend or foe.*** ■ a familiar or helpful thing: *he settled for that old friend the compensation grant.* ■ (often as a polite form of address or in ironic reference) an acquaintance or a stranger one comes across: *my friends, let me introduce myself.* ■ (**Friend**) a member of the Religious Society of Friends; a Quaker.
▸*v.* [*trans.*] *archaic* or *poetic/literary* befriend (someone). ▷Old English *frēond*, of Germanic origin; related to Dutch *vriend* and German *Freund*, from an Indo-European root meaning 'to love,' shared by **FREE**. —**friend·less** *adj.*
▸*PHRASES* □ **be** (or **make**) **friends with** be (or become) on good or affectionate terms with (someone). □ **a friend at court** a person in a position to use their influence on one's behalf. □ **a friend in need is a friend indeed** *proverb* a person who helps at a difficult time is a truly reliable person. □ **friends in high places** people in senior positions who are able and willing to use their influence on one's behalf.

friend·ly /ˈfrendlē/ ▸*adj.* (**-li·er, -li·est**) kind and pleasant: *they were* ***friendly to*** *me* | *she gave me a friendly smile.* ■ [*predic.*] (of a person) on good or affectionate terms: *I was* ***friendly with*** *one of the local farmers.* ■ (of a contest) not seriously or unpleasantly competitive or divisive: *friendly rivalry between the two schools.* ■ *Soccer* (of a match) not affecting a team's league standings. ■ [in *combination*] denoting something that is adapted for or is not harmful to a specified thing: *an environment-friendly agronomic practice.* ■ favorable or serviceable: *trees providing a friendly stage on which seedlings begin to grow.* ■ *Military* (of troops or equipment) of, belonging to, or in alliance with one's own forces.
▸*adv.* (also **friend·li·ly** /-ləlē/) in a friendly manner. —**friend·li·ness** *n.*

friend·ly fire ▸*n. Military* weapon fire coming from one's own side, esp. fire that causes accidental injury or death to one's own forces.

Friend·ly Is·lands another name for **TONGA**.

friend of Dor·o·thy ▸*n.* (*pl.* **friends of Dor·o·thy**) *informal* a gay man. ▷from the name of *Dorothy*, a character played by the actress Judy Garland (a gay icon) in the movie *The Wizard of Oz* (1939).

friend·ship /ˈfrendˌSHip/ ▸*n.* the emotions or conduct of friends; the state of being friends. ■ a relationship between friends: *she formed close friendships with women.* ■ a state of mutual trust and support between allied nations. ▷Old English *frēondscipe* (see **FRIEND, -SHIP**).

Friends of the Earth (abbr.: **FoE**) an international pressure group established in 1971 to campaign for a better awareness of and response to environmental problems.

fri·er ▸*n.* variant spelling of **FRYER**.

Fries·land /ˈfrēzlənd/ the western part of the ancient region of Frisia. ■ a northern province in the Netherlands, bounded on the west and north by the IJsselmeer and the North Sea; capital, Leeuwarden.

frieze[1] /frēz/ ▸*n.* a broad horizontal band of sculpted or painted decoration, esp. on a wall near the ceiling. ■ a horizontal paper strip mounted on a wall to give a similar effect. ■ *Architecture* the part of an entablature between the architrave and the cornice. ▷mid 16th cent.: from French *frise*, from medieval Latin *frisium*, variant of *frigium*, from Latin *Phrygium (opus)* '(work) of Phrygia.'

frieze[2] ▸*n.* heavy, coarse woolen cloth with a nap, usually on one side only. ▷late Middle English: from French *frise*, from medieval Latin *frisia*, 'Frisian wool.'

frig[1] /frig/ *vulgar slang* ▸*v.* (**frigged, frig·ging**) [*trans.*] used as a euphemism for 'fuck.' ■ masturbate.
▸*phrasal v.* □ **frig around** spend time doing unimportant or trivial things.
▸*exclam.* expressing extreme anger, annoyance, or contempt. ▷late Middle English: of unknown origin. The original sense was 'move restlessly, wriggle,' later 'rub, chafe,' hence 'masturbate' (late 17th cent.).

frig[2] /frij/ (also **'frig**) ▸*n. informal* short for **REFRIGERATOR**.

frig·ate /ˈfrigit/ ▸*n.* a warship with a mixed armament, generally heavier than a destroyer (in the U.S. Navy) and of a kind originally introduced for convoy escort work. ■ *historical* a sailing warship of a size and armament just below that of a ship of the line. ▷late 16th cent. (denoting a light, fast boat that was rowed or sailed): from French *frégate*, from Italian *fregata*, of unknown origin.

frig·ate bird ▸*n.* a predatory tropical seabird with dark plumage, long narrow wings, a deeply forked tail, and a long hooked bill. Also called **MAN-O'-WAR BIRD** (see **MAN-OF-WAR**). • Family Fregatidae and genus *Fregata*: five species.

Frig·ga /ˈfrigə/ *Scandinavian Mythology* the wife of Odin and goddess of married love and of the hearth, often identified with Freya. Friday is named after her.

frig·ging /ˈfrigən; -iNG/ (often **frig·gin'**) ▸*adj.* & *adv. vulgar slang* used for emphasis, esp. to express anger, annoyance, contempt, or surprise.

fright /frīt/ ▸*n.* **1** a sudden intense feeling of fear: *I jumped up in fright.* ■ an experience that causes one to feel sudden intense fear: *she's had a nasty fright* | *I got* ***the fright of my life*** *seeing that woman in the hotel.* **2** a person or thing looking grotesque or ridiculous.
▸*v.* [*trans.*] *archaic* frighten: *come, be comforted, he shan't fright you.* ▷Old English *fryhto*, *fyrhto* (noun), of Germanic origin; related to Dutch *furcht* and German *Furcht*.
▸*PHRASES* □ **look a fright** *informal* have a disheveled or grotesque appearance. □ **take fright** suddenly become frightened or panicked.

fright·en /ˈfrītn/ ▸*v.* [*trans.*] make (someone) afraid or anxious: *the savagery of his thoughts frightened him* | *people were no longer easily* ***frightened into*** *docility.* ■ (**frighten someone/something off**) deter someone or something from involvement or action by making them afraid. ■ [*intrans.*] (of a person) become afraid or anxious: *at his age, I guess he doesn't frighten any more.* —**fright·en·er** /ˈfrītn-ər/ *n.* —**fright·en·ing·ly** /ˈfrītn-iNGlē/ *adv.*

fright·ened /ˈfrītnd/ ▸*adj.* afraid or anxious: *a frightened child.*

fright·ful /ˈfrītfəl/ ▸*adj.* very unpleasant, serious, or shocking: *there's been a frightful accident.* ■ *informal* used for emphasis, esp. of something bad: *her hair was a frightful mess.* —**fright·ful·ness** *n.*

fright·ful·ly /ˈfrītfəlē/ ▸*adv.* [as *submodifier*] *Brit. dated* very (used for emphasis): *it was frightfully hot* | *I'm frightfully sorry.*

fright wig ▸*n.* a wig with the hair arranged standing up or sticking out, as worn by a clown or similar performer.

frig·id /ˈfrijid/ ▸*adj.* very cold in temperature: *frigid water.* ■ (esp. of a woman) unable or unwilling to be sexually aroused and responsive. ■ showing no friendliness or enthusiasm; stiff or formal in behavior or style: *Henrietta looked back with a frigid calm.* ▷late Middle English: from Latin *frigidus*, from *frigere* 'be cold,' from *frigus* (noun) 'cold.' —**fri·gid·i·ty** /frə'jidətē/ *n.* —**frig·id·ly** *adv.* —**frig·id·ness** *n.*

frig·id zone ▶*n.* (also **Frig·id Zone**) each of the two areas of the earth respectively north of the Arctic Circle and south of the Antarctic Circle. ■ *informal* a range of extremely cold temperatures: *winter temperatures can dip into the frigid zone.*

fri·jol /'frēhōl; frē'hōl/ ▶*n.* (*pl.* **-jo·les** /-hōlz; 'hōlāz; -lēz/) a bean, esp. a red kidney bean or cowpea, used as a staple in Mexican cooking.

fri·jo·les /frē'hōlēz/ ▶*plural n.* (in Mexican cooking) beans. ▷Spanish, plural of *frijol* 'bean.'

fri·jo·les re·fri·tos /rā'frētōs/ ▶ *n.* Spanish term for **REFRIED BEANS.**

frill /fril/ ▶*n.* a strip of gathered or pleated material sewn by one side onto a garment or larger piece of material as a decorative edging or ornament. ■ a thing resembling such a strip in appearance or function: *a frill of silver hair surrounded a shining bald pate.* ■ a natural fringe of feathers or hair on a bird or other animal. ■ *Paleontology* an upward-curving bony plate extending behind the skull of many ceratopsian dinosaurs. ■ (usu. **frills**) *figurative* an unnecessary extra feature or embellishment: *it was just a comfortable apartment with no frills.* ▷late 16th cent.: from or related to Flemish *frul.* —**frilled** *adj.* —**frill·er·y** /'frilərē/ *n.*

frilled liz·ard (also **frill-necked lizard**) ▶*n.* a large northern Australian lizard with a membrane around the neck that can be erected to form a ruff for defensive display. When disturbed, it runs away on its hind legs. • *Chlamydosaurus kingii*, family Agamidae.

frilled lizard

frilled shark ▶*n.* an elongated deep-sea shark of snakelike appearance, with prominent gill covers that give the appearance of a frill around the neck. • *Chlamydoselachus anguineus*, the only member of the family Clamydoselachidae.

frill·y /'frilē/ ▶*adj.* (**frill·i·er, frill·i·est**) decorated with frills or similar ornamentation: *a frilly apron.* ■ overelaborate or showy in character or style: *seafood dishes that avoid being too frilly or rich.*
▶*plural n.* (**frillies**) *informal* an item of women's underwear. —**frill·i·ness** /'frilēnis/ *n.*

Fri·maire /frē'mer/ ▶*n.* the third month of the French Republican calendar (1793–1805), originally running from November 21 to December 20. ▷French, from *frimas* 'hoarfrost.'

fringe /frinj/ ▶*n.* **1** an ornamental border of threads left loose or formed into tassels or twists, used to edge clothing or material. **2** chiefly British term for **BANGS** (see **BANG**[1] sense 2). ■ a natural border of hair or fibers in an animal or plant. **3** (often **the fringes**) the outer, marginal, or extreme part of an area, group, or sphere of activity: *his uncles were on the fringes of crooked activity.* ■ (**the fringe**) the unconventional, extreme, or marginal wing of a group or sphere of activity: *the lunatic fringe of American political life | rap music is no longer something **on the fringe**.* **4** a band of contrasting brightness or darkness produced by diffraction or interference of light. ■ a strip of false color in an optical image. **5** short for **FRINGE BENEFIT.**
▶*adj.* [*attrib.*] not part of the mainstream; unconventional, peripheral, or extreme: *fringe theater.*
▶*v.* [*trans.*] decorate (clothing or material) with a fringe: *a rich robe of gold, **fringed with** black velvet.* ■ (often **be fringed**) form a border around (something): *the sea is fringed by palm trees.* ■ [as *adj.*] (**fringed**) (of a plant or animal) having a natural border of hair or fiber. ▷Middle English: from Old French *frenge*, based on late Latin *fimbria*, earlier a plural noun meaning 'fibers, shreds.' —**fringe·less** *adj.* —**fring·y** /'frinjē/ *adj.*

fringe ben·e·fit ▶*n.* an extra benefit supplementing an employee's salary, for example, a company car, subsidized meals, health insurance, etc.

fringed or·chid ▶*n.* a North American orchid with a flower that has a fringed lip. • Genus *Habenaria*, family Orchidaceae: many species.

fring·ing reef ▶*n.* a coral reef that lies close to the shore.

frip·per·y /'fripərē/ ▶*n.* (*pl.* **-per·ies**) showy or unnecessary ornament in architecture, dress, or language. ■ a tawdry or frivolous thing. ▷mid 16th cent. (denoting old or secondhand clothes): from French *friperie*, from Old French *freperie*, from *frepe* 'rag,' of unknown ultimate origin.

Fris. ▶*abbr.* Frisian.

Fris·bee /'frizbē/ (also **fris·bee**) ▶*n.* *trademark* a concave plastic disk designed for skimming through the air as an outdoor game or amusement. ■ the game or amusement of skimming such a disk. ▷1950s: said to be named after the *Frisbie* bakery (Bridgeport, Connecticut), whose pie tins could be used similarly.

Frisch[1] /frisн/, Karl von (1886–1982), Austrian zoologist. He worked mainly on honeybees, studying particularly their vision, navigation, and communication. He showed that they perform an elaborate dance in the hive to indicate the direction and distance of food. Nobel Prize in Physiology or Medicine (1973, shared with Lorenz and Nikolaas Tinbergen).

Frisch[2], Otto Robert (1904–79), British physicist; born in Austria. With his aunt, Lise Meitner, he recognized that Otto Hahn's experiments with uranium had produced a new type of nuclear reaction, which Frisch called nuclear fission. He also indicated the explosive potential of its chain reaction.

Frisch[3], Ragnar (Anton Kittil) (1895–1973), Norwegian economist; a pioneer of econometrics. Nobel Prize for Economics (1969, shared with Jan Tinbergen).

fri·sée /frē'zā/ ▶*n.* the curly endive (see **ENDIVE** sense 1). ▷French, from *chicorée frisée* 'curly endive.'

Fri·sia /'frizнə; 'frēzнə/ an ancient region in northwestern Europe. It included the Frisian Islands and parts of the mainland corresponding to the modern provinces of Friesland and Groningen in the Netherlands and the regions of Ostfriesland and Nordfriesland in northwestern Germany.

Fri·sian /'frizнən; 'frē-/ ▶*adj.* of or relating to Frisia or Friesland, its people, or language.
▶*n.* **1** a native or inhabitant of Frisia or Friesland. **2** the West Germanic language of Frisia or Friesland, the language most closely related to English. ▷late 16th cent.: from Latin *Frisii* 'Frisians' (from Old Frisian *Frīsa, Frēsa*) + **-IAN.**

Fri·sian Is·lands a chain of islands that lie off the coast of northwestern Europe and extend from the IJsselmeer in the Netherlands to Jutland. The **West Frisian Islands** form part of the Netherlands, the **East Frisian Islands** form part of Germany, and the **North Frisian Islands** are divided between Germany and Denmark.

frisk /frisk/ ▶*v.* **1** [*trans.*] (of a police officer or other official) pass the hands over (someone) in a search for hidden weapons, drugs, or other items. **2** [*intrans.*] (of an animal or person) skip or leap playfully; frolic: *this did not deter the foal from **frisking about**.* ■ [*trans.*] (of an animal) move or wave (its tail or legs) playfully: *a horse was frisking his back legs like a colt.*
▶*n.* **1** [in *sing.*] an act of frisking someone. **2** a playful skip or leap. ▷early 16th cent. (sense 2): from obsolete *frisk* 'lively, frisky,' from Old French *frisque* 'alert, lively, merry,' perhaps of Germanic origin. Sense 1, originally a slang term, dates from the late 18th cent. —**frisk·er** *n.*

fris·ket /'friskit/ ▶*n.* *Printing* a thin metal frame keeping the paper in position during printing on a hand press. ■ fluid or adhesive paper used in painting or crafts to cover areas of a surface on which paint is not wanted.
▶*v.* [*trans.*] apply such a fluid or adhesive paper to (a surface): *the first step was to frisket all the panels.* ▷late 17th cent.: from French *frisquette*, from Provençal *frisqueto*, from Spanish *frasqueta.*

frisk·y /'friskē/ ▶*adj.* (**frisk·i·er, frisk·i·est**) playful and full of energy: *he bounds about like a frisky pup.* —**frisk·i·ly** /'friskəlē/ *adv.* —**frisk·i·ness** *n.*

fris·son /frē'sôɴ/ ▶*n.* a sudden strong feeling of excitement or fear; a thrill: *a frisson of excitement.* ▷late 18th cent.: French, literally 'a shiver or thrill.'

frit /frit/ ▶*n.* the mixture of silica and fluxes that is fused at high temperature to make glass. ■ a similar calcined and pulverized mixture used to make soft-paste porcelain or ceramic glazes.
▶*v.* (**frit·ted, frit·ting**) [*trans.*] make into frit. ▷mid 17th cent.: from Italian *fritta*, feminine past participle of *friggere* 'to fry.'

frites /frēt(s)/ ▶*plural n.* short for **POMMES FRITES.**

frit fly ▶*n.* a very small black fly whose larvae are a serious pest of cereal crops and golf-course turf. • *Oscinella frit*, family Chloropidae. ▷late 19th cent.: from Latin *frit* 'particle on an ear of grain.'

frith /friтн/ ▶*n.* archaic spelling of **FIRTH.**

frit·il·lar·y /'fritl,erē/ ▶*n.* **1** a Eurasian plant of the lily family, with hanging bell-like flowers. • Genus *Fritillaria*, family Liliaceae: numerous species. **2** a butterfly with orange-brown wings that are checkered with black. • Subfamilies Argynninae and Melitaeinae, family Nymphalidae: *Argynnis, Speyeria*, and other genera, and numerous species, including the North American **great spangled fritillary** (*S. cybele*). ▷mid 17th cent.: from modern Latin *fritillaria*, from Latin *fritillus* 'dice box' (probably with reference to the checkered corolla of the snake's-head fritillary).

great spangled fritillary

frit·ta·ta /frē'tätə/ ▶*n.* an Italian dish made with fried beaten eggs, resembling a Spanish omelet. ▷Italian, from *fritto*, past participle of *friggere* 'to fry.' Compare with **FRITTER**[2].

frit·ter[1] /'fritər/ ▶*v.* [*trans.*] **1** (**fritter something away**) waste time, money, or energy on trifling matters: *I wish we hadn't frittered the money away so easily.* ■ [*intrans.*] dwindle; diminish: *the day fritters.* **2** *archaic* divide (something) into small pieces: *they become frittered into minute tatters.* ▷early 18th cent.: based on obsolete *fitter* 'break into fragments, shred'; perhaps related to German *Fetzen* 'rag, scrap.' —**frit·ter·er** *n.*

frit·ter[2] ▶*n.* a piece of fruit, vegetable, or meat that is coated in batter and deep-fried. ▷late Middle English: from Old French *friture*, based on Latin *frigere* (see **FRY**[1]). Compare with **FRITTATA.**

frit·to mi·sto /,frētō 'mēstō/ ▶*n.* a dish of various foods, typically seafood, deep-fried in batter. ▷Italian, 'mixed fry.'

fritz /frits/ ▶*n.* (in phrase **go** or **be on the fritz**) *informal* (of a machine) stop working properly. ▷early 20th cent.: said to be a use of *Fritz*, with allusion to cheap German imports into the U.S. before World War I.

Fri·u·li /frē'o͞olē/ a historic region in southeastern Europe now divided between Slovenia and the Italian region of Friuli-Venezia Giulia. —**Fri·u·li·an** /-'o͞olēən/ *adj.* & *n.*

Fri·u·li-Ve·ne·zia Giu·lia /frē'o͞olē vä'netsēə 'jo͞olyə/ a region in northeastern Italy, on the border with Slovenia and Austria; capital, Trieste.

friv·ol /'frivəl/ ▶*v.* (**friv·oled, friv·ol·ing**; *Brit.* **friv·olled, friv·ol·ling**) [*intrans.*] behave in a frivolous way. ▷mid 19th cent.: back-formation from **FRIVOLOUS.**

friv·o·lous /'frivələs/ ▶*adj.* not having any serious purpose or value: *rules to stop frivolous lawsuits.* ■ (of a person) carefree and not serious. ▷late Middle English: from Latin *frivolus* 'silly, trifling' + **-OUS.** —**fri·vol·i·ty** /fri'välətē/ *n.* —**friv·o·lous·ly** *adv.* —**friv·o·lous·ness** *n.*

frizz /friz/ ▶*v.* [*trans.*] form (hair) into a mass of small, tight curls or tufts: *her hair was frizzed up in a style that seemed matronly.* ■ [*intrans.*] (of hair) form itself into such a mass: *his hair had frizzed out symmetrically.*
▶*n.* the state of being formed into such a mass of curls or tufts: *a perm designed to add curl without frizz.* ▷late Middle English (in the sense 'dress leather with pumice'): from French *friser*. The sense 'form hair into a mass of curls' dates from the late 16th cent.

friz·zan·te /frit'säntā/ ▸*adj.* (of wine) semisparkling. ▷Italian.

friz·zle[1] /'frizəl/ ▸*v.* [*intrans.*] fry or grill with a sizzling noise: *Elsie had the fat frizzling in the frying pan.* ■ [*trans.*] fry until crisp, shriveled, or burned: [as *adj.*] (**frizzled**) *add diced frizzled salt pork to taste.*
▸*n.* [in *sing.*] the sound or act of frying: *the frizzle of the pan.* ▷mid 18th cent.: from **FRY**[1], probably influenced by **SIZZLE**.

friz·zle[2] ▸*v.* [*trans.*] form (hair) into tight curls.
▸*n.* a tight curl in hair. ▷mid 16th cent.: from **FRIZZ** + **-LE**[4]. **—friz·zly** /'friz(ə)lē/ *adj.*

friz·zy /'frizē/ ▸*adj.* (**-zi·er**, **-zi·est**) formed of a mass of small, tight curls or tufts: *frizzy red hair.* **—friz·zi·ness** *n.*

fro /frō/ ▸*adv.* see **TO AND FRO**. ▷Middle English: from Old Norse *frá* (see **FROM**).

Fro·bish·er /'frōbishər/, Sir Martin (*c.*1535–94), English explorer. In 1576, he led an unsuccessful expedition in search of the Northwest Passage. Frobisher served in Sir Francis Drake's Caribbean expedition of 1585–86 and took part in the defeat of the Spanish Armada.

frock /fräk/ ▸*n.* **1** a woman's or girl's dress. **2** a loose outer garment, in particular: ■ a long gown with flowing sleeves worn by monks, priests, or clergy. ■ *historical* a field laborer's smock. ■ short for **FROCK COAT**. **3** [in *sing.*] *archaic* priestly office: *such words as these cost the preacher his frock.*
▸*v.* [*trans.*] provide with or dress in a frock: [as *adj.*, in *combination*] *a black-frocked Englishman.* ■ *archaic* invest (someone) with priestly office. Compare with **DEFROCK**. ▷late Middle English: from Old French *froc*, of Germanic origin. The sense 'priest's or monk's gown' is preserved in *defrock*.

frock coat ▸*n.* a man's double-breasted, long-skirted coat, now worn chiefly on formal occasions.

F

froe /frō/ ▸*n.* a cleaving tool with a handle at right angles to the blade. ▷late 16th cent.: abbreviation of obsolete *frower*, from **FROWARD** in the sense 'turned away.'

Froe·bel /'frœbəl/, Friedrich (Wilhelm August) (1782–1852), German educator and founder of the kindergarten system.

frog[1] /frôg; fräg/ ▸*n.* **1** a tailless amphibian with a short squat body, moist smooth skin, and very long hind legs for leaping. • Frogs are found in most families of the order Anura, but the 'true frogs' are confined to the large family Ranidae. ■ *informal* a person regarded as repulsive in character or appearance. **2** (**Frog**) *informal, offensive* a French person.
▸*v.* [*intrans.*] hunt for or catch frogs. ▷Old English *frogga*, of Germanic origin; related to Dutch *vors* and German *Frosch*. Used as a general term of abuse in Middle English, the term was applied specifically to the Dutch in the 17th cent.; its application to the French (late 18th cent.) is partly alliterative, partly from the reputation of the French for eating frogs' legs. **—frog·ger** *n.* **—frog·gy** *adj.*
▸*PHRASE* □ **have a frog in one's throat** *informal* lose one's voice or find it hard to speak because of hoarseness.

frog[2] ▸*n.* a thing used to hold or fasten something, in particular: ■ an ornamental coat fastener or braid consisting of a spindle-shaped button and a loop through which it passes. ■ an attachment to a belt for holding a sword, bayonet, or similar weapon. ■ a perforated or spiked device for holding the stems of flowers in an arrangement. ■ the piece into which the hair is fitted at the lower end of the bow of a stringed instrument. ■ a grooved metal plate for guiding the wheels of a railroad vehicle at an intersection. ▷early 18th cent.: perhaps a use of **FROG**[1], influenced by synonymous Italian *forchetta* or French *fourchette* 'small fork,' because of the shape.

frog[3] ▸*n.* an elastic horny pad growing in the sole of a horse's hoof, helping to absorb the shock when the hoof hits the ground. ■ a raised or swollen area on a surface. ▷early 17th cent.: perhaps from **FROG**[2].

frog·fish /'frôg,fish/ ▸*n.* (*pl.* same or **-fish·es**) an anglerfish that typically lives on the seabed, where its warty skin and color provide camouflage. • Families Antennariidae (numerous species, including *Antennaria hispidus* of the Indo-Pacific), and Brachionichthyidae (four Australian species).

frogged /'frôgd; frägd/ ▸*adj.* (of a coat) having an ornamental braid or fastening consisting of a spindle-shaped button and a loop.

frog·ging /'frôging; fräg-/ ▸*n.* ornamental braid or coat fastenings consisting of spindle-shaped buttons and loops.

frog·hop·per /'frôg,häpər; fräg-/ ▸*n.* a jumping, plant-sucking bug, the larva of which produces a frothy mass on plants. Also called **SPITTLEBUG**. • Family Cercopidae, suborder Homoptera: several genera.

frog kick ▸*n.* a movement used in swimming, esp. in the breast stroke, in which the legs are brought toward the body with the knees bent and the feet together and then kicked outward before being brought together again, all in one continuous movement.

frog·let /'frôglət; 'fräg-/ ▸*n.* **1** a small kind of frog. • Several genera, including *Crinia* of Australia (family Myobatrachidae), and *Philautus* of Malaysia (family Rhacophoridae). **2** a tiny frog that has recently developed from a tadpole.

frog·man /'frôg,man; 'fräg-; -mən/ ▸*n.* (*pl.* **-men**) a person who swims underwater wearing a rubber suit, flippers, and an oxygen supply. Also called **SCUBA DIVER**.

frog·march /'frôg,märch; 'fräg-/ ▸*v.* [*trans.*] force (someone) to walk forward by holding and pinning their arms from behind: *the cop frogmarched him down the steep stairs.*

frog·mouth /'frôg,mouth; 'fräg-/ ▸*n.* a nocturnal bird resembling a nightjar, occurring in Southeast Asia and Australasia. • Family Podargidae: two genera and several species, in particular the **tawny frogmouth** (*Podargus strigoides*) of Australia.

frog or·chid ▸*n.* a small orchid with inconspicuous green flowers, growing chiefly on calcareous grassland in north temperate regions. • *Coeloglossum viride*, family Orchidaceae.

frog's-bit ▸*n.* a floating freshwater plant with creeping stems that bear clusters of small rounded leaves. • Two species in the family Hydrocharitaceae: **Eurasian frog's-bit** (*Hydrocharis morsus-ranae*) and **American frog's-bit** (*Limnobium spongia*).

frog·spawn /'frôg,spôn; 'fräg-/ ▸*n.* the eggs of a frog, which are surrounded by transparent jelly.

frog spit ▸*n.* another term for **CUCKOO SPIT**.

froi·deur /frwä'dər/ ▸*n.* coolness or reserve between people. ▷French, from *froid* 'cold.'

frol·ic /'frälik/ ▸*v.* (**frol·icked**, **frol·ick·ing**) [*intrans.*] (of an animal or person) play and move about cheerfully, excitedly, or energetically: *Edward* ***frolicked on*** *the sand.* ■ play about with someone in a flirtatious or sexual way: *he denied allegations that he* ***frolicked with*** *a secretary.*
▸*n.* (often **frolics**) a playful action or movement: *his injuries were inflicted by the frolics of a young filly | the days of fun and frolic were gone for good.* ■ flirtatious or sexual activity or actions: *her poolside frolics.*
▸*adj. archaic* cheerful, merry, or playful: *a thousand forms of frolic life.* ▷early 16th cent. (as an adjective): from Dutch *vrolijk* 'merry, cheerful.' **—frol·ick·er** *n.*

frol·ic·some /'fräliksəm/ ▸*adj.* lively and playful. **—frol·ic·some·ly** *adv.* **—frol·ic·some·ness** *n.*

from /frəm/ ▸*prep.* **1** indicating the point in space at which a journey, motion, or action starts: *she began to walk away from him | I leapt from my bed | figurative he was turning the committee away from appeasement.* ■ indicating the distance between a particular place and another place used as a point of reference: *the ambush occurred 50 yards from a checkpoint.* **2** indicating the point in time at which a particular process, event, or activity starts: *the show will run from 10 to 2.* **3** indicating the source or provenance of someone or something: *I'm from Hartford | she phoned him from the hotel | she demanded the keys from her husband.* ■ indicating the date at which something was created: *a document dating from the thirteenth century.* **4** indicating the starting point of a specified range on a scale: *men who ranged in age* ***from*** *seventeen* ***to*** *eighty-four.* ■ indicating one extreme in a range of conceptual variations: *anything* ***from*** *geography* ***to*** *literature.* **5** indicating the point at which an observer is placed: *you can see the island from here | figurative the ability to see things from another's point of view.* **6** indicating the raw material out of which something is manufactured: *a varnish made from copal.* **7** indicating separation or removal: *the party was ousted from power after sixteen years.* **8** indicating prevention: *the story of how he was saved from death.* **9** indicating a cause: *a child suffering from asthma.* **10** indicating a source of knowledge or the basis for one's judgment: *information obtained from papers, books, and presentations.* **11** indicating a distinction: *the courts view him in a different light from that of a manual worker.* ▷Old English *fram*, *from*, of Germanic origin; related to Old Norse *frá* (see **FRO**).
▸*PHRASES* □ **as from** see **AS**[1]. □ **from day to day** (or **hour to hour**, etc.) daily (or hourly, etc.); as the days (or hours, etc.) pass. □ **from now** (or **then**, etc.) **on** now (or then, etc.) and in the future: *they were friends from that day on.* □ **from time to time** occasionally.

fro·mage blanc /frō,mäzh 'bläNgk/ ▸*n.* a type of soft French cheese made from cow's milk and having a creamy sour taste. ▷French, literally 'white cheese.'

Fromm /främ/, Erich (1900–80), U.S. psychoanalyst and social philosopher; born in Germany. His works, which include *Escape from Freedom* (1941), *Man for Himself* (1947), and *The Sane Society* (1955), emphasize the role of culture in neurosis and strongly criticize materialist values.

frond /fränd/ ▸*n.* the leaf or leaflike part of a palm, fern, or similar plant: *fronds of bracken | figurative her hair escaped in wayward fronds.* ▷late 18th cent.: from Latin *frons*, *frond-* 'leaf.' **—frond·ed** *adj.*

Fronde /fränd; frôNd/ a series of civil wars in France 1648–53, in which the nobles rose in rebellion against Mazarin and the court during the minority of Louis XIV. Although some concessions were obtained, the nobles were not successful in curbing the power of the monarchy. ▷late 18th cent.: French, from the name for a type of sling used in a children's game played in the streets of Paris at this time.

fron·deur /,frôN'dər/ ▸*n. rare* a political rebel. ▷mid 19th cent.: French, literally 'slinger,' used to denote a member of the **FRONDE**.

frons /fränz/ ▸*n.* (*pl.* **fron·tes** /'fräntēz/) *Zoology* the forehead or equivalent part of an animal, esp. the middle part of an insect's face between the eyes and above the clypeus. ▷mid 19th cent.: from Latin, 'front, forehead.'

front /frənt/ ▸*n.* **1** the side or part of an object that presents itself to view or that is normally seen or used first; the most forward part of something: *a page at the front of the book had been torn out | he sealed the envelope and wrote on the front.* ■ [in *sing.*] the position directly ahead of someone or something; the most forward position or place: *she quickly turned her head to face the front.* ■ the forward-facing part of a person's body, on the opposite side to their back. ■ the part of a garment covering this: *oatmeal slopped from the tray on to his shirt front.* ■ *informal* a woman's bust or cleavage. ■ any face of a building, esp. that of the main entrance: *the west front of the cathedral.* ■ *chiefly Brit.* short for **SEAFRONT** or **WATERFRONT**. **2** the foremost line or part of an armed force; the furthest position that an army has reached and where the enemy is or may be engaged: *his regiment was immediately sent to the front.* ■ the direction toward which a line of troops faces when formed. ■ a particular formation of troops for battle. ■ a particular situation or sphere of operation: *there was some good news on the jobs front.* ■ [often in *names*] an organized political group: *the Palestinian Liberation Front.* ■ *Meteorology* the forward edge of an advancing mass of air. See **COLD FRONT**, **OCCLUDED FRONT**, **WARM FRONT**. **3** [in *sing.*] an appearance or form of behavior assumed by a person to conceal their genuine feelings: *she put on a brave front.* ■ a person or organization serving as a cover for subversive or illegal activities: *the CIA identified the company as* ***a front for*** *a terrorist group.* ■ a well-known or prestigious person who acts as a representative, rather than an active member, of an organization. See also **FRONTMAN**. **4** boldness and confidence of manner: *he's got a bit of talent and a lot of front.* **5** *archaic* a person's face or forehead.
▸*adj.* [*attrib.*] **1** of or at the front: *the front cover of the magazine | she was in the front yard.* **2** *Phonetics* (of a vowel sound) formed by raising the body of the tongue, excluding the blade and tip, toward the hard palate.
▸*v.* [*trans.*] **1** (of a building or piece of land) have the front facing or directed toward: *the houses that front Beacon Street | [intrans.] we sold the uphill land that* ***fronted on*** *the road.* ■ be or stand in front of: *they reached the hedge fronting the garden.* ■ *archaic* stand face to face with; confront: *Tom fronted him with unwavering eyes.* **2** (usu. **be fronted**) provide (something) with a front or facing of a particular type or material: *a metal box fronted by an alloy panel |* [as *adj.*, in *combination*] (**-fronted**) *a glass-fronted bookcase.* **3** lead or be the most prominent member in (an organization, activity, or group of musicians): *the group is fronted by two girl singers.* ■ present or host (a television or radio program). ■ [*intrans.*] act as a front or cover for someone or something acting illegally or wishing to conceal something: *he* ***fronted for*** *them in illegal property deals.* **4** *Phonetics* articulate (a vowel sound) with the tongue further forward: [as *adj.*] (**fronted**) *all speakers*

use raised and fronted variants more in spontaneous speech. **5** *Linguistics* place (a sentence element) at the beginning of a sentence instead of in its usual position, typically for emphasis or as feature of some dialects, as in *horrible it was.*
▸*exclam.* used to summon someone to the front or to command them to assume a forward-facing position, as in calling a bellhop to the front desk or giving orders to troops on parade: *scouts,* ***front and center!*** ▷Middle English (denoting the forehead): from Old French *front* (noun), *fronter* (verb), from Latin *frons, front-* 'forehead, front.' **—fron·ting** /'frəntiNG/ *n.* **—front·less** *adj.* **—front·ward** /-wərd/ *adj.* & *adv.* **—front·wards** /-wərdz/ *adv.*
▸**PHRASES** □ **in front 1** in a position just ahead of or further forward than someone or something else: *the car in front stopped suddenly.* ■ in the lead in a game or contest: *the Reds were in front until the eighth inning.* **2** on the part or side that normally first presents itself to view: *a house with a wide porch in front.* □ **in front of 1** in a position just ahead or at the front part of someone or something else: *the lawn in front of the house.* ■ in a position facing someone or something: *she sat in front of the mirror.* **2** in the presence of: *the teacher didn't want his authority challenged in front of the class.* □ **out front** at or to the front; in front: *two station wagons stopped out front.* ■ in the auditorium of a theater. □ **up front 1** at or near the front: *the floor plan has an open living area up front.* **2** in advance: *every fee must be paid up front.* **3** open and direct; frank: *I vowed to be up front with her.*

front·age /'frəntij/ ▸*n.* the facade of a building. ■ the direction this faces: *beautiful homes with river frontage.* ■ a strip or extent of land abutting on a street or water: *the houses have a narrow* ***frontage*** *to the street | our lot has a frontage of 153 feet, with a depth of 170 feet.*

front·age road ▸*n.* a subsidiary road running parallel to a main road and giving access to houses, and businesses. Also called SERVICE ROAD.

fron·tal[1] /'frəntl/ ▸*adj.* of or at the front: *the frontal view misses the octagonal tower.* ■ (of an attack) delivered directly on the front, not the side or back: *a frontal assault upon the Iraqi fortifications.* ■ of or relating to the forehead or front part of the skull: *the frontal sinuses.* ▷mid 17th cent. (in the sense 'relating to the forehead'): from modern Latin *frontalis,* from Latin *frons, front-* 'front, forehead.' **—fron·tal·ly** /'frəntl-ē/ *adv.*

fron·tal[2] ▸*n.* a decorative cloth for covering the front of an altar. ▷Middle English (denoting a band or ornament worn on the forehead): from Old French *frontel,* from Latin *frontale,* from *frons, front-* 'front, forehead.'

fron·tal bone ▸*n.* the bone that forms the front part of the skull and the upper part of the eye sockets. ■ either of the pair of bones from which this is formed by fusion in infancy.

fron·tal lobe ▸*n.* each of the paired lobes of the brain lying immediately behind the forehead, including areas concerned with behavior, learning, personality, and voluntary movement.

fron·tal lo·bot·o·my ▸*n.* lobotomy of the frontal lobe of the cerebrum to sever the white connecting fibers.

front-and-center ▸*adj.* prominent; at the forefront: *a list of society's front-and-center concerns.* **—front and center** *adv. Arizona's Lute Olson stands front and center, making his presence known to every hopeful wearing a triple-digit number on his back.*

front bench ▸*n.* (in the UK) the foremost seats in the House of Commons, occupied by the members of the cabinet and shadow cabinet. **—front·bench·er** /,frənt'benCHər/ *n.*

front bot·tom ▸*n. chiefly Brit. informal* used euphemistically to refer to the female genitalia: *these are women who insist on a "no front bottom" clause.*

front burn·er ▸*n. figurative* the focus of attention: *a revamp of the 1872 Mining Law is next up* ***on the front burner.*** Compare with BACK BURNER.

front court ▸*n.* the part of a basketball court where each team tries to score against its opponent. ■ the players on a team who usually play closest to the other team's basket when trying to score.

Front de Lib·ér·a·tion Na·tion·ale /,frôN də ,libə,räs-'yôN ,näsyənäl/ (abbr.: **FLN**) a revolutionary political party in Algeria that supported the war of independence against France 1954–62. ▷French, 'National Liberation Front.'

front desk ▸*n.* the main desk at a hotel or motel, for checking in or out and handling requests from guests.

Fron·te·nac /'frontə,nak; frônt(ə)'näk/, Louis de Buade, Comte de (1622–98), French politician. He served as governor of New France 1672–82, 1689–98.

front-end ▸*adj.* [*attrib.*] of or relating to the front of a car or other vehicle: *front-end styling.* ■ *informal* (of money) paid or charged at the beginning of a transaction: *a front-end fee.* ■ *Computing* (of a device or program) directly accessed by the user and allowing access to further devices, programs, or databases.
▸*n. Computing* a part of a computer or program that allows access to other parts.

front-end load ▸*n.* the deduction of commission fees and expenses from mutual fund shares at the time of purchase.

front-end load·er ▸*n.* a machine with a scoop or bucket on an articulated arm at the front for digging and loading earth. ■ a hydraulic bucket or scoop that fits on to the front of a tractor.

fron·tes /'fräntēz/ ▸ plural form of FRONS.

front-fanged ▸*adj.* (of a snake such as a cobra or viper) having the front pair of teeth modified as fangs, with grooves or canals to conduct the venom. Compare with BACK-FANGED.

fron·tier /,frən'ti(ə)r/ ▸*n.* a line or border separating two countries. ■ the district near such a line. ■ the extreme limit of settled land beyond which lies wilderness, esp. referring to the western U.S. before Pacific settlement: *his novel of the American frontier.* ■ the extreme limit of understanding or achievement in a particular area: *the success of science in extending the frontiers of knowledge.* ▷late Middle English: from Old French *frontiere,* based on Latin *frons, front-* 'front.' **—fron·tier·less** *adj.*

fron·tiers·man /,frən'ti(ə)rzmən/ ▸*n.* (*pl.* **-men**) a person, esp. a man, living in the region of a frontier, esp. that between settled and unsettled country.

fron·tiers·wom·an /,frən'ti(ə)rz,wo͝omən/ ▸*n.* (*pl.* **-women**) a woman living in the region of a frontier, esp. that between settled and unsettled country.

fron·tis·piece /'frəntis,pēs/ ▸*n.* **1** an illustration facing the title page of a book. **2** *Architecture* the principal face of a building. ■ a decorated entrance. ■ a pediment over a door or window. ▷late 16th cent. (sense 2): from French *frontispice* or late Latin *frontispicium* 'facade,' from Latin *frons, front-* 'front' + *specere* 'to look.' The change in the ending (early in the word's history) was by association with PIECE.

front·let /'frəntlət/ ▸*n.* **1** an ornamental piece of cloth hanging over the upper part of an altar frontal. **2** *dated* a decorative band or ornament worn on the forehead. ■ another term for PHYLACTERY. ■ a piece of armor or harness for an animal's forehead. ▷late 15th cent. (sense 2): from Old French *frontelet,* diminutive of *frontel* (see FRONTAL[2]).

front line (also **front·line**) ▸*n.* (usu. **the front line**) the military line or part of an army that is closest to the enemy: [as *adj.*] *the front-line troops.* ■ the most important or influential position in a debate or movement: *it is doctors who are on the front line of the euthanasia debate.*

front-line state ▸*plural n.* a country that borders on an area troubled by a war or other crisis: *Germany will no longer be a front-line state with little strategic depth.*

front-load ▸*v.* [*trans.*] to incur the greater share of expenses in (a project) at the beginning or early stages.

front·man /'frənt,man; -mən/ ▸*n.* (*pl.* **-men**) a person who leads or represents a group or organization, in particular: ■ the leader of a group of musicians, esp. the lead singer of a pop group. ■ (also **front**) a person who represents an illegal or disreputable organization to give it an air of legitimacy.

front mat·ter ▸*n.* the pages preceding the main text of a book, including the title, table of contents, and preface.

front mon·ey ▸*n.* money received at the beginning of the period of a contract, or money spent in advance of a business operation before income can be obtained: *sought investors willing to put up front money to stage the Broadway musical.*

front of·fice ▸*n.* the management or administrative officers of a business or other organization.

fron·ton /'frän,tän/ ▸*n.* **1** a building where pelota or jai alai is played. **2** another term for PEDIMENT. ▷late 17th cent.: from French, from Italian *frontone,* from *fronte* 'forehead,' from Latin *frons, front-* 'front, forehead.'

front-page ▸*adj.* appearing on the first page of a newspaper or similar publication and containing important or remarkable news: *they ran a front-page story headlined "White-Collar Chic."* ■ worthy of being printed on the first page of a newspaper, etc.: *dishonest research has become front-page news.*
▸*v.* [*trans.*] print (a story) on the first page of a newspaper, etc.: *the paper had front-paged a 1988 discovery at one of his nearby digs.*

Front Range the easternmost range of the Rocky Mountains, chiefly in Colorado, that reaches 14,270 feet (4,349 m) at Grays Peak; also home to Pikes Peak.

front run·ner ▸*n.* the contestant that is leading in a race or other competition. ■ an athlete or horse that runs best when in the front of the field.

front-run·ning ▸*adj.* ahead in a race or other competition. ■ (of an athlete or horse) running best when in front of the field.
▸*n.* **1** *Stock Market* the practice by market makers of dealing on advance information provided by their brokers and investment analysts, before their clients have been given the information. **2** the practice of giving one's support to a competitor because they are in front.

front·side /'frənt,sīd/ ▸*adj.* [*attrib.*] denoting a maneuver in surfing and other board sports that is done counterclockwise for a regular rider and clockwise for a goofy rider.

front-wheel drive ▸*n.* a transmission system that provides power to the front wheels of a motor vehicle.

frore /frôr/ ▸*adj. poetic/literary* frozen; frosty. ▷Middle English: archaic past participle of FREEZE.

Frost /frôst/, Robert (Lee) (1874–1963), U.S. poet, noted for his ironic tone and simple language. Much of his poetry reflects his ties to New England, including the collections *North of Boston* (1914) and *New Hampshire* (1923). He won Pulitzer Prizes in 1924, 1931, and 1937.

frost /frôst/ ▸*n.* a deposit of small white ice crystals formed on the ground or other surfaces when the temperature falls below freezing. ■ a period of cold weather when such deposits form: *when the hard frosts had set in.* ■ *figurative* a chilling or dispiriting quality, esp. one conveyed by a cold manner: *there was a light frost of anger in Jack's tone.* ■ [in *sing.*] *informal, chiefly Brit.* a failure.
▸*v.* [*trans.*] cover (something) with or as if with small ice crystals; freeze: *each windowpane was frosted along its edges.* ■ [*intrans.*] become covered with small ice crystals: *a mustache that* ***frosts up*** *when he's ice-climbing.* ■ decorate (a cake, cupcake, or other baked item) with icing. ■ tint hair strands to change the color of isolated strands. ■ injure (a plant) by freezing weather. ■ *informal* anger or annoy: *such discrimination frosted her no end.* ▷Old English *frost, forst,* of Germanic origin; related to Dutch *vorst* and German *Frost,* also to FREEZE. **—frost·less** *adj.*

frost·bite /'frôs(t),bīt/ ▸*n.* injury to body tissues caused by exposure to extreme cold, typically affecting the nose, fingers, or toes and sometimes resulting in gangrene.

frost·ed /'frôstid/ ▸*adj.* covered with or as if with frost: *I stood looking out on the frosted garden.* ■ (of glass or a window) having a translucent textured surface so that it is difficult to see through. ■ (of food) decorated or dusted with icing or sugar. ■ (of hair) having isolated strands tinted a light color.

frost flow·er ▸*n.* any of a group of delicate clusters of ice crystals that form directly from water vapor, typically on the surface of sea ice.

frost-free ▸*adj.* free of a buildup of ice without defrosting: *a frost-free freezer*

frost heave ▸*n.* the uplift of water-saturated soil or other surface deposits due to expansion on freezing. ■ a mound formed in this way, esp. when broken through the pavement of a road. **—frost heav·ing** *n.*

frost·ing /'frôstiNG/ ▸*n.* **1** icing. **2** a roughened matte finish on otherwise shiny material such as glass or steel.

frost line ▸*n.* [in *sing.*] the maximum depth of ground below which the soil does not freeze in winter.

frost·work /'frôst,wərk/ ▸*n.* attractive patterns made by frost on a window or other surface.

frost·y /'frôstē/ ▸*adj.* (**frost·i·er, frost·i·est**) **1** (of the weather) very cold with frost forming on surfaces: *a cold and frosty morning.* ■ covered with or as if with frost: *the dog crouched in the frosty grass.* **2** cold and

F

Pronunciation Key ə *ago*; ər *over*; 'ə or ,ə *up*; 'ər or ,ər *fur*; a *hat*; ā *rate*; ä *car*; CH *chew*; e *let*; ē *see*; e(ə)r *air*; i *fit*; ī *by*; i(ə)r *ear*; NG *sing*; ō *go*; ô *for*; oi *boy*; o͝o *good*; o͞o *goo*; ou *out*; SH *she*; TH *thin*; TH *then*; (h)w *why*; ZH *vision*

unfriendly in manner: *Sam gave her a frosty look.* **—frost·i·ly** /ˈfrôstəlē/ *adv.* **—frost·i·ness** /-stēnis/ *n.*

froth /frôTH/ ▸*n.* a mass of small bubbles in liquid caused by agitation, fermentation, etc.; foam: *leave the yeast until there is a good head of froth.* ■ impure matter that rises to the surface of liquid: *skim off any surface froth.* ■ *figurative* a thing that rises or overflows in a soft, light mass: *her skirt swirled in a froth of black lace.* ■ worthless or insubstantial talk, ideas, or activities: *the froth of party politics.*
▸*v.* [*intrans.*] form or contain a rising or overflowing mass of small bubbles: *he took a quick sip of beer as it frothed out of the can* | [as *adj.*] (**frothing**) *scooping salmon out of the frothing gorge.* ■ *figurative* rise or overflow in a soft, light mass: *she wore an ivory silk blouse, frothing at neck and cuffs.* ■ [*trans.*] agitate (a liquid) so as to produce a mass of small bubbles. ▷late Middle English: from Old Norse *frotha, frauth.*
▸*PHRASE* □ **froth at the mouth** emit a large amount of saliva from the mouth in a bodily seizure. ■ *figurative* display intense anger: *one can barely read a word about them without frothing at the mouth.*

froth·y /ˈfrôTHē; -T͟Hē/ ▸*adj.* (**froth·i·er, froth·i·est**) full of or covered with a mass of small bubbles: *steaming mugs of frothy coffee.* ■ light and entertaining but of little substance: *lots of frothy interviews.* **—froth·i·ly** /-THəlē; T͟Həlē/ *adv.* **—froth·i·ness** /-THēnis; T͟Hēnis/ *n.*

frot·tage /frôˈtäZH/ ▸*n.* **1** *Art* the technique or process of taking a rubbing from an uneven surface to form the basis of a work of art. ■ a work of art produced in this way. **2** the practice of touching or rubbing against the clothed body of another person in a crowd as a means of obtaining sexual gratification. ▷1930s: French, 'rubbing, friction.' **—frot·teur** /-ˈtər/ *n.* (*pl.* same) (in sense 2). **—frot·teur·ism** /-ˈtərˌizəm/ *n.* (in sense 2).

frot·to·la /ˈfrätl-ə/ ▸*n.* (*pl.* **frot·to·le** /ˈfrätl-ā/) *Music* a form of Italian comic or amorous song, esp. from the 15th and 16th centuries. ▷Italian, literally 'fib, tall tale.'

F

Froude num·ber /froud/ ▸*n.* a dimensionless number used in hydrodynamics to indicate how well a particular model works in relation to a real system. ▷mid 19th cent.: named after William *Froude* (1810–79), English civil engineer.

frou·frou /ˈfro͞oˌfro͞o/ (also **frou-frou**) ▸*n.* a rustling noise made by someone walking in a dress. ■ frills or other ornamentation, particularly of women's clothes: [as *adj.*] *a little froufrou skirt.* ▷late 19th cent.: from French, imitative.

frounce /frouns/ ▸*n. Falconry* a form of trichomoniasis affecting hawks, resulting in a sore with a cheesy secretion in the mouth or throat. ▷late Middle English: of unknown origin.

fro·ward /ˈfrō(w)ərd/ ▸*adj.* (of a person) difficult to deal with; contrary. ▷late Old English *frāward* 'leading away from, away,' based on Old Norse *frá* (see **FRO, FROM**). **—fro·ward·ly** *adv.* **—fro·ward·ness** *n.*

frown /froun/ ▸*v.* [*intrans.*] furrow one's brow in an expression of disapproval, displeasure, or concentration: *he frowned as he reread the letter.* ■ (**frown on/upon**) disapprove of: *the old Russian rural system frowned on private enterprise.*
▸*n.* a facial expression or look characterized by such a furrowing of one's brows: *a frown of disapproval.* ▷late Middle English: from Old French *froignier*, from *froigne* 'surly look,' of Celtic origin. **—frown·er** *n.* **—frown·ing·ly** *adv.*

frowst /froust/ *informal, chiefly Brit.* ▸*n.* [in *sing.*] a warm stuffy atmosphere in a room.
▸*v.* [*intrans.*] lounge about in such an atmosphere: *don't frowst by the fire all day.* ▷late 19th cent.: back-formation from **FROWSTY**. **—frowst·er** *n.*

frowst·y /ˈfroustē/ ▸*adj.* (**frowst·i·er, frowst·i·est**) *Brit.* having a stale, warm, and stuffy atmosphere: *a small, frowsty office.* ▷mid 19th cent. (originally dialect): variant of **FROWZY**. **—frowst·i·ness** *n.*

frowz·y /ˈfrouzē/ (also **frows·y**) ▸*adj.* (**frowz·i·er, frowz·i·est**) scruffy and neglected in appearance. ■ dingy and stuffy: *a frowzy nightclub.* ▷late 17th cent. (originally dialect): of unknown origin. **—frowz·i·ness** /-zēnis/ *n.*

fro·yo /ˈfrō ˌyō/ ▸*n. informal* frozen yogurt. ▷blend.

froze /frōz/ ▸ past of **FREEZE**.

fro·zen /ˈfrōzən/ ▸ past participle of **FREEZE**.
▸*adj. Billiards* (of a ball) resting against another ball or a cushion.

fro·zen shoul·der ▸the common name for **ADHESIVE CAPSULITIS**.

fro·zen smoke ▸*n.* another term for **AEROGEL**.

FRS ▸*abbr.* ■ Federal Reserve System. ■ (in the UK) Fellow of the Royal Society.

frt. ▸*abbr.* freight.

Fruc·ti·dor /ˌfro͝oktəˈdôr; fryk-/ ▸*n.* the twelfth month of the French Republican calendar (1793–1805), originally running from August 18 to September 16. ▷French, from Latin *fructus* 'fruit' + Greek *dōron* 'gift.'

fruc·ti·fi·ca·tion /ˌfrəktəfiˈkāSHən/ ▸*n.* the process of fructifying. ■ *Botany* a spore-bearing or fruiting structure, esp. in a fungus. ▷late 15th cent.: from late Latin *fructificatio(n-)*, from Latin *fructificare* 'fructify,' from *fructus* 'fruit.'

fruc·ti·fy /ˈfrəktəˌfī/ ▸*v.* (**-fies, -fied**) [*trans.*] *formal* make (something) fruitful or productive. ■ [*intrans.*] bear fruit or become productive. ▷Middle English: from Old French *fructifier*, from Latin *fructificare*, from *fructus* 'fruit.'

fruc·tose /ˈfrəkˌtōs; ˈfro͝ok-; -ˌtōz/ ▸*n. Chemistry* a hexose sugar found esp. in honey and fruit. ▷mid 19th cent.: from Latin *fructus* 'fruit' + **-OSE**[2].

fruc·tu·ous /ˈfrəkCHo͞oəs; ˈfro͝ok-/ ▸*adj. formal* full of or producing a great deal of fruit. ▷late Middle English: from Latin *fructuosus*, from *fructus* 'fruit.'

frug /fro͞og/ ▸*n.* a vigorous dance to pop music, popular in the mid-1960s.
▸*v.* (**frugged, frug·ging**) [*intrans.*] perform such a dance. ▷of unknown origin.

fru·gal /ˈfro͞ogəl/ ▸*adj.* sparing or economical with regard to money or food: *he led a remarkably frugal existence.* See note at **ECONOMICAL**. ■ simple and plain and costing little: *a frugal meal.* ▷mid 16th cent.: from Latin *frugalis*, from *frugi* 'economical, thrifty,' from *frux, frug-* 'fruit.' **—fru·gal·i·ty** /fro͞oˈgalətē/ *n.* **—fru·gal·ly** *adv.* **—fru·gal·ness** *n.*

fru·giv·o·rous /fro͞oˈjivərəs/ ▸*n. Zoology* (of an animal) feeding on fruit. ▷mid 20th cent.: from Latin *frux, frug-* 'fruit' + *-vore* (see **-VOROUS**). **—fru·gi·vore** /ˈfro͞ojiˌvôr/ *n.*

fruit /fro͞ot/ ▸*n.* **1** the sweet and fleshy product of a tree or other plant that contains seed and can be eaten as food: *tropical fruits such as mangoes and papaya* | *eat plenty of fresh fruit and vegetables.* ■ *Botany* the seed-bearing structure of a plant, e.g., an acorn. ■ the result or reward of work or activity: *the pupils began to appreciate the fruits of their labors* | *the journal was* ***the first fruit*** *of the creative partnership.* ■ *archaic or poetic/literary* natural produce that can be used for food: *we give thanks for the fruits of the earth.* ■ *archaic* offspring: *she couldn't bear not to see the fruit of her womb.* **2** *informal, offensive* a male homosexual.
▸*v.* [*intrans.*] (of a tree or other plant) produce fruit, typically at a specified time: *the trees fruit very early* | [as *n.*] (**fruiting**) *cover strawberries with cloches to encourage early fruiting.* ▷Middle English: from Old French, from Latin *fructus* 'enjoyment of produce, harvest,' from *frui* 'enjoy,' related to *fruges* 'fruits of the earth,' plural (and most common form) of *frux, frug-* 'fruit.'
▸*PHRASES* □ **bear fruit** have good results: *their efforts finally bore fruit in 1993 in a surprise decision by the Supreme Court.* □ **in fruit** (of a tree or plant) at the stage of producing fruit. □ **old fruit** *Brit., informal, dated* a friendly form of address used by one man to another.

fruit ac·id ▸*n.* another term for **ALPHA-HYDROXY ACID**.

fruit·age /ˈfro͞otij/ ▸*n. archaic or poetic/literary* fruit collectively.

fruit·ar·i·an /fro͞oˈte(ə)rēən/ ▸*n.* a person who eats only fruit. ▷late 19th cent.: from **FRUIT**, on the pattern of *vegetarian.* **—fruit·ar·i·an·ism** /-ˌnizəm/ *n.*

fruit bat ▸*n.* a bat with a long snout and large eyes, feeding chiefly on fruit or nectar and found mainly in the Old World tropics. • Family Pteropodidae: many genera and numerous species. See also **FLYING FOX**.

fruit bod·y ▸*n.* another term for **FRUITING BODY**.

fruit·cake /ˈfro͞otˌkāk/ ▸*n.* a cake containing dried fruit and nuts. ■ *informal* an eccentric or insane person. [compare with *nutty as a fruitcake* (see **NUTTY**).]

fruit cock·tail ▸*n.* a finely chopped fruit salad, often commercially produced in cans.

fruit cup ▸*n.* a salad made of chopped fruit and served in a glass dish as an appetizer or dessert.

fruit drop ▸*n.* the shedding of unripe fruit from a tree.

fruit·ed /ˈfro͞otid/ ▸*adj.* [usu. in *combination*] (of a tree or plant) producing fruit, esp. of a specified kind: *heavy-fruited plants like tomatoes.*

fruit·er /ˈfro͞otər/ ▸*n.* a tree producing fruit at a specified time or in a specified manner: *the wet-season fruiters.*

fruit·er·er /ˈfro͞otərər/ ▸*n.* a retailer of fruit. ▷late Middle English: from **FRUITER** + **-ER**[1]; the reason for the addition of the suffix is unclear.

fruit fly ▸*n.* a small fly that feeds on fruit in both its adult and larval stages. • Families Drosophilidae and Tephritidae: many genera. See also **DROSOPHILA**.

fruit·ful /ˈfro͞otfəl/ ▸*adj.* (of a tree, a plant, or land) producing much fruit; fertile. See note at **FERTILE**. ■ producing good or helpful results; productive: *years of fruitful collaboration* | *the two days of talks had been fruitful.* ■ (of a person) producing many offspring. **—fruit·ful·ly** *adv.* **—fruit·ful·ness** *n.*

fruit·ing bod·y ▸*n. Botany* the spore-producing organ of a fungus, often seen as a mushroom or toadstool.

fru·i·tion /fro͞oˈiSHən/ ▸*n.* **1** the point at which a plan or project is realized: *the plans have* ***come to fruition*** *sooner than expected.* ■ [in *sing.*] the realization of a plan or project: *new methods will come with the fruition of that research.* **2** *poetic/literary* the state or action of producing fruit. ▷late Middle English (in the sense 'enjoyment'): via Old French from late Latin *fruitio(n-)*, from *frui* 'enjoy' (see **FRUIT**); the current senses (dating from the late 19th cent.) arose by association with **FRUIT**.

fruit·less /ˈfro͞otləs/ ▸*adj.* **1** failing to achieve the desired results; unproductive or useless: *his fruitless attempts to publish poetry.* **2** (of a tree or plant) not producing fruit. **—fruit·less·ly** *adv.* **—fruit·less·ness** *n.*

fruit·let /ˈfro͞otlət/ ▸*n.* an immature or small fruit. ■ *Botany* another term for **DRUPELET**.

fruit ma·chine ▸*n.* British term for **SLOT MACHINE**.

fruit pi·geon ▸*n.* a fruit-eating pigeon occurring in the Old World tropics. • a relative of the imperial pigeons occurring in New Guinea (genus *Ducula*, family Columbidae). • a green pigeon occurring in Africa (genus *Treron*, family Columbidae).

fruit sal·ad ▸*n.* a mixture of different types of chopped fruit served in syrup or juice. ■ *military slang* a display of medals and other decorations.

fruit sug·ar ▸*n.* another term for **FRUCTOSE**.

fruit tree ▸*n.* a tree grown for its edible fruit.

fruit·wood /ˈfro͞otˌwo͝od/ ▸*n.* [usu. as *adj.*] the wood of a fruit tree, esp. when used in furniture: *a fruitwood dressing table.*

fruit·y /ˈfro͞otē/ ▸*adj.* (**fruit·i·er, fruit·i·est**) **1** (esp. of food or drink) of, resembling, or containing fruit: *a light and fruity Beaujolais.* **2** (of a voice or sound) mellow, deep, and rich: *Jeff had a wonderfully fruity voice.* ■ *Brit., informal* sexually suggestive in content or style. **3** *informal, offensive* relating to or associated with homosexuals. **4** *informal* eccentric or crazy: *a kind of fruity professor.* **—fruit·i·ly** /ˈfro͞otl-ē/ *adv.* **—fruit·i·ness** /ˈfro͞otēnəs/ *n.*

fru·men·ty /ˈfro͞oməntē/ (also **fur·me·ty**) ▸*n. Brit.* an old-fashioned dish consisting of hulled wheat boiled in milk and seasoned with cinnamon and sugar. ▷late Middle English: from Old French *frumentee*, from *frument*, from Latin *frumentum* 'corn.'

frump /frəmp/ ▸*n.* an unattractive woman who wears dowdy old-fashioned clothes. ▷mid 16th cent.: probably a contraction of late Middle English *frumple* 'wrinkle,' from Middle Dutch *verrompelen*. The word originally denoted a mocking speech or action; later (in the plural) ill humor, the sulks; hence a bad-tempered, (later) dowdy woman (early 19th cent.). **—frump·i·ly** /ˈfrəmpəlē/ *adv.* **—frump·i·ness** /ˈfrəmpēnis/ *n.* **—frump·ish** *adj.* **—frump·ish·ly** *adv.* **—frump·y** *adj.*

Frun·ze /ˈfro͞onzə/ former name (1926–91) of **BISHKEK**.

fru·se·mide /ˈfro͞osəˌmīd; -zə-/ ▸*n.* variant spelling of **FUROSEMIDE**.

frus·ta /ˈfrəstə/ ▸ plural form of **FRUSTUM**.

frus·trate /ˈfrəsˌtrāt/ ▸*v.* [*trans.*] prevent (a plan or attempted action) from progressing, succeeding, or being fulfilled: *his attempt to frustrate the merger.* ■ prevent (someone) from doing or achieving something: *an increasingly popular way to frustrate car thieves.* See note at **THWART**. ■ cause (someone) to feel upset or annoyed, typically as a result of being unable to change or achieve something: [as *adj.*] (**frustrating**) *it can be very frustrating to find that the size you want isn't there.*
▸*adj. archaic* frustrated. ▷late Middle English: from Latin *frustrat-* 'disappointed,' from the verb *frustrare*, from *frustra* 'in vain.' **—frus·trat·er** *n.* **—frus·trat·ing·ly** *adv.* [as *submodifier*] *progress turned out to be frustratingly slow.*

frus·trat·ed /ˈfrəsˌtrātid/ ▸*adj.* feeling or expressing distress and annoyance, esp. because of inability to change or achieve something: *young people get* ***frustrated with*** *the system.* ■ [*attrib.*] (of a person) unable to follow or be successful in a particular career: *a frustrated actor.* ■ [*attrib.*] prevented from progressing, succeeding, or being fulfilled: *our parents may want us to fulfill their own frustrated dreams.* ■ (of a person or sexual desire) unfulfilled sexually: *jealousies and frustrated passions.* —**frus·trat·ed·ly** *adv.*

frus·tra·tion /frəˈstrāsʜən/ ▸*n.* the feeling of being upset or annoyed, esp. because of inability to change or achieve something: *I sometimes feel like screaming with frustration.* ■ an event or circumstance that causes one to have such a feeling: *the inherent frustrations of assembly line work.* ■ the prevention of the progress, success, or fulfillment of something: *the frustration of their wishes.* ▷mid 16th cent.: from Latin *frustratio(n-)*, from *frustrare* 'disappoint' (see **FRUSTRATE**).

frus·tule /ˈfrəsˌᴄʜo͞ol/ ▸*n. Botany* the silicified cell wall of a diatom, consisting of two valves or overlapping halves. ▷mid 19th cent.: from Latin *frustulum*, diminutive of *frustum* (see **FRUSTUM**).

frus·tum /ˈfrəstəm/ ▸*n.* (*pl.* **-ta** /-tə/ or **-tums**) *Geometry* the portion of a cone or pyramid that remains after its upper part has been cut off by a plane parallel to its base, or that is intercepted between two such planes. ▷mid 17th cent.: from Latin, 'piece cut off.'

fru·ti·cose /ˈfro͞otiˌkōs; -ˌkōz/ ▸*adj. Botany* (of a lichen) having upright or pendulous branches. ▷mid 17th cent.: from Latin *fruticosus*, from *frutex, frutic-* 'bush, shrub.'

Fry /frī/, Christopher (Harris) (1907–), English playwright. He is known chiefly for his comic verse dramas, esp. *The Lady's not for Burning* (1948) and *Venus Observed* (1950).

fry[1] /frī/ ▸*v.* (**fries, fried**) [*trans.*] cook (food) in hot fat or oil, typically in a shallow pan. Compare with **DEEP FRY**. ■ [*intrans.*] (of food) be cooked in such a way: *put half a dozen steaks to fry in a pan.* ■ [*intrans.*] *informal* (of a person) burn or overheat: *with the sea and sun and wind you'll fry if you don't take care.* ■ *informal* execute or be executed by electrocution.
▸*n.* (*pl.* **fries**) [in *sing.*] a meal of meat or other food cooked in such a way. ■ a social gathering where fried food is served: *you'll explore islands and stop for a fish fry.* ■ (**fries**) another term for **FRENCH FRIES**. ▷Middle English: from Old French *frire*, from Latin *frigere*.

fry[2] ▸*plural n.* young fish, esp. when newly hatched. ■ the young of other animals produced in large numbers, such as frogs. ▷Middle English: from Old Norse *frjó*.

fry·er /ˈfrīər/ (also **fri·er**) ▸*n.* **1** a large, deep container for frying food. **2** a small young chicken suitable for frying.

fry·ing pan (also **fry·pan**) ▸*n.* a shallow pan with a long handle, used for cooking food in hot fat or oil.
▸*PHRASE* □ **out of the frying pan into the fire** from a bad situation to one that is worse.

fry-up ▸*n. Brit., informal* a dish of various types of fried food.

FSBO ▸*abbr.* for sale by owner; designating some aspect of sales of private homes by their owners: *FSBO sellers.*

FSH ▸*abbr.* follicle-stimulating hormone.

FSLIC ▸Federal Savings and Loan Insurance Corporation.

f. sp. ▸*abbr.* a taxonomic category, esp. of fungi, below that of species and defined by physiological characteristics, esp. as they affect pathogenicity. The abbreviation is used in binomial names, between the species name and a special qualifier. ▷abbreviation of Latin *forma specialis*, 'special form.'

FST ▸*abbr.* flat-screen television.

f-stop ▸*n. Photography* a camera setting corresponding to a particular f-number.

FT ▸*abbr.* ■ *Basketball* free throw. ■ full-time.

Ft. ▸*abbr.* Fort: *Ft. Lauderdale.*

ft. ▸*abbr.* foot; feet.

FTA ▸*abbr.* Free Trade Agreement, used to refer to that signed in 1988 between the U.S. and Canada.

FTC ▸*abbr.* Federal Trade Commission.

ft-c ▸*abbr.* foot-candle.

fth. ▸*abbr.* fathom.

FT in·dex ▸ another term for **FTSE INDEX**.

ft-lb ▸*abbr.* foot-pound.

FTP *Computing* ▸*abbr.* file transfer protocol, a standard for the exchange of program and data files across a network.
▸*v.* (**FTP'd** or **FTPed, FTPing**) [*trans.*] *informal* transfer (a file) from one computer or system to another, esp. on the Internet.

FTSE in·dex a figure (published by the *Financial Times*) indicating the relative prices of shares on the London Stock Exchange, esp. (also **FTSE 100 index**) one calculated on the basis of Britain's one hundred largest public companies. ▷*FTSE*, abbreviation of *Financial Times Stock Exchange.*

Fu·ad /fo͞oˈäd/ the name of two kings of Egypt: ■ **Fuad I** (1868–1936), reigned 1922–36. Formerly sultan of Egypt 1917–22, he became Egypt's first king after independence. ■ **Fuad II** (1952–), grandson of Fuad I; reigned 1952–53. Named king as an infant on the forced abdication of his father, Farouk, he was deposed when Egypt became a republic.

fu·bar /ˈfo͞oˌbär/ ▸*adj.* out of working order; seriously, perhaps irreparably, damaged: *the clock in the hall is fubar.* ▷1940s: acronym from *fucked up beyond all recognition* (or *repair*).

fub·sy /ˈfəbzē/ ▸*adj.* (**fub·si·er, fub·si·est**) *Brit., informal* fat and squat. ▷late 18th cent.: from dialect *fubs* 'small fat person,' perhaps a blend of **FAT** and **CHUB**.

FUBU /ˈfo͞oˌbo͞o/ (also **Fubu**) ▸*n. trademark* a brand of designer and sports clothing marketed mainly at young consumers of hip-hop culture: [*attrib.*] *a powder-blue Fubu football jersey.* ▷1990s: acronym from 'For Us, By Us.'

Fuchs[1] /fo͝oks/, (Emil) Klaus (Julius) (1911–88), British physicist; born in Germany. A communist who fled Nazi persecution, he passed secret information regarding the atom bomb to the Soviet Union during the 1940s.

Fuchs[2], Sir Vivian (Ernest) (1908–99), English geologist and explorer. He made the first overland crossing of the Antarctic 1955–58. His party met Sir Edmund Hillary's New Zealand contingent, approaching from the opposite direction, at the South Pole.

fuch·sia /ˈfyo͞osʜə/ ▸*n.* **1** a shrub with pendulous tubular flowers that are typically of two contrasting colors. They are native to America and New Zealand and are commonly grown as ornamentals. • Genus *Fuchsia*, family Onagraceae: many cultivars. **2** a vivid purplish-red color like that of the sepals of a typical fuchsia flower.
▸*adj.* like the sepals of a fuchsia flower in color; purplish red. ▷modern Latin, named in honor of Leonhard *Fuchs* (1501–66), German botanist.

fuch·sin /ˈfyo͞oksən; -ˌsēn/ (also **fuch·sine**) ▸*n.* a deep red synthetic dye used as a biological stain and disinfectant. • A chloride of rosaniline; chem. formula: $C_{20}H_{20}N_3Cl$. ▷mid 19th cent.: from German *Fuchs* 'fox,' translating French *Renard* (the name of the chemical company that first produced fuchsin commercially) + **-IN**[1].

fu·ci /ˈfyo͞osī; -sē/ ▸ plural form of **FUCUS**.

fuck /fək/ *vulgar slang* ▸*v.* [*trans.*] **1** have sexual intercourse with (someone). ■ [*intrans.*] (of two people) have sexual intercourse. **2** ruin or damage (something).
▸*phrasal v.* □ **fuck around** spend time doing unimportant or trivial things. ■ have sexual intercourse with a variety of partners. ■ (**fuck around with**) meddle with. □ **fuck off** [usu. in *imperative*] (of a person) go away. □ **fuck someone over** treat someone in an unfair or humiliating way. □ **fuck someone up** damage or confuse someone emotionally. □ **fuck something up** (or **fuck up**) do something badly or ineptly.
▸*n.* an act of sexual intercourse. ■ [with *adj.*] a sexual partner.
▸*exclam.* used alone or as a noun (**the fuck**) or a verb in various phrases to express anger, annoyance, contempt, impatience, or surprise, or simply for emphasis. ▷early 16th cent.: of Germanic origin (compare Swedish dialect *focka* and Dutch dialect *fokkelen*); possibly from an Indo-European root meaning 'strike,' shared by Latin *pugnus* 'fist.' —**fuck·a·ble** *adj.*
▸*PHRASES* □ **go fuck yourself** an exclamation expressing anger or contempt for, or rejection of, someone. □ **not give a fuck** (**about**) used to emphasize indifference or contempt.

USAGE Despite the wideness and proliferation of its use in many sections of society, the word **fuck** remains (and has been for centuries) one of the most taboo words in English. Until relatively recently, it rarely appeared in print; even today, there are a number of euphemistic ways of referring to it in speech and writing, e.g., **the F-word, f*****, or **f—k**.

fuck·er /ˈfəkər/ ▸*n. vulgar slang* a contemptible or stupid person (often used as a general term of abuse).

fuck·head /ˈfəkˌhed/ ▸*n. vulgar slang* a stupid or contemptible person (often used as a general term of abuse).

fuck·ing /ˈfəkiɴɢ/ ▸*adj.* [*attrib.*] & *adv.* [as *submodifier*] *vulgar slang* used for emphasis or to express anger, annoyance, contempt, or surprise.

fuck-me ▸*adj. vulgar slang* (of clothing, esp. shoes) inviting or perceived as inviting sexual interest.

fuck-up ▸*n. vulgar slang* a mess or muddle. ■ a person who has a tendency to make a mess of things.

fuck·wit /ˈfəkˌwit/ ▸*n. chiefly Brit., vulgar slang* a stupid or contemptible person (often used as a general term of abuse).

fu·coid /ˈfyo͞oˌkoid/ *Botany* ▸*n.* a brown seaweed or fossil plant of a group to which bladderwrack belongs. • Order Fucales, class Phaeophyceae, including genus *Fucus.*
▸*adj.* of, relating to, or resembling a brown seaweed, esp. a fucoid. ▷mid 19th cent.: from **FUCUS** + **-OID**.

fu·co·xan·thin /ˌfyo͞okōˈzanᴛʜin/ ▸*n. Chemistry* a brown carotenoid pigment occurring in and generally characteristic of the brown algae. ▷late 19th cent.: from **FUCUS** + *xanthin*, variant of **XANTHINE**.

fu·cus /ˈfyo͞okəs/ ▸*n.* (*pl.* **fu·ci** /ˈfyo͞osī; -sē/) a seaweed of a large genus of brown algae having flat leathery fronds. • Genus *Fucus*, class Phaeophyceae. ▷early 17th cent. (denoting a cosmetic): from Latin, 'rock lichen, red dye, rouge,' from Greek *phukos* 'seaweed,' of Semitic origin. —**fu·coid** /-ˌkoid/ *adj.*

FUD /fəd/ ▸*n.* fear, uncertainty and doubt, usually evoked intentionally in order to put a competitor at a disadvantage: [as *adj.*] *the FUD factor.* ▷acronym.

fud·dle /ˈfədl/ ▸*v.* [*trans.*] [usu. as *adj.*] (**fuddled**) confuse or stupefy (someone), esp. with alcohol: *my head was aching and my brain seemed fuddled.* ■ [*intrans.*] *archaic* go on a drinking bout.
▸*n.* [in *sing.*] a state of confusion or intoxication: *through the fuddle of wine he heard some of the conversation.* ■ *archaic* a drinking bout. ▷late 16th cent. (in the sense 'go on a drinking bout'): of unknown origin.

fud·dy-dud·dy /ˈfədē ˌdədē/ ▸*n.* (*pl.* **-dies**) *informal* a person who is old-fashioned and fussy: *he probably thinks I'm an* ***old fuddy-duddy.*** ▷early 20th cent. (originally dialect): of unknown origin.

fudge /fəj/ ▸*n.* **1** a soft candy made from sugar, butter, and milk or cream. ■ rich chocolate, used esp. as a filling for cakes or a sauce on ice cream: *chocolate cake filled with whipped cream and topped with* ***hot fudge*** | [as *adj.*] *a fudge cake.* **2** an instance of faking or ambiguity: *the new settlement is a fudge rushed out to win cheers at the conference.* ■ *archaic* nonsense. **3** a piece of late news inserted in a newspaper page.
▸*v.* [*trans.*] present or deal with (something) in a vague, noncommittal, or inadequate way, esp. so as to conceal the truth or mislead: *a temptation to* ***fudge the issue*** *and nudge grades up.* ■ adjust or manipulate (facts or figures) so as to present a desired picture.
▸*exclam. dated* nonsense (expressing disbelief or annoyance). ▷early 17th cent.: probably an alteration of obsolete *fadge* 'to fit.' Early usage was as a verb in the sense 'turn out as expected,' also 'merge together': this probably gave rise to its use in confectionery. In the late 17th cent. the verb came to mean 'fit together in a clumsy or underhanded manner,' which included facts or figures being cobbled together in a superficially convincing way: this led to the exclamation 'fudge!' and to noun sense 3.

fudge fac·tor ▸*n. informal* a figure included in a calculation to account for error or unanticipated circumstances, or to ensure a desired result.

fueh·rer /ˈfyo͝orər/ ▸*n.* variant spelling of **FÜHRER**.

fu·el /ˈfyo͞oəl/ ▸*n.* material such as coal, gas, or oil that is burned to produce heat or power. ■ short for **NUCLEAR FUEL**. ■ food, drink, or drugs as a source of energy: *any protein intake can also be used as fuel.* ■ a thing that sustains or inflames passion, argument, or other emotion or activity: *the remuneration packages will add fuel to the debate about top-level rewards.*
▸*v.* (**fu·eled, fu·el·ing**; *Brit.* **fu·elled, fu·el·ling**) [*trans.*] **1** supply or power (an industrial plant, vehicle, or machine) with fuel: *the plan includes a hydroelectric plant to fuel a paper factory* | *figurative a big novel that is fueled by anger and revenge.* ■ fill up (a vehicle, aircraft, or ship) with oil or gasoline. ■ [*intrans.*] (**fuel up**) (of a person) eat a meal: *arrive straight from work and fuel up on the complimentary buffet.* **2** cause (a fire) to burn more intensely. ■ sustain or inflame (a

feeling or activity): *his rascal heart and private pain fuel his passion as an actor.* ▷Middle English: from Old French *fouaille*, based on Latin *focus* 'hearth' (in late Latin 'fire').

▸*PHRASE* □ **add fuel to the fire** (or **flames**) *figurative* cause a situation or conflict to become more intense, esp. by provocative comments.

fu·el cell ▸*n.* a cell producing an electric current directly from a chemical reaction.

fu·el el·e·ment ▸*n.* an element consisting of nuclear fuel and other materials for use in a reactor.

fu·el in·jec·tion ▸*n.* the direct introduction of fuel under pressure into the combustion units of an internal combustion engine. —**fu·el-in·ject·ed** *adj.*

fu·el oil ▸*n.* oil used as fuel in an engine or furnace.

fu·el rod ▸*n.* a rod-shaped fuel element in a nuclear reactor.

fu·el·wood /ˈfyo͞oəlˌwo͝od/ ▸*n.* wood used as fuel.

Fuen·tes /ˈfwentās/, Carlos (1928–), Mexican writer. Notable works: *Where the Air is Clear* (1958), *Terra Nostra* (1975), and *The Old Gringo* (1984).

fu·fu /ˈfo͞oˌfo͞o/ (also **foo-foo**) ▸*n.* dough made from boiled and ground plantain or cassava, used as a staple food in parts of western and central Africa. ▷mid 18th cent.: from Twi *fufuu*.

fug /fəg/ ▸*n.* [in *sing.*] *Brit., informal* a warm stuffy or smoky atmosphere in a room: *the cozy fug of the music halls.* ▷late 19th cent. (originally dialect and schoolchildren's slang): of unknown origin. —**fug·gy** *adj.*

fu·ga·cious /fyo͞oˈgāsHəs/ ▸*adj. poetic/literary* tending to disappear; fleeting: *she was acutely conscious of her fugacious youth.* ▷mid 17th cent.: from Latin *fugax*, *fugac-* (from *fugere* 'flee') + -IOUS. —**fu·ga·cious·ly** *adv.* —**fu·ga·cious·ness** *n.*

fu·gac·i·ty /fyo͞oˈgasətē/ ▸*n.* **1** *poetic/literary* the quality of being fleeting or evanescent. **2** *Chemistry* a thermodynamic property of a real gas that, if substituted for the pressure or partial pressure in the equations for an ideal gas, gives equations applicable to the real gas.

fu·gal /ˈfyo͞ogəl/ ▸*adj.* of the nature of a fugue: *the virtuosity of the fugal finale.* —**fu·gal·ly** *adv.*

fu·ga·to /f(y)o͞oˈgätō/ *Music* ▸*adj.* & *adv.* in the style of a fugue, but not in strict or complete fugal form.
▸*n.* (*pl.* **-tos**) a passage in this style. ▷Italian.

-fuge ▸*comb. form* expelling or dispelling either a specified thing or in a specified way: *vermifuge* | *centrifuge.* ▷from modern Latin *-fugus*, from Latin *fugare* 'cause to flee.'

fu·gi·tive /ˈfyo͞ojətiv/ ▸*n.* a person who has escaped from a place or is in hiding, esp. to avoid arrest or persecution: *fugitives from justice* [as *adj.*] *fugitive criminals.* ■ [as *adj.*] *figurative* quick to disappear; fleeting: *he entertained a fugitive idea that Barbara needed him.* ▷late Middle English: from Old French *fugitif, -ive*, from Latin *fugitivus*, from *fugere* 'flee.'

fu·gle·man /ˈfyo͞ogəlmən/ ▸*n.* (*pl.* **-men**) *historical* a soldier placed in front of a regiment or company while drilling to demonstrate the motions and time. ■ *figurative* a leader, organizer, or spokesman: *fuglemen of the ideological right.* ▷early 19th cent.: from German *Flügelmann* 'leader of the file,' from *Flügel* 'wing' + *Mann* 'man.'

fu·gu /ˈf(y)o͞ogo͞o/ ▸*n.* a puffer fish that is eaten as a Japanese delicacy, after some highly poisonous parts have been removed. ▷mid 20th cent.: from Japanese.

fugue /fyo͞og/ ▸*n.* **1** *Music* a contrapuntal composition in which a short melody or phrase (the subject) is introduced by one part and successively taken up by others and developed by interweaving the parts. **2** *Psychiatry* a state or period of loss of awareness of one's identity, often coupled with flight from one's usual environment, associated with certain forms of hysteria and epilepsy. ▷late 16th cent.: from French, or from Italian *fuga*, from Latin *fuga* 'flight,' related to *fugere* 'flee.' —**fugu·ist** /ˈfyo͞ogist/ *n.*

füh·rer /ˈfyo͞orər/ (also **fueh·rer**) ▸*n.* a ruthless, tyrannical leader. ▷mid 20th cent.: from German *Führer* 'leader,' part of the title *Führer und Reichskanzler* 'Leader and Chancellor of the Empire' assumed in 1934 by Adolf HITLER.

Fu·jai·rah /fo͞oˈjīrə/ (also **Al Fu·jay·rah**) one of the seven member states of the United Arab Emirates; pop. 76,000.

Fu·ji, Mount /ˈfo͞ojē/ a dormant volcano on the island of Honshu in Japan. Japan's highest mountain, it rises to 12,385 feet (3,776 m). It is regarded as sacred by the Japanese. Also called FUJIYAMA /ˌfo͞ojēˈyämə/.

Fu·jian /ˈfo͞oˈjyän/ (also **Fu·kien** /ˈfo͞oˈkyen/) a province in southeastern China, on the China Sea; capital, Fuzhou.

Fu·ji·ta scale /fo͞oˈjētə/ (also **Fujita-Pearson scale**) ▸*Meteorology n.* a scale of tornado severity with numbers from 0 to 6, based on the degree of observed damage. ▷mid 20th cent.: named after Dr. Tetsuya Theodore *Fujita* (1920–1988), the meteorologist who chiefly devised it.

Fu·ji·ya·ma /ˌfo͞ojē(y)ämə/ another name for MOUNT FUJI.

Fu·ku·o·ka /ˌfo͞oko͞oˈōkə/ an industrial city and port in southern Japan, capital of Kyushu island; pop. 1,237,000.

-ful ▸*suffix* **1** (forming adjectives from nouns) full of: *sorrowful.* ■ having the qualities of: *masterful.* **2** forming adjectives from adjectives or from Latin stems with little change of sense: *grateful.* **3** (forming adjectives from verbs) apt to; able to; accustomed to: *forgetful* | *watchful.* **4** (*pl.* **-fuls**) forming nouns denoting the amount needed to fill the specified container, holder, etc.: *bucketful* | *handful.* ▷from FULL[1].

> *USAGE* The combining form **-ful** is used to form nouns meaning 'the amount needed to fill' (*cupful, spoonful*, etc.). The plural form of such words is *cupfuls, spoonfuls*, etc. *Three cups full* would denote the individual cups rather than a quantity measured in cups: *on the sill were three cups full of milk; add three cupfuls of milk to the batter.*

Fu·la /ˈfo͞olə/ ▸*n.* the Benue-Congo language of the Fulani people, spoken as a first language by about 10 million people and widely used in West Africa as a lingua franca. Also called FUL, FULANI.

Fu·la·ni /fo͞oˈlänē/ ▸*n.* (*pl.* same) **1** a member of a people living in a region of West Africa from Senegal to northern Nigeria and Cameroon. They are traditionally nomadic cattle herders of Muslim faith. **2** another term for FULA.
▸*adj.* of or relating to this people or their language. ▷the name in Hausa.

Ful·bright /ˈfo͝olˌbrīt/, (James) William (1905–95), U.S. senator. He sponsored the Fulbright Act of 1946, which authorized funds from the sale of surplus war materials overseas to be used to finance exchange programs of students and teachers between the U.S. and other countries. The program now is supported by federal grants.

ful·crum /ˈfo͝olkrəm; ˈfəl-/ ▸*n.* (*pl.* **-cra** /-krə/ or **-crums**) the point on which a lever rests or is supported and on which it pivots. ■ a thing that plays a central or essential role in an activity, event, or situation: *research is the fulcrum of the academic community.* ▷late 17th cent. (originally in the general sense 'a prop or support'): from Latin, literally 'post of a couch,' from *fulcire* 'to prop up.'

ful·fill /fo͝olˈfil/ (*Brit.* **ful·fil**) ▸*v.* **1** bring to completion or reality; achieve or realize (something desired, promised, or predicted): *he wouldn't be able to fulfill his ambition to visit Naples.* ■ (**fulfill oneself**) gain happiness or satisfaction by fully developing one's abilities or character. ■ *archaic* complete (a period of time or piece of work). **2** carry out (a task, duty, or role) as required, pledged, or expected: *some officials were dismissed because they could not fulfill their duties.* ■ satisfy or meet (a requirement or condition): *goods must fulfill three basic conditions.* ▷late Old English *fullfyllan* 'fill up, make full' (see FULL[1], FILL). —**ful·fill·a·ble** *adj.* —**ful·fill·er** *n.*

ful·filled /fo͝olˈfild/ ▸*adj.* satisfied or happy because of fully developing one's abilities or character.

ful·fill·ing /fo͝olˈfiliNG/ ▸*adj.* making someone satisfied or happy because of fully developing their character or abilities: *a fulfilling and rewarding career.*

ful·fill·ment /fo͝olˈfilmənt/ (*Brit.* **ful·fil·ment**) ▸*n.* **1** satisfaction or happiness as a result of fully developing one's abilities or character: *she did not believe that marriage was the key to happiness and fulfillment.* **2** the achievement of something desired, promised, or predicted: *winning the championship was the fulfillment of a childhood dream.* ■ the meeting of a requirement or condition: *the fulfillment of statutory requirements.* ■ the performance of a task, duty, or role as required, pledged, or expected.

ful·gent /ˈfəljənt/ ▸*adj. poetic/literary* shining brightly. ▷late Middle English: from Latin *fulgent-* 'shining,' from the verb *fulgere*.

ful·gu·ra·tion /ˌfo͝olg(y)əˈrāsHən/ ▸*n.* **1** *Medicine* the destruction of small growths or areas of tissue using diathermy. **2** *poetic/literary* a flash like that of lightning. ▷mid 17th cent. (usually plural in the sense 'flashes of lightning'): from Latin *fulguratio(n-)* 'sheet lightning,' from *fulgur* 'lightning.' Sense 1 dates from the early 20th cent. —**ful·gu·rant** *adj.* (in sense 2). —**ful·gu·rate** *v.* (in sense 2). —**ful·gu·rous** *adj.* (in sense 2).

ful·gu·rite /ˈfo͝olg(y)əˌrīt/ ▸*n. Geology* vitreous material formed of sand or other sediment fused by lightning. ■ a piece of such material. ▷mid 19th cent.: from Latin *fulgur* 'lightning' + -ITE[1].

fu·lig·i·nous /fyo͞oˈlijənəs/ ▸*adj.* sooty; dusky. ▷late 16th cent. (originally describing a vapor as 'thick and noxious'): from late Latin *fuliginosus*, from *fuligo*, *fuligin-* 'soot.'

Fu·ling /ˈfo͞oˈliNG/ a city in Sichuan province, in central China, on the Yangtze River at its junction with the Wu River; pop. 986,000.

full[1] /fo͝ol/ ▸*adj.* **1** containing or holding as much or as many as possible; having no empty space: *wastebaskets full of rubbish* | *she could only nod, for her mouth was full.* ■ having eaten or drunk to one's limits or satisfaction. See also FULL UP below. ■ [*predic.*] (**full of**) containing or holding much or many; having a large number of: *his diary is full of entries about her.* ■ [*predic.*] (**full of**) having a lot of (a particular quality): *she was full of confidence.* ■ [*predic.*] (**full of**) completely engrossed with; unable to stop talking or thinking about: *Anna had been full of her day, saying how Mitch had described England to her.* ■ filled with intense emotion: *she picked at her food, her heart too full to eat.* ■ involving a lot of activities: *he lived a full life.* **2** [*attrib.*] not lacking or omitting anything; complete: *fill in your full name below* | *full details on request.* ■ (often used for emphasis) reaching the utmost limit; maximum: *he reached for the engine control and turned it up to full power* | *John made full use of all the tuition provided.* ■ having all the privileges and status attached to a particular position: *the country applied for full membership in the European Community.* ■ (of a report or account) containing as much detail or information as possible. ■ used to emphasize an amount or quantity: *he kept his fast pace going for the full 14-mile distance.* ■ [*attrib.*] (of a covering material in bookbinding) used for the entire cover: *bound in full cloth.* **3** (of a person or part of their body) plump or rounded: *she had full lips* | *the fuller figure.* ■ (of the hair) having body. ■ (of a garment) made using much material arranged in folds or gathers, or generously cut so as to fit loosely: *the dress has a square neck and a full skirt.* ■ (of a sound) strong and resonant. ■ (of a flavor or color) rich or intense.
▸*adv.* **1** straight; directly: *she turned her head and looked full into his face.* **2** very: *he **knew full well** she was too polite to barge in.* ■ *archaic* entirely (used to emphasize an amount or quantity): *they talked for full half an hour.*
▸*n.* (**the full**) *archaic* the period, point, or state of the greatest fullness or strength; the height of a period of time. ■ the state or time of full moon. ■ *archaic* or *Irish* the whole.
▸*v.* **1** [*trans.*] *black English* make (something) full; fill up: *he **full up** the house with bawling.* **2** [*trans.*] gather or pleat (fabric) so as to make a garment full. **3** [*intrans.*] (of the moon or tide) become full. ▷Old English, of Germanic origin; related to Dutch *vol* and German *voll*.

▸*PHRASES* □ **full and by** *Sailing* close-hauled but with sails filling. □ **full of beans** see BEAN. □ **full of oneself** very self-satisfied and with an exaggerated sense of self-worth. □ **full of years** *archaic* having lived to a considerable age. □ **full on 1** running at or providing maximum power or capacity: *he had the heater full on.* **2** so as to make a direct or significant impact: *the recession has hit us full on.* ■ (**full-on**) *informal* (of an activity or thing) not diluted in nature or effect: *this is full-on ballroom boogie.* □ **full out 1** as much or as far as possible; with maximum effort or power: *he held his foot to the floor until the car raced full out.* **2** *Printing* flush with the margin. □ **full steam** (or **speed**) **ahead** used to indicate that one should proceed with as much speed or energy as possible. □ **full to the brim** see BRIM. □ **full up** filled to capacity. ■ having eaten or drunk so much that one is replete. □ **in full** with nothing omitted: *I shall expect your life story in full.* ■ to the full amount due: *their relocation costs would be paid in full.* ■ to the utmost; completely: *the textbooks have failed to exploit in full the opportunities offered.* □ **to the full** to the greatest possible extent: *enjoy your free trip to Europe to the full.*

full[2] ▸*v.* [*trans.*] [often as *n.*] (**fulling**) clean, shrink, and felt (cloth) by heat, pressure, and moisture. ▷Middle English: probably a back-formation from *fuller*, influenced by Old French *fouler* 'press hard upon' or medieval Latin *fullare*, based on Latin *fullo* 'fuller.' —**full·er** *n.*

full·back /ˈfo͝olˌbak/ ▸*n.* **1** *Football* an offensive player in the backfield. ■ an offensive position in the backfield: *he played fullback against us last year.* **2** (in a game such as soccer or field hockey) a player in a defensive position near the goal. ■ a defensive position near the goal: *Louis switched from wing to fullback.*

full-blood·ed ▸*adj.* **1** [*attrib.*] of unmixed race: *a full-blooded Cherokee.* ■ *figurative* genuine; pure: *his belief in full-blooded socialism.* **2** vigorous, enthusiastic, and without compromise: *a full-blooded argument.* **—full blood** *n.* (in sense 1). **—full-blood·ed·ly** *adv.* **—full-blood·ed·ness** *n.*

full-blown ▸*adj.* fully developed: *the onset of full-blown AIDS in persons infected with HIV.* ■ (of a flower) in full bloom.

full-bod·ied ▸*adj.* rich and satisfying in flavor or sound: *a spicy, full-bodied white wine.*

full bore ▸*adv.* at full speed or maximum capacity: *the boat came full bore toward us.*
▸*adj.* [*attrib.*] denoting firearms of relatively large caliber: *full-bore handguns.* ■ *figurative* complete; thoroughgoing: *a full-bore leftist.*

full-bot·tomed ▸*adj.* (of a wig) long at the back.

full broth·er ▸*n.* a brother born of the same mother and father.

full col·or ▸*n.* the full range of colors: *lively illustrations* **in full color**.

full-court press ▸*n.* *Basketball* a defensive tactic in which members of a team cover their opponents throughout the court and not just near their own basket. ■ *figurative* an instance of aggressive pressure: *if the president were to mount a full-court press for the space station.*

full dress ▸*n.* clothes worn on ceremonial or formal occasions.
▸*adj.* [*attrib.*] denoting an event, activity, or process that is treated with complete seriousness or that possesses all the characteristics of a genuine example of the type: *shuttle diplomacy might be better than a full-dress conference.*

full dress u·ni·form ▸*n.* a military uniform worn on ceremonial occasions.

full em·ploy·ment ▸*n.* the condition in which virtually all who are able and willing to work are employed: *a target of full employment.*

Ful·ler[1] /ˈfo͝olər/, (Sarah) Margaret (1810–50), U.S. literary critic and social reformer. An advocate of cultural education for women, she conducted "Conversations," a popular series of discussion groups in the Boston area before becoming literary critic of the *New York Tribune* 1844–46. Among her books is *Woman in the Nineteenth Century* (1845).

Ful·ler[2], Melville Weston (1833–1910), U.S. Supreme Court associate justice 1888–1910. He was also a member of the Court of International Arbitration 1900–1910 in The Hague, Netherlands.

Full·er[3] /ˈfo͝olər/, R. Buckminster (1895–1983), U.S. designer and architect; full name *Richard Buckminster Fuller.* He is best known for his invention of the geodesic dome and also for his ideals of using the world's resources with maximum purpose and least waste.

full·er[1] /ˈfo͝olər/ ▸*n.* a person who fulls cloth. ▷Old English *fullere*, from Latin *fullo*, of unknown origin.

full·er[2] ▸*n.* a grooved or rounded tool on which iron is shaped. ■ a groove made by this, esp. in a horseshoe.
▸*v.* [*trans.*] stamp (iron) with a such a tool. ▷early 19th cent. (as a verb): of unknown origin.

full·er·ene /ˌfo͝oləˈrēn/ ▸*n.* *Chemistry* a form of carbon having a large spheroidal molecule consisting of a hollow cage of atoms, of which buckminsterfullerene was the first known example. ▷late 20th cent.: contraction of BUCKMINSTERFULLERENE.

full·er's earth ▸*n.* a type of clay used in fulling cloth and as an adsorbent.

full·er's tea·sel ▸*n.* a teasel with stiff bracts that curve backward from the prickly flowerhead. • *Dipsacus sativus*, family Dipsacaceae. ▷so named because it was formerly dried and used for raising the nap on woven cloth.

Ful·ler·ton /ˈfo͝olərtən/ a city in southwestern California, southeast of Los Angeles; pop. 114,144.

full face ▸*adv.* with all of the face visible; facing directly at someone or something: *she looked full face at the mirror.*
▸*adj.* [*attrib.*] **1** showing all of the face: *a full-face mug shot.* **2** covering all of the face: *a full-face motorcycle helmet.*

full-fash·ioned ▸*adj.* (of women's clothing, esp. hosiery) shaped and seamed to fit the body: *full-fashioned stockings.* ■ (of a knitted garment) shaped by increasing or decreasing the number of loops made along the fabric length without alteration of the stitch.

full-fig·ured ▸*adj.* (of women's clothing) designed for large women.

full-fledged ▸*adj.* completely developed or established; of full status: *coldlike symptoms that never quite develop into full-fledged colds.*

full flood ▸*n.* the tide or a river at its highest. ■ (**in full flood**) speaking enthusiastically and volubly: *she was in full flood about the glories of bicycling.*

full-fron·tal ▸*adj.* (of nudity or a nude figure) with full exposure of the front of the body. ■ with nothing concealed or held back: *they put a full-frontal guitar assault to clever lyrics.*

full gain·er ▸*n.* *Sports* (in diving) a dive in which a complete backwards somersault is performed before entering the water feet first.

full-grown ▸*adj.* having reached maturity.

full growth ▸*n.* the greatest size that a plant or animal naturally attains; maturity.

full-heart·ed ▸*adj.* with great enthusiasm and commitment; full of sincere feeling: *full-hearted consent of the electorate.* **—full-heart·ed·ly** *adv.* **—full-heart·ed·ness** *n.*

full house ▸*n.* [in *sing.*] **1** an audience, or a group of people attending a meeting, that fills the venue for the event to capacity. **2** a poker hand with three of a kind and a pair, beating a flush and losing to four of a kind. ■ a winning card at bingo in which all the numbers have been successfully marked off.

full-length ▸*adj.* of the standard length: *a full-length Disney cartoon.* ■ (of a garment or curtain) extending to, or almost to, the ground. ■ (of a mirror or portrait) showing the whole human figure.
▸*adv.* (usu. **full length**) (of a person) with the body lying stretched out and flat: *Lucy flung herself full length on the floor.*

full marks ▸*plural n.* the maximum award in an examination or assessment. ■ praise for someone's intelligence, hard work, or other quality: *she had to give him full marks for originality.*

full meas·ure ▸*n.* the total amount or extent: *the full measure of their worth.*

full moon ▸*n.* the phase of the moon in which its whole disk is illuminated. ■ the time when this occurs: *it was several days after full moon.*

full-mo·tion vid·e·o (abbr.: **FMV**) ▸*n.* digital video data that is transmitted or stored on video discs for real-time reproduction on a computer (or other multimedia system) at a rate of not less than 25 frames per second.

full-mouthed /ˈmouT͟Hd; ˈmouTHt/ ▸*adj.* **1** (of cattle, sheep, etc.) having a full set of adult teeth. **2** spoken loudly or vigorously.

full nel·son ▸*n.* see NELSON.

full·ness /ˈfo͝olnəs/ (also **ful·ness**) ▸*n.* **1** the state of being filled to capacity: *scores of cans in different states of fullness.* ■ the state of having eaten enough or more than enough and feeling full: *the feeling of fullness you acquire from eating brown rice.* ■ the state of being complete or whole: *the honesty and fullness of the information they provide.* ■ (in or alluding to biblical use) all that is contained in the world: *God's green earth in all its fullness is for the people.* **2** (of a person's body or part of it) the state of being filled out so as to produce a rounded shape: *the childish fullness of his cheeks.* ■ (of a garment or the hair) the condition of having been cut or designed to give a full shape. ■ richness or intensity of flavor, sound, or color: *the coffee is of a luxurious fullness.*
▸*PHRASES* □ **the fullness of one's** (or **the**) **heart** *poetic/literary* overwhelming emotion. □ **in the fullness of time** after a due length of time has elapsed; eventually: *he'll tell us in the fullness of time.*

full page ▸*n.* [usu. as *adj.*] an entire page of a newspaper or magazine: *full-page advertisements.*

full pro·fes·sor ▸*n.* see PROFESSOR. **—full pro·fes·sor·ship** *n.*

full-rigged ▸*adj.* (of a sailing ship) having three or more masts that all carry square sails.

full-scale ▸*adj.* of the same size as the thing represented: *a huge tank containing two full-scale pirate ships.* ■ unrestricted in size, extent, or intensity; complete and thorough: *a full-scale invasion of the mainland.*

full score ▸*n.* a score of a musical composition giving the parts for all performers on separate staves.

full sis·ter ▸*n.* a sister born of the same mother and father.

full-size ▸*adj.* **1** of normal size for its type: *she was still a puppy, not yet full-size.* ■ (of a bed) having the dimensions suitable for two people, specifically 54 inches by 75 inches. **2** enlarged: *click on any item to see a full-size picture.* (Also **full-sized.**)

full stop ▸*n.* *chiefly Brit.* another term for PERIOD (sense 2).

full term ▸*n.* see TERM (sense 2).

full tilt ▸*adv.* see TILT.

full-time ▸*adj.* occupying or using the whole of someone's available working time, typically 40 hours in a week: *a full-time job.*
▸*adv.* on a full-time basis: *both parents were employed full-time.*

full-tim·er ▸*n.* a person who does a full-time job.

ful·ly /ˈfo͝olē/ ▸*adv.* **1** completely or entirely; to the furthest extent: *I fully understand the fears of the workers.* ■ without lacking or omitting anything: *this issue is discussed more fully in chapter seven* | [as *submodifier*] *a fully equipped gymnasium.* **2** no less or fewer than (used to emphasize an amount): *fully 65 percent of all funerals are by cremation.* ▷Old English *fullīce* (see FULL[1], -LY[2]).

-fully ▸*suffix* forming adverbs corresponding to adjectives ending in *-ful* (such as *sorrowfully* corresponding to *sorrowful*).

ful·ly-fash·ioned ▸*adj.* another term for FULL-FASHIONED.

ful·ly-fledged ▸*adj.* British term for FULL-FLEDGED.

ful·mar /ˈfo͝olmər; -ˌmär/ ▸*n.* a gull-sized gray and white seabird of the petrel family, with a stocky body and tubular nostrils. • Genus *Fulmarus*, family Procellariidae: two species, in particular the **northern fulmar** (*F. glacialis*) of the arctic. ▷late 17th cent.: from Hebridean Norn dialect, from Old Norse *fúll* 'stinking, foul' (because of its habit of regurgitating its stomach contents when disturbed) + *már* 'gull.'

ful·mi·nant /ˈfo͝olmənənt; ˈfəl-/ ▸*adj.* *Medicine* (of a disease or symptom) severe and sudden in onset. ▷early 17th cent.: from French, or from Latin *fulminant-* 'striking with lightning,' from the verb *fulminare* (see FULMINATE).

ful·mi·nate /ˈfo͝oləˌnāt; ˈfəl-/ ▸*v.* [*intrans.*] express vehement protest: *all* **fulminated against** *the new curriculum.* ■ *poetic/literary* explode violently or flash like lightning: *thunder fulminated around the house.* ■ [usu. as *adj.*] *Medicine* (**fulminating**) (of a disease or symptom) develop suddenly and severely: *fulminating appendicitis.*
▸*n.* *Chemistry* a salt or ester of fulminic acid. ▷late Middle English: from Latin *fulminat-* 'struck by lightning,' from *fulmen, fulmin-* 'lightning.' The earliest sense (derived from medieval Latin *fulminare*) was 'denounce formally,' later 'issue formal censures' (originally said of the pope). A sense 'emit thunder and lightning,' based on the original Latin meaning, arose in the early 17th cent., and hence 'explode violently' (late 17th cent.).

ful·mi·nate of mer·cu·ry ▸*n.* a white or grayish crystalline powder that when dry is extremely volatile when exposed to heat or pressure and is used as an explosive.

ful·mi·na·tion /ˌfo͝oləˈnāSHən; -fəl-/ ▸*n.* (usu. **fulminations**) an expression of vehement protest: *the fulminations of media moralists.* ■ a violent explosion or a flash like lightning.

ful·min·ic ac·id /fo͝olˈminik; fəl-/ ▸*n.* *Chemistry* a very unstable acid isomeric with cyanic acid. • Chem. formula: HONC. ▷early 19th cent.: *fulminic* from Latin *fulmen, fulmin-* 'lightning' + -IC.

ful·ness /ˈfo͝olnəs/ ▸*n.* variant spelling of FULLNESS.

ful·some /ˈfo͝olsəm/ ▸*adj.* **1** complimentary or flattering to an excessive degree: *they are almost embarrassingly fulsome in their appreciation.* **2** of large size or quantity; generous or abundant: *a fulsome harvest.* ▷Middle English (in the sense 'abundant'): from FULL[1] + -SOME[1]. **—ful·some·ly** *adv.* **—ful·some·ness** *n.*

USAGE The earliest recorded use of **fulsome**, in the 13th century, had the meaning 'abundant,' but in modern use this is held by many to be incorrect. The correct current meaning is 'disgusting because overdone, excessive.' The word is still often used to mean 'abundant, copious,' but this use can give rise to ambiguity: for one speaker, **fulsome praise** may be a genuine compliment; for others, it will be interpreted as an insult. For this reason alone, it is best to avoid the word altogether if the context is likely to be sensitive.

Ful·ton /ˈfo͝oltn/, Robert (1765–1815), U.S. inventor; pioneer of the steamship. He constructed a steam-propelled "diving-boat" in 1800, which he submerged to a depth of 25 feet (7.6 m). In 1806, he built the first successful paddle steamer, the *Clermont*. Eighteen other steamships were subsequently built, inaugurating the era of commercial steam navigation.

ful·vic ac·id /ˈfəlvik; ˈfo͝ol-/ ▸*n.* a highly soluble organic phenol found in humus that chelates elemental mineral nutrients.

ful·vous /ˈfo͝olvəs; ˈfəl-/ ▸*adj.* reddish yellow; tawny. ▷mid 17th cent.: from Latin *fulvus* + **-ous**.

Fu Man·chu /ˈfo͞o manˈcʜo͞o/ (in full **Fu Manchu mustache**) ▸*n.* a long narrow mustache in which the ends taper and droop down to the chin. ▷mid 20th cent.: the kind of mustache worn by *Fu Manchu*, a master criminal in the novels of British writer Sax Rohmer (1883-1959).

Fu Manchu

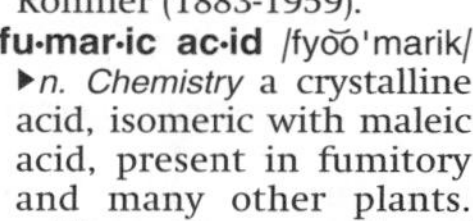

fu·mar·ic ac·id /fyo͝oˈmarik/ ▸*n. Chemistry* a crystalline acid, isomeric with maleic acid, present in fumitory and many other plants. • Alternative name: ***trans*-butenedioic acid**; chem. formula: HOOCCH=CHCOOH. ▷mid 19th cent.: *fumaric* from modern Latin *Fumaria* 'fumitory' + **-ic**. —**fu·ma·rate** /ˈfyo͞oməˌrāt/ *n.*

fu·ma·role /ˈfyo͞oməˌrōl/ ▸*n.* an opening in or near a volcano, through which hot sulfurous gases emerge. ▷early 19th cent.: from obsolete Italian *fumaruolo*, from late Latin *fumariolum* 'vent, hole for smoke,' a diminutive based on Latin *fumus* 'smoke.' —**fu·ma·rol·ic** /ˌfyo͞oməˈrōlik/ *adj.*

fum·ble /ˈfəmbəl/ ▸*v.* [*intrans.*] use the hands clumsily while doing or handling something: *she* ***fumbled with*** *the lock.* ■ (of the hands) do or handle something clumsily: *her hands fumbled with the waistband of his trousers.* ■ (**fumble around/about**) move clumsily in various directions using the hands to find one's way: *Greg fumbled around in the closet and found his black jacket.* ■ [*trans.*] use the hands clumsily to move (something) as specified: *she fumbled a cigarette from her bag.* ■ [*trans.*] *Football* drop or lose control of (the ball), sometimes causing a turnover: *he seldom fumbled a ball.* ■ [*trans.*] (in other ball games) fail to catch or field (the ball, a pass, a shot, etc.) cleanly. ■ express oneself or deal with something clumsily or nervously: *asked for explanations, Michael had fumbled for words.*
▸*n.* [usu. in *sing.*] an act of using the hands clumsily while doing or handling something: *just one fumble during a tire change could separate the winners from the losers.* ■ *Football* an act of dropping or losing control of the ball, sometimes causing a turnover: *his fumble was recovered on the 6-yard line.* ■ (in other ball games) an act of failing to catch or field the ball cleanly. ■ an act of managing or dealing with something clumsily: *we are not talking about subtle errors of judgment, but major fumbles.* ▷late Middle English: from Low German *fommeln* or Dutch *fommelen*. —**fum·bler** /ˈfəmb(ə)lər/ *n.* —**fum·bling·ly** /ˈfəmb(ə)liɴɢlē/ *adv.*

fume /fyo͞om/ ▸*n.* (usu. **fumes**) gas, smoke, or vapor that smells strongly or is dangerous to inhale: *clouds of exhaust fumes spewed by cars.* ■ a pungent odor of a particular thing or substance: *he breathed* ***fumes of*** *wine into her face.* ■ *poetic/literary* a watery vapor, steam, or mist rising from the earth or sea.
▸*v.* [*intrans.*] **1** emit gas, smoke, or vapor: *fragments of lava hit the ground, fuming and sizzling.* ■ [*trans.*] [usu. as *adj.*] (**fumed**) expose (esp. wood) to ammonia fumes in order to produce dark tints: *the fumed oak sideboard.* **2** feel, show, or express great anger: *he is fuming over the interference in his work.* ▷late Middle English: from Old French *fumer* (verb), from Latin *fumare* 'to smoke.' —**fum·ing·ly** /ˈfyo͞omiɴɢlē/ *adv.* —**fum·y** /ˈfyo͞omē/ *adj.*

fume hood ▸*n.* a ventilated enclosure in a chemistry laboratory, in which harmful volatile chemicals can be used or kept.

fu·met /fyo͞oˈmā; ˈfyo͞omət/ ▸*n.* a concentrated stock, esp. of game or fish, used as flavoring. ▷early 18th cent. (in the senses 'smell of game' and 'game flavor'): from French, from *fumer* 'to smoke.' The current sense dates from the early 20th cent.

fu·mi·gate /ˈfyo͞oməˌgāt/ ▸*v.* [*trans.*] apply the fumes of certain chemicals to (an area) to disinfect it or to rid it of vermin. ▷mid 16th cent. (in the sense 'to perfume'): from Latin *fumigat-* 'fumigated,' from the verb *fumigare*, from *fumus* 'smoke.' —**fu·mi·gant** /-gənt/ *n.* —**fu·mi·ga·tion** /ˌfyo͞oməˈgāsʜən/ *n.* —**fu·mi·ga·tor** /-ˌgātər/ *n.*

fu·mi·to·ry /ˈfyo͞oməˌtôrē/ ▸*n.* an Old World plant with spikes of small tubular pink or white flowers and finely divided grayish leaves, often considered a weed. • Genus *Fumaria*, family Fumariaceae. ▷late Middle English: from Old French *fumeterre*, from medieval Latin *fumus terrae* 'smoke of the earth' (because of its grayish leaves).

fun /fən/ ▸*n.* enjoyment, amusement, or lighthearted pleasure: *the children were* ***having fun*** *in the play area* | *anyone who turns up can join in the fun.* ■ a source of this: *people-watching is great fun.* ■ playful behavior or good humor: *she's full of fun.* ■ behavior or an activity that is intended purely for amusement and should not be interpreted as having serious or malicious purposes: *it was nothing serious; they just enjoyed having some harmless fun.* ■ [*attrib.*] (of a place or event) providing entertainment or leisure activities for children: *a 33-acre movie-themed fun park.*
▸*adj.* (**fun·ner fun·nest**) *informal* amusing, entertaining, or enjoyable: *it was a fun evening* | *what's the funnest part of wakeboarding for you?*
▸*v. informal* joke or tease: [*intrans.*] *no need to get sore—I was only funning* | [*trans.*] *they are just funning you.* ▷late 17th cent. (denoting a trick or hoax): from obsolete *fun* 'to cheat or hoax,' dialect variant of late Middle English *fon* 'make a fool of, be a fool,' related to *fon* 'a fool,' of unknown origin. Compare with **fond**.
▸*PHRASES* □ **for fun** (or **for the fun of it**) in order to amuse oneself and not for any more serious purpose. □ **fun and games** amusing and enjoyable activities: *teaching isn't all fun and games.* □ **someone's idea of fun** used to emphasize one's dislike for an activity or to mock someone else's liking for it: *being stuck behind a desk all day* ***isn't my idea of fun.*** □ **in fun** not intended seriously; as a joke: *remember when you meet the press to say that your speech was all in fun.* □ **like fun** *dated* an ironic exclamation of contradiction or disbelief in response to a statement. □ **make fun of** (or **poke fun at**) tease, laugh at, or joke about (someone) in a mocking or unkind way. □ **not much** (or **a lot of**) **fun** used to indicate that something strikes one as extremely unpleasant and depressing: *it can't be much fun living next door to him.* □ **what fun!** used to convey that an activity or situation sounds amusing or enjoyable.

USAGE The use of **fun** as an adjective meaning 'enjoyable,' as in *we had a fun evening*, is not fully accepted in standard English and should only be used in informal contexts. There are signs, however, that this situation is changing, given the recent appearance in U.S. English of comparative and superlative forms **funner** and **funnest**, formed as if **fun** were a normal adjective. The adjectival forms **funner** and **funnest** have not 'arrived' in all the dictionaries, however, and if employed at all, they should be used sparingly and not in formal written English.

Fu·na·ba·shi /ˌfo͞onäˈbäsʜē/ a city in central Japan, on eastern Honshu Island, a suburb of Tokyo; pop. 533,000.

Fu·na·fu·ti /ˌf(y)o͞onəˈf(y)o͞otē/ the capital of Tuvalu, on an island of the same name; pop. 2,500.

fu·nam·bu·list /fyo͞oˈnambyəlist/ ▸*n.* a tightrope walker. ▷late 18th cent.: from French *funambule* or Latin *funambulus* (from *funis* 'rope' + *ambulare* 'to walk') + **-ist**.

Fun·chal /fo͞onˈsʜäl; fən-/ the capital and chief port of Madeira, on the south coast of the island; pop. 110,000.

func·tion /ˈfəɴɢksʜən/ ▸*n.* **1** an activity or purpose natural to or intended for a person or thing: *bridges perform the function of providing access across water* | *Vitamin A is required for good eye function.* ■ practical use or purpose in design: *building designs that prioritize style over function.* ■ a basic task of a computer, esp. one that corresponds to a single instruction from the user. **2** *Mathematics* a relationship or expression involving one or more variables: *the function (bx + c).* ■ a variable quantity regarded in relation to one or more other variables in terms of which it may be expressed or on which its value depends. ■ *Chemistry* a functional group. **3** a thing dependent on another factor or factors: *class shame is a function of social power.* **4** a large or formal social event or ceremony: *he was obliged to attend party functions.*
▸*v.* [*intrans.*] work or operate in a proper or particular way: *her liver is functioning normally.* ■ (**function as**) fulfill the purpose or task of (a specified thing): *the museum intends to function as an educational and study center.* ▷mid 16th cent.: from French *fonction*, from Latin *functio(n-)*, from *fungi* 'perform.' —**func·tion·less** *adj.*

func·tion·al /ˈfəɴɢksʜənl/ ▸*adj.* **1** of or having a special activity, purpose, or task; relating to the way in which something works or operates: *there are important functional differences between left and right brain.* ■ designed to be practical and useful, rather than attractive: *she had assumed the apartment would be functional and simple.* ■ working or operating: *the museum will be fully functional from the opening of the festival.* ■ (of a disease) affecting the operation, rather than the structure, of an organ: *functional diarrhea.* ■ (of a mental illness) having no discernible organic cause: *functional psychosis.* **2** *Mathematics* of or relating to a variable quantity whose value depends on one or more other variables. —**func·tion·al·ly** *adv.* [*sentence adverb*] *functionally, the role of the library service is clearly educational.*

func·tion·al food ▸*n. chiefly Brit.* another term for **nutraceutical**.

func·tion·al gram·mar ▸*n.* a theory of grammar concerned with how the social, cognitive, and pragmatic functions of language relate to structure.

func·tion·al group ▸*n. Chemistry* a group of atoms responsible for the characteristic reactions of a particular compound.

func·tion·al il·lit·er·ate ▸*n.* a person whose level of ability to read and write is below that needed to do the ordinary tasks required to function normally in society.

func·tion·al·ism /ˈfəɴɢksʜənlˌizəm/ ▸*n.* belief in or stress on the practical application of a thing, in particular: ■ (in the arts) the doctrine that the design of an object should be determined solely by its function, rather than by aesthetic considerations, and that anything practically designed will be inherently beautiful. ■ (in the social sciences) the theory that all aspects of a society serve a function and are necessary for the survival of that society. ■ (in the philosophy of mind) the theory that mental states can be sufficiently defined by their cause, their effect on other mental states, and their effect on behavior. —**func·tion·al·ist** *n.* & *adj.*

func·tion·al·i·ty /ˌfəɴɢksʜəˈnalətē/ ▸*n.* **1** the quality of being suited to serve a purpose well; practicality: *I like the feel and functionality of this bakeware.* ■ the purpose that something is designed or expected to fulfill: *manufacturing processes may be affected by the functionality of the product.* **2** the range of operations that can be run on a computer or other electronic system: *new software with additional functionality.*

func·tion·al med·i·cine ▸*n.* medical practice or treatments that focus on optimal functioning of the body and its organs, usually involving systems of holistic or alternative medicine: *you don't have to have a disease to benefit from functional medicine.*

func·tion·al shift ▸*n.* a shift in the use of a word to a new grammatical function, such as the use of the nouns *contact* and *impact* as verbs.

func·tion·ar·y /ˈfəɴɢksʜəˌnerē/ ▸*n.* (*pl.* **-ar·ies**) a person who has to perform official functions or duties; an official.

func·tion key ▸*n. Computing* a button on a computer keyboard, distinct from the main alphanumeric keys, to which software can assign a particular function.

func·tion word ▸*n. Linguistics* a word whose purpose is more to signal grammatical relationship than the lexical meaning of a sentence, e.g., *do* in *do you live here?*.

func·tor /ˈfəɴɢktər/ ▸*n. Logic & Mathematics* a function; an operator. ■ *Linguistics* another term for **function word**. ▷1930s: from **function**, on the pattern of words such as *factor*.

fund /fənd/ ▸*n.* a sum of money saved or made available for a particular purpose: *he had set up a fund to coordinate economic investment.* ■ (**funds**) financial resources: *the misuse of public funds.* ■ a large stock or supply of something: *a vast* ***fund of*** *information.* ■ (**the funds**) *Brit.* the stock of the national debt (as a mode of investment). ■ an organization set up for the administration and management of a monetary fund.
▸*v.* [*trans.*] provide with money for a particular purpose: *the World Bank refused to fund the project* | [*in combination*] *government-funded research.* ▷mid 17th cent.: from Latin *fundus* 'bottom, piece of landed

property.' The earliest sense was 'the bottom or lowest part,' later 'foundation or basis'; the association with money has perhaps arisen from the idea of landed property being a source of wealth.
▸*PHRASE* □ **in funds** *Brit.* having money to spend.

fun·dal /ˈfəndəl/ ▸*adj. Medicine* of or relating to the fundus of an organ, esp. of the stomach, uterus, or eyeball.

fun·da·ment /ˈfəndəmənt/ ▸*n.* **1** the foundation or basis of something. **2** *humorous* a person's buttocks. ▷Middle English (also denoting the base of a building, or the founding of a building or institution): from Old French *fondement*, from Latin *fundamentum*, from *fundare* 'to found.'

fun·da·men·tal /ˌfəndəˈmentl/ ▸*adj.* forming a necessary base or core; of central importance: *the protection of fundamental human rights | interpretation of evidence is* **fundamental to** *the historian's craft.* ■ affecting or relating to the essential nature of something or the crucial point about an issue: *the fundamental problem remains that of the housing shortage.* ■ so basic as to be hard to alter, resolve, or overcome: *the theories are based on a fundamental error.*
▸*n.* (usu. **fundamentals**) a central or primary rule or principle on which something is based: *two courses cover the fundamentals of microbiology.* ■ a fundamental note, tone, or frequency. ▷late Middle English: from French *fondamental*, or late Latin *fundamentalis*, from Latin *fundamentum*, from *fundare* 'to found.' **—fun·da·men·tal·i·ty** /ˌfəndəmənˈtalətē/ *n.*

fun·da·men·tal fre·quen·cy ▸*n. Physics* the lowest frequency produced by the oscillation of the whole of an object, as distinct from the harmonics of higher frequency.

fun·da·men·tal·ism /ˌfəndəˈmentlˌizəm/ ▸*n.* a form of Protestant Christianity that upholds belief in the strict and literal interpretation of the Bible, including its narratives, doctrines, prophecies, and moral laws. ■ strict maintenance of ancient or fundamental doctrines of any religion or ideology, notably Islam.

Modern Christian fundamentalism arose from American millenarian sects of the 19th century, and has become associated with reaction against social and political liberalism and rejection of the theory of evolution. Islamic fundamentalism appeared in the 18th and 19th centuries as a reaction to the disintegration of Islamic political and economic power, asserting that Islam is central to both state and society and advocating strict adherence to the Koran (*Qur'an*) and to Islamic law (*sharia*), supported if need be by jihad or holy war.

—fun·da·men·tal·ist *n. & adj.*

fun·da·men·tal·ly /ˌfəndəˈmentl-ē/ ▸*adv.* [often as *submodifier*] in central or primary respects: *two fundamentally different concepts of democracy.* ■ [*sentence adverb*] used to make an emphatic statement about the basic truth of something: *fundamentally, this is a matter for doctors.*

fun·da·men·tal note ▸*n. Music* the lowest note of a chord in its original (uninverted) form.

fun·da·men·tal par·ti·cle ▸*n.* another term for **ELEMENTARY PARTICLE**.

fun·da·men·tal tone ▸*n. Music* the tone that represents the fundamental frequency of a vibrating object such as a string or bell.

fun·da·men·tal u·nit ▸*n.* one of a set of unrelated units of measurement, which are arbitrarily defined and from which other units are derived. For example, in the SI system the fundamental units are the meter, kilogram, and second. ■ a thing that is or is perceived as being the smallest part into which a complex whole can be analyzed: *the house is the fundamental unit of Basque society.*

fund·ed debt ▸*n.* debt in the form of securities with long-term or indefinite redemption. Compare with **FLOATING DEBT**.

fun·di /ˈfənˌdī; -ˌdē/ ▸ plural form of **FUNDUS**.

fund·ie /ˈfəndē/ ▸*n.* (*pl.* **-ies**) *informal chiefly Brit.* a fundamentalist, esp. a Christian fundamentalist. ▷1980s: from German, abbreviation of *Fundamentalist* 'fundamentalist.'

fund·ing /ˈfəndiNG/ ▸*n.* money provided, esp. by an organization or government, for a particular purpose. ■ the action or practice of providing such money.

fund man·ag·er ▸*n.* an employee or department of a large institution (such as a bank, pension fund, or insurance company) that manages the investment of money on its own behalf or on that of an outside client.

fund-rais·er ▸*n.* a person whose job or task is to seek financial support for a charity, institution, or other enterprise. ■ an event held to generate financial support for such an enterprise. **—fund-raise** *v.* **—fund-rais·ing** *n.*

fun·dus /ˈfəndəs/ ▸*n.* (*pl.* **-di** /-dī; -dē/) *Anatomy* the part of a hollow organ (such as the uterus or the gallbladder) that is farthest from the opening. ■ the upper part of the stomach, which forms a bulge higher than the opening of the esophagus (farthest from the pylorus). ■ the part of the eyeball opposite the pupil. ▷mid 18th cent.: from Latin, literally 'bottom.'

Fun·dy, Bay of /ˈfəndē/ an arm of the Atlantic Ocean between the Canadian provinces of New Brunswick and Nova Scotia. Its fast-running tides, which are used to generate electricity, are the highest in the world and reach 50–80 feet (12–15 m).

fu·ner·al /ˈfyo͞on(ə)rəl/ ▸*n.* the ceremonies honoring a dead person, typically involving burial or cremation. ■ *rare* a sermon delivered at such a ceremony. ■ *archaic or poetic/literary* a procession of mourners at a burial. ▷late Middle English: from Old French *funeraille*, from medieval Latin *funeralia*, neuter plural of late Latin *funeralis*, from Latin *funus, funer-* 'funeral, death, corpse.'
▸*PHRASE* □ **it's** (or **that's**) **someone's funeral** *informal* used to warn someone that an unwise act or decision is their responsibility: *"I won't discuss it." "Don't then—it's your funeral."*

fu·ner·al di·rec·tor ▸*n.* an undertaker.

fu·ner·al home (also **funeral parlor**) ▸*n.* an establishment where the dead are prepared for burial or cremation.

fu·ner·al pyre ▸*n.* a pile of wood on which a corpse is burned as part of a funeral ceremony in some traditions.

fu·ner·ar·y /ˈfyo͞onəˌrerē/ ▸*adj.* relating to a funeral or the commemoration of the dead: *funerary ceremonies.* ▷late 17th cent.: from late Latin *funerarius*, from *funus, funer-* 'funeral.'

fu·ne·re·al /fyəˈni(ə)rēəl; fyo͞o-/ ▸*adj.* having the mournful, somber character appropriate to a funeral: *Lincoln's funereal gloominess was legendary.* ▷early 18th cent.: from Latin *funereus* (from *funus, funer-* 'funeral') + **-AL**. **—fu·ne·re·al·ly** *adv.*

fun·fair /ˈfənˌfer/ ▸*n. chiefly Brit.* a fair consisting of rides, sideshows, and other amusements.

fun·gal /ˈfəNGgəl/ ▸*adj.* of or caused by a fungus or fungi: *fungal diseases such as mildew.*

fun·gi /ˈfənˌjī; -ˌgī/ ▸ plural form of **FUNGUS**.

fun·gi·ble /ˈfənjəbəl/ ▸*adj. Law* (of goods contracted for without an individual specimen being specified) able to replace or be replaced by another identical item; mutually interchangeable: *money is fungible—money that is raised for one purpose can easily be used for another.* ▷late 17th cent.: from medieval Latin *fungibilis*, from *fungi* 'perform, enjoy,' with the same sense as *fungi vice* 'serve in place of.' **—fun·gi·bil·i·ty** /ˌfənjəˈbilətē/ *n.*

fun·gi·cide /ˈfənjəˌsīd; ˈfəNGgə-/ ▸*n.* a chemical that destroys fungus. **—fun·gi·cid·al** /ˌfənjəˈsīdl; ˌfəNGgə-/ *adj.*

fun·gi·form /ˈfənjəˌfôrm; ˈfəNGgəˌ-/ ▸*adj.* having the shape of or resembling a fungus or mushroom.

fun·gi·stat·ic /ˌfənjəˈstatik; ˌfəNGgə-/ ▸*adj.* inhibiting the growth of fungi. **—fun·gi·stat·i·cal·ly** /-ik(ə)lē/ *adv.*

fun·giv·or·ous /ˌfənˈjivərəs; -ˈgiv-/ ▸*adj.* feeding on fungi or mushrooms.

fun·go /ˈfəNGgō/ ▸*n.* (also **fun·go fly**) (*pl.* **-goes** or **-gos**) *Baseball* a fly ball hit for fielding practice. ■ (also **fungo bat** or **stick**) a long lightweight bat for hitting practice balls to fielders. ▷mid 19th cent.: of unknown origin.

fun·goid /ˈfəNGˌgoid/ ▸*adj.* of or caused by a fungus or fungi: *she suffered from a fungoid disease of her feet.* ■ resembling a fungus in shape, texture, or speed of growth: *his skin looked moist and fungoid.*
▸*n.* a fungoid plant.

fun·gous /ˈfəNGgəs/ ▸*adj.* resembling, caused by, or having the nature of a fungus. ▷late Middle English: from Latin *fungosus*, from *fungus* (see **FUNGUS**).

fun·gus /ˈfəNGgəs/ ▸*n.* (*pl.* **-gi** /-jī; -gī/ or **-gus·es**) any of a group of unicellular, multicellular, or syncytial spore-producing organisms feeding on organic matter, including molds, yeast, mushrooms, and toadstools. ■ fungal infection (esp. on fish). ■ [in *sing.*] used to describe something that has appeared or grown rapidly and is considered unpleasant or unattractive: *there was a fungus of outbuildings behind the house.*

Fungi lack chlorophyll and are therefore incapable of photosynthesis. Many play an ecologically vital role in breaking down dead organic matter; some are an important source of antibiotics or are used in fermentation, and others cause disease. The familiar mushrooms and toadstools are merely the fruiting bodies of organisms that exist mainly as a threadlike mycelium in the soil. Some fungi form associations with other plants, growing with algae to form lichens, or in the roots of higher plants to form mycorrhizas. Fungi are now often classified as a separate kingdom distinct from the green plants.

▷late Middle English: from Latin, perhaps related to Greek *spongos, sphongos* (see **SPONGE**).

fun·gus bee·tle ▸*n.* a small beetle that feeds chiefly on fungi and is typically black with red or yellow markings. • Families Mycetophagidae, Erotylidae, and others: several genera.

fun·gus gar·den ▸*n. Entomology* a growth of fungus cultivated by certain ants or termites as a source of food.

fun·gus gnat ▸*n.* a slender and delicate fly whose larvae feed chiefly on fungi. • Family Mycetophilidae: numerous species.

fun·house /ˈfənˌhous/ ▸*n.* (in an amusement park) a building equipped with trick mirrors, shifting floors, and other devices designed to scare or amuse people as they walk through.

fu·ni·cle /ˈfyo͞onikəl/ ▸*n. Botany* a filamentous stalk attaching a seed or ovule to the placenta. Also called **FUNICULUS**. ■ *Entomology* a filamentous section of an insect's antenna, supporting the club. ▷mid 17th cent.: anglicized form of Latin *funiculus* (see **FUNICULUS**).

fu·nic·u·lar /fyo͞oˈnikyələr/ ▸*adj.* **1** (of a railroad, esp. one on a mountainside) operating by cable with ascending and descending cars counterbalanced. **2** of or relating to a rope or its tension.
▸*n.* a railroad operating in such a way. ▷mid 17th cent. (in the sense 'of or like a cord or thread'): from Latin *funiculus* (diminutive of *funis* 'rope') + **-AR**[1].

fu·nic·u·lus /fyo͞oˈnikyələs/ ▸*n.* (*pl.* **-li** /-ˌlī; -ˌlē/) *Anatomy* a bundle of nerve fibers enclosed in a sheath of connective tissue, or forming one of the main tracts of white matter in the spinal cord. ■ another term for **FUNICLE**. ▷mid 17th cent.: from Latin, diminutive of *funis* 'rope.'

Funk /fo͞oNGk; fəNGk/, Casimir (1884–1967), U.S. biochemist; born in Poland. He showed that a number of diseases, including scurvy, rickets, beriberi, and pellagra, were each caused by the deficiency of a particular dietary component. He coined the term *vitamins* for the chemicals concerned.

funk[1] /fəNGk/ *informal* ▸*n.* **1** (also **blue funk**) [in *sing.*] a state of depression: *I sat absorbed in my own blue funk.* ■ *chiefly Brit.* a state of great fear or panic: *are you in a blue funk about running out of things to say?* **2** *dated, chiefly Brit.* a coward.
▸*v.* [*trans.*] *chiefly Brit.* avoid (a task or thing) out of fear: *I could have seen him this morning but I* **funked it**. ▷mid 18th cent. (first recorded as slang at Oxford University in Oxford, England): perhaps from **FUNK**[2] in the slang sense 'tobacco smoke,' or from obsolete Flemish *fonck* 'disturbance, agitation.'

funk[2] ▸*n.* **1** a style of popular dance music of U.S. black origin, based on elements of blues and soul and having a strong rhythm that typically accentuates the first beat in the bar. **2** [in *sing.*] *informal, dated* a strong musty smell of sweat or tobacco. ▷early 17th cent. (in the sense 'musty smell'): perhaps from French dialect *funkier* 'blow smoke on,' based on Latin *fumus* 'smoke.'
▸*phrasal v.* □ **funk something up** give music elements of such a style.

funk·a·del·ic /ˌfəNGkəˈdelik/ ▸*adj.* denoting a type of dance music that combines funk with elements (such as the use of highly amplified guitars and a heavy drumbeat) derived from rock. ▷1970s: from the name of a pop group, formed *c.*1970, from **FUNK**[2] + a shortened form of **PSYCHEDELIC**. **—funkadelia** /-ˈdēlēə/ *n.*

funk·ster /ˈfəNGkstər/ ▸*n. informal* a performer or fan of funky music.

funk·y[1] /ˈfəNGkē/ ▸*adj.* (**funk·i·er**, **funk·i·est**) *informal* **1** (of music) having or using a strong dance rhythm, in particular that of funk: *some excellent funky beats.* ■ modern and stylish in an unconventional or striking way: *she likes wearing funky clothes.* **2** strongly musty: *cooked greens make the kitchen smell really funky.* ▷late 18th cent. (in the sense 'smelling strong or bad'): from FUNK[2]. —**funk·i·ly** /ˈfəNGkəlē/ *adv.* —**funk·i·ness** *n.*

funk·y[2] ▸*adj.* (**funk·i·er, funk·i·est**) *Brit., archaic or informal* frightened, panicky, or cowardly. ▷mid 19th cent.: from FUNK[1].

fun·nel /ˈfənl/ ▸*n.* a tube or pipe that is wide at the top and narrow at the bottom, used for guiding liquid or powder into a small opening. ■ a thing resembling such a tube or pipe in shape or function: *a funnel of light fell from a circular ceiling.* ■ a metal chimney on a ship or steam engine.

▸*v.* (**funneled, funneling;** *Brit.* **funnelled, funnelling**) [with *obj.* and *adverbial of direction*] guide or channel (something) through or as if through a funnel: *some $12.8 billion was **funneled through** the Marshall Plan.* ■ [*no obj.*, with *adverbial of direction*] move or be guided through or as if through a funnel: *the wind **funneled down** through the valley.* ■ [*intrans.*] assume the shape of a funnel by widening or narrowing at the end: *the crevice **funneled out.*** ▷late Middle English: apparently via Old French from Provençal *fonilh*, from late Latin *fundibulum*, from Latin *infundibulum*, from *infundere*, from *in-* 'into' + *fundere* 'pour.' —**fun·nel·like** /-ˌlīk/ *adj.*

fun·nel cake ▸*n.* a cake made of batter that is poured through a funnel into hot fat or oil, deep-fried until crisp, and served sprinkled with sugar, of Pennsylvania Dutch origin.

fun·nel cloud ▸*n.* a rotating funnel-shaped cloud forming the core of a tornado or waterspout.

fun·nel neck ▸*n.* a neck for a knit garment similar to a turtleneck but shorter and without a fold. Compare with MOCK TURTLENECK.

fun·nel-web spi·der ▸*n.* any of a number of spiders that build a funnel-shaped web, in particular: • a large and dangerously venomous Australian spider (genera *Atrax* and *Hadronyche*, family Dipluridae, suborder Mygalomorphae). • a spider of the family Agelenidae.

fun·ni·ly /ˈfənl-ē/ ▸*adv.* in a strange or amusing way: *you do talk funnily.* ■ [*sentence adverb*] (**funnily enough**) used to admit that a situation or fact is surprising or curious: *funnily enough, I was starting to like the idea.*

fun·ny /ˈfənē/ ▸*adj.* (**-ni·er, -ni·est**) **1** causing laughter or amusement; humorous: *a funny story | the play is hilariously funny.* ■ [*predic.*] expressing a speaker's objection to another's laughter or mockery: *She started to laugh. "What's so funny?" he asked.* ■ [*predic.*] [with *negative*] *informal* used to emphasize that something is unpleasant or wrong and should be regarded seriously or avoided: *stealing other people's work isn't funny.* **2** difficult to explain or understand; strange: *I had a funny feeling you'd be around | a **funny thing**, democracy.* ■ unusual or odd; curious: *Bev has a funny little stammer.* ■ unusual in such a way as to arouse suspicion: *there was something funny going on.* ■ used to draw attention to or express surprise at a curious or interesting fact or occurrence: ***that's funny!**—that vase of flowers has been moved.* ■ *informal* (of a person or part of the body) not in wholly good health or order; slightly ill: *suddenly my stomach felt funny.*

▸*n.* (*pl.* **-nies**) (**funnies**) *informal* ■ the comic strips in newspapers: *I read the sports page, funnies, and editorial.* —**fun·ni·ness** /ˈfənēnis/ *n.*

▸*PHRASES* □ **see the funny side (of something)** appreciate the humorous aspect of a situation or experience. □ **(oh) very funny!** *informal* used ironically to indicate that a speaker does not share another's joke or amusement.

fun·ny bone ▸*n. informal* the part of the elbow over which the ulnar nerve passes. A knock on the funny bone may cause numbness and pain along the forearm and hand. ■ a person's sense of humor, as located in an imaginary physical organ: *photographs to jostle the mind and the funny bone.*

fun·ny busi·ness ▸*n.* deceptive, disobedient, or lecherous behavior: *they sent a big strong farmer's lad to make sure there was no funny business.*

fun·ny farm ▸*n. informal, offensive* a psychiatric hospital: *he should be taken off to **the funny farm**.*

fun·ny man ▸*n.* a professional comedian or clown.

fun·ny mon·ey ▸*n. informal* currency that is forged or otherwise worthless.

fun·ny pa·pers ▸*plural n.* a section of a newspaper containing comics and humorous matter.

fun run ▸*n. informal* a noncompetitive run, esp. for sponsored runners in support of a charity.

fun·ster /ˈfənstər/ ▸*n. informal* a person who makes fun; a joker.

fur /fər/ ▸*n.* **1** the short, fine, soft hair of certain animals: *a long, lean, muscular cat with sleek fur.* ■ the skin of an animal with such hair on it. ■ skins of this type, or fabrics resembling these, used as material for making, trimming, or lining clothes: *jackets made out of yak fur | [as adj.] a fur coat.* ■ a garment made of, trimmed, or lined with fur: *she pulled the fur around her* ■ *Heraldry* any of several heraldic tinctures representing animal skins in stylized form (e.g., ermine, vair). **2** *Brit.* a coating formed by hard water on the inside surface of a pipe, kettle, or other container. ■ a coating formed on the tongue as a symptom of sickness.

▸*v.* (**furred, fur·ring**) [*trans.*] **1** [as *adj.*, often in *combination*] (**furred**) covered with or made from a particular type of fur: *silky-furred lemurs.* **2** *Brit.* coat or clog with a deposit: *the stuff that **furs up** coronary arteries.* **3** level (floor or wall timbers) by inserting strips of wood. ▷Middle English (as a verb): from Old French *forrer* 'to line, sheathe,' from *forre* 'sheath,' of Germanic origin. —**fur·less** *adj.*

▸*PHRASES* □ **fur and feather** game mammals and birds. □ **make the fur fly** *informal* cause serious, perhaps violent, trouble.

fur. ▸*abbr.* furlong(s).

fu·ran /ˈfyo͝orˌan; fyo͝oˈran/ ▸*n. Chemistry* a colorless volatile liquid with a planar unsaturated five-membered ring in its molecule. • Chem. formula: C_4H_4O. ■ any substituted derivative of this. ▷late 19th cent.: from synonymous *furfuran.*

fur·bear·er /ˈfərˌbe(ə)rər/ ▸*n.* an animal whose fur is valued commercially.

fur·be·low /ˈfərbəˌlō/ ▸*n.* a gathered strip or pleated border of a skirt or petticoat. ■ (**furbelows**) showy ornaments or trimmings: ***frills and furbelows** just made her look stupid.*

▸*v.* [*trans.*] [usu. as *adj.*] (**furbelowed**) *poetic/literary* adorn with trimmings. ▷late 17th cent.: from French *falbala* 'trimming, flounce,' of unknown ultimate origin.

fur·bish /ˈfərbisH/ ▸*v.* [*trans.*] [usu. as *adj.*] (**furbished**) give a fresh look to (something old or shabby); renovate: *the newly furbished church.* ■ *archaic* brighten up (a weapon) by polishing it. ▷late Middle English: from Old French *forbiss-*, lengthened stem of *forbir*, of Germanic origin. —**fur·bish·er** *n.*

fur·ca /ˈfərkə/ ▸*n.* (*pl.* **-cae** /-kī; -sē;/) *Zoology* a forked appendage or projection in an arthropod, in particular: ■ an ingrowth of the thorax of many insects. ■ the furcula of a springtail. ▷early 17th cent.: from Latin, literally 'fork.' —**fur·cal** /ˈfərkəl/ *adj.*

fur·cate *technical* ▸*v.* /ˈfərˌkāt; fərˈkāt/ [*intrans.*] divide into two or more branches; fork: *lines of descent furcating from a common source.*

▸*adj.* /ˈfərˌkāt; -kit/ divided into two or more branches; forked. ▷early 19th cent.: from late Latin *furcatus* 'cloven,' from Latin *furca* 'fork.' —**fur·ca·tion** /fərˈkāsHən/ *n.*

fur·cu·la /ˈfərkyələ/ ▸*n.* (*pl.* **-lae** /-ˌlē; -ˌlī/) *Zoology* a forked organ or structure, in particular: ■ the wishbone of a bird. ■ the forked appendage at the end of the abdomen in a springtail, by which the insect jumps. ▷mid 19th cent.: from Latin, diminutive of *furca* 'fork.' —**fur·cu·lar** *adj.*

fur·fu·ra·ceous /ˌfərf(y)əˈrāsHəs/ ▸*adj. Botany & Medicine* covered with or characterized by branlike scales. ▷mid 17th cent.: from late Latin *furfuraceus* (from Latin *furfur* 'bran') + -OUS.

fur·fur·al /ˈfərf(y)əˌral/ ▸*n. Chemistry* a colorless liquid used in synthetic resin manufacture, originally obtained by distilling bran. • An aldehyde derived from furan; chem. formula: C_4H_3OCHO. ▷late 19th cent.: from obsolete *furfurol* (in the same sense) + -AL.

fur·fur·al·de·hyde /ˌfərf(y)əˈraldəˌhīd/ ▸*n. Chemistry* another term for FURFURAL.

fu·ri·o·so /ˌfyo͝orēˈōsō; -zō/ ▸*adv. & adj. Music* (esp. as a direction) furiously and wildly. ▷Italian.

fu·ri·ous /ˈfyo͝orēəs/ ▸*adj.* extremely angry: *she was **furious** at this attempt to manipulate her.* ■ full of anger or energy; violent or intense: *he drove at a furious speed.* ▷late Middle English: from Old French *furieus*, from Latin *furiosus*, from *furia* 'fury.' —**fu·ri·ous·ly** *adv.* —**fu·ri·ous·ness** *n.*

furl /fərl/ ▸*v.* [*trans.*] roll or fold up and secure neatly (a flag, sail, umbrella, or other piece of fabric): *he shouted to the crew to furl sails | [as adj.]* (**furled**) *a furled umbrella.* ■ [*intrans.*] *poetic/literary* become rolled up; curl: [as *adj.*] (**furled**) *the plant sends up cones of furled leaves.* ▷late 16th cent.: from French *ferler*, from Old French *fer, ferm* 'firm' + *lier* 'bind' (from Latin *ligare*). —**furl·a·ble** *adj.*

fur·long /ˈfərˌlôNG; -ˌläNG/ ▸*n.* an eighth of a mile, 220 yards. ▷Old English *furlang*, from *furh* 'furrow' + *lang* 'long.' The word originally denoted the length of a furrow in a common field (formally regarded as a square of ten acres). It was also used as the equivalent of the Roman *stadium*, one eighth of a Roman mile, whence the current sense. Compare with STADIUM.

fur·lough /ˈfərlō/ ▸*n.* leave of absence, esp. that granted to a member of the armed services: *a civil servant home on furlough | a six-week furlough in Australia.* ■ a temporary release of a convict from prison: *a system that allowed murderers to leave prison for weekend furloughs.* ■ a layoff, esp. a temporary one, from a place of employment.

▸*v.* [*trans.*] grant such leave of absence to. ■ lay off (workers), esp. temporarily: *President Reagan furloughed "nonessential" employees | [as adj.]* (**furloughed**) *factories are apt to recall some furloughed workers.* ▷early 17th cent.: from Dutch *verlof*, modeled on German *Verlaub*, of West Germanic origin and related to LEAVE[2].

fur·me·ty /ˈfərmitē/ ▸*n.* variant of FRUMENTY.

furn. ▸*abbr.* furnished.

fur·nace /ˈfərnəs/ ▸*n.* an enclosed structure in which material can be heated to very high temperatures, e.g., for smelting metals. ■ an appliance fired by gas, oil, or wood in which air or water is heated to be circulated throughout a building in a heating system. ■ used to describe a very hot place: *her car was a furnace.* ▷Middle English: from Old French *fornais(e)*, from Latin *fornax, fornac-*, from *fornus* 'oven.'

Fur·neaux Is·lands /ˈfərnō/ a group of islands off the coast of northeastern Tasmania, in Australia, in the Bass Strait. The largest island is Flinders Island.

fur·nish /ˈfərnisH/ ▸*v.* [*trans.*] provide (a house or room) with furniture and fittings: *the proprietor has furnished the bedrooms in a variety of styles.* ■ (**furnish someone with**) supply someone with (something); give (something) to someone: *she was able to furnish me with details of the incident.* ■ be a source of; provide: *fish furnish an important source of protein.* ▷late Middle English (in the general sense 'provide or equip with what is necessary or desirable'): from Old French *furniss-*, lengthened stem of *furnir*, ultimately of West Germanic origin. —**fur·nish·er** *n.*

fur·nished /ˈfərnisHt/ ▸*adj.* (of accommodations) available to be rented with furniture.

fur·nish·ing /ˈfərnisHiNG/ ▸*n.* **1** (usu. **furnishings**) furniture, fittings, and other decorative accessories, such as curtains and carpets, for a house or room. **2** the action of decorating a house or room and providing it with furniture and fittings.

▸*adj.* denoting fabrics used for curtains, upholstery, or floor coverings: *they create historic furnishing textiles for the finest museums.*

fur·ni·ture /ˈfərnicHər/ ▸*n.* **1** large movable equipment, such as tables and chairs, used to make a house, office, or other space suitable for living or working. ■ *figurative* a person's habitual attitude, outlook, and way of thinking: *the mental furniture of the European.* **2** [usu. with *adj.*] small accessories or fittings for a particular use or piece of equipment: *computer hardware, software, and furniture.* ■ the mountings of a rifle. ■ *Printing* pieces of wood or metal placed around or between metal type to make blank spaces and fasten the matter in the chase. ▷early 16th cent. (denoting the action of furnishing): from French *fourniture*, from *fournir*, from Old French *furnir* 'to furnish.'

▸*PHRASE* □ **part of the furniture** *informal* a person or thing that has been somewhere so long as to seem a permanent, unquestioned, or invisible feature.

fu·ror /ˈfyo͝orˌôr; -ər/ (also *chiefly Brit.* **fu·rore**) ▸*n.* [in *sing.*] an outbreak of public anger or excitement: *the article raised a furor among mathematicians.* ■ *archaic* a wave of enthusiastic admiration; a craze. ▷late 18th cent.: from Italian *furore*, from Latin *furor*, from *furere* 'be mad, rage.'

fu·ro·se·mide /fyo͝oˈrōsəˌmīd/ (*chiefly Brit.* also **fru·se·mide**) ▸*n. Medicine* a synthetic compound with a strong diuretic action, used esp. in the treatment of edema. • Chem. formula: $C_{12}H_{11}ClN_2O_5S$. ▷1960s: from *fur-* (alteration of *fur(yl)*, denoting a radical derived from furan) + *-o-* + *sem-* (of unknown origin) + -IDE.

fur·ri·er /ˈfərēər/ ▸*n.* a person who prepares or deals in furs. ▷Middle English: from Old French *forreor*, from *forrer* 'to line, sheathe' (see FUR). The change in the ending in the 16th cent. was due to association with -IER.

fur·ri·er·y /ˈfərēərē/ ▶n. the art or trade of dressing and preparing furs.

fur·ring strip /ˈfəriNG/ ▶n. a length of wood tapering to nothing, used in roofing and other construction work.

fur·row /ˈfərō; ˈfə-rō/ ▶n. a long narrow trench made in the ground by a plow, esp. for planting seeds or for irrigation. ■ a rut, groove, or trail in the ground or another surface: *truck wheels had dug furrows in the sand.* ■ a line or wrinkle on a person's face: *there were deep furrows in his brow.*
▶v. [trans.] make a rut, groove, or trail in (the ground or the surface of something): *gorges furrowing the deep-sea floor.* ■ (with reference to the forehead or face) mark or be marked with lines or wrinkles caused by frowning, anxiety, or concentration: [trans.] *a look of concern furrowed his brow* | [intrans.] *her brow furrowed* | [as adj.] (**furrowed**) *he stroked his furrowed brow.* ■ (with reference to the eyebrows) tighten or be tightened and lowered in anxiety, concentration, or disapproval, so wrinkling the forehead: [intrans.] *his brows furrowed in concentration* | [trans.] *she furrowed her brows, thinking hard.* ■ [usu. as adj.] (**furrowed**) use a plow to make a long narrow trench in (land or earth): *furrowed fields.* ▷Old English *furh*, of Germanic origin; related to Dutch *voor* and German *Furche*, from an Indo-European root shared by Latin *porca* 'ridge between furrows.' —**fur·row·y** adj.

fur·ry /ˈfərē/ ▶adj. (-ri·er, -ri·est) covered with fur: *furry creatures in fields.* ■ having a soft surface like fur: *it has soft and furry apple-green leaves.* —**fur·ri·ness** /ˈfərēnis/ n.

fur seal ▶n. a gregarious eared seal that frequents the coasts of the Pacific and southern oceans, the male of which is substantially larger than the female. The thick fur on the underside is used commercially as sealskin. • Two genera in the family Otariidae: the **northern fur seal** (*Callorhinus ursinus*) and the **southern fur seal** (genus *Arctocephalus*).

fur·ther /ˈfərTHər/ ▶ used as comparative of FAR.
▶adv. **1** (also **far·ther** /ˈfärTHər/) at, to, or by a greater distance (used to indicate the extent to which one thing or person is or becomes distant from another): *for some time I had wanted to move farther from Lynne* | *figurative the committee seems to have moved further away from its original aims.* ■ [with negative] used to emphasize the difference between a supposed or suggested fact or state of mind and the truth: *as for her being a liar, nothing could be further from the truth* | *nothing could be further from his mind than marrying.* **2** (also **far·ther** /ˈfär-/) over a greater expanse of space or time; for a longer way: *we had walked further than I realized* | *figurative wages have been driven down even further.* ■ beyond the point already reached or the distance already covered: *Emily decided to drive further up the coast* | *before going any further we need to define our terms.* **3** beyond or in addition to what has already been done: *we are investigating ways to further increase customer satisfaction* | *this theme will be developed further in Chapter 6* | *I shall not trouble you any further.* ■ [sentence adverb] used to introduce a new point relating to or reinforcing a previous statement: *Ethnic minorities are more prone to unemployment. Further, this disadvantage extends to other areas of life.* ■ at or to a more advanced, successful, or desirable stage: *at the end of three years they were no further on.*
▶adj. **1** (also **far·ther** /ˈfär-/) more distant in space than something else of the same kind: *two men were standing at the further end of the clearing.* ■ more remote from a central point: *the museum is in the further reaches of the town.* **2** additional to what already exists or has already taken place, been done, or been accounted for: *cook for a further ten minutes.*
▶v. [trans.] help the progress or development of (something); promote: *he had depended on using them to further his own career.* ▷Old English *furthor* (adverb), *furthra* (adjective), *fyrthrian* (verb), of Germanic origin; related to FORTH. —**fur·ther·er** n.
▶PHRASES □ **not go any further** (of a secret) not be told to anyone else. □ **until further notice** used to indicate that a situation will not change until another announcement is made: *the museum is closed to the public until further notice.* □ **until further orders** used to indicate that a situation is only to change when another command is received: *they were to be kept in prison until further orders.*

USAGE On the differences between **further** and **farther**, see **usage** at FARTHER.

fur·ther·ance /ˈfərTHərəns/ ▶n. the advancement of a scheme or interest: *acts in furtherance of an industrial dispute.*

fur·ther·more /ˈfərTHərˌmôr/ ▶adv. [sentence adverb] in addition; besides (used to introduce a fresh consideration in an argument): *this species has a quiet charm and, furthermore, is an easy garden plant.*

fur·ther·most /ˈfərTHərˌmōst/ ▶adj. variant form of FARTHERMOST.

fur·thest /ˈfərTHist/ ▶adj. & adv. variant form of FARTHEST.

USAGE On the differences between **furthest** and **farthest**, see **usage** at FARTHER.

fur·tive /ˈfərtiv/ ▶adj. attempting to avoid notice or attention, typically because of guilt or a belief that discovery would lead to trouble; secretive: *they spent a furtive day together* | *he stole a furtive glance at her.* See note at SECRET. ■ suggestive of guilty nervousness: *the look in his eyes became furtive.* ▷early 17th cent.: from French *furtif, -ive* or Latin *furtivus*, from *furtum* 'theft.' —**fur·tive·ly** adv. —**fur·tive·ness** n.

fu·run·cle /ˈfyo͝orˌəNGkəl/ ▶n. technical term for BOIL2. ▷late Middle English: from Latin *furunculus*, literally 'petty thief,' also 'knob on a vine' (regarded as stealing the sap), from *fur* 'thief.' —**fu·run·cu·lar** /fyo͝oˈrəNGkyələr/ adj. —**fu·run·cu·lous** /fyo͝oˈrəNGkyələs/ adj.

fu·run·cu·lo·sis /fyo͝oˌrəNGkyəˈlōsəs/ ▶n. **1** Medicine the simultaneous or repeated occurrence of boils on the skin. **2** a bacterial disease of salmon and trout. ▷late 19th cent.: from FURUNCLE + -OSIS.

fu·ry /ˈfyo͝orē/ ▶n. (pl. -ries) **1** wild or violent anger: *tears of fury and frustration* | *Rachel shouted, beside herself with fury.* ■ (**a fury**) a surge of violent anger or other feeling: *in a fury, he lashed the horse on.* ■ [in sing.] violence or energy displayed in natural phenomena or in someone's actions: *the fury of a gathering storm* | *she was paddling with a new fury.* **2** (**Fury**) Greek Mythology a spirit of punishment, often represented as one of three goddesses who executed the curses pronounced upon criminals, tortured the guilty with stings of conscience, and inflicted famines and pestilences. The Furies were identified at an early date with the Eumenides. ■ dated used to convey a woman's anger or aggression by comparing her to such a spirit: *she turned on him like a vengeful fury.* ▷late Middle English: from Old French *furie*, from Latin *furia*, from *furiosus* 'furious,' from *furere* 'be mad, rage.'
▶PHRASE □ **like fury** informal with great energy or effort: *she fought like fury in his arms.*

furze /fərz/ ▶n. another term for GORSE. ▷Old English *fyrs*, of unknown origin. —**furz·y** adj.

fu·sain /ˈfyo͞oˌzān/ ▶n. Geology a crumbly, porous type of coal resembling wood charcoal, used in drawing. ▷late 19th cent.: from French, literally 'spindle tree,' also 'fine charcoal' (made from the spindle tree).

fu·sar·i·um /fyo͞oˈzerēəm/ ▶n. a mold of a large genus, many of which cause plant diseases, esp. wilting. • Genus *Fusarium*, subdivision Deuteromycotina. ■ infestation with any of these or related molds. ▷early 20th cent.: modern Latin, from Latin *fusus* 'spindle.'

fus·cous /ˈfəskəs/ ▶adj. technical or poetic/literary dark and somber in color. ▷mid 17th cent.: from Latin *fuscus* 'dusky' + -OUS.

fuse1 /fyo͞oz/ ▶n. a safety device consisting of a strip of wire that melts and breaks an electric circuit if the current exceeds a safe level.
▶v. **1** [trans.] join or blend to form a single entity: *intermarriage had fused the families into a large unit.* ■ [intrans.] (of groups of atoms or cellular structures) join or coalesce: *the two nuclei move together and fuse into one nucleus.* ■ melt (a material or object) with intense heat, esp. so as to join it with something else: *powdered glass was fused to a metal base.* **2** [trans.] provide (a circuit or electrical appliance) with a fuse: [as adj.] (**fused**) *a fused plug.* **3** [intrans.] Brit. (of an electrical appliance) stop working when a fuse melts: *the crew were left in darkness after the lights fused.* ■ [trans.] cause (an electrical appliance) to stop working in such a way. ▷late 16th cent.: from Latin *fus-* 'poured, melted,' from the verb *fundere*.
▶PHRASE □ **blow a fuse** use too much power in an electrical circuit, causing a fuse to melt. ■ informal lose one's temper: *it was only a suggestion—there's no need to blow a fuse.*

fuse2 (also **fuze**) ▶n. a length of material along which a small flame moves to explode a bomb or firework, meanwhile allowing time for those who light it to move to a safe distance. ■ a device in a bomb, shell, or mine that makes it explode on impact, after an interval, at set distance from the target, or when subjected to magnetic or vibratory stimulation.
▶v. [trans.] fit a fuse to (a bomb, shell, or mine): *the bomb was fused to go off during a charity performance.* ▷mid 17th cent.: from Italian *fuso*, from Latin *fusus* 'spindle.' —**fuse·less** adj.
▶PHRASES □ **light the** (or **a**) **fuse** set something tense or exciting in motion: *the event lit the fuse for the revolution.* □ **a short fuse** a tendency to lose one's temper quickly: *watch your tongue—he's got a very short fuse.* ■ (**on a short fuse**) likely to lose one's temper or explode.

fuse box ▶n. a box housing the fuses for circuits in a building.

fused sil·i·ca ▶n. an extremely transparent glass made from fusing silica, commonly used in optical lenses.

fu·see /fyo͞oˈzē/ (also **fu·zee**) ▶n. **1** a conical pulley or wheel, esp. in a watch or clock. **2** a large-headed match capable of staying lit in strong wind. **3** a railroad signal flare. ▷late 16th cent. (denoting a spindle-shaped figure): from French *fusée* 'spindleful,' based on Latin *fusus* 'spindle.'

fu·se·lage /ˈfyo͞osəˌläzH; -zə-/ ▶n. the main body of an aircraft. ▷early 20th cent.: from French, from *fuseler* 'shape into a spindle,' from *fuseau* 'spindle.'

fu·sel oil /ˈfyo͞ozəl/ ▶n. a mixture of several alcohols (chiefly amyl alcohol) produced as a byproduct of alcoholic fermentation. ▷mid 19th cent.: from German *Fusel* 'bad liquor,' probably related to *fuseln* 'to bungle.'

Fu·shun /ˈfo͞oˈSHo͞on/ a coal-mining city in northeastern China, in the province of Liaoning; pop. 1,330,000.

fu·si·ble /ˈfyo͞ozəbəl/ ▶adj. able to be fused or melted easily. ▷late Middle English: from Old French, or from medieval Latin *fusibilis*, from *fundere* 'pour, melt.' —**fu·si·bil·i·ty** /ˌfyo͞ozəˈbilətē/ n.

fu·si·form /ˈfyo͞ozəˌfôrm/ ▶adj. Botany & Zoology tapering at both ends; spindle-shaped. ▷mid 18th cent.: from Latin *fusus* 'spindle' + -IFORM.

fu·sil1 /ˈfyo͞ozəl/ ▶n. historical a light flintlock musket. ▷late 16th cent. (denoting a flint in a tinderbox): from French, ultimately from Latin *focus* 'hearth, fire.'

fu·sil2 ▶n. Heraldry an elongated lozenge. ▷late Middle English: from Old French *fusel*, from a diminutive of Latin *fusus* 'spindle.'

fu·sil·ier /ˌfyo͞ozəˈli(ə)r/ (also **fu·sil·eer**) ▶n. (usu. **Fusiliers**) a member of any of several British regiments formerly armed with fusils: *the Royal Scots Fusiliers.* ■ historical a soldier armed with a fusil. ▷late 17th cent.: from French, from *fusil* (see FUSIL1).

fu·sil·lade /ˈfyo͞osəˌläd; -ˌlād/ ▶n. a series of shots fired or missiles thrown all at the same time or in quick succession: *marchers had to dodge a fusillade of missiles* | *figurative a fusillade of accusations.*
▶v. [trans.] archaic attack (a place) or shoot down (someone) by a series of shots fired at the same time or in quick succession. ▷early 19th cent.: from French, from *fusiller* 'to shoot,' from *fusil* (see FUSIL1) + -ADE1.

fu·sil·li /fyo͞oˈsilē; -ˈsēlē/ ▶n. pasta pieces in the form of short spirals. ▷Italian, literally 'little spindles,' diminutive of *fuso*.

fu·si·mo·tor /ˈfyo͞ozəˌmōtər/ ▶adj. Anatomy relating to or denoting the motor neurons with slender fibers that innervate muscle spindles.

fu·sion /ˈfyo͞ozHən/ ▶n. the process or result of joining two or more things together to form a single entity: *a fusion of an idea from anthropology and an idea from psychology* | *malformation or fusion of the three bones in the middle ear.* ■ Physics short for NUCLEAR FUSION. ■ the process of causing a material or object to melt with intense heat, esp. so as to join with another: *the fusion of resin and glass fiber in the molding process.* ■ music that is a mixture of different styles, esp. jazz and rock.
▶adj. referring to food or cooking that incorporates elements of diverse cuisines: *their fusion fare includes a sushi-like roll of gingery rice and eel wrapped in marinated Greek grape leaves.* ▷mid 16th cent.: from Latin *fusio(n-)*, from *fundere* 'pour, melt.' —**fu·sion·al** /-zHənl/ adj.

fu·sion bomb ▶n. a bomb deriving its energy from nuclear fusion, esp. a hydrogen bomb.

fu·sion·ist /ˈfyo͞ozHənist/ ▶n. **1** a person who strives for coalition between political parties or factions.

F

2 a player or fan of music that is mixture of two modern styles. **—fu·sion·ism** /-,nizəm/ *n.*

fuss /fəs/ ▸*n.* [in *sing.*] a display of unnecessary or excessive excitement, activity, or interest: *I don't know what all the fuss is about.* ■ a protest or dispute of a specified degree or kind: *he didn't put up too much of a fuss.* ■ elaborate or complex procedures; trouble or difficulty: *they settled in with very little fuss.*
▸*v.* [*intrans.*] show unnecessary or excessive concern about something: *she's always fussing about her food.* ■ move around or busy oneself restlessly: *beside him Kelly was fussing with sheets of paper.* ■ [*trans.*] *Brit.* disturb or bother (someone): *when she cries in her sleep, try not to fuss her.* ▷early 18th cent.: perhaps Anglo-Irish. **—fuss·er** *n.*
▸*PHRASES* □ **make a fuss** become angry and complain. □ **make a fuss over** (or *Brit.* **of**) treat (a person or animal) with excessive attention or affection.

fussed /fəst/ ▸*adj.* [*predic.*] *Brit., informal* (of a person) feeling concern, distress, or annoyance; having strong feelings about something: *it'd be great to be there but* **I'm not** *that* **fussed**.

fuss·pot /ˈfəs,pät/ ▸*n. informal* a fussy person.

fuss·y /ˈfəsē/ ▸*adj.* (**fuss·i·er, fuss·i·est**) (of a person) fastidious about one's needs or requirements; hard to please: *he is very fussy about what he eats.* ■ showing excessive or anxious concern about detail: *Eleanor patted her hair with quick, fussy movements.* ■ full of unnecessary detail or decoration: *I hate fussy clothes.* **—fuss·i·ly** /ˈfəsəlē/ *adv.* **—fuss·i·ness** *n.*

fus·ta·nel·la /,fəstəˈnelə/ ▸*n.* a stiff white kilt, worn by men in Albania and Greece. ▷mid 19th cent.: from Italian, from modern Greek *phoustani, phoustanela*, probably from Italian *fustagno*, from medieval Latin *fustaneum* (see **FUSTIAN**).

fus·tian /ˈfəsCHən/ ▸*n.* **1** thick, durable twilled cloth with a short nap, usually dyed in dark colors. **2** pompous or pretentious speech or writing: *a smoke screen of fustian and fantasy.* ▷Middle English: from Old French *fustaigne*, from medieval Latin *fustaneum*, from (*pannus*) *fustaneus* 'cloth from *Fostat*,' a suburb of Cairo; sense 2 perhaps from the fact that fustian was sometimes used to cover pillows and cushions, implying that the language was "padded"; compare with **BOMBAST**.

fus·tic /ˈfəstik/ ▸*n.* **1** *archaic* a yellow dye obtained from either of two kinds of timber, esp. that of old fustic. **2** (also **old fustic**) a tropical American tree with heartwood that yields dyes and other products. See also **YOUNG FUSTIC**. • *Madura* (or **Chlorophora**) *tinctoria*, family Moraceae. ▷late Middle English: via French from Spanish *fustoc*, from Arabic *fustuk*, from Greek *pistakē* 'pistachio tree.'

fus·ty /ˈfəstē/ ▸*adj.* (**fus·ti·er, fus·ti·est**) smelling stale, damp, or stuffy: *the fusty odor of decay.* ■ old-fashioned in attitude or style: *grammar in the classroom became a fusty notion.* ▷late 15th cent.: from Old French *fuste* 'smelling of the cask,' from *fust* 'cask, tree trunk,' from Latin *fustis* 'cudgel.' **—fus·ti·ly** /ˈfəstəlē/ *adv.* **—fus·ti·ness** *n.*

fut. ▸*abbr.* future.

fu·thark /ˈfo͞o,THärk/ (also **fu·thorc** /-,THôrk/, **fu·thork**) ▸*n.* the runic alphabet. ▷mid 19th cent.: from its first six letters: *f, u, th, a* (or *o*), *r, k.*

fu·tile /ˈfyo͞otl; -,til/ ▸*adj.* incapable of producing any useful result; pointless: *a futile attempt to keep fans from mounting the stage.* ▷mid 16th cent.: from Latin *futilis* 'leaky, futile,' apparently from *fundere* 'pour.' **—fu·tile·ly** *adv.* **—fu·til·i·ty** /fyo͞oˈtilətē/ *n.*

fu·til·i·tar·i·an /fyo͞o,tiləˈterēən/ ▸*adj.* devoted to futile pursuits.
▸*n.* a person devoted to futile pursuits.

fu·ton /ˈfo͞o,tän/ ▸*n.* a Japanese quilted mattress rolled out on the floor for use as a bed. ■ a type of low wooden sofa bed having such a mattress. ▷late 19th cent.: Japanese.

fut·tock /ˈfətək/ ▸*n.* each of the curved timber pieces forming the lower part of a ship's frame. ▷Middle English: perhaps from Middle Low German, or from **FOOT + HOOK**.

fu·ture /ˈfyo͞oCHər/ ▸*n.* **1** (usu. **the future**) the time or a period of time following the moment of speaking or writing; time regarded as still to come: *we plan on getting married in the near future | work on the building will be halted for the foreseeable future.* ■ events that will or are likely to happen in the time to come: *nobody can predict the future.* ■ used to refer to what will happen to someone or something in the time to come: *a blueprint for the future of American fast food.* ■ a prospect of success or happiness: *he'd decided that there was no future in the gang | I began to believe I might have a future as an artist.* ■ *Grammar* a tense of verbs expressing events that have not yet happened. **2** (**futures**) *Finance* short for **FUTURES CONTRACT**.
▸*adj.* [*attrib.*] at a later time; going or likely to happen or exist: *the needs of future generations.* ■ (of a person) planned or destined to hold a specified position: *his future wife.* ■ existing after death: *expectation of a future life.* ■ *Grammar* (of a tense) expressing an event yet to happen. ▷late Middle English: via Old French from Latin *futurus*, future participle of *esse* 'be' (from the stem *fu-*, ultimately from a base meaning 'grow, become'). **—fu·ture·less** *adj.*
▸*PHRASES* □ **for future reference** see **REFERENCE**. □ **in future** *chiefly Brit.* from now on: *she would be more careful in future.*

fu·ture his·to·ry ▸*n.* (in science fiction) a narration of imagined future events.

fu·ture life ▸*n.* a future state or existence, esp. seen as very different from the present: *he became confident of a future life as a student.* ■ (in Hinduism and some other religions) a reincarnated existence. ■ [in *sing.*] (in Christianity and some other religions) the afterlife: *heaven and the future life with Christ.*

fu·ture per·fect ▸*n. Grammar* a tense of verbs expressing expected completion in the future, in English exemplified by *will have done.*

fu·ture-proof ▸*adj. Brit.* (of a product) unlikely to become obsolete. **—fu·ture-proofed** *adj.* **—fu·ture-proof·ing** *n.*

fu·tures con·tract ▸*n. Finance* an agreement traded on an organized exchange to buy or sell assets, esp. commodities or shares, at a fixed price but to be delivered and paid for later. Compare with **FORWARD CONTRACT**.

fu·ture shock ▸*n.* a state of distress or disorientation due to rapid social or technological change. ▷1970s: popularized by the 1970 book *Future Shock* by Alvin Toffler (1928–).

fu·tur·ism /ˈfyo͞oCHə,rizəm/ ▸*n.* concern with events and trends of the future or which anticipate the future. ■ (**Futurism**) an artistic movement begun in Italy in 1909 that violently rejected traditional forms so as to celebrate and incorporate into art the energy and dynamism of modern technology. Launched by Filippo Marinetti, it had effectively ended by 1918 but was widely influential, particularly in Russia on figures such as Malevich and Mayakovsky. ▷from **FUTURE + -ISM**, translating Italian *futurismo*, French *futurisme*.

fu·tur·ist /ˈfyo͞oCHərist/ ▸*n.* **1** (**Futurist**) an adherent of futurism. **2** a person who studies the future and makes predictions about it based on current trends. **3** *Theology* a person who believes that eschatological prophecies are still to be fulfilled.
▸*adj.* **1** (often **Futurist**) of or relating to futurism or the Futurists. **2** relating to a vision of the future, esp. one involving the development of technology: *the grim urban setting of the novel would have been a futurist nightmare.*

fu·tur·is·tic /,fyo͞oCHəˈristik/ ▸*adj.* having or involving modern technology or design: *a swimming pool and futuristic dome.* ■ (of a film or book) set in the future, typically in a world of advanced or menacing technology. ■ *dated* of or characteristic of Futurism. **—fu·tur·is·ti·cal·ly** *adv.*

fu·tu·ri·ty /fyo͞oˈto͝orətē; -ˈCHo͝orətē/ ▸*n.* (*pl.* **-ties**) the future time: *the tremendous shadows that futurity casts upon the present.* ■ a future event. ■ renewed or continuing existence: *the snowdrops were a promise of futurity.* ■ short for **FUTURITY RACE**.

fu·tu·ri·ty race (also **futurity stakes**) ▸*n.* a horse race for young horses for which entries are made long in advance, sometimes before the horses are born.

fu·tur·ol·o·gy /,fyo͞oCHəˈräləjē/ ▸*n.* systematic forecasting of the future, esp. from present trends in society. **—fu·tur·o·log·i·cal** /-rəˈläjikəl/ *adj.* **—fu·tur·ol·o·gist** /-jist/ *n.*

futz /fəts/ ▸*v.* [*intrans.*] *informal* waste time; idle or busy oneself aimlessly: *mother* **futzed around** *in the kitchen.* ■ (**futz around with**) deal with (something) in a trifling way; fiddle with: *Mick was futzing around with his camera equipment.* ▷1930s: perhaps an alteration of Yiddish *arumfartzen* 'fart around.'

Fu·xin /ˈfo͞oˈSHin/ (also **Fou-hsin**) an industrial city in northeastern China, in Liaoning province; pop. 743,000.

fuze /fyo͞oz/ ▸*n.* variant spelling of **FUSE**[2].

fu·zee ▸*n.* variant spelling of **FUSEE**.

Fu·zhou /ˈfo͞oˈjō/ (also **Foo·chow**) a port in southeastern China, capital of Fujian province; pop. 1,270,000.

fuzz[1] /fəz/ ▸*n.* a fluffy or frizzy mass of hair or fiber: *a fuzz of black hair | his face was covered with white fuzz.* ■ a blurred image or area: *she saw Jess surrounded by a fuzz of sunlight.* ■ a buzzing or distorted sound, esp. one deliberately produced as an effect on an electric guitar.
▸*v.* **1** make or become blurred or indistinct: [*trans.*] *snow fuzzes the outlines of the signs* | [*intrans.*] *tiny detail can be enlarged to poster size without* **fuzzing out**. **2** [*intrans.*] (of hair) become fluffy or frizzy: *her hair* **fuzzed out** *uncontrollably in the heat.* ▷late 16th cent.: probably of Low German or Dutch origin; compare with Dutch *voos*, Low German *fussig* 'spongy.'

fuzz[2] ▸*n.* (**the fuzz**) *informal* the police. ▷1920s: of unknown origin.

fuzz·ball /ˈfəz,bôl/ ▸*n.* a ball of fuzz: *a black and white puppy that looks like a laundered fuzzball.* ■ another term for **PUFFBALL** (sense 1).

fuzz·box /ˈfəz,bäks/ ▸*n.* a device that adds a distorted buzzing quality to the sound of an electric guitar or other instrument.

fuzzed /fəzd/ ▸*adj.* (of popular music or electric instruments) having or producing a distorted buzzing tone: *fuzzed guitars.*

fuzz·y /ˈfəzē/ ▸*adj.* (**fuzz·i·er, fuzz·i·est**) **1** having a frizzy, fluffy, or frayed texture or appearance: *a girl with fuzzy dark hair.* **2** difficult to perceive clearly or understand and explain precisely; indistinct or vague: *the picture is very fuzzy | that fuzzy line between right and wrong.* ■ (of a person or the mind) unable to think clearly; confused: *my mind felt fuzzy.* ■ another term for **FUZZED**. **3** *Computing & Logic* of or relating to a form of set theory and logic in which predicates may have degrees of applicability, rather than simply being true or false. It has important uses in artificial intelligence and the design of control systems. **—fuzz·i·ly** /ˈfəzəlē/ *adv.* **—fuzz·i·ness** *n.*
▸*PHRASE* □ **warm fuzzy** (or **warm and fuzzy**) *informal* used to refer to a sentimentally emotional response or something designed to evoke such a response: *babies require a lot of attention, not just momentary warm fuzzies.*

fuz·zy-head·ed /ˈfəzē,hedid/ ▸*adj.* **1** muddled in thought or conception: *fuzzyheaded liberals.* **2** slightly dizzy or giddy: *a strange musky scent in the air made her feel fuzzyheaded and distracted.*

fuzz·y-wuzz·y /ˈfəzē ˈwəzē/ ▸*n.* (*pl.* **-zies**) *Brit., informal, offensive* a black person, esp. one with tightly curled hair. ▷late 19th cent.: reduplication of **FUZZY**.

f.v. ▸*abbr. Latin* folio verso (on the back of the page).

FWB ▸*abbr.* four-wheel brake.

FWD ▸*abbr.* ■ four-wheel drive. ■ front-wheel drive.

fwd. ▸*abbr.* forward.

F-word ▸*n. informal* used instead of or in reference to the word "fuck" because of its taboo nature.

FX ▸*abbr.* ■ unusual (visual or sound) effects: *computer FX may allow him to redefine cinema.* ■ foreign exchange. ▷from the pronunciation of the two letters forming the two syllables of *effects*.

FY ▸*abbr.* fiscal year.

-fy ▸*suffix* **1** (added to nouns) forming verbs denoting making or producing: *speechify.* ■ denoting transformation or the process of making into: *deify | petrify.* **2** forming verbs denoting the making of a state defined by an adjective: *amplify | falsify.* **3** forming verbs expressing a causative sense: *horrify.* ▷from French *-fier*, from Latin *-ficare, -facere*, from *facere* 'do, make.'

FYI ▸*abbr.* for your information.

fyke /fīk/ (also **fyke net**) ▸*n.* a bag net for catching fish. ▷mid 19th cent.: from Dutch *fuik* 'fish trap.'

fyl·fot /ˈfil,fät/ ▸*n.* a swastika. ▷late 15th cent.: perhaps from *fill-foot* 'pattern filling the foot of a painted window.'

fyn·bos /ˈfān,bäs/ ▸*n.* a distinctive type of vegetation found only on the southern tip of Africa. It includes a wide range of plant species, particularly small heatherlike trees and shrubs. ▷Afrikaans, literally 'fine bush.'

fytte ▸*n.* variant spelling of **FIT**[3].

FZS ▸*abbr.* Fellow of the Zoological Society.

F

Gg

G1 /jē/ (also **g**) ▸*n.* (*pl.* **Gs** or **G's**) **1** the seventh letter of the alphabet. ■ denoting the next after F in a set of items, categories, etc. ■ (**g**) *Chess* denoting the seventh file from the left, as viewed from White's side of the board. **2** *Music* the fifth note in the diatonic scale of C major. ■ a key based on a scale with G as its keynote.

G2 ▸*abbr.* ■ *Physics* gauss. ■ German. ■ [in *combination*] (in units of measurement) giga- (10^9). ■ good. ■ *informal* grand (a thousand dollars). ■ a unit of gravitational force equal to that exerted by the earth's gravitational field.
▸*symbol* ■ *Chemistry* Gibbs free energy. ■ general audiences, a rating in the Voluntary Movie Rating System that all ages may be admitted. ■ *Physics* the gravitational constant, equal to 6.67×10^{-11} N m^2 kg^{-2}. ■ *Physics* conductance.

g ▸*abbr.* ■ *Chemistry* gas. ■ gelding. ■ gram(s). ■ *Physics* denoting quantum states or wave functions that do not change sign on inversion through the origin. The opposite of **U**. [from German *gerade* 'even.']
▸*symbol Physics* the acceleration due to gravity, equal to 9.81 m s^{-2}.

G7 ▸*abbr.* Group of Seven.

G8 ▸*abbr.* Group of Eight.

GA ▸*abbr.* ■ Gamblers Anonymous. ■ General Assembly. ■ general aviation. ■ General of the Army. ■ Georgia (in official postal use).

Ga1 /gä/ ▸*symbol* the chemical element gallium.

Ga2 ▸*abbr. Bible* Galatians.

Ga. ▸*abbr.* Georgia.

gab /gab/ *informal* ▸*v.* (**gabbed**, **gab·bing**) [*intrans.*] talk, typically at length, about trivial matters: *Franny walked right past a woman gabbing on the phone.*
▸*n.* talk; chatter. ▷early 18th cent.: variant of **GOB1**.

GABA ▸*abbr.* gamma-aminobutyric acid.

gab·ar·dine /ˈgabərˌdēn/ (*chiefly Brit.* also **gab·er·dine**) ▸*n.* a smooth, durable twill-woven cloth, typically of worsted or cotton. ■ *Brit.* a raincoat made of such cloth. ■ (usu. **gaberdine**) *historical* a loose long upper garment, worn particularly by Jewish men. ▷early 16th cent.: from Old French *gauvardine*, earlier *gallevardine*, perhaps from Middle High German *wallevart* 'pilgrimage' and originally 'a garment worn by a pilgrim.' The textile sense is first recorded in the early 20th cent.

gab·ble /ˈgabəl/ ▸*v.* [*intrans.*] talk rapidly and unintelligibly; utter meaningless sounds: *he gabbled on in a panicky way until he was dismissed.*
▸*n.* rapid, unintelligible talk. ▷late 16th cent.: from Dutch *gabbelen*, of imitative origin. **—gab·bler** /ˈgablər/ *n.*

gab·bro /ˈgabrō/ ▸*n.* (*pl.* **-bros**) *Geology* a dark, coarse-grained plutonic rock of crystalline texture, consisting mainly of pyroxene, plagioclase feldspar, and often olivine. ▷mid 19th cent.: from Italian, from Latin *glaber*, *glabr-* 'smooth.' **—gab·bro·ic** /gəˈbrō-ik/ *adj.* **—gab·broid** /-broid/ *adj.*

gab·by /ˈgabē/ ▸*adj.* (**gab·bi·er**, **gab·bi·est**) *informal* excessively or annoyingly talkative.

gab·er·dine /ˈgabərˌdēn/ ▸*n.* chiefly British spelling of **GABARDINE**.

gab·fest /ˈgabˌfest/ ▸*n. informal* a conference or other gathering with prolonged talking: *these summits are merely empty gabfests.* ■ a prolonged conversation.

ga·bi·on /ˈgābēən/ ▸*n.* a wirework container filled with rock, broken concrete, or other material, used in the construction of dams, retaining walls, etc. ■ *historical* a similar container of wickerwork, filled with earth or stone and used in fortifications. ▷mid 16th cent.: via French from Italian *gabbione*, from *gabbia* 'cage,' from Latin *cavea*. **—ga·bi·on·age** /ˈgābēəˌnäZH/ *n.*

Ga·ble /ˈgābəl/, (William) Clark (1901–60), U.S. actor. He was noted for movies such as *It Happened One Night* (1934), for which he won an Academy Award, and *Gone with the Wind* (1939). His last movie, *The Misfits*, was released posthumously in 1961.

Clark Gable

ga·ble /ˈgābəl/ ▸*n.* the part of a wall that encloses the end of a pitched roof. ■ (also **gable end**) a wall topped with a gable. ■ a gable-shaped canopy over a window or door. ▷Middle English: via Old French from Old Norse *gafl*, of Germanic origin; related to Dutch *gaffel* and German *Gabel* 'fork' (the point of the gable originally being the fork of two crossed timbers supporting the end of the rooftree). **—ga·bled** *adj.*

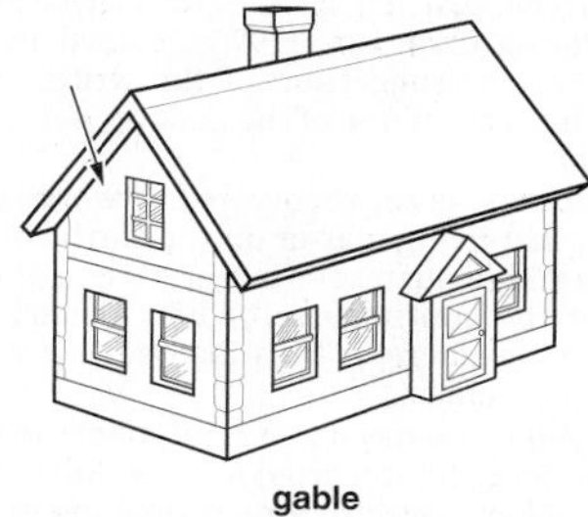

gable

ga·ble roof ▸*n.* a roof with two sloping sides and a gable at each end.

Ga·bon /gäˈbôN/ a country in West Africa, on the Atlantic coast; pop. 1,355,000; capital, Libreville; languages, French (official) and West African languages. **—Gab·o·nese** /ˌgabəˈnēz; -ˈnēs/ *adj.* & *n.*

Gabon became a French territory in 1888. Part of French Equatorial Africa from 1910 to 1958, it declared independence in 1960.

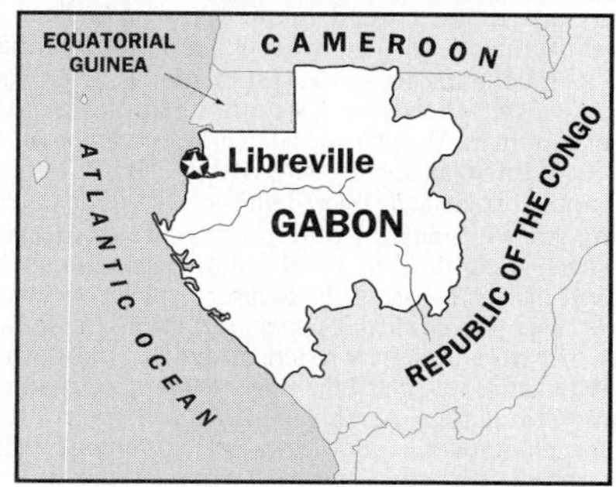

ga·boon /gəˈbo͞on/ (also **gaboon mahogany**) ▸*n.* a tropical West African hardwood tree valued for its timber. Also called **OKOUME**. • *Aucoumea klaineana*, family Burseraceae. ▷early 20th cent.: from *Gaboon* (now **GABON**).

Ga·boon vi·per ▸*n.* a large, thick-bodied venomous African snake with a pair of hornlike scales on the snout, and the scales richly patterned with brown, purple, and cream. • *Bitis gabonica*, family Viperidae. ▷early 20th cent.: named after *Gaboon* (now **GABON**).

Ga·bor /gəˈbôr; ˈgäbôr/, Dennis (1900–79), British electrical engineer; born in Hungary. He conceived the idea of holography. Nobel Prize for Physics (1971).

Ga·bo·ro·ne /ˌgäbəˈrōnā/ the capital of Botswana, in the southern part of the country near the border with South Africa; pop. 133,000.

Ga·bri·el /ˈgābrēəl/ (in the Bible) the archangel who foretold the birth of Jesus to the Virgin Mary (Luke 1:26–38), and who also appeared to Zacharias, father of John the Baptist, and to Daniel; (in Islam) the archangel who revealed the Koran to the Prophet Muhammad.

Gad1 /gad/ (in the Bible) a Hebrew patriarch, son of Jacob and Zilpah (Gen. 30:9–11). ■ the tribe of Israel traditionally descended from him.

Gad2 ▸*interj.* used to express dismay or surprise. ▷late 15th cent.: euphemistic alteration of **GOD**.

gad /gad/ ▸*v.* (**gad·ded**, **gad·ding**) [*intrans.*] *informal* go around from one place to another, in the pursuit of pleasure or entertainment: *help out around the house and not be* ***gadding about*** *the countryside.* ▷late Middle English: back-formation from obsolete *gadling* 'wanderer, vagabond,' (earlier) 'companion,' of Germanic origin.

gad·a·bout /ˈgadəˌbout/ ▸*n.* a habitual pleasure-seeker.

Gad·a·rene /ˈgadəˌrēn/ ▸*adj.* involving or engaged in a headlong or potentially disastrous rush to do something. ▷early 19th cent. (in the current sense): from New Testament Greek *Gadarēnos* 'inhabitant of *Gadara*' (see Matt. 8:28–32).

Gad·da·fi /gəˈdäfē/ (also **Qad·da·fi** /kə-/), Mu'ammer Muhammad al (1942–), Libyan statesman; head of state since 1970. After leading a coup that overthrew King Idris in 1969, he established the Libyan Arab Republic and has pursued a policy of Islamic fundamentalism blended with Arab nationalism. He has been accused of supporting international terrorism.

Gad·dis /ˈgadis/, William (1922–98) U.S. writer. He is noted for the novels *JR* (1975), *Carpenter's Gothic* (1985), and *A Frolic of His Own* (1994).

gad·fly /ˈgadˌflī/ ▸*n.* (*pl.* **-flies**) a fly that bites livestock, esp. a horsefly, warble fly, or botfly. ■ *figurative* an annoying person, esp. one who provokes others into action by criticism. ▷late 16th cent.: from **GAD1**, or obsolete *gad* 'goad, spike,' from Old Norse *gaddr*, of Germanic origin; related to **YARD1**.

gadg·et /ˈgajit/ ▸*n.* a small mechanical device or tool, esp. an ingenious or novel one: *a state-of-the-art kitchen with every conceivable gadget.* ▷late 19th cent. (originally in nautical use): probably from French *gâchette* 'lock mechanism' or from the French dialect word *gagée* 'tool.' **—gadg·e·teer** /ˌgajiˈti(ə)r/ *n.* **—gadg·et·ry** /-trē/ *n.* **—gadg·et·y** *adj.*

ga·did /ˈgādid/ ▸*n. Zoology* a fish of the cod family

(Gadidae). ▷late 19th cent.: from modern Latin *Gadidae* (plural), from *gadus* 'cod.'

ga·doid /ˈgādoid/ ▶*n. Zoology* a bony fish of an order (Gadiformes) that comprises the cods, hakes, and their relatives. ▷mid 19th cent.: from modern Latin *gadus* (from Greek *gados* 'cod') + **-OID**.

gad·o·lin·ite /ˈgadl-əˌnīt/ ▶*n.* a rare dark brown or black mineral, consisting of a silicate of iron, beryllium, and rare earths. ▷early 19th cent.: named after Johan *Gadolin* (1760–1852), the Finnish mineralogist who first identified it.

gad·o·lin·i·um /ˌgadlˈinēəm/ ▶*n.* the chemical element of atomic number 64, a soft silvery-white metal of the lanthanide series. (Symbol: **Gd**) ▷late 19th cent.: from **GADOLINITE**.

ga·droon /gəˈdro͞on/ ▶*n.* a decorative edging on metal or wood, typically formed by inverted flutings. ▷late 17th cent.: from French *godron*, probably related to *goder* 'to pucker,' also to **GODET**. —**ga·drooned** *adj.* —**ga·droon·ing** *n.*

Gads·den /ˈgadzdən/ an industrial city in northeastern Alabama; pop. 38,978.

Gads·den Pur·chase /ˈgadzdən/ an area in New Mexico and Arizona, near the Rio Grande, that covers an area of more than 30,000 square miles (77,700 sq km). It was purchased from Mexico in 1853 by U.S. diplomat James Gadsden (1788–1858) with the intention of ensuring a southern railroad route to the Pacific Ocean.

gad·wall /ˈgadˌwôl/ ▶*n.* (*pl.* same or **-walls**) a brownish-gray freshwater duck found across Eurasia and North America. • *Anas strepera*, family Anatidae. ▷mid 17th cent.: of unknown origin.

Gad·zooks /ˌgadˈzo͝oks/ (also **gad·zooks**) ▶*exclam. dated* or *humorous* an exclamation of surprise or annoyance. ▷late 17th cent.: alteration of *God's hooks*, i.e., the nails by which Jesus Christ was fastened to the cross; see **GAD2**.

Gae·a /ˈjēə/ variant spelling of **GAIA** (sense 1).

Gael /gāl/ ▶*n.* a Gaelic-speaking person. ■ a person whose ancestors spoke Gaelic. ▷from Scottish Gaelic *Gaidheal*. —**Gael·dom** /-dəm/ *n.*

Gael·ic /ˈgālik/ ▶*adj.* of or relating to the Goidelic languages, particularly the Celtic language of Scotland, and the culture associated with speakers of these languages and their descendants.

▶*n.* (also **Scottish Gaelic**) a Goidelic language brought from Ireland in the 5th and 6th centuries AD and spoken in the highlands and islands of western Scotland. ■ (also **Irish Gaelic**) another term for **IRISH** (the language).

Gael·tacht /ˈgāltəKHt/ (**the Gaeltacht**) regions in Ireland, primarily the western coast, where the vernacular language is Irish. ▷Irish, earlier *Gaedhealtacht*, from *Gaedheal* 'Gael' + *tacht* 'talk, speech.'

gaff1 /gaf/ ▶*n.* **1** a stick with a hook, or a barbed spear, for landing large fish. **2** *Sailing* a spar to which the head of a fore-and-aft sail is bent.

▶*v.* [*trans.*] seize or impale with a gaff. ▷Middle English: from Provençal *gaf* 'hook'; related to **GAFFE**.

gaff2 ▶*n.* rough treatment; criticism: *if wages increase, perhaps we can* ***stand the gaff***. ▷early 19th cent. (in the senses 'outcry; nonsense' and in the phrase *blow the gaff* 'let out a secret'): of unknown origin.

gaff3 ▶*n. Brit., informal* a house, apartment, or other building, esp. as being a person's home: *John's new gaff is on McDonald Road.* ▷1930s: of unknown origin.

gaffe /gaf/ ▶*n.* an unintentional act or remark causing embarrassment to its originator; a blunder: *an unforgivable social gaffe.* ▷early 20th cent.: from French, literally 'boat hook' (from Provençal *gaf*: see **GAFF1**), used colloquially to mean 'blunder.'

gaf·fer /ˈgafər/ ▶*n.* **1** the chief electrician in a motion-picture or television production unit. **2** *informal* an old man. **3** *Brit., informal* a person in charge of others; a boss. ▷late 16th cent.: probably a contraction of **GODFATHER**; compare with **GAMMER**.

gag1 /gag/ ▶*n.* a thing, typically a piece of cloth, put in or over a person's mouth to prevent speaking or crying out. ■ *figurative* a restriction on freedom of speech or dissemination of information: *they lobbied hard for a gag on doctors and nurses.* ■ a device for keeping the patient's mouth open during a dental or surgical operation.

▶*v.* (**gagged, gag·ging**) **1** [*trans.*] (often **be gagged**) put a gag on (someone): *she was bound and gagged by robbers in her home.* ■ *figurative* (of a person or body with authority) prevent (someone) from speaking freely or disseminating information: *the administration is trying to gag its critics.* **2** [*intrans.*] choke or retch: *he* ***gagged on*** *the sourness of the wine.* ▷Middle English: perhaps related to Old Norse *gagháls* 'with the neck thrown back,' or imitative of a person choking.

gag2 ▶*n.* a joke or an amusing story or scene, esp. one forming part of a comedian's act or in a film or play.

▶*v.* [*intrans.*] tell jokes. ▷mid 19th cent. (originally theatrical slang): of unknown origin.

ga·ga /ˈgäˌgä/ ▶*adj. informal* overexcited or irrational, typically as a result of infatuation or excessive enthusiasm; mentally confused; senile. ▷early 20th cent.: from French, 'senile, a senile person,' reduplication based on *gâteux*, variant of *gâteur*, hospital slang in the sense 'bed wetter.'

Ga·ga·rin /gəˈgärin/, Yury (Alekseyevich) (1934–68), Russian cosmonaut. In 1961, he made the first manned space flight, completing a single orbit of the earth in 108 minutes.

gage1 /gāj/ *archaic* ▶*n.* a valued object deposited as a guarantee of good faith. ■ a pledge, esp. a glove, thrown down as a symbol of a challenge to fight.

▶*v.* [*trans.*] offer (a thing or one's life) as a guarantee of good faith. ▷Middle English: from Old French *gage* (noun), *gager* (verb), of Germanic origin; related to **WAGE** and **WED**.

gage2 ▶*n.* & *v.* variant spelling of **GAUGE**.

gage3 ▶*n.* another term for **GREENGAGE**.

gag·ger /ˈgagər/ ▶*n.* a person or thing that gags, in particular: ■ a piece of iron used in a foundry mold to keep the core in place.

gag·gle /ˈgagəl/ ▶*n.* a flock of geese. ■ *informal* a disorderly or noisy group of people: *the* ***gaggle of*** *reporters and photographers that dogged his every step.* ▷Middle English (as a verb): imitative of the noise that a goose makes; compare with Dutch *gaggelen* and German *gackern*.

gag·man /ˈgagˌman/ (also **gag man**) ▶*n.* a writer or performer of gags.

gag or·der ▶*n. Law* a judge's order that a case may not be discussed in public.

gag rule ▶*n.* a regulation or directive that prohibits public discussion of a particular matter, in particular: ■ a regulation preventing the staff of government-funded family-planning clinics from offering patients information about abortion. ■ a U.S. government policy preventing U.S. aid to foreign family-planning organizations unless they agree not to promote or perform abortions.

gag·ster /ˈgagstər/ ▶*n.* another term for **GAGMAN**.

Gai·a /ˈgīə/ **1** (also **Gae·a, Ge**) *Greek Mythology* the Earth personified as a goddess, daughter of Chaos. She was the mother and wife of Uranus (Heaven); their offspring included the Titans and the Cyclopes. [Greek, 'Earth.'] **2** the earth viewed as a vast self-regulating organism. [1970s: coined by James Lovelock, at the suggestion of the writer William Golding, from the name of the goddess *Gaia*.] —**Gai·an** *n.* & *adj.*

Gai·a hy·poth·e·sis the theory, put forward by James Lovelock, that living matter on the earth collectively defines and regulates the material conditions necessary for the continuance of life. The planet, or rather the biosphere, is thus likened to a vast self-regulating organism.

gai·e·ty /ˈgāitē/ (also **gay·e·ty**) ▶*n.* (*pl.* **-ties**) the state or quality of being lighthearted or cheerful: *the sudden gaiety of children's laughter.* ■ merrymaking or festivity: *he seemed to be a part of the gaiety, having a wonderful time.* ■ (**gaieties**) *dated* entertainments or amusements. ▷mid 17th cent.: from French *gaieté*, from *gai* (see **GAY**).

gai·jin /gīˈjin/ ▶*n.* (*pl.* same) (in Japan) a foreigner. ▷Japanese, contraction of *gaikoku-jin*, from *gaikoku* 'foreign country' + *jin* 'person.'

gail·lar·di·a /gəˈlärdēə/ ▶*n.* an American plant of the daisy family, cultivated for its bright red and yellow flowers. • Genus *Gaillardia*, family Compositae. ▷modern Latin, named in memory of *Gaillard* de Marentonneau, 18th-cent. French amateur botanist.

gai·ly /ˈgālē/ ▶*adv.* in a cheerful or lighthearted way: *he waved gaily to the crowd.* ■ without thinking of the consequences: *she plunged gaily into speculation on the stock market.* ■ [as *submodifier*] with a bright or cheerful appearance: *gaily colored sailboats dot the lake.*

gain /gān/ ▶*v.* [*trans.*] **1** obtain or secure (something desired, favorable, or profitable): *a process that has gained the confidence of the industry* | [with *two objs.*] *their blend of acoustic folk pop gained them several chart hits.* See note at **GET**. ■ reach or arrive at (a desired destination): *we gained the ridge.* ■ [*intrans.*] (**gain on**) come closer to (a person or thing pursued): *a huge bear gaining on him with every stride.* ■ *archaic* bring over to one's interest or views; win over: *to gratify the queen and gain the court.* **2** increase the amount or rate of (something, typically weight or speed): *she had gradually gained weight since her wedding.* ■ [*intrans.*] increase in value: *stocks also gained for the third day in a row.* ■ [*intrans.*] (**gain in**) improve or advance in some respect: *canoeing is gaining in popularity.* ■ (of a clock or watch) become fast by (a specific amount of time): *this atomic clock will neither gain nor lose a second in the next 1 million years.*

▶*n.* an increase in wealth or resources: *the mayor was accused of using municipal funds for personal gain.* ■ a thing that is achieved or acquired: *a balance between water loss and water gain.* ■ the factor by which power or voltage is increased in an amplifier or other electronic device, usually expressed as a logarithm. ▷late 15th cent. (as a noun, originally in the sense 'booty'): from Old French *gaigne* (noun), *gaignier* (verb), of Germanic origin. —**gain·a·ble** *adj.* —**gain·er** *n.*

Gaines·ville /ˈgānzˌvil; -vəl/ a city in north central Florida, home to the University of Florida; pop. 95,447.

gain·ful /ˈgānfəl/ ▶*adj.* [*attrib.*] serving to increase wealth or resources: *he soon found* ***gainful employment***. —**gain·ful·ly** *adv.* —**gain·ful·ness** *n.*

gain·say /ˌgānˈsā; ˈgānˌsā/ ▶*v.* (*past* and *past part.* **-said**) [*trans.*] [with *negative*] *formal* deny or contradict (a fact or statement): *the impact of the railroads cannot be gainsaid.* ■ speak against or oppose (someone). ▷Middle English: from obsolete *gain-* 'against' + **SAY**. —**gain·say·er** *n.*

Gains·bor·ough /ˈgānzbərə/, Thomas (1727–88), English painter. He was known for his society portraits, including *Mr. and Mrs. Andrews* (1748) and *The Blue Boy* (c.1770), and for landscapes such as *The Watering Place* (1777).

gain·shar·ing /ˈgānˌSHe(ə)riNG/ ▶*n.* an incentive plan in which employees or customers receive benefits directly as a result of cost-saving measures that they initiate or participate in: [as *modifier*] *the company's gainsharing program ties bonuses directly to team performance.*

'gainst /genst/ ▶*prep. poetic/literary* short for **AGAINST**.

gait /gāt/ ▶*n.* a person's manner of walking: *the easy gait of an athlete.* ■ the paces of an animal, esp. a horse or dog.

▶*v.* [*intrans.*] (of a dog or horse) walk in a trained gait, as at a show: *the dogs are gaiting in a circle.* ▷late Middle English (originally Scots).

gai·ta /ˈgītə/ ▶*n.* a kind of bagpipe played in northern Spain and Portugal. ▷Spanish and Portuguese.

gait·er /ˈgātər/ ▶*n.* (usu. **gaiters**) a garment similar to leggings, worn to cover or protect the ankle and lower leg. ■ a shoe or overshoe extending to the ankle or above. ■ a garment of this kind worn as part of the traditional costume of an Anglican bishop. ▷early 18th cent.: from French *guêtre*, probably of Germanic origin and related to **WRIST**. —**gait·ered** *adj.*

Gai·thers·burg /ˈgāTHərzˌbərg/ a city in west central Maryland, northwest of Washington, DC; pop. 52,613.

gal1 /gal/ ▶*n. informal* a girl or young woman. ▷late 18th cent.: representing a pronunciation.

gal2 ▶*n. Physics* a unit of gravitational acceleration equal to one centimeter per second per second. ▷early 20th cent.: named after **GALILEO GALILEI**.

Gal. ▶*abbr. Bible* Galatians.

gal. ▶*abbr.* gallon(s).

ga·la /ˈgālə; ˈgalə/ ▶*n.* a social occasion with special entertainments or performances: [as *adj.*] *a black-tie gala that begins with a cocktail reception.* ▷early 17th cent. (in the sense 'showy dress'): via Italian and Spanish from Old French *gale* 'rejoicing.'

ga·lac·ta·gogue /gəˈlaktəˌgäg/ ▶*n. Medicine* a food or drug that promotes or increases the flow of a mother's milk. ▷mid 19th cent.: from Greek *gala, galakt-* 'milk' + *agōgos* 'leading.'

ga·lac·tic /gəˈlaktik/ ▶*adj.* of or relating to a galaxy or galaxies, esp. the Milky Way galaxy. ■ *Astronomy* measured relative to the galactic equator. ▷mid 19th cent.: from Greek *galaktias* (variant of *galaxias* 'galaxy') + **-IC**.

ga·lac·tic e·qua·tor ▶*n. Astronomy* the great circle passing as closely as possible through the densest parts of the Milky Way.

ga·lac·tic noise ▶*n.* unidentified radio-frequency radiation coming from beyond the solar system.

ga·lac·tor·rhe·a /gəˌlaktəˈrēə/ ▶*n. Medicine* excessive or inappropriate production of milk. ▷mid 19th

gaits of a horse

cent.: from Greek *gala, galakt-* 'milk' + *rhoia* 'flux, flow.'

ga·lac·tos·a·mine /gəlak'täsə,mēn; -min; -'tōsə-/ ▸*n.* an amino acid derived from the sugar galactose and typically found in glycolipids. ▷early 20th cent.: from German *Galaktosamin.*

ga·lac·tose /gə'laktōs/ ▸*n. Chemistry* a sugar of the hexose class that is a constituent of lactose and many polysaccharides. ▷mid 19th cent.: from Greek *gala, galakt-* 'milk' + **-OSE**[2].

ga·lac·to·si·dase /gə'laktōsi,dās; -,dāz; -lak'tō-/ ▸*n.* an enzyme, such as lactase, that is involved in the hydrolytic breakdown of a galactoside.

ga·lac·to·side /gə'laktə,sīd/ ▸*n.* a glycoside yielding galactose on hydrolysis.

ga·la·go /gə'lāgō; -'lägō/ ▸*n.* (*pl.* **-gos**) another term for **BUSH BABY**. ▷modern Latin (genus name).

ga·lah /gə'lä/ ▸*n.* a small Australian cockatoo with a gray back and rosy pink head and underparts, abundant and regarded as a pest. • *Eulophus roseicapillus,* family Cacatuidae (or Psittacidae). ▷mid 19th cent.: from Yuwaalaraay (an Aboriginal language of New South Wales).

Gal·a·had /'galə,had/ (also **Sir Galahad**) the noblest of King Arthur's legendary knights; renowned for immaculate purity and destined to find the Holy Grail.

ga·lan·gal /gə'lanGgəl/ (also **ga·lin·gale** /'galin,gāl/) ▸*n.* an Asian plant of the ginger family, the aromatic rhizome of which is widely used in cooking and herbal medicine. • Genera *Alpinia* and *Kaempferia,* family Zingiberaceae. ▷Middle English *galingale,* via Old French from Arabic *kalanjān,* perhaps from Chinese *gāoliángjiāng,* from *gāoliáng* (the name of a district in Guangdong Province, China) + *jiāng* 'ginger.'

ga·lant /gə'länt/ ▸*adj.* of, relating to, or denoting a light and elegant style of 18th-century music. ▷French and German (see **GALLANT**).

gal·an·tine /'galən,tēn/ ▸*n.* a dish of white meat or fish that is boned, cooked, pressed, and served cold in aspic. ▷Middle English (in the sense 'sauce for fish'): from Old French, alteration of *galatine,* from medieval Latin *galatina;* the current sense dates from the early 18th cent.

Ga·la·pa·gos Is·lands /gə'läpəgəs; -'lap-/ a Pacific Ocean archipelago on the equator, about 650 miles (1,045 km) west of Ecuador, to which it belongs; pop. 9,750. Noted for giant tortoises and many other endemic species, they were the site of Charles Darwin's 1835 observations, which helped him to form his theory of natural selection. Spanish name **ARCHIPIÉLAGO DE COLÓN**.

Gal·a·te·a /,galə'tēə/ **1** *Greek Mythology* a sea nymph courted by the Cyclops Polyphemus, who in jealousy killed his rival Acis. **2** the name given to the statue fashioned by Pygmalion and brought to life.

Ga·la·ți /gä'läts; -'lätsē/ an industrial city in eastern Romania, a port on the lower Danube River; pop. 324,000.

Ga·la·tia /gə'lāsH(ē)ə/ an ancient region in central Asia Minor, settled by invading Gauls (the Galatians) in the 3rd century BC. It later became a province of the Roman Empire. **—Ga·la·tian** *adj.* & *n.*

Ga·la·tians /gə'lāsHənz/ a book of the New Testament, an epistle of St. Paul to the Church in Galatia.

gal·ax·y /'galəksē/ ▸*n.* (*pl.* **-ax·ies**) a system of millions or billions of stars, together with gas and dust, held together by gravitational attraction. ■ (**the Galaxy**) the galaxy of which the solar system is a part; the Milky Way. ■ *figurative* a large or impressive group of people or things: *a* **galaxy of** *boundless young talent.*

The Galaxy in which the earth is located is a disk-shaped spiral galaxy with approximately 100,000 million stars. The sun is located about two thirds of the way out from the center.

▷late Middle English (originally referring to the Milky Way): via Old French from medieval Latin *galaxia,* from Greek *galaxias (kuklos)* 'milky (vault),' from *gala, galakt-* 'milk.'

Gal·ba /'galbə/ (*c.*3 BC–AD 69), Roman emperor AD 68–69; full name *Servius Sulpicius Galba.* The successor to Nero, he aroused hostility because of his severity and parsimony and was murdered in a conspiracy organized by Otho.

gal·ba·num /'galbənəm/ ▸*n.* a bitter aromatic resin produced from kinds of ferula. ▷Middle English: via Latin from Greek *khalbanē,* probably of Semitic origin.

Gal·braith /'gal,brāTH/, John Kenneth (1908–), U.S. economist; born in Canada. Well known for his criticism of consumerism and of the power of large multinational corporations, he wrote *The Affluent Society* (1958) and *The New Industrial State* (1967).

gale /gāl/ ▸*n.* a very strong wind: *it was almost blowing a gale* | [as *adj.*] *gale-force winds.* ■ *Meteorology* a wind of force 7 to 10 on the Beaufort scale (28-55 knots or 32-63 mph). ■ a storm at sea. ■ (**a gale of/gales of**) *figurative* a burst of sound, esp. of laughter: *she collapsed into* **gales of** *laughter.* ▷mid 16th cent.: perhaps related to Old Norse *galinn* 'mad, frantic.'

ga·le·a /'gālēə/ ▸*n.* (*pl.* **-le·ae** /-lē,ē/ or **-le·as**) *Botany & Zoology* a structure shaped like a helmet. ▷mid 19th cent.: from Latin, literally 'helmet.'

Ga·len /'gālən/ (129–199), Greek physician; full name *Claudios Galenos;* Latin name *Claudius Galenus.* While attempting to systematize medicine, he made important discoveries in anatomy and physiology. **—Ga·len·ism** /-,nizəm/ *n.* **—Ga·len·ist** /-nist/ *adj.* & *n.*

ga·le·na /gə'lēnə/ ▸*n.* a bluish, gray, or black mineral of metallic appearance, consisting of lead sulfide. It is the chief ore of lead. ▷late 17th cent.: from Latin, 'lead ore' (in a partly purified state).

Ga·len·ic /gā'lenik; gə-/ ▸*adj. Medicine* of or relating to Galen or his methods. ■ (usu. **galenic**) (of a medicine) galenical.

ga·len·i·cal /gā'lenikəl; gə-/ *Medicine* ▸*adj.* (of a medicine) made of natural rather than synthetic components. ■ (usu. **Galenical**) of or relating to Galen.
▸*n.* a medicine of this type.

ga·lère /ga'ler/ ▸*n.* a group or coterie: *the repulsive galère of Lolita's admirers.* ▷mid 18th cent.: French, literally 'galley.' The term was used in Molière's play *Scapin* meaning 'coterie.'

Gales·burg /'gālz,bərg/ a commercial and industrial city in west central Illinois; pop. 33,530.

ga·lette /gə'let/ ▸*n.* a flat round cake. ■ a pancake made from potatoes or buckwheat. ▷French, from Old French *galet* 'pebble.'

gal Fri·day ▸*n.* informal term for **GIRL FRIDAY**.

ga·li·a mel·on /'gälēə/ ▸*n.* a small rounded melon of a variety with rough skin and fragrant orange flesh.

Ga·li·bi /gə'lēbē/ ▸*n.* another term for **CARIB** (sense 2). ▷Carib, literally 'strong man.'

Ga·li·cia /gə'lisHə/ **1** an autonomous region and former kingdom in northwestern Spain; capital, Santiago de Compostela. **2** a region in eastern central Europe, north of the Carpathian Mountains. A former province of Austria, it now forms part of southeastern Poland and western Ukraine.

Ga·li·ci·an /gə'lisHən/ ▸*adj.* **1** of or relating to Galicia in northwestern Spain, its people, or their language. **2** of or relating to Galicia in east central Europe.
▸*n.* **1** a native or inhabitant of Galicia in northwestern Spain. **2** the Romance language of Galicia in northwestern Spain, closely related to Portuguese. **3** a native or inhabitant of Galicia in east central Europe.

Gal·i·le·an[1] /,galə'lēən/ ▸*adj.* of or relating to Galileo or his methods.

Gal·i·le·an[2] ▸*adj.* of or relating to Galilee. ■ *archaic, derogatory* Christian.
▸*n.* a native of Galilee. ■ *archaic, derogatory* a Christian.

Gal·i·le·an sat·el·lites *Astronomy* the four largest moons of Jupiter (Callisto, Europa, Ganymede, and Io), discovered by Galileo in 1610 and independently by the German astronomer Simon Marius (1573–1624).

Gal·i·le·an tel·e·scope ▸*n.* an astronomical telescope of the earliest type, with a biconvex objective and biconcave eyepiece.

Gal·i·lee /'galə,lē/ a northern region of ancient Palestine, west of the Jordan River, associated with the ministry of Jesus. It is now part of Israel.

Gal·i·lee, Sea of a lake in northern Israel. The Jordan River flows through it from north to south. Also called **TIBERIAS, LAKE, KINNERET, LAKE.**

gal·i·lee /'galə,lē/ ▸*n.* a chapel or porch at the entrance to some English churches. ▷Middle English: from Old French, from medieval Latin *galilea* 'Galilee.' Compare with **GALLERY**.

Gal·i·le·o /,galə'lāō/ an American space probe to Jupiter launched in 1989. It reached the vicinity of Jupiter in 1995 and released a probe which descended into Jupiter's atmosphere.

Gal·i·le·o Ga·li·lei /,galə'lāō ,galə'lāē/ (1564–1642), Italian astronomer and physicist. He discovered the constancy of a pendulum's swing, formulated the law of uniform acceleration of falling bodies, and described the parabolic trajectory of projectiles. He applied the telescope to astronomy and observed craters on the moon, sunspots, Jupiter's moons, and the phases of Venus.

gal·in·gale /'galin,gāl/ ▸*n.* **1** a Eurasian sedge with an aromatic rhizome, formerly used in perfumes. [late 16th cent.: variant of **GALANGAL**.] • *Cyperus longus,* family Cyperaceae. **2** variant spelling of **GALANGAL**.

gal·i·pot /'galə,pät/ ▸*n.* hardened resin deposits formed on the stem of certain species of pine, in particular the maritime pine. ▷late 18th cent.: from French, of unknown origin.

gall[1] /gôl/ ▸*n.* **1** bold, impudent behavior: *the bank*

Pronunciation Key ə *ago;* ər *over;* 'ə *or* ,ə *up;* 'ər *or* ,ər *fur;* a *hat;* ā *rate;* ä *car;* CH *chew;* e *let;* ē *see;* e(ə)r *air;* i *fit;* ī *by;* i(ə)r *ear;* NG *sing;* ō *go;* ô *for;* oi *boy;* o͝o *good;* o͞o *goo;* ou *out;* SH *she;* TH *thin;* T͟H *then;* (h)w *why;* ZH *vision*

G

had the gall to demand a fee. See note at TEMERITY. **2** the contents of the gallbladder; bile (proverbial for its bitterness). ■ an animal's gallbladder. ■ used to refer to something bitter or cruel: *accept life's gall without blaming somebody else.* ▷Old English *gealla* (denoting bile), of Germanic origin; related to Dutch *gal*, German *Galle* 'gall,' from an Indo-European root shared by Greek *kholē* and Latin *fel* 'bile.'

gall2 ▶*n.* **1** annoyance; irritation: *he imagined Linda's gall as she found herself still married and not rich.* **2** (esp. of a horse) a sore on the skin made by chafing.
▶*v.* [*trans.*] **1** make (someone) feel annoyed: *he knew he was losing, and it galled him.* **2** make sore by rubbing: *the straps galled their shoulders.* ▷Old English *gealle* 'sore on a horse,' perhaps related to GALL1; superseded in Middle English by forms from Middle Low German or Middle Dutch.

gall3 ▶*n.* an abnormal growth formed on plants and trees, esp. oaks, in response to the presence of insect larvae, mites, or fungi. ■ [as *adj.*] denoting insects or mites that produce such growths: *gall flies.* ▷Middle English: via Old French from Latin *galla.*

Gal·la /ˈgalə/ ▶*n.* & *adj.* another term for OROMO. ▷of unknown origin.

gal·lant ▶*adj.* **1** /ˈgalənt/ (of a person or their behavior) brave; heroic: *she had made gallant efforts to pull herself together.* ■ *archaic* grand; fine: *they made a gallant array as they marched off.* **2** /ˈgalənt/ (of a man or his behavior) giving special attention and respect to women; chivalrous.
▶*n.* /gəˈlant; -ˈlänt; ˈgalənt/ *dated* or *literary* a man who pays special attention to women. ■ a dashing man of fashion; a fine gentleman.
▶*v.* /gəˈlant; -ˈlänt/ [*trans.*] *archaic* (of a man) flirt with (a woman). ▷Middle English (in the sense 'finely dressed'): from Old French *galant*, from *galer* 'have fun, make a show,' from *gale* 'pleasure, rejoicing.' —**gal·lant·ly** /ˈgaləntlē/ *adv.*

gal·lant·ry /ˈgaləntrē/ ▶*n.* (*pl.* **-ries**) **1** courageous behavior, esp. in battle: *a medal awarded for outstanding gallantry during the raid.* **2** polite attention or respect given by men to women. ■ (**gallantries**) actions or words used when paying such attention. ▷late 16th cent. (in the sense 'splendor, ornamentation'): from French *galanterie*, from *galant* (see GALLANT).

G

Gal·lau·det /ˌgaləˈdet/, Thomas Hopkins (1787–1851), U.S. educator. In 1817, he founded the first free American school for the deaf in Hartford, Connecticut. Gallaudet College in Washington, DC, is named for him.

gall·ber·ry /ˈgôlˌberē/ (also **gallberry holly**) ▶*n.* (*pl.* **-ries**) a North American holly with shiny leaves and white flowers: • Genus *Ilex*, family Aquifoliaceae: the **tall gallberry** (*I. coriacea*) of the southeastern U.S., and the more widespread **low gallberry** (*I. glabra*), with black berries and nearly spineless leaves.

gall·blad·der /ˈgôlˌbladər/ (also **gall blad·der**) ▶*n.* the small sac-shaped organ beneath the liver, in which bile is stored after secretion by the liver and before release into the intestine.

gal·le·on /ˈgalēən; ˈgalyən/ ▶*n.* a sailing ship in use (esp. by Spain) from the 15th through 17th centuries, originally as a warship, later for trade. Galleons were mainly square-rigged and usually had three or more decks and masts. ▷early 16th cent.: either via Middle Dutch from French *galion*, from *galie* 'galley,' or from Spanish *galeón.*

galleon

gal·le·ri·a /ˌgaləˈrēə/ ▶*n.* a covered or enclosed area, esp. one with commercial establishments for shopping, dining, etc. ▷Italian (see GALLERY).

gal·ler·y /ˈgalərē/ ▶*n.* (*pl.* **-ler·ies**) **1** a room or building for the display or sale of works of art. ■ a collection of pictures. **2** a balcony, esp. a platform or upper floor, projecting from the back or sidewall inside a church or hall, providing space for an audience or musicians. ■ (**the gallery**) the highest of such balconies in a theater, containing the cheapest seats. ■ a group of spectators, esp. those at a golf tournament. **3** a long room or passage, typically one that is partly open at the side to form a portico or colonnade. ■ a horizontal underground passage, esp. in a mine. ▷late Middle English (sense 3): via Old French from Italian *galleria* 'gallery,' formerly also 'church porch,' from medieval Latin *galeria*, perhaps an alteration of *galilea* (see GALILEE). —**gal·ler·ied** *adj.*
▶*PHRASE* □ **play to the gallery** act in an exaggerated or theatrical manner, esp. to appeal to popular taste.

gal·ley /ˈgalē/ ▶*n.* (*pl.* **-leys**) **1** *historical* a low, flat ship with one or more sails and up to three banks of oars, chiefly used for warfare, trade, and piracy. ■ a long rowboat used as a ship's boat. **2** the kitchen in a ship or aircraft. **3** (also **galley proof**) a printer's proof in the form of long single-column strips, not in sheets or pages. [*galley* from French *galée* denoting an oblong tray for holding setup type.] ▷Middle English: via Old French from medieval Latin *galea*, from medieval Greek *galaia*, of unknown origin.

gal·ley slave ▶*n.* *historical* a person condemned to row in a galley.

Gal·lia·no /galˈyänō/ ▶*n.* a golden-yellow Italian liqueur flavored with herbs. ▷named after Major Giuseppe *Galliáno*, noted for halting Ethiopian forces in the war of 1895–96.

gal·liard /ˈgalyərd/ ▶*n.* *historical* a lively dance in triple time for two people, including complicated turns and steps. ▷late Middle English (as an adjective meaning 'valiant, sturdy' and 'lively, brisk'): from Old French *gaillard* 'valiant,' of Celtic origin. The current sense dates from the mid 16th cent.

Gal·lic /ˈgalik/ ▶*adj.* **1** French or typically French. **2** of or relating to the Gauls. ▷late 17th cent.: from Latin *Gallicus*, from *Gallus* 'a Gaul.' —**Gal·li·cize** /ˈgaləˌsīz/ *v.*

gal·lic ac·id /ˈgalik; ˈgôlik/ ▶*n.* *Chemistry* an acid extracted from oak galls and other vegetable products, formerly used in making ink. • Alternative name: **3, 4, 5-trihydroxybenzoic acid**; chem. formula: $C_6H_2(OH)_3COOH$. ▷late 18th cent.: *gallic* from Latin *galla* 'oak gall' (see GALL3) + -IC. —**gal·late** /ˈgalāt; ˈgôlāt/ *n.*

Gal·li·can /ˈgalikən/ ▶*adj.* **1** of or relating to the ancient Church of Gaul or France. **2** of or holding a doctrine (reaching its peak in the 17th century) that asserted the freedom of the Roman Catholic Church in France and elsewhere from the ecclesiastical authority of the papacy. Compare with ULTRAMONTANE.
▶*n.* an adherent of the Gallican doctrine. ▷late Middle English: from Old French *gallican*, or from Latin *Gallicanus*, from *Gallicus* (see GALLIC). —**Gal·li·can·ism** /-ˌnizəm/ *n.*

Gal·li·cism /ˈgaliˌsizəm/ ▶*n.* a French expression, esp. one adopted by speakers of another language. ▷mid 17th cent.: from French *gallicisme*, from Latin *Gallicus* (see GALLIC).

Gal·lic Wars Julius Caesar's campaigns 58–51 BC, which established Roman control over Gaul north of the Alps and west of the Rhine River (Transalpine Gaul). During this period Caesar twice invaded Britain (55 and 54 BC).

gal·li·gas·kins /ˌgaliˈgaskinz/ ▶*plural n.* *Brit., historical* loose-fitting breeches, trousers, or gaiters. ▷late 16th cent.: perhaps an alteration (influenced by *galley* and *Gascon*) of obsolete French *gargesque*, from Italian *grechesca*, feminine of *grechesco* 'Greek.'

gal·li·mau·fry /ˌgaləˈmôfrē/ ▶*n.* (*pl.* **-fries**) a confused jumble or medley of things. ■ a dish made from diced or minced meat, esp. a hash or ragout. ▷mid 16th cent.: from archaic French *galimafrée* 'unappetizing dish,' perhaps from Old French *galer* 'have fun' + Picard *mafrer* 'eat copious quantities.'

gal·li·mi·mus /ˌgaliˈmīməs/ ▶*n.* an ostrich dinosaur of the late Cretaceous period. • Genus *Gallimimus*, infraorder Ornithomimosauria, suborder Theropoda. ▷modern Latin, from Latin *galli* 'of a cockerel' (genitive of *gallus*) + *mimus* 'mime, pretense.'

gal·li·na·ceous /ˌgaləˈnāsHəs/ ▶*adj.* *dated* of or relating to birds of an order (Galliformes) which includes domestic poultry and game birds. ▷late 18th cent.: from Latin *gallinaceus* (from *gallina* 'hen,' from *gallus* 'cock') + -OUS.

gall·ing /ˈgôliNG/ ▶*adj.* annoying; humiliating: *the loss was particularly galling.* —**gall·ing·ly** *adv.*

gal·li·nule /ˈgaləˌn(y)o͞ol/ ▶*n.* a marsh bird of the rail family, with mainly black, purplish-blue, or dark green plumage, and a red bill. • Genera *Porphyrio* and *Porphyrula* (or *Gallinula*), family Rallidae: several species, including the **purple gallinule** (*Porphyrula martinica*), found from the southeastern U.S. to Argentina. See also MOORHEN. ▷late 18th cent.: from modern Latin *Gallinula* (genus term), diminutive of Latin *gallina* 'hen,' from *gallus* 'cock.'

gal·li·ot /ˈgalēət/ ▶*n.* *historical* a single-masted Dutch cargo boat or fishing vessel. ■ a small fast galley, esp. in the Mediterranean. ▷Middle English: from Old French *galiote* or Dutch *galjoot*, from a diminutive of medieval Latin *galea* 'galley.'

Gal·lip·o·li /gəˈlipəlē/ a major campaign of World War I that took place on the Gallipoli peninsula, on the European side of the Dardanelles in 1915–16. The Allies (with heavy involvement of troops from Australia and New Zealand) hoped to gain control of the strait, but the campaign reached stalemate after each side suffered heavy casualties.

gal·li·pot /ˈgaləˌpät/ ▶*n.* *historical* a small pot made from glazed earthenware or metal, used by pharmacists to hold medicines or ointments. ▷late Middle English: probably from GALLEY + POT1 (because gallipots were brought from the Mediterranean in galleys).

gal·li·um /ˈgalēəm/ ▶*n.* the chemical element of atomic number 31, a soft, silvery-white metal that melts at about 30°C, just above room temperature. (Symbol: **Ga**) ▷late 19th cent.: modern Latin, from Latin *Gallia* 'France' or *gallus* 'cock'; named (either patriotically or as a translation of his own name) by Paul-Émile *Lecoq de Boisbaudran* (1838–1912), the French chemist who discovered it in 1875.

gal·li·um ar·sen·ide ▶*n.* a dark-gray crystalline compound containing gallium and arsenic, used in the manufacture of microelectronic components, such as solar cells and semiconductors.

gal·li·vant /ˈgaləˌvant/ ▶*v.* [*intrans.*] *informal* go around from one place to another in the pursuit of pleasure or entertainment: *she quit her job to go gallivanting around the globe.* ▷early 19th cent.: perhaps an alteration of GALLANT.

gal·li·wasp /ˈgaləˌwäsp/ ▶*n.* a marsh lizard found in Central America and the Caribbean. • Genus *Diploglossus*, family Anguidae: many species, in particular *D. monotropis* of the West Indies. ▷late 17th cent.: of unknown origin.

gall midge ▶*n.* a small, delicate midge that induces gall formation in plants or may cause other damage to crops. • Family Cecidomyiidae: numerous genera and species.

gall mite ▶*n.* a minute mite that is parasitic on plants, typically living inside buds and causing them to form hard galls. • Family Eriophyidae, order Prostigmata: numerous species, in particular *Cecidophyopsis ribis*, which affects black-currant bushes, causing big bud and transmitting the reversion virus.

Gallo- ▶*comb. form* French; French and . . . : *Gallo-German.* ■ relating to France. ▷from Latin *Gallus* 'a Gaul.'

gal·lon /ˈgalən/ ▶*n.* **1** a unit of volume for liquid measure equal to four quarts, in particular: ■ *U.S.* equivalent to 3.79 liters. ■ (also **imperial gallon**) *Brit.* (also used for dry measure) equivalent to 4.55 liters. **2** (**gallons of**) *informal* a large volume: *gallons of fake blood.* ▷Middle English: from Anglo-Norman French *galon*, from the base of medieval Latin *galleta*, *galletum* 'pail, liquid measure,' perhaps of Celtic origin. —**gal·lon·age** /-nij/ *n.*

gal·loon /gəˈlo͞on/ ▶*n.* a narrow ornamental strip of fabric, typically a silk braid or piece of lace, used to trim clothing or finish upholstery. ▷early 17th cent.: from French *galon*, from *galonner* 'to trim with braid,' of unknown ultimate origin.

gal·lop /ˈgaləp/ ▶*n.* [in *sing.*] the fastest pace of a horse or other quadruped, with all the feet off the ground together in each stride: *the horse broke into a furious gallop | riding at full gallop.* ■ a ride on a horse at this pace: *Will went for a gallop on the beach.* ■ a very fast pace of running or moving.
▶*v.* (**gal·loped, gal·lop·ing**) [*intrans.*] (of a horse) go at the pace of a gallop. ■ [*trans.*] make (a horse) gallop: *Fred galloped the horse off to the start.* ■ (of a person) run fast and rather boisterously. ■ *figurative* (of a process or time) progress rapidly in a seemingly uncontrollable manner: *panic about the deadline galloping toward them* | [as *adj.*] (**galloping**) *galloping inflation.* ▷early 16th cent.: from Old French *galop* (noun), *galoper* (verb), variants of Old Northern French *walop*, *waloper* (see WALLOP). —**gal·lop·er** *n.*

Gal·lo·way /ˈgaləˌwā/ ▶*n.* an animal of a breed of cattle that originated in Galloway, Scotland. They are hornless and black and are raised for beef.

gal·lows /ˈgalōz/ ▶*plural n.* [usu. treated as *sing.*] a structure, typically of two uprights and a crosspiece, for the hanging of criminals. ■ (**the gallows**) execution by hanging: *saved from the gallows by a last-minute reprieve.* ▷Old English *galga, gealga*, of Germanic origin; related to Dutch *galg* and German *Galgen*; reinforced in Middle English by Old Norse *gálgi*.

gal·lows hu·mor ▶*n.* grim and ironic humor in a desperate or hopeless situation.

gal·lows tree ▶*n.* another term for GALLOWS.

gall·stone /ˈgôlˌstōn/ ▶*n.* a small, hard crystalline mass formed abnormally in the gallbladder or bile ducts from bile pigments, cholesterol, and calcium salts. Gallstones can cause severe pain and blockage of the bile duct.

Gal·lup /ˈgaləp/, George Horace (1901–84) U.S. statistician. A pioneer of public opinion polls, he founded the American Institute of Public Opinion in 1935.

Gal·lup poll /ˈgaləp/ ▶*n. trademark* an assessment of public opinion by the questioning of a statistically representative sample. ▷1940s: named after George H. *Gallup* (1901–84), U.S. statistician who devised the method.

gal·lus·es /ˈgaləsiz/ ▶*plural n. informal* suspenders for trousers. ▷mid 19th cent.: plural of *gallus*, variant of GALLOWS.

gall wasp ▶*n.* a small winged insect of antlike appearance. The female lays its egg in plant tissue, which swells to form a gall when the larva hatches. • Superfamily Cynipoidea, order Hymenoptera: several genera.

Ga·lois /gälˈwä/, Évariste (1811–32), French mathematician. His memoir on the conditions for solubility of polynomial equations was posthumously published in 1846.

Ga·lois the·o·ry *Mathematics* a method of applying group theory to the solution of algebraic equations.

ga·loot /gəˈlo͞ot/ ▶*n. informal* a clumsy or oafish person (often as a term of abuse). ▷early 19th cent. (originally in nautical use meaning 'an experienced marine'): of unknown origin.

gal·op /ˈgaləp/ ▶*n.* a lively ballroom dance in duple time, popular in the late 18th century. ▷mid 19th cent.: French, literally 'gallop.'

ga·lore /gəˈlôr/ ▶*adj.* [*postpositive*] in abundance: *there were prizes galore for everything.* ▷early 17th cent.: from Irish *go leor*, literally 'to sufficiency.'

ga·losh /gəˈläsʜ/ ▶*n.* (usu. **galoshes**) a waterproof overshoe, typically made of rubber. ▷Middle English (denoting a type of clog): via Old French from late Latin *gallicula*, diminutive of Latin *gallica (solea)* 'Gallic (shoe).' The current sense dates from the mid 19th cent.

Gals·wor·thy /ˈgôlzˌwərT͟Hē/, John (1867–1933), British novelist and playwright. He is noted for *The Forsyte Saga* (1906–28), a series of novels. Nobel Prize for Literature (1932).

Gal·ton /ˈgôltn/, Sir Francis (1822–1911), English scientist. He founded eugenics and introduced methods of measuring human mental and physical abilities. He also pioneered the use of fingerprints as a means of identification. He was a cousin of Charles Darwin.

ga·lumph /gəˈləmf/ ▶*v.* [*intrans.*] *informal* move in a clumsy, ponderous, or noisy manner: *she galumphed along beside him* | [as *adj.*] (**galumphing**) *a galumphing tortoise.* ▷1871 (in the sense 'prance in triumph'): coined by Lewis Carroll in *Through the Looking Glass*; perhaps a blend of GALLOP and TRIUMPH.

galv. ▶*abbr.* galvanic.

Gal·va·ni /gälˈvänē/, Luigi (1737–98), Italian anatomist. He is noted for his discovery of the twitching of frogs' legs in an electric field.

gal·van·ic /galˈvanik/ ▶*adj.* **1** relating to or involving electric currents produced by chemical action. **2** sudden and dramatic: *hurry with awkward galvanic strides.* ▷late 18th cent.: from French *galvanique*, from GALVANI. —**gal·van·i·cal·ly** /-ik(ə)lē/ *adv.*

gal·van·ic skin re·sponse (also **galvanic skin reflex**) (abbr.: **GSR**) ▶*n.* a change in the electrical resistance of the skin caused by emotional stress, measurable with a sensitive galvanometer, e.g., in lie-detector tests.

gal·va·nism /ˈgalvəˌnizəm/ ▶*n. historical* **1** electricity produced by chemical action. **2** the therapeutic use of electric currents. ▷late 18th cent.: from French *galvanisme*, from GALVANI.

gal·va·nize /ˈgalvəˌnīz/ ▶*v.* [*trans.*] **1** shock or excite (someone), typically into taking action: *the urgency of his voice* **galvanized** *them* **into** *action.* **2** [often as *adj.*] (**galvanized**) coat (iron or steel) with a protective layer of zinc: *an old galvanized bucket.* ▷early 19th cent. (in the sense 'stimulate by electricity'): from French *galvaniser* (see GALVANI). —**gal·va·ni·za·tion** /ˌgalvəniˈzāsʜən/ *n.* —**gal·va·niz·er** *n.*

gal·va·no·mag·net·ic /ˌgalvənōmagˈnetik; galˈvanō-/ ▶*adj.* of or relating to the production of an electromagnetic field within a conductor or semiconductor through which a current is flowing.

gal·va·nom·e·ter /ˌgalvəˈnämitər/ ▶*n.* an instrument for detecting and measuring small electric currents. —**gal·va·no·met·ric** /-nəˈmetrik/ *adj.*

gal·va·no·scope /ˈgalvənəˌskōp/ ▶*n.* a galvanometer that works by measuring the deflection of a needle in the magnetic field induced by the electric current. —**gal·va·no·scop·ic** /ˌgalvənəˈskäpik/ *adj.*

Gal·ves·ton /ˈgalvəstən/ a port in southeastern Texas, southeast of Houston; pop. 59,070. It is situated on Galveston Bay, an inlet of the Gulf of Mexico.

Gal·way /ˈgôlˌwā/ a county in the Republic of Ireland, on the western coast of Connacht Province. ■ its county town, a seaport at the head of Galway Bay; pop. 51,000.

Gal·way Bay an inlet of the Atlantic Ocean on the western coast of Ireland.

gam1 /gam/ ▶*n. informal* a leg, esp. in reference to the shapeliness of a woman's leg. ▷late 18th cent.: probably a variant of the heraldic term *gamb*, which denotes a charge representing an animal's leg, from Old Northern French *gambe* 'leg.'

gam2 ▶*n.* **1** a school of whales, porpoises, or dolphins. **2** a social meeting or informal conversation (originally one among whalers at sea).

Ga·ma, Vas·co da see DA GAMA.

Ga·may /gaˈmā; ˈgamā/ ▶*n.* a variety of black wine grape native to the Beaujolais district of France. ■ a fruity red wine made from this grape. ■ (also **Gamay-Beaujolais**) a red wine with a similar flavor. ▷from the name of a hamlet in Burgundy, eastern France.

gam·ba /ˈgämbə; ˈgam-/ ▶*n.* short for VIOLA DA GAMBA.

gam·ba·do1 /gamˈbādō; -ˈbä-/ (also **gam·bade** /-ˈbād; -ˈbäd/) ▶*n.* (*pl.* **-dos** or **-does**) a leap or bound, esp. an exaggerated one. ▷early 19th cent.: from Spanish *gambada*, from *gamba* 'leg.'

gam·ba·do2 ▶*n.* (*pl.* **-dos** or **-does**) a gaiter, typically one attached to a saddle to protect a rider's leg from the weather. ▷mid 17th cent.: from Italian *gamba* 'leg' + -ADO.

Gam·bi·a /ˈgambēə; ˈgäm-/ a river in West Africa that rises near Labé in Guinea and flows for 500 miles (800 km) through Senegal and Gambia to meet the Atlantic Ocean at Banjul.

Gam·bi·a, The /ˈgambēə; ˈgäm-/ ▶a country on the coast of West Africa; pop. 900,000; capital, Banjul; languages, English (official), Malinke and other indigenous languages, and Creole.

The Gambia consists of a narrow strip of territory on either side of the Gambia River that forms an enclave in Senegal. It was created as a British colony in 1843 and became an independent member of the Commonwealth of Nations in 1965 and a republic in 1970.

—**Gam·bi·an** *adj.* & *n.*

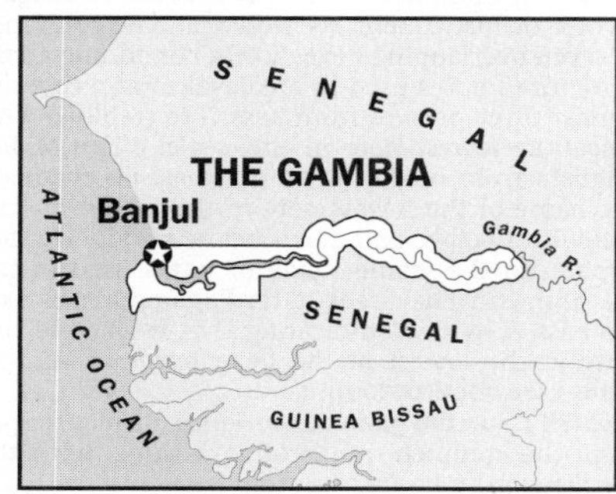

gam·bier /ˈgambi(ə)r/ (also **gam·bir**) ▶*n.* an astringent extract of a tropical Asiatic plant, used in tanning. • The chief source of gambier is the climber *Uncaria gambier*, family Rubiaceae. ▷early 19th cent.: from Malay *gambir*, the name of the plant.

Gam·bier Is·lands /ˈgamˌbir/ a group of coral islands in the South Pacific Ocean, part of French Polynesia.

gam·bit /ˈgambit/ ▶*n.* (in chess) an opening in which a player makes a sacrifice, typically of a pawn, for the sake of some compensating advantage. ■ a device, action, or opening remark, typically one entailing a degree of risk, that is calculated to gain an advantage: *his resignation was a tactical gambit.* ▷mid 17th cent.: originally *gambett*, from Italian *gambetto*, literally 'tripping up,' from *gamba* 'leg.'

gam·ble /ˈgambəl/ ▶*v.* [*intrans.*] play games of chance for money; bet: *she was fond of* **gambling on** *cards and horses.* ■ [*trans.*] bet (a sum of money) in such a way: *he was gambling every penny he had on the spin of a wheel.* ■ *figurative* take risky action in the hope of a desired result: [with *clause*] *the British could only gamble that something would turn up.*

▶*n.* [usu. in *sing.*] an act of gambling; an enterprise undertaken or attempted with a risk of loss and a chance of profit or success. ▷early 18th cent.: from obsolete *gamel* 'play games,' or from the verb GAME1. —**gam·bler** /-blər/ *n.*

gam·boge /gamˈbōj; -ˈbo͞ozʜ/ ▶*n.* a gum resin produced by various eastern Asian trees, used as a yellow pigment and in medicine as a purgative. ▷early 18th cent. (earlier in the Latin form): from modern Latin *gambaugium*, from CAMBODIA.

gam·bol /ˈgambəl/ ▶*v.* (**-boled**, **-bol·ing**; *Brit.* **-bolled**, **-bol·ling**) [*intrans.*] run or jump about playfully: *the mare gamboled toward Connie.*

▶*n.* [usu. in *sing.*] an act of running or jumping about playfully. ▷early 16th cent.: alteration of obsolete *gambade*, via French from Italian *gambata* 'trip up,' from *gamba* 'leg.'

gam·brel /ˈgambrəl/ (also **gambrel roof**) ▶*n.* a roof with two sides, each of which has a shallower slope above a steeper one. ■ a hip roof with a small gable forming the upper part of each end. ▷mid 16th cent. (in the sense 'bent piece of wood or iron used by butchers to hang carcasses on'): from Old Northern French *gamberel*, from *gambier* 'forked stick,' from *gambe* 'leg.' The sense 'hip roof' (mid 19th cent.) is based on an earlier meaning 'joint in the upper part of a horse's hind leg,' the shape of which the roof resembles.

gam·bu·sia /gamˈbyo͞ozʜə/ ▶*n.* another term for MOSQUITOFISH. ▷modern Latin, alteration of American Spanish *gambusino*.

game1 /gām/ ▶*n.* **1** a form of play or sport, esp. a competitive one played according to rules and decided by skill, strength, or luck. ■ a complete episode or period of play, typically ending in a definite result: *a baseball game.* ■ a single portion of play forming a scoring unit in a match, esp. in tennis. ■ *Bridge* a score of 100 points for tricks bid and made (the best of three games constituting a rubber). ■ a person's performance in a game; a person's standard or method of play: *he will attempt to raise his game to another level.* ■ (**games**) a meeting for sporting contests, esp. track and field: *the Olympic Games.* ■ (**games**) *Brit.* sports and athletic activities as organized in a school. ■ the equipment for a game, esp. a board game or a computer game. **2** a type of activity or business, esp. when regarded as a game: *this was a game of shuttle diplomacy at which I had become adept.* ■ a secret and clever plan or trick: *I was on to his little game, but I didn't want him to know.* ■ [often with *negative*] a thing that is frivolous or amusing: *a Tarot reading is not a game or a stunt.* **3** wild mammals or birds hunted for sport or food. ■ the flesh of these mammals or birds, used as food.

▶*adj.* eager and willing to do something new or challenging: *they were* **game for** *anything after the traumas of Monday.*

▶*v.* [*intrans.*] [often as *adj.*] (**gaming**) play games of chance for money: *the gaming tables of Monte Carlo.* ■ play video or computer games. ▷Old English *gamen* 'amusement, fun,' *gamenian* 'play, amuse oneself,' of Germanic origin. —**game·ly** *adv.* —**game·ness** *n.* —**game·ster** /-stər/ *n.*

▶*PHRASES* □ **ahead of the game** ahead of one's competitors or peers in the same sphere of activity. □ **beat someone at their own game** use someone's own methods to outdo them in their chosen activity. □ **game over** *informal* said when a situation is regarded as hopeless or irreversible. □ **make (a) game of** *archaic* mock; taunt. □ **make a game of it** *Sports* make a contest more closely competitive. □ **off** (or **on**) **one's game** playing badly (or well). □ **the only**

game in town *informal* the best, the most important, or the only thing worth considering. □ **play the game** behave in a fair or honorable way; abide by the rules or conventions. □ **play games** deal with someone or something in a way that lacks due seriousness or respect: *Don't play games with me!*

game bird ▶*n.* **1** a bird hunted for sport or food. **2** a bird of a large group that includes pheasants, grouse, quails, guineafowl, guans, etc. • Order Galliformes: several families.

game·cock /ˈgām,käk/ ▶*n.* a rooster bred and trained for cockfighting. Also called **game fowl**.

game face ▶*n.* a sports player's neutral or serious facial expression, displaying determination and concentration.

game fish (also **game·fish** /ˈgām,fisн/) ▶*n.* (*pl.* same) a fish caught by anglers for sport, esp. (in fresh water) salmon and trout and (in the sea) billfish, shark, bass, and many members of the mackerel family.

game·keep·er /ˈgām,kēpər/ ▶*n.* a person employed to breed and protect game, typically for a large estate. **—game·keep·ing** /-,kēpiɴɢ/ *n.*

gam·e·lan /ˈgamə,lan/ ▶*n.* a traditional instrumental ensemble of Indonesia, typically including many bronze percussion instruments. ▷early 19th cent.: from Javanese.

game mis·con·duct ▶*n. Ice Hockey* a punitive suspension of a player for the remainder of a game, with a substitution permitted.

game plan ▶*n.* a strategy worked out in advance, esp. in sports, politics, or business.

game·play /ˈgām,plā/ ▶*n.* the tactical aspects of a computer game, such as its plot and the way it is played, as distinct from the graphics and sound effects.

game point ▶*n.* (in tennis and other sports) a point that, if won by one contestant, will also win the game.

gam·er /ˈgāmər/ ▶*n.* a person who plays a game or games, typically a participant in a computer or role-playing game. ■ (esp. in sports) a person known for consistently making a strong effort.

game room ▶*n.* a room for relaxing or socializing in a house or public building, typically furnished with a pool table, Ping- Pong table, dart board, or other recreational amenities.

game show ▶*n.* a television program in which people compete to win prizes.

games·man·ship /ˈgāmzmən,sнip/ ▶*n.* the art of winning games by using various ploys and tactics to gain a psychological advantage. **—games·man** *n.* (*pl.* **-men**).

game·some /ˈgāmsəm/ ▶*adj.* playful and merry. **—game·some·ly** *adv.* **—game·some·ness** *n.*

gam·e·tan·gi·um /,gaməˈtanjēəm/ ▶*n.* (*pl.* **-gi·a** /-jēə/) *Botany* a specialized organ or cell in which gametes are formed in algae, ferns, and some other plants. ▷late 19th cent.: from modern Latin *gameta* (see **GAMETE**) + Greek *angeion* 'vessel' + **-IUM**.

gam·ete /ˈgamēt; gəˈmēt/ ▶*n. Biology* a mature haploid male or female germ cell that is able to unite with another of the opposite sex in sexual reproduction to form a zygote. ▷late 19th cent.: from modern Latin *gameta*, from Greek *gametē* 'wife,' *gametēs* 'husband,' from *gamos* 'marriage.' **—ga·met·ic** /gəˈmetik/ *adj.*

game the·o·ry (also **games the·o·ry**) ▶*n.* the branch of mathematics concerned with the analysis of strategies for dealing with competitive situations where the outcome of a participant's choice of action depends critically on the actions of other participants. Game theory has been applied to contexts in war, business, and biology. Compare with **DECISION THEORY**.

gameto- ▶*comb. form Biology* representing **GAMETE**.

ga·me·to·cyte /gəˈmētə,sīt/ ▶*n. Biology* a cell that divides (by meiosis) to form gametes.

gam·e·to·gen·e·sis /gə,mētəˈjenəsis/ ▶*n. Biology* the process in which cells undergo meiosis to form gametes. **—ga·me·to·gen·ic** /-ˈjenik/ *adj.* **—gam·e·tog·e·ny** /,gaməˈtäjənē/ *n.*

ga·me·to·phyte /gəˈmētə,fit/ ▶*n. Botany* (in the life cycle of plants with alternating generations) the gamete-producing and usually haploid phase, producing the zygote from which the sporophyte arises. It is the dominant form in bryophytes. **—ga·me·to·phyt·ic** /gə,mētəˈfitik/ *adj.*

game war·den ▶*n.* a person who is employed to supervise game and hunting in a particular area.

gam·ey ▶*adj.* variant spelling of **GAMY**.

gam·in /ˈgamin/ ▶*n. dated* a street urchin. ▷mid 19th cent.: French, originally an eastern dialect word, of unknown origin.

gam·ine /ˈgamēn/ ▶*n.* a girl with mischievous or boyish charm. ■ *dated* a female street urchin.
▶*adj.* characteristic of or relating to such a girl. ▷late 19th cent.: French, feminine of *gamin* (see **GAMIN**).

gam·ma /ˈgamə/ ▶*n.* the third letter of the Greek alphabet (Γ, γ), transliterated as 'g.' • The combinations γγ, γκ, and γχ are usually transliterated as 'ng,' 'nc' or 'nk,' and 'nch' or 'nkh.' ■ [as *adj.*] denoting the third in a series of items, categories, etc. ■ [as *adj.*] relating to gamma rays: *gamma detector*. ■ (**Gamma**) [followed by Latin genitive] *Astronomy* the third (usually third-brightest) star in a constellation: *Gamma Orionis*. ■ *Physics* (*pl.* same) a unit of magnetic field strength equal to 10^{-5} oersted.

gam·ma-a·mi·no·bu·tyr·ic ac·id /ə,mēnōbyo͞oˈtirik/ ▶*n. Biochemistry* an amino acid that acts to inhibit the transmission of nerve impulses in the central nervous system. • Chem. formula: $H_2NCH_2CH_2CH_2COOH$. ▷early 20th cent.: *gamma* indicating the relative position of amino on the third carbon away from the acid group.

gam·ma glob·u·lin /ˈgläbyələn/ ▶*n.* see **GLOBULIN**.

gam·ma-HCH ▶*n.* another term for **LINDANE**. ▷*HCH* from *hexachlorocyclohexane*.

gam·ma ra·di·a·tion ▶*n.* gamma rays.

gam·ma rays ▶*plural n.* penetrating electromagnetic radiation of shorter wavelength than X-rays.

gam·mer /ˈgamər/ ▶*n. archaic* an old countrywoman. ▷late 16th cent.: probably a contraction of **GODMOTHER**; see also **GAFFER**.

gam·mon[1] /ˈgamən/ ▶*n.* ham that has been cured or smoked like bacon. ■ the bottom piece of a side of bacon, including a hind leg. ▷late 15th cent. (denoting the haunch of a pig): from Old Northern French *gambon*, from *gambe* 'leg.'

gam·mon[2] ▶*n.* a victory in backgammon (carrying a double score) in which the winner removes all their pieces before the loser has removed any.
▶*v.* [*trans.*] defeat (a backgammon opponent) in such a way. ▷mid 18th cent.: apparently from Old English *gamen* or *gamenian* (see **GAME**[1]), with survival of the *-n* ending.

gam·mon[3] *informal, dated, chiefly Brit.* ▶*n.* nonsense; rubbish.
▶*v.* [*trans.*] hoax or deceive (someone). ▷early 18th cent.: origin uncertain; the term was first used as criminals' slang in *give gammon to* 'give cover to (a pickpocket)' and *keep in gammon* 'distract (a victim) for a pickpocket.'

gam·my /ˈgamē/ ▶*adj. Brit., informal* (of part of a person's body, esp. the leg) unable to function normally because of injury or chronic pain. ▷mid 19th cent. (in the sense 'bad, false'): dialect form of **GAME**[2].

Gam·ow /ˈgamôf/, George (1904–68), U.S. physicist; born in Russia. A proponent of the big bang theory, he also suggested the triplet code of bases in DNA, which governs the synthesis of amino acids.

gamp /gamp/ ▶*n. Brit., dated* an umbrella, esp. a large unwieldy one. ▷mid 19th cent.: named after Mrs. *Gamp*, in Charles Dickens's *Martin Chuzzlewit*, who carried such an umbrella.

gam·ut /ˈgamət/ ▶*n.* (**the gamut**) **1** the complete range or scope of something: *the whole gamut of human emotion*. See note at **RANGE**. **2** *Music* a complete scale of musical notes; the compass or range of a voice or instrument. ■ *historical* a scale consisting of seven overlapping hexachords, containing all the recognized notes used in medieval music, covering almost three octaves from bass G to treble E. ■ *historical* the lowest note in this scale. ▷late Middle English: from medieval Latin *gamma ut*, originally the name of the lowest note in the medieval scale (bass G an octave and a half below middle C), then applied to the whole range of notes used in medieval music. The Greek letter Γ (gamma) was used for bass G, with *ut* indicating that it was the first note in the lowest of the hexachords or six-note scales (see **SOLMIZATION**).
▶*PHRASE* □ **run the gamut** experience, display, or perform the complete range of something: *wines that run the gamut from dry to sweet*.

gam·y /ˈgāmē/ (also **gam·ey**) ▶*adj.* (**gam·i·er, gam·i·est**) (of meat) having the strong flavor or smell of game, esp. when it is slightly tainted. ■ racy; disreputable: *gamy language*. **—gam·i·ly** /ˈgāməlē/ *adv.* **—gam·i·ness** *n.*

ga·nache /gəˈnasн/ ▶*n.* a whipped filling of chocolate and cream, used in desserts such as cakes and truffles. ▷French.

Ga·na·pa·ti /,gənəˈpətē/ *Hinduism* another name for **GANESH**.

Gän·cä /gänˈjä/ an industrial city in Azerbaijan; pop. 281,000. The city was formerly called Elizavetpol 1804–1918 and Kirovabad 1935–89. Russian name **GYANDZHE**.

Gand /gän/ French name of **GHENT**.

Gan·da /ˈgändə/ ▶*n.* & *adj.* another term for **BAGANDA**.

Gan·der /ˈgandər/ a town on the island of Newfoundland, on Lake Gander; pop. 10,339. Its airport served the first regular transatlantic flights during World War II.

gan·der /ˈgandər/ ▶*n.* **1** a male goose. **2** [in *sing.*] *informal* a look or glance: *take a gander at that luggage*. [from criminals' slang.] ▷Old English *gandra*, of Germanic origin; related to Dutch *gander*, also to **GANNET**.

Gan·dhi[1] /ˈgändē/, Indira (1917–84), Indian stateswoman; prime minister 1966–77 and 1980–84. The daughter of Jawaharlal Nehru, she sought to establish a secular state and to lead India out of poverty. She was assassinated by her own Sikh bodyguards following prolonged religious disturbance.

Gan·dhi[2], Mahatma (1869–1948), Indian nationalist and spiritual leader; full name *Mohandas Karamchand Gandhi*. Prominent in the opposition to British rule in India, he pursued a policy of nonviolent civil disobedience. Although he never held government office, he was regarded as the country's supreme political and spiritual leader. Gandhi was assassinated by a Hindu following his agreement to the creation of the state of Pakistan.

Gan·dhi[3], Rajiv (1944–91), Indian statesman; prime minister 1984–89. The eldest son of Indira Gandhi, he became prime minister after his mother's assassination. His premiership was marked by continuing unrest, and he was assassinated during an election campaign. His widow, **Sonia,** (b. 1946), born in Italy, entered the political arena in 1998 and was elected head of the Congress Party, leading the party to victory in the 2004 elections.

Gan·dhi·na·gar /,gəndiˈnəgər/ a city in western India, capital of the state of Gujarat; pop. 122,000.

gan·dy danc·er /ˈgandē/ ▶*n. informal* a track maintenance worker on a railroad. ▷early 20th cent.: of unknown origin.

ga·nef /ˈgänəf/ ▶ *n.* a variant spelling of **GONIF**.

Ga·nesh /gəˈnäsн/ (also **Ga·ne·sha** /-ˈnäsнə/) *Hinduism* an elephant-headed deity, son of Shiva and Parvati. Worshiped as the remover of obstacles and patron of learning, he is usually depicted colored red, with a potbelly and one broken tusk, riding a rat. Also called **GANAPATI**. ▷from Sanskrit *Gaṇeśa* 'lord of the ganas' (Shiva's attendants).

gang[1] /gaɴɢ/ ▶*n.* **1** an organized group of criminals. ■ a group of young people involved in petty crime or violence. ■ *informal* a group of people, esp. young people, who regularly associate together. ■ an organized group of people doing manual work: *ninety days of hard labor on the road gang*. **2** a set of switches, sockets, or other electrical or mechanical devices grouped together.
▶*v.* **1** [*intrans.*] (**gang together**) (of a number of people) form a group or gang: *the smaller supermarket chains are ganging together to beat the big boys*. ■ (**gang up**) (of a number of people) join together, typically in order to intimidate someone: *he is being unfairly ganged up on*. **2** [*trans.*] (often **be ganged**) arrange (electrical devices or machines) together to work in coordination. ▷Old English, from Old Norse *gangr, ganga* 'gait, course, going,' of Germanic origin; related to **GANG**[2]. The original meaning was 'going, a journey,' later in Middle English 'a way, passage,' also 'set of things or people that go together.'

gang[2] ▶*v.* [*intrans.*] *Scottish* go; proceed: *gang to your bed, lass*.
▶*phrasal v.* □ **gang agley** (of a plan) go wrong. [1786: from Robert Burns's 'The best laid schemes o' Mice an' Men, Gang aft agley' (*Poems and Songs*).] ▷Old English *gangan*, of Germanic origin; related to **GO**[1].

Gan·ga /ˈgəɴɢgə/ Hindi name for **GANGES**.

gang·bang /ˈgaɴɢ,baɴɢ/ ▶*n. informal* **1** the successive rape of one person by a group of other people. ■ a sexual orgy involving changes of partner. **2** an instance of violence, esp. a shooting, involving members of a criminal gang.
▶*v.* [*intrans.*] participate in a gangbang. ■ [*trans.*] victimize (someone) by such participation. **—gang·bang·er** *n.*

gang·bust·er /ˈgaNG,bəstər/ ▸*n. informal* a police officer or other person who takes part in breaking up criminal gangs. ■ [as *adj.*] very successful, esp. commercially: *the restaurant did a gangbuster business.*
▸*PHRASE* □ **go** (or **like**) **gangbusters** used to refer to great vigor, speed, or success: *the real estate market was going gangbusters | it's growing like gangbusters.*

gang·er /ˈgaNGər/ ▸*n. Brit.* the foreman of a gang of laborers.

Gan·ges /ˈgan,jēz/ a river in northern India and Bangladesh that rises in the Himalayas and flows southwest for about 1,678 miles (2,700 km) to the Bay of Bengal, where it forms the world's largest delta. The river is regarded by Hindus as sacred. Hindi name **GANGA**. —**Gan·get·ic** /ganˈjetik/ *adj.*

gang·land /ˈgaNG,land/ ▸*n.* the world of criminal gangs: [as *adj.*] *he was the victim of a gangland killing.*

gan·gle /ˈgaNGgəl/ ▸*v.* [*intrans.*] move ungracefully. ▷mid 20th cent.: back-formation from **GANGLING**.

gan·gling /ˈgaNGgliNG/ ▸*adj.* (of a person) tall, thin, and awkward in movements or bearing. ▷early 19th cent.: from the verb **GANG**[2] + **-LE**[4] + **-ING**[2].

gan·gli·on /ˈgaNGglēən/ ▸*n.* (*pl.* **-gli·a** /-glēə/ or **-gli·ons**) **1** *Anatomy* a structure containing a number of nerve cell bodies, typically linked by synapses, and often forming a swelling on a nerve fiber. ■ a network of cells forming a nerve center in the nervous system of an invertebrate. ■ a well-defined mass of gray matter within the central nervous system. See also **BASAL GANGLIA**. **2** *Medicine* an abnormal benign swelling on a tendon sheath. ▷late 17th cent.: from Greek *ganglion* 'tumor on or near sinews or tendons,' used by Galen to denote the complex nerve centers. —**gan·gli·on·ic** /,gaNGglēˈänik/ *adj.*

gan·gli·o·side /ˈgaNGglēə,sīd/ ▸*n. Biochemistry* any of a group of complex lipids that are present in the gray matter of the human brain. ▷1940s: from **GANGLION** + *-oside* (see **-OSE**[2], **-IDE**).

gan·gly /ˈgaNGglē/ ▸*adj.* (**gan·gl·ier**, **gan·gl·iest**) another term for **GANGLING**.

Gang of Four (in China) a group of four associates, including Mao Zedong's wife, involved in implementing the Cultural Revolution. They were among the groups competing for power on Mao's death in 1976, but were arrested and imprisoned.

gang·plank /ˈgaNG,plaNGk/ ▸*n.* a movable plank used as a ramp to board or disembark from a ship or boat.

gang·plow /ˈgaNG,plou/ ▸*n.* a type of plow with several blades for turning two or more furrows at one time.

gang rape ▸*n.* the rape of one person by a group. —**gang-rape** *v.*

gan·grene /ˈgaNGgrēn; gaNGˈgrēn/ ▸*n. Medicine* localized death and decomposition of body tissue, resulting from either obstructed circulation or bacterial infection.
▸*v.* [*intrans.*] become affected with gangrene. ▷mid 16th cent.: via French from Latin *gangraena*, from Greek *gangraina*. —**gan·gre·nous** /ˈgaNGgrənəs/ *adj.*

gang·sta /ˈgaNGstə/ ▸*n.* **1** *informal* a gang member. **2** (also **gangsta rap**) a type of rap music featuring aggressive lyrics, often with reference to gang violence. ▷1980s: alteration of **GANGSTER**.

gang·ster /ˈgaNGstər/ ▸*n.* a member of a gang of violent criminals. —**gang·ster·ism** /-,rizəm/ *n.*

Gang·tok /ˈgəNG,tôk/ a city in northern India, in the foothills of the Kanchenjunga Mountains, capital of the state of Sikkim; pop. 25,000.

gangue /gaNG/ ▸*n.* the commercially valueless material in which ore is found. ▷early 19th cent.: from French, from German *Gang* 'course, lode'; related to **GANG**[1].

gang·way ▸*n.* /ˈgaNG,wā/ a raised platform or walkway providing a passage. ■ *Brit.* a passage between rows of seats, esp. in a theater or aircraft. ■ a movable bridge linking a ship to the shore. ■ an opening in the bulwarks by which a ship is entered or left. ■ a temporary arrangement of planks for crossing muddy or difficult ground on a building site.
▸*exclam.* /ˈgaNGˈwā/ make way!; get out of the way!

gan·is·ter /ˈganəstər/ ▸*n.* a close-grained, hard siliceous rock, or a similar synthetic product, used esp. for lining furnaces. ▷early 19th cent.: of unknown origin.

gan·ja /ˈgänjə/ ▸*n.* marijuana. ▷early 19th cent.: from Hindi *gāṁjā*.

gan·net /ˈganit/ ▸*n.* **1** a large seabird with mainly white plumage, known for catching fish by plunge-diving. • Genus *Morus* (or *Sula*), family Sulidae: three species, in particular the **northern gannet** (*M. bassanus*) of the North Atlantic (also called **SOLAN GOOSE** (see **SOLAN**).) **2** *Brit., informal* a greedy person. ▷Old English *ganot*, of Germanic origin; related to Dutch *gent* 'gander,' also to **GANDER**.

gan·net·ry /ˈganitrē/ ▸*n.* (*pl.* **-ries**) a breeding colony of gannets, usually on an isolated rock.

gan·oid /ˈganoid/ *Zoology* ▸*adj.* (of fish scales) hard and bony with a shiny enamellike surface. Compare with **CTENOID** and **PLACOID**. ■ (of a fish) having ganoid scales.
▸*n.* a primitive fish that has ganoid scales, e.g., a bichir, sturgeon, or freshwater garfish. ▷mid 19th cent.: from French *ganoïde*, from Greek *ganos* 'brightness.'

Gan·su /ˈgänˈsoo; ˈgan-/ (also **Kan·su**) a province in northwestern central China, between Mongolia and Tibet; capital, Lanzhou. This narrow, mountainous province forms a corridor through which the Silk Road passed.

gant·let /ˈgantlit; ˈgônt-/ ▸*n.* variant spelling of **GAUNTLET**[2].

gan·try /ˈgantrē/ ▸*n.* (*pl.* **-tries**) a bridgelike overhead structure with a platform supporting equipment such as a crane, railroad signals, lights, or cameras. ■ a movable framework for supporting and servicing a rocket prior to launching. ▷late Middle English (denoting a wooden stand for barrels): probably from dialect *gawn* (contraction of **GALLON**) + **TREE**.

Gantt chart /gant/ ▸*n.* a chart in which a series of horizontal lines shows the amount of work done or production completed in certain periods of time in relation to the amount planned for those periods. ▷early 20th cent.: named after Henry L. *Gantt* (1861–1919), American management consultant.

Gan·y·mede /ˈganə,mēd/ **1** *Greek Mythology* a Trojan youth who was so beautiful that he was carried off by Zeus to be the cupbearer for the Olympic gods. **2** *Astronomy* one of the Galilean moons of Jupiter, the seventh closest satellite to the planet and the largest satellite in the solar system with a diameter of 3,268 miles (5,260 km).

ganz·feld /ˈgänz,feld; ˈgans-/ (also **Ganz·feld**) ▸*n.* a technique of controlled sensory input used in parapsychology with the aim of improving results in tests of telepathy and other paranormal phenomena. ▷late 20th cent.: from German, literally 'whole field.'

GAO ▸*abbr.* General Accounting Office, a body that undertakes investigations for Congress.

gaol ▸*n. Brit.* variant spelling of **JAIL**. —**gaol·er** *n.*

gap /gap/ ▸*n.* **1** a break or hole in an object or between two objects: *he came through the gap in the hedge.* ■ a pass or way through a range of hills. **2** an unfilled space or interval; a break in continuity: *there are many gaps in our understanding of what happened.* ■ a difference, esp. an undesirable one, between two views or situations: *the media were **bridging the gap** between government and people.* ▷Middle English: from Old Norse, 'chasm'; related to **GAPE**. —**gapped** *adj.* —**gap·py** *adj.*

GAPA ▸*abbr.* ground-to-air pilotless aircraft.

gape /gāp/ ▸*v.* [*intrans.*] stare with one's mouth open wide, typically in amazement or wonder: *they **gaped at** her as if she were an alien.* ■ be or become wide open: [with *complement*] *a large duffel bag gaped open by her feet* | [as *adj.*] (**gaping**) *there was a gaping hole in the wall.*
▸*n.* a wide opening or breach: *a gape of the jaws.* ■ an open-mouthed stare: *she climbed into her sports car to the gapes of passersby.* ■ a widely open mouth or beak: *juvenile birds with yellow gapes.* ■ (**the gapes**) a disease of birds with gaping of the mouth as a symptom, caused by infestation with gapeworm. ▷Middle English: from Old Norse *gapa*; related to **GAP**. —**gap·ing·ly** *adv.*

gap·er /ˈgāpər/ ▸*n.* **1** a person who stares, typically in amazement or wonder. **2** a burrowing bivalve mollusk, the shell valves of which have an opening at one or both ends. • Genus *Mya*, family Myidae.

gape·worm /ˈgāp,wərm/ ▸*n.* a parasitic nematode worm that infests the trachea and bronchi of birds, causing the gapes. • *Syngamus trachea*, class Phasmida.

gap·ping /ˈgapiNG/ ▸*n. Grammar* the omission of a verb in the second of two coordinate clauses, as in *I went by bus and Mary by car.*

gap-toothed ▸*adj.* having or showing gaps between the teeth.

gap year ▸*n. chiefly Brit.* a period, typically an academic year, taken by a student as a break between secondary school and higher education.

gar /gär/ ▸*n.* the freshwater garfish of North America. ▷mid 18th cent.: abbreviation.

ga·rage /gəˈräzh; -ˈräj/ ▸*n.* **1** a building or shed for housing a motor vehicle or vehicles. ■ an establishment that provides services and repairs for motor vehicles. **2** (also **garage rock**) [*mass noun*] a style of unpolished energetic rock music associated with suburban amateur bands. [as *adj.*] *garage band.*
▸*v.* [*trans.*] put or keep (a motor vehicle) in a garage. ▷early 20th cent.: from French, from *garer* 'to shelter.'

ga·rage sale ▸*n.* a sale of miscellaneous household goods, often held in the garage or front yard of someone's house.

ga·ram ma·sa·la /,gärəm məˈsälə/ ▸*n.* a spice mixture used in Indian cooking. ▷from Urdu *garam maṣālaḥ*, from *garam* 'hot, pungent' + *maṣālaḥ* 'spice.'

Gar·a·mond /ˈgarə,mänd/ ▸*n.* a typeface much used in books. ▷mid 19th cent.: named after Claude *Garamond* (1499–1561), French type founder.

garb[1] /gärb/ ▸*n.* clothing or dress, esp. of a distinctive or special kind: *the black and brown garb of a Franciscan friar.*
▸*v.* [*trans.*] (usu. **be garbed**) dress in distinctive clothes: *she was **garbed in** Indian shawls.* ▷late 16th cent.: via French from Italian *garbo* 'elegance,' of Germanic origin; related to **GEAR**.

garb[2] ▸*n. Heraldry* a sheaf of wheat. ▷early 16th cent.: from Old Northern French *garbe*; compare with French *gerbe*.

gar·bage /ˈgärbij/ ▸*n.* wasted or spoiled food and other refuse, as from a kitchen or household. ■ a thing that is considered worthless or meaningless: *a store full of overpriced garbage.* ▷late Middle English (in the sense 'offal'): from Anglo-Norman French, of unknown ultimate origin.
▸*PHRASE* □ **garbage in, garbage out** (abbr.: **GIGO**) used to express the idea that in computing and other spheres, incorrect or poor quality input will always produce faulty output.

gar·bage can (also **garbage bin**) ▸*n.* a container, typically plastic or metal, for household refuse.

gar·ban·zo /gärˈbänzō/ (also **garbanzo bean**) ▸*n.* (*pl.* **-zos**) a chickpea. ▷mid 18th cent.: from Spanish.

gar·ble /ˈgärbəl/ ▸*v.* [*trans.*] reproduce (a message, sound, or transmission) in a confused and distorted way: *the connection was awful and kept garbling his voice* | [as *adj.*] (**garbled**) *I got a garbled set of directions.*
▸*n.* a garbled account or transmission. ▷late Middle English (in the sense 'sift out, cleanse'): from Anglo-Latin and Italian *garbellare*, from Arabic *garbala* 'sift,' perhaps from late Latin *cribellare* 'to sieve,' from Latin *cribrum* 'sieve.' —**gar·bler** /-b(ə)lər/ *n.*

Gar·bo /ˈgär,bō/, Greta (1905–90), U.S. actress; born in Sweden; born *Greta Gustafsson*. Notable movies: *Anna Christie* (1930), *Mata Hari* (1931), and *Anna Karenina* (1935). After her retirement in 1941, she lived as a recluse.

Greta Garbo

gar·board /ˈgär,bôrd/ (also **garboard strake**) ▸*n.* the first range of planks or plates laid on a ship's bottom next to the keel. ▷early 17th cent.: from Dutch *gaarboord*, perhaps from *garen* 'gather' + *boord* 'board.'

gar·bol·o·gy /gärˈbäləjē/ ▸*n.* the study of a community or culture by analyzing its waste. ▷1960s: from **GARBAGE** + **-LOGY**. —**gar·bol·o·gist** /-jist/ *n.*

Gar·ci·a /gärˈsēə/, Jerry (1942–95), U.S. rock singer and guitarist; full name *Jerome John Garcia*. He was

Pronunciation Key ə *ago*; ər *over*; ˈə or ,ə *up*; ˈər or ,ər *fur*; a *hat*; ā *rate*; ä *car*; CH *chew*; e *let*; ē *see*; e(ə)r *air*; i *fit*; ī *by*; i(ə)r *ear*; NG *sing*; ō *go*; ô *for*; oi *boy*; o͝o *good*; o͞o *goo*; ou *out*; SH *she*; TH *thin*; T͟H *then*; (h)w *why*; ZH *vision*

the central figure of the Grateful Dead, a group formed *c.*1966. Mixing psychedelic rock with country and blues influences in lengthy improvisations, the band toured extensively until Garcia's death.

Gar·cí·a Lor·ca /gär'sēə 'lôrkə/ see **LORCA**.

Gar·cí·a Már·quez /gär'sēə 'märkes/, Gabriel (1928–), Colombian novelist. His works include *One Hundred Years of Solitude* (1967) and *Chronicle of a Death Foretold* (1981). Nobel Prize for Literature (1982).

gar·çon /gär'sôN/ ▸*n.* a waiter in a French restaurant or hotel. ▷French, literally 'boy.'

gar·çon·nière /,gärsə'nyer/ ▸*n.* a bachelor's apartment. ▷French, from *garçon* 'boy.'

Gar·da /'gärdə/ ▸*n.* [treated as *sing.* or *pl.*] the state police force of the Irish Republic. ■ (*pl.* **-dai** /-'dē/) a member of the Irish police force. ▷from Irish *Garda Síochána* 'Civic Guard.'

Gar·da, Lake /'gärdə/ a lake in northeastern Italy that lies between Lombardy and Venetia.

gar·den /'gärdn/ ▸*n.* **1** a piece of ground, often near a house, used for growing flowers, fruit, or vegetables. ■ (**gardens**) ornamental grounds laid out for public enjoyment and recreation: *botanical gardens.* **2** [in *names*] a large public hall: *Madison Square Garden.*
▸*v.* [*intrans.*] cultivate or work in a garden. ▷Middle English: from Old Northern French *gardin*, variant of Old French *jardin*, of Germanic origin; related to **YARD**[2].

Gar·de·na /gär'dēnə/ a city in southwestern California, south of Los Angeles; pop. 49,847.

gar·den a·part·ment ▸*n.* **1** a low-rise apartment complex with landscaped gardens or lawns. **2** a ground-floor unit of an apartment building, with access to a garden or lawn.

Gar·den Cit·y **1** a city in southwestern Kansas, on the Arkansas River; pop. 28,451. **2** a commercial village in the town of Hempstead on Long Island in New York; pop. 21,686.

gar·den cress ▸*n.* a type of cress that is usually grown as a sprouting vegetable, often mixed with sprouting mustard, and used in salads. • *Lepidium sativum*, family Brassicaceae.

gar·den eel ▸*n.* an eel of warm seas that lives in a community or "garden." Each individual occupies a burrow from which its head and foreparts protrude, enabling it to catch passing food. • Several genera and species, family Congridae.

gar·den·er /'gärdnər/ ▸*n.* a person who tends and cultivates a garden as a pastime or for a living: *cultivars grown by amateur gardeners | a topiary gardener.* ▷Middle English: from Old French *gardinier*, from *gardin* (see **GARDEN**). **—gar·den·ing** /'gärdniNG; -dn-iNG/ *n.*

Gar·den Grove a city in southwestern California, southeast of Los Angeles; pop. 143,050.

gar·de·nia /gär'dēnyə/ ▸*n.* a tree or shrub of the bedstraw family, with large fragrant white or yellow flowers. Native to warm climates, it is widely cultivated. • Genus *Gardenia*, family Rubiaceae: several species, in particular the Cape jasmine. ▷modern Latin, named in honor of Dr. Alexander *Garden* (1730–91), Scottish naturalist.

Gar·den of E·den see **EDEN**[2].

Gar·den of Geth·sem·a·ne see **GETHSEMANE, GARDEN OF.**

gar·den par·ty ▸*n.* a social event held outdoors on a lawn or in a garden.

Gar·den State a nickname for the state of **NEW JERSEY.**

gar·den-va·ri·e·ty ▸*adj.* [*attrib.*] of the usual or ordinary type; commonplace: *they are your everyday, garden-variety Americans.*

gar·den war·bler ▸*n.* a migratory Eurasian songbird with drab plumage, frequenting woodlands. • *Sylvia borin*, family Sylviidae.

garde·robe /'gärd,rōb/ ▸*n.* a toilet in a medieval building. ■ a wardrobe or small storeroom, esp. in a medieval building. ▷late Middle English: French, from *garder* 'to keep' + *robe* 'robe, dress'; compare with **WARDROBE.**

Gard·ner[1] /'gärdnər/, Ava (Lavinia) (1922–90), U.S. actress. Notable movies: *The Killers* (1946), *Bhowani Junction* (1956), and *The Night of the Iguana* (1964).

Gard·ner[2], Erle Stanley (1899–1970), U.S. novelist and short-story writer. He practiced as a defense lawyer before writing novels that feature lawyer-detective Perry Mason.

Gar·field /'gär,fēld/, James Abram (1831–81), 20th president of the U.S. March–September 1881. He fought for the Union during the Civil War, resigning his command to enter Congress as a Republican. He served in the U.S. House of Representatives 1863–80. Although his presidency was shortened by an assassin, his battle against corruption succeeded in breaking the stronghold of New York senator Roscoe Conkling (1829–88) over the New York Customs House—the U.S.'s principal port of entry.

James A. Garfield

gar·fish /'gär,fiSH/ ▸*n.* (*pl.* same or **-fish·es**) any of a number of long, slender fish with elongated beaklike jaws containing sharply pointed teeth: • a marine fish (family Belonidae, in particular the common European *Belone belone*). Also called **NEEDLEFISH** or **GARPIKE.** • a freshwater fish (family Lepisosteidae and genus *Lepisosteus*). Also called **GAR** or **GARPIKE.** ▷Middle English: apparently from Old English *gār* 'spear' + **FISH**[1].

gar·ga·ney /'gärgənē/ ▸*n.* (*pl.* same or **-neys**) a small Eurasian duck, the male of which has a dark brown head with a white stripe from the eye to the neck. • *Anas querquedula*, family Anatidae. ▷mid 17th cent.: from Italian dialect *garganei*, of imitative origin.

gar·gan·tu·a /gär'ganCHōōə/ ▸*n.* a person of great size; a giant.

gar·gan·tu·an /gär'ganCHōōən/ ▸*adj.* enormous: *a gargantuan appetite.* ▷late 16th cent.: from *Gargantua*, the name of a voracious giant in Rabelais' book of the same name (1534), + **-AN.**

gar·get /'gärgit/ ▸*n.* inflammation of a cow's or ewe's udder. ▷early 18th cent.: perhaps a special use of Old French *gargate* 'throat'; related to **GARGOYLE.** The term was used earlier to denote inflammation of the throat in cattle.

gar·gle /'gärgəl/ ▸*v.* [*intrans.*] wash one's mouth and throat with a liquid kept in motion by exhaling through it: *instruct patients to gargle with warm water.*
▸*n.* an act or instance or the sound of gargling: *a swig and gargle of mouthwash.* ■ [usu. in *sing.*] a liquid used for gargling. ▷early 16th cent.: from French *gargouiller* 'gurgle, bubble,' from *gargouille* 'throat' (see **GARGOYLE**).

gar·goyle /'gär,goil/ ▸*n.* a grotesque carved human or animal face or figure projecting from the gutter of a building, typically acting as a spout to carry water clear of a wall. ▷Middle English: from Old French *gargouille* 'throat,' also 'gargoyle' (because of the water passing through the throat and mouth of the figure); related to Greek *gargarizein* 'to gargle' (imitating the sounds made in the throat). **—gar·goyled** *adj.*

gargoyle

gar·goyl·ism /'gärgoi,lizəm/ ▸*n.* another term for **HURLER'S SYNDROME.** ▷early 20th cent.: from **GARGOYLE** (because the deformities that characterize the syndrome were thought to resemble Gothic gargoyles) + **-ISM.**

Gar·i·bal·di /,garə'bôldē/, Giuseppe (1807–82), Italian patriot and military leader of the Risorgimento (unification of Italy). With his volunteer force of "Red Shirts," he captured Sicily and southern Italy from the Austrians in 1860–61, thereby playing a key role in the establishment of a united kingdom of Italy.

gar·i·bal·di /,garə'bôldē/ ▸*n.* (*pl.* **-dis**) **1** *historical* a woman's or children's loose blouse, originally bright red in imitation of the shirts worn by Garibaldi and his followers. **2** a small bright orange marine fish found off California. • *Hypsypops rubicundus*, family Pomacentridae. ▷mid 19th cent.: named after G. **GARIBALDI.**

gar·ish /'gariSH/ ▸*adj.* obtrusively bright and showy; lurid: *garish shirts in all sorts of colors.* ▷mid 16th cent.: of unknown origin. **—gar·ish·ly** *adv.* **—gar·ish·ness** *n.*

Gar·land[1] /'gärlənd/ a city in northeastern Texas, northeast of Dallas; pop. 215,768.

Gar·land[2], Judy (1922–69), U.S. singer and actress; born *Frances Gumm.* Her most well known movie role was in *The Wizard of Oz* (1939), in which she played Dorothy and sang "Over the Rainbow." Other notable movies: *Meet Me in St. Louis* (1944) and *A Star is Born* (1954). She is the mother of actress and singer Liza Minelli.

gar·land /'gärlənd/ ▸*n.* a wreath of flowers and leaves, worn on the head or hung as a decoration. ■ *dated* a prize or distinction. ■ *archaic* a literary anthology or miscellany.
▸*v.* [*trans.*] adorn or crown with a garland: *they were garlanded with flowers.* ▷Middle English: from Old French *garlande*, of unknown origin.

gar·lic /'gärlik/ ▸*n.* **1** a strong-smelling pungent-tasting bulb, used as a flavoring in cooking and in herbal medicine. **2** the plant, closely related to the onion, that produces this bulb. • *Allium sativum*, family Liliaceae (or Alliaceae). ▷Old English *gārlēac*, from *gār* 'spear' (because the shape of a clove resembles the head of a spear) + *lēac* 'leek.' **—gar·lick·y** *adj.*

gar·lic chives ▸*plural n.* another term for **CHINESE CHIVES.**

gar·lic mus·tard ▸*n.* a European mustard plant with medicinal and culinary uses that is also an aggressive woodland invader in most of the eastern U.S. • *Alliaria petiolata*, family Brassicaceae.

gar·lic press ▸*n.* a hand-held device for crushing cloves of garlic through a sievelike receptacle.

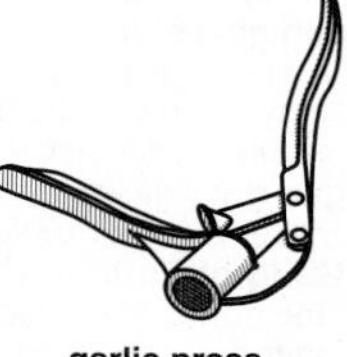

garlic press

gar·ment /'gärmənt/ ▸*n.* an item of clothing. ▷Middle English: from Old French *garnement* 'equipment,' from *garnir* 'equip' (see **GARNISH**).

gar·ment bag ▸ *n.* a large zippered bag incorporating a hanger on which garments may be hung to prevent wrinkling during travel or storage.

Gar·mo, Mount /'gär,mō/ former name (until 1933) of **COMMUNISM PEAK.**

Gar·ner[1] /'gärnər/, Errol (Louis) (1923–77) U.S. jazz pianist and composer. He formed his own trio and also recorded with Charlie Parker. He wrote many songs, including "Misty."

Gar·ner[2], John Nance (1868–1967) U.S. vice president 1933–41; known as **Cactus Jack.** A member of the U.S. House of Representatives from Texas 1903–33, he served as speaker from 1931 until 1933.

gar·ner /'gärnər/ ▸*v.* [*trans.*] gather or collect (something, esp. information or approval): *the police struggled to garner sufficient evidence.* ■ *archaic* store; deposit: *the crop was ready to be reaped and garnered.*
▸*n. archaic* a storehouse; a granary. ▷Middle English (originally as a noun meaning 'granary'): from Old French *gernier*, from Latin *granarium* 'granary,' from *granum* 'grain.'

gar·net /'gärnit/ ▸*n.* a precious stone consisting of a deep red vitreous silicate mineral. ■ *Mineralogy* any of a class of silicate minerals including this, which belong to the cubic system and have the general chemical formula $A_3B_2(SiO_4)_3$ (A and B being respectively divalent and trivalent metals). ▷Middle English: probably via Middle Dutch from Old French *grenat*, from medieval Latin *granatus*, perhaps from *granatum* (see **POMEGRANATE**), because the garnet is similar in color to the pulp of the fruit.

gar·ni·er·ite /'gärnēə,rīt/ ▸*n.* a bright green amorphous mineral consisting of a hydrated silicate of nickel and magnesium. ▷1875: named after Jules *Garnier* (1839–1904), French geologist.

gar·nish /'gärniSH/ ▸*v.* [*trans.*] **1** decorate or embellish (something, esp. food): *salad garnished with an orange slice.* **2** *Law* serve with a garnishment. ■ seize (money, esp. part of a person's salary) to settle a debt or claim: *the IRS garnished his earnings.*
▸*n.* a decoration or embellishment for something, esp. food. ▷Middle English (in the sense 'equip, arm'): from Old French *garnir*, probably of

Germanic origin and related to WARN. Sense 1 dates from the late 17th cent.

gar·nish·ee /ˌgärniˈshē/ *Law* ▸*n.* a third party who is served notice by a court to surrender money in settlement of a debt or claim: [as *adj.*] *a garnishee order.* ▸*v.* (**-ees, -eed**) another term for GARNISH (sense 2).

gar·nish·ment ▸*n.* **1** a decoration or embellishment. **2** *Law* a court order directing that money or property of a third party (usually wages paid by an employer) be seized to satisfy a debt owed by a debtor to a plaintiff creditor.

gar·ni·ture /ˈgärnichər; -ˌcho͝or/ ▸*n.* a set of decorative vases. ■ decorative accessories. ▷late 15th cent.: from French, from *garnir* 'to garnish.'

Ga·ronne /gəˈrän; gəˈrôn/ a river in southwestern France that rises in the Pyrenees Mountains and flows northwest for 400 miles (645 km) through Toulouse and Bordeaux to join the Dordogne River at the Gironde estuary.

ga·rotte ▸*v.* & *n.* variant spelling of GARROTE.

gar·pike /ˈgärˌpīk/ ▸*n.* another term for GARFISH. ▷late 18th cent.: from GAR + PIKE[1].

gar·ret /ˈgarit/ ▸*n.* a top-floor or attic room, esp. a small dismal one (traditionally inhabited by an artist). ▷Middle English (in the sense 'watchtower'): from Old French *garite*, from *garir* (see GARRISON).

Gar·rick /ˈgarik/, David (1717–79), English actor and playwright. A versatile actor, he managed the Drury Lane Theatre.

Gar·ri·son /ˈgarəsən/, William Lloyd (1805–79) U.S. social liberal and spearhead for New England abolitionism. He published *The Liberator* 1831–65 and was a founder of the American Anti-Slavery Society in 1833.

gar·ri·son /ˈgarəsən/ ▸*n.* the troops stationed in a fortress or town to defend it. ■ the building occupied by such troops. ▸*v.* [*trans.*] provide (a place) with a body of troops: *troops are garrisoned in the various territories.* ■ [*trans.*] station (troops) in a particular place: *Soviet forces were garrisoned in Lithuania.* ▷Middle English (in the sense 'safety, means of protection'): from Old French *garison*, from *garir* 'defend, provide,' of Germanic origin.

gar·ri·son cap ▸*n.* a cap without a brim, esp. one worn as part of a military uniform.

gar·ri·son town ▸*n.* a town that has troops permanently stationed in it.

gar·ron /ˈgarən/ ▸*n.* a small, sturdy workhorse of a breed originating in Ireland and Scotland. ▷mid 16th cent.: from Scottish Gaelic *gearran*, Irish *gearrán*.

gar·rote /gəˈrät; -ˈrōt/ (also **gar·rotte** or **ga·rotte**) ▸*v.* [*trans.*] kill (someone) by strangulation, typically with an iron collar or a length of wire or cord: *he had been garroted with piano wire.* ▸*n.* a wire, cord, or apparatus used for such a killing. ▷early 17th cent.: via French from Spanish, 'a cudgel, a garrote,' perhaps of Celtic origin.

gar·ru·lous /ˈgar(y)ələs/ ▸*adj.* excessively talkative, esp. on trivial matters: *Polonius is portrayed as a foolish, garrulous old man.* See note at TALKATIVE. ▷early 17th cent.: from Latin *garrulus* (from *garrire* 'to chatter, prattle') + -OUS. —**gar·ru·li·ty** /gəˈro͞olitē/ *n.* —**gar·ru·lous·ly** *adv.* —**gar·ru·lous·ness** *n.*

Gar·son /ˈgärsən/, Greer (1908–96) U.S. actress; born in Ireland. She starred in movies such as *Mrs. Miniver* (Academy Award, 1942), *Adventure* (1946), and *Sunrise at Campobello* (1960).

gar·ter /ˈgärtər/ ▸*n.* **1** a band worn around the leg to keep up a stocking or sock. ■ a band worn on the arm to keep a shirtsleeve up. ■ a suspender for a sock or stocking. **2** (**the Garter**) short for ORDER OF THE GARTER. ■ the badge or membership of this order. ▷Middle English: from Old French *gartier*, from *garet* 'bend of the knee, calf of the leg,' probably of Celtic origin. —**gar·tered** *adj.*

gar·ter belt ▸*n.* a belt with attached garters or fasteners, worn as an undergarment to hold up stockings.

gar·ter snake ▸*n.* **1** a common, harmless North American snake that typically has well-defined longitudinal stripes and favors damp habitats. It is occasionally kept as a pet. • Genus *Thamnophis*, family Colubridae: several species, in particular *T. sirtalis*. **2** a venomous burrowing African snake that is typically dark with lighter bands. • Genus *Elapsoidea*, family Elapidae: several species.

gar·ter stitch ▸*n.* knitting in which all of the rows are knitted in knit (plain) stitch, rather than alternating with purl rows.

garth /gärTH/ ▸*n. Brit.* an open space surrounded by cloisters. ■ *archaic* a yard or garden. ▷Middle English (also, in early use, denoting a hollow): from Old Norse *garthr*; related to YARD[2].

Gar·u·da /gəˈro͞odə/ *Hinduism* an eaglelike being that Vishnu rides as his mount. ▷from Sanskrit *garuḍa*.

Gar·vey /ˈgärvē/, Marcus (Mosiah) (1887–1940), Jamaican political activist and black nationalist leader. He advocated the establishment of an African homeland for black Americans. His thinking was later an important influence on Rastafarianism.

Gar·y /ˈgarē; ˈge(ə)rē/ an industrial city in northwestern Indiana, on Lake Michigan, southeast of Chicago; pop. 102,746.

gas /gas/ ▸*n.* (*pl.* **gas·es** or **gas·ses**) **1** an airlike fluid substance which expands freely to fill any space available, irrespective of its quantity: *hot balls of gas that become stars | poisonous gases.* ■ *Physics* a substance of this type that cannot be liquefied by the application of pressure alone. Compare with VAPOR. ■ a flammable substance of this type used as a fuel. ■ a gaseous anesthetic such as nitrous oxide, used in dentistry. ■ gas or vapor used as a poisonous agent to kill or disable an enemy in warfare. ■ gas generated in the alimentary canal; flatulence. ■ *Mining* an explosive mixture of firedamp with air. **2** *informal* short for GASOLINE. **3** (**a gas**) *informal* a person or thing that is entertaining or amusing: *the party would be a gas.* ▸*v.* (**gas·es, gassed, gas·sing**) [*trans.*] **1** attack with or expose to poisonous gas. ■ kill by exposure to poisonous gas. ■ [*intrans.*] (of a storage battery or dry cell) give off gas. **2** fill the tank of (an engine or motor vehicle) with gasoline: *after **gassing up** the car, he went into the restaurant.* **3** [*intrans.*] *informal* talk, esp. excessively, idly, or boastfully: *I thought you'd never stop gassing.* ▷mid 17th cent.: invented by J. B. van Helmont (1577–1644), Belgian chemist, to denote an occult principle that he believed to exist in all matter; suggested by Greek *khaos* 'chaos,' with Dutch *g* representing Greek *kh*.
▸*PHRASES* □ **run out of gas** *informal* run out of energy; lose momentum. □ **step on the gas** *informal* press on the accelerator to make a car go faster.

gas·bag /ˈgasˌbag/ ▸*n.* **1** *informal* a person who talks too much, typically about unimportant things. **2** the container holding the gas in a balloon or airship.

gas burn·er ▸*n.* a nozzle or jet through which gas is released to burn, e.g., on a stove.

gas cham·ber ▸*n.* an airtight room that can be filled with poisonous gas as a means of execution.

gas chro·mat·o·graph ▸*n.* a device or apparatus used in gas chromatography to separate the constituents of a volatile substance.

gas chro·ma·tog·ra·phy ▸*n.* chromatography employing a gas as the moving carrier medium. Compare with GAS-LIQUID CHROMATOGRAPHY.

Gas·cogne /gäsˈkôn(yə)/ French name for GASCONY.

Gas·con /ˈgaskən/ ▸*n.* **1** a native or inhabitant of Gascony. **2** (**gascon**) *archaic* a person who boasts about their achievements or possessions. [with allusion to the perceived character of natives of Gascony.] ▸*adj.* of or relating to Gascony or its people. ▷via Old French from Latin *Vasco, Vascon-*; related to BASQUE.

gas·con·ade /ˌgaskəˈnād/ ▸*n. poetic/literary* extravagant boasting. ▷mid 17th cent.: from French *gasconnade*, from *gasconner* 'talk like a Gascon, brag.'

gas con·stant (Symbol: **R**) ▸*n. Chemistry* the constant of proportionality in the gas equation. It is equal to 8.314 joule kelvin^{-1} mole^{-1}.

Gas·co·ny /ˈgaskənē/ a region and former province in southwestern France, in the northern foothills of the Pyrenees Mountains. French name GASCOGNE.

gas·e·ous /ˈgasēəs; ˈgasHəs/ ▸*adj.* of, relating to, or having the characteristics of a gas: *gaseous emissions from motor vehicles | gaseous oxygen.* —**gas·e·ous·ness** *n.*

gas e·qua·tion ▸*n. Chemistry* the equation of state of an ideal gas, $PV = nRT$, where P = pressure, V = volume, T = absolute temperature, R = the gas constant, and n = the number of moles of gas.

gas-fired ▸*adj.* using a combustible gas as its fuel: *gas-fired central heating.*

gas fit·ter ▸*n.* a person trained to connect, disconnect, and service gas fittings and appliances.

gas gan·grene ▸*n.* rapidly spreading gangrene occurring in dirty wounds infected by bacteria that give off a foul-smelling gas. • This disease is usually caused by anaerobic bacteria of the genus *Clostridium*.

gas gi·ant ▸*n. Astronomy* a large planet of relatively low density consisting predominantly of hydrogen and helium, such as Jupiter, Saturn, Uranus, or Neptune.

gas guz·zler /ˈgəz(ə)lər/ ▸*n. informal* an automobile with high fuel consumption.

gash /gasH/ ▸*n.* **1** a long deep slash, cut, or wound: *a bad gash in one leg became infected.* ■ a cleft made as if by a slashing cut: *the blast ripped a 25-foot gash in the hull.* **2** *vulgar slang* the vulva. ■ *offensive* women collectively regarded in sexual terms. ▸*v.* [*trans.*] make a gash in; cut deeply: *the jagged edges gashed their fingers.* ▷Middle English *garse*, from Old French *garcer* 'to chap, crack,' perhaps based on Greek *kharassein* 'sharpen, scratch, engrave.' The current spelling is recorded from the mid 16th cent.

gas·i·fy /ˈgasəˌfī/ ▸*v.* (**-fies, -fied**) [*trans.*] (often **be gasified**) convert (a solid or liquid, esp. coal) into gas: *5 million tons of coal have been gasified.* ■ [*intrans.*] become a gas: *if PVC is overheated it will gasify.* —**gas·i·fi·ca·tion** /ˌgasəfiˈkāsHən/ *n.*

gas jet ▸*n.* **1** another term for GAS BURNER. **2** a flame of illuminated gas from a gas burner.

Gas·kell /ˈgaskəl/, Mrs. Elizabeth (Cleghorn) (1810–65), English novelist. An active humanitarian from a Unitarian background, she wrote *Mary Barton* (1848), *Cranford* (1853), and *North and South* (1855), which display her interest in social concerns. She also wrote a biography (1857) of her friend Charlotte Brontë.

gas·ket /ˈgaskit/ ▸*n.* **1** a shaped piece or ring of rubber or other material sealing the junction between two surfaces in an engine or other device. **2** a cord securing a furled sail to the yard, boom, or gaff of a sailing vessel. ▷early 17th cent. (sense 2): perhaps from French *garcette* 'thin rope' (originally 'little girl'), diminutive of *garce*, feminine of *gars* 'boy.'
▸*PHRASE* □ **blow a gasket** **1** *informal* lose one's temper. **2** suffer a leak in a gasket of an engine.

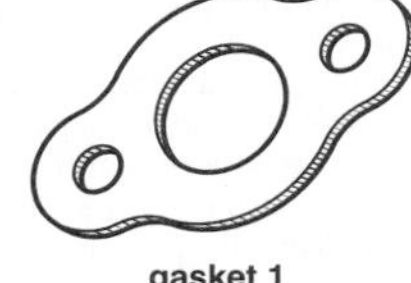

gasket 1

gas·kin /ˈgaskin/ ▸*n.* the muscular part of the hind leg of a horse between the stifle and the hock. ▷late 16th cent.: perhaps from GALLIGASKINS (the original sense).

gas laws ▸*plural n. Chemistry* the physical laws that describe the properties of gases, including Boyle's and Charles' laws.

gas·light /ˈgasˌlīt/ ▸*n.* a type of lamp in which an incandescent mantle is heated by a jet of burning gas. ■ the light produced by such a lamp: *in the gaslight she looked paler than ever.* —**gas·lit** /-ˌlit/ *adj.*

gas-liq·uid chro·ma·tog·ra·phy ▸*n.* chromatography employing a gas as the moving carrier medium and a liquid as the stationary medium.

gas log ▸*n.* a gas-burning appliance consisting of a gas burner made to resemble a log, used in a fireplace to simulate the effect of a burning log.

gas·man /ˈgasˌman/ ▸*n.* (*pl.* **-men**) a person who installs or services gas appliances or reads gas meters.

gas man·tle ▸*n.* see MANTLE[1] (sense 1).

gas mask ▸*n.* a protective mask used to cover a person's face as a defense against poisonous gas.

gas·o·hol /ˈgasəˌhôl; -ˌhäl/ ▸*n.* a mixture of gasoline and ethyl alcohol used as fuel in internal combustion engines. ▷1970s: blend of GAS and ALCOHOL.

gas oil ▸*n.* a type of fuel oil distilled from petroleum.

gas·o·line /ˌgasəˈlēn; ˈgasəlēn/ (*dated* also **gas·o·lene**) ▸*n.* refined petroleum used as fuel for internal combustion engines. ▷mid 19th cent.: from GAS + -OL + -INE[4] (or -ENE).

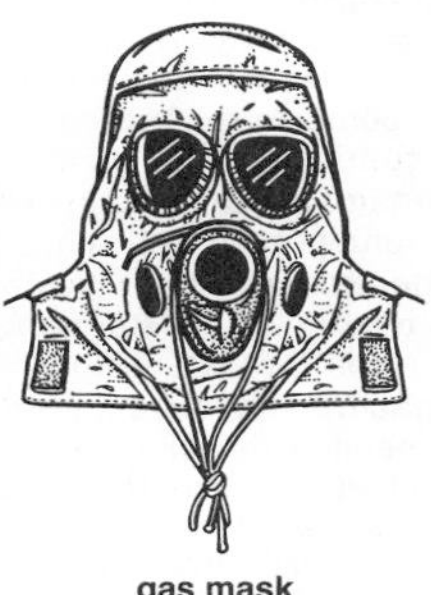

gas mask

gas·om·e·ter /gasˈämitər/ ▸*n.* a tank for storing and measuring gas. ▷late 18th cent. (in the sense 'container for holding or measuring a gas'): from French *gazomètre*, from *gaz* 'gas' + *-mètre* '(instrument) measuring.'

gasp /gasp/ ▸*v.* [*intrans.*] inhale suddenly with the mouth open, out of pain or astonishment: *a woman gasped in horror at the sight of him.* ■ [*trans.*] say (something) while catching one's breath, esp. as a result of strong emotion: *Jeremy **gasped out** an apology* | [with *direct speech*] *"It's beautiful!," she gasped, much impressed.* ■ strain to take a deep breath: *she surfaced and **gasped for** air.*

▸*n.* a convulsive catching of breath: *his breath was coming in gasps.* ▷late Middle English: from Old Norse *geispa* 'to yawn.'

▸*PHRASE* □ **one's** (or **the**) **last gasp** the point of exhaustion, death, or completion: *the last gasp of the Cold War.*

Gas·pé Pen·in·su·la /gas'pā/ a region in southeastern Quebec in Canada, between the St. Lawrence River and New Brunswick.

gas-per·me·a·ble ▸*adj.* (of a contact lens) allowing the diffusion of gases into and out of the cornea.

gas plant ▸*n.* an aromatic Eurasian plant of the rue family, with showy white flowers and fragrant leaves that emit a flammable vapor. This can sometimes be ignited without harming the plant. Also called **BURNING BUSH, DITTANY, FRAXINELLA.** • *Dictamnus* (formerly **Fraxinella**) *albus*, family Rutaceae.

Gas·ser /'gasər/, Herbert Spencer (1888–1963), U.S. physiologist. In collaboration with Joseph Erlanger, he used an oscilloscope to show that the velocity of a nerve impulse is proportional to the diameter of the fiber. Nobel Prize for Physiology or Medicine (1944, shared with Erlanger).

gas·ser /'gasər/ ▸*n. informal* **1** an idle talker; a chatterer. **2** a very attractive or impressive person or thing: *that story you wrote for me is a gasser!*

Gas·sion /gäs'yōN/, Edith Giovanna, see **PIAF**.

gas sta·tion ▸*n.* a service station.

gas·sy /'gasē/ ▸*adj.* (**-si·er, -si·est**) **1** of, like, or full of gas: *the carbonated water has a gassy, soda-pop character* | *gassy planets like Jupiter.* **2** *informal* (of people or language) inclined to be verbose: *a long and gassy book.* **3** (of people) flatulent. **—gas·si·ness** *n.*

Gast·ar·beit·er /'gäst,ärbītər/ ▸*n.* (*pl.* same or **-beit·ers**) German term for **GUEST WORKER.** ▷German, from *Gast* 'guest' + *Arbeiter* 'worker.'

G

gast·haus /'gäst,hous/ (also **Gast·haus**) ▸*n.* (*pl.* **-haus·es** or **-häus·er** /-,hoizər/) a small inn or hotel in a German-speaking country or region. ▷from German, from *Gast* 'guest' + *Haus* 'house.'

gas-tight ▸*adj.* sealed so as to prevent the leakage of gas.

Gas·to·nia /ga'stōnēə/ an industrial city in southwestern North Carolina; pop. 66,277.

gastr- ▸*comb. form* variant spelling of **GASTRO-** shortened before a vowel (as in *gastrectomy*).

gas·trec·to·my /ga'strektəmē/ ▸*n.* (*pl.* **-mies**) surgical removal of a part or the whole of the stomach.

gas·tric /'gastrik/ ▸*adj.* of the stomach. ▷mid 17th cent.: from modern Latin *gastricus*, from Greek *gastēr, gastr-* 'stomach.'

gas·tric juice ▸*n.* a thin, clear, virtually colorless acidic fluid secreted by the stomach glands and active in promoting digestion.

gas·trin /'gastrin/ ▸*n. Biochemistry* a hormone that stimulates secretion of gastric juice, and is secreted into the bloodstream by the stomach wall in response to the presence of food. ▷early 20th cent.: from **GASTRIC + -IN**[1].

gas·tri·tis /ga'strītis/ ▸*n. Medicine* inflammation of the lining of the stomach.

gastro- (also **gastr-** before a vowel) ▸*comb. form* of or relating to the stomach: *gastrectomy* | *gastroenteritis.* ▷from Greek *gastēr, gastr-* 'stomach.'

gas·troc·ne·mi·us /,gastrō(k)'nēmēəs/ (also **gastrocnemius muscle**) ▸*n.* (*pl.* **-mi·i** /-mē,ī/) *Anatomy* the chief muscle of the calf of the leg, which flexes the knee and foot. It runs to the Achilles tendon from two heads attached to the femur. ▷late 17th cent.: modern Latin, from Greek *gastroknēmia* 'calf of the leg,' from *gastēr, gastr-* 'stomach' + *knēmē* 'leg' (from the bulging shape of the calf).

gas·tro·col·ic /,gastrō'kälik/ ▸*adj.* [*attrib.*] of or relating to the stomach and the colon.

gas·tro·en·ter·i·tis /,gastrō,entə'rītis/ ▸*n.* inflammation of the stomach and intestines, typically resulting from bacterial toxins or viral infection and causing vomiting and diarrhea.

gas·tro·en·ter·ol·o·gy /,gastrō,entə'räləjē/ ▸*n.* the branch of medicine that deals with disorders of the stomach and intestines. **—gas·tro·en·ter·o·log·i·cal** /-tərə'läjikəl/ *adj.* **—gas·tro·en·te·rol·o·gist** /-jist/ *n.*

gas·tro·in·tes·ti·nal /,gastrōin'testənl/ ▸*adj.* of or relating to the stomach and the intestines.

gas·tro·lith /'gastrə,liTH/ ▸*n.* **1** *Medicine* a hard concretion in the stomach. **2** *Zoology* a small stone swallowed by a bird, reptile, or fish, to aid digestion in the gizzard.

gas·tro·nome /'gastrə,nōm/ (also **gas·tron·o·mer** /ga'stränəmər/ or **gas·tron·o·mist** /ga'stränə,mist/) ▸*n.* a gourmet. ▷early 19th cent.: from French, from *gastronomie* (see **GASTRONOMY**).

gas·tron·o·my /ga'stränəmē/ ▸*n.* the practice or art of choosing, cooking, and eating good food. ■ the cooking of a particular area: *traditional American gastronomy.* ▷early 19th cent.: from French *gastronomie*, from Greek *gastronomia*, alteration of *gastrologia* (see **GASTRO-, -LOGY**). **—gas·tro·nom·ic** /,gastrə'nämik/ *adj.* **—gas·tro·nom·i·cal** /,gastrə'nämikəl/ *adj.* **—gas·tro·nom·i·cal·ly** /,gastrə'nämik(ə)lē/ *adv.*

Gas·trop·o·da /,gastrə'pōdə/ *Zoology* a large class of mollusks which includes snails, slugs, whelks, and all terrestrial kinds. They have a large muscular foot for movement and (in many kinds) a single asymmetrical spiral shell. ▷modern Latin (plural), from Greek *gastēr, gastr-* 'stomach' + *pous, pod-* 'foot.' **—gas·tro·pod** /'gastrə,päd/ *n.*

gas·tro·pub /'gastrə,pəb/ ▸*n. Brit.* a pub that specializes in serving high-quality food. ▷1990s: blend of *gastronomy* and *pub*.

gas·tro·scope /'gastrə,skōp/ ▸*n.* an optical instrument used for inspecting the interior of the stomach. **—gas·tro·scop·ic** /,gastrə'skäpik/ *adj.* **—gas·tros·co·py** /ga'sträskəpē/ *n.*

gas·tros·to·my /ga'strästəmē/ ▸*n.* (*pl.* **-mies**) an opening into the stomach from the abdominal wall, made surgically for the introduction of food. ■ a surgical operation for making such an opening.

Gas·trot·ri·cha /gas'trätrikə/ *Zoology* a small phylum of minute aquatic wormlike animals that bear bristles and cilia. They are thought to be related to the nematode worms and rotifers. ▷modern Latin (plural), from Greek *gastēr, gastr-* 'stomach' + *thrix, trikh-* 'hair.' **—gas·tro·trich** /'gastrə,trik/ *n.*

gas·tru·la /'gastrōōlə/ ▸*n.* (*pl.* **-lae** /-,lē/) *Embryology* an embryo at the stage following the blastula, when it is a hollow cup-shaped structure having three layers of cells. ▷late 19th cent.: modern Latin, from Greek *gastēr, gastr-* 'stomach' + the Latin diminutive ending *-ula*. **—gas·tru·la·tion** /,gastrə'lāSHən/ *n.*

gas tur·bine ▸*n.* a turbine driven by expanding hot gases produced by burning fuel, as in a jet engine.

gas·works /'gas,wərks/ ▸*plural n.* [treated as *sing.*] a place where gas is manufactured and processed.

gat[1] /gat/ ▸*n. informal* a revolver or pistol. ▷early 20th cent.: abbreviation of **GATLING GUN.**

gat[2] ▸ archaic past of **GET.**

gate /gāt/ ▸*n.* **1** a hinged barrier used to close an opening in a wall, fence, or hedge. ■ a gateway: *she went out through the gate.* ■ *figurative* a means of entrance or exit: *they were opening the gates of their country wide to the enemy.* ■ an exit from an airport building to an aircraft. ■ [in *names*] a mountain pass or other natural passage: *the Golden Gate.* **2** the number of people who pay to enter a sports facility, exhibition hall, etc., for any one event: [as *adj.*] *gate receipts.* ■ the money taken for admission. **3** a device resembling a gate in structure or function, in particular: ■ a hinged or sliding barrier for controlling the flow of water: *a sluice gate.* ■ *Skiing* an opening through which a skier must pass in a slalom course, typically marked by upright poles. ■ a device for holding each frame of a movie film in position behind the lens of a camera or projector. **4** an electric circuit with an output that depends on the combination of several inputs: *a logic gate.* ■ the part of a field-effect transistor to which a signal is applied to control the resistance of the conductive channel of the device.

▸*v.* [*trans.*] *Brit.* (usu. **be gated**) confine (a student) to school or college: *he was gated for the rest of term.* ▷Old English *gæt, geat*, plural *gatu*, of Germanic origin; related to Dutch *gat* 'gap, hole, breach.'

▸*PHRASE* □ **get** (or **be given**) **the gate** *informal* be dismissed from a job.

-gate ▸*comb. form* in nouns denoting an actual or alleged scandal, esp. one involving a cover-up: *Irangate.* ▷early 1970s: suggested by the *Watergate* scandal, 1972.

gate ar·ray ▸*n. Computing* a regular arrangement of logic gates. ■ an electronic chip consisting of such an arrangement.

ga·teau /gä'tō; ga-/ ▸*n.* (*pl.* **-teaux** *pronunc.* same or /-'tōz/) a rich cake, typically one containing layers of cream or fruit. ▷mid 19th cent.: from French *gâteau* 'cake.'

gate-crash·er ▸*n.* a person who attends a party or other gathering without an invitation or ticket. **—gate-crash** *v.*

gat·ed com·mu·ni·ty ▸*n.* a residential area with roads that have gates to control the movement of traffic and people into and out of the area.

gate·fold /'gāt,fōld/ ▸*n.* an oversized page in a book or magazine folded to the same size as the other pages but intended to be opened out for reading.

gate·house /'gāt,hous/ ▸*n.* a house or enclosure near a gateway.

gate·keep·er /'gāt,kēpər/ ▸*n.* an attendant at a gate who is employed to control who goes through it. ■ *figurative* a person or thing that controls access to something: *the primary-care doctor serves as the gatekeeper to specialists.*

gate·keep·ing /'gāt,kēpiNG/ ▸*n.* **1** the activity of controlling, and usually limiting, general access to something: *Wal-Mart's cultural gatekeeping has served to narrow the mainstream for entertainment offerings.* **2** *Computing* a function or system that controls access or operations to files, computers, networks, or the like: [as *modifier*] *a gatekeeping mechanism that allows reads under some circumstances and blocks them under others.*

gate·leg ta·ble /'gāt,leg/ ▸*n.* a table with hinged legs that swing out from the frame to support the drop leaves that make the surface of the table larger. **—gate·legged** /'gāt,legəd/ *adj.*

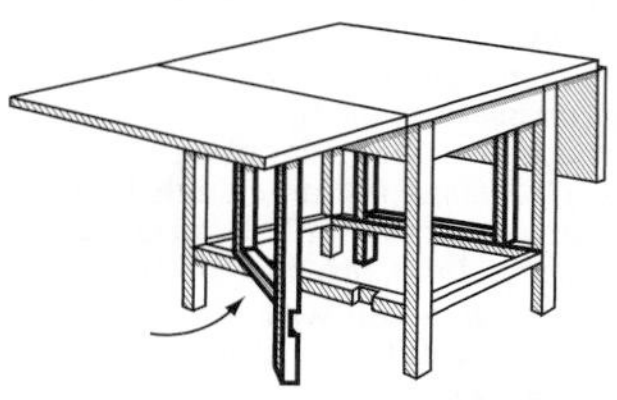

gateleg table

gate·post /'gāt,pōst/ ▸*n.* a post on which a gate is hinged, or against which it shuts.

▸*PHRASE* □ **between you and me and the gatepost** see **BEDPOST.**

Gates[1] /gāts/, Bill (1955–), U.S. computer entrepreneur; full name *William Henry Gates.* He cofounded Microsoft, a computer software company. Overseas expansion and successful marketing of the MS-DOS and Windows operating systems for personal computers made the firm a leading multinational computer company by 1990. He became the youngest multibillionaire in U.S. history.

Bill Gates

Gates[2], Horatio (1728–1806), American army officer; born in England. Originally an officer in the British army, he sided with the colonials when the American Revolution broke out. He commanded the Saratoga campaign 1777.

Gates·head /'gāts,hed/ an industrial town in northeastern England, on the southern bank of the Tyne River, opposite Newcastle; pop. 196,000.

gate valve ▸*n.* a valve with a sliding part that controls the extent of the aperture.

gate·way /'gāt,wā/ ▸*n.* an opening that can be closed

by a gate: *we turned into a gateway leading to a small cottage.* ■ a frame or arch built around or over a gate: *a big house with a wrought-iron gateway.* ■ a means of access or entry to a place: *Mombasa, the* ***gateway to*** *East Africa.* ■ a means of achieving a state or condition: *the Christian symbolism of death as the gateway to life.* ■ *Computing* a device used to connect two different networks, esp. a connection to the Internet.

Gate·way Arch a colossal arch built along the west bank of the Mississippi River in St. Louis, Missouri. The stainless steel arch, 630 feet (192 m) wide and rising 630 feet (192 m) above the banks of the river, was designed by Eero Saarinen and was built 1963-65.

Gateway Arch

gate·way drug ▸*n.* a habit-forming drug that, while not itself addictive, may lead to the use of other addictive drugs: *many believe that alcohol and cigarettes are gateway drugs that increase the risk of subsequent involvement with illegal drugs.*

Ga·tha /ˈgätə; -ˌtä/ ▸*n.* any of 17 poems attributed to Zoroaster that are the most ancient texts of the Avesta. ▷from Avestan *gāthā.*

gath·er /ˈgat͟hər/ ▸*v.* **1** [*intrans.*] come together; assemble or accumulate: *a crowd gathered in the square.* **2** [*trans.*] bring together and take in from scattered places or sources: *we have gathered the information.* ■ pick up from the ground or a surface: *they* ***gathered up*** *the dirty plates and cups.* ■ collect (grain or other crops) as a harvest. ■ collect (plants, fruits, etc.) for food. ■ draw together or toward oneself: *she gathered the child in her arms.* ■ draw and hold together (fabric or a part of a garment) by running thread through it: *the front is gathered at the waist.* **3** [*trans.*] infer; understand: *her clients were, I gathered, a prosperous group.* **4** [*trans.*] develop a higher degree of: *the green movement is gathering pace.* **5** [*trans.*] summon up (a mental or physical attribute such as one's thoughts or strength) for a purpose: *he lay gathering his thoughts together | he* ***gathered himself*** *for a tremendous leap.*
▸*n.* (**gathers**) a part of a garment that is gathered or drawn in. ▷Old English *gaderian*; related to Dutch *gaderen*, also to TOGETHER. **—gath·er·er** *n.*
▸*PHRASE* □ **gather way** (of a ship) begin to move.

THE RIGHT WORD **assemble, collect, congregate, convene, gather, marshal, muster**

Gather is the most general of these terms meaning to come or bring together. It implies bringing widely scattered things or people to one place but with no particular arrangement (*to gather shells at the beach; to gather the family in the living room*).

Collect, on the other hand, implies both selectivity (*to collect evidence for the trial*) and organization (*to collect butterflies as a hobby*). To *gather* one's thoughts means to bring them together because they have been previously scattered; to *collect* one's thoughts is to organize them.

Assemble pertains to objects or people who are brought together for a purpose (*to assemble data for a report; to assemble Congress so that legislation will be passed*), while **congregate** may be more spontaneous, done as a free choice (*people congregated in front of the palace, hoping to catch a glimpse of the queen*).

Convene is a formal word meaning to *assemble* or meet in a body (*to convene an international conference on the subject of global warming*).

Marshal and **muster** are usually thought of as military terms. *Muster* implies bringing together the parts or units of a force (*troops mustered for inspection*), and *marshal* suggests a very orderly and purposeful arrangement (*to marshal the allied forces along the battle front*).

gath·er·ing /ˈgat͟həriNG/ ▸*n.* **1** an assembly or meeting, esp. a social or festive one or one held for a specific purpose: *a family gathering.* **2** a set of printed signatures of a book, gathered for binding.

Gat·i·neau /ˌgatn'ō; ga-tē'nō/ a city in southwestern Quebec in Canada, a largely French-speaking suburb across the Ottawa River from Ottawa in Ontario. Pop. 92,284.

Gat·ling gun /ˈgatliNG/ (also **Gat·ling**) ▸*n.* a rapid-fire, crank-driven gun with a cylindrical cluster of several barrels. The first practical machine gun, it was officially adopted by the U.S. Army in 1866. ▷named after Richard J. *Gatling* (1818–1903), its American inventor.

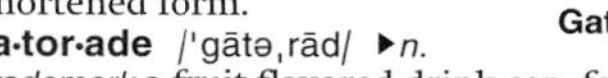

Gatling gun

ga·tor /ˈgātər/ ▸*n. informal* an alligator. ▷mid 19th cent.: shortened form.

Ga·tor·ade /ˈgātəˌrād/ ▸*n. trademark* a fruit-flavored drink esp. for athletes, designed to supply the body with carbohydrates and to replace fluids and sodium lost during exercise.

GATT /gat/ General Agreement on Tariffs and Trade, an international treaty (1948–94) to promote trade and economic development by reducing tariffs and other restrictions. It was superseded by the establishment of the World Trade Organization in 1995.

gauche /gōSH/ ▸*adj.* lacking ease or grace; unsophisticated and socially awkward. ▷mid 18th cent.: French, literally 'left.' **—gauche·ly** *adv.* **—gauche·ness** *n.*

gau·che·rie /ˌgōSHəˈrē/ ▸*n.* awkward, embarassing, or unsophisticated ways: *she had long since gotten over gaucheries such as blushing.* ▷late 18th cent.: French, from *gauche* (see GAUCHE).

Gau·cher's dis·ease /gōˈSHāz/ ▸*n.* a hereditary disease in which the metabolism and storage of fats is abnormal. It results in bone fragility, neurological disturbance, anemia, and enlargement of the liver and spleen. ▷mid 20th cent.: named after Phillippe C. E. *Gaucher* (1854–1918), French physician.

gau·cho /ˈgouCHō/ ▸*n.* (*pl.* **-chos**) a cowboy of the South American pampas. ▷Latin American Spanish, probably from Araucanian *kauču* 'friend.'

gaud /gôd/ ▸*n. archaic* a showy and purely ornamental thing: *displays of overpriced gauds.* ▷Middle English (denoting a trick or pretense): perhaps via Anglo-Norman French from Old French *gaudir* 'rejoice,' from Latin *gaudere*. Current senses may have been influenced by obsolete *gaud* 'a large ornamental bead in a rosary.'

gaud·er·y /ˈgôdərē/ ▸*n.* **1** gaudy articles or decoration, esp. clothing or jewelry. **2** tasteless or extravagant display of such articles.

Gau·dí /ˈgoudē/, Antonio (1853–1926), Spanish architect; full name *Antonio Gaudí y Cornet*. He was a leading but idiosyncratic exponent of art nouveau who worked chiefly in Barcelona and is known mainly for his ornate and extravagant church of the Sagrada Familia in Barcelona.

gaud·y[1] /ˈgôdē/ ▸*adj.* (**gaud·i·er**, **gaud·i·est**) extravagantly bright or showy, typically so as to be tasteless: *silver bows and gaudy ribbons.* ▷late 15th cent.: probably from GAUD + -Y[1]. **—gaud·i·ly** /-dəlē/ *adv.* **—gaud·i·ness** *n.*

gaud·y[2] ▸*n.* (*pl.* **gaud·ies**) *Brit.* a celebratory reunion dinner or entertainment held by a college. ▷mid 16th cent. (in the sense 'rejoicing, a celebration'): from Latin *gaudium* 'joy,' or from *gaude* 'rejoice!,' imperative of *gaudere*.

gauge /gāj/ (*chiefly technical* also **gage**) ▸*n.* **1** an instrument or device for measuring the magnitude, amount, or contents of something, typically with a visual display of such information. ■ a tool for checking whether something conforms to a desired dimension. ■ *figurative* a means of estimating something; a criterion or test: *emigration is perhaps the best* ***gauge of*** *public unease.* **2** the thickness, size, or capacity of something, esp. as a standard measure, in particular: ■ the diameter of a string, fiber, tube, etc.: [as *adj.*] *a fine 0.018-inch gauge wire.* ■ [*in combination*] a measure of the diameter of a gun barrel, or of its ammunition, expressed as the number of spherical pieces of shot of the same diameter as the barrel that can be made from 1 pound (454 g) of lead: [as *adj.*] *a 12-gauge shotgun.* ■ [*in combination*] the thickness of sheet metal or plastic: [as *adj.*] *500-gauge polyethylene.* ■ the distance between the rails of a line of railroad track: *the line was laid to a gauge of 2 ft. 9 in.* **3** (usu. **the gage**) *historical Nautical* the position of a sailing vessel to windward (**weather gage**) or leeward (**lee gage**) of another.
▸*v.* [*trans.*] **1** estimate or determine the magnitude, amount, or volume of: *astronomers can gauge the star's intrinsic brightness.* ■ form a judgment or estimate of (a situation, mood, etc.): *she is unable to gauge his mood.* **2** measure the dimensions of (an object) with a gauge: *when dry, the assemblies can be gauged exactly and planed to width.* ■ [as *adj.*] (**gauged**) made in standard dimensions: *gauged sets of strings.* ▷Middle English (denoting a standard measure): from Old French *gauge* (noun), *gauger* (verb), variant of Old Northern French *jauge* (noun), *jauger* (verb), of unknown origin. **—gauge·a·ble** *adj.* **—gaug·er** *n.*

gauge the·o·ry ▸*n. Physics* a quantum theory using mathematical functions to describe subatomic interactions in terms of particles that are not directly detectable.

Gau·guin /gōˈgaN/, (Eugène Henri) Paul (1848–1903), French painter. He lived mainly in Tahiti from 1891, painting in a post-Impressionist style that was influenced by primitive art. Notable works: *The Vision after the Sermon* (1888) and *Faa Iheihe* (1898).

Gau·ha·ti /gouˈhätē/ an industrial city in northeastern India, in Assam, a port on the Brahmaputra River; pop. 578,000.

Gaul[1] /gôl/ an ancient region in Europe that corresponds to modern France, Belgium, the southern Netherlands, southwestern Germany, and northern Italy. The area south of the Alps was conquered in 222 BC by the Romans, who called it **Cisalpine Gaul**. The area north of the Alps, known as **Transalpine Gaul**, was taken by Julius Caesar between 58 and 51 BC.

Gaul[2] ▸*n.* a native or inhabitant of ancient Gaul. ▷from Latin *Gallus*, probably of Celtic origin.

Gau·lei·ter /ˈgouˌlītər/ ▸*n.* **1** *historical* a political official governing a district under Nazi rule. **2** an overbearing official. ▷1930s: German, from *Gau* 'administrative district' + *Leiter* 'leader.'

Gaul·ish /ˈgôliSH/ ▸*adj.* of, relating to, or denoting the ancient Gauls.
▸*n.* the Celtic language of the ancient Gauls.

Gaulle, Charles de, see DE GAULLE.

Gaull·ism /ˈgôˌlizəm/ ▸*n.* the principles and policies of Charles de Gaulle, characterized by their conservatism, nationalism, and advocacy of centralized government. ▷1940s: from French *Gaullisme*. **—Gaull·ist** *n.* & *adj.*

Gaunt[1] /gônt/ former name of GHENT.

Gaunt[2], John of, see JOHN OF GAUNT.

gaunt /gônt/ ▸*adj.* (of a person) lean and haggard, esp. because of suffering, hunger, or age. See note at THIN. ■ (of a building or place) grim or desolate in appearance. ▷late Middle English: of unknown origin. **—gaunt·ly** *adv.* **—gaunt·ness** *n.*

gaunt·let[1] /ˈgôntlit; ˈgänt-/ ▸*n.* a stout glove with a long loose wrist. ■ *historical* an armored glove, as worn by a medieval knight. ■ the part of a glove covering the wrist. ▷late Middle English: from Old French *gantelet*, diminutive of *gant* 'glove,' of Germanic origin.
▸*PHRASE* □ **take up** (or **throw down**) **the gauntlet** accept (or issue) a challenge. [from the medieval custom of issuing a challenge by throwing one's gauntlet to the ground; whoever picked it up was deemed to have accepted the challenge.]

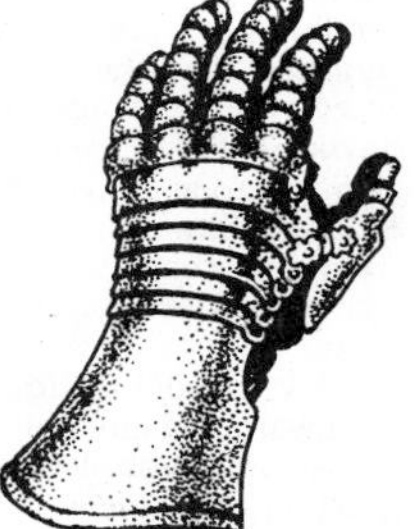

knight's gauntlet

gaunt·let[2] (also **gant·let** /ˈgantlit; ˈgônt-/) ▸*n.* (in phrase **run the gauntlet**) **1** go through an intimidating or dangerous crowd, place, or experience in order to reach a goal: *they had to run the gauntlet of television cameras.* **2** *historical* undergo the military punishment of receiving blows while running between two rows of men with sticks. ▷mid 17th cent.: alteration of *gantlope* (from Swedish *gatlopp*, from *gata* 'lane' + *lopp* 'course') by association with GAUNTLET[1].

gaur /gou(ə)r/ ▸*n.* a large wild ox native to India and Malaysia. Also called **INDIAN BISON, SELADANG.** • *Bos gaurus*, family Bovidae. ▹early 19th cent.: from Sanskrit *gaura*; related to **COW**[1].

Gauss /gous/, Karl Friedrich (1777–1855), German mathematician, astronomer, and physicist. He laid the foundations of number theory.

gauss /gous/ (abbr.: **G**) ▸*n.* (*pl.* same or **gauss·es**) a unit of magnetic induction, equal to one ten-thousandth of a tesla. ▹late 19th cent.: named after K. **GAUSS**.

Gauss·i·an dis·tri·bu·tion /ˈgousēən/ ▸*n. Statistics* another term for **NORMAL DISTRIBUTION.** ▹early 20th cent.: named after K. **GAUSS**, who described it.

Gau·ta·ma /ˈgôtəmə; ˈgou-/, Siddhartha, see **BUDDHA**.

gauze /gôz/ ▸*n.* a thin translucent fabric of silk, linen, or cotton. ■ (also **wire gauze**) a very fine wire mesh. ■ *Medicine* thin, loosely woven cloth used for dressing and swabs. ■ [in *sing.*] *figurative* a transparent haze or film: *they saw the grasslands through a gauze of golden dust.* ▹mid 16th cent.: from French *gaze*, perhaps from *Gaza*, the name of a town in Palestine. **—gauz·i·ly** /-zəlē/ *adv.* **—gauz·i·ness** *n.* **—gauz·y** *adj.*

ga·vage /gəˈväzʜ/ ▸*n.* the administration of food or drugs by force, esp. to an animal, typically through a tube leading down the throat to the stomach. ▹late 19th cent.: French, from *gaver* 'force-feed,' from a base meaning 'throat.'

gave /gāv/ ▸ past of **GIVE**.

gav·el /ˈgavəl/ ▸*n.* a small mallet with which an auctioneer, a judge, or the chair of a meeting hits a surface to call for attention or order.
▸*v.* (**gav·eled, gav·el·ing;** *Brit.* **gav·elled, gav·el·ling**) [*trans.*] bring (a hearing or person) to order by use of such a mallet: *he gaveled the convention to order.* ▹early 19th cent. (originally U.S. in the sense 'stonemason's mallet'): of unknown origin.

gav·el·kind /ˈgavəlˌkīnd/ ▸*n. historical* a system of inheritance in which a deceased person's land is divided equally among all male heirs. ▹Middle English: from obsolete *gavel* 'payment, rent' + **KIND**[1].

gav·el-to-gav·el ▸*adj.* lasting from beginning to end of a formal session or meeting, such as a political convention: *uninterrupted gavel-to-gavel coverage without commentary.*

ga·vi·al /ˈgāvēəl/ ▸*n.* variant spelling of **GHARIAL.** ▹from French, the *-v-* probably being substituted for *-r-* by scribal error.

ga·votte /gəˈvät/ ▸*n.* a medium-paced French dance, popular in the 18th century. ■ a piece of music accompanying or in the rhythm of such a dance, composed in common time beginning on the third beat of the bar. ▹French, from Provençal *gavoto* 'dance of the mountain people,' from *Gavot* 'a native of the Alps.'

GAW (or **G.A.W.**) ▸*abbr.* guaranteed annual wage.

Ga·wain /gəˈwān; ˈgäˌwān; ˈgäwən/ (in Arthurian legend) one of the knights of the Round Table who quested after the Holy Grail. He is the hero of the medieval poem *Sir Gawain and the Green Knight.*

gawk /gôk/ ▸*v.* [*intrans.*] stare openly and stupidly: *they were* **gawking at** *some pinup.*
▸*n.* an awkward or shy person. ▹late 17th cent. (as a noun): perhaps related to obsolete *gaw* 'to gaze,' from Old Norse *gá* 'heed.' **—gawk·er** *n.* **—gawk·ish** *adj.*

gawk·y /ˈgôkē/ ▸*adj.* (**gawk·i·er, gawk·i·est**) nervously awkward and ungainly: *a gawky teenager.* **—gawk·i·ly** /-kəlē/ *adv.* **—gawk·i·ness** *n.*

gawp /gôp/ ▸*v.* [*intrans.*] *informal* stare openly in a stupid or rude manner: *what are you gawping at?* ▹late 17th cent.: perhaps an alteration of **GAPE**. **—gawp·er** *n.*

Gay /gā/, John (1685–1732), English poet and playwright. He is chiefly known for *The Beggar's Opera* (1728).

gay /gā/ ▸*adj.* (**gay·er, gay·est**) **1** (of a person, esp. a man) homosexual: *that friend of yours, is he gay?* ■ relating to or used by homosexuals: *feminist, black, and gay perspectives.* **2** lighthearted and carefree: *Nan had a gay disposition and a very pretty face.* ■ characterized by cheerfulness or pleasure: *we had a gay old time.* ■ brightly colored; showy; brilliant: *a gay profusion of purple and pink sweet peas.*
▸*n.* a homosexual, esp. a man. ▹Middle English (sense 2): from Old French *gai*, of unknown origin. **—gay·ness** *n.*

USAGE Gay meaning 'homosexual,' dating back to the 1930s (if not earlier), became established in the 1960s as the term preferred by homosexual men to describe themselves. It is now the standard accepted term throughout the English-speaking world. As a result, the centuries-old other senses of gay meaning either 'carefree' or 'bright and showy,' once common in speech and literature, are much less frequent. The word gay cannot be readily used unselfconsciously today in these older senses without sounding old-fashioned or arousing a sense of double entendre, despite concerted attempts by some to keep them alive.
Gay in its modern sense typically refers to men (**lesbian** being the standard term for homosexual women), but in some contexts it can be used of both men and women.

Ga·ya /gəˈyä/ a city in northeastern India, in the state of Bihar, south of Patna; pop. 291,000. It is a place of Hindu pilgrimage.

gay·dar /ˈgāˌdär/ ▸*n. informal, humorous* the putative ability of homosexuals to recognize one another intuitively or by means of very slight indications. ■ the similar ability of heterosexuals to discern the homosexuality of others. ▹1990s: blend of *gay* and *radar.*

Gaye /gā/, Marvin (1939–84), U.S. soul singer, composer, and musician. After signing a contract with Motown in 1961, he began recording as a solo singer. Best known for "I Heard It Through the Grapevine" (1968), he later recorded the albums *Let's Get It On* (1973) and *Midnight Love* (1982). He was shot to death by his father during a quarrel.

gay·e·ty ▸*n.* variant spelling of **GAIETY**.

gay lib·er·a·tion ▸*n.* a movement to eliminate social and legal discrimination against homosexuals.

Gay-Lus·sac's law /ˌgā ləˈsak/ *Chemistry* a law stating that the volumes of gases undergoing a reaction at constant pressure and temperature are in a simple ratio to each other and to that of the product. ▹early 19th cent.: named after Joseph L. *Gay-Lussac* (1778–1850), French chemist and physicist.

gay pride ▸*n.* a sense of dignity and satisfaction in connection with the public acknowledgment of one's own homosexuality.

gay rights ▸*plural n.* equal civil and social rights for homosexuals compared with heterosexuals.

gaz. ▸*abbr.* ■ gazette. ■ gazetteer.

ga·za·ni·a /gəˈzānēə/ ▸*n.* a tropical herbaceous plant of the daisy family, with showy flowers that are typically orange or yellow. • Genus *Gazania*, family Compositae. ▹modern Latin, named after Theodore of *Gaza* (1398–1478), Greek scholar.

Ga·za Strip /ˈgäzə; ˈgazə/ a strip of territory in Palestine, on the southeastern Mediterranean coast, including the town of Gaza; pop. 748,000. Administered by Egypt from 1949 and occupied by Israel from 1967, it became a self-governing enclave under the PLO–Israeli accord of 1994 and elected its own legislative council in 1996.

gaze /gāz/ ▸*v.* [*intrans.*] look steadily and intently, esp. in admiration, surprise, or thought: *he could only gaze at her in astonishment.*
▸*n.* a steady intent look: *he turned, following her gaze | offices screened from the public gaze.* ■ [in *sing.*] (in literary theory) a particular perspective taken to embody certain aspects of the relationship between observer and observed, esp. as reflected in the way in which an author or film director (unconsciously or otherwise) directs attention: *the male gaze.* ▹late Middle English: perhaps related to obsolete *gaw* (see **GAWK**). **—gaz·er** *n.*

ga·ze·bo /gəˈzēbō/ ▸*n.* (*pl.* **-bos** or **-boes**) a roofed structure that offers an open view of the surrounding area, typically used for relaxation or entertainment. ▹mid 18th cent.: perhaps humorously from **GAZE**, in imitation of Latin future tenses ending in *-ebo*: compare with **LAVABO**.

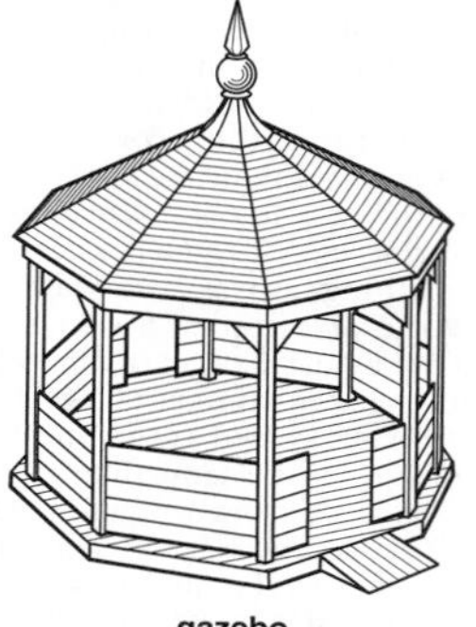
gazebo

ga·zelle /gəˈzel/ ▸*n.* (*pl.* same or **-zelles**) a small slender antelope that typically has curved horns and a yellowish-brown coat with white underparts, found in open country in Africa and Asia. • *Gazella* and other genera, family Bovidae: several species. ▹early 17th cent.: from French, probably via Spanish from Arabic *ghazāl*.

gaze track·ing ▸*n.* another term for **EYE TRACKING**.

ga·zette /gəˈzet/ ▸*n.* **1** (used in the names of periodicals) a journal or newspaper. **2** *Brit.* the official publication of a government organization or institution, listing appointments and other public notices.
▸*v.* [*trans.*] *Brit.* announce or publish in an official gazette. ▹early 17th cent.: via French from Italian *gazzetta*, originally Venetian *gazeta de la novità* 'a halfpennyworth of news' (because the news-sheet sold for a *gazeta*, a Venetian coin of small value).

gaz·et·teer /ˌgaziˈti(ə)r/ ▸*n.* a geographical index or dictionary. ▹early 17th cent. (in the sense 'journalist'): via French from Italian *gazzettiere*, from *gazzetta* (see **GAZETTE**). The current sense comes from a late 17th-cent. gazetteer called *The Gazetteer's: or, Newsman's Interpreter: Being a Geographical Index.*

Ga·zi·an·tep /ˌgäzē-änˈtep/ a city in southern Turkey, near the border with Syria; pop. 603,000. Former name (until 1921): **AINTAB**.

ga·zil·lion /gəˈzilyən/ (also **ka·zil·lion**) ▸*cardinal number informal* a very large number or quantity (used jocularly or for emphasis): *I'd like to sell* **gazillions of** *books.* ▹late 20th cent.: fanciful formation on the pattern of *billion* and *million.*

gaz·pa·cho /gäˈspäcʜō/ ▸*n.* (*pl.* **-chos**) a Spanish-style soup made from tomatoes and other vegetables and spices, served cold. ▹Spanish.

ga·zump /gəˈzəmp/ ▸*v.* [*trans.*] *Brit.* **1** (of a seller) raise the contracted price of a property after having informally accepted a lower offer (from an intending buyer). **2** *archaic* swindle (someone). ▹1920s (sense 2): from Yiddish *gezumph* 'overcharge.' Sense 1 dates from the 1970s. **—ga·zump·er** *n.*

ga·zund·er /gəˈzəndər/ ▸*v.* [*trans.*] *Brit.* (of a buyer) lower the amount of an offer made on a property and accepted by (a seller) at the time of final negotiations. ▹late 1980s: humorous blend of **GAZUMP** and **UNDER**.

GB ▸*abbr.* ■ *Computing* (also **Gb**) gigabyte(s). ■ Great Britain.

GBH ▸*abbr.* grievous bodily harm.

Gbyte ▸*abbr.* gigabyte(s).

GCB ▸*abbr.* (in the UK) Knight or Dame Grand Cross of the Order of the Bath.

gcd ▸*abbr. Mathematics* greatest common divisor.

gcf ▸*abbr. Mathematics* greatest common factor.

GCT ▸*abbr.* Greenwich Civil Time.

GD ▸*abbr.* Grand Duchy.

Gd ▸*symbol* the chemical element gadolinium.

gd. ▸*abbr.* ■ good. ■ guard.

Gdańsk /gəˈdänsk; -ˈdansk/ an industrial port and shipbuilding center in northern Poland, on an inlet of the Baltic Sea; pop. 465,000. Disputed between Prussia and Poland during the 19th century, it was a free city under a League of Nations mandate 1919–39, when it was annexed by Nazi Germany, which precipitated hostilities with Poland and the outbreak of World War II. German name **DANZIG**.

g'day /gəˈdā/ ▸*exclam. Austral./NZ* good day.

GDP ▸*abbr.* gross domestic product.

GDR *historical* ▸*abbr.* German Democratic Republic. See **GERMANY**.

gds. ▸*abbr.* goods.

Gdy·nia /gəˈdinēə/ a port and naval base in northern Poland, on the Baltic Sea, northwest of Gdańsk; pop. 251,500.

Ge[1] ▸*symbol* the chemical element germanium.

Ge[2] /gā/ *Greek Mythology* another name for **GAIA**.

ge·an·ti·cline /jēˈantiˌklīn/ ▸*n. Geology* a large-scale anticline or upward fold of stratified rock. ▹late 19th cent.: from Greek *gē* 'earth' + **ANTICLINE**.

gear /gi(ə)r/ ▸*n.* **1** (often **gears**) one of a set of toothed wheels that work together to alter the relation between the speed of a driving mechanism (such as the engine of a vehicle or the crank of a bicycle) and the speed of the driven parts (the wheels). ■ a particular function or state of adjustment of engaged gears: *he was tooling along in fifth gear.* **2** *informal* equipment that is used for a particular purpose. ■ a person's personal possessions and clothes. ■ clothing, esp. of a specified kind: *designer gear.* ■ *Nautical* a ship's rigging.

▶*v.* [*trans.*] design or adjust the gears in (a machine) to give a specified speed or power output: *it's geared too high for serious off-road use.* ■ (**gear something to**) adjust or adapt something to suit a special purpose or need.

▶*phrasal v.* □ **gear down** (or **up**) change to a lower (or higher) gear. □ **gear for** make ready or prepared: *a nation geared for war.* □ **gear up** equip or prepare oneself: *the region started to* **gear up for** *the tourist season.* ▷Middle English: of Scandinavian origin; compare with Old Norse *gervi*. Early senses expressed the general meaning 'equipment or apparatus,' later 'mechanism': hence sense 1 (early 19th cent.).

▶*PHRASE* □ **in gear** with a gear engaged: *the captain revved the engines and put them in gear.* ■ *figurative* done with more energy or effort: *I've got to get my act in gear.*

gear·box /ˈgi(ə)rˌbäks/ ▶*n.* a set of gears with its casing, esp. in a motor vehicle; the transmission.

gear·ing /ˈgi(ə)riNG/ ▶*n.* **1** the set or arrangement of gears in a machine: *the mill's internal waterwheel and gearing survive.* **2** British term for LEVERAGE (sense 2).

gear lev·er (also **gear·stick**) ▶*n. Brit.* another term for GEARSHIFT.

gear ra·ti·o ▶*n.* (in a gearbox, transmission, etc.) the ratio between the rates at which the last and first gears rotate.

gear·shift /ˈgi(ə)rˌSHift/ ▶*n.* a device used to engage or disengage gears in a transmission or similar mechanism.

gear·wheel /ˈgi(ə)rˌ(h)wēl/ ▶*n.* a toothed wheel in a set of gears. ■ (on a bicycle) a cogwheel driven directly by the chain.

geas /gesh/ ▶*n.* (*pl.* **geas·a** /ˈgeSHə/) (in Irish folklore) an obligation or prohibition magically imposed on a person. ▷Irish.

geck·o /ˈgekō/ ▶*n.* (*pl.* **-os** or **-oes**) a nocturnal and often highly vocal lizard that has adhesive pads on the feet to assist in climbing on smooth surfaces. It is widespread in warm regions. • Gekkonidae and related families: numerous genera and species. ▷late 18th cent.: from Malay dialect *geko, gekok*, imitative of its cry.

GED ▶*abbr.* general equivalency degree (or diploma).

gee[1] /jē/ (also **gee-whiz** /ˈjē ˈ(h)wiz/) ▶*exclam. informal* a mild expression, typically of surprise, enthusiasm, or sympathy: *Gee, Linda looks great at fifty!* ▷mid 19th cent.: perhaps an abbreviation of JESUS.

gee[2] ▶*exclam.* (**gee up**) a command to a horse to go faster.

▶*v.* (**gees, geed, gee·ing**) [*trans.*] command (a horse) to go faster. ■ encourage (someone) to work more quickly: *I was running around geeing people up.* ▷early 17th cent.: of unknown origin.

gee[3] ▶*n. informal* a thousand dollars: *we paid five gees.* ▷1930s: representing the initial letter of GRAND.

gee·bung /ˈjēbəNG/ ▶*n.* an Australian shrub or small tree that bears creamy-yellow flowers and small green fruit. • Genus *Persoonia*, family Proteaceae. ▷early 19th cent.: from Dharuk.

Gee·chee /ˈgēCHē/ ▶*n.* term used of the Gullah dialect, or a speaker of this dialect. ▷possibly from the name of the *Ogeechee* River, in Georgia.

geek /gēk/ ▶*n. informal* **1** an unfashionable or socially inept person. ■ [with *adj.*] a person with an eccentric devotion to a particular interest: *a computer geek.* **2** a carnival performer who does wild or disgusting acts. ▷late 19th cent.: from the related English dialect *geck* 'fool,' of Germanic origin; related to Dutch *gek* 'mad, silly.' —**geek·y** *adj.*

Gee·long /jēˈlôNG/ a port and oil-refining center on the southern coast of Australia, in the state of Victoria; pop. 126,000.

geese /gēs/ ▶ plural form of GOOSE.

gee-string ▶*n.* variant spelling of G-STRING.

gee-whiz *informal* ▶*exclam.* another term for GEE[1].

▶*adj.* [*attrib.*] characterized by or causing naive astonishment or wonder, in particular at new technology: *this era of gee-whiz gadgetry.*

Ge'ez /gēˈez/ ▶*n.* an ancient Semitic language of Ethiopia, which survives as the liturgical language of the Ethiopian Orthodox Church. It is the ancestor of the modern Ethiopian languages such as Amharic. Also called ETHIOPIC. ▷of Ethiopic origin.

geez ▶*exclam.* variant spelling of JEEZ.

gee·zer /ˈgēzər/ ▶*n. informal* an old man (used as a disparaging term). ▷late 19th cent.: representing a dialect pronunciation of earlier *guiser* 'mummer.'

ge·fil·te fish /gəˈfiltə/ ▶*n.* a dish of stewed or baked stuffed fish, or of fish cakes boiled in a fish or vegetable broth and usually served chilled. ▷late 19th cent.: Yiddish, 'stuffed fish,' from *filn* 'to fill' + FISH[1].

ge·gen·schein /ˈgāgənˌSHīn/ ▶*n. Astronomy* a patch of very faint nebulous light sometimes seen in the night sky opposite the position of the sun. It is thought to be the image of the sun reflected from gas and dust outside the atmosphere. ▷late 19th cent.: German *Gegenschein*, from *gegen* 'opposite' + *Schein* 'glow, shine.'

Ge·hen·na /gəˈhenə/ (in Judaism and the New Testament) hell. ▷via ecclesiastical Latin from Greek *geenna*, from Hebrew *gē' hinnōm* 'hell,' literally 'valley of Hinnom,' a place near Jerusalem where children were sacrificed to Baal (Jer. 19:5,6).

Geh·rig /ˈgerig/, Lou (1903–41), U.S. baseball player; full name *Henry Louis Gehrig*; known as **the Iron Horse**. He played a then-record 2,130 consecutive major league games for the New York Yankees from 1925 to 1939; his stamina earned him his nickname. He died from amyotrophic lateral sclerosis (ALS), often called Lou Gehrig's disease.

Lou Gehrig

Gei·ger /ˈgīgər/, Hans (Johann) Wilhelm (1882–1945), German nuclear physicist. In 1908, he developed a prototype radiation counter for detecting alpha particles.

Gei·ger count·er (also **Gei·ger-Mül·ler count·er** /ˈmələr; ˈmyōōlər/) ▶*n.* a device for measuring radioactivity by detecting and counting ionizing particles.

Gei·sel /ˈgīzəl/, Theodor (Seuss) (1904–91) U.S. writer and illustrator; known as Dr. Seuss. His numerous children's books include *And to Think That I Saw It on Mulberry Street* (1937), *Horton Hatches the Egg* (1940), *The Cat in the Hat* (1957), and *Green Eggs and Ham* (1960). His books for adults include *You're Only Old Once!* (1986) and *Oh, the Places You'll Go!* (1990).

gei·sha /ˈgāSHə; ˈgē-/ (also **geisha girl**) ▶*n.* (*pl.* same or **-shas**) a Japanese hostess trained to entertain men with conversation, dance, and song. ▷late 19th cent.: Japanese, 'entertainer,' from *gei* 'performing arts' + *sha* 'person.'

Geiss·ler tube /ˈgīslər/ ▶*n.* a sealed tube of glass or quartz with a central constriction, filled with vapor for the production of a luminous electrical discharge. ▷mid 19th cent.: named after Heinrich *Geissler* (1814–79), the German mechanic and glassblower who invented it.

Geist /gīst/ ▶*n.* [in *sing.*] the spirit of an individual or group. ▷German; related to GHOST.

gei·to·nog·a·my /ˌgītnˈägəmē/ ▶*n. Botany* the fertilization of a flower by pollen from another flower on the same (or a genetically identical) plant. Compare with XENOGAMY. ▷late 19th cent.: from Greek *geitōn, geitono-* 'neighbor' + *-gamos* 'marrying.' —**gei·to·nog·a·mous** /-məs/ *adj.* .

Ge·jiu /ˈgeˈjōō/ (also **Ge·ju**) a city in southern China, near the border with Vietnam; pop. 384,000.

gel[1] /jel/ ▶*n.* a jellylike substance containing a cosmetic, medicinal, or other preparation: *try rubbing some teething gel onto sore gums.* ■ a substance of this consistency used for setting the hair. ■ *Chemistry* a semisolid colloidal suspension of a solid dispersed in a liquid. ■ *Biochemistry* a semirigid slab or cylinder of an organic polymer used as a medium for the separation of macromolecules.

▶*v.* (**gelled, gel·ling**) [*intrans.*] *Chemistry* form into a gel: *the mixture gelled at 7 degrees Celsius.* ■ [*trans.*] treat (the hair) with gel. ▷late 19th cent.: abbreviation of GELATIN.

gel[2] ▶*v.* (**gelled, gel·ling**) *chiefly Brit.* variant spelling of JELL. ▷late 19th cent.: from GEL[1].

gel·a·da /jəˈlädə/ (also **gelada baboon**) ▶*n.* (*pl.* same or **-das**) a brownish baboon with a long mane and naked red rump, native to Ethiopia. • *Theropithecus gelada*, family Cercopithecidae. ▷mid 19th cent.: from Amharic *č'äallada*.

ge·la·ti /jəˈlätē/ ▶ plural form of GELATO.

gel·a·tin /ˈjelətn/ (also *chiefly dated* **gel·a·tine**) ▶*n.* a virtually colorless and tasteless water-soluble protein prepared from collagen and used in food preparation as the basis of jellies, in photographic processes, and in glue. ■ (usu. **blasting gelatin**) a high explosive consisting chiefly of a gel of nitroglycerine with added cellulose nitrate. ▷early 19th cent.: from French *gélatine*, from Italian *gelatina*, from *gelata*, from Latin (see JELLY).

ge·lat·i·nize /jəˈlatnˌīz; ˈjelətnˌīz/ ▶*v.* make or become gelatinous or jellylike. ■ [*trans.*] [usu. as *adj.*] (**gelatinized**) coat with gelatin: *gelatinized glass microscope slides.* —**ge·lat·i·ni·za·tion** /jeˌlatniˈzāSHən/ *n.*

ge·lat·i·nous /jəˈlatn-əs/ ▶*adj.* having a jellylike consistency: *a sweet, gelatinous drink.* ■ of or like the protein gelatin: *tooth enamel is coated with a gelatinous layer of protein.* —**ge·lat·i·nous·ly** *adv.*

ge·la·tion[1] /jeˈlāSHən/ ▶*n. technical* solidification by freezing. ▷mid 19th cent.: from Latin *gelatio(n-)*, from *gelare* 'freeze.'

ge·la·tion[2] ▶*n. Chemistry* the process of forming a gel.

ge·la·to /jəˈlätō/ ▶*n.* (*pl.* **-ti** /-tē/) an Italian-style ice cream. ▷Italian.

gel·cap ▶*n.* a gelatin capsule containing liquid medication or other substance to be taken orally.

gel·coat /ˈjelˌkōt/ ▶*n.* the smooth, hard surface layer of polyester resin in a fiberglass structure.

geld /geld/ ▶*v.* [*trans.*] castrate (a male animal). ■ *figurative* deprive of vitality or vigor: *the English version of the book has been gelded.* ▷Middle English: from Old Norse *gelda*, from *geldr* 'barren.'

Gel·der·land /ˈgeldərˌlänt; ˈKHel-/ a province in the Netherlands, on the border with Germany; capital, Arnhem.

geld·ing /ˈgeldiNG/ ▶*n.* a castrated animal, esp. a male horse. ▷late Middle English: from Old Norse *geldingr*, from *geldr* 'barren.'

gel·id /ˈjelid/ ▶*adj.* icy; extremely cold: *the gelid pond* | *figurative she gave a gelid reply.* ▷early 17th cent.: from Latin *gelidus*, from *gelu* 'frost, intense cold.'

gel·ig·nite /ˈjeligˌnīt/ ▶*n.* a high explosive made from a gel of nitroglycerine and nitrocellulose in a base of wood pulp and sodium or potassium nitrate, used particularly for rock blasting. ▷late 19th cent.: probably from GELATIN + Latin *(l)ignis* 'wood' + -ITE[1].

Gell-Mann /ˌgel ˈmän/, Murray (1929–), U.S. theoretical physicist. He coined the word *quark* and proposed the concept of strangeness in quarks. Nobel Prize for Physics (1969).

gel pen ▶*n.* a pen that uses a gel-based ink, combining the permanence of oil-based ballpoint ink and the smooth glide of water-based ink.

gel·se·mi·um /jelˈsēmēəm/ ▶*n.* **1** a preparation of the rhizome of yellow jasmine, used in homeopathy to treat flulike symptoms. **2** a plant of a genus that includes the yellow jasmine. • Genus *Gelsemium*, family Loganiaceae. ▷late 19th cent.: modern Latin, from Italian *gelsomino* 'jasmine.'

Gel·sen·kir·chen /ˌgelzənˈki(ə)rKHən/ an industrial city in western Germany, in North Rhine-Westphalia, northeast of Essen; pop. 294,000.

gelt /gelt/ ▶*n. informal* money. ▷early 16th cent. (originally often used to refer to the pay of a German army): from German *Geld* 'money.'

GEM ▶*abbr.* ground-effect machine.

gem /jem/ ▶*n.* a precious or semiprecious stone, esp. when cut and polished or engraved. ■ a person or thing considered to be outstandingly good or special in some respect: *this architectural gem of a palace.* ■ used in names of some brilliantly colored hummingbirds, e.g., **mountain gem**.

▶*v.* (**gemmed, gem·ming**) [*trans.*] [usu. as *adj.*] (**gemmed**) *rare* decorate with or as with gems. ▷Old English *gim*, from Latin *gemma* 'bud, jewel'; influenced in Middle English by Old French *gemme*. —**gem·like** /-ˌlīk/ *adj.*

Ge·ma·ra /gəˈmärə/ ▶*n.* (**the Gemara**) a rabbinical commentary on the Mishnah, forming the second part of the Talmud. ▷from Aramaic *gĕmārā* 'completion.'

Pronunciation Key ə *ago*; ər *over*; ˈə or ˌə *up*; ˈər or ˌər *fur*; a *hat*; ā *rate*; ä *car*; CH *chew*; e *let*; ē *see*; e(ə)r *air*; i *fit*; ī *by*; i(ə)r *ear*; NG *sing*; ō *go*; ô *for*; oi *boy*; ŏŏ *good*; ōō *goo*; ou *out*; SH *she*; TH *thin*; TH *then*; (h)w *why*; ZH *vision*

ge·ma·tri·a /gəˈmätrēə/ ▶*n.* a Kabbalistic method of interpreting the Hebrew scriptures by computing the numerical value of words, based on those of their constituent letters. ▷mid 17th cent.: from Aramaic *gīmaṭrēyā*, from Greek *gēometria* (see GEOMETRY).

Ge·may·el /jəˈmīəl/, Pierre (1905–84), Lebanese political leader. A Maronite Christian, he founded the right-wing Phalange Party in 1936 and served as a member of parliament 1960–84. His youngest son, **Bashir** (1947–82), was assassinated while president-elect; his eldest son, **Amin** (1942–), served as president 1982–88.

Ge·mein·schaft /gəˈmīnˌsHäft; -ˌsHaft/ ▶*n.* social relations between individuals, based on close personal and family ties; community. Contrasted with GESELLSCHAFT. ▷German, from *gemein* 'common' + *-schaft* (see -SHIP).

ge·mel·li /jəˈmelē/ ▶*n.* pasta in the form of two short rods twisted around each other. ▷Italian, literally 'twins'.

gem·i·nal /ˈjemənl/ ▶*adj. Chemistry* denoting substituent atoms or groups, esp. protons, attached to the same atom in a molecule. ▷late 20th cent.: from Latin *geminus* 'twin' + -AL. —**gem·i·nal·ly** *adv.*

gem·i·nate *Phonetics* ▶*adj.* /ˈjemənit/ consisting of identical adjacent speech sounds, esp. consonants; doubled.
▶*v.* /ˈjeməˌnāt/ [*trans.*] double or repeat (a speech sound). ▷late Middle English: from Latin *geminatus*, past participle of *geminare* 'double, pair with,' from *geminus* 'twin.' —**gem·i·na·tion** /ˌjeməˈnāsHən/ *n.*

Gem·i·ni /ˈjeməˌnī; -ˌnē/ **1** *Astronomy* a northern constellation (the Twins), said to represent the mythological twins Castor and Pollux, whose names are given to its two brightest stars. See DIOSCURI. ■ [as *genitive*] (**Gem·i·no·rum** /ˌjeməˈnôrəm/) used with a preceding letter or numeral to designate a star in this constellation: *the star Eta Geminorum.* **2** *Astrology* the third sign of the zodiac, which the sun enters about May 21. ■ (**a Gemini**) (*pl.* **-nis**) a person born when the sun is in this sign. **3** a series of twelve manned orbiting space missions, launched by the U.S. in the 1960s in preparation for the Apollo program. ▷Latin, plural of *geminus* 'twin.' —**Gem·i·ni·an** /-ˌnīən/ *n.* & *adj.* (in sense 2).

Gem·i·nids /ˈjemənidz/ *Astronomy* an annual meteor shower with a radiant in the constellation Gemini, reaching a peak about December 13.

gem·ma /ˈjemə/ ▶*n.* (*pl.* **gem·mae** /ˈjemē/) *Biology* a small cellular body or bud that can separate to form a new organism. ■ another term for CHLAMYDOSPORE. ▷late 18th cent. (denoting a leaf bud, as distinct from a flower bud): from Latin, literally 'bud, jewel.'

gem·ma·tion /jeˈmāsHən/ ▶*n. Biology* asexual reproduction by the production of gemmae; budding. ▷mid 18th cent.: from French, from *gemmer* 'to bud,' from *gemme* 'bud,' from Latin *gemma*.

gem·mip·a·rous /jeˈmipərəs/ ▶*adj. Biology* (of a plant or animal) reproducing by gemmation. ▷late 18th cent.: from modern Latin *gemmiparus*, from Latin *gemma* 'bud, jewel' + *parere* 'produce, give birth to.'

gem·mule /ˈjemyo͞ol/ ▶*n. Zoology* a tough-coated dormant cluster of embryonic cells produced by a freshwater sponge for development in more favorable conditions. ▷mid 19th cent.: from French, from Latin *gemmula*, diminutive of *gemma* 'bud, jewel.' —**gem·mu·la·tion** /ˌjemyəˈlāsHən/ *n.*

gem·ol·o·gy /jeˈmäləjē/ (also **gem·mol·o·gy**) ▶*n.* the study of precious stones. ▷early 19th cent.: from Latin *gemma* 'bud, jewel' + -LOGY. —**gem·o·log·i·cal** /ˌjeməˈläjikəl/ *adj.* —**gem·ol·o·gist** /-jist/ *n.*

gems·bok /ˈgemzˌbäk/ ▶*n.* a large antelope that has a gray coat, distinctive black-and-white head markings, and long straight horns, native to southwestern and East Africa. • *Oryx gazella*, family Bovidae. See also ORYX. ▷late 18th cent.: via Afrikaans from Dutch, literally 'chamois,' from *gems* 'chamois' + *bok* 'buck.'

Gem State a nickname for IDAHO.

gem·stone /ˈjemˌstōn/ ▶*n.* a precious or semiprecious stone, esp. one cut, polished, and used in a piece of jewelry.

ge·müt·lich /gəˈmo͞otlik/ ▶*adj.* pleasant and cheerful. ▷mid 19th cent.: German.

ge·müt·lich·keit /gəˈmo͞otlikˌkīt/ (also **Ge·müt·lich·keit**) ▶*n.* geniality; friendliness. ▷mid 19th cent.: German.

Gen. ▶*abbr.* ■ General: *Gen. Eisenhower.* ■ *Bible* Genesis.

-gen ▶*comb. form* **1** *Chemistry* denoting a substance that produces something: *oxygen* | *allergen.* **2** *Botany* denoting a substance or plant that is produced: *cultigen.* ▷via French *-gène* from Greek *genēs* '-born, of a specified kind,' from *gen-* (root of *gignomai* 'be born, become,' *genos* 'a kind').

ge·na /ˈjēnə/ ▶*n.* (*pl.* **-nae** /-nē/) *Zoology* the lateral part of the head of an insect or other arthropod below the level of the eyes. ▷early 19th cent.: Latin, literally 'cheek.' —**ge·nal** *adj.*

gen·darme /ˈzHändärm/ ▶*n.* **1** an armed police officer in France and other French-speaking countries. **2** a rock pinnacle on a mountain, occupying and blocking an arête. ▷mid 16th cent. (originally denoting a mounted officer in the French army): French, from *gens d'armes* 'men of arms.' Sense 1 dates from the late 18th cent.

gen·dar·me·rie /zHänˈdärmərē/ ▶*n.* a force of gendarmes. ■ the headquarters of such a force. ▷mid 16th cent.: French (see GENDARME).

gen·der /ˈjendər/ ▶*n.* **1** *Grammar* (in languages such as Latin, Greek, Russian, and German) each of the classes (typically masculine, feminine, common, neuter) of nouns and pronouns distinguished by the different inflections that they have and require in words syntactically associated with them. Grammatical gender is only very loosely associated with natural distinctions of sex. ■ the property (in nouns and related words) of belonging to such a class: *adjectives usually agree with the noun in gender and number.* **2** the state of being male or female (typically used with reference to social and cultural differences rather than biological ones): *traditional concepts of gender* | [as *adj.*] *gender roles.* ■ the members of one or other sex: *differences between the genders are encouraged from an early age.* ▷late Middle English: from Old French *gendre* (modern *genre*), based on Latin *genus* 'birth, family, nation.' The earliest meanings were 'kind, sort, genus' and 'type or class of noun, etc.' (which was also a sense of Latin *genus*).

USAGE The word **gender** has been used since the 14th century primarily as a grammatical term, referring to the classes of noun in Latin, Greek, German, and other languages designated as *masculine, feminine,* or *neuter*. It has also been used since the 14th century in the sense 'the state of being male or female,' but this did not become a common standard use until the mid 20th century. Although the words **gender** and **sex** both have the sense 'the state of being male or female,' they are typically used in slightly different ways: **sex** tends to refer to biological differences, while **gender** tends to refer to cultural or social ones.

gen·der bend·er ▶*n. informal* **1** a person who dresses and behaves in a way characteristic of the opposite sex. **2** *Electronics* a device for changing an electrical or electronic connector from male to female, or from female to male.

gen·der chang·er ▶*n.* an electrical adaptor which allows two male or two female connectors to be connected to each other.

gen·der dys·pho·ri·a ▶*n. Medicine* the condition of feeling one's emotional and psychological identity as male or female to be opposite to one's biological sex. —**gen·der dys·phor·ic** *adj.* & *n.*

gen·dered /ˈjendərd/ ▶*adj.* of, specific to, or biased toward the male or female sex: *gendered occupations.*

gen·der gap ▶*n.* the discrepancy in opportunities, status, attitudes, etc., between men and women.

gen·der-neu·tral ▶*adj.* **1** denoting a word that cannot be taken to refer to one sex only, e.g., *firefighter* (as opposed to *fireman*). **2** (of language or a piece of writing) using gender-neutral words wherever appropriate.

gene /jēn/ ▶*n. Biology* (in informal use) a unit of heredity that is transferred from a parent to offspring and is held to determine some characteristic of the offspring: *proteins coded directly by genes.* ■ (in technical use) a distinct sequence of nucleotides forming part of a chromosome, the order of which determines the order of monomers in a polypeptide or nucleic acid molecule which a cell (or virus) may synthesize. ▷early 20th cent.: from German *Gen*, from *Pangen*, a supposed ultimate unit of heredity (from Greek *pan-* 'all' + *genos* 'race, kind, offspring').

ge·ne·a·log·i·cal /ˌjēnēəˈläjikəl/ ▶*adj.* of or relating to the study or tracing of lines of family descent: *genealogical research.* ▷late 16th cent.: from French *généalogique*, via medieval Latin from Greek *genealogikos*, from *genealogia* (see GENEALOGY). —**ge·ne·a·log·i·cal·ly** /-ik(ə)lē/ *adv.*

ge·ne·a·log·i·cal tree ▶*n.* a diagram showing the lines of descent of a human family or of an animal species, so named because its typical construction is like that of an inverted branching tree.

ge·ne·al·o·gy /ˌjēnēˈäləjē; -ˈal-/ ▶*n.* (*pl.* **-gies**) a line of descent traced continuously from an ancestor: *combing through the birth records and genealogies.* ■ the study and tracing of lines of descent or development. ■ a plant's or animal's line of evolutionary development from earlier forms. ▷Middle English: via Old French and late Latin from Greek *genealogia*, from *genea* 'race, generation' + *-logia* (see -LOGY). —**ge·ne·al·o·gist** /-jist/ *n.* —**ge·ne·al·o·gize** /-ˌjīz/ *v.*

gene-al·tered ▶*adj.* (especially in journalism) genetically modified: *the much ballyhooed, vine-ripened, gene-altered, rot-resistant tomato.*

gene am·pli·fi·ca·tion /ˌampləfiˈkāsHən/ ▶*n.* the multiple replication of a section of the genome, which occurs during a single cell cycle and results in the production of many copies of a specific sequence of the DNA molecule.

gene ex·pres·sion ▶*n.* see EXPRESSION (sense 1).

gene fre·quen·cy ▶*n.* the ratio of a particular allele to the total of all other alleles of the same gene in a given population.

gene map ▶*n.* **1** a record of the DNA sequence of a gene: *a cancer gene map.* **2** a genome map.

gene pool ▶*n.* the stock of different genes in an interbreeding population.

gen·er·a /ˈjenərə/ ▶ plural form of GENUS.

gen·er·al /ˈjenərəl/ ▶*adj.* **1** affecting or concerning all or most people, places, or things; widespread: *books of general interest.* See note at UNIVERSAL. ■ not specialized or limited in range of subject, application, activity, etc.: *brush up on your general knowledge.* ■ (of a rule, principle, etc.) true for all or most cases. ■ normal or usual: *it is not general practice to confirm or deny such reports.* **2** considering or including the main features or elements of something, and disregarding exceptions; overall: *they fired in the general direction of the enemy* | *a general introduction to the subject.* **3** [often in *titles*] chief or principal: *a general manager.*
▶*n.* **1** a commander of an army, or an army officer of very high rank. ■ an officer in the U.S. Army, Air Force, or Marine Corps ranking above lieutenant general. ■ the head of a religious order organized on quasi-military lines, e.g., the Jesuits, the Dominicans, or the Salvation Army. **2** (**the general**) *archaic* the general public. ▷Middle English: via Old French from Latin *generalis*, from *genus, gener-* 'class, race, kind.' The noun primarily denotes a person having overall authority: the sense 'army commander' is an abbreviation of *captain general*, from French *capitaine général* 'commander in chief.'
▶***PHRASES*** □ **as a general rule** in most cases. □ **in general 1** usually; mainly: *in general, Alexander was a peaceful, loving man.* **2** as a whole: *our understanding of culture in general and of literature in particular.*

Gen·er·al A·mer·i·can ▶*n.* (in nontechnical use) the variety of English spoken in the greater part of the U.S., particularly with reference to the lack of regional characteristics.

gen·er·al an·es·the·sia ▶*n.* anesthesia that affects the whole body and usually induces a loss of consciousness: *he had the operation* ***under general anesthesia.*** Compare with LOCAL ANESTHESIA.

Gen·er·al Bap·tist ▶*n.* a member of an Arminian Baptist congregation who rejects the Calvinist doctrine of predestination. Compare with PARTICULAR BAPTISTS

gen·er·al court-mar·tial ▶*n.* a court-martial for trying serious offenses, consisting of at least five officers with the authority to impose a sentence of dishonorable discharge or death.

gen·er·al·cy /ˈjenərəlsē/ ▶*n.* the rank, office, or tenure of a general.

gen·er·al de·liv·er·y ▶*n.* mail delivery to a post office for pickup by the addressee.

gen·er·al e·lec·tion ▶*n.* a regular election of candidates for office, as opposed to a primary election. ■ a regular election for statewide or national offices.

gen·er·al e·quiv·a·len·cy de·gree (also **gen·er·al e·quiv·a·len·cy di·plo·ma**) (abbr.: **GED**) ▶*n.* a diploma signifying high school graduation, awarded to those who successfully complete a required examination.

gen·er·al head·quar·ters ▶*n.* [treated as *sing.* or *pl.*] the headquarters of a military commander.

gen·er·al·is·si·mo /ˌjenərəˈlisəˌmō/ ▶*n.* (*pl.* **-mos**) the commander of a combined military force consisting of army, navy, and air force units. ▷early 17th cent.:

Italian, 'having greatest authority,' superlative of *generale* (see **GENERAL**).

gen·er·al·ist /'jenərəlist/ ▸*n.* a person competent in several different fields or activities: *with a generalist's education and some specific skills.*
▸*adj.* able to carry out a range of activities, or adapt to different situations: *a generalist doctor.*

gen·er·al·i·ty /,jenə'ralitē/ ▸*n.* (*pl.* **-ties**) **1** a statement or principle having general rather than specific validity or force: *he confined his remarks to generalities.* ■ the quality or state of being general: *policy should be formulated at an appropriate level of generality.* **2** (**the generality**) the majority: *appropriate to the generality of laymen.* ▷late Middle English: from Old French *generalite*, from late Latin *generalitas*, from *generalis* (see **GENERAL**).

gen·er·al·i·za·tion /,jenərəli'zāsHən/ ▸*n.* a general statement or concept obtained by inference from specific cases: *he was making sweeping generalizations.* ■ the action of generalizing: *such anecdotes cannot be a basis for generalization.*

gen·er·al·ize /'jenərə,līz/ ▸*v.* **1** [*intrans.*] infer general principles from specific cases: *it is tempting to generalize from these conclusions.* ■ make general or broad statements: *it is not easy to* **generalize about** *the poor.* ■ make or become more widely or generally applicable: [*trans.*] *most of what we have observed in this field can be generalized to other fields* | [*intrans.*] *many of the results generalize to multibody structures.* **2** [*trans.*] make (something) more widespread or common: *attempts to generalize an elite education.* ■ make for wide general use or application: [as *adj.*] (**generalized**) *generalized information pertinent to anyone.* ■ [as *adj.*] (**generalized**) *Medicine* (of a disease) affecting much or all of the body; not localized: *a generalized rash and fever.* ▷Middle English (in the sense 'reduce to a general statement'): from **GENERAL** + **-IZE**. —**gen·er·al·iz·a·bil·i·ty** /,jenərə,līzə'bilitē/ *n.* —**gen·er·al·iz·a·ble** *adj.* —**gen·er·al·iz·er** *n.*

gen·er·al·ly /'jenərəlē/ ▸*adv.* **1** [*sentence adverb*] in most cases; usually: *the term of a lease is generally 99 years.* **2** in general terms; without regard to particulars or exceptions: *a decade when France was moving generally to the left.* **3** widely: *the best scheme is generally reckoned to be the Canadian one.*

gen·er·al meet·ing ▸*n.* a meeting open to all members of an organization.

gen·er·al of·fi·cer ▸*n.* an officer ranking above colonel in the U.S. Army, Air Force, or Marine Corps.

gen·er·al of the air force ▸*n.* an officer of the highest rank in the U.S. Air Force, ranking above general (awarded only in wartime).

gen·er·al of the ar·my ▸*n.* an officer of the highest rank in the U.S. Army, above general (awarded only in wartime).

gen·er·al prac·ti·tion·er (abbr.: **GP**) ▸*n.* a medical doctor who is trained to provide primary health care to patients of either sex and any age.

gen·er·al-pur·pose ▸*adj.* having a range of potential uses; not specialized in function or design: *a general-purpose detergent.*

Ge·ne·ral San Mar·tín /,KHānā'räl ,sän mär'tēn/ (also **San Martín**) a city in eastern Argentina, northwest of Buenos Aires; pop. 408,000.

Ge·ne·ral San·tos /,KHānā'räl 'säntōs/ (also called **Dadiangas**) a port city in the Philippines, on southern Mindanao Island, on Saragani Bay; pop. 250,000.

Ge·ne·ral Sar·mien·to /,KHānā'räl ,sär'myentō/ (also **Sar·mien·to** or **San Mi·guel**) a city in eastern Argentina, west of Buenos Aires; pop. 647,000.

gen·er·al se·man·tics ▸*plural n.* [usu. treated as *sing.*] a system of linguistic philosophy developed by Alfred Korzybski (1879–1950), which explores the arbitrary nature of words and symbols and attempts to refine ways of using language.

gen·er·al·ship /'jenərəl,sHip/ ▸*n.* the skill or practice of exercising military command.

gen·er·al staff ▸*n.* [treated as *sing.* or *pl.*] the staff assisting a military commander in planning and executing operations.

gen·er·al strike ▸*n.* a strike of workers in all or most industries.

Gen·er·al Syn·od ▸*n.* the highest governing body of the Church of England, an elected assembly of three houses (bishops, clergy, and laity).

gen·er·al the·o·ry of rel·a·tiv·i·ty ▸*n.* see **RELATIVITY** (sense 2).

gen·er·ate /'jenə,rāt/ ▸*v.* [*trans.*] cause (something, esp. an emotion or situation) to arise or come about: *changes that are likely to generate controversy* | *generate more jobs in the economy.* ■ produce (energy, esp. electricity). ■ produce (a set or sequence of items) by performing specified mathematical or logical operations on an initial set. ■ *Linguistics* produce (a sentence or other unit, esp. a well-formed one) by the application of a finite set of rules to lexical or other linguistic input. ■ *Mathematics* form (a line, surface, or solid) by notionally moving a point, line, or surface. ▷early 16th cent. (in the sense 'beget, procreate'): from Latin *generat-* 'created,' from the verb *generare*, from *genus*, *gener-* 'stock, race.' —**gen·er·a·ble** /'jenərəbəl/ *adj.*

gen·er·a·tion /,jenə'rāsHən/ ▸*n.* **1** all of the people born and living at about the same time, regarded collectively: *one of his generation's finest songwriters.* ■ the average period, generally considered to be about thirty years, during which children are born and grow up, become adults, and begin to have children of their own. ■ a set of members of a family regarded as a single step or stage in descent: [as *adj.*, in *combination*] *a third-generation Canadian.* ■ a single stage in the development of a type of product: *a new generation of rear-engined sports cars.* **2** the production of something: *methods of electricity generation* | *the generation of wealth.* ■ the propagation of living organisms; procreation. ▷Middle English: via Old French from Latin *generatio(n-)*, from the verb *generare* (see **GENERATE**). —**gen·er·a·tion·al** /-sHənl/ *adj.* —**gen·er·a·tion·al·ly** /-sHənl-ē/ *adv.*

gen·er·a·tion gap ▸*n.* (usu. **the generation gap**) differences of outlook or opinion between people of different generations.

gen·er·a·tion-skip·ping tax (abbr. **GST**) ▸*n.* an estate tax imposed on beneficiaries who are two or more generations removed from the testator: *a married couple has a total generation-skipping tax exemption of transfers of up to $2,000,000.*

Gen·er·a·tion X ▸*n.* the generation born after that of the baby boomers (roughly from the early 1960s to mid 1970s), often perceived to be disaffected and directionless. —**Gen·er·a·tion X·er** /'eksər/ *n.*

gen·er·a·tive /'jenərətiv; -,rātiv;/ ▸*adj.* of or relating to reproduction. ■ able to produce: *the generative power of the life force.* ■ *Linguistics* applying principles of generative grammar. ▷late Middle English: from late Latin *generativus*, from *generare* 'beget' (see **GENERATE**).

gen·er·a·tive cell ▸*n.* a reproductive cell, esp. a cell of an angiosperm pollen grain that divides to produce two male gamete nuclei.

gen·er·a·tive gram·mar ▸*n.* *Linguistics* a type of grammar that describes a language in terms of a set of logical rules formulated so as to be capable of generating the infinite number of possible sentences of that language and providing them with the correct structural description. ■ a set of rules of this kind.

gen·er·a·tor /'jenə,rātər/ ▸*n.* a thing that generates something, in particular: ■ a dynamo or similar machine for converting mechanical energy into electricity. ■ an apparatus for producing gas, steam, or another product. ■ a facility that generates electrical power. ■ [with *adj.*] *Computing* a routine that constructs other routines or subroutines using given parameters, for specific applications: *a report generator.* ■ *Mathematics* a point, line, or surface regarded as moving and so notionally forming a line, surface, or solid.

gen·er·a·trix /,jenə'rātriks/ ▸*n.* (*pl.* **-tri·ces** /-trə,sēz/) *Mathematics* another term for **GENERATOR**. ▷mid 19th cent.: from Latin (feminine).

ge·ner·ic /jə'nerik/ ▸*adj.* **1** characteristic of or relating to a class or group of things; not specific: *chèvre is a generic term for all goat's milk cheese.* See note at **UNIVERSAL**. ■ (of goods, esp. medicinal drugs) having no brand name; not protected by a registered trademark: *generic aspirin.* **2** *Biology* of or relating to a genus.
▸*n.* a consumer product having no brand name or registered trademark: *substituting generics for brand-name drugs.* ▷late 17th cent.: from French *générique*, from Latin *genus*, *gener-* 'stock, race.' —**ge·ner·i·cal·ly** /-ik(ə)lē/ *adv.*

gen·er·os·i·ty /,jenə'räsitē/ ▸*n.* the quality of being kind and generous: *I was overwhelmed by the generosity of friends and neighbors.* ■ the quality or fact of being plentiful or large: *diners certainly cannot complain about the generosity of portions.* ▷late Middle English (denoting nobility of birth): from Latin *generositas*, from *generosus* 'magnanimous' (see **GENEROUS**). Current senses date from the 17th cent.

gen·er·ous /'jenərəs/ ▸*adj.* (of a person) showing a readiness to give more of something, as money or time, than is strictly necessary or expected: *she was* **generous with** *her money.* ■ showing kindness toward others: *it was generous of them to ask her along.* ■ (of a thing) larger or more plentiful than is usual or necessary: *a generous sprinkle of pepper.* ▷late 16th cent.: via Old French from Latin *generosus* 'noble, magnanimous,' from *genus*, *gener-* 'stock, race.' The original sense was 'of noble birth,' hence 'characteristic of noble birth, courageous, magnanimous, not mean' (a sense already present in Latin). —**gen·er·ous·ly** *adv.* —**gen·er·ous·ness** *n.*

Gen·e·see Riv·er /,jenə'sē; 'jenə,sē/ a river that flows for 144 miles (232 km) from northwestern Pennsylvania through western New York into Lake Ontario at Rochester.

Gen·e·sis /'jenəsis/ the first book of the Bible, which includes the stories of the creation of the world, Noah's Ark, the Tower of Babel, and the patriarchs Abraham, Isaac, Jacob, and Joseph. ▷late Old English, via Latin from Greek, 'generation, creation, nativity, horoscope,' from the base of *gignesthai* 'be born or produced.' The name was given to the first book of the Old Testament in the Greek translation (the Septuagint), hence in the Latin translation (the Vulgate).

gen·e·sis /'jenəsis/ ▸*n.* [in *sing.*] the origin or mode of formation of something: *this tale had its genesis in fireside stories.* ▷early 17th cent.: from Greek (see **GENESIS**).

Ge·net /jə'nā/, Jean (1910–86), French novelist, poet, and playwright. Much of his work portrayed life in the criminal and homosexual underworlds, of which he was a part. Notable works: *Our Lady of the Flowers* (novel, 1944), *The Maids* (play, 1947), and *The Thief's Journal* (autobiography, 1949).

gen·et[1] /'jenit/ ▸*n.* a nocturnal, catlike mammal of the civet family with short legs, spotted fur, and a long bushy ringed tail, found in Africa, southwestern Europe, and Arabia. • Genus *Genetta*, family Viverridae: several species, in particular the **common** (or **small-spotted**) **genet** (*G. genetta*). ■ the fur of the genet. ▷Middle English (used in the plural meaning 'genet skins'): from Old French *genete*, probably via Catalan, Portuguese, or Spanish from Arabic *jarnaiṭ*.

gen·et[2] /'jenit/ ▸*n.* another term for **JENNET** (sense 2).

gene ther·a·py ▸*n.* the transplantation of normal genes into cells in place of missing or defective ones in order to correct genetic disorders.

ge·net·ic /jə'netik/ ▸*adj.* **1** of or relating to genes or heredity: *all the cells in the body contain the same genetic information.* ■ of or relating to genetics: *an attempt to control mosquitoes by genetic techniques.* **2** of or relating to origin; arising from a common origin: *the genetic relations between languages.* ▷mid 19th cent. (sense 2): from **GENESIS**, on the pattern of pairs such as *antithesis*, *antithetic*. —**ge·net·i·cal** *adj.* —**ge·net·i·cal·ly** /-ik(ə)lē/ *adv.*

ge·net·i·cal·ly mod·i·fied /jə'netik(ə)lē 'mädə,fīd/ (abbreviation: **GM**) ▸*adj.* (of an organism or crop) containing genetic material that has been artificially altered so as to produce a desired characteristic: *genetically modified viruses to insert new genes into growing plants.*

ge·net·ic blue·print ▸*n.* (not in technical use) a gene map, or a genome map.

ge·net·ic code ▸*n.* the nucleotide triplets of DNA and RNA molecules that carry genetic information in living cells. See **TRIPLET CODE**.

ge·net·ic coun·sel·ing ▸*n.* the giving of advice to prospective parents concerning the chances of genetic disorders in a future child.

ge·net·ic drift ▸*n.* *Biology* variation in the relative frequency of different genotypes in a small population, owing to the chance disappearance of particular genes as individuals die or do not reproduce.

ge·net·ic en·gi·neer·ing ▸*n.* the deliberate modification of the characteristics of an organism by manipulating its genetic material.

ge·net·ic fin·ger·print·ing (also **genetic profiling**) ▸*n.* another term for **DNA FINGERPRINTING**.

ge·net·ic load ▸*n.* *Biology* the presence of unfavorable genetic material in the genes of a population.

ge·net·ic map ▸*n.* a graphic representation of a chromosome including the position of its genes. —**ge·net·ic map·ping** *n.*

ge·net·ic mark·er ▸*n.* a gene or short sequence of

DNA used to identify a chromosome or to locate other genes on a genetic map.

ge·net·ic pol·lu·tion ▸*n.* the spread of altered genes from genetically engineered organisms to other, nonengineered organisms, especially by cross-pollination.

ge·net·ics /jəˈnetiks/ ▸*plural n.* [treated as *sing.*] the study of heredity and the variation of inherited characteristics. ■ [treated as *sing.* or *pl.*] the genetic properties or features of an organism, characteristic, etc.: *the effects of family genetics on the choice of career.* —**ge·net·i·cist** /-ˈnetəsist/ *n.*

ge·net·ic test·ing ▸*n.* the sequencing of human DNA in order to discover genetic differences, anomalies, or mutations that may prove pathological: *genetic testing to identify HLA status in the fetuses of 49 couples considered at risk.*

Ge·ne·va /jəˈnēvə/ a city in southwestern Switzerland, on Lake Geneva; pop. 167,000. It is headquarters of international bodies such as the Red Cross, various organizations of the United Nations, and the World Health Organization. French name **GENÈVE**.

Ge·ne·va, Lake a lake in southwestern central Europe, between the Jura Mountains and the Alps. Its southern shore forms part of the border between France and Switzerland. French name **LAC LÉMAN**.

Ge·ne·va bands ▸*plural n.* two white cloth strips attached to the collar of some Protestants' clerical dress. ▷late 19th cent.: from the place name **GENEVA**, where they were originally worn by Calvinists.

Ge·ne·va Bi·ble ▸*n.* an English translation of the Bible published in 1560 by Protestant scholars working in Europe.

Ge·ne·va Con·ven·tion an international agreement first made at Geneva in 1864 and later revised, governing the status and treatment of captured and wounded military personnel and civilians in wartime.

Ge·ne·va cross ▸*n.* a red cross on a white background, used to identify medical equipment and facilities, esp. in war, and as a sign of neutrality.

Ge·ne·va Pro·to·col any of various protocols drawn up in Geneva, esp. that of 1925 limiting chemical and bacteriological warfare.

Ge·nève /ZHəˈnev; -ˈnāv/ French name for **GENEVA**.

ge·ne·ver /jəˈnēvər/ (also *poetic/literary* **ge·ne·va** /-ˈnēvə/) ▸*n.* Dutch gin. ▷early 18th cent.: from Dutch, from Old French *genevre*, from an alteration of Latin *juniperus* (gin being flavored with juniper berries). The variant spelling is due to association with **GENEVA**.

Gen·ghis Khan /ˌgeNGgis ˈkän; ˌjeNG-/ (1162–1227), founder of the Mongol empire; born *Temujin.* He took the name Genghis Khan ("ruler of all") in 1206 after uniting the nomadic Mongol tribes. When he died, his empire extended from China to the Black Sea. His grandson Kublai Khan completed the conquest of China.

ge·ni·al[1] /ˈjēnyəl; -nēəl/ ▸*adj.* friendly and cheerful: *waved to them in genial greeting.* ■ (esp. of air or climate) pleasantly mild and warm. ▷mid 16th cent.: from Latin *genialis* 'nuptial, productive,' from *genius* (see **GENIUS**). The Latin sense was adopted into English; hence the senses 'mild and conducive to growth' (mid 17th cent.), later 'cheerful, kindly' (mid 18th cent.). —**ge·ni·al·i·ty** /ˌjēnēˈalitē/ *n.* —**gen·ial·ly** *adv.*

ge·ni·al[2] ▸*adj. Anatomy, rare* of or relating to the chin. ▷mid 19th cent.: from Greek *geneion* 'chin' (from *genus* 'jaw') + **-AL**.

gen·ic /ˈjenik/ ▸*adj.* [*attrib.*] *Biology* of or relating to genes: *a genic mutation.*

-genic ▸*comb. form* **1** producing: *carcinogenic.* ■ produced by: *iatrogenic.* **2** well suited to: *mediagenic.* [on the pattern of words such as *(photo)genic.*] ▷from **-GEN** + **-IC**.

-genically ▸*suffix* forming adverbs corresponding to adjectives ending in *-genical,* (such as *iatrogenically* corresponding to *iatrogenic*).

ge·nic·u·late /jəˈnikyəlit; -ˌlāt/ ▸*adj. Anatomy* bent at a sharp angle. ▷mid 17th cent.: from Latin *geniculatus*, from *geniculum* 'small knee, joint (of a plant).'

ge·nic·u·late bod·y (also **geniculate nucleus**) ▸*n. Anatomy* either of two protuberances on the inferior surface of the thalamus that relay auditory and visual impulses respectively to the cerebral cortex.

ge·nie /ˈjēnē/ ▸*n.* (*pl.* **-nies** or **-ni·i** /-nēˌī/) a spirit of Arabian folklore, as traditionally depicted imprisoned within a bottle or oil lamp, and capable of granting wishes when summoned. Compare with **JINN**. ▷mid 17th cent. (denoting a guardian or protective spirit): from French *génie*, from Latin *genius* (see **GENIUS**). *Génie* was adopted in the current sense by the 18th-cent. French translators of *The Arabian Nights' Entertainments*, because of its resemblance in form and sense to Arabic *jinnī* 'jinni.'

ge·ni·i /ˈjēnēˌī/ ▸ plural form of **GENIE, GENIUS**.

ge·nip /gəˈnip/ ▸*n.* **1** the edible fruit of a tropical American tree. **2** (also **gen·i·pap tree** /ˈjenəˌpap/) either of two tropical American trees that yield this fruit: • (also **gui·nep** /giˈnep/) a large spreading tree (*Melicoccus bijugatus*, family Sapindaceae). • another term for **GENIPAPO**. ▷mid 18th cent.: from American Spanish *quenepo* 'guinep tree,' *quenepa*, denoting the fruit.

gen·i·pa·po /ˌjenəˈpapō/ (also **gen·i·pap tree** /ˈjenəˌpap/) ▸*n.* a tropical American tree of the bedstraw family that yields useful timber. Its fruit has a jelly-like pulp that is used for flavoring drinks and to make a black dye. Also called **GENIP**. • *Genipa americana*, family Rubiaceae. ■ a drink, flavoring, or dye made from this fruit. ▷early 17th cent.: from Portuguese *jenipapo*, from Tupi.

genit. ▸*abbr. Grammar* genitive.

gen·i·tal /ˈjenitl/ ▸*adj.* of or relating to the human or animal reproductive organs: *conditions of the lower genital tract.* ■ *Psychoanalysis* (in Freudian theory) relating to or denoting the final stage of psychosexual development reached in adulthood.
▸*n.* (**genitals**) a person or animal's external organs of reproduction. ▷late Middle English: from Old French, or from Latin *genitalis*, from *genitus*, past participle of *gignere* 'beget.'

gen·i·tal her·pes ▸*n.* a disease characterized by blisters in the genital area, caused by a variety of the herpes simplex virus.

gen·i·ta·li·a /ˌjeniˈtālēə; -ˈtālyə/ ▸*plural n. formal* or *technical* the genitals. ▷late 19th cent.: from Latin, neuter plural of *genitalis* (see **GENITAL**).

gen·i·tal wart ▸*n.* a small growth occurring in the anal or genital areas, caused by a virus that is spread esp. by sexual contact.

gen·i·tive /ˈjenitiv/ *Grammar* ▸*adj.* relating to or denoting a case of nouns and pronouns (and words in grammatical agreement with them) indicating possession or close association.
▸*n.* a word in the genitive case. ■ (**the genitive**) the genitive case. ▷late Middle English: from Old French *genitif, -ive* or Latin *genitivus (casus)* '(case) of production or origin,' from *gignere* 'beget.' —**gen·i·ti·val** /ˌjeniˈtīvəl/ *adj.* —**gen·i·ti·val·ly** /ˌjeniˈtīvəlē/ *adv.*

gen·i·tor /ˈjenitər/ ▸*n. Anthropology* a person's biological father. Often contrasted with **PATER**. ▷late Middle English (in the sense 'father'): from Old French *geniteur* or Latin *genitor*, from the root of *gignere* 'beget.' The current sense dates from the mid 20th cent.

gen·i·to·u·ri·nar·y /ˌjenitōˈyŏŏrəˌnerē/ ▸*adj.* [*attrib.*] *chiefly Medicine* of or relating to the genital and urinary organs.

gen·i·ture /ˈjeniCHər; -ˌCHŏŏrCHgettysbur/ ▸*n. archaic* a person's birth or parentage. ▷late Middle English: from Old French *geniture* or Latin *genitura*, from the root of *gignere* 'beget.'

gen·ius /ˈjēnyəs/ ▸*n.* (*pl.* **gen·ius·es**) **1** exceptional intellectual or creative power or other natural ability: *she was a teacher of genius | Gardner had a real* **genius for** *tapping wealth.* **2** a person who is exceptionally intelligent or creative, either generally or in some particular respect: *one of the great musical geniuses of the 20th century.* **3** (*pl.* **gen·i·i** /ˈjēnēˌī/) (in some mythologies) a guardian spirit associated with a person, place, or institution. ■ a person regarded as exerting a powerful influence over another for good or evil: *he sees Adams as the man's evil genius.* **4** (*pl.* **gen·i·i**) the prevalent character or spirit of something such as a nation or age: *Boucher's paintings did not suit the austere genius of neoclassicism.* ▷late Middle English: from Latin, 'attendant spirit present from one's birth, innate ability or inclination,' from the root of *gignere* 'beget.' The original sense 'tutelary spirit attendant on a person' gave rise to a sense 'a person's characteristic disposition' (late 16th cent.), which led to a sense 'a person's natural ability,' and finally 'exceptional natural ability' (mid 17th cent.).

ge·ni·us lo·ci /ˈjēnēəs ˈlōsī; -kī/ ▸*n.* [in *sing.*] the prevailing character or atmosphere of a place. ■ the presiding god or spirit of a place. ▷early 17th cent.: Latin, literally 'spirit of the place.'

genl. ▸*abbr.* general.

gen·lock /ˈjenˌläk/ ▸*n.* a device for maintaining synchronization between two different video signals, or between a video signal and a computer or audio signal, enabling video images and computer graphics to be mixed.
▸*v.* [*intrans.*] maintain synchronization between two signals using the genlock technique. ▷1960s: from **GENERATOR** + the verb **LOCK**[1].

Gen·o·a /ˈjenō-ə/ a seaport on the northwestern coast of Italy, capital of Liguria region; pop. 701,000. It was the birthplace of Christopher Columbus. Italian name **GENOVA**. —**Gen·o·ese** /ˌjenōˈēz; -ˈēs/ *adj.* & *n.*

gen·o·a /ˈjenō-ə/ ▸*n.* (also **genoa jib**) *Sailing* a large jib or foresail whose foot extends aft of the mast, used esp. on racing yachts. ▷late 19th cent.: so named because of association with the city of **GENOA**.

gen·o·cide /ˈjenəˌsīd/ ▸*n.* the deliberate killing of a large group of people, esp. those of a particular ethnic group or nation. ▷1940s: from Greek *genos* 'race' + **-CIDE**. —**gen·o·cid·al** /ˌjenəˈsīdl/ *adj.*

ge·noise /ZHəˈnwäz/ ▸ *n.* a sponge cake with melted butter incorporated into the batter: *the genoise au chocolat paired moist cake layers with a truffle-like filling.*

ge·nome /ˈjēˌnōm/ ▸*n. Biology* the haploid set of chromosomes in a gamete or microorganism, or in each cell of a multicellular organism. ■ the complete set of genes or genetic material present in a cell or organism. ▷1930s: blend of **GENE** and **CHROMOSOME**. —**ge·no·mic** /jēˈnämik; -ˈnō-; ji-/ *adj.*

ge·nome map ▸*n.* a record of the entire genome of an organism, consisting of correctly ordered gene maps.

ge·no·mics /jēˈnōmiks; -ˈnäm-/, ▸*plural n.* [treated as *sing.*] the branch of molecular biology concerned with the structure, function, evolution, and mapping of genomes. ▷1980s: from *genome* 'the complete set of genes present in an organism' + *-ics*.

gen·o·type /ˈjenəˌtīp; ˈjē-/ ▸*n. Biology* the genetic constitution of an individual organism. Often contrasted with **PHENOTYPE**.
▸*v.* [*trans.*] investigate the genetic constitution of (an individual organism): *the person appointed will be responsible for maintaining and genotyping many different lines of zebra fish.* ▷early 20th cent.: from German *Genotypus*, from Greek *genos* 'race, offspring' + *-tupos* 'type.' —**gen·o·typ·ic** /ˌjenəˈtipik; ˌjē-/ *adj.*

-genous ▸*comb. form* **1** producing; inducing: *erogenous.* **2** originating in: *endogenous.* ▷from **-GEN** + **-OUS**.

Ge·no·va /ˈjenəvə/ Italian name for **GENOA**.

gen·re /ˈZHänrə/ ▸*n.* a category of artistic composition, as in music or literature, characterized by similarities in form, style, or subject matter. ▷early 19th cent.: French, literally 'a kind' (see **GENDER**).

gen·re paint·ing ▸*n.* a style of painting depicting scenes from ordinary life, esp. domestic situations. Genre painting is associated particularly with 17th-century Dutch and Flemish artists. —**gen·re paint·er** *n.*

gens /jenz/ ▸*n.* (*pl.* **gen·tes** /ˈjentēz/) **1** a group of families in ancient Rome who shared a name and claimed a common origin. **2** *Anthropology* a group of people who are related through their male ancestors. ▷Latin, from the root of *gignere* 'beget.'

Gent /KHent/ Flemish name for **GHENT**.

gent /jent/ ▸*n. informal* a gentleman. ■ (**the Gents**) *Brit.* a men's public toilet. ▷mid 16th cent.: originally a standard written abbreviation; a colloquial usage since the early 19th cent.

gen·ta·mi·cin /ˌjentəˈmīsin/ ▸*n.* a broad-spectrum antibiotic used chiefly for severe systemic infections. • This antibiotic is derived from bacteria of the genus *Micromonospora.* ▷mid 20th cent.: from *genta-* (of unknown origin) + *-micin* (alteration of **-MYCIN**).

gen·teel /jenˈtēl/ ▸*adj.* polite, refined, or respectable, often in an affected or ostentatious way. See note at **URBANE**. ▷late 16th cent. (in the sense 'fashionable, stylish'): from French *gentil* 'well-born.' From the 17th cent. to the 19th cent. the word was used in such senses as 'of good social position,' 'having the manners of a well-born person,' 'well-bred.' The ironic or derogatory implication dates from the 19th cent. —**gen·teel·ly** *adv.* —**gen·teel·ness** *n.*

gen·teel·ism /jenˈtēlizəm/ ▸*n.* a word or expression used because it is thought to be socially more acceptable than the everyday word: *in German usage "sister" was the accepted genteelism for "mistress."*

gen·tes /ˈjentēz/ ▸ plural form of **GENS**.

gen·tian /ˈjenCHən/ ▸*n.* a plant of temperate and mountainous regions, typically with violet or vivid blue trumpet-shaped flowers. Many kinds are cultivated as ornamentals, esp. as arctic alpines, and some are of medicinal use. • Genera *Gentiana* and

G

Gentianella, family Gentianaceae: numerous species, including the four-petaled **fringed gentian** (*Gentiana crinita*) of North America. ■ a tonic liquor formerly extracted from the root of the gentian. ▷late Middle English: from Latin *gentiana*, according to Pliny named after *Gentius*, king of Illyria, who is said to have discovered the medicinal properties of a common species.

fringed gentian

gen·tian vi·o·let ▶*n.* a synthetic violet dye derived from rosaniline, used as an antiseptic.

gen·tile /ˈjentīl/ ▶*adj.* **1** (**Gentile**) not Jewish: *Christianity spread from Jewish into Gentile cultures.* ■ (of a person) not belonging to one's own religious community. ■ (in the Mormon church) non-Mormon. **2** *chiefly Anthropology* of, relating to, or indicating a nation or clan, esp. a gens.
▶*n.* (**Gentile**) a person who is not Jewish. ▷late Middle English: from Latin *gentilis* 'of a family or nation, of the same clan' (used in the Vulgate to refer to non-Jews), from *gens*, *gent-* 'family, race,' from the root of *gignere* 'beget.'

Gen·ti·le da Fa·bri·a·no /jenˈtēlā də ˌfäbrēˈänō/ (*c.*1370–1427), Italian painter. His major surviving work is *The Adoration of the Magi* (1423), an altarpiece.

gen·til·i·ty /jenˈtilitē/ ▶*n.* social superiority as demonstrated by genteel manners, behavior, or appearances: *her grandmother's pretensions to gentility.* ■ genteel manners, behavior, or appearances. ▷Middle English (in the sense 'honorable birth'): from Old French *gentilite*, from *gentil* (see GENTLE).

gen·tle /ˈjentl/ ▶*adj.* (**gen·tler**, **gen·tlest**) **1** (of a person) mild in temperament or behavior; kind or tender: *he was a gentle, sensitive man.* ■ *archaic* (of a person) noble or having the qualities attributed to noble birth; courteous; chivalrous. **2** moderate in action, effect, or degree; not harsh or severe: *a little gentle persuasion* | *a gentle breeze.* ■ (of a slope) gradual: *a gentle embankment.*
▶*v.* make or become gentle; calm or pacify: [*intrans.*] *Cobb's tone gentled a little.* ■ [*trans.*] touch gently: *her lips were gentling his cheek.* ■ [*trans.*] make (an animal) docile by gentle handling: *a bird that has been gentled enough to sit on the hand.* ▷Middle English: from Old French *gentil* 'highborn, noble,' from Latin *gentilis* 'of the same clan' (see GENTILE). The original sense was 'nobly born,' hence 'courteous, chivalrous,' later 'mild, moderate in action or disposition' (mid 16th cent.). —**gen·tle·ness** *n.* —**gen·tly** /-tlē/ *adv.*

gen·tle breeze ▶*n.* a light wind of force 3 on the Beaufort scale (7–10 knots or 8–12 mph).

gent·le·folk /ˈjentl͵fōk/ ▶*plural n. archaic* people of high social position.

gen·tle·la·dy ▶*n.* a polite form of a address for a woman, used esp. to a congresswoman during a congressional debate.

gent·le·man /ˈjentlmən/ ▶*n.* (*pl.* **-men**) **1** a chivalrous, courteous, or honorable man: *he behaved like a perfect gentleman.* ■ a man of good social position, esp. one of wealth and leisure. ■ (in the UK) a man of noble birth attached to a royal household. **2** a polite or formal way of referring to a man: *opposite her an old gentleman sat reading.* ■ (**gentlemen**) used as a polite form of address to a group of men: *"Can I help you, gentlemen?"* ■ used as a courteous designation for a male fellow member of the U.S. House of Representatives. ▷Middle English (in the sense 'man of noble birth'): from GENTLE + MAN, translating Old French *gentilz hom.* In later use the term denoted a man of a good family (esp. one entitled to a coat of arms) but not of the nobility.

gen·tle·man-at-arms ▶*n.* (*pl.* **gen·tle·men-at-arms**) one of the bodyguards of the British monarch on ceremonial occasions.

gen·tle·man farm·er ▶*n.* (*pl.* **gen·tle·men farm·ers**) a well-to-do man who runs a farm for pleasure.

gen·tle·man·ly /ˈjentlmənlē/ ▶*adj.* (of a man) befitting a gentleman; chivalrous, courteous, or honorable: *a paragon of gentlemanly conduct.* —**gen·tle·man·li·ness** *n.*

gen·tle·man's a·gree·ment (also **gen·tle·men's a·gree·ment**) ▶*n.* an arrangement or understanding which is based upon the trust of both or all parties, rather than being legally binding.

gen·tle·man's gen·tle·man ▶*n.* a valet.

gen·tle·peo·ple ▶*plural n.* a polite or formal way of addressing or referring to a group of people.

gen·tle·wom·an /ˈjentl͵wo͝omən/ ▶*n.* (*pl.* **-wom·en**) *archaic* a woman of high social standing.

gen·too /ˈjento͞o/ (also **gentoo penguin**) ▶*n.* a tall penguin with a white triangular patch above the eye, breeding on subantarctic islands. • *Pygoscelis papua*, family Spheniscidae. ▷mid 19th cent.: perhaps from Anglo-Indian *Gentoo* 'a Hindu,' from Portuguese *gentio* 'gentile.'

gen·tri·fy /ˈjentrə͵fī/ ▶*v.* (**-fies**, **-fied**) [*trans.*] renovate and improve (esp. a house or district) so that it conforms to middle-class taste. ■ [usu. as *adj.*] (**gentrified**) make (someone or their way of life) more refined or dignified. —**gen·tri·fi·ca·tion** /͵jentrəfiˈkāshən/ *n.* —**gen·tri·fi·er** *n.*

gen·try /ˈjentrē/ ▶*n.* (often **the gentry**) people of good social position, specifically (in the UK) the class of people next below the nobility in position and birth: *a member of the landed gentry.* ■ [with *adj.*] people of a specified class or group: *a New Orleans family of Creole gentry.* ▷late Middle English (in the sense 'superiority of birth or rank'): from Anglo-Norman French *genterie*, based on *gentil* (see GENTLE).

ge·nu /ˈjēn(y)o͞o; ˈjen(y)o͞o/ ▶*n.* (*pl.* **gen·u·a** /ˈjen(y)o͞oə/) *Anatomy* the knee. ■ *Anatomy & Biology* a part of certain structures resembling a knee, in particular a bend in the corpus callosum of mammals. ▷mid 19th cent.: from Latin.

gen·u·flect /ˈjenyə͵flekt/ ▶*v.* [*intrans.*] lower one's body briefly by bending one knee to the ground, typically in worship or as a sign of respect: *she genuflected and crossed herself.* ■ [with *adverbial*] *figurative* show deference or servility: *politicians had to genuflect to the far left to advance their careers.* ▷mid 17th cent. (in the sense 'bend (the knee)'): from ecclesiastical Latin *genuflectere*, from Latin *genu* 'knee' + *flectere* 'to bend.' —**gen·u·flec·tion** /͵jenyəˈflekshən/ *n.* —**gen·u·flec·tor** /-tər/ *n.*

gen·u·ine /ˈjenyo͞oin/ ▶*adj.* truly what something is said to be; authentic: *each book is bound in genuine leather.* ■ (of a person, emotion, or action) sincere: *she had no doubts as to whether Tom was genuine* | *a genuine attempt to delegate authority.* ▷late 16th cent. (in the sense 'natural or proper'): from Latin *genuinus*, from *genu* 'knee' (with reference to the Roman custom of a father acknowledging paternity of a newborn child by placing it on his knee); later associated with *genus* 'birth, race, stock.' —**gen·u·ine·ly** *adv.* —**gen·u·ine·ness** *n.*

THE RIGHT WORD **actual, authentic, bona fide, genuine, legitimate, veritable**

A car salesperson might claim that the seats of that pricey sedan you're considering are made from **genuine** leather, a word that applies to anything that is really what it is claimed or represented to be.

If you're in the market for a Model T Ford, however, you'll want to make sure that the car is **authentic**, which emphasizes formal proof or documentation that an object is what it is claimed to be.

Use **bona fide** when sincerity is involved (*a bona fide offer*), and **legitimate** when you mean lawful or in accordance with established rules, principles, and standards (*a legitimate business*).

Veritable implies correspondence with the truth but not necessarily a literal or strict correspondence with reality (*a veritable supermarket for car-buyers*).

How will it feel to drive that Mercedes out of the showroom? You won't know until you're the **actual** owner of the car—a word that means existing in fact rather than in the imagination.

ge·nus /ˈjēnəs/ ▶*n.* (*pl.* **gen·e·ra** /ˈjenərə/ or **ge·nus·es**) *Biology* a grouping of organisms having common characteristics distinct from those of other such groupings. The genus is a principal taxonomic category that ranks above species and below family, and is denoted by a capitalized Latin name, e.g., *Leo.* ■ (in philosophical and general use) a class of things that have common characteristics and that can be divided into subordinate kinds. ▷mid 16th cent.: from Latin, 'birth, race, stock.'

Gen-X·er /ˈjen ˈeksər/ ▶*n.* a member of Generation X (born in the 1960s and 1970s). Also called XER.

-geny ▶*comb. form* denoting the mode by which something develops or is produced: *orogeny* | *organogeny.* ▷related to French *-génie*; both forms derive from Greek *-geneia*, from *gen-* (root of *gignomai* 'be born, become' and *genos* 'a kind').

Geo. *dated* ▶*abbr.* George.

geo- ▶*comb. form* of or relating to the earth: *geocentric* | *geochemistry.* ▷from Greek *gē* 'earth.'

ge·o·bot·a·ny /͵jēōˈbätn-ē/ ▶*n.* another term for PHYTOGEOGRAPHY. —**ge·o·bo·tan·i·cal** /-bəˈtanikəl/ *adj.* —**ge·o·bot·a·nist** /-ˈbätn-ist/ *n.*

ge·o·cach·ing /ˈjēō͵kashiNG/ ▶*n.* the recreational activity of hunting for and finding a hidden object by means of GPS coordinates posted on a Web site. ▷from *geo(graphical)* +*cache* + *-ing*.

ge·o·cen·tric /͵jēōˈsentrik/ ▶*adj.* having or representing the earth as the center, as in former astronomical systems. Compare with HELIOCENTRIC. ■ *Astronomy* measured from or considered in relation to the center of the earth. —**ge·o·cen·tri·cal·ly** /-trik(ə)lē/ *adv.* —**ge·o·cen·trism** /-trizəm/ *n.*

ge·o·chem·is·try /͵jēōˈkeməstrē/ ▶*n.* the study of the chemical composition of the earth and its rocks and minerals. —**ge·o·chem·i·cal** /-ˈkemikəl/ *adj.* —**ge·o·chem·ist** /-ˈkemist/ *n.*

ge·o·chro·nol·o·gy /͵jēōkrəˈnäləjē/ ▶*n.* the branch of geology concerned with the dating of rock formations and geological events. —**ge·o·chron·o·log·i·cal** /-͵kränəˈläjikəl/ *adj.* —**ge·o·chro·nol·o·gist** /-jist/ *n.*

ge·o·chron·o·met·ric /͵jēō͵kränəˈmetrik/ ▶*adj.* of or relating to geochronological measurement. —**ge·o·chro·nom·e·try** /-krəˈnämətrē/ *n.*

ge·o·code /ˈjēə͵kōd/ ▶*n.* the characterization of a region, neighborhood, etc., based on population statistics such as the average age or income of its inhabitants, used esp. for marketing purposes.

ge·ode /ˈjēōd/ ▶*n.* a small cavity in rock lined with crystals or other mineral matter. ■ a rock containing such a cavity. ▷late 17th cent.: via Latin from Greek *geōdēs* 'earthy,' from *gē* 'earth.' —**ge·od·ic** /jēˈädik/ *adj.*

ge·o·des·ic /͵jēəˈdesik; -ˈdē-/ ▶*adj.* **1** of, relating to, or denoting the shortest possible line between two points on a sphere or other curved surface. **2** another term for GEODETIC.
▶*n.* a geodesic line or structure.

ge·o·des·ic dome ▶*n.* a dome constructed of short struts following geodesic lines and forming an open framework of triangles or polygons. The principles of its construction were described by Buckminster Fuller.

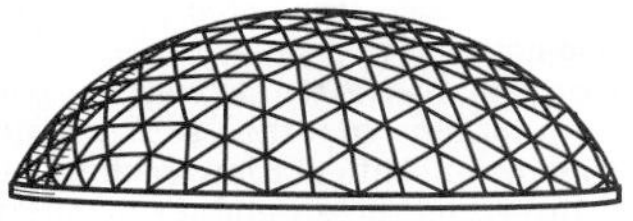

geodesic dome

ge·od·e·sy /jēˈädəsē/ ▶*n.* the branch of mathematics dealing with the shape and area of the earth or large portions of it. ▷late 16th cent.: from modern Latin *geodaesia*, from Greek *geōdaisia*, from *gē* 'earth' + *daiein* 'to divide.' —**ge·od·e·sist** /-sist/ *n.*

ge·o·det·ic /͵jēəˈdetik/ ▶*adj.* of or relating to geodesy, esp. as applied to land surveying. ▷late 17th cent.: from Greek *geōdaitēs* 'land surveyor,' from *geōdaisia* (see GEODESY).

ge·o·det·ic sur·vey ▶*n.* a land survey with corrections made to account for the curvature of the earth's surface.

ge·o·duck /ˈgo͞oē͵dək/ ▶*n.* a giant mud-burrowing bivalve mollusk occurring on the west coast of North America, where it is collected for food. Its shell valves are not large enough to enclose its body and very long siphon. • *Panopea generosa*, family Hyatellidae. ▷late 19th cent.: from Puget Sound Salish.

ge·o·ec·o·nom·ics /͵jēō͵ekəˈnämiks; -͵ēkə-/ ▶*plural n.* [treated as *sing.*] **1** the study of the economic trends and conditions of the world's countries and how they are related; economics considered on the broadest global scale. **2** the economic policies or conditions of a country as seen in a global perspective.

Geof·frey of Mon·mouth /ˈjefrē əv ˈmänˌməTH/ (*c.*1100–*c.*54), Welsh chronicler. His *Historia Regum Britanniae* (*c.*1139; first printed in 1508), an account of the kings of Britain, was a major source for English literature, especially for the tales of King Arthur.

Pronunciation Key ə *ago*; ər *over*; ˈə *or* ͵ə *up*; ˈər *or* ͵ər *fur*; a *hat*; ā *rate*; ä *car*; CH *chew*; e *let*; ē *see*; e(ə)r *air*; i *fit*; ī *by*; i(ə)r *ear*; NG *sing*; ō *go*; ô *for*; oi *boy*; o͝o *good*; o͞o *goo*; ou *out*; SH *she*; TH *thin*; T͟H *then*; (h)w *why*; ZH *vision*

geog. ▸*abbr.* ■ geographer. ■ geographic. ■ geographical. ■ geography.

ge·o·graph·i·cal /ˌjēəˈgrafikəl/ ▸*adj.* of or relating to geography. ▷mid 16th cent.: from French *géographique* or late Latin *geographicus*, from Greek *geōgraphikos*, from *geōgraphos* 'geographer,' from *gē* 'earth' + *graphein* 'write, draw.' **—ge·o·graph·ic** *adj.* **—ge·o·graph·i·cal·ly** /-ik(ə)lē/ *adv.*

ge·o·graph·i·cal mile ▸*n.* a distance equal to one minute of longitude or latitude at the equator (about 1,850 meters).

ge·og·ra·phy /jēˈägrəfē/ ▸*n.* the study of the physical features of the earth and its atmosphere, and of human activity as it affects and is affected by these, including the distribution of populations and resources, land use, and industries. ■ [usu. in *sing.*] the nature and relative arrangement of places and physical features: *knowing the geography and topology of the battlefield.* ▷late 15th cent.: from French *géographie* or Latin *geographia*, from Greek *geōgraphia*, from *gē* 'earth' + *-graphia* 'writing.' **—ge·og·ra·pher** /-fər/ *n.*

ge·oid /ˈjē-oid/ ▸*n.* (**the geoid**) the hypothetical shape of the earth, coinciding with mean sea level and its imagined extension under (or over) land areas. ▷late 19th cent.: from Greek *geoeidēs*, from *gē* 'earth' + *-oeidēs* (see **-OID**).

geol. ▸*abbr.* ■ geologic. ■ geological. ■ geologist. ■ geology.

ge·o·log·i·cal sur·vey ▸*n.* a detailed and systematic study of the topography, geology, and mineral resources of an area or country.

ge·ol·o·gy /jēˈäləjē/ ▸*n.* the science that deals with the earth's physical structure and substance, its history, and the processes that act on it. ■ the geological features of an area: *the geology of the Outer Hebrides.* ■ the geological features of a planetary body: *the geology of the surface of Mars.* ▷late 18th cent.: from modern Latin *geologia*, from Greek *gē* 'earth' + *-logia* (see **-LOGY**). **—ge·o·log·ic** /ˌjēəˈläjik/ *adj.* **—ge·o·log·i·cal** /ˌjēəˈläjikəl/ *adj.* **—ge·o·log·i·cal·ly** /ˌjēəˈläjik(ə)lē/ *adv.* **—ge·ol·o·gist** /-jist/ *n.* **—ge·ol·o·gize** /-ˌjīz/ *v.*

geom. ▸*abbr.* ■ geometric. ■ geometrical. ■ geometry.

ge·o·mag·net·ic e·qua·tor ▸*n.* a notional circle on the earth's surface, the plane of which is equidistant between the north and south magnetic poles and perpendicular to the magnetic field.

ge·o·mag·net·ism /ˌjēōˈmagniˌtizəm/ ▸*n.* the branch of geology concerned with the magnetic properties of the earth. **—ge·o·mag·net·ic** /-ˌmagˈnetik/ *adj.* **—ge·o·mag·net·i·cal·ly** /-ˌmagˈnetik(ə)lē/ *adv.*

ge·o·man·cy /ˈjēəˌmansē/ ▸*n.* **1** the art of placing or arranging buildings or other sites auspiciously. **2** divination from configurations seen in a handful of earth thrown on the ground, or by interpreting lines or textures on the ground. **—ge·o·man·cer** /-sər/ *n.* **—ge·o·man·tic** /ˌjēəˈmantik/ *adj.*

ge·o·mat·ics /ˌjēəˈmatiks/ ▸*plural n.* [treated as *sing.*] the application of computerization to information in geography and related fields. ▷1980s: blend of *geography* and *informatics*. **—ge·o·mat·ic** *adj.*

ge·om·e·ter /jēˈämitər/ ▸*n.* **1** a person skilled in geometry. **2** (also **geometer moth**) *Entomology* a geometrid moth or its caterpillar. ▷late Middle English: from late Latin *geometra*, based on Greek *geōmetrēs*, from *gē* 'earth' + *metrēs* 'measurer.'

ge·o·met·ric /ˌjēəˈmetrik/ ▸*adj.* **1** of or relating to geometry, or according to its methods. **2** (of a design) characterized by or decorated with regular lines and shapes: *traditional Hopi geometric forms.* ■ (**Geometric**) *Archaeology* of or denoting a period of Greek culture (around 900–700 BC) characterized by geometrically decorated pottery. ▷mid 17th cent.: via French from Latin *geometricus*, from Greek *geōmetrikos*, from *geōmetrēs* (see **GEOMETER**). **—ge·o·met·ri·cal** *adj.* **—ge·o·met·ri·cal·ly** /-ik(ə)lē/ *adv.*

ge·o·met·ric i·so·mer (also **ge·o·met·ri·cal i·so·mer**) ▸*n. Chemistry* each of two or more compounds that differ from each other in the arrangement of groups with respect to a double bond, ring, or other rigid structure. **—ge·o·met·ric i·som·er·ism** *n.*

ge·o·met·ric mean ▸*n.* the central number in a geometric progression (e.g., *9* in *3, 9, 27*), also calculable as the *n*th root of a product of *n* numbers.

ge·o·met·ric pro·gres·sion ▸*n.* a progression of numbers with a constant ratio between each number and the one before (e.g., each subsequent number is increased by a factor of 3 in the progression *1, 3, 9, 27, 81*).

ge·o·met·rics /ˌjēəˈmetriks/ ▸*plural n.* straight lines and simple geometric shapes, e.g., circles and squares, used together to form a design or pattern: *their high-quality sheets in florals, classic solids, and bold geometrics can transform the look and feel of a room.*

ge·o·met·ric se·ries ▸*n.* a series of numbers or quantities in geometric progression.

ge·om·e·trid /jēˈämətrid/ ▸*n.* a moth of a large family (Geometridae), distinguished by having twiglike caterpillars that move by arching and straightening the body. Also called **GEOMETER**. ▷late 19th cent.: from modern Latin *Geometridae* (plural), from the genus name *Geometra*, from Latin *geometres* (see **GEOMETER**).

ge·om·e·try /jēˈämətrē/ ▸*n.* the branch of mathematics concerned with the properties and relations of points, lines, surfaces, solids, and higher dimensional analogs. ■ (*pl.* **-tries**) a particular mathematical system describing such properties: *non-Euclidean geometries.* ■ [in *sing.*] the shape and relative arrangement of the parts of something: *the geometry of spiders' webs.* ▷Middle English: via Old French from Latin *geometria*, from Greek, from *gē* 'earth' + *metria* (see **-METRY**).

ge·o·mor·phic /ˌjēəˈmôrfik/ ▸*adj.* of or relating to the form of the landscape and other natural features of the earth's surface.

ge·o·mor·phol·o·gy /ˌjēōˌmôrˈfäləjē/ ▸*n.* the study of the physical features of the surface of the earth and their relation to its geological structures. **—ge·o·mor·pho·log·i·cal** /-ˌmôrfəˈläjikəl/ *adj.* **—ge·o·mor·phol·o·gist** /-jist/ *n.*

ge·oph·a·gy /jēˈäfəjē/ ▸*n.* the practice of eating earth, esp. chalk or clay in famine-stricken regions. ▷mid 19th cent.: from **GEO-** 'earth' + Greek *phagia* 'eating, feeding' (from *phagein* 'eat').

ge·o·phys·ics /ˌjēōˈfiziks/ ▸*plural n.* [treated as *sing.*] the physics of the earth. **—ge·o·phys·i·cal** /-ˈfizikəl/ *adj.* **—ge·o·phys·i·cist** /-ˈfizisist/ *n.*

ge·o·pol·i·tics /ˌjēōˈpäləˌtiks/ ▸*plural n.* [treated as *sing.* or *pl.*] politics, esp. international relations, as influenced by geographical factors. ■ [treated as *sing.*] the study of politics of this type. **—ge·o·po·lit·i·cal** /-pəˈlitikəl/ *adj.* **—ge·o·po·lit·i·cal·ly** /-pəˈlitik(ə)lē/ *adv.* **—ge·o·pol·i·ti·cian** /-ˌpäləˈtisHən/ *n.*

Geor·die /ˈjôrdē/ *Brit., informal* ▸*n.* a person from Tyneside, an area in northeastern England. ■ the English dialect or accent typical of people from Tyneside.
▸*adj.* of or relating to Tyneside, its people, or their accent or dialect: *Geordie humor.* ▷mid 19th cent.: diminutive of the given name *George*.

George /jôrj/ the name of four kings of Great Britain and Ireland, one of Great Britain and Ireland (from 1920, of the United Kingdom), and one of the United Kingdom: ■ **George I** (1660–1727), great-grandson of James I; reigned 1714–27; elector of Hanover 1698–1727. The first British sovereign of the house of Hanover, he was unpopular in

Circles

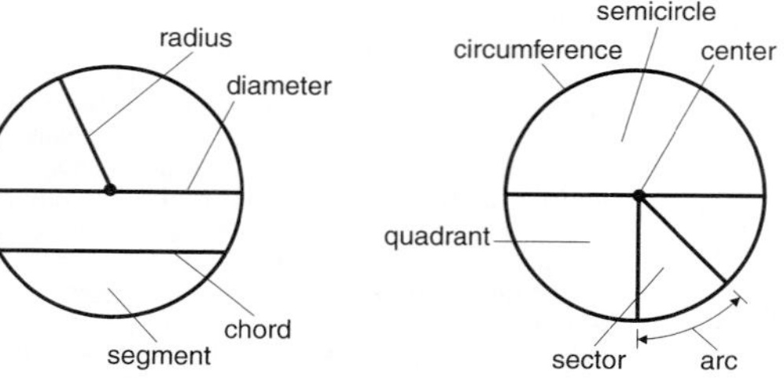

Quadrilaterals

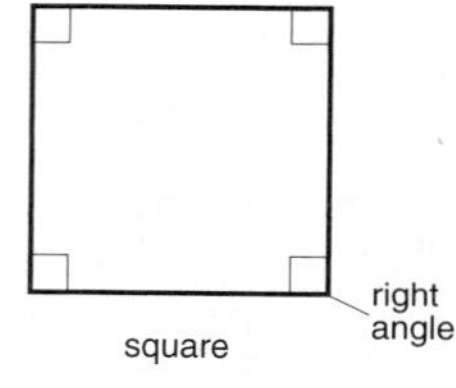

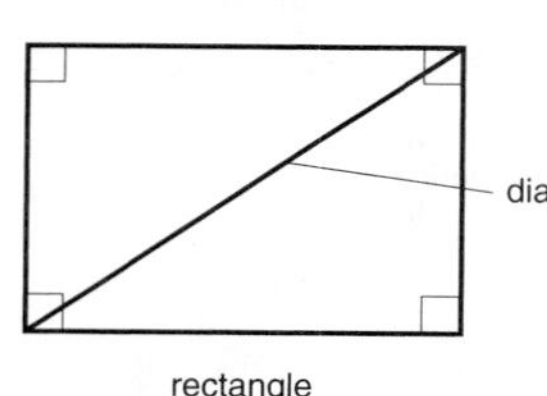

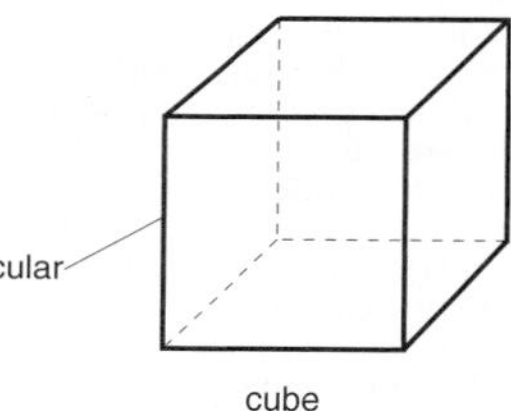

Triangles

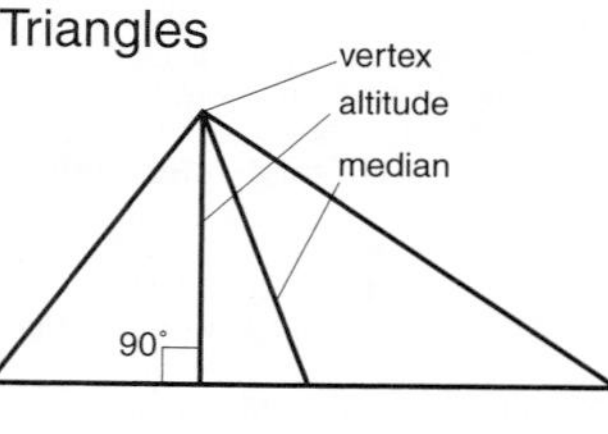

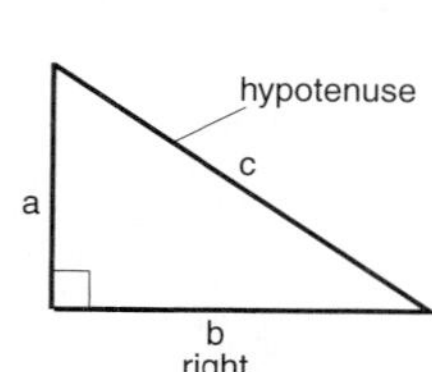

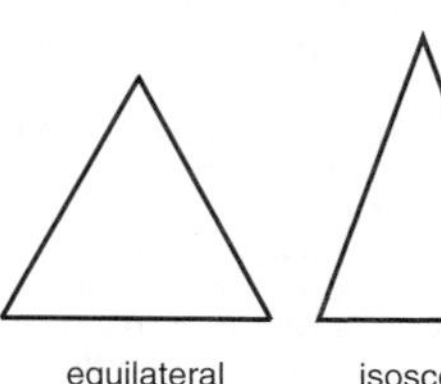

Types of Triangles

Conic Sections

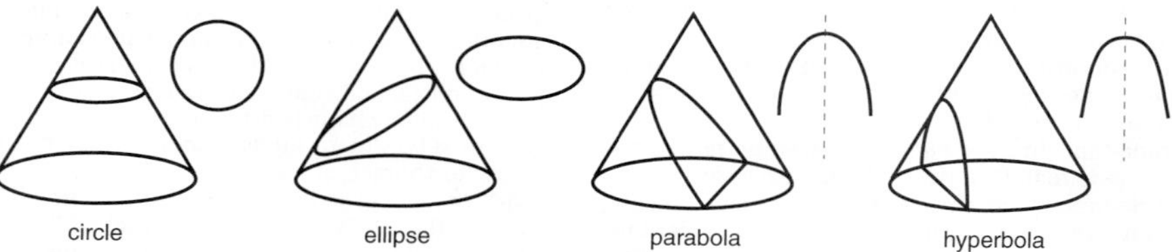

geometric shapes and forms

England because of his German manners and his inability to speak English. ■ **George II** (1683–1760), son of George I; reigned 1727–60; elector of Hanover 1727–60. He took an active part in the War of the Austrian Succession 1740–48. ■ **George III** (1738–1820), grandson of George II; reigned 1760–1820; elector of Hanover 1760–1815; king of Hanover 1815–20. He reigned during the time of the American Revolution and the War of 1812. His political influence declined from 1788 after bouts of mental illness. ■ **George IV** (1762–1830), son of George III; reigned 1820–30. Known as a patron of the arts and *bon viveur*, he had a bad reputation that was further damaged by his attempt to divorce his estranged wife Caroline of Brunswick just after coming to the throne. ■ **George V** (1865–1936), son of Edward VII; reigned 1910–36. He exercised restrained but important influence over British politics and played a significant role in the formation of the government in 1931. During World War I he changed the name of the royal house to Windsor. ■ **George VI** (1894–1952), son of George V; reigned 1936–52. He came to the throne when his older brother Edward VIII abdicated.

George, Lake /jôrj/ a resort lake in northeastern New York, northeast of Albany, near the Vermont border, scene of many 18th-century military actions.

George, St., patron saint of England. He is reputed in legend to have slain a dragon and may have been martyred near Lydda in Palestine some time before the reign of Constantine. Feast day, April 23.

Geor·ges Bank /ˈjôrjəz/ underwater rise in the Atlantic Ocean, between Massachusetts and Nova Scotia, site of important U.S. and Canadian fishing zones.

George·town /ˈjôrj,toun/ **1** the capital of Guyana, a port at the mouth of the Demerara River; pop. 188,000. **2** an affluent section of northwestern Washington, DC, home to government officials, shopping districts, and Georgetown University.

George Town **1** the capital of the Cayman Islands, on the island of Grand Cayman; pop. 12,000. **2** the chief port of Malaysia and capital of the state of Penang, on Penang Island; pop. 219,000. Also called PENANG.

geor·gette /jôrˈjet/ ▶*n.* a thin silk or crepe dress material. ▷early 20th cent.: named after *Georgette* de la Plante (*c.*1900), French dressmaker.

Geor·gia /ˈjôrjə/ **1** a country in southwestern Asia, on the eastern shore of the Black Sea; pop. 4,693,000; capital, Tbilisi; languages, Georgian (official), Russian, and Armenian.

An independent kingdom in medieval times, Georgia became part of the Russian empire in the 19th century and then was absorbed into the Soviet Union. When the Soviet Union broke up in 1991, Georgia became an independent republic outside of the Commonwealth of Independent States. Since then, separatist movements among the Abkhazian and South Ossetian minorities have led to outbreaks of ethnic conflict.

2 a state in the southeastern U.S., on the Atlantic coast; pop. 8,186,453; capital, Atlanta; statehood, Jan. 2, 1788 (4). Founded as an English colony in 1732 and named after George II, it was one of the original thirteen states. It was the site of General Sherman's "March to the Sea" in 1864 during the Civil War.

Geor·gia, Strait of /ˈjôrjə/ an ocean passage between Vancouver Island and the mainland of British Columbia and Washington.

Geor·gian[1] /ˈjôrjən/ ▶*adj.* **1** of or characteristic of the reigns of the British kings George I–IV (1714–1830). ■ of or relating to British architecture of this period that was characterized esp. by restrained elegance and the use of neoclassical styles. **2** of or characteristic of the reigns of the British kings George V and VI (1910–52). ■ of or relating to British literature of 1910–20, in particular pastoral poetry of a type strongly attacked by the early modernists.

Geor·gian[2] ▶*adj.* of or relating to the country of Georgia, its people, or their language.
▶*n.* **1** a native or national of Georgia, or a person of Georgian descent. **2** the South Caucasian (or Kartvelian) language, having its own alphabet, that is the official language of Georgia.

Geor·gian[3] ▶*adj.* of or relating to the state of Georgia in the U.S.
▶*n.* a native of Georgia.

geor·gic /ˈjôrjik/ ▶*n.* a poem or book dealing with agriculture or rural topics. ■ (**Georgics**) the title of a didactic poem on farming by the Roman poet Virgil.
▶*adj. poetic/literary* rustic; pastoral. ▷early 16th cent.: via Latin from Greek *geōrgikos*, from *geōrgos* 'farmer.'

ge·o·sci·ence /ˌjēōˈsīəns; ˈjēō,sīəns/ ▶*n.* (also **geosciences**) earth sciences, esp. geology. —**ge·o·sci·en·tist** /ˌjēōˈsīəntist; ˈjēō,sīəntist/ *n.*

ge·o·spa·tial /ˌjēōˈspāsʜəl/ ▶*adj. Geography* relating to or denoting data that is associated with a particular location.

ge·o·sphere /ˈjēə,sfir/ ▶*n.* any of the almost spherical concentric regions of matter that make up the earth and its atmosphere, as the lithosphere and hydrosphere.

ge·o·sta·tion·ar·y /ˌjēōˈstāsʜə,nerē/ ▶*adj.* (of an artificial satellite of the earth) moving in a geosynchronous orbit in the plane of the equator, so that it remains stationary in relation to a fixed point on the surface. This orbit is achieved at an altitude of 22,300 miles (35,900 km.) above the earth. It is used by communication and meteorological satellites.

ge·o·stroph·ic /ˌjēəˈsträfik/ ▶*adj. Meteorology & Oceanography* relating to or denoting the component of a wind or current that arises from a balance between pressure gradients and Coriolis forces. ▷early 20th cent.: from GEO- 'of the earth' + Greek *strophē* 'a turning' (from *strephein* 'to turn').

ge·o·syn·chro·nous /ˌjēōˈsiNGkrənəs/ ▶*adj.* (of an earth satellite or its orbit) having a period of rotation synchronous with that of the earth's rotation.

ge·o·syn·cline /ˌjēōˈsin,klīn/ ▶*n. Geology* a large-scale depression in the earth's crust containing very thick deposits.

ge·o·tax·is /ˌjēōˈtaksis/ ▶*n. Biology* the motion of a motile organism or cell in response to the force of gravity. —**ge·o·tac·tic** /-ˈtaktik/ *adj.*

ge·o·tech·nics /ˌjēōˈtekniks/ ▶*plural n.* [treated as *sing.*] the branch of civil engineering concerned with the study and modification of soil and rocks. —**ge·o·tech·nic** *adj.* —**ge·o·tech·ni·cal** /-nikəl/ *adj.*

ge·o·tec·ton·ic /ˌjēōtekˈtänik/ ▶*adj.* another term for TECTONIC.

ge·o·ther·mal /ˌjēōˈᴛʜərməl/ (also **ge·o·ther·mic** /-ˈᴛʜərmik/) ▶*adj.* of, relating to, or produced by the internal heat of the earth: *some 70% of Iceland's energy needs are met from geothermal sources.*

ge·ot·ro·pism /jēˈätrə,pizəm/ ▶*n. Botany* the growth of the parts of plants with respect to the force of gravity. The upward growth of plant shoots is an instance of **negative geotropism**; the downward growth of roots is **positive geotropism**. ▷late 19th cent.: from GEO- 'earth' + Greek *tropē* 'turning' + -ISM. —**ge·o·trop·ic** /ˌjēəˈträpik; -ˈtrō-/ *adj.*

ger. ▶*abbr. Grammar* ■ gerund. ■ gerundive.

Ge·ra /ˈgārä/ an industrial city in eastern central Germany, in Thuringia; pop. 127,000.

ge·ra·ni·al /jəˈrānēəl/ ▶*n. Chemistry* a fragrant oil present in lemongrass oil and used in perfumery. • an isomer of citral; chem. formula: $C_{10}H_{16}O$. ▷late 19th cent.: from German, contraction of *Geranialdehyde.*

ge·ra·ni·ol /jəˈrānē,ôl; -,äl/ ▶*n. Chemistry* a fragrant liquid present in some floral oils and used in perfumery. • A terpenoid alcohol; chem. formula: $C_{10}H_{18}O$. ▷late 19th cent.: from German, from GERANIUM + -OL.

ge·ra·ni·um /jəˈrānēəm/ ▶*n.* a herbaceous plant or small shrub of a genus that comprises the cranesbills and their relatives. Geraniums bear a long narrow fruit that is said to be shaped like the bill of a crane. • Genus *Geranium*, family Geraniaceae. ■ (in general or informal use) a cultivated pelargonium. ■ the scarlet color of many cultivated pelargoniums. ▷modern Latin, from Greek *geranion*, from *geranos* 'crane.'

ger·ber·a /ˈgərbərə/ ▶*n.* a plant of the daisy family, native to Asia and Africa, with large brightly colored flowers. • Genus *Gerbera*, family Compositae: many species, in particular the widely cultivated Transvaal daisy. ▷modern Latin, named after Traugott *Gerber* (died 1743), German naturalist.

ger·bil /ˈjərbəl/ ▶*n.* **1** a burrowing mouselike rodent that is specially adapted to living in arid conditions, found in Africa and Asia. • Subfamily Gerbillinae, family Muridae: several genera, in particular *Gerbillus*. **2** another term for JIRD. ▷mid 19th cent.: from French *gerbille*, from modern Latin *gerbillus*, diminutive of *gerboa* (see JERBOA).

ger·e·nuk /ˈgerə,no͝ok/ ▶*n.* a slender East African antelope with a long neck, often browsing on tall bushes by standing on its hind legs. • *Litocranius walleri*, family Bovidae. ▷late 19th cent.: from Somali.

ger·i·at·ric /ˌjerēˈatrik/ ▶*adj.* [*attrib.*] of or relating to old people, esp. with regard to their health care: *a geriatric hospital.*
▶*n.* an old person, esp. one receiving special care: *a rest home for geriatrics.* ▷1920s: from Greek *gēras* 'old age' + *iatros* 'doctor,' on the pattern of *pediatric*.

USAGE Geriatric is the normal, semiofficial term used in the U.S. and Britain when referring to the health care of old people (*a geriatric ward; geriatric patients*). When used outside such contexts, however, it typically carries overtones of being worn out and decrepit and can therefore be offensive.

ger·i·at·rics /ˌjerēˈatriks/ ▶*plural n.* [treated as *sing.* or *pl.*] the branch of medicine or social science dealing with the health and care of old people. —**ger·i·a·tri·cian** /ˌjerēəˈtrisʜən/ *n.*

Gé·ri·cault /ˌᴢʜerēˈkō/, (Jean Louis André) Théodore (1791–1824), French painter. His most noted work, *The Raft of the Medusa* (1819), depicts the survivors of a famous 1816 shipwreck.

germ /jərm/ ▶*n.* **1** a microorganism, esp. one that causes disease. **2** a portion of an organism capable of developing into a new one or part of one. Compare with GERM CELL. ■ the embryo in a cereal grain or other plant seed. Compare with WHEAT GERM. ■ an initial stage from which something may develop: ***the germ of** a brilliant idea.* ▷late Middle English (sense 2): via Old French from Latin *germen* 'seed, sprout.' Sense 1 dates from the late 19th cent. —**germ·y** *adj.* (*informal*, in sense 1).

Ger·man /ˈjərmən/ ▶*n.* **1** a native or national of Germany. ■ a person of German descent: *Sudeten Germans.* **2** a West Germanic language used in Germany, Austria, and parts of Switzerland, and by communities in the U.S. and elsewhere. See also HIGH GERMAN, LOW GERMAN. **3** (in full **German cotillion**) a complex dance in which one couple leads the other couples through a variety of figures and there is a continual change of partners.
▶*adj.* of or relating to Germany, its people, or their language. ▷from Latin *Germanus*, used to designate related peoples of central and northern Europe, a name perhaps given by Celts to their neighbors; compare with Old Irish *gair* 'neighbor.'

ger·man /ˈjərmən/ ▶*adj. archaic* germane. ■ [*postpositive*] (of a sibling) having the same parents: *my brothers-german.* ▷Middle English: from Old French *germain*, from Latin *germanus* 'genuine, of the same parents.'

Ger·man cock·roach ▶*n.* a small, brown, common indoor cockroach found worldwide. • *Blatella germanica*, order Dictyoptera.

Ger·man Dem·o·crat·ic Re·pub·lic (abbr.: **GDR, DDR**) official name for the former state of **East Germany** (see GERMANY).

ger·man·der /jərˈmandər/ ▶*n.* a widely distributed plant of the mint family. Some kinds are cultivated as ornamentals and some are used in herbal medicine. • Genus *Teucrium*, family Labiatae: many species, including the **American germander** (*T. canadense*) and the European **wall germander** (*T. chamaedrys*). ▷late Middle English: from medieval Latin *germandra*, based on Greek *khamaidrus*, literally 'ground oak,' from *khamai* 'on the ground' + *drus* 'oak' (because the leaves of some species were thought to resemble those of the oak).

ger·man·der speed·well ▶*n.* a speedwell with bright blue flowers and leaves resembling those of the germander, native to Eurasia but now common in North America. • *Veronica chamaedrys*, family Scrophulariaceae.

ger·mane /jərˈmān/ ▶*adj.* relevant to a subject under

G

consideration: *that is not germane to our theme.* ▷early 17th cent.: variant of GERMAN, with which it was synonymous from Middle English. The current sense has arisen from a usage in Shakespeare's *Hamlet.* **—ger·mane·ly** *adv.* **—ger·mane·ness** *n.*

Ger·man East Af·ri·ca a former German protectorate in East Africa 1891–1918 that corresponds to present-day Tanzania, Rwanda, and Burundi.

Ger·man Em·pire an empire in German-speaking central Europe, created by Bismarck in 1871 after the Franco-Prussian War by the union of twenty-five German states under the Hohenzollern king of Prussia. Also called **SECOND REICH.**

Forming an alliance with Austria–Hungary, the German Empire became the greatest industrial power in Europe and engaged in colonial expansion in Africa, China, and the Far East. Tensions arising with other colonial powers led to World War I, after which the German Empire collapsed and the Weimar Republic was created.

Ger·man·ic /jər'manik/ ▶*adj.* **1** of, relating to, or denoting the branch of the Indo-European language family that includes English, German, Dutch, Frisian, the Scandinavian languages, and Gothic. ■ of, relating to, or denoting the peoples of ancient northern and western Europe speaking such languages. **2** having characteristics of or attributed to Germans or Germany: *she had an almost Germanic regard for order.*
▶*n.* the Germanic languages collectively. See also **EAST GERMANIC, NORTH GERMANIC, WEST GERMANIC.** ■ the unrecorded ancient language from which these developed, thought to have been spoken on the shores of the Baltic Sea in the 3rd millennium BC. Also called **PROTO-GERMANIC.** ▷mid 17th cent.: from Latin *Germanicus*, from *Germanus* (see **GERMAN**).

Ger·man·ist /'jərmənist/ ▶*n.* an expert in or student of the language, literature, and civilization of Germany, or of Germanic languages.

ger·ma·ni·um /jər'mānēəm/ ▶*n.* the chemical element of atomic number 32, a shiny gray semimetal. Germanium was important in the making of transistors and other semiconductor devices, but has been largely replaced by silicon. (Symbol: **Ge**) ▷late 19th cent.: modern Latin, from Latin *Germanus* (see **GERMAN**).

Ger·man·ize /'jərmə,nīz/ ▶*v.* [*trans.*] make German; cause to adopt German language and customs: *the Poles had Germanized their family names.* **—Ger·man·i·za·tion** /,jərməni'zāsʜən/ *n.*

Ger·man mea·sles ▶*plural n.* [usu. treated as *sing.*] another term for **RUBELLA.**

Germano- ▶*comb. form* German; German and . . . : *Germanophile.* ■ relating to Germany: *Germanocentric.*

Ger·man·o·phile /jər'manə,fīl/ ▶*n.* a person who is fond of or greatly admires Germany or German people or culture.

Ger·man shep·herd (also **German shepherd dog**) ▶*n.* a large dog of a breed often used as guard dogs or guide dogs or for police work.

German shepherd

Ger·man sil·ver ▶*n.* a white alloy of nickel, zinc, and copper.

Ger·man South West Af·ri·ca a former German protectorate 1884–1918 in southwestern Africa that corresponds to present-day Namibia.

Ger·man·town /'jərmən,toun/ **1** a city in southwestern Tennessee, a southeastern suburb of Memphis; pop. 37,348. **2** a historic residential section of northwestern Philadelphia in Pennsylvania, scene of a 1777 battle.

Ger·ma·ny /'jərmənē/ a country in central Europe, on the Baltic Sea in the north; pop. 84,424,000; capital, Berlin; seat of government, Bonn; official language, German. German name **DEUTSCHLAND.**

The multiplicity of small German states achieved real unity only with the rise of Prussia and the formation of the German Empire in the mid 19th century. After being defeated in World War I, Germany was taken over in the 1930s by the Nazi dictatorship that led to a policy of expansionism and eventually to complete defeat in World War II. Germany was occupied for a time by the victorious Allies and was partitioned. The western part (including West Berlin), which was occupied by the U.S., Britain, and France, became the Federal Republic of Germany or **West Germany**, with its capital at Bonn. The eastern part, occupied by the Soviet Union, became the German Democratic Republic or **East Germany**, with its capital in East Berlin. West Germany emerged as a major European industrial power and was a founder member of the EEC, while the East remained under Soviet domination. After the general collapse of communism in eastern Europe, East and West Germany reunited on October 3, 1990.

germ cell ▶*n. Biology* a cell containing half the number of chromosomes of a somatic cell and able to unite with one from the opposite sex to form a new individual; a gamete. ■ an embryonic cell with the potential of developing into a gamete.

ger·mi·cide /'jərmə,sīd/ ▶*n.* a substance or other agent that destroys harmful microorganisms; an antiseptic. **—ger·mi·cid·al** /,jərmə'sīdl/ *adj.*

Ger·mi·nal /'jərmənl/ ▶*n.* the seventh month of the French Republican calendar (1793–1805), originally running from March 21 to April 19.

ger·mi·nal /'jərmənl/ ▶*adj.* [*attrib.*] relating to or of the nature of a germ cell or embryo. ■ in the earliest stage of development. ■ providing material for future development: *the subject was revived in a germinal article by Charles Ferguson.* ▷early 19th cent.: from Latin *germen, germin-* 'sprout, seed' + **-AL.** **—ger·mi·nal·ly** *adv.*

ger·mi·nal disk (also **ger·mi·nal disc**) ▶*n.* another term for **BLASTODISK.**

ger·mi·nate /'jərmə,nāt/ ▶*v.* [*intrans.*] (of a seed or spore) begin to grow and put out shoots after a period of dormancy. ■ [*trans.*] cause (a seed or spore) to sprout in such a way. ■ *figurative* come into existence and develop: *the idea germinated and slowly grew into an obsession.* ▷late 16th cent.: from Latin *germinat-* 'sprouted forth, budded,' from the verb *germinare*, from *germen, germin-* 'sprout, seed.' **—ger·mi·na·ble** /-nəbəl/ *adj.* **—ger·mi·na·tion** /,jərmə'nāsʜən/ *n.* **—ger·mi·na·tive** /-,nātiv/ *adj.* **—ger·mi·na·tor** /-,nātər/ *n.*

Ger·mis·ton /'jərməstən/ a city in South Africa, southeast of Johannesburg; pop. 134,000. It is the site of a large gold refinery.

germ lay·er ▶*n. Embryology* each of the three layers of cells (ectoderm, mesoderm, and endoderm) that are formed in the early embryo.

germ line ▶*n. Biology* a series of germ cells each descended or developed from earlier cells in the series, regarded as continuing through successive generations of an organism.

germ plasm ▶*n. Biology* germ cells, collectively. ■ the genetic material of such cells.

germ war·fare ▶*n.* another term for **BIOLOGICAL WARFARE.**

Ge·ron·i·mo[1] /jə'ränə,mō/ (*c.*1829–1909), Apache chief. He resisted white encroachment on tribal

Geronimo

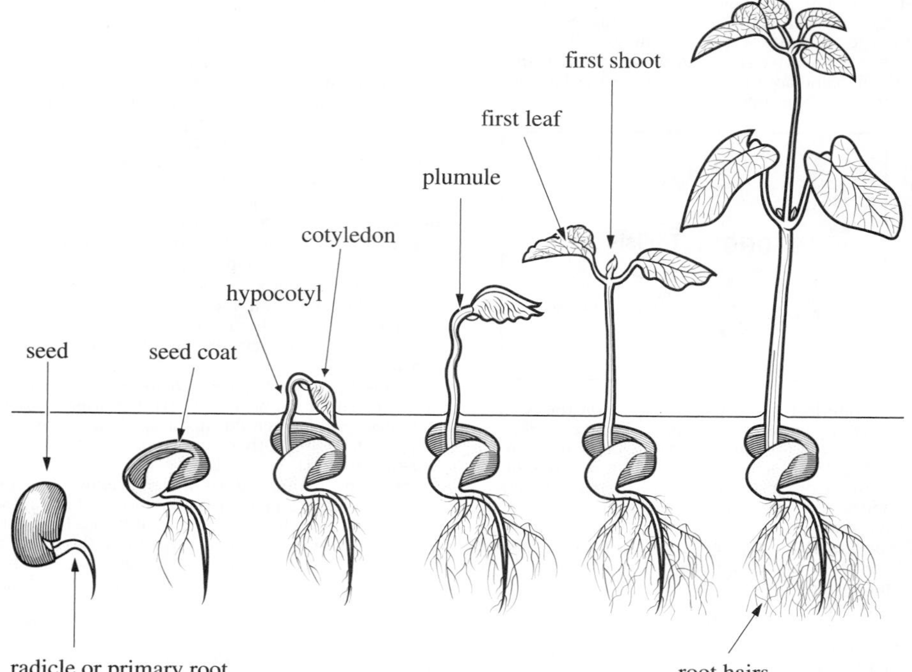

germination of a bean

lands in Arizona by leading his people in raids on settlers and U.S. troops before he surrendered in 1886.

Ge·ron·i·mo[2] ▸*exclam.* used to express exhilaration, esp. when leaping from a great height or moving at a high speed. ▷World War II: by association with **Geronimo**[1], adopted as a slogan by American paratroopers.

ge·ron·tic /jəˈräntik/ ▸*adj.* of or relating to old age, elderly people, or senescent animals or plants. ▷late 19th cent.: from Greek *gerōn, geront-* 'old man' + **-ic**.

ger·on·toc·ra·cy /ˌjerənˈtäkrəsē/ ▸*n.* a state, society, or group governed by old people. ■ government based on rule by old people. ▷mid 19th cent.: from Greek *gerōn, geront-* 'old man' + **-cracy**. **—ge·ron·to·crat** /jəˈräntəˌkrat/ *n.* **—ge·ron·to·crat·ic** /jəˌräntəˈkratik/ *adj.*

ger·on·tol·o·gy /ˌjerənˈtäləjē/ ▸*n.* the scientific study of old age, the process of aging, and the particular problems of old people. ▷early 20th cent.: from Greek *gerōn, geront-* 'old man' + **-logy**. **—ge·ron·to·log·i·cal** /jəˌräntlˈäjikəl/ *adj.* **—ger·on·tol·o·gist** /-jist/ *n.*

-gerous ▸*comb. form* bearing (a specified thing): *armigerous.* ▷from Latin *-ger* 'bearing' (from the root of *gerere* 'to bear, carry') + **-ous**.

Ger·ry /ˈjerē/, Elbridge (1744–1814) U.S. politician. A signer of the Declaration of Independence in 1776 and vice president of the U.S. 1813–14, his political maneuvering in Massachusetts gave rise to the term "gerrymander."

ger·ry·man·der /ˈjerēˌmandər/ ▸*v.* [*trans.*] [often as *n.*] (**gerrymandering**) manipulate the boundaries of (an electoral constituency) so as to favor one party or class. ■ achieve (a result) by such manipulation: *a total freedom to gerrymander the results they want.* ▸*n.* an instance of such a practice. ▷early 19th cent.: from the name of Governor Elbridge *Gerry* of Massachusetts + **salamander**, from the supposed similarity between a salamander and the shape of a new voting district on a map drawn when he was in office (1812), the creation of which was felt to favor his party: the map (with claws, wings, and fangs added), was published in the Boston *Weekly Messenger*, with the title *The Gerry-Mander*. **—ger·ry·man·der·er** *n.*

Gersh·win /ˈgərˌshwin/, George (1898–1937), U.S. composer and pianist; born *Jacob Gershovitz*. He achieved success in 1919 with the song "Swanee" and went on to compose many successful songs and musicals, as well as *Rhapsody in Blue* (1924) and *American in Paris* (1928) for orchestra and an opera, *Porgy and Bess* (1935). The lyrics for many of these were written by his brother **Ira Gershwin** (1896–1983).

ger·und /ˈjerənd/ ▸*n. Grammar* a form that is derived from a verb but that functions as a noun, in English ending in *-ing*, e.g., *asking* in *do you mind my asking you?*. ▷early 16th cent.: from late Latin *gerundium*, from *gerundum*, variant of *gerendum*, the gerund of Latin *gerere* 'do.'

ger·un·dive /jəˈrəndiv/ ▸*n. Grammar* (in Latin) a form that is derived from a verb but that functions as an adjective, denoting something "that should or must be done." ▷Middle English (in the sense 'gerund'): from late Latin *gerundivus (modus)* 'gerundive (mood),' from *gerundium* (see **gerund**).

Ge·sell·schaft /gəˈzelˌshäft; -ˌshaft/ ▸*n.* social relations based on impersonal ties, as duty to a society or organization. Contrasted with **Gemeinschaft**. ▷German, from *Gesell(e)* 'companion' + *-schaft* (see **-ship**).

ges·ne·ri·ad /gesˈni(ə)rēˌad; jes-/ ▸*n.* a tropical plant of a family that includes African violets, gloxinias, and their relatives. • Family Gesneriaceae. ▷mid 19th cent.: from modern Latin *Gesneria* (genus name), from the name of Conrad von *Gesner* (1516–65), Swiss naturalist, + **-ad**[1].

ges·so /ˈjesō/ ▸*n.* (*pl.* **-soes**) a hard compound of plaster of Paris or whiting in glue, used in sculpture or as a base for gilding or painting on wood. ▷late 16th cent.: Italian, from Latin *gypsum* (see **gypsum**). **—ges·soed** *adj.*

ge·stalt /gəˈshtält; -ˈshtôlt/ (also **Ge·stalt**) ▸*n.* (*pl.* **-stalt·en** /-ˈshtältn; -ˈshtôltn/ or **-stalts**) *Psychology* an organized whole that is perceived as more than the sum of its parts. ▷1920s: from German *Gestalt*, literally 'form, shape.' **—ge·stalt·ism** *n.* **—ge·stalt·ist** *n.*

Ge·stalt psy·chol·o·gy ▸*n.* a movement in psychology founded in Germany in 1912, seeking to explain perceptions in terms of gestalts rather than by analyzing their constituents.

Ge·stalt ther·a·py ▸*n.* a psychotherapeutic approach developed by Fritz Perls (1893–1970). It focuses on insight into gestalts in patients and their relations to the world, and often uses role-playing to aid the resolution of past conflicts.

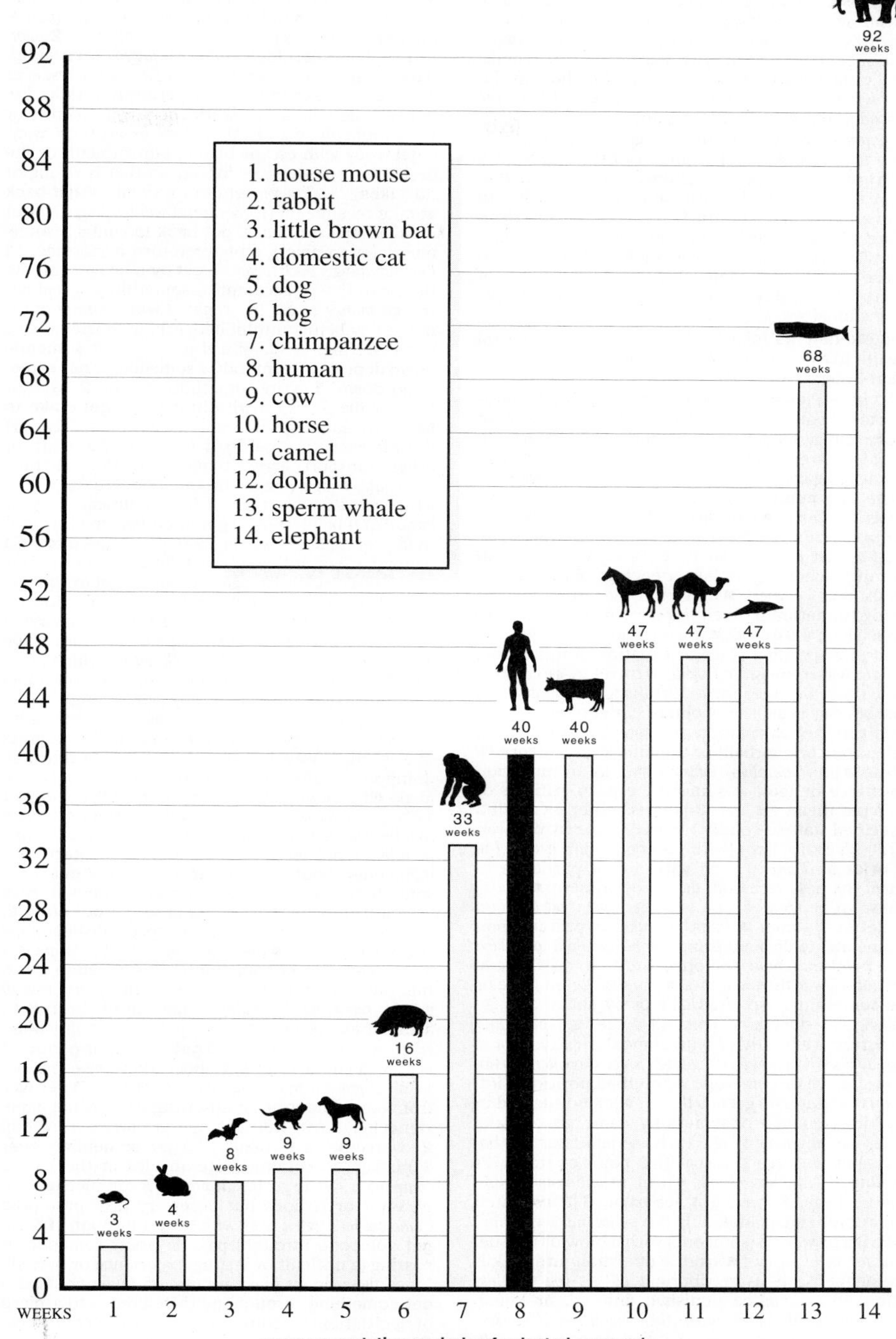

average gestation periods of selected mammals

Ge·sta·po /gəˈstäpō/ the German secret police under Nazi rule. It ruthlessly suppressed opposition to the Nazis in Germany and occupied Europe and sent Jews and others to concentration camps. From 1936 it was headed by Heinrich Himmler. ▷German, from *Geheime Staatspolizei* 'secret state police.'

ges·tate /ˈjeˌstāt/ ▸*v.* [*trans.*] carry (a fetus) in the womb from conception to birth: *these individuals gestate male-based litters* | [*intrans.*] *rabbits gestate for approximately twenty-eight days.* ■ [*intrans.*] (of a fetus) undergo gestation. ■ *figurative* develop (something) in the mind over a long period: *a research trip he made while gestating his new book.* ▷mid 19th cent.: from Latin *gestat-* 'carried in the womb,' from the verb *gestare*. **—ges·ta·tive** /jeˈstātiv; ˈjestətiv/ *adj.*

ges·ta·tion /jeˈstāshən/ ▸*n.* the process of carrying or being carried in the womb between conception and birth. ■ the duration of such a process. ■ *figurative* the development of something over a period of time: *various ideas are in the process of gestation.* ▷mid 16th cent. (denoting an excursion on horseback, in a carriage, etc., considered as exercise): from Latin *gestatio(n-)*, from *gestare* 'carry, carry in the womb,' frequentative of *gerere* 'carry.' **—ges·ta·tion·al** /-shənl/ *adj.*

ges·tic·u·late /jeˈstikyəˌlāt/ ▸*v.* [*intrans.*] use gestures, esp. dramatic ones, instead of speaking or to emphasize one's words: *they were shouting and gesticulating frantically at drivers who did not slow down.* ▷early 17th cent.: from Latin *gesticulat-* 'gesticulated,' from the verb *gesticulari*, from *gesticulus*, diminutive of *gestus* 'action.' **—ges·tic·u·la·tion** /jeˌstikyəˈlāshən/ *n.* **—ges·tic·u·la·tive** /-ˌlātiv/ *adj.* **—ges·tic·u·la·tor** /-ˌlātər/ *n.* **—ges·tic·u·la·to·ry** /-ləˌtôrē/ *adj.*

ges·ture /ˈjesCHər/ ▸*n.* a movement of part of the body, esp. a hand or the head, to express an idea or meaning: *Alex made a gesture of apology | so much is conveyed by gesture.* ■ an action performed to convey one's feelings or intentions: *Maggie was touched by the kind gesture.* ■ an action performed for show in the knowledge that it will have no effect: *I hope the amendment will not be just a gesture.*
▸*v.* [*intrans.*] make a gesture: *she gestured meaningfully with the pistol.* ■ [*trans.*] express (something) with a gesture or gestures: *he gestured his dissent at this.* ■ [*trans.* or *infinitive*] direct or invite (someone) to move somewhere specified: *he gestured her to a chair.* ▷late Middle English: from medieval Latin *gestura,* from Latin *gerere* 'bear, wield, perform.' The original sense was 'bearing, deportment,' hence 'the use of posture and bodily movements for effect in oratory.' —**ges·tur·al** *adj.*

ge·sund·heit /gəˈzo͝ontīt/ ▸*exclam.* used to wish good health to a person who has just sneezed. ▷from German *Gesundheit* 'health.'

get /get/ ▸*v.* (**get·ting**; *past* **got** /gät/; *past part.* **got** or **got·ten** /ˈgätn/) **1** [*trans.*] come to have or hold (something); receive: *I got the impression that she wasn't happy.* ■ experience, suffer, or be afflicted with (something bad): *I got a sudden pain in my left eye.* ■ receive as a punishment or penalty: *I'll get the sack if things go wrong.* ■ contract (a disease or ailment): *I might be getting the flu.* ■ receive (a communication): *I got a letter from my fiancé.* **2** [*trans.*] succeed in attaining, achieving, or experiencing; obtain: *I need all the sleep I can get.* ■ move in order to pick up or bring (something); fetch: *get another chair* [with *two objs.*] *I'll get you a drink.* ■ [*trans.*] tend to meet with or find in a specified place or situation: *it was nothing like the winters we get in Florida.* ■ travel by or catch (a bus, train, or other form of transport): *I'll get a taxi and be home in an hour.* ■ obtain (a figure or answer) as a result of calculation. ■ respond to a ring of (a telephone or doorbell) or the knock on (a door): *I'll get it!* ■ [in *imperative*] *informal* said as an invitation to notice or look at someone, esp. to criticize or ridicule them: *get her!* **3** [*intrans.*] enter or reach a specified state or condition; become: *he got very worried | it's getting late |* [with *past part.*] *you'll get used to it.* ■ [as *auxiliary v.*] used with a past participle to form the passive mood: *the cat got groomed.* ■ [*trans.*] cause to be treated in a specified way: *get the form signed by a doctor.* ■ [*trans.*] induce or prevail upon (someone) to do something: *Sophie got Beth to make a fire.* ■ [*intrans.*] have the opportunity to do: *he got to try out a few of these new cars.* ■ [*intrans.*] begin to be or do something, esp. gradually or by chance: *we got talking one evening.* **4** [*intrans.*] come, go, or make progress eventually or with some difficulty: *I got to the airport | they weren't going to get anywhere.* ■ [*intrans.*] move or come into a specified position, situation, or state: *she got into the car.* ■ [*trans.*] succeed in making (someone or something) come, go, or make progress: *my honesty often gets me into trouble.* ■ [*intrans.*] *informal* reach a specified point or stage: ***it's getting so** I can't even think.* ■ [usu. in *imperative*] *informal* go away. **5** (**have got**) see HAVE. **6** [*trans.*] catch or apprehend (someone): *the police have got him.* ■ strike or wound (someone) with a blow or missile: *you got me in the eye!* ■ *informal* punish, injure, or kill (someone), esp. as retribution: *I'll get you for this!* ■ (**get it**) *informal* be punished, injured, or killed: *wait until Dad comes home, then you'll get it!* ■ (**get mine, his,** etc.) *informal* be killed or appropriately punished or rewarded: *I'll get mine, you get yours, we'll all get wealthy.* ■ *informal* annoy or amuse (someone) greatly: *cleaning the same things all the time, that's what gets me.* ■ *informal* baffle (someone): *"What's a 'flowery boundary tree'?" "You got me."* **7** [*trans.*] *informal* understand (an argument or the person making it): *What do you mean? I don't get it.* **8** [*trans.*] *archaic* acquire (knowledge) by study; learn: *knowledge which is gotten at school.*
▸*phrasal v.* □ **get something across** manage to communicate an idea clearly. □ **get ahead** become successful in one's life or career: *how to get ahead in advertising.* □ **get along 1** have a harmonious or friendly relationship: *they seem to get along pretty well.* **2** manage to live or survive: *don't worry, we'll get along without you.* □ **get around 1** coax or persuade (someone) to do or allow something that they initially do not want to. **2** deal successfully with (a problem). ■ evade (a regulation or restriction) without contravening it: *the company changed its name to get around the law.* □ **get around to** (or *chiefly Brit.* **round to**) deal with (a task) in due course: *I didn't get around to putting all the photos in frames.* □ **get at 1** reach or gain access to (something): *it's difficult to get at the screws.* ■ bribe or unfairly influence (someone): *he had been got at by government officials.* **2** *informal* imply (something): *I can see what you're getting at.* □ **get away** escape: *Stevie was caught, but the rest of us got away | he was very lucky to **get away with** his life.* ■ leave one's home or work for a time of rest or recreation; go on a vacation: *it will be nice to get away.* □ **get away with** escape blame, punishment, or undesirable consequences for (an act that is wrong or mistaken): *you'll never get away with this.* □ **get back at** take revenge on (someone): *I wanted to get back at them for what they did.* □ **get back to** contact (someone) later to give a reply or return a message: *I'll find out and get back to you.* □ **get by** manage with difficulty to live or accomplish something: *he had just enough money to get by.* □ **get down** *informal* enjoy oneself by being uninhibited, esp. with friends in a social setting: *get down and party!* □ **get someone down** depress or demoralize someone. □ **get something down 1** write something down. **2** swallow food or drink, esp. with difficulty. □ **get down to** begin to do or give serious attention to: *let's get down to business.* □ **get in 1** (of a train, aircraft, or other transport) arrive at its destination: *the train got in late.* ■ (of a person) arrive at one's destination: *what time did you get in?* **2** (of a political party or candidate) be elected. □ **get in on** become involved in (a profitable or exciting activity). □ **get into** (of a feeling) affect, influence, or take control of (someone): *I don't know what's got into him.* □ **get in with** become friendly with (someone), esp. in order to gain an advantage: *I hope he doesn't get in with the wrong crowd.* □ **get off 1** *informal* escape a punishment; be acquitted: *she got off lightly | you'll **get off with** a warning.* **2** *vulgar slang* have an orgasm. □ **get off on** *informal* be excited or aroused by (something): *he was obviously getting off on the adrenaline of performing before the crowd.* □ **get on 1** perform or make progress in a specified way: *how are you getting on?* ■ continue doing something, esp. after an interruption: *I've got to **get on with** this job.* **2** *chiefly Brit.* another way of saying GET ALONG (sense 1). **3** (**be getting on**) *informal* be old or comparatively old: *we are both getting on a bit.* □ **get on to** *chiefly Brit.* make contact with (someone) about a particular topic. □ **get out 1** (of something previously secret) become known: *news got out that we were coming.* **2** (also **get out of here**) *informal* [in *imperative*] used to express disbelief: *get out, you're a liar.* ■ [usu. in *imperative*] *informal* go away; leave. □ **get something out** succeed in uttering, publishing, or releasing something: *we need to get this report out by Friday.* □ **get out of** contrive to avoid or escape (a duty or responsibility): *they wanted to get out of paying.* □ **get something out of** achieve benefit from (an undertaking or exercise): *we never got any money out of it.* □ **get over 1** recover from (an ailment or an upsetting or startling experience): *the trip will help him get over Sal's death.* **2** overcome (a difficulty). □ **get something over 1** manage to communicate an idea or theory: *the company is keen to get the idea over.* **2** complete an unpleasant or tedious but necessary task promptly: *Come on, let's **get it over with**.* □ **get through 1** (also **get someone through**) pass or assist someone in passing (a difficult or testing experience or period): *I need these lessons to get me through my exam.* ■ (also **get something through**) (with reference to a piece of legislation) become or cause to become law. **2** make contact by telephone: *after an hour of busy signals, I finally got through.* ■ succeed in communicating with someone in a meaningful way: *I just don't think anyone can **get through to** these kids.* □ **get to 1** *informal* annoy or upset (someone) by persistent action: *he started crying—we were getting to him.* **2** another way of saying GET AROUND TO above. □ **get together** gather or assemble socially or to cooperate. □ **get up 1** (also **get someone up**) rise or cause to rise from bed after sleeping. **2** (of wind or the sea) become strong or agitated. □ **get something up 1** prepare or organize a project or piece of work: *we used to get up little plays.* **2** enhance or refine one's knowledge of a subject.
▸*n.* **1** *Tennis* a successful return of a difficult ball. **2** *dated* an animal's offspring: *he passes this on to his get.* **3** *Brit., informal dialect* a person whom the speaker dislikes or despises. ▷Middle English: from Old Norse *geta* 'obtain, beget, guess'; related to Old English *gietan* (in *begietan* 'beget,' *forgietan* 'forget'), from an Indo-European root shared by Latin *praeda* 'booty, prey,' *praehendere* 'get hold of, seize,' and Greek *khandanein* 'hold, contain, be able.' —**get·ta·ble** *adj.*
▸*PHRASES* □ (**as**) —— **as all get out** *informal* to a great or extreme extent: *he was stubborn as all get out.* □ **be out to get someone** be determined to punish or harm someone, esp. in retaliation: *he thinks the media are out to get him.* □ **get in there** *informal* take positive action to achieve one's aim (often said as an exhortation): *you get in there, son, and you work.* □ **get it on** *informal* have sexual intercourse. □ **get it up** *vulgar slang* (of a man) achieve an erection. □ **get-rich-quick** *derogatory* designed or concerned to make a lot of money fast: *another one of your get-rich-quick schemes.* □ **get-up-and-go** *informal* energy, enthusiasm, and initiative.

USAGE The verb **get** is in the top five of the most common verbs in the English language. Because of **get**'s commonness, some writers think it unfit for formal writing. This may be so in some senses and contexts, where *receive* or *understand* or even *murder* would be more exact, but many writers known for their precision and elegance of style use **get** with ease and confidence: *There's no **getting around it*** (Jacques Barzun); *Mr. Head began to get out his tickets* (Flannery O'Connor); *She would **get home** just in time* (James Baldwin); *They got into automobiles which bore them out to Long Island* (F. Scott Fitzgerald).
For a discussion of **got** and **gotten**, see **usage** at GOTTEN.

THE RIGHT WORD **acquire, attain, gain, get, obtain, procure, secure**
Get is a very broad term meaning to come into possession of. You can *get* something by fetching it (*get some groceries*), by receiving it (*get a birthday gift*), by earning it (*get interest on a bank loan*), or by any of a dozen other familiar means.
Substituting **obtain** sounds less colloquial. But it can also sound pretentious (*all employees were required to obtain an annual physical exam*) and should be reserved for contexts where the emphasis is on seeking something out (*to obtain blood samples*).
Acquire often suggests a continued, sustained, or cumulative acquisition (*to acquire poise as one matures*), but it can also hint at deviousness (*to acquire the keys to the safe*).
Use **procure** if you want to emphasize the effort involved in bringing something to pass (*procure a mediated divorce settlement*) or if you want to imply maneuvering to possess something (*procure a reserved parking space*). But beware: *Procure* is so often used to describe the act of obtaining partners to gratify the lust of others (*to procure a prostitute*) that it has acquired somewhat unsavory overtones.
Gain also implies effort, usually in *getting* something advantageous or profitable (*gain entry; gain victory*).
In a similar vein, **secure** underscores the difficulty involved in bringing something to pass and the desire to place it beyond danger (*secure a permanent peace; secure a lifeline*).
Attain should be reserved for achieving a high goal or desirable result (*If she attains the summit of Mt. Everest, she will secure for herself a place in mountaineering history*).

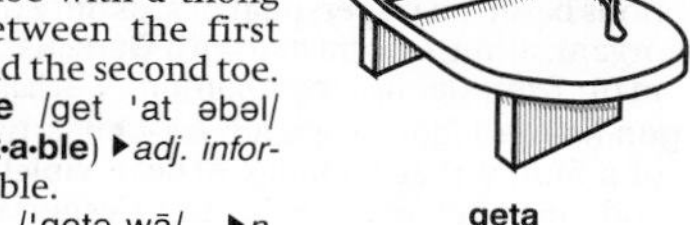
geta

ge·ta /ˈgetə; ˈgeˌtä/ ▸*adj.* (*pl.* same or **ge·tas**) a Japanese wooden shoe with a thong to pass between the first (big) toe and the second toe.

get-at-a·ble /get ˈat əbəl/ (also **get·at·a·ble**) ▸*adj. informal* accessible.

get·a·way /ˈgetəˌwā/ ▸*n.* **1** an escape or quick departure, esp. after committing a crime: *the thugs made their getaway |* [as *adj.*] *a getaway car.* ■ a fast start by a racing car: *the driver made a poor getaway.* **2** *informal* a vacation: *a perfect family getaway.* ■ the destination or accommodations for a vacation: *a popular island getaway.*

get-go (also **git-go**) ▸*n.* the very beginning: *Lawrence knew **from the get-go** that he could count on me to tell him the truth.*

Geth·sem·a·ne, Gar·den of /geTHˈseməne͞/ a garden between Jerusalem and the Mount of Olives, where Jesus went with his disciples after the Last Supper and was betrayed (Matt. 26:36–46). ▷from Hebrew *gath-shemen* 'oil press.'

get·ter /ˈgetər/ ▸*n.* **1** [usu. in *combination*] a person or thing that gets a specified desirable thing: *an attention-getter | a vote-getter.* **2** *Electronics & Physics* a substance used to remove residual gas from a vacuum tube, or impurities or defects from a semiconductor crystal.

get·to·geth·er ▸*n.* an informal gathering. ■ a sociable meeting or conference.

get-tough ▸*adj. informal* designating an approach or attitude characterized by assertiveness, firmness, or aggressiveness: *the administration is implementing get-tough changes in the juvenile system | France's get-tough policy on illegal immigrants.*

Get·ty /ˈgetē/, Jean Paul (1892–1976), U.S. industrialist. He made a fortune in the oil industry and was also a noted art collector. He founded the J. Paul Getty Museum in Los Angeles, California.

Get·tys·burg /ˈgetēzˌbərg; -iz-/ a historic agricultural and commercial borough in south central Pennsylvania, scene of a critical Civil War battle in July 1863; pop. 7,025.

Get·tys·burg, Battle of a decisive battle of the Civil War, fought near the town of Gettysburg in Pennsylvania in July 1863. A Union army under General Meade repulsed the Confederate army of General Lee and forced him to abandon his invasion of the north.

Get·tys·burg Ad·dress a speech delivered on November 18, 1863, by President Abraham Lincoln at the dedication of the national cemetery on the site of the Battle of Gettysburg.

get·up /ˈgetəp/ (also **get-up**) ▸*n. informal* a style or arrangement of dress, esp. an elaborate or unusual one: *she looks ridiculous in that getup.*

Getz /gets/, Stan (1927–91), U.S. jazz saxophonist; born *Stanley Gayetsky.* A leader of the "cool" school of jazz, his recordings include "Early Autumn" (1948) and "The Girl from Ipanema" (1963). His *Jazz Samba* album (1962) with Charlie Parker launched the samba and bossa nova movements of the 1960s.

ge·um /ˈjēəm/ ▸*n.* a plant of a genus that comprises the avens. • Genus *Geum,* family Rosaceae. ▷modern Latin, variant of Latin *gaeum.*

GeV ▸*abbr.* gigaelectronvolt, equivalent to 10^9 electron-volts.

gew·gaw /ˈg(y)o͞oˌgô/ ▸*n.* (usu. **gewgaws**) a showy thing, esp. one that is useless or worthless. ▷Middle English: of unknown origin.

Ge·würz·tra·mi·ner /gəˈvo͝ortstrəˌmēnər/ ▸*n.* a variety of white grape grown mainly in the Alsace, Austria, and the Rhine valley. ■ a wine made from this grape. ▷German, from *Gewürz* 'spice' + **Traminer.**

gey·ser /ˈgīzər/ ▸*n.* **1** a hot spring in which water intermittently boils, sending a tall column of water and steam into the air. ■ a jet or stream of liquid: *the pipe sent up* ***a geyser of*** *sewer water into the street.* **2** *Brit.* a gas-fired water heater through which water flows as it is rapidly heated.
▸*v.* [*intrans.*] (esp. of water or steam) gush or burst out with great force: *yellow smoke geysered upward.* ▷late 18th cent.: from Icelandic *Geysir,* the name of a particular spring in Iceland; related to *geysa* 'to gush.'

gey·ser·ite /ˈgīzəˌrīt/ ▸*n.* a hard opaline siliceous deposit occurring around geysers and hot springs. ▷early 19th cent.: from **geyser** + **-ite**[1].

GFE ▸*abbr.* government-furnished equipment.

GFWC ▸*abbr.* General Federation of Women's Clubs.

GGPA ▸*abbr.* graduate grade-point average.

Gha·ga·ra Ri·ver /gəˈgärə; ˈgägərə/ (also **Gogra**; Nepalese **Karnali**)a river in south central Asia that flows for 570 miles (900 km) from southwestern Tibet through Nepal into India, where it joins the Ganges River.

Gha·na /ˈgänə/ a country in West Africa, with a southern coastline that borders on the Atlantic Ocean; pop. 20,750,000; capital, Accra; languages, English (official) and West African languages.

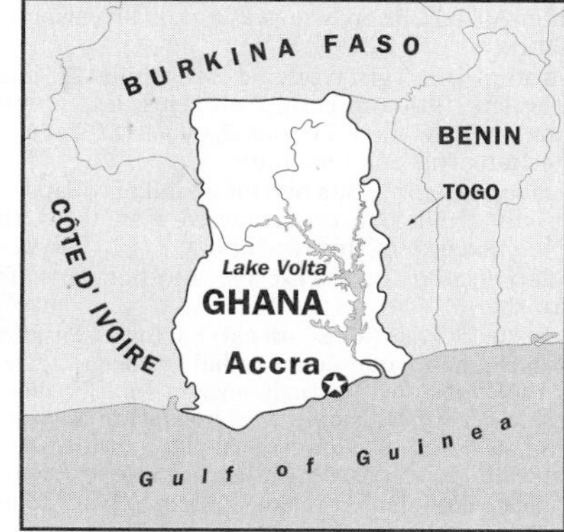

Former name (until 1957) **Gold Coast.** —**Gha·na·ian** /gəˈnāən; gəˈnīən/ *adj. & n.*

Formerly a center of the slave trade, the area became the British colony of Gold Coast in 1874. In 1957, it gained independence as a member of the Commonwealth of Nations under the leadership of Kwame Nkrumah. It was the first British colony to become independent.

gha·ri·al /ˈgərēəl/ (also **ga·vi·al** /ˈgāvēəl/) ▸*n.* a large fish-eating crocodile with a long narrow snout that widens at the nostrils, native to the Indian subcontinent. See also **false gharial.** • *Gavialis gangeticus,* the only member of the family Gavialidae. ▷early 19th cent.: from Hindi *ghaṛiyāl.* The spelling *gavial* (from French) is an alteration probably due to scribal error.

ghast·ly /ˈgastlē/ ▸*adj.* (**-li·er, -li·est**) **1** causing great horror or fear; frightful or macabre: *she was overcome with horror at the ghastly spectacle.* ■ *informal* objectionable; unpleasant: *we had to wear ghastly old-fashioned dresses.* **2** extremely unwell: *he always felt ghastly first thing in the morning.* ■ deathly white or pallid: *a ghastly pallor* | [as *submodifier*] *he turned ghastly pale and rushed to the bathroom.* ▷Middle English: from obsolete *gast* 'terrify,' from Old English *gǣstan,* of Germanic origin; related to **ghost.** The *gh* spelling is by association with **ghost.** The sense 'objectionable' dates from the mid 19th cent. —**ghast·li·ness** *n.*

ghat /gôt; gät/ (also **ghaut**) ▸*n.* **1** (in the Indian subcontinent) a flight of steps leading down to a river. **2** (in the Indian subcontinent) a mountain pass. ▷from Hindi *ghāṭ.*

Ghats /gôts/ two mountain ranges in central and southern India. Known as **the Eastern Ghats** and **the Western Ghats,** they run parallel to the coast on either side of the Deccan plateau and meet at the southern tip of India.

gha·zal /ˈgəzəl/ ▸*n.* (in Middle Eastern and Indian literature and music) a lyric poem with a fixed number of verses and a repeated rhyme, typically on the theme of love, and normally set to music. ▷via Persian from Arabic *ġazal.*

gha·zi /ˈgäzē/ (also, esp. as an honorific title, **Gha·zi**) ▸*n.* (*pl.* **gha·zis**) a Muslim fighter against non-Muslims. ▷from Arabic *al-ġāzī,* participle of *ġazā* 'invade, raid.'

Gha·zi·a·bad /ˈgäzēəˌbäd/ a city in northern India, in Uttar Pradesh, east of Delhi; pop. 461,000.

GHB ▸*abbr.* (sodium) gamma-hydroxybutyrate, a designer drug with anesthetic properties. • Chem. formula: $CH_2OH(CH_2)_2COONa$.

ghee /gē/ ▸*n.* clarified butter made from the milk of a buffalo or cow, used in Indian cooking. ▷from Hindi *ghī,* from Sanskrit *ghṛtá* 'sprinkled.'

Ghent /gent/ a city in Belgium, capital of the province of East Flanders, on the Scheldt River; pop. 230,200. Flemish name **Gent,** French name **Gand.**

gher·kin /ˈgərkin/ ▸*n.* **1** a small variety of cucumber, or a young green cucumber used for pickling. ■ a pickle made from such a cucumber. **2** a trailing plant with cucumberlike fruits used for pickling. • *Cucumis anguria,* family Cucurbitaceae. ■ the fresh or pickled fruit of this plant. ▷early 17th cent.: from Dutch *augurkje, gurkje,* diminutive of *augurk, gurk,* from Slavic, based on medieval Greek *angourion* 'cucumber.'

ghet·to /ˈgetō/ ▸*n.* (*pl.* **-tos** or **-toes**) a part of a city, esp. a slum area, occupied by a minority group or groups. ■ *historical* the Jewish quarter in a city: *the Warsaw Ghetto.* ■ an isolated or segregated group or area: *the relative security of the gay ghetto.*
▸*v.* (**-toes, -toed**) [*trans.*] put in or restrict to an isolated or segregated area or group. ▷early 17th cent.: perhaps from Italian *getto* 'foundry' (because the first ghetto was established in 1516 on the site of a foundry in Venice), or from Italian *borghetto,* diminutive of *borgo* 'borough.'

ghet·to blast·er ▸*n. informal* a large portable radio and cassette or CD player.

ghet·to·ize /ˈgetōˌīz/ ▸*v.* [*trans.*] put in or restrict to an isolated or segregated place, group, or situation: *the Arabs are ghettoized and have few rights.* —**ghet·to·i·za·tion** /ˌgetō-iˈzāsнən/ *n.*

Ghib·el·line /ˈgibəˌlēn; -ˌlīn; -lin/ ▸*n.* a member of one of the two great political factions in Italian medieval politics, traditionally supporting the Holy Roman Emperor against the pope and his supporters, the Guelphs. ▷from Italian *Ghibellino,* perhaps from German *Waiblingen,* an estate belonging to Hohenstaufen emperors.

Ghi·ber·ti /gēˈbertē/, Lorenzo (1378–1455), Italian sculptor and goldsmith.

ghil·lie ▸*n.* variant spelling of **gillie.**

Ghir·lan·da·io /ˌgi(ə)rlənˈdīō/ (*c.*1448–94), Italian painter; born *Domenico di Tommaso Bigordi.* He is noted for his religious frescoes, particularly *Christ Calling Peter and Andrew* (1482–84) in the Sistine Chapel in Rome.

ghost /gōst/ ▸*n.* an apparition of a dead person that is believed to appear or become manifest to the living, typically as a nebulous image: *the building is haunted by the ghost of a monk* | *figurative the ghosts of communism returned to haunt the living.* ■ [as *adj.*] appearing or manifesting but not actually existing: *the Flying Dutchman is the most famous ghost ship.* ■ a faint trace of something: *she gave the* ***ghost of*** *a smile.* ■ *archaic* a spirit or soul. ■ a faint secondary image produced by a fault in an optical system or on a cathode-ray screen, e.g., by faulty television reception or internal reflection in a mirror or camera.
▸*v.* **1** [*trans.*] act as ghostwriter of (a work): *his memoirs were smoothly ghosted by a journalist.* **2** [*intrans.*] glide smoothly and effortlessly: *they ghosted up the river.* ▷Old English *gāst* (in the sense 'spirit, soul'), of Germanic origin; related to Dutch *geest* and German *Geist.* The *gh-* spelling occurs first in Caxton, probably influenced by Flemish *gheest.* —**ghost·like** /-ˌlīk/ *adj.*
▸***PHRASES*** □ **the ghost in the machine** *Philosophy* the mind viewed as distinct from the body (usually used in a derogatory fashion by critics of dualism). [coined by the philosopher Gilbert Ryle (1949).] □ **give up the ghost** die. ■ (of a machine) stop working. □ **look as if you have seen a ghost** look very pale and shocked. □ **not stand a ghost of a chance** have no chance at all.

ghost·bust·er /ˈgōstˌbəstər/ *informal* ▸*n.* **1** a person who claims to be able to banish ghosts and poltergeists. ■ a parapsychologist. **2** an investigator of tax fraud.

ghost crab ▸*n.* a pale yellowish crab that lives in a burrow in the sand above the high-water mark and goes down to the sea at night to feed. • Genus *Ocypode,* family Ocypodidae.

Ghost Dance an American Indian religious cult of the second half of the 19th century, based on the performance of a ritual dance that, it was believed, would drive away white people and restore the traditional lands and way of life. Advocated by the Sioux chief Sitting Bull, the cult was central to the uprising that was crushed at the Battle of Wounded Knee.

ghost·ing /ˈgōstiNG/ ▸*n.* the appearance of a ghost or secondary image on a television or other display screen.

ghost·ly /ˈgōstlē/ ▸*adj.* (**-li·er, -li·est**) of or like a ghost in appearance or sound; eerie and unnatural: *a ghostly figure with a hood.* ▷Old English *gāstlic,* from *gāst* 'ghost.' —**ghost·li·ness** *n.*

ghost moth (also **ghost swift**) ▸*n.* a medium to large swift moth, the male of which has white wings. • Family Hepialidae. See **swift** (sense 2).

ghost sto·ry ▸*n.* a story involving ghosts or ghostly circumstances, intended to be suspenseful and scary.

ghost town ▸*n.* a deserted town with few or no remaining inhabitants.

ghost word ▸*n.* a word that is not actually used but is recorded in a dictionary or other reference work.

ghost·writ·er /ˈgōstˌrītər/ ▸*n.* a person whose job it is to write material for someone else who is the named author. —**ghost·write** *v.*

ghoul /go͞ol/ ▸*n.* an evil spirit or phantom, esp. one supposed to rob graves and feed on dead bodies. ■ a person morbidly interested in death or disaster. ▷late 18th cent.: from Arabic *ġūl,* 'a desert demon believed to rob graves and devour corpses.' —**ghoul·ish** *adj.* —**ghoul·ish·ly** *adv.* —**ghoul·ish·ness** *n.*

GHQ ▸*abbr.* general headquarters.

Ghul·ghu·leh /go͞olˈgo͞olē/ an ancient city in central Afghanistan. It was destroyed by Genghis Khan *c.*1221.

Ghz (or **GHz**) ▸*abbr.* gigahertz.

GI ▸*n.* (*pl.* **GIs**) a private soldier in the U.S. Army. ▷1930s (originally denoting equipment supplied to U.S. forces): abbreviation of *galvanized iron;* later misinterpreted as an abbreviation of *government* (or *general*) *issue.*

Pronunciation Key ə *ago;* ər *over;* ˈə or ˌə *up;* ˈər or ˌər *fur;* a *hat;* ā *rate;* ä *car;* CH *chew;* e *let;* ē *see;* e(ə)r *air;* i *fit;* ī *by;* i(ə)r *ear;* NG *sing;* ō *go;* ô *for;* oi *boy;* o͝o *good;* o͞o *goo;* ou *out;* SH *she;* TH *thin;* T͟H *then;* (h)w *why;* ZH *vision*

gi /gē/ ▶*n.* (*pl.* **gis**) a lightweight two-piece white garment worn in judo and other martial arts. A gi typically consists of loose-fitting pants and a jacket that is closed with a cloth belt. ▷Japanese.

gi

Gia·co·met·ti /ˌjäkəˈmetē/, Alberto (1901–66), Swiss sculptor and painter. His most typical works are of emaciated and extremely elongated human forms, such as *Invisible Object* (1934–35), and *Pointing Man* (1947).

gi·ant /ˈjīənt/ ▶*n.* **1** an imaginary or mythical being of human form but superhuman size. ■ (in Greek mythology) any of the beings of this kind who rebelled unsuccessfully against the gods of Olympus. ■ an abnormally tall or large person, animal, or plant. ■ a very large company or organization. ■ a person of exceptional talent or qualities: *a giant among sportsmen.* **2** *Astronomy* a star of relatively great size and luminosity compared to ordinary stars of the main sequence, and 10–100 times the diameter of the sun.
▶*adj.* [*attrib.*] of very great size or force; gigantic: *giant multinational corporations | a giant transport plane | a giant meteorite.* ■ used in names of very large animals and plants, e.g., **giant hogweed**, **giant tortoise**. ▷Middle English *geant* (with the first syllable later influenced by Latin *gigant-*), from Old French, via Latin from Greek *gigas, gigant-*. **—gi·ant·like** /-ˌlīk/ *adj.*

gi·ant ant·eat·er ▶*n.* a large insectivorous mammal with long coarse fur, large claws, an elongated snout, and a long tongue for catching ants. It is native to Central and South America. • *Myrmecophaga tridactyla*, family Myrmecophagidae, order Xenartha (or Edentata).

giant anteater

gi·ant clam ▶*n.* a very large bivalve mollusk that occurs in the tropical Indo-Pacific. • Family Tridacnidae: several species, including *Tridacna gigas*, which is the largest living shelled mollusk.

gi·ant deer ▶*n.* another term for **IRISH ELK**.

gi·ant·ess /ˈjīəntis/ ▶*n.* a female giant.

gi·ant gou·ra·mi ▶*n.* a large edible freshwater fish that is native to Asia. It is widely farmed there and has been introduced elsewhere. • Family Osphronemidae and genus *Osphronemus*, in particular *O. goramy*.

gi·ant ground·sel ▶*n.* a large treelike plant of the daisy family, having a thick stem and a few short branches tipped with broad leaves, growing chiefly on high mountains in central and eastern Africa. • Genus *Senecio* (or *Dendrosenecio*), family Compositae.

gi·ant·ism /ˈjīənˌtizəm/ ▶*n.* a tendency toward abnormally large size; gigantism.

gi·ant-kill·er ▶*n.* a person or team that defeats a seemingly much more powerful opponent. **—gi·ant-kill·ing** *n.*

gi·ant or·der ▶*n. Architecture* an order whose columns extend through more than one story.

gi·ant pan·da ▶*n.* see **PANDA**.

gi·ant pet·rel ▶*n.* the largest petrel, which is found around southern oceans, has a massive bill, and scavenges from carcasses. • Genus *Macronectes*, family Procellariidae: two species.

gi·ant puff·ball ▶*n.* a European fungus that produces a spherical white fruiting body with a diameter of up to 32 inches (80 cm), edible when young. • *Langermannia gigantea*, family Lycoperdaceae, class Gasteromycetes.

gi·ant reed ▶*n.* a fast-growing perennial grass native to India that is a principal source for reeds used in musical instruments. In the U.S. it threatens some native plant habitats because of its spreading and dispersal habits. • *Arundo donax*, family Poaceae.

gi·ant sal·a·man·der ▶*n.* a very large salamander that is native to North America and eastern Asia, in particular: • a permanently aquatic salamander (three species in the family Cryptobranchidae), e.g., the American hellbender. • a terrestrial salamander (three species in the family Dicamptodontidae), of western North America.

gi·ant se·quoi·a ▶*n.* another term for **GIANT REDWOOD** (see **REDWOOD**).

gi·ant silk moth ▶*n.* see **SILKWORM MOTH**.

gi·ant sla·lom ▶*n.* a long-distance slalom with fast, wide turns.

gi·ant squid ▶*n.* a deep-sea squid that is the largest known invertebrate, reaching a length of 59 feet (18 m) or more. • Genus *Architeuthis*, order Teuthoidea.

gi·ant toad ▶*n.* another term for **CANE TOAD**.

gi·ant tor·toise ▶*n.* a very large tortoise with a long lifespan, occurring on several tropical oceanic islands. • Genus *Geochelone*, family Testudinidae: *G. nigra* (Galapagos Islands) and *G. gigantea* (Aldabra and the Seychelles).

giaour /ˈjou(ə)r/ ▶*n. archaic, derogatory* a non-Muslim, esp. a Christian. ▷from Turkish *gâvur*, from Persian *gaur*, probably from Arabic *kāfir* (see **KAFFIR**).

Giap /zyäp/, Vo Nguyen (1912–), Vietnamese military and political leader. As North Vietnamese vice-premier and defense minister, he was responsible for the strategy leading to the withdrawal of U.S. forces from South Vietnam in 1973 and the subsequent reunification of the country in 1976.

gi·ar·di·a·sis /ˌjēärˈdīəsis; järˈdī-/ ▶*n.* infection of the intestine with a flagellate protozoan, which causes diarrhea and other symptoms. • The protozoan is *Giardia lamblia*, phylum Metamonada, kingdom Protista. ▷early 20th cent.: from modern Latin *Giardia* (from the name of Alfred M. *Giard* (1846–1908), French biologist) + **-ASIS**.

gib /gib/ ▶*n.* a wood or metal bolt, wedge, or pin for holding part of a machine or structure in place, usually adjusted by a screw or key: [as *adj.*] *gib screws.*
▶*v.* [*trans.*] fasten (parts) together with a gib. ▷late 18th cent.: of unknown origin.

gib·ber /ˈjibər/ ▶*v.* [*intrans.*] speak rapidly and unintelligibly, typically through fear or shock: *they shrieked and gibbered as flames surrounded them* | [as *adj.*] (**gibbering**) *a gibbering idiot.* ▷early 17th cent.: imitative.

gib·ber·el·lic ac·id /ˌjibəˈrelik/ ▶*n.* a gibberellin that is used commercially, notably in germinating barley for malt. ▷1950s: *gibberellic* from modern Latin *Gibberella* (see **GIBBERELLIN**) + **-IC**.

gib·ber·el·lin /ˌjibəˈrelin/ ▶*n.* any of a group of plant hormones that stimulate stem elongation, germination, and flowering. ▷1930s: from modern Latin *Gibberella* (from *Gibberella fujikuroi*, the fungus from which one of the gibberellins was first extracted), diminutive of the genus name *Gibbera*, from Latin *gibber* 'hump,' + **-IN**[1].

gib·ber·ish /ˈjibərisʜ/ ▶*n.* unintelligible or meaningless speech or writing; nonsense: *he talks gibberish.* ▷early 16th cent.: perhaps from **GIBBER** (but recorded earlier) + the suffix **-ISH**[1] (denoting a language as in *Spanish, Swedish*, etc.).

gib·bet /ˈjibit/ *historical* ▶*n.* a gallows. ■ an upright post with an arm on which the bodies of executed criminals were left hanging as a warning or deterrent to others. ■ (**the gibbet**) execution by hanging: *the four ringleaders were sentenced to the gibbet.*
▶*v.* (**-bet·ed, -bet·ing**) [*trans.*] hang up (a body) on a gibbet. ■ execute (someone) by hanging. ■ *archaic or figurative* hold up to contempt: *poor Melbourne is gibbeted in the Times.* ▷Middle English: from Old French *gibet* 'staff, cudgel, gallows,' diminutive of *gibe* 'club, staff,' probably of Germanic origin.

Gib·bon /ˈgibən/, Edward (1737–94), English historian. He is best known for his multivolume work, *The History of the Decline and Fall of the Roman Empire* (1776–88).

gib·bon /ˈgibən/ ▶*n.* a small, slender tree-dwelling ape with long powerful arms and loud hooting calls, native to the forests of Southeast Asia. See also **WHITE-HANDED GIBBON**. • Family Hylobatidae and genus *Hylobates*: several species. ▷late 18th cent.: from French, from an Indian dialect word.

gib·bous /ˈgibəs/ ▶*adj.* (of the moon) having the observable illuminated part greater than a semicircle and less than a circle. ■ convex or protuberant: *gibbous eyes.* ▷late Middle English: from late Latin *gibbosus*, from Latin *gibbus* 'hump.' **—gib·bos·i·ty** /giˈbäsitē/ *n.* **—gib·bous·ly** *adv.* **—gib·bous·ness** *n.*

Gibbs /gibz/, Josiah Willard (1839–1903), U.S. physical chemist. He pioneered in chemical thermodynamics and statistical mechanics.

Gibbs free en·er·gy ▶*n. Chemistry* a thermodynamic quantity equal to the enthalpy (of a system or process) minus the product of the entropy and the absolute temperature. (Symbol: **G**) ▷named after J. W. *Gibbs* (see **GIBBS**).

gibbs·ite /ˈgibzīt/ ▶*n.* a colorless mineral consisting of aluminum hydroxide, occurring chiefly as a constituent of bauxite or in encrustations. ▷early 19th cent.: named after George *Gibbs* (1776–1833), American mineralogist, + **-ITE**[1].

gibe /jīb/ (also **jibe**) ▶*n.* an insulting or mocking remark; a taunt: *a gibe at his old rivals.*
▶*v.* [*intrans.*] make insulting or mocking remarks; jeer: *some cynics in the media might gibe.* ▷mid 16th cent. (as a verb): perhaps from Old French *giber* 'handle roughly' (in modern dialect 'kick'); compare with **JIB**[2].

gib·lets /ˈjiblits/ ▶*plural n.* the liver, heart, gizzard, and neck of a chicken or other fowl, usually removed before the bird is cooked, and often used to make gravy, stuffing, or soup. ▷Middle English (in the sense 'an inessential appendage,' later 'garbage, offal'): from Old French *gibelet* 'game bird stew,' probably from *gibier* 'birds or mammals hunted for sport.'

Gi·bral·tar /jəˈbrôltər/ a British dependency near the southern tip of the Iberian peninsula, at the eastern end of the Strait of Gibraltar; pop. 28,000. Occupying a site of great strategic importance, Gibraltar consists of a fortified town and a military base at the foot of a rocky headland called the **Rock of Gibraltar**. Britain captured it during the War of the Spanish Succession in 1704 and is responsible for its defense, external affairs, and internal security. **—Gi·bral·tar·i·an** /jəˌbrôlˈte(ə)rēən; ˌjibˌrôl-/ *adj. & n.*

Gi·bral·tar, Strait of a channel between the southern tip of the Iberian peninsula and North Africa that forms the only outlet of the Mediterranean Sea to the Atlantic Ocean. It is about 38 miles (60 km) long and varies in width from 15 to 25 miles (24 to 40 km).

Gib·ran /jiˈbrän/ (also **Jub·ran**), Khalil (1883–1931), U.S. writer and artist; born in Lebanon. His writings in both Arabic and English are deeply romantic, displaying his religious and mystical nature. He is especially known for *The Prophet* (1923).

Gib·son[1] /ˈgibsən/, Althea (1927–), U.S. tennis player. She was the first black player to succeed at the highest level of tennis, winning all of the major world women's singles titles in the late 1950s.

Gib·son[2], Bob (1935–) U.S. baseball player; full name Robert Gibson. A pitcher, he played for the St. Louis Cardinals 1959–75. Baseball Hall of Fame (1981).

Gib·son[3], Charles Dana (1867–1944) U.S. artist. A magazine illustrator, he created the "Gibson Girl," typifying a standard of fashion for the times.

Gib·son[4], Mel (1956–), Australian actor and director; born in the U.S.; born in *Mel Columcille Gerard Gibson*. Notable movie appearances: the *Lethal Weapon* trilogy (1987, 1989, and 1992), and *Braveheart* (1995), which he also directed and which won five Academy Awards. In 2004 he produced and directed the controversial film *The Passion of the Christ*.

Gib·son[5] ▶*n.* a dry martini cocktail garnished with a pickled onion.

Gib·son Des·ert /ˈgibsən/ a desert region in western Australia, southeast of the Great Sandy Desert, in eastern central Western Australia. The first European to cross it was Ernest Giles in 1876. He named it after Alfred Gibson, who was lost on an earlier expedition.

Gib·son girl ▶*n.* a girl typifying the fashionable ideal of the late 19th and early 20th centuries. ▷represented in the work of Charles D. *Gibson* (1867–1944), American artist and illustrator.

gi·bus /ˈjībəs/ (also **gibus hat**) ▶*n.* a kind of collapsible top hat. ▷mid 19th cent.: named after *Gibus*, the French inventor of this type of hat.

gid·dap /gidˈəp; -ˈap/ ▶*exclam.* another term for **GIDDY-UP**.

gid·dy /ˈgidē/ ▶*adj.* (**-di·er, -di·est**) having a sensation of whirling and a tendency to fall or stagger; dizzy: *I felt giddy and had to steady myself | Luke felt almost **giddy with** relief.* ■ disorienting and alarming, but exciting: *he has risen to the giddy heights of master.* ■ excitable and frivolous: *her giddy young sister-in-law.*
▶*v.* (**-dies, -died**) [*trans.*] make (someone) feel excited to the point of disorientation: [as *adj.*] *the giddying*

G

speed of the revolving doors. ▷Old English *gidig* 'insane,' literally 'possessed by a god,' from the base of GOD. Current senses date from late Middle English. **—gid·di·ly** /ˈgidəlē/ *adv.* **—gid·di·ness** *n.*

gid·dy-up /ˌgidēˈəp/ (also **gid·dap**) ▸*exclam.* used to get a horse to start moving or go faster. ▷1920s (as *giddap*): reproducing a pronunciation of *get up.*

Gide /ZHēd/, André (Paul Guillaume) (1869–1951), French novelist, essayist, and critic; regarded as the father of modern French literature. His notable works include *The Immoralist* (1902), *Strait Is the Gate* (1909), *The Counterfeiters* (1927), and *Journal* (1939–50). Nobel Prize for Literature (1947).

Gid·e·on /ˈgidēən/ **1** (in the Bible) an Israelite leader, described in Judges 6:11. **2** a member of Gideons International.

Gid·e·ons In·ter·na·tion·al an international Christian organization of business and professional people, founded in 1899 in the U.S. with the aim of spreading the Christian faith by placing bibles in hotel rooms and hospital wards.

gie /gē/ ▸*v.* (**gies, gie·ing;** *past* **gied;** *past part.* **gied** or **gien** /gēn/) Scottish form of GIVE.

Giel·gud /ˈgēlˌgo͝od/, Sir (Arthur) John (1904–2000), English actor and director. A notable Shakespearean actor, particularly remembered for his interpretation of the role of Hamlet, he has also appeared in contemporary plays and movies and won an Academy Award for his role as the butler in *Arthur* (1980).

GIF /jif/ ▸*n. Computing* a popular format for image files, with built-in data compression. ■ (also **gif**) a file in this format. ▷late 20th cent.: acronym from *graphic interchange format.*

GIFT /gift/ ▸*n. Medicine* gamete intrafallopian transfer, a technique for assisting conception by introducing mixed ova and sperm into a Fallopian tube. ▷1980s: acronym.

gift /gift/ ▸*n.* **1** a thing given willingly to someone without payment; a present: *a Christmas gift* | [as *adj.*] *a gift shop.* See note at PRESENT. ■ an act of giving something as a present: *his mother's gift of a pen.* ■ *informal* a very easy task or unmissable opportunity: *that touchdown was an absolute gift.* **2** a natural ability or talent: *he has a* **gift for** *comedy.*
▸*v.* [*trans.*] give (something) as a gift, esp. formally or as a donation or bequest: *the company gifted 2,999 shares to a charity.* ■ present (someone) with a gift or gifts: *the director* **gifted** *her* **with** *a heart-shaped brooch.* ■ (**gift someone with**) endow someone with (something): *she was gifted with a powerful clairvoyance.* ▷Middle English: from Old Norse *gipt*; related to GIVE.
▸**PHRASES** □ **the gift of tongues** see TONGUE. □ **look a gift horse in the mouth** find fault with something that has been received as a gift or favor. [earlier as *look a given horse in the mouth.*]

gift cer·tif·i·cate ▸*n.* a voucher given as a present that is exchangeable for a specified cash value of goods or services from a particular place of business.

gift·ed /ˈgiftid/ ▸*adj.* having exceptional talent or natural ability: *a gifted amateur musician.* ■ having exceptional intelligence: *scholarships for gifted students.* **—gift·ed·ness** *n.*

gift of gab (*chiefly Brit.* also **gift of the gab**) ▸*n.* the ability to speak with eloquence and fluency.

gift·ware /ˈgiftˌwe(ə)r/ ▸*n.* goods sold as being suitable as gifts.

gift wrap ▸*n.* decorative paper for wrapping presents. Also called **gift-wrapping**.
▸*v.* (**gift-wrap**) [*trans.*] [usu. as *adj.*] (**gift-wrapped**) wrap (a present) in decorative paper. ■ *figurative* hand over (something) as if a gift: *his first on-screen role came gift-wrapped.*

Gi·fu /ˈgēfo͞o/ a city in central Japan, on the island of Honshu; pop. 410,000.

gig[1] /gig/ ▸*n.* **1** *chiefly historical* a light two-wheeled carriage pulled by one horse. **2** a light, fast, narrow boat adapted for rowing or sailing.
▸*v.* [*intrans.*] travel in a gig. ▷late 18th cent.: apparently a transferred sense of obsolete *gig* 'a flighty girl,' which was also applied to various objects or devices that whirled.

gig[2] *informal* ▸*n.* a live performance by or engagement for a musician or group playing popular or jazz music. ■ a job, esp. one that is temporary or that has an uncertain future: *he secured his first gig as an NFL coach.*
▸*v.* (**gigged, gig·ging**) [*intrans.*] perform a gig or gigs. ■ [*trans.*] use (a piece of musical equipment) at a gig. ▷1920s: of unknown origin.

gig[3] ▸*n.* a harpoonlike device used for catching fish or frogs.
▸*v.* (**gigged, gig·ging**) [*intrans.*] catch fish or frogs using such a device. ▷early 18th cent.: shortening of earlier (rarely used) *fizgig*, probably from Spanish *fisga* 'harpoon.'

gig[4] ▸*n. informal Computing* short for GIGABYTE.

giga- ▸*comb. form* used in units of measurement: **1** denoting a factor of 10^9: *gigahertz.* **2** *Computing* denoting a factor of 2^{30}. ▷from Greek *gigas* 'giant.'

gig·a·bit /ˈgigəˌbit; ˈjig-/ ▸*n. Computing* a unit of information equal to one billion (10^9) or, strictly, 2^{30} bits.

gig·a·byte /ˈgigəˌbīt; ˈjig-/ (abbr.: **GB**) ▸*n. Computing* a unit of information equal to one billion (10^9) or, strictly, 2^{30} bytes.

gig·a·flop /ˈgigəˌfläp/ ▸*n. Computing* a unit of computing speed equal to one billion floating-point operations per second. ▷1970s: back-formation from *gigaflops* (see GIGA-, -FLOP).

gi·gan·tesque /ˌjīgənˈtesk/ ▸*adj.* like or appropriate to a giant: *these figures, gigantesque and caricatured, haunted my dreams* | *a gigantesque feat.* ▷early 19th cent.: from French, from Italian *gigantesco*, from Greek *gigas, gigant-* (see GIANT).

gi·gan·tic /jīˈgantik/ ▸*adj.* of very great size or extent; huge or enormous: *a gigantic concrete tower.* ▷early 17th cent. (in the sense 'like or suited to a giant'): from Latin *gigas, gigant-* (see GIANT) + -IC. **—gi·gan·ti·cal·ly** /-ik(ə)lē/ *adv.*

gi·gan·tism /jīˈgantizəm/ ▸*n. chiefly Biology* unusual or abnormal largeness. ■ *Medicine* excessive growth due to hormonal imbalance. ■ *Botany* excessive size in plants due to polyploidy.

gi·gan·tom·a·chy /ˌjīgənˈtäməkē/ ▸*n.* (in Greek mythology) the struggle between the gods and the giants. ▷late 16th cent.: from Greek *gigantomakhia*, from *gigas, gigant-* (see GIANT) + *-makhia* 'fighting.'

Gi·gan·to·pi·the·cus /jīˌgantəˈpiTHəkəs/ ▸*n.* a very large fossil Asian ape of the late Miocene to early Pleistocene epochs. • Genus *Gigantopithecus*, family Pongidae. ▷modern Latin, from Greek *gigas, gigant-* (see GIANT) + *pithēkos* 'ape.'

gig·a·ton /ˈgigəˌtən; ˈjig-/ ▸*n.* a unit of explosive force equal to one billion (10^9) tons of trinitrotoluene (TNT).

gig·a·watt /ˈgigəˌwät; ˈjig-/ ▸*n.* (abbrev. **GW**) a unit of electric power equal to one billion (10^9) watts.

gig·gle /ˈgigəl/ ▸*v.* [*intrans.*] laugh lightly in a nervous, affected, or silly manner: *they giggled at some private joke* | [as *adj.*] (**giggling**) *three giggling girls.*
▸*n.* a laugh of such a kind. ■ (**the giggles**) continuous uncontrollable giggling: *I got a fit of the giggles.* ▷early 16th cent.: imitative. **—gig·gler** *n.* **—gig·gly** *adj.* (**-gli·er, -gli·est**).

GIGO /ˈgiˌgō/ *chiefly Computing* ▸*abbr.* garbage in, garbage out. See GARBAGE.

gig·o·lo /ˈjigəˌlō/ ▸*n.* (*pl.* **-los**) *chiefly derogatory* a young man paid or financially supported by an older woman to be her escort or lover. ■ a professional male dancing partner or escort. ▷1920s (in the sense 'dancing partner'): from French, formed as the masculine of *gigole* 'dance hall woman,' from colloquial *gigue* 'leg.'

gig·ot /ˈjigət/ ▸*n.* a leg of mutton or lamb. ▷French, diminutive of colloquial *gigue* 'leg,' from *giguer* 'to hop, jump,' of unknown origin.

gig·ot sleeve ▸*n.* a leg-of-mutton sleeve.

gigue /ZHēg/ ▸*n. Music* a lively piece of music in the style of a dance, typically of the Renaissance or baroque period, and usually in compound time. ▷late 17th cent.: French, literally 'jig.'

Gi·jón /KHēˈKHōn/ a port and industrial city in northern Spain, on the Bay of Biscay; pop. 260,000.

Gi·la mon·ster /ˈhēlə/ ▸*n.* a venomous lizard native to the southwestern U.S. and Mexico. • *Heloderma suspectum*, family Helodermatidae. ▷late 19th cent.: named after *Gila*, a river in New Mexico and Arizona.

Gila monster

Gi·la Riv·er /ˈhēlə/ a river that flows for 645 miles (1,045 km) from New Mexico across southern Arizona to the Colorado River. Phoenix is in its valley.

Gil·bert[1] /ˈgilbərt/, Cass (1859–1934) U.S. architect. He designed the Woolworth building in New York City 1908–13, the annex to the U.S. Treasury building 1918–19, and the U.S. Supreme Court building 1935.

Gil·bert[2], Sir Humphrey (*c.*1539–83), English explorer. He claimed Newfoundland for Elizabeth I in 1583.

Gil·bert[3], William (1544–1603), English physician and physicist. He discovered how to make magnets and coined the term *magnetic pole.*

Gil·bert[4], Sir W. S. (1836–1911), English playwright; full name *William Schwenck Gilbert*. He is best known as a librettist who collaborated on light operas with composer Sir Arthur Sullivan. Notable works: *HMS Pinafore* (1878), *The Pirates of Penzance* (1879), and *The Mikado* (1885).

Gil·bert and El·lice Is·lands /ˈgilbərt and ˈeləs/ a former British colony 1915–75 in the central Pacific Ocean that consisted of two groups of islands: the Gilbert Islands, now a part of Kiribati, and the Ellice Islands, now Tuvalu.

Gil·bert Is·lands a group of islands in the central Pacific Ocean that forms part of Kiribati. The islands straddle the equator and lie immediately west of the International Date Line. They were formerly part of the British colony of the Gilbert and Ellice Islands.

gild[1] /gild/ ▸*v.* [*trans.*] cover thinly with gold. ■ give a specious or false brilliance to: *the useless martyrs' deaths of the pilots gilded the operation.* ▷Old English *gyldan*, of Germanic origin; related to GOLD. **—gild·er** *n.*
▸**PHRASE** □ **gild the lily** try to improve what is already beautiful or excellent. [misquotation, from 'To gild refined gold, to paint the lily; to throw perfume on the violet, ... is wasteful, and ridiculous excess' (Shakespeare's *King John* VI. ii. 11).]

gild[2] ▸*n.* archaic spelling of GUILD.

gild·ed /ˈgildid/ ▸*adj.* covered thinly with gold leaf or gold paint: *an elegant gilded birdcage.* ■ wealthy and privileged: *he saw plain, decent boys transformed to gilded, roistering youths.*

gild·ing /ˈgildiNG/ ▸*n.* the process of applying gold leaf or gold paint. ■ the material used in, or the surface produced by, this process.

gi·let /ZHiˈlā/ ▸*n.* (*pl.* **-lets** *pronunc.* same) a light sleeveless padded jacket. ▷late 19th cent.: French, 'waistcoat,' from Spanish *jileco*, from Turkish *yelek.*

Gil·ga·mesh /ˈgilgəˌmesH/ a legendary king of the Sumerian city-state of Uruk who is supposed to have ruled sometime during the first half of the 3rd millennium BC. He is the hero of the Babylonian epic of Gilgamesh, which recounts his exploits in an ultimately unsuccessful quest for immortality.

Gill /gil/, (Arthur) Eric (Rowton) (1882–1940), English sculptor, engraver, and typographer. He did the relief carvings *Stations of the Cross* (1914–18) at Westminster Cathedral and the *Prospero and Ariel* (1931) on Broadcasting House in London. He also designed the first sans serif typeface, Gill Sans.

gill[1] /gil/ ▸*n.* (often **gills**) **1** the paired respiratory organ of fishes and some amphibians, by which oxygen is extracted from water flowing over surfaces within or attached to the walls of the pharynx. ■ an organ of similar function in an invertebrate animal. **2** the vertical plates arranged radially on the underside of mushrooms and many toadstools. **3** the wattles or dewlap of a fowl. ■ (**gills**) the flesh below a person's jaws and ears: *we stuffed ourselves* **to the gills** *with scrambled eggs and toast.*
▸*v.* [*trans.*] **1** gut or clean (a fish). **2** catch (a fish) in a gill net. ▷Middle English: from Old Norse. **—gilled** *adj.* [in *combination*] *a six-gilled shark.*
▸**PHRASE** □ **green around** (or **at**) **the gills** (of a person) sickly-looking.

gill[2] /jil/ ▸*n.* a unit of liquid measure, equal to a quarter of a pint. ▷Middle English: from Old French *gille* 'measure or container for wine,' from late Latin *gillo* 'water pot.'

gill[3] /gil/ ▸*n. Brit.* a deep ravine, esp. a wooded one. ■ a narrow mountain stream. ▷Middle English: from Old Norse *gil* 'deep glen.'

gill[4] /jil/ (also **jill**) ▸*n.* **1** *archaic* a young woman; a sweetheart. **2** a female ferret. Compare with HOB[2]

Pronunciation Key ə *ago*; ər *over*; ˈə or ˌə *up*; ˈər or ˌər *fur*; a *hat*; ā *rate*; ä *car*; CH *chew*; e *let*; ē *see*; e(ə)r *air*; i *fit*; ī *by*; i(ə)r *ear*; NG *sing*; ō *go*; ô *for*; oi *boy*; o͝o *good*; o͞o *goo*; ou *out*; SH *she*; TH *thin*; TH *then*; (h)w *why*; ZH *vision*

(sense 1). ▷late Middle English: abbreviation of the given name *Gillian*.

gill arch ▸*n.* any of a series of bony or cartilaginous curved bars along the pharynx, supporting the gills of fish and amphibians. ■ any of the corresponding rudimentary structures in the embryos of higher vertebrates.

gill cov·er ▸*n.* a flap of skin protecting a fish's gills, typically stiffened by bony plates. Also called OPERCULUM.

Gil·les·pie /gəˈlespē/, Dizzy (1917–93), U.S. jazz trumpet player and bandleader; born *John Birks Gillespie*. As a virtuoso trumpet player and a leading exponent of bebop style, he formed his own group in 1944 and toured the world.

gil·lie /ˈgilē/ (also **ghil·lie**) ▸*n.* **1** (in Scotland) a man or boy who attends someone on a hunting or fishing expedition. ■ *historical* a Highland chief's attendant. **2** (usu. **ghillie**) a type of shoe with laces along the instep and no tongue, esp. those used for Scottish country dancing. ▷late 16th cent.: from Scottish Gaelic *gille* 'lad, servant.' The word was also found in the term *gilliewetfoot*, denoting a servant who carried the chief over a stream, used as a contemptuous name by Lowlanders for the follower of a Highland chief. Sense 2 dates from the 1930s.

gill net ▸*n.* a fishing net that is hung vertically so that fish get trapped in it by their gills. **—gill-net·ter** *n.*

gill-o·ver-the-ground ▸*n.* another term for GROUND IVY.

gill slit /gil/ ▸*n.* **1** any of a series of openings between the gill arches of a fish, through which water passes from the pharynx to the exterior, bathing the gills in the process. **2** any of a similar set of grooves found in embryos of higher vertebrates.

gil·ly·flow·er /ˈjilē,flou(-ə)r/ (also **gil·li·flow·er**) ▸*n.* any of a number of fragrant flowers, such as the wallflower, clove pink, or white stock. ▷Middle English *gilofre* (in the sense 'clove'), from Old French *gilofre, girofle*, via medieval Latin from Greek *karuophullon* (from *karuon* 'nut' + *phullon* 'leaf'). The ending was altered by association with FLOWER, but *gilliver* survived in dialect.

Gil·son·ite /ˈgilsə,nīt/ ▸*n. trademark* a very pure, shiny black, brittle form of asphalt, used in making inks, paints, and varnishes. ▷late 19th cent.: named after Samuel H. *Gilson*, 19th-cent. American mineralogist, + -ITE[1].

gilt[1] /gilt/ ▸*adj.* covered thinly with gold leaf or gold paint. ■ gold-colored.
▸*n.* gold leaf or gold paint applied in a thin layer to a surface. ▷Middle English: archaic past participle of GILD[1].

gilt[2] ▸*n.* a young sow. ▷Middle English: from Old Norse *gyltr*.

gilt-edged ▸*adj.* (esp. of paper or a book) having a gilded edge or edges. ■ relating to or denoting stocks or other securities that are regarded as extremely reliable investments. ■ of very high quality.

gim·bal /ˈgimbəl; ˈjim-/ ▸*n.* (often **gimbals**) a contrivance, typically consisting of rings pivoted at right angles, for keeping an instrument such as a compass or chronometer horizontal in a moving vessel or aircraft. ▷late 16th cent. (used in the plural denoting connecting parts in machinery): variant of earlier *gimmal*, itself a variant of late Middle English *gemel* 'twin, hinge, finger ring that can be divided into two rings,' from Old French *gemel* 'twin,' from Latin *gemellus*, diminutive of *geminus*. **—gim·baled** (or **gim·balled**) *adj.*

gim·crack /ˈjim,krak/ ▸*adj.* flimsy or poorly made but deceptively attractive: *plastic gimcrack cookware.*
▸*n.* a cheap and showy ornament; a knickknack. ▷Middle English *gibecrake*, of unknown origin. Originally a noun, the term denoted some kind of inlaid work in wood, later a fanciful notion or mechanical contrivance, hence a knickknack. **—gim·crack·er·y** /-,krakərē/ *n.*

gim·let /ˈgimlit/ ▸*n.* **1** a small T-shaped tool with a screw-tip for boring holes. **2** a cocktail of gin (or sometimes vodka) and lime juice. ▷Middle English: from Old French *guimbelet*, diminutive of *guimble* 'drill,' ultimately of Germanic origin.

gimlet 1

gim·let eye ▸*n.* an eye with a piercing stare. **—gim·let-eyed** *adj.*

gim·me /ˈgimē/ *informal* ▸*contraction of* give me (not acceptable in standard use): *just gimme the damn thing.*
▸*n.* a thing that is very easy to perform or obtain, esp. in a game or sport: *the kick would hardly be a gimme in that wind.*

gim·me cap (also **gim·me hat**) ▸*n. informal* a baseball cap that bears a company name or slogan and is given away for publicity purposes.

gim·mick /ˈgimik/ ▸*n.* a trick or device intended to attract attention, publicity, or business.
▸*v.* [*trans.*] provide with a gimmick; alter or tamper with: *motels and restaurants* ***gimmicked up*** *like barns and country stores.* ▷1920s (originally U.S.): of unknown origin but possibly an approximate anagram of *magic*, the original sense being 'a piece of magicians' apparatus.' **—gim·mick·y** *adj.*

gim·mick·ry /ˈgimikrē/ ▸*n.* gimmicks collectively; the use of gimmicks: *it does what it says it does, with no design gimmickry.*

gimp[1] /gimp/ ▸*n.* **1** twisted silk, worsted, or cotton with cord or wire running through it, used chiefly as upholstery trimming. ■ (in lacemaking) coarser thread that forms the outline of the design in some techniques. **2** fishing line made of silk bound with wire. ▷mid 17th cent.: from Dutch, of unknown ultimate origin.

gimp[2] *informal, often offensive* ▸*n.* a physically handicapped or lame person. ■ a limp. ■ a feeble or contemptible person.
▸*v.* [*intrans.*] limp; hobble: *she gimped around thereafter on an artificial leg.* ▷1920s (originally U.S.): of unknown origin. **—gimp·y** *adj.*

gin[1] /jin/ ▸*n.* **1** a clear alcoholic spirit distilled from grain or malt and flavored with juniper berries. **2** (also **gin rummy**) a two-handed form of the card game rummy in which players are dealt ten cards each and attempt to produce a hand in which the point value of unmatched cards adds up to ten or less. ▷early 18th cent.: abbreviation of GENEVER.

gin[2] ▸*n.* **1** a machine for separating cotton from its seeds. **2** a machine for raising and moving heavy weights. **3** (also **gin trap**) a snare for catching game.
▸*v.* (**ginned, gin·ning**) [*trans.*] **1** treat (cotton) in a gin. **2** trap (a person or animal) in a gin. ▷Middle English (in the sense 'a tool or device, a trick'): from Old French *engin* (see ENGINE). **—gin·ner** *n.*

gin·ger /ˈjinjər/ ▸*n.* **1** a hot fragrant spice made from the rhizome of a plant. It is chopped or powdered for cooking, preserved in syrup, or candied. ■ spirit; mettle: *he had more ginger than her first husband.* **2** a Southeast Asian plant, which resembles bamboo in appearance, from which this rhizome is taken. • *Zingiber officinale*, family Zingiberaceae. **3** a light reddish-yellow color.
▸*adj.* (chiefly of hair or fur) of a light reddish-yellow color. ■ (of a person or animal) having ginger hair or fur.
▸*v.* [*trans.*] **1** [usu. as *adj.*] (**gingered**) flavor with ginger: *gingered chicken wings.* **2** (**ginger someone/something up**) stimulate; enliven: *she slapped his hand lightly to ginger him up.* ▷late Old English *gingifer*, conflated in Middle English with Old French *gingimbre*, from medieval Latin *gingiber*, from Greek *zingiberis*, from Pali *siṅgivera*, of Dravidian origin. **—gin·ger·y** *adj.*

gin·ger ale ▸*n.* a clear, effervescent nonalcoholic drink flavored with ginger extract.

gin·ger beer ▸*n.* a cloudy, effervescent mildly alcoholic drink, made by fermenting a mixture of ginger and syrup. ■ a nonalcoholic commercial variety of this.

gin·ger·bread /ˈjinjər,bred/ ▸*n.* cake made with molasses and flavored with ginger. ■ fancy decoration, esp. on a building: [as *adj.*] *a high-gabled gingerbread house.* ▷Middle English (originally denoting preserved ginger), from Old French *gingembrat*, from medieval Latin *gingibratum*, from *gingiber* (see GINGER). The change in the ending in the 15th cent. was due to association with BREAD.

gin·ger jar ▸*n.* a small ceramic jar with a high rim over which a lid fits.

gin·ger·ly /ˈjinjərlē/ ▸*adv.* in a careful or cautious manner: *Jackson sat down very gingerly.*
▸*adj.* showing great care or caution: *with strangers the preliminaries are taken at a gingerly pace.* ▷early 16th cent. (in the sense 'daintily, mincingly'): perhaps from Old French *gensor* 'delicate,' comparative of *gent* 'graceful,' from Latin *genitus* 'well-born.' **—gin·ger·li·ness** *n.*

gin·ger snap ▸*n.* a thin brittle cookie flavored with ginger.

ging·ham /ˈgiNGəm/ ▸*n.* lightweight plain-woven cotton cloth, typically checked in white and a bold color: [as *adj.*] *gingham curtains.* ▷early 17th cent.: from Dutch *gingang*, from Malay *genggang* (originally an adjective meaning 'striped').

gin·gi·va /jinˈjīvə; ˈjinjəvə/ ▸*n.* (*pl.* **gin·gi·vae** /jinˈjīvē; ˈjinjə,vē/) *Medicine* the gum. ▷mid 17th cent.: Latin, 'gum.' **—gin·gi·val** *adj.*

gin·gi·vi·tis /,jinjəˈvītis/ ▸*n. Medicine* inflammation of the gums.

ging·ko ▸*n.* variant spelling of GINKGO.

gin·gly·mus /ˈjiNGgləməs; ˈgiNG-/ ▸*n.* (*pl.* **-mi** /-,mī; -,mē/) *Anatomy* a hingelike joint, such as the elbow or knee, that allows movement in only one plane. ▷late 16th cent.: modern Latin, from Greek *ginglumos* 'hinge.'

Ging·rich /ˈgiNG(g)riCH/, Newt(on Leroy) (1943–) U.S. politician. A representative to Congress from Georgia 1979–98, he served as Speaker of the House from 1995 until his resignation in 1998. A conservative, he was noted for his "Contract with America," which outlined Republican goals for the first 100 days of the Congress of 1995.

gink /giNGk/ ▸*n. informal* a foolish or contemptible person. ▷early 20th cent. (originally U.S.): of unknown origin.

gink·go /ˈgiNGkō/ (also **ging·ko**) ▸*n.* (*pl.* **-goes** or **-gos**) a deciduous Chinese tree related to the conifers, with fan-shaped leaves and yellow flowers. It has a number of primitive features and is similar to some Jurassic fossils. Also called MAIDENHAIR TREE. • *Ginkgo biloba*, the only living member of the family Ginkgoaceae and order Ginkgoales, class Coniferopsida. ▷late 18th cent.: from Japanese *ginkyō*, from Chinese *yínxing*.

gin mill ▸*n. informal* a run-down or seedy nightclub or bar.

gi·nor·mous /jiˈnôrməs; jī-/ ▸*adj. informal, humorous* extremely large; enormous: *a ginormous five-volume treatment of Greek and Arabic medicine.* ▷blend of *gigantic* and *enormous*.

gin rum·my ▸*n.* see GIN[1].

Gins·berg[1] /ˈginzbərg/, Allen (1926–97), U.S. poet. Part of the beat generation and later influential in the hippie movement of the 1960s, he is noted for *Howl and Other Poems* (1956), in which he attacked society for its materialism and complacency.

Gins·burg[2], Ruth Bader (1933–) U.S. Supreme Court associate justice 1993– . Appointed to the Court by President Clinton, she is one of the more liberal voices on the court.

gin·seng /ˈjinseNG/ ▸*n.* **1** a plant tuber credited with various tonic and medicinal properties, esp. in the Far East. **2** the plant from which this tuber is obtained, native to eastern Asia and North America. • Genus *Panax*, family Araliaceae: several species, in particular the Asian *P. pseudoginseng* and the North American *P. quinquefolius*. ▷mid 17th cent.: from Chinese *rénshēn*, from *rén* 'man' + *shēn*, a kind of herb (because of the supposed resemblance of the forked root to a person).

gin·zo /ˈginzō/ *informal, offensive* ▸*n.* (*pl.* **-zoes**) an Italian; a person of Italian descent.
▸*adj.* Italian. ▷mid 20th cent.: perhaps from U.S. slang *Guinea*, denoting an Italian or Spanish immigrant.

Gior·gio·ne /jôrˈjōnē/ (*c.*1478–1510), Italian painter; also called **Giorgio Barbarelli** or **Giorgio da Castelfranco**. He introduced the small easel picture in oils that was intended for private collectors. Notable works: *The Tempest* (*c.*1505) and *Sleeping Venus* (*c.*1510).

Giot·to[1] /ˈjôtō/ (*c.*1267–1337), Italian painter; full name *Giotto di Bondone*. He introduced a naturalistic style showing human expression. His name is associated with the legend of "Giotto's O," in which he is said to have proven his mastery to the pope by drawing a perfect circle freehand. His works include the frescoes in the Arena Chapel in Padua (1305–08) and the church of Santa Croce in Florence (*c.*1320).

Giot·to[2] a European space probe that photographed the nucleus of Halley's Comet in March 1986.

Gio·van·ni de' Me·di·ci /jōˈvānē də ˈmediCHē/ the name of the Pope Leo X (see LEO[1]).

gip /jip/ ▸*n.* variant spelling of GYP[1].

gip·sy ▸*n.* variant spelling of GYPSY.

gi·raffe /jəˈraf/ ▸*n.* (*pl.* same or **-raffes**) a large African mammal with a very long neck and forelegs, having a coat patterned with brown patches separated by lighter lines. It is the tallest living animal. • *Giraffa camelopardalis*, family Giraffidae. ■ (**the Giraffe**) the constellation Camelopardalis. ▷late 16th cent.: from French *girafe*, Italian *giraffa*, or Spanish and Portuguese *girafa*, based on Arabic *zarāfa*. The animal was known in Europe in the medieval period, and isolated instances of names for it based on the Arabic are recorded in Middle English, when it was commonly called the CAMELOPARD.

giraffe

gir·an·dole /ˈjirənˌdōl/ ▸*n.* **1** a branched support for candles or other lights, which either stands on a surface or projects from a wall. **2** an earring or pendant with a large central stone surrounded by small ones. ▷mid 17th cent. (denoting a revolving cluster of fireworks): from French, from Italian *girandola*, from *girare* 'gyrate, turn,' from Latin *gyrare* (see GYRATE).

gir·a·sol /ˈjirəˌsôl; -ˌsäl/ (also **gir·a·sole** /-ˌsōl/) ▸*n.* **1** a kind of opal reflecting a reddish glow. **2** another term for JERUSALEM ARTICHOKE. ▷late 16th cent. (in the sense 'sunflower'): from French, or from Italian *girasole*, from *girare* 'to turn' + *sole* 'sun' (because the sunflower turns to follow the path of the sun).

gird[1] /gərd/ ▸*v.* (*past* and *past part.* **gird·ed** or **girt** /gərt/) [*trans.*] *poetic/literary* encircle (a person or part of the body) with a belt or band: *a young man was to be* ***girded with*** *the belt of knighthood.* ■ secure (a garment or sword) on the body with a belt or band: *a white robe girded with a magenta sash.* ■ surround; encircle: *the mountains girding Kabul.*
▸*phrasal v.* □ **gird oneself for** prepare oneself for (dangerous or difficult future actions). ▷Old English *gyrdan*, of Germanic origin; related to Dutch *gorden* and German *gürten*, also to GIRDLE and GIRTH.
▸PHRASE □ **gird (up) one's loins** prepare and strengthen oneself for what is to come.

gird[2] *archaic* ▸*v.* [*intrans.*] make cutting or critical remarks: *they* ***girded at*** *the committee.*
▸*n.* a cutting or critical remark; a taunt. ▷Middle English (in the sense 'strike, stab'): of unknown origin.

gird·er /ˈgərdər/ ▸*n.* a large iron or steel beam or compound structure used for building bridges and the framework of large buildings. ▷early 17th cent.: from GIRD[1] in the archaic sense 'brace, strengthen.'

gir·dle /ˈgərdl/ ▸*n.* a belt or cord worn around the waist. ■ a woman's elasticized corset extending from waist to thigh. ■ a thing that surrounds something like a belt or girdle: *a communications girdle around the world.* ■ *Anatomy* either of two sets of bones encircling the body, to which the limbs are attached. See PECTORAL GIRDLE, PELVIC GIRDLE. ■ the part of a cut gem dividing the crown from the base and embraced by the setting. ■ a ring around a tree made by removing bark.
▸*v.* [*trans.*] **1** encircle (the body) with or as a girdle or belt: *the Friar loosened the rope that girdled his waist.* ■ surround; encircle: *the chain of volcanoes that girdles the Pacific.* **2** cut through the bark all the way around (a tree or branch), typically in order to kill it or to kill a branch to make the tree more fruitful. ▷Old English *gyrdel*, of Germanic origin; related to Dutch *gordel* and German *Gürtel*, also to GIRD[1] and GIRTH.

gir·dler /ˈgərd(ə)lər/ ▸*n.* **1** *archaic* a maker of girdles. **2** a person or thing that girdles. ■ an insect that removes rings of bark from trees: [in *combination*] *a twig-girdler.*

girl /gərl/ ▸*n.* **1** a female child. ■ a person's daughter, esp. a young one: *he was devoted to his little girl.* **2** a young or relatively young woman. ■ [with *adj.*] a young woman of a specified kind or having a specified job: *a career girl | a chorus girl.* ■ (**girls**) *informal* women who mix socially or belong to a particular group, team, or profession: *I look forward to having lunch with the girls.* ■ a person's girlfriend: *his girl eloped with an accountant.* ■ *dated* a female servant. ▷Middle English (denoting a child or young person of either sex): perhaps related to Low German *gör* 'child.'

girl Fri·day ▸*n.* a female helper, esp. a junior office worker or a personal assistant to a business executive. ▷1940s: on the pattern of *man Friday.*

girl·friend /ˈgərlˌfrend/ ▸*n.* a regular female companion with whom a person has a romantic or sexual relationship: *his girlfriend is Australian.* ■ a woman's female friend.

Girl Guide ▸*n. chiefly Brit.* a member of the Guides Association.

girl·hood /ˈgərlˌho͝od/ ▸*n.* the state or time of being a girl: *they had been friends since girlhood.*

girl·ie /ˈgərlē/ ▸*n.* (also **girl·y**) (*pl.* **-ies**) *offensive* a girl or young woman (often used as a term of address).
▸*adj.* **1** (usu. **girly**) *often derogatory* like, characteristic of, or appropriate to a girl or young woman: *men aren't afraid to be soft, girly, and foppish.* **2** [*attrib.*] depicting or featuring nude or partially nude young women in erotic poses: *girlie magazines.*

girl·ish /ˈgərlisн/ ▸*adj.* of, like, or characteristic of a girl: *girlish giggles.* **—girl·ish·ly** *adv.* **—girl·ish·ness** *n.*

Girl Scout ▸*n.* a member of an organization of girls, esp. the **Girl Scouts of America**, that promotes character, outdoor activities, good citizenship, and service to others.

gi·ro /ˈjīrō/ ▸*n.* (*pl.* **-ros**) short for AUTOGIRO.

Gi·ronde /zнēˈrônd/ an estuary in southwestern France, formed at the junction of the Garonne and Dordogne rivers, north of Bordeaux. It flows northwest for 45 miles (72 km) into the Bay of Biscay.

Gi·ron·dist /jəˈrändist; zнə-/ (also **Gi·ron·din** /-din/) ▸*n.* a member of the French moderate republican party in power 1791–93 during the French Revolution, so called because the party leaders were the deputies from the department of the Gironde. ▷from archaic French *Girondiste* (now *Girondin*).

girt[1] /gərt/ ▸ past participle of GIRD[1].

girt[2] ▸*n.* old-fashioned term for GIRTH.

girth /gərтн/ ▸*n.* **1** the measurement around the middle of something, esp. a person's waist. ■ a person's middle or stomach, esp. when large. **2** a band attached to a saddle, used to secure it on a horse by being fastened around its belly.
▸*v.* [*trans.*] *archaic* surround; encircle: *the four seas that girth Britain.* ▷Middle English (sense 2): from Old Norse *gjǫrth.*

GIS ▸*abbr.* geographic information system, a system for storing and manipulating geographical information on computer.

Gis·card d'És·taing /zнēˈskär deˈstaɴɢ/, Valéry (1926–), French statesman; president 1974–81. As secretary of state for finance 1959–62 and finance minister 1962–66 under President Charles de Gaulle, he was responsible for the policies that formed the basis for France's economic growth. He was a member of the European Parliament 1989–93 and was leader of the center-right Union pour la démocratie française from 1988.

Gish /gisн/, Lillian (1896–1993), U.S. actress. She and her sister **Dorothy** (1898–1968) appeared in a number of D. W. Griffith's movies, including *Hearts of the World* (1918) and *Orphans of the Storm* (1922).

Lillian Gish

gis·mo ▸*n.* variant spelling of GIZMO.

gist /jist/ ▸*n.* [in *sing.*] **1** the substance or essence of a speech or text: *she noted the gist of each message.* **2** *Law* the real point of an action: *damage is the gist of the action and without it the plaintiff must fail.* ▷early 18th cent.: from Old French, third person singular present tense of *gesir* 'to lie,' from Latin *jacere*. The Anglo-French legal phrase *cest action gist* 'this action lies' denoted that there were sufficient grounds to proceed; *gist* was adopted into English denoting the grounds themselves (sense 2).

git /git/ ▸*n. Brit., informal* an unpleasant or contemptible person. ▷1940s: variant of the noun GET (see sense 3).

Gi·ta /ˈgētə/ ▸*n.* short for BHAGAVADGITA.

gîte /zнēt/ ▸*n.* a small furnished vacation house in France, typically in a rural district. ▷French, from Old French *giste*; related to *gésir* 'to lie.'

Gi·te·ga /gēˈtāgə/ a commercial town in central Burundi, east of Bujumbura; pop. 102,000.

Git·mo /ˈgitˌmō/ ▸*n. informal* the U.S. naval base or detention facility at Guantánamo Bay, Cuba. ▷representing a pronunciation of *GTMO*, an abbreviation of *Guantanamo.*

git·tern /ˈgitərn/ ▸*n. historical* a lutelike medieval stringed instrument, forerunner of the guitar. ▷late Middle English: from Old French *guiterne*; perhaps related to CITTERN and GUITAR.

Giu·li·a·ni /ˌjo͞olēˈänē/, Rudolph (1944–) U.S. politician. The moderate Republican mayor of New York City 1993–2001, he worked to combat and reduce crime in the city and to reduce the number of people on the welfare rolls. He attained national prominence through his strong leadership after the attacks of September 11, 2001. He served as U.S. attorney for the Southern District of New York 1983–1989.

give /giv/ ▸*v.* (*past* **gave** /gāv/; *past part.* **giv·en** /ˈgivən/) **1** [with *two objs.*] freely transfer the possession of (something) to (someone); hand over to: *they gave her water to drink | the check* ***given to*** *the jeweler proved worthless | [trans.] he* ***gave*** *the papers* ***back.*** ■ bestow (love, affection, or other emotional support): *his parents gave him the encouragement he needed to succeed* | [as *adj.*] (**giving**) *he was very giving and supportive.* ■ administer (medicine): *she was given antibiotics.* ■ hand over (an amount) in exchange or payment; pay: *how much did you give for that?* ■ (**give something for**) place a specified value on (something): *he never* ***gave*** *anything* ***for*** *French painting or for abstraction.* ■ [*trans.*] used hyperbolically to express how greatly one wants to have or do something: *I'd* ***give*** *anything* ***for*** *a cup of tea |* ***I'd give my right arm*** *to be in* Othello. ■ communicate or impart (a message) to (someone): *give my love to all the girls.* ■ [*trans.*] commit, consign, or entrust: *a baby* ***given into*** *their care by the accident of her birth.* ■ freely devote, set aside, or sacrifice for a purpose: *all who have* ***given*** *thought* ***to*** *the matter agree* | [*intrans.*] *committee members who* ***give*** *so generously* ***of*** *their time and effort.* ■ [*trans.*] (of a man) sanction the marriage of (his daughter) to someone: *he* ***gave her in marriage*** *to an English noble.* ■ (**give oneself to**) *dated* consent to have sexual intercourse with (someone). ■ pass on (an illness or infection) to (someone): *I hope I don't give you my cold.* ■ [usu. in *imperative*] make a connection to allow (someone) to speak to (someone else) on the telephone: *give me the police.* ■ cite or present when making a toast or introducing a speaker or entertainer: *for your entertainment this evening I give you . . . Mister Albert DeNiro!* **2** [with *two objs.*] cause or allow (someone or something) to have (something, esp. something abstract); provide or supply with: *you gave me such a fright* | [*trans.*] *this leaflet gives our opening times.* ■ allot or assign (a score) to: *I gave it five out of ten.* ■ sentence (someone) to (a specified penalty): *for the first offense I was given a fine.* ■ concede or yield (something) as valid or deserved in respect of (someone): *give him his due.* ■ allow (someone) to have (a specified amount of time) for an activity or undertaking: *give me a second to bring the car around* | [*trans.*] *I'll give you until tomorrow morning.* ■ *informal* predict that (an activity, undertaking, or relationship) will last no longer than (a specified time): *this is a place that will not improve with time—I give it three weeks.* ■ [*trans.*] yield as a product or result: *milk is sometimes added to give a richer cheese.* ■ [*trans.*] (**give something off/out/forth**) emit odor, vapor, or similar substances: *it can be burned without giving off toxic fumes.* **3** [*trans.*] carry out or perform (a specified action): *I gave a bow* | [with *two objs.*] *he gave the counter a polish.* ■ utter or produce (a sound): *he gave a gasp.* ■ provide (a party or social meal) as host or hostess: *a dinner given in honor of a Canadian diplomat* | [with *two objs.*]

Korda gave him a going-away party. **4** [*trans.*] state or put forward (information or argument): *he did not give his name.* ■ pledge or assign as a guarantee: [with *two objs.*] *I give you my word.* ■ [with *two objs.*, usu. with *negative*] say to (someone) as an excuse or inappropriate answer: *don't give me any of your back talk.* ■ deliver (a judgment) authoritatively: *I gave my verdict.* ■ present (an appearance or impression): *he gave no sign of life.* ■ [*intrans.*] *informal* tell what one knows: *okay, give—what's that all about?* **5** [*intrans.*] alter in shape under pressure rather than resist or break: *that chair doesn't give.* ■ yield or give way to pressure: *the heavy door didn't give until the fifth push* | *figurative when two people who don't get on are thrust together, something's got to give.* ■ [*intrans.*] *informal* concede defeat; surrender: *I give!*

▸*phrasal v.* □ **give someone away** **1** reveal the true identity of someone: *his strangely shaped feet gave him away.* ■ reveal information that incriminates someone. **2** hand over a bride ceremonially to her bridegroom as part of a wedding ceremony. □ **give something away** reveal something secret or concealed. □ **give in** cease fighting or arguing; yield; surrender: *he reluctantly* **gave in to** *the pressure.* □ **give on to** (or **into**) *Brit.* (of a window, door, corridor, etc.) overlook or lead into: *a plate glass window gave on to the roof.* □ **give out** be completely used up: *her energy was on the verge of giving out.* ■ stop functioning; break down: *he curses and swears till his voice gives out.* □ **give something out** distribute or broadcast something: *I've been giving out leaflets.* □ **give over** [often in *imperative*] *Brit., informal* stop doing something. ■ used to express vehement disagreement or denial: *I suggested her salary might be £100,000. "Give over!"* □ **give up** cease making an effort; resign oneself to failure. □ **give it up** [usu. in *imperative*] *informal* applaud a performer or entertainer. □ **give oneself up to** **1** surrender oneself to law-enforcement agents. **2** *dated* allow oneself to be taken over by (an emotion or addiction): *he gave himself up to pleasure.* □ **give someone up** **1** deliver a wanted person to authority: *a voice told him to come out and* **give himself up**. **2** *dated* stop hoping that someone is still going to arrive: *oh, it's you—we'd almost given you up.* ■ pronounce a sick person incurable. □ **give something up** part with something that one would prefer to keep: *she would have given up everything for love.* ■ stop the habitual doing or consuming of something: *I've decided to give up drinking.* □ **give up on** stop having faith or belief in: *they weren't about to give up on their heroes so easily.*

▸*n.* capacity to bend or alter in shape under pressure; elasticity: *plastic pots that have enough give to accommodate the vigorous roots.* ■ *figurative* ability to adapt or comply; flexibility: *there is no give at all in the British position.* ▷Old English *giefan, gefan*, of Germanic origin; related to Dutch *geven* and German *geben.* **—giv·er** *n.*

▸*PHRASES* □ **give oneself airs** act pretentiously or snobbishly. □ **give and take** mutual concessions and compromises. ■ [as *v.*] make concessions and compromises. □ **give as good as one gets** respond with equal force or vehemence when attacked. □ **give the** (**whole**) **game** (or **show**) **away** inadvertently reveal something secret or concealed. □ **give it to someone** *informal* scold or punish someone. □ **give me ——** I prefer or admire ——: *give me the mainland any day!* □ **give me a break** *informal* used to express exasperation, protest, or disbelief. □ **give or take ——** *informal* to within —— (used to express the degree or accuracy of a figure): *three hundred and fifty years ago, give or take a few.* ■ apart from: *give or take the odd aircraft bit, there are few new products.* □ **give rise to** cause or induce to happen: *decisions which give rise to arguments.* □ **give someone to understand** (or **believe** or **know**) inform someone in a formal and rather indirect way: *I was given to understand that I had been invited.* □ **give up the ghost** see GHOST. □ **give someone what for** *informal dated* punish or scold someone severely. □ **not give a damn** (or **hoot**, etc.) *informal* not care at all: *people who don't give a damn about the environment.* □ **what gives?** *informal* what's the news?; what's happening? (frequently used as a friendly greeting).

THE RIGHT WORD **afford, award, bestow, confer, donate, give, grant**

You **give** a birthday present, **grant** a favor, **bestow** charity, and **confer** an honor. While all of these verbs mean to convey something or transfer it from one's own possession to that of another, the circumstances surrounding that transfer dictate which word is the best one.

Give is the most general, meaning to pass over, deliver, or transmit something (*give him encouragement*).

Grant implies that a request or desire has been expressed, and that the receiver is dependent on the giver's discretion (*grant permission for the trip*).

Award suggests that the giver is in some sense a judge, and that the thing given is deserved (*award a scholarship*), while *bestow* implies that something is given as a gift and may imply condescension on the part of the giver (*bestow a large sum of money on a needy charity*).

To *confer* is to give an honor, a privilege, or a favor; it implies that the giver is a superior (*confer a knighthood; confer a college degree*).

Donate implies that the giving is to a public cause or charity (*donate a painting to the local art museum*), and to **afford** is to give or bestow as a natural consequence (the window afforded a fine view of the mountains).

give·a·way /ˈgivəˌwā/ *informal* ▸*n.* **1** a thing that is given free, esp. for promotional purposes: *a preelection tax giveaway.* **2** a thing that makes an inadvertent revelation: *the shape of the parcel was a dead giveaway.*

▸*adj.* [*attrib.*] **1** free of charge: *giveaway goodies.* ■ (of prices) very low. **2** revealing: *small giveaway mannerisms.*

give·back /ˈgivˌbak/ ▸*n.* an agreement by workers to surrender benefits and conditions previously agreed upon in return for new concessions or awards.

giv·en /ˈgivən/ ▸ past participle of GIVE.

▸*adj.* **1** specified or stated: *our level of knowledge on* **any given** *subject.* **2** [*predic.*] (**given to**) inclined or disposed to: *she was not often given to anger.* **3** conferred or bestowed as a gift: *she squandered what was a given opportunity.* **4** *archaic Law* (of a document) signed and dated: *given under my hand this eleventh day of April.*

▸*prep.* taking into account: *given the complexity of the task, they were able to do a good job.*

▸*n.* a known or established fact or situation: *at a couture house, attentive service is a given.*

giv·en name ▸*n.* another term for FIRST NAME.

Gi·za /ˈgēzə/ a city southwest of Cairo in northern Egypt, on the western bank of the Nile River, site of the Pyramids and the Sphinx; pop. 2,156,000. Also called **EL GIZA**; Arabic name **AL JIZAH**.

giz·mo /ˈgizmō/ (also **gis·mo**) ▸*n.* (*pl.* **-mos**) *informal* a gadget, esp. one whose name the speaker does not know or cannot recall: *the latest multimedia gizmo.* ▷1940s (originally U.S.): of unknown origin.

giz·zard /ˈgizərd/ ▸*n.* a muscular, thick-walled part of a bird's stomach for grinding food, typically with grit. Also called VENTRICULUS. ■ a muscular stomach of some fish, insects, mollusks, and other invertebrates. ■ *informal* a person's stomach or throat. ▷late Middle English *giser*: from Old French, based on Latin *gigeria* 'cooked entrails of fowl.' The final *-d* was added in the 16th cent.

gjet·ost /ˈyetôst; ˈjet-/ ▸*n.* a very sweet, firm, golden-brown Norwegian cheese, traditionally made with goat's milk. ▷Norwegian, from *gjet, geit* 'goat' + *ost* 'cheese.'

gl. ▸*abbr.* gloss.

GLA ▸*abbr.* gamma linolenic acid.

gla·bel·la /gləˈbelə/ ▸*n.* (*pl.* **-bel·lae** /-ˈbelē/) *Anatomy* the smooth part of the forehead above and between the eyebrows. ▷early 19th cent.: modern Latin, from Latin *glabellus* (adjective), diminutive of *glaber* 'smooth.' **—gla·bel·lar** /-ˈbelər/ *adj.*

gla·brous /ˈglābrəs/ ▸*adj. technical* (chiefly of the skin or a leaf) free from hair or down; smooth. ▷mid 17th cent.: from Latin *glaber, glabr-* 'hairless, smooth' + -OUS.

gla·cé /glaˈsā/ ▸*adj.* [*attrib.*] **1** (of fruit) having a glossy surface due to preservation in sugar: *a glacé cherry.* **2** (of cloth or leather) smooth and highly polished.

▸*v.* (**-cés, -céed** /-ˈsād/ or **-céd, -cé·ing**) [*trans.*] glaze with a thin sugar-based coating: [as *adj.*] *glacéed cape gooseberries.* ▷mid 19th cent.: French, literally 'iced,' past participle of *glacer*, from *glace* 'ice.'

gla·cé ic·ing ▸*n.* icing made with powdered sugar and water.

gla·cial /ˈglāshəl/ ▸*adj.* **1** relating to, resulting from, or denoting the presence or agency of ice, esp. in the form of glaciers: *thick glacial deposits* | *a glacial lake.* **2** of ice; icy: *the glacial mountains of New Zealand* | *figurative glacial blue eyes.* ■ extremely cold: *glacial temperatures.* ■ *Chemistry* denoting pure organic acids (esp. acetic acid) that form icelike crystals on freezing. ■ extremely slow (like the movement of a glacier): *an official described progress in the talks as glacial.*

▸*n. Geology* a glacial period. ▷mid 17th cent.: from French, or from Latin *glacialis* 'icy,' from *glacies* 'ice.' **—gla·cial·ly** *adv.*

gla·cial pe·ri·od ▸*n.* a period in the earth's history when polar and mountain ice sheets were unusually extensive across the earth's surface.

gla·ci·at·ed /ˈglāshēˌātid/ ▸*adj.* covered or having been covered by glaciers or ice sheets: *a glaciated valley.* ▷mid 19th cent.: past participle of obsolete *glaciate*, from Latin *glaciare* 'freeze,' from *glacies* 'ice.'

gla·ci·a·tion /ˌglāshēˈāshən/ ▸*n. Geology* the process, condition, or result of being covered by glaciers or ice sheets. ■ a glacial period.

gla·cier /ˈglāshər/ ▸*n.* a slowly moving mass or river of ice formed by the accumulation and compaction of snow on mountains or near the poles. ▷mid 18th cent.: from French, from *glace* 'ice,' based on Latin *glacies.*

Gla·cier Bay Na·tion·al Park a national park in southeastern Alaska, on the Pacific coast. It covers an area of 4,975 square feet (12,880 sq km).

gla·ci·ol·o·gy /ˌglāshēˈäləjē/ ▸*n.* the study of the internal dynamics and effects of glaciers. ▷late 19th cent.: from Latin *glacies* 'ice' + -LOGY. **—gla·ci·o·log·i·cal** /-shēəˈläjikəl/ *adj.* **—gla·ci·ol·o·gist** /-jist/ *n.*

gla·cis /ˈglāsis; ˈglas-/ ▸*n.* (*pl.* same or **-cis·es**) a gently sloping bank, in particular one that slopes down from a fort, exposing attackers to the defenders' missiles. ▷late 17th cent.: from French, from Old French *glacier* 'to slip,' from *glace* 'ice,' based on Latin *glacies.*

glad[1] /glad/ ▸*adj.* (**glad·der, glad·dest**) [*predic.*] pleased; delighted: *she was alive, which was something to be glad about* | [with *infinitive*] *I'm really glad to hear that.* ■ happy for someone's good fortune: *I'm so* **glad for** *you.* ■ [*attrib.*] causing happiness: *glad tidings.* ■ grateful: *he was* **glad for** *the excuse to put it off.* ■ [with *infinitive*] willing and eager (to do something): *he will be glad to carry your bags.*

▸*v.* (**glad·ded, glad·ding**) [*trans.*] *poetic/literary* make happy; please: *Albion's lessening shore could grieve or glad mine eye.* ▷Old English *glæd* (originally in the sense 'bright, shining'), of Germanic origin; related to Old Norse *glathr* 'bright, joyous' and German *glatt* 'smooth,' also to Latin *glaber* 'smooth, hairless.' **—glad·ly** *adv.* **—glad·ness** *n.*

glad[2] ▸*n. informal* a gladiolus. ▷1920s: abbreviation.

glad·den /ˈgladn/ ▸*v.* [*trans.*] make glad: *it was a sound that gladdened her heart.*

glade /glād/ ▸*n.* an open space in a forest. ▷late Middle English: of unknown origin; perhaps related to GLAD[1] or GLEAM, with reference to the comparative brightness of a clearing (obsolete senses of *glade* include 'a gleam of light' and 'a bright space between clouds').

glad-hand ▸*v.* [*trans.*] (esp. of a politician) greet or welcome warmly or with the appearance of warmth: *they had been taking every free minute to glad-hand loyal supporters.*

▸*n.* (**glad-hand**) [in *sing.*] a warm and hearty, but often insincere, greeting or welcome. **—glad-hand·er** *n.*

glad·i·a·tor /ˈgladēˌātər/ ▸*n.* **1** (in ancient Rome) a man trained to fight with weapons against other men or wild animals in an arena. **2** a person defending or opposing a cause; a controversialist: *he chose not to be a gladiator in the presidential arena.* ▷late Middle English: from Latin, from *gladius* 'sword.' **—glad·i·a·to·ri·al** /ˌgladēəˈtôrēəl/ *adj.*

glad·i·o·lus /ˌgladēˈōləs/ ▸*n.* (*pl.* **-li** /-lī/ or **-lus·es**) an Old World plant of the iris family, with sword-shaped leaves and spikes of brightly colored flowers, popular in gardens and as a cut flower. • Genus *Gladiolus*, family Iridaceae: many species. ▷Old English (originally denoting the *gladdon*, a purple-flowered iris), from Latin, diminutive of *gladius* 'sword' (used as a plant name by Pliny).

glad rags ▸*plural n. informal* clothes for a special occasion; one's best clothes.

glad·some /ˈgladsəm/ ▸*adj. poetic/literary* (of a person) having a cheerful, joyful disposition. ■ (of a feeling, look, or action) filled with, marked by, or causing joy. ■ (of nature) full of brightness or beauty; cheering.

Glad·stone /ˈgladˌstōn/, William Ewart (1809–98), British statesman; prime minister 1868–74, 1880–85, 1886, and 1892–94. At first a Conservative minister, he later joined the Liberal Party and became its leader in 1867. Elementary education, the Irish Land and the third Reform acts, and the campaign for Irish home rule were introduced during his administrations.

Glad·stone bag ▸*n.* a bag like a briefcase having two equal compartments joined by a hinge. ▷late 19th cent.: named after W. E. GLADSTONE, who was noted for the amount of traveling he undertook when electioneering.

Glag·o·lit·ic /ˌglagəˈlitik/ ▸*adj.* denoting or relating to an alphabet based on Greek minuscules, formerly used in writing some Slavic languages.
▸*n.* this alphabet.

The Glagolitic alphabet is of uncertain origin and was introduced in the 9th century at about the same time as the Cyrillic alphabet, which has superseded it except in some Orthodox Church liturgies.

▷from modern Latin *glagoliticus*, from *glagòljica*, the name in Serbo-Croat of the Glagolitic alphabet, from Old Church Slavic *glagolŭ* 'word.'

glair /gle(ə)r/ ▸*n.* a preparation made from egg white, used esp. as an adhesive for bookbinding and gilding. ■ *dated* egg white. ▷Middle English: from Old French *glaire*, based on Latin *clara*, feminine of *clarus* 'clear.' **—glair·y** *adj.*

glaive /glāv/ ▸*n. poetic/literary* a sword. ▷Middle English (denoting a lance or halberd): from Old French, apparently from Latin *gladius* 'sword.'

glam /glam/ *informal* ▸*adj.* glamorous: *a magician and his glam assistant.* ■ relating to or denoting glam rock.
▸*n.* glamour: *sass, panache, and a dash of glam.* ■ glam rock.
▸*v.* (**glammed**, **glam·ming**) [*intrans.*] (**glam up**) make oneself look glamorous. ▷1930s: abbreviation.

glam·a·zon /ˈglaməˌzän; -zən/ ▸*n. informal* a glamorous, powerfully assertive woman. ▷1990s: from *glam* + *Amazon*.

glam·or·ize /ˈglaməˌrīz/ (also **glam·our·ize**) ▸*v.* [*trans.*] make (something) seem glamorous or desirable, esp. spuriously so: *the lyrics glamorize drugs.* **—glam·or·i·za·tion** /ˌglaməriˈzāsʜən/ *n.*

glam·or·ous /ˈglamərəs/ ▸*adj.* having glamour: *one of the world's most glamorous women.* **—glam·or·ous·ly** *adv.*

glam·our /ˈglamər/ (also **glam·or**) ▸*n.* the attractive or exciting quality that makes certain people or things seem appealing or special: *the glamour of Monte Carlo* | [as *adj.*] *the glamour days of Old Hollywood.* ■ beauty or charm that is sexually attractive: *George had none of his brother's glamour.* ■ *archaic* enchantment; magic: *that maiden, made by glamour out of flowers.* ▷early 18th cent. (originally Scots in the sense 'enchantment, magic'): alteration of GRAMMAR. Although *grammar* itself was not used in this sense, the Latin word *grammatica* (from which it derives) was often used in the Middle Ages to mean 'scholarship, learning,' including the occult practices popularly associated with learning.

glam·our puss ▸*n. dated, informal* a glamorous person, esp. a woman.

glam rock ▸*n.* a style of rock music first popular in the early 1970s, characterized by male performers wearing exaggeratedly flamboyant clothes and makeup.

glance[1] /glans/ ▸*v.* [*intrans.*] **1** take a brief or hurried look: *Ginny glanced at her watch.* ■ (**glance at/through**) read quickly or cursorily: *I glanced through your personnel file last night.* **2** hit something at an angle and bounce off obliquely: *he saw a stone* **glance off** *a crag and hit Tom on the head.* ■ (esp. of light) reflect off something with a brief flash: *sunlight* **glanced off** *the curved body of a dolphin.* ■ [*trans.*] (in ball games) deflect (the ball) slightly with a delicate contact: *he glanced the ball into the right corner of the net.*
▸*n.* **1** a brief or hurried look: *Sean and Michael exchanged glances.* **2** *poetic/literary* a flash or gleam of light. ▷late Middle English (in the sense 'rebound obliquely'): probably a nasalized form of obsolete *glace* in the same sense, from Old French *glacier* 'to slip,' from *glace* 'ice,' based on Latin *glacies*. **—glanc·ing·ly** *adv.*
▸*PHRASES* □ **at a glance** immediately upon looking: *she saw at a glance what had happened.* □ **at first glance** when seen or considered for the first time, esp. briefly: *good news, at first glance, for frequent travelers.* □ **glance one's eye** *archaic* look briefly: *glancing his severe eye around the group.*

glance[2] ▸*n.* a shiny sulfide ore of lead, copper, or other metal. ▷late Middle English: from German *Glanz* 'brightness, luster'; compare with Dutch *glanserts* 'glance ore.'

glanc·ing /ˈglansiɴɢ/ ▸*adj.* [*attrib.*] striking someone or something at an angle rather than directly and with full force: *he was struck a glancing blow.*

gland[1] /gland/ ▸*n.* an organ in the human or animal body that secretes particular chemical substances for use in the body or for discharge into the surroundings. ■ a structure resembling this, esp. a lymph node. ■ *Botany* a secreting cell or group of cells on or within a plant structure. ▷late 17th cent.: from French *glande*, alteration of Old French *glandre*, from Latin *glandulae* 'throat glands.'

gland[2] ▸*n.* a sleeve used to produce a seal around a piston rod or other shaft. ▷early 19th cent.: probably a variant of Scots *glam* 'a vice or clamp'; related to CLAMP.

gland·ers /ˈglandərz/ ▸*plural n.* [usu. treated as *sing.*] a rare contagious disease that mainly affects horses, characterized by swellings below the jaw and mucous discharge from the nostrils. • This disease is caused by the bacterium *Pseudomonas mallei*. ▷late 15th cent.: from Old French *glandre* (see GLAND[1]).

glan·du·lar /ˈglanjələr/ ▸*adj.* of, relating to, or affecting a gland or glands. ▷mid 18th cent.: from French *glandulaire*, from *glandule* 'gland,' from Latin *glandulae* (see GLAND[1]).

glans /glanz/ ▸*n.* (*pl.* **glan·des** /ˈglandēz/) *Anatomy* the rounded part forming the end of the penis (**glans penis**) or clitoris (**glans clitoridis**). ▷mid 17th cent.: from Latin, literally 'acorn.'

glare /gle(ə)r/ ▸*v.* [*intrans.*] **1** stare in an angry or fierce way: *she* **glared at** *him, her cheeks flushing.* ■ [*trans.*] express (a feeling, esp. defiance) by staring in such a way: *he glared defiance at the pistols pointing down at him.* **2** [with *adverbial*] (of the sun or an electric light) shine with a strong or dazzling light: *the sun glared out of a clear blue sky.*
▸*n.* **1** a fierce or angry stare. **2** strong and dazzling light: *Murray narrowed his eyes against the glare of the sun.* ■ *figurative* oppressive public attention or scrutiny: *he carried on his life in the full* **glare of** *publicity.* ■ *archaic* dazzling or showy appearance; tawdry brilliance: *the pomp and glare of rhetoric.* ▷Middle English (in the sense 'shine brilliantly or dazzlingly'): from Middle Dutch and Middle Low German *glaren* 'to gleam, glare': perhaps related to GLASS. The sense 'stare' occurred first in the adjective *glaring* (late Middle English). **—glar·y** *adj.*

glare ice ▸*n.* smooth, glassy ice. ▷mid 19th cent.: probably from obsolete *glare* 'frost'; perhaps related to GLARE.

glar·ing /ˈgle(ə)riɴɢ/ ▸*adj.* **1** [*attrib.*] giving out or reflecting a strong or dazzling light: *the glaring sun.* ■ staring fiercely or fixedly: *their glaring eyes.* **2** highly obvious or conspicuous: *there is a glaring omission in the above data.* **—glar·ing·ly** *adv.*

Glas·gow /ˈglasgō; ˈglaz-/ a city in Scotland, on the Clyde River; pop. 655,000. It is the largest city in Scotland.

Glash·ow /ˈglasʜō/, Sheldon Lee (1932–), U.S. theoretical physicist. He independently developed a unified theory to explain electromagnetic interactions and the weak nuclear force, and he extended the quark theory of Murray Gell-Mann. Nobel Prize for Physics (1979, shared with Abdus Salam and Steven Weinberg).

glas·nost /ˈglazˌnōst; ˈglas-; ˈgläz-; ˈgläs-/ ▸*n.* (in the former Soviet Union) the policy or practice of more open consultative government and wider dissemination of information, initiated by leader Mikhail Gorbachev from 1985. ▷from Russian *glasnost'*, literally 'the fact of being public,' from *glasnyy* 'public, open' + *-nost'* '-ness.'

glass /glas/ ▸*n.* **1** a hard, brittle substance, typically transparent or translucent, made by fusing sand with soda, lime, and sometimes other ingredients and cooling rapidly. It is used to make windows, drinking containers, and other articles: *a piece of glass* | [as *adj.*] *a glass door.* ■ any similar substance that has solidified from a molten state without crystallizing. **2** a thing made from, or partly from, glass, in particular: ■ a container to drink from: *a beer glass.* ■ glassware. ■ greenhouses or cold frames considered collectively. ■ *chiefly Brit.* a mirror. ■ *archaic* an hourglass. **3** a lens, or an optical instrument containing a lens or lenses, in particular a monocle or a magnifying lens. **4** the liquid or amount of liquid contained in a glass; a glassful: *a glass of lemonade* | *I'll have another glass, please.*
▸*v.* [*trans.*] **1** cover or enclose with glass: *the inn has a long balcony, now* **glassed in**. **2** (esp. in hunting) scan (one's surroundings) with binoculars: *the first day was spent glassing the rolling hills.* **3** *poetic/literary* reflect in or as if in a mirror: *the opposite slopes* **glassed themselves** *in the deep dark water.* ▷Old English *glæs*, of Germanic origin; related to Dutch *glas* and German *Glas*. **—glass·ful** /-ˌfo͝ol/ *n.* (*pl.* **-fuls.**) **—glass·less** *adj.* **—glass·like** /-ˌlīk/ *adj.*
▸*PHRASE* □ **people (who live) in glass houses shouldn't throw stones** *proverb* you shouldn't criticize others when you have similar faults of your own.

glass·blow·ing /ˈglasˌblō-iɴɢ/ ▸*n.* the craft of making glassware by blowing air through a tube of semi-molten glass. **—glass·blow·er** /-ˌblōər/ *n.*

glass case ▸*n.* an exhibition display case made mostly from glass.

glass ceil·ing ▸*n.* [usu. in *sing.*] an unofficially acknowledged barrier to advancement in a profession, esp. affecting women and members of minorities.

glass cut·ter ▸*n.* a tool that scores a line on a piece of glass, allowing the glass to be snapped along the line. ■ a person who cuts glass. **—glass cut·ting** *n.*

glassed-in ▸*adj.* (of a building or part of a building) covered or enclosed with glass.

glass eel ▸*n.* an elver at the time that it first enters brackish or fresh water, when it is translucent.

glass·es /ˈglasiz/ ▸*plural n.* a pair of lenses set in a frame resting on the nose and ears, used to correct or assist defective eyesight or protect the eyes. ■ a pair of binoculars.

glass eye ▸*n.* an artificial eye made from glass.

glass fi·ber ▸*n.* a filament of glass. ■ *chiefly Brit.* a strong plastic, textile, or other material containing embedded glass filaments for reinforcement.

glass har·mon·i·ca ▸*n.* a musical instrument in which the sound is made by a row of rotating, concentric glass bowls, kept moist and pressed with the fingers or with keys. It was invented in 1761 by Benjamin Franklin and was popular until about 1830.

glass·house /ˈglasˌhous/ ▸*n. Brit.* a greenhouse.

glass·ine /glaˈsēn/ ▸*n.* [usu. as *adj.*] a glossy transparent paper: *glassine envelopes.* ▷early 20th cent.: from GLASS + -INE[4].

glass jaw ▸*n. informal Boxing* a weak jaw that is easily broken, esp. as an indication of a fighter's vulnerability to an opponent's punches.

glass liz·ard ▸*n.* a legless burrowing lizard of snakelike appearance, with smooth shiny skin and an easily detached tail, native to Eurasia, Africa, and America. Also called GLASS SNAKE. • Genus *Ophisaurus*, family Anguidae: several species.

glass·mak·ing /ˈglasˌmākiɴɢ/ ▸*n.* the manufacture of glass. **—glass·mak·er** /-ˌmākər/ *n.*

glass snake ▸*n.* another term for GLASS LIZARD.

glass·ware /ˈglasˌwe(ə)r/ ▸*n.* ornaments and articles made from glass.

glass wool ▸*n.* glass in the form of fine fibers used for packing and insulation.

glass·work /ˈglasˌwərk/ ▸*n.* **1** the business or technique of cutting and installing glass for windows and doors; glazing. **2** the manufacture of glass and glassware. **3** ornaments and articles made of glass; glassware.

glass·works /ˈglasˌwərks/ ▸*n.* [treated as *sing.* or *pl.*] a factory where glass and glass articles are made.

glass·wort /ˈglasˌwərt; -ˌwôrt/ ▸*n.* a widely distributed salt-marsh plant with fleshy scalelike leaves. The ashes of the burned plant were formerly used in glassmaking. Also called SAMPHIRE. • Genus *Salicornia*, family Chenopodiaceae: several species.

glass shapes

G

glass·y /ˈglasē/ ▸*adj.* (**glass·i·er**, **glass·i·est**) **1** of or resembling glass in some way, in particular: ■ having the physical properties of glass; vitreous: *glassy lavas.* ■ (of water) having a smooth surface. ■ (of sound) resembling the sharp or ringing noise made when glass is struck: *a glassy clink.* ■ (of a building) having glass walls. **2** (of a person's eyes or expression) showing no interest or animation; dull and glazed. **—glass·i·ly** /ˈglasəlē/ *adv.* **—glass·i·ness** *n.*

Glas·ton·bur·y /ˈglastənb(ə)rē; -ˌberē/ a town in southwestern England; pop. 7,000. It is the legendary burial place of King Arthur and Queen Guinevere and the site of a ruined abbey held by legend to have been founded by Joseph of Arimathea.

Glas·we·gian /glazˈwējən; -jēən; glas-/ ▸*adj.* of or relating to Glasgow.
▸*n.* a native of Glasgow. ■ the dialect or accent of people from Glasgow. ▷from GLASGOW, on the pattern of words such as *Norwegian.*

Glat·zer Neisse /ˈglätsər ˌnīsə/ German name for NEISSE (sense 2).

Glau·ber's salt /ˈgloubərz/ ▸*n.* (also **Glau·ber's salts**) a crystalline hydrated form of sodium sulfate, used chiefly as a laxative. ▷mid 18th cent.: named after Johann R. *Glauber* (1604–1668), the German chemist who first produced the substance artificially.

glau·co·ma /glôˈkōmə/ ▸*n. Medicine* a condition of increased pressure within the eyeball, causing gradual loss of sight. ▷mid 17th cent.: via Latin from Greek *glaukōma,* based on *glaukos* 'bluish-green, bluish-gray' (because of the gray-green haze in the pupil). **—glau·co·ma·tous** /-mətəs/ *adj.*

glau·co·nite /ˈglôkəˌnīt/ ▸*n.* a greenish clay mineral of the illite group, found chiefly in marine sands. ▷mid 19th cent.: from German *Glaukonit,* from Greek *glaukon* (neuter of *glaukos* 'bluish-green') + -ITE[1]. **—glau·co·nit·ic** /ˌglôkəˈnitik/ *adj.*

glau·co·phane /ˈglôkəˌfān/ ▸*n.* a bluish sodium-containing mineral of the amphibole group, found chiefly in schists and other metamorphic rocks. ▷mid 19th cent.: from German *Glaukophan,* from Greek *glaukos* 'bluish-green' + *-phanēs* 'shining.'

glau·cous /ˈglôkəs/ ▸*adj. technical* or *poetic/literary* **1** of a dull grayish-green or blue color. **2** covered with a powdery bloom like that on grapes. ▷late 17th cent.: via Latin from Greek *glaukos* 'bluish-green' + -OUS.

glaze /glāz/ ▸*v.* [*trans.*] **1** fit panes of glass into (a window or doorframe or similar structure): *windows can be glazed using laminated glass.* ■ enclose or cover with glass: *the verandas were* ***glazed in.*** **2** (often **be glazed**) cover with a glaze or similar finish: *new potatoes that had been glazed in mint-flavored butter.* **3** [*intrans.*] lose brightness and animation: *the prospect makes my eyes* ***glaze over*** *with boredom* | [as *adj.*] (**glazed**) *she had that glazed look in her eyes again.*
▸*n.* [usu. in *sing.*] **1** a substance used to give a smooth, shiny surface to something, in particular: ■ a vitreous substance fused on to the surface of pottery to form a hard, impervious decorative coating. ■ a liquid such as milk or beaten egg, used to form a smooth shiny coating on food. ■ *chiefly Art* a thin topcoat of transparent paint used to modify the tone of an underlying color. **2** a smooth, shiny surface formed esp. by glazing: *the glaze of the white cups.* ■ a thin, glassy coating of ice on the ground or the surface of water. ▷late Middle English *glase,* from GLASS. **—glaz·er** *n.*

gla·zier /ˈglāZHər/ ▸*n.* a person whose profession is fitting glass into windows and doors.

glazier's point // ▸*n.* a small triangle of sheet metal, used to hold glass in a window frame until the putty dries.

glaz·ing /ˈglāziNG/ ▸*n.* the action of installing windows. ■ glass windows: *sealed protective glazing.* ■ a material used to produce a glaze.

GLBT ▸*abbr.* gay, lesbian, bisexual, and transgendered: [usu. as *modifier*] *a planned GLBT cable channel.*

GLC ▸*abbr. Chemistry* gas–liquid chromatography.

gld. ▸*abbr.* guilder.

gleam /glēm/ ▸*v.* [*intrans.*] shine brightly, esp. with reflected light: *light gleamed on the china cats* | *her eyes gleamed with satisfaction.* ■ (of a smooth surface or object) reflect light because well polished: *Victor buffed the glass until it gleamed* | [as *adj.*] (**gleaming**) *sleek and gleaming black limousines.* ■ (of an emotion or quality) appear or be expressed through the brightness of someone's eyes or expression: *a hint of mischief gleaming in her eyes.*
▸*n.* [usu. in *sing.*] a faint or brief light, esp. one reflected from something: *the gleam of a silver tray.* ■ a brief or faint instance of a quality or emotion, esp. a desirable one: *the gleam of hope vanished.* ■ a brightness in a person's eyes taken as a sign of a particular emotion: *she saw an unmistakable* ***gleam of*** *triumph in his eyes.* ▷Old English *glǣm* 'brilliant light,' of Germanic origin. **—gleam·ing·ly** *adv.* **—gleam·y** *adj.* (*archaic*).
▸*PHRASE* □ **a gleam in someone's eye** see EYE.

glean /glēn/ ▸*v.* [*trans.*] extract (information) from various sources: *the information is* ***gleaned from*** *press clippings.* ■ collect gradually and bit by bit: *objects gleaned from local markets.* ■ *historical* gather (leftover grain or other produce) after a harvest: [as *n.*] (**gleaning**) *the conditions of farm workers in the 1890s made gleaning essential.* ▷late Middle English: from Old French *glener,* from late Latin *glennare,* probably of Celtic origin. **—glean·er** *n.* **—glean·ing** *n.*

glean·ings /ˈglēniNGz/ ▸*plural n.* things, esp. facts, that are gathered or collected from various sources rather than acquired as a whole. ■ *historical* grain or other produce that is gathered after a harvest: *the gleanings of your harvest are plentiful.*

Glea·son /ˈglēsən/, Jackie (1916–87) U.S. entertainer; born *Herbert John Gleason*; known as **the Great One**. He is best known for his comedic work on television on "The Jackie Gleason Show" (1952–55, 1956–59, 1961–70) and as bus driver Ralph Kramden on "The Honeymooners" (1955–56). He also appeared on Broadway in *Take Me Along* (1959) and in movies such as *The Hustler* (1961) and *Nothing in Common* (1986).

glebe /glēb/ ▸*n. historical* a piece of land serving as part of a clergyman's benefice and providing income. ■ *archaic* land; fields. ▷late Middle English: from Latin *gleba, glaeba* 'clod, land, soil.'

glee /glē/ ▸*n.* **1** great delight: *his face lit up with impish glee.* **2** a song for men's voices in three or more parts, usually unaccompanied, of a type popular esp. *c.*1750–1830. ▷Old English *glēo* 'entertainment, music, fun,' of Germanic origin. Sense 2 dates from the mid 17th cent.

glee club ▸*n.* a group organized to sing short choral works, esp. part-songs.

glee·ful /ˈglēfəl/ ▸*adj.* exuberantly or triumphantly joyful: *she gave a gleeful chuckle.* **—glee·ful·ly** *adv.* **—glee·ful·ness** *n.*

glee·man /ˈglēmən/ ▸*n.* (*pl.* **-men**) *historical* a professional entertainer, esp. a singer.

glee·some /ˈglēsəm/ ▸*adj. archaic* gleeful.

gleet /glēt/ ▸*n. Medicine* a watery discharge from the urethra caused by gonorrheal infection. ▷Middle English (denoting mucus formed in the stomach): from Old French *glette* 'slime, secretion,' of unknown origin. **—gleet·y** *adj.*

Gleich·schal·tung /ˈglīkˌSHältoŏNG/ ▸*n.* the standardization of political, economic, and social institutions as carried out in authoritarian states. ▷German, from *gleich* 'same' + *schalten* 'force or bring into line.'

glen /glen/ ▸*n.* a narrow valley. ▷late Middle English: from Scottish Gaelic and Irish *gleann* (earlier *glenn*).

Glen·dale **1** a city in south central Arizona, northwest of Phoenix; pop. 218,812. **2** a city in southwestern California, north of Los Angeles; pop. 194,973.

Glen·do·ra /glenˈdôrə/ a city in southwestern California, northeast of Los Angeles; pop. 47,828.

glen·gar·ry /glenˈgarē/ ▸*n.* (*pl.* **-ries**) a brimless boat-shaped hat with a cleft down the center, typically having two ribbons hanging at the back, worn as part of Scottish Highland dress. ▷mid 19th cent.: from *Glengarry,* the name of a valley in the Highlands of Scotland.

glengarry

Glen More /glen ˈmôr/ another name for GREAT GLEN.

Glenn /glen/, John Herschel, Jr. (1921–) U.S. astronaut and politician. In 1962, he became the first American to orbit the earth. An Ohio Democrat, he served four terms in the U.S. Senate 1975–99. In 1998, in his late 70s, he joined the crew of the space shuttle in order to help study the effects of space travel on older people.

gle·noid fos·sa /ˈglēnoid ˈfäsə/ (also **glenoid cavity**) ▸*n. Anatomy* a shallow depression on a bone into which another bone fits to form a joint, esp. that on the scapula into which the head of the humerus fits. ▷early 18th cent.: *glenoid* from French *glénoïde,* from Greek *glēnoeidēs,* from *glēnē* 'socket.'

gley /glā/ ▸*n. Soil Science* a sticky waterlogged soil lacking in oxygen, typically gray to blue in color. ▷1920s: from Ukrainian, literally 'sticky blue clay'; related to CLAY.

gli·a /ˈglēə; ˈglīə/ ▸*n. Anatomy* the connective tissue of the nervous system, consisting of several different types of cell associated with neurons. Also called NEUROGLIA. ▷late 19th cent.: from Greek, literally 'glue.' **—gli·al** *adj.*

glib /glib/ ▸*adj.* (**glib·ber**, **glib·best**) (of words or the person speaking them) fluent and voluble but insincere and shallow: *she was careful not to let the answer sound too glib.* See note at TALKATIVE. ▷late 16th cent. (also in the sense 'smooth, unimpeded'): ultimately of Germanic origin; related to Dutch *glibberig* 'slippery' and German *glibberig* 'slimy.' **—glib·ly** *adv.* **—glib·ness** *n.*

glide /glīd/ ▸*v.* **1** [*intrans.*] move with a smooth continuous motion, typically with little noise: *a few gondolas glided past.* ■ [*trans.*] cause to move with a smooth continuous motion. **2** [*intrans.*] make an unpowered flight, either in a glider or in an aircraft with engine failure. ■ (of a bird) fly through the air with very little movement of the wings.
▸*n.* [in *sing.*] **1** a smooth continuous movement. ■ an unpowered maneuver in an aircraft. ■ a flight in a glider or unpowered aircraft. ■ a smooth continuous step in ballroom dancing. **2** *Phonetics* a sound produced as the vocal organs move toward or away from articulation of a vowel or consonant, for example /y/ in *mute* /myoōt/ . ▷Old English *glīdan,* of Germanic origin; related to Dutch *glijden* and German *gleiten.*

glide path ▸*n.* an aircraft's line of descent to land, esp. as indicated by ground radar.

glid·er /ˈglīdər/ ▸*n.* **1** a light aircraft that is designed to fly for long periods without using an engine. **2** a person or thing that glides: *the flying lemur is an efficient glider as well as climber.* **3** a long swinging seat suspended from a frame in a porch.

glide re·flec·tion ▸*n. Mathematics* a transformation consisting of a translation combined with a reflection about a plane parallel to the direction of the translation.

glid·ing /ˈglīdiNG/ ▸*n.* the sport of flying in a glider.

glim /glim/ ▸*n. archaic, informal* a candle or lantern. ▷late Middle English (denoting brightness): perhaps an abbreviation of GLIMMER. The current sense dates from the late 17th cent.

glim·mer /ˈglimər/ ▸*v.* [*intrans.*] shine faintly with a wavering light: *the moonlight glimmered on the lawn* | [as *adj.*] (**glimmering**) *pools of glimmering light.*
▸*n.* a faint or wavering light. ■ a faint sign of a feeling or quality, esp. a desirable one: *there is one glimmer of hope for Becky.* ▷late Middle English: probably of Scandinavian origin; related to Swedish *glimra* and Danish *glimre.* **—glim·mer·ing·ly** *adv.*

glim·mer·ing /ˈglimәriNG/ ▸*n.* a glimmer: *the glimmering of an idea.*

glimpse /glimps/ ▸*n.* a momentary or partial view: *she* ***caught a glimpse*** *of the ocean* | *a glimpse into the world of the wealthy.*
▸*v.* [*trans.*] see or perceive briefly or partially: *he glimpsed a figure standing in the shade.* ■ [*intrans.*] *archaic* shine or appear faintly or intermittently: *glowworms glimpsing in the dark.* ▷Middle English (in the sense 'shine faintly'): probably of Germanic origin; related to Middle High German *glimsen,* also to GLIMMER.

Glin·ka /ˈgliNGkə/, Mikhail (Ivanovich) (1804–57), Russian composer. He is considered the father of the Russian national school of music. Notable operas: *A Life for the Czar* (1836) and *Russlan and Ludmilla* (1842).

glint /glint/ ▸*v.* [*intrans.*] give out or reflect small flashes of light: *her glasses were glinting in the firelight.* ■ (of a person's eyes) shine with a particular emotion: *his eyes glinted angrily.*
▸*n.* a small flash of light, esp. as reflected from a shiny surface: *the glint of gold in his teeth.* ■ [in *sing.*] a brightness in someone's eyes seen as a sign of enthusiasm or a particular emotion: *she saw the glint of excitement in his eyes.* ▷Middle English (in the sense 'move quickly or obliquely'): variant of dialect *glent,* probably of Scandinavian origin and related to Swedish dialect *glänta, glinta* 'to slip, slide, gleam.'

gli·o·blas·to·ma /ˌglīōblaˈstōmə/ ▸*n.* (*pl.* **-mas** or **-ma·ta** /-mətə/) *Medicine* a highly invasive glioma in the brain.

gli·o·ma /glīˈōmə/ ▸*n.* (*pl.* **-mas** or **-ma·ta** /-mətə/)

Medicine a malignant tumor of the glial tissue of the nervous system. ▷late 19th cent.: from Greek *glia* 'glue' + **-OMA**.

glis·sade /gli'säd; -'sād/ ▶*n.* **1** a way of sliding down a steep slope of snow or ice, typically on the feet with the support of an ice ax. **2** *Ballet* a movement, typically used as a joining step, in which one leg is brushed outward from the body, which then takes the weight while the second leg is brushed in to meet it.
▶*v.* [*intrans.*] slide down a steep slope of snow or ice with the support of an ice ax. ▷mid 19th cent.: French, from *glisser* 'to slip, slide.'

glis·san·do /gli'sändō/ ▶*n.* (*pl.* **-di** /-dē/ or **-dos**) *Music* a continuous slide upward or downward between two notes. ▷Italian, from French *glissant*, present participle of *glisser* 'to slip, slide.'

glis·sé /glə'sā; glē-/ ▶*n.* (*pl.* same) *Ballet* a movement in which weight is transferred from one foot, which is slid outward from the body and briefly extended off the ground, to the other, which is then brought to meet it. ▷early 20th cent.: French, literally 'slipped, glided'.

glis·ten /'glisən/ ▶*v.* [*intrans.*] (of something wet or greasy) shine; glitter: *his cheeks glistened with tears* | [as *adj.*] (**glistening**) *the glistening swimming pool.*
▶*n.* [in *sing.*] a sparkling light reflected from something wet: *there was a glisten of perspiration across her top lip.* ▷Old English *glisnian*, of Germanic origin; related to Middle Low German *glisen*. The noun dates from the mid 19th cent. **—glis·ten·ing·ly** *adv.*

glis·ter /'glistər/ *poetic/literary* ▶*v.* [*intrans.*] sparkle; glitter.
▶*n.* a sparkle. ▷late Middle English: probably from Middle Low German *glistern* or Middle Dutch *glisteren*.

glitch /glicн/ *informal* ▶*n.* a sudden, usually temporary malfunction or irregularity of equipment: *a draft version was lost in a computer glitch.* ■ an unexpected setback in a plan: *this has been the first real glitch they've encountered in a three months' tour.* ■ *Astronomy* a brief irregularity in the rotation of a pulsar.
▶*v.* [*intrans.*] suffer a sudden malfunction or irregularity: *her job involves troubleshooting when systems glitch.* ▷1960s (originally U.S.): of unknown origin. The original sense was 'a sudden surge of current,' hence 'malfunction, hitch' in astronautical slang. **—glitch·y** *adj.*

glit·ter /'glitər/ ▶*v.* [*intrans.*] shine with a bright, shimmering, reflected light: *trees and grass glittered with dew.* ■ shine as a result of strong feeling: *her eyes were glittering with excitement.*
▶*n.* [in *sing.*] bright, shimmering, reflected light: *the blue glitter of the sea.* ■ tiny pieces of sparkling material used for decoration: *sneakers trimmed with sequins and glitter.* ■ *figurative* an attractive, exciting, often superficial, quality: *he avoids the glitter of show business.* ■ a glint in a person's eye indicating a particular emotion: *the scathing glitter in his eyes.* ▷late Middle English: from Old Norse *glitra.* **—glit·ter·y** *adj.*
▶PHRASE □ **all that glitters is not gold** *proverb* the attractive external appearance of something is not a reliable indication of its true nature.

glit·te·ra·ti /,glitə'rätē/ ▶*plural n. informal* the fashionable set of people engaged in show business or some other glamorous activity. ▷1950s (originally U.S.): blend of **GLITTER** and **LITERATI**.

glit·ter·ing /'glitəriNG/ ▶*adj.* [*attrib.*] shining with a shimmering or sparkling light: *glittering chandeliers.* ■ *figurative* impressively successful or elaborate: *a glittering military career.* **—glit·ter·ing·ly** *adv.*

glitz /glits/ *informal* ▶*n.* extravagant but superficial display: *the glitz and sophisticated night life of Ibiza.*
▶*v.* [*trans.*] make (something) glamorous or showy: *we need to* **glitz up** *the program.* ▷1970s (originally a North American usage): back-formation from **GLITZY**.

glitz·y /'glitsē/ ▶*adj.* (**glitz·i·er, glitz·i·est**) *informal* ostentatiously attractive (often used to suggest superficial glamour): *I wanted something glitzy to wear to the launch party.* ▷1960s (originally a North American usage): from **GLITTER**, suggested by **RITZY**, and perhaps also by German *glitzerig* 'glittering.' **—glitz·i·ly** /-səlē/ *adv.* **—glitz·i·ness** *n.*

Gli·wi·ce /gli'vētsə/ a mining and industrial city in southern Poland, near the border with the Czech Republic; pop. 214,000.

gloam·ing /'glōmiNG/ ▶*n.* (**the gloaming**) *poetic/literary* twilight; dusk. ▷Old English *glōmung*, from *glōm* 'twilight,' of Germanic origin; related to **GLOW**.

gloat /glōt/ ▶*v.* [*intrans.*] contemplate or dwell on one's own success or another's misfortune with smugness or malignant pleasure: *his enemies* **gloated over** *his death.*
▶*n.* [in *sing.*] *informal* an act of gloating. ▷late 16th cent.: of unknown origin; perhaps related to Old Norse *glotta* 'to grin' and Middle High German *glotzen* 'to stare.' The original sense was 'give a sideways or furtive look,' hence 'cast amorous or admiring glances'; the current sense dates from the mid 18th cent. **—gloat·er** *n.* **—gloat·ing·ly** *adv.*

glob /gläb/ ▶*n. informal* a lump of a semiliquid substance: *thick* **globs of** *melted mozzarella cheese.* ▷early 20th cent.: perhaps a blend of **BLOB** and **GOB**[2].

glob·al /'glōbəl/ ▶*adj.* of or relating to the whole world; worldwide: *the downturn in the global economy.* ■ of or relating to the entire earth as a planet: *global environmental change.* ■ relating to or embracing the whole of something, or of a group of things: *some students may prefer to be given a global picture of what is involved in the task.* ■ *Computing* operating or applying through the whole of a file, program, etc: *global searches.* **—glob·al·ly** *adv.*

glo·bal com·mon ▶*n.* any of the earth's ubiquitous and unowned natural resources, such as the oceans, the atmosphere, and space: [usually *plural*] *financial speculators and other abusers of our global commons.*

glob·al·ist /'glōbəlist/ ▶*n.* a person who advocates the interpretation or planning of economic and foreign policy in relation to events and developments throughout the world. ■ a person or organization advocating or practicing operations across national divisions. **—glob·al·ism** /-,lizəm/ *n.*

glob·al·ize /'glōbə,līz/ ▶*v.* develop or be developed so as to make possible international influence or operation: [*trans.*] *communication globalizes capital markets* [*intrans.*] *building facilities overseas is part of the strategy of every company that aims to globalize.* **—glob·al·i·za·tion** /,glōbəli'zāsнən/ *n.*

Glob·al Sur·vey·or (in full **Mars Global Surveyor**) an unmanned American spacecraft that went into orbit around Mars in 1997 to begin detailed photography and mapping of the surface.

glob·al vil·lage ▶*n.* the world considered as a single community linked by telecommunications.

glob·al warm·ing ▶*n.* the gradual increase in the overall temperature of the earth's atmosphere due to the greenhouse effect caused by increased levels of carbon dioxide, chlorofluorocarbons, and other pollutants. See **CLIMATE CHANGE**.

globe /glōb/ ▶*n.* **1** (**the globe**) the earth: *collecting goodies from all over the globe.* ■ a spherical representation of the earth or of the constellations with a map on the surface. **2** a spherical or rounded object: *orange trees clipped into giant globes.* ■ a glass sphere protecting a light. ■ a drinking glass shaped approximately like a sphere: *a brandy globe.* ■ a golden orb as an emblem of sovereignty.
▶*v.* [*trans.*] *poetic/literary* form (something) into a globe. ▷late Middle English (in the sense 'spherical object'): from Old French, or from Latin *globus*. **—globe·like** /-,līk/ *adj.* **—glo·boid** /'glōboid/ *adj.* & *n.* **—glo·bose** /'glōbōs/ *adj.*

globe ar·ti·choke ▶*n.* see **ARTICHOKE** (sense 1).

globe·fish /'glōb,fisн/ ▶*n.* (*pl.* same or **-fish·es**) **1** a pufferfish or a porcupine fish. **2** an ocean sunfish. See **SUNFISH** (sense 1).

globe·flow·er /'glōb,flou(-ə)r/ ▶*n.* a plant of the buttercup family with globular yellow or orange flowers, native to north temperate regions. • Genus *Trollius*, family Ranunculaceae.

Globe The·a·tre a theater in Southwark, London, erected in 1599, where many of Shakespeare's plays were first publicly performed.The theater's site was rediscovered in 1989, and a reconstruction of the original theater was opened in 1997.

globe this·tle ▶*n.* an Old World thistle with globe-shaped heads of metallic blue-gray flowers. • Genus *Echinops*, family Compositae.

globe-trot·ter (also **globe·trot·ter**) ▶*n. informal* a person who travels widely. **—globe-trot** *v.* **—globe-trot·ting** *n.* & *adj.*

glo·big·er·i·na /glō,bijə'rīnə; -'rēnə/ ▶*n.* (*pl.* **-nas** or **-nae** /-nē/) a planktonic marine protozoan with a calcareous shell. The shells collect as a deposit (**globigerina ooze**) over much of the ocean floor. • Genus *Globigerina*, order Foraminiferida, kingdom Protista. ▷modern Latin, from Latin *globus* 'spherical object, globe' (because of the globular chambers in its shell) + *-ger* 'carrying' + **-INA**.

glob·u·lar /'gläbyələr/ ▶*adj.* **1** globe-shaped; spherical. See note at **ROUND**. **2** composed of globules.
▶*n. Astronomy* short for **GLOBULAR CLUSTER**.

glob·u·lar clus·ter ▶*n. Astronomy* a large compact spherical star cluster, typically of old stars in the outer regions of a galaxy.

glob·ule /'gläbyōōl/ ▶*n.* a small round particle of a substance; a drop: **globules of** *fat.* ■ *Astronomy* a small dark cloud of gas and dust seen against a brighter background such as a luminous nebula. ▷mid 17th cent.: from French, or from Latin *globulus*, diminutive of *globus* 'spherical object, globe.' **—glob·u·lous** /-yələs/ *adj.*

glob·u·lin /'gläbyəlin/ ▶*n. Biochemistry* any of a group of simple proteins soluble in salt solutions and forming a large fraction of blood serum protein. The three principal subsets of globulin are **alpha globulin**, **beta globulin**, and **gamma globulin**, which are distinguished by their respective degrees of electrophoretic mobility (alpha having the greatest and gamma having the least). ▷mid 19th cent.: from **GLOBULE** (in the archaic sense 'blood corpuscle') + **-IN**[1].

glo·bus pal·li·dus /'glōbəs 'palidəs/ ▶*n. Anatomy* the median part of the lentiform nucleus in the brain. ▷late 18th cent.: from Latin, 'pale globus.'

glo·chid /'glōkid/ ▶*n. Botany* a barbed bristle on the areole of some cacti. ▷late 19th cent.: from Greek *glōkhis*, *glōkhid-* 'arrowhead.'

glo·chid·i·um /glō'kidēəm/ ▶*n.* (*pl.* **-chid·i·a** /-'kidēə/) *Zoology* a parasitic larva of certain freshwater bivalve mollusks, which attaches itself by hooks and suckers to the fins or gills of fish. ▷late 19th cent.: modern Latin, based on Greek *glōkhis* 'arrowhead.'

glock·en·spiel /'gläkən,spēl; -,sнpēl/ ▶*n.* a musical percussion instrument having a set of tuned metal pieces mounted in a frame and struck with small hammers. ▷early 19th cent. (denoting an organ stop imitating the sound of bells): from German *Glockenspiel*, literally 'bell-play.'

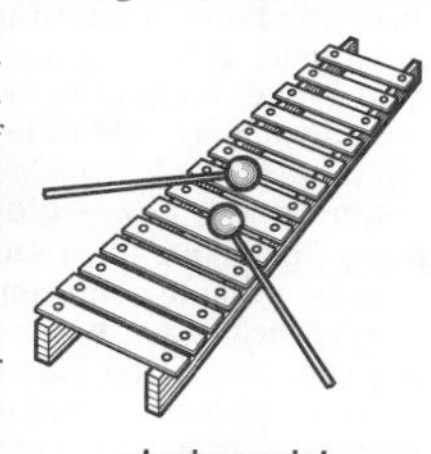

glockenspiel

glom /gläm/ ▶*v.* (**glommed, glom·ming**) *informal* [*trans.*] steal: *I thought he was about to glom my wallet.* ■ [*intrans.*] (**glom onto**) become stuck or attached to. ▷early 20th cent.: variant of Scots *glaum*, of unknown origin.

glo·mer·u·lo·ne·phri·tis /glō,meryəlō,nə'frītis/ ▶*n. Medicine* acute inflammation of the kidney, typically caused by an immune response.

glo·mer·u·lus /glō'meryələs/ ▶*n.* (*pl.* **-li** /-,lī/) *Anatomy & Biology* a cluster of nerve endings, spores, or small blood vessels, in particular: ■ a cluster of capillaries around the end of a kidney tubule, where waste products are filtered from the blood. ▷mid 19th cent.: modern Latin, diminutive of Latin *glomus*, *glomer-* 'ball of thread.' **—glo·mer·u·lar** /-lər/ *adj.*

gloom /glōōm/ ▶*n.* **1** partial or total darkness: *he strained his eyes peering into the gloom.* ■ *poetic/literary* a dark or shady place. **2** a state of depression or despondency: *a year of economic gloom for the car industry* | *his gloom deepened.*
▶*v.* [*intrans.*] **1** *poetic/literary* have a dark or somber appearance: *the black gibbet glooms beside the way.* ■ [*trans.*] cover with gloom; make dark or dismal: *a black yew gloom'd the stagnant air.* **2** be or look depressed or despondent: *Charles was always glooming about money.* ▷late Middle English (as a verb): of unknown origin.
▶PHRASE □ **gloom and doom** see **DOOM**.

gloom·y /'glōōmē/ ▶*adj.* (**gloom·i·er, gloom·i·est**) dark or poorly lit, esp. so as to appear depressing or frightening: *a gloomy corridor.* ■ feeling distressed or pessimistic: *I am by no means gloomy about the prospects for domestic industry.* ■ causing distress or depression: *a gloomy atmosphere.* **—gloom·i·ly** /-məlē/ *adv.* **—gloom·i·ness** *n.*

gloop /glōōp/ ▶*n. informal* another term for **GLOP**. ▷late 20th cent.: the letters *gl*, *o*, and *p* are said to be symbolic of semiliquid matter (compare with **GLOP**). **—gloop·i·ness** *n.* **—gloop·y** *adj.* (**gloop·i·er, gloop·i·est**).

glop /gläp/ ▶*n. informal* a sticky and amorphous substance, typically something unpleasant: *the snow was sun-softened glop.* ■ a soft, shapeless lump of

Pronunciation Key ə *ago*; ər *over*; 'ə or ,ə *up*; 'ər or ,ər *fur*; a *hat*; ā *rate*; ä *car*; cн *chew*; e *let*; ē *see*; e(ə)r *air*; i *fit*; ī *by*; i(ə)r *ear*; NG *sing*; ō *go*; ô *for*; oi *boy*; ŏŏ *good*; ōō *goo*; ou *out*; sн *she*; тн *thin*; <u>тн</u> *then*; (h)w *why*; zн *vision*

something: *a* ***glop*** *of creamy dressing.* ■ *figurative* worthless or overly sentimental writing, music, or other material: *commercialized glop, not worth thinking about.* ▷1940s: symbolic (see GLOOP). —**glop·py** *adj.* (**-pi·er, -pi·est**).

Glo·ri·a /ˈglôrēə/ ▸*n.* a Christian liturgical hymn or formula beginning (in the Latin text) with *Gloria*, in particular: ■ the hymn beginning *Gloria in excelsis Deo* (Glory be to God in the highest), forming a set part of the Mass. ■ a musical setting of this: *Vivaldi's Gloria.* ■ the doxology beginning *Gloria Patris* (Glory be to the Father), used after psalms and in formal prayer (e.g., in the rosary). ▷Middle English: Latin, 'glory.'

Glo·ri·a·na /ˌglôrēˈänə/ the nickname of Queen Elizabeth I.

glo·ri·fied /ˈglôrəˌfīd/ ▸*adj.* **1** [*attrib.*] (esp. of something or someone ordinary or unexceptional) represented in such a way as to appear more elevated or special: *all Peter will be is a sort of glorified secretary.* **2** (in religious contexts) made glorious: *the transformed and glorified Jesus.*

glo·ri·fy /ˈglôrəˌfī/ ▸*v.* (**-fies, -fied**) [*trans.*] **1** reveal or make clearer the glory of (God) by one's actions: *God can be glorified through a life of scholarship.* ■ give praise to (God). **2** describe or represent as admirable, esp. unjustifiably or undeservedly: *a football video glorifying violence.* ▷Middle English: from Old French *glorifier*, from ecclesiastical Latin *glorificare*, from late Latin *glorificus*, from Latin *gloria* 'glory.' —**glo·ri·fi·ca·tion** /ˌglôrəfiˈkāsʜən/ *n.* —**glo·ri·fi·er** *n.*

glo·ri·ous /ˈglôrēəs/ ▸*adj.* **1** having, worthy of, or bringing fame or admiration: *the most glorious victory of all time.* **2** having a striking beauty or splendor that evokes feelings of delighted admiration: *a glorious autumn day.* ▷Middle English: from Old French *glorieus*, from Latin *gloriosus*, from *gloria* 'glory.' —**glo·ri·ous·ly** *adv.* —**glo·ri·ous·ness** *n.*

glo·ry /ˈglôrē/ ▸*n.* (*pl.* **-ries**) **1** high renown or honor won by notable achievements: *to fight and die for the glory of one's nation.* ■ praise, worship, and thanksgiving offered to God. **2** magnificence; great beauty: *the train has been restored to all its former glory.* ■ (often **glories**) a thing that is beautiful or distinctive; a special cause for pride, respect, or delight: *the glories of Paris.* ■ the splendor and bliss of heaven: *with the saints in glory.* **3** a luminous ring or halo, esp. as depicted around the head of Jesus Christ or a saint.

▸*v.* [*intrans.*] (**glory in**) take great pride or pleasure in: *they were individuals who gloried in their independence.* ■ exult in unpleasantly or boastfully: *readers tended to defend their paper or even to glory in its bias.* ▷Middle English: from Old French *glorie*, from Latin *gloria*.

▸*PHRASES* □ **glory be!** expressing enthusiastic piety. ■ *informal* used as an exclamation of surprise or delight. ■ (**Glory Be**) [as *n.*] (esp. in Roman Catholic use) the doxology beginning "Glory be to the Father." □ **go to glory** die; be destroyed. □ **in one's glory** *informal* in a state of extreme joy or exaltation.

glo·ry days ▸*plural n.* a time in the past regarded as being better than the present: *his glory days as a high school basketball star | the glory days of tourism.*

glo·ry hole ▸*n.* **1** a small furnace used to keep glass malleable for handworking. **2** *dated, informal* an untidy storage place, esp. a room or cupboard. **3** *informal* a hole in a wall through which fellatio or masturbation is conducted incognito. ▷early 19th cent.: of unknown origin.

glo·ry-of-the-snow ▸*n.* another term for CHIONODOXA.

gloss[1] /gläs; glôs/ ▸*n.* shine or luster on a smooth surface: *hair with a healthy gloss.* See note at POLISH. ■ see LIPGLOSS. ■ (also **gloss paint**) a type of paint that dries to a bright shiny surface. ■ [in *sing.*] a superficially attractive appearance or impression: *beneath the gloss of success was a tragic private life.*

▸*v.* [*trans.*] apply a cosmetic gloss to. ■ apply gloss paint to. ■ (**gloss over**) try to conceal or disguise (something embarrassing or unfavorable) by treating it briefly or representing it misleadingly: *the social costs of this growth are glossed over.* ▷mid 16th cent.: of unknown origin. —**gloss·er** *n.*

gloss[2] ▸*n.* a translation or explanation of a word or phrase. ■ an explanation, interpretation, or paraphrase: *the chapter acts as a helpful* ***gloss on*** *Pynchon's general method.*

▸*v.* [*trans.*] (usu. **be glossed**) provide an explanation, interpretation, or paraphrase for (a text, word, etc.). ■ [*intrans.*] (**gloss on/upon**) *archaic* write or make comments, esp. unfavorable ones, about (something): *those laws, which they assumed the liberty of interpreting and glossing upon.* ▷mid 16th cent.: alteration of the noun *gloze*, from Old French *glose* (see GLOZE), suggested by medieval Latin *glossa* 'explanation of a difficult word,' from Greek *glōssa* 'word needing explanation, language, tongue.'

gloss. ▸*abbr.* glossary.

glos·sa /ˈgläsə; ˈglô-/ ▸*n.* (*pl.* **-sae** /-sē/ or **-sas**) a tonguelike structure in the labium of an insect's mouthparts.

glos·sal /ˈgläsəl; ˈglô-/ ▸*adj. rare Anatomy* of the tongue; lingual. ▷early 19th cent.: from Greek *glōssa* 'tongue' + -AL.

glos·sa·ry /ˈgläsərē; ˈglô-/ ▸*n.* (*pl.* **-ries**) an alphabetical list of terms or words found in or relating to a specific subject, text, or dialect, with explanations; a brief dictionary. ▷late Middle English: from Latin *glossarium*, from *glossa* (see GLOSS[2]). —**glos·sar·i·al** /gläˈse(ə)rēəl; glô-/ *adj.* —**glos·sa·rist** /-rist/ *n.*

glos·sa·tor /ˈgläˌsātər; ˈglô-; gläˈsātər; glô-/ ▸*n. chiefly historical* a person who writes glosses, esp. a scholarly commentator on the texts of classical, civil, or canon law. ▷late Middle English: from medieval Latin, from *glossare*, from Latin *glossa* (see GLOSS[2]).

glos·si·tis /gläˈsītis; glô-/ ▸*n. Medicine* inflammation of the tongue. ▷early 19th cent.: from Greek *glōssa* 'tongue' + -ITIS.

glos·sog·ra·pher /gläˈsägrəfər; glô-/ ▸*n.* a writer of glosses or commentaries.

glos·sog·ra·phy /gläˈsägrəˌfē/ ▸*n.* **1** the writing of glosses or commentaries. **2** the compiling of glossaries.

glos·so·la·li·a /ˌgläsəˈlālēə; ˌglô-/ ▸*n.* the phenomenon of (apparently) speaking in an unknown language, esp. in religious worship. It is practiced esp. by Pentecostal and charismatic Christians. ▷late 19th cent.: from Greek *glōssa* 'language, tongue' + *lalia* 'speech.' —**glos·so·la·lic** /-ˌlālik/ *adj.*

glos·so·pha·ryn·ge·al nerve /ˌgläsōfəˈrinjēəl; ˌglô-/ ▸*n. Anatomy* each of the ninth pair of cranial nerves, supplying the tongue and pharynx.

gloss·y /ˈgläsē; ˈglô-/ ▸*adj.* (**gloss·i·er, gloss·i·est**) shiny and smooth: *thick, glossy, manageable hair.* ■ (of a magazine or photograph) printed on high-quality smooth shiny paper. ■ superficially attractive and stylish, and suggesting wealth or expense: *glossy TV miniseries and soaps.*

▸*n.* (*pl.* **gloss·ies**) *informal* a magazine printed on glossy paper, expensively produced with many color photographs. ■ a photograph printed on glossy paper. —**gloss·i·ly** /-səlē/ *adv.* —**gloss·i·ness** *n.*

glot·tal /ˈglätl/ ▸*adj.* [*attrib.*] of or produced by the glottis.

glot·tal stop ▸*n.* a consonant formed by the audible release of the airstream after complete closure of the glottis. It is widespread in some nonstandard English accents, and in some other languages, such as Arabic, it is a standard consonant.

glot·tis /ˈglätis/ ▸*n.* the part of the larynx consisting of the vocal cords and the slitlike opening between them. It affects voice modulation through expansion or contraction. ▷late 16th cent.: modern Latin, from Greek *glōttis*, from *glōtta*, variant of *glōssa* 'tongue.' —**glot·tic** /ˈglätik/ *adj.*

glot·to·chro·nol·o·gy /ˌglätōkrəˈnäləjē/ ▸*n.* the use of statistical data to date the divergence of languages from their common sources. —**glot·to·chron·o·log·i·cal** /-ˌkränəˈläjikəl/ *adj.*

Glouces·ter /ˈglôstər; ˈgläs-/ **1** a city in southwestern England, the county town of Gloucestershire; pop. 93,000. **2** a city in northeastern Massachusetts, on Cape Ann, noted as a fishing and resort center; pop. 28,716.

Glouces·ter·shire /ˈglôstərsʜər; ˈgläs-; -ˌsʜi(ə)r/ a county in southwestern England; county town, Gloucester.

glove /gləv/ ▸*n.* a covering for the hand worn for protection against cold or dirt and typically having separate parts for each finger and the thumb. ■ a padded protective covering for the hand used in boxing, baseball, and other sports.

▸*v.* [*trans.*] *informal* (of a baseball catcher) catch, deflect, or touch (the ball) with one's glove. ▷Old English *glōf*, of Germanic origin. —**gloved** *adj.* —**glove·less** *adj.*

▸*PHRASES* □ **fit like a glove** (of clothes) fit exactly. □ **the gloves are off** (or **with the gloves off** or **take the gloves off**) used to express the notion that something will be done in an uncompromising or brutal way, without compunction or hesitation: *for the banks chasing this growing business, the gloves are now definitely off.*

glove box (also **glove·box**) ▸*n.* **1** another term for GLOVE COMPARTMENT. **2** a closed chamber into which a pair of gloves projects from openings in the side, used esp. in laboratories and incubators in hospitals to prevent contamination.

glove com·part·ment ▸*n.* a recess with a hinged door in the dashboard of a motor vehicle, used for storing small items.

glov·er /ˈgləvər/ ▸*n.* a maker of gloves.

glow /glō/ ▸*v.* [*intrans.*] give out steady light without flame: *the tips of their cigarettes glowed in the dark.* ■ have an intense color and a slight shine: [with *complement*] *faces that glowed red with the cold.* ■ have a heightened color or a bloom on the skin as a result of warmth or health: *he was glowing with health.* ■ feel deep pleasure or satisfaction and convey it through one's expression and bearing: *Katy always glowed when he praised her.*

▸*n.* [in *sing.*] a steady radiance of light or heat: *the setting sun cast a deep red glow over the city.* ■ a feeling of warmth in the face or body; the visible effects of this as a redness of the cheeks: *he could feel the brandy filling him with a warm glow.* ■ a strong feeling of pleasure or well-being: *with a* ***glow of*** *pride, Mildred walked away.* ▷Old English *glōwan*, of Germanic origin; related to Dutch *gloeien* and German *glühen*.

glow dis·charge ▸*n.* a luminous sparkless electrical discharge from a pointed conductor in a gas at low pressure.

glow·er /ˈglouər/ ▸*v.* [*intrans.*] have an angry or sullen look on one's face; scowl: *she* ***glowered at*** *him suspiciously.*

▸*n.* [in *sing.*] an angry or sullen look. ▷late 15th cent.: perhaps a Scots variant of synonymous dialect *glore*, or from obsolete *glow* 'to stare,' both possibly of Scandinavian origin. —**glow·er·ing** *adj.* —**glow·er·ing·ly** *adv.*

glow·fly /ˈglōˌflī/ ▸ another term for FIREFLY.

glow·ing /ˈglōiɴɢ/ ▸*adj.* [*attrib.*] expressing great praise: *he received a glowing report from his teachers.* —**glow·ing·ly** *adv.*

glow·worm /ˈglōˌwərm/ ▸*n.* a soft-bodied beetle with luminescent organs in the abdomen, esp. the larvalike wingless female, which emits light to attract the flying male. • Families Lampyridae and Phengodidae: several genera numerous species including the American *Zarhipis integripennis*.

glox·in·i·a /gläkˈsinēə/ ▸*n.* a tropical American plant with large, velvety, bell-shaped flowers. • Genera *Gloxinia* and *Sinningia*, family Gesneriaceae: several species, in particular the florists' gloxinia (*S. speciosa*), which is a popular houseplant. ▷modern Latin, named after Benjamin P. *Gloxin*, the 18th-cent. German botanist who first described it.

gloze /glōz/ ▸*v.* [*trans.*] *rare* make excuses for: *the demeanor of Mathews is rather* ***glozed over.*** ■ [*intrans.*] *archaic* use ingratiating or fawning language. ■ [*intrans.*] *archaic* make a comment or comments. ▷Middle English: from Old French *gloser*, from *glose* 'a gloss, comment,' based on Latin *glossa* (see GLOSS[2]).

gluc- ▸*comb. form.* variant of GLUCO- before a vowel: *glucasil.*

glu·ca·gon /ˈglo͞okəˌgän/ ▸*n. Biochemistry* a hormone formed in the pancreas that promotes the breakdown of glycogen to glucose in the liver. ▷1920s: from Greek *glukus* 'sweet' + *agōn* 'leading, bringing.'

Gluck /glo͝ok/, Christoph Willibald von (1714–87), German composer. His first operas were in the traditional Italian style, but with *Orfeo ed Euridice* (1762), he initiated a new style in which he united dramatic, musical, and emotional elements, revolutionizing opera. Later works include *Alceste* (1767), *Iphigénie en Aulide* (1774), and *Iphigénie en Tauride* (1779).

glu·co·cor·ti·coid /ˌglo͞okōˈkôrtiˌkoid/ ▸*n. Biochemistry* any of a group of corticosteroids (e.g., hydrocortisone) that are involved in the metabolism of carbohydrates, proteins, and fats and have anti-inflammatory activity.

glu·co·sa·mine /glo͞oˈkōsəˌmēn; -min/ ▸*n.* a natural component of human cartilage. ■ a synthesized form of this, taken as a dietary supplement to relieve arthritis pain.

glu·cose /ˈglo͞okōs/ ▸*n. Biochemistry* a simple sugar that is an important energy source in living organisms and is a component of many carbohydrates. • A hexose; chem. formula: $C_6H_{12}O_6$. ■ a syrup containing glucose and other sugars, made by hydrolysis of starch and used in the food industry. ▷mid 19th cent.: from French, from Greek *gleukos* 'sweet wine,' related to *glukus* 'sweet.'

glu·co·side /ˈglo͞okəˌsīd/ ▸*n. Biochemistry* a glycoside derived from glucose. —**glu·co·sid·ic** /ˌglōōkəˈsidik/ *adj.*

glu·cu·ron·ic ac·id /ˌglōōkyəˈränik/ ▸*n. Biochemistry* an acid derived from glucose, occurring naturally as a constituent of hyaluronic acid and other glycosaminoglycans. • A uronic acid; chem. formula: $HOOC(CHOH)_4CHO$.

glue /glōō/ ▸*n.* an adhesive substance used for sticking objects or materials together.
▸*v.* (**glues, glued, glu·ing** or **glue·ing**) [*trans.*] fasten or join with or as if with glue: *the wood is cut up into small pieces which are then glued together.* ■ (**be glued to**) *informal* be paying very close attention to (something, esp. a television or computer screen): *I was glued to the television when the Olympics were on.* ▷Middle English: from Old French *glu* (noun), *gluer* (verb), from late Latin *glus, glut-*, from Latin *gluten.* —**glue·like** /-ˌlīk/ *adj.* —**glue·y** *adj.*

glue·pot /ˈglōōˌpät/ ▸*n.* a pot with an outer container holding water, used to heat glue that sets when it cools.

glue sniff·ing ▸*n.* the practice of inhaling intoxicating fumes from the solvents in adhesives. —**glue sniff·er** *n.*

glug /gləg/ *informal* ▸*v.* (**glugged, glug·ging**) [*trans.*] drink or pour (liquid) with a hollow gurgling sound: *he* ***glugs down*** *half his beer.*
▸*n.* a hollow gurgling sound or series of sounds as of liquid being poured from a bottle. ■ an amount of liquid poured from a bottle: *a couple of good* ***glugs*** *of Dubonnet.* ▷late 17th cent.: imitative.

glum /gləm/ ▸*adj.* (**glum·mer, glum·mest**) looking or feeling dejected; morose: *they looked glum but later cheered up.* ▷mid 16th cent.: related to dialect *glum* 'to frown,' variant of **GLOOM**. —**glum·ly** *adv.* —**glum·ness** *n.*

THE RIGHT WORD **doleful, dour, glum, lugubrious, melancholy, saturnine, sullen**

All happy people are alike, to paraphrase Tolstoy, but each unhappy person is unhappy in his or her own way.

A **sullen** person is gloomy, untalkative, and ill-humored by nature.

A **glum** person is usually silent because of low spirits or depressing circumstances (*to be glum in the face of a plummeting stock market*).

Melancholy suggests a more or less chronic sadness (*her melancholy was the result of an unhappy childhood*), while a person who is **saturnine** has a forbiddingly gloomy and taciturn nature (*his request was met with a saturnine and scornful silence*).

Dour refers to a grim and bitter outlook or disposition (*a dour old woman who never smiled*), and **doleful** implies a mournful sadness (*the child's doleful expression as his parents left*).

Someone or something described as **lugubrious** is mournful or gloomy in an affected or exaggerated way (*lugubrious songs about lost love*).

glume /glōōm/ ▸*n. Botany* each of two membranous bracts surrounding the spikelet of a grass (forming the husk of a cereal grain) or one surrounding the florets of a sedge. ▷late 18th cent.: from Latin *gluma* 'husk.'

glu·on /ˈglōōän/ ▸*n. Physics* a subatomic particle of a class that is thought to bind quarks together. ▷1970s: from **GLUE** + **-ON**.

glut /glət/ ▸*n.* an excessively abundant supply of something: *there is a glut of cars on the market.*
▸*v.* (**glut·ted, glut·ting**) [*trans.*] (usu. **be glutted**) supply or fill to excess: *the factories for recycling paper are glutted* | *he was* ***glutting himself*** *on junk food.* ■ *archaic* satisfy fully: *he planned a treacherous murder to glut his desire for revenge.* ▷Middle English: probably via Old French from Latin *gluttire* 'to swallow'; related to **GLUTTON**.

glu·ta·mate /ˈglōōtəˌmāt/ ▸*n. Biochemistry* a salt or ester of glutamic acid. ■ glutamic acid, its salts, or its anion. ■ short for **MONOSODIUM GLUTAMATE**.

glu·tam·ic ac·id /glōōˈtamik/ ▸*n. Biochemistry* an acidic amino acid that is a constituent of many proteins. • Chem. formula: $HOOC(CH_2)_2(NH_2)COOH$. ▷late 19th cent.: from **GLUTEN** + **AMINE** + **-IC**.

glu·ta·mine /ˈglōōtəˌmēn/ ▸*n. Biochemistry* a hydrophilic amino acid that is a constituent of most proteins. • An amide of glutamic acid; chem. formula: $H_2NCOCH_2CH_2(NH_2)COOH$. ▷late 19th cent.: blend of **GLUTAMIC ACID** and **AMINE**.

glu·ta·thi·one /ˌglōōtəˈTHīōn/ ▸*n. Biochemistry* a compound involved as a coenzyme in oxidation–reduction reactions in cells. It is a tripeptide derived from glutamic acid, cysteine, and glycine.

glute /glōōt/ ▸*n.* (usu. **glutes**) *informal* short for **GLUTEUS**.

glu·te·al /ˈglōōtēəl/ ▸*n.* (usually **gluteals**) a gluteus muscle in the buttocks: *reshaping the gluteals isn't a matter of doing 25 more leg lifts.* ▷late 18th cent.: from *gluteus* + *-al.*

glu·ten /ˈglōōtn/ ▸*n.* a substance present in cereal grains, esp. wheat, that is responsible for the elastic texture of dough. A mixture of two proteins, it causes illness in people with celiac disease. ▷late 16th cent. (originally denoting protein from animal tissue): via French from Latin, literally 'glue.'

glu·te·us /ˈglōōtēəs/ (also **gluteus muscle**) ▸*n.* (*pl.* **-te·i** /-tēˌī/) any of three muscles in each buttock that move the thigh, the largest of which is the **gluteus maximus**. ▷late 17th cent.: modern Latin, from Greek *gloutos* 'buttock.' —**glu·te·al** /-tēəl/ *adj.*

glu·ti·nous /ˈglōōtn-əs/ ▸*adj.* like glue in texture; sticky: *glutinous mud.* ▷late Middle English: from Old French *glutineux* or Latin *glutinosus*, from *gluten* 'glue.' —**glu·ti·nous·ly** *adv.* —**glu·ti·nous·ness** *n.*

glut·ton /ˈglətn/ ▸*n.* **1** an excessively greedy eater. ■ a person who is excessively fond of or always eager for something: *a* ***glutton for*** *adventure.* **2** another term for **WOLVERINE**, esp. the European species. [translation of German *Vielfrass* 'glutton,' from Middle Low German *velvratze, velevras* 'wolverine.'] ▷Middle English: from Old French *gluton*, from Latin *glutton-*, related to *gluttire* 'to swallow,' *gluttus* 'greedy,' and *gula* 'throat.' —**glut·ton·ize** /-ˌīz/ *v.* —**glut·ton·ous** /-əs/ *adj.* —**glut·ton·ous·ly** /-əslē/ *adv.*
▸***PHRASE*** □ **a glutton for punishment** a person who is always eager to undertake hard or unpleasant tasks.

glut·ton·y /ˈglətn-ē/ ▸*n.* habitual greed or excess in eating. ▷Middle English: from Old French *glutonie*, from *gluton* 'glutton.'

gly·ce·mic index /glīˈsēmik/ ▸*n.* a system that ranks foods on a scale from 1 to 100 based on their effect on blood-sugar levels.

glyc·er·ide /ˈglisəˌrīd/ ▸*n.* a fatty acid ester of glycerol.

glyc·er·in /ˈglisərin/ (also **glyc·er·ine** /-rin; -ˌrēn; ˌglisəˈrēn/) ▸*n.* another term for **GLYCEROL**. ▷mid 19th cent.: from French *glycerin*, from Greek *glukeros* 'sweet.'

glyc·er·ol /ˈglisəˌrôl; -ˌräl/ ▸*n.* a colorless, sweet, viscous liquid formed as a byproduct in soap manufacture. It is used as an emollient and laxative, and for making explosives and antifreeze. • A trihydric alcohol; chem. formula: $CH_2(OH)CH(OH)CH_2(OH)$. ▷late 19th cent.: from **GLYCERIN** + **-OL**.

glyc·er·yl /ˈglisəˌril/ ▸*n.* [as *adj.*] *Chemistry* of or denoting a radical derived from glycerol by replacement of one or more hydrogen atoms: *glyceryl trinitrate.* ▷mid 19th cent.: from **GLYCERIN** + **-YL**.

gly·cine /ˈglīsēn/ ▸*n. Biochemistry* the simplest naturally occurring amino acid. It is a constituent of most proteins. • Chem. formula: H_2NCH_2COOH. ▷mid 19th cent.: from Greek *glukus* 'sweet' + **-INE**[4].

glyco- ▸*comb. form* of, relating to, or producing sugar: *glycogenesis* | *glycoside.* ▷from Greek *glukus* 'sweet.'

gly·co·bi·ol·o·gy /ˌglīkōbīˈäləjē/ ▸*n.* the scientific study of carbohydrates and their role in biology. ■ this field limited to the study of sugars.

gly·co·gen /ˈglīkəjən/ ▸*n. Biochemistry* a substance deposited in bodily tissues as a store of carbohydrates. It is a polysaccharide that forms glucose on hydrolysis. —**gly·co·gen·ic** /ˌglīkəˈjenik/ *adj.*

gly·co·gen·e·sis /ˌglīkəˈjenəsis/ ▸*n. Biochemistry* the formation of glycogen from sugar.

gly·col /ˈglīkôl; -kōl/ ▸*n.* short for **ETHYLENE GLYCOL**. ■ *Chemistry* another term for **DIOL**. ▷mid 19th cent. (applied to ethylene glycol): from **GLYCERIN** + **-OL** (originally intended to designate a substance intermediate between glycerine and alcohol).

gly·col·ic ac·id /glīˈkälik/ ▸*n.* a colorless, translucent, crystalline compound, $C_2H_4O_3$, that occurs in cane sugar, unripe grapes, and sugar beets and has numerous industrial uses, esp. in dyeing leather and textiles and in the manufacture of pesticides.

gly·col·y·sis /glīˈkäləsis/ ▸*n. Biochemistry* the breakdown of glucose by enzymes, releasing energy and pyruvic acid. —**gly·co·lyt·ic** /ˌglīkəˈlitik/ *adj.*

gly·co·pro·tein /ˌglīkōˈprōtēn/ ▸*n. Biochemistry* any of a class of proteins that have carbohydrate groups attached to the polypeptide chain. Also called **glycopeptide**.

gly·cos·a·mi·no·gly·can /ˌglīkōsəˌmēnōˈglīkan/ ▸*n. Biochemistry* any of a group of compounds occurring chiefly as components of connective tissue. They are complex polysaccharides containing amino groups. Formerly called **MUCOPOLYSACCHARIDE**.

gly·co·side /ˈglīkəˌsīd/ ▸*n. Biochemistry* a compound formed from a simple sugar and another compound by replacement of a hydroxyl group in the sugar molecule. Many drugs and poisons derived from plants are glycosides. ▷late 19th cent.: from **GLYCO-** 'relating to sugar,' on the pattern of *glucoside.* —**gly·co·sid·ic** /ˌglīkəˈsidik/ *adj.*

gly·cos·u·ri·a /ˌglīkōsyŏŏˈrēə/ ▸*n. Medicine* a condition characterized by an excess of sugar in the urine, typically associated with diabetes or kidney disease. ▷mid 19th cent.: from French *glycosurie*, from *glucos* 'glucose.' —**gly·cos·u·ric** /-ˈsyŏŏrik/ *adj.*

glyph /glif/ ▸*n.* **1** a hieroglyphic character or symbol; a pictograph: *flanges painted with esoteric glyphs.* ■ strictly, a sculptured symbol (e.g., as forming the ancient Mayan writing system). ■ *Computing* a small graphic symbol. **2** *Architecture* an ornamental carved groove or channel, as on a Greek frieze. ▷late 18th cent. (sense 2): from French *glyphe*, from Greek *gluphē* 'carving.' —**glyph·ic** /ˈglifik/ *adj.*

gly·phos·ate /ˈglīfəˌsāt/ ▸*n.* a synthetic compound that is a nonselective systemic herbicide, particularly effective against perennial weeds. • Alternative name: ***N*-(phosphonomethyl) glycine**; chem. formula: $C_3H_8NO_5P$.

glyp·tic /ˈgliptik/ ▸*adj.* of or concerning carving or engraving.
▸*n.* (usu. **glyptics**) the art of carving or engraving, esp. on precious stones. ▷early 19th cent.: from French *glyptique* or Greek *gluptikos*, from *gluptēs* 'carver,' from *gluphein* 'carve.'

glyp·to·dont /ˈgliptəˌdänt/ ▸*n.* a fossil South American edentate mammal of the Cenozoic era, related to armadillos but much larger. Glyptodonts had fluted teeth and a body covered in a thick bony carapace. • Family Glyptodontidae, order Xenarthra (or Edentata): several genera, including *Glyptodon.* ▷mid 19th cent.: from Greek *gluptos* 'carved' (from *gluphein* 'carve') + *odous, odont-* 'tooth.'

glyp·tog·ra·phy /glipˈtägrəfē/ ▸*n.* the art or scientific study of gem engraving. ▷late 18th cent.: from Greek *gluptos* 'carved' (from *gluphein* 'carve') + **-GRAPHY**.

GM ▸*abbr.* ■ general manager. ■ *Chess* grand master. ■ genetically modified. ■ General Motors.

gm ▸*abbr.* gram(s).

G-man ▸*n.* (*pl.* **G-men**) *informal* an FBI agent. ▷1930s: probably an abbreviation of *Government man.*

GMAT ▸*abbr.* ■ Graduate Management Admissions Test. ■ Greenwich Mean Astronomical Time.

GMP ▸*abbr.* guanosine monophosphate.

GMT ▸*abbr.* Greenwich Mean Time.

GMW ▸*abbr.* gram-molecular weight.

gn ▸*abbr.* guinea(s).

gnar /När/ ▸*v.* [*intrans.*] (**gnarred gnar·ring**) snarl, growl: *my Norwegian friend gnarred—that's the only word for what he did—he gnarred.* ▷Imit.: compare Middle Low German *gnarren*, German *knarren* 'creak,' *knurren* 'snarl.'

gnarl /närl/ ▸*n.* a rough, knotty protuberance, esp. on a tree. ▷early 19th cent.: back-formation from **GNARLED**.

gnarled /närld/ ▸*adj.* knobbly, rough, and twisted, esp. with age: *the gnarled old oak tree.* ▷early 17th cent.: variant of *knarled*, from **KNAR**.

gnarl·y /ˈnärlē/ ▸*adj.* (**gnarl·i·er, gnarl·i·est**) **1** gnarled. **2** *informal* difficult, dangerous, or challenging: *she battled through the gnarly first sequence.* [originally surfers' slang, perhaps from the appearance of rough sea.] ■ unpleasant; unattractive: *train stations can be pretty gnarly places.*

gnash /naSH/ ▸*v.* [*trans.*] grind (one's teeth) together, typically as a sign of anger: *no doubt he is gnashing his teeth in rage.* ■ [*intrans.*] (of teeth) strike together; grind: *the dog's jaws were primed to gnash.* ▷late Middle English: perhaps related to Old Norse *gnastan* 'a gnashing.'

gnat /nat/ ▸*n.* a small two-winged fly that resembles a mosquito. Gnats include both biting and nonbiting forms, and they typically form large swarms. • Several families, including Simuliidae (black flies) and Ceratopogonidae. ■ a person or thing seen as tiny or insignificant, esp. in comparison with something larger or more important: *I was only a gnat in the affair.* ▷Old English *gnætt*, of Germanic origin; related to German *Gnitze.*

gnat·catch·er /ˈnat,kaCHər; -,keCHər/ ▸*n.* a tiny gray-backed New World songbird, with a long tail that is often cocked. • Genus *Polioptila*, family Polioptilidae (or Sylviidae): several species.

gnath·ic /ˈnaTHik/ ▸*adj. rare* of or relating to the jaws. ▷late 19th cent.: from Greek *gnathos* 'jaw' + **-IC**.

Gna·thos·to·mu·li·da /nə,THästəˈmyo͞olədə/ *Zoology* a minor phylum of minute marine worms that appear to be intermediate between coelenterates and flatworms. ▷modern Latin (plural), from Greek *gnathos* 'jaw' + *stoma* 'mouth.' **—gna·thos·to·mu·lid** /,naTHə ˈstōmyəlid; ,nā-/ *n.* & *adj.*

gnaw /nô/ ▸*v.* [*intrans.*] bite at or nibble something persistently: *picking up the pig's foot, he* **gnawed at** *it.* ■ [*trans.*] bite at or nibble (something): *she sat gnawing her underlip.* ■ *figurative* (of something painful to the mind or body) cause persistent and wearing distress or anxiety: *the doubts continued to* **gnaw at** *me* | [as *adj.*] (**gnawing**) *that gnawing pain in her stomach.* ▷Old English *gnagan*, of Germanic origin; related to German *nagen*, ultimately imitative. **—gnaw·ing·ly** *adv.*

gnd. ▸*abbr.* ground.

gneiss /nīs/ ▸*n.* a metamorphic rock with a banded or foliated structure, typically coarse-grained and consisting mainly of feldspar, quartz, and mica. ▷mid 18th cent.: from German, from Old High German *gneisto* 'spark' (because of the rock's sheen). **—gneiss·ic** /-sik/ *adj.* **—gneiss·oid** /-soid/ *adj.*

gnoc·chi /ˈnäkē/ ▸*plural n.* (in Italian cooking) small dumplings made from potato, semolina, or flour, usually served with a sauce. ▷Italian, plural of *gnocco*, alteration of *nocchio* 'knot in wood.'

gnome[1] /nōm/ ▸*n.* a legendary dwarfish creature supposed to guard the earth's treasures underground. ■ *informal* a small ugly person. ■ *informal* a person regarded as having secret or sinister influence, esp. in financial matters: *the gnomes of Zurich.* ■ (also **garden gnome**) a small garden ornament in the form of a bearded man with a pointed hat. ▷mid 17th cent.: from French, from modern Latin *gnomus*, a word used by Paracelsus as a synonym of *Pygmaeus*, denoting a mythical race of very small people said to inhabit parts of Ethiopia and India (compare with **PYGMY**). **—gnom·ish** *adj.*

gnome[2] ▸*n.* a short statement encapsulating a general truth; a maxim. ▷late 16th cent.: from Greek *gnōmē* 'thought, opinion' (related to *gignōskein* 'know').

gno·mic /ˈnōmik/ ▸*adj.* expressed in or of the nature of short, pithy maxims or aphorisms: *that most gnomic form, the aphorism.* ■ enigmatic; ambiguous: *I had to have the gnomic response interpreted for me.* ▷early 19th cent.: from Greek *gnōmikos* (perhaps via French *gnomique*), from *gnōmē* 'thought, judgment,' (plural) *gnōmai* 'sayings, maxims,' related to *gignōskein* 'know.' **—gno·mi·cal·ly** /-ik(ə)lē/ *adv.*

gno·mon /ˈnōmän/ ▸*n.* **1** the projecting piece on a sundial that shows the time by the position of its shadow. **2** *Geometry* the part of a parallelogram left when a similar parallelogram has been taken from its corner. ▷mid 16th cent.: via Latin from Greek *gnōmōn* 'indicator, carpenter's square' (related to *gignōskein* 'know'). **—gno·mon·ic** /nōˈmänik/ *adj.*

gno·mon·ics /nōˈmäniks/ ▸*plural n.* [*treated as sing.*] the art of constructing and using dials and sundials.

gno·sis /ˈnōsis/ ▸*n.* knowledge of spiritual mysteries. ▷late 16th cent.: from Greek *gnōsis* 'knowledge' (related to *gignōskein* 'know').

gnos·tic /ˈnästik/ ▸*adj.* of or relating to knowledge, esp. esoteric mystical knowledge. ■ (**Gnostic**) of or relating to Gnosticism.
▸*n.* (**Gnostic**) an adherent of Gnosticism. ▷late 16th cent. (as a noun): via ecclesiastical Latin from Greek *gnōstikos*, from *gnōstos* 'known' (related to *gignōskein* 'know').

Gnos·ti·cism /ˈnästə,sizəm/ ▸*n.* a prominent heretical movement of the 2nd-century Christian Church, partly of pre-Christian origin. Gnostic doctrine taught that the world was created and ruled by a lesser divinity, the demiurge, and that Christ was an emissary of the remote supreme divine being, esoteric knowledge (gnosis) of whom enabled the redemption of the human spirit.

gno·to·bi·ot·ic /,nōtōbīˈätik/ ▸*adj. Biology* of, relating to, or denoting an environment for rearing or culturing organisms in which all the microorganisms are either known or excluded. ▷1940s: from Greek *gnōtos* 'known' + **BIOTIC**.

GNP ▸*abbr.* gross national product.

GnRH ▸*abbr.* gonadotropin-releasing hormone.

gns ▸*abbr.* guineas.

gnu /n(y)o͞o/ ▸*n.* a large dark antelope with a long head, a beard and mane, and a sloping back. Also called **WILDEBEEST**. • Genus *Connochaetes*, family Bovidae: two species, in particular the abundant **brindled gnu** or blue wildebeest (*C. taurinus*). ▷late 18th cent.: from Khoikhoi and San, perhaps imitative of the sound made by the animal when alarmed.

go[1] /gō/ ▸*v.* (**goes, go·ing**; *past* **went** /went/; *past part.* **gone** /gôn; gän/) **1** [*intrans.*] move from one place or point to another; travel: *he* **went out** *to the store* | *she longs to* **go back** *home* | *we've got a long way to go.* ■ travel a specified distance: *you just have to go a few miles to get to the road.* ■ travel or move in order to engage in a specified activity or course of action: *let's* **go and** *have a beer* | [with *infinitive*] *we* **went to** *see her* | [with *present participle*] *she used to go hunting.* ■ (**go to**) attend or visit for a particular purpose: *we went to the movies* | *he went to Brown University.* ■ (**go to**) provide access to: *that door goes to the garage.* ■ [in *imperative*] begin motion (used in a starter's order to begin a race): *ready, set, go!* ■ (**go to**) (of a rank or honor) be allotted or awarded: *the top prize went to a twenty-four-year-old sculptor.* ■ (**go into/to/toward**) (of a thing) contribute to or be put into (a whole); be used for or devoted to: *considerable effort went into making the operation successful.* ■ pass a specified amount of time in a particular way or under particular circumstances: *sometimes they* **went for** *two months without talking.* ■ used to indicate how many people a supply of food, money, or another resource is sufficient for or how much can be achieved using it: *the sale will* **go a long way toward** *easing the huge debt burden* | *a little luck can* **go a long way.** ■ (of a thing) lie or extend in a certain direction: *the scar started just above her ankle and went all the way up inside her leg.* ■ change in level, amount, or rank in a specified direction: *prices* **went up** *by 15 percent.* ■ *informal* used to emphasize the speaker's annoyance at a specified action or event: *then he* **goes** *and spoils it all* | [with *present participle*] *don't go poking your nose where you shouldn't.* ■ *informal* said in various expressions when angrily or contemptuously dismissing someone: *go and get stuffed.* **2** [*intrans.*] leave; depart: *I really must go.* ■ (of time) pass or elapse: *the hours* **went by** | *three years* **went past.** ■ come to an end; cease to exist: *a golden age that has now gone for good* | *11,500 jobs are due to go by next year.* ■ leave or resign from a post: *I tried to persuade the Chancellor not to go.* ■ be lost or stolen: *when he returned minutes later, his equipment was gone.* ■ die (used euphemistically): *I'd like to see my grandchildren before I go.* ■ (of a thing) be sold: *all the produce* **went to** *the farmers' market in Germantown.* ■ (of money) be spent, esp. in a specified way: *the rest of his money* **went into** *medical expenses.* **3** (**be going to be/do something**) intend or be likely or intended to be or do something; be about to (used to express a future tense): *I'm going to be late for work* | *she's going to have a baby.* **4** [*intrans.*] pass into a specified state, esp. an undesirable one: *the food is going bad* | *her mind immediately went blank* | *he's gone crazy.* ■ (**go to/into**) enter into a specified state, institution, or course of action: *she turned over and went back to sleep* | *the car went into a spin.* ■ happen, proceed, or be for a time in a specified condition: *no one went hungry in our house.* ■ make a sound of a specified kind: *the engine went bang.* ■ (of a bell or similar device) make a sound in functioning: *I heard the buzzer go four times.* ■ [with *direct speech*] *informal* say: *the kids go, "Yeah, sure."* ■ (**go by/under**) be known or called by (a specified name): *he now goes under the name Charles Perez.* **5** [*intrans.*] proceed in a specified way or have a specified outcome; turn out: *how did the weekend go?* | *it all* **went off** *smoothly.* ■ be successful, esp. in being enjoyable or exciting: *the hosts had to struggle to make things go.* ■ be acceptable or permitted: *underground events where* **anything goes.** ■ (of a song, account, verse, etc.) have a specified content or wording: *if you haven't heard it, the story goes like this.* **6** [*intrans.*] be harmonious, complementary, or matching: *rosemary* **goes with** *roast lamb* | *the earrings and the scarf don't really go.* ■ be found in the same place or situation; be associated: *cooking and eating* **go together.** **7** [*intrans.*] (of a machine or device) function: *my car won't go.* ■ continue in operation or existence: *the committee was* **kept going** *even when its existence could no longer be justified.* **8** [*intrans.*] (of an article) be regularly kept or put in a particular place: *remember which card goes in which slot.* ■ fit or be able to be accommodated in a particular place or space: *you're trying to fit a round peg into a square hole, and it just won't go.* **9** [*intrans.*] *informal* use a toilet; urinate or defecate. **10** [*trans.*] bid, bet, or pay.
▸*phrasal v.* □ **go about 1** begin or carry on work at (an activity); busy oneself with: *you are going about this in the wrong way.* **2** *Sailing* change to the opposite tack. □ **go against** oppose or resist: *he refused to go against the unions.* ■ be contrary to (a feeling or principle): *these tactics go against many of our instincts.* ■ (of a judgment, decision, or result) be unfavorable for: *the tribunal's decision went against them.* □ **go ahead** proceed or be carried out without hesitation: *the project will go ahead.* □ **go along with** give one's consent or agreement to (a person or their views): *the group has decided to go along with the committee's proposal.* □ **go around 1** (*chiefly Brit.* **go round**) spin: revolve: *the wheels were going around.* **2** (*chiefly Brit.* **go round**) (esp. of food) be sufficient to supply everybody present: *there was barely enough food to go around.* **3** (of an aircraft) abort an approach to landing and prepare to make a fresh approach. □ **go around with** be regularly in the company of: *he goes around with some of the neighborhood kids.* □ **go at** energetically attack or tackle: *he went at things with a daunting eagerness.* □ **go back 1** (of a clock) be set to an earlier standard time, esp. at the end of daylight saving time. **2** (of two people) have known each each for a specified, typically long, period of time: *Victor and I go back longer than I care to admit.* □ **go back on** fail to keep (a promise): *he wouldn't go back on his word.* □ **go down 1** (of a ship or aircraft) sink or crash: *he saw eleven B-17s go down.* ■ be defeated in a contest: *they went down 2–1.* **2** (of a person, period, or event) be recorded or remembered in a particular way: *his name will now* **go down in history.** **3** be swallowed: *solids can sometimes go down much easier than liquids.* **4** (of a person, action, or work) elicit a specified reaction: *my slide shows went down reasonably well.* **5** *informal* happen: *you really don't know what's going down?* **6** *Brit., informal* leave a university, esp. Oxford or Cambridge, after finishing one's studies: *Dobbins went down last spring.* **7** *vulgar slang* have sexual intercourse (said by a male of a female). □ **go down on** *vulgar slang* perform oral sex on. □ **go down with** *Brit.* begin to suffer from (a specified illness): *I went down with an attack of bronchitis.* □ **go for 1** decide on; choose: *I wished that we had gone for plan B.* ■ tend to find (a particular type of person) attractive: *Dionne went for the outlaw type.* **2** attempt to gain or attain: *he went for a job as a delivery driver.* ■ (**go for it**) strive to the utmost to gain or achieve something (frequently said as an exhortation): *sounds like a good idea—go for it!* **3** launch oneself at (someone); attack: *she went for him with clawed hands.* **4** end up having a specified value or effect: *my good intentions* **went for nothing.** **5** apply to; have relevance for: *the same goes for money-grubbing lawyers.* □ **go forward** (of a clock) be set to a later standard time, esp. daylight saving time. □ **go in for** like or habitually take part in (something, esp. an activity): *I don't go in for partying as much as Jesse and Rachel do.* □ **go into 1** take up in study or as an occupation: *he went into bankruptcy law.* **2** investigate or inquire into (something): *there's no need to go into it now.* **3** (of a whole number) be capable of dividing another, typically without a remainder: *six will go into eighteen, but not into five.* □ **go off 1** (of a gun, bomb, or similar device) explode or fire. ■ (of an alarm) begin to sound. ■ *informal* become suddenly angry; lose one's temper: *if you got in an argument with him, he'd just go off.* **2** *chiefly Brit.* (esp. of food) begin to decompose; become unfit for consumption. **3** *informal, chiefly Brit.* begin to dislike: *I went off men after my husband left me.* **4** go to sleep: *I went off as soon as my head hit the pillow.* □ **go on 1** [often with *present participle*] continue or persevere: *I can't go on protecting you.* ■ talk at great length, esp. tediously or angrily: *she* **went on about** *how lovely it would be to escape from the city.* ■ continue speaking or doing something after a short pause: [with *direct speech*] *"I don't understand," she went on.* ■ *informal* said when encouraging someone or expressing disbelief: *go on, tell him!* **2** happen; take place: *God knows what went on there.* **3** [often with *infinitive*] proceed to do: *she went on to do postgraduate work.* □ **go out 1** (of a fire or light) be extinguished. ■ cease operating or functioning: *the power went out on our block last night.* **2** (of the tide) ebb; recede to low tide. **3** leave one's home to go to an entertainment or social event, typically in the evening: *I'm going out for dinner.* ■ carry on a regular romantic, and sometimes sexual, relationship: *he was* **going out with** *her best friend.* **4** used to convey someone's deep sympathy or similar feeling: *the boy's heart went out to the pitiful figure.* **5** *Golf* play the first nine holes in a round of eighteen

holes. Compare with **COME HOME** (see **HOME**). **6** (in some card games) be the first to dispose of all the cards in one's hand. □ **go over 1** examine, consider, or check the details of (something): *I want to go over these plans with you again.* **2** change one's allegiance or religion: *he* **went over to** *the Democratic Party.* **3** (esp. of an action or performance) be received in a specified way: *his earnestness would go over well in a courtroom.* □ **go round** *chiefly Brit.* See **GO AROUND.** □ **go through 1** undergo (a difficult or painful period or experience): *the country is going through a period of economic instability.* **2** search through or examine carefully or in sequence: *she started to go through the bundle of letters.* **3** (of a proposal or contract) be officially approved or completed: *the sale of the building is set to go through.* **4** *informal* use up or spend (available money or other resources). **5** (of a book) be successively published in (a specified number of editions): *within two years it went through thirty-one editions.* □ **go through with** perform (an action or process) to completion despite difficulty or unwillingness: *he bravely went through with the ceremony.* □ **go under** (of a business) become bankrupt. ■ (of a person) die or suffer an emotional collapse. □ **go up 1** (of a building or other structure) be built: *housing developments went up.* **2** explode or suddenly burst into flames: *last night two factories* **went up in flames**. **3** *Brit., informal* begin one's studies at a university, esp. Oxford or Cambridge. □ **go with 1** give one's consent or agreement to (a person or their views). **2** have a romantic or sexual relationship with (someone). □ **go without** suffer lack or deprivation: *I like to give my children what they want, even if I have to go without.*

▶*n.* (*pl.* **goes**) *informal* **1** an attempt or trial at something: *I thought I'd* **give it a go**. ■ *chiefly Brit.* a state of affairs: *this seems a rum sort of go.* ■ *chiefly Brit.* an attack of illness: *he's had this nasty go of dysentery.* ■ a project or undertaking that has been approved: *tell them the project is a go.* ■ *chiefly Brit.* used in reference to a single item, action, or spell of activity: *he put it to his lips then knocked it back in one go.* **2** *dated* spirit, animation, or energy: *there's no go in me at all these days.* ■ vigorous activity: *it's* **all go** *around here.*

▶*adj.* [*predic.*] *informal* functioning properly: *all systems go.* ▷Old English *gān*, of Germanic origin; related to Dutch *gaan* and German *gehen*; the form *went* was originally the past tense of **WEND**.

▶*PHRASES* □ **as** (or **so**) **far as it goes** bearing in mind its limitations (said when qualifying praise of something): *the book is a useful catalog as far as it goes.* □ **as —— go** compared to the average or typical one of the specified kind: *as castles go, it is small and old.* □ **from the word go** *informal* from the very beginning. □ **go figure!** *informal* said to express the speaker's belief that something is amazing or incredible. □ **go great guns** see **GUN**. □ **go halves** share something equally. □ **going!, (going!,) gone!** an auctioneer's announcement that bidding is closing or closed. □ **going on ——** (*Brit.* also **going on for ——**) approaching a specified time, age, or amount: *I was going on fourteen when I went to my first gig.* □ **go (to) it** *Brit., informal* act in a vigorous, energetic, or dissipated way: *Go it, Dad! Give him what for!* □ **go it alone** see **ALONE**. □ **go to show** (or **prove**) (of an occurrence) serve as evidence or proof of something specified. □ **have a go at 1** make an attempt at; try: *let me have a go at straightening the rim.* **2** *chiefly Brit.* attack or criticize (someone): *she's always having a go at me.* □ **have —— going for one** *informal* used to indicate how much someone has in their favor or to their advantage: *Why did she do it? She had so much going for her.* □ **make a go of** *informal* be successful in (something): *he's determined to make a go of his marriage.* □ **on the go** *informal* very active or busy: *he's been on the go all evening.* □ **to go** (of food or drink from a restaurant or cafe) to be eaten or drunk off the premises: *order one large cheese-and-peppers pizza, to go.* □ **what goes around comes around** *proverb* the consequences of one's actions will have to be dealt with eventually. □ **who goes there?** said by a sentry as a challenge.

USAGE 1 The use of go followed by **and**, as in *I must* **go and** *change* (rather than *I must go to change*), is extremely common but is regarded by some grammarians as an oddity. For more details, see **usage** at **AND**.

2 Go used in the sense of *say* (*She goes, "No way!"*) is informal, on a par with *I'm like, "No way!"*

go[2] ▶*n.* a Japanese board game of territorial possession and capture. ▷late 19th cent.: Japanese, literally 'small stone,' also the name of the game.

Go·a /'gōə/ a state on the western coast of India; capital, Panaji. Formerly a Portuguese territory, it was seized by India in 1961. It formed a Union Territory with Daman and Diu until 1987, when it was made a state. **—Go·an** *adj.* & *n.* **—Go·a·nese** /gōə'nēz; -'nēs/ *adj.* & *n.*

goad /gōd/ ▶*n.* a spiked stick used for driving cattle. ■ a thing that stimulates someone into action: *for him the visit was a goad to renewed effort.*

▶*v.* [*trans.*] provoke or annoy (someone) so as to stimulate some action or reaction: *he* **goaded** *her* **on** *to more daring revelations.* ■ [*trans.*] drive or urge (an animal) on with a goad. ▷Old English *gād*, of Germanic origin.

go-a·head *informal* ▶*n.* (usu. **the go-ahead**) permission to proceed: *the government had given the go-ahead for the power station.*

▶*adj.* **1** enthusiastic about new projects; enterprising: *a young and go-ahead managing director.* **2** [*attrib.*] denoting the run, score, etc., that gives a team the lead in a game.

goal /gōl/ ▶*n.* **1** (in football, soccer, rugby, hockey, and some other games) a pair of posts linked by a crossbar and often with a net attached behind it, forming a space into or over which the ball has to be sent in order to score. ■ an instance of sending the ball into or over this space, esp. as a unit of scoring in a game: *the decisive opening goal* | *we won by three goals to two.* ■ a cage or basket used similarly in other sports. **2** the object of a person's ambition or effort; an aim or desired result: *going to law school has become the most important goal in his life.* ■ the destination of a journey: *the aircraft bumped toward our goal some 400 miles to the west.* ■ *poetic/literary* a point marking the end of a race. ▷Middle English (in the sense 'limit, boundary'): of unknown origin. **—goal·less** *adj.*

▶*PHRASE* □ **in goal** in the position of goalkeeper.

goal·hang·er ▶*n.* *Soccer derogatory* a player who spends much of the game near the opposing team's goal in the hope of scoring easy goals.

goal·ie /'gōlē/ ▶*n.* informal term for **GOALTENDER** or **GOALKEEPER**.

goal·keep·er /'gōl,kēpər/ ▶*n.* *chiefly Brit.* another term for **GOALTENDER**. **—goal·keep·ing** /-,kēpiNG/ *n.*

goal kick ▶*n.* *Soccer* a free kick taken by the defending side from within their goal area after attackers send the ball over the end line outside the goal.

goal line ▶*n.* *Sports* a line between each pair of goals or goalposts, extended across the playing field to form the end boundary of the field of play. ■ *Football* either of two lines, one at each end of the football field, across which the ball must be carried or caught for a touchdown.

goal·mouth /'gōl,mouTH/ ▶*n.* the area just in front of a goal in soccer, lacrosse, or hockey.

goal·post /'gōl,pōst/ ▶*n.* either of the two upright posts of a goal.

▶*PHRASE* □ **move the goalposts** unfairly alter the conditions or rules of a procedure during its course.

goal·tend·er /'gōl,tendər/ ▶*n.* **1** **2** a player in soccer or hockey whose special role is to stop the ball or puck from entering the goal.

goal·tend·ing /'gōl,tendiNG/ ▶*n.* **1** *Soccer* & *Hockey* the action of stopping the ball or puck from entering the goal. **2** *Basketball* a violation in which a defensive player interferes with a shot when it is on its downward arc or is on or over the rim.

goal to go ▶*n.* *Football* the situation in which an offensive team gets a first down within ten yards of the goal line, and thus cannot advance for another first down.

go·an·na /gō'anə/ ▶*n.* Australian term for **MONITOR** (sense 4). ▷mid 19th cent.: alteration of **IGUANA**.

go-a·round (also **go-round**) ▶*n.* **1** a flight path typically taken by an aircraft after an aborted approach to landing. **2** *informal* a confrontation; an argument: *they had one go-around after another.*

goat /gōt/ ▶*n.* **1** a hardy domesticated ruminant animal that has backward curving horns and (in the male) a beard. It is kept for its milk and meat and is noted for its lively and frisky behavior. • *Capra hircus*, family Bovidae, descended from the wild bezoar. ■ a wild mammal related to this, such as the ibex, markhor, and tur. See also **MOUNTAIN GOAT.** ■ (**the Goat**) the zodiacal sign Capricorn or the constellation Capricornus. **2** a person likened to a goat, in particular: ■ a lecherous man. ■ a scapegoat. ▷Old English *gāt* 'nanny goat,' of Germanic origin; related to Dutch *geit* and German *Geiss*, also to Latin *haedus* 'kid.' **—goat·ish** *adj.* **—goat·y** *adj.*

▶*PHRASE* □ **get someone's goat** *informal* irritate someone: *I've tried to get along with her, but sometimes she really gets my goat.*

goat·an·te·lope ▶*n.* a ruminant mammal of a group that combines the characteristics of both goats and antelopes. • Subfamily Caprinae, family Bovidae: tribes Rupicaprini (the chamois, goral, serow, and mountain goat) and Ovibonini (the musk ox and takin).

goat·ee /gō'tē/ (also **goatee beard**) ▶*n.* a small pointed beard. ▷early 19th cent.: so named because of its resemblance to the tuft on a goat's chin. **—goat·eed** *adj.*

goatee

goat·fish /'gōt,fiSH/ ▶*n.* (*pl.* same or **-fish·es**) another term for **RED MULLET**.

goat·herd /'gōt,hərd/ ▶*n.* a person who tends goats. ▷Old English, from **GOAT** + obsolete *herd* 'herdsman.'

goat's-beard (also **goats·beard**) ▶*n.* **1** a plant of the daisy family, with slender grasslike leaves, yellow flowers that typically close at about midday, and downy fruits that resemble those of a dandelion. Native to Eurasia, it has become established in eastern North America. • *Tragopogon pratensis*, family Compositae. **2** a plant of the rose family, with long plumes of white flowers, found in both Eurasia and North America. • *Aruncus vulgaris*, family Rosaceae. ▷mid 16th cent.: translating Greek *tragopōgon* or Latin *Barba Capri*.

goat·skin /'gōt,skin/ ▶*n.* the skin of a goat. ■ such a skin, or leather made from it, as a material. ■ a garment or object made out of goatskin.

goat's-rue ▶*n.* a herbaceous plant of the pea family, which was formerly used in medicine, esp. as a vermifuge. • Two species in the family Leguminosae: a bushy Eurasian plant that is cultivated as an ornamental (*Galega officinalis*), and a North American plant with pink and yellow flowers and that smells of goats (*Tephrosia virginiana*).

goat·suck·er /'gōt,səkər/ ▶*n.* another term for **NIGHTJAR**. ▷early 17th cent.: so named because the bird was thought to suck goats' udders.

goat wil·low ▶*n.* a common European willow with broad leaves and soft fluffy catkins. Also called **great sallow**.

G

gob[1] /gäb/ *informal* ▶*n.* **1** a lump or clot of a slimy or viscous substance: *a gob of phlegm.* ■ a small lump. **2** (**gobs of**) a lot of: *he wants to make gobs of money selling cassettes.* ▷late Middle English: from Old French *gobe* 'mouthful, lump,' from *gober* 'to swallow, gulp,' perhaps of Celtic origin.

gob[2] ▶*n.* *informal, dated* an American sailor. ▷early 20th cent.: of unknown origin.

gob[3] ▶*n.* *informal, chiefly Brit.* a person's mouth: *Jean told him to shut his big gob.* ▷mid 16th cent.: perhaps from Scottish Gaelic *gob* 'beak, mouth.'

gob·bet /'gäbit/ ▶*n.* a piece or lump of flesh, food, or other matter: *they lobbed* **gobbets of** *fresh bonito off the side of the boat.* ▷Middle English: from Old French *gobet*, diminutive of *gobe* (see **GOB**[2]).

gob·ble[1] /'gäbəl/ ▶*v.* [*trans.*] eat (something) hurriedly and noisily: *one man* **gobbled up** *a burger.* | [*intrans.*] *they don't eat, they gobble.* ■ use a large amount of (something) very quickly: *these old houses just* **gobble up** *money.* ■ (of a large organization or other body) incorporate or take over (a smaller one): *he amassed his packaging empire by* **gobbling up** *National Can Corporation.* ▷early 17th cent.: probably from **GOB**[2].

gob·ble[2] ▶*v.* [*intrans.*] (of a male turkey) make a characteristic swallowing sound in the throat. ■ (of a person) make such a sound when speaking, esp. when excited or angry: *she was gobbling to herself faintly in her distress.*

▶*n.* the gurgling sound made in the throat by a male turkey. ▷late 17th cent.: imitative, perhaps influenced by **GOBBLE**[1].

gob·ble·dy·gook /'gäbəldē,go͝ok; -,go͞ok/ (also **gob·ble·de·gook**) ▶*n.* *informal* language that is meaningless or is made unintelligible by excessive use of abstruse technical terms; nonsense. ▷1940s (originally U.S.): probably imitating a turkey's gobble.

gob·bler[1] /'gäblər/ ▶*n.* a person who eats greedily and noisily.

gob·bler[2] ▶*n.* *informal* a turkey cock.

Gob·e·lin /ˈgōbəlin; ˈgäb-/ (also **Gobelin tapestry**) ▸*n.* a tapestry made at the Gobelins factory in Paris, or in imitation of one.

Gob·e·lins /ˈgōbəlinz; ˈgäb-/ a tapestry and textile factory in Paris, established by the Gobelin family *c.*1440 and taken over by the French Crown in 1662. It was highly successful in the late 17th and 18th centuries, using designs by leading French painters, and tapestry panels became used as alternatives to oil paintings.

go-be·tween ▸*n.* an intermediary or negotiator.

Go·bi Des·ert /ˈgōbē/ a barren plateau in southern Mongolia and northern China.

Go·bin·eau /ˈgäbəˌnō/, Joseph Arthur, Comte de (1816–82), French writer and anthropologist. His stated view that the races are innately unequal and that the white Aryan race is superior to all others later influenced the ideology and policies of the Nazis.

gob·let /ˈgäblit/ ▸*n.* a drinking glass with a foot and a stem. ■ *archaic* a metal or glass bowl-shaped drinking cup, sometimes with a foot and a cover. ▷late Middle English: from Old French *gobelet*, diminutive of *gobel* 'cup,' of unknown origin.

gob·let cell ▸*n. Anatomy* a column-shaped cell found in the respiratory and intestinal tracts, which secretes the main component of mucus.

gob·lin /ˈgäblin/ ▸*n.* a mischievous, ugly, dwarflike creature of folklore. ▷Middle English: from Old French *gobelin*, possibly related to German *Kobold* (see KOBOLD) or to Greek *kobalos* 'mischievous goblin.' In medieval Latin *Gobelinus* occurs as the name of a mischievous spirit, said to haunt Évreux in northern France in the 12th cent.

go·bo[1] /ˈgōbō/ ▸*n.* (*pl.* **-bos**) a dark plate or screen used to shield a lens from light. ■ *Theater* a partial screen used in front of a spotlight to project a shape. ■ a shield used to mask a microphone from extraneous noise. ▷1930s: of unknown origin, perhaps from *go between*.

go·bo[2] ▸*n.* a vegetable root used chiefly in Japanese and Hawaiian cooking. ▷Japanese.

go·bo·ny /gəˈbōnē/ ▸*adj. Heraldry* another term for COMPONY.

gob·smacked /ˈgäbˌsmakt/ ▸*adj. Brit., informal* utterly astonished; astounded. ▷1980s: from GOB[1] + SMACK[1], with reference to being shocked by a blow to the mouth, or to clapping a hand to one's mouth in astonishment. **—gob·smack·ing** /-ˌsmakiNG/ *adj.*

gob·stop·per /ˈgäbˌstäpər/ ▸*n. chiefly Brit.* a jawbreaker.

go·by /ˈgōbē/ ▸*n.* (*pl.* **-bies**) a small, usually marine fish that typically has a sucker on the underside. • Family Gobiidae: numerous genera and species. ▷mid 18th cent.: from Latin *gobius*, from Greek *kōbios*, denoting some kind of small fish.

go-by ▸*n.* (in phrase **give someone the go-by**) *informal, dated* avoid or snub someone. ■ end a romantic relationship with someone: *her young man's given her the go-by.*

go-cart ▸*n.* **1** variant spelling of GO-KART. **2** a handcart. ■ a stroller. ■ *archaic* a baby walker. ▷late 17th cent. (denoting a baby walker): from GO[1] (in the obsolete sense 'walk') + CART.

God /gäd/ ▸*n.* **1** [without *article*] (in Christianity and other monotheistic religions) the creator and ruler of the universe and source of all moral authority; the supreme being. **2** (**god**) (in certain other religions) a superhuman being or spirit worshiped as having power over nature or human fortunes; a deity: *a moon god | an incarnation of the god Vishnu.* ■ an image, idol, animal, or other object worshiped as divine or symbolizing a god. ■ used as a conventional personification of fate: *he dialed the number and, the gods relenting, got through at once.* **3** (**god**) an adored, admired, or influential person: *he has little time for the fashion victims for whom he is a god.* ■ a thing accorded the supreme importance appropriate to a god: *don't make money your god.* **4** (**the gods**) *informal* the gallery in a theater. ■ the people sitting in this area.
▸*exclam.* used to express a range of emotions such as surprise, anger, and distress: *God, what did I do to deserve this? | my God! Why didn't you tell us sooner?* ■ to give emphasis to a statement or declaration: *God, how I hate that woman!* ▷Old English, of Germanic origin; related to Dutch *god* and German *Gott*. **—god·hood** /-ˌhŏŏd/ *n.* **—god·ship** /-ˌSHip/ *n.* **—god·ward** /-wərd/ *adj.* & *adv.* **—god·wards** /-wərdz/ *adv.*
▸PHRASES □ **for God's sake!** see SAKE[1] (sense 3). □ **God bless** an expression of good wishes on parting. □ **God damn** (**you**, **him**, etc) may (you, he, etc.) be damned. □ **God the Father** (in Christian doctrine) the first person of the Trinity, God as creator and supreme authority. □ **God forbid** see FORBID. □ **God grant** used to express a wish that something should happen: *God grant he will soon regain his freedom.* □ **God help** (**you**, **him**, etc.) used to express the belief that someone is in a difficult, dangerous, or hopeless situation: *God help anyone who tried to cheer me out of my bad mood.* □ **God the Son** (in Christian doctrine) Christ regarded as the second person of the Trinity; God as incarnate and resurrected savior. □ **God willing** used to express the wish that one will be able to do as one intends or that something will happen as planned: *one day, God willing, she and John might have a daughter.* □ **in God's name** used in questions to emphasize anger or surprise: *what in God's name are you doing up there?* □ **play God** behave as if all-powerful or supremely important. □ **please God** used to emphasize a strong wish or hope: *please God the money will help us find a cure.* □ **thank God** see THANK. □ **to God** used after a verb to emphasize a strong wish or hope: *I hope to God you've got something else to put on.* □ **with God** dead and in heaven.

God Al·might·y (also **God·al·might·y**) ▸*exclam.* used to express esp. surprise, anger, or exasperation.

Go·dard /gōˈdär(d)/, Jean-Luc (1930–), French movie director. A leading figure of the *nouvelle vague*, his movies include *Breathless* (1960), *Alphaville* (1965), and *Wind from the East* (1969).

Go·da·va·ri /gəˈdävərē/ a river in central India that rises in the state of Maharashtra and flows southeast for about 900 miles (1,440 km) across the Deccan plateau to the Bay of Bengal.

god·aw·ful /ˈgädˈôfəl/ (also **god-aw·ful** or **God-aw·ful**) ▸*adj. informal* extremely unpleasant: *it had been the most godawful forty-eight hours.*

god·child /ˈgädˌCHīld/ ▸*n.* (*pl.* **-child·ren** /-ˌCHildrən/) a person in relation to a godparent.

god·damn /ˈgädˈdam/ (also **god·dam** or **god·damned**) ▸*adj., adv.,* & *n. informal* used for emphasis, esp. to express anger or frustration: [as *adj.*] *we're sick of this goddamn weather* | [as *n.*] *I don't give a goddamn what you do!* ▷mid 17th cent.: abbreviation of *God damn (me)*.

God·dard /ˈgädərd/, Robert Hutchings (1882–1945), U.S. physicist. He designed and built the first successful liquid-fueled rocket. The National Aeronautics and Space Administration's (NASA) Goddard Space Flight Center is named for him.

god·daugh·ter /ˈgädˌdôtər/ ▸*n.* a female godchild.

god·dess /ˈgädis/ ▸*n.* a female deity: *a temple to Athena Nike, goddess of victory.* ■ a woman who is adored, esp. for her beauty: *he had an affair with a screen goddess.*

Gö·del /ˈgōdl/, Kurt (1906–78), U.S. mathematician; born in Austria. Among his important contributions to mathematical logic is the incompleteness theorem.

Gö·del's in·com·plete·ness the·o·rem see INCOMPLETENESS THEOREM.

go·det /gōˈdet/ ▸*n.* a triangular piece of material inserted in a dress, shirt, or glove to make it flared or for ornamentation. ▷late 19th cent.: from French.

go·de·tia /gəˈdēSHə/ ▸*n.* a North American plant with showy lilac to red flowers. • Genus *Clarkia* (or *Godetia*), family Onagraceae. ▷modern Latin, named after Charles H. *Godet* (1797–1879), Swiss botanist.

go-dev·il ▸*n. chiefly historical* a gadget used in farming, logging, or drilling for oil, in particular: ■ a crude sled, used chiefly for dragging logs. ■ a jointed apparatus for cleaning pipelines.

god·fa·ther /ˈgädˌfäTHər/ ▸*n.* **1** a male godparent. **2** a man who is influential in a movement or organization, through providing support for it or through playing a leading or innovatory part in it: *the godfather of alternative comedy.* ■ a person directing an illegal organization, esp. a leader of a Mafia family.

God-fear·ing ▸*adj.* earnestly religious: *an honest, God-fearing woman.*

god·for·sak·en /ˈgädfərˌsākən/ ▸*adj.* lacking any merit or attraction; dismal: *what are you doing in this godforsaken place?*

God·frey /ˈgädfrē/, Arthur (Michael) (1903–83) U.S. entertainer. He starred in radio and television variety shows, heard on radio in "Arthur Godfrey Time" 1945–72 (also televised 1952–59) and appearing on television on "Arthur Godrey's Talent Scouts" 1948–58, and "Arthur Godrey and His Friends" 1949–59.

God-giv·en ▸*adj.* received from God: *the God-given power to work miracles.* ■ possessed without question, as if by divine authority: *the union man's God-given right to strike.*

God·havn /ˈgōTHˌhoun/ a town in western Greenland, on the south coast of the island of Disko.

god·head /ˈgädˌhed/ ▸*n.* (usu. **the Godhead**) God. ■ divine nature. ■ *informal* an adored, admired, or influential person; an idol.

Go·di·va /gəˈdīvə/, Lady (died 1080), English noblewoman; wife of Leofric, Earl of Mercia. According to legend, she agreed to her husband's proposition that he would reduce unpopular taxes only if she rode naked on horseback through Coventry's marketplace. According to later versions of the story, nobody watched except peeping Tom, who was struck blind in punishment.

god·less /ˈgädlis/ ▸*adj.* not recognizing or obeying God: *the godless forces of communism.* ■ without a god: *humanity coming to terms with a godless world.* ■ profane; wicked. **—god·less·ness** *n.*

god·like /ˈgädˌlīk/ ▸*adj.* resembling God or a god in qualities such as power, beauty, or benevolence: *our parents are godlike figures to our childish eyes.* ■ befitting or appropriate to a god: *we act as though we have godlike powers to decide our own destiny.*

god·ly /ˈgädlē/ ▸*adj.* (**-li·er**, **-li·est**) devoutly religious; pious: *how to live the godly life.* **—god·li·ness** *n.*

god·man ▸*n.* **1** *Indian* a holy man; a guru. **2** an incarnation of a god in human form. ■ (**God-man**) Jesus Christ.

god·moth·er /ˈgädˌməTHər/ ▸*n.* a female godparent. ■ a woman who is influential in a movement or organization, through providing support for it or through playing a leading or innovatory part in it: *she has been called the godmother of Quebec business.*

go·down /ˈgōdoun; gōˈdoun/ ▸*n.* (in eastern Asia, esp. India) a warehouse. ▷late 16th cent.: from Portuguese *gudão*, from Tamil *kiṭaṅku*, Malayalam *kiṭaṅṅu*, or Kannada *gadaṅgu* 'store, warehouse.'

god·par·ent /ˈgädˌpe(ə)rənt; -ˌpar-/ ▸*n.* a person who presents a child at baptism and responds on the child's behalf, promising to take responsibility for the child's religious education.

God's a·cre ▸*n. archaic* a churchyard. ▷early 17th cent.: from German *Gottesacker*, Dutch *Godsakker*.

God Save the Queen (or **King**) ▸*n.* the British national anthem. ▷evidence suggests a 17th-cent. origin for the complete words and tune of the anthem. The ultimate origin is obscure: the phrase "God save the King" occurs in various passages in the Old Testament, while as early as 1545 it was a watchword in the English navy, with "long to reign over us" as a countersign.

God's coun·try ▸*n.* [in *sing.*] an area or region, esp. a peaceful, rural one, supposedly favored by God.

god·send /ˈgädˌsend/ ▸*n.* a very helpful or valuable event, person, or thing: *this highway is* ***a godsend to*** *the local community.* ▷early 19th cent.: from *God's send* 'what God has sent.'

God's gift ▸*n.* the ideal or best possible person or thing for someone or something (used chiefly ironically or in negative statements): *he thought he was* ***God's gift*** *to women.*

god·son /ˈgädˌsən/ ▸*n.* a male godchild.

God·speed /ˈgädˈspēd/ ▸*exclam. dated* an expression of good wishes to a person starting a journey. ▷Middle English: from *God speed you* 'may God help you prosper.'

God Squad ▸*n. informal* used to refer to evangelical Christians, typically suggesting intrusive moralizing and proselytizing.

God's truth ▸*n.* the absolute truth: *it's done more harm than good, and that's* ***the God's truth.***

Godt·håb /ˈgôtˌhôp/ former name (until 1979) of NUUK.

Go·du·nov /ˈgädnˌôf/, Boris (1550–1605), tsar of Russia 1598–1605. His reign was marked by famine, doubts over his involvement in the earlier death of Ivan the Terrible's eldest son, and the appearance of pretender False Dmitri.

God·win /ˈgädwən/, William (1756–1836), English social philosopher and novelist; the husband of Mary Wollstonecraft and the father of Mary Wollstonecraft Shelley.

God·win-Aus·ten, Mount /ˈgädwən ˈôstən/ former name for **K2**.

god·wit /ˈgädwit/ ▸*n.* a large, long-legged wader with a long, slightly upturned or straight bill, and typically a reddish-brown head and breast in the breeding male. • Genus *Limosa*, family Scolopacidae: four species. ▷mid 16th cent.: of unknown origin.

God·zil·la /gädˈzilə/ ▸*n. informal, humorous* **1** a particularly enormous example (of something): *a Godzilla of a condominium tower.* **2** a person or thing likened to a frightful and menacing creature: *Don't let Nurse Godzilla catch you. She'll raise holy hell.* ▷from the name of a huge prehistoric monster featured in a series of Japanese films from 1955.

Goeb·bels /'gəbəlz/ (also **Göb·bels**), (Paul) Joseph (1897–1945), German Nazi leader and politician. From 1933, he was Adolf Hitler's minister of propaganda. He committed suicide rather than surrender to the Allies.

go·er /'gōər/ ▸*n.* **1** a person or thing that goes: *the natives are friendly to tourists, whom they call "comers and goers."* **2** [in *combination*] a person who attends a specified place or event, esp. regularly: *a churchgoer* | *conference-goers.* **3** [with *adj.*] *informal* a person or thing that goes in a specified way: *horse no. 7 is a fast goer.* ■ a project likely to be accepted or to succeed: *if the business is a goer, the entrepreneur moves on.*

Goe·ring /'gəriNG/, Hermann Wilhelm (1893–1946), German Nazi leader and politician. He was responsible for the German rearmament program, founder of the Gestapo, and director of the German economy. Sentenced to death at the Nuremberg war trials, he committed suicide in his cell.

Goes /go͞os/, Hugo van der (*fl. c.*1467–82), Flemish painter; born in Ghent. His best-known work is the *Portinari Altarpiece* (1475), commissioned for a church in Florence, Italy.

goes /gōz/ ▸ third person singular present of **GO**[1].

go·est /'gō-ist/ ▸ archaic second person singular present of **GO**[1].

go·eth /'gō-iTH/ ▸ archaic third person singular present of **GO**[1].

Goe·thals /'gōTHəlz/, George Washington (1858–1928) U.S. army officer and engineer. As chief engineer and chairman of the Panama Canal Commission 1907, he oversaw construction of the Panama Canal, which was completed in 1914, and then served as the Canal Zone's governor 1914–17.

Goe·the /'gə(r)tə; 'gœtə/, Johann Wolfgang von (1749–1832), German poet, playwright, novelist, philosopher, and scientist. Involved at first with the *Sturm und Drang* movement, he changed to a more classical style, as in the "Wilhelm Meister" novels 1796–1829. Notable dramas: *Götz von Berlichingen* (1773), *Tasso* (1790), and *Faust* (1808–32).

goe·thite /'gōTHīt/ ▸*n.* a dark reddish-brown or yellowish-brown mineral consisting of oxyhydroxide iron, occurring typically as masses of fibrous crystals. ▷early 19th cent.: from the name of J.W. von **GOETHE** + **-ITE**[1].

go·fer /'gōfər/ (also **go·pher**) ▸*n. informal* a person who runs errands, esp. on a movie set or in an office. ▷1960s: from *go for* (i.e., go and fetch).

gof·fer /'gäfər/ (also **gauf·fer** /'gôfər; 'gäf-/) ▸*v.* [*trans.*] [usu. as *adj.*] (**goffered**) treat (a lace edge or frill) with heated irons in order to crimp or flute it: *a goffered frill.* ■ [as *adj.*] (**goffered**) (of the gilt edges of a book) embossed with a repeating design.
▸*n.* an iron used to crimp or flute lace. ▷late 16th cent.: from French *gaufrer* 'stamp with a patterned tool,' from *gaufre* 'honeycomb,' from Middle Low German *wāfel* (see **WAFFLE**[2]).

go fish ▸*n.* a card game in which each player in turn asks an opponent for a particular card and is told to "go fish" from the undealt deck if denied.

Gog and Ma·gog /gôg and mə'gäg/ **1** in the Bible, the names of enemies of God's people. In Ezek. 38–9, Gog is apparently a ruler from the land of Magog, while in Rev. 20:8, Gog and Magog are nations under the dominion of Satan. **2** (in medieval legend) opponents of Alexander the Great, living north of the Caucasus. **3** two giant statues standing in Guildhall, London, representing either the last two survivors of a race of giants supposed to have inhabited Britain before Roman times, or Gogmagog, chief of the giants, and Corineus, a Roman invader.

Go·ge·bic Range /gō'gēbik/ a range of iron-bearing hills in the western Upper Peninsula in Michigan and adjacent areas in Wisconsin.

go-get·ter ▸*n. informal* an aggressively enterprising person. **—go-get·ting** *adj.*

gog·gle /'gägəl/ ▸*v.* [*intrans.*] look with wide open eyes, typically in amazement or wonder: *"What in the world are you goggling at"?* ■ (of the eyes) protrude or open wide.
▸*adj.* [*attrib.*] (of the eyes) protuberant or rolling.
▸*n.* **1** (**goggles**) close-fitting eyeglasses with side shields, for protecting the eyes from glare, dust, water, etc. ■ *informal* eyeglasses. **2** [in *sing.*] a stare with protruding eyes. ▷Middle English (in the sense 'look to one side, squint'): probably from a base symbolic of oscillating movement. **—gog·gled** *adj.*

gog·gle-eye ▸*n.* any of a number of edible fishes with large eyes that occur widely on reefs in tropical and subtropical seas: • a nocturnal fish related to the bigeye (*Priacanthus hamrur*, family Priacanthidae). • (also **goggle-eye jack**) a fish often found in shoals (*Selar crumenophthalmus*, family Carangidae).

gog·gle-eyed ▸*adj.* having staring or protuberant eyes, esp. through astonishment.

go-go ▸*adj.* [*attrib.*] **1** relating to or denoting an unrestrained and erotic style of dancing to popular music: *a go-go bar* | *go-go dancers.* **2** assertively dynamic: *the go-go bravado of the 1980s.* ▷1960s: reduplication of **GO**[1], perhaps influenced by **A GOGO**.

Go·gol /'gōgəl/, Nikolai (Vasilevich) (1809–52), Russian novelist, playwright, and short-story writer; born in Ukraine. His writings are satirical and often explore themes of fantasy and the supernatural. Notable works: *The Government Inspector* (1836), *Notes of a Madman* (1835), and *Dead Souls* (1842).

Goi·â·nia /goi'anēə/ a city in southern central Brazil, capital of the state of Goiás; pop. 998,000. It was founded as a new city in 1933.

Goi·del·ic /goi'delik/ ▸*adj.* of, relating to, or denoting the northern group of Celtic languages, including Irish, Scottish Gaelic, and Manx. Compare with **BRYTHONIC**. Also called **Q-CELTIC**.
▸*n.* these languages collectively.

go·ing /'gōiNG/ ▸*n.* **1** an act or instance of leaving a place; a departure: *his going left an enormous gap in each of their lives.* **2** [in *sing.*] the condition of the ground viewed in terms of suitability for walking, riding, or other travel (used esp. in the context of horse racing): *the going was ideal here, with short turf and a level surface.* ■ progress affected by such a condition: *the paths were covered with drifting snow and the going was difficult.* ■ conditions for, or progress in, an endeavor: *when the going gets tough, the tough get going.*
▸*adj.* **1** [*predic.*] *chiefly Brit.* existing or available; to be had: *he asked if there were any other jobs going.* **2** [*attrib.*] (esp. of a price) generally accepted as fair or correct; current: *people willing to work for the going rate.*

go·ing a·way ▸*adj.* [*attrib.*] marking or celebrating a departure: *a going-away party.*
▸*adv. informal* with victory assured before the end of a race or other sporting contest: *Jordan finished the game with 20 points and Detroit won going away.*

go·ing-o·ver ▸*n.* [in *sing.*] *informal* a thorough treatment, esp. in cleaning or inspection: *give the place a going-over with the vacuum cleaner.* ■ a beating.

go·ings-on ▸*plural n.* events or behavior, esp. of an unusual or suspect nature.

goi·ter /'goitər/ (*Brit.* **goi·tre**) ▸*n.* a swelling of the neck resulting from enlargement of the thyroid gland: *a woman with a goiter* | *the belief that amber necklaces were good for curing goiter.* ▷early 17th cent.: from French, a back-formation from *goitreux* 'having a goiter,' or from Old French *goitron* 'gullet,' both based on Latin *guttur* 'throat.' **—goi·tered** *adj.* **—goi·trous** /'goitrəs/ *adj.*

go-kart (also **go-cart**) ▸*n.* a small racing car with a lightweight or skeleton body. ▷1950s: *kart*, alteration of **CART**. **—go-kart·ing** *n.*

Go·lan Heights /'gō,län; -lən/ a range of hills on the border between Syria and Israel, northeast of the Sea of Galilee. Formerly under Syrian control, the area was occupied by Israel in 1967 and annexed in 1981. Negotiations for the withdrawal of Israeli troops from the region began in 1992.

Gol·con·da /gäl'kändə/ ▸*n.* a source of wealth, advantages, or happiness: *the posters calling emigrants from Europe to the Golconda of the American West.* ▷late 19th cent.: from the name of a city near Hyderabad, India, famous for its diamonds.

gold /gōld/ ▸*n.* **1** a yellow precious metal, the chemical element of atomic number 79, valued esp. for use in jewelry and decoration, and to guarantee the value of currencies. (Symbol: **Au**) ■ [with *adj.*] an alloy of this: *9-carat gold.*

Gold is quite widely distributed in nature, but economical extraction is only possible from deposits of the native metal or sulfide ores or as a byproduct of copper and lead mining.The use of the metal in coins is now limited, but it is also used in electrical contacts and (in some countries) as a filling for teeth.

2 a deep lustrous yellow or yellow-brown color: *her eyes were light green and flecked with gold.* **3** coins or articles made of gold: *her ankles and wrists were glinting with gold.* ■ money in large sums; wealth: *he proved to be a rabid seeker for gold and power.* ■ a thing that is precious, beautiful, or brilliant: *they scout continents in search of the new green gold.* ■ short for **GOLD MEDAL**. ▷Old English, of Germanic origin; related to Dutch *goud* and German *Gold*, from an Indo-European root shared by **YELLOW**.
▸*PHRASES* □ **go gold** (of a recording) achieve sales meriting a gold disk. □ **pot** (or **crock**) **of gold** a large but distant or imaginary reward. [with allusion to the story of a crock of gold supposedly to be found by anyone reaching the end of a rainbow.]

gol·darn /'gäl'därn/ ▸*adj., adv., & n. informal* used as a euphemism for **GODDAMN**.

gold·beat·er /'gōld,bētər/ ▸*n.* a person who beats gold out into gold leaf.

gold·beat·er's skin ▸*n.* an animal membrane used to separate leaves of gold during beating.

gold bee·tle (also **gold·bug**) ▸*n.* a leaf beetle with metallic gold coloration. • Several species in the family Chrysomelidae, in particular *Metriona bicolor*.

Gold·berg[1] /'gōld,bərg/, Arthur Joseph (1908–90) U.S. Supreme Court associate justice 1962–65. He served as U.S. ambassador to the UN 1965–68 but resigned because he did not agree with the escalation of the Vietnam War.

Gold·berg[2], Rube (1883–1970) U.S. cartoonist; full name *Reuben Lucius Goldberg*. As creator of the comic strip characters Professor Lucifer Gorgonzola Butts (an inventor of complex mechanical devices to achieve simple tasks), Boob McNutt, and Lala Palooza, he satirized American folkways and modern technology.

Gold·berg[3], Whoopi (1955–) U.S. actress; born *Caryn Johnson*. She appeared in many movies, including *The Color Purple* (1985), *Ghost* (Academy Award, 1990), and *Sister Act* (1992).

gold brick *informal* ▸*n.* a thing that looks valuable, but is in fact worthless. ■ (also **gold·brick** or **gold·brick·er**) a con man. ■ a lazy person: [as *adj.*] *hard-working Amos and goldbrick Andy.*
▸*v.* (usu. **goldbrick**) [*intrans.*] invent excuses to avoid a task; shirk: *he wasn't goldbricking; he was really sick.* ■ [*trans.*] swindle (someone).

gold·bug /'gōld,bəg/ (also **gold bug**) ▸*n.* **1** *informal* an advocate of a single gold standard for currency. ■ a person favoring gold as an investment. **2** another term for **GOLD BEETLE**.

gold card ▸*n.* a charge card or credit card issued to people with a high credit rating and giving benefits not available with the standard card.

Gold Coast former name (until 1957) of **GHANA**. ■ (also **gold coast**) *informal* any coastal area noted for luxurious living and expensive homes.

gold dig·ger ▸*n. informal* a person who dates others purely to extract money from them, in particular a woman who strives to marry a wealthy man.

gold dust ▸*n.* **1** fine particles of gold. **2** another term for **BASKET-OF-GOLD**.

gold·en /'gōldən/ ▸*adj.* **1** colored or shining like gold: *curls of glossy golden hair* | *bake until golden.* **2** made or consisting of gold: *a golden crown.* **3** rare and precious, in particular: ■ (of a period) very happy and prosperous: *those golden days before World War I.* ■ (of an opportunity) very favorable: *a golden opportunity to boost foreign trade.* ■ (of a person) popular, talented, and successful: *Einstein was* ***the golden boy*** *of the "Second Scientific Revolution."* **4** (of a voice) rich and smooth: *a choir of young golden voices.* **5** denoting the fiftieth year of something: *the American Ballet Theater's golden anniversary extravaganza.* **—gold·en·ly** *adv.*

gold·en age ▸*n.* an idyllic, often imaginary past time of peace, prosperity, and happiness. ■ the period when a specified art, skill, or activity is at its peak: *the golden age of cinema.* ▷mid 16th cent.: the Greek and Roman poets' name for the first period of history, when the human race lived in an ideal state.

gold·en ag·er ▸*n.* used euphemistically or humorously to refer to an old person.

gold·en calf ▸*n.* (in the Bible) an image of gold in the shape of a calf, made by Aaron in response to the Israelites' plea for a god while they awaited Moses' return from Mount Sinai, where he was receiving the Ten Commandments (Exod. 32). ■ a false god, esp. wealth as an object of worship.

gold·en cat ▸*n.* a small forest-dwelling cat found in

G

Africa and Asia. • Genus *Felis*, family Felidae: the African *F. aurata*, with a chestnut to silver-gray coat, and the Asiatic *F. temmincki*, with a golden-brown coat and striped head.

Gold·en De·li·cious ▸*n.* a widely grown dessert apple of a greenish-yellow, soft-fleshed variety.

gold·en ea·gle ▸*n.* a large Eurasian and North American eagle with yellow-tipped head feathers in the mature adult. • *Aquila chrysaetos*, family Acciptridae.

gold·en·eye /ˈgōldən,ī/ ▸*n.* (*pl.* same or **-eyes**) a migratory northern diving duck, the male of which has a dark head with a white cheek patch and yellow eyes. • Genus *Bucephala*, family Anatidae: two species, in particular the **common goldeneye** (*B. clangula*).

Gold·en Fleece *Greek Mythology* the fleece of a golden ram, guarded by an unsleeping dragon, that was sought and won by Jason with the help of Medea. ■ a goal that is highly desirable but difficult to achieve.

Gold·en Gate a deep channel that connects San Francisco Bay with the Pacific Ocean. It is spanned by the Golden Gate suspension bridge, which was completed in 1937.

Golden Gate Bridge

gold·en glow ▸*n.* another term for GREEN-HEADED CONEFLOWER (see CONEFLOWER).

gold·en goose ▸*n.* a continuing source of wealth or profit that may be exhausted if it is misused: *they were killing the golden goose of tourism.* See also KILL THE GOOSE THAT LAYS THE GOLDEN EGG at EGG[1].

gold·en ham·ster ▸*n.* see HAMSTER.

gold·en hand·cuffs ▸*plural n. informal* used to refer to benefits, typically deferred payments, provided by an employer to discourage an employee from taking employment elsewhere.

gold·en hand·shake ▸*n. informal* a payment given to someone who is laid off or retires early.

Gold·en Hind the ship in which Francis Drake circumnavigated the globe in 1577–80. ▷named by Drake in honor of his patron, Sir Christopher Hatton (1540–91), whose crest was a golden hind.

Gold·en Horde the Tartar and Mongol army, led by descendants of Genghis Khan, that overran Asia and parts of eastern Europe in the 13th century and maintained an empire until around 1500 (so called from the richness of the leader's camp).

Gold·en Horn a curved inlet of the Bosporus that forms the harbor of Istanbul. Turkish name HALIÇ.

gold·en hour ▸*n. Medicine* the first hour after the occurrence of a traumatic injury, considered the most critical for successful emergency treatment.

gold·en ju·bi·lee ▸*n.* the fiftieth anniversary of a significant event.

gold·en mean ▸*n.* [in *sing.*] **1** the ideal moderate position between two extremes. **2** another term for GOLDEN SECTION.

gold·en num·ber ▸*n.* the number showing a year's place in the Metonic lunar cycle and used to fix the date of Easter for that year.

gold·en old·ie ▸*n. informal* an old song or movie that is still well known and popular.

gold·en par·a·chute ▸*n. informal* a large payment or other financial compensation guaranteed to a company executive should the executive be dismissed as a result of a merger or takeover.

gold·en plov·er ▸*n.* a northern Eurasian and North American plover, with a gold-speckled back and black face and underparts in the breeding season. • Genus *Pluvialis*, family Charadriidae: three species, in particular *P. apricaria* of Europe and *P. dominica* of Canada.

gold·en rai·sin ▸*n.* a raisin made from a white grape.

gold·en re·triev·er ▸*n.* a retriever of a breed with a thick golden-colored coat.

golden retriever

gold·en rice ▸*n.* a genetically modified variety of rice containing large amounts of the orange or red plant pigment betacarotene, a substance important in the human diet as a precursor of vitamin A.

gold·en·rod /ˈgōldən,räd/ ▸*n.* a plant of the daisy family that bears tall spikes of small bright yellow flowers. • Genus *Solidago*, family Compositae: numerous species, including **tall goldenrod** (*S. altissima*) with plumelike flower clusters, **downy goldenrod** (*S. puberula*) with erect, wandlike flower clusters, and **lance-leaved goldenrod** (*S. graminifolia*) with flat-topped flower clusters.

gold·en rule ▸*n.* a basic principle that should be followed to ensure success in general or in a particular activity: *one of the golden rules in this class is punctuality.* ■ (often **Golden Rule**) the biblical rule of "do unto others as you would have them do unto you" (Matt. 7:12).

gold·en·seal /ˈgōldən,sēl/ ▸*n.* a North American woodland plant of the buttercup family, with a bright yellow root that is used in herbal medicine. • *Hydrastis canadensis*, family Ranunculaceae.

gold·en sec·tion ▸*n.* the division of a line so that the whole is to the greater part as that part is to the smaller part (i.e., in a ratio of 1 to $\frac{1}{2}(\sqrt{5}+1)$), a proportion that is considered to be particularly pleasing to the eye.

Gold·en State a nickname for the state of CALIFORNIA.

gold·en syr·up ▸*n. British* a thick syrup with a buttery aroma, made from cane sugar.

gold·en wat·tle ▸*n.* an Australian acacia with golden flowers. • Genus *Acacia*, family Leguminosae: *A. pycnatha*, whose flowers are used as Australia's national emblem, and *A. longifolia*.

gold·en wed·ding (also **golden wedding anniversary**) ▸*n.* the fiftieth anniversary of a wedding.

gold·field /ˈgōld,fēld/ ▸*n.* a district in which gold is found as a mineral.

gold-filled ▸*adj.* (esp. of jewelry) consisting of a base metal covered in a thin layer of gold.

gold·finch /ˈgōld,fincн/ ▸*n.* a brightly colored finch with yellow feathers in the plumage. • Genus *Carduelis*, family Fringillidae: four species, esp. the **American goldfinch** (*C. tristis*)and the **Eurasian goldfinch** (*C. carduelis*). ▷late Old English *goldfinc* (see GOLD, FINCH).

gold·fish /ˈgōld,fisн/ ▸*n.* (*pl.* same or **-fish·es**) a small reddish-golden Eurasian carp, popular in ponds and aquariums. A long history of breeding in China and Japan has resulted in many varieties of form and color. • *Carassius auratus*, family Cyprinidae.

gold·fish bowl ▸*n.* a spherical glass container for goldfish. ■ *figurative* a place or situation lacking privacy: *a goldfish bowl of publicity.*

gold·i·locks /ˈgōldē,läks/ ▸*n. informal* a person with golden hair.

Gold·ing /ˈgōldiɴg/, Sir William (Gerald) (1911–93), English novelist. His first novel *Lord of the Flies* (1954) told of boys stranded on a desert island who revert to savagery. Other notable works: *Rites of Passage* (1980) and *Fire Down Below* (1989). Nobel Prize for Literature (1983).

gold leaf ▸*n.* gold that has been beaten into a very thin sheet, used in gilding.

Gold·man /ˈgōldmən/, Emma (1869–1940), U.S. political activist; born in Lithuania. She was involved in New York's anarchist movement and was an opponent of U.S. conscription. Notable works: *Anarchism and Other Essays* (1910) and *My Disillusionment in Russia* (1923).

gold med·al ▸*n.* a medal made of or colored gold, customarily awarded for first place in a race or competition. **—gold med·al·ist** *n.*

gold mine ▸*n.* a place where gold is mined. ■ *figurative* a source of wealth, valuable information, or resources: *this book is a gold mine of information.* **—gold min·er** *n.*

gold plate ▸*n.* a thin layer of gold, electroplated or otherwise applied as a coating to another metal. ■ objects coated with gold. ■ plates, dishes, etc., made of gold.
▸*v.* (**gold-plate**) [*trans.*] cover (something) with a thin layer of gold.

gold-plat·ed ▸*adj.* covered with a thin layer of gold: *a gold-plated tiepin.* ■ *figurative* likely to prove profitable; secure: *houses are no longer the gold-plated investment they were.*

gold re·serve ▸*n.* a quantity of gold held by a central bank to support the issue of currency.

gold rush ▸*n.* a rapid movement of people to a newly discovered goldfield. The first major gold rush, to California in 1848–49, was followed by others in the U.S., Australia (1851–53), South Africa (1884), and Canada (Klondike, 1897–98).

Golds·bor·o /ˈgōldz,bərō/ a city in eastern North Carolina, a noted tobacco center; pop. 40,709.

Gold·smith /ˈgōld,smiтн/, Oliver (1728–74), Irish novelist, poet, essayist, and playwright. Notable works: *The Vicar of Wakefield* (1766), *The Deserted Village* (1770), and *She Stoops to Conquer* (1773).

gold·smith /ˈgōld,smiтн/ ▸*n.* a person who makes gold articles. ▷late Old English (see GOLD, SMITH).

gold stand·ard ▸*n. historical* the system by which the value of a currency was defined in terms of gold, for which the currency could be exchanged. The gold standard was generally abandoned in the Depression of the 1930s. Compare with SILVER STANDARD. ■ *figurative* the best, most reliable, or most prestigious thing of its type: *you can't rely on lab tests as being the gold standard.*

gold·stone /ˈgōld,stōn/ ▸*n.* a variety of aventurine containing sparkling gold-colored particles.

gold·thread /ˈgōld,тнred/ ▸*n.* a plant of the buttercup family that yields a yellow dye and is used in herbal medicine as a treatment for mouth ulcers. It grows in North America and northeastern Asia. • Genus *Coptis*, family Ranunculaceae: several species, in particular *C. groenlandica* and *C. trifolia*.

Gold·wa·ter /ˈgōld,wôtər; -,wä-/, Barry Morris (1909–98) U.S. politician. A conservative, he was a member of the U.S. Senate from Arizona 1953–65, 1969–87 and a Republican presidential candidate in 1964.

Gold·wyn /ˈgōldwən/, Samuel (1882–1974), U.S. movie producer; born in Poland; born *Schmuel Gelbfisz*, changed to *Samuel Goldfish*, then *Goldwyn*. He produced his first movie in 1913 and, with Louis B. Mayer, founded Metro-Goldwyn-Mayer (MGM) in 1924.

go·lem /ˈgōləm/ ▸*n.* (in Jewish legend) a clay figure brought to life by magic. ■ an automaton or robot. ▷late 19th cent.: from Yiddish *goylem*, from Hebrew *gōlem* 'shapeless mass.'

golf /gälf; gôlf/ ▸*n.* **1** a game played on a large open-air course, in which a small hard ball is struck with a club into a series of small holes in the ground, the object being to use the fewest possible strokes to complete the course.

A golf course usually has 18 holes, each set in a smooth lawn (a green) separated from the others by stretches of smooth grass (fairways), rough ground, sand-filled bunkers, and other hazards. Various clubs are used to hit the ball from a tee toward the green and then putt it into the hole.

2 a code word representing the letter G, used in radio communication.
▸*v.* [*intrans.*] play golf: [as *n.*] (**golfing**) *a week's golfing.* ▷late Middle English (originally Scots): perhaps related to Dutch *kolf* 'club, bat,' used as a term in several Dutch games; *golf*, however, is recorded before these games. **—golf·er** *n.*

golf bag ▸*n.* a tall cylindrical bag used for carrying golf clubs and balls.

golf ball ▸*n.* a small hard ball used in the game of golf.

golf cart ▸*n.* a small motorized vehicle for golfers and their equipment.

golf club ▸*n.* **1** a club used to hit the ball in golf, with a heavy wooden or metal head on a slender shaft. **2** an organization of members for playing golf. ■ the premises used by such an organization.

golf course ▸*n.* a course on which golf is played.

golf links ▸*plural n.* see LINKS.

golf shirt ▸*n.* a light, short-sleeved shirt with a

collar, typically of a knitted fabric and with buttons at the neck only. See also **POLO SHIRT**.

Gol·gi /ˈgôljē/, Camillo (1844–1926), Italian histologist and anatomist. He devised a staining technique to investigate nerve tissue, classified types of nerve cells, and described the structure in the cytoplasm of most cells, now named after him. Nobel Prize for Physiology or Medicine (1906, shared with Ramon y Cajal).

Gol·gi ap·pa·rat·us (also **Golgi body**) ▸*n. Biology* a complex of vesicles and folded membranes within the cytoplasm of most eukaryotic cells, involved in secretion and intracellular transport.

Gol·go·tha /ˈgälgəTHə; gôlˈgäTHə/ the site of the crucifixion of Jesus; Calvary. ▷from late Latin, via Greek from an Aramaic form of Hebrew *gulgoleth* 'skull' (see Matt. 27:33).

Go·li·ath /gəˈlīəTH/ (in the Bible) a Philistine giant, according to legend slain by David (1 Sam. 17), but according to another tradition slain by Elhanan (2 Sam. 21:19).

go·li·ath bee·tle ▸*n.* a very large, boldly marked tropical beetle related to the chafers, the male of which has a forked horn on the head. • Genus *Goliathus*, family Scarabaeidae: several species, in particular *G. giganteus* of Africa, which is the largest known beetle.

gol·li·wog /ˈgälē,wäg/ (also **gol·li·wogg**) ▸*n.* **1** a soft doll with bright clothes, a black face, and fuzzy hair. **2** *derogatory* a grotesque person. ▷late 19th cent.: from *Golliwogg*, the name of a doll character in books by Bertha Upton (died 1912), American writer, and Florence K. Upton (died 1922), American illustrator; perhaps suggested by **GOLLY** and **POLLIWOG**.

gol·ly /ˈgälē/ (also **by golly**) ▸*exclam. informal, dated* used to express surprise or delight: *"Golly! Is that the time?"* ▷late 18th cent.: euphemism for **GOD**.

Go·mel /gôˈm(y)el/ Russian name for **HOMEL**.

go·mer /ˈgōmər/ ▸*n.* **1** *military slang* an inept or stupid colleague, especially a trainee. **2** *informal* (used mainly by doctors) a troublesome patient, especially an elderly or homeless one. ▷1960s: origin uncertain; sense 1 perhaps from the television character *Gomer* Pyle, a bungling Marine Corps enlistee; sense 2 perhaps an acronym from *get out of my emergency room.*

Go·mor·rah /gəˈmôrə/ a town in ancient Palestine, probably south of the Dead Sea. According to Gen. 19:24, it was destroyed by fire from heaven, along with Sodom, for the wickedness of its inhabitants.

Gom·pers /ˈgämpərz/, Samuel (1850–1924) U.S. labor leader; born in England. He helped to found the Federation of Organized Trades and Labor Unions in 1881. When it was reorganized as the American Federation of Labor in 1886, he served as its president until his death and did much to win respect for organized labor.

-gon ▸*comb. form* in nouns denoting plane figures with a specified number of angles: *hexagon | pentagon.* ▷from Greek *-gōnos* '-angled.'

go·nad /ˈgōnad/ ▸*n. Physiology & Zoology* an organ that produces gametes; a testis or ovary. ▷late 19th cent.: from modern Latin *gonades*, plural of *gonas*, from Greek *gonē* 'generation, seed.' **—go·nad·al** /gōˈnadl/ *adj.*

go·nad·o·trop·ic hor·mone /gō,nadəˈträpik; -ˈtrōpik/ (*chiefly Brit.* also **gonadotrophic hormone** /-ˈträfik; -ˈtrōfik/) ▸*n.* another term for **GONADOTROPIN**.

go·nad·o·tro·pin /gō,nadəˈtrōpin/ (*chiefly Brit.* also **go·nad·o·tro·phin** /-ˈtrōfin/) ▸*n. Biochemistry* any of a group of hormones secreted by the pituitary that stimulate the activity of the gonads.

Gon·court /gônˈko͝or/, Edmond de (1822–96) and Jules de (1830–70), French novelists and critics. In his will, Edmond provided for the establishment of the Académie Goncourt, which awards the annual Prix Goncourt.

Gond /gänd/ (also **Gon·di** /ˈgändē/) ▸*n.* (*pl.* same) **1** a member of an indigenous people living in the hill forests of central India. **2** the Dravidian language of this people.
▸*adj.* of or relating to the Gonds or their language. ▷from Sanskrit *gonḍa*.

Gon·dar /ˈgändər/ (also **Gonder**) a commercial city in northwestern Ethiopia, in Amhara province; pop. 112,000. A historic center for both Christians and Jews (Falashas), it was the capital of Ethiopia before 1855.

gon·do·la /ˈgändələ; gänˈdōlə/ ▸*n.* a light flat-bottomed boat used on Venetian canals, having a high point at each end and worked by one oar at the stern. ■ a cabin on a suspended ski lift. ■ (also **gondola car**) an open railroad freight car. ■ an enclosed compartment suspended from an airship or balloon. ▷mid 16th cent.: from Venetian Italian, from Rhaeto-Romanic *gondolà* 'to rock, roll.'

gondola

gon·do·lier /,gändlˈi(ə)r/ ▸*n.* a person who propels and steers a gondola. ▷early 17th cent.: via French from Italian *gondoliere*, from *gondola* (see **GONDOLA**).

Gond·wa·na /gänˈdwänə/ (also **Gond·wa·na·land**) a vast continental area believed to have existed in the southern hemisphere and to have resulted from the breakup of Pangaea in Mesozoic times. It comprised the present Arabia, Africa, South America, Antarctica, Australia, and the peninsula of India. ▷late 19th cent. (originally denoting any of a series of rocks in India, esp. fluviatile shales and sandstones): from the name of a region in central northern India, from Sanskrit *gonḍavana* 'forest of Gond.'

gone /gôn/ ▸ past participle of **GO**[1].
▸*adj.* [*predic.*] **1** no longer present; departed: *while you were gone | the bad old days are gone.* ■ no longer in existence; dead or extinct: *an aunt of mine, long since gone.* ■ no longer available: *all 35,000 tickets will be gone by next weekend.* ■ *informal* in a trance or stupor, esp. through exhaustion, drink, or drugs: *she sat, half-gone, on a folding chair.* ■ [*attrib.*] lost; hopeless: *spending time and effort on a gone sucker like Galindez.* ■ *dated* excellent; inspired: *a bunch of real gone cats.* **2** *informal* having reached a specified time in a pregnancy: *she is now four months gone.*
▸*prep. Brit.* (of time) past: *it's gone half past eleven.* ■ (of age) older than: *she was gone sixty by then.*
▸*PHRASE* □ **be gone on** *informal* be infatuated with: *I always knew he was gone on you.*

gon·er /ˈgônər/ ▸*n. informal* a person or thing that is doomed or cannot be saved.

gon·fa·lon /ˈgänfələn/ ▸*n.* a banner or pennant, esp. one with streamers, hung from a crossbar. ■ *historical* such a banner as the standard of some Italian republics. ▷late 16th cent.: from Italian *gonfalone*, from a Germanic compound whose second element is related to **VANE**.

gon·fa·lon·ier /,gänfələˈni(ə)r/ ▸*n.* the bearer of a gonfalon, a standard-bearer.

gong /gäNG; gôNG/ ▸*n.* a metal disk with a turned rim, giving a resonant note when struck: *a dinner gong.*
▸*v.* [*intrans.*] sound a gong or make a sound like that of a gong being struck. ▷early 17th cent.: from Malay *gong, gung*, of imitative origin.

go·ni·a·tite /ˈgōnēə,tīt/ ▸*n.* an ammonoid fossil of an early type found chiefly in the Devonian and Carboniferous periods, typically with simple angular suture lines. Compare with **AMMONITE** and **CERATITE**. • Typified by the genus *Goniatites*, order Goniatitida. ▷mid 19th cent.: from modern Latin *Goniatites*, from Greek *gōnia* 'angle.'

gon·if /ˈgänəf/ (also **gon·iff, gan·ef**) ▸*n. informal* a disreputable or dishonest person (often used as a general term of abuse). ▷mid 19th cent.: from Yiddish *ganev*, from Hebrew *gannāḇ* 'thief.'

go·ni·om·e·ter /,gōnēˈämitər/ ▸*n.* an instrument for the precise measurement of angles, esp. one used to measure the angles between the faces of crystals. ▷mid 18th cent.: from French *goniomètre*, from Greek *gōnia* 'angle' + French *-mètre* '(instrument) measuring.' **—go·ni·o·met·ric** /-nēəˈmetrik/ *adj.* **—go·ni·o·met·ri·cal** /-nēəˈmetrikəl/ *adj.* **—go·ni·om·e·try** /-trē/ *n.*

gon·na /ˈgônə; ˈgənə/ *informal* ▸*contraction of* going to: *we're gonna win this game.*

gon·o·coc·cus /,gänəˈkäkəs/ ▸*n.* (*pl.* **-coc·ci** /-ˈkäk,sī/) a bacterium that causes gonorrhea. • *Neisseria gonorrhoeae*, a Gram-negative diplococcus. ▷late 19th cent.: from *gono-* (as in **GONORRHEA**) + **COCCUS**. **—gon·o·coc·cal** /-ˈkäkəl/ *adj.*

go-no-go /ˈgō ˈnō ,gō/ ▸*adj.* **1** designating a situation in which one must decide whether or not to continue with a particular course of action, or the moment when such a decision must be made. **2** designating the decision to continue with or abandon a course of action.

gon·or·rhe·a /,gänəˈrēə/ (*Brit.* **gon·or·rhoe·a**) ▸*n.* a venereal disease involving inflammatory discharge from the urethra or vagina. ▷early 16th cent.: via late Latin from Greek *gonorrhoia*, from *gonos* 'semen' + *rhoia* 'flux.' **—gon·or·rhe·al** *adj.*

Gon·za·lez /gənˈzälis/, Henry B. (1916–2000) U.S. politician. A Democrat from Texas, he was a member of the U.S. House of Representatives 1961–98 where he championed the rights of minorities and fought for tighter restrictions on the savings and loan industry during the 1980s.

gon·zo /ˈgänzō/ ▸*adj. informal* of or associated with journalistic writing of an exaggerated, subjective, and fictionalized style. ■ bizarre or crazy: *the woman was either gonzo or stoned.* ▷1970s: perhaps from Italian *gonzo* 'foolish' or Spanish *ganso* 'goose, fool.'

goo /go͞o/ ▸*n. informal* **1** a sticky or slimy substance: *he tipped the grayish goo from the test tube.* **2** sickly sentiment. ▷early 20th cent. (originally U.S.): perhaps from *burgoo*, a nautical slang term for porridge, based on Persian *bulġ ūr* 'bruised grain.'

goo·ber /ˈgo͞obər/ ▸*informal* **1** (also **goo·ber pea**) a peanut. **2** *often offensive* a person from the southeastern U.S., esp. Georgia or Arkansas. ■ *offensive* an unsophisticated person; a yokel.

Goo·ber State a nickname for the state of **GEORGIA**.

good /go͝od/ ▸*adj.* (**bet·ter** /ˈbetər/, **best** /best/) **1** to be desired or approved of: *we live at peace with each other, which is good | a good quality of life.* ■ pleasing and welcome: *she was pleased to hear good news about him.* ■ expressing approval: *the play had good reviews.* **2** having the qualities required for a particular role: *the schools here are good.* ■ functioning or performed well: *good health | either she was feeling chastened or she was doing a good act.* ■ appropriate to a particular purpose: *this is a good month for planting seeds.* ■ (of language) with correct grammar and pronunciation: *she speaks good English.* ■ strictly adhering to or fulfilling all the principles of a particular cause, religion, or party: *a good Catholic girl.* ■ (of a ticket) valid: *the ticket is* **good for** *travel from May to September.* **3** possessing or displaying moral virtue: *I've met many good people who made me feel ashamed of my own shortcomings* | [as *plural n.*] (**the good**) *the rich and the good shared the same fate as the poor and the bad.* ■ showing kindness: *you are good—thank you.* ■ obedient to rules or conventions: *accustom the child to being rewarded for good behavior.* ■ used to address or refer to people, esp. in a patronizing or humorous way: *the good people of the city were disconcerted.* ■ commanding respect: *he was concerned with establishing and maintaining his good name.* ■ belonging or relating to a high social class: *he comes from a good family.* **4** giving pleasure; enjoyable or satisfying: *the streets fill up with people looking for a good time.* ■ pleasant to look at; attractive: *you're looking pretty good.* ■ (of food and drink) having a pleasant taste: *the scampi was very good.* ■ (of clothes) smart and suitable for formal wear: *he went upstairs to change out of his good suit.* **5** [*attrib.*] thorough: *the attic needed a good cleaning | have a good look around.* ■ used to emphasize that a number is at least as great as one claims: *they're a good twenty years younger.* ■ used to emphasize a following adjective: *we had a good long hug.* ■ fairly large: *a good crowd | figurative there's a good chance that we may be able to help you.* **6** used in conjunction with the name of God or a related expression as an exclamation of extreme surprise or anger: *good heavens!*
▸*n.* **1** that which is morally right; righteousness: *a mysterious balance of good and evil.* **2** benefit or advantage to someone or something: *he is* **too clever for his own good.** **3** (**goods**) merchandise or possessions: *imports of luxury goods.* ■ *Brit.* things to be transported, as distinct from passengers: *a means of transporting passengers as well as goods* | [as *adj.*] *a goods train.* ■ (**the goods**) *informal* the genuine article.
▸*adv. informal* well: *my mother could never cook this good.* ▷Old English *gōd*, of Germanic origin; related to Dutch *goed* and German *gut*.
▸*PHRASES* □ **all to the good** to be welcomed without qualification: □ **as good as ——** very nearly ——: *she's as good as here.* ■ used of a result which will inevitably follow: *if we pass on the information, he's as good as dead.* □ **be any** (or **no** or **much**) **good** have some (or none or much) merit: *tell me whether that picture is any good.* ■ be of some (or none or much) help in dealing with a situation: *it was no good trying*

G

to ward things off. □ **be so good as** (or **be good enough**) **to do something** used to make a polite request: *would you be so good as to answer.* □ **be —— to the good** have a specified net profit or advantage: *I came out $7 to the good.* □ **come up with** (or **deliver**) **the goods** *informal* do what is expected or required of one. □ **do good 1** act virtuously, esp. by helping others. **2** make a helpful contribution to a situation: *could the discussion do any good?* □ **do someone good** be beneficial to someone, esp. to their health: *the walk will do you good.* □ **for good** (**and all**) forever; definitively: *the experience almost frightened me away for good.* □ **get** (or **have**) **the goods on** *informal* obtain (or possess) information about (someone) that may be used to their detriment. □ **good and ——** *informal* used as an intensifier before an adjective or adverb: *it'll be good and dark by then.* □ (**as**) **good as gold** (esp. of a child) extremely well behaved. □ (**as**) **good as new** in a very good condition or state, close to the original state again after damage, injury, or illness: *the skirt looked as good as new.* □ **the Good Book** the Bible. □ **good for 1** having a beneficial effect on: *smoking is not good for the lungs.* **2** reliably providing: *they found him good for a laugh.* ■ sufficient to pay for: *his money was good for a bottle of whiskey.* □ **good for** (or **him, her,** etc.) **!** used as an exclamation of approval toward a person, esp. for something that they have achieved: *"I'm taking my driving test next month." "Good for you!"* □ **the Good Shepherd** a name for Jesus. [with biblical allusion to John 10: 1-16.] □ **good wine needs no bush** see WINE. □ **a good word** words in recommendation or defense of a person: *I hoped you might* ***put in a good word for*** *me with your friends.* □ **have a good mind to do something** see MIND. □ **in someone's good books** see BOOK. □ **in good time 1** with no risk of being late: *I arrived in good time.* **2** (also **all in good time**) in due course but without haste: *you shall have a puppy all in good time.* □ **make good** be successful: *a college friend who made good in Hollywood.* □ **make something good 1** compensate for loss, damage, or expense: *if I scratched the table, I'd make good the damage.* ■ repair or restore after damage: *make good the wall where you have buried the cable.* **2** fulfill a promise or claim: *I challenged him to make good his boast.* □ **one good turn deserves another** see TURN. □ **put a good face on something** see FACE. □ **take something in good part** not be offended by something: *he took her abruptness in good part.* □ **up to no good** doing something wrong.

USAGE The adverb corresponding to the adjective **good** is **well**: *she is a good swimmer who performs well in meets.* Confusion sometimes arises because **well** is also an adjective meaning 'in good health, healthy,' for which **good** is widely used informally as a substitute: *I feel well,* meaning 'I feel healthy'—versus the informal *I feel good,* meaning either 'I feel healthy' or 'I am in a good mood.'
See also **usage** at BAD.

good af·ter·noon ▸*exclam.* expressing good wishes on meeting or parting in the afternoon.

Good·all /ˈgo͝od,ôl/, Jane (1934–), English zoologist. After working with Louis Leakey in Tanzania from 1957, she made prolonged and intimate studies of chimpanzees at the Gombe Stream Reserve at Lake Tanganyika from 1970.

good·bye /,go͝odˈbī/ (also **good-bye** or **good·by** or **good-by**) ▸*exclam.* used to express good wishes when parting or at the end of a conversation.
▸*n.* (*pl.* **-byes** or **-bys**) an instance of saying "goodbye"; a parting: *a final goodbye.* ▷late 16th cent.: contraction of *God be with you!*, with *good* substituted on the pattern of phrases such as *good morning.*

good eve·ning ▸*exclam.* expressing good wishes on meeting or parting during the evening.

good faith ▸*n.* honesty or sincerity of intention: *the details contained in this brochure have been published* ***in good faith.***

good·fel·la /ˈgo͝od,felə/ ▸*n. informal* a gangster, esp. a member of a Mafia family.

good form ▸*n.* what complies with current social conventions: *it wasn't considered* ***in good form*** *to show too much enthusiasm.*

good-for-noth·ing ▸*adj.* (of a person) worthless: *his good-for-nothing son.*
▸*n.* a worthless person.

Good Fri·day ▸*n.* the Friday before Easter Sunday, on which the Crucifixion of Jesus Christ is commemorated in the Christian Church. It is traditionally a day of fasting and penance. ▷from GOOD, in the sense 'holy, observed as a holy day.'

good-heart·ed ▸*adj.* kind and well meaning. —**good-heart·ed·ly** *adv.* —**good-heart·ed·ness** *n.*

Good Hope, Cape of see CAPE OF GOOD HOPE.

good hu·mor ▸*n.* a genial disposition or mood: *I admire your dignity and good humor.*

good-hu·mored ▸*adj.* genial; cheerful. —**good-hu·mored·ly** *adv.*

good·ie ▸*n.* variant spelling of GOODY[1].

good·ish /ˈgo͝odish/ ▸*adj.* fairly good: *in goodish working order.* ■ fairly large: *a goodish portion.*

Good-King-Hen·ry (also **Good King Henry**) ▸*n.* an edible plant of the goosefoot family, with large dark green leaves and insignificant clusters of flowers. Native to Europe, it has become naturalized in North America. • *Chenopodium bonus-henricus,* family Chenopodiaceae. ▷late 16th cent.: of unknown origin.

good-look·ing ▸*adj.* (chiefly of a person) attractive. —**good-look·er** *n.*

good·ly /ˈgo͝odlē/ ▸*adj.* (**-li·er, -li·est**) **1** considerable in size or quantity: *we ran up a goodly bar bill.* **2** *archaic* attractive, excellent, or admirable. ▷Old English *gōdlic* (see GOOD, -LY[1]). —**good·li·ness** *n.*

Good·man /ˈgo͝odmən/, Benny (1909–86), U.S. jazz clarinetist and bandleader; full name *Benjamin David Goodman;* known as **the King of Swing**. In 1934, he formed his own band, which was the first big band to include both black and white musicians.

good·man /ˈgo͝odmən/ ▸*n.* (*pl.* **-men**) *archaic, chiefly Scottish* the male head of a household.

good mon·ey ▸*n.* money that might usefully be spent elsewhere; hard-earned money: *I'm not going to pay good money for it.* ■ *informal* high wages: *I earn good money.*

good morn·ing ▸*exclam.* expressing good wishes on meeting or parting during the morning.

good na·ture ▸*n.* a kind and unselfish disposition: *your boy has a good nature.* —**good-na·tured** *adj.* —**good-na·tured·ly** *adv.*

good·ness /ˈgo͝odnis/ ▸*n.* the quality of being good, in particular: ■ virtue; moral excellence: *a belief in the basic goodness of mankind.* ■ kindness; generosity: *he did it out of the goodness of his heart.* ■ the beneficial or nourishing element of food.
▸*exclam.* (as a substitution for "God") expressing surprise, anger, etc.: *goodness knows what her rent will be.* ▷Old English *gōdnes* (see GOOD, -NESS).
▸*PHRASES* □ **for goodness' sake** see SAKE[1]. □ **goodness of fit** *Statistics* the extent to which observed data match the values expected by theory. □ **have the goodness to do something** used in exaggeratedly polite requests: *have the goodness to look at me when I'm speaking to you!*

THE RIGHT WORD **goodness, morality, probity, rectitude, virtue**
Of all these words denoting moral excellence, **goodness** is the broadest in meaning. It describes an excellence so well established that it is thought of as inherent or innate and is associated with kindness, generosity, helpfulness, and sincerity (*she has more goodness in her little finger than most people have in their whole body*).
Morality, on the other hand, is moral excellence based on a code of ethical conduct or religious teaching (*his behavior was kept in line by fear of punishment rather than morality*).
Although it is often used as a synonym for *goodness,* **virtue** suggests moral excellence that is acquired rather than innate and that is consciously or steadfastly maintained, often in spite of temptations or evil influences (*her virtue was as unassailable as her noble character*).
Rectitude is used to describe strict adherence to the rules of just or right behavior and carries strong connotations of sternness and self-discipline (*he had a reputation for rectitude and insisted on absolute truthfulness*).
Probity describes an honesty or integrity that has been tried and proved (*as mayor, she displayed a probity that was rare in a politician*).

Good News Bi·ble ▸*n.* a translation of the Bible in simple everyday English, published 1966–76 by the United Bible Societies.

good night (also **good·night** or **good-night**) ▸*exclam.* expressing good wishes on parting at night or before going to bed.

good old boy ▸*n.* a man who embodies some or all of the qualities considered characteristic of many white men of the southern U.S., including an unpretentious, convivial manner, conservative or intolerant attitudes, and a strong sense of fellowship with and loyalty to other members of his peer group.

goods and chat·tels ▸*plural n. chiefly Law* all kinds of personal possessions.

good-sized ▸*adj.* of ample size; fairly large: *a good-sized garden.*

good-tem·pered ▸*adj.* not easily irritated or made angry. —**good-tem·pered·ly** *adv.*

good-time ▸*adj.* [*attrib.*] (of a person) recklessly pursuing pleasure: *a good-time party girl | he's just a* ***good-time Charlie.***

good·wife /ˈgo͝od,wīf/ ▸*n.* (*pl.* **-wives**) *archaic, chiefly Scottish* the female head of a household.

good·will /,go͝odˈwil/ (also **good will**) ▸*n.* **1** friendly, helpful, or cooperative feelings or attitude: *the plan is dependent on goodwill between the two sides* | [as *adj.*] *a goodwill gesture.* **2** the established reputation of a business regarded as a quantifiable asset, e.g., as represented by the excess of the price paid at a takeover for a company over its fair market value.

Good·win /ˈgo͝odwin/, Doris Kearns (1943–) U.S. journalist, historian, and writer. Her works include *Lyndon Johnson and the American Dream* (1976), *The Fitzgeralds and the Kennedys* (1989), and *No Ordinary Time* (1995).

good works ▸*plural n.* charitable acts.

good·y[1] /ˈgo͝odē/ ▸*n.* (also **good·ie**) (*pl.* **good·ies**) *informal* (usu. **goodies**) something attractive or desirable, esp. something tasty or pleasant to eat.
▸*exclam.* expressing childish delight: *goody, we can have a party.*

good·y[2] ▸*n.* (*pl.* **good·ies**) *archaic* (often as a title prefixed to a surname) an elderly woman of humble station: *the tale of Goody Blake and Harry Gill.* ▷mid 16th cent.: pet form of GOODWIFE; compare with HUSSY.

Good·year /ˈgo͝od,yi(ə)r/, Charles (1800–60), U.S. inventor. He developed the process of the vulcanization of rubber after accidentally dropping some rubber mixed with sulfur and white lead on a hot stove.

good·y-good·y *informal* ▸*n.* a smug or obtrusively virtuous person.
▸*adj.* smug or obtrusively virtuous.

good·y two-shoes ▸ *n.* a smugly or obtrusively virtuous person; a goody-goody. ▷from the nickname of the the heroine of the *History of Little Goody Two-Shoes* (1766).

goo·ey /ˈgo͞oē/ ▸*adj.* (**goo·i·er, goo·i·est**) *informal* soft and sticky. ■ mawkishly sentimental: *you can love somebody without going all gooey.* —**goo·ey·ness** *n.*

goof /go͞of/ *informal* ▸*n.* **1** a mistake: *he made one of the most embarrassing goofs of his tenure.* See note at MISTAKE. **2** a foolish or stupid person.
▸*v.* [*intrans.*] **1** spend time idly or foolishly; fool around: *I was* ***goofing around*** *and broke my arm.* ■ (**goof off**) evade a duty; idle or shirk: *he was* ***goofing off from*** *his math homework.* ■ (**goof on**) make fun of; ridicule: *Lew and I started goofing on Alison's friend.* **2** make a mistake; blunder: *you're scared to say yes in case you* ***goof up.*** ▷early 20th cent.: of unknown origin.

goof·ball /ˈgo͞of,bôl/ ▸*n. informal* **1** a naive, silly, or stupid person. **2** a narcotic drug in pill form, esp. a barbiturate.
▸*adj. informal* foolish; silly: *Yvonne and her goofball antics.*

goof-off ▸*n. informal* a person who is habitually lazy or does less than their fair share of work.

goof·proof /ˈgo͞of,pro͞of/ ▸*adj.* (of a product, procedure, etc.) designed to be simple enough for anyone to use or implement: *each comes with complete instructions and detailed illustrations that make the installation nearly goof-proof.*
▸*v.* [*trans.*] design or adapt (a product, procedure, etc.) so that it is simple for anyone to use: *these simple steps can goof-proof your 1040.*

goof-up ▸*n. informal* a stupid mistake.

goof·us /ˈgo͞ofəs/ ▸*n. informal* a foolish or stupid person (often used as a general term of abuse). ▷1920s: based on GOOF.

goof·y /ˈgo͞ofē/ ▸*adj.* (**goof·i·er, goof·i·est**) *informal* **1** foolish; harmlessly eccentric. **2** (in surfing and other board sports) with the right leg in front of the left on the board. —**goof·i·ly** /-fəlē/ *adv.* —**goof·i·ness** *n.*

goo·gle /ˈgo͞ogəl/ (also **Goo·gle**) ▸*v. informal* [*intrans.*] use an Internet search engine, particularly Google.com: *she spent the afternoon googling aimlessly.* ■ [*trans.*] search for the name of (someone) on the Internet to find out information about them: *you meet someone, swap numbers, fix a date, then Google them through 1,346,966,000 Web pages.* ▷from *Google,* the proprietary name of a popular Internet search engine.

goo·gle bomb·ing ▸*n.* the activity of designing Internet links that will bias search engine results so as to create an inaccurate impression of the search target. **—google bomb** *n.* **—google-bomb** *v.* [*trans.*]

goog·ly /ˈgōōglē/ ▸*n.* (*pl.* **-lies**) *Cricket* a ball bowled with a deceptive bounce. ▷early 20th cent.: of unknown origin.

goo·gol /ˈgōō,gôl/ ▸*cardinal number* equivalent to ten raised to the power of a hundred (10^{100}). ▷1940s: said to have been coined by the nine-year-old nephew of E. Kasner (1878–1955), American mathematician, at Kasner's request.

goo·gol·plex /ˈgōōgôl,pleks/ ▸*cardinal number* equivalent to ten raised to the power of a googol. ▷1940s: from GOOGOL + *-plex* as in *multiplex*.

goo-goo *informal* ▸*adj.* **1** amorously adoring: *making goo-goo eyes at him.* **2** (of speech or vocal sounds) childish or meaningless: *making soothing goo-goo noises.* ▷early 20th cent.: possibly related to GOGGLE.

gook[1] /gōōk; gŏŏk/ ▸*n. informal, offensive* a foreigner, esp. a person of Philippine, Korean, or Vietnamese descent. ▷1930s: of unknown origin.

gook[2] ▸*n. informal* a sloppy wet or viscous substance: *all that gook she kept putting on her face.* ▷1970s: variant of GUCK.

Goo·la·gong /ˈgōōlə,gäNG/, Evonne, see CAWLEY.

goom·bah /ˈgōōmbä; gōōmˈbä/ ▸*n. informal* an associate or accomplice, esp. a senior member of a criminal gang. ▷1960s: probably a dialect alteration of Italian *compàre* 'godfather, friend, accomplice.'

goom·bay /ˈgōōmbā; ˈgōōm-/ ▸*n. W. Indian* a goatskin drum with a round or squared top, played with the hands. ■ the calypso-style music associated with the playing of such drums. ■ a dance to such drums. ■ (chiefly in the Bahamas) a festival or season of such music and dance. ▷perhaps from Kikongo *ngoma*, denoting a type of drum.

goon /gōōn/ ▸*n. informal* **1** a silly, foolish, or eccentric person. **2** a bully or thug, esp. one hired to terrorize or do away with opposition: *a squad of goons waving pistols.* ▷mid 19th cent.: perhaps from dialect *gooney* 'booby'; influenced by the subhuman cartoon character 'Alice the *Goon*,' created by E. C. Segar (1894–1938), American cartoonist.

goon·ey bird /ˈgōōnē/ (also **goon·y bird**) ▸*n.* **1** another term for an albatross of the North Pacific. • Genus *Diomedea*, family Diomedeidae: the Laysan albatross (*D. immutabilis*) and the black-footed albatross (*D. nigripes*). **2** *informal* a foolish or inept person; a goon. ▷mid 19th cent.: of unknown origin.

goop /gōōp/ ▸*n. informal* sloppy or sticky semifluid matter, typically something unpleasant. ■ mawkish sentiment. ▷1970s: the sounds *g*, *oo*, and *p* are said to be symbolic of semiliquid matter; compare with GLOOP. **—goop·i·ness** /-pēnis/ *n.* **—goop·y** *adj.*

goos·an·der /gōōˈsandər/ ▸*n.* (*pl.* same or **-ders**) British term for COMMON MERGANSER (see MERGANSER). ▷early 17th cent.: probably from GOOSE + *-ander* as in dialect *bergander* 'shelduck' (the coloring of the male common merganser resembling that of the shelduck).

goose /gōōs/ ▸*n.* (*pl.* **geese** /gēs/) **1** a large waterbird with a long neck, short legs, webbed feet, and a short broad bill. Generally geese are larger than ducks and have longer necks and shorter bills. • Several genera in the family Anatidae, esp. *Anser* and *Branta*; most domesticated geese are descended from the greylag. ■ the female of such a bird. ■ the flesh of a goose as food. **2** *informal* a foolish person: *"Silly goose," he murmured fondly.* **3** (*pl.* **goos·es**) a tailor's smoothing iron.
▸*v.* [*trans.*] *informal* **1** poke (someone) between the buttocks. **2** give (something) a boost; invigorate; increase: *the director* **goosed up** *the star's grosses by making him funny.* ▷Old English *gōs*, of Germanic origin; related to Dutch *gans* and German *Gans*, from an Indo-European root shared by Latin *anser* and Greek *khēn*.
▸*PHRASE* □ **cook someone's goose** see COOK.

goose bar·na·cle (also **goose·neck bar·na·cle**) ▸*n.* a stalked barnacle that hangs down from driftwood or other slow-moving floating objects, catching passing prey with its feathery legs. • Genus *Lepas*, class Cirripedia.

goose·ber·ry /ˈgōōs,berē/ ▸*n.* (*pl.* **-ries**) **1** a round edible yellowish-green or reddish berry with a thin translucent hairy skin. **2** the thorny shrub that bears this fruit. • *Ribes grossularia*, family Grossulariaceae. ▷mid 16th cent.: the first element perhaps from GOOSE, or perhaps based on Old French *groseille*, altered because of an unexplained association with the bird.

goose·bumps /ˈgōōs,bəmps/ ▸*plural n.* another term for GOOSE PIMPLES.

Goose Creek // a city in southeastern South Carolina, a northwestern suburb of Charleston; pop. 29,208.

goose egg *informal* ▸*n.* **1** zero, esp. a zero score in a game: *once again, our team goes home with a big goose egg.* **2** a lump, typically on the head, from a blow. ▷late 19th cent.: with reference to the shape of the zero.

goose·fish /ˈgōōs,fisH/ ▸*n.* (*pl.* same or **-fish·es**) a bottom-dwelling anglerfish. Also called MONKFISH. • Family Lophiidae: several species, in particular *Lophius americanus* of North American waters.

goose·flesh /ˈgōōs,flesH/ ▸*n.* a pimply state of the skin with the hairs erect, produced by cold or fright. ▷early 19th cent.: so named because the skin resembles that of a plucked goose.

goose·foot /ˈgōōs,fŏŏt/ ▸*n.* (*pl.* **-foots**) a plant of temperate regions with divided leaves that are said to resemble the foot of a goose. Some kinds are edible and many are common weeds. • Genus *Chenopodium*, family Chenopodiaceae.

goose·grass /ˈgōōs,gras/ ▸*n.* another term for CLEAVERS.

goose·neck /ˈgōōs,nek/ ▸*n.* a support or pipe curved like a goose's neck: [as *adj.*] *a gooseneck lamp.* ■ *Sailing* a metal fitting at the end of a boom, connecting it to a pivot or ring near the base of the mast.

goose pim·ples ▸*plural n.* the pimples that form gooseflesh.

goose step ▸*n.* a military marching step in which the legs are not bent at the knee.
▸*v.* (**goose-step**) [*intrans.*] march with such a step: *East German soldiers goose-stepped outside the monument.*

goose·y /ˈgōōsē/ (also **goos·y**) ▸*adj.* (**goos·i·er, goos·i·est**) having or showing a quality considered to be characteristic of a goose, esp. foolishness or nervousness. ■ *informal* exhibiting gooseflesh: *I've gone all goosey.*

GOP ▸*abbr.* Grand Old Party (Republican Party).

go·pak /ˈgōpak/ (also **ho·pak**) ▸*n.* an energetic Ukrainian dance in duple time, traditionally performed by men. ▷1920s: via Russian, from Ukrainian *hopak*.

go·pher[1] /ˈgōfər/ ▸*n.* **1** (also **pocket gopher**) a burrowing rodent with fur-lined pouches on the outside of the cheeks, found in North and Central America. • Family Geomyidae: several genera and species. ■ *informal* another term for GROUND SQUIRREL. **2** (also **gopher tortoise**) a tortoise of dry sandy regions that excavates tunnels as shelter from the sun, native to the southern U.S. • *Gopherus polyphemus*, family Testudinidae. **3** (also **Gopher**) *Computing* a menu-based system that allows users of the Internet to search for and retrieve documents on topics of interest. [1990s: named after the gopher mascot of the University of Minnesota, where the system was invented.] ▷late 18th cent.: perhaps from Canadian French *gaufre* 'honeycomb' (because the gopher "honeycombs" the ground with its burrows).

go·pher[2] ▸*n.* variant spelling of GOFER.

go·pher ball ▸*n. Baseball* a pitch that is hit for a home run.

go·pher snake ▸*n.* a large harmless yellowish-cream snake with darker markings, native to western North America. • *Pituophis catenifer*, family Colubridae. ■ (also **blue gopher snake**) another term for INDIGO SNAKE.

Go·pher State a nickname for the state of MINNESOTA.

go·pher wood ▸*n.* **1** (in biblical use) the timber from which Noah's ark was made, from an unidentified tree (Gen. 6:14). **2** (**go·pher·wood**) either of two North American trees: • STINKING CEDAR. • YELLOWWOOD. ▷early 17th cent.: *gopher* from Hebrew *gōper*.

go·pik /ˈgōpik/ ▸*n.* (*pl.* same or **-piks**) a monetary unit of Azerbaijan, equal to one hundredth of a manat.

Go·rakh·pur /ˈgôrək,pŏŏr/ an industrial city in northeastern India, in Uttar Pradesh, near the border with Nepal; pop. 490,000.

go·ral /ˈgôrəl/ ▸*n.* a long-haired goat-antelope with backward curving horns, found in mountainous regions of eastern Asia. • Genus *Nemorhaedus*, family Bovidae: two species. ▷mid 19th cent.: a local word in the Himalayas.

Gor·ba·chev /ˈgôrbə,CHôf/, Mikhail (Sergeevich) (1931–), Soviet statesman, general secretary of the Communist Party of the Soviet Union 1985–91 and president 1988–91. His foreign policy helped bring about an end to the Cold War, while within the Soviet Union he introduced major reforms (*glasnost* and *perestroika*), both in the economy and in freedom of information. He resigned following an attempted coup and at a time of the Soviet republics' desire for autonomy. Nobel Peace Prize (1990).

gor·bli·mey /gôrˈblīmē/ *Brit., informal* ▸*exclam.* an expression of surprise or indignation.
▸*adj.* [*attrib.*] common; lower class. ▷late 19th cent.: alteration of *God blind me*; also in use as a noun in the early 20th cent. to denote various kinds of unusual clothing.

Gor·di·an knot /ˈgôrdēən/ ▸*n.* an extremely difficult or involved problem. ▷mid 16th cent.: from the legend that *Gordius*, king of Gordium, tied an intricate knot and prophesied that whoever untied it would become the ruler of Asia. It was cut through with a sword by Alexander the Great.
▸*PHRASE* □ **cut the Gordian knot** solve or remove a problem in a direct or forceful way, rejecting gentler or more indirect methods.

gor·di·an worm ▸*n.* another term for HORSEHAIR WORM.

Gor·di·mer /ˈgôrdəmər/, Nadine (1923–), South African novelist and short-story writer. Her experience with the effects of apartheid underlies much of her work. Notable novels: *The Conservationist* (Booker Prize, 1974) and *Burger's Daughter* (1979). Nobel Prize for Literature (1991).

Nadine Gordimer

Gor·di·um /ˈgôrdēəm/ an ancient city in Asia Minor (now northwestern Turkey), the capital of Phrygia in the 8th and 9th centuries BC.

Gor·don /ˈgôrdn/, Charles George (1833–85), British general and colonial administrator. He is noted for crushing the Taiping Rebellion (1863–64) in China and for fighting Mahdist forces in Sudan in 1884.

Gor·don set·ter ▸*n.* a setter of a black-and-tan breed, used as a gun dog. ▷mid 19th cent.: named after the 4th Duke of *Gordon* (1743–1827), who promoted the breed.

Gor·dy /ˈgôrdē/, Berry, Jr. (1929–), U.S. recording company and popular music producer. He founded Motown Records in 1959 and had huge success in the 1960s and 1970s, popularizing black rhythm-and-blues and soul music.

Gore /gôr/ Al(bert Arnold, Jr.) (1948–) U.S. vice president 1993–2001. A Tennessee Democrat, he served in the U.S. House of Representatives 1977–85 and U.S. Senate 1985–93. The Democratic nominee in the 2000 presidential election, he bowed to George

Al Gore

Pronunciation Key ə *ago*; ər *over*; ˈə or ˌə *up*; ˈər or ˌər *fur*; a *hat*; ā *rate*; ä *car*; CH *chew*; e *let*; ē *see*; e(ə)r *air*; i *fit*; ī *by*; i(ə)r *ear*; NG *sing*; ō *go*; ô *for*; oi *boy*; ŏŏ *good*; ōō *goo*; ou *out*; SH *she*; TH *thin*; T̲H̲ *then*; (h)w *why*; ZH *vision*

W. Bush in one of the closest and most controversial elections in U.S. history. Noted for his commitment to environmental issues, he wrote *Earth in the Balance* (1992).

gore[1] /gôr/ ▸*n.* blood that has been shed, esp. as a result of violence: *the film omitted the* **blood and gore** *in order to avoid controversy.* ▷Old English *gor* 'dung, dirt,' of Germanic origin; related to Dutch *goor*, Swedish *gorr* 'muck, filth.' The current sense dates from the mid 16th cent.

gore[2] ▸*v.* [*trans.*] (of an animal such as a bull) pierce or stab with a horn or tusk. ▷late Middle English (in the sense 'stab, pierce'): of unknown origin.

gore[3] ▸*n.* a triangular or tapering piece of material used in making a garment, sail, or umbrella. ■ a small, triangular piece of land, esp. one lying in the fork of a road.

▸*v.* [*trans.*] make with a gore-shaped piece of material: [as *adj.*] (**gored**) *a gored skirt.* ▷Old English *gāra* 'triangular piece of land,' of Germanic origin; related to Dutch *geer* and German *Gehre*, also probably to Old English *gār* 'spear' (a spear-head being triangular).

gore[3]

Gó·rec·ki /gə'retskē/, Henryk (Mikołaj) (1933–), Polish composer. His works include the Third Symphony (1976), known as the *Symphony of Sorrowful Songs*.

Gö·re·me /,gœrā'mā/ a valley in Cappadocia in central Turkey, noted for its cave dwellings hollowed out of soft tufa rock. In the Byzantine era, these caves contained hermits' cells, monasteries, and more than 400 churches.

Gore-Tex /'gôr ,teks/ ▸*n. trademark* a synthetic waterproof fabric permeable to air and water vapor, used in outdoor and sports clothing.

gorge /gôrj/ ▸*n.* **1** a narrow valley between hills or mountains, typically with steep rocky walls and a stream running through it. **2** *archaic* the throat. ■ the contents of the stomach. **3** *Architecture* the neck of a bastion or other outwork; the rear entrance to a fortification. **4** a mass of ice obstructing a narrow passage, esp. a river.

▸*v.* [*intrans.*] eat a large amount greedily; fill oneself with food: *the river comes alive during March when fish* **gorge on** *caddisworms | we used to go to all the little restaurants there and* **gorge ourselves**. ▷Middle English (as a verb): from Old French *gorger*, from *gorge* 'throat,' based on Latin *gurges* 'whirlpool.' The noun originally meant 'throat' and is from Old French *gorge*; sense 1 dates from the mid 18th cent. **—gorg·er** *n.*

▸*PHRASE* □ **one's gorge rises** one is sickened or disgusted: *looking at it, Wendy felt her gorge rise.*

gorged /gôrjd/ ▸*adj.* [*postpositive*] *Heraldry* having the neck encircled by a coronet or collar, esp. of a specified tincture. ▷early 17th cent.: from French *gorge* 'throat' + **-ED**[1].

gor·geous /'gôrjəs/ ▸*adj.* beautiful; very attractive: *gorgeous colors and exquisite decoration.* ■ *informal* very pleasant: *a short but gorgeous hot summer.* ▷late 15th cent. (describing sumptuous clothing): from Old French *gorgias* 'fine, elegant,' of unknown origin. **—gor·geous·ly** *adv.* **—gor·geous·ness** *n.*

gor·get /'gôrjit/ ▸*n.* **1** *historical* an article of clothing that covered the throat. ■ a piece of armor for the throat. ■ a wimple. **2** a patch of color on the throat of a bird or other animal, esp. a hummingbird. ▷late Middle English (denoting a piece of armor protecting the throat): from Old French *gorgete*, from *gorge* 'throat' (see **GORGE**).

gor·gio /'gôrjēō/ ▸*n.* (*pl.* **-gios**) the gypsy name for a nongypsy. ▷from Romany *gorjo*.

Gor·gon /'gôrgən/ (also **gor·gon**) ▸*n. Greek Mythology* each of three sisters, Stheno, Euryale, and Medusa, with snakes for hair, who had the power to turn anyone who looked at them to stone. ■ a fierce, frightening, or repulsive woman. ▷via Latin from Greek *Gorgō*, from *gorgos* 'terrible.'

gor·go·nei·on /,gôrgə'nēän/ ▸*n.* (*pl.* **-nei·a** /-'nēə/) a representation of a Gorgon's head. ▷Greek, neuter of *gorgoneios* 'of or relating to a Gorgon' (see **GORGON**).

gor·go·ni·an /gôr'gōnēən/ *Zoology* ▸*n.* a colonial coral of an order distinguished by a horny, treelike skeleton, including the sea fans and precious red coral. Also called **HORNY CORAL.** • Order Gorgonacea, class Anthozoa.

▸*adj.* of or relating to Gorgons or gorgonians. ▷mid 19th cent.: from modern Latin *Gorgonia*, from Latin *Gorgo* (see **GORGON**), with reference to its petrifaction, + **-AN.**

Gor·gon·zo·la /,gôrgən'zōlə/ ▸*n.* a type of rich, strong-flavored Italian cheese with bluish-green veins. ▷named after *Gorgonzola*, a village in northern Italy, where it was originally made.

go·ril·la /gə'rilə/ ▸*n.* a powerfully built great ape with a large head and short neck, found in the forests of central Africa. It is the largest living primate. • *Gorilla gorilla*, family Pongidae: three races (two **lowland gorillas** and the **mountain gorilla**). ■ *informal* a heavily built, aggressive-looking man. ▷from an alleged African word for a wild or hairy person, found in the Greek account of the voyage of the Carthaginian explorer Hanno in the 5th or 6th cent. BC; adopted in 1847 as the specific name of the ape.

mountain gorilla

Gor·ky[1] /'gôrkē/ former name (1932–91) for **NIZHNI NOVGOROD.**

Gor·ky[2], Arshile (1904–48), U.S. painter; born in Turkey. An exponent of abstract expressionism, he is best known for his work of the early 1940s, such as *Waterfall* (1943).

Gor·ky[3], Maxim (1868–1936), Russian writer and revolutionary; pseudonym of *Aleksei Maksimovich Peshkov*. After the Russian Revolution, he was proclaimed the founder of the new, officially sanctioned socialist realism. Notable works: *The Lower Depths* (1901) and an autobiographical trilogy (1915–23).

Gor·lov·ka /gôr'läfkə/ Russian name for **HORLIVKA**

gor·mand·ize ▸*v.* variant spelling of **GOURMANDIZE. —gor·mand·iz·er** *n.*

Gor·no-Al·tai /'gôrnə äl'tī/ an autonomous republic in south central Russia, on the border with Mongolia; pop. 192,000; capital, Gorno-Altaisk.

gorp /gôrp/ ▸*n. informal* another term for **TRAIL MIX.**

gorse /gôrs/ ▸*n.* a yellow-flowered shrub of the pea family, the leaves of which are modified to form spines, native to western Europe and North Africa. • Genus *Ulex*, family Leguminosae: several species, in particular the very spiny *U. europaeus*, which was introduced to North America. ▷Old English *gors*, *gorst*, from an Indo-European root meaning 'rough, prickly,' shared by German *Gerste* and Latin *hordeum* 'barley.' **—gors·y** *adj.*

gor·y /'gôrē/ ▸*adj.* (**gor·i·er**, **gor·i·est**) involving or showing violence and bloodshed: *a gory horror film.* ■ covered in blood. **—gor·i·ly** /-rəlē/ *adv.* **—gor·i·ness** *n.*

▸*PHRASE* □ **the gory details** *humorous* the explicit details of something: *she told him the gory details of her past.*

gosh /gäsн/ ▸*exclam. informal* used to express surprise or give emphasis: *gosh, we envy you.* ■ used as a euphemism for "God": *a gosh-awful team.* ▷mid 18th cent.: euphemism for **GOD.**

gos·hawk /'gäs,hôk/ ▸*n.* a large, short-winged hawk resembling a large sparrow hawk. • Genus *Accipiter*, family Accipitridae: several species, in particular the **northern goshawk** (*A. gentilis*) of Eurasia and North America. ▷Old English *gōshafoc*, from *gōs* 'goose' + *hafoc* 'hawk.'

gosht /gōsнt/ ▸*n. Indian* red meat (beef, lamb, or mutton): [as *adj.*] *gosht biryani.* ▷from Hindi *gośt*.

gos·ling /'gäzliNG/ ▸*n.* a young goose. ▷Middle English (originally *gesling*): from Old Norse *gæslingr*, from *gás* 'goose' + **-LING**, later altered by association with **GOOSE.**

go-slow ▸*adj.* (of a proposal or course of action) cautious and prudent: *a go-slow policy for the building of nuclear plants.*

▸*n. chiefly Brit.* a strategy or tactic, esp. a form of protest, in which work or progress is delayed or slowed down: *a reported go-slow by mechanics.*

go south ▸*v. phrase* (**goes south, go·ing south;** *past* **went south** *past part* **gone south**) *informal* fall in value, deteriorate, or fail: *my stock portfolio hasn't exactly gone south, but it's seen better days | don't drink that milk—it went south a few days ago.*

gos·pel /'gäspəl/ ▸*n.* **1** the teaching or revelation of Christ: *it is the Church's mission to preach the gospel.* ■ (also **gospel truth**) a thing that is absolutely true: *they say it's sold out, but don't take that as gospel.* ■ a set of principles or beliefs: *the new economics unit has produced what it reckons to be the approved gospel.* **2** (**Gospel**) the record of Jesus' life and teaching in the first four books of the New Testament. ■ each of these books. ■ a portion from one of these read at a church service.

The four Gospels ascribed to St. Matthew, St. Mark, St. Luke, and St. John all give an account of the ministry, crucifixion, and resurrection of Christ, although the Gospel of John differs greatly from the other three. There are also several later, apocryphal accounts that are recorded as Gospels.

3 (also **gospel music**) a fervent style of black American evangelical religious singing, developed from spirituals sung in Southern Baptist and Pentecostal churches: [as *adj.*] *gospel singers.* ▷Old English *gōdspel*, from *gōd* 'good' + *spel* 'news, a story' (see **SPELL**[2]), translating ecclesiastical Latin *bona annuntiatio* or *bonus nuntius*, used to gloss ecclesiastical Latin *evangelium*, from Greek *euangelion* 'good news' (see **EVANGEL**); after the vowel was shortened in Old English, the first syllable was mistaken for *god* 'God.'

gos·pel·er /'gäspələr/ (*Brit.* **gos·peller**) ▸*n.* a person who zealously teaches or professes faith in the gospel. ■ (in church use) the reader of the Gospel in a Communion service.

gos·pel·ize /'gäspə,līz/ ▸*v.* **1** [*trans.*] *rare* preach the Gospel to; convert to Christianity. **2** convert (a piece of music) to the style of gospel music: *she gospelizes the hymn "Let There Be Peace."*

Gos·pel side ▸*n.* (in a church) the north side of the altar, at which the Gospel is read.

gos·sa·mer /'gäsəmər/ ▸*n.* a fine, filmy substance consisting of cobwebs spun by small spiders, which is seen esp. in autumn. ■ used to refer to something very light, thin, and insubstantial or delicate: *in the light from the table lamp, his hair was blond gossamer.*

▸*adj.* [*attrib.*] made of or resembling gossamer: *gossamer wings.* ▷Middle English: apparently from **GOOSE** + **SUMMER**[1], perhaps from the time of year around St. Martin's summer, i.e., early November, when geese were eaten (gossamer being common then). **—gos·sa·mer·y** *adj.*

gos·san /'gäsən; 'gäz-/ ▸*n. Geology & Mining* an iron-containing secondary deposit, largely consisting of oxides and typically yellowish or reddish, occurring above a deposit of a metallic ore. ▷late 18th cent.: of unknown origin.

gos·sip /'gäsəp/ ▸*n.* casual or unconstrained conversation or reports about other people, typically involving details that are not confirmed as being true: *he became the subject of much local gossip.* ■ *chiefly derogatory* a person who likes talking about other people's private lives.

▸*v.* (**-siped, -sip·ing**) [*intrans.*] engage in gossip: *they would start* **gossiping about** *her as soon as she left.* ▷late Old English *godsibb* 'godfather, godmother, baptismal sponsor,' literally 'a person related to one in God,' from *god* 'God' + *sibb* 'a relative' (see **SIB**). In Middle English the sense was 'a close friend, a person with whom one gossips,' hence 'a person who gossips,' later (early 19th cent.) 'idle talk' (from the verb, which dates from the early 17th cent.). **—gos·sip·er** *n.* **—gos·sip·y** *adj.*

gos·sip col·umn ▸*n.* a section of a newspaper devoted to gossip about well-known people. **—gos·sip col·um·nist** *n.*

gos·sip·mon·ger /'gäsəp,məNGgər; -,mäNG-/ ▸*n. derogatory* a person who habitually passes on confidential information or spreads rumors.

gos·soon /gä'so͞on/ ▸*n. Irish* a lad. ▷late 17th cent.: from French *garçon* 'boy.'

gos·sy·pol /'gäsə,pôl; -,päl/ ▸*n. Chemistry* a toxic crystalline compound present in cottonseed oil. • A polycyclic phenol; chem. formula: $C_{30}H_{30}O_8$. ▷late 19th cent.: from modern Latin *Gossypium* (genus name), from Latin *gossypinum*, *-pion* 'cotton plant' (of unknown origin) + **-OL.**

got /gät/ ▸ past and past participle of **GET.**

USAGE See usage at **GOTTEN.**

got·cha /'gäcнə/ *informal* ▸*exclam.* I have got you (used to express satisfaction at having captured or defeated someone or uncovered their faults).

▸*n.* an instance of publicly tricking someone or exposing them to ridicule, esp. by means of an elaborate deception. ▷1930s: representing a pronunciation.

go-team ▸*n.* a group of investigators who can be dispatched immediately to investigate accidents, attacks, and the like: *a go-team from the National Transportation Safety Board is en route to the scene.*

Gö·te·borg /ˈyœtəˌbôr(yə)/ Swedish name of GOTHENBURG.

Goth /gäTH/ ▸*n.* **1** a member of a Germanic people that invaded the Roman Empire from the east between the 3rd and 5th centuries. The eastern division, the Ostrogoths, founded a kingdom in Italy, while the Visigoths went on to found one in Spain. **2** (**goth**) a style of rock music derived from punk, typically with apocalyptic or mystical lyrics. ■ a member of a subculture favoring black clothing, white and black makeup, and goth music. ▷Old English *Gota*, superseded in Middle English by the adoption of late Latin *Gothi* (plural), from Greek *Gothoi*, from Gothic *Gutthiuda* 'the Gothic people.'

Goth. ▸*abbr.* Gothic.

Go·tham /ˈgäTHəm/ a nickname for New York City, used originally by Washington Irving and now associated with the Batman stories.

Goth·en·burg /ˈgäTHənˌbərg/ a seaport in southwestern Sweden, on the Kattegat strait; pop. 433,000. It is the second largest city in Sweden. Swedish name GÖTEBORG.

Goth·ic /ˈgäTHik/ ▸*adj.* **1** of or relating to the Goths or their extinct East Germanic language, which provides the earliest manuscript evidence of any Germanic language (4th–6th centuries AD). **2** of or in the style of architecture prevalent in western Europe in the 12th–16th centuries, characterized by pointed arches, rib vaults, and flying buttresses, together with large windows and elaborate tracery. **3** (also *pseudoarchaic* **Gothick**) belonging to or redolent of the Dark Ages; portentously gloomy or horrifying: *19th-century Gothic horror.* **4** (of lettering) of or derived from the angular style of handwriting with broad vertical downstrokes used in western Europe from the 13th century, including Fraktur and black-letter typefaces. **5** (**gothic**) of or relating to goths or their rock music.
▸*n.* **1** the language of the Goths. **2** the Gothic style of architecture. **3** Gothic type. ▷from French *gothique* or late Latin *gothicus*, from *Gothi* (see GOTH). It was used in the 17th and 18th centuries to mean 'not classical' (i.e., not Greek or Roman), and hence to refer to medieval architecture that did not follow classical models (sense 2) and a typeface based on medieval handwriting (sense 4). **—Goth·i·cal·ly** /-ik(ə)lē/ *adv.* **—Goth·i·cism** /ˈgäTHəˌsizəm/ *n.*

goth·ic nov·el ▸*n.* an English genre of fiction popular in the 18th to early 19th centuries, characterized by an atmosphere of mystery and horror and having a pseudomedieval setting.

Got·land /ˈgätˌland; ˈgôtˌlänt/ an island and province of Sweden, in the Baltic Sea; pop. 57,000

go-to guy /ˈgō ˈto͞o/ ▸*n. informal* a person who can be relied upon for help or support: *a relentlessly hands-on manager who is the go-to guy for any issues related to the 17-day festival.* ■ *Sports* a member of a sports team who can be relied on to score points if given the opportunity.

got·ta /ˈgätə/ ▸*contraction of* have got to (not acceptable in standard use): *you gotta be careful.*

got·ten /ˈgätn/ ▸ past participle of GET.

USAGE As past participles of **get**, the words **got** and **gotten** both date back to Middle English. In North American English, **got** and **gotten** are not identical in use. **Gotten** usually implies the process of obtaining something (*he has* **gotten** *two tickets for the show*, while **got** implies the state of possession or ownership (*he hasn't* **got** *any money*).

Göt·ter·däm·mer·ung /ˌgätərˈdaməro͞oNG/ (in Germanic mythology) the downfall of the gods. ▷German, literally 'twilight of the gods,' popularized by Wagner's use of the word as the title of the last opera of the Ring cycle.

Göt·ting·en /ˈgœtiNGən/ a town in northern central Germany, on the Leine River; pop. 124,000. It is noted for its university.

gouache /gwäSH; go͞oˈäSH/ ▸*n.* a method of painting using opaque pigments ground in water and thickened with a gluelike substance. ■ paint of this kind; opaque watercolor. ■ a picture painted in this way. ▷late 19th cent.: French, from Italian *guazzo.*

Gou·da /ˈgo͞odə/ ▸*n.* a flat round cheese with a yellow rind, originally made in the town of Gouda in the Netherlands.

gouge /gouj/ ▸*n.* **1** a chisel with a concave blade, used in carpentry, sculpture, and surgery. **2** an indentation or groove made by gouging.
▸*v.* [*trans.*] **1** make (a groove, hole, or indentation) with or as if with a gouge: *the channel had been gouged out by the ebbing water.* ■ make a rough hole or indentation in (a surface), esp. so as to mar or disfigure it: *he had wielded the blade inexpertly, gouging the grass in several places.* ■ (**gouge something out**) cut or force something out roughly or brutally: *one of his eyes had been gouged out.* **2** *informal* overcharge; swindle: *the airline ends up gouging the very passengers it is supposed to assist.* ▷late Middle English: from Old French, from late Latin *gubia, gulbia*, perhaps of Celtic origin; compare with Old Irish *gulba* 'beak' and Welsh *gylf* 'beak, pointed instrument.' **—goug·er** *n.*

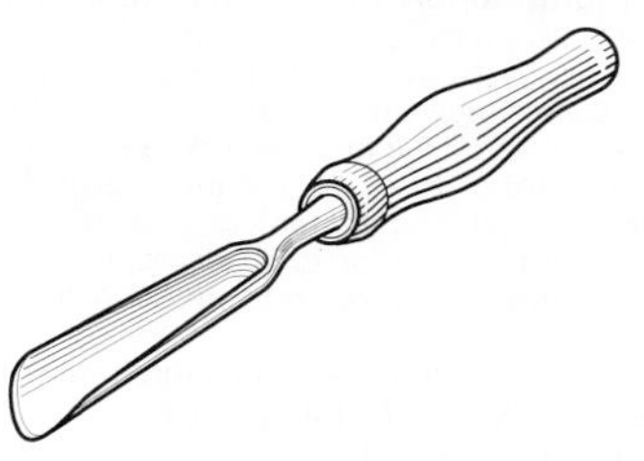

gouge 1

gou·gère /go͞oˈZHe(ə)r/ ▸*n.* a puff of choux pastry flavored with cheese (usually Gruyère), often stuffed with a savory filling. ▷French.

gou·lash /ˈgo͞oˌläSH/ ▸*n.* **1** a highly seasoned Hungarian soup or stew of meat and vegetables, flavored with paprika. **2** (in informal bridge) a redealing of the four hands (unshuffled, with each hand arranged in suits and order of value) after no player has bid. The cards are usually dealt in batches of five, five, and three, and the resulting hands may have very uneven distributions. ▷from Hungarian *gulyás-hús*, from *gulyás* 'herdsman' + *hús* 'meat'; sense 2 (dating from the 1920s) is an extended use.

Gould[1] /go͞old/, Glenn (Herbert) (1932–82), Canadian pianist and composer. Best known for his performances of works by Bach, he retired from the concert platform in 1964 to concentrate on recording and broadcasting.

Gould[2], Jay (1836–92) U.S. financier. With James Fisk and Daniel Drew 1797–1879, he gained control of the Erie Railroad in 1868 through stock manipulation. With Fisk, he attempted to corner the gold market, an effort that created the Black Friday panic on September 24, 1869.

Gould[3], Stephen Jay (1941–2002), U.S. paleontologist. A noted popularizer of science, he studied modifications of Darwinian evolutionary theory, proposed the concept of punctuated equilibrium, and wrote on the social context of scientific theory. Notable works: *Ever Since Darwin* (1977), *Bully for Brontosaurus* (1992), *The Lying Stones of Marrakesh: Penultimate Reflections in Natural History* (2000), and *The Structure of Evolutionary Theory* (2002).

Gou·nod /go͞oˈnō/, Charles François (1818–93), French composer, conductor, and organist. He is best known for his opera *Faust* (1859).

gou·ra·mi /go͞oˈrämē/ ▸*n.* (*pl.* same or **-mis**) a small, brightly colored Asian labyrinth fish, popular in aquariums. It builds a nest of bubbles, which is typically guarded by the male. • Belontiidae and related families: several species. ▷late 19th cent.: from Malay *gurami.*

gourd /gôrd; go͝ord/ ▸*n.* **1** a fleshy, typically large fruit with a hard skin, some varieties of which are edible. ■ a drinking container, water container, or ornament made from the hard hollowed and dried skin of this fruit. **2** a climbing or trailing plant that bears this fruit. • Family Cucurbitaceae (the **gourd family**): several genera and species, including the colored **ornamental gourds** (*Cucurbita pepo* var. *ovifera*). The gourd family also includes the marrows, squashes, pumpkins, melons, and cucumbers. ▷Middle English: from Old French *gourde*, based on Latin *cucurbita.* **—gourd·ful** /-ˌfo͝ol/ *n.* (*pl.* **-fuls**).
▸*PHRASE* □ **out of one's gourd** *informal* out of one's mind; crazy. ■ under the influence or alcohol or drugs: *he was obviously stoned out of his gourd.*

gourde /go͝ord/ ▸*n.* the basic monetary unit of Haiti, equal to 100 centimes. ▷the Franco-American name for a dollar.

gour·mand /go͝orˈmänd/ ▸*n.* a person who enjoys eating and often eats too much. ■ a connoisseur of good food. See **usage** below. ▷late Middle English: from Old French, of unknown origin. **—gour·man·dism** /ˈgo͝orm ənˌdizəm/ *n.*

USAGE The words **gourmand** and **gourmet** overlap in meaning but are not identical. Both mean 'a connoisseur of good food,' but **gourmand** more usually means 'a person who enjoys eating and often overeats.'

gour·man·dize /ˈgo͝orm ənˌdīz/ ▸*v.* [*intrans.*] indulge in good eating; eat greedily.
▸*n.* the action of indulging in or being a connoisseur of good eating. ▷late Middle English (as a noun): from French *gourmandise*, from *gourmand*; the verb dates from the mid 16th cent.

gour·met /ˌgôrˈmā; ˌgo͝or-/ ▸*n.* a connoisseur of good food; a person with a discerning palate. ■ [as *adj.*] of a kind or standard suitable for a gourmet: *a gourmet meal.* ▷early 19th cent.: French, originally meaning 'wine taster,' influenced by GOURMAND.

USAGE On the distinction between **gourmet** and **gourmand**, see usage at GOURMAND.

gout /gout/ ▸*n.* **1** a disease in which defective metabolism of uric acid causes arthritis, esp. in the smaller bones of the feet, deposition of chalkstones, and episodes of acute pain. **2** *poetic/literary* a drop or spot, esp. of blood, smoke, or flame: *gouts of flame and phlegm.* ▷Middle English: from Old French *goute*, from medieval Latin *gutta*, literally 'drop' (because gout was believed to be caused by the dropping of diseased matter from the blood into the joints). **—gout·i·ness** /-tēnis/ *n.* **—gout·y** *adj.*

gout·weed /ˈgoutˌwēd/ ▸*n.* ground elder, which was formerly used to treat gout.

gov. ▸*abbr.* ■ government. ■ governor.

gov·ern /ˈgəvərn/ ▸*v.* [*trans.*] **1** conduct the policy, actions, and affairs of (a state, organization, or people): *he was incapable of governing the country* | [as *adj.*] (**governing**) *the governing coalition.* ■ control, influence, or regulate (a person, action, or course of events): *the future of Jamaica will be governed by geography, not history.* ■ (**govern oneself**) conduct oneself, esp. with regard to controlling one's emotions: *the rabbinic system that delineates how a devout Jew governs himself.* ■ regulate the speed of (a motor or engine) by a governor. **2** constitute a law, rule, standard, or principle for: *constant principles govern the poetic experience.* ■ serve to decide (a legal case). **3** *Grammar* (of a word) require that (another word or group of words) be in a particular case: *the Latin preposition "cum" governs nouns in the ablative.* **4** regulate the speed of (a motor or machine) with a governor. ▷Middle English: from Old French *governer*, from Latin *gubernare* 'to steer, rule,' from Greek *kubernan* 'to steer.' **—gov·ern·a·bil·i·ty** /ˌgəvərnəˈbilitē/ *n.* **—gov·ern·a·ble** *adj.*

gov·ern·ance /ˈgəvərnəns/ ▸*n.* the action or manner of governing: *a more responsive system of governance will be required.* ■ *archaic* sway; control: *what, shall King Henry be a pupil still,* **under** *the surly Gloucester's governance?* ▷Middle English: from Old French, from *governer* (see GOVERN).

gov·ern·ess /ˈgəvərnis/ ▸*n.* a woman employed to teach children in a private household. ▷Middle English (originally *governeress*, denoting a female ruler): from Old French *governeresse*, feminine of *governeour* 'governor,' from Latin *gubernator*, from *gubernare* (see GOVERN).

gov·ern·ing bod·y ▸*n.* a group of people who formulate the policy and direct the affairs of an institution in partnership with the managers, esp. on a voluntary or part-time basis: *the school's governing body.*

gov·ern·ment /ˈgəvər(n)mənt/ ▸*n.* **1** [treated as *sing.* or *pl.*] the governing body of a nation, state, or community: *an agency of the federal government* | [as *adj.*] *government controls.* ■ the system by which a nation, state, or community is governed: *a secular, pluralistic, democratic government.* ■ the action or manner of controlling or regulating a nation, organization, or people: *rules for the government of the infirmary.* ■ the group of persons in office at a particular time; administration: *the election of the new government.* ■ another term for POLITICAL SCIENCE. ■ (governments) all bonds issued by the U.S. Treasury or other federal agencies. **2** *Grammar* the relation between a governed and a governing word. ▷Middle English: from Old French *governement*, from *governer* (see GOVERN). **—gov·ern·men·tal** /ˌgəvər(n)ˈmentl/ *adj.* **—gov·ern·men·tal·ly** /ˌgəvər(n)ˈmentl-ē/ *adv.*

Pronunciation Key ə *ago*; ər *over*; ˈə *or* ˌə *up*; ˈər *or* ˌər *fur*; a *hat*; ā *rate*; ä *car*; CH *chew*; e *let*; ē *see*; e(ə)r *air*; i *fit*; ī *by*; i(ə)r *ear*; NG *sing*; ō *go*; ô *for*; oi *boy*; o͝o *good*; o͞o *goo*; ou *out*; SH *she*; TH *thin*; TH *then*; (h)w *why*; ZH *vision*

Gov·ern·ment House ▶*n. Brit.* the official residence of a governor, esp. in a colony or Commonwealth state that regards the British monarch as head of state.

gov·ern·ment-is·sue ▶*adj.* (of equipment) provided by the government.

gov·ern·ment se·cu·ri·ties ▶*plural n.* bonds or other promissory certificates issued by the government.

gov·ern·ment sur·plus ▶*n.* unused equipment sold by the government.

gov·ern·ment·wide /ˈgəvər(n)mənt,wīd/ ▶*adj. & adv.* affecting or involving all areas and departments of government: *a governmentwide program to determine if work in the nation's forests could be done better by private contractors.*

gov·er·nor /ˈgəvə(r)nər/ ▶*n.* **1** the elected executive head of a state of the U.S. ■ an official appointed to govern a town or region. ■ the representative of the British Crown in a colony or in a Commonwealth state that regards the monarch as head of state. **2** *Brit.* the head of a public institution: *the governor of the Bank of England.* ■ a member of a governing body. **3** *Brit., informal* the person in authority; one's employer. **4** a device automatically regulating the supply of fuel, steam, or water to a machine, ensuring uniform motion or limiting speed. ▷Middle English: from Old French *governeour,* from Latin *gubernator,* from *gubernare* (see GOVERN). **—gov·er·nor·ship** /-,SHip/ *n.*

gov·er·nor gen·er·al ▶*n.* (*pl.* **gov·er·nors gen·er·al**) the chief representative of the Crown in a Commonwealth country of which the British monarch is head of state. ■ *chiefly historical* an analogous representative of another Crown.

govt. ▶*abbr.* government: *local govt.*

gow·an /ˈgouən/ ▶*n. Scottish & N. English* a wild white or yellow flower, esp. a daisy. ▷mid 16th cent.: probably a variant of dialect *gollan,* denoting various yellow-flowered plants, perhaps related to Old English *golde* 'marigold.'

gowk /gouk/ ▶*n. Brit. dialect* **1** an awkward or foolish person (often as a general term of abuse). **2** a cuckoo. ▷Middle English (sense 2): from Old Norse *gaukr.*

gown /goun/ ▶*n.* a long dress, typically having a close-fitting bodice and a flared or flowing skirt, worn on formal occasions: *a silk ball gown.* ■ a nightgown. ■ a dressing gown. ■ a protective garment worn in a hospital, either by a staff member during surgery or by a patient. ■ a loose cloak indicating one's profession or status, worn by a lawyer, teacher, academic, or college. ■ the members of a college as distinct from the permanent residents of the college town: *efforts are underway to improve town-gown relations.* Often contrasted with TOWN.

▶*v.* (**be gowned**) be dressed in a gown: *she was gowned in luminous silk.* ▷Middle English: from Old French *goune,* from late Latin *gunna* 'fur garment'; probably related to Byzantine Greek *gouna* 'fur, fur-lined garment.'

Go·won /ˈgōwən/, Yakubu (1934–), Nigerian general and statesman, head of state 1966–75.

goy /goi/ ▶*n.* (*pl.* **goy·im** /ˈgoi-im/ or **goys**) *informal, often offensive* a Jewish name for a non-Jew. ▷from Hebrew *gōy* 'people, nation.' **—goy·ish** *adj.*

Go·ya /ˈgoiə/ (1746–1828), Spanish painter and etcher; full name *Francisco José de Goya y Lucientes.* He is known for his works concerning the French occupation of Spain 1808–14, including *The Shootings of May 3rd 1808* (1814) and *The Disasters of War* (1810–14), depicting the cruelty and horror of war.

Go·zo /ˈgōzō/ an island in northwest Malta, to the northwest of the main island of Malta.

GP ▶*abbr.* ■ general practitioner: *talk over any worries with your GP.*

GPA ▶*abbr.* grade point average.

g.p.d. (also **GPD** or **gpd**) ▶*abbr.* gallons per day.

gph ▶*abbr.* gallons per hour.

gpm ▶*abbr.* gallons per minute.

GPO ▶*abbr.* ■ general post office. ■ Government Printing Office.

GPRS ▶*abbr.* general packet radio services, a technology for radio transmission of small packets of data, especially between cellular phones and the Internet.

GPS ▶*abbr.* Global Positioning System, an accurate worldwide navigational and surveying facility based on the reception of signals from an array of orbiting satellites.

g.p.s. (also **GPS** or **gps**) ▶*abbr.* gallons per second.

GPU a Soviet secret police agency 1922–23. See also OGPU. ▷abbreviation of Russian *Gosudarstvennoe politicheskoe upravlenie* 'State Political Directorate.'

GQ ▶*abbr.* general quarters.

gr (also **gr.**) ▶*abbr.* ■ grain(s). ■ gram(s). ■ gray. ■ gross.

Graaf·i·an fol·li·cle /ˈgräfēən/ ▶*n. Physiology* a fluid-filled structure in the mammalian ovary within which an ovum develops before ovulation. ▷mid 19th cent.: named after R. de *Graaf* (1641–73), Dutch anatomist.

grab /grab/ ▶*v.* (**grabbed, grab·bing**) [*trans.*] **1** grasp or seize suddenly and roughly: *she grabbed him by the shirt collar | she grabbed her keys and rushed out.* ■ [*intrans.*] (**grab at/for**) make a sudden snatch at: *he grabbed at the handle, missed, and nearly fell.* ■ *informal* obtain or get (something) quickly or opportunistically, sometimes unscrupulously: *I'll grab another drink while there's still time | someone's grabbed my seat.* ■ [*intrans.*] (of a brake on a vehicle) grip the wheel harshly or jerkily: *the brakes grabbed very badly.* **2** [usu. with *negative* or in *questions*] *informal* attract the attention of; make an impression on: *how does that grab you?*

▶*n.* **1** [in *sing.*] a quick, sudden clutch or attempt to seize: *he **made a grab at** the pistol.* ■ an act of obtaining something opportunistically or unscrupulously: *they used the law to effect a land grab.* **2** a mechanical device for clutching, lifting, and moving things, esp. materials in bulk. ■ [as *adj.*] denoting a bar or strap for people to hold on to for support or in a moving vehicle: *for elderly people, grab rails at strategic places are likely to prevent accidents.* **3** [usu. with *modifier*] *Computing* a frame of video or television footage, digitized and stored as a still image in a computer memory for subsequent display, printing, or editing: *a screen grab from Wednesday's program.* ▷late 16th cent.: from Middle Low German and Middle Dutch *grabben;* perhaps related to GRIP, GRIPE, and GROPE. **—grab·ber** *n.*

▶*PHRASE* □ **up for grabs** *informal* available; obtainable: *great prizes up for grabs.*

grab bag ▶*n.* a container from which a person chooses a wrapped item at random, without knowing the contents. ■ an assortment of miscellaneous items.

grab·ble /ˈgrabəl/ ▶*v.* [*intrans.*] *archaic* feel or search with the hands; grope about. ■ sprawl or tumble on all fours. ▷late 16th cent.: probably from Dutch *grabbelen* 'scramble for a thing,' from Middle Dutch *grabben* (see GRAB).

grab·by /ˈgrabē/ ▶*adj.* (**-bi·er, -bi·est**) *informal* having or showing a selfish desire for something; greedy. ■ attracting attention; arousing people's interest: *a grabby angle on a news story.*

gra·ben /ˈgräbən/ ▶*n.* (*pl.* same or **gra·bens**) *Geology* an elongated block of the earth's crust lying between two faults and displaced downward relative to the blocks on either side, as in a rift valley. ▷late 19th cent.: from German *Graben* 'a ditch.'

grace /grās/ ▶*n.* **1** simple elegance or refinement of movement: *she moved through the water with effortless grace.* ■ courteous goodwill: *at least he has the grace to admit his debt to her.* ■ (**graces**) an attractively polite manner of behaving: *she has all **the social graces**.* **2** (in Christian belief) the free and unmerited favor of God, as manifested in the salvation of sinners and the bestowal of blessings. ■ a divinely given talent or blessing: *the graces of the Holy Spirit.* ■ the condition or fact of being favored by someone: *he fell from grace because of drug use at the Olympics.* **3** (also **grace period**) a period officially allowed for payment of a sum due or for compliance with a law or condition, esp. an extended period granted as a special favor: *another three days' grace.* **4** a short prayer of thanks said before or after a meal: *before dinner the Reverend Newman said grace.* **5** (**His, Her,** or **Your Grace**) used as forms of description or address for a duke, duchess, or archbishop: *His Grace, the Duke of Atholl.*

▶*v.* [*trans.*] do honor or credit to (someone or something) by one's presence: *she bowed out from the sport she has graced for two decades.* ■ [*trans.*] (of a person or thing) be an attractive presence in or on; adorn: *Ms. Pasco has graced the front pages of magazines like* Elle *and* Vogue. ▷Middle English: via Old French from Latin *gratia,* from *gratus* 'pleasing, thankful'; related to GRATEFUL.

▶*PHRASES* □ **be in someone's good** (or **bad**) **graces** be regarded by someone with favor (or disfavor). □ **there but for the grace of God (go I)** used to acknowledge one's good fortune in avoiding another's mistake or misfortune. □ **the (Three) Graces** *Greek Mythology* three beautiful goddesses (Aglaia, Thalia, and Euphrosyne), daughters of Zeus. They were believed to personify and bestow charm, grace, and beauty. □ **with good** (or **bad**) **grace** in a willing and happy (or reluctant and resentful) manner.

grace-and-fa·vor ▶*adj.* [*attrib.*] *Brit.* denoting accommodations occupied by permission of a sovereign or government.

grace·ful /ˈgrāsfəl/ ▶*adj.* having or showing grace or elegance: *she was a tall girl, slender and graceful.* **—grace·ful·ly** *adv.* **—grace·ful·ness** *n.*

grace·less /ˈgrāslis/ ▶*adj.* lacking grace, elegance, or charm. **—grace·less·ly** *adv.* **—grace·less·ness** *n.*

grace note ▶*n. Music* an extra note added as an embellishment and not essential to the harmony or melody.

Gra·cias a Di·os, Cape /ˈgräsyäs ä ˈdē-ōs/ a cape that forms the eastern end of the Mosquito Coast in Central America, on the border between Nicaragua and Honduras.

grac·ile /ˈgrasəl; ˈgras,īl/ ▶*adj. Anthropology* (of a hominid species) of slender build. ■ (of a person) slender or thin, esp. in a charming or attractive way. ▷early 17th cent.: from Latin *gracilis* 'slender.'

grac·i·lis /ˈgrasəlis/ (also **gracilis muscle**) ▶*n. Anatomy* a slender superficial muscle of the inner thigh. ▷early 17th cent.: from Latin, literally 'slender.'

gra·cil·i·ty /grəˈsilitē; grə-/ ▶*n. formal* **1** the state of being gracefully slender. **2** (with reference to a literary style) plain simplicity.

gra·ci·o·so /,gräSHēˈōsō; ,gräsē-/ ▶*n.* (*pl.* **-sos**) (in Spanish comedy) a buffoon or clown. ▷Spanish, literally 'gracious.'

gra·cious /ˈgrāSHəs/ ▶*adj.* **1** courteous, kind, and pleasant: *smiling and gracious in defeat.* ■ pleasantly indulgent, esp. toward an inferior. ■ elegant and tasteful, esp. as exhibiting wealth or high social status: *the British painter specialized in gracious Victorian interiors | gracious living.* **2** (in Christian belief) showing divine grace: *I am saved by God's gracious intervention on my behalf.* **3** *Brit.* a polite epithet used of royalty or their acts: *the accession of Her present gracious Majesty.*

▶*exclam.* expressing polite surprise. ▷Middle English: via Old French from Latin *gratiosus,* from *gratia* 'esteem, favor' (see GRACE). **—gra·cious·ly** *adv.* **—gra·cious·ness** *n.*

grack·le /ˈgrakəl/ ▶*n.* **1** a songbird of the American blackbird family, the male of which has shiny black plumage with a blue-green sheen. • Several genera and species, family Icteridae, in particular the **common grackle** (*Quiscalus quiscula*). **2** another term for an Asian mynah or starling, with mainly black plumage. • *Gracula* and other genera, family Sturnidae; **southern grackle** is another term for HILL MYNAH (see MYNAH). ▷late 18th cent.: from modern Latin *Gracula,* from Latin *graculus* 'jackdaw.'

grad[1] /grad/ ▶*n.* informal term for GRADUATE.

grad. ▶*abbr.* ■ gradient. ■ graduate. ■ graduated.

grad·a·ble /ˈgrādəbəl/ ▶*adj. Grammar* denoting an adjective that can be used in the comparative and superlative and take a submodifier. Contrasted with CLASSIFYING. **—grad·a·bil·i·ty** /,grādəˈbilitē/ *n.*

gra·date /ˈgrādāt/ ▶*v.* pass or cause to pass by gradations from one shade of color to another: [*intrans.*] *the black background gradated toward a dark purple.* ■ [*trans.*] arrange in steps or grades of size, amount, or quality: [as *adj.*] (**gradated**) *the Temple compound became a series of concentric circles of gradated purity.* ▷mid 18th cent.: back-formation from GRADATION.

gra·da·tion /grāˈdāSHən/ ▶*n.* a scale or a series of successive changes, stages, or degrees: *within the woodpecker family, there is a gradation of drilling ability.* ■ a stage or change in a such a scale or series: *minute gradations of distance.* ■ a minute change from one shade, tone, or color to another: *amorphous shapes in subtle gradations of green and blue.* ■ (in historical linguistics) another term for ABLAUT. ▷mid 16th cent.: from Latin *gradatio(n-),* based on *gradus* 'step.' **—gra·da·tion·al** /-SHənl/ *adj.* **—gra·da·tion·al·ly** /-SHənl-ē/ *adv.*

grade /grād/ ▶*n.* **1** a particular level of rank, quality, proficiency, intensity, or value: *sea salt is usually available in coarse or fine grades.* ■ a level in a salary or employment structure. ■ a mark indicating the quality of a student's work: *I got good grades last semester.* ■ *Brit.* an examination, esp. in music: *I took grade five and got a distinction.* ■ (with specifying ordinal number) those students in a school or school system who are grouped by age or ability for teaching at a particular level for a year: *she teaches first grade.* ■ a level of quality or size for food or other products: *grade AA butter.* ■ (in historical linguistics) one in a series of related root forms exhibiting ablaut. ■ *Zoology* a group of animals at a similar evolutionary level. **2** a gradient or slope: *just over the crest of a long seven*

percent grade. **3** [usu. as *adj.*] a variety of cattle produced by crossing with a superior breed: *grade stock.*
▶*v.* [*trans.*] (usu. **be graded**) **1** arrange in or allocate to grades; class or sort: *they are graded according to thickness* | [as *adj.*] (**graded**) *carefully graded exercises.* ■ give a mark to (a student or a piece of work). **2** [*intrans.*] pass gradually from one level, esp. a shade of color, into another: *the sky graded from blue to white on the horizon.* **3** reduce (a road) to an easy gradient. **4** cross (livestock) with a superior breed. ▷early 16th cent.: from French, or from Latin *gradus* 'step.' Originally used as a unit of measurement of angles (a degree of arc), the term later referred to degrees of merit or quality.
▶*PHRASES* □ **at grade** on the same level: *the crossing at grade of two streets.* □ **make the grade** *informal* succeed; reach the desired standard.

grade cross·ing ▶*n.* a place where a railroad and a road, or two railroad lines, cross at the same level.

grade point ▶*n.* a numerical value assigned to a letter grade received in a course at a college or university, multiplied by the number of credits awarded for the course.

grade point av·er·age (abbr.: **GPA**) ▶*n.* an indication of a student's academic achievement at a college or university, calculated as the total number of grade points received over a given period divided by the total number of credits awarded.

grad·er /ˈgrādər/ ▶*n.* **1** a person or thing that grades. ■ a wheeled machine for leveling the ground, esp. in making roads. **2** [in *combination*] a student of a specified grade in a school: *first-grader.*

grade school ▶*n.* an elementary school. **—grade school·er** *n.* .

gra·di·ence /ˈgrādēəns/ ▶*n. Linguistics* the absence of a clear-cut boundary between one category and another, for example between *cup* and *mug* in semantics.

gra·di·ent /ˈgrādēənt/ ▶*n.* **1** an inclined part of a road or railway; a slope: *fail-safe brakes for use on steep gradients.* ■ the degree of such a slope: *the path becomes very rough as the gradient increases.* ■ *Mathematics* the degree of steepness of a graph at any point. **2** *Physics* an increase or decrease in the magnitude of a property (e.g., temperature, pressure, or concentration) observed in passing from one point or moment to another. ■ the rate of such a change. ■ *Mathematics* the vector formed by the operator ∇ acting on a scalar function at a given point in a scalar field. ▷mid 19th cent.: from **GRADE**, on the pattern of *salient.*

gra·dine /grəˈdēn/ (also **gra·din** /ˈgrādin/) ▶*n. archaic* a low step or ledge, esp. one at the back of an altar. ▷mid 19th cent.: from Italian *gradino*, diminutive of *grado* 'step.'

gra·di·om·e·ter /ˌgrādēˈämitər/ ▶*n.* a surveying instrument used for setting out or measuring the gradient of a slope. ■ *Physics* an instrument for measuring the gradient of an energy field, esp. the horizontal gradient of the earth's gravitational or magnetic field.

grad·u·al /ˈgrajo͞oəl/ ▶*adj.* taking place or progressing slowly or by degrees: *the gradual introduction of new methods.* ■ (of a slope) not steep or abrupt.
▶*n.* (in the Western Christian Church) a response sung or recited between the Epistle and Gospel in the Mass. ■ a book of plainsong for the Mass. ▷late Middle English: from medieval Latin *gradualis*, from Latin *gradus* 'step.' The original sense of the adjective was 'arranged in degrees'; the noun refers to the altar steps in a church, from which the antiphons were sung. **—grad·u·al·ly** *adv.* **—grad·u·al·ness** *n.*

grad·u·al·ism /ˈgrajo͞oəˌlizəm/ ▶*n.* a policy of gradual reform rather than sudden change or revolution. ■ *Biology* the hypothesis that evolution proceeds chiefly by the accumulation of gradual changes (in contrast to the punctuationist model). **—grad·u·al·ist** *n.* **—grad·u·al·is·tic** /ˌgrajəwəˈlistik/ *adj.*

grad·u·ate ▶*n.* /ˈgrajo͞oit/ **1** a person who has successfully completed a course of study or training, esp. a person who has been awarded an undergraduate academic degree. ■ a person who has received a high school diploma: *she is 19, a graduate of Lincoln High.* **2** a graduated cup, tube, flask, or measuring glass, used esp. by chemists and pharmacists.
▶*v.* /ˈgrajo͞oˌāt/ **1** [*intrans.*] successfully complete an academic degree, course of training, or high school: *I* **graduated from** *West Point in 1965.* ■ [*trans.*] *informal* receive an academic degree from: *she graduated college in 1970.* ■ [*trans.*] confer a degree or other academic qualification on: *the school graduated more than one hundred arts majors in its first year.* ■ (**graduate to**) move up to (a more advanced level or position): *he started with motorbikes but now he's graduated to his first car.* **2** [*trans.*] arrange in a series or according to a scale: [as *adj.*] (**graduated**) *a graduated tax.* ■ mark out (an instrument or container) in degrees or other proportionate divisions: *the stem was graduated with marks for each hour* [as *adj.*] *graduated cylinders.* **3** [*trans.*] change (something, typically color or shade) gradually or step by step: *the color is graduated from the middle of the frame to the top.*
▶*adj.* /ˈgrajo͞oit/ [*attrib.*] relating to graduate school education: *the graduate faculty.* ■ having graduated from a school or academic program: *a graduate electrical engineer.* ▷late Middle English: from medieval Latin *graduat-* 'graduated,' from *graduare* 'take a degree,' from Latin *gradus* 'degree, step.'

USAGE The traditional use is "be graduated from": *she will be graduated from medical school in June.* However, it is now more common to say "graduate from": *she will graduate from medical school in June.* The use of **graduate** as a transitive verb, as in *he graduated high school last week*, is increasingly common, especially in speech, but is considered incorrect by most traditionalists.

grad·u·ate school ▶*n.* a division of a university offering advanced programs beyond the bachelor's degree.

grad·u·a·tion /ˌgrajo͞oˈāsʜən/ ▶*n.* **1** the receiving or conferring of an academic degree or diploma. ■ the ceremony at which degrees are conferred. **2** the action of dividing into degrees or other proportionate divisions on a graduated scale. ■ a mark on a container or instrument indicating a degree of quantity.

gra·dus /ˈgrādəs/ ▶*n.* (*pl.* **-dus·es**) *historical* a manual of classical prosody formerly used in schools to help in writing Greek and Latin verse. ▷mid 18th cent.: Latin, from *Gradus ad Parnassum* 'Step(s) to Parnassus,' the title of one such manual.

Grae·cism ▶*n. chiefly Brit.* variant spelling of **GRECISM**.

Graeco- ▶*comb. form chiefly Brit.* variant spelling of **GRECO-**. ▷from Latin *Graecus* (see **GREEK**).

Grae·co-Ro·man ▶*adj. chiefly Brit.* variant spelling of **GRECO-ROMAN**.

Graf /graf/, Steffi (1969–), German tennis player; full name *Stephanie Graf.* She won the Grand Slam in 1988 and continued to win major tennis tournaments through the 1990s.

graf·fi·ti /grəˈfētē/ ▶*plural n.* (*sing.* **-to** /-tō/) [treated as *sing.* or *pl.*] writing or drawings scribbled, scratched, or sprayed illicitly on a wall or other surface in a public place: *the walls were covered with graffiti* | [as *adj.*] *a graffiti artist.*
▶*v.* [*trans.*] write or draw graffiti on (something): *he and another artist graffitied an entire train.* ■ write (words or drawings) as graffiti. ▷mid 19th cent.: from Italian (plural), from *graffio* 'a scratch.' **—graf·fi·tist** /-tist/ *n.*

USAGE In Italian, the word **graffiti** is a plural noun, and its singular form is **graffito**. Traditionally, the same distinction has been maintained in English, so that **graffiti**, being plural, would require a plural verb: *the* ***graffiti were*** *all over the wall.* By the same token, the singular would require a singular verb: *there* ***was*** *a* ***graffito*** *on the wall.* Today these distinctions survive in some specialist fields such as archaeology, but sound odd to most native speakers. The most common modern use is to treat **graffiti** as if it were a mass noun, similar to a word like **writing**, and not to use **graffito** at all. In this case, **graffiti** takes a singular verb, as in *the* ***graffiti was*** *all over the wall.* Such uses are now widely accepted as standard and may be regarded as part of the natural development of the language, rather than as mistakes. A similar process is going on with other words such as **agenda**, **data**, and **media**.

graft[1] /graft/ ▶*n.* **1** *Horticulture* a shoot or scion inserted into a slit of stock, from which it receives sap. ■ an instance of inserting a shoot or scion in this way. **2** *Medicine* a piece of living tissue that is transplanted surgically. ■ a surgical operation in which tissue is transplanted.
▶*v.* [*trans.*] **1** *Horticulture* insert (a scion) as a graft: *it was common to graft different varieties onto a single tree trunk.* ■ insert a graft on (a stock). **2** *Medicine* transplant (living tissue) as a graft: *they can graft a new hand onto the arm.* ■ *figurative* insert or fix (something) permanently to something else, typically in a way considered inappropriate: *western-style government could not easily be* ***grafted onto*** *a profoundly different country.* ▷late Middle English *graff*, from Old French *grafe*, via Latin from Greek *graphion* 'stylus, writing implement' (with reference to the tapered tip of the scion), from *graphein* 'write.' The final *-t* is typical of phonetic confusion between *-f* and *-ft* at the end of words; compare with **TUFT**.

graft[2] ▶*n.* practices, esp. bribery, used to secure illicit gains in politics or business; corruption: *sweeping measures to curb official graft.* ■ such gains: *government officials grow fat off bribes and graft.*
▶*v.* [*intrans.*] make money by shady or dishonest means. ▷mid 19th cent.: of unknown origin. **—graft·er** *n.*

graft[3] *Brit., informal* ▶*n.* hard work: *turning those dreams into reality was sheer hard graft.*
▶*v.* [*intrans.*] work hard: *I need people prepared to go out and graft.* ▷mid 19th cent.: perhaps related to the phrase *spade's graft* 'the amount of earth that one stroke of a spade will move,' based on Old Norse *groftr* 'digging.' **—graft·er** *n.*

graft·age /ˈgraftij/ ▶ *n. Horticulture* the practice, process, or technique of grafting.

graft un·ion ▶*n.* the point on a plant where the graft is joined to the rootstock.

Gra·ham[1] /gram; ˈgrāəm/, Billy (1918–), U.S. evangelical preacher and author; full name *William Franklin Graham.* A minister of the Southern Baptist Church, he is known for his large evangelistic crusades.

Gra·ham[2], Katherine Meyer (1917–2001), U.S. publisher. She was married to Philip Graham, who headed the communications empire started by her father that included *Newsweek* magazine and the *Washington Post.* She became the company's president upon her husband's death in 1963 and supported the reporting of Carl Bernstein and Bob Woodward that led to the exposure of the Watergate scandal.

Gra·ham[3], Martha (1893–1991), U.S. dancer, teacher, and choreographer. She evolved a new dance language using more flexible movements intended to express psychological complexities and emotional power.

Gra·ham[4], Otto (Everett, Jr.) (1921–), U.S. football player. A quarterback for the Cleveland Browns 1946–55, he led the team to the championship of the All–America Football Conference 1946–49 and then to the championship of the NFL 1950, 1954–55. Football Hall of Fame (1965).

gra·ham /gram; ˈgrāəm/ (also **Gra·ham**) ▶*adj.* [*attrib.*] denoting unbolted whole-wheat flour, or cookies or bread made from this: *a box of* ***graham crackers.*** ▷mid 19th cent.: named after Sylvester *Graham* (1794–1851), an American advocate of dietary reform.

Gra·hame /ˈgrāəm; gram/, Kenneth (1859–1932), Scottish writer; known for the children's classic *The Wind in the Willows* (1908).

Gra·ham Land /ˈgrāəm; gram/ the northern part of the Antarctic Peninsula, the only part of Antarctica that lies outside of the Antarctic Circle. Discovered in 1831–32 by English navigator John Biscoe (1794–1843), it now forms part of British Antarctic Territory, but is claimed also by Chile and Argentina.

Gra·ham's law *Chemistry* a law stating that the rates of diffusion and effusion of a gas are inversely proportional to the square root of the density of the gas. ▷mid 19th cent.: named after T. *Graham* (1805–1869).

Grail /grāl/ (also **Holy Grail**) ▶*n.* (in medieval legend) the cup or platter used by Jesus at the Last Supper, and in which Joseph of Arimathea received Christ's blood at the Cross. Quests for it undertaken by medieval knights are described in versions of the Arthurian legends written from the early 13th century onward. ■ (also **grail**) *figurative* a thing that is being earnestly pursued or sought after: *profit has become the holy grail.* ▷from Old French *graal*, from medieval Latin *gradalis* 'dish.'

grain /grān/ ▶*n.* **1** wheat or any other cultivated cereal crop used as food. ■ the seeds of such cereals: [as *adj.*] *grain exports.* **2** a single fruit or seed of a cereal: *a few* ***grains of*** *corn.* ■ a small hard particle of a substance such as salt or sand: *a* ***grain of*** *salt.* ■ the smallest possible quantity or amount of a quality: *there wasn't* ***a grain of truth*** *in what he said.* ■ a discrete particle or crystal in a metal, igneous rock, etc., typically visible only when a surface is magnified. ■ a piece of solid propellant for use in a rocket engine. **3** (abbr.: **gr.**) the smallest unit of weight in the troy and avoirdupois systems, equal to 1/5760 of a pound troy and 1/7000 of a pound avoirdupois (approximately 0.0648 grams). [because originally the weight was equivalent to that of a grain of wheat.] **4** the longitudinal arrangement or pattern of fibers in wood, paper, etc.: *he scored **along the grain** of the table with the knife.* ■ roughness in texture of wood, stone, etc.; the arrangement and size of constituent particles: *the lighter, finer grain of the wood is attractive.* ■ the rough or textured outer surface of leather, or of a similar artificial material. ■ *Mining* lamination or planes of cleavage in materials such as stone and coal. ■ *Photography* a granular appearance of a photograph or negative, which is in proportion to the size of the emulsion particles composing it. **5** *archaic* a person's character or natural tendency. **6** *historical* kermes or cochineal, or dye made from either of these. [the kermes was thought to consist of grains.]

▸*v.* [*trans.*] **1** (usu. **be grained**) give a rough surface or texture to: *her fingers were **grained with** chalk dust.* ■ [*intrans.*] form into grains: *if the sugar does grain up, add more water.* **2** [usu. as *n.*] (**graining**) paint (esp. furniture or interior surfaces) in imitation of the grain of wood or marble: *the art of graining and marbling.* **3** remove hair from (a hide): [as *adj.*] (**grained**) *the boots were of best grained leather.* **4** feed (a horse) on grain. ▷Middle English (originally in the sense 'seed, grain of wheat'): from Old French *grain*, from Latin *granum*. **—grained** *adj.* [usu. in *combination*] *coarse-grained sandstone.* **—grain·er** *n.* **—grain·less** *adj.*

▸*PHRASES* □ **against the grain** contrary to the natural inclination or feeling of someone or something: *it **goes against the grain** to tell outright lies.* [from the fact that wood is easier to cut along the line of the grain.] □ **in grain** thorough, genuine, by nature, or downright; indelible. [from *dyed in the grain.*]

grain bee·tle ▸*n.* a small beetle that infests grain stores and warehouses. • Cucujidae and other families: several species, in particular the tropical **saw-toothed grain beetle** (*Oryzaephilus surinamensis*), now found worldwide.

grain bor·er ▸*n.* a beetle that feeds on grain and rice and is a common pest of granaries and flour mills. • Family Bostrichidae: several species, including the tropical **lesser grain borer** (*Rhizopertha dominica*), now found worldwide.

grain leath·er ▸*n.* leather dressed with the grain side outward.

grain side ▸*n.* the side of a hide on which the hair was.

grains of par·a·dise ▸*plural n.* the seeds of a West African plant of the ginger family, resembling those of cardamom and used as a spice and in herbal medicine. Also called MALAGUETTA. • The plant is *Aframomum melegueta*, family Zingiberaceae.

grain wee·vil ▸*n.* a weevil that is a common pest of stored grain, which is eaten by the larvae. • *Sitophilus granarius*, family Curculionidae.

grain whis·key ▸*n.* whiskey made mainly from corn and malted and unmalted barley.

grain·y /'grānē/ ▸*adj.* (**grain·i·er, grain·i·est**) **1** granular: *a juicy, grainy texture.* ■ *Photography* showing visible grains of emulsion, as characteristic of old photographs or modern high-speed film. ■ (of sound, esp. recorded music or a voice) having a rough or gravelly quality: *the grainy sound of bootleg cassettes.* ■ (of food) containing whole grains: *a good grainy loaf.* **2** (of wood) having prominent grain. **—grain·i·ness** *n.*

gral·loch /'graləkl/ ▸*n.* the viscera of a dead deer.

▸*v.* [*trans.*] disembowel (a deer that has been shot). ▷mid 19th cent.: from Scottish Gaelic *grealach* 'entrails.'

gram[1] /gram/ (*Brit.* also **gramme**) (abbr.: **g**) ▸*n.* a metric unit of mass equal to one thousandth of a kilogram. ▷late 18th cent.: from French *gramme*, from late Latin *gramma* 'a small weight,' from Greek.

gram[2] ▸*n.* chickpeas or other legumes used as food. ▷early 18th cent.: from Portuguese *grão*, from Latin *granum* 'grain.'

gram[3] ▸*n.* short for GRANDMA.

-gram[1] ▸*comb. form* in nouns denoting something written or recorded (esp. in a certain way): *cryptogram* | *heliogram.* ▷from Greek *gramma* 'thing written, letter of the alphabet,' from *graphein* 'write.'

-gram[2] ▸*comb. form* in nouns denoting a novelty greeting or message as a humorous or embarrassing surprise for the recipient: *kissogram.* ▷on the pattern of *telegram.*

gram·i·ci·din /ˌgramə'sīdn/ ▸*n. Medicine* an antibiotic with a wide range of activity, used in many medicinal preparations. • This antibiotic is obtained from the bacterium *Bacillus brevis.*

gram·i·na·ceous /ˌgramə'nāsHəs/ ▸*adj. Botany* of, relating to, or denoting plants of the grass family (Gramineae). ▷mid 19th cent.: from Latin *gramen*, *gramin-* 'grass' + -ACEOUS.

gram·i·niv·o·rous /ˌgramə'nivərəs/ ▸*adj. Zoology* (of an animal) feeding on grass. ▷mid 18th cent.: from Latin *gramen*, *gramin-* 'grass' + -VOROUS.

gram·ma /'gramə/ ▸*n. informal* one's grandmother.

gram·ma·logue /'graməˌläg/ ▸*n.* (in shorthand) a word represented by a single sign or symbol. ▷mid 19th cent.: formed irregularly from Greek *gramma* 'letter of the alphabet, thing written' + *logos* 'word,' on the pattern of words such as *catalogue*.

gram·mar /'gramər/ ▸*n.* the whole system and structure of a language or of languages in general, usually taken as consisting of syntax and morphology (including inflections) and sometimes also phonology and semantics. ■ [usu. with *adj.*] a particular analysis of the system and structure of language or of a specific language. ■ a book on grammar: *my old Latin grammar.* ■ a set of actual or presumed prescriptive notions about correct use of a language: *it was not bad grammar, just dialect.* ■ the basic elements of an area of knowledge or skill: *the grammar of wine.* ■ *Computing* a set of rules governing what strings are valid or allowable in a language or text. ▷late Middle English: from Old French *gramaire*, via Latin from Greek *grammatikē* (*tekhnē*) '(art) of letters,' from *gramma*, *grammat-* 'letter of the alphabet, thing written.'

gram·mar·i·an /grə'me(ə)rēən/ ▸*n.* a person who studies and writes about grammar. ▷Middle English: from Old French *gramarien*, from *gramaire* (see GRAMMAR).

gram·mar school ▸*n.* **1** another term for ELEMENTARY SCHOOL. **2** (in the UK) a state secondary school to which pupils are admitted on the basis of ability. Since 1965 most have been absorbed into the comprehensive school system. ■ a school founded in or before the 16th century for teaching Latin, later becoming a secondary school teaching academic subjects.

-grammatic ▸*comb. form* in adjectives corresponding to nouns ending in *-gram* (such as *cryptogrammatic* corresponding to *cryptogram*).

gram·mat·i·cal /grə'matikəl/ ▸*adj.* of or relating to grammar: *grammatical analysis* | *the grammatical function of a verb.* ■ well formed; in accordance with the productive rules of the grammar of a language: *a grammatical sentence.* ▷early 16th cent.: from late Latin *grammaticalis*, via Latin from Greek *grammatikos*, from *gramma*, *grammat-* 'letter of the alphabet, thing written.' **—gram·mat·i·cal·i·ty** /-ˌmati'kalitē/ *n.* **—gram·mat·i·cal·ly** /-ik(ə)lē/ *adv.* **—gram·mat·i·cal·ness** *n.*

gram·mat·i·cal·ize /grə'matikəˌlīz/ ▸*v.* [*trans.*] *Linguistics* change (an element) from one having lexical meaning into one having a largely grammatical function. **—gram·mat·i·cal·i·za·tion** /-ˌmatikəli'zāsHən/ *n.*

gramme ▸*n. Brit.* variant spelling of GRAM[1].

gram-mo·lec·u·lar weight (abbr.: **GMW**) ▸*n.* the quantity of a chemical compound equal to its molecular weight in grams; now usu. replaced by the mole. Also called **gram molecule**. See MOLE[4].

Gram·my /'gramē/ ▸*n.* (*pl.* **-mys** or **-mies**) each of a number of annual awards given by the American National Academy of Recording Arts and Sciences for achievement in the record industry. ▷1950s: blend of GRAMOPHONE and EMMY.

Gram-neg·a·tive /gram/ ▸*adj.* see GRAM STAIN.

gram·o·phone /'graməˌfōn/ ▸*n.* old-fashioned term for RECORD PLAYER. ▷late 19th cent.: formed by inversion of elements of *phonogram* 'sound recording.'

gram·o·phone rec·ord ▸*n.* old-fashioned term for RECORD (sense 4).

gramp /gramp/ (also **gramps, gramp·y** /'gramˌpē/) ▸*n. dialect* or *informal* one's grandfather. ▷late 19th cent.: contraction of GRANDPAPA.

Gram·pi·an /'grampēən/ a former local government region in northeastern Scotland, dissolved in 1996.

Gram·pi·an Moun·tains (also **the Gram·pi·ans**) **1** a mountain range in northern central Scotland. Its southern edge forms a natural boundary between the Highlands and the Lowlands. **2** a mountain range in southeastern Australia, in Victoria. It forms a spur of the Great Dividing Range at its western end.

Gram-pos·i·tive ▸*adj.* see GRAM STAIN.

gram·pus /'grampəs/ ▸*n.* (*pl.* **-pus·es**) a cetacean of the dolphin family, in particular: ■ another term for RISSO'S DOLPHIN. ■ another term for ORCA. ▷early 16th cent.: alteration (by association with GRAND 'big') of Old French *grapois*, from medieval Latin *craspiscis*, from Latin *crassus piscis* 'fat fish.'

Gram stain ▸*n. Medicine* a staining technique for the preliminary identification of bacteria, in which a violet dye is applied, followed by a decolorizing agent and then a red dye. The cell walls of certain bacteria (denoted **Gram-positive**) retain the first dye and appear violet, while those that lose it (denoted **Gram-negative**) appear red. Also called **Gram's method**. ▷late 19th cent.: named after Hans C. J. *Gram* (1853–1938), the Danish physician who devised the method.

gran /gran/ ▸*n. informal, chiefly Brit.* one's grandmother. ▷mid 19th cent.: abbreviation.

gra·na /'grānə/ ▸*plural n.* (*sing.* **-num** /-nəm/) *Botany* the stacks of thylakoids embedded in the stroma of a chloroplast. ▷late 19th cent.: plural of Latin *granum* 'grain.'

Gra·na·da /grə'nädə/ **1** a city in southern Spain; pop. 287,000. Founded in the 8th century, it became the capital of the Moorish kingdom of Granada in 1238. **2** a city in Nicaragua, on the northwestern shore of Lake Nicaragua; pop. 89,000. Founded by the Spanish in 1523, it is the oldest city in the country.

gran·a·dil·la /ˌgranə'dilə; -dēyə/ (also **gren·a·dil·la**) ▸*n.* a passion fruit, or the fruit of a related plant. • This fruit comes from plants of the genus *Passiflora*, family Passifloraceae, including the **giant granadilla** (*P. quadrangularis*), which has large pale fruits. ▷late 16th cent.: Spanish, diminutive of *granada* 'pomegranate.'

gra·na·ry /'grānərē; 'gran-/ ▸*n.* (*pl.* **-ries**) a storehouse for threshed grain. ■ a region producing large quantities of corn. ▷late 16th cent.: from Latin *granarium*, from *granum* 'grain.'

Gran Ca·na·ria /ˌgrän kə'närēə/ a volcanic island off the northwestern coast of Africa, one of the Canary Islands. Its chief town, Las Palmas,is the capital of the Canary Islands.

Gran Cha·co /grän 'CHäkō/ (also **Cha·co**) a lowland plain in central South America, that extends from southern Bolivia through Paraguay to northern Argentina.

grand /grand/ ▸*adj.* **1** magnificent and imposing in appearance, size, or style: *a grand country house* | *the dinner party was very grand.* ■ designed to impress through scale or splendor: *a grand gesture.* ■ (of a person) of high rank and with an appearance and manner appropriate to it: *she was such a grand lady.* ■ large or ambitious in scope or scale: *his grand design for the future of Europe* | *collecting on a grand scale.* ■ used in names of places or buildings to suggest size or splendor: *the Grand Canyon* | *the Grand Hotel.* **2** [*attrib.*] denoting the largest or most important item of its kind: *the grand entrance.* ■ of the highest rank (used esp. in official titles): *the grand duke.* ■ *Law* (of a crime) serious: *grand theft.* Compare with PETTY (sense 2). **3** *informal* very good or enjoyable; excellent: *we had a grand day.* **4** [in *combination*] (in names of family relationships) denoting one generation removed in ascent or descent: *a grand-niece.*

▸*n.* **1** (*pl.* same) *informal* a thousand dollars or pounds: *he gets thirty-five grand a year.* **2** a grand piano. ▷Middle English: from Old French *grant*, *grand*, from Latin *grandis* 'full-grown, big, great.' The original uses were to denote family relationships (sense 4, following Old French usage) and as a title (*the Grand*, translating Old French *le Grand*); hence the senses 'of the highest rank,' 'of great importance.' **—grand·ly** *adv.* **—grand·ness** *n.*

▸*PHRASE* □ **a** (or **the**) **grand old man of** a man long and highly respected in (a particular field): *the grand old man of the Republican Party.*

gran·dad /'granˌdad/ ▸*n.* variant spelling of GRANDDAD.

grand·dad·dy /'granˌdadē/ (also **gran·dad·dy**) ▸*n.* (*pl.* **-dies**) another term for GRANDDAD. ■ (**the granddaddy of**) used to denote a person or thing that is considered to be the best, largest, or most notable of a particular kind: *that young fellow is going to have the granddaddy of all headaches.*

gran·dam /'granˌdam; -dəm/ (also **grand·dam, gran·dame**) ▸*n.* archaic term for GRANDMOTHER. ■ an old woman. ■ a female ancestor. ▷Middle English: from Anglo-Norman French *graund dame* (see GRAND,

DAME). Of the English terms of relationship formed with *grand*, this is the oldest.

grand a·part·heid ▶*n. historical* (in South Africa) a form of apartheid, prevalent in the 1960s and 1970s, that involved comprehensive racial segregation and measures such as the removal of black people from white areas and the creation of black homelands.

grand·aunt /ˈgrand,ant; -,änt/ ▶*n.* another term for GREAT-AUNT.

grand·ba·by /ˈgran(d),bābē/ ▶*n.* (*pl.* **-bies**) a grandchild who is still a baby.

Grand Banks a submarine plateau of the continental shelf off the southeastern coast of Newfoundland, Canada. It is where the warm Gulf Stream and the cold Labrador Current meet; this promotes the growth of plankton, which makes the waters an important feeding area for fish.

grand batte·ment /ˈgrän bätˈmäɴ/ ▶*n. Ballet* a movement in which both legs are kept straight and one leg is kicked outward from the body and in again.

Grand Ca·nal 1 a series of waterways in eastern China that extend south from Beijing to Hangzhou, a distance of 1,060 miles (1,700 km). Built in stages between 486 BC and AD 1327, its original purpose was to transport rice from the river valleys to the cities. **2** the main waterway of Venice, Italy. It is lined on each side by palaces and spanned by the Rialto Bridge.

Grand Can·yon a deep gorge in Arizona, formed by the Colorado River. It is about 277 miles (440 km) long, 5–15 miles (8–24 km) wide, and, in places, 6,000 feet (1,800 m) deep. The area was designated a national park in 1919.

Grand Canyon

Grand Can·yon State a nickname for the state of ARIZONA.

grand·child /ˈgran(d),CHīld/ ▶*n.* (*pl.* **-child·ren** /-,CHildrən/) a child of one's son or daughter.

Grand Cou·lee Dam /ˈkōōlē/ a dam on the Columbia River in east central Washington, completed in 1942.

grand cross ▶*n. Astrology* an arrangement of four planets in which each is in opposition to one other planet and square to the other two, forming a cross.

grand cru /,gräɴ ˈkry/ ▶*n.* (*pl.* **grands crus** *pronunc.* same) (chiefly in French official classifications) a wine of the most superior grade, or the vineyard that produces it. Compare with PREMIER CRU. ▷early 20th cent.: French, literally 'great growth.'

grand·dad /ˈgran,dad/ (also **gran·dad**) ▶*n. informal* one's grandfather.

grand·daugh·ter /ˈgran,dôtər/ ▶*n.* a daughter of one's son or daughter.

grand duch·ess ▶*n.* the wife or widow of a grand duke. ■ a princess or noblewoman ruling over a territory in certain European countries. ■ *historical* a daughter (or son's daughter) of a Russian tsar.

grand duch·y ▶*n.* a state or territory ruled by a grand duke or duchess.

grand duke ▶*n.* a prince or nobleman ruling over a territory in certain European countries. ■ *historical* a son (or son's son) of a Russian tsar.

Grande Co·more /,gränd kəˈmôr/ the largest of the islands of the Comoros, off the northwestern coast of Madagascar; pop. 233,500; chief town, Moroni.

grande dame /ˈgran ˈdam; ˈgrän ˈdäm/ ▶*n.* a woman of influential position within a particular sphere: *the grande dame of British sculpture.* ▷mid 18th cent.: French, literally 'grand lady.'

gran·dee /granˈdē/ ▶*n.* a Spanish or Portuguese nobleman of the highest rank. ■ a person of high rank or eminence: *several city grandees and eminent lawyers.* ▷late 16th cent.: from Spanish and Portuguese *grande* 'grand,' used as a noun. The change of ending was due to association with -EE.

grande hor·i·zon·tale /ˈgrand ,ôrizänˈtäl/ ▶*n.* (*pl.* **grandes hor·i·zon·tales** *pronunc.* same) *humorous* a prostitute. ▷late 19th cent.: French, literally 'great horizontal.'

gran·deur /ˈgranjər; ˈgran,dyōōr/ ▶*n.* splendor and impressiveness, esp. of appearance or style: *the austere grandeur of mountain scenery.* ■ high rank or social importance: *for all their grandeur, the chancellors were still officials of the household.* ▷late 16th cent. (denoting tall stature): from French, from *grand* 'great, grand' (see GRAND).

grand·fa·ther /ˈgran(d),fäTHər/ ▶*n.* the father of one's father or mother. ■ the person who founded or originated something: *Freud is often called* **the grandfather** *of psychoanalysis.*
▶*v.* [*trans.*] *informal* exempt (someone or something) from a new law or regulation: *smokers who worked here before the ban have been grandfathered.* —**grand·fa·ther·ly** *adj.*

grand·fa·ther clause ▶*n. informal* a clause exempting certain classes of people or things from the requirements of a piece of legislation affecting their previous rights, privileges, or practices. . ▷early 20th cent.: so called because under constitutional clauses in some southern states, permitting whites to vote and disenfranchising blacks, the descendants of those voting before 1867 were permitted to vote without having to meet certain stringent conditions.

grand·fa·ther clock ▶*n.* a clock in a tall freestanding wooden case, driven by weights.

Grand Fleet *historical* the main British naval fleet, either that based at Spithead in the 18th century or that based at Scapa Flow in World War I.

Grand Forks a city in northeastern North Dakota, on the Red River of the North; pop. 49,321.

Grand Gui·gnol /gräɴ gēnˈyôl/ ▶*n.* a dramatic entertainment of a sensational or horrific nature, originally a sequence of short pieces as performed at the Grand Guignol theater in Paris. ▷French, literally 'Great Punch.'

gran·di·flo·ra /,grandəˈflôrə/ ▶*adj.* [*attrib.*] (of a cultivated plant) bearing large flowers.
▶*n.* a grandiflora plant. ▷early 20th cent.: modern Latin (often used in specific names of large-flowered plants), from Latin *grandis* 'great' + *flos, flor-* 'flower.'

gran·dil·o·quent /granˈdiləkwənt/ ▶*adj.* pompous or extravagant in language, style, or manner, esp. in a way that is intended to impress: *a grandiloquent celebration of Spanish glory.* ▷late 16th cent.: from Latin *grandiloquus,* literally 'grand-speaking,' from *grandis* 'grand' + *loqui* 'speak.' The ending was altered in English by association with ELOQUENT. —**gran·dil·o·quence** *n.* —**gran·dil·o·quent·ly** *adv.*

Grand In·quis·i·tor ▶*n. historical* the director of the court of Inquisition, esp. in Spain and Portugal.

gran·di·ose /ˈgrandē,ōs; ,grandēˈōs/ ▶*adj.* impressive or magnificent in appearance or style, esp. pretentiously so: *the court's grandiose facade.* ■ excessively grand or ambitious: *grandiose plans to reform the world.* ▷mid 19th cent.: from French, from Italian *grandioso,* from *grande* 'grand.' —**gran·di·ose·ly** *adv.* —**gran·di·os·i·ty** /,grandēˈäsitē/ *n.*

Grand Is·land a commercial and industrial city in south central Nebraska; pop. 42,940.

grand je·té /ˈgrän ZHəˈtā/ ▶*n. Ballet* a jump in which a dancer springs from one foot to land on the other with one leg forward of their body and the other stretched backward while in the air.

Grand Junc·tion a city in western Colorado, at the junction of the Colorado (formerly the Grand) and Gunnison rivers; pop. 41,986.

grand ju·ry ▶*n. Law* a jury, normally of twenty-three jurors, selected to examine the validity of an accusation before trial.

grand lar·ce·ny ▶*n. Law* (in many U.S. states and formerly in Britain) theft of personal property having a value above a legally specified amount.

grand·ma /ˈgran(d),mä; ˈgram-/ ▶*n. informal* one's grandmother.

grand mal /,gran(d) ˈmäl; ˈmal/ ▶*n.* a serious form of epilepsy with muscle spasms and prolonged loss of consciousness. Compare with PETIT MAL. ■ an epileptic fit of this kind. ▷late 19th cent.: from French, literally 'great sickness.'

grand·ma·ma /ˈgran(d),mämə; -mə,mä; ˈgram-/ (also **grand·mam·ma**) ▶*n.* archaic form of GRANDMA.

Grand·ma Mo·ses see MOSES[2].

grand man·ner ▶*n.* (**the grand manner**) a style considered appropriate for noble and stately matters: *formal dining in the grand manner.* ■ (**the Grand Manner**) the lofty and rhetorical manner of historical painting exemplified by Raphael and Poussin.

Grand Mar·nier /ˈgräɴ märˈnyā/ ▶*n. trademark* an orange-flavored cognac-based liqueur. ▷French.

grand mas·ter ▶*n.* **1** (usu. **grandmaster**) a chess player of the highest class, esp. one who has won an international tournament. **2** (**Grand Master**) the head of an order of chivalry or of Freemasons.

grand·moth·er /ˈgran(d),məTHər/ ▶*n.* the mother of one's father or mother. —**grand·moth·er·ly** *adj.*
▶*PHRASE* □ **teach one's grandmother to suck eggs** presume to advise a more experienced person.

grand·moth·er clock ▶*n.* a clock similar to a grandfather clock but about two-thirds the size.

grand·neph·ew /ˈgran(d),nefyōō/ ▶*n.* another term for GREAT-NEPHEW.

grand·niece /ˈgran(d),nēs/ ▶*n.* another term for GREAT-NIECE.

grand op·er·a ▶*n.* an opera on a serious theme in which the entire libretto (including dialogue) is sung. ■ the genre of such opera.

grand·pa /ˈgran(d),pä; ˈgram-/ ▶*n. informal* one's grandfather.

grand·pa·pa /ˈgran(d),päpə; -pə,pä; ˈgram-/ ▶*n.* old-fashioned term for GRANDFATHER.

grand·pap·py /ˈgran(d),papē; ˈgram-/ ▶*n.* (*pl.* **-pies**) dialect term for GRANDFATHER.

grand·par·ent /ˈgran(d),pe(ə)rənt; -,par-/ ▶*n.* a parent of one's father or mother; a grandmother or grandfather. —**grand·pa·ren·tal** /,gran(d)pəˈrentl/ *adj.* —**grand·par·ent·hood** /-,hōōd/ *n.*

grand pi·an·o ▶*n.* a large, full-toned piano that has the body, strings, and soundboard arranged horizontally and in line with the keys and is supported by three legs.

Grand Prai·rie an industrial city in northeastern Texas, between Dallas and Fort Worth; pop. 99,616.

Grand Prix /,gräɴ ˈprē; ,gran/ ▶*n.* (*pl.* **Grands Prix** *pronunc.* same) an important sporting event in which participants compete for a major prize. ■ any of a series of auto-racing or motorcycling contests forming part of a world championship series, held in various countries under international rules. ■ (in full **Grand Prix de Paris**) an international horse race for three-year-olds, founded in 1863 and run annually in June at Longchamps, Paris. ▷mid 19th cent.: French, literally 'great or chief prize.'

Grand Rap·ids an industrial city in southwestern Michigan, on the Grand River, noted for furniture production; pop. 197,800.

grand sei·gneur /,gräɴ sānˈyər/ ▶*n.* a man whose rank or position allows him to command others. ▷early 17th cent.: French, literally 'great lord.'

grand siè·cle /ˈgrän sēˈeklə/ ▶*n.* the reign of Louis XIV, seen as France's period of political and cultural preeminence. ▷mid 19th cent.: French, literally 'great century or age.'

grand·sire /ˈgrand,sīr/ ▶*n.* archaic term for GRANDFATHER.

grand slam ▶*n.* the winning of each of a group of major championships or matches in a particular sport in the same year, in particular in tennis or golf. ■ *Bridge* the bidding and winning of all thirteen tricks. ■ *Baseball* a home run hit when each of the three bases is occupied by a runner, thus scoring four runs. ▷early 19th cent. (as a term in cards, esp. bridge): from SLAM[2].

grand·son /ˈgran(d),sən/ ▶*n.* the son of one's son or daughter.

grand·stand /ˈgran(d),stand/ ▶*n.* the main seating area, usually roofed, commanding the best view for spectators at racetracks or sports stadiums.
▶*v.* [*intrans.*] [usu. as *n.*] (**grandstanding**) *derogatory* seek to attract applause or favorable attention from spectators or the media: *they accused him of political grandstanding.*

Grand Strand a name for the northeastern coast of South Carolina, site of many resorts including Myrtle Beach.

Grand Te·ton Na·tion·al Park /ˈtē,tän/ a preserve in northwestern Wyoming, just south of Yellowstone National Park, named for the highest of its peaks. Jackson Hole is here.

grand to·tal ▶*n.* the final amount after everything is added up; the sum of other totals.

grand tour ▶*n. historical* a cultural tour of Europe conventionally undertaken, esp. in the 18th century, by a young man of the upper classes as a part of his education. ■ a guided inspection or tour of a building, exhibit, or institution.

grand trine /trīn/ ▸*n. Astrology* an arrangement of three planets in which each planet is in trine with the other two, forming an equilateral triangle.

grand·un·cle /ˈgrand,əNGkəl/ ▸*n.* another term for GREAT-UNCLE.

grand u·ni·fied the·o·ry ▸*n. Physics* a theory attempting to give a single explanation of the strong, weak, and electromagnetic interactions between subatomic particles.

Grange /grānj/, Red (1903–91) U.S. football player; born Harold Edward Grange; known as the **Galloping Ghost**. He played professionally, mostly with the Chicago Bears, from 1925 until he retired in 1934. Football Hall of Fame (1963).

grange /grānj/ ▸*n.* **1** [usu. in *names*] *Brit.* a country house with farm buildings attached: *Biddulph Grange.* ■ *historical* an outlying farm with tithe barns, belonging to a monastery or feudal lord. ■ *archaic* a barn. **2** (**the Grange**) (in the U.S.) a farmers' association organized in 1867. The Grange sponsors social activities, community service, and political lobbying. Officially called the ORDER OF PATRONS OF HUSBANDRY. ■ a local lodge of this association. ▹Middle English (in the sense 'granary, barn'): from Old French, from medieval Latin *granica (villa)* 'grain house or farm,' based on Latin *granum* 'grain.'

grang·er·ize /ˈgrānjə,rīz/ ▸*v.* [*trans.*] [usu. as *adj.*] (**grangerized**) illustrate (a book) by later insertion of material, esp. prints cut from other works. ▹late 19th cent.: from the name J. *Granger* (1723–76), English biographer. **—grang·er·i·za·tion** /,grānjərəˈzāSHən/ *n.*

gran·i·fer·ous /grəˈnifərəs/ ▸*adj. Botany* (of a plant) producing grain or a grainlike seed. ▹mid 17th cent.: from Latin *granum* 'grain' + -FEROUS.

gra·ni·ta /grəˈnētə/ ▸*n.* (*pl.* **-te** /-tā/) a coarse, Italian-style flavored ice. ■ a drink made with crushed ice. ▹Italian.

gran·ite /ˈgranit/ ▸*n.* a very hard, granular, crystalline, igneous rock consisting mainly of quartz, mica, and feldspar and often used as a building stone. ■ used in similes and metaphors to refer to something very hard and impenetrable: [as *adj.*] *a man with granite determination.* ▹mid 17th cent.: from Italian *granito*, literally 'grained,' from *grano* 'grain,' from Latin *granum*. **—gra·nit·ic** /grəˈnitik/ *adj.* **—gran·it·oid** /ˈgrani,toid/ *adj.* & *n.*

Gran·ite State a nickname for the state of NEW HAMPSHIRE.

gran·ite·ware /ˈgranit,we(ə)r/ ▸*n.* a speckled form of earthenware imitating the appearance of granite. ■ a kind of enameled ironware.

gran·it·ize /ˈgrani,tīz/ ▸*v.* [*trans.*] [usu. as *adj.*] (**granitized**) *Geology* alter (rock) so as to give it a granitic character. **—gran·it·i·za·tion** /,granitiˈzāSHən/ *n.*

gra·niv·o·rous /grəˈnivərəs/ ▸*adj. Zoology* (of an animal) feeding on grain. ▹mid 17th cent.: from Latin *granum* 'grain' + -VOROUS. **—gra·ni·vore** /ˈgranə,vôr/ *n.*

gran·ny /ˈgranē/ (also **gran·nie**) ▸*n.* (*pl.* **-nies**) *informal* one's grandmother. ▹mid 17th cent.: from *grannam* (representing a colloquial pronunciation of GRANDAM) + -Y[2].

gran·ny flat ▸*n. informal* a part of a house made into self-contained accommodations suitable for an elderly relative.

gran·ny gear ▸*n. informal* the lowest gear on a bicycle.

gran·ny glass·es ▸*plural n. informal* round, steel-rimmed or gold-rimmed glasses.

gran·ny knot ▸*n.* a square knot with the ends crossed the wrong way and therefore liable to slip or jam.

Gran·ny Smith ▸*n.* a dessert apple of a bright green variety with crisp, sharp-flavored flesh, originating in Australia. ▹late 19th cent.: named after Maria Ann (*Granny*) *Smith* (*c.*1801–1870), who first produced such apples.

gran·o·di·or·ite /,granəˈdīə,rīt/ ▸*n. Geology* a coarse-grained, plutonic rock containing quartz and plagioclase, between granite and diorite in composition. ▹late 19th cent.: from GRANITE + DIORITE.

gra·no·la /grəˈnōlə/ ▸*n.* a kind of breakfast cereal consisting typically of rolled oats, brown sugar or honey, dried fruit, and nuts. ■ [as *adj.*] *chiefly derogatory* denoting those with liberal or environmentalist political views, typified as eating health foods. ▹late 19th cent. (as a trademark): from *gran-* (representing GRANULAR or GRAIN) + *-ola*. The current term dates from the 1970s.

gran·o·lith·ic /,granəˈliTHik/ ▸*adj.* (of concrete) containing fine granite chippings or crushed granite, used to render floors and surfaces. ■ (of a floor or surface) rendered with such concrete. ▸*n.* granolithic concrete or rendering. ▹late 19th cent.: from *grano-* (irregular combining form from Latin *granum* 'grain') + Greek *lithos* 'stone' + -IC.

gran·o·phyre /ˈgranə,fī(ə)r/ ▸*n. Geology* a granitic rock consisting of intergrown feldspar and quartz crystals in a medium- to fine-grained groundmass. ▹late 19th cent.: from German *Granophyr*, from *Granit* 'granite'+ *Porphyr* (see PORPHYRY). **—gran·o·phy·ric** /,granəˈfirik/ *adj.*

Grant[1] /grant/, Cary (1904–86), U.S. actor; born in Britain; born *Alexander Archibald Leach*. He made his Hollywood screen debut in *This Is the Night* (1932) after appearing in Broadway musicals. He acted in more than 70 movies usually as the debonair male lead, including *Holiday* (1938) and *The Philadelphia Story* (1940).

Grant[2], Duncan (James Corrow) (1885–1978), Scottish painter and designer; a member of the Bloomsbury Group.

Grant[3], Ulysses Simpson (1822–85), 18th president of the U.S. 1869–77; born *Hiram Ulysses Grant*. As supreme commander of the Union army, he defeated the Confederate army in 1865 with a policy of attrition. As a popular general elected to the presidency, he lacked political experience and was unable to check widespread political corruption and inefficiency. During his first administration, the 15th Amendment was ratified (giving all qualified male citizens the right to vote) and the national park system was established.

Ulysses S. Grant

grant /grant/ ▸*v.* [with *two objs.*] **1** agree to give or allow (something requested) to: *a letter granting them permission to smoke.* See note at GIVE. ■ give (a right, power, property, etc.) formally or legally to: *the amendment that granted women the right to vote.* **2** agree or admit to (someone) that (something) is true: *he hasn't made much progress, I'll grant you that.*
▸ **1** *n.* a sum of money given by an organization, esp. a government, for a particular purpose. ■ *formal* the action of granting something: *we had to recommend the grant or refusal of broadcasting licenses.* ■ *Law* a legal conveyance or formal conferment: *a grant of land | a grant of probate.* **2** a geographical subdivision in New Hampshire, Vermont, and Maine. ▹Middle English: from Old French *granter* 'consent to support,' variant of *creanter* 'to guarantee,' based on Latin *credere* 'entrust.' **—grant·a·ble** *adj.* **—grant·er** *n.*
▸*PHRASE* □ **take someone/something for granted** fail to appreciate someone or something that is very familiar or obvious: *the comforts that people take for granted | she took him for granted.* **take something for granted** assume that something is true without questioning it: *people no longer took for granted everything about Christianity.*

grant·ed /ˈgrantid/ ▸*adv.* [*sentence adverb*] admittedly; it is true (used to introduce a factor that is opposed to the main line of argument but is not regarded as so strong as to invalidate it): *granted, sitting around the house may not be your idea of the perfect retirement, but what's your choice when inflation is eroding the value of your nest egg?*
▸*conj.* (**granted that**) even assuming that: *granted that officers were used to making decisions, they still couldn't be expected to understand.*

gran·tee /granˈtē/ ▸*n. chiefly Law* a person to whom a grant or conveyance is made.

Granth /grənt/ short for ADI GRANTH.

Gran·tha /ˈgrəntə/ ▸*n.* a southern Indian alphabet dating from the 5th century AD, used by Tamil Brahmans when writing Sanskrit transcriptions of their sacred books. ▹from Sanskrit *grantha* (see GRANTH).

Granth Sa·hib /ˈgrənt ˈsä(h)ib/ another term for ADI GRANTH.

grant-in-aid ▸*n.* (*pl.* **grants-in-aid**) an amount of money given to a local government, an institution, or a particular scholar.

gran·tor /granˈtôr; ˈgrantər/ ▸*n. chiefly Law* a person or institution that makes a grant or conveyance.

grants·man·ship /ˈgrantsmən,SHip/ ▸*n.* the skill or practice of obtaining grants-in-aid, esp. for research. **—grants·man** *n.*

gran tu·ris·mo /,gran to͝oˈrizmō/ (abbr.: **GT**) ▸*n.* (*pl.* **-mos**) a high-performance model of automobile. ▹mid 20th cent.: Italian, literally 'great touring.'

gran·u·lar /ˈgranyələr/ ▸*adj.* **1** resembling or consisting of small grains or particles. ■ having a roughened surface or structure. **2** *technical* characterized by a high level of granularity: *a granular database.* ▹late 18th cent.: from late Latin *granulum* (see GRANULE) + -AR[1].

gran·u·lar·i·ty /,granyəˈlaritē/ ▸*n.* **1** the quality or condition of being granular. **2** *technical* the scale or level of detail present in a set of data or other phenomenon: *the granularity of this war is not the sand that covers most of the country, but these details that have proved so elusive.*

gran·u·late /ˈgranyə,lāt/ ▸*v.* **1** [*trans.*] [usu. as *adj.*] (**granulated**) form (something) into grains or particles: *granulated sugar.* ■ [*intrans.*] (of a substance) take the form of grains or particles: *the syrup would not granulate properly.* **2** [*intrans.*] [often as *adj.*] (**granulating**) *Medicine* (of a wound or lesion) form a grainy surface as part of the healing process. ■ [as *adj.*] (**granulated**) *chiefly Biology* having a roughened surface: *the skin is densely granulated.* **—gran·u·la·tion** /,granyəˈlāSHən/ *n.* **—gran·u·la·tor** /-,lātər/ *n.*

gran·u·la·tion tis·sue ▸*n.* new vascular tissue in granular form on an ulcer or the healing surface of a wound.

gran·ule /ˈgranyo͞ol/ ▸*n.* **1** a small compact particle of a substance: *coffee granules.* **2** a small convective cell on the surface of the sun with temperatures a few hundred degrees hotter than the surrounding regions, and lasting a few minutes. ▹mid 17th cent.: from late Latin *granulum*, diminutive of Latin *granum* 'grain.'

gran·u·lite /ˈgranyə,līt/ ▸*n. Geology* a fine-grained, granular metamorphic rock in which the main component minerals are typically feldspars and quartz. ▹mid 19th cent.: from GRANULE + -ITE[1]. **—gran·u·lit·ic** /,granyəˈlitik/ *adj.*

gran·u·lo·cyte /ˈgranyələ,sīt/ ▸*n. Physiology* a white blood cell with secretory granules in its cytoplasm, e.g., an eosinophil or a basophil. ▹early 20th cent.: from late Latin *granulum* 'granule' + -CYTE. **—gran·u·lo·cyt·ic** /,granyələˈsitik/ *adj.*

gran·u·lo·ma /,granyəˈlōmə/ ▸*n.* (*pl.* **-mas** or **-ma·ta** /-mətə/) *Medicine* a mass of granulation tissue, typically produced in response to infection, inflammation, or the presence of a foreign substance. **—gran·u·lom·a·tous** /-ˈlämətəs/ *adj.*

gran·u·lo·met·ric /,granyələˈmetrik/ ▸*adj.* relating to the size distribution or measurement of grain sizes in sand, rock, or other deposits.

gran·u·lose /ˈgranyə,lōs/ ▸*adj.* consisting of or covered with small grains or granules.

gra·num /ˈgrānəm/ ▸ singular form of GRANA.

grape /grāp/ ▸*n.* **1** a berry, typically green (classified as white), purple, red, or black, growing in clusters on a grapevine, eaten as fruit, and used in making wine. ■ (**the grape**) *informal* wine: *an exploration of the grape.* **2** a dark purplish red color. **3** short for GRAPESHOT. ▹Middle English (also in the Old French sense): from Old French, 'bunch of grapes,' probably from *graper* 'gather (grapes),' from *grap* 'hook' (denoting an implement used in harvesting grapes), of Germanic origin. **—grap·ey** (also **grap·y**) *adj.* (**grap·i·er, grap·i·est**)

grape·fruit /ˈgrāp,fro͞ot/ ▸*n.* (*pl.* same) **1** a large, round, yellow citrus fruit with an acid, juicy pulp. **2** the tree bearing this fruit. • *Citrus paradisi*, family Rutaceae. ▹early 19th cent.: from GRAPE + FRUIT (probably because the fruits grow in clusters).

grape hy·a·cinth ▸*n.* a small Eurasian plant of the lily family, with clusters of small, globular blue flowers, cultivated as an ornamental or for use in perfume. • Genus *Muscari*, family Liliaceae.

grape i·vy ▸*n.* an evergreen climbing plant of the grape family that is grown as a houseplant. • Genus *Cissus,* family Vitaceae: several species, in particular *C. rhombifolia.*

grape·seed oil /ˈgrāpˌsēd/ ▸*n.* oil extracted from the residue of grapes that have been juiced.

grape·shot /ˈgrāpˌshät/ ▸*n. historical* ammunition consisting of a number of small iron balls fired together from a cannon.

grape sug·ar ▸*n.* dextrose present in or derived from grapes.

grape·vine /ˈgrāpˌvīn/ ▸*n.* **1** a vine native to both Eurasia and North America, esp. one bearing fruit (grapes) used for eating or winemaking. Numerous cultivars and hybrids have been developed for the winemaking industry. • Genus *Vitis,* family Vitaceae: many species, in particular *V. vinifera* and the American *V. labrusca.* **2** *informal* used to refer to the circulation of rumors and unofficial information: *I'd heard **through the grapevine** that the business was nearly settled.*

graph[1] /graf/ ▸*n.* a diagram showing the relation between variable quantities, typically of two variables, each measured along one of a pair of axes at right angles. ■ *Mathematics* a collection of points whose coordinates satisfy a given relation.
▸*v.* [*trans.*] plot or trace on a graph. ▷late 19th cent.: abbreviation of *graphic formula.*

graph[2] ▸*n. Linguistics* a visual symbol representing a unit of sound or other feature of speech. Graphs include not only letters of the alphabet but also punctuation marks. ▷1930s: from Greek *graphē* 'writing.'

-graph ▸*comb. form* **1** in nouns denoting something written or drawn in a specified way: *autograph.* **2** in nouns denoting an instrument that records: *seismograph.* ▷from French *-graphe,* based on Greek *graphos* 'written, writing.'

graph·eme /ˈgrafēm/ ▸*n. Linguistics* the smallest meaningful contrastive unit in a writing system. Compare with **PHONEME.** ▷1930s: from **GRAPH**[2] + **-EME.** —**gra·phe·mic** /grafˈēmik/ *adj.* —**gra·phe·mi·cal·ly** /grəˈfēmik(ə)lē/ *adv.* —**gra·phe·mics** /grəˈfēmiks/ *n.*

-grapher ▸*comb. form* indicating a person concerned with a subject denoted by a noun ending in *-graphy* (such as *geographer* corresponding to *geography*). ▷from Greek *-graphos* 'writer' + **-ER**[1].

graph·ic /ˈgrafik/ ▸*adj.* **1** of or relating to visual art, esp. involving drawing, engraving, or lettering: *his mature graphic work.* ■ giving a vivid picture with explicit detail: *he gave a graphic description of the torture.* ■ *Computing* of, relating to, or denoting a visual image: *graphic information such as charts and diagrams.* **2** of or in the form of a graph. **3** [*attrib.*] *Geology* of or denoting rocks having a surface texture resembling cuneiform writing.
▸*n. Computing* a graphical item displayed on a screen or stored as data. ▷mid 17th cent.: via Latin from Greek *graphikos,* from *graphē* 'writing, drawing.' —**graph·i·cal·ly** /-ik(ə)lē/ *adv.*

THE RIGHT WORD **graphic, pictorial, picturesque, vivid**

A photograph of a car accident on the front page of a newspaper might be described as **graphic,** while a photograph of a mountain village would be called **picturesque.** Both adjectives are used to describe things that have visual impact or that produce a strong, clear impression, but *graphic* means having the power to evoke a strikingly lifelike representation, whether it is in pictures or in words (*the driving instructor gave them a graphic description of what happens in a 50-mph head-on collision*).

Vivid is a more general term suggesting something that is felt, seen, heard, or apprehended with a sense of intense reality (*the vivid colors of the landscape; a vivid memory of the horrors of war*).

Something that is **pictorial** aims to present a vivid picture (*a pictorial writing style*), while **picturesque** usually applies to scenes, pictures, etc., that are visually striking because they are panoramic, quaint, or unusual (*from a distance the village looked picturesque, but up close it was seen to be rundown*).

-graphic ▸*comb. form* in adjectives corresponding to nouns ending in *-graphy* (such as *demographic* corresponding to *demography*). ▷from or suggested by Greek *-graphikos,* from *graphē* 'writing, drawing'; partly from **-GRAPHY** or **-GRAPH** + **-IC.**

graph·i·cal /ˈgrafikəl/ ▸*adj.* **1** of, relating to, or in the form of a graph: *flowcharts are graphical presentations.* **2** of or relating to visual art or computer graphics: *a high-resolution graphical display.* —**graph·i·cal·ly** /-ik(ə)lē/ *adv.*

-graphical ▸*comb. form* equivalent to **-GRAPHIC.**

-graphically ▸*comb. form* in adverbs corresponding to nouns ending in *-graphic* (such as *demographically* corresponding to *demographic*).

graph·i·cal us·er in·ter·face (abbr.: **GUI**) ▸*n. Computing* a visual way of interacting with a computer using items such as windows, icons, and menus, used by most modern operating systems.

graph·ic arts ▸*plural n.* the visual arts based on the use of line and tone rather than three-dimensional work or the use of color. ■ (**graphic art**) the activity of practicing these arts, esp. as a subject of study. —**graph·ic art·ist** *n.*

graph·ic de·sign ▸*n.* the art or skill of combining text and pictures in advertisements, magazines, or books. —**graph·ic de·sign·er** *n.*

graph·ic e·qual·iz·er ▸*n.* an electronic device or computer program that allows the separate control of the strength and quality of selected frequency bands.

graph·ic nov·el ▸*n.* a novel in comic-strip format.

graph·ics /ˈgrafiks/ ▸*plural n.* [usu. treated as *sing.*] **1** the products of the graphic arts, esp. commercial design or illustration. **2** the use of diagrams in calculation and design. **3** (also **computer graphics**) [treated as *pl.*] visual images produced by computer processing. ■ [treated as *sing.*] the use of computers linked to display screens to generate and manipulate visual images.

graph·ics card ▸*n. Computing* a printed circuit board that controls the output to a display screen.

graph·ics tab·let ▸*n. Computing* an input device consisting of a flat, pressure-sensitive pad that the user draws on or points at with a special stylus, to guide a pointer displayed on the screen.

graph·ite /ˈgraˌfīt/ ▸*n.* a gray, crystalline, allotropic form of carbon that occurs as a mineral in some rocks and can be made from coke. It is used as a solid lubricant, in pencils, and as a moderator in nuclear reactors. ▷late 18th cent.: coined in German (*Graphit*), from Greek *graphein* 'write' (because of its use as pencil "lead"). —**gra·phit·ic** /grəˈfitik/ *adj.*

graph·i·tize /ˈgrafiˌtīz/ ▸*v. technical* convert or be converted into graphite. —**graph·i·ti·za·tion** /ˌgrafitiˈzāshən/ *n.*

graph·ol·o·gy /graˈfäləjē/ ▸*n.* **1** the study of handwriting, for example, as used to infer a person's character. **2** *Linguistics* the study of written and printed symbols and of writing systems. ▷mid 19th cent.: from Greek *graphē* 'writing' + **-LOGY.** —**graph·o·log·i·cal** /ˌgrafəˈläjikəl/ *adj.* —**graph·ol·o·gist** /-jist/ *n.*

graph pa·per ▸*n.* paper printed with a network of small squares to assist the drawing of graphs or other diagrams.

graph the·o·ry ▸*n.* the mathematical theory of the properties and applications of graphs.

-graphy ▸*comb. form* in nouns denoting: **1** a descriptive science: *geography.* **2** a technique of producing images: *radiography.* **3** a style or method of writing or drawing: *calligraphy.* ■ writing about (a specified subject): *hagiography.* ■ a written or printed list: *filmography.* ▷from or suggested by Greek *-graphia* 'writing.'

grap·nel /ˈgrapnəl/ ▸*n.* a grappling hook. ■ a small anchor with several flukes. ▷late Middle English: from an Anglo-Norman French diminutive of Old French *grapon,* of Germanic origin.

grapnel (anchor)

grap·pa /ˈgräpə/ ▸*n.* a brandy distilled from the fermented residue of grapes after they have been pressed in winemaking. ▷Italian, literally 'grape stalk,' of Germanic origin.

grap·ple /ˈgrapəl/ ▸*v.* **1** [*intrans.*] engage in a close fight or struggle without weapons; wrestle: *passersby **grappled with** the man after the knife attack.* ■ [*trans.*] seize hold of (someone). ■ (**grapple with**) struggle with or work hard to deal with or overcome (a difficulty or challenge): *other towns are still grappling with the problem.* **2** [*trans.*] *archaic* seize or hold with a grapnel.
▸*n.* an act of grappling. ■ *informal* a wrestling match. ■ an instrument for catching hold of or seizing something; a grappling hook. ▷Middle English (as a noun denoting a grapnel): from Old French *grapil,* from Provençal, diminutive of *grapa* 'hook,' of Germanic origin; related to **GRAPE.** The verb dates from the mid 16th cent. —**grap·pler** /ˈgrapl(ə)r/ *n.*

grap·pling /ˈgrapliNG/ ▸*n.* **1** a grappling hook or grappling iron. **2** a small anchor; a grapnel.

grap·pling hook /ˈgrapliNG/ (also **grappling iron**) ▸*n.* a device with iron claws, attached to a rope and used for dragging or grasping.

grap·to·lite /ˈgraptəˌlīt/ ▸*n.* an extinct marine invertebrate animal of the Paleozoic era, forming mainly planktonic colonies and believed to be related to the pterobranchs. • Class Graptolithina, phylum Hemichordata. ▷mid 19th cent.: from Greek *graptos* 'marked with letters' + **-LITE**: so named because of the impressions left on hard shales, resembling markings with a slate pencil.

GRAS ▸*abbr.* generally recognized as safe; an FDA label for substances not known to be health hazards.

grasp /grasp/ ▸*v.* [*trans.*] seize and hold firmly: *she grasped the bottle.* ■ [*intrans.*] (**grasp at**) try to seize hold of: *they grasped at each other with numbed fingers | they had grasped at any means to overthrow him.* ■ get mental hold of; comprehend fully: *the way in which children could grasp complex ideas.* ■ act decisively to the advantage of (something): *we must grasp the opportunities offered.*
▸*n.* [in *sing.*] a firm hold or grip: *the child slipped from her grasp.* ■ a person's power or capacity to attain something: *he knew success was within his grasp.* ■ a person's understanding: *meanings that are beyond my grasp | his grasp of detail.* ▷late Middle English: perhaps related to **GROPE.** —**grasp·a·ble** *adj.* —**grasp·er** *n.*
▸***PHRASES*** □ **grasp at straws** (or **a straw**) see **STRAW.** □ **grasp the nettle** *Brit.* tackle a difficulty boldly. [because a nettle stings when touched lightly, but not when grasped firmly.]

grasp·ing /ˈgraspiNG/ ▸*adj.* greedy; avaricious: *grasping, power-hungry individuals.* —**grasp·ing·ly** *adv.* —**grasp·ing·ness** *n.*

Grass /gräs/, Günter (Wilhelm) (1927–), German novelist, poet, and playwright. His works are intellectual and experimental and often reflect his socialist views. Notable works: *The Tin Drum* (1959), *The Plebeians Rehearse the Uprising* (1966), and *The Flounder* (1977). Nobel Prize for Literature (1999).

grass /gras/ ▸*n.* **1** vegetation consisting of typically short plants with long narrow leaves, growing wild or cultivated on lawns and pasture, and as a fodder crop. ■ ground covered with grass: *he sat down on the grass.* ■ pastureland: *the farms were mostly given over to grass.* **2** the mainly herbaceous plant that constitutes such vegetation, which has jointed stems and spikes of small, wind-pollinated flowers.

Grasses belong to the large family Gramineae (or Poaceae; the **grass family**), and form the dominant vegetation of many areas of the world. The possession of a growing point that is mainly at ground level makes grasses suitable as the food of many grazing animals, and for use in lawns and playing fields.

3 *informal* marijuana. **4** *Brit., informal* a police informer. [perhaps related to the 19th-cent. rhyming slang *grasshopper* 'copper.']
▸*v.* [*trans.*] **1** (usu. **be grassed**) cover (an area of ground) with grass: *hillsides so closely **grassed over,** they seem to be painted green.* ■ feed (livestock) with grass. **2** [*intrans.*] *Brit., informal* inform the police of criminal activity or plans: *someone had **grassed on** the thieves.* ▷Old English *græs,* of Germanic origin; related to Dutch *gras,* German *Gras,* also ultimately to **GREEN** and **GROW.** —**grass·less** *adj.* —**grass·like** /-ˌlīk/ *adj.*
▸***PHRASES*** □ **the grass is always greener on the other side of the fence** *proverb* other people's lives or situations always seem better than one's own. □ **not let the grass grow under one's feet** not delay in acting or taking an opportunity.

grass carp ▸*n.* a large Chinese freshwater fish, farmed for food in Southeast Asia and introduced elsewhere to control the growth of vegetation in waterways. • *Ctenopharyngodon idella,* family Cyprinidae.

grass·cloth /ˈgrasˌklôTH/ ▸*n.* a fine, light cloth

resembling linen, woven from the fibers of the inner bark of the ramie plant.

grass·cy·cling /ˈgras,sīkliNG/ ▸*n.* the leaving of chopped grass clippings on a mowed lawn as a fertilizer: *grasscycling is the easiest, most environmentally beneficial method of dealing with grass clippings.* **—grass·cy·cle** *v.*

grass·hop·per /ˈgras,häpər/ ▸*n.* a plant-eating insect with long hind legs that are used for jumping and for producing a chirping sound. It frequents grassy places and low vegetation. • Family Acrididae, order Orthoptera: many genera.

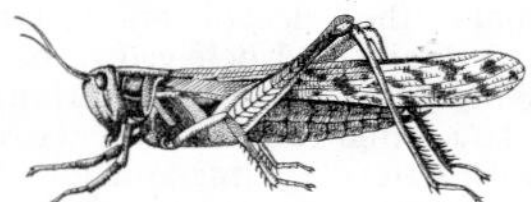

American grasshopper

grass·hop·per mouse ▸*n.* a mainly carnivorous North American mouse with a stout body, gray or brownish fur, and a short white-tipped tail. • Genus *Onychomys*, family Muridae: three species.

grass·land /ˈgras,land/ ▸*n.* (also **grasslands**) a large open area of country covered with grass, esp. one used for grazing: *rough grassland.*

grass of Par·nas·sus ▸*n.* a herbaceous plant of north temperate regions that bears a solitary white flower. • Genus *Parnassia*, family Saxifragaceae: several species, including *P. glauca* and *P. palustris.*

grass par·rot (also **grass parakeet**) ▸*n.* *Austral.* a small parrot frequenting grassy country. • Family Psittacidae: several genera, in particular *Psephotus* and *Neophema.*

grass pea ▸*n.* a plant of the pea family which is cultivated as food for animals and humans, though excessive consumption can lead to lathyrism. Also called CHICKLING PEA. • *Lathyrus sativus*, family Leguminosae.

grass·quit /ˈgras,kwit/ ▸*n.* a small Caribbean and tropical American songbird related to the buntings, the male being partly or mainly black. • Family Emberizidae (subfamily Emberizinae): three genera, in particular *Tiaris*, and several species.

G

grass roots (also **grass·roots** /ˈgras,ro͞ots/) ▸*plural n.* the most basic level of an activity or organization: *the whole campaign would be conducted **at the grass roots.*** | [as *adj.*] *trying to improve the sport's image **at the grass-roots level.*** ■ ordinary people regarded as the main body of an organization's membership: *you have lost touch with the grass roots of the party.*

grass ski ▸*n.* each of a pair of short skis with rollers on the bottom, for going down grass-covered slopes. **—grass ski·ing** *n.*

grass skirt ▸*n.* a skirt made of long grass and leaves fastened to a waistband, associated esp. with female dancers from some Pacific islands.

grass snake ▸*n.* a common harmless Eurasian snake that typically has a yellowish band around the neck and is often found in or near water. • *Natrix natrix*, family Colubridae. ■ another term for GREEN SNAKE.

grass tet·a·ny ▸*n.* a disease of livestock caused by magnesium deficiency, occurring esp. when there is a change from indoor feeding to outdoor grazing.

grass wid·ow ▸*n.* a woman whose husband is away often or for a prolonged period. ▹early 16th cent. (denoting an unmarried woman with a child): from GRASS + WIDOW, perhaps from the idea of the couple having lain on the grass instead of in bed. The current sense dates from the mid 19th cent.; compare with Dutch *grasweduwe* and German *Strohwitwe* 'straw widow.'

grass·y /ˈgrasē/ ▸*adj.* (**grass·i·er, grass·i·est**) of or covered with grass: *grassy slopes.* ■ characteristic of grass: *an intense grassy green.* ■ tasting or smelling like grass: *try the pleasant, grassy Chablis.* **—grass·i·ness** *n.*

grate[1] /grāt/ ▸*v.* **1** [*trans.*] reduce (something, esp. food) to small shreds by rubbing it on a grater: *peel and roughly grate the carrots* | [as *adj.*] (**grated**) *grated cheese.* **2** [*intrans.*] make an unpleasant rasping sound: *the hinges of the door grated.* ■ (**grate against**) rub against something with such a sound: *his helmet grated against the top of the door.* ■ have an irritating effect: *he had a juvenile streak that **grated on** her nerves.* ▹late Middle English: from Old French *grater*, of Germanic origin; related to German *kratzen* 'to scratch.'

grate[2] ▸*n.* **1** the recess of a fireplace or furnace. ■ a metal frame confining fuel in a fireplace or furnace. **2** a grating. ▹Middle English (meaning 'a grating'): from Old French, based on Latin *cratis* 'hurdle.'

grate·ful /ˈgrātfəl/ ▸*adj.* feeling or showing an appreciation of kindness; thankful: *I'm very grateful to you for all your help.* ■ *archaic* received or experienced with gratitude; welcome: *enjoying the grateful shade.* ▹mid 16th cent.: from obsolete *grate* 'pleasing, agreeable, thankful' (from Latin *gratus*) + -FUL. **—grate·ful·ly** *adv.* **—grate·ful·ness** *n.*

grat·er /ˈgrātər/ ▸*n.* a device having a surface covered with holes edged by slightly raised cutting edges, used for grating cheese and other foods. ■ a device in which blades are moved manually (by turning a handle), used for grating cheese and other foods.

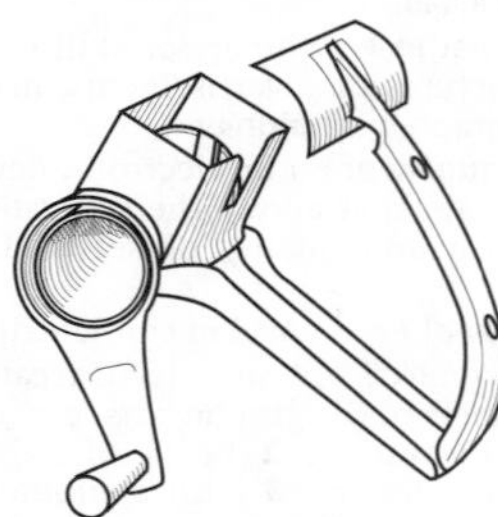

cheese grater

grat·i·cule /ˈgratə,kyo͞ol/ ▸*n.* *technical* a network of lines representing meridians and parallels, on which a map or plan can be represented. ▹late 19th cent.: from French, from medieval Latin *graticula* 'a little grating,' from Latin *craticula* 'gridiron,' diminutive of *cratis* 'hurdle.'

grat·i·fy /ˈgratə,fī/ ▸*v.* (**-fies, -fied**) [*trans.*] (often **be gratified**) give (someone) pleasure or satisfaction: *I was gratified to see the coverage in May's issue* | [as *adj.*] (**gratifying**) *the results were gratifying.* ■ indulge or satisfy (a desire): *not all the sexual impulses can be gratified.* ▹late Middle English (in the sense 'make pleasing'): from French *gratifier* or Latin *gratificari* 'give or do as a favor,' from *gratus* 'pleasing, thankful.' **—grat·i·fi·ca·tion** /,gratəfiˈkāSHən/ *n.* **—grat·i·fi·er** *n.* **—gra·ti·fy·ing·ly** *adv.*

grat·in /ˈgrätn; ˈgratn/ ▸*n.* a dish with a light browned crust of breadcrumbs or melted cheese. ▹French, from *gratter*, earlier *grater* 'to grate.'

gra·ti·né /,grätnˈā; ,gra-/ (also **gra·ti·née**) ▸*adj.* [*postpositive*] another term for AU GRATIN. ▹French, past participle of *gratiner* 'cook au gratin.' **—gra·ti·néed** *adj.*

grat·ing[1] /ˈgrātiNG/ ▸*adj.* sounding harsh and unpleasant: *her high, grating voice.* ■ irritating: *a smarty-pants tone that I found grating.* **—grat·ing·ly** *adv.*

grat·ing[2] ▸*n.* a framework of parallel or crossed bars, typically preventing access through an opening while permitting communication or ventilation. ■ (also **diffraction grating**) *Optics* a set of equally spaced parallel wires, or a surface ruled with equally spaced parallel lines, used to produce spectra by diffraction.

grat·is /ˈgratis/ ▸*adv.* without charge; free: *a monthly program was issued gratis.*
▸*adj.* given or done for nothing; free: *gratis copies.* ▹late Middle English: from Latin, contraction of *gratiis* 'as a kindness,' from *gratia* 'grace, kindness.'

grat·i·tude /ˈgratə,t(y)o͞od/ ▸*n.* the quality of being thankful; readiness to show appreciation for and to return kindness: *she expressed her gratitude to the committee for their support.* ▹late Middle English: from Old French, or from medieval Latin *gratitudo*, from Latin *gratus* 'pleasing, thankful.'

gra·tu·i·tous /grəˈt(y)o͞oitəs/ ▸*adj.* **1** uncalled for; lacking good reason; unwarranted: *gratuitous violence.* **2** given or done free of charge: *solicitors provide a form of gratuitous legal advice.* ▹mid 17th cent.: from Latin *gratuitus* 'given freely, spontaneous' + -OUS. **—gra·tu·i·tous·ly** *adv.* **—gra·tu·i·tous·ness** *n.*

gra·tu·i·ty /grəˈt(y)o͞oitē/ ▸*n.* (*pl.* **-ties**) money given in return for some service or favor, in particular: See note at PRESENT. ■ *formal* a tip given to a waiter, taxicab driver, etc. ▹late 15th cent. (denoting graciousness or favor): from Old French *gratuité* or medieval Latin *gratuitas* 'gift,' from Latin *gratus* 'pleasing, thankful.'

Grau /grou/, Shirley Ann (1929–) U.S. writer. Her works include *The Keepers of the House* (1964), *The Condor Passes* (1971), and *Roadwalkers* (1994).

gra·va·men /grəˈvāmən/ ▸*n.* (*pl.* **-vam·i·na** /-ˈvamənə/) *chiefly Law* the essence or most serious part of a complaint or accusation. ■ a grievance. ▹early 17th cent. (as an ecclesiastical term denoting formal presentation of a grievance): from late Latin, literally 'physical inconvenience,' from Latin *gravare* 'to load,' from *gravis* 'heavy.'

grave[1] /grāv/ ▸*n.* a place of burial for a dead body, typically a hole dug in the ground and marked by a stone or mound: *the coffin was lowered into the grave.* ■ (**the grave**) used as an allusive term for death: *life beyond the grave.* ■ a place where a broken piece of machinery or other discarded object lies: *lift the aircraft from its watery grave.* ▹Old English *græf*, of Germanic origin; related to Dutch *graf* and German *Grab.*

▸*PHRASES* □ **dig one's own grave** do something foolish that causes one to fail or be ruined. □ (**as**) **silent** (or **quiet**) **as the grave** extremely quiet. □ **take the** (or **one's**, etc.) **secret to the grave** die without revealing a secret. □ **turn** (also **turn over**) **in one's grave** used to express the opinion that something would have caused anger or distress to someone who is now dead: *Bach must be turning in his grave at the vulgarities of the twentieth century.*

grave[2] ▸*adj.* giving cause for alarm; serious: *a matter of grave concern.* ■ serious or solemn in manner or appearance; somber: *his face was grave.*
▸*n.* also /gräv/ another term for GRAVE ACCENT. ▹late 15th cent. (originally of a wound in the sense 'severe, serious'): from Old French *grave* or Latin *gravis* 'heavy, serious.' **—grave·ly** *adv.* **—grave·ness** *n.*

grave[3] ▸*v.* (*past part.* **grav·en** /ˈgrāvən/ or **graved**) [*trans.*] *archaic* engrave (an inscription or image) on a surface. ■ *poetic/literary* fix (something) indelibly in the mind: *the times are graven on my memory.* ▹Old English *grafan* 'dig,' of Germanic origin; related to German *graben*, Dutch *graven* 'dig' and German *begraben* 'bury,' also to GRAVE[1] and GROOVE.

grave[4] ▸*v.* [*trans.*] *historical* clean (a ship's bottom) by burning off the accretions and then tarring it. ▹late Middle English: perhaps from French dialect *grave*, variant of Old French *greve* 'shore' (because originally the ship would have been run aground).

gra·ve[5] /ˈgrä,vā/ ▸*adj.* *Music* slowly; with solemnity. ▹Italian: *grave* 'slowly.'

grave ac·cent /gräv; grāv/ ▸*n.* a mark (\`) placed over certain letters in some languages to indicate an alteration of a sound, as of quality, quantity, or pitch. ▹early 17th cent.: French *grave* (see GRAVE[2]).

grave·dig·ger /ˈgrāv,digər/ ▸*n.* a person who digs graves.

grav·el /ˈgravəl/ ▸*n.* a loose aggregation of small water-worn or pounded stones. ■ a mixture of such stones with coarse sand, used for paths and roads and as an aggregate. ■ a stratum or deposit of such stones. ■ *Medicine* aggregations of crystals formed in the urinary tract.
▸*v.* (**grav·eled, grav·el·ing**; *Brit.* **grav·elled, grav·el·ling**) [*trans.*] **1** cover (an area of ground) with gravel. **2** *informal* make (someone) angry or annoyed: *this was a bad strike, and it graveled him to involve himself in it.* ■ *archaic* make (someone) feel confused or puzzled. ▹Middle English: from Old French, diminutive of *grave* (see GRAVE[4]).

grav·el-blind ▸*adj.* *archaic* almost completely blind. ▹early 17th cent.: originally as *high-gravel-blind*, a humorous usage meaning 'more than sand-blind (= half-blind),' with reference to Shakespeare's *Merchant of Venice.*

gra·vel·ly /ˈgravəlē/ ▸*adj.* resembling, containing, or consisting of gravel: *a dry gravelly soil.* ■ (of a voice) deep and rough-sounding.

grav·en /ˈgrāvən/ ▸ past participle of GRAVE[3].

grav·en im·age ▸*n.* a carved idol or representation of a god used as an object of worship. ▹with biblical allusion to Exod. 20:4.

Gra·ven·stein /ˈgrävən,stīn/ ▸*n.* a widely grown apple of a large variety having yellow, red-streaked skin, used for cooking and as a dessert apple. ▹early 19th cent.: the German form of *Graasten*, a village in Denmark formerly in Schleswig-Holstein, Germany.

grav·er /ˈgrāvər/ ▸*n.* a burin or other engraving tool. ■ *archaic* a person who engraves or carves.

Graves[1] /ˈgrāvz/, Robert (Ranke) (1895–1985), English poet, novelist, and critic; professor of poetry at Oxford University 1961–66. Notable prose works: *Goodbye to All That* (1929), *I, Claudius* (1934), and *The White Goddess* (1948).

Graves[2] /ˈgrävz; gräv/ ▸*n.* a red or white wine from the district of Graves, to the south of Bordeaux in France.

Graves' dis·ease ▸*n.* a swelling of the neck and protrusion of the eyes resulting from an overactive thyroid gland. Also called **EXOPHTHALMIC GOITER.** ▷mid 19th cent.: named after Robert J. Graves (1796–1853), the Irish physician who first identified it.

grave·side /ˈgrāv,sīd/ ▸*n.* the ground around the edge of a grave.

grave·site /ˈgrāv,sīt/ ▸*n.* the location of a person's grave.

grave·stone /ˈgrāv,stōn/ ▸*n.* an inscribed headstone marking a grave.

Gra·vett·i·an /grəˈvetēən/ ▸*adj. Archaeology* of, relating to, or denoting an Upper Paleolithic culture in Europe following the Aurignacian, dated to about 28,000–19,000 years ago. ■ [as *n.*] (**the Gravettian**) the Gravettian culture or period. ▷1930s: from *la Gravette*, an archaeological site in southwestern France, where objects from this culture were found.

grave·yard /ˈgrāv,yärd/ ▸*n.* a burial ground, esp. one beside a church.

grave·yard shift ▸*n.* a work shift that runs through the early morning hours, typically covering the period between midnight and 8 a.m.

grav·id /ˈgravid/ ▸*adj. technical* pregnant; carrying eggs or young. ■ *figurative* full of meaning or a specified quality: *the scene is gravid with unease.* ▷late 16th cent.: from Latin *gravidus* 'laden, pregnant,' from *gravis* 'heavy.'

gra·vim·e·ter /grəˈvimitər/ ▸*n.* an instrument for measuring the difference in the force of gravity from one place to another. ▷late 18th cent.: from French *gravimètre*, from *grave* 'heavy' (from Latin *gravis*) + *-mètre* '(instrument) measuring.'

grav·i·met·ric /,gravəˈmetrik/ ▸*adj.* of or relating to the measurement of weight. ■ (of chemical analysis) based on weighing reagents and products.

gra·vim·e·try /grəˈvimətrē/ ▸*n. Physics* the measurement of weight.

grav·ing dock ▸*n.* another term for **DRY DOCK.** ▷early 19th cent.: *graving* from **GRAVE**[4].

grav·i·tas /ˈgravi,täs/ ▸*n.* dignity, seriousness, or solemnity of manner: *a post for which he has the expertise and the gravitas.* ▷Latin, from *gravis* 'serious.'

grav·i·tate /ˈgravi,tāt/ ▸*v.* [*intrans.*] move toward or be attracted to a place, person, or thing: *they gravitated to the Catholic faith in their hour of need.* ■ *Physics* move, or tend to move, toward a center of gravity or other attractive force. ■ *archaic* descend or sink by the force of gravity. ▷mid 17th cent.: from modern Latin *gravitat-*, from the verb *gravitare*, from Latin *gravitas* 'weight.'

grav·i·ta·tion /,graviˈtāsʜən/ ▸*n.* movement, or a tendency to move, toward a center of attractive force, as in the falling of bodies to the earth. ■ *Physics* a force of attraction exerted by each particle of matter in the universe on every other particle: *the law of universal gravitation.* Compare with **GRAVITY.** ■ *figurative* movement toward or attraction to something: *a tentative gravitation toward the prices that we saw before the announcement.* ▷mid 17th cent.: from modern Latin *gravitatio(n-)*, from the verb *gravitare* (see **GRAVITATE**). —**grav·i·ta·tion·al** /-sʜənl/ *adj.* —**grav·i·ta·tion·al·ly** /-sʜənl-ē/ *adv.*

grav·i·ta·tion·al con·stant (abbr.: **G**) ▸*n. Physics* the constant in Newton's law of gravitation relating gravity to the masses and separation of particles, equal to 6.67×10^{-11}N m^2 kg^{-2}.

grav·i·ta·tion·al field ▸*n. Physics* the region of space surrounding a body in which another body experiences a force of gravitational attraction.

grav·i·ta·tion·al lens ▸*n. Astronomy* a region of space containing a massive object whose gravitational field distorts electromagnetic radiation passing through it in a similar way to a lens, sometimes producing a multiple image of a remote object.

grav·i·ton /ˈgravi,tän/ ▸*n. Physics* a hypothetical quantum of gravitational energy, regarded as a particle. ▷1940s: from **GRAVITATION** + **-ON.**

grav·i·ty /ˈgravitē/ ▸*n.* **1** *Physics* the force that attracts a body toward the center of the earth, or toward any other physical body having mass. For most purposes Newton's laws of gravity apply, with minor modifications to take the general theory of relativity into account. ■ the degree of intensity of this, measured by acceleration. **2** extreme or alarming importance; seriousness: *crimes of the utmost gravity.* ■ seriousness or solemnity of manner: *has the poet ever spoken with greater eloquence or gravity?* ▷late 15th cent. (sense 2): from Old French, or from Latin *gravitas* 'weight, seriousness,' from *gravis* 'heavy.' Sense 1 dates from the 17th cent.

grav·i·ty feed ▸*n.* a supply system making use of gravity to maintain the flow of material. —**grav·i·ty-fed** *adj.*

grav·i·ty wave ▸*n. Physics* **1** a hypothetical wave carrying gravitational energy, postulated by Einstein to be emitted when a massive body is accelerated. **2** a wave propagated on a liquid surface or in a fluid through the effects of gravity.

grav·lax /ˈgräv,läks/ ▸*n.* a Scandinavian dish of dry-cured salmon marinated in herbs. ▷Swedish, from *grav* 'trench' + *lax* 'salmon' (from the former practice of burying the salmon in salt in a hole in the ground).

gra·vure /grəˈvyŏŏr/ ▸*n.* an image produced from etching a plate through an intaglio process and producing a print from it. ■ the production of prints in this way.

gra·vy /ˈgrāvē/ ▸*n.* (*pl.* **-vies**) **1** the fat and juices exuding from meat during cooking. ■ a sauce made from these juices together with stock and other ingredients. **2** *informal* unearned or unexpected money. ▷Middle English (denoting a spicy sauce): perhaps from a misreading (as *gravé*) of Old French *grané*, probably from *grain* 'spice,' from Latin *granum* 'grain.'

gra·vy boat ▸*n.* a boat-shaped vessel used for serving gravy or sauce; sauceboat.

gra·vy train ▸*n. informal* used to refer to a situation in which someone can make a lot of money for very little effort: *come to Hollywood and get on the gravy train.*

Gray[1] /grā/, Asa (1810–88), U.S. botanist. Finding no conflict between evolution and his view of divine design in nature, he supported Darwin's theories at a time when they were unpopular.

Gray[2], Elisha (1835–1901) U.S. inventor. A rival of Alexander Graham Bell for the telephone patent, his small business eventually became the Western Electric Company.

Gray[3], Horace (1828–1902) U.S. Supreme Court associate justice 1881–1902. Appointed to the Court by President Arthur, he had served as Massachusett's chief justice 1873–81.

Gray[4], Thomas (1716–71), English poet; known for "Elegy Written in a Country Church-Yard" (1751).

gray[1] /grā/ (*Brit.* **grey**) ▸*adj.* **1** of a color intermediate between black and white, as of ashes or an overcast sky: *gray flannel trousers.* ■ (of hair) turning gray or white with age: *a gray beard.* ■ (of a person) having gray hair: *a gray, fatherly gentleman.* ■ *informal* relating to old people, esp. when seen as an oppressed group: *gray power.* ■ (of the weather) cloudy and dull; without sun: *a cold, gray November day.* ■ (of a person's face) pale, as through tiredness, age, or illness: *a few people, their faces gray and bitter.* **2** dull and nondescript; without interest or character: *gray, faceless men | the gray daily routine.* **3** (of financial or trading activity) not accounted for in official statistics: *the gray economy.*

▸*n.* **1** gray color or pigment: *dirty intermediate tones of gray.* ■ gray clothes or material: *the gentleman in gray.* ■ gray hair: *he sighed at the amount of gray at his temple.* ■ (usu. **Gray**) the Confederate army in the Civil War, or a member of that army. **2** a gray thing or animal, in particular a gray or white horse.

▸*v.* [*intrans.*] (esp. of hair) become gray with age: *he had put on weight and grayed somewhat* | [as *adj.*] (**graying**) *a man of about fifty with graying hair.* ■ (of a person or group) become older; age: [as *adj.*] (**graying**) *a graying workforce.*

▸*phrasal v.* □ **gray something out** display a menu option in a light font to indicate that it is not available: [*usually passive*] *all the property fields on the Shortcut tab are either missing or grayed out.* ▷Old English *grǣg*, of Germanic origin; related to Dutch *grauw* and German *grau.* —**gray·ish** *adj.* —**gray·ly** *adv.* —**gray·ness** *n.*

gray[2] (abbr.: **Gy**) ▸*n. Physics* the SI unit of the absorbed dose of ionizing radiation, corresponding to one joule per kilogram. ▷1970s: named after Louis H. Gray (1905–65), English radiobiologist.

gray a·re·a ▸*n.* an ill-defined situation or field not readily conforming to a category or to an existing set of rules: *gray areas in the legislation have still to be clarified.*

gray·beard /ˈgrā,bi(ə)rd/ (*Brit.* **grey·beard**) ▸*n.* **1** *humorous* or *derogatory* an old man. **2** *archaic* a large stoneware jug used for holding spirits.

Gray code ▸*n.* a numerical code used in computing in which consecutive integers are represented by binary numbers differing in only one digit. ▷mid 20th cent.: named after Frank Gray (1887–1969), American physicist.

gray em·i·nence ▸*n.* another term for **ÉMINENCE GRISE.**

Gray Fri·ar ▸*n.* a Franciscan friar. ▷Middle English: so named because of the color of the order's habit.

gray goods /ˈgrā ,gŏŏdz/ ▸*plural n.* **1** newly manufactured fabrics that have not been subjected to whitening processes. **2** goods traded in a gray market.

gray goose ▸*n.* a goose of a group distinguished by having mainly gray plumage. • Genus *Anser*, family Anatidae: several species, e.g., graylag and white-fronted geese.

gray jay ▸*n.* a fluffy, long-tailed jay with dark gray upper parts and a whitish face, found in Canada and the northwestern U.S. • *Perisoreus canadensis*, family Corvidae.

gray kan·ga·roo ▸*n.* a large forest-dwelling kangaroo native to Australia. • Genus *Macropus*, family Macropodidae: the eastern *M. giganteus* (also called **FORESTER**), with silvery-gray fur, and the western *M. fuliginosus*, with brownish fur.

gray·lag /ˈgrā,lag/ (also **graylag goose**) ▸*n.* a large goose with mainly gray plumage, which is native to Eurasia and is the ancestor of the domestic goose. • *Anser anser*, family Anatidae. ▷early 18th cent.: probably from **GRAY**[1] + dialect *lag* 'goose,' of unknown origin.

gray·ling /ˈgrāliɴɢ/ ▸*n.* **1** an edible freshwater fish of Eurasia and North America that is silvery-gray with horizontal violet stripes and has a long, high dorsal fin. • Genus *Thymallus*, family Salmonidae: several species. **2** a mainly brown European butterfly that has wings with bright eyespots and grayish undersides. • *Hipparchia semele*, subfamily Satyrinae, family Nymphalidae. ▷Middle English: from **GRAY**[1] + **-LING.**

gray·mail /ˈgrā,māl/ ▸*n.* a tactic used by the defense in a spy trial, involving the threat to expose government secrets unless charges against the defendant are dropped.

gray mar·ket ▸*n.* an unofficial market or trade in something, esp. unissued shares or controlled or scarce goods: *the discounting of bonds in the gray market* | [as *adj.*] *a gray market price.*

gray mat·ter ▸*n.* the darker tissue of the brain and spinal cord, consisting mainly of nerve cell bodies and branching dendrites. Compare with **WHITE MATTER.** ■ *informal* intelligence: *I wish I had a little of her gray matter.*

gray mul·let ▸*n.* a thick-bodied, blunt-headed fish that typically lives in inshore or estuarine waters and is a valued food fish. • Family Mugilidae: several genera and species.

gray par·rot (also **African gray parrot**) ▸*n.* a parrot of western equatorial Africa, with gray plumage and a red tail, widely kept as a pet for its mimicking abilities. • *Psittacus erithacus*, family Psittacidae.

gray·scale /ˈgrā,skāl/ ▸*n. Computing* a range of gray shades from white to black, as used in a monochrome display or printout: [as *adj.*] *a grayscale scanner.*

gray seal ▸*n.* a large seal with a spotted, grayish coat and a convex profile, found commonly in the North Atlantic. Also called **ATLANTIC SEAL.** • *Halichoerus grypus*, family Phocidae.

gray squir·rel ▸*n.* an American tree squirrel with mainly gray fur. • Genus *Sciurus*, family Sciuridae: four species, in particular *Sciurus carolinensis*, native to eastern North America and introduced to Britain and elsewhere.

gray·wacke /ˈgrā,wak; -,wakə/ (*Brit.* **grey·wacke**) ▸*n. Geology* a dark coarse-grained sandstone containing more than 15 percent clay. ▷late 18th cent. (as *grauwacke*): from German *Grauwacke*, from *grau* 'gray' + **WACKE.** The anglicized form dates from the early 19th cent.

gray wa·ter ▸*n. technical* the relatively clean waste water from baths, sinks, washing machines, and other kitchen appliances. Compare with **BLACK WATER.**

gray whale ▸*n.* a mottled gray baleen whale that typically has heavy encrustations of barnacles on the skin, commonly seen in coastal waters of the northeastern Pacific. • *Eschrichtius robustus*, the only member of the family Eschrichtiidae.

gray wolf ▸*n.* another term for **TIMBER WOLF.**

Graz /gräts/ a city in southern Austria, on the Mur

Pronunciation Key ə *ago;* ər *over;* ˈə or ,ə *up;* ˈər or ,ər *fur;* a *hat;* ā *rate;* ä *car;* ch *chew;* e *let;* ē *see;* e(ə)r *air;* i *fit;* ī *by;* i(ə)r *ear;* ɴɢ *sing;* ō *go;* ô *for;* oi *boy;* ŏŏ *good;* o͞o *goo;* ou *out;* sʜ *she;* th *thin;* th *then;* (h)w *why;* zʜ *vision*

G

River; pop. 232,000. It is the second largest city in Austria.

graze[1] /grāz/ ▸*v.* [*intrans.*] (of cattle, sheep, etc.) eat grass in a field: *cattle* ***graze on*** *the open meadows.* ■ [*trans.*] (of an animal) feed on (grass or land covered by grass): *llamas graze the tufts of grass.* ■ [*trans.*] put (cattle, sheep, etc.) to feed on land covered by grass: *shepherds who grazed animals on common land.* ■ *informal* (of a person) eat small quantities of food at frequent but irregular intervals: *advertisers should not encourage children to* ***graze on*** *snacks or sweets.* ■ *informal* casually sample something: *we grazed up and down the channels.* ▷Old English *grasian*, from *græs* 'grass.' —**graz·er** *n.*

graze[2] ▸*v.* [*trans.*] scrape the skin of (a part of the body) so as to break the surface but cause little or no bleeding: *she fell down and grazed her knees.* ■ touch or scrape lightly in passing: *his hands just grazed hers.*
▸*n.* a slight injury where the skin is scraped: *it'll be fine, it's only a graze.* ▷late 16th cent.: perhaps a specific use of GRAZE[1].

gra·zier /'grāZHər/ ▸*n. Brit.* a person who rears or fattens cattle or sheep for market. ▷Middle English: from GRASS + -IER.

graz·ing /'grāziNG/ ▸*n.* grassland suitable for pasturage: *pastures and rough grazing.*

grease ▸*n.* /grēs/ oily or fatty matter, in particular: ■ a thick oily substance used as a lubricant: *axle grease.* ■ oil or fat used or produced in cooking. ■ oily matter in the hair, esp. when used for styling. ■ the oily matter in unprocessed wool; lanolin.
▸*v.* /grēs; grēz/ [*trans.*] smear or lubricate with grease: [as *adj.*] (**greased**) *place on a greased baking sheet.* ▷Middle English: from Old French *graisse*, based on Latin *crassus* 'thick, fat.' —**grease·less** *adj.*
▸*PHRASES* □ **grease the palm of** *informal* bribe (someone). □ **grease the skids** *informal* help matters run smoothly: *his mission was to use his budgetary skills to grease the skids for new projects.* □ **grease the wheels** help something go smoothly: *it is inadequate to grease the wheels of recovery.* □ **like greased lightning** *informal* extremely fast: *you come up with plans faster than greased lightning.*

grease·ball /'grēs,bôl/ ▸*n. informal, offensive* a foreigner, esp. one of Mediterranean or Latin American origin.

G

grease gun ▸*n.* a device for pumping grease under pressure to a particular point.

grease mon·key ▸*n. informal, derogatory* a mechanic.

grease·paint /'grēs,pānt/ ▸*n.* a waxy substance used as makeup by actors.

grease pen·cil ▸*n.* a pencil made of grease colored with a pigment, used esp. for marking glossy surfaces.

greas·er /'grēsər; -zər/ ▸*n.* **1** a mechanic. ■ an unskilled member of a ship's engine-room crew. ■ *informal* a rough young man, esp. one who greases his hair back and is a member of a motorcycle gang. **2** *informal, offensive* a Hispanic American, esp. a Mexican. **3** *informal* a gentle landing of an aircraft.

grease·wood /'grēs,wo͝od/ ▸*n.* **1** a resinous dwarf shrub of the goosefoot family, which yields hard yellow wood used chiefly for fuel. It grows in dry areas of the western U.S. and is toxic to livestock if eaten in large quantities. • *Sarcobatus vermiculatus*, family Chenopodiaceae. **2** another term for CHAMISE.

greas·y /'grēsē; -zē/ ▸*adj.* (**greas·i·er, greas·i·est**) covered with an oily substance: *he wiped his greasy fingers.* ■ producing more body oils than average: *greasy skin.* ■ containing or cooked with too much oil or fat: *greasy food.* ■ of or like grease: *their moisturizers don't feel greasy.* ■ slippery: *the floor was greasy.* ■ *figurative* (of a person or their manner) effusively polite in a way that is felt to be insincere and repulsive: *the greasy little man from the newspaper.* —**greas·i·ly** /-səlē; -zəlē/ *adv.* —**greas·i·ness** *n.*

greas·y pole ▸*n. informal* a pole covered with an oily substance to make it more difficult to climb or walk along, used esp. as a form of entertainment. ■ used to refer to the difficult route to the top of someone's profession: *he steadily climbed the greasy pole toward the job he coveted most.*

greas·y spoon ▸*n. informal* a cheap, run-down cafe or restaurant serving fried foods.

great /grāt/ ▸*adj.* **1** of an extent, amount, or intensity considerably above the normal or average: *the article was of great interest | she showed great potential as an actor.* ■ very large and imposing: *a great ocean between them.* ■ [*attrib.*] used to reinforce another adjective of size or extent: *a great big grin.* ■ [*attrib.*] used to express surprise, admiration, or contempt, esp. in exclamations: *you great oaf!* ■ (also **greater**) [*attrib.*] used in names of animals or plants that are larger than similar kinds, e.g., **great auk, greater flamingo.** ■ (**Greater**) [*attrib.*] (of a city) including adjacent urban areas: *Greater Cleveland.* **2** of ability, quality, or eminence considerably above the normal or average: *the great Italian conductor | we obeyed our great men and leaders | great art has the power to change lives.* ■ (**the Great**) a title denoting the most important person of the name: *Alexander the Great.* ■ *informal* very good or satisfactory; excellent: *this has been another great year | what a great guy | wouldn't it be great to have him back?* | [as *exclam.*] *"Great!" said Tom.* ■ [*predic.*] *informal* (of a person) very skilled or capable in a particular area: *a brilliant man, great at mathematics.* **3** [*attrib.*] denoting the element of something that is the most important or the most worthy of consideration: *the great thing is the challenge.* ■ used to indicate that someone or something particularly deserves a specified description: *I was a great fan of Hank's.* **4** [in *combination*] (in names of family relationships) denoting one degree further removed upward or downward: *great-aunt | great-granddaughter | great-great-grandfather.*
▸*n.* **1** a great or distinguished person: *the Beatles, Bob Dylan, all the greats.* ■ [as *plural n.*] (**the great**) great people collectively: *the lives of the great, including Churchill and Newton.* **2** (**Greats**) *Brit., informal* another term for LITERAE HUMANIORES.
▸*adv. informal* excellently; very well: *we played awful, they played great.* ▷Old English *grēat* 'big'; related to Dutch *groot* and German *gross.*
▸*PHRASES* □ **great and small** of all sizes, classes, or types: *all creatures great and small.* □ **a great deal** see DEAL[1]. □ **a great many** see MANY. □ **a great one for** a habitual doer of; an enthusiast for: *my father was a great one for buying gadgets.* □ **Great Scott!** expressing surprise or amazement. [arbitrary euphemism for *Great God!*] □ **to a great extent** in a substantial way; largely: *we are all to a great extent the product of our culture.*

great ape ▸*n.* a large ape of a family closely related to humans, including the gorilla, orangutan, and chimpanzees, but excluding the gibbons; an anthropoid ape. • Family Pongidae, order Primates.

Great At·trac·tor *Astronomy* a massive grouping of galaxies in the direction of the constellations Hydra and Centaurus, whose gravitational pull is thought to be responsible for deviations in the velocity of other galaxies.

great auk ▸*n.* a large, extinct, flightless auk of the North Atlantic, resembling a giant razorbill. The great auk was the original "penguin"; many were taken for food, and the last individuals were killed on an islet off Iceland in 1844. • *Alca* (or **Pinguinus**) *impennis*, family Alcidae.

great-aunt ▸*n.* an aunt of one's father or mother.

Great Aus·tra·lian Bight a wide bay on the southern coast of Australia, part of the southern Indian Ocean.

Great Bar·ri·er Reef a coral reef in the western Pacific Ocean, off the coast of Queensland, Australia. It extends for about 1,250 miles (2,000 km), roughly parallel to the coast, and is the largest coral reef in the world.

Great Ba·sin an arid region in the western U.S. between the Sierra Nevada and the Rocky Mountains that includes most of Nevada and parts of the adjacent states.

Great Bear *Astronomy* the constellation Ursa Major.

Great Bear Lake a large lake in western Northwest Territories, Canada. It drains into the Mackenzie River via the Great Bear River.

Great Bi·ble *n.* the edition of the English Bible that Thomas Cromwell ordered in 1538 to be set up in every parish church in England. It was the work of Miles Coverdale and was first issued in 1539.

Great Brit·ain /'britn/ England, Wales, and Scotland considered as a unit. The name is also often used loosely to refer to the United Kingdom.

USAGE **Great Britain** is the name for the island that comprises England, Scotland, and Wales. The term came into official use in 1603, when King James I (who was also James VI of Scotland) acceded to the throne of England and Wales. Scotland joined this legislative union in 1707.
The **United Kingdom** includes Great Britain and Northern Ireland. The **British Isles** include the United Kingdom and surrounding, smaller islands. The all-encompassing adjective *British* is unlikely to offend anyone from any of these places. *Welsh, Scottish,* and *English* should be used only if you are sure of a person's specific origin.

Great Char·ter another name for MAGNA CARTA.

great circle ▸*n.* a circle on the surface of a sphere that lies in a plane passing through the sphere's center. As it represents the shortest distance between any two points on a sphere, a great circle of the earth is the preferred route taken by a ship or aircraft.

great·coat /'grāt,kōt/ ▸*n.* a long heavy overcoat.

greatcoat

great crest·ed grebe ▸*n.* a large grebe with a crest and ear ruffs in the breeding season, found from Europe to New Zealand. • *Podiceps cristatus*, family Podicipedidae.

Great Dane ▸*n.* a dog of a very large, powerful, short-haired breed.

Great Dane

Great De·pres·sion see DEPRESSION.

Great Dis·mal Swamp (also **Dismal Swamp**) an area of swampland in southeastern Virginia and northeastern North Carolina.

great di·vide ▸*n.* a distinction regarded as significant and very difficult to ignore or overcome: *the great divide between workers and management.* ■ an event, date, or place seen as the point at which significant and irrevocable change occurs: *to our parents, the war was the great divide.* ■ the boundary between life and death: *she is still on the human side of the great divide.* ■ (**Great Divide**) another name for CONTINENTAL DIVIDE or GREAT DIVIDING RANGE.

Great Di·vid·ing Range a mountain system in eastern Australia. Curving roughly parallel to the coast,

it extends from eastern Victoria to northern Queensland. Also called **Great Divide**.

great e·gret ▸*n.* a large white heron of North and South America. Its yellow bill turns orange when breeding. Also called **American egret**. • *Casmerodius albus*, family Ardeidae.

great egret

Great·er An·til·les /an'tilēz/ see **Antilles**.

great·er cel·an·dine /'selən ˌdīn; -ˌdēn/ ▸*n.* a yellow-flowered Eurasian plant of the poppy family. Its toxic orange sap has long been used in herbal medicine, esp. for disorders of the eyes and skin. • *Chelidonium majus*, family Papaveraceae.

Great·er Sun·da Is·lands / 'səndə; 'sŏŏndə/ see **Sunda Islands**.

Great Ex·hi·bi·tion the first international exhibition of the products of industry, promoted by Prince Albert and held in the Crystal Palace in London in 1851.

Great Falls an industrial city in north central Montana, on the Missouri River; pop. 56,690.

Great Glen a large fault valley in Scotland that extends southwest for 60 miles (97 km) from the Moray Firth to Loch Linnhe. It contains Loch Ness. Also calledGlen More.

great-heart·ed ▸*adj. dated* having a noble, generous, and courageous spirit. —**great-heart·ed·ness** *n.*

great horned owl ▸*n.* a large owl found throughout North and South America, with hornlike ear tufts. • *Bubo virginianus*, family Strigidae.

great horned owl

Great In·di·an Des·ert another name for **Thar Desert**.

Great Lakes a group of five large interconnected lakes in central North America that consist of lakes Superior, Michigan, Huron, Erie, and Ontario, and constitute the largest area of fresh water in the world. Lake Michigan is wholly within the U.S., and the others lie on the Canada–U.S. border. Connected to the Atlantic Ocean by the St. Lawrence Seaway, the Great Lakes form an important commercial waterway.

Great Lake State a nickname for the state of **Michigan**.

Great Land a nickname for the state of **Alaska**.

Great Leap For·ward an unsuccessful attempt made under Mao Zedong in China 1958–60 to hasten the process of industrialization and improve agricultural production by reorganizing the population into large rural collectives and adopting labor-intensive industrial methods.

great·ly /'grātlē/ ▸*adv.* by a considerable amount; very much: *I admire him greatly* | [as *submodifier*] *they now have greatly increased powers.*

Great Moth·er ▸*n.* another name for **mother goddess**.

Great Neb·u·la *Astronomy* **1** (also **Great Nebula in Andromeda**) the Andromeda Galaxy. **2** (also **Great Nebula in Orion**) a bright emission nebula in Orion, visible to the naked eye.

great-neph·ew ▸*n.* a son of one's nephew or niece.

great·ness /'grātnəs/ ▸*n.* the quality of being great, distinguished, or eminent: *Elgar's greatness as a composer.*

great-niece ▸*n.* a daughter of one's nephew or niece.

great north·ern div·er ▸*n. chiefly Brit.* another term for **common loon** (see **loon**[2]).

great or·gan ▸*n.* the chief keyboard in a large organ and its related pipes and mechanism.

Great Ouse /ŏŏz/ another name for **Ouse** (sense 1).

Great Plague a serious outbreak of bubonic plague in England in 1665–6, in which about one fifth of the population of London died. It was the last major outbreak in Britain.

Great Plains a vast area of plains east of the Rocky Mountains in North America that extend from the valleys of the Mackenzie River in Canada to southern Texas.

Great Pyrenees ▸*n.* a large heavily built dog of a white breed, with a thick shaggy double coat.

Great Red Spot *Astronomy* a weather system on the planet Jupiter which measures over 6,200 miles (10,000 km) across and has persisted at least since the beginning of telescopic observations.

Great Rift Val·ley a large system of rift valleys in eastern Africa and the Middle East, the largest in the world, that runs for about 3,000 miles (4,285 km) from the Jordan valley in Syria into Mozambique. It is marked by a chain of lakes and a series of volcanoes, including Mount Kilimanjaro.

great room ▸*n.* a large room in a modern house that combines features of a living room with those of a dining room or family room.

Great Rus·sian ▸*adj.* & *n.* former term for **Russian** (language and people), as distinguished from other peoples and languages of the Russian Empire.

Great St. Ber·nard Pass see **St. Bernard Pass**.

Great Salt Lake a salt lake in northern Utah, near Salt Lake City. With an area of about 1,000 square miles (2,590 sq km), it is the largest salt lake in North America.

Great Sand Sea an area of desert in northeastern Africa, on the border between Libya and Egypt.

Great Sand·y Des·ert **1** a large desert in northwestern Australia, in north central Western Australia. **2** another name for **Rub' al Khali**.

Great Schism /'s(k)izəm/ **1** the breach between the Eastern and the Western Churches, traditionally dated to 1054 and becoming final in 1472. **2** the period 1378–1417, when the Western Church was divided by the creation of antipopes.

Great Seal ▸*n.* a seal used for the authentication of state documents of the highest importance, held by the Secretary of State.

great sku·a /'skyōōə/ ▸*n.* a large North Atlantic skua with mainly brown plumage, feeding by robbing other seabirds. • *Catharacta skua*, family Stercorariidae.

Great Slave Lake a large lake in southwestern Northwest Territories, Canada. The deepest lake in North America, it reaches a depth of 2,015 feet (615 m). The Mackenzie River flows out of it.

Great Smok·y Moun·tains (also **Smoky Mountains** or **Smokies**) a range of the Appalachian Mountains in southwestern North Carolina and eastern Tennessee. They are named for a frequent haze.

Great So·ci·e·ty ▸*n.* a domestic program in the administration of President Lyndon B. Johnson that instituted federally sponsored social welfare programs.

great tit ▸*n.* a tit (songbird) with a black head and white cheeks, occurring in many different races from western Europe to eastern Asia. • *Parus major*, family Paridae.

Great Trek the northward migration 1835–37 of large numbers of Boers, discontented with British rule in the Cape, to the areas where they eventually founded the Transvaal Republic and Orange Free State.

great-un·cle ▸*n.* an uncle of one's mother or father.

Great Vic·to·ri·a Des·ert /vik'tôrēə/ a desert region in Australia that straddles the boundary between Western Australia and South Australia.

Great Wall of Chi·na a fortified wall in northern China, extending some 2,400 km (1,500 miles) from Kansu province to the Yellow Sea north of Beijing. It was first built *c.*210 BC, as a protection against nomad invaders. The present wall dates from the Ming dynasty.

Great Wall of China

Great War another name for **World War I**.

great white shark ▸*n.* a large, aggressive shark of warm seas, with a brownish or gray back, white underparts, and large triangular teeth. Also called **white pointer**. • *Carcharodon carcharias*, family Lamnidae.

Great White Way a nickname for **Broadway**.

greave /grēv/ ▸*n. historical* a piece of armor used to protect the shin. ▹Middle English: from Old French *greve* 'shin, greave,' of unknown origin.

grebe /grēb/ ▸*n.* a diving waterbird with a long neck, lobed toes, and almost no tail, typically having bright breeding plumage used in display. • Family Podicipedidae: several genera. The several North American species include the **western grebe** (*Aechmorphorus occidentalis*) and the **pied-billed grebe** (*Podilymbus podiceps*). ▹mid 18th cent.: from French *grèbe* (term used in the Savoy region), of unknown origin.

pied-billed grebe

Gre·cian /'grēsʜən/ ▸*adj.* of or relating to ancient Greece, esp. its architecture. ▹late Middle English: from Old French *grecien*, from Latin *Graecia* 'Greece.'

Gre·cian nose ▸*n.* a straight nose that continues the line of the forehead without a dip.

Gre·cism /'grēsizəm/ (also *chiefly Brit.* **Grae·cism**) ▸*n.* a Greek idiom or grammatical feature, esp. as imitated in another language. ■ the Greek spirit, style, or mode of expression, esp. as imitated in a work of art. ▹late 16th cent.: from French *grécisme* or medieval Latin *Graecismus*, from *Graecus* (see **Greek**).

Gre·co /'grekō/, José (1918–2001) U.S. dancer and choreographer; born in Italy. He had his own dance company from 1931 and also appeared in movies such as *Around the World in 80 Days* (1956).

Greco- (also *chiefly Brit.* **Graeco-**) ▸*comb. form* Greek; Greek and . . . : *Grecophile* | *Greco-Turkish.* ■ relating to Greece.

Gre·co, El see **El Greco**.

Gre·co-Ro·man /'grekō/ (also *chiefly Brit.* **Grae·co-Ro·man**) ▸*adj.* of or relating to the ancient Greeks and Romans. ■ denoting a style of wrestling in which holds below the waist are prohibited.

Greece /grēs/ a country in southeastern Europe; pop. 10,647,000; official language, Greek; capital, Athens.

The age of the classical city-states, of which the most prominent were Athens and Sparta, reached its peak in the 5th century BC, after which Greece fell to Macedonia and then became part of the Roman and Byzantine Empires. It was conquered by the Ottoman Turks in 1466 and remained under

Turkish rule until the war of independence from 1821 until 1830, after which it became a kingdom. The monarchy was overthrown in a military coup in 1967, and a civilian republic was established in 1974. Greece joined the EC (now the EU) in 1981.

greed /grēd/ ▸*n.* intense and selfish desire for something, esp. wealth, power, or food. ▷late 16th cent.: back-formation from GREEDY.

greed·y /ˈgrēdē/ ▸*adj.* (**greed·i·er**, **greed·i·est**) having or showing an intense and selfish desire for something, esp. wealth or power: *greedy thieves who plundered a defense contractor.* ■ having an excessive desire or appetite for food. ▷Old English *grǣdig*, of Germanic origin. —**greed·i·ly** /-dəlē/ *adv.* —**greed·i·ness** *n.*

THE RIGHT WORD **acquisitive, avaricious, covetous, gluttonous, greedy, rapacious**

The desire for money and the things it can buy is often associated with Americans. But not all Americans are **greedy**, which implies an insatiable desire to possess or acquire something, beyond what one needs or deserves (*greedy for profits*). *Greedy* is especially dergatory when the object of longing is itself evil or when it cannot be possessed without harm to oneself or others (*a reporter greedy for information*).

Someone who is *greedy* for food might be called **gluttonous**, which emphasizes consumption as well as desire (*a gluttonous appetite for sweets*).

A *greedy* child may grow up to be an **avaricious** adult, which implies a fanatical greediness for money or other valuables.

Rapacious is an even stronger term, with an emphasis on taking things by force (*so rapacious in his desire for land that he forced dozens of families from their homes*).

Acquisitive, on the other hand, is a more neutral word suggesting a willingness to exert effort in acquiring things (*an acquisitive woman who filled her house with antiques and artwork*), and not necessarily material things (*a probing, acquisitive mind*).

Covetous, in contrast to *acquisitive*, implies an intense desire for something as opposed to the act of acquiring or possessing it. It is often associated with the Ten Commandments (*Thou shalt not covet thy neighbor's wife*) and suggests a longing for something that rightfully belongs to another.

G

Greek /grēk/ ▸*adj.* of or relating to Greece, its people, or their language. Compare with HELLENIC.
▸*n.* **1** a native or national of modern Greece, or a person of Greek descent. ■ a Greek-speaking person in the ancient world, typically a native of one of the city-states of Greece and the eastern Mediterranean. **2** the ancient or modern language of Greece, the only representative of the Hellenic branch of the Indo-European family.

The ancient form of Greek was spoken in the southern Balkan peninsula from the 2nd millennium BC. The Greek alphabet, used from the 1st millennium BC onwards, was adapted from the Phoenician alphabet. The dialect of classical Athens formed the basis of the standard dialect (*koinē*) from the 3rd century BC onwards, and this remained as a literary language during the periods of the Byzantine Empire and Turkish rule (see KATHAREVOUSA). The colloquial language, however, continued to evolve independently (see DEMOTIC).

3 a member of a fraternity or sorority having a Greek-letter name. ▷Old English *Grēcas* 'the Greeks,' from Latin *Graeci*, the name given by the Romans to the people who called themselves the Hellenes, from Greek *Graikoi*, which according to Aristotle was the prehistoric name of the Hellenes. —**Greek·ness** *n.*
▸***PHRASES*** □ **beware of Greeks bearing gifts** *proverb* if a rival or enemy shows one generosity or kindness, one should be suspicious of their motives. [with allusion to Virgil's *Aeneid* (ii. 49).] □ **it's (all) Greek to me** *informal* I can't understand it at all.

Greek Cath·o·lic ▸*n.* **1** a member of the Eastern Orthodox Church. **2** a Uniate member of a church observing the Greek rite.

Greek Church another term for GREEK ORTHODOX CHURCH.

Greek cof·fee ▸*n.* very strong black coffee served with the fine grounds in it.

Greek cross ▸*n.* a cross of which all four arms are of equal length.

Greek fire ▸*n.* *historical* a combustible compound emitted by a flame-throwing weapon and used to set light to enemy ships. It was first used by the Greeks besieged in Constantinople (673–78). It ignited on contact with water, and was probably based on naphtha and quicklime.

Greek key ▸*n.* a pattern of interlocking right-angled spirals.

Greek Or·tho·dox Church (also **Greek Church**) the Eastern Orthodox Church, which uses the Byzantine rite in Greek, in particular the national Church of Greece. See ORTHODOX CHURCH.

Greek re·vi·val ▸*n.* a neoclassical style of architecture inspired by and incorporating features of Greek temples from the 5th century BC, popular in the U.S. and Europe in the first half of the 19th century.

Greek sal·ad ▸*n.* a salad consisting of tomatoes, olives, and feta cheese.

Gree·ley[1] /ˈgrēlē/ an agricultural and commercial city in north central Colorado; pop. 76,930.

Gree·ley[2], Horace (1811–72) U.S. journalist and political leader. He founded the *New York Tribune* in 1841. An abolitionist and supporter of the Free Soil movement, he became known for his advice "Go West, young man."

green /grēn/ ▸*adj.* **1** of the color between blue and yellow in the spectrum; colored like grass or emeralds: *the leaves are bright green.* ■ consisting of fresh vegetables of this color: *a green salad.* ■ denoting a light or flag of this color used as a signal to proceed. ■ (of a ski run) of the lowest level of difficulty, as indicated by colored markers on the run. ■ *Physics* denoting one of three colors of quark. **2** covered with grass, trees, or other plants: *proposals that would smother green fields with development.* ■ (usu. **Green**) concerned with or supporting protection of the environment as a political principle: *a Green candidate for the European parliament.* ■ (of a product) not harmful to the environment. **3** (of a plant or fruit) young or unripe: *green shoots.* ■ (of wood) unseasoned. ■ (of food or leather) not dried, smoked, or tanned. ■ (of a person) inexperienced, naive, or gullible: *a green recruit fresh from college.* ■ (of a memory) not fading: *clubs devoted to keeping green the memory of Sherlock Holmes.* ■ still strong or vigorous: *first there was green old age, hardly different from middle age.* ■ *archaic* (of a wound) fresh; not healed. **4** (of the complexion or a person) pale and sickly-looking: *"Are you all right?—You look absolutely green."* ■ as a sign of jealousy or envy.
▸*n.* **1** green color or pigment: *major roads are marked in green.* ■ green clothes or material: *two girls in red and green.* ■ green foliage or growing plants: *that lovely canopy of green over Puritan Road.* ■ *informal, dated* money: *you'll save yourself some green.* **2** a green thing, in particular: ■ a green light. **3** a piece of public or common grassy land, esp. in the center of a town: *a house overlooking the green.* ■ an area of smooth, very short grass immediately surrounding a hole on a golf course. **4** (**greens**) green leafy vegetables: *salad greens | collard greens.* **5** (usu. **Green**) a member or supporter of an environmentalist group or party.
▸*v.* make or become green, in particular: ■ [*trans.*] make (an urban or desert area) more verdant by planting or encouraging trees or other greenery: *greening the desert.* ■ [*trans.*] make less harmful or more sensitive to the environment: *the importance of greening this industry.* ■ [*intrans.*] become green in color, through age or by becoming covered with plants: *the roof was greening with lichen.* ▷Old English *grēne* (adjective), *grēnian* (verb), of Germanic origin; related to Dutch *groen*, German *grün*, also to GRASS and GROW. —**green·ish** *adj.* —**green·ly** *adv.* —**green·ness** *n.*

green al·gae ▸*plural n.* photosynthetic algae that contain chlorophyll and store starch in discrete chloroplasts. They are eukaryotic and most live in fresh water, ranging from unicellular flagellates to more complex multicellular forms. • Treated either as plants (division Chlorophyta) or as protozoans (phylum Chlorophyta, kingdom Protista). The classification of green algae is complex and under review.

Green·a·way /ˈgrēnəˌwā/, Kate (1846–1901), English artist; full name *Catherine Greenaway*. She is known esp. for her illustrations of children's books such as *Mother Goose* (1881).

green·back /ˈgrēnˌbak/ ▸*n.* **1** *informal* a dollar bill; a dollar: *the pot she purchased with our last greenback.* **2** *informal* an animal with a green back, esp. a race of the cutthroat trout found only in Colorado.

Green Bay an industrial port city in northeastern Wisconsin, on Green Bay; pop. 102,313.

green bean ▸*n.* the immature pod of any of various bean plants, eaten as a vegetable. See also STRING BEAN.

green belt ▸*n.* **1** a green belt marking a level of proficiency in judo, karate, or other martial arts below that of a brown belt. ■ a person qualified to wear this. **2** (**greenbelt**) an area of open land around a city, on which building is restricted.

Green Be·ret ▸*n.* *informal* a member of the U.S. Army Special Forces.

green·bot·tle /ˈgrēnˌbätl/ ▸*n.* a metallic green fly that sometimes lays eggs in wounds on sheep or other animals. • Genus *Lucilia*, family Calliphoridae: several species, in particular the common *L. caesar*.

green·bri·er /ˈgrēnˌbrīər/ (also **green·bri·ar**) ▸*n.* a green-stemmed North American vine of the lily family, typically prickly and with blue-black berries. Also called CATBRIER. • Genus *Smilax*, family Liliaceae: several species, in particular the woody and thorny *S. rotundifolia*.

green·bul /ˈgrēnˌbo͝ol/ ▸*n.* an African bulbul with an olive-green back. • Family Pycnonotidae: several genera, in particular *Phyllastrephus* and *Pycnonotus*, and numerous species.

green card ▸*n.* **1** (in the U.S.) a permit allowing a foreign national to live and work permanently in the U.S. **2** (in the UK) an international insurance document for motorists.

green chan·nel ▸*n.* (at a customs area in an airport or port) the passage that should be taken by arriving passengers who have no goods to declare.

green cheese ▸*n.* unripened or unmatured cheese.

green·chop /ˈgrēnˌchäp/ ▸*v.* [*trans.*] cut (grass) in order to bring to cattle or store as silage.

green corn ▸*n.* the tender ears of young sweet corn, suitable for cooking and eating.

green crab (also **European green crab**) ▸*n.* a name for the COMMON SHORE CRAB, in its capacity as an invasive species in the U.S.

green drag·on ▸*n.* a North American arum with a large divided leaf, a greenish-cream spathe, and a very long white spadix. Also called DRAGON ARUM. • *Arisaema dracontium*, family Araceae.

green dragon

Greene[1] /grēn/, (Henry) Graham (1904–91), English novelist. The moral paradoxes he saw in his Roman Catholic faith underlie much of his work. Notable works: *Brighton Rock* (1938), *The Power and the Glory* (1940), and *The Third Man* (movie 1949; novel 1950).

Greene[2], Nathanael (1742–86) American general. Noted as a military strategist, he forced the British out of Georgia and the Carolinas in a series of battles (1781) during the American Revolution.

green earth ▸*n.* another term for TERRE VERTE.

Green·er /ˈgrēnər/ ▸*n.* a type of shotgun. ▷late 19th cent.: named after William Greener (1806–69) or his son William W. *Greener*, gunsmiths and authors.

green·er·y /ˈgrēnərē/ ▸*n.* green foliage, growing plants, or vegetation.

green·eye /ˈgrēnˌī/ ▸*n.* a small, slender-bodied fish with iridescent pale green eyes, occurring in deep waters of the western Atlantic. • Family Chlorophthalmidae: two genera and several species.

green-eyed mon·ster ▸*n.* (**the green-eyed monster**) *informal, humorous* jealousy personified. ▷from Shakespeare's *Othello* (III. 3. 166).

green fat ▸*n.* the green, gelatinous part of a turtle, highly regarded by gourmets.

green fee ▸*n.* another term for GREENS FEE.

green·field /ˈgrēnˌfēld/ ▸*adj.* [*attrib.*] relating to or denoting previously undeveloped sites for commercial development or exploitation. Compare with BROWNFIELD.
▸*n.* an undeveloped site, esp. one being evaluated and considered for commercial development or exploitation.

green·finch /ˈgrēnˌfinch/ ▸*n.* a Eurasian finch with green and yellow plumage. • Genus *Carduelis*, family Fringillidae: three species, in particular the common *C. chloris* of Europe and the Middle East.

green fin·gers ▸*plural n.* British term for **GREEN THUMB.**

green·fly /ˈgrēnˌflī/ ▸*n.* (*pl.* same or **-flies**) a green aphid that is a common pest of crops and garden plants. • Several species in the family Aphididae.

green·gage /ˈgrēnˌgāj/ ▸*n.* **1** (also **greengage plum**) a sweet, greenish fruit resembling a small plum. Also called **GAGE**[3]. **2** the tree bearing this fruit. • *Prunus domestica* subsp. *italica* (or *P. italica*), family Rosaceae. ▷early 18th cent.: named after Sir William *Gage* (1657–1727), the English botanist who introduced it to England.

Green God·dess ▸*n.* a salad dressing made with mayonnaise, garlic, and anchovies, and colored with parsley and green onions.

green goose ▸*n.* a goose that is killed when under four months old and eaten without stuffing.

green·gro·cer /ˈgrēnˌgrōsər/ ▸*n. Brit.* a retailer of fruit and vegetables. **—green·gro·cer·y** /-ˌgrōs(ə)rē/ *n.*

green·heart /ˈgrēnˌhärt/ ▸*n.* a South American evergreen tree of the laurel family, yielding hard greenish timber that is used for marine work because of its resistance to marine borers. • *Ocotea rodiaei*, family Lauraceae. ■ this timber, or similar timber from various other tropical trees.

green·horn /ˈgrēnˌhôrn/ ▸*n. informal* a person who is new to or inexperienced at a particular activity.

green·house /ˈgrēnˌhous/ ▸*n.* a glass building in which plants are grown that need protection from cold weather.

green·house ef·fect ▸*n.* the trapping of the sun's warmth in a planet's lower atmosphere due to the greater transparency of the atmosphere to visible radiation from the sun than to infrared radiation emitted from the planet's surface.

It is theorized that on earth the increasing quantity of atmospheric carbon dioxide from the burning of fossil fuels, together with the release of other gases, is causing an increased greenhouse effect and leading to global warming. A greenhouse effect involving CO_2 is also responsible for the very high surface temperature of Venus.
See also **GLOBAL WARMING.**

green·house gas ▸*n.* a gas that contributes to the greenhouse effect by absorbing infrared radiation, e.g. carbon dioxide and chlorofluorocarbons.

green·ie /ˈgrēnē/ ▸*n. informal, often derogatory* a person who campaigns for protection of the environment.

Green·ing /ˈgrēniNG/ ▸*n.* an apple of a variety that is green when ripe. ▷early 17th cent. (originally denoting a kind of pear): probably from Middle Dutch *groeninc*, a kind of apple, from *groen* 'green.'

green jer·sey ▸*n.* (in a cycling race involving stages) a green knit shirt worn each day by the rider accumulating the highest number of points, and presented at the end of the race to the rider with the highest overall points total.

green·keep·er /ˈgrēnˌkēpər/ ▸*n.* another term for **GREENSKEEPER.**

Green·land /ˈgrēnlənd/ a large island that lies to the northeast of North America, mostly within the Arctic Circle; pop. 56,300; capital, Godthåb (Nuuk). Danish name **GRØNLAND**; called in Inuit **KALAALLIT NUNAAT. —Green·land·er** *n.*

Only 5 percent of Greenland is habitable; the population is largely Inuit. Formerly a Norse and a Danish settlement, Greenland became a dependency of Denmark in 1953 with internal autonomy in 1979. It withdrew from the European Community in 1985.

Green·land hal·i·but ▸*n.* an edible halibut with a black or dark brown upper side that is found in cold, deep waters of the north. • *Reinhardtius hippoglossoides*, family Pleuronectidae.

Green·land·ic /grēnˈlandik/ ▸*n.* a dialect of the Inuit (Eskimo) language that is one of the official languages of Greenland, the other being Danish.

USAGE See usage at **INUIT**

Green·land right whale (also **Greenland whale**) ▸*n.* another term for **BOWHEAD.**

Green·land Sea a sea that lies between the east coast of Greenland and the Svalbard archipelago, part of the Arctic Ocean.

green·let /ˈgrēnlit/ ▸*n.* a small warblerlike vireo with drab plumage, found in Central and South America. • Genus *Hylophilus*, family Vireonidae: several species.

green light ▸*n.* a green traffic light giving permission to proceed. ■ *figurative* permission to go ahead with a project: *the commission has* **given the green light** *for a wind-farm development.*
▸*v.* (**green-light**) [*trans.*] give permission to go ahead with (a project, esp. a movie).

green·ling /ˈgrēnliNG/ ▸*n.* (*pl.* same or **-lings**) a spiny-finned, edible fish of the North Pacific. • Family Hexagrammidae: two genera and several species, including the lingcod.

green liz·ard ▸*n.* a lizard that is typically green with (esp. in the male) a blue throat, native to Europe and southwestern Asia. • *Lacerta viridis*, family Lacertidae.

green·mail /ˈgrēnˌmāl/ ▸*n. Stock Market* the practice of buying enough shares in a company to threaten a takeover, forcing the owners to buy them back at a higher price in order to retain control. ▷1980s: blend of **GREEN** and **BLACKMAIL. —green·mail·er** *n.*

green man ▸*n. historical* a man dressed up in greenery to represent a wild man of the woods or seasonal fertility. ■ a carved image of this, often seen in medieval English churches as a human face with branches and foliage growing out of the mouth.

green ma·nure ▸*n.* a fertilizer consisting of growing plants that are plowed back into the soil.

green mon·key ▸*n.* a common African guenon with greenish-brown upper parts and a black face. Compare with **GRIVET** and **VERVET.** • *Cercopithecus aethiops*, family Cercopithecidae, in particular the race *C. a. sabaeus* of West Africa, which is often tamed.

green monkey disease ▸*n.* another term for **MARBURG DISEASE.**

Green Moun·tains a range of the Appalachian Mountains that extends north to south through Vermont and reaches 4,393 feet (1,340 m) at Mount Mansfield.

Green Moun·tain State a nickname for the state of **VERMONT.**

green·ock·ite /ˈgrēnəˌkīt/ ▸*n.* a mineral consisting of cadmium sulfide and typically occuring as a yellow crust on zinc ores. ▷mid 19th cent.: from the name of Lord *Greenock*, who later became Earl Cathcart (1783–1859), + **-ITE**[1].

green on·ion ▸*n.* an onion taken from the ground before the bulb has formed, typically eaten raw in salad; a scallion.

Green Par·ty ▸*n.* an environmentalist political party.

green pep·per ▸*n.* the unripe fruit of a sweet pepper, which is mild in flavor and widely used in cooking. ■ the plant that yields this fruit. See **CAPSICUM.**

green pi·geon ▸*n.* a fruit-eating pigeon with mainly green plumage occurring in the Old World tropics. • Genus *Treron*, family Columbidae: many species. See also **FRUIT PIGEON.**

green plov·er ▸*n. Brit.* the northern lapwing.

green rev·o·lu·tion ▸*n.* a large increase in crop production in developing countries achieved by the use of fertilizers, pesticides, and high-yield crop varieties.

Green Riv·er 1 a river that flows for 730 miles (1,130 km) from Wyoming through Colorado and Utah into the Colorado River. **2** a city in southwestern Wyoming, on the Green River, southwest of Rock Springs; pop. 11,808.

green room ▸*n.* a room in a theater or studio in which performers can relax when they are not performing.

green·sand /ˈgrēnˌsand/ ▸*n. Geology* a greenish kind of sandstone, often loosely consolidated.

Greens·boro /ˈgrēnzˌbərə/ a city in north central North Carolina; pop. 223,891.

greens fee (also **green fee**) ▸*n.* a charge for playing one round or session on a golf course.

green·shank /ˈgrēnˌSHaNGk/ ▸*n.* a large sandpiper with long, greenish legs and gray plumage, breeding in northern Eurasia and North America. • Genus *Tringa*, family Scolopacidae: two species, in particular *T. nebularia.*

greens·keep·er /ˈgrēnzˌkēpər/ (also **green·keep·er**) ▸*n.* a person employed to look after a golf course.

green snake ▸*n.* a harmless American snake with a green back and white or yellowish underparts. • Genus *Opheodrys*, family Colubridae: two species.

green space ▸*n.* an area of grass, trees, or other vegetation set apart for recreational or aesthetic purposes in an otherwise urban environment.

Green·span /ˈgrēnˌspan/, Alan (1926–) U.S. economist. As chairman of the National Commission on Social Security Reform 1981–83, he helped to prevent the bankruptcy of the Social Security system. He served as chairman of the Federal Reserve Board from 1987.

green·stick frac·ture /ˈgrēnˌstik/ ▸*n.* a fracture of the bone, occurring typically in children, in which one side of the bone is broken and the other only bent.

green·stone /ˈgrēnˌstōn/ ▸*n. Geology* a greenish igneous rock containing feldspar and hornblende. ■ *chiefly NZ* a variety of nephrite.

green·sward /ˈgrēnˌswôrd/ ▸*n. archaic* or *poetic/literary* grass-covered ground.

green·tail·ing /ˈgrēnˌtāliNG/ ▸*n.* the sale of goods that are not harmful to the environment or were produced in conformity with environmental standards: *organic gardening is part of our commitment to greentailing.* ▷blend of *green* 'not ecologically harmful' and *retailing.*

green tea ▸*n.* tea that is made from unfermented leaves and is pale in color and slightly bitter in flavor, produced mainly in China and Japan. Compare with **BLACK TEA.**

green thumb ▸*n. informal* natural talent for growing plants: *you don't need a green thumb to grow them.*

green tur·tle ▸*n.* a sea turtle with an olive-brown shell, often living close to the coast and extensively hunted for food. • *Chelonia mydas*, family Cheloniidae.

green turtle

Green·ville /ˈgrēnˌvil; -vəl/ **1** a city in northwestern Mississippi, in the Delta; pop. 41,633. **2** a city in eastern North Carolina, near the Pamlico River; pop. 60,476. **3** an industrial city in northwestern South Carolina; pop. 56,002.

green vit·ri·ol ▸*n. archaic* crystalline ferrous sulfate.

green·ware /ˈgrēnˌwe(ə)r/ ▸*n.* unfired pottery.

green·wash /ˈgrēnˌwäSH; -ˌwôSH/ (also **green·wash·ing**) ▸*n.* disinformation disseminated by an organization so as to present an environmentally responsible public image: *the recycling bins in the cafeteria are just feeble examples of their corporate greenwash.* ▷1980s: from *green* 'not ecologically harmful,' on the pattern of *whitewash.* **—green·wash·er** *n.*

green·way /ˈgrēnˌwā/ ▸*n.* a strip of undeveloped land near an urban area, set aside for recreational use or environmental protection.

green·weed /ˈgrēnˌwēd/ ▸ see **DYER'S GREENWEED.**

Green·wich /ˈgrinij; ˈgren-; -iCH/ **1** a London borough on the southern bank of the Thames River. **2** a town in southwestern Connecticut, on Long Island Sound, an affluent suburb of New York City; pop. 61,101.

Green·wich Mean Time (abbr.: **GMT**) (also **Green·**

wich time) the mean solar time at the Greenwich meridian, adopted as the standard time in a zone that includes the British Isles.

Green·wich me·rid·i·an ▸*n.* the prime meridian, which passes through the former Royal Observatory at Greenwich, England, adopted internationally as the earth's zero of longitude in 1884.

Green·wich Vil·lage a district of New York City on the lower west side of Manhattan, traditionally associated with writers, artists, and musicians.

green·wood /ˈgrēn,wo͝od/ ▸*n. archaic* a wood or forest in leaf (regarded as the typical scene of medieval outlaw life).

green wood·peck·er ▸*n.* a large green and yellow woodpecker with a red crown and a laughing call, found from Europe to central Asia. • *Picus viridis*, family Picidae.

green·y /ˈgrēnē/ ▸*adj.* [often in *combination*] slightly green: *the greeny-brown surface of the stone.*

Greer /gri(ə)r/, Germaine (1939–), Australian feminist and writer. She first wrote *The Female Eunuch* (1970), an analysis of women's subordination in a male-dominated society. Other books include *The Change* (1991) about social attitudes toward female aging.

greet[1] /grēt/ ▸*v.* [*trans.*] give a polite word or sign of welcome or recognition to (someone) on meeting. ■ [*trans.*] receive or acknowledge (something) in a specified way: *everyone present greeted this idea warmly.* ■ (of a sight or sound) become apparent to or be noticed by (someone) on arrival somewhere: *flowers and cheers greeted the shipyard workers.* ▷Old English *grētan* 'approach, attack, or salute'; related to Dutch *groeten* and German *grüssen* 'greet.'

greet[2] ▸*v.* [*intrans.*] *Scottish* weep; cry: *he sat down on the armchair and started to greet.* ▷Old English, partly from *grētan* 'cry out, rage,' partly from *grēotan* 'lament,' both of Germanic origin.

greet·er /ˈgrētər/ ▸*n.* a person who greets people entering a store, church service, or other public place.

greet·ing /ˈgrētiNG/ ▸*n.* a polite word or sign of welcome or recognition: *Mandy shouted a greeting.* ■ the action of giving such a sign: *she raised her hand* **in** *greeting.* ■ (usu. **greetings**) a formal expression of goodwill, said on meeting or in a written message: *warm greetings to you all.*

greet·ing card (*Brit.* **greet·ings card**) ▸*n.* a decorative card sent to convey good wishes on some occasion.

greg·a·rine /ˈgregə,rīn/ *Zoology* ▸*adj.* of or relating to a group of microscopic, wormlike protozoans that are internal parasites of insects, annelids, and other invertebrates. ■ (of movement) slow and gliding, as seen in these protozoans.
▸*n.* a gregarine protozoan. • Class Gregarina (or subclass Gregarinidia), phylum Sporozoa, kingdom Protista. ▷mid 19th cent.: from modern Latin *Gregarina*, from Latin *gregarius* (see **GREGARIOUS**).

gre·gar·i·ous /griˈge(ə)rēəs/ ▸*adj.* (of a person) fond of company; sociable: *he was a popular and gregarious man.* ■ (of animals) living in flocks or loosely organized communities: *gregarious species forage in flocks from colonies or roosts.* ■ (of plants) growing in open clusters or in pure associations. ▷mid 17th cent.: from Latin *gregarius* (from *grex, greg-* 'a flock') + **-OUS**. **—gre·gar·i·ous·ly** *adv.* **—gre·gar·i·ous·ness** *n.*

Gre·go·ri·an cal·en·dar /grəˈgôrēən/ ▸*n.* the calendar introduced in 1582 by Pope Gregory XIII, as a modification of the Julian calendar.

To bring the calendar back into line with the solar year, 10 days were suppressed, and centenary years were made leap years only if they were divisible by 400. England did not adopt the reformed calendar until 1752, by which time 11 days had to be suppressed. At the same time, New Year's Day was changed from March 25 to January 1, and dates using the new calendar were designated 'New Style.'

Gre·go·ri·an chant ▸*n.* church music sung as a single vocal line in free rhythm and a restricted scale (plainsong), in a style developed for the medieval Latin liturgy. ▷mid 18th cent.: named after St. Gregory the Great (in Latin *Gregorius*), who is said to have standardized it.

Gre·go·ri·an tel·e·scope ▸*n.* an early reflecting telescope in which light reflected from a concave elliptical secondary mirror passes through a hole in the primary mirror. It was rendered obsolete by the introduction of Newtonian and Cassegrain telescopes. ▷mid 18th cent.: named after James *Gregory* (1638–75), the Scottish mathematician who invented it.

Greg·o·ry, St. /ˈgregərē/ (*c.*540–604), pope (as Gregory I) 590–604 and doctor of the Church; known as **St. Gregory the Great**. He sent St. Augustine to England to lead the country's conversion to Christianity. He is also credited with the introduction of Gregorian chant. Feast day, March 12.

Greg·o·ry VIII (1502–85) pope 1572–85; born in Italy. He was a major sponsor of numerous educational programs and institutes. The Gregorian calendar, still in use, was introduced in 1582 as a result of his efforts to correct the errors in the Julian calendar.

Greg·o·ry of Na·zi·an·zus, St. /,nāzēˈanəs/ (329–89), doctor of the Church; bishop of Constantinople. He upheld orthodoxy against the Arian and Apollinarian heresies, and he was influential in restoring adherence to the Nicene Creed. Feast day, (Eastern Church) January 25 and 30; (Western Church) January 2 (formerly May 9).

Greg·o·ry of Nys·sa, St. /ˈnisə/ (*c.*330–*c.*395), doctor of the Eastern Church; bishop of Nyssa in Cappadocia. The brother of St. Basil, he joined with St. Basil and St. Gregory of Nazianzus to oppose Arianism. Feast day, March 9.

Greg·o·ry of Tours, St. /to͝or/ (*c.*540–594), Frankish bishop and historian. He was elected bishop of Tours in 573. Feast day, November 17.

grei·sen /ˈgrīzən/ ▸*n. Geology* a light-colored rock containing quartz, mica, and fluorine-rich minerals, resulting from the alteration of granite by hot vapor from magma. ▷late 19th cent.: from German, probably a dialect word, from *greis* 'gray with age.'

grem·lin /ˈgremlin/ ▸*n. informal* an imaginary mischievous sprite regarded as responsible for an unexplained problem or fault, esp. a mechanical or electronic one: *a gremlin in my computer omitted a line.* ■ such a problem or fault. ▷1940s: perhaps suggested by **GOBLIN**.

Gre·nache /grəˈnäsH/ ▸*n.* a variety of black wine grape native to the Languedoc-Roussillon region of France. ■ a sweet red dessert wine made from this grape. ▷French.

Gre·na·da /grəˈnādə/ a country in the southern Windward Islands, in the Caribbean Sea, that consists of the island of Grenada and the southern Grenadine Islands; pop. 84,800; capital, St. George's; languages, English (official) and English Creole. **—Gre·na·di·an** /-dēən/ *adj.* & *n.*

The island of Grenada was sighted in 1498 by Columbus. Colonized by the French, it was ceded to Britain in 1763, recaptured by the French, and restored to Britain in 1783. It became an independent Commonwealth of Nations state in 1974. Seizure of power by a left-wing military group in 1983 prompted an invasion by the U.S. and some Caribbean countries; they withdrew in 1985.

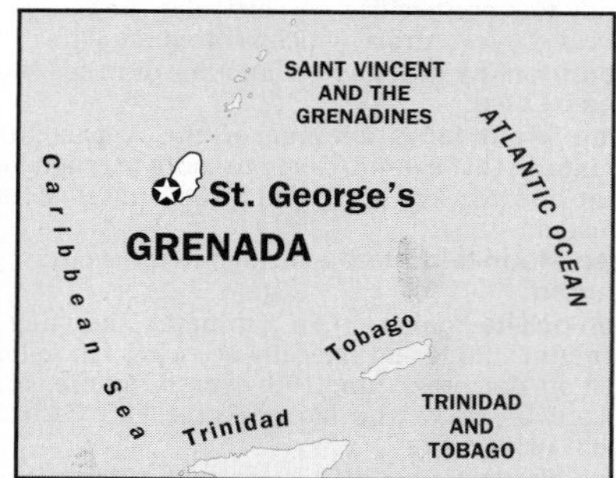

gre·nade /grəˈnād/ ▸*n.* a small bomb thrown by hand or launched mechanically. ■ a glass receptacle containing chemicals that are released when the receptacle is thrown and broken, used for testing drains and extinguishing fires. ▷mid 16th cent. (in the sense 'pomegranate'): from French, alteration of Old French *(pome) grenate* (see **POMEGRANATE**), on the pattern of Spanish *granada*. The bomb was so named because of its shape, supposedly resembling a pomegranate.

gren·a·dier /,grenəˈdi(ə)r/ ▸*n.* **1** a soldier armed with grenades or a grenade launcher. ■ (**Grenadiers** or **Grenadier Guards**) (in the UK) the first regiment of the royal household infantry. **2** a common bottom-dwelling fish with a large head, a long tapering tail, and typically a luminous gland on the belly. Also called **RAT-TAIL**. • Family Macrouridae: numerous genera and species. ▷late 17th cent.: from French, from *grenade* (see **GRENADE**).

gren·a·dil·la /,grenəˈdilə; -ˈdēyə/ ▸*n.* variant spelling of **GRANADILLA**.

gren·a·dine[1] /ˈgrenə,dēn; ,grenəˈdēn/ ▸*n.* a sweet syrup made from pomegranates. ▷French, from *grenade* 'pomegranate' (see **GRENADE**).

gren·a·dine[2] ▸*n.* dress fabric of loosely woven silk or silk and wool. ▷mid 19th cent.: from French (earlier *grenade*), 'grained silk,' from *grenu* 'grained,' from *grain* 'grain.'

Gren·a·dine Is·lands /,grenəˈdēn/ (also **the Gren·a·dines**) a chain of small islands in the Caribbean Sea, part of the Windward Islands. They are divided administratively between the islands of St. Vincent and Grenada.

Gren·del /ˈgrendl/ the water monster killed by Beowulf in the Old English epic poem *Beowulf.*

Gre·no·ble /grəˈnōbəl; grəˈnôbl(ə)/ a city in southeastern France; pop. 153,970.

Gren·ville /ˈgrenvəl/, George (1712–70), British statesman; prime minister 1763–65. The Stamp Act (1765), which aroused great opposition in the North American colonies, was passed during his term of office.

grep /grep/ ▸*n.* a Unix command used to search files for the occurrence of a string of characters that matches a specified pattern, and to output all the matching lines: *Use grep to extract all the lines in textdata.txt that contain either "deleted" or "suspended".*
▸*v.* (**grepped, grep·ping**) search for a string of characters using grep.: from the initial letters of global(ly) search regular expression print.

Gresh·am /ˈgresHəm/ a city in northwestern Oregon, east of Portland; pop. 90,205.

Gresh·am's law *Economics* the tendency for money of lower intrinsic value to circulate more freely than money of higher intrinsic and equal nominal value (often expressed as "Bad money drives out good").

Gret·na Green /ˈgretnə/ a village in Scotland just north of the English border, near Carlisle, formerly a popular place for young runaway couples from England to be married without the parental consent required.

Gretz·ky /ˈgretskē/, Wayne (1961–), Canadian hockey player. The leading scorer in the National Hockey League, he was voted most valuable player nine times. He made his professional debut in 1978 with the Indianapolis Racers and soon moved to the Edmonton Oilers. He retired in April 1999 and was elected to the Hockey Hall of Fame in November of that year.

gre·vil·le·a /griˈvilēə/ ▸*n.* an evergreen tree or shrub bearing conspicuous flowers that lack petals, most kinds of which are native to Australia. • Genus *Grevillea*, family Proteaceae. ▷modern Latin, named after Charles F. *Greville* (1749–1809), Scottish horticulturalist.

grew /gro͞o/ ▸ past of **GROW**.

Grey[1] /grā/, Charles, 2nd Earl (1764–1845), British statesman; prime minister 1830–34.

Grey[2], Lady Jane (1537–54), niece of Henry VIII; queen of England July 9–19, 1553. In 1553, to ensure a Protestant succession, John Dudley, the Duke of Northumberland, forced Jane to marry his son and persuaded the dying Edward VI to name Jane as his successor. She was deposed by forces loyal to Edward's (Catholic) sister Mary and was executed the following year.

Grey[3], Zane (1872–1939), U.S. writer; born *Pearl Grey*. He wrote 54 westerns in a romanticized and formulaic style that sold over 13 million copies during his lifetime.

grey ▸*adj.* British spelling of **GRAY**[1].

grey·beard ▸*n.* British spelling of **GRAYBEARD**.

grey·hen /ˈgrā,hen/ ▸*n.* the female of the black grouse.

grey·hound /ˈgrā,hound/ ▸*n.* a dog of a tall, slender breed having keen sight and capable of high speed, used since ancient times for hunting small game and now chiefly in racing and coursing. ▷Old English *grīghund*; the first element, related to Old Norse *grey* 'bitch,' is of unknown origin.

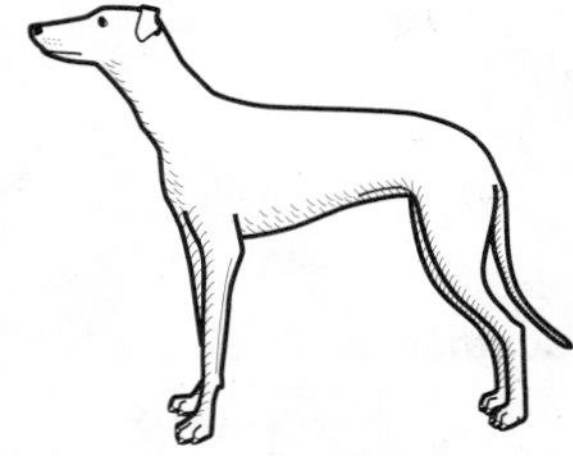

greyhound

grey·hound rac·ing ▸*n.* a sport in which greyhounds race around a circular or oval track in pursuit of a moving dummy hare and spectators bet on the outcome.

grey·lag ▸*n.* British spelling of GRAYLAG.

grey·scale ▸*n.* British spelling of GRAYSCALE.

grey·wacke ▸*n.* British spelling of GRAYWACKE.

grib·ble /ˈgribəl/ ▸*n.* a small marine isopod that bores into submerged wooden structures, often causing damage to pier timbers. • *Limnoria lignorum*, order Isopoda. ▷late 18th cent.: perhaps related to the verb GRUB.

grid /grid/ ▸*n.* **1** a framework of spaced bars that are parallel to or cross each other; a grating: *the metal grids had been pulled across the foyer.* **2** a network of lines that cross each other to form a series of squares or rectangles: *a grid of tree-lined streets.* ■ a football field. ■ a network of cables or pipes for distributing power, esp. high-voltage transmission lines for electricity: *the second reactor was not connected to the grid until 1985.* ■ a network of regularly spaced lines on a map that cross one another at right angles and are numbered to enable the precise location of a place. ■ a pattern of lines marking the starting places on a auto-racing track: *first away from the grid.* ■ *Electronics* an electrode placed between the cathode and anode of a thermionic tube or cathode-ray tube, serving to control or modulate the flow of electrons. **3** a number of computers linked together via the Internet so that their combined power may be harnessed to work on difficult problems.
▸*v.* [*trans.*] [usu. as *adj.*] (**gridded**) put into or set out as a grid: *a well-planned core of gridded streets.* ▷mid 19th cent.: back-formation from GRIDIRON.

grid bi·as ▸*n.* *Electronics* a fixed voltage applied between the cathode and the control grid of a thermionic tube in order to determine the grid's operating conditions.

grid·der /ˈgridər/ ▸*n.* a football player.

grid·dle /ˈgridl/ ▸*n.* **1** a heavy, flat iron plate that is heated and used for cooking food. **2** *historical* a miner's wire-bottomed sieve.
▸*v.* [*trans.*] **1** cook on a griddle: [as *adj.*] (**griddled**) *griddled corn cakes.* **2** *historical* screen (ore) with a griddle: *black copper ore is generally* **griddled out**. ▷Middle English (denoting a gridiron): from Old French *gredil*, from Latin *craticula*, diminutive of *cratis* 'hurdle'; related to CRATE, GRATE[2], and GRILL[1].

grid·i·ron /ˈgridˌīərn/ ▸*n.* **1** a frame of parallel bars or beams, typically in two sets arranged at right angles, in particular: ■ a frame of parallel metal bars used for grilling meat or fish over an open fire. ■ a frame of parallel beams for supporting a ship in dock. ■ (in the theater) a framework over a stage supporting scenery and lighting. **2** a field for football, marked with regularly spaced parallel lines. ■ the game of football: [as *adj.*] *the national gridiron season* . **3** another term for GRID (sense 2). ▷Middle English *gredire*, alteration of *gredile* 'griddle' by association with IRON.

grid·lock /ˈgridˌläk/ ▸*n.* **1** a traffic jam affecting a whole network of intersecting streets. **2** another term for DEADLOCK (sense 1). —**grid·locked** *adj.*

grid ref·er·ence ▸*n.* a map reference indicating a location in terms of a series of vertical and horizontal grid lines identified by numbers or letters.

grief /grēf/ ▸*n.* deep sorrow, esp. that caused by someone's death: *she was overcome with grief.* ■ *informal* trouble or annoyance: *they won't give you any grief in the next few days.* ▷Middle English: from Old French *grief*, from *grever* 'to burden' (see GRIEVE).
▸*PHRASES* □ **come to grief** have an accident; meet with disaster: *many a ship has come to grief along this shore.* □ **good grief!** an exclamation of irritation, frustration, or surprise.

grief-strick·en ▸*adj.* overcome with deep sorrow.

Grieg /grēg/, Edvard (1843–1907), Norwegian composer, conductor, and violinist. Notable works: Piano Concerto in A minor (1869) and the incidental music to Henrik Ibsen's play *Peer Gynt* (1876).

Grier /ˈgri(ə)r/, Robert Cooper (1794–1870) U.S. Supreme Court associate justice 1846–70. Appointed to the Court by President Polk, he was a strong advocate for the Union before, during, and after the Civil War.

griev·ance /ˈgrēvəns/ ▸*n.* a real or imagined wrong or other cause for complaint or protest, esp. unfair treatment: *failure to redress genuine grievances.* ■ an official statement of a complaint over something believed to be wrong or unfair: *three pilots have filed grievances against the company.* ■ a feeling of resentment over something believed to be wrong or unfair: *he was nursing a grievance.* ▷Middle English (also in the sense 'injury'): from Old French *grevance*, from *grever* 'to burden' (see GRIEVE).

grieve /grēv/ ▸*v.* [*intrans.*] suffer grief: *she* **grieved for** *her father.* ■ [*trans.*] feel grief for or because of: *she did not have the opportunity to grieve her mother's death.* See note at MOURN. ■ [*trans.*] cause great distress to (someone): *what grieves you, my son?* | [*trans.*] *it grieves me to think of you in that house alone.* ▷Middle English (also in the sense 'harm, oppress'): from Old French *grever* 'burden, encumber,' based on Latin *gravare*, from *gravis* 'heavy, grave' (see GRAVE[2]). —**griev·er** *n.*

griev·ous /ˈgrēvəs/ ▸*adj.* *formal* (of something bad) very severe or serious: *his death was a grievous blow* | *the American fleet suffered grievous losses.* ▷Middle English: from Old French *greveus*, from *grever* (see GRIEVE). —**griev·ous·ly** *adv.* —**griev·ous·ness** *n.*

USAGE Do not pronounce this word as though it had an extra syllable, as /ˈgrēvē-əs/ .

griev·ous bod·i·ly harm (abbr.: **GBH**) ▸*n.* *Law* serious physical injury inflicted on a person by the deliberate action of another.

Grif·fey /ˈgrifē/, Ken, Jr. (1969–) U.S. baseball player; full name *George Kenneth Griffey, Jr.*; known as **Junior**. He played centerfield for the Seattle Mariners 1989–1999 before moving to the Cincinnati Reds in 2000.

grif·fin /ˈgrifin/ (also **gryph·on**, **grif·fon** /ˈgrifən/) ▸*n.* a mythical creature with the head and wings of an eagle and the body of a lion, typically depicted with pointed ears and with the eagle's legs taking the place of the forelegs. ▷Middle English: from Old French *grifoun*, based on late Latin *gryphus*, via Latin from Greek *grups*, *grup-*.

griffin

Grif·fith /ˈgrifiтн/, D. W. (1875–1948), U.S. movie director; full name *David Lewelyn Wark Griffith*. A pioneer in movies, he is responsible for introducing many cinematic techniques, including flashback and fade-out. Notable films: *The Birth of a Nation* (1915), *Intolerance* (1916), and *Broken Blossoms* (1919).

Grif·fith Joy·ner /ˈjoinər/, Florence (1959–98) U.S. track and field athlete; called *Flojo*. She won three gold medals and established world records in the 100– and 200–meter and 4 x 100–meter races at the 1988 Olympic Games.

grif·fon /ˈgrifən/ ▸*n.* **1** a dog of any of several terrier-like breeds originating in northwestern Europe. ■ (also **Brussels griffon**) a dog of a toy breed with a flat face and upturned chin. **2** (also **griffon vulture**) a large Old World vulture with predominantly pale brown plumage. • Genus *Gyps*, family Accipitridae: four species, in particular the Eurasian *G. fulvus* and the African **Ruppell's griffon** (*G. ruepelli*). **3** variant spelling of GRIFFIN. ▷Middle English (in senses 2 and 3): variant of GRIFFIN; sense 1 was adopted from French in the 18th cent.

grift /grift/ *informal* ▸*v.* [*intrans.*] engage in petty swindling.
▸*n.* a petty swindle. ▷early 20th cent.: alteration of GRAFT[2]. —**grift·er** *n.*

grig /grig/ ▸*n.* *Brit., dialect* **1** a small eel. **2** a grasshopper or cricket. ▷Middle English (in the sense 'dwarf'): of unknown origin.
▸*PHRASE* □ **(as) merry** (or **lively**) **as a grig** full of fun; extravagantly lively.

grill[1] /gril/ ▸*n.* a metal framework used for cooking food over an open fire; a gridiron. ■ a portable device for cooking outdoors, consisting of such a framework placed over charcoal or gas fuel. ■ a large griddle. ■ a dish of food, esp. meat, cooked using a grill. ■ (also **grill room**) a restaurant serving grilled food.
▸*v.* **1** [*trans.*] cook (something) using a grill: *grill the trout for about five minutes.* **2** [*trans.*] *informal* subject (someone) to intense questioning or interrogation: *my father grilled us about what we had been doing* | [as *n.*] (**grilling**) *they faced a grilling over the latest results.* ▷mid 17th cent.: from French *gril* (noun), *griller* (verb), from Old French *graille* 'grille.' —**grill·er** *n.*

grill[2] ▸*n.* variant spelling of GRILLE.

gril·lade /griˈläd; grēˈyäd/ ▸*n.* (often **grillades**) a kind of meat stew usually made with beef steak, typical of French regional and Cajun cooking. ▷mid 17th cent.: French, literally 'something grilled.'

gril·lage /ˈgrilij/ ▸*n.* a heavy framework of cross-timbering or metal beams forming a foundation for building, esp. on soft, wet, or unstable ground. ▷late 18th cent.: from French (see GRILLE, -AGE).

grille /gril/ (also **grill**) ▸*n.* a grating or screen of metal bars or wires, placed in front of something as protection or to allow ventilation or discreet observation. ■ a grating at the front of a motor vehicle allowing air to circulate to the radiator to cool it. ▷mid 17th cent.: from French, from medieval Latin *craticula*, diminutive of *cratis* 'hurdle'; related to CRATE, GRATE[2], and GRIDDLE.

grill room ▸*n.* see GRILL[1].

grill·work /ˈgrilˌwərk/ ▸*n.* metal bars or wires arranged to form a grille.

grilse /grils/ ▸*n.* a salmon that has returned to fresh water after a single winter at sea. ▷late Middle English: of unknown origin.

grim /grim/ ▸*adj.* (**grim·mer**, **grim·mest**) forbidding or uninviting: *his grim expression* | *long rows of grim, dark housing developments.* ■ (of humor) lacking genuine levity; mirthless; black: *some moments of grim humor.* ■ depressing or worrying to consider: *the grim news of the murder.* ■ allowing no compromise; stern; relentless: *grim determination to succeed.* ■ unrelentingly harsh; merciless or severe: *few creatures are able to thrive in this grim and hostile land.* ▷Old English, of Germanic origin; related to Dutch *grim* and German *grimm*. —**grim·ly** *adv.* —**grim·ness** *n.*
▸*PHRASE* □ **like grim death** with great determination: *we had to hold on like grim death.*

grim·ace /ˈgriməs; griˈmās/ ▸*n.* an ugly, twisted expression on a person's face, typically expressing disgust, pain, or wry amusement: *she gave a grimace of pain.*
▸*v.* [*intrans.*] make a grimace: *I sipped the coffee and grimaced.* ▷mid 17th cent.: from French, from Spanish *grimazo* 'caricature,' from *grima* 'fright.'

Gri·mal·di /grəˈmäldē; -ˈmôl-/, Francesco Maria (1618–63), Italian physicist and astronomer.

gri·mal·kin /griˈmôkin; -ˈmal-/ ▸*n.* *archaic* a cat (used esp. in reference to its characteristically feline qualities). ■ a spiteful old woman. ▷late 16th cent.: from GRAY[1] + *Malkin* (nickname for the given name *Matilda*).

grime /grīm/ ▸*n.* dirt ingrained on the surface of something, esp. clothing, a building, or the skin.
▸*v.* [*trans.*] (usu. **be grimed**) blacken or make dirty with grime: *the beaches are grimed with a foul foam.* ▷Middle English: from Middle Low German and Middle Dutch.

Grim·ke /ˈgrimkē/ a family of U.S. reformers, abolitionists, and feminists that included sisters **Sarah Moore** (1792–1872) and **Angelina Emily** (1805–79). They wrote for the American Anti-Slavery Society. Sarah later wrote pamphlets for women's rights and with Theodore Dwight Weld (1803–95), Angelina's husband, *American Slavery as It Is: Testimony of a Thousand Witnesses* (1839).

Grimm /grim/, Jacob (Ludwig Carl) (1785–1863) and Wilhelm (Carl) (1786–1859), German philologists and folklorists. In 1852, they inaugurated a dictionary of German on historical principles, which was eventually completed by other scholars in 1960. They also compiled an anthology of German fairy tales, which appeared in three volumes between 1812 and 1822.

Grimm's law *Linguistics* the observation that certain Indo-European consonants (mainly stops) undergo regular changes in the Germanic languages that are not seen in non-Germanic languages such as Greek or Latin. Examples include *p* becoming *f* so that Latin *pedem* corresponds to English *foot* and German *Fuss*. The principle was set out by Jacob Grimm in his German grammar (2nd edition, 1822).

gri·moire /grimˈwär/ ▸*n.* a book of magic spells and invocations. ▷mid 19th cent.: French, alteration of *grammaire* 'grammar.'

Grim Reap·er ▸*n.* a personification of death in the form of a cloaked skeleton wielding a large scythe.

Pronunciation Key ə *ago*; ər *over*; ˈə or ˌə *up*; ˈər or ˌər *fur*; a *hat*; ā *rate*; ä *car*; CH *chew*; e *let*; ē *see*; e(ə)r *air*; i *fit*; ī *by*; i(ə)r *ear*; NG *sing*; ō *go*; ô *for*; oi *boy*; o͝o *good*; o͞o *goo*; ou *out*; SH *she*; TH *thin*; T͟H *then*; (h)w *why*; ZH *vision*

grim·y /ˈgrīmē/ ▸*adj.* (**grim·i·er, grim·i·est**) covered with or characterized by grime: *the grimy industrial city.* —**grim·i·ly** /-məlē/ *adv.* —**grim·i·ness** *n.*

grin /grin/ ▸*v.* (**grinned, grin·ning**) [*intrans.*] smile broadly, esp. in an unrestrained manner and with the mouth open: *Dennis appeared, grinning cheerfully.* See note at SMILE. ■ [*trans.*] express with a broad smile. ■ grimace or appear to grimace grotesquely in a way that reveals the teeth: [as *adj.*] (**grinning**) *a grinning skull.*
▸*n.* a broad smile: *"OK," he said with a grin.* ▷Old English *grennian* 'bare the teeth in pain or anger,' of Germanic origin; probably related to GROAN. —**grin·ner** *n.* —**grin·ning·ly** *adv.*
▸*PHRASE* □ **grin and bear it** suffer pain or misfortune in a stoical manner.

grinch ▸*n. informal* a person who is mean-spirited and unfriendly. ▷mid 20th cent.: from the name of the title character in Dr. Seuss's book *How the Grinch Stole Christmas!* (1957)

grind /grīnd/ ▸*v.* (*past* **ground** /ground/) **1** [*trans.*] reduce (something) to small particles or powder by crushing it: *grind some black pepper over the salad | they **grind up** fish for fertilizer.* ■ [*intrans.*] (of a mill or machine) work with a crushing action: *the old mill was grinding again.* ■ sharpen, smooth, or produce (something) by crushing or by friction: *power from a waterwheel was used to grind cutlery.* ■ operate (a mill or machine) by turning the handle: *she was grinding a coffee mill.* **2** rub or cause to rub together gratingly: [*intrans.*] *tectonic plates that inexorably grind against each other* | [*trans.*] *he keeps me awake at night, grinding his teeth.* ■ [*intrans.*] move noisily and laboriously, esp. against a countering force: *the truck was grinding slowly up the hill.* **3** [*intrans.*] *informal* (of a dancer) rotate the hips: *go-go girls grinding to blaring disco.*
▸*phrasal v.* □ **grind away** work or study hard. □ **grind someone down** wear someone down with continuous harsh or oppressive treatment: *mundane everyday things which just grind people down.* □ **grind on** continue for a long time in a wearying or tedious way: *the rail talks grind on.* □ **grind something out** produce something dull or tedious slowly and laboriously: *I must grind out some more fiction.*
▸*n.* [in *sing.*] **1** a crushing or grating sound or motion: *the crunch and grind of bulldozers | figurative the slow grind of the U.S. legal system.* ■ hard dull work: *relief from the daily grind.* See note at LABOR. ■ *informal* an excessively hard-working student. ■ the size of ground particles: *only the right grind gives you all the fine flavor.* **2** *informal* a dancer's rotary movement of the hips: *a bump and grind.* ▷Old English *grindan*, probably of Germanic origin. Although no cognates are known, it may be distantly related to Latin *frendere* 'rub away, gnash.'
▸*PHRASE* □ **grind to a halt** (or **come to a grinding halt**) move more and more slowly and then stop.

grind·er /ˈgrīndər/ ▸*n.* **1** a machine used for grinding something: *a coffee grinder.* ■ a person employed to grind cutlery, tools, or cereals. **2** a molar tooth. ■ (**grinders**) *informal* the teeth. **3** *informal* another term for SUBMARINE SANDWICH.

grind·ing /ˈgrīndiNG/ ▸*adj.* [*attrib.*] **1** (of a state) oppressive, tedious, and seemingly without end: *grinding poverty.* **2** (of a sound or motion) harsh and grating: *the group's grinding, ear-splitting guitar.* —**grind·ing·ly** *adv.*

grind·ing wheel ▸*n.* a wheel used for cutting, grinding, or finishing metal or other objects, and typically made of abrasive particles bonded together.

grind·stone /ˈgrīnd,stōn/ ▸*n.* a thick disk of stone or other abrasive material mounted so as to revolve, used for grinding, sharpening, or polishing metal objects. ■ *rare* another term for MILLSTONE.
▸*PHRASE* □ **keep one's nose to the grindstone** work hard and continuously.

grin·go /ˈgriNGgō/ ▸*n.* (*pl.* **-gos**) *informal, often offensive* a white person from an English-speaking country (used in Spanish-speaking regions, chiefly Latin America). ▷mid 19th cent.: Spanish, literally 'foreign, foreigner, or gibberish,' perhaps an alteration of *griego* 'Greek.'

gri·ot /grē'ō; ˈgrēō/ ▸*n.* a member of a class of traveling poets, musicians, and storytellers who maintain a tradition of oral history in parts of West Africa. ▷French, earlier *guiriot*, perhaps from Portuguese *criado.*

grip /grip/ ▸*v.* (**gripped, grip·ping**) [*trans.*] **1** take and keep a firm hold of; grasp tightly: *his knuckles were white as he gripped the steering wheel.* ■ [*intrans.*] maintain a firm contact, esp. by friction: *a sole that really grips well on wet rock.* **2** (of a feeling or emotion) deeply affect (someone): *she was gripped by a feeling of excitement.* ■ (of an illness or unwelcome situation) afflict strongly: *the country was gripped by recession.* ■ compel the attention or interest of: [as *adj.*] (**gripping**) *a gripping TV thriller.*
▸*n.* **1** [in *sing.*] a firm hold; a tight grasp or clasp: *his arm was held in a vicelike grip | figurative the icy grip of winter.* ■ a manner of grasping or holding something: *I've changed my grip and my backswing.* ■ the ability of something, esp. a wheel or shoe, to maintain a firm contact with a surface: *these shoes have got no grip.* ■ [in *sing.*] an effective form of control over something: *our firm **grip on** inflation.* ■ [in *sing.*] an intellectual understanding of something: *you've got a pretty good **grip on** what's going on.* **2** a part or attachment by which something is held in the hand: *handlebar grips.* **3** a traveling bag: *a grip crammed with new clothes.* **4** an assistant in a theater; a stagehand. ■ a member of a camera crew responsible for moving and setting up equipment. ▷Old English *grippa* (verb), *gripe* 'grasp, clutch' (noun), *gripa* 'handful, sheath'; related to GRIPE. —**grip·per** *n.* —**grip·ping·ly** *adv.*
▸*PHRASES* □ **come** (or **get**) **to grips with** engage in combat with: *they never came to grips with the enemy.* ■ begin to deal with or understand: *a real tough problem to come to grips with.* □ **get a grip** [usu. in *imperative*] *informal* keep or recover one's self-control: *get a grip, guys!* □ **get a grip on** take control of: *the Fed will have to act to get a grip on inflation.* □ **in the grip of** dominated or affected by something undesirable or adverse: *people caught in the grip of a drug problem.* □ **lose one's grip** become unable to understand or control one's situation: *an elderly person who seems to be losing his grip.*

gripe /grīp/ ▸*v.* **1** [*reporting verb*] *informal* express a complaint or grumble about something, esp. something trivial: [*intrans.*] *they gripe about the busywork* | [with *direct speech*] *"Holidays make no difference to Simon," Pat griped.* ■ [*trans.*] *dated* distress; annoy: *there's something griping you.* **2** [*trans.*] affect with gastric or intestinal pain: *it gripes my belly like a green apple* | [as *adj.*] (**griping**) *then the griping pains started.* **3** [*trans.*] *archaic* grasp tightly; clutch: *Hilyard griped his dagger.* **4** [*trans.*] *Nautical* secure (a boat) with gripes. **5** [*intrans.*] *Sailing* (of a ship) turn to face the wind in spite of the helm.
▸*n.* **1** *informal* a complaint, esp. a trivial one: *his biggest gripe is that he has lost his sense of privacy.* **2** (usu. **gripes**) gastric or intestinal pain; colic. **3** *archaic* an act of grasping tightly. **4** (**gripes**) *Nautical* lashings securing a boat in its place on deck or in davits. ▷Old English *grīpan* 'grasp, clutch,' of Germanic origin; related to Dutch *grijpen*, German *greifen* 'seize,' also to GRIP and GROPE. Sense 2 dates from the 17th cent.; sense 1, of U.S. origin, dates from the 1930s. —**grip·er** *n.*

grippe /grip/ ▸*n.* old-fashioned term for INFLUENZA. ▷late 18th cent.: French, from *gripper* 'seize.' —**grip·py** /ˈgripē/ *adj.*

grip·py /ˈgripē/ ▸*adj.* (of a wheel or shoe) able to grip a surface well: *grippy, quiet tires.*

Gri·qua /ˈgrēkwə/ ▸*n.* (*pl.* same or **-quas**) a member of a people of mixed European and Khoikhoi origin, living mainly in the Cape Province of South Africa. ▷the name in Nama.

Gris /grēs/, Juan (1887–1927), Spanish painter; born *José Victoriano Gonzales.* A main contributor to the development of the later phase of synthetic cubism, his work features the use of collage and paint in simple fragmented shapes.

gri·saille /gri'zī; -'zāl/ ▸*n. Art* a method of painting in gray monochrome, typically to imitate sculpture. ■ a painting or stained-glass window in this style. ▷mid 19th cent.: French, from *gris* 'gray.'

gris·e·o·ful·vin /,grizēə'fōōlvin/ ▸*n. Medicine* an antibiotic used against fungal infections of the hair and skin. • This antibiotic is obtained from the mold *penicillium griseovulvum.* ▷1930s: from the modern Latin binomial, from medieval Latin *griseus* 'grayish' + Latin *fulvus* 'reddish yellow.'

gri·sette /gri'zet/ ▸*n.* **1** a common edible woodland mushroom with a brown or gray cap, a slender stem, and white gills. • *Amanita vaginata* and *A. fulva*, family Amanitaceae, class Hymenomycetes. **2** *dated* a young working-class Frenchwoman. ▷French, from *gris* 'gray' + the diminutive suffix *-ette*; in sense 2 the term derives from the gray dress material typically worn by such women; sense 1 is an extended use.

gris-gris /ˈgrē,grē/ ▸*n.* (*pl.* same) an African or Caribbean charm or amulet. ■ the use of such charms esp. in voodoo: [as *adj.*] *the New Orleans gris-gris traditions.* ▷late 17th cent.: from French *grisgris*, of West African origin.

Grish·am /ˈgrisHəm/, John (1955–) U.S. writer and lawyer. His many novels include *A Time to Kill* (1988), *The Firm* (1991), *The Testament* (1999), and *The Brethren* (2000).

gris·kin /ˈgriskin/ ▸*n. Brit.* the lean part of a loin of pork. ▷late 17th cent.: perhaps from archaic *grice* 'pig' + -KIN.

gris·ly /ˈgrizlē/ ▸*adj.* (**-li·er, -li·est**) causing horror or disgust: *the town was shaken by a series of grisly crimes.* ▷Old English *grislic* 'terrifying,' of Germanic origin; related to Dutch *griezelig.* —**gris·li·ness** *n.*

gri·son /ˈgrizən/ ▸*n.* a weasellike mammal with dark fur and a white stripe across the forehead, found in Central and South America. • Genus *Galictis*, family Mustelidae: two species. ▷late 18th cent.: from French, from *gris* 'gray.'

gris·si·ni /gri'sēnē/ ▸*plural n.* thin, crisp Italian breadsticks. ▷Italian.

Gris·som /ˈgrisəm/, Gus (1926–67) U.S. astronaut; full name *Virgil Ivan Grissom.* Part of the original Project Mercury astronaut team in 1959, he was killed in a flash fire in the *Apollo I* capsule along with fellow astronauts **Edward H. White** (1930–67) and **Roger B. Chaffee** (1935–67).

grist /grist/ ▸*n.* grain that is ground to make flour. ■ malt crushed to make mash for brewing. ■ *figurative* useful material, esp. to back up an argument: *the research provided the most sensational grist for opponents of tobacco.* ▷Old English, 'grinding,' of Germanic origin; related to GRIND.
▸*PHRASE* □ **grist for the mill** useful experience, material, or knowledge.

gris·tle /ˈgrisəl/ ▸*n.* cartilage, esp. when found as tough, inedible tissue in meat. ▷Old English, of unknown origin. —**gris·tly** /ˈgris(ə)lē/ *adj.*

grist·mill /ˈgrist,mil/ ▸*n.* a mill for grinding grain.

grit /grit/ ▸*n.* **1** small, loose particles of stone or sand: *she had a bit of grit in her eye.* ■ [as *adj.*] (with numeral) indicating the grade of fineness of an abrasive: *220-grit paper.* ■ (also **grit·stone**) a coarse sandstone: *layers of impervious shales and grits.* **2** courage and resolve; strength of character: *he displayed the **true grit** of the navy pilot.*
▸*v.* (**grit·ted, grit·ting**) [*trans.*] **1** clench (the teeth), esp. in order to keep one's resolve when faced with an unpleasant or painful duty: *figurative Congress must grit its teeth and take action* | [as *adj.*] (**gritted**) *"Not here," he said through gritted teeth.* **2** [*intrans.*] move with or make a grating sound: *fine red dust that gritted between the teeth.* ▷Old English *grēot* 'sand, gravel,' of Germanic origin; related to German *Griess*, also to GROATS.

grits /grits/ ▸*plural n.* [also treated as *sing.*] a dish of coarsely ground corn kernels boiled with water or milk. ■ coarsely ground corn kernels from which this dish is made. ▷Old English *grytt, grytte* 'bran, mill dust,' of Germanic origin: related to Dutch *grutten*, German *Grütze*, also to GROATS.

grit·ty /ˈgritē/ ▸*adj.* (**grit·ti·er, grit·ti·est**) **1** containing or covered with grit. **2** showing courage and resolve: *a gritty pioneer woman.* ■ tough and uncompromising: *a gritty look at urban life.* —**grit·ti·ly** /ˈgritəlē/ *adv.* —**grit·ti·ness** *n.*

griv·et /ˈgrivit/ (also **grivet monkey**) ▸*n.* a common African guenon with greenish-brown upper parts and a black face. Compare with GREEN MONKEY and VERVET. • *Cercopithecus aethiops*, family Cercopithecidae, in particular the race *C. a. aethiops* of Ethiopia and Sudan, with long white cheek tufts. ▷mid 19th cent.: from French, of unknown origin.

griz·zle[1] /ˈgrizəl/ ▸*adj.* [often in *combination*] (esp. of hair or fur) having dark and white hairs mixed: *grizzle-haired.*
▸*n.* a mixture of dark and white hairs. ▷Middle English: from Old French *grisel*, from *gris* 'gray.'

griz·zle[2] ▸*v.* [*intrans.*] *informal, chiefly Brit.* (of a child) cry fretfully: [as *adj.*] (**grizzling**) *a grizzling baby* | [as *n.*] (**grizzling**) *no grizzling, now!* ■ complain; grumble. ▷mid 18th cent. (in the sense 'show the teeth, grin'): of unknown origin. —**griz·zler** /ˈgriz(ə)lər/ *n.*

griz·zled /ˈgrizəld/ ▸*adj.* having or streaked with gray hair: *grizzled hair.* ▷late Middle English: from the adjective GRIZZLE[1] + -ED[1].

griz·zly /ˈgrizlē/ ▸*n.* (*pl.* **-zlies**) (also **griz·zly bear**) an animal of a large race of the brown bear native to North America. • *Ursus arctos horribilis*, family Ursidae.

▸adj. (**-zli·er, -zli·est**) gray or gray-haired. ▹early 19th cent.: *grizzly* from GRIZZLE2.

gro. ▸abbr. gross.

groan /grōn/ ▸v. [intrans.] make a deep inarticulate sound in response to pain or despair: *Marty groaned and pulled the blanket over his head.* ■ [with direct speech] say something in a despairing or miserable tone: *"Oh God!" I groaned.* ■ complain; grumble: *they were* **moaning and groaning** *about management.* ■ (of a thing) make a low creaking or moaning sound when pressure or weight is applied: *James slumped back into his chair, making it groan and bulge.* ■ (**groan under/beneath**) figurative be oppressed by: *families groaning under mortgage increases.* ■ (**groan with/under**) be heavily loaded with: *tables groan with smoking joints of venison.*

▸n. a deep, inarticulate sound made in pain or despair. ■ a complaint: *to listen with sincerity to everyone's moans and groans.* ■ a low creaking or moaning sound made by an object or device under pressure: *the protesting groan of timbers.* ▹Old English *grānian*, of Germanic origin; related to German *greinen* 'cry, whine,' *grinsen* 'grin,' also probably to GRIN. **—groan·er** n. **—groan·ing·ly** adv.

▸PHRASE □ **groan inwardly** feel like groaning at something but remain silent: *everything has a tepid inevitability, and even as you smile you may be groaning inwardly.*

groat /grōt/ ▸n. historical any of various medieval European coins, in particular an English silver coin worth four old pence, issued between 1351 and 1662. ■ [in sing.] [with negative] archaic a small sum: *I do not care a groat.* ▹from Middle Dutch *groot* or Middle Low German *grōte* 'great, thick,' hence 'thick penny'; compare with GROSCHEN.

groats /grōts/ ▸plural n. hulled or crushed grain, esp. oats. ▹late Old English *grotan* (plural): related to GRIT and GRITS.

gro·cer /ˈgrōsər/ ▸n. a person who sells food and small household goods. ▹Middle English (originally 'a person who sold things in the gross' (i.e., in large quantities)): from Old French *grossier*, from medieval Latin *grossarius*, from late Latin *grossus* 'gross.'

gro·cer·y /ˈgrōs(ə)rē/ ▸n. (pl. **-cer·ies**) (also **grocery store**) a grocer's store or business. ■ (**groceries**) items of food sold in such a store.

Grod·no /ˈgrôdnə/ Russian name of HRODNA.

grog /gräg/ ▸n. spirits (originally rum) mixed with water. ■ informal, alcoholic drink, esp. beer. ■ crushed unglazed pottery or brick used as an additive in plaster or clay. ▹mid 18th cent.: said to be from *Old Grog*, the reputed nickname (because of his grogram cloak) of Admiral Vernon (1684–1757), who in 1740 first ordered diluted (instead of neat) rum to be served out to sailors.

grog·gy /ˈgrägē/ ▸adj. (**-gi·er, -gi·est**) dazed, weak, or unsteady, esp. from illness, intoxication, sleep, or a blow: *the sleeping pills had left her feeling groggy.* **—grog·gi·ly** /ˈgrägəlē/ adv. **—grog·gi·ness** n.

grog·ram /ˈgrägrəm/ ▸n. a coarse fabric made of silk, often combined with mohair or wool and stiffened with gum. ▹mid 16th cent.: from French *gros grain* 'coarse grain' (see also GROSGRAIN).

groin1 /groin/ ▸n. **1** the area between the abdomen and the thigh on either side of the body. ■ informal the region of the genitals. **2** Architecture a curved edge formed by two intersecting vaults. ▹late Middle English *grynde*, perhaps from Old English *grynde* 'depression, abyss.'

groin2 (also **groyne**) ▸n. a low wall or sturdy timber barrier built out into the sea from a beach to check erosion and drifting. ▹late 16th cent.: from dialect *groin* 'snout,' from Old French *groign*, from late Latin *grunium* 'pig's snout,' from Latin *grunnire* 'to grunt.'

groined /groind/ ▸adj. Architecture (of a vault) formed by the intersection of two barrel vaults, usually with plain groins without ribs.

grok /gräk/ ▸v. (**grokked, grok·king**) [trans.] informal understand (something) intuitively or by empathy: *because of all the commercials, children grok things immediately.* ■ [intrans.] empathize or communicate sympathetically; establish a rapport. ▹mid 20th cent.: a word coined by Robert Heinlein (1907–88), American science fiction writer, in *Stranger in a Strange Land.*

grom·met /ˈgrämit/ ▸n. **1** an eyelet placed in a hole in a sheet or panel to protect or insulate a rope or cable passed through it or to prevent the sheet or panel from being torn. **2** Medicine a tube surgically implanted in the eardrum to drain fluid from the middle ear. **3** informal a young or inexperienced skier, snowboarder, surfer, or skateboarder: *mega moves that make gods out of grommets.* ▹early 17th cent. (in nautical use in the sense 'a circle of rope used as a fastening'): from obsolete French *grommette*, from *gourmer* 'to curb,' of unknown ultimate origin. Current senses date from the mid 20th cent.

Gro·my·ko /grəˈmēkō/, Andrei (Andreevich) (1909–89), Soviet statesman; foreign minister 1957–1985; president of the Soviet Union 1985–88. His appointment to the presidency, largely a formal position, by Mikhail Gorbachev was widely interpreted as a maneuver to reduce Gromyko's influence and to make an ending of the Cold War possible.

Gro·ning·en /ˈgrōniNGən/ a city in the northern Netherlands, capital of a province with the same name; pop. 169,000.

Grøn·land /ˈgrœn,län/ Danish name for GREENLAND.

groom /gro͞om; gro͝om/ ▸v. [trans.] **1** look after the coat of (a horse, dog, or other animal) by brushing and cleaning it: *you must be prepared to spend time grooming your dog.* ■ (of an animal) clean the fur or skin of: *their main preoccupation is licking and* **grooming themselves.** ■ give a neat and tidy appearance to (someone): [as n.] (**grooming**) *she pays great attention to makeup, grooming, and clothes.* ■ look after (a lawn, ski slope, or other surface). **2** prepare or train (someone) for a particular purpose or activity: *star pupils who are* **groomed for** *higher things.*

▸n. **1** a person employed to take care of horses. **2** a bridegroom. **3** Brit. any of various officials of the royal household. ▹Middle English (in the sense 'boy,' later 'man, male servant'): of unknown origin.

grooms·man /ˈgro͞omzmən; ˈgro͝omz-/ ▸n. (pl. **-men**) a male friend officially attending the bridegroom at a wedding.

groove /gro͞ov/ ▸n. **1** a long, narrow cut or depression, esp. one made to guide motion or receive a corresponding ridge. ■ a spiral track cut in a phonograph record, into which the stylus fits. ■ Climbing an indentation where two planes of rock meet at an angle of more than 120°. **2** an established routine or habit: *his thoughts were slipping* **into a** *familiar* **groove.** **3** informal a rhythmic pattern in popular or jazz music: *the groove laid down by the drummer and bassist is tough and funky.*

▸v. **1** [trans.] make a groove or grooves in: *deep lines grooved her face.* **2** [intrans.] informal dance or listen to popular or jazz music, esp. that with an insistent rhythm: *they were* **grooving to** *Motown.* ■ dated play such music in an accomplished and stylish manner: *the rhythm section grooves in the true Basie manner.* ■ enjoy oneself: *Harley relaxed and began to groove.* **3** [trans.] informal Baseball pitch (a ball) in the center of the strike zone. ■ (in the context of other sports) kick or throw (the ball) successfully; score (a goal) with stylish ease: *the San Diego kicker grooved the winning field goal.* ▹Middle English (denoting a mine or shaft): from Dutch *groeve* 'furrow, pit'; related to GRAVE1.

▸PHRASE □ **in** (or **into**) **the groove** informal performing consistently well or confidently: *it might take me a couple of races to get back into the groove.* ■ indulging in relaxed and spontaneous enjoyment, esp. dancing: *get into the groove!*

grooved /gro͞ovd/ ▸adj. provided with or having a groove or grooves.

groov·ing saw ▸n. a circular saw used for cutting grooves.

groov·y /ˈgro͞ovē/ ▸adj. (**groov·i·er, groov·i·est**) informal, dated or humorous fashionable and exciting: *sporting a groovy new haircut.* ■ enjoyable and excellent: *he played all the remarkably groovy guitar parts himself.* **—groov·i·ly** /-vəlē/ adv. **—groov·i·ness** n.

grope /grōp/ ▸v. **1** [intrans.] feel about or search blindly or uncertainly with the hands: *she got up and* **groped for** *her spectacles.* ■ (**grope for**) search mentally with hesitation or uncertainty for (a word or answer): *she was groping for the words which would express what she thought* | [as adj.] (**groping**) *their groping attempts to create a more meaningful existence.* ■ move along with difficulty by feeling objects as one goes: *she blew out the candle and* **groped her way** *to the door.* **2** [trans.] informal feel or fondle (someone) for sexual pleasure, esp. against their will: *he was accused of groping office girls.*

▸n. an act of fondling someone for sexual pleasure: *she and Steve sneaked off for a quick grope.* ▹Old English *grāpian*; related to GRIPE. **—grop·ing·ly** adv.

Gro·pi·us /ˈgrōpēəs/, Walter (1883–1969), U.S. architect; born in Germany. He was the first director of the Bauhaus School of Design 1919–28 and a pioneer of the international style. He was one of the designers of the Pan American Building (1962) in New York.

gros·beak /ˈgrōs,bēk/ ▸n. a finch or related songbird with a stout conical bill and typically brightly colored plumage. • Several genera in the family Fringillidae and subfamily Cardinalinae (family Emberizidae); the **white-fronted grosbeak** or **grosbeak weaver** (*Amblyospiza albifrons*) belongs to the family Ploceidae. ▹late 17th cent.: from French *grosbec*, from *gros* 'big, fat' + *bec* 'beak.'

gro·schen /ˈgrōsHən/ ▸n. (pl. same) a monetary unit of Austria (until the introduction of the euro), equal to one hundredth of a schilling. ■ historical a small German silver coin. ■ informal a German ten-pfennig piece. ▹German, from Middle High German *grosse*, from medieval Latin *(denarius) grossus* 'thick (penny)'; compare with GROAT.

gros·grain /ˈgrō,grān/ ▸n. a heavy, ribbed fabric, typically of silk or rayon. ▹mid 19th cent.: French, 'coarse grain' (see also GROGRAM).

gros point /grō/ ▸n. a type of needlepoint embroidery consisting of stitches crossing two or more threads of the canvas in each direction. ▹mid 19th cent.: French, literally 'large stitch,' from *gros point de Venise*, a type of lace originally from Venice, worked in bold relief. The current sense dates from the 1930s.

gross /grōs/ ▸adj. **1** unattractively large or bloated: *I feel fat, gross—even my legs feel flabby.* ■ large-scale; not fine or detailed: *at the gross anatomical level.* ■ complete; blatant: *a gross exaggeration.* ■ vulgar; unrefined: *the duties we felt called upon to perform toward our inferiors were only gross, material ones.* ■ informal very unpleasant; repulsive: *it's disgusting and gross, but it's a fact.* **2** (of income, profit, or interest) without deduction of tax or other contributions; total: *the gross amount of the gift was $1,000* | *the current rate of interest is about 6.1 percent gross.* Often contrasted with NET2 (sense 1). ■ (of weight) including all contents, fittings, wrappings, or other variable items; overall: *a projected gross takeoff weight of 500,000 pounds.* ■ (of a score in golf) as actually played, without taking handicap into account.

▸adv. without tax or other contributions having been deducted.

▸v. [trans.] produce or earn (an amount of money) as gross profit or income: *the film went on to gross $8 million in the U.S.*

▸phrasal v. □ **gross someone out** informal disgust someone, typically with repulsive or obscene behavior or appearance.

▸n. **1** (pl. same) an amount equal to twelve dozen; 144: *fifty-five gross of tins of processed milk.* [From French *grosse douzaine*, literally 'large dozen.'] **2** (pl. **gross·es**) a gross profit or income: *the box-office grosses mounted.* ▹Middle English (in the sense 'thick, massive, bulky'): from Old French *gros, grosse* 'large,' from late Latin *grossus.* **—gross·ly** adv. [as submodifier] *Freda was grossly overweight.* **—gross·ness** n.

▸PHRASE □ **by the gross** figurative in large numbers or amounts: *impoverished Mexicans who were arrested here by the gross.*

gross a·nat·o·my ▸n. the branch of anatomy that deals with the structure of organs and tissues that are visible to the naked eye.

gross do·mes·tic prod·uct (abbr.: **GDP**) ▸n. the total value of goods produced and services provided in a country during one year. Compare with GROSS NATIONAL PRODUCT.

gross na·tion·al prod·uct (abbr.: **GNP**) ▸n. the total value of goods produced and services provided by a country during one year, equal to the gross domestic product plus the net income from foreign investments.

gross-out ▸n. informal something disgusting or repellent: [as adj.] *the movie features several gross-out scenes.*

gross ton ▸n. see TON1 (sense 1).

gros·su·lar /ˈgräsyələr/ ▸n. a mineral of the garnet group, consisting essentially of calcium aluminum silicate. ▹early 19th cent.: from modern Latin *grossularia* 'gooseberry.' The yellow-green variety is sometimes known as *gooseberry garnet.*

Gros Ventre /ˈgrō ,vänt/ n. (pl. **Gros Ventres** pronunc. same) **1** (also **Gros Ventres of the Missouri**) another term for HIDATSA. **2** (also **Gros Ventres of the**

Prai·ries) another term for **ATSINA**. ▷French, literally 'big belly.'

grosz /grôSH/ ▶*n.* (*pl.* **gros·zy** /'grôSHē/) a monetary unit of Poland, equal to one hundredth of a zloty. ▷Polish; compare with **GROSCHEN**.

grot /grät/ ▶*n. poetic/literary* a grotto. ▷early 16th cent.: from French *grotte*, from Italian *grotta*, via Latin from Greek *kruptē* 'vault, crypt.'

gro·tesque /grō'tesk/ ▶*adj.* comically or repulsively ugly or distorted: *grotesque facial distortions.* ■ incongruous or inappropriate to a shocking degree: *a lifestyle of grotesque luxury.*

▶*n.* **1** a very ugly or comically distorted figure, creature, or image: *the rods are carved in the form of a series of gargoyle faces and grotesques.* ■ (**the grotesque**) that which is grotesque: *images of the macabre and the grotesque.* ■ a style of decorative painting or sculpture consisting of the interweaving of human and animal forms with flowers and foliage. **2** *Printing* a family of 19th-century sans serif typefaces. ▷mid 16th cent. (as noun): from French *crotesque* (the earliest form in English), from Italian *grottesca*, from *opera* or *pittura grottesca* 'work or painting resembling that found in a grotto'; "grotto" here probably denoted the rooms of ancient buildings in Rome that had been revealed by excavations and contained murals in the grotesque style. **—gro·tesque·ly** *adv.* **—gro·tesque·ness** *n.*

gro·tes·quer·ie /grō'teskərē/ (also **gro·tes·quer·y**) ▶*n.* (*pl.* **-quer·ies**) grotesque quality or grotesque things collectively: *living in a world of grotesquerie and make-believe.* ■ a grotesque figure, object, or action. ▷late 17th cent.: French (see **GROTESQUE**).

Gro·ti·us /'grōSH(ē)əs/, Hugo (1583–1645), Dutch jurist and diplomat; Latinized name of *Huig de Groot.* His legal treatise, *De Jure Belli et Pacis* (1625), established the basis of modern international law.

Grot·on /'grätn/ a town in southeastern Connecticut, on the Thames River and Long Island Sound, a submarine manufacturing center; pop. 45,144.

grot·to /'grätō/ ▶*n.* (*pl.* **-toes** or **-tos**) a small picturesque cave, esp. an artificial one in a park or garden. ■ an indoor structure resembling a cave. ▷early 17th cent.: from Italian *grotta*, via Latin from Greek *kruptē* (see **CRYPT**). **—grot·toed** *adj.*

grot·ty /'grätē/ ▶*adj.* (**-ti·er**, **-ti·est**) *Brit., informal* unpleasant and of poor quality: *a grotty little hotel.* ■ [*as complement*] unwell: *if the person feels very grotty, it is probably true influenza.* ▷1960s: from **GROTESQUE** + **-Y**[1]. **—grot·ti·ness** *n.*

grouch /groucH/ ▶*n.* a habitually grumpy person: *rock's foremost poet and ill-mannered grouch.* ■ a complaint or grumble: *my only real grouch was that the children's chorus was far less easy on the ear.* ■ a fit of grumbling or sulking: *he's in a thundering grouch.*

▶*v.* [*intrans.*] voice one's discontent in an ill-tempered manner; grumble: *there's not a lot to grouch about.* ▷late 19th cent.: variant of obsolete *grutch*, from Old French *grouchier* 'to grumble, murmur,' of unknown origin. Compare with **GRUDGE**.

grouch·y /'groucHē/ ▶*adj.* (**grouch·i·er**, **grouch·i·est**) irritable and bad-tempered; grumpy; complaining: *the old man grew sulky and grouchy.* **—grouch·i·ly** /-CHəlē/ *adv.* **—grouch·i·ness** *n.*

ground[1] /ground/ ▶*n.* **1** [in *sing.*] the solid surface of the earth: *he lay on the ground.* ■ a limited or defined extent of the earth's surface; land: *an adjoining area of ground had been purchased.* ■ land of a specified kind: *my feet squelched over marshy ground.* ■ an area of land or sea used for a specified purpose: *shore dumping can pollute fishing grounds and beaches.* ■ (**grounds**) an area of enclosed land surrounding a large house or other building: *the house stands in seven acres of grounds.* ■ [as *adj.*] (in aviation) of or relating to the ground rather than the air (with particular reference to the maintenance and servicing of an aircraft on the ground): *ground staff | ground crew.* ■ [as *adj.*] (of an animal) living on or in the ground. ■ [as *adj.*] (of a fish) bottom-dwelling. ■ [as *adj.*] (of a plant) low-growing, esp. in relation to similar plants. **2** an area of knowledge or subject of discussion or thought: *third-year courses typically* **cover** *less* **ground** *and go into more depth | he shifted the argument onto theoretical grounds of his own choosing.* **3** (**grounds**) factors forming a basis for action or the justification for a belief: *there are some* **grounds for** *optimism | they called for a retrial* **on the grounds of** *the new evidence.* **4** *chiefly Art* a prepared surface to which paint is applied. ■ a substance used to prepare a surface for painting. ■ (in embroidery or ceramics) a plain surface to which decoration is applied. ■ a piece of wood fixed to a wall as a base for boards, plaster, or woodwork. **5** *Music* short for **GROUND BASS**. **6** (**grounds**) solid particles, esp. of ground coffee, that form a residue; sediment. **7** electrical connection of a circuit or conductor to the earth.

▶*v.* [*trans.*] **1** (often **be grounded**) prohibit or prevent (a pilot or an aircraft) from flying: *a bitter wind blew from the northeast, and the bombers were grounded.* ■ *informal* (of a parent) refuse to allow (a child) to go out socially as a punishment: *he was grounded for hitting her on the head.* **2** run (a ship) aground: *rather than be blown up, Muller grounded his ship on a coral reef and surrendered.* ■ [*intrans.*] (of a ship) go aground: *the larger ships grounded on the riverbed at low tide.* **3** (usu. **be grounded in**) give (something abstract) a firm theoretical or practical basis: *the study of history must be grounded in a thorough knowledge of the past.* ■ instruct (someone) thoroughly in a subject: *they were grounded in the classics, in history, and in literature.* **4** place or lay (something) on the ground or hit the ground with it: *he was penalized two strokes for grounding his club in a bunker.* **5** connect (an electrical device) with the ground. **6** [*intrans.*] *Baseball* (of a batter) hit a pitched ball so that it bounces on the ground: *he* **grounded to** *second.* ■ (**ground out**) (of a batter) be put out by hitting a ball on the ground to a fielder who throws it to or touches first base before the batter touches that base: *he* **grounded out to** *shortstop.* ▷Old English *grund*, of Germanic origin; related to Dutch *grond* and German *Grund.*

▶*PHRASES* □ **be thick** (or **thin**) **on the ground** existing (or not existing) in large numbers or amounts: *new textbooks on particle physics are thin on the ground.* □ **break ground 1** do preparatory digging or other work prior to building or planting something. **2** another term for **BREAK NEW GROUND** below. □ **break new** (or **fresh**) **ground** do something innovative that is considered an advance or positive benefit. □ **cut the ground from under someone's feet** do something that leaves someone without a reason or justification for their actions or opinions. □ **from the ground up** *informal* connect completely or complete: *they needed to learn the business from the ground up.* □ **gain ground** become more popular or accepted: *new moral attitudes are gaining ground.* □ **gain ground on** get closer to someone or something one is pursuing or with whom one is competing: *the dollar gained ground on all other major currencies.* □ **get off the ground** (or **get something off the ground**) start or cause to start happening or functioning successfully: *he doesn't appreciate the steps he must take to get the negotiations off the ground.* □ **give** (or **lose**) **ground** retreat or lose one's advantage during a conflict or competition: *he refused to give ground on this issue.* □ **go to ground** (of a fox or other animal) enter its earth or burrow. ■ *figurative* (of a person) hide or become inaccessible, esp. for a long time: *he had gone to ground following the presidential coup.* □ **hold** (or **stand**) **one's ground** not retreat or lose one's advantage during a conflict or competition: *you will be able to hold your ground and resist the enemy's attack.* □ **make up ground** get closer to someone ahead in a race or competition. □ **on the ground** in a place where real, practical work is done: *the troops on the ground are cynical.* □ **on one's own ground** in one's own territory or concerning one's own range of knowledge or experience: *I feel reasonably relaxed if I'm interviewed on my own ground.* □ **prepare the ground** make it easier for something to occur or be developed: *congress approved a series of measures intended to* **prepare the ground for** *the new economic structure.* □ **run someone/something to ground** see **RUN**. □ **work** (or **run**) **oneself into the ground** exhaust oneself by working or running very hard.

ground[2] ▶ past and past participle of **GRIND**.

▶*adj.* [*attrib.*] reduced to fine particles by crushing or mincing: *ground cumin.* ■ shaped, roughened, or polished by grinding: *the thick opaque ground perimeter of the lenses.*

▶*PHRASE* □ **ground down** exhausted or worn down.

ground ball ▶*n. Baseball* a ball hit along the ground.

ground bass /bās/ ▶*n. Music* a short theme, usually in the bass, that is constantly repeated as the other parts of the music vary.

ground bee·tle ▶*n.* any of a number of beetles that live mainly on or near the ground, in particular a fast-running predatory beetle of the family Carabidae.

ground·break·ing /'ground,brākiNG/ ▶*adj.* breaking new ground; innovative; pioneering. **—ground·break·er** /-,brākər/ *n.*

ground cher·ry ▶*n.* an American plant of the nightshade family that resembles the cape gooseberry. • Genus *Physalis*, family Solanaceae: several species, in particular *P. pruinosa*, which yields edible fruit.

ground cloth (also **ground·cloth**) ▶*n.* a waterproof cloth spread under a sleeping bag, directly on the ground or inside a tent. Also called **GROUNDSHEET**.

ground clut·ter ▶*n.* noise in a radar echo caused by untargeted built or natural landscape features.

ground con·trol ▶*n.* [treated as *sing.* or *pl.*] the ground-based personnel and equipment that monitor and direct the flight and landing of aircraft or spacecraft. **—ground con·trol·ler** *n.*

ground cov·er ▶*n.* low-growing, spreading plants that help to stop weeds from growing.

ground crew ▶*n.* [treated as *sing.* or *pl.*] a team of people who maintain and service an aircraft on the ground.

ground dove /dəv/ ▶*n.* a small dove that spends much of its time on the ground, feeding and frequently nesting there. • *Columbina, Gallicolumba*, and related genera, family Columbidae: several species, including the **common ground dove** (*C. passerina*) of North and Central America.

ground·ed /'groundid/ ▶*adj.* **1** well balanced and sensible: *the kids have money and a rock-star dad, but they seem grounded.* **2** (of a pilot or an aircraft) prohibited or prevented from flying: *you don't taunt a grounded flier, especially after he's had a few beers.* ■ *informal* (of a child being punished) not allowed to participate in social or recreational activities: *the problem is, I've got more grounded friends than available friends.*

ground ef·fect ▶*n.* the effect of added aerodynamic buoyancy produced by a cushion of air below a vehicle moving close to the ground.

ground el·der ▶*n.* a common weed of the parsley family, native to Europe, with leaves that resemble those of the elder and spreading, underground stems. • *Aegopodium podagraria*, family Umbelliferae: a variegated cultivar is sometimes grown as ground cover.

ground·er /'groundər/ ▶*n. Baseball* a ground ball.

ground floor ▶*n.* the floor of a building at ground level.

▶*PHRASE* □ **get in on the ground floor** *informal* become part of an enterprise in its early stages.

ground game ▶*n. Football* play consisting of running from scrimmage to advance the ball.

ground glass ▶*n.* **1** glass with a smooth ground surface that renders it nontransparent while retaining its translucency. **2** glass ground into an abrasive powder.

ground·hog /'ground,häg; -,hôg/ ▶*n.* another term for **WOODCHUCK**.

Ground·hog Day ▶*n.* February 2, when the groundhog is said to come out of its hole at the end of hibernation. If the animal sees its shadow—i.e., if the weather is sunny—it is said to portend six weeks more of winter weather.

ground·hop·per /'ground,häpər/ ▶*n.* a small, predominantly brown insect that resembles a grasshopper and has well-developed wings. • Family Tetrigidae, order Orthoptera: several species.

ground·ing /'groundiNG/ ▶*n.* [in *sing.*] basic training or instruction in a subject: *every child needs* **a** *good* **grounding in** *science and technology.*

ground i·vy ▶*n.* a creeping plant of the mint family, with bluish-purple flowers. Native to Europe, it has become established in eastern North America. Also called **GILL-OVER-THE-GROUND, CREEPING CHARLIE.** • *Glechoma hederacea*, family Labiatae.

ground·less /'ground-lis/ ▶*adj.* not based on any good reason: *your fears are quite groundless.* ▷Old English *grundlēas* (see **GROUND**[1], **-LESS**). **—ground·less·ly** *adv.* **—ground·less·ness** *n.*

ground lev·el ▶*n.* **1** the level of the ground: [as *adj.*] *ground-level ozone pollution.* ■ the ground floor of a building. **2** *Physics* another term for **GROUND STATE**.

ground·ling /'groundliNG/ ▶*n.* **1** a spectator or reader of inferior taste, such as a member of a theater audience who traditionally stood in the pit beneath the stage: *Dante is not for groundlings.* [with reference to Shakespeare's *Hamlet* III. ii. 11.] **2** a person on the ground as opposed to one in a spacecraft or aircraft. **3** a fish that lives at the bottom of lakes and streams, esp. a gudgeon or loach. **4** a creeping or dwarf plant. ▷early 17th cent. (denoting a fish): from **GROUND**[1] + **-LING**; compare with Dutch *grondeling*, German *Gründling* 'gudgeon.'

ground loop ▶*n.* **1** a violent, uncontrolled swinging movement of an aircraft while landing, taking off, or taxiing. **2** an unwanted electric current path in a circuit resulting in stray signals or interference,

occurring, e.g., when two earthed points in the same circuit have different potentials.
▶*v.* (**ground-loop**) [*intrans.*] (of an aircraft) make a ground loop.

ground·mass /ˈground,mas/ ▶*n.* [in *sing.*] *Geology* the compact, finer-grained material in which the crystals are embedded in a porphyritic rock.

ground·nut /ˈground,nət/ ▶*n.* **1** another term for PEANUT. **2** a North American twining vine of the pea family, which bears clusters of fragrant brownish or maroon flowers and which yields a sweet edible tuber. • Genus *Apios*, family Leguminosae: several species, in particular *A. americana*.

ground·out /ˈground,out/ ▶*n. Baseball* a play in which a batter is put out by hitting a ball on the ground to a fielder who throws it to or touches first base before the batter touches that base.

ground pine ▶*n.* **1** a small, yellow-flowered Eurasian plant of the mint family that resembles a pine seedling in appearance and smell. • *Ajuga chamaepitys*, family Labiatae. **2** a North American club moss with small, shiny leaves, resembling a miniature conifer and growing typically in coniferous woodland. • Genus *Lycopodium*, family Lycopodiaceae: several species, in particular *L. obscurum* and *L. tristachyum*.

ground plan ▶*n.* the plan of a building at ground level as imagined seen from above. ■ the general outline or basis of a plan.

ground rule ▶*n.* (usu. **ground rules**) a basic principle: *some ground rules for assessing new machines.* ■ *Baseball* a rule pertaining to the limits of play on a particular field.

ground run ▶*n.* the movement of an aircraft along the ground just before takeoff or just after landing.

ground·sel /ˈgroun(d)səl/ ▶*n.* **1** a widely distributed plant of the daisy family, with yellow rayless flowers. • Genus *Senecio*, family Compositae: several species, in particular the **common groundsel** (*S. vulgaris*), which is a common weed. See also GIANT GROUNDSEL. **2** variant spelling of GROUNDSILL. ▷Old English *gundæswelgiæ* (later *grundeswylige*), probably from *gund* 'pus' + *swelgan* 'to swallow' (with reference to its use in poultices). The later form may be by association with GROUND[1], and refer to the plant's rapid growth.

ground·sheet /ˈgroun(d),SHēt/ ▶*n.* another term for GROUND CLOTH.

ground·sill (also **ground·sel**) ▶*n.* the horizontal beam or timber in a building that is secured to the foundation and is the base for the rest of the structure.

grounds·keep·er /ˈgroun(d)z,kēpər/ ▶*n.* a person who maintains an athletic field, a park, or the grounds of a school or other institution.

ground sloth ▶*n.* an extinct terrestrial edentate mammal of the Cenozoic era in America, typically of very large size. • Order Xenarthra (or Edentata). See MEGATHERIUM, MYLODON.

grounds·man /ˈgroun(d)zmən/ ▶*n.* (*pl.* **-men**) British term for GROUNDSKEEPER.

ground·speed /ˈground,spēd/ ▶*n.* an aircraft's speed relative to the ground. Compare with AIRSPEED.

ground squir·rel ▶*n.* a burrowing squirrel that is typically highly social, found chiefly in North America and northern Eurasia, where it usually hibernates in winter. Also called GOPHER. • *Spermophilus* and other genera, family Sciuridae: many species, including the sousliks and chipmunks.

ground state ▶*n. Physics* the lowest energy state of an atom or other particle.

ground·stroke /ˈground,strōk/ ▶*n. Tennis* a stroke played after the ball has bounced, as opposed to a volley.

ground·swell /ˈgroun(d),swel/ ▶*n.* [in *sing.*] **1** a buildup of opinion or feeling in a large section of the population: *an unexpected groundswell of opposition developed.* **2** a large or extensive swell in the sea.

ground tack·le ▶*n.* the equipment used to anchor or moor a boat or ship.

ground·wa·ter /ˈground,wôtər; -,wätər/ ▶*n.* water held underground in the soil or in pores and crevices in rock.

ground wave ▶*n.* a radio wave that reaches a receiver from a transmitter directly, without reflection from the ionosphere.

ground·work /ˈground,wərk/ ▶*n.* preliminary or basic work: *a manned space station is needed to* **lay the groundwork for** *a colony on the moon.*

ground ze·ro ▶*n.* [in *sing.*] the point on the earth's surface directly above or below an exploding nuclear bomb. ■ the site of the former World Trade Center in New York City in the wake of the terrorist attacks of September 11, 2001. ■ *figurative* a starting point or base for some activity: *if you're starting at ground zero in terms of knowledge, go to the library.*

group /groōp/ ▶*n.* [treated as *sing.* or *pl.*] a number of people or things that are located close together or are considered or classed together: *these bodies fall into four distinct groups.* ■ a number of people who work together or share certain beliefs: *I now belong to my local drama group.* ■ a commercial organization consisting of several companies under common ownership. ■ a number of musicians who play popular music together. ■ *Military* a unit of the U.S. Air Force, consisting of two or more squadrons. ■ *Military* a unit of the U.S. Army, consisting of two or more battalions. ■ *Art* two or more figures or objects forming a design. ■ *Chemistry* a set of elements occupying a column in the periodic table and having broadly similar properties arising from their similar electronic structure. ■ *Chemistry* a combination of atoms having a recognizable identity in a number of compounds. ■ *Mathematics* a set of elements, together with an associative binary operation, that contains an inverse for each element and an identity element. ■ *Geology* a stratigraphic division consisting of two or more formations.
▶*v.* [*trans.*] (often **be grouped**) put together or place in a group or groups: *three wooden chairs were grouped around a dining table.* ■ put into categories; classify: *we* **group** *them* **into** *species merely as a convenience.* ■ [*intrans.*] form a group or groups: *many growers began to group together to form cooperatives.* ▷late 17th cent.: from French *groupe*, from Italian *gruppo*, of Germanic origin; related to CROP.

group dy·nam·ics ▶*plural n.* [also treated as *sing.*] *Psychology* the processes involved when people in a group interact with each other, or the study of these.

group·er /ˈgroōpər/ ▶*n.* a large or very large heavy-bodied fish of the sea bass family, with a big head and wide mouth, found in warm seas. • Family Serranidae: several genera, in particular *Epinephelus* and *Mycteroperca*. The **Nassau grouper** (*E. striatus*) is the most economically important fish of the Bahamas. ▷early 17th cent.: from Portuguese *garoupa*, probably from a local term in South America.

Nassau grouper

group home ▶*n.* a home where a small number of unrelated people in need of care, support, or supervision, such as the elderly or the mentally ill, can live together.

group·ie /ˈgroōpē/ ▶*n. informal* a person, esp. a young woman, who regularly follows a pop music group or other celebrity in the hope of meeting or getting to know them. ■ [with *adj.*] *often derogatory* an enthusiastic or uncritical follower: *the contemporary art groupie.*

group·ing /ˈgroōpiNG/ ▶*n.* a set of people acting together with a common interest or purpose, esp. within a larger organization: *a grouping of Protestant churches.* ■ the arrangement or formation of people or things in a group or groups: *an alternative form of ability grouping.*

Group of Eight /ˈgroōp əv ˈāt/ (abbr.: **G8**) *n.* the eight leading industrial nations (U.S., Japan, Germany, France, UK, Italy, Canada, and Russia), whose heads of government meet regularly.

Group of Sev·en 1 (abbr.: **G7**) a group of seven leading industrial nations outside the former communist bloc, consisting of the U.S., Japan, Germany (originally West Germany), France, the UK, Italy, and Canada. **2** a group of Canadian landscape painters, officially established in 1920, who formed the first major national movement in Canadian art. Their work exhibited a bold and colorful expressionistic style.

group prac·tice ▶*n.* a medical practice run by several doctors.

group ther·a·py ▶*n.* a form of psychotherapy in which a group of patients meet to describe and discuss their problems together under the supervision of a therapist.

group·think /ˈgroōp,THiNGk/ ▶*n.* the practice of thinking or making decisions as a group in a way that discourages creativity or individual responsibility: *there's always a danger of groupthink when two leaders are so alike.* ▷late 20th cent.: on the pattern of *doublethink.*

grou·pus·cule /groōˈpəs,kyoōl/ ▶*n.* a political or religious splinter group. ▷mid 20th cent.: from French, diminutive of *groupe* 'group.'

group ve·loc·i·ty ▶*n. Physics* the speed at which the energy of a wave travels.

group·ware /ˈgroōp,we(ə)r/ ▶*n. Computing* software designed to facilitate collective working by a number of different users.

group work ▶*n. Brit.* work done by a group in collaboration.

grouse[1] /grous/ ▶*n.* (*pl.* same) a medium to large game bird with a plump body and feathered legs, the male being larger and more conspicuously colored than the female. • Family Tetraonidae (or Phasianidae): several genera, esp. *Lagopus* and *Tetrao*. The family also includes ptarmigans, capercaillies, and prairie chickens. ■ the flesh of this bird as food. ▷early 16th cent.: perhaps related to medieval Latin *gruta* or to Old French *grue* 'crane.'

grouse[2] ▶*v.* [*intrans.*] complain pettily; grumble: *she heard him grousing about his assistant.*
▶*n.* a grumble or complaint: *our biggest grouse was about the noise of the construction work.* ▷early 19th cent.: of unknown origin; compare with GROUCH. **—grous·er** *n.*

grout[1] /grout/ ▶*n.* a mortar or paste for filling crevices, esp. the gaps between wall or floor tiles.
▶*v.* [*trans.*] fill in with grout: *the gaps are grouted afterward.* ▷mid 17th cent.: perhaps from obsolete *grout* 'sediment,' (plural) 'dregs,' or related to French dialect *grouter* 'grout a wall.'

grout[2] ▶*n.* (**grouts**) *archaic* sediment; dregs; grounds: *old women told fortunes in grouts of tea.* ▷Old English *grūt*, of Germanic origin; related to Dutch *gruit* 'dregs,' German *Grauss* 'grain, weak beer,' also to GRITS and GROATS. The original meaning was 'coarse meal, groats,' also denoting the infusion of malt that was fermented to make beer, hence, in Middle English, 'sediment.'

grout·er /ˈgroutər/ ▶*n.* a tool used for grouting tiles.

grout·ing /ˈgroutiNG/ ▶*n.* grout, esp. when hardened.

Grove[1] /grōv/, Sir George (1820–1900), English musicologist. He was the founder and first editor of the multivolume *Dictionary of Music and Musicians* (1879–89), which is now named for him in its later editions, and served as the first director of the Royal College of Music 1883–94.

Grove[2], Lefty (1900–1975) U.S. baseball player; full name *Robert Moses Grove*. A pitcher, he played for the Philadelphia Athletics 1925–34 and the Boston Red Sox 1935–41. He led the American League in strikeouts 7 times and had a career total of 2,217. Baseball Hall of Fame (1947).

grove /grōv/ ▶*n.* a small wood, orchard, or group of trees: *an olive grove* | [in *place names*] *Ocean Grove.* ▷Old English *grāf*, of Germanic origin. **—grovy** *adj.*

grov·el /ˈgrävəl; ˈgrə-/ ▶*v.* (**grov·eled**, **grov·el·ing**; *Brit.* **grov·elled**, **grov·el·ling**) [*intrans.*] lie or move abjectly on the ground with one's face downward: *she was groveling on the floor in fear.* ■ act in an obsequious manner in order to obtain someone's forgiveness or favor: *everyone expected me to grovel with gratitude* | [as *adj.*] (**groveling**) *his groveling references to "great" historians and their "brilliant" works.* ▷Middle English: back-formation from the obsolete adverb *grovelling*, from obsolete *groof*, *grufe* 'the face or front' (in the phrase *on grufe*, from Old Norse *á grúfu* 'face downward') + the suffix *-ling*. **—grov·el·er** *n.* **—grov·el·ing·ly** *adv.*

groves of Ac·a·deme ▶*plural n.* the academic world. ▷translating Horace's *silvas Academi.*

grow /grō/ ▶*v.* (*past* **grew** /groō/; *past part.* **grown** /grōn/) [*intrans.*] **1** (of a living thing) undergo natural development by increasing in size and changing physically; progress to maturity: *he would watch Nick grow to manhood* | [as *adj.*] (**growing**) *the linguistic skills acquired by the growing child* | [as *adj.*] (**grown**) *the stupidity of grown men hitting a ball with a stick.* ■ (of a plant) germinate and develop: *seaweed grows in the ocean.* ■ [*trans.*] produce by cultivation: *more and more land*

G

was needed to grow crops for export. ■ [trans.] allow or cause (a part of the body) to grow or develop: [trans.] *she grew her hair long.* ■ (of something abstract) come into existence and develop: *the Vietnamese diaspora* ***grew out of*** *their national tragedy.* **2** become larger or greater over a period of time; increase: *turnover grew to more than $100,000 within three years* | [as adj.] (**growing**) *a growing number of people are coming to realize this.* ■ [trans.] cause (something, esp. a business) to expand or increase. See **usage** below. **3** [with complement] become gradually or increasingly: *sharing our experiences, we grew braver.* ■ [with infinitive] (of a person) come to feel or know something over time: *she grew to like the friendly, quiet people at the farm.* ■ (**grow apart**) (of two or more people) become gradually estranged.

▸*phrasal v.* □ **grow into** become as a result of natural development or gradual increase: *Swampscott grew into a fishing village of about three hundred people by the 1850s.* ■ become large enough to wear (a garment) comfortably. □ **grow on** become gradually more appealing to (someone): *a house has to grow on you.* □ **grow out** disappear because of normal growth: *Colette's old perm had almost grown out.* □ **grow out of** become too large to wear (a garment): *blazers that they grew out of.* ■ become too mature to retain (a childish habit): *most children grow out of tantrums by the time they're three.* □ **grow up** advance to maturity; spend one's childhood and adolescence: *a young Muslim woman who grew up in Philadelphia.* ■ [often in imperative] begin to behave or think sensibly and realistically: *grow up, sister, and come into the real world.* ■ arise; develop: *a school of painting grew up in Cuzco.* ▷Old English *grōwan* (originally referring chiefly to plants), of Germanic origin; related to Dutch *groeien*, also to **GRASS** and **GREEN**. —**grow·a·ble** *adj.*

▸*PHRASE* □ **grow on trees** [usu. with *negative*] *informal* be plentiful or easily obtained: *money doesn't grow on trees.*

USAGE Although **grow** is typically intransitive, as in *he grew two inches taller over the summer*, its use as a transitive verb has long been standard in such phrases as *grow crops* and *grow a beard.*
Recently, however, **grow** has extended its transitive sense and has become trendy in business, economics, and government contexts: *growing the industry, growing your business, growing your investment*, and so on. Many people stumble over this extended sense and label it 'jargon.'

G

grow·er /ˈgrōər/ ▸*n.* **1** a person who grows a particular type of crop: *a fruit grower.* **2** [with adj.] a plant that grows in a specified way: *a fast grower.*

grow·ing pains ▸*plural n.* neuralgic pains that occur in the limbs of some young children. ■ *figurative* the difficulties experienced in the early stages of an enterprise: *the growing pains of a young republic.*

grow·ing point ▸*n.* the point at which growth originates. ■ *Botany* the meristem region at the apex of a plant shoot at which continuous cell division and differentiation occur.

grow·ing sea·son ▸*n.* the part of the year during which rainfall and temperature allow plants to grow: *a short growing season.*

growl /groul/ ▸*v.* [intrans.] (of an animal, esp. a dog) make a low guttural sound of hostility in the throat: *the dogs yapped and growled about his heels.* ■ [with direct speech] (of a person) say something in a low grating voice, typically in a threatening manner: *"Keep out of this," he growled.* ■ (of a thing) make a low or harsh rumbling sound, typically one that is felt to be threatening: *thunder growls without warning from a summer sky.*
▸*n.* a low guttural sound made in the throat, esp. by a dog. ■ a similar sound made by a person, esp. to express hostility or anger. ■ [in sing.] a low throaty sound made by a machine or engine: *the growl of diesel engines.* ▷mid 17th cent.: probably imitative. —**growl·ing·ly** *adv.*

growl·er /ˈgroulər/ ▸*n.* **1** a person or thing that growls. **2** a small iceberg that rises little above the water. **3** *informal* a pail or other container used for carrying drink, esp. draft beer. **4** an electromagnet with two poles designed to test for short circuits in the windings of an armature. **5** *archaic, informal* a four-wheeled hansom cab.

grown /grōn/ ▸ past participle of **GROW**.

grown-up ▸*adj.* adult: *Joe is married with two grown-up daughters.* ■ suitable for or characteristic of an adult: *it seems a grown-up thing to do.*
▸*n.* an adult (esp. a child's word): *I don't like it when grown-ups get all serious.*

growth /grōth/ ▸*n.* **1** the process of increasing in physical size: *the upward growth of plants* | *the growth of the city affects the local climate.* ■ the process of developing or maturing physically, mentally, or spiritually: *keeping a journal can be a vital step in our personal growth.* ■ the increase in number and spread of small or microscopic organisms: *some additives slow down the growth of microorganisms.* ■ the process of increasing in amount, value, or importance: *the rates of population growth are lowest in the north.* ■ increase in economic value or activity: *the government aims to get growth back into the economy.* **2** something that has grown or is growing: *a day's growth of unshaven stubble on his chin.* ■ *Medicine & Biology* a tumor or other abnormal formation. **3** a vineyard or crop of grapes of a specified classification of quality, or a wine from it.

growth com·pa·ny ▸*n.* a company that is growing rapidly in comparison to other companies in its field or the economy as a whole.

growth fac·tor ▸*n. Biology* a substance, such as a vitamin or hormone, that is required for the stimulation of growth in living cells.

growth fund ▸*n.* a mutual fund that invests primarily in stocks that are expected to increase in capital value rather than yield high income.

growth hor·mone ▸*n.* a hormone that stimulates growth in animal or plant cells, esp. (in animals) a hormone secreted by the pituitary gland.

growth in·dus·try ▸*n.* an industry that is developing particularly rapidly.

growth ring ▸*n.* a concentric layer of wood, shell, or bone developed during an annual or other regular period of growth.

growth stock ▸*n.* a company stock that tends to increase in capital value rather than yield high income.

groyne ▸*n.* variant spelling of **GROIN**2.

groz·ing i·ron /ˈgrōziNG/ ▸*n. chiefly historical* a pair of pliers for clipping the edges of pieces of glass. ■ *historical* a tool for smoothing soldered joints in lead pipes. ▷Middle English: *grozing* from Middle Dutch, from the stem of *gruizen* 'crush, trim glass,' from *gruis* 'fragments.'

Groz·ny /ˈgrôznē; ˈgräznē/ a city in southwestern Russia, near the border with Georgia, capital of Chechnya; pop. 401,000.

GRP ▸*abbr.* glass-reinforced plastic.

grrrl ▸*n.* see **RIOT GRRRL**.

grt ▸*abbr.* gross registered tonnage, a measure of a ship's size found by dividing the volume of the space enclosed by its hull (measured in cubic feet) by one hundred.

grub /grəb/ ▸*n.* **1** the larva of an insect, esp. a beetle. ■ a maggot or small caterpillar. **2** *informal* food: *a popular bar serving excellent grub.*
▸*v.* (**grubbed**, **grub·bing**) [intrans.] **1** dig or poke superficially at the earth; dig shallowly in soil: *the damage done to pastures by badgers* ***grubbing for*** *worms.* ■ [trans.] remove (something) from the earth by digging it up: *all the vines are* ***grubbed up*** *and the land left fallow for a few years.* ■ [trans.] clear (the ground) of roots and stumps: [as n.] (**grubbing**) *construction operations including clearing and grubbing.* **2** search for something in a clumsy and unmethodical manner; rummage: *I began grubbing about in the wastepaper basket to find the envelope.* ■ do demeaning or humiliating work in order to achieve something: *she has achieved material independence without having to* ***grub for*** *it.* ■ [trans.] achieve or acquire (something) in such a way: *they were grubbing a living from garbage pails.* ▷Middle English: perhaps related to Dutch *grobbelen*, also to **GRAVE**1. —**grub·ber** *n.*

grub·by /ˈgrəbē/ ▸*adj.* (**-bi·er**, **-bi·est**) dirty; grimy: *the grubby face of a young boy.* ■ *figurative* disreputable; sordid: *grubby little moneylenders.* —**grub·bi·ly** /-bəlē/ *adv.* —**grub·bi·ness** *n.*

grub·stake /ˈgrəbˌstāk/ *informal* ▸*n.* an amount of material, provisions, or money supplied to an enterprise (originally a prospector for ore) in return for a share in the resulting profits.
▸*v.* [trans.] provide with a grubstake.

Grub Street /grəb/ ▸*n.* used in reference to a world or class of impoverished journalists and writers. ▷the name of a street (later Milton Street) in Moorgate, London, England, inhabited by such authors in the 17th cent.

grudge /grəj/ ▸*n.* a persistent feeling of ill will or resentment resulting from a past insult or injury: *she* ***held a grudge against*** *her former boss.*
▸*v.* [trans.] be resentfully unwilling to give, grant, or allow (something): *he grudged the work and time that the meeting involved.* ■ [with *two objs.*] [usu. with *negative*] feel resentful that (someone) has achieved (something): *I don't grudge him his moment of triumph.* ▷late Middle English: variant of obsolete *grutch* 'complain, murmur, grumble,' from Old French *grouchier*, of unknown origin. Compare with **GROUCH**. —**grudg·er** *n.*

▸*PHRASE* □ **bear** (or **owe**) **someone a grudge** maintain a feeling of ill will or resentment toward someone.

grudge match ▸*n.* a contest or other competitive situation based on personal antipathy between the participants.

grudg·ing /ˈgrəjiNG/ ▸*adj.* given, granted, or allowed only reluctantly or resentfully: *a grudging apology.* ■ (of a person) reluctant or resentfully unwilling to give, grant, or allow something: *Oliver was grudging about accepting Wickham's innocence.* —**grudg·ing·ly** *adv.* —**grudg·ing·ness** *n.*

gruel /ˈgroo͞əl/ ▸*n.* a thin liquid food of oatmeal or other meal boiled in milk or water. ▷Middle English: from Old French, of Germanic origin.

gruel·ing /ˈgroo͞əliNG/ (*Brit.* **gruel·ling**) ▸*adj.* extremely tiring and demanding: *a grueling schedule.* ▷mid 19th cent.: from the verb *gruel* 'exhaust, punish,' from an old phrase *get one's gruel* 'receive one's punishment.' —**gruel·ing·ly** *adv.*

grue·some /ˈgroo͞səm/ ▸*adj.* causing repulsion or horror; grisly: *a most gruesome murder.* ■ *informal* extremely unpleasant: *gruesome working hours.* ▷late 16th cent.: from Scots *grue* 'to feel horror, shudder' (of Scandinavian origin) + **-SOME**1. Rare before the late 18th cent., the word was popularized by Sir Walter Scott. —**grue·some·ly** *adv.* —**grue·some·ness** *n.*

gruff /grəf/ ▸*adj.* abrupt or taciturn in manner: *penetrate a gruff exterior and you will find him affable.* See note at **BRUSQUE**. ■ (of a voice) rough and low in pitch: *she spoke with a gruff, masculine voice.* ▷late 15th cent. (in the sense 'coarse-grained'): from Flemish and Dutch *grof* 'coarse, rude,' of West Germanic origin. —**gruff·ly** *adv.* —**gruff·ness** *n.*

grum·ble /ˈgrəmbəl/ ▸*v.* [reporting verb] complain or protest about something in a bad-tempered but typically muted way: [with clause] *his father was grumbling that he hadn't heard a word from him* | [trans.] *he grumbled something about the decision being unnecessary.* ■ [intrans.] make a low rumbling sound: *thunder was grumbling somewhere in the distance.* ■ [intrans.] (of an internal organ) give intermittent discomfort: *your stomach is grumbling.*
▸*n.* a complaint: *the main grumble is that he spends too much time away.* ■ a low rumbling sound. ▷late 16th cent.: from obsolete *grumme* (probably of Germanic origin and related to Dutch *grommen*) + **-LE**4. —**grum·bler** /-blər/ *n.* —**grum·bling·ly** /-bliNGlē/ *adv.* —**grum·bly** /-blē/ *adj.*

grump /grəmp/ *informal* ▸*n.* a grumpy person. ■ a fit of sulking: *he walks off in a grump to the other end of the meadow.*
▸*v.* [intrans.] act in a sulky, grumbling manner: *he grumped at me when I moved the papers.* ▷early 18th cent.: imitating inarticulate sounds expressing displeasure. —**grump·ish** *adj.* —**grump·ish·ly** *adv.*

grump·y /ˈgrəmpē/ ▸*adj.* (**grump·i·er**, **grump·i·est**) bad-tempered and sulky. —**grump·i·ly** /-pəlē/ *adv.* —**grump·i·ness** *n.*

Grun·dy /ˈgrəndē/ ▸*n.* see **MRS. GRUNDY**.

Grü·ne·wald /ˈgroo͞nˌväld/, Mathias (*c.*1460–1528), German painter; born *Mathis Nithardt*; also called **Mathis Gothardt** /ˈgätˌhärt/ . His most noted work is the nine-panel *Isenheim Altar* (completed 1516).

grunge /grənj/ ▸*n.* **1** grime; dirt. **2** (also **grunge rock**) a style of rock music characterized by a raucous guitar sound and lazy vocal delivery. ■ the fashion associated with this music, including loose, layered clothing and ripped jeans. ▷1970s: back-formation from *grungy*, perhaps suggested by **GRUBBY** and **DINGY**. —**grun·gi·ness** *n.* —**grun·gy** *adj.*

grun·ion /ˈgrənyən/ ▸*n.* a small, slender Californian fish that swarms onto beaches at night to spawn. The eggs are buried in the sand, and the young fish are swept out to sea on the following spring tide. • *Leuresthes tenuis*, family Atherinidae. ▷early 20th cent.: probably from Spanish *gruñón* 'grunter.'

grunt /grənt/ ▸*v.* [intrans.] (of an animal, esp. a pig) make a low, short guttural sound. ■ (of a person) make a low inarticulate sound resembling this, typically to express effort or indicate assent: *Graham grunted and heaved as he helped the masons fit a huge slab of stone into place.* ■ [trans.] utter with a low, short guttural sound.
▸*n.* **1** a low, short guttural sound made by an animal

or a person. **2** *informal* a low-ranking or unskilled soldier or other worker: *he went from grunt to senior executive vice-president in less than five years* | [as *adj.*] *grunt work.* [alteration of *ground*, from *ground man* (with reference to unskilled railroad work before progressing to lineman).] ■ a common soldier. **3** a dessert made of fruit topped with cookie dough: *blueberry grunt.* **4** an edible shoaling fish of tropical inshore waters and coral reefs, able to make a loud noise by grinding its teeth and amplifying the sound in the swim bladder. • Family Pomadasyidae: numerous genera and species. ▷Old English *grunnettan*, of Germanic origin and related to German *grunzen*; probably originally imitative.

grunt·er /ˈgrəntər/ ▸*n.* a fish that makes a grunting noise, esp. when caught, in particular: • a mainly marine fish of warm waters (family Theraponidae: several genera). • another term for **GRUNT** (sense 4).

grun·tled /ˈgrəntld/ ▸*adj. humorous* pleased, satisfied, and contented. ▷1930s: back-formation from **DISGRUNTLED**.

Grus /grəs; gro͞os/ *Astronomy* a small southern constellation (the Crane), south of Piscis Austrinus. ■ [as *genitive*] (**Gruis** /ˈgro͞oəs/) used with a preceding letter or numeral to designate a star in this constellation: *the star Delta Gruis.* ▷Latin.

Gru·yère /gro͞oˈyer; grē-/ ▸*n.* a firm, tangy cheese. ▷named after *Gruyère*, a district in Switzerland, where it was first made.

gr. wt. ▸*abbr.* gross weight.

gryph·on ▸*n.* variant spelling of **GRIFFIN**.

grys·bok /ˈgrīsˌbäk/ ▸*n.* a small mainly nocturnal antelope with small vertical horns and a slightly arched back, found in southwestern Africa. • Genus *Raphicerus*, family Bovidae: two species. ▷late 18th cent.: from Afrikaans, from Dutch *grijs* 'gray' + *bok* 'buck.'

GSA ▸*abbr.* ■ General Services Administration. ■ Girl Scouts of America.

GSC ▸*abbr.* General Staff Corps.

GSM ▸*abbr.* Global System (or Standard) for Mobile, a standardized international system for digital mobile telecommunication.

gsm ▸*abbr.* grams per square meter, a measure of weight for paper: *100 gsm paper.*

GSO ▸*abbr.* general staff officer.

GSOH ▸*abbr.* good sense of humor (used in personal advertisements).

G-spot ▸*n.* a sensitive area of the anterior wall of the vagina believed by some to be highly erogenous and capable of ejaculation. ▷1944: *G* from *Gräfenberg*, because first described by Gräfenberg and Dickinson in the *Western Journal of Surgery*.

GSR ▸*abbr.* galvanic skin response.

GST ▸*abbr.* generation-skipping tax

Gstaad /gəˈshtät/ a winter-sports resort in western Switzerland.

G-string (also **gee-string**) ▸*n.* a garment consisting of a narrow strip of cloth that covers the genitals and is attached to a waistband, worn as underwear or by striptease performers.

G-suit (also **an·ti-G suit**) ▸*n.* a garment with pressurized pouches that are inflatable with air or fluid, worn by fighter pilots and astronauts to enable them to withstand high forces of acceleration. ▷1940s: from g (symbol of *gravity*) + **SUIT**.

GT ▸*adj.* denoting a high-performance car: *GT cars.* ▸*n.* a high-performance car. ▷1960s: abbreviation of Italian **GRAN TURISMO**.

gt. ▸*abbr.* ■ gilt. ■ great.

G.T.C. ▸*abbr.* ■ good till canceled. ■ good till countermanded.

gtd. ▸*abbr.* guaranteed.

GTi ▸*adj.* denoting a high-performance car with a fuel-injected engine: *a Peugeot 205 GTi.* ▸*n.* a car of this type. ▷late 20th cent.: from **GT** + *i* for *injection*.

GTP ▸*abbr.* guanosine triphosphate.

GTS ▸*abbr. Nautical* gas turbine ship.

gtt. ▸*abbr. Pharmacology* guttae.

GU ▸*abbr.* ■ genitourinary. ■ Guam. .

gua·ca·mo·le /ˌgwäkəˈmōlē/ ▸*n.* a dish of mashed avocado mixed with chopped onion, tomatoes, chili peppers, and seasoning. ▷Latin American Spanish, from Nahuatl *ahuacamolli*, from *ahuacatl* 'avocado' + *molli* 'sauce.'

gua·cha·ro /ˈgwächəˌrō/ ▸*n.* (*pl.* **-ros**) a large, nocturnal, fruit-eating bird that resembles a nightjar and lives in caves in Central and South America. ▷early 19th cent.: from Spanish *guácharo*, of South American origin.

Gua·da·la·ja·ra /ˌgwädl-əˈhärə/ a city in western central Mexico, capital of the state of Jalisco; pop. 2,846,720.

Gua·dal·ca·nal /ˌgwädlkəˈnal/ an island in the western Pacific Ocean, the largest of the Solomon Islands; pop. 71,000. During World War II, it was the scene of the first major U.S. offensive against the Japanese in August 1942.

Gua·dal·quiv·ir /ˌgwädlkiˈvir/ a river in southern Spain, in Andalusia. It flows for 410 miles (657 km) through Cordoba and Seville to reach the Atlantic Ocean northwest of Cadiz.

Gua·da·lu·pe Moun·tains /ˈgwädlˌo͞op; -ˈo͞opē/ a range in western Texas and southern New Mexico. Guadalupe Peak at 8,749 feet (2,668 m) is the highest point in Texas. The Carlsbad Caverns are in the New Mexico section.

Gua·de·loupe /ˌgwädl-ˈo͞op/ a group of islands in the Lesser Antilles that form an overseas department of France; pop. 387,000; capital, Basse-Terre. **—Gua·de·lou·pi·an** /-ēən/ *adj.* & *n.*

Gua·dia·na /gwädˈyänə/ a river in Spain and Portugal. Rising in a plateau region southeast of Madrid, it flows southwest for about 350 miles (580 km) before entering the Atlantic Ocean at the Gulf of Cadiz. For the last part of its course, it forms the border between Spain and Portugal.

guai·ac /ˈgwīak/ ▸*n.* brown resin obtained from guaiacum trees, used as a flavoring and in varnishes. It was formerly used medicinally and as a test for traces of blood.

guai·a·col /ˈgwīəˌkôl; -ˌkōl/ ▸*n. Chemistry* an oily yellow liquid with a penetrating odor, obtained by distilling wood tar or guaiac, used as a flavoring and an expectorant. • Alternative name: ***o*-methoxyphenol**; chem. formula: $HOC_6H_4OCH_3$. ▷mid 19th cent.: from **GUAIACUM** + **-OL**.

guai·a·cum /ˈgwīəkəm/ ▸*n.* an evergreen tree of the Caribbean and tropical America, formerly important for its hard, heavy, oily timber but now scarce. Also called **LIGNUM VITAE**. • *Guaiacum officinale* and *G. sanctum*, family Zygophyllaceae. ■ another term for **GUAIAC**. ▷mid 16th cent.: modern Latin, via Spanish from Taino *guayacan*.

guai·fen·e·sin /gwīˈfenəsin/ ▸*n.* an expectorant used in cough syrups and sometimes for pain relief from fibromyalgia.

Guam /gwäm/ the largest and most southern of the Mariana Islands, administered as an unincorporated territory of the U.S.; pop. 166,000; capital, Agaña. Guam was ceded to the U.S. by Spain in 1898. It was the site of fighting between the Japanese and the U.S. during World War II. **—Gua·ma·ni·an** /gwäˈmānēən/ *adj.* & *n.*

guan /gwän/ ▸*n.* a large, pheasantlike, tree-dwelling bird of tropical American rain forests. • Family

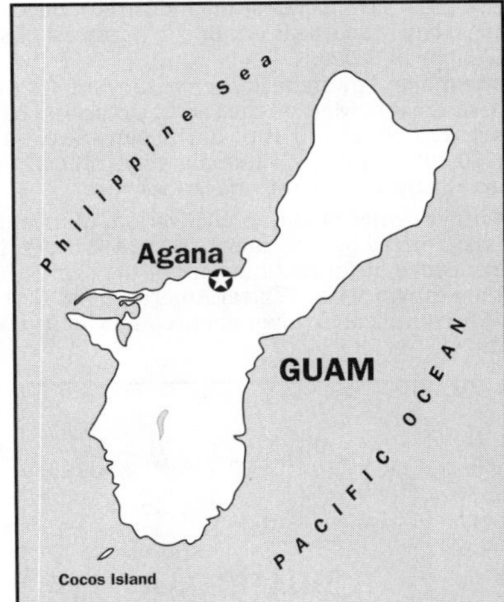

Cracidae (the **guan family**): several genera, esp. *Penelope*. The guan family also includes curassows and chachalacas. ▷late 17th cent.: via American Spanish from Miskito *kwamu*.

gua·na·co /gwəˈnäkō/ ▸*n.* (*pl.* **-cos**) a wild Andean mammal similar to the domestic llama, which is probably derived from it. It has a valuable pale brown pelt. • *Lama guanicoe*, family Camelidae. ▷early 17th cent.: via Spanish from Quechua *huanacu*.

Gua·na·jua·to /ˌgwänəˈ(h)wätō/ a state in central Mexico. ■ its capital city; pop. 45,000.

Guan·che /ˈgwänchä/ ▸*n.* a member of an aboriginal people speaking a Berber language who formerly inhabited the Canary Islands, and were absorbed after the Spanish conquest in the 15th century. ▷Spanish.

Guang·dong /ˈgwängˈdo͝ong/ (also **Kwang·tung**) a province in southern China, on the South China Sea; capital, Guangzhou (Canton).

Guang·xi Zhuang /ˈgwängˈshē ˈjwäng/ (also **Kwang·si Chuang**) an autonomous region in southern China, on the Gulf of Tonkin; capital, Nanning.

Guang·zhou /ˈgwängˈjō/ (also **Kwang·chow**) a city in southern China, the capital of Guangdong province; pop. 3,918,000. It is the leading industrial and commercial center of southern China. Also called **CANTON**.

guan·i·dine /ˈgwänəˌdēn/ ▸*n. Chemistry* a strongly basic crystalline compound, used in organic synthesis. • An imide derived from urea; chem. formula: $HNC(NH_2)_2$. ▷mid 19th cent.: from **GUANO** + **-IDE** + **-INE**[4].

gua·nine /ˈgwänēn/ ▸*n. Biochemistry* a compound that occurs in guano and fish scales, and is one of the four constituent bases of nucleic acids. A purine derivative, it is paired with cytosine in double-stranded DNA. • Alternative name: **6-oxy-2-aminopurine**; chem. formula: $C_5H_5N_5O$. ▷mid 19th cent.: from **GUANO** + **-INE**[4].

gua·no /ˈgwänō/ ▸*n.* (*pl.* **-nos**) the excrement of seabirds, occurring in thick deposits notably on the islands off Peru and Chile, and used as fertilizer. ■ an artificial fertilizer resembling natural guano, esp. one made from fish. ▷early 17th cent.: from Spanish, or from Latin American Spanish *huano*, from Quechua *huanu* 'dung.'

gua·no·sine /ˈgwänəˌsēn/ ▸*n. Biochemistry* a compound consisting of guanine combined with ribose, a nucleoside unit in RNA. ▷early 20th cent.: from **GUANINE**, with the insertion of **-OSE**[2].

gua·no·sine tri·phos·phate /trīˈfäsfāt/ (abbr.: **GTP**) ▸*n.* a nucleotide composed of guanine, ribose, and three phosphate groups, which participates in various metabolic reactions, including protein synthesis.

Guan·tá·na·mo Bay /gwänˈtänəmō/ a bay on the southeastern coast of Cuba, the site of a U.S. naval base that was established in 1903.

G

Guan Yin /ˈgwän ˈyin/ (in Chinese Buddhism) the goddess of compassion.

Gua·po·ré /ˌgwäpəˈrā/ a river that flows northwest for 1,090 miles (1,745 km) from southwestern Brazil, forming much of the Brazil-Bolivia border, to the Mamoré River.

guar /gwär/ ▸*n.* a drought-resistant plant of the pea family, which is grown as a vegetable and fodder crop and as a source of guar gum, native to dry regions of Africa and Asia. Also called **CLUSTER BEAN**. • *Cyamopsis tetragonoloba*, family Leguminosae. ■ (also **guar gum** or **guar flour**) a fine powder obtained by grinding guar seeds, which has numerous commercial applications, esp. in the food industry, where it is used as a thickener and a binder. ▷late 19th cent.: from Hindi *guār*.

guar. ▸*abbr.* guaranteed.

gua·ra·che ▸*n.* variant spelling of **HUARACHE**.

gua·ra·na /gwəˈränə/ ▸*n.* **1** a substance prepared from the seeds of a Brazilian shrub, used as a tonic or stimulant. **2** the shrub (*Paullinia cupana*) of the soapberry family that yields guarana. ▷mid 19th cent.: from Tupi.

Gua·ra·ni /gwärəˈnē/ ▸*n.* (*pl.* same) **1** a member of an American Indian people of Paraguay and adjacent regions. **2** the language of this people, one of the main divisions of the Tupi-Guarani language family and a national language of Paraguay. **3** (**gua·ra·ni**) the basic monetary unit of Paraguay, equal to 100 centimos. ▸*adj.* of or relating to the Guarani or their language. ▷Spanish.

guar·an·tee /ˌgarənˈtē/ ▸*n.* a formal promise or assurance (typically in writing) that certain conditions will be fulfilled, esp. that a product will be repaired or replaced if not of a specified quality and durability: *we offer a 10-year **guarantee against** rusting.* ■ something that gives a certainty of outcome: *past performance is no **guarantee of** future results.* ■ variant

Pronunciation Key ə ago; ər over; ˈə or ˌə up; ˈər or ˌər fur; a hat; ā rate; ä car; ch chew; e let; ē see; e(ə)r air; i fit; ī by; i(ə)r ear; ng sing; ō go; ô for; oi boy; o͝o good; o͞o goo; ou out; sh she; th thin; th then; (h)w why; zh vision

spelling of GUARANTY. ■ less common term for GUARANTOR.

▸*v.* (-tees, -teed, -tee·ing) [*intrans.*] provide a formal assurance or promise, esp. that certain conditions shall be fulfilled relating to a product, service, or transaction: [with *clause* or *infinitive*] *the con artist guarantees that the dirt pile will yield at least 20 ounces of gold.* ■ [*trans.*] provide such an assurance regarding (something, esp. a product): *the repairs will be guaranteed for three years* | [as *adj.*] (**guaranteed**) *the guaranteed bonus is not very high.* ■ [*trans.*] provide financial security for; underwrite: *a demand that $100,000 be deposited to guarantee their costs.* ■ [*trans.*] promise with certainty: *no one can guarantee a profit on stocks.* ▷late 17th cent. (in the sense 'guarantor'): perhaps from Spanish *garante*, corresponding to French *garant* (see WARRANT), later influenced by French *garantie* 'guaranty.'

guar·an·tee fund ▸*n.* a sum of money pledged as a contingent indemnity for loss.

guar·an·tor /ˌgarənˈtôr; ˈgarəntər/ ▸*n.* a person, organization, or thing that guarantees something: *the role of the police as guarantors of public order.* ■ *Law* a person or organization who provides a guaranty.

guar·an·ty /ˈgarənˌtē/ (also **guar·an·tee**) ▸*n.* (*pl.* **-ties**) a formal pledge to pay another person's debt or to perform another person's obligation in the case of default. ■ a thing serving as security for a such a pledge. ▷early 16th cent.: from Old French *garantie*, from *garantir*; related to WARRANT.

guard /gärd/ ▸*v.* [*trans.*] watch over to keep safe: *they were sent to* **guard** *villagers* **from** *attack by bandits.* ■ watch over in order to control entry and exit: *the gates were guarded by uniformed soldiers.* ■ watch over (someone) to prevent them from escaping: *police officers were guarding inmates who could not be accommodated in prison.* ■ [*intrans.*] (**guard against**) take precautions against: *farmers must guard against sudden changes in the market.* ■ protect against damage or harm: *the company fiercely guarded its independence.* ■ *Basketball* stay close to (an opponent) in order to prevent a good shot, pass, or drive. ■ cover or equip (a part of a machine) with a device to protect the operator.

▸*n.* **1** a person who keeps watch, esp. a soldier or other person formally assigned to protect a person or to control access to a place: *a security guard* | [as *adj.*] *he distracted the soldier on guard duty.* ■ [treated as *sing.* or *pl.*] a body of soldiers serving to protect a place or person: *the hound belonged to a member of the castle's guard.* ■ (**Guards**) the household troops of the British army. ■ a prison warder. ■ *Brit.* an official who rides on and is in general charge of a train. ■ *Football* each of two offensive players positioned either side of the center. ■ *Basketball* each of two backcourt players chiefly responsible for running the team's offense. **2** a device worn or fitted to prevent injury or damage: *a retractable blade guard.* ■ a chain attached to a watch or bracelet to prevent loss. ■ a ring worn to prevent another ring from falling off the finger. ■ a piece of metal placed to protect an operator from the potentially dangerous parts of a machine. **3** a defensive posture adopted in a boxing, fencing, or martial arts contest or in a fight: *this kick can curl around an otherwise effective guard.* ■ a state of caution, vigilance, or preparedness against adverse circumstances: *he let his guard slip enough to make some unwise comments.* ▷late Middle English (in the sense 'care, custody'): from Old French *garde* (noun), *garder* (verb), of West Germanic origin. Compare with WARD.

▸*PHRASES* □ **keep** (or **stand**) **guard** act as a guard. □ **lower** (or **let down**) **one's guard** relax one's defensive posture, leaving oneself vulnerable to attack: *if you lower your guard or take a step backward, I will throw in the towel.* ■ reduce one's level of vigilance or caution: *she was not ready to let down her guard and confide in him.* □ **off guard** unprepared for some surprise or difficulty: *the government was caught off guard by the unexpected announcement.* □ **on guard** on duty to protect or defend something. ■ (also **on one's guard**) prepared for any contingency; vigilant: *we must be* **on guard against** *such temptation.* □ **put up one's guard** adopt a defensive posture. □ **under guard** being guarded: *he was held in an empty stable under guard.*

guard·ant /ˈgärdnt/ ▸*adj.* [usu. *postpositive*] *Heraldry* (esp. of an animal) depicted with the body sideways and the face toward the viewer: *three lions passant guardant.* ▷late 16th cent.: from French *gardant* 'guarding,' from *garder* 'to guard.'

guard cell ▸*n.* *Botany* each of a pair of curved cells that surround a stoma, becoming larger or smaller according to the pressure within the cells.

guard·ed /ˈgärdid/ ▸*adj.* cautious and having possible reservations: *he has given a guarded welcome to the idea.* ■ (of a person's medical condition) serious and of uncertain outcome: *the surviving crewman was in stable but guarded condition.* **—guard·ed·ly** *adv.* **—guard·ed·ness** *n.*

guard hair ▸*n.* long, coarse hair forming an animal's outer fur.

guard·house /ˈgärdˌhous/ ▸*n.* a building used to accommodate a military guard or to detain military prisoners. ■ a building accommodating a guard who controls entrance to the grounds of a house, housing development, school, or other facility: *the prestigious islands have opted for guardhouses, where the license plate numbers of visitors are copied down.*

guard·i·an /ˈgärdēən/ ▸*n.* a defender, protector, or keeper: *self-appointed guardians of public morality.* ■ a person who looks after and is legally responsible for someone who is unable to manage their own affairs, esp. an incompetent or disabled person or a child whose parents have died. ■ the superior of a Franciscan convent. ▷late Middle English: from Old French *garden*, of Germanic origin; compare with WARD and WARDEN. The ending was altered by association with -IAN. **—guard·i·an·ship** /-ˌship/ *n.*

guard·i·an an·gel ▸*n.* a spirit that is believed to watch over and protect a person or place.

Guard·mem·ber /ˈgärdˌmembər/ ▸*n.* a person who serves in the National Guard.

guard of hon·or ▸*n.* a group of soldiers ceremonially welcoming an important visitor or escorting a casket in a funeral. Also called HONOR GUARD.

guard·rail /ˈgärdˌrāl/ ▸*n.* a rail that prevents people from falling off or being hit by something. ■ a strong fence at the side of a road or in the middle of an expressway, intended to reduce the risk of serious accidents.

guard ring ▸*n.* **1** a ring preventing another ring from slipping off a finger. **2** a ring-shaped electrode used to limit the extent of an electric field, esp. in a capacitor.

guard·room /ˈgärdˌro͞om; -ˌro͝om/ ▸*n.* a room in a military base used to accommodate a guard or detain prisoners.

guards·man /ˈgärdzmən/ ▸*n.* (*pl.* **-men**) (in the U.S.) a member of the National Guard. ■ (in the UK) a soldier of a regiment of Guards.

Guar·ne·ri /ˌgwärˈne(ə)rē/, Giuseppe (1687–1744), Italian violin-maker; known as **del Gesù**. He is the most well known of a family of three generations of violin-makers based in Cremona.

Guar·ne·ri·us /gwärˈne(ə)rēəs/ ▸*n.* a violin made by a member of the Guarneri family of Cremona, Italy, during the 17th and 18th centuries.

Gua·ru·lhos /gwäˈro͞olyo͞os/ an industrial and commercial city in southeastern Brazil, northeast of São Paulo; pop. 973,000.

Gua·te·ma·la /ˌgwätəˈmälə/ a country in Central America that borders on the Pacific Ocean and has a short coastline on the Caribbean Sea; pop. 14,280,200; capital, Guatemala City; official language, Spanish. **—Gua·te·ma·lan** *adj.* & *n.*

A former center of Mayan civilization, Guatemala was conquered by the Spanish in 1523–24. After independence, it formed the core of the short-lived United Provinces of Central America 1828–38 before becoming an independent republic in its own right.

Gua·te·ma·la Cit·y the capital of Guatemala; pop. 1,167,000. At an altitude of 4,920 feet (1,500 m) in the central highlands, it was founded in 1776 to replace the former capital, Antigua Guatemala, which was destroyed by an earthquake in 1773.

gua·va /ˈgwävə/ ▸*n.* **1** an edible pale orange tropical fruit with pink, juicy flesh and a strong, sweet aroma. **2** the small tropical American tree that bears this fruit. • Genus *Psidium*, family Myrtaceae: several species, in particular *P. guajava.* ▷mid 16th cent.: from Spanish *guayaba*, probably from Taino.

Gua·via·re Riv·er /gwävˈyärā/ a river that flows east for 650 miles (1,040 km) from the Andes Mountains in Colombia to join the Orinoco River at the Venezuelan border.

guay·a·ber·a /ˌgīəˈberə/ ▸*n.* a lightweight open-necked Cuban or Mexican shirt with two breast pockets and two pockets over the hips, typically having short sleeves and worn untucked. ▷1970s: Cuban Spanish, apparently originally from the name of the *Yayabo* river, influenced by Spanish *guayaba* 'guava.'

Gua·ya·quil /ˌgīəˈkēl/ a seaport in western Ecuador, the country's principal port and second largest city; pop. 1,877,000.

Guay·na·bo /gwīˈnäbō/ a community in northeastern Puerto Rico, south of San Juan; pop. 73,385.

gua·yu·le /(g)wäˈyo͞olē/ ▸*n.* a silver-leaved Mexican shrub of the daisy family that yields large amounts of latex. • *Parthenium argentatum*, family Compositae. ■ a rubber substitute made from this latex. ▷early 20th cent.: via Latin American Spanish from Nahuatl *cuauhuli.*

gu·ber·na·to·ri·al /ˌgo͞obərnəˈtôrēəl/ ▸*adj.* of or relating to a state governor or the office of state governor: *a gubernatorial election.* ▷mid 18th cent.: from Latin *gubernator* 'governor' (from *gubernare* 'steer, govern,' from Greek *kubernan* 'to steer') + -IAL.

guck /gək/ ▸*n.* *informal* a slimy, dirty, or otherwise unpleasant substance: *he got mud and cow guck all over his white jersey.* ▷possibly a blend of GOO and MUCK.

gudg·eon[1] /ˈgəjən/ ▸*n.* **1** a small, edible, European freshwater fish, often used as bait by anglers. • *Gobio gobio*, family Cyprinidae. **2** *archaic* a credulous or easily fooled person. ▷late Middle English: from Old French *goujon*, from Latin *gobio(n-)*, from *gobius* 'goby.'

gudg·eon[2] ▸*n.* a pivot or spindle on which a bell or other object swings or rotates. ■ the tubular part of a hinge into which the pin fits to unite the joint. ■ a socket at the stern of a vessel, into which a rudder is fitted. ■ a pin holding two blocks of stone together. ▷Middle English: from Old French *goujon*, diminutive of *gouge* (see GOUGE).

gudg·eon pin ▸*n.* a pin holding a piston rod and a connecting rod together.

Gud·run /ˈgo͝odro͞on/ (in Norse legend) the Norse equivalent of Kriemhild, wife of Sigurd and later of Atli (Attila the Hun).

guel·der rose /ˈgeldər/ ▸*n.* a deciduous Eurasian shrub of the honeysuckle family with flattened heads of fragrant, creamy-white flowers, followed by clusters of bitter translucent red berries. Similar to the closely related highbush cranberry, it is widely cultivated in North America. • *Viburnum opulus*, family Caprifoliaceae. See also SNOWBALL BUSH. ▷late 16th cent.: from Dutch *geldersche roos* 'rose of *Gelderland*' (see GELDERLAND).

Guelph /gwelf/ ▸*n.* **1** a member of one of two great factions in Italian medieval politics, traditionally supporting the pope against the Holy Roman Emperor. Compare with GHIBELLINE. **2** a member of a princely family of Swabian origin from which the British royal house is descended through George I. ▷from Italian *Guelfo*, from Middle High German *Welf*, the name of the founder of one of the two great rival dynasties in the Holy Roman Empire. **—Guelph·ic** /-fik/ *adj.*

gue·non /gəˈnōn/ ▸*n.* an African monkey found mainly in forests, with a long tail and typically a brightly colored coat. The male is much larger than the female. • Genus *Cercopithecus*, family Cercopithecidae: several species, including the vervet, mona, and Diana monkeys. ▷mid 19th cent.: from French, of unknown origin.

guer·don /ˈgərdn/ *chiefly archaic* ▸*n.* a reward or recompense.

▸*v.* [*trans.*] give a reward to (someone): *there might come a time in which he should guerdon them.* ▷late Middle English: from Old French, from medieval Latin *widerdonum*, alteration (by association with Latin *donum* 'gift') of a West Germanic compound represented by Old High German *widarlōn* 'repayment.'

Gue·rick·e /ˈgerikə/, Otto von (1602–86), German engineer and physicist. He was the first to investigate the properties of a vacuum, and he devised the

Magdeburg hemispheres to demonstrate atmospheric pressure.

gue·ril·la the·a·ter (also **guer·ril·la the·a·ter**) ▸*n.* the dramatization of political and social issues, typically performed outdoors, e.g. in the street or a park, as a means of protest or propaganda.

Guern·sey[1] /ˈgərnzē/ an island in the English Channel, northwest of Jersey; pop. 59,000; capital, St. Peter Port.

Guern·sey[2] ▸*n.* (*pl.* **-seys**) **1** an animal of a breed of dairy cattle from Guernsey, noted for producing rich, creamy milk. **2** (**guernsey**) a thick sweater made with oiled navy blue wool and originally worn by fishermen.

Guern·sey lil·y ▸*n.* a nerine with large heads of pink lilylike flowers. Native to South Africa, it has long been cultivated and was first described in Guernsey, England. • *Nerine sarniensis*, family Liliaceae (or Amaryllidaceae).

Guer·re·ro /gəˈrerō/ a state in southwestern central Mexico, on the Pacific coast; capital, Chilpancingo.

guer·ril·la /gəˈrilə/ (also **gue·ril·la**) ▸*n.* a member of a small independent group taking part in irregular fighting, typically against larger regular forces: *this small town fell to the guerrillas* | [as *adj.*] *guerrilla warfare.* ▷early 19th cent. (introduced during the Peninsular War (1808–14): from Spanish, diminutive of *guerra* 'war.'

guer·ril·la mar·ket·ing ▸*n.* innovative, unconventional, and low-cost marketing techniques aimed at obtaining maximum exposure for a product.

Guess /ges/, George, see **SEQUOYA**.

guess /ges/ ▸*v.* [*trans.*] estimate or suppose (something) without sufficient information to be sure of being correct: *she guessed the child's age to be 14 or 15* | [with *clause*] *he took her aside, and I guessed that he was offering her a job.* ■ (**guess at**) make a conjecture about: *their motives he could only guess at.* ■ correctly conjecture or perceive: [with *clause*] *she's guessed where we're going.* ■ [in *imperative*] used to introduce something considered surprising or exciting: *guess what I've just seen!* ■ (**I guess**) *informal* used to indicate that although one thinks or supposes something, it is without any great conviction or strength of feeling: [with *clause*] *I guess I'd better tell you everything.*
▸*n.* an estimate or conjecture: *my guess is that within a year we will have a referendum.* ▷Middle English: origin uncertain; perhaps from Dutch *gissen*, and probably related to **GET**. **—guess·a·ble** *adj.* **—guess·er** *n.*
▸*PHRASES* □ **anybody's** (or **anyone's**) **guess** very difficult or impossible to determine: *how well the system will work is anybody's guess.* □ **keep someone guessing** *informal* leave someone uncertain or in doubt as to one's intentions or plans.

guess·ti·mate (also **gues·ti·mate**) *informal* ▸*n.* /ˈgestəmit/ an estimate based on a mixture of guesswork and calculation.
▸*v.* /ˈgestəˌmāt/ [*trans.*] form such an estimate of: *the task is to guesstimate the total vote.* ▷1930s: blend of **GUESS** and **ESTIMATE**.

guess·work /ˈgesˌwərk/ ▸*n.* the process or results of guessing.

guest /gest/ ▸*n.* a person who is invited to visit the home of or take part in a function organized by another: *I have two guests coming to dinner tonight* | [as *adj.*] *a guest bedroom.* ■ a person invited to participate in an official event: *the bishop went to Cuba as a guest of the Catholic Church* | [as *adj.*] *a guest speaker.* ■ a person invited to take part in a radio or television program, sports event, or other entertainment: *a regular guest on the morning show* | [as *adj.*] *a guest appearance.* ■ a person lodging at a hotel or boardinghouse: *a reduction for guests staying seven nights or more.* ■ a customer at a restaurant. ■ *Entomology* a small invertebrate that lives unharmed within an ants' nest.
▸*v.* [*intrans.*] *informal* appear as a guest: *he* ***guested on*** *one of her early albums.* ▷Middle English: from Old Norse *gestr*, of Germanic origin; related to Dutch *gast* and German *Gast*, from an Indo-European root shared by Latin *hostis* 'enemy' (originally 'stranger').
▸*PHRASES* □ **be my guest** *informal* please do: *May I choose the restaurant? Be my guest!* □ **guest of honor** the most important guest at an occasion.

guest book (also **guest·book**) ▸*n.* a book in which visitors to a public building or to a private home write their names and addresses, and sometimes remarks. ■ a Web page where visitors to a site may leave their names and comments.

guest house (also **guest·house**) ▸*n.* a private house offering accommodations to paying guests. ■ a small, separate house on the grounds of a larger house or establishment, used for accommodating guests.

gues·ti·mate ▸*n.* & *v.* variant spelling of **GUESSTIMATE**.

guest work·er ▸*n.* a person with temporary permission to work in another country, esp. in Germany. ▷1960s: translation of the German *Gastarbeiter*.

Gue·va·ra /gəˈvärə/, Che (1928–67), Argentine revolutionary and guerrilla leader; full name *Ernesto Guevara de la Serna*. He played a significant part in the Cuban revolution 1956–59 and became a government minister under Fidel Castro. He was captured and executed by the Bolivian army while training guerrillas for a planned uprising in Bolivia.

guff /gəf/ ▸*n. informal* trivial, worthless, or insolent talk or ideas. ▷early 19th cent. (in the sense 'puff, whiff of a bad smell'): imitative.

guf·faw /gəˈfô/ ▸*n.* a loud and boisterous laugh.
▸*v.* [*intrans.*] laugh in such a way: *both men guffawed at the remark.* ▷early 18th cent. (originally Scots): imitative.

Gug·gen·heim /ˈgo͝ogənˌhīm; ˈgo͞o-/, Meyer (1828–1905), U.S. industrialist; born in Switzerland. With his seven sons he established large mining and metal-processing companies. His son **Solomon** (1861–1949) set up several foundations that supported the arts, including the Guggenheim Museum in New York.

gug·gul /ˈgo͝ogəl/ ▸*n.* an herbal preparation made from the sticky gum of various myrrh trees that has been alleged to aid in lowering serum cholesterol. • The trees providing the main source are *Commiphora mukul* and *Commiphora wightii*, family Burseraceae.

GUI /ˈgo͞oē/ *Computing* ▸*abbr.* graphical user interface.

Gui·a·na /gēˈänə; gīˈanə/ a region in northern South America, bounded by the Orinoco, Negro, and Amazon rivers and the Atlantic Ocean. It now includes Guyana, Suriname, French Guiana, and the Guiana Highlands.

Gui·a·na High·lands a mountainous plateau region in northern South America that lies between the Orinoco and Amazon river basins, largely in southeastern Venezuela and northern Brazil.

guid·ance /ˈgīdəns/ ▸*n.* **1** advice or information aimed at resolving a problem or difficulty, esp. as given by someone in authority: *he looked to his father for inspiration and guidance.* **2** the directing of the motion or position of something, esp. a missile: *a surface-to-air missile guidance system.*

guide /gīd/ ▸*n.* **1** a person who advises or shows the way to others: *this lady is going to act as our guide for the rest of the tour.* ■ a professional mountain climber in charge of a group. **2** a thing that helps someone to form an opinion or make a decision or calculation: *here is a* ***guide to*** *the number of curtain hooks you will need.* ■ a principle or standard of comparison: *as a guide, there are roughly six glasses to a bottle.* ■ a book, document, or display providing information on a subject or about a place: *a guide to baby and toddler care.* **3** a structure or marking that directs the motion or positioning of something: *the guides for the bolt needed straightening.* **4** a soldier, vehicle, or ship whose position determines the movements of others.
▸*v.* **1** [*trans.*] show or indicate the way to (someone): *he guided her to the front row and sat beside her.* ■ [*trans.*] direct the motion or positioning of (something): *the groove in the needle guides the thread.* **2** [*trans.*] direct or have an influence on the course of action of (someone or something): *he guided the team to a second successive win in the tournament.* ▷late Middle English: from Old French *guide* (noun), *guider* (verb), of Germanic origin; related to **WIT**[2]. **—guid·a·ble** *adj.* **—guid·er** *n.*

guide·book /ˈgīdˌbo͝ok/ ▸*n.* a book of information about a place, designed for the use of visitors or tourists.

guid·ed /ˈgīdid/ ▸*adj.* conducted by a guide: *a guided tour of the castle.* ■ directed by remote control or by internal equipment: *a guided missile.*

guid·ed im·age·ry ▸*n.* the use of words and music to evoke positive imaginary scenarios in a subject with a view to bringing about some beneficial effect. ■ particular images used in this exercise.

guide dog ▸*n.* a dog trained to lead a blind person.

guide·line /ˈgīdˌlīn/ ▸*n.* a general rule, principle, or piece of advice.

guide num·ber ▸*n. Photography* a measure of the power of a flashgun expressed in meters or feet.

guide·post /ˈgīdˌpōst/ ▸*n.* another term for **SIGNPOST**.

guide rope ▸*n.* a rope used to guide the movement of the load of a crane.

Guides As·so·ci·a·tion (in the UK) an organization for girls, founded in 1910.

guide·way /ˈgīdˌwā/ ▸*n.* a groove or track along which something moves.

gui·don /ˈgīdn/ ▸*n.* a pennant that narrows to a point or fork at the free end, esp. one used as the standard of a light cavalry regiment. ▷mid 16th cent.: from French, from Italian *guidone*, from *guida* 'a guide.'

Gui·gnol /gēnˈyôl/ the bloodthirsty chief character in a French puppet show of that name that is similar to Punch and Judy. See also **GRAND GUIGNOL**.

guild /gild/ (also **gild**) ▸*n.* a medieval association of craftsmen or merchants, often having considerable power. ■ an association of people for mutual aid or the pursuit of a common goal. ■ *Ecology* a group of species that have similar requirements and play a similar role within a community. ▷late Old English: probably from Middle Low German and Middle Dutch *gilde*, of Germanic origin; related to **YIELD**.

guild·er /ˈgildər/ ▸*n.* (*pl.* same or **-ers**) the basic monetary unit of the Netherlands (until the introduction of the euro), equal to 100 cents. ■ *historical* a gold or silver coin formerly used in the Netherlands, Germany, and Austria. ▷alteration of Dutch *gulden* (see **GULDEN**).

guild·hall /ˈgildˌhôl/ ▸*n.* a building used as the meeting place of a guild or corporation. ■ *Brit.* a town hall. ■ (**the Guildhall**) the hall of the Corporation of the City of London, used for ceremonial occasions.

guile /gīl/ ▸*n.* sly or cunning intelligence: *he used all his guile and guts to free himself from the muddle he was in.* ▷Middle English: from Old French, probably from Old Norse; compare with **WILE**. **—guile·ful** /-fəl/ *adj.* **—guile·ful·ly** /-fəlē/ *adv.*

guile·less /ˈgīllis/ ▸*adj.* devoid of guile; innocent and without deception: *his face, once so open and guileless.* **—guile·less·ly** *adv.* **—guile·less·ness** *n.*

Gui·lin /ˈgwāˈlin/ (also **Kwei·lin**) a city in southern China, on the Li River, in the autonomous region of Guangxi Zhuang; pop. 552,000.

Guil·lain–Bar·ré syn·drome /gēˈyan bəˈrā/ ▸*n. Medicine* an acute form of polyneuritis, often preceded by a respiratory infection, causing weakness and often paralysis of the limbs. ▷1916: named after Georges *Guillain* (1876–1961) and Jean *Barré* (1880–1967), two of those who first described the syndrome.

guil·le·mot /ˈgiləˌmät/ ▸*n.* a black-breasted auk with a narrow pointed bill, typically nesting on cliff ledges. • Family Alcidae, genus *Cepphus*: several species, in particular the North Atlantic **black guillemot** (*C. grylle*), with a white wing patch in summer and pale plumage in winter. ▷late 17th cent.: from French, diminutive of *Guillaume* 'William.'

guil·loche /giˈlōsʜ/ ▸*n.* architectural ornamentation resembling braided or interlaced ribbons. ▷mid 19th cent.: from French *guillochis*, denoting the ornamentation, or *guilloche*, a carving tool.

guil·lo·tine /ˈgiləˌtēn; ˈgēə-/ ▸*n.* a machine with a heavy blade sliding vertically in grooves, used for beheading people. ■ a device for cutting that incorporates a descending or sliding blade, used typically for cutting paper, card, or sheet metal. ■ a surgical instrument with a sliding blade used typically for the removal of the tonsils. ■ *Brit.* (in parliament) a procedure used to prevent delay in the discussion of a legislative bill by fixing times at which various parts of it must be voted on: [as *adj.*] *a guillotine motion.*

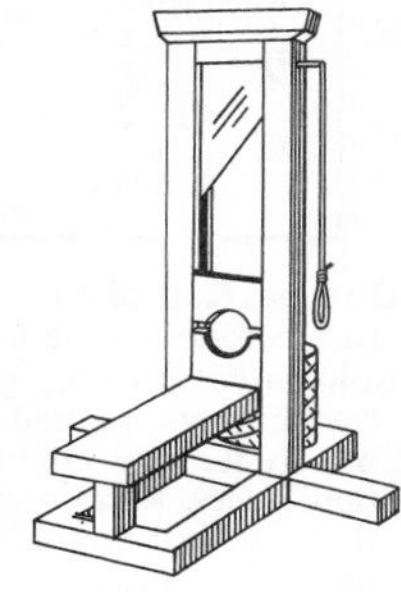
guillotine

▸*v.* [*trans.*] execute (someone) by guillotine. ■ *Brit.* (in parliament) end discussion by applying a guillotine to (a bill or debate). ▷late 18th cent.: from French, named after Joseph-Ignace *Guillotin* (1738–1814), the French physician who recommended its use for executions in 1789.

guilt /gilt/ ▸*n.* the fact of having committed a specified or implied offense or crime: *it is the duty of the*

prosecution to prove the prisoner's guilt. ■ a feeling of having done wrong or failed in an obligation: *he remembered with sudden guilt the letter from his mother that he had not yet read.*
▸*v.* [*trans.*] *informal* make (someone) feel guilty, especially in order to induce them to do something: *Celeste had been **guilted into** going by her parents.* ▷Old English *gylt*, of unknown origin.
▸*PHRASE* □ **guilt by association** guilt ascribed to someone not because of any evidence but because of their association with an offender.

guilt·less /ˈgiltlis/ ▸*adj.* having no guilt; innocent: *you don't need a pardon if you're guiltless.* —**guilt·less·ly** *adv.* —**guilt·less·ness** *n.*

guilt trip ▸*n.* an experience of feeling guilty about something, esp. when such guilt is excessive, self-indulgent, or unfounded: *let's skip the guilt trip and talk real, rational reasons.*
▸*v.* (**guilt-trip**) [*trans.*] make (someone) feel guilty, esp. in order to induce them to do something: *a pay increase will not guilt-trip them into improvements.*

guilt·y /ˈgiltē/ ▸*adj.* (**guilt·i·er**, **guilt·i·est**) culpable of or responsible for a specified wrongdoing: *the police will soon discover who the guilty party is | he was found **guilty of** manslaughter | he found them **guilty on** a lesser charge.* See also **FIND**, **PLEAD**. ■ justly chargeable with a particular fault or error: *she was guilty of a serious error of judgment.* ■ conscious of or affected by a feeling of guilt: *John felt guilty at having deceived the family | she wrestled with a guilty conscience after her adultery.* ■ involving a feeling or a judgment of guilt: *I have no guilty secret to reveal | a guilty verdict.* ▷Old English *gyltig* (see **GUILT**, **-Y**[1]). —**guilt·i·ly** /-təlē/ *adv.* —**guilt·i·ness** *n.*
▸*PHRASE* □ **not guilty** innocent, esp. of a formal charge: *he pled not guilty to murder.*

USAGE See usage at **INNOCENT** and **PLEAD**.

guimpe /gimp/ (also **guimp**) ▸*n. historical* a high-necked blouse or undergarment worn showing beneath a low-necked dress. ▷mid 19th cent.: from French; related to German *Wimpel*, Dutch *wimpel* 'pennant, streamer,' also to **WIMPLE** and the rare word *gimp* 'nun's neckerchief.'

Guin·ea /ˈginē/ a country on the west coast of Africa; pop. 9,246,000; capital, Conakry; languages, French (official), Fulani, Malinke, and others. —**Guin·e·an** /-ēən/ *adj.* & *n.*

Part of a feudal Fulani empire from the 16th century, Guinea was colonized by France as part of French West Africa. It became an independent republic in 1958.

Guin·ea, Gulf of a large inlet of the Atlantic Ocean that borders on the southern coast of West Africa.

guin·ea /ˈginē/ (abbr.: **gn.**) ▸*n. Brit.* the sum of £1.05 (21 shillings in predecimal currency), now used mainly for determining professional fees and auction prices. ■ *historical* a former British gold coin that was first minted in 1663 from gold imported from West Africa, with a value that was later fixed at 21 shillings. It was replaced by the sovereign from 1817. ▷named after **GUINEA** in West Africa.

Guin·ea-Bis·sau /ˈginē biˈsou/ a country on the western coast of Africa, between Senegal and Guinea; pop. 1,300,000; capital, Bissau; languages, Portuguese (official), West African languages, Creoles.

The area, a center of the slave trade, was explored by the Portuguese in the 15th century. Formerly called Portuguese Guinea, it became a colony in 1879 and the independent republic of Guinea-Bissau in 1974. A military coup in 1980 brought continuing unrest.

guin·ea fowl ▸*n.* (*pl.* same) a large African game bird with slate-colored, white-spotted plumage and a loud call. It is sometimes domesticated. • Family Numididae (or Phasianidae): several genera and species, e.g., the **helmeted guineafowl** (*Numida meleagris*).

guin·ea pig ▸*n.* a domesticated, tailless South American cavy, originally raised for food. It no longer occurs in the wild and is now typically kept as a pet or for laboratory research. • *Cavia porcellus*, family Caviidae. ■ a person or thing used as a subject for experiment.

guin·ea worm ▸*n.* a very long parasitic nematode worm that lives under the skin of infected humans and other mammals in rural Africa and Asia. • *Dracunculus medinensis*, class Phasmida.

gui·nep /giˈnep/ ▸*n.* variant spelling of **GENIP** (sense 2).

Guin·e·vere /ˈgwinəˌvi(ə)r/ (in Arthurian legend) the wife of King Arthur and mistress of Lancelot.

Guin·ness /ˈginis/, Sir Alec (1914–2000), English actor. He performed in movies, such as *Bridge on the River Kwai* (1957) and *Star Wars* (1977), and as espionage chief George Smiley in television versions of John Le Carré's novels.

gui·pure /giˈpyo͝or/ ▸*n.* a heavy lace consisting of embroidered motifs held together by large connecting stitches. ▷mid 19th cent.: from French, from *guiper* 'cover with silk,' of Germanic origin.

gui·ro /ˈgwi(ə)rō/ ▸*n.* (*pl.* **-ros**) a musical instrument with a serrated surface that gives a rasping sound when scraped with a stick, originally made from an elongated gourd and used in Latin American music. ▷late 19th cent.: Spanish, literally 'gourd.'

guise /gīz/ ▸*n.* an external form, appearance, or manner of presentation, typically concealing the true nature of something: *he visited **in the guise of** an inspector | telemarketing and selling **under the guise of** market research.* ▷Middle English: from Old French, of Germanic origin; related to **WISE**[2].

gui·tar /giˈtär/ ▸*n.* a stringed musical instrument with a fretted fingerboard, typically incurved sides, and six or twelve strings, played by plucking or strumming with the fingers or a plectrum. See also **ELECTRIC GUITAR**. ▷early 17th cent.: from Spanish *guitarra* (partly via French), from Greek *kithara*, denoting an instrument similar to the lyre. —**gui·tar·ist** /-rist/ *n.*

electric guitar acoustic guitar

guitar

gui·tar·fish /giˈtärˌfisн/ ▸*n.* (*pl.* same or **-fish·es**) a fish of shallow warm seas, related to the rays and having a guitarlike body shape. • Several species in the family Rhinobatidae, including *Rhinobatus rhinobatus*, common in European waters, and the **Chinese guitarfish** (*Platyrhina sinensis*, family Platyrhinidae).

Gui·yang /ˈgwāˈyäNG/ (also **Kwei·yang**) an industrial city in southern China, capital of Guizhou province; pop. 1,490,000.

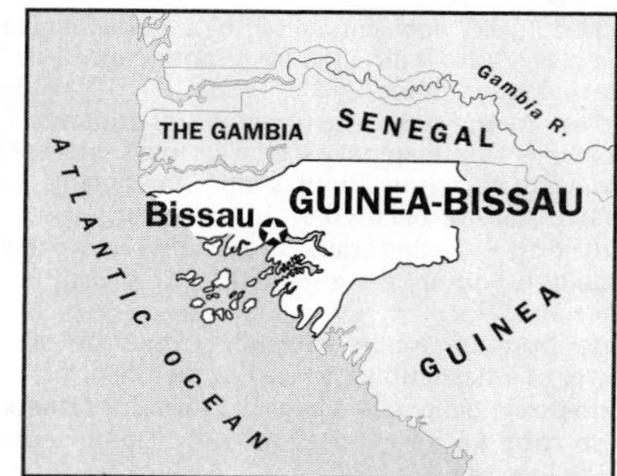

Gui·zhou /ˈgwāˈjō/ (also **Kwei·chow**) a province in southern China; capital, Guiyang.

Gu·ja·rat /ˌgo͞ojəˈrät; ˌgo͞oj-/ a state in western India, on the Arabian Sea; capital, Gandhinagar. Formed in 1960 from the northern and western parts of the former state of Bombay, it is one of the most industrialized parts of the country. A catastrophic earthquake in January 2001 left many thousands of people dead.

Gu·ja·ra·ti /ˌgo͞ojəˈrätē/ (also **Gu·je·ra·ti**) ▸*n.* (*pl.* **-tis** /-tēz/) **1** a native or inhabitant of Gujarat. **2** the Indic language of the Gujaratis.
▸*adj.* of or relating to this people or their language.

Guj·ran·wa·la /ˌgo͞ojrənˈwälə; ˌgo͞oj-/ a city in northeastern Pakistan, in Punjab province, northwest of Lahore; pop. 597,000. It was an important center of Sikh influence in the early 19th century.

Guj·rat /ˈgo͞ojˌrät/ a city in northeastern Pakistan, in Punjab province, north of Lahore; pop. 154,000.

Gu·lag /ˈgo͞oläg/ ▸*n.* [in *sing.*] a system of labor camps maintained in the Soviet Union from 1930 to 1955 in which many people died. ■ (**gulag**) a camp in this system, or any political labor camp: *the imprisonment of dissidents in a massive gulag.* ▷Russian, from *G(lavnoe) u(pravlenie ispravitel'no-trudovykh) lag(ereĭ)* 'Chief Administration for Corrective Labor Camps.'

gu·lar /ˈg(y)o͞olər/ *Zoology* ▸*adj.* of, relating to, or situated on the throat of an animal, esp. a reptile, fish, or bird.
▸*n.* a plate or scale on the throat of a reptile or fish. ▷early 19th cent.: from Latin *gula* 'throat' + **-AR**[1].

Gul·bar·ga /ˈgo͞olbərˌgä/ a city in southern central India, in the state of Karnataka; pop. 303,000. It was formerly the seat of the Bahmani kings of the Deccan (1347–*c.*1424).

gulch /gəlcн/ ▸*n.* a narrow and steep-sided ravine marking the course of a fast stream. ▷mid 19th cent.: perhaps from dialect *gulch* 'to swallow.'

gul·den /ˈgo͞oldən/ ▸*n.* (*pl.* same or **-dens**) another term for **GUILDER**. ▷late 19th cent.: Dutch and German, literally 'golden.'

gules /gyo͞olz/ ▸*n.* red, as a heraldic tincture: [*postpositive*] *sword and long cross gules.* ▷Middle English: from Old French *goles* (plural of *gole* 'throat,' from Latin *gula*) used to denote pieces of red-dyed fur used as a neck ornament.

gulf /gəlf/ ▸*n.* **1** a deep inlet of the sea almost surrounded by land, with a narrow mouth. ■ (**the Gulf**) informal name for **PERSIAN GULF**. **2** a deep ravine, chasm, or abyss. ■ *figurative* a large difference or division between two people or groups, or between viewpoints, concepts, or situations: *a **wide gulf** between theory and practice.* ▷late Middle English: from Old French *golfe*, from Italian *golfo*, based on Greek *kolpos* 'bosom, gulf.'

Gulf In·tra·coast·al Wa·ter·way a route that allows sheltered boat passage along the coast of the Gulf of Mexico between Key West in Florida and Brownsville in Texas.

Gulf of A·den, Gulf of Boo·thia, etc. see **ADEN, GULF OF**; **BOOTHIA, GULF OF**, etc.

Gulf·port /ˈgəlfˌpôrt/ a city in southern Mississippi, on the Gulf of Mexico, west of Biloxi; pop. 71,127.

Gulf States **1** the countries bordering on the Persian Gulf (Iran, Iraq, Kuwait, Saudi Arabia, Bahrain, Qatar, the United Arab Emirates, and Oman). **2** the U.S. states that border on the Gulf of Mexico (Florida, Alabama, Mississippi, Louisiana, and Texas).

Gulf Stream a warm ocean current that flows from the Gulf of Mexico parallel with the U.S. coast toward Newfoundland, Canada, and then continues across the Atlantic Ocean toward northwestern Europe as the North Atlantic Drift.

Gulf War **1** another name for **IRAN–IRAQ WAR**. **2** the war of January and February 1991 in which an international coalition of forces assembled in Saudi Arabia under the auspices of the United Nations forced the withdrawal of Saddam Hussein's Iraqi forces from Kuwait, which they had invaded and occupied in August 1990.

Gulf War syn·drome ▸*n.* a medical condition affecting many veterans of the 1991 Gulf War, causing fatigue, chronic headaches, and skin and respiratory disorders. Its origin is uncertain, though it has been attributed to exposure to a combination of pesticides, vaccines, and other chemicals.

gulf·weed /ˈgəlfˌwēd/ ▸*n.* another term for **SARGASSUM**.

gull[1] /gəl/ ▸*n.* a long-winged, web-footed seabird with a raucous call, typically having white plumage with a gray or black mantle. • Family Laridae: several genera, in particular *Larus*, and numerous species. ▷late Middle English: of Celtic origin; related to Welsh *gwylan* and Breton *gwelan*.

gull[2] ▸*v.* [*trans.*] fool or deceive (someone): *workers had been* **gulled into** *inflicting poverty and deprivation upon themselves.*
▸*n.* a person who is fooled or deceived. ▷late 16th cent.: of unknown origin.

Gul·lah /ˈgələ/ ▸*n.* **1** a member of a black people living on the coast of South Carolina and nearby islands. **2** the Creole language of this people, having an English base with elements from various West African languages. It has about 125,000 speakers.
▸*adj.* of or relating to this people or their language. ▷perhaps a shortening of *Angola*, or from *Gola*, the name of an agricultural people of Liberia and Sierra Leone.

gull·er·y /ˈgələrē/ ▸*n.* (*pl.* **-er·ies**) a breeding colony, breeding place, or roost of gulls.

gul·let /ˈgəlit/ ▸*n.* the passage by which food passes from the mouth to the stomach; the esophagus. ▷late Middle English: from Old French *goulet*, diminutive of *goule* 'throat,' from Latin *gula*.

gul·ley /ˈgəlē/ ▸*n.* (*pl.* **-leys**) variant spelling of GULLY.

gul·li·ble /ˈgələbəl/ ▸*adj.* easily persuaded to believe something; credulous: *an attempt to persuade a gullible public to spend their money.* ▷early 19th cent.: from GULL[2] + -IBLE. **—gul·li·bil·i·ty** /ˌgələˈbilitē/ *n.* **—gul·li·bly** /-blē/ *adv.*

> ***THE RIGHT WORD*** **callow, credulous, gullible, ingenuous, naive, trusting, unsophisticated**
>
> Some people will believe anything. Those who are truly **gullible** are the easiest to deceive, which is why they so often make fools of themselves.
>
> Those who are merely **credulous** might be a little too quick to believe something, but they usually aren't stupid enough to act on it.
>
> **Trusting** suggests the same willingness to believe (*a trusting child*), but it isn't necessarily a bad way to be (*a person so trusting he completely disarmed his enemies*).
>
> No one likes to be called **naive** because it implies a lack of street smarts (*she's so naive she'd accept a ride from a stranger*), but when applied to things other than people, it can describe a simplicity and absence of artificiality that is quite charming (*the naive style in which nineteenth-century American portraits were often painted*).
>
> Most people would rather be thought of as **ingenuous**, meaning straightforward and sincere (*an ingenuous confession of the truth*), because it implies the simplicity of a child without the negative overtones.
>
> **Callow**, however, comes down a little more heavily on the side of immaturity and almost always goes hand-in-hand with youth.
>
> Whether young or old, someone who is **unsophisticated** lacks experience in worldly and cultural matters.

gull wing ▸*n.* [as *adj.*] (of a door on a car or aircraft) opening upward: *gull-wing doors.*

gul·ly /ˈgəlē/ (also **gul·ley**) ▸*n.* (*pl.* **-lies**) a water-worn ravine. ■ a deep artificial channel serving as a gutter or drain.
▸*v.* [*trans.*] [usu. as *adj.*] (**gullied**) erode gullies into (land) by water action: *he began to pick his way over the gullied landscape.* ▷mid 16th cent. (in the sense 'gullet'): from French *goulet* (see GULLET).

gulp /gəlp/ ▸*v.* [*trans.*] swallow (drink or food) quickly or in large mouthfuls, often audibly: *he smiled and gulped his milk.* ■ breathe (air) deeply and quickly: *we emerged to gulp great lungfuls of cold night air.* ■ [*intrans.*] make effortful breathing or swallowing movements, typically in response to strong emotion: *fumes seeped in until she was forced to gulp for air | she* **gulped back** *the tears.*
▸*n.* an act of gulping food or drink: *she swallowed the rest of the coffee with a gulp.* ■ a large mouthful of liquid hastily drunk: *Titch took a gulp of beer and wiped his mouth on his sleeve.* ■ a large quantity of air breathed in. ■ a swallowing movement of the throat: *the chairman gave an audible gulp.* ▷Middle English: probably from Middle Dutch *gulpen*, of imitative origin. **—gulpy** *adj.*
▸*PHRASE* □ **at a gulp** with one gulp: *having emptied his glass at a gulp, Roger pulled out a cigar.*

gulp·er /ˈgəlpər/ (also **gulper eel**) ▸*n.* a deep-sea eel with very large jaws that open to give an enormous gape and with eyes near the tip of the snout. • Order Saccopharyngiformes: several families.

GUM ▸*abbr.* genitourinary medicine.

gum[1] /gəm/ ▸*n.* **1** a viscous secretion of some trees and shrubs that hardens on drying but is soluble in water, and from which adhesives and other products are made. Compare with RESIN. ■ glue that is used for sticking paper or other light materials together. ■ short for CHEWING GUM or BUBBLEGUM. ■ a gum tree, esp. a eucalyptus. See also SWEET GUM. **2** *dated* a long rubber boot.
▸*v.* (**gummed, gum·ming**) [*trans.*] cover with gum or glue: [as *adj.*] (**gummed**) *gummed paper.* ■ [*trans.*] fasten with gum or glue: *I was gumming small green leaves to a paper tree.* ■ (**gum something up**) clog up a mechanism and prevent it from working properly: *open and close the valves to make sure they don't get gummed up. | figurative there was no winner and they debated the factors that could have* **gummed up the works**. ▷Middle English: from Old French *gomme*, based on Latin *gummi*, from Greek *kommi*, from Egyptian *kemai*.

gum[2] ▸*n.* the firm area of flesh around the roots of the teeth in the upper or lower jaw: *a tooth broken off just above the gum* | [as *adj.*] *gum disease.*
▸*v.* (**gummed, gum·ming**) [*trans.*] chew with toothless gums: *some grandmother gumming a meal.* ▷Old English *gōma* 'inside of the mouth or throat,' of Germanic origin; related to German *Gaumen* 'roof of the mouth.'

gum[3] ▸*n.* (in phrase **by gum!**) an exclamation used for emphasis. ▷early 19th cent.: euphemistic alteration of *God*.

gum ar·a·bic ▸*n.* a gum exuded by some kinds of acacia and used as an emulsifier, in glue, as the binder for watercolor paints, and in incense.

gum ben·ja·min /ˈbenjəmən/ ▸*n.* another term for BENZOIN (sense 1).

gum ben·zo·in ▸*n.* see BENZOIN (sense 1).

gum·bo /ˈgəmbō/ ▸*n.* (*pl.* **-bos**) **1** okra, esp. the gelatinous pods used in cooking. ■ (in Cajun cooking) a spicy chicken or seafood soup thickened typically with okra or rice. **2** (**Gumbo**) a French-based patois spoken by some blacks and Creoles in Louisiana. **3** a fine, clayey soil that becomes sticky and impervious when wet. **4** a type of Cajun music consisting of a lively blend of styles and sounds: *New Orleans syncopated gumbo.* ▷early 19th cent.: from the Angolan word *kingombo* 'okra.'

gum·boil /ˈgəmˌboil/ ▸*n.* a small swelling formed on the gum over an abscess at the root of a tooth.

gum·boot /ˈgəmˌbo͞ot/ ▸*n.* (usu. **gumboots**) chiefly British term for GUM[1] (sense 2).

gum·drop /ˈgəmˌdräp/ ▸*n.* a firm, jellylike, translucent candy made with gelatin or gum arabic.

gum·ma /ˈgəmə/ ▸*n.* (*pl.* **gum·mas** or **gum·ma·ta** /ˈgəmətə/) *Medicine* a small, soft swelling that is characteristic of the late stages of syphilis and occurs in the connective tissue of the liver, brain, testes, and heart. ▷early 18th cent.: modern Latin, from Latin *gummi* (see GUM[1]). **—gum·ma·tous** /ˈgəmətəs/ *adj.*

gum·mo·sis /gəˈmōsis/ ▸*n.* the copious production and exudation of gum by a diseased or damaged tree, esp. as a symptom of a disease of fruit trees.

gum·my[1] /ˈgəmē/ ▸*adj.* (**-mi·er, -mi·est**) viscous; sticky. ■ covered with or exuding a viscous substance: *his eyes are all gummy.* **—gum·mi·ness** *n.*

gum·my[2] ▸*adj.* (**-mi·er, -mi·est**) toothless: *a gummy grin.*
▸*n.* (*pl.* **-mies**) (also **gummy shark**) a small, edible shark of Australasian coastal waters, with rounded teeth that it uses to crush hard-shelled prey. • *Mustelus antarcticus*, family Triakidae. **—gum·mi·ly** /ˈgəməlē/ *adv.*

gum o·lib·a·num /ōˈlibənəm/ ▸*n.* another term for FRANKINCENSE.

gump·tion /ˈgəmpsHən/ ▸*n. informal* shrewd or spirited initiative and resourcefulness: *she* **had the gumption to** *put her foot down and head Dan off from those crazy schemes.* ▷early 18th cent. (originally Scots): of unknown origin.

gum res·in ▸*n.* a plant secretion consisting of resin mixed with gum.

gum san·da·rac ▸*n.* see SANDARAC.

gum·shoe /ˈgəmˌsHo͞o/ ▸*n. informal* a detective. ▷early 20th cent.: from *gumshoes* in the sense 'sneakers,' suggesting stealth.

gum trag·a·canth ▸*n.* see TRAGACANTH.

gum tree ▸*n.* a tree that exudes gum, esp. a eucalyptus.

gum tur·pen·tine ▸*n.* see TURPENTINE.

gun /gən/ ▸*n.* a weapon incorporating a metal tube from which bullets, shells, or other missiles are propelled by explosive force, typically making a characteristic loud, sharp noise. ■ a device for discharging something (e.g., insecticide, grease, or electrons) in a required direction. ■ a gunman: *a hired gun.* ■ (**guns**) *dated Nautical slang* used as a nickname for a ship's gunnery officer. ■ a starting pistol used in track and field events. ■ the firing of a piece of artillery as a salute or signal: *the boom of the one o'clock gun echoed across the river.*
▸*v.* (**gunned, gun·ning**) [*trans.*] **1** (**gun someone down**) shoot someone with a gun: *they were gunned down by masked snipers.* **2** *informal* cause (an engine) to race: *as Neil gunned the engine, the boat jumped forward.* ■ [*trans.*] accelerate (a vehicle): *he gunned the car away from the curb.*
▸*phrasal v.* □ **gun for** pursue or act against (someone) with hostility: *the Republican candidate was gunning for his rival over campaign finances.* ■ seek out or strive for (something) determinedly: *he had been gunning for a place in the squad.* ▷Middle English *gunne, gonne*, perhaps from a nickname for the Scandinavian name *Gunnhildr*, from *gunnr* + *hildr*, both meaning 'war.' **—gun·less** *adj.* **—gunned** *adj.* [in *combination*] *a heavy-gunned ship.*
▸*PHRASES* □ **big gun** *informal* an important or powerful person. □ **go great guns** *informal* proceed forcefully, vigorously, or successfully: *the film industry has been going great guns recently.* □ **jump the gun** *informal* act before the proper time. □ **stick to one's guns** *informal* refuse to compromise or change, despite criticism: *we have stuck to our guns on that issue.* □ **top gun** a (or the) most important person: *the top guns in contention for the coveted post of chairman.* □ **under the gun** *informal* under great pressure: *manufacturers are under the gun to offer alternatives.*

gu·na /ˈgo͞onə/ ▸*n.* (in Vedanta) any of the three interdependent modes or qualities of prakriti: sattva, rajas, or tamas.

gun·boat /ˈgənˌbōt/ ▸*n.* a small, fast ship mounting guns, for use in shallow coastal waters and rivers.

gun·boat di·plo·ma·cy ▸*n.* foreign policy that is supported by the use or threat of military force.

gun car·riage ▸*n.* a wheeled support for a piece of artillery.

gun·cot·ton /ˈgənˌkätn/ ▸*n.* a highly nitrated form of nitrocellulose, used as an explosive.

gun deck ▸*n.* a deck on a vessel on which guns are placed.

gun·di /ˈgəndē/ ▸*n.* (*pl.* **-dis**) a small, gregarious rodent living on rocky outcrops in the deserts of North and East Africa. • Family Ctenodactylidae: four genera and several species. ▷late 18th cent.: from North African Arabic.

gun dog ▸*n.* a dog trained to retrieve game for a hunter.

gun·fight /ˈgənˌfīt/ ▸*n.* a fight involving an exchange of fire with guns. **—gun·fight·er** *n.*

gun·fire /ˈgənˌfīr/ ▸*n.* the repeated firing of a gun or guns: *they'd been caught up in gunfire in Beirut.*

gun·flint /ˈgənˌflint/ ▸*n.* a small piece of flint that is used to ignite the gunpowder in a flintlock gun.

gunge /gənj/ *Brit., informal* ▸*n.* a sticky, viscous, and unpleasantly messy material.
▸*v.* (**gunged, gunge·ing**) [*trans.*] (**gunge something up**) clog or obstruct with gunge. ▷1960s: perhaps suggested by GOO and GUNK. **—gun·gy** *adj.*

gung-ho /ˈgəNG ˈhō/ ▸*adj.* unthinkingly enthusiastic and eager, esp. about taking part in fighting or warfare: *the gung-ho soldier who wants all the big military toys.* ▷World War II: from Chinese *gōnghé*, taken to mean 'work together' and adopted as a slogan by U.S. Marines.

gun·ite /ˈgənīt/ ▸*n.* a mixture of cement, sand, and water applied through a pressure hose, producing a dense hard layer of concrete used in building for lining tunnels and structural repairs. ▷early 20th cent.: from GUN + -ITE[1].

gunk /gəNGk/ ▸*n. informal* unpleasantly sticky or messy substance. ▷1930s: the proprietary name of a detergent.

gunk·hole /ˈgəNGkˌhōl/ *informal* ▸*n.* a shallow inlet or cove that is difficult or dangerous to navigate.
▸*v.* [*intrans.*] cruise in and out of such inlets or coves: *they were gunkholing through the coral archipelago.* ▷early 20th cent.: of unknown origin.

gun·lock /ˈgənˌläk/ ▸*n.* a mechanism by which the charge of a gun is exploded.

gun·mak·er /ˈgənˌmākər/ ▸*n.* a manufacturer of guns.

gun·man /ˈgənmən/ ▸*n.* (*pl.* **-men**) a man who uses a gun to commit a crime or terrorist act: *a gang of masked gunmen.* ■ one who has to do with guns or is engaged in their manufacture.

gun·met·al /ˈgənˌmetl/ ▸*n.* a gray, corrosion-resistant form of bronze containing zinc, formerly used for making cannon. ■ (also **gunmetal gray**) a dark blue-brown gray color: [as *adj.*] *the river glinted brass under a gunmetal sky.*

gun mi·cro·phone ▸*n.* a highly directional microphone with an elongated barrel that can be directed from a distance at a localized sound source.

gun moll ▸*n. informal* another term for **MOLL** (sense 1).

gun·nel[1] /ˈgənl/ ▸*n.* an elongated laterally compressed fish with a dorsal fin that runs along most of the back and reduced or absent pelvic fins. It occurs in cool inshore waters of the northern hemisphere. • Family Pholidae: two genera and several species. ▷late 17th cent.: of unknown origin.

gun·nel[2] ▸*n.* variant spelling of **GUNWALE**.

gun·ner /ˈgənər/ ▸*n.* **1** a serviceman who operates or specializes in guns, in particular: ■ *historical* a naval warrant officer in charge of a ship's guns, gun crews, and ordnance stores. ■ a member of an aircraft crew who operates a gun, esp. (formerly) in a gun turret on a bomber. **2** a person who hunts game with a gun.

gun·ner·a /ˈgənərə/ ▸*n.* a South American plant that has extremely large leaves resembling rhubarb and that is grown as a waterside ornamental. • Genus *Gunnera*, family Gunneraceae: several species, in particular *G. manicata* and *G. tinctoria*. ▷modern Latin, named after Johann E. *Gunnerus* (1718–73), Norwegian botanist.

gun·ner·y /ˈgənərē/ ▸*n.* the design, manufacture, or firing of heavy guns: *a pioneer of naval gunnery.*

gun·ner·y ser·geant ▸*n.* a noncommissioned officer in the U.S. Marine Corps ranking above staff sergeant and below master sergeant.

Gun·ni·son Riv·er /ˈgənəsən/ a river that flows for 180 miles (290 km) through western Colorado to the Colorado River. It is noted for its "Black Canyon."

gun·ny /ˈgənē/ ▸*n.* coarse fabric, typically made of jute fiber and used esp. for sacks. ▷early 18th cent.: from Marathi *gōnī*, from Sanskrit *goṇī* 'sack.'

gun·play /ˈgənˌplā/ ▸*n.* the use of guns: *the struggle started with skirmishes and some scattered gunplay.*

gun·point /ˈgənˌpoint/ ▸*n.* (in phrase **at gunpoint**) while threatening someone or being threatened with a gun: *two robbers **held** a family **at gunpoint** while they searched their house.*

gun·port /ˈgənˌpôrt/ ▸*n.* see **PORT**[4].

gun·pow·der /ˈgənˌpoudər/ ▸*n.* **1** an explosive consisting of a powdered mixture of saltpeter, sulfur, and charcoal. The earliest known propellant explosive, gunpowder has now largely been superseded by high explosives, although it is still used for quarry blasting and in fuses and fireworks. **2** (also **gunpowder tea**) a fine green China tea of granular appearance.

Gun·pow·der Plot a conspiracy by a small group of Catholic extremists to blow up James I and his Parliament on November 5, 1605.

The plot is commemorated by the traditional searching of the vaults before the opening of each session of Parliament, and by bonfires and fireworks, with the burning of an effigy of Guy Fawkes, one of the conspirators, annually on November 5.

gun·room /ˈgənˌro͞om; -ˌro͝om/ ▸*n.* **1** a room used for storing sporting guns in a house. **2** *Brit., dated* a set of quarters for midshipmen or other junior officers in a warship.

gun·run·ner /ˈgənˌrənər/ ▸*n.* a person engaged in the illegal sale or importing of firearms. —**gun·run·ning** /-ˌrəniNG/ *n.*

gun·sel /ˈgənsəl/ ▸*n. informal, dated* a criminal carrying a gun. ▷early 20th cent. (denoting a homosexual youth): from Yiddish *gendzel* 'little goose,' influenced in sense by **GUN**.

gun·ship /ˈgənˌSHip/ ▸*n.* an airplane or a helicopter heavily armed with machine guns or with machine guns and cannon, providing air support for ground troops in combat.

gun·shot /ˈgənˌSHät/ ▸*n.* a shot fired from a gun. ■ *archaic* the range of a gun: *we bore down and came nearly within gunshot.*

gun-shy ▸*adj.* (esp. of a hunting dog) alarmed at the report of a gun. ■ *figurative* nervous and apprehensive.

gun·sight /ˈgənˌsīt/ ▸*n.* a device on a gun that enables it to be aimed accurately.

gun·sling·er /ˈgənˌsliNGər/ ▸*n. informal* a man who carries a gun and shoots well. ■ *figurative* a forceful and adventurous participant in a particular sphere: *the heroes of Wall Street were hip young gunslingers.* —**gun·sling·ing** /-ˌsliNGiNG/ *adj.*

gun·smith /ˈgənˌsmiTH/ ▸*n.* a person who makes, sells, and repairs small firearms.

gun·stock /ˈgənˌstäk/ ▸*n.* the stock or support to which the barrel of a gun is attached.

gun·ter /ˈgəntər/ ▸*n. Sailing* a fore-and-aft sail whose spar is nearly vertical, so that the sail is nearly triangular. ■ (also **gunter rig**) *historical* a type of rig in which the topmast slides up and down the lower mast on rings. ▷late 18th cent.: named after E. *Gunter* (see **GUNTER'S CHAIN**). —**gun·ter-rigged** *adj.*

Gun·ter's chain /ˈgəntərz/ ▸*n. Surveying* a former measuring instrument 66 feet (20.1 m) long, subdivided into 100 links, each of which is a short section of wire connected to the next link by a loop. It has now been superseded by the steel tape and electronic equipment. ■ this length as a unit, equal to $1/10$ furlong or $1/80$ mile. Also called **CHAIN**. ▷late 17th cent.: named after Edmund *Gunter* (1581–1626), the English mathematician who devised it.

Gun·ther /ˈgo͝ontər/ (in the Nibelungenlied) the husband of Brunhild and brother of Kriemhild, by whom he was beheaded in revenge for Siegfried's murder.

Gun·tur /go͝onˈto͝or/ a city in eastern India, in Andhra Pradesh; pop. 471,000.

gun·wale /ˈgənl/ (also **gun·nel**) ▸*n.* (often **gunwales**) the upper edge of the side of a boat or ship. ▷late Middle English: from **GUN** + **WALE** (because it was formerly used to support guns).

▸PHRASE □ **to the gunwales** *informal* so as to be almost overflowing: *the car is stuffed to the gunwales with camera equipment.*

Guo·min·dang /ˈgwōˈminˈdäNG/ variant spelling of **KUOMINTANG**.

gup·pie /ˈgəpē/ ▸*n.* (*pl.* **-pies**) *informal* a homosexual yuppie. ▷1980s: blend of **GAY** and **YUPPIE**.

gup·py /ˈgəpē/ ▸*n.* (*pl.* **-pies**) a small, livebearing freshwater fish widely kept in aquariums. Native to tropical America, it has been introduced elsewhere to control mosquito larvae. • *Poecilia reticulata*, family Poeciliidae. ▷1920s: named after R. J. Lechmere *Guppy* (1836–1916), a Trinidadian clergyman who sent the first specimen to the British Museum.

Gup·ta /ˈgo͝optə/ a Hindu dynasty established in AD 320 by Chandragupta I in Bihar. At one stage it ruled most of the north of the Indian subcontinent, but it began to disintegrate toward the end of the 5th century. —**Gup·tan** *adj.*

Gur /go͝or/ ▸*n.* a branch of the Niger–Congo family of languages, including Senufo, spoken in parts of West Africa. Also called **VOLTAIC**.

▸*adj.* of, relating to, or denoting this group of languages.

gur·dwa·ra /ˌgərˈdwärə/ ▸*n.* a Sikh place of worship. ▷from Punjabi *gurduārā*, from Sanskrit *guru* 'teacher' + *dvāra* 'door.'

gur·gle /ˈgərgəl/ ▸*v.* [*intrans.*] make a hollow bubbling sound like that made by water running out of a bottle: *my stomach gurgled* | [as *adj.*] (**gurgling**) *a faint gurgling noise.* ■ [with *adverbial of direction*] (of a liquid) run or flow with such a sound: *chemicals gurgle down a drain straight into the sewers.*

▸*n.* a gurgling sound: *Catherine gave a gurgle of laughter.* ▷late Middle English: imitative, or directly from Dutch *gorgelen*, German *gurgeln*, or medieval Latin *gurgulare*, all from Latin *gurgulio* 'gullet.'

Gur·kha /ˈgo͝orkə/ ▸*n.* a member of any of several peoples of Nepal noted for their military prowess. ■ a member of units of the British army established specifically for Nepalese recruits in the mid 19th century. ▷name of a locality, from Sanskrit *gorakṣa* 'cowherd' (from *go* 'cow' + *rakṣ-* 'protect'), used as an epithet of their patron deity.

Gur·mu·khi /ˈgo͝orməˌkē/ ▸*n.* the script used by Sikhs for writing Punjabi. ■ the Punjabi language as written in this script. ▷Punjabi, from Sanskrit *guru* (see **GURU**) + *mukha* 'mouth.'

gurn /gərn/ ▸*v.* [*intrans.*] *chiefly Brit.* make a grotesque face: [as *n.*] (**gurning**) *gurning is one of the fair's most popular competitions.* ▷early 20th cent.: dialect variant of **GRIN**. —**gurn·er** *n.*

gur·nard /ˈgərnərd/ ▸*n.* a bottom-dwelling fish of coastal waters, with a heavily boned head and three fingerlike pectoral rays, which it uses for searching for food and for walking on the seabed. • Family Triglidae: several genera and many species, including the common European *Eutrigla gurnardus*. ▷Middle English: from Old French *gornart*, from *grondir* 'to grunt,' from Latin *grundire, grunnire*.

gur·ney /ˈgərnē/ ▸*n.* (*pl.* **-neys**) a wheeled stretcher used for transporting hospital patients. ▷late 19th cent.: apparently named after J. T. *Gurney* of Boston, Massachusetts, patentee of a new cab design in 1883.

gur·ry /ˈgərē/ ▸*n.* fish or whale offal. ▷late 18th cent.: of unknown origin.

gu·ru /ˈgo͞oro͞o; go͞oˈro͞o/ ▸*n.* (*pl.* **-rus**) (in Hinduism and Buddhism) a spiritual teacher, esp. one who imparts initiation. ■ each of the ten first leaders of the Sikh religion. ■ an influential teacher or popular expert: *a management guru.* ▷from Hindi and Punjabi, from Sanskrit *guru* 'weighty, grave' (compare with Latin *gravis*), hence 'elder, teacher.'

gush /gəSH/ ▸*v.* [*intrans.*] **1** [with *adverbial of direction*] (of a liquid) flow out in a rapid and plentiful stream, often suddenly: *William watched the murky liquid **gushing out*** | *figurative millions of dollars **gushed out** of that office.* ■ [*trans.*] send out in a rapid and plentiful stream. **2** speak or write with effusiveness or exaggerated enthusiasm: *a nice old lady reporter who covers the art openings and **gushes about** everything.*

▸*n.* **1** a rapid and plentiful stream or burst. **2** exaggerated effusiveness or enthusiasm. ▷late Middle English: probably imitative. —**gush·ing·ly** *adv.*

gush·er /ˈgəSHər/ ▸*n.* **1** an oil well from which oil flows profusely without being pumped. ■ a thing from which a liquid flows profusely. **2** an effusive person: *the earnest, ingratiating gusher of numerous television interviews.*

gush·y /ˈgəSHē/ ▸*adj.* (**gush·i·er, gush·i·est**) excessively effusive: *her gushy manner.* —**gush·i·ly** /-SHəlē/ *adv.* —**gush·i·ness** *n.*

gus·set /ˈgəsit/ ▸*n.* a piece of material sewn into a garment to strengthen or enlarge a part of it, such as the collar of a shirt or the crotch of an undergarment. ■ a bracket strengthening an angle of a structure. ▷late Middle English: from Old French *gousset*, diminutive of *gousse* 'pod, shell,' of unknown origin. —**gusseted** *adj.*

gus·sy /ˈgəsē/ ▸*v.* (**-sies, -sied**) [*trans.*] (**gussy someone/something up**) *informal* make more attractive, esp. in a showy or gimmicky way: *shopkeepers gussied up their window displays.* ▷1940s: perhaps from *Gussie*, nickname for the given name *Augustus*.

gust /gəst/ ▸*n.* a brief, strong rush of wind. ■ a burst of something such as rain, sound, or emotion: ***gusts of** rain lashed down the narrow alleys.*

▸*v.* [*intrans.*] (of the wind) blow in gusts: *the wind was gusting through the branches of the tree.* ▷late 16th cent.: from Old Norse *gustr*, related to *gjósa* 'to gush.'

gus·ta·tion /gəˈstāSHən/ ▸*n. formal* the action or faculty of tasting. ▷late 16th cent.: from Latin *gustatio(n-)*, from *gustare* 'to taste,' from *gustus* 'taste.' —**gus·ta·tive** /ˈgəstətiv/ *adj.*

gus·ta·to·ry /ˈgəstəˌtôrē/ ▸*adj. formal* concerned with tasting or the sense of taste: *gustatory delights.*

Gus·ta·vus Adol·phus /gəˈstävəs əˈdôlfəs/ (1594–1632), king of Sweden 1611–32. His domestic reforms laid the foundation for the modern Swedish state.

gus·to /ˈgəstō/ ▸*n.* (*pl.* **-tos** or **-toes**) **1** enjoyment or vigor in doing something; zest: *she sang it with gusto.* ■ [in *sing.*] *archaic* a relish or liking: *he had **a** particular **gusto for** those sort of performances.* **2** *archaic* style of artistic execution. ▷early 17th cent.: from Italian, from Latin *gustus* 'taste.'

gust·y /ˈgəstē/ ▸*adj.* (**gust·i·er, gust·i·est**) **1** characterized by or blowing in gusts: *a gusty morning.* **2** having or showing gusto: *gusty female vocals.* —**gust·i·ly** /ˈgəstəlē/ *adv.* —**gust·i·ness** *n.*

gut /gət/ ▸*n.* **1** (also **guts**) the stomach or belly: *a painful stabbing feeling in his gut.* ■ *Medicine & Biology* the lower alimentary canal or a part of this; the intestine: *microbes which naturally live in the human gut.* ■ (**guts**) entrails that have been removed or exposed in violence or by a butcher. ■ (**guts**) the internal parts or essence of something: *the guts of a modern computer.* **2** (**guts**) *informal* personal courage and determination; toughness of character: *she had both more brains and more guts than her husband* | *you just haven't got the guts to admit it.* ■ [as *adj.*] *informal* (of a feeling or reaction) based on a deep-seated emotional response rather than considered thought; instinctive: *a gut feeling.* **3** fiber made from the intestines of animals, used esp. for violin or racket strings or for surgical use: [as *adj.*] *gut strings.* **4** a narrow passage or strait.

▸*v.* (**gut·ted**, **gut·ting**) [*trans.*] take out the intestines and other internal organs of (a fish or other animal) before cooking it. ■ remove or destroy completely the internal parts of (a building or other structure): *the fire gutted most of the factory.* ■ remove or extract the most important parts of (something) in a damaging or destructive manner: *a mine shutdown gutted the town's economy.* ▷Old English *guttas* (plural), probably related to *gēotan* 'pour.'

▸*PHRASES* □ **bust a gut** *informal* make a strenuous effort: *a problem which nobody is going to bust a gut trying to solve.* □ **—— one's guts out** used to indicate that the specified action is done or performed as hard as possible: *he ran his guts out and finished fourth.* □ **hate someone's guts** *informal* feel a strong hatred for someone.

gut·buck·et /ˈgət,bəkit/ *informal* ▸*n.* [as *adj.*] *informal* (of jazz or blues) raw and spirited in style: *his gutbucket guitar solos.* ▷early 20th cent.: perhaps from the earlier denotation of a one-stringed plucked instrument, with reference to its construction, or referring to the bucket that caught *gutterings* (streams of liquid) from beer barrels in low-class saloons where such music was played.

gut course ▸*n. informal* a college or university course requiring little work or intellectual ability.

Gu·ten·berg /ˈgōōtn,bərg/, Johannes (*c.*1400–68), German printer. He was the first in the West to print by using movable type and to use a press. By *c.*1455, he had produced what later became known as the Gutenberg Bible.

Gu·ten·berg Bi·ble ▸*n.* the edition of the Bible (Vulgate version) completed by Johannes Gutenberg in about 1455 in Mainz, Germany. It is the first complete book extant in the West and is also the earliest to be printed from movable type.

gut flo·ra ▸*plural n.* another term for **INTESTINAL FLORA.**

Guth·rie /ˈgəTHrē/, Woody (1912–1967), U.S. folk singer and songwriter; full name *Woodrow Wilson Guthrie.* His radical politics, as well as the hardships of the Depression, inspired many of his songs.

Guth·rie test ▸*n. Medicine* a routine blood test carried out on babies a few days after birth to detect the condition phenylketonuria. ▷named after Robert *Guthrie* (born 1916), American microbiologist.

gut·less /ˈgətləs/ ▸*adj. informal* lacking courage or determination. —**gut·less·ly** *adv.* —**gut·less·ness** *n.*

guts·y /ˈgətsē/ ▸*adj.* (**guts·i·er**, **guts·i·est**) *informal* showing courage, determination, and spirit: *she gave a gutsy performance in the tennis tournament.* ■ (of food or drink) strongly flavorsome: *a smooth Bordeaux that is gutsy enough to accompany steak.* —**guts·i·ly** /-səlē/ *adv.* —**guts·i·ness** *n.*

gut·ta-per·cha /,gətə ˈpərCHə/ ▸*n.* a hard, tough thermoplastic substance that is the coagulated latex of certain Malaysian trees. It consists chiefly of a hydrocarbon isomeric with rubber and is now used chiefly in dentistry and for electrical insulation. • This substance is obtained from trees of the genus *Palaquium*, family Sapotaceae, in particular *P. gutta.* ▷mid 19th cent.: from Malay *getah perca*, from *getah* 'gum' + *perca* 'strips of cloth' (which it resembles), altered by association with obsolete *gutta* 'gum,' from Latin *gutta* 'a drop.'

gut·tate /ˈgət,āt/ ▸*adj. chiefly Biology* having drops or droplike markings. ■ in the form of or resembling drops. ▷early 19th cent.: from Latin *guttatus* 'speckled,' from *gutta* 'a drop.'

gut·ta·tion /gəˈtāSHən/ ▸*n.* the secretion of droplets of water from the pores of plants. ▷late 19th cent.: from Latin *gutta* 'drop' + **-ATION.**

gut·ter /ˈgətər/ ▸*n.* a shallow trough fixed beneath the edge of a roof for carrying off rainwater. ■ a channel at the side of a street for carrying off rainwater. ■ (**the gutter**) used to refer to a poor or squalid background or environment: *only moneyed privilege had kept him out of the gutter.* ■ *technical* a groove or channel for flowing liquid. ■ the blank space between facing pages of a book or between adjacent columns of type or stamps in a sheet. ■ a channel on either side of a lane in a bowling alley.

▸*v.* **1** [*intrans.*] (of a candle or flame) flicker and burn unsteadily: *the candles had almost* **guttered out.** **2** [*trans.*] *archaic* channel or furrow with something such as streams or tears: *my cheeks are guttered with tears.* ■ [*intrans.*] (**gutter down**) stream down: *the raindrops gutter down her visage.* ▷Middle English: from Old French *gotiere*, from Latin *gutta* 'a drop'; the verb dates from late Middle English, originally meaning 'cut grooves in' and later (early 18th cent.) used of a candle that melts rapidly because it has become channeled on one side.

gut·ter ball ▸*n.* (in tenpin bowling) a nonscoring ball that enters the gutter before reaching the pins.

gut·ter·ing /ˈgətəriNG/ ▸*n. chiefly Brit.* the gutters of a building. ■ material used to make gutters.

gut·ter press ▸*n.* (**the gutter press**) *chiefly Brit.* reporters or newspapers engaging in sensational journalism, esp. accounts of the private lives of public figures.

gut·ter·snipe /ˈgətər,snīp/ ▸*n. derogatory* a street urchin.

gut·tur·al /ˈgətərəl/ ▸*adj.* (of a speech sound) produced in the throat; harsh-sounding. ■ (of a manner of speech) characterized by the use of such sounds: *his parents' guttural central European accent.*

▸*n.* a guttural consonant (e.g., *k, g*) or other speech sound. ▷late 16th cent.: from French, or from medieval Latin *gutturalis*, from Latin *guttur* 'throat.' —**gut·tur·al·ly** *adv.*

gut·tur·al·ize /ˈgətərə,līz/ ▸*v.* [*trans.*] **1** say or pronounce in a harsh-sounding guttural manner. **2** articulate (a speech sound) by moving the back of the tongue toward the velum.

gut·ty /ˈgətē/ ▸*adj.* (**-ti·er**, **-ti·est**) *informal* gutsy.

gut-wrench·ing ▸*adj. informal* extremely unpleasant or upsetting: *the film is a gut-wrenching portrait of domestic violence.*

guv /gəv/ ▸*n. Brit., informal* (as a form of address) sir: *"Excuse me, guv," he began.* ▷late 19th cent.: abbreviation of **GUV'NOR.**

guv'nor /ˈgəvnər/ ▸*n. Brit., informal* a man in a position of authority such as one's employer or father (often used as a term of address): *I had a lecture from* **the guv'nor.** ▷mid 19th cent.: representing a nonstandard or colloquial pronunciation.

guy[1] /gī/ ▸*n.* **1** *informal* a man: *he's a nice guy.* [mid 19th cent.] ■ (**guys**) people of either sex: *you guys want some coffee?* **2** *Brit.* a figure representing Guy Fawkes, burned on a bonfire on Guy Fawkes' Night, and often displayed by children begging for money for fireworks.

▸*v.* [*trans.*] make fun of; ridicule: *he didn't realize I was guying the whole idea.* ▷early 19th cent. (sense 2): named after *Guy* Fawkes (see **GUNPOWDER PLOT**).

guy[2] ▸*n.* a rope or line fixed to the ground to secure a tent or other structure.

▸*v.* [*trans.*] secure with a line or lines: *it was set on concrete footings and guyed with steel cable.* ▷late Middle English: probably of Low German origin; related to Dutch *gei* 'brail' and German *Geitaue* 'brails.'

Guy·a·na /gīˈänə; gīˈanə/ a country on the northeastern coast of South America; pop. 705,000; capital, Georgetown; languages, English (official), English Creole, and Hindi. Official name **COOPERATIVE REPUBLIC OF GUYANA.** ▷from an American Indian word meaning 'land of waters.' —**Guy·a·nese** /,gīəˈnēz; -ˈnēs/ *adj.* & *n.*

The Spanish explored the area in 1499, and the Dutch settled here in the 17th century. It was occupied by the British from 1796 and established, with adjacent areas, as the colony of British Guiana in 1831. In 1966, it became an independent state of the Commonwealth of Nations.

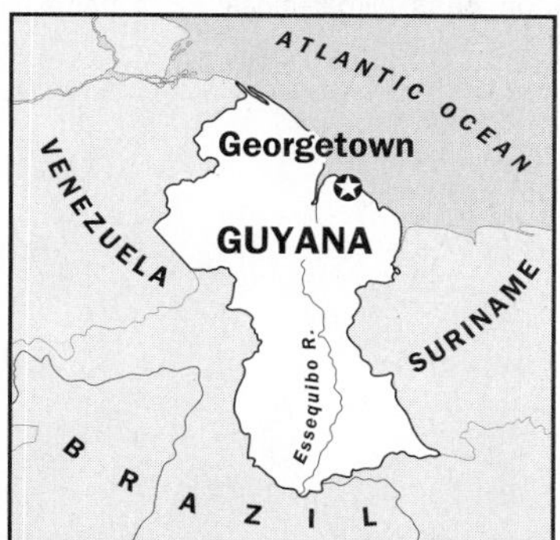

guy·ot /gēˈō/ ▸*n. Geology* a seamount with a flat top. ▷1940s: named after Arnold H. *Guyot* (1807–84), Swiss geographer.

guz·zle /ˈgəzəl/ ▸*v.* [*trans.*] eat or drink (something) greedily: *we guzzle our beer and devour our pizza* | (*figurative*) *this car guzzles gas.* ▷late 16th cent.: perhaps from Old French *gosillier* 'chatter, vomit,' from *gosier* 'throat,' from late Latin *geusiae* 'cheeks.' —**guz·zler** /-z(ə)lər/ *n.*

Gvoth /gvôt/, Stanislav, see **MIKITA.**

Gvozdena Vrata /ˈgvôzdənə ˈvrätə/ Serbo-Croat name for **IRON GATE.**

GVW ▸*abbr.* gross vehicle weight.

GW ▸*abbr.* gigawatt.

Gwa·li·or /ˈgwälē,ôr/ a city in central India, in a district of the same name in Madhya Pradesh; pop. 693,000.

Gwynn /gwin/, Nell (1650–87), English actress; full name *Eleanor Gwynn.* A comedienne at London's Theatre Royal, she was a mistress of Charles II.

Gy *Physics* ▸*abbr.* gray(s).

Gyan·dzhe /gyänˈjə/ Russian name for **GÄNCÄ.**

gybe ▸*v.* & *n.* variant spelling of **JIBE**[2].

gym /jim/ ▸*n. informal* **1** a gymnasium. **2** a membership organization that provides a range of facilities designed to improve and maintain physical fitness and health: *we got guest passes to Suzanne's gym.* **3** physical education: *I'm taking just one more semester of gym.* ▷late 19th cent.: abbreviation.

gym. ▸*abbr. Sports* gymnastics.

gym·kha·na /jimˈkänə/ ▸*n.* a day event comprising races and other competitions between horse riders or car drivers. ▷mid 19th cent.: from Urdu *gendkānah* 'racket court,' from Hindi *geṁd* 'ball' + Persian *kānah* 'house,' altered by association with **GYMNASTIC.**

gym·na·si·um /jimˈnāzēəm/ ▸*n.* (*pl.* **-si·ums** or **-si·a** /-zēə/) **1** a room or building equipped for gymnastics, games, and other physical exercise. **2** /gimˈnäzē,ōōm/ a school in Germany, Scandinavia, or central Europe that prepares pupils for university entrance. ▷late 16th cent.: via Latin from Greek *gumnasion*, from *gumnazein* 'exercise naked,' from *gumnos* 'naked.' —**gym·na·si·al** /-zēəl/ *adj.* (in sense 2).

gym·nast /ˈjimnist/ ▸*n.* a person trained in or skilled in gymnastics. ▷late 16th cent.: from French *gymnaste* or Greek *gumnastēs* 'trainer of athletes,' from *gumnazein* 'exercise naked' (see **GYMNASIUM**).

gym·nas·tic /jimˈnastik/ ▸*adj.* of or relating to gymnastics: *a gymnastic display.* —**gym·nas·ti·cal·ly** /-ik(ə)lē/ *adv.*

gym·nas·tics /jimˈnastiks/ ▸*plural n.* [also treated as *sing.*] exercises developing or displaying physical agility and coordination. The modern sport of gymnastics typically involves exercises on uneven bars, balance beam, floor, and vaulting horse (for women), and horizontal and parallel bars, rings, floor, and pommel horse (for men). ■ [with *adj.*] other physical or mental agility of a specified kind: *these vocal gymnastics make the music unforgettable.*

gymno- ▸*comb. form* bare; naked: *gymnosophist* | *gymnosperm.* ▷from Greek *gumnos* 'naked.'

gym·nos·o·phist /jimˈnäsəfist/ ▸*n.* a member of an ancient Indian sect that wore very little clothing and was given to asceticism and contemplation. ▷late Middle English: from French *gymnosophiste*, via Latin from Greek *gumnosophistai* (plural), from *gumnos* 'naked' + *sophistēs* 'teacher of philosophy, sophist' (see **SOPHIST**). —**gym·nos·o·phy** /-fē/ *n.*

gym·no·sperm /ˈjimnə,spərm/ ▸*n. Botany* a plant that has seeds unprotected by an ovary or fruit. Gymnosperms include the conifers, cycads, and ginkgo. Compare with **ANGIOSPERM.** • Subdivision Gymnospermae, division Spermatophyta. —**gym·no·sper·mous** /,jimnəˈspərməs/ *adj.*

gym·nure /ˈjim,nyōōr/ ▸*n.* another term for **MOONRAT.** ▷late 19th cent.: from modern Latin *Gymnura* (former genus name), from Greek *gumnos* 'naked' + *oura* 'tail.'

gyn. ▸*abbr.* ■ gynecological. ■ gynecologist. ■ gynecology.

gynaeco- *chiefly Brit.* ▸ variant spelling of **GYNECO-.** ▷from Greek *gunē, gunaik-* 'woman, female.'

gy·nan·dro·morph /gīˈnandrə,môrf; jinˈan-/ ▸*n. Zoology & Medicine* an abnormal individual, esp. an insect, having some male and some female characteristics. ▷late 19th cent.: from Greek *gunandros* 'of doubtful sex' (see **GYNANDROUS**) + *morphē* 'form.' —**gy·nan·dro·mor·phic** /gī,nandrəˈmôrfik; jin,an-/ *adj.* —**gy·nan·dro·mor·phy** /-fē/ *n.*

gy·nan·drous /gīˈnandrəs; jinˈan-/ ▸*adj. Botany* (of a flower) having stamens and pistil united in one column, as in orchids. ■ (of a person or animal) hermaphrodite. ▷early 19th cent.: from Greek *gunandros* 'of doubtful sex' (from *gunē* 'woman' + *anēr, andr-* 'man, male') + **-OUS.**

gyn·ar·chy /ˈgīˌnärkē; ˈjinˌär-/ ▸*n.* (*pl.* **-chies**) rule by women or a woman.

gyneco- ▸*comb. form comb. form* relating to women; female: *gynecocracy* | *gynecophobia.*

gyn·e·coc·ra·cy /ˌginəˈkäkrəsē; ˌjinə-/ (*Brit.* **gyn·ae·coc·ra·cy**) ▸*n.* another term for GYNARCHY.

gy·ne·coid /ˈjiniˌkoid; ˈgīni-; ˈjīni-/ ▸*adj.* relating to or characteristic of a woman: *people with a pear-shaped figure—also known as the gynecoid pattern because it is more common in women—tend to carry extra weight on their thighs and buttocks.*

gynecol. ▸*abbr.* ■ gynecological. ■ gynecology.

gy·ne·col·o·gy /ˌgīnəˈkäləjē; ˌjinə-/ (*Brit.* **gy·nae·col·o·gy**) ▸*n.* the branch of physiology and medicine that deals with the functions and diseases specific to women and girls, esp. those affecting the reproductive system. **—gyn·e·co·log·ic** /-kəˈläjik/ *adj.* **—gyn·e·co·log·i·cal** /-kəˈläjikəl/ *adj.* **—gyn·e·co·log·i·cal·ly** /-kəˈläjik(ə)lē/ *adv.* **—gy·ne·col·o·gist** /-jist/ *n.*

gyn·e·co·mas·ti·a /ˌgīnəkōˈmastēə/ (*Brit.* **gyn·ae·co·mas·ti·a**) ▸*n. Medicine* enlargement of a man's breasts, usually due to hormone imbalance or hormone therapy.

gyn·e·co·pho·bi·a /ˌgīnəkōˈfōbēə/ (*Brit.* **gyn·ae·co·pho·bi·a**) ▸*n.* another term for GYNOPHOBIA.

gy·no·cen·tric /ˌgīnəˈsentrik/ ▸*adj.* centered on or concerned exclusively with women; taking a female (or specifically a feminist) point of view.

gy·noe·ci·um /jiˈnēshēəm; gī-; -sēəm/ ▸*n.* (*pl.* **-ci·a** /-shēə; -sēə/) *Botany* the female part of a flower, consisting of one or more carpels. ▷mid 19th cent.: modern Latin, from Greek *gunaikeion* 'women's apartments,' from *gunē, gunaik-* 'woman, female' + *oikos* 'house.'

gy·no·pho·bi·a /ˌgīnəˈfōbēə; ˌjinə-/ ▸*n.* extreme or irrational fear of women or of the female. **—gy·no·pho·bic** /-bik/ *adj.*

-gynous ▸*comb. form Botany* having female organs or pistils of a specified kind or number: *epigynous.* ▷based on modern Latin *-gynus* (from Greek *-gunos*, from *gunē* 'woman') + **-OUS**.

gyo·za /ˈgyōzə/ ▸*n.* a Japanese dish consisting of wonton wrappers stuffed with pork and cabbage. ▷Japanese, from Chinese *jiaozi.*

G

gyp[1] /jip/ *informal* ▸*v.* (**gypped, gyp·ping**) [*trans.*] cheat or swindle (someone): *that's salesmanship, you have to gyp people into buying stuff they don't like.*
▸*n.* (also **gip**) an act of cheating; a swindle. ▷late 19th cent.: of unknown origin.

gyp[2] ▸*n. Brit.* a college servant at the Universities of Cambridge and Durham. ▷mid 18th cent.: perhaps from obsolete *gippo* 'menial kitchen servant,' originally denoting a man's short tunic, from obsolete French *jupeau.*

gyp joint ▸*n. informal* **1** a business establishment, esp. a store, that has a reputation for cheating customers by charging exorbitant prices for inferior goods or services: *a 42nd Street gyp joint.* **2** a gambling establishment in which the games are run dishonestly.

gyp·po /ˈjipō/ ▸*n.* (*pl.* **-pos**) *informal, derogatory* a gypsy.

gyp·soph·i·la /jipˈsäfələ/ ▸*n.* a plant of the genus *Gypsophila* in the pink family, esp. (in gardening) baby's breath. ▷modern Latin, from Greek *gupsos* 'chalk, gypsum' + *philos* 'loving.'

gyp·sum /ˈjipsəm/ ▸*n.* a soft white or gray mineral consisting of hydrated calcium sulfate. It occurs chiefly in sedimentary deposits and is used to make plaster of Paris and fertilizers, and in the building industry. ▷late Middle English: from Latin, from Greek *gupsos.* **—gyp·sif·er·ous** /jipˈsifərəs/ *adj.*

gyp·sum board ▸*n.* another term for PLASTERBOARD.

gyp·sy /ˈjipsē/ (also **gip·sy**) ▸*n.* (*pl.* **-sies**) a member of a traveling people with dark skin and hair who speak Romany and traditionally live by seasonal work, itinerant trade, and fortune-telling. Gypsies are now found mostly in Europe, parts of North Africa, and North America, but are believed to have originated in the Indian subcontinent. ■ the language of the gypsies; Romany. ■ a person who leads an unconventional life. ■ a person who moves from place to place as required by employment.
▸*adj.* (of a business or business person) nonunion or unlicensed: *gypsy trucking firms.* ▷mid 16th cent.: originally *gipcyan,* short for EGYPTIAN (because gypsies were popularly supposed to have come from Egypt). **—gyp·sy·ish** *adj.*

gyp·sy moth ▸*n.* a tussock moth having a brown male and larger white female. The caterpillar can be a serious pest of orchards and woodland. • *Lymantria dispar*, family Lymantriidae.

gy·ral /ˈjīrəl/ ▸*adj. chiefly Anatomy* of or relating to a gyrus or gyri.

gy·rate /ˈjīrāt/ ▸*v.* move or cause to move in a circle or spiral, esp. quickly: [*intrans.*] *their wings gyrate through the water like paddle wheels.* ■ [*intrans.*] dance in a wild or suggestive manner: *strippers gyrated to rock music on a low stage.* ▷early 19th cent.: from Latin *gyrat-* 'revolved,' from the verb *gyrare*, from Greek *guros* 'a ring.' **—gy·ra·tion** /jīˈrāshən/ *n.* **—gy·ra·tor** /-ˌrātər/ *n.*

gy·ra·to·ry /ˈjīrəˌtôrē/ ▸*adj.* of or involving circular or spiral motion.

gyre /jīr/ ▸*v.* [*intrans.*] *poetic/literary* whirl; gyrate: *a swarm of ghosts gyred around him.*
▸*n.* a spiral; a vortex. ■ *Geography* a circular pattern of currents in an ocean basin: *the central North Pacific gyre.* ▷late Middle English (in the sense 'whirl (someone or something) around)': from late Latin *gyrare*, from Latin *gyrus* 'a ring,' from Greek *guros.* The noun is from Latin *gyrus.*

gyr·fal·con /ˈjərˌfalkən; -ˌfôl-/ ▸*n.* the largest falcon, found in arctic regions and occurring in several color forms, one of which is mainly white. • *Falco rusticolus*, family Falconidae. ▷Middle English: from Old French *gerfaucon*, of Germanic origin. The first element is probably related to Old High German *gēr* 'spear'; the spelling *gyr-* arose from a mistaken idea that the bird's name came from Latin *gyrare* 'revolve.'

gy·ri /ˈjīrī/ ▸ plural form of GYRUS.

gy·ro[1] /ˈjīrō/ ▸*n.* (*pl.* **-ros**) short for GYROSCOPE or GYROCOMPASS.

gy·ro[2] /ˈyērō; ˈzhirō/ ▸*n.* (*pl.* **-ros**) a sandwich made with slices of spiced meat cooked on a spit, served with salad in pita bread. ▷1970s: from modern Greek *guros* 'turning.'

gyro- ▸*comb. form* **1** relating to rotation: *gyromagnetic.* **2** gyroscopic: *gyrostabilizer.* ▷from Greek *guros* 'a ring.'

gy·ro·com·pass /ˈjīrōˌkəmpəs/ ▸*n.* a nonmagnetic compass in which the direction of true north is maintained by a continuously driven gyroscope whose axis is parallel to the earth's axis of rotation.

gy·ro·cop·ter /ˈjīrəˌkäptər/ ▸*n.* a small, light single-seater autogiro. ▷from GYRO- 'relating to rotation,' on the pattern of *helicopter.*

gy·ro·mag·net·ic /ˌjīrōmagˈnetik/ ▸*adj.* **1** *Physics* of or relating to the magnetic and mechanical properties of a rotating charged particle. **2** (of a compass) combining a gyroscope and a normal magnetic compass.

gy·ron /ˈjīrən/ ▸*n. Heraldry* a triangular ordinary formed by two lines from the edge of the shield meeting at the fess point at 45 degrees. ▷late 16th cent.: from Old French *giron* 'gusset.'

gy·ron·ny /jīˈränē/ ▸*adj. Heraldry* (of a shield) divided into eight gyrons by straight lines all crossing at the fess point. ▷late Middle English: from French *gironné*, from *giron* (see GYRON).

gy·ro·pi·lot /ˈjīrəˌpīlət/ ▸*n.* a gyrocompass used to provide automatic steering for a ship or aircraft.

gy·ro·plane /ˈjīrəˌplān/ ▸*n.* an autogiro or similar aircraft.

gy·ro·scope /ˈjīrəˌskōp/ ▸*n.* a device consisting of a wheel or disk mounted so that it can spin rapidly about an axis that is itself free to alter in direction. The orientation of the axis is not affected by tilting of the mounting; so gyroscopes can be used to provide stability or maintain a reference direction in navigation systems, automatic pilots, and stabilizers. ▷mid 19th cent.: from French, from Greek *guros* 'a ring' + modern Latin *scopium* (see -SCOPE). **—gy·ro·scop·ic** /ˌjīrəˈskäpik/ *adj.* **—gy·ro·scop·i·cal·ly** /ˌjīrəˈskäpik(ə)lē/ *adv.*

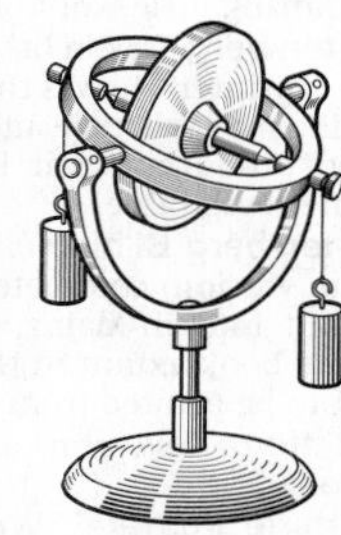
gyroscope

gy·ro·sta·bi·lized /ˌjīrōˈstābəˌlīzd/ ▸*adj.* **1** (of a vessel) stabilized by a gyrostabilizer. **2** (of cameras, binoculars, and other optical devices) capable of securing a steady view by means of an electronic device that corrects for movement.

gy·ro·sta·bi·liz·er /ˌjīrōˈstābəˌlīzər/ ▸*n.* a gyroscopic device for maintaining the equilibrium of something such as a ship, aircraft, or platform.

gy·rus /ˈjīrəs/ ▸*n.* (*pl.* **gy·ri** /ˈjīrī/) *Anatomy* a ridge or fold between two clefts on the cerebral surface in the brain. ▷mid 19th cent.: from Latin, from Greek *guros* 'a ring.'

GySgt ▸*abbr.* gunnery sergeant.

gyt·tja /ˈyiˌchä/ ▸*n. Geology* sediment rich in organic matter deposited at the bottom of a eutrophic lake. ▷late 19th cent.: Swedish, literally 'mud, ooze.'

Gyum·ri /ˈgyōōmrē/ an industrial city in northwestern Armenia, close to the border with Turkey; pop. 123,000. The city was destroyed by an earthquake in 1926 and again in 1988. It was formerly called Aleksandropol(1840–1924) and Leninakan (1924–91). Russian name KUMAYRI.

gyve /jīv/ ▸*n.* (usu. **gyves**) *archaic* a fetter or shackle. ▷Middle English: of unknown origin. **—gyved** *adj.*

Hh

H[1] /āCH/ (also **h**) ▸*n.* (*pl.* **Hs** or **H's** /ˈāCHiz/) **1** the eighth letter of the alphabet. ■ denoting the next after G in a set of items, categories, etc. ■ (**h**) *Chess* denoting the file on the right-hand edge of the board, as viewed from White's side. **2** (**H**) a shape like that of a capital H. **3** (**H**) *Music* (in the German system) the note B natural.

H[2] ▸*abbr.* ■ hard (used in describing grades of pencil lead): *a 2H pencil.* ■ height (in giving the dimensions of an object). ■ *Physics* henry(s). ■ *informal* heroin.
▸*symbol* ■ *Chemistry* enthalpy. ■ the chemical element hydrogen. ■ *Physics* magnetic field strength.

h /āCH/ ▸*abbr.* ■ (in measuring the height of horses) hand(s). ■ [*in combination*] (in units of measurement) hecto-: *wine production reached 624,000 hl last year.* ■ horse. ■ (esp. with reference to water) hot: *nine rooms, all with h & c.* ■ hour(s): *breakfast at 0700 h.*
▸*symbol* ■ *Physics* Planck's constant.

ha[1] /hä/ (also **hah**) ▸*exclam.* used to express surprise, suspicion, triumph, or some other emotion. ▷natural utterance: first recorded in Middle English.

ha[2] ▸*abbr.* hectare(s).

Haar·lem /ˈhärləm/ a city in western Netherlands, near Amsterdam; pop. 148,000. It is the commercial center of the Dutch bulb industry.

Hab. ▸*abbr. Bible* Habakkuk.

Ha·bak·kuk /ˈhabəˌko͝ok; həˈbakək/ a Hebrew minor prophet, probably of the 7th century BC. ■ a book of the Bible containing his prophecies.

ha·ba·ne·ra /ˌhäbəˈne(ə)rə; -ˈny(ə)rə/ ▸*n.* a Cuban dance in slow duple time. ▷late 19th cent.: Spanish, short for *danza habanera* 'dance of Havana.'

Ha·ba·ne·ro /ˌhäbəˈne(ə)rō; -ˈnye(ə)rō/ (also **ha·ba·ne·ro**) ▸*n.* a small chili pepper that is the hottest variety available. Also called **SCOTCH BONNET**. ▷Spanish, literally 'of Havana.'

Hab·da·lah /ˌhävdäˈlä; hävˈdôlə/ ▸*n.* variant spelling of **HAVDALAH**.

ha·be·as cor·pus /ˈhābēəs ˈkôrpəs/ ▸*n. Law* a writ requiring a person under arrest to be brought before a judge or into court, esp. to secure the person's release unless lawful grounds are shown for their detention. ■ the legal right to apply for such a writ. ▷late Middle English: Latin, literally 'you shall have the body (in court).'

ha·ben·dum /həˈbendəm/ ▸*n. Law* the part of a deed or conveyance that states the estate or quantity of interest to be granted, e.g., the term of a lease. ▷early 17th cent.: Latin, literally '(that is) to be had'.

hab·er·dash·er /ˈhabərˌdaSHər/ ▸*n.* **1** a dealer in men's clothing. **2** *Brit.* a dealer in goods for dressmaking and sewing. ▷Middle English: probably based on Anglo-Norman French *hapertas*, perhaps the name of a fabric, of unknown origin. In early use the term denoted a dealer in a variety of household goods, later also specifically a hatter. Current senses date from the early 17th cent.

hab·er·dash·er·y /ˈhabərˌdaSHərē/ ▸*n.* (*pl.* **-er·ies**) the goods and wares sold by a haberdasher. ■ the shop of a haberdasher.

hab·er·geon /ˈhabərjən; həˈbərjən/ ▸*n. historical* a sleeveless coat of mail or scale armor. ▷Middle English: from Old French *haubergeon*, from *hauberc* (see **HAUBERK**), originally denoting a garment protecting the neck; compare with Dutch *halsberg*.

Ha·ber proc·ess /ˈhäbər/ (also **Ha·ber–Bosch proc·ess** /ˈhäbər ˈbäSH/) ▸*n.* an industrial process for producing ammonia from nitrogen and hydrogen, using an iron catalyst at high temperature and pressure. ▷named after Fritz Haber (1868–1934) and Carl Bosch (1874–1940), German chemists.

hab·ile /ˈhabəl/ ▸*adj. rare* deft; skillful. ▷late Middle English: variant of **ABLE**. The spelling change in the 16th and 17th centuries was due to association with French *habile* and Latin *habilis*.

ha·bil·i·ment /həˈbiləmənt/ ▸*n.* (usu. **habiliments**) *archaic* clothing. ▷late Middle English (in the general sense 'outfit, attire'): from Old French *habillement*, from *habiller* 'fit out,' from Latin *habilis* (see **ABLE**).

ha·bil·i·tate /həˈbiləˌtāt/ ▸*v.* **1** [*trans.*] fit out the workings of (a mine). **2** [*intrans.*] qualify for office, esp. as a teacher in a German university. ▷early 17th cent.: from medieval Latin *habilitat-* 'made able,' from the verb *habilitare*, from *habilitas* (see **ABILITY**). **—ha·bil·i·ta·tion** /həˌbiləˈtāSHən/ *n.*

hab·it /ˈhabit/ ▸*n.* **1** a settled or regular tendency or practice, esp. one that is hard to give up: *this can develop into **a bad habit** | we stayed together **out of habit**.* ■ *informal* an addictive practice, esp. one of taking drugs: *a cocaine habit.* ■ *Psychology* an automatic reaction to a specific situation. ■ general shape or mode of growth, esp. of a plant or a mineral: *a shrub of spreading habit.* **2** a long, loose garment worn by a member of a religious order or congregation. ■ short for **RIDING HABIT**. ■ *archaic* dress; attire. **3** *archaic* a person's bodily condition or constitution: *a victim to a consumptive habit.*
▸*v.* [*trans.*] (usu. **be habited**) *archaic* dress; clothe: *a boy habited as a serving lad.* ▷Middle English: from Old French *abit*, *habit*, from Latin *habitus* 'condition, appearance,' from *habere* 'have, consist of.' The term originally meant 'dress, attire,' later coming to denote physical or mental constitution.
▸PHRASE □ **break** (or *informal* **kick**) **the habit** stop engaging in a habitual practice.

hab·it·a·ble /ˈhabitəbəl/ ▸*adj.* suitable or good enough to live in. ▷late Middle English: via Old French from Latin *habitabilis*, from *habitare* 'possess, inhabit.' **—hab·it·a·bil·i·ty** /ˌhabətəˈbilətē/ *n.*

hab·i·tant /ˈhabitənt; ˈhabətnt/ ▸*n.* **1** [often as *adj.*] an early French settler in Canada (esp. Quebec) or Louisiana: *the habitant farmhouses of old Quebec.* **2** *archaic* an inhabitant. ▷late Middle English (sense 2): from Old French, from *habiter*, from Latin *habitare* 'inhabit.'

hab·i·tat /ˈhabiˌtat/ ▸*n.* the natural home or environment of an animal, plant, or other organism: *wild chimps in their natural habitat.* ■ a particular type of environment regarded as a home for organisms: *Long Point was internationally recognized for its unique Great Lakes coastal habitat.* ■ *informal* a person's usual or preferred surroundings. ▷late 18th cent.: from Latin, literally 'it dwells,' from *habitare* (see **HABITABLE**).

hab·i·ta·tion /ˌhabiˈtāSHən/ ▸*n.* the state or process of living in a particular place: *signs of human habitation.* ■ *formal* a place in which to live; a house or home. ▷late Middle English: via Old French from Latin *habitatio(n-)*, from *habitare* 'inhabit.' **—hab·i·ta·tive** /ˈhabitəˌtiv/ *adj.*

hab·it-form·ing ▸*adj.* (of a drug or activity) addictive.

ha·bit·u·al /həˈbiCHo͞oəl/ ▸*adj.* done or doing constantly or as a habit: *a habitual late sleeper | this pattern of behavior can become habitual.* ■ regular; usual: *his habitual dress.* ▷late Middle English (in the sense 'part of one's character'): from medieval Latin *habitualis*, from *habitus* 'condition, appearance' (see **HABIT**). **—ha·bit·u·al·ly** *adv.*

ha·bit·u·ate /həˈbiCHo͞oˌāt/ ▸*v.* make or become accustomed or used to something: [*trans.*] *she had habituated the chimps to humans.* ▷late 15th cent.: from late Latin *habituat-* 'accustomed,' from the verb *habituare*, from *habitus* (see **HABIT**).

ha·bit·u·a·tion /həˌbiCHo͞oˈāSHən/ ▸*n.* the action of habituating or the condition of being habituated. ■ *Psychology* the diminishing of a physiological or emotional response to a frequently repeated stimulus. ▷late Middle English (in the sense 'formation of habit'): from French or from Latin *habitatio(n)-*, from late Latin *habituare* (see **HABITUATE**).

hab·i·tude /ˈhabiˌt(y)o͞od/ ▸*n. rare* a habitual tendency or way of behaving. ▷late Middle English: via Old French from Latin *habitudo*, from *habere* 'have' (compare with **HABIT**).

ha·bit·u·é /həˈbiCHo͞oˌā/ ▸*n.* a resident of or frequent visitor to a particular place: *his uncle was a habitué of the French theater.* ▷early 19th cent.: French, literally 'accustomed,' past participle of *habituer*.

hab·i·tus /ˈhabitəs/ ▸*n. chiefly Medicine & Psychology* general constitution, esp. bodily build. ▷late 19th cent.: from Latin.

ha·boob /həˈbo͞ob/ ▸*n.* a violent and oppressive wind blowing in summer, esp. in Sudan, bringing sand from the desert. ▷late 19th cent.: from Arabic *habūb* 'blowing furiously.'

Habs·burg /ˈhapsbərg; ˈhäpsˌbo͝ork/ (also **Haps·burg**) one of the principal dynasties of central Europe from medieval to modern times.

The family established a hereditary monarchy in Austria in 1282 and secured the title of Holy Roman Emperor from 1452. Austrian and Spanish branches were created when Charles divided the territories between his son Philip II and his brother Ferdinand; the Habsburgs ruled Spain 1504–1700, while Habsburg rule in Austria ended with the collapse of Austria–Hungary in 1918.

ha·ček /ˈhaˌCHek/ (also **há·ček**) ▸*n.* a diacritic mark (ˇ) placed over a letter to indicate modification of the sound in Slavic and other languages. ▷Czech, diminutive of *hák* 'hook.'

ha·cen·da·do /ˌäsenˈdädō/ (also **ha·cien·da·do** /ˌäsyen-/) ▸*n.* (*pl.* **-dos**) the owner of a hacienda. ▷Spanish.

Ha·chi·o·ji /ˌhäCHēˈōjē/ an industrial city in east central Japan, on east central Honshu Island, west of Tokyo, noted for silk-weaving; pop. 466,000.

ha·chures /haˈSHo͝orz; ˈhaSHərz/ ▸*plural n.* short parallel lines used in hill-shading on maps, their closeness indicating steepness of gradient. ▷mid 19th cent.: from French, from *hacher* (see **HATCH**[3]). **—ha·chured** /haˈSHo͝ord; ˈhaSHərd/ *adj.*

ha·ci·en·da /ˌhäsēˈendə/ ▸*n.* (in Spanish-speaking regions) a large estate or plantation with a dwelling house. ■ the main house on such an estate. ▷Spanish, from Latin *facienda* 'things to be done,' from *facere* 'make, do' (see **FAZENDA**).

hack[1] /hak/ ▸*v.* **1** [*trans.*] cut with rough or heavy blows: ***hack off** the dead branches* | [*intrans.*] *a fishmonger **hacked at** it with a cleaver.* **2** [*intrans.*] use a computer to gain unauthorized access to data in a system: *they **hacked into** a bank's computer.* ■ [*trans.*] gain unauthorized access to (data in a computer): *hacking private information from computers.* **3** [usu. with *negative*] (**hack it**) *informal* manage; cope: *lots of people leave because they **can't hack it**.*
▸*phrasal v.* □ **hack around** pass one's time idly or with no definite purpose. □ **hack someone off** *informal* annoy or infuriate someone.
▸*n.* **1** a rough cut, blow, or stroke: *he was sure one of us was going to take a hack at him.* ■ (in sports) a kick or hit inflicted on another player. ■ a cut or gash. ■ a tool for rough striking or cutting, e.g., a mattock or a miner's pick. **2** *informal* an act of computer hacking. ■ a piece of computer code that performs some

Pronunciation Key ə *ago*; ər *over*; ˈə or ˌə *up*; ˈər or ˌər *fur*; a *hat*; ā *rate*; ä *car*; CH *chew*; e *let*; ē *see*; e(ə)r *air*; i *fit*; ī *by*; i(ə)r *ear*; NG *sing*; ō *go*; ô *for*; oi *boy*; o͝o *good*; o͞o *goo*; ou *out*; SH *she*; TH *thin*; TH *then*; (h)w *why*; ZH *vision*

function, esp. an unofficial alternative or addition to a commercial program: *freeware and shareware hacks.* ▷Old English *haccian* 'cut in pieces'; related to Dutch *hakken* and German *hacken.*

▸*PHRASE* □ **hacking cough** a short, dry, frequent cough.

hack[2] ▸*n.* **1** a writer or journalist producing dull, unoriginal work: [as *adj.*] *a hack scriptwriter.* ■ a person who does dull routine work. **2** a horse for ordinary riding. ■ a good-quality lightweight riding horse, esp. one used in the show ring. ■ a ride on a horse. ■ an inferior or worn-out horse. ■ a horse rented out for riding. **3** a taxicab.

▸*v.* [*intrans.*] [usu. as *n.*] (**hacking**) ride a horse for pleasure or exercise. ▷Middle English (sense 2): abbreviation of **HACKNEY**. Sense 1 dates from the late 17th cent. **—hack·er·y** /ˈhakərē/ *n.* (in sense 1)

hack[3] ▸*n.* **1** *Falconry* a board on which a hawk's meat is laid. **2** a wooden frame for drying bricks, cheeses, etc. ■ a pile of bricks stacked up to dry before firing. ▷late Middle English (denoting the lower half of a divided door): variant of **HATCH**[1].

▸*PHRASE* □ **at hack** (of a young hawk) given partial liberty but not yet allowed to hunt for itself.

hack·a·more /ˈhakəˌmôr/ ▸*n.* a bitless bridle that operates by exerting pressure on the horse's nose. ▷mid 19th cent.: perhaps from Spanish *jaquima*, earlier *xaquima* 'halter.'

hack·ber·ry /ˈhakˌberē/ ▸*n.* (*pl.* **-ries**) a tree of the elm family that has leaves resembling those of nettles, found in both tropical and temperate regions. See also **NETTLE TREE**. • Genus *Celtis*, family Ulmaceae: several species, in particular the **North American hackberry** (*C. occidentalis*), which bears edible purple berries and whose bark becomes ridged and covered with warty knobs. ■ the berry of this tree. ▷mid 18th cent.: variant of northern English dialect *hagberry*, of Scandinavian origin.

Hack·en·sack /ˈhakənˌsak/ a city in northeastern New Jersey, east of Paterson; pop. 37,049.

hack·er /ˈhakər/ ▸*n.* **1** *informal* an enthusiastic and skillful computer programmer or user. ■ a person who uses computers to gain unauthorized access to data. **2** a person or thing that hacks or cuts roughly. **3** a person who plays amateur sports without talent or skill: *for the weekend hacker, a set of basic golf clubs should suffice.*

hack·ette /haˈket/ ▸*n. Brit., informal, chiefly derogatory* a female journalist.

hack·ing jack·et ▸*n.* a riding jacket, often tweed, with a tight waist, flared skirt, slits at the side or back, and slanted pockets with flaps.

hack·le /ˈhakəl/ ▸*n.* **1** (**hackles**) erectile hairs along the back of a dog or other animal that rise when it is angry or alarmed. ■ the hairs on the back of a person's neck, thought of as being raised when the person is angry or hostile: *off-road vehicles have long* ***raised the hackles*** *of environmentalists.* **2** (often **hackles**) a long, narrow feather on the neck or saddle of a domestic rooster or other bird. ■ *Fishing* a feather wound around a fishing fly so that its filaments are splayed out. ■ such feathers collectively. ■ a bunch of feathers in a military headdress. **3** a steel comb for separating flax fibers.

▸*v.* [*trans.*] dress or comb with a hackle. ▷late Middle English (sense 2): variant of **HATCHEL**.

Hack·man /ˈhakmən/, Gene (1930–) U.S. actor. His notable movies include *The French Connection* (Academy Award, 1971), *Superman* (1978), *Mississippi Burning* (1988), and *Unforgiven* (Academy Award, 1992).

hack·ma·tack /ˈhakməˌtak/ ▸*n.* any of a number of North American coniferous trees, in particular the tamarack. ▷late 18th cent.: perhaps from Western Abnaki *akemantak* 'snowshoe-conifer.'

hack·ney /ˈhaknē/ ▸*n.* (*pl.* **-neys**) *historical* a horse or pony of a light breed with a high-stepping trot, used in harness. ■ [usu. as *adj.*] a horse-drawn vehicle kept for hire: *a hackney coach.* ▷Middle English: probably from *Hackney* in East London, England, where horses were pastured. The term originally denoted an ordinary riding horse (as opposed to a warhorse or draft horse), esp. one available for hire: hence *hackney carriage* or *coach*, and the verb *hackney* meaning 'use (a horse) for general purposes,' later 'make commonplace by overuse' (see **HACKNEYED**).

hack·ney car·riage ▸*n. Brit.* a taxicab.

hack·neyed /ˈhaknēd/ ▸*adj.* (of a phrase or idea) lacking significance through having been overused; unoriginal and trite: *hackneyed old sayings.*

hack·saw /ˈhakˌsô/ ▸*n.* a saw with a narrow fine-toothed blade set in a frame, used esp. for cutting metal.

▸*v.* (*past part.* **-sawn** or **-sawed**) [*trans.*] cut (something) using a hacksaw.

hack·tiv·ist /ˈhaktəˌvist/ ▸*n.* a computer hacker whose activity is aimed at promoting a social or political cause. ▷1990s: blend of *hacker* and *activist.* **—hack·tiv·ism** /-ˌvizəm/ *n.*

had /had/ ▸ past and past participle of **HAVE**.

ha·da·da /ˈhädəˌdä/ (**ha·da·da i·bis**) ▸*n.* a large gray-brown African ibis with iridescent patches on the wings and a loud, harsh call. • *Bostrychia* (or **Hagedashia**) *hagedash*, family Threskiornithidae. ▷late 18th cent.: imitative of its call.

ha·dal /ˈhādl/ ▸*adj.* of or relating to the zone of the sea greater than approximately 20,000 feet (6,000 m) in depth (chiefly oceanic trenches). ▷mid 20th cent.: from **HADES** + **-AL**.

had·da /ˈhadə/ *informal* ▸*contraction of* had to.

had·dock /ˈhadək/ ▸*n.* (*pl.* same) a silvery-gray bottom-dwelling fish of North Atlantic coastal waters, related to the cod. It is popular as a food fish and is of great commercial value. • *Melanogrammus aeglefinus*, family Gadidae. ▷Middle English: from Anglo-Norman French *hadoc*, from Old French *hadot*, of unknown origin.

hade /hād/ *Geology* ▸*n.* the inclination of a mineral vein or fault from the vertical.

▸*v.* [*intrans.*] (of a shaft, vein, or fault) incline from the vertical: *it was hading eighteen inches for every fathom in depth.* ▷late 17th cent.: perhaps a dialect form of the verb **HEAD**.

Ha·des /ˈhādēz/ *Greek Mythology* the underworld; the abode of the spirits of the dead. ■ the god of the underworld, one of the sons of Cronus. Roman equivalent **PLUTO**. ▷from Greek *Haidēs*, of unknown origin. **—Ha·de·an** /ˈhādēən/ *adj.*

Ha·dith /həˈdēᴛʜ/ ▸*n.* (*pl.* same or **-diths**) a collection of traditions containing sayings of the prophet Muhammad that, with accounts of his daily practice (the Sunna), constitute the major source of guidance for Muslims apart from the Koran. ■ one of these sayings. ▷from Arabic *ḥadīṯ* 'tradition.'

hadj ▸*n.* variant spelling of **HAJJ**.

hadj·i ▸*n.* variant spelling of **HAJI**.

Had·ley cell /ˈhadlē / ▸*n. Meteorology* a large-scale atmospheric convection cell in which air rises at the equator and sinks at medium latitudes, typically about 30° north or south. ▷1950s: named after George *Hadley* (1685–1768), English scientific writer.

had·n't /ˈhadnt/ ▸*contraction of* had not.

Ha·dri·an /ˈhādrēən/ (AD 76–138), Roman emperor 117–138; full name *Publius Aelius Hadrianus.* The adopted successor of Trajan, he toured the provinces of the empire and secured the frontiers.

Ha·dri·an's Wall /ˈhādrēənz / a Roman defensive wall across northern England, stretching from the Solway Firth in the west to the mouth of the Tyne River in the east (about 74 miles; 120 km). It was begun in AD 122, after the emperor Hadrian's visit, to defend the province of Britain against invasions by tribes from the north.

had·ron /ˈhadˌrän/ ▸*n. Physics* a subatomic particle of a type including the baryons and mesons that can take part in the strong interaction. ▷1960s: from Greek *hadros* 'bulky' + **-ON**. **—ha·dron·ic** /hadˈränik/ *adj.*

had·ro·saur /ˈhadrəˌsôr/ (also **had·ro·sau·rus** /ˌhadrəˈsôrəs/) ▸*n.* a large, herbivorous, mainly bipedal dinosaur of the middle to late Cretaceous period, with jaws flattened like the bill of a duck. Also called **DUCK-BILLED DINOSAUR**. • Family Hadrosauridae, infraorder Ornithopoda, order Ornithischia. ▷late 19th cent.: from modern Latin *Hadrosaurus* (genus name), from Greek *hadros* 'thick, stout' + *sauros* 'lizard.' **—had·ro·sau·ri·an** *adj.*

hadst /hadst/ ▸ archaic second person singular past of **HAVE**.

haec·ce·i·ty /hakˈsēətē/ ▸*n. Philosophy* that property or quality of a thing by virtue of which it is unique or describable as "this (one)." ■ the property of being a unique and individual thing. ▷mid 17th cent.: from medieval Latin *haecceitas*, from Latin *haec*, feminine of *hic* 'this.'

Haeck·el /ˈhekəl/, Ernst Heinrich (1834–1919), German biologist and philosopher. He popularized Darwin's theories and saw evolution as providing a framework for describing the world, with the German Empire representing the highest evolved form of a civilized nation.

Hae·ju /ˈhīˈjo͞o/ an industrial port city in southwestern North Korea, on the Yellow Sea; pop. 195,000.

haem ▸*n.* British spelling of **HEME**.

hae·mag·glu·ti·na·tion, etc. ▸*n.* British spelling of **HEMAGGLUTINATION**, etc.

hae·mal ▸*adj.* British spelling of **HEMAL**.

haemato- ▸*comb. form* British spelling of **HEMATO-**.

-haemia ▸*comb. form chiefly Brit.* variant spelling of **-EMIA**.

haemo- ▸*comb. form* British spelling of **HEMO-**.

ha·fiz /ˈhäfiz/ ▸*n.* a Muslim who knows the Koran by heart. ▷Persian, from Arabic *ḥāfiẓ* 'guardian,' from *ḥafiẓa* 'guard, know by heart.'

haf·ni·um /ˈhafnēəm/ ▸*n.* the chemical element of atomic number 72, a hard silver-gray metal of the transition series, resembling and often occurring with zirconium. (Symbol: **Hf**) ▷1920s: modern Latin, from *Hafnia*, Latinized form of Danish *Havn*, former name of Copenhagen.

haft /haft/ ▸*n.* the handle of a knife, ax, or spear.

▸*v.* [*trans.*] [often as *adj.*] (**hafted**) provide (a blade, ax head, or spearhead) with a haft. ▷Old English *hæft*, of Germanic origin: related to Dutch *heft, hecht* and German *Heft*, also to **HEAVE**.

Haf·to·rah /ˌhäftäˈrä; häfˈtôrə/ (also **Haph·ta·rah** or **Haph·to·rah**) ▸*n.* (*pl.* **-to·roth** /-täˈrôt, -ˈtôrōs/) *Judaism* a short reading from the Prophets that follows the reading from the Law in a synagogue. ▷from Hebrew *hapṭārāh* 'dismissal.'

hag[1] /hag/ ▸*n.* **1** a witch, esp. one in the form of an ugly old woman (often used as a term of disparagement for a woman): *a fat* ***old hag*** *in a dirty apron.* **2** short for **HAGFISH**. ▷Middle English: perhaps from Old English *hægtesse, hegtes*, related to Dutch *heks* and German *Hexe* 'witch,' of unknown ultimate origin. **—hag·gish** *adj.*

hag[2] ▸*n. Scottish & N. English* **1** (also **peat hag**) an overhang of peat. **2** a soft place on a moor or a firm place in a bog. ▷Middle English (denoting a gap in a cliff): from Old Norse *hǫgg* 'gap,' from *hǫggva* 'hack, hew.'

Hag. ▸*abbr. Bible* Haggai.

Ha·gar /ˈhägər/ (in the Bible and in Islamic tradition) the mother of Ishmael (Ismail), son of Abraham.

Ha·gen /ˈhägən/ an industrial city in northwestern Germany, in North Rhine-Westphalia; pop. 214,000.

Ha·gers·town /ˈhägərzˌtoun/ a city in northwestern Maryland; pop. 36,687.

hag·fish /ˈhagˌfisʜ/ ▸*n.* (*pl.* same or **-fish·es**) a primitive jawless marine vertebrate distantly related to the lampreys, with a slimy eellike body, a slitlike mouth surrounded by barbels, and a rasping tongue used for feeding on dead or dying fish. • Class Myxini and family Myxinidae: several genera, in particular *Myxine*, and numerous species. ▷early 17th cent.: from **HAG**[1] + **FISH**[1].

Hag·ga·dah /hägäˈdä; həˈgädə/ (also **Ag·ga·dah** /ägäˈdä; əˈgädə/) ▸*n.* (*pl.* **-doth** or **-dot** /-ˈdôt/) *Judaism* **1** the text recited at the Seder on the first two nights of the Jewish Passover, including a narrative of the Exodus. **2** a legend, parable, or anecdote used to illustrate a point of the Law in the Talmud. ■ this (nonlegal) element of the Talmud. Compare with **HALACHA**. ▷mid 18th cent.: from Hebrew *Haggāḏāh* 'tale, parable,' from *higgīḏ* 'tell, expound.' **—Hag·gad·ic** /həˈgädik/ *adj.* **—Hag·ga·dist** /həˈgädist/ *n.*

Hag·gai /ˈhagēˌī; ˈhagī/ a Hebrew minor prophet of the 6th century BC. ■ a book of the Bible containing his prophecies of a glorious future in the Messianic age.

hag·gard /ˈhagərd/ ▸*adj.* **1** looking exhausted and unwell, esp. from fatigue, worry, or suffering: *I trailed on behind, haggard and disheveled.* **2** (of a hawk) caught for training as a wild adult of more than twelve months. Compare with **PASSAGE HAWK**.

▸*n.* a haggard hawk. ▷mid 16th cent. (used in falconry): from French *hagard*; perhaps related to **HEDGE**; later influenced by **HAG**[1]. **—hag·gard·ly** *adv.* **—hag·gard·ness** *n.*

hag·gis /ˈhagis/ ▸*n.* (*pl.* same) a Scottish dish consisting of a sheep's or calf's offal mixed with suet, oatmeal, and seasoning and boiled in a bag, traditionally one made from the animal's stomach. ▷late Middle English: probably from earlier *hag* 'hack, hew,' from Old Norse *hǫggva.*

hag·gle /ˈhagəl/ ▸*v.* [*intrans.*] dispute or bargain persistently, esp. over the cost of something: *the two sides are* ***haggling over*** *television rights.*

▸*n.* a period of such bargaining. ▷late 16th cent. (in the sense 'hack, mangle'): from Old Norse *hǫggva* 'hew.' **—hag·gler** /ˈhaglər/ *n.*

hagio- ▸*comb. form* relating to saints or holiness: *hagiographer.* ▷from Greek *hagios* 'holy.'

Hag·i·og·ra·pha /ˌhagēˈägrəfə; ˌhägē-/ ▸*plural n.* the books of the Bible comprising the last of the three major divisions of the Hebrew scriptures, other than the Law and the Prophets. The books of the Hagiographa are: Ruth, Psalms, Job, Proverbs, Ecclesiastes, Song of Solomon, Lamentations, Daniel, Esther, Ezra, Nehemiah, and Chronicles. Also called THE WRITINGS (see WRITING). ▷via late Latin from Greek.

hag·i·og·ra·pher /ˌhagēˈägrəfər; ˌhāgē-/ ▶*n.* **1** a writer of the lives of the saints. ■ *derogatory* a person who writes in an adulatory way about someone else, esp. in a biography. **2** *Theology* a writer of any of the Hagiographa.

hag·i·og·ra·phy /ˌhagēˈägrəfē; ˌhāgē-/ ▶*n.* the writing of the lives of saints. ■ *derogatory* adulatory writing about another person. ■ a biography idealizing its subject. **—hag·i·o·graph·ic** /ˌhagēəˈgrafik; ˌhāgēə-/ *adj.* **—hag·i·o·graph·i·cal** /ˌhagēəˈgrafəkəl; ˌhāgēə-/ *adj.*

hag·i·ol·a·try /ˌhagēˈälətrē; ˌhāgē-/ ▶*n.* the worship of saints. ■ *derogatory* undue veneration of a famous person.

hag·i·ol·o·gy /ˌhagēˈäləjē; ˌhāgē-/ ▶*n.* literature dealing with the lives and legends of saints. **—hag·i·o·log·i·cal** /ˌhagēəˈläjəkəl; ˌhāgēə-/ *adj.* **—hag·i·ol·o·gist** /-jist/ *n.*

hag·i·o·scope /ˈhagēəˌskōp; ˈhāgēə-/ ▶*n.* another term for SQUINT (sense 3).

hag·rid·den /ˈhagˌridn/ ▶*adj.* afflicted by nightmares or anxieties: *it once made parents and doctors hagridden.*

Hague /hāg/ **(The Hague)** the seat of government and administrative center of the Netherlands, on the North Sea coast, capital of the province of South Holland; pop. 444,000. The International Court of Justice is based here. Dutch name **DEN HAAG**; also called **'s-GRAVENHAGE**.

hah ▶*exclam.* variant spelling of HA[1].

ha-ha /ˈhä ˌhä; ˌhä ˈhä/ ▶*n.* a ditch with a wall on its inner side below ground level, forming a boundary to a park or garden without interrupting the view. ▷early 18th cent.: from French, said to be from the cry of surprise on suddenly encountering such an obstacle.

ha ha ▶*exclam.* used to represent laughter or amusement. ▷natural utterance: first recorded in Old English (compare with HA[1]).

ha·ham /ˈhähəm/ ▶*n.* variant spelling of CHACHAM.

Hahn /hän/, Otto (1879–1968), German chemist, codiscoverer of nuclear fission. Together with Lise Meitner, he discovered the element protactinium in 1917. The pair discovered nuclear fission in 1938 with **Fritz Strassmann** (1902–80). Nobel Prize for Chemistry (1944, shared with Strassmann).

hahn·i·um /ˈhänēəm/ ▶*n.* the name formerly proposed by the American Chemical Society for the chemical element of atomic number 105 (**dubnium**), and by IUPAC for element 108 (**hassium**). ▷1970s: named in honor of O. **HAHN**.

Hai·da /ˈhīdə/ ▶*n.* (*pl.* same or **-das**) **1** a member of an American Indian people of coastal British Colombia and southeastern Alaska. **2** the language of this people, of unknown affinity.
▶*adj.* of or relating to this people or their language. ▷mid 19th cent.: the name in Haida, literally 'people.'

Hai·fa /ˈhīfə/ the chief port in Israel, in the northwestern part of the country, on the Mediterranean coast; pop. 248,000.

Haight-Ash·bury /ˈhāt ˈashˌberē/ a residential and commercial section of central San Francisco in California, associated with youth culture of the 1960s.

haik /hīk/ (also **haick**) ▶*n.* a large outer wrap, typically white, worn by people from North Africa. ▷early 18th cent.: from Arabic *ḥā'ik*.

Hai·kou /ˈhīˈkō/ the capital of Hainan autonomous region, a port on the northeastern coast of Hainan island; pop. 280,000.

hai·ku /ˈhīˌko͞o; ˌhīˈko͞o/ ▶*n.* (*pl.* same or **-kus**) a Japanese poem of seventeen syllables, in three lines of five, seven, and five, traditionally evoking images of the natural world. ■ an English imitation of this. ▷Japanese, contracted form of *haikai no ku* 'light verse.'

hail[1] /hāl/ ▶*n.* pellets of frozen rain that fall in showers from cumulonimbus clouds. ■ [in *sing.*] a large number of things hurled forcefully through the air, esp. with intent to harm: *a hail of bullets.*
▶*v.* [*intrans.*] **(it hails, it is hailing,** etc.) hail falls: *it hailed so hard we had to stop.* ▷Old English *hagol, hægl* (noun), *hagalian* (verb), of Germanic origin; related to Dutch *hagel* and German *Hagel.*

hail[2] ▶*v.* **1** [*trans.*] call out to (someone) to attract attention: *the crew hailed a fishing boat.* ■ signal (an approaching taxicab) to stop: *she raised her hand to hail a cab.* **2** [*trans.*] (often **be hailed**) acclaim enthusiastically as being a specified thing: *he has been **hailed as** the new James Dean.* **3** [*intrans.*] **(hail from)** have one's home or origins in (a place): *he hails from Pittsburgh.*
▶*exclam. archaic* expressing greeting or acclaim: *hail, Caesar!*
▶*n.* a shout or call used to attract attention. ▷Middle English: from the obsolete adjective *hail* 'healthy' (occurring in greetings and toasts, such as *wæs hæil*: see WASSAIL), from Old Norse *heill*, related to HALE[1] and WHOLE. **—hail·er** *n.*
▶PHRASE □ **within hail** (or **within hailing distance**) at a distance within which someone may be called to; within earshot.

Ha'il /hīl/ (also **Hail; Hayel**) a city in northwestern Saudi Arabia, on the pilgrimage route from Iraq to Mecca; pop. 177,000.

Hai·le Se·las·sie /ˈhīlē səˈlasē/ (1892–1975), emperor of Ethiopia 1930–74; born *Tafari Makonnen.* In exile in Britain during the Italian occupation of Ethiopia 1936–41, he was restored to the throne by the Allies and ruled until he was deposed by a military coup.

hail-fel·low-well-met ▶*adj.* showing excessive familiarity: *Harold was accustomed to hail-fellow-well-met salesmen.*

Hail Mar·y ▶*n.* (*pl.* **Hail Ma·rys**) **1** a prayer to the Virgin Mary used chiefly by Roman Catholics, beginning with part of Luke 1:28. Also called **AVE MARIA**. ■ a recitation of such a devotional phrase or prayer: *muttering Hail Marys under her breath.* **2** [usu. as *adj.*] *Football* a desperation long pass to try to score late in the game, typically unsuccessful: *they beat the 49ers on a Hail Mary pass in the final seconds.* ■ any attempt with a small chance of success: *a Hail Mary plan.*

hail·stone /ˈhālˌstōn/ ▶*n.* a pellet of hail.

hail·storm /ˈhālˌstôrm/ ▶*n.* a storm of heavy hail.

Hai·nan /ˈhīˈnän/ an island in the South China Sea that forms an autonomous region of China; pop. 6,420,000; capital, Haikou.

Hai·naut /(h)āˈnō/ a province in southern Belgium; capital, Mons.

Hai·phong /ˈhīˈfông; -ˈfäng/ a port in northern Vietnam, on the Gulf of Tonkin, at the delta of the Red River; pop. 783,000.

hair /he(ə)r/ ▶*n.* **1** any of the fine threadlike strands growing from the skin of humans, mammals, and some other animals. ■ a similar strand growing from the epidermis of a plant, or forming part of a living cell. ■ **(a hair)** a very small quantity or extent: *his magic takes him a hair above the competition.* **2** such strands collectively, esp. those growing on a person's head: *a woman with shoulder-length fair hair* | [as *adj.*] *a hair salon.* ■ the styling or dressing of a person's hair: *hair and makeup by Terry.* ▷Old English *hǣr*, of Germanic origin; related to Dutch *haar* and German *Haar.* **—haired** *adj.* [in *combination*] *a curly-haired boy.* **—hair·less** *adj.* **—hair·like** *adj.*
▶PHRASES □ **hair of the dog** *informal* an alcoholic drink taken to cure a hangover. [from *hair of the dog that bit you*, formerly recommended as an efficacious remedy for the bite of a mad dog.] □ **a hair's breadth** a very small amount or margin: *you escaped death **by a hair's breadth**.* □ **in** (or **out of**) **someone's hair** *informal* annoying (or ceasing to annoy) someone: *I'm glad he's out of my hair.* □ **let one's hair down** *informal* behave in an uninhibited or relaxed manner: *let your hair down and just have some fun.* □ **make someone's hair stand on end** alarm or horrify someone. □ **not a hair out of place** (of a person) extremely neat and tidy in appearance. □ **not turn a hair** remain apparently unmoved or unaffected: *the old woman didn't turn a hair; she just sat quietly rocking.* □ **put hair on one's chest** *informal* (of an alcoholic drink) be very strong. □ **split hairs** make small and overfine distinctions.

hair·band /ˈhe(ə)rˌband/ ▶*n.* a band for securing or tying back one's hair.

hair·breadth /ˈhe(ə)rˌbre(d)th/ ▶*n.* see A HAIR'S BREADTH at HAIR.

hair·brush /ˈhe(ə)rˌbrəsh/ ▶*n.* a brush for arranging or smoothing a person's hair.

hair·cloth /ˈhe(ə)rˌklôth/ ▶*n.* stiff cloth woven with a cotton or linen warp and horsehair weft.

hair·cut /ˈheərˌkət/ ▶*n.* **1** the style in which a person's hair is cut. ■ an act of cutting a person's hair. **2** a reduction in the stated value of an asset in order to determine the collateral or market value. **3** the amount, usually a percentage, by which an asset is reduced: *what is the haircut on Foreign Denominated Securities Positions for the Euro?* ■ any ad hoc reduction in value: *if you paid in dollars, they were going to give you a haircut of about 20 percent.*

hair·do /ˈhe(ə)rˌdo͞o/ ▶*n.* (*pl.* **-dos**) *informal* the style of a person's hair. ■ an act of styling a person's hair (used esp. of a woman's hair).

hair·dress·er /ˈhe(ə)rˌdresər/ ▶*n.* a person who cuts and styles hair as an occupation. **—hair·dress·ing** /-ˌdresing/ *n.*

hair dry·er (also **hair dri·er**) ▶*n.* an electrical device for drying a person's hair by blowing warm air over it.

hair grass (also **hair-grass**) ▶*n.* a slender-stemmed grass of temperate and cool regions. • *Deschampsia, Aira,* and other genera, family Gramineae.

hair·line /ˈhe(ə)rˌlīn/ ▶*n.* **1** the edge of a person's hair, esp. on the forehead. **2** a very thin or fine line: *the boards fitted so tightly together, there was only a hairline between them* | [as *adj.*] *a hairline fracture.*

hair·net /ˈhe(ə)rˌnet/ ▶*n.* a piece of fine mesh fabric for confining the hair.

hair·piece /ˈhe(ə)rˌpēs/ ▶*n.* a quantity or switch of detached hair used to augment a person's natural hair.

hair·pin /ˈhe(ə)rˌpin/ ▶*n.* a U-shaped pin for fastening the hair. ■ a sharp U-shaped curve in a road.
▶*adj.* shaped like a hairpin; forming a U: *up the steep cliff along a slippery hairpin path.*

hair·rais·ing ▶*adj.* extremely alarming, astonishing, or frightening: *hair-raising adventures.* **—hair-rais·er** *n.*

hair shirt ▶*n.* a shirt of haircloth, formerly worn by penitents and ascetics.
▶*adj.* **(hair-shirt** or **hair-shirt·ed)** austere and self-sacrificing: *a hair-shirted existence advocated by ecofundamentalists.*

hair space ▶*n. Printing* a very thin space between letters or words.

hair·split·ting /ˈhe(ə)rˌspliting/ ▶*adj.* characterized by or fond of small and overfine distinctions: *legal experts have a particularly hairsplitting mentality.*
▶*n.* the action of making small and overfine distinctions; quibbling. **—hair·split·ter** /-ˌsplitər/ *n.*

hair spray (also **hair·spray**) /ˈhe(ə)rˌsprā/ ▶*n.* a solution sprayed onto a person's hair to keep it in place.

hair·spring /ˈhe(ə)rˌspring/ ▶*n.* a slender flat coiled spring regulating the movement of the balance wheel in a watch.

hair·streak /ˈhe(ə)rˌstrēk/ ▶*n.* a butterfly with a narrow streak or row of dots on the underside of the hind wing and a small taillike projection on the hind wing. • Many genera in the family Lycaenidae.

hair·style /ˈhe(ə)rˌstīl/ ▶*n.* a particular way in which a person's hair is cut or arranged.

hair·styl·ist /ˈhe(ə)rˌstīlist/ (also **hair styl·ist**) ▶*n.* a person who cuts and styles people's hair professionally. **—hair·styl·ing** /-ˌstīling/ *n.*

hair trig·ger ▶*n.* a trigger of a firearm set for release at the slightest pressure. ■ [as *adj.*] *figurative* liable to change suddenly and violently: *a hair-trigger temper.*

hair·weav·ing /ˈhe(ə)rˌwēving/ ▶*n.* the process of interweaving a hairpiece with one's own hair.

hair worm ▶*n.* another term for HORSEHAIR WORM.

hair·y /ˈhe(ə)rē/ ▶*adj.* **(hair·i·er, hair·i·est) 1** covered with hair, esp. thick or long hair: *a hairy chest.* ■ having a rough feel or appearance suggestive of coarse hair: *a hairy tweed coat and skirt.* **2** *informal* alarming and difficult: *we drove up yet another hairy mountain road.* **—hair·i·ly** /ˈhe(ə)rəlē/ *adv.* **—hair·i·ness** *n.*

Hai·ti /ˈhātē/ a country in the Caribbean Sea that occupies the western third of the island of Hispaniola; pop. 7,600,000; capital, Port-au-Prince; official languages, Haitian Creole and French.

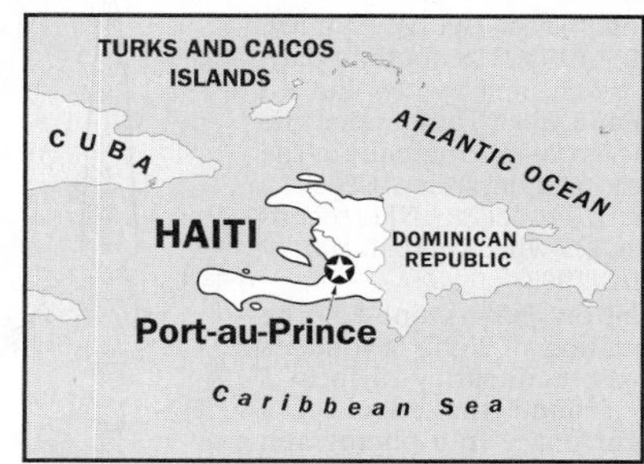

The area was ceded to France by Spain in 1697, and many slaves were imported from West Africa to work on sugar plantations. In 1791, the slaves rose in rebellion under Toussaint L'Ouverture, and the colony was proclaimed an independent state in 1804, under the name of Haiti. It was administered by the U.S. 1915–34 after a succession of corrupt dictatorships. Then, from 1957 until 1986, the country was under the oppressive dictatorship of the Duvalier family. Haiti's first democratically chosen president was elected in 1990 but was overthrown by the military the following year; democracy was restored by U.S. and UN intervention in 1994. Political upheaval occurred again in 2004, resulting in the ouster of the president. Haiti is the poorest country in the Western Hemisphere.

Hai·tian /'hāsHən/ ▸*adj.* of or relating to Haiti, its inhabitants, or their language.
▸*n.* **1** a native or inhabitant of Haiti. **2** (also **Haitian Creole**) the French-based Creole language spoken in Haiti.

Hai·tink /'hī,tiNGk/, Bernard (Johann Herman) (1929–), Dutch musical director and orchestra conductor.

haj·i /'hajē/ (also **haj·ji** or **had·ji**) ▸*n.* (*pl.* **haj·is**) a Muslim who has been to Mecca as a pilgrim: [as *title*] *Haji Hadi.* ▷from Persian and Turkish *hājjī*, *hājī*, from Arabic *ḥajj* (see **HAJJ**).

hajj /haj/ (also **haj** or **hadj**) ▸*n.* the Muslim pilgrimage to Mecca that takes place in the last month of the year, and that all Muslims are expected to make at least once during their lifetime. ▷from Arabic *(al-) ḥajj* '(the Great) Pilgrimage.'

ha·ka·ma /'hakəmə/ ▸*n.* [treated as *sing.* or *pl.*] loose trousers with many pleats in the front, forming part of Japanese formal dress. ▷mid 19th cent.: Japanese.

hake /hāk/ (*pl.* same or **hakes**) ▸*n.* **1** a large-headed elongated fish with long jaws and strong teeth. It is a valuable commercial food fish. • Family Merlucciidae and genus *Merluccius*: several species. **2** any of a number of similar fishes related to the true hakes. • Species in several families, esp. in the northwestern Atlantic genus *Urophycis* (family Phycidae). ▷Middle English: perhaps from Old English *haca* 'hook.'

ha·kim /hə'kēm/ ▸*n.* **1** a physician using traditional remedies in India and Muslim countries. [from Arabic *ḥakīm* 'wise man, physician.'] **2** a judge, ruler, or governor in India and Muslim countries. [from Arabic *ḥākim* 'ruler.']

Hak·ka /'häkə/ ▸*n.* **1** a member of a people of southeastern China, esp. Canton, Taiwan, and Hong Kong, who migrated from the north during the 12th century. **2** the dialect of Chinese spoken by this people.
▸*adj.* of or relating to this people or their language. ▷from Chinese (Cantonese dialect) *haàk ka* 'stranger.'

H

Ha·ko·da·te /,häkō'dätā/ a port in northern Japan, on the southern tip of the island of Hokkaido; pop. 307,000.

Ha·la·cha /,hälä'KHä; hälô'KHə/ (also **Ha·la·kah**) ▸*n.* Jewish law and jurisprudence, based on the Talmud. ▷from Hebrew *hălāḵāh* 'law.' —**Ha·la·chic** /hə'läKHik; hə'lakik/ *adj.*

ha·lal /hə'läl; hə'lal/ ▸*adj.* denoting or relating to meat prepared as prescribed by Muslim law: *halal butchers.* ■ religiously acceptable according to Muslim law: *halal banking.*
▸*n.* halal meat. ▷mid 19th cent.: from Arabic *ḥalāl* 'according to religious law.'

ha·la·la /hə'lälə/ ▸*n.* (*pl.* same or **-las**) a monetary unit of Saudi Arabia, equal to one hundredth of a riyal. ▷Arabic.

Hal·as /'haləs/, George (Stanley) (1895–1983), U.S. football player, coach, and owner; known as **Papa Bear**. He founded the Chicago Bears (originally as the Decatur Staleys) in 1920. As a coach, he set an NFL record with 325 wins. Football Hall of Fame (1963).

ha·la·tion /hā'lāsHən/ ▸*n.* the spreading of light beyond its proper boundaries to form a fog around the edges of a bright image in a photograph or on a television screen. ▷mid 19th cent.: formed irregularly from **HALO** + **-ATION**.

halberd

hal·berd /'halbərd; 'hôl-/ (also **hal·bert** /-bərt/) ▸*n.* *historical* a combined spear and battle-ax. ▷late 15th cent.: from French *hallebarde*, from Italian *alabarda*, from Middle High German *helmbarde* (from *helm* 'handle' + *barde* 'hatchet').

hal·berd·ier /,halbər'dir; ,hôlbər-/ ▸*n.* *historical* a man armed with a halberd. ▷early 16th cent.: from French *hallebardier*, from *hallebarde* (see **HALBERD**).

hal·cy·on /'halsēən/ ▸*adj.* denoting a period of time in the past that was idyllically happy and peaceful: *the halcyon days of the mid-1980s, when profits were soaring.* See note at **CALM**.
▸*n.* **1** a tropical Asian and African kingfisher with brightly colored plumage. • Genus *Halcyon*, family Alcedinidae: many species. **2** a mythical bird said by ancient writers to breed in a nest floating at sea at the winter solstice, charming the wind and waves into calm. ▷late Middle English (in the mythological sense): via Latin from Greek *alkuōn* 'kingfisher' (also *halkuōn*, by association with *hals* 'sea' and *kuōn* 'conceiving').

Hale[1] /hāl/, Edward Everett (1822–1909), U.S. clergyman, writer, and philanthropist. A Unitarian minister, he wrote the story "A Man Without a Country" (1863).

Hale[2], George Ellery (1868–1938), U.S. astronomer. He discovered that sunspots are associated with strong magnetic fields and invented the spectroheliograph. He also initiated the construction of the 200-inch (5-meter) Hale reflector at Mount Palomar in California.

Hale[3], Nathan (1755–76), American hero. He volunteered in 1776 during the American Revolution to spy behind British lines on Long Island. Disguised as a schoolmaster, he was captured by the British and hanged without trial. His last words are said to have been, "I only regret that I have but one life to lose for my country."

hale[1] /hāl/ ▸*adj.* (of a person, esp. an elderly one) strong and healthy: *only just sixty, very* **hale and hearty**. ▷Old English, variant of *hāl* 'whole.'

hale[2] ▸*v.* [*trans.*] *archaic* drag or draw forcibly: *he haled an old man out of the audience.* ▷Middle English: from Old French *haler*, from Old Norse *hala*.

Ha·le·a·ka·la /,hälä,äkə'lä/ a dormant volcano on eastern Maui in Hawaii.

Hale–Bopp /'hāl'bäp/ a periodic comet that passed close to the sun in the spring of 1997 and was one of the brightest of the 20th century. ▷named after Alan *Hale* and Thomas *Bopp*, the American astronomers who discovered it (independently of each other).

ha·ler /'hälər/ ▸*n.* (*pl.* same or **-le·ru** /-lə,ro͞o/) a monetary unit of the Czech Republic and Slovakia, equal to one hundredth of a koruna. ▷from Czech *haléř*, from Middle High German *haller*, from *Schwäbisch Hall*, a town in Germany where coins were minted.

Ha·ley[1] /'hālē/, Alex(ander Murray Palmer) (1921–92) U.S. writer. His best-selling work *Roots: The Saga of an American Family* (1976) chronicled the ancestors of his African-American family. The book and subsequent television miniseries in 1977 each won a Pulitzer Prize. He also wrote *The Autobiography of Malcolm X* (1965) and *Queen* (published posthumously, 1993).

Ha·ley[2], Bill (1925–81), U.S. rock-and-roll singer; full name *William John Clifton Haley*. His song, "Rock Around the Clock" (1954), helped to establish the popularity of rock and roll.

half /haf/ ▸*n.* (*pl.* **halves** /havz/) either of two equal or corresponding parts into which something is or can be divided: *the northern half of the island* | *two and a half years* | *divided* **in half** | *reduced* **by half**. ■ either of two equal periods of time into which a sports game or a performance is divided. ■ *Baseball* either of the two parts of one inning: *the top half of the third.* ■ *Golf* a score for an individual hole that is the same as one's opponent's. ■ short for **HALFBACK**.
▸*predeterminer, pron.* & *adj.* an amount equal to a half: [as *predeterminer*] *half an hour* | *almost half the children turned up* | [as *pron.*] **half of** *the lectures are delivered by him* | [as *adj.*] *the last half century.* ■ amounting to a part thought of as roughly a half: [as *predeterminer*] *half the letters were sent first class* | [as *pron.*] **half of** *them are gate-crashers.*
▸*adv.* to the extent of half: *the glass was half full.* ■ [often in *combination*] to a certain extent; partly: *the chicken is half-cooked.* ▷Old English *half*, *healf*, of Germanic origin; related to Dutch *half* and German *halb* (adjectives). The earliest meaning of the Germanic base was 'side,' also a noun sense in Old English.
▸*PHRASES* □ **a —— and a half** *informal* used to indicate that one considers a particular person or thing to be an impressive example of their kind: *Aunt Edie was a woman and a half.* □ **at half cock** see **HALF COCK**. □ **go halves** share something equally: *she promised to* **go halves with** *him.* □ **half the battle** see **BATTLE**. □ **half a chance** *informal* the slightest opportunity: *given half a chance, he can make anything work.* □ **half an eye** see **EYE**. □ **the half of it** [usu. with *negative*] *informal* the most important part or aspect of something: *you don't know the half of it.* □ **half past one** (**two**, etc.) thirty minutes after one (two, etc.) o'clock. □ **half the time** see **TIME**. □ **not do things by halves** do things thoroughly or extravagantly. □ **not half 1** not nearly: *he is not half such a fool as they thought.* **2** *informal* not at all: *the players are not half bad.* □ **too —— by half** used to emphasize something bad: *the idea seems too superstitious by half.*

half a doz·en ▸*n.* another term for **HALF-DOZEN**.

half-and-half ▸*adv.* & *adj.* in equal parts: [as *adv.*] *views were split almost exactly half-and-half* | [as *adj.*] *a half-and-half mixture.*
▸*n.* a mixture of milk and cream. ■ a mixture of equal parts of beer and stout or of ale and porter.

half-assed (also **half-ass**, *Brit.* **half-arsed**) ▸*adj.* *vulgar slang* (of a completed task) inadequate; poorly done. ■ (of a person) incompetent.

half·back /'haf,bak/ ▸*n.* *Football* an offensive back usually positioned behind the quarterback and to the side of the fullback. ■ a usually defensive player in a ball game such as soccer or field hockey whose position is between the line or the forward.

half-baked ▸*adj.* (of an idea or philosophy) not fully thought through; lacking a sound basis: *half-baked notions of Teutonic superiority.* ■ foolish: *half-baked visionaries without a mission.*

half·beak /'haf,bēk/ ▸*n.* a slender shoaling fish of coastal areas, with small pectoral fins and the lower jaw lengthened into a beak. It is related to the flying fishes and often skitters along the surface. • Several genera and species in the family Exocoetidae, including the widely distributed *Euleptorhamphus viridis*.

half bind·ing ▸*n.* a type of bookbinding in which the spine and corners are bound in one material (typically leather) and the rest of the cover in another. —**half-bound** *adj.*

half blood ▸*n.* **1** *dated* the relationship between people having one parent in common: *brothers and sisters of the half blood.* ■ a person related to another in this way. **2** (**half-blood**) *offensive* another term for **HALF-BREED**. —**half-blood·ed** *adj.* (in sense 2).

half boot ▸*n.* a boot that reaches up to the calf.

half-bot·tle ▸*n.* a bottle that is half the standard size.

half-bred ▸*adj.* (of an animal) having only one purebred parent.
▸*n.* an animal of this kind.

half-breed ▸*n.* *offensive* a person whose parents are of different races, esp. the offspring of an American Indian and a person of white European ancestry.
▸*adj.* denoting a person of such ancestry.

half-broth·er (also **half broth·er**) ▸*n.* a brother with whom one has only one parent in common.

half-caste ▸*n.* *offensive* a person whose parents are of different races, in particular, with a European father and an Indian mother.
▸*adj.* denoting such a person.

half cock ▸*n.* the partly raised position of the cock of a gun.

half-cocked ▸*adj.* (of a gun) with the cock partly raised.
▸*adv.* *figurative* when only partly ready; prematurely: *not* **going off half-cocked** *and selling the company.*

half crown (also **half-crown** or **half a crown**) ▸*n.* a former British coin and monetary unit equal to two shillings and sixpence.

half-cut ▸*adj.* *Brit.*, *informal* drunk.

half deck ▸*n.* a deck reaching half the length of a ship or boat, fore or aft. —**half-decked** *adj.*

half dol·lar (also **half-dol·lar**) ▸*n.* a U.S. or Canadian coin worth fifty cents. ■ the sum of fifty cents.

half-door ▸*n.* a door of half the usual size, typically covering the bottom half of an opening (e.g., in a stable).

half-doz·en (also **half a dozen**) ▸*n.* a set or group of six: *a half-dozen slices of smoked salmon.* ■ *informal* approximately six.

half-du·plex ▸*adj.* (of a communications system or computer circuit) allowing the transmission of signals in both directions but not simultaneously.

half gai·ner /'gānər/ ▸*n.* a dive in which the diver leaves the diving board facing forward, does a half-somersault backward, and enters the water head first facing the board.

half-har·dy ▸*adj. chiefly Brit.* (of a plant) able to grow outdoors at all times except in severe frost: *a half-hardy annual.*

half·heart·ed /ˈhafˈhärtid/ ▸*adj.* without enthusiasm or energy: *after two years of halfhearted effort, he dropped out of school.* **—half·heart·ed·ly** *adv.* **—half·heart·ed·ness** *n.*

half hitch ▸*n.* a knot formed by passing the end of a rope around its standing part and then through the loop, often used in pairs: *the rope was tied with two half hitches to a long tape.*

half hour ▸*n.* (also **half an hour**) a period of thirty minutes: *a slide show presented every half hour.* ■ a point in time thirty minutes after any full hour of the clock: *the library clock struck the half hour.* **—half-hour·ly** *adj.* & *adv.*

half-in·te·ger ▸*n.* a number obtained by dividing an odd integer by two (½, 1½, 2½, etc.). **—half-in·te·gral** *adj.*

half-land·ing ▸*n. Brit.* an area of floor approximately halfway up a flight of stairs, typically where it turns a corner.

half-length ▸*adj.* of approximately half the normal length. ■ (of a painting or sculpture) showing a person down to the waist.
▸*n.* a painting or sculpture of a person down to the waist.

half-life ▸*n.* the time taken for the radioactivity of a specified isotope to fall to half its original value. ■ the time required for any specified property (e.g., the concentration of a substance in the body) to decrease by half.

half-light ▸*n.* dim light such as at dusk: *the trees had a slightly spooky look in the half-light.*

half-mast ▸*n.* the position of a flag that is being flown some way below the top of its staff as a mark of respect for a person who has died. ■ *chiefly humorous* a position lower than normal or acceptable, esp. for clothes: *the zipper on his fly always riding* ***at half-mast.***

half meas·ure ▸*n.* (usu. **half measures**) an action or policy that is not forceful or decisive enough: *there are* ***no half measures*** *with this company.*

half-moon ▸*n.* the moon when only half of its illuminated surface is visible from the earth; the first or last quarter. ■ the time when this occurs. ■ a semicircular or crescent-shaped object: [as *adj.*] *half-moon spectacles.*

half-move ▸*n. Chess* a move made by one player (esp. in the context of the analysis of play made by a chess-playing computer program).

half nel·son ▸*n.* see **NELSON**.

half note (*Brit.* **min·im**) ▸*n. Music* a note having the time value of two quarter notes or half of a whole note, represented by a ring with a stem.

half pay ▸*n.* half of a person's normal or previous salary or wages: *a sabbatical year during which he would receive half pay from Fordham University.*

half·pen·ny /ˈhāp(ə)nē; ˈhafˌpenē/ (also **ha'pen·ny**) ▸*n.* (*pl.* for separate coins **-pen·nies**, for a sum of money **-pence** /-pəns/) a former British coin equal to half an old or new penny. The last halfpenny was withdrawn in 1984.

half·pen·ny·worth /ˈhāpniˌwərTH; ˈhafˌpenē-/ (also **ha'p'orth**) ▸*n. Brit.* as much as could be bought for a halfpenny. ■ [usu. with *negative*] (**ha'p'orth**) *informal* a negligible amount: *he's never been a ha'p'orth of bother.*

half pint (also **half-pint**) ▸*n.* **1** half of a pint. **2** *informal* a small or insignificant person or animal.
▸*adj. informal* very small; diminutive.

half-pipe ▸*n.* a channel made of concrete or cut into the snow with a U-shaped cross section, used by skateboarders, rollerbladers, or snowboarders to perform jumps and other maneuvers.

half-price ▸*adj.* & *adv.* costing half the normal price: [as *adj.*] *half-price admission.*
▸*n.* half the usual price: *many shoes* ***at half price.***

half-round ▸*adj.* semicircular in cross section.

half seas o·ver ▸*adj.* [*predic.*] *Brit., informal* or *dated* fairly drunk.

half-sis·ter (also **half sis·ter**) ▸*n.* a sister with whom one has only one parent in common.

half sov·er·eign (also **half-sov·er·eign**) ▸*n.* a former British gold coin worth ten shillings.

half step ▸*n.* **1** *Music* a semitone. **2** a military marching pace approximately half the speed of the quick march.

half-test·er ▸*n. historical* a canopy extending over half the length of a bed. ■ a bed with such a canopy.

half-tim·bered ▸*adj.* having walls with a timber frame and a brick or plaster filling. **—half-tim·ber·ing** /ˈtimb(ə)riNG/ *n.*

half·time /ˈhafˌtīm/ ▸*n.* the time at which half of a game or contest is completed, esp. when marked by an intermission: *the most pressure he felt was at halftime when he looked up and saw the score* | [as *adj.*] *a Super Bowl halftime show.*

half ti·tle ▸*n.* the title of a book, printed on the right-hand page before the title page. ■ the title of a section of a book printed on the right-hand page before the section begins. ■ a page on which a title of either of these kinds is printed.

half·tone /ˈhafˌtōn/ ▸*n.* [usu. as *adj.*] a reproduction of a photograph or other image in which the various tones of gray or color are produced by variously sized dots of ink: *halftone illustrations.*

half-track ▸*n.* a military or other vehicle with wheels at the front and caterpillar tracks at the rear.

half-truth ▸*n.* a statement that conveys only part of the truth, esp. one used deliberately in order to deceive someone.

half-vol·ley ▸*n.* (in ball games, esp. tennis) a strike of the ball made immediately after it bounces off the ground.

half·way /ˈhafˈwā/ ▸*adv.* & *adj.* at or to a point equidistant between two others: [as *adv.*] *he stopped halfway down the passage* | [as *adj.*] *she reached the halfway point.* ■ in the middle of a period of time: [as *adv.*] *halfway through the night.* ■ [as *adv.*] to some extent: *I'm incapable of doing anything even halfway decent.*
▸PHRASE □ **meet someone halfway** compromise; concede some points in order to gain others: *I'm willing to compromise and meet him halfway.*

half·way house ▸*n.* a center for helping former drug addicts, prisoners, psychiatric patients, or others to adjust to life in general society. ■ the halfway point in a progression: *suspension of the talks was only a halfway house toward complete termination.* ■ *historical* an inn midway between two towns.

half·wit /ˈhafˌwit/ ▸*n. informal* a foolish or stupid person. **—half-wit·ted** *adj.* **—half-wit·ted·ly** *adv.* **—half-wit·ted·ness** *n.*

half-year·ly ▸*adj.* & *adv. chiefly Brit.* at intervals of six months.

hal·i·but /ˈhaləbət/ ▸*n.* (*pl.* same) a northern marine fish that is the largest of the flatfishes and important as a food fish. • Genus *Hippoglossus*, family Pleuronectidae: *H. hippoglossus* of the Atlantic and *H. stenolepis* of the Pacific. ▷late Middle English: from *haly* 'holy' + obsolete *butt* 'flatfish' (because it was often eaten on holy days).

Ha·liç /häˈlēCH/ Turkish name of **GOLDEN HORN**.

Hal·i·car·nas·sus /ˌhaləˈkärnasəs/ an ancient Greek city on the southwestern coast of Asia Minor, at what is now the Turkish city of Bodrum. It is the site of the Mausoleum of Halicarnassus, one of the Seven Wonders of the World.

hal·ide /ˈhaˌlīd; ˈhā-/ ▸*n. Chemistry* a binary compound of a halogen with another element or group.

Hal·i·fax /ˈhaləˌfaks/ the capital of Nova Scotia, Canada; pop. 67,800 (1991). It is Canada's principal ice-free port on the Atlantic coast.

hal·ite /ˈhaˌlīt; ˈhāˌlīt/ ▸*n.* sodium chloride as a mineral, typically occurring as colorless cubic crystals; rock salt. ▷mid 19th cent.: from Greek *hals* 'salt' + **-ITE**[1].

hal·i·to·sis /ˌhaliˈtōsəs/ ▸*n.* technical term for **BAD BREATH**. ▷late 19th cent.: from Latin *halitus* 'breath' + **-OSIS**.

Hall[1] /hôl/, Diane see **KEATON**.

Hall[2], Gus (1910–2000) U.S. Communist Party leader; born *Arvo Custa Halberg.* He joined the Communist Party in the U.S. in 1934 and served as national secretary 1950–59 before becoming general secretary. He was the U.S. Communist Party's presidential candidate in four elections from 1972 to 1984.

Hall[3], Lyman (1724–90) American leader. He was a member of the Continental Congress 1775–78, 1780 and a signer of the Declaration of Independence in 1776.

hall /hôl/ ▸*n.* **1** an area in a building onto which rooms open; a corridor. ■ the room or space just inside the front entrance of a house or apartment: *an entrance hall.* **2** a large room for meetings, concerts, or other events: [in *names*] *Carnegie Hall.* ■ a large public room in a mansion or palace used for receptions and banquets. ■ *Brit.* the room used for meals in a college, university, or school: *he dined* ***in hall.*** ■ a college or university building containing classrooms, residences, or rooms for other purposes. ■ the principal living room of a medieval house. **3** [usu. in *names*] *Brit.* a large country house, esp. one with a landed estate: *Darlington Hall.* ▷Old English *hall, heall* (originally denoting a roofed space, located centrally, for the communal use of a tribal chief and his people); of Germanic origin and related to German *Halle*, Dutch *hall*, also to Norwegian and Swedish *hall.*

Hal·lan·dale /ˈhalənˌdāl/ a resort city in southeastern Florida, north of Miami; pop. 30,996.

Hal·le /ˈhälə/ a city in eastern central Germany, on the Saale River, in Saxony-Anhalt; pop. 303,000.

Hal·lé /ˈhälə/, Sir Charles (1819–95), German pianist and conductor; born *Karl Halle.* He founded the Hallé Orchestra 1858.

Hall ef·fect ▸*n. Physics* the production of a potential difference across an electrical conductor when a magnetic field is applied in a direction perpendicular to that of the flow of current. ▷early 20th cent.: named after Edwin H. Hall (1855–1938), American physicist.

Hal·lel /häˈlāl; ˈhäˌlāl/ ▸*n.* (usu. **the Hallel**) a portion of the service for certain Jewish festivals, consisting of Psalms 113–118: [as *adj.*] *the Hallel psalms.* ▷from Hebrew *hallēl* 'praise.'

hal·le·lu·jah /ˌhaləˈlo͞oyə/ (also **al·le·lu·ia**) ▸*exclam.* God be praised (uttered in worship or as an expression of rejoicing): *He is risen! Alleluia!*
▸*n.* an utterance of the word "hallelujah" as an expression of worship or rejoicing. ■ (usu. **alleluia**) a piece of music or church liturgy containing this: *the Gospel comes after the Alleluia verse.* ▷Old English, via ecclesiastical Latin *alleluia* from Greek *allēlouia* (in the Septuagint), or (from the 16th century) directly from Hebrew *hallĕlūyāh* 'praise ye the Lord.'

Hal·ley /ˈhalē; ˈhā-/, Edmond (1656–1742), English astronomer and mathematician. He is best known for identifying a bright comet (later named after him) and for successfully predicting its return.

Hal·ley's Com·et /ˈhalēz; ˈhā-/ a periodical comet with an orbital period of about 76 years, its reappearance in 1758–59 having been predicted by Edmond Halley. It was first recorded in 240 BC and last appeared, rather faintly, in 1985–86.

Hal·li·day /ˈhaləˌdā/, Michael Alexander Kirkwood (1925–), English linguist.

hall·mark /ˈhôlˌmärk/ ▸*n.* a mark stamped on articles of gold, silver, or platinum in Britain, certifying their standard of purity. ■ a distinctive feature, esp. one of excellence: *the tiny bubbles are the hallmark of fine champagnes.*
▸*v.* [*trans.*] stamp with a hallmark. ■ designate as distinctive, esp. for excellence. ▷early 18th cent. (as a noun): from *Goldsmiths' Hall* in London, England, where articles were tested and stamped with such a mark.

hal·lo /həˈlō/ ▸*exclam., n.,* & *v.* variant spelling of **HELLO**. ■ variant of **HALLOO**.

hal·loa /həˈlō; ha-/ ▸*exclam., n., v.* variant of **HALLOO**.

Hall of Fame a national memorial in New York City containing busts and memorials honoring the achievements of famous Americans. ■ [as *n.*] a similar establishment commemorating the achievements of a particular group of people, esp. athletes in a specified sport: *he was inducted into the Hockey Hall of Fame.* **—Hall of Fam·er** *n.*

hal·loo /həˈlo͞o/ ▸*exclam.* used to attract someone's attention. ■ used to incite dogs to the chase during a hunt.
▸*n.* a cry of "halloo."
▸*v.* (**-loos, -looed**) [*intrans.*] cry or shout "halloo" to attract attention or to give encouragement to dogs in hunting. ■ [*trans.*] shout to (someone) to attract their attention. ▷mid 16th cent.: probably from the rare verb *hallow* 'pursue or urge on with shouts,' from imitative Old French *haloer.*

hal·lou·mi /häˈlo͞omē/ ▸*n.* a mild, firm, white Cypriot cheese made from goats' or ewes' milk, used especially in cooked dishes. ▷1990s: from Egyptian Arabic *ḥalūm*, probably from Arabic *ḥaluma* 'to be mild.'

hal·low /ˈhalō/ ▸*v.* [*trans.*] honor as holy: *the Ganges is hallowed as a sacred, cleansing river* | [as *adj.*] (**hallowed**) *hallowed ground.* ■ *formal* make holy; consecrate. ■ [as *adj.*] (**hallowed**) greatly revered or respected: *in keeping with a hallowed family tradition.*

▸*n. archaic* a saint or holy person. ▷Old English *hālgian* (verb), *hālga* (noun), of Germanic origin; related to Dutch and German *heiligen*, also to HOLY.

Hal·low·een /ˌhaləˈwēn; ˌhälə-; -ōˈēn/ (also **Hal·low·e'en**) ▸*n.* the night of October 31, the eve of All Saints' Day, commonly celebrated by children who dress in costume and solicit candy or other treats door-to-door. ▷late 18th cent.: contraction of *All Hallow Even* (see HALLOW, EVEN[2]).

Hall·statt /ˈhälˌsʜtät/ ▸*n.* [usu. as *adj.*] *Archaeology* a cultural phase of the late Bronze Age and early Iron Age in Europe (*c.*1200–600 BC in temperate continental areas), preceding the La Tène period and associated with the early Celts. ▷mid 19th cent.: the name of a village in Austria, site of a burial ground of this period.

hall tree ▸*n.* a coatrack in the hall of a house.

hal·lu·ces /ˈhal(y)əˌsēz/ ▸ plural form of HALLUX.

hal·lu·ci·nate /həˈlo͞osənˌāt/ ▸*v.* [*intrans.*] experience a seemingly real perception of something not actually present, typically as a result of a mental disorder or of taking drugs: *people sense themselves going mad and hallucinate about spiders.* ■ [*trans.*] experience a hallucination of (something): *I don't care if they're hallucinating purple snakes.* ▷mid 17th cent. (in the sense 'be deceived, have illusions'): from Latin *hallucinat-* 'gone astray in thought,' from the verb *hallucinari*, from Greek *alussein* 'be uneasy or distraught.' —**hal·lu·ci·nant** /-sənənt/ *adj.* & *n.* —**hal·lu·ci·na·tor** /-ˌātər/ *n.*

hal·lu·ci·na·tion /həˌlo͞osənˈāsʜən/ ▸*n.* an experience involving the apparent perception of something not present: *he continued to suffer from horrific hallucinations.*

hal·lu·ci·na·to·ry /həˈlo͞osənəˌtôrē/ ▸*adj.* of or resembling a hallucination: *a hallucinatory fantasy.* ■ inducing hallucinations: *a hallucinatory drug.*

hal·lu·ci·no·gen /həˈlo͞osənəˌjən/ ▸*n.* a drug that causes hallucinations, such as LSD. —**hal·lu·ci·no·gen·ic** /həˌlo͞osənəˈjenik/ *adj.*

hal·lux /ˈhaləks/ ▸*n.* (*pl.* **hal·lu·ces** /ˈhal(y)əˌsēz/) *Anatomy* a person's big toe. ■ *Zoology* the innermost digit of the hind foot of vertebrates. ▷mid 19th cent.: modern Latin alteration of medieval Latin *allex*, Latin *hallus*.

hall·way /ˈhôlˌwā/ ▸*n.* another term for HALL (sense 1).

ha·lo /ˈhālō/ ▸*n.* (*pl.* **-loes** or **-los**) a disk or circle of light shown surrounding or above the head of a saint or holy person to represent their holiness. ■ *figurative* the glory associated with an idealized person or thing: *he has long since lost his halo for many ordinary Russians.* ■ a circle or ring of something resembling a halo: *their frizzy haloes of hair.* ■ a circle of white or colored light around the sun, moon, or other luminous body caused by refraction through ice crystals in the atmosphere. ■ *Astronomy* a tenuous sphere of hot gas and old stars surrounding a spiral galaxy.
▸*v.* (**-loes, -loed**) [*trans.*] (usu. **be haloed**) surround with or as if with a halo. ▷mid 16th cent. (denoting a circle of light around the sun, etc.): from medieval Latin, from Latin *halos*, from Greek *halōs* 'disk of the sun or moon.'

halo- ▸*comb. form* **1** relating to salinity: *halophile.* [from Greek *hals, halo-* 'salt.'] **2** representing HALOGEN.

hal·o·car·bon /ˈhaləˌkärbən/ ▸*n. Chemistry* a chlorofluorocarbon or other compound in which the hydrogen of a hydrocarbon is replaced by halogens.

ha·lo ef·fect ▸*n.* the tendency for an impression created in one area to influence opinion in another area: *the convertible furnishes a sporty image and provides a halo effect for other cars in the showrooms.*

hal·o·form /ˈhaləˌfôrm/ ▸*n. Chemistry* a compound derived from methane by substituting three hydrogen atoms for halogen atoms, e.g., chloroform. ▷1930s: from HALOGEN, on the pattern of *chloroform*.

hal·o·gen /ˈhaləjən/ ▸*n. Chemistry* any of the elements fluorine, chlorine, bromine, iodine, and astatine, occupying group VIIA (17) of the periodic table. They are reactive nonmetallic elements that form strongly acidic compounds with hydrogen, from which simple salts can be made. ■ [as *adj.*] denoting lamps and radiant heat sources using a filament surrounded by the vapor of iodine or another halogen: *halogen headlights.* ▷mid 19th cent.: from Greek *hals, halo-* 'salt' + -GEN. —**hal·o·gen·ic** /ˌhaləˈjenik/ *adj.*

hal·o·gen·ate /ˈhaləjəˌnāt; haˈläjə-/ ▸*v.* [*trans.*] [usu. as *adj.*] (**halogenated**) *Chemistry* introduce one or more halogen atoms into (a compound or molecule), usually in place of hydrogen. —**hal·o·gen·a·tion** /ˌhaləjəˈnāsʜən; həˌläjə-/ *n.*

hal·on /ˈhāˌlän/ ▸*n.* any of a number of unreactive gaseous compounds of carbon with bromine and other halogens, used in fire extinguishers, but now known to damage the ozone layer. ▷1960s: from HALOGEN + -ON.

hal·o·per·i·dol /ˌhalōˈperəˌdôl; -däl/ ▸*n. Medicine* a synthetic antidepressant drug used chiefly in the treatment of psychotic conditions. ▷1960s: blend of HALOGEN and PIPERIDINE + -OL.

hal·o·phile /ˈhaləˌfīl/ ▸*n. Ecology* an organism, esp. a microorganism, that grows in or can tolerate saline conditions. —**hal·o·phil·ic** /ˌhaləˈfilik/ *adj.*

hal·o·phyte /ˈhaləˌfīt/ ▸*n. Botany* a plant adapted to growing in saline conditions, as in a salt marsh.

hal·o·thane /ˈhaləˌᴛʜān/ ▸*n. Medicine* a volatile synthetic organic compound used as a general anesthetic. • Chem. formula: $CF_3CHBrCl$. ▷1950s: blend of HALOGEN and ETHANE.

Hals /hälz/, Frans (*c.*1580–1666), Dutch portrait and genre painter. He endowed his portraits with vitality and humor. Notable works: *The Banquet of the Officers of the St. George Militia Company* (1616) and *The Laughing Cavalier* (1624).

Hal·sey /ˈhôlzē/, William Frederick (1882–1959) U.S. naval officer; known as **Bull**. He was commander of Allied naval forces in the South Pacific 1942–44 and of the U.S. Third Fleet 1944–45. He became a fleet admiral in 1945.

Häl·sing·borg /ˈhelsiɴɢˌbôr(yə)/ Swedish name of HELSINGBORG.

halt[1] /hôlt/ ▸*v.* bring or come to an abrupt stop: [*trans.*] *there is growing pressure to halt the bloodshed* | [*intrans.*] *she halted in mid-sentence.* ■ [in *imperative*] used as a military command to bring marching soldiers to a stop: *company, halt!*
▸*n.* a suspension of movement or activity, typically a temporary one: *a halt in production* | *a bus screeched* **to a halt**. ▷late 16th cent.: originally in the phrase *make halt*, from German *haltmachen*, from *halten* 'to hold.'
▸*PHRASE* □ **call a halt** demand or order a stop: *he decided to* **call a halt** *to all further discussion.*

halt[2] *archaic* ▸*adj.* lame.
▸*v.* [*intrans.*] walk with a limp: *he halted slightly in his walk.* ■ hesitate; waver: *that night the ingénue halted in her lines and put no heart into her work.* ▷Old English *healtian* (verb), *halt, healt* (adjective), of Germanic origin.

halt·er[1] /ˈhôltər/ ▸*n.* **1** a rope or strap with a noose or headstall placed around the head of a horse or other animal, used for leading or tethering it. ■ *archaic* a rope with a noose for hanging a person. **2** [usu. as *adj.*] a strap by which the bodice of a sleeveless dress or top is fastened or held behind at the neck, leaving the shoulders and back bare: [as *adj.*] *tourists in* **halter tops** *and shorts.* ■ a top with such a neck.
▸*v.* [*trans.*] put a halter on (an animal). ■ *archaic* hang (someone). ▷Old English *hælftre*, of Germanic origin, meaning 'something to hold things by'; related to German *Halfter*, also to HELVE.

halter top

hal·ter[2] /ˈhalˌti(ə)r/ (also **hal·tere**) ▸*n.* (usu. **halteres**) *Entomology* the balancing organ of a two-winged fly, seen as either of a pair of knobbed filaments that take the place of the hind wings, vibrating during flight. ▷mid 16th cent. (originally plural, denoting a pair of weights like dumbbells held in the hands to give impetus when jumping): from Greek *haltēres* (plural), from *hallesthai* 'to leap.'

halt·er-break ▸*v.* [*trans.*] accustom (a young horse) to wearing and being handled in a halter.

halt·ing /ˈhôltiɴɢ/ ▸*adj.* slow and hesitant, esp. through lack of confidence; faltering: *she speaks halting English with a heavy accent.* —**halt·ing·ly** *adv.*

hal·vah /ˈhälvä/ (also **hal·va**) ▸*n.* a Middle Eastern confection made of sesame flour and honey. ▷Yiddish, or from Turkish *helva*, from Arabic and Persian *ḥalwā* 'sweetmeat.'

halve /hav; häv/ ▸*v.* [*trans.*] **1** divide into two parts of equal or roughly equal size: *peel and halve the pears.* ■ reduce or be reduced by half: [*intrans.*] *profits are expected to halve after a tail-off in new customers* | [*trans.*] *his pledge to halve the deficit over the next four years.* ■ share (something) equally with another person: *she insisted on halving the bill.* ■ *Golf* use the same number of strokes as one's opponent and thus tie (a hole or match). **2** [usu. as *n.*] (**halving**) fit (crossing timbers) together by cutting out half the thickness of each. ▷Middle English: from HALF.

halves /havz; hävz/ ▸ plural form of HALF.

hal·wa /ˈhälwä/ (also **hal·wah**) ▸*n.* a sweet Indian dish consisting of carrots or semolina boiled with milk, almonds, sugar, butter, and cardamom. ▷from Arabic, literally 'sweetmeat.'

hal·yard /ˈhalyərd/ ▸*n.* a rope used for raising and lowering a sail, spar, flag, or yard on a sailing ship. ▷late Middle English *halier*, from HALE[2] + -IER. The change in the ending in the 18th cent. was due to association with YARD[1].

Ham /ham/ (in the Bible) a son of Noah (Gen. 10:1), traditional ancestor of the Hamites.

ham[1] /ham/ ▸*n.* **1** meat from the upper part of a pig's leg salted and dried or smoked: *thin slices of ham* | *a honey-baked ham.* **2** (**hams**) the backs of the thighs or the thighs and buttocks: *he squatted down on his hams.* ▷Old English *ham, hom* (originally denoting the back of the knee), from a Germanic base meaning 'be crooked.' In the late 15th cent. the term came to denote the back of the thigh, hence the thigh or hock of an animal.

ham[2] ▸*n.* **1** an excessively theatrical actor: *nobody gets to emote more than a ham on the witness stand.* ■ excessively theatrical acting. **2** *informal* an amateur radio operator.
▸*v.* (**hammed, ham·ming**) [*intrans.*] *informal* overact: *he was* **hamming it up**, *doing all the voices and the effects.* ▷late 19th cent. : perhaps from the first syllable of AMATEUR; compare with the slang term *hamfatter* 'inexpert performer.' Sense 2 dates from the early 20th cent.

Ha·ma /ˈhämə/ (also **Ha·mah**) an industrial city in western Syria, on the Orontes River; pop. 229,000. Much of the city was destroyed during an unsuccessful uprising against the government in 1982.

ha·ma·chi /həˈmäcʜē/ ▸*n.* the Japanese name for Pacific yellowtail, especially when used in sushi and sashimi.

Ha·ma·da /həˈmädə/, Shoji (1894–1978), Japanese potter. He worked mainly in stoneware to produce utilitarian items of unpretentious simplicity.

Ha·ma·dan /ˌhäməˈdän; ˈhaməˌdan/ a commercial city in western Iran, in the Zagros Mountains between Tehran and Bakhtaran; pop. 350,000. It is on the site of the ancient city of Ecbatana, which became the capital of the kingdom of Media in the 6th century BC.

ham·a·dry·ad /ˌhaməˈdrīəd/ ▸*n.* **1** (also **Hamadryad**) *Greek & Roman Mythology* a nymph who lives in a tree and dies when the tree dies. **2** another term for KING COBRA. ▷via Latin from Greek *hamadruas*, from *hama* 'together' + *drus* 'tree.'

ham·a·dry·as ba·boon /ˌhaməˈdrīəs/ ▸*n.* a large Arabian and northeastern African baboon, the male of which has a silvery-gray cape of hair and a naked red face and rump. It was held sacred in ancient Egypt. Also called SACRED BABOON. • *Papio hamadryas*, family Cercopithecidae. ▷1930s: modern Latin (see HAMADRYAD).

Ha·mah /ˈhämä/ variant spelling of HAMA.

Ha·ma·ma·tsu /ˌhäməˈmätso͞o/ an industrial city in Japan, on the southern coast of the island of Honshu; pop. 535,000.

ham·a·mel·is /ˌhaməˈmēlis/ ▸*n.* technical name for WITCH HAZEL. ▷mid 18th cent.: modern Latin (genus name), from Greek *hamamēlis* 'medlar.'

ham-and-egg·er /ˈegər/ ▸*n. informal* an ordinary person of little consequence. ▷originally used in boxing, in the sense 'an average boxer who earns only enough to pay for his meals.'

ha·mar·ti·a /ˌhämärˈtēə/ ▸*n.* a fatal flaw leading to the downfall of a tragic hero or heroine. ▷late 18th cent.: Greek, 'fault, failure, guilt'; the term was used in Aristotle's *Poetics* with reference to ancient Greek tragedy.

Ha·mas /häˈmäs/ a Palestinian Islamic fundamentalist movement that has become a focus for Arab resistance in the Israeli-occupied territories. It opposes peace with Israel and has come into conflict with the more moderate Palestine Liberation Organization.

ha·mate /ˈhāˌmāt/ (also **hamate bone**) ▸*n. Anatomy* a carpal bone situated on the lower outside edge of the hand. It has a hook-shaped projection on the palmar side to which muscles of the little finger are attached. ▷early 18th cent.: from Latin *hamatus* 'hooked,' from *hamus* 'hook.'

ham·bone /ˈham,bōn/ ▸*n. informal* an inferior actor or performer, esp. one who uses a spurious black accent.

Ham·burg /ˈham,bərg; ˈhäm,bo͝ork/ **1** a port in northern Germany, on the Elbe River; pop. 1,669,000. Founded by Charlemagne in the 9th century, it is now the largest port in Germany. **2** a town in western New York, south of Buffalo; pop. 53,735.

ham·burg /ˈhambərg/ ▸*n.* (also **Hamburg steak**) another term for HAMBURGER. ▷from HAMBURG.

ham·burg·er /ˈham,bərgər/ ▸*n.* a round patty of ground beef, fried or grilled and typically served on a bun or roll and garnished with various condiments. ■ ground beef. ▷late 19th cent. (originally U.S.): from German, from HAMBURG.

ham·burg·er bun ▸*n.* a flattish soft bread roll, often topped with sesame seeds, designed to be filled with a hamburger.

Ham·burg·er Hill a name given to a mountain in central Vietnam, near the border with Laos, where hundreds of U.S. soldiers were killed in a 1969 assault during the Vietnam War.

Ham·den /ˈhamdən/ a town in south central Connecticut, north of New Haven; pop. 56,913.

Ha·meln /ˈhäməln/ (also **Ham·e·lin** /ˈham(ə)lən/) a town in northwestern Germany, in Lower Saxony, on the Weser River; pop. 57,000. A medieval market town, it is the setting of the legend of the Pied Piper of Hamelin.

ha·mer·kop ▸*n.* variant spelling of HAMMERKOP.

hames /hāmz/ ▸*plural n.* two curved pieces of iron or wood forming or attached to the collar of a draft horse, to which the traces are attached. ▷Middle English: from Middle Dutch.

ham·fat·ter /ˈham,fatər/ (also **ham·fat**) ▸*n. informal* an inexpert or amateurish performer, esp. a mediocre jazz musician: [as *adj.*] *recordings loaded with that "hamfat" band sound.* ▷late 19th cent.: perhaps an alteration of AMATEUR.

ham-fist·ed /ˈham ,fistid/ ▸*adj.* another term for HAM-HANDED. **—ham-fist·ed·ly** *adv.* **—ham-fist·ed·ness** *n.*

ham-hand·ed ▸*adj. informal* clumsy; bungling: *a ham-handed attempt.* **—ham-hand·ed·ly** *adv.* **—ham-hand·ed·ness** *n.*

Ham·hung /ˈhäm,ho͝oNG/ an industrial city in eastern North Korea; pop. 775,000. It was the center of government of northeastern Korea during the Yi dynasty 1392–1910.

Ha·mil·car /həˈmil,kär/ (*c.*270–229 BC), Carthaginian general, father of Hannibal. He fought Rome in the first Punic War and negotiated the terms of peace after the defeat of the Carthaginians.

Ham·il·ton[1] /ˈhamәltәn; -әltn/ **1** a port and industrial city in southern Canada, at the western end of Lake Ontario, in Ontario; pop. 318,499. **2** a city on North Island in New Zealand; pop. 149,000. **3** a town in southern Scotland, near Glasgow; pop. 50,000. **4** the capital of Bermuda; pop. 1,100. **5** a township in west central New Jersey, southeast of Trenton; pop. 87,109. **6** an industrial city in southwestern Ohio, north of Cincinnati; pop. 60,690.

Ham·il·ton[2] /ˈhamәltәn/, Alexander (*c.*1757–1804), U.S. politician. He established the U.S. central banking system as secretary of the treasury 1789–95 under President George Washington and advocated a strong central government. He was killed in a duel with Aaron Burr.

Alexander Hamilton

Ham·il·ton[3], Lady Emma (*c.*1765–1815), English mistress of Lord Horatio Nelson; born *Amy Lyon*.

Ham·il·ton[4], Sir William Rowan (1806–65), Irish mathematician and theoretical physicist. Hamilton made influential contributions to optics and to the foundations of algebra and quantum mechanics.

Ham·il·to·ni·an /,hamәlˈtōnēәn/ ▸*adj.* **1** *Physics & Mathematics* of, relating to, or invented by the mathematician Sir W. R. Hamilton, esp. denoting concepts employed in the wave-mechanical description of particles. **2** of or relating to the American statesman Alexander Hamilton or his doctrines.
▸*n.* **1** (also **hamiltonian**) *Physics & Mathematics* a Hamiltonian operator or function. **2** a follower or adherent of Alexander Hamilton or his doctrines. **—Ham·il·to·ni·an·ism** /-izәm/ *n.* (in sense 2).

Ham·ite /ˈha,mīt/ ▸*n.* a member of a group of North African peoples, including the ancient Egyptians and Berbers, supposedly descended from Ham, son of Noah.

Ham·it·ic /həˈmitik/ ▸*adj. historical* of or denoting a hypothetical language family formerly proposed to comprise Berber, ancient Egyptian, the Cushitic languages, and the Chadic languages. These are now recognized as independent branches of the Afro-Asiatic family. ▷from *Ham* (the name of a son of Noah) + -ITE[1] + -IC.

Ham·i·to-Se·mit·ic /ˈhami,tō səˈmitik/ ▸*adj.* former term for AFRO-ASIATIC.

Ham·let /ˈhamlit/ a legendary prince of Denmark, hero of a tragedy by Shakespeare.
▸*PHRASE* □ **Hamlet without the Prince** a performance or event taking place without the principal actor or central figure.

ham·let /ˈhamlit/ ▸*n.* a small settlement, generally one smaller than a village. ▷Middle English: from Old French *hamelet*, diminutive of *hamel* 'little village'; related to HOME (*hām* in Old English).

Ham·lisch /ˈhamlisн/, (Frederick) Marvin (1944–) U.S. composer. He composed the music for movies such as *The Way We Were* (Academy Award, 1973) and *The Sting* (Academy Award, 1973), and Broadway shows such as *A Chorus Line* (1975).

Hamm[1] /häm/ an industrial city in northwestern Germany, in North Rhine-Westphalia, on the Lippe River; pop. 180,000.

Hamm[2], Mia (1972–) U.S. soccer player; full name *Mariel Margret Hamm*. She began to play for the U.S. national women's soccer team in 1987, the youngest player ever be a member of the team. She was part of the U.S. team that won the Women's World Cup in 1999, the silver medal at the 2000 Olympic games, and the gold medal at the 1996 and 2004 games.

Ham·mar·skjöld /ˈhamәr,sнōld; ˈhäm-; -,sнәld/, Dag (Hjalmar Agne Carl) (1905–61), Swedish diplomat and politician. As secretary-general of the UN 1953–61, he was influential in the establishment of the UN emergency force in Sinai and Gaza 1956 and also initiated peace moves in the Middle East 1957–58. He was killed in a plane crash while on a peace mission in Congo. Nobel Peace Prize (1961, posthumously).

Dag Hammarskjöld

ham·mer /ˈhamәr/ ▸*n.* **1** a tool with a heavy metal head mounted at right angles at the end of a handle, used for jobs such as breaking things and driving in nails. ■ a machine with a metal block for giving a heavy blow to something. ■ an auctioneer's mallet for indicating by a sharp tap that an article is sold. ■ a part of a mechanism that hits another part to make it work, such as one exploding the charge in a gun or one striking the strings of a piano. **2** a metal ball, typically weighing 16 pounds (7.3 kg), attached to a wire for throwing in an athletic contest. ■ (**the hammer**) the sport of throwing such a ball. **3** another term for MALLEUS.
▸*v.* [*trans.*] **1** hit or beat (something) with a hammer or similar object: *they are made by heating and hammering pieces of iron.* ■ [*intrans.*] strike or knock at or on something violently with one's hand or with a hammer or other object: *she* ***hammered on*** *his door.* ■ [*intrans.*] (**hammer away**) work hard and persistently: *for six months I have been* ***hammering away at*** *a plot.* ■ [*trans.*] drive or secure (something) by striking with or as if with a hammer: *he hammered the tack in | he was hammering leather soles onto a pair of small boots.* ■ (**hammer something in/into**) instill (an attitude, idea, or habit) forcefully or repeatedly: *it has been hammered into people's heads that communists are the bad guys.* **2** *informal* attack or criticize forcefully and relentlessly: *he got hammered for an honest mistake.* ■ utterly defeat in a game or contest: *they hammered St. Louis 6–0.*
▸*phrasal v.* □ **hammer something out 1** make something by shaping metal with a hammer. **2** laboriously work out the details of a plan or agreement: *a deal was being hammered out with the Dutch museums.* **3** play a tune loudly or clumsily, esp. on the piano. ▷Old English *hamor*, *hamer*, of Germanic origin: related to Dutch *hamer*, German *Hammer*, and Old Norse *hamarr* 'rock.' The original sense was probably 'stone tool.' **—ham·mer·er** *n.* **—ham·mer·less** *adj.*
▸*PHRASES* □ **come** (or **go**) **under the hammer** be sold at an auction. □ **hammer and tongs** *informal* energetically, enthusiastically, or with great vehemence: *all the way to the bottom, Larry could hear them clanging away, hammer and tongs.* □ **hammer something home** see HOME.

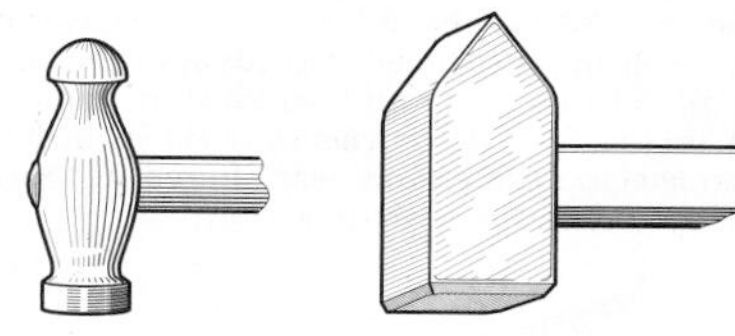

ball-peen hammer sledgehammer

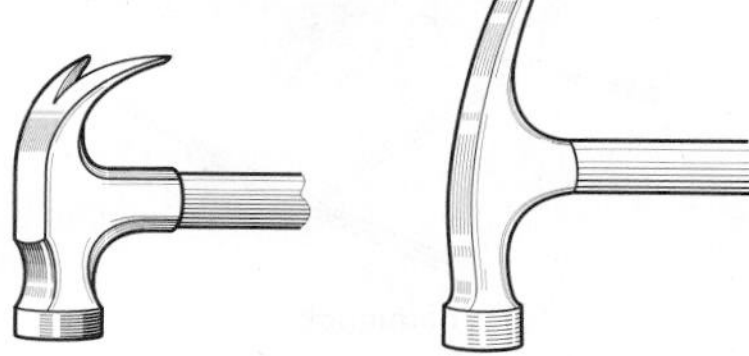

claw hammer tack hammer

hammer 1

ham·mer and sick·le ▸*n.* the symbols of the industrial worker and the peasant used as the emblem of the former Soviet Union and of international communism.

hammer and sickle

ham·mer·beam /ˈhamәr,bēm/ (also **ham·mer beam**) ▸*n.* a short wooden beam (typically carved) projecting from a wall to support either a principal rafter or one end of an arch.

ham·mer drill ▸*n.* a power drill that works by delivering a rapid succession of blows, used chiefly for drilling in masonry or rock.

Ham·mer·fest /ˈhämәr,fest/ a port in northern Norway, on North Kvaløy island; pop. 7,000. It is the most northern town in Europe.

ham·mer·head /ˈhamәr,hed/ ▸*n.* **1** (also **hammerhead shark**) a shark of tropical and temperate oceans that has flattened bladelike extensions on either side of the head, with the eyes and nostrils placed at or near the ends. • Family Sphyrnidae and genus *Sphyrna*: several species. **2** a brown African marsh bird related to the storks, having a crest that looks like a backward projection of the head, and constructing an enormous nest. Also called HAMMERKOP. • *Scopus umbretta*, the only member of the family Scopidae. **3** the striking head of a hammer.

ham·mer·ing /'haməriNG/ ▶*n.* **1** the sound or action of hammering something. **2** *informal* a heavy defeat: *the 7–0 hammering by the Yankees.*

▶*PHRASE* □ **take a hammering** be subjected to a heavy defeat or harsh treatment.

ham·mer·kop /'hamər,käp/ (also **ham·er·kop**) ▶*n.* another term for HAMMERHEAD (sense 2). ▷mid 19th cent.: from Afrikaans *hamerkop*, from *hamer* 'hammer' + *kop* 'head.'

ham·mer·lock /'hamər,läk/ ▶*n.* an armlock in which a person's arm is bent up behind the back.

ham·mer price ▶*n.* the price realized by an item sold at auction.

Ham·mer·stein /'hamər,stīn/, Oscar (1895–1960), U.S. librettist; full name *Oscar Hammerstein II*. He collaborated with various composers, including Jerome Kern, with whom he wrote *Showboat* (1927), and most notably Richard Rodgers, with whom he wrote *Oklahoma!* (1943), *South Pacific* (1949), and *The Sound of Music* (1959).

ham·mer·toe /'hamər,tō/ ▶*n.* a toe that is bent permanently downward, typically as a result of pressure from footwear.

Ham·mett /'hamət/, (Samuel) Dashiell (1894–1961), U.S. novelist. He developed the hard-boiled style of detective fiction in works such as *The Maltese Falcon* (1930) and *The Thin Man* (1932), both of which were made into successful movies. He lived for many years with Lillian Hellman; they were both persecuted for their left-wing views during the McCarthy era.

ham·mock /'hamək/ ▶*n.* a bed made of canvas or of rope mesh and suspended by cords at the ends, used as garden furniture or on board a ship. ▷mid 16th cent. (in the Spanish form *hamaca*): via Spanish from Taino *hamaka*; the ending was altered in the 16th cent. by association with -OCK.

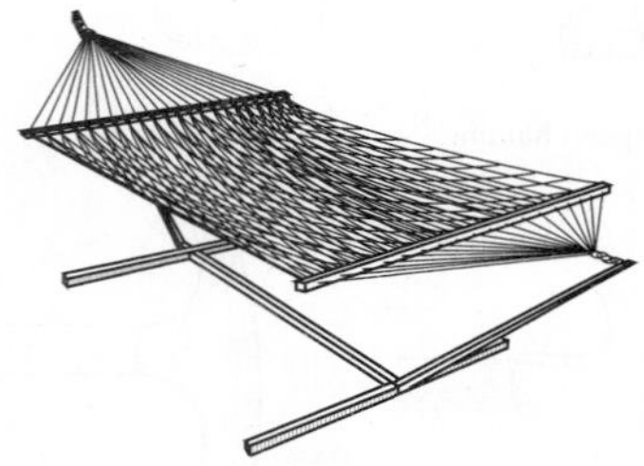

hammock

Ham·mond /'hamənd/ an industrial port city in northwestern Indiana, on Lake Michigan, southeast of Chicago in Illinois; pop. 83,048.

Ham·mond or·gan /'hamənd/ ▶*n. trademark* a type of electronic organ. ▷1930s: named after Laurens *Hammond* (1895–1973), American mechanical engineer.

Ham·mu·ra·bi /,hamə'räbē; ,hä-/ (died 1750 BC), the sixth king of the first dynasty of Babylonia, reigned 1792–1750 BC. He extended the Babylonian empire and instituted one of the earliest known collections of laws.

ham·my /'hamē/ ▶*adj.* (**-mi·er, -mi·est**) *informal* (of acting or an actor) exaggerated or overtheatrical: *there is some hammy acting.* **—ham·mi·ly** /'hamәlē/ *adv.* **—ham·mi·ness** *n.*

ham·per[1] /'hampər/ ▶*n.* a large basket with a lid used for laundry: *a laundry hamper.* ■ a basket with a carrying handle and a hinged lid, used for food, cutlery, and plates on a picnic: *a picnic hamper.* ▷Middle English (denoting any large case or casket): from Anglo-Norman French *hanaper* 'case for a goblet,' from Old French *hanap* 'goblet,' of Germanic origin.

ham·per[2] ▶*v.* [*trans.*] (often **be hampered**) hinder or impede the movement or progress of: *their work is hampered by lack of funds.* See note at HINDER.

▶*n. Nautical* necessary but cumbersome equipment on a ship. ▷late Middle English (in the sense 'shackle, entangle, catch'): perhaps related to German *hemmen* 'restrain.'

Hamp·shire[1] /'ham(p)SHər/ a county on the coast of southern England; county town, Winchester.

Hamp·shire[2] /'ham(p)SHi(ə)r/ ▶*n.* a pig of a black breed with a white saddle and prick ears.

Hamp·ton[1] /'ham(p)tən/ a city in southeastern Virginia, on the harbor of Hampton Roads, on Chesapeake Bay; pop. 146,437.

Hamp·ton[2], Lionel Leo (1909–2002), U.S. jazz vibraphonist, drummer, pianist, singer, and bandleader. He played with Benny Goodman in small ensembles before forming his own big band in 1942.

Hamp·ton Roads a deep-water estuary in southeastern Virginia, 4 miles (6 km) long, that is formed by the James River where it joins Chesapeake Bay. It is the site of the battle between the ships *Merrimac* and *Monitor* in 1862 during the Civil War.

Hamp·tons /'ham(p)tənz/ (**the Hamptons**) a cluster of resort villages in eastern Long Island in New York that include Southampton, East Hampton, and Westhampton Beach.

ham·ster /'hamstər/ ▶*n.* a solitary burrowing rodent with a short tail and large cheek pouches for carrying food, native to Europe and northern Asia. • Subfamily Cricetinae, family Muridae: several genera and species, in particular the **golden hamster** (*Mesocricetus auratus*), often kept as a pet or laboratory animal, and the **common hamster** (*Cricetus cricetus*). ▷early 17th cent.: from German, from Old High German *hamustro* 'weevil.'

ham·string /'ham,striNG/ ▶*n.* any of five tendons at the back of a person's knee: *he pulled a hamstring.* ■ the great tendon at the back of a quadruped's hock.

▶*v.* (*past* and *past part.* **-strung**) [*trans.*] cripple (a person or animal) by cutting their hamstrings. ■ (usu. **be hamstrung**) severely restrict the efficiency or effectiveness of: *we were hamstrung by a total lack of knowledge.*

Ham·sun /'hämsən/, Knut (1859–1952), Norwegian novelist; pseudonym of *Knut Pedersen*. Notable works: *Hunger* (1890) and *Growth of the Soil* (1917). Nobel Prize for Literature (1920).

ham·u·lus /'hamyələs/ ▶*n.* (*pl.* **-li** /-,lī; -,lē/) *Anatomy & Zoology* a small hook or hooklike projection, esp. one of a number linking the fore- and hind wings of a bee or wasp. ▷early 18th cent.: from Latin, diminutive of *hamus* 'hook.'

ham·za /'hamzə/ ▶*n.* (in Arabic script) a symbol representing a glottal stop. ■ such a sound. ▷early 19th cent.: Arabic, literally 'compression.'

Han /han/ **1** the Chinese dynasty that ruled from 206 BC until AD 220 with only a brief interruption. During this period Chinese rule was extended over Mongolia, Confucianism was recognized as the state philosophy, and detailed historical records were kept. **2** the dominant ethnic group in China.

Han·cock[1] /'han,käk/, John (1737–93), American revolutionary and politician. Noted as the first signer of the Declaration of Independence in 1776, he was a member of the Continental Congress 1775–80, 1785, 1786 and its first president 1775–77. He was later governor of Massachusetts 1780–85, 1787–93.

Han·cock[2], Winfield Scott (1824–86), U.S. army officer. A Union general, he was noted for his defense of Cemetery Ridge at the Battle of Gettysburg 1863. He was the 1880 Democratic presidential candidate, narrowly losing to Garfield.

han·cock /'han,käk/ ▶*v.* [*trans.*] *informal* put one's signature to (a document): *Secretary Richardson hancocked a memorandum written to managers across the weapons-complex with the Department's goal spelled out.* ▷from *John Hancock*, 'autograph signature.'

Hand /hand/, (Billings) Learned (1872–1961), U.S. jurist and writer. He wrote over 2,000 opinions as judge of the U.S. Court of Appeals, 2nd Circuit 1924–51. He authored *The Spirit of Liberty* (1952) and *The Bill of Rights* (1958).

hand /hand/ ▶*n.* **1** the end part of a person's arm beyond the wrist, including the palm, fingers, and thumb: *she placed the money on the palm of her hand* | *he was leading her by the hand.* ■ a similar prehensile organ forming the end part of a limb of various mammals, such as that on all four limbs of a monkey. ■ [as *adj.*] operated by or held in the hand: *hand luggage.* ■ [as *adj.* or in *combination*] done or made manually rather than by machine: *hand signals* | *a hand-stitched quilt.* ■ [in *sing.*] *informal* a round of applause: *his fans gave him **a big hand**.* ■ *dated* a pledge of marriage by a woman: *he wrote to request the hand of her daughter in marriage.* **2** something resembling a hand in form or position, in particular: ■ a pointer on a clock or watch indicating the passing of units of time: *the second hand.* ■ a bunch of bananas. **3** (**hands**) used in reference to the power to direct something: *the day-to-day running of the house was in her hands* | *taking the law into their own hands.* ■ (usu. **a hand**) an active role in influencing something: *he **had** a big **hand in** organizing the event.* ■ (usu. **a hand**) help in doing something: *do you need a hand?* ■ (usu. **hands**) (in sports) skill and dexterity: *he's a receiver with very good hands.* ■ a person's workmanship, esp. in artistic work: *this should be a clue in attributing other work to his hand.* ■ a person's handwriting: *he inscribed the statement in a bold hand.* ■ [with *adj.*] a person who does something to a specified standard: *I'm a great **hand at** inventing.* **4** a person who engages in manual labor, esp. in a factory, on a farm, or on board a ship: *a factory hand* | *the ship was lost with all hands.* **5** the set of cards dealt to a player in a card game. ■ a round or short spell of play in a card game: *his idea of a good time would be **a hand of** bridge.* ■ *Bridge* the cards held by declarer as opposed to those in the dummy. **6** a unit of measurement of a horse's height, equal to 4 inches (10.16 cm). [denoting the breadth of a hand, formerly used as a more general lineal measure and taken to equal three inches.] **7** the feel of goods, esp. textiles, when handled: *fabrics with a softer hand.*

▶*v.* **1** [with *two objs.*] pick (something) up and give to (someone): *he handed each man a glass* | *I handed the trowel back to him.* ■ *informal* make (abusive, untrue, or otherwise objectionable) remarks to (someone): *all the yarns she'd been handing me.* ■ *informal* make (something) easily obtainable for (someone): *it was a win handed to him on a plate.* **2** [*trans.*] hold the hand of (someone) in order to help them move in the specified direction: *he handed him into a carriage.* **3** [*trans.*] *Sailing* take in or furl (a sail): ***hand in** the main!*

▶*phrasal v.* □ **hand something down 1** pass something on to a younger person or a successor: *songs are handed down from mother to daughter.* **2** announce something, esp. a judgment or sentence, formally or publicly. □ **hand something in** give something to a person in authority for their attention. □ **hand something on** pass something to the next person in a series or succession: *he had handed on the family farm to his son.* ■ pass responsibility for something to someone else; delegate. □ **hand something out 1** give a share of something or one of a set of things to each of a number of people; distribute: *they handed out free drinks to everyone.* **2** impose or inflict a penalty or misfortune on someone. □ **hand over** pass responsibility to someone else: *he will soon **hand over to** a new director.* □ **hand someone/something over** give someone or something, or the responsibility for someone or something, to someone else: *hand the matter over to the police.* □ **hand something around** offer something to each of a number of people in turn: *a big box of chocolates was handed around.* ▷Old English *hand*, *hond*, of Germanic origin; related to Dutch *hand* and German *Hand*. **—hand·less** *adj.*

▶*PHRASES* □ **at hand** nearby: *keep the manual close at hand.* ■ readily accessible when needed. ■ close in time; about to happen: *a breakthrough in combating the disease may be at hand.* □ **at** (or **by**) **the hands** (or **hand**) **of** through the agency of: *tests he would undergo at the hands of a senior neurologist.* □ **bind** (or **tie**) **someone hand and foot** tie someone's hands and feet together. □ **by hand** by a person and not a machine: *the crop has to be harvested by hand.* □ **give** (or **lend**) **a hand** assist in an action or enterprise. □ **hand in glove** in close collusion or association: *they were working **hand in glove with** our enemies.* □ **hand in hand** (of two people) with hands joined, esp. as a mark of affection. ■ *figurative* closely associated: *she had the confidence that usually **goes hand in hand with** experience.* □ (**from**) **hand to mouth** satisfying only one's immediate needs because of lack of money for future plans and investments: *they were flat broke and living hand to mouth* | [as *adj.*] *a hand-to-mouth existence.* □ **hands down** easily and decisively; without question: *winning the debate hands down.* □ **hands off** used as a warning not to touch or interfere with something: *hands off that cake!* ■ [as *adj.*] (**hands-off**) not involving or requiring direct control or intervention: *a hands-off management style.* □ **hands-on** involving or offering active participation rather than theory: *hands-on practice to gain experience.* ■ *Computing* involving or requiring personal operation at a keyboard. □ **hands up!** used as an instruction to raise one's hands in surrender or to signify assent or participation: *Hands up! Who saw the program?* □ **have one's hands full** have as much work as one can do. □ **have one's hands tied** *informal* be unable to act freely. □ **have to hand it to someone** *informal* used to acknowledge the merit or achievement of someone: *I've got to hand it to you—you've got the magic touch.* □ **in hand 1** receiving or requiring immediate attention: *he threw himself into the work in hand.* ■ in progress: *negotiations are now well in hand.* **2** ready for use if required; in reserve:

he had $1,000 of borrowed cash in hand. **3** under one's control: *the police had the situation well in hand.* ■ (of land) farmed directly by its owner and not let to tenants. □ **in safe hands** protected by someone trustworthy from harm or damage: *the future of the cathedral is in safe hands.* □ **keep one's hand in** become (or remain) practiced in something. □ **make** (or **lose** or **spend**) **money hand over fist** *informal* make (or lose or spend) money very rapidly. □ **off someone's hands** not having to be dealt with or looked after by the person specified: *they just want the problem off their hands.* □ **on every hand** all around: *new technologies were springing up on every hand.* □ **on hand** present, esp. for a specified purpose: *her trainer was on hand to give advice.* ■ readily available. ■ needing to be dealt with: *they had many urgent and pressing matters on hand.* □ **on someone's hands** used to indicate that someone is responsible for dealing with someone or something: *he has a difficult job on his hands.* ■ used to indicate that someone is to blame for something: *he has my son's blood on his hands.* ■ at someone's disposal: *since I retired I've had more time on my hands.* □ **on the one** (or **the other**) **hand** used to present factors that are opposed or that support opposing opinions: *a conflict between their rationally held views on the one hand and their emotions and desires on the other.* □ **out of hand 1** not under control. **2** without taking time to think: *they rejected negotiations out of hand.* □ **the right hand doesn't know what the left hand is doing** used to convey that there is a state of confusion within a group or organization. □ **set** (or **put**) **one's hand to** start work on. □ **stay someone's hand** restrain someone from acting. □ **take a hand** become influential in determining something; intervene: *fate was about to* ***take a hand in*** *the outcome of the championship.* □ **to hand** within easy reach: *have a pen and paper to hand.* □ **turn one's hand to** undertake (an activity different from one's usual occupation): *a music teacher who turned his hand to writing books.* □ **wait on someone hand and foot** attend to all someone's needs or requests, esp. when this is regarded as unreasonable. □ **with one hand** (**tied**) **behind one's back** with serious limitations or restrictions: *at the moment, the police are tackling record crime rates with one hand tied behind their back.* ■ used to indicate that one could do something without any difficulty: *I could do her job with one hand tied behind my back.*

Han·dan /ˈhänˈdän/ industrial city in southern Hebei province in eastern China, a communications and transportation hub on the Fuyang River north of Anyang; pop. 1,110,000.

hand·bag /ˈhan(d),bag/ ▶*n.* a woman's purse.

hand·ball /ˈhan(d),bôl/ ▶*n.* **1** a game similar to squash in which a ball is hit with the hand in a walled court. ■ (also **team handball**) a team game similar to soccer in which the ball is thrown or hit with the hands rather than kicked. ■ the ball used in these games. **2** *Soccer* touching of the ball with the hand or arm, constituting a foul.

hand·bar·row /ˈhand,barō/ ▶*n.* a rectangular frame with poles at each end for being carried by two people.

hand·bell /ˈhan(d),bel/ ▶*n.* a small bell with a handle or strap, esp. one of a set tuned to a range of notes and played by a group of people.

hand·bill /ˈhan(d),bil/ ▶*n.* a small printed advertisement or other notice distributed by hand.

hand·blown /ˈhand,blōn/ ▶*adj.* (of glassware) made by a glassblower with a hand-held blowpipe.

hand·book /ˈhan(d),bo͝ok/ ▶*n.* a book giving information such as facts on a particular subject or instructions for operating a machine.

hand·brake /ˈhan(d),brāk/ ▶*n.* the emergency or parking brake on a motor vehicle. ■ a brake operated by hand, as on a bicycle.

hand·car /ˈhan(d),kär/ ▶*n.* a light railroad vehicle propelled by pushing cranks or levers and used by workers for inspecting the track.

hand·cart /ˈhan(d),kärt/ ▶*n.* a small cart pushed or drawn by hand.

hand·clap /ˈhan(d),klap/ ▶*n.* a clap of the hands: *the switch is sensitive enough to be activated by a handclap.*

hand·clasp /ˈhand,klasp/ ▶*n.* the act of clasping someone else's hand; handshake.

hand·craft /ˈhan(d),kraft/ ▶*v.* [*trans.*] [usu. as *adj.*] (**handcrafted**) make skillfully by hand: *a handcrafted rocking chair.*
▶*n.* another term for HANDICRAFT.

hand crank ▶*n.* a crank that is turned by hand.
▶*v.* (**hand-crank**) [*trans.*] operate (a device) by turning a crank by hand.

hand cream ▶*n.* a moisturizing cream for the hands.

hand·cuff /ˈhan(d),kəf/ ▶*n.* (**handcuffs**) a pair of lockable linked metal rings for securing a prisoner's wrists.
▶*v.* [*trans.*] put handcuffs on (someone): *he was led into court* ***handcuffed to*** *a policeman.* ■ *figurative* restrain; hamper: *he will not allow his training to handcuff his creativity.*

-handed ▶*comb. form* **1** for or involving a specified number of hands: *a two-handed back-hand.* **2** chiefly using or designed for use by the hand specified: *a right-handed batter | a left-handed guitar.* **3** relating to capability, means, or result, esp. of failure: *empty-handed | heavy-handed.*

-handedly ▶*comb. form* in adverbs corresponding to adjectives ending in *-handed* (such as *heavy-handedly* corresponding to *heavy-handed*).

-handedness ▶*comb. form* in nouns corresponding to adjectives ending in *-handed* (such as *left-handedness* corresponding to *left-handed*).

Han·del /ˈhandl/, George Frederick (1685–1759), German composer and organist, resident in Britain from 1712; born *Georg Friedrich Händel.* He is chiefly remembered for his oratorio *Messiah* (1742), his *Water Music* suite (*c.*1717), and his *Music for the Royal Fireworks* (1749).

hand·ful /ˈhan(d),fo͝ol/ ▶*n.* (*pl.* **-fuls**) **1** a quantity that fills the hand: *a small* ***handful of*** *fresh coriander.* ■ a small number or amount: *one of* ***a handful of*** *attorneys in the Southwest who specialize in water-rights laws.* **2** *informal* a person who is very difficult to deal with or control: *the kids could be such a handful.*

hand gal·lop ▶*n.* [in *sing.*] an easily controlled gallop.

hand gre·nade ▶*n.* a hand-thrown grenade.

hand·grip /ˈhan(d),grip/ ▶*n.* **1** a handle for holding onto something. **2** a grasp with the hand, esp. considered in terms of its strength, as in a handshake.

hand·gun /ˈhan(d),gən/ ▶*n.* a gun designed for use by one hand, chiefly either a pistol or a revolver.

hand-held (also **handheld**) ▶*adj.* designed to be held in the hand: *a hand-held computer.*

hand·hold /ˈhand,hōld/ ▶*n.* something for a hand to grip: *the rock is steep and there are few handholds.* ■ a secure grip with a hand or the hands: *he was able to jump to catch a handhold.*

hand·hold·ing /ˈhand,hōldiNG/ ▶*n.* the provision of careful attention, support, or reassurance to another. ■ the giving of simple, detailed, step-by-step instructions.

hand·i·cap /ˈhandē,kap/ ▶*n.* a condition that markedly restricts a person's ability to function physically, mentally, or socially: *he was born with a significant visual handicap.* ■ a circumstance that makes progress or success difficult: *a criminal conviction is a handicap and a label that may stick forever.* ■ a disadvantage imposed on a superior competitor in sports such as golf, horse racing, and competitive sailing in order to make the chances more equal. ■ a race or contest in which such a disadvantage is imposed: [in *names*] *the trophy for the $75,000 Ak-Sar-Ben Handicap.* ■ the extra weight to be carried in a race by a racehorse on the basis of its previous performance to make its chances of winning the same as those of the other horses. ■ the number of strokes by which a golfer normally exceeds par for a course (used as a method of enabling players of unequal ability to compete with each other): [in *combination*] *his game struggles along in the 20-handicap range.*
▶*v.* (**-capped**, **-cap·ping**) [*trans.*] act as an impediment to: *lack of funding has handicapped the development of research.* ■ place (someone) at a disadvantage: *without a good set of notes you will handicap yourself when it comes to exams.* ▷mid 17th cent.: from the phrase *hand in cap*; originally a pastime in which one person claimed an article belonging to another and offered something in exchange, any difference in value being decided by an umpire. All three deposited forfeit money in a cap; the two opponents showed their agreement or disagreement with the valuation by bringing out their hands either full or empty. If both were the same, the umpire took the forfeit money; if not, it went to the person who accepted the valuation. The term *handicap race* was applied (late 18th cent.) to a horse race in which an umpire decided the weight to be carried by each horse, the owners showing acceptance or dissent in a similar way: hence in the late 19th cent. *handicap* came to mean the extra weight given to the superior horse.

hand·i·capped /ˈhandē,kapt/ ▶*adj.* having a condition that markedly restricts one's ability to function physically, mentally, or socially: *a special school for handicapped children* | [as *plural n.*] (**the handicapped**) *a home for the handicapped.*

> ***USAGE*** **Handicapped** in the sense referring to a person's mental or physical disabilities is first recorded in the early 20th century. For a brief period in the second half of the 20th century, it looked as if **handicapped** would be replaced by **disabled**, but both words are now acceptable and interchangeable in standard American English, and neither word has been overtaken by newer coinages such as *differently abled* or *physically challenged*. See also **usage** at LEARNING DISABILITY.

hand·i·cap·per /ˈhandē,kapər/ ▶*n.* a person appointed to assign or assess a competitor's handicap, esp. in golf or horse racing. ■ [usu. in *combination*] a person or horse having a specified handicap: *a three-handicapper.*

hand·i·craft /ˈhandē,kraft/ ▶*n.* (often **handicrafts**) a particular skill of making decorative objects by hand: *the traditional handicrafts of this region | teachers of drawing, design, and handicraft* | [as *adj.*] *handicraft workshops.* ■ an object made using a skill of this kind: *pottery and handicrafts decorate the rooms and hallways.* ▷Middle English: alteration of HANDCRAFT, on the pattern of *handiwork.*

hand·i·work /ˈhandē,wərk/ ▶*n.* **1** (**one's handiwork**) something that one has made or done: *the dressmakers stood back to survey their handiwork.* **2** making things by hand, considered as a subject of instruction: *they taught young women reading, writing, and handiwork.* ▷Old English *handgeweorc*, from HAND + *geweorc* 'something made,' interpreted in the 16th cent. as *handy* + *work.*

hand job (also **hand·job**) ▶*n.* *vulgar slang* an act of male masturbation, esp. as performed on a man by someone else.

hand·ker·chief /ˈhaNGkərCHif; -CHēf/ ▶*n.* a square of cotton or other finely woven material, typically carried one's pocket and intended for blowing or wiping one's nose. ▷mid 16th cent.: from HAND + KERCHIEF.

han·dle /ˈhandl/ ▶*v.* [*trans.*] **1** feel or manipulate with the hands: *heavy paving slabs can be difficult to handle | people who handle food.* ■ drive or control (a vehicle): *where did you learn to handle a boat?* ■ [*intrans.*] (of a vehicle) respond in a specified manner when being driven or controlled: *a roadworthy bicycle that also handles well off the pavement.* **2** manage (a situation or problem): *a lawyer's ability to handle a case properly.* ■ *informal* deal with (someone or something): *I don't think I could handle it if they turned me down.* ■ have the resources to cope with: *more orders than I can handle.* ■ control or manage commercially: *the advertising company that is handling the account.* ■ [with *adverbial*] (**handle oneself**) conduct oneself in a specified manner: *he handled himself with considerable aplomb.* ■ (**handle oneself**) *informal* defend oneself physically or verbally: *I can handle myself in a fight.* **3** process: *the airport expects to handle almost 250,000 passengers this weekend.*
▶*n.* **1** the part by which a thing is held, carried, or controlled: *the pan features helpful lifting handles.* ■ (**a handle on**) *figurative* a means of understanding, controlling, or approaching a person or situation: *it'll give people some kind of handle on these issues |* ***get a handle on*** *your life.* **2** *informal* the name of a person or place: *that's some handle for a baby.* **3** [in *sing.*] *informal* the total amount of money bet over a particular time (typically at a casino) or at a particular sporting event: *the monthly handle of a couple of casinos in Las Vegas.* ▷Old English *handle* (noun), *handlian* (verb), from HAND. —**han·dle·a·bil·i·ty** /,handl-əˈbilitē/ *n.* —**han·dle·a·ble** *adj.* —**han·dled** *adj.* [in *combination*] *a rope-handled canvas bag.* —**han·dle·less** *adj.*

han·dle·bar /ˈhandl,bär/ ▶*n.* (usu. **handlebars**) the steering bar of a bicycle, motorcycle, scooter, or other vehicle, with a handgrip at each end.

han·dle·bar mus·tache ▶*n.* a wide, thick mustache with the ends curving slightly upward.

handlebar mustache

han·dler /ˈhandlər/ ▶*n.* **1** [usu. with *adj.*] a person who handles or deals with certain articles or commodities: *a baggage handler | a food handler.* ■ a device that handles certain articles or substances. **2** a person who trains or has charge of an animal: *the performance of dog and handler in the ring must be accurate and correct.* **3** a person who trains or manages another person, in particular: ■ a person who trains and acts as second to a boxer. ■ a publicity agent. ■ a person who advises on and directs the activities of a politician or other public figure.

hand·ling /ˈhandl-iNG/ ▸*n.* the act of taking or holding something in the hands. ■ the packaging and labeling of something to be shipped.

hand·made /ˈhan(d)ˈmād/ ▸*adj.* made by hand, not by machine, and typically therefore of superior quality: *his expensive handmade leather shoes.*

hand·maid·en /ˈhan(d),mādn/ (also **hand·maid**) ▸*n.* a female servant. ■ a subservient partner or element: *shipping will continue to be the handmaiden of world trade.*

hand-me-down ▸*n.* (often **hand-me-downs**) a garment or other item that has been passed on from another person.
▸*adj.* [*attrib.*] (of a garment or other item) passed on from another person: *he ran in the cold with no mittens and a hand-me-down coat.*

hand·off /ˈhand,ôf; -,äf/ ▸*n.* *Football* an exchange made by handing the ball to a teammate.

hand·out /ˈhand,out/ ▸*n.* **1** something given free to a needy person or organization: *hundreds of thousands of refugees subsist on international handouts.* **2** printed information provided free of charge, esp. to accompany a lecture or advertise something: *she was shocked when she saw a one-page handout condemning her campaign.*

hand·o·ver /ˈhand,ōvər/ ▸*n.* *chiefly Brit.* an act or instance of handing something over.

hand·phone /ˈhand,fōn/ ▸*n.* *SE Asian* a cordless or cellular phone.

hand·pick /ˈhandˈpik/ (also **hand-pick**) ▸*v.* [*trans.*] select carefully with a particular purpose in mind: *the board's executive director handpicked the review panel to ensure the vote* | [as *adj.*] (**handpicked**) *a handpicked team.*

hand press ▸*n.* a printing press that is operated by hand.

hand·print /ˈhand,print/ ▸*n.* the mark left by the impression of a hand.

hand·print·ed /ˈhandˈprintid/ ▸*adj.* **1** written by hand with the letters individually formed. **2** of or bearing a design printed by hand.

hand pup·pet ▸*n.* a puppet operated by putting one's hand inside it.

hand·rail /ˈhan(d),rāl/ ▸*n.* a rail fixed to posts or a wall for people to hold onto for support.

hand·saw /ˈhan(d),sô/ ▸*n.* a wood saw worked by one hand.

hand·sel /ˈhansəl/ ▸*n.* & *v.* variant spelling of HANSEL.

hand·sel·ling /ˈhandˈseliNG/ ▸*n.* the practice of promoting books by personal recommendation rather than by publisher-sponsored marketing. —**hand·sell** *v.* [*trans.*]

hand·set /ˈhan(d),set/ ▸*n.* the part of a telephone that is held up to speak into and listen to. ■ a hand-held controller for a piece of electronic equipment, such as a television or video recorder.

hands-free ▸*adj.* (of a telephone or other electronic device) designed to be operated without using the hands.

hand·shake /ˈhan(d),SHāk/ ▸*n.* an act of shaking a person's hand with one's own, used as a greeting or to finalize an agreement. ■ a person's particular way of doing this: *her handshake was warm and firm.* ■ *Computing* an exchange of standardized signals between devices in a computer network regulating the transfer of data. —**hand·shak·ing** /-SHākiNG/ *n.*

hand·some /ˈhansəm/ ▸*adj.* (**-som·er, -som·est**) **1** (of a man) good-looking. ■ (of a woman) striking and imposing in good looks rather than conventionally pretty. ■ (of a thing) well made, imposing, and of obvious quality: *handsome cookbooks | a handsome country town.* **2** (of a number, sum of money, or margin) substantial: *elected by a handsome majority.* ■ generous; liberal: *a handsome gift.* ▷Middle English: from HAND + -SOME[1]. The original sense was 'easy to handle or use,' hence 'suitable' and 'apt, clever' (mid 16th cent.), giving rise to the current appreciatory senses (late 16th cent.). —**hand·some·ly** *adv.* —**hand·some·ness** *n.*
▸*PHRASE* □ **handsome is as handsome does** *proverb* character and behavior are more important than appearance.

hand·span /ˈhand,span/ ▸*n.* the width of a person's hand, as measured from the tip of the thumb to the tip of the little finger, when the fingers and thumb are spread out.

hand·spike /ˈhand,spīk/ ▸*n.* *historical* a wooden rod with an iron tip, used as a lever on board ship and by artillery soldiers.

hand·spring /ˈhand,spriNG/ ▸*n.* an acrobatic jump through the air onto one's hands followed by springing onto one's feet.

hand·stand /ˈhand,stand/ ▸*n.* an act of balancing on one's hands with one's feet in the air or against a wall.

hand-to-hand ▸*adj.* (of fighting) at close quarters: *training in* ***hand-to-hand combat.***

hand tool ▸*n.* a tool held in the hand and operated without electricity or other power.

hand-wav·ing ▸*n.* the use of gestures and insubstantial language meant to impress or convince: *their patriotic hand-waving lacked sincerity* | [as *adj.*] *her path of logic and hand-waving explanations.*

hand·work /ˈhand,wərk/ ▸*n.* work done with the hands: *the transition from handwork to machine production.* —**hand·worked** *adj.*

hand·wo·ven /ˈhandˈwōvən/ ▸*adj.* made on a hand-operated loom: *handwoven linens.* ■ woven by hand.

hand·wring·ing /ˈhand,riNGiNG/ ▸*n.* the clasping together and squeezing of one's hands, esp. when distressed or worried. ■ an excessive display of concern or distress: *his customary handwringing about the need for more local aid.*

hand·writ·ing /ˈhan(d),rītiNG/ ▸*n.* writing with a pen or pencil. ■ a person's particular style of writing: *her handwriting was small and neat.*

hand·writ·ten /ˈhan(d),ritn/ ▸*adj.* written with a pen, pencil, or other hand-held implement.

Han·dy /ˈhandē/, W. C. (1873–1958), U.S. composer and musician; full name *William Christopher Handy;* known as the **Father of the Blues.** As a cornettist he led the Mahara Minstrels band 1896–1903. Many of his works, including "St. Louis Blues" and "Memphis Blues," were multistrain jazz compositions that utilized elements of the blues.

hand·y /ˈhandē/ ▸*adj.* (**hand·i·er, hand·i·est**) **1** convenient to handle or use; useful: *a handy desktop encyclopedia | handy for everyday use.* **2** close at hand: *keep credit cards handy.* ■ placed or occurring conveniently: *a hotel in a handy central location.* **3** skillful: *he's* ***handy with*** *a needle.* —**hand·i·ly** /ˈhandl-ē; ˈhandəlē/ *adv.* —**hand·i·ness** *n.*
▸*PHRASE* □ **come in handy** *informal* turn out to be useful: *the sort of junk that might come in handy one day.*

hand·y·man /ˈhandē,man/ ▸*n.* (*pl.* **-men**) a person able or employed to do occasional domestic repairs and minor renovations.

Han·ford /ˈhanfərd/ a government reservation in Richland in southeastern Washington, a former U.S. plutonium-production site.

hang /haNG/ ▸*v.* (*past* **hung** /həNG/ except in sense 2) **1** suspend or be suspended from above with the lower part dangling free: [*trans.*] *that's where people are supposed to hang their wash* | [*intrans.*] *a chain hanging freely over two pegs.* ■ attach or be attached to a wall: [*trans.*] *we could just hang the pictures on the walls* | [*intrans.*] *the room in which the pictures will hang.* ■ (**be hung with**) be adorned with pictures or other decorations: *the walls of her hall were hung with examples of her work.* ■ exhibit or be exhibited, as in a museum. ■ attach or be attached so as to allow free movement about the point of attachment: [*trans.*] *a long time was spent hanging a couple of doors.* ■ [*intrans.*] droop: *she just sat with her mouth hanging open.* ■ [*intrans.*] (of fabric or a garment) be arranged in folds so as to droop in a specified way: *this blend of silk and wool hangs well and resists creases.* ■ [*trans.*] paste (wallpaper) to a wall. ■ informal way of saying HANG AROUND (sense 2) or HANG OUT (sense 3). **2** (*past* **hanged**) [*trans.*] kill (someone) by tying a rope attached from above around the neck and removing the support from beneath (used as a form of capital punishment): *he was hanged for murder | she hanged herself in her cell.* ■ [*intrans.*] be killed in such a way: *both men were sentenced to hang.* ■ *dated* used in expressions as a mild oath: [*intrans.*] *they could all go hang* | [*trans.*] *I'm hanged if I know.* **3** [*intrans.*] remain static in the air: *a haze of smoke hung below the ceiling.* ■ be present or imminent, esp. oppressively or threateningly: *a sense of dread hung over him for days.* ■ [*trans.*] *Baseball* deliver (a breaking pitch) that does not change direction as intended. **4** [*trans.*] (of a juror) prevent (a jury) from reaching a verdict by a dissenting vote. **5** *Computing* come or cause to come unexpectedly to a state in which no further operations can be carried out.
▸*phrasal v.* □ **hang around 1** loiter; wait around: *undercover officers spent most of their time hanging around bars.* **2** (**hang around with**) associate with (someone): *he never hangs around with that gang.* □ **hang back** remain behind: *Stephen hung back for fear of being seen.* ■ show reluctance to act or move: *they were hanging back, each unwilling to speak first.* □ **hang in** *informal* remain persistent and determined in difficult circumstances: *in the second half, we just had to* ***hang in there.*** □ **hang on 1** hold tightly: *he hung on to the back of her coat.* ■ *informal* remain firm or persevere, esp. in difficult circumstances: *we must hang on as best we can.* ■ (**hang on to**) keep; retain: *he is determined to hang on to his job.* **2** *informal* wait for a short time: *hang on a minute—do you think I might have left anything out?* ■ (on the telephone) remain connected until one is able to talk to a particular person. **3** be contingent or dependent on: *the future of Europe should not hang on a referendum by the French.* **4** listen closely to: *she hung on his every word.* □ **hang something on** *informal* attach the blame for something to (someone). □ **hang out 1** (of laundry) hang from a clothesline to dry. **2** (of a shirttail or other piece of clothing) protrude and hang loosely downward: *with the front tucked in and the tail hanging out.* **3** *informal* spend time relaxing or enjoying oneself: *musicians hang out with their own kind.* □ **hang together 1** make sense; be consistent: *it helps the speech to hang together.* **2** (of people) remain associated; help or support each other. □ **hang up 1** hang from a hook, hanger, etc.: *his good shirt's ironed and hanging up.* **2** end a telephone conversation by cutting the connection. ■ (**hang up on**) end a telephone conversation with (someone) by abruptly cutting the connection. □ **hang up something** hang something on a hook: *a closet where he could hang up his clothes.* ■ *informal* cease or retire from the activity associated with the garment or object specified: *he will soon have to hang up his referee's whistle for good.*
▸*n.* [in *sing.*] a downward droop or bend: *the bullish hang of his head.* ■ the way in which something hangs: *the hang of one's clothes.* ■ the way in which pictures are displayed in an exhibition. ▷Old English *hangian* (intransitive verb), related to Dutch and German *hangen*, reinforced by the Old Norse transitive verb *hanga.*
▸*PHRASES* □ **get the hang of** *informal* learn how to operate or do (something): *it's quite simple when you get the hang of it.* □ **hang by a thread** see THREAD. □ **hang fire** delay or be delayed in taking action or progressing. □ **hang one's hat** *informal* be resident. □ **hang heavily** (or **heavy**) (of time) pass slowly. □ **hang in the air** remain unresolved: *the question that has been hanging in the air.* □ **hang a left** (or **right**) *informal* make a left (or right) turn. □ **hang loose** see LOOSE. □ **hang someone out to dry** *informal* leave someone in a difficult or vulnerable situation. □ **hang ten** *Surfing* ride a surfboard with all ten toes curled over the board's front edge. □ **hang tough** be or remain inflexible or firmly resolved. □ **let it all hang out** *informal* be very relaxed or uninhibited. □ **not care** (or **give**) **a hang** *informal* not care at all: *people just don't give a hang about plants.*

USAGE In modern English, **hang** has two past tense and past participle forms: **hanged** and **hung.** **Hung** is the normal form in most general uses (*they* ***hung*** *out the wash; she* ***hung*** *around for a few minutes; he had* ***hung*** *the picture over the fireplace*), but **hanged** is the form normally used in reference to execution by hanging (*the outlaw was* ***hanged***).

hang·ar /ˈhaNGər/ ▸*n.* a large building with extensive floor area, typically for housing aircraft.
▸*v.* [*trans.*] (usu. **be hangared**) place or store in a hangar: *the army choppers that were hangared out at Springs.* ▷late 17th cent. (in the sense 'shelter'): from French; probably from Germanic bases meaning 'hamlet' and 'enclosure.' —**hang·ar·age** /-rij/ *n.*

Hang·chow /ˈhaNGˈCHou; ˈhängˈjō/ variant of HANGZHOU.

hang·dog /ˈhaNG,dôg; -,däg/ ▸*adj.* having a dejected or guilty appearance; shamefaced: *the boys wore hangdog looks as the police marched them down the steps.*

hang·er /ˈhaNGər/ ▸*n.* **1** [in *combination*] a person who hangs something: *a wallpaper hanger.* **2** (also **coat hanger**) a shaped piece of wood, plastic, or metal with a hook at the top, from which clothes may be hung in order to keep them in shape and free of creases. **3** something from which another thing hangs, such as a hook. **4** *historical* a short sword that hung from a belt.

hang·er-on ▸*n.* (*pl.* **hang·ers-on**) a person who associates with another person or a group in a sycophantic manner or for the purpose of gaining some personal advantage: *he was a hanger-on who used to come around and drink with Father.*

hang glid·er ▸*n.* an unpowered flying apparatus for a single person, consisting of a frame with a fabric airfoil stretched over it. The operator is suspended from a harness below and controls flight by body movement. ■ a person flying such an apparatus. **—hang-glide** *v.* **—hang glid·ing** *n.*

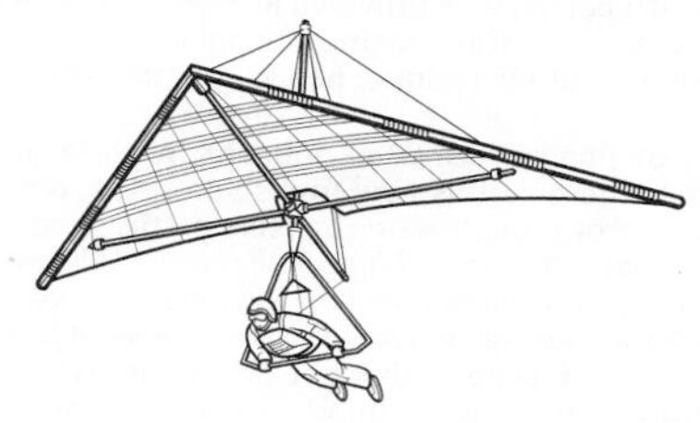
hang glider

hang·ing /ˈhaNGiNG/ ▸*n.* **1** the practice of hanging condemned people as a form of capital punishment. **2** a decorative piece of fabric or curtain hung on the wall of a room or around a bed: *a beautiful wall hanging.*
▸*adj.* [*attrib.*] suspended in the air: *hanging palls of smoke.* ■ situated or designed so as to appear to hang down: *hanging gardens.*

hang·ing bas·ket ▸*n.* a basket or similar container that can be suspended from a building by a small rope or chain and in which decorative flowering plants are grown.

Hang·ing Gar·dens of Bab·y·lon legendary terraced gardens at Babylon, watered by pumps from the Euphrates, whose construction was ascribed to Nebuchadnezzar (*c.*600 BC). They were one of the Seven Wonders of the World.

hang·ing in·dent ▸*n.* indentation of a paragraph in which all lines except the first are indented.

hang·ing val·ley ▸*n.* a valley that is cut across by a deeper valley or a cliff.

hang·ing wall ▸*n. Geology* the block of rock that lies above an inclined fault or an ore body. Compare with FOOTWALL.

hang·man /ˈhaNGmən; -ˌman/ ▸*n.* (*pl.* **-men**) an executioner who hangs condemned people. ■ a game for two in which one player tries to guess the letters of a word, and failed attempts are recorded by drawing a gallows and someone hanging on it, line by line.

hang·nail /ˈhaNGˌnāl/ ▸*n.* a piece of torn skin at the root of a fingernail. ▷late 17th cent.: alteration of *agnail* 'painful swelling around a nail' (from Old English *angnægl*, denoting a corn on the toe), influenced by HANG.

hang·out /ˈhaNGˌout/ ▸*n. informal* a place one frequently visits: *I nursed a beer at a favorite college hangout.*

hang·o·ver /ˈhaNGˌōvər/ ▸*n.* a severe headache or other after effects caused by drinking an excess of alcohol. ■ a thing that has survived from the past: *a hangover from the sixties.*

Hang Seng in·dex /ˈhaNG ˈseNG/ a figure indicating the relative price of shares on the Hong Kong Stock Exchange. ▷named after the *Hang Seng Bank* in Hong Kong, where it was devised.

hang time ▸*n. Football* the number of seconds during which a punted ball is in the air.

hang-up ▸*n. informal* an emotional problem or inhibition: *people with hang-ups about their age.*

Hang·zhou /ˈhängˈjō/ (also **Hang·chow**) a city in eastern China, the capital of Zhejiang province, on an inlet of the Yellow Sea called Hangzhou Bay, at the southern end of the Grand Canal; pop. 2,589,500.

hank /haNGk/ ▸*n.* **1** a coil or skein of yarn, hair, rope, or other material: *a thick hank of her blonde hair.* **2** a measurement of the length per unit mass of cloth or yarn, which varies according to the type being measured. For example, a hank is equal to 840 yards for cotton yarn and 560 yards for worsted. **3** *Sailing* a ring for securing a staysail to the stay. ▷Middle English: from Old Norse *hǫnk*; compare with Swedish *hank* 'string' and Danish *hank* 'handle.'

hank·er /ˈhaNGkər/ ▸*v.* [*intrans.*] (**hanker after/for/to do something**) feel a strong desire for or to do something: *to have his wife accuse him of hankering after adultery | she hankered to go back |* [as *n.*] (**hankering**) *you have a hankering for the sea.* ▷early 17th cent.: probably related to HANG; compare with Dutch *hunkeren.* **—hank·er·er** *n.*

Hanks /haNGks/, Tom (1956–), U.S. actor, director, and producer; full name *Thomas J. Hanks.* Lighthearted films such as *Splash!* (1984) and *Big* (1988) brought him international success. He won Academy Awards for his performances in *Philadelphia* (1993) and *Forrest Gump* (1994). Other films include *Saving Private Ryan* (1998) and *The Terminal* (2004).

han·ky /ˈhaNGkē/ (also **han·kie**) ▸*n.* (*pl.* **-kies**) *informal* a handkerchief. ▷late 19th cent.: abbreviation.

han·ky-pan·ky /ˈpaNGkē/ ▸*n. informal, humorous* behavior, in particular sexual or legally dubious behavior, considered improper but not seriously so: *there's no hanky-panky involved, no dating of customers | suspicions of financial hanky-panky.* ▷mid 19th cent.: perhaps an alteration of HOKEY-POKEY.

Han·ni·bal[1] /ˈhanəbəl/ a port city in northeastern Missouri, on the Mississippi River, the boyhood home of Mark Twain; pop. 18,004.

Han·ni·bal[2] /ˈhanəbəl/ (247–182 BC), Carthaginian general. In the second Punic War he attacked Italy by crossing the Alps. He repeatedly defeated the Romans, although he failed to take Rome itself. After being recalled to Africa he was defeated at Zama by Scipio Africanus in 202.

Ha·noi /haˈnoi; hə-/ the capital of Vietnam, on the Red River, in the northern part of the country; pop. 1,090,000. It was the capital of French Indo-China 1887–1946 and of North Vietnam before the reunification of North and South Vietnam.

Han·o·ver /ˈhanˌōvər; ˈhän-/ **1** an industrial city in northwestern Germany, the capital of Lower Saxony, on the Mittelland Canal; pop. 517,000. German name **HANNOVER** ■ a former state and province in northern Germany. In 1714 the Elector of Hanover succeeded to the British throne as George I, and from then until the accession of Victoria (1837) the same monarch ruled both Britain and Hanover. ■ the British royal house from 1714 to the death of Queen Victoria in 1901. **2** a town in west central New Hampshire, on the Connecticut River, home to Dartmouth College; pop. 9,212.

Han·o·ve·ri·an /ˌhanəˈve(ə)rēən/ ▸*adj.* of or relating to the royal house of Hanover.
▸*n.* **1** (usu. **the Hanoverians**) any of the British sovereigns from George I to Victoria. **2** a medium-built horse of a German breed, developed for use both as a riding horse and in harness.

Han Riv·er /hän/ 1 (Chinese name **Han Shui**) a river in eastern China that flows southeast for 952 miles (1,532 km) from southwestern Shaanxi province to the Yangtze River in Hubei province. 2 (Chinese name **Han Jiang**) river in south China that rises in southeastern Fujian province and flows south for 210 miles (338 km) to the South China Sea at Shantou in Guangdong province.

Han·sard /ˈhansərd/ ▸*n.* the official verbatim record of debates in the British, Canadian, Australian, or New Zealand parliament. ▷late 19th cent.: named after Thomas C. *Hansard* (1776–1833), an English printer whose company originally printed it.

Hans·ber·ry /ˈhanzˌberē/, Lorraine (1930–65) U.S. playwright and civil rights activist. Her *A Raisin in the Sun* (1959) was the first play by an African-American woman to be produced on Broadway. It was made into a movie in 1961.

Hanse /hans; ˈhänzə/ ▸*n.* a medieval guild of merchants. ■ (**the Hanse**) the Hanseatic League. ■ a fee payable to a guild of merchants. ▷Middle English: from Old French *hanse* 'guild, company,' from Old High German *hansa* 'company, troop.'

Han·se·at·ic League /ˌhansēˈatik/ a medieval association of northern German cities, formed in 1241 and surviving until the 19th century. In the later Middle Ages it included over 100 towns and functioned as an independent political power. ▷*Hanseatic* from medieval Latin *Hanseaticus*, from *hansa* (see HANSE).

han·sel /ˈhansəl/ (also **hand·sel**) ▸*n.* a gift given for good luck at the beginning of the year or to mark an acquisition or the start of an enterprise. ■ the first installment of a payment.
▸*v.* (**-seled, -sel·ing**; *Brit.* **-selled, -sel·ling**) [*trans.*] give a hansel to. ■ inaugurate (something), esp. by being the first to try it: *a floodlit fixture to officially hansel the completed stadium.* ▷Middle English (denoting luck): apparently related to late Old English *handselen* 'giving into a person's hands,' and Old Norse *handsal* 'giving of the hand to seal a promise,' from HAND + an element related to SELL; the notion of 'luck,' however, is not present in these words.

Han·sen's dis·ease /ˈhansənz/ ▸*n.* another name for LEPROSY. ▷1930s: named after Gerhard H. A. *Hansen* (1841–1912), the Norwegian physician who discovered the causative agent of the disease.

han·som /ˈhansəm/ (also **han·som cab**) ▸*n. historical* a two-wheeled horse-drawn carriage accommodating two inside, with the driver seated behind. ▷mid 19th cent.: named after Joseph A. *Hansom* (1803–82), English architect, patentee of such a cab in 1834.

hansom

han·ta·vi·rus /ˈhantəˌvīrəs/ ▸*n.* a virus of a genus carried by rodents and causing various febrile hemorrhagic diseases, often with kidney damage or failure. ▷1980s: from *Hantaan* (the name of a river in Korea where the virus was first isolated) + VIRUS.

Ha·nuk·kah /ˈKHänəkə; ˈhänəkə/ (also **Cha·nu·kah**) ▸*n.* a lesser Jewish festival, lasting eight days from the 25th day of Kislev (in December) and commemorating the rededication of the Temple in 165 BC by the Maccabees after its desecration by the Syrians. It is marked by the successive kindling of eight lights. ▷from Hebrew *ḥănukkāh* 'consecration.'

han·u·man /ˈhənŏŏˌmän/ ▸*n.* **1** (also **hanuman langur**) a pale-colored langur monkey of the Indian subcontinent, venerated by Hindus. • *Presbytis entellus*, family Cercopithecidae. **2** *Hinduism* (**Hanuman**) a semidivine being of monkeylike form, whose exploits are described in the Ramayana. ▷from Sanskrit *hanumant* 'large-jawed.'

Han·zhong /ˈhänˈjŏŏNG/ a city in Shaanxi province, in central China, southwest of Xi'an on the northern bank of the Han River; pop. 420,000.

hao·ma /ˈhoumə/ ▸*n.* variant of HOM.

Hao·ra variant spelling of HOWRAH.

hap /hap/ *archaic* ▸*n.* luck; fortune. ■ a chance occurrence, esp. an event that is considered unlucky.
▸*v.* (**happed, hap·ping**) [*intrans.*] come about by chance: *what can hap to him worthy to be deemed evil?* ■ [with *infinitive*] have the fortune or luck to do something: *where'er I happ'd to roam.* ▷Middle English: from Old Norse *happ.*

hap·ax le·go·me·non /ˈhapaks ləˈgäməˌnän/ ▸*n.* (*pl.* **hap·ax le·go·me·na** /ləˈgämənə/) a term of which only one instance of use is recorded. ▷mid 17th cent.: Greek, 'a thing said once,' from *hapax* 'once' and the passive participle of *legein* 'to say.'

ha'·pen·ny ▸*n.* variant spelling of HALFPENNY.

hap·haz·ard /ˌhapˈhazərd/ ▸*adj.* lacking any obvious principle of organization: *the kitchen drawers contained a haphazard collection of silver souvenir spoons.* ▷late 16th cent.: from HAP + HAZARD. **—hap·haz·ard·ly** *adv.* **—hap·haz·ard·ness** *n.*

Haph·ta·rah /ˌhäftäˈrä; häfˈtôrə/ (also **Haph·to·rah**) ▸*n.* (*pl.* **-ta·roth** /-täˈrôt; -ˈtôrōs/) variant spelling of HAFTORAH.

hap·ki·do /häpˈkēdō/ ▸*n.* a comprehensive Korean martial art that stresses domination of one's opponent through the eclectic use of joint-locks, throws, choking, tackling, kicking, and punching. ▷Korean: 'way of gathered strength.'

hap·less /ˈhaplis/ ▸*adj.* (esp. of a person) unfortunate: *if you're one of the many hapless car buyers who've been shafted.* ▷late Middle English: from HAP (in the early sense 'good fortune') + -LESS. **—hap·less·ly** *adv.* **—hap·less·ness** *n.*

haplo- ▸*comb. form* single; simple: *haplography | haploid.* ▷from Greek *haploos* 'single.'

hap·lo·chro·mine /ˌhaplōˈkrōˌmēn/ *Zoology* ▸*adj.* of, relating to, or denoting cichlid fishes of a large and diverse group that are particularly abundant in the large lakes of East Africa.

▸*n.* a haplochromine fish. • *Haplochromis* and related genera, family Cichlidae. ▷from the modern Latin genus name.

hap·lo·dip·loid /ˌhaplōˈdiploid/ ▸*adj.* *Biology* denoting or possessing a genetic system in which females develop from fertilized (diploid) eggs and males from unfertilized (haploid) ones.

hap·log·ra·phy /hapˈlägrəfē/ ▸*n.* the inadvertent omission of a repeated letter or letters in writing (e.g., writing *philogy* for *philology*). ▷late 19th cent.: from Greek *haploos* 'single' + -GRAPHY.

hap·loid /ˈhapˌloid/ *Genetics* ▸*adj.* (of a cell or nucleus) having a single set of unpaired chromosomes. Compare with DIPLOID. ■ (of an organism or part) composed of haploid cells.
▸*n.* a haploid organism or cell. ▷early 20th cent.: from Greek *haploos* 'single' + -OID. **—hap·loi·dy** *n.*

hap·lol·o·gy /hapˈläləjē/ ▸*n.* the omission of an occurrence of a sound or syllable that is repeated within a word, e.g., in *probly* for *probably*. ▷late 19th cent.: from Greek *haploos* 'single' + -LOGY.

hap·lon·tic /hapˈläntik/ ▸*adj.* *Genetics* (chiefly of an alga or other lower plant) having a life cycle in which the main form is haploid, with a diploid zygote being formed only briefly. Compare with DIPLONTIC and DIPLOHAPLONTIC. **—hap·lont** /ˈhapˌlänt/ *n.*

hap·lo·sis /hapˈlōsis/ ▸*n.* *Biology* the halving of the number of chromosomes in a diploid cell during meiosis, resulting in two haploid cells.

ha'p'orth /ˈhāpərTH/ ▸*n.* variant spelling of HALFPENNYWORTH.

hap·pen /ˈhapən/ ▸*v.* [*intrans.*] **1** take place; occur: *the afternoon when the disturbance happened.* ■ ensue as an effect or result of an action or event: *this is what happens when the mechanism goes wrong.* ■ [with *infinitive*] chance to do something or come about: *we just happened to meet Paul | there happens to be a clash of personalities.* ■ [with *clause*] come about by chance: ***it just so happened that** she turned up that afternoon.* ■ (**happen on**) find or come across by chance: *Mike played football as a boy and happened on cycling by accident.* ■ [with *infinitive*] used as a polite formula in questions: *do you happen to know who her doctor is?* **2** (**happen to**) be experienced by (someone); befall: *the same thing happened to me.* ■ become of: *I don't care what happens to the money.* ▷late Middle English (superseding the verb *hap*): from the noun HAP + -EN[1].
▸*PHRASE* □ **as it happens** actually; as a matter of fact: *we've got a room vacant, as it happens.*

THE RIGHT WORD **befall, chance, happen, occur, transpire**

When things **happen**, they come to pass either for a reason or by chance (*it happened the day after school started; she happened upon the scene of the accident*), but the verb is more frequently associated with chance (*it happened to be raining when we got there*).

Occur can also refer either to something that comes to pass either accidentally or as planned, but it should be used interchangeably with *happen* only when the subject is a definite or actual event (*the tragedy occurred last winter*). Unlike *happen*, *occur* also carries the implication of something that presents itself to sight or mind (*it never occurred to me that he was lying*).

Transpire is a more formal (and some would say undesirable) word meaning to *happen* or *occur*, and it conveys the sense that something has leaked out or become known (*he told her exactly what had transpired while she was away*).

While things that *happen*, *occur*, or *transpire* can be either positive or negative, when something **befalls** it is usually unpleasant (*he had no inkling of the disaster that would befall him when he got home*).

hap·pen·ing /ˈhap(ə)niNG/ ▸*n.* **1** an event or occurrence: *altogether it was an eerie happening.* ■ a noteworthy or exciting event: *an all-star, superstar, megastar happening.* **2** a partly improvised or spontaneous piece of theatrical or other artistic performance, typically involving audience participation: *a multimedia happening.*
▸*adj.* *informal* fashionable; trendy: *nightclubs for the young are the happening thing.*

hap·pen·stance /ˈhapənˌstans/ ▸*n.* coincidence: *it was just happenstance that I happened to be there | an untoward happenstance for Trudy.* ▷late 19th cent.: blend of HAPPEN and CIRCUMSTANCE.

hap·pi /ˈhapē/ (also **hap·pi coat**) ▸*n.* (*pl.* **-pis**) a loose informal Japanese coat. ▷late 19th cent.: Japanese.

hap·pi·ly /ˈhapəlē/ ▸*adv.* in a happy way: *Eleanor giggled happily.* ■ [*sentence adverb*] it is fortunate that: *happily, today's situation is very different.*

hap·py /ˈhapē/ ▸*adj.* (**-pi·er, -pi·est**) **1** feeling or showing pleasure or contentment: *Melissa came in looking happy and excited* | [with *clause*] *we're just happy that he's still alive* | [with *infinitive*] *they are happy to see me doing well.* ■ [*predic.*] (**happy about**) having a sense of confidence in or satisfaction with (a person, arrangement, or situation): *I was never very happy about the explanation | I can't say they looked too happy about it, but a deal's a deal.* ■ [*predic.*] (**happy with**) satisfied with the quality or standard of: *I'm happy with his performance.* ■ [with *infinitive*] willing to do something: *we will be happy to advise you.* ■ (of an event or situation) characterized by happiness: *we had a very happy, relaxed time.* ■ [*attrib.*] used in greetings: *happy birthday.* ■ [*attrib.*] fortunate and convenient: *he had the happy knack of making people like him.* **2** [in *combination*] *informal* inclined to use a specified thing excessively or at random: *our litigation-happy society.* ▷Middle English (in the sense 'lucky'): from the noun HAP + -Y[1]. **—hap·pi·ness** *n.*
▸*PHRASES* □ (**as**) **happy as a clam** (**at high tide**) extremely happy. □ **happy hunting ground** a place where success or enjoyment is obtained. [originally referring to the optimistic hope of American Indians for good hunting grounds in the afterlife.]

hap·py-go-luck·y ▸*adj.* cheerfully unconcerned about the future: *a happy-go-lucky, relaxed attitude.*

hap·py hour ▸*n.* a period of the day when drinks are sold at reduced prices in a bar or restaurant.

hap·py me·di·um ▸*n.* a satisfactory compromise: *you have to **strike a happy medium between** looking like royalty and looking like a housewife.*

Haps·burg /ˈhapsbərg; ˈhäpsˌbo͝ork/ variant spelling of **HABSBURG**.

hap·ten /ˈhapˌten/ ▸*n.* *Physiology* a small molecule that, when combined with a larger carrier such as a protein, can elicit the production of antibodies that bind specifically to it (in the free or combined state). ▷early 20th cent.: from Greek *haptein* 'fasten.'

hap·tic /ˈhaptik/ ▸*adj.* *technical* of or relating to the sense of touch, in particular relating to the perception and manipulation of objects using the senses of touch and proprioception. ▷late 19th cent.: from Greek *haptikos* 'able to touch or grasp,' from *haptein* 'fasten.'

hap·to·glo·bin /ˌhaptəˈglōbən/ ▸*n.* *Biochemistry* a protein present in blood serum that binds to and removes free hemoglobin from the bloodstream. ▷1940s: from Greek *haptein* 'fasten' + *(hemo)globin*.

ha·ra-ki·ri /ˌhärə ˈki(ə)rē; ˌharə-; ˌharē ˈkarē/ ▸*n.* ritual suicide by disembowelment with a sword, formerly practiced in Japan by samurai as an honorable alternative to disgrace or execution. ■ *figurative* ostentatious or ritualized self-destruction: *you may wonder why you find this software hard to navigate, painfully slow, and prone to hara-kiri.* ▷mid 19th cent.: colloquial Japanese, from *hara* 'belly' + *kiri* 'cutting.'

ha·ram /ˈhe(ə)rəm; ˈharəm/ ▸*adj.* forbidden or proscribed by Islamic law. ▷from Arabic *ḥarām* 'forbidden.'

ha·rangue /həˈraNG/ ▸*n.* a lengthy and aggressive speech.
▸*v.* [*trans.*] lecture (someone) at length in an aggressive and critical manner: *the kind of guy who **harangued** total strangers **about** PCB levels in whitefish.* ▷late Middle English: from Old French *arenge*, from medieval Latin *harenga*, perhaps of Germanic origin. The spelling was later altered to conform with French *harangue* (noun), *haranguer* (verb). **—ha·rangu·er** *n.*

Ha·rap·pa /həˈrapə/ an ancient city of the Indus valley civilization (*c.*2600–1700 BC), in northern Pakistan. The site of the ruins was discovered in 1920.

Ha·ra·re /həˈrärē; -ˈrärā/ the capital of Zimbabwe; pop. 1,184,000. Former name (until 1982) **SALISBURY**[1].

ha·rass /həˈras; ˈharəs/ ▸*v.* [*trans.*] subject to aggressive pressure or intimidation: *a warning to men harassing girls at work.* ■ make repeated small-scale attacks on (an enemy): *the squadron's task was to harass the retreating enemy forces.* ■ [as *adj.*] (**harassed**) feeling or looking strained by having too many demands made on one. ▷early 17th cent.: from French *harasser*, from *harer* 'set a dog on,' from Germanic *hare*, a cry urging a dog to attack. **—ha·rass·er** *n.* **—ha·rass·ing·ly** *adv.* **—ha·rass·ment** *n.*

USAGE Traditionally, the word **harass** has been pronounced with stress on the first syllable, as "HAR-uhs." But the newer pronunciation that puts the stress on the second syllable is increasingly more widespread and is considered standard. This pronunciation fact is also true for **harassment**.

Har·bin /härˈbin; ˈhärbin/ a city in northeastern China, the capital of Heilongjiang province, on the Songhua River; pop. 3,597,000.

har·bin·ger /ˈhärbənjər/ ▸*n.* a person or thing that announces or signals the approach of another: *witch hazels are the harbingers of spring.* ■ a forerunner of something: *these works were not yet opera, but they were the most important harbinger of opera.* ▷Middle English: from Old French *herbergere*, from *herbergier* 'provide lodging for,' from *herberge* 'lodging,' from Old Saxon *heriberga* 'shelter for an army, lodging' (from *heri* 'army' + a Germanic base meaning 'fortified place'), related to HARBOR. The term originally denoted a person who provided lodging, later one who went ahead to find lodgings for an army or for a nobleman and his retinue, hence, a herald (mid 16th cent.).

har·bor /ˈhärbər/ (*Brit.* **har·bour**) ▸*n.* a place on the coast where vessels may find shelter, esp. one protected from rough water by piers, jetties, and other artificial structures: *fishing in the harbor | the westerly wind kept us **in harbor** until the following afternoon.* ■ *figurative* a place of refuge: *the offered harbor of his arms.*
▸*v.* [*trans.*] **1** keep (a thought or feeling, typically a negative one) in one's mind, esp. secretly: *she started to harbor doubts about the wisdom of their journey.* **2** give a home or shelter to: *woodlands that once harbored a colony of red deer.* ■ shelter or hide (a criminal or wanted person): *he was suspected of harboring an escaped prisoner.* ■ carry the germs of (a disease). **3** [*intrans.*] *archaic* (of a ship or its crew) moor in a harbor: *he might have harbored in San Francisco.* ▷late Old English *herebeorg* 'shelter, refuge,' *herebeorgian* 'occupy shelter,' of Germanic origin; related to Dutch *herberge* and German *Herberge*, also to French *auberge* 'inn'; see also HARBINGER. **—har·bor·er** *n.* **—har·bor·less** *adj.*

har·bor·mas·ter /ˈhärbərˌmastər/ (also **harbor master**) ▸*n.* an official in charge of a harbor.

har·bor por·poise ▸*n.* a porpoise with a dark gray back shading to white underparts, found in the coastal waters of North America and northern Europe. Also called COMMON PORPOISE. • *Phocoena phocoena*, family Phocoenidae.

har·bor seal ▸*n.* a seal with a mottled gray-brown coat and a concave profile, found along North Atlantic and North Pacific coasts. • *Phoca vitulina*, family Phocidae.

hard /härd/ ▸*adj.* **1** solid, firm, and resistant to pressure; not easily broken, bent, or pierced: *a hard mattress | ground frozen hard as a rock.* ■ (of a person) not showing any signs of weakness; tough: *the hard, tough, honest cop.* ■ (of information) reliable, esp. because based on something true or substantiated: *hard facts about the underclass are maddeningly elusive.* ■ (of a subject of study) dealing with precise and verifiable facts: *efforts to turn psychology into hard science.* ■ (of water) containing mineral salts that make lathering difficult. ■ (of prices of stock, commodities, etc.) stable or firm in value. ■ (of science fiction) scientifically accurate rather than purely fantastic or whimsical: *a hard SF novel.* ■ (of a consonant) pronounced as *c* in *cat* or *g* in *go*. **2** requiring a great deal of endurance or physical or mental effort: *stooping over all day was hard work* | [with *infinitive*] *she found it hard to believe that he could be involved.* ■ putting a lot of energy into an activity: *he'd been a hard worker all his life.* ■ difficult to bear; causing suffering: *times were hard at the end of the war | he'd had a hard life.* ■ not showing sympathy or affection; strict: *he can be such a hard taskmaster.* ■ (of a season or the weather) severe: *it's been a long, hard winter.* ■ harsh or unpleasant to the senses: *the hard light of morning.* ■ (of wine) harsh or sharp to the taste, esp. because of tannin. **3** done with a great deal of force or strength: *a hard blow to the head.* **4** potent, powerful, or intense, in particular: ■ (of liquor) strongly alcoholic; denoting distilled spirits rather than beer or wine. ■ (of apple cider) having alcoholic content from fermentation. ■ (of a drug) potent and addictive. ■ denoting an extreme or dogmatic faction within a political party: *the hard left.* ■ (of radiation) highly penetrating. ■ (of pornography) highly obscene and explicit.
▸*adv.* **1** with a great deal of effort: *they work hard at school.* ■ with a great deal of force; violently: *it was raining hard.* **2** so as to be solid or firm: *the mortar has set hard.* **3** to the fullest extent possible: *put the wheel **hard over** to starboard.* ▷Old English *hard, heard*, of Germanic origin; related to Dutch *hard* and German *hart*. **—hard·ish** *adj.* **—hard·ness** *n.*
▸*PHRASES* □ **be hard on 1** treat or criticize (someone) severely: *you're being too hard on her.* **2** be diffi-

cult for or unfair to: *I think the war must have been hard on her.* **3** be likely to hurt or damage: *the monitor flickers, which is hard on the eyes.* □ **be hard put** [usu. with *infinitive*] find it very difficult: *you'll be hard put to find a better compromise.* □ **give someone a hard time** *informal* deliberately make a situation difficult for someone. □ **go hard with** *dated* turn out to (someone's) disadvantage: *it would go hard with the poor.* □ **hard and fast** (of a rule or a distinction made) fixed and definitive: *it is impossible to lay down any hard and fast rules.* □ **hard as nails** see NAIL. □ **hard at it** *informal* busily working or occupied: *they were hard at it with brooms and mops.* □ **hard by** close to: *he lived hard by the cathedral.* □ **hard done by** *Brit.* harshly or unfairly treated: *she would be justified in feeling hard done by.* □ **hard feelings** [usu. with *negative*] feelings of resentment: *there are* ***no hard feelings,*** *and we wish him well.* □ **hard going** difficult to understand or enjoy: *the studying is at times hard going.* □ **hard hit** badly affected: *hard hit by falling oil prices.* □ **a hard nut to crack** *informal* a person or thing that is difficult to understand or influence. □ **hard of hearing** not able to hear well. □ **hard on** (or **upon**) close to; following soon after: *we followed hard on their tracks.* □ **hard up** *informal* short of money: *I'm too hard up to buy fancy clothes.* □ **the hard way** through suffering or learning from the unpleasant consequences of mistakes: *his reputation was earned the hard way.* □ **play hard to get** *informal* deliberately adopt an aloof or uninterested attitude, typically in order to make oneself more attractive or interesting.

THE RIGHT WORD **arduous, difficult, hard, laborious, trying**

For the student who doesn't read well, homework is **hard** work, which means that it demands great physical or mental effort.

An English assignment to write an essay might be particularly **difficult**, meaning that it not only requires effort but skill. Where *hard* suggests toil, *difficult* emphasizes complexity (*a difficult math problem*).

Memorizing long lists of vocabulary words would be **laborious**, which is even more restrictive than *hard* and suggests prolonged, wearisome toil with no suggestion of the skill required and no reference to the complexity of the task.

Reading *War and Peace*, however, would be an **arduous** task, because it would require a persistent effort over a long period of time.

A school assignment may be *difficult*, but is usually not *arduous*; that is, it may require skill rather than perseverance. It may also be *arduous* without being particularly *difficult*, as when a student is asked to write "I will not throw spitballs" five hundred times.

A student who is new to a school may find it especially **trying**, which implies that it taxes someone's patience, skill, or capabilities.

hard·back /ˈhärd,bak/ ▸*adj.* & *n.* another term for HARDCOVER.

hard·ball /ˈhärd,bôl/ ▸*n.* baseball, esp. as contrasted with softball. ■ *Baseball* a very competitive pitching and playing style. ■ *informal* uncompromising and ruthless methods or dealings, esp. in politics: *the leadership* ***played hardball*** *to win the vote.*

hard-bit·ten (also **hard·bit·ten**) ▸*adj.* tough and cynical: *joining the hard-bitten reporting veterans at the presidential debate.*

hard·board /ˈhärd,bôrd/ ▸*n.* stiff board made of compressed and treated wood pulp.

hard·bod·y /ˈhärd,bädē/ ▸*n.* (*pl.* **-bod·ies**) *informal* a person with very toned or well-developed muscles: *you're in the cockpit of a ragtop Testarossa with a tanned, blond hardbody at your side.* —**hard·bod·ied** *adj.*

hard-boiled ▸*adj.* **1** (of an egg) boiled until the white and the yolk are solid. **2** (of a person) tough and cynical. ■ denoting a tough, realistic style of detective fiction set in a world permeated by corruption and deceit: *a hard-boiled thriller.* —**hard-boil** *v.* (in sense 1).

hard case ▸*n.* *informal* a tough or intractable person.

hard cash ▸*n.* negotiable coins and paper money as opposed to other forms of payment.

hard charg·er ▸*n.* someone with an aggressive, domineering personality. ■ (in car racing) someone who gains a considerably better position during the course of a race.

hard cheese ▸*n.* see CHEESE[1].

hard clam ▸*n.* another term for QUAHOG.

hard coal ▸*n.* another term for ANTHRACITE.

hard-code ▸*v.* [*trans.*] *Computing* fix (data or parameters) in a program in such a way that they cannot easily be altered by the user.

hard-cooked ▸*adj.* another term for HARD-BOILED (sense 1).

hard cop·y ▸*n.* a printed version on paper of data held in a computer.

hard core ▸*n.* the most active, committed, or doctrinaire members of a group or movement: *there is always a hard core of trusty stalwarts* | [as *adj.*] *a hard core following.* ■ popular music that is experimental in nature and typically characterized by high volume and aggressive presentation. ■ pornography of an explicit kind: [as *adj.*] *hard-core porn.*

hard court ▸*n.* a tennis court surfaced with asphalt or another hard material: [as *adj.*] *former national hard court champion.*

hard·cov·er /ˈhärd,kəvər/ ▸*adj.* (of a book) bound between rigid boards covered in cloth, paper, leather, or film: *hardcover and paperback editions.*
▸*n.* a hardcover book.
▸*PHRASE* □ **in hardcover** in a hardcover edition.

hard cur·ren·cy ▸*n.* currency that is not likely to depreciate suddenly or to fluctuate greatly in value.

hard disk ▸*n.* *Computing* a rigid nonremovable magnetic disk with a large data storage capacity, as distinct from the smaller capacity floppy disk.

hard drive ▸*n.* *Computing* a high-capacity, self-contained storage device containing a read-write mechanism plus one or more hard disks, inside a sealed unit. Also called HARD DISK DRIVE.

hard-earned ▸*adj.* having taken a great deal of effort to earn or acquire: *my few hard-earned dollars mean a lot to my family.*

hard-edge ▸*adj.* of or relating to a style of abstract painting characterized by geometric shapes with sharply defined edges and often in bright colors. —**hard-edge** *n.* a painting in hard-edge style.

hard-edged ▸*adj.* **1** having sharply defined edges. **2** having an intense, tough, or sharp quality: *hard-edged urban films.*

hard·en /ˈhärdn/ ▸*v.* make or become hard or harder: [*intrans.*] *wait for the glue to harden* | [*trans.*] *bricks that seem to have been hardened by firing.* ■ make or become more severe and less sympathetic: [*trans.*] *she hardened her heart.* ■ make or become tougher and more clearly defined: [*intrans.*] *suspicion* ***hardened into*** *certainty.* ■ [*intrans.*] (of prices of stocks, commodities, etc.) rise and remain steady at a higher level.
▸*phrasal v.* □ **harden something off** inure a plant to cold by gradually increasing its exposure to it. —**hard·en·er** *n.*
▸*PHRASE* □ **hardening of the arteries** another term for ARTERIOSCLEROSIS.

hard·ened /ˈhärdnd/ ▸*adj.* **1** having become or been made hard or harder: *hardened steel.* ■ strengthened or made secure against attack, esp. by nuclear weapons: *the silos are* ***hardened against*** *air attack.* **2** [*attrib.*] experienced in a particular job or activity and therefore not easily upset by its more unpleasant aspects: *hardened police officers* | [in *combination*] *a battle-hardened veteran.* ■ utterly fixed in a habit or way of life seen as bad: *hardened criminals* | *a hardened liar.*

hard er·ror ▸*n.* *Computing* an error or hardware fault causing failure of a program or operating system, esp. one that gives no option of recovery.

hard fern ▸*n.* a European fern of heathy places, with long, narrow, leathery fronds consisting of a row of thin lobes on each side of the stem. • *Blechnum spicant*, family Blechnaceae.

hard·gain·er /ˈhärd'gānər/ ▸*n.* (in bodybuilding) a person who does not find it easy to gain muscle through exercise.

hard hat ▸*n.* a rigid protective helmet, as worn by factory and building workers. ■ *informal* a worker who wears a hard hat. ■ *informal* a person with reactionary or conservative views.

hard·head /ˈhärd,hed/ ▸*n.* (also **hardhead catfish**) a marine catfish, the male of which incubates the eggs inside its mouth. It occurs along the Atlantic coast of North America. • *Arius felis*, family Ariidae.

hard·head·ed /ˈhärd,hedid/ ▸*adj.* practical and realistic; not sentimental: *as experienced and hardheaded a bunch of legislators as has ever entered Congress.* —**hard·head·ed·ly** *adv.* —**hard·head·ed·ness** *n.*

hard·heads /ˈhärd,hedz/ ▸*plural n.* [treated as *sing.*] another term for KNAPWEED, esp. the black knapweed.

hard-heart·ed ▸*adj.* incapable of being moved to pity or tenderness; unfeeling. —**hard-heart·ed·ly** *adv.* —**hard-heart·ed·ness** *n.*

hard-hit·ting ▸*adj.* **1** uncompromisingly direct and honest, esp. in revealing unpalatable facts: *some of this season's more hard-hitting episodes deal with urban violence.* **2** (of an athlete or athletes) aggressive and physical: *the game's grunting, hard-hitting defense.*

har·di·hood /ˈhärdē,ho͝od/ ▸*n.* *dated* boldness; daring.

Har·ding /ˈhärdiNG/, Warren (Gamaliel) (1865–1923), 29th president of the U.S. 1921–23. A Republican, he served in the U.S. Senate 1915–21 before becoming president. His administration was marked by corruption and scandal, in particular, the Teapot Dome scandal, in which his secretary of the interior accepted money in return for leasing the Teapot Dome oil reserves in Wyoming to private oil producers. Harding died in office while on a trip to California.

Warren G. Harding

hard la·bor ▸*n.* heavy manual work as a punishment.

hard land·ing ▸*n.* a clumsy or rough landing of an aircraft. ■ an uncontrolled landing in which a spacecraft crashes onto the surface of a planet or moon and is destroyed.

hard line ▸*n.* an uncompromising adherence to a firm policy: *he is known to* ***take a hard line on*** *sentencing policy for murder.*
▸*adj.* uncompromising; strict: *a hard-line party activist.*

hard-lin·er ▸*n.* a member of a group, typically a political group, who adheres uncompromisingly to a set of ideas or policies.

hard-luck sto·ry ▸*n.* an account of one's problems intended to gain sympathy or help.

hard·ly /ˈhärdlē/ ▸*adv.* **1** scarcely (used to qualify a statement by saying that it is true to an insignificant degree): *it is hardly bigger than a credit card.* ■ only a very short time before: *the party had hardly started when the police arrived.* ■ only with great difficulty: *she could hardly sit up straight.* ■ no or not (suggesting surprise at or disagreement with a statement): *I hardly think so.* **2** *archaic* harshly: *the rule worked hardly.*
▸*PHRASES* □ **hardly any** almost no: *they sold hardly any books.* ■ almost none: *hardly any had previous convictions.* □ **hardly ever** very rarely: *we hardly ever see them.*

USAGE 1 Words like **hardly**, **scarcely**, and **rarely** should not be used with negative constructions. Thus, it is correct to say *I* ***can hardly*** *wait* but incorrect to say *I* ***can't hardly*** *wait.* This is because adverbs like **hardly** are treated as if they were negatives, and it is a well-known grammatical rule of standard English that double negatives are not acceptable. Words like **hardly** behave as negatives in other respects as well, as for example in combining with terms such as **any** or **at all**, which normally occur only where a negative is present (thus, standard usage is *I've got* ***hardly any*** *money*, but not *I've got* ***any*** *money*). See also **usage** at DOUBLE NEGATIVE.

2 **Hardly . . . than** versus **hardly . . . when**: the conjunction *than* is best left to work with comparative adjectives and adverbs (*lovelier than; more quickly than*). Consider a construction such as *Sheila had hardly recovered from the flu when she lost her beloved beagle*: in speech, one might tend to use **than** as the complement to **hardly**, but in careful writing, since time is the point, the word to use is **when**. In a more formal context, however, the idea would be better conveyed: *No sooner had Sheila recovered from the flu than she lost her beloved beagle.* In this sentence, *than* does belong because it is the natural conjunction after the comparative adjective *sooner*.

3 As synonyms, *hardly*, *barely*, and *scarcely* are almost indistinguishable.

hard-nosed ▸*adj. informal* realistic and determined; tough-minded: *the hard-nosed, tough approach.*

hard nut ▸*n. Brit., informal* a tough, aggressive, or insensitive person.

hard-on ▸*n. vulgar slang* an erection of the penis.

hard pal·ate ▸*n.* the bony front part of the palate.

hard·pan /ˈhärd,pan/ ▸*n.* a hardened impervious layer, typically of clay, occurring in or below the soil and impairing drainage and plant growth.

hard-paste ▸*adj.* denoting true porcelain made of fusible and infusible materials (usually kaolin and china stone) fired at a high temperature. Developed in early medieval China, it was not made in Europe until the early 18th century.

hard-pressed ▸*adj.* **1** closely pursued: *the hard-pressed French infantry.* **2** burdened with urgent business: *training centers are hard-pressed and insufficient in numbers.* ■ (also **hard pressed**) in difficulties: *creating jobs in the hard-pressed construction industry* | [with infinitive] *many families will* **be hard pressed to** *support their elderly relations.*

hard rock ▸*n.* highly amplified rock music with a heavy beat.

hard roe ▸*n.* see ROE.

hard sauce ▸*n.* a sauce of butter and sugar, typically with brandy, rum, or vanilla added.

hard·scape /ˈhärd,skāp/ ▸*n.* the nonliving or manmade fixtures of a planned outdoor area: *before you begin to implement your plan, consider the hardscape of your ornamental garden.*

hard·scap·ing /ˈhärd,skāpiNG/ ▸*n.* the placement of nonplant elements such as fences, walkways, paving, and lighting in a planned outdoor area.

hard·scrab·ble /ˈhärd,skrabəl/ ▸*adj.* **1** returning little in exchange for great effort: *her uncle's hardscrabble peanut farm.* **2** characterized by chronic poverty and hardship: *the hardscrabble coal town of Grundy, Virginia.*

hard sell ▸*n.* a policy or technique of aggressive salesmanship or advertising: *they invited 1,000 participants and gave them* **the hard sell.**

hard-shell ▸*adj.* [*attrib.*] **1** having a hard shell or outer casing: *hard-shell helmets.* **2** rigid or uncompromising, esp. in fundamentalist religious belief: *I am a hard-shell Baptist.*

hard-shell clam ▸*n.* another term for QUAHOG.

hard·ship /ˈhärd,SHip/ ▸*n.* severe suffering or privation: *intolerable levels of hardship* | *the shared hardships of wartime.*

hard·stand·ing /ˈhärdˈstandiNG/ ▸*n. Brit.* ground surfaced with a hard material for parking vehicles on.

hard stuff ▸*n.* (**the hard stuff**) *informal* strong liquor.

hard·tack /ˈhärd,tak/ ▸*n.* hard dry bread or biscuit, esp. as rations for sailors.

hard·top /ˈhärd,täp/ ▸*n.* a motor vehicle with a rigid roof that in some cases is detachable. ■ a roof of this type.

Har·dwar /ˈhär,dwär/ a city in northern India, in Uttar Pradesh, on the Ganges River; pop. 189,000. It is a place of Hindu pilgrimage.

hard·ware /ˈhärd,we(ə)r/ ▸*n.* tools, machinery, and other durable equipment: *tanks and other military hardware.* ■ the machines, wiring, and other physical components of a computer or other electronic system. Compare with SOFTWARE. ■ tools, implements, and other items used in home life and activities such as gardening.

hard·wear·ing /ˈhärd,we(ə)riNG/ (also **hard-wear·ing**) ▸*adj.* able to stand much wear: *casual loafer shoe with hardwearing sole and heel.*

hard wheat ▸*n.* wheat of a variety having a hard grain rich in gluten.

hard-wired ▸*adj. Electronics* involving or achieved by permanently connected circuits. ■ *informal* genetically determined or compelled: *fear is hard-wired in our brain.* —**hard-wire** *v.* & *adj.*

hard·wir·ing /ˈhärdˈwī(ə)riNG/ ▸*n.* **1** electronic connection by means of wires: *to achieve effective automation of a line of this type, you have had to use extensive hardwiring.* **2** a predisposition for a particular kind of learning on behavior, thought to be based on structures within the brain or nervous system.

hard·wood /ˈhärd,wo͝od/ ▸*n.* **1** the wood from a broad-leaved tree (such as oak, ash, or beech) as distinguished from that of conifers. ■ a tree producing such wood. **2** (in gardening) mature growth on shrubs and other plants from which cuttings may be taken.

hard·work·ing (also **hard-work·ing**) ▸*adj.* (of a person) tending to work with energy and commitment; diligent.

Har·dy[1] /ˈhärdē/, Oliver, see LAUREL AND HARDY.

Har·dy[2], Thomas (1840–1928), English novelist and poet. Much of his work deals with the struggle against the indifferent force that inflicts the sufferings and ironies of life. Notable works: *The Mayor of Casterbridge* (1886), *Tess of the D'Urbervilles* (1891), and *Jude the Obscure* (1896).

har·dy /ˈhärdē/ ▸*adj.* (**-di·er, -di·est**) robust; capable of enduring difficult conditions. ■ (of a plant) able to survive outside during winter. ▷Middle English (in the sense 'bold, daring'): from Old French *hardi*, past participle of *hardir* 'become bold,' of Germanic origin; related to HARD. —**har·di·ly** /-dəlē/ *adv.* —**har·di·ness** /-dēnis/ *n.*

hare /he(ə)r/ ▸*n.* a fast-running, long-eared mammal that resembles a large rabbit, having long hind legs and occurring typically in grassland or open woodland. • *Lepus* and other genera, family Leporidae: several species. ■ (also **electric hare**) a dummy hare propelled around the track in greyhound racing.
▸*v.* [*intrans.*] *chiefly Brit.* run with great speed: *he hared off between the trees.* ▷Old English *hara*, of Germanic origin: related to Dutch *haas* and German *Hase*.
▸*PHRASE* □ **run with the hare and hunt with the hounds** *Brit.* try to remain on good terms with both sides in a conflict or dispute.

hare and hounds ▸*n.* a game in which a group of people (the "hounds") chases across the countryside another person or group (the "hares"), who leave pieces of paper (the "scent") behind them.

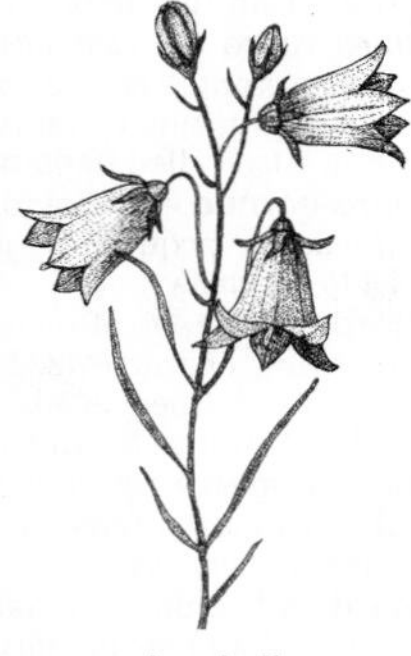
harebell

hare·bell /ˈhe(ə)r,bel/ ▸*n.* a widely distributed bellflower with slender stems and pale blue flowers in late summer. Also called BLUEBELL, esp. in Scotland. • *Campanula rotundifolia*, family Campanulaceae. ▷Middle English: probably so named because it is found growing in places frequented by hares.

hare·brained /ˈhe(ə)r,brānd/ ▸*adj.* rash; ill-judged: *a harebrained scheme.*

Ha·re·di /KHäreˈdē; häˈrādē/ ▸*n.* (*pl.* **-dim** /-ˈdēm/) a member of any of various Orthodox Jewish sects characterized by strict adherence to the traditional form of Jewish law and rejection of modern secular culture, many of whom do not recognize the modern state of Israel as a spiritual authority. ▷Hebrew, literally 'one who trembles (in awe at the word of God).'

Hare·foot /ˈhe(ə)r,fo͝ot/, Harold, see HAROLD.

Ha·re Krish·na /,härē ˈkrisHnə; ,harē/ ▸*n.* a member of the International Society for Krishna Consciousness, a religious sect based mainly in the U.S. and other Western countries. Its devotees typically wear saffron robes, favor celibacy, practice vegetarianism, and chant mantras based on the name of the Hindu god Krishna. ■ this sect. ▷1960s: Sanskrit, literally 'O Vishnu Krishna,' the words of a devotional chant.

hare·lip /ˈhe(ə)r,lip/ ▸*n. offensive* another term for CLEFT LIP. ▷mid 16th cent.: from a perceived resemblance to the mouth of a hare. —**hare·lipped** *adj.*

USAGE See usage at CLEFT LIP.

har·em /ˈhe(ə)rəm; ˈhar-/ ▸*n.* **1** the separate part of a Muslim household reserved for wives, concubines, and female servants. **2** the wives (or concubines) of a polygamous man. ■ a group of female animals sharing a single mate. ▷mid 17th cent. (sense 1): from Arabic *ḥaram*, *ḥarīm*, literally 'prohibited, prohibited place' (hence 'sanctuary, women's quarters, women'), from *ḥarama* 'be prohibited.'

hare's-tail (also **hare's-tail grass**) ▸*n.* a Mediterranean grass with white silky flowering heads and woolly gray-green leaves, widely grown as an ornamental, used esp. when dried. • *Lagurus ovatus*, family Gramineae.

hare wal·la·by ▸*n.* a small, agile, fast-moving Australian wallaby with orange rings of fur around the eyes. • Genera *Lagorchestes* and *Lagostrophus*, family Macropodidae: several species.

Har·gei·sa /härˈgāsə/ (also **Har·gey·sa**) a city in northwestern Somalia; pop. 400,000.

Har·greaves /ˈhär,grēvz/, James (1720–78), English inventor who invented the spinning jenny around 1764.

har·i·cot /ˈhari,kō/ (also **har·i·cot bean**) ▸*n.* **1** a bean of a variety with small white seeds, esp. the kidney bean. **2** the dried seed of this bean used as a vegetable. ▷mid 17th cent.: French, perhaps from Aztec *ayacotli*.

har·i·cot vert /ˈve(ə)r(t)/ ▸a green bean with a very narrow edible pod and very small seeds. ▷French, 'green bean.'

Har·i·jan /ˈharə,jan/ ▸*n.* a member of a hereditary Hindu group of the lowest social and ritual status. See UNTOUCHABLE. ▷from Sanskrit *harijana*, literally 'a person dedicated to Vishnu,' from *Hari* 'Vishnu' + *jana* 'person.' The term was adopted and popularized by Gandhi.

ha·ris·sa /həˈrēsə/ ▸*n.* a hot sauce or paste used in North African cuisine, made from chili peppers, paprika, and olive oil. ▷from Arabic.

hark /härk/ ▸*v.* [*intrans.*] *poetic/literary* listen: *Hark! He knocks.*
▸*phrasal v.* □ **hark back** mention or remember something from the past: *if it was such a rotten vacation, why hark back to it?* [originally a hunting term, used of hounds retracing their steps to find a lost scent.] □ **hark back to** evoke (an older style or genre): *paintings that hark back to Constable and Turner.* ▷Middle English: of Germanic origin; related to German *horchen*, also to HEARKEN.

hark·en ▸*v.* variant spelling of HEARKEN.

Har·lan /ˈhärlən/ U.S. jurists. **John Marshall Harlan** (1833–1911), U.S. Supreme Court associate justice 1877–1911. A strong defender of civil rights, he declared in *Plessy v. Ferguson* (1896) in a dissenting opinion that the Constitution is "color-blind." His grandson and namesake, **John Marshall Harlan** (1899–1971), generally conservative, was also a U.S. Supreme Court associate justice 1955–71.

Har·lem /ˈhärləm/ a district in New York City, north of 96th Street in northeastern Manhattan. It has a large black population and in the 1920s and 1930s was noted for its nightclubs and jazz bands.

Har·lem Ren·ais·sance a literary movement in the 1920s that centered on Harlem and was an early manifestation of black consciousness in the U.S. The movement included writers such as Langston Hughes and Zora Neale Hurston.

har·le·quin /ˈhärlik(w)ən/ ▸*n.* **1** (**Harlequin**) a mute character in traditional pantomime, typically masked and dressed in a diamond-patterned costume. ■ *historical* a stock comic character in Italian *commedia dell'arte*. **2** (also **harlequin duck**) a small duck of fast-flowing streams around the Arctic and North Pacific, the male having mainly gray-blue plumage with bold white markings. • *Histrionicus histrionicus*, family Anatidae.
▸*adj.* in varied colors; variegated. ▷late 16th cent.: from obsolete French, from earlier *Herlequin* (or *Hellequin*), the name of the leader of a legendary troop of demon horsemen; perhaps ultimately related to Old English *Herla cyning* 'King Herla,' a mythical figure sometimes identified with Woden.

har·le·quin·ade /,härlik(w)əˈnād/ ▸*n. historical* the section of a traditional pantomime in which Harlequin played a leading role. ■ *dated* a piece of buffoonery. ▷late 18th cent.: from French *arlequinade*, from *(h)arlequin* (see HARLEQUIN).

Har·lin·gen /ˈhärlinjən/ a city in southern Texas, northwest of Brownsville; pop. 48,735.

har·lot /ˈhärlət/ ▸*n. archaic* a prostitute or promiscuous woman. ▷Middle English (denoting a vagabond or beggar, later a lecherous man or woman): from Old French *harlot*, *herlot* 'young man, knave, vagabond.' —**har·lot·ry** /-trē/ *n.*

Har·low /ˈhärlō/, Jean (1911–37), U.S. movie actress; born *Harlean Carpenter*. The movie *Hell's Angels* (1930)

Jean Harlow

launched her career, and her platinum blonde hair and sex appeal brought her immediate success. Her six movies with Clark Gable included *Red Dust* (1932) and *Saratoga* (1937).

harm /härm/ ▸*n.* physical injury, esp. that which is deliberately inflicted: *it's fine as long as no one is inflicting harm on anyone else.* ■ material damage: *it's unlikely to do much harm to the engine.* ■ actual or potential ill effect or danger: *I can't see any harm in it.*
▸*v.* [*trans.*] physically injure: *the villains didn't harm him.* ■ damage the health of: *smoking when pregnant can harm your baby.* ■ have an adverse effect on: *this could harm his Olympic prospects.* ▷Old English *hearm* (noun), *hearmian* (verb), of Germanic origin; related to German *Harm* and Old Norse *harmr* 'grief, sorrow.'
▸*PHRASES* □ **come to no harm** be unhurt or undamaged. □ **do more harm than good** inadvertently make a situation worse rather than better. □ **do (someone) no harm** used to indicate that a situation or action will not hurt someone, whether or not it will provide any benefit: *the diet of milk and zwieback certainly did him no harm.* □ **mean no harm** not intend to cause damage or insult: *this was cruel, but they meant no harm by it.* □ **no harm done** used to reassure someone that what they have done has caused no real damage. □ **out of harm's way** in a safe place.

har·mat·tan /ˌhärmə'tän/ ▸*n.* a dry, dusty easterly or northeasterly wind on the West African coast, occurring from December to February. ▷late 17th cent.: from Twi *haramata.*

harm·ful /'härmfəl/ ▸*adj.* causing or likely to cause harm: *shield the planet from harmful cosmic rays* | *sugars that can be* **harmful to** *the teeth.* **—harm·ful·ly** *adv.* **—harm·ful·ness** *n.*

harm·less /'härmlis/ ▸*adj.* not able or likely to cause harm: *the venom of most spiders is* **harmless to** *humans.* ■ inoffensive: *as an entertainer, he's pretty harmless.* **—harm·less·ly** *adv.* **—harm·less·ness** *n.*

har·mo·lod·ics /ˌhärmə'lädiks/ ▸*plural n.* [treated as *sing.*] a form of free jazz in which musicians improvise simultaneously on a melodic line at various pitches. ▷1970s: coined by the American saxophonist Ornette Coleman (b. 1930) and said to be a blend of *harmony, movement,* and *melodic.* **—harmolodic** *adj.*

har·mon·ic /här'mänik/ ▸*adj.* **1** of, relating to, or characterized by musical harmony: *a basic four-chord harmonic sequence.* ■ *Music* relating to or denoting a harmonic or harmonics. **2** *Mathematics* of or relating to a harmonic progression. ■ *Physics* of or relating to component frequencies of a complex oscillation or wave. ■ *Astrology* using or produced by the application of a harmonic: *harmonic charts.*
▸*n.* **1** *Music* an overtone accompanying a fundamental tone at a fixed interval, produced by vibration of a string, column of air, etc., in an exact fraction of its length. ■ a note produced on a musical instrument as an overtone, e.g., by lightly touching a string while sounding it. **2** *Physics* a component frequency of an oscillation or wave. ■ *Astrology* a division of the zodiacal circle by a specified number, used in the interpretation of a birth chart. ▷late 16th cent. (in the sense 'relating to music, musical'): via Latin from Greek *harmonikos,* from *harmonia* (see HARMONY). **—har·mon·i·cal·ly** /-ik(ə)lē/ *adv.*

har·mon·i·ca /här'mänikə/ ▸*n.* a small rectangular wind instrument with a row of metal reeds along its length, held against the lips and moved from side to side to produce different notes by blowing or sucking. Also called MOUTH ORGAN. ▷mid 18th cent.: from Latin, feminine singular or neuter plural of *harmonicus* 'musical' (see HARMONIC).

har·mon·ic mi·nor (also **harmonic minor scale**) ▸*n.* *Music* a scale containing a minor third, minor sixth, and major seventh, forming the basis of conventional harmony in minor keys.

har·mon·ic mo·tion ▸*n.* another term for SIMPLE HARMONIC MOTION.

har·mon·ic pro·gres·sion ▸*n.* **1** *Music* a series of chord changes forming the underlying harmony of a piece of music. **2** *Mathematics* a sequence of quantities whose reciprocals are in arithmetic progression (e.g., 1, 1/3, 1/5, 1/7, etc.).

har·mon·ic se·ries ▸*n.* **1** *Music* a set of frequencies consisting of a fundamental and the harmonics related to it by an exact fraction. **2** *Mathematics* a series of values in harmonic progression.

har·mo·ni·ous /här'mōnēəs/ ▸*adj.* tuneful; not discordant: *harmonious music.* ■ forming a pleasing or consistent whole: *the decor is a harmonious blend of traditional and modern.* ■ free from disagreement or dissent: *harmonious relationships.* **—har·mo·ni·ous·ly** *adv.* **—har·mo·ni·ous·ness** *n.*

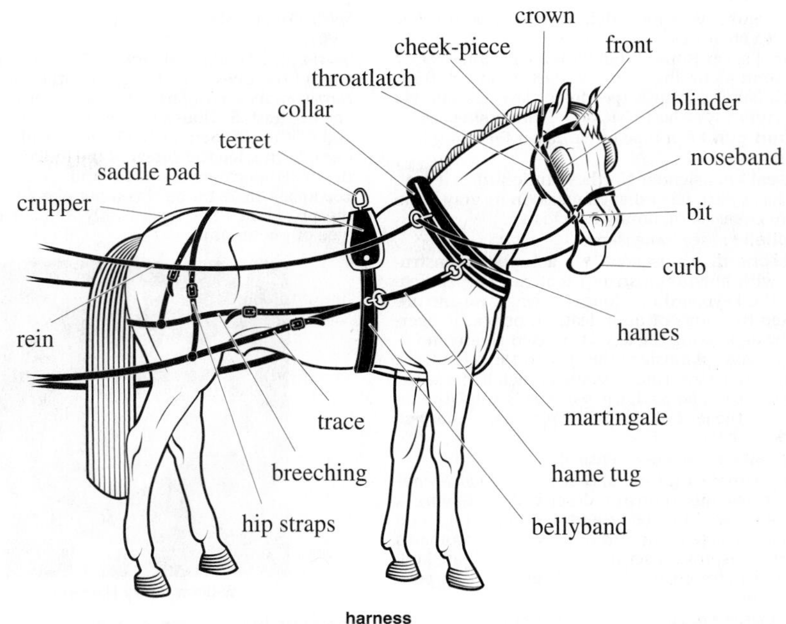

harness

har·mo·nist /'härmənist/ ▸*n.* a person skilled in musical harmony.

har·mo·ni·um /här'mōnēəm/ ▸*n.* a keyboard instrument in which the notes are produced by air driven through metal reeds by foot-operated bellows. ▷mid 19th cent.: from French, from Latin *harmonia* (see HARMONY) or Greek *harmonios* 'harmonious.'

har·mo·nize /'härməˌnīz/ ▸*v.* [*trans.*] add notes to (a melody) to produce harmony. ■ [*intrans.*] sing in harmony: *she scats and harmonizes simultaneously.* ■ [*intrans.*] produce a pleasing visual combination: *the containers harmonize in color, texture, and shape with the flowers they display.* ■ make consistent: *the economic group founded to harmonize national development plans.* ▷late 15th cent. (in the sense 'sing or play in harmony'): from French *harmoniser,* from *harmonie* (see HARMONY). **—har·mo·ni·za·tion** /ˌhärmənə'zāsʜən/ *n.*

har·mo·ny /'härmənē/ ▸*n.* (*pl.* **-nies**) **1** the combination of simultaneously sounded musical notes to produce chords and chord progressions having a pleasing effect: *four-part harmony in the barbershop style* | *the note played on the fourth beat anticipates the harmony of the following bar.* ■ the study or composition of musical harmony. ■ the quality of forming a pleasing and consistent whole: *delightful cities where old and new blend in harmony.* ■ an arrangement of the four Gospels, or of any parallel narratives, that presents a single continuous narrative text. **2** agreement or concord: *man and machine in perfect harmony.* ▷late Middle English: via Old French from Latin *harmonia* 'joining, concord,' from Greek, from *harmos* 'joint.'
▸*PHRASE* □ **harmony of the spheres** see SPHERE.

har·ness /'härnis/ ▸*n.* a set of straps and fittings by which a horse or other draft animal is fastened to a cart, plow, etc., and is controlled by its driver. ■ an arrangement of straps for fastening something to a person's body, such as a parachute, or for restraining a young child.
▸*v.* [*trans.*] **1** put a harness on (a horse or other draft animal). ■ (**harness something to**) attach a draft animal to (something) by a harness: *the horse was harnessed to two long shafts.* **2** control and make use of (natural resources), esp. to produce energy: *attempts to harness solar energy* | *figurative harnessing the creativity of graduates.* ▷Middle English: from Old French *harneis* 'military equipment,' from Old Norse, from *herr* 'army' + *nest* 'provisions.' **—har·ness·er** *n.*
▸*PHRASE* □ **in harness** (of a horse or other animal) used for driving or draft work. ■ in the routine of daily work: *a man who died in harness far beyond the normal age of retirement.* ■ working closely with someone to achieve something: *local and central government should work in harness.*

har·ness rac·ing ▸*n.* racing for trotting horses pulling a two-wheeled vehicle (a sulky) and driver. Also called TROTTING. **—har·ness race** *n.*

Har·ney Peak /'härnē/ a peak in the Black Hills of southwestern South Dakota, 7,242 feet (2,209 m) tall, the highest in the U.S. east of the Rocky Mountains.

Har·old /'harəld/ the name of two kings of England: ■ **Harold I** (died 1040), reigned 1035–40; known as **Harold Harefoot** /'herˌfo͝ot/ . An illegitimate son of Canute, he came to the throne when his half-brother Hardecanute (Canute's legitimate heir) was king of Denmark and thus absent when Canute died. ■ **Harold II** (*c.*1019–66), reigned 1066, the last Anglo-Saxon king of England. He was killed and his army defeated by William of Normandy at the Battle of Hastings.

Ha·roun-al-Ra·schid /hä'ro͞on äl rä'sʜēd/ variant spelling of HARUN AR-RASHID.

harp /härp/ ▸*n.* **1** a musical instrument, roughly triangular in shape, consisting of a frame supporting a graduated series of parallel strings, played by plucking with the fingers. The modern orchestral harp has an upright frame, with pedals that enable the strings to be retuned to different keys. **2** another term for HARMONICA: *Papa had been teaching him to play the blues harp.* [short for *mouth harp.*] **3** (also **harp shell** or **harp snail**) a marine mollusk that has a large vertically ribbed shell with a wide aperture, found chiefly in the Indo-Pacific. • Family Harpidae, class Gastropoda.
▸*v.* [*intrans.*] **1** talk or write persistently and tediously on a particular topic: *guys who are constantly* **harping on about** *the war.* **2** *archaic* play on a harp. ▷Old English *hearpe,* of Germanic origin; related to Dutch *harp* and German *Harfe.*

harp 1

harp·er /'härpər/ ▸*n.* a musician, esp. a folk musician, who plays a harp.

Har·pers Fer·ry /'härpərz/ a small town in far northeastern West Virginia, at the junction of the Potomac and Shenandoah rivers. It is noted for a raid in October 1859 in which John Brown and a group of abolitionists captured a Federal arsenal located here.

harp·ist /'härpist/ ▸*n.* a musician who plays a harp.

Har·poc·ra·tes /här'päkrəˌtēz/ Greek name for HORUS.

har·poon /ˌhär'po͞on/ ▸*n.* a barbed spearlike missile attached to a long rope and thrown by hand or fired

from a gun, used for catching whales and other large sea creatures.
▸*v.* [*trans.*] spear (something) with a harpoon. ▹early 17th cent. (denoting a barbed dart or spear): from French *harpon*, from *harpe* 'dog's claw, clamp,' via Latin from Greek *harpē* 'sickle.' —**har·poon·er** *n.*

har·poon gun ▸*n.* a type of gun used for firing harpoons.

harp seal ▸*n.* a slender North Atlantic seal that typically has a dark harp-shaped mark on its gray back. • *Phoca groenlandica*, family Phocidae.

harp shell ▸*n.* see **HARP** (sense 3).

harp·si·chord /ˈhärpsiˌkôrd/ ▸*n.* a keyboard instrument with horizontal strings that run perpendicular to the keyboard in a long tapering case and are plucked by points of quill, leather, or plastic operated by depressing the keys. It is used chiefly in European classical music of the 16th to 18th centuries. ▹early 17th cent.: from obsolete French *harpechorde*, from late Latin *harpa* 'harp' + *chorda* 'string' (the insertion of the letter *s* being unexplained). —**harp·si·chord·ist** /-ist/ *n.*

harp snail ▸*n.* see **HARP** (sense 3).

har·py /ˈhärpē/ ▸*n.* (*pl.* **-pies**) *Greek and Roman Mythology* a rapacious monster described as having a woman's head and body and a bird's wings and claws or depicted as a bird of prey with a woman's face. ■ a grasping, unscrupulous woman. ▹late Middle English: from Latin *harpyia*, from Greek *harpuiai* 'snatchers.'

har·py ea·gle ▸*n.* a large crested eagle of tropical rain forests, often preying on monkeys. • Family Accipitridae: *Harpia harpyja* of South America, the largest eagle, and *Harpyopsis novaeguineae* of New Guinea.

har·que·bus /ˈ(h)ärk(w)əbəs/ (also **ar·que·bus**) ▸*n. historical* an early type of portable gun supported on a tripod or a forked rest. ▹mid 16th cent.: from French *harquebuse*, based on Middle Low German *hakebusse*, from *hake* 'hook' + *busse* 'gun.'

har·ri·dan /ˈharidn/ ▸*n.* a strict, bossy, or belligerent old woman: *a bullying old harridan.* ▹late 17th cent. (originally slang): perhaps from French *haridelle* 'old horse.'

har·ri·er[1] /ˈharēər/ ▸*n.* a person who engages in persistent attacks on others or incursions into their land.

har·ri·er[2] ▸*n.* a hound of a breed used for hunting hares. ■ a cross-country runner. ▹late Middle English *hayrer*, from **HARE** + **-ER**[1]. The spelling change was due to association with **HARRIER**[1].

har·ri·er[3] ▸*n.* a long-winged, slender-bodied bird of prey with low quartering flight. • Genus *Circus*, family Accipitridae: several species. ▹mid 16th cent. (as *harrower*): from *harrow* 'harry, rob' (variant of **HARRY**). The spelling change in the 17th cent. was due to association with **HARRIER**[1].

har·ri·er hawk ▸*n.* an African bird of prey with a bare yellow face, resembling a goshawk but flying like a harrier. • Genus *Polyboroides*, family Accipitridae: two species, in particular *P. typus*.

Har·ri·man /ˈharəmən/, (William) Averell (1891–1986), U.S. diplomat and financier. The chairman of the board of the Union Pacific Railroad 1932–46, he was U.S. secretary of commerce 1946–48 and governor of New York 1955–59. He also served as ambassador to the Soviet Union 1943–46, to Britain 1946, and at-large 1968–69.

Har·ris /ˈharəs/, Joel Chandler (1848–1908), U.S. writer. He is best known for his Brer Rabbit and Brer Fox stories as told by the fictional Uncle Remus.

Har·ris·burg /ˈharəsˌbərg/ the capital of Pennsylvania, in the southeastern central part of the state, on the Susquehanna River; pop. 52,376. The nearby nuclear power station at Three Mile Island suffered a serious accident in 1979.

Har·ri·son[1] /ˈharəsən/, Benjamin (1833–1901), 23rd president of the U.S. 1889–93; the grandson of William Henry Harrison. An Indiana Republican, he served as a U.S. senator 1881–87. During his administration, Oklahoma was settled and the way was paved for the annexation of Hawaii. Due to deterioration of the economy and labor unrest, he was not reelected.

Har·ri·son[2], George (1943–2001), English musician and songwriter. He was the lead guitarist of the Beatles, for which he occasionally wrote songs, such as "Something" (1969). His fascination with India was reflected in his solo career after the group's breakup in 1970. See photograph at **LENNON**.

Har·ri·son[3], Sir Rex (1908–90), English actor; full name *Reginald Carey Harrison*. Notable movies: *Blithe Spirit* (1944), *My Fair Lady* (1964), and *Dr. Dolittle* (1967).

Har·ri·son[4], William Henry (1773–1841), 9th president of the U.S., 1841; the grandfather of Benjamin Harrison. As a Whig from Ohio, he became a member of the U.S. House of Representatives 1817–19 and of the U.S. Senate 1825–28. Already a military hero, having led the defeat of the Indians at the Battle of Tippecanoe in 1811 and of Indian chief Tecumseh in 1813, he was a popular candidate for the presidency but served only 32 days before he died of pneumonia.

William Henry Harrison

Har·ri·son·burg /ˈharəsənˌbərg/ a commercial and academic city in northern Virginia, in the Shenandoah Valley; pop. 40,468.

Har·ris's hawk (also **Har·ris hawk**) ▸*n.* a large chocolate-brown buteo with chestnut shoulder patches and a conspicuous white rump and tail band. Popular with falconers, it occurs in arid country from the southwestern U.S. to South America and frequently nests in tall cacti. • *Parabuteo unicinctus*, family Accipitridae.

Har·ris tweed ▸*n. trademark* handwoven tweed made in the Outer Hebrides in Scotland, esp. on the island of Lewis and Harris.

Har·rods·burg /ˈharədzˌbərg/ a historic city in central Kentucky, the first English settlement (1774) west of the Allegheny Mountains; pop. 7,335.

Har·ro·vi·an /həˈrōvēən/ ▸*n.* a past or present member of Harrow School. ▹early 19th cent.: from modern Latin *Harrovia* 'Harrow' + **-AN**.

har·row /ˈharō/ ▸*n.* an implement consisting of a heavy frame set with teeth or tines that is dragged over plowed land to break up clods, remove weeds, and cover seed.
▸*v.* [*trans.*] **1** draw a harrow over (land). **2** cause distress to: *Todd could take it, whereas I'm harrowed by it* | [as *adj.*] (**harrowing**) *a harrowing film about racism and violence.* ▹Middle English: from Old Norse *herfi*; obscurely related to Dutch *hark* 'rake.' —**har·row·er** *n.* —**har·row·ing·ly** *adv.*

Har·row·ing of Hell (in medieval Christian theology) the defeat of the powers of evil and the release of its victims by the descent of Christ into hell after his death. ▹Middle English: *harrowing* from *harrow*, byform of the verb **HARRY**.

Har·row School /ˈharō/ a boys' preparatory school in northwest London, founded under Queen Elizabeth I in 1571.

har·rumph /həˈrəmf/ ▸*v.* [*intrans.*] clear the throat noisily. ■ grumpily express dissatisfaction or disapproval: *skeptics tend to harrumph at case histories like this.*
▸*n.* a noisy clearing of the throat. ■ a grumpy expression of dissatisfaction or disapproval. ▹1930s: imitative.

Benjamin Harrison

har·ry /ˈharē/ ▸*v.* (**-ries**, **-ried**) [*trans.*] persistently carry out attacks on (an enemy or an enemy's territory). ■ persistently harass: *he bought the house for Jenny, whom he harries into marriage* | [as *adj.*] (**harried**) *harried reporters are frequently forced to invent what they cannot find out.* ▹Old English *herian*, *hergian*, of Germanic origin, probably influenced by Old French *harier*, in the same sense.

harsh /härsʜ/ ▸*adj.* **1** unpleasantly rough or jarring to the senses: *drenched in a harsh white neon light* | *harsh guttural shouts.* **2** cruel or severe: *a time of harsh military discipline.* ■ (of a climate or conditions) difficult to survive in; hostile: *the harsh environment of the desert.* ■ (of reality or a fact) grim and unpalatable: *the harsh realities of the world news.* ■ having an undesirably strong effect: *she finds soap too harsh and drying.* ▹Middle English: from Middle Low German *harsch* 'rough,' literally 'hairy,' from *haer* 'hair.' —**harsh·en** /-sʜən/ *v.* —**harsh·ly** *adv.* —**harsh·ness** *n.*

hars·let /ˈhärslit/ ▸*n.* variant spelling of **HASLET**.

Hart[1] /härt/, Frederick E. (1943–1999) U.S. sculptor. He sculpted and cast in bronze the *Three Soldiers* or *Three Fighting Men* statue (1984) that stands at the Vietnam Veterans Memorial in Washington, DC. His work also includes the front entrance to the National Cathedral that was completed and dedicated in 1990.

Hart[2], Lorenz (Milton) (1895–1943) U.S. lyricist. His collaborations with composer Richard Rodgers include the scores for the Broadway shows *Babes in Arms* (1937), *The Boys from Syracuse* (1938) and *Pal Joey* (1940). Songs for which he wrote the lyrics include "Blue Moon" (1934) and "My Funny Valentine" (1937).

Hart[3], Moss (1904–61) U.S. playwright and director. His collaborations with George S. Kaufman include the plays *You Can't Take It with You* (1936) and *The Man Who Came to Dinner* (1939). He also wrote the movie script for *Gentlemen's Agreement* (Academy Award, 1947).

hart /härt/ ▸*n.* an adult male deer, esp. a red deer over five years old. ▹Old English *heorot*, *heort*, of Germanic origin; related to Dutch *hert* and German *Hirsch*.

Harte /härt/, (Francis) Bret (1836–1902), U.S. short-story writer and poet. He is chiefly remembered for his stories about life in a California gold-mining town. Notable works: *The Luck of Roaring Camp and Other Sketches* (1870) and *Tales of the Argonauts* (1875).

har·te·beest /ˈhärt(ə)ˌbēst/ ▸*n.* a large African antelope with a long head and sloping back, related to the gnus. • Genera *Alcelaphus*, *Damaliscus*, and *Sigmoceros*, family Bovidae: three or four species, in particular the **red hartebeest** (*A. buselaphus*), which typically has a reddish-brown coat. ▹late 18th cent.: from South African Dutch, from Dutch *hert* 'hart' + *beest* 'beast.'

Hart·ford /ˈhärtfərd/ the capital of Connecticut, in the center of the state, on the Connecticut River; pop. 121,578.

harts·horn /ˈhärtsˌhôrn/ (also **spirit of hartshorn**) ▸*n. archaic* aqueous ammonia solution used as smelling salts, formerly prepared from the horns of deer. ▹Old English *heortes horn* (see **HART**, **HORN**).

hart's tongue (also **hart's tongue fern**) ▸*n.* a common European fern whose long, narrow undivided fronds are said to resemble the tongues of deer. • *Phyllitis* (or **Asplenium**) *scolopendrium*, family Aspleniaceae.

har·um-scar·um /ˈhe(ə)rəm ˈske(ə)rəm/ ▸*adj.* reckless; impetuous: *she shall be frightened out of her wits by your harum-scarum ways.*
▸*n.* such a person.
▸*adv.* in a harum-scarum manner: *the tables were scattered harum-scarum around a small room.* ▹late 17th cent. (as an adverb): reduplication based on **HARE** and **SCARE**.

Ha·run ar-Ra·shid /häˈro͞on är räˈsʜēd/ (also **Ha·roun-al-Ras·chid** /äl/) (763–809), fifth Abbasid caliph of Baghdad 786–809.

ha·rus·pex /həˈrəsˌpeks; ˈharəˌspeks/ ▸*n.* (*pl.* **ha·rus·pi·ces** /həˈrəspəˌsēz/) (in ancient Rome) a religious official who interpreted omens by inspecting the entrails of sacrificial animals. ▹Latin, from an unrecorded element meaning 'entrails' (related to Sanskrit *hirā* 'artery') + *-spex* (from *specere* 'look at'). —**ha·rus·pi·cy** /həˈrəspəsē/ *n.*

Har·vard clas·si·fi·ca·tion /ˈhärvərd/ ▸*n. Astronomy* a system of classification of stars based on their spectral types, the chief classes (O, B, A, F, G, K, M) forming a series from hot bluish-white stars to cool dull red stars. ▷1960s: named after the observatory at **HARVARD UNIVERSITY**, where it was devised.

Har·vard U·ni·ver·si·ty an Ivy League university in Cambridge, Massachusetts, founded in 1636. It is the oldest American university. ▷named after John *Harvard* (1607–38), an English settler who bequeathed his library and half his estate to the university.

har·vest /'härvist/ ▸*n.* the process or period of gathering in crops: *helping with the harvest.* ■ the season's yield or crop: *a poor harvest.* ■ a quantity of animals caught or killed for human use: *a limited harvest of wild mink.* ■ *figurative* the product or result of an action: *in terms of science, Apollo yielded a meager harvest.*
▸*v.* [*trans.*] gather (a crop) as a harvest: [as *n.*] (**harvesting**) *after harvesting, most of the crop is stored in large buildings.* ■ catch or kill (animals) for human consumption or use. ■ remove (cells, tissue, or an organ) from a person or animal for transplantation or experimental purposes. ■ *figurative* gain (something) as the result of an action: *the movie has harvested $105.7 million overseas.* ▷Old English *hærfest* 'autumn,' of Germanic origin; related to Dutch *herfst* and German *Herbst*, from an Indo-European root shared by Latin *carpere* 'pluck' and Greek *karpos* 'fruit.' —**har·vest·a·ble** *adj.* —**har·vest·er** *n.*

har·ves·ter ant ▸*n.* an ant that gathers and stores seeds and grain as a communal food source for the colony. • *Messor* and other genera, family Formicidae.

har·vest home ▸*n.* the gathering in of the final part of the year's harvest. ■ a festival marking the end of the harvest period.

har·vest·man /'härvəstmən/ ▸*n.* (*pl.* **-men**) another term for **DADDY LONGLEGS** (sense 1).

har·vest mite ▸*n.* another term for **CHIGGER** (sense 1).

har·vest moon ▸*n.* the full moon that is seen nearest to the time of the autumnal equinox.

har·vest mouse ▸*n.* **1** a nocturnal mouse found in North and Central America. • Genus *Reithrodontomys*, family Muridae: several species. **2** a small northern Eurasian mouse with a prehensile tail, nesting among the stalks of growing grains and other vegetation. • *Micromys minutus*, family Muridae.

Har·vey[1] /'härvē/, Anne see **SEXTON**.

Har·vey[2], William (1578–1657), English physician, who first described how blood circulates.

Har·vey Wall·bang·er /'härvē 'wôl,baNGər/ ▸*n.* a cocktail made from vodka or gin, orange juice, and Galliano.

Ha·ry·a·na /,härē'änə/ a state in northern India; capital, Chandigarh. It was formed in 1966, largely from Hindi-speaking parts of the former state of Punjab.

harz·burg·ite /'härtsbər,gīt/ ▸*n. Geology* a plutonic rock of the peridotite group consisting largely of orthopyroxene and olivine. ▷late 19th cent.: from *Harzburg*, the name of a town in Germany, + **-ITE**[1].

Harz Moun·tains /härts/ a range of mountains in central Germany, the highest of which is the Brocken.

has /haz/ ▸ third person singular present of **HAVE**.

has-been ▸*n. informal, derogatory* a person or thing considered to be outmoded or no longer of any significance: *a political has-been* | [as *adj.*] *a has-been film star.*

hash[1] /hasH/ ▸*n.* a dish of cooked meat cut into small pieces and recooked, usually with potatoes. ■ a finely chopped mixture: *a hash of raw tomatoes, chilies, and coriander.* ■ a mixture of jumbled incongruous things; a mess.
▸*v.* [*trans.*] **1** make (meat or other food) into a hash. ■ chop (meat or vegetables). **2** (**hash something out**) come to agreement on something after lengthy and vigorous discussion: *they went to the diner to hash out ideas.* ▷late 16th cent. (as a verb): from French *hacher*, from *hache* (see **HATCHET**).
▸*PHRASES* □ **make a hash of** *informal* make a mess of; bungle: *listening to other board members make a hash of things.* □ **settle someone's hash** *informal* deal with and subdue someone in no uncertain manner. □ **sling hash** see **SLING**[1].

hash[2] ▸*n. informal* short for **HASHISH**.

hash[3] (also **hash sign**) ▸*n.* the sign #. ▷1980s: probably from **HATCH**[3], altered by folk etymology.

hash browns (also **hashed browns**) ▸*plural n.* a dish of cooked potatoes, typically with onions added, that have been chopped into small pieces and fried until brown.

Hash·e·mite /'hasHə,mīt/ ▸*n.* a member of an Arab princely family claiming descent from Hashim, great-grandfather of Muhammad.
▸*adj.* of or relating to this family.

Hash·e·mite King·dom of Jor·dan official name for **JORDAN**[1] (sense 1).

hash house ▸*n. informal* a cheap restaurant.

Ha·shi·mo·to's dis·ease /,hasHi'mōtōz/ ▸*n.* an autoimmune disease causing chronic inflammation and consequential failure of the thyroid gland. ▷1930s: named after Hakaru *Hashimoto* (1881–1934), Japanese surgeon.

hash·ish /'ha,sHēsH/ ▸*n.* an extract of the cannabis plant, containing concentrations of the psychoactive resins. ▷late 16th cent.: from Arabic *ḥašīš* 'dry herb, powdered hemp leaves.'

hash mark ▸*n.* **1** a service stripe worn on the left sleeve of an enlisted person's uniform to indicate three years of service in the army or four years in the navy. ■ a similar stripe on any uniform. **2** *Football* one of a series of marks made along parallel lines that delineate the middle of the field, used to spot the ball after a play ends outside these lines. **3** the symbol #, used esp. for tallying.

Ha·sid /KHä'sēd; 'KHäsid; 'häsid/ (also **Cha·sid**, **Chas·sid**, or **Has·sid**) ▸*n.* (*pl.* **Ha·si·dim** /,KHäsē'dēm; hä'sēdim/) **1** a member of a strictly orthodox Jewish sect in Palestine in the 3rd and 2nd centuries BC that opposed Hellenizing influences on their faith and supported the Maccabean revolt. **2** an adherent of Hasidism. ▷from Hebrew *ḥāsīd* 'pious.' —**Ha·sid·ic** /KHä'sedik; häsēdik/ *adj.*

Has·i·dism /'hasi,dizəm/ (also **Cha·si·dism**, **Chas·si·dism**, or **Has·si·dism**) ▸*n.* an influential mystical Jewish movement founded in Poland in the 18th century in reaction to the rigid academicism of rabbinical Judaism.The movement declined sharply in the 19th century, but fundamentalist communities developed from it, and Hasidism is still a force in Jewish life, particularly in Israel and New York.

has·let /'haslət; 'hāz-/ (also **hars·let**) ▸*n.* a cold meat preparation consisting of chopped or minced pork offal compressed into a loaf before being cooked. ▷late Middle English (originally denoting meat for roasting): from Old French *hastelet*, diminutive of *haste* 'roast meat, spit,' probably of Germanic origin and related to Dutch *harst* 'sirloin.'

Has·mo·ne·an /,hazmə'nēən/ ▸*adj.* of or relating to the Jewish dynasty established by the Maccabees.
▸*n.* a member of this dynasty. ▷from modern Latin *Asmonaeus* (from Greek *Asamonaios*, the grandfather of Mattathias, head of the Maccabees in the 2nd cent. BC) + **-AN**.

has·n't /'haznt/ ▸*contraction of* has not.

hasp /hasp/ ▸*n.* a slotted hinged metal plate that forms part of a fastening for a door or lid and is fitted over a metal loop and secured by a pin or padlock. ■ a similar metal plate on a trunk or suitcase with a projecting piece that is secured by the lock.
▸*v.* [*trans.*] *archaic* lock (a door, window, or lid) by securing the hasp over the loop of the fastening. ▷Old English *hæpse*, *hæsp*, of Germanic origin; related to Dutch *haspel* and German *Haspe*.

hasp

Has·sid ▸*n.* variant spelling of **HASID**.

Has·sid·ism ▸*n.* variant spelling of **HASIDISM**.

has·si·um /'hasēəm/ ▸*n.* the chemical element of atomic number 108, a very unstable element made by high-energy atomic collisions. (Symbol: **Hs**) See also **HAHNIUM**. ▷modern Latin, from Latin *Hassias* 'Hesse' (the German state); it was discovered in Darmstadt in 1984.

has·sle /'hasəl/ *informal* ▸*n.* irritating inconvenience: *the hassle of losing a high security key* | *traveling can be a hassle.* ■ deliberate harassment: *if they give you any hassle, just tell them it's for me.* ■ a disagreement; a quarrel: *an election-year hassle with farmers.*
▸*v.* [*trans.*] harass; pester: *squeegee men who hassle drivers for change at stoplights.* ▷late 19th cent. (originally dialect in the sense 'hack or saw at'): of unknown origin, perhaps a blend of **HAGGLE** and **TUSSLE**.

has·sock /'hasək/ ▸*n.* **1** a thick, firmly padded cushion, in particular: ■ a footstool. ■ *chiefly Brit.* a cushion for kneeling on in church. **2** a firm clump of grass or matted vegetation in marshy or boggy ground. ▷Old English *hassuc* (sense 2), of unknown origin.

hast /hast/ ▸ archaic second person singular present of **HAVE**.

has·tate /'ha,stāt/ ▸*adj. Botany* (of a leaf) having a narrow triangular shape like that of a spearhead. ▷late 18th cent.: from Latin *hastatus*, from *hasta* 'spear.'

haste /hāst/ ▸*n.* excessive speed or urgency of movement or action; hurry: *working with feverish haste* | *I write in haste.*
▸*v.* archaic term for **HASTEN**. ▷Middle English: from Old French *haste* (noun), *haster* (verb), of Germanic origin.
▸*PHRASES* □ **make haste** *dated* hurry; hasten: *I make haste to seal this.* □ **more haste, less speed** *proverb* you make better progress with a task if you don't try to do it too quickly.

has·ten /'hāsən/ ▸*v.* [*intrans.*] be quick to do something: *he hastened to refute the assertion.* ■ [with *adverbial of direction*] move or travel hurriedly: *we hastened back to Paris.* ■ [*trans.*] cause (something) to happen sooner than it otherwise would: *a move that could hasten peace talks.* ▷mid 16th cent.: extended form of **HASTE**, on the pattern of verbs in **-EN**[1].

Has·tings /'hāstiNGz/ a city in southern Nebraska, directly south of Grand Island; pop. 24,064.

Has·tings, Bat·tle of a decisive battle that took place in 1066 just north of the town of Hastings, East Sussex. William the Conqueror defeated the forces of the Anglo-Saxon king Harold II; Harold died in the battle, leaving the way open for the Norman Conquest of England.

hast·y /'hāstē/ ▸*adj.* (**hast·i·er**, **hast·i·est**) done or acting with excessive speed or urgency; hurried: *a hasty attempt to defuse the situation* | *hasty decisions.* See note at **SUPERFICIAL**. ■ *archaic* quick-tempered. ▷Middle English: from Old French *hasti*, *hastif*, from *haste* (see **HASTE**). —**hast·i·ly** /'hāstəlē/ *adv.* —**hast·i·ness** *n.*

hast·y pud·ding ▸*n.* a mush containing cornmeal or (in Britain) wheat flour stirred to a thick batter in boiling milk or water.

hat /hat/ ▸*n.* a shaped covering for the head worn for warmth, as a fashion item, or as part of a uniform. ■ used to refer to a particular role or occupation of someone who has more than one: *wearing her scientific hat, she is director of a pharmacology research group.* ▷Old English *hætt*, of Germanic origin; related to Old Norse *hǫttr* 'hood,' also to **HOOD**[1]. —**hat·ful** /-,fōōl/ *n.* (*pl.* **-fuls.**) —**hat·less** *adj.* —**hat·ted** *adj.* [in *combination*] *a white-hatted cowboy.*
▸*PHRASES* □ **hat in hand** used to indicate an attitude of humility: *standing on the stoop of his ex-wife's house, hat in hand.* □ **keep something under one's hat** keep something a secret. □ **pass the hat** collect contributions of money from a number of people for a specific purpose. □ **pick something out of a hat** select something, esp. the winner of a contest, at random. □ **take one's hat off to** (or **hats off to**) used to state one's admiration for (someone who has done something praiseworthy): *I take my hat off to anyone who makes it work* | *hats off to emergency services for prompt work in the wake of the storms.* □ **talk through one's hat** see **TALK**. □ **throw one's hat in** (or **into**) **the ring** express willingness to take up a challenge, esp. to enter a political race.

hat·band /'hat,band/ ▸*n.* a decorative ribbon encircling a hat, held in position above the brim.

hat·box /'hat,bäks/ ▸*n.* a large cylindrical box used to protect a hat when being transported or stored.

hatch[1] /hacH/ ▸*n.* an opening of restricted size allowing for passage from one area to another, in particular: ■ a door in an aircraft, spacecraft, or submarine. ■ an opening in the deck of a boat or ship leading to the cabin or a lower level, esp. a hold: *a cargo hatch.* ■ an opening in a ceiling leading to a loft. ■ an opening in a kitchen wall for serving or selling food through: *a service hatch.* ■ the rear door of a hatchback car. ■ short for **HATCHBACK**. ▷Old English *hæcc* (denoting the lower half of a divided door), of Germanic origin; related to Dutch *hek* 'paling, screen.'
▸*PHRASE* □ **down the hatch** *informal* used in a toast; drink up.

hatch[2] ▸*v.* **1** [*intrans.*] (of a young bird, fish, or reptile) emerge from its egg: *ten little chicks* ***hatched out.*** ■ (of an egg) open and produce a young animal: *eggs need to be put in a warm place to hatch.* ■ [*trans.*] incubate (an egg): *the eggs are best hatched under broody* *hens or in incubators.* ■ [*trans.*] cause (a young animal) to emerge from its egg: *our penguins were hatched and hand-reared here.* **2** [*trans.*] conspire to devise (a plot or plan): *the little plot that you and Sylvia* ***hatched up*** *last night.*

▸*n.* a newly hatched brood: *a hatch of mayflies.* ▷Middle English *hacche*; related to Swedish *häcka* and Danish *hække*.

hatch3 ▸*v.* [*trans.*] (in fine art and technical drawing) shade (an area) with closely drawn parallel lines: [as *n.*] (**hatching**) *the miniaturist's use of hatching and stippling.* ▷late 15th cent. (in the sense 'inlay with strips of metal'): from Old French *hacher*, from *hache* (see HATCHET).

hatch·back /ˈhaCH,bak/ ▸*n.* a car with a door across the full width at the back end that opens upward to provide easy access for loading.

hat·check /ˈhat,CHek/ ▸*adj.* of or employed in a checkroom for hats, coats, and other personal items.

hatch·el /ˈhaCHəl/ ▸*n.* another term for HACKLE (sense 3).

▸*v.* another term for HACKLE. ▷Middle English *hechele*, related to HOOK.

hatch·er·y /ˈhaCHərē/ ▸*n.* (*pl.* **-er·ies**) a place where the hatching of fish or poultry eggs is artificially controlled for commercial purposes.

hatch·et /ˈhaCHit/ ▸*n.* a small ax with a short handle for use in one hand. ■ a tomahawk. ▷Middle English: from Old French *hachette*, diminutive of *hache* 'ax,' from medieval Latin *hapia*, of Germanic origin.

hatch·et-faced ▸*adj. informal* with a narrow face and sharp features.

hatch·et·fish /ˈhaCHit,fiSH/ ▸*n.* (*pl.* same or **-fish·es**) a deep-bodied laterally compressed tropical freshwater fish of the New World. It is able to fly short distances above the surface of the water by beating its broad pectoral fins. • Family Gasteropelecidae: three genera, in particular *Gasteropelecus*, and several species.

hatch·et job ▸*n. informal* a fierce attack on someone or their work, esp. in print: *the author's attempted hatchet job on the judge was totally unjustified and irresponsible.*

hatch·et man ▸*n. informal* a person employed to carry out controversial or disagreeable tasks, such as the dismissal of a number of people from employment. ■ a person who writes fierce attacks on others or their work. ▷late 19th cent.: figuratively, from an early use denoting a hired Chinese assassin.

hatch·ling /ˈhaCHliNG/ ▸*n.* a young animal that has recently emerged from its egg.

hatch·ment /ˈhaCHmənt/ ▸*n.* a large tablet, typically diamond-shaped, bearing the coat of arms of someone who has died, displayed in their honor. ▷early 16th cent.: probably from obsolete French *hachement*, from Old French *acesmement* 'adornment.'

hatch·way /ˈhaCH,wā/ ▸*n.* an opening or hatch, esp. in a ship's deck.

hate /hāt/ ▸*v.* [*trans.*] feel intense or passionate dislike for (someone): *the boys hate each other* | *he was particularly hated by the extreme right.* ■ have a strong aversion to (something): *he hates flying* | [with *infinitive*] *I'd hate to live there.* ■ [with *infinitive*] used politely to express one's regret or embarrassment at doing something: *I hate to bother you.*

▸*n.* intense or passionate dislike: *feelings of hate and revenge.* ■ [as *adj.*] denoting hostile actions motivated by intense dislike or prejudice: *a hate campaign.* ▷Old English *hatian* (verb), *hete* (noun), of Germanic origin; related to Dutch *haten* (verb) and German *hassen* (verb), *Hass* 'hatred.' **—hat·a·ble** /ˈhātəbəl/ (also **hate·a·ble**) *adj.* **—hat·er** *n.*

hate crime ▸*n.* a crime motivated by racial, sexual, or other prejudice, typically one involving violence.

hate·ful /ˈhātfəl/ ▸*adj.* arousing, deserving of, or filled with hatred: *hateful letters of abuse that had come unsigned.* ■ *informal* very unpleasant: *I don't have to stay in this hateful place.* **—hate·ful·ly** *adv.* **—hate·ful·ness** *n.*

hate mail ▸*n.* hostile and sometimes threatening letters sent, usually anonymously, to an individual or group.

hath /haTH/ ▸ archaic third person singular present of HAVE.

Hath·a·way /ˈhaTHə,wā/, Anne (*c.*1557–1623), the wife of Shakespeare, whom she married in 1582.

hath·a yo·ga /ˈhäTHə/ ▸*n.* a yoga system of physical exercises and breathing control. ▷from Sanskrit *haṭha* 'force' and YOGA.

Hath·or /ˈhaTHôr/ *Egyptian Mythology* a sky goddess, the patron of love and joy, represented variously as a cow, with a cow's head or ears, or with a solar disk between a cow's horns.

hat·pin /ˈhat,pin/ ▸*n.* a long pin, typically with an ornamental head, that holds a woman's hat in position by securing it to her hair.

hat·rack /ˈhat,rak/ ▸*n.* a tall freestanding post fitted with large hooks for hanging hats on.

ha·tred /ˈhātrid/ ▸*n.* intense dislike or ill will: *racial hatred* | *his murderous hatred of his brother.* ▷Middle English: from HATE + *-red* (from Old English *rǣden* 'condition').

Hat·shep·sut /hatˈSHep,so͞ot/ (died 1482 BC), Egyptian queen of the 18th dynasty, reigned *c.*1503–1482 BC. On the death of her husband, Tuthmosis II, she became regent for her nephew, Tuthmosis III. She then named herself pharaoh and was often portrayed as male.

hat·stand /ˈhat,stand/ ▸*n.* British term for HATRACK.

hat·ter /ˈhatər/ ▸*n.* a person who makes and sells hats.

Hat·ter·as, Cape /ˈhatərəs/ a peninsula in eastern North Carolina, often called "the Graveyard of the Atlantic" because of the treacherous waters around.

Hat·ties·burg /ˈhatēz,bərg/ an industrial, commercial, and academic city in southeastern Mississippi; pop. 44,779.

hat trick ▸*n.* three successes of the same kind, esp. consecutive ones within a limited period: *the band completes the trilogy, making for a dubious musical hat trick.* ■ (chiefly in ice hockey or soccer) the scoring of three goals in a game by one player. ■ (in cricket) the taking of three wickets by the same bowler with successive balls. ▷late 19th cent.: originally referring to the club presentation of a new hat (or some equivalent) to a bowler taking three wickets successively.

hau·berk /ˈhôbərk/ ▸*n. historical* a piece of armor originally covering only the neck and shoulders but later consisting of a full-length coat of mail or military tunic. ▷Middle English: from Old French *hauberc*, *hausberc*, originally denoting protection for the neck, of Germanic origin.

haugh·ty /ˈhôtē/ ▸*adj.* (**haugh·ti·er**, **haugh·ti·est**) arrogantly superior and disdainful: *a look of haughty disdain* | *a haughty aristocrat.* ▷mid 16th cent.: extended form of obsolete *haught*, earlier *haut*, from Old French, from Latin *altus* 'high.' **—haugh·ti·ly** /-təlē/ *adv.* **—haugh·ti·ness** *n.*

haul /hôl/ ▸*v.* **1** [*trans.*] (of a person) pull or drag with effort or force: *he hauled his bike out of the shed.* ■ *Nautical* pull on (a rope). ■ (**haul oneself**) propel or pull oneself with difficulty: *he hauled himself along the cliff face.* ■ *informal* force (someone) to appear for reprimand or trial: *they will be hauled into court next week.* ■ [*intrans.*] (of a person) pull hard: *she* ***hauled on*** *the reins.* **2** [*trans.*] (of a vehicle) pull (an attached trailer or load) behind it: *the train was hauling a cargo of liquid chemicals.* ■ transport in a truck or cart: *Bennie hauls trash in North Philadelphia.* **3** [*intrans.*] (esp. of a sailing ship) make an abrupt change of course.

▸*n.* **1** an amount of something gained or acquired: *the movie increased $59,177 over its haul from the previous week.* ■ a quantity of something that was stolen or is possessed illegally: *they escaped with a haul of antiques.* ■ the number of points, medals, or titles won by a person or team in a sporting event or over a period. ■ a number of fish caught. **2** a distance to be traversed: *the thirty-mile haul to Tallahassee.* See also LONG HAUL, SHORT HAUL. ▷mid 16th cent. (originally in the nautical sense 'trim sails for sailing closer to the wind'): variant of HALE2.

▸*PHRASES* □ **haul ass** *informal* move or leave fast. □ **haul off** *informal* leave; depart. ■ withdraw a little in preparation for some action: *he hauled off and smacked the kid.*

haul·age /ˈhôlij/ ▸*n.* the action or process of hauling. ■ the commercial transport of goods: *road haulage.* ■ a charge for such transport.

haul·er /ˈhôlər/ ▸*n.* a person or company employed in the transport of goods or materials by road: *private haulers collect the bagged or bundled waste.* ■ a truck used for the transport of goods or materials.

haul·ier /ˈhôlēər/ ▸*n.* British term for HAULER.

haulm /hôm/ *chiefly Brit.* ▸*n.* a stalk or stem. ■ the stalks or stems collectively of peas, beans, or potatoes without the pods or tubers, as used for bedding: *potato haulm.* ▷Old English *healm*, *halm*, of Germanic origin; related to Dutch *halm* and German *Halm*, from an Indo-European root shared by Latin *culmus* 'stalk' and Greek *kalamos* 'reed.'

haunch /hônCH; hänCH/ ▸*n.* **1** a buttock and thigh considered together, in a human or animal. ■ the leg and loin of an animal, such as a deer, as food: *haunch of caribou meat.* **2** *Architecture* the side of an arch, between the crown and the pier. ▷Middle English: from Old French *hanche*, of Germanic origin.

▸*PHRASE* □ **sit on one's haunches** squat with the haunches resting on the backs of the heels.

haunt /hônt; hänt/ ▸*v.* [*trans.*] (of a ghost) manifest itself at (a place) regularly: *a gray lady who haunts the chapel.* ■ (of a person) frequent (a place): *he haunts used book stores.* ■ be persistently and disturbingly present in (something): *cities haunted by the shadow of cholera.* ■ be persistently in the mind of (someone): *the sight haunted me for years.*

▸*n.* a place frequented by a specified person or group of people: *I revisited my* ***old haunts*** | *Greenwich Village has been home to a number of literary haunts.* ▷Middle English (in the sense 'frequent (a place)'): from Old French *hanter*, of Germanic origin; distantly related to HOME. **—haunt·er** *n.*

haunt·ed /ˈhôntid; ˈhän-/ ▸*adj.* (of a place) frequented by a ghost: *it looked like a classic haunted mansion.* ■ having or showing signs of mental anguish or torment: *the hollow cheeks, the haunted eyes.*

haunt·ing /ˈhôntiNG; ˈhän-/ ▸*adj.* poignant and evocative; difficult to ignore or forget: *the melodies were elaborate and of haunting beauty.* **—haunt·ing·ly** *adv.*

Haupt·mann /ˈhoupt,män/, Gerhart (1862–1946), German playwright. An early pioneer of naturalism, he is known for *Before Sunrise* (1889) and *The Ascension of Joan* (1893). Nobel Prize for Literature (1912).

hau·ri·ent /ˈhôrēənt/ ▸*adj.* [*postpositive*] *Heraldry* (of a fish or marine creature) depicted swimming vertically, typically with the head upward. ▷late 16th cent.: from Latin *haurient-* 'drawing in (air, water, etc.),' from the verb *haurire*.

Hau·sa /ˈhousə; ˈhouzə/ ▸*n.* (*pl.* same or **-sas**) **1** a member of a people of northern Nigeria and adjacent regions. **2** the Chadic language of this people, spoken mainly in Nigeria and Niger, and widely used as a lingua franca in parts of West Africa.

▸*adj.* of or relating to this people or their language. ▷the name in Hausa.

haus·frau /ˈhous,frou/ ▸*n.* a German housewife. ■ *informal* a woman regarded as overly domesticated or efficient. ▷late 18th cent.: from German, from *Haus* 'house' + *Frau* 'woman, wife.'

Hauss·mann /ˈhousmən/, Jacques see HOUSEMAN.

haus·tel·lum /hôˈsteləm/ ▸*n.* (*pl.* **haus·tel·la** /hôˈstelə/) *Zoology* the sucking organ or proboscis of an insect or crustacean. ▷early 19th cent.: modern Latin diminutive of *haustrum* 'scoop,' from *haust-* 'drawn in,' from the verb *haurire*. **—haus·tel·late** /hôˈstelit; ˈhôstə,lāt/ *adj.*

haus·to·ri·um /hôˈstôrēəm/ ▸*n.* (*pl.* **haus·to·ri·a** /hôˈstôrēə/) *Botany* a slender projection from the root of a parasitic plant, such as a dodder, or from the hyphae of a parasitic fungus, enabling the parasite to penetrate the tissues of its host and absorb nutrients from it. ▷late 19th cent.: modern Latin, from Latin *haustor* 'thing that draws in,' from the verb *haurire*. **—haus·to·ri·al** /hôstôrēəl/ *adj.*

haut·boy /ˈ(h)ō,boi/ (also **haut·bois** /-,boi/) ▸*n.* archaic form of OBOE. ▷mid 16th cent.: from French *hautbois*, from *haut* 'high' + *bois* 'wood.'

haute /ōt/ (or **haut**) ▸*adj.* fashionably elegant or high-class.

haute bour·geoi·sie /,ōt bo͝ozHwäˈzē/ ▸*n.* (**the haute bourgeoisie**) [treated as *sing.* or *pl.*] the upper middle class. ▷late 19th cent.: French, literally 'high bourgeoisie.'

haute cou·ture /,ōt ,ko͞oˈto͝or/ ▸*n.* the designing and making of high-quality fashionable clothes by leading fashion houses, esp. to order. ■ fashion houses that engage in such work. ■ clothes of this kind. ▷early 20th cent.: French, literally 'high dressmaking.'

haute cui·sine /,ōt ,kwəˈzēn/ ▸*n.* the preparation and cooking of high-quality food following the style of traditional French cuisine. ■ food produced in such a way. ▷early 20th cent.: French, literally 'high cookery.'

haute é·cole /,ōt eˈkôl/ ▸*n.* the art or practice of advanced classical dressage. ▷mid 19th cent.: French, literally 'high school.'

Haute-Nor·man·die /,ōt ,nôrmänˈdē/ a region in

northern France, on the coast of the English Channel.

hau·teur /hō'tər/ ▶*n.* haughtiness of manner; disdainful pride. ▷French, from *haut* 'high.'

haut monde /ō 'mônd; 'mänd/ ▶*n.* (**the haut monde**) fashionable society. ▷mid 19th cent.: French, literally 'high world.'

Ha·va·na¹ /hə'vanə/ the capital of Cuba, on the northern coast; pop. 2,160,000. It was founded in 1515 by Diego Velázquez de Cuéllar. Spanish name **La Habana**.

Ha·van·a² /hə'vanə; hə'vänə/ ▶*n.* a cigar made in Cuba or from Cuban tobacco.

Ha·va·su, Lake /'havə,so͞o/ a reservoir and recreational site on the Colorado River between Arizona and southeastern California.

Hav·da·lah /,hävdä'lä; häv'dôlə/ (also **Hab·da·lah**) ▶*n.* a Jewish religious ceremony or formal prayer marking the end of the Sabbath. ▷from Hebrew *haḇdālāh* 'separation, division.'

have /hav/ ▶*v.* (**has** /haz; (h)əz/; *past* **had** /had; (h)əd/) [*trans.*] **1** (also **have got**) possess, own, or hold: *he had a new car and a boat | have you got a job yet? | I don't have that much money on me | he's got the equipment with him.* ■ possess or be provided with (a quality, characteristic, or feature): *the ham had a sweet, smoky flavor | she's got blue eyes | the house has gas heat.* ■ (**have oneself**) *informal* provide or indulge oneself with (something): *he had himself two highballs.* ■ be made up of; comprise: *in 1989 the party had 10,000 members.* ■ used to indicate a particular relationship: *he's got three children | do you have a client named Pedersen?* ■ be able to make use of (something available or at one's disposal): *how much time have I got for the presentation?* ■ have gained (a qualification): *he's got a BA in English.* ■ possess as an intellectual attainment; know (a language or subject): *he knew Latin and Greek; I had only a little French.* **2** experience; undergo: *I went to a few parties and had a good time | I was having difficulty in keeping awake.* ■ (also **have got**) suffer from (an illness, ailment, or disability): *I've got a headache.* ■ (also **have got**) let (a feeling or thought) come into one's mind; hold in the mind: *he had the strong impression that someone was watching him | we've got a few ideas we're kicking around | I've no doubt he's as busy as I am.* ■ [with *past part.*] experience or suffer the specified action happening or being done to (something): *she had her bag stolen.* ■ [*trans.*] cause (someone or something) to be in a particular state or condition: *I want to have everything ready in good time | I had the TV on with the sound turned down.* ■ (also **have got**) *informal* have put (someone) at a disadvantage in an argument (said either to acknowledge that one has no answer to a point or to show that one knows one's opponent has no answer): *you've got me there; I've never given the matter much thought.* ■ [with *past part.*] cause (something) to be done for one by someone else: *it is advisable to have your carpet laid by a professional.* ■ tell or arrange for something to be done: [*trans.*] *she had her long hair cut | always having the builders in to do something.* ■ (usu. **be had**) *informal* cheat or deceive (someone): *I realized I'd been had.* ■ *vulgar slang* engage in sexual intercourse with (someone). **3** (**have to do something** or **have got to do something**) be obliged or find it necessary to do the specified thing: *you don't have to accept this situation | we've got to plan for the future.* ■ [*trans.*] need or be obliged to do (something): *he's got a lot to do.* ■ be strongly recommended to do something: *if you think that place is great, you have to try our summer house.* ■ be certain or inevitable to happen or be the case: *there has to be a catch.* **4** perform the action indicated by the noun specified (used esp. in spoken English as an alternative to a more specific verb): *he had a look around | the color green has a restful effect.* ■ organize and bring about: *are you going to have a party?* ■ eat or drink: *I'll have the vegetable plate.* ■ give birth to or be due to give birth to: *she's going to have a baby.* **5** (also **have got**) show (a personal attribute or quality) by one's actions or attitude: *he had little patience with technological gadgetry | [trans.] if you've got the drive to finish your degree.* ■ [often in *imperative*] exercise or show (mercy, pity, etc.) toward another person: *God have mercy on me!* ■ [with *negative*] not accept; refuse to tolerate: *I can't have you insulting Tom like that.* **6** (also **have got**) [*trans.*] place or keep (something) in a particular position: *Mary had her back to me | I soon had the trout in a net.* ■ hold or grasp (someone or something) in a particular way: *he had me by the throat.* **7** be the recipient of (something sent, given, or done): *she had a letter from Mark.* ■ take or invite into one's home so as to provide care or entertainment, esp. for a limited period: *we're having the children for the weekend.*

▶*auxiliary v.* used with a past participle to form the perfect, pluperfect, and future perfect tenses, and the conditional mood: *I have finished | he had asked her | she will have left by now | I could have helped, had I known | "Have you seen him?" "Yes, I have."*

▶*phrasal v.* □ **have at** attempt or attack forcefully or aggressively. □ **have someone on** *Brit., informal* try to make someone believe something that is untrue, esp. as a joke: *that's just too neat—you're having me on.* □ **have (got) something on 1** be wearing something: *she had a blue dress on.* **2** *Brit.* be committed to an arrangement: *I've got a lot on at the moment.* □ **have something out** undergo an operation to extract the part of the body specified: *she had her wisdom teeth out.*

▶*n.* (**the haves**) *informal* people with plenty of money and possessions: *an increasing gap between the haves and have-nots.* ▷Old English *habban*, of Germanic origin; related to Dutch *hebben* and German *haben*, also probably to **heave**.

▶*PHRASES* □ **have a care** (or **an eye**, etc.) see **care**, **eye**, etc. □ **have got it bad** *informal* be very powerfully affected emotionally, esp. by love. ■ be in a situation where one is treated badly or exploited: *if you think you've got it bad now, how would you like to be paid to collect pebbles?* □ **have had it** *informal* **1** be in a very poor condition; be beyond repair or past its best: *the car had had it.* ■ be extremely tired: *tomorrow she would drive on through Germany, but for today, she'd had it.* ■ have lost all chance of survival: *the Cold War is ended—Marxism's had it.* **2** be unable to tolerate someone or something any longer: ***I've had it with*** *him—he's humiliated me once too often!* □ **have it 1** [with *clause*] express the view that (used to indicate that the speaker is reporting something that they do not necessarily believe to be fact): *rumor had it that although he lived in a derelict house, he was really very wealthy.* **2** win a decision, esp. after a vote: *the ayes have it.* **3** have found the answer to something: *"I have it!" Rosa exclaimed.* □ **have it away** (or **off**) *Brit., vulgar slang* have sexual intercourse. □ **have it both ways** see **both**. □ **have it coming** deserve punishment or downfall. □ **have (got) it in for** *informal* feel a particular dislike of (someone) and behave in a hostile manner toward them. □ **have (got) it in one (to do something)** *informal* have the capacity or potential (to do something): *everyone thinks he has it in him to produce a literary classic.* □ **have it out** *informal* attempt to resolve a contentious matter by confronting someone and engaging in a frank discussion or argument: *give her the chance of a night's rest before you* ***have it out with*** *her.* □ **have a nice day** used to express good wishes when parting. □ **have (got) nothing on** *informal* **1** be not nearly as good as (someone or something), esp. in a particular respect: *bright though his three sons were, they had nothing on Sally.* **2 have nothing** (or **something**) **on someone** know nothing (or something) discreditable or incriminating about someone: *I am not worried—they've got nothing on me.* □ **have nothing to do with** see **do**¹. □ **have one too many** see **many**. □ **have (got) something to oneself** be able to use, occupy, or enjoy something without having to share it with anyone else. □ **have —— to do with** see **do**¹.

USAGE 1 **Have** and **have got**: there is a great deal of debate on the difference between these two forms. A traditional view is that **have got** is chiefly British, but not correct in formal writing, while **have** is chiefly American. Actual usage is more complicated: **have got** is in fact also widely used in U.S. English. In both U.S. and British usage, **have** is more formal than **have got**, and it is more appropriate in writing to use constructions such as **don't have** (or **do not have**) rather than **haven't got**. See also **usage** at **gotten**.

2 A common mistake is to write the word of instead of **have** or **'ve**: *I* ***could of*** *told you that* instead of *I* ***could've*** *told you that.* The reason for the mistake is that the pronunciation of **have** in unstressed contexts is the same as that of **of**, and the two words are confused when it comes to writing them down. The error was recorded as early as 1837 and, although common, is unacceptable in standard English.

3 Another controversial issue is the insertion of **have** where it is superfluous, as, for example, *I might have missed it if you* ***hadn't have*** *pointed it out* (rather than the standard ... *if you* ***hadn't*** *pointed it out*). This construction has been around since at least the 15th century, but only where a hypothetical situation is presented (e.g., statements starting with **if**). More recently, there has been speculation among grammarians and linguists that this insertion of **have** may represent a kind of subjunctive and is actually making a useful distinction in the language. However, it is still regarded as an error in standard English.

Ha·vel /'hävəl/, Václav (1936–), Czech playwright and statesman; president of Czechoslovakia 1989–92 and of the Czech Republic 1993–2003. His plays, such as *The Garden Party* (1963), were critical of totalitarianism, and he was twice imprisoned as a dissident.

ha·ve·li /,həvə'lē/ ▶*n.* (*pl.* **havelis**) *Indian* a mansion. ▷via Hindi from Arabic *havelī*.

have·lock /'hav,läk/ ▶*n.* a cloth covering for a military cap that extends downward to protect the neck from sun and weather. ▷mid 19th cent.: named after Sir Henry *Havelock* (1795–1857), an English general who served in India.

havelock

ha·ven /'hāvən/ ▶*n.* a place of safety or refuge: *a haven for wildlife.* ■ an inlet providing shelter for ships or boats; a harbor or small port. ▷late Old English *hæfen*, from Old Norse *hǫfn*; related to Dutch *haven*, German *Hafen* 'harbor.'

have-nots ▶*plural n.* (usu. **the have-nots**) *informal* economically disadvantaged people: *lack of access to information will perpetuate the division between the* ***haves and have-nots***.

have·n't /'havənt/ ▶*contraction of* have not.

ha·ver /'hāvər/ ▶*v.* [*intrans.*] *Scottish* talk foolishly; babble: *Tom havered on.* ■ *Brit.* act in a vacillating or indecisive manner: [as *n.*] (**havering**) *most people giggle at their havering and indecision.*

▶*n.* (also **havers**) *Scottish* foolish talk; nonsense. ▷early 18th cent.: of unknown origin.

Ha·ver·hill /'hāv(ə)rəl/ an industrial city in northeastern Massachusetts, on the Merrimack River; pop. 51,418.

hav·er·sack /'havər,sak/ ▶*n.* a small, sturdy bag carried on the back or over the shoulder, used esp. by soldiers and hikers. ▷mid 18th cent.: from French *havresac*, from obsolete German *Habersack*, denoting a bag used by soldiers to carry oats as horse feed, from dialect *Haber* 'oats' + *Sack* 'sack, bag.'

Ha·ver·sian ca·nal /hə'vərzнən/ ▶*n.* *Anatomy* any of the minute tubes that form a network in bone and contain blood vessels. ▷mid 19th cent.: named after Clopton *Havers* (1650–1702), English anatomist.

Hav·li·cek /'havlə,cнek/ John (1940–) U.S. basketball player; nickname **Hondo**. He played for the Boston Celtics 1962–78, during which time they won eight NBA titles 1963–66, 1968–69, 1974, 1976. Basketball Hall of Fame (1983).

hav·oc /'havək/ ▶*n.* widespread destruction: *the hurricane ripped through Florida, causing havoc.* ■ great confusion or disorder: *schoolchildren* ***wreaking havoc*** *in the classroom.*

▶*v.* (**hav·ocked**, **hav·ocking**) [*trans.*] *archaic* lay waste to; devastate. ▷late Middle English: from Anglo-Norman French *havok*, alteration of Old French *havot*, of unknown origin. The word was originally used in the phrase *cry havoc* (Old French *crier havot*) 'to give an army the order *havoc*,' which was the signal for plundering.

▶*PHRASE* □ **play havoc with** completely disrupt; cause serious damage to: *shift work plays havoc with the body clock.*

haw¹ /hô/ ▶*n.* the red fruit of the hawthorn. ▷Old English *haga*, of Germanic origin; probably related to **hedge** (compare with Dutch *haag* 'hedge').

haw² ▶*n.* the third eyelid or nictitating membrane in certain mammals, esp. dogs and cats. ▷late Middle English (denoting a discharge from the eye): of unknown origin.

haw³ ▶*v.* see **hem and haw** at **hem**².

Ha·wai·i /hə'wī(y)ē; -'wä(y)ē; -'wô(y)ē/ a state in the U.S. that is comprised of a group of islands in the North Pacific Ocean, about 3,000 miles (4,830 km) west of mainland U.S.; pop. 1,211,537; capital, Honolulu (on Oahu); statehood, Aug. 21, 1959 (50). First settled by Polynesians, Hawaii was discovered by Captain James Cook in 1778. It was annexed by the U.S. in 1898 and is a popular vacation destination. Former name **SANDWICH ISLANDS**. ■ the largest island in the state of Hawaii.

Ha·wai·i-A·leu·tian Stand·ard Time (abbr.: **HST**) ▸*n.* the standard time in a zone including the Hawaiian Islands and the western Aleutian Islands, specifically: ■ standard time based on the mean solar time at longitude 150° W., ten hours behind GMT. Also called **Hawaiian Standard Time**.

Ha·wai·ian /hə'wīən; -'woi-ən/ ▸*n.* **1** a native or inhabitant of Hawaii. **2** the Austronesian language of Hawaii.
▸*adj.* of or relating to Hawaii, its people, or their language. ■ *Geology* relating to or denoting a type of volcanic eruption in which fluid basaltic lava is produced, as is typical of volcanoes in Hawaii.

Ha·wai·ian goose ▸*n.* a rare goose native to Hawaii, now breeding chiefly in captivity. Also called **NENE**. • *Branta savdvicensis*, family Anatidae.

Ha·wai·ian gui·tar ▸*n.* a steel-stringed guitar in which a characteristic glissando effect is produced by sliding a metal bar along the strings as they are plucked.

Ha·wai·ian hon·ey·creep·er ▸*n.* see **HONEYCREEPER** (sense 2).

ha·wa·la /hə'wälə; -'välə/ ▸*n.* a system or agency for transferring money traditionally used in the Muslim world, whereby the money is paid to an agent who then instructs a remote associate to pay the final recipient. ▹from Arabic, literally 'change, transform.'

haw·finch /'hô,finCH/ ▸*n.* a large Old World finch with a massive bill for cracking open cherrystones and other hard seeds. • Genus *Coccothraustes*, family Fringillidae: three species, in particular the widespread *C. coccothraustes*. ▹late 17th cent.: from **HAW**[1] + **FINCH**.

hawk[1] /hôk/ ▸*n.* **1** a diurnal bird of prey with broad rounded wings and a long tail, typically taking prey by surprise with a short chase. Compare with **FALCON**. • Family Accipitridae: several genera, esp. *Accipiter*, which includes the Cooper's hawk and goshawk. ■ a bird of prey related to the buteos. ■ *Falconry* any diurnal bird of prey used in falconry. **2** a person who advocates an aggressive or warlike policy, esp. in foreign affairs. Compare with **DOVE**[1] (sense 2).
▸*v.* [*intrans.*] **1** (of a person) hunt game with a trained hawk: *he spent the afternoon hawking.* **2** (of a bird or dragonfly) hunt on the wing for food: *swifts hawked low over the water* | [*trans.*] *dragonflies hawk and feed on flies.* ▹Old English *hafoc, heafoc*, of Germanic origin; related to Dutch *havik* and German *Habicht*. **—hawk·ish** *adj.* **—hawk·ish·ly** *adv.* **—hawk·ish·ness** *n.* **—hawk·like** /-,līk/ *adj.*
▸*PHRASES* □ **have eyes like a hawk** miss nothing of what is going on around one. □ **watch someone like a hawk** keep a vigilant eye on someone, esp. to check that they do nothing wrong.

hawk[2] ▸*v.* [*trans.*] carry around and offer (goods) for sale, typically advertising them by shouting: *street traders were hawking costume jewelry.* ▹late 15th cent.: back-formation from **HAWKER**[1].

hawk[3] ▸*v.* [*intrans.*] clear the throat noisily: *he hawked and spat into the flames.* ■ [*trans.*] (**hawk something up**) bring phlegm up from the throat. ▹late 16th cent.: probably imitative.

hawk[4] ▸*n.* a plasterer's square board with a handle underneath for carrying plaster or mortar. ▹late Middle English: of unknown origin.

hawk ea·gle ▸*n.* a small tropical eagle with broad wings and a long tail, and typically a crest. • Genera *Spizaetus* and *Spizastur*, family Accipitridae: several species.

Hawke Bay a bay on the eastern coast of North Island, in New Zealand.

hawk·er[1] /'hôkər/ ▸*n.* a person who travels around selling goods, typically advertising them by shouting. ▹early 16th cent.: probably from Low German or Dutch and related to **HUCKSTER**.

hawk·er[2] ▸*n.* a falconer. ▹Old English *hafocere*, from *hafoc* 'hawk.'

hawk-eyed ▸*adj.* having very good eyesight. ■ watching carefully; vigilant: *a hawk-eyed policeman saved the lives of dozens of shoppers.*

Hawk·eye State /'hô,kī/ a nickname for the state of **IOWA**.

hawk·fish /'hôk,fiSH/ ▸*n.* (*pl.* same or **-fish·es**) a small tropical marine fish found chiefly in the Indo-Pacific region. It typically lives in shallow water and adopts a distinctive perching or "hovering" position just above coral. • Family Cirrhitidae: three genera and several species.

Hawk·ing /'hôkiNG/, Stephen (William) (1942–), English theoretical physicist. His main work has been with space-time, quantum mechanics, and black holes. His book *A Brief History of Time* (1988) was a best seller.

Hawk·ing ra·di·a·tion ▸*n. Physics* electromagnetic radiation that, according to theory, should be emitted by a black hole. The radiation is due to the black hole capturing one of a particle-antiparticle pair created spontaneously near to the event horizon.

Haw·kins /'hôkənz/, Coleman (Randolph) (1904–69), U.S. jazz saxophonist. During the 1920s and 1930s he was influential in making the tenor saxophone popular as a jazz instrument. He played with the Fletcher Henderson band 1923–34.

hawk moth (also **hawk·moth**) ▸*n.* a large swift-flying moth with a stout body and narrow forewings, typically feeding on nectar while hovering. Also called **SPHINX**. See also **HORNWORM**. • Family Sphingidae: several genera and many species.

hawk moth

hawk-nosed ▸*adj.* (of a person) having a nose that is curved like a hawk's beak.

hawk owl ▸*n.* a hawklike owl with a small head and long tail, and typically an obscure facial disk. • Family Strigidae: three genera, including *Ninox* (several species in Asia and Australasia) and *Surnia*, in particular the diurnal *S. ulula* of northern coniferous forests.

Hawks /hôks/, Howard (Winchester) (1896–1977), U.S. movie director, producer, and screenwriter. He wrote and directed the screenplay for his first movie in 1926 and also directed such movies as *The Big Sleep* (1946), *Gentlemen Prefer Blondes* (1953), and *Rio Bravo* (1959).

hawks·beard /'hôks,bērd/ (also **hawk's beard**) ▸*n.* a plant of the daisy family that resembles a dandelion but has a branched stem with several flowers. • Genus *Crepis*, family Compositae: several species, including the **western hawksbeard** (*C. occidentalis*), found in the rocky areas of the western and southwestern U.S., and the **slender hawksbeard** (*C. atribarba*), found in the open areas of western North America .

hawks·bill /'hôks,bil/ (also **hawksbill turtle**) ▸*n.* a small tropical sea turtle with hooked jaws and overlapping horny plates on the shell, extensively hunted as the traditional source of tortoiseshell. • *Eretmochelys imbricata*, family Cheloniidae.

hawksbill

hawk·shaw /'hôk,SHô/ ▸*n. informal, dated* a detective. ▹early 20th cent.: from the name of a detective in the play *The Ticket-of-Leave Man* by Tom Taylor (1817–80), English dramatist; also portrayed in the comic strip *Hawkshaw the Detective* by Augustus Charles ("Gus") Mager (1878–1956), American cartoonist.

hawk·weed /'hôk,wēd/ ▸*n.* a widely distributed plant of the daisy family, typically having small yellow dandelionlike flowerheads and often growing as a weed. • Genus *Hieracium*, family Compositae. ▹late Old English, rendering Latin *hieracium*, based on Greek *hierax* 'hawk.'

Ha·worth /'hou,wərTH/, Sir Walter Norman (1883–1950), English organic chemist. A pioneer in carbohydrate chemistry, he was the first person to make a vitamin artificially when he synthesized vitamin C. Nobel Prize for Chemistry (1937, shared with Paul Karrer 1889-1971).

hawse /hôz/ ▸*n.* the part of a ship's bows through which the anchor cables pass. ■ the space between the head of an anchored vessel and the anchors. ▹late Middle English *halse*, probably from Old Norse *háls* 'neck, ship's bow.'

hawse·hole /'hôz,hōl/ ▸*n.* a hole in the deck of a ship through which an anchor cable passes.

hawse·pipe /'hôz,pīp/ ▸*n.* an inclined pipe leading from a hawsehole to the side of a ship, containing the shank of the anchor when the anchor is raised.

haw·ser /'hôzər/ ▸*n.* a thick rope or cable for mooring or towing a ship. ▹Middle English: from Anglo-Norman French *haucer*, from Old French *haucier* 'to hoist,' based on Latin *altus* 'high.'

haw·ser-laid ▸*adj.* **1** another term for **CABLE-LAID**. **2** *chiefly historical* denoting the ordinary type of rope commonly used in ships' rigging, typically made of three left-handed strands twisted together right-handed.

haw·thorn /'hô,THôrn/ ▸*n.* a thorny shrub or tree of the rose family, with white, pink, or red blossoms and small dark red fruits (haws). Native to north temperate regions, it is commonly used for hedges. Also called **MAY**[2], **QUICKTHORN**, or **WHITETHORN**. • Genus *Crataegus*, family Rosaceae: many species, in particular the European **common hawthorn** (*C. monogyna*). ▹Old English *hagathorn*, probably meaning literally 'hedge thorn' (see **HAW**[1], **THORN**); related to Dutch *haagdoorn*, German *Hagedorn*.

Haw·thorne[1] /'hô,THôrn/ a city in southwestern California, south of Los Angeles; pop. 71,349.

Haw·thorne[2] /'hô,THôrn/, Nathaniel (1804–64), U.S. novelist and short-story writer. Much of his fiction explores guilt, sin, and morality. Notable works: *The Scarlet Letter* (1850), *The House of Seven Gables* (1851), and *The Marble Faun* (1860).

Haw·thorne ef·fect ▸*n.* the alteration of behavior by the subjects of a study due to their awareness of being observed. ▹1960s: from *Hawthorne*, the name of one of the Western Electric Company's plants in Chicago, where the phenomenon was first observed in the 1920s.

Hay /hā/, John Milton (1838–1905) U.S. diplomat and writer. He was U.S. ambassador to Great Britain 1897–98, and then, as U.S. secretary of state 1898–1905, he negotiated the Hay–Pauncefote Treaty 1901 that made possible the construction of the Panama Canal.

hay[1] /hā/ ▸*n.* grass that has been mown and dried for use as fodder. ▹Old English *hēg, hīeg, hīg*, of Germanic origin; related to Dutch *hooi* and German *Heu*, also to **HEW**.
▸*PHRASES* □ **hit the hay** *informal* go to bed. □ **make hay (while the sun shines)** *proverb* make good use of an opportunity while it lasts.

hay[2] ▸*n.* a country dance with interweaving steps similar to a reel. ■ a winding figure in such a dance. ▹early 16th cent.: from an obsolete sense 'a kind of dance' of French *haie* 'hedge,' figuratively 'row of people lining the route of a procession.'

hay·box /'hā,bäks/ ▸*n. historical* a box stuffed with hay in which heated food was left to continue cooking.

hay·cock /'hā,käk/ ▸*n.* a conical heap of hay in a field.

Hay·dn /'hīdn/, Franz Joseph (1732–1809), Austrian composer. A major exponent of the classical style, he was musical director to the household of Hungary's Prince Esterházy 1761–90. His work includes 104 symphonies, chamber and keyboard music, and the oratorio *The Creation* (1796–98).

Ha·yek /'hīək/, Friedrich August von (1899–1992), British economist; born in Austria. Strongly opposed to Keynesian economics, he was a leading advocate of the free market. Nobel Prize for Economics (1974, shared with Gunnar Myrdal).

Hayes[1] /hāz/, Helen (1900–1993) U.S. actress; born Helen Hayes Brown; known as **the first lady of the American theater**. Her Broadway career spanned seven decades and included Tony-winning roles in *Happy Birthday* (1946) and *Time Remembered* (1957). She also appeared in movies such as *The Sin of*

Madelon Claudet (Academy Award, 1932) and *Airport* (Academy Award, 1970).

Hayes[2], Rutherford B(irchard) (1822–93), 19th president of the U.S. 1877–81. A Republican, he served in the U.S. House of Representatives 1865–68 and as governor of Ohio 1868–72 and 1876–77 before succeeding Ulysses S. Grant to the presidency. During his administration, Reconstruction in the South came to an end. His use of federal troops during the railroad strikes of 1877 cost him the popular support of the people.

Rutherford B. Hayes

hay fe·ver ▸*n.* an allergy caused by pollen or dust in which the mucous membranes of the eyes and nose are itchy and inflamed, causing a runny nose and watery eyes.

hay·field /ˈhāˌfēld/ ▸*n.* a field where hay is being or is to be made.

hay·fork /ˈhāˌfôrk/ ▸*n.* a hand tool for lifting hay; pitchfork. ■ a machine for lifting hay.

hay·ing /ˈhāiNG/ ▸*n.* the activity of mowing and drying grass to make hay.

hay·lage /ˈhālij/ ▸*n.* silage made from grass that has been partially dried. ▷1960s: blend of HAY[1] and SILAGE.

hay·loft /ˈhāˌlôft/ ▸*n.* a loft over a stable or barn used for storing hay or straw.

hay·mak·er /ˈhāˌmākər/ ▸*n.* **1** a person who is involved in making hay, esp. one who tosses and spreads it to dry after mowing. ■ an apparatus for shaking and drying hay. **2** *informal* a forceful blow: *he caught him on the side of the head with a stinging haymaker.* **—hay·mak·ing** *n.*

Hay·mar·ket Square /ˈhāˌmärkit/ a historic site in Chicago, in Illinois, site of an 1886 bombing during a labor demonstration.

hay·mow /ˈhāˌmō/ ▸*n.* a stack of hay. ■ a part of a barn in which hay is stored.

hay·rick /ˈhāˌrik/ ▸*n.* another term for HAYSTACK.

hay·ride /ˈhāˌrīd/ ▸*n.* a ride taken for pleasure in a wagon carrying hay.

hay·seed /ˈhāˌsēd/ ▸*n.* **1** grass seed obtained from hay. **2** *informal* a person from the country, esp. a simple, unsophisticated one.

hay·stack /ˈhāˌstak/ ▸*n.* a packed pile of hay, typically with a pointed or ridged top.

Hay·ward[1] /ˈhāwərd/ a city in north central California, south of Oakland, on San Francisco Bay; pop. 111,498.

Hay·ward[2], Susan (1919–75) U.S. actress; born *Edythe Marrener*. Her most well-known movie was *I Want to Live* (Academy Award, 1958).

hay·wire /ˈhāˌwīr/ ▸*adj. informal* erratic; out of control: *her imagination had* **gone haywire**. ▷early 20th cent. (originally U.S.): from HAY[1] + WIRE, from the use of hay-baling wire in makeshift repairs.

Hay·worth /ˈhāˌwərTH/, Rita (1918–87), U.S. actress and dancer; born *Margarita Carmen Cansino*. She achieved stardom in movie musicals such as *Cover Girl* (1944) before going on to play roles in *film noir*, notably in *Gilda* (1946) and *The Lady from Shanghai* (1948).

haz·ard /ˈhazərd/ ▸*n.* **1** a danger or risk: *the hazards of smoking.* ■ a potential source of danger: *a fire hazard | a health hazard.* ■ a permanent feature of a golf course that presents an obstruction to playing a shot, such as a bunker or stream. **2** *poetic/literary* chance; probability. **3** a gambling game using two dice, in which the chances are complicated by arbitrary rules.

▸*v.* [*trans.*] **1** venture to say (something): *he hazarded a guess.* **2** put (something) at risk of being lost: *the cargo business is too risky to hazard money on.* ▷Middle English (sense 3): from Old French *hasard*, from Spanish *azar*, from Arabic *az-zahr* 'chance, luck,' from Persian *zār* or Turkish *zar* 'dice.'

haz·ard light ▸*n.* each of a pair of flashing lights on a vehicle, warning that it is stationary or unexpectedly slowing down or reversing.

haz·ard·ous /ˈhazərdəs/ ▸*adj.* risky; dangerous: *we work in hazardous conditions | it is* **hazardous to** *personal safety.* ▷mid 16th cent.: from French *hasardeux*, from *hasard* 'chance' (see HAZARD). **—haz·ard·ous·ly** *adv.* **—haz·ard·ous·ness** *n.*

haze[1] /hāz/ ▸*n.* a slight obscuration of the lower atmosphere, typically caused by fine suspended particles. ■ a tenuous cloud of something such as vapor or smoke in the air: *a faint haze of steam.* ■ [in *sing.*] *figurative* a state of mental obscurity or confusion: *through an alcoholic haze.* ▷early 18th cent. (originally denoting fog or hoarfrost): probably a back-formation from HAZY.

haze[2] ▸*v.* **1** [*trans.*] force (a new or potential recruit to the military, a college fraternity, etc.) to perform strenuous, humiliating, or dangerous tasks: *rookies were mercilessly hazed.* **2** [*trans.*] drive (cattle) in a specified direction while on horseback. ▷late 17th cent. (originally Scots and dialect in the sense 'frighten, scold, or beat'): perhaps related to obsolete French *haser* 'tease or insult.'

ha·zel /ˈhāzəl/ ▸*n.* **1** a temperate shrub or small tree with broad leaves, bearing prominent male catkins in spring and round hard-shelled edible nuts in autumn. • Genus *Corylus*, family Betulaceae: several species, in particular the common **Eurasian hazel** (*C. avellana*), formerly widely managed as coppice. **2** a reddish-brown or greenish-brown color, esp. of someone's eyes. ▷Old English *hæsel*, of Germanic origin; related to Dutch *hazelaar* 'hazel tree,' *hazelnoot* 'hazelnut,' and German *Hasel*, from an Indo-European root shared by Latin *corylus*.

ha·zel grouse ▸*n.* a small Eurasian woodland grouse with mainly grayish plumage. • *Bonasa bonasia*, family Tetraonidae (or Phasianidae).

ha·zel·nut /ˈhāzəlˌnət/ ▸*n.* a round brown hard-shelled nut that is the edible fruit of the hazel.

haz·ing /ˈhāziNG/ ▸*n.* the imposition of strenuous, often humiliating, tasks as part of a program of rigorous physical training and initiation: *army cadets were hospitalized for injuries caused by hazing.* ■ humiliating and sometimes dangerous initiation rituals, esp. as imposed on college students seeking membership to a fraternity or sorority: *seven officers of the fraternity were charged with hazing.*

Haz·litt /ˈhazlət/, William (1778–1830), English essayist and critic. Notable works: *Table Talk* (1821) and *The Spirit of the Age* (1825).

ha·zy /ˈhāzē/ ▸*adj.* (**ha·zi·er**, **ha·zi·est**) covered by a haze: *the sky was hazy from irrigation evaporation.* ■ vague, indistinct, or ill-defined: *hazy memories | the picture we have of him as a man is extremely hazy.* ▷early 17th cent. (in nautical use in the sense 'foggy'): of unknown origin. **—ha·zi·ly** /-zilē/ *adv.* **—ha·zi·ness** *n.*

haz·zan /KHäˈzän; ˈKHäzən/ ▸*n.* (*pl.* **haz·za·nim** /ˌKHäzäˈnēm; KHäˈzônim/) another term for CANTOR (sense 1). ▷mid 17th cent.: from Hebrew *ḥazzān* 'cantor,' possibly from Assyrian *hazannu* 'mayor, village headman.'

HB ▸*abbr.* ■ half board. ■ (also **hb**) hardback. ■ hard black (used in describing a medium grade of pencil lead). ■ the political wing of the Basque separatist organization ETA. [abbreviation of Basque *Herri Batasuna* 'United People.']

Hb ▸*symbol* hemoglobin.

HBM *Brit.* ▸*abbr.* Her or His Britannic Majesty (or Majesty's).

H-bomb ▸*n.* another term for HYDROGEN BOMB. ▷1950s: from H[2] (denoting hydrogen) + BOMB.

HBP ▸*abbr. Baseball* (in box scores, of a batter) hit by a pitch.

HC ▸*abbr.* ■ Holy Communion. ■ (in the UK) House of Commons. ■ hydrocarbon: *increasing fuel efficiency decreases the levels of HC.*

h.c. ▸*abbr.* honoris causa.

HCF ▸*abbr. Mathematics* highest common factor.

HCFC ▸*abbr.* hydrochlorofluorocarbon.

HCG ▸*abbr.* human chorionic gonadotropin.

H.D. see DOOLITTLE.

hd. ▸*abbr.* ■ hand. ■ head.

hdbk. ▸*abbr.* handbook.

HDD *Computing* ▸*abbr.* hard disk drive.

hdkf. ▸*abbr.* handkerchief.

HDL ▸*abbr.* high-density lipoprotein.

hdqrs. ▸*abbr.* headquarters.

HDTV ▸*abbr.* high-definition television, using more lines per frame to give a sharper image than a conventional television.

hdwe. ▸*abbr.* hardware.

HE ▸*abbr.* ■ high explosive. ■ His Eminence. ■ His or Her Excellency.

He ▸*symbol* the chemical element helium.

he /hē/ ▸*pron.* [*third person singular*] used to refer to a man, boy, or male animal previously mentioned or easily identified: *everyone liked my father—he was the perfect gentleman.* ■ used to refer to a person or animal of unspecified sex (in modern use, now chiefly replaced by "he or she" or "they": (see **usage** below): *every child needs to know that he is loved.* ■ any person (in modern use, now chiefly replaced by "anyone" or "the person"): *he who is silent consents.*

▸*n.* [in *sing.*] a male; a man: *is that a he or a she?* ■ [in *combination*] male: *a he-goat.* ▷Old English *he*, *hē*, of Germanic origin; related to Dutch *hij*.

USAGE 1 For a discussion of *I am older than* **he** versus *I am older than* **him**, see **usage** at PERSONAL PRONOUN and THAN.

2 Until recently, **he** was used uncontroversially to refer to a person of unspecified sex, as in *every child needs to know that* **he** *is loved*. This use has become problematic and is a hallmark of old-fashionedness and sexism in language. Use of **they** as an alternative to **he** in this sense *(everyone needs to feel that* **they** *matter)* has been in use since the 16th century in contexts where it occurs after an indefinite pronoun such as **everyone** or **someone**. It is becoming more and more accepted both in speech and in writing and is used as the norm in this dictionary. Another acceptable alternative is **he or she**, although this can become tiresomely long-winded when used frequently.

See also **usage** at SHE, THEY and EVERYBODY.

Head /hed/, Edith (1907–81), U.S. costume designer. She worked on a wide range of movies, winning Academy Awards for costume design in *All About Eve* (1950), *The Sting* (1973), and others.

head /hed/ ▸*n.* **1** the upper part of the human body, or the front or upper part of the body of an animal, typically separated from the rest of the body by a neck, and containing the brain, mouth, and sense organs. ■ the head regarded as the location of intellect, imagination, and memory: *whatever comes into my head.* ■ (**head for**) an aptitude for or tolerance of: *she had a good head for business.* ■ *informal* a headache, esp. one resulting from intoxication. ■ the height or length of a head as a measure: *a dazzling woman half a head taller than he was.* ■ [usu. in *combination*] a habitual user of an illicit drug: *a large group of young adults and potheads.* ■ [usu. in *combination*] a fan or enthusiast: *a producer known for his work with metalheads and rappers.* ■ (**heads**) the obverse side of a coin (used when tossing a coin): *heads or tails?* ■ the antlers of a deer. **2** a thing having the appearance of a head either in form or in relation to a whole, in particular: ■ the cutting, striking, or operational end of a tool, weapon, or mechanism. ■ the flattened or knobbed end of a nail, pin, screw, or match. ■ the ornamented top of a pillar or column. ■ a compact mass of leaves or flowers at the top of a stem, esp. a capitulum: *huge heads of fluffy cream flowers.* ■ the edible leafy part at the top of the stem of such green vegetables as cabbage and lettuce. ■ one saleable unit of certain vegetables, such as cabbage or cauliflower. **3** the front, forward, or upper part or end of something, in particular: ■ the upper end of a table or bed: *he sat down at the head of the cot.* ■ the flat end of a cask or drum. ■ the front of a line or procession. ■ the top of a page. ■ short for HEADLINE. ■ the top of a flight of stairs or steps. ■ the source of a river or stream. ■ the end of a lake or inlet at which a river enters. ■ [usu. in *place names*] a promontory: *Beachy Head.* ■ the top of a ship's mast. ■ the bows of a ship. ■ the fully developed top of a pimple, boil, or abscess. ■ the foam on top of a glass of beer, or the cream on the top of milk. ■ short for CYLINDER HEAD. **4** a person in charge of something; a director or leader: *the head of the Dutch Catholic Church.* ■ *Brit.* short for HEADMASTER or HEADMISTRESS. **5** *Grammar* the word that governs all the other words in a phrase in which it is used, having the same grammatical function as the whole phrase. **6** a person considered as a numerical unit: *they paid fifty dollars a head.* ■ [treated as *pl.*] a number of cattle or game as specified: *seventy head of dairy cattle.* **7** a component in an audio, video, or information system by which information is transferred from an electrical signal to the recording medium, or vice versa. ■ short for PRINTHEAD. **8** a body of water kept at a particular height in order to provide a supply at sufficient pressure: *an 8 m head of water in the shafts.* ■ the pressure exerted by such water or by a confined body of steam: *a good head of steam on the gauge.* **9** *Nautical, slang* a toilet, esp. on a boat or ship. **10** *Geology* a superficial deposit of rock fragments, formed at the edge of an ice sheet by repeated freezing and thawing and then moved downhill.

▸*adj.* [*attrib.*] chief; principal: *the head waiter.*

▸*v.* [*trans.*] **1** be in the leading position on: *the Palm Sunday procession was headed by the crucifer.* ■ be in charge of: *an organizational unit headed by a line manager | she* ***headed up*** *the Centennial program.* **2** (usu. **be headed**) give a title or caption to: *an article headed "The Protection of Human Life."* ■ [as *adj.*] (**headed**) having a printed heading, typically the name and address of a person or organization: *headed notepaper.* **3** [*intrans.*] (also **be headed**) move in a specified direction: *he was* ***heading for*** *the exit | we were headed in the wrong direction.* ■ (**head for**) appear to be moving inevitably toward (something, esp. something undesirable): *the economy is heading for recession.* ■ [*trans.*] direct or steer in a specified direction: *she headed the car toward them.* **4** *Soccer* shoot or pass (the ball) with the head: *a corner kick that he headed into the net.* **5** lop off the upper part or branches of (a plant or tree). **6** [*intrans.*] (of a lettuce or cabbage) form a head.

▸*phrasal v.* □ **head someone/something off** intercept and turn aside: *he ran up the road to head off approaching cars.* ■ forestall: *they headed off a fight by ordering further study of both plans.* □ **head up** *Sailing* steer toward the wind. ▷Old English *hēafod*, of Germanic origin; related to Dutch *hoofd* and German *Haupt.* **—head·ed** *adj.* [in *combination*] *bald-headed men | wooly-headed New Age thinking.* **—head·less** *adj.*

▸*PHRASES* □ **be banging** (or **knocking**) **one's head against a brick wall** be doggedly attempting the impossible and suffering in the process. □ **bang** (or **knock**) **people's heads together** reprimand people severely, esp. in an attempt to stop their arguing. □ **be hanging over someone's head** (of something unpleasant) threaten to affect someone at any moment. □ **be on someone's** (**own**) **head** be someone's sole responsibility. □ **bite** (or **snap**) **someone's head off** reply sharply and brusquely to someone. □ (**down**) **by the head** *Nautical* (of a boat or ship) deeper in the water forward than astern: *the Boy Andrew went down by the head.* □ **come to a head** reach a crisis: *the violence came to a head with the deaths of six youths.* ■ suppurate; fester: *abscesses should be allowed to come to a head.* □ **enter someone's head** [usu. with *negative*] occur to someone: *such an idea never entered my head.* □ **from head to toe** (or **foot**) all over one's body: *I was shaking from head to toe.* □ **get one's head around** (or **round**) [usu. with *negative*] *informal* understand or come to terms with something: *I just can't get my head around this idea.* □ **give someone his** (or **her**) **head** allow someone complete freedom of action. □ **give someone head** *vulgar slang* perform oral sex on someone. □ **go to someone's head** (of alcohol) make someone dizzy or slightly drunk. ■ (of success) make someone conceited. □ **get something into one's** (or **someone's**) **head** come or cause (someone) to realize or understand: *when will you get it into your head that it's the project that counts not me?* □ **head of hair** the hair on a person's head, regarded in terms of its appearance or quantity: *he had a fine head of hair.* □ **—— one's head off** talk, laugh, etc., unrestrainedly: *he was drunk as a skunk and singing his head off.* □ **head over heels 1** turning over completely in forward motion, as in a somersault. **2** (also **head over heels in love**) madly in love: *I immediately* ***fell head over heels for*** *Don.* □ **a head start** an advantage granted or gained at the beginning of something: *our fine traditions give us a* ***head start on*** *the competition.* □ **heads will roll** people will be dismissed or forced to resign. □ **head to head** in open, direct conflict or competition: *the governor and the senator went head to head in a spontaneous debate.* □ **in one's head** by mental process without use of physical aids: *the piece he'd already written in his head.* □ **keep one's head** remain calm. □ **keep one's head above water** avoid succumbing to difficulties, typically debt. □ **keep one's head down** remain inconspicuous in difficult or dangerous times. □ **lose one's head** lose self-control; panic. □ **make head or tail of** (or **heads or tails**) [usu. with *negative*] understand at all: *we couldn't make head or tail of his answer.* □ **off** (or **out of**) **one's head** *informal* crazy: *my old man's* ***going off his head***, *you know.* ■ extremely drunk or severely under the influence of drugs. □ **off the top of one's head** without careful thought or investigation. □ **over someone's head 1** (also **above someone's head**) beyond someone's ability to understand: *the discussion was over my head, I'm afraid.* **2** without someone's knowledge or involvement, esp. when they have a right to it: *the deal was struck over the heads of the regions concerned.* ■ with disregard for someone else's (stronger) claim: *his promotion over the heads of more senior colleagues.* □ **put their** (or **our** or **your**) **heads together** consult and work together: *they forced the major banks to put their heads together to sort it out.* □ **put something into someone's head** suggest something to someone: *who's being putting ideas into your head?* □ **take it into one's head to do something** impetuously decide to do something. □ **turn someone's head** make someone conceited. □ **turn heads** attract a great deal of attention or interest: *she recently turned heads with a nude scene.*

-head[1] ▸*suffix* equivalent to -HOOD. ▷Middle English *-hed, -hede.*

-head[2] ▸*comb. form* **1** denoting the front, forward, or upper part or end of a specified thing: *spearhead | masthead.* **2** in nouns used informally to express disparagement of a person: *airhead | dumbhead.* **3** in nouns used informally to denote an addict or habitual user of a specified drug: *crackhead.*

head·ache /ˈhedˌāk/ ▸*n.* a continuous pain in the head. ■ *informal* a thing or person that causes worry or trouble; a problem: *an administrative headache.* **—head·ach·y** /-ˌākē/ *adj.*

head·band /ˈhedˌband/ ▸*n.* **1** a band of fabric worn around the head as a decoration or to keep the hair or perspiration off the face. **2** an ornamental strip of colored silk fastened to the top of the spine of a book.

head·bang·er /ˈhedˌbaNGər/ ▸*n. informal* a fan or performer of heavy metal music. Also called METALHEAD.

head·board /ˈhedˌbôrd/ ▸*n.* an upright panel forming or placed behind the head of a bed.

head-butt /ˈhedˌbət/ ▸*n.* an aggressive and forceful thrust with the top of the head, esp. into the face or body of another person.

▸*v.* [*trans.*] attack (someone) with such a thrust of the head.

head case ▸*n. informal* a mentally ill or unstable person.

head·cheese /ˈhedˌCHēz/ ▸*n.* meat from a pig's or calf's head that is cooked and pressed into a loaf with aspic.

head cold ▸*n.* a common cold characterized by congested nasal passages, sneezing, and headache.

head count ▸*n.* an instance of counting the number of people present: *a U.S. Marine turns up missing at a head count.* ■ a total number of people, esp. the number of people employed in a particular organization: *you may decide that by reducing your head count you can reach this quarter's goals.*

head·dress /ˈhedˌdres/ ▸*n.* an ornamental covering or band for the head, esp. one worn on ceremonial occasions.

American Indian headdress

head·end /ˈhedˌend/ ▸*n.* a control center in a cable television system where various signals are brought together and monitored before being introduced into the cable network.

head·er /ˈhedər/ ▸*n.* **1** *Soccer* a shot or pass made with the head. **2** *informal* a headlong fall or dive. **3** a brick or stone laid at right angles to the face of a wall. Compare with STRETCHER (sense 4). **4** a line or block of text appearing at the top of each page of a book or document. Compare with FOOTER (sense 2). **5** (also **header tank**) a raised tank of water maintaining pressure in a plumbing system. **6** a beam crossing and supporting the ends of joists, studs, or rafters.

head first ▸*adj. & adv.* with the head in front of the rest of the body: [as *adv.*] *she dived head first into the water* | [as *attrib. adj.*] *a head-first slide.* ■ without sufficient forethought.

head·ful /ˈhedˌfo͝ol/ ▸*n.* **1** a quantity sufficient to cover the head: *a headful of tight curls.* **2** a great amount (of knowledge or information): *a headful of things to worry about.*

head gas·ket ▸*n.* the gasket that fits between the cylinder head and the cylinders or cylinder block in an internal combustion engine.

head·gear /ˈhedˌgi(ə)r/ ▸*n.* hats, helmets, and other items worn on the head: *protective headgear.* ■ orthodontic equipment worn on the head and attached to braces on the teeth. ■ the parts of a harness around a horse's head.

head·hunt·er /ˈhedˌhəntər/ ▸*n.* a person who identifies and approaches suitable candidates employed elsewhere to fill business positions: *a headhunter offering you a wonderful new position at a higher salary.* ■ a member of a society that collects the heads of dead enemies as trophies. **—head·hunt** *v.* **—head·hunt·ing** /-ˌhəntiNG/ *n.*

head·ing /ˈhediNG/ ▸*n.* **1** a title at the head of a page or section of a book: *chapter headings.* ■ a division or section of a subject; a class or category: *this topic falls under four main headings.* **2** a direction or bearing: *he crawled on a heading of 90 degrees until he came to the track.* **3** a horizontal passage made in preparation for building a tunnel. ■ *Mining* another term for DRIFT (sense 4). **4** a strip of cloth at the top of a curtain above the hooks or wire that suspend the curtain.

head·land /ˈhedlənd; ˈhedˌland/ ▸*n.* **1** a narrow piece of land that projects from a coastline into the sea. **2** a strip of land left unplowed at the end of a field.

head·light /ˈhedˌlīt/ (also **head·lamp**) ▸*n.* a powerful light at the front of a motor vehicle or railroad engine.

head·line /ˈhedˌlīn/ ▸*n.* a heading at the top of an article or page in a newspaper or magazine: *a front-page headline.* ■ (**the headlines**) the most important items of news in a newspaper or in a broadcast news bulletin: *issues that are never long out of the headlines.*

▸*v.* **1** [*trans.*] provide with a headline: *a feature that was headlined "Invest in Your Future."* **2** [*trans.*] appear as the star performer at (a concert): *an acoustic jam headlined by rappers L.L. Cool J and De La Soul.*

head·lin·er /ˈhedˌlīnər/ ▸*n.* a performer or act that is promoted as the star attraction on a program or advertisement.

head·lock /ˈhedˌläk/ ▸*n.* a method of restraining someone by holding an arm firmly around their head, esp. as a hold in wrestling.

head·long /ˈhedˌlôNG; -ˌläNG/ ▸*adv. & adj.* **1** [as *adv.*] with the head foremost: *he fell headlong into the tent.* **2** in a rush; with reckless haste: [as *attrib. adj.*] *a headlong dash through the house* | [as *adv.*] *those who rush headlong to join in the latest craze.* ▷Middle English *headling* (from HEAD + the adverbial suffix *-ling*), altered in late Middle English by association with -LONG.

head louse ▸*n.* a louse that infests the scalp and hair of the human head and is especially common among schoolchildren. • *Pediculus humanus capitis*, family Pediculidae, order Anoplura. See also BODY LOUSE.

head·man /ˈhedmən/ ▸*n.* (*pl.* **-men**) the chief or leader of a community or tribe.

head·mas·ter /ˈhedˌmastər/ ▸*n.* (esp. in private schools) the man in charge of a school; the principal. **—head·mas·ter·ly** *adj.*

head·mis·tress /ˈhedˌmistris/ ▸*n.* (esp. in private schools) the woman in charge of a school; the principal.

head·note /ˈhedˌnōt/ ▸*n.* a note inserted at the head of an article, reported law case, or other document, summarizing or commenting on the content. ■ *Law* a summary of a decided case prefixed to the case report, setting out the principles behind the decision and an outline of the facts.

head of state ▸*n.* the chief public representative of a country, such as a president or monarch, who may also be the head of government.

head-on ▸*adj. & adv.* **1** with or involving the front of a vehicle: [as *attrib. adj.*] *a head-on collision* | [as *adv.*] *they hit a bus head-on.* **2** with or involving direct confrontation: [as *attrib. adj.*] *trying to avoid a head-on clash.*

head·phones /ˈhed,fōnz/ ▸*plural n.* a pair of earphones typically joined by a band placed over the head, for listening to audio signals such as music or speech.

headphones

head·piece /ˈhed,pēs/ ▸*n.* **1** a device worn on the head as an ornament or to serve a function: *her headpiece was a wreath of silk flowers | headpieces for carrying water.* **2** an illustration or ornamental motif printed at the head of a chapter in a book. **3** the part of a halter or bridle that fits over the top of a horse's head behind the ears.

head·quar·ter /ˈhed,kwôrtər/ ▸*v.* [*trans.*] (usu. **be headquartered**) provide (an organization) with headquarters at a specified location: *UNESCO is headquartered in Paris.*

head·quar·ters /ˈhed,kwôrtərz/ ▸*n.* [treated as *sing.* or *pl.*] the premises occupied by a military commander and the commander's staff. ■ the place or building serving as the managerial and administrative center of an organization.

head·rail /ˈhed,rāl/ ▸*n.* a horizontal rail at the top of something.

head·rest /ˈhed,rest/ ▸*n.* a padded part extending from or fixed to the back of a seat or chair, designed to support the head.

head·room /ˈhed,rōōm; -,rŏŏm/ ▸*n.* the space above a driver's or passenger's head in a vehicle. ■ the space or clearance between the top of a vehicle and the underside of a bridge or other structure above it.

head·sail /ˈhed,sāl/ ▸*n.* a sail on a ship's foremast or bowsprit.

head·scarf /ˈhed,skärf/ ▸*n.* (*pl.* **-scarves**) a square of fabric worn as a covering for the head, often folded into a triangle and knotted under the chin.

head·set /ˈhed,set/ ▸*n.* **1** a set of headphones, typically with a microphone attached, used esp. in telephone and radio communication. **2** the bearing assembly that links the front fork of a bicycle to its frame.

head·ship /ˈhed,sʜip/ ▸*n.* the position of leader or chief. ■ *chiefly Brit.* the position of head teacher in a school.

head shop ▸*n.* a store that sells drug-related paraphernalia.

head·shot /ˈhed,sʜät/ ▸*n.* **1** a photograph of a person's head. ■ a frame, or a sequence of frames, of videotape or motion-picture film that captures a close-up of a person's head. **2** a bullet or gunshot aimed at the head.

head·shrink·er /ˈhed,sʜriNGkər/ ▸*n. historical* a headhunter who preserved and shrank the heads of his dead enemies. ■ *informal* a clinical psychiatrist, psychologist, or psychotherapist. Compare with **SHRINK**.

heads·man /ˈhedzmən/ ▸*n.* (*pl.* **-men**) *historical* a man who was responsible for beheading condemned prisoners.

head·space /ˈhed,spās/ ▸*n.* the unfilled space above the contents of a closed container.

head·spring /ˈhed,spriNG/ ▸*n.* **1** a spring that is the main source of a stream. **2** a somersault similar to a handspring, except that the performer lands on the head as well as the hands.

head·stall /ˈhed,stôl/ ▸*n.* **1** the part of a bridle or halter that fits around a horse's head. **2** another term for **HEADPIECE** (sense 3).

head·stand /ˈhed,stand/ ▸*n.* the act of balancing on one's head and hands with the feet in the air.

head·stand·er /ˈhed,standər/ ▸*n.* a small deep-bodied freshwater fish of the Amazon region, popular in aquariums. It swims and feeds at an oblique angle with the head down. • Genus *Abramites*, family Anostomidae: two species.

head·stay /ˈhed,stā/ ▸*n.* a forestay, esp. in a small vessel.

head·stock /ˈhed,stäk/ ▸*n.* **1** a set of bearings in a machine, supporting a revolving part. **2** the widened piece at the end of the neck of a guitar, to which the tuning pegs are fixed. **3** the horizontal end member of the underframe of a railroad vehicle.

head·stone /ˈhed,stōn/ ▸*n.* a slab of stone set up at the head of a grave, typically inscribed with the name of the dead person.

head·stream /ˈhed,strēm/ ▸*n.* a headwater stream.

head·strong /ˈhed,strôNG/ ▸*adj.* self-willed and obstinate: *I am headstrong and like getting my own way.*

heads-up *informal* ▸*n.* an advance warning of something: *the heads-up came just in time to stop the tanks from launching the final assault.*
▸*adj.* [*attrib.*] showing alertness or perceptiveness: *they played a very heads-up game.*

head tax ▸*n.* a uniform tax imposed on each person: *a 50 cent head tax imposed on departing ferry passengers.*

head-to-head ▸*adj.* & *adv.* involving two parties confronting each other: [as *adj.*] *a head-to-head battle with discounters.*
▸*n.* a conversation, confrontation, or contest between two parties.

head-trip ▸*n.* **1** an intellectually stimulating experience. **2** an act performed primarily for self-gratification.

head-turn·ing ▸*adj.* extremely noticeable or attractive: *her skimpy, head-turning costumes.*

head-up dis·play (also **heads-up dis·play**) ▸*n.* a display of instrument readings in an aircraft or vehicle that can be seen without lowering the eyes, typically through being projected onto the windshield or visor.

head voice ▸*n.* [in *sing.*] one of the high registers of the voice in speaking or singing, above chest voice.

head·ward /ˈhedwərd/ ▸*adj.* in the region or direction of the head. ■ *Geology* denoting erosion by a stream or river occurring progressively upstream from the original source.
▸*adv.* (also **head·wards**) toward the head.

head·wa·ter /ˈhed,wôtər; -,wätər/ ▸*n.* (usu. **headwaters**) a tributary stream of a river close to or forming part of its source: *these paths follow rivers right up into their headwaters.*

head·way /ˈhed,wā/ ▸*n.* **1** forward movement or progress: *they appear to be **making headway** in bringing the rebels under control | the ship was making very little headway against heavy seas.* **2** the average interval of time between vehicles moving in the same direction on the same route.

head·wear /ˈhed,we(ə)r/ ▸*n.* coverings for the head, such as hats, caps, and scarves.

head·wind /ˈhed,wind/ ▸*n.* a wind blowing from directly in front, opposing forward motion.

head·word /ˈhed,wərd/ ▸*n.* a word that begins a separate entry in a reference work such as a dictionary.

head·work /ˈhed,wərk/ ▸*n.* **1** activities taxing the mind; mental work. **2** (**headworks**) apparatus for controlling the flow of water in a river or canal.

head·y /ˈhedē/ ▸*adj.* (**head·i·er**, **head·i·est**) (of liquor) potent; intoxicating: *several bottles of heady local wine.* ■ having a strong or exhilarating effect: *the heady days of the birth of the women's movement | a heady, exotic perfume.* —**head·i·ly** /ˈhedl-ē/ *adv.* —**head·i·ness** *n.*

heal /hēl/ ▸*v.* [*trans.*] (of a person or treatment) cause (a wound, injury, or person) to become sound or healthy again: *his concern is to heal sick people* | [as *adj.*] (**healing**) *a healing effect on the entire body* | [as *n.*] (**healing**) *the gift of healing.* ■ [*intrans.*] become sound or healthy again: *he would have to wait until his knee had healed.* ■ alleviate (a person's distress or anguish): *time can heal the pain of grief.* ■ correct or put right (an undesirable situation): *the rift between them was never really healed.* ▷Old English *hǣlan* (in the sense 'restore to sound health'), of Germanic origin; related to Dutch *heelen* and German *heilen*, also to **WHOLE**. —**heal·a·ble** *adj.* —**heal·er** *n.*

heal-all ▸*n.* a universal remedy; a panacea. ■ *informal* any of a number of medicinal plants, esp. self-heal.

health /helTH/ ▸*n.* the state of being free from illness or injury: *he was restored to health* | [as *adj.*] *a health risk.* ■ a person's mental or physical condition: *bad health forced him to retire.* ■ *figurative* soundness, esp. financial or moral: *a standard for measuring the financial health of a company.* ■ used to express friendly feelings toward one's companions before drinking. ▷Old English *hǣlth*, of Germanic origin; related to **WHOLE**.

health·care /ˈhelTH,ke(ə)r/ (also **health care**) ▸*n.* the maintenance and improvement of physical and mental health, esp. through the provision of medical services: [as *adj.*] *healthcare workers.*

health cen·ter ▸*n.* a building or establishment housing local medical services or the practice of a group of doctors.

health farm ▸*n. chiefly Brit.* a residential establishment where people seek improved health by a regimen of dieting, exercise, and treatment.

health food ▸*n.* natural food that is thought to have health-giving qualities.

health·ful /ˈhelTHfəl/ ▸*adj.* having or conducive to good health: *healthful methods of cooking vegetables.* See note at **SANITARY**. —**health·ful·ly** *adv.* —**health·ful·ness** *n.*

health main·te·nance or·ga·ni·za·tion (abbr.: **HMO**) ▸*n.* a health insurance organization to which subscribers pay a predetermined fee in return for a range of medical services from physicians and healthcare workers registered with the organization.

health phys·ics ▸*plural n.* [treated as *sing.*] the branch of radiology that deals with the health of people working with radioactive materials.

health sav·ings ac·count ▸*n.* a savings account used in conjunction with a high-deductible health insurance policy that allows users to save money tax-free against medical expenses. (abbr. **HSA**).

health serv·ice ▸*n.* a public service providing medical care.

health tour·ism ▸*n.* travel to a tourist destination with the main purpose of receiving some therapeutic treatment. —**health tour·ist** *n.*

health·y /ˈhelTHē/ ▸*adj.* (**health·i·er**, **health·i·est**) in good health: *feeling fit and healthy.* ■ (of a part of the body) not diseased: *healthy cells.* ■ indicative of, conducive to, or promoting good health: *a healthy appetite | a healthy balanced diet.* ■ (of a person's attitude) sensible and well balanced: *a healthy contempt for authority.* ■ *figurative* in a good condition: *the family is the basis of any healthy society.* ■ desirable; beneficial: *healthy competition.* ■ of a satisfactory size or amount: *making a healthy profit.* —**health·i·ly** /ˈhelTHəlē/ *adv.* —**health·i·ness** *n.*

Hea·ney /ˈhēnē/, Seamus (Justin) (1939–), Irish poet; born in Northern Ireland. He became an Irish citizen in 1972 . Notable works: *North* (1975) and *The Haw Lantern* (1987). In 1999 he published an acclaimed new translation of *Beowulf.* Nobel Prize for Literature (1995).

heap /hēp/ ▸*n.* an untidy collection of things piled up haphazardly: *she rushed out, leaving her clothes in a heap on the floor.* ■ a mound or pile of a particular substance: ***a heap of** gravel.* ■ *informal* an untidy or dilapidated place or vehicle: *they climbed back in the heap and headed home.* ■ (**a heap of/heaps of**) *informal* a large amount or number of something: *we have heaps of room.*
▸*adv.* (**heaps**) *informal* a great deal: *"How do you like Maggie?" "I like you heaps better!"*
▸*v.* [*trans.*] put in a pile or mound: *she heaped logs on the fire | **heaped up** in one corner was a pile of junk.* ■ (**heap something with**) load something copiously with: *he heaped his plate with rice.* ■ (**heap something on/upon**) bestow praise, abuse, or criticism liberally on: *they had once heaped praise on her.* ■ [*intrans.*] form a heap: *clouds heaped higher in the west.* ▷Old English *hēap* (noun), *hēapian* (verb), of Germanic origin; related to Dutch *hoop* and German *Haufen*.
▸**PHRASES** □ **at the top** (or **bottom**) **of the heap** (of a person) at the highest (or lowest) point of a society or organization: *she had come up the hard way from the very bottom of the heap.* □ **be struck all of a heap** *informal* be extremely disconcerted. □ **heap coals of fire on someone's head** □ go out of one's way to cause someone remorse. [with biblical allusion to Rom. 12:20.] □ **in a heap** (of a person) with the body completely limp: *he landed in a heap at the bottom of the stairs.*

hear /hi(ə)r/ ▸*v.* (*past* **heard** /hərd/) [*trans.*] perceive with the ear the sound made by (someone or something): *behind her she could hear men's voices* | [*trans.*] *she had never been heard to complain* | [*intrans.*] *he did not hear very well.* ■ be told or informed of: *have you heard the news?* | [with *clause*] *they heard that I had moved* | [*intrans.*] *I was shocked to **hear of** her death.* ■ [*intrans.*] (**have heard of**) be aware of; know of the existence of: *nobody had ever heard of my college.* ■ [*intrans.*] (**hear from**) be contacted by (someone), esp. by letter or telephone: *if you would like to join the committee, we would love to hear from you.* ■ listen or pay attention to: [with *clause*] *she just doesn't hear what I'm telling her.* ■ (**hear someone out**) listen to all that someone has to say: *Joseph gravely heard them out but never offered advice.* ■ [*intrans.*] (**will/would not hear of**) will or would not allow or agree to: *I won't hear of such idiocy.* ■ *Law* listen to and judge (a case or plaintiff): *an all-woman jury heard the case.* ■ listen to and grant (a prayer): *our Heavenly Father has heard our prayers.* ▷Old English *hīeran, hēran*, of Germanic origin; related to Dutch *hooren* and German *hören*. **—hear·a·ble** *adj.* **—hear·er** *n.*

▸*PHRASES* □ **be hearing things** see **THING**. □ **be unable to hear oneself think** *informal* used to complain about very loud noise or music: *I hate bars where you can't hear yourself think.* □ **hear! hear!** used to express one's wholehearted agreement, esp. with something said in a speech. □ **hear tell of** (or **that**) be informed of (or that): *I heard tell that he went out west.*

Heard and Mc·Don·ald Is·lands /hərd and mək'dänəld/ a group of uninhabited islands in the southern Indian Ocean, administered by Australia since 1947 as an external territory.

hear·ing /'hi(ə)riNG/ ▸*n.* **1** the faculty of perceiving sounds: *people who have very acute hearing.* ■ the range within which sounds may be heard; earshot: *she had moved out of hearing.* **2** an opportunity to state one's case: *I think I had a fair hearing.* ■ *Law* an act of listening to evidence in a court of law or before an official, esp. a trial before a judge without a jury.

hear·ing aid ▸*n.* a small device that fits in or on the ear, worn by a partially deaf person to amplify sound.

hear·ing dog ▸*n.* a dog trained to alert the deaf or hard of hearing to such sounds as the ringing of an alarm, doorbell, or telephone.

heark·en /'härkən/ (also **hark·en**) ▸*v.* [*intrans.*] *archaic* listen: *he refused to* **hearken to** *Thomas's words of wisdom.*

▸*phrasal v.* □ **hearken back** another way of saying **HARK BACK** (see **HARK**). ▷Old English *heorcnian*; probably related to **HARK**. The spelling with *ea* (dating from the 16th cent.) is due to association with **HEAR**.

hear·say /'hi(ə)r,sā/ ▸*n.* information received from other people that one cannot adequately substantiate; rumor: *according to hearsay, Bob had managed to break his arm.* ■ *Law* the report of another person's words by a witness, usually disallowed as evidence in a court of law: *everything they had told him would have been ruled out as hearsay* | [as *adj.*] *hearsay evidence.*

hearse /hərs/ ▸*n.* a vehicle for conveying the coffin at a funeral. ▷Middle English: from Anglo-Norman French *herce* 'harrow, frame,' from Latin *hirpex* 'a kind of large rake,' from Oscan *hirpus* 'wolf' (with reference to the teeth). The earliest recorded sense in English is 'latticework canopy placed over the coffin (while in church) of a distinguished person,' but this probably arose from the late Middle English sense 'triangular frame (shaped like the ancient harrow) for carrying candles at certain services.' The current sense dates from the mid 17th cent.

Hearst[1] /hərst/, Patty (1954–) U.S. newspaper heiress; full name *Patricia Campbell Hearst*; granddaughter of William Randolph Hearst. Kidnapped by the Symbionese Liberation Army in 1974, she was brainwashed, took the name of Tania, and joined them in their criminal activities. After being found by the FBI in 1975, she was tried and convicted of bank robbery in 1976 and served three years of her sentence. In 2001, she was pardoned by President Clinton.

Hearst[2], William Randolph (1863–1951), U.S. newspaper publisher and tycoon. His introduction of features such as large headlines and sensational crime reporting revolutionized U.S. journalism. He was the model for the central character of Orson Welles's movie *Citizen Kane* (1941).

heart /härt/ ▸*n.* **1** a hollow muscular organ that pumps the blood through the circulatory system by rhythmic contraction and dilation. In vertebrates there may be up to four chambers (as in humans), with two atria and two ventricles. ■ the region of the chest above the heart: *holding hand on heart for the Pledge of Allegiance.* ■ the heart regarded as the center of a person's thoughts and emotions, esp. love or compassion: *hardening his heart, he ignored her entreaties* | *he poured out his heart to me* | *he has no heart.* ■ one's mood or feeling: *they had a change of heart.* ■ courage or enthusiasm: *they may* **lose heart** *as the work mounts up* | *Mary* **took heart** *from the encouragement handed out* | *I put my* **heart and soul** *into it and then got fired.* **2** the central or innermost part of something: *right in the heart of the city.* ■ the vital part or essence: *the heart of the matter.* ■ the close compact head of a cabbage or lettuce. **3** a conventional representation of a heart with two equal curves meeting at a point at the bottom and a cusp at the top. ■ (**hearts**) one of the four suits in a conventional pack of playing cards, denoted by a red figure of such a shape. ■ a card of this suit. ■ (**hearts**) a card game similar to whist, in which players attempt to avoid taking tricks containing a card of this suit. **4** [usu. with *adj.*] the condition of agricultural land as regards fertility. ▷Old English *heorte*, of Germanic origin; related to Dutch *hart* and German *Herz*, from an Indo-European root shared by Latin *cor, cord-* and Greek *kēr, kardia*. **—heart·ed** *adj.* [in *combination*] *a generous-hearted woman.*

▸*PHRASES* □ **after one's own heart** of the type that one likes or understands best; sharing one's tastes: *a man after God's own heart.* □ **at heart** in one's real nature, in contrast to how one may appear: *he's a good guy at heart.* □ **break someone's heart** overwhelm someone with sadness. □ **by heart** from memory. □ **close** (or **dear**) **to** (or **near**) **one's heart** of deep interest and concern to one. □ **from the** (**bottom of one's**) **heart** with sincere feeling: *their warmth and hospitality is right from the heart.* □ **give** (or **lose**) **one's heart to** fall in love with. □ **have a heart** [often in *imperative*] be merciful; show pity. □ **have a heart of gold** have a generous nature. □ **have the heart to do something** [usu. with *negative*] be insensitive or hard-hearted enough to do something: *I don't have the heart to tell her.* □ **have** (or **put**) **one's heart in** be (or become) keenly involved in or committed to (an enterprise). □ **have one's heart in one's mouth** be greatly alarmed or apprehensive. □ **have one's heart in the right place** be sincere or well intentioned. □ **heart of stone** a stern or cruel nature. □ **hearts and flowers** used in allusion to extreme sentimentality. □ **hearts and minds** used in reference to emotional and intellectual support or commitment: *a campaign to win the hearts and minds of America's college students.* □ **one's heart's desire** a person or thing that one greatly wishes for. □ **one's heartstrings** used in reference to one's deepest feelings of love or compassion: *the kitten's pitiful little squeak* **tugged at** *her* **heartstrings**. □ **in one's heart of hearts** in one's inmost feelings. □ **take something to heart** take criticism seriously and be affected or upset by it. □ **wear one's heart on one's sleeve** make one's feelings apparent. □ **with all one's heart** (or **one's whole heart**) sincerely; completely. □ **with one's heart in one's boots** in a state of great depression or trepidation: *I had to follow her with my heart in my boots.*

heart·ache /'härt,āk/ ▸*n.* emotional anguish or grief, typically caused by the loss or absence of someone loved.

heart at·tack ▸*n.* a sudden and sometimes fatal occurrence of coronary thrombosis, typically resulting in the death of part of a heart muscle.

heart·beat /'härt,bēt/ ▸*n.* the pulsation of the heart. ■ (usu. **heartbeats**) a single pulsation of the heart: *her heartbeats steadied.* ■ *figurative* a person or thing providing or representing an animating or vital unifying force: *conflict is the essential heartbeat of fiction.*

▸*PHRASE* □ **a heartbeat away from** very close to; on the verge of: *the man who is just a heartbeat away from the presidency.*

heart·break /'härt,brāk/ ▸*n.* overwhelming distress: *an unforgettable tale of joy and heartbreak.*

heart·break·er /'härt,brākər/ ▸*n.* **1** a person who is very attractive but who is irresponsible in emotional relationships. **2** a story or event that causes overwhelming distress.

heart·break·ing /'härt,brākiNG/ ▸*adj.* causing overwhelming distress; very upsetting. **—heart·break·ing·ly** *adv.* [as *submodifier*] *a heartbreakingly lonely place.*

heart·bro·ken /'härt,brōkən/ ▸*adj.* (of a person) suffering from overwhelming distress; very upset: *he was* **heartbroken at** *the thought of leaving the house.*

heart·burn /'härt,bərn/ ▸*n.* a form of indigestion felt as a burning sensation in the chest, caused by acid regurgitation into the esophagus.

heart·en /'härtn/ ▸*v.* [*trans.*] (usu. **be heartened**) make more cheerful or confident: [*trans.*] *she was heartened to observe that the effect was faintly comic* | [as *adj.*] (**heartening**) *this is the most heartening news of all.* See note at **ENCOURAGE**. **—heart·en·ing·ly** *adv.*

heart fail·ure ▸*n.* severe failure of the heart to function properly, esp. as a cause of death: *her mother had died of heart failure.*

heart·felt /'härt,felt/ ▸*adj.* (of a feeling or its expression) sincere; deeply and strongly felt: *our heartfelt thanks.*

hearth /härTH/ ▸*n.* the floor of a fireplace: *the crackling blaze on the hearth.* ■ the area in front of a fireplace: *they were sitting around the hearth.* ■ used as a symbol of one's home: *he left* **hearth and home** *to train in Denmark.* ■ the base or lower part of a furnace, where molten metal collects. ▷Old English *heorth*; related to Dutch *haard* and German *Herd*.

hearth·rug /'härTH,rəg/ ▸*n.* a rug laid in front of a fireplace to protect the carpet or floor.

hearth·side /'härTH,sīd/ ▸*n.* the area around a hearth or fireplace; fireside.

hearth·stone /'härTH,stōn/ ▸*n.* a flat stone forming a hearth or part of a hearth.

heart·i·ly /'härtl-ē/ ▸*adv.* **1** in a hearty manner: *she laughed heartily* | *they dined heartily.* **2** [as *submodifier*] very; to a great degree (esp. with reference to personal feelings): *they were heartily sick of the whole subject.*

heart·land /'härt,land/ ▸*n.* the central or most important part of a country, area, or field of activity. ■ the center of support for a belief or movement: *the heartland of the rebel cause.* ■ (**the heartland**) the central part of the U.S.; the Midwest: *a recession that battered the coasts while sparing the heartland.*

heart·less /'härtlis/ ▸*adj.* displaying a complete lack of feeling or consideration: *heartless thieves stole the stroller of a two-year-old boy.* **—heart·less·ly** *adv.* **—heart·less·ness** *n.*

heart line ▸*n.* (in palmistry) the upper of the two horizontal lines that cross the palm of the hand, linked to a person's physical health and ability to form emotional relationships.

heart-lung ma·chine ▸*n.* a machine that temporarily takes over the functions of the heart and lungs, esp. during heart surgery.

heart mas·sage ▸*n.* another term for cardiac massage.

Heart of Dix·ie a nickname for the state of **ALABAMA**.

heart of palm ▸*n.* the edible bud of a palm tree.

heart-rend·ing ▸*adj.* (of a story or event) causing great sadness or distress. **—heart-rend·ing·ly** *adv.*

heart's-blood ▸*n.* *archaic* the blood, as being necessary for life.

heart-search·ing ▸*n.* thorough, typically painful examination of one's feelings and motives: *I began to write, but not without much heart-searching.*

hearts·ease /'härts,ēz/ (also **heart's-ease**) ▸*n.* a wild European pansy that typically has purple and yellow flowers. It has given rise to the hybrids from which most garden pansies were developed. • *Viola tricolor*, family Violaceae. ▷late Middle English: origin uncertain, the term being applied by herbalists to both the pansy and the wallflower in the 16th cent.

heart·sick /'härt,sik/ ▸*adj.* despondent, typically from grief or loss of love. **—heart·sick·ness** *n.*

heart·sore /'härt,sôr/ ▸*adj.* *poetic/literary* grieving; heartsick.

heart-stop·ping ▸*adj.* thrilling; full of suspense. **—heart-stop·per** *n.* **—heart-stop·ping·ly** *adv.*

heart·throb /'härt,THräb/ ▸*n.* *informal* a man, typically a celebrity, whose good looks excite immature romantic feelings in women.

heart-to-heart ▸*adj.* (of a conversation) candid, intimate, and personal: *a heart-to-heart chat.*

▸*n.* such a conversation: *they had seemed engrossed in a heart-to-heart.*

heart ur·chin ▸*n.* a heart-shaped burrowing sea urchin that has a thick covering of fine spines on the shell, giving it a furry appearance. • Class Echinoidea, order Spatangoida.

heart·warm·ing /'härt,wôrmiNG/ ▸*adj.* emotionally rewarding or uplifting.

heart·wood /'härt,wŏŏd/ ▸*n.* the dense inner part of a tree trunk, yielding the hardest timber.

heart·y /'härtē/ ▸*adj.* (**heart·i·er, heart·i·est**) **1** (of a person or their behavior) loudly vigorous and cheerful: *a hearty and boisterous character* | *he sang in a hearty baritone.* ■ (of a feeling or an opinion) heartfelt: *hearty congratulations.* ■ (of a person) strong and healthy: *a white-bearded but hearty man.* **2** (of food) wholesome and substantial: *a hearty meal cooked over open flames.* ■ (of a person's appetite) robust and healthy: *Jim goes for a long walk to work up a hearty appetite for dinner.*

▸*n. Brit., informal* **1** a vigorously cheerful and sporty person. **2** (usu. **me hearties**) a form of address ascribed to sailors. **—heart·i·ness** *n.*

heat /hēt/ ▸*n.* **1** the quality of being hot; high temperature: *it is sensitive to both heat and cold.* ■ hot weather conditions: *the oppressive heat was making both men sweat.* ■ a source or level of heat for cooking: *remove from the heat and beat in the butter.* ■ a spicy quality in food that produces a burning sensation in the mouth: *chili peppers add taste and heat to food.* ■ *Physics* heat seen as a form of energy arising from the random motion of the molecules of bodies, which may be transferred by conduction, convection, or radiation. ■ *technical* the amount of heat that is needed to cause a specific process or is evolved in such a process: *the heat of formation.* ■ *technical* a single operation of heating something, esp. metal in a furnace. **2** intensity of feeling, esp. of anger or excitement: *words few men would dare use to another, even in the heat of anger.* ■ (**the heat**) *informal* intensive and unwelcome pressure or criticism, esp. from the authorities: *a flurry of legal proceedings* ***turned up the heat*** *in the dispute.* **3** a preliminary round in a race or contest: *the 200-meter heats.*

▸*v.* make or become hot or warm: [*trans.*] *the room faces north and is difficult to heat* | [*intrans.*] *the pipes expand as they* ***heat up.*** ■ [*intrans.*] (**heat up**) (of a person) become excited or impassioned. ■ [*intrans.*] (**heat up**) become more intense and exciting: *the action really begins to heat up.* ■ [*trans.*] *archaic* inflame; excite: *this discourse had heated them.* ▷Old English *hǣtu* (noun), *hǣtan* (verb), of Germanic origin; related to Dutch *hitte* (noun) and German *heizen* (verb), also to **HOT**.

▸*PHRASES* □ **if you can't stand the heat, get out of the kitchen** *proverb* if you can't deal with the pressures and difficulties of a situation or task, you should leave others to deal with it rather than complaining. □ **in the heat of the moment** while temporarily angry, excited, or engrossed, and without stopping for thought. □ **in heat** (of a female mammal) in the receptive period of the sexual cycle; in estrus.

heat bar·ri·er ▸*n.* the limitation of the speed of an aircraft or other flying object by heat resulting from air friction.

heat ca·pac·i·ty ▸*n.* the number of heat units needed to raise the temperature of a body by one degree.

heat death ▸*n. Physics* a state of uniform distribution of energy, esp. viewed as a possible fate of the universe. It is a corollary of the second law of thermodynamics.

heat·ed /ˈhētid/ ▸*adj.* **1** made warm or hot: *a heated swimming pool.* **2** inflamed with passion or conviction: *she had a heated argument with an official.* **—heat·ed·ly** *adv.*

heat en·gine ▸*n.* a device for producing motive power from heat, such as a gasoline engine or steam engine.

heat·er /ˈhētər/ ▸*n.* **1** a person or thing that heats, in particular a device for warming the air or water: *a wall-mounted electric heater* | *a gas water heater.* ■ *Electronics* a conductor used for indirect heating of the cathode of a thermionic tube. **2** *Baseball* a fastball. **3** *informal, dated* a gun.

heat ex·chang·er ▸*n.* a device for transferring heat from one medium to another.

Heath /hēTH/, Sir Edward (Richard George) (1916–), British statesman; prime minister 1970–74. He negotiated Britain's entry into the European Economic Community.

heath /hēTH/ ▸*n.* **1** an area of open uncultivated land, esp. in Britain, with characteristic vegetation of heather, gorse, and coarse grasses. ■ *Ecology* vegetation dominated by dwarf shrubs of the heath family: [as *adj.*] *heath vegetation.* **2** a dwarf shrub with small leathery leaves and small pink or purple bell-shaped flowers, characteristic of heathland and moorland. • *Erica* and related genera, family Ericaceae (the **heath family**): many species, including the common European **cross-leaved heath** (*E. tetralix*). ▷Old English *hǣth*, of Germanic origin; related to Dutch *heide* and German *Heide.* **—heath·y** *adj.*

heat haze ▸*n.* an obscuration of the atmosphere in hot weather, esp. a shimmering in the air near the ground that distorts distant views.

heath·en /ˈhēT͟Hən/ ▸*n. chiefly derogatory* a person who does not belong to a widely held religion (esp. one who is not a Christian, Jew, or Muslim) as regarded by those who do: *bringing Christianity to the heathens.* ■ a follower of a polytheistic religion; a pagan. ■ (**the heathen**) heathen people collectively, esp. (in biblical use) those who did not worship the God of Israel. ■ *informal* an unenlightened person; a person regarded as lacking culture or moral principles.

▸*adj.* of or relating to heathens: *heathen gods.* ■ *informal* unenlightened or uncivilized: *they dismiss the idea of a sauce of simply melted butter as somewhat heathen.* ▷Old English *hǣthen*, of Germanic origin; related to Dutch *heiden* and German *Heide*; generally regarded as a specifically Christian use of a Germanic adjective meaning 'inhabiting open country,' from the base of **HEATH**. **—heath·en·dom** /-dəm/ *n.* **—heath·en·ish** *adj.* **—heath·en·ism** /-ˌnizəm/ *n.*

heath·er /ˈheT͟Hər/ ▸*n.* a purple-flowered Eurasian heath that grows abundantly on moorland and heathland. Many ornamental varieties have been developed. Also called **LING**². • *Calluna vulgaris*, family Ericaceae. This family includes the rhododendrons and azaleas as well as the blueberries and many other berry-bearing dwarf shrubs. ■ *informal* any similar plant of this family; a heath. ▷Old English *hadre, hedre* (recorded in place names), of unknown origin. The word was chiefly Scots until the 16th cent.; the change in the first syllable in the 18th cent. was due to association with **HEATH**. **—heath·er·y** *adj.*

heath·land /ˈhēTHˌland/ ▸*n.* (also **heathlands**) an extensive area of heath: *1,000 acres of heathland.*

heat in·dex ▸*n.* a quantity expressing the discomfort felt as a result of the combined effects of the temperature and humidity of the air.

heat·ing /ˈhētiNG/ ▸*n.* the imparting or generation of heat. ■ equipment or devices used to provide heat, esp. to a building: *baseboard heating.*

heat lamp ▸*n.* an electrical device with a bulb that emits mainly heat rather than light, used as a heat source.

heat light·ning ▸*n.* a flash or flashes of light seen near the horizon, esp. on warm evenings, believed to be the reflection of distant lightning on high clouds.

Heat-Moon, William Least (1939–) U.S. writer; also known as **William Trogdon**. Part Osage Indian, he wrote *Blue Highways* (1982), *PrairyErth* (1991), and *River-Horse* (1999).

heat·proof /ˈhētˌpro͞of/ ▸*adj.* able to resist great heat.

heat pump ▸*n.* a device that transfers heat from a colder area to a hotter area by using mechanical energy, as in a refrigerator.

heat rash ▸*n.* another term for **PRICKLY HEAT**.

heat-re·sist·ant ▸*adj.* another term for **HEATPROOF**. ■ not easily becoming hot: *fondue forks with heat-resistant handles.*

heat-seek·ing /ˈhētˌsēkiNG/ ▸*adj.* (of a missile) able to detect and home in on infrared radiation emitted by a target, such as the exhaust vent of a jet aircraft.

heat shield ▸*n.* a device or coating for protection from excessive heat. ■ an outer covering on a spacecraft, esp. on the nose cone and leading edges, to protect it from the heat generated during reentry into the earth's atmosphere.

heat sink ▸*n.* a device or substance for absorbing excessive or unwanted heat.

heat·stroke /ˈhētˌstrōk/ ▸*n.* a condition marked by fever and often by unconsciousness, caused by failure of the body's temperature-regulating mechanism when exposed to excessively high temperatures.

heat treat·ment ▸*n.* **1** the use of heat for therapeutic purposes in medicine. **2** the use of heat to modify the properties of a material, esp. in metallurgy. **—heat-treat** *v.*

heat wave ▸*n.* a prolonged period of abnormally hot weather.

heave /hēv/ ▸*v.* (*past* **heaved** or *chiefly Nautical* **hove** /hōv/) **1** [*trans.*] lift or haul (a heavy thing) with great effort: *she heaved the sofa back into place* | *he* ***heaved himself*** *out of bed.* ■ *Nautical* pull, raise, or move (a boat or ship) by hauling on a rope or ropes. ■ *informal* throw (something heavy): *she heaved half a brick at him.* **2** [*trans.*] produce (a sigh): *he heaved a euphoric sigh of relief.* **3** [*intrans.*] rise and fall rhythmically or spasmodically: *his shoulders heaved as he panted.* ■ make an effort to vomit; retch: *my stomach heaved.*

▸*phrasal v.* □ **heave to** *Nautical* (of a boat or ship) come to a stop, esp. by turning across the wind leaving the headsail backed: *he hove to and dropped anchor.*

▸*n.* **1** an act of heaving, esp. a strong pull. ■ *Geology* a sideways displacement in a fault. **2** (**the heaves**) *informal* a case of retching or vomiting: *waiting for the heaves to subside.* **3** (**heaves**) a disease of horses, with labored breathing. ▷Old English *hebban*, of Germanic origin; related to Dutch *heffen* and German *heben* 'lift up.' **—heav·er** *n.*

▸*PHRASE* □ **heave in sight** (or **into view**) *chiefly Nautical* come into view: *the three canoes hove into view.*

heave-ho ▸*exclam.* a cry emitted when doing in unison actions that take physical effort.

▸*n.* such an exclamation. ■ (**the heave-ho**) expulsion or elimination from an institution, association, or contest: *conjecture over who'll* ***get the heave-ho.*** ▷late Middle English: from *heave!* (imperative) + **HO**², originally in nautical use when hauling a rope.

heav·en /ˈhevən/ ▸*n.* **1** a place regarded in various religions as the abode of God (or the gods) and the angels, and of the good after death, often traditionally depicted as being above the sky. ■ God (or the gods): *Constantine was persuaded that disunity in the Church was displeasing to heaven.* ■ *Theology* a state of being eternally in the presence of God after death. ■ *informal* a place, state, or experience of supreme bliss: *lying by the pool with a good book is my idea of heaven.* ■ used in various exclamations as a substitute for "God": *Heaven knows!* | *good heavens!* **2** (often **heavens**) *poetic/literary* the sky, esp. perceived as a vault in which the sun, moon, stars, and planets are situated. *Galileo used a telescope to observe the heavens.* ▷Old English *heofon*, of Germanic origin; related to Dutch *hemel* and German *Himmel.* **—heav·en·ward** /-wərd/ *adj. & adv.* **—heav·en·wards** /-wərdz/ *adv.*

▸*PHRASES* □ **the heavens open** it suddenly starts to rain heavily. □ **in seventh heaven** in a state of ecstasy. □ **move heaven and earth to do something** make extraordinary efforts to do a specified thing: *if he had truly loved her he would have moved heaven and earth to get her back.* □ **stink** (or **smell**) **to high heaven** have a very strong and unpleasant odor.

heav·en·ly /ˈhevənlē/ ▸*adj.* **1** of heaven; divine: *heavenly Father.* **2** of the heavens or sky: *heavenly constellations.* **3** *informal* very pleasing; wonderful: *their shampoos smell heavenly* | *it was a heavenly morning for a ride.* ▷Old English *heofonlic* (see **HEAVEN**, **-LY**¹). **—heav·en·li·ness** *n.*

heav·en·ly bod·y ▸*n.* a planet, star, or other celestial body.

heav·en·ly host ▸*n.* a literary or biblical term for the angels.

heav·en-sent ▸*adj.* (of an event or opportunity) occurring at a favorable time; opportune.

heav·i·er-than-air ▸*adj.* (of an aircraft) weighing more than the air it displaces.

heav·ing /ˈhēviNG/ ▸*adj. Brit., informal* (of a place) extremely crowded: *the foyer was absolutely heaving with people.*

heav·ing line ▸*n.* a lightweight line with a weight at the end, made to be thrown between a ship and the shore, or from one ship to another, and used to pull a heavier line across.

Heav·i·side /ˈhevēˌsīd/, Oliver (1850–1925), English physicist and electrical engineer. In 1902, he suggested the existence of a layer in the atmosphere responsible for reflecting radio waves back to earth.

Heav·i·side lay·er (also **Heav·i·side–Ken·nel·ly lay·er** /ˈkenl-ē/) ▸*n.* another name for **E LAYER**. ▷early 20th cent.: named after O. **HEAVISIDE** and A. E. **KENNELLY**.

heav·y /ˈhevē/ ▸*adj.* (**heav·i·er, heav·i·est**) **1** of great weight; difficult to lift or move: *the pan was too heavy for me to carry.* ■ used in questions about weight: *how heavy is it?* ■ [*attrib.*] (of a class of thing) above the average weight; large of its kind: *heavy artillery.* ■ [*predic.*] weighed down; full of something: *branches* ***heavy with*** *blossoms.* ■ (of a person's head or eyes) feeling weighed down by weariness: *a heavy head.* ■ *Physics* of or containing atoms of an isotope of greater than the usual mass. See also **HEAVY WATER**. **2** of great density; thick or substantial: *heavy gray clouds* | *a heavy blanket.* ■ (of food or a meal) hard to digest; too filling. ■ (of ground or soil) hard to travel over or work with because muddy or full of clay. ■ not delicate or graceful; coarse: *he had a big mustache and heavy features.* ■ moving slowly or with difficulty: *steering that is heavy when parking.* ■ *Aviation, informal* (of a large aircraft) leaving a large amount of turbulence behind in its flight. ■ (of a smell) overpowering: *the air was heavy with the sweet odor of apples.* ■ (of the sky) full of dark clouds; oppressive: *a heavy thundery sky.* **3** of more than the usual size, amount, or force: *rush hour traffic was heavy and I was delayed.* ■ doing something to excess: *a heavy smoker.* ■ (**heavy on**) using a lot of: *stories heavy on melodrama.* **4** striking or falling with force: *a heavy blow to the head* | *we had heavy overnight rain.* ■ causing a strong impact: *a heavy fall.* ■ (of music, esp. rock) having a strong bass component and a forceful rhythm. **5** needing much physical effort: *long hours and heavy work.* ■ mentally oppressive; hard to endure: *a heavy burden of responsibility.* ■ important or serious: *a heavy discussion.* ■ (of a literary work) hard to read or understand because overly serious or difficult. ■ feeling or expressing grief: *I left him with a heavy heart.* ■ *informal* (of a situation) serious and hard to deal with: *things were getting pretty heavy.*

■ *informal* (of a person) strict or harsh: *the police were really getting heavy.*
▶*n.* (*pl.* **heav·ies**) **1** a thing, such as a vehicle, that is large or heavy of its kind. ■ *informal* a large, strong man, esp. one hired for protection: *I needed money to pay off the heavies.* ■ an important person: *music business heavies.* ■ (**heavies**) *Brit., informal* serious newspapers: *reporters from the Sunday heavies.* **2** a villainous role or actor in a book, movie, etc.: *we've got to have this guy play the heavy.* **3** *chiefly Scottish* strong beer, esp. bitter: *a pint of heavy.*
▶*adv.* heavily: *his words hung heavy in the air* | [in *combination*] *heavy-laden.* ▷Old English *hefig,* of Germanic origin; related to Dutch *hevig,* also to HEAVE. —**heav·i·ly** /ˈhevəlē/ *adv.* —**heav·i·ness** *n.* —**heav·y·ish** *adj.*
▶*PHRASES* □ **heavy with child** pregnant. □ **make heavy weather of** see WEATHER.

THE RIGHT WORD **burdensome, cumbersome, heavy, massive, ponderous, weighty**

Trying to move a refrigerator out of a third-floor apartment is difficult because it is **cumbersome**, which means that it is so heavy and bulky that it becomes unwieldy or awkward to handle.

Cartons filled with books, on the other hand, are merely **heavy**, which implies greater density and compactness than the average load.

A huge oak dining table might be described as **massive**, which stresses largeness and solidity rather than weight, while something that is **ponderous** is too large or too massive to move, or to be moved quickly (*a ponderous printing press*).

Most of these terms can be used figuratively as well. *Heavy*, for example, connotes a pressing down on the mind, spirits, or senses (*heavy with fatigue; a heavy heart*), and *ponderous* implies a dull and labored quality (*a novel too ponderous to read*).

Burdensome, which refers to something that is not only *heavy* but must be carried or supported, is even more likely to be used in an abstract way to describe something that is difficult but can, with effort, be managed (*a burdensome task*).

Both a package and a problem may be described as **weighty**, meaning actually (as opposed to relatively) heavy; but it is more commonly used to mean very important or momentous (*weighty matters to discuss*).

heav·y breath·ing ▶*n.* breathing that is audible through being deep or labored, esp. in sleep or as a result of exertion. ■ *figurative* sexual desire or arousal: *it's the caller who's supposed to do the heavy breathing, she thought, not the callee.*

heav·y chain ▶*n. Biochemistry* the protein subunit that, as one of a pair, makes up the major part of an immunoglobulin molecule.

heav·y chem·i·cals ▶*plural n.* bulk chemicals used in industry and agriculture.

heav·y cream ▶*n.* thick cream that contains a lot of butterfat.

heav·y-du·ty ▶*adj.* (of material or an article) designed to withstand the stresses of demanding use: *heavy-duty rubber gloves.* ■ *informal* intense, important, or abundant: *she did some heavy-duty cleaning.*

heav·y-foot·ed ▶*adj.* slow and laborious in movement: *the whole occasion could resemble a heavy-footed hippo dance in mud.*

heav·y go·ing ▶*n.* a person or situation that is difficult or boring: *she found the technical manuals heavy going.*

heav·y-hand·ed ▶*adj.* clumsy or insensitive: *this heavy-handed prose is merely tiresome.* ■ overly forceful or oppressive: *the government's most heavy-handed efforts to muzzle social protest.* —**heav·y-hand·ed·ly** *adv.* —**heav·y-hand·ed·ness** *n.*

heav·y-heart·ed ▶*adj.* feeling depressed or melancholy.

heav·y hit·ter ▶*n. informal* **1** an important or powerful person: *a high-profile national issue pitting heavy hitters in the Senate against the Department of Agriculture.* **2** a high-scoring athlete.

heav·y horse ▶*n.* a large, strong, heavily built horse of a type or breed used for draft work.

heav·y hy·dro·gen ▶*n.* another term for DEUTERIUM.

heav·y in·dus·try ▶*n.* the manufacture of large, heavy articles and materials in bulk.

heav·y-lift ▶*adj.* [*attrib.*] (of a vehicle) capable of lifting or transporting extremely heavy loads: *a heavy-lift helicopter.*

heav·y lift·ing ▶*n.* the lifting of heavy objects. ■ *figurative* hard or difficult work: *the heavy lifting in this business is in designing external distribution systems.*

heav·y met·al ▶*n.* **1** a type of highly amplified harsh-sounding rock music with a strong beat, characteristically using violent or fantastic imagery. **2** a metal of relatively high density, or of high relative atomic weight.

heav·y oil ▶*n.* any of the relatively dense hydrocarbons (denser than water) derived from petroleum, coal tar, and similar materials.

heav·y pet·ting ▶*n.* erotic contact between two people involving stimulation of the genitals but stopping short of intercourse.

heav·y·set /ˈhevēˌset/ ▶*adj.* having a stocky or stout build.

heav·y sleep·er ▶*n.* a person who sleeps deeply and is difficult to wake up.

heav·y wa·ter ▶*n.* water in which the hydrogen in the molecules is partly or wholly replaced by the isotope deuterium, used esp. as a moderator in nuclear reactors.

heav·y·weight /ˈhevēˌwāt/ ▶*n.* **1** a weight in boxing and other sports, typically the heaviest category. In the amateur boxing scale it ranges from 178 to 200 pounds (81 to 91 kg). ■ a boxer or other competitor of this weight. **2** a person or thing of above-average weight. ■ [often with *adj.*] a person of influence or importance, esp. in a particular sphere: *a political heavyweight with national recognition.*
▶*adj.* of above-average weight. ■ serious, important, or influential: *heavyweight news coverage.*

Heb. ▶*abbr.* ■ *Bible* Hebrews. ■ Hebrew.

heb·dom·a·dal /hebˈdämədl/ ▶*adj. formal* weekly (used esp. of organizations that meet weekly): *forced to eke out a meager living scribbling hebdomadal feuilletons.* ▷early 17th cent. (in the sense 'lasting seven days'): from late Latin *hebdomadalis,* from Greek *hebdomas, hebdomad-* 'the number seven, seven days,' from *hepta* 'seven.'

He·be[1] /ˈhēbē/ *Greek Mythology* the daughter of Hera and Zeus, and cupbearer of the gods. ▷from Greek *hēbē* 'youthful beauty.'

Hebe[2] /hēb/ ▶*n. informal, offensive* a Jewish person. ▷early 20th cent.: abbreviation of HEBREW.

He·bei /ˈhəˈbā/ (also **Ho·peh** /ˈhəˈbā; ˈhō-/) a province in northeastern central China; capital, Shijiazhuang.

he·be·phre·ni·a /ˌhēbəˈfrēnēə/ ▶*n.* a form of chronic schizophrenia involving disordered thought, inappropriate emotions, hallucinations, and bizarre behavior. ▷late 19th cent. (originally associated with behavior in puberty): from HEBE[1] + Greek *phrēn* 'mind' + -IA[1]. —**he·be·phren·ic** /-ˈfrenik/ *adj.* & *n.*

heb·e·tude /ˈhebəˌt(y)o͞od/ ▶*n. poetic/literary* the state of being dull or lethargic. ▷early 17th cent.: from late Latin *hebetudo,* from *hebes, hebet-* 'blunt.'

Hebr. ▶*abbr.* ■ Hebrew or Hebrews.

He·bra·ic /hēˈbrāik/ ▶*adj.* of Hebrew or the Hebrews: *a student of Hebraic religious literature.* ▷via Christian Latin from late Greek *Hebraikos,* from *Hebraios* (see HEBREW). —**He·bra·i·cal·ly** /-ik(ə)lē/ *adv.*

He·bra·ism /ˈhēbrāˌizəm/ ▶*n.* **1** a Hebrew idiom or expression. **2** the Jewish religion, culture, or character. ▷late 16th cent.: from French *hébraïsme* or modern Latin *Hebraismus,* from late Greek *Hebraïsmos,* from *Hebraios* (see HEBREW). —**He·bra·is·tic** /ˌhēbrāˈistik/ *adj.* —**He·bra·ize** /-ˌīz/ *v.*

He·bra·ist /ˈhēbrāist/ ▶*n.* a scholar of the Hebrew language. ■ a student or adherent of the Jewish religion, culture, or character.

He·brew /ˈhēbro͞o/ ▶*n.* **1** a member of an ancient people living in what is now Israel and Palestine and, according to biblical tradition, descended from the patriarch Jacob, grandson of Abraham. After the Exodus (*c.*1300 BC) they established the kingdoms of Israel and Judah, and their scriptures and traditions form the basis of the Jewish religion. ■ old-fashioned and sometimes offensive term for JEW. **2** the Semitic language of this people, in its ancient or modern form.
▶*adj.* **1** of the Hebrews or the Jews. **2** of or in Hebrew. ▷from Old French *Ebreu,* via Latin from late Greek *Hebraios,* from Aramaic *ʿibray,* based on Hebrew *ʿibrî* understood to mean 'one from the other side (of the river).'

Hebrew is written from right to left in a characteristic alphabet of twenty-two consonants, the vowels sometimes being marked by additional signs. From about AD 500 it was almost entirely restricted to Jewish religious use, but it was revived as a spoken language in the 19th century and, with a vocabulary extended by borrowing from contemporary languages, is now the official language of the state of Israel.

He·brew Bi·ble the sacred writings of Judaism, called by Christians the Old Testament, and comprising the Law (Torah), the Prophets, and the Hagiographa or Writings.

He·brews /ˈhēbro͞oz/ a book of the New Testament, traditionally included among the letters of St. Paul but now generally held to be non-Pauline.

Heb·ri·des /ˈhebrəˌdēz/ a group of about 500 islands off the northwestern coast of Scotland. The **Inner Hebrides** are separated from the **Outer Hebrides** by the Little Minch. Also called WESTERN ISLES. —**Heb·ri·de·an** /ˌhebrəˈdēən/ *n.* & *adj.*

He·bron /ˈhēbrən/ a Palestinian city on the West Bank of the Jordan River; pop. 75,000. As the home of Abraham, it is a holy city of both Judaism and Islam. Israeli forces withdrew from all but a small part of the city in 1997.

Heb·ros /ˈhēbrəs/ (also **Heb·rus**) ancient Greek name for MARITSA.

Hec·a·te /ˈhekətē/ *Greek Mythology* a goddess of dark places, often associated with ghosts and sorcery. She is frequently identified with Artemis and Selene.

hec·a·tomb /ˈhekəˌtōm/ ▶*n.* (in ancient Greece or Rome) a great public sacrifice, originally of a hundred oxen. ■ *figurative* an extensive loss of life for some cause. ▷late 16th cent.: via Latin from Greek *hekatombē* (from *hekaton* 'hundred' + *bous* 'ox').

Hecht /hekt/, Ben (1894–1964) U.S. writer and playwright. He wrote the screenplays for *Underworld* (Academy Award, 1927) and *The Scoundrel* (Academy Award, 1935) and co-wrote *The Front Page* (1928).

heck /hek/ ▶*exclam.* expressing surprise, frustration, or dismay: *oh heck, I can't for the life of me remember.* ■ (**the heck**) used for emphasis in questions and exclamations: *what the heck's the matter?* ▷late 19th cent. (originally dialect): euphemistic alteration of HELL.
▶*PHRASE* □ **a heck of a ——** used for emphasis in various statements or exclamations: *it was a heck of a lot of money.*

heck·el·phone /ˈhekəlˌfōn/ ▶*n.* a woodwind instrument resembling a large oboe, with a range about an octave lower. ▷early 20th cent.: from German *Heckelphon,* named after Wilhelm *Heckel* (1856–1909), German instrument maker, on the pattern of *saxophone.*

heck·le /ˈhekəl/ ▶*v.* [*trans.*] **1** (often **be heckled**) interrupt (a public speaker) with derisive or aggressive comments or abuse: *he was booed and heckled when he tried to address the demonstrators* | [*intrans.*] *he is merely heckling from the sidelines.* **2** dress (flax or hemp) to split and straighten the fibers for spinning.
▶*n.* a heckling comment: *the meeting regularly dissolved into heckles.* ▷Middle English (sense 2): from *heckle* 'flax comb,' a northern and eastern form of HACKLE. The sense 'interrupt (a public speaker) with aggressive questions' arose in the mid 17th cent.; for the development in sense, compare with TEASE. —**heck·ler** /ˈhek(ə)lər/ *n.*

heck·uv·a /ˈhekəvə/ ▶ nonstandard spelling of HECK OF A (see HECK): *a heckuva lot of people.*

hec·tare /ˈhekˌte(ə)r/ (abbr.: **ha**) ▶*n.* a metric unit of square measure, equal to 100 ares (2.471 acres or 10,000 square meters). ▷early 19th cent.: from French, formed irregularly from Greek *hekaton* 'hundred' + ARE[2]. —**hec·tar·age** /ˈhektərij/ *n.*

hec·tic /ˈhektik/ ▶*adj.* **1** full of incessant or frantic activity: *a hectic business schedule.* **2** *archaic Medicine* relating to, affected by, or denoting a regularly recurrent fever typically accompanying tuberculosis, with flushed cheeks and hot, dry skin.
▶*n. Medicine, archaic* a hectic fever or flush. ■ a patient suffering from such a fever. ▷late Middle English *etik,* via Old French from late Latin *hecticus,* from Greek *hektikos* 'habitual,' from *hexis* 'habit, state of mind or body.' The original specific association with the symptoms of tuberculosis (*hectic fever*) gave rise to the early 20th-cent. sense 'characterized by feverish activity.' —**hec·ti·cal·ly** /-tik(ə)lē/ *adv.*

hecto- ▶*comb. form* (used commonly in units of measurement) a hundred: *hectometer.* ▷from French, formed irregularly by contraction of Greek *hekaton* 'hundred.'

hec·to·coty·lus /ˌhektōˈkätl-əs/ ▶*n.* (*pl.* **-coty·li** /-ˈkätlˌī/) *Zoology* a modified arm used by male octopuses and some other cephalopods to transfer sperm to the female. ▷mid 19th cent.: modern Latin, from HECTO- 'hundred' + Greek *kotulē* 'hollow thing,' a name given by Cuvier to what he mistakenly took to be a genus of parasitic worms.

hec·to·gram /ˈhektəˌgram/ (*Brit.* also **hec·to·gramme**) (abbr.: **hg**) ▸*n.* a metric unit of mass equal to one hundred grams.

hec·to·graph /ˈhektəˌgraf/ ▸*n.* an apparatus for copying documents by the use of a gelatin plate that receives an impression of the master copy.

hec·to·li·ter /ˈhektəˌlētər/ (*Brit.* **hec·to·li·tre**) (abbr.: **hl**) ▸*n.* a metric unit of capacity equal to one hundred liters, used esp. for wine, beer, grain, and other agricultural produce.

hec·to·me·ter /ˈhektəˌmētər/ (*Brit.* **hec·to·me·tre**) (abbr.: **hm**) ▸*n.* a metric unit of length equal to one hundred meters.

Hec·tor /ˈhektər/ *Greek Mythology* a Trojan warrior, son of Priam and Hecuba and husband of Andromache. He was killed by Achilles, who dragged his body behind his chariot three times around the walls of Troy.

hec·tor /ˈhektər/ ▸*v.* [*trans.*] talk to (someone) in a bullying way: *she doesn't hector us about giving up things* | [as *adj.*] (**hectoring**) *a brusque, hectoring manner.* ▷late Middle English: from the Greek name HECTOR. Originally denoting a hero, the sense later became 'braggart or bully' (applied in the late 17th cent. to a member of a gang of youths in London, England), hence 'talk to in a bullying way.' **—hec·tor·ing·ly** /ˈhekt(ə)riNGlē/ *adv.*

Hec·u·ba /ˈhekyəbə/ *Greek Mythology* the queen of Troy, wife of Priam and mother of children including Hector, Paris, Cassandra, and Troilus.

he'd /hēd/ ▸*contraction of* ■ he had: *he'd seen all he wanted.* ■ he would: *he'd like to see you.*

hed·dle /ˈhedl/ ▸*n.* one of a set of looped wires or cords in a loom, with an eye in the center through which a warp yarn is passed before going through the reed to control its movement and divide the threads. ▷early 16th cent.: apparently from an alteration of Old English *hefeld.*

he·der /ˈKHādər; ˈhādər/ ▸*n.* (*pl.* **he·da·rim** /KHəˈdärim/ or **he·ders**) variant spelling of CHEDER.

hedge /hej/ ▸*n.* a fence or boundary formed by closely growing bushes or shrubs: *she was standing barefoot in a corner of the lawn, trimming the hedge.* ■ a contract entered into or asset held as a protection against possible financial loss: *inflation hedges such as real estate and gold.* ■ a word or phrase used to allow for additional possibilities or to avoid overprecise commitment, for example, *etc., often, usually,* or *sometimes.*
▸*v.* [*trans.*] **1** (often **be hedged**) surround or bound with a hedge: *a garden hedged with yews.* ■ (**hedge something in**) enclose. **2** limit or qualify (something) by conditions or exceptions: *experts usually hedge their predictions, just in case.* ■ [*intrans.*] avoid making a definite decision, statement, or commitment: *she hedged around the one question she wanted to ask.* **3** protect (one's investment or an investor) against loss by making balancing or compensating contracts or transactions: *the company hedged its investment position on the futures market.* ▷Old English *hegg,* of Germanic origin; related to Dutch *heg* and German *Hecke.* **—hedg·er** *n.*
▸*PHRASE* □ **hedge one's bets** avoid committing oneself when faced with a difficult choice.

hedge fund ▸*n.* a limited partnership of investors that uses high risk methods, such as investing with borrowed money, in hopes of realizing large capital gains.

hedge·hog /ˈhejˌhôg; -ˌhäg/ ▸*n.* a nocturnal insectivorous Old World mammal with a spiny coat and short legs, able to roll itself into a ball for defense. • Family Erinaceidae: four genera and several species, including the **common hedgehog** (*Erinaceus europaeus*) of western and northern Europe. ■ any other animal covered with spines, esp. a porcupine. ▷late Middle English: from HEDGE (from its habitat) + HOG (from its piglike snout).

common hedgehog

hedge·hop /ˈhejˌhäp/ ▸*v.* [*intrans.*] fly an aircraft at a very low altitude. **—hedge·hop·per** *n.*

hedge·row /ˈhejˌrō/ ▸*n.* a hedge of wild shrubs and trees, typically bordering a road or field. ▷Old English: from HEDGE + obsolete *rew* 'hedgerow,' assimilated to ROW[1].

hedge trim·mer ▸*n.* an electric tool resembling a chainsaw used for cutting back bushes, shrubs, and hedges.

he·don·ic /hēˈdänik/ ▸*adj. technical* relating to or considered in terms of pleasant (or unpleasant) sensations. ▷mid 17th cent.: from Greek *hēdonikos,* from *hēdonē* 'pleasure.'

he·don·ism /ˈhēdnˌizəm/ ▸*n.* the pursuit of pleasure; sensual self-indulgence. ■ the ethical theory that pleasure (in the sense of the satisfaction of desires) is the highest good and proper aim of human life. ▷mid 19th cent.: from Greek *hēdonē* 'pleasure' + -ISM. **—he·don·ist** *n.* **—he·don·is·tic** /ˌhēdnˈistik/ *adj.* **—he·don·is·ti·cal·ly** /ˌhēdnˈistik(ə)lē/ *adv.*

-hedral ▸*comb. form* in adjectives corresponding to nouns ending in *-hedron* (such as *dodecahedral* corresponding to *dodecahedron*).

-hedron ▸*comb. form* (*pl.* **-hedra** or **-hedrons**) in nouns denoting geometric solids having a specified number of plane faces: *decahedron.* ■ denoting geometric solids having faces of a specified shape: *rhombohedron.* ▷from Greek *hedra* 'seat, base.'

hee·bie-jee·bies /ˈhēbē ˈjēbēz/ ▸*plural n.* (**the heebie-jeebies**) *informal* a state of nervous fear or anxiety: *it takes a lot more than a measly poltergeist to* **give me the heebie-jeebies.** ▷1920s: coined by W. B. DeBeck (1890–1942), American cartoonist, in his comic strip *Barney Google.*

heed /hēd/ ▸*v.* [*trans.*] pay attention to; take notice of: *he should have heeded the warnings.*
▸*n.* careful attention: *if he heard, he* **paid** *no* **heed** | *we must* **take heed of** *the suggestions.* ▷Old English *hēdan* (originally intransitive); related to Dutch *hoeden* and German *hüten.*

heed·ful /ˈhēdfəl/ ▸*adj.* aware of and attentive to: *he is* **heedful of** *his own intuitions.* **—heed·ful·ly** *adv.* **—heed·ful·ness** *n.*

heed·less /ˈhēdlis/ ▸*adj.* showing a reckless lack of care or attention: *"Elaine!" she shouted,* **heedless of** *attracting unwanted attention* | *his heedless impetuosity.* **—heed·less·ly** *adv.* **—heed·less·ness** *n.*

hee-haw /ˈhē ˌhô/ ▸*n.* the loud, harsh cry of a donkey or mule. ■ [as *adj.*] *informal* relating to or denoting unsophisticated rural humor and attitudes: *hee-haw manners.*
▸*v.* [*intrans.*] make the loud, harsh cry of a donkey or mule. ▷early 19th cent.: imitative.

heel[1] /hēl/ ▸*n.* **1** the back part of the foot below the ankle. ■ a corresponding part of the foot in vertebrate animals. ■ the part of the palm of the hand next to the wrist: *he rubbed the heel of his hand against the window.* ■ the part of a shoe or boot supporting the heel: *shoes with low heels.* ■ the part of a sock covering the heel. ■ (**heels**) high-heeled shoes. **2** a thing resembling a heel in form or position, in particular: ■ the end of a violin bow at which it is held. ■ the part of the head of a golf club nearest the shaft. ■ a crusty end of a loaf of bread, or the rind of a cheese. ■ a piece of the main stem of a plant left attached to the base of a cutting. **3** *informal* an inconsiderate or untrustworthy person: *what kind of a heel do you think I am?* **4** [as *exclam.*] a command to a dog to walk close behind its owner.
▸*v.* [*trans.*] **1** fit or renew a heel on (a shoe or boot). **2** (of a dog) follow closely behind its owner: *these dogs are born with the instinctive urge to heel.* **3** [*intrans.*] touch the ground with the heel when dancing. **4** *Golf* strike (the ball) with the heel of the club. ▷Old English *hēla, hǣla,* of Germanic origin; related to Dutch *hiel.* **—heeled** /hēld/ *adj.* [in *combination*] *high-heeled shoes.* **—heel·less** *adj.*
▸*PHRASES* □ **at** (or **to**) **heel** (of a dog) close to and slightly behind its owner. □ **at the heels of** (or **at someone's heels**) following closely behind: *he headed off with Sammy at his heels.* □ **bring someone to heel** bring someone under control. □ **down at heel** (of a shoe) with the heel worn down. ■ having a poor, shabby appearance. □ **kick up one's heels** have a lively, enjoyable time. □ **on the heels of** following closely after: *September frosts would be on the heels of the dog days of August.* □ **set someone back on their heels** astonish or discomfit someone. □ **turn on one's heel** turn sharply around. □ **under the heel of** dominated or controlled by: *the Greeks spent several centuries under the heel of the Ottoman Empire.*

heel[2] ▸*v.* [*intrans.*] (of a boat or ship) be tilted temporarily by the pressure of wind or by an uneven distribution of weight on board. Compare with LIST[2]. ■ [*trans.*] cause (a boat or ship) to lean over in such a way.
▸*n.* an instance of a ship leaning over in such a way. ■ the degree of incline of a ship's leaning measured from the vertical. ▷late 16th cent.: from obsolete *heeld, hield* 'incline,' of Germanic origin; related to Dutch *hellen.*

heel·ball /ˈhēlˌbôl/ ▸*n.* a mixture of hard wax and lampblack used by shoemakers for polishing. ■ this or a similar mixture used in brass rubbing.

heel bone ▸*n.* the calcaneus.

heel·tap /ˈhēlˌtap/ ▸*n.* **1** one of the layers of leather or other material of which a shoe heel is made. **2** *dated* an amount of liquor left at the bottom of a glass after drinking.

He·fei /ˈhəˈfā/ (also **Ho·fei**) an industrial city in eastern China, capital of Anhui province; pop. 1,541,000.

Hef·lin /ˈheflin/, Van (1910–71) U.S. actor; full name *Emmett Evan Heflin, Jr.* He appeared in many movies, including *Johnny Eager* (Academy Award, 1942), *The Strange Love of Martha Ivers* (1946), *Shane* (1953), and *Stagecoach* (1966).

Hef·ner /ˈhefnər/, Hugh (Marston) (1926–) U.S. publisher. He founded *Playboy* magazine in 1953 and Playboy Clubs International, Inc., in 1959.

heft /heft/ ▸*v.* [*trans.*] lift or carry (something heavy): *Donald hefted another pair of sandbags from the stack.* ■ lift or hold (something) in order to test its weight: *Eileen hefted the gun in her hand.*
▸*n.* the weight of someone or something. ■ *figurative* ability or influence: *his colleagues wonder if he has the intellectual heft for his new job.* ▷late Middle English (as a noun): probably from HEAVE, on the pattern of words such as *cleft* and *weft.*

heft·y /ˈheftē/ ▸*adj.* (**heft·i·er, heft·i·est**) large, heavy, and powerful: *a hefty young chap.* ■ (of a number or amount) impressively large: *a hefty 10 million* | *hefty Christmas bonuses.* **—heft·i·ly** /-təlē/ *adv.* **—heft·i·ness** *n.*

He·gang /ˈhəˈgäNG/ a city in Heilongjiang province, in northeastern China, northeast of Harbin; pop. 650,000.

He·gel /ˈhāgəl/, Georg Wilhelm Friedrich (1770–1831), German philosopher. In *Science of Logic* (1812–16) he described the three-stage process of dialectical reasoning, on which Marx based his theory of dialectical materialism. **—He·ge·li·an** /həˈgālēən/ *adj.* & *n.* **—He·ge·li·an·ism** /həˈgālēəˌnizəm/ *n.*

heg·e·mon·ic /ˌhegəˈmänik/ ▸*adj.* ruling or dominant in a political or social context: *the bourgeoisie constituted the hegemonic class.* ▷mid 17th cent.: from Greek *hēgemonikos* 'capable of commanding,' from *hēgemōn* (see HEGEMONY).

he·gem·o·ny /həˈjemənē; ˈhejəˌmōnē/ ▸*n.* leadership or dominance, esp. by one country or social group over others: *Germany was united under Prussian hegemony after 1871.* ▷mid 16th cent.: from Greek *hēgemonia,* from *hēgemōn* 'leader,' from *hēgeisthai* 'to lead.'

He·gi·ra /hiˈjīrə; ˈhejərə/ (also **He·ji·ra** or **Hij·ra** /ˈhijrə/) ▸*n.* Muhammad's departure from Mecca to Medina in AD 622, prompted by the opposition of the merchants of Mecca and marking the consolidation of the first Muslim community. ■ the Muslim era reckoned from this date: *the second century of the Hegira.* See also **AH.** ■ (**hegira**) an exodus or migration. ▷via medieval Latin from Arabic *hijra* 'departure,' from *hajara* 'emigrate.'

hei·au /ˈheˌēˌou/ ▸*n.* (*pl.* same or **hei·aus**) an ancient Hawaiian temple or sacred site. ▷Hawaiian.

Hei·deg·ger /ˈhīdəgər/, Martin (1889–1976), German philosopher. In *Being and Time* (1927), he examined the ontology of Being, in particular, human existence as involvement with a world of objects (*Dasein*).

Hei·del·berg /ˈhīdlˌbərg/ a city in southwestern Germany, on the Neckar River, in Baden-Württemberg; pop. 139,000. Its university is the oldest in Germany.

Hei·del·berg man ▸*n.* a fossil hominid of the early middle Pleistocene period, identified by only a jawbone found near Heidelberg in 1907. • an early form of *Homo erectus* (formerly *H. heidelbergensis*), family Hominidae.

Hei·den /ˈhīdn/, Eric (1958–) U.S. speed skater. He was the world champion in speed skating in 1977,

1978, and 1979 before he won five gold medals (500–, 1000–, 1500–, 5000–, and 10,000–meter races) at the 1980 Olympic games.

heif·er /ˈhefər/ ▸*n.* a young female cow that has not borne a calf. ▷Old English *heahfore*, of unknown origin.

Hei·fetz /ˈhīfits/, Jascha (1901–87) U.S. violinist; born in Lithuania. Recognized as a musical prodigy at age three, he made his U.S. debut at Carnegie Hall in 1917 and went on to become one of the most celebrated violinists of the century.

heigh /hī; hā/ ▸*exclam. archaic* expressing encouragement or inquiry. ▷natural utterance: first recorded in Middle English.

heigh-ho ▸*exclam. informal* expressing boredom, resignation, or jollity: *it was like talking to a brick wall. Heigh-ho! | how pleasant it is to have money, heigh-ho!*

height /hīt/ ▸*n.* **1** the measurement from base to top or (of a standing person) from head to foot: *columns rising to 65 feet* ***in height*** *| both men were of average height.* ■ elevation above ground or a recognized level (typically sea level): *the glider is gaining height.* ■ the quality of being tall or high: *his height seems to work to his advantage.* **2** a high place or area: *he's terrified of heights.* **3** the most intense part or period of something: ***the height of*** *the tourist season |* ***at the height of*** *his career | they* ***took*** *consumerism* ***to new heights.*** ■ an extreme instance or example of something: *it would be* ***the height of*** *bad manners not to attend the wedding.* ▷Old English *hēhthu* (in the sense 'top of something'), of Germanic origin; related to Dutch *hoogte*, also to **HIGH**.

height·en /ˈhītn/ ▸*v.* [*trans.*] make (something) higher. ■ make or become more intense: [*trans.*] *the pleasure was heightened by the sense of guilt that accompanied it |* [*intrans.*] *concern over CFCs has heightened |* [as *adj.*] (**heightened**) *the heightened color of her face.*

height·ism /ˈhītizəm/ ▸*n.* prejudice or discrimination against someone on the basis of their height. —**height·ist** *adj.* & *n.*

height of land ▸*n.* a watershed.

Heil·bronn /ˈhīlˌbrän; -ˌbrôn/ a city in southwestern Germany, on the Neckar River, in Baden-Württemberg; pop. 117,000.

Hei·long /ˈhāˈlôNG/ Chinese name of **AMUR**.

Hei·long·jiang /ˈhāˈlôNGjēˈäNG/ (also **Hei·lung·kiang** /-ˈlo͝oNG-/) a province in northeastern China, on the Russian frontier; capital, Harbin.

Heim·lich ma·neu·ver /ˈhīmlik; ˈhīmliKH/ ▸*n.* a first-aid procedure for dislodging an obstruction from a person's windpipe in which a sudden strong pressure is applied on the abdomen, between the navel and the rib cage. ▷1970s: named after Henry J. *Heimlich* (born 1920), the American doctor who developed the procedure.

hei·nie /ˈhīnē/ ▸*n. informal* a person's buttocks. ▷1960s: alteration of **HINDER**[2], variant of **HIND**[1].

hei·nous /ˈhānəs/ ▸*adj.* (of a person or wrongful act, esp. a crime) utterly odious or wicked: *a battery of heinous crimes.* ▷late Middle English: from Old French *haineus*, from *hair* 'to hate,' of Germanic origin. —**hei·nous·ly** *adv.* —**hei·nous·ness** *n.*

Heinz /hīnz/, Henry John (1844–1919), U.S. food manufacturer. In 1869 he established a family firm for the manufacture and sale of processed foods. Heinz devised the marketing slogan "57 Varieties" in 1896 and erected New York City's first electric sign to promote his company's pickles in 1900.

heir /e(ə)r/ ▸*n.* a person legally entitled to the property or rank of another on that person's death: *his eldest son and heir | she aspired to marry the heir to the throne.* ■ *figurative* a person inheriting and continuing the legacy of a predecessor: *they saw themselves as the true heirs of the Enlightenment.* ▷Middle English: via Old French from Latin *heres*. —**heir·dom** /-dəm/ *n.* —**heir·less** *adj.* —**heir·ship** /-ˌSHip/ *n.*

heir ap·par·ent ▸*n.* (*pl.* **heirs ap·par·ent**) an heir whose claim cannot be set aside by the birth of another heir. Compare with **HEIR PRESUMPTIVE**. ■ *figurative* a person who is most likely to succeed to the place of another: *he was once considered heir apparent to the chairman.*

heir-at-law ▸*n.* (*pl.* **heirs-at-law**) an heir by right of blood, esp. to the real property of a person who dies intestate.

heir·ess /ˈe(ə)ris/ ▸*n.* a female heir, esp. to vast wealth: *an oil heiress.*

heir·loom /ˈe(ə)rˌlo͞om/ ▸*n.* a valuable object that has belonged to a family for several generations. ▷late Middle English: from **HEIR** + **LOOM**[1] (which formerly had the senses 'tool, heirloom').

heir pre·sump·tive ▸*n.* (*pl.* **heirs pre·sump·tive**) an heir whose claim could be set aside by the birth of another heir. Compare with **HEIR APPARENT**.

Hei·sen·berg /ˈhīzənˌbərg/, Werner Karl (1901–76), German mathematical physicist and philosopher. He developed a system of quantum mechanics based on matrix algebra in which he states his well-known uncertainty principle (1927). Nobel Prize for Physics (1932).

Heis·man Tro·phy /ˈhīsmən/ ▸*n.* an annual award given to the outstanding college football player in the U.S. by the Downtown Athletic Club of New York City. ▷named in honor of football pioneer John W. Heisman (1869–1936).

heist /hīst/ *informal* ▸*n.* a robbery: *a diamond heist.* ▸*v.* [*trans.*] steal: *he heisted a Pontiac.* ▷mid 19th cent.: representing a local pronunciation of **HOIST**.

He·jaz /hēˈjaz; -ˈZHäz/ (also **Hi·jaz**) a coastal region in western Saudi Arabia that borders the Red Sea.

He·ji·ra ▸*n.* variant spelling of **HEGIRA**.

He·La cells /ˈhelə/ ▸*plural n.* human epithelial cells of a strain maintained in tissue culture since 1951 and used in research, esp. in virology. ▷1950s: from the name of *Henrietta Lacks*, whose cervical carcinoma provided the original cells.

held /held/ ▸ past and past participle of **HOLD**[1].

hel·den·ten·or /ˈheldəntəˌnôr; ˈheldnˌtenər/ ▸*n.* a powerful tenor voice suitable for heroic roles in opera. ■ a singer with such a voice. ▷1920s: German, literally 'hero tenor.'

Hel·en /ˈhelən/ *Greek Mythology* the daughter of Zeus and Leda, born from an egg. In the Homeric poems she was the outstandingly beautiful wife of Menelaus, and her abduction by Paris (to whom she had been promised, as a bribe, by Aphrodite) led to the Trojan War.

Hel·e·na /ˈhelənə/ the capital of Montana, in the western central part of the state; pop. 25,780.

Hel·e·na, St. /ˈhelənə/ (*c.*255–*c.*330), Roman empress and mother of Constantine the Great. In 326 she founded basilicas on the Mount of Olives and at Bethlehem and is credited with finding the cross on which Jesus Christ was crucified. Feast day (in the Eastern Church) May 21; (in the Western Church) August 18.

he·len·i·um /həˈlēnēəm/ ▸*n.* an American plant of the daisy family that bears many red to yellow flowers, each having a prominent central disk. • Genus *Helenium*, family Compositae: many species, esp. the sneezeweeds. ▷modern Latin, from Greek *helenion*. The term originally denoted the herb *elecampane*, possibly in commemoration of Helen of Troy (said to have planted elecampane on the island of Pharos); the current designation was adopted by Linnaeus in the 18th cent.

heli- ▸*comb. form* relating to helicopters: *heli-skiing | helipad.*

he·li·a·cal /həˈlīəkəl/ ▸*adj. Astronomy* relating to or near the sun. ▷mid 16th cent.: via late Latin from Greek *hēliakos* (from *hēlios* 'sun') + **-AL**.

he·li·a·cal ris·ing ▸*n.* the rising of a celestial object at the same time or just before the sun, or its first visible rising after a period of invisibility due to conjunction with the sun. The last setting before such a period is the **heliacal setting**. ▷early 17th cent.: *heliacal*, via late Latin from Greek *hēliakos* (from *hēlios* 'sun') + **-AL**.

he·li·an·the·mum /ˌhēlēˈanTHəməm/ ▸*n.* a rockrose of the genus *Helianthemum*. ▷modern Latin, from Greek *hēlios* 'sun' + *anthemon* 'flower' (because the flowers open in sunlight).

he·li·an·thus /ˌhēlēˈanTHəs/ ▸*n.* a plant of the genus *Helianthus* in the daisy family, esp. (in gardening) a sunflower. ▷modern Latin, from Greek *hēlios* 'sun' + *anthos* 'flower.'

hel·i·cal /ˈhelikəl; ˈhē-/ ▸*adj.* having the shape or form of a helix; spiral: *helical molecules.* —**hel·i·cal·ly** /-ik(ə)lē/ *adv.*

hel·i·ces /ˈhēləˌsēz/ ▸ plural form of **HELIX**.

hel·i·chry·sum /ˌheləˈkrīsəm/ ▸*n.* an Old World plant of the daisy family. Some kinds are grown as everlastings, retaining their shape and color when dried. Compare with **STRAWFLOWER**. • Genus *Helichrysum*, family Compositae. ▷Latin, from Greek *helikhrusos*, from *helix* 'spiral' + *khrusos* 'gold.' It originally denoted a yellow-flowered plant, possibly *Helichrysum stoechas*.

he·lic·i·ty /həˈlisitē/ ▸*n.* **1** *chiefly Biochemistry* helical character, esp. of DNA. **2** *Physics* a combination of the spin and the linear motion of a subatomic particle. ▷1950s (sense 2): from Latin *helix*, *helic-* 'spiral' + **-ITY**.

hel·i·coid /ˈheliˌkoid/ ▸*n.* an object of spiral or helical shape. ■ *Geometry* a surface formed by simultaneously moving a straight line along an axis and rotating it around it (like a screw thread). ▸*adj.* of the form of a helix or helicoid. ▷late 17th cent.: from Greek *helikoeidēs* 'of spiral form,' from *helix*, *helik-* (see **HELIX**). —**hel·i·coi·dal** /ˌheliˈkoidəl/ *adj.*

Hel·i·con, Mount /ˈheləˌkän; -ikən/ a mountain in Boeotia, in central Greece, north of the Gulf of Corinth, that rises to 5,741 feet (1,750 m). It was believed by the ancient Greeks to be the home of the Muses.

hel·i·con /ˈheliˌkän; -kən/ ▸*n.* a large spiral bass tuba played encircling the player's head and resting on the shoulder. ▷late 19th cent.: from Latin, associated with **HELIX**.

hel·i·co·nia /ˌheliˈkōnēə/ ▸*n.* a large-leaved tropical American plant that bears spectacular flowers with brightly colored bracts. • Genus *Heliconia*, family Heliconiaceae (formerly Musaceae): many species, including the lobster claw.

hel·i·cop·ter /ˈheliˌkäptər/ ▸*n.* a type of aircraft that derives both lift and propulsion from one or two sets of horizontally revolving overhead rotors. It is capable of moving vertically and horizontally, the direction of motion being controlled by the pitch of the rotor blades. Compare with **AUTOGIRO**. ▸*v.* [*trans.*] transport by helicopter: *the Coast Guard helicoptered a compressor to one ship.* ■ [*intrans.*] fly somewhere in a helicopter: *the inspection team helicoptered ashore.* ▷late 19th cent.: from French *hélicoptère*, from Greek *helix* 'spiral' + *pteron* 'wing.'

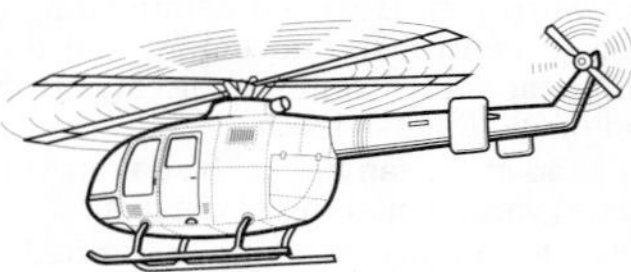

helicopter

he·lic·tite /həˈliktīt; ˈhelikˌtīt/ ▸*n. Geology* a distorted form of stalactite, typically resembling a twig. ▷late 19th cent.: from Greek *heliktos* 'twisted,' on the pattern of *stalactite*.

helio- ▸*comb. form* of or relating to the sun: *heliogravure | heliostat.* ▷from Greek *hēlios* 'sun.'

he·li·o·cen·tric /ˌhēlēəˈsentrik/ ▸*adj.* having or representing the sun as the center, as in the accepted astronomical model of the solar system. Compare with **GEOCENTRIC**. ■ *Astronomy* measured from or considered in relation to the center of the sun: *heliocentric distance.* —**he·li·o·cen·tri·cal·ly** /-trik(ə)lē/ *adv.*

He·lio·gab·a·lus /ˌhēlēōˈgabələs/ (also **El·a·gab·a·lus** /ˌeləˈgabələs/) (AD 204–222), Roman emperor 218–222; born *Varius Avitus Bassianus*. He was notorious for his dissipated lifestyle and neglect of state affairs.

he·li·o·gram /ˈhēlēəˌgram/ ▸*n.* a message sent by reflecting sunlight in flashes from a movable mirror.

he·li·o·graph /ˈhēlēəˌgraf/ ▸*n.* **1** a signaling device by which sunlight is reflected in flashes from a movable mirror. ■ a message sent in such a way; a heliogram. **2** a telescopic apparatus for photographing the sun. **3** *historical* a type of early photographic engraving made using a sensitized silver plate and an asphalt or bitumen varnish. ▸*v.* [*trans.*] **1** *dated* send (a message) by heliograph. **2** *historical* take a heliographic photograph of. —**he·li·o·graph·ic** /ˌhēlēəˈgrafik/ *adj.* —**he·li·og·ra·phy** /ˌhēlēˈägrəfē/ *n.*

he·li·o·gra·vure /ˌhēlēōgrəˈvyo͝or/ ▸*n.* another term for **PHOTOGRAVURE**.

he·li·om·e·ter /ˌhēlēˈämitər/ ▸*n. historical Astronomy* a refracting telescope with a split objective lens, used for finding the angular distance between two stars. ▷mid 18th cent.: from **HELIO-** 'of the sun' + **-METER** (because it was originally used for measuring the diameter of the sun).

he·li·o·pause /ˈhēlēəˌpôz/ ▸*n. Astronomy* the boundary of the heliosphere.

He·li·op·o·lis /ˌhēlēˈäpələs/ **1** an ancient Egyptian city located near the apex of the Nile delta at what is now Cairo. It was the original site of the obelisks known as Cleopatra's Needles. **2** ancient Greek name for **BAALBEK**. ▷from Greek *hēlios* 'sun' + *polis* 'city.'

He·li·os /ˈhēlēˌäs/ *Greek Mythology* the sun personified as a god, father of Phaethon. He is generally represented as a charioteer driving daily from east to west across the sky. ▷Greek *hēlios* 'sun.'

he·li·o·sphere /ˈhēlēə,sfi(ə)r/ ▸*n.* *Astronomy* the region of space, encompassing the solar system, in which the solar wind has a significant influence. —**he·li·o·spher·ic** /,hēlēəˈsferik; -ˈsfi(ə)rik/ *adj.*

he·li·o·stat /ˈhēlēə,stat/ ▸*n.* an apparatus containing a movable or driven mirror, used to reflect sunlight in a fixed direction. See also **COELOSTAT**.

he·li·o·ther·a·py /,hēlēəˈTHerəpē/ ▸*n.* the therapeutic use of sunlight.

he·li·o·trope /ˈhēlēə,trōp/ ▸*n.* a plant of the borage family, cultivated for its fragrant purple or blue flowers, which are used in perfume. • Genus *Heliotropium*, family Boraginaceae. ■ a light purple color, similar to that typical of heliotrope flowers. ▷Old English *eliotropus* (originally applied to various plants whose flowers turn toward the sun), via Latin from Greek *hēliotropion* 'plant turning its flowers to the sun,' from *hēlios* 'sun' + *trepein* 'to turn.' The spelling was influenced by French *héliotrope*.

he·li·ot·ro·pism /,hēlēˈätrə,pizəm; ,hēlēəˈtrōpizəm/ ▸*n.* *Botany* the directional growth of a plant in response to sunlight. Compare with **PHOTOTROPISM**. ■ *Zoology* the tendency of an animal to move toward light. —**he·li·o·trop·ic** /,hēlēəˈträpik; -ˈtrōpik/ *adj.*

He·li·o·zo·a /,hēlēəˈzōə/ *Zoology* a class of single-celled aquatic animals that are related to the radiolarians. They have a spherical shell with fine radiating needlelike projections. • Class Heliozoa, phylum Actinopoda, kingdom Protista. ▷modern Latin (plural), from Greek *hēlios* 'sun' + *zōion* 'animal.' —**he·li·o·zo·an** *n.* & *adj.*

hel·i·pad /ˈhelə,pad/ ▸*n.* a landing and takeoff area for helicopters.

hel·i·port /ˈhelə,pôrt/ ▸*n.* an airport or landing place for helicopters. ▷1940s: from **HELI-** + **PORT**[1], on the pattern of *airport*.

hel·i-ski·ing /ˈheli ,skē-iNG/ ▸*n.* skiing in which the skier is taken up the mountain by helicopter. —**hel·i-ski** *v.* —**hel·i-ski·er** *n.*

he·li·um /ˈhēlēəm/ ▸*n.* the chemical element of atomic number 2, an inert gas that is the lightest member of the noble gas series. (Symbol: **He**)

Helium occurs in traces in air and more abundantly in natural gas deposits. It is used as a lifting gas for balloons and airships, and liquid **helium** (boiling point: 4.2 kelvins, −268.9°C) is used as a coolant. **Helium** is produced in stars as the main product of the thermonuclear fusion of hydrogen and is the second most abundant element in the universe after hydrogen.

▷late 19th cent.: modern Latin, from Greek *hēlios* 'sun,' because its existence was inferred from an emission line in the sun's spectrum.

he·lix /ˈhēliks/ ▸*n.* (*pl.* **-li·ces** /-lə,sēz/) an object having a three-dimensional shape like that of a wire wound uniformly in a single layer around a cylinder or cone, as in a corkscrew or spiral staircase. ■ *Geometry* a curve on a conical or cylindrical surface that would become a straight line if the surface were unrolled into a plane. ■ *Biochemistry* an extended spiral chain of atoms in a protein, nucleic acid, or other polymeric molecule. ■ *Architecture* a spiral ornament. ■ *Anatomy* the rim of the external ear. ▷mid 16th cent. (in the architectural sense 'spiral ornament'): via Latin from Greek.

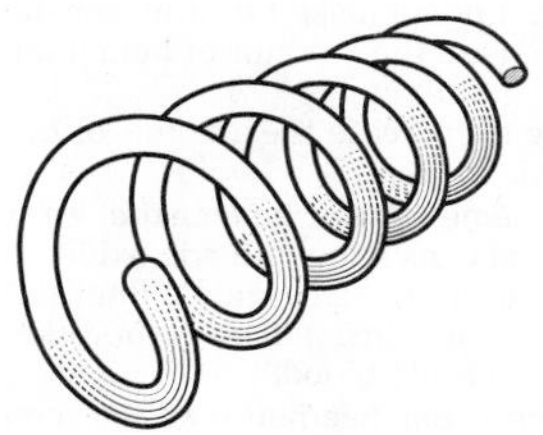

helix

hell /hel/ ▸*n.* a place regarded in various religions as a spiritual realm of evil and suffering, often traditionally depicted as a place of perpetual fire beneath the earth where the wicked are punished after death. ■ a state or place of great suffering; an unbearable experience: *I've been through hell | he made her life hell.*
▸*exclam.* used to express annoyance or surprise or for emphasis: *oh, hell—where will this all end? | hell, no, we were all married.* ■ (**the hell**) *informal* expressing anger, contempt, or disbelief: *who the hell are you? | the hell you are!* ▷Old English *hel, hell*, of Germanic origin; related to Dutch *hel* and German *Hölle*, from an Indo-European root meaning 'to cover or hide.' —**hell·ward** /-wərd/ *adv.* & *adj.*
▸*PHRASES* □ **all hell broke loose** *informal* suddenly there was pandemonium. □ (**as**) —— **as hell** *informal* used for emphasis: *he's as guilty as hell.* □ **be hell on** *informal* be very unpleasant or harmful to: *a sensitive liberal mentality can be hell on a marriage.* □ **catch** (or **get**) **hell** *informal* be severely reprimanded: *Paul kept his mouth shut and looked apologetic—we got hell.* □ **come hell or high water** whatever difficulties may occur. □ **for the hell of it** *informal* just for fun: *she walked on window ledges for the hell of it.* □ —— **from hell** *informal* an extremely unpleasant or troublesome instance or example of something: *I've got a hangover from hell.* □ **get the hell out** (**of**) *informal* escape quickly from (a place or situation): *let's all get the hell out of here.* □ **give someone hell** *informal* severely reprimand or make things very unpleasant for someone. □ **go to hell** *informal* used to express angry rejection of someone or something. □ **go to** (or **through**) **hell and back** endure an extremely unpleasant or difficult experience. □ **go to hell in a handbasket** *informal* undergo a rapid process of deterioration. □ **hell for leather** as fast as possible. □ **hell's bells** *informal* an exclamation of annoyance or anger. □ **hell hath no fury like a woman scorned** *proverb* a woman who has been rejected by a man can be ferociously angry and vindictive. □ **a** (or **one**) **hell of a ——** *informal* used to emphasize something very bad or great: *it cost us a hell of a lot of money.* □ **hell's half acre** a great distance. □ **hell on wheels** a disastrous situation. □ **like hell** *informal* **1** very fast, much, hard, etc. (used for emphasis): *it hurts like hell.* **2** used in ironic expressions of scorn or disagreement: *like hell, he thought.* □ **not a hope in hell** *informal* no chance at all. □ **play hell** *informal* make a fuss; create havoc. ■ cause damage: *the rough road* ***played hell with*** *the tires.* □ **the road to hell is paved with good intentions** *proverb* promises and plans must be put into action, or else they are useless. □ **there will be hell to pay** *informal* serious trouble will occur as a result of a previous action. □ **to hell** used for emphasis: *damn it to hell.* □ **to hell with** *informal* expressing one's scorn or lack of concern for (someone or something): *to hell with the consequences.* □ **until** (or **till**) **hell freezes over** for an extremely long time or forever. □ **what the hell** *informal* it doesn't matter.

he'll /hēl/ ▸*contraction of* he shall; he will.

hel·la·cious /heˈlāSHəs/ ▸*adj.* *informal* very great, bad, or overwhelming: *there was this hellacious hailstorm.* ▷1930s: from **HELL** + **-ACIOUS**, perhaps suggested by *bodacious*. —**hel·la·cious·ly** *adv.*

Hel·lad·ic /heˈladik/ ▸*adj.* *Archaeology* of, relating to, or denoting the Bronze Age cultures of mainland Greece (*c.*3000–1050 BC), of which the latest period is equivalent to the Mycenaean age. ▷early 19th cent.: from Greek *Helladikos*, from *Hellas, Hellad-* 'Greece.'

Hel·las /ˈheləs/ Greek name for **GREECE**.

hell·bend·er /ˈhel,bendər/ ▸*n.* an aquatic giant salamander with grayish skin and a flattened head, native to North America. • *Cryptobranchus alleganiensis*, family Cryptobranchidae.

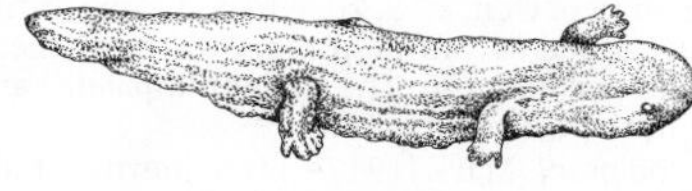

hellbender

hell-bent ▸*adj.* [*predic.*] determined to achieve something at all costs: *why are you* ***hell-bent on*** *leaving?*

hell·cat /ˈhel,kat/ ▸*n.* a spiteful, violent woman.

hel·le·bore /ˈhelə,bôr/ ▸*n.* a poisonous winter-flowering Eurasian plant of the buttercup family, typically having coarse divided leaves and large white, green, or purplish flowers. • Genus *Helleborus*, family Ranunculaceae. ■ another term for **FALSE HELLEBORE**. ▷Old English (denoting any of various plants supposed to cure madness), from Old French *ellebre, elebore* or medieval Latin *eleborus*, via Latin from Greek *helleboros*.

hel·leb·o·rine /ˈheləbə,rīn; həˈlebərən/ ▸*n.* a mainly woodland orchid occurring chiefly in north temperate regions. • Two genera in the family Orchidaceae: *Epipactis* (with greenish or reddish flowers that are sometimes self-fertilized) and *Cephalanthera* (with larger white or pink flowers). ▷late 16th cent.: French or Latin, from Greek *helleborinē*, a plant like hellebore, from *helleboros* 'hellebore.'

Hel·len /ˈhelən/ *Greek Mythology* the son or brother of Deucalion and ancestor of all the Hellenes or Greeks.

Hel·lene /ˈhelēn/ ▸*n.* an ancient Greek. ■ a native of modern Greece (chiefly in the title of the now exiled royal family): *the King of the Hellenes.* ▷from Greek *Hellēn* 'a Greek.' Compare with **HELLEN**.

Hel·len·ic /heˈlenik/ ▸*adj.* Greek. ■ *Archaeology* relating to or denoting Iron Age and Classical Greek culture (between Helladic and Hellenistic).
▸*n.* the branch of the Indo-European language family comprising classical and modern Greek. ■ the Greek language. ▷from Greek *Hellēnikos*, from *Hellēn* (see **HELLENE**).

Hel·len·ism /ˈhelə,nizəm/ ▸*n.* the national character or culture of Greece, esp. ancient Greece. ■ the study or imitation of ancient Greek culture. ▷early 17th cent. (denoting a Greek phrase or idiom): from Greek *Hellēnismos*, from *Hellēnizein* 'speak Greek, make Greek,' from *Hellēn* 'a Greek.' —**Hel·len·ist** *n.* —**Hel·len·i·za·tion** /,heləniˈzāSHən/ *n.* —**Hel·len·ize** /-,nīz/ *v.* —**Hel·len·iz·er** /-,nīzər/ *n.*

Hel·len·is·tic /,heləˈnistik/ ▸*adj.* of or relating to Greek history, language, and culture from the death of Alexander the Great to the defeat of Cleopatra and Mark Antony by Octavian in 31 BC. During this period Greek culture flourished, spreading through the Mediterranean and into the Near East and Asia and centering on Alexandria in Egypt and Pergamum in Turkey.

Hel·ler /ˈhelər/, Joseph (1923–99), U.S. novelist. His experiences in the U.S. Army Air Force during World War II inspired his best-known novel *Catch-22* (1961), an absurd black comedy that satirized war and was the source of the expression "catch-22." He also wrote *Something Happened* (1974), *God Knows* (1984), *Picture This* (1988), and *Closing Time* (1994).

hel·ler /ˈhelər/ ▸*n.* (*pl.* same or **hel·lers**) a former German or Austrian coin of low value. ■ another term for **HALER**. ▷from German *Heller*, earlier *haller* (see **HALER**).

Hel·ler·work /ˈhelər,wərk/ ▸*n.* a type of bodywork that combines some techniques of Rolfing with verbal dialogue and movement exercises. ▷1970s: after Joseph *Heller* (1940–), its inventor.

Hel·les·pont /ˈhelə,spänt/ the ancient name for the Dardanelles, named after the legendary Helle, who fell into the strait and was drowned while escaping with her brother Phrixus from their stepmother, Ino, on a golden-fleeced ram.

hell·fire /ˈhel,fīr/ ▸*n.* the fire or fires regarded as existing in hell: *threats of hellfire and damnation.*

hell·gram·mite /ˈhelgrə,mīt/ ▸*n.* the aquatic larva of a dobsonfly, often used as fishing bait. ▷mid 19th cent.: of unknown origin.

hell·hole /ˈhel,hōl/ ▸*n.* an oppressive or unbearable place.

hell·hound /ˈhel,hound/ ▸*n.* a demon in the form of a dog. ▷Old English: originally referring especially to Cerberus, the watchdog of Hades in Greek mythology.

hel·lion /ˈhelyən/ ▸*n.* *informal* a rowdy, mischievous, or troublemaking person, esp. a child. ▷mid 19th cent.: perhaps from dialect *hallion* 'a worthless fellow,' changed by association with **HELL**.

hell·ish /ˈheliSH/ ▸*adj.* of or like hell: *an unearthly, hellish landscape.* ■ *informal* extremely difficult or unpleasant: *it had been a hellish week.*
▸*adv.* [*as submodifier*] *Brit., informal* extremely (used for emphasis): *it was hellish expensive.* —**hell·ish·ly** *adv.* [*as submodifier*] *a hellishly dull holiday.* —**hell·ish·ness** *n.*

Hell·man /ˈhelmən/, Lillian (Florence) (1907–84), U.S. playwright. Her plays, such as *The Children's Hour* (1934), *The Little Foxes* (1939), and *Watch on the Rhine* (1941), often reflected her socialist and feminist concerns. She lived with the detective-story writer Dashiell Hammett, and both were blacklisted during the McCarthy era.

hel·lo /həˈlō; heˈlō; ˈhelō/ (also **hal·lo** or *chiefly Brit.* **hul·lo**) ▸*exclam.* used as a greeting: *hello there, Katie!* ■ used to begin a telephone conversation: *Hello? Connor speaking.* ■ *Brit.* used to express surprise: *hello, what's all this then?* ■ used as a cry to attract

H

someone's attention: *"Hello below!" he cried.* ■ /hə'lō; he'lō/ [often pronounced with a rising–falling intonation pattern and a prolonged final vowel] expressing sarcasm or anger: *hello! did you even get what the play was about?*
▶*n.* (*pl.* **-los**) an utterance of "hello"; a greeting: *she was getting polite nods and hellos from people.*
▶*v.* (**-loes, -loed**) [*intrans.*] say or shout "hello"; greet someone. ▷late 19th cent.: variant of earlier *hollo;* related to **HOLLA**.

USAGE The pronunciation given above for the sense 'expressing sarcasm or anger' shows an unusual instance in English of intonation conveying meaning. Another example would be the lengthening of the 'ṷ' vowel in the expression "excuse me" to indicate sarcasm.

hell-rais·er ▶*n.* a person who causes trouble by drinking, being violent, or otherwise behaving outrageously. **—hell-rais·ing** *adj.* & *n.*

Hell's An·gel ▶*n.* a member of any of a number of gangs ("chapters") of male motorcycle enthusiasts, first formed in California in the 1950s and originally notorious for lawless behavior.

Hell's Can·yon a chasm in Idaho, cut by the Snake River, that forms the deepest gorge in the U.S. Flanked by the Seven Devils Mountains, the canyon drops to a depth of 7,900 feet (2,433 m).

hell·uv·a /'heləvə/ ▶ nonstandard spelling of **HELL OF A** (see **HELL**): *I'm in a helluva mess.*

helm[1] /helm/ ▶*n.* (**the helm**) a tiller or wheel and any associated equipment for steering a ship or boat: *she stayed at the helm, alert for tankers.* ■ *figurative* a position of leadership: *they are family-run empires whose founders remain **at the helm**.* ■ *Nautical* a helmsman.
▶*v.* [*trans.*] steer (a boat or ship). ■ *figurative* manage the running of: *the magazine he helmed in the late eighties.* ▷Old English *helma;* probably related to **HELVE**.

helm[2] ▶*n. archaic* a helmet. ▷Old English, of Germanic origin; related to Dutch *helm* and German *Helm,* also to **HELMET**, from an Indo-European root meaning 'to cover or hide.' **—helmed** *adj.*

Hel·mand /'helmənd/ the longest river in Afghanistan. Rising in the Hindu Kush, it flows southwest for 700 miles (1,125 km) before emptying into marshland near the Iran–Afghanistan frontier.

helm·er /'helmər/ ▶*n. informal* a film director.

hel·met /'helmit/ ▶*n.* **1** a hard or padded protective hat, various types of which are worn by soldiers, police officers, firefighters, motorcyclists, athletes, and others. **2** *Botany* the arched upper part (galea) of the corolla in some flowers, esp. those of the mint and orchid families. **3** (also **helmet shell**) a predatory mollusk with a squat heavy shell, living in tropical and temperate seas and preying chiefly on sea urchins. • Family Cassidae, class Gastropoda. ▷late Middle English: from Old French, diminutive of *helme,* of Germanic origin; related to **HELM**[2]. **—hel·met·ed** *adj.*

helmet 1

hel·minth /'helmənTH/ ▶*n.* a parasitic worm; a fluke, tapeworm, or nematode. ▷mid 19th cent.: from Greek *helmins, helminth-* 'intestinal worm.' **—hel·min·thic** /hel'minTHik/ *adj.*

hel·min·thi·a·sis /ˌhelmən'THīəsis/ ▶*n. Medicine* infestation with parasitic worms.

hel·min·thol·o·gy /ˌhelmən'THäləjē/ ▶*n.* the study of parasitic worms. **—hel·min·tho·log·i·cal** /helˌminTHə'läjikəl/ *adj.* **—hel·min·thol·o·gist** /-jist/ *n.*

Hel·mont /'helmänt/, Jan Baptista van (1577–1644), Belgian chemist and physician. He made early studies on the conservation of matter, was the first to distinguish gases, and coined the word *gas.*

Helms /helmz/, Jesse (1921–), U.S. politician. Noted for his conservatism, he served as a senator from North Carolina 1973–2003.

helms·man /'helmzmən/ ▶*n.* (*pl.* **-men**) a person who steers a ship or boat.

Hé·lo·ïse /'(h)eləˌwēz/ (1098–1164), French abbess. She is known for her tragic love affair with the theologian Abelard. She later became abbess of the community of Paraclete.

hel·ot /'helət/ ▶*n.* a member of a class of serfs in ancient Sparta, intermediate in status between slaves and citizens. ■ a serf or slave. ▷via Latin from Greek *Heilōtes* (plural), traditionally taken as referring to *Helos,* a Laconian town whose inhabitants were enslaved. **—hel·ot·age** /-ˌtij/ *n.* **—hel·ot·ism** /-ˌtizəm/ *n.* **—hel·ot·ry** /-trē/ *n.*

help /help/ ▶*v.* [*trans.*] **1** make it easier for (someone) to do something by offering one's services or financial or material aid: *Roger's companion helped him with the rent* | [*trans.*] *she helped him find a buyer* | [*intrans.*] *the teenager **helped out** in the corner store.* ■ improve (a situation or problem); be of benefit to: *upbeat comments about prospects helped confidence* | [*intrans.*] *legislation to fit all new cars with catalytic converters will help.* ■ [*trans.*] assist (someone) to move in a specified direction: *I helped her up.* ■ (**help someone on/off with**) assist someone to put on or take off (a garment). ■ relieve the symptoms of (an ailment): *sore throats can be helped by gargling.* **2** (**help someone to**) serve someone with (food or drink): *she **helped herself** to a cookie.* ■ (**help oneself**) take something without permission: *he **helped himself to** the wages she had brought home.* **3** (**can/could not help**) cannot or could not avoid: *he could not help laughing* | *you **can't help but** agree.* ■ (**can/could not help oneself**) cannot or could not stop oneself from acting in a certain way: *she couldn't help herself; she burst into tears.*
▶*n.* assistance: *I asked for help from my neighbors* | *thank you for your help.* ■ [in *sing.*] a person or thing that helps: *he was a great help.* ■ a domestic servant or employee. ■ [as *plural n.*] (**the help**) a group of such employees working for one employer. ■ [as *adj.*] giving assistance to a computer user in the form of displayed instructions: *a help menu.*
▶*exclam.* used as an appeal for urgent assistance: *Help! I'm drowning!* ▷Old English *helpan* (verb), *help* (noun), of Germanic origin; related to Dutch *helpen* and German *helfen.* **—help·er** *n.*
▶*PHRASES* □ **so help me** (**God**) used to emphasize that one means what one is saying. □ **there is no help for it** there is no way of avoiding or remedying a situation.

help desk ▶*n.* a service providing information and support to the users of a computer network.

help·er cell /'helpər/ (also **helper T cell**) ▶*n. Physiology* a T cell that influences or controls the differentiation or activity of other cells of the immune system.

help·ful /'helpfəl/ ▶*adj.* giving or ready to give help: *people are friendly and helpful* | *helpful staff.* ■ useful: *we find it very helpful to receive comments.* **—help·ful·ly** *adv.* **—help·ful·ness** *n.*

help·ing /'helpiNG/ ▶*n.* a portion of food served to one person: *there will be enough for six to eight helpings* | *she asked for a second helping of spinach.*

help·ing hand ▶*n.* (**a helping hand**) assistance: *she was always ready to lend a helping hand.*

help·less /'helplis/ ▶*adj.* unable to defend oneself or to act without help: *the cubs are born blind and helpless.* ■ uncontrollable: *they burst into helpless laughter.* **—help·less·ly** *adv.* **—help·less·ness** *n.*

help·line /'helpˌlīn/ ▶*n.* a telephone service providing help with problems.

Help·mann /'helpmən/, Sir Robert (Murray) (1909–86), Australian ballet dancer, choreographer, director, and actor. He began a long partnership with Margot Fonteyn in 1935.

help·mate /'helpˌmāt/ (also **help·meet** /-ˌmēt/) ▶*n.* a helpful companion or partner, esp. one's husband or wife. ▷late 17th cent. (as *helpmeet*): from an erroneous reading of Gen. 2:18, 20, where Adam's future wife is described as "an help meet for him" (i.e., a suitable helper for him). The variant *helpmate* came into use in the early 18th cent.

Hel·prin /'helprən/, Mark (1947–) U.S. journalist and writer. His works of fiction include *Winter's Tale* (1983), *A Soldier of the Great War* (1991), and *Memoir from Antproof Case* (1995).

Hel·sing·borg /'helsiNGˌbôrg(yə)/ a port in southern Sweden, on the Øresund opposite Elsinore in Denmark; pop. 109,000. Swedish name **HÄLSINGBORG**.

Hel·sing·fors /'helsiNGˌfôrz/ Swedish name of **HELSINKI**.

Hel·sing·ør /ˌhelseNG'œr/ Danish name of **ELSINORE**.

Hel·sin·ki /hel'siNGkē; 'helsiNGkē/ the capital of Finland, a port in the southern part of the country, on the Gulf of Finland; pop. 492,000. Swedish name **HELSINGFORS**

hel·ter-skel·ter /'heltər 'skeltər/ ▶*adj.* & *adv.* in disorderly haste or confusion: [as *adj.*] *she had blamed her grogginess on a helter-skelter lifestyle* | [as *adv.*] *hurtling helter-skelter down the pavement.*
▶*n.* **1** [in *sing.*] disorder; confusion: *the helter-skelter of a school day.* **2** *Brit.* a tall spiral slide winding around a tower at a fair. ▷late 16th cent. (as an adverb): a rhyming jingle of unknown origin, perhaps symbolic of running feet or from Middle English *skelte* 'hasten.'

helve /helv/ ▶*n.* the handle of a weapon or tool. ▷Old English *helfe,* of Germanic origin; related to **HALTER**[1].

Hel·ve·tia /hel'vēSHə/ Latin name of **SWITZERLAND**.

Hel·ve·tian /hel'vēSHən/ *chiefly historical* ▶*adj.* Swiss.
▶*n.* a native of Switzerland.

Hel·vet·ic /hel'vetik/ ▶*adj.* & *n.* another term for **HELVETIAN**.

Hel·ve·ti·i /hel'vēSHēˌī/ ▶*plural n.* an ancient Celtic people living in what is now western Switzerland.

hem[1] /hem/ ▶*n.* the edge of a piece of cloth or clothing that has been turned under and sewn.
▶*v.* (**hemmed, hem·ming**) [*trans.*] **1** turn under and sew the edge of (a piece of cloth or clothing). **2** (**hem someone/something in**) (usu. **be hemmed in**) surround and restrict the space or movement of: *he was hemmed in by the tables.* ▷Old English, 'the border of a piece of cloth.' The verb senses date from the mid 16th cent.

hem[2] ▶*exclam.* used in writing to indicate a sound made when coughing or clearing the throat to attract someone's attention or express hesitation.
▶*n.* an utterance of such a sound.
▶*v.* (**hemmed, hem·ming**) [*intrans.*] *archaic* make such a sound when hesitating or as a signal. ▷late 15th cent.: imitative.
▶*PHRASE* □ **hem and haw** hesitate; be indecisive: *I waste a lot of time hemming and hawing before going into action.*

he·mag·glu·ti·na·tion /ˌhēməˌglōōtn'āSHən/ (*Brit.* **hae·mag·glu·ti·na·tion**) ▶*n. Medicine & Biology* the clumping together of red blood cells. **—he·mag·glu·ti·nate** /-'glōōtnˌāt/ *v.*

he·mag·glu·ti·nin /ˌhēmə'glōōtn-in/ (*Brit.* **hae·mag·glu·ti·nin**) ▶*n. Medicine & Biology* a substance, such as a viral protein, that causes hemagglutination.

he·mal /'hēməl/ (*Brit.* **hae·mal**) ▶*adj. Physiology* of or concerning the blood. ■ *Zoology* situated on the same side of the body as the heart and major blood vessels (i.e., in chordates, ventral). ▷mid 19th cent.: from Greek *haima* 'blood' + **-AL**.

he-man ▶*n. informal* a well-built, muscular man, esp. one who is ostentatiously so.

he·man·gi·o·ma /hiˌmanjē'ōmə/ (*Brit.* **hae·man·gi·o·ma**) ▶*n.* (*pl.* **-o·mas** or **-o·ma·ta** /-'ōmətə/) *Medicine* a benign tumor of blood vessels, often forming a red birthmark.

he·ma·te·in /ˌhēmə'tē-in; 'hēməˌtēn/ ▶*n.* a reddish-brown crystalline dye obtained from logwood and used as a stain and indicator. • Chem. formula $C_{16}H_{12}O_6$.

he·ma·tem·e·sis /ˌhēmə'teməsis/ (*Brit.* **hae·ma·tem·e·sis**) ▶*n. Medicine* the vomiting of blood. ▷early 19th cent.: from **HEMATO-** 'of blood' + Greek *emesis* 'vomiting.'

he·mat·ic /hē'matik/ (*Brit.* **hae·mat·ic**) ▶*adj. dated Medicine* of, relating to, or affecting the blood. ▷mid 19th cent.: from Greek *haimatikos,* from *haima, haimat-* 'blood.'

he·ma·tin /'hēməˌtin/ (*Brit.* **hae·ma·tin**) ▶*n. Biochemistry* a bluish-black compound derived from hemoglobin by removal of the protein part and oxidation of the iron atom. ▷mid 19th cent.: from Greek *haima, haimat-* 'blood' + **-IN**[1].

he·ma·tin·ic /ˌhēmə'tinik/ ▶*n.* any substance that tends to increase the amount of hemoglobin in the blood.
▶*adj.* tending to increase the amount of hemoglobin in the blood.

he·ma·tite /'hēməˌtīt/ (*Brit.* **hae·ma·tite**) ▶*n.* a reddish-black mineral consisting of ferric oxide. It is an important ore of iron. ▷late Middle English: via Latin from Greek *haimatitēs (lithos)* 'bloodlike (stone),' from *haima, haimat-* 'blood.'

hemato- (*chiefly Brit.* **haemato-**) ▶*comb. form* of or relating to the blood: *hematoma.* ▷from Greek *haima, haimat-* 'blood.'

he·mat·o·blast /hi'matəˌblast/ ▶*n.* an immature blood cell.

he·mat·o·cele /hi'matəˌsēl/ (*Brit.* **hae·mat·o·cele**) ▶*n. Medicine* a swelling caused by blood collecting in a body cavity.

he·mat·o·crit /hi'matəˌkrit/ (*Brit.* **hae·mat·o·crit**) ▶*n. Physiology* the ratio of the volume of red blood cells to the total volume of blood. ■ an instrument for measuring this, typically by centrifugation. ▷late

19th cent.: from HEMATO- 'of blood' + Greek *kritēs* 'judge.'

he·mat·o·gen·e·sis /ˌhēmətəˈjenəsis; hiˌmatə-/ ▸*n.* another term for HEMOPOIESIS.

he·ma·tog·e·nous /ˌhēməˈtäjənəs/ (*Brit.* **hae·ma·tog·e·nous**) ▸*adj. Medicine* originating in or carried by the blood.

he·ma·tol·o·gy /ˌhēməˈtäləjē/ (*Brit.* **hae·ma·tol·o·gy**) ▸*n.* the study of the physiology of the blood. **—he·ma·to·log·ic** /-təˈlajik/ *adj.* **—he·ma·to·log·i·cal** /-təˈlajikəl/ *adj.* **—he·ma·tol·o·gist** /-jist/ *n.*

he·ma·tol·y·sis /hēməˈtäləsis/ ▸*n.* another term for HEMOLYSIS.

he·ma·to·ma /ˌhēməˈtōmə/ (*Brit.* **hae·ma·to·ma**) ▸*n.* (*pl.* **-to·mas** or **-to·ma·ta** /-ˈtōmətə/) *Medicine* a solid swelling of clotted blood within the tissues.

he·ma·toph·a·gous /ˌhēməˈtäfəgəs/ (*Brit.* **hae·ma·toph·a·gous**) ▸*adj.* (of an animal, esp. an insect or tick) feeding on blood.

he·mat·o·poi·e·sis /ˌhēmətōpoiˈēsis; hiˌmatə-/ (*Brit.* **hae·mat·o·poi·e·sis**) ▸*n.* another term for HEMOPOIESIS. **—he·ma·to·poi·et·ic** /-poiˈetik/ *adj.*

he·ma·tox·y·lin /ˌhēməˈtäksəlin/ (*Brit.* **hae·ma·tox·y·lin**) ▸*n. Chemistry* a colorless compound present in logwood that is easily converted into blue, red, or purple dyes and is used as a biological stain. • A phenol; chem. formula: $C_{16}H_{14}O_6$. ▷mid 19th cent.: from modern Latin *Haematoxylum* (genus name), from *haemato-*, variant of HEMATO- 'of blood,' + Greek *xulon* 'wood.'

he·mat·o·zo·on /hiˌmatəˈzōən; ˌhēmətə-/ ▸*n.* (*pl.* **-zo·a** /-ˈzōə/) any parasitic organism that lives in the blood.

he·ma·tu·ri·a /ˌhēməˈt(y)ŏŏrēə/ (*Brit.* **hae·ma·tu·ri·a**) ▸*n. Medicine* the presence of blood in urine.

heme /hēm/ (*Brit.* **haem**) ▸*n. Biochemistry* an iron-containing compound of the porphyrin class that forms the nonprotein part of hemoglobin and some other biological molecules. ▷1920s: back-formation from HEMOGLOBIN.

hem·er·o·cal·lis /ˌhemərōˈkaləs/ ▸*n.* (*pl.* same) a plant of a genus that comprises the daylilies. • Genus *Hemerocallis*, family Liliaceae. ▷modern Latin, from Greek *hēmerokallis* 'a lily that flowers for a day,' from *hēmera* 'day' + *kallos* 'beauty.'

hemi- ▸*prefix* half: *hemicylindrical* | *hemiplegia*. ▷from Greek *hēmi-*; related to Latin *semi-*.

-hemia ▸*comb. form* variant spelling of **-EMIA**.

hem·i·al·gi·a /ˌhemēˈalj(ē)ə/ ▸*n.* pain affecting one half of the body.

hem·i·a·nop·si·a /ˌhēmēəˈnäpsēə/ (also **hem·i·a·no·pi·a** /-ˈnōpēə/) ▸*n.* blindness over half the field of vision.

he·mic /hēmik/ ▸*adj.* of or relating to the blood or the circulatory system.

hem·i·cel·lu·lose /ˌhemiˈselyəlōs; -lōz/ ▸*n. Biochemistry* any of a class of substances that occur as constituents of the cell walls of plants and are polysaccharides of simpler structure than cellulose. ▷late 19th cent.: coined in German from HEMI- + CELLULOSE.

Hem·i·chor·da·ta /ˌhemikôrˈdātə/ *Zoology* a small phylum of marine invertebrates that comprises the acorn worms. ▷modern Latin (see HEMI-, CHORDATA). **—hem·i·chor·date** /-ˈkôrdāt; -ˈkôrdit/ *n.* & *adj.*

hem·i·cy·cle /ˈhemiˌsīkəl/ ▸*n.* a semicircular shape or structure.

hem·i·cy·lin·dri·cal /ˌhemisəˈlindrikəl/ ▸*adj.* having the shape of half a cylinder (divided lengthways).

hem·i·dem·i·sem·i·qua·ver /ˌhemēˌdemēˈsemēˌkwāvər/ ▸*n. Music, chiefly Brit.* a note with the time value of half a demisemiquaver; a sixty-fourth note.

hem·i·he·dral /ˌheməˈhēdrəl/ ▸*adj. Crystallography* having half the number of planes required for symmetry of the holohedral form.

hem·i·hy·drate /ˌhemiˈhīdrāt/ ▸*n. Chemistry* a crystalline hydrate containing one molecule of water for every two molecules of the compound in question.

hem·i·me·tab·o·lous /ˌhemiməˈtabələs/ ▸*adj. Entomology* (of an insect) having no pupal stage in the transition from larva to adult. **—hem·i·met·a·bol·ic** /ˌheməˌmetəˈbälik/ *adj.*

hem·i·mor·phite /ˌheməˈmôrfīt/ ▸*n.* a mineral consisting of hydrated zinc silicate, typically occurring as flat white prisms.

Hem·ings /ˈhemiNGz/, Sally (1773–1835), U.S. slave. A slave at Thomas Jefferson's estate, Monticello, she was reported to be his mistress in the *Richmond Recorder* 1802. Further, more recent evidence has shown that they probably had children together.

Hem·ing·way /ˈhemiNGˌwā/, Ernest (Miller) (1899–1961), U.S. novelist, short-story writer, and journalist. He achieved success with *The Sun Also Rises* (1926), which reflected the disillusionment of the postwar "lost generation." In World War II, he joined in the D-Day landings as a war correspondent. Other notable works: *A Farewell to Arms* (1929), *For Whom the Bell Tolls* (1940), and *The Old Man and the Sea* (1952, Pulitzer Prize 1953). Nobel Prize for Literature (1954).

Ernest Hemingway

hem·i·o·la /ˌhemēˈōlə/ ▸*n. Music* a musical figure in which, typically, two groups of three beats are replaced by three groups of two beats, giving the effect of a shift between triple and duple meter. ▷late Middle English: via medieval Latin from Greek *hēmiolia* 'in the ratio of one and a half to one' (from *hēmi-* 'half' + *holos* 'whole').

hem·i·par·a·site /ˌheməˈparəˌsīt/ ▸*n. Botany* a plant that obtains or may obtain part of its food by parasitism, e.g., mistletoe, which also photosynthesizes.

hem·i·pa·re·sis /ˌhemәpәˈrēsis/ ▸*n.* another term for HEMIPLEGIA.

hem·i·pe·nis /ˈhemiˌpēnis/ ▸*n.* (*pl.* **-pe·nes** /-ˌpēnēz/) *Zoology* each of the paired male reproductive organs in snakes and lizards.

hem·i·ple·gi·a /ˌheməˈplēj(ē)ə/ ▸*n. Medicine* paralysis of one side of the body. ▷early 17th cent.: modern Latin, from Greek *hēmiplēgia*, from *hemi-* 'half' + *plēgē* 'stroke.' **—hem·i·ple·gic** /-ˈplējik/ *n.* & *adj.*

He·mip·ter·a /həˈmiptərə/ *Entomology* a large order of insects that comprises the true bugs, which include aphids, cicadas, leafhoppers, and many others. They have piercing and sucking mouthparts and incomplete metamorphosis. See also HETEROPTERA, HOMOPTERA. ■ [as *plural n.*] (**hemiptera**) insects of this order; true bugs. ▷modern Latin (plural), from Greek *hemi-* 'half' + *pteron* 'wing' (because of the forewing structure, partly hardened at the base and partly membranous). **—he·mip·ter·an** *n.* & *adj.* **—he·mip·ter·ous** /-tərəs/ *adj.*

hem·i·sphere /ˈheməˌsfi(ə)r/ ▸*n.* a half of a sphere. ■ a half of the earth, usually as divided into northern and southern halves by the equator, or into western and eastern halves by an imaginary line passing through the poles. ■ a half of the celestial sphere. ■ (also **cerebral hemisphere**) each of the two parts of the cerebrum (left and right) in the brain of a vertebrate. ▷late Middle English (in the sense 'half the celestial sphere, the sky'): from Old French *emisphere*, via Latin from Greek *hēmisphairion*, from *hēmi-* 'half' + *sphaira* 'sphere.' **—hem·i·spher·ic** /ˌheməˈsfi(ə)rik; -ˈsferik/ *adj.* **—hem·i·spher·i·cal** *adj.* **—hem·i·spher·i·cal·ly** *adv.*

hem·i·stich /ˈheməˌstik/ ▸*n.* (chiefly in Old English verse) a half of a line of verse. ▷late 16th cent.: via late Latin from Greek *hēmistikhion*, from *hemi-* 'half' + *stikhos* 'row, line of verse.'

Hem·kund, Lake /hemˈkŏŏnd/ a lake in northern India, in the Himalayan foothills, in Uttar Pradesh. It is regarded as holy by the Sikhs.

hem·line /ˈhemˌlīn/ ▸*n.* the level of the lower edge of a garment such as a skirt, dress, or coat: *a long jacket with a lowered hemline at the back.*

hem·lock /ˈhemˌläk/ ▸*n.* **1** a highly poisonous European plant of the parsley family, with a purple-spotted stem, fernlike leaves, small white flowers, and an unpleasant smell. • *Conium maculatum*, family Umbelliferae. ■ a sedative or poisonous potion obtained from this plant. Such a potion was said to have been used to poison Socrates. **2** (also **hemlock fir** or **spruce**) a coniferous North American tree with dark green foliage that is said to smell like hemlock when crushed, grown chiefly for timber and pulp production, and also grown in Europe as an ornamental. • Genus *Tsuga*, family Pinaceae: several species, in particular **eastern hemlock** (*T. canadensis*) and **Carolina hemlock** (*T. caroliniana*). ▷Old English *hymlice, hemlic*, of unknown origin.

hemo- (*chiefly Brit.* **haemo-**) ▸*comb. form* equivalent to HEMATO-. ▷from Greek *haima* 'blood.'

he·mo·chro·ma·to·sis /ˌhēməˌkrōməˈtōsis/ (*Brit.* **hae·mo·chro·ma·to·sis**) ▸*n. Medicine* a hereditary disorder in which iron salts are deposited in the tissues, leading to liver damage, diabetes mellitus, and bronze discoloration of the skin.

he·mo·coel /ˈhēməˌsēl/ (*Brit.* **hae·mo·coel**) ▸*n. Zoology* the primary body cavity of most invertebrates, containing circulatory fluid. ▷late 19th cent.: from HEMO- 'of blood' + Greek *koilos* 'hollow, cavity.'

he·mo·cy·a·nin /ˌhēməˈsīənən/ (*Brit.* **hae·mo·cy·a·nin**) ▸*n. Biochemistry* a protein containing copper, responsible for transporting oxygen in the blood plasma of arthropods and mollusks. ▷mid 19th cent.: from HEMO- 'of blood' + CYAN + -IN[1].

he·mo·cyte /ˈhēməˌsīt/ ▸*n.* a blood cell, esp. in an invertebrate.

he·mo·cy·tom·e·ter /ˌhēməsīˈtämitər/ (also **he·ma·cy·tom·e·ter**) (*Brit.* **hae·mo·cy·tom·e·ter**) ▸*n.* an instrument for visual counting of the number of cells in a blood sample or other fluid under a microscope.

he·mo·di·al·y·sis /ˌhēməˌdīˈaləsis/ (*Brit.* **hae·mo·di·al·y·sis**) ▸*n.* (*pl.* **-ses** /-ˌsēz/) *Medicine* kidney dialysis.

he·mo·dy·nam·ic /ˌhēmōdīˈnamik/ (*Brit.* **hae·mo·dy·nam·ic**) ▸*adj. Physiology* of or relating to the flow of blood within the organs and tissues of the body. **—he·mo·dy·nam·i·cal·ly** /-ik(ə)lē/ *adv.* **—he·mo·dy·nam·ics** *n.*

he·mo·flag·el·late /ˌhēməˈflajəˌlāt; -lit/ ▸*n.* any parasitic flagellate protozoan that lives in the bloodstream.

he·mo·glo·bin /ˈhēməˌglōbin/ (*Brit.* **hae·mo·glo·bin**) ▸*n. Biochemistry* a red protein responsible for transporting oxygen in the blood of vertebrates. Its molecule comprises four subunits, each containing an iron atom bound to a heme group. ▷mid 19th cent.: a contracted form of *hematoglobulin*, in the same sense.

he·mo·glo·bin·op·a·thy /ˌhēməˌglōbəˈnäpəTHē/ (*Brit.* **hae·mo·glo·bin·op·a·thy**) ▸*n.* (*pl.* **-thies**) *Medicine* a hereditary condition involving an abnormality in the structure of hemoglobin.

he·mo·glo·bi·nu·ri·a /ˌhēməˌglōbəˈn(y)ŏŏrēə/ (*Brit.* **hae·mo·glo·bi·nu·ri·a**) ▸*n. Medicine* excretion of free hemoglobin in the urine.

he·mo·lymph /ˈhēməˌlim(p)f/ (*Brit.* **hae·mo·lymph**) ▸*n.* a fluid equivalent to blood in most invertebrates, occupying the hemocoel.

he·mol·y·sin /hiˈmälisin; ˌhēməˈlī-/ ▸*n.* a substance in the blood that destroys red blood cells and liberates hemoglobin.

he·mol·y·sis /hēˈmäləsis/ (*Brit.* **hae·mol·y·sis**) ▸*n.* the rupture or destruction of red blood cells. Also called HEMATOLYSIS.

he·mo·lyt·ic /ˌhēməˈlitik/ (*Brit.* **hae·mo·lyt·ic**) ▸*adj. Medicine* relating to or involving the rupture or destruction of red blood cells: *hemolytic anemia.*

he·mo·lyt·ic dis·ease of the new·born ▸*n. Medicine* a severe form of anemia caused in a fetus or newborn infant by incompatibility with the mother's blood type, typically when the mother is Rhesus negative and produces antibodies that attack Rhesus positive fetal blood through the placenta. Also called ERYTHROBLASTOSIS.

he·mo·phil·i·a /ˌhēməˈfilēə/ (*Brit.* **hae·mo·phil·i·a**) ▸*n.* a medical condition in which the ability of the blood to clot is severely reduced, causing the sufferer to bleed severely from even a slight injury. The condition is typically caused by a hereditary lack of a coagulation factor, most often factor VIII. **—he·mo·phil·i·ac** /-ˈfilēˌak/ *n.* **—he·mo·phil·ic** /-ˈfilik/ *adj.*

he·mo·poi·e·sis /ˌhēməpoiˈēsis/ (*Brit.* **hae·mo·poi·e·sis**) ▸*n.* the production of blood cells and platelets, which occurs in the bone marrow. Also called HEMATOGENESIS. ▷early 20th cent.: from HEMO- 'of blood' + Greek *poiēsis* 'making.' **—he·mo·poi·et·ic** /-poiˈetik/ *adj.*

he·mop·ty·sis /hēˈmäptəsis/ (*Brit.* **hae·mop·ty·sis**) ▸*n.* the coughing up of blood. ▷mid 17th cent.: modern Latin, from HEMO- 'of blood' + Greek *ptusis* 'spitting.'

H

hem·or·rhage /ˈhem(ə)rij/ (*Brit.* **haem·or·rhage**) ▸*n.* an escape of blood from a ruptured blood vessel, esp. when profuse. ■ a damaging loss of valuable people or resources suffered by an organization, group, or country: *a hemorrhage of highly qualified teachers.*
▸*v.* [*intrans.*] (of a person) suffer a hemorrhage: *he had begun hemorrhaging in the night.* ■ [*trans.*] expend (money) in large amounts in a seemingly uncontrollable manner: *the business was hemorrhaging cash.* ▷late 17th cent. (as a noun): alteration of obsolete *hemorrhagy*, via Latin *haemorrhagia* from Greek *haimorrhagia*, from *haima* 'blood' + the stem of *rhēgnunai* 'burst.'

hem·or·rhag·ic /ˌheməˈrajik/ (*Brit.* **haem·or·rhag·ic**) ▸*adj.* accompanied by or produced by hemorrhage: *a viral hemorrhagic fever | hemorrhagic colitis.*

hem·or·rhoid /ˈhem(ə)ˌroid/ (*Brit.* **haem·or·rhoid**) ▸*n.* (usu. **hemorrhoids**) a swollen vein or group of veins in the region of the anus. Also (collectively) called **PILES**. ▷late Middle English: via Old French and Latin from Greek *haimorrhoides (phlebes)* 'bleeding (veins),' from *haima* 'blood' + an element related to *rhein* 'to flow.' **—hem·or·rhoi·dal** /ˌhem(ə)ˈroidl/ *adj.*

he·mo·sta·sis /ˌhēməˈstāsəs; heme-/ (*Brit.* **hae·mo·sta·sis**) ▸*n. Medicine* the stopping of a flow of blood. **—he·mo·stat·ic** /-ˈstatik/ *adj.*

he·mo·stat /ˈhēməˌstat/ (*Brit.* **hae·mo·stat**) ▸*n. Medicine* an instrument for preventing the flow of blood from an open blood vessel by compression of the vessel.

hemp /hemp/ ▸*n.* (also **Indian hemp**) the cannabis plant, esp. when grown for fiber. ■ the fiber of this plant, extracted from the stem and used to make rope, stout fabrics, fiberboard, and paper. ■ used in names of other plants that yield fiber, e.g., **Manila hemp**. ■ marijuana. ▷Old English *henep, hænep*, of Germanic origin; related to Dutch *hennep* and German *Hanf*, also to Greek *kannabis.*

hemp ag·ri·mo·ny ▸*n.* an erect Eurasian plant of the daisy family, resembling a valerian, with clusters of pale purple flowers and hairy stems. • *Eupatorium cannabinum*, family Compositae.

hemp·en /ˈhempən/ ▸*adj.* [*attrib.*] made from hemp fiber: *hempen rope.*

hemp net·tle ▸*n.* a nettlelike plant of the mint family, native to Eurasia but introduced elsewhere. • Genus *Galeopsis*, family Labiatae: several species, including *G. tetrahit*, found in waste areas of southern Canada and the northern U.S.

hemp·seed /ˈhempˌsēd/ ▸*n.* the seed of hemp, particularly as used for fishing bait.

Hemp·stead /ˈhem(p)ˌsted/ **1** a town on western Long Island in southeastern New York state, on the eastern boundary of Queens in New York City, that includes the villages of Hempstead, Rockville Centre, Levittown, and many others; pop. 725,639. **2** a village on western Long Island in the town of Hempstead; pop. 56,554.

hem·stitch /ˈhemˌstiCH/ ▸*n.* a decoration used on woven fabric, esp. alongside a hem, in which several adjacent threads are pulled out and the crossing threads are tied into bunches, making a row of small openings.
▸*v.* [*trans.*] incorporate such a decoration in the hem of (a piece of cloth or clothing).

hen /hen/ ▸*n.* a female bird, esp. of a domestic fowl. ■ (**hens**) domestic fowls of either sex. ■ used in names of birds, esp. waterbirds of the rail family, e.g., **moorhen**. ■ a female lobster, crab, or salmon. ▷Old English *henn*, of Germanic origin; related to Dutch *hen* and German *Henne.*
▸*PHRASE* □ **as rare** (or **scarce**) **as hen's teeth** extremely rare.

He·nan /ˈhəˈnän/ (also **Ho·nan** /ˈhōˈnän/) a province in northeastern central China; capital, Zhengzhou.

hen and chick·ens ▸*n.* any of a number of plants producing additional small flowerheads or offshoots. • Several species, esp. the houseleeks (family Crassulaceae).

hen·bane /ˈhenˌbān/ ▸*n.* a coarse and poisonous Eurasian plant of the nightshade family, with sticky hairy leaves and an unpleasant smell. • *Hyoscyamus niger*, family Solanaceae. ■ a psychoactive drink prepared from this plant.

hen·bit /ˈhenˌbit/ ▸*n.* a dead-nettle with purple flowers and partly prostrate stems, native to Eurasia, several kinds of which have become widely naturalized in North America. • Genus *Lamium*, family Labiatae: several species, in particular *L. amplexicaule*. ▷late 16th cent.: apparently a translation of Low German or Dutch *hoenderbeet.*

hence /hens/ ▸*adv.* **1** as a consequence; for this reason: *a stiff breeze and hence a high windchill.* **2** in the future (used after a period of time): *two years hence they might say something quite different.* **3** (also **from hence**) *archaic* from here: *hence, be gone.* ▷Middle English *hennes* (sense 3): from earlier *henne* (from Old English *heonan*, of Germanic origin, related to **HE**) + **-S**[3] (later respelled *-ce* to denote the unvoiced sound).

hence·forth /ˈhensˌfôrTH/ (also **hence·for·ward** /hensˈfôrwərd/) ▸*adv.* from this time on or from that time on: *the company announced that it would henceforth charge royalties.*

hench·man /ˈhenCHmən/ ▸*n.* (*pl.* **-men**) *chiefly derogatory* a faithful follower or political supporter, esp. one prepared to engage in crime or dishonest practices by way of service. ■ *historical* a squire or page of honor to a person of rank. ▷Middle English, from Old English *hengest* 'male horse' + **MAN**, the original sense being probably 'groom.'

hen·coop /ˈhenˌko͞op/ ▸*n.* a cage or pen for keeping poultry in.

hendeca- ▸*comb. form* eleven; having eleven: *hendecasyllable.* ▷from Greek *hendeka* 'eleven.'

hen·dec·a·gon /henˈdekəˌgän/ ▸*n.* a plane figure with eleven straight sides and angles. ▷early 18th cent.: from **HENDECA-** 'eleven' + **-GON**, on the pattern of words such as *polygon.* **—hen·de·cag·o·nal** /ˌhendəˈkagənl/ *adj.* .

hen·dec·a·syl·la·ble /henˈdekəˌsiləbəl; -ˌdekəˈsiləbəl/ ▸*n. Prosody* a line of verse containing eleven syllables. **—hen·dec·a·syl·lab·ic** /henˌdekəsəˈlabik/ *adj.*

Hen·der·son /ˈhendərsən/ **1** a city in northwestern Kentucky, on the Ohio River; pop. 27,373. **2** a city in southeastern Nevada, southeast of Las Vegas; pop. 175,381.

Hen·der·son·ville /ˈhendərsənˌvil/ a city in north central Tennessee, a northeastern suburb of Nashville; pop. 40,620.

hen·di·a·dys /henˈdīədəs/ ▸*n. Rhetoric* the expression of a single idea by two words connected with "and," e.g., *nice and warm*, when one could be used to modify the other, as in *nicely warm.* ▷late 16th cent.: via medieval Latin from Greek *hen dia duoin* 'one thing by two.'

Hen·drix /ˈhendriks/, Jimi (1942–70), U.S. rock musician; full name *James Marshall Hendrix.* Remembered for the flamboyance and originality of his improvisations, he greatly widened the scope of the electric guitar. Notable songs: "Purple Haze" (1967) and "All Along the Watchtower" (1968).

hen·e·quen /ˈhenək(w)ən/ ▸*n.* **1** a fiber resembling sisal, chiefly used for twine and paper pulp. **2** a Central American agave from which such fiber is obtained. • *Agave fourcroydes*, family Agavaceae. ▷early 17th cent.: from Spanish *jeniquen*, from a local word.

henge /henj/ ▸*n.* a prehistoric monument consisting of a circle of stone or wooden uprights. ▷mid 18th cent.: back-formation from **STONEHENGE**.

hen·house /ˈhenˌhous/ ▸*n.* a small shed for keeping poultry in.

Hen·ie /ˈhenē/, Sonja (1912–69),U.S. figure skater; born in Norway. She won ten consecutive world championships 1927–36 and three Olympic gold medals 1928, 1932, 1936. She starred in movies such as *One in a Million* (1936) and *Sun Valley Serenade* (1941) and toured professionally with her own ice show until 1952.

Hen·le's loop /ˈhenlēz/ ▸*n.* another term for **LOOP OF HENLE**.

Hen·ley /ˈhenlē/ (in full **Henley Royal Regatta**) the oldest rowing regatta in Europe, inaugurated in 1839 at Henley-on-Thames, England, and held annually in the first week in July.

hen·na /ˈhenə/ ▸*n.* **1** the powdered leaves of a tropical shrub, used as a dye to color the hair and decorate the body. **2** the Old World shrub that produces these leaves, with small pink, red, or white flowers. • *Lawsonia inermis*, family Lythraceae.
▸*v.* (**hen·nas, hen·naed** /ˈhenəd/, **hen·na·ing**) [*trans.*] dye (hair) with henna.
▸*adj.* reddish-brown: *girls with henna hair and burgundy nails.* ▷early 17th cent.: from Arabic *ḥinnā'.*

Hen·ne·pin /ˈhenəpən/, Louis (1640–*c.*1701) French missionary, explorer, and writer. He accompanied La Salle as his chaplain through the Great Lakes in 1679, explored the surrounding territory that included the Mississippi River, and described his discoveries in writing.

hen·o·the·ism /ˈhenōTHēˌizəm; ˌhenōˈTHē-/ ▸*n.* adherence to one particular god out of several, esp. by a family, tribe, or other group. ▷mid 19th cent.: from Greek *heis, hen-* 'one' + *theos* 'god' + **-ISM**.

hen par·ty ▸*n. informal, often derogatory* a social gathering of women.

hen·peck /ˈhenˌpek/ ▸*v.* [*trans.*] [usu. as *adj.*] (**henpecked**) (of a woman) continually criticize and give orders to (her husband or other male partner): *henpecked husbands.*

Hen·ri /ˈhenrē/, Robert (1865–1929), U.S. painter. An advocate of realism, he believed that an artist must be a social force. The Ashcan School of painters was formed largely as a result of his influence.

Hen·ri·cian /henˈrisHēən/ ▸*adj.* of or relating to the reign and policies of Henry VIII of England.

Hen·ry[1] /ˈhenrē/ the name of eight kings of England: ■ **Henry I** (1068–1135), youngest son of William I; reigned 1100–35. He conquered Normandy in 1105. ■ **Henry II** (1133–89), son of Matilda; reigned 1154–89. The first Plantagenet king, he restored order and extended his kingdom. ■ **Henry III** (1207–72), son of John; reigned 1216–72. ■ **Henry IV** (1367–1413), son of John of Gaunt; reigned 1399–1413; known as **Henry Bolingbroke**. He overthrew Richard II, establishing the Lancastrian dynasty. ■ **Henry V** (1387–1422), son of Henry IV; reigned 1413–22. He renewed the Hundred Years War soon after coming to the throne and defeated the French at Agincourt in 1415. ■ **Henry VI** (1421–71), son of Henry V; reigned 1422–61 and 1470–71. ■ **Henry VII** (1457–1509), the first Tudor king; son of Edmund Tudor, Earl of Richmond; reigned 1485–1509; known as **Henry Tudor**. He defeated Richard III at Bosworth Field and eventually established an unchallenged Tudor dynasty. ■ **Henry VIII** (1491–1547), son of Henry VII; reigned 1509–47. Henry had six wives (Catherine of Aragon, Anne Boleyn, Jane Seymour, Anne of Cleves, Catherine Howard, Katherine Parr) and three children (Mary I, with Catherine of Aragon; Elizabeth I, with Anne Boleyn; and Edward VI, with Jane Seymour). His first divorce, from Catherine of Aragon, was opposed by the pope, leading to England's break with the Roman Catholic Church.

Henry VIII

Hen·ry[2] (1394–1460), Portuguese prince; known as **Henry the Navigator**. The third son of John I of Portugal, he organized many voyages of exploration, most notably south along the African coast, thus laying the foundation for Portuguese imperial expansion around Africa to the Far East.

Hen·ry[3] the name of seven kings of the Germans, six of whom were also Holy Roman Emperors: ■ **Henry I** (*c.*876–936), reigned 919–936; known as **Henry the Fowler**. He waged war successfully against the Slavs in Brandenburg, the Magyars, and the Danes. ■ **Henry II** (973–1024), reigned 1002–24; Holy Roman Emperor 1014–24; also known as **Saint Henry**. ■ **Henry III** (1017–56), reigned 1039–56; Holy Roman Emperor 1046–56. He brought stability and prosperity to the empire, defeating the Czechs and fixing the frontier between Austria and Hungary. ■ **Henry IV** (1050–1106), son of Henry III; reigned 1056–1105; Holy Roman Emperor 1084–1105. Increasing conflict with Pope Gregory VII led Henry to call a council in 1076 to depose the pope, who excommunicated Henry. ■ **Henry V** (1086–1125), reigned 1099–1125; Holy Roman Emperor 1111–25. ■ **Henry VI** (1165–97), reigned 1169–97; Holy Roman Emperor 1191–97. ■ **Henry VII** (*c.*1269/74–1313), reigned 1308–13; Holy Roman Emperor 1312–13.

Hen·ry[4], O (1862–1910), U.S. short-story writer; pseudonym of *William Sydney Porter.* Jailed for embezzlement in 1898, he started writing in prison. His humorous, ironic stories of everyday life depend on coincidence and twists. Collections of his works include *Cabbages and Kings* (1904), *The Voice of the City* (1908), and *Waifs and Strays* (published posthumously in 1917).

Hen·ry[5], Patrick (1736–99) American revolutionary. As a member of the Continental Congress 1774–76, he was noted as an orator. He is best remembered for an impassioned speech in which he urged the colonies into readiness with the statement "Give me liberty, or give me death."

Patrick Henry

hen·ry /'henrē/ (abbr.: **H**) ▸*n.* (*pl.* **hen·ries** or **hen·rys**) *Physics* the SI unit of inductance, equal to an electromotive force of one volt in a closed circuit with a uniform rate of change of current of one ampere per second. ▷late 19th cent.: named after Joseph *Henry* (1797–1878), the American physicist who discovered the phenomenon.

Hen·ry IV (1553–1610), king of France 1589–1610; known as **Henry of Navarre**. Although leader of Huguenot forces in the latter stages of the French Wars of Religion, on succeeding the Catholic Henry III, he became Catholic himself in order to guarantee peace. He established religious freedom with the Edict of Nantes (1598) and restored order after the prolonged civil war.

Hen·ry Bo·ling·broke /'bôliNG,brŏŏk; 'bōliNG,brŏk/, Henry IV of England (see **HENRY**[1]).

Hen·ry's law *Chemistry* a law stating that the mass of a dissolved gas in a given volume of solvent at equilibrium is proportional to the partial pressure of the gas. ▷late 19th cent.: named after William *Henry* (1774–1836), English chemist.

Hen·ry the Fow·ler /'foulər/, Henry I, king of the Germans (see **HENRY**[3]).

Hen·ry Tu·dor /'to͞odər/, Henry VII of England (see **HENRY**[1]).

Hen·son[1] /'hensən/, Jim (1936–90) U.S. puppeteer; full name *James Maury Henson*. He created the Muppets, the most commercially successful puppets in history, who became well known as the principal characters on television's "Sesame Street" (1969–) and "The Muppet Show" (1976–81).

Hen·son[2], Matthew (Alexander) (1866–1955) U.S. explorer. He accompanied Peary as his valet when their party became the first to reach the North Pole in 1909. He wrote *A Black Explorer at the North Pole* (1912).

hep /hep/ ▸*adj.* old-fashioned term for **HIP**[3].

hep·a·rin /'hepərin/ ▸*n. Biochemistry* a compound occurring in the liver and other tissues that inhibits blood coagulation. A sulfur-containing polysaccharide, it is used as an anticoagulant in the treatment of thrombosis. ▷early 20th cent.: via late Latin from Greek *hēpar* 'liver' + **-IN**[1].

hep·a·rin·ize /'hepərə,nīz/ ▸*v.* [*trans.*] add heparin to (blood or a container about to be filled with blood) to prevent it from coagulating. **—hep·a·rin·i·za·tion** /,hepərənə'zāsHən/ *n.*

he·pat·ic /hə'patik/ ▸*adj.* of or relating to the liver: *right and left hepatic ducts.*

▸*n. Botany* less common term for **LIVERWORT**. ▷late Middle English: via Latin from Greek *hēpatikos*, from *hēpar, hēpat-* 'liver.'

he·pat·i·ca /hə'patikə/ ▸*n.* a plant of the buttercup family, with anemonelike flowers, native to north temperate regions. • Genus *Hepatica*, family Ranunculaceae. ▷from medieval Latin *hepatica (herba)* 'plant having liver-shaped parts, or one used to treat liver diseases,' feminine of *hepaticus* (see **HEPATIC**).

he·pat·ic por·tal vein ▸*n.* see **PORTAL VEIN**.

hep·a·ti·tis /,hepə'tītis/ ▸*n.* a disease characterized by inflammation of the liver. ▷early 18th cent.: modern Latin, from Greek *hēpar, hēpat-* 'liver' + **-ITIS**.

hep·a·ti·tis A ▸*n.* a form of viral hepatitis transmitted in food, causing fever and jaundice.

hep·a·ti·tis B ▸*n.* a severe form of viral hepatitis transmitted in infected blood, causing fever, debility, and jaundice.

hep·a·ti·tis C ▸*n.* a form of viral hepatitis transmitted in infected blood, causing chronic liver disease. It was formerly called non-A, non-B hepatitis.

hepato- ▸*comb. form* of or relating to the liver. ▷from Greek *hēpar, hēpat-* 'liver.'

hep·a·to·cyte /'hepətə,sīt; hə'patə-/ ▸*n. Physiology* a liver cell.

hep·a·to·ma /,hepə'tōmə/ ▸*n.* (*pl.* **-to·mas** or **-to·ma·ta** /-'tōmətə/) *Medicine* a cancer of the cells of the liver.

hep·a·to·meg·a·ly /,hepətō'megəlē/ ▸*n. Medicine* abnormal enlargement of the liver.

hep·a·to·pan·cre·as /,hepətō'panGkrēəs; -'pankrēəs/ ▸*n. Zoology* technical term for **DIGESTIVE GLAND**.

hep·a·to·tox·ic /,hepətō'täksik/ ▸*adj.* damaging or destructive to liver cells. **—hep·a·to·tox·ic·i·ty** /-,täk'sisətē/ *n.* **—hep·a·to·tox·in** /-'täksən/ *n.*

Hep·burn[1] /'hep,bərn/, Audrey (1929–93), U.S. actress; born in Belgium; born *Edda Kathleen van Heemstra Hepburn-Ruston*. After pursuing a career as a stage and movie actress in Britain, she moved to Hollywood, where she starred in such movies as *Roman Holiday* (1953), for which she won an Academy Award; *Sabrina* (1954); *Breakfast at Tiffany's* (1961); and *My Fair Lady* (1964).

Hep·burn[2], Katharine (1909–2003), U.S. actress; full name *Katharine Houghton Hepburn*. Making her screen debut in 1932, she starred in a wide range of movies, often opposite Spencer Tracy. Her movies include *Morning Glory* (1933); *Guess Who's Coming to Dinner* (1967); *The Lion in Winter* (1968); and *On Golden Pond* (1981), for all of which she won Academy Awards.

Katharine Hepburn

hep·cat /'hep,kat/ ▸*n. informal, dated* a stylish or fashionable person, esp. in the sphere of jazz or popular music. ▷1930s: from **HEP** + **CAT**[1].

He·phaes·tus /hi'festəs/ *Greek Mythology* the god of fire and of craftsmen, son of Zeus and Hera; husband of Aphrodite. He was a divine metalworker who was lame as the result of having interfered in a quarrel between his parents. Roman equivalent **VULCAN**.

Hep·ple·white /'hepəl,(h)wīt/, George (died 1786), English cabinetmaker and furniture designer. The posthumously published book of his designs, *The Cabinetmaker and Upholsterer's Guide* (1788), contains almost 300 designs.

hepta- ▸*comb. form* seven; having seven: *heptagon* | *heptathlon.* ▷from Greek *hepta* 'seven.'

hep·ta·chlor /'heptə,klôr/ ▸*n.* a chlorinated hydrocarbon used as an insecticide. • Chem. formula: $C_{10}H_5Cl_7$.

hep·tad /'hep,tad/ ▸*n. technical* a group or set of seven. ▷mid 17th cent.: from Greek *heptas, heptad-*, from *hepta* 'seven.'

hep·ta·gon /'heptə,gän/ ▸*n.* a plane figure with seven straight sides and angles. ▷late 16th cent.: from Greek *heptagōnon*, neuter (used as a noun) of *heptagōnos* 'seven-angled.' **—hep·tag·o·nal** /hep'tagənl/ *adj.*

hep·ta·he·dron /heptəhēdrən/ ▸*n.* (*pl.* **-he·drons** or **-he·dra** /-'hēdrə/) a solid figure with seven plane faces. ▷late 17th cent.: from **HEPTA-** 'seven' + **-HEDRON**, on the pattern of words such as *polyhedron.* **—hep·ta·he·dral** /-'hēdrəl/ *adj.*

hep·tam·er·ous /hep'tamərəs/ ▸*adj. Botany & Zoology* having parts arranged in groups of seven. ■ consisting of seven joints or parts.

hep·tam·e·ter /hep'tamitər/ ▸*n. Prosody* a line of verse consisting of seven metrical feet. ▷late 19th cent.: via late Latin from Greek *heptametron*, from *hepta-* 'seven' + *metron* 'measure.'

hep·tane /'hep,tān/ ▸*n. Chemistry* a colorless liquid hydrocarbon of the alkane series, obtained from petroleum. • Chem. formula: C_7H_{16}; several isomers, esp. the straight-chain isomer (***n*-heptane**). ▷late 19th cent.: from **HEPTA-** 'seven' (denoting seven carbon atoms) + **-ANE**[2].

hep·tar·chy /'hep,tärkē/ ▸*n.* (*pl.* **-chies**) a country or region consisting of seven smaller, autonomous regions. ■ the seven kingdoms of the Angles and the Saxons believed to have been established in Britain in the 7th–8th century. ■ government by seven rulers. ▷late 16th cent.: from **HEPTA-** 'seven' + Greek *arkhia* 'rule,' on the pattern of *tetrarchy.* **—hep·tar·chic** /hep'tärkik/ *adj.* **—hep·tar·chi·cal** /hep'tärkikəl/ *adj.*

Hep·ta·teuch /'heptə,t(y)o͞ok/ ▸*n.* the first seven books of the Bible (Genesis to Judges) collectively. ▷late 17th cent.: via late Latin from Greek *heptateukhos*, from *hepta* 'seven' + *teukhos* 'book, volume.'

hep·tath·lon /hep'taTH,län/ ▸*n.* a track and field event, in particular one for women, in which each competitor takes part in the same prescribed seven events (100-meter hurdles, high jump, shot put, 200-meter dash, long jump, javelin, and 800-meter run). ▷1970s: from **HEPTA-** 'seven' + Greek *athlon* 'contest,' on the pattern of words such as *decathlon.* **—hep·tath·lete** /-'taTHlēt/ *n.*

hep·ta·va·lent /'heptəvālənt/ ▸*adj. Chemistry* having a valence of seven.

hep·tyl /'heptəl/ ▸*n.* [as *adj.*] *Chemistry* of or denoting an alkyl radical $-C_7H_{15}$, derived from heptane.

Hep·worth /'hepwərTH/, Dame (Jocelyn) Barbara (1903–75), English sculptor. She worked in wood, stone, and bronze and is noted for her simple monumental works in landscape and architectural settings, including *The Family of Man* (nine-piece group, 1972).

her /hər/ ▸*pron.* [*third person singular*] **1** used as the object of a verb or preposition to refer to a female person or animal previously mentioned or easily identified: *she knew I hated her* | *I told Hannah I would wait for her.* Compare with **SHE**. ■ referring to a ship, country, or other inanimate thing regarded as female: *the crew tried to sail her through a narrow gap.* ■ often used in place of "she" after the verb "to be" and after "than" or "as" to refer to a female person or animal: *it must be her* | *he was younger than her.* See **usage** below. **2** *archaic* or *dialect* herself: *peevishly she flung her on her face.*

▸*possessive adj.* **1** belonging to or associated with a female person or animal previously mentioned or easily identified: *Patricia loved her job* | *how the mother crane treats her babies.* ■ belonging to or associated with a ship, country, or other inanimate thing regarded as female. **2** (**Her**) used in titles: *Her Royal Highness.* ▷Old English *hire*, genitive and dative of *hīo, hēo* 'she.'

USAGE On whether **her** or **she** is the correct pronoun in a comparative construction ("younger than her" or "younger than she"?), see **usage** at **PERSONAL PRONOUN** and **THAN**.

He·ra /'herə/ *Greek Mythology* a powerful goddess, the wife and sister of Zeus and the daughter of Cronus and Rhea. She was worshiped as the queen of heaven and as a marriage goddess. Roman equivalent **JUNO**. ▷from Greek *Hēra* 'lady,' feminine of *hērōs* 'hero,' perhaps used as a title.

Her·a·cles /'herəklēz/ (also **Her·a·kles**) Greek equivalent of **HERCULES**.

Her·a·cli·tus /,herə'klītəs/ (*c.*500 BC), Greek philosopher. He believed that fire is the origin of all things and that permanence is an illusion, everything being in a process of constant change.

He·rak·li·on /he'raklēən/ the capital of Crete, a port on the northern coast of the island; pop. 117,000. Greek name **IRÁKLION**.

her·ald /'herəld/ ▸*n.* **1** an official messenger bringing news. **2** a person or thing viewed as a sign that something is about to happen: *they considered the first*

H

primroses as the herald of spring. **3** *historical* an official employed to oversee state ceremony, precedence, and the use of armorial bearings, and to make proclamations, carry ceremonial messages, and oversee tournaments.

▸*v.* [*trans.*] be a sign that (something) is about to happen: *the speech heralded a change in policy.* ■ (usu. **be heralded**) acclaim: *the band **has been heralded as** the industrial supergroup of the '90s.* ▷Middle English: from Old French *herault* (noun), *herauder* (verb), of Germanic origin.

he·ral·dic /hə'raldik/ ▸*adj.* of or relating to heraldry. **—he·ral·di·cal·ly** /-ik(ə)lē/ *adv.*

her·ald·ry /'herəldrē/ ▸*n.* the system by which coats of arms and other armorial bearings are devised, described, and regulated. ■ armorial bearings or other heraldic symbols. ■ colorful ceremony: *all the pomp and heraldry provided a splendid pageant.* **—her·ald·ist** /'herəldist/ *n.*

Her·alds' Col·lege /'herəldz/ informal name for **College of Arms**.

He·rat /hə'rät; he-/ a city in western Afghanistan; pop. 177,000.

herb /(h)ərb/ ▸*n.* **1** any plant with leaves, seeds, or flowers used for flavoring, food, medicine, or perfume: *bundles of dried herbs* | [as *adj.*] *a formal herb garden.* ■ a part of such a plant as used in cooking: *a potato base topped with tomatoes, cheese, and herbs.* **2** *Botany* any seed-bearing plant that does not have a woody stem and dies down to the ground after flowering. ▷Middle English: via Old French from Latin *herba* 'grass, green crops, herb.' Although *herb* has always been spelled with an *h*, pronunciation without it was usual in British English until the 19th cent. and is still standard in the U.S.

her·ba·ceous /(h)ər'bāshəs/ ▸*adj.* of, denoting, or relating to herbs (in the botanical sense). ▷mid 17th cent.: from Latin *herbaceus* 'grassy' (from *herba* 'grass, herb') + **-ous**.

her·ba·ceous bor·der ▸*n.* a garden border containing herbaceous, typically perennial, flowering plants.

her·ba·ceous per·en·ni·al ▸*n.* a plant whose growth dies down annually but whose roots or other underground parts survive.

herb·age /'(h)ərbij/ ▸*n.* herbaceous vegetation. ■ the succulent part of this vegetation, used as pasture. ■ *historical* the right of pasture on another person's land. ▷late Middle English: from Old French *erbage*, based on Latin *herba* 'herb, grass, crops.'

herb·al /'(h)ərbəl/ ▸*adj.* relating to or made from herbs, esp. those used in cooking and medicine: *herbal remedies.*

▸*n.* a book that describes herbs and their culinary and medicinal properties. ▷early 16th cent. (as a noun): from medieval Latin *herbalis* (adjective), from Latin *herba* 'grass, herb.'

her·bal·ism /'(h)ərbə,lizəm/ ▸*n.* the study or practice of the medicinal and therapeutic use of plants, now esp. as a form of alternative medicine.

herb·al·ist /'(h)ərbəlist/ ▸*n.* a practitioner of herbalism. ■ a dealer in medicinal herbs. ■ an early botanical writer.

her·bar·i·um /(h)ər'be(ə)rēəm/ ▸*n.* (*pl.* **-bar·i·ums** or **-bar·i·a** /-'be(ə)rēə/) a systematically arranged collection of dried plants. ■ a room or building housing such a collection. ■ a box, cabinet, or other receptacle in which dried plants are kept. ▷late 18th cent.: from late Latin, from Latin *herba* 'grass, herb.'

herb·a·ry /'(h)ərbərē/ ▸*n.* (*pl.* **-ries**) *archaic* an herb garden.

herbed /(h)ərbd/ ▸*adj.* (of food) cooked, flavored, or seasoned with herbs.

Her·bert[1] /'hərbərt/ George (1593–1633), English metaphysical poet and clergyman. His poems, collected in *The Temple,* express a sweet and trusting friendliness with God.

Her·bert [2] /'hərbərt/, Victor (1859–1924) U.S. composer, conductor, and cellist; born in Ireland. Among his light operas, or operettas, are included *Babes in Toyland* (1903) and *Naughty Marietta* (1910). He conducted the Pittsburgh Symphony 1889–1904.

herb·i·cide /'(h)ərbə,sīd/ ▸*n.* a substance that is toxic to plants and is used to destroy unwanted vegetation.

her·bi·vore /'(h)ərbə,vôr/ ▸*n.* an animal that feeds on plants. ▷mid 19th cent.: from Latin *herba* 'herb' + *-vore* (see **-vorous**). **—her·biv·o·rous** /(h)ər'biv(ə)rəs/ *adj.*

her·biv·o·ry /(h)ə'bivərē/ ▸*n.* the eating of plants, especially ones that are still living: *in response to herbivory, plants defend themselves with arrays of structural and chemical weapons.* ▷mid 20th cent.: from *herbivor(ous)* + *-y*.

herb Par·is ▸*n.* a European woodland plant of the lily family, with a single unbranched stem bearing a green and purple flower above four unstalked leaves. • *Paris quadrifolia*, family Liliaceae (or Trilliaceae). ▷translating medieval Latin *herba paris*, probably literally 'herb of a pair,' referring to the resemblance of the four leaves to a true-love knot.

herb Rob·ert ▸*n.* a common cranesbill with pungent-smelling red-stemmed leaves and pink flowers, native to north temperate regions. • *Geranium robertianum*, family Geraniaceae. ▷translating medieval Latin *herba Roberti*, variously supposed to refer to *Robert* Duke of Normandy, St. *Robert*, or St. Rupert.

herb·y /'(h)ərbē/ ▸*adj.* (**herb·i·er**, **herb·i·est**) (of food or drink) containing or tasting or smelling of herbs.

Her·ce·go·vi·na variant spelling of **Herzegovina**.

Her·cu·la·ne·um /,hərkyə'lānēəm/ an ancient Roman town, near Naples, on the lower slopes of Mount Vesuvius. The volcano's eruption in AD 79 buried it, along with Pompeii, deeply under volcanic ash and thus largely preserved it until its accidental rediscovery by a well-digger in 1709.

Her·cu·le·an /,hərkyə'lēən; hər'kyo͞olēən/ ▸*adj.* requiring great strength or effort: *a Herculean task.* ■ (of a person) muscular and strong. ▷late 16th cent. (in the sense 'relating to Hercules'): from Latin *Herculeus* 'Hercules' + **-an**.

Her·cu·les /'hərkyə,lēz/ **1** *Greek & Roman Mythology* a hero of superhuman strength and courage who performed twelve immense tasks or "labors" imposed on him and who after death was ranked among the gods. Greek name **Heracles** or **Herakles**. ■ [as *n.*] (**a Hercules**) a man of exceptional strength or size. **2** *Astronomy* a large northern constellation, said to represent the kneeling figure of Hercules. It contains the brightest globular cluster in the northern hemisphere, but no bright stars. ■ [as *genitive*] (**Herculis**) used with a preceding letter or numeral to designate a star in this constellation: *the star Delta Herculis.* ▷Latin, from Greek *Hēraklēs*.

Her·cu·les bee·tle ▸*n.* a large tropical American rhinoceros beetle, the male of which has two long curved horns extending from the head and one from the thorax. • Genus *Dynastes*, family Scarabaeidae: several species, including the **eastern Hercules beetle** (*D. tityus*) of the southeastern U.S.

Her·cu·les-club ▸*n.* either of two tall prickly shrubs or small trees of the U.S.: • the **southern prickly-ash** (*Zanthoxylum clava-herculis*, family Rutaceae), a tree of the rue family with knobby, corky protrusions on its trunk. • the **devil's walking stick** (*Aralia spinosa*, family Araliaceae), a tree of the ginseng family, with large leaves and black berries. Also called **angelica tree**.

Her·cy·ni·an /hər'sinēən/ ▸*adj. Geology* of, relating to, or denoting a prolonged mountain-forming period (orogeny) in western Europe, eastern North America, and the Andes in the Upper Paleozoic era, esp. the Carboniferous and Permian periods. ■ [as *n.*] (**the Hercynian**) the Hercynian orogeny. ▷late 16th cent.: from Latin *Hercynia silva*; originally used by the ancient writers to designate an area of forested mountains in central Germany; later (from the late 19th cent.) applied in geology to the Harz Mountains formed in the Hercynian period.

herd /hərd/ ▸*n.* a large group of animals, esp. hoofed mammals, that live, feed, or migrate together or are kept together as livestock: ***a herd of** elephants* | *large farms with big dairy herds.* ■ *derogatory* a large group of people, typically with a shared characteristic: *I dodged **herds of** joggers and cyclists* | *he is not of **the common herd**.*

▸*v.* [with *adverbial of direction*] move in a particular direction: [*trans.*] *Nick herded me through the baggage claim and into his Jaguar* | [*intrans.*] *we all herded into a storage room.* ■ [*trans.*] keep or look after (livestock): *Hunter and Tripp herded sheep.* ▷Old English *heord*, of Germanic origin; related to German *Herde*.

herd·boy /'hərd,boi/ ▸*n.* a boy who looks after a herd of livestock.

herd·er /'hərdər/ ▸*n.* a person who looks after a herd of livestock or makes a living from keeping livestock, esp. in open country.

herd im·mu·ni·ty ▸*n.* general immunity to a pathogen in a population based on the acquired immunity to it by a high proportion of members over time.

herd in·stinct ▸*n.* an inclination in people or animals to behave or think like the majority.

herds·man /'hərdzmən/ ▸*n.* (*pl.* **-men**) the owner or keeper of a herd of domesticated animals. ■ (**the Herdsman**) the constellation Boötes.

here /hi(ə)r/ ▸*adv.* **1** in, at, or to this place or position: *they have lived here most of their lives* | *come here and let me look at them* | [after *prep.*] *I'm getting out of here* | *it's too hot in here.* ■ used when pointing or gesturing to indicate the place in mind: *sign here* | *I have here a letter from the chief of police.* ■ used to draw attention to someone or something that has just arrived: ***here's** my brother* | ***here comes** the bus.* ■ [with *infinitive*] used to indicate one's role in a particular situation: *I'm here to help you* | *we're not here to mess around.* ■ used to refer to existence in the world in general: *what are we all doing here?* **2** (usu. **here is/are**) used when introducing something or someone: *here's a dish that is simple and quick to make* | *here's what you have to do.* ■ used when giving something to someone: *here's the money I promised you* | *here is my address.* **3** used when indicating a time or situation that has arrived or is happening: *here is your opportunity* | *here comes summer.* ■ used to refer to a particular point or aspect reached in an argument, situation, or activity: *here lies the key to the recovery* | *here we encounter the main problem.*

▸*exclam.* **1** used to attract someone's attention: *here, let me hold it.* **2** indicating one's presence in a roll call. ▷Old English *hēr*, of Germanic origin; related to Dutch and German *hier*, also to **he**.

▸*PHRASES* □ **here and now** at this very moment; at the present time: *we're going to settle this here and now* | [as *n.*] *our obsession with **the here and now**.* □ **here and there** in various places: *small bushes scattered here and there.* □ **here goes** an expression indicating that one is about to start something difficult or exciting. □ **here's to someone/something** used to wish health or success before drinking: *here's to us!* | *here's to your safe arrival.* □ **here today, gone tomorrow** soon over or forgotten; short-lived. □ **here we are** said on arrival at one's destination. □ **here we go again** said to indicate that the same events, typically undesirable ones, are recurring. □ **neither here nor there** of no importance or relevance.

here·a·bouts /'hirə,bouts/ (also **here·a·bout**) ▸*adv.* near this place: *there is little natural water hereabouts.*

here·af·ter /hi(ə)r'aftər/ ▸*adv. formal* from now on: *nothing I say hereafter is intended to relate to the second decision.* ■ at some time in the future: *this court is in no way prejudging any such defense which may hereafter be raised.* ■ after death: *a sermon about hope of life hereafter.*

▸*n.* (**the hereafter**) life after death: *suffering is part of our preparation for the hereafter.*

here·at /,hi(ə)r'at/ ▸*adv. archaic* as a result of this: *greatly distressed hereat, they declared themselves to deserve a fine.*

here·by /,hi(ə)r'bī; 'hi(ə)r,bī/ ▸*adv. formal* as a result of this document or utterance: *the Port Authority hereby solicits proposals from developers.*

he·red·i·ta·ble /hə'reditəbəl/ ▸*adj.* less common term for **heritable**. ▷late Middle English: from Old French, or from medieval Latin *hereditabilis*, from ecclesiastical Latin *hereditare* 'inherit,' from Latin *heres, hered-* 'heir.'

her·e·dit·a·ment /,herə'ditəmənt/ ▸*n. dated Law* any item of property, either a **corporeal hereditament** (such as land or a building) or an **incorporeal hereditament** (such as a rent or a right of way). ■ an item of inheritance. ▷late Middle English: from medieval Latin *hereditamentum*, from ecclesiastical Latin *hereditare* 'inherit,' from Latin *heres, hered-* 'heir.'

he·red·i·tar·i·an /hə,redi'te(ə)rēən/ ▸*adj.* of or relating to the theory that heredity is the primary influence on human behavior, intelligence, or other characteristics.

▸*n.* an advocate of such a view. **—he·red·i·tar·i·an·ism** /-ə,nizəm/ *n.*

he·red·i·tar·y /hə'redi,terē/ ▸*adj.* (of a title, office, or right) conferred by or based on inheritance: *members of the ancient Polish aristocracy who had hereditary right to elect the king.* ■ [*attrib.*] (of a person) holding a position by inheritance: *I am the hereditary chief of the Piscataway people.* ■ (of a characteristic or disease) determined by genetic factors and therefore able to be passed on from parents to their offspring or descendants: *cystic fibrosis is our most common fatal hereditary disease.* ■ of or relating to inheritance: *a form of hereditary succession and dynastic rule became standard practice.* ■ *Mathematics* (of a set) defined such that every element that has a given relation to a member of the set is also a member of the set. ▷late Middle English: from Latin *hereditarius*, from *hereditas* (see HEREDITY). —**he·red·i·tar·i·ly** /hə,redi'te(ə)rəlē/ *adv.* —**he·red·i·tar·i·ness** /hə,redi'te(ə)rēnis/ *n.*

he·red·i·ty /hə'reditē/ ▶*n.* **1** the passing on of physical or mental characteristics genetically from one generation to another: *few scientists dispute that heredity can create a susceptibility to alcoholism.* ■ a person's ancestry: *he wears a Cossack tunic to emphasize his Russian heredity.* **2** inheritance of title, office, or right: *membership is largely based on heredity.* ▷late 18th cent.: from French *hérédité*, from Latin *hereditas* 'heirship,' from *heres, hered-* 'heir.'

Her·e·ford /'hərfərd; 'herə-/ ▶*n.* an animal of a breed of red and white beef cattle. ▷early 19th cent.: named after *Hereford*, England, where it originated.

here·in /,hi(ə)r'in/ ▶*adv. formal* in this document or book: *the author herein recounts his travel adventures.* ■ in this matter; arising from this: *the statues are sensual to the point of erotic and herein lies their interest.*

here·in·af·ter /,hi(ə)rin'aftər/ ▶*adv. formal* further on in this document: *grievous bodily harm (hereinafter GBH).*

here·in·be·fore /,hi(ə)rinbi'fôr/ ▶*adv. formal* before this point in this document.

here·of /,hi(ə)r'əv/ ▶*adv. formal* of this document: *in accordance with section 17 hereof.*

He·re·ro /hə're(ə)rō/ ▶*n.* (*pl.* same or **-ros**) **1** a member of a people living in Namibia, Angola, and Botswana. **2** the Bantu language of this people.
▶*adj.* of or relating to the Herero or their language. ▷a local name, from *Otshi-Herero*, the Herero word for the language.

he·re·si·arch /hə'rēzē,ärk; 'herəsē-/ ▶*n.* the founder of a heresy or the leader of a heretical sect. ▷mid 16th cent.: via ecclesiastical Latin from ecclesiastical Greek *hairesiarkhēs* 'leader of a sect,' from *hairesis* 'heretical sect, heresy' + *arkhēs* 'ruler.'

her·e·sy /'herəsē/ ▶*n.* (*pl.* **-sies**) belief or opinion contrary to orthodox religious (esp. Christian) doctrine: *Huss was burned for heresy | the doctrine was denounced as a heresy by the pope.* ■ opinion profoundly at odds with what is generally accepted: *cutting capital gains taxes is heresy | the politician's heresies became the conventional wisdom of the day.* ▷Middle English: from Old French *heresie*, based on Latin *haeresis*, from Greek *hairesis* 'choice' (in ecclesiastical Greek 'heretical sect'), from *haireisthai* 'choose.'

her·e·tic /'herətik/ ▶*n.* a person believing in or practicing religious heresy. ■ a person holding an opinion at odds with what is generally accepted. ▷Middle English: from Old French *heretique*, via ecclesiastical Latin from Greek *hairetikos* 'able to choose' (in ecclesiastical Greek, 'heretical'), from *haireisthai* 'choose.' —**he·ret·i·cal** /hə'retikəl/ *adj.* —**he·ret·i·cal·ly** *adv.*

here·to /,hi(ə)r'to͞o/ ▶*adv. formal* to this matter or document: *the written consent of each of the parties hereto | hereto is appended an estimate of the cost.*

here·to·fore /'hi(ə)rtə,fôr/ ▶*adv. formal* before now: *diseases that heretofore were usually confined to rural areas.*

here·un·der /,hi(ə)r'əndər/ ▶*adv. formal* as provided for under the terms of this document: *all expenses incurred hereunder by the bank shall be recoverable.* ■ further on in a document.

here·un·to /hi(ə)r'ən,to͞o; 'hi(ə)r,ən'to͞o/ ▶*adv. archaic* or *formal* to this document: *signed in the presence of us both who have hereunto subscribed our names as witnesses.*

here·up·on /,hi(ə)rə'pän/ ▶*adv.* after or as a result of this.

here·with /,hir'wiTH; -'wiTH/ ▶*adv. formal* with this letter: *I send you herewith fifteen dollars.*

her·i·ot /'hereēət/ ▶*n. Brit., historical* a tribute paid to a lord out of the belongings of a tenant who died, often consisting of a live animal or, originally, military equipment that he had been lent during his lifetime. ▷Old English *heregeatwa*, from *here* 'army' + *geatwa* 'trappings.'

her·it·a·ble /'heritəbəl/ ▶*adj.* able to be inherited, in particular: ■ *Biology* (of a characteristic) transmissible from parent to offspring. ■ *Law* (of property) capable of being inherited by heirs-at-law. Compare with MOVABLE (sense 2). ▷late Middle English: from Old French *heriter* 'inherit,' from ecclesiastical Latin *hereditare*, from Latin *heres, hered-* 'heir.' —**her·it·a·bil·i·ty** /,heritə'bilitē/ *n.* —**her·it·a·bly** /-blē/ *adv.*

her·it·age /'heritij/ ▶*n.* [in *sing.*] **1** property that is or may be inherited; an inheritance. ■ valued objects and qualities such as cultural traditions, unspoiled countryside, and historic buildings that have been passed down from previous generations: *the richness of our diverse cultural heritage | a sense of history and heritage.* ■ [as *adj.*] (of a plant variety) not hybridized with another; old-fashioned: *heritage roses.* **2** *archaic* a special or individual possession; an allotted portion. ■ God's chosen people (the people of Israel, or the Christian Church). ▷Middle English: from Old French *heritage*, from *heriter* 'inherit' (see HERITABLE).

her·i·tor /'heritər/ ▶*n.* a person who inherits. ▷late Middle English: from Anglo-Norman French *heriter*, based on Latin *hereditarius* (see HEREDITARY). The spelling change in the 16th cent. was by association with words ending in -OR[1].

herk·y-jerk·y /'hərkē 'jərkē/ ▶*adj. informal* characterized by or moving in sudden stops and starts: *there were no windup toys, no herky-jerky contraptions.* ▷late 20th cent.: reduplication of JERKY[1].

herl /hərl/ ▶*n.* a barb or filament of a feather used in dressing a fishing fly. ▷late Middle English: apparently of Germanic origin and related to Middle Low German *harle*.

herm /hərm/ ▶*n.* a squared stone pillar with a carved head on top (typically of Hermes), used in ancient Greece as a boundary marker or a signpost. ▷from the Greek name HERMES.

Her·man /'hərmən/, Woody (1913–87), U.S. jazz clarinetist, saxophonist, and bandleader; full name *Woodrow Charles Herman*; known as **the Boy Wonder of the Clarinet**. He led several big bands that were all called Thundering Herds and became known for the song "Woodchoppers' Ball" (1939). "Ebony Concerto" was written for him by Stravinsky and first performed at Carnegie Hall in 1946.

her·maph·ro·dite /hər'mafrədit/ ▶*n.* a person or animal having both male and female sex organs or other sexual characteristics, either abnormally or (in the case of some organisms) as the natural condition. ■ *Botany* a plant having stamens and pistils in the same flower. ■ *archaic* a person or thing combining opposite qualities or characteristics.
▶*adj.* of or denoting a person, animal, or plant of this kind: *hermaphrodite creatures in classical sculpture.* ▷late Middle English: via Latin from Greek *hermaphroditos* (see HERMAPHRODITUS). —**her·maph·ro·dit·ic** /-,mafrə'ditik/ *adj.* —**her·maph·ro·dit·i·cal** /-,mafrə'ditikəl/ *adj.* —**her·maph·ro·dit·ism** /hər'mafrədi,tizəm/ (or **her·maph·ro·dism** /-,dizəm/) *n.*

her·maph·ro·dite brig ▶*n.* a two-masted sailing ship with a square-rigged foremast and, on the mainmast, a square topsail above a fore-and-aft gaff mainsail.

Her·maph·ro·dit·us /hər,mafrə'dītəs/ *Greek Mythology* a son of Hermes and Aphrodite, with whom the nymph Salmacis fell in love and prayed to be forever united. As a result Hermaphroditus and Salmacis became joined in a single body that retained characteristics of both sexes.

her·me·neu·tic /,hərmə'n(y)o͞otik/ ▶*adj.* concerning interpretation, esp. of the Bible or literary texts.
▶*n.* a method or theory of interpretation. ▷late 17th cent.: from Greek *hermēneutikos*, from *hermēneuein* 'interpret.' —**her·me·neu·ti·cal** *adj.* —**her·me·neu·ti·cal·ly** /-(ə)lē/ *adv.*

her·me·neu·tics /,hərmə'n(y)o͞otiks/ ▶*plural n.* [usu. treated as *sing.*] the branch of knowledge that deals with interpretation, esp. of the Bible or literary texts.

Her·mes /'hərmēz/ *Greek Mythology* the son of Zeus and Maia, the messenger of the gods, and god of merchants, thieves, and oratory. He was portrayed as a herald equipped for traveling, with broad-brimmed hat, winged shoes, and a winged rod. Roman equivalent MERCURY. ▷probably from Greek *herma* 'heap of stones': from early times he was represented by a carved stock or stone and was identified with THOTH.

Her·mes Tris·me·gis·tus /,trismə'jistəs/ a legendary figure regarded by Neoplatonists and others as the author of certain works on astrology, magic, and alchemy. ▷Latin, 'thrice-greatest Hermes,' in reference to THOTH, identified with HERMES.

her·met·ic /hər'metik/ ▶*adj.* **1** (of a seal or closure) complete and airtight: *a hermetic seal that ensures perfect waterproofing.* ■ insulated or protected from outside influences: *a hermetic society.* **2** (also **Her·met·ic**) of or relating to an ancient occult tradition encompassing alchemy, astrology, and theosophy. ■ esoteric; cryptic: *obscure and hermetic poems.* ▷mid 17th cent. (sense 2): from modern Latin *hermeticus*, from HERMES, identified with THOTH, regarded as the founder of alchemy and astrology. —**her·met·i·cal·ly** /hər'metiklē; -ik(ə)lē/ *adv.* —**her·met·i·cism** /hər'meti,sizəm/ *n.*

her·mit /'hərmit/ ▶*n.* **1** a person living in solitude as a religious discipline. ■ any person living in solitude or seeking to do so. **2** a hummingbird found in the shady lower layers of tropical forests, foraging along a regular route. • *Phaethornis* and other genera, family Trochilidae: several species. ▷Middle English: from Old French *hermite*, from late Latin *eremita*, from Greek *erēmitēs*, from *erēmos* 'solitary.' —**her·mit·ic** /hər'mitik/ *adj.*

her·mit·age /'hərmitij/ ▶*n.* **1** the dwelling of a hermit, esp. when small and remote. **2** (**the Hermitage**) /,ermi'täZH/ a major art museum in St. Petersburg, Russia, containing among its collections those begun by Catherine the Great. [named with reference to the "retreat" in which the empress displayed her treasures to her friends.] **3** (**the Hermitage**) /'hərmitij/ an estate, the home of Andrew Jackson, in central Tennessee, northeast of Nashville. ▷Middle English: from Old French, from *hermite* (see HERMIT).

her·mit crab ▶*n.* a crab with a soft asymmetrical abdomen that lives in a castoff mollusk shell for protection. In several kinds, the shell becomes covered with sponges, sea anemones, or bryozoans. • Superfamily Paguroidea.

Her·mi·tian /hər'misHən/ ▶*adj. Mathematics* denoting or relating to a matrix in which those pairs of elements that are symmetrically placed with respect to the principal diagonal are complex conjugates. ▷early 20th cent.: from the name of Charles *Hermite* (1822–1905), French mathematician, + -IAN.

her·mit thrush ▶*n.* a small migratory North American thrush, noted for its melodious song. • *Catharus guttatus*, subfamily Turdinae, family Muscicapidae.

hermit thrush

Her·mo·sil·lo /,ermō'sē(y)ō/ a city in northwestern Mexico, capital of the state of Sonora; pop. 449,000.

her·ni·a /'hərnēə/ ▶*n.* (*pl.* **-ni·as** or **-ni·ae** /-nē,ē/) a condition in which part of an organ is displaced and protrudes through the wall of the cavity containing it (often involving the intestine at a weak point in the abdominal wall). ▷late Middle English: from Latin. —**her·ni·al** *adj.*

her·ni·ate /'hərnē,āt/ ▶*v.* [*intrans.*] [usu. as *adj.*] (**herniated**) (of an organ) suffer a hernia: *a herniated bowel.* —**her·ni·a·tion** /hərnē'āsHən/ *n.*

He·ro[1] /'hi(ə)rō/ *Greek Mythology* a priestess of Aphrodite at Sestos on the European shore of the Hellespont, whose lover Leander, a youth of Abydos on the opposite shore, swam the strait nightly to visit her. One stormy night he was drowned, and Hero in grief threw herself into the sea.

He·ro[2] /'hi(ə)rō; 'hē,rō/ (1st century), Greek mathematician and inventor; known as **Hero of Alexandria**. He described a number of hydraulic, pneumatic, and other mechanical devices, including elementary applications of the power of steam.

he·ro /'hi(ə)rō/ ▶*n.* (*pl.* **-roes**) a person, typically a man, who is admired or idealized for courage, outstanding achievements, or noble qualities: *a war hero.* ■ the chief male character in a book, play, or movie, who is typically identified with good qualities, and with whom the reader is expected to sympathize. ■ (in mythology and folklore) a person of superhuman qualities and often semidivine origin, in particular one of those whose exploits and dealings with the gods were the subject of ancient Greek myths and legends. ■ (also **hero sandwich**) another term for SUBMARINE SANDWICH. ▷Middle English (with mythological reference): via Latin from Greek *hērōs*.

Her·od /'herəd/ the name of four rulers of ancient Palestine: ■ **Herod the Great** (*c.*74–4 BC), ruled 37–4 BC. According to the New Testament, Jesus was born during his reign, and he ordered the massacre of the innocents (Matt. 2:16). ■ **Herod Antipas** (22 BC–*c.*AD 40), son of Herod the Great, tetrarch of Galilee and Peraea 4 BC–AD 40. He married Herodias and was responsible for the beheading of John the Baptist. According to the New Testament (Luke 23:7), Pilate sent Jesus to be questioned by him before the Crucifixion. ■ **Herod Agrippa I**

Pronunciation Key ə *ago*; ər *over*; 'ə or ,ə *up*; 'ər or ,ər *fur*; a *hat*; ā *rate*; ä *car*; CH *chew*; e *let*; ē *see*; e(ə)r *air*; i *fit*; ī *by*; i(ə)r *ear*; NG *sing*; ō *go*; ô *for*; oi *boy*; o͝o *good*; o͞o *goo*; ou *out*; SH *she*; TH *thin*; TH *then*; (h)w *why*; ZH *vision*

(10 BC–AD 44), grandson of Herod the Great; king of Judaea AD 41–44. He imprisoned St. Peter and put St. James the Great to death. ■ **Herod Agrippa II** (AD 27–*c.*93), son of Herod Agrippa I; king of various territories in northern Palestine 50–*c.*93. He presided over the trial of St. Paul (Acts 25:13 ff.). —**He·ro·di·an** /hə'rōdēən/ *adj.* & *n.*

He·rod·o·tus /hə'rädətəs/ (5th century BC), Greek historian. Known as "the Father of History," he was the first historian to collect his materials systematically, test their accuracy to a certain extent, and arrange them in a well-constructed and vivid narrative.

he·ro·ic /hə'rōik/ ▸*adj.* having the characteristics of a hero or heroine; very brave: *heroic deeds | a few heroic individuals.* ■ of or representing heroes or heroines: *early medieval heroic poetry.* ■ (of language or a work of art) grand or grandiose in scale or intention: *one passes under pyramids and obelisks, all on a heroic scale.* ■ *Sculpture* (of a statue) larger than life-size but less than colossal.
▸*n.* (**heroics**) **1** behavior or talk that is bold or dramatic, esp. excessively or unexpectedly so: *the makeshift team performed heroics.* **2** short for HEROIC VERSE. ▷late Middle English: from Old French *heroique* or Latin *heroicus*, from Greek *hērōikos* 'relating to heroes,' from *hērōs* 'hero.' —**he·ro·i·cal·ly** /-ik(ə)lē/ *adv.*

he·ro·ic cou·plet ▸*n.* (in verse) a pair of rhyming iambic pentameters, much used by Chaucer and the poets of the 17th and 18th centuries such as Alexander Pope.

he·ro·ic stan·za ▸*n.* a rhyming quatrain in heroic verse. Also called **heroic quatrain**. ■ (in English poetry) a quatrain in iambic pentameter rhyming *abab* or *abba*. Compare with ELEGIAC STANZA.

he·ro·ic verse ▸*n.* a type of verse used for epic or heroic subjects, such as the dactylic hexameter, iambic pentameter, or alexandrine. Also called **heroic meter**.

her·o·in /'herō-in/ ▸*n.* a highly addictive analgesic drug derived from morphine, often used illicitly as a narcotic producing euphoria. • Alternative name: **diacetylmorphine**; chem. formula: $C_{17}H_{17}NO(C_2H_3O_2)_2$. ▷late 19th cent.: from German *Heroin*, from Latin *heros* 'hero' (because of its effects on the user's self-esteem).

her·o·ine /'herō-in/ ▸*n.* a woman admired or idealized for her courage, outstanding achievements, or noble qualities: *she was the heroine of a materialist generation.* ■ the chief female character in a book, play, or movie, who is typically identified with good qualities, and with whom the reader is expected to sympathize. ■ (in mythology and folklore) a woman of superhuman qualities and often semidivine origin, in particular one whose dealings with the gods were the subject of ancient Greek myths and legends. ▷mid 17th cent. (in the sense 'demigoddess, venerated woman'): from French *héroïne* or Latin *heroina*, from Greek *hērōinē*, feminine of *hērōs* 'hero.'

her·o·ism /'herō,izəm/ ▸*n.* great bravery. ▷early 18th cent.: from French *héroïsme*, from *héros*, from Latin *heros* (see HERO).

her·o·ize /'hi(ə)rō,īz/ ▸*v.* [*trans.*] (often **be heroized**) treat or represent as a hero: *the father is heroized for long forbearance.*

her·on /'herən/ ▸*n.* a large fish-eating wading bird with long legs, a long S-shaped neck, and a long pointed bill. • Family Ardeidae (the **heron family**): several genera and numerous species, including the **great blue heron** (*Ardea herodias*). ▷Middle English: from Old French, of Germanic origin.

great blue heron

her·on·ry /'herənrē/ ▸*n.* (*pl.* **-ries**) a breeding colony of herons, typically in a group of trees.

He·roph·i·lus /hə'räfələs/ (4th–3rd centuries BC), Greek anatomist. He is considered the father of human anatomy for his fundamental discoveries concerning the anatomy of the brain, eye, and reproductive organs.

he·ro's wel·come ▸*n.* an enthusiastic welcome for someone who has done something brave or praiseworthy.

he·ro-wor·ship ▸*n.* excessive admiration for someone. ■ (in ancient Greece) the worship of superhuman heroes.
▸*v.* [*trans.*] admire (someone) excessively. —**he·ro-wor·ship·er** *n.*

herp /hərp/ ▸*n.* short for HERPTILE.

her·pes /'hərpēz/ ▸*n.* any of a group of viral diseases caused by herpes viruses, affecting the skin (often with blisters) or the nervous system. ▷late Middle English (originally used also of other skin conditions): via Latin from Greek *herpēs* 'shingles,' literally 'creeping,' from *herpein* 'to creep.' —**her·pet·ic** /hər'petik/ *adj.*

her·pes sim·plex ▸*n.* a viral infection, caused by a group of herpes viruses, that may produce cold sores, genital inflammation, or conjunctivitis.

her·pes·vi·rus /'hərpēz,vīrəs/ ▸*n.* *Medicine* any of a group of DNA viruses causing herpes and other diseases.

her·pes zos·ter /'zästər/ ▸*n.* medical name for SHINGLES. ■ a herpesvirus that causes shingles and chicken pox. ▷late Middle English: from HERPES and Latin *zoster*, from Greek *zōstēr* 'girdle, shingles.'

her·pe·to·fau·na /'hərpitō,fônə/ ▸*n.* *Zoology* the reptiles and amphibians of a particular region, habitat, or geological period. ▷modern Latin, from Greek *herpeton* 'creeping thing, reptile' + FAUNA. —**her·pe·to·fau·nal** /-fônəl/ *adj.*

her·pe·tol·o·gy /,hərpə'täləjē/ ▸*n.* the branch of zoology concerned with reptiles and amphibians. ▷early 19th cent.: from Greek *herpeton* 'reptile' (from *herpein* 'to creep') + -LOGY. —**her·pe·to·log·i·cal** /-tə'läjəkəl/ *adj.* —**her·pe·tol·o·gist** /-jist/ *n.*

herp·tile /,hərp'tīl/ ▸*n.* a reptile or amphibian. ▷blend of HERPETOLOGY and REPTILE.

Herr /he(ə)r/ ▸*n.* (*pl.* **Herr·en** /'he(ə)rən/) a title or form of address used of or to a German-speaking man, corresponding to *Mr.* and also used before a rank or occupation: *good morning, Herr Weber | my trip with the Herr Doktor was postponed.* ■ a German man. ▷German, from Old High German *hērro*, comparative of *hēr* 'exalted.'

Her·ren·volk /'herən,fōk; -,fōlk/ ▸*n.* the German nation as considered by the Nazis to be innately superior to others. ▷mid 20th cent.: German, 'master race,' from *Herr* 'master' + *Volk* 'people, folk.'

her·ring /'heriNG/ ▸*n.* a silvery fish that is most abundant in coastal waters and is of great commercial importance as a food fish in many parts of the world. • *Clupea* and other genera, family Clupeidae (the **herring family**): several species, in particular (*C. harengus*), of the North Atlantic. The herring family also includes the sprats, shads, and pilchards. ▷Old English *hǣring*, *hēring*; related to Dutch *haring* and German *Hering*.

her·ring·bone /'heriNG,bōn/ ▸*n.* [usu. as *adj.*] **1** an arrangement or design consisting of columns of short parallel lines, with all the lines in one column sloping one way and all the lines in the next column sloping the other way so as to resemble the bones in a fish, used esp. in the weave of cloth or the placing of bricks: *a brown wool herringbone jacket.* ■ (also **herringbone stitch**) a cross-stitch with a pattern resembling such an arrangement, used in embroidery or for securing an edge. **2** *Skiing* a method of ascending a slope by walking forward in alternate steps with each ski angled outward.
▸*v.* **1** [*trans.*] mark with a herringbone pattern. ■ work with a herringbone stitch. **2** [*intrans.*] *Skiing* ascend a slope using the herringbone technique: *we learned how to herringbone up the hills and swoosh down them.*

herringbone 1

her·ring gull ▸*n.* a gull with gray black-tipped wings, abundant and widespread in both Eurasia and North America. • *Larus argentatus*, family Laridae.

Her·ri·ot /'herēət/, James (1916–1995), English short-story writer and veterinary surgeon; pseudonym of *James Alfred Wight*. His experiences as a veterinarian inspired a series of stories including *All Creatures Great and Small* (1972).

Herrn·hut·er /'he(ə)rn,hōōtər/ ▸*n.* a member of a Moravian Church. ▷mid 18th cent.: German, from *Herrnhut* (literally 'the Lord's keeping'), the name of the first German settlement of the Moravian Church.

hers /hərz/ ▸*possessive pron.* used to refer to a thing or things belonging to or associated with a female person or animal previously mentioned: *his eyes met hers | the choice was hers | friends of hers warned her.*

Her·schel /'hərSHəl/, Sir (Frederick) William (1738–1822), English astronomer; born in Germany. His cataloguing of the skies resulted in the discovery of the planet Uranus.

her·self /hər'self/ ▸*pron.* [*third person singular*] **1** [*reflexive*] used as the object of a verb or preposition to refer to a female person or animal previously mentioned as the subject of the clause: *she had to defend herself | Jo made herself a cup of tea.* **2** [*emphatic*] she or her personally (used to emphasize a particular female person or animal mentioned): *she told me herself.* ▷Old English (see HER, SELF).
▸*PHRASES* □ (**not**) **be herself** see BE ONESELF, NOT BE ONESELF at BE. □ **by herself** see BY ONESELF at BY.

Her·sey /'hərsē/, John Richard (1914–93) U.S. writer; born in China of U.S. missionary parents. Among his works are *A Bell for Adano* (1944) and *Hiroshima* (1946).

Her·shey[1] /'hərSHē/ a village in southeastern Pennsylvania, created by chocolate manufacturer Milton Hershey (1857–1945); pop. 11,860.

Her·shey[2], Alfred D. see DELBRÜCK.

her·sto·ry /'hərstərē/ ▸*n.* (*pl.* **-ries**) history viewed from a female or specifically feminist perspective. ▷1970s: from HER + STORY[1], analogous formation based on the form *history*.

Hertz /hərts/, Heinrich Rudolf (1857–94), German physicist and pioneer in radio communication. He continued the work of Maxwell on electromagnetic waves and was the first to broadcast and receive radio waves.

hertz /hərts/ (abbr.: **Hz**) ▸*n.* (*pl.* same) the SI unit of frequency, equal to one cycle per second. ▷late 19th cent.: named after H. R. HERTZ.

Hertz·i·an wave /'hərtsēən/ ▸*n.* former term for RADIO WAVE.

Hertz·sprung–Rus·sell di·a·gram /'herts,sprōōNG 'rəsəl/ ▸*n.* *Astronomy* a two-dimensional graph, devised independently by Ejnar Hertzsprung (1873–1967) and Henry Norris Russell (1877–1957), in which the absolute magnitudes of stars are plotted against their spectral types. Stars are found to occupy only certain regions of such a diagram.

He·rut /KHe'rōōt; he-/ a right-wing Israeli political party founded by Menachem Begin in 1948 from the remains of the Irgun group and one of the parties that combined to form the Likud coalition in 1973. ▷Hebrew, 'freedom.'

Her·ze·go·vi·na /,hərtsə'gōvənə; ,hert-; -gō'vēnə/ (also **Her·ce·go·vi·na**) a region in the Balkans that forms the southern part of Bosnia–Herzegovina and is separated from the Adriatic Sea by part of Croatia. Its chief town is Mostar. —**Her·ze·go·vi·ni·an** /-gō'vinēən; -gō'vēnēən/ *adj.* & *n.*

Her·zl /'hərtsəl/, Theodor (1860–1904), Hungarian journalist, playwright, and Zionist leader. The founder of the Zionist movement in 1897, he worked for most of his life as a writer and journalist in Vienna.

he's /hēz/ ▸*contraction of* ■ he is: *he's going to speak.* ■ he has: *he's given up his job.*

Hesh·van /'KHeSHvän; 'heSHvən/ ▸*n.* variant spelling of HESVAN.

He·si·od /'hesēəd/ (*c.*700 BC), Greek poet. One of the earliest known Greek poets, he wrote the *Theogony*, an epic poem on the genealogies of the gods.

hes·i·tant /'hezitənt/ ▸*adj.* tentative, unsure, or slow in acting or speaking: *clients are hesitant about buying | her slow, hesitant way of speaking.* ▷late Middle English: from Latin *haesitant-* 'being undecided,' from the verb *haesitare* (see HESITATE). —**hes·i·tance** *n.* —**hes·i·tan·cy** /-tənsē/ *n.* —**hes·i·tant·ly** *adv.*

hes·i·tate /'hezi,tāt/ ▸*v.* [*intrans.*] pause before saying or doing something, esp. through uncertainty: *she hesitated, unsure of what to say.* ■ [with *infinitive*] be reluctant to do something: *he hesitated to spoil the mood by being inquisitive.* ▷early 17th cent.: from Latin *haesitat-* 'stuck fast, left undecided,' from the verb *haesitare*, from *haerere* 'stick, stay.' —**hes·i·tat·er** /-,tātər/ *n.* —**hes·i·tat·ing·ly** /-,tātiNGlē/ *adv.*
▸*PHRASE* □ **he who hesitates is lost** *proverb* delay or vacillation may have unfortunate or disastrous consequences.

hes·i·ta·tion /,hezi'tāSHən/ ▸*n.* the action of pausing or hesitating before saying or doing something: *she answered without hesitation.*

Hes·pe·ri·a /he'spi(ə)rēə/ a city in southern California, north of San Bernardino; pop. 50,418.

Hes·pe·ri·an /he'spi(ə)rēən/ ▸*adj. Greek Mythology* of or concerning the Hesperides. ■ *poetic/literary* western. ▷late 15th cent.: from Latin *hesperius* (from Greek *hesperios*, from *Hesperia* 'land of the west,' from *hesperos* 'western' (see **HESPERUS**)) + **-AN**.

Hes·per·i·des /he'sperə,dēz/ *Greek Mythology* a group of nymphs who were guardians, with the aid of a watchful dragon, of a tree of golden apples in a garden located beyond the Atlas Mountains at the western border of Oceanus, the river encircling the world. One of the labors of Hercules was to fetch the golden apples.

hes·per·id·i·um /,hespə'ridēəm/ ▸*n.* (*pl.* **hes·per·id·i·a** /-,hespə'ridēə/) *Botany* a fruit with sectioned pulp inside a separable rind, e.g., an orange or grapefruit. ▷mid 19th cent.: based on *Hesperideae*, former name of an order of plants containing citrus fruits, named after the golden apples of the Hesperides (see **HESPERIDES**) + **-IUM**.

Hes·per·us /'hespərəs/ ▸*n. poetic/literary* the planet Venus. ▷Latin, from Greek *hesperos* 'western,' (as a noun) 'the evening star,' related to Latin *vesper* 'evening (star)' (see **VESPER**.)

Hess1 /hes/, Dame Myra (1890–1965), English pianist. She was noted for her performances of the music of Schumann, Beethoven, Mozart, and Bach.

Hess2, (Walther Richard) Rudolf (1894–1987), German politician, deputy leader of the Nazi Party 1934–41. In 1941, secretly and on his own initiative, he parachuted into Scotland to negotiate peace with Britain. He was imprisoned for the duration of the war and, at the Nuremberg war trials, sentenced to life imprisonment in Spandau prison, Berlin, where he died.

Hess3, Victor Francis (1883–1964), U.S. physicist; born in Austria; born *Victor Franz Hess*. He showed that some ionizing radiation (later termed cosmic rays) was extraterrestrial in origin but did not come from the sun. Nobel Prize for Physics (1936, shared with C. D. Anderson).

Hes·se1 /hes; 'hesə/ a state in western Germany; capital, Wiesbaden. German name **HESSEN** . **—Hes·sian** /'hesʜən/ *adj.* & *n.*

Hes·se2 /'hesə/, Hermann (1877–1962), Swiss novelist and poet, born in Germany. His work reflects his interest in spiritual values as expressed in Eastern religion and his involvement in Jungian analysis. Notable works: *Siddhartha* (1922), *Steppenwolf* (1927), and *The Glass Bead Game* (1943). Nobel Prize for Literature (1946).

hes·sian /'hesʜən/ ▸*n.* a strong, coarse fabric made from hemp or jute, used for sacks. ▷late 19th cent.: from *Hesse* (see **HESSE**1) + **-IAN**.

Hes·sian boot ▸*n.* a high tasseled leather boot, originally worn by Hessian troops.

Hes·sian fly ▸*n.* a gall midge whose larvae are a pest of cereal crops, occurring in wheat-growing areas. • *Mayetiola destructor*, family Cecidomyiidae. ▷late 18th cent.: so named because it was supposed (erroneously) to have been carried to America by Hessian troops during the American Revolution.

hest /hest/ ▸*n.* archaic form of **BEHEST**. ▷Old English *hǣs*, of Germanic origin; related to **HIGHT**. The spelling change in Middle English was by association with abstract nouns ending in *-t*.

Hes·ton /'hestən/, Charlton (1924–), U.S. actor and social activist. His movies include *The Ten Commandments* (1956), *Ben-Hur* (Academy Award, 1959), and *Planet of the Apes* (1968). He headed the National Rifle Association (NRA) 1998–2003.

Hes·van /'ᴋʜesʜvän; 'hesvən/ (also **Ches·van**, **Hesh·van**) ▸*n.* (in the Jewish calendar) the second month of the civil and eighth of the religious year, usually coinciding with parts of October and November. ▷from Hebrew *ḥešwān*.

Hes·y·chast /'hesi,kast/ ▸*n. historical* a member of a movement dedicated to contemplation, originating among the Orthodox monks of Mount Athos in the 14th century. ▷mid 19th cent.: from late Greek *hēsukhastēs* 'hermit,' from *hēsukhazein* 'be still,' from *hēsukhos* 'still.'

het /het/ ▸*adj.* & *n. informal* short for **HETEROSEXUAL**.

he·tae·ra /hi'ti(ə)rə/ (also **he·tai·ra** /-'tīrə/) ▸*n.* (*pl.* **-tae·ras** or **-tae·rae** /-'ti(ə)rē/) a courtesan or mistress, esp. one in ancient Greece akin to the modern geisha. ▷from Greek *hetaira*, feminine of *hetairos* 'companion.'

het·er·o /'hetərō/ ▸*adj.* & *n. informal* short for **HETEROSEXUAL**.

hetero- ▸*comb. form* other; different: *heteropolar* | *heterosexual*. Often contrasted with **HOMO-**. ▷from Greek *heteros* 'other.'

het·er·o·ar·o·mat·ic /,hetərō,arə'matik/ ▸*adj. Chemistry* denoting an organic compound with a ring structure that is both heterocyclic and aromatic.

het·er·o·at·om /,hetərō'atəm/ ▸*n.* an atom in the ring of a cyclic compound other than a carbon atom. **—het·er·o·a·tom·ic** /-ə'tämik/ *adj.*

het·er·o·cer·cal /,hetərō'sərkəl/ ▸*adj. Zoology* (of a fish's tail) having unequal upper and lower lobes, usually with the vertebral column passing into the upper. Contrasted with **DIPHYCERCAL**, **HOMOCERCAL**. ▷mid 19th cent.: from **HETERO-** 'other' + Greek *kerkos* 'tail.'

het·er·o·chro·mat·ic /,hetərōkrə'matik/ ▸*adj.* **1** of several different colors or (in physics) wavelengths. **2** *Biochemistry* of or relating to heterochromatin.

het·er·o·chro·ma·tin /,hetərō'krōmətin/ ▸*n. Biology* chromosome material of different density from normal (usually greater), in which the activity of the genes is modified or suppressed. Compare with **EUCHROMATIN**.

het·er·o·chro·mo·some /,hetərō'krōmə,sōm/ ▸*n.* another term for **SEX CHROMOSOME**.

het·er·o·clite /'hetərə,klīt/ *formal* ▸*adj.* abnormal or irregular.
▸*n.* an abnormal thing or person. ■ an irregularly declined word, esp. a Greek or Latin noun. ▷late 15th cent.: via late Latin from Greek *heteroklitos*, from *heteros* 'other' + *-klitos* 'inflected' (from *klinein* 'to lean, inflect'). **—het·er·o·clit·ic** /,hetərə'klitik/ *adj.*

het·er·o·cy·clic /,hetərō'sīklik; -'siklik/ ▸*adj. Chemistry* denoting a compound whose molecule contains a ring of atoms of at least two elements (one of which is generally carbon).

het·er·o·cyst /'hetərə,sist/ ▸*n.* a large, transparent, thick-walled cell found in the filaments of certain blue-green algae and in certain fungi.

het·er·o·dox /'hetərə,däks/ ▸*adj.* not conforming with accepted or orthodox standards or beliefs: *heterodox views*. ▷early 17th cent. (originally as a noun denoting an unorthodox opinion): via late Latin from Greek *heterodoxos*, from *heteros* 'other' + *doxa* 'opinion.' **—het·er·o·dox·y** *n.*

het·er·o·dyne /'hetərə,dīn/ *Electronics* ▸*adj.* of or relating to the production of a lower frequency from the combination of two almost equal high frequencies, as used in radio transmission.
▸*v.* [*trans.*] combine (a high-frequency signal) with another to produce a lower frequency in this way. ▷early 20th cent.: from **HETERO-** 'other' + *-dyne*, suffix formed irregularly from Greek *dunamis* 'power.'

het·er·oe·cious /,hetə'rēsʜəs/ ▸*adj.* parasitic on different and often unrelated species of host at different stages of life. Compare with **HOMOECIOUS**.

het·er·o·ga·met·ic /,hetərōgə'metik/ ▸*adj. Biology* denoting the sex that has sex chromosomes that differ in morphology, resulting in two different kinds of gamete, e.g., (in mammals) the male and (in birds) the female. The opposite of **HOMOGAMETIC**.

het·er·og·a·my /,hetə'rägəmē/ ▸*n.* **1** *chiefly Zoology* the alternation of generations, esp. between sexual and parthenogenetic generations. **2** *Botany* a state in which the flowers of a plant are of two or more types. Compare with **HOMOGAMY** (sense 2). ■ another term for **ANISOGAMY**. **3** marriage between people from different sociological or educational backgrounds. Compare with **HOMOGAMY** (sense 1). **—het·er·og·a·mous** /-'rägəməs/ *adj.*

het·er·o·ge·ne·ous /,hetərə'jēnēəs/ ▸*adj.* diverse in character or content: *a large and heterogeneous collection*. ■ *Chemistry* of or denoting a process involving substances in different phases (solid, liquid, or gaseous). ■ *Mathematics* incommensurable through being of different kinds, degrees, or dimensions. ▷early 17th cent.: from medieval Latin *heterogeneus*, from Greek *heterogenēs*, from *heteros* 'other' + *genos* 'a kind.' **—het·er·o·ge·ne·i·ty** /-jə'nēətē/ *n.* **—het·er·o·ge·ne·ous·ly** *adv.* **—het·er·o·ge·ne·ous·ness** *n.*

USAGE The correct spelling for the word meaning 'diverse in character or content' is **heterogeneous**, but a fairly common misspelling is **heterogenous**. The reason for the error probably relates to the pronunciation, which, in rapid speech, often skims over the fifth syllable as if to skip the **e**. Take care to note that **heterogenous** is a different word, which is used in specialized medical and biological senses and means 'originating outside the organism.'

het·er·og·e·nous /,hetə'räjənəs/ ▸*adj. Medicine* originating outside the organism: *present in the urine are heterogenous proteins*.

USAGE See usage at **HETEROGENEOUS**.

het·er·o·glos·si·a /,hetərō'gläsēə/ ▸*n.* the presence of two or more voices or expressed viewpoints in a text or other artistic work.

het·er·o·graft /'hetərō,graft/ ▸*n.* another term for **XENOGRAFT**.

het·er·og·y·nous /,hetə'räjənəs/ ▸*adj.* having females of two kinds, fertile and neuter, as in bees and ants.

het·er·ol·o·gous /,hetə'räləgəs/ ▸*adj. chiefly Medicine Biology* not homologous. **—het·er·ol·o·gy** /-'räləjē/ *n.*

het·er·ol·y·sis /,hetə'räləsis; -rō'līsis/ ▸*n.* **1** *Biology* the dissolution of cells by lysins or enzymes from different species. **2** *Chemistry* the breakdown of a compound into oppositely charged ions. **—het·er·o·lyt·ic** *adj.*

het·er·om·er·ous /,hetə'rämərəs/ ▸*adj. Biology* having or composed of parts that differ in number or position.

het·er·o·mor·phic /,hetərə'môrfik/ ▸*adj. Biology* occurring in two or more different forms, esp. at different stages in the life cycle. **—het·er·o·morph** /'hetərə,môrf/ *n.* —/'hetərə,môrfē/ **het·er·o·mor·phy** *n.*

het·er·o·mor·phism /,hetərə'môrfizəm/ ▸*n. Biology* the quality or condition of existing in various forms: *chromosomal heteromorphism*.

het·er·on·o·mous /,hetə'ränəməs/ ▸*adj.* subject to a law or standard external to itself. ■ (in Kantian moral philosophy) acting in accordance with one's desires rather than reason or moral duty. Compare with **AUTONOMOUS**. ■ subject to different laws. **—het·er·on·o·my** /-'ränəmē/ *n.*

het·er·o·nym /'hetərə,nim/ ▸*n. Linguistics* **1** each of two or more words that are spelled identically but have different sounds and meanings, such as *tear* meaning "rip" and *tear* meaning "liquid from the eye." **2** each of two or more words that are used to refer to the identical thing in different geographical areas of a speech community, such as *submarine sandwich*, *hoagie*, and *grinder*. **3** each of two words having the same meaning but derived from unrelated sources, for example *preface* and *foreword*. Contrasted with **PARONYM**. **—het·er·o·nym·ic** /,hetərə'nimik/ *adj.* **—het·er·on·y·mous** /,hetə'ränəməs/ *adj.*

het·er·o·phyte /'heərə,fīt/ ▸*n. Botany* a plant that derives its nourishment from other organisms. **—het·er·o·phyt·ic** /-rō'fitik/ *adj.*

het·er·o·plas·ty /'hetərə,plastē/ ▸*n.* the operation of grafting tissue between two individuals of the same or different species. **—het·er·o·plas·tic** /'hetərə'plastik/ *adj.*

het·er·o·po·lar /,hetərō'pōlər/ ▸*adj. chiefly Physics* characterized by opposite or alternating polarity. ■ (esp. of an electric motor) with an armature passing north and south magnetic poles alternately.

Het·er·op·ter·a /,hetə'räptərə/ *Entomology* a group of true bugs in which the forewings are nonuniform, having a thickened base and membranous tip. The predatory and water bugs belong to this group, as well as many plant bugs. Compare with **HOMOPTERA**. • Suborder Heteroptera, order Hemiptera. ■ [as *plural n.*] (**heteroptera**) bugs of this group. ▷modern Latin (plural), from Greek *heteros* 'other' + *pteron* 'wing.' **—het·er·op·ter·an** /-'räptərən/ *n.* & *adj.* **—het·er·op·ter·ous** /-'räptərəs/ *adj.*

het·er·o·sex·ism /,hetərō'sek,sizəm/ ▸*n.* discrimination or prejudice against homosexuals on the assumption that heterosexuality is the normal sexual orientation. **—het·er·o·sex·ist** *adj.*

het·er·o·sex·u·al /,hetərō'seksʜo͞oəl/ ▸*adj.* (of a person) sexually attracted to people of the opposite sex. ■ involving or characterized by sexual activity between people of the opposite sex: *heterosexual relationships*.
▸*n.* a heterosexual person. **—het·er·o·sex·u·al·i·ty** /-,seksʜo͞o'alitē/ *n.* **—het·er·o·sex·u·al·ly** *adv.*

het·er·o·sis /,hetə'rōsəs/ ▸*n. Genetics* the tendency of a crossbred individual to show qualities superior to those of both parents. Also called **HYBRID VIGOR**. ▷early 20th cent.: from Greek *heterōsis* 'alteration,' from *heteros* 'other.'

het·er·os·po·rous /,hetə'räspərəs; -ərə'spôrəs/ ▸*adj. Biology* producing two different kinds of spores. **—het·er·os·po·ry** *n.*

het·er·o·sty·ly /'hetərə,stīlē/ ▸*n. Botany* the condition

Pronunciation Key ə *ago*; ər *over*; 'ə or ,ə *up*; 'ər or ,ər *fur*; a *hat*; ā *rate*; ä *car*; ᴄʜ *chew*; e *let*; ē *see*; e(ə)r *air*; i *fit*; ī *by*; i(ə)r *ear*; ɴɢ *sing*; ō *go*; ô *for*; oi *boy*; o͝o *good*; o͞o *goo*; ou *out*; sʜ *she*; ᴛʜ *thin*; T̲H̲ *then*; (h)w *why*; ᴢʜ *vision*

(e.g., in primroses) of having styles of different lengths relative to the stamens in the flowers of different individual plants, to reduce self-fertilization. ▷late 19th cent.: from HETERO- 'different' + Greek *stulos* 'column' + -Y3. —**het·er·o·sty·lous** /ˌhetərə ˈstīləs/ *adj.*

het·er·ot·ic /ˌhetəˈrätik/ ▸*adj.* **1** *Biology* of or relating to heterosis (hybrid vigor). **2** *Physics* of or relating to a theory of cosmic strings that combines elements of two earlier models.

het·er·o·trans·plant /ˌheterōˈtransˌplant/ ▸*n.* another term for XENOGRAFT.

het·er·o·troph /ˈhetərəˌträf; -trōf/ ▸*n.* *Biology* an organism deriving its nutritional requirements from complex organic substances. Compare with AUTOTROPH. ▷early 20th cent.: from HETERO- 'other' + Greek *trophos* 'feeder.' —**het·er·o·troph·ic** /ˌhetərəˈträfik; -ˈtrō-/ *adj.* —**het·er·ot·ro·phy** /ˌhetəˈrätrəfē/ *n.*

het·er·o·typ·ic /ˌhetərōˈtipik/ ▸*adj.* different in form, arrangement, or type. ■ *Biology* of or relating to the first of the two nuclear divisions of meiosis.

het·er·o·zy·go·sis /ˌhetərōzīˈgōsis/ ▸*n.* *Genetics* the state of being a heterozygote. ■ *Biology* the formation of a zygote through the fusion of genetically different gametes.

het·er·o·zy·gote /ˌhetərōˈzīgət; -ˈzīgōt/ ▸*n.* *Genetics* an individual having two different alleles of a particular gene or genes, and so giving rise to varying offspring. Compare with HOMOZYGOTE. —**het·er·o·zy·gos·i·ty** /-zīˈgäsitē/ *n.* —**het·er·o·zy·gous** /-ˈzīgəs/ *adj.*

het·man /ˈhetmən/ ▸*n.* (*pl.* **-men**) a Polish or Cossack military commander. ▷Polish, probably from German *Hauptmann* 'captain.'

het up /ˌhet ˈəp/ ▸*adj.* [*predic.*] *informal* angry and agitated: *her husband is all* **het up about** *something.* ▷mid 19th cent.: from dialect *het* 'heated, hot,' surviving in Scots.

heu·cher·a /ˈhyo͞okərə/ ▸*n.* a North American plant with dark green round or heart-shaped leaves and slender stems of tiny flowers. • Genus *Heuchera*, family Saxifragaceae: many species, including the white-flowered **alpine heuchera** (*H. glabra*) of the Pacific Northwest. See also ALUMROOT, CORAL BELLS. ▷modern Latin, named after Johann H. von *Heucher* (1677–1747), German botanist.

heu·rig·er /ˈhoirigər/ (also **heu·rig·e** /-rigə/) ▸*n.* (*pl.* **-rig·en** /-rigən/) (esp. in Austria) wine from the latest harvest. ■ an establishment where this is served. ▷mid 20th cent.: Austrian German, literally 'this year's (wine).'

heu·ris·tic /hyo͞oˈristik/ ▸*adj.* enabling a person to discover or learn something for themselves: *a "hands-on" or interactive heuristic approach to learning.* ■ *Computing* proceeding to a solution by trial and error or by rules that are only loosely defined.
▸*n.* a heuristic process or method. ■ (**heuristics**) [usu. treated as *sing.*] the study and use of heuristic techniques. ▷early 19th cent.: formed irregularly from Greek *heuriskein* 'find.' —**heu·ris·ti·cal·ly** *adv.*

he·ve·a /ˈhēvēə/ ▸*n.* a South American tree of a genus that comprises the rubber trees. • Genus *Hevea*, family Euphorbiaceae. ▷modern Latin, from Quechua *hyeve*.

He·ve·sy /ˈhevəshē/, George Charles de (1885–1966), Hungarian radiochemist. He studied radioisotopes and invented the technique of labeling with isotopic tracers. Hevesy was also codiscoverer of the element hafnium in 1923. Nobel Prize for Chemistry (1943).

HEW ▸*abbr.* (Department of) Health, Education, and Welfare.

hew /hyo͞o/ ▸*v.* (*past part.* **hewn** /hyo͞on/ or **hewed**) **1** [*trans.*] chop or cut (something, esp. wood) with an ax, pick, or other tool: *we have finished hauling and hewing timber.* ■ (usu. **be hewn**) make or shape (something) by cutting or chopping a material such as wood or stone: *a seat* **hewn out of** *a fallen tree trunk.* **2** [*intrans.*] (**hew to**) conform or adhere to: *some artists took photographs that hewed to more traditional ideas of art.* ▷Old English *hēawan*, of Germanic origin; related to Dutch *houwen* and German *hauen*.

hew·er /ˈhyo͞oər/ ▸*n.* *dated* a person who cuts wood, stone, or other materials. ■ a miner who cuts coal from a seam.
▸*PHRASE* □ **hewers of wood and drawers of water** menial drudges; laborers. [with biblical allusion to Josh. 9:21.]

Hew·lett /ˈhyo͞olit/, William R. (1913–2001) U.S. electrical engineer, inventor, and businessman. He invented an audio oscillator and with David Packard (1912–96) cofounded the Hewlett–Packard Company in 1939.

hex1 /heks/ ▸*v.* [*trans.*] cast a spell on; bewitch: *he hexed her with his fingers.*
▸*n.* a magic spell; a curse: *a death hex.* ■ a witch. ▷mid 19th cent. (as a verb): from Pennsylvania Dutch *hexe* (verb), *Hex* (noun), from German *hexen* (verb), *Hexe* (noun).

hex2 ▸*adj.* & *n.* **1** short for HEXADECIMAL. **2** short for HEXAGONAL (see HEXAGON).

hexa- (also **hex-** before a vowel) ▸*comb. form* six; having six. ▷from Greek *hex* 'six.'

hex·a·chlor·o·phene /ˌheksəˈklôrəˌfēn/ ▸*n.* a white, odorless compound used as an antibacterial agent. Chem. formula: $(C_6HCl_3OH)_2CH_2$

hex·a·chord /ˈheksəˌkôrd/ ▸*n.* a musical scale of six notes with a half step between the third and fourth. An overlapping series of seven such scales starting on G, C, and F formed the basis of medieval music theory.

hex·ad /ˈhekˌsad/ ▸*n.* *technical* a group or set of six. ▷mid 17th cent. (denoting a series of six numbers): from Greek *hexas, hexad-*, from *hex* 'six.'

hex·a·dec·i·mal /ˌheksəˈdes(ə)məl/ ▸*adj.* *Computing* relating to or using a system of numerical notation that has 16 rather than 10 as its base. —**hex·a·dec·i·mal·ly** *adv.*

hex·a·gon /ˈheksəˌgän/ ▸*n.* a plane figure with six straight sides and angles. ▷late 16th cent.: via late Latin from Greek *hexagōnon*, neuter (used as a noun) of *hexagōnos* 'six-angled.'

hex·ag·o·nal /hekˈsagənl/ ▸*adj.* of or pertaining to a hexagon. ■ (of a solid) having a section that is a hexagon; constructed on a base that is a hexagon. ■ designating or pertaining to a crystal system in which three coplanar axes of equal length are separated by 60° and a fourth axis of a different length is at right angles to these. ■ (of a mineral) crystallizing in this system. —**hex·ag·o·nal·ly** *adv.*

hex·a·gram /ˈheksəˌgram/ ▸*n.* a figure formed of six straight lines, in particular: ■ a star-shaped figure formed by two intersecting equilateral triangles. ■ any of a set of sixty-four figures made up of six parallel whole or broken lines, occurring in the ancient Chinese *I Ching*. ▷mid 19th cent.: from HEXA- 'six' + Greek *gramma* 'line.'

hex·a·he·dron /ˌheksəˈhēdrən/ ▸*n.* (*pl.* **-drons** or **-dra** /-drə/) a solid figure with six plane faces. ▷late 16th cent.: from Greek *hexaedron*, neuter (used as a noun) of *hexaedros* 'six-faced.' —**hex·a·he·dral** /-drəl/ *adj.*

hex·am·er·ous /hekˈsamərəs/ ▸*n.* *Botany & Zoology* having parts arranged in groups of six. ■ consisting of six joints or parts.

hex·am·e·ter /hekˈsamitər/ ▸*n.* *Prosody* a line of verse consisting of six metrical feet, esp. of six dactyls. ▷late Middle English: from Latin, from Greek *hexametros* 'of six measures' (from *hex* 'six' + *metron* 'measure'). —**hex·a·met·ric** /ˌheksəˈmetrik/ *adj.*

hex·ane /ˈhekˌsān/ ▸*n.* *Chemistry* a colorless liquid hydrocarbon of the alkane series. • Chem. formula: C_6H_{14}; five isomers, esp. the straight-chain isomer (***n*-hexane**). ▷late 19th cent.: from HEXA- 'six' (denoting six carbon atoms) + -ANE2.

hex·a·pla /ˈheksəplə/ ▸*n.* a sixfold text in parallel columns, esp. of the Old Testament. ▷early 17th cent. (originally referring to Origen's edition of the Old Testament): from Greek, neuter plural of *hexaploos* 'sixfold,' from *hex* 'six' + *ploos* '-fold.'

hex·a·ploid /ˈheksəˌploid/ *Genetics* ▸*adj.* (of a cell or nucleus) containing six homologous sets of chromosomes. ■ (of an organism or species) composed of hexaploid cells.
▸*n.* a hexaploid organism, variety, or species. —**hex·a·ploi·dy** *n.*

Hex·ap·o·da /ˌheksəˈpōdə/ *Entomology* a class of six-legged arthropods that comprises the insects. The name is used as another term for *Insecta*, esp. when the primitive apterygotes are not considered to be true insects. ▷modern Latin (plural), from Greek *hexapous, hexapod-*, from *hex* 'six' + *pous* 'foot.' —**hex·a·pod** /ˈheksəˌpäd/ *n.*

hex·a·style /ˈheksəˌstīl/ *Architecture* ▸*n.* a six-columned portico.
▸*adj.* (of a portico) having six columns. ▷early 18th cent.: from Greek *hexastulos*, from *hex* 'six' + *stulos* 'column.'

Hex·a·teuch /ˈheksəˌt(y)o͞ok/ ▸*n.* the first six books of the Bible (Genesis to Joshua) collectively. ▷late 19th cent.: from HEXA- 'six' + Greek *teukhos* 'book.'

hex·a·va·lent /ˌheksəˈvālənt/ ▸*adj.* *Chemistry* having a valence of six.

hex·ose /ˈhekˌsōs/ ▸*n.* *Chemistry* any of the class of simple sugars whose molecules contain six carbon atoms, such as glucose and fructose. They generally have the chemical formula $C_6H_{12}O_6$. ▷late 19th cent.: from HEXA- 'six' + -OSE2.

hex sign ▸*n.* a design usually in the shape of a star, wheel, or rosette on a circular field. Formerly, hex signs were painted on barns, esp. by the Pennsylvania Dutch, and were thought to ward off evil.

hex·yl /ˈheksəl/ ▸*n.* [as *adj.*] *Chemistry* of or denoting an alkyl radical $-C_6H_{13}$, derived from hexane.

hey /hā/ ▸*exclam.* used to attract attention, to express surprise, interest, or annoyance, or to elicit agreement: *hey, what's going on here? | hey, don't I know it!* ■ hi; hello: *hey, how you doing?* ▷natural exclamation: first recorded in Middle English.
▸*PHRASE* □ **what the hey** *informal* used as a euphemism for "what the hell."

hey·day /ˈhāˌdā/ ▸*n.* (usu. **one's heyday**) the period of a person's or thing's greatest success, popularity, or vigor: *the paper has lost millions of readers since its heyday in 1964.* ▷late 16th cent. (denoting good spirits or passion): from archaic *heyday!*, an exclamation of joy, surprise, etc.

Hey·er·dahl /ˈhāərˌdäl/, Thor (1914–2002), Norwegian anthropologist. He is noted for his ocean voyages in primitive craft to demonstrate his theories of cultural diffusion, the best known of which was that of the balsa raft *Kon-Tiki* from Peru to the islands east of Tahiti in 1947. In 1969, he successfully crossed from Morocco to Central America in a papyrus boat (*Ra II*).

hey pres·to ▸*exclam.* *chiefly Brit.* & *Canadian* another way of saying PRESTO.

Hez·bol·lah /ˌhezbəˈlä; hezˈbälə/ (also **Hiz·bul·lah**) an extremist Shiite Muslim group that has close links with Iran, created after the Iranian revolution of 1979 and active esp. in Lebanon. ▷from Arabic *ḥizbullāh* 'Party of God,' from *ḥezb* 'party' + *'allāh* (see ALLAH).

HF *Physics* ▸*abbr.* high frequency.

Hf ▸*symbol* the chemical element hafnium.

hf ▸*abbr.* half.

HFC ▸*abbr.* hydrofluorocarbon.

hfs ▸*abbr.* hyperfine structure.

HG *Brit.* ▸*abbr.* Her or His Grace.

Hg ▸*symbol* the chemical element mercury. ▷abbreviation of modern Latin *hydrargyrum*.

hg ▸*abbr.* hectogram(s).

hgb. ▸*abbr.* hemoglobin.

HGH ▸*abbr.* human growth hormone.

hgt. ▸*abbr.* height.

hgwy. ▸*abbr.* highway.

HH ▸*abbr.* ■ *Brit.* Her or His Highness. ■ His Holiness. ■ (used in describing grades of pencil lead) extra hard.

hh. ▸*abbr.* hands (as a unit of measurement of a horse's height).

hhd ▸*abbr.* hogshead(s).

HHFA ▸*abbr.* Housing and Home Finance Agency.

H-hour ▸*n.* the time of day at which an attack, landing, or other military operation is scheduled to begin. ▷World War I: from *H* (for *hour*) + HOUR.

HHS ▸*abbr.* Department of Health and Human Services.

HI ▸*abbr.* Hawaii (in official postal use).

hi /hī/ ▸*exclam.* *informal* used as a friendly greeting or to attract attention: *"Hi there. How was the flight?"* ▷natural exclamation: first recorded in late Middle English.

Hi·a·le·ah /ˌhīəˈlēə/ a city in southeastern Florida, northwest of Miami; pop. 226,419.

hi·a·tus /hīˈātəs/ ▸*n.* (*pl.* **-tus·es**) [usu. in *sing.*] a pause or gap in a sequence, series, or process: *there was a brief hiatus in the war with France.* ■ *Prosody & Grammar* a break between two vowels coming together but not in the same syllable, as in *the ear* and *cooperate.* ▷mid 16th cent. (originally denoting a physical gap or opening): from Latin, literally 'gaping,' from *hiare* 'gape.' —**hi·a·tal** /-ˈātəl/ *adj.*

hi·a·tus her·ni·a (also **hi·a·tal her·ni·a**) ▸*n.* *Medicine* the protrusion of an organ, typically the stomach, through the esophageal opening in the diaphragm.

Hi·a·wath·a1 /ˌhīəˈwäTHə/ (*fl.* *c.*1570), legendary American Indian chief; meaning of name "He Makes Rivers." A member of the Mohawk tribe, he is credited with establishing an Iroquois confederacy—comprised of Onondaga, Mohawk, Oneida, Cayuga, and Seneca tribes—the Five Nations League. His name was used for the hero of Longfellow's poem, "The Song of Hiawatha."

Hi·a·wath·a[2] a fictional Chippewa hero who lived on Lake Superior and who was the hero of a narrative poem by Henry Wadsworth Longfellow called *The Song of Hiawatha* (1855).

hi·ba /ˈhēbə/ ▸*n.* a Japanese conifer with evergreen scalelike leaves that form flattened sprays of foliage, widely planted as an ornamental and yielding durable timber. • *Thujopsis dolabrata*, family Cupressaceae. ▷Japanese.

hi·ba·chi /həˈbäCHē/ ▸*n.* (*pl.* **-chis**) a portable cooking apparatus consisting of a small grill over a brazier. ■ (in Japan) a large earthenware pan or brazier in which charcoal is burned to provide indoor heating. ▷mid 19th cent.: Japanese *hibachi, hi-hachi*, from *hi* 'fire' + *hachi* 'bowl, pot.'

hi·ba·ku·sha /ˌhēbəˈko͞oSHə; hēˈbäko͞oˌSHä/ ▸*n.* (*pl.* same) (in Japan) a survivor of either of the atomic explosions at Hiroshima or Nagasaki in 1945. ▷mid 20th cent.: Japanese, from *hi* 'suffer' + *baku* 'explosion' + *sha* 'person.'

Hib·bing /ˈhibiNG/ a city in northeastern Minnesota, a mining center in the Mesabi Range; pop. 18,046.

hi·ber·nate /ˈhībərˌnāt/ ▸*v.* [*intrans.*] (of an animal or plant) spend the winter in a dormant state. ■ *figurative* (of a person) remain inactive or indoors for an extended period: *the pilots who have been hibernating during the winter months get their gliders out again.* ▷early 19th cent.: from Latin *hibernare*, from *hiberna* 'winter quarters,' from *hibernus* 'wintry.' **—hi·ber·na·tion** /ˌhībərˈnāSHən/ *n.* **—hi·ber·na·tor** /-ˌnātər/ *n.*

Hi·ber·ni·an /hīˈbərnēən/ ▸*adj.* of or concerning Ireland (now chiefly used in names): *the Royal Hibernian Academy.*
▸*n.* a native of Ireland (now chiefly used in names): *the Ancient Order of Hibernians.* ▷from Latin *Hibernia* (alteration of *Iverna*, from Greek *I(w)ernē*, of Celtic origin; related to Irish *Éire*, *Éirinn* 'Ireland': see **EIRE, ERIN**) + **-AN**.

Hi·ber·ni·an·ism /hīˈbərnēəˌnizəm/ (also **Hi·ber·ni·cism** /-niˌsizəm/) ▸*n.* an Irish idiom or expression.

Hiberno- ▸*comb. form* Irish; Irish and . . . : *Hiberno-English.* ■ relating to Ireland. ▷from medieval Latin *Hibernus* 'Irish'; see also **HIBERNIAN**.

hi·bis·cus /hīˈbiskəs/ ▸*n.* a plant of the mallow family, grown in warm climates for its large brightly colored flowers or for products such as fiber or timber. • Genus *Hibiscus*, family Malvaceae: many species, including the rose mallow. ▷Latin, from Greek *hibiskos*, which Dioscorides identified with the marsh mallow.

hic /hik/ ▸*exclam.* used in writing to express the sound of a hiccup, esp. a drunken one. ▷late 19th cent.: imitative.

hic·cup /ˈhikəp/ (also **hic·cough**) ▸*n.* an involuntary spasm of the diaphragm and respiratory organs, with a sudden closure of the glottis and a characteristic sound like that of a cough. ■ (**hiccups**) an attack of such spasms occurring repeatedly for some time: *he* ***got the hiccups.*** ■ a temporary or minor difficulty or setback: *just a little hiccup in our usual wonderful service.*
▸*v.* (**-cuped, -cup·ing**) [*intrans.*] suffer from or make the sound of a hiccup or series of hiccups. ▷late 16th cent.: imitative; the form *hiccough* arose by association with **COUGH**. **—hic·cup·y** *adj.*

hic ja·cet /ˈhik ˈjāsət/ ▸*n. poetic/literary* an epitaph. ▷early 17th cent.: Latin, 'here lies,' the first two words of a Latin epitaph.

hick /hik/ ▸*n. informal, chiefly derogatory* a person who lives in the country, regarded as being unintelligent or provincial: *wondering what a hick from the sticks was doing there* | [as *adj.*] *a hick town.* ▷mid 16th cent.: nickname for the given name *Richard.*

hick·ey /ˈhikē/ ▸*n.* (*pl.* **-eys**) **1** *informal* a gadget. **2** *informal* a skin blemish, esp. a mark caused by a lover biting or sucking the skin. ■ a blemish in printing, esp. an uninked area in a solid, caused by a piece of dirt. ▷early 20th cent.: of unknown origin.

Hick·ok /ˈhikäk/, James Butler (1837–76), U.S. frontiersman and marshal; known as **Wild Bill Hickok**. The legend of his invincibility became something of a challenge to gunmen, and he was eventually murdered at Deadwood, South Dakota.

Hick·o·ry /ˈhik(ə)rē/ a city in west central North Carolina, noted for its furniture industry; pop. 28,301.

hick·o·ry /ˈhik(ə)rē/ ▸*n.* a chiefly North American tree of the walnut family that yields useful timber and typically bears edible nuts. • Genus *Carya*, family Juglandaceae: several species, including the **shagbark hickory** (*C. ovata*), with shaggy peeling bark. See also **PECAN, PIGNUT**. ■ a stick made of hickory wood. ▷late 17th cent.: abbreviation of *pohickery*, the local Virginian name, from Algonquian *pawcohiccora.*

Hicks /hiks/, Sir John Richard (1904–89), English economist. He did pioneering work on general economic equilibrium, the theory that economic forces tend to balance one another rather than simply reflect cyclical trends. Nobel Prize in Economics (1972, shared with K. J. Arrow).

Hicks·ville /ˈhiksˌvil/ a village in central Long Island in New York; pop. 40,174.

hid /hid/ ▸ past of **HIDE**[1].

Hi·dal·go /ēˈdälgō/ a state in southern Mexico; capital, Pachuca de Soto.

hi·dal·go /hiˈdälgō/ ▸*n.* (*pl.* **-gos**) (in Spanish-speaking regions) a gentleman. ▷late 16th cent.: Spanish, from *hijo de algo*, literally 'son of something' (i.e., of an important person).

Hi·dat·sa /hēˈdätsä/ ▸*n.* (*pl.* same or **-sas**) **1** a member of an American Indian people living on the upper Missouri River in North Dakota. **2** the Siouan language of this people.
▸*adj.* of or relating to this people or their language. ▷a Hidatsa village name.

hid·den /ˈhidn/ ▸ past participle of **HIDE**[1].
▸*adj.* kept out of sight; concealed: *hidden dangers* | *her hidden feelings.* **—hid·den·ness** *n.*

hid·den a·gen·da ▸*n.* a secret or ulterior motive for something.

hid·den·ite /ˈhidnˌīt/ ▸*n.* a rare green gem variety of spodumene. ▷late 19th cent.: named after William E. Hidden (1832–1918), U.S. mineralogist.

hid·den re·serves ▸*plural n.* a company's funds that are not declared on its balance sheet. ■ mental or physical capabilities beyond those normally available to someone: *hidden reserves of power.*

hide[1] /hīd/ ▸*v.* (*past* **hid** /hid/; *past part.* **hid·den** /ˈhidn/) [*trans.*] put or keep out of sight; conceal from the view or notice of others: *he hid the money in the house* | *the sacred relic had been* ***hidden away*** *in a sealed cavern.* ■ (of a thing) prevent (someone or something) from being seen: *clouds hid the moon.* ■ keep secret or unknown: *Hal could hardly hide his dislike.* ■ [*intrans.*] conceal oneself: *Juliet's first instinct was to hide under the blankets* | *he had a little money and could* ***hide out*** *until the end of the month.* ■ [*intrans.*] (**hide behind**) use (someone or something) to protect oneself from criticism or punishment, esp. in a way considered cowardly or unethical: *companies and manufacturers with poor security can hide behind the law.*
▸*n. Brit.* a camouflaged shelter used to get a close view of wildlife. ▷Old English *hȳdan*. **—hid·er** *n.*
▸*PHRASES* □ **hide one's head** cover up one's face or keep out of sight, esp. from shame. □ **hide one's light under a bushel** keep quiet about one's talents or accomplishments. [with biblical allusion to Matt. 15.]

hide[2] ▸*n.* the skin of an animal, esp. when tanned or dressed. ■ used to refer to a person's ability to withstand criticisms or insults: *"I'm sorry I called you a pig." "My hide's thick enough; it didn't bother me."* ▷Old English *hȳd*, of Germanic origin; related to Dutch *huid* and German *Haut*. **—hid·ed** *adj.*
▸*PHRASES* □ **hide or hair of someone** [with *negative*] the slightest sight or trace of someone: *I could find neither hide nor hair of him.* □ **save someone's hide** see **SAVE**[1]. □ **tan** (or **whip**) **someone's hide** beat or flog someone. ■ punish someone severely.

hide[3] ▸*n.* a former measure of land used in England, typically equal to between 60 and 120 acres, being the amount that would support a family and its dependents. ▷Old English *hīd, hīgid*, from the base of *hīgan, hīwan* 'household members,' of Germanic origin.

hide-and-seek ▸*n.* a children's game in which one player tries to find other players who have hidden themselves.

hide·a·way /ˈhīdəˌwā/ ▸*n.* a place used as a retreat or a hiding place: *an intimate hideaway overlooking the bay.*
▸*adj.* designed to be concealed when not in use: *a hideaway bed.*

hide·bound /ˈhīdˌbound/ ▸*adj.* unwilling or unable to change because of tradition or convention: *you are hidebound by your petty laws.* ■ (of cattle) with their skin clinging close to their back and ribs as a result of bad feeding. ■ (of a tree) having the bark so tightly adherent as to impede growth. ▷mid 16th cent. (as a noun denoting a condition of cattle): from **HIDE**[2] + **BOUND**[4]. The earliest sense of the adjective (of cattle) was extended to emaciated human beings, and then applied figuratively in the sense 'narrow, cramped, or bigoted in outlook.'

hid·e·ous /ˈhidēəs/ ▸*adj.* ugly or disgusting to look at: *his smile made him look more hideous than ever.* ■ extremely unpleasant: *the whole hideous story.* ▷Middle English: from Old French *hidos, hideus*, from *hide, hisde* 'fear,' of unknown origin. **—hid·e·ous·ly** *adv.* [as *submodifier*] *a hideously expensive camera.* **—hid·e·ous·ness** *n.*

hide·out /ˈhīdˌout/ ▸*n.* a hiding place, esp. one used by someone who has broken the law.

hid·ey-hole /ˈhīdē ˌhōl/ ▸*n. informal* a place for hiding something or oneself in, esp. as a retreat from other people.

hid·ing[1] /ˈhīdiNG/ ▸*n. informal* a physical beating: *they took off after him, caught him, and gave him a hiding.* ■ *figurative* a severe defeat: *if they'd played badly, they would have expected a hiding.* ▷early 19th cent.: from **HIDE**[2] + **-ING**[1].
▸*PHRASE* □ **be on a hiding to nothing** *Brit.* be unlikely to succeed, or be unlikely to gain much advantage if one does.

hid·ing[2] ▸*n.* the action of concealing someone or something. ■ the state of being hidden: *the shipowner had gone* ***into hiding.*** ▷Middle English: from **HIDE**[1] + **-ING**[1].

hi·dro·sis /hiˈdrōsəs; hī-/ ▸*n. Medicine* sweating. ▷mid 19th cent.: from Greek *hidrōsis*, from *hidrōs* 'sweat.' **—hi·drot·ic** /hiˈdrätik; hī-/ *adj.*

hie /hī/ ▸*v.* (**hies, hied, hie·ing** or **hy·ing**) [*intrans.*] go quickly: *I hied down to New Orleans* | *I* ***hied myself*** *to a screenwriters' conference.* ▷Middle English: from Old English *hīgian* 'strive, pant,' of unknown origin.

hi·er·arch /ˈhī(ə)ˌrärk/ ▸*n.* a chief priest, archbishop, or other leader. ▷late Middle English: via medieval Latin from Greek *hierarkhēs*, from *hieros* 'sacred' + *arkhēs* 'ruler.'

hi·er·ar·chi·cal /ˌhī(ə)ˈrärkikəl/ ▸*adj.* of the nature of a hierarchy; arranged in order of rank: *the hierarchical bureaucracy of a local authority.* **—hi·er·ar·chi·cal·ly** *adv.*

hi·er·ar·chy /ˈhī(ə)ˌrärkē/ ▸*n.* (*pl.* **-chies**) a system or organization in which people or groups are ranked one above the other according to status or authority. ■ (**the hierarchy**) the upper echelons of a hierarchical system; those in authority: *the magazine was read quite widely even by some of the hierarchy.* ■ an arrangement or classification of things according to relative importance or inclusiveness: *a taxonomic hierarchy of phyla, classes, orders, families, genera, and species.* ■ (**the hierarchy**) the clergy of the Catholic or Episcopal Church; the religious authorities. ■ *Theology* the traditional system of orders of angels and other heavenly beings. ▷late Middle English: via Old French and medieval Latin from Greek *hierarkhia*, from *hierarkhēs* 'sacred ruler' (see **HIERARCH**). The earliest sense was 'system of orders of angels and heavenly beings'; the other senses date from the 17th cent. **—hi·er·ar·chic** /ˌhī(ə)ˈrärkik/ *adj.* **—hi·er·ar·chi·za·tion** /ˌhī(ə)ˌrärkəˈzāSHən/ *n.* **—hi·er·ar·chize** /-ˌkīz/ *v.*

hi·er·at·ic /ˌhī(ə)ˈratik/ ▸*adj.* of or concerning priests: *he raised both his arms in an outlandish hieratic gesture.* ■ of or in the ancient Egyptian writing of abridged hieroglyphics used by priests. Compare with **DEMOTIC**. ■ of or concerning Egyptian or Greek styles of art adhering to early methods as laid down by religious tradition. ▷mid 17th cent. (earlier as *hieratical*): via Latin from Greek *hieratikos*, from *hierasthai* 'be a priest,' from *hiereus* 'priest,' *hieros* 'sacred.' **—hi·er·at·i·cal·ly** /-ik(ə)lē/ *adv.*

hiero- ▸*comb. form* sacred; holy. ▷from Greek *hieros* 'sacred.'

hi·er·oc·ra·cy /ˌhī(ə)ˈräkrəsē/ ▸*n.* (*pl.* **-cies**) rule by priests. ■ a ruling body composed of priests. **—hi·er·o·crat·ic** /ˌhī(ə)rəˈkratik/ *adj.*

hi·er·o·glyph /ˈhī(ə)rəˌglif/ ▸*n.* a stylized picture of an object representing a word, syllable, or sound, as found in ancient Egyptian and other writing systems. ▷late 16th cent.: back-formation from **HIEROGLYPHIC**.

hi·er·o·glyph·ic /ˌhī(ə)rəˈglifik/ ▸*n.* (**hieroglyphics**) writing consisting of hieroglyphs. ■ enigmatic or incomprehensible symbols or writing: *tattered notebooks filled with illegible hieroglyphics.*

▸*adj.* of or written in hieroglyphs. ■ (esp. in art) stylized, symbolic, or enigmatic in effect. ▷late 16th cent.: from French *hiéroglyphique*, from Greek *hieroglyphikos*, from *hieros* 'sacred' + *gluphē* 'carving.' **—hi·er·o·glyph·i·cal** *adj.* **—hi·er·o·glyph·i·cal·ly** *adv.*

hi·er·o·gram /ˈhī(ə)rəˌgram/ ▸*n.* a sacred inscription or symbol.

hieroglyphics

hi·er·ol·a·try /ˌhī(ə)ˈrälətrē/ ▸*n.* the worship of saints or sacred things.

hi·er·ol·o·gy /ˌhī(ə)ˈräləjē/ ▸*n.* sacred literature or lore.

hi·er·o·phant /ˈhī(ə)rəˌfant/ ▸*n.* a person, esp. a priest in ancient Greece, who interprets sacred mysteries or esoteric principles. ▷late 17th cent.: via late Latin from Greek *hierophantēs*, from *hieros* 'sacred' + *phainein* 'show, reveal.' **—hi·er·o·phan·tic** /ˌhī(ə)rəˈfantik/ *adj.*

hi-fi /ˈhī ˈfī/ *informal* ▸*adj.* of, used for, or relating to the reproduction of music or other sound with high fidelity.

▸*n.* (*pl.* **-fis**) a set of equipment for high-fidelity sound reproduction, esp. a radio or phonograph. ▷1950s: abbreviation of **HIGH FIDELITY**.

hig·gle /ˈhigəl/ ▸*v.* archaic spelling of **HAGGLE**.

hig·gle·dy-pig·gle·dy /ˈhigəldē ˈpigəldē/ ▸*adv.* & *adj.* in confusion or disorder: [as *adv.*] *bits of paper hanging higgledy-piggledy on the furniture and walls* | [as *adj.*] *a higgledy-piggledy mountain of newspapers.* ▷late 16th cent.: rhyming jingle, probably with reference to the irregular herding together of pigs.

hig·gler /ˈhiglər/ ▸*n.* *W. Indian* a person who travels around selling small items; a peddler.

Higgs /higz/ (also **Higgs boson** or **Higgs particle**) ▸*n.* *Physics* a subatomic particle whose existence is predicted by the theory that unified the weak and electromagnetic interactions. ▷1970s: named after Peter W. Higgs (1929–), English physicist.

high /hī/ ▸*adj.* **1** of great vertical extent: *the top of a high mountain* | *the mast was higher than the tallest building in the city.* ■ (after a measurement and in questions) measuring a specified distance from top to bottom: *a tree forty feet high* | *how high is the fence?* ■ far above ground, sea level, or another point of reference: *a fortress high up on a hill.* ■ extending above the normal or average level: *a round face with a high forehead.* ■ [*attrib.*] (of territory or landscape) inland and well above sea level: *high prairies.* ■ near to the top of a real or notional list in order of rank or importance: *financial security is* ***high on*** *your list of priorities.* ■ [*attrib.*] performed at, to, or from a considerable height: *high diving.* ■ *Baseball* (of a pitched ball) above a certain level, such as the batter's armpits, as it crosses home plate, and thus outside the strike zone. **2** great, or greater than normal, in quantity, size, or intensity: *a high temperature* | *fudge is* ***high in*** *calories.* ■ of large numerical or monetary value: *they had been playing for high stakes.* ■ very favorable: *nature had provided him with an admirably high opinion of himself.* ■ extreme in religious or political views: *the high Christology of the Christian creeds.* ■ (of a period or movement) at its peak: *high summer.* ■ (of latitude) close to 90°; near the North or South Pole: *high southern latitudes.* **3** great in rank or status: *he held high office in professional organizations.* ■ ranking above others of the same kind: *they announced the High Commissioner's retirement.* ■ morally or culturally superior: *they believed that nature was driven by something higher than mere selfishness.* **4** (of a sound or note) having a frequency at the upper end of the auditory range: *a high, squeaky voice.* ■ (of a singer or instrument) producing notes of relatively high pitch: *a high soprano voice.* **5** [*predic.*] *informal* excited; euphoric: *he was high on an idea.* ■ intoxicated with drugs: *some of them were already* ***high on*** *alcohol and Ecstasy.* **6** [*predic.*] unpleasantly strong-smelling, in particular (of food) beginning to go bad. ■ (of game) slightly decomposed and so ready to cook. **7** *Phonetics* (of a vowel) produced with the tongue relatively near the palate.

▸*n.* **1** a high point, level, or figure: *commodity prices were at a rare high.* ■ a notably happy or successful moment: *the highs and lows of life.* ■ a high-frequency sound or musical note. ■ an area of high atmospheric pressure; an anticyclone. **2** [usu. in *sing.*] *informal* a state of high spirits or euphoria: *the highs I got from cocaine always ended in despair* | *the team is still* ***on a high*** *from Saturday's victory.* **3** *informal* high school (chiefly used in names): *I enjoyed my years at McKinley High.* **4** a high power setting: *the vent blower was* ***on high.*** ■ top gear in a motor vehicle.

▸*adv.* **1** at or to a considerable or specified height: *the sculpture stood about five feet high.* **2** highly: *he ranked high among the pioneers of twentieth-century chemical technology.* ■ at a high price: *buying shares low and selling them high.* **3** (of a sound) at or to a high pitch. ▷Old English *hēah*, of Germanic origin; related to Dutch *hoog* and German *hoch*.

▸*PHRASES* □ **ace** (or **king** or **queen**, etc.) **high** (in card games) having the ace (or another specified card) as the highest-ranking. □ **from on high** from a very high place. ■ from remote high authority or heaven: *government programs coming down from on high.* □ **high and dry** out of the water, esp. the sea as it retreats: *when the tide goes out, a lot of boats are* ***left high and dry.*** ■ in a difficult position, esp. without resources: *when the plant shut down, hundreds of workers found themselves high and dry.* □ **high and low** in many different places: *we* ***searched high and low*** *for a new teacher.* □ **high and mighty** *chiefly derogatory* important and influential: *the accursed high and mighty elite.* ■ *informal* thinking or acting as though one is more important than others. □ **a high old time** *informal* a most enjoyable time: *they had a high old time at the clambake.* □ **high, wide, and handsome** *informal* expansive and impressive. [from *Arizona Nights* by Stewart E. White (1873–1946), U.S. author.] □ **it is high time that ——** it is past the time when something should have happened or been done: *it was high time that she faced the facts.* □ **on high** in or to heaven or a high place: *a spotter plane circling on high.* □ **on one's high horse** *informal* used to refer to someone's behaving in an arrogant or pompous manner: *get down off your high horse.* □ **run high** (of a river) be full and close to overflowing, with a strong current. ■ (of feelings) be intense: *passions run high when marriages break up.*

high·ball /ˈhīˌbôl/ ▸*n.* **1** a drink consisting of whiskey and a mixer such as soda or ginger ale, served with ice in a tall glass. **2** *informal* a railroad signal to proceed.

▸*v.* [*intrans.*] *informal* travel fast: *they highballed north.*

high-band ▸*adj.* relating to or denoting a video system using a relatively high carrier frequency, which allows more bandwidth for the signal.

high beam ▸*n.* the brightest setting of a vehicle's headlights. ■ (**high beams**) the headlights of a vehicle when set on high beam: *glare from the high beams of a car coming up behind them.*

high·bind·er /ˈhīˌbīndər/ ▸*n.* *informal* an unscrupulous person, esp. a corrupt politician. ■ an assassin, esp. one belonging to a Chinese-American criminal organization. ▷early 19th cent.: first recorded as *Highbinders*, the name of a New York gang.

high·born /ˈhīˌbôrn/ ▸*adj.* having noble parents: *the highborn man who inherited wealth and dutifully flaunted it.*

high·boy /ˈhīˌboi/ ▸*n.* a tall chest of drawers on legs.

high·bred /ˈhīˌbred/ ▸*adj.* **1** bred from superior stock. **2** having or showing good breeding or manners; well-bred.

high·brow /ˈhīˌbrou/ ▸*adj.* *often derogatory* scholarly or rarefied in taste: *innovatory art had a small, mostly highbrow following.*

▸*n.* a person of this type.

high·bush cran·ber·ry /ˈhīˌbo͝osh/ ▸*n.* a shrub of the honeysuckle family, with round clusters of white flowers followed by red berries. Compare with **GUELDER ROSE**. • *Viburnum trilobum*, family Caprifoliaceae.

high chair ▸*n.* a small chair with long legs for a baby or small child, fitted with a tray that is used as a table at mealtimes.

High Church ▸*adj.* of or adhering to a tradition within the Anglican Church emphasizing ritual, priestly authority, sacraments, and historical continuity with Catholic Christianity. Compare with **LOW CHURCH**, **BROAD CHURCH**.

▸*n.* [treated as *sing.* or *pl.*] the principles or adherents of this tradition. **—High Church·man** *n.*

high-class ▸*adj.* of a high standard, quality, or social class: *a high-class boarding school.*

high col·or (also **high col·or·ing**) ▸*n.* a flushed complexion: *he had a high color to his cheeks.*

high com·e·dy ▸*n.* comedy employing sophisticated wit and often satirizing the upper classes. Compare with **LOW COMEDY**.

high com·mand ▸*n.* the commander in chief and associated senior staff of an army, navy, or air force.

high com·mis·sion ▸*n.* an embassy of one British Commonwealth country in another. **—high com·mis·sion·er** *n.*

high con·cept ▸*n.* (especially in a movie or television plot) emphasis on a striking and easily communicable idea: *for mainstream media companies, the focus has shifted from high concept to hard cash* | [as *adj.*] *a series of high-concept videos.*

high-coun·try ▸*adj.* of or relating to land above the piedmont and below the timberline: *the high-country snowpack often exceeds 10 feet.*

high court ▸*n.* a supreme court of justice. ■ the U.S. Supreme Court. ■ (in the U.S.) the supreme court in a state. ■ (in some U.S. states) a superior court. ■ (in full **High Court of Justice**) (in England and Wales) the court of unlimited civil jurisdiction forming part of the Supreme Court and comprising three divisions: Queen's Bench, Chancery, and the Family Division.

high day ▸*n.* *Brit.* the day of a religious festival.

▸*PHRASE* □ **high days and holidays** *informal* special occasions: *the drawing room is used only on high days and holidays.*

high-den·si·ty li·po·pro·tein ▸(abbr.: **HDL**) *n.* a lipoprotein that removes cholesterol from the blood and is associated with a reduced risk of atherosclerosis and heart disease. Compare with **LOW-DENSITY LIPOPROTEIN**.

high-end ▸*adj.* [*attrib.*] denoting the most expensive of a range of products.

high·er an·i·mals ▸*plural n.* animals of relatively advanced or developed characteristics, such as mammals and other vertebrates.

high·er court ▸*n.* *Law* a court that can overrule the decision of another.

high·er crit·i·cism ▸*n.* the study of the literary methods and sources discernible in a text, esp. as applied to biblical writings.

high·er ed·u·ca·tion ▸*n.* education beyond high school, esp. at a college or university.

high·er law ▸*n.* a moral or religious principle that is believed to overrule secular constitutions and laws.

high·er learn·ing ▸*n.* education and learning at the college or university level.

high·er math·e·mat·ics ▸*plural n.* [usu. treated as *sing.*] advanced mathematics, such as number theory and topology.

high·er plants ▸*plural n.* plants of relatively complex or advanced characteristics, esp. vascular plants (including flowering plants).

high·er-up ▸*n.* *informal* a senior person in an organization: *he was looking for a way to impress the higher-ups.*

high·est com·mon fac·tor (abbr.: **HCF**) ▸*n.* the highest number that can be divided exactly into each of two or more numbers.

high ex·plo·sive ▸*n.* a chemical explosive that is rapid and destructive, used in shells and bombs.

high·fa·lu·tin /ˌhīfəˈlo͞otn/ (also **high·fa·lu·ting** /-ˈlo͞otiNG/) ▸*adj.* *informal* (esp. of speech, writing, or ideas) pompous or pretentious: *you don't want any highfalutin jargon.* ▷mid 19th cent.: perhaps from **HIGH** + *fluting* (present participle of **FLUTE**).

high fash·ion ▸*n.* another term for **HAUTE COUTURE**.

high fi·del·i·ty ▸*n.* the reproduction of sound with little distortion, giving a result very similar to the original.

high fi·nance ▸*n.* financial transactions involving large amounts of money.

high five *informal* ▸*n.* a gesture of celebration or greeting in which two people slap each other's palms with their arms raised: *they gave each other an exuberant high five in the middle of the press center.*

▸*v.* (**high-five**) [*trans.*] greet with such a gesture.

high·fli·er /ˈhīflīər/ (also **high-fli·er**) ▸*n.* a person who is or has the potential to be very successful, esp. academically or in business: *the company cannot expect to recruit many highfliers.* —**high·fly·ing** /-ˈflī-iNG/ *adj.*

high-flown ▸*adj.* (esp. of language or ideas) extravagant and lofty.

high fre·quen·cy ▸*n.* (in radio) a frequency of 3–30 megahertz.

high gear ▸*n.* a gear that causes a wheeled vehicle to move fast, owing to a high ratio between the speed of the wheels and that of the mechanism driving them: *pull away* ***in high gear*** | *figurative the war against the Mafia has gone into high gear.*

High Ger·man ▸*n.* the standard literary and spoken form of German, originally used in the highlands in the south of Germany. The establishment of this form as a standard language owes much to the biblical translations of Martin Luther in the 16th century. See also **Middle High German, Old High German.**

high-grade ▸*adj.* of very good quality: *high-grade printing papers.* ■ (of ore) rich in metal value and commercially profitable.

high ground ▸*n.* **1** land that is higher than the surrounding area, esp. that which stays dry: *they decided to climb to high ground and serve as lookouts.* **2** (**the high ground**) a position of superiority in a debate: *if he turns it down, he will have lost the* ***moral high ground*** *to the president.*

high-hand·ed ▸*adj.* using power or authority without considering the feelings of others: *they oppose this cruel and high-handed takeover.* —**high-hand·ed·ly** *adv.* —**high-hand·ed·ness** *n.*

high hat ▸*n.* **1** a tall hat, esp. a top hat. ■ *informal* a snobbish or supercilious person. **2** (**high-hat**) variant spelling of **hi-hat.**
▸*adj.* (**high-hat**) *informal* snobbish.
▸*v.* (**high-hat**) (**-hat·ted, -hat·ting**) [*trans.*] *informal* act in a snobbish or supercilious manner toward (someone).

high heels ▸*plural n.* tall, thin heels on women's shoes. ■ women's shoes with heels of this type. —**high-heeled** /ˈhī ˈˌhēld/ *adj.*

High Hol·i·days (also **High Holy Days**) ▸*plural n.* the Jewish holy days of Yom Kippur and Rosh Hashanah. Also called **Days of Awe.**

high hur·dles ▸*plural n.* [treated as *sing.*] a race in which runners jump over hurdles 42 inches (107 cm) high. —**high hur·dler** *n.*

high-im·pact ▸*adj.* [*attrib.*] **1** (of plastic or a similar substance) able to withstand great impact without breaking. **2** denoting exercises, typically aerobics, that place a great deal of harmful stress on the body.

high·jack ▸*v.* variant spelling of **hijack.**

high jinks /jiNGks/ ▸*plural n.* boisterous fun: *high jinks behind the wheel of a car.* ▷late 17th cent.: see **jink.**

high jump ▸*n.* (**the high jump**) an athletic event in which competitors jump over a bar that is raised until only one competitor can jump over it without dislodging it. —**high jump·er** *n.*
▸*PHRASE* □ **be for the high jump** *Brit., informal* be about to be severely reprimanded or punished.

high-key (also **high-keyed**) ▸*adj.* **1** emotionally taut; high-strung. **2** *Art & Photography* having a predominance of light or bright tones.

high kick ▸*n.* a kick with the foot high in the air, for example in dancing or martial arts.
▸*v.* [*intrans.*] (**high-kick**) make such a kick. —**high-kick·ing** *adj.*

high·land /ˈhīlənd/ ▸*n.* **1** (also **high·lands**) an area of high or mountainous land: *the highlands of Madagascar* | [as *adj.*] *a highland region of Vietnam.* **2** (**the Highlands**) the mountainous part of Scotland, north of Glasgow, often associated with Gaelic culture: [as *adj.*] *a Highland regiment.* ▷Old English *hēahlond* 'a high promontory' (see **high, land**). —**high·land·er** *n.* —**high·land·man** *n.* (*pl.* **-men**).

High·land cat·tle ▸*plural n.* animals of a shaggy-haired breed of cattle with long, curved, widely spaced horns.

High·land dress ▸*n.* clothing in the traditional style of the Scottish Highlands, including the kilt, now chiefly worn on formal occasions.

High·land fling ▸*n.* a vigorous Scottish dance consisting of a series of complex steps performed solo, originally to celebrate victory.

High·land Games ▸*plural n.* a meeting for athletic events, playing of the bagpipes, and dancing, held in the Scottish Highlands or by Scots elsewhere.

high·land moc·ca·sin ▸*n.* the North American copperhead.

high-lev·el ▸*adj.* at or of a level above that which is normal or average: *a high-level cistern* | *high-level crop production.* ■ relating to or involving people of high administrative rank or great authority: *high-level negotiations.* ■ *Computing* denoting a programming language (e.g., BASIC or Pascal) that is relatively accessible to the user, having instructions that resemble an existing language such as English. ■ (of nuclear waste) highly radioactive and requiring long-term storage in isolation.

high life ▸*n.* **1** (also **high liv·ing**) an extravagant social life as enjoyed by the wealthy. **2** (usu. **high·life**) a style of dance music of West African origin, influenced by rock and jazz.

high·light /ˈhīˌlīt/ ▸*n.* **1** an outstanding part of an event or period of time: *he views that season as the highlight of his career.* ■ (**highlights**) the best parts of a sporting or other event edited for broadcasting or recording: *he never watches TV highlights of games he has umpired.* **2** a bright or reflective area in a painting, picture, or design. ■ (usu. **highlights**) a bright tint in the hair, esp. one produced by bleaching or dyeing.
▸*v.* [*trans.*] **1** (often **be highlighted**) pick out and emphasize: *the issues highlighted by the report* | *speakers at the conference highlighted additional problems faced by women with AIDS.* ■ make visually prominent: *a vast backdrop with the colorful logo highlighted with lasers.* ■ mark with a highlighter: *a photocopy with sections highlighted in green.* **2** create highlights in (hair).

high·light·er /ˈhīˌlītər/ ▸*n.* **1** a broad felt-tipped pen used to overlay transparent fluorescent color on text or a part of an illustration, leaving it legible and emphasized. **2** a cosmetic that is lighter than the wearer's foundation or skin, used to emphasize features such as the eyes or cheekbones.

high-low ▸*n.* **1** *historical* a lace-up boot with a low heel, reaching to the ankle, worn by military personnel in the 18th and early 19th centuries. **2** a poker game in which the high and low hands split the pot. **3** *Bridge* a signal given to one's partner to lead a suit by playing a high card and then a lower card of the same suit.

high-low-jack ▸*n.* a card game in which points are won for the high trump, low trump, jack of trumps, and either the ten of trumps or the most points.

high·ly /ˈhīlē/ ▸*adv.* to a high degree: [as *submodifier*] *a highly dangerous substance* | *highly paid people.* ■ high in a hierarchy: *a highly placed official.* ■ favorably: *he was highly regarded by his colleagues.* ▷Old English *hēalīce* (see **high, -ly**[1]).

high-main·te·nance ▸*adj.* needing a lot of work to keep in good condition. ■ *informal* (of a person or relationship) demanding a lot of attention.

High Mass ▸*n.* (in the Roman Catholic Church) formerly, a mass with full ceremonial, including music and incense and typically having the assistance of a deacon and subdeacon.

high-mind·ed ▸*adj.* having strong moral principles: *high-minded notions of what good persons want to be.* —**high-mind·ed·ly** *adv.* —**high-mind·ed·ness** *n.*

high muck-a-muck /ˈhī ˈmək ə ˌmək/ (also **high muck·e·ty-muck**) ▸*n.* *informal* a person in a position of authority, esp. one who is overbearing or conceited: *he was once a high muckety-muck at the CIA.* ▷mid 19th cent.: perhaps from Chinook *hiyu* 'plenty' + *muckamuck* 'food,' from Nootka *ḥayo* 'ten' + *ma·ho·maq-* 'choice wheatmeal,' with *high* substituted for *hiyu.*

high·ness /ˈhīnis/ ▸*n.* **1** the state of being high: *the highness of her cheekbones.* **2** (**His/Your**, etc., **Highness**) a title given to a person of royal rank, or used in addressing them: *I am most grateful, Your Highness.* ▷Old English *hēanes* (see **high, -ness**).

high noon ▸*n.* **1** midday. **2** an event or confrontation that is likely to decide the final outcome of a situation: *the high noon of his quest for the presidential nomination.* [popularized by the film *High Noon* (1952).]

high note ▸*n.* a successful point in an event or period of time: *he wants to end his managerial career* ***on a high note.***

high-oc·tane ▸*adj.* denoting gasoline having a high octane number and thus good anti-knock properties. ■ *figurative* powerful or dynamic: *a high-octane forty-year-old.*

high-pass ▸*adj.* *Electronics* (of a filter) transmitting all frequencies above a certain value.

high-pitched ▸*adj.* **1** (of a sound) high in pitch. **2** (of a roof) steep. **3** (of a battle or dispute) intense.

high plac·es ▸*plural n.* positions of power or authority: *people* ***in high places*** *were taking note.*

High Point an industrial city in north central North Carolina, noted for furniture manufacturing; pop. 85,839.

high point ▸*n.* the most enjoyable or significant part of an experience or period of time: ***the high point of*** *her life had been a trip she took to Vancouver.*

high pol·y·mer ▸*n.* a polymer having a high molecular weight, such as those used in plastics and resins.

high-pow·ered (also **high-pow·er**) ▸*adj.* (of a machine or device) having greater than normal strength or capabilities: *a high-powered rifle.* ■ dynamic and capable: *a high-powered delegation.*

high-pres·sure ▸*adj.* **1** involving a high degree of activity and exertion; stressful: *he worked in a high-pressure advertising job.* ■ (of a salesperson or sales pitch) employing a high degree of coercion; insistent: *high-pressure marketing tactics.* **2** involving or using much physical force: *high-pressure jets of freezing water.* **3** denoting a condition of the atmosphere with the pressure above average (e.g., in an anticyclone).

high priest ▸*n.* a chief priest of a non-Christian religion, in particular: ■ the chief priest of the historic Jewish religion. ■ the head of a religious cult or similar group. ■ *figurative* a chief advocate of a belief or practice: *the high priest of the drug culture.*

high priest·ess ▸*n.* a female high priest.

high pro·file ▸*n.* [in *sing.*] a position of attracting much attention or publicity: *people who have a high profile in the community.*
▸*adj.* attracting much attention or publicity: *a high-profile military presence.*

high re·lief ▸*n.* see **relief** (sense 4).

High Ren·ais·sance see **Renaissance.**

high-res ▸*adj.* variant spelling of **hi-res.**

high-rise ▸*adj.* (of a building) having many stories: *office towers and high-rise apartments.* ■ taller or set higher than normal: *high-rise handlebars.*
▸*n.* a building with many stories.

high road ▸*n.* a main road: *Chris avoided the high road and took a roundabout way through the woods.* ■ *figurative* a morally superior approach toward something: *he is winning support for* ***taking the high road*** *in refusing to be drawn into negative campaigning.* ■ a direct or certain route or course.

high roll·er ▸*n.* *informal* a person who gambles or spends large amounts of money. ▷with reference to rolling dice. —**high-roll·ing** *adj.*

high school ▸*n.* a school that typically comprises grades 9 through 12, attended after primary school or middle school. —**high school·er** *n.*

high seas ▸*plural n.* (**the high seas**) the open ocean, esp. that not within any country's jurisdiction.

high sea·son ▸*n.* *chiefly Brit.* the most popular time of year at a resort, hotel, or tourist attraction, when prices are highest.

high sign ▸*n.* *informal* a surreptitious gesture, often prearranged, giving warning or indicating that all is well: *I'm getting the high sign from my secretary—gotta go.*

High·smith /ˈhīˌsmiTH/, Patricia (1921–95), U.S. writer of detective fiction; born *Patricia Plangman.* Her novels are noted for their black humor, particularly those featuring Tom Ripley, an amoral anti-hero living in France. Notable works: *Strangers on a Train* (1949), *The Talented Mr. Ripley* (1956), and *Ripley Under Water* (1991).

high so·ci·e·ty ▸*n.* see **society** (sense 1).

high-sound·ing ▸*adj.* (of language or ideas) extravagant and lofty.

high-speed ▸*adj.* moving, operating, or happening very quickly: *high-speed travel.* ■ (of photographic film) needing little light or only short exposure. ■ (of steel) suitable for drill bits and other tools that cut fast enough to become red-hot.

high spir·its ▸*plural n.* lively and cheerful behavior or mood: *the team returned* ***in high spirits.*** —**high-spir·it·ed** *adj.* —**high-spir·it·ed·ness** *n.*

high spot ▸*n.* the most enjoyable or significant part of an experience or period of time: *perhaps that summer will mark the high spot of my life.*
▸*PHRASE* □ **hit the high spots** *informal* visit the most exciting places in town.

high-stick ▸*v.* [*intrans.*] [usu. as *n.*] (**high-sticking**) *Ice Hockey* strike an opponent on or above the

H

shoulders with one's stick, for which a penalty may be assessed.

high street ▸*n. Brit.* the main street of a town, esp. as the traditional site for most stores, banks, and other businesses. ■ [as *adj.*] (of retail goods) catering to the needs of the ordinary public: *high-street fashion.*

high-strung ▸*adj.* nervous and easily upset: *a high-strung racing thoroughbred.*

hight /hīt/ ▸*adj.* [*predic.*] *archaic* or *poetic/literary* named: *a little pest, hight Tommy Moore.* ▷Middle English, from Old English *heht,* past tense of *hātan* 'command, call, or name,' of Germanic origin; related to Dutch *heten* and German *heissen.*

high ta·ble ▸*n. Brit.* a table in a dining hall, typically on a platform, for the most important people, such as the fellows of a college: *I sat* **at high table**.

high·tail /ˈhīˌtāl/ ▸*v.* [*intrans.*] *informal* move or travel fast: *I cut my trip short and* **hightailed it** *home.*

high tea ▸*n. Brit.* a meal eaten in the late afternoon or early evening, typically consisting of a cooked dish, bread and butter, and tea.

high-tech (also **hi-tech**) ▸*adj.* employing, requiring, or involved in high technology: *a high-tech security system.* ■ (chiefly in architecture and interior design) using styles and materials, such as steel, glass, and plastic, that are more usual in industry.
▸*n.* (**high tech**) short for HIGH TECHNOLOGY.

high tech·nol·o·gy ▸*n.* advanced technological development, esp. in electronics: [as *adj.*] *high-technology weapons.*

high-ten·sile ▸*adj.* (of metal) very strong under tension: *high-tensile steel.*

high ten·sion ▸*n.* another term for HIGH VOLTAGE.

high-test ▸*adj.* (of gasoline) high-octane. ■ meeting very high standards: *a high-test office.*

high-tick·et ▸*adj.* another term for BIG-TICKET.

high tide ▸*n.* the state of the tide when at its highest level: **at high tide** *you have to go inland.* ■ the highest point of something: **the high tide of** *nationalism.*

high-toned ▸*adj.* stylish or superior: *she's getting high-toned and putting on airs.*

high-top (also **high·top**) ▸*adj.* denoting a sneaker with a laced upper that extends some distance above the wearer's ankle.
▸*n.* (**high-tops**) a pair of such sneakers.

high trea·son ▸*n.* see TREASON.

high-up ▸*n. informal* a senior person in an organization.

high volt·age ▸*n.* an electrical potential large enough to cause injury or damage.

high wa·ter ▸*n.* **1** another term for HIGH TIDE. **2** the highest level reached by any body of water, esp. a river: *high water from early January flooding has receded.*

high-wa·ter mark ▸*n.* the level reached by the sea at high tide, or by a lake or river at its highest stand. ■ a maximum recorded level or value: *unemployment and crime both stand at a high-water mark.*

high·way /ˈhīˌwā/ ▸*n.* a main road, esp. one connecting major towns or cities: *a six-lane highway* | *figurative the highway to success.* ■ another term for EXPRESSWAY. ■ (chiefly in official use) a public road. ■ *Computing* a pathway connecting parts of one computer system or between different systems.

high·way·man /ˈhīˌwāmən/ ▸*n.* (*pl.* **-men**) *historical* a man, typically on horseback, who held up travelers at gunpoint in order to rob them.

high wine ▸*n.* a type of liquor containing a high percentage of alcohol.

high wire ▸*n.* a high tightrope. ■ [as *adj.*] *figurative* requiring great skill or judgment: *it will take a financial high-wire balancing act to fund the requirements.*

high words ▸*plural n. archaic* angry words: *high words passed between them.*

high yel·low ▸*adj. offensive* denoting a mulatto or a light-skinned black person.
▸*n.* person of this kind.

HIH *Brit.* ▸*abbr.* Her or His Imperial Highness.

hi-hat (also **high-hat**) ▸*n.* a pair of foot-operated cymbals forming part of a drum kit.

hi·jab /hiˈjäb/ ▸*n.* a head covering worn in public by some Muslim women. ■ the religious code that governs the wearing of such clothing. ▷from Persian, from Arabic *ḥajaba* 'to veil.'

hi·jack /ˈhīˌjak/ (also **high·jack**) ▸*v.* [*trans.*] illegally seize (an aircraft, ship, or vehicle) in transit and force it to go to a different destination or use it for one's own purposes: *three armed men hijacked a white van* | [as *n.*] (**hijacking**) *an eight-hour hijacking.* ■ steal (goods) by seizing them in transit. ■ take over (something) and use it for a different purpose: *the organization had been hijacked by extremists.*
▸*n.* an incident or act of hijacking. ▷1920s (originally U.S.): of unknown origin. —**hi·jack·er** *n.*

Hi·jaz variant spelling of HEJAZ.

hi·ji·ki /hēˈjēkē/ ▸*n.* Japanese seaweed sold in dried black strips. ▷Japanese.

Hij·ra /ˈhijrə/ ▸*n.* variant spelling of HEGIRA.

hike /hīk/ ▸*n.* **1** a long walk, esp. in the country or wilderness. ■ *informal* a long distance. **2** a sharp increase, esp. in price: *fears of* **a hike in** *interest rates.* **3** *Football* a snap: *he takes the hike, drops back, and fakes to his right.*
▸*v.* **1** [*intrans.*] walk for a long distance, esp. across country or in the woods: *we planned to hike another mile up a steep trail.* | [as *n.*] (**hiking**) *she enjoys hiking and climbing in her spare time.* **2** [*trans.*] pull or lift up (something, esp. clothing): *he* **hiked up** *his sweatpants and marched to the door.* ■ increase (something, esp. a price) sharply: *some of the local merchants hiked the price of goods.* **3** *Football* snap (a football). ▷early 19th cent. (originally dialect, as a verb): of unknown origin. —**hik·er** *n.*
▸*PHRASE* □ **take a hike** [usu. in *imperative*] *informal* go away (used as an expression of irritation or annoyance).

hi·la /ˈhīlə/ ▸ plural form of HILUM.

hi·lar /ˈhīlər/ ▸*adj. Anatomy & Botany* of or relating to a hilus or hilum.

hi·lar·i·ous /həˈle(ə)rēəs/ ▸*adj.* extremely amusing: *a hilarious dialogue from characters we never meet again.* ■ boisterously merry: *an old man was in hilarious conversation with three young men.* ▷early 19th cent.: from Latin *hilaris* (from Greek *hilaros* 'cheerful') + -OUS. The sense 'exceedingly amusing' dates from the 1920s. —**hi·lar·i·ous·ly** *adv.*

hi·lar·i·ty /həˈle(ə)ritē/ ▸*n.* extreme amusement, esp. when expressed by laughter: *his incredulous expression was the cause of much hilarity.* ■ boisterous merriment: *the noisy hilarity of the streets.* ▷late Middle English (in the sense 'cheerfulness'): from French *hilarité,* from Latin *hilaritas* 'cheerfulness, merriment,' from *hilaris* (see HILARIOUS).

Hil·a·ry, St. /ˈhilərē/ (*c.*315–*c.*367), French bishop. As bishop of Poitiers, he opposed Arianism. Feast day, January 13.

Hil·bert space /ˈhilbərt/ ▸*n. Mathematics* an infinite-dimensional analog of Euclidean space. ▷early 20th cent.: named after David *Hilbert* (1862–1943), German mathematician.

Hil·da, St. /ˈhildə/ (614–680), English abbess. Related to the Anglo-Saxon kings of Northumbria, she founded a monastery for both men and women at Whitby around 658. Feast day, November 17.

Hil·de·gard of Bin·gen, St. (1098–1179), German abbess, scholar, composer, and mystic. A nun of the Benedictine order, she wrote scientific works, poetry, and music, and described her mystical experiences in *Scivias.*

Hil·des·heim /ˈhildəsˌhīm/ an industrial city in northwestern Germany, in Lower Saxony; pop. 106,000.

Hil·i·gay·non /ˌhiliˈgīnən/ ▸*n.* (*pl.* same or **-nons**) **1** a member of a people inhabiting Panay, Negros, and other islands in the central Philippines. **2** the Austronesian language of this people.
▸*adj.* of or relating to this people or their language.

Hill /hil/, Benny (1925–92), English comedian; born *Alfred Hawthorne.* His risqué humor, as seen in the series *The Benny Hill Show* (1957–66), had an international appeal.

hill /hil/ ▸*n.* **1** a naturally raised area of land, not as high or craggy as a mountain. ■ a sloping piece of road or trail: *they were climbing a steep hill in low gear.* ■ a heap or mound of something: **a hill of** *sliding shingle.* **2** (**the Hill**) *informal* short for CAPITOL HILL.
▸*v.* [*trans.*] form (something) into a heap. ■ bank up (a plant) with soil: *if frost threatens our new plants, we* **hill** *them* **up**. ▷Old English *hyll,* of Germanic origin; from an Indo-European root shared by Latin *collis* and Greek *kolōnos* 'hill.'
▸*PHRASES* □ **a hill of beans** [with *negative*] *informal* a thing of little value: *the problems of one old actor don't amount to a hill of beans.* □ **as old as the hills** see OLD. □ **over the hill** *informal* old and past one's prime. □ **up hill and down dale** see UP.

Hil·la·ry /ˈhilərē/, Sir Edmund (Percival) (1919–), New Zealand mountaineer and explorer. In 1953, Hillary and Tenzing Norgay, as members of a British expedition, were the first people to reach the summit of Mount Everest.

hill·bil·ly /ˈhilˌbilē/ ▸*n.* (*pl.* **-lies**) **1** *informal, chiefly derogatory* an unsophisticated country person, associated originally with the remote regions of the Appalachians. **2** old-fashioned term for COUNTRY MUSIC. ▷early 20th cent.: from HILL + *Billy* (nickname for the given name *William*).

hill climb ▸*n.* a race for vehicles up a steep, often winding, hill. —**hill-climb·er** *n.* —**hill-climb·ing** *n.*

hill·ock /ˈhilək/ ▸*n.* a small hill or mound. —**hill·ock·y** *adj.*

Hills·bo·ro /ˈhilzˌbərō/ a commercial and industrial city in northwestern Oregon; pop. 70,186.

hill·side /ˈhilˌsīd/ ▸*n.* the sloping side of a hill.

hill sta·tion ▸*n.* a town in the low mountains of the Indian subcontinent, popular as a holiday resort during the hot season.

hill·top /ˈhilˌtäp/ ▸*n.* the summit of a hill.

hill·walk·ing /ˈhilˌwôkiNG/ ▸*n.* the pastime of walking in hilly country. —**hill·walk·er** /-ˌwôkər/ *n.*

hill·y /ˈhilē/ ▸*adj.* (**hill·i·er, hill·i·est**) having many hills. —**hill·i·ness** *n.*

Hi·lo /ˈhēlō/ a port community in Hawaii, on the northern coast of the island of Hawaii; pop. 40,759.

hilt /hilt/ ▸*n.* the handle of a weapon or tool, esp. a sword, dagger, or knife. ▷Old English *hilt, hilte,* of Germanic origin. —**hilt·ed** *adj.*
▸*PHRASE* □ (**up**) **to the hilt** completely: *we're mortgaged to the hilt.*

Hil·ton /ˈhiltn/, Conrad (Nicholson) (1887–1979) U.S. businessman. After buying up different hotels during the 1920s, 1930s, and 1940s, he formed the Hilton Hotels Corporation in 1946 and Hilton International in 1948.

Hil·ton Head Is·land a resort town in southeastern South Carolina, on one of the Sea Islands in the Atlantic Ocean, northeast of Savannah in Georgia; pop. 33,862.

hi·lum /ˈhīləm/ ▸*n.* (*pl.* **hi·la** /ˈhīlə/) *Botany* the scar on a seed marking the point of attachment to its seed vessel. ■ a point in a starch granule around which the layers of starch are deposited. ■ *Anatomy* another term for HILUS. ▷mid 17th cent. (in the Latin sense): from Latin, literally 'little thing, trifle,' once thought to mean 'that which sticks to a bean,' hence the current sense (mid 18th cent.).

hi·lus /ˈhīləs/ ▸*n.* (*pl.* **hi·li** /ˈhīlī; -lē/) *Anatomy* an indentation in the surface of a kidney, spleen, or other organ, where blood vessels, ducts, nerve fibers, etc., enter or leave it. ▷mid 19th cent.: modern Latin, alteration of HILUM.

HIM *Brit.* ▸*abbr.* Her or His Imperial Majesty.

him /him/ ▸*pron.* [*third person singular*] **1** used as the object of a verb or preposition to refer to a male person or animal previously mentioned or easily identified: *his wife survived him* | *he took the children with him.* Compare with HE. ■ referring to a person or animal of unspecified sex (in modern use chiefly replaced by "him or her" or "them"): *withdrawing your child from school to educate him at home may seem drastic.* ■ often used in place of "he" after the verb "to be" and after "than" or "as" to refer to a male person or animal: *that's him all right* | *I could never be as good as him.* See **usage** below. **2** *archaic* or *dialect* himself: *in the depths of him, he too didn't want to go.* ▷Old English, dative singular form of *he, hē* 'he' and *hit* 'it.'

USAGE On whether **him** or **he** is the correct pronoun in a comparative construction (*smarter than* **him** or *smarter than* **he**?), see **usage** at PERSONAL PRONOUN and THAN.
See also **usage** at HE.

Hi·ma·chal Pra·desh /həˈmäCHəl prəˈdāsh; -ˈdesh/ a mountainous state in northern India; capital, Simla.

Him·a·la·yan /ˌhiməˈlāən/ ▸*adj.* of or relating to the Himalayas: *the Himalayan foothills.*
▸*n.* a cat of a long-haired breed having blue eyes and a pale coat with dark points, developed by crossing Persian and Siamese cats.

Him·a·la·yas /ˌhiməˈlāəz; həˈmäl(ə)yəz/ a vast mountain system in southern Asia that extends for 1,500 miles (2,400 km) from Kashmir east to Assam. The Himalayas consist of a series of parallel ranges that rise up from the Ganges River basin to the Tibetan plateau. The backbone is the Great Himalayan Range, the highest mountain range in the world, with several peaks rising to over 25,000 feet (7,700 m), the highest being Mount Everest. ▷from Sanskrit *Himālaya,* from *hima* 'snow' + *ālaya* 'abode.'

hi·mat·i·on /həˈmatēˌän/ ▸*n.* an outer garment worn by the ancient Greeks over the left shoulder and under the right. ▷Greek.

him·bo /ˈhimbō/ ▸*n.* (*pl.* **-bos**) *informal, humorous* an attractive but unintelligent man. ▷1980s: analogous form of *bimbo.*

H

Himm·ler /'himlər/, Heinrich (1900–45), German leader; chief of the SS (Nazi special police force) 1929–45 and of the Gestapo 1936–45. He established and oversaw the systematic genocide of over 6,000,000 Jews and other disfavored groups between 1941 and 1945. Captured by British forces in 1945, he committed suicide.

Hims /himz; hims/ variant form of **HOMS**.

him·self /him'self/ ▶*pron.* [*third person singular*] **1** [*reflexive*] used as the object of a verb or preposition to refer to a male person or animal previously mentioned as the subject of the clause: *the steward introduced himself as Pete | he ought to be ashamed of himself.* **2** [*emphatic*] he or him personally (used to emphasize a particular male person or animal mentioned): *Thomas himself laid down what we should do | he said so himself.* ■ *chiefly Irish* a third party of some importance, esp. the master of the house: *I'll mention it to himself.* ▷Old English (see **HIM**, **SELF**).
▶*PHRASES* □ **(not) be himself** see **BE ONESELF, NOT BE ONESELF** at **BE**. □ **by himself** see **BY ONESELF** at **BY**.

Him·yar·ite /'himyə,rīt/ ▶*n.* a member of an ancient people of the southwestern part of the Arabian peninsula, who ruled much of southern Arabia before the 6th century AD.
▶*adj.* of or relating to this people. ▷from the name *Himyar* (the name of a traditional king of Yemen) + **-ITE**[1].

hin /hin/ ▶*n.* a Hebrew unit of liquid capacity equal to approximately 5.5 quarts (5 l). ▷late Middle English: from biblical Hebrew *hīn*.

Hi·na·ya·na /,hēnə'yänə/ (also **Hinayana Buddhism**) ▶*n.* a pejorative name given by the followers of Mahayana Buddhism to the more conservative schools of early Buddhism. The tradition died out in India, but it survived in Sri Lanka (Ceylon) as the Theravada school and was taken from there to other regions of Southeast Asia. See **THERAVADA**. ▷from Sanskrit *hīna* 'lesser' + *yāna* 'vehicle.'

hind[1] /hīnd/ ▶*adj.* [*attrib.*] (esp. of a bodily part) situated at the back; posterior: *he snagged a calf by the hind leg.* ▷Middle English: perhaps shortened from Old English *behindan* (see **BEHIND**).
▶*PHRASE* □ **on one's hind legs** see **LEG**.

hind[2] ▶*n.* **1** a female deer, esp. a red deer or sika in and after its third year. **2** any of several large edible groupers with spotted markings. ▷Old English, of Germanic origin; related to Dutch *hinde* and German *Hinde*, from an Indo-European root meaning 'hornless,' shared by Greek *kemas* 'young deer.'

hind[3] ▶*n. archaic, chiefly Scottish* a skilled farm worker. ■ a peasant or rustic. ▷late Old English *hīne* 'household servants,' apparently from *hīgna, hīna*, genitive plural of *hīgan, hīwan* 'family members.'

Hind. ▶*abbr.* ■ Hindi. ■ Hindu. ■ Hindustan. ■ Hindustani.

hind- ▶*comb. form* (added to nouns) at the back; posterior: *hindquarters | hindbrain.*

hind·brain /'hīn(d),brān/ ▶*n.* the lower part of the brainstem, comprising the cerebellum, pons, and medulla oblongata. Also called **RHOMBENCEPHALON**.

Hin·den·burg[1] /'hindən,bərg; -,bŏŏrk/ former German name (1915–45) of **ZABRZE**.

Hin·den·burg[2] /'hindənbərg/, Paul Ludwig von Beneckendorff und von (1847–1934), German field marshal and statesman; president of the Weimar Republic 1925–34.

Hin·den·burg Line /'hindənbərg/ (in World War I) a German fortified line of defense on the Western Front to which Paul von Hindenburg directed retreat and which was not breached until near the end of the war. Also called **SIEGFRIED LINE**.

hind·er[1] /'hindər/ ▶*v.* [*trans.*] create difficulties for (someone or something), resulting in delay or obstruction: *various family stalemates were hindering communication.* See note at **PROHIBIT**. ▷Old English *hindrian* 'injure or damage,' of Germanic origin; related to German *hindern*, also to **BEHIND**.

THE RIGHT WORD **encumber, hamper, hinder, impede, obstruct, prevent**

If you're about to set off on a cross-country trip by car and wake up to find that a foot of snow has fallen overnight, it would be correct to say that the weather has **hindered** you.

But if you're trying to drive through a snowstorm and are forced to creep along at a snail's pace behind a snowplow, it would be correct to say you were **impeded**.

To *hinder* is to delay or hold something back, especially something that is under way or is about to start (*she entered college but was hindered by poor study habits*); it connotes a thwarting of progress, either deliberate or accidental.

Impede, on the other hand, means to slow the progress of someone or something by a deliberate act; it implies that the obstacles are more serious and suggests that movement or progress is so slow that it is painful or frustrating (*the shoes were so tight they impeded his circulation*).

Both **hamper** and **encumber** involve hindering by outside forces. To *hamper* is to impede by placing restraints on someone or something so as to make action difficult (*hampered by family responsibilities*), while *encumber* means to hinder by the placing of a burden (*encumbered with several heavy suitcases*).

To **obstruct** is to place obstacles in the way, often bringing progress or movement to a complete halt (*obstruct traffic; obstruct justice*).

Prevent suggests precautionary or restraining measures (*the police prevented him from entering the burning building*) and is also used to describe a nonhuman agency or cause that hinders something (*the snow prevented us from leaving that day*).

hind·er[2] /'hīndər/ ▶*adj.* [*attrib.*] (esp. of a bodily part) rear; hind: *the hinder end of its body.* ▷Middle English: perhaps from Old English *hinderweard* 'backward,' related to **BEHIND**.

Hin·di /'hindē/ ▶*n.* a form of Hindustani written in Devanagari and with many loanwords from Sanskrit, an official language of India, and the most widely spoken language of northern India.
▶*adj.* of or relating to Hindi. ▷from Urdu *hindī*, from *Hind* 'India.' See **INDUS**[1], **SINDHI**.

hind limb (also **hind·limb**) ▶*n.* either of the back limbs of an animal.

hind·most /'hīn(d),mōst/ ▶*adj.* furthest back: *the hindmost part of the frog's food canal.*

Hin·doo /'hindōō/ ▶*n.* & *adj.* archaic spelling of **HINDU**.

hind·quar·ters /'hīn(d),kwôrtərz/ ▶*plural n.* the hind legs and adjoining parts of a quadruped.

hin·drance /'hindrəns/ ▶*n.* a thing that provides resistance, delay, or obstruction to something or someone: ***a hindrance to** the development process | the visitor can wander around without hindrance.*

hind·sight /'hīn(d),sīt/ ▶*n.* understanding of a situation or event only after it has happened or developed: ***with hindsight,** I should never have gone.*

Hin·du /'hindōō/ ▶*n.* (*pl.* **-dus**) a follower of Hinduism.
▶*adj.* of or relating to Hindus or Hinduism. ▷Urdu, from Persian *hindū*, from *Hind* 'India.'

Hin·du·ism /'hindōō,izəm/ ▶*n.* a major religious and cultural tradition of the Indian subcontinent, developed from Vedic religion.

Hinduism is practiced primarily in India, Bangladesh, Sri Lanka, and Nepal. It is a diverse family of devotional and ascetic cults and philosophical schools, all sharing a belief in reincarnation and involving the worship of one or more of a large pantheon of gods and goddesses, including Shiva and Vishnu (incarnate as Rama and Krishna), Kali, Durga, Parvati, and Ganesh. Hindu society was traditionally based on a caste system.

—**Hin·du·ize** /-,īz/ *v.*

Hin·du Kush /'hindōō 'kōōsh/ a mountain range in northern Pakistan and Afghanistan that forms a western continuation of the Himalayas. Several peaks exceed 20,000 feet (6,150 m), the highest being Tirich Mir.

Hin·du·stan /,hindōō'stan; -'stän/ *historical* the Indian subcontinent in general, more specifically that part of India north of the Deccan, esp. the plains of the Ganges and Jumna rivers.

Hin·du·sta·ni /,hindōō'stänē/ ▶*n.* a group of Indic dialects spoken in northwestern India, principally Hindi and Urdu. ■ the Delhi dialect of Hindi, widely used throughout India as a lingua franca.
▶*adj.* of or relating to the culture of northwestern India: *Hindustani classical music.*

USAGE **Hindustani** was the usual term in the 18th and 19th centuries for the native language of northwestern India. The usual modern term is **Hindi** (or **Urdu** in Muslim contexts), although **Hindustani** is still used to refer to the dialect of Hindi spoken around Delhi.

Hin·dut·va /hin'dətvə/ ▶*n. Indian* a strong or aggressive sense of Hindu identity, seeking the creation of a Hindu state. ▷Hindi.

hind wing (also **hind·wing**) ▶*n.* either of the two back wings of a four-winged insect.

Hines[1] /hīnz/, Earl (Kenneth) (1905–83) U.S. jazz pianist and band leader; known as **Fatha Hines**. He originated the "trumpet style" of piano playing.

Hines[2], Gregory (1946–2003) U.S. dancer, choreographer, and actor. He appeared in movies such as *The Cotton Club* (1984), *White Nights* (1985), *The Preacher's Wife* (1996), and *The Tic Code* (2000), as well as on Broadway in such shows as *Jelly's Last Jam* (1992) and on television in "The Gregory Hines Show" 1997–98.

hinge /hinj/ ▶*n.* a movable joint or mechanism on which a door, gate, or lid swings as it opens and closes, or that connects linked objects. ■ *Biology* a natural joint that performs a similar function, for example that of a bivalve shell. ■ a central point or principle on which everything depends: *this period can be called the hinge of history.* ■ a small piece of gummed transparent paper used to affix a stamp to a page in an album.

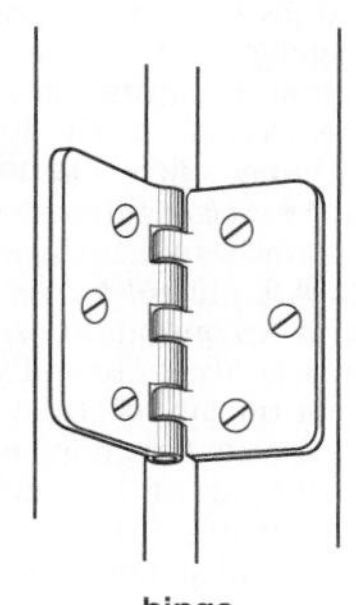
hinge

▶*v.* (**hing·ing**) [*trans.*] (usu. **be hinged**) attach or join with or as if with a hinge: *the ironing board was set into the wall and hinged at the bottom* | [as *adj.*] (**hinged**) *a pocket watch with a hinged lid.* ■ [*intrans.*] (of a door or part of a structure) hang and turn on a hinge: *the skull's jaw hinged down.* ■ [*intrans.*] (**hinge on**) depend entirely on: *the future of the industry could hinge on the outcome of next month's election.* ▷Middle English *henge*; related to **HANG**. —**hinge·less** *adj.*

Hin·gis /'hiNGəs/, Martina (1981–) Swiss tennis player. She won five Grand Slam singles titles: Wimbledon 1997; Australian Open 1997, 1998, 1999; U.S. Open 1997.

hink·y /'hiNGkē/ ▶*adj.* (**hink·i·er, hink·i·est**) *informal* (of a person) dishonest or suspect: *he knew the guy was hinky.* ■ (of an object) unreliable: *my brakes are a little hinky.* ▷1950s: of obscure origin.

hin·ny /'hinē/ ▶*n.* (*pl.* **-nies**) the offspring of a female donkey and a male horse. ▷early 17th cent.: via Latin from Greek *hinnos*.

hi·no·ki /hi'nōkē/ ▶*n.* **1** the valuable timber of a Japanese cypress. **2** (also **hinoki cypress**) the tall slow-growing tree that yields this timber and has bright green scalelike leaves. • *Chamaecyparis obtusa*, family Cupressaceae. ▷early 18th cent.: from Japanese.

hint /hint/ ▶*n.* a slight or indirect indication or suggestion: *he has given no **hint of** his views.* ■ a small piece of practical information or advice: *handy hints about what to buy.* ■ a very small trace of something: *Randy smiled with **a hint of** mockery.*
▶*v.* [*intrans.*] suggest or indicate something indirectly or covertly: *there were those who **hinted at** doctored evidence* | [with *clause*] *Edwards has hinted that he will dispose of his majority shareholding.* ■ (**hint at**) (of a thing) be a slight or possible indication of: *the restrained fronts of the terraced houses only hinted at the wealth within.* ▷early 17th cent. (in the sense 'occasion, opportunity'): apparently from obsolete *hent* 'grasp, get hold of,' from Old English *hentan*, of Germanic origin; related to **HUNT**. The basic notion is 'something that may be taken advantage of.'
▶*PHRASES* □ **drop a hint** see **DROP**. □ **take a** (or **the**) **hint** understand and act on a hint: *she tried to put him off but he didn't take the hint.*

hin·ter·land /'hintər,land/ (also **hin·ter·lands**) ▶*n.* the often uncharted areas beyond a coastal district or a river's banks: *early settlers were driven from the coastal areas into the hinterland.* ■ an area surrounding a town or port and served by it: *the city had grown prosperous by exploiting its local western hinterland.* ■ the remote areas of a region: *the mountain hinterland.* ■ *figurative* an area lying beyond what is visible or known: *in the hinterland of his mind these things rose, dark and ominous.* ▷late 19th cent.: from German, from *hinter* 'behind' + *Land* 'land.'

hip[1] /hip/ ▶*n.* **1** a projection of the pelvis and upper thigh bone on each side of the body in human beings and quadrupeds. ■ (**hips**) the circumference of the body at the buttocks: *a sweater tied around the hips.* ■ a person's hip joint: *she ran into a fence and dislocated her hip.* **2** the sharp edge of a roof from the ridge to the eaves where two sides meet. ▷Old English *hype*, of Germanic origin; related to Dutch *heup* and German *Hüfte*, also to HOP[1].

▸PHRASE □ **on the hip** *archaic* at a disadvantage.

hip[2] (also **rose hip**) ▸*n.* the fruit of a rose, esp. a wild kind. ▷Old English *hēope, hīope*; related to Dutch *joop* and German *Hiefe*.

hip[3] ▸*adj.* (**hip·per, hip·pest**) *informal* following the latest fashion, esp. in popular music and clothes: *it's becoming hip to be environmentally conscious.* ■ understanding; aware: *he's trying to show how* ***hip*** *he is to Americana.* ▷early 20th cent.: of unknown origin. —**hip·ly** *adv.* —**hip·ness** *n.*

hip[4] ▸*exclam.* introducing a communal cheer: *hip, hip, hooray!* ▷mid 18th cent.: of unknown origin.

HIPAA /ˈhip,ô/ ▸*abbr.* Health Insurance Portability and Accountability Act, a 1996 Federal law that restricts access to individuals' private medical information: [as *adj.*] *HIPAA regulations.*

hip·bone /ˈhip,bōn/ ▸*n.* a large bone forming the main part of the pelvis on each side of the body and consisting of the fused ilium, ischium, and pubis. Also called INNOMINATE BONE.

hip boot ▸*n.* a waterproof boot that reaches the hip.

hip flask ▸*n.* a small flask for liquor, of a kind intended to be carried in a hip pocket.

hip-hop ▸*n.* a style of popular music of U.S. black and Hispanic origin, featuring rap with an electronic backing. ▷1980s: reduplication probably based on HIP[3].

hip-hug·gers (also **hip·hug·gers**) ▸*plural n.* pants hanging from the hips rather than from the waist.

hip joint ▸*n.* the ball-and-socket joint connecting a leg to the trunk of the body, in which the head of the thigh bone fits into the socket of the ilium.

Hip·par·chus /hiˈpärkəs/ (*c.*170–after 126 BC), Greek astronomer and geographer. He is best known for his discovery of the precession of the equinoxes and is credited with the invention of trigonometry.

hipped[1] /hipt/ ▸*adj.* **1** [*in combination*] (of a person or animal) having hips of a specified kind: *a thin-hipped girl.* **2** (of a roof) having a sharp edge from the ridge to the eaves where two sides meet.

hipped[2] ▸*adj.* [*predic.*] (**hipped on**) *informal* obsessed or infatuated with: *why are you suddenly hipped on discipline?* ▷1920s.: from HIP[3], or as the past participle of *hip* 'make someone hip (i.e., aware).'

hipped roof ▸*n.* another term for HIP ROOF.

hip·pie /ˈhipē/ (also **hip·py**) ▸*n.* (esp. in the 1960s) a person of unconventional appearance, typically having long hair and wearing beads, associated with a subculture involving a rejection of conventional values and the taking of hallucinogenic drugs.
▸*adj.* of or relating to hippies or the subculture associated with them: *he epitomized the hippie biker.* ▷1950s: from HIP[3] + -IE (sense 1). —**hip·pie·dom** /-dəm/ *n.* —**hip·pi·ness** *n.* —**hip·py·ish** /ˈhipē-ish/ *adj.*

hip·po /ˈhipō/ ▸*n.* (*pl.* same or **-pos**) informal term for HIPPOPOTAMUS.

hip·po·cam·pus /,hipəˈkampəs/ ▸*n.* (*pl.* **-cam·pi** /-ˈkampī; -ˈkampē/) *Anatomy* the elongated ridges on the floor of each lateral ventricle of the brain, thought to be the center of emotion, memory, and the autonomic nervous system. ▷late 16th cent.: via Latin from Greek *hippokampos*, from *hippos* 'horse' + *kampos* 'sea monster.'

hip pock·et ▸*n.* a pocket in the back of a pair of pants.

▸PHRASE □ **in someone's hip pocket** completely under someone's control.

hip·po·cras /ˈhipə,kras/ ▸*n.* *historical* wine flavored with spices. ▷late Middle English: from Old French *ipocras* 'Hippocrates' (see HIPPOCRATES), translating medieval Latin *vinum Hippocraticum* 'Hippocratic wine' (because it was strained through a filter called a *Hippocrates' sleeve*).

Hip·poc·ra·tes /hiˈpäkrətēz/ (*c.*460–377 BC), Greek physician, traditionally regarded as the father of medicine. His name is associated with the medical profession's Hippocratic oath because of his attachment to a body of ancient Greek medical writings, probably none of which was written by him.

Hip·po·crat·ic oath /ˈhipəˈkratik/ ▸*n.* an oath stating the obligations and proper conduct of doctors, formerly taken by those beginning medical practice. Parts of the oath are still used in most medical schools. ▷mid 18th cent.: *Hippocratic* from medieval Latin *Hippocraticus* 'relating to Hippocrates' (see HIPPOCRATES).

Hip·po·crene /ˈhipə,krēn; ,hipəˈkrēnē/ ▸*n.* *poetic/literary* used to refer to poetic or literary inspiration. ▷early 17th cent.: via Latin from Greek *Hippokrēnē*, *Hippou krēnē*, literally 'fountain of the horse' (from *hippos* 'horse' + *krēnē* 'fountain'), the name of a fountain on Mount Helicon sacred to the Muses, which according to legend was produced by a stroke of Pegasus' hoof.

hip·po·drome /ˈhipə,drōm/ ▸*n.* **1** an arena used for equestrian or other sporting events. **2** (in ancient Greece or Rome) a course for chariot or horse races. ▷late 16th cent. (sense 2): from French, via Latin from Greek *hippodromos*, from *hippos* 'horse' + *dromos* 'race, course.' The early sense led to the term's use as a grandiose name for a modern circus, later applied to other places of popular entertainment (late 19th cent.).

hip·po·griff /ˈhipə,grif/ (also **hip·po·gryph**) ▸*n.* a mythical creature with the body of a horse and the wings and head of an eagle, born of the union of a male griffin and a filly. ▷mid 17th cent.: from French *hippogriffe*, from Italian *ippogrifo*, from Greek *hippos* 'horse' + Italian *grifo* 'griffin.'

hip point·er ▸*n.* a sports injury in which the point of the hip is deeply bruised and painful.

Hip·pol·y·tus /hiˈpälətəs/ *Greek Mythology* the son of Theseus, banished and cursed by his father after being falsely accused by Phaedra, his father's wife, of rape. He was killed when a sea monster, sent by Poseidon in response to the curse, frightened his horses as he drove his chariot along a seashore.

hip·po·pot·a·mus /,hipəˈpätəməs/ ▸*n.* (*pl.* **-mus·es** or **-mi** /-,mī; -,mē/) a large thick-skinned semiaquatic African mammal, with massive jaws and large tusks. • Family Hippopotamidae: the very large *Hippopotamus amphibius*, frequenting rivers and lakes, and the smaller **pygmy hippopotamus** (*Choeropsis liberiensis*), frequenting forests near fresh water in West Africa. ▷Middle English: via Latin from Greek *hippopotamos*, earlier *hippos ho potamios* 'river horse' (from *hippos* 'horse,' *potamos* 'river').

Hip·po Re·gi·us /ˈhipō ˈrējēəs/ see ANNABA.

hip·pus /ˈhipəs/ ▸*n.* *Medicine* spasmodic or rhythmic contraction of the pupil of the eye, a symptom of some neurological conditions. ▷late 17th cent.: modern Latin, from Greek *hippos* 'tremor of the eyes.'

hip·py[1] ▸*n.* & *adj.* variant spelling of HIPPIE.

hip·py[2] ▸*adj.* having large hips.

hip·py-dip·py /ˈhipē ˈdipē/ ▸*adj.* *informal* rejecting conventional practices or behavior in a way perceived to be vague and unconsidered or foolishly idealistic: *despite her hippy-dippy reputation, discipline seems to be the key to her success.*

hip roof (also **hipped roof**) ▸*n.* a roof with the ends inclined, as well as the sides.

hip·shot /ˈhip,shät/ ▸*adj.* & *adv.* having a dislocated hip. ■ [as *adv.*] having a posture with one hip lower than the other.

hip·ster[1] /ˈhipstər/ ▸*n.* *informal* a person who follows the latest trends and fashions. ▷1940s (used originally as an equivalent term to HEPCAT): from HIP[3] + -STER. —**hip·ster·ism** /-,rizəm/ *n.*

hip·ster[2] ▸*adj.* (of a garment) having the waistline at the hips rather than the waist.
▸*n.* (**hipsters**) pants having such a waistline; hip-huggers.

hi·ra·ga·na /,hi(ə)rəˈgänə/ ▸*n.* the more cursive and more widely used form of kana (syllabic writing) used in Japanese, esp. used for function words and inflections. Compare with KATAKANA. ▷Japanese, 'plain kana.'

hir·cine /ˈhər,sīn; -sən/ ▸*adj.* *archaic* of or resembling a goat. ▷mid 17th cent.: from Latin *hircinus*, from *hircus* 'he-goat.'

hire /hīr/ ▸*v.* [*trans.*] **1** employ (someone) for wages: *management hired and fired labor in line with demand.* ■ employ for a short time to do a particular job: *don't hire a babysitter who's under 16* | [as *adj.*] (**hired**) *a hired assassin.* ■ (**hire oneself out**) make oneself available for temporary employment: *he hired himself out as a laborer.* **2** *chiefly Brit.* obtain the temporary use of (something) for an agreed payment; rent: *she had to hire a dress for the wedding.* ■ (**hire something out**) grant the temporary use of something for an agreed payment.
▸*n.* **1** the action of hiring someone or something. **2** a recently recruited employee: *new hires go through six months of training.* ▷Old English *hȳrian* 'employ (someone) for wages,' *hȳr* 'payment under contract for the use of something'; related to Dutch *huren* (verb), *huur* (noun). —**hire·a·ble** (also **hir·a·ble**) *adj.* —**hir·er** *n.*

▸PHRASE □ **for** (or **on**) **hire** available to be hired.

hire car ▸*n.* *Brit.* a rental car.

hired girl ▸*n.* a female domestic servant.

hired gun ▸*n.* *informal* **1** an expert brought in to resolve complex problems or to lobby for a cause: *it is a chance for an insurance company's hired gun to find some excuse to deny your benefits.* **2** a hired bodyguard, mercenary, or assassin.

hired hand ▸*n.* a person hired to do short-term manual work.

hired man ▸*n.* a male domestic servant. ■ another term for HIRED HAND.

hire·ling /ˈhīrling/ ▸*n.* *chiefly derogatory* a person employed to undertake menial work, esp. on a casual basis. ▷mid 16th cent.: from HIRE + -LING, on the pattern of Dutch *huurling*.

hire pur·chase ▸*n.* British term for INSTALLMENT PLAN.

hi-res /ˈhī ˈrez/ (also **high-res**) ▸*adj.* *informal* (of a display or a photograph or video image) showing a large amount of detail. ▷late 20th cent.: from *high-resolution*.

Hi·ro·hi·to /,hi(ə)rəˈhētō/ (1901–89), emperor of Japan 1926–89; full name *Michinomiya Hirohito*. Regarded as the 124th direct descendant of Jimmu, he refrained from involvement in politics, although he was instrumental in obtaining Japan's agreement to the unconditional surrender that ended World War II. In 1946, the new constitution imposed by the U.S. obliged him to renounce his divinity and become a constitutional monarch.

Hirohito

Hi·ro·shi·ma /,hi(ə)rəˈshēmə; hiˈrōshəmə/ a city in southwestern Japan, on the southern coast of the island of Honshu; pop. 1,086,000. It was the target of the first atom bomb, which was dropped by the U.S. on August 6, 1945, and resulted in the deaths of about one third of the city's population of 300,000. This, with a second attack on Nagasaki three days later, led to Japan's surrender and to the end of World War II.

Hirsch·sprung's dis·ease /ˈhirsh,proongz/ ▸*n.* a congenital condition in which the rectum and part of the colon fail to develop a normal system of nerves, and consequently feces accumulate in the colon following birth. ▷early 20th cent.: named after Harald *Hirschprung* (1830–1916), Danish pediatrician.

hir·sute /ˈhər,soot; hərˈsoot; ˈhi(ə)r,soot/ ▸*adj.* hairy: *their hirsute chests.* ▷early 17th cent.: from Latin *hirsutus*. —**hir·sute·ness** *n.*

hir·sut·ism /ˈhərsoo,tizəm; hərˈsoo-; ˈhi(ə)r,soo-/ ▸*n.* *Medicine* abnormal growth of hair on a person's face and body, esp. on a woman.

Hirt /hərt/, Al(ois Maxwell) (1922–99) U.S. trumpeter. At first noted for his Dixieland jazz, he later, during the 1960s, turned to playing more nonjazz music, such as in his Grammy-winning song "Java" (1964). From the 1970s he was based in New Orleans, his hometown, and performed in his own nightclub when not on tour. Albums of his music put together after his death include *Music to Watch Girls By* (2000) and *Cocktail Hour* (2000).

hir·un·dine /hiˈrəndin; -,dīn/ ▸*n.* *Ornithology* a songbird of the swallow family (Hirundinidae). ▷mid 19th cent.: from Latin *hirundo* 'swallow' + -INE[1].

his /hiz/ ▸*possessive adj.* **1** belonging to or associated with a male person or animal previously mentioned or easily identified: *James sold his business.* ■ belonging to or associated with a person or animal of unspecified sex (in modern use chiefly replaced by "his or her" or "their"): *any child with delayed speech should*

have his hearing checked. **2** (**His**) used in titles: *His Honor* | *His Lordship.*
▸*possessive pron.* used to refer to a thing or things belonging to or associated with a male person or animal previously mentioned: *he took my hand in his* | *some friends of* ***his.*** ▷Old English, genitive singular form of *he, hē* 'he' and *hit* 'it.'
▸*PHRASE* □ **his and hers** (of matching items) for husband and wife, or men and women: *his and hers towels.*

USAGE See **usage** at **HE**.

His·pan·ic /hiˈspanik/ ▸*adj.* of or relating to Spain or to Spanish-speaking countries, esp. those of Latin America. ■ of or relating to Spanish-speaking people or their culture, esp. in the U.S.
▸*n.* a Spanish-speaking person living in the U.S., esp. one of Latin American descent. ▷from Latin *Hispanicus*, from *Hispania* 'Spain.' —**His·pan·i·cize** /hiˈspaniˌsiz/ *v.*

USAGE In the U.S., **Hispanic** is the standard accepted term when referring to Spanish-speaking people living in the U.S. Other, more specific, terms such as **Latino** and **Chicano** are also used where occasion demands.
See also **usage** at **CHICANO**.

His·pan·ic A·mer·i·can ▸*n.* a U.S. citizen or resident of Hispanic descent.
▸*adj.* of or relating to Hispanic Americans.

His·pan·io·la /ˌhispənˈyōlə/ an island in the Greater Antilles in the Caribbean Sea, divided into the countries of Haiti and the Dominican Republic. After its European discovery by Columbus in 1492, Hispaniola was colonized by the Spaniards, who ceded the western part (now Haiti) to France in 1697.

His·pan·ist /hiˈspanist/ (also **His·pa·n·icist** /-əsist/) ▸*n.* an expert in or student of the language, literature, and civilization of Spain and the Spanish-speaking countries of Latin America.

His·pan·o /hiˈspanō; -ˈspänō/ ▸*n.* (*pl.* **-pan·os**) a person descended from Spanish settlers in the Southwest before it was annexed to the U.S. ■ a Hispanic.

Hispano- ▸*comb. form* Spanish; Spanish and . . . : *Hispano-Argentine.* ■ relating to Spain. ▷from Latin *Hispanus* 'Spanish.'

His·pan·o·phobe /hiˈspanəˌfōb/ ▸*n.* a person who dislikes or fears Spanish-speaking peoples or countries.

his·pid /ˈhispid/ ▸*adj. Botany & Zoology* covered with stiff hair or bristles. ▷mid 17th cent.: from Latin *hispidus.*

Hiss /his/, Alger (1904–96), U.S. public official. In 1948 he was accused by journalist Whittaker Chambers of passing State Department documents to a Soviet agent.

hiss /his/ ▸*v.* [*intrans.*] make a sharp sibilant sound as of the letter *s*: *the escaping gas was now hissing.* ■ (of a person) make such a sound as a sign of disapproval or derision: *the audience hissed loudly at the mention of his name.* ■ [*trans.*] express disapproval of (someone) by making such a sound: *he was hissed off the stage.* ■ [*reporting verb*] whisper something in an urgent or angry way: *he hissed at them to be quiet* | [with *direct speech*] *"Get back!" he hissed.*
▸*n.* a sharp sibilant sound: *the spit and hiss of a cornered cat.* ■ a sound such as this used as an expression of disapproval or derision: *a hiss of annoyance.* ■ electrical interference at audio frequencies: *tape hiss.* ▷late Middle English (as a verb): imitative.

his·self /hiˈself; hiz-/ ▸*pron.* nonstandard spelling of **HIMSELF**, used in representing informal or dialect speech.

his·sy /ˈhisē/ (also **his·sy fit**) ▸*n.* an angry outburst or tantrum.

hist /hist/ ▸*exclam. archaic* used to attract attention or call for silence. ▷natural exclamation: first recorded in English in the late 16th cent.

hist. ▸*abbr.* ■ histology. ■ historian. ■ historical. ■ history.

hist- ▸*comb. form* variant spelling of **HISTO-** shortened before a vowel (as in *histidine*).

his·ta·mine /ˈhistəˌmēn; -ˌmin/ ▸*n. Biochemistry* a compound that is released by cells in response to injury and in allergic and inflammatory reactions, causing contraction of smooth muscle and dilation of capillaries. • A heterocyclic amine; chem. formula: $C_5H_9N_3$. ▷early 20th cent.: blend of **HISTIDINE** and **AMINE**. —**his·ta·min·ic** /ˌhistəˈminik/ *adj.*

his·ti·dine /ˈhistəˌdēn/ ▸*n. Biochemistry* a basic amino acid that is a constituent of most proteins. It is an essential nutrient in the diet of vertebrates, and is the source from which histamine is derived in the body. • Chem. formula: $C_6H_9N_3O_2$. ▷late 19th cent.: from Greek *histos* 'web, tissue' + **-IDE** + **-INE**[4].

his·ti·o·cyte /ˈhistēəˌsīt/ ▸*n. Physiology* a stationary phagocytic cell present in connective tissue. ▷early 20th cent.: from Greek *histion* (diminutive of *histos* 'tissue, web') + **-CYTE**.

histo- (also **hist-** before a vowel) ▸*comb. form Biology* relating to organic tissue: *histochemistry* | *histocompatibility.* ▷from Greek *histos* 'web, tissue.'

his·to·chem·is·try /ˌhistəˈkeməstrē/ ▸*n.* the branch of science concerned with the identification and distribution of the chemical constituents of tissues by means of stains, indicators, and microscopy. —**his·to·chem·i·cal** /-ˈkemikəl/ *adj.* —**his·to·chem·i·cal·ly** /-ˈkemik(ə)lē/ *adv.*

his·to·com·pat·i·bil·i·ty /ˌhistōkəmˌpatəˈbilitē/ ▸*n. Medicine* compatibility between the tissues of different individuals, so that one accepts a graft from the other without having an immune reaction.

his·to·gen·e·sis /ˌhistəˈjenəsis/ ▸*n. Biology* the differentiation of cells into specialized tissues and organs during growth. —**his·to·ge·net·ic** /ˌhistəjəˈnetik/ *adj.*

his·to·gram /ˈhistəˌgram/ ▸*n. Statistics* a diagram consisting of rectangles whose area is proportional to the frequency of a variable and whose width is equal to the class interval. ▷late 19th cent.: from Greek *histos* 'mast, web' + **-GRAM**[1].

his·tol·o·gy /hiˈstäləjē/ ▸*n. Biology* the study of the microscopic structure of tissues. —**his·to·log·ic** /ˌhistəˈläjik/ *adj.* —**his·to·log·i·cal** /ˌhistəˈläjikəl/ *adj.* —**his·tol·o·gist** /-jist/ *n.*

his·tol·y·sis /hiˈstäləsis/ ▸*n. Biology* the breaking down of tissues (e.g., during animal metamorphosis). —**his·to·lyt·ic** /ˌhistəˈlitik/ *adj.*

his·tone /ˈhiˌstōn/ ▸*n. Biochemistry* any of a group of basic proteins found in chromatin. ▷late 19th cent.: coined in German, perhaps from Greek *histanai* 'arrest' or from *histos* 'web, tissue.'

his·to·pa·thol·o·gy /ˌhistōpəˈTHäləjē/ ▸*n.* the study of changes in tissues caused by disease. —**his·to·path·o·log·i·cal** /ˌhistōˌpaTHəˈläjikəl/ *adj.* —**his·to·pa·thol·o·gist** /-jist/ *n.*

his·to·plas·mo·sis /ˌhistōplazˈmōsis/ ▸*n. Medicine* infection by a fungus found in the droppings of birds and bats in humid areas. It is not serious if confined to the lungs but can be fatal if spread throughout the body. • The fungus is *Histoplasma capsulatum.*

his·to·ri·an /hiˈstôrēən/ ▸*n.* an expert in or student of history, esp. that of a particular period, geographical region, or social phenomenon: *a military historian.* ▷late Middle English: from Old French *historien*, from Latin *historia* (see **HISTORY**).

his·to·ri·at·ed /hiˈstôrēˌātid/ ▸*adj.* (of an initial letter in an illuminated manuscript) decorated with designs representing scenes from the text. ▷late 19th cent.: from French *historié*, past participle of *historier* in an obsolete sense 'illustrate,' from medieval Latin *historiare*, from *historia* (see **HISTORY**).

his·tor·ic /hiˈstôrik; -ˈstär-/ ▸*adj.* **1** famous or important in history, or potentially so: *we are standing on a historic site* | *a time of historic change.* ■ *archaic* of or concerning history; of the past: *eruptions in historic times.* **2** *Grammar* (of a tense) used in the narration of past events, esp. Latin and Greek imperfect and pluperfect. ▷early 17th cent. (in the sense 'relating to or in accordance with history'): via Latin from Greek *historikos*, from *historia* 'narrative, knowing by inquiry' (see **HISTORY**).

USAGE 1 On the use of *an historic moment* or *a historic moment*, see **usage** at **AN**.
2 In general, **historic** means 'notable in history, significant in history,' as in a Supreme Court decision, a battlefield, or a great discovery. **Historical** means 'relating to history or past events': (*historical society; historical documents*). To write **historic** instead of **historical** may imply a greater significance than is warranted: a **historical** lecture may simply tell about something that happened, whereas a **historic** lecture would in some way change the course of human events. It would be correct to say, *Professor Suarez's historical lecture on the Old Southwest was given at the historic mission church.*

his·tor·i·cal /hiˈstôrikəl; -ˈstär-/ ▸*adj.* of or concerning history; concerning past events: *the historical background to such studies.* ■ belonging to the past, not the present: *famous historical figures.* ■ (esp. of a novel or movie) set in the past. ■ (of the study of a subject) based on an analysis of its development over a period: *for the Darwinians, biogeography became a historical science.* ▷late Middle English: via Latin from Greek *historikos* (see **HISTORIC**).

USAGE 1 On the difference between **historical** and **historic**, see **usage** at **HISTORIC**.
2 On the use of *an historical event* or *a historical event*, see **usage** at **AN**.

his·tor·i·cal lin·guis·tics ▸*plural n.* [treated as *sing.*] the study of the history and development of languages.

his·tor·i·cal·ly /hiˈstôrik(ə)lē; -ˈstär-/ ▸*adv.* with reference to past events: *a historically accurate picture of the time.* ■ [*sentence adverb*] in the past: *historically, government policy has favored urban dwellers.*

his·tor·i·cal ma·te·ri·al·ism ▸*n.* another term for **DIALECTICAL MATERIALISM**.

his·tor·i·cism /hiˈstôrəˌsizəm; -ˈstär-/ ▸*n.* **1** the theory that social and cultural phenomena are determined by history. ■ the belief that historical events are governed by laws. **2** the tendency to regard historical development as the most basic aspect of human existence. **3** *chiefly derogatory* (in artistic and architectural contexts) excessive regard for past styles. ▷late 19th cent.: from **HISTORIC**, translating German *Historismus.* —**his·tor·i·cist** *n.*

his·to·ric·i·ty /ˌhistəˈrisitē/ ▸*n.* historical authenticity: *an effort to assert the historicity of poetry and the political power of poets.*

his·tor·i·cize /hisˈstôrəˌsiz; -ˈstär-/ ▸*v.* [*trans.*] treat or represent as historical. —**his·tor·i·ci·za·tion** /hiˌstôrəsəˈzāSHən; -ˌstär-/ *n.*

his·tor·ic pres·ent /ˈprezənt/ ▸*n. Grammar* the present tense used instead of the past in vivid narrative, esp. in titles, such as *The Empire Strikes Back*, and informally in speech, e.g., "so I say to him."

his·to·ri·og·ra·phy /hiˌstôrēˈägrəfē; -ˌstär-/ ▸*n.* the study of historical writing. ■ the writing of history. ▷mid 16th cent.: via medieval Latin from Greek *historiographia*, from *historia* 'narrative, history' + *graphia* 'writing.' —**his·to·ri·og·ra·pher** /-ˈägrəfər/ *n.* —**his·to·ri·o·graph·ic** /-əˈgrafik/ *adj.* —**his·to·ri·o·graph·i·cal** /-əˈgrafikəl/ *adj.*

his·to·ry /ˈhist(ə)rē/ ▸*n.* (*pl.* **-ries**) **1** the study of past events, particularly in human affairs: *medieval European history.* ■ the past considered as a whole: *letters that have changed the course of history.* **2** the whole series of past events connected with someone or something: *the history of Aegean painting.* ■ an eventful past: *the group has quite a history.* ■ a past characterized by a particular thing: *his family had a history of insanity.* **3** a continuous, typically chronological, record of important or public events or of a particular trend or institution: *a history of the labor movement.* ■ a historical play: *Shakespeare's comedies, histories, and tragedies.* ▷late Middle English (also as a verb): via Latin from Greek *historia* 'finding out, narrative, history,' from *histōr* 'learned, wise man,' from an Indo-European root shared by **WIT**[2].
▸*PHRASES* □ **be history** be perceived as no longer relevant to the present: *the mainframe will soon be history* | *I was making a laughingstock of myself, but that's history now.* ■ *informal* used to indicate imminent departure, dismissal, or death: *an inch either way and you'd be history.* □ **go down in history** be remembered or recorded in history. □ **make history** do something that is remembered in or influences the course of history. □ **the rest is history** used to indicate that the events succeeding those already related are so well known that they need not be recounted again: *they teamed up, discovered that they could make music, and the rest is history.*

his·to·sol /ˈhistəˌsôl; -ˌsäl/ ▸*n. Soil Science* a soil of an order comprising peaty soils, with a deep surface layer of purely organic material.

his·tri·on·ic /ˌhistrēˈänik/ ▸*adj.* overly theatrical or melodramatic in character or style: *a histrionic outburst.* ■ *formal* of or concerning actors or acting: *histrionic talents.* ■ *Psychiatry* denoting a personality disorder marked by shallow, volatile emotions, and attention-seeking behavior.
▸*n.* **1** (**histrionics**) exaggerated dramatic behavior designed to attract attention: *discussions around the issue have been based as much in histrionics as in history.* ■ dramatic performance; theater. **2** *archaic* an actor. ▷mid 17th cent. (in the sense 'dramatically exaggerated, hypocritical'): from late Latin *histrionicus*, from Latin *histrio(n-)* 'actor.' —**his·tri·on·i·cal·ly** /-ik(ə)lē/ *adv.*

hit /hit/ ▸*v.* (**hit·ting**; *past* **hit**) [*trans.*] **1** bring one's

Pronunciation Key ə *ago*; ər *over*; ˈə or ˌə *up*; ˈər or ˌər *fur*; a *hat*; ā *rate*; ä *car*; CH *chew*; e *let*; ē *see*; e(ə)r *air*; i *fit*; ī *by*; i(ə)r *ear*; NG *sing*; ō *go*; ô *for*; oi *boy*; o͝o *good*; o͞o *goo*; ou *out*; SH *she*; TH *thin*; TH *then*; (h)w *why*; ZH *vision*

H

hand or a tool or weapon into contact with (someone or something) quickly and forcefully: *the woman hit the mugger with her umbrella* | [*intrans.*] *use your words, but do not hit the police* **hit out** *with billy clubs.* ■ accidentally strike (part of one's body) against something, often causing injury: *she fainted and* **hit** *her head* **on** *the metal bedstead.* ■ (of a moving object or body) come into contact with (someone or something stationary) quickly and forcefully: *a car hit the barrier.* ■ *informal* touch or press (part of a machine or other device) in order to work it: *he picked up the phone and hit several buttons.* **2** cause harm or distress to: *the area has been badly hit by business closures.* ■ [*intrans.*] (**hit out**) make a strongly worded criticism or attack: *he* **hit out at** *suppliers for hyping their products.* ■ (of a disaster) occur in and cause damage to (an area) suddenly: *the country was hit by a major earthquake.* ■ *informal* attack and rob or kill: *if they're cops, maybe it's not a good idea to have them hit.* ■ *informal* be affected by (an unfortunate and unexpected circumstance or event): *the opening of the town center hit a snag.* **3** (of a missile or a person aiming one) strike (a target): *the sniper fired and hit a third man.* ■ *informal* reach (a particular level, point, or figure): *his career hit rock bottom.* ■ arrive at (a place): *it was still night when we hit the outskirts of Chicago.* ■ *informal* go to (a place): *we hit a diner for coffee and doughnuts.* ■ be suddenly and vividly realized by: [*trans.*] *it hit her that I wanted to settle down here.* ■ [*intrans.*] *informal* (of a piece of music, film, or play) be successful: *actors are promised a pay increase if a show hits.* ■ [*intrans.*] take effect: *we sat waiting for the caffeine to hit.* ■ *informal* give (someone) a dose of a drug or an alcoholic drink. ■ *informal* (of a product) become available and make an impact on: *the latest board game to hit the market.* ■ *informal* used to express the idea that someone is taking up a pursuit or taking it seriously: *more and more teenagers are hitting the books.* ■ (**hit someone for/up for**) *informal* ask someone for: *she was waiting for the right moment to hit her mother for some cash.* **4** propel (a ball) with a bat, racket, stick, etc., to score or attempt to score runs or points in a game. ■ score (runs or points) in this way: *he had hit 25 home runs.* ■ *Baseball* [*intrans.*] (of a batter) make a base hit.

▸*phrasal v.* □ **hit on** (or **upon**) **1** discover or think of, esp. by chance: *she hit on a novel idea for fund-raising.* **2** *informal* make sexual advances toward. **hit up** attempt to get something, typically money, from (someone): *he hit up some family members.*

▸*n.* **1** an instance of striking or being struck: *few structures can withstand a hit from a speeding car.* ■ a verbal attack: *he could not resist a* **hit at** *his friend's religiosity.* ■ *informal* a murder, typically one planned and carried out by a criminal organization. ■ *Baseball* short for BASE HIT. **2** an instance of striking the target aimed at: *one of the bombers had scored a direct hit.* ■ a successful venture, esp. in entertainment: *he was the director of many big hits* | [as *adj.*] *a hit comedy.* ■ a successful pop record or song. ■ *informal* a successful and popular person or thing: *handsome, smiling, and smart, he was an immediate hit.* ■ *Computing* an instance of identifying an item of data that matches the requirements of a search. ■ an instance of a particular Web site being accessed by a user: *the site gets an average 350,000 hits per day.* **3** *informal* a dose of a psychoactive drug. ▷late Old English *hittan* (in the sense 'come upon, find'), from Old Norse *hitta* 'come upon, meet with,' of unknown origin. **—hit·ter** *n.*

▸*PHRASES* □ **hit-and-miss** done or occurring at random: *picking a remedy can be a bit hit-and-miss.* □ **hit someone below the belt** *Boxing* give one's opponent an illegal low blow. ■ behave unfairly, esp. so as to gain an unfair advantage. □ **hit the bottle** see BOTTLE. □ **hit the ground running** *informal* start something and proceed at a fast pace with enthusiasm. □ **hit the hay** □ see HAY[1]. □ **hit home** see HOME. □ **hit it off** *informal* be naturally friendly or well suited. □ **hit the jackpot** see JACKPOT. □ **hit the mark** be successful in an attempt or accurate in a guess. □ **hit the nail on the head** find exactly the right answer. □ **hit-or-miss** /ˈ,hid ôr ˈmis/ as likely to be unsuccessful as successful: *her work can be hit-or-miss.* □ **hit the right note** see NOTE. □ **hit the road** (or **trail**) *informal* set out on a journey. □ **hit the roof** see ROOF. □ **hit the sack** see SACK[1]. □ **hit the spot** see SPOT. □ **make a hit** be successful or popular: *you made a big hit with her.*

hit-and-run (also **hit and run**) ▸*adj.* denoting a motor accident in which the vehicle or vessel involved does not stop, or a driver, victim, vehicle, vessel, etc., involved in such an accident: *a hit-and-run boating accident* | *a man on a bicycle had been struck and killed by a hit-and-run driver.* ■ designating an attack or an attacker using swift action followed by immediate withdrawal: *a hit-and-run guerrilla war in the streets of Mogadishu.* ■ done or intended for quickness of effect rather than for permanency: *hit-and-run agents who sign rookies to huge bonuses and buy themselves getaway cars* | *the average hit-and-run fragrance has a life span of two or three years.* ■ *Baseball* designating an offensive play in which a base runner, not attempting to steal a base, runs before the pitch is thrown, in an attempt to advance further in case of a hit. **—hit-and-run** (also **hit and run**) *n.*, *v.*

hitch /hiCH/ ▸*v.* **1** [*trans.*] move (something) into a different position with a jerk: *she hitched the blanket around him* | *he* **hitched** *his pants* **up**. **2** [*intrans.*] *informal* travel by hitchhiking. ■ [*trans.*] obtain (a ride) by hitchhiking. **3** [*trans.*] fasten or tether with a rope: *he returned to where he had hitched his horse.* ■ harness (a draft animal or team): *Thomas* **hitched** *the pony* **to** *his cart.*

▸*n.* **1** a temporary interruption or problem: *everything went* **without a hitch**. **2** a knot used for fastening a rope to another rope or something else. ■ a device for attaching one thing to another, esp. the tow bar of a motor vehicle: *a trailer hitch.* **3** *informal* an act of hitchhiking. **4** *informal* a period of service: *his 12-year hitch in the navy.* ▷Middle English (in the sense 'lift up with a jerk'): of unknown origin.

▸*PHRASES* □ **get hitched** *informal* marry. □ **hitch one's wagon to a star** try to succeed by forming a relationship with someone who is already successful.

Hitch·cock /ˈhiCH,käk/, Sir Alfred (Joseph) (1899–1980), English movie director. Acclaimed in Britain for movies such as *The Thirty-Nine Steps* (1935), he moved to Hollywood in 1939. Among his later works, notable for their suspense and their technical ingenuity, are the thrillers *Strangers on a Train* (1951), *Psycho* (1960), and *The Birds* (1963).

Alfred Hitchcock

hitch·er /ˈhiCHər/ ▸*n.* a hitchhiker.

hitch·hike /ˈhiCH,hīk/ ▸*v.* [*intrans.*] travel by getting free rides in passing vehicles: *he dropped out in 1976 and hitchhiked west.*

▸*n.* a journey made by hitchhiking. **—hitch·hik·er** *n.*

hi-tech /ˈhī ˈtek/ ▸*adj.* variant spelling of HIGH-TECH.

hith·er /ˈhiT͟Hər/ ▸*adv.* *archaic* or *poetic/literary* to or toward this place: *I little knew then that such calamity would summon me hither!*

▸*adj.* *archaic* situated on this side: *on the hither side of the service road.* ▷Old English *hider*, of Germanic origin; related to HE and HERE.

hith·er and thith·er (also **hith·er and yon**) ▸*adv.* in various directions, esp. in a disorganized way: *the entire household ran hither and thither.*

hith·er·to /ˈhiT͟Hər,to͞o; ,hiT͟Hərˈto͞o/ ▸*adv.* until now or until the point in time under discussion: *there is a need to replace what has hitherto been a haphazard method of payment.*

hith·er·ward /ˈhiT͟Hərwərd/ ▸*adv.* *archaic* to or toward this place.

Hit·ler /ˈhitlər/, Adolf (1889–1945), German leader, born in Austria; chancellor of Germany 1933–45. He cofounded the National Socialist German Workers' (Nazi) Party in 1919 and came to prominence through his powers of oratory. He wrote *Mein Kampf* (1925), an exposition of his political ideas, while in prison. He established the totalitarian Third Reich in 1933. His expansionist foreign policy precipitated World War II, while his fanatical anti-Semitism led to the Holocaust. ■ [as *n.*] (**a Hitler**) a person with authoritarian or tyrannical characteristics: *little Hitlers in the classroom.* **—Hit·ler·i·an** /hitˈle(ə)rēən/ *adj.* **—Hit·ler·ite** /-,rīt/ *n.* & *adj.*

Hit·ler·ism /ˈhitlə,rizəm/ ▸*n.* the political principles or policy of the Nazi Party in Germany 1933–45. ▷named after Adolf HITLER.

Hit·ler mus·tache ▸*n.* a small square mustache like that worn by Adolf Hitler.

Hit·ler sa·lute ▸*n.* another term for NAZI SALUTE.

hit list ▸*n.* a list of people to be killed for criminal or political reasons: *a terrorist hit list.* ■ a list of things to be attacked or opposed: *one of a dozen "corporate welfare" schemes on a Washington hit list.*

hit man ▸*n.* *informal* a person who is paid to kill someone, esp. for a criminal or political organization.

hit pa·rade ▸*n.* *dated* a weekly listing of the current best-selling pop records. ■ any list of popular things: *at the top of the intellectual hit parade among pundits.*

hit squad ▸*n.* a team of assassins.

Hitt. ▸*abbr.* Hittite.

Hit·tite /ˈhitīt/ ▸*n.* **1** a member of an ancient people who established an empire in Asia Minor and Syria that flourished from *c.*1700 to *c.*1200 BC. ■ a subject of this empire or one of their descendants, including the members of a Canaanite or Syrian people mentioned in the Bible (11th to 8th century BC). **2** the Anatolian language of the Hittites, the earliest attested Indo-European language. Written in both hieroglyphic and cuneiform scripts, it was deciphered in the early 20th century.

▸*adj.* of or relating to the Hittites, their empire, or their language. ▷from Hebrew *Ḥittīm*, ultimately from Hittite *Ḫatti*.

HIV ▸*abbr.* human immunodeficiency virus, a retrovirus that causes AIDS.

hive /hīv/ ▸*n.* a beehive. ■ the bees in a hive. ■ a thing that has the domed shape of a beehive. ■ *figurative* a place in which people are busily occupied: *the kitchen became a hive of activity.*

▸*v.* [*trans.*] place (bees) in a hive. ■ [*intrans.*] (of bees) enter a hive.

▸*phrasal v.* □ **hive something off** *chiefly Brit.* (esp. in business) separate something from a larger group or organization, esp. from public to private ownership: *the weekly magazine hived off by the BBC.* ▷Old English *hȳf*, of Germanic origin.

hive bee ▸*n.* another term for HONEYBEE.

hives /hīvz/ ▸*plural n.* [treated as *sing.* or *pl.*] another term for URTICARIA. ▷early 16th cent. (originally Scots, denoting various conditions causing a rash, esp. in children): of unknown origin.

HIV-pos·i·tive ▸*adj.* having had a positive result in a blood test for the AIDS virus HIV.

hiya /ˈhīə/ ▸*exclam.* an informal greeting. ▷1940s: alteration of *how are you?*

Hiz·bul·lah ▸ variant spelling of HEZBOLLAH.

HK ▸*abbr.* Hong Kong.

HL ▸*abbr.* (in the UK) House of Lords.

hl ▸*abbr.* hectoliter(s).

hld. ▸*abbr.* hold.

hlqn ▸*abbr.* harlequin.

HM ▸*abbr.* ■ headmaster or headmistress. ■ (in the UK) Her (or His) Majesty('s): *HM Forces.*

hm ▸*abbr.* hectometer(s).

hmm /(h)m/ (also **h'm**) ▸*exclam.* & *n.* variant spelling of HEM[2], HUM[2].

HMO ▸*abbr.* health maintenance organization.

Hmong /hmôNG/ ▸*n.* (*pl.* same) **1** a member of a people living traditionally in isolated mountain villages throughout Southeast Asia. Large numbers have emigrated to the U.S. **2** the language of this people, occurring in a large number of highly distinct dialects.

▸*adj.* relating to or denoting this people or their language.

HMS ▸*abbr.* Her or His Majesty's Ship, used in the names of ships in the British navy: *HMS Ark Royal.*

HN ▸*abbr.* head nurse.

hny ▸*abbr.* honey.

Ho ▸*symbol* the chemical element holmium.

ho[1] /hō/ (also **hoe**) ▸*n.* (*pl.* **hos** or **hoes**) *black slang* a prostitute. ■ *derogatory* a woman. ▷1960s: representing a dialect pronunciation of WHORE.

ho[2] /hō/ ▸*exclam.* **1** an expression of surprise, admiration, triumph, or derision: *Ho! I'll show you.* ■ [in *combination*] used as the second element of various exclamations: *what ho!* | *heave ho.* **2** used to call for attention: *ho there!* ■ [in *combination*] *dated, chiefly Nautical* used to draw attention to something seen: *land ho!* ▷natural exclamation: first recorded in Middle English.

ho. ▸*abbr.* house.

hoa·gie /ˈhōgē/ ▸*n.* (also **hoa·gy**) (*pl.* **-gies**) another term for SUBMARINE SANDWICH. ▷of unknown origin.

Hoag·land /ˈhōglənd/, Edward (Morley) (1932–) U.S. writer. His novels include *Seven Rivers West* (1986). He also wrote short stories such as those collected in *The Final Fate of Alligators* (1992) and travel books, which include *African Calliope* (1979).

hoar /hôr/ *archaic poetic/literary* ▸*adj.* grayish white; gray or gray-haired with age.
▸*n.* hoarfrost. ▷Old English *hār*, of Germanic origin; related to German *hehr* 'majestic, noble.'

hoard /hôrd/ ▸*n.* a stock or store of money or valued objects, typically one that is secret or carefully guarded: *he came back to rescue his little* ***hoard of*** *gold.* ■ an ancient store of coins or other valuable artifacts: *a* ***hoard of*** *Romano-British bronzes.* ■ an amassed store of useful information or facts, retained for future use: *a* ***hoard of*** *secret information about his work.*
▸*v.* [*trans.*] amass (money or valued objects) and hide or store away: *thousands of antiques hoarded by a compulsive collector.* ■ accumulate a supply of (something) in a time of scarcity: *many of the boat people had hoarded rations.* ■ reserve in the mind for future use: [as *adj.*] (**hoarded**) *a year's worth of hoarded resentments and grudges.* ▷Old English *hord* (noun), *hordian* (verb), of Germanic origin; related to German *Hort* (noun), *horten* (verb). **—hoard·er** *n.*

USAGE Take care not to confuse the same-sounding words **hoard** and **horde**. A **hoard** is 'a secret stock or store of something' (*a* ***hoard*** *of treasure*), while a **horde** is a disparaging word for 'a large group of people' (***hordes*** *of fans descended on the stage*). One way to remember the difference is to think of *stashing your* ***hoard*** *behind the loose* ***board*** (note the spelling likeness of **hoard** and **board**).

hoard·ing /ˈhôrdiNG/ ▸*n. Brit.* a large board in a public place, used to display advertisements; a billboard. ■ a temporary board fence erected around a building site. ▷early 19th cent.: from obsolete *hoard* in the same sense (probably based on Old French *hourd*; related to HURDLE) + -ING[1].

hoar·frost /ˈhôr,frôst; -,fräst/ ▸*n.* a grayish-white crystalline deposit of frozen water vapor formed in clear still weather on vegetation, fences, etc.

hoar·hound /ˈhôrˈ,hound/ ▸*n.* variant spelling of HOREHOUND.

hoarse /hôrs/ ▸*adj.* (of a person's voice) sounding rough and harsh, typically as the result of a sore throat or of shouting: *a hoarse whisper* | [as *complement*] *he shouted himself hoarse.* ▷Old English *hās*, of Germanic origin; related to Dutch *hees*. The spelling with *r* was influenced in Middle English by an Old Norse cognate. **—hoarse·ly** *adv.* **—hoars·en** /ˈhôrsən/ *v.* **—hoarse·ness** *n.*

hoar·y /ˈhôrē/ ▸*adj.* (**hoar·i·er**, **hoar·i·est**) **1** grayish-white: *hoary cobwebs.* ■ (of a person) having gray or white hair; aged: *a hoary old fellow with a face of white stubble.* ■ [*attrib.*] used in names of animals and plants covered with whitish fur or short hairs, e.g., **hoary bat**, **hoary cress**. **2** old and trite: *that hoary American notion that bigger is better.* **—hoar·i·ly** /ˈhôrəlē/ *adv.* **—hoar·i·ness** *n.*

hoar·y mar·mot /ˈhôrē ˈmärmət/ ▸*n.* a large stocky grayish-brown marmot with a whistling call, found in the mountains of northwestern North America. • *Marmota caligata*, family Sciuridae.

ho·at·zin /wätˈsēn/ ▸*n.* a large tree-dwelling tropical American bird with weak flight. Young hoatzins have hooked claws on their wings, enabling them to climb around among the branches. • *Opisthocomus hoazin*, the only member of the family Opisthocomidae (order Galliformes or Cuculiformes). ▷mid 17th cent.: from American Spanish, from Nahuatl *uatzin*, probably imitative of its call.

hoax /hōks/ ▸*n.* a humorous or malicious deception: *they recognized the plan as a hoax* | [as *adj.*] *he was accused of making hoax calls.*
▸*v.* [*trans.*] deceive with a hoax. ▷late 18th cent. (as a verb): probably a contraction of HOCUS. **—hoax·er** *n.*

hob[1] /häb/ ▸*n.* **1** a flat metal shelf at the side or back of a fireplace, having its surface level with the top of the grate and used esp. for heating pans. **2** a machine tool used for cutting gears or screw threads. ▷late 16th cent. Sense 1 dates from the late 17th cent.

hob[2] ▸*n.* **1** a male ferret. Compare with GILL[4] (sense 2). **2** *archaic* or *dialect* a sprite or hobgoblin. ▷late Middle English (in the sense 'country fellow'): nickname for *Rob*, short for *Robin* or *Robert*, often referring specifically to ROBIN GOODFELLOW.
▸*PHRASE* □ **play** (or **raise**) **hob** cause mischief.

Ho·ban /ˈhōbən/, James (1762–1831), U.S. architect; born in Ireland. He designed the White House in Washington, DC 1793–1801 and, after it was burned in the War of 1812, supervised its restoration and redesign 1815–29.

Ho·bart /ˈhō,bärt/ the capital and chief port of Tasmania, on the southeastern part of the island; pop. 127,100.

Hobbes /häbz/, Thomas (1588–1679), English philosopher. He believed that human action was motivated entirely by selfish concerns, notably fear of death. He is best known for his treatise *Leviathan, or the Matter, Form, and Power of a Commonwealth, Ecclesiastical and Civil* (1651). **—Hobbes·i·an** /ˈhäbzēən/ *adj.*

hob·bit /ˈhäbit/ ▸*n.* a member of an imaginary race similar to humans, of small size and with hairy feet, in stories by J. R. R. Tolkien. ▷1937: invented by Tolkien in his book *The Hobbit*, and said by him to mean 'hole-dweller.'

hob·ble /ˈhäbəl/ ▸*v.* **1** [*intrans.*] walk in an awkward way, typically because of pain from an injury: *he was hobbling around on crutches.* ■ *figurative* proceed haltingly in action or speech: *inertia and habit will keep it hobbling along.* **2** [*trans.*] (often **be hobbled**) tie or strap together (the legs of a horse or other animal) to prevent it from straying. [variant of HOPPLE.] ■ cause (a person or animal) to limp: *Johnson was still hobbled slightly by an ankle injury.* ■ *figurative* be or cause a problem for: *cotton farmers hobbled by low prices.*
▸*n.* **1** [in *sing.*] an awkward way of walking, typically due to pain from an injury: *he finished the game almost reduced to a hobble.* **2** a rope or strap used for hobbling a horse or other animal. ▷Middle English: probably of Dutch or Low German origin and related to Dutch *hobbelen* 'rock from side to side.' **—hob·bler** /ˈhäb(ə)lər/ *n.*

hob·ble·bush /ˈhäbəl,bŏŏSH/ ▸*n.* a North American viburnum that bears clusters of white or pink flowers and purple-black berries. • *Viburnum alnifolium*, family Caprifoliaceae.

hob·ble·de·hoy /ˈhäbəldē,hoi/ *informal, dated* ▸*n.* a clumsy or awkward youth.
▸*adj.* awkward or clumsy: *his hobbledehoy hands.* ▷mid 16th cent.: of unknown origin.

hob·ble skirt ▸*n.* a style of skirt so narrow at the hem as to impede walking, popular in the 1910s.

Hobbs /häbz/ a city in southeastern New Mexico, just west of the Texas border, southeast of Roswell; pop. 28,657.

hob·by[1] /ˈhäbē/ ▸*n.* (*pl.* **-bies**) **1** an activity done regularly in one's leisure time for pleasure: *her hobbies are reading and gardening.* **2** *archaic* a small horse or pony. ■ *historical* an early type of velocipede. ▷late Middle English *hobyn*, *hoby*, from nicknames for the given name *Robin*. Originally in sense 2 (compare with DOBBIN), it later came to denote a toy horse or hobbyhorse, hence 'a pastime, something done for pleasure.'

hob·by[2] ▸*n.* (*pl.* **-bies**) a migratory Old World falcon with long narrow wings, catching dragonflies and birds on the wing. • Genus *Falco*, family Falconidae: four species, e.g., the (**northern**) **hobby** (*F. subbuteo*) of Eurasia. ▷late Middle English: from Old French *hobet*, diminutive of *hobe* 'falcon.'

hob·by·horse /ˈhäbē,hôrs/ ▸*n.* **1** a child's toy consisting of a stick with a model of a horse's head at one end. ■ a rocking horse. ■ a model of a horse or a horse's head, typically of wicker, used in morris dancing or pantomime. **2** a preoccupation; a favorite topic: *one of her favorite hobbyhorses was about how people had to care for "the child inside."*

hob·by·ist /ˈhäbēist/ ▸*n.* a person who pursues a particular hobby: *a computer hobbyist.*

hob·gob·lin /ˈhäb,gäblən/ ▸*n.* (in mythology and fairy tales) a mischievous imp or sprite. ■ a fearsome mythical creature. ▷mid 16th cent.: from HOB[2] + GOBLIN.

hob·nail /ˈhäb,nāl/ ▸*n.* a short heavy-headed nail used to reinforce the soles of boots. ■ a blunt projection, esp. in cut or molded glassware. ■ glass decorated with such projections. ▷late 16th cent.: from HOB[1] + NAIL. **—hob·nailed** *adj.*

hob·nail liv·er (also **hob·nailed liv·er**) ▸*n.* a liver having many small knobby projections due to cirrhosis.

hob·nob /ˈhäb,näb/ ▸*v.* (**-nobbed**, **-nob·bing**) [*intrans.*] *informal* mix socially, esp. with those of higher social status: *a select few who* ***hobnob with*** *the biggest celebrities the country has to offer.* ▷early 19th cent. (in the sense 'drink together'): from archaic *hob or nob*, *hob and nob*, probably meaning 'give and take,' used by two people drinking to each other's health, from dialect *hab nab* 'have or not have.'

ho·bo /ˈhō,bō/ ▸*n.* (*pl.* **-boes** or **-bos**) a homeless person; a tramp. ■ a migrant worker. ▷late 19th cent.: of unknown origin.

Ho·bo·ken /ˈhō,bōkən/ an industrial city in northeastern New Jersey, on the Hudson River, opposite New York City; pop. 33,397.

Hob·son's choice /ˈhäbsənz/ ▸*n.* a choice of taking what is available or nothing at all. ▷mid 17th cent.: named after Thomas *Hobson* (1554–1631), a livery stable owner in Cambridge, England, who gave the customer the "choice" of the horse nearest the door or none at all.

Ho Chi Minh /ˈhō ˈCHē ˈmin/ (1890–1969), Vietnamese communist statesman; president of North Vietnam 1954–69; born *Nguyen That Thanh*. He led the Vietminh against the Japanese during World War II, fought the French until they were defeated in 1954 and Vietnam was divided into North and South Vietnam, and deployed his forces in the guerrilla struggle that became the Vietnam War.

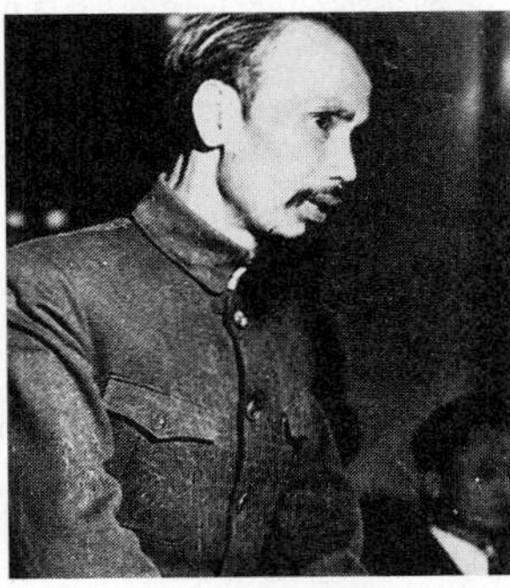

Ho Chi Minh

Ho Chi Minh Cit·y a city and port on the southern coast of Vietnam; pop 3,016,000. As Saigon, it was the capital of the French colony established in Vietnam in the 19th century and became the capital of South Vietnam in the partition of 1954. The name was changed to Ho Chi Minh City in 1975.

Ho Chi Minh Trail a covert system of trails along Vietnam's western frontier, a major supply route for North Vietnamese forces during the Vietnam War.

hock[1] /häk/ ▸*n.* **1** the joint in a quadruped's hind leg between the knee and the fetlock, the angle of which points backward. **2** a knuckle of meat, esp. of pork or ham. ▷late Middle English.

hock[2] ▸*v.* [*trans.*] informal term for PAWN[2]. ▷mid 19th cent. (in the phrase *in hock*): from Dutch *hok* 'hutch, prison, debt.'
▸*PHRASE* □ **in hock** having been pawned. ■ in debt: *East European states* ***in hock to*** *Western bankers.*

hock[3] ▸*n. Brit.* a dry white wine from the German Rhineland. ▷abbreviation of obsolete *hockamore*, alteration of German *Hochheimer (Wein)* '(wine) from Hochheim.'

hock·et /ˈhäkit/ ▸*n. Music* a spasmodic or interrupted effect in medieval and contemporary music, produced by dividing a melody between two parts, notes in one part coinciding with rests in the other. ▷late 18th cent.: from French *hoquet* 'hiccup'; in Old French the sense was 'hitch, sudden interruption,' which also existed in Middle English. **—hock·et·ing** *n.*

hock·ey /ˈhäkē/ ▸*n.* **1** short for ICE HOCKEY. **2** short for FIELD HOCKEY. ▷early 16th cent.: of unknown origin.

Hock·ney /ˈhäknē/, David (1937–), English painter. He is best known for his California work of the mid 1960s, which depicts flat, almost shadowless architecture, lawns, and swimming pools.

ho·cus /ˈhōkəs/ ▸*v.* (**-cused**, **-cus·ing** or *Brit.* **-cussed**, **-cus·sing**) [*trans.*] *archaic* deceive (someone): *these people have been hocussed and cheated by the government.* ▷late 17th cent.: from an obsolete noun *hocus* 'trickery,' from HOCUS-POCUS.

ho·cus-po·cus /ˈpōkəs/ ▸*n.* meaningless talk or activity, often designed to draw attention away from and disguise what is actually happening: *some people*

still view psychology as a lot of hocus-pocus. ■ a form of words often used by a person performing magic tricks. ■ deception; trickery.
▸*v.* (**-po·cused**, **-po·cus·ing** or *Brit.* **-po·cussed**, **-po·cus·sing**) [*intrans.*] play tricks. ■ [*trans.*] play tricks on, deceive. ▷early 17th cent.: from *hax pax max Deus adimax*, a pseudo-Latin phrase used as a magic formula by conjurors.

hod /häd/ ▸*n.* a builder's V-shaped open trough on a pole, used for carrying bricks and other building materials. ■ a coal scuttle. ▷late 16th cent.: variant of northern English dialect *hot* 'a basket for carrying earth,' from Old French *hotte* 'pannier,' probably of Germanic origin.

hod·den /'hädn/ ▸*n. chiefly Scottish N. English* a coarse woolen cloth. ▷late 16th cent.: of unknown origin.

Ho·dei·da /hō'dādə/ the chief port of Yemen, on the Red Sea; pop. 246,000. Arabic name **AL-HUDAYDA**.

hodge·podge /'häj,päj/ (*Brit.* **hotch·potch**) ▸*n.* [in *sing.*] a confused mixture: *Rob's living room was* ***a hodgepodge of*** *modern furniture and antiques.* See note at **JUMBLE**. ▷late Middle English: alteration of **HOTCHPOTCH** by association with *Hodge* (a nickname for the given name *Roger*), an archaic British term used as a name for a typical agricultural worker.

Hodg·kin[1] /'häjkin/, Sir Alan Lloyd (1914–1998), English physiologist. With Andrew Huxley he demonstrated the role of sodium and potassium ions in the transmission of nerve impulses between cells. Nobel Prize for Physiology or Medicine (1963, shared with John C. Eccles and A. F. Huxley).

Hodg·kin[2], Dorothy (Crowfoot) (1910–94), British chemist. She developed Sir Lawrence Bragg's X-ray diffraction technique for investigating the structure of crystals and applied it to complex organic compounds. She determined the structures of penicillin, vitamin B_{12}, and insulin. Nobel Prize for Chemistry (1964).

Hodg·kin's dis·ease /'häjkinz/ ▸*n.* a malignant but often curable disease of lymphatic tissues typically causing painless enlargement of the lymph nodes, liver, and spleen. ▷mid 19th cent.: named after Thomas *Hodgkin* (1798–1866), the English physician who first described it.

ho·di·er·nal /,hōdē'ərnl; ,hädē-/ ▸*adj. rare* of or relating to the present day. ▷mid 17th cent.: from Latin *hodiernus* (from *hodie* 'today') + **-AL**.

hod·o·graph /'hädə,graf/ ▸*n. Mathematics* a curve, the radius vector of which represents in magnitude and direction the velocity of a moving object. ▷mid 19th cent.: from Greek *hodos* 'way' + **-GRAPH**.

ho·do·scope /'hädə,skōp/ ▸*n. Physics* an instrument for observing the paths of subatomic particles, esp. those arising from cosmic rays. ▷early 20th cent. (denoting a microscope for examination of light paths in crystals): from Greek *hodos* 'way' + **-SCOPE**. The current sense dates from the 1950s.

Hoe /hō/, Richard March (1812–86), U.S. inventor and industrialist. In 1846, he developed a successful rotary press, which greatly increased the speed of printing.

hoe[1] /hō/ ▸*n.* a long-handled gardening tool with a thin metal blade, used mainly for weeding and breaking up soil.
▸*v.* (**hoes**, **hoed**, **hoe·ing**) [*trans.*] use a hoe to dig (earth) or thin out or dig up (plants). ■ [*intrans.*] use a hoe. ▷Middle English: from Old French *houe*, of Germanic origin; related to German *Haue*, also to **HEW**. **—ho·er** *n.*

hoe[2] ▸*n.* variant spelling of **HO**[1].

hoe·cake /'hō,kāk/ ▸*n.* a coarse cake made of cornmeal, originally baked on the blade of a hoe.

hoe·down /'hō,doun/ ▸*n.* a social gathering at which lively folk dancing takes place. ■ a lively folk dance.

Ho·fei variant of **HEFEI**.

Hof·fa /'häfə/, Jimmy (1913–*c.*1975), U.S. trade union leader; full name *James Riddle Hoffa*. President of the Teamsters from 1957, he was imprisoned 1967–71 for attempted bribery of a federal court judge, fraud, and looting pension funds. His sentence was commuted by President Nixon and he was given parole in 1971 on condition that he resign as president of the union. He disappeared in 1975 and is thought to have been murdered.

Hoff·man /'häfmən/, Dustin (Lee) (1937–), U.S. actor. A versatile method actor, he won Academy Awards for *Kramer vs Kramer* (1979), about a couple battling for child custody, and *Rain Man* (1989), in which he plays an autistic adult. Other notable movies: *The Graduate* (1967) and *Tootsie* (1983).

Hoff·mann /'häfmən/, E. T. A. (1776–1822), German novelist, short-story writer, and music critic; full name *Ernst Theodor Amadeus Hoffmann*. His extravagantly fantastic stories provided the inspiration for Offenbach's opera *Tales of Hoffmann* (1881).

Hof·mann /'hôfmän/, Hans (1880–1966) U.S. artist; born in Germany. He was a leader in the style of abstract expressionism.

Hof·manns·thal /'hōfmən,stäl/, Hugo von (1874–1929), Austrian poet and playwright. He wrote the libretti for many of Richard Strauss's operas, including *Elektra* (1909) and *Der Rosenkavalier* (1911). With Strauss and Max Reinhardt, he helped found the Salzburg Festival.

hog /hôg; häg/ ▸*n.* **1** a domesticated pig, esp. one over 120 pounds (54 kg) and reared for slaughter. ■ a feral pig. ■ a wild animal of the pig family, for example, a warthog. ■ *informal* a greedy person. **2** *informal* a large, heavy motorcycle. **3** (also **hogg**) *Brit.* a young sheep before the first shearing.
▸*v.* (**hogged**, **hog·ging**) **1** [*trans.*] *informal* keep or use all of (something) for oneself in an unfair or selfish way: *he never hogged the limelight.* **2** (with reference to a ship) bend or become bent convex upward along its length as a result either of the hull being supported in the middle and not at the ends (as in a heavy sea) or the vessel's being loaded more heavily at the ends. Compare with **SAG**. ▷late Old English *hogg*, *hocg*, perhaps of Celtic origin and related to Welsh *hwch* and Cornish *hoch* 'pig, sow.' **—hog·ger** *n.* **—hog·ger·y** /'hôgərē; 'häg-/ *n.* **—hog·gish** *adj.* **—hog·gish·ly** *adv.* **—hog·like** /-,līk/ *adj.*
▸*PHRASES* □ **go (the) whole hog** *informal* do something completely or thoroughly. [of several origins suggested, one interprets *hog* as a slang term for a ten-cent piece; another refers the idiom to one of Cowper's poems (1779), which discusses Muslim uncertainty about which parts of the pig are acceptable as food, leading to the 'whole hog' being eaten, because of confusion over Muhammad's teaching.] □ **live high on** (or **off**) **the hog** *informal* have a luxurious lifestyle.

Ho·gan /'hōgən/, Ben (1912–97) U.S. golfer; full name *William Benjamin Hogan*. His numerous championship titles include the Masters (1951, 1953), the PGA (1946, 1948), the U.S. Open (1948, 1950, 1951, 1953), and the British Open (1953).

ho·gan /'hō,gän; -gən/ ▸*n.* a traditional Navajo hut of logs and earth. ▷Navajo.

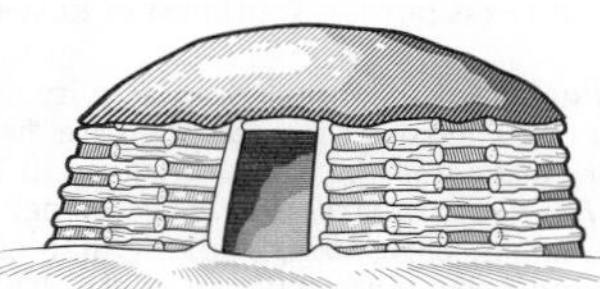

hogan

Ho·garth /'hō,gärTH/, William (1697–1764), English painter and engraver. Notable works include his series of engravings on "modern moral subjects," such as *A Rake's Progress* (1735). **—Ho·garth·i·an** /hō'gärTHēən/ *adj.*

hog·back /'hôg,bak; 'häg-/ ▸*n.* a long hill or mountain ridge with steep sides.

hog deer ▸*n.* a short-legged heavily built deer having a yellow-brown coat with darker underparts, found in grasslands and paddy fields in Southeast Asia. • *Cervus porcinus*, family Cervidae.

hog·fish /'hôg,fiSH; 'häg-/ ▸*n.* (*pl.* same or **-fish·es**) a colorful wrasse that occurs chiefly in the warm waters of the western Atlantic, often acting as a cleaner fish for other species. • Several genera and species in the family Labridae, in particular the large edible *Lachnolaimus maximus*.

hogg /hôg; häg/ ▸*n.* variant spelling of **HOG** (sense 3).

Hog·gar Moun·tains /'hägər; ,hə'gär/ a mountain range in the Saharan desert in southern Algeria that rises to a height of 9,573 feet (2,918 m) at Tahat. Also called **AHAGGAR MOUNTAINS**.

hog heav·en ▸*n.* a state of complete happiness: *Bryan stood on the pitcher's mound, knowing he was* ***in hog heaven.***

hog line ▸*n. Curling* a line marked across either end of a curling rink. No sweeping is allowed until a stone has crossed the first line.

Hog·ma·nay /'hägmə,nā/ ▸*n.* (in Scotland) New Year's Eve, and the celebrations that take place at this time. ▷early 17th cent.: perhaps from *hoguinané*, Norman French form of Old French *aguillanneuf* 'last day of the year, new year's gift.'

hog-nosed bat ▸*n.* a tiny insectivorous bat with a piglike nose and no tail, native to Thailand. It is the smallest known bat. • *Craseonycteris thonglongyai*, the only member of the family Craseonycteridae.

hog-nosed skunk ▸*n.* an American skunk with a bare elongated snout and a black face, found in rugged terrain. • Genus *Conepatus*, family Mustelidae: several species.

hog·nose snake /'hôg,nōz; 'häg-/ (also **hog-nosed snake**) ▸*n.* a harmless burrowing American snake with an upturned snout. When threatened it inflates itself with air and hisses, and may feign death. Also called **PUFF ADDER** in North America. • Genus *Heterodon*, family Colubridae: several species.

hog plum ▸*n.* a tropical tree that bears edible plumlike fruit, in particular: • a Caribbean tree (also called **yellow mombin**) with yellow fruit (*Spondias mombin*, family Anacardiaceae). • a tropical American tree (also called **tallowwood**) with bitter fruit and timber that is used as a sandalwood substitute (*Ximenia americana*, family Olacaceae). ▷late 17th cent.: so named because the fruit is common food for hogs in the West Indies and Brazil.

hogs·head /'hôgz,hed; 'hägz-/ (abbr.: **hhd**) ▸*n.* a large cask. ■ a measure of capacity for wine, equal to 63 gallons (238.7 liters). ■ a measure of capacity for beer, equal to 64 gallons (245.5 liters). ▷Middle English: from **HOG** + **HEAD**; the reason for the term is unknown.

hog-tie (also **hog·tie**) ▸*v.* [*trans.*] secure by fastening together the hands and feet (of a person) or all four feet (of an animal): *they gagged him and hog-tied him to the front pew.* ■ *figurative* impede or hinder greatly: *an economy hog-tied by entrenched Stalinism.*

hog·wash /'hôg,wôSH; 'häg,wäSH/ ▸*n. informal* nonsense. ▷mid 15th cent.: from **HOG** + **WASH**; the original sense was 'kitchen swill for pigs.'

hog·weed /'hôg,wēd; 'häg-/ ▸*n.* a large, coarse, white-flowered weed of the parsley family, native to north temperate regions and formerly used as forage for pigs. • Genus *Heracleum*, family Umbelliferae: several species, in particular the common European *H. sphondylium* and the introduced **giant hogweed** (*H. mantegazzianum*).

hog-wild (also **hog wild**) ▸*adj. informal* extremely enthusiastic; out of control: *I'm not hog-wild about this job.*
▸*PHRASE* □ **go hog-wild** act in an unrestrained manner: *Congress will go hog-wild in its spending.*

Ho·hen·stau·fen /,hōən'stoufən; -'SHtou-/ a German dynastic family, some of whom ruled as Holy Roman Emperors between 1138 and 1254, among them Frederick I (Barbarossa).

Ho·hen·zol·lern /'hōən,zälərn/ a German dynastic family from which came the kings of Prussia from 1701 to 1918 and German emperors from 1871 to 1918.

Hoh·hot /'hə'hôt/ (also **Hu·he·hot** /'ho͞o'hā'hōt/) the capital of Inner Mongolia autonomous region, in northeastern China; pop. 1,206,000. Former name (until 1954) **KWEISUI**.

ho ho /'hō 'hō/ ▸*exclam.* representing deep, exuberant laughter. ■ used to express triumph, esp. at discovery: *Ho ho! A stranger in our midst!* ▷mid 16th cent.: reduplication of **HO**[2].

ho-hum /'hō 'həm/ ▸*exclam.* used to express boredom or resignation.
▸*adj.* boring: *a ho-hum script.* ▷1920s: imitative of a yawn.

hoick /hoik/ *informal* ▸*v.* [*trans.*] lift or pull abruptly or with effort: *she hoicked her bag on to the desk.*
▸*n.* an abrupt pull. ▷late 19th cent.: perhaps a variant of **HIKE**.

hoicks /hoiks/ ▸*exclam.* variant of **YOICKS**.

hoi pol·loi /'hoi pə,loi/ ▸*plural n.* (usu. **the hoi polloi**) *derogatory* the masses; the common people: *avoid mixing with the hoi polloi.* ▷mid 17th cent.: Greek, literally 'the many.'

USAGE 1 **Hoi** is the Greek word for **the**, and the phrase **hoi polloi** means 'the many.' This has led some traditionalists to insist that **hoi polloi** should not be used in English with **the**, since that would be to state the word **the** twice. But, once established in English, expressions such as **hoi polloi** are typically treated as fixed units and are subject to the rules and conventions of English. Evidence shows that use with **the** has now become an accepted part of standard English usage: *they kept to themselves, away from the hoi polloi* (rather than *. . . away from hoi polloi*).
2 **Hoi polloi** is sometimes used incorrectly to

mean 'upper class'—that is, the exact opposite of its normal meaning. It seems likely that the confusion arose by association with the similar-sounding but otherwise unrelated word **hoity-toity**.

hoi·sin /'hoisin; hoi'sin/ (also **hoisin sauce**) ▸*n.* a sweet, spicy, dark red sauce made from soybeans, vinegar, sugar, garlic, and various spices, widely used in southern Chinese cooking.

hoist /hoist/ ▸*v.* [*trans.*] raise (something) by means of ropes and pulleys: *high overhead great cranes hoisted girders.* ■ [*trans.*] raise or haul up: *she hoisted her backpack onto her shoulder.*
▸*n.* **1** an act of raising or lifting something. ■ *figurative* an act of increasing something: *the government's interest rate hoist.* ■ an apparatus for lifting or raising something. **2** the part of a flag nearest the staff; the vertical dimension of a flag. **3** a group of flags raised as a signal. ▷late 15th cent.: alteration of dialect *hoise*, probably from Dutch *hijsen* or Low German *hiesen*, but recorded earlier. **—hoist·er** *n.*
▸*PHRASES* □ **hoist one's flag** (of an admiral) take up command. □ **hoist the flag** stake one's claim to discovered territory by displaying a flag. □ **hoist by one's own petard** see PETARD.

hoi·ty-toi·ty /'hoitē 'toitē/ ▸*adj.* **1** haughty; snobbish: *the moneyed, hoity-toity inhabitants of the island.* **2** *archaic* frolicsome. ▷mid 17th cent. (in the sense 'boisterous or silly behavior'): from obsolete *hoit* 'indulge in riotous mirth,' of unknown origin.

Ho·kan /'hōkən/ ▸*adj.* relating to or denoting a group of American Indian languages of California and western Mexico, considered as a possible language family and including Yuman, Mojave, and several other languages now extinct or nearly so.
▸*n.* this hypothetical language family. ▷from Hokan *hok* 'about two' + **-AN**.

hoke /hōk/ ▸*v.* [*trans.*] *informal* (of an actor) act (a part) in an insincere, sentimental, or melodramatic manner: *just try it straight—don't* **hoke it up**. ▷early 20th cent.: back-formation from HOKUM.

hok·ey /'hōkē/ ▸*adj.* (**hok·i·er**, **hok·i·est**) *informal* mawkishly sentimental: *a good-hearted, slightly hokey song.* ■ noticeably contrived: *a hokey country-western accent.* ▷1940s: from HOKUM + -Y[1]. **—hok·ey·ness** (also **hok·i·ness**) *n.*

ho·key-po·key ▸*n. informal* **1** (**the hokey-pokey**) a circle dance with a synchronized shaking of the limbs in turn, accompanied by a simple song. **2** hocus-pocus; trickery. **3** *dated* ice cream sold on the street, esp. by Italian street vendors. ▷late 19th cent.: of unknown origin.

Hok·kai·do /hä'kīdō/ the most northern of the four main islands of Japan; pop. 5,644,000; capital, Sapporo.

hok·ku /'hō,ko͞o; 'hä-/ ▸*n.* (*pl.* same) another term for HAIKU. ▷late 19th cent.: Japanese, literally 'opening verse' (of a linked sequence of comic verses).

ho·kum /'hōkəm/ ▸*n. informal* nonsense: *they dismissed such corporate homilies as boardroom hokum.* ■ trite, sentimental, or unrealistic situations and dialogue in a movie, play, or piece of writing: *classic B-movie hokum.* ▷early 20th cent.: of unknown origin.

Ho·ku·sai /'hōkə,sī/, Katsushika (1760–1849), Japanese painter and wood engraver. He represented aspects of everyday Japanese life in his woodcuts.

Hol·arc·tic /häl'ärktik; hō'lärk-; -'ärtik/ ▸*adj. Zoology* of, relating to, or denoting a zoogeographical region comprising the Nearctic and Palearctic regions combined. The two continents have been linked intermittently by the Bering land bridge, and the faunas are closely related. ■ [as *n.*] (**the Holarctic**) the Holarctic region. ▷late 19th cent.: from HOLO- 'whole' + ARCTIC.

Hol·bein /'hōl,bīn/, Hans (1497–1543), German painter and engraver; known as **Holbein the Younger**. He was commissioned by Henry VIII to supply portraits of the king's prospective brides.

hold[1] /hōld/ ▸*v.* (*past* **held** /held/) **1** [*trans.*] grasp, carry, or support with one's arms or hands: *she was holding a brown leather suitcase* | [*intrans.*] *he* **held onto** *the back of a chair.* ■ [*trans.*] keep or sustain in a specified position: *I held the door open for him figurative the people are* **held down** *by a repressive military regime.* ■ embrace (someone): *Mark pulled her into his arms and held her close.* ■ (**hold something up**) support and prevent from falling: *concrete pillars hold up the elevated section of the railroad.* ■ be able to bear (the weight of a person or thing): *I reached up to the nearest branch that seemed likely to hold my weight.* ■ (of a vehicle) maintain close contact with (the road), esp. when driven at speed: *the car holds the corners very well.* ■ (of a ship or an aircraft) continue to follow (a particular course): *the ship is holding a southeasterly course.* ■ [*intrans.*] *archaic* keep going in a particular direction: *he* **held on his way**, *close behind his friend.* **2** [*trans.*] keep or detain (someone): *the police were holding him on a murder charge* | [*trans.*] *she was held prisoner for two days.* ■ keep possession of (something), typically in the face of a challenge or attack: *the rebels held the town for many weeks* | [*intrans.*] *White managed to* **hold onto** *his lead.* ■ keep (someone's interest or attention). ■ (of a singer or musician) sustain (a note). ■ stay or cause to stay at a certain value or level: [*intrans.*] *the savings rate held at 5%* | [*trans.*] *he is determined to hold down inflation.* **3** [*intrans.*] remain secure, intact, or in position without breaking or giving way: *the boat's anchor would not hold.* ■ (of a favorable condition or situation) continue without changing: *let's hope her luck holds.* ■ be or remain valid or available: *I'll have that coffee now, if the offer still holds.* ■ (of an argument or theory) be logical, consistent, or convincing: *their views still seem to* **hold up** *extremely well.* ■ (**hold to**) refuse to abandon or change (a principle or opinion). ■ [*trans.*] (**hold someone to**) cause someone to adhere to (a commitment). **4** [*trans.*] contain or be capable of containing (a specified amount): *the tank held twenty-four gallons.* ■ be able to drink (a reasonable amount of alcohol) without becoming drunk or suffering any ill effects: *I can hold my liquor as well as anyone.* ■ have or be characterized by: *I don't know what the future holds.* **5** [*trans.*] have in one's possession: *the managing director still holds fifty shares in the company.* ■ [*intrans.*] *informal* be in possession of illegal drugs: *he was holding, and the police hauled him off to jail.* ■ have or occupy (a job or position). ■ have or adhere to (a belief or opinion): *I feel nothing but pity for someone who holds such chauvinistic views* | [with *clause*] *they hold that all literature is empty of meaning.* ■ [*trans.*] consider (someone) to be responsible or liable for a particular situation: *you can't hold yourself responsible for what happened.* ■ (**hold someone/something in**) regard someone or something with (a specified feeling): *the speed limit is held in contempt by many drivers.* ■ [with *clause*] (of a judge or court) rule; decide: *the Court of Appeals held that there was no evidence to support the judge's assessment.* **6** [*trans.*] keep or reserve for someone: *a reservation can be held for twenty-four hours.* ■ prevent from going ahead or occurring: *hold your fire!* ■ maintain (a telephone connection) until the person one has telephoned is free to speak: *please hold, and I'll see if he's available* | [*intrans.*] *will you hold?* ■ *informal* refrain from adding or using (something, typically an item of food or drink): *a strawberry margarita, but hold the tequila.* ■ (**hold it**) *informal* used as a way of exhorting someone to wait or to stop doing something: *hold it right there, pal!* ■ [*intrans.*] *archaic* restrain oneself. **7** [*trans.*] arrange and take part in (a meeting or conversation): *a meeting was held at the church.*
▸*phrasal v.* □ **hold something against** allow past actions or circumstances to have a negative influence on one's present attitude toward (someone): *he knew that if he failed her, she would hold it against him forever.* □ **hold back** hesitate to act or speak: *he held back, remembering the mistake he had made before.* □ **hold someone/something back** prevent or restrict the advance, progress, or development of someone or something: *Jane struggled to hold back her laughter.* ■ (**hold something back**) refuse or be unwilling to make something known: *you're not holding anything back from me, are you?* □ **hold something down** *informal* succeed in keeping a job or position for a period of time. □ **hold forth** talk lengthily, assertively, or tediously about a subject: *he was* **holding forth on** *the merits of the band's debut album.* □ **hold off** (of bad weather) fail to occur. ■ delay or postpone an action or decision. □ **hold someone/something off** resist an attacker or challenge: *he held off a late challenge by Vose to win by thirteen seconds.* □ **hold on 1** [often in *imperative*] wait; stop: *hold on a minute, I'll be right back!* **2** endure or keep going in difficult circumstances: *if only they could hold on a little longer.* □ **hold on to** keep: *the industry is trying to hold on to experienced staff.* □ **hold out** resist or survive in dangerous or difficult circumstances: *Russian troops* **held out against** *constant attacks.* ■ continue to be sufficient: *we can stay here for as long as our supplies hold out.* □ **hold out for** continue to demand (a particular thing), refusing to accept what has been offered: *he is holding out for a guaranteed 7 percent raise.* □ **hold out on** *informal* refuse to give something, typically information, to (someone). □ **hold something out** offer a chance or hope: *a new drug may hold out hope for patients with lung cancer.* □ **hold something over 1** postpone something. **2** use a fact or piece of information to threaten or intimidate (someone). □ **hold together** (or **hold something together**) remain or cause to remain united: *if your party holds together, you will probably win.* □ **hold up** remain strong or vigorous: *the dollar held up well against the yen.* □ **hold someone/something up 1** delay or block the movement or progress of someone or something: *our return flight was held up for seven hours.* **2** rob someone or something using the threat of force or violence: *a masked gunman held up the post office.* **3** present or expose someone or something as an example or for particular treatment: *they were* **held up to** *public ridicule.* **4** *Bridge* refrain from playing a winning card for tactical reasons. □ **hold with** [with *negative*] *informal* approve of: *I don't hold with fighting or violence.*
▸*n.* **1** an act or manner of grasping something; a grip: *he* **caught hold of** *her arm* | *he lost his hold and fell.* ■ a particular way of grasping or restraining someone, esp. an opponent in wrestling or judo. ■ a place where one can grip with one's hands or feet while climbing: *he felt carefully with his feet for a hold and swung himself up.* ■ a way of influencing someone: *he discovered that Tom had some kind of* **hold over** *his father.* ■ a degree of power or control: *military forces tightened their* **hold on** *the capital.* **2** *archaic* a fortress. ▷Old English *haldan, healdan*, of Germanic origin; related to Dutch *houden* and German *halten*; the noun is partly from Old Norse *hald* 'hold, support, custody.' **—hold·a·ble** *adj.*
▸*PHRASES* □ **be left holding the bag** (or **baby**) *informal* be left with an unwelcome responsibility, typically without warning. □ **don't hold your breath** see BREATH. □ **get hold of** grasp (someone or something) physically. ■ grasp (something) intellectually; understand. ■ *informal* obtain: *if you can't get hold of ripe tomatoes, add some tomato purée.* ■ *informal* find or manage to contact (someone): *I'll try and get hold of Mark.* □ **hold someone/something at bay** see BAY[5]. □ **hold one's breath** see BREATH. □ **hold someone/something cheap** *archaic* have a low opinion of someone or something. □ **hold court** be the center of attention amid a crowd of one's admirers. □ **hold someone/something dear** care for or value someone or something greatly: *fidelity is something most of us hold dear.* □ **hold fast** remain tightly secured: *the door held fast, obviously locked.* ■ continue to believe in or adhere to an idea or principle: *it is important that we* **hold fast to** *the policies.* □ **hold the fort** take responsibility for a situation while another person is temporarily absent. □ **hold one's ground** see GROUND[1]. □ **hold someone's hand** give a person comfort, guidance, or moral support in a difficult situation. □ **hold hands** (of two or more people) clasp each other by the hand, typically as a sign of affection. □ **hold someone/something harmless** *Law* indemnify someone or something. □ **hold one's horses** [usu. as *imperative*] *informal* wait a moment. □ **hold the line** not yield to the pressure of a difficult situation: *France's central bank would hold the line.* □ **hold one's nose** squeeze one's nostrils with one's fingers in order to avoid inhaling an unpleasant smell. □ **hold one's own** see OWN. □ **hold one's peace** see PEACE. □ **hold (one's) serve** (or **service**) (in tennis and other racket sports) win a game in which one is serving. □ **hold the stage** see STAGE. □ **hold sway** see SWAY. □ **hold someone to bail** *Law* bind by bail. □ **hold one's tongue** [often in *imperative*] *informal* remain silent. □ **hold someone/something to ransom** see RANSOM. □ **hold true** (or **good**) remain true or valid: *his views still hold true today.* □ **hold up one's head** (or **hold one's head high**) see HEAD. □ **hold water** [often with *negative*] (of a statement, theory, or line of reasoning) appear to be valid, sound, or reasonable: *this argument just does not hold water.* □ **no holds barred** (in wrestling) with no restrictions on the kinds of holds that are used. ■ *figurative* used to convey that no rules or restrictions apply in a conflict or dispute: *no-holds-barred military action.* □ **on hold** waiting to be connected while making a telephone call. ■ temporarily not being dealt with or pursued: *he* **put** *his career* **on hold**. □ **take hold** start to have an effect: *the reforms of the late nineteenth century had taken hold.* □ **there is no holding someone back** used to convey that someone is particularly determined or cannot be prevented from

Pronunciation Key ə ago; ər over; 'ə or ,ə up; 'ər or ,ər fur; a hat; ā rate; ä car; CH chew; e let; ē see; e(ə)r air; i fit; ī by; i(ə)r ear; NG sing; ō go; ô for; oi boy; o͝o good; o͞o goo; ou out; SH she; TH thin; T͟H then; (h)w why; ZH vision

H

doing something: *there's no holding you back these days.*

hold[2] ▸*n.* a large space in the lower part of a ship or aircraft in which cargo is stowed. ▷late 16th cent.: from obsolete *holl*, from Old English *hol* (see HOLE). The addition of *-d* was due to association with HOLD[1].

hold·all /ˈhōld,ôl/ ▸*n. Brit.* a large rectangular bag with handles and a shoulder strap, used for carrying clothes and other personal belongings.

hold·back /ˈhōl(d),bak/ ▸*n.* a thing serving to hold something else in place: *a curtain holdback.* ■ a sum of money withheld under certain conditions.

hold but·ton ▸*n.* a button on a telephone that temporarily interrupts a call so that another call may be taken.

Hol·den /ˈhōldən/, William (1918–81) U.S. actor; born *William Beadle.* His movies include *Stalag 17* (Academy Award, 1953), *Picnic* (1955), *Bridge on the River Kwai* (1957), and *Towering Inferno* (1974). He also campaigned for animal preservation in Africa.

hold·er /ˈhōldər/ ▸*n.* **1** a device or implement for holding something: *a cigarette holder.* **2** a person who holds something: *U.S. passport holders | holders of two American hostages.* ■ the possessor of a trophy, championship, or record: [with *adj.*] *the record holder in the 100-meter dash.* **3** *Brit.* a smallholder.

hold·fast /ˈhōl(d),fast/ ▸*n.* a firm grip. ■ a staple or clamp securing an object to a wall or other surface. ■ *Biology* a stalked organ by which an alga or other simple aquatic plant or animal is attached to a substrate.

hold·ing /ˈhōldiNG/ ▸*n.* **1** an area of land held by lease. ■ the tenure of such land. **2** (**holdings**) stocks, property, and other financial assets in someone's possession: *commercial property holdings.* ■ books, periodicals, and other material in a library. **3** (in certain team sports such as football, basketball, and ice hockey) an illegal move that prevents an opponent from moving freely. **4** a court's ruling on a matter of law essential to a judicial decision. ■ the legal principle drawn from such a ruling.

hold·ing com·pa·ny ▸*n.* a company created to buy and possess the shares of other companies, which it then controls.

hold·ing ground ▸*n. Nautical* an area of seabed where an anchor will hold.

hold·ing pat·tern ▸*n.* the flight path maintained by an aircraft awaiting permission to land. ■ a state or period of no progress or change: *stock markets settled down yesterday into a holding pattern.*

hold·ing tank ▸*n.* a large container in which liquids are temporarily held.

hold·out /ˈhōld,out/ ▸*n.* an act of resisting something or refusing to accept what is offered: *a defiant holdout against a commercial culture.* ■ a person or organization acting in such a way.

hold·o·ver /ˈhōld,ōvər/ ▸*n.* a person or thing surviving from an earlier time, esp. someone surviving in office or remaining on a sports team: *he purged the party of holdovers from the communist days.*

hold·up /ˈhōld,əp/ ▸*n.* **1** a situation that causes delay, esp. to a journey. **2** a robbery conducted with the use of threats or violence: *three dead in armored car holdup.*

hole /hōl/ ▸*n.* **1** a hollow place in a solid body or surface: *he dug out a small hole in the snow.* ■ an animal's burrow. ■ an aperture passing through something: *he had a hole in his sock.* ■ a cavity or receptacle on a golf course, typically one of eighteen or nine, into which the ball must be hit. ■ a cavity of this type as representing a division of a golf course or of play in golf: *Stephen lost the first three holes to Eric.* ■ *Physics* a position from which an electron is absent, esp. one regarded as a mobile carrier of positive charge in a semiconductor. ■ [in *place names*] a valley: *Jackson Hole.* **2** *informal* a small or unpleasant place: *she had wasted a whole lifetime in this hole of a town.* ■ *informal* an awkward situation: *get yourself out of a hole.*

▸*v.* [*trans.*] **1** make a hole or holes in: *a fuel tank was holed by the attack and a fire started.* **2** *Golf* hit (the ball) so that it falls into a hole: *alternate shots from each partner until the ball is holed* [*intrans.*] *he* **holed in one** *at the third.*

▸*phrasal v.* □ **hole out** *Golf* send the ball into a hole. □ **hole up** *informal* hide oneself: *I holed up for two days in a tiny cottage in Pennsylvania.* ▷Old English *hol* (noun), *holian* (verb), of Germanic origin; related to Dutch *hol* (noun) 'cave,' (adjective) 'hollow,' and German *hohl* 'hollow,' from an Indo-European root meaning 'cover, conceal.' —**hol·ey** /ˈhōlē/ *adj.*

▸PHRASES □ **blow a hole in** ruin the effectiveness of (something): *the amendment could blow a hole in the legislation.* □ **in the hole** *informal* in debt: *we're still three thousand dollars in the hole.* □ **in holes** worn so much that holes have formed: *my clothes are in holes.* □ **make a hole in** use a large amount of: *holidays can make a big hole in your savings.* □ **need something like a hole in the head** *informal* used to emphasize that someone has absolutely no need or desire for something. □ **a square peg in a round hole** see PEG.

hole-and-cor·ner ▸*adj.* attempting to avoid public notice; secret: *a hole-and-corner wedding.*

hole card ▸*n.* (in stud or other forms of poker) a card that has been dealt face down. ■ *figurative* a thing that is kept secret until it can be used to one's own advantage.

hole in one ▸*n.* (*pl.* **holes in one**) *Golf* a shot that enters the hole from the tee with no intervening shots.

hole in the heart ▸*n. Medicine* a congenital defect in the heart septum, resulting in inadequate circulation of oxygenated blood (a cause of blue baby syndrome).

hole in the wall ▸*n. informal* **1** a small dingy place, esp. a bar or restaurant: *even though the gallery was only a hole in the wall, I couldn't have afforded it* | [as *adj.*] *hole-in-the wall bars.* **2** *Brit.* an automatic cash dispenser installed in the outside wall of a bank.

hole saw ▸*n.* a tool for making circular holes, consisting of a metal cylinder with a toothed edge.

Ho·li /ˈhōlē/ ▸*n.* a Hindu spring festival celebrated in February or March in honor of Krishna. ▷via Hindi from Sanskrit *holī.*

Hol·i·day /ˈhälə,dā/, Billie (1915–59), U.S. jazz singer; born *Eleanora Fagan.* She began her recording career with Benny Goodman's band in 1933 and then went on to perform with many small jazz groups. Her autobiography, *Lady Sings the Blues* (1956), was made into a movie in 1972.

hol·i·day /ˈhäli,dā/ ▸*n.* a day of festivity or recreation when no work is done: *December 25 is an official public holiday.* ■ [as *adj.*] characteristic of a holiday; festive: *a holiday atmosphere.* ■ *chiefly Brit.* (often **holidays**) a vacation: *I spent my summer holidays on a farm | Fred was* **on holiday** *in Spain.*

▸*v.* [*intrans.*] *chiefly Brit.* spend a holiday in a specified place: *he is* **holidaying in** *Italy.* ▷Old English *hāligdæg* 'holy day.'

hol·i·day camp ▸*n. Brit.* a site for vacationers with accommodations, entertainment, and leisure facilities.

hol·i·day·mak·er /ˈhälidā,mākər/ ▸*n. Brit.* a person on vacation away from home.

hol·i·day sea·son ▸*n.* the period of time from Thanksgiving until New Year, including such festivals as Christmas, Hanukkah, and Kwanzaa.

ho·li·er-than-thou ▸*adj.* characterized by an attitude of moral superiority: *they had quite a critical, holier-than-thou approach.*

ho·li·ness /ˈhōlēnis/ ▸*n.* the state of being holy: *a life of holiness and total devotion to God.* ■ (**His/Your Holiness**) a title given to the pope, Orthodox patriarchs, and the Dalai Lama, or used in addressing them. ■ [as *adj.*] denoting a Christian renewal movement originating in the mid 19th century among Methodists in the U.S., emphasizing the Wesleyan doctrine of the sanctification of believers. ▷Old English *hālignes* (see HOLY, -NESS).

ho·lism /ˈhōl,izəm/ ▸*n. chiefly Philosophy* the theory that parts of a whole are in intimate interconnection, such that they cannot exist independently of the whole, or cannot be understood without reference to the whole, which is thus regarded as greater than the sum of its parts. Holism is often applied to mental states, language, and ecology. The opposite of ATOMISM. ■ *Medicine* the treating of the whole person, taking into account mental and social factors, rather than just the physical symptoms of a disease. ▷1920s: from HOLO- 'whole' + -ISM; coined by J. C. Smuts to designate the tendency in nature to produce organized "wholes" (bodies or organisms) from the ordered grouping of units. —**ho·list** *adj.* & *n.*

ho·lis·tic /hōˈlistik/ ▸*adj. chiefly Philosophy* characterized by comprehension of the parts of something as intimately interconnected and explicable only by reference to the whole. ■ *Medicine* characterized by the treatment of the whole person, taking into account mental and social factors, rather than just the physical symptoms of a disease. —**ho·lis·ti·cal·ly** /-ik(ə)lē/ *adv.*

hol·la /ˈhälə/ ▸*exclam. archaic* used to call attention to something: *"Holla! what storm is this?"* ▷early 16th cent. (as an order to stop or cease): from French *holà*, from *ho* 'ho!' + *là* 'there.'

Hol·land /ˈhälənd/ **1** another name for the NETHERLANDS. **2** a city in southwestern Michigan, noted for its Dutch heritage; pop. 30,745.

hol·land /ˈhälənd/ ▸*n.* a kind of smooth, durable linen fabric, used chiefly for window shades and furniture covering. ▷Middle English: from HOLLAND, the name of a former province of the Netherlands where the cloth was made, from Dutch, earlier *Holtlant* (from *holt* 'wood' + *-lant* 'land').

hol·lan·daise sauce /ˈhälən,dāz/ ▸*n.* a creamy sauce of melted butter, egg yolks, and lemon juice or vinegar, served esp. with fish. ▷French *hollandaise*, feminine of *hollandais* 'Dutch,' from *Hollande* 'Holland.'

Hol·land·er /ˈhäləndər/ ▸*n. dated* a native of the Netherlands.

Hol·lands /ˈhäləndz/ ▸*n. archaic* Dutch gin. ▷from archaic Dutch *hollandsch genever* (earlier form of *hollands jenever*) 'Dutch gin.'

hol·ler /ˈhälər/ *informal* ▸*v.* [*intrans.*] (of a person) give a loud shout or cry: *he hollers when he wants feeding* | [with *direct speech*] *"I can't get down," she hollered.*

▸*n.* a loud cry or shout. ■ (also **field holler**) a melodic cry with abrupt or swooping changes of pitch, used originally by black slaves at work in the fields and later contributing to the development of the blues. ▷late 17th cent. (as a verb): variant of the rare verb *hollo*; related to HALLOO.

Hol·ler·ith /ˈhälə,riTH/, Herman (1860–1929), U.S. engineer. He invented a tabulating machine using punched cards for computation, an important precursor of the electronic computer, and he founded a company that later expanded to become the IBM Corporation.

hol·low /ˈhälō/ ▸*adj.* **1** having a hole or empty space inside: *each fiber has a hollow core.* ■ (of a thing) having a depression in its surface; concave: *hollow cheeks.* ■ (of a sound) echoing, as though made in or on an empty container: *a hollow cough.* **2** without significance: *the result was a hollow victory.* ■ insincere: *a hollow promise.*

▸*n.* a hole or depression in something: *a hollow at the base of a large tree.* ■ a small valley: *the house fell behind as they climbed out of the hollow.*

▸*v.* [*trans.*] form by making a hole: *a tunnel was* **hollowed out** *in a mountain range.* ■ make a depression in. ▷Old English *holh* 'cave'; obscurely related to HOLE. —**hol·low·ly** *adv.* —**hol·low·ness** *n.*

▸PHRASES □ **beat someone hollow** defeat or surpass someone completely or thoroughly. □ **in the hollow of one's hand** entirely in one's power: *great events lay in the hollow of his hand.*

hol·low at·om ▸*n.* an atom in which inner-shell electrons are missing, usually as a result of electrical excitation.

hol·low-eyed ▸*adj.* (of a person) having deeply sunken eyes, typically as a result of illness or tiredness.

hol·low-heart·ed ▸*adj. archaic* insincere; false.

hol·low square ▸*n. historical* a body of infantry drawn up in a square with a space in the middle.

hol·low·ware /ˈhälō,we(ə)r/ ▸*n.* serving dishes and accessories, esp. of silver, that are hollow or concave. Contrast with FLATWARE.

Hol·ly /ˈhälē/, Buddy (1936–59), U.S. rock-and-roll singer, guitarist, and songwriter; born *Charles Hardin Holley.* He recorded such hits as "That'll be the Day" with his band, The Crickets, before going solo in 1958. He was killed in an airplane crash.

hol·ly /ˈhälē/ ▸*n.* a widely distributed shrub, typically having prickly dark green leaves, small white flowers, and red berries. There are several deciduous species of holly but the evergreen hollies are more typical and familiar. • Genus *Ilex*, family Aquifoliaceae: many species, in particular the **American holly** (*I. opaca*), known as the "Christmas holly." See also GALLBERY, WINTERBERRY, YAUPON. ■ the branches, foliage, and berries of this plant used as Christmas decorations. ▷Middle English *holi*, shortened form of Old English *holegn, holen*, of Germanic origin; related to German *Hulst.*

hol·ly fern ▸*n.* a small shield fern that has narrow glossy fronds with a double row of stiff bristle-edged lobes, found chiefly in mountainous areas of both Eurasia and North America. • Several species in the genus *Polystichum*, family Dryopteridaceae, in particular the widespread *P. lonchitis*.

hol·ly·hock /ˈhälē,häk/ ▸*n.* a tall Eurasian plant of the mallow family, widely cultivated for its large showy flowers. • *Alcea rosea*, family Malvaceae. ▷Middle English: from **HOLY** + obsolete *hock* 'mallow,' of unknown origin. It originally denoted the marsh mallow, which has medicinal uses (hence, perhaps, the use of 'holy'); the current sense dates from the mid 16th cent.

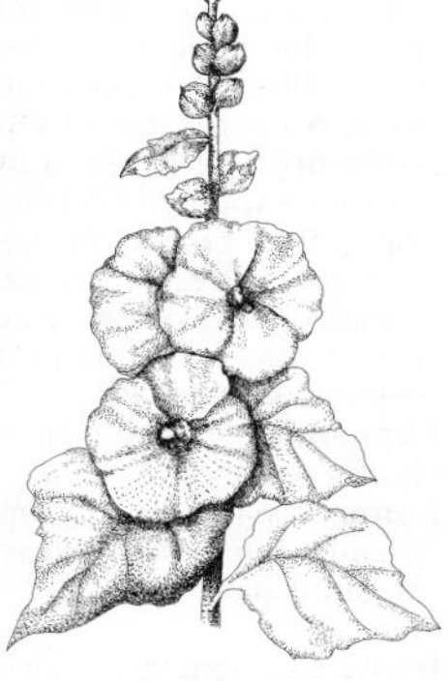
hollyhock

hol·ly oak ▸*n.* the holm oak or the kermes oak, both of which have tough evergreen leaves that are reminiscent of holly leaves.

Hol·ly·wood /ˈhälē,wo͝od/ **1** a resort city in southeastern Florida, north of Miami, on the Atlantic Ocean; pop. 139,357. **2** a district in Los Angeles, the principal center of the U.S. movie industry. ■ the U.S. movie industry and the lifestyles of the people associated with it: *he was never seduced by the glitz and money of Hollywood.*

Hol·ly·wood bed ▸*n.* a bed consisting of a mattress on a box spring supported on short legs, often with an upholstered headboard.

Holm /hōm/, Celeste (1919–) U.S. actress. She starred in movies such as *Gentleman's Agreement* (Academy Award, 1947), *Come to the Stable* (1949), and *All about Eve* (1950).

holm /hōm/ (also **holme**) ▸*n. Brit.* an islet, esp. in a river or near a mainland. ■ a piece of flat ground by a river that is submerged in time of flood. ▷Old English, from Old Norse *holmr*.

Holmes[1] /hōmz/, Oliver Wendell (1809–94), U.S. physician, poet, and essayist; father of U.S. Supreme Court justice Oliver Wendell Holmes. His main contribution to medicine was an essay, written in 1843, on contagion as one cause of puerperal fever. His best-known literary works are the humorous essays known as "table talks," which began with *The Autocrat of the Breakfast Table* (1857–58).

Holmes[2], Oliver Wendell (1841–1935) U.S. Supreme Court associate justice 1902–32; the son of physician and essayist Oliver Wendell Holmes. He became well known for his strong, articulate, and often dissenting opinons.

Holmes[3], Sherlock, an extremely perceptive private detective in stories by Sir Arthur Conan Doyle. **—Holmes·i·an** /-zēən/ *adj.*

hol·mi·um /ˈhōlmēəm/ ▸*n.* the chemical element of atomic number 67, a soft silvery-white metal of the lanthanide series. (Symbol: **Ho**) ▷late 19th cent.: modern Latin, from *Holmia*, Latinized form of *Stockholm*, the capital of Sweden (because many minerals of the yttrium group, to which holmium belongs, are found in that area); discovered by P.T. Cleve, Swedish chemist.

holm oak /hōm/ ▸*n.* an evergreen southern European oak, with dark green glossy leaves. Also called **EVERGREEN OAK** or **ILEX**. • *Quercus ilex*, family Fagaceae. ▷late Middle English: *holm*, alteration of dialect *hollin*, from Old English *holen* 'holly.'

hol·o /ˈhälō/ ▸*n.* (*pl.* **hol·os**) *informal* a hologram.

holo- ▸*comb. form* whole; complete: *holocaust* | *holophytic.* ▷from Greek *holos* 'whole.'

ho·lo·blas·tic /,häləˈblastik; ,hōlə-/ ▸*adj.* (of an ovum) having cleavage planes that divide the egg into separate blastomeres.

hol·o·caust /ˈhälə,kôst; ˈhōlə-/ ▸*n.* **1** destruction or slaughter on a mass scale, esp. caused by fire or nuclear war: *a nuclear holocaust* | *the threat of imminent holocaust.* ■ (**the Holocaust**) the mass murder of Jews under the German Nazi regime during the period 1941–45. More than 6 million European Jews, as well as members of other persecuted groups, such as gypsies and homosexuals, were murdered at concentration camps such as Auschwitz. **2** *historical* a Jewish sacrificial offering that is burned completely on an altar. ▷Middle English: from Old French *holocauste*, via late Latin from Greek *holokauston*, from *holos* 'whole' + *kaustos* 'burned' (from *kaiein* 'burn').

Hol·o·caust de·ni·al ▸*n.* the belief or assertion that the Holocaust did not happen or was greatly exaggerated. **—Hol·o·caust de·ni·er** *n.*

Hol·o·cene /ˈhälə,sēn; ˈhōlə-/ ▸*adj. Geology* of, relating to, or denoting the present epoch, which is the second epoch in the Quaternary period and followed the Pleistocene. Also called **RECENT.** ■ [as *n.*] (**the Holocene**) the Holocene epoch or the system of deposits laid down during this time.

> The Holocene epoch has lasted from about 10,000 years ago to the present day. It covers the period since the ice retreated after the last glaciation and is sometimes regarded as just another interglacial period.

▷late 19th cent.: coined in French from **HOLO-** 'whole' + Greek *kainos* 'new.'

hol·o·en·zyme /,häləˈen,zīm; ,hōlō-/ ▸*n. Biochemistry* a biochemically active compound formed by the combination of an enzyme with a coenzyme.

Hol·o·fer·nes /,häləˈfərnēz/ (in the Apocrypha) the Assyrian general of Nebuchadnezzar's forces, who was killed by Judith (Judith 4:1 ff.).

hol·o·gram /ˈhälə,gram; ˈhōlə-/ ▸*n.* a three-dimensional image formed by the interference of light beams from a laser or other coherent light source. ■ a photograph of an interference pattern that, when suitably illuminated, produces a three-dimensional image.

hol·o·graph /ˈhälə,graf; ˈhōlə-/ ▸*n.* a manuscript handwritten by the person named as its author: [as *adj.*] *a holograph letter by Abraham Lincoln.* ▷early 17th cent.: from French *holographe*, or via late Latin from Greek *holographos*, from *holos* 'whole' + *-graphos* 'written, writing.'

hol·og·ra·phy /hōˈlägrəfē/ ▸*n.* the study or production of holograms. **—hol·o·graph·ic** /,häləˈgrafik; ,hōlə-/ *adj.* **—hol·o·graph·i·cal·ly** /,häləˈgrafik(ə)lē; ,hōlə-/ *adv.*

hol·o·he·dral /,häləˈhēdrəl; ,hōlə-/ ▸*adj. Crystallography* having the full number of planes required by the symmetry of a crystal system.

Ho·lon /ˈhō,län; KHôˈlôn/ a manufacturing town in west central Israel, part of the Tel Aviv-Jaffa metropolitan area; pop. 164,000.

ho·loph·ra·sis /həˈläfrəsis/ ▸*n.* the expression of a whole phrase in a single word, for example *howdy* for *how do you do.* ■ the learning of linguistic elements as whole chunks by very young children acquiring their first language, for example *it's all gone* learned as *allgone.* **—hol·o·phrase** /ˈhälə,frāz; ˈhōlə-/ *n.* **—hol·o·phras·tic** /,häləˈfrastik; hōlə-/ *adj.*

hol·o·phyt·ic /,häləˈfitik; ,hōlə-/ ▸*adj. Biology* (of a plant or protozoan) able to synthesize complex organic compounds by photosynthesis.

hol·o·thu·ri·an /,häləˈTHo͝orēən; ,hōlə-/ ▸*n. Zoology* a sea cucumber. ▷mid 19th cent.: from the modern Latin genus name *Holothuria* (from Greek *holothourion*, denoting a kind of zoophyte) + **-AN**.

Hol·o·thu·roi·de·a /,hälōTHo͝orˈoidēə; ,hōlō-/ *Zoology* a class of echinoderms that comprises the sea cucumbers. ▷modern Latin (plural), based on Greek *holothourion* (see **HOLOTHURIAN**). **—hol·o·thu·roid** /-ˈTHo͝or,oid/ *n.* & *adj.*

hol·o·type /ˈhälə,tīp; ˈhōlə-/ ▸*n. Botany & Zoology* a single type specimen upon which the description and name of a new species is based. Compare with **SYNTYPE**.

hols /hälz/ ▸*plural n. Brit., informal* holidays. ▷early 20th cent.: abbreviation.

Hol·stein /ˈhōl,stān; -,stēn/ ▸*n.* an animal of a typically black-and-white breed of large dairy cattle.

hol·ster /ˈhōlstər/ ▸*n.* a holder for carrying a handgun or other firearm, typically made of leather and worn on a belt or under the arm: *the Luger slid easily from the holster.* ▸*v.* [*trans.*] put (a gun) into its holster. ▷mid 17th cent.: corresponding to and contemporary with Dutch *holster*, of unknown origin.

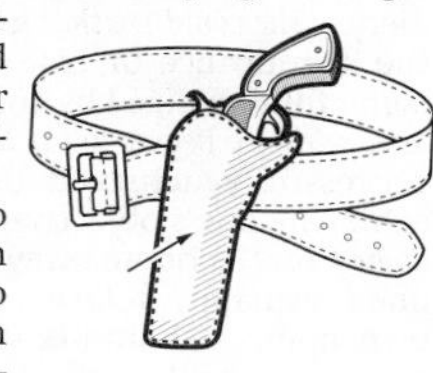
holster

holt[1] /hōlt/ ▸*n.* the den of an animal, esp. that of an otter. ▷late Middle English (sense 2): variant of **HOLD**[1].

holt[2] ▸*n. archaic* or *dialect* a wood or wooded hill. ▷Old English, of Germanic origin; related to Middle Dutch *hout* and German *Holz*, from an Indo-European root shared by Greek *klados* 'twig.'

ho·lus-bo·lus /ˈhōləs ˈbōləs/ ▸*adv.* all at once: *swallowing every proposal that is made holus-bolus.* ▷mid 19th cent. (originally dialect): perhaps pseudo-Latin for 'whole bolus, whole lump.'

ho·ly /ˈhōlē/ ▸*adj.* (**ho·li·er**, **ho·li·est**) **1** dedicated or consecrated to God or a religious purpose; sacred: *the Holy Bible* | *the holy month of Ramadan.* See note at **DIVINE.** ■ (of a person) devoted to the service of God: *saints and holy men.* ■ morally and spiritually excellent: *I do not lead a holy life.* **2** *informal* used as an intensifier: *having a holy good time.* **3** *dated* or *humorous* used in exclamations of surprise or dismay: *holy smoke!* ▷Old English *hālig*, of Germanic origin; related to Dutch and German *heilig*, also to **WHOLE**. **—ho·li·ly** /ˈhōləlē/ *adv.*

Ho·ly Al·li·ance a loose alliance of European powers pledged to uphold the principles of the Christian religion. It was proclaimed at the Congress of Vienna (1814–15) by the emperors of Austria and Russia and the king of Prussia and was joined by most other European monarchs.

Ho·ly Ark ▸*n.* see **ARK** (sense 2).

ho·ly bas·il ▸*n.* a kind of basil that is venerated by Hindus as a sacred plant. Also called **TULSI**. • *Ocimum sanctum*, family Labiatae.

ho·ly cit·y ▸*n.* a city held sacred by the adherents of a religion. ■ (**the Holy City**) Jerusalem. ■ (**the Holy City**) (in Christian tradition) Heaven.

Ho·ly Com·mun·ion ▸*n.* see **COMMUNION** (sense 2).

ho·ly day ▸*n.* a day on which a religious observance is held.

holy day of obligation /ˈhōlē dā əv; ə ,äbləˈgāSHən/ ▸*n.* (in the Roman Catholic Church) a day on which Roman Catholics are required to attend Mass.

Ho·ly Fam·i·ly Jesus as a child with Mary and Joseph (and often also others such as John the Baptist or St. Anne), esp. as a subject for a painting.

Ho·ly Fa·ther ▸*n.* a title of the pope.

Ho·ly·field /ˈhōlē,fēld/, Evander (1962–) U.S. boxer. He was a four-time world heavyweight champion 1990–92, 1993–94, 1996–99, 2000–2001.

ho·ly fool ▸*n.* a person who appears untelligent and unsophisticated but who has other redeeming qualities.

Ho·ly Ghost ▸*n.* another term for **HOLY SPIRIT**.

Ho·ly Grail ▸*n.* see **GRAIL**.

Ho·ly In·no·cents' Day ▸*n.* see **INNOCENTS' DAY**.

Ho·ly Joe ▸*n. informal* a sanctimonious or pious man. ■ a clergyman. ▷late 19th cent.: originally nautical slang.

Ho·ly Land a region on the eastern shore of the Mediterranean Sea, in what is now Israel and Palestine, revered by Christians as the place in which Jesus Christ lived and taught, by Jews as the land given to the people of Israel, and by Muslims. ■ a region similarly revered, for example, Arabia in Islam.

Ho·ly League any of various European alliances sponsored by the papacy during the 15th, 16th, and 17th centuries. They include the League of 1511–13, formed by Pope Julius II to expel Louis XII of France from Italy, and the French Holy League (also called the Catholic League) of 1576 and 1584, a Catholic extremist league formed during the French Wars of Religion.

Ho·ly Name ▸*n.* (esp. in the Catholic Church) the name of Jesus as an object of formal devotion.

Ho·ly Of·fice the ecclesiastical court of the Roman Catholic Church established as the final court of appeal in trials of heresy. Formed in 1542 as part of the Inquisition, it was renamed the Sacred Congregation for the Doctrine of the Faith in 1965.

ho·ly of ho·lies /ˈhōlē əv ˈhōlēz/ ▸*n.* the inner chamber of the sanctuary in the Jewish Temple in Jerusalem, separated by a veil from the outer chamber. It was reserved for the presence of God and could be entered only by the High Priest on the Day of Atonement. ■ a place regarded as most sacred or special: *she had done the wrong thing, venturing into this holy of holies.*

Hol·yoke /ˈhōlē,ōk; ˈhō(l),yōk/ an industrial city in west central Massachusetts, northwest of Springfield; pop. 43,704.

ho·ly or·ders ▸*plural n.* the sacrament or rite of ordination as a member of the Christian clergy, esp. in the grades of bishop, priest, or deacon.
▸*PHRASES* □ **in holy orders** having the status of an

Pronunciation Key ə *ago*; ər *over*; ˈə or ,ə *up*; ˈər or ,ər *fur*; a *hat*; ā *rate*; ä *car*; CH *chew*; e *let*; ē *see*; e(ə)r *air*; i *fit*; ī *by*; i(ə)r *ear*; NG *sing*; ō *go*; ô *for*; oi *boy*; o͝o *good*; o͞o *goo*; ou *out*; SH *she*; TH *thin*; T͟H *then*; (h)w *why*; ZH *vision*

ordained member of the clergy. □ **take holy orders** become an ordained member of the clergy.

ho·ly place ▶*n.* a place revered as holy, typically one to which religious pilgrimage is made. ■ *historical* the outer chamber of the sanctuary in the Jewish Temple in Jerusalem.

Ho·ly Roll·er ▶*n. informal, derogatory* a member of an evangelical Christian group that expresses religious fervor by frenzied excitement or trances.

Ho·ly Ro·man Em·pire the empire set up in western Europe following the coronation of Charlemagne as emperor in the year 800. It was created by the medieval papacy in an attempt to unite Christendom under one rule. At times the territory of the empire was extensive and included Germany, Austria, Switzerland, and parts of Italy and the Netherlands.

Ho·ly Sat·ur·day *n.* the Saturday preceding Easter Sunday.

Ho·ly Scrip·ture ▶*n.* the sacred writings of Christianity contained in the Bible.

Ho·ly See the papacy or the papal court; those associated with the pope in the government of the Roman Catholic Church at the Vatican. Also called SEE OF ROME.

Ho·ly Sep·ul·chre the place in which the body of Jesus was laid after being taken down from the Cross. ■ the church in Jerusalem erected over the traditional site of this tomb.

Ho·ly Spir·it ▶*n.* (in Christianity) the third person of the Trinity; God as spiritually active in the world.

Ho·ly Spir·it As·so·ci·a·tion for the U·ni·fi·ca·tion of World Chris·ti·an·i·ty another name for UNIFICATION CHURCH.

ho·ly·stone /ˈhōlē,stōn/ *chiefly historical* ▶*n.* a piece of soft sandstone used for scouring the decks of ships. ▶*v.* [*trans.*] scour (a deck) with a holystone. ▷early 19th cent.: probably from HOLY + STONE. Sailors called the stones "bibles" or "prayer books," perhaps because they scrubbed the decks on their knees.

ho·ly ter·ror ▶*n.* see TERROR (sense 2).

Ho·ly Thurs·day *n.* **1** (chiefly in the Roman Catholic Church) Maundy Thursday. **2** *dated* (in the Anglican Church) Ascension Day.

Ho·ly Trin·i·ty ▶*n.* see TRINITY.

ho·ly war ▶*n.* a war declared or waged in support of a religious cause.

ho·ly wa·ter ▶*n.* water blessed by a priest and used in religious ceremonies.

Ho·ly Week ▶*n.* the week before Easter, starting on Palm Sunday.

Ho·ly Writ ▶*n.* the Bible. ■ writings or sayings of unchallenged authority.

Ho·ly Year ▶*n.* (in the Roman Catholic Church) a period of remission from the penal consequences of sin, granted under certain conditions for a year usually at intervals of twenty-five years.

hom /hōm/ (also **ho·ma** /ˈhōmə/, **hao·ma** /ˈhoumə/) ▶*n.* the soma plant, a leafless vine of eastern India. • *Sarcostemma acidum*, family Asclepiadaceae ■ the sour, milky juice of this plant, consumed as a sacred drink of the Parsees. See also SOMA². ▷mid 19th cent.: from Persian *hūm* or Avestan *haoma*.

hom·age /ˈ(h)ämij/ ▶*n.* special honor or respect shown publicly: *they* ***paid homage to*** *the local boy who became president | a masterly work written* ***in homage to*** *Beethoven.* See note at HONOR. ■ *historical* formal public acknowledgment of feudal allegiance: *a man doing* ***homage*** *to his personal lord.* ▷Middle English: Old French, from medieval Latin *hominaticum*, from Latin *homo, homin-* 'man' (the original use of the word denoted the ceremony by which a vassal declared himself to be his lord's "man").

hom·bre /ˈämbrā; -brē/ ▶*n. informal* a man, esp. one of a particular type: *the Raiders quarterback is one tough hombre.* ▷mid 19th cent. (originally denoting a man of Spanish descent): Spanish, 'man,' from Latin *homo, homin-*.

hom·burg /ˈhämbərg/ ▶*n.* a man's felt hat having a narrow curled brim and a tapered crown with a lengthwise indentation. ▷late 19th cent.: named after *Homburg*, a town in western Germany, where such hats were first worn.

homburg

home /hōm/ ▶*n.* **1** the place where one lives permanently, esp. as a member of a family or household: *I was nineteen when I left home and went to college | they have made Provence their home.* ■ the family or social unit occupying such a place: *he came from a good home and was well educated.* ■ a house or an apartment considered as a commercial property: *low-cost homes for first-time buyers.* ■ a place where something flourishes, is most typically found, or from which it originates: *Piedmont is the home of Italy's finest red wines.* ■ *informal* a place where an object is kept. **2** an institution for people needing professional care or supervision: *an old people's home.* **3** *Sports* the goal or end point. ■ the place where a player is free from attack. ■ (in lacrosse) each of the three players stationed nearest their opponents's goal. ■ *Baseball* short for HOME PLATE. ■ a game played or won by a team on their own ground. ▶*adj.* [*attrib.*] **1** of or relating to the place where one lives: *I don't have your home address.* ■ made, done, or intended for use in the place where one lives: *traditional home cooking.* ■ relating to one's own country and its domestic affairs: *Japanese competitors are selling cars for lower prices in the U.S. than in their home market.* **2** (of a sports team or player) belonging to the country or locality in which a sporting event takes place: *the home team.* ■ played on or connected with a team's own ground: *their first home game of the season.* **3** denoting the administrative center of an organization: *the company has moved its home office.* ▶*adv.* to the place where one lives: *what time did he get home last night?* ■ in or at the place where one lives: *I stayed home with the kids.* ■ to the end or conclusion of a race or something difficult: *the favorite romped home six lengths clear.* ■ *Baseball* to or toward home plate. ■ to the intended or correct position: *he drove the bolt home noisily.* ▶*v.* [*intrans.*] **1** (of an animal) return by instinct to its territory after leaving it: *a dozen geese homing to their summer nesting grounds.* ■ (of a pigeon bred for long-distance racing) fly back to or arrive at its loft after being released at a distant point. **2** (**home in on**) move or be aimed toward (a target or destination) with great accuracy: *more than 100 missiles were launched, homing in on radar emissions.* ■ focus attention on: *a teaching style that homes in on what is of central importance for each student.* ▷Old English *hām*, of Germanic origin; related to Dutch *heem* and German *Heim*. —**home·like** /ˈhōm,līk/ *adj.*

▶*PHRASES* □ **at home** in one's own house. ■ in one's own neighborhood, town, or country: *he has been consistently successful both at home and abroad.* ■ comfortable and at ease in a place or situation: *sit down and* ***make yourself at home.*** ■ confident or relaxed about doing or using something: *he was quite at home talking about Eisenstein or Brecht.* ■ ready to receive and welcome visitors: *she took to her room and was not* ***at home to*** *friends.* ■ (with reference to sports fixtures) at a team's own ground: *Houston lost at home to Phoenix.* □ **bring something home to someone** make someone realize the full significance of something: *her first-hand account brought home to me the pain of the experience.* □ **close** (or **near**) **to home** (of a remark or topic of discussion) relevant or accurate to the point that one feels uncomfortable or embarrassed. □ **come home** *Golf* play the second nine holes in a round of eighteen holes. Compare with GO OUT (see GO¹). □ **come home to someone** (of the significance of something) become fully realized by someone: *the full enormity of what was happening came home to Sara.* □ **drive** (or **hammer** or **press** or **ram**) **something home** make something clearly and fully understood by the use of repeated or forcefully direct arguments. □ **hit** (or **strike**) **home** (of a blow or a missile) reach an intended target. ■ (of words) have the intended, esp. unsettling or painful, effect on their audience: *she could see that her remark had hit home.* ■ (of the significance or true nature of a situation) become fully realized by someone: *the full impact of life as a celebrity began to hit home.* □ **home free** having successfully achieved or being within sight of achieving one's objective: *at 7–0 they should have been home free.* □ **a home away from home** a place where one is as happy, relaxed, or comfortable as in one's own home. □ **home is where the heart is** *proverb* your home will always be the place for which you feel the deepest affection, no matter where you are. □ **home sweet home** used as an expression of one's pleasure or relief at being in or returning to one's own home.

home bank·ing ▶*n.* a system of banking whereby transactions are performed directly by telephone or via a computer and modem.

home base ▶*n.* a place from which operations or activities are carried out; headquarters. ■ the objective toward which players progress in certain games.

home·bod·y /ˈhōm,bädē/ ▶*n.* (*pl.* **-bod·ies**) *informal* a person who likes to stay at home, esp. one who is perceived as unadventurous.

home·boy /ˈhōm,boi/ ▶*n. informal* a young acquaintance from one's own town or neighborhood, or from the same social background. ■ (esp. among urban black people) a member of a peer group or gang. ■ a performer of rap music.

home-bred ▶*adj.* bred or raised at home. ■ lacking in worldly experience; unsophisticated.

home brew ▶*n.* beer or other alcoholic drink brewed at home: *I observed the town's bootlegger deliver three bottles of home brew.* ■ [as *adj.*] *informal* made at home, rather than in a store or factory: *home-brew software.* —**home-brewed** *adj.*

home·buy·er /ˈhōm,bīər/ ▶*n.* a person who buys a house or condominium.

home·com·ing /ˈhōm,kəmiNG/ ▶*n.* an instance of returning home. ■ a high school, college, or university game, dance, or other event to which alumni are invited.

home ec /ˈhōm ˈek/ ▶*n. informal* short for HOME ECONOMICS.

home ec·o·nom·ics ▶*plural n.* [often treated as *sing.*] cooking and other aspects of household management, esp. as taught at school.

home farm ▶*n.* a main farm where the owner or farmer lives. ■ *chiefly Brit. S. African* a farm on an estate that is set aside to provide produce for the owner of the estate.

home fries (also **home-fried potatoes**) ▶*plural n.* fried sliced potatoes.

home front ▶*n.* the civilian population and activities of a nation whose armed forces are engaged in war abroad.

home·girl /ˈhōm,gərl/ ▶*n.* a female equivalent of a homeboy.

home·grown /ˈhōmˈgrōn/ ▶*adj.* grown or produced in one's own garden or country: *a basket of homegrown fruit.* ■ belonging to one's own particular locality or country: *a jazz concert featuring homegrown artists.*

home key ▶*n.* **1** *Music* the basic key in which a work is written; the tonic key. **2** a key on a computer or typewriter keyboard that acts as the base position for one's fingers in touch-typing.

Ho·mel /hô'm(y)el/ an industrial city in southeastern Belarus; pop. 506,000. Russian name GOMEL.

home·land /ˈhōm,land/ ▶*n.* a person's or a people's native land: *migrants who departed from their Asian homeland.* ■ an autonomous or semiautonomous state occupied by a particular people: *their political aim is a separate Tamil homeland.* ■ *historical* any of ten partially self-governing areas in South Africa designated for particular indigenous African peoples under the former policy of apartheid.

home·less /ˈhōmlis/ ▶*adj.* (of a person) without a home, and therefore typically living on the streets: *the plight of young homeless people* | [as *n.*] (**the homeless**) *charities for the homeless.* —**home·less·ness** *n.*

home loan ▶*n.* a loan advanced to a person to assist in buying a house or condominium.

home·ly /ˈhōmlē/ ▶*adj.* (**home·li·er, home·li·est**) **1** (of a person) unattractive in appearance. **2** *Brit.* (of a place or surroundings) simple but cozy and comfortable, as in one's own home: *a modern hotel with a homely atmosphere.* ■ unsophisticated and unpretentious: *homely pleasures.* —**home·li·ness** *n.*

home·made /ˈhō(m)ˈmād/ ▶*adj.* made at home, rather than in a store or factory: *homemade apple pies | it sounds like the homemade album that it is.*

home·mak·er /ˈhōm,mākər/ ▶*n.* a person, esp. a housewife, who manages a home.

home·mak·ing /ˈhōm,mākiNG/ ▶*n.* the creation and management of a home, esp. as a pleasant place in which to live.

home mov·ie ▶*n.* a film made at home or without professional equipment or expertise, esp. a movie featuring one's own activities.

ho·me·o·box /ˈhōmēō,bäks/ ▶*n. Genetics* any of a class of closely similar sequences that occur in various genes and are involved in regulating embryonic development in a wide range of species. ▷1980s: from *homeotic* (see HOMEOSIS) + the noun BOX¹; first discovered in homeotic genes of *Drosophila* fruit flies.

Home Of·fice the British government department dealing with domestic affairs, including law and order, immigration, and broadcasting, in England and Wales.

ho·me·o·mor·phism /ˌhōmēəˈmôrˌfizəm/ ▸*n.* *Mathematics* an instance of topological equivalence to another space or figure. —**ho·me·o·mor·phic** /-ˈmôrfik/ *adj.*

ho·me·o·path /ˈhōmēəˌpaTH/ (also **ho·me·op·a·thist** /ˌhōmēˈäpəTHist/, *Brit.* **ho·moe·o·path**) ▸*n.* a person who practices homeopathy. ▷mid 19th cent.: from German *Homöopath* (see HOMEOPATHY).

ho·me·op·a·thy /ˌhōmēˈäpəTHē/ (*Brit.* **ho·moe·op·a·thy**) ▸*n.* the treatment of disease by minute doses of natural substances that in a healthy person would produce symptoms of disease. Often contrasted with ALLOPATHY. ▷early 19th cent.: coined in German from Greek *homoios* 'like' + *patheia* (see -PATHY). —**ho·me·o·path·ic** /ˌhōmēəˈpaTHik/ *adj.* —**ho·me·o·path·i·cal·ly** /ˌhōmēəˈpaTHik(ə)lē/ *adv.*

ho·me·o·sis /ˌhōmēˈōsis/ ▸*n.* (*pl.* **-ses** /-ˌsēz/) *Biology* the replacement of part of one segment of an insect or other segmented animal by a structure characteristic of a different segment, esp. through mutation. ▷late 19th cent.: from Greek *homoiōsis* 'becoming like,' from *homoios* 'like.' —**ho·me·ot·ic** /-ˈätik/ *adj.*

ho·me·o·sta·sis /ˌhōmēəˈstāsis/ ▸*n.* (*pl.* **-ses** /-sēz/) the tendency toward a relatively stable equilibrium between interdependent elements, esp. as maintained by physiological processes. ▷1920s: modern Latin, from Greek *homoios* 'like' + -STASIS. —**ho·me·o·stat·ic** /-ˈstatik/ *adj.*

ho·me·o·therm /ˈhōmēəˌTHərm/ (also **ho·moi·o·therm**) ▸*n.* *Zoology* an organism that maintains its body temperature at a constant level, usually above that of the environment, by its metabolic activity. Often contrasted with POIKILOTHERM; compare with WARM-BLOODED. ▷late 19th cent.: modern Latin, from Greek *homoios* 'like' + *thermē* 'heat.' —**ho·me·o·ther·mal** /ˌhōmēəˈTHərməl/ *adj.* —**ho·me·o·ther·mic** /ˌhōmēəˈTHərmik/ *adj.* —**ho·me·o·ther·my** *n.*

home·own·er /ˈhōmˌōnər/ ▸*n.* a person who owns their own home. —**home·own·er·ship** /-SHip/ *n.*

home page (also **home·page**) ▸*n.* *Computing* the introductory document of an individual's or organization's Web site. It typically serves as a table of contents to the site's other pages or provides links to other sites.

home plate ▸*n.* *Baseball* the five-sided flat white rubber base next to which the batter stands and over which the pitcher must throw the ball for a strike. A runner must touch home plate after having reached all the other bases to score a run.

home port ▸*n.* the port from which a ship originates or in which it is registered.

home·port /ˈhōmˌpôrt/ ▸*v.* [*trans.*] assign (a vessel) to a particular port as its home: *Guam's strategic location makes it the logical place to homeport an aircraft carrier.*

Ho·mer[1] /ˈhōmər/ (8th century BC), Greek epic poet. He is traditionally held to be the author of the *Iliad* and the *Odyssey*, although modern scholarship has revealed the place of the Homeric poems in a preliterate oral tradition. In later antiquity, Homer was regarded as the greatest poet, and his poems were constantly used as a model and source by others.

▸*PHRASE* □ **Homer sometimes nods** *proverb* even the most gifted person occasionally makes mistakes.

Ho·mer[2], Winslow (1836–1910), U.S. painter. He is noted for his seascapes, such as *Cannon Rock* (1895), painted in a vigorous naturalistic style that combines imagination and strength and is considered an expression of the American pioneering spirit.

ho·mer /ˈhōmər/ ▸*n.* **1** *Baseball* a home run. **2** a homing pigeon. **3** *informal* a referee or official who is thought to favor the team playing at home.

▸*v.* [*intrans.*] *Baseball* hit a home run: *he homered for the sixth time in seven games.*

home range ▸*n.* *Zoology* an area over which an animal or group of animals regularly travels in search of food or mates, and that may overlap with those of neighboring animals or groups of the same species.

Ho·mer·ic /hōˈmerik/ ▸*adj.* of or in the style of Homer or the epic poems ascribed to him. ■ of Bronze Age Greece as described in these poems: *the mists of the Homeric age.* ■ epic and large-scale: *some of us exert a Homeric effort.* ▷via Latin from Greek *Homērikos*, from *Homēros* (see HOMER[1]).

home rule ▸*n.* the government of a colony, dependent country, or region by its own citizens.

home run ▸*n.* *Baseball* a fair hit that allows the batter to make a complete circuit of the bases without stopping and score a run.

home·school·ing /ˈhōmˈskōōliNG/ (also **home-school·ing**) ▸*n.* the education of children at home by their parents. —**home·school** *v.* —**home·school·er** /ˈskōōlər/ *n.*

Home Sec·re·tar·y ▸*n.* (in the UK) the Secretary of State in charge of the Home Office.

home shop·ping ▸*n.* shopping carried out from one's own home by ordering goods advertised in a catalog or on a television channel, or by using various electronic media. —**home shop·per** *n.*

home·sick /ˈhōmˌsik/ ▸*adj.* experiencing a longing for one's home during a period of absence from it: *he was homesick for America after five weeks in Europe.* —**home·sick·ness** *n.*

home·site /ˈhōmˌsīt/ ▸*n.* a building plot for a house: *previously undevelopable areas are being eyed for homesites.*

home·spun /ˈhōmˌspən/ ▸*adj.* **1** simple and unsophisticated: *homespun philosophy.* **2** (of cloth or yarn) made or spun at home. ■ denoting a coarse handwoven fabric similar to tweed.

▸*n.* cloth of this type: *clad in homespun.*

home stand ▸*n.* a series of consecutive games played at a team's home stadium, field, or court.

Home·stead /ˈhōmˌsted/ an agricultural and suburban city in southeastern Florida, southwest of Miami; pop. 28,866.

home·stead /ˈhōmˌsted/ ▸*n.* **1** a house, esp. a farmhouse, and outbuildings. **2** *Law* a person's or family's residence, which comprises the land, house, and outbuildings, and in most states is exempt from forced sale for collection of debt. **3** *historical* (as provided by the federal Homestead Act of 1862) an area of public land in the West (usually 160 acres) granted to any U.S. citizen willing to settle on and farm the land for at least five years. **4** (in southern Africa) a hut or cluster of huts occupied by one family or clan, standing alone or as part of a traditional African village. ▷Old English *hāmstede* 'a settlement' (see HOME, STEAD). —**home·stead·er** *n.*

Home·stead Act ▸*n.* see HOMESTEAD (sense 3)

home·stead·ing /ˈhōmˌstediNG/ ▸*n.* life as a settler on a homestead. ■ the granting of homesteads to settlers.

home·stretch /ˈhōmˈstreCH/ (also **home stretch**) ▸*n.* the concluding straight part of a racecourse: *he drifted in back of the pack halfway down the homestretch.* ■ *figurative* the last part of an activity or campaign: *this was his last term, the home stretch.*

home stud·y ▸*n.* **1** a course of study carried out at home, rather than in a traditional classroom setting. **2** an assessment of prospective adoptive parents to see if they are suitable for adopting a child.

home·style /ˈhōmˌstīl/ ▸*adj.* [*attrib.*] such as would be made or provided at home; simple and unpretentious. ■ (of a meal in a restaurant) brought to the table in serving dishes from which each plate is served, rather than in individual portions.

home the·a·ter ▸*n.* television and video equipment designed to reproduce at home the experience of being in a movie theater, typically including stereo speakers and a big-screen television set.

home·town /ˈhōmˈtoun/ ▸*n.* the town where one was born or grew up, or the town of one's present fixed residence.

home truth ▸*n.* (usu. **home truths**) an unpleasant fact about oneself, esp. as pointed out by another person: *what he needed was someone to tell him a few home truths.*

home vid·e·o ▸*n.* a film on videotape for viewing at home.

home·ward /ˈhōmwərd/ ▸*adv.* (also **home·wards** /-wərdz/) toward home: *setting off homeward.*

▸*adj.* going or leading toward home: *their homeward journey.* ▷Old English *hāmweard* (see HOME, -WARD).

home·work /ˈhōmˌwərk/ ▸*n.* schoolwork that a student is required to do at home. ■ work or study done in preparation for a certain event or situation: *he had evidently* **done his homework** *and read his predecessor's reports.* ■ paid work carried out in one's own home, esp. low-paid piecework.

USAGE See usage at SCHOOLWORK.

home·work·er /ˈhōmˌwərkər/ ▸*n.* a person who works from home, esp. doing low-paid piecework.

hom·ey[1] /ˈhōmē/ (also **hom·y**) ▸*adj.* (**hom·i·er**, **hom·i·est**) (of a place or surroundings) pleasantly comfortable and cozy. ■ unsophisticated; unpretentious: *an idealized vision of traditional peasant life as simple and homey.* —**hom·ey·ness** (also **hom·i·ness**) *n.*

hom·ey[2] ▸*n.* (*pl.* **hom·eys**) variant spelling of HOMIE.

hom·i·cid·al /ˌhäməˈsīdl; ˌhōmə-/ ▸*adj.* of, relating to, or tending toward murder: *he had homicidal tendencies.*

hom·i·cide /ˈhäməˌsīd; ˈhōmə-/ ▸*n.* the deliberate and unlawful killing of one person by another; murder: *he was charged with homicide | two thirds of homicides in the county were drug-related.* ■ (**Homicide**) the police department that deals with such crimes: *a detective from Homicide.* ■ *dated* a murderer. ▷Middle English: from Old French, from Latin *homicidium*, from *homo*, *homin-* 'man.'

hom·ie /ˈhōmē/ (also **hom·ey**) ▸*n.* (*pl.* **hom·ies**) *informal* a homeboy or homegirl.

hom·i·let·ic /ˌhäməˈletik/ ▸*adj.* of the nature of or characteristic of a homily: *homiletic literature.*

▸*n.* (**homiletics**) the art of preaching or writing sermons: *the teaching of homiletics.* ▷mid 17th cent.: via late Latin from Greek *homilētikos*, from *homilein* 'converse with, consort,' from *homilia* (see HOMILY).

ho·mil·i·ar·y /häˈmilēˌerē/ ▸*n.* (*pl.* **-ar·ies**) *historical* a book of homilies. ▷mid 19th cent.: from medieval Latin *homiliarius*, from ecclesiastical Latin *homilia* (see HOMILY).

hom·i·ly /ˈhäməlē/ ▸*n.* (*pl.* **-lies**) a religious discourse that is intended primarily for spiritual edification rather than doctrinal instruction; a sermon. ■ a tedious moralizing discourse: *she delivered her homily about the need for patience.* ▷late Middle English: via Old French from ecclesiastical Latin *homilia*, from Greek, 'discourse, conversation' (in ecclesiastical use, 'sermon'), from *homilos* 'crowd.' —**hom·i·list** /-list/ *n.*

hom·ing /ˈhōmiNG/ ▸*adj.* relating to an animal's ability to return to a place or territory after traveling a distance away from it: *a strong homing instinct.* ■ (of a pigeon) trained to fly home from a great distance and bred for long-distance racing. ■ (of a weapon or piece of equipment) fitted with an electronic device that enables it to find and hit a target.

hom·i·nid /ˈhäməˌnid/ ▸*n.* *Zoology* a primate of a family (Hominidae) that includes humans and their fossil ancestors. ▷late 19th cent.: from modern Latin *Hominidae* (plural), from Latin *homo*, *homin-* 'man.'

hom·i·noid /ˈhäməˌnoid/ *Zoology* ▸*n.* a primate of a group that includes humans, their fossil ancestors, and the great apes. • Superfamily Hominoidea: families Hominidae and Pongidae.

▸*adj.* of or relating to primates of this group; hominid or pongid. ▷early 20th cent.: from Latin *homo*, *homin-* 'human being' + -OID.

hom·i·ny /ˈhämənē/ ▸*n.* coarsely ground corn used to make grits: [as *adj.*] *hominy grits.* ▷early 17th cent.: shortened from Virginia Algonquian *uskatahomen*.

Ho·mo /ˈhōmō/ the genus of primates of which modern humans (*Homo sapiens*) are the present-day representatives. ■ [with Latin or pseudo-Latin *adj.*] denoting kinds of modern human, often humorously: *a textbook example of Homo neuroticus.* ▷Latin, 'man.'

The genus *Homo* is believed to have existed for at least two million years, and modern humans (*H. sapiens sapiens*) first appeared in the Upper Paleolithic. Among several extinct species are *H. habilis*, *H. erectus*, and *H. neanderthalensis*.

ho·mo /ˈhōˌmō/ *offensive* ▸*n.* (*pl.* **-mos**) a homosexual man.

▸*adj.* homosexual. ▷1920s: abbreviation.

homo- ▸*comb. form* **1** same: *homogametic.* **2** relating to homosexual love: *homoerotic.* Often contrasted with HETERO-. ▷from Greek *homos* 'same.'

ho·mo·cen·tric[1] /ˌhōmōˈsentrik/ ▸*adj.* having the same center. ▷early 17th cent.: from Greek HOMO- 'same' + -CENTRIC

ho·mo·cen·tric[2] ▸*adj.* another term for ANTHROPOCENTRIC. ▷early 20th cent.: from Latin *homo* 'human being, man' + -CENTRIC.

ho·mo·cer·cal /ˌhōməˈsərkəl/ ▸*adj.* *Zoology* (of a fish's tail) appearing outwardly symmetrical but with the backbone passing into the upper lobe, as in all higher fish. Contrasted with DIPHYCERCAL, HETEROCERCAL. ▷mid 19th cent.: from HOMO- 'same' + Greek *kerkos* 'tail' + -AL.

ho·mo·cys·teine /ˌhōməˈsistēn/ ▸*n.* *Biochemistry* an amino acid that occurs in the body as an intermediate in the metabolism of methionine and cysteine. • Chem. formula: $HSCH_2CH_2CH(NH_2)COOH$.

ho·moe·cious /hōˈmēSHəs; hä-/ ▸*adj.* parasitic on a single host throughout life. Compare with HETEROECIOUS.

ho·moe·o·path ▸*n. Brit.* variant spelling of **HOMEOPATH**.

ho·moe·op·a·thy ▸*n. Brit.* variant spelling of **HOMEOPATHY**.

ho·mo·e·rot·ic /ˌhōmō-iˈrätik/ ▸*adj.* concerning or arousing sexual desire centered on a person of the same sex: *homoerotic images.* **—ho·mo·e·rot·i·cism** /-ˌsizəm/ *n.*

ho·mo·ga·met·ic /ˌhōmōgəˈmetik/ ▸*adj. Biology* denoting the sex that has sex chromosomes that do not differ in morphology, resulting in only one kind of gamete, e.g., (in mammals) the female and (in birds) the male. The opposite of **HETEROGAMETIC**.

ho·mog·a·my /hōˈmägəmē; hä-/ ▸*n.* **1** *Biology* inbreeding, esp. as a result of isolation. ■ marriage between people from similar sociological or educational backgrounds. Compare with **HETEROGAMY** (sense 3). **2** *Botany* a state in which the flowers of a plant are all of one type (either hermaphrodite or of the same sex). Compare with **HETEROGAMY** (sense 2). **3** *Botany* the simultaneous ripening of the stamens and pistils of a flower, ensuring self-pollination. Compare with **DICHOGAMY**. ▷late 19th cent.: from **HOMO-** 'same' + Greek *gamos* 'marriage.' **—ho·mog·a·mous** /-ˈmägəməs/ *adj.*

ho·mog·e·nate /həˈmäjəˌnāt; -nət/ ▸*n. Biology* a suspension of cell fragments and cell constituents obtained when tissue is homogenized.

ho·mo·ge·ne·ous /ˌhōməˈjēnēəs/ ▸*adj.* of the same kind; alike: *timbermen prefer to deal with homogeneous woods.* ■ consisting of parts all of the same kind: *culturally speaking the farmers constitute an extremely homogeneous group.* ■ *Mathematics* containing terms all of the same degree. ▷early 17th cent. (as *homogeneity*): from medieval Latin *homogeneus*, from Greek *homogenēs*, from *homos* 'same' + *genos* 'race, kind.' **—ho·mo·ge·ne·i·ty** /ˌhōməjəˈnēitē; ˌhämə-/ *n.* **—ho·mo·ge·ne·ous·ly** *adv.* **—ho·mo·ge·ne·ous·ness** *n.*

USAGE **Homogeneous**, 'of the same kind,' should not be confused with the more specialized biological term **homogenous**, 'having a common descent,' which has been largely replaced by the term **homologous**.
See also **usage** at **HETEROGENEOUS**.

ho·mog·e·nize /həˈmäjəˌnīz/ ▸*v.* [*trans.*] **1** subject (milk) to a process in which the fat droplets are emulsified and the cream does not separate: [as *adj.*] (**homogenized**) *homogenized milk.* ■ *Biology* prepare a suspension of cell constituents from (tissue) by physical treatment in a liquid. **2** make uniform or similar. **—ho·mog·e·ni·za·tion** /həˌmäjənīˈzāsʜən/ *n.* **—ho·mog·e·niz·er** *n.*

ho·mog·e·nous /həˈmäjənəs/ ▸*adj. Biology* old-fashioned term for **HOMOLOGOUS**. ▷late 19th cent. (in sense 1): from **HOMO-** 'same' + Greek *genos* 'race, kind' + **-OUS**. Sense 2 (mid 20th cent.) is an alteration of *homogeneous*, probably after *homogenize*.

USAGE See **usage** at **HOMOGENEOUS**.

ho·mog·e·ny /həˈmäjənē/ ▸*n. Biology* a variant of *homogeneity* (see **HOMOEGENEOUS**).

ho·mo·graft /ˈhōməˌgraft; ˈhämə-/ ▸*n.* a tissue graft from a donor of the same species as the recipient. Compare with **ALLOGRAFT**.

hom·o·graph /ˈhäməˌgraf; ˈhōmə-/ ▸*n.* each of two or more words spelled the same but not necessarily pronounced the same and having different meanings and origins (e.g., **BOW**[1] and **BOW**[2]). **—hom·o·graph·ic** /ˌhäməˈgrafik; ˌhōmə-/ *adj.*

ho·moi·o·therm /hōˈmoiəˌᴛʜərm/ ▸*n.* variant spelling of **HOMEOTHERM**.

ho·moi·ou·si·an /ˌhōmoiˈo͞ozʜən/ ▸*n. historical* in the fourth-century Arian controversy, a person who held that God the Father and God the Son are of like but not identical substance. Compare with **HOMOOUSIAN**. ▷late 17th cent. (as an adjective in the sense 'of similar but not identical substance'): via ecclesiastical Latin from Greek *homoiousios*, from *homoios* 'like' + *ousia* 'essence, substance.' The noun dates from the mid 18th cent.

ho·mo·log ▸*n.* variant spelling of **HOMOLOGUE**.

ho·mol·o·gate /hōˈmäləˌgāt; hə-/ ▸*v.* [*trans.*] *formal* express agreement with or approval of: *one body of patrons elected the teacher, the others afterward homologating the appointment.* ■ approve (a car, boat, or engine) for sale in a particular market or use in a particular class of racing. ▷late 16th cent.: from medieval Latin *homologat-* 'agreed,' from the verb *homologare*, from Greek *homologein* 'confess.' **—ho·mol·o·ga·tion** /hōˌmäləˈgāsʜən; hə-/ *n.*

ho·mol·o·gize /hōˈmäləˌjīz; hə-/ ▸*v.* [*trans.*] *formal* make or show to have the same relation, relative position, or structure.

ho·mol·o·gous /hōˈmäləgəs; hə-/ ▸*adj.* having the same relation, relative position, or structure, in particular: ■ *Biology* (of organs) similar in position, structure, and evolutionary origin but not necessarily in function: *a seal's flipper is* **homologous with** *the human arm.* Often contrasted with **ANALOGOUS**. ■ *Biology* (of chromosomes) pairing at meiosis and having the same structural features and pattern of genes. ■ *Chemistry* (of a series of chemical compounds) having the same functional group but differing in composition by a fixed group of atoms. ▷mid 17th cent.: via medieval Latin from Greek *homologos* 'agreeing, consistent,' from *homos* 'same' + *logos* 'ratio, proportion.'

ho·mo·logue /ˈhōməˌlôg; -ˌläg/ (also **ho·mo·log**) ▸*n. technical* a homologous thing. ▷mid 19th cent.: from French, from Greek *homologos* (see **HOMOLOGOUS**).

ho·mol·o·gy /hōˈmäləjē; hə-/ ▸*n.* the quality or condition of being homologous. ■ *Biology* similarity in sequence of a protein or nucleic acid between organisms of the same or different species.

ho·mo·mor·phic /ˌhōməˈmôrfik/ ▸*adj. technical* of the same or similar form. ■ *Mathematics* of, relating to, or of the nature of a homomorphism. **—ho·mo·mor·phi·cal·ly** /ˌhōməˈmôrfik(ə)lē/ *adv.*

ho·mo·mor·phism /ˌhōməˈmôrˌfizəm/ ▸*n. Mathematics* a transformation of one set into another that preserves in the second set the relations between elements of the first.

hom·o·nym /ˈhäməˌnim; ˈhōmə-/ ▸*n.* each of two words having the same pronunciation but different meanings, origins, or spelling (e.g., **TO**, **TOO**, and **TWO**); a homophone. ■ each of two or more words having the same spelling but different meanings and origins (e.g., **POLE**[1] and **POLE**[2]); a homograph. ■ *Biology* a Latin name that is identical to that of a different organism, the newer of the two names being invalid. ▷late 17th cent.: via Latin from Greek *homōnumon*, neuter of *homōnumos* 'having the same name,' from *homos* 'same' + *onoma* 'name.' **—hom·o·nym·ic** /ˌhäməˈnimik; ˌhōmə-/ *adj.* **—ho·mon·y·mous** /hōˈmänəməs/ *adj.* **—ho·mon·y·my** /hōˈmänəmē/ *n.*

ho·mo·ou·si·an /ˌhōmōˈo͞osēən; -zēən/ (also **ho·mou·si·an**) ▸*n. historical* in the fourth-century Arian controversy, a person who held that God the Father and God the Son are of the same substance. Compare with **HOMOIOUSIAN**. ▷mid 16th cent.: from ecclesiastical Latin *homousianus*, from *homousius*, from Greek *homoousios*, from *homos* 'same' + *ousia* 'essence, substance.'

ho·mo·phile /ˈhōməˌfīl/ ▸*n.* a homosexual man or woman. ■ a person active in supporting the rights of homosexuals.
▸*adj.* of or relating to homosexuals. ■ active in supporting the rights of homosexuals.

ho·mo·pho·bi·a /ˌhōməˈfōbēə/ ▸*n.* an extreme and irrational aversion to homosexuality and homosexual people. ▷1960s: from **HOMOSEXUAL** + **-PHOBIA**. **—ho·mo·phobe** /ˈhōməˌfōb/ *n.* **—ho·mo·pho·bic** /-ˈfōbik/ *adj.*

ho·mo·phone /ˈhäməˌfōn; ˈhōmə-/ ▸*n.* each of two or more words having the same pronunciation but different meanings, origins, or spelling, e.g., **NEW** and **KNEW**. ■ each of a set of symbols denoting the same sound or group of sounds.

ho·mo·phon·ic /ˌhäməˈfänik; ˌhōmə-/ ▸*adj.* **1** *Music* characterized by the movement of accompanying parts in the same rhythm as the melody. Often contrasted with **POLYPHONIC**. **2** another term for **HOMOPHONOUS**. **—ho·mo·phon·i·cal·ly** /-ik(ə)lē/ *adv.*

ho·moph·o·nous /hōˈmäfənəs; hə-/ ▸*adj.* (of a word or words) having the same pronunciation as another or others but different meaning, origin, or spelling. **—ho·moph·o·ny** /-ˈmäfənē/ *n.*

ho·mo·po·lar /ˌhäməˈpōlər; ˌhōmə-/ ▸*adj.* having equal or constant electrical polarity. ■ (of an electric generator) producing direct current without the use of commutators.

Ho·mop·ter·a /hōˈmäptərə/ *Entomology* a group of true bugs comprising those in which the forewings are uniform in texture. Plant bugs such as aphids, whitefly, scale insects, and cicadas belong to this group. Compare with **HETEROPTERA**. • Suborder Homoptera, order Hemiptera. ■ [as *plural n.*] (**homoptera**) bugs of this group. ▷modern Latin (plural), from **HOMO-** 'equal' + Greek *pteron* 'wing.' **—ho·mop·ter·an** *n.* & *adj.* **—ho·mop·ter·ous** /-tərəs/ *adj.*

ho·mor·gan·ic /ˌhōmôrˈganik/ ▸*adj.* denoting sets of speech sounds that are produced using the same vocal organs, e.g., *p*, *b*, and *m*.

Ho·mo sa·pi·ens /ˈhōmō ˈsāpēənz/ the primate species to which modern humans belong; humans regarded as a species. See also **HOMO**. ■ a member of this species. ▷Latin, literally 'wise man.'

ho·mo·sex·u·al /ˌhōməˈseksʜo͞oəl/ ▸*adj.* (of a person) sexually attracted to people of one's own sex. ■ involving or characterized by sexual attraction between people of the same sex: *homosexual desire.*
▸*n.* a person who is sexually attracted to people of their own sex. ▷late 19th cent.: from **HOMO-** 'same' + **SEXUAL**. **—ho·mo·sex·u·al·i·ty** /-ˌseksʜo͞oˈalitē/ *n.* **—ho·mo·sex·u·al·ly** *adv.*

ho·mo·so·cial /ˌhōməˈsōsʜəl/ ▸*adj.* of or relating to social interaction between members of the same sex, typically men.

ho·mo·trans·plant /ˌhōmōˈtransˌplant/ ▸*n.* another term for **ALLOGRAFT**.

ho·mo·u·si·an /ˌhōmōˈo͞osēən; -zēən/ ▸*n.* variant spelling of **HOMOOUSIAN**.

ho·mo·zy·gote /ˌhōmōˈzīgōt/ ▸*n. Genetics* an individual having two identical alleles of a particular gene or genes and so breeding true for the corresponding characteristic. Compare with **HETEROZYGOTE**. **—ho·mo·zy·gos·i·ty** /-zīˈgäsitē/ *n.* **—ho·mo·zy·gous** /-ˈzīgəs/ *adj.*

Homs /hôms/ (also **Hims** /hims/) an industrial city in western Syria, on the Orontes River; pop. 537,000. It was named in 636 by the Muslims and occupies the site of the ancient city of Emesa.

ho·mun·cu·lus /həˈmənɢkyələs; hō-/ ▸*n.* (*pl.* **-li** /-ˌlī/ or **-les** /-ˌlēz/) a very small human or humanoid creature. ■ *historical* a supposed microscopic but fully formed human being from which a fetus was formerly believed to develop. ▷mid 17th cent.: from Latin, diminutive of *homo*, *homin-* 'man.'

hom·y ▸*adj.* variant spelling of **HOMEY**[1].

hon /hən/ ▸*n. informal* short for **HONEY** (as a form of address): *It wouldn't interest you, hon.*

Hon. ▸*abbr.* ■ (in official job titles) Honorary: *the Hon. Secretary.* ■ (in titles of some government officials and judges) Honorable: *the Hon. Charles Rothschild.*

Ho·nan /ˈhōˈnan; ˈhōˌnän/ **1** variant of **HENAN**. **2** former name for **LUOYANG**.

hon·cho /ˈhänᴄʜō/ *informal* ▸*n.* (*pl.* **-chos**) a leader or manager; the person in charge: *the company's* **head honcho** *in the U.S.*
▸*v.* (**-choes**, **-choed**) [*trans.*] be in charge of (a project or situation): *the task at hand was to honcho an eighteen-wheeler to St. Louis.* ▷1940s: from Japanese *hanchō* 'group leader,' a term brought back to the U.S. by servicemen stationed in Japan during the occupation following World War II.

Hon·da /ˈhändə/, Soichiro (1906–92), Japanese motor manufacturer. Opening his first factory in 1934, he began motorcycle manufacture in 1948 and expanded into automobile production during the 1960s.

Hon·du·ras /hänˈd(y)o͝orəs/ a country in Central America that borders on the Caribbean Sea and also has a short coastline on the Pacific Ocean; pop. 6,283,000; capital, Tegucigalpa; official language, Spanish. **—Hon·du·ran** /-rən/ *adj.* & *n.*

At the southern limit of the Mayan empire, it was visited by Columbus in 1502 and became a Spanish colony. In 1821, Honduras became an independent republic.

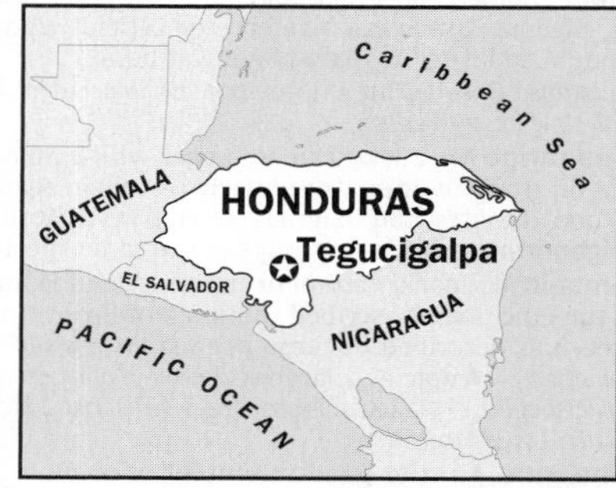

hone /hōn/ ▸*v.* [*trans.*] sharpen with a whetstone. ■ (usu. **be honed**) make sharper or more focused or efficient: *their appetites were honed by fresh air and exercise.*
▸*n.* a whetstone, esp. one used to sharpen razors. ■ the stone of which whetstones are made. ▷Middle

English: from Old English *hān* 'stone,' of Germanic origin; related to Old Norse *hein*.

Ho·neck·er /ˈhōnekər/, Erich (1912–94), East German statesman; head of state 1976–89. His repressive regime was marked by a close allegiance to the Soviet Union. He was ousted in 1989 as communism collapsed throughout Eastern Europe.

hon·est /ˈänist/ ▸*adj.* free of deceit and untruthfulness; sincere: *I haven't been totally honest with you.* ■ morally correct or virtuous: *I did the only right and honest thing.* ■ [*attrib.*] fairly earned, esp. through hard work: *struggling to make an honest living.* ■ (of an action) blameless or well intentioned even if unsuccessful or misguided: *he'd made an honest mistake.* ■ [*attrib.*] simple, unpretentious, and unsophisticated: *good honest food with no gimmicks.*
▸*adv.* [*sentence adverb*] *informal* used to persuade someone of the truth of something: *you'll like it when you get there, honest.* ▷Middle English (originally in the sense 'held in or deserving of honor'): via Old French from Latin *honestus*, from *honos* (see HONOR).
▸*PHRASES* □ **make an honest woman of** *dated* or *humorous* marry a woman, esp. to avoid scandal if she is pregnant. [*honest* here originally meant 'respectable,' but was probably associated with the archaic sense 'chaste, virtuous.'] □ **to be honest** speaking frankly: *I've never been much of a movie buff, to be honest.*

hon·est bro·ker ▸*n.* an impartial mediator in international, industrial, or other disputes. ▷late 19th cent.: translating German *ehrlicher Makler* with reference to BISMARCK2, under whom Germany was united.

hon·est·ly /ˈänistlē/ ▸*adv.* **1** in a truthful, fair, or honorable way: *he'd come by the money honestly.* **2** used to emphasize the sincerity of an opinion, belief, or feeling: *she honestly believed that she was making life easier for Jack.* ■ [*sentence adverb*] used to emphasize the sincerity or truthfulness of a statement: *honestly, darling, I'm not upset.* ■ [*sentence adverb*] used to indicate the speaker's disapproval, annoyance, or impatience: *honestly, that man is the absolute limit!*

hon·est-to-God *informal* ▸*adj.* [*attrib.*] genuine; real: *an honest-to-God celebrity.*
▸*adv.* genuinely; really: [as *exclam.*] *"You mean you didn't know?" "Honest to God!"*

hon·est-to-good·ness ▸*adj.* [*attrib.*] genuine and straightforward: *an honest-to-goodness family vacation in the sun.*

hon·es·ty /ˈänistē/ ▸*n.* **1** the quality of being honest: *they spoke with convincing honesty about their fears | it was not, in all honesty, an auspicious debut.* **2** a European plant with purple or white flowers and round, flat, translucent seedpods that are used for indoor flower arrangements. Also called MONEY PLANT. • Genus *Lunaria*, family Brassicaceae. ▷Middle English: from Old French *honeste*, from Latin *honestas*, from *honestus* (see HONEST). The original sense was 'honor, respectability,' later 'decorum, virtue, chastity.' The plant is so named from its seedpods, translucency symbolizing lack of deceit.

hone·wort /ˈhōnˌwərt; -ˌwôrt/ ▸*n.* a wild plant of the parsley family. • Two species in the family Umbelliferae: *Cryptotaenia canadensis*, a native of North America and eastern Asia that is cultivated for food in Japan, and *Trinia glauca*, a small European plant. ▷mid 17th cent.: from obsolete *hone* 'swelling' (for which the plant was believed to be a remedy) + WORT.

hon·ey /ˈhənē/ ▸*n.* (*pl.* **-eys**) **1** a sweet, sticky, yellowish-brown fluid made by bees and other insects from nectar collected from flowers. ■ this substance used as food, typically as a sweetener: *his pancake is sometimes smeared with jam or honey.* ■ a yellowish-brown or golden color: [as *adj.*] *her honey skin.* ■ any sweet substance similar to bees' honey. **2** *informal* an excellent example of something: *it's one* **honey of** *an adaptation.* ■ darling; sweetheart (usually as a form of address): *hi, honey!* ▷Old English *hunig*, of Germanic origin; related to Dutch *honig* and German *Honig*.

hon·ey ant ▸*n.* an ant that stores large amounts of honeydew and nectar in its elastic abdomen, which becomes greatly distended. This is then fed to nest mates by regurgitation. • *Myrmecocystus* and other genera, family Formicidae.

hon·ey badg·er ▸*n.* another term for RATEL.

hon·ey·bee /ˈhənēˌbē/ ▸*n.* (also **hive bee**) a stinging winged insect that collects nectar and pollen, produces wax and honey, and lives in large communities. It was domesticated for its honey around the end of the Neolithic period and is usually kept in hives. • Four species in the genus *Apis*, family Apidae, in particular the widespread *A. mellifera*.

hon·ey buck·et ▸*n. informal* a toilet that does not use water and has to be emptied manually.

hon·ey·bunch /ˈhənēˌbənCH/ (also **hon·ey·bun** /-ˌbən/) ▸*n. informal* darling (used as a form of address).

hon·ey·comb /ˈhənēˌkōm/ ▸*n.* **1** a structure of hexagonal cells of wax, made by bees to store honey and eggs. **2** a structure of adjoining cavities or cells: *a honeycomb of caves.* ■ a mass of cavities produced by corrosion or dissolution: [as *adj.*] *honeycomb weathering.* ■ a raised hexagonal or cellular pattern on the face of a fabric. **3** tripe from the second stomach of a ruminant.

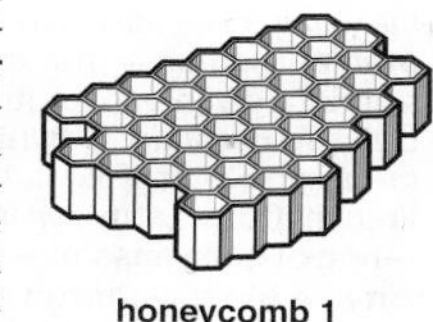
honeycomb 1

▸*v.* [*trans.*] fill with cavities or tunnels: *whole hillsides were honeycombed with mines.* ■ corrode (something) internally, forming small cavities in it. ■ *figurative* infiltrate and undermine: *their men honeycombed the army.* ▷Old English *hunigcamb* (see HONEY, COMB).

hon·ey·creep·er /ˈhənēˌkrēpər/ ▸*n.* **1** a tropical American tanager with a long curved bill, feeding on nectar and insects. • Genera *Cyanerpes* and *Chlorophanes*, family Emberizidae (subfamily Thraupinae): five species. **2** (also **Hawaiian honeycreeper**) a Hawaiian songbird of variable appearance and with a specialized bill, several kinds of which are now endangered. • Family Drepanididae (or Fringillidae): several genera and species, often with Hawaiian names such as the iiwi and ou.

hon·ey·dew /ˈhənēˌd(y)o͞o/ ▸*n.* **1** a sweet, sticky substance excreted by aphids and often deposited on leaves and stems. ■ *poetic/literary* an ideally sweet substance. **2** (also **honeydew melon**) a melon of a variety with smooth pale skin and sweet green flesh.

hon·ey·eat·er /ˈhənēˌētər/ ▸*n.* an Australasian songbird with a long brushlike tongue for feeding on nectar. • Family Meliphagidae: numerous species and genera.

hon·eyed /ˈhənēd/ (also **hon·ied**) ▸*adj.* (of food) containing or coated with honey. ■ having a rich sweetness of taste or smell: *as the wine matures, it becomes more honeyed.* ■ having a golden or warm yellow color. ■ *figurative* (of a person's words or tone of voice) soothing, soft, and intended to please or flatter: *he wooed her with honeyed words.*

hon·ey fun·gus ▸*n.* another term for HONEY MUSHROOM.

hon·ey·guide /ˈhənēˌgīd/ ▸*n.* a small bird of the Old World tropics, typically having drab plumage and feeding chiefly on beeswax and bee grubs. Two African kinds attract humans and other mammals, esp. ratels, to bee nests. • Family Indicatoridae: four genera, esp. *Indicator*.

hon·ey lo·cust ▸*n.* a tree of the pea family with long branched thorns, although a thornless variety has been cultivated and is typically grown as an ornamental for its fernlike foliage. • Genus *Gleditsia*, family Leguminosae: several species, in particular the North American *G. triacanthos*, the pods of which contain a sweet pulp.

hon·ey·moon /ˈhənēˌmo͞on/ ▸*n.* a vacation spent together by a newly married couple: *romantic handholding breakfasts together* ***on their honeymoon.*** ■ [often as *adj.*] *figurative* an initial period of enthusiasm or goodwill, typically at the start of a new job: *the new president's honeymoon period.*
▸*v.* [*intrans.*] spend a honeymoon: *they are* ***honeymooning in*** *the south of France.* ▷mid 16th cent. (originally denoting the period of time following a wedding): from HONEY + MOON. The original reference was to affection waning like the moon, but later the sense became 'the first month after marriage.' —**hon·ey·moon·er** *n.*

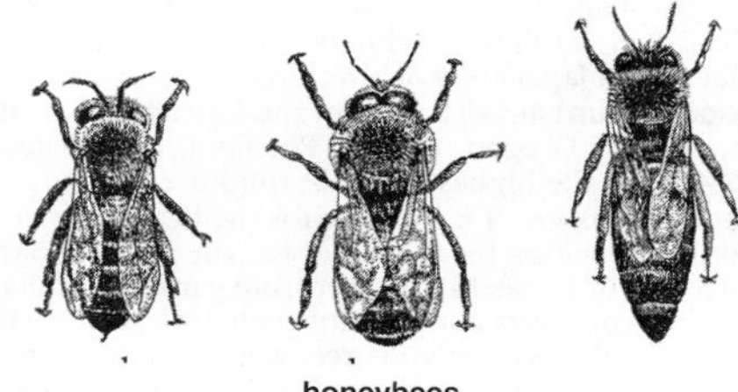
honeybees

hon·ey mush·room ▸*n.* a widespread parasitic fungus that produces clumps of honey-colored toadstools at the base of trees. The black stringlike hyphae invade a tree, causing decay or death and spreading out to other trees. Also called HONEY FUNGUS. • *Armillaria mellea*, family Tricholomataceae, class Hymenomycetes.

hon·ey pos·sum ▸*n.* a tiny shrewlike marsupial with a long pointed snout and a prehensile tail, found only in southwestern Australia, where it feeds exclusively upon nectar and pollen. • *Tarsipes rostratus*, the only member of the family Tarsipedidae.

hon·ey·pot /ˈhənēˌpät/ ▸*n.* a container in which honey is kept. ■ *figurative* a place to which many people are attracted: *its elegant shops make Florence a global honeypot.* ■ *vulgar slang* a woman's genitals.

hon·ey·pot ant ▸*n.* another term for HONEY ANT.

hon·ey·suck·er /ˈhənēˌsəkər/ ▸*n.* any of a number of long-billed birds that feed on nectar, esp. (in South Africa) a sunbird.

hon·ey·suck·le /ˈhənēˌsəkəl/ ▸*n.* a widely distributed climbing shrub with tubular flowers that are typically fragrant and of two colors or shades, opening in the evening for pollination by moths. • Genera *Lonicera* and *Diervilla*, family Caprifoliaceae (the **honeysuckle family**): many species, including the common **Japanese honeysuckle** (*L. japonica*), the **trumpet honeysuckle** (*L. sempervirens*), and the **northern bush honeysuckle** (*D. lonicera*). The honeysuckle family also includes such berry-bearing shrubs as guelder rose, elder, and snowberry. ▷Middle English *honysoukil*, extension of *honysouke*, from Old English *hunigsūce* (see HONEY, SUCK). It originally denoted tubular flowers, such as the red clover, which are sucked for their nectar.

hon·ey·trap /ˈhənēˌtrap/ (also **hon·ey trap**) ▸*n.* a stratagem in which irresistible bait is used to lure a victim. ■ the bait so used: *the house was a honeytrap, fitted out with a gaming machine, a sauna, plenty of videos and drink and drugs and anything else that might persuade a wandering boy to come in off the streets.*

hon·ey·wort /ˈhənˌwərt; -ˌwôrt/ ▸*n.* a Mediterranean plant of the borage family with grayish-green leaves and tubular yellow or purple flowers that are a favored source of nectar for bees. • Genus *Cerinthe*, family Boraginaceae: several species, in particular the yellow-flowered *C. major*.

hong·i /ˈhäNGē/ ▸*n. NZ* (usu. **the hongi**) a traditional Maori greeting in which people press their noses together. ▷Maori.

Hong Kong /ˈhäNG ˈkäNG; ˈhôNG ˈkôNG/ a former British dependency on the southeastern coast of China that was returned to China in 1997; pop. 6,850,000. The area comprises Hong Kong Island, ceded by China in 1841; the Kowloon peninsula, ceded in 1860; and the New Territories, additional areas of the mainland that were leased for 99 years in 1898. Hong Kong has become one of the world's major financial and manufacturing centers.

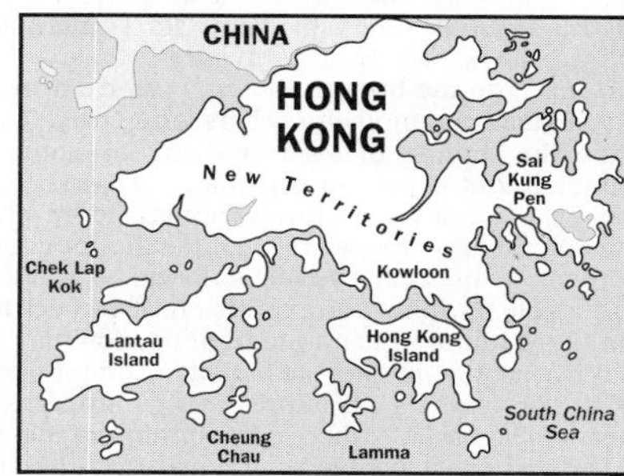

Ho·ni·a·ra /ˌhōnēˈärə/ the capital of the Solomon Islands, a port on the northwestern coast of the island of Guadalcanal; pop. 35,000.

hon·ied /ˈhənēd/ ▸*adj.* variant spelling of HONEYED.

ho·ni soit qui mal y pense /ˌônē ˈswä kē ˌmäl ē ˈpäNs/ ▸*exclam.* shame on him who thinks evil of it (the motto of the Order of the Garter). ▷French.

honk /häNGk; hôNGk/ ▸*n.* the cry of a wild goose. ■ the harsh sound of a car horn. ■ any similar sound.
▸*v.* **1** [*intrans.*] emit such a cry or sound. ■ [*trans.*] cause (a car horn) to make such a sound. ■ [*trans.*] express by sounding a car horn: *taxi drivers honking their*

Pronunciation Key ə *ago*; ər *over*; ˈə or ˌə *up*; ˈər or ˌər *fur*; a *hat*; ā *rate*; ä *car*; CH *chew*; e *let*; ē *see*; e(ə)r *air*; i *fit*; ī *by*; i(ə)r *ear*; NG *sing*; ō *go*; ô *for*; oi *boy*; o͝o *good*; o͞o *goo*; ou *out*; SH *she*; TH *thin*; T͟H *then*; (h)w *why*; ZH *vision*

support. **2** *Brit., informal* vomit. ▷mid 19th cent.: imitative.

honk·er /ˈhäNGkər; ˈhôNG-/ ▸*n.* a person or thing that honks. ■ *informal* a wild goose.

hon·ky /ˈhäNGkē; ˈhôNG-/ ▸*n.* (*pl.* **-kies**) *informal, often offensive* a contemptuous term used by black people for a white person or for white people collectively. ▷1960s: of unknown origin.

hon·ky-tonk /ˈhäNGkē ˌtäNGk; ˈhôNGkē ˌtôNGk/ ▸*n. informal* **1** a cheap or disreputable bar, club, or dancehall, typically where country music is played: *country bands at highway honky-tonks.* ■ [as *adj.*] squalid and disreputable: *a honky-tonk beach resort.* **2** country music: *good-time urban cowboy fare with a hint of honky-tonk and a healthy measure of rock.* **3** [often as *adj.*] ragtime piano music.
▸*v.* [*intrans.*] listen to or dance to country music: *come on, let's go honky-tonking.* ▷late 19th cent.: of unknown origin.

hon·nête homme /ô'net ˈôm/ ▸*n.* a decent, cultivated man of the world; a gentleman. ▷mid 17th cent.: French, literally 'honest man.'

Ho·no·lu·lu /ˌhänlˈo͞olo͞o; ˌhōn-/ the capital of Hawaii, a principal port on the southeastern coast of the island of Oahu; pop. 371,657.

hon·or /ˈänər/ (*Brit.* **hon·our**) ▸*n.* **1** high respect; esteem: *his portrait hangs in the place of honor.* ■ [in *sing.*] a person or thing that brings credit: *you are* ***an honor to*** *our profession.* ■ adherence to what is right or to a conventional standard of conduct: *I must as a matter of honor avoid any taint of dishonesty.* **2** a privilege: *the great poet of whom it is my honor to speak tonight.* ■ an exalted position: *the honor of being horse of the year.* ■ a thing conferred as a distinction, esp. an official award for bravery or achievement: *the highest military honors.* ■ (**honors**) a special distinction for proficiency in an examination: *she passed with honors.* ■ (**honors**) a class or course of degree studies more specialized than that of the ordinary level: [as *adj.*] *an honors degree in mathematics.* ■ (**His, Your,** etc., **Honor**) a title of respect given to or used in addressing a judge or a mayor. ■ *Golf* the right of teeing off first, having won the previous hole. **3** *dated* a woman's chastity or her reputation for this: *she died defending her honor.* **4** *Bridge* an ace, king, queen, or jack. ■ (**honors**) possession in one's hand of at least four of the ace, king, queen, and jack of trumps, or of all four aces in no trumps, for which a bonus is scored. ■ (in whist) an ace, king, queen, or jack of trumps.
▸*v.* [*trans.*] **1** regard with great respect: *Joyce has now learned to honor her father's memory* | [as *adj.*] (**honored**) *an honored guest.* ■ (often **be honored**) pay public respect to: *talented writers were honored at a special ceremony.* ■ grace; privilege: *the Princess* ***honored*** *the ball* ***with*** *her presence* | [as *adj.*] (**honored**) *I felt honored to be invited.* ■ (in square dancing) salute (another dancer) with a bow. **2** fulfill (an obligation) or keep (an agreement): *make sure the franchisees honor the terms of the contract.* ■ accept (a bill) or pay (a check) when due: *the bank informed him that the check would not be honored.* ▷Middle English: from Old French *onor* (noun), *onorer* (verb), from Latin *honor.*
▸*PHRASES* □ **do the honors** *informal* perform a social duty or small ceremony for others (often used to describe the serving of food or drink to a guest). □ **honor bright** *dated* "on my honor": *I'll never do it again, honor bright, I won't.* [from Thomas Moore's *Tom Cribb's Memorial to Congress* (1819).] □ **in honor bound** another way of saying ON ONE'S HONOR. □ **in honor of** as a celebration of or expression of respect for. □ **on one's honor** under a moral obligation: *they are on their honor as gentlemen not to cheat.* □ **on** (or **upon**) **my honor** used as an expression of sincerity: *I promise on my honor.* □ **there's honor among thieves** *proverb* dishonest people may have certain standards of behavior that they will respect.

THE RIGHT WORD **deference, homage, honor, obeisance, reverence**

The Ten Commandments instruct us to "Honor thy father and mother." But what does *honor* entail? While all of these nouns describe the respect or esteem that one shows to another, *honor* implies acknowledgment of a person's right to such respect (*honor one's ancestors; honor the dead*).

Homage is honor with praise or tributes added, and it connotes a more worshipful attitude (*pay homage to the king*).

Reverence combines profound respect with love or devotion (*he treated his wife with reverence*), while **deference** suggests courteous regard for a superior, often by yielding to the person's status or wishes (*show deference to one's elders*).

Obeisance is a show of honor or reverence by an act or gesture of submission or humility, such as a bow or a curtsy (*the schoolchildren were instructed to pay obeisance when the queen arrived*).

hon·or·a·ble /ˈänərəbəl/ (*Brit.* **hon·our·a·ble**) ▸*adj.* **1** bringing or worthy of honor: *this is the only honorable course* | *a decent and honorable man.* See note at MORAL. ■ *formal* or *humorous* (of the intentions of a man courting a woman) directed toward marriage: *the young man's intentions had been honorable.* **2** (**Honorable**) used as a title indicating eminence or distinction, given esp. to judges and certain high officials: *the Honorable Richard Morris Esquire, chief justice of the supreme court of our state.* ▷Middle English: via Old French from Latin *honorabilis,* from *honor* 'honor.' —**hon·or·a·ble·ness** *n.* —**hon·or·a·bly** *adv.*

hon·or·a·ble dis·charge ▸*n.* discharge from military service with a favorable record.

hon·or·a·ble men·tion ▸*n.* a commendation given to a candidate in an examination or competition who is not awarded a prize.

hon·or·and /ˈänərənd; -ˌrand/ ▸*n.* a person to be publicly honored, esp. with an honorary degree. ▷1950s: from Latin *honorandus* 'to be honored,' gerundive of *honorare* 'to honor,' from *honor* 'honor.'

hon·o·rar·i·um /ˌänəˈre(ə)rēəm/ ▸*n.* (*pl.* **-rar·i·ums** or **-rar·i·a** /-ˈre(ə)rēə/) a payment given for professional services that are rendered nominally without charge. ▷mid 17th cent.: from Latin, denoting a gift made on being admitted to public office, from *honorarius* (see HONORARY).

hon·or·ar·y /ˈänəˌrerē/ ▸*adj.* **1** conferred as an honor, without the usual requirements or functions: *an honorary doctorate.* ■ (of a person) holding such a title or position: *an honorary member of the club.* **2** *Brit.* (of an office or its holder) unpaid: *Honorary Secretary of the Association.* ▷early 17th cent.: from Latin *honorarius,* from *honor* 'honor.'

hon·o·ree /ˌänəˈrē/ ▸*n.* a person who receives an honor.

hon·or guard ▸ another term for GUARD OF HONOR.

hon·or·if·ic /ˌänəˈrifik/ ▸*adj.* given as a mark of respect: *an honorific award for military valor.* ■ (of an office or position) given as a mark of respect, but having few or no duties. ■ denoting a form of address showing high status, politeness, or respect: *an honorific title for addressing women.*
▸*n.* a title or word implying or expressing high status, politeness, or respect: *he will be able to put the honorific after his name:* licenciado, *"college graduate."* ▷mid 17th cent.: from Latin *honorificus,* from *honor* 'honor.' —**hon·or·if·i·cal·ly** /ik(ə)lē/ *adv.*

ho·no·ris cau·sa /äˈnôros ˈkôzə; ˈkousə/ ▸*adv.* (esp. of a degree awarded without examination) as a mark of esteem: *the artist has been awarded the degree honoris causa.* ▷early 17th cent.: Latin, literally 'for honor's sake.'

hon·or point ▸*n.* *Heraldry* the point halfway between the top of a shield and the fess point.

hon·ors list ▸*n.* a publicly issued list of people and the distinctions they are to be awarded.

hon·or so·ci·e·ty ▸*n.* an organization for high-school or college students of high academic achievement.

hon·ors of war ▸*plural n.* privileges granted to a capitulating force, for example,that of marching out with colors flying.

hon·or sys·tem ▸*n.* [in *sing.*] a system of payment or examination that relies solely on the honesty of those concerned.

hon·our ▸*n.* & *v.* British spelling of HONOR.

hon·our·a·ble ▸*adj.* British spelling of HONORABLE.

Hon·shu /ˈhänsHo͞o/ the largest of the four main islands of Japan; pop 99,254,000.

Hooch, Pieter de, see DE HOOCH.

hooch 1 /ho͞ocH/ (also **hootch**) ▸*n. informal* alcoholic liquor, esp. inferior or illicit whiskey. ▷late 19th cent.: abbreviation of *Hoochinoo,* the name of an Alaskan Indian people who made liquor.

hooch2 /ho͞ocH/ ▸*n. informal* a shelter or improvised dwelling. ▷1950s (originally military slang): perhaps from Japanese *uchi* 'dwelling.'

Hood, Mount /ho͝od/ a peak in the Cascade Range in northwest Oregon, east of Portland, 11,239 feet (3,426 m), the highest point in the state.

hood1 /ho͝od/ ▸*n.* **1** a covering for the head and neck with an opening for the face, typically forming part of a coat or sweatshirt. ■ a separate garment similar to this worn over a university gown or a surplice to indicate the wearer's degree. ■ *Falconry* a leather covering for a hawk's head. **2** a thing resembling a hood in shape or use, in particular: ■ a metal part covering the engine of an automobile. ■ a canopy to protect users of machinery or to remove fumes from it. ■ a hoodlike structure or marking on the head or neck of an animal. ■ the upper part of the flower of a plant such as a dead-nettle. ■ a tubular attachment to keep stray light out of a camera lens: *a lens hood.* ■ *Brit.* a folding waterproof cover of an automobile, baby carriage, etc.
▸*v.* [*trans.*] put a hood on or over. ▷Old English *hōd;* related to Dutch *hoed,* German *Hut* 'hat,' also to HAT. —**hood·less** *adj.* —**hood·like** /-ˌlīk/ *adj.*

hood2 ▸*n. informal* a gangster or similar violent criminal. ▷1930s: abbreviation of HOODLUM.

hood3 (also **'hood**) ▸*n. informal* a neighborhood, esp. one's own neighborhood: *I've lived in the hood for 15 years.* ▷1970s: shortening of NEIGHBORHOOD.

-hood ▸*suffix* forming nouns: **1** denoting a condition or quality: *falsehood* | *womanhood.* **2** denoting a collection or group: *brotherhood.* ▷Old English *-hād,* originally an independent noun meaning 'person, condition, quality.'

hood·ed /ˈho͝odid/ ▸*adj.* (of an article of clothing) having a hood: *a hooded cape in violet silk.* ■ (of a person) wearing a hood: *a hooded figure.* ■ (of eyes) having thick, drooping upper eyelids resembling hoods: *a dark man with hooded eyes.* ■ (of an animal) having a hoodlike structure or marking on the head or neck: *hooded cranes* | *hooded mergansers.*

hood·ed crow ▸*n.* a bird of the northern and eastern European race of the carrion crow, having a gray body with a black head, wings, and tail. • *Corvus corone cornix,* family Corvidae.

hood·ed seal ▸*n.* a seal with a gray and white blotched coat, found in the Arctic waters of the North Atlantic. The male has a nasal sac that is inflated into a hood during display. • *Cystophora cristata,* family Phocidae.

hood·i·a /ˈho͝odēə/ ▸*n.* a southern African cactus that contains a highly effective appetite suppressant • Genus *Hoodia,* family Asclepiadaceae;about 20 species. ▷from modern Latin *Hoodia,* from *Hood,* the name of an English plant grower.

hood·ie /ˈho͝odē/ (also **hood·y**) ▸*n.* [*pl.* **-ies**] *informal* a hooded sweatshirt or jacket: *a phalanx of boys suited in NBN hoodies.* ▷from *hood* + *-ie* or *-y.*

hood·lum /ˈho͞odləm; ˈho͝od-/ ▸*n.* a person who engages in crime and violence; a hooligan or gangster. ▷late 19th cent. (originally U.S.): of unknown origin.

hood mold (also **hood mold·ing**) ▸*n.* *Architecture* another term for DRIPSTONE (sense 1).

hoo·doo /ˈho͞oˌdo͞o/ ▸*n.* **1** voodoo; witchcraft. ■ a run of bad luck associated with a person or activity: *when is this hoodoo going to end?* ■ a person or thing that brings or causes bad luck. **2** a column or pinnacle of weathered rock: *a towering sandstone hoodoo.*
▸*v.* (**-doos, -dooed**) [*trans.*] bewitch: *she's hoodooed you.* ■ bring bad luck to: *a fine player, but repeatedly hoodooed.* ▷late 19th cent. (originally U.S.): apparently an alteration of VOODOO. It originally denoted a person who practiced voodoo, hence a hidden cause of bad luck (sense 1). Sense 2 is apparently due to the resemblance of the rock column to a strange human form, often topped by an overhanging "hat" of harder rock.

hood·wink /ˈho͝odˌwiNGk/ ▸*v.* [*trans.*] deceive or trick (someone): *an attempt to hoodwink the public.* ▷mid 16th cent. (originally in the sense 'to blindfold'): from the noun HOOD1 + an obsolete sense of WINK 'close the eyes.'

hoo·ey /ˈho͞oē/ ▸*n. informal* nonsense: *your interest is just a lot of hooey and I know it.* ▷1920s (originally U.S.): of unknown origin.

hoof /ho͝of; ho͞of/ ▸*n.* (*pl.* **hoofs** or **hooves** /ho͝ovz; ho͞ovz/) the horny part of the foot of an ungulate animal, esp. a horse: *there was a clatter of hoofs as a rider came up to them.*
▸*v.* [*trans.*] *informal* (**hoof it**) go on foot: *it was awfully hot, but we hoofed it all the way back.* ■ dance: *we hoof it reasonably fancily, and no one guffaws.* ▷Old English *hōf,* of Germanic origin; related to Dutch *hoef* and German *Huf.* —**hoofed** *adj.*
▸*PHRASE* □ **on the hoof** **1** (of livestock) not yet slaughtered. **2** *informal* without great thought or preparation: *policy was made on the hoof.*

hoof-and-mouth dis·ease ▸*n.* another term for FOOT-AND-MOUTH DISEASE.

hoof·er /ˈho͝ofər; ˈho͞ofər/ ▸*n. informal* a professional dancer.

Hoo·ghly /ˈho͞oglē/ (also **Hu·gli**) the most western of the rivers in the Ganges delta, in West Bengal, India.

It flows for 120 miles (192 km) into the Bay of Bengal and is navigable to Calcutta.

hoo-ha /ˈho͞o ˌhä/ ▸*n.* [in *sing.*] *informal* a commotion; a fuss: *the book was causing such a hoo-ha.* ▷1930s: of unknown origin.

hook /ho͝ok/ ▸*n.* **1** a piece of metal or other material, curved or bent back at an angle, for catching hold of or hanging things on: *a picture hook.* ■ (also **fishhook**) a bent piece of metal, typically barbed and baited, for catching fish. ■ a cradle on which a telephone receiver rests. ■ *figurative* a thing designed to catch people's attention: *companies are looking for a sales hook.* ■ a chorus or repeated instrumental passage in a piece of music, esp. a pop or rock song, that gives it immediate appeal and makes it easy to remember. **2** a curved cutting instrument, esp. as used for reaping or shearing. **3** a short swinging punch made with the elbow bent, esp. in boxing: *a perfectly timed right hook to the chin.* ■ *Golf* a stroke that makes the ball deviate in flight in the direction of the follow-through (from right to left for a right-handed player), typically inadvertently. Compare with SLICE. **4** a curved stroke in handwriting, esp. as made in learning to write. ■ *Music* an added stroke transverse to the stem in the symbol for an eighth note or other note. **5** [usu. in *place names*] a curved promontory or sand spit.
▸*v.* **1** [*trans.*] attach or fasten with a hook or hooks: *the truck had a red lamp hooked to its tailgate | she tried to* **hook up** *her bra.* ■ [*intrans.*] be or become attached with a hook: *a ladder that hooks over the roof ridge.* ■ bend or be bent into the shape of a hook so as to fasten around or to an object: [*trans.*] *he hooked his thumbs in his belt* | [*intrans.*] *her legs hooked around mine.* **2** [*trans.*] catch with a hook: *he hooked a 24-lb pike.* ■ (usu. **be hooked**) *informal* captivate: *I was hooked by John's radical zeal.* ■ *archaic, informal* steal. **3** [*trans.*] *Golf* strike (the ball) or play (a stroke) so that the ball deviates in the direction of the follow-through, typically inadvertently. ■ [*intrans.*] *Boxing* punch one's opponent with the elbow bent. **4** [*trans.*] *Rugby* push (the ball) backward with the foot from the front line in a scrum. ■ [intrans.] (of a player) hook the ball.
▸*phrasal v.* □ **hook someone/something up** (or **hook up**) link or be linked to electronic equipment: *Ali was hooked up to an electrocardiograph.* ▷Old English *hōc*, of Germanic origin; related to Dutch *hoek* 'corner, angle, projecting piece of land,' also to German *Haken* 'hook.' **—hook·less** *adj.* **—hook·let** /-lit/ *n.* **—hook·like** /-ˌlīk/ *adj.*
▸**PHRASES** □ **by hook or by crook** by any possible means: *the government intends, by hook or by crook, to hold on to the land.* □ **get one's hooks into** *informal* get hold of: *they were going to move out rather than let Mel get his hooks into them.* □ **get** (or **give someone**) **the hook** *informal* be dismissed (or dismiss someone) from a job. □ **hook, line, and sinker** used to emphasize that someone has been completely deceived or tricked: *he fell hook, line, and sinker for this year's April Fool joke.* [with allusion to the taking of bait by a fish.] □ **off the hook 1** *informal* no longer in difficulty or trouble: *I lied to get him off the hook.* **2** (of a telephone receiver) not on its rest, and so preventing incoming calls. □ **on the hook for** *informal* (in a financial context) responsible for: *he's on the hook for about $9.5 million.* □ **on one's own hook** *informal, dated* on one's own account; by oneself.

hookah

hook·ah /ˈho͝okə; ˈho͞okə/ ▸*n.* an oriental tobacco pipe with a long, flexible tube that draws the smoke through water contained in a bowl. ▷mid 18th cent.: from Urdu, from Arabic *ḥukka* 'casket, jar.'

hook and eye ▸*n.* a small metal hook and loop used together as a fastener on a garment.

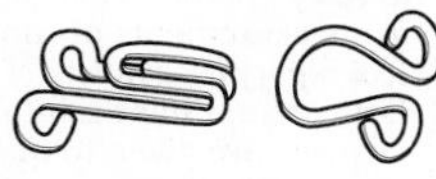
hook and eye

hook-and-lad·der truck ▸*n.* a fire engine that carries extension ladders and other firefighting and rescue equipment.

Hooke /ho͝ok/, Robert (1635–1703), English scientist. He formulated the law of elasticity (Hooke's law), proposed an undulating theory of light, introduced the term *cell* to biology, postulated elliptical orbits for the earth and moon, and proposed the inverse square law of gravitational attraction.

hooked /ho͝okt/ ▸*adj.* **1** having a hook or hooks: *a hooked gold earring.* ■ curved like a hook: *a golden eagle with hooked beak.* **2** *informal* captivated; absorbed: *he was* **hooked on** *a video game.* ■ addicted: *a girl who got* **hooked on** *cocaine.* **3** (of a rug or mat) made by pulling yarn through canvas with a hook.

Hook·er[1] /ˈho͝okər/, Sir Joseph Dalton (1817–1911), English botanist and pioneer in phytogeography. He applied Darwin's theories to plants and, with **George Bentham** (1800–84), he produced a work on classification, *Genera Plantarum* (1862–83).

Hook·er[2], Thomas (*c.*1586–1647) American clergyman; born in England. A founding settler of Hartford, Connecticut, in 1636, he helped to write the *Fundamental Orders* (1639), which was Connecticut's original constitution.

hook·er[1] /ˈho͝okər/ ▸*n.* **1** *informal* a prostitute. **2** *Rugby* the player in the middle of the front row of the scrum, who tries to hook the ball.

hook·er[2] ▸*n.* a one-masted sailboat of a kind used esp. in Ireland for fishing. ■ *informal Nautical* an old boat. ▷mid 17th cent.: from Dutch *hoeker*, from *hoek* 'hook' (used earlier in *hoekboot*, denoting a two-masted Dutch fishing vessel).

hook·er[3] ▸*n.* *informal* a glass or drink of undiluted brandy, whiskey, or other liquor. ▷mid 19th cent.: of unknown origin.

Hooke's law /ho͝oks/ *Physics* a law stating that the strain in a solid is proportional to the applied stress within the elastic limit of that solid.

hook·ey ▸*n.* variant spelling of HOOKY[1].

hook-nosed ▸*adj.* having a prominent aquiline nose.

hook shot ▸*n.* *Basketball* a one-handed shot in which a player extends one arm out to the side and over the head toward the basket.

hook·tip /ˈho͝okˌtip/ ▸*n.* a slender moth that has hooked tips to the forewings. The caterpillar tapers to a point at the rear and rests with both ends raised. • Family Drepanidae: *Drepana* and other genera.

hook·up /ˈho͝okˌəp/ ▸*n.* a connection to a public electric, water, or sewer line, or to a similar service: *the campground has 70 sites with water and sewer hookups.* ■ an interconnection of broadcasting equipment for special transmissions: *he reached a global audience on the satellite hookup.*

hook·worm /ˈho͝okˌwərm/ ▸*n.* a parasitic nematode worm that inhabits the intestines of humans and other animals. It has hooklike mouthparts with which it attaches itself to the wall of the gut, puncturing the blood vessels and feeding on the blood. • *Ancylostoma, Uncinaria, Necator*, and other genera, class Phasmida, including *N. americanus*, which infects millions of people in the tropics. ■ a disease caused by an infestation of hookworms, often resulting in severe anemia.

hook·y[1] /ˈho͝okē/ (also **hook·ey**) ▸*n.* (in phrase **play hooky**) *informal* stay away from school or work without permission or explanation. ▷mid 19th cent. (originally U.S.): of unknown origin.

hook·y[2] ▸*adj.* (of a tune or a component of a tune) having immediate appeal and easy to remember: *a hooky bass line.*

hoo·li·gan /ˈho͞oləgin/ ▸*n.* a violent young troublemaker, typically one of a gang. ▷late 19th cent.: perhaps from *Hooligan*, the surname of a fictional rowdy Irish family in a music-hall song of the 1890s, also of a character in a cartoon. **—hoo·li·gan·ism** /-ˌnizəm/ *n.*

hoo·lock /ˈho͞oˌläk/ (also **hoolock gibbon**) ▸*n.* a gibbon with white eyebrows, the male of which has black fur and the female golden, found from northeastern India to Myanmar (Burma). • *Hylobates hoolock*, family Hylobatidae. ▷early 19th cent.: perhaps from Bengali and imitative of the animal's cry.

hoop /ho͞op/ ▸*n.* a circular band of metal, wood, or similar material, esp. one used for binding the staves of barrels or forming part of a framework. ■ the round metal rim from which a basketball net is suspended. ■ (**hoops**) *informal* the game of basketball. ■ a large ring used as a toy by being bowled along. ■ a large ring, typically with paper stretched over it, for circus performers to jump through. ■ one of a pair of rings that hold fabric taut while it is being embroidered. ■ *historical* a circle of flexible material used for expanding a woman's petticoat or skirt. ■ short for HOOP PETTICOAT. ■ *chiefly Brit.* a croquet wicket.
▸*v.* [*trans.*] bind or encircle with or as with hoops. ▷late Old English *hōp*; related to Dutch *hoep*. **—hooped** *adj.*
▸**PHRASES** □ **jump through hoops** perform a difficult and grueling series of tests at someone else's request or command: *we had to jump through all sorts of hoops to win accreditation.* □ **shoot hoops** play basketball.

hoop·er /ˈho͞opər/ ▸*n.* old-fashioned term for COOPER. ▷Middle English: from HOOP.

hoop·head ▸*n.* *informal* a basketball player or devoted fan.

hoop i·ron ▸*n.* flattened iron in long thin strips used for binding together the staves of casks or tubs.

hoop·la /ˈho͞oplä; ˈho͞opˌlä/ ▸*n.* **1** *informal* excitement surrounding an event or situation, esp. when considered to be unnecessary fuss: *the hoopla and ceremony of international competition.* **2** *Brit.* a game in which rings are thrown from behind a line in an attempt to encircle one of several prizes.

hoo·poe /ˈho͞oˌpō; -ˌpo͞o/ ▸*n.* a salmon-pink Eurasian bird with a long down-curved bill, a large erectile crest, and black and white wings and tail. • *Upupa epops*, the only member of the family Upupidae. ▷mid 17th cent.: alteration of obsolete *hoop*, from Old French *huppe*, from Latin *upupa*, imitative of the bird's call.

hoop pet·ti·coat ▸*n.* *historical* a petticoat expanded with hoops of flexible material.

hoop skirt ▸*n.* *historical* a skirt worn over a series of hoops that make it spread out.

hoo·ray /həˈrā; ho͞o-/ ▸*exclam.* another term for HURRAH.

hoose·gow /ˈho͞osˌgou/ ▸*n.* *informal* a prison. ▷early 20th cent.: via Latin American Spanish from Spanish *juzgado* 'tribunal,' from Latin *judicatum* 'something judged,' neuter past participle of *judicare*.

Hoo·sier /ˈho͞ozHər/ ▸*n.* a native or inhabitant of Indiana. ▷early 19th cent.: of unknown origin.

Hoo·sier State a nickname for the state of INDIANA.

hoot /ho͞ot/ ▸*n.* a deep or medium-pitched musical sound, often wavering or interrupted, that is the typical call of many kinds of owl. ■ a similar but typically more raucous sound made by a horn, siren, or steam whistle. ■ a shout expressing scorn or disapproval: *there were* **hoots of** *derision.* ■ a short outburst of laughter: *the audience broke into hoots of laughter.* ■ (**a hoot**) *informal* an amusing situation or person: *your mom's a real hoot.*
▸*v.* [*intrans.*] (of an owl) utter a hoot. ■ (of a person) make loud sounds of scorn, disapproval, or merriment: *she began to hoot with laughter.* ■ [*trans.*] (**hoot something down**) express loud scornful disapproval of something: *his questions were hooted down or answered obscenely.* ■ (of a horn, siren, etc.) make a hoot. ■ [*trans.*] (of the driver of a vehicle) sound (the horn). ▷Middle English (in the sense 'make sounds of derision'): perhaps imitative.
▸**PHRASE** □ **not care** (or **give**) **a hoot** (or **two hoots**) *informal* not care at all.

hootch /ho͞ocH/ ▸*n.* variant spelling of HOOCH.

hoot·en·an·ny /ˈho͞otnˌanē/ ▸*n.* (*pl.* **-nies**) *informal* an informal gathering with folk music and sometimes dancing. ▷1920s (originally U.S., denoting a gadget or 'thingamajig'): of unknown origin.

hoot·er /ˈho͞otər/ ▸*n.* **1** *informal* a person's nose. **2** (**hooters**) *vulgar slang* a woman's breasts. **3** *Brit.* a siren or steam whistle, esp. one used as a signal for work to begin or cease. ■ the horn of a motor vehicle.

Hoo·ver[1] /ˈho͞ovər/ a city in north central Alabama, south of Birmingham; pop. 62,742.

Hoo·ver[2], Herbert (Clark) (1874–1964), 31st president of the U.S. 1929–33. After serving as secretary of commerce 1921–29 under Presidents Harding and Coolidge, he was elected to the presidency on the Republican ballot. As president, he was faced with the long-term problems of the Depression. Unable to keep his campaign promise of prosperity and to improve his poor record in international affairs, he was defeated for reelection by Democrat Franklin D. Roosevelt in 1932.

Hoo·ver[3], J. Edgar (1895–1972), U.S. government official; director of the FBI 1924–72; full name *John Edgar Hoover*. He reorganized the FBI into an efficient, scientific law-enforcement agency, but came under criticism for the organization's role during the McCarthy era and for its reactionary political stance in the 1960s.

Herbert Clark Hoover

Hoo·ver4, William (Henry) (1849–1932), U.S. industrialist; manufacturer of vacuum cleaners.

Hoo·ver·ville /ˈhōōvər,vil/ ▸*n.* a shantytown built by unemployed and destitute people during the Depression of the early 1930s. ▷named after H.C. HOOVER1, during whose presidency such accommodations were built (see also -VILLE).

hooves /hōōvz; hōōvz/ ▸ plural form of HOOF.

hop1 /häp/ ▸*v.* (**hopped, hop·ping**) [*intrans.*] (of a person) move by jumping on one foot. ■ (of a bird or other animal) move by jumping with two or all feet at once: *a blackbird was hopping around in the sun.* ■ spring or leap a short distance with one jump: *he hopped down from the rock.* ■ [*trans.*] jump over (something): *the cow hopped the fence.* ■ *informal* make a quick trip: *let's hop over to the bar.* ■ make a quick change of position, location, or activity: *over the years he hopped from one department to another.* ■ [*in combination*] visit a succession of things or places: *regulars liked to table-hop.* ■ [*trans.*] *informal* board (a bus, airplane, or other mode of transportation): *she hopped a train in Winnipeg.* ■ [*trans.*] *informal* jump onto (a moving vehicle): *ex-soldiers looking for work hopped freight trains heading west.* ■ [usu. as *n.* in *combination*] (**-hopping**) (of an aircraft or ferry) pass quickly from one place to another: *two-week island-hopping packages.* ■ (**hop it**) *Brit., informal* go away quickly.
▸*phrasal v.* □ **hop in** (or **out**) *informal* get into (or out of) a car: *hop in then and we'll be off.*
▸*n.* **1** a hopping movement. ■ a short journey or distance: *a short hop by cab from Soho.* **2** an informal dance. ▷Old English *hoppian*, of Germanic origin; related to German dialect *hopfen* and German *hopsen.*
▸**PHRASES** □ **hop, skip, and (a) jump** **1** old-fashioned term for TRIPLE JUMP. **2** *informal* a short distance: *it's just a hop, skip, and a jump from my hometown.* □ **hop the twig** (or **stick**) *Brit., informal* depart suddenly or die. □ **hop to it** begin a task quickly; get busy: *I shall have the experience of snapping my fingers and having people hop to it.* □ **on the hop** *Brit., informal* **1** unprepared: *he was* **caught on the hop.** **2** bustling around; busy: *we were always kept on the hop.*

hop2 ▸*n.* a twining climbing plant native to north temperate regions, cultivated for the conelike flowers borne by the female plant, which are used in brewing beer. • *Humulus lupulus*, family Cannabaceae (or Cannabidaceae). ■ (**hops**) the dried conelike flowers of this plant, used in brewing to give a bitter flavor and as a mild sterilant.
▸*v.* (**hopped, hop·ping**) **1** [*trans.*] flavor with hops: *a strong dark beer, heavily hopped.* **2** (**be hopped up**) *informal* be stimulated or intoxicated by or as if by a psychoactive drug. ▷late Middle English *hoppe* (in the sense 'ripened hop cones for flavoring malt liquor'), from Middle Low German or Middle Dutch. **—hop·py** *adj.*

ho·pak /ˈhōpak/ ▸*n.* variant spelling of GOPAK.

Hope /hōp/, Bob (1903–2003), U.S. comedian; born in Britain; born *Leslie Townes Hope.* He often portrayed a cowardly incompetent, cheerfully failing to become a romantic hero, as in the series of *Road* movies (1940–62), in which he starred with Bing Crosby and Dorothy Lamour. He is also noted for his annual Christmas television specials 1953–94, many of which telecast the USO shows that he brought to U.S. troops stationed around the world.

hope /hōp/ ▸*n.* **1** a feeling of expectation and desire for a certain thing to happen: *he looked through her belongings in the hope of coming across some information | I had high hopes of making the Olympic team.* ■ a person or thing that may help or save someone: *their only hope is surgery.* ■ grounds for believing that something good may happen: *he does see some hope for the future.* **2** *archaic* a feeling of trust.
▸*v.* [*intrans.*] want something to happen or be the case: *he's* **hoping for** *an offer of compensation* | [with *clause*] *I hope that the kids are OK.* ■ [with *infinitive*] intend if possible to do something: *we're hoping to address all these issues.* ▷late Old English *hopa* (noun), *hopian* (verb), of Germanic origin; related to Dutch *hoop* (noun), *hopen* (verb), and German *hoffen* (verb). **—hop·er** *n.*
▸**PHRASES** □ **hope against hope** cling to a mere possibility: *they were hoping against hope that he would find a way out.* □ **hope for the best** hope for a favorable outcome. □ **hope springs eternal (in the human breast)** *proverb* it is human nature to always find fresh cause for optimism. □ **in hopes of** with the aim of: *I lay on a towel in the park in hopes of getting a tan.* □ **in hopes that** hoping that: *they are screaming in hopes that a police launch will pick us up.* □ **not a hope** *informal* no chance at all.

hope chest ▸*n.* a chest containing household linen and clothing stored by a woman in preparation for her marriage.

hope·ful /ˈhōpfəl/ ▸*adj.* feeling or inspiring optimism about a future event: *a hopeful sign* | [with *clause*] *he remained hopeful that something could be worked out.*
▸*n.* a person likely or hoping to succeed: *a leading gubernatorial hopeful.* **—hope·ful·ness** *n.*

hope·ful·ly /ˈhōpfəlē/ ▸*adv.* **1** in a hopeful manner: *he rode on hopefully.* **2** [*sentence adverb*] it is to be hoped that: *hopefully, it should be finished by next year.*

USAGE The traditional sense of **hopefully**, 'in a hopeful manner' (*he stared hopefully at the trophy*), has been used since 1593. The first recorded use of **hopefully** as a sentence adverb, meaning 'it is to be hoped that' (*hopefully, we'll see you tomorrow*), appears in 1702 in the *Magnalia Christi Americana*, written by Massachusetts theologian and writer Cotton Mather. This use of **hopefully** is now the most common one. Sentence adverbs in general (*frankly, honestly, regrettably, seriously*) are found in English since at least the 1600s, and their use has become common in recent decades. However, most traditionalists take the view that all sentence adverbs are inherently suspect. Although they concede that the battle over **hopefully** is lost on the popular front, they continue to withhold approval of its use as a sentence adverb. Attentive ears are particularly bothered when the sentence that follows does not match the promise of the introductory adverb, as when *frankly* is followed not by an expression of honesty but by a self-serving proclamation (*frankly, I don't care if you go or not*).
See also **usage** at SENTENCE ADVERB and THANKFULLY.

Ho·peh /ˈhōˈpā/ variant of HEBEI.

hope·less /ˈhōplis/ ▸*adj.* **1** feeling or causing despair about something: *his situation was obviously hopeless | Jessica looked at him in mute hopeless appeal.* **2** inadequate; incompetent: *I'm* **hopeless at** *names.* **—hope·less·ly** *adv.* **—hope·less·ness** *n.*

hop·head /ˈhäp,hed/ ▸*n. informal* a drug addict. ▷early 20th cent.: from HOP2 + HEAD.

hop horn·beam ▸*n.* see HORNBEAM.

Ho·pi /ˈhōpē/ ▸*n.* (*pl.* same or **Ho·pis**) **1** a member of a Pueblo Indian people living chiefly in northeastern Arizona. **2** the Uto-Aztecan language of this people.
▸*adj.* of or relating to this people or their language. ▷the name in Hopi.

Hop·kins1 /ˈhäpkənz/, Sir (Philip) Anthony (1937–), Welsh actor. He won an Academy Award for his performance in *The Silence of the Lambs* (1991). Other notable movies: *The Elephant Man* (1980), *The Remains of the Day* (1993), and *Hannibal* (2001).

Hop·kins2 Sir Frederick Gowland (1861–1947), English biochemist. He carried out pioneering work on "accessory food factors" essential to the diet, later called vitamins. Nobel Prize for Physiology or Medicine (1929, shared with Christiaan Eijkman).

Hop·kins3, Gerard Manley (1844–89), English poet. A shipwreck inspired him to write "The Wreck of the Deutschland," which makes use of his "sprung rhythm" technique.

Hop·kins4, Mark (1802–87), U.S. philosopher and educator. He taught moral philosophy 1830–87 at Williams College and was that institution's president 1836–72. He also served as president of the American Board of Commissioners for Foreign Missions 1857–87.

Hop·kin·son /ˈhäpkənsən/, Francis (1737–91), U.S. public official, musician, and writer. He was a signer of the Declaration of Independence in 1776 and helped to design the first U.S. flag in 1777. A harpsichordist, he is considered the first native-born American composer of classical music.

Hop·kins·ville /ˈhäpkinz,vil/ a city in southwestern Kentucky, southwest of Bowling Green; pop. 30,089.

hop·lite /ˈhäp,līt/ ▸*n.* a heavily armed foot soldier of ancient Greece. ▷from Greek *hoplitēs*, from *hoplon* 'weapon.'

Hop·per1 /ˈhäpər/, Edward (1882–1967), U.S. realist painter. He is best known for his mature works, such as *Early Sunday Morning* (1930) and *Nighthawks* (1942), often depicting isolated figures in bleak scenes from everyday urban life.

Hop·per2, Grace Murray (1906–92), U.S. admiral, mathematician, and computer scientist. She taught mathematics at Vassar College 1931–44 before serving in the U.S. Navy 1943–86 where she became the highest ranked female officer. From 1959 until 1971, she worked as a computer programmer for the Sperry Rand Corporation.

hop·per /ˈhäpər/ ▸*n.* **1** a container for a bulk material such as grain, rock, or trash, typically one that tapers downward and is able to discharge its contents at the bottom. ■ *chiefly historical* a tapering container, working with a hopping motion, through which grain passed into a mill. ■ (in full **hopper car**) a railroad car able to discharge coal or other bulk material through its floor. ■ a barge for carrying away mud or sediment from a dredging machine and discharging it. ■ (also **hopper head**) a container at the top of a vertical pipe that receives water from a gutter or waste pipe. ■ a box in which bills are put for consideration by a legislature. **2** a person or thing that hops. ■ *informal* a person who makes a series of short trips: *an island hopper.* ■ a hopping insect, esp. a grasshopper.

hop·ping /ˈhäpiNG/ ▸*adj. informal* very active or lively: *the delis do a hopping lunch business.*
▸**PHRASE** □ **hopping mad** *informal* extremely angry.

hop·ping john ▸*n.* (in the southern U.S. and Caribbean) a stew of rice with black-eyed peas, often also containing bacon and red peppers.

hop·ple /ˈhäpəl/ ▸*v.* & *n. Riding* another term for HOBBLE (sense 2). ▷late 16th cent.: probably of Low German origin and related to early Flemish *hoppelen* and Middle Dutch *hobelen* 'jump, dance'; compare with HOBBLE.

hop·sack /ˈhäp,sak/ ▸*n.* a coarse fabric of a loose plain weave, used for clothing. ■ a coarse hemp sack used for hops.

hop·scotch /ˈhäp,skäCH/ ▸*n.* a children's game in which each child by turn hops into and over squares marked on the ground to retrieve a marker thrown into one of these squares.
▸*v.* [*intrans.*] skip from place to place; move erratically: *the blackouts hopscotched around eight Western states | he hopscotched from Indonesia to Hong Kong to Australia to Japan.* ▷early 19th cent.: from HOP1 + SCOTCH1.

hop·tree /ˈhäp,trē/ (also **hop tree**) ▸*n.* a North American shrub or small tree of the rue family, with bitter fruit that was formerly used in brewing as a substitute for hops. • *Ptelea trifoliata*, family Rutaceae.

hor. ▸*abbr.* ■ horizon. ■ horizontal. ■ horology.

ho·ra /ˈhôrə; ˈhōrə/ (also **ho·rah**) ▸*n.* a Romanian or Israeli dance in which the performers form a ring. ▷late 19th cent.: from Romanian *horă*, Hebrew *hōrāh.*

Hor·ace /ˈhôrəs/ (65–68 BC), Roman poet of the Augustan period; full name *Quintus Horatius Flaccus.* A well-known satirist and literary critic, he is noted for his *Odes.* Other works include *Satires* and *Ars Poetica.*

ho·ral /ˈhôrəl/ ▸*adj.* of or relating to an hour or hours; hourly. ▷early 18th cent.: from late Latin *horalis*, from Latin *hora* 'hour.'

ho·ra·ry /ˈhôrərē/ ▸*adj. archaic* of or relating to hours as measurements of time. ■ occurring every hour: *I took horary observations of the barometer.* ■ *Astrology* relating to or denoting a branch of astrology in which answers are given to questions using a chart drawn up for the time a question is posed. ▷early 17th cent.: from medieval Latin *horarius*, from Latin *hora* 'hour.'

Ho·ra·tian /həˈrāsHən/ ▸*adj.* of or relating to the Roman poet Horace or his work. ■ (of an ode) of several stanzas, each of the same metrical pattern.

hor·cha·ta /ôr'CHätə/ ▸*n.* (in Spain and Latin American countries) an almond-flavored soft drink. ▷Spanish.

horde /hôrd/ ▸*n.* **1** *chiefly derogatory* a large group of people: *he was surrounded by* ***a horde of*** *tormenting relatives.* ■ an army or tribe of nomadic warriors: *Tartar hordes.* **2** *Anthropology* a loosely knit small social group typically consisting of about five families. ▷mid 16th cent. (originally denoting a tribe or troop of Tartar or other nomads): from Polish *horda*, from Turkish *ordu* '(royal) camp.'

USAGE The words **hoard** and **horde** are quite distinct; see **usage** at **HOARD**.

hore·hound /'hôr,hound/ (also **hoar·hound**) ▸*n.* a strong-smelling hairy plant of the mint family, with a tradition of use in medicine. • Two species in the family Labiatae: **white horehound** (*Marrubium vulgare*), a widely distributed plant traditionally used as a medicinal herb, and **black horehound** (*Ballota nigra*), a Eurasian plant that has become naturalized in North America and was formerly reputed to cure the bite of a mad dog. ■ the bitter aromatic juice of white horehound, used esp. in the treatment of coughs and colds. ▷Old English *hāre hūne*, from *hār* (see **HOAR**) + *hūne*, the name of the white horehound, also applied to related plants.

Hor·gan /'hôrgən/, Paul (1903–95) U.S. writer; full name *Paul George Vincent O'Shaughnessy Horgan*. His works, mostly about the southwestern U.S., include *Great River* (1954) and *Lamy of Santa Fe* (1975).

ho·ri·zon /hə'rīzən/ ▸*n.* **1** [usu. in *sing.*] the line at which the earth's surface and the sky appear to meet: *the sun rose above the horizon.* ■ (also **apparent** or **visible horizon**) the circular boundary of the part of the earth's surface visible from a particular point, ignoring irregularities and obstructions. ■ (also **celestial horizon**) *Astronomy* a great circle of the celestial sphere, the plane of which passes through the center of the earth and is parallel to that of the apparent horizon of a place. **2** (often **horizons**) the limit of a person's mental perception, experience, or interest: *she wanted to leave home and broaden her horizons.* **3** *Geology* a layer of soil or rock, or a set of strata, with particular characteristics. ■ *Archaeology* a level of an excavated site representing a particular period. ▷late Middle English: via Old French from late Latin *horizon*, from Greek *horizōn (kuklos)* 'limiting (circle).'

▸*PHRASE* □ **on the horizon** just imminent or becoming apparent: *trouble could be on the horizon.*

hor·i·zon·tal /,hôrə'zän(t)l/ ▸*adj.* **1** parallel to the plane of the horizon; at right angles to the vertical: *a horizontal line.* ■ (of machinery) having its parts working in a horizontal direction: *a horizontal steam engine.* **2** combining companies engaged in the same stage or type of production: *a horizontal merger.* ■ involving social groups of equal status: *horizontal class loyalties.* **3** of or at the horizon: *the horizontal moon.*

▸*n.* a horizontal line, plane, etc. ▷mid 16th cent. (sense 3): from French, or from modern Latin *horizontalis*, from late Latin *horizon*, *horizont-* (see **HORIZON**). **—hor·i·zon·tal·i·ty** /-,zän'talitē/ *n.* **—hor·i·zon·tal·ly** *adv.*

hor·i·zon·tal sta·bi·liz·er ▸*n.* a horizontal airfoil at the tail of an aircraft.

Hork·heim·er /'hôrk,hīmər/, Max (1895–1973), German philosopher and sociologist; a leading figure of the Frankfurt School.

Hor·liv·ka /'hôrləfkə/ an industrial city in southeastern Ukraine, in the Donets Basin; pop. 338,000. Russian name **GORLOVKA**.

hor·mone /'hôr,mōn/ ▸*n.* *Physiology* a regulatory substance produced in an organism and transported in tissue fluids such as blood or sap to stimulate specific cells or tissues into action. ■ a synthetic substance with a similar effect. ■ (**hormones**) a person's sex hormones as held to influence behavior or mood. ▷early 20th cent.: from Greek *hormōn*, present participle of *horman* 'impel, set in motion.' **—hor·mo·nal** /hôr'mōnl/ *adj.*

hor·mone re·place·ment ther·a·py (abbr.: **HRT**) ▸*n.* treatment with estrogens with the aim of alleviating menopausal symptoms or osteoporosis.

Hor·muz /hôr'mo͞oz; 'hôr,məz/ (also **Or·muz** /ôr'mo͞oz; 'ôr,məz/) an Iranian island at the mouth of the Persian Gulf, in the Strait of Hormuz. It is the site of an ancient city that was an important center of commerce in the Middle Ages.

Hor·muz, Strait of a strait that links the Persian Gulf with the Gulf of Oman and that leads to the Arabian Sea and separates Iran from the Arabian peninsula. It is of strategic and economic importance as a waterway through which sea traffic to and from the oil-rich countries of the gulf must pass.

Horn, Cape /hôrn/ the most southern point of South America, on a Chilean island south of Tierra del Fuego. The region is notorious for its storms and, until the opening of the Panama Canal in 1914, constituted the only sea route between the Atlantic and Pacific oceans. Also called **the Horn**. ▷named after *Hoorn*, the birthplace of the Dutch navigator William C. Schouten (*c.*1580–1625), who sailed around it in 1616.

horn /hôrn/ ▸*n.* **1** a hard permanent outgrowth, often curved and pointed, found in pairs on the heads of cattle, sheep, goats, giraffes, etc., and consisting of a core of bone encased in keratinized skin. ■ a woolly keratinized outgrowth, occurring singly or one behind another, on the snout of a rhinoceros. ■ a deer's antler. ■ a hornlike projection on the head of another animal, e.g., a snail's tentacle or the tuft of a horned owl. ■ (**horns**) *archaic* a pair of horns as an emblem of a cuckold. **2** the substance of which horns are composed: *powdered rhino horn.* ■ a receptacle or instrument made of horn, such as a drinking container or powder flask. **3** a thing resembling or compared to a horn in shape. ■ a horn-shaped projection. ■ a sharp promontory or mountain peak. ■ a raised projection on the pommel of a Western saddle: *slung from the horn of his saddle was a leather bag.* ■ (**the Horn**) Cape Horn. ■ an arm or branch of a river or bay. ■ the extremity of the moon or other crescent. ■ *Brit., vulgar slang* an erect penis. **4** a wind instrument, conical in shape or wound into a spiral, originally made from an animal horn (now typically brass) and played by lip vibration. ■ short for **FRENCH HORN**. **5** an instrument sounding a warning or other signal: *a car horn.*

▸*v.* [*trans.*] (of an animal) butt or gore with the horns.

▸*phrasal v.* □ **horn in** *informal* intrude; interfere. ▷Old English, of Germanic origin; related to Dutch *hoorn* and German *Horn*, from an Indo-European root shared by Latin *cornu* and Greek *keras*. **—horn·ist** /-ist/ *n.* (in sense 4). **—horn·less** *adj.* **—horn·like** /-,līk/ *adj.*

▸*PHRASES* □ **blow** (or **toot**) **one's own horn** *informal* talk boastfully about oneself or one's achievements. □ **draw** (or **pull**) **in one's horns** become less assertive or ambitious. □ **on the horn** *informal* on the telephone: *she got on the horn to complain.* □ **on the horns of a dilemma** faced with a decision involving equally unfavorable alternatives.

horn·beam /'hôrn,bēm/ ▸*n.* a deciduous tree of north temperate regions, with oval serrated leaves, inconspicuous drooping flowers, and tough winged nuts. It yields hard pale timber. • Genera *Carpinus* and *Ostrya*, family Betulaceae: several species, including the **American hornbeam** (*C. caroliniana*), the **eastern** (or **hop**) **hornbeam** (*O. virginiana*), and the **European hornbeam** (*C. betulus*). ▷late Middle English: so named because of the tree's hard, close-grained wood.

horn·bill /'hôrn,bil/ ▸*n.* a medium to large tropical Old World bird, having a very large curved bill that typically has a large horny or bony casque. The male often seals up the female inside the nest hole. • Family Bucerotidae: several genera and numerous species, e.g., the **great Indian hornbill** (*Buceros bicornis*).

horn·blende /'hôrn,blend/ ▸*n.* a dark brown, black, or green mineral of the amphibole group consisting of a hydroxyl alumino-silicate of calcium, magnesium, and iron, occurring in many igneous and metamorphic rocks. ▷late 18th cent.: from German, from *Horn* 'horn' + *blende* (see **BLENDE**).

horn·book /'hôrn,bo͝ok/ ▸*n.* *historical* a teaching aid consisting of a leaf of paper showing the alphabet, and often the ten digits and the Lord's Prayer, mounted on a wooden tablet and protected by a thin plate of horn. ■ *Law* a one-volume treatise summarizing the law in a specific field.

Horne /hôrn/, Lena (Calhoun) (1917–) U.S. singer and actress. In the early 1940s, she became the first African American to have a long-term contract with a Hollywood studio. Her movies include *Stormy Weather* (1943) and *Till the Clouds Roll By* (1946). In 1981, she opened on Broadway in *Lena Horne: The Lady and Her Music.*

horned /hôrnd/ ▸*adj.* **1** having a horn or horns: *horned cattle* | [in *combination*] *a long-horned bison.* **2** [*attrib.*] *poetic/literary* crescent-shaped: *the horned moon.*

horned grebe ▸*n.* a North American and northern Eurasian grebe with reddish underparts and a black and gold crest. • *Podiceps auritus*, family Podicipedidae.

horned lark ▸*n.* a widespread lark of open country, esp. the Arctic and mountains, the male having a black and white head pattern and two small black hornlike crests. • Genus *Eremophila*, family Alaudidae: two species, in particular *E. alpestris*. British name: **shorelark**.

horned liz·ard ▸*n.* an American lizard that somewhat resembles a toad, with spiny skin and large spines on the head, typically occurring in dry open country. Also called **HORNED TOAD**. • Genus *Phrynosoma*, family Iguanidae: several species, in particular the **Texas horned lizard** (*P. cornutum*) and the **regal horned lizard** (*P. solare*).

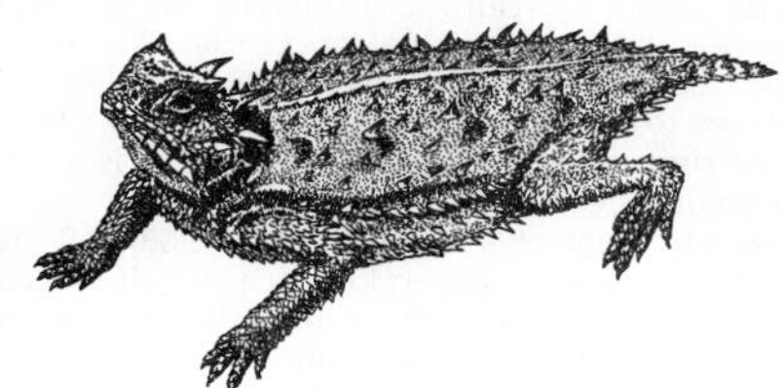

regal horned lizard

horned pop·py (also **horn pop·py**) ▸*n.* a Eurasian poppy with grayish-green lobed leaves, large flowers, and a long curved seed capsule. • Genus *Glaucium*, family Papaveraceae: several species, in particular the **yellow horned poppy** (*G. flavum*), which has become naturalized in the U.S., esp. along the coast from Massachusetts to Virginia.

horned toad ▸*n.* **1** another term for **HORNED LIZARD**. **2** a large toad with horn-shaped projections of skin over the eyes, in particular: • a Southeast Asian toad (*Megophrys* and other genera, family Peltobatidae). • a South American toad (*Ceratophrys* and other genera, family Leptodactylidae).

horned vi·per ▸*n.* a venomous nocturnal snake with an upright projection over each eye, native to the sandy deserts of North Africa and Arabia. It moves in the same way as the sidewinder. • *Cerastes cerastes*, family Viperidae.

hor·ne·ro /hôr'ne(ə)rō/ ▸*n.* (*pl.* **-ros**) a tropical American bird of the ovenbird family, often building its ovenlike mud nest on the top of a fence post. Also called **OVENBIRD**. • Genus *Furnarius*, family Furnariidae: several species, in particular the **rufous hornero** (*F. rufus*). ▷late 19th cent.: from Spanish, literally 'baker.'

Hor·ner's syn·drome /'hôrnərz/ ▸*n.* *Medicine* a condition marked by a contracted pupil, drooping upper eyelid, and local inability to sweat on one side of the face, caused by damage to sympathetic nerves on that side of the neck. ▷early 20th cent.: named after Johann F. *Horner* (1831–86), Swiss ophthalmologist.

hor·net /'hôrnit/ ▸*n.* a large stinging wasp that typically nests in hollow trees. • *Vespa* and other genera, family Vespidae: several species, including the **giant hornet** (*V. crabro*) and the **bald-faced** (or **white-faced**) **hornet** (*V. maculata*). ▷Old English *hyrnet*, of Germanic origin; related to German *Hornisse*. The form of the word was probably influenced by Middle Dutch and Middle Low German *hornte*.

bald-faced hornet

▸*PHRASE* □ **a hornets' nest** a situation fraught with difficulties or complications: *the move has* ***stirred up a hornet's nest*** *of academic fear and loathing.*

hor·net moth ▸*n.* a clearwing moth that resembles a hornet, with larvae that burrow under tree bark. • Several species in the family Sesiidae, including *Sesia apiformis*, which can be a pest of poplars.

Hor·ney /'hôr,nī/, Karen (Danielsen) (1885–1952) U.S. psychoanalyst; born in Germany. Expelled from the New York Psychoanalytic Institute for her critique of Freudian practices 1941, she was the founder of the Association for Advancement of Psychoanalysis and the American Institute for Psychoanalysis that same year.

horn·fels /ˈhôrn,felz/ ▸*n.* a dark, fine-grained metamorphic rock consisting largely of quartz, mica, and particular feldspars. ▷mid 19th cent.: from German, literally 'horn rock.'

Horn of Af·ri·ca a peninsula in northeastern Africa that includes Somalia and parts of Ethiopia. It lies between the Gulf of Aden and the Indian Ocean. Also called **Somali Peninsula**.

horn of plen·ty ▸*n.* **1** a cornucopia. **2** an edible woodland mushroom with a funnel-shaped cap that bears spores on its grayish outer surface, found in both Eurasia and North America. • *Craterellus cornucopiodes*, family Cantharellaceae, class Hymenomycetes.

horn·pipe /ˈhôrn,pīp/ ▸*n.* a lively dance associated with sailors, typically performed by one person. ■ a piece of music for such a dance. ▷late Middle English (denoting a wind instrument made of horn, played to accompany dancing): from **horn** + **pipe**.

horn-rimmed ▸*adj.* (of glasses) having rims made of horn or a similar substance.

Horns·by /ˈhôrnzbē/, Rogers (1896–1963) U.S. baseball player and manager; known as **Rajah**. A second baseman, he was known for his batting prowess and played mainly for the St. Louis Cardinals 1915–26, 1932. Baseball Hall of Fame (1942).

horn shell ▸*n.* a mollusk with a long tapering shell, occurring in brackish and marine waters. • Families Potamididae and Cerithidae, class Gastropoda.

horn·swog·gle /ˈhôrn,swägəl/ ▸*v.* [*trans.*] (usu. **be hornswoggled**) *informal* get the better of (someone) by cheating or deception: *you mean to say you were hornswoggled?* ▷early 19th cent. (originally U.S.): of unknown origin.

horn·tail /ˈhôrn,tāl/ ▸*n.* a large wasplike sawfly that deposits its eggs inside trees and timber. It has a long egg-laying tube but no sting. Also called **wood-wasp**. • Family Siricidae, suborder Symphyta, order Hymenoptera: several species.

horn·worm /ˈhôrn,wərm/ ▸*n.* the caterpillar of a hawk moth, having a spike or "horn" on its tail. • Family Sphingidae: several genera and many species, in particular pests like the **tobacco hornworm** (*Manduca sexta*) and the **tomato hornworm** (*M. quinquemaculata*).

horn·wort /ˈhôrn,wərt; -,wôrt/ ▸*n.* a submerged aquatic plant with narrow forked leaves that become translucent and horny as they age, occurring worldwide. • Genus *Ceratophyllum*, family Ceratophyllaceae: two or more species, in particular *C. demersum*.

horn·y /ˈhôrnē/ ▸*adj.* (**horn·i·er**, **horn·i·est**) **1** of or resembling horn: *a horny beak | horny nails.* ■ hard and rough: *horny, dry skin.* **2** *informal* feeling or arousing sexual excitement. **—horn·i·ness** *n.*

horn·y cor·al ▸*n.* see **coral** (sense 2).

horol. ▸*abbr.* horology.

hor·o·loge /ˈhôrə,läj/ ▸*n. archaic* a timepiece. ▷late Middle English: from Old French, via Latin from Greek *hōrologion*, from *hōra* 'time' + *-logos* '-telling.'

Hor·o·lo·gi·um /,hôrə,lōjēəm/ *Astronomy* a faint southern constellation (the Clock), between Hydrus and Eridanus. ■ [as *genitive*] (**Horologii** /-jē,ī/) used with a preceding letter or numeral to designate a star in this constellation: *the star R Horologii.* ▷Latin.

ho·rol·o·gy /həˈräləjē/ ▸*n.* the study and measurement of time. ■ the art of making clocks and watches. ▷early 19th cent.: from Greek *hōra* 'time' + **-logy**. **—ho·rol·o·ger** /-jər/ *n.* **—hor·o·log·ic** /,hôrəˈläjik/ *adj.* **—hor·o·log·i·cal** /,hôrəˈläjikəl/ *adj.* **—ho·rol·o·gist** /-jist/ *n.*

ho·rop·ter /ˈhô,räptər; həˈräptər/ ▸*n. Optics* a line or surface containing all those points in space whose images fall on corresponding points of the retinas of the two eyes. ▷early 18th cent.: from Greek *horos* 'limit' + *optēr* 'person who looks.'

hor·o·scope /ˈhôrə,skōp; ˈhärə-/ ▸*n. Astrology* a forecast of a person's future, typically including a delineation of character and circumstances, based on the relative positions of the stars and planets at the time of that person's birth. ■ a short forecast for people born under a particular sign, esp. as published in a newspaper or magazine. ■ a birth chart. See **chart**. ▷Old English: via Latin from Greek *hōroskopos*, from *hōra* 'time' + *skopos* 'observer.' **—hor·o·scop·ic** /,hôrəˈskäpik; ,härə-/ *adj.* **—ho·ros·co·py** /həˈräskəpē/ *n.*

Hor·o·witz /ˈhôrə,wits/, Vladimir (1904–89), U.S. pianist, born in Russia. He first toured the U.S. in 1928 and settled there soon afterward. A leading international virtuoso, he was best known for his performances of Scarlatti, Liszt, Scriabin, and Prokofiev.

hor·ren·dous /həˈrendəs; hô-/ ▸*adj.* extremely unpleasant, horrifying, or terrible: *she suffered horrendous injuries.* ▷mid 17th cent.: from Latin *horrendus* (gerundive of *horrere* '(of hair) stand on end') + **-ous**. **—hor·ren·dous·ly** *adv.*

hor·rent /ˈhôrənt/ ▸*adj. poetic/literary* **1** (of a person's hair) standing on end. **2** feeling or expressing horror: *a horrent cry.* ▷mid 17th cent.: from Latin *horrent-* '(of hair) standing on end,' from the verb *horrere*.

hor·ri·ble /ˈhôrəbəl; ˈhär-/ ▸*adj.* causing or likely to cause horror; shocking: *a horrible massacre.* ■ *informal* very unpleasant: *the tea tasted horrible.* ▷Middle English: via Old French from Latin *horribilis*, from *horrere* 'tremble, shudder' (see **horrid**). **—hor·ri·ble·ness** *n.* **—hor·ri·bly** /-blē/ *adv.* [as *submodifier*] *the plan had gone horribly wrong.*

hor·rid /ˈhôrid; ˈhär-/ ▸*adj.* **1** causing horror: *a horrid nightmare.* ■ *informal* very unpleasant or disagreeable: *the teachers at school were horrid | a horrid brown color.* **2** *poetic/literary* rough; bristling. ▷late 16th cent. (in the sense 'rough, bristling'): from Latin *horridus*, from *horrere* 'tremble, shudder, (of hair) stand on end.' **—hor·rid·ly** *adv.* **—hor·rid·ness** *n.*

hor·rif·ic /hôˈrifik; hə-/ ▸*adj.* causing horror: *horrific injuries.* ▷mid 17th cent.: from Latin *horrificus*, from *horrere* 'tremble, shudder' (see **horrid**). **—hor·rif·i·cal·ly** /ik(ə)lē/ *adv.*

hor·ri·fy /ˈhôrə,fī; ˈhär-/ ▸*v.* (**-fies, -fied**) [*trans.*] (usu. **be horrified**) fill with horror; shock greatly: *they were horrified by the very idea | [as adj.] (**horrified**) the horrified spectators | [as adj.] (**horrifying**) a horrifying incident.* ▷late 18th cent.: from Latin *horrificare*, from *horrificus* (see **horrific**). **—hor·ri·fi·ca·tion** /hô,rifiˈkāshən; hə-/ *n.* **—hor·ri·fied·ly** /-,fī(ə)dlē/ *adv.* **—hor·ri·fy·ing·ly** *adv.* [as *submodifier*] *horrifyingly flimsy boats.*

hor·rip·i·la·tion /hô,ripəˈlāshən; hə-/ ▸*n. poetic/literary* the erection of hairs on the skin due to cold, fear, or excitement. ▷mid 17th cent.: from late Latin *horripilatio(n-)*, from Latin *horrere* 'stand on end' (see **horrid**) + *pilus* 'hair.' **—hor·rip·i·late** /hôˈripə,lāt; hə-/ *v.*

hor·ror /ˈhôrər; ˈhär-/ ▸*n.* **1** an intense feeling of fear, shock, or disgust: *children screamed in horror.* ■ a thing causing such a feeling: *photographs showed the horror of the tragedy | the horrors of civil war.* ■ a literary or film genre concerned with arousing such feelings: [as *adj.*] *a horror movie.* ■ intense dismay: *to her horror she found that a thief had stolen the machine.* ■ [as *exclam.*] (**horrors**) *chiefly humorous* used to express dismay: *horrors, two buttons were missing!* ■ [in *sing.*] intense dislike: *many have a **horror of** consulting a dictionary.* ■ (**the horrors**) an attack of extreme nervousness or anxiety: *the mere thought of it gives me the horrors.* **2** *informal* a bad or mischievous person, esp. a child: *that little horror Zach was around.* ▷Middle English: via Old French from Latin *horror*, from *horrere* 'tremble, shudder' (see **horrid**).

hor·ror-struck (also **hor·ror-strick·en**) ▸*adj.* (of a person) briefly paralyzed with horror or shock.

hor·ror va·cui /ˈvakyə,wī/ ▸*n.* [in *sing.*] a fear or dislike of leaving empty spaces, esp. in an artistic composition. ▷mid 19th cent.: modern Latin, literally 'horror of a vacuum.'

hors con·cours /,ôr kôNˈkōōr/ ▸*adj.* **1** unrivaled; unequaled: *most husbands are fools, but that one was hors concours.* **2** *formal* (of an exhibit or exhibitor) not competing for a prize. ▷late 19th cent.: French, literally 'out of the competition.'

hors de com·bat /,ôr də kämˈbä/ ▸*adj.* out of action due to injury or damage: *their pilots had been rendered temporarily hors de combat.* ▷mid 18th cent.: French, literally 'out of the fight.'

hors d'oeuvre /ôr ˈdərv; ˈdœvrə/ ▸*n.* (*pl.* same or **hors d'oeuvres** *pronunc.* same or /ˈdərvz/) a small savory dish, typically one served as an appetizer at the beginning of a meal. ▷mid 18th cent.: French, literally 'outside the work.'

horse /hôrs/ ▸*n.* **1** a solid-hoofed plant-eating domesticated mammal with a flowing mane and tail, used for riding, racing, and to carry and pull loads. • *Equus caballus*, family Equidae (the **horse family**), descended from the wild Przewalski's horse. The horse family also includes the asses and zebras. ■ an adult male horse; a stallion or gelding. ■ a wild mammal of the horse family. ■ [treated as *sing.* or *pl.*] cavalry: *forty horse and sixty foot.* **2** a frame or structure on which something is mounted or supported, esp. a sawhorse. ■ *Nautical* a horizontal bar, rail, or rope in the rigging of a sailing ship for supporting something. ■ short for **pommel horse** or **vaulting horse**. **3** *informal* heroin. **4** *informal* a unit of horsepower: *the huge 63-horse 701-cc engine.* **5** *Mining* an obstruction in a vein.
▸*v.* [*trans.*] (usu. **be horsed**) provide (a person or vehicle) with a horse or horses.
▸*phrasal v.* □ **horse around** *informal* fool around: *schoolkids laughing and horsing around.* ▷Old English *hors*, of Germanic origin; related to Dutch *ros* and German *Ross*. **—horse·less** *adj.* **—horse·like** /-,līk/ *adj.*
▸*PHRASES* □ **don't change horses in midstream** *proverb* choose a sensible moment to change your mind. □ **from the horse's mouth** (of information) from the person directly concerned or another authoritative source. □ **horses for courses** *Brit., proverb* different people are suited to different things or situations. □ **to horse** (as a command) mount your horses! □ **you can lead** (or **take**) **a horse to water but you can't make him drink** *proverb* you can give someone an opportunity, but you can't force them to take it.

horse-and-bug·gy ▸*adj.* [*attrib.*] old-fashioned: *horse-and-buggy technology.* ■ of a time when horses and buggies were a common mode of transportation: *he had lived in the horse-and-buggy era and lived to see them put a man on the moon.*

horse·back /ˈhôrs,bak/ ▸*adj.* & *adv.* mounted on a horse: [as *adj.*] *a horseback rider* | [as *adv.*] *they rode horseback along the trail.*
▸*PHRASE* □ **on** (or **by**) **horseback** mounted on a horse.

horse·bean /ˈhôrs,bēn/ (also **horse bean**) ▸*n.* another term for **broad bean**.

horse chest·nut ▸*n.* a deciduous tree with large leaves of five leaflets, conspicuous sticky winter buds, and upright conical clusters of white, pink, or red flowers. Unrelated to true chestnuts, the horse chestnut bears unpalatable nuts enclosed in fleshy, thorny husks. • Genus *Aesculus*, family Hippocastanaceae: several species, in particular *A. hippocastanum*, native east of the Balkans and widely planted over much of Europe and North America. ■ the fruit or seed of this tree. ▷late 16th cent.: translating (now obsolete) botanical Latin *Castanea equina*; its fruit is said to have been an Eastern remedy for chest diseases in horses.

horse cloth ▸*n.* a cloth used to cover a horse, or as part of its trappings.

horse-drawn ▸*adj.* (of a vehicle) pulled by a horse or horses: *a horse-drawn carriage.*

horse·feath·ers /ˈhôrs,feT͟Hərz/ ▸*exclam.* used to express disagreement, disbelief, or frustration.

horse·flesh /ˈhôrs,flesH/ ▸*n.* horses considered collectively. ■ the flesh of a horse, esp. when used as food.

horse·fly /ˈhôrs,flī/ ▸*n.* (*pl.* **-flies**) a stoutly built fly, the female of which is a bloodsucker and inflicts painful bites on horses and other mammals, including humans. • Genus *Tabanus*, family Tabanidae: numerous species.

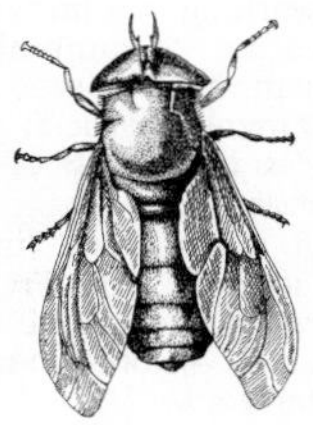
horsefly

Horse Guards ▸*plural n.* a mounted brigade from the household troops of the British monarch, used for ceremonial occasions.

horse·hair /ˈhôrs,he(ə)r/ ▸*n.* hair from the mane or tail of a horse, typically used in furniture for padding.

horse·hair worm ▸*n.* a long slender worm related to the nematodes, the larvae being parasites of arthropods and the adults living in water or damp soil. • Phylum Nematomorpha: two classes.

Horse·head Neb·u·la /ˈhôrs,hed/ *Astronomy* a dust nebula in the shape of a horse's head, forming a dark silhouette against a bright emission nebula in Orion.

horse·hide /ˈhôrs,hīd/ ▸*n.* **1** the skin of a horse. ■ leather made from the skin of a horse. **2** *informal* a baseball. [so named because, until replaced by cowhide in late 20th century, the traditional covering of a baseball was horsehide.]

horse lat·i·tudes ▸*plural n.* a belt of calm air and sea occurring in both the northern and southern hemispheres between the trade winds and the westerlies. ▷late 18th cent.: of uncertain origin.

horse·laugh /ˈhôrs,laf/ (also **horse-laugh**) ▸*n.* a loud, coarse laugh.

horse·leech /ˈhôrs,lēcH/ ▸*n.* a large predatory leech of freshwater and terrestrial habitats that feeds on carrion and small invertebrates. • Genus *Haemopis*, family Hirudidae.

horse·less /ˈhôrslis/ ▸*adj.* [*attrib.*] (of a vehicle) not drawn by a horse or horses: *a horseless cabriolet.*

horse·less car·riage ▸*n. archaic, humorous* an automobile.

horse mack·er·el ▸*n.* a shoaling edible fish of the eastern Atlantic, commercially fished in southern African waters. Also called SCAD. • *Trachurus trachurus*, family Carangidae.

horse·man /ˈhôrsmən/ ▸*n.* (*pl.* **-men**) a rider on horseback, esp. a skilled one.

horse·man·ship /ˈhôrsmən,ship/ ▸*n.* the art or practice of riding on horseback.

horse·mint /ˈhôrs,mint/ ▸*n.* a tall coarse kind of mint. • Genera *Mentha* and *Monarda*, family Labiatae: several species and hybrids, including the European *Mentha longifolia* and the North American *Monarda punctata*. ▷Middle English: from HORSE (often used in the names of plants to denote a coarse variety) + MINT[1].

horse mush·room ▸*n.* a large edible mushroom with a creamy-white cap and pinkish-gray gills, found in grassland in both Eurasia and North America. • *Agaricus arvensis*, family Agaricaceae, class Hymenomycetes.

horse op·er·a ▸*n. informal* a western movie.

horse pis·tol ▸*n. historical* a large pistol carried at the pommel of the saddle by a rider.

horse·play /ˈhôrs,plā/ ▸*n.* rough, boisterous play.

horse·play·er /ˈhôrs,plāər/ ▸*n.* a person who regularly bets on horse races.

horse·pow·er /ˈhôrs,pou(-ə)r/ (abbr.: **hp**) ▸*n.* (*pl.* same) a unit of power equal to 550 foot-pounds per second (745.7 watts). ■ the power of an engine measured in terms of this: *a strong 140-horsepower engine.* See also BRAKE HORSEPOWER. ■ power; ability to perform strenuous tasks: *other software improvements include more analytical horsepower.*

horse race ▸*n.* **1** a race between two or more horses ridden by jockeys. **2** a very close contest: *eight hours after the polls closed, the election was still a horse race.*

horse rac·ing ▸*n.* the sport in which horses and their riders take part in races, typically with substantial betting on the outcome.

horse·rad·ish /ˈhôrs,radish/ ▸*n.* a European plant of the cabbage family, with long docklike leaves, grown for its pungent root. • *Armoracia rusticana*, family Brassicaceae. ■ this root, which is scraped or grated as a condiment and often made into a sauce.

horse sense ▸*n. informal* common sense.

horse·shit /ˈhôr(s),shit/ ▸*n. vulgar slang* **1** horse dung. **2** nonsense.

horse·shoe /ˈhôr(s),shōō/ ▸*n.* a shoe for a horse formed of a narrow band of iron in the form of an extended circular arc and secured to the hoof with nails. ■ a shoe of this kind or a representation of one, regarded as bringing good luck. ■ something resembling this in shape: [as *adj.*] *a horseshoe bend.* ■ (**horseshoes**) [treated as *sing.*] a game in which horseshoes are thrown at a stake in the ground.

horse·shoe bat ▸*n.* an insectivorous Old World bat with a horseshoe-shaped ridge on the nose. • Family Rhinolophidae and genus *Rhinolophus*: numerous species.

horse·shoe crab ▸*n.* a large marine arthropod with a domed horseshoe-shaped shell, a long tail-spine, and ten legs, little changed since the Devonian. • Class Merostomata, subphylum Chelicerata: four species, in particular the North American *Limulus polyphemus*.

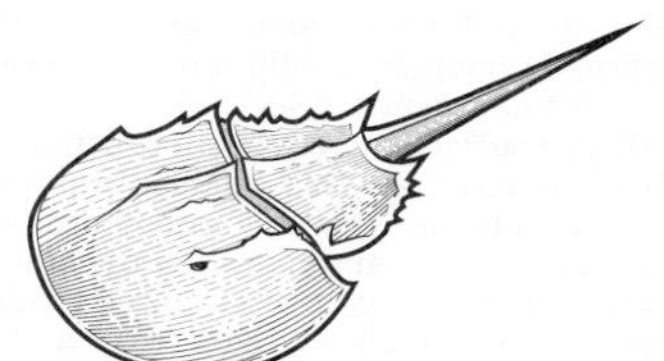

horseshoe crab

Horse·shoe Falls ▸ see NIAGARA FALLS.

horse's neck ▸*n. informal* a drink consisting of ginger ale, a twist of lemon peel, and liquor, typically brandy.

horse·tail /ˈhôrs,tāl/ ▸*n.* a nonflowering plant with a hollow jointed stem that bears whorls of narrow leaves, producing spores in cones at the tips of the shoots. • Genus *Equisetum*, the only surviving genus of the family Equisetaceae and class Sphenopsida, division Pteridophyta.

horse-trad·ing (also **horse trad·ing**) ▸*n.* the buying and selling of horses. ■ hard and shrewd bargaining, typically in politics. **—horse-trade** *v.* **—horse-trad·er** *n.*

horse·whip /ˈhôrs,(h)wip/ ▸*n.* a long whip used for driving and controlling horses.
▸*v.* (**-whipped**, **-whip·ping**) [*trans.*] beat with such a whip: *she would horsewhip them mercilessly.*

horse·wom·an /ˈhôrs,wŏŏmən/ ▸*n.* (*pl.* **-wom·en**) a woman who rides on horseback, esp. a skilled one.

hors·ey /ˈhôrsē/ (also **hors·y**) ▸*adj.* (**hors·i·er**, **hors·i·est**) **1** of or resembling a horse: *wide eyes and big, horsey teeth.* **2** concerned with or devoted to horses or horse racing: *the horsey fraternity.* **—hors·i·ly** /ˈhôrsəlē/ *adv.* **—hors·i·ness** *n.*

horst /hôrst/ ▸*n. Geology* a raised elongated block of the earth's crust lying between two faults. ▷late 19th cent.: from German *Horst* 'heap.'

Horst Wes·sel Song /ˈhôrst ˈvesəl/ the official song of the Nazi Party in Germany. The words were written by Horst Wessel (1907–30), a member of Hitler's Storm Troops killed by political enemies and regarded as a Nazi martyr.

hort. ▸*abbr.* ■ horticulture or horticultural.

Hor·ta /ˈhôrtə/, Victor (1861–1947), Belgian architect. His work is notable for its innovative use of iron and glass, and he is considered the originator of Art Nouveau.

hor·ta·to·ry /ˈhôrtə,tôrē/ ▸*adj.* tending or aiming to exhort: *the central bank relied on hortatory messages and voluntary compliance.* ▷late 16th cent.: from Latin *hortatorius*, from *hortari* 'exhort.' **—hor·ta·tion** /,hôrˈtāshən/ *n.* **—hor·ta·tive** /ˈhôrtətiv/ *adj.*

hor·ti·cul·ture /ˈhôrti,kəlchər/ ▸*n.* the art or practice of garden cultivation and management. ▷late 17th cent.: from Latin *hortus* 'garden,' on the pattern of *agriculture*. **—hor·ti·cul·tur·al** /,hôrtiˈkəlchərəl/ *adj.* **—hor·ti·cul·tur·al·ist** /,hôrtiˈkəlchərəlist/ *n.* **—hor·ti·cul·tur·ist** /,hôrtəˈkəlchərist/ *n.*

hor·tus sic·cus /ˈhôrtəs ˈsikəs/ ▸*n.* (*pl.* **hor·ti sic·ci** /ˈhôrtī ˈsikī; ˈsikē/) an arranged collection of dried plants; a herbarium. ▷late 17th cent.: Latin, literally 'dry garden.'

Ho·rus /ˈhôrəs/ *Egyptian Mythology* a god regarded as the protector of the monarchy, typically represented as a falcon-headed man. He assumed various aspects: in the myth of Isis and Osiris he was the posthumous son of the latter, whose murder he avenged.

Hos. ▸*abbr. Bible* Hosea.

ho·san·na /hōˈzanə; -ˈzä-/ (also **ho·san·nah**) ▸*exclam.* (esp. in biblical, Judaic, and Christian use) used to express adoration, praise, or joy.
▸*n.* an expression of adoration, praise, or joy. ▷Old English, via late Latin from Greek *hōsanna*, from Rabbinical Hebrew *hōšaʿnā*, abbreviation of biblical *hōšīʿā-nnā* 'save, we pray' (Ps. 118:25).

hose /hōz/ ▸*n.* **1** a flexible tube conveying water, used esp. for watering plants and in firefighting. **2** [treated as *pl.*] stockings, socks, and tights (esp. in commercial use): *a chorus girl's fishnet hose.* ■ *historical* breeches: *Elizabethan doublet and hose.*
▸*v.* [*trans.*] water, spray, or drench with a hose: *he was* **hosing down** *the driveway.* ▷Old English *hosa*, of Germanic origin; related to Dutch *hoos* 'stocking' and German *Hosen* 'trousers.' Originally singular, the term denoted a covering for the leg, sometimes including the foot but sometimes reaching only as far as the ankle.

Ho·se·a /hōˈzāə; -ˈzēə/ a Hebrew minor prophet of the 8th century BC. ■ a book of the Bible containing his prophecies.

ho·sel /ˈhōzəl/ ▸*n.* the socket of a golf club head into which the shaft fits. ▷late 16th cent.: diminutive of HOSE, in the dialect sense 'sheathing.'

hose·pipe /ˈhōz,pīp/ ▸*n.* British term for HOSE (sense 1).

ho·sier /ˈhōzhər/ ▸*n.* a manufacturer or seller of hosiery.

ho·sier·y /ˈhōzhərē/ ▸*n.* stockings, socks, and tights collectively.

hosp. ▸*abbr.* hospital.

hos·pice /ˈhäspis/ ▸*n.* a home providing care for the sick, esp. the terminally ill. ■ *archaic* a lodging for travelers, esp. one run by a religious order. ▷early 19th cent.: from French, from Latin *hospitium*, from *hospes*, *hospit-* (see HOST[1]).

hos·pi·ta·ble /häˈspitəbəl; ˈhäspitəbəl/ ▸*adj.* friendly and welcoming to strangers or guests: *two friendly, hospitable brothers run the hotel.* ■ (of an environment) pleasant and favorable for living in: *the Sonoran desert is one of the least hospitable places on earth.* ▷late 16th cent.: from French, from obsolete *hospiter* 'receive a guest,' from medieval Latin *hospitare* 'entertain,' from *hospes*, *hospit-* (see HOST[1]). **—hos·pi·ta·bly** /-blē/ *adv.*

hos·pi·tal /ˈhä,spitl/ ▸*n.* **1** an institution providing medical and surgical treatment and nursing care for sick or injured people. **2** *historical* a hospice, esp. one run by the Knights Hospitallers. **3** [usu. in *names*] *Brit. Law* a charitable institution for the education of the young. ▷Middle English (sense 2): via Old French from medieval Latin *hospitale*, neuter of Latin *hospitalis* 'hospitable,' from *hospes*, *hospit-* (see HOST[1]).

hos·pi·tal cor·ners ▸*plural n.* overlapping folds used to tuck sheets neatly and securely under the mattress at the corners, in a manner typically used by nurses.

hos·pi·tal·er /ˈhä,spitl-ər/ (also **hos·pi·tal·ler**) ▸*n.* a member of a charitable religious order, originally the Knights Hospitalers. ▷Middle English: from Old French *hospitalier*, from medieval Latin *hospitalarius*, from *hospitale* (see HOSPITAL).

Hos·pi·ta·let /,äspitlˈet; ,ōspētäˈlet/ (also **Hos·pi·ta·let de Llo·bre·gat** /dā ,(l)yōbriˈgät/) a city and southern suburb of Barcelona in northeastern Spain; pop. 269,000.

hos·pi·tal fe·ver ▸*n. historical* louse-borne typhus acquired in overcrowded, insanitary conditions in an old-fashioned hospital.

hos·pi·tal·ism /ˈhä,spitl,izəm/ ▸*n.* the adverse effects of a prolonged stay in the hospital, such as developmental retardation in children.

hos·pi·tal·ist /ˈhäspitl-ist/ ▸*n.* a dedicated in-patient physician who works exclusively in a hospital.

hos·pi·tal·i·ty /,häspiˈtalitē/ ▸*n.* the friendly and generous reception and entertainment of guests, visitors, or strangers.
▸*adj.* denoting a suite or room in a hotel where visitors are entertained, typically at a convention: *liquor flowed most freely in the hospitality suites of thirteen candidates.* ■ relating to or denoting the business of housing or entertaining visitors: *the hospitality industry.* ▷late Middle English: from Old French *hospitalite*, from Latin *hospitalitas*, from *hospitalis* 'hospitable' (see HOSPITAL).

hos·pi·tal·ize /ˈhäspitl,īz/ ▸*v.* [*trans.*] (usu. **be hospitalized**) admit or cause (someone) to be admitted to a hospital for treatment: *Casey was hospitalized for chest pains.* **—hos·pi·tal·i·za·tion** /,häspitl-iˈzāshən/ *n.*

hos·pi·tal·ler ▸*n.* British spelling of HOSPITALER.

hos·pi·tal ship ▸*n.* a ship that functions as a hospital, esp. to receive or take home sick or wounded military personnel.

hos·po·dar /ˈhäspə,där/ ▸*n. historical* a governor of Wallachia and Moldavia under the Ottoman Porte. ▷from Romanian, from Ukrainian *hospodar*; related to Russian *gospodar'*, from *gospod'* 'lord.'

hoss /hôs/ ▸*n.* nonstandard spelling of HORSE, used in representing dialect or informal speech.

host[1] /hōst/ ▸*n.* **1** a person who receives or entertains other people as guests: *a dinner-party host.* ■ a person, place, or organization that holds and organizes an event to which others are invited: *Innsbruck once* **played host to** *the Winter Olympics.* ■ an area in which particular living things are found: *Australia is* **host to** *some of the world's most dangerous animals.* ■ *often humorous* the landlord or landlady of a pub: ***mine host*** *raised his glass of whiskey.* ■ the moderator or emcee of a television or radio program. **2** *Biology* an animal or plant on or in which a parasite or commensal organism lives. ■ (also **host cell**) a living cell in which a virus multiplies. ■ a person whose immune system has been invaded by a pathogenic organism. ■ a person or animal that has received transplanted tissue or a transplanted organ. **3** (also **host computer**) a computer that mediates multiple access to databases mounted on it or provides other services to a computer network.
▸*v.* [*trans.*] act as host at (an event) or for (a television or radio program). ■ [*intrans.*] act as host. ▷Middle English: from Old French *hoste*, from Latin *hospes*, *hospit-* 'host, guest.'

host[2] ▸*n.* (**a host of** or **hosts of**) a large number of people or things: *a host of memories rushed into her* mind. ▪ *archaic* an army. ▪ *poetic/literary* (in biblical use) the sun, moon, and stars: *the starry host of heaven.* ▪ another term for HEAVENLY HOST. See also LORD OF HOSTS at LORD. ▷Middle English: from Old French *ost, hoost,* from Latin *hostis* 'stranger, enemy' (in medieval Latin 'army').

host³ ▸*n.* (usu. **the Host**) the bread consecrated in the Eucharist: *the elevation of the Host.* ▷Middle English: from Old French *hoiste,* from Latin *hostia* 'victim.'

hos·ta /ˈhōstə; ˈhästə/ ▸*n.* an eastern Asian plant cultivated in the West for its shade-tolerant foliage and loose clusters of tubular mauve or white flowers. Also called PLANTAIN LILY. • Genus *Hosta* (formerly *Funkia*), family Liliaceae. ▷modern Latin, named after Nicolaus T. *Host* (1761–1834), Austrian physician.

hos·tage /ˈhästij/ ▸*n.* a person seized or held as security for the fulfillment of a condition: *the kidnapper had instructed the hostage's family to drop the ransom at noon.* ▷Middle English: from Old French, based on late Latin *obsidatus* 'the state of being a hostage' (the earliest sense in English), from Latin *obses, obsid-* 'hostage.'

▸*PHRASES* □ **hold** (or **take**) **someone hostage** seize and keep someone as a hostage: *they were held hostage by armed rebels | taken hostage at gunpoint.* □ **a hostage to fortune** an act, commitment, or remark that is regarded as unwise because it invites trouble or could prove difficult to live up to: *making objectives explicit is to give a hostage to fortune.*

hos·tel /ˈhästl/ ▸*n.* an establishment that provides cheap food and lodging for a specific group of people, such as students, workers, or travelers. ▪ short for YOUTH HOSTEL. ▪ *archaic* an inn providing accommodations. ▷Middle English (in the general sense 'lodging, place to stay'): from Old French, from medieval Latin *hospitale* (see HOSPITAL).

hos·tel·ing /ˈhästl-iNG/ (*Brit.* **hos·tel·ling**) ▸*n.* the practice of staying in youth hostels when traveling. —**hos·tel·er** /ˈhästl-ər/ *n.*

hos·tel·ry /ˈhästl-rē/ ▸*n.* (*pl.* **-ries**) *archaic* or *humorous* an inn. ▷late Middle English: from Old French *hostelerie,* from *hostelier* 'innkeeper,' from *hostel* (see HOSTEL).

host·ess /ˈhōstis/ ▸*n.* a woman who receives or entertains guests: *the perfect dinner-party hostess.* ▪ a woman employed at a restaurant to welcome and seat customers. ▪ a woman employed to entertain customers at a nightclub, bar, or dance hall. ▪ a stewardess on an aircraft, train, etc. ▪ a woman who introduces a television or radio program: *a game-show hostess.*

▸*v.* [*trans.*] act as a hostess at (an event): *she was welcome to hostess the evening, if she chose.* ▪ [*intrans.*] act as a hostess. ▷Middle English: from Old French *(h)ostesse,* feminine of *(h)oste* (see HOST¹).

hos·tile /ˈhästl; ˈhä,stīl/ ▸*adj.* unfriendly; antagonistic: *a hostile audience | he wrote a ferociously hostile attack.* ▪ of or belonging to a military enemy: *hostile aircraft.* ▪ [*predic.*] opposed: *people are very* ***hostile to*** *the idea.* ▪ (of a takeover bid) opposed by the company to be bought. ▷late 16th cent.: from French, or from Latin *hostilis,* from *hostis* 'stranger, enemy.' —**hos·tile·ly** *adv.*

THE RIGHT WORD **adverse, bellicose, belligerent, hostile, inimical**

Few people have trouble recognizing hostility when confronted with it. Someone who is **hostile** displays an attitude of intense ill will and acts like an enemy (*the audience grew hostile after waiting an hour for the show to start*).

Both **bellicose** and **belligerent** imply a readiness or eagerness to fight, but the former is used to describe a state of mind or temper (*after drinking all night, he was in a bellicose mood*), while the latter is normally used to describe someone who is actively engaged in hostilities (*the belligerent brothers were at it again*).

While *hostile* and *belligerent* usually apply to people, **adverse** and **inimical** are used to describe tendencies or influences. *Inimical* means having an antagonistic tendency (*remarks that were inimical to everything she believed in*), and *adverse* means turned toward something in opposition (*an adverse wind; under adverse circumstances*). Unlike *hostile, adverse* and *inimical* need not connote the involvement of human feeling.

hos·tile wit·ness ▸*n.* *Law* a witness who is antagonistic to the party calling them and, being unwilling to tell the truth, may have to be cross-examined by the party.

hos·til·i·ty /häˈstilitē/ ▸*n.* (*pl.* **-ties**) hostile behavior; unfriendliness or opposition: *their* ***hostility to*** *all outsiders.* ▪ (**hostilities**) acts of warfare: *he called for an immediate cessation of hostilities.* ▷late Middle English: from French *hostilité* or late Latin *hostilitas,* from Latin *hostilis* (see HOSTILE).

hos·tler /ˈ(h)äslər/ (also **os·tler**) ▸*n.* *historical* a man employed to look after the horses of people staying at an inn. ▷late Middle English: from Old French *hostelier* 'innkeeper,' from *hostel* (see HOSTEL).

hot /hät/ ▸*adj.* (**hot·ter, hot·test**) **1** having a high degree of heat or a high temperature: *it was hot inside the hall | basking under a hot sun.* ▪ feeling or producing an uncomfortable sensation of heat: *she felt hot and her throat was parched.* ▪ (of food or drink) prepared by heating and served without cooling. ▪ *informal* (of an electric circuit) at a high voltage; live. ▪ *informal* radioactive. **2** (of food) containing or consisting of pungent spices or peppers that produce a burning sensation when tasted: *a very hot dish cooked with green chili.* **3** passionately enthusiastic, eager, or excited: *the idea had been nurtured in his hot imagination.* ▪ lustful, amorous, or erotic: *steamy bed scenes that may be too hot for young fans.* ▪ angry, indignant, or upset: *her reply came boiling out of her, hot with rage.* ▪ (of music, esp. jazz) strongly rhythmical and excitingly played: *hot salsa and lambada dancing.* **4** involving much activity, debate, or intense feeling: *the environment has become a very hot issue.* ▪ (esp. of news) fresh or recent and therefore of great interest: *have I got some hot gossip for you!* ▪ currently popular, fashionable, or in demand: *they know the hottest dance moves.* ▪ difficult to deal with; awkward or dangerous: *he found my story simply too hot to handle.* ▪ (of a hit or return in ball games) difficult for an opponent to deal with: *fielding a hot grounder at third.* ▪ *Hunting* (of the scent) fresh and strong, indicating that the quarry has passed recently. ▪ *informal* (of goods) stolen and difficult to dispose of because easily identifiable. ▪ *informal* (of a person) wanted by the police. ▪ [*predic.*] (in children's games) very close to finding or guessing something. **5** *informal* knowledgeable or skillful: *Tony is very* ***hot on*** *local history.* ▪ [*predic.*] [usu. with *negative*] good; promising: *this is not so* ***hot for*** *business.* ▪ [*predic.*] (**hot on**) *informal* considering as very important; strict about: *local customs officers are hot on confiscations.*

▸*phrasal v.* □ **hot up** (or **hot something up**) *Brit., informal* become or make hot: *he hotted up the flask in Daisy's hand.* ▪ become or make more active, lively, or exciting: *the championship contest hotted up.* ▷Old English *hāt,* of Germanic origin; related to Dutch *heet* and German *heiss.* —**hot·ness** *n.* —**hot·tish** *adj.*

▸*PHRASES* □ **get hot** (of an athlete or team) suddenly become effective: *he got hot at the right time and found himself in the title match.* □ **have the hots for** *informal* be sexually attracted to. □ **hot and bothered** see BOTHER. □ **hot and heavy** *informal* intense; with intensity: *the competition became very hot and heavy.* □ **hot on the heels of** following closely: *the two new species come hot on the heels of the discovery of the Vu Quang ox.* □ **hot to trot** *informal* ready and eager to engage in an activity. □ **hot under the collar** *informal* angry, resentful, or embarrassed. □ **in hot pursuit** following closely and eagerly. □ **in hot water** *informal* in a situation of difficulty, trouble, or disgrace: *he is in hot water for insensitive remarks he made.* □ **make it** (or **things**) **hot for someone** *informal* make things unpleasant for someone; persecute.

hot air ▸*n.* *informal* empty talk that is intended to impress: *they dismissed the theory as a load of hot air.*

hot·bed /ˈhät,bed/ ▸*n.* a bed of earth heated by fermenting manure, for raising or forcing plants. ▪ an environment promoting the growth of something, esp. something unwelcome: *the country was* ***a hotbed of*** *revolt and dissension.*

hot-blood·ed ▸*adj.* lustful; passionate: *hot-blooded, pulse-pounding passion.*

hot box (also **hot·box**) ▸*n.* *Railroad* an overheated axle box or journal box.

hot but·ton ▸*n.* *informal* [often as *adj.*] a topic or issue that is highly charged emotionally or politically: *the hot-button issue of nuclear waste disposal.*

hot cath·ode ▸*n.* a cathode designed to be heated in order to emit electrons.

hotch·pot /ˈhäCH,pät/ ▸*n.* *Law* the reunion and blending together of properties for the purpose of securing equal division, esp. of the property of an intestate parent. ▷late Middle English (in the sense 'hodgepodge'): from Anglo-Norman French and Old French *hochepot,* from *hocher* 'to shake' (probably of Low German origin) + *pot* 'pot.'

hotch·potch /ˈhäCH,päCH/ ▸*n.* *Brit.* variant of HODGEPODGE. ▪ a mutton stew with mixed vegetables. ▷late Middle English: variant of HOTCHPOT.

hot cross bun ▸*n.* a bun marked with a cross and containing dried fruit, traditionally eaten during Lent.

hot dark mat·ter ▸*n.* see DARK MATTER.

hot-desk·ing ▸*n.* the practice in an office of allocating desks to workers when they are required or on a rotating system, rather than giving each worker their own desk.

hot dog ▸*n.* **1** a hot sausage served in a long, soft roll and typically topped with various condiments. **2** *informal* a person who shows off, esp. a skier or surfer who performs stunts or tricks.

▸*exclam.* *informal* used to express delight or enthusiastic approval: *hot dog! I've finally found something I can do that you can't.*

▸*v.* (**hot-dog**) (**-dogged, -dog·ging**) [*intrans.*] *informal* perform stunts or tricks; show off: *he chastised the dancers who'd been hotdogging.* —**hot·dog·ger** *n.*

ho·tel /hōˈtel/ ▸*n.* **1** an establishment providing accommodations, meals, and other services for travelers and tourists. **2** a code word representing the letter H, used in radio communication. ▷mid 18th cent.: from French *hôtel,* from Old French *hostel* (see HOSTEL).

USAGE The normal pronunciation of **hotel** sounds the **h-**, which means that the preceding indefinite article is **a**. However, the older pronunciation without the **h-** is still sometimes heard, and gives rise to the preceding indefinite article being **an**. See also **usage** at AN.

hô·tel de ville /ō'tel də 'vēl/ ▸*n.* (*pl.* **hô·tels de ville** *pronunc.* same) (in France) a city hall or town hall.

ho·te·lier /,ôtel'yā; hōtl'i(ə)r/ ▸*n.* a person who owns or manages a hotel. ▷early 20th cent.: from French *hôtelier,* from Old French *hostelier* 'innkeeper' (see HOSTELRY).

ho·tel·ing /hōˈteliNG/ ▸*n.* the short-term provision of office space to a temporary worker. ▪ the short-term letting of surplus office space to employees from other companies. ▷from *hotel* + *-ing.*

hot flash ▸*n.* a sudden feeling of feverish heat, typically as a symptom of menopause.

hot flush ▸*n.* British term for HOT FLASH.

hot·foot /ˈhät,fo͝ot/ ▸*n.* a practical joke in which a match is inserted into the victim's shoe and then lit.

▸*v.* [*trans.*] (**hotfoot it**) [with *adverbial of direction*] walk or run quickly and eagerly: *we hotfooted it after him.*

▸*adv.* in eager haste: *he rushed hotfoot to the planning office to object.*

hot·head /ˈhät,hed/ (also **hot-head**) ▸*n.* a person who is impetuous or who easily becomes angry and violent. —**hot·head·ed** *adj.* —**hot·head·ed·ly** *adv.* —**hot·head·ed·ness** *n.*

hot·house /ˈhät,hous/ ▸*n.* a heated building, typically made largely of glass, for rearing plants out of season or in a climate colder than is natural for them. ▪ *figurative* an environment that encourages the rapid growth or development of someone or something, esp. in a stifling or intense way: [as *adj.*] *the hothouse atmosphere of the college.*

▸*v.* [*trans.*] educate (a child) to a high level at an earlier age than is usual.

hot key ▸*n.* *Computing* a key or a combination of keys providing quick access to a particular function within a program.

hot·line /ˈhät,līn/ (also **hot line**) ▸*n.* a direct telephone line set up for a specific purpose, esp. for use in emergencies or for communication between heads of government. ▪ a telephone line to a source of information or emergency help: *a domestic violence hotline | a technical support hotline.*

hot link *Computing* ▸*n.* a connection between documents or applications that enables material from one source to be incorporated into another, in particular a facility that automatically updates material in a document when an alteration is made to the document from which it originated. ▪ a hypertext link.

▸*v.* (**hot-link**) [*trans.*] connect (two documents) by means of a hot link.

hot·list /ˈhät,list/ ▸*n.* *Computing* a personal list of favorite or most frequently accessed Web sites compiled by an Internet user.

hot·ly /ˈhätlē/ ▸*adv.* in a passionate, excited, or angry way: *the rumors were hotly denied | hotly debated issues.* ▪ closely and with determination: *a hotly contested tournament | he rushed out, hotly pursued by Boris.*

hot met·al ▸*n.* a typesetting technique in which type

is newly made each time from molten metal, cast by a composing machine.

hot mon·ey ▶*n.* capital that is frequently transferred between financial institutions in an attempt to maximize interest or capital gain.

hot pants ▶*plural n.* tight, brief women's shorts, worn as a fashion garment. ■ *informal* strong sexual desire.

hot pep·per ▶*n.* any of several varieties of pungent pepper used dried or chopped as a condiment.

hot plate ▶*n.* a flat heated surface (or a set of these), typically portable, used for cooking food or keeping it hot.

hot pot (also **hot·pot**) ▶*n. Brit.* a casserole of meat and vegetables, typically with a covering layer of sliced potato.

hot po·ta·to ▶*n. informal* a controversial issue or situation that is awkward or unpleasant to deal with: *dog registration has become a political hot potato.*

hot press ▶*n.* a device in which paper or cloth is pressed between glazed boards and hot metal plates in order to produce a smooth or glossy surface. ■ a similar apparatus used in making plywood.
▶*v.* (**hot-press**) [*trans.*] press with such a device.

hot rod ▶*n.* a motor vehicle that has been specially modified to give it extra power and speed.
▶*v.* (**hot-rod**) (**-rod·ded, -rod·ding**) **1** [*intrans.*] drive a hot rod. **2** [*trans.*] modify (a vehicle or other device) to make it faster or more powerful. —**hot rod·der** (also **hot-rod·der**) *n.*

hot seat ▶*n.* (**the hot seat**) *informal* **1** the position of a person who carries full responsibility for something, including facing criticism or being answerable for decisions or actions: *it's been a bad week for the men **in the hot seat.*** **2** the electric chair.

hot shoe ▶*n. Photography* a socket on a camera with direct electrical contacts for an attached flashgun or other accessory.

hot·shot /ˈhät,sʜät/ ▶*n. informal* an important or exceptionally able person: *these three hotshots decide what's what at the firm.* ■ a show-off; an exhibitionist: *the hotshots whizz by on their snowboards.*
▶*adj.* aggressive and skillful: *a hotshot broker angling for a partnership.*

hot spot ▶*n.* a small area or region with a relatively hot temperature in comparison to its surroundings. ■ *Geology* an area of volcanic activity, esp. where this is isolated. ■ *figurative* a place of significant activity or danger: *the hotel was the hot spot in town, with its all-night coffee shop.* ■ (also **hot·spot**) *Computing* an area on the screen that can be clicked on to start an operation such as loading a file.

hot spring ▶*n.* a spring of naturally hot water, typically heated by subterranean volcanic activity.

Hot Springs a spa city in central Arkansas; pop. 35,750.

Hot·spur /ˈhät,spər/ the nickname of Sir Henry Percy (see **Percy**).

hot·spur /ˈhät,spər/ ▶*n. archaic* a rash, impetuous person. ▷late Middle English: literally 'a person whose spur is hot from rash or constant riding.'

hot-stove ▶*adj.* [*attrib.*] denoting a discussion about a favorite sport carried on during the off-season: *hot-stove speculation | these postseason fans—known as the hot-stove league—will be in here all winter arguing about the strike zone.* ▷1950s: by association with discussions conducted around a heater in the winter.

hot-stove league ▶*n. informal* sports fans, esp. baseball fans in the off season, who discuss players, teams, and the upcoming season.

hot stuff ▶*n. informal* used to refer to a person or thing of outstanding quality, interest, or talent: *he's hot stuff at arithmetic.* ■ used to refer to a sexually exciting person, movie, book, etc.: *Jill was reputed to be hot stuff.*

hot-swap ▶*v.* [*trans.*] *informal* fit or replace (a computer part) with the power still connected. —**hot-swap·pa·ble** *adj.*

hot·sy-tot·sy /ˈhätsē ˈtätsē/ ▶*adj.* **1** *informal, dated* used as a term of approval: *hotsy-totsy rhythms thrill the air.* **2** another term for **hoity-toity**. ▷early 20th cent.: reduplication of **hot**, a fanciful formation by Billie de Beck (died 1942), U.S. cartoonist.

hot-tem·pered ▶*adj.* easily angered; quick-tempered.

Hot·ten·tot /ˈhätn,tät/ ▶*n.* & *adj.* used to refer to Khoikhoi peoples. ▷Afrikaans.

hot tick·et ▶*n. informal* a person or thing that is much in demand: *he's the current hot ticket on the hard-core hip-hop block* | [as *adj.*] *a hot-ticket invitation.*

hot·tie /ˈhätē/ (also **hot·ty**) ▶*n.* (*pl.* **hot·ties**) *informal* a sexually attractive person: *a former high school hottie who married a prom queen.* ▷from *hot* + *-ie* or *-y*.

hot tub ▶*n.* a large tub filled with hot aerated water used for recreation or physical therapy.

hot war ▶*n.* a war with active military hostilities.

hot-wa·ter bot·tle (also **hot-water bag**) ▶*n.* a flat, oblong container, typically made of rubber, that is filled with hot water and used for warmth.

hot-wire ▶*v.* [*trans.*] *informal* start the engine of (a vehicle) by bypassing the ignition system, typically in order to steal it.
▶*adj.* [*attrib.*] (of an electrical instrument) depending on the expansion of a wire when heated or on a change in the electrical resistance of a wire when heated or cooled: *a hot-wire detector.*

hou·ba·ra /ho͞oˈbärə/ (also **houbara bustard**) ▶*n.* a bustard of arid open country and semidesert, found from the Canary Islands to central Asia and threatened by hunting. • *Chlamydotis undulata*, family Otidae. ▷early 19th cent.: modern Latin, from Arabic *ḥubārā*.

Hou·di·ni /ho͞oˈdēnē/, Harry (1874–1926), U.S. magician and escape artist; born in Hungary; born *Erik Weisz*. In the early 1900s, he became known for his ability to escape from all kinds of bonds and containers, from prison cells to aerially suspended straitjackets. ■ [as *n.*] a person skilled at escaping: *you're a regular Houdini.* ■ an ingenious escape: *he will have to **do a Houdini** to escape from me.*

Harry Houdini

Hou·ma a city in southeastern Louisiana, in the Cajun Country, southwest of New Orleans; pop. 32,393.

houm·mos /ˈho͝oməs/ ▶*n.* variant spelling of **hummus**.

hound /hound/ ▶*n.* a dog of a breed used for hunting, esp. one able to track by scent. ■ any dog. ■ [with *adj.*] a person who avidly pursues something: *he has a reputation as a publicity hound.* ■ *informal, dated* a despicable or contemptible man. ■ used in names of dogfishes, e.g., **nurse hound**, **smooth hound**.
▶*v.* [*trans.*] harass or persecute (someone) relentlessly: *a tenacious attorney general who had hounded Jimmy Hoffa and other labor bosses | his opponents used the allegations to **hound** him **out of office**.* ■ pursue relentlessly: *he led the race from start to finish but was hounded all the way by Phillips.* ▷Old English *hund* (in the general sense 'dog'), of Germanic origin; related to Dutch *hond* and German *Hund*, from an Indo-European root shared by Greek *kuōn, kun-* 'dog.'
▶*PHRASE* □ **ride to hounds** see **ride**.

hound's-tongue ▶*n.* a tall plant of the borage family that has a mousy smell and bears long silky hairs, small purplish flowers, and tongue-shaped leaves. • *Cynoglossum officinale*, family Boraginaceae.

hounds·tooth /ˈhoun(d)z-,to͞otʜ/ ▶*n.* a large checked pattern with notched corners suggestive of a canine tooth, typically used in cloth for jackets and suits.

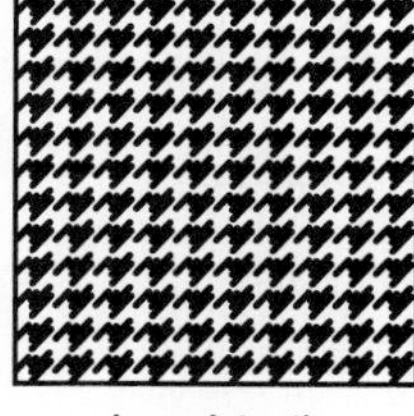

houndstooth

houn·gan /ˈho͞oɴɢgən/ ▶*n.* a voodoo priest. ▷early 20th cent.: from Fon, from *hun*, a deity represented by a fetish, + *ga* 'chief.'

hour /ou(ə)r/ ▶*n.* **1** a period of time equal to a twenty-fourth part of a day and night and divided into 60 minutes: *an extra hour of daylight | rates have ranged from $9 to $32 an hour* | [as *adj.*, usu. with preceding numeral] *a two-hour operation.* ■ a less definite period of time: *during the early hours of the morning.* ■ the distance traveled in one hour: *Ocean City is less than an hour away.* **2** a point in time: *I wondered if my last hour had come.* ■ a time of day or night: *you can't turn him away at this hour.* ■ a time of day specified as an exact number of hours from midnight or midday: *the clock in the sitting room **struck the hour**.* ■ (**hours**) [with preceding numeral] a time so specified on the 24-hour clock: *the first bomb fell at 0051 hours.* ■ the time as formerly reckoned from sunrise: *it was about the ninth hour.* ■ the appropriate time for some specific action: *now that the hour had come, David decided he could not face it.* **3** [usu. with *adj.*] a period set aside for some purpose or marked by some activity: *leisure hours.* ■ (**hours**) a fixed period of time for an activity, such as work, use of a building, etc.: *shortened working hours.* **4** (usu. **hours**) (in the Western Church) a short service of psalms and prayers to be said at a particular time of day, esp. in religious communities. **5** *Astronomy* 15° of longitude or right ascension (one twenty-fourth part of a circle). ▷Middle English: from Anglo-Norman French *ure*, via Latin from Greek *hōra* 'season, hour.'
▶*PHRASES* □ **all hours** any time, esp. outside the time considered usual for something: *intruders had access at all hours | teenagers expect to be allowed to stay out **to all hours**.* □ **keep late hours** get up and go to bed late. □ **keep regular hours** do the same thing at the same time every day. □ **on the hour** at an exact hour, or on each hour, of the day or night: *news bulletins on the hour.* □ **within the hour** after less than an hour.

hour·glass /ˈou(ə)r,glas/ ▶*n.* an invertible device with two connected glass bulbs containing sand that takes an hour to pass from the upper to the lower bulb. ■ [as *adj.*] shaped like such a device: *her hourglass figure.*

hourglass

hour hand ▶*n.* the hand on a clock or watch that indicates the hour.

hou·ri /ˈho͝orē/ ▶*n.* (*pl.* **-ris**) a beautiful young woman, esp. one of the virgin companions of the faithful in the Muslim Paradise. ▷mid 18th cent.: from French, from Persian *ḥūrī*, from Arabic *ḥūr*, plural of *'aḥwar* 'having eyes with a marked contrast of black and white.'

hour-long (also **hour·long**) ▶*adj.* [*attrib.*] lasting for one hour.

hour·ly /ˈou(ə)rlē/ ▶*adj.* **1** done or occurring every hour: *there is an hourly bus service.* ■ (with numeral or fraction) occurring at intervals measured in hours: *diamorphine was prescribed at four-hourly doses | trains run at half-hourly intervals.* **2** reckoned hour by hour: *to introduce standard fees instead of hourly rates.*
▶*adv.* **1** every hour: *sunscreens should be applied hourly | a train runs hourly from 7 a.m. to 8 p.m.* ■ (with numeral or fraction) at intervals measured in hours: *temperature should be recorded four-hourly.* **2** by the hour: *hourly paid workers.* **3** frequently; continually: *her curiosity was mounting hourly.*

Hou·sa·ton·ic River /,ho͞osəˈtänik/ a river that flows for 130 miles (210 km) from the Berkshire Hills in western Massachusetts through Connecticut to Long Island Sound.

house ▶*n.* /hous/ (*pl.* **hous·es** /ˈhouziz/) **1** a building for human habitation, esp. one that is lived in by a family or small group of people. ■ the people living in such a building; a household: *do you want the whole house woken up?* ■ (often **House**) a family or family lineage, esp. a noble or royal one; a dynasty: *the power and prestige of **the house of** Stewart.* ■ [with *adj.*] a building in which animals live or in which things are kept: *a reptile house.* **2** a building in which people meet for a particular activity: *a house of prayer.* ■ a business or institution: *he had purchased a publishing house.* ■ a restaurant or inn: [as *adj.*] *I ordered a bottle of their house wine.* ■ a residential hall at a school or college, or its residents. ■ a gambling establishment or its management. ■ a host or proprietor: *help yourself to a drink, compliments of the house!* ■ a theater: *a hundred musicians performed in front of a full house.* ■ an audience in a theater or concert venue: *the house*

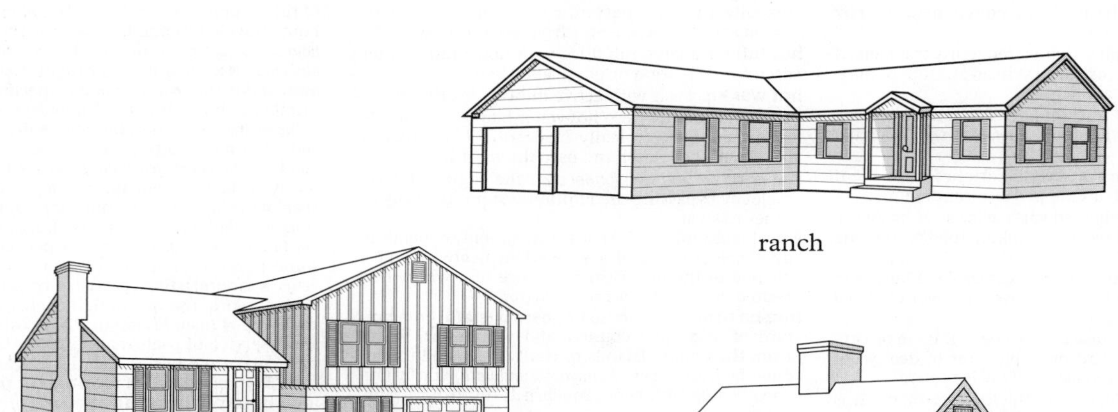
ranch

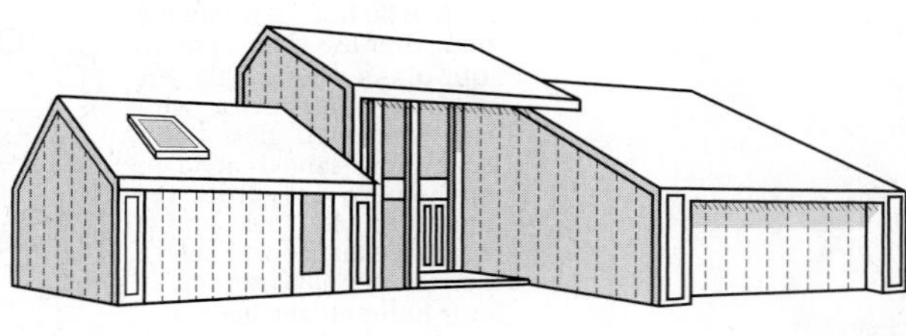
split level

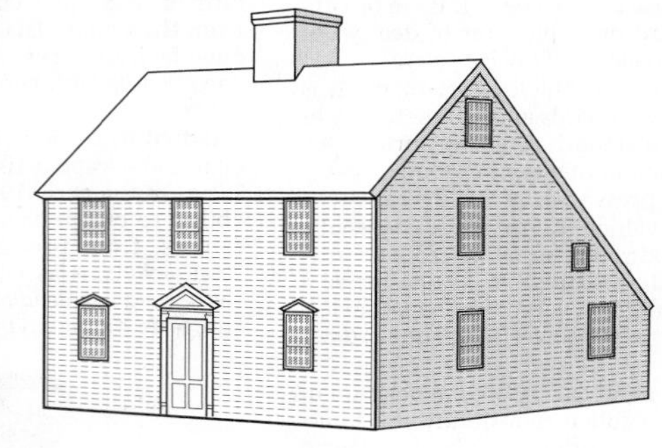
saltbox

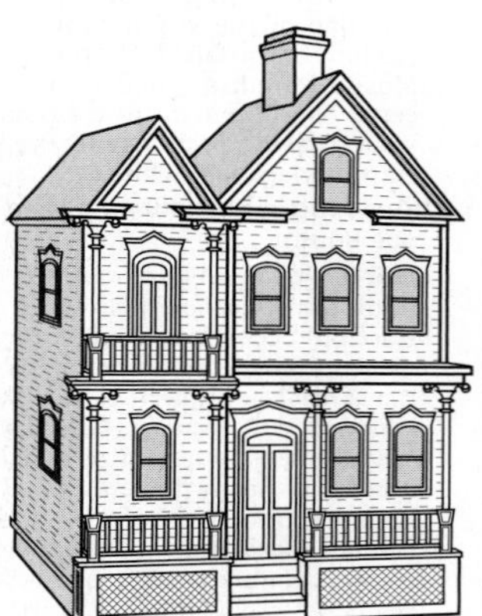
contemporary

Tudor

Victorian

colonial

Cape Cod

house styles

burst into applause. ■ a religious community that occupies a particular building: *the Cistercian house at Clairvaux.* ■ *dated* a brothel. ■ *Brit., formal* a college of a university. **3** a legislative or deliberative assembly: *the sixty-member National Council, the country's upper house.* ■ (**the House**) the House of Representatives or (in the UK or Canada) the House of Commons or Lords. **4** (also **house mu·sic**) a style of popular dance music typically using synthesized drum and bass lines, sparse repetitive vocals, and a fast beat. **5** *Astrology* any of the twelve divisions of the celestial sphere, based on the positions of the ascendant and midheaven at a given time and place, and determined by any of a number of methods. ■ such a division represented as a sector on an astrological chart, used in allocating elements of character and circumstance to different spheres of human life.

▸*adj.* /hous/ [*attrib.*] **1** (of an animal or plant) kept in, frequenting, or infesting buildings. **2** of or relating to resident medical staff at a hospital. **3** of or relating to a business, institution, or society: *a house journal.* ■ (of a band or group) resident or regularly performing in a club or other venue.

▸*v.* /houz/ [*trans.*] **1** provide (a person or animal) with shelter or living quarters: *attempts by the government to house the poor.* **2** provide space for; accommodate: *the museum houses a collection of Roman sculpture.* ■ enclose or encase (something): *the radar could be housed in a pod beneath the engine.* ■ insert or fix (something) in a socket or mortise. ▷Old English *hūs* (noun), *hūsian* (verb), of Germanic origin; related to Dutch *huis*, German *Haus* (nouns), and Dutch *huizen*, German *hausen* (verbs). **—house·ful** /-ˌfo͝ol/ *n.* (*pl.* **-fuls**) **—house·less** *adj.*

▸*PHRASES* □ **like a house on fire** (or **afire**) *informal* vigorously; furiously. ■ excellently: *Ben and my aunt got along like a house on fire.* □ **house and home** a person's home (used for emphasis): *some people sell house and home to sit in a boat writing books.* □ **a house divided cannot stand** *proverb* a group or organization weakened by internal dissensions will be unable to withstand external pressures. □ **house of cards** a structure built out of playing cards precariously balanced together. ■ an insubstantial or insecure situation or scheme: *his case was a house of cards until Attorney Jabowski stepped in.* □ **keep house** do the cooking, cleaning, and other tasks involved in the running of a household. □ **on the house** (of a drink or meal in a bar or restaurant) at the management's expense; free. □ **play house** (of a child) play at being a family in their home. □ **put** (or **set** or **get**) **one's house in order** make necessary reforms: *to get their own economic house in order.* □ **set up house** make one's home in a specified place.

house a·gent ▸*n.* British term for REAL ESTATE AGENT.

house ar·rest ▸*n.* the state of being kept as a prisoner in one's own house, rather than in a prison: *she was placed* ***under house arrest.***

house·boat /ˈhousˌbōt/ ▸*n.* a boat that is or can be moored for use as a dwelling.

house·bound /ˈhousˌbound/ ▸*adj.* unable to leave one's house, typically due to illness or old age.

house·boy /ˈhousˌboi/ ▸*n.* a boy or man employed to undertake domestic duties.

house brand ▸*n.* a brand name used exclusively by a retailer (or a selected group of retailers) for a product or line of products that are typically sold for prices lower than that of comparable items with manufacturer brand names. ■ a product bearing such a name: *don't get the expensive coffee, get the house brand.*

house·break /ˈhousˌbrāk/ (*past* **-broke**; *past part.* **-brok·en**) ▸*v.* [*trans.*] train (a pet) to urinate and defecate outside the house or only in a special place: *an elephant is exceedingly difficult to housebreak* | [as *adj.*] (**housebroken**) *wolves are almost never housebroken.* ■ *informal* or *humorous* teach (someone) good manners or neatness.

house·break·ing /ˈhousˌbrākiNG/ ▸*n.* the action of breaking into a building, esp. in daytime, to commit a crime. **—house·break·er** /-ˌbrākər/ *n.*

house·carl /ˈhousˌkärl/ (also **house·carle**) ▸*n. historical* a member of the bodyguard of a Danish or English king or noble. ▷late Old English *hūscarl*, from Old Norse *húskarl* 'manservant,' (plural) 'retinue, bodyguard,' from *hús* 'house' + *karl* 'man.'

house church ▸*n.* **1** a charismatic church independent of traditional denominations. **2** a group meeting for Christian worship in a private house.

house·clean·ing /ˈhousˌklēniNG/ ▸*n.* **1** the cleaning of the interior of a dwelling. **2** the removal of unwanted or superfluous items, practices, conditions, or personnel: *the new owner's housecleaning cost a lot of people their jobs.* **—house·clean** *v.* **—house·clean·er** *n.*

house·coat /ˈhousˌkōt/ ▸*n.* a woman's long, loose, lightweight robe for informal wear around the house.

house crick·et ▸*n.* a chiefly nocturnal cricket with a birdlike warble, native to North Africa and southwestern Asia. It has become established in heated buildings. • *Acheta domesticus*, family Gryllidae.

house·dress /ˈhousˌdres/ ▸*n.* a simple, usually washable, dress suitable for wearing while doing housework.

house·fa·ther /ˈhousˌfäT͟Hər/ ▸*n.* a man in charge of and living in a boarding school dormitory or other group residence.

house finch ▸*n.* a red-breasted brown finch, now common from Canada to Mexico and sometimes regarded as a pest. • *Carpodacus mexicanus*, family Fringillidae.

house flag ▸*n.* a flag indicating the company that a ship belongs to.

house·fly /ˈhousˌflī/ (also **house fly**) ▸*n.* (*pl.* **-flies**) a common small fly occurring worldwide in and around human habitation. Its eggs are laid in decaying material, and the fly can be a health hazard due to its contamination of food. • *Musca domestica*, family Muscidae.

house geck·o ▸*n.* a large-eyed nocturnal gecko of the Old World tropics, occupying a range of habitats including houses. • *Hemidactylus, Gehyra*, and other genera, family Gekkonidae: several species, including *H. mabouia* of Africa and tropical America, and *G. mutilata* of Asia.

house guest (also **house·guest**) ▸*n.* a guest staying for some days in a private house.

house·hold /ˈhousˌ(h)ōld/ ▸*n.* a house and its occupants regarded as a unit: *the whole household was asleep* | *ten percent of households had a television.* ■ the affairs related to keeping a house: *it is mostly women who are responsible for running households* | [as *adj.*] *household appliances.*

House·hold Cav·al·ry (in the British army) the two cavalry regiments with responsibility for guarding the monarch and royal palaces (and otherwise acting as part of the Royal Armoured Corps).

house·hold·er /ˈhousˌ(h)ōldər/ ▸*n.* a person who owns or rents a house; the head of a household.

house·hold gods ▸*plural n.* gods presiding over a household, esp. (in Roman History) the lares and penates. ■ *figurative* possessions held in esteem: *the Fairley household gods—portraits and an assortment of silver.*

house·hold name (also **house·hold word**) ▸*n.* a person or thing that is well known by the public: *I'd like to sell gazillions of books and become a household name.*

house·hold troops ▸*plural n.* troops employed to guard a sovereign.

house-hunt ▸*v.* [*intrans.*] seek a house to buy or rent and live in. **—house-hunt·er** *n.* **—house-hunt·ing** *n.*

house·hus·band /ˈhousˌhəzbənd/ ▸*n.* a man who lives with a partner and carries out household duties traditionally done by a housewife rather than working outside the home.

house·keep·er /ˈhousˌkēpər/ ▸*n.* a person, typically a woman, employed to manage a household. **—house·keep** *v.* (*dated*).

house·keep·ing /ˈhousˌkēpiNG/ ▸*n.* **1** the management of household affairs. ■ money set aside or given for such a purpose: *writing barely pays my part of the housekeeping.* ■ a department within a hotel or other residential facility that oversees the cleaning of rooms and the provision of necessities such as towels and glassware: *you'll never have to nag housekeeping for a set of dry towels.* **2** operations such as record-keeping or maintenance in an organization or a computer that make work possible but do not directly constitute its performance. ■ *Biology* the regulation of metabolic functions that are common to all cells: [as *adj.*] *housekeeping genes.*

▸*adj.* (of cabins, cottages, or other rental properties) having basic facilities such as a stove and refrigerator: *completely equipped housekeeping cabins.*

house·leek /ˈhousˌlēk/ ▸*n.* a succulent plant with rosettes of fleshy leaves and small pink flowers. Houseleeks grow on walls and roofs, and are popular cultivated plants. • *Sempervivum* and related genera, family Crassulaceae: several species, in particular *S. tectorum.*

house lights (also **house·lights**) ▸*plural n.* the lights in the area of a theater where the audience sits: *the show ended and the house lights came up.*

house·maid /ˈhousˌmād/ ▸*n.* a female domestic employee, esp. one who cleans reception rooms and bedrooms.

house·maid's knee ▸*n.* inflammation of the fluid-filled cavity covering the kneecap, often due to excessive kneeling; bursitis.

House·man /ˈhousmən/, John (1902–88) U.S. actor, producer, and director; born in Romania; born *Jacques Haussmann.* His movies include *The Paper Chase* (Academy Award, 1973).

house·man /ˈhousmən/ ▸*n.* (*pl.* **-men**) **1** another term for HOUSEBOY. **2** *Brit.* a hospital intern.

house·mas·ter /ˈhousˌmastər/ ▸*n.* a teacher, typically male, in charge of a dormitory at a boarding school.

house·mis·tress /ˈhousˌmistris/ ▸*n.* a female teacher in charge of a dormitory at a boarding school.

house·moth·er /ˈhousˌməT͟Hər/ ▸*n.* a woman in charge of and living in a boarding school dormitory or children's home.

house mouse ▸*n.* a grayish-brown mouse found abundantly as a scavenger in human dwellings. It is widely kept as a pet or experimental animal and has been bred in many varieties. • *Mus musculus*, family Muridae.

house mu·sic ▸*n.* see HOUSE (sense 4).

House of Bur·gess·es ▸*n.* the lower house of the colonial Virginia legislature.

House of Com·mons (in the UK and Canada) the elected chamber of Parliament.

house of cor·rec·tion ▸*n.* an institution for the short-term confinement of minor offenders.

house of·fi·cer ▸*n.* *Brit.* a medical intern.

house of God ▸*n.* a place of religious worship, esp. a church.

house of ill fame (also **house of ill repute**) ▸*n. archaic* or *humorous* a brothel.

House of Lords (in the UK) the nonelective chamber of Parliament composed of peers and bishops. ■ a committee of specially qualified members of this, appointed as the ultimate judicial appeal court of England and Wales.

House of Rep·re·sent·a·tives the lower house of the U.S. Congress and other legislatures, including most U.S. state governments.

house or·gan ▸*n.* a periodical published by a company to be read by its employees and other interested parties and dealing mainly with its own activities.

house·par·ent /ˈhousˌpe(ə)rənt; -ˌparənt/ ▸*n.* a housemother or housefather.

house par·ty ▸*n.* a party at which the guests stay at a house overnight or for a few days.

house·plant /ˈhousˌplant/ (also **house plant**) ▸*n.* a plant grown indoors.

house-proud ▸*adj.* attentive to, or preoccupied with, the care and appearance of one's home.

house rat ▸*n.* another term for BLACK RAT.

house·room /ˈhousˌro͞om; -ˌro͝om/ ▸*n.* space or accommodations in one's house: *she refused to give houseroom to the canvas her brother had bought.*

house-sit (also **house·sit**) ▸*v.* [*intrans.*] live in and look after a house while its owner is away. **—house-sit·ter** *n.* **—house-sit·ting** *n.*

Hous·es of Par·lia·ment (in the UK) the Houses of Lords and Commons regarded together, or the building where they meet (the Palace of Westminster).

Houses of Parliament

house spar·row ▸*n.* a brown and gray sparrow that nests in the eaves and roofs of houses, common from Europe to southern Asia and introduced elsewhere. Also called ENGLISH SPARROW. • *Passer domesticus*, family Passeridae (or Ploceidae).

house style ▸*n.* a company's preferred manner of presentation and layout of written material: *the document will automatically be set out according to the house style.*

house-to-house ▸*adj.* & *adv.* performed at or taken to each house in turn: [as *adj.*] *a veteran salesman took a rookie on house-to-house canvassing* | [as *adv.*] *troops searched house to house for agitators.*

house·top /ˈhousˌtäp/ ▸*n.* the outer surface of the roof of a house.
▸*PHRASE* □ **shout something from the housetops** old-fashioned way of saying SHOUT SOMETHING FROM THE ROOFTOPS (see SHOUT).

house-train ▸*v. chiefly Brit.* another term for HOUSEBREAK.

House Un-A·mer·i·can Ac·tiv·i·ties Com·mit·tee (abbr.: **HUAC**) a committee of the U.S. House of Representatives established in 1938 to investigate subversives. It became notorious for its zealous investigations of alleged communists, particularly in the late 1940s, although it was originally intended to pursue Fascists also.

house·warm·ing /ˈhousˌwôrmiNG/ ▸*n.* [usu. as *adj.*] a party celebrating a move to a new home: *a housewarming gift.*

house·wife /ˈhousˌwīf/ ▸*n.* (*pl.* **-wives**) **1** a married woman whose main occupation is caring for her family, managing household affairs, and doing housework. **2** a small case for needles, thread, and other small sewing items. ▷Middle English *husewif* (see HOUSE, WIFE). —**house·wife·ly** *adj.* —**house·wif·er·y** /-ˌwifərē/ *n.*

house·work /ˈhousˌwərk/ ▸*n.* regular work done in housekeeping, such as cleaning, shopping, and cooking.

house·y /ˈhousē/ ▸*adj. Brit., informal* in the style of house music.

hous·ing[1] /ˈhouziNG/ ▸*n.* **1** houses and apartments considered collectively: *affordable housing* | [as *adj.*] *a housing development.* ■ the provision of accommodations: *the sector that offers housing to the poorest.* **2** a rigid casing that encloses and protects a piece of moving or delicate equipment. ■ a structure that supports and encloses the bearings at the end of an axle or shaft. **3** a recess or groove cut in one piece of wood to allow another piece to be attached to it. ■ *Nautical* the part of a mast below the deck.

hous·ing[2] ▸*n. archaic* a cloth covering put on a horse for protection or ornament. ▷late Middle English (in the general sense 'covering'): from Old French *houce*, from medieval Latin *hultia*, of Germanic origin.

hous·ing de·vel·op·ment (*Brit.* **hous·ing estate**) ▸*n.* a residential area in which the houses have all been planned and built at the same time.

hous·ing start ▸*n.* the beginning of construction of a new house. ■ (**housing starts**) the number of new houses begun during a particular period, used as an indicator of economic conditions.

Hous·man /ˈhousmən/, A. E. (1859–1936), English poet and classical scholar; full name *Alfred Edward Housman*. He is chiefly remembered for his poems collected in *A Shropshire Lad* (1896).

Hous·ton[1] /ˈ(h)yo͞ostən/ an inland port in Texas, linked to the Gulf of Mexico by the Houston Ship Canal; pop. 1,953,631. Since 1961, it has been a center for space research and manned space flight; it is the site of the NASA Space Center. ▷named after Samuel *Houston*.

Hous·ton[2], Samuel (1793–1863) U.S. soldier and politician. He led the struggle to win control of Texas and to make it part of the U.S. He was the first president of the republic of Texas 1836–38, 1841–44 and the first U.S. senator from the state of Texas 1846–59. The governor of Texas 1859–61, he was ousted for refusing to swear allegiance to the Confederacy during the Civil War.

Samuel Houston

Hous·ton[3], Whitney (1963–) U.S. singer and actress. Her songs, a blend of gospel, ballad, pop, rock, and rhythm and blues, include "Saving All My Love for You" (1985) and "I Wanna Dance with Somebody" (1987). She starred in the movies *The Bodyguard* (1992), *Waiting to Exhale* (1995), and *The Preacher's Wife* (1996).

hove /hōv/ *chiefly Nautical* ▸ past of HEAVE.

hov·el /ˈhəvəl; ˈhävəl/ ▸*n.* **1** a small, squalid, unpleasant, or simply constructed dwelling. ■ *archaic* an open shed or outbuilding, used for sheltering cattle or storing grain or tools. **2** *historical* a conical building enclosing a kiln. ▷late Middle English: of unknown origin.

hov·er /ˈhəvər/ ▸*v.* [*intrans.*] remain in one place in the air: *army helicopters hovered overhead.* ■ remain poised in one place, typically with slight but undirected movement: *her hand* **hovered over** *the console.* ■ (of a person) wait or linger close at hand in a tentative or uncertain manner: *she hovered anxiously in the background.* ■ remain at or near a particular level: *inflation will hover around the 4 percent mark.* ■ remain in a state that is between two specified states or kinds of things: *his expression* **hovered between** *cynicism and puzzlement.*
▸*n.* [in *sing.*] an act of remaining in the air in one place. ▷late Middle English: from archaic *hove* 'hover, linger,' of unknown origin. —**hov·er·er** *n.*

hov·er·craft /ˈhəvərˌkraft/ ▸*n.* (*pl.* same) a vehicle or craft that travels over land or water on a cushion of air provided by a downward blast. A design was first patented by Christopher Cockerell (1910–) in 1955.

hov·er·port /ˈhəvərˌpôrt/ ▸*n.* a terminal for hovercraft.

hov·er·train /ˈhəvərˌtrān/ ▸*n.* a train that travels on a cushion of air.

how[1] /hou/ ▸*adv.* [usu. *interrog. adv.*] **1** in what way or manner; by what means: *how does it work?* | *he did not know how he ought to behave* | [with *infinitive*] *he showed me how to adjust the focus.* **2** used to ask about the condition or quality of something: *how was your vacation?* | *how did they play?* ■ used to ask about someone's physical or mental state: *how are the children?* | *I asked how he was doing.* **3** [with *adj.* or *adv.*] used to ask about the extent or degree of something: *how old are you?* | *how long will it take?* | *I wasn't sure how fast to go.* ■ used to express a strong feeling such as surprise about the extent of something: *how kind it was of him* | *how I wish I had been there!* **4** [*relative adv.*] the way in which; that: *she told us how she had lived out of a suitcase for a week.* ■ in any way in which; however: *I'll do business how I like.* ▷Old English *hū*; related to Dutch *hoe*, also to WHO and WHAT.
▸*PHRASES* □ **and how!** *informal* very much so (used to express strong agreement): *"Did you miss me?" "And how!"* □ **here's how!** *dated* said when drinking to someone's health. □ **how about 1** used to make a suggestion or offer: *how about a drink?* **2** used when asking for information or an opinion on something: *how about your company?* □ **the how and why** the methods and reasons for doing something: *tonight's edition demystifies the how and why of television ratings.* □ **how come?** see COME. □ **how do?** an informal greeting. □ **how do you do?** a formal greeting. □ **how many** what number: *how many books did you sell?* □ **how much** what amount or price: *just how much did it cost?* □ **how now?** *archaic* what is the meaning of this? □ **how so?** how can you show that that is so? □ **how's that for ——?** isn't that a remarkable instance of ——?: *how's that for stereotypical thinking?*

how[2] ▸*exclam.* a greeting attributed to North American Indians (used in humorous imitation). ▷early 19th cent.: perhaps from Sioux *háo* or Omaha *hou*.

How·ard[1] /ˈhou-ərd/, Catherine (*c.*1521–42), fifth wife of Henry VIII. Accused of infidelity, she confessed and was beheaded.

How·ard[2], Curly see THREE STOOGES, THE.

How·ard[3], John (Winston) (1939–), Australian statesman; prime minister from 1996.

How·ard[4], Leslie (1893–1943), English actor; born *Leslie Howard Stainer*. He was best known for his roles as the archetypal British gentleman in movies such as *The Scarlet Pimpernel* (1935) and *Pygmalion* (1938). Other notable movies include *Gone with the Wind* (1939).

How·ard[5], Moe see THREE STOOGES, THE.

How·ard[6], Shemp see THREE STOOGES, THE.

How·ard[7], Trevor (Wallace) (1916–88), English actor. He starred in *Brief Encounter* (1945) and *The Third Man* (1949) and later played character roles in movies such as *Gandhi* (1982).

how·be·it /houˈbēit/ ▸*adv. archaic* nevertheless; however: *howbeit, I've no proof of the thing.*

how·dah /ˈhoudə/ ▸*n.* (in the Indian subcontinent) a seat for riding on the back of an elephant or camel, typically with a canopy and accommodating two or more people. ▷from Urdu *haudah*, from Arabic *hawdaj* 'litter.'

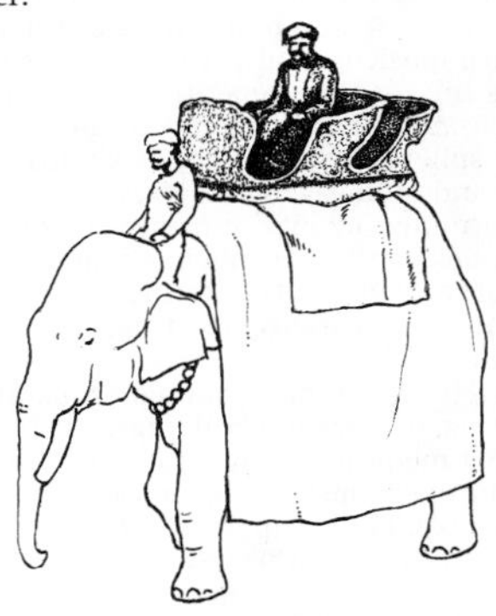
howdah

how-do-you-do /ˌhou də yə ˈdo͞o/ (also **how-de-do** or **how-d'ye-do**) ▸*n.* [in *sing.*] *informal* an awkward, messy, or annoying situation: *a fine how-do-you-do that would be!*

how·dy /ˈhoudē/ ▸*exclam.* an informal friendly greeting, particularly associated with the western states: *howdy, stranger.* ▷early 19th cent.: alteration of *how d'ye*.

Howe[1] /hou/, Elias (1819–67), U.S. inventor. In 1846, he patented the first sewing machine. Its principles were adapted by Isaac Merrit Singer and others in violation of Howe's patent rights, and it took a seven-year litigation battle to secure the royalties.

Howe[2], Gordie (1928–) Canadian hockey player; full name *Gordon Howe*. A prolific scorer, he played for the Omaha Knights 1945–46, the Detroit Red Wings 1946–71, the Houston Aeros 1973–77, and the New England Whalers 1977–80. Hockey Hall of Fame (1972).

how·e'er /houˈe(ə)r/ *poetic/literary* ▸*contraction of* however.

How·ells /ˈhou-əlz/, William Dean (1837–1920) U.S. writer and critic. He was editor-in-chief of *Atlantic Monthly* magazine 1871–81. His novels include *The Rise of Silas Lapham* (1885) and *A Hazard of New Fortunes* (1890).

how·ev·er /houˈevər/ ▸*adv.* **1** used to introduce a statement that contrasts with or seems to contradict something that has been said previously: *People tend to put on weight in middle age. However, gaining weight is not inevitable.* **2** [*relative adv.*] in whatever way; regardless of how: *however you look at it, you can't criticize that.* ■ [with *adj.* or *adv.*] to whatever extent: *he was hesitant to take the risk, however small.*

USAGE When **ever** is used as an intensifier after *how, what, when, where,* or *why*, it should be separated by a space. Thus, ***how ever** did you find her?* could be rephrased, with no change of meaning, ***how did you ever** find her?* This rule tends to be more often followed—or more widely understood—in Britain than in the U.S.
However in the sense of 'no matter how' (*however gently you correct him, Peter always takes offense*) should be spelled as one word. See also **usage** at WHATEVER.

how·itz·er /ˈhouətsər/ ▸*n.* a short gun for firing shells on high trajectories at low velocities. ▷late 17th cent.: from Dutch *houwitser*, from German *Haubitze*, from Czech *houfnice* 'catapult.'

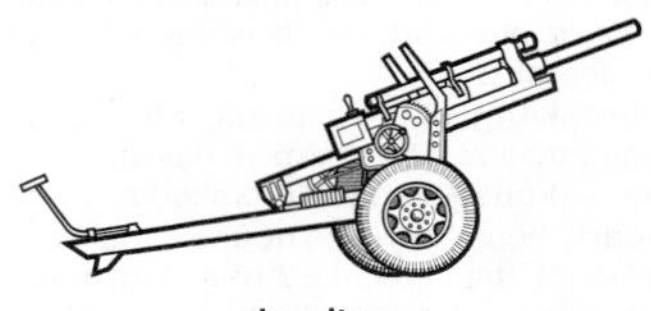
howitzer

howl /houl/ ▸*n.* a long, loud, doleful cry uttered by an animal such as a dog or wolf. ■ a loud cry of pain, fear, anger, amusement, or derision: *he let out a* **howl** *of anguish* | *figurative I got* **howls of** *protest from readers.* ■ [in *sing.*] a prolonged wailing noise such as that

made by a strong wind: *they listened to* **the howl of** *the gale.* ■ *Electronics* a wailing noise in a loudspeaker due to electrical or acoustic feedback.
▸*v.* [*intrans.*] make a howling sound: *he howled in agony | the wind howled around the house.* ■ weep and cry out loudly: *a baby started to howl.* ■ [*trans.*] (**howl someone down**) shout in disapproval in order to prevent a speaker from being heard: *they howled me down and called me a chauvinist.* ▷Middle English *houle* (verb), probably imitative.

howl·er /ˈhoulər/ ▸*n.* **1** *informal* a stupid or glaring mistake, esp. an amusing one. **2** a person or animal that howls. **3** (also **howler monkey**) a fruit-eating monkey with a prehensile tail and a loud howling call, native to the forests of tropical America. • Genus *Alouatta*, family Cebidae: several species.

howl·ing /ˈhouliNG/ ▸*adj.* [*attrib.*] **1** producing a long, loud, doleful cry or wailing sound. ■ *archaic* filled with or characterized by such sounds: *the howling wilderness.* **2** *informal* extreme; great: *the meal was a howling success.*

How·rah /ˈhourə/ (also **Hao·ra**) a city in eastern India, on the Hooghly River, opposite Calcutta; pop. 947,000.

how·so·e'er /ˌhousōˈe(ə)r/ *poetic/literary* ▸*contraction of* howsoever.

how·so·ev·er /ˌhousōˈevər/ *formal* or *archaic* ▸*adv.* [with *adj.* or *adv.*] to whatever extent: *any quantity howsoever small.*
▸*conj.* in whatever way; regardless of how: *howsoever it came into being, it is good to look at.*

how-to *informal* ▸*adj.* [*attrib.*] providing detailed and practical advice: *read a how-to book.*
▸*n.* (*pl.* **-tos**) a book, video, or training session that provides such advice. ■ (**how-tos**) the correct procedures for a particular activity: *you will discover the how-tos of freehand drawing.*

Hox·ha /ˈhôjə/, Enver (1908–85), Albanian statesman; founder of the Albanian Communist Party in 1941; prime minister 1944–54, and first secretary of the Albanian Communist Party 1954–85. He rigorously isolated Albania from Western influences and implemented a Stalinist program of nationalization and collectivization.

hoy[1] /hoi/ ▸*exclam.* used to attract someone's attention: *"Hoy! Look!"* ▷natural exclamation: first recorded in late Middle English.

hoy[2] ▸*n.* *historical* a small coastal sailing vessel, typically carrying one mast rigged fore-and-aft. ▷Middle English: from Middle Dutch *hoei*, of unknown origin.

hoy·a /ˈhoiə/ ▸*n.* a climbing or sprawling evergreen shrub with ornamental foliage and waxy flowers, native to Southeast Asia and the Pacific and grown as a greenhouse or indoor plant. • Genus *Hoya*, family Asclepiadaceae. ▷modern Latin, named after Thomas *Hoy* (*c.*1750–*c.*1821), English gardener.

hoy·den /ˈhoidn/ ▸*n.* *dated* a boisterous girl. ▷late 16th cent. (denoting a rude or ignorant man): probably from Middle Dutch *heiden* (see HEATHEN). **—hoy·den·ish** *adj.*

Hoyle[1] /hoil/, Sir Fred (1915–2001), English astrophysicist and writer. He was one of the proponents of the steady state theory of cosmology, and, mainly with U.S. physicist **William A. Fowler** (1911–95), described the processes of nucleosynthesis inside stars.

Hoyle[2] /hoil/ ▸*n.* (in phrase **according to Hoyle**) according to plan or the rules. ▷early 20th cent.: from the name of Edmond *Hoyle* (1672–1769), English writer on card games.

h.p. (also **HP**) ▸*abbr.* ■ high pressure. ■ *Brit.* hire purchase. ■ horsepower.

HPF ▸*abbr.* highest possible frequency.

HPV ▸*abbr.* human papilloma virus.

HQ ▸*abbr.* headquarters.

HR ▸*abbr.* ■ House of Representatives. ■ human resources.

hr ▸*abbr.* hour.

Hr. ▸*abbr.* Herr.

Hra·dec Krá·lo·vé /ˈ(h)rädˌets ˈkrälôˌve/ a town in the northern Czech Republic, on the Elbe River; pop. 162,000. German name KÖNIGGRÄTZ.

HRE ▸*abbr.* ■ Holy Roman Empire or Emperor.

H. Rept. ▸*abbr.* House Report.

H. Res. ▸*abbr.* House Resolution.

HRH *Brit.* ▸*abbr.* Her or His Royal Highness (as a title): *HRH Prince Philip.*

Hrod·na /ˈKHrôdnə/ a city in western Belarus, on the Neman River, near the borders with Poland and Lithuania; pop. 277,000. Russian name GRODNO.

hrs ▸*abbr.* hours.

HRT ▸*abbr.* hormone replacement therapy.

Hr·vat·ska /ˈKH(ə)rvatskä; ˈhərvätskä/ Croatian name for CROATIA.

hryv·na /ˈ(h)rivnyə; -nē; həˈriv-/ (also **hryv·nia**) ▸*n.* the basic monetary unit of Ukraine, equal to 100 kopiykas. ▷from Ukrainian *gryvnya* '3-kopek coin of pre-independent Ukraine,' from Old Russian *grivina* 'necklace, ring, coin.'

Hs ▸*symbol* the chemical element hassium.

HSA ▸*abbr.* HEALTH SAVINGS ACCOUNT.

HSGT ▸*abbr.* high speed ground transit.

HSH ▸*abbr.* Her or His Serene Highness (as a title): *HSH Prince Rainer.*

Hsia·men variant spelling of XIAMEN.

Hsian variant spelling of XIAN.

Hsiang ▸ variant spelling of XIANG.

Hsi·ning variant spelling of XINING.

HST ▸*abbr.* ■ hypersonic transport. ■ Hubble Space Telescope.

Hsu-chou variant spelling of XUZHOU.

HT ▸*abbr.* ■ halftime. ■ (electrical) high tension.

HTLV ▸*abbr.* human T cell lymphotropic virus.

HTLV-I ▸*abbr.* ■ T-cell lymphotrophic virus type I. ■ human lymphotropic virus, type 1.

HTLV-III ▸*abbr.* ■ human T-cell lymphotropic virus, type III.

HTML ▸*n.* *Computing* Hypertext Markup Language, a standardized system for tagging text files to achieve font, color, graphic, and hyperlink effects on World Wide Web pages.

Hts. ▸*abbr.* Heights.

HTTP *Computing* ▸*abbr.* Hypertext Transfer (or Transport) Protocol, the data transfer protocol used on the World Wide Web.

HUAC /ˈhyo͞o-ak/ ▸*abbr.* House Un-American Activities Committee.

Huai·bei /ˈhwīˈbā/ an industrial city in northern Anhui province, in eastern China, southwest of Xuzhou; pop. 1,308,000.

Huai·nan /ˈhwīˈnän/ a city in east central China, in the province of Anhui; pop. 1,228,000.

Hual·la·ga /wäˈyägä/ a river in central Peru, one of the headwaters of the Amazon River. Rising in the central Andes, it flows northeast for 700 miles (1,100 km) to the Amazon Basin at Lagunas.

Huam·bo /ˈwämbō/ a city in the mountains in western Angola; pop. 400,000. Founded in 1912, it was known by its Portuguese name of Nova Lisboa until 1978.

Huang Hai /ˈhwäNG ˈhī/ Chinese name for YELLOW SEA.

Huang Ho /ˈhō/ (also **Huang He** /ˈhə/) Chinese name for YELLOW RIVER.

Huang·shi /ˈhwäNGˈSHē/ (formerly **Hwangshih**) an industrial city in Hubei province, in east central China, on the Yangtze River, south of Wuhan; pop. 458,000.

hua·ra·che /wəˈräCHē/ (also **gua·ra·che**) ▸*n.* a leather-thonged sandal, originally worn by Mexican Indians. ▷late 19th cent.: Mexican Spanish.

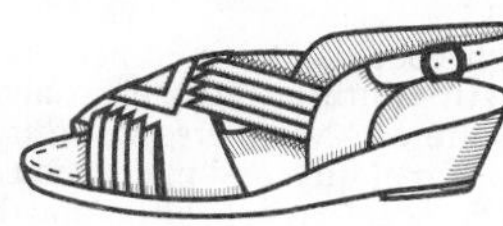

huarache

Huas·ca·rán /ˌwäskəˈrän/ an extinct volcano in the Peruvian Andes, in western central Peru, that rises to 22,205 feet (6,768 m). It is the highest peak in Peru.

hub /həb/ ▸*n.* the central part of a wheel, rotating on or with the axle, and from which the spokes radiate. ■ a place or thing that forms the effective center of an activity, region, or network: *the kitchen was* **the hub** *of family life.* ▷early 16th cent. (denoting a shelf at the side of a fireplace used for heating pans): of unknown origin (compare with HOB[1]).
▸*PHRASE* □ **hub-and-spoke** denoting a system of air transportation in which local airports offer flights to a central airport where international or long-distance flights are available.

hub·ba hub·ba /ˈhəbə ˈhəbə/ ▸*exclam.* *informal* used to express approval, excitement, or enthusiasm, esp. with regard to a person's appearance: *In walks the willowy Juanita. Hubba hubba!* | [as *adj.*] *they parodied her hubba-hubba image.* ▷1940s: of unknown origin.

Hub·bard squash /ˈhəbərd/ ▸*n.* a winter squash of a variety with a green or yellow rind and yellow flesh.

Hub·ble /ˈhəbəl/, Edwin Powell (1889–1953), U.S. astronomer. He studied galaxies and devised a classification scheme for them. In 1929, he proposed what is now known as Hubble's law with its constant of proportionality (Hubble's constant). The Hubble Space Telescope, deployed in space in 1990, is named for him.

hub·ble-bub·ble /ˈhəbəl ˌbəbəl/ ▸*n.* a hookah. ▷mid 17th cent.: imitative repetition of BUBBLE.

Hub·ble clas·si·fi·ca·tion *Astronomy* a simple method of describing the shapes of galaxies, using subdivisions of each of four basic types (elliptical, spiral, barred spiral, and irregular). Hubble's suggestion that they form an evolutionary sequence is no longer accepted.

Hub·ble's con·stant *Astronomy* the ratio of the speed of recession of a galaxy (due to the expansion of the universe) to its distance from the observer. The reciprocal of the constant is called **Hubble time** and represents the length of time for which the universe has been expanding, and hence the age of the universe.

Hub·ble's law *Astronomy* a law stating that the redshifts in the spectra of distant galaxies (and hence their speeds of recession) are proportional to their distance.

Hub·ble Space Tel·e·scope an orbiting astronomical observatory launched in 1990. The telescope's high-resolution images are far better than can be obtained from the earth's surface.

hub·bub /ˈhəbəb/ ▸*n.* [in *sing.*] a chaotic din caused by a crowd of people: *a hubbub of laughter and shouting.* ■ a busy, noisy situation: *she fought through the hubbub.* ▷mid 16th cent.: perhaps of Irish origin; compare with the Irish exclamations *ababú*, *abú*, used in battle cries.

hub·by /ˈhəbē/ ▸*n.* (*pl.* **-bies**) *informal* a husband. ▷late 17th cent.: familiar abbreviation.

hub·cap /ˈhəbˌkap/ ▸*n.* a metal or plastic cover for the hub of a motor vehicle's wheel.

Hu·bei /ˈho͞oˈbā/ (also **Hu·peh**) a province in eastern China; capital, Wuhan.

Hub·li /ˈho͞oblē/ (also **Hub·li-Dhar·wad** /därˈwäd/, **Hub·li-Dhar·war** /därˈwär/) a city in southwestern India; pop. 648,000. It was united with the adjacent city of Dharwad in 1961.

hu·bris /ˈ(h)yo͞obris/ ▸*n.* excessive pride or self-confidence. ■ (in Greek tragedy) excessive pride toward or defiance of the gods, leading to nemesis. ▷Greek. **—hu·bris·tic** /(h)yo͞oˈbristik/ *adj.*

hu·chen /ˈho͞okən/ ▸*n.* (*pl.* same) a large, slender, nonmigratory fish of the salmon family that lives only in the Danube River system. • *Hucho hucho*, family Salmonidae. ▷early 20th cent.: from German.

huck·a·back /ˈhəkəˌbak/ ▸*n.* a strong linen or cotton fabric with a rough surface, used for toweling. ▷late 17th cent.: of unknown origin.

huck·le·ber·ry /ˈhəkəlˌberē/ ▸*n.* **1** a small, round, edible blue-black berry related to the blueberry. **2** the low-growing North American shrub of the heath family that bears this fruit. • Genus *Gaylussacia*, family Ericaceae: several species, including the common **black huckleberry** (*G. baccata*). ▷late 16th cent.: probably originally a dialect name for the blueberry (though early evidence is lacking), from dialect *huckle* 'hip, haunch' (because of the plant's jointed stems).

huck·ster /ˈhəkstər/ ▸*n.* a person who sells small items, either door-to-door or from a stall or small store. ■ a mercenary person eager to make a profit out of anything. ■ a publicity agent or advertising copywriter, esp. for radio or television.
▸*v.* [*trans.*] promote or sell (something, typically a product of questionable value). ■ [*intrans.*] bargain; haggle. ▷Middle English (in the sense 'retailer at a stall, hawker'): probably of Low German origin. **—huck·ster·ism** /-izəm/ *n.*

HUD /həd / ▸*abbr.* ■ (Department of) Housing and Urban Development. ■ head-up display.

Hud·ders·field /ˈhədərzˌfēld/ a town in northern England, formerly in Yorkshire; pop. 149,000.

hud·dle /ˈhədl/ ▸*v.* [*intrans.*] crowd together; nestle closely: *they* **huddled together** *for warmth.* ■ curl one's body into a small space: *the watchman remained, huddled under his canvas shelter.* ■ draw together for an

Pronunciation Key ə *ago*; ər *over*; ˈə or ˌə *up*; ˈər or ˌər *fur*; a *hat*; ā *rate*; ä *car*; CH *chew*; e *let*; ē *see*; e(ə)r *air*; i *fit*; ī *by*; i(ə)r *ear*; NG *sing*; ō *go*; ô *for*; oi *boy*; o͝o *good*; o͞o *goo*; ou *out*; SH *she*; TH *thin*; TH *then*; (h)w *why*; ZH *vision*

H

informal, private conversation: *selection committee members huddled with attorneys.* ■ [*trans.*] *Brit.* heap together in a disorderly manner: *a man with his clothes all huddled on anyhow.*
▸*n.* a crowded or confused mass of people or things: *a **huddle of** barns and outbuildings.* ■ a brief gathering of players during a game to receive instructions, esp. in football. ■ a small group of people holding an informal, private conversation. ■ *archaic* confusion; bustle. ▷late 16th cent. (in the sense 'conceal'): perhaps of Low German origin.

Hud·son1 /ˈhədsən/ a town in southern New Hampshire, on the Merrimack River; pop. 22,928.

Hud·son2, Henry (*c.*1565–1611), English explorer. He discovered the North American bay, river, and strait that bear his name. In 1610, he attempted to winter in Hudson Bay, but his crew mutinied and set Hudson and a few companions adrift, never to be seen again.

Hud·son Bay an inland sea—the largest in the world—in northeastern Canada. It is connected to the North Atlantic Ocean via Hudson Strait. ▷named after the explorer Henry *Hudson*, who discovered it in 1610.

Hud·so·ni·an /hədˈsōnēən/ ▸*adj.* of or relating to Hudson Bay and the surrounding land. ■ *Biology* denoting a biogeographical zone represented by the territory around the bay (north of the tree line from Labrador to Alaska).

Hud·son Riv·er a river in eastern New York, that rises in the Adirondack Mountains and flows south for 350 miles (560 km) into the Atlantic Ocean at New York City. ▷named after Henry *Hudson*, who in 1609 sailed 150 miles (240 km) up the river as far as Albany.

Hud·son's Bay blan·ket (also **Hud·son Bay blan·ket**) ▸*n. Canadian* a durable woolen blanket, typically with wide colored stripes. ▷late 19th cent.: originally sold by the *Hudson's Bay* Company and frequently used as material for coats.

Hud·son's Bay Com·pa·ny a British colonial trading company set up in 1670 and granted all lands draining into Hudson Bay for purposes of commercial exploitation, principally trade in fur.

Hué /(h)wā/ a city in central Vietnam; pop. 219,000.

hue /(h)yo͞o/ ▸*n.* a color or shade: *her face lost its golden hue | verdigris is greenish-yellow in hue.* ■ the attribute of a color by virtue of which it is discernible as red, green, etc., and which is dependent on its dominant wavelength, and independent of intensity or lightness. ■ *figurative* character; aspect: *men of all political hues submerged their feuds.* ▷Old English *hīw, hēow* (also 'form, appearance,' obsolete except in Scots), of Germanic origin; related to Swedish *hy* 'skin, complexion.' The sense 'color, shade' dates from the mid 19th cent. —**hued** *adj.* [*in combination*] *rainbow-hued.* —**hue·less** *adj.*

hue and cry ▸*n.* a loud clamor or public outcry. ■ *historical* a loud cry calling for the pursuit and capture of a criminal. In former English law the cry had to be raised by the inhabitants of a hundred in which a robbery had been committed if they were not to become liable for the damages suffered by the victim. ▷late Middle English: from the Anglo-Norman French legal phrase *hu e cri*, literally 'outcry and cry,' from Old French *hu* 'outcry' (from *huer* 'to shout').

Hue·co Moun·tains /ˈwākō/ a range in southern New Mexico and western Texas, near El Paso, that rises to 6,717 feet (2,049 m).

hue·vos ran·che·ros /ˈwāvōs ranˈcherōs; rän-/ ▸*n.* a dish of fried or poached eggs served on a tortilla with a spicy tomato sauce.

huff /həf/ ▸*v.* [*intrans.*] **1** blow out loudly; puff: *he was huffing under a heavy load.* ■ [*trans.*] express (one's annoyance or offense): *he huffed out his sudden irritation.* **2** [*trans.*] sniff fumes from (gasoline or solvents) for a euphoric effect, the consequences of which may be lethal: *kids that are huffing spray paint like crazy.*
▸*n.* [usu. in *sing.*] a fit of petty annoyance: *she walked off **in a huff**.* ▷late 16th cent.: imitative of the sound of blowing. —**huff·ish** *adj.*
▸*PHRASE* □ **huff and puff** breathe heavily with exhaustion. ■ express one's annoyance in an obvious or threatening way.

huff·y /ˈhəfē/ ▸*adj.* (**huff·i·er, huff·i·est**) annoyed or irritated and quick to take offense at petty things: *ask writers for more than a second draft and they get huffy.* —**huff·i·ly** /ˈhəfəlē/ *adv.* —**huff·i·ness** *n.*

hug /həg/ ▸*v.* (**hugged, hug·ging**) [*trans.*] squeeze (someone) tightly in one's arms, typically to express affection: *he hugged her close to him | people kissed and hugged each other.* ■ hold (something) closely or tightly around or against part of one's body: *he hugged his knees to his chest.* ■ fit tightly around: *a pair of jeans that hugged the contours of his body.* ■ keep close to: *I headed north, hugging the coastline all the way.* ■ (**hug oneself**) congratulate or be pleased with oneself: *she hugged herself with secret joy.* ■ cherish or cling to (something such as a belief): *a boy hugging a secret.*
▸*n.* an act of holding someone tightly in one's arms, typically to express affection: *there were hugs and tears as they were reunited.* ■ a squeezing grip in wrestling. ▷mid 16th cent.: probably of Scandinavian origin and related to Norwegian *hugga* 'comfort, console.' —**hug·ga·ble** *adj.*

huge /(h)yo͞oj/ ▸*adj.* (**hug·er, hug·est**) extremely large; enormous: *a huge area | he made a huge difference to the team.* ▷Middle English: shortening of Old French *ahuge*, of unknown origin. —**huge·ness** *n.*

huge·ly /ˈ(h)yo͞ojlē/ ▸*adv.* [often as *submodifier*] very much; to a great extent: *a hugely expensive house.*

hug·ger-mug·ger /ˈhəgər ˌməgər/ ▸*adj.* **1** confused; disorderly: *a spirit of careless frivolity where all was hugger-mugger.* **2** secret; clandestine.
▸*n.* **1** confusion; muddle. **2** secrecy. ▷early 16th cent. (sense 2 of the *noun*): probably related to HUDDLE and to dialect *mucker* 'hoard money, conceal.' This is one of a number of similar formations from late Middle English to the 16th cent., including *hucker-mucker* and *hudder-mudder*, with the basic sense 'secrecy, concealment.'

Hughes1 /hyo͞oz/, Charles Evans (1862–1948) U.S. chief justice 1930–41 and politician. He was a U.S. Supreme Court associate justice 1910–16 and unsuccessfully ran against Democrat Woodrow Wilson for the presidency 1916 before becoming chief justice.

Hughes2, Howard (Robard) (1905–76), U.S. industrialist, movie producer, and aviator. He made his fortune through the Hughes Tool Company, made his debut as a movie director in 1926, and from 1935 to 1938 broke many world aviation records. He lived as a recluse for the last 25 years of his life. Notable movies: *Hell's Angels* (1930) and *The Outlaw* (1941).

Hughes3, (James Mercer) Langston (1902–67), U.S. writer. A leading voice of the Harlem Renaissance, he began a prolific literary career with *The Weary Blues* (1926), a series of poems on black themes, using blues and jazz rhythms. Other poetry collections include *The Negro Mother* (1931) and *Shakespeare in Harlem* (1941).

Hughes4, Ted (1930–98), English poet; full name *Edward James Hughes*. His vision of the natural world as a place of violence, terror, and beauty pervades his work. He served as Britain's poet laureate 1984–98. Hughes was married to Sylvia Plath, a marriage he recounted in *Birthday Letters* (1998). Other notable works: *The Hawk in the Rain* (1957) and *Crow* (1970).

Hug·li variant spelling of HOOGHLY.

Hu·go /ˈ(h)yo͞ogō/ Victor (1802–85), French poet, novelist, and playwright; full name *Victor-Marie Hugo*. His belief that theater should express both the grotesque and the sublime of human existence overturned existing conventions. Notable works: *Hernani* (drama, 1830), *Les Feuilles d'automne* (poems, 1831), *Notre-Dame de Paris* (1831), and *Les Misérables* (novel, 1862).

Hu·gue·not /ˈhyo͞ogəˌnät/ ▸*n.* a French Protestant of the 16th–17th centuries. Largely Calvinist, the Huguenots suffered severe persecution at the hands of the Catholic majority, and many thousands emigrated from France. ▷French, alteration (by association with the name of a Geneva burgomaster, Besançon *Hugues*) of *eiguenot*, from Dutch *eedgenot*, from Swiss German *Eidgenoss* 'confederate,' from *Eid* 'oath' + *Genoss* 'associate.'

huh /hə/ ▸*exclam.* used to express scorn, anger, disbelief, surprise, or amusement: *"Huh," she snorted, "Over my dead body!"* ■ used in questions to invite agreement or further comment or to express a lack of understanding: *pretty devastating, huh?* ▷natural utterance: first recorded in English in the early 17th cent.

Hu·he·hot /ˈho͞ohāˌhōt/ variant of HOHHOT.

hui /ˈho͞o-ē/ ▸*n.* (*pl.* **huisor huies**) (in Hawaii) a club or association. ▷Maori and Hawaiian.

hu·ia /ˈho͞oyə/ ▸*n.* an extinct New Zealand wattlebird with glossy black plumage, the female having a much longer and more curved bill than the male. The tail feathers were formerly prized by Maoris, and the last huia was seen in 1907. • *Heteralocha acutirostris*, family Callaeidae. ▷mid 19th cent.: from Maori, imitative of its cry.

hui·sa·che /wēˈsächē/ ▸*n.* an acacia tree with violet-scented flowers that yield an essential oil used in perfumery, native to warm regions of America and cultivated elsewhere. Also called SWEET ACACIA and SPONGE TREE. • *Acacia farnesiana*, family Leguminosae.

huit·la·co·che /ˌwētləˈkōchā/ ▸*n.* a fungus that grows on corn, considered a delicacy in Mexico where cooks use it to flavor food.

hu·la /ˈho͞olə/ (also **hu·la-hu·la**) ▸*n.* a dance performed by Hawaiian women, characterized by six basic steps, undulating hips, and gestures symbolizing or imitating natural phenomena or historical or mythological subjects. ▷early 19th cent.: Hawaiian.

hu·la hoop (also *trademark* **Hu·la-Hoop**) ▸*n.* a large hoop spun around the body by gyrating the hips, for play or exercise.

hu·la skirt ▸*n.* a long grass skirt as worn by a hula dancer.

hulk /həlk/ ▸*n.* **1** an old ship stripped of fittings and permanently moored, esp. for use as storage or (formerly) as a prison. ■ any large disused structure: *hulks of abandoned machinery.* **2** a large or unwieldy boat or other object. ■ a large, clumsy-looking person: *a six-foot **hulk of a man**.*
▸*v.* [*intrans.*] appear large or threatening: *mile-high cliffs, hulking above wild-rushing glacial streams.* ■ move heavily or clumsily: *a single figure hulking across the screen, stopping to kick or stab.* ▷Old English *hulc* 'fast ship,' probably reinforced in Middle English by Middle Low German and Middle Dutch *hulk*; probably of Mediterranean origin and related to Greek *holkas* 'cargo ship.'

hulk·ing /ˈhəlking/ ▸*adj. informal* (of a person or object) large, heavy, or clumsy: *a hulking young man.*

Hull1 /həl/ a city and port in northeastern England, situated at the junction of the Hull and Humber rivers; pop. 252,000. Official name KINGSTON-UPON-HULL.

Hull2, Bobby (1939–) Canadian hockey player; full name *Robert Marvin Hull, Jr.* He played for the Chicago Blackhawks 1957–72, the Winnipeg Jets 1972–79, and the Hartford Whalers 1980–81. Hockey Hall of Fame (1983).

Hull3, Cordell (1871–1955) U.S. statesman. He served as a member of the U.S. House of Representatives 1907–21, 1923–31, U.S. senator 1931–33, and as U.S. secretary of state 1933–44. Nobel Peace Prize (1945).

hull1 /həl/ ▸*n.* the main body of a ship or other vessel, including the bottom, sides, and deck but not the masts, superstructure, rigging, engines, and other fittings.
▸*v.* [*trans.*] (usu. **be hulled**) hit and pierce the hull of (a ship) with a shell or other missile. ▷Middle English: perhaps the same word as HULL2, or related to HOLD2. —**hulled** *adj.* [*in combination*] *a wooden-hulled narrowboat.*

hull2 ▸*n.* the outer covering of a fruit or seed, esp. the pod of peas and beans, or the husk of grain. ■ the green calyx of a strawberry or raspberry.
▸*v.* [*trans.*] [usu. as *adj.*] (**hulled**) remove the hulls from (fruit, seeds, or grain). ▷Old English *hulu*, of Germanic origin; related to Dutch *huls*, German *Hülse* 'husk, pod,' and German *Hülle* 'covering,' also to HEEL3.

hul·la·ba·loo /ˈhələbəˌlo͞o; ˌhələbəˈlo͞o/ ▸*n.* [in *sing.*] *informal* a commotion; a fuss: *remember all the hullabaloo over the golf ball?* ▷mid 18th cent.: reduplication of *hallo, hullo*, etc.

hul·lo /həˈlō/ ▸*exclam.* variant spelling of HELLO. ▷first recorded, in this form, in T. Hughes' *Tom Brown's Schooldays* (1857).

hum1 /həm/ ▸*v.* (**hummed, hum·ming**) [*intrans.*] **1** make a low, steady continuous sound like that of a bee: *the computers hummed.* ■ sing with closed lips: *he hummed softly to himself | [trans.] she was humming a cheerful tune.* ■ (of a place) be filled with a low, steady continuous sound: *the room **hummed with** an expectant murmur.* ■ *informal* be in a state of great activity: *the repair shops are humming as the tradesmen set about their various tasks.* **2** *Brit., informal* smell unpleasant: *when the wind drops this stuff really hums.*
▸*n.* [in *sing.*] a low, steady, continuous sound: *the hum of insects | a low hum of conversation.* ■ an unwanted low-frequency noise in an amplifier caused by variation of electric current, esp. the alternating frequency of the power lines. ▷late Middle English: imitative. —**hum·ma·ble** *adj.* —**hum·mer** *n.*

hum2 ▸*exclam.* used to express hesitation or dissent: *"Ah, hum, Elaine, isn't it ?"* ▷mid 16th cent.: imitative; related to the verb HUM1.

hu·man /ˈ(h)yo͞omən/ ▸*adj.* of, relating to, or

characteristic of people or human beings: *the human body | the survival of the human race.* ■ of or characteristic of people as opposed to God or animals or machines, esp. in being susceptible to weaknesses: *they are only human, and therefore mistakes do occur | the risk of human error.* ■ of or characteristic of people's better qualities, such as kindness or sensitivity: *the human side of politics is getting stronger.* ■ *Zoology* of or belonging to the genus *Homo.*
▸*n.* a human being, esp. a person as distinguished from an animal or (in science fiction) an alien. ▷late Middle English *humaine,* from Old French *humain(e),* from Latin *humanus,* from *homo* 'man, human being.' The present spelling became usual in the 18th cent.; compare with HUMANE. —**hu·man·ness** *n.*

USAGE See usage at HUMANITARIAN.

hu·man be·ing ▸*n.* a man, woman, or child of the species *Homo sapiens,* distinguished from other animals by superior mental development, power of articulate speech, and upright stance.

hu·man cap·i·tal ▸*n.* the skills, knowledge, and experience possessed by an individual or population, viewed in terms of their value or cost to an organization or country.

hu·man chain ▸*n.* a line of people formed for passing things quickly from one site to another. ■ a line or circle of people linking hands in a protest or demonstration.

hu·man cho·ri·on·ic go·nad·o·tro·pin /ˌkôrēˈänik ˌgōˌnadəˈtrōpin/ (abbr.: **HCG**) ▸*n.* a hormone produced in the human placenta that maintains the corpus luteum during pregnancy.

hu·mane /(h)yo͞oˈmān/ ▸*adj.* **1** having or showing compassion or benevolence: *regulations ensuring the humane treatment of animals.* ■ inflicting the minimum of pain: *humane methods of killing.* **2** *formal* (of a branch of learning) intended to have a civilizing or refining effect on people: *the center emphasizes economics as a humane discipline.* ▷late Middle English: the earlier form of HUMAN, restricted to the senses above in the 18th cent. —**hu·mane·ly** *adv.* —**hu·mane·ness** *n.*

hu·man e·col·o·gy ▸*n.* see ECOLOGY.

hu·man en·gi·neer·ing ▸*n.* the management of industrial labor, esp. with regard to relationships between people and machines; ergonomics.

Hu·man Ge·nome Pro·ject an international project to study the entire genetic material of a human being.

hu·man ge·og·ra·phy ▸*n.* the branch of geography dealing with how human activity affects or is influenced by the earth's surface.

hu·man in·ter·est ▸*n.* the aspect of a story in the media that interests people because it describes the experiences or emotions of individuals: *the conflict was not lacking in human interest* | [as *adj.*] *dry and distant matters are often treated from a human-interest angle.*

hu·man·ism /ˈ(h)yo͞oməˌnizəm/ ▸*n.* an outlook or system of thought attaching prime importance to human rather than divine or supernatural matters. Humanist beliefs stress the potential value and goodness of human beings, emphasize common human needs, and seek solely rational ways of solving human problems. ■ (often **Humanism**) a Renaissance cultural movement that turned away from medieval scholasticism and revived interest in ancient Greek and Roman thought. ■ (among some contemporary writers) a system of thought criticized as being centered on the notion of the rational, autonomous self and ignoring the unintegrated and conditioned nature of the individual. —**hu·man·ist** *n.* & *adj.* —**hu·man·is·tic** /ˌ(h)yo͞oməˈnistik/ *adj.* —**hu·man·is·ti·cal·ly** /ˌ(h)yo͞oməˈnistik(ə)lē/ *adv.*

hu·man·i·tar·i·an /(h)yo͞oˌmaniˈte(ə)rēən/ ▸*adj.* concerned with or seeking to promote human welfare: *groups sending humanitarian aid | a humanitarian organization.*
▸*n.* a person who seeks to promote human welfare; a philanthropist. —**hu·man·i·tar·i·an·ism** /-ˌnizəm/ *n.*

USAGE **Humanitarian** is not synonymous with **human,** but usage often belies this fact, as evident in this sentence: *Red Cross volunteers rushed to the scene of what may be the the worst* **humanitarian** *disaster this country has seen.* This use of **humanitarian** to mean **human** is quite common, esp. in 'live reports' on television, but is not generally considered good English style. Strictly speaking, it could be argued that *a humanitarian disaster* would more accurately refer to "a catastrophe to which no relief agencies responded."

hu·man·i·ty /(h)yo͞oˈmanitē/ ▸*n.* (*pl.* **-ties**) **1** the human race; human beings collectively: *appalling crimes against humanity.* ■ the fact or condition of being human; human nature: *a few moments when Soviets and Canadians shared their common humanity.* **2** humaneness; benevolence: *he praised them for their standards of humanity, care, and dignity.* **3** (**humanities**) learning or literature concerned with human culture, esp. literature, history, art, music, and philosophy. ▷Middle English: from Old French *humanite,* from Latin *humanitas,* from *humanus* (see HUMAN).

hu·man·ize /ˈ(h)yo͞oməˌnīz/ ▸*v.* [*trans.*] **1** make (something) more humane or civilized: *his purpose was to humanize prison conditions.* **2** give (something) a human character. ▷early 17th cent.: from French *humaniser,* from Latin *humanus* (see HUMAN). —**hu·man·i·za·tion** /ˌhyo͞oməniˈzāSHən/ *n.*

hu·man·kind /ˈ(h)yo͞omənˌkīnd/ ▸*n.* human beings considered collectively (used as a neutral alternative to "mankind"): *the origin of humankind.*

USAGE See usage at MAN.

hu·man·ly /ˈ(h)yo͞omənlē/ ▸*adv.* **1** from a human point of view; in a human manner: *they can grow both humanly and spiritually.* ■ by human means; within human ability: *we did all that was humanly possible.* **2** *chiefly archaic* with human feeling or kindness.

hu·man na·ture ▸*n.* the general psychological characteristics, feelings, and behavioral traits of humankind, regarded as shared by all humans: *he had a poor opinion of human nature.*

hu·man·oid /ˈ(h)yo͞oməˌnoid/ ▸*adj.* having an appearance or character resembling that of a human.
▸*n.* (esp. in science fiction) a being resembling a human in its shape.

hu·man re·la·tions ▸*plural n.* relations with or between people, particularly the treatment of people in a professional context.

hu·man re·sourc·es ▸*plural n.* the personnel of a business or organization, esp. when regarded as a significant asset. ■ the department of a business or organization that deals with the administration, management, and training of personnel: *director of human resources at the company.*

hu·man right ▸*n.* (usu. **human rights**) a right that is believed to belong justifiably to every person: *a flagrant disregard for basic human rights | communication is a fundamental human right.*

hu·man shield ▸*n.* a person or group of people held near a potential target to deter attack.

hu·man T cell lym·pho·trop·ic vi·rus /ˌlimfōˈträpik; -ˈtrōpik/ (abbr.: **HTLV**) ▸*n.* any of a group of retroviruses that cause disease by attacking T cells.

Hum·ber /ˈhəmbər/ an estuary in northeastern England that is formed at the junction of the Ouse and Trent rivers near Goole and that flows east for 38 miles (60 km) to enter the North Sea at Spurn Head. It has the major port of Hull on its northern bank and is spanned by the world's largest suspension bridge, which opened in 1981 and has a span of 4,626 feet (1,410 m).

hum·ble /ˈhəmbəl/ ▸*adj.* (**hum·bler, hum·blest**) **1** having or showing a modest or low estimate of one's own importance: *he was humble about his stature as one of rock history's most influential guitarists.* ■ (of an action or thought) offered with or affected by such an estimate of one's own importance: *my humble apologies.* **2** of low social, administrative, or political rank: *she came from a humble, unprivileged background.* ■ (of a thing) of modest pretensions or dimensions: *he built the business empire from humble beginnings.*
▸*v.* [*trans.*] lower (someone) in dignity or importance: *I knew he had* **humbled himself** *to ask for my help.* ■ (usu. **be humbled**) decisively defeat (another team or competitor, typically one that was previously thought to be superior): *humbled by his political opponents.* ▷Middle English: from Old French, from Latin *humilis* 'low, lowly,' from *humus* 'ground.' —**hum·ble·ness** *n.* —**hum·bly** /-blē/ *adv.*
▸*PHRASES* □ **eat humble pie** make a humble apology and accept humiliation. [*humble pie* is from a pun based on UMBLES 'offal,' considered inferior food.] □ **my humble abode** used to refer to one's home with an ironic or humorous show of modesty or humility. □ **your humble servant** *archaic* or *humorous* used at the end of a letter or as a form of ironic courtesy: *your most humble servant, George Porter.*

THE RIGHT WORD **abase, debase, degrade, demean, humble, humiliate**

While all of these verbs mean to lower in one's own estimation or in the eyes of others, there are subtle distinctions among them.

Humble and **humiliate** sound similar, but *humiliate* emphasizes shame and the loss of self-respect and usually takes place in public (*humiliated by her tearful outburst*), while *humble* is a milder term implying a lowering of one's pride or rank (*to humble the arrogant professor by pointing out his mistake*).

Abase suggests groveling or a sense of inferiority and is usually used reflexively (*got down on his knees and abased himself before the king*), while **demean** is more likely to imply a loss of dignity or social standing (*refused to demean herself by marrying a common laborer*).

When used to describe things, **debase** means a deterioration in the quality or value of something (*a currency debased by the country's political turmoil*), but in reference to people it connotes a weakening of moral standards or character (*debased himself by accepting bribes*).

Degrade is even stronger, suggesting the destruction of a person's character through degenerate or shameful behavior (*degraded by long association with criminals*).

hum·ble-bee ▸*n.* another term for BUMBLEBEE. ▷late Middle English: probably from Middle Low German *hummelbē,* from *hummel* 'to buzz' + *bē* 'bee.'

Hum·boldt Cur·rent /ˈhəmˌbōlt/ another name for PERUVIAN CURRENT.

hum·bug /ˈhəmˌbəg/ ▸*n.* **1** deceptive or false talk or behavior: *his comments are sheer humbug.* ■ a hypocrite: *you see what a humbug I am.* **2** *Brit.* a hard candy, esp. one flavored with peppermint.
▸*v.* (**-bugged, -bug·ging**) [*trans.*] deceive; trick: *to humbug his humble neighbors was not difficult.* ■ [*intrans.*] *dated* act like a fraud or sham. ▷mid 18th cent. (in the senses 'hoax, trick' and 'deceiver'): of unknown origin. —**hum·bug·ger·y** /-ˌbəg(ə)rē/ *n.*

hum·ding·er /ˈhəmˈdiNGər/ ▸*n. informal* a remarkable or outstanding person or thing of its kind: *a humdinger of a funny story.* ▷early 20th cent. (originally U.S.): of unknown origin.

hum·drum /ˈhəmˌdrəm/ ▸*adj.* lacking excitement or variety; dull; monotonous: *humdrum routine work.*
▸*n.* dullness; monotony: *an escape from the humdrum of his life.* ▷mid 16th cent.: probably a reduplication of HUM[1].

Hume /hyo͞om/, David (1711–76), Scottish philosopher, economist, and historian. He rejected the possibility of certainty in knowledge. Notable works: *A Treatise of Human Nature* (1739–40) and *History of England* (1754–62). —**Hum·e·an** /ˈhyo͞omēən/ *adj.* & *n.*

hu·mec·tant /(h)yo͞oˈmektənt/ ▸*adj.* retaining or preserving moisture.
▸*n.* a substance, esp. a skin lotion or a food additive, used to reduce the loss of moisture. ▷early 19th cent. (denoting a moistening agent): from Latin *humectant-* 'moistening,' from the verb *humectare,* from *humectus* 'moist, wet,' from *humere* 'be moist.'

hu·mer·al /ˈ(h)yo͞omərəl/ ▸*adj.* [*attrib.*] **1** of or relating to the humerus of a human or other vertebrate: *a humeral fracture.* ■ *Entomology* of, relating to, or in the region of the humerus on the wing of an insect: *a humeral lobe.* **2** (in Catholic use) denoting a plain vestment worn around the shoulders when administering the sacrament. ▷late 16th cent.: from French, or from late Latin *humeralis,* from Latin *humerus* (see HUMERUS).

hu·mer·us /ˈ(h)yo͞omərəs/ ▸*n.* (*pl.* **-meri** /-məˌrī/) *Anatomy* the bone of the upper arm or forelimb, forming joints at the shoulder and the elbow. ■ *Entomology* a structure in an insect involving, or in the region of, the front basal corners of the wings or wing cases. ▷late Middle English: from Latin, 'shoulder.'

hu·mic /ˈ(h)yo͞omik/ ▸*adj.* [*attrib.*] relating to or consisting of humus: *humic acids.*

hu·mid /ˈ(h)yo͞omid/ ▸*adj.* marked by a relatively high level of water vapor in the atmosphere: *a hot and humid day.* ▷late Middle English: from French *humide* or Latin *humidus,* from *humere* 'be moist.' —**hu·mid·ly** *adv.*

hu·mid·i·fi·er /(h)yo͞oˈmidəˌfī(ə)r/ ▸*n.* a device for keeping the atmosphere moist in a room.

hu·mid·i·fy /(h)yo͞oˈmidəˌfī/ ▸*v.* (**-fies, -fied**) [*trans.*] [often as *adj.*] (**humidified**) increase the level of moisture in (air): *a regulated flow of humidified air.* —**hu·mid·i·fi·ca·tion** /-ˌmidəfiˈkāSHən/ *n.*

hu·mid·i·stat /(h)yo͞oˈmidiˌstat/ ▸*n.* a machine or

H

device that automatically regulates the humidity of the air in a room or building.

hu·mid·i·ty /(h)yo͞o'miditē/ ▸*n.* (*pl.* **-ties**) the state or quality of being humid. ■ a quantity representing the amount of water vapor in the atmosphere or a gas: *the temperature is seventy-seven, the humidity in the low thirties.* ■ atmospheric moisture. ▷late Middle English: from Old French *humidite* or Latin *humiditas*, from *humidus* (see **HUMID**).

hu·mi·dor /'(h)yo͞omi,dôr/ ▸*n.* an airtight container for keeping cigars or tobacco moist. ▷early 20th cent.: from **HUMID**, on the pattern of *cuspidor*.

hu·mi·fy /'(h)yo͞omə,fī/ ▸*v.* (**-fies, -fied**) [*trans.*] convert (plant remains) into humus. **—hu·mi·fi·ca·tion** /,(h)yo͞omifi'kāsʜən/ *n.*

hu·mil·i·ate /(h)yo͞o'milē,āt/ ▸*v.* [*trans.*] make (someone) feel ashamed and foolish by injuring their dignity and self-respect, esp. publicly: *you'll humiliate me in front of the whole school!* | [as *adj.*] (**humiliating**) *a humiliating election defeat.* See note at **HUMBLE**. ▷mid 16th cent. (in the sense 'bring low'): from late Latin *humiliat-* 'made humble,' from the verb *humiliare*, from *humilis* (see **HUMBLE**). The current sense dates from the mid 18th cent. **—hu·mil·i·at·ing·ly** /-,ātiɴɢlē/ *adv.* **—hu·mil·i·a·tion** /-,milē'āsʜən/ *n.* **—hu·mil·i·a·tor** /-,ātər/ *n.*

hu·mil·i·ty /(h)yo͞o'militē/ ▸*n.* a modest or low view of one's own importance; humbleness. ▷Middle English: from Old French *humilite*, from Latin *humilitas*, from *humilis* (see **HUMBLE**).

hu·mint /'(h)yo͞omint/ ▸*n.* covert intelligence-gathering by agents or others. ▷late 20th cent.: from *human intelligence*.

Hum·mel /'həməl/, Berta (1909–46) German artist and nun; also known as **Sister Maria Innocentia**. She created the sketches upon which M. I. Hummel figurines, made by the Franz Goebel Company, are based.

hum·mer /'həmər/ ▸*n. informal* a **HUMVEE**. ▷by shortening and alteration.

hum·ming·bird /'həmiɴɢ,bərd/ ▸*n.* a small nectar-feeding tropical American bird that is able to hover and fly backward, typically having colorful iridescent plumage. • Family Trochilidae: many genera and numerous species, including the **ruby-throated hummingbird** (*Archilochus colubris*) of the eastern U.S., and the red-crowned **Anna's hummingbird** (*Calypte anna*), found chiefly along the Pacific coast of the U.S. ▷mid 17th cent.: so named because of the humming sound produced by the rapid vibration of the bird's wings.

ruby-throated hummingbird

hum·ming·bird hawk moth (also **hummingbird moth**) ▸*n.* a migratory day-flying hawk moth that makes an audible hum while hovering in front of flowers to feed on nectar. • Family Sphingidae.

hum·mock /'həmək/ ▸*n.* a hillock, knoll, or mound. ■ a hump or ridge in an ice field. ■ a piece of forested ground rising above a marsh. ▷mid 16th cent. (originally in nautical use denoting a small hillock on the coast): of unknown origin. **—hum·mock·y** *adj.*

hum·mus /'ho͝oməs; 'həm-/ (also **houm·mos** or **hum·ous**) ▸*n.* a thick paste or spread made from ground chickpeas and sesame seeds, olive oil, lemon, and garlic, made originally in the Middle East. ▷from Arabic *ḥummuṣ*.

hu·mon·gous /(h)yo͞o'mäɴɢgəs; -'məɴɢ-/ (also **hu·mun·gous**) ▸*adj. informal* huge; enormous: *a humongous steak.* ▷1970s (originally U.S.): possibly based on **HUGE** and **MONSTROUS**, influenced by the stress pattern of *stupendous*.

hu·mor /'(h)yo͞omər/ (*Brit.* **hu·mour**) ▸*n.* **1** the quality of being amusing or comic, esp. as expressed in literature or speech: *his tales are full of humor.* See note at **WIT**. ■ the ability to perceive or express humor or to appreciate a joke: *their inimitable brand of humor* | *she has a great* **sense of humor**. **2** a mood or state of mind: *her* **good humor** *vanished* | *the clash hadn't improved his humor.* ■ *archaic* an inclination or whim. **3** (also **cardinal humor**) *historical* each of the four chief fluids of the body (blood, phlegm, yellow bile [choler], and black bile [melancholy]) that were thought to determine a person's physical and mental qualities by the relative proportions in which they were present.
▸*v.* [*trans.*] comply with the wishes of (someone) in order to keep them content, however unreasonable such wishes might be: *she was always humoring him to prevent trouble.* ■ *archaic* adapt or accommodate oneself to (something). ▷Middle English (as *humour*): via Old French from Latin *humor* 'moisture,' from *humere* (see **HUMID**). The original sense was 'bodily fluid' (surviving in *aqueous humor* and *vitreous humor*, fluids in the eyeball); it was used specifically for any of the cardinal humors (sense 3), whence 'mental disposition' (thought to be caused by the relative proportions of the humors). This led, in the 16th cent., to the senses 'state of mind, mood' (sense 2) and 'whim, fancy,' hence *to humor someone* 'to indulge a person's whim.' Sense 1 dates from the late 16th cent. **—hu·mor·less** *adj.* **—hu·mor·less·ly** *adv.* **—hu·mor·less·ness** *n.*
▸*PHRASE* □ **out of humor** in a bad mood.

hu·mor·al /'(h)yo͞omərəl/ ▸*adj. Medicine* of or relating to the body fluids, esp. with regard to immune responses involving antibodies in body fluids as distinct from cells (see **CELL-MEDIATED**). ■ *historical* of or relating to the four bodily humors. ■ *historical Medicine* (of diseases) caused by or attributed to a disordered state of body fluids or (formerly) the bodily humors. ▷late Middle English (in the general sense 'relating to bodily fluids'): from Old French, or from medieval Latin *humoralis*, from Latin *humor* 'moisture' (see **HUMOR**).

hu·mor·esque /,(h)yo͞omə'resk/ ▸*n.* a short, lively piece of music. ▷late 19th cent.: from German *Humoreske*, from *Humor* 'humor.'

hu·mor·ist /'(h)yo͞omərist/ ▸*n.* a humorous writer, performer, or artist.

hu·mor·ous /'(h)yo͞omərəs/ ▸*adj.* causing lighthearted laughter and amusement; comic: *a humorous and entertaining talk.* ■ having or showing a sense of humor: *his humorous gray eyes.* **—hu·mor·ous·ly** *adv.* **—hu·mor·ous·ness** *n.*

hu·mour ▸*n.* British spelling of **HUMOR**.

hu·mous ▸*n.* variant spelling of **HUMMUS**.

hump /həmp/ ▸*n.* a rounded protuberance found on the back of a camel or other animal or as an abnormality on a person's back. ■ a rounded raised mass of earth or land. ■ a mound over which railroad vehicles are pushed so as to run by gravity to the required place in a switchyard.
▸*v.* **1** [*trans.*] *informal* lift or carry (a heavy object) with difficulty: *he continued to hump cases up and down the hotel corridor.* ■ [*intrans.*] move heavily and awkwardly: *an elephant seal was a vast mound of flesh, humping along the ground in waves of blubber.* **2** [*trans.*] make hump-shaped: *the cat humped himself into a different shape and purred.* **3** [*intrans.*] *vulgar slang* have sexual intercourse. ■ [*trans.*] have sexual intercourse with (someone). ▷early 18th cent.: probably related to Low German *humpe* 'hump,' also to Dutch *homp*, Low German *humpe* 'lump, hunk (of bread).' **—humped** *adj. a humped back.* **—hump·less** *adj.* **—hump·y** *adj.* (**hump·i·er, hump·i·est**).
▸*PHRASE* □ **over the hump** over the worst or most difficult part of something.

hump·back /'həmp,bak/ ▸*n.* **1** (also **humpback whale**) a baleen whale that has a hump (instead of a dorsal fin) and long white flippers. It is noted for its lengthy vocalizations or "songs." • *Megaptera novaeangliae*, family Balaenopteridae. **2** (also **humpback salmon**) another term for **PINK SALMON**. **3** another term for **HUNCHBACK**. **—hump·backed** *adj.*

Hum·per·dinck /'həmpər,diɴɢk/, Engelbert (1854–1921), German composer who wrote the opera *Hänsel und Gretel* (1893).

humph /həmf/ ▸*exclam.* used to express slightly scornful doubt or dissatisfaction. ▷natural utterance: first recorded in English in the mid 16th cent.

Hum·phrey /'həmfrē/, Hubert Horatio (1911–78), U.S. politician. He was a U.S. senator from Minnesota 1949–64 before becoming U.S. vice president 1965–69. A Democratic presidential candidate in 1968, he again served in the Senate 1971–78.

Hump·ty Dump·ty /'həm(p)tē 'dəm(p)tē/ (also **hump·ty dump·ty**) ▸*n.* (*pl.* **Hump·ty Dump·ties**) *informal* **1** a fat, rotund person: [as *adj.*] *he was a Humpty Dumpty figure of a man.* **2** a person or thing that once overthrown cannot be restored. ▷late 18th cent.: from the egglike nursery-rhyme character *Humpty Dumpty*, who fell off a wall and could not be put together again.

hu·mun·gous ▸*adj.* variant spelling of **HUMONGOUS**.

hu·mus /'(h)yo͞oməs/ ▸*n.* the organic component of soil, formed by the decomposition of leaves and other plant material by soil microorganisms. ▷late 18th cent.: from Latin, literally 'soil.'

Hum·vee /'həm'vē/ ▸*n. trademark* a modern military vehicle. ▷late 20th cent.: alteration, from the initials of *high-mobility multipurpose vehicle*.

Hun /hən/ ▸*n.* **1** a member of a warlike Asiatic nomadic people who ravaged Europe in the 4th–5th centuries. ■ a reckless or uncivilized destroyer of something. **2** *informal, derogatory* a German (esp. in military contexts during World War I and World War II). ■ (**the Hun**) Germans collectively. ▷Old English *Hūne, Hūnas* (plural), from late Latin *Hunni*, from Greek *Hounnoi*, of Middle Iranian origin. **—Hun·nish** *adj.*

Hu·nan /'ho͞o'nän/ a province in eastern central China; capital, Changsha.

hunch /həncʜ/ ▸*v.* [*trans.*] raise (one's shoulders) and bend the top of one's body forward: *he thrust his hands in his pockets, hunching his shoulders* | [*intrans.*] *he* **hunched over** *his glass.* ■ [*intrans.*] bend one's body into a huddled position: *I* **hunched up** *as small as I could.* ■ shove or push; nudge: *she hunched me and winked.*
▸*n.* **1** a feeling or guess based on intuition rather than known facts: *she was acting* **on a hunch**. **2** a humped position or thing: *the hunch of his back.* **3** *chiefly dialect* a thick piece; a hunk: ***a hunch of** bread.* ▷late 15th cent.: of unknown origin. The original meaning was 'push, shove' (noun and verb), a sense retained now in Scots as a noun, and in U.S. dialect as a verb. Sense 1 of the noun probably derives from the sense 'nudge someone in order to draw attention to something.'

hunch·back /'həncʜ,bak/ ▸*n.* a back deformed by a sharp forward angle, forming a hump, typically caused by collapse of a vertebra. ■ *often offensive* a person with such a deformity. **—hunch·backed** *adj.*

hun·dred /'həndrid/ ▸*cardinal number* (*pl.* **-dreds** or (with numeral or quantifying word) **-dred**) (**a/one hundred**) the number equivalent to the product of ten and ten; ten more than ninety; 100: *a hundred yards away* | *there are just a hundred of us here.* (Roman numeral: **c** or **C.**) ■ (**hundreds**) the numbers from 100 to 999: *an unknown number, probably in the hundreds, had already been lost.* ■ (**hundreds**) several hundred things or people: *it cost hundreds of dollars.* ■ (usu. **hundreds**) *informal* an unspecified large number: *hundreds of letters poured in.* ■ (**the —— hundreds**) the years of a specified century: *the early nineteen hundreds.* ■ one hundred years old: *you must be over a hundred!* ■ one hundred miles per hour. ■ a hundred-dollar bill. ■ (chiefly in spoken English) used to express whole hours in the twenty-four-hour system: *thirteen hundred hours.*
▸*n. Brit., historical* a subdivision of a county or shire, having its own court. ▷late Old English, from *hund* 'hundred' (from an Indo-European root shared with Latin *centum* and Greek *hekaton*) + a second element meaning 'number'; of Germanic origin and related to Dutch *honderd* and German *hundert*. The noun sense 'subdivision of a county' is of uncertain origin: it may originally have been equivalent to a hundred hides of land (see **HIDE**[3]). **—hun·dred·fold** /-,fōld/ *adj.* & *adv.* **—hun·dredth** /'həndridᴛʜ; 'həndriᴛʜ/ *ordinal number*.
▸*PHRASE* □ **a** (or **one**) **hundred percent** entirely;

Hubert H. Humphrey

H

completely: *I'm one hundred percent sure.* ■ [usu. with *negative*] *informal* completely fit and healthy: *I wasn't exactly one hundred percent.* ■ *informal* maximum effort and commitment: *he always gave one hundred percent for the team.*

Hun·dred Flow·ers a period of debate in China 1956–57, when, under the slogan "Let a hundred flowers bloom and a hundred schools of thought contend," citizens were invited to voice their opinions of the communist regime. It was forcibly ended after social unrest and fierce criticism of the government, with those who had voiced their opinions being prosecuted.

hun·dred·weight /ˈhəndrid,wāt/ (abbr.: **cwt**) ▸*n.* (*pl.* same or **-weights**) a unit of weight equal to one twentieth of a ton, in particular: ■ (also **short hun·dred·weight**) (in the U.S.) equal to 100 lb avoirdupois (about 45.4 kg). ■ (also **metric hundredweight**) (in the metric system) equal to 50 kg. ■ (also **long hun·dredweight**) (in the UK) equal to 112 lb avoirdupois (about 50.8 kg).

Hun·dred Years War a war between France and England, conventionally dated 1337–1453.

The war consisted of a series of conflicts in which successive English kings attempted to dominate France and included an early string of English military successes, most notably Crécy and Poitiers. In 1415 England, under Henry V, delivered a crushing victory at Agincourt and occupied much of northern France, but, with the exception of Calais, all English conquests had been lost by 1453.

hung /həNG/ ▸ past and past participle of HANG.
▸*adj.* **1** (of a jury) unable to agree on a verdict. ■ (in the UK and Canada) (of an elected body) having no political party with an overall majority: *a hung parliament.* **2** [*predic.*] (**hung up**) *informal* emotionally confused or disturbed: *people are hung up in all sorts of ways.* ■ (**hung up about/on**) have a psychological or emotional obsession or problem about: *guys are so hung up about the way they look.* ■ delayed or detained: *my mother was probably hung up in traffic.* **3** [*predic.*] *vulgar slang* used esp. in similes to refer to the size of a man's penis: *he's hung like a horse.*

Hun·gar·i·an /həNGˈge(ə)rēən/ ▸*adj.* of or relating to Hungary, its people, or their language.
▸*n.* **1** a native or national of Hungary. ■ a person of Hungarian descent. **2** an Ugric language, the official language of Hungary, spoken also in Romania. Also called MAGYAR. ▹from medieval Latin *Hungarī* + -AN.

Hun·ga·ry /ˈhəNGgərē/ a country in central Europe; pop. 10,032,000; capital, Budapest official language, Hungarian; Hungarian name MAGYARORSZÁG. ▹from medieval Latin *Hungaria* (see also HUNGARIAN).

Hungary was conquered by the Habsburgs in the 17th century and became an equal partner in the Austro-Hungarian empire in 1867. Following the collapse of the empire in 1918, it became an independent kingdom. After participation in World War II on the Axis side, Hungary was occupied by the Soviet Union and became a communist state. Although a liberal reform movement was crushed by Soviet troops in 1956, the communist system was abandoned in 1989, and the first multiparty elections were held in 1990. Hungary joined NATO in 1999 and the EU in 2004.

hun·ger /ˈhəNGgər/ ▸*n.* a feeling of discomfort or weakness caused by lack of food, coupled with the desire to eat: *she was faint with hunger.* ■ a severe lack of food: *they died from cold and hunger.* ■ a strong desire or craving: *her* **hunger for** *knowledge.*
▸*v.* [*intrans.*] **1** (**hunger after/for**) have a strong desire or craving for: *all actors hunger for such a role.* **2** *archaic* feel or suffer hunger through lack of food. ▹Old English *hungor* (noun), *hyngran* (verb), of Germanic origin; related to Dutch *honger* and German *Hunger.*

hun·ger strike ▸*n.* a prolonged refusal to eat, carried out as a protest, typically by a prisoner. —**hun·ger strik·er** *n.*

hung·o·ver /ˈhəNGˈōvər/ (also **hung over**) ▸*adj.* suffering from a hangover after drinking alcohol.

hun·gry /ˈhəNGgrē/ ▸*adj.* (**-gri·er**, **-gri·est**) feeling or displaying the need for food: *I was feeling ravenously hungry | children with hungry looks on their faces.* ■ [*attrib.*] causing hunger: *I always find art galleries hungry work.* ■ having a strong desire or craving: *he was* **hungry for** *any kind of excitement* | [in *combination*] *grasping, power-hungry individuals.* ▹Old English *hungrig*; related to Dutch *hongerig*, German *hungrig*, also to HUNGER. —**hun·gri·ly** /-grəlē/ *adv.* —**hun·gri·ness** *n.*

Hun·jiang /ˈhŏŏNGˈjyäNG/ an industrial city in Jilin province, in northeastern China, near the border with North Korea; pop. 694,000.

hunk /həNGk/ ▸*n.* **1** a large piece of something, esp. one of food cut or broken off a larger piece: *a hunk of bread.* **2** *informal* a sexually attractive man, esp. a large, strong one. ▹early 19th cent.: probably of Dutch or Low German origin. —**hunk·y** *adj.* (**hunk·i·er**, **hunk·i·est**).

hunk·er /ˈhəNGkər/ ▸*v.* [*intrans.*] squat or crouch down low: *he* **hunkered down** *beside her.* ■ take shelter in a defensive position: *the best way to deal with your father is to* **hunker down** *and let it blow over.* ■ hunch; bend: *burly workers* **hunkered over** *the menu of the day.* ■ *figurative* apply oneself seriously to a task: *students* **hunkered down** *to prepare for the examinations.* ▹early 18th cent.: probably related to Dutch *huiken* and German *hocken.*

hun·kers /ˈhəNGkərz/ ▸*plural n. informal* haunches: *sitting on his hunkers.* ▹mid 18th cent. (originally Scots): from HUNKER.

hunk·y-do·ry /ˈhəNGkē ˈdôrē/ ▸*adj. informal* fine; going well: *everything is hunky-dory.* ▹mid 19th cent. (originally U.S.): *hunky* from Dutch *honk* 'home, base' (in games); the origin of *dory* is unknown.

Hunt[1] /hənt/, (William) Holman (1827–1910), English painter, cofounder of the Pre-Raphaelite Brotherhood. Notable works: *The Light of the World* (1854) and *The Scapegoat* (1855).

Hunt[2], Ward (1810–86) U.S. Supreme Court associate justice 1873–82. Appointed to the Court by President Grant, he previously served as a judge and then chief judge of the New York state court of appeals 1865–73.

hunt /hənt/ ▸*v.* **1** [*trans.*] pursue and kill (a wild animal) for sport or food: *in the autumn they hunted deer* | [*intrans.*] *they hunted and fished.* ■ (of an animal) chase and kill (its prey): *mice are hunted by weasels and foxes* | [*intrans.*] *lionesses hunt in groups.* ■ [*intrans.*] try to find someone or something by searching carefully: *he desperately* **hunted for** *a new job.* ■ (**hunt something out/up**) search for something until it is found. ■ [*trans.*] (of the police) search for (a criminal): *the gang is being hunted by police* | [*intrans.*] *police are* **hunting for** *her attacker.* ■ (**hunt someone down**) pursue and capture someone. **2** [*intrans.*] (of a machine, instrument needle, or system) oscillate around a desired speed, position, or state. ■ (of an aircraft or rocket) oscillate around a mean flight path. ■ (of an automatic transmission in a motor vehicle) keep shifting between gears because of improperly designed shift logic. **3** [*intrans.*] (**hunt down/up**) (in change-ringing) move the place of a bell in a simple progression.
▸*n.* **1** an act of hunting wild animals or game. ■ an association of people who meet regularly to hunt, esp. with hounds. ■ an area where hunting takes place. ■ a search: *police launched a* **hunt for** *the killer.* **2** an oscillating motion around a desired speed, position, or state. ▹Old English *huntian*, of Germanic origin. The sense in change-ringing dates from the late 17th cent., and is probably based on the idea of the bells pursuing one another; it gave rise to the sense 'oscillate around a desired speed' (late 19th cent.).

hunt-and-peck ▸*adj.* denoting or using an inexpert form of typing in which only one or two fingers are used: *hunt-and-peck computer users.*

hunt·ed /ˈhəntid/ ▸*adj.* being pursued or searched for: *they ran like hunted hares.* ■ appearing worn or harassed as if one is being pursued: *his eyes had a hunted look.*

hunt·er /ˈhən(t)ər/ ▸*n.* **1** a person or animal that hunts: *a deer hunter.* ■ a person searching for something: *a bargain hunter.* ■ a horse of a breed developed for stamina in fox hunting and ability to jump obstacles. ■ (**the Hunter**) the constellation Orion. **2** a watch with a hinged cover protecting the glass.

hunt·er-gath·er·er ▸*n.* a member of a nomadic people who live chiefly by hunting, fishing, and harvesting wild food.

hunt·er-kill·er ▸*adj.* (of a naval vessel, esp. a submarine) equipped to locate and destroy enemy vessels, esp. other submarines.

hunt·er's moon ▸*n.* the first full moon after a harvest moon.

hunt·ing /ˈhəntiNG/ ▸*n.* **1** the activity of hunting wild animals or game, esp. for food or sport. **2** (also **plain hunting**) *Bell-ringing* a simple system of changes in which bells move through the order in a regular progression.

hunt·ing dog ▸*n.* **1** a dog of a breed developed for hunting. **2** (also **Cape hunting dog**) an African wild dog that has a dark coat with pale markings and a white-tipped tail, living and hunting in packs. • *Lycaon pictus*, family Canidae. Also called: **African wild dog.**

hunt·ing ground ▸*n.* a place used or suitable for hunting. ■ *figurative* a place where people can observe or acquire what they want: *the circuit is a favorite hunting ground for talent scouts.*

hunt·ing horn ▸*n.* a horn blown to give signals during hunting.

Hun·ting·ton /ˈhəntiNGtən/ **1** a town in northern Long Island in New York that includes Huntington, Cold Spring Harbor, and other villages; pop. 191,474. **2** a city in southwestern West Virginia, on the Ohio River; pop. 51,475.

Hun·ting·ton Beach a city in southern California, on the Pacific coast, south of Long Beach; pop. 181,519.

Hun·ting·ton's cho·re·a /ˈhəntiNGtənz kəˈrēə/ ▸*n.* a hereditary disease marked by degeneration of the brain cells and causing chorea and progressive dementia. ▹late 19th cent.: named after George *Huntington* (1851–1916), the U.S. neurologist who first described it.

Hunt·ley /ˈhəntlē/, Chet (1911–74) U.S. television journalist; born *Chester Robert Huntley.* With David Brinkley he coanchored "The Huntley–Brinkley Report" 1956–70.

hunt·ress /ˈhəntris/ ▸*n.* a woman who hunts.

hunts·man /ˈhəntsmən/ ▸*n.* (*pl.* **-men**) a person who hunts. ■ a hunt official in charge of hounds.

Hunts·ville /ˈhənts,vil/ **1** a city in northern Alabama; pop. 158,216. It is a center for space exploration and solar energy research. **2** a city in eastern Texas, north of Houston; pop. 27,925.

hun·yak /ˈhənyak/ ▸*n. informal, offensive* a person of Hungarian or central European origin, esp. an immigrant. ▹early 20th cent.: alteration of HUNGARIAN, on the pattern of *Polack.*

Hu·on pine /ˈ(h)yŏŏ-än/ ▸*n.* a tall Tasmanian conifer that has yewlike berries and fragrant red timber. • *Dacrydium franklinii*, family Podocarpaceae. ▹early 19th cent.: from *Huon*, the name of a river in the south of Tasmania.

hup /həp/ ▸*exclam.* used as a way of encouraging a marching rhythm: *hup, two, three!*

Hu·peh /ˈhŏŏˈpā/ variant of HUBEI.

hur·dle /ˈhərdl/ ▸*n.* **1** an upright frame, typically one of a series, that athletes in a race must jump over. ■ (**hurdles**) a hurdle race: *the women's 100-meter hurdles.* **2** an obstacle or difficulty: *there are many hurdles to overcome.* **3** *chiefly Brit.* a portable rectangular frame strengthened with willow branches or wooden bars, used as a temporary fence. ■ a horse race over a series of such frames: *a handicap hurdle.* ■ *historical* a frame on which traitors were dragged to execution.
▸*v.* **1** [*intrans.*] [often as *n.*] (**hurdling**) take part in a

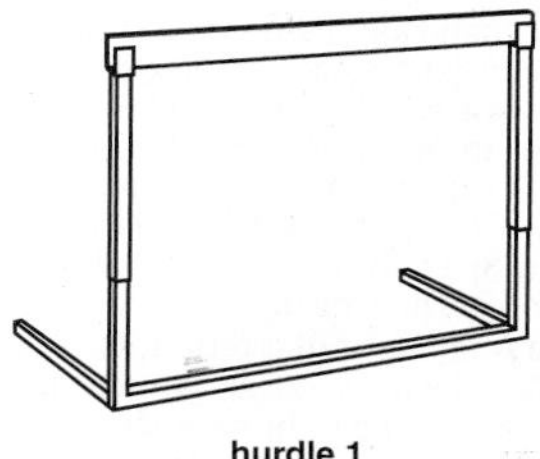
hurdle 1

race that involves jumping hurdles. ■ [*trans.*] jump over (a hurdle or other obstacle) while running. **2** [*trans.*] enclose or fence off with hurdles. ▷Old English *hyrdel* 'temporary fence,' of Germanic origin; related to Dutch *horde* and German *Hürde*.

hur·dler /ˈhərdlər/ ▶*n.* an athlete, dog, or horse that runs in hurdle races.

hur·dy-gur·dy /ˈhərdē ˌgərdē/ ▶*n.* (*pl.* **-dies**) a musical instrument with a droning sound played by turning a handle, which is typically attached to a rosined wheel sounding a series of drone strings, with keys worked by the left hand. ■ *informal* a barrel organ. ▷mid 18th cent.: probably imitative of the sound of the instrument.

hurl /hərl/ ▶*v.* [*trans.*] throw (an object) with great force: *rioters hurled a brick through the windshield of a car.* ■ push or impel (someone) violently: *I seized Nathan and hurled him into the lobby | figurative he hurled himself into the job with enthusiasm.* ■ utter (abuse) vehemently: *they were hurling insults over a back fence.* ■ [*intrans.*] *informal* vomit: *it made me want to hurl.* ▷Middle English: probably imitative, but corresponding in form and partly in sense with Low German *hurreln*.

hurl·er /ˈhərlər/ ▶*n.* **1** *informal* a baseball pitcher. **2** a player of hurling.

Hurl·er's syn·drome /ˈhərlərz/ ▶*n.* *Medicine* a defect in metabolism arising from congenital absence of an enzyme, causing accumulation of lipids and glycosaminoglycans, and resulting in mental retardation, a protruding abdomen, and bone deformities including an abnormally large head. Also called GARGOYLISM. ▷1930s: named after Gertrud *Hurler* (1889–1965), the Austrian pediatrician who first described it.

hurl·ey /ˈhərlē/ ▶*n.* a stick used in the game of hurling. ■ another term for HURLING. ▷early 19th cent.: from the verb HURL.

hurl·ing /ˈhərliNG/ ▶*n.* an Irish game resembling field hockey, played with a shorter stick with a broader oval blade. It is the national game of Ireland and may date back to the 2nd millennium BC.

hurl·y-burl·y /ˈhərlē ˈbərlē/ ▶*n.* busy, boisterous activity: *the hurly-burly of school life.* ▷Middle English: reduplication based on HURL.

Hu·ron /ˈhyo͝oˌrän/ ▶*n.* (*pl.* same or **-rons**) **1** a member of a confederation of native North American peoples formerly living in the region east of Lake Huron and now settled mainly in Oklahoma and Quebec. **2** the extinct Iroquoian language of any of these peoples.

▶*adj.* of or relating to these peoples or their language. ▷French, literally 'having hair standing in bristles on the head,' from Old French *hure* 'head of a wild boar,' of unknown ultimate origin.

Hu·ron, Lake /ˈ(h)yo͝orən; ˈ(h)yo͝orˌän/ the second largest of the five Great Lakes of North America, on the border between Canada and the U.S.

hur·rah /ho͝oˈrä; hə-/ (also **hoo·ray, hur·ray** /-ˈrā/) ▶*exclam.* used to express joy or approval: *Hurrah! She's here at last!*

▶*n.* an utterance of the word "hurrah."

▶*v.* [*intrans.*] shout "hurrah." ▷late 17th cent.: alteration of archaic *huzza*; perhaps originally a sailors' cry when hauling.

Hur·ri /ˈho͝orē/ ▶*plural n.* the Hurrian people collectively. ▷the name in Hittite and Akkadian.

Hur·ri·an /ˈho͝orēən/ ▶*adj.* of, relating to, or denoting an ancient people, originally from Armenia, who settled in Syria and northern Mesopotamia during the 3rd–2nd millennia BC and were later absorbed by the Hittites and Assyrians.

▶*n.* **1** a member of this people. **2** the language of the Hurrians, written in cuneiform and of unknown affinity .

hur·ri·cane /ˈhəriˌkān; ˈhə-ri-/ ▶*n.* a storm with a violent wind, in particular a tropical cyclone in the Caribbean. ■ a wind of force 12 on the Beaufort scale (equal to or exceeding 64 knots or 74 mph). ■ *figurative* a violent uproar or outburst: *the manager resigned in a hurricane of disagreement.* ▷mid 16th cent.: from Spanish *huracán*, probably from Taino *hurakán* 'god of the storm.'

Hur·ri·cane Alley a popular term for areas of the U.S. and the Caribbean, such as Florida and the Gulf Coast, that are prone to hurricanes.

hur·ri·cane deck ▶*n.* a covered deck at or near the top of a ship's superstructure.

hur·ri·cane lamp ▶*n.* an oil lamp with a glass chimney, designed to protect the flame even in high winds.

hur·ri·cane tape ▶*n.* a strong type of adhesive tape used on windows to keep the glass in place if it is broken by strong winds.

hur·ry /ˈhərē; ˈhə-rē/ ▶*v.* (**-ries, -ried**) [*intrans.*] move or act with haste; rush: *we'd better hurry | servants hurried around.* ■ [often in *imperative*] (**hurry up**) do something more quickly: *hurry up and finish your meal.* ■ [*trans.*] cause to move or proceed with haste: *she hurried him across the landing.* ■ [*trans.*] (often **be hurried**) do or finish (something) quickly, typically too quickly: *formalities were hurried over* | [as *adj.*] (**hurried**) *I ate a hurried breakfast.*

▶*n.* great haste: *in my hurry to leave, I knocked over a pile of books.* ■ [with *negative* and in *questions*] a need for haste; urgency: *there's no hurry to get back | relax, what's the hurry?* ▷late 16th cent. (as a verb): imitative. **—hur·ried·ly** *adv.* **—hur·ried·ness** *n.*

▶*PHRASE* □ **in a hurry** rushed; in a rushed manner: *the city offers fast food if you're in a hurry.* ■ eager to get a thing done quickly: *no one seemed in a hurry for the results.* ■ [usu. with *negative*] *informal* easily; readily: *an experience you won't forget in a hurry.*

hur·ry-scur·ry *archaic* ▶*n.* disorderly haste; confused hurrying.

▶*adj.* & *adv.* with hurry and confusion. ▷mid 18th cent.: reduplication of HURRY.

hur·ry-up ▶*adj.* [*attrib.*] *informal* showing, involving, or requiring haste or urgency: *the hurry-up atmosphere of the court contributed to the mistake.*

hurst /hərst/ ▶*n.* a hillock. ■ a sandbank in the sea or a river. ■ [usu. in *place names*] a wood or wooded rise. ▷Old English *hyrst*, of Germanic origin; related to German *Horst*.

Hurs·ton /ˈhərstən/, Zora Neale (1901–60), U.S. novelist. Her novels reflect her interest in folklore, esp. that of the Deep South. Notable works: *Jonah's Gourd Vine* (1934), *Dust Tracks on a Road* (autobiography, 1942), and *Seraph on the Suwanee* (1948).

hurt /hərt/ ▶*v.* (*past* and *past part.* **hurt**) [*trans.*] cause physical pain or injury to: *Ow! You're hurting me!* | [*intrans.*] *does acupuncture hurt?* ■ [*intrans.*] (of a part of the body) suffer pain: *my back hurts.* ■ cause mental pain or distress to (a person or their feelings): *she didn't want to hurt his feelings.* ■ [*intrans.*] (of a person) feel mental pain or distress: *he was hurting badly, but he smiled through his tears.* ■ be detrimental to: *high interest rates are hurting the local economy.* ■ [*intrans.*] (**hurt for**) *informal* have a pressing need for: *Frank wasn't hurting for money.*

▶*n.* physical injury; harm. ■ mental pain or distress: *the hurt of being constantly ignored | wariness that masked a hurt.* ▷Middle English (originally in the senses 'to strike' and 'a blow'): from Old French *hurter* (verb), *hurt* (noun), perhaps ultimately of Germanic origin.

hurt·ful /ˈhərtfəl/ ▶*adj.* causing distress to someone's feelings: *his hurtful remarks.* **—hurt·ful·ly** *adv.* **—hurt·ful·ness** *n.*

hur·tle /ˈhərtl/ ▶*v.* [*intrans.*] move at a great speed, typically in a wildly uncontrolled manner: *a runaway car hurtled toward them.* ■ [*trans.*] cause to move in such a way: *the branch flew off and hurtled us into a ditch.* ▷Middle English (in the sense 'strike against, collide with'): frequentative of HURT.

Hu·sain variant spelling of HUSSEIN[2], HUSSEIN[3].

Hu·sák /ˈho͞osäk/, Gustáv (1913–91), Czech statesman, leader of the Communist Party of Czechoslovakia 1969–87 and president 1975–89.

hus·band /ˈhəzbənd/ ▶*n.* a married man considered in relation to his wife: *she and her husband are both retired.*

▶*v.* [*trans.*] use (resources) economically; conserve: *the need to husband his remaining strength.* ▷late Old English (in the senses 'male head of a household' and 'manager, steward'), from Old Norse *húsbóndi* 'master of a house,' from *hús* 'house' + *bóndi* 'occupier and tiller of the soil.' The original sense of the verb was 'till, cultivate.' **—hus·band·er** *n.* (*rare*). **—hus·band·hood** /-ˌho͝od/ *n.* **—hus·band·less** *adj.* **—hus·band·ly** *adj.*

hus·band·man /ˈhəzbəndmən/ ▶*n.* (*pl.* **-men**) *archaic* a person who cultivates the land; a farmer. ▷Middle English (originally in northern English use denoting the holder of a *husbandland*, i.e., manorial tenancy): from HUSBAND in the obsolete sense 'farmer' + MAN.

hus·band·ry /ˈhəzbəndrē/ ▶*n.* **1** the care, cultivation, and breeding of crops and animals: *crop husbandry.* **2** management and conservation of resources. ▷Middle English: from HUSBAND in the obsolete sense 'farmer' + -RY; compare with HUSBANDMAN.

hush /həSH/ ▶*v.* [*trans.*] make (someone) be quiet or stop talking: *he placed a finger before pursed lips to hush her.* ■ [*intrans.*] be quiet: *Hush! Someone will hear you.* ■ (**hush something up**) suppress public mention of something: *management took steps to hush up the dangers.*

▶*n.* [in *sing.*] a silence: *a hush descended over the crowd.* ▷mid 16th cent.: back-formation from obsolete *husht* 'silent, hushed' (taken to be a past participle), from an interjection *husht* 'quiet!'

hush·a·by /ˈhəSHəˌbī/ (also **hush·a·bye**) ▶*exclam.* *archaic* used to calm a child.

hushed /həSHt/ ▶*adj.* having a calm and still silence: *he addressed the hushed courtroom.* ■ (of a voice or conversation) quiet and serious: *the nurses were talking in hushed voices.*

hush-hush ▶*adj.* *informal* (esp. of an official plan or project) highly secret or confidential: *a hush-hush research unit.*

hush mon·ey ▶*n.* *informal* money paid to someone to prevent them from disclosing embarrassing or discreditable information.

hush pup·py ▶*n.* cornmeal dough that has been quickly deep-fried.

husk /həsk/ ▶*n.* the dry outer covering of some fruits or seeds. ■ a dry or rough outer layer or coating, esp. when empty of its contents: *the husks of dead bugs | figurative I expect whatever husk of a person emerges from the car to be sheet-white.*

▶*v.* **1** [*trans.*] remove the husk or husks from. **2** [with *direct speech*] say something in a husky voice: *"Help me," husked Miles.* ▷late Middle English: probably from Low German *hūske* 'sheath,' literally 'little house.'

husk·ing bee ▶*n.* another term for CORNHUSKING.

husk·y[1] /ˈhəskē/ ▶*adj.* (**husk·i·er, husk·i·est**) **1** (of a voice or utterance) sounding low-pitched and slightly hoarse. **2** strong; hefty: *Patrick looked a husky, strong guy.* **3** like or consisting of a husk or husks. **—husk·i·ly** /ˈhəskəlē/ *adv.* **—husk·i·ness** *n.*

husk·y[2] (also **hus·kie**) ▶*n.* (*pl.* **husk·ies**) a powerful dog of a breed with a thick double coat that is typically gray, used in the Arctic for pulling sleds. ▷mid 19th cent. (originally denoting the Eskimo language or an Eskimo): abbreviation of obsolete *Ehuskemay* or Newfoundland dialect *Huskemaw* 'Eskimo,' probably from Montagnais (see ESKIMO). The term replaced the 18th-cent. term *Eskimo dog*.

Huss /həs; ho͞os/, John (*c.*1372–1415), Bohemian religious reformer; Czech name *Jan Hus*. He supported the views of Wyclif, attacked ecclesiastical abuses, and was excommunicated in 1411. He was later tried and burned at the stake. See also HUSSITE.

hus·sar /həˈzär/ ▶*n.* *historical* (in the 15th century) a Hungarian light horseman. ■ a soldier in a light cavalry regiment that had adopted a dress uniform modeled on that of the Hungarian hussars. ▷from Hungarian *huszár*, from Old Serbian *husar*, from Italian *corsaro* (see CORSAIR).

Hus·sein[1], Abdullah ibn, see ABDULLAH IBN HUSSEIN.

Hus·sein[2] /ho͞oˈsān/ (also **Hu·sain**), ibn Talal (1935–99), king of Jordan 1953–99. Hussein sought to maintain good relations both with the West and with other Arab nations, but his moderate policies created problems with Palestinian refugees from Israel within Jordan. During the Gulf War, he supported Iraq, but in 1994 he signed a treaty that normalized relations with Israel. He was succeeded by his son ABDULLAH.

Hus·sein[3] (also **Hu·sain**), Saddam (1937–), Iraqi president; prime minister and head of the armed forces 1979–2003; full name *Saddam bin Hussein at-Takriti*. During his presidency, Iraq fought a war with Iran 1980–88 and invaded Kuwait 1990, from which Iraqi forces were expelled in the Gulf War of 1991. His regime was known for its brutality, and the UN imposed economic sanctions against the country in 1990. Believing that Saddam was developing weapons of mass destruction, the U.S., with coalition forces, invaded Iraq in March 2003. Saddam was captured and imprisoned in December 2003.

Huss·ite /ˈhəsīt/ ▶*n.* a member or follower of the religious movement begun by John Huss. After Huss's execution the Hussites took up arms against the Holy Roman Empire and demanded a set of reforms that anticipated the Reformation. Most of the demands were granted 1436, and a church was established that remained independent of the Roman Catholic Church until 1620.

▶*adj.* of or relating to the Hussites. **—Huss·it·ism** /ˈhəsīˌtizəm/ *n.*

hus·sy /ˈhəsē; ˈhəzē/ ▶*n.* (*pl.* **-sies**) an impudent or immoral girl or woman: *that brazen little hussy!* ▷late Middle English: contraction of HOUSEWIFE (the original sense); the current sense dates from the mid 17th cent.

hust·ings /ˈhəstiNGz/ ▸n. (pl. same) a meeting at which candidates in an election address potential voters. ■ the campaigning associated with an election: *a formidable political operator at his best* ***on the hustings.*** ▷late Old English *husting* 'deliberative assembly, council,' from Old Norse *hústhing* 'household assembly held by a leader,' from *hús* 'house' + *thing* 'assembly, parliament'; *hustings* was applied in Middle English to the highest court of the City of London, England. Subsequently it denoted the platform where the Lord Mayor and aldermen presided and (early 18th cent.) a temporary platform on which parliamentary candidates were nominated; hence the sense 'electoral proceedings.'

hus·tle /ˈhəsəl/ ▸v. **1** [trans.] force (someone) to move hurriedly or unceremoniously in a specified direction: *they hustled him into the back of a horse-drawn wagon.* ■ [trans.] push roughly; jostle: *they were hissed and hustled as they went in.* ■ [intrans.] hurry; bustle: *he had to retag second base and hustle back to first.* **2** [trans.] informal obtain by forceful action or persuasion: *the brothers headed to New York to try and hustle a record deal.* ■ (**hustle someone into**) coerce or pressure someone into doing or choosing something: *don't be hustled into anything.* ■ sell aggressively: *he hustled his company's oil around the country.* ■ obtain by illicit action; swindle; cheat: *Linda hustled money from men she met.* **3** [intrans.] informal engage in prostitution.
▸n. **1** busy movement and activity: *the* ***hustle and bustle*** *of the big cities.* ■ energetic effort: *he forced a turnover with his hustle, diving after a loose ball.* **2** informal a fraud or swindle. ▷late 17th cent. (originally in the sense 'shake, toss'): from Middle Dutch *hutselen.* Sense 3 dates from the early 20th cent.
▸PHRASE □ **hustle one's butt** (or vulgar slang **ass**) informal move or act quickly.

hus·tler /ˈhəslər/ ▸n. informal an aggressively enterprising person; a go-getter. ■ an enterprising and often dishonest person, esp. one trying to sell something. ■ an expert player, esp. at pool or billiards, who pretends to be less skillful than they are and lures or challenges less skilled, esp. amateur, players into games in order to win money from them. ■ a female prostitute. ■ a male prostitute, esp. for homosexual clients.

Hus·ton /ˈhyo͞ostən/, John (1906–87), U.S. movie director; an Irish citizen from 1964. After a varied background as a boxer, cavalryman, journalist, and actor, he made his debut as a movie director in 1941 with *The Maltese Falcon.* Other notable movies include *The African Queen* (1951) and *Prizzi's Honor* (1985). His father, **Walter** (1884–1950) was an actor who won an Academy Award for his performance in *Treasure of the Sierra Madre* (1948), and his daughter, **Anjelica** (1951–) had leading roles in such movies as *Prizzi's Honor* (Academy Award, 1985), *The Addams Family* (1991), and *The Royal Tenenbaums* (2001).

hut /hət/ ▸n. a small single-story building of simple or crude construction, serving as a poor, rough, or temporary house or shelter.
▸v. (**hut·ted, hut·ting**) [trans.] provide with huts: [as adj.] (**hutted**) *a hutted encampment.* ▷mid 16th cent. (in the sense 'temporary wooden shelter for troops'): from French *hutte,* from Middle High German *hütte.* —**hut·like** /-ˌlīk/ adj.

hutch /həCH/ ▸n. **1** a box or cage, typically with a wire mesh front, for keeping rabbits, ferrets, or other small domesticated animals: *a rabbit hutch.* **2** a storage chest. ■ a cupboard or dresser typically with open shelves above. ▷Middle English: from Old French *huche,* from medieval Latin *hutica,* of unknown origin. The original sense was 'storage chest' (sense 2).

Hutch·in·son[1] /ˈhəCHənsən/ a city in south central Kansas; pop. 40,787.

Hutch·in·son[2], Anne Marbury (1591–1643) American religious leader; born in England. She was banished from Massachusetts Bay Colony in 1637 for her liberal views on grace and salvation. First moving to Rhode Island and then settling in New York in 1642, she and most of her family were killed by Indians.

hut·ment /ˈhətmənt/ ▸n. Military an encampment of huts.

Hut·son /ˈhətsən/, Don (1913–97) U.S. football player. He was a receiver as well as a safety and a kicker for the Green Bay Packers 1935–45. Football Hall of Fame (1963).

Hut·ter·ite /ˈhətəˌrīt/ ▸n. a member of either an Anabaptist Christian sect established in Moravia in the early 16th century, or a North American community holding similar beliefs and practicing an old-fashioned communal way of life.
▸adj. of or relating to Hutterites or their beliefs and practices. ▷from the name of Jacob *Hutter* (died 1536), a Moravian Anabaptist, + **-ITE**[1].

Hut·ton /ˈhətn/, James (1726–97), Scottish geologist. Although controversial at the time, his description of the processes that have shaped the surface of the earth is now accepted as showing that it is very much older than had previously been believed.

Hu·tu /ˈho͞otoo͞/ ▸n. (pl. same or **Hu·tus** or **Ba·hu·tu** /bəˈho͞oto͞o/) a member of a Bantu-speaking people forming the majority population in Rwanda and Burundi. They are traditionally a farming people and were historically dominated by the Tutsi people; the antagonism between the peoples led in 1994 to large-scale ethnic violence, esp. in Rwanda.
▸adj. of or relating to this people. ▷a local name.

Hux·ley[1] /ˈhəkslē/, Aldous (Leonard) (1894–1963), English novelist and essayist. After writing *Antic Hay* (1923) and *Brave New World* (1932), he moved to California in 1937, where he experimented with psychedelic drugs in 1953 and wrote of his experiences in *The Doors of Perception* (1954).

Hux·ley[2], Andrew Fielding (1917–), British physiologist, the grandson of Thomas Henry Huxley. He worked with Sir Alan Hodgkin on the physiology of nerve transmission. Nobel Prize for Physiology or Medicine (1963, shared with John C. Eccles and A. L. Hodgkin).

Hux·ley[3], Thomas Henry (1825–95), English biologist. A surgeon and leading supporter of Darwinism, he coined the word *agnostic* to describe his own beliefs.

Huy·gens /ˈhoigənz/, Christiaan (1629–95), Dutch physicist, mathematician, and astronomer. His wave theory of light enabled him to explain reflection and refraction.

huz·zah /həˈzä/ (also **huz·za**) archaic ▸exclam. used to express approval or delight; hurrah.
▸v. [intrans.] cry "huzzah." ▷late 16th cent.: perhaps used originally as a sailor's cry when hauling.

HV (also **h.v.**) ▸abbr. ■ high velocity. ■ high voltage.

hvy. ▸abbr. heavy.

HW ▸abbr. ■ hardwood. ■ high water. ■ hot water (heat).

HWM ▸abbr. high-water mark.

hwy ▸abbr. highway.

hy·a·cinth /ˈhīəˌsinTH/ ▸n. **1** a bulbous plant of the lily family, with straplike leaves and a compact spike of bell-shaped fragrant flowers. Native to western Asia, hyacinths are cultivated outdoors and as houseplants. • Genus *Hyacinthus,* family Liliaceae: several species, in particular *H. orientalis,* from which the common large-flowered cultivars are derived. ■ a light purplish-blue color typical of some hyacinth flowers. **2** another term for **JACINTH**. ▷mid 16th cent. (denoting a gem): from French *hyacinthe,* via Latin from Greek *huakinthos,* denoting any of various plants identified with the flower in the myth of **HYACINTHUS**, and a gem (perhaps the sapphire). The current sense dates from the late 16th cent. —**hy·a·cin·thine** /ˌhīəˈsinTHin; -ˌTHīn/ adj.

hyacinth

hy·a·cinth bean ▸n. a tropical Asian plant of the pea family, widely grown as an ornamental or for its edible seeds and pods and as a fodder crop. • *Lablab purpureus* (or *Dolichos lablab*), family Leguminosae.

Hy·a·cin·thus /ˌhīəˈsinTHəs/ Greek Mythology a beautiful boy whom the god Apollo loved but killed accidentally with a discus. From his blood Apollo caused the hyacinth to spring up.

Hy·a·des /ˈhīˌdēz/ Astronomy an open star cluster in the constellation Taurus, appearing to surround the bright star Aldebaran. ▷from Greek *Huades,* by folk etymology from *huein* 'to rain,' but perhaps from *hus* 'pig,' the Latin name of the constellation being *Suculae* 'little pigs.'

hy·ae·na ▸n. variant spelling of **HYENA**.

hy·a·lin /ˈhīəlin/ ▸n. Physiology a clear substance produced esp. by the degeneration of epithelial or connective tissues. ▷mid 19th cent.: via Latin from Greek *hualinos,* from *hualos* 'glass.'

hy·a·line /ˈhīəlin; -ˌlīn/ ▸adj. Anatomy & Zoology having a glassy, translucent appearance. ■ relating to, consisting of, or characterized by hyaline material.
▸n. **1** (**the hyaline**) poetic/literary a thing that is clear and translucent like glass, esp. a smooth sea or a clear sky. **2** another term for **HYALIN**. ▷mid 17th cent.: from Latin *hyalinus* (see **HYALIN**).

hy·a·line car·ti·lage ▸n. a translucent bluish-white type of cartilage present in the joints, the respiratory tract, and the immature skeleton.

hy·a·line mem·brane dis·ease ▸n. a condition in newborn babies in which the lungs are deficient in surfactant, preventing their proper expansion and causing the formation of hyaline material in the lung spaces. Also called **RESPIRATORY DISTRESS SYNDROME**.

hy·a·lite /ˈhīəˌlīt/ ▸n. a translucent, colorless variety of opal. ▷late 18th cent.: from Greek *hualos* 'glass' + **-ITE**[1].

hy·a·loid /ˈhīəˌloid/ ▸adj. Anatomy glassy; transparent. ▷mid 19th cent.: from French *hyaloïde,* or via late Latin from Greek *hualoeidēs* 'like glass,' from *hualos* 'glass.'

hy·a·loid mem·brane ▸n. a thin transparent membrane enveloping the vitreous humor of the eye.

hy·a·lu·ron·ic ac·id /ˌhīəlo͞oˈränik/ ▸n. Biochemistry a viscous fluid carbohydrate present in connective tissue, synovial fluid, and the humors of the eye. ▷1930s: *hyaluronic* from a blend of **HYALOID** and **URONIC ACID**. —**hy·a·lu·ro·nate** /hīəˈlo͝orəˌnāt/ n.

Hy·an·nis /hīˈanis/ a commercial village in southeastern Massachusetts, on Cape Cod; pop. 14,120.

hy·brid /ˈhīˌbrid/ ▸n. a thing made by combining two different elements; a mixture: *the final text is a* ***hybrid of*** *the stage play and the film.* ■ Biology the offspring of two plants or animals of different species or varieties, such as a mule (a hybrid of a donkey and a horse): *a* ***hybrid of*** *wheat and rye.* ■ offensive a person of mixed racial or cultural origin. ■ a word formed from elements taken from different languages, for example *television* (*tele-* from Greek, *vision* from Latin). ■ a hybrid car.
▸adj. of mixed character; composed of mixed parts: *Mexico's hybrid postconquest culture.* ■ bred as a hybrid from different species or varieties: *a hybrid variety | hybrid offspring.* ▷early 17th cent. (as a noun): from Latin *hybrida* 'offspring of a tame sow and wild boar, child of a freeman and slave, etc.' —**hy·brid·ism** /ˈhībrəˌdizəm/ n. —**hy·brid·i·ty** /hīˈbriditē/ n.

hy·brid car ▸n. a car with a gasoline engine and an electric motor, each of which can propel it.

hy·brid·ize /ˈhībriˌdīz/ ▸v. **1** [trans.] crossbreed (individuals of two different species or varieties). ■ [intrans.] (of an animal or plant) breed with an individual of another species or variety. **2** [intrans.] Biochemistry form a double-stranded nucleic acid structure from a single-stranded mixture by complementary base pairing. —**hy·brid·iz·a·ble** adj. —**hy·brid·i·za·tion** /ˌhībrədiˈzāSHən/ n.

hy·brid vig·or ▸n. another term for **HETEROSIS**.

hyd. ▸abbr. ■ hydraulics. ■ hydrostatics.

hy·dan·to·in /hīˈdantō-ən/ ▸n. Chemistry a crystalline compound present in sugar beet and used in the manufacture of some anticonvulsant drugs. • A cyclic derivative of urea; chem. formula: $C_3H_4N_2O_2$. ▷mid 19th cent.: from Greek *hudōr* 'water' + *allantoic* (see **ALLANTOIS**) + **-IN**[1].

hy·da·thode /ˈhīdəˌTHōd/ ▸n. Botany a modified pore, esp. on a leaf, that exudes drops of water. ▷late 19th cent.: from Greek *hudōr, hudat-* 'water' + *hodos* 'way.'

hy·da·tid /ˈhīdətid/ ▸n. Medicine a cyst containing watery fluid. ■ such a cyst formed by and containing a tapeworm larva. ■ a tapeworm larva. ▷late 17th cent.: from modern Latin *hydatis,* from Greek *hudatis, hudatid-* 'watery vesicle,' from *hudōr, hudat-* 'water.'

hy·da·tid·i·form mole /ˌhīdəˈtitəˌfôrm/ ▸n. Medicine a cluster of fluid-filled sacs formed in the uterus by the degeneration of chorionic tissue around an aborting embryo.

Hyde[1] /hīd/, Edward, see **CLARENDON**.

Hyde[2], Mr., see **JEKYLL**[1].

Hyde Park /hīd/ **1** a town in southeastern New York, on the Hudson River, north of Poughkeepsie,

Pronunciation Key ə *ago;* ər *over;* ˈə or ˌə *up;* ˈər or ˌər *fur;* a *hat;* ā *rate;* ä *car;* CH *chew;* e *let;* ē *see;* e(ə)r *air;* i *fit;* ī *by;* i(ə)r *ear;* NG *sing;* ō *go;* ô *for;* oi *boy;* o͝o *good;* o͞o *goo;* ou *out;* SH *she;* TH *thin;* T͟H *then;* (h)w *why;* ZH *vision*

H

associated with the family of Franklin D. Roosevelt; pop. 21,320. **2** a park in western central London, England.

Hy·der·a·bad /ˈhīd(ə)rəˌbad; -ˌbäd/ **1** a city in central India, capital of the state of Andhra Pradesh; pop. 3,005,000. **2** a former large princely state in southern central India, divided in 1956 between Maharashtra, Mysore, and Andhra Pradesh. **3** a city in southeastern Pakistan, in the province of Sind, on the Indus River; pop. 1,000,000.

hydr- ▸*comb. form* variant spelling of HYDRO- shortened before a vowel (as in *hydraulic*).

Hy·dra /ˈhīdrə/ **1** *Greek Mythology* a many-headed snake whose heads grew again as they were cut off, killed by Hercules. ■ [as *n.*] (**hydra**) a thing that is hard to overcome or resist because of its pervasive or enduring quality or its many aspects. **2** *Astronomy* the largest constellation (the Water Snake or Sea Monster), said to represent the beast slain by Hercules. Its few bright stars are close to the celestial equator. Compare with HYDRUS. ■ [as *genitive*] (**Hydrae** /-drē/) used with a preceding letter or numeral to designate a star in this constellation: *the star Beta Hydrae.* ▷via Latin from Greek *hudra.*

hy·dra /ˈhīdrə/ ▸*n.* a minute freshwater coelenterate with a stalklike tubular body and a ring of tentacles around the mouth. • Genus *Hydra*, class Hydrozoa. ▷via Latin from Greek *hudra* 'water snake' (see HYDRA), named by Linnaeus because, if cut into pieces, each section can grow into a whole animal.

hy·dram·ni·os /hīˈdramnēˌäs/ ▸*n. Medicine* a condition in which excess amniotic fluid accumulates during pregnancy.

hy·dran·gea /hīˈdrānjə/ ▸*n.* a shrub or climbing plant with rounded or flattened flowering heads of small florets, the outer ones of which are typically infertile. Hydrangeas are native to Asia and America. • Genus *Hydrangea*, family Hydrangeaceae: many species, in particular **late** (or **panicled**) **hydrangea** (*H. paniculata*), an ornamental shrub that blooms in late summer, and **bigleaf hydrangea** (*H. macrophylla*), commonly grown for florists and as a houseplant. ▷modern Latin, from Greek *hudro-* 'water' + *angeion* 'vessel' (from the cup shape of its seed capsule).

hydrangea

hy·drant /ˈhīdrənt/ ▸*n.* an upright water pipe, esp. one in a street, with a nozzle to which a fire hose can be attached. ▷early 19th cent. (originally U.S.): formed irregularly from HYDRO- 'relating to water' + -ANT.

hy·drate /ˈhīˌdrāt/ ▸*n. Chemistry* a compound, typically a crystalline one, in which water molecules are chemically bound to another compound or an element.
▸*v.* [*trans.*] cause to absorb water. ■ *Chemistry* combine chemically with water molecules: [as *adj.*] (**hydrated**) *hydrated silicate crystals.* ▷early 19th cent.: coined in French from Greek *hudōr* 'water.' —**hy·drat·a·ble** *adj.* —**hy·dra·tion** /hīˈdrāshən/ *n.* —**hy·dra·tor** /-tər/ *n.*

hy·drau·lic /hīˈdrôlik/ ▸*adj.* **1** denoting, relating to, or operated by a liquid moving in a confined space under pressure: *hydraulic fluid* | *hydraulic lifting gear.* **2** of or relating to the science of hydraulics. **3** (of cement) hardening under water. ▷early 17th cent.: via Latin from Greek *hudraulikos*, from *hudro-* 'water' + *aulos* 'pipe.' —**hy·drau·li·cal·ly** /-(ə)lē/ *adv.*

hy·drau·lic frac·tur·ing ▸*n.* the forcing open of fissures in subterranean rocks by introducing liquid at high pressure, esp. to extract oil or gas.

hy·drau·lic ram ▸*n.* an automatic pump in which a large volume of water flows through a valve that it periodically forces shut, the sudden pressure change being used to raise a smaller volume of water to a higher level.

hy·drau·lics /hīˈdrôliks/ ▸*plural n.* **1** [usu. treated as *sing.*] the branch of science and technology concerned with the conveyance of liquids through pipes and channels, esp. as a source of mechanical force or control. **2** hydraulic systems, mechanisms, or forces.

hy·dra·zine /ˈhīdrəˌzēn/ ▸*n. Chemistry* a colorless volatile alkaline liquid with powerful reducing properties, used in chemical synthesis and in some kinds of rocket fuels. • Chem. formula: N_2H_4. ▷late 19th cent.: from HYDROGEN + AZO- + -INE[4].

hy·dric /ˈhīdrik/ ▸*adj. Ecology* (of an environment or habitat) containing plenty of moisture; very wet. Compare with MESIC[1] and XERIC. ▷early 20th cent.: from HYDRO- + -IC.

hy·dride /ˈhīˌdrīd/ ▸*n. Chemistry* a binary compound of hydrogen with a metal.

hy·dri·od·ic ac·id /ˌhīdrēˈädik/ ▸*n. Chemistry* a strongly acidic solution of the gas hydrogen iodide in water. • Chem. formula: HI. ▷early 19th cent.: *hydriodic* from a blend of HYDROGEN and IODINE.

hy·dro /ˈhīdrō/ ▸*n.* (*pl.* **-dros**) **1** a hydroelectric power plant. ■ hydroelectricity. ■ *Canadian* electricity. **2** *Brit.* a hotel or clinic originally providing hydropathic treatment.
▸*adj.* relating to or denoting hydroelectricity: *hydro and steam energy.* ▷late 19th cent.: abbreviation.

hydro- (also **hydr-**) ▸*comb. form* **1** water; relating to water: *hydraulic* | *hydrocolloid.* ■ *Medicine* affected with an accumulation of serous fluid: *hydrocephalus.* **2** *Chemistry* combined with hydrogen: *hydrocarbon.* ▷from Greek *hudōr* 'water.'

hy·dro·bro·mic ac·id /ˌhīdrəˈbrōmik/ ▸*n. Chemistry* a strongly acidic solution of the gas hydrogen bromide in water. • Chem. formula: HBr.

hy·dro·car·bon /ˈhīdrəˌkärbən/ ▸*n. Chemistry* a compound of hydrogen and carbon, such as any of those that are the chief components of petroleum and natural gas.

hy·dro·cele /ˈhīdrəˌsēl/ ▸*n. Medicine* the accumulation of serous fluid in a body sac.

hy·dro·ceph·a·lus /ˌhīdrōˈsefələs/ ▸*n. Medicine* a condition in which fluid accumulates in the brain, typically in young children, enlarging the head and sometimes causing brain damage. ▷late 17th cent.: modern Latin, from Greek *hudrokephalon*, from *hudro-* 'water' + *kephalē* 'head.' —**hy·dro·ce·phal·ic** /ˌhīdrōsəˈfalik/ *adj.* —**hy·dro·ceph·a·ly** /-ˈsefəlē/ *n.*

hy·dro·chlo·ric ac·id /ˌhīdrəˈklôrik/ ▸*n. Chemistry* a strongly acidic solution of the gas hydrogen chloride in water. • Chem. formula: HCl.

hy·dro·chlo·ride /ˌhīdrəˈklôˌrīd/ ▸*n. Chemistry* a compound of a particular organic base with hydrochloric acid: [with *adj.*] *cocaine hydrochloride.*

hy·dro·chlo·ro·fluor·o·car·bon /ˌhīdrōˌklôrōˈflo͝orōˌkärbən/ (abbr.: **HCFC**) ▸*n. Chemistry* any of a class of inert compounds of carbon, hydrogen, hydrocarbons, chlorine, and fluorine, used in place of chlorofluorocarbons as being somewhat less destructive to the ozone layer.

hy·dro·col·loid /ˌhīdrōˈkäˌloid/ ▸*n.* a substance that forms a gel in the presence of water, examples of which are used in surgical dressings and in various industrial applications.

hy·dro·cor·ti·sone /ˌhīdrəˈkôrtiˌzōn/ ▸*n. Biochemistry* a steroid hormone produced by the adrenal cortex and used medicinally to treat inflammation resulting from eczema and rheumatism.

hy·dro·cy·an·ic ac·id /ˌhīdrōsīˈanik/ ▸*n. Chemistry* a highly poisonous acidic solution of hydrogen cyanide in water.

hy·dro·dy·nam·ics /ˌhīdrōdīˈnamiks/ ▸*plural n.* [treated as *sing.*] the branch of science concerned with forces acting on or exerted by fluids (esp. liquids). ▷late 18th cent.: from modern Latin *hydrodynamica*, from Greek *hudro-* 'water' + *dunamikos* (see DYNAMIC). —**hy·dro·dy·nam·ic** *adj.* —**hy·dro·dy·nam·i·cal** /-ˈnamikəl/ *adj.* —**hy·dro·dy·nam·i·cist** /-ˈnamisist/ *n.*

hy·dro·e·lec·tric /ˌhīdrōəˈlektrik/ ▸*adj.* relating to or denoting the generation of electricity using flowing water (typically from a reservoir held behind a dam or other barrier) to drive a turbine that powers a generator. —**hy·dro·e·lec·tric·i·ty** /-ˌelekˈtrisitē/ *n.*

hy·dro·fluor·ic ac·id /ˌhīdrəˌflo͝orik/ ▸*n. Chemistry* an acidic and extremely corrosive solution of the liquid hydrogen fluoride in water. • Chem. formula: HF.

hy·dro·fluor·o·car·bon /ˌhīdrōˈflo͝orəˌkärbən/ (abbr.: **HFC**) ▸*n. Chemistry* any of a class of partly chlorinated and fluorinated hydrocarbons, used as an alternative to chlorofluorocarbons in foam production, refrigeration, and other processes.

hy·dro·foil /ˈhīdrəˌfoil/ ▸*n.* a boat whose hull is fitted underneath with shaped vanes (foils) that lift the hull clear of the water to increase the boat's speed. ■ another term for FOIL[4]. ▷1920s: from HYDRO- 'relating to water' + FOIL[4].

hy·dro·frac·tur·ing /ˈhīdrəˌfrakCHəriNG/ ▸*n.* another term for HYDRAULIC FRACTURING.

hy·dro·gel /ˈhīdrəˌjel/ ▸*n.* a gel in which the liquid component is water.

hy·dro·gen /ˈhīdrəjən/ ▸*n.* a colorless, odorless, highly flammable gas, the chemical element of atomic number 1. (Symbol: **H**)

Hydrogen is the lightest of the chemical elements and has the simplest atomic structure, a single electron orbiting a nucleus consisting of a single proton. It is by far the commonest element in the universe, although not on the earth, where it occurs chiefly combined with oxygen as water.

▷late 18th cent.: coined in French from Greek *hudro-* 'water' + *-genēs* (see -GEN). —**hy·drog·e·nous** /hīˈdräjənəs/ *adj.*

hy·drog·e·nase /ˈhīdrəjəˌnās; hīˈdräjə-/ ▸*n.* [usu. with *adj.*] *Biochemistry* an enzyme that catalyzes the reduction of a particular substance by hydrogen.

hy·dro·gen·ate /ˈhīdrəjəˌnāt; hīˈdräjənāt/ ▸*v.* [*trans.*] [often as *adj.*] (**hydrogenated**) charge with or cause to combine with hydrogen. —**hy·dro·gen·a·tion** /ˌhīdrəjəˈnāSHən; hīˌdräjə-/ *n.*

hy·dro·gen bomb ▸*n.* an immensely powerful bomb whose destructive power comes from the rapid release of energy during the nuclear fusion of isotopes of hydrogen (deuterium and tritium), using an atom bomb as a trigger. Compare with ATOM BOMB.

hy·dro·gen bond ▸*n. Chemistry* a weak bond between two molecules resulting from an electrostatic attraction between a proton in one molecule and an electronegative atom in the other.

hy·dro·gen cy·a·nide ▸*n. Chemistry* a highly poisonous gas or volatile liquid with an odor of bitter almonds, made by the action of acids on cyanides. • Chem. formula: HCN.

hy·dro·gen per·ox·ide ▸*n. Chemistry* a colorless, viscous, unstable liquid with strong oxidizing properties, commonly used in diluted form in disinfectants and bleaches. • Chem. formula: H_2O_2.

hy·dro·gen sul·fide ▸*n. Chemistry* a colorless poisonous gas with a smell of rotten eggs, made by the action of acids on sulfides. • Chem. formula: H_2S.

hy·dro·ge·ol·o·gy /ˌhīdrəjēˈäləjē/ ▸*n.* the branch of geology concerned with water occurring underground or on the surface of the earth. —**hy·dro·ge·o·log·i·cal** /-ˌjēəˈläjikəl/ *adj.* —**hy·dro·ge·ol·o·gist** /-jist/ *n.*

hy·drog·ra·phy /hīˈdrägrəfē/ ▸*n.* the science of surveying and charting bodies of water, such as seas, lakes, and rivers. —**hy·drog·ra·pher** /-fər/ *n.* —**hy·dro·graph·ic** /ˌhīdrəˈgrafik/ *adj.* —**hy·dro·graph·i·cal** /ˌhīdrəˈgrafikəl/ *adj.* —**hy·dro·graph·i·cal·ly** /ˌhīdrəˈgrafik(ə)lē/ *adv.*

hy·droid /ˈhīˌdroid/ *Zoology* ▸*n.* a coelenterate of an order that includes the hydras. They are distinguished by the dominance of the polyp phase. • Order Hydroida, class Hydrozoa.
▸*adj.* of or relating to coelenterates of this group. ■ another term for POLYPOID (sense 1). ▷mid 19th cent.: from HYDRA + -OID.

hy·dro·lase /ˈhīdrəˌlās; -ˌlāz/ ▸*n.* [usu. with *adj.*] *Biochemistry* an enzyme that catalyzes the hydrolysis of a particular substrate.

hy·drol·o·gy /hīˈdräləjē/ ▸*n.* the branch of science concerned with the properties of the earth's water, esp. its movement in relation to land. —**hy·dro·log·ic** /ˌhīdrəˈläjik/ *adj.* —**hy·dro·log·i·cal** /ˌhīdrəˈläjikəl/ *adj.* —**hy·dro·log·i·cal·ly** /ˌhīdrəˈläjik(ə)lē/ *adv.* —**hy·drol·o·gist** /-jist/ *n.*

hy·drol·y·sate /hīˈdräləˌsāt/ ▸*n. Chemistry* a substance produced by hydrolysis.

hy·drol·y·sis /hīˈdräləsis/ ▸*n. Chemistry* the chemical breakdown of a compound due to reaction with water. —**hy·dro·lyt·ic** /ˌhīdrəˈlitik/ *adj.*

hy·dro·lyze /ˈhīdrəˌlīz/ (*Brit.* **hy·dro·lyse**) ▸*v.* [*trans.*] *Chemistry* break down (a compound) by chemical reaction with water. ■ [*intrans.*] undergo this process.

hy·dro·mag·net·ics /ˌhīdrōmagˈnetiks/ ▸*plural n.* another term for MAGNETOHYDRODYNAMICS. —**hy·dro·mag·net·ic** *adj.*

hy·dro·man·cy /ˈhīdrəˌmansē/ ▸*n.* divination by means of signs derived from the appearance of water and its movements.

hydrofoil

hy·dro·mas·sage /ˌhīdrōmə'säzh; -'säj/ ▸ *n.* massage using jets of water, as a health or beauty treatment.

hy·dro·me·chan·ics /ˌhīdrōmə'kaniks/ ▸ *plural n.* [treated as *sing.*] the mechanics of liquids; hydrodynamics, esp. in relation to mechanical applications. —**hy·dro·me·chan·i·cal** /-'kanikəl/ *adj.*

hy·dro·me·du·sa /ˌhīdrōmə'd(y)o͞osə; -zə/ ▸ *n.* (*pl.* **-sae** /-ˌsē; -ˌzē/) *Zoology* the medusoid phase of a hydroid coelenterate.

hy·dro·mel /'hīdrəˌmel/ ▸ *n. historical* a drink similar to mead, made with fermented honey and water. ▷late Middle English: from Latin, from Greek *hudromeli*, from *hudro-* 'water' + *meli* 'honey.'

hy·dro·me·te·or /ˌhīdrō'mētēər/ ▸ *n. Meteorology* an atmospheric phenomenon or entity involving water or water vapor, such as rain or a cloud.

hy·drom·e·ter /hī'drämitər/ ▸ *n.* an instrument for measuring the density of liquids. —**hy·dro·met·ric** /ˌhīdrə'metrik/ *adj.* —**hy·drom·e·try** /-itrē/ *n.*

hy·dron·ic /hī'dränik/ ▸ *adj.* denoting a cooling or heating system in which heat is transported using circulating water.

hy·dro·ni·um i·on /hī'drōnēəm/ ▸ *n. Chemistry* the ion H_3O^+, consisting of a protonated water molecule and present in all aqueous acids. ▷early 20th cent.: *hydronium*, from German (a contraction).

hy·drop·a·thy /hī'dräpəTHē/ ▸ *n.* the treatment of illness through the use of water, either internally or through external means such as steam baths (not now a part of orthodox medicine). Compare with **HYDROTHERAPY**. ▷mid 19th cent.: from **HYDRO-** 'of water,' on the pattern of *allopathy* and *homeopathy*. —**hy·dro·path·ic** /ˌhīdrə'paTHik/ *adj.* —**hy·drop·a·thist** /-THist/ *n.*

hy·dro·phil·ic /ˌhīdrə'filik/ ▸ *adj.* having a tendency to mix with, dissolve in, or be wetted by water. The opposite of **HYDROPHOBIC**. —**hy·dro·phi·lic·i·ty** /-fə'lisitē/ *n.*

hy·droph·i·lous /hī'dräfələs/ ▸ *adj. Botany* (of a plant) water-pollinated. —**hy·droph·i·ly** /-'dräfəlē/ *n.*

hy·dro·pho·bi·a /ˌhīdrə'fōbēə/ ▸ *n.* extreme or irrational fear of water, esp. as a symptom of rabies in humans. ■ rabies, esp. in humans. ▷late Middle English: via late Latin from Greek *hudrophobia*, from *hudro-* 'water' + *phobos* 'fear.'

hy·dro·pho·bic /ˌhīdrə'fōbik/ ▸ *adj.* **1** tending to repel or fail to mix with water. The opposite of **HYDROPHILIC**. **2** of or suffering from hydrophobia. —**hy·dro·pho·bic·i·ty** /-fō'bisitē/ *n.*

hy·dro·phone /'hīdrəˌfōn/ ▸ *n.* a microphone that detects sound waves under water.

hy·dro·phyte /'hīdrəˌfīt/ ▸ *n. Botany* a plant that grows only in or on water. —**hy·dro·phyt·ic** /ˌhīdrə'fitik/ *adj.*

hy·dro·plane /'hīdrəˌplān/ ▸ *n.* **1** a light fast motorboat designed to skim over the surface of water. **2** a finlike attachment that enables a moving submarine to rise or fall in the water. **3** a seaplane.
▸ *v.* [*intrans.*] **1** (of a vehicle) slide uncontrollably on the wet surface of a road: *a motorist whose car hydroplaned and crashed into a tree.* **2** (of a boat) skim over the surface of water with its hull lifted.

hy·dro·pon·ics /ˌhīdrə'päniks/ ▸ *plural n.* [treated as *sing.*] the process of growing plants in sand, gravel, or liquid, with added nutrients but without soil. ▷1930s: from **HYDRO-** 'of water' + Greek *ponos* 'labor' + **-ICS**. —**hy·dro·pon·ic** *adj.* —**hy·dro·pon·i·cal·ly** /-'pänik(ə)lē/ *adv.*

hy·dro·pow·er /'hīdrəˌpouər/ ▸ *n.* hydroelectric power.

hy·dro·qui·none /ˌhīdrōkwi'nōn; -'kwinˌōn/ ▸ *n. Chemistry* a crystalline compound made by the reduction of benzoquinone. • Alternative name: **benzene-1,4-diol**; chem. formula: $C_6H_4(OH)_2$.

hy·dro·sphere /'hīdrəˌsfir/ ▸ *n.* (usu. **the hydrosphere**) all the waters on the earth's surface, such as lakes and seas, and sometimes including water over the earth's surface, such as clouds.

hy·dro·stat·ic /ˌhīdrə'statik/ ▸ *adj.* relating to or denoting the equilibrium of liquids and the pressure exerted by liquid at rest. ▷late 17th cent.: probably from Greek *hudrostatēs* 'hydrostatic balance,' from *hudro-* 'water' + *statikos* (see **STATIC**). —**hy·dro·stat·i·cal** *adj.* —**hy·dro·stat·i·cal·ly** /ik(ə)lē/ *adv.*

hy·dro·stat·ics /ˌhīdrə'statiks/ ▸ *plural n.* [treated as *sing.*] the branch of mechanics concerned with the hydrostatic properties of liquids.

hy·dro·sul·fite /ˌhīdrō'səlˌfīt/ ▸ *n.* another term for **DITHIONITE**.

hy·dro·ther·a·py /ˌhīdrə'THerəpē/ ▸ *n.* another term for **HYDROPATHY**. ■ the use of exercises in a pool as part of treatment for conditions such as arthritis or partial paralysis. —**hy·dro·ther·a·pist** /-pist/ *n.*

hy·dro·ther·mal /ˌhīdrə'THərməl/ ▸ *adj.* of, relating to, or denoting the action of heated water in the earth's crust. —**hy·dro·ther·mal·ly** *adv.*

hy·dro·ther·mal vent ▸ *n.* an opening in the sea floor out of which heated mineral-rich water flows.

hy·dro·tho·rax /ˌhīdrə'THôˌraks/ ▸ *n.* the condition of having fluid in the pleural cavity.

hy·drot·ro·pism /ˌhī'drätrəˌpizəm/ ▸ *n. Botany* the growth or turning of plant roots toward or away from moisture.

hy·drous /'hīdrəs/ ▸ *adj. chiefly Chemistry Geology* containing water as a constituent: *a hydrous lava flow.* ▷early 19th cent.: from Greek *hudro-* 'water' + **-OUS**.

hy·drox·ide /hī'dräkˌsīd/ ▸ *n. Chemistry* a compound of a metal with the hydroxide ion OH^- (as in many alkalis) or the group −OH.

hy·drox·o·ni·um i·on /ˌhīdräk'sōnēəm/ ▸ *n. Chemistry* another term for **HYDRONIUM ION**. ▷1920s: *hydroxonium* from **HYDRO-** (relating to hydrogen) + **OXY-**[2] + the suffix *-onium* (from **AMMONIUM**).

hydroxy- ▸ *comb. form Chemistry* representing **HYDROXYL** or **HYDROXIDE**: *hydroxyapatite.*

hy·drox·y·a·pa·tite /hīˌdräksē'apəˌtīt/ ▸ *n.* a mineral of the apatite group that is the main inorganic constituent of tooth enamel and bone, although it is rare in rocks.

hy·drox·yl /hī'dräksəl/ ▸ *n.* [as *adj.*] *Chemistry* of or denoting the radical −OH, present in alcohols and many other organic compounds: *a hydroxyl group.* ▷mid 19th cent.: from a blend of **HYDROGEN** and **OXYGEN**, + **-YL**.

hy·drox·yl·ate /hī'dräksəˌlāt/ ▸ *v.* [*trans.*] [often as *adj.*] (**hydroxylated**) *Chemistry* introduce a hydroxyl group into (a molecule or compound). —**hy·drox·y·la·tion** /hiˌdräksə'lāSHən/ *n.*

Hy·dro·zo·a /ˌhīdrə'zōə/ *Zoology* a class of coelenterates that includes hydras and Portuguese men-of-war. Many of them are colonial, and some kinds have both polypoid and medusoid phases. ▷modern Latin (plural), from **HYDRO-** 'water' + Greek *zōion* 'animal.' —**hy·dro·zo·an** *n.* & *adj.*

Hy·drus /'hīdrəs/ *Astronomy* an inconspicuous southern constellation (the Water Snake), between the star Achernar and the south celestial pole. Compare with **HYDRA** (sense 2). ■ [as *genitive*] (**Hydri** /-drī/) used with a preceding letter or numeral to designate a star in this constellation: *the star Delta Hydri.* ▷Latin, from Greek *hudros*.

hy·e·na /hī'ēnə/ ▸ *n.* a doglike African mammal with forelimbs that are longer than the hind limbs and an erect mane. Hyenas are noted as scavengers but most are also effective hunters. • Family Hyaenidae: two genera, in particular *Hyaena*, and three species. ▷Middle English: via Latin from Greek *huaina*, feminine of *hus* 'pig' (the transference of the term probably being because the animal's mane was thought to resemble a hog's bristles).

hy·giene /'hīˌjēn/ ▸ *n.* conditions or practices conducive to maintaining health and preventing disease, esp. through cleanliness: *poor standards of food hygiene | personal hygiene.* ▷late 16th cent.: via French from modern Latin *hygieina*, from Greek *hugieinē (tekhnē)* '(art) of health,' from *hugiēs* 'healthy.'

hy·gi·en·ic /hī'jenik; -'jē-/ ▸ *adj.* conducive to maintaining health and preventing disease, esp. by being clean; sanitary: *hygienic conditions.* See note at **SANITARY**. —**hy·gi·en·i·cal·ly** /-(ə)lē/ *adv.*

hy·gien·ist /hī'jenəst; -jē-/ ▸ *n.* **1** a specialist in the promotion of clean conditions for the preservation of health: *an industrial hygienist.* **2** short for **DENTAL HYGIENIST**.

hygro- ▸ *comb. form* relating to moisture: *hygrometer.* ▷from Greek *hugros* 'wet.'

hy·grom·e·ter /hī'grämitər/ ▸ *n.* an instrument for measuring the humidity of the air or a gas. —**hy·gro·met·ric** /ˌhīgrə'metrik/ *adj.* —**hy·grom·e·try** /-trē/ *n.*

hy·groph·il·ous /hī'gräfələs/ ▸ *adj. Botany* (of a plant) growing in damp conditions.

hy·gro·phyte /'hīgrəˌfīt/ ▸ *n. Botany* a plant that grows in wet conditions.

hy·gro·scope /'hīgrəˌskōp/ ▸ *n.* an instrument that gives an indication of the humidity of the air.

hy·gro·scop·ic /ˌhīgrə'skäpik/ ▸ *adj.* (of a substance) tending to absorb moisture from the air. ■ relating to humidity or its measurement. —**hy·gro·scop·i·cal·ly** /-(ə)lē/ *adv.*

hy·ing /'hī-iNG/ ▸ present participle of **HIE**.

Hyk·sos /'hikˌsäs; -ˌsōs/ ▸ *plural n.* a people of mixed Semitic and Asian descent who invaded Egypt and settled in the Nile delta *c.*1640 BC. They formed the 15th and 16th dynasties of Egypt and ruled a large part of the country until driven out *c.*1532 BC. ▷from Greek *Huksōs* (interpreted by Manetho as 'shepherd kings' or 'captive shepherds'), from Egyptian *heqa khoswe* 'foreign rulers.'

hy·la /'hīlə/ ▸ *n.* a tree frog of a widespread genus, typically bright green in color. • Genus *Hyla*, family Hylidae: many species. ▷modern Latin, from Greek *hulē* 'timber.'

hy·lic /'hīlik/ ▸ *adj. rare* of matter; material. The opposite of **PSYCHIC** (sense 2). ▷mid 19th cent.: via late Latin from Greek *hulikos*, from *hulē* 'matter.'

hylo- ▸ *comb. form* of or relating to matter: *hylozoism.* ▷from Greek *hulē* 'matter.'

hy·lo·mor·phism /ˌhīlə'môrˌfizəm/ ▸ *n. Philosophy* the doctrine that physical objects result from the combination of matter and form. ▷late 19th cent.: from **HYLO-** 'matter' + Greek *morphē* 'form.' —**hy·lo·mor·phic** /-fik/ *adj.*

hy·lo·zo·ism /ˌhīlə'zōˌizəm/ ▸ *n. Philosophy* the doctrine that all matter has life. ▷late 17th cent.: from **HYLO-** 'matter' + Greek *zōē* 'life.'

hy·men /'hīmən/ ▸ *n.* a membrane that partially closes the opening of the vagina and whose presence is traditionally taken to be a mark of virginity. ▷mid 16th cent.: via late Latin from Greek *humēn* 'membrane.' —**hy·men·al** /'hīmənl/ *adj.*

hy·me·ne·al /ˌhīmə'nēəl/ ▸ *adj. poetic/literary* of or concerning marriage. ▷early 17th cent.: from Latin *hymenaeus*, from *Hymen* (from Greek *Humēn*), the name of the god of marriage, + **-AL**.

hy·me·ni·um /hī'mēnēəm/ ▸ *n.* (*pl.* **-nia** /-nēə/) *Botany* (in higher fungi) a surface consisting mainly of spore-bearing structures (asci or basidia). ▷early 19th cent.: from Greek *humenion*, diminutive of *humēn* 'membrane.' —**hy·me·ni·al** /-nēəl/ *adj.*

Hy·me·nop·ter·a /ˌhīmə'näptərə/ *Entomology* a large order of insects that includes the bees, wasps, ants, and sawflies. These insects have four transparent wings and the females often have a sting. ■ [as *plural n.*] (**hymenoptera**) insects of this order. ▷modern Latin (plural), from Greek *humenopteros* 'membrane-winged,' from *humēn* 'membrane' + *pteron* 'wing.' —**hy·me·nop·ter·an** *n.* & *adj.* —**hy·me·nop·ter·ous** /-tərəs/ *adj.*

Hy·mie /'hīmē/ ▸ *n. informal, offensive* a Jewish person. ▷1980s: colloquial abbreviation of the Jewish male given name *Hyman*.

hymn /him/ ▸ *n.* a religious song or poem, typically of praise to God or a god: *a Hellenistic* **hymn to** *Apollo.* ■ a formal song sung during Christian worship, typically by the whole congregation. ■ a song, text, or other composition praising or celebrating someone or something: *a most unusual passage like a* **hymn to** *the great outdoors.*
▸ *v.* **1** [*trans.*] praise or celebrate (something): *Johnson's reply hymns education.* **2** [*intrans.*] *rare* sing hymns. ▷Old English, via Latin from Greek *humnos* 'ode or song in praise of a god or hero,' used in the Septuagint to translate various Hebrew words, and hence in the New Testament and other Christian writings. —**hym·nic** /'himnik/ *adj.*

hym·nal /'himnəl/ ▸ *n.* a book of hymns.
▸ *adj.* of hymns: *hymnal music.* ▷late 15th cent.: from medieval Latin *hymnale*, from Latin *hymnus* (see **HYMN**).

hym·na·ry /'himnərē/ ▸ *n.* (*pl.* **-ries**) another term for **HYMNAL**.

hym·no·dy /'himnədē/ ▸ *n.* the singing or composition of hymns. ▷early 18th cent.: via medieval Latin from Greek *humnōidia*, from *humnos* 'hymn.' —**hym·no·dist** /-dist/ *n.*

hym·nog·ra·pher /him'nägrəfər/ ▸ *n.* a writer of hymns. ▷early 17th cent.: from Greek *humnographos*, from *humnos* 'hymn' + *graphos* 'writer.' —**hym·nog·ra·phy** /-'nägrəfē/ *n.*

hym·nol·o·gy /him'näləjē/ ▸ *n.* the study or composition of hymns. ▷mid 17th cent.: originally from Greek *humnologia* 'hymn-singing,' the early sense until the mid 19th cent. —**hym·no·log·i·cal** /ˌhimnə'läjikəl/ *adj.* —**hym·nol·o·gist** /-jist/ *n.*

hy·oid /'hīˌoid/ *Anatomy & Zoology* ▸ *n.* (also **hyoid bone**) a U-shaped bone in the neck that supports the tongue.
▸ *adj.* of or relating to this bone or structures associated with it. ▷early 19th cent.: via French from modern Latin *hyoïdes*, from Greek *huoeidēs* 'shaped like the letter upsilon (υ).'

Pronunciation Key ə *ago*; ər *over*; 'ə *or* ˌə *up*; 'ər *or* ˌər *fur*; a *hat*; ā *rate*; ä *car*; CH *chew*; e *let*; ē *see*; e(ə)r *air*; i *fit*; ī *by*; i(ə)r *ear*; NG *sing*; ō *go*; ô *for*; oi *boy*; o͝o *good*; o͞o *goo*; ou *out*; SH *she*; TH *thin*; T͟H *then*; (h)w *why*; ZH *vision*

H

hy·os·cine /ˈhīəˌsēn/ ▸*n.* another term for **SCOPOLAMINE**. ▷late 19th cent.: from modern Latin *hyoscyamus* (see **HYOSCYAMINE**) + **-INE**[4].

hy·os·cy·a·mine /ˌhīəˈsīəmin; -ˌmēn/ ▸*n. Chemistry* a poisonous compound present in henbane, with similar properties to hyoscine. • Chem. formula: $C_{17}H_{23}NO_3$. ▷mid 19th cent.: from modern Latin *hyoscyamus* (from Greek *huoskuamos* 'henbane,' from *hus, huos* 'pig' + *kuamos* 'bean') + **-INE**[4].

hyp. ▸*abbr.* ■ hypotenuse. ■ hypothesis or hypothetical.

hyp- ▸*comb. form* variant spelling of **HYPO-** shortened before a vowel or *h* (as in *hypesthesia*).

hyp·aes·the·sia ▸*n.* British spelling of **HYPESTHESIA**.

hy·pae·thral ▸*adj.* variant spelling of **HYPETHRAL**.

hy·pal·la·ge /hīˈpaləjē; hi-/ ▸*n. Rhetoric* a transposition of the natural relations of two elements in a proposition, for example in the sentence "*Melissa shook her doubtful curls.*" ▷late 16th cent.: via late Latin from Greek *hupallagē*, from *hupo* 'under' + *allassein* 'to exchange.'

hy·pa·lon /ˈhīpəˌlän/ (also *trademark* **Hy·pa·lon**) ▸*n.* a kind of synthetic rubber made of chlorinated and sulfonated polyethylene. ▷mid 20th cent.: of unknown origin.

hy·pan·thi·um /hiˈpanTHēəm; hī-/ ▸*n.* (*pl.* **-thi·a** /-THēə/) *Botany* a cuplike or tubular enlargement of the receptacle of a flower, loosely surrounding the gynoecium or united with it.

Hy·pa·tia /hīˈpāSHə; -patēə/ (*c.*370–415), Greek philosopher, astronomer, and mathematician. She was the head of the Neoplatonist school in Alexandria and was famous for her eloquence and learning. She was murdered by a mob of Christians incited by Cyril, the bishop of Alexandria.

hype[1] /hīp/ *informal* ▸*n.* extravagant or intensive publicity or promotion: *she relied on hype and headlines to stoke up interest in her music.* ■ a deception carried out for the sake of publicity.
▸*v.* [*trans.*] promote or publicize (a product or idea) intensively, often exaggerating its importance or benefits: *an industry quick to hype its products.* ▷1920s (originally in the sense 'shortchange, cheat,' or 'person who cheats, etc.'): of unknown origin.

hype[2] *informal* ▸*n.* a hypodermic needle or injection. ■ a drug addict.
▸*v.* [*trans.*] (usu. **be hyped up**) stimulate or excite (someone): *I was hyped up because I wanted to do well.* ▷1920s (originally U.S.): abbreviation of **HYPODERMIC**.

hy·per /ˈhīpər/ ▸*adj. informal* hyperactive or unusually energetic: *eating sugar makes you hyper.* ▷1940s: abbreviation of **HYPERACTIVE**.

H

hyper- ▸*prefix* **1** over; beyond; above: *hypernym.* ■ exceeding: *hypersonic.* ■ excessively; above normal: *hyperthyroidism.* **2** relating to hypertext: *hyperlink.* ▷from Greek *huper* 'over, beyond.'

hy·per·ac·tive /ˌhīpərˈaktiv/ ▸*adj.* abnormally or extremely active: *a hyperactive pituitary gland.* ■ (of a child) showing constantly active and sometimes disruptive behavior. **—hy·per·ac·tiv·i·ty** /-ˌakˈtivitē/ *n.*

hy·per·ae·mi·a ▸*n.* British spelling of **HYPEREMIA**.

hy·per·aes·the·sia ▸*n.* British spelling of **HYPERESTHESIA**.

hy·per·al·ge·si·a /ˌhīpəralˈjēzēə; -ˈjēsēə/ ▸*n. Medicine* abnormally heightened sensitivity to pain. **—hy·per·al·ge·sic** /-ˈjēzik; -ˈjēsik/ *adj.*

hy·per·al·i·men·ta·tion /ˌhīpərˌaləmənˈtāSHən/ ▸*n. Medicine* artificial supply of nutrients, typically intravenously.

hy·per·bar·ic /ˌhīpərˈbarik/ ▸*adj.* of or involving a gas at a pressure greater than normal. ▷1960s: from **HYPER-** 'above normal' + Greek *baros* 'heavy.'

hy·per·ba·ton /hīˈpərbəˌtän/ ▸*n. Rhetoric* an inversion of the normal order of words, esp. for the sake of emphasis, as in the sentence "*this I must see.*" ▷mid 16th cent.: via Latin from Greek *huperbaton* 'overstepping' (from *huper* 'over, above' + *bainein* 'go, walk').

hy·per·bo·la /hīˈpərbələ/ ▸*n.* (*pl.* **-bo·las** or **-bo·lae** /-bəlē/) a symmetrical open curve formed by the intersection of a cone with a plane at a smaller angle with its axis than the side of the cone. ■ *Mathematics* the pair of such curves formed by the intersection of a plane with two equal cones on opposites of the same vertex. ▷mid 17th cent.: modern Latin, from Greek *huperbolē* 'excess' (from *huper* 'above' + *ballein* 'to throw').

hy·per·bo·le /hīˈpərbəlē/ ▸*n.* exaggerated statements or claims not meant to be taken literally. ▷late Middle English: via Latin from Greek *huperbolē* (see **HYPERBOLA**). **—hy·per·bol·i·cal** /ˌhīpərˈbälikəl/ *adj.* **—hy·per·bol·i·cal·ly** /ˌhīpərˈbälik(ə)lē/ *adv.* **—hy·per·bo·lism** /-ˌlizəm/ *n.*

hy·per·bol·ic /ˌhīpərˈbälik/ ▸*adj.* **1** of or relating to a hyperbola. ■ *Mathematics* (of a function, e.g., a cosine) having the same relation to a rectangular hyperbola as the unqualified function does to a circle. **2** (of language) exaggerated; hyperbolical.

hy·per·bol·ic pa·rab·o·loid ▸*n. Mathematics* a surface whose section parallel to one properly oriented coordinate plane is a hyperbola and whose sections parallel to the other two coordinate planes are parabolas.

hy·per·bo·loid /hīˈpərbəˌloid/ ▸*n.* a solid or surface having plane sections that are hyperbolas, ellipses, or circles. **—hy·per·bo·loi·dal** /hīˌpərbəˈloidl/ *adj.*

hy·per·bo·re·an /ˌhīpərˈbôrēən; -bəˈrēən/ *poetic/literary* ▸*n.* an inhabitant of the extreme north. ■ (**Hyperborean**) *Greek Mythology* a member of a race worshiping Apollo and living in a land of sunshine and plenty beyond the north wind.
▸*adj.* of or relating to the extreme north. ▷late Middle English: from late Latin *hyperboreanus*, from Greek *huperboreos*, from *huper* 'beyond' + *boreas* 'north wind.'

hy·per·cap·ni·a /ˌhīpərˈkapnēə/ ▸*n. Pathology* excessive carbon dioxide in the bloodstream, typically caused by inadequate respiration.

hy·per·cho·les·ter·ol·e·mi·a /ˌhīpərkəˌlestərəˈlēmēə/ (*Brit.* **hy·per·cho·les·ter·ol·ae·mi·a**) ▸*n. Medicine* an excess of cholesterol in the bloodstream. ▷late 19th cent.: from **HYPER-** 'above normal' + **CHOLESTEROL** + **-EMIA**.

hy·per·con·scious /ˌhīpərˈkänSHəs/ ▸*adj.* acutely or excessively aware: *placing so much emphasis on willpower as to become hyperconscious, if not sometimes even inhibited.*

hy·per·cor·rec·tion /ˌhīpərkəˈrekSHən/ ▸*n.* the erroneous use of a word form or pronunciation based on a false analogy with a correct or prestigious form, such as *between you and I* for the standard *between you and me.* **—hy·per·cor·rect** /-ˈrekt/ *adj.*

hy·per·crit·i·cal /ˌhīpərˈkritikəl/ ▸*adj.* excessively and unreasonably critical, esp. of small faults. **—hy·per·crit·i·cal·ly** /-ik(ə)lē/ *adv.*

hy·per·cube /ˈhīpərˌkyo͞ob/ ▸*n.* a geometric figure in four or more dimensions that is analogous to a cube in three dimensions.

hy·per·drive /ˈhīpərˌdrīv/ ▸*n.* (in science fiction) a propulsion system for travel in hyperspace.

hy·per·e·mi·a /ˌhīpəˈrēmēə/ (*Brit.* **hy·per·ae·mi·a**) ▸*n. Medicine* an excess of blood in the vessels supplying an organ or other part of the body. ▷mid 19th cent.: from **HYPER-** 'above normal' + **-EMIA**. **—hy·per·e·mic** /-ˈrēmik/ *adj.*

hy·per·es·the·sia /ˌhīpərəsˈTHēZHə/ (*Brit.* **hy·per·aes·the·si·a**) ▸*n. Medicine* excessive physical sensitivity, esp. of the skin. ▷mid 19th cent.: from **HYPER-** 'above normal' + Greek *aisthēsis* 'sensation.' **—hy·per·es·thet·ic** /-ˈTHetik/ *adj.*

hy·per·ex·tend /ˌhīpərikˈstend/ ▸*v.* [*trans.*] forcefully extend (a limb or joint) beyond its normal limits, either in exercise or therapy or so as to cause injury. **—hy·per·ex·ten·sion** /-ˈstenSHən/ *n.*

hy·per·fli·er /ˈhīpərˌflīər/ ▸*n. informal* a person who travels a great deal, especially for business. ▷1990s: from *hyper-* 'excessively, above normal' + *flier.*

hy·per·fo·cal dis·tance /ˌhīpərˈfōkəl/ ▸*n.* the distance between a camera lens and the closest object that is in focus when the lens is focused at infinity.

hy·per·ga·my /hīˈpərgəmē/ ▸*n.* the action of marrying a person of a superior caste or class. ▷late 19th cent.: from **HYPER-** 'above' + Greek *gamos* 'marriage.'

hy·per·gly·ce·mi·a /ˌhīpərglīˈsēmēə/ (*Brit.* **hy·per·gly·cae·mi·a**) ▸*n. Medicine* an excess of glucose in the bloodstream, often associated with diabetes mellitus. ▷late 19th cent.: from **HYPER-** 'above normal' + **GLYCO-** + **-EMIA**. **—hy·per·gly·ce·mic** /-ˈsēmik/ *adj.*

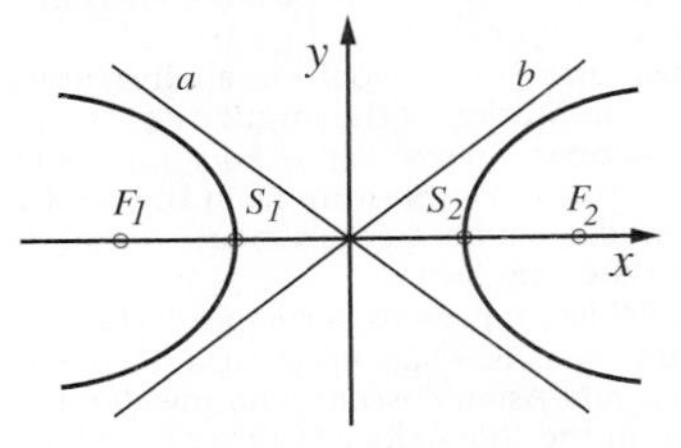

hyperbola

hy·per·gol·ic /ˌhīpərˈgälik/ ▸*adj.* (of a rocket propellant) igniting spontaneously on mixing with another substance. ▷1940s: from German *Hypergol*, probably from **HYPER-** 'beyond' + Greek *ergon* 'work' + **-OL**.

hy·per·i·cin /hīˈperəsin/ ▸*n.* a substance found in St. John's wort, credited with chemical and pharmacological properties similar to those of antidepressants. • A polycyclic quinone; chem. formula: $C_{30}H_{14}O_8$. ▷early 20th cent.: from *hypericum* 'a yellow-flowered plant' + *-in*, chemical suffix.

hy·per·i·cum /hīˈperikəm/ ▸*n.* a yellow-flowered plant of a genus that includes the St. John's worts and rose of Sharon. • Genus *Hypericum*, family Guttiferae. ▷Latin, from Greek *hupereikon*, from *huper* 'over, above' + *ereikē* 'heath.'

hy·per·im·mune /ˌhīpəriˈmyo͞on/ ▸*adj. Medicine* having a high concentration of antibodies produced in reaction to repeated injections of an antigen. **—hy·per·im·mu·nized** /-ˈimyəˌnīzd/ *adj.*

hy·per·in·fla·tion /hīpərinˈflāSHən/ ▸*n.* monetary inflation occurring at a very high rate.

hy·per·in·stru·ment /ˈhīpərˌinstrəmənt/ ▸*n.* a musical instrument designed or adapted to be used with electronic sensors whose output controls the computerized generation or transformation of the sound.

Hy·pe·ri·on /hīˈpi(ə)rēən/ *Astronomy* a satellite of Saturn, the sixteenth closest to the planet, discovered in 1848. It has an irregular shape, with a diameter of 159 miles (255 km). ▷named after a Titan of Greek mythology.

hy·per·ker·a·to·sis /ˌhīpərˌkerəˈtōsis/ ▸*n. Medicine* abnormal thickening of the outer layer of the skin.

hy·per·ki·ne·sis /ˌhīpərkiˈnēsis/ (also **hy·per·ki·ne·sia** /-ˈnēZHə/) ▸*n.* **1** *Medicine* muscle spasm. **2** *Psychiatry* a disorder of children marked by hyperactivity and inability to concentrate. ▷mid 19th cent.: from **HYPER-** 'above normal' + Greek *kinēsis* 'motion.'

hy·per·ki·net·ic /ˌhīpərkəˈnetik/ ▸*adj.* frenetic; hyperactive. ■ of or affected with hyperkinesis.

hy·per·link /ˈhīpərˌliNGk/ *Computing* ▸*n.* a link from a hypertext file or document to another location or file, typically activated by clicking on a highlighted word or image on the screen.
▸*v.* [*trans.*] link (a file) in this way: *thumbnail images that are hyperlinked to a larger image.*

hy·per·li·pe·mi·a /ˌhīpərləˈpēmēə/ (*Brit.* **hy·per·li·pae·mi·a**) ▸*n.* another term for **HYPERLIPIDEMIA**. **—hy·per·li·pe·mic** /-ˈpēmik/ *adj.*

hy·per·lip·i·de·mi·a /ˌhīpərˌlipiˈdēmēə/ (*Brit.* **hy·per·lip·i·dae·mi·a**) ▸*n. Medicine* an abnormally high concentration of fats or lipids in the blood. **—hy·per·lip·i·de·mic** /-ˈdēmik/ *adj.*

hy·per·mar·ket /ˈhīpərˌmärkit/ ▸*n. chiefly Brit.* a very large store with a wide range of goods and a large parking lot, typically situated outside a town. ▷1970s: translation of French *hypermarché*, from **HYPER-** 'beyond, exceeding'+ *marché* 'market.'

hy·per·me·di·a /ˌhīpərˈmēdēə/ ▸*n. Computing* an extension to hypertext providing multimedia facilities, such as those handling sound and video. ▷1960s: from **HYPER-** 'above, beyond' + **MEDIA**[1].

hy·per·me·tro·pi·a /ˌhīpərməˈtrōpēə/ ▸*n.* another term for **HYPEROPIA**. ▷mid 19th cent.: from Greek *hupermetros* 'beyond measure' (from *huper* 'over, above' + *metron* 'measure') + *ōps* 'eye.' **—hy·per·me·tro·pic** /-ˈträpik; -ˈtrō-/ *adj.*

hy·perm·ne·sia /ˌhīpərmˈnēZHə/ ▸*n.* unusual power or enhancement of memory, typically under abnormal conditions such as trauma, hypnosis, or narcosis.

hy·per·mu·ta·ble /ˌhīpərˈmyo͞otəbəl/ ▸*adj. Genetics* of or in a state in which mutation is abnormally frequent. **—hy·per·mu·ta·tion** /-myo͞oˈtāSHən/ *n.*

hy·per·nym /ˈhīpərˌnim/ ▸*n.* a word with a broad meaning that more specific words fall under; a superordinate. For example, *color* is a hypernym of *red.* Contrasted with **HYPONYM**. ▷1970s: from **HYPER-** 'beyond,' on the pattern of *hyponym.*

hy·per·on /ˈhīpəˌrän/ ▸*n. Physics* an unstable subatomic particle classified as a baryon, heavier than the neutron and proton. ▷1950s: from **HYPER-** 'beyond, over' + **-ON**.

hy·per·o·pi·a /ˌhīpəˈrōpēə/ ▸*n.* farsightedness. ▷late 19th cent.: from **HYPER-** 'beyond' + Greek *ōps* 'eye.' **—hy·per·op·ic** /-ˈräpik/ *adj.*

hy·per·par·a·site /ˌhīpərˈparəˌsīt/ ▸*n. Biology* a parasite whose host is itself a parasite. **—hy·per·par·a·sit·ic** /-ˌparəˈsitik/ *adj.* **—hy·per·par·a·sit·ism** /-sīˌtizəm; -si-/ *n.*

hy·per·par·a·thy·roid·ism /ˌhīpərˌparəˈTHīroiˌdizəm/

▸*n. Medicine* an abnormally high concentration of parathyroid hormone in the blood, resulting in weakening of the bones through loss of calcium. **—hy·per·par·a·thy·roid** *adj.*

hy·per·phys·i·cal /ˌhīpərˈfizikəl/ ▸*adj.* supernatural. **—hy·per·phys·i·cal·ly** /-ik(ə)lē/ *adv.*

hy·per·pla·sia /ˌhīpərˈplāZHə/ ▸*n. Medicine & Biology* the enlargement of an organ or tissue caused by an increase in the reproduction rate of its cells, often as an initial stage in the development of cancer. ▷mid 19th cent.: from **HYPER-** 'beyond' + Greek *plasis* 'formation.'

hy·per·re·al /ˌhīpə(r)ˈrēəl/ ▸*adj.* **1** exaggerated in comparison to reality. **2** (of artistic representation) extremely realistic in detail. **—hy·per·re·al·ism** /-ˌlizəm/ *n.* **—hy·per·re·al·ist** /-ist/ *adj.* **—hy·per·re·al·is·tic** /ˌhīpə(r)ˌrēəˈlistik/ *adj.* **—hy·per·re·al·i·ty** /ˌhīpə(r)rēˈalitē/ *n.*

hy·per·sen·si·tive /ˌhīpərˈsensitiv/ ▸*adj.* abnormally or excessively sensitive, either psychologically or in physical response. **—hy·per·sen·si·tive·ness** *n.* **—hy·per·sen·si·tiv·i·ty** /-ˌsensiˈtivitē/ *n.*

hy·per·son·ic /ˌhīpərˈsänik/ ▸*adj.* **1** relating to speeds of more than five times the speed of sound (Mach 5). **2** relating to sound frequencies above about a thousand million hertz. ▷1930s (sense 2): from **HYPER-** 'beyond, exceeding,' on the pattern of *supersonic* and *ultrasonic*. **—hy·per·son·i·cal·ly** /-ik(ə)lē/ *adv.*

hy·per·space /ˈhīpərˌspās/ ▸*n.* space of more than three dimensions. ■ (in science fiction) a notional space-time continuum in which it is possible to travel faster than light. **—hy·per·spa·tial** /ˌhīpərˈspāSHəl/ *adj.*

hy·per·sphere /ˈhīpərˌsfi(ə)r/ ▸*n.* a sphere that exhibits more than three dimensions.

hy·per·sthene /ˈhīpərˌsTHēn/ ▸*n.* a greenish rock-forming mineral of the orthopyroxene class, consisting of a magnesium iron silicate. ▷early 19th cent.: coined in French, from **HYPER-** 'exceeding' + Greek *sthenos* 'strength' (because it is harder than hornblende).

hy·per·ten·sion /ˌhīpərˈtenSHən/ ▸*n. Medicine* abnormally high blood pressure. ■ a state of great psychological stress.

hy·per·ten·sive /ˌhīpərˈtensiv/ ▸*adj.* exhibiting hypertension.
▸*n. Medicine* a person with high blood pressure.

hy·per·text /ˈhīpərˌtekst/ ▸*n. Computing* a software system that links topics on the screen to related information and graphics, which are typically accessed by a point-and-click method. ■ a document presented on a computer in this way.

hy·per·ther·mi·a /ˌhīpərˈTHərmēə/ ▸*n. Medicine* the condition of having a body temperature greatly above normal. ▷late 19th cent.: from **HYPER-** 'beyond' + Greek *thermē* 'heat.' **—hy·per·ther·mic** /-ˈTHərmik/ *adj.*

hy·per·thy·roid·ism /ˌhīpərˈTHīroiˌdizəm/ ▸*n. Medicine* overactivity of the thyroid gland, resulting in a rapid heartbeat and an increased rate of metabolism. Also called **THYROTOXICOSIS**. **—hy·per·thy·roid** *adj.* **—hy·per·thy·roid·ic** /-THīˈroidik/ *adj.*

hy·per·ton·ic /ˌhīpərˈtänik/ ▸*adj.* having increased pressure or tone, in particular: ■ *Biology* having a higher osmotic pressure than a particular fluid, typically a body fluid or intracellular fluid. ■ *Physiology* of or in a state of abnormally high muscle tone. **—hy·per·to·ni·a** /-ˈtōnēə/ *n.* (OF MUSCLES). **—hy·per·to·nic·i·ty** /ˌhīpərtəˈnisitē/ *n.*

hy·per·tro·phy /hīˈpərtrəfē/ ▸*n. Physiology* the enlargement of an organ or tissue from the increase in size of its cells. ■ excessive growth.
▸*v.* (**-phies, -phied**) [*intrans.*] (of a body or an organ) become enlarged due to an increase in cell size. ▷mid 19th cent.: from **HYPER-** 'beyond, exceeding' + Greek *-trophia* 'nourishment.' **—hy·per·troph·ic** /ˌhīpərˈtrāfik; -ˈtrō-/ *adj.* **—hy·per·troph·ied** /-trəfēd/ *adj.*

hy·per·ven·ti·late /ˌhīpərˈventlˌāt/ ▸*v.* [*intrans.*] breathe at an abnormally rapid rate, so increasing the rate of loss of carbon dioxide: *she started to hyperventilate under stress.* ■ [*trans.*] (usu. **be hyperventilated**) cause to breathe in such a way: *the patients were hyperventilated for two minutes.* ■ [as *adj.*] (**hyperventilated**) *figurative* inflated or pretentious in style; overblown: *hyperventilated prose.* **—hy·per·ven·ti·la·tion** /-ˌventlˈāSHən/ *n.*

hyp·es·the·sia /ˌhipəsˈTHēZHə; ˌhīpəs-/ (*Brit.* **hyp·aes·the·sia**) ▸*n.* a diminished capacity for physical sensation, esp. of the skin. ▷late 19th cent.: from **HYPO-** 'below' + Greek *aisthēsis* 'sensation.' **—hyp·es·thet·ic** /-ˈTHetik/ *adj.*

hy·pe·thral /hiˈpēTHrəl; hī-/ (also **hy·pae·thral**) ▸*adj.* (of a classical building) having no roof; open to the sky: *the hypethral temple.* ▷late 18th cent.: via Latin from Greek *hupaithros* (from *hupo* 'under' + *aithēr* 'air') + **-AL**.

hy·pha /ˈhīfə/ ▸*n.* (*pl.* **-phae** /-fē/) *Botany* each of the branching filaments that make up the mycelium of a fungus. ▷mid 19th cent.: modern Latin, from Greek *huphē* 'web.' **—hy·phal** *adj.*

Hyph·a·sis /ˈhifəsis/ ancient Greek name for **BEAS**.

hy·phen /ˈhīfən/ ▸*n.* the sign (-) used to join words to indicate that they have a combined meaning or that they are linked in the grammar of a sentence (as in *pick-me-up, rock-forming*), to indicate the division of a word at the end of a line, or to indicate a missing or implied element (as in *short- and long-term*).
▸*v.* another term for **HYPHENATE**. ▷early 17th cent.: via late Latin from Greek *huphen* 'together,' from *hupo* 'under' + *hen* 'one.'

hy·phen·ate /ˈhīfəˌnāt/ ▸*v.* [*trans.*] write with a hyphen: [as *adj.*] (**hyphenated**) *a hyphenated surname.*
▸*n.* a person who is active in more than one occupation or sphere: *as a supreme hyphenate, she was prepared to carry a heavy load as the director-producer-star of her new film.* **—hy·phen·a·tion** /ˌhīfəˈnāSHən/ *n.*

hy·phen·at·ed A·mer·i·can ▸*n. informal* an American citizen who can trace their ancestry to another, specified part of the world, such as an African American or an Irish American (so called because terms like *African American* are often written with a hyphen).

hyp·na·gog·ic /ˌhipnəˈgäjik; -ˈgō-/ (also **hyp·no·gog·ic**) ▸*adj. Psychology* of or relating to the state immediately before falling asleep. ▷late 19th cent.: from French *hypnagogique*, from Greek *hupnos* 'sleep' + *agōgos* 'leading' (from *agein* 'to lead'). **—hyp·na·gog·i·a** *n.*

hypno- ▸*comb. form* relating to sleep: *hypnopedia.* ■ relating to hypnosis: *hypnotherapy.* ▷from Greek *hupnos* 'sleep.'

hyp·no·gog·ic ▸ a variant spelling of **HYPNAGOGIC**. **—hyp·no·gog·i·a** *n.*

hyp·no·pe·di·a /ˌhipnōˈpēdēə/ (*Brit.* **hyp·no·pae·di·a**) ▸*n.* learning by hearing while asleep or under hypnosis.

hyp·no·pho·bi·a /ˌhipnəˈfōbēə/ ▸*n.*
▸an abnormal fear of falling asleep. **—hyp·no·pho·bic** *adj.*

hyp·no·pom·pic /ˌhipnəˈpämpik/ ▸*adj. Psychology* of or relating to the state immediately preceding waking up. ▷early 20th cent.: from Greek *hupnos* 'sleep' + *pompē* 'sending away' + **-IC**.

Hyp·nos /ˈhipˌnäs/ *Greek Mythology* the god of sleep, son of Nyx (Night). ▷from Greek *hupnos* 'sleep.'

hyp·no·sis /hipˈnōsis/ ▸*n.* the induction of a state of consciousness in which a person apparently loses the power of voluntary action and is highly responsive to suggestion or direction. Its use in therapy, typically to recover suppressed memories or to allow modification of behavior by suggestion, has been revived but is still controversial. ■ this state of consciousness. ▷late 19th cent.: from Greek *hupnos* 'sleep' + **-OSIS**.

hyp·no·ther·a·py /ˌhipnōˈTHerəpē/ ▸*n.* the use of hypnosis as a therapeutic technique. **—hyp·no·ther·a·pist** /-pist/ *n.*

hyp·not·ic /hipˈnätik/ ▸*adj.* **1** of, producing, or relating to hypnosis: *a hypnotic state.* ■ exerting a compelling, fascinating, or soporific effect: *her voice had a hypnotic quality.* **2** *Medicine* (of a drug) sleep-inducing.
▸*n.* **1** *Medicine* a sleep-inducing drug. **2** a person under or open to the influence of hypnotism. ▷early 17th cent.: from French *hypnotique*, via late Latin from Greek *hupnōtikos* 'narcotic, causing sleep,' from *hupnoun* 'put to sleep,' from *hupnos* 'sleep.' **—hyp·not·i·cal·ly** /-(ə)lē/ *adv.*

hyp·no·tism /ˈhipnəˌtizəm/ ▸*n.* the study or practice of hypnosis. **—hyp·no·tist** *n.*

hyp·no·tize /ˈhipnəˌtīz/ ▸*v.* (often **be hypnotized**) [*trans.*] produce a state of hypnosis in (someone): *a witness had been hypnotized to enhance his memory.* ■ capture the whole attention of (someone); fascinate: *hypnotized by the rain, Eric stared across the street.* **—hyp·no·tiz·a·ble** /-ˌtīzəbəl; ˌhipnəˈtīzəbəl/ *adj.*

hy·po[1] /ˈhīpō/ ▸*n. Photography* the chemical sodium thiosulphate (formerly called hyposulphite) used as a photographic fixer. ▷mid 19th cent.: abbreviation of *hyposulphite*.

hy·po[2] ▸*n.* (*pl.* **-pos**) informal term for **HYPODERMIC**. ▷early 20th cent.: abbreviation.

hypo- (also **hyp-**) ▸*prefix* under: *hypodermic.* ■ below normal: *hypoglycemia.* ■ slightly: *hypomanic.* ■ *Chemistry* containing an element with an unusually low valence: *hypochlorous.* ▷from Greek *hupo* 'under.'

hy·po·al·ler·gen·ic /ˌhīpōalərˈjenik/ ▸*adj.* (esp. of cosmetics and textiles) relatively unlikely to cause an allergic reaction.

hy·po·blast /ˈhīpəˌblast/ ▸*n. Biology* former term for **ENDODERM**.

hy·po·cal·ce·mi·a /ˌhīpōkalˈsēmēə/ (*Brit.* **hy·po·cal·cae·mi·a**) ▸*n. Medicine* deficiency of calcium in the bloodstream.

hy·po·caust /ˈhīpəˌkôst/ ▸*n.* a hollow space under the floor of an ancient Roman building, into which hot air was sent for heating a room or bath. ▷from Latin *hypocaustum*, from Greek *hupokauston* 'place heated from below,' from *hupo* 'under' + *kau-* (base of *kaiein* 'to burn').

hy·po·cen·ter /ˈhīpəˌsentər/ ▸*n.* **1** the underground focus point of an earthquake. Compare with **EPICENTER**. **2** another term for **GROUND ZERO**.

hy·po·chlo·rous ac·id /ˌhīpəˈklôrəs/ ▸*n. Chemistry* a weak acid with oxidizing properties formed when chlorine dissolves in cold water, used in bleaching and water treatment. • Chem. formula: $HOCl$. ▷mid 19th cent.: *hypochlorous* from **HYPO-** (denoting an element in a low valency) + **CHLORINE** + **-OUS**. **—hy·po·chlo·rite** /-ˌrīt/ *n.*

hy·po·chon·dri·a /ˌhīpəˈkändrēə/ ▸*n.* abnormal anxiety about one's health, esp. with an unwarranted fear that one has a serious disease. ▷late Middle English (in the Greek sense): via late Latin from Greek *hupokhondria*, denoting the soft body area below the ribs, from *hupo* 'under' + *khondros* 'sternal cartilage.' Melancholy was originally thought to arise from the liver, gallbladder, spleen, etc.

hy·po·chon·dri·ac /ˌhīpəˈkändrēˌak/ ▸*n.* a person who is abnormally anxious about their health.
▸*adj.* another term for **HYPOCHONDRIACAL**. ▷late 16th cent.: coined in French from Greek *hupokhondriakos*, from *hupokhondria* (see **HYPOCHONDRIA**).

hy·po·chon·dri·a·cal /ˌhīpōkənˈdrīəkəl/ ▸*adj.* of or affected by hypochondria.

hy·po·chon·dri·a·sis /ˌhīpōkənˈdrīəsis/ ▸*n.* technical term for **HYPOCHONDRIA**.

hy·po·co·ris·tic /ˌhīpəkəˈristik/ ▸*adj.* denoting, or of the nature of, a pet name or diminutive form of a name.
▸*n.* a hypocoristic name or form. ▷mid 19th cent.: from Greek *hupokorisma*, from *hupokorizesthai* 'play the child,' from *hupo* 'under' + *korē* 'child.' **—hy·poc·o·rism** /hīˈpäkəˌrizəm; hi-/ *n.*

hy·po·cot·yl /ˈhīpəˌkätl; ˌhīpəˈkätl/ ▸*n. Botany* the part of the stem of an embryo plant beneath the stalks of the seed leaves, or cotyledons, and directly above the root.

hy·po·cre·tin /hīpəˈkrētn/ ▸another name for **OREXIN**.

hy·poc·ri·sy /hiˈpäkrisē/ ▸*n.* (*pl.* **-sies**) the practice of claiming to have moral standards or beliefs to which one's own behavior does not conform; pretense. ▷Middle English: from Old French *ypocrisie*, via ecclesiastical Latin, from Greek *hupokrisis* 'acting of a theatrical part,' from *hupokrinesthai* 'play a part, pretend,' from *hupo* 'under' + *krinein* 'decide, judge.'

hyp·o·crite /ˈhipəˌkrit/ ▸*n.* a person who indulges in hypocrisy. ▷Middle English: from Old French *ypocrite*, via ecclesiastical Latin from Greek *hupokritēs* 'actor,' from *hupokrinesthai* (see **HYPOCRISY**). **—hyp·o·crit·i·cal** /ˌhipəˈkritikəl/ *adj.* **—hyp·o·crit·i·cal·ly** /ˌhipəˈkritik(ə)lē/ *adv.*

hy·po·cy·cloid /ˌhīpəˈsīˌkloid/ ▸*n. Mathematics* the curve traced by a point on the circumference of a circle that is rolling on the interior of another circle. **—hy·po·cy·cloi·dal** /ˌhīpəˈsīˌkloidl/ *adj.*

hy·po·der·mic /ˌhīpəˈdərmik/ ▸*adj.* [*attrib.*] *Medicine* of or relating to the region immediately beneath the skin. ■ (of a needle or syringe) used to inject a drug or other substance beneath the skin. ■ (of a drug or other substance or its application) injected beneath the skin.
▸*n.* a hypodermic syringe or injection. **—hy·po·der·mi·cal·ly** /-(ə)lē/ *adv.*

hy·po·gas·tri·um /ˌhīpəˈgastrēəm/ ▸*n.* (*pl.* **-tri·a** /-trēə/) *Anatomy* the part of the central abdomen that is situated below the region of the stomach. ▷late 17th cent.: modern Latin, from Greek *hupogastrion*, from

Pronunciation Key ə *ago*; ər *over*; ˈə or ˌə *up*; ˈər or ˌər *fur*; a *hat*; ā *rate*; ä *car*; CH *chew*; e *let*; ē *see*; e(ə)r *air*; i *fit*; ī *by*; i(ə)r *ear*; NG *sing*; ō *go*; ô *for*; oi *boy*; o͝o *good*; o͞o *goo*; ou *out*; SH *she*; TH *thin*; T͟H *then*; (h)w *why*; ZH *vision*

H

hupo 'under' + *gastēr* 'belly.' —**hy·po·gas·tric** /-trik/ *adj.*

hy·po·ge·al /ˌhīpəˈjēəl/ (also **hy·po·ge·an**) ▸*adj. Botany* underground; subterranean. Compare with EPIGEAL. ■ (of seed germination) with the seed leaves remaining below the ground. ▷late 17th cent.: via late Latin from Greek *hupogeios* (from *hupo* 'under' + *gē* 'earth') + -AL.

hy·po·gene /ˈhīpəˌjēn/ ▸*adj. Geology* producing or occurring under the surface of the earth. ▷mid 19th cent.: from HYPO- 'under' + Greek *genēs* '-born, of a certain kind.' —**hy·po·gen·ic** /ˌhīpəˈjenik/ *adj.*

hy·po·ge·um /ˌhīpəˈjēəm/ ▸*n.* (*pl.* **-ge·a** /-ˈjēə/) an underground chamber. ▷mid 17th cent.: from Latin, from Greek *hupogeion*, neuter of *hupogeios* 'underground.'

hy·po·glos·sal nerve /ˌhīpəˈgläsəl/ ▸*n. Anatomy* each of the twelfth pair of cranial nerves, supplying the muscles of the tongue. ▷mid 19th cent.: *hypoglossal* from HYPO- 'under' + Greek *glōssa* 'tongue' + -AL.

hy·po·gly·ce·mi·a /ˌhīpōglīˈsēmēə/ (*Brit.* **hy·po·gly·cae·mi·a**) ▸*n. Medicine* deficiency of glucose in the bloodstream. ▷late 19th cent.: from HYPO- 'below' + GLYCO- + -EMIA. —**hy·po·gly·ce·mic** /-ˈsēmik/ *adj.*

hy·po·gon·ad·ism /ˌhīpōˈgōnaˌdizəm/ ▸*n. Medicine* reduction or absence of hormone secretion or other physiological activity of the gonads (testes or ovaries). —**hy·po·go·nad·al** /ˌhīpəˌgōˈnadl/ *adj.* —**hy·po·go·nad·ic** /ˌhīpəgōˈnadik/ *n. & adj.*

hy·pog·y·nous /hīˈpäjənəs/ ▸*adj. Botany* (of a plant or flower) having the stamens and other floral parts situated below the carpels (or gynoecium). Compare with EPIGYNOUS, PERIGYNOUS. ▷early 19th cent.: from modern Latin *hypogynus*, from HYPO- 'below' + *gunē* 'woman' (used to represent 'pistil') + -OUS. —**hy·pog·y·ny** /-ˈpäjənē/ *n.*

hy·poid /ˈhīˌpoid/ (also **hypoid gear**) ▸*n.* a bevel wheel with teeth engaging with a spiral pinion mounted at right angles to the wheel's axis, used to connect nonintersecting shafts in vehicle transmissions and other mechanisms. ▷1920s: perhaps a contraction of HYPERBOLOID.

hy·po·ka·le·mi·a /ˌhīpōkāˈlēmēə/ (*Brit.* **hy·po·ka·lae·mi·a**) ▸*n. Medicine* deficiency of potassium in the bloodstream. ▷1940s: from HYPO- 'below' + modern Latin *kalium* 'potassium.' —**hy·po·ka·le·mic** /-ˈlēmik/ *adj.*

hy·po·lim·ni·on /ˌhīpəˈlimnēˌän; -nēən/ ▸*n.* (*pl.* **-ni·a** /-nēə/) the lower layer of water in a stratified lake, typically cooler than the water above and relatively stagnant. ▷early 20th cent.: from HYPO- 'below' + Greek *limnion* (diminutive of *limnē* 'lake').

hy·po·mag·ne·se·mi·a /ˌhīpəˌmagnəˈsēmēə/ (*Brit.* **hy·po·mag·ne·sae·mi·a**) ▸*n. Medicine & Veterinary Medicine* deficiency of magnesium in the blood, significant in cattle as the cause of grass tetany. —**hy·po·mag·ne·se·mic** /-ˈsēmik/ *adj.*

hy·po·ma·ni·a /ˌhīpəˈmānēə/ ▸*n. Psychiatry* a mild form of mania, marked by elation and hyperactivity. —**hy·po·man·ic** /-ˈmanik/ *adj.*

hy·po·nym /ˈhīpəˌnim/ ▸*n.* a word of more specific meaning than a general or superordinate term applicable to it. For example, *spoon* is a hyponym of *cutlery*. Contrasted with HYPERNYM. —**hy·pon·y·my** /hīˈpänəmē/ *n.*

hy·po·par·a·thy·roid·ism /ˌhīpōˌparəˈTHīroiˌdizəm/ ▸*n. Medicine* diminished concentration of parathyroid hormone in the blood, which causes deficiencies of calcium and phosphorus compounds in the blood and results in muscular spasms. —**hy·po·par·a·thy·roid** *adj.*

hy·poph·y·sis /hīˈpäfəsis/ ▸*n.* (*pl.* **-ses** /-ˌsēz/) *Anatomy* technical term for PITUITARY. ▷late 17th cent.: modern Latin, from Greek *hupophusis* 'offshoot,' from *hupo* 'under' + *phusis* 'growth.' —**hy·po·phys·e·al** /ˌhīpəˈfizēəl; hīˌpäfəˈsēəl/ (also **hy·po·phys·i·al**) *adj.*

hy·po·pi·tu·i·ta·rism /ˌhīpōˌpiˈt(y)o͞o-itəˌrizəm/ ▸*n. Medicine* diminished hormone secretion by the pituitary gland, causing dwarfism in children and premature aging in adults. —**hy·po·pi·tu·i·tar·y** /ˌhīpōpəˈt(y)o͞oiˌterē/ *adj.*

hy·po·pne·a /hīˈpäpnēə; hi-/ ▸*n.* abnormally slow or shallow breathing.

hy·po·rhe·ic ▸*adj.* denoting an area or ecosystem beneath the bed of a river or stream that is saturated with water and that supports invertebrate fauna which play a role in the larger ecosystem: *the hyporheic zone.*

hy·po·sen·si·tiv·i·ty /ˈhīpōˌsensiˈtivitē/ ▸*n.* a lower than normal sensitivity to stimuli.

hy·po·sen·si·tize /ˌhīpōˈsensiˌtīz/ ▸*v.* [*trans.*] reduce the sensitivity of (a hypersensitive person) to an allergen by frequently injecting small amounts of the allergen; desensitize. —**hy·po·sen·si·ti·za·tion** /ˈhīpōˌsensitiˈzāSHən/ *n.*

hy·po·spa·di·as /ˌhīpəˈspādēəs; ˌhipə-/ ▸*n. Medicine* a congenital condition in males in which the opening of the urethra is on the underside of the penis. ▷early 19th cent.: from Greek *hupospadias* 'person having hypospadias.'

hy·po·spray /ˈhīpōˌsprā/ ▸*n.* (chiefly in science fiction) a device used to introduce a drug or other substance into the body through the skin without puncturing it.

hy·pos·ta·sis /hīˈpästəsis/ ▸*n.* (*pl.* **-ses** /-ˌsēz/) **1** *Medicine* the accumulation of fluid or blood in the lower parts of the body or organs under the influence of gravity, as occurs in cases of poor circulation or after death. **2** *Philosophy* an underlying reality or substance, as opposed to attributes or that which lacks substance. ■ *Theology* (in Trinitarian doctrine) each of the three persons of the Trinity, as contrasted with the unity of the Godhead. ■ [in *sing.*] *Theology* the single person of Christ, as contrasted with his dual human and divine nature. ▷early 16th cent. (in theological use): via ecclesiastical Latin from Greek *hupostasis* 'sediment,' later 'essence, substance,' from *hupo* 'under' + *stasis* 'standing.'

hy·pos·ta·size /hīˈpästəˌsīz/ ▸*v.* another term for HYPOSTATIZE.

hy·po·stat·ic /ˌhīpəˈstatik/ ▸*adj. Theology* relating to the persons of the Trinity. —**hy·po·stat·i·cal** *adj.*

hy·po·stat·ic un·ion ▸*n. Theology* the combination of divine and human natures in the single person of Christ.

hy·pos·ta·tize /hīˈpästəˌtīz/ ▸*v.* [*trans.*] *formal* treat or represent (something abstract) as a concrete reality.

hy·po·sthe·ni·a /ˌhīpäsˈTHēnēə/ ▸*n.* an abnormal lack of strength.

hy·po·style /ˈhīpəˌstīl/ ▸*adj. Architecture* (of a building) having a roof supported by pillars, typically in several rows.

▸*n.* a building having such a roof. ▷mid 19th cent.: from Greek *hupostulos*, from *hupo* 'under' + *stulos* 'column.'

hy·po·tax·is /ˌhīpəˈtaksis/ ▸*n. Grammar* the subordination of one clause to another. Contrasted with PARATAXIS. ▷late 19th cent.: from Greek *hupotaxis*, from *hupo* 'under' + *taxis* 'arrangement.' —**hy·po·tac·tic** /ˌhīpəˈtaktik/ *adj.*

hy·po·ten·sion /ˌhīpəˈtenSHən/ ▸*n.* abnormally low blood pressure.

hy·po·ten·sive /ˌhīpōˈtensiv/ ▸*adj.* lowering the blood pressure: *hypotensive drugs.* ■ relating to or suffering from abnormally low blood pressure.

hy·pot·e·nuse /hīˈpätnˌ(y)o͞os/ ▸*n.* the longest side of a right triangle, opposite the right angle. ▷late 16th cent.: via Latin *hypotenusa* from Greek *hupoteinousa (grammē)* 'subtending (line),' from the verb *hupoteinein* (from *hupo* 'under' + *teinein* 'stretch').

hypoth. ▸*abbr.* ■ hypothesis or hypothetical.

hy·po·thal·a·mus /ˌhīpəˈTHaləməs/ ▸*n.* (*pl.* **-mi** /-ˌmī/) *Anatomy* a region of the forebrain below the thalamus that coordinates both the autonomic nervous system and the activity of the pituitary, controlling body temperature, thirst, hunger, and other homeostatic systems, and involved in sleep and emotional activity. —**hy·po·tha·lam·ic** /ˌhīpōˌTHəˈlamik/ *adj.*

hy·poth·e·cate /həˈpäTHiˌkāt; hī-/ ▸*v.* [*trans.*] pledge (money) by law to a specific purpose. ▷early 17th cent.: from medieval Latin *hypothecat-* 'given as a pledge,' from the verb *hypothecare*, based on Greek *hupothēkē*. —**hy·poth·e·ca·tion** /həˌpäTHiˈkāSHən; hī-/ *n.*

hy·po·ther·mal /ˌhīpəˈTHərməl/ ▸*adj.* not very hot; tepid. ■ relating to or suffering from hypothermia. ■ *Geology* of or relating to mineral deposits formed at relatively high temperature and pressure. —**hy·po·ther·mic** /-ˈTHərmik/ *adj.*

hy·po·ther·mi·a /ˌhīpəˈTHərmēə/ ▸*n.* the condition of having an abnormally low body temperature, typically one that is dangerously low. ▷late 19th cent.: from HYPO- 'below' + Greek *thermē* 'heat.'

hy·poth·e·sis /hīˈpäTHəsis/ ▸*n.* (*pl.* **-ses** /-ˌsēz/) a supposition or proposed explanation made on the basis of limited evidence as a starting point for further investigation: *professional astronomers attacked him for popularizing an unconfirmed hypothesis.* ■ *Philosophy* a proposition made as a basis for reasoning, without any assumption of its truth. ▷late 16th cent.: via late Latin from Greek *hupothesis* 'foundation,' from *hupo* 'under' + *thesis* 'placing.'

hy·poth·e·sis test·ing ▸*n. Statistics* the theory, methods, and practice of testing a hypothesis by comparing it with the null hypothesis. The null hypothesis is only rejected if its probability falls below a predetermined significance level, in which case the hypothesis being tested is said to have that level of significance.

hy·poth·e·size /hīˈpäTHəˌsīz/ ▸*v.* [*trans.*] put (something) forward as a hypothesis: *it was reasonable to hypothesize a viral causality* | [with *clause*] *they hypothesize that the naturally high insulin levels result from a "thrifty gene."* —**hy·poth·e·siz·er** *n.*

hy·po·thet·i·cal /ˌhīpəˈTHetikəl/ ▸*adj.* of, based on, or serving as a hypothesis: *that option is merely hypothetical at this juncture.* ■ supposed but not necessarily real or true: *the hypothetical tenth planet.* ■ *Logic* denoting or containing a proposition of the logical form *if p then q*.

▸*n.* (usu. **hypotheticals**) a hypothetical proposition or statement: *Finn talked in hypotheticals, tossing what-if scenarios to Rosen.* —**hy·po·thet·i·cal·ly** /-ik(ə)lē/ *adv.* [*sentence adverb*] *hypothetically, varying interpretations of the term are possible.*

hy·po·thet·i·co-de·duc·tive /ˌhīpəˈTHetiˌkō diˈdəktiv/ ▸*adj. Philosophy* of or relating to the testing of the consequences of hypotheses, to determine whether the hypotheses themselves are false or acceptable.

hy·po·thy·roid·ism /ˌhīpōˈTHīroiˌdizəm/ ▸*n. Medicine* abnormally low activity of the thyroid gland, resulting in retardation of growth and mental development in children and adults. —**hy·po·thy·roid** *n. & adj.*

hy·po·ton·ic /ˌhīpəˈtänik/ ▸*adj.* having reduced pressure or tone, in particular: ■ *Biology* having a lower osmotic pressure than a particular fluid, typically a body fluid or intracellular fluid. ■ *Physiology* of or in a state of abnormally low muscle tone. —**hy·po·to·ni·a** /-ˈtōnēə/ *n.* —**hy·po·to·nic·i·ty** /ˌhīpōtōˈnisitē/ *n.*

hy·pot·ro·phy /hīˈpätrəfē/ ▸*n.* (*pl.* **-phies**) a degeneration of an organ or tissue caused by a loss of cells.

hy·po·ven·ti·la·tion /ˌhīpōˌventlˈāSHən/ ▸*n. Medicine* breathing at an abnormally slow rate, resulting in an increased amount of carbon dioxide in the blood.

hy·po·vo·le·mi·a /ˌhīpōvəˈlēmēə/ (*Brit.* **hy·po·vo·lae·mi·a**) ▸*n. Medicine* a decreased volume of circulating blood in the body. ▷early 20th cent.: from HYPO- 'under' + VOLUME + Greek *haima* 'blood.' —**hy·po·vo·le·mic** /-ˈlēmik/ *adj.*

hy·po·xan·thine /ˌhīpōˈzanˌTHēn/ ▸*n. Biochemistry* a compound that is an intermediate in the metabolism of purines in animals and occurs in plant tissues. • Alternative name: **6-hydroxypurine**; chem. formula: $C_5H_4N_4O$.

hy·pox·e·mi·a /ˌhīpäkˈsēmēə/ (*Brit.* **hy·pox·ae·mi·a**) ▸*n. Medicine* an abnormally low concentration of oxygen in the blood. ▷late 19th cent.: from HYPO- (denoting an element in a low valency) + OXYGEN + -EMIA.

hy·pox·i·a /hīˈpäksēə/ ▸*n. Medicine* deficiency in the amount of oxygen reaching the tissues. ■ oxygen deficiency in a biotic environment leading to this: *aquatic hypoxia.* ▷1940s: from HYPO- (denoting an element in a low valency) + OXYGEN + -IA[1]. —**hy·pox·ic** /-sik/ *adj.*

hyp·si·loph·o·dont /ˌhipsəˈläfəˌdänt/ (also **hyp·si·loph·o·don·tid** /-ˌläfəˈdäntid/) ▸*n.* a small bipedal herbivorous dinosaur of the middle Jurassic to late Cretaceous periods, adapted for swift running. • Family Hypsilophodontidae, infraorder Ornithopoda, order Ornithischia. ▷late 19th cent.: from modern Latin *Hypsilophodontidae*, from Greek *hupsilophos* 'high-crested' + *odous, odont-* 'tooth.'

hypso- ▸*comb. form* relating to height or elevation: *hypsometer.* ▷from Greek *hupsos* 'height.'

hyp·sog·ra·phy /hipˈsägrəfē/ ▸*n.* the branch of geography concerned with the determination and mapping of the relative elevation of areas of land. —**hyp·so·graph·ic** /ˌhipsəˈgrafik/ *adj.* —**hyp·so·graph·i·cal** /ˌhipsōˈgrafikəl/ *adj.*

hyp·som·e·ter /hipˈsämitər/ ▸*n.* a device for calibrating thermometers at the boiling point of water at a known height above sea level or for estimating height above sea level by finding the temperature at which water boils.

hyp·so·met·ric /ˌhipsōˈmetrik/ ▸*adj.* of or relating to the use of the hypsometer; hypsographic.

Hy·ra·coi·de·a /ˌhīrəˈkoidēə/ *Zoology* a small order of mammals that comprises the hyraxes. ▷modern Latin (plural), based on Greek *hurax, hurak-* (see HYRAX). —**hy·ra·coid** /ˈhīrəˌkoid/ *n. & adj.*

hy·ra·co·the·ri·um /ˌhīrəkōˈTHi(ə)rēəm/ ▸*n.* the earliest fossil ancestor of the horse. It was a small forest animal of the Eocene epoch, with four toes on the front feet and three on the back. Also called EOHIPPUS. • Genus *Hyracotherium*, family Equidae. ▷modern Latin: from *hyraco-* (combining form from HYRAX) + Greek *thērion* 'wild animal.'

hy·rax /ˈhīˌraks/ ▸*n.* a small herbivorous mammal with a compact body and a very short tail, found in arid country in Africa and Arabia. The nearest relatives to hyraxes are the elephants and other subungulates. • Family Procaviidae and order Hyracoidea: three genera and several species. ▷mid 19th cent.: modern Latin, from Greek *hurax* 'shrewmouse.'

hy·son /ˈhīsən/ ▸*n.* a type of green China tea. ▷mid 18th cent.: from Chinese *xīchūn*, literally 'bright spring.'

hys·sop /ˈhisəp/ ▸*n.* **1** a small bushy aromatic plant of the mint family, the bitter minty leaves of which are used in cooking and herbal medicine. • *Hyssopus officinalis*, family Labiatae. **2** (in biblical use) a wild shrub of uncertain identity whose twigs were used for sprinkling in ancient Jewish rites of purification. ▷Old English *hysope* (reinforced in Middle English by Old French *ysope*), via Latin from Greek *hyssōpos*, of Semitic origin.

hys·ter·ec·to·mize /ˌhistəˈrektəˌmīz/ ▸*v.* [*trans.*] perform a hysterectomy on (a woman or a female animal).

hys·ter·ec·to·my /ˌhistəˈrektəmē/ ▸*n.* (*pl.* **-mies**) a surgical operation to remove all or part of the uterus. ▷late 19th cent.: from Greek *hustera* 'womb' + -ECTOMY.

hys·ter·e·sis /ˌhistəˈrēsis/ ▸*n.* *Physics* the phenomenon in which the value of a physical property lags behind changes in the effect causing it, as for instance when magnetic induction lags behind the magnetizing force. ▷late 19th cent.: from Greek *husterēsis* 'shortcoming, deficiency,' from *husterein* 'be behind,' from *husteros* 'late.'

hys·te·ri·a /hiˈsterēə; -ˈsti(ə)rēə/ ▸*n.* exaggerated or uncontrollable emotion or excitement, esp. among a group of people: *the mass hysteria that characterizes the week before Christmas.* ■ *Psychiatry* a psychological disorder (not now regarded as a single definite condition) whose symptoms include conversion of psychological stress into physical symptoms (somatization), selective amnesia, shallow volatile emotions, and overdramatic or attention-seeking behavior. The term has a controversial history as it was formerly regarded as a disease specific to women. ▷early 19th cent.: from Latin *hystericus* (see HYSTERIC).

hys·ter·ic /hiˈsterik/ ▸*n.* **1** (**hysterics**) *informal* a wildly emotional and exaggerated reaction: *the child has been seized with regular fits of hysterics at bedtime.* ■ uncontrollable laughter: *this started them both giggling and they fled upstairs* ***in hysterics.*** **2** a person suffering from hysteria.
▸*adj.* another term for HYSTERICAL (sense 2). ▷mid 17th cent. (as an adjective): via Latin from Greek *husterikos* 'of the womb,' from *hustera* 'womb' (hysteria being thought to be specific to women and associated with the womb), related to UTERUS.

hys·ter·i·cal /hiˈsterikəl/ ▸*adj.* **1** deriving from or affected by uncontrolled extreme emotion: *hysterical laughter | the band was mobbed by hysterical fans.* ■ *informal* extremely funny: *her attempts to teach them to dance were hysterical.* **2** *Psychiatry* relating to, associated with, or suffering from hysteria: *the doctor thinks the condition is partly hysterical.* ■ another term for HISTRIONIC (denoting personality disorder). **—hys·ter·i·cal·ly** *adv.* [as *submodifier*] *isn't it hysterically funny?*

hys·ter·i·cal re·al·ism ▸*n.* realistic fiction that is characterized by overblown prose and intellectual digressions.

hys·ter·on prot·er·on /ˈhistəˌrän ˈprätəˌrän/ ▸*n.* *Rhetoric* a figure of speech in which what should come last is put first, i.e., an inversion of the natural order, for example "*I die! I faint! I fail!*" ▷mid 16th cent.: late Latin, from Greek *husteron proteron* 'the latter (put in place of) the former.'

Hys·tri·co·mor·pha /ˌhistrikōˈmôrfə/ *Zoology* a major division of the rodents that includes the guinea pigs, porcupines, coypu, and their relatives. They occur chiefly in South America. • Suborder Hystricomorpha, order Rodentia. ▷modern Latin (plural), from Latin *hystrix, hystric-* 'porcupine' (from Greek *hustrix*) + *morphē* 'form.' **—hys·tri·co·morph** /ˈhistrikōˌmôrf/ *n.* & *adj.*

Hy·trel /ˈhīˌtrel/ ▸*n.* *trademark* a strong, flexible synthetic resin used in shoes, sports equipment, and other manufactured articles.

Hz ▸*abbr.* hertz.

Ii

I[1] /ī/ (also **i**) ▸*n.* (*pl.* **Is** or **I's**) **1** the ninth letter of the alphabet. ■ denoting the next after H in a set of items, categories, etc. **2** the Roman numeral for one.
▸*PHRASE* □ **dot the i's and cross the t's** see DOT[1].

I[2] ▸*pron.* [*first person singular*] used by a speaker to refer to himself or herself: *accept me for what I am.*
▸*n.* (**the I**) *Philosophy* (in metaphysics) the subject or object of self-consciousness; the ego. ▷Old English, of Germanic origin; related to Dutch *ik* and German *ich*, from an Indo-European root shared by Latin *ego* and Greek *egō*.

USAGE On whether it is correct to say *between you and I* or *between you and* **me**, see **usage** at BETWEEN and PERSONAL PRONOUN.
On whether it is correct to say *Rachel and I went to Paris* or *Rachel and* **me** *went to Paris*, see **usage** at PERSONAL PRONOUN.

I[3] ▸*abbr.* ■ Independent. ■ (preceding a highway number) Interstate. ■ (**I.**) Island(s) or Isle(s) (chiefly on maps).
▸*symbol* ■ electric current: $V = I/R$. ■ the chemical element iodine.

i ▸*symbol* (*i*) *Mathematics* the imaginary quantity equal to the square root of minus one. Compare with J.

-i[1] ▸*suffix* forming the plural: **1** of nouns adopted from Latin ending in *-us*: *foci* | *timpani.* **2** of nouns adopted from Italian ending in *-e* or *-o*: *dilettanti.*

USAGE The suffix **-i** is one of several suffixes in the English language that form foreign plurals (*-a* and *-ae* are two others). Many nouns derived from a foreign language retain their foreign plural, at least when they first enter English and particularly if they belong to a specialized field. Over time, however, it is quite normal for a word in general use to acquire a regular English plural. This may coexist with the foreign plural (e.g., there are two equally acceptable plurals of **cactus**: the Latin form **cacti** and the English form **cactuses**), or it may actually oust a foreign plural (e.g., there is now one standard plural of **octopus**: the English form **octopuses**, which has supplanted the Greek form **octopodes**).

-i[2] ▸*suffix* forming adjectives from names of countries or regions in the Near or Middle East: *Azerbaijani* | *Pakistani.* ▷from Semitic and Indo-Iranian adjectival endings.

-i- ▸*suffix* a connecting vowel chiefly forming words ending in *-ana, -ferous, -fic, -form, -fy, -gerous, -vorous.* Compare with **-O-**.

IA ▸*abbr.* Iowa (in official postal use).

Ia. ▸*abbr.* Iowa.

i.a. ▸*abbr.* in absentia.

-ia[1] ▸*suffix* **1** forming nouns adopted unchanged from Latin or Greek (such as *mania, militia*), and modern Latin or Greek terms (such as *utopia*). **2** forming names of: ■ *Medicine* states and disorders: *anemia* | *diphtheria.* ■ *Botany & Zoology* genera and higher groups: *dahlia* | *Latimeria.* **3** forming names of countries: *India.* ▷representing Latin or Greek endings.

-ia[2] ▸*suffix* forming noun plurals: **1** from Greek neuter nouns ending in *-ion* or from those in Latin ending in *-ium* or *-e*: *paraphernalia* | *regalia.* **2** *Zoology* in the names of classes: *Reptilia.*

IAA *Biochemistry* ▸*abbr.* indoleacetic acid.

IAAF ▸*abbr.* International Amateur Athletic Federation.

IABA ▸*abbr.* International Amateur Boxing Association.

Ia·coc·ca /ˌīəˈkōkə/, Lee (1924–) U.S. industrialist; full name *Lido Anthony Iacocca.* He was president of Ford Motor Company 1970–78 before leading the Chrysler Corporation 1978–92. He told his success story in *Iacocca* (1984).

IADB ▸*abbr.* ■ Inter-American Defense Board. ■ Inter-American Development Bank.

IAEA ▸*abbr.* International Atomic Energy Agency.

-ial ▸*suffix* forming adjectives such as *celestial, primordial.* ▷from French *-iel* or Latin *-ialis.*

IALC ▸*abbr.* instrument approach and landing chart.

IAMAW ▸*abbr.* International Association of Machinists and Aerospace Workers.

i·amb /ˈīˌam(b)/ ▸*n. Prosody* a metrical foot consisting of one short (or unstressed) syllable followed by one long (or stressed) syllable.

i·am·bic /īˈambik/ ▸*adj. Prosody* of or using iambs: *iambic pentameters.*
▸*n.* a verse using iambs. ■ (**iambics**) verse of this kind. ▷mid 16th cent.: from French *iambique*, via late Latin from Greek *iambikos*, from *iambos* (see IAMBUS).

i·am·bus /īˈambəs/ ▸*n.* (*pl.* **-bus·es** or **-bi** /-bī/) *Prosody* another term for IAMB. ▷late 16th cent.: Latin, from Greek *iambos* 'iambus, lampoon,' from *iaptein* 'attack verbally' (because the iambic trimeter was first used by Greek satirists).

-ian /ēən; ən/ ▸*suffix* forming adjectives and nouns such as *antediluvian* and *Christian.* Compare with **-AN**. ▷from French *-ien* or Latin *-ianus.*

IAP ▸*abbr.* international airport.

I·ap·e·tus /īˈapetəs; ēˈap-/ *Astronomy* a satellite of Saturn, the seventeenth closest to the planet, discovered by Cassini in 1671. It has one bright icy side and one very dark side and a diameter of 907 miles (1,460 km). ▷named after a Titan of Greek mythology, son of Uranus (Heaven) and Gaia (Earth).

IAQ ▸*abbr.* indoor air quality.

IARU ▸*abbr.* International Amateur Radio Union.

IAS ▸*abbr.* ■ indicated air speed. ■ Institute for Advanced Studies.

Ia·şi /yäsн/ a city in eastern Romania; pop. 338,000. From 1565 to 1859 it was the capital of the principality of Moldavia. German name **JASSY**.

-iasis ▸*suffix* a common form of **-ASIS**.

IATA /īˈätə/ ▸*abbr.* International Air Transport Association.

iatro- ▸*comb. form* relating to a physician or to medical treatment: *iatrogenic.* ▷from Greek *iatros* 'physician,' from *iasthai* 'heal.'

i·at·ro·chem·is·try /īˌatrəˈkemistrē/ ▸*n. historical* a school of thought of the 16th and 17th centuries that sought to understand medicine and physiology in terms of chemistry. **—i·at·ro·chem·i·cal** *adj.* **—i·at·ro·chem·ist** *n.*

i·at·ro·gen·ic /īˌatrəˈjenik/ ▸*adj.* of or relating to illness caused by medical examination or treatment. **—i·at·ro·gen·e·sis** /-ˈjenisis/ *n.*

IAU ▸*abbr.* ■ International Association of Universities. ■ International Astronomical Union.

ib. ▸*adv.* short for IBID.

I·ba·ban /ēˈbädn/ the second largest city in Nigeria, 100 miles (160 km) northeast of Lagos; pop. 1,295,000.

I·ba·gué /ˌēbəˈgā/ a city in west central Colombia, capital of Tolima department; pop. 334,000.

I·bá·rru·ri Gó·mez /iˈbärərē ˈgōmez/, Dolores (1895–1989), Spanish politician and leader of the Republicans during the Spanish Civil War; known as **La Pasionaria**.

I-beam ▸*n.* a girder that has the shape of an I when viewed in section.

I·be·ri·a /īˈbi(ə)rēə/ the ancient name of the Iberian peninsula. ▷Latin, literally 'the country of the *Iberi* or *Iberes*,' from Greek *Ibēres* 'Spaniards.'

I·be·ri·an /īˈbi(ə)rēən/ ▸*adj.* relating to or denoting Iberia, or the countries of Spain and Portugal.
▸*n.* **1** a native of Iberia, esp. in ancient times. **2** the extinct Romance language spoken in the Iberian peninsula in late classical times. It forms an intermediate stage between Latin and modern Spanish, Catalan, and Portuguese. Also called **IBERO-ROMANCE**. **3** the extinct Celtic language spoken in the Iberian peninsula in ancient times, known only from a few inscriptions, place names, and references by Latin authors. Also called **CELTIBERIAN**.

I·be·ri·an pen·in·su·la the extreme southwestern peninsula of Europe that contains Spain and Portugal.

Ibero- ▸*comb. form* Iberian; Iberian and . . . : *Ibero-Roman.* ■ relating to Iberia.

I·be·ro-Ro·mance /īˈbi(ə)rō rōˈmans/ ▸*n.* another term for **IBERIAN** (sense 2).

i·bex /ˈīˌbeks/ ▸*n.* (*pl.* **i·bex·es**) a wild goat with long, thick ridged horns and a beard, found in the mountains of the Alps, Pyrenees, central Asia, and Ethiopia. • Genus *Capra*, family Bovidae: the widespread *C. ibex*, and the **Spanish ibex** (*C. pyrenaica*) of the Pyrenees. ▷early 17th cent.: from Latin.

IBF ▸*abbr.* International Boxing Federation.

I·bi·bi·o /iˈbibēō; ibəˈbēō/ ▸*n.* (*pl.* same or **-i·os**) **1** a member of a people of southern Nigeria. **2** the Benue-Congo language of this people, closely related to Efik.
▸*adj.* of or relating to this people or their language. ▷the name in Ibibio.

ibid. /ˈibid/ (also **ib.**) ▸*adv.* in the same source (used to save space in textual references to a quoted work that has been mentioned in a previous reference). ▷abbreviation of Latin *ibidem* 'in the same place.'

-ibility ▸*suffix* forming nouns corresponding to adjectives ending in *-ible* (such as *accessibility* corresponding to *accessible*). ▷from French *-ibilité* or Latin *-ibilitas.*

i·bis /ˈībis/ ▸*n.* (*pl.* **i·bis·es**) a large wading bird with a long down-curved bill, long neck, and long legs. • Family Threskiornithidae: several genera and species, including the **sacred ibis** and **white ibis**. ▷late Middle English: via Latin from Greek.

i·bis·bill /ˈībisˌbil/ ▸*n.* an upland wading bird of central Asia, with a long, down-curved bill and black, white, and blue-gray plumage on the head and breast. • *Ibidorhyncha struthersii*, the only member of the family Ibidorhynchidae.

I·bi·za /iˈbēтнə; iˈvēтнə/ the most western of the Balearic Islands, a popular resort. ■ its capital city and port; pop. 25,000. **—I·bi·zan** *adj.* & *n.*

I·bi·zan hound /iˈbēzən/ ▸*n.* a dog of a breed of hound from Ibiza, characterized by large, pointed, pricked ears and white, yellowish-, or reddish-brown coloring.

-ible /əbəl; ibəl/ ▸*suffix* forming adjectives: **1** able to be: *audible* | *defensible.* **2** suitable for being: *reversible* | *edible.* **3** causing: *terrible* | *horrible.* **4** having the quality to: *descendible* | *passible.* ▷from French *-ible* or Latin *-ibilis.*

-ibly ▸*suffix* forming adverbs corresponding to adjectives ending in *-ible* (such as *audibly* corresponding to *audible*).

IBM ▸*abbr.* International Business Machines, a leading U.S. computer manufacturer.

Ibn Ba·tu·ta /ˌibən bəˈto͞otə/ (*c.*1304–68), Arab explorer. From 1325 to 1354, he traveled through northern and western Africa, India, and China and wrote a vivid account of his journey in the *Rihlah.*

ibn Hus·sein, Abdullah, see **ABDULLAH IBN HUSSEIN**.

Ibn Sa·ud /ˌibən säˈo͞od/ (*c.*1880–1953) king of Saudi Arabia 1932–53; full name *Abd al-Aziz ibn Abd ar-Rahman ibn Faysal ibn Turki Abd Allah ibn Muhammad Al Saud.* A powerful Muslim leader, he founded Saudi

Arabia 1932 after having unified the various domains over which he had assumed sovereignty.

I·bo /ˈēbō/ (also **Ig·bo**) /ˈigˌbō/ ▸*n.* (*pl.* same or **I·bos**) **1** a member of a people of southeastern Nigeria. **2** the Kwa language of this people.

▸*adj.* of or relating to this people or their language. ▷a local name.

i·bo·ga·ine /iˈbōgəˌēn/ ▸*n.* a hallucinogenic compound derived from the roots of a West African shrub, sometimes used as a treatment for heroin or cocaine addiction. • The shrub is *Tabernanthe iboga*, family Apocynaceae. ▷from a blend of *iboga* (local name for the compound) and COCAINE.

IBRD ▸*abbr.* International Bank for Reconstruction and Development.

IBS ▸*abbr.* irritable bowel syndrome.

Ib·sen /ˈibsən/, Henrik (1828–1906), Norwegian playwright. He was the first major playwright to write tragedy about ordinary people in prose. Notable works: *Peer Gynt* (1867), *A Doll's House* (1879), *Ghosts* (1881), and *The Master Builder* (1892).

i·bu·pro·fen /ˌībyo͞oˈprōfən/ ▸*n.* a synthetic compound used widely as an analgesic and anti-inflammatory drug. • Alternative name: **2-(4-isobutylphenyl) propionic acid**; chem. formula: $C_{13}H_{18}O_2$. ▷1960s: from elements of the chemical name.

IC ▸*abbr.* ■ integrated circuit. ■ intensive care. ■ internal combustion: *the IC engine.*

i/c ▸*abbr.* ■ (esp. in military contexts) in charge of: *the quartermaster general is i/c rations.* ■ in command: *2 i/c = second in command*

-ic ▸*suffix* **1** forming adjectives such as *Islamic, terrific.* **2** forming nouns such as *lyric, mechanic.* **3** denoting a particular form or instance of a noun ending in *-ics*: *aesthetic | dietetic | tactic.* **4** *Chemistry* denoting an element in a higher valence: *ferric | sulfuric.* Compare with **-ous**. ▷from French *-ique*, Latin *-icus*, or Greek *-ikos*.

-ical /ikəl/ ▸*suffix* forming adjectives: **1** corresponding to nouns or adjectives usually ending in *-ic* (such as *comical* corresponding to *comic*). **2** corresponding to nouns ending in *-y* (such as *pathological* corresponding to *pathology*).

-ically ▸*suffix* forming adverbs corresponding to adjectives ending in *-ic* or *-ical* (such as *tactically* corresponding to *tactical*).

ICANN ▸*abbr.* Internet Committee for Assigned Names and Numbers, the nonprofit organization that oversees the use of Internet domains.

ICAO ▸*abbr.* International Civil Aviation Organization.

Ic·a·rus /ˈikərəs/ *Greek Mythology* the son of Daedalus, who escaped from Crete using wings made by his father but was killed when he flew too near the sun and the wax attaching his wings melted. **—I·car·i·an** /iˈke(ə)rēən; īˈke(ə)r-/ *adj.*

ICBM ▸*abbr.* intercontinental ballistic missile.

ICC ▸*abbr.* ■ Interstate Commerce Commission. ■ International Chamber of Commerce. ■ International Criminal Court.

ICE ▸*abbr.* internal combustion engine.

ice /īs/ ▸*n.* frozen water, a brittle, transparent crystalline solid: *the pipes were blocked with ice.* ■ a frozen mixture of fruit juice or flavored water and sugar. ■ *informal* diamonds. ■ *figurative* complete absence of friendliness or affection in manner or expression: *the ice in his voice was only to hide the pain.* ■ *informal* an illegal profit made from scalping tickets. ■ *informal* money paid in graft or bribery. ■ *informal* methamphetamine.

▸*v.* [*trans.*] **1** decorate (a cake) with icing. **2** *informal* clinch (something such as a victory or deal). **3** *informal* kill: *a man had been iced by the police.* **4** *Ice Hockey* shoot (the puck) so as to commit icing.

▸*phrasal v.* □ **ice over** (of water or an object) become completely covered with ice. □ **ice up** (of an object) become coated with or blocked by ice. ▷Old English *īs*, of Germanic origin; related to Dutch *ijs* and German *Eis*.

▸*PHRASES* □ **break the ice** do or say something to relieve tension or get conversation going at the start of a party or when people meet for the first time. □ **on ice 1** (of wine or food) kept chilled by being surrounded by ice. ■ *figurative* (esp. of a plan or proposal) held in reserve for future consideration: *the recommendation was put on ice.* **2** (of an entertainment) performed by skaters: *Cinderella on Ice.* □ **on thin ice** in a precarious or risky situation: *you're skating on thin ice.*

-ice ▸*suffix* forming nouns such as *service, police,* and abstract nouns such as *avarice, justice.* ▷from Old French *-ice*, from Latin *-itia, -itius, -itium,* or from other sources by assimilation.

ice age ▸*n.* a glacial episode during a past geological period. See GLACIAL PERIOD. ■ (**the Ice Age**) the series of glacial episodes during the Pleistocene period.

ice ax (also **ice axe**) ▸*n.* an ax used by climbers for cutting footholds in ice, having a head with one pointed and one flattened end, and a spike at the foot.

ice bag ▸*n.* another term for ICE PACK (sense 1).

ice beer ▸*n.* a type of strong lager brewed at subzero temperatures so that ice crystals form. These are then strained off to remove impurities and excess water.

ice·berg /ˈīsˌbərg/ ▸*n.* a large floating mass of ice detached from a glacier or ice sheet and carried out to sea. ▷late 18th cent.: from Dutch *ijsberg*, from *ijs* 'ice' + *berg* 'hill.'

▸*PHRASE* □ **the tip of the iceberg** the small, perceptible part of a much larger situation or problem that remains hidden: *the statistics represent just the tip of the iceberg.*

ice·berg let·tuce ▸*n.* a lettuce of a variety having a dense, round head of crisp, pale leaves.

ice·blink /ˈīsˌbliNGk/ ▸*n.* a bright appearance of the sky caused by reflection from a distant ice sheet.

ice blue ▸*n.* a very pale blue color.

ice·boat /ˈīsˌbōt/ ▸*n.* **1** a light, wind-driven vehicle with sails and runners, used for traveling on ice. **2** a boat used for breaking ice on a waterway; an icebreaker.

ice·bound /ˈīsˌbound/ ▸*adj.* completely surrounded or covered by ice: *the lake was icebound.*

ice·box /ˈīsˌbäks/ ▸*n.* a chilled box or cupboard for keeping something cold, esp. food. ■ *dated* a refrigerator.

ice·break·er /ˈīsˌbrākər/ ▸*n.* a ship designed for breaking a channel through ice. ■ a thing that serves to relieve inhibitions or tension between people, or start a conversation. ■ a thing that breaks up moving ice so as to lessen its impact, esp. a structure protecting the upstream end of a bridge pier.

ice buck·et ▸*n.* a cylindrical container holding chunks of ice, either ready to serve in drinks or for chilling a bottle of wine in.

ice cap (also **icecap**) ▸*n.* a covering of ice over a large area, esp. on the polar region of a planet.

ice chest ▸*n.* a chilled box for keeping something cold, esp. food and beverages.

ice climb·ing ▸*n.* the sport or activity of climbing glaciers. **—ice climb·er** *n.*

ice-cold ▸*adj.* (esp. of a liquid) very cold; as cold as ice: *there is plenty of ice-cold beer.* ■ *figurative* unemotional or dispassionate; unfeeling: *he is the epitome of ice-cold judgment.*

ice cream ▸*n.* a soft frozen food made with sweetened and flavored milk fat. ■ a serving of this, typically in a bowl or a wafer cone or on a stick. ▷mid 18th cent.: alteration of *iced cream.*

ice cube ▸*n.* a small block of ice made in a freezer, esp. for adding to drinks.

iced /īst/ ▸*adj.* [*attrib.*] **1** (of a drink or other liquid) cooled in or mixed with pieces of ice: *iced coffee.* ■ (of a surface or object) covered or coated with ice: *I've played ice hockey on rivers, ponds, and iced barnyards.* **2** (of a cake or cookie) decorated with icing.

ice danc·ing ▸*n.* a form of ice skating incorporating choreographed dance moves, typically performed by skaters in pairs. **—ice dance** *n.* **—ice danc·er** *n.*

iced tea (also **ice tea**) ▸*n.* a chilled drink of sweetened tea, typically flavored with lemon.

ice·fall /ˈīsˌfôl/ ▸*n.* **1** a steep part of a glacier that looks like a frozen waterfall. **2** a fall of loose ice; an avalanche of ice.

ice field ▸*n.* a wide flat expanse of floating ice, esp. in polar regions.

ice·fish /ˈīsˌfiSH/ ▸*n.* (*pl.* same or **-fish·es**) **1** another name for CAPELIN. **2** a scaleless Antarctic fish of pallid appearance with spiny gill covers and a snout shaped like a duck's bill. • *Chaenocephalus aceratus*, family Chaenichthyidae.

ice-fish ▸*v.* [*intrans.*] fish through holes in the ice on a lake or river: *ice-fish for perch.* **—ice fish·ing** *n.*

ice floe ▸*n.* see FLOE.

ice fog ▸*n.* fog formed of minute ice crystals.

ice front ▸*n.* the lower edge of a glacier.

ice hock·ey ▸*n.* a fast contact sport played on an ice rink between two teams of six skaters, who attempt to drive a small rubber disk (the puck) into the opposing goal with hooked or angled sticks. It developed in Canada in the 19th century.

ice·house /ˈīsˌhous/ (also **ice house** or **ice-house**) ▸*n.* a building for storing ice, typically one situated partly or wholly underground.

Ice·land /ˈīslənd/ an island country in the North Atlantic Ocean, just south of the Arctic Circle, at the northern end of the Mid-Atlantic Ridge, volcanically active, only about 20 percent habitable; pop. 300,000; capital, Reykjavik; official language, Icelandic. Icelandic name ÍSLAND.

First settled by Norse colonists in the 9th century, Iceland was under Norwegian rule from 1262 to 1380, when it passed to Denmark. Granted internal self-government in 1874, it became a fully fledged independent republic in 1944.

Ice·land·er /ˈīsləndər/ ▸*n.* a native or national of Iceland. ■ a person of Icelandic descent.

Ice·lan·dic /īsˈlandik/ ▸*adj.* of or relating to Iceland or its language.

▸*n.* the North Germanic language of Iceland, which is very similar to Old Norse.

Ice·land moss (also **Iceland lichen**) ▸*n.* a brown, branching lichen with stiff spines along the margins of the fronds, growing in mountain and moorland habitats. It can be boiled to produce an edible jelly. • *Cetraria islandica*, order Parmeliales.

Ice·land pop·py (also **Ice·lan·dic pop·py**) ▸*n.* a tall poppy that is widely cultivated for its colorful flowers and suitability for cutting, native to arctic and north temperate regions. • *Papaver nudicaule*, family Papaveraceae.

Ice·land spar ▸*n.* a transparent variety of calcite, showing strong double refraction.

ice·man /ˈīsmən/ ▸*n.* (*pl.* **-men**) a man who sells or delivers ice.

ice milk ▸*n.* a sweet frozen food similar to ice cream but containing less butterfat.

ice pack ▸*n.* **1** a bag filled with ice and applied to the body to reduce swelling or lower temperature. **2** another term for PACK ICE.

ice pick ▸*n.* a sharp, straight, pointed implement with a handle, used to break ice into small pieces for chilling food and drinks.

ice plant ▸*n.* either of two succulent plants that are widely cultivated for their flowers: • a South African plant that has leaves covered with glistening fluid-filled hairs that resemble ice crystals (genera *Mesembryanthemum* and *Dorotheanthus*, family Aizoaceae, in particular *M. crystallinum*). • an Asian stonecrop that bears domed heads of tiny pink flowers (*Sedum spectabile*, family Crassulaceae).

ice rink ▸*n.* see RINK.

ice sheet ▸*n.* a permanent layer of ice covering an extensive tract of land, esp. a polar region.

ice shelf ▸*n.* a floating sheet of ice permanently attached to a landmass.

ice show ▸*n.* an entertainment performed by ice skaters.

ice skate ▸*n.* a boot with a blade attached to the bottom, used for skating on ice.

figure skate

hockey skate

ice skates

Pronunciation Key ə *ago;* ər *over;* ˈə *or* ˌə *up;* ˈər *or* ˌər *fur;* a *hat;* ā *rate;* ä *car;* CH *chew;* e *let;* ē *see;* e(ə)r *air;* i *fit;* ī *by;* i(ə)r *ear;* NG *sing;* ō *go;* ô *for;* oi *boy;* o͝o *good;* o͞o *goo;* ou *out;* SH *she;* TH *thin;* T͟H *then;* (h)w *why;* ZH *vision*

▸*v.* [*intrans.*] skate on ice as a sport or pastime. —**ice skat·er** *n.*

ice skat·ing (also **ice-skat·ing**) ▸*n.* skating on ice as a sport or pastime. Ice skating became a recognized sport in 1876. Skaters are marked for technical and artistic excellence in performing a series of prescribed patterns and free skating (**figure skating**) or a choreographed series of dance moves (**ice dancing**).

ice storm ▸*n.* a storm of freezing rain that leaves a coating of ice.

ice tea ▸*n.* another term for ICED TEA.

ice wa·ter ▸*n.* water melted from ice or with ice added to cool it.

ice wine ▸*n.* a sweet, concentrated wine made from grapes that froze on the vine.

I Ching /'ē 'CHING; 'jing/ ▸*n.* an ancient Chinese manual of divination based on eight symbolic trigrams and sixty-four hexagrams, interpreted in terms of the principles of yin and yang. It was included as one of the "five classics" of Confucianism. English name BOOK OF CHANGES. ▷from Chinese *yijing* 'book of changes.'

ich·neu·mon /ik'n(y)ōōmən/ ▸*n.* **1** (also **ichneumon wasp** or **ichneumon fly**) a slender parasitic wasp with long antennae that deposits its eggs in, on, or near the larvae of other insects. • Family Ichneumonidae, order Hymenoptera: numerous genera and species. **2** another term for EGYPTIAN MONGOOSE. ▷late 15th cent. (sense 2): via Latin from Greek *ikhneumōn* 'tracker,' from *ikhneuein* 'to track,' from *ikhnos* 'track, footstep.'

ich·nog·ra·phy /ik'nägrəfē/ ▸*n.* (*pl.* **-phies**) a ground plan of a building or map of a region. ▷late 16th cent.: from French *ichnographie*, or via Latin from Greek *ikhnographia*, from *ikhnos* 'track' + *-graphia* (see -GRAPHY).

i·chor /'ī,kôr/ ▸*n.* *Greek Mythology* the fluid that flows like blood in the veins of the gods. ■ *poetic/literary* any bloodlike fluid: *tomatoes drooled ichor from their broken skins.* ■ *archaic* a watery, fetid discharge from a wound. ▷mid 17th cent.: from Greek *ikhōr*. —**i·chor·ous** /'īkərəs/ *adj.*

ichth. ▸*abbr.* ichthyology.

ich·thus /'ikTHəs/ ▸*n.* an image of a fish used as a symbol of Christianity. ▷from Greek *ikhthus* 'fish' : the initial letters of the word are sometimes taken as short for *I*esous *Ch*ristos, *Th*eou *U*ios, *S*oter (Jesus Christ, Son of God, Savior).

ich·thy·ic /'ikTHē-ik/ ▸*adj. archaic* fishlike. ▷mid 19th cent.: from Greek *ikhthuïkos* 'fishy,' from *ikhthus* 'fish.'

ichthyo- ▸*comb. form* relating to fish; fishlike: *ichthyosaur.* ▷from Greek *ikhthus* 'fish.'

ich·thy·ol·o·gy /,ikTHē'äləjē/ ▸*n.* the branch of zoology that deals with fishes. —**ich·thy·o·log·i·cal** /-ə'läjikəl/ *adj.* —**ich·thy·ol·o·gist** /-jist/ *n.*

ich·thy·oph·a·gous /,ikTHē'äfəgəs/ ▸*adj. formal* fish-eating: *Americans are more ichthyophagous than ever.* —**ich·thy·oph·a·gy** /-'äfəjē/ *n.*

ich·thy·orn·is /,ikTHē'ôrnis/ ▸*n.* an extinct, gull-like, fish-eating bird of the late Cretaceous period, with large toothed jaws. • Genus *Ichthyornis*, order Ichthyornithiformes. ▷modern Latin, from ICHTHYO- + Greek *ornis* 'bird.'

ich·thy·o·saur /'ikTHēə,sôr/ (also **ich·thy·o·sau·rus** /,ikTHēə'sôrəs/) ▸*n.* an extinct marine reptile of the Mesozoic era resembling a dolphin, with a long pointed head, four flippers, and a vertical tail. • Order Ichthyosauria, subclass Diapsida: numerous genera, including *Ichthyosaurus.* ▷mid 19th cent.: from ICHTHYO- 'fish' + Greek *sauros* 'lizard.' —**ich·thy·o·sau·ri·an** /,ikTHēə'sôrēən/ *adj.*

ich·thy·o·sis /,ikTHē'ōsis/ ▸*n. Medicine* a congenital skin condition that causes the epidermis to become dry and rough like fish scales. —**ich·thy·ot·ic** /-'ätik/ *adj.*

I-chun variant of YICHUN.

-ician ▸*suffix* (forming nouns) denoting a person skilled in or concerned with a field or subject (often corresponding to a noun ending in *-ic* or *-ics*): *politician | statistician.* ▷from French *-icien*.

i·ci·cle /'īsikəl/ ▸*n.* a hanging, tapering piece of ice formed by the freezing of dripping water. ■ a thin, shiny strip of plastic or foil hung on a Christmas tree for decoration. ▷Middle English: from ICE + dialect *ickle* 'icicle' (from Old English *gicel*).

ic·ing /'īsiNG/ ▸*n.* **1** a mixture of sugar with liquid or butter, typically flavored and colored, and used as a coating for cakes or cookies. **2** the formation of ice on an aircraft, ship, or other vehicle, or in an engine. **3** *Ice Hockey* the action of shooting the puck from one's own end of the rink to the other but not into the goal, for which the referee calls a face-off in one's own end.

▸*PHRASE* □ **the icing** (or **frosting**) **on the cake** an attractive but inessential addition or enhancement: *being a scientist is enjoyable, and winning a Nobel is icing on the cake.*

ic·ing sug·ar ▸*n.* British term for CONFECTIONERS' SUGAR.

-icist ▸*suffix* equivalent to -ICIAN. ▷based on forms ending in -IC, + -IST.

-icity ▸*suffix* forming abstract nouns esp. from adjectives ending in *-ic* (such as *authenticity* from *authentic*). ▷based on forms ending in -IC, + -ITY.

ICJ ▸*abbr.* International Court of Justice.

ick /ik/ ▸*exclam.* used to express disgust: *oatmeal—ick!* ▸*n. informal* a sticky or congealed substance, typically regarded with disgust: *she scrubbed the ick off the back of the stove.* ▷1940s: probably imitative.

-ick ▸*suffix archaic* variant spelling of -IC.

Ick·es /'ikəs/, Harold LeClair (1874–1952) U.S. lawyer and public official. He served as head of the federal Public Works Administration 1933–39 and as U.S. secretary of the interior 1933–46.

ick·y /'ikē/ ▸*adj.* (**ick·i·er**, **ick·i·est**) *informal* sticky, esp. unpleasantly so. ■ distastefully sentimental: *a romantic subplot that is just plain icky.* ■ nasty or repulsive (used as a general term of disapproval): *icky boys with all their macho strutting.* ▷1930s: perhaps related to SICK[1] or to the child's word *ickle* 'little.' —**ick·i·ness** *n.*

i·con /'ī,kän/ ▸*n.* a painting of Jesus Christ or another holy figure, typically in a traditional style on wood, venerated and used as an aid to devotion in the Byzantine and other Eastern Churches. ■ a person or thing regarded as a representative symbol of something: *this iron-jawed icon of American manhood.* ■ *Computing* a symbol or graphic representation on a video display terminal of a program, option, or window, esp. one of several for selection. ■ *Linguistics* a sign whose form directly reflects the thing it signifies, for example, the word *snarl* pronounced in a snarling way. ▷mid 16th cent. (in the sense 'simile'): via Latin from Greek *eikōn* 'likeness, image.' Current senses date from the mid 19th cent. onward.

i·con·ic /ī'känik/ ▸*adj.* of, relating to, or of the nature of an icon: *language is not in general an iconic sign system.* ■ (of a classical Greek statue) depicting a victorious athlete in a conventional style. ▷mid 17th cent.: from Latin *iconicus*, from Greek *eikonikos*, from *eikōn* 'likeness, image.' —**i·con·i·cal·ly** /-ik(ə)lē/ *adv.* —**i·co·nic·i·ty** /,īkə'nisitē/ *n.* (esp. in linguistics).

i·con·i·fy /ī'känə,fī/ ▸*v.* (**-fies**, **-fied**) [*trans.*] *Computing* reduce (a window on a video display terminal) to a small symbol or graphic representation of itself so as to make room on the screen for other windows.

i·con·ize /'īkə,nīz/ ▸*v.* [*trans.*] **1** *Computing* reduce (a window on a video display terminal) to a small symbol or graphic. **2** treat as an icon: *they iconized him as an iron-jawed symbol of American manhood.*

icono- ▸*comb. form* **1** of an image or likeness: *iconology.* **2** relating to icons: *iconoclast.* ▷from Greek *eikōn* 'likeness.'

i·con·o·clasm /ī'känə,klazəm/ ▸*n.* **1** the action of attacking or assertively rejecting cherished beliefs and institutions or established values and practices. **2** the rejection or destruction of religious images as heretical; the doctrine of iconoclasts. ▷late 18th cent.: from ICONOCLAST, on the pattern of pairs such as *enthusiast, enthusiasm.*

i·con·o·clast /ī'känə,klast/ ▸*n.* **1** a person who attacks cherished beliefs or institutions. **2** a destroyer of images used in religious worship, in particular: ■ *historical* a supporter of the 8th- and 9th-century movement in the Byzantine Church that sought to abolish the veneration of icons and other religious images. ■ *historical* a Puritan of the 16th or 17th century. ▷mid 17th cent. (sense 2): via medieval Latin from ecclesiastical Greek *eikonoklastēs*, from *eikōn* 'likeness' + *klan* 'to break.' —**i·con·o·clas·tic** /ī,känə'klastik/ *adj.* —**i·con·o·clas·ti·cal·ly** /ī,känə'klastik(ə)lē/ *adv.*

i·co·nog·ra·phy /,īkə'nägrəfē/ ▸*n.* **1** (*pl.* **-phies**) the use or study of images or symbols in visual arts. ■ the visual images, symbols, or modes of representation collectively associated with a person, cult, or movement: *the iconography of pop culture.* **2** the illustration of a subject by drawings or figures. ■ a collection of illustrations or portraits. ▷early 17th cent. (denoting a drawing or plan): from Greek *eikonographia* 'sketch, description,' from *eikōn* 'likeness' + *-graphia* 'writing.' —**i·co·nog·ra·pher** /-fər/ *n.* —**i·con·o·graph·ic** /ī,känə'grafik/ *adj.* —**i·con·o·graph·i·cal** /ī,känə'grafikəl/ *adj.* —**i·con·o·graph·i·cal·ly** /ī,känə'grafik(ə)lē/ *adv.*

i·co·nol·a·try /,īkə'nälətrē/ ▸*n. chiefly derogatory* the worship of icons. ▷early 17th cent.: from ecclesiastical Greek *eikonolatreia*, from *eikōn* 'likeness' + *-latria* 'worship.'

i·co·nol·o·gy /,īkə'näləjē/ ▸*n.* the study of visual imagery and its symbolism and interpretation, esp. in social or political terms. ■ symbolism: *the iconology of a work of art.* —**i·con·o·log·i·cal** /ī,känə'läjikəl/ *adj.*

i·co·nos·ta·sis /,īkə'nästəsis/ ▸*n.* (*pl.* **-ses** /-,sēz/) a screen bearing icons, separating the sanctuary of many Eastern churches from the nave. ▷mid 19th cent.: from modern Greek *eikonostasis*, from *eikōn* 'likeness' + *stasis* 'standing, stopping.'

i·co·sa·he·dron /ī,kōsə'hēdrən; ī,käsə-/ ▸*n.* (*pl.* **-drons** or **-dra** /-drə/) a solid figure with twenty plane faces, esp. equilateral triangular ones. ▷late 16th cent.: via late Latin from Greek *eikosaedron*, neuter (used as a noun) of *eikosaedros* 'twenty-faced.' —**i·co·sa·he·dral** /-drəl/ *adj.*

ICRC ▸*abbr.* International Committee of the Red Cross.

-ics ▸*suffix* (forming nouns) denoting arts or sciences, branches of study, or profession: *classics | politics.* ▷from French *-iques*, Latin *-ica*, or Greek *-ika*, plural forms.

> *USAGE* A noun ending in **-ics** meaning 'a subject of study or branch of knowledge' will usually take a singular rather than a plural verb: ***politics* is** *a blood sport;* ***classics* is** *hardly studied at all these days.* However, the same word may take a plural verb in cases where the sense is plural: *many of the* ***classics were*** *once regarded with disdain.*

ICT ▸*abbr.* information and computing technology.

ic·tal /'iktl/ ▸*adj. Medicine* of or relating to a seizure. ▷1950s: from ICTUS + -AL.

ic·ter·us /'iktərəs/ ▸*n. Medicine* technical term for JAUNDICE. ▷early 18th cent.: via Latin from Greek *ikteros.* The Latin term denoted jaundice, also a yellowish-green bird (the sight of which was thought to cure jaundice). —**ic·ter·ic** /ik'terik/ *adj.*

Ic·ti·nus /ik'tīnəs/ (5th century BC), Greek architect. He is said to have designed the Parthenon in Athens with architect Callicrates and sculptor Phidias between 448 and 437 BC.

ic·tus /'iktəs/ ▸*n.* (*pl.* same or **ic·tus·es**) **1** *Prosody* a rhythmical or metrical stress. **2** *Medicine* a stroke or seizure; a fit. ▷early 18th cent. (denoting the beat of the pulse): from Latin, literally 'blow'.

ICU ▸*abbr.* intensive care unit.

i·cy /'īsē/ ▸*adj.* (**i·ci·er**, **i·ci·est**) covered with or consisting of ice: *there were icy patches on the roads.* ■ very cold: *an icy wind.* ■ *figurative* (of a person's tone or manner) very unfriendly; hostile: *her voice was icy.* —**i·ci·ly** /'īsilē/ *adv.* —**i·ci·ness** *n.*

ID ▸*abbr.* ■ Idaho (in official postal use). ■ identification or identity: *they weren't carrying any ID* | [as *adj.*] *an ID card.*

Id ▸*n.* variant spelling of EID.

I'd /īd/ ▸*contraction of* ■ I would or I should: *I'd like a bath.* ■ I had: *I'd agreed to go.*

id /id/ ▸*n. Psychoanalysis* the part of the mind in which innate instinctive impulses and primary processes are manifest. Compare with EGO and SUPEREGO. ▷1920s: from Latin, literally 'that,' translating German *es.* The term was first used in this sense by Freud, following use in a similar sense by his contemporary, Georg Groddeck.

id. ▸*abbr.* idem.

-id[1] ▸*suffix* forming adjectives such as *putrid, torrid.* ▷from French *-ide*, from Latin *-idus.*

-id[2] ▸*suffix* **1** forming nouns such as *chrysalid, pyramid.* **2** *Biology* forming names of structural constituents: *plastid.* **3** *Botany* forming names of plants belonging to a family with a name ending in *-idaceae*: *orchid.* ▷from or suggested by French *-ide*, via Latin *-idis* from Greek *-is, -id-*.

-id[3] ▸*suffix* forming nouns: **1** *Zoology* denoting an animal belonging to a family with a name ending in *-idae* or to a class with a name ending in *-ida*: *carabid | arachnid.* **2** denoting a member of a specified dynasty or family: *Achaemenid | Sassanid.* **3** *Astronomy* denoting a meteor in a shower radiating from a specified constellation: *Geminids.* ■ denoting a star of a class like one in a specified constellation:

cepheid. ▷from or suggested by Latin *-ides* (plural *-idae, -ida*), from Greek.

IDA ▸*abbr.* International Development Association.

I·da /ˈīdə/ **1** a mountain in central Crete, associated in classical times with the god Zeus. Rising to 8,058 ft. (2,456 m.), it is the highest peak on the island. **2** *Astronomy* asteroid 243, which is 52 km. long and has a tiny moon (Dactyl), which is about 1.5 km. across.

I·da·ho /ˈīdəˌhō/ a state in the northwestern U.S. that borders on the Canadian province of British Columbia on the north and that includes part of the Rocky Mountains; pop. 1,293,953; capital, Boise; statehood, July 3, 1890 (43). It was explored by Lewis and Clark in 1805 and was crossed by the Oregon Trail that ended at Fort Vancouver in Washington. **—I·da·ho·an** /-ˌhōən/ *n. & adj.*

I·da·ho Falls a city in southeastern Idaho, on the Snake River; pop. 50,730.

IDDD ▸*abbr.* international direct distance dialing.

id·dings·ite /ˈidiNGˌzīt/ ▸*n.* a brownish mineral deposit consisting of a mixture of silicates, formed by alteration of olivine. ▷late 19th cent.: from the name of Joseph P. *Iddings* (1857–1920), American geologist, + **-ITE**[1].

IDE *Computing* ▸*abbr.* Integrated Drive Electronics, a standard for interfacing computers and their peripherals.

-ide ▸*suffix Chemistry* forming nouns: denoting binary compounds of a nonmetallic or more electronegative element or group: *cyanide | sodium chloride.* ■ denoting various other compounds: *peptide | saccharide.* ■ denoting elements of a series in the periodic table: *lanthanide.* ▷originally used in *oxide.*

i·de·a /īˈdēə/ ▸*n.* **1** a thought or suggestion as to a possible course of action: *they don't think it's a very good idea.* ■ a concept or mental impression: *our menu list will give you some idea of how interesting a low-fat diet can be.* ■ an opinion or belief: *nineteenth-century ideas about drinking.* ■ a feeling that something is probable or possible: *he had an idea that she must feel the same.* **2** (**the idea**) the aim or purpose: *I took a job with* ***the idea of*** *getting some money together.* **3** *Philosophy* (in Platonic thought) an eternally existing pattern of which individual things in any class are imperfect copies. ■ (in Kantian thought) a concept of pure reason, not empirically based in experience. ▷late Middle English (sense 3): via Latin from Greek *idea* 'form, pattern,' from the base of *idein* 'to see.'

▸*PHRASES* □ **get** (or **give someone**) **ideas** *informal* become (or make someone) ambitious, bigheaded, or tempted to do something against someone else's will, esp. make a sexual advance: *Mac began to get ideas about turning pro.* □ **have** (**got**) **no idea** *informal* not know at all: *she had no idea where she was going.* □ **not someone's idea of** *informal* not what someone regards as: *it's not my idea of a happy ending.* □ **put ideas into someone's head** suggest ambitions or thoughts that a person would not otherwise have had. □ **that's an idea** *informal* that suggestion or proposal is worth considering. □ **that's the idea** *informal* used to confirm to someone that they have understood something or they are doing something correctly: *"A sort of bodyguard?" "That's the idea."* □ **the very idea!** *informal* an exclamation of disapproval or disagreement.

THE RIGHT WORD **concept, conception, idea, impression, notion, thought**

If you have an **idea** it might refer to something perceived through the senses (*I had no idea it was so cold out*), to something visualized (*the idea of a joyous family outing*), or to something that is the product of the imagination (*a great idea for raising money*). *Idea* is a comprehensive word that applies to almost any aspect of mental activity.

A **thought**, on the other hand, is an idea that is the result of meditation, reasoning, or some other intellectual activity (*she hadn't given much thought to the possibility of losing*).

A **notion** is a vague or capricious idea, often without any sound basis (*he had a notion that he could get there by hitchhiking*).

A widely held idea of what something is or should be is a **concept** (*the concept of loyalty was beyond him*), while a **conception** is a concept that is held by a person or small group and that is often colored by imagination and feeling (*her conception of marriage as a romantic ideal*).

An idea that is triggered by something external is an **impression**, a word that suggests a half-formed mental picture or superficial view (*he made a good impression; she had the impression that everything would be taken care of*).

i·de·al /īˈdē(ə)l/ ▸*adj.* **1** satisfying one's conception of what is perfect; most suitable: *the swimming pool is* ***ideal for*** *a quick dip | this is an ideal opportunity to save money.* **2** [*attrib.*] existing only in the imagination; desirable or perfect but not likely to become a reality: *in an ideal world, we might have made a different decision.* ■ representing an abstract or hypothetical optimum: *mathematical modeling can determine theoretically ideal conditions.*

▸*n.* a person or thing regarded as perfect: *you're my ideal of how a man should be.* See note at **MODEL.** ■ a standard of perfection; a principle to be aimed at: *tolerance and freedom, the liberal ideals.* ▷late Middle English (as a term in Platonic philosophy, in the sense 'existing as an archetype'): from late Latin *idealis*, from Latin *idea* (see **IDEA**). **—i·de·al·ly** *adv.*

i·de·al gas ▸*n. Chemistry* a hypothetical gas whose molecules occupy negligible space and have no interactions, and that consequently obeys the gas laws exactly.

i·de·al·ism /īˈdē(ə)ˌlizəm/ ▸*n.* **1** the practice of forming or pursuing ideals, esp. unrealistically: *the idealism of youth.* Compare with **REALISM.** ■ (in art or literature) the representation of things in ideal or idealized form. Often contrasted with **REALISM** (sense 2). **2** *Philosophy* any of various systems of thought in which the objects of knowledge are held to be in some way dependent on the activity of mind. Often contrasted with **REALISM** (sense 3). ▷late 18th cent. (sense 2): from French *idéalisme* or German *Idealismus*, from late Latin *idealis* (see **IDEAL**). **—i·de·al·ist** *n.* **—i·de·al·is·tic** /īˌdē(ə)ˈlistik/ *adj.* **—i·de·al·is·ti·cal·ly** /īˌdē(ə)ˈlistik(ə)lē/ *adv.*

i·de·al·i·ty /ˌīdēˈalitē/ ▸*n.* (*pl.* **-ties**) *formal* the state or quality of being ideal: *the ideality of the island of Aran.* ■ the quality of expressing or being characterized by ideals: *the loftiness and ideality of the Gettysburg Address.* ■ *archaic* an ideal or idealized thing: *they commenced their married life with idealities about love.*

i·de·al·ize /īˈdē(ə)ˌlīz/ ▸*v.* [*trans.*] [often as *adj.*] (**idealized**) regard or represent as perfect or better than in reality: *Helen's idealized accounts of their life together.* **—i·de·al·i·za·tion** /īˌdē(ə)liˈzāSHən/ *n.* **—i·de·al·iz·er** *n.*

i·de·ate /ˈīdēˌāt/ ▸*v.* [*trans.*] [often as *adj.*] (**ideated**) form an idea of; imagine or conceive: *the arc whose ideated center is a nodal point in the composition.* ■ [*intrans.*] form ideas; think. ▷late 17th cent.: from medieval Latin *ideat-* 'formed as an idea,' from the verb *ideare*, from Latin *idea* (see **IDEA**).

i·de·a·tion /ˌīdēˈāSHən/ ▸*n. Psychology* the formation of ideas or concepts: *paranoid ideation.* **—i·de·a·tion·al** /-SHənl/ *adj.* **—i·de·a·tion·al·ly** /-SHənl-ē/ *adv.*

i·deb·e·none /īˈdebəˌnōn/ ▸*n.* a benzoquinone compound with strong antioxidant properties. It has therapeutic uses in age-related cognitive dysfunction and skin rejuvenation, owing to its ability to stimulate nerve growth.

i·dée fixe /ēdā ˈfēks/ ▸*n.* (*pl.* **i·dées fixes** *pronunc.* same) an idea or desire that dominates the mind; an obsession. ▷mid 19th cent.: French, literally 'fixed idea.'

i·dée re·çue /ēdā rəˈsoo/ ▸*n.* (*pl.* **i·dées re·çues** /ēdā rəˈsooz/) a generally accepted concept or idea. ▷mid 20th cent.: French, literally 'received idea.'

i·dem /ˈīˌdem; ˈidem/ ▸*adv.* used in citations to indicate an author or work that has just been mentioned: *Marianne Elliott,* Partners in Revolution, *1982; idem,* Wolfe Tone, *1989.* ▷late Middle English: Latin, literally 'the same.'

i·dem·po·tent /ˈīdemˌpōtənt/ *Mathematics* ▸*adj.* denoting an element of a set that is unchanged in value when multiplied or otherwise operated on by itself.

▸*n.* an element of this type. ▷late 19th cent.: from Latin *idem* 'same' + **POTENT**[1].

ident /īˈdent/ ▸*n.* short for **IDENTIFICATION**, esp. in informal or technical use.

i·den·ti·cal /īˈdentikəl/ ▸*adj.* **1** similar in every detail; exactly alike: *four girls in identical green outfits | the passage on the second floor was* ***identical to*** *the one below.* See note at **SAME.** ■ (of twins) developed from a single fertilized ovum, and therefore of the same sex and usually very similar in appearance. Compare with **FRATERNAL** (sense 2). ■ [*attrib.*] (of something encountered on separate occasions) the same: *she stole a suitcase from the identical station at which she had been arrested before.* **2** *Logic & Mathematics* expressing an identity: *an identical proposition.* ▷late 16th cent. (sense 2): from medieval Latin *identicus*, from late Latin *identitas* (see **IDENTITY**). **—i·den·ti·cal·ly** /-ik(ə)lē/ *adv.*

USAGE See **usage** at **SAME.**

i·den·ti·fi·ca·tion /īˌdentəfiˈkāSHən/ ▸*n.* the action or process of identifying someone or something or the fact of being identified: *each child was tagged with a number for identification | it may be impossible for relatives to make positive identifications.* ■ a means of proving a person's identity, esp. in the form of official papers: *I asked to see his identification.* ■ a person's sense of identity with someone or something: *children's* ***identification with*** *storybook characters.* ■ the association or linking of one thing with another: *the traditional Russian identification of democracy with anarchy.* ▷mid 17th cent.: originally from medieval Latin *identificat-* 'identified,' from the verb *identificare*; later from **IDENTIFY.**

i·den·ti·fi·er /īˈdentəˌfīər/ ▸*n.* a person or thing that identifies something: *the new number is to be known as the "unique patient identifier."* ■ *Computing* a sequence of characters used to identify or refer to a program or an element, such as a variable or a set of data, within it.

i·den·ti·fy /īˈdentəˌfī/ ▸*v.* (**-fies, -fied**) [*trans.*] **1** (often **be identified**) establish or indicate who or what (someone or something) is: *the judge ordered that the girl not be identified | the contact would* ***identify*** *himself simply* ***as*** *Cobra.* ■ recognize or distinguish (esp. something considered worthy of attention): *a system that ensures that the student's real needs are identified.* **2** (**identify someone/something with**) associate (someone) closely with; regard (someone) as having strong links with: *he was equivocal about being identified too closely with the peace movement.* ■ equate (someone or something) with: *because of my upstate accent, people identified me with a homely farmer's wife.* ■ [*intrans.*] (**identify with**) regard oneself as sharing the same characteristics or thinking as someone else: *I liked Fromm and identified with him.* ▷mid 17th cent. (in the sense 'treat as being identical with'): from medieval Latin *identificare*, from late Latin *identitas* (see **IDENTITY**) + Latin *-ficare* (from *facere* 'make'). **—i·den·ti·fi·a·ble** /-ˌfīəbəl/ *adj.* **—i·den·ti·fi·a·bly** /-ˌfīəblē/ *adv.*

i·den·ti·kit /īˈdentiˌkit/ ▸*n. trademark* a picture of a person, esp. one sought by the police, reconstructed from typical facial features according to witnesses' descriptions: [as *adj.*] *an identikit photograph.* ▷1960s: blend of **IDENTITY** and **KIT**[1].

i·den·ti·ty /īˈdentitē/ ▸*n.* (*pl.* **-ties**) **1** the fact of being who or what a person or thing is: *he knows the identity of the bombers | she believes she is the victim of mistaken identity.* ■ the characteristics determining this: *attempts to define a distinct Canadian identity.* ■ [as *adj.*] *chiefly Brit.* (of an object) serving to establish who the holder, owner, or wearer is by bearing their name and often other details such as a signature or photograph: *an identity card.* **2** a close similarity or affinity: *the initiative created an identity between the city and the suburbs.* **3** *Mathematics* (also **identity operation**) a transformation that leaves an object unchanged. ■ (also **identity element**) an element of a set that, if combined with another element by a specified binary operation, leaves that element unchanged. **4** *Mathematics* the equality of two expressions for all values of the quantities expressed by letters, or an equation expressing this, e.g., $(x + 1)^2 = x^2 + 2x + 1$. ▷late 16th cent. (in the sense 'quality of being identical'): from late Latin *identitas*, from Latin *idem* 'same.'

i·den·ti·ty cri·sis ▸*n. Psychiatry* a period of uncertainty and confusion in which a person's sense of identity becomes insecure, typically due to a change in their expected aims or role in society.

i·den·ti·ty ma·trix ▸*n. Mathematics* a square matrix in which all the elements of the principal diagonal are ones and all other elements are zeros. The effect of multiplying a given matrix by an identity matrix is to leave the given matrix unchanged.

i·den·ti·ty pa·rade (also **i·den·ti·fi·ca·tion pa·rade**) ▸*n. Brit.* a police lineup.

i·den·ti·ty pol·i·tics ▸*plural n.* [treated as *sing.*] a tendency for people of a particular religion, race, social background, etc., to form exclusive political alliances, moving away from traditional broad-based party politics.

i·den·ti·ty theft ▸*n.* the fraudulent acquisition and use of a person's private identifying information, usually for financial gain.

id·e·o·gram /ˈidēəˌgram; ˈīdēə-/ ▸*n.* a written

Pronunciation Key ə *ago*; ər *over*; ˈə or ˌə *up*; ˈər or ˌər *fur*; a *hat*; ā *rate*; ä *car*; CH *chew*; e *let*; ē *see*; e(ə)r *air*; i *fit*; ī *by*; i(ə)r *ear*; NG *sing*; ō *go*; ô *for*; oi *boy*; o͝o *good*; o͞o *goo*; ou *out*; SH *she*; TH *thin*; T͟H *then*; (h)w *why*; ZH *vision*

I

character symbolizing the idea of a thing without indicating the sounds used to say it, e.g., numerals and Chinese characters. ▷mid 19th cent.: from Greek *idea* 'form' + -GRAM[1].

Chinese character for Earth

III

Roman numeral three

Wheelchair access sign

Biohazard sign

ideograms

id·e·o·graph /ˈidēəˌgraf; ˈīdēə-/ ▸*n.* another term for IDEOGRAM. ▷mid 19th cent.: from Greek *idea* 'form' + -GRAPH. —**id·e·o·graph·ic** /ˌidēəˈgrafik; ˌīdēə-/ *adj.* —**id·e·og·ra·phy** /ˌidēˈägrəfē; ˌīdē-/ *n.*

i·de·o·logue /ˈīdēəˌlôg; -ˌläg; ˈidēə-/ ▸*n.* an adherent of an ideology, esp. one who is uncompromising and dogmatic: *a Nazi ideologue.* ▷early 19th cent.: from French *idéologue*; see also IDEOLOGY.

i·de·ol·o·gy /ˌīdēˈäləjē; ˌidē-/ ▸*n.* **1** (*pl.* **-gies**) a system of ideas and ideals, esp. one that forms the basis of economic or political theory and policy: *the ideology of republicanism.* ■ the ideas and manner of thinking characteristic of a group, social class, or individual: *a critique of bourgeois ideology.* ■ *archaic* visionary speculation, esp. of an unrealistic or idealistic nature. **2** *archaic* the science of ideas; the study of their origin and nature. ▷late 18th cent. (sense 2): from French *idéologie*, from Greek *idea* 'form, pattern' + *-logos* (denoting discourse or compilation). —**i·de·o·log·i·cal** /-əˈläjikəl/ *adj.* —**i·de·o·log·i·cal·ly** /-əˈläjik(ə)lē/ *adv.* —**i·de·ol·o·gist** /-jist/ *n.*

ides /īdz/ ▸*plural n.* (in the ancient Roman calendar) a day falling roughly in the middle of each month (the 15th day of March, May, July, and October, and the 13th of other months), from which other dates were calculated. Compare with NONES, CALENDS. ▷late Old English: from Old French, from Latin *idus* (plural), of unknown origin.

i·dig·bo /iˈdigbō/ ▸*n.* a West African tree that has a distinctive pagodalike shape and yields weather-resistant timber. • *Terminalia ivorensis*, family Combretaceae. ▷a local name.

idio- ▸*comb. form* distinct; private; personal; own: *idiotype.* ▷from Greek *idios* 'own, distinct.'

id·i·o·cy /ˈidēəsē/ ▸*n.* (*pl.* **-cies**) extremely stupid behavior: *the idiocy of decimating rain forests | every aspect of public administration throws up its own idiocies.* ▷early 16th cent. (originally denoting low intelligence): from IDIOT, probably on the pattern of pairs such as *lunatic, lunacy.*

id·i·o·graph·ic /ˌidēəˈgrafik/ ▸*adj.* of or relating to the study or discovery of particular scientific facts and processes, as distinct from general laws. Often contrasted with NOMOTHETIC.

id·i·o·lect /ˈidēəˌlekt/ ▸*n.* the speech habits peculiar to a particular person. ▷1940s: from IDIO- 'own, personal' + *-lect* as in *dialect.*

id·i·om /ˈidēəm/ ▸*n.* **1** a group of words established by usage as having a meaning not deducible from those of the individual words (e.g., *rain cats and dogs, see the light*). ■ a form of expression natural to a language, person, or group of people: *he had a feeling for phrase and idiom.* ■ the dialect of a people or part of a country. **2** a characteristic mode of expression in music or art: *they were both working in a neo-Impressionist idiom.* ▷late 16th cent.: from French *idiome*, or via late Latin from Greek *idiōma* 'private property, peculiar phraseology,' from *idiousthai* 'make one's own,' from *idios* 'own, private.'

id·i·o·mat·ic /ˌidēəˈmatik/ ▸*adj.* **1** using, containing, or denoting expressions that are natural to a native speaker: *distinctive idiomatic dialogue.* **2** appropriate to the style of art or music associated with a particular period, individual, or group: *a short Bach piece containing lots of idiomatic motifs.* ▷early 18th cent.: from Greek *idiōmatikos* 'peculiar, characteristic,' from *idiōma* (see IDIOM). —**id·i·o·mat·i·cal·ly** /-ik(ə)lē/ *adv.*

id·i·o·path·ic /ˌidēəˈpaTHik/ ▸*adj. Medicine* relating to or denoting any disease or condition that arises spontaneously or for which the cause is unknown.

id·i·op·a·thy /ˌidēˈäpəTHē/ ▸*n.* (*pl.* **-thies**) *Medicine* a disease or condition that arises spontaneously or for which the cause is unknown. ▷late 17th cent.: from modern Latin *idiopathia*, from Greek *idiopatheia*, from *idios* 'own, private' + *-patheia* 'suffering.'

id·i·o·phone /ˈidēəˌfōn/ ▸*n. technical Music* an instrument the whole of which vibrates to produce a sound when struck, shaken, or scraped, such as a bell, gong, or rattle.

id·i·o·syn·cra·sy /ˌidēəˈsiNGkrəsē/ ▸*n.* (*pl.* **-sies**) (usu. **idiosyncrasies**) a mode of behavior or way of thought peculiar to an individual: *one of his little idiosyncrasies was always preferring to be in the car first.* ■ a distinctive or peculiar feature or characteristic of a place or thing: *the idiosyncrasies of the prison system.* ■ *Medicine* an abnormal physical reaction by an individual to a food or drug. ▷early 17th cent. (originally in the sense 'physical constitution peculiar to an individual'): from Greek *idiosunkrasia*, from *idios* 'own, private' + *sun* 'with' + *krasis* 'mixture.'

id·i·o·syn·crat·ic /ˌidēəsiNGˈkratik; ˌidē-ō-/ ▸*adj.* of or relating to idiosyncrasy; peculiar or individual: *she emerged as one of the great idiosyncratic talents of the Nineties.* ▷late 18th cent.: from IDIOSYNCRASY, on the pattern of Greek *sunkratikos* 'mixed together.' —**id·i·o·syn·crat·i·cal·ly** /-ik(ə)lē/ *adv.*

id·i·ot /ˈidēət/ ▸*n. informal* a stupid person. ■ *archaic Medicine* a mentally handicapped person. ▷Middle English (denoting a person of low intelligence): via Old French from Latin *idiota* 'ignorant person,' from Greek *idiōtēs* 'private person, layman, ignorant person,' from *idios* 'own, private.' —**id·i·ot·ic** /ˌidēˈätik/ *adj.* —**id·i·ot·i·cal·ly** /ˌidēˈätik(ə)lē/ *adv.*

id·i·ot board (also **idiot card**) ▸*n. informal* a board displaying a television script to a speaker as an aid to memory.

id·i·ot box ▸*n. informal* a television set.

id·i·ot light ▸*n. informal* a warning light that goes on when a fault occurs in a device, esp. a light on the instrument panel of a motor vehicle.

id·i·ot sa·vant ▸*n.* (*pl.* **id·i·ot sa·vants** or **id·i·ots sa·vants** *pronunc.* same) a person who is considered to be mentally handicapped but displays brilliance in a specific area, esp. one involving memory. ▷late 20th cent.: French, literally 'learned idiot.'

id·i·o·type /ˈidēəˌtīp/ ▸*n. Biology* the set of genetic determinants of an individual. ■ *Immunology* a set of antigen-binding sites that characterizes the antibodies produced by a particular clone of antibody-producing cells.

I·di·ta·rod Riv·er /īˈditəˌräd/ a river in western Alaska, scene of a 1908 gold rush, route of the Iditarod dogsled race that goes from Anchorage to Nome.

i·dle /ˈīdl/ ▸*adj.* (**i·dler**, **i·dlest**) **1** (esp. of a machine or factory) not active or in use: *assembly lines* ***standing idle*** *for lack of spare parts.* ■ (of a person) not working; unemployed. ■ (of a person) avoiding work; lazy. ■ [*attrib.*] (of time) characterized by inaction or absence of significant activity: *at no time in the day must there be an idle moment.* ■ (of money) held in cash or in accounts paying no interest. **2** without purpose or effect; pointless: *he did not want to waste valuable time in idle chatter.* ■ (esp. of a threat or boast) without foundation: *I knew Ellen did not make idle threats.* ▸*v.* [*intrans.*] (of a person) spend time doing nothing; be idle: *four men were idling outside the shop.* See note at LOITER. ■ [*intrans.*] move aimlessly or lazily: *Cal idled past MetroHealth at a stately pace.* ■ (of an engine) run slowly while disconnected from a load or out of gear: *the car is noisily idling in the street.* ■ [*trans.*] cause (an engine) to idle. ■ [*trans.*] take out of use or employment: *he will close the newspaper, idling 2,200 workers.*
▸*phrasal v.* □ **idle something away** spend one's time doing nothing or very little. ▷Old English *īdel* 'empty, useless'; related to Dutch *ijdel* 'vain, frivolous, useless' and German *eitel* 'bare, worthless.' —**i·dle·ness** *n.*

i·dler /ˈīdlər/ ▸*n.* **1** a habitually lazy person. ■ a person who is doing nothing in particular, typically while waiting for something. **2** a pulley that transmits no power but guides or tensions a belt or rope. ■ an idle wheel.

i·dle wheel ▸*n.* an intermediate wheel between two geared wheels, esp. when its purpose is to allow them to rotate in the same direction.

i·dly /ˈīdlē/ ▸*adv.* with no particular purpose, reason, or foundation: *"How was the game?" Katie asked idly.* ■ in an inactive or lazy way: *I can no longer stand idly by and let him take the blame.*

I·do /ˈēdō/ ▸*n.* an artificial universal language developed from Esperanto. ▷early 19th cent.: Ido, literally 'offspring.'

i·do·crase /ˈīdəˌkrās; -ˌkrāz; ˈidə-/ ▸*n.* a mineral consisting of a silicate of calcium, magnesium, and aluminum, occurring typically as dark green to brown prisms in metamorphosed limestone. ▷early 19th cent.: from Greek *eidos* 'form' + *krasis* 'mixture.'

i·dol /ˈīdl/ ▸*n.* an image or representation of a god used as an object of worship. ■ a person or thing that is greatly admired, loved, or revered: *movie idol Robert Redford.* ▷Middle English: from Old French *idole*, from Latin *idolum* 'image, form' (used in ecclesiastical Latin in the sense 'idol'), from Greek *eidōlon*, from *eidos* 'form, shape.'

i·dol·a·ter /īˈdälətər/ ▸*n.* a person who worships an idol or idols. ▷late Middle English: from Old French *idolatre*, based on Greek *eidōlolatrēs*, from *eidōlon* (see IDOL) + *-latrēs* 'worshiper.'

i·dol·a·trous /īˈdälətrəs/ ▸*adj.* worshiping idols: *the idolatrous peasantry.* ■ treating someone or something as an idol: *America's idolatrous worship of the auto.*

i·dol·a·try /īˈdälətrē/ ▸*n.* worship of idols. ■ extreme admiration, love, or reverence for something or someone: *we must not allow our idolatry of art to obscure issues of political significance.* ▷Middle English: from Old French *idolatrie*, based on Greek *eidōlolatreia*, from *eidōlon* (see IDOL) + *-latreia* 'worship.'

i·dol·ize /ˈīdlˌīz/ ▸*v.* [*trans.*] admire, revere, or love greatly or excessively: *he idolized his mother.* See note at REVERE. —**i·dol·i·za·tion** /ˌīdl-iˈzāSHən/ *n.* —**i·dol·iz·er** *n.*

I·dom·e·neus /īˈdämən(y)o͞os; īˌdäməˈnēəs/ *Greek Mythology* king of Crete, son of Deucalion and descendant of Minos. He was forced to kill his son after vowing to sacrifice the first living thing that he met on his return from the Trojan War.

IDP ▸*abbr.* ■ integrated data processing. ■ International Driving Permit.

Id ul-A·dha /ˈid äl ˈäT͟Hä/ see EID.

Id ul-Fi·tr /ˈid äl ˈfētər/ see EID.

i·dyll /ˈīdl/ (also **i·dyl**) ▸*n.* an extremely happy, peaceful, or picturesque episode or scene, typically an idealized or unsustainable one: *the rural idyll remains strongly evocative in most industrialized societies.* ■ a short description in verse or prose of a picturesque scene or incident, esp. in rustic life. ▷late 16th cent. (in the Latin form): from Latin *idyllium*, from Greek *eidullion*, diminutive of *eidos* 'form, picture.'

i·dyl·lic /īˈdilik/ ▸*adj.* (esp. of a time or place) like an idyll; extremely happy, peaceful, or picturesque: *an attractive hotel in an idyllic setting.* —**i·dyl·li·cal·ly** /-ik(ə)lē/ *adv.*

IE ▸*abbr.* Indo-European.

i.e. ▸*abbr.* that is to say (used to add explanatory information or to state something in different words): *a walking boot that is synthetic, i.e., not leather or suede.* ▷from Latin *id est* 'that is.'

-ie ▸*suffix* **1** variant spelling of -Y[2] (as in *auntie*). **2** *archaic* variant spelling of -Y[1], -Y[3]. ▷earlier form of *-y.*

IEA ▸*abbr.* International Energy Agency.

IED ▸*n.* an improvised explosive device, such as a car bomb.

IEEE ▸*abbr.* Institute of Electrical and Electronics Engineers.

IEEE 802.11 ▸*n. Computing* a standard for communication over a wireless network. See also WI-FI. ▷1990s an abbreviation of *Institute of Electrical and Electronics Engineers.*

IEEE 1394 (also **FireWire**) ▸*n. Computing* a standard for high-speed connection and data exchange between computers and peripherals: *both front and rear IEEE 1394 ports.* ▷1990s an abbreviation of *Institute of Electrical and Electronics Engineers.*

Ie·per /ˈyāpər/ Flemish name of YPRES.

-ier ▸*suffix* forming personal nouns denoting an occupation or interest: **1** pronounced with stress on the preceding element: *glazier.* [Middle English: variant of -ER[1].] **2** pronounced with stress on the final element: *brigadier | cashier.* [from French *-ier*, from Latin *-arius.*]

IF ▸*abbr.* intermediate frequency.

if /if/ ▸*conj.* **1** introducing a conditional clause: ■ on the condition or supposition that; in the event that: *if you have a complaint, write to the director | if you like, I'll* *put in a word for you.* ■ (with past tense) introducing a hypothetical situation: *if you had stayed, this would never have happened.* ■ whenever; every time: *if I go out, she gets nasty.* **2** despite the possibility that; no matter whether: *if it takes me seven years, I shall do it.* **3** (often used in indirect questions) whether: *he asked if we would like some coffee | see if you can track it down.* **4** [with *modal*] expressing a polite request: *if I could trouble you for your names? | if you wouldn't mind giving him a message?* **5** expressing an opinion: *that's an awfully long walk, if you don't mind my saying so | if you ask me, he's in love.* **6** expressing surprise or regret: *well,* ***if it isn't*** *Frank! | if I could just be left alone.* **7** with implied reservation: ■ and perhaps not: *the new leaders have little if any control.* ■ used to admit something as being possible but regarded as relatively insignificant: *if there was any weakness, it was naiveté | so what if he did?* ■ despite being (used before an adjective or adverb to introduce a contrast): *she was honest, if a little brutal.*

▸*n.* a condition or supposition: *there are so many* ***ifs and buts*** *in the policy.* ▷Old English *gif*, of Germanic origin; related to Dutch *of* and German *ob*.

▸*PHRASES* □ **if and only if** used to introduce a condition that is necessary as well as sufficient: *witches are real if and only if there are criteria for identifying witches.* □ **if and when** at a future time (should it arise): *if and when the film gets the green light, be sure you've read the book first.* □ **if anything** used to suggest tentatively that something may be the case (often the opposite of something previously implied): *I haven't made much of this—if anything, I've played it down.* □ **if I were you** used to accompany a piece of advice: *I would go to see him if I were you.* □ **if not** perhaps even (used to introduce a more extreme term than one first mentioned): *hundreds if not thousands of germs.* □ **if only 1** even if for no other reason than: *Willy would have to tell George more, if only to keep him from pestering.* **2** used to express a wish, esp. regretfully: *if only I had listened to you.* □ **if so** if that is the case.

USAGE **If** and **whether** are more or less interchangeable in sentences like *I'll see* ***if*** *he left an address* and *I'll see* ***whether*** *he left an address*, although **whether** is generally regarded as more formal and suitable for written use. But, although **if** and **whether** are often interchangeable, a distinction worth noting is that **if** is also used in conditional constructions and **whether** in expressing an alternative or possibility. Thus, *tell me if you're going to be in town next week* could be strictly interpreted as 'you need not reply if you are *not* going to be in town,' whereas *tell me whether you're going to be in town next week* clearly means 'a reply is desired one way or the other.'

IFAD ▸*abbr.* International Fund for Agricultural Development.

IFC ▸*abbr.* International Finance Corporation.

Ife /'ēfā/ an industrial city in southwestern Nigeria; pop. 241,000.

-iferous ▸*comb. form* common form of **-FEROUS**.

iff /if/ ▸*conj. Logic & Mathematics* if and only if. ▷1950s: arbitrary extension of *if*.

if·fy /'ifē/ ▸*adj.* (**if·fi·er**, **if·fi·est**) *informal* full of uncertainty; doubtful: *the prospect for classes resuming next Wednesday seems iffy.* ■ of doubtful quality or legality: *a good wine merchant will change the iffy bottles for sound ones.*

-ific ▸*suffix* common form of **-FIC**.

-ification ▸*suffix* common form of **-FICATION**.

IFO ▸*abbr.* identified flying object.

-iform ▸*comb. form* common form of **-FORM**.

IFR ▸*abbr.* instrument flight rules, used to regulate the flying and navigating of an aircraft using instruments alone.

If·tar /'if,tär/ ▸*n.* the meal eaten by Muslims after sunset during Ramadan.

IFV ▸*abbr.* infantry fighting vehicle.

Ig ▸*abbr.* immunoglobulin.

I.G. ▸*abbr.* ■ Indo-Germanic. ■ Inspector General.

Ig·bo /'igbō/ ▸*n.* & *adj.* see **IBO**.

Igle·sias /ē'gläsēəs/, Julio (1943–), Spanish singer. He is noted for his love songs and ballads.

ig·loo /'iglōō/ ▸*n.* a dome-shaped Eskimo house, typically built from blocks of solid snow. ▷mid 19th cent.: from Inuit *iglu* 'house.'

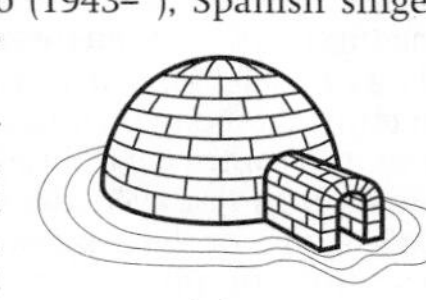

igloo

ign. ▸*abbr.* ignition.

Ig·na·tius Loy·o·la, St. /ig'nāsн(ē)əs loi'ōlə/ (1491–1556), Spanish theologian and founder of the Society of Jesus (the Jesuit order). His *Spiritual Exercises* (1548), an ordered scheme of meditations, is still used in Jesuit training programs. Feast day, July 31.

ig·ne·ous /'ignēəs/ ▸*adj. Geology* (of rock) having solidified from lava or magma. ■ relating to or involving volcanic processes: *igneous activity.* ■ *rare* of fire; fiery. ▷mid 17th cent.: from Latin *igneus* (from *ignis* 'fire') + **-OUS**.

ig·nim·brite /'ignim,brīt/ ▸*n. Geology* a volcanic rock consisting essentially of pumice fragments, formed by the consolidation of material deposited by pyroclastic flows. ▷1930s: from Latin *ignis* 'fire' + *imber, imbr-* 'shower of rain, storm cloud' + **-ITE**[1].

ig·nis fat·u·us /'ignəs 'facнōōəs/ ▸*n.* (*pl.* **ig·nes fat·u·i** /'ignēz 'facнōō,ī/) a phosphorescent light seen hovering or floating at night on marshy ground, thought to result from the combustion of natural gases. ■ something deceptive or deluding. ▷mid 16th cent.: modern Latin, literally 'foolish fire' (because of its erratic movement).

ig·nite /ig'nīt/ ▸*v.* catch fire or cause to catch fire: [*intrans.*] *furniture can give off lethal fumes when it ignites |* [*trans.*] *sparks flew out and ignited the dry scrub.* ■ [*trans.*] *figurative* arouse (an emotion): *the words ignited new fury in him.* ■ [*trans.*] *figurative* inflame or instigate (a situation): *they were about to ignite the European socialist revolution.* ▷mid 17th cent. (in the sense 'make intensely hot'): from Latin *ignire* 'set on fire,' from *ignis* 'fire.' **—ig·nit·a·bil·i·ty** /ig,nītə'bilitē/ *n.* **—ig·nit·a·ble** *adj.*

ig·ni·ter /ig'nītər/ ▸*n.* **1** a device for igniting a fuel mixture in an engine. **2** a device for causing an electric arc.

ig·ni·tion /ig'nisнən/ ▸*n.* the action of setting something on fire or starting to burn: *three minutes after ignition, the flames were still growing.* ■ the process of starting the combustion of fuel in the cylinders of an internal combustion engine. ■ (usu. **the ignition**) the mechanism for bringing this about, typically activated by a key or switch: *he put the key in the ignition.* ▷early 17th cent. (denoting the heating of a substance to the point of combustion or chemical change): from medieval Latin *ignitio(n-)*, from the verb *ignire* 'set on fire' (see **IGNITE**).

ig·ni·tron /'igni,trän/ ▸*n.* a kind of rectifier with a mercury cathode, able to carry large electric currents. ▷1930s: from **IGNITE** or **IGNITION** + **-TRON**.

ig·no·ble /ig'nōbəl/ ▸*adj.* (**-no·bler**, **-no·blest**) **1** not honorable in character or purpose: *ignoble feelings of intense jealousy.* **2** of humble origin or social status: *ignoble savages.* ▷late Middle English (sense 2): from French, or from Latin *ignobilis*, from *in-* 'not' + *gnobilis*, older form of *nobilis* 'noble.' **—ig·no·bil·i·ty** /,ignō'bilitē/ *n.* **—ig·no·bly** /-blē/ *adv.*

ig·no·min·i·ous /,ignə'minēəs/ ▸*adj.* deserving or causing public disgrace or shame: *no other party risked ignominious defeat.* ▷late Middle English: from French *ignominieux*, or Latin *ignominiosus*, from *ignominia* (see **IGNOMINY**). **—ig·no·min·i·ous·ly** *adv.* **—ig·no·min·i·ous·ness** *n.*

ig·no·min·y /'ignə,minē; ig'nämінē/ ▸*n.* public shame or disgrace: *the ignominy of being imprisoned.* ▷mid 16th cent.: from French *ignominie* or Latin *ignominia*, from *in-* 'not' + a variant of *nomen* 'name.'

ig·no·ra·mus /,ignə'rāməs; -'raməs/ ▸*n.* (*pl.* **-mus·es**) an ignorant or stupid person. ▷late 16th cent.: Latin, literally 'we do not know' (in legal use 'we take no notice of it'), from *ignorare* (see **IGNORE**). The modern sense may derive from the name of a character in George Ruggle's *Ignoramus* (1615), a satirical comedy exposing lawyers' ignorance.

ig·no·rance /'ignərəns/ ▸*n.* lack of knowledge or information: *he acted in* ***ignorance of*** *basic procedures.* ▷Middle English: via Old French from Latin *ignorantia*, from *ignorant-* 'not knowing' (see **IGNORANT**).

ig·no·rant /'ignərənt/ ▸*adj.* lacking knowledge or awareness in general; uneducated or unsophisticated: *he was told constantly that he was ignorant and stupid.* ■ [*predic.*] lacking knowledge, information, or awareness about something in particular: *they were* ***ignorant of*** *astronomy.* ■ *informal* discourteous or rude: *this ignorant, pin-brained receptionist.* ■ *black English* easily angered: *I is an ignorant man—even police don't meddle with me.* ▷late Middle English: via Old French from Latin *ignorant-* 'not knowing,' from the verb *ignorare* (see **IGNORE**). **—ig·no·rant·ly** *adv.*

THE RIGHT WORD **ignorant, illiterate, uneducated, uninformed, unlearned, unlettered, untutored**

Someone who knows nothing about growing things might be called **ignorant** by a farmer who never went to high school but has spent his life in the fields. Although all of these adjectives refer to a lack of knowledge, *ignorant* refers to a lack of knowledge in general (*a foolish, ignorant person*) or to a lack of knowledge of some particular subject (*ignorant of the fine points of financial management*).

A professor of art history might refer to someone who doesn't know how to look at a painting as **uneducated** or **untutored**, both of which refer to a lack of formal education in schools (*she was very bright but basically uneducated, and completely untutored in the fine arts*).

Someone who cannot read or write is **illiterate**, a term that may also denote a failure to display civility or cultivated behavior (*the professor routinely referred to his students as illiterate louts*).

Someone who is **unlettered** lacks a knowledge of fine literature (*a scientist who was highly trained but unlettered*); it also implies being able to read and write, but with no skill in either of these areas.

Unlearned is similar to *ignorant* in that it refers to a lack of learning in general or in a specific subject (*an unlearned man who managed to become a millionaire*), but it does not carry the same negative connotations.

Uninformed refers to a lack of definite information or data. For example, one can be highly intelligent and well educated but still *uninformed* about the latest developments in earthquake prediction.

ig·no·ra·ti·o e·len·chi /,ignə'rāsнēō i'lenGkī; -kē/ ▸*n.* (*pl.* **ig·no·ra·ti·o·nes e·len·chi** /,ignə,rāsнē'ōnēz/) *Philosophy* a logical fallacy that consists in apparently refuting an opponent while actually disproving something not asserted. ▷late 16th cent.: Latin, literally 'ignorance of the elenchus.'

ig·nore /ig'nôr/ ▸*v.* [*trans.*] refuse to take notice of or acknowledge; disregard intentionally: *he ignored her outraged question.* See note at **NEGLECT**. ■ fail to consider (something significant): *direct satellite broadcasting ignores national boundaries.* ■ *Law* (of a grand jury) reject (an indictment) as groundless. ▷late 15th cent. (in the sense 'be ignorant of'): from French *ignorer* or Latin *ignorare* 'not know, ignore,' from *in-* 'not' + *gno-*, a base meaning 'know.' Current senses date from the early 19th cent. **—ig·nor·a·ble** *adj.* **—ig·nor·er** *n.*

ig·no·tum per ig·no·tius /ig'nōtəm pər ig'nōsнəs/ ▸*n.* the action of offering an explanation that is harder to understand than the thing it is meant to explain. ▷late Latin, literally 'the unknown through the more unknown.'

I·gua·çu /,ēgwə'sōō/ a river in southern Brazil. It rises in the Serra do Mar in southeastern Brazil and flows west for 800 miles (1,300 km) to the Paraná River, which it joins just below Iguaçu Falls, a spectacular series of waterfalls. Spanish name **IGUAZÚ**

i·gua·na /i'gwänə/ ▸*n.* a large, arboreal, tropical American lizard with a spiny crest along the back and greenish coloration, occasionally kept as a pet. • Genus *Iguana*, family Iguanidae: two species, in particular the common **green iguana** (*I. iguana*). ■ any iguanid lizard. ▷mid 16th cent.: from Spanish, from Arawak *iwana*.

i·gua·nid /i'gwänid/ ▸*n. Zoology* a lizard of the iguana family (Iguanidae). Iguanids are found mainly in the New World but also occur in Madagascar and on some Pacific islands. ▷late 19th cent.: from modern Latin *Iguanidae* (plural), from the genus name *Iguana* (see **IGUANA**).

i·guan·o·don /i'gwänə,dän/ ▸*n.* a large, partly bipedal, herbivorous dinosaur of the early to mid Cretaceous period, with a broad, stiff tail and the thumb developed into a spike. • Genus *Iguanodon*, infraorder Ornithopoda, order Ornithischia. ▷modern Latin, from **IGUANA** + Greek *odous, odont-* 'tooth' (because its teeth resemble those of the iguana). **—i·guan·o·dont** /-,dänt/ *adj.*

IGY ▸*abbr.* International Geophysical Year.

i.h.p. ▸*abbr.* indicated horsepower.

IHS ▸*abbr.* Jesus. ▷Middle English: from late Latin, representing Greek *ΙΗΣ* as an abbreviation of *Iēsous* 'Jesus' used in manuscripts and also as a symbolic or ornamental monogram, but later often taken as an abbreviation of various Latin phrases, notably *Iesus Hominum Salvator* 'Jesus Savior of Men,' *In Hoc Signo (vinces)* 'in this sign (thou shalt conquer),' and *In Hac Salus* 'in this (cross) is salvation.'

i·i·wi /ē'ē,wē/ ▸*n.* (*pl.* same or **i·i·wis**) a Hawaiian honeycreeper with a long, down-curved bill and mainly bright red plumage. • *Vestiaria coccinea,* family Drepanididae (or Fringillidae). ▷late 18th cent.: from Hawaiian.

IJs·sel /'īsəl/ a river in the Netherlands. In part, it is a distributary of the Rhine River, which it leaves at Arnhem to join the Oude IJssel ("Old IJssel") a few miles downstream and then flows north for 72 miles (115 km) through the eastern Netherlands to the IJsselmeer.

IJs·sel·meer /'īsəl,mer/ a shallow lake in the northwestern Netherlands that was created in 1932 when a dam was built across the entrance to the old Zuider Zee. Large areas have since been reclaimed as polders.

i·kat /'ēkät/ ▸*n.* fabric made using an Indonesian decorative technique in which warp or weft threads, or both, are tie-dyed before weaving. ▷1930s: Malay, literally 'fasten, tie.'

i·ke·ba·na /,ikə'bänə; ,ēke-/ ▸*n.* the art of Japanese flower arrangement, with formal display according to strict rules. ▷early 20th cent.: Japanese, literally 'living flowers,' from *ikeru* 'keep alive' + *hana* 'flower.'

Ikh·na·ton /ik'nätn/ variant form of **AKHENATEN**.

i·kon ▸*n.* variant spelling of **ICON**.

Ik·san /'ēk,sän/ a commercial city in southwestern South Korea; pop. 323,000.

IL ▸*abbr.* Illinois (in official postal use).

il- ▸*prefix* **1** variant spelling of **IN-**[1], **IN-**[2] **2** assimilated before *l* (as in *illustrate, illogical*).

-il ▸*suffix* forming adjectives and nouns such as *civil* and *fossil.* ▷from Old French, from Latin *-ilis.*

ILA ▸*abbr.* ■ International Law Association. ■ International Longshoremen's Association.

i·lang-i·lang ▸*n.* variant spelling of **YLANG-YLANG**.

-ile ▸*suffix* forming adjectives and nouns such as *agile* and *juvenile.* ■ *Statistics* forming nouns denoting a value of a variate that divides a population into the indicated number of equal-sized groups, or one of the groups itself: *decile | percentile.* ▷variant of **-IL** especially in adoptions from French.

il·e·a /'ilēə/ ▸ plural form of **ILEUM**.

Île-de-France /,ēl də 'fräNs/ a region of north central France, incorporating the city of Paris.

il·e·i·tis /,ilē'ītis/ ▸*n. Medicine* inflammation of the ileum.

il·e·os·to·my /,ilē'ästəmē/ ▸*n.* (*pl.* **-mies**) a surgical operation in which a piece of the ileum is diverted to an artificial opening in the abdominal wall. ■ an opening so formed. ▷late 19th cent.: from **ILEUM** + Greek *stoma* 'mouth.'

Iles du Vent /,ēl dy 'väN/ French name for **WINDWARD ISLANDS** (sense 2).

I·le·sha /ē'lāSHə/ a city in southwestern Nigeria; pop. 342,000.

il·e·um /'ilēəm/ ▸*n.* (*pl.* **il·e·a** /'ilēə/) *Anatomy* the third portion of the small intestine, between the jejunum and the cecum. ▷late 17th cent.: from medieval Latin, variant of **ILIUM**. **—il·e·ac** /-,ak/ *adj.* **—il·e·al** /-əl/ *adj.*

il·e·us /'ilēəs/ ▸*n. Medicine* a painful obstruction of the ileum or other part of the intestine. ▷late 17th cent.: from Latin, from Greek *eileos, ilios* 'colic,' apparently from *eilein* 'to roll.'

i·lex /'ī,leks/ ▸*n.* **1** another term for **HOLM OAK**. **2** a tree or shrub of a genus that includes holly and its relatives. • Genus *Ilex,* family Aquifoliaceae. ▷late Middle English: from Latin, 'holm oak.'

ILGWU ▸*abbr.* International Ladies' Garment Workers' Union.

il·i·a /'ilēə/ ▸ plural form of **ILIUM**.

il·i·ac /'ilē,ak/ ▸*adj.* of or relating to the ilium or the nearby regions of the lower body: *the iliac artery.* ▷early 16th cent.: from late Latin *iliacus,* from *ilia* 'entrails.'

i·li·a·cus /i'līəkəs/ (also **iliacus muscle**) ▸*n. Anatomy* a triangular muscle that passes from the pelvis through the groin on either side and, together with the psoas, flexes the hip. ▷early 17th cent.: from late Latin.

Il·i·ad /'ilēəd; -,ad/ a Greek hexameter epic poem in twenty-four books, traditionally ascribed to Homer, telling how Achilles killed Hector at the climax of the Trojan War.

Il·i·um /'ilēəm/ the alternative name of **TROY**, esp. the 7th-century BC Greek city.

il·i·um /'ilēəm/ ▸*n.* (*pl.* **il·i·a** /'ilēə/) the large broad bone forming the upper part of each half of the pelvis. ▷late 16th cent.: from Latin, singular of *ilia* 'flanks, entrails.'

ilk /ilk/ ▸*n.* [in *sing.*] a type of people or things similar to those already referred to: *the veiled suggestions that reporters* ***of his ilk*** *seem to be so good at | fascists, racists, and others of that ilk.* ■ (**of that ilk**) *Scottish, chiefly archaic* of the place or estate of the same name: *Sir Iain Moncreiffe* ***of that ilk.*** ▷Old English *ilca* 'same,' of Germanic origin; related to **ALIKE**.

USAGE In modern use, **ilk** is used in phrases such as ***of his ilk, of that ilk,*** to mean 'type' or 'sort.' The use arose out of a misunderstanding of the earlier, Scottish use in the phrase **of that ilk**, where it means 'of the same name or place.' For this reason, some traditionalists regard the modern use as incorrect. It is, however, the only common current use and is now part of standard English.

ill /il/ ▸*adj.* **1** not in full health; sick: *her daughter is seriously ill* | [with *submodifier*] *a terminally ill patient.* **2** [*attrib.*] poor in quality: *ill judgment dogs the unsuccessful.* ■ harmful: *she had a cup of the same wine and suffered no ill effects.* ■ hostile: *I bear you no ill will.* ■ (esp. of fortune) not favorable: *no one less deserved such ill fortune than McStay.*

▸*adv.* **1** [usu. in *combination*] badly, wrongly, or imperfectly: *some of his premises seem ill-chosen | it ill becomes one so beautiful to be gloomy.* ■ unfavorably or unpropitiously: *something which boded ill for unwary golfers.* **2** only with difficulty; hardly: *she could ill afford the cost of new curtains.*

▸*n.* **1** [as *plural n.*] (**the ill**) people who are ill: *a day center for the mentally ill.* **2** (usu. **ills**) a problem or misfortune: *a lengthy work on the ills of society.* ■ evil; harm: *how could I wish him ill?* ▷Middle English (in the senses 'wicked,' 'malevolent,' 'harmful,' and 'difficult'): from Old Norse *illr* 'evil, difficult,' of unknown origin.

▸***PHRASES*** □ **ill at ease** uncomfortable or embarrassed. □ **speak** (or **think**) **ill of** say (or think) something critical about.

USAGE On the punctuation of **ill** in compound adjectives, see **usage** at **WELL**[1], as the same rules apply.

I'll /īl/ ▸*contraction of* I shall; I will: *I'll arrange it.*

Ill. ▸*abbr.* Illinois.

ill-ad·vised ▸*adj.* (of a person) unwise or imprudent: *you would be ill-advised to go on your own.* ■ badly thought out: *ill-advised financial ventures.* **—ill-ad·vis·ed·ly** *adv.*

ill-af·fect·ed ▸*adj. archaic* not inclined to be friendly or sympathetic.

ill-as·sort·ed ▸*adj.* not well matched: *ill-assorted furniture.*

il·la·tion /ə'lāSHən/ ▸*n. archaic* the action of inferring or drawing a conclusion. ■ an inference. ▷mid 16th cent.: from Latin *illatio(n-),* from *illat-* 'brought in,' from the verb *inferre* (see **INFER**).

il·la·tive /'ilətiv; i'lātiv/ ▸*adj.* **1** of the nature of or stating an inference. ■ proceeding by inference. **2** *Grammar* relating to or denoting a case of nouns in some languages used to express motion into something.

▸*n.* the illative case, or a word in this case. ▷late 16th cent.: from Latin *illativus,* from *illat-* 'brought in' (see **ILLATION**). **—il·la·tive·ly** *adv.*

Il·la·war·ra /,ilə'wärə; -'wôrə/ ▸*n.* (also **Illawarra shorthorn**) an animal of an Australian breed of red or roan dairy cattle. ▷early 20th cent.: from the name of a coastal district south of Sydney, where the breed was developed.

ill-bred ▸*adj.* badly brought up or rude. **—ill breed·ing** *n.*

ill-con·ceived ▸*adj.* not carefully planned or considered: *ill-conceived schemes.*

ill-con·sid·ered ▸*adj.* badly thought out: *an ill-considered remark.*

ill-dis·posed ▸*adj.* unfriendly or unsympathetic: *this fact was ignored by ill-disposed critics.*

il·le·gal /i(l)'lēgəl/ ▸*adj.* contrary to or forbidden by law, esp. criminal law: *illegal drugs.*

▸*n.* an illegal immigrant. ▷early 17th cent.: from French *illégal* or medieval Latin *illegalis,* from Latin *in-* 'not' + *legalis* 'according to the law.' **—il·le·gal·i·ty** /,i(l)li'galitē/ *n.* (*pl.* **-ties**) **—il·le·gal·ly** *adv.*

il·leg·i·ble /i(l)'lejəbəl/ ▸*adj.* not clear enough to be read: *his handwriting is totally illegible.* **—il·leg·i·bil·i·ty** /i(l),lejə'bilitē/ *n.* **—il·leg·i·bly** /-blē/ *adv.*

il·le·git·i·mate /,i(l)lə'jitəmit/ ▸*adj.* not authorized by the law; not in accordance with accepted standards or rules: *an illegitimate exercise of power by the military.* ■ (of a child) born of parents not lawfully married to each other.

▸*n.* a person who is illegitimate by birth. ▷mid 16th cent.: from late Latin *illegitimus* (from *in-* 'not' + *legitimus* 'lawful'), suggested by **LEGITIMATE**. **—il·le·git·i·ma·cy** /-məsē/ *n.* **—il·le·git·i·mate·ly** *adv.*

ill-fat·ed ▸*adj.* destined to fail or have bad luck: *an ill-fated expedition.*

ill-fa·vored (*Brit.* **ill-fa·voured**) ▸*adj.* unattractive or offensive: *he was by anyone's reckoning ill-favored and homely.*

ill-found·ed ▸*adj.* (esp. of an idea or belief) not based on fact or reliable evidence: *ill-founded criticism | her fear may be ill-founded.*

ill-got·ten ▸*adj.* acquired by illegal or unfair means: *the Mafiosi launder their* ***ill-gotten gains.***

ill hu·mor ▸*n.* irritability or bad temper. **—ill-hu·mored** *adj.*

il·lib·er·al /i(l)'lib(ə)rəl/ ▸*adj.* **1** opposed to liberal principles; restricting freedom of thought or behavior: *illiberal and anti-democratic policies.* **2** *rare* uncultured or unrefined. **3** *rare* not generous; mean. ▷mid 16th cent. (in the sense 'vulgar, ill-bred'): from French *illibéral,* from Latin *illiberalis* 'mean, sordid,' from *in-* 'not' + *liberalis* (see **LIBERAL**). **—il·lib·er·al·i·ty** /-,libə'ralitē/ *n.* **—il·lib·er·al·ly** *adv.*

Il·lich /'iliCH/, Ivan (1926–), U.S. educator and writer; born in Austria. He advocated the deinstitutionalization of education, religion, and medicine. Notable works: *Deschooling Society* (1971) and *Limits to Medicine* (1978).

il·lic·it /i(l)'lisit/ ▸*adj.* forbidden by law, rules, or custom: *illicit drugs | illicit sex.* ▷early 16th cent.: from French, or from Latin *illicitus,* from *in-* 'not' + *licitus* (see **LICIT**). **—il·lic·it·ly** *adv.* **—il·lic·it·ness** *n.*

il·lim·it·a·ble /i(l)'limitəbəl/ ▸*adj.* without limits or an end: *the illimitable human capacity for evil.* **—il·lim·it·a·bil·i·ty** /-,limitə'bilitē/ *n.* **—il·lim·it·a·bly** /-blē/ *adv.*

Il·li·noi·an /,ili'noi-ən/ ▸*adj. Geology* of, relating to, or denoting a Pleistocene glaciation in North America, preceding the Wisconsin and approximating to the Saale of northern Europe. ■ [as *n.*] (**the Illinoian**) the Illinoian glaciation or the system of deposits laid down during it. ▷mid 19th cent.: from **ILLINOIS** + **-AN**.

Il·li·nois /,ilə'noi; -'noiz/ a state in the eastern central U.S.; pop. 12,419,293; capital, Springfield; statehood, Dec. 3, 1818 (21). Colonized by the French in the 1600s and ceded to Britain in 1763, it was acquired by the U.S. in 1783. **—Il·li·nois·an** /-'noiən; -'noizən/ *n.* & *adj.*

Il·li·nois Riv·er a river that flows southwest for 273 miles (440 km) through Illinois to the Mississippi River.

il·liq·uid /i(l)'likwid/ ▸*adj.* (of assets) not easily converted into cash: *illiquid assets.* ■ (of a market) with few participants and a low volume of activity. **—il·li·quid·i·ty** /,i(l)li'kwiditē/ *n.*

il·lite /'ilīt/ ▸*n.* a clay mineral of the muscovite mica group, with a lattice structure that does not expand on absorption of water. ▷1930s: from **ILLINOIS** + **-ITE**[1].

il·lit·er·ate /i(l)'litərit/ ▸*adj.* unable to read or write: *his parents were illiterate.* ■ [with *submodifier*] ignorant in a particular subject or activity: *the extent to which voters are politically illiterate.* ■ uncultured or poorly educated: *the ignorant, illiterate town council.* See note at **IGNORANT**. ■ (esp. of a piece of writing) showing a lack of education, esp. an inability to read or write well.

▸*n.* a person who is unable to read or write. ▷late Middle English: from Latin *illitteratus,* from *in-* 'not' + *litteratus* (see **LITERATE**). **—il·lit·er·a·cy** /-əsē/ *n.* **—il·lit·er·ate·ly** *adv.* **—il·lit·er·ate·ness** *n.*

▸***PHRASE*** □ **functionally illiterate** lacking the literacy necessary for coping with most jobs and many everyday situations.

ill-judged ▸*adj.* lacking careful consideration; unwise: *an ill-judged decision.*

ill na·ture ▸*n. dated* meanness and irritability. **—ill-na·tured** *adj.* **—ill-na·tured·ly** *adv.*

ill·ness /'ilnis/ ▸*n.* a disease or period of sickness affecting the body or mind: *he died after a long illness | I've never missed a day's work through illness.*

il·lo·cu·tion /,ilə'kyo͞oSHən/ ▸*n.* an action performed by saying or writing something, e.g., ordering, warning, or promising. **—il·lo·cu·tion·ar·y** /-,nerē/ *adj.*

il·log·ic /i(l)ˈläjik/ ▸*n.* reasoning or thought that is not logical.

il·log·i·cal /i(l)ˈläjikəl/ ▸*adj.* lacking sense or clear, sound reasoning: *an illogical fear of the supernatural.* **—il·log·i·cal·i·ty** /i(l),läjiˈkalitē/ *n.* (*pl.* **-ties**) **—il·log·i·cal·ly** /-ik(ə)lē/ *adv.*

ill-o·mened ▸*adj.* attended by bad omens: *ill-omened birds of prey.*

ill-starred ▸*adj.* destined to fail or have many difficulties; unlucky: *an ill-starred expedition.*

ill tem·per ▸*n.* irritability; anger. **—ill-tem·pered** *adj.*

ill-treat ▸*v.* [*trans.*] act cruelly toward (a person or animal). **—ill-treat·ment** *n.*

il·lude /iˈlo͞od/ ▸*v.* [*trans.*] *poetic/literary* trick; delude: *he had allowed his imagination to illude him.* ▷late Middle English: from Latin *illudere* 'to mock.'

il·lume /iˈlo͞om/ ▸*v.* [*trans.*] *poetic/literary* light up; illuminate: *sparks from candles illume our faces.* ▷late Middle English: abbreviation of **ILLUMINE**.

il·lu·mi·nance /iˈlo͞omənəns/ ▸*n. Physics* the amount of luminous flux per unit area.

il·lu·mi·nant /iˈlo͞omənənt/ ▸*n. technical* a means of lighting or source of light: *until 1880, oil was the only illuminant in use.*
▸*adj.* giving off light. ▷mid 17th cent.: from Latin *illuminant-* 'illuminating,' from the verb *illuminare* (see **ILLUMINATE**).

il·lu·mi·nate /iˈlo͞omə,nāt/ ▸*v.* [*trans.*] light up: *a flash of lightning illuminated the house* | *figurative his face was illuminated by a smile.* ■ decorate (a building or structure) with lights for a special occasion. ■ [often as *adj.*] (**illuminated**) decorate (a page or initial letter in a manuscript) with gold, silver, or colored designs. ■ [usu. as *adj.*] (**illuminating**) *figurative* help to clarify or explain (a subject or matter): *a most illuminating discussion.* ■ enlighten (someone) spiritually or intellectually. ▷late Middle English: from Latin *illuminat-* 'illuminated,' from the verb *illuminare*, from *in-* 'upon' + *lumen, lumin-* 'light.' **—il·lu·mi·nat·ing·ly** *adv.* **—il·lu·mi·na·tive** /-,nātiv; -nətiv/ *adj.* **—il·lu·mi·na·tor** /-,nātər/ *n.*

il·lu·mi·na·ti /i,lo͞oməˈnätē/ ▸*plural n.* people claiming to possess special enlightenment or knowledge of something: *some mysterious standard known only to the illuminati of the organization.* ■ (**Illuminati**) a sect of 16th-century Spanish heretics who claimed special religious enlightenment. ■ (**Illuminati**) a Bavarian secret society founded in 1776, organized like the Freemasons. ▷late 16th cent.: plural of Italian *illuminato* or Latin *illuminatus* 'enlightened,' past participle of *illuminare* (see **ILLUMINATE**). **—il·lu·mi·nism** /iˈlo͞omə,nizəm/ *n.* **—il·lu·mi·nist** /iˈlo͞omənist/ *n.*

il·lu·mi·na·tion /i,lo͞oməˈnāsʜən/ ▸*n.* lighting or light: *higher levels of illumination are needed for reading.* ■ (often **illuminations**) a display of lights on a building or other structure. ■ *Physics* another term for **ILLUMINANCE**. ■ *figurative* spiritual or intellectual enlightenment. ■ *figurative* clarification: *these books form the most sustained analysis and illumination of the subject.* ■ the art of illuminating a manuscript. ■ an illuminated design in a manuscript. ▷Middle English: via Old French from late Latin *illuminatio(n-)*, from the verb *illuminare* (see **ILLUMINATE**).

il·lu·mine /iˈlo͞omən/ ▸*v.* [*trans.*] *poetic/literary* light up; brighten: *the lamplight illumined her pale features.* ■ enlighten (someone) spiritually or intellectually: *he assures himself that he is illumined and not deluded.* ▷Middle English: from Old French *illuminer*, from Latin *illuminare* (see **ILLUMINATE**).

illus. ▸*abbr.* ■ illustrated or illustration.

ill-use /ˈil ˈyo͞oz/ ▸*v.* [*trans.*] (usu. **be ill-used**) ill-treat (someone).
▸*n.* (**ill use**) ill-treatment.

il·lu·sion /iˈlo͞ozʜən/ ▸*n.* a false idea or belief: *he had no illusions about the trouble she was in.* ■ a deceptive appearance or impression: *the illusion of family togetherness* | *the tension between illusion and reality.* ■ a thing that is or is likely to be wrongly perceived or interpreted by the senses: *Zollner's illusion makes parallel lines seem to diverge by placing them on a zigzag-striped background.* ▷Middle English (in the sense 'deceiving, deception'): via Old French from Latin *illusio(n-)*, from *illudere* 'to mock,' from *in-* 'against' + *ludere* 'play.' **—il·lu·sion·al** /-zʜənl/ *adj.*
▸*PHRASES* □ **be under the illusion that** believe mistakenly that: *the world is under the illusion that the original painting still hangs in the Winter Palace.* □ **be under no illusion** (or **illusions**) be fully aware of the true state of affairs.

il·lu·sion·ism /iˈlo͞ozʜə,nizəm/ ▸*n.* the principle or technique by which artistic representations are made to resemble real objects or to give an appearance of space by the use of perspective. **—il·lu·sion·is·tic** /i,lo͞ozʜəˈnistik/ *adj.*

il·lu·sion·ist /iˈlo͞ozʜənist/ ▸*n.* a person who performs tricks that deceive the eye; a magician.

il·lu·sive /iˈlo͞osiv/ ▸*adj. chiefly poetic/literary* deceptive; illusory: *that illusive haven.* ▷early 17th cent.: from medieval Latin *illusivus*, from Latin *illus-* 'mocked,' from the verb *illudere* (see **ILLUSION**).

il·lu·so·ry /iˈlo͞osərē; -zərē/ ▸*adj.* based on illusion; not real: *she knew the safety of her room was illusory.* See note at **OSTENSIBLE**. **—il·lu·so·ri·ly** /-rəlē/ *adv.* **—il·lu·so·ri·ness** *n.*

il·lus·trate /ˈilə,strāt/ ▸*v.* [*trans.*] provide (a book, newspaper, etc.) with pictures: *the guide is illustrated with full-color photographs.* ■ explain or make (something) clear by using examples, charts, pictures, etc.: *the results are illustrated in Figure 7.* ■ serve as an example of: *a collection of pieces that illustrate Bach's techniques.* ▷early 16th cent. (in the sense 'illuminate, shed light on'): from Latin *illustrat-* 'lit up,' from the verb *illustrare*, from *in-* 'upon' + *lustrare* 'illuminate.'

il·lus·tra·tion /,iləˈstrāsʜən/ ▸*n.* a picture illustrating a book, newspaper, etc.: *an illustration of a yacht.* ■ an example serving to clarify or prove something: *this accident is a graphic illustration of the disaster that's waiting to happen.* ■ the action or fact of illustrating something, either pictorially or by exemplification: *by way of illustration, I refer to the following case.* ▷late Middle English (in the sense 'illumination; spiritual or intellectual enlightenment'): via Old French from Latin *illustratio(n-)*, from the verb *illustrare* (see **ILLUSTRATE**). **—il·lus·tra·tion·al** /-sʜənl/ *adj.*

il·lus·tra·tive /iˈləstrətiv; ˈilə,strātiv/ ▸*adj.* serving as an example or explanation: *this timetable is provided for illustrative purposes only.* **—il·lus·tra·tive·ly** *adv.*

il·lus·tra·tor /ˈilə,strātər/ ▸*n.* a person who draws or creates pictures for magazines, books, advertising, etc.

il·lus·tri·ous /iˈləstrēəs/ ▸*adj.* well known, respected, and admired for past achievements: *his illustrious predecessor* | *an illustrious career.* ▷mid 16th cent.: from Latin *illustris* 'clear, bright' + **-OUS**. **—il·lus·tri·ous·ly** *adv.* **—il·lus·tri·ous·ness** *n.*

il·lu·vi·a·tion /i,lo͞ovēˈāsʜən/ ▸*n. Soil Science* the introduction of salts or colloids into one soil horizon from another by percolating water. ▷early 20th cent.: from **IL-** 'in' + *-luvial* (on the pattern of *alluvial*) + **-ATION**. **—il·lu·vi·al** /iˈlo͞ovēəl; -vyəl/ *adj.* **—il·lu·vi·at·ed** /iˈlo͞ovē,ātid/ *adj.*

ill will ▸*n.* animosity or bitterness: *he didn't bear his estranged wife any ill will.*

Il·lyr·i·a /iˈli(ə)rēə/ an ancient region along the eastern coast of the Adriatic Sea that included Dalmatia and what is now Montenegro and northern Albania. **—Il·lyr·i·an** *adj.* & *n.*

Il·lyr·i·an /iˈli(ə)rēən/ ▸*n.* a native or inhabitant of ancient Illyria. ■ the branch of the Indo-European family of languages possibly represented by modern Albanian.
▸*adj.* of or relating to the ancient region of Illyria or its language.

il·men·ite /ˈilmə,nīt/ ▸*n.* a black mineral consisting of iron titanium oxide, of which it is the main ore. ▷early 19th cent.: named after the *Ilmen* mountains in the Urals + **-ITE**[1].

ILO ▸*abbr.* International Labor Organization.

I·lo·ca·no /,ēlōˈkänō/ ▸*n.* (*pl.* same or **-nos**) **1** a member of a people inhabiting northwestern Luzon in the Philippines. **2** the Austronesian language of this people.
▸*adj.* of or relating to this people or their language. ▷Philippine Spanish, from *Ilocos*, the name of two provinces in the Philippines.

I·lo·i·lo /,ēlōˈēlō/ a port on the southern coast of Panay in the Philippines; pop. 310,000.

I·lo·rin /iˈlôrin/ a city in western Nigeria; pop. 390,000.

ILS ▸*abbr.* instrument landing system, a system in which an aircraft's instruments interact with ground-based electronics to enable the pilot to land the aircraft safely in poor visibility.

il·va·ite /ˈilvə,īt/ ▸*n.* a mineral consisting of a basic silicate of calcium and iron, typically occurring as black prisms. ▷early 19th cent.: from Latin *Ilva* 'Elba'(an Italian island in the Mediterranean) + **-ITE**[1].

-ily ▸*suffix* forming adverbs corresponding to adjectives ending in *-y* (such as *happily* corresponding to *happy*). ▷see **-Y**[1], **-LY**[2].

IM ▸*abbr. Computing* ■ instant message. ■ instant messaging.

IM ▸*v.* (**IM's, IM'd, IM'ing**) [*trans.*] send a message to (someone) by using an instant messaging system: *I was being IM'd by a tireless horde of hot-blooded all-American testosterone-crazed males.*

I'm /īm/ ▸*contraction of* I am: *I'm a busy woman.*

im- ▸*prefix* variant spelling of **IN-**[1], **IN-**[2] assimilated before *b, m, p* (as in *imbibe, immure, impart*).

im·age /ˈimij/ ▸*n.* a representation of the external form of a person or thing in sculpture, painting, etc. See note at **EMBLEM**. ■ a visible impression obtained by a camera, telescope, microscope, or other device, or displayed on a video screen. ■ an optical appearance or counterpart produced by light or other radiation from an object reflected in a mirror or refracted through a lens. ■ *Mathematics* a point or set formed by mapping from another point or set. ■ a mental representation or idea: *he had an image of Uncle Walter throwing his crutches away.* ■ a simile or metaphor: *he uses the image of a hole to describe emotional emptiness.* ■ the general impression that a person, organization, or product presents to the public: *she strives to project an image of youth.* ■ [in *sing.*] a person or thing that closely resembles another: *he's **the image of** his father.* ■ [in *sing.*] semblance or likeness: *we are made **in the image of** God.* ■ (in biblical use) an idol.
▸*v.* [*trans.*] make a representation of the external form of: *artworks that imaged women's bodies.* ■ (usu. **be imaged**) make a visual representation of (something) by scanning it with a detector or electromagnetic beam: *every point on the Earth's surface was imaged by the satellite* | [as *n.*] (**imaging**) *medical imaging.* ■ form a mental picture or idea of: *it is possible for us to image a society in which no one committed crime.* ▷Middle English: from Old French, from Latin *imago*; related to **IMITATE**. **—im·age·less** *adj.*

im·age in·ten·si·fi·er ▸*n.* a device used to make a brighter version of an image on a photoelectric screen.

im·age-mak·er ▸*n.* a person employed to identify and create a favorable public image for a person, organization, or product.

im·age proc·ess·ing ▸*n.* the analysis and manipulation of a digitized image, esp. in order to improve its quality. **—im·age proc·es·sor** *n.*

im·ag·er /ˈimijər/ ▸*n.* an electronic or other device that records images of something: *a thermal imager.*

im·age·ry /ˈimij(ə)rē/ ▸*n.* visually descriptive or figurative language, esp. in a literary work: *Tennyson uses imagery to create a lyrical emotion.* ■ visual images collectively: *the impact of computer-generated imagery on contemporary art.* ■ visual symbolism: *the film's religious imagery.* ▷Middle English (in the senses 'statuary, carved images collectively'): from Old French *imagerie*, from *imager* 'make an image,' from *image* (see **IMAGE**).

im·age·set·ter /ˈimij,setər/ ▸*n. Computing* a very high-quality type of color printer used to print glossy magazines, newsletters, or other documents.

im·ag·i·na·ble /iˈmaj(ə)nəbəl/ ▸*adj.* possible to be thought of or believed: *the most spectacular views imaginable.* ▷late Middle English: from late Latin *imaginabilis*, from Latin *imaginare* 'form an image of, represent,' from *imago, imagin-* 'image.' **—i·mag·i·na·bly** /-blē/ *adv.*

i·ma·gi·nal ▸*adj.* **1** /iˈmaj(ə)nəl/ of or relating to an image: *imaginal education methods.* **2** /iˈmāgənəl; iˈmä-/ *Entomology* of or relating to an adult insect or imago. ▷late 19th cent.: from Latin *imago, imagin-* 'image' + **-AL**.

i·ma·gi·nal disk /iˈmāgənəl; iˈmä-/ ▸*n. Entomology* a thickening of the epidermis of an insect larva, which, on pupation, develops into a particular organ of the adult insect.

im·ag·i·nar·y /iˈmajə,nerē/ ▸*adj.* **1** existing only in the imagination: *Chris had imaginary conversations with her.* **2** *Mathematics* (of a number or quantity) expressed in terms of the square root of a negative number (usually the square root of −1, represented by *i* or *j*). See also **COMPLEX**. ▷late Middle English: from Latin *imaginarius*, from *imago, imagin-* 'image.' **—im·ag·i·nar·i·ly** /i,majəˈne(ə)rəlē/ *adv.*

USAGE **Imaginary** means 'product of the imagination, unreal.' **Imaginative** means 'showing imagination, original.' Science fiction, for example, deals with **imaginary** people, places, and events; how **imaginative** it is depends on the writer's ability.

Pronunciation Key ə *ago*; ər *over*; ˈə or ,ə *up*; ˈər or ,ər *fur*; a *hat*; ā *rate*; ä *car*; ch *chew*; e *let*; ē *see*; e(ə)r *air*; i *fit*; ī *by*; i(ə)r *ear*; ng *sing*; ō *go*; ô *for*; oi *boy*; o͝o *good*; o͞o *goo*; ou *out*; sh *she*; th *thin*; t͟h *then*; (h)w *why*; zh *vision*

im·ag·i·na·tion /i,majə'nāSHən/ ▸*n.* the faculty or action of forming new ideas, or images or concepts of external objects not present to the senses: *she'd never been blessed with a vivid imagination.* ■ the ability of the mind to be creative or resourceful: *technology gives workers the chance to use their imagination.* ■ the part of the mind that imagines things: *a girl who existed only in my imagination.* ▷Middle English: via Old French from Latin *imaginatio(n-)*, from the verb *imaginari* 'picture to oneself,' from *imago, imagin-* 'image.'

im·ag·i·na·tive /i'maj(ə)nətiv/ ▸*adj.* having or showing creativity or inventiveness: *making imaginative use of computer software | he was imaginative beyond all other architects.* See note at CREATIVE. **—i·mag·i·na·tive·ly** *adv.* **—i·mag·i·na·tive·ness** *n.*

USAGE See usage at IMAGINARY.

im·ag·ine /i'majən/ ▸*v.* [*trans.*] **1** form a mental image or concept of: *imagine a road trip from Philadelphia to Chicago* | [with *clause*] *I couldn't imagine what she expected to tell them.* ■ [often as *adj.*] (**imagined**) believe (something unreal or untrue) to exist or be so: *they suffered from ill health, real or imagined, throughout their lives.* **2** [with *clause*] suppose or assume: *after Ned died, everyone imagined that Mabel would move away.* ■ [as *exclam.*] just suppose: *imagine! to outwit Heydrich!* ▷Middle English: from Old French *imaginer*, from Latin *imaginare* 'form an image of, represent' and *imaginari* 'picture to oneself,' both from *imago, imagin-* 'image.' **—i·mag·in·er** *n.*

im·ag·i·neer /i,majə'ni(ə)r/ ▸*n.* a person who devises and implements a new or highly imaginative concept or technology, in particular one who devises the attractions in Walt Disney theme parks.
▸*v.* [*trans.*] [often as *n.*] (**imagineering**) devise and implement (such a concept or technology): *theme parks are benefiting from a new era of imagineering.* ▷1940s: from IMAGINE, on the pattern of *engineer.*

im·ag·ines /i'māgə,nēz; i'mä-/ ▸ plural form of IMAGO.

im·ag·in·ings /i'majəniNGz/ ▸*plural n.* thoughts or fantasies: *this was quite beyond his worst imaginings.*

im·ag·ism /'imə,jizəm/ ▸*n.* a movement in early 20th-century English and American poetry that sought clarity of expression through the use of precise images. The movement derived in part from the aesthetic philosophy of T. E. Hulme and involved Ezra Pound, James Joyce, Amy Lowell, and others. **—im·ag·ist** *n.* **—im·ag·is·tic** /,imə'jistik/ *adj.*

i·ma·go /i'māgō; i'mä-/ ▸*n.* (*pl.* **i·ma·gos, i·ma·goes** or **i·ma·gi·nes** /i'māgə,nēz/) **1** *Entomology* the final and fully developed adult stage of an insect, typically winged. **2** *Psychoanalysis* an unconscious, idealized mental image of someone, esp. a parent, that influences a person's behavior. ▷late 18th cent. (sense 1): modern Latin use of Latin *imago* 'image.' Sense 2 dates from the early 20th cent.

i·mam /i'mäm/ ▸*n.* the person who leads prayers in a mosque. ■ (**Imam**) a title of various Muslim leaders, esp. of one succeeding Muhammad as leader of Shiite Islam: *Imam Khomeini.* ▷from Arabic *'imām* 'leader,' from *'amma* 'lead the way.' **—i·mam·ate** /-,māt/ *n.*

IMAP /'ī,map/ ▸*abbr. Computing* Internet Mail Access Protocol.

I·ma·ri /i'märē/ ▸*n.* [usu. as *adj.*] a type of richly decorated Japanese porcelain: *an Imari vase.* ▷late 19th cent.: from the name of a port in northwestern Kyushu, Japan, from which it was shipped.

IMAX /'ī,maks/ ▸*n. trademark* a technique of widescreen cinematography that produces an image approximately ten times larger than that from standard 35 mm film: [as *adj.*] *IMAX theaters.* ▷1960s: from *i-* (probably representing a pronunciation of EYE) + *max* (short for MAXIMUM).

im·bal·ance /im'baləns/ ▸*n.* lack of proportion or relation between corresponding things: *tension is generated by the imbalance of power | the condition is caused by a hormonal imbalance.*

im·be·cile /'imbəsəl; -,sil/ ▸*n. informal* a stupid person.
▸*adj.* [*attrib.*] stupid; idiotic: *try not to make imbecile remarks.* ▷mid 16th cent. (as an adjective in the sense 'physically weak'): via French from Latin *imbecillus*, literally 'without a supporting staff,' from *in-* (expressing negation) + *baculum* 'stick, staff.' The current sense dates from the early 19th cent. **—im·be·cil·ic** /,imbə'silik/ *adj.* **—im·be·cil·i·ty** /,imbə'silitē/ *n.* (*pl.* **-ties**).

im·bed ▸*v.* variant spelling of EMBED.

im·bibe /im'bīb/ ▸*v.* [*trans.*] *formal, often humorous* drink (alcohol): *they were imbibing far too many pitchers of beer* | [*intrans.*] *having imbibed too freely, he fell over.* ■ *figurative* absorb or assimilate (ideas or knowledge): *the Bolshevist propaganda that you imbibed in your youth.* ■ *chiefly Botany* (esp. of seeds) absorb (water) into ultramicroscopic spaces or pores. ■ *Botany* place (seeds) in water in order to absorb it. ▷late Middle English (in the senses 'absorb or cause to absorb moisture' and 'take into solution'): from Latin *imbibere*, from *in-* 'in' + *bibere* 'to drink.' **—im·bib·er** *n.* **—im·bi·bi·tion** /,imbə'bisHən/ *n.* (*chiefly Botany*).

im·bri·cate /'imbri,kāt/ *chiefly Zoology Botany* ▸*v.* [usu. as *adj.*] (**imbricated**) arrange (scales, sepals, plates, etc.) so that they overlap like roof tiles: *these molds have spherical bodies composed of imbricated triangular plates.* ■ [*intrans.*] [usu. as *adj.*] (**imbricating**) overlap: *a coating of imbricating scales.*
▸*adj.* (of scales, sepals, plates, etc.) having adjacent edges overlapping. Compare with VALVATE. ▷early 17th cent. (in the sense 'shaped like a pantile'): from Latin *imbricat-* 'covered with roof tiles,' from the verb *imbricare*, from *imbrex, imbric-* 'roof tile' (from *imber* 'shower of rain'). **—im·bri·ca·tion** /,imbri'kāSHən/ *n.*

im·bro·glio /im'brōlyō/ ▸*n.* (*pl.* **-glios**) an extremely confused, complicated, or embarrassing situation: *the Watergate imbroglio.* ■ *archaic* a confused heap. ▷mid 18th cent.: Italian, from *imbrogliare* 'confuse'; related to EMBROIL.

Im·bros /'ēm,brôs/ a Turkish island in the Aegean Sea, near the entrance to the Dardanelles. Turkish name IMROZ.

im·brue /im'bro͞o/ (also **em·brue** /em-/) ▸*v.* (**-brues, -brued, -bru·ing**) [*trans.*] *archaic & poetic/literary* stain (something, esp. one's hands or sword): *they were unwilling to imbrue their hands in his blood.* ▷late Middle English: from Old French *embruer* 'bedaub, bedabble,' ultimately of Germanic origin and related to BROTH.

im·bue /im'byo͞o/ ▸*v.* (**-bues, -bued, -bu·ing**) [*trans.*] (often **be imbued with**) inspire or permeate with a feeling or quality: *he was imbued with a deep Christian piety.* ▷late Middle English (in the sense 'saturate'): from French *imbu* 'moistened,' from Latin *imbutus*, past participle of *imbuere* 'moisten.'

IMD ▸*abbr.* intermodulation distortion.

IMF ▸*abbr.* International Monetary Fund.

IMHO ▸*abbr.* in my humble opinion (used esp. in electronic mail).

Im·ho·tep /im'hō,tep/ (*fl.* 27th century BC), Egyptian architect and scholar, who was later deified. It is thought that he designed the step pyramid built at Saqqara for third-dynasty pharaoh Djoser.

im·id·az·ole /,imi'dazōl/ ▸*n. Chemistry* a colorless crystalline compound with mildly basic properties, present as a substituent in the amino acid histidine. • a heterocyclic compound; chem. formula: $C_3H_4N_2$. ▷late 19th cent.: from IMIDE + AZO- + -OLE.

im·ide /'imīd/ ▸*n. Chemistry* an organic compound containing the group −CONHCO−, related to ammonia by replacement of two hydrogen atoms by acyl groups. ▷mid 19th cent.: from French, arbitrary alteration of AMIDE.

i·mine /i'mēn; 'imin/ ▸*n. Chemistry* an organic compound containing the group −C=NH or −C=NR where R is an alkyl or other group. ▷late 19th cent.: from AMINE, on the pattern of the pair *amide, imide.*

im·ip·ra·mine /i'miprə,mēn/ ▸*n.* a synthetic compound used to treat depression. • A tricyclic amine; chem. formula: $C_{19}H_{24}N_2$. ▷1950s: from *imi(ne)* + *pr(opyl)* + AMINE.

imit. ▸*abbr.* ■ imitation or imitative.

im·i·tate /'imi,tāt/ ▸*v.* (often **be imitated**) take or follow as a model: *his style was imitated by many other writers.* ■ copy (a person's speech or mannerisms), esp. for comic effect: *she imitated my Scottish accent.* ■ copy or simulate: *synthetic fabrics can now imitate everything from silk to rubber.* ▷mid 16th cent.: from Latin *imitat-* 'copied,' from the verb *imitari*; related to *imago* 'image.' **—im·i·ta·ble** /'imitəbəl/ *adj.* **—im·i·ta·tor** /-,tātər/ *n.*

THE RIGHT WORD **ape, copy, imitate, impersonate, mimic, mock**

A young girl might **imitate** her mother by answering the phone in exactly the same tone of voice, while a teenager who deliberately *imitates* the way her mother talks for the purpose of irritating her would more accurately be said to **mimic** her. *Imitate* implies following something as an example or model (*he imitated the playing style of his music teacher*), while *mimic* suggests imitating someone's mannerisms for fun or ridicule (*they liked to mimic the teacher's southern drawl*).

To **copy** is to imitate or reproduce something as closely as possible (*he copied the style of dress and speech used by the other gang members*).

When someone assumes another person's appearance or mannerisms, sometimes for the purpose of perpetrating a fraud, he or she is said to **impersonate** (*arrested for impersonating a police officer; a comedian well known for impersonating political figures*).

Ape and **mock** both imply an unflattering imitation. Someone who mimics in a contemptuous way is said to *ape* (*he entertained everyone in the office by aping the boss's phone conversations with his wife*), while someone who imitates with the intention of belittling or irritating is said to *mock* (*the students openly mocked their teacher's attempt to have a serious discussion about sex*).

im·i·ta·tion /,imi'tāSHən/ ▸*n.* a thing intended to simulate or copy something else: [as *adj.*] *an imitation diamond.* ■ the action of using someone or something as a model: *a child learns to speak by imitation.* ■ an act of imitating a person's speech or mannerisms, esp. for comic effect: *he attempted an atrocious imitation of my English accent.* ■ *Music* the repetition of a phrase or melody in another part or voice, usually at a different pitch. ▷late Middle English: from Latin *imitatio(n-)*, from the verb *imitari* (see IMITATE).
▸*PHRASE* □ **imitation is the sincerest form of flattery** *proverb* copying someone or something is an implicit way of paying them a compliment.

im·i·ta·tive /'imi,tātiv/ ▸*adj.* **1** copying or following a model or example: *the derring-do of our film heroes inspired us to imitative feats.* ■ following a model or example without any attempt at originality: *an ill-conceived and imitative addition to the museum.* **2** (of a word) reproducing a natural sound (e.g., *fizz*) or pronounced in a way that is thought to correspond to the appearance or character of the object or action described (e.g., *blob*). **—im·i·ta·tive·ly** *adv.* **—im·i·ta·tive·ness** *n.*

im·mac·u·late /i'makyəlit/ ▸*adj.* (esp. of a person or their clothes) perfectly clean, neat, or tidy: *an immaculate white suit.* ■ free from flaws or mistakes; perfect: *an immaculate safety record.* ■ *Theology* (in the Roman Catholic Church) free from sin. ■ *Botany & Zoology* uniformly colored without spots or other marks. ▷late Middle English (in the sense 'free from moral stain'): from Latin *immaculatus*, from *in-* 'not' + *maculatus* 'stained' (from *macula* 'spot'). **—im·mac·u·la·cy** /-ləsē/ *n.* **—im·mac·u·late·ly** *adv.* **—im·mac·u·late·ness** *n.*

Im·mac·u·late Con·cep·tion ▸*n.* the doctrine that God preserved the Virgin Mary from the taint of original sin from the moment she was conceived; it was defined as a dogma of the Roman Catholic Church in 1854. ■ the feast commemorating the Immaculate Conception on December 8.

im·ma·nent /'imənənt/ ▸*adj.* existing or operating within; inherent: *the protection of liberties is **immanent** in constitutional arrangements.* ■ (of God) permanently pervading and sustaining the universe. Often contrasted with TRANSCENDENT. ▷mid 16th cent.: from late Latin *immanent-* 'remaining within,' from *in-* 'in' + *manere* 'remain.' **—im·ma·nence** *n.* **—im·ma·nen·cy** *n.* **—im·ma·nent·ism** /-,tizəm/ *n.* **—im·ma·nent·ist** /-tist/ *n.*

USAGE See usage at EMINENT.

Im·man·u·el variant spelling of EMMANUEL.

im·ma·te·ri·al /,i(m)mə'ti(ə)rēəl/ ▸*adj.* **1** unimportant under the circumstances; irrelevant: *so long as the band kept the beat, what they played was immaterial.* **2** *Philosophy* spiritual, rather than physical: *we have immaterial souls.* ▷late Middle English (sense 2): from late Latin *immaterialis*, from *in-* 'not' + *materialis* 'relating to matter.' **—im·ma·te·ri·al·i·ty** /-,ti(ə)rē'alitē/ *n.* **—im·ma·te·ri·al·ly** *adv.*

USAGE **Immaterial** and **irrelevant** are familiar in legal, esp. courtroom, use. **Immaterial** means 'unimportant because not adding anything to the point.' **Irrelevant**, a much more common word, means 'beside the point, not speaking to the point.' Courts have long ceased to demand precise distinctions, and evidence is often objected to as "immaterial, irrelevant, and incompetent ('offered by a witness who is not qualified to offer it')."

im·ma·te·ri·al·ism /,i(m)mə'ti(ə)rēə,lizəm/ ▸*n.* the belief that material things have no objective existence. **—im·ma·te·ri·al·ist** *n.*

im·ma·ture /,imə'CHo͝or; -'t(y)o͝or/ ▸*adj.* not fully developed: *many of the fish caught are immature | immature fruit.* See note at YOUTHFUL. ■ (of a person or their behavior) having or showing emotional or intellectual development appropriate to someone younger: *his immature sense of humor.* ▷mid 16th cent. (in the sense 'premature,' referring to death): from Latin *immaturus* 'untimely, unripe,' from *in-* 'not' + *maturus* 'ripe' (see MATURE). **—im·ma·ture·ly** *adv.* **—im·ma·tu·ri·ty** /-itē/ *n.*

im·meas·ur·a·ble /i'mezHərəbəl/ ▶*adj.* too large, extensive, or extreme to measure: *immeasurable suffering.* **—im·meas·ur·a·bil·i·ty** /-ˌmezHərə'bilitē/ *n.* **—im·meas·ur·a·bly** *adv.*

im·me·di·a·cy /i'mēdēəsē/ ▶*n.* the quality of bringing one into direct and instant involvement with something, giving rise to a sense of urgency or excitement: *electronic mail works because it has the immediacy of a scribbled memo.*

im·me·di·ate /i'mēdē-it/ ▶*adj.* **1** occurring or done at once; instant: *the authorities took no immediate action* | *the book's success was immediate.* ■ relating to or existing at the present time: *the immediate concern was how to avoid taxes.* **2** nearest in time, relationship, or rank: *a funeral with only the immediate family in attendance.* ■ nearest or next to in space: *roads in the immediate vicinity of the port.* ■ (of a relation or action) without an intervening medium or agency; direct: *coronary thrombosis was the immediate cause of death.* **3** *Philosophy* (of knowledge or reaction) gained or shown without reasoning; intuitive. ▷late Middle English (in the sense 'nearest in space or order'): from Old French *immediat,* or from late Latin *immediatus,* from *in-* 'not' + *mediatus* 'intervening,' past participle of *mediare* (see MEDIATE). **—im·me·di·ate·ness** *n.*

im·me·di·ate con·stit·u·ent ▶*n. Linguistics* each of the constituents of a syntactic unit at the next level down in the hierarchy.

im·me·di·ate·ly /i'mēdē-itlē/ ▶*adv.* **1** at once; instantly: *I called immediately for an ambulance.* **2** without any intervening time or space: *she was sitting immediately behind me.* ■ in direct or very close relation: *they would be the states most immediately affected by any such action.* ▶*conj. chiefly Brit.* as soon as: *let me know immediately she arrives.*

im·med·i·ca·ble /i'medikəbəl/ ▶*adj. archaic* unable to be healed or treated; incurable. ▷mid 16th cent.: from Latin *immedicabilis,* from *in-* 'not' + *medicabilis* (see MEDICABLE).

Im·mel·mann /'iməlmən; -ˌmän/ (also **Immelmann turn**) ▶*n.* an aerobatic maneuver in which an airplane performs a half loop followed by a half roll, resulting in reversal of direction and increased height. ▷early 20th cent.: named after Max *Immelmann* (1890–1916), German fighter pilot.

im·me·mo·ri·al /ˌi(m)mə'môrēəl/ ▶*adj.* originating in the distant past; very old: *an immemorial custom.* ▷early 17th cent.: from medieval Latin *immemorialis,* from *in-* 'not' + *memorialis* 'relating to the memory.' **—im·me·mo·ri·al·ly** *adv.*

im·mense /i'mens/ ▶*adj.* extremely large or great, esp. in scale or degree: *the cost of restoration has been immense* | *an immense apartment building.* ▷late Middle English: via French from Latin *immensus* 'immeasurable,' from *in-* 'not' + *mensus* 'measured' (past participle of *metiri*). **—im·men·si·ty** /-sitē/ *n.*

im·mense·ly /i'menslē/ ▶*adv.* to a great extent; extremely: [as *submodifier*] *the president was immensely popular.*

im·merse /i'mərs/ ▶*v.* **1** dip or submerge in a liquid: ***immerse** the paper **in** water for twenty minutes.* ■ baptize (someone) by immersion in water. **2** (**immerse oneself** or **be immersed**) *figurative* involve oneself deeply in a particular activity or interest: *she immersed herself in her work* | *she was still immersed in her thoughts.* ▷early 17th cent.: from Latin *immers-* 'dipped into,' from the verb *immergere,* from *in-* 'in' + *mergere* 'to dip.'

im·mer·sion /i'mərzHən; -sHən/ ▶*n.* the action of immersing someone or something in a liquid: *his back was still raw from **immersion in** the icy Atlantic Ocean.* ■ deep mental involvement: *his total **immersion in** Marxism.* ■ a method of teaching a foreign language by the exclusive use of that language, usually at a special school. ■ baptism by immersing a person bodily (but not necessarily completely) in water. ■ *rare Astronomy* the disappearance of a celestial body in the shadow of or behind another. See also EMERSION. ▷late 15th cent.: from late Latin *immersio(n-),* from *immergere* 'dip into' (see IMMERSE).

im·mer·sion heat·er ▶*n.* an electric heating element that is positioned in the liquid to be heated.

im·mer·sive /i'mərsiv/ ▶*adj.* (of a computer display or system) generating a three-dimensional image that appears to surround the user.

im·mi·grant /'imigrənt/ ▶*n.* a person who comes to live permanently in a foreign country. ■ *Biology* an animal or plant living or growing in a region to which it has migrated. ▷late 18th cent.: from Latin *immigrant-* 'immigrating,' from the verb *immigrare,* on the pattern of *emigrant.*

im·mi·grate /'imiˌgrāt/ ▶*v.* [*intrans.*] come to live permanently in a foreign country: *the Mennonites immigrated to western Canada in the 1870s.* ▷early 17th cent.: from Latin *immigrat-* 'immigrated,' from the verb *immigrare,* from *in-* 'into' + *migrare* 'migrate.'

USAGE See usage at EMIGRATE.

im·mi·gra·tion /ˌimi'grāsHən/ ▶*n.* the action of coming to live permanently in a foreign country: *a barrier to control illegal immigration from Mexico.* ■ the place at an airport or country's border where government officials check the documents of people entering that country.

im·mi·nent /'imənənt/ ▶*adj.* **1** about to happen: *they were in imminent danger of being swept away.* **2** *archaic* overhanging. ▷late Middle English: from Latin *imminent-* 'overhanging, impending,' from the verb *imminere,* from *in-* 'upon, toward' + *minere* 'to project.' **—im·mi·nence** *n.* **—im·mi·nent·ly** *adv.*

USAGE See usage at EMINENT.

im·mis·ci·ble /i(m)'misəbəl/ ▶*adj.* (of liquids) not forming a homogeneous mixture when added together: *water is **immiscible with** suntan oil.* ▷late 17th cent.: from late Latin *immiscibilis,* from *in-* 'not' + *miscibilis* (see MISCIBLE). **—im·mis·ci·bil·i·ty** /-ˌmisə'bilitē/ *n.* **—im·mis·ci·bly** /-blē/ *adv.*

im·mis·er·a·tion /i(m)ˌmizə'rāsHən/ ▶*n.* economic impoverishment. ▷1940s: translating German *Verelendung.* **—im·mis·er·ate** /-'mizəˌrāt/ *v.*

im·mis·er·i·za·tion /i(m)ˌmizərə'zāsHən/ ▶*n.* another term for IMMISERATION. **—im·mis·er·ize** /-'mizəˌrīz/ *v.*

im·mit·i·ga·ble /i(m)'mitigəbəl/ ▶*adj. archaic* unable to be made less severe or serious: *the pain was immitigable.* ▷late 16th cent.: from late Latin *immitigabilis,* from *in-* 'not' + *mitigabilis* 'able to be mitigated.' **—im·mit·i·ga·bly** /-blē/ *adv.*

im·mit·tance /i(m)'mitns/ ▶*n. Physics* admittance and impedance (as a combined concept). ▷1950s: blend of IMPEDANCE and ADMITTANCE.

im·mix·ture /i'mikscHər/ ▶*n. archaic* the process of mixing or being involved with something.

im·mo·bile /i(m)'mōbəl; -bēl; -bīl/ ▶*adj.* not moving; motionless: *she sat immobile for a long time.* ■ incapable of moving or being moved: *an immobile work force.* ▷Middle English: from Old French, from Latin *immobilis,* from *in-* 'not' + *mobilis* (see MOBILE). **—im·mo·bil·i·ty** /ˌi(m)mō'bilitē/ *n.*

im·mo·bil·ism /i(m)'mōbəˌlizəm/ ▶*n.* deep-seated resistance to political change.

im·mo·bi·lize /i(m)'mōbəˌlīz/ ▶*v.* [*trans.*] prevent (something or someone) from moving or operating as normal: *I want you to immobilize their vehicle* | *fear had immobilized her.* ■ restrict the movements of (a limb or patient) to allow healing: *other children in the ward were immobilized in traction.* ▷late 19th cent.: from French *immobiliser,* from *immobile* (see IMMOBILE). **—im·mo·bi·li·za·tion** /-ˌmōbəli'zāsHən/ *n.*

im·mod·er·ate /i(m)'mädərit/ ▶*adj.* not sensible or restrained; excessive: *immoderate drinking.* ▷late Middle English: from Latin *immoderatus,* from *in-* 'not' + *moderatus* 'reduced, controlled' (past participle of *moderare*). **—im·mod·er·ate·ly** *adv.* **—im·mod·er·a·tion** /-ˌmädə'rāsHən/ *n.*

im·mod·est /i(m)'mädist/ ▶*adj.* lacking humility or decency: *she thought Western clothes were ugly and immodest.* ▷late 16th cent.: from French *immodeste* or Latin *immodestus,* from *in-* 'not' + *modestus* (see MODEST). **—im·mod·est·ly** *adv.* **—im·mod·es·ty** *n.*

im·mo·late /'iməˌlāt/ ▶*v.* [*trans.*] kill or offer as a sacrifice, esp. by burning. ▷mid 16th cent.: from Latin *immolat-* 'sprinkled with sacrificial meal,' from the verb *immolare,* from *in-* 'upon' + *mola* 'meal.' **—im·mo·la·tion** /ˌimə'lāsHən/ *n.* **—im·mo·la·tor** /-ˌlātər/ *n.*

im·mor·al /i(m)'môrəl; -'märəl/ ▶*adj.* not conforming to accepted standards of morality: *an immoral and unwinnable war.* **—im·mo·ral·i·ty** /ˌimə'ralitē; ˌimô-/ *n.* (*pl.* **-ties**) **—im·mor·al·ly** *adv.*

USAGE Immoral means 'failing to adhere to moral standards.' **Amoral** is a more neutral, impartial word meaning 'without, or not concerned with, moral standards.' An **immoral** person commits acts that violate society's moral norms. An **amoral** person has no understanding of these norms, or no sense of right and wrong; the word may refer to a 'social deviant.' **Amoral** may also mean 'not concerned with, or outside the scope of morality' (following the pattern of *apolitical, asexual*). **Amoral,** then, may refer to a judicial ruling that is concerned only with narrow legal or financial issues. Whereas **amoral** may be simply descriptive, **immoral** is judgmental.

im·mor·al·ism /i'môrəˌlizəm; -'mär-/ ▶*n.* a system of thought or behavior that does not accept moral principles. ▷early 20th cent.: suggested by German *Immoralismus.* **—im·mor·al·ist** *n.*

im·mor·tal /i(m)'môrtl/ ▶*adj.* living forever; never dying or decaying: *our mortal bodies are inhabited by immortal souls.* ■ deserving to be remembered forever: *the immortal children's classic, "The Adventures of Tom Sawyer."*
▶*n.* an immortal being, esp. a god of ancient Greece or Rome. ■ a person of enduring fame: *he will always be one of the immortals of hockey.* ■ (**Immortals**) *historical* the royal bodyguard of ancient Persia. ■ (**Immortal**) a member of the French Academy. ▷late Middle English: from Latin *immortalis,* from *in-* 'not' + *mortalis* (see MORTAL). **—im·mor·tal·i·ty** /ˌi(m)môr'talitē/ *n.* **—im·mor·tal·ly** *adv.*

im·mor·tal·ize /i(m)'môrtlˌīz/ ▶*v.* [*trans.*] (usu. **be immortalized in**) confer enduring fame upon: *he will be forever immortalized in the history books.* **—im·mor·tal·i·za·tion** /-ˌmôrtl-i'zāsHən/ *n.*

im·mor·telle /ˌi,môr'tel/ ▶*n.* **1** another term for EVERLASTING (sense 2). **2** *W. Indian* a Caribbean tree of the pea family, with a spiny trunk and clusters of red, orange, or pinkish flowers. • Genus *Erythrina,* family Leguminosae: two species. ▷mid 19th cent.: French, literally 'everlasting.'

im·mo·tile /i(m)'mōtl/ ▶*adj. Biology* not motile.

im·mov·a·ble /i(m)'mo͞ovəbəl/ ▶*adj.* not able to be moved: *lock your bike to something immovable like a lamp post.* ■ (of a person) not yielding to argument or pressure. ■ (esp. of a principle) fixed or unchangeable: *an immovable article of faith.* ■ *Law* (of property) consisting of land, buildings, or other permanent items.
▶*n.* (**immovables**) *Law* immovable property. **—im·mov·a·bil·i·ty** /-ˌmo͞ovə'bilitē/ *n.* **—im·mov·a·bly** /-blē/ *adv.*

immun. ▶*abbr.* ■ immunity or immunization.

im·mune /i'myo͞on/ ▶*adj.* resistant to a particular infection or toxin owing to the presence of specific antibodies or sensitized white blood cells: *they were naturally **immune to** hepatitis B.* ■ protected or exempt, esp. from an obligation or the effects of something: *they are **immune from** legal action.* ■ [*predic.*] not affected or influenced by something: *no one is **immune to** his immense charm.* ■ [*attrib.*] *Biology* of or relating to immunity: *the body's immune system.* ▷late Middle English (in the sense 'free from (a liability)'): from Latin *immunis* 'exempt from public service or charge,' from *in-* 'not' + *munis* 'ready for service.' Senses relating to physiological resistance date from the late 19th cent.

im·mune de·fi·cien·cy ▶*n.* another term for IMMUNODEFICIENCY.

im·mune re·sponse ▶*n.* the reaction of the cells and fluids of the body to the presence of a substance that is not recognized as a constituent of the body itself.

im·mu·ni·ty /i'myo͞onitē/ ▶*n.* (*pl.* **-ties**) the ability of an organism to resist a particular infection or toxin by the action of specific antibodies or sensitized white blood cells: ***immunity to** typhoid seems to have increased spontaneously.* ■ protection or exemption from something, esp. an obligation or penalty: *the rebels were given **immunity from** prosecution.* ■ *Law* officially granted exemption from legal proceedings. ■ (**immunity to**) lack of susceptibility, esp. to something unwelcome or harmful: *products must have an adequate level of immunity to interference* | *exercises designed to build an immunity to fatigue.* ▷late Middle English (in the sense 'exemption (from a liability)'): from Latin *immunitas,* from *immunis* (see IMMUNE).

im·mu·nize /'imyəˌnīz/ ▶*v.* [*trans.*] make (a person or animal) immune to infection, typically by inoculation: *the vaccine is used to **immunize** children **against** measles.* **—im·mu·ni·za·tion** /ˌimyəni'zāsHən/ *n.* **—im·mu·niz·er** *n.*

immuno- ▶*comb. form Medicine* representing IMMUNE, IMMUNITY, or IMMUNOLOGY.

Pronunciation Key ə *ago;* ər *over;* 'ə *or* ˌə *up;* 'ər *or* ˌər *fur;* a *hat;* ā *rate;* ä *car;* CH *chew;* e *let;* ē *see;* e(ə)r *air;* i *fit;* ī *by;* i(ə)r *ear;* NG *sing;* ō *go;* ô *for;* oi *boy;* o͝o *good;* o͞o *goo;* ou *out;* SH *she;* TH *thin;* TH *then;* (h)w *why;* ZH *vision*

im·mu·no·as·say /ˌimyənō'asā; iˌmyo͞o-/ ▸*n. Biochemistry* a procedure for detecting or measuring specific proteins or other substances through their properties as antigens or antibodies: *these general principles can be applied to all immunoassays | the uses of immunoassay in industry.*

im·mu·no·blot·ting /ˌimyənō'blätiNG; iˌmyo͞o-/, ▸*n.* a technique for analyzing or identifying proteins in a mixture, involving separation by electrophoresis followed by staining with antibodies.

im·mu·no·chem·is·try /ˌimyənō'kemistrē; iˌmyo͞o-/ ▸*n.* the branch of biochemistry concerned with immune responses and systems.

im·mu·no·com·pe·tent /ˌimyənō'kämpitənt; iˌmyo͞o-/ ▸*adj. Medicine* having a normal immune response. —**im·mu·no·com·pe·tence** *n.*

im·mu·no·com·pro·mised /ˌimyənō'kämprəˌmīzd; iˌmyo͞o-/ ▸*adj. Medicine* having an impaired immune system.

im·mu·no·cy·to·chem·is·try /ˌimyənōˌsītō'kemistrē; iˌmyo͞o-/ ▸*n.* the range of microscopic techniques used in the study of the immune system. —**im·mu·no·cy·to·chem·i·cal** /-'kemәkəl/ *adj.*

im·mu·no·de·fi·cien·cy /ˌimyənōdə'fisHənsē; iˌmyo͞o-/ ▸*n.* failure of the immune system to protect the body adequately from infection, due to the absence or insufficiency of some component process or substance.

im·mu·no·dif·fu·sion /ˌimyənōdi'fyo͞oZHən; iˌmyo͞o-/ ▸*n. Biochemistry* a technique for detecting or measuring antibodies and antigens by their precipitation when diffused together through a gel or other medium.

im·mu·no·e·lec·tro·pho·re·sis /ˌimyənō-iˌlektrōfə'rēsis; i'myo͞o-/ ▸*n. Biochemistry* a technique for the identification of proteins in serum or other fluid by electrophoresis and subsequent immunodiffusion.

im·mu·no·fluo·res·cence /ˌimyənōˌflo͝o'resəns; -flô-; iˌmyo͞o-/ ▸*n. Biochemistry* a technique for determining the location of an antigen (or antibody) in tissues by reaction with an antibody (or antigen) labeled with a fluorescent dye. —**im·mu·no·fluo·res·cent** *adj.*

im·mu·no·gen·ic /ˌimyənō'jenik; iˌmyo͞o-/ ▸*adj.* relating to or denoting substances able to produce an immune response. —**im·mu·no·ge·nic·i·ty** /-jə'nisitē/ *n.*

im·mu·no·glob·u·lin /ˌimyənō'gläbyələn; iˌmyo͞o-/ ▸*n. Biochemistry* any of a class of proteins present in the serum and cells of the immune system, that function as antibodies.

im·mu·nol·o·gy /ˌimyə'näləjē/ ▸*n.* the branch of medicine and biology concerned with immunity. —**im·mu·no·log·ic** /ˌimyənə'läjik; iˌmyo͞o-/ *adj.* —**im·mu·no·log·i·cal** /ˌimyənə'läjikəl; iˌmyo͞o-/ *adj.* —**im·mu·no·log·i·cal·ly** /ˌimyənə'läjik(ə)lē; iˌmyo͞o-/ *adv.* —**im·mu·nol·o·gist** /-jist/ *n.*

im·mu·no·sorb·ent /ˌimyənō'sôrbənt; -'zôr-; iˌmyo͞o-/ ▸*adj. Biochemistry* relating to or denoting techniques making use of the absorption of antibodies by insoluble preparations of antigens.

im·mu·no·sup·pres·sion /ˌimyənōsə'presHən; iˌmyo͞o-/ ▸*n. Medicine* the partial or complete suppression of the immune response of an individual. It is induced to help the survival of an organ after a transplant operation. —**im·mu·no·sup·pres·sant** /-sə'presənt/ *n.* —**im·mu·no·sup·pressed** /-sə'prest/ *adj.*

im·mu·no·sup·pres·sive /ˌimyənōsə'presiv; iˌmyo͞o-/ ▸*adj. Medicine* (chiefly of drugs) partially or completely suppressing the immune response of an individual.
▸*n.* a drug of this kind.

im·mu·no·ther·a·py /ˌimyənō'THerəpē; iˌmyo͞o-/ ▸*n. Medicine* the prevention or treatment of disease with substances that stimulate the immune response.

im·mure /i'myo͝or/ ▸*v.* [*trans.*] (usu. **be immured**) enclose or confine (someone) against their will: *her brother was immured in a lunatic asylum.* ▷late 16th cent.: from French *emmurer* or medieval Latin *immurare*, from *in-* 'in' + *murus* 'wall.' —**im·mure·ment** *n.*

im·mu·ta·ble /i'myo͞otəbəl/ ▸*adj.* unchanging over time or unable to be changed: *an immutable fact.* ▷late Middle English: from Latin *immutabilis*, from *in-* 'not' + *mutabilis* (see **MUTABLE**). —**im·mu·ta·bil·i·ty** /iˌmyo͞otə'bilitē/ *n.* —**im·mu·ta·bly** /-blē/ *adv.*

IMO ▸*abbr.* International Maritime Organization.

i-Mode /'ī ˌmōd/ ▸*n. trademark* a proprietary technology that allows data to be transferred to and from Internet sites via cellular phones. ▷early 21st cent.: from *I* (referring to the user's ability to interact directly with the Internet) + *mode.*

IMP /imp/ ▸*abbr. Bridge* International Match Point.

imp /imp/ ▸*n.* a mischievous child: *a cheeky young imp.* ■ a small, mischievous devil or sprite.
▸*v.* [*trans.*] repair a damaged feather in (the wing or tail of a trained hawk) by attaching part of a new feather. ▷Old English *impa, impe* 'young shoot, scion,' *impian* 'to graft,' based on Greek *emphuein* 'to implant.' In late Middle English, the noun denoted a descendant, esp. of a noble family, and later a child of the devil or a person regarded as such; hence a 'little devil' or mischievous child (early 17th cent.).

imp. ▸*abbr.* ■ imperative. ■ imperfect. ■ imperial. ■ impersonal. ■ implement. ■ import or imported or importer. ■ important. ■ imprimatur. ■ in the first place. [from Latin *imprimis.*] ■ imprint. ■ improper. ■ improved or improvement.

im·pact ▸*n.* /'imˌpakt/ the action of one object coming forcibly into contact with another: *there was the sound of a third impact | bullets that expand and cause devastating injury on impact.* ■ the effect or influence of one person, thing, or action, on another: *our regional measures have had a significant **impact on** unemployment.*
▸*v.* /im'pakt/ **1** [*intrans.*] come into forcible contact with another object: *the shell impacted twenty yards away.* ■ [*trans.*] come into forcible contact with: *an asteroid impacted the earth some 60 million years ago.* ■ have a strong effect: *high interest rates have **impacted on** retail spending | [trans.] the move is not expected to impact the company's employees.* **2** [*trans.*] press firmly: *the animals' feet do not impact and damage the soil as cows' hooves do.* ▷early 17th cent. (as a verb in the sense 'press closely, fix firmly'): from Latin *impact-* 'driven in,' from the verb *impingere* (see **IMPINGE**).

> *USAGE* The phrasal verb **impact on**, as in *when produce is lost, it always **impacts on** the bottom line*, has been in the language since the 1960s. Many people disapprove of it despite its relative frequency, saying that **make an impact on** or other equivalent wordings should be used instead. This may be partly because, in general, new formations of verbs from nouns (as in the case of **impact**) are regarded as somehow inferior. As a verb, **impact** remains rather vague and rarely carries the noun's original sense of forceful collision. Careful writers are advised to use more exact verbs that will leave their readers in no doubt about the intended meaning. In addition, since the use of **impact** is associated with business and commercial writing, it has a peripheral status of 'jargon,' which makes it doubly disliked.

im·pact cra·ter ▸*n.* a crater on a planet or moon caused by the impact of a meteorite or other object, typically circular with a raised rim.

im·pact·ed /im'paktid/ ▸*adj.* **1** *chiefly Medicine* pressed firmly together, in particular: ■ (of a tooth) wedged between another tooth and the jaw. ■ (of a fractured bone) having the parts crushed together. ■ (of feces) lodged in the intestine. **2** strongly affected by something: *grandiose planning projects have had deleterious effects on impacted social groups.*

im·pac·tion /im'paksHən/ ▸*n. Medicine* the condition of being or process of becoming impacted, esp. of feces in the intestine.

im·pac·tive /im'paktiv/ ▸*adj.* having a strong effect or influence; making an impression: *impactive color radiates from the sculptures.*

im·pac·tor /im'paktər/ ▸*n. chiefly Astronomy* an object (such as a meteorite) that collides with another body.

im·pair /im'pe(ə)r/ ▸*v.* [*trans.*] weaken or damage (esp. a human faculty or function): *drug use that impairs job performance.* ▷Middle English *enpeire*, from Old French *empeirier*, based on late Latin *pejorare* (from Latin *pejor* 'worse'). The current spelling is due to association with words derived from Latin beginning with *im-*.

im·paired /im'pe(ə)rd/ ▸*adj.* having a disability of a specified kind: [in *combination*] *hearing-impaired children.*

im·pair·ment /im'pe(ə)rmənt/ ▸*n.* the state or fact of being impaired, esp. in a specified faculty: *a degree of physical or mental impairment | memory impairment.*

im·pal·a /im'palə; -'pälə/ ▸*n.* (*pl.* same) a graceful antelope often seen in large herds in open woodland in southern and East Africa. • *Aepyceros melampus*, family Bovidae. ▷late 19th cent.: from Zulu *i-mpala.*

impala

im·pale /im'pāl/ ▸*v.* [*trans.*] **1** pierce or transfix with a sharp instrument: *his head was **impaled on** a pike and exhibited for all to see.* **2** *Heraldry* display (a coat of arms) side by side with another on the same shield, separated by a vertical line: [as *adj.*] (**impaled**) *the impaled arms of her husband and her father.* ■ (of a coat of arms) adjoin (another coat of arms) in this way. ▷mid 16th cent. (in the sense 'enclose with stakes or pales'): from French *empaler* or medieval Latin *impalare*, from Latin *in-* 'in' + *palus* 'a stake.' —**im·pale·ment** *n.* —**im·pal·er** *n.*

im·pal·pa·ble /im'palpəbəl/ ▸*adj.* unable to be felt by touch: *an impalpable ghost.* ■ not easily comprehended: *something so impalpable as personhood.* ▷early 16th cent.: from French, or from late Latin *impalpabilis*, from *in-* 'not' + *palpabilis* (see **PALPABLE**). —**im·pal·pa·bil·i·ty** /-ˌpalpə'bilitē/ *n.* —**im·pal·pa·bly** /-blē/ *adv.*

im·pa·na·tion /ˌimpə'nāsHən/ ▸*n. Theology* the medieval and Reformation doctrine that the body of Christ is present within the Eucharistic bread and does not replace it. Compare with **CONSUBSTANTIATION**. ▷mid 16th cent.: from medieval Latin *impanatio(n-)*, from *impanare* 'embody in bread,' from *in-* 'in' + *panis* 'bread.' —**im·pa·nate** /'impəˌnāt; im'panit/ *adj.*

im·pan·el /im'panl/ (also **em·pan·el**) ▸*v.* (**-pan·eled, -pan·el·ing**; *Brit.* **-pan·elled, -pan·el·ling**) [*trans.*] enlist or enroll (a jury). ■ enroll (someone) on to a jury: *several of her friends have been impaneled.* ▷late Middle English (originally as *empanel*): from Anglo-Norman French *empaneller*, from *em-* 'in' + Old French *panel* 'panel.' —**im·pan·el·ment** *n.*

im·park /im'pärk/ ▸*v.* [*trans.*] *historical* enclose (animals) in a park. ■ enclose (land) to make it into a park. ▷late Middle English: from Old French *emparquer*, from *em-* 'within' + *parc* 'park.'

im·part /im'pärt/ ▸*v.* [*trans.*] make (information) known; communicate: *teachers had a duty to **impart** strong morals **to** their students.* ■ bestow (a quality): *its main use has been to **impart** a high surface gloss **to** finished articles.* ▷late Middle English (in the sense 'give a share of'): from Old French *impartir*, from Latin *impartire*, from *in-* 'in' + *pars, part-* 'part.' —**im·par·ta·tion** /ˌimpär'tāsHən/ *n.*

im·par·tial /im'pärsHəl/ ▸*adj.* treating all rivals or disputants equally; fair and just: *independent and impartial advice.* —**im·par·ti·al·i·ty** /-ˌpärsHē'alitē/ *n.* —**im·par·tial·ly** *adv.*

im·pass·a·ble /im'pasəbəl/ ▸*adj.* impossible to travel along or over: *the narrow channels are **impassable to** oceangoing ships.* —**im·pass·a·bil·i·ty** /-ˌpasə'bilitē/ *n.* —**im·pass·a·ble·ness** *n.* —**im·pass·a·bly** /-blē/ *adv.*

im·passe /'imˌpas; im'pas/ ▸*n.* a situation in which no progress is possible, esp. because of disagreement; a deadlock: *the current political impasse.* ▷mid 19th cent.: from French, from *im-* (expressing negation) + the stem of *passer* 'to pass.'

im·pas·si·ble /im'pasəbəl/ ▸*adj. chiefly Theology* incapable of suffering or feeling pain: *belief in an impassible God.* ▷Middle English: via Old French from ecclesiastical Latin *impassibilis*, from Latin *in-* 'not' + *passibilis* (see **PASSIBLE**). —**im·pas·si·bil·i·ty** /-ˌpasə'bilitē/ *n.* —**im·pas·si·bly** /-blē/ *adv.*

im·pas·sion /im'pasHən/ ▸*v.* [*trans.*] make passionate: *her body had once pleased and impassioned him.* ▷late 16th cent.: from Italian *impassionare*, from *im-* (expressing intensive force) + *passione* 'passion,' from Christian Latin *passio* (see **PASSION**).

im·pas·sioned /im'pasHənd/ ▸*adj.* filled with or showing great emotion: *she made an impassioned plea for help.*

im·pas·sive /im'pasiv/ ▸*adj.* not feeling or showing emotion: *impassive passersby ignore the performers.* —**im·pas·sive·ly** *adv.* —**im·pas·sive·ness** *n.* —**im·pas·siv·i·ty** /ˌimpə'sivitē/ *n.*

im·pas·to /im'pastō; -'pästō/ ▸*n. Art* the process or technique of laying on paint or pigment thickly so that it stands out from a surface. ■ paint applied thickly. ▷late 18th cent.: from Italian, from *impastare*, from *im-* 'upon' + *pasta* 'a paste,' from late Latin.

im·pa·tiens /im'pāsHənz/ ▸*n.* an East African plant with abundant red, pink, or white flowers. It is often grown as a houseplant, and its many hybrids are grown as bedding plants. • Genus *Impatiens*, family Balsaminaceae. ▷late 18th cent.: modern Latin, from Latin, literally 'impatient' (because the capsules of the plant readily burst open when touched).

im·pa·tient /im'pāsHənt/ ▸*adj.* **1** having or showing a tendency to be quickly irritated or provoked: *an* *impatient motorist blaring his horn | she was* ***impatient with*** *any restriction.* ■ [*predic.*] (**impatient of**) intolerant of: *a man impatient of bureaucracy.* **2** restlessly eager: *they are* ***impatient for*** *change* | [with *infinitive*] *he was impatient to be on his way.* ▷late Middle English (in the senses 'lacking patience' and 'unbearable'): via Old French from Latin *impatient-* 'not bearing, impatient,' from *in-* 'not' + *pati* 'suffer, bear'. **—im·pa·tience** *n.* **—im·pa·tient·ly** *adv.*

im·peach /im'pēCH/ ▶*v.* [*trans.*] call into question the integrity or validity of (a practice): *there is no basis to Searle's motion to impeach the verdict.* ■ charge (the holder of a public office) with misconduct: *the governor served only one year before being impeached and convicted for fiscal fraud.* ■ *Brit.* charge with treason or another crime against the state. ▷late Middle English (also in the sense 'hinder, prevent'; earlier as *empeche*): from Old French *empecher* 'impede,' from late Latin *impedicare* 'catch, entangle' (based on *pedica* 'a fetter,' from *pes, ped-* 'foot'). Compare with IMPEDE. **—im·peach·a·ble** *adj.* **—im·peach·ment** *n.*

im·pec·ca·ble /im'pekəbəl/ ▶*adj.* (of behavior, performance, or appearance) in accordance with the highest standards of propriety; faultless: *a man of impeccable character.* ■ *rare Theology* not liable to sin. ▷mid 16th cent. (in the theological sense): from Latin *impeccabilis,* from *in-* 'not' + *peccare* 'to sin.' **—im·pec·ca·bil·i·ty** /-ˌpekə'bilitē/ *n.* **—im·pec·ca·bly** /-blē/ *adv.*

im·pe·cu·ni·ous /ˌimpə'kyo͞onēəs/ ▶*adj.* having little or no money: *a titled but impecunious family.* ▷late 16th cent.: from IN-[1] 'not' + obsolete *pecunious* 'having money, wealthy' (from Latin *pecuniosus,* from *pecunia* 'money'). **—im·pe·cu·ni·os·i·ty** /-ˌkyo͞onē'äsitē/ *n.* **—im·pe·cu·ni·ous·ness** *n.*

im·ped·ance /im'pēdns/ ▶*n.* the effective resistance of an electric circuit or component to alternating current, arising from the combined effects of ohmic resistance and reactance. See also ACOUSTIC IMPEDANCE. • Impedance is usually expressed as a complex quantity $Z = R + jX$, where R is resistance, X is reactance, and j is the imaginary square root of -1.

USAGE **Impedance** is a specialized electrical term (as defined above), while **impediment** is an everyday term meaning 'a hindrance or obstruction': *a low-**impedance** power supply; interpreting his handwriting was an **impediment** to getting business done.*

im·pede /im'pēd/ ▶*v.* [*trans.*] delay or prevent (someone or something) by obstructing them; hinder: *the sap causes swelling that can impede breathing.* See note at HINDER. ▷late 16th cent.: from Latin *impedire* 'shackle the feet of,' based on *pes, ped-* 'foot.' Compare with IMPEACH.

im·ped·i·ment /im'pedəmənt/ ▶*n.* a hindrance or obstruction in doing something: *a serious* ***impediment to*** *scientific progress.* ■ (also **speech impediment**) a defect in a person's speech, such as a lisp or stammer. ▷late Middle English: from Latin *impedimentum,* from *impedire* (see IMPEDE). **—im·ped·i·men·tal** /-ˌpedə'mentl/ *adj.*

USAGE See usage at IMPEDANCE.

im·ped·i·men·ta /imˌpedə'mentə/ ▶*plural n.* equipment for an activity or expedition, esp. when considered as bulky or an encumbrance. ▷early 17th cent.: from Latin, plural of *impedimentum* 'impediment,' from *impedire* (see IMPEDE).

im·pel /im'pel/ ▶*v.* (**-pelled, -pel·ling**) [*trans.*] drive, force, or urge (someone) to do something: *financial difficulties* ***impelled*** *him* ***to*** *desperate measures* | [*trans.*] *a lack of equality impelled the oppressed to fight.* ■ drive forward; propel: *vital energies impel him in unforeseen directions.* ▷late Middle English (in the sense 'propel'): from Latin *impellere,* from *in-* 'toward' + *pellere* 'to drive.'

im·pel·ler /im'pelər/ ▶*n.* the rotating part of a centrifugal pump, compressor, or other machine designed to move a fluid by rotation. ■ a similar device turned by the flow of water past a ship's hull, used to measure speed or distance traveled.

im·pend /im'pend/ ▶*v.* [*intrans.*] [usu. as *adj.*] (**impending**) be about to happen: *my impending departure.* ■ (of something bad) loom: *danger of collision impends.* ▷late 16th cent.: from Latin *impendere,* from *in-* 'toward, upon' + *pendere* 'hang.'

im·pen·e·tra·ble /im'penətrəbəl/ ▶*adj.* **1** impossible to pass through or enter: *a dark, impenetrable forest.* ■ (of a club or group) secretive and exclusive: *an impenetrable clique.* ■ impervious to new ideas or influences: *his career shows just how impenetrable European assumptions were.* ■ *Physics* (of matter) incapable of occupying the same space as other matter at the same time. **2** impossible to understand: *impenetrable interviews with French intellectuals.* ▷late Middle English: via French from Latin *impenetrabilis,* from *in-* 'not' + *penetrabilis* 'able to be pierced,' from the verb *penetrare* (see PENETRATE). **—im·pen·e·tra·bil·i·ty** /-ˌpenətrə'bilitē/ *n.* **—im·pen·e·tra·bly** /-blē/ *adv.*

im·pen·i·tent /im'penitnt/ ▶*adj.* not feeling shame or regret about one's actions or attitudes. ▷late Middle English: from ecclesiastical Latin *impaenitent-* 'not repenting,' from Latin *in-* 'not' + *paenitere* 'repent.' **—im·pen·i·tence** *n.* **—im·pen·i·ten·cy** *n.* **—im·pen·i·tent·ly** *adv.*

im·per·a·tive /im'perətiv/ ▶*adj.* **1** of vital importance; crucial: *immediate action was imperative* | [with *clause*] *it is imperative that standards be maintained.* **2** giving an authoritative command; peremptory: *the bell pealed again, a final imperative call.* ■ *Grammar* denoting the mood of a verb that expresses a command or exhortation, as in *come here!*

▶*n.* **1** an essential or urgent thing: *free movement of labor was an economic imperative.* ■ a factor or influence making something necessary: *the change came about through a financial imperative.* ■ a thing felt as an obligation: *the moral imperative of aiding Third World development.* **2** *Grammar* a verb or phrase in the imperative mood. ■ (**the imperative**) the imperative mood. ▷late Middle English (as a grammatical term): from late Latin *imperativus* (literally 'specially ordered,' translating Greek *prostatikē enklisis* 'imperative mood'), from *imperare* 'to command,' from *in-* 'toward' + *parare* 'make ready.' **—im·per·a·ti·val** /-ˌperə'tīvəl/ *adj.* **—im·per·a·tive·ly** *adv.* **—im·per·a·tive·ness** *n.*

im·pe·ra·tor /ˌimpə'rätər; -ˌtôr/ ▶*n. Roman History* commander (a title conferred under the Republic on a victorious general and under the Empire on the emperor). ▷Latin, from *imperare* 'to order, command.' **—im·per·a·to·ri·al** /imˌperə'tôrēəl/ *adj.*

im·per·cep·ti·ble /ˌimpər'septəbəl/ ▶*adj.* impossible to perceive: *his head moved in an almost imperceptible nod.* ▷late Middle English: from French, or from medieval Latin *imperceptibilis,* from *in-* 'not' + *perceptibilis,* from the verb *percipere* (see PERCEIVE). **—im·per·cep·ti·bil·i·ty** /-ˌseptə'bilitē/ *n.* **—im·per·cep·ti·bly** /-blē/ *adv.*

im·per·cep·tive /ˌimpər'septiv/ ▶*adj.* lacking in perception or insight: *she dismissed the statement as juvenile or at least imperceptive.*

im·per·cip·i·ent /ˌimpər'sipēənt/ ▶*adj.* failing to perceive something. **—im·per·cip·i·ence** *n.*

im·per·fect /im'pərfikt/ ▶*adj.* **1** not perfect; faulty: *an imperfect grasp of English.* ■ not fully formed or done; incomplete: *imperfect census records* | *smoke due to imperfect combustion.* **2** *Grammar* (of a tense) denoting a past action in progress but not completed at the time in question. **3** *Music* (of a cadence) ending on the dominant chord. **4** *Law* (of a gift, title, etc.) transferred without all the necessary conditions or requirements being met.

▶*n.* (**the imperfect**) *Grammar* the imperfect tense. ▷Middle English *imparfit, imperfet,* from Old French *imparfait,* from Latin *imperfectus,* from *in-* 'not' + *perfectus* (see PERFECT). The spelling change in the 16th cent. was due to association with the Latin form. **—im·per·fect·ly** *adv.*

im·per·fect com·pe·ti·tion ▶*n.* the situation prevailing in a market in which elements of monopoly allow individual producers or consumers to exercise some control over market prices.

im·per·fec·tion /ˌimpər'fekSHən/ ▶*n.* a fault, blemish, or undesirable feature: *the imperfections and injustices in our political system.* ■ the state of being faulty or incomplete: *he accepted me without question, in all my imperfection.* ▷late Middle English: via Old French from late Latin *imperfectio(n-),* from *imperfectus* (see IMPERFECT).

im·per·fec·tive /ˌimpər'fektiv/ *Grammar* ▶*adj.* relating to or denoting an aspect of verbs, esp. in Slavic languages, that expresses action without reference to its completion. The opposite of PERFECTIVE.

▶*n.* the imperfective aspect, or an imperfective form of a verb.

im·per·fect rhyme ▶*n.* a rhyme in which there is only a partial matching of sounds (e.g., *love* and *move*). See also PARARHYME.

im·per·fo·rate /im'pərfərit/ ▶*adj.* not perforated, in particular: ■ *Anatomy & Zoology* lacking the normal opening: *unicellular spores of these parasites have an imperforate wall.* ■ (of a postage stamp or a block or sheet of stamps) lacking perforations, esp. as an error.

im·pe·ri·al /im'pi(ə)rēəl/ ▶*adj.* **1** of or relating to an empire: *Britain's imperial era.* ■ of or relating to an emperor: *the imperial family.* ■ majestic; magnificent: *the bedroom is huge and imperial.* ■ imperious or domineering: *the party and its autocratic—many would say imperial—ways.* **2** of, relating to, or denoting the system of nonmetric weights and measures (the ounce, pound, stone, inch, foot, yard, mile, acre, pint, gallon, etc.) formerly used for all measures in the UK, and still used for some. **3** *chiefly historical* (of a size of paper) measuring roughly 762 × 559 mm (30 × 22 inches).

▶*n.* a small pointed beard growing below the lower lip (associated with Napoleon III of France). ▷late Middle English: via Old French from Latin *imperialis,* from *imperium* 'command, authority, empire'; related to *imperare* 'to command.' Compare with EMPEROR, EMPIRE, also with IMPERIOUS. **—im·pe·ri·al·ly** *adv.*

im·pe·ri·al gal·lon ▶*n.* see GALLON (sense 1).

im·pe·ri·al·ism /im'pi(ə)rēəˌlizəm/ ▶*n.* a policy of extending a country's power and influence through diplomacy or military force: *the struggle against imperialism (figurative) French ministers protested at U.S. cultural imperialism.* ■ *chiefly historical* rule by an emperor. **—im·pe·ri·al·is·tic** /-ˌpi(ə)rēə'listik/ *adj.* **—im·pe·ri·al·is·ti·cal·ly** *adv.*

im·pe·ri·al·ist /im'pi(ə)rēəlist/ ▶*adj.* of, relating to, supporting, or practicing imperialism: *an imperialist regime.*

▶*n. chiefly derogatory* a person who supports or practices imperialism.

im·pe·ri·al·ize /im'pi(ə)rēəˌlīz/ ▶*v.* [*trans.*] [usu. as *adj.*] (**imperialized**) subject to imperial rule or influence: *people of an imperialized culture.*

im·pe·ri·al pi·geon ▶*n.* a tropical, fruit-eating pigeon that typically has a pale grayish head and breast and a dark back, occurring in Australasia, Indonesia, and South Asia. • Genus *Ducula,* family Columbidae.

Im·pe·ri·al Val·ley an irrigated section of the Colorado Desert, in southeastern California.

im·per·il /im'perəl/ ▶*v.* (**-per·iled, -per·il·ing;** *Brit.* **-per·illed, -per·il·ling**) [*trans.*] put at risk of being harmed, injured, or destroyed: *white-band disease imperils coral reefs.* ▷late Middle English: from PERIL, probably on the pattern of *endanger.* **—im·per·il·ment** *n.*

im·pe·ri·ous /im'pi(ə)rēəs/ ▶*adj.* assuming power or authority without justification; arrogant and domineering: *his imperious demands.* ▷mid 16th cent.: from Latin *imperiosus,* from *imperium* 'command, authority, empire'; related to *imperare* 'to command.' Compare with IMPERIAL. **—im·pe·ri·ous·ly** *adv.* **—im·pe·ri·ous·ness** *n.*

im·per·ish·a·ble /im'periSHəbəl/ ▶*adj.* enduring forever: *imperishable truths.* **—im·per·ish·a·bil·i·ty** /-ˌperiSHə'bilitē/ *n.* **—im·per·ish·a·ble·ness** *n.* **—im·per·ish·a·bly** *adv.*

im·pe·ri·um /im'pi(ə)rēəm/ ▶*n.* absolute power: *it was the high noon of the imperium, an age when there was something empowering about being an American.* ▷mid 17th cent.: from Latin, 'command, authority, empire'; related to *imperare* 'to command.'

im·per·ma·nent /im'pərmənənt/ ▶*adj.* not permanent. **—im·per·ma·nence** *n.* **—im·per·ma·nen·cy** *n.* **—im·per·ma·nent·ly** *adv.*

im·per·me·a·ble /im'pərmēəbəl/ ▶*adj.* not allowing fluid to pass through: *an impermeable membrane.* ■ not liable to be affected by pain or distress; insusceptible or imperturbable: *women who appear* ***impermeable to*** *pain.* ▷late 17th cent.: from French *imperméable,* or from late Latin *impermeabilis,* from *in-* 'not' + *permeabilis* (see PERMEABLE). **—im·per·me·a·bil·i·ty** /-ˌpərmēə'bilitē/ *n.*

im·per·mis·si·ble /ˌimpər'misəbəl/ ▶*adj.* too bad to be allowed: *the prosecution made impermissible use of the testimony.* **—im·per·mis·si·bil·i·ty** /-ˌmisə'bilitē/ *n.*

im·per·son·al /im'pərsənl/ ▶*adj.* **1** not influenced by, showing, or involving personal feelings: *the impersonal march of progress.* ■ (of a place or organization) large, featureless, and anonymous: *large, impersonal institutions.* ■ not betraying any personal information about the user or subject: *the room was bare, cramped, and impersonal.* **2** not existing as a person; having no personality: *he gradually came to believe in an impersonal God.* **3** *Grammar* (of a verb) used only with a formal subject (in English usually *it*) and expressing an action not attributable to a definite subject (as in *it is snowing*). ▷late Middle English (sense 3): from late Latin *impersonalis,* from Latin *in-* 'not' +

personalis (see PERSONAL). **—im·per·son·al·i·ty** /-ˌpərsəˈnalitē/ *n.* **—im·per·son·al·ly** *adv.*

im·per·son·al pro·noun ▶*n.* the pronoun *it* when used without definite reference or antecedent, as in *it was snowing* and *it seems hard to believe.*

im·per·son·ate /imˈpərsəˌnāt/ ▶*v.* [*trans.*] pretend to be (another person) as entertainment or in order to deceive someone: *it's a very serious offense to impersonate a police officer.* See note at IMITATE. ▷early 17th cent. (in the sense 'personify'): from IN-[2] 'into' + Latin *persona* 'person,' on the pattern of *incorporate.* **—im·per·son·a·tion** /-ˌpərsəˈnāsʜən/ *n.* **—im·per·son·a·tor** /-ˌnātər/ *n.*

im·per·ti·nent /imˈpərtn-ənt/ ▶*adj.* **1** not showing proper respect; rude: *an impertinent question.* **2** *formal* not pertinent to a particular matter; irrelevant: *talk of "rhetoric" and "strategy" is* **impertinent to** *this process.* ▷late Middle English (sense 2): from Old French, or from late Latin *impertinent-* 'not having reference to,' from Latin *in-* 'not' + *pertinere* 'pertain.' **—im·per·ti·nence** *n.* **—im·per·ti·nent·ly** *adv.*

THE RIGHT WORD **impertinent, impudent, insolent, intrusive, meddlesome, obtrusive**

All of these adjectives mean "exceeding the bounds of propriety"; the easiest way to distinguish **impertinent** from the others is to think of its root: *impertinent* behavior is not pertinent—in other words, it is out of place. The *impertinent* person has a tendency to be rude or presumptuous toward those who are entitled to deference or respect (*it was an impertinent question to ask a woman who had just lost her husband*).

The **intrusive** person is unduly curious about other people's affairs (*her constant questions about the state of their marriage were intrusive and unwelcome*), while **obtrusive** implies objectionable actions rather than an objectionable disposition. The *obtrusive* person has a tendency to thrust himself or herself into a position where he or she is conspicuous and apt to do more harm than good (*they tried to keep him out of the meeting because his presence would be obtrusive*).

To be **meddlesome** is to have a prying or inquisitive nature and a tendency to interfere in an annoying way in other people's affairs (*a meddlesome neighbor*).

Impudent and **insolent** are much stronger words for inappropriate behavior. Young people are often accused of being *impudent*, which means to be impertinent in a bold and shameless way (*an impudent young man who had a lot to learn about tact*).

Anyone who is guilty of insulting and contemptuously arrogant behavior might be called *insolent* (*he was so insolent to the arresting officer that he was handcuffed*).

im·per·turb·a·ble /ˌimpərˈtərbəbəl/ ▶*adj.* unable to be upset or excited; calm: *an imperturbable tranquility.* ▷late Middle English: from late Latin *imperturbabilis*, from *in-* 'not' + *perturbare* (see PERTURB). **—im·per·turb·a·bil·i·ty** /-tərbəˈbilitē/ *n.* **—im·per·turb·a·bly** *adv.*

im·per·vi·ous /imˈpərvēəs/ ▶*adj.* not allowing fluid to pass through: *an impervious layer of basaltic clay.* ■ [*predic.*] (**impervious to**) unable to be affected by: *he worked, apparently impervious to the heat.* ▷mid 17th cent.: from Latin *impervius* (from *in-* 'not' + *pervius* 'pervious') + -OUS. **—im·per·vi·ous·ly** *adv.* **—im·per·vi·ous·ness** *n.*

im·pe·ti·go /ˌimpiˈtīgō; -tē-/ ▶*n.* a contagious bacterial skin infection forming pustules and yellow, crusty sores. • This disease is caused by the bacteria *Streptococcus pyogenes* or *S. aureus.* ▷late Middle English: from Latin, from *impetere* 'to assail, attack.'

im·pe·trate /ˈimpəˌtrāt/ ▶*v.* [*trans.*] *archaic* beseech or beg for: *a slight testimonial which I thought fit to impetrate from that worthy nobleman.* ▷late 15th cent.: from Latin *impetrat-* 'brought to pass,' from the verb *impetrare* (based on *patrare* 'bring to pass').

im·pet·u·ous /imˈpecʜōōəs/ ▶*adj.* acting or done quickly and without thought or care: *her friend was headstrong and impetuous.* ■ moving forcefully or rapidly: *an impetuous but controlled flow of water.* ▷late Middle English: from Old French *impetueux*, from late Latin *impetuosus*, from *impetere* 'to assail, attack.' **—im·pet·u·os·i·ty** /-ˌpecʜōōˈäsitē/ *n.* **—im·pet·u·ous·ly** *adv.* **—im·pet·u·ous·ness** *n.*

im·pe·tus /ˈimpitəs/ ▶*n.* the force or energy with which a body moves: *hit the booster coil before the flywheel loses all its impetus.* ■ the force that makes something happen or happen more quickly: *the crisis of the 1860s provided the original* **impetus for** *the settlements.* ▷mid 17th cent.: from Latin, 'assault, force,' from *impetere* 'assail,' from *in-* 'toward' + *petere* 'seek.'

Imp·hal /ˈimˌpəl/ a city in northeastern India, the capital of the state of Manipur, that lies close to the border with Myanmar (Burma); pop. 157,000. It was the scene of an important victory in 1944 by Anglo-Indian forces over the Japanese.

im·pi /ˈimpē/ ▶*n.* (*pl.* **im·pis**) a body of Zulu warriors. ■ an armed band of Zulus involved in urban or rural conflict. ▷mid 19th cent.: Zulu, literally 'regiment, armed band.'

im·pi·e·ty /imˈpī-itē/ ▶*n.* (*pl.* **-ties**) lack of piety or reverence, esp. for a god: *he blamed the fall of the city on the impiety of the people | one impiety will cost me my eternity in Paradise.* ▷Middle English: from Old French *impiete* or Latin *impietas*, from *impius* 'impious.'

im·pinge /imˈpinj/ ▶*v.* (**-ping·ing**) [*intrans.*] have an effect or impact, esp. a negative one: *Nora was determined that the tragedy would* **impinge** *as little as possible* **on** *Constance's life.* ■ advance over an area belonging to someone or something else; encroach: *the site* **impinges on** *a greenbelt area.* ■ (**impinge on/upon**) *Physics* strike: *the gases impinge on the surface of the liquid.* ▷mid 16th cent.: from Latin *impingere* 'drive something in or at,' from *in-* 'into' + *pangere* 'fix, drive.' The word originally meant 'thrust at forcibly,' then 'come into forcible contact'; hence 'encroach on' (mid 18th cent.). **—im·pinge·ment** *n.* **—im·ping·er** *n.*

im·pi·ous /ˈimpēəs; imˈpī-/ ▶*adj.* not showing respect or reverence, esp. for a god: *the emperor's impious attacks on the Church.* ■ (of a person or act) wicked: *impious villains.* ▷mid 16th cent.: from Latin *impius* (from *in-* 'not' + *pius*: see PIOUS) + -OUS. **—im·pi·ous·ly** *adv.* **—im·pi·ous·ness** *n.*

imp·ish /ˈimpisʜ/ ▶*adj.* inclined to do slightly naughty things for fun; mischievous: *he had an impish look about him.* **—imp·ish·ly** *adv.* **—imp·ish·ness** *n.*

im·plac·a·ble /imˈplakəbəl/ ▶*adj.* unable to be placated: *he was an implacable enemy of Ted's.* ■ relentless; unstoppable: *the implacable advance of the enemy.* ▷late Middle English: from Latin *implacabilis*, from *in-* 'not' + *placabilis* (see PLACABLE). **—im·plac·a·bil·i·ty** /-ˌplakəˈbilitē/ *n.* **—im·plac·a·bly** /-blē/ *adv.*

im·plant ▶*v.* /imˈplant/ [*trans.*] insert or fix (tissue or an artificial object) in a person's body, esp. by surgery: *electrodes had been* **implanted in** *his brain.* ■ (**implant someone/something with**) provide someone or something with (something) by such insertion: *rats implanted with amphetamine pellets.* ■ [*intrans.*] (of a fertilized egg) become attached to the wall of the uterus. ■ *figurative* establish or fix (an idea) in a person's mind.

▶*n.* /ˈimˌplant/ a thing implanted in something else, esp. a piece of tissue, prosthetic device, or other object implanted in the body: *a silicone breast implant.* ▷late Middle English: from late Latin *implantare* 'engraft,' from Latin *in-* 'into' + *plantare* 'to plant.'

im·plant·able /imˈplantəbəl/ ▶*adj.* capable of or designed for being implanted in living tissue: *an implantable defibrillator.*

im·plan·ta·tion /ˌimplanˈtāsʜən/ ▶*n.* the action of implanting or state of being implanted. ■ *Zoology & Medicine* (in a mammal) the attachment of the fertilized egg or blastocyst to the wall of the uterus at the start of pregnancy, often delayed in some mammals by several months. Also called NIDATION. ▷late 16th cent.: from French, from *implanter* 'to implant.'

im·plau·si·ble /imˈplôzəbəl/ ▶*adj.* (of an argument or statement) not seeming reasonable or probable; failing to convince: *this is a blatantly implausible claim.* **—im·plau·si·bil·i·ty** /-ˌplôzəˈbilitē/ *n.* **—im·plau·si·bly** /-blē/ *adv.*

im·ple·ment ▶*n.* /ˈimpləmənt/ a tool, utensil, or other piece of equipment, esp. as used for a particular purpose: *agricultural implements.* See note at TOOL.

▶*v.* /-ˌment/ [*trans.*] put (a decision, plan, agreement, etc.) into effect: *the regulations implement a 1954 treaty.* ▷late Middle English (in the sense 'article of furniture, equipment, or dress'): partly from medieval Latin *implementa* (plural), partly from late Latin *implementum* 'filling up, fulfillment,' both from Latin *implere* 'fill up' (later 'employ'), from *in-* 'in' + *plere* 'fill.' The verb dates from the early 18th cent. **—im·ple·men·ta·tion** /ˌimpləmənˈtāsʜən/ *n.* **—im·ple·ment·er** (also **im·ple·men·tor** /-ˌmentər/) *n.*

im·pli·cate /ˈimpliˌkāt/ ▶*v.* [*trans.*] **1** show (someone) to be involved in a crime: *police claims* **implicated** *him* **in** *many more killings.* ■ (**be implicated in**) bear some of the responsibility for (an action or process, esp. a criminal or harmful one): *the team believes he is heavily implicated in the bombing | a chemical implicated in ozone depletion.* ■ involve (something) in a necessary way: *cable franchise activities plainly implicate First Amendment interests.* **2** [with *clause*] convey (a meaning or intention) indirectly through what one says, rather than stating it explicitly; imply: *by saying that coffee would keep her awake, Mary implicated that she didn't want any.*

▶*n. chiefly Logic* a thing implied. ▷late Middle English: from Latin *implicatus* 'folded in,' past participle of *implicare* (see IMPLY). The original sense was 'entwine, entangle'; compare with EMPLOY and IMPLY. The earliest modern sense (sense 2) dates from the early 17th cent., but appears earlier in IMPLICATION. **—im·pli·ca·tive** /ˈimpliˌkātiv; imˈplikətiv/ *adj.* **—im·pli·ca·tive·ly** *adv.*

im·pli·ca·tion /ˌimpliˈkāsʜən/ ▶*n.* **1** the conclusion that can be drawn from something, although it is not explicitly stated: *the implication is that no one person at the bank is responsible.* ■ a likely consequence of something: *a victory that had important political implications.* **2** the action or state of being involved in something: *our implication in the problems.* ▷late Middle English (in the sense 'entwining, being entwined'): from Latin *implicatio(n-)*, from the verb *implicare* (see IMPLICATE). **—im·pli·ca·tion·al** /-sʜənl/ *adj.*

▶***PHRASE*** □ **by implication** by what is implied or suggested rather than by formal expression: *he criticized her and, by implication, her country.*

im·pli·ca·ture /ˈimplikəcʜər/ ▶*n.* the action of implying a meaning beyond the literal sense of what is explicitly stated, e.g., saying *the frame is nice* and implying *I don't like the picture in it.* ■ a meaning so implied.

im·plic·it /imˈplisit/ ▶*adj.* **1** implied though not plainly expressed: *comments seen as implicit criticism of the policies.* ■ [*predic.*] (**implicit in**) essentially or very closely connected with; always to be found in: *the values implicit in the school ethos.* **2** with no qualification or question; absolute: *an implicit faith in God.* **3** *Mathematics* (of a function) not expressed directly in terms of independent variables. ▷late 16th cent.: from French *implicite* or Latin *implicitus*, later form of *implicatus* 'entwined,' past participle of *implicare* (see IMPLY). **—im·plic·it·ly** *adv.* **—im·plic·it·ness** *n.*

im·plode /imˈplōd/ ▶*v.* collapse or cause to collapse violently inward: [*intrans.*] *the windows on both sides of the room had imploded* | [*trans.*] *these forces would implode the pellet to a density 100 times higher than that of lead.* ■ [*intrans.*] *figurative* suffer sudden economic or political collapse: *can any amount of aid save the republics from imploding?* ■ *Phonetics* [*trans.*] utter or pronounce (a consonant) with a sharp intake of air. ▷late 19th cent.: from IN-[2] 'within' + Latin *plodere*, *plaudere* 'to clap,' on the pattern of *explode.* **—im·plo·sion** /-zʜən/ *n.*

im·plore /imˈplôr/ ▶*v.* [*reporting verb*] beg someone earnestly or desperately to do something: [*trans.*] *he implored her to change her mind* | [with *direct speech*] *"Please don't talk that way," Ellen implored.* See note at BEG. ■ [*trans.*] *archaic* beg earnestly for: *I implore mercy.* ▷early 16th cent.: from French *implorer* or Latin *implorare* 'invoke with tears.' **—im·plor·ing·ly** *adv.*

im·plo·sive /imˈplōsiv/ ▶*adj.* formed by implosion; tending to implode. ■ *Phonetics* denoting a type of consonant produced in the glottis with an ingressive air flow.

im·ply /imˈplī/ ▶*v.* (**-plies, -plied**) [*trans.*] strongly suggest the truth or existence of (something not expressly stated): *the salesmen who uses jargon to imply his superior knowledge* | [with *clause*] *the report implies that two million jobs might be lost.* ■ (of a fact or occurrence) suggest (something) as a logical consequence: *the forecasted traffic increase implied more roads and more air pollution.* ▷late Middle English: from Old French *emplier*, from Latin *implicare*, from *in-* 'in' + *plicare* 'to fold.' The original sense was 'entwine, entangle'; in the 16th and 17th centuries the word also meant 'employ.' Compare with EMPLOY and IMPLICATE. **—im·pli·ed·ly** /-ˈplī-idlē/ *adv.*

USAGE **Imply** and **infer** do not mean the same thing and should not be used interchangeably: see usage at INFER.

im·pol·der /imˈpōldər/ ▶*v.* [*trans.*] make (an area of the seabed) into a polder by reclaiming it from the sea. ▷late 19th cent.: from Dutch *impolderen.*

im·po·lite /ˌimpəˈlīt/ ▶*adj.* not having or showing good manners; rude: *it would have been impolite to refuse.* ▷early 17th cent. (in the sense 'unpolished'): from Latin *impolitus*, from *in-* 'not' + *politus* (see POLITE). **—im·po·lite·ly** *adv.* **—im·po·lite·ness** *n.*

im·pol·i·tic /imˈpäliˌtik/ ▶*adj.* failing to possess or display prudence; unwise: *it was impolitic to pay the slightest tribute to the enemy.* **—im·pol·i·tic·ly** *adv.*

im·pon·der·a·ble /im'pändərəbəl/ ▸*n.* a factor that is difficult or impossible to estimate or assess: *there are too many imponderables for an overall prediction.*
▸*adj.* **1** difficult or impossible to estimate, assess, or answer: *an imponderable problem of metaphysics.* **2** *archaic or poetic/literary* very light. **—im·pon·der·a·bil·i·ty** /-,pändərə'bilitē/ *n.* **—im·pon·der·a·bly** /-blē/ *adv.*

im·port ▸*v.* /im'pôrt/ [*trans.*] **1** bring (goods or services) into a country from abroad for sale: *Japan's reluctance to import more cars.* ■ introduce (an idea) from a different place or context: *new beliefs were often imported by sailors.* ■ *Computing* transfer (data) into a file or document. **2** *archaic* indicate or signify: *having thus seen, what is imported in a Man's trusting his Heart.* ■ express or make known: [with *clause*] *they passed a resolution importing that they relied on His Majesty's gracious promise.*
▸*n.* /'im,pôrt/ **1** (usu. **imports**) a commodity, article, or service brought in from abroad for sale. ■ (**imports**) sales of goods or services brought in from abroad, or the revenue from such sales: *this surplus pushes up the yen, which ought to boost imports.* ■ the action or process of importing goods or services: *the import of live cattle from Canada.* **2** [in *sing.*] the meaning or significance of something, esp. when not directly stated: *the import of her message is clear.* ■ great significance; importance: *pronouncements of world-shaking import.* ▷late Middle English (in the sense 'signify'): from Latin *importare* 'bring in' (in medieval Latin 'imply, mean, be of consequence'), from *in-* 'in' + *portare* 'carry.' **—im·port·a·ble** *adj.* **—im·por·ta·tion** /,impôr'tāsʜən/ *n.* **—im·port·er** *n.*

im·por·tance /im'pôrtns/ ▸*n.* the state or fact of being of great significance or value: *the importance of democracy | the relative importances of the external and internal causes.* ▷early 16th cent.: from French, from medieval Latin *importantia,* from *important-* 'being of consequence,' from the verb *importare* (see IMPORT).
▸PHRASE □ **full of one's own importance** having a very high opinion of oneself; self-important.

im·por·tant /im'pôrtnt/ ▸*adj.* of great significance or value; likely to have a profound effect on success, survival, or well-being: *important habitats for wildlife | it is important to avoid monosyllabic answers |* [*sentence adverb*] *the speech had passion and, more important, compassion.* ■ (of a person) having high rank or status. ■ (of an artist or artistic work) significantly original and influential. ▷late Middle English: from medieval Latin *important-* 'being of consequence,' from the verb *importare* (see IMPORT).

im·por·tant·ly /im'pôrtnt-lē/ ▸*adv.* **1** [*sentence adverb*] used to emphasize a significant point or matter: *a nondrinking, nonsmoking, and, importantly, nonpolitical sportsman.* **2** in a manner designed to draw attention to one's importance: *Kruger strutted forward importantly.*

im·por·tu·nate /im'pôrcʜənit/ ▸*adj.* persistent, esp. to the point of annoyance or intrusion: *importunate creditors.* ▷early 16th cent.: from Latin *importunus* 'inconvenient, unseasonable,' based on *Portunus,* the name of the god who protected harbors (from *portus* 'harbor'); compare with OPPORTUNE. **—im·por·tu·nate·ly** *adv.* **—im·por·tu·ni·ty** /,impôr't(y)o͞onitē/ *n.* (*pl.* **-ties**).

im·por·tune /,impôr't(y)o͞on; im'pôrcʜən/ ▸*v.* [*trans.*] ask (someone) pressingly and persistently for or to do something: *if he were alive now, I should importune him with my questions.* See note at BEG. ■ approach (someone) to offer one's services as a prostitute. ▷mid 16th cent.: from French *importuner* or medieval Latin *importunari,* from Latin *importunus* 'inconvenient, unseasonable' (see IMPORTUNATE).

im·pose /im'pōz/ ▸*v.* **1** [*trans.*] force (something unwelcome or unfamiliar) to be accepted or put in place: *the decision was theirs and was not* ***imposed on*** *them by others.* ■ forcibly put (a restriction) in place: *sanctions imposed on South Africa.* ■ require (a duty, charge, or penalty) to be undertaken or paid. ■ (**impose oneself**) exert firm control over something: *the director was unable to* ***impose himself on*** *the production.* **2** [*intrans.*] take advantage of someone by demanding their attention or commitment: *she realized that she had* ***imposed on*** *Miss Hatherby's kindness.* **3** [*trans.*] *Printing* arrange (pages of type) so that they will be in the correct order after printing and folding. ▷late 15th cent. (in the sense 'impute'): from French *imposer,* from Latin *imponere* 'inflict, deceive' (from *in-* 'in, upon' + *ponere* 'put'), but influenced by *impositus* 'inflicted' and Old French *poser* 'to place.'

im·pos·ing /im'pōziɴɢ/ ▸*adj.* grand and impressive in appearance: *an imposing 17th-century manor house.* **—im·pos·ing·ly** *adv.*

im·po·si·tion /,impə'zisʜən/ ▸*n.* **1** the action or process of imposing something or of being imposed: *the imposition of martial law.* **2** a thing that is imposed, in particular: ■ an unfair or resented demand or burden. ■ a tax or duty. ■ an unsuitable addition to an artistic or other work. ■ *Christian Church* the laying-on of hands, as in blessing or ordination. **3** *Printing* the imposing of pages of type. ■ a particular arrangement of imposed pages: *some samples of 16-page impositions.* ▷late Middle English: from Latin *impositio(n-),* from the verb *imponere* (see IMPOSE).

im·pos·si·bil·ism /im'päsəbə,lizəm/ ▸*n.* belief in ideas or policy, esp. on social reform, that are held to be unrealizable or impractical. **—im·pos·si·bil·ist** *n.*

im·pos·si·bil·i·ty /im,päsə'bilitē/ ▸*n.* (*pl.* **-ties**) the state or fact of being impossible: *the impossibility of walking anywhere in this jungle.* ■ an impossible thing or situation: *they believe that a world at peace is an impossibility.* ▷late Middle English: from French *impossibilité* or Latin *impossibilitas,* from *impossibilis,* from *in-* 'not' + *possibilis* (see POSSIBLE).

im·pos·si·ble /im'päsəbəl/ ▸*adj.* not able to occur, exist, or be done: *a seemingly impossible task |* [with *infinitive*] *it was almost impossible to keep up with him.* ■ very difficult to deal with: *she was in an impossible situation.* ■ *informal* (of a person) very unreasonable: *"Impossible woman!" the doctor complained.* ▷Middle English: from Old French, or from Latin *impossibilis,* from *in-* 'not' + *possibilis* (see POSSIBLE).

im·pos·si·bly /im'päsəblē/ ▸*adv.* [*sentence adverb*] used to describe an event or action that is so difficult or unlikely one would not expect it to be possible: *he held her and, impossibly, she fell asleep.* ■ [as *submodifier*] so as to be impossible: *impossibly high standards.* ■ [as *submodifier*] possessing the specified quality to an unbelievably high degree: *impossibly blond hair.*

im·post[1] /'im,pōst/ ▸*n.* a tax or similar compulsory payment. ■ *Horse Racing* the weight carried by a horse as a handicap. ▷mid 16th cent.: from French (earlier form of *impôt*), from medieval Latin *impostus,* from Latin *impositus,* past participle of *imponere* (see IMPOSE).

im·post[2] ▸*n.* *Architecture* the top course of a pillar that supports an arch. ▷late 15th cent.: from Italian *imposta,* feminine past participle of *imporre,* from Latin *imponere* (see IMPOSE).

im·pos·tor /im'pästər/ (also **im·post·er**) ▸*n.* a person who pretends to be someone else in order to deceive others, esp. for fraudulent gain. See note at QUACK. ▷late 16th cent. (in early use spelled *imposture,* and sometimes confused with IMPOSTURE in meaning): from French *imposteur,* from late Latin *impostor,* contraction of *impositor,* from Latin *imponere* (see IMPOSE).

im·pos·ture /im'päscʜər/ ▸*n.* an instance of pretending to be someone else in order to deceive others. ▷mid 16th cent.: via French from late Latin *impostura,* from Latin *imposit-* 'imposed upon,' from the verb *imponere* (see IMPOSE).

im·po·tent /'impətnt/ ▸*adj.* **1** unable to take effective action; helpless or powerless: *he was seized with an impotent anger.* **2** (of a man) abnormally unable to achieve a sexual erection. ■ (of a male animal) unable to copulate. ▷late Middle English: via Old French from Latin *impotent-* 'powerless,' from *in-* 'not' + *potent-* (see POTENT[1]). **—im·po·tence** *n.* **—im·po·ten·cy** *n.* **—im·po·tent·ly** *adv.*

im·pound /im'pound/ ▸*v.* [*trans.*] **1** seize and take legal custody of (something, esp. a vehicle, goods, or documents) because of an infringement of a law or regulation: *vehicles parked where they cause an obstruction will be impounded.* **2** shut up (domestic animals) in a pound or enclosure. ■ (of a dam) hold back or confine (water). **—im·pound·a·ble** *adj.* **—im·pound·er** *n.* **—im·pound·ment** *n.*

im·pov·er·ish /im'päv(ə)risʜ/ ▸*v.* [*trans.*] make (a person or area) poor: *they discourage investment and impoverish their people |* [as *adj.*] (**impoverished**) *impoverished peasant farmers.* ■ exhaust the strength, vitality, or natural fertility of: *the soil was impoverished by annual burning |* [as *adj.*] (**impoverished**) *figurative an impoverished and debased language.* ▷late Middle English (formerly also as *empoverish*): from Old French *empoveriss-,* lengthened stem of *empoverir,* based on *povre* 'poor.' **—im·pov·er·ish·ment** *n.*

im·prac·ti·ca·ble /im'praktikəbəl/ ▸*adj.* (of a course of action) impossible in practice to do or carry out: *it was impracticable to widen the road here.* **—im·prac·ti·ca·bil·i·ty** /-,praktikə'bilitē/ *n.* **—im·prac·ti·ca·bly** /-blē/ *adv.*

USAGE **Impracticable** and **impractical** are sometimes confused. **Impracticable** means 'impossible to carry out' and is normally used of a specific procedure or course of action: *poor visibility made the task difficult, even* ***impracticable.*** **Impractical,** on the other hand, tends to be used in more general senses, often to mean simply 'unrealistic' or 'not sensible': *in windy weather an umbrella is* ***impractical.*** In describing a person, **impractical** may be used, but **impracticable** would not make sense.

im·prac·ti·cal /im'praktikəl/ ▸*adj.* **1** (of an object or course of action) not adapted for use or action; not sensible or realistic: *impractical high heels | his impractical romanticism.* ■ (of a person) not skilled or interested in practical matters: *Paul was impractical and dreamy.* **2** impossible to do; impracticable. **—im·prac·ti·cal·i·ty** /-,prakti'kalitē/ *n.* **—im·prac·ti·cal·ly** /-ik(ə)lē/ *adv.*

USAGE On the differences in the use of **impractical** and **impracticable,** see usage at IMPRACTICABLE.

im·pre·cate /'impri,kāt/ ▸*v.* [*trans.*] *archaic* utter (a curse) or invoke (evil) against someone or something. ▷early 17th cent.: from Latin *imprecat-* 'invoked,' from the verb *imprecari.*

im·pre·ca·tion /,impri'kāsʜən/ ▸*n.* *formal* a spoken curse: *she hurled her imprecations at anyone who might be listening.* ▷late Middle English: from Latin *imprecatio(n-),* from *imprecari* 'invoke (evil),' from *in-* 'toward' + *precari* 'pray.' **—im·pre·ca·to·ry** /'imprikə,tôrē/ *adj.*

im·pre·cise /,impri'sīs/ ▸*adj.* lacking exactness and accuracy of expression or detail: *the witness could give only vague and imprecise descriptions.* **—im·pre·cise·ly** *adv.* **—im·pre·cise·ness** *n.* **—im·pre·ci·sion** /-'sizʜən/ *n.*

im·preg·na·ble /im'preg-nəbəl/ ▸*adj.* (of a fortified position) unable to be captured or broken into: *an impregnable wall of solid sandstone figurative the companies are impregnable to takeovers.* ■ unable to be defeated or destroyed; unassailable: *the case against Hastings would have been almost impregnable.* ▷late Middle English: from Old French *imprenable,* from *in-* 'not' + *prendre* 'take' (from Latin *prehendere*). The current spelling arose in the 16th cent., perhaps influenced by Old French variants. **—im·preg·na·bil·i·ty** /-,pregnə'bilitē/ *n.* **—im·preg·na·bly** /-blē/ *adv.*

im·preg·nate /im'preg,nāt/ ▸*v.* [*trans.*] **1** make (a woman or female animal) pregnant. ■ *Biology* fertilize (a female reproductive cell or ovum). **2** (usu. **be impregnated with**) soak or saturate (something) with a substance: *wood that had been impregnated with preservative.* ■ imbue with feelings or qualities: *an atmosphere impregnated with tension.* ▷early 17th cent. (in the sense 'fill'): from late Latin *impregnat-* 'made pregnant,' from the verb *impregnare.* **—im·preg·na·tion** /,impreg'nāsʜən/ *n.*

im·pre·sa·ri·o /,imprə'sārē,ō; -'se(ə)r-/ ▸*n.* (*pl.* **-ri·os**) a person who organizes and often finances concerts, plays, or operas. ■ *chiefly historical* the manager of a musical, theatrical, or operatic company. ▷mid 18th cent.: from Italian, from *impresa* 'undertaking.'

im·pre·scrip·ti·ble /,impri'skriptəbəl/ ▸*adj.* *Law* (of rights) unable to be taken away by prescription or by lapse of time. ▷late 16th cent.: from medieval Latin *imprescriptibilis,* from *in-* 'not' + Latin *praescript-* (from *praescribere* 'prescribe').

im·press[1] ▸*v.* /im'pres/ [*trans.*] **1** make (someone) feel admiration and respect: *they immediately impressed the judges |* [*intrans.*] *he has to put on an act to impress.* **2** make a mark or design on (an object) using a stamp or seal; imprint: *she impressed the damp clay with her seal.* ■ apply (a mark) to something with pressure: *a revenue stamp was embossed or* ***impressed on*** *the instrument.* ■ (**impress something on**) *figurative* fix an idea in (someone's mind): *nobody impressed on me the need to save.* **3** apply (an electric current or potential) from an external source.
▸*n.* /'im,pres/ [in *sing.*] an act of making an impression or mark: *bluish marks made by the impress of his fingers.* ■ a mark made by a seal or stamp. ■ *figurative* the characteristic mark or quality of a person or attribute: *his desire to put his own impress on the films he made.* ▷late Middle English (in the sense 'apply with pressure'): from Old French *empresser,* from *em-* 'in' + *presser* 'to press,' influenced by Latin *imprimere* (see

Pronunciation Key ə *ago;* ər *over;* 'ə or ,ə **up;** 'ər or ,ər *fur;* a *hat;* ā *rate;* ä *car;* cʜ *chew;* e *let;* ē *see;* e(ə)r *air;* i *fit;* ī *by;* i(ə)r *ear;* ɴɢ *sing;* ō *go;* ô *for;* oi *boy;* o͝o *good;* o͞o *goo;* ou *out;* sʜ *she;* ᴛʜ *thin;* T͟H *then;* (h)w *why;* zʜ *vision*

IMPRINT). Sense 1 dates from the mid 18th cent. **—im·press·i·ble** *adj.*

im·press2 ▸*v.* [*trans.*] *historical* force (someone) to serve in an army or navy: *a number of Poles, impressed into the German army.* ■ commandeer (goods or equipment) for public service. ▷late 16th cent.: from IN-2 'into' + PRESS2. **—im·press·ment** *n.*

im·pres·sion /im'presHən/ ▸*n.* **1** an idea, feeling, or opinion about something or someone, esp. one formed without conscious thought or on the basis of little evidence: *his first impressions of Manchester were very positive | they give the impression that all is sweetness and light.* See note at IDEA. ■ an effect produced on someone: *her courtesy and quick wit had made a good impression.* ■ a difference made by the action or presence of someone or something: *the floor was too dirty for the mop to make much impression.* **2** an imitation of a person or thing, esp. one done to entertain: *he did an impression of Frank Sinatra.* ■ a graphic or pictorial representation of someone or something: *the police have issued an artist's impression of the attacker.* **3** a mark impressed on a surface by something: *the impression of his body on the leaves.* ■ *Dentistry* a negative copy of the teeth or mouth made by pressing them into a soft substance. **4** the printing of a number of copies of a book, periodical, or picture for issue at one time. ■ [usu. with *adj.*] a particular printed version of a book or other publication, esp. one reprinted from existing type, plates, or film with no or only minor alteration. Compare with EDITION. ■ a print taken from an engraving. **5** an instance of a pop-up or other Web advertisement being seen on computer users' monitors: *Nielsen/NetRatings reported Web publishers served 7.3 billion pop-up ad impressions.* ▷late Middle English: via Old French from Latin *impressio(n-)*, from *impress-* 'pressed in,' from the verb *imprimere* (see IMPRINT). **—im·pres·sion·al** /-sHənl/ *adj.*

▸PHRASE □ **under the impression that** believing, mistakenly or on the basis of little evidence, that something is the case: *he was under the impression that they had become friends.*

im·pres·sion·a·ble /im'presH(ə)nəbəl/ ▸*adj.* easily influenced because of a lack of critical ability: *a girl of eighteen is highly impressionable.* ▷mid 19th cent.: from French, from *impressionner*, from Latin *impressio(n-)*, from the verb *imprimere* 'press into' (see IMPRINT). **—im·pres·sion·a·bil·i·ty** /-presH(ə)nə'bilitē/ *n.* **—im·pres·sion·a·bly** /-blē/ *adv.*

Im·pres·sion·ism /im'presHə,nizəm/ ▸*n.* a style or movement in painting originating in France in the 1860s, characterized by a concern with depicting the visual impression of the moment, esp. in terms of the shifting effect of light and color. ■ a literary or artistic style that seeks to capture a feeling or experience rather than to achieve accurate depiction. ■ *Music* a style of composition (associated esp. with Debussy) in which clarity of structure and theme is subordinate to harmonic effects, characteristically using the whole-tone scale.

> The Impressionist painters repudiated both the precise academic style and the emotional concerns of Romanticism, and their interest in objective representation, especially of landscape, was influenced by early photography. Impressionism met at first with suspicion and scorn, but soon became deeply influential. Its chief exponents included Monet, Renoir, Pissarro, Cézanne, Degas, and Sisley.

▷from French *impressionnisme*, from *impressionniste*, originally applied unfavorably with reference to Monet's painting *Impression: Soleil levant* (1872).

Im·pres·sion·ist /im'presHənist/ ▸*n.* a painter, writer, or composer who is an exponent of Impressionism. ▸*adj.* of or relating to Impressionism or its exponents.

im·pres·sion·ist /im'presHənist/ ▸*n.* an entertainer who impersonates famous people.

im·pres·sion·is·tic /im,presHə'nistik/ ▸*adj.* **1** based on subjective reactions presented unsystematically: *a personal and impressionistic view of the war.* **2** (**Impressionistic**) in the style of Impressionism: *an Impressionistic portrait.* **—im·pres·sion·is·ti·cal·ly** /-ik(ə)lē/ *adv.*

im·pres·sive /im'presiv/ ▸*adj.* evoking admiration through size, quality, or skill: grand, imposing, or awesome: *an impressive view of the mountains | impressive achievements in science.* **—im·pres·sive·ly** *adv.* **—im·pres·sive·ness** *n.*

im·prest /'im,prest/ ▸*n.* a fund used by a business for small items of expenditure and restored to a fixed amount periodically. ■ an advance of money made to someone engaged in some business with the state, enabling them to carry out the business. ■ a sum of money advanced to a person for a particular purpose. ▷mid 16th cent.: from the earlier phrase *in prest* 'as a loan,' influenced by Italian or medieval Latin *imprestare* 'lend.'

im·pri·ma·tur /,imprə'mätər; -'mātər/ ▸*n.* an official license by the Roman Catholic Church to print an ecclesiastical or religious book. ■ [in *sing.*] a person's acceptance or guarantee that something is of a good standard: *the original LP enjoyed the imprimatur of the composer.* ▷mid 17th cent.: from Latin, 'let it be printed' from the verb *imprimere* (see IMPRINT).

im·print ▸*v.* /im'print/ **1** [*trans.*] (usu. **be imprinted**) impress or stamp (a mark or outline) on a surface or body: *tire marks were **imprinted in** the snow.* ■ make an impression or mark on (something): *clothes **imprinted with** the logos of sports teams.* ■ *figurative* fix (an idea) firmly in someone's mind: *he would always have this ghastly image **imprinted on** his mind.* **2** [*intrans.*] (**imprint on**) *Zoology* (of a young animal) come to recognize (another animal, person, or thing) as a parent or other object of habitual trust.

▸*n.* /'imprint/ **1** a mark made by pressing something on to a softer substance so that its outline is reproduced: *he made imprints of the keys in bars of soap.* ■ *figurative* a lasting impression or effect: *years in the colonies had left their imprint.* **2** a printer's or publisher's name, address, and other details in a book or other printed item. ■ a brand name under which books are published, typically the name of a former publishing house that is now part of a larger group. ▷late Middle English (originally as *emprint*): from Old French *empreinter*, based on Latin *imprimere*, from *in-* 'into' + *premere* 'to press.'

im·pris·on /im'prizən/ ▸*v.* [*trans.*] (usu. **be imprisoned**) put or keep in prison or a place like a prison: *he was imprisoned for six months for contempt of court.* ▷Middle English *emprison*, from Old French *emprisoner*, from *em-* 'in' + *prison*. **—im·pris·on·ment** *n.*

im·prob·a·ble /im'präbəbəl/ ▸*adj.* not likely to be true or to happen: *this account of events was seen by the jury as most improbable.* ■ unexpected and apparently inauthentic: *the characters have improbable names.* ▷late 16th cent.: from French, or from Latin *improbabilis* 'hard to prove,' from *in-* 'not' + *probabilis* (see PROBABLE). **—im·prob·a·bil·i·ty** /-,präbə'bilitē/ *n.* (*pl.* **-ties**) **—im·prob·a·bly** /-blē/ *adv.*

im·pro·bi·ty /im'prōbitē/ ▸*n.* *formal* wickedness or dishonesty. ▷late 16th cent.: from Latin *improbitas*, from *improbus* 'wicked,' from *in-* 'not' + *probus* 'good.' Compare with PROBITY.

im·promp·tu /im'präm(p),t(y)o͞o/ ▸*adj.* & *adv.* done without being planned, organized, or rehearsed: [as *adj.*] *an impromptu press conference* | [as *adv.*] *he spoke impromptu.* See note at SPONTANEOUS.

▸*n.* (*pl.* **-tus**) a short piece of instrumental music, esp. a solo, that is reminiscent of an improvisation. ▷mid 17th cent. (as an adverb): from French, from Latin *in promptu* 'in readiness,' from *promptus* (see PROMPT).

im·prop·er /im'präpər/ ▸*adj.* not in accordance with accepted rules or standards, esp. of morality or honesty: *he was accused of improper behavior in his business dealings.* ■ lacking in modesty or decency: *it was thought improper for elderly women to wear bright colors.* ▷late Middle English: from French *impropre* or Latin *improprius*, from *in-* 'not' + *proprius* 'one's own, proper.' **—im·prop·er·ly** *adv.*

im·prop·er frac·tion ▸*n.* a fraction in which the numerator is greater than the denominator, such as $^5/_4$.

im·pro·pri·ate /im'prōprē,āt/ ▸*v.* [*trans.*] [usu. as *adj.*] (**impropriated**) grant (an ecclesiastical benefice) to a corporation or person as their property. ■ place (tithes or ecclesiastical property) in lay hands. ▷early 16th cent.: from Anglo-Latin *impropriat-* 'appropriated,' from the verb *impropriare*, based on Latin *proprius* 'one's own, proper.' **—im·pro·pri·a·tion** /-,prōprē'āsHən/ *n.*

im·pro·pri·a·tor /im'prōprē,ātər/ ▸*n.* a person to whom a benefice is granted as their property.

im·pro·pri·e·ty /,imprə'prī-itē/ ▸*n.* (*pl.* **-ties**) a failure to observe standards or show due honesty or modesty; improper language, behavior, or character: *she was scandalized at the impropriety of the question | there are no demonstrable legal improprieties.* ▷early 17th cent. (also in the sense 'inaccuracy, incorrectness'): from French *impropriété* or Latin *improprietas*, from *improprius* (see IMPROPER).

im·prov /'im,präv/ ▸*n.* *informal* improvisation, esp. as a theatrical technique.

im·prove /im'pro͞ov/ ▸*v.* make or become better: [*trans.*] *efforts to improve relations with China and Pakistan* | [as *adj.*] (**improved**) *improved road and rail links* | [*intrans.*] *his condition improved after glass was removed from his arm.* ■ [*trans.*] develop or increase in mental capacity by education or experience: *I subscribed to two magazines to improve my mind.* ■ [*intrans.*] (**improve on/upon**) achieve or produce something better than: *they are trying to improve on the tired old style.* ■ increase the value of (real property) by renovation, construction, landscaping, etc.: [as *adj.*] (**improved**) *improved property in an urban renewal project area.* ▷early 16th cent. (as *emprowe* or *improwe*): from Anglo-Norman French *emprower* (based on Old French *prou* 'profit,' ultimately from Latin *prodest* 'is of advantage'); *-owe* was changed to *-ove* under the influence of PROVE. The original sense was 'make a profit, increase the value of'; subsequently 'make greater in amount or degree.' **—im·prov·a·bil·i·ty** /-,pro͞ovə'bilitē/ *n.* **—im·prov·a·ble** *adj.* **—im·prov·er** *n.*

im·prove·ment /im'pro͞ovmənt/ ▸*n.* an example or instance of improving or being improved: *an improvement in East–West relations.* ■ the action of improving or being improved: *there's still **room for improvement**.* ■ a thing that makes something better or is better than something else: *home improvements | it's **an improvement on** the last cake I made.* ▷late Middle English *emprowement* (in the sense 'profitable management or use; profit'), from Anglo-Norman French, from *emprower* (see IMPROVE).

im·prov·i·dent /im'prävidənt/ ▸*adj.* not having or showing foresight; spendthrift or thoughtless: *improvident and undisciplined behavior.* **—im·prov·i·dence** *n.* **—im·prov·i·dent·ly** *adv.*

im·pro·vise /'imprə,vīz/ ▸*v.* [*trans.*] create and perform (music, drama, or verse) spontaneously or without preparation: *the ability to improvise operatic arias in any given style* | [*intrans.*] *he was improvising to a backing of guitar chords* | [as *adj.*] (**improvised**) *improvised humor.* ■ produce or make (something) from whatever is available: *I improvised a costume for myself out of an old blue dress* | [as *adj.*] (**improvised**) *we camped out, sleeping on improvised beds.* ▷early 19th cent.: from French *improviser* or its source, Italian *improvvisare*, from *improvviso* 'extempore,' from Latin *improvisus* 'unforeseen,' based on *provisus*, past participle of *providere* 'make preparation for.' **—im·prov·i·sa·tion** /im,prävi'zāsHən/ *n.* **—im·prov·i·sa·tion·al** /im,prävi'zāsHənl/ *adj.* **—im·prov·i·sa·to·ri·al** /im,prävizə'tôrēəl/ *adj.* **—im·pro·vi·sa·to·ry** /im'prävizə,tôrē/ *adj.* **—im·pro·vis·er** *n.*

im·pru·dent /im'pro͞odnt/ ▸*adj.* not showing care for the consequences of an action; rash: *it would be imprudent to leave her winter coat behind.* ▷late Middle English: from Latin *imprudent-* 'not foreseeing,' from *in-* 'not' + *prudent-* (see PRUDENT). **—im·pru·dence** *n.* **—im·pru·dent·ly** *adv.*

im·pu·dent /'impyəd(ə)nt/ ▸*adj.* not showing due respect for another person; impertinent: *he could have strangled this impudent upstart.* See note at IMPERTINENT. ▷late Middle English (in the sense 'immodest, indelicate'): from Latin *impudent-*, from *in-* 'not' + *pudent-* 'ashamed, modest' (from *pudere* 'be ashamed'). **—im·pu·dence** *n.* **—im·pu·dent·ly** *adv.*

im·pu·dic·i·ty /,impyə'disitē/ ▸*n.* *formal* lack of modesty. ▷early 16th cent.: from French *impudicité*, from Latin *impudicitia*, from *impudicus* 'shameless,' from *in-* 'not' + *pudere* 'be ashamed.'

im·pugn /im'pyo͞on/ ▸*v.* [*trans.*] dispute the truth, validity, or honesty of (a statement or motive); call into question: *the father does not impugn her capacity as a good mother.* ▷late Middle English (also in the sense 'assault, attack physically'): from Latin *impugnare* 'assail,' from *in-* 'toward' + *pugnare* 'fight.' **—im·pugn·a·ble** *adj.* **—im·pugn·ment** *n.*

im·pu·is·sant /im'pwisənt; -'pyo͞o-isənt/ ▸*adj.* *poetic/literary* unable to take effective action; powerless. ▷early 17th cent.: French, from *im-* 'not' + *puissant* 'powerful.' **—im·pu·is·sance** *n.*

im·pulse /'im,pəls/ ▸*n.* **1** a sudden strong and unreflective urge or desire to act: *I had an almost irresistible impulse to giggle* | [as *adj.*] *impulse buying.* ■ the tendency to act in this way: *he was a man of impulse, not premeditation.* **2** a driving or motivating force; an impetus: *an added impulse to this process of renewal.* **3** a pulse of electrical energy; a brief current: *nerve impulses | a spiral is used to convert radio waves into electrical impulses.* **4** *Physics* a force acting briefly on a body and producing a finite change of momentum. ■ a change of momentum so produced, equivalent to the average value of the force multiplied by the time during which it acts. ▷early 17th cent. (as a verb in the sense 'give an impulse to'): the verb from Latin *impuls-* 'driven on,' the noun from *impulsus* 'impulsion, outward pressure,' both from the verb *impellere* (see IMPEL).

▸*PHRASE* □ **on impulse** (or **on an impulse**) suddenly and without forethought; impulsively.

im·pul·sion /im'pəlsHən/ ▸*n.* a strong urge to do something; an impulse: *the impulsion of the singers to govern the pace.* ■ the force or motive behind an action or process: *attitudes changed under the impulsion of humanitarian considerations.* ▷late Middle English (in the sense 'the act or an instance of impelling'): via Old French from Latin *impulsio(n-)*, from the verb *impellere* (see IMPEL).

im·pul·sive /im'pəlsiv/ ▸*adj.* **1** acting or done without forethought: *they had married as young impulsive teenagers | perhaps he's regretting his impulsive offer.* See note at SPONTANEOUS. **2** *Physics* acting as an impulse. ▷late Middle English (in the sense 'tending to impel'): from French *impulsif, -ive* or late Latin *impulsivus*, from Latin *impuls-* 'driven onward' (see IMPULSE). Sense 1 dates from the mid 18th cent. **—im·pul·sive·ly** *adv.* **—im·pul·sive·ness** *n.* **—im·pul·siv·i·ty** /ˌimˌpəl'sivitē/ *n.*

im·pu·ni·ty /im'pyo͞onitē/ ▸*n.* exemption from punishment or freedom from the injurious consequences of an action: *the impunity enjoyed by military officers implicated in civilian killings | protesters burned flags on the streets* ***with impunity.*** ▷mid 16th cent.: from Latin *impunitas*, from *impunis* 'unpunished,' from *in-* 'not' + *poena* 'penalty' or *punire* 'punish.'

im·pure /im'pyo͝or/ ▸*adj.* **1** mixed with foreign matter; adulterated: *bullets cast from an impure lead.* ■ dirty: *a parasite that thrives in impure water.* ■ (of a color) mixed with another color. **2** morally wrong, esp. in sexual matters: *citizens suspected of harboring impure thoughts.* ■ defiled or contaminated according to ritual prescriptions: *the perception of woman as impure.* ▷late Middle English (in the sense 'dirty, containing offensive matter'): from Latin *impurus*, from *in-* 'not' + *purus* 'pure.' **—im·pure·ly** *adv.* **—im·pure·ness** *n.*

im·pu·ri·ty /im'pyo͝oritē/ ▸*n.* (*pl.* **-ties**) the quality or condition of being impure. ■ a thing or constituent that impairs the purity of something: *aluminum and lead are impurities frequently found in tap water.* ■ *Electronics* a trace element deliberately added to a semiconductor; a dopant. ▷late Middle English: from French *impurité* or Latin *impuritas*, from *impurus* (see IMPURE).

im·pute /im'pyo͞ot/ ▸*v.* [*trans.*] represent (something, esp. something undesirable) as being done, caused, or possessed by someone; attribute: *the crimes imputed to Richard.* ■ *Finance* assign (a value) to something by inference from the value of the products or processes to which it contributes: [as *adj.*] (**imputed**) *recovering the initial outlay plus imputed interest.* ■ *Theology* ascribe (righteousness, guilt, etc.) to someone by virtue of a similar quality in another: *Christ's righteousness has been imputed to us.* ▷late Middle English: from Old French *imputer*, from Latin *imputare* 'enter in the account,' from *in-* 'in, toward' + *putare* 'reckon.' **—im·put·a·ble** *adj.* **—im·pu·ta·tion** /ˌimpyə'tāsHən/ *n.*

Im·roz /əm'rôz/ Turkish name of IMBROS.

IN ▸*abbr.* Indiana (in official postal use).

In ▸*symbol* the chemical element indium.

in /in/ ▸*prep.* **1** expressing the situation of something that is or appears to be enclosed or surrounded by something else: *living in Deep River | dressed in their Sunday best | soak it in warm soapy water | she saw it in the rearview mirror.* ■ expressing motion with the result that something ends up within or surrounded by something else: *don't put dye in the bathtub | he got in his car and drove off.* **2** expressing a period of time during which an event takes place or a situation remains the case: *they met in 1885 | at one o'clock in the morning | I hadn't seen him in years.* **3** expressing the length of time before a future event is expected to take place: *I'll see you in fifteen minutes.* **4** (often followed by a noun without a determiner) expressing a state or condition: *to be in love | I've got to put my affairs in order | a woman in her thirties | laid out in a straight line.* ■ indicating the quality or aspect with respect to which a judgment is made: *no discernible difference in quality.* **5** expressing inclusion or involvement: *I read it in a book | acting in a film.* **6** indicating someone's occupation or profession: *she works in publishing.* **7** indicating the language or medium used: *say it in Polish | put it in writing.* ■ indicating the key in which a piece of music is written: *Mozart's Piano Concerto in E flat.* **8** [with *verbal n.*] as an integral part of (an activity): *in planning public expenditure it is better to be prudent.*
▸*adv.* **1** expressing movement with the result that someone or something becomes enclosed or surrounded by something else: *come in | bring it in | presently the admiral breezed in.* **2** expressing the situation of being enclosed or surrounded by something: *we were locked in.* **3** expressing arrival at a destination: *the train got in very late.* **4** (of the tide) rising or at its highest level. **5** *Baseball* (of an infielder or outfielder) playing closer to home plate than usual: *looking for a force, they brought the infield in.* ■ (of a pitch) very close to the batter: *he threw a fastball in and up a little.*
▸*adj.* **1** [*predic.*] (of a person) present at one's home or office: *we knocked at the door but there was no one in.* **2** *informal* fashionable: *pastels and light colors are in this year | the in thing to do.* **3** [*predic.*] (of the ball in tennis and similar games) landing within the designated playing area.
▸*n.* a position of influence: *he would ensure an in with the nominee.* ▷Old English *in* (preposition), *inn, inne* (adverb), of Germanic origin; related to Dutch and German *in* (preposition), German *ein* (adverb), from an Indo-European root shared by Latin *in* and Greek *en*.
▸*PHRASES* □ **be in for** have good reason to expect (typically something unpleasant): *it looks as if we're in for a storm.* ■ (**be in for it**) have good reason to expect trouble or retribution. □ **have it in for someone** see HAVE. □ **in all** see ALL. □ **in and out of** being a frequent visitor to (a house) or frequent inmate of (an institution): *he was in and out of jail for most of his twenties.* □ **in on** privy to (a secret): *they were in on the conspiracy.* □ **in so far as** see INSOFAR. □ **in that** for the reason that (used to specify the respect in which a statement is true): *I was fortunate in that I had friends.* □ **in with** *informal* enjoying friendly relations with: *I was in demand because I was in with the right people.* □ **the ins and outs** *informal* all the details (of something).

in. ▸*abbr.* inch(es).

in-[1] ▸*prefix* **1** (added to adjectives) not: *inanimate | intolerant.* **2** (added to nouns) without; lacking: *inadvertence | inappreciation.* ▷from Latin.

> ***USAGE*** The prefix **in-** (as defined for both IN-[1] above and IN-[2] below) is also found assimilated in the following forms: **il-** before *l*; **im-** before *b*, *m*, or *p*; **ir-** before *r*.

in-[2] ▸*prefix* in; into; toward; within: *induce | influx | inborn.* ▷representing IN or the Latin preposition *in*.

-in[1] ▸*suffix Chemistry* forming names of organic compounds, pharmaceutical products, proteins, etc.: *insulin | penicillin | dioxin.* ▷alteration of -INE[4].

-in[2] ▸*comb. form* denoting a gathering of people having a common purpose, typically as a form of protest: *sit-in | sleep-in | love-in.*

-ina ▸*suffix* **1** denoting feminine names and titles: *czarina.* **2** denoting names of musical instruments: *concertina.* **3** denoting names of plant and animal groups: *globigerina.* ▷from Italian, Spanish, or Latin.

in·a·bil·i·ty /ˌinə'bilitē/ ▸*n.* [with *infinitive*] the state of being unable to do something: *his inability to accept new ideas | the inability of the soldiers to understand an alien culture.*

in ab·sen·tia /ˌin əb'sensH(ē)ə/ ▸*adv.* while not present at the event being referred to: *two foreign suspects will be tried in absentia.* ▷late 19th cent.: Latin, literally 'in absence.'

in·ac·tion /in'aksHən/ ▸*n.* lack of action where some is expected or appropriate: *future generations will condemn us for inaction.*

---

in·a·bil·i·ty *n.*
in·ac·ces·si·ble *adj.*
  in·ac·ces·si·bil·i·ty *n.*
  in·ac·ces·si·bly *adv.*
in·ac·cu·rate *adj.*
  in·ac·cu·ra·cy *n.*
  in·ac·cu·rate·ly *adv.*
in·ac·tive *adj.*
  in·ac·tiv·i·ty *n.*
in·ad·e·quate *adj.*
  in·ad·e·qua·cy *n.*
  in·ad·e·quate·ly *adv.*
in·ad·mis·si·ble *adj.*
  in·ad·mis·si·bil·i·ty *n.*
  in·ad·mis·si·bly *adv.*
in·ad·vis·a·ble *adj.*
  in·ad·vis·a·bil·i·ty *n.*
in·ap·po·site *adj.*
  in·ap·po·site·ly *adv.*
  in·ap·po·site·ness *n.*
in·ap·pre·ci·a·ble *adj.*
  in·ap·pre·ci·a·bly *adv.*
in·ap·pre·ci·a·tive *adj.*
  in·ap·pre·ci·a·tion *n.*
in·ap·pro·pri·ate *adj.*
  in·ap·pro·pri·ate·ly *adv.*
in·apt *adj.*
  in·ap·ti·tude *n.*
  in·apt·ly *adv.*
in·ar·gu·a·ble *adj.*
  in·ar·gu·a·bly *adv.*
in·ar·tis·tic *adj.*
  in·ar·tis·ti·cal·ly *adj.*
in·at·ten·tive *adj.*
  in·at·ten·tion *n.*
  in·at·ten·tive·ly *adv.*
  in·at·ten·tive·ness *n.*
in·au·di·ble *adj.*
  in·au·di·bly *adv.*
in·aus·pi·cious *adj.*
  in·aus·pi·cious·ly *adv.*
in·ca·pa·ble *adj.*
  in·ca·pa·bil·i·ty *n.*
  in·ca·pa·bly *adv.*
in·cau·tious *adj.*
  in·cau·tion *n.*
  in·cau·tious·ly *adv.*
  in·cau·tious·ness *n.*
in·ci·vil·i·ty *n.*
in·cog·ni·zant *adj.*
  in·cog·ni·zance *n.*
in·com·mu·ni·ca·ble *adj.*
  in·com·mu·ni·ca·bil·i·ty *n.*
  in·com·mu·ni·ca·ble·ness *n.*
  in·com·mu·ni·ca·bly *adv.*
in·com·mu·ni·ca·tive *adj.*
  in·com·mu·ni·ca·tive·ly *adv.*
  in·com·mu·ni·ca·tive·ness *n.*
in·com·plet·a·ble *adj.*
  in·com·plet·a·bil·i·ty *n.*
in·com·pre·hen·si·ble *adj.*
  in·com·pre·hen·si·bil·i·ty *n.*
  in·com·pre·hen·si·ble·ness *n.*
  in·com·pre·hen·si·bly *adv.*
in·com·put·a·ble *adj.*
in·con·den·sa·ble *adj.*
in·con·sec·u·tive *adj.*
  in·con·sec·u·tive·ly *adv.*
in·cor·rect *adj.*
  in·cor·rect·ly *adv.*
  in·cor·rect·ness *n.*
in·cur·a·ble *adj.*
  in·cur·a·bil·i·ty *n.*
  in·cur·a·bly *adv.*
in·dec·o·rous *adj.*
  in·dec·o·rous·ly *adv.*
  in·dec·o·rous·ness *n.*
in·de·fin·a·ble *adj.*
  in·de·fin·a·bly *adv.*
in·dis·cern·i·ble *adj.*
  in·dis·cern·i·bil·i·ty *n.*
  in·dis·cern·i·bly *adv.*
in·dis·put·a·ble *adj.*
  in·dis·put·a·bil·i·ty *n.*
  in·dis·put·a·bly *adv.*
in·dis·so·ci·a·ble *adj.*
in·dis·tinct *adj.*
  in·dis·tinct·ly *adv.*
  in·dis·tinct·ness *n.*
in·dis·tinc·tive *adj.*
  in·dis·tinc·tive·ly *adv.*
  in·dis·tinc·tive·ness *n.*
in·dis·tin·guish·a·ble *adj.*
  in·dis·tin·guish·a·bly *adv.*
in·di·vis·i·ble *adj.*
  in·di·vis·i·bil·i·ty *n.*
  in·di·vis·i·bly *adv.*
in·ed·i·ble *adj.*
  in·ed·i·bil·i·ty *n.*
in·ed·u·ca·ble *adj.*
  in·ed·u·ca·bil·i·ty *n.*
in·ef·fec·tive *adj.*
  in·ef·fec·tive·ly *adv.*
  in·ef·fec·tive·ness *n.*
in·ef·fi·ca·cious *adj.*
  in·ef·fi·ca·cious·ly *adv.*
  in·ef·fi·ca·cious·ness *n.*
in·ef·fi·ca·cy *n.*
in·e·las·tic *adj.*
in·el·i·gi·ble *adj.*
in·ex·act *adj.*
in·ex·pe·di·ent *adj.*
  in·ex·pe·di·ence *n.*
  in·ex·pe·di·en·cy *n.*
in·ex·pen·sive *adj.*
  in·ex·pen·sive·ly *adv.*
in·ex·plic·it *adj.*
  in·ex·plic·it·ly *adv.*
  in·ex·plic·it·ness *n.*
in·ex·ten·si·ble *adj.*
in·fea·si·ble *adj.*
  in·fea·si·bil·i·ty *n.*
in·fu·si·ble *adj.*
  in·fu·si·bil·i·ty *n.*
in·hu·mane *adj.*
in·ju·di·cious *adj.*
in·op·por·tune *adj.*
  in·op·por·tune·ly *adv.*
in·suf·fi·cient *adj.*
  in·suf·fi·cient·ly *adv.*
in·sus·cep·ti·ble *adj.*
in·vi·a·ble *adj.*
  in·vi·a·bil·i·ty *n.*
in·vol·a·tile *adj.*

in·ac·ti·vate /in'aktə,vāt/ ▸v. [trans.] make inactive or inoperative: *household bleach does not inactivate the virus* | [as adj.] (**inactivated**) *an inactivated polio vaccine.* —**in·ac·ti·va·tion** /-,aktə'vāsʜən/ n. —**in·ac·ti·va·tor** /-,vātər/ n.

in·ad·vert·ent /,inəd'vərtnt/ ▸adj. not resulting from or achieved through deliberate planning: *many French leaders cannot accept at all that American dominance is inadvertent.* ■ (of a mistake) made through lack of care. ▷mid 17th cent.: from IN-[1] 'not' + Latin *advertent-* 'turning the mind to' (from the verb *advertere*). The noun *inadvertence* dates from late Middle English. —**in·ad·vert·ence** n. —**in·ad·vert·en·cy** n. —**in·ad·vert·ent·ly** adv.

in·al·ien·a·ble /in'ālēənəbəl/ ▸adj. unable to be taken away from or given away by the possessor: *freedom of religion, the most inalienable of all human rights.* —**in·al·ien·a·bil·i·ty** /-,ālēənə'bilitē/ n. —**in·al·ien·a·bly** /-blē/ adv.

in·al·ter·a·ble /in'ôltərəbəl/ ▸adj. unable to be changed. —**in·al·ter·a·bil·i·ty** /-,ôltərə'bilitē/ n. —**in·al·ter·a·bly** /-blē/ adv.

in·am·o·ra·ta /in,amə'rätə/ ▸n. a person's female lover. ▷mid 17th cent.: Italian, literally 'enamored,' feminine of *inamorato* (see INAMORATO).

in·am·o·ra·to /in,amə'rä,tō/ ▸n. (pl. **-tos**) a person's male lover. ▷late 16th cent.: Italian, literally 'enamored,' past participle of the verb *inamorare*, based on Latin *amor* 'love.'

in-and-out ▸adj. informal **1** involving inward and outward movement, esp. rapid entrance and exit: *smuggling drugs was a quick in-and-out operation.* **2** inconsistent and unreliable: *this horse is a notoriously in-and-out performer.*

in·ane /i'nān/ ▸adj. silly; stupid: *don't constantly badger people with inane questions.* ▷mid 16th cent.: from Latin *inanis* 'empty, vain.' —**in·ane·ly** adv. —**in·ane·ness** n. —**in·an·i·ty** /i'nanitē/ n. (pl. **-ties**).

in·an·i·mate /in'anəmit/ ▸adj. not alive, esp. not in the manner of animals and humans: *inanimate objects like stones.* ■ showing no sign of life; lifeless: *he was completely inanimate, and it was difficult to see if he was breathing.* ▷late Middle English: from late Latin *inanimatus* 'lifeless,' from *in-* 'not' + *animatus* (see ANIMATE). —**in·an·i·mate·ly** adv.

in·a·ni·tion /,inə'nisʜən/ ▸n. lack of mental or spiritual vigor and enthusiasm: *she was thinking that old age bred inanition.* ■ exhaustion caused by lack of nourishment. ▷late Middle English: from late Latin *inanitio(n-)*, from Latin *inanire* 'make empty,' from *inanis* 'empty, vain.'

in·ap·par·ent /,inə'parənt; -'pe(ə)r-/ ▸adj. Medicine causing no noticeable signs or symptoms: *clinically inapparent hepatitis.*

in·ap·pe·tence /in'apətəns/ ▸n. chiefly Veterinary Medicine lack of appetite. —**in·ap·pe·tent** adj.

in·ap·pli·ca·ble /in'aplikəbəl; ,inə'plik-/ ▸adj. not relevant or appropriate: *the details are likely to be **inapplicable to** other designs.* —**in·ap·pli·ca·bil·i·ty** /-,aplikə'bilitē/ n. —**in·ap·pli·ca·bly** /-blē/ adv.

in·arch /in'ärcʜ/ ▸v. [trans.] Horticulture graft (a plant) by connecting a growing branch without separating it from its parent stock. ▷early 17th cent. (formerly also as *enarch*): from EN-[1], IN-[2] 'into' + the verb ARCH[1].

in·ar·tic·u·late /,inär'tikyəlit/ ▸adj. **1** unable to speak distinctly or express oneself clearly: *he was inarticulate with abashment and regret.* ■ not clearly expressed or pronounced: *inarticulate complaints of inadequate remuneration.* ■ having no distinct meaning; unintelligible: *lurching up and down uttering inarticulate cries.* ■ not expressed; unspoken: *mention of her mother filled her with inarticulate irritation.* **2** without joints or articulations. ■ Zoology denoting a brachiopod in which the valves of the shell have no hinge and are held together by muscles. ▷early 17th cent.: from IN-[1] 'not' + the adjective ARTICULATE; the sense 'not clearly pronounced' corresponds to that of late Latin *inarticulatus.* —**in·ar·tic·u·la·cy** /-ləsē/ n. —**in·ar·tic·u·late·ly** adv. —**in·ar·tic·u·late·ness** n.

in·as·much /,inəz'məcʜ/ ▸adv. (**inasmuch as**) to the extent that; insofar as: *these provisions apply only inasmuch as trade between Member States is affected.* ■ considering that; since (used to specify the respect in which a statement is true): *a most unusual astronomer inasmuch as he was deaf-mute.* ▷Middle English: originally as *in as much*, translating Old French *en tant (que)* 'in so much (as).'

in·au·gu·ral /in'ôg(y)ərəl/ ▸adj. [attrib.] marking the beginning of an institution, activity, or period of office: *his inaugural concert as music director.*
▸n. an inaugural speech, esp. one made by an incoming U.S. president. ■ an inaugural ceremony: *the ball before the inaugural.* ▷late 17th cent.: from French (from *inaugurer* 'inaugurate,' from Latin *inaugurare*) + -AL.

in·au·gu·rate /in'ôg(y)ə,rāt/ ▸v. [trans.] begin or introduce (a system, policy, or period): *he inaugurated a new policy of trade and exploration.* ■ admit (someone) formally to public office: *the new president will be inaugurated on January 20.* ■ mark the beginning or first public use of (an organization or project): *the museum was inaugurated on September 12.* ▷late 16th cent.: from Latin *inaugurat-* 'interpreted as omens (from the flight of birds),' based on *augurare* 'to augur.' —**in·au·gu·ra·tion** /-ôg(y)ə'rāsʜən/ n. —**in·au·gu·ra·tor** n. —**in·au·gu·ra·to·ry** /-ə,tôrē/ adj.

in·au·then·tic /,inô'tʜentik/ ▸n. not in fact what it is said to be: *the Holy Shroud of Turin is thought to have been proved inauthentic by radiocarbon dating.* ■ not genuinely belonging to a style or period: *baroque harpsichord pieces played on the decidedly inauthentic modern Steinway.* ■ lacking full reality or sincerity: *people close to death could not waste time being inauthentic.* —**in·au·then·ti·cal·ly** /-ik(ə)lē/ adv. —**in·au·then·tic·i·ty** /-ôtʜən'tisitē/ n.

inbd. ▸abbr. inboard.

in-be·tween informal ▸adj. situated somewhere between two extremes or recognized categories; intermediate: *I am not unconscious, but in some in-between state.*
▸n. an intermediate thing: *successes, failures and in-betweens.* —**in-be·tween·er** n.

in·board /'in,bôrd/ ▸adv. & adj. within a ship, aircraft, or vehicle: [as adv.] *the spray was coming inboard now* | [as adj.] *the uncovered inboard engine.* ■ toward the center of a ship, aircraft, or vehicle: [as adv.] *move the clew inboard along the boom* | [as adj.] *the inboard ailerons on the wings were dead.*
▸n. a boat's engine housed inside its hull. ■ a boat with such an engine.

in·born /'in'bôrn/ ▸adj. existing from birth: *an inborn defect in the formation of collagen.* ■ natural to a person or animal: *people think doctors have inborn compassion.* See note at INHERENT.

in·bound /'in,bound/ ▸adj. & adv. traveling toward a particular place, esp. when returning to the original point of departure: [as adj.] *inbound traffic* | [as adv.] *we have three enemy planes inbound on bearing two ninety.*
▸v. [trans.] Basketball throw (the ball) from out of bounds, putting it into play.

in·bounds /'in,boundz/ ▸adj. Basketball denoting or relating to a throw that puts the ball into play from out of bounds: *an inbounds pass.*

in-box ▸n. a box on someone's desk for letters addressed to them and other documents that they have to deal with. ■ Computing the window in which an individual user's received e-mail messages and similar electronic communications are displayed.

in·breathe /'in'brēt͟h/ ▸v. [trans.] poetic/literary breathe in or absorb: *he felt himself inbreathing power from on high.*

in·bred /'in,bred/ ▸adj. **1** produced by inbreeding: *a classic inbred Englishman.* **2** existing in a person, animal, or plant from birth; congenital: *inbred disease resistance in crops.*

in·breed /'in,brēd/ ▸v. (past and past part. **-bred**) [intrans.] [often as n.] (**inbreeding**) breed from closely related people or animals, esp. over many generations: *persistent inbreeding has produced an unusually high frequency of sufferers from this disease.*

in·built /'in,bilt/ ▸adj. existing as an original or essential part of something or someone: *the body's inbuilt ability to heal itself.*

Inc. /ingk/ ▸abbr. ■ incorporated: *Northeast Airlines Inc.* ■ (also **inc.**) incomplete.

In·ca /'ingkə/ ▸n. **1** a member of a South American Indian people living in the central Andes before the Spanish conquest.

> The Incas arrived in the Cuzco valley in Peru c.AD 1200. When the Spanish invaded in the early 1530s, the Inca empire covered most of modern Ecuador and Peru, much of Bolivia, and parts of Argentina and Chile. Inca technology and architecture were highly developed. Their descendants, speaking Quechua, still make up about half of Peru's population.

2 the supreme ruler of this people. ▷late 16th cent.: the name in Quechua, literally 'lord, royal person.' —**In·ca·ic** /in'kāik; ing-/ adj. —**In·can** adj.

in·ca /'ingkə/ ▸n. a South American hummingbird having mainly blackish or bronze-colored plumage with one or two white breast patches. • Genus *Coeligena*, family Trochilidae: four species.

in·cal·cu·la·ble /in'kalkyələbəl; ing-/ ▸adj. **1** too great to be calculated or estimated: *an archive of incalculable value.* **2** not able to be calculated or estimated: *the cost is incalculable but colossal.* ■ (of a person or their character) unpredictable: *under the pressure of anxiety his temper became incalculable.* —**in·cal·cu·la·bil·i·ty** /-,kalkyələ'bilitē/ n. —**in·cal·cu·la·bly** /-blē/ adv.

in cam·er·a ▸adv. see CAMERA[2].

in·can·desce /,inkən'des/ ▸v. [intrans.] glow with heat: *the lights of the town lay incandescing across the prairie.* ▷late 19th cent.: back-formation from INCANDESCENT.

in·can·des·cent /,inkən'desənt/ ▸adj. emitting light as a result of being heated: *plumes of incandescent liquid rock.* ■ (of an electric light) containing a filament that glows white-hot when heated by a current passed through it. ■ extremely angry: *she was incandescent at the way the IRS acted.* ■ of outstanding and exciting quality; brilliant: *Mravinsky's incandescent performance of Siegfried's Funeral March.* ▷late 18th cent.: from French, from Latin *incandescent-* 'glowing,' from the verb *incandescere*, from *in-* (expressing intensive force) + *candescere* 'become white' (from *candidus* 'white'). —**in·can·des·cence** n. —**in·can·des·cent·ly** adv.

in·cant /in'kant/ ▸v. [trans.] chant or intone: *priests were incanting psalms around her body.* ▷mid 16th cent. (in the sense 'use enchantment on'): from Latin *incantare* 'to chant, charm,' from *in-* (expressing intensive force) + *cantare* 'sing.' The current sense dates from the mid 20th cent.

in·can·ta·tion /,inkan'tāsʜən/ ▸n. a series of words said as a magic spell or charm: *an incantation to raise the dead.* ■ the use of such words: *there was no magic in such incantation* | *incantations of old slogans.* ▷late Middle English: via Old French from late Latin *incantatio(n-)*, from *incantare* 'chant, bewitch' (see INCANT). —**in·can·ta·to·ry** /-'kantə,tôrē/ adj.

in·ca·pac·i·tate /,inkə'pasi,tāt/ ▸v. [trans.] prevent from functioning in a normal way: *he was incapacitated by a heart attack.* ■ Law deprive (someone) of their legal capacity. ▷mid 17th cent.: from INCAPACITY + -ATE[3]. —**in·ca·pac·i·tant** /-'pasətnt/ n. —**in·ca·pac·i·ta·tion** /-,pasi'tāsʜən/ n.

in·ca·pac·i·ty /,inkə'pasitē/ ▸n. (pl. **-ties**) physical or mental inability to do something or to manage one's affairs: *they can be fired only for incapacity or misbehavior.* ■ legal disqualification: *they are not subject to any legal incapacity.* ▷early 17th cent.: from French *incapacité* or late Latin *incapacitas*, from *in-* (expressing negation) + *capacitas* (see CAPACITY).

in·car·cer·ate /in'kärsə,rāt/ ▸v. [trans.] (usu. **be incarcerated**) imprison: *many are incarcerated for property offenses.* ■ [trans.] confine (someone) in a particular place: *he spent a long evening incarcerated below decks.* ▷mid 16th cent.: from medieval Latin *incarcerat-* 'imprisoned,' from the verb *incarcerare*, from *in-* 'into' + Latin *carcer* 'prison.' —**in·car·cer·a·tion** /-,kärsə'rāsʜən/ n. —**in·car·cer·a·tor** /-,rātər/ n.

in·car·na·dine /in'kärnə,din; -,dēn/ poetic/literary ▸n. a bright crimson or pinkish-red color.
▸adj. of a crimson or pinkish-red color.
▸v. [trans.] color (something) a bright crimson or pinkish-red. ▷late 16th cent.: from French *incarnadin(e)*, from Italian *incarnadino*, variant of *incarnatino* 'flesh color,' based on Latin *incarnare* (see INCARNATE).

in·car·nate ▸adj. /in'kärnit; -,nāt/ [often postpositive] (esp. of a deity or spirit) embodied in flesh; in human form: *God incarnate* | *he chose to be incarnate as a man.* ■ [postpositive] represented in the ultimate or most extreme form: *here is capitalism incarnate.*
▸v. /-,nāt/ [trans.] embody or represent (a deity or spirit) in human form: *the idea that God incarnates himself in man.* ■ put (an idea or other abstract concept) into concrete form: *a desire to make things which will incarnate their personality.* ■ (of a person) be the living embodiment of (a quality): *the man who incarnates the suffering which has affected every single Mozambican.* ▷late Middle English: from ecclesiastical Latin *incarnat-* 'made flesh,' from the verb *incarnare*, from *in-* 'into' + *caro, carn-* 'flesh.'

in·car·na·tion /,inkär'nāsʜən/ ▸n. **1** a person who embodies in the flesh a deity, spirit, or abstract quality: *Rama was Vishnu's incarnation on earth.* ■ (**the Incarnation**) (in Christian theology) the embodiment of God the Son in human flesh as Jesus Christ. **2** (with reference to reincarnation) one of a series of lifetimes that a person spends on earth: *in my next incarnation, I'd like to be the Secretary of Fun.* ■ the form in which a person spends such a lifetime. ▷Middle English (as a term in Christian theology): via Old French from ecclesiastical Latin *incarnatio(n-)*, from the verb *incarnare* (see INCARNATE).

in·case ▶*v.* variant spelling of ENCASE.

in·cen·di·ar·y /in'sendē,erē/ ▶*adj.* (of a device or attack) designed to cause fires: *incendiary grenades.* ■ tending to stir up conflict: *incendiary rhetoric | an incendiary slogan.* ■ very exciting: *an incendiary live performer.*
▶*n.* (*pl.* **-ar·ies**) an incendiary bomb or device. ■ a person who starts fires, esp. in a military context. ■ a person who stirs up conflict. ▷late Middle English: from Latin *incendiarius*, from *incendium* 'conflagration,' from *incendere* 'set fire to.' **—in·cen·di·a·rism** /-dēə,rizəm/ *n.*

in·cense¹ ▶*n.* /'in,sens/ a gum, spice, or other substance that is burned for the sweet smell it produces. ■ the smoke or perfume of such a substance.
▶*v.* /in'sens/ [*trans.*] perfume with incense or a similar fragrance: *the aroma of cannabis incensed the air.* ▷Middle English (originally as *encense*): from Old French *encens* (noun), *encenser* (verb), from ecclesiastical Latin *incensum* 'something burned, incense,' neuter past participle of *incendere* 'set fire to,' from *in-* 'in' + the base of *candere* 'to glow.' **—in·cen·sa·tion** /,insen'sāsʜən/ *n.*

in·cense² /in'sens/ ▶*v.* [*trans.*] (usu. **be incensed**) make very angry: *she was incensed by the accusations.* ▷late Middle English (in the general sense 'inflame or excite someone with a strong feeling'): from Old French *incenser*, from Latin *incendere* 'set fire to.'

in·cense ce·dar ▶*n.* a columnar cedar with scalelike leaves that smell of turpentine when crushed, found chiefly in mountainous areas of California and Oregon and grown as an ornamental in Europe. • *Calocedrus decurrens*, family Cupressaceae.

in·cen·so·ry /in'sensərē/ ▶*n.* (*pl.* **-ries**) another term for CENSER. ▷early 17th cent. (denoting a burnt offering, or an altar for it): from medieval Latin *incensorium*, from *incensum* (see INCENSE¹).

in·cen·ter /'in,sentər/ (*Brit.* **in·cen·tre**) ▶*n. Geometry* the center of the incircle of a triangle or other figure.

in·cen·tive /in'sentiv/ ▶*n.* a thing that motivates or encourages one to do something: *there is no incentive for customers to conserve water* ■ a payment or concession to stimulate greater output or investment: *tax incentives for investing in depressed areas* | [as *adj.*] *incentive payments.* ▷late Middle English: from Latin *incentivum* 'something that sets the tune or incites,' from *incantare* 'to chant or charm.'

in·cen·tiv·ize /in'sentə,vīz/ ▶*v.* [*trans.*] provide (someone) with an incentive for doing something: *this is likely to incentivize management to find savings.*

in·cept /in'sept/ ▶*v.* [*intrans.*] *Brit., historical* graduate from a university with an academic degree. ▷mid 16th cent. (in the sense 'undertake, begin'): from Latin *incept-* 'begun,' from the verb *incipere*. The current sense dates from the mid 19th cent. **—in·cep·tor** /-tər/ *n.*

in·cep·tion /in'sepsʜən/ ▶*n.* [in *sing.*] the establishment or starting point of an institution or activity: *she has been on the board since its inception two years ago.* See note at ORIGIN. ▷late Middle English: from Latin *inceptio(n-)*, from *incipere* 'begin.'

in·cep·ti·sol /in'septi,sôl; -,säl/ ▶*n. Soil Science* a soil of an order comprising freely draining soils in which the formation of distinct horizons is not far advanced, such as brown earth. ▷1960s: from Latin *inceptum* 'beginning' (from the verb *incipere*) + -SOL.

in·cep·tive /in'septiv/ ▶*adj.* relating to or marking the beginning of something; initial. ■ *Grammar* (of a verb) expressing the beginning of an action; inchoative.
▶*n. Grammar* an inceptive verb. ▷early 17th cent. (as a noun): from late Latin *inceptivus*, from *incept-* 'begun,' from the verb *incipere*.

in·cer·ti·tude /in'sərti,t(y)o͞od/ ▶*n.* a state of uncertainty or hesitation: *some schools broke down under the stresses of policy incertitude.* ▷late Middle English: from Old French, or from late Latin *incertitudo*, from *in-* (expressing negation) + *certitudo* (see CERTITUDE).

in·ces·sant /in'sesənt/ ▶*adj.* (of something regarded as unpleasant) continuing without pause or interruption: *the incessant beat of the music.* ▷late Middle English: via Old French from late Latin *incessant-*, from *in-* 'not' + Latin *cessant-* 'ceasing' (from the verb *cessare*). **—in·ces·san·cy** *n.* **—in·ces·sant·ly** *adv.* **—in·ces·sant·ness** *n.*

in·cest /'in,sest/ ▶*n.* sexual relations between people classed as being too closely related to marry each other. ■ the crime of having sexual intercourse with a parent, child, sibling, or grandchild. ▷Middle English: from Latin *incestus*, *incestum* 'unchastity, incest,' from *in-* 'not' + *castus* 'chaste.'

in·ces·tu·ous /in'sesCHo͞oəs/ ▶*adj.* **1** involving or guilty of incest: *the child of an incestuous relationship.* **2** (of human relations generally) excessively close and resistant to outside influence: *the incestuous nature of literary journalism.* ▷early 16th cent.: from late Latin *incestuosus*, from Latin *incestus* (see INCEST). **—in·ces·tu·ous·ly** *adv.* **—in·ces·tu·ous·ness** *n.*

inch¹ /inCH/ ▶*n.* **1** a unit of linear measure equal to one twelfth of a foot (2.54 cm): *the toy train is four inches long | eighteen inches of thread.* (Symbol: ") ■ [often with *negative*] a very small amount or distance: *I had no intention of budging an inch.* **2** a unit used to express other quantities, in particular: ■ (as a unit of rainfall) a quantity that would cover a horizontal surface to a depth of one inch. ■ (also **inch of mercury**) (as a unit of atmospheric pressure) an amount that would support a column of mercury one-inch high in a barometer (equal to 33.86 millibars, 29.5 inches being equal to one bar).
▶*v.* [*intrans.*] move slowly and carefully in a specified direction: *the 2,000 mourners inched along narrow country lanes | figurative the stock market inched ahead today.* ■ [*trans.*] cause (something) to move in this manner: *he inched the car forward.* ▷late Old English *ynce*, from Latin *uncia* 'twelfth part,' from *unus* 'one' (probably denoting a unit). Compare with OUNCE¹.
▶*PHRASES* □ **by inches 1** only just: *the shot missed her by inches.* **2** very slowly and gradually; bit by bit: *you can't let him die by inches like this.* □ **every inch 1** the whole surface, distance, or area: *between them they know every inch of the country.* **2** entirely; very much so: *he's every inch the gentleman.* □ **give someone an inch and he** (or **she**) **will take a mile** *proverb* once concessions have been made to someone they will demand a great deal. □ **inch by inch** gradually; bit by bit: *inch by inch he crept along the wall.* □ **within an inch of** very close to: *her mouth was within an inch of his chin.* □ **(to) within an inch of one's life** almost to the point of death: *he was beaten within an inch of his life.*

inch² ▶*n.* [in *place names*] *chiefly Scottish* a small island or a small area of high land: *Inchkeith.* ▷Middle English: from Scottish Gaelic *innis.*

inch·meal /'inCH,mēl/ ▶*adv.* by inches; little by little: *inchmeal he advanced up the slope.* ▷mid 16th cent.: from INCH¹ + *-meal* from Old English *mǣlum*, in the sense 'measure, quantity taken at one time.'

in·cho·ate /in'kō-it; -āt/ ▶*adj.* just begun and so not fully formed or developed; rudimentary: *a still inchoate democracy.* ■ *Law* (of an offense, such as incitement or conspiracy) anticipating a further criminal act. ▷mid 16th cent.: from Latin *inchoatus*, past participle of *inchoare*, variant of *incohare* 'begin.' **—in·cho·ate·ly** *adv.* **—in·cho·ate·ness** *n.*

USAGE Because **inchoate** means 'just begun and so not fully formed or developed,' a sense of 'disorder' may be implied. But to extend the usage of **inchoate** to mean 'chaotic, confused, incoherent' (*he speaks in an inchoate manner*) is incorrect, although not uncommon. Perhaps even more common are incorrect pronunciations of **inchoate**, such as /in'CHōt/, which assumes two syllables (rather than three) and a *ch* sound like that of *chair* or *chosen* (rather than a *k* sound like that of *charisma* or *chorus*).

in·cho·a·tive /in'kō-itiv/ ▶*adj. Grammar* denoting an aspect of a verb expressing the beginning of an action, typically one occurring of its own accord. In many English verbs, inchoative uses alternate systematically with causative uses. Compare with ERGATIVE.
▶*n.* an inchoative verb.

In·chon /'in'CHän/ a port on the western coast of South Korea, on the Yellow Sea, near Seoul; pop. 1,818,000. It was the site of a successful invasion by U.S. troops in 1950 that enabled them to return Seoul to South Korea.

inch·worm /'inCH,wərm/ ▶*n.* a caterpillar of a geometrid moth, which moves forward by arching and straightening its body. Also called LOOPER, MEASURING WORM, or SPANWORM.

in·ci·dence /'insidəns/ ▶*n.* **1** the occurrence, rate, or frequency of a disease, crime, or something else undesirable: *an increased incidence of cancer.* ■ the way in which the burden of a tax falls upon the population: *the entire incidence falls on the workers.* **2** *Physics* the intersection of a line, or something moving in a straight line, such as a beam of light, with a surface. See also ANGLE OF INCIDENCE. ▷late Middle English (denoting a casual or subordinate event or circumstance): from Old French, or from medieval Latin *incidentia*, from Latin *incidere* 'fall upon, happen to' (see INCIDENT). Sense 1 dates from the early 19th cent.

USAGE **Incidence** and **incidents** sound the same, but **incidence** is more often used in technical contexts, referring to the frequency with which something occurs: *increased ultraviolet light is likely to cause increased incidence of skin cancer.* **Incidents** is simply the plural of **incident**, an event: *the police are supposed to investigate any incidents of domestic violence.* The form **incidences** should be avoided.

in·ci·dent /'insidənt/ ▶*n.* an event or occurrence: *several amusing incidents.* ■ a violent event, such as a fracas or assault: *one person was stabbed in the incident.* ■ a hostile clash between forces of rival countries. ■ (**incident of**) a case or instance of something happening: *a single incident of rudeness does not support a finding of contemptuous conduct.* ■ the occurrence of dangerous or exciting things: *the winter passed without incident.* ■ a distinct piece of action in a play or a poem.
▶*adj.* **1** [*predic.*] (**incident to**) likely to happen because of; resulting from: *the changes incident to economic development.* ■ *Law* attaching to: *the costs properly incident to a suit for foreclosure or redemption.* **2** (esp. of light or other radiation) falling on or striking something: *when an ion beam is* **incident on** *a surface.* ■ of or relating to incidence: *the incident angle.* ▷late Middle English: via Old French from Latin *incident-* 'falling upon, happening to,' from the verb *incidere*, from *in-* 'upon' + *cadere* 'to fall.'

USAGE On the difference between **incidents** and **incidence**, see usage at INCIDENCE.

in·ci·den·tal /,insi'dentl/ ▶*adj.* **1** accompanying but not a major part of something: *for the fieldworker who deals with real problems, paperwork is incidental | incidental expenses.* ■ occurring by chance in connection with something else: *the incidental catch of dolphins in the pursuit of tuna.* See note at ACCIDENTAL. **2** [*predic.*] (**incidental to**) liable to happen as a consequence of (an activity): *the ordinary risks incidental to a fireman's job.*
▶*n.* (usu. **incidentals**) an incidental detail, expense, event, etc.: *an allowance to cover meals, taxis, and other incidentals.* ▷early 17th cent.: originally from medieval Latin *incidentalis*, from Latin *incident-* 'falling upon, happening to' (from the verb *incidere*).

in·ci·den·tal·ly /,insi'dent(ə)lē/ ▶*adv.* **1** [*sentence adverb*] used when a person has something more to say, or is about to add a remark unconnected to the current subject; by the way: *incidentally, it was many months before the whole truth was discovered.* **2** in an incidental manner; as a chance occurrence: *the infection was discovered only incidentally at a postmortem examination.*

in·ci·den·tal mu·sic ▶*n.* music used in a film or play as a background to create or enhance a particular atmosphere.

in·cin·er·ate /in'sinə,rāt/ ▶*v.* [*trans.*] (often **be incinerated**) destroy (something, esp. waste material) by burning: *such garbage must be incinerated at the hospital.* ▷late 15th cent.: from medieval Latin *incinerat-* 'burned to ashes,' from the verb *incinerare*, from *in-* 'into, toward' + *cinis*, *ciner-* 'ashes.' **—in·cin·er·a·tion** /-,sinə'rāsʜən/ *n.*

in·cin·er·a·tor /in'sinə,rātər/ ▶*n.* an apparatus for burning waste material, esp. industrial waste, at high temperatures until it is reduced to ash.

in·cip·i·ent /in'sipēənt/ ▶*adj.* in an initial stage; beginning to happen or develop: *he could feel incipient anger building up | an incipient black eye.* ■ (of a person) developing into a specified type or role: *we seemed more like friends than incipient lovers.* ▷late 16th cent. (as a noun denoting a beginner): from Latin *incipient-* 'undertaking, beginning,' from the verb *incipere*, from *in-* 'into, toward' + *capere* 'take.' **—in·cip·i·ence** *n.* **—in·cip·i·en·cy** *n.* **—in·cip·i·ent·ly** *adv.*

in·ci·pit /'insipit/ ▶*n.* the opening words of a text, manuscript, early printed book, or chanted liturgical text. Compare with EXPLICIT. ▷late 19th cent.: Latin, literally '(here) begins.'

in·cir·cle /'in,sərkəl/ ▶*n. Geometry* a circle inscribed in a triangle or other figure so as to touch (but not cross) each side.

Pronunciation Key ə *ago*; ər *over*; 'ə or ,ə *up*; 'ər or ,ər *fur*; a *hat*; ā *rate*; ä *car*; CH *chew*; e *let*; ē *see*; e(ə)r *air*; i *fit*; ī *by*; i(ə)r *ear*; NG *sing*; ō *go*; ô *for*; oi *boy*; o͝o *good*; o͞o *goo*; ou *out*; SH *she*; TH *thin*; TH *then*; (h)w *why*; ZH *vision*

in·cise /in'sīz/ ▶*v.* [*trans.*] (usu. **be incised**) mark or decorate (an object or surface) with a cut or a series of cuts: *a button incised with a skull.* ■ cut (a mark or decoration) into a surface: *figures incised on upright stones.* ■ cut (skin or flesh) with a surgical instrument: *the wound was incised and drained.* ▷mid 16th cent.: from French *inciser*, from Latin *incis-* 'cut into, engraved,' from the verb *incidere*, from *in-* 'into' + *caedere* 'to cut.'

in·cised me·an·der ▶*n. Geology* a river meander that has been cut abnormally deeply into the landscape because uplift of the land has led to renewed downward erosion by the river.

in·ci·sion /in'sizHən/ ▶*n.* a surgical cut made in skin or flesh: *an abdominal incision.* ■ a mark or decoration cut into a surface: *a block of marble delicately decorated with incisions.* ■ the action or process of cutting into something: *the method is associated with less blood loss during incision.* ▷late Middle English: from late Latin *incisio(n-)*, from Latin *incidere* 'cut into' (see INCISE). —**in·ci·sion·al** /-zHənl/ *adj.*

in·ci·sive /in'sīsiv/ ▶*adj.* (of a person or mental process) intelligently analytical and clear-thinking: *she was an incisive critic.* ■ (of an account) accurate and sharply focused: *the songs offer incisive pictures of American ways.* ▷late Middle English (in the sense 'cutting, penetrating'): from medieval Latin *incisivus*, from Latin *incidere* 'cut into' (see INCISE). —**in·ci·sive·ly** *adv.* —**in·ci·sive·ness** *n.*

in·ci·sor /in'sīzər/ ▶*n.* (also **incisor tooth**) a narrow-edged tooth at the front of the mouth, adapted for cutting. In humans there are four incisors in each jaw. ▷late 17th cent.: from medieval Latin, literally 'cutter,' from Latin *incis-* (see INCISE).

in·cis·ure /in'sizHər; -'sī-/ (also **in·ci·su·ra** /ˌinˌsī'zHŏŏrə/) ▶*n.* (*pl.* **-cis·ures** or **-cis·u·rae** /-'sizHərē/) *Anatomy* a deep indentation or notch in an edge or surface.

in·cite /in'sīt/ ▶*v.* [*trans.*] encourage or stir up (violent or unlawful behavior): *the offense of inciting racial hatred.* ■ urge or persuade (someone) to act in a violent or unlawful way: *he* **incited** *loyal subjects* **to** *rebellion.* ▷late 15th cent.: from French *inciter*, from Latin *incitare*, from *in-* 'toward' + *citare* 'rouse.' —**in·ci·ta·tion** /ˌinsī'tāsHən/ *n.* —**in·cite·ment** *n.* —**in·cit·er** *n.*

> ***THE RIGHT WORD*** **arouse, exhort, foment, incite, instigate, provoke**
> The best way to start a riot is to **incite** one, which means to urge or stimulate to action, either in a favorable or an unfavorable sense.
> If you **instigate** an action, however, it implies that you are responsible for initiating it and that the purpose is probably a negative or evil one (*the man who instigated the assassination plot*).
> **Foment** suggests agitation or incitement over an extended period of time (*foment a discussion; foment the rebellion that leads to war*). An instigator, in other words, is someone who initiates the idea, while a fomenter is someone who keeps it alive.
> You can **provoke** a riot in the same way that you instigate one, but the emphasis here is on spontaneity rather than on conscious design (*her statement provoked an outcry from animal rights activists*). To **arouse** is to awaken a feeling or elicit a response (*my presence in the junkyard aroused suspicion*), or to open people's eyes to a situation (*we attempted to arouse public awareness*).
> But once you've aroused people, you may have to **exhort** them, meaning to urge or persuade them, by appealing to their sympathy or conscience, to take constructive action.

incl. ▶*abbr.* ■ including. ■ inclusive.

in·clem·ent /in'klemənt/ ▶*adj.* (of the weather) unpleasantly cold or wet. ▷early 17th cent.: from French *inclément* or Latin *inclement-*, from *in-* 'not' + *clement-* 'clement.' —**in·clem·en·cy** *n.* (*pl.* **-cies**).

in·cli·na·tion /ˌinklə'nāsHən; ˌiNGklə-/ ▶*n.* **1** a person's natural tendency or urge to act or feel in a particular way; a disposition or propensity: *John was a scientist by training and inclination | he was free to follow his inclinations.* ■ (**inclination for/to/toward**) an interest in or liking for (something): *Burger King and Wendy's didn't show any inclination to jump into a price war with McDonald's.* **2** a slope or slant: *changes in inclination of the line on the graph.* ■ a bending of the body or head in a bow: *the questioner's inclination of his head.* ■ the dip of a magnetic needle. **3** the angle at which a straight line or plane is inclined to another. ■ *Astronomy* the angle between the orbital plane of a planet, comet, etc., and the ecliptic, or between the orbital plane of a satellite and the equatorial plane of its primary. ■ *Astronomy* the angle between the axis of an astronomical object and a fixed reference angle. ▷late Middle English: from Latin *inclinatio(n-)*, from *inclinare* 'bend toward' (see INCLINE).

in·cline ▶*v.* /in'klīn/ **1** (**be inclined to/toward/to do something**) feel willing or favorably disposed toward (an action, belief, or attitude): *he was inclined to accept the offer | Lucy was inclined to a belief in original sin.* ■ [with *infinitive*] (esp. as a polite formula) tend toward holding a specified opinion: *I'm inclined to agree with you.* ■ [*trans.*] make (someone) willing or disposed to do something: *his prejudice inclines him to overlook obvious facts.* ■ [*intrans.*] feel favorably disposed to someone or something: *I* **incline to** *the view that this conclusion is untenable.* **2** (**be inclined to/to do something**) have a tendency to do something: *she's inclined to gossip with complete strangers.* ■ [with *adverbial*] have a specified disposition or talent: *some people are very mathematically inclined.* **3** [*intrans.*] lean or turn away from a given plane or direction, esp. the vertical or horizontal: *the bunker doors incline outward* | [as *adj.*] (**inclined**) *an inclined ramp.* ■ [*trans.*] bend (one's head) forward and downward.
▶*n.* /'inˌklīn/ an inclined surface or slope, esp. on a road, path, or railway: *the road climbs a long incline through a forest.* ■ an inclined plane: *the Hay Incline was built to raise boats from one canal level to another.* ▷Middle English (originally in the sense 'bend (the head, the body, or oneself) toward something'; formerly also as *encline*): from Old French *encliner*, from Latin *inclinare*, from *in-* 'toward' + *clinare* 'to bend.' —**in·clin·a·ble** *adj.* —**in·clin·er** *n.*

in·clined plane ▶*n.* a plane inclined at an angle to the horizontal. ■ a sloping ramp up which heavy loads can be raised by ropes or chains.

in·cli·nom·e·ter /ˌinklə'nämitər/ ▶*n.* a device for measuring the angle of inclination of something, esp. from the horizontal. ▷mid 19th cent.: from Latin *inclinare* 'to incline' + -METER.

in·close ▶*v.* variant spelling of ENCLOSE.

in·clo·sure ▶*n.* variant spelling of ENCLOSURE.

in·clude /in'klo͞od/ ▶*v.* [*trans.*] **1** comprise or contain as part of a whole: *the price includes dinner, bed, and breakfast | other changes included the abolition of the death penalty.* **2** make part of a whole or set: *we have included some hints for beginners in this section.* ■ allow (someone) to share in an activity or privilege: *there were doubts as to whether she was included in the invitation.* ▷late Middle English (also in the sense 'shut in'): from Latin *includere*, from *in-* 'into' + *claudere* 'to shut.'

> ***USAGE*** **Include** has a broader meaning than **comprise**. In the sentence *the accommodations* ***comprise*** *two bedrooms, bathroom, kitchen, and living room*, the word **comprise** implies that there are no accommodations other than those listed. **Include** can be used in this way too, but it is also used in a nonrestrictive way, implying that there may be other things not specifically mentioned that are part of the same category, as in *the price* ***includes*** *a special welcome pack.* Careful writers will avoid superfluous uses of "including . . . and more," commonly imitated from advertising. The 'and more' is superfluous because **including** or **includes** implies that there is more than what is listed.

in·clud·ed /in'klo͞odid/ ▶*adj.* [*postpositive*] contained as part of a whole being considered: *all of Europe (Russia included) | service tax included.* ■ *Botany* (of a style or stamen) not protruding beyond the corolla.

in·clud·ing /in'klo͞odiNG/ ▶*prep.* containing as part of the whole being considered: *languages including Welsh, Cornish, and Breton | weapons were recovered from the house, including a shotgun.*

in·clu·sion /in'klo͞ozHən/ ▶*n.* **1** the action or state of including or of being included within a group or structure: *the inclusion of handicapped pupils in regular classrooms.* ■ a person or thing that is included within a larger group or structure: *the exhibition features such inclusions as the study of the little girl.* **2** *Biology, Geology, Metallurgy* a body or particle recognizably distinct from the substance in which it is embedded. ▷early 17th cent.: from Latin *inclusio(n-)*, from *includere* 'shut in.'

in·clu·sion·a·ry /in'klo͞ozHəˌnerē/ ▶*adj.* designed or intended to accommodate diversity in age, income, race, or some other category: *several clubs prefer not to adhere to the new, inclusionary policies.* ▷on the pattern of *exclusionary*.

in·clu·sive /in'klo͞osiv/ ▶*adj.* including or covering all the services, facilities, or items normally expected or required: *the price is inclusive, with few incidentals.* ■ [*predic.*] (**inclusive of**) containing (a specified element) as part of a whole: *all prices are inclusive of taxes.* ■ [*postpositive*] with the inclusion of the extreme limits stated: *between the ages of 55 and 59 inclusive.* ■ not excluding any section of society or any party involved in something: *only an inclusive peace process will end the conflict.* ■ (of language) deliberately nonsexist, esp. avoiding the use of masculine pronouns to refer to both men and women. ▷late 16th cent.: from medieval Latin *inclusivus*, from Latin *includere* (see INCLUDE). —**in·clu·sive·ly** *adv.* —**in·clu·sive·ness** *n.*

in·clu·sive fit·ness ▶*n. Genetics* the ability of an individual organism to pass on its genes to the next generation, taking into account the shared genes passed on by the organism's close relatives.

in·clu·siv·i·ty /ˌinklo͞o'sivitē/ ▶*n.* an intention or policy of including people who might otherwise be excluded or marginalized, such as the handicapped, learning-disabled, or racial and sexual minorities: *you will need a thorough understanding of inclusivity and the needs of special education pupils.* ▷on the pattern of *exclusivity*.

in·cog /in'käg/ ▶*adj., adv., & n. informal, dated* short for INCOGNITO.

in·cog·ni·to /ˌinkäg'nētō; in'kägniˌtō/ ▶*adj. & adv.* (of a person) having one's true identity concealed: [as *adj.*] *in order to observe you have to be incognito* | [as *adv.*] *he is now operating incognito.*
▶*n.* (*pl.* **-tos**) an assumed or false identity. ▷mid 17th cent.: from Italian, literally 'unknown,' from Latin *incognitus*, from *in-* 'not' + *cognitus* (past participle of *cognoscere* 'know').

in·co·her·ent /ˌinkō'hi(ə)rənt; ˌiNG-; -'her-/ ▶*adj.* **1** (of spoken or written language) expressed in an incomprehensible or confusing way; unclear: *he screamed some incoherent threat.* ■ (of a person) unable to speak intelligibly: *I splutter several more times before becoming incoherent.* ■ (of an ideology, policy, or system) internally inconsistent; illogical: *the film is ideologically incoherent.* **2** *Physics* (of waves) having no definite or stable phase relationship. —**in·co·her·ence** *n.* —**in·co·her·en·cy** *n.* (*pl.* **-cies**) —**in·co·her·ent·ly** *adv.*

in·com·bus·ti·ble /ˌinkəm'bəstəbəl/ ▶*adj.* (esp. of a building material or component) consisting or made of material that does not burn if exposed to fire. ▷late 15th cent.: from medieval Latin *incombustibilis*, from *in-* 'not' + *combustibilis* (see COMBUSTIBLE). —**in·com·bus·ti·bil·i·ty** /-ˌbəstə'bilitē/ *n.*

in·come /'inˌkəm; 'iNG-/ ▶*n.* money received, esp. on a regular basis, for work or through investments: *he has a nice home and an adequate income | figures showed an overall increase in income this year.* ▷Middle English (in the sense 'entrance, arrival,' now only Scots): in early use from Old Norse *innkoma*, later from IN + COME. The current sense dates from the late 16th cent.

in·come group ▶*n.* a section of the population classified according to their level of income.

in·come tax ▶*n.* tax levied by a government directly on income, esp. an annual tax on personal income.

in·com·ing /'inˌkəmiNG/ ▶*adj.* in the process of coming in: *incoming passengers | the incoming tide.* ■ (of a message or communication) being received rather than sent: *an incoming call.* ■ (of an official or administration) having just been elected or appointed to succeed another: *the incoming president.* ■ approaching with hostile intent; attacking: *incoming jets* | [*postpositive*] *"Missile incoming!" blared the bridge.*
▶*n.* (**incomings**) revenue; income: *keep an account of your incomings and outgoings.*

in·com·men·su·ra·ble /ˌinkə'mensərəbəl; -sHər-/ ▶*adj.* **1** not able to be judged by the same standard as something; having no common standard of measurement: *the two types of science are incommensurable.* **2** *Mathematics* (of numbers) in a ratio that cannot be expressed as a ratio of integers. ■ irrational.
▶*n.* (usu. **incommensurables**) an incommensurable quantity. ▷mid 16th cent. (in the mathematical sense): from late Latin *incommensurabilis*, from *in-* 'not' + *commensurabilis* (see COMMENSURABLE). —**in·com·men·su·ra·bil·i·ty** /-ˌmensərə'bilitē; -sHər-/ *n.* —**in·com·men·su·ra·bly** *adv.*

in·com·men·su·rate /ˌinkə'mensərit; -sHə-/ ▶*adj.* **1** [*predic.*] (**incommensurate with**) out of keeping or proportion with: *man's influence on the earth's surface seems incommensurate with his scale.* **2** another term for INCOMMENSURABLE (sense 1). —**in·com·men·su·rate·ly** *adv.* —**in·com·men·su·rate·ness** *n.*

in·com·mode /ˌinkə'mōd/ ▶*v.* [*trans.*] *formal* inconvenience (someone): *they are incommoded by the traffic.* ▷late 16th cent.: from French *incommoder* or Latin *incommodare*, from *in-* 'not' + *commodus* 'convenient.'

in·com·mo·di·ous /ˌinkəˈmōdēəs/ ▸*adj.* *formal or dated* causing inconvenience or discomfort. —**in·com·mo·di·ous·ly** *adv.* —**in·com·mo·di·ous·ness** *n.*

in·com·mu·ni·ca·ble /ˌinkəˈmyo͞onikəbəl/ ▸*adj.* not able to be communicated to others: *the pain of separation took the form of an incommunicable depression.* ▷mid 16th cent. (in the sense 'incommunicative'): from late Latin *incommunicabilis* 'not to be imparted,' from *in-* 'not' + *communicabilis* (see COMMUNICABLE). —**in·com·mu·ni·ca·bil·i·ty** /-ˌmyo͞onikəˈbilitē/ *n.* —**in·com·mu·ni·ca·ble·ness** *n.* —**in·com·mu·ni·ca·bly** *adv.*

in·com·mu·ni·ca·do /ˌinkəˌmyo͞oniˈkädō/ ▸*adj.* not able, wanting, or allowed to communicate with other people: *they were separated and detained incommunicado.* ▷mid 19th cent.: from Spanish *incomunicado*, past participle of *incomunicar* 'deprive of communication.'

in·com·mut·a·ble /ˌinkəˈmyo͞otəbəl/ ▸*adj.* not capable of being changed or exchanged. ▷late Middle English: from Latin *incommutabilis*, from *in-* 'not' + *commutabilis* (see COMMUTABLE). —**in·com·mut·a·bly** /-blē/ *adv.*

in·com·pa·ny ▸*adj.* occurring or existing within a company: *in-company training programs.*

in·com·pa·ra·ble /inˈkämp(ə)rəbəl/ ▸*adj.* **1** without an equal in quality or extent; matchless: *the incomparable beauty of Venice.* **2** unable to be compared; totally different in nature or extent: *censorship still exists, but now it's absolutely* **incomparable with** *what it was.* ▷late Middle English: via Old French from Latin *incomparabilis*, from *in-* 'not' + *comparabilis* (see COMPARABLE). —**in·com·pa·ra·bil·i·ty** /-ˌkämp(ə)rəˈbilitē/ *n.* —**in·com·pa·ra·bly** /-blē/ *adv.*

in·com·pat·i·ble /ˌinkəmˈpatəbəl; ˌiNG-/ ▸*adj.* (of two things) so opposed in character as to be incapable of existing together: *cleverness and femininity were seen as incompatible.* ■ (of two people) unable to live together harmoniously. ■ [*predic.*] (**incompatible with**) (of one thing or person) not consistent or able to coexist with (another): *long hours are simply incompatible with family life.* ■ (of equipment, machinery, computer programs, etc.) not capable of being used in combination: *all four prototype camcorders used special tapes and were incompatible with one another.* ▷late Middle English: from medieval Latin *incompatibilis*, from *in-* 'not' + *compatibilis* (see COMPATIBLE). —**in·com·pat·i·bil·i·ty** /-ˌpatəˈbilitē/ *n.* —**in·com·pat·i·bly** /-blē/ *adv.*

in·com·pe·tent /inˈkämpətənt; iNG-/ ▸*adj.* not having or showing the necessary skills to do something successfully: *a forgetful and utterly incompetent assistant.* ■ *Law* not qualified to act in a particular capacity: *the patient is deemed legally incompetent.* ■ *Medicine* (esp. of a valve or sphincter) not able to perform its function.
▸*n.* an incompetent person. ▷late 16th cent. (in the sense 'not legally competent'): from French, or from late Latin *incompetent-*, from *in-* 'not' + Latin *competent-* 'being fit or proper' (see COMPETENT). —**in·com·pe·tence** *n.* —**in·com·pe·ten·cy** *n.* —**in·com·pe·tent·ly** *adv.*

in·com·plete /ˌinkəmˈplēt; ˌiNG-/ ▸*adj.* not having all the necessary or appropriate parts: *the records are patchy and incomplete.* ■ not full or finished: *the analysis remains incomplete.* ▷late Middle English: from late Latin *incompletus*, from Latin *in-* 'not' + *completus* 'filled, finished' (see COMPLETE). —**in·com·plete·ly** *adv.* —**in·com·plete·ness** *n.*

in·com·plete·ness the·o·rem (also **Gödel's incompleteness theorem**) ▸*n.* *Logic* the theorem that in any sufficiently powerful, logically consistent formulation of logic or mathematics there must be true formulas that are neither provable nor disprovable. The theorem entails the corollary that the consistency of a logical system cannot be proved within that system.

in·com·ple·tion /ˌinkəmˈplēSHən; ˌiNG-/ ▸*n.* **1** the state of lacking something or of having failed to complete something: *humans with their profound sense of incompletion.* **2** *Football* a forward pass that is not completed.

in·com·pre·hen·sion /ˌinkämprəˈhenSHən; inˌkäm-/ ▸*n.* failure to understand something: *they gave him a look of complete incomprehension.*

in·com·press·i·ble /ˌinkəmˈpresəbəl/ ▸*adj.* not able to be compressed. —**in·com·press·i·bil·i·ty** /-ˌpresəˈbilitē/ *n.*

in·con·ceiv·a·ble /ˌinkənˈsēvəbəl/ ▸*adj.* not capable of being imagined or grasped mentally; unbelievable: [with *clause*] *it seemed inconceivable that the president had been unaware of what was going on they behaved with inconceivable cruelty.* —**in·con·ceiv·a·bil·i·ty** /-ˌsēvəˈbilitē/ *n.* —**in·con·ceiv·a·ble·ness** *n.* —**in·con·ceiv·a·bly** /-blē/ *adv.* [as *submodifier*] *a crisis of inconceivably devastating proportions.*

in·con·clu·sive /ˌinkənˈklo͞osiv; ˌiNG-/ ▸*adj.* not leading to a firm conclusion; not ending doubt or dispute: *the medical evidence is inconclusive.* —**in·con·clu·sive·ly** *adv.* —**in·con·clu·sive·ness** *n.*

In·co·nel /ˈiNGkəˌnel/ ▸*n.* *trademark* an alloy of nickel containing chromium and iron, resistant to corrosion at high temperatures. ▷1930s: apparently from *I(nternational) N(ickel) Co(mpany)*, on the pattern of *nickel.*

in·con·gru·ent /inˈkäNGgro͞oənt; ˌinkənˈgro͞o-/ ▸*adj.* incongruous; incompatible. ■ *Chemistry* (of melting, dissolution, or other process) affecting the components of an alloy or other substance differently. ▷late Middle English: from Latin *incongruent-*, from *in-* 'not' + *congruent-* 'meeting together' (see CONGRUENT). —**in·con·gru·ence** *n.* —**in·con·gru·ent·ly** *adv.*

in·con·gru·ous /inˈkäNGgro͞oəs/ ▸*adj.* not in harmony or keeping with the surroundings or other aspects of something: *the duffel coat looked incongruous with the black dress she wore underneath.* ▷early 17th cent.: from Latin *incongruus* (from *in-* 'not' + *congruus* 'agreeing, suitable,' from the verb *congruere*) + -OUS. —**in·con·gru·i·ty** /ˌinkənˈgro͞o-itē; ˌiNG-; -käNG-/ *n.* (*pl.* **-ties**) —**in·con·gru·ous·ly** *adv.*

in·con·nu /ˌinkəˈn(y)o͞o; aNkôˈny/ ▸*n.* **1** an unknown person or thing. **2** (*pl.* same) an edible predatory freshwater whitefish that is related to the salmon. It lives in Eurasian and North American lakes close to the Arctic Circle. • *Stenodus leucichthys*, family Salmonidae. ▷early 19th cent.: French, literally 'unknown.'

in·con·se·quent /inˈkänsəˌkwent; -ˌkwənt/ ▸*adj.* not connected or following logically; irrelevant: *people say the most stupid, inconsequent things when surprised.* ■ another term for INCONSEQUENTIAL. ▷late 16th cent.: from Latin *inconsequent-*, from *in-* 'not' + *consequent-* 'overtaking, following closely' (see CONSEQUENT). —**in·con·se·quence** *n.* —**in·con·se·quent·ly** *adv.*

in·con·se·quen·tial /ˌinkänsəˈkwenCHəl/ ▸*adj.* not important or significant: *they talked about inconsequential things.* —**in·con·se·quen·ti·al·i·ty** /-ˌkwenCHēˈalitē/ *n.* (*pl.* **-ties**) —**in·con·se·quen·tial·ly** *adv.* —**in·con·se·quen·tial·ness** *n.*

in·con·sid·er·a·ble /ˌinkənˈsidərəbəl/ ▸*adj.* [usu. with *negative*] of small size, amount, or extent: *a not inconsiderable amount of money.* ■ unimportant or insignificant: *a not inconsiderable artist.* ▷late 16th cent. (in the sense 'impossible to imagine'): from French, or from late Latin *inconsiderabilis*, from *in-* 'not' + *considerabilis* 'worthy of consideration' (see CONSIDERABLE).

in·con·sid·er·ate /ˌinkənˈsidərit/ ▸*adj.* thoughtlessly causing hurt or inconvenience to others: *it's* **inconsiderate of** *her to go away without telling us.* ▷late Middle English (originally in the sense 'not properly considered'): from Latin *inconsideratus*, from *in-* 'not' + *consideratus* 'examined, considered' (see CONSIDERATE). —**in·con·sid·er·ate·ly** *adv.* —**in·con·sid·er·ate·ness** *n.* —**in·con·sid·er·a·tion** /-ˌsidəˈrāSHən/ *n.*

in·con·sist·en·cy /ˌinkənˈsistənsē/ ▸*n.* (*pl.* **-cies**) the fact or state of being inconsistent: *inconsistency between his expressed attitudes and his actual behavior.* ■ an inconsistent element or an instance of being inconsistent: *the single glaring inconsistency in the argument.* ▷mid 17th cent.: from INCONSISTENT, on the pattern of *consistency.*

in·con·sist·ent /ˌinkənˈsistənt/ ▸*adj.* not staying the same throughout; having self-contradictory elements: *police interpretation of the law was often inconsistent.* ■ acting at variance with one's own principles or former conduct: *parents can become inconsistent and lacking in control over their children.* ■ (**inconsistent with**) not compatible or in keeping with: *he had done nothing inconsistent with his morality.* ■ erratic in behavior or action: *we're too inconsistent to win the league.* —**in·con·sist·ent·ly** *adv.*

in·con·sol·a·ble /ˌinkənˈsōləbəl/ ▸*adj.* (of a person or their grief) not able to be comforted or alleviated: *his widow, Jane, was inconsolable.* ▷late 16th cent.: from French, or from Latin *inconsolabilis*, from *in-* 'not' + *consolabilis* 'able to be consoled,' from the verb *consolari* (see CONSOLE[1]). —**in·con·sol·a·bil·i·ty** /-ˌsōləˈbilitē/ *n.* —**in·con·sol·a·bly** /-blē/ *adv.*

in·con·so·nant /inˈkänsənənt/ ▸*adj.* *rare* not in agreement or harmony; not compatible. —**in·con·so·nance** *n.* —**in·con·so·nant·ly** *adv.*

in·con·spic·u·ous /ˌinkənˈspikyo͞oəs/ ▸*adj.* not clearly visible or attracting attention; not conspicuous: *an inconspicuous red-brick building.* ▷early 17th cent. (in the sense 'invisible, indiscernible'): from Latin *inconspicuus* (from *in-* 'not' + *conspicuus* 'clearly visible') + -OUS. —**in·con·spic·u·ous·ly** *adv.* —**in·con·spic·u·ous·ness** *n.*

in·con·stant /inˈkänstənt/ ▸*adj.* frequently changing; variable or irregular: *their exact dimensions aren't easily measured since they are inconstant.* ■ (of a person or their behavior) not faithful and dependable. ▷late Middle English: via Old French from Latin *inconstant*, from *in-* 'not' + *constant-* 'standing firm' (see CONSTANT). —**in·con·stan·cy** *n.* (*pl.* **-cies**) —**in·con·stant·ly** *adv.*

in·con·test·a·ble /ˌinkənˈtestəbəl/ ▸*adj.* not able to be disputed. ▷late 17th cent.: from French, or from medieval Latin *incontestabilis*, from *in-* 'not' + *contestabilis* 'able to be called upon in witness,' from the verb *contestari* (see CONTEST). —**in·con·test·a·bil·i·ty** /-ˌtestəˈbilitē/ *n.* —**in·con·test·a·bly** /-blē/ *adv.*

in·con·ti·nent /inˈkäntənənt; -ˈkäntn-ənt/ ▸*adj.* **1** having no or insufficient voluntary control over urination or defecation. **2** lacking self-restraint; uncontrolled: *the incontinent hysteria of the fans.* ▷late Middle English (sense 2): from Old French, or from Latin *incontinent-*, from *in-* 'not' + *continent-* 'holding together' (see CONTINENT[2]). Sense 1 dates from the early 19th cent. —**in·con·ti·nence** *n.* —**in·con·ti·nent·ly** *adv.*

in·con·tro·vert·i·ble /inˌkäntrəˈvərtəbəl/ ▸*adj.* not able to be denied or disputed: *incontrovertible proof.* —**in·con·tro·vert·i·bil·i·ty** /-ˌvərtəˈbilitē/ *n.* —**in·con·tro·vert·i·bly** /-blē/ *adv.*

in·con·ven·ience /ˌinkənˈvēn-yəns/ ▸*n.* trouble or difficulty caused to one's personal requirements or comfort: *the inconvenience of having to change trains.* ■ a cause or instance of such trouble: *the inconveniences of life in a remote city.*
▸*v.* [*trans.*] cause such trouble or difficulty to: *noise and fumes from traffic would inconvenience residents.* ▷late Middle English (originally in the sense 'incongruity, inconsistency,' also in the general sense 'unsuitability'): via Old French from late Latin *inconvenientia* 'incongruity, inconsistency,' from *in-* 'not' + Latin *convenient-* 'agreeing, fitting' (see CONVENIENT).

in·con·ven·ient /ˌinkənˈvēn-yənt/ ▸*adj.* causing trouble, difficulties, or discomfort: *she telephoned frequently, usually at inconvenient times.* ▷late Middle English (originally in the sense 'incongruous' or 'unsuitable'): via Old French from Latin *inconvenient*, from *in-* 'not' + *convenient-* 'agreeing, fitting' (see CONVENIENT). Current senses date from the mid 17th cent. —**in·con·ven·ient·ly** *adv.*

in·con·vert·i·ble /ˌinkənˈvərtəbəl/ ▸*adj.* not able to be changed in form, function, or character. ■ (of currency) not able to be converted into another form on demand. ▷mid 17th cent.: from French, or from late Latin *inconvertibilis*, from *in-* 'not' + *convertibilis* (see CONVERTIBLE). —**in·con·vert·i·bil·i·ty** /-ˌvərtəˈbilitē/ *n.* —**in·con·vert·i·bly** /-blē/ *adv.*

in·co·or·di·na·tion /ˌinkōˌôrdnˈāSHən/ ▸*n.* *technical* lack of coordination, esp. the inability to use different parts of the body together smoothly and efficiently.

in·cor·po·rate ▸*v.* /inˈkôrpəˌrāt/ [*trans.*] **1** put or take in (something) as part of a whole; include: *he has* **incorporated in** *his proposals a large number of measures | territories that had been* **incorporated into** *the Japanese Empire.* ■ contain or include (something) as part of a whole: *the guide incorporates all the recent changes in legislation.* ■ combine (ingredients) into one substance: *add the cheeses and butter and process briefly to incorporate them.* **2** (often **be incorporated**) constitute (a company, city, or other organization) as a legal corporation.
▸*adj.* /-ˈkôrp(ə)rit/ *archaic* **1** another term for INCORPORATED. **2** *poetic/literary* having a bodily form; embodied. ▷late Middle English: from late Latin *incorporat-* 'embodied,' from the verb *incorporare*, from *in-* 'into' + Latin *corporare* 'form into a body' (from *corpus*, *corpor-* 'body'). —**in·cor·po·ra·tion** /-ˌkôrpəˈrāSHən/ *n.* —**in·cor·po·ra·tor** /-ˌrātər/ *n.*

in·cor·po·rat·ed /inˈkôrpəˌrātid/ ▸*adj.* (of a company or other organization) formed into a legal corporation: *the Incorporated Society of Musicians* | [*postpositive*] *Adobe Systems Incorporated.*

in·cor·po·ra·tive /inˈkôrpəˌrātiv/ ▸*adj.* tending to incorporate or include things.

I

in·cor·po·re·al /ˌinkôrˈpôrēəl/ ▸*adj.* not composed of matter; having no material existence: *millions believe in a supreme but incorporeal being they call God.* ■ *Law* having no physical existence. ▷late Middle English: from Latin *incorporeus*, from *in-* 'not' + *corporeus* (from *corpus, corpor-* 'body') + **-AL**. —**in·cor·po·re·al·i·ty** /-ˌpôrēˈalitē/ *n.* —**in·cor·po·re·al·ly** *adv.* —**in·cor·po·re·i·ty** /-pəˈrēitē/ *n.*

in·cor·ri·gi·ble /inˈkôrijəbəl; -ˈkär-/ ▸*adj.* (of a person or their tendencies) not able to be corrected, improved, or reformed: *she's an incorrigible flirt.*
▸*n.* a person of this type. ▷Middle English: from Old French, or from Latin *incorrigibilis*, from *in-* 'not' + *corrigibilis* (see **CORRIGIBLE**). —**in·cor·ri·gi·bil·i·ty** /-ˌkôrijəˈbilitē; -ˌkär-/ *n.* —**in·cor·ri·gi·ble·ness** *n.* —**in·cor·ri·gi·bly** /-blē/ *adv.* [as *submodifier*] *the incorrigibly macho character of news-gathering operations.*

in·cor·rupt /ˌinkəˈrəpt/ ▸*adj. rare* (esp. of a human body) not having undergone decomposition. ▷late Middle English: from Latin *incorruptus*, from *in-* 'not' + *corruptus* 'destroyed, marred' (see **CORRUPT**).

in·cor·rupt·i·ble /ˌinkəˈrəptəbəl/ ▸*adj.* **1** not susceptible to corruption, esp. by bribery. **2** not subject to death or decay; everlasting. ▷Middle English: from Old French, or from ecclesiastical Latin *incorruptibilis*, from *in-* 'not' + *corruptibilis* 'corruptible, liable to decay.' —**in·cor·rupt·i·bil·i·ty** /-ˌrəptəˈbilitē/ *n.* —**in·cor·rupt·i·bly** /-blē/ *adv.*

in-coun·try ▸*adj.* & *adv.* in a country rather than operating from outside but in relation to it: [as *adv.*] *the people we're putting in-country will get instructions from satellite radios.*

incr. ▸*abbr.* ■ increase or increased or increasing.

in·cras·sate /inˈkrasit; -ˌsāt/ ▸*adj. rare* thickened in form or consistency. ▷late 15th cent.: from late Latin *incrassatus* 'made thick,' past participle of *incrassare*. —**in·cras·sat·ed** *adj.*

in·crease ▸*v.* /inˈkrēs/ become or make greater in size, amount, intensity, or degree: [*intrans.*] *car use is increasing at an alarming rate* | [*trans.*] *we are aiming to increase awareness of social issues* | [as *adj.*] (**increasing**) *the increasing numbers of students.*
▸*n.* /ˈinˌkrēs/ an instance of growing or making greater: *an increase from sixteen to eighteen clubs* | *some increase in inflation.* ▷Middle English (formerly also as *encrease*): from Old French *encreistre*, from Latin *increscere*, from *in-* 'into' + *crescere* 'grow.' —**in·creas·a·ble** *adj.* —**in·creas·ing·ly** *adv.* [*sentence adverb*] *increasingly, attention is paid to health and lifestyle* | [as *submodifier*] *an increasingly difficult situation.*
▸**PHRASE** □ **on the increase** becoming greater, more common, or more frequent.

in·cre·ate /ˌinkrēˈāt; inˈkrē-it/ ▸*adj. poetic/literary* not yet created. ▷late Middle English: from ecclesiastical Latin *increatus*, from Latin *in-* 'not' + *creatus* (past participle of *creare* 'create').

in·cred·i·ble /inˈkredəbəl/ ▸*adj.* **1** impossible to believe: *an almost incredible tale of triumph and tragedy.* **2** difficult to believe; extraordinary: *the noise from the crowd was incredible.* ■ *informal* amazingly good or beautiful: *I was mesmerized: she looked so incredible.* ▷late Middle English: from Latin *incredibilis*, from *in-* 'not'+ *credibilis* (see **CREDIBLE**). —**in·cred·i·bil·i·ty** /-ˌkredəˈbilitē/ *n.*

USAGE Believability is at the heart of both **incredible** and **incredulous**, but there is an important distinction in the respective uses of these two adjectives. **Incredible** means 'unbelievable' or 'not convincing' and can be applied to a situation, statement, policy, or threat to a person: *I find this testimony incredible.* **Incredulous** means 'disinclined to believe, skeptical'—the opposite of *credulous, gullible*—and is usually applied to a person's attitude: *you shouldn't be surprised that I'm incredulous after all your lies.*

in·cred·i·bly /inˈkredəblē/ ▸*adv.* **1** [as *submodifier*] to a great degree; extremely or unusually: *Michele was incredibly brave.* **2** [*sentence adverb*] used to introduce a statement that is hard to believe; strangely: *incredibly, he was still alive.*

in·cre·du·li·ty /ˌinkrəˈd(y)o͞olitē/ ▸*n.* the state of being unwilling or unable to believe something: *he stared down the street in incredulity.*

in·cred·u·lous /inˈkrejələs/ ▸*adj.* (of a person or their manner) unwilling or unable to believe something: *an incredulous gasp.* ▷late 16th cent.: from Latin *incredulus* (from *in-* 'not' + *credulus* 'believing, trusting,' from *credere* 'believe') + **-OUS**. —**in·cred·u·lous·ly** *adv.* —**in·cred·u·lous·ness** *n.*

USAGE See usage at **INCREDIBLE**.

in·cre·ment /ˈiNGkrəmənt; ˈin-/ ▸*n.* an increase or addition, esp. one of a series on a fixed scale: *the inmates' pay can escalate in five-cent increments to a maximum of 90 cents an hour.* ■ a regular increase in salary on such a scale: *he had waived his right to the second increment of $18 million so that it could be distributed among 40 employees.* ■ *Mathematics* a small positive or negative change in a variable quantity or function. ▷late Middle English: from Latin *incrementum*, from the stem of *increscere* 'grow' (see **INCREASE**). —**in·cre·men·tal** /ˌiNGkrəˈmentl; ˌin-/ *adj.* —**in·cre·men·tal·ly** /ˌiNGkrəˈmentl-ē; ˌin-/ *adv.*

in·cre·men·tal back·up ▸*n. Computing* a security copy that contains only those files that have been altered since the last full backup.

in·cre·men·tal·ism /ˌiNGkrəˈmentlˌizəm; ˌin-/ ▸*n.* belief in or advocacy of change by degrees; gradualism. —**in·cre·men·tal·ist** *n.* & *adj.*

in·crim·i·nate /inˈkriməˌnāt/ ▸*v.* [*trans.*] make (someone) appear guilty of a crime or wrongdoing; strongly imply the guilt of (someone): *he refused to answer questions in order not to incriminate himself* | [as *adj.*] (**incriminating**) *incriminating evidence.* ▷mid 18th cent.: from late Latin *incriminat-* 'accused,' from the verb *incriminare*, from *in-* 'into, toward' + Latin *crimen* 'crime.' —**in·crim·i·na·tion** /-ˌkriməˈnāSHən/ *n.* —**in·crim·i·na·to·ry** /-nəˌtôrē/ *adj.*

in-crowd ▸*n.* (**the in-crowd**) *informal* a small group of people perceived by others to be particularly fashionable, informed, or popular.

in·crust ▸*v.* variant spelling of **ENCRUST**.

in·crus·ta·tion ▸*n.* variant spelling of **ENCRUSTATION**.

in·cu·bate /ˈinkyəˌbāt; ˈiNG-/ ▸*v.* [*trans.*] (of a bird) sit on (eggs) in order to keep them warm and bring them to hatching. ■ (esp. in a laboratory) keep (eggs, cells, bacteria, embryos, etc.) at a suitable temperature so that they develop: *the samples were incubated at 80°C for three minutes.* ■ (**be incubating something**) have an infectious disease developing inside one before symptoms appear: *the possibility that she was incubating early syphilis.* ■ [*intrans.*] develop slowly without outward or perceptible signs: *unfortunately the BSE bug incubates for around three years.* ▷mid 17th cent.: from Latin *incubat-* 'lain on,' from the verb *incubare*, from *in-* 'upon' + *cubare* 'to lie.'

in·cu·ba·tion /ˌinkyəˈbāSHən; ˌiNG-/ ▸*n.* the process of incubating eggs, cells, bacteria, a disease, etc.: *the chick hatches after a month's incubation.* ▷early 17th cent.: from Latin *incubatio(n-)* 'brooding,' from the verb *incubare* (see **INCUBATE**). —**in·cu·ba·tive** /ˈinkyəˌbātiv; ˈiNG-/ *adj.* —**in·cu·ba·to·ry** /inˈkyo͞obəˌtôrē; iNG-/ *adj.*

in·cu·ba·tion pe·ri·od ▸*n.* the period over which eggs, cells, etc., are incubated. ■ the period between exposure to an infection and the appearance of the first symptoms.

in·cu·ba·tor /ˈinkyəˌbātər; ˈiNG-/ ▸*n.* an enclosed apparatus providing a controlled environment for the care and protection of premature or unusually small babies. ■ an apparatus used to hatch eggs or grow microorganisms under controlled conditions. ■ a place, esp. with support staff and equipment, made available at low rent to new small businesses.

in·cu·bous /ˈiNGkyo͞obəs/ ▸*adj. Botany* (of a liverwort) having leaves that point forward so that their upper edges overlap the lower edges of the leaves above. Often contrasted with **SUCCUBOUS**. ▷mid 19th cent.: from Latin *incubare* 'lie on' + **-OUS**.

in·cu·bus /ˈiNGkyəbəs; ˈin-/ ▸*n.* (*pl.* **-bi** /-ˌbī/) a male demon believed to have sexual intercourse with sleeping women. ■ *figurative* a cause of distress or anxiety: *debt is a big incubus in developing countries.* ■ *archaic* a nightmare. ▷Middle English: late Latin form of Latin *incubo* 'nightmare,' from *incubare* 'lie on' (see **INCUBATE**).

in·cu·des /inˈkyo͞oˌdēz/ ▸ plural form of **INCUS**.

in·cul·cate /inˈkəlˌkāt; ˈinkəl-/ ▸*v.* [*trans.*] instill (an attitude, idea, or habit) by persistent instruction: *the failures of the churches to inculcate a sense of moral responsibility.* ■ teach (someone) an attitude, idea, or habit by such instruction: *they will try to* **inculcate** *you* **with** *a respect for culture.* ▷mid 16th cent.: from Latin *inculcat-* 'pressed in,' from the verb *inculcare*, from *in-* 'into' + *calcare* 'to tread' (from *calx, calc-* 'heel'). —**in·cul·ca·tion** /ˌinkəlˈkāSHən/ *n.* —**in·cul·ca·tor** /-ˌkātər/ *n.*

in·cul·pate /inˈkəlˌpāt; ˈinkəl-/ ▸*v.* [*trans.*] *archaic* accuse or blame. ■ incriminate: *someone placed the pistol in your room in order to inculpate you.* ▷late 18th cent.: from late Latin *inculpat-* 'made culpable,' from the verb *inculpare*, from *in-* 'upon, toward' + *culpare* 'to blame' (from *culpa* 'fault'). —**in·cul·pa·tion** /ˌinkəlˈpāSHən/ *n.* —**in·cul·pa·to·ry** /inˈkəlpəˌtôrē/ *adj.*

in·cul·tu·ra·tion ▸*n.* variant spelling of **ENCULTURATION**.

in·cum·ben·cy /inˈkəmbənsē/ ▸*n.* (*pl.* **-cies**) the holding of an office or the period during which one is held.

in·cum·bent /inˈkəmbənt/ ▸*adj.* **1** [*predic.*] (**incumbent on/upon**) necessary for (someone) as a duty or responsibility: *it is incumbent on all decent people to concentrate on destroying this evil.* **2** [*attrib.*] (of an official or regime) currently holding office: *the incumbent president had been defeated.*
▸*n.* the holder of an office or post. ▷late Middle English (as a noun): from Anglo-Latin *incumbens, incumbent-*, from Latin *incumbere* 'lie or lean on,' from *in-* 'upon' + a verb related to *cubare* 'lie.'

in·cu·na·ble /inˈkyo͞onəbəl/ ▸*n.* one book in a collection of incunabula.

in·cu·nab·u·la /ˌinkəˈnab-yələ; ˌiNG-/ ▸*n.* (*sing.* **in·cu·nab·u·lum** /ˌinkəˈnabyələm; ˌiNG-/ or **in·cu·na·ble** /inˈkyo͞onəbəl/) early printed books, esp. those printed before 1501. ■ *archaic* the early stages of the development of something. ▷early 19th cent.: Latin (neuter plural), 'swaddling clothes, cradle,' from *in-* 'into' + *cunae* 'cradle.' —**in·cu·nab·u·list** /-list/ *n.*

in·cur /inˈkər; iNG-/ ▸*v.* (**-curred, -cur·ring**) [*trans.*] become subject to (something unwelcome or unpleasant) as a result of one's own behavior or actions: *I will pay any expenses incurred.* ▷late Middle English: from Latin *incurrere*, from *in-* 'toward' + *currere* 'run.' —**in·cur·rence** /-əns/ *n.*

in·cu·ri·ous /inˈkyo͝orēəs/ ▸*adj.* (of a person or their manner) not eager to know something; lacking curiosity. ▷late 16th cent. (in the sense 'careless'): partly from Latin *incuriosus* 'careless, indifferent,' from *in-* 'not' + *curiosus* 'careful' (see **CURIOUS**); partly from **IN-**[1] 'not' + **CURIOUS**. —**in·cu·ri·os·i·ty** /-ˌkyo͝orēˈäsitē/ *n.* —**in·cu·ri·ous·ly** *adv.* —**in·cu·ri·ous·ness** *n.*

in·cur·rent /inˈkərənt; -ˈkə-rənt/ ▸*adj. chiefly Zoology* (of a vessel or opening) conveying fluid inward. The opposite of **EXCURRENT**. ▷late 16th cent. (in the sense 'falling within (a period)'): from Latin *incurrent-* 'running in,' from the verb *incurrere* (see **INCUR**).

in·cur·sion /inˈkərZHən/ ▸*n.* an invasion or attack, esp. a sudden or brief one: *incursions into enemy territory.* ▷late Middle English (formerly also as *encursion*): from Latin *incursio(n-)*, from the verb *incurrere* (see **INCUR**). —**in·cur·sive** /-siv/ *adj.*

in·cur·vate /inˈkərˌvāt; ˈinkər-/ ▸*v.* [*intrans.*] [usu. as *adj.*] (**incurvated**) curve inward.
▸*adj.* curved inward. ▷late Middle English (as an adjective): from Latin *incurvat-* 'bent into a curve,' from the verb *incurvare*. —**in·cur·va·tion** /ˌinkərˈvāSHən/ *n.*

in·curve /inˈkərv/ ▸*v.* [*intrans.*] [usu. as *adj.*] (**incurved**) curve inward: *incurved horns.* ▷late Middle English: from Latin *incurvare*, from *in-* 'in, toward' + *curvare* 'to curve.'

in·cus /ˈiNGkəs/ ▸*n.* (*pl.* **in·cu·des** /inˈkyo͞oˌdēz/) *Anatomy* a small anvil-shaped bone in the middle ear, transmitting vibrations between the malleus and stapes. ▷mid 17th cent.: from Latin, literally 'anvil.'

in·cuse /inˈkyo͞oz; -ˈkyo͞os/ ▸*n.* an impression hammered or stamped on a coin.
▸*v.* [*trans.*] mark (a coin) with a figure by impressing it with a stamp.
▸*adj.* hammered or stamped on a coin. ▷early 19th cent.: from Latin *incusus* 'forged with a hammer,' past participle of *incudere*, from *in-* 'into' + *cudere* 'to forge.'

Ind. ▸*abbr.* ■ Independent. ■ India. ■ Indian. ■ Indiana.

in·debt·ed /inˈdetid/ ▸*adj.* owing money: *heavily indebted countries.* ■ owing gratitude for a service or favor: *I am* **indebted to** *her for her help in indexing my book.* ▷Middle English *endetted*, from Old French *endette* 'involved in debt,' past participle of *endetter*. The spelling change in the 16th cent. was due to association with medieval Latin *indebitare* (based on Latin *debitum* 'debt'). —**in·debt·ed·ness** *n.*

in·de·cen·cy /inˈdēsənsē/ ▸*n.* (*pl.* **-cies**) indecent behavior: *a law governing indecency on cable television.* ■ an indecent act, gesture, or expression.

in·de·cent /inˈdēsənt/ ▸*adj.* not conforming with generally accepted standards of behavior or propriety; obscene: *the film was grossly indecent.* ■ not appropriate or fitting: *they leaped on the suggestion with indecent haste.* ▷late 16th cent.: from French *indécent* or Latin *indecent-*, from *in-* 'not' + *decent-* 'being fitting' (see **DECENT**). —**in·de·cent·ly** *adv.*

in·de·cent as·sault ▸*n.* see **SEXUAL ASSAULT**.

in·de·cent ex·po·sure ▸*n.* the crime of intentionally showing one's sexual organs in public. ■ the act of outraging public decency by being naked in a public place.

in·de·ci·pher·a·ble /ˌindiˈsīfərəbəl/ ▸*adj.* not able to be read or understood: *indecipherable scrawls.*

in·de·ci·sion /ˌindiˈsizHən/ ▸*n.* the inability to make a decision quickly. ▷mid 18th cent.: from French *indécision,* from *in-* (expressing negation) + *décision,* from Latin *decisio(n-),* from the verb *decidere* (see **DECIDE**).

in·de·ci·sive /ˌindiˈsīsiv/ ▸*adj.* **1** not settling an issue: *these experimental results are indecisive.* **2** (of a person) not having or showing the ability to make decisions quickly and effectively. —**in·de·ci·sive·ly** *adv.* —**in·de·ci·sive·ness** *n.*

in·de·clin·a·ble /ˌindiˈklīnəbəl/ ▸*adj. Grammar* (of a noun, pronoun, or adjective in a highly inflected language) having no inflections. ▷late Middle English: via French from Latin *indeclinabilis,* from *in-* 'not' + *declinabilis* 'able to be inflected' (see **DECLINE**).

in·de·com·pos·a·ble /ˌindēkəmˈpōzəbəl/ ▸*adj. Mathematics* unable to be expressed as a product of factors or otherwise decomposed into simpler elements.

in·de·co·rum /ˌindiˈkôrəm/ ▸*n.* failure to conform to good taste, propriety, or etiquette. ▷late 16th cent. (denoting an indecorous act): from Latin, neuter of *indecorus* (see **INDECOROUS**).

in·deed /inˈdēd/ ▸*adv.* **1** used to emphasize a statement or response confirming something already suggested: *it was not expected to last long, and indeed it took less than three weeks | "She should have no trouble hearing him." "No indeed."* ■ used to emphasize a description, typically of a quality or condition: *it was a very good buy indeed | thank you very much indeed.* **2** used to introduce a further and stronger or more surprising point: *the idea is attractive to many men and indeed to many women.* **3** used in a response to express interest, incredulity, or contempt: *"His neck was broken." "Indeed?" | Nice boys, indeed—they were going to smash his head in!* ■ expressing interest of an ironical kind with repetition of a question just asked: *"Who'd believe it?" "Who indeed?"* ▷Middle English: originally as *in deed.*

in·deed·y /inˈdēdē/ ▸*adv.* informal term for **INDEED** (sense 1): *Yes, indeedy! That was a good question.*

indef. ▸*abbr.* indefinite.

in·de·fat·i·ga·ble /ˌindəˈfatigəbəl/ ▸*adj.* (of a person or their efforts) persisting tirelessly: *an indefatigable defender of human rights.* ▷early 17th cent.: from French, or from Latin *indefatigabilis,* from *in-* 'not' + *de-* 'away, completely' + *fatigare* 'wear out.' —**in·de·fat·i·ga·bil·i·ty** /-ˌfatigəˈbilitē/ *n.* —**in·de·fat·i·ga·bly** /-blē/ *adv.*

in·de·fea·si·ble /ˌindəˈfēzəbəl/ ▸*adj. chiefly Law & Philosophy* not able to be lost, annulled, or overturned: *an indefeasible right.* —**in·de·fea·si·bil·i·ty** /-ˌfēzəˈbilitē/ *n.* —**in·de·fea·si·bly** /-blē/ *adv.*

in·de·fect·i·ble /ˌindəˈfektəbəl/ ▸*adj. rare* not liable to fail, end, or decay. ■ perfect; faultless.

in·de·fen·si·ble /ˌindəˈfensəbəl/ ▸*adj.* **1** not justifiable by argument: *the policy of apartheid was morally indefensible.* **2** not able to be protected against attack: *the towns were tactically indefensible.* —**in·de·fen·si·bil·i·ty** /-ˌfensəˈbilitē/ *n.* —**in·de·fen·si·bly** /-blē/ *adv.*

in·def·i·nite /inˈdefənit/ ▸*adj.* lasting for an unknown or unstated length of time: *they may face indefinite detention.* ■ not clearly expressed or defined; vague: *their status remains indefinite.* ■ *Grammar* (of a word, inflection, or phrase) not determining the person, thing, time, etc., referred to. ▷mid 16th cent.: from Latin *indefinitus,* from *in-* 'not' + *definitus* 'defined, set within limits' (see **DEFINITE**). —**in·def·i·nite·ness** *n.*

in·def·i·nite ar·ti·cle ▸*n. Grammar* a determiner (*a* and *an* in English) that introduces a noun phrase and implies that the thing referred to is nonspecific (as in *she bought me a book; government is an art; he went to a public school*). Typically, the indefinite article is used to introduce new concepts into a discourse. Compare with **DEFINITE ARTICLE**.

in·def·i·nite in·te·gral ▸*n. Mathematics* an integral expressed without limits, and so containing an arbitrary constant.

in·def·i·nite·ly /inˈdefənitlē/ ▸*adv.* for an unlimited or unspecified period of time: *talks cannot go on indefinitely.* ■ [as *submodifier*] to an unlimited or unspecified degree or extent: *an indefinitely large number of channels.*

in·def·i·nite pro·noun ▸*n. Grammar* a pronoun that does not refer to any person, amount, or thing in particular, e.g., *anything, something, anyone, everyone.*

in·de·his·cent /ˌindiˈhisənt/ ▸*adj. Botany* (of a pod or fruit) not splitting open to release the seeds when ripe. —**in·de·his·cence** *n.*

in·del·i·ble /inˈdeləbəl/ ▸*adj.* (of ink or a pen) making marks that cannot be removed. ■ not able to be forgotten or removed: *his story made an indelible impression on me.* ▷late 15th cent. (as *indeleble*): from French, or from Latin *indelebilis,* from *in-* 'not' + *delebilis* (from *delere* 'efface, delete'). The ending was altered under the influence of **-IBLE**. —**in·del·i·bil·i·ty** /-ˌdeləˈbilitē/ *n.* —**in·del·i·bly** /-blē/ *adv.*

in·del·i·cate /inˈdelikit/ ▸*adj.* having or showing a lack of sensitive understanding or tact: *forgive me asking an indelicate question, but how are you for money?* ■ slightly indecent: *an earthy, often indelicate sense of humor.* —**in·del·i·ca·cy** /-kəsē/ *n.* (*pl.* **-cies**) —**in·del·i·cate·ly** *adv.*

in·dem·ni·fy /inˈdemnəˌfī/ ▸*v.* (**-fies, -fied**) [*trans.*] compensate (someone) for harm or loss: *the amount of insurance that may be carried to indemnify the owner in the event of a loss.* ■ secure (someone) against legal responsibility for their actions: *the newspaper could not be forced to* **indemnify** *the city* **for** *personal-injury liability that might result from accidents involving newsracks.* ▷early 17th cent.: from Latin *indemnis* 'unhurt, free from loss or damage,' from *in-* (expressing negation) + *damnum* 'loss, damage.' —**in·dem·ni·fi·ca·tion** /-ˌdemnəfiˈkāsHən/ *n.* —**in·dem·ni·fi·er** *n.*

in·dem·ni·ty /inˈdemnitē/ ▸*n.* (*pl.* **-ties**) security or protection against a loss or other financial burden: *no indemnity will be given for loss of cash.* ■ security against or exemption from legal responsibility for one's actions: *a deed of indemnity | even warranties and indemnities do not provide complete protection.* ■ a sum of money paid as compensation, esp. a sum exacted by a victor in war as one condition of peace. ▷late Middle English: from French *indemnite,* from late Latin *indemnitas,* from *indemnis* 'unhurt, free from loss.'

in·de·mon·stra·ble /ˌindəˈmänstrəbəl; inˈdemən-/ ▸*adj.* not able to be proved or demonstrated. ■ *Philosophy* (of a truth) axiomatic and hence unprovable.

in·dene /ˈinˌdēn/ ▸*n. Chemistry* a colorless liquid hydrocarbon, obtained from coal tar and used in making synthetic resins. • A bicyclic aromatic compound; chem. formula: C_9H_8. ▷late 19th cent.: from **INDOLE** + **-ENE**.

in·dent[1] ▸*v.* /inˈdent/ [*trans.*] **1** start (a line of text) or position (a block of text, table, etc.) further from the margin than the main part of the text. **2** (usu. **be indented**) form deep recesses in (a line or surface): *a coastline indented by many fjords.* ■ make toothlike notches in: *it has rounded leaves indented at the tip.* **3** [*intrans.*] *Brit.* make a requisition or written order for something. **4** *historical* divide (a document drawn up in duplicate) into its two copies with a zigzag line, thus ensuring identification. ■ draw up (a legal document) in exact duplicate.
▸*n.* /inˈdent; ˈinˌdent/ **1** a space left by indenting a line or block of text. **2** an indentation: *every indent in the coastline.* **3** *Brit.* an official order or requisition for specified goods or stores. **4** an indenture. ▷late Middle English (as a verb in the sense 'give a zigzag outline to, divide by a zigzag line'): from Anglo-Norman French *endenter* or medieval Latin *indentare,* from *en-, in-* 'into' + Latin *dens, dent-* 'tooth.' —**in·den·tor** /-tər/ *n.*

in·dent[2] ▸*v.* [*trans.*] make a dent or depression in (something): *his chin was firm and slightly indented.* ■ impress (a mark) on something.

in·den·ta·tion /ˌindenˈtāsHən/ ▸*n.* **1** the action of indenting or the state of being indented: *paragraphs are marked off by indentation | an indentation for each change of speaker.* **2** a deep recess in a surface or coastline: *the indentation between the upper lip and the nose.* ■ a toothlike notch: *the leaves are covered in indentations.*

in·den·ta·tion test ▸*n.* a test for determining the hardness of a solid by making an indentation in a sample under standard conditions and measuring the size of the indentation or the distance moved by the indenter.

in·dent·ed /inˈdentid/ ▸*adj. Heraldry* divided or edged with a zigzag line.

in·dent·er /inˈdentər/ ▸*n.* a small hard object used for producing an indentation in a solid in an indentation test.

in·den·tion /inˈdencHən/ ▸*n.* archaic term for **INDENTATION**.

in·den·ture /inˈdencHər/ ▸*n.* a formal legal agreement, contract, or document, in particular: ■ *historical* a deed of contract of which copies were made for the contracting parties with the edges indented for identification. ■ a formal list, certificate, or inventory. ■ an agreement binding an apprentice to a master: *the 30 apprentices have received their indentures on completion of their training.* ■ *historical* a contract by which a person agreed to work for a set period for a landowner in a British colony in exchange for passage to the colony. ■ the fact of being bound to service by such an agreement: *men in their first year after* **indenture to** *the Company of Watermen and Lightermen.*
▸*v.* [*trans.*] (usu. **be indentured to**) *chiefly historical* bind (someone) by an indenture as an apprentice or laborer: [as *adj.*] (**indentured**) *landowners tried to get their estates cultivated by indentured laborers.* ▷late Middle English *endenture,* via Anglo-Norman French from medieval Latin *indentura,* from *indentatus,* past participle of *indentare* (see **INDENT**[1]). —**in·den·ture·ship** /-ˌsHip/ *n.*

In·de·pend·ence /ˌindəˈpendəns/ a historic city in northwestern Missouri, east of Kansas City; pop. 113,288.

in·de·pend·ence /ˌindəˈpendəns/ ▸*n.* the fact or state of being independent: *Argentina gained independence from Spain in 1816 | I've always valued my independence.* See note at **LIBERTY**. ▷mid 17th cent.: from **INDEPENDENT**, partly on the pattern of French *indépendance.*

In·de·pend·ence Day ▸*n.* another term for **FOURTH OF JULY**. ■ a day celebrating the anniversary of national independence.

In·de·pend·ence Hall a building in Philadelphia where the U.S. Declaration of Independence was proclaimed and outside which the Liberty Bell is kept.

in·de·pend·en·cy /ˌindəˈpendənsē/ ▸*n.* (*pl.* **-cies**) **1** *rare* an independent or self-governing state. **2** archaic term for **INDEPENDENCE**.

in·de·pend·ent /ˌindəˈpendənt/ ▸*adj.* **1** free from outside control; not depending on another's authority: *the study is totally* **independent of** *central government | Canada's largest independent investment firm.* ■ (of a country) self-governing: *India became independent in 1947.* ■ not belonging to or supported by a political party: *the independent candidate.* ■ (of broadcasting, a school, etc.) not supported by public funds. ■ not influenced or affected by others; impartial: *a thorough and independent investigation of the case.* ■ (**Independent**) *historical* Congregational. **2** not depending on another for livelihood or subsistence: *I wanted to remain independent in old age.* ■ capable of thinking or acting for oneself: *advice for independent travelers.* ■ (of income or resources) making it unnecessary to earn one's living: *a woman of independent means.* **3** not connected with another or with each other; separate: *we need two independent witnesses to testify | the legislature and the judicature are* **independent of** *each other.* ■ not depending on something else for strength or effectiveness; freestanding: *an independent electric shower.* ■ *Mathematics* (of one of a set of axioms, equations, or quantities) incapable of being expressed in terms of, or derived or deduced from, the others.
▸*n.* an independent person or body. ■ an independent political candidate, voter, etc. ■ (**Independent**) *historical* a Congregationalist. ▷early 17th cent. (as an adjective): partly on the pattern of French *indépendant.* —**in·de·pend·ent·ly** *adv.*

in·de·pend·ent sus·pen·sion ▸*n.* a form of vehicle suspension in which each wheel is supported independently of the others.

in·de·pend·ent var·i·a·ble ▸*n. Mathematics* a variable (often denoted by *x*) whose variation does not depend on that of another.

in-depth ▸*adj.* comprehensive and thorough: *in-depth interviews.*

in·de·scrib·a·ble /ˌindiˈskrībəbəl/ ▸*adj.* too unusual, extreme, or indefinite to be adequately described: *most prisoners suffered indescribable hardship.* —**in·de·scrib·a·bil·i·ty** /-ˌskrībəˈbilitē/ *n.* —**in·de·scrib·a·bly** /-blē/ *adv.*

in·de·struct·i·ble /ˌindiˈstrəktəbəl/ ▸*adj.* not able to be destroyed: *indestructible plastic containers.* —**in·de·struct·i·bil·i·ty** /-ˌstrəktəˈbilitē/ *n.* —**in·de·struct·i·bly** /-blē/ *adv.*

in·de·ter·mi·na·ble /ˌindiˈtərmənəbəl/ ▸*adj.* not able to be definitely ascertained, calculated, or identified: *a woman of indeterminable age.* ■ (of a dispute or difficulty) not able to be resolved. ▷late 15th cent. (in the sense 'unable to be limited'): from late Latin *indeterminabilis,* from *in-* 'not' + *determinabilis* (see **DETERMINABLE**). —**in·de·ter·mi·na·bly** /-blē/ *adv.*

Pronunciation Key ə *ago;* ər *over;* ˈə or ˌə *up;* ˈər or ˌər *fur;* a *hat;* ā *rate;* ä *car;* CH *chew;* e *let;* ē *see;* e(ə)r *air;* i *fit;* ī *by;* i(ə)r *ear;* NG *sing;* ō *go;* ô *for;* oi *boy;* o͝o *good;* o͞o *goo;* ou *out;* SH *she;* TH *thin;* T̲H̲ *then;* (h)w *why;* ZH *vision*

in·de·ter·mi·na·cy prin·ci·ple /ˌindiˈtərmənəsē/ ▶*n.* another term for UNCERTAINTY PRINCIPLE.

in·de·ter·mi·nate /ˌindiˈtərmənit/ ▶*adj.* not certain, known, or established: *the date of manufacture is indeterminate.* ■ left doubtful; vague: *many felt that the ending rendered the story incomplete, or at least indeterminate.* ■ (of a judicial sentence) such that the convicted person's conduct determines the date of release. ■ *Mathematics* (of a quantity) having no definite or definable value. ■ *Medicine* (of a condition) from which a diagnosis of the underlying cause cannot be made: *indeterminate colitis.* ■ *Botany* (of a plant shoot) not having all the axes terminating in a flower bud and so producing a shoot of indefinite length. ▷early 17th cent.: from late Latin *indeterminatus,* from *in-* 'not' + Latin *determinatus* 'limited, determined' (see DETERMINATE). **—in·de·ter·mi·na·cy** /-nəsē/ *n.* **—in·de·ter·mi·nate·ly** *adv.* **—in·de·ter·mi·nate·ness** *n.*

in·de·ter·mi·nate vow·el ▶*n. Phonetics* the vowel heard in "*a* mom*e*nt *a*go"; a schwa.

in·de·ter·mi·na·tion /ˌindiˌtərməˈnāshən/ ▶*n.* the state of being uncertain or undecided.

in·de·ter·min·ism /ˌindiˈtərməˌnizəm/ ▶*n.* **1** *Philosophy* the doctrine that not all events are wholly determined by antecedent causes. **2** the state of being uncertain or undecided. **—in·de·ter·min·ist** *n.* **—in·de·ter·min·is·tic** /-ˌtərməˈnistik/ *adj.*

in·dex /ˈinˌdeks/ ▶*n.* (*pl.* **-dex·es** or esp. in technical use **-di·ces** /-dəˌsēz/) **1** an alphabetical list of names, subjects, etc., with references to the places where they occur, typically found at the end of a book. ■ an alphabetical list by title, subject, author, or other category of a collection of books or documents, e.g., in a library. ■ *Computing* a set of items each of which specifies one of the records of a file and contains information about its address. **2** an indicator, sign, or measure of something: *exam results may serve as an* **index of** *the teacher's effectiveness.* ■ a figure in a system or scale representing the average value of specified prices, shares, or other items as compared with some reference figure: *the hundred-shares index closed down 9.3.* ■ a pointer on an instrument, showing a quantity, a position on a scale, etc. ■ [with *adj.*] a number giving the magnitude of a physical property or another measured phenomenon in terms of a standard: *the oral hygiene index was calculated as the sum of the debris and calculus indices.* **3** *Mathematics* an exponent or other superscript or subscript number appended to a quantity. **4** *Printing* a symbol shaped like a pointing hand, typically used to draw attention to a note. **5** (**the Index**) short for INDEX LIBRORUM PROHIBITORUM.
▶*v.* [*trans.*] **1** record (names, subjects, etc.) in an index: *the list indexes theses under regional headings.* ■ provide an index to. **2** link the value of (prices, wages, or other payments) automatically to the value of a price index: *the Supreme Soviet passed legislation* **indexing** *wages* **to** *prices.* **3** [*intrans.*] [often as *n.*] (**indexing**) (of a machine or part of one) rotate or otherwise move from one predetermined position to another in order to carry out a sequence of operations. ▷late Middle English: from Latin *index, indic-* 'forefinger, informer, sign,' from *in-* 'toward' + a second element related to *dicere* 'say' or *dicare* 'make known'; compare with INDICATE. The original sense 'index finger' (with which one points) came to mean 'pointer' (late 16th cent.), and figuratively something that serves to point to a fact or conclusion; hence a list of topics in a book ("pointing" to their location). **—in·dex·a·ble** *adj.* **—in·dex·a·tion** /ˌindekˈsāshən/ *n.* **—in·dex·er** *n.* **—in·dex·i·ble** *adj.*

in·dex case ▶*n. Medicine* the first identified case in a group of related cases of a particular communicable or heritable disease.

in·dex fin·ger ▶*n.* the finger next to the thumb; the forefinger.

in·dex fos·sil ▶*n. Geology* a fossil that is useful for dating and correlating the strata in which it is found.

in·dex·i·cal /inˈdeksikəl/ *Linguistics* ▶*adj.* another term for DEICTIC.
▶*n.* an indexical word or expression. ▷early 20th cent.: coined in this sense by the American philosopher C. S. Peirce.

In·dex Li·bro·rum Pro·hib·i·to·rum /ˈinˌdeks lĭˈbrôrəm ˌprōhibəˈtôrəm/ an official list of books that Roman Catholics were forbidden to read or that were to be read only in expurgated editions, as contrary to Catholic faith or morals. The first Index was issued in 1557; it was revised at intervals until abolished in 1966. ▷Latin, 'index of forbidden books.'

In·di·a /ˈindēə/ a country in southern Asia that occupies the greater part of the Indian subcontinent; pop. 1,065,000,000; capital, New Delhi; official languages, Hindi and English (14 other languages are recognized as official in certain regions; of these, Bengali, Gujarati, Marathi, Tamil, Telugu, and Urdu have the most first-language speakers). Hindi name BHARAT. ■ a code word representing the letter I, used in radio communication. ▷via Latin from Greek *India,* from *Indos,* the name of the Indus River, from Persian *Hind,* from Sanskrit *sindhu* 'river,' specifically 'the Indus,' also 'the region around the Indus' (compare with SINDHI). Both the Greeks and the Persians extended the name to include all the country east of the Indus. Compare with HINDI and HINDU.

Much of India was united under a Muslim sultanate based around Delhi from the 12th century until incorporated in the Mogul empire in the 16th century. Colonial intervention began in the late 17th century, particularly by the British; in 1765, the East India Company acquired the right to administer Bengal. In 1858, after the Indian Mutiny, Britain took over the company's authority, and in 1876 Queen Victoria was proclaimed Empress of India. Independence was won in 1947, at which time India was partitioned, and Pakistan was created from mainly Muslim territories in the northeast (now Bangladesh) and the northwest. A member of the Commonwealth of Nations, India is the second most populous country in the world.

In·di·a ink ▶*n.* deep black ink containing dispersed carbon particles, used esp. in drawing and technical graphics. ▷mid 17th cent.: originally applied to Chinese and Japanese pigments prepared in solid blocks and imported to Europe via India.

In·di·a·man /ˈindēəmən/ ▶*n.* (*pl.* **-men**) *historical* a ship engaged in trade with India or the East or West Indies, esp. an East Indiaman. ▷early 18th cent.: from INDIA + *-man* from MAN-OF-WAR.

In·di·an /ˈindēən/ ▶*adj.* **1** of or relating to the indigenous peoples of America. **2** of or relating to India or to the subcontinent comprising India, Pakistan, and Bangladesh.
▶*n.* **1** an American Indian. **2** a native or national of India, or a person of Indian descent. **—In·di·an·i·za·tion** /ˌindēəniˈzāshən/ *n.* **—In·di·an·ize** /-ˌnīz/ *v.* **—In·di·an·ness** *n.*

USAGE **Indian**, meaning 'native of America before the arrival of Europeans,' is objected to by many who now favor **Native American**. There are others (including many members of these ethnic groups), however, who see nothing wrong with **Indian** or **American Indian**, which are long-established terms, although the preference where possible is to refer to specific peoples, as **Apache**, **Delaware**, and so on. The terms **Amerind** and **Amerindian**, once proposed as alternatives to **Indian**, are used in linguistics and anthropology, but have never gained widespread use. Newer alternatives, not widely used or established, include **First Nation** (esp. in Canada) and the more generic **aboriginal peoples**. It should be noted that **Indian** is held by many not to include some American groups, for example, Aleuts and Eskimos. A further consideration is that **Indian** also (and in some contexts primarily) refers to inhabitants of India or their descendants, who may be referred to as "Asian Indians" to prevent misunderstanding.
See also **usage** at AMERICAN INDIAN .

In·di·an·a /ˌindēˈanə/ a state in the eastern central U.S.; pop. 6,080,485; capital, Indianapolis; statehood, Dec. 11, 1816 (19). It was colonized by the French in the early 1700s and ceded to Britain in 1763. It passed to the U.S. in 1783 by the Treaty of Paris. **—In·di·an·an** *n.* & *adj.*

In·di·an·ap·o·lis /ˌindēəˈnapələs/ the capital of Indiana, in the central part of the state; pop. 791,926. The city hosts the Indy 500, an annual 500-mile (804.5-km) car race.

In·di·an bi·son ▶*n.* another term for GAUR.

In·di·an burn ▶*n. informal* an act of placing both hands on a person's arm and then twisting it with a wringing motion to produce a burning sensation.

In·di·an club ▶*n.* each of a pair of bottle-shaped clubs swung to exercise the arms in gymnastics or to perform juggling tricks.

In·di·an co·bra ▶*n.* another term for SPECTACLED COBRA.

In·di·an corn ▶*n.* any primitive corn with colorful variegated kernels, dried and used for decoration. ■ another term for CORN[1].

In·di·an de·fense ▶*n.* [usu. with *adj.*] *Chess* a defense in which Black responds to White's advance of the queen's pawn by moving the king's knight to the *f6* square, usually following with a fianchetto.

In·di·an el·e·phant ▶*n.* the elephant of southern Asia, which is smaller than the African elephant, with smaller ears and only one lip to the trunk. It is often tamed as a beast of burden in India. Also called **ASIAN ELEPHANT.** • *Elephas maximus*, family Elephantidae.

In·di·an file ▶*n.* another term for **SINGLE FILE.** ▷mid 18th cent.: so called because it was believed that North American Indians usually marched in this order.

In·di·an hemp ▶*n.* see **HEMP.**

In·di·an ink ▶*n.* British term for **INDIA INK.**

In·di·an·ism /ˈindēəˌnizəm/ ▶*n.* **1** devotion to or adoption of the customs and culture of North American Indians. **2** a word or idiom characteristic of Indian English or North American Indians.

In·di·an meal ▶*n.* meal ground from corn.

In·di·an Mu·ti·ny a revolt of Indians against British rule, 1857–58. Also called **SEPOY MUTINY.**

Discontent with British administration resulted in widespread mutinies in British garrison towns, with accompanying massacres of white soldiers and inhabitants. After a series of sieges (most notably that of Lucknow) and battles, the revolt was put down; it was followed by the institution of direct rule by the British Crown in place of the East India Company administration.

In·di·an Na·tion·al Con·gress a broad-based political party in India, founded in 1885 and the principal party in government since independence in 1947. Following splits in the party, the Indian National Congress (I), formed by Indira Gandhi as a breakaway group, (the I standing for Indira) was confirmed in 1981 as the official Congress Party.

In·di·an O·cean an ocean south of India that extends from the eastern coast of Africa to the East Indies and Australia.

In·di·an paint·brush ▶*n.* see **PAINTBRUSH** (sense 2).

In·di·an pipe ▶*n.* a plant with a yellowish stem that bears a single drooping flower, native to North America and northeastern Asia. It lacks chlorophyll and obtains nourishment via symbiotic fungi in its roots. • *Monotropa uniflora*, family Monotropaceae.

Indian pipe

In·di·an poke ▶*n.* see **POKE**[3] (sense 2).

In·di·an red ▶*n.* a red ferric oxide pigment made typically by roasting ferrous salts.

In·di·an rhi·noc·er·os ▶*n.* a large one-horned rhinoceros with prominent skin folds and a prehensile upper lip, found in northeastern India and Nepal. • *Rhinoceros unicornis*, family Rhinocerotidae.

In·di·an rope-trick ▶*n.* the supposed feat, performed in the Indian subcontinent, of climbing an upright, unsupported length of rope.

In·di·an run·ner ▶*n.* a duck of a slender upright breed, typically with white or yellowish-brown plumage, kept for egg laying.

In·di·an shot ▶*n.* see **CANNA.**

In·di·an sign ▶*n. dated* a magic spell or curse.

In·di·an sub·con·ti·nent the part of Asia south of the Himalayas that forms a peninsula, which extends into the Indian Ocean between the Arabian Sea and the Bay of Bengal. Historically forming the whole territory of greater India, the region is now divided among India, Pakistan, and Bangladesh.

In·di·an sum·mer ▶*n.* a period of unusually dry, warm weather occurring in late autumn. ■ a period of happiness or success occurring late in life.

In·di·an yel·low ▶*n.* an orange-yellow pigment originally obtained from the urine of cows fed on mango leaves.

In·di·a pa·per ▶*n.* soft, absorbent paper, originally imported from China and used for proofs of engravings. ■ very thin, tough, opaque printing paper, used esp. for Bibles.

In·di·a rub·ber ▶*n.* natural rubber.

In·di·a rub·ber tree ▶*n.* another term for **RUBBER TREE.**

In·dic /ˈindik/ ▶*adj.* relating to or denoting the group of Indo-European languages comprising Sanskrit and the modern Indian languages that are its descendants.
▶*n.* this language group. ▷via Latin from Greek *Indikos*, from *India* (see **INDIA**).

indic. ▶*abbr.* ■ indicating. ■ indicative. ■ indicator.

in·di·can /ˈindiˌkan/ ▶*n. Biochemistry* a potassium salt present in urine, in which it occurs as a product of the metabolism of indole. • Alternative name: **potassium indoxylsulphate**; chem. formula $C_8H_6NOSO_2OH$. ▷mid 19th cent.: from Latin *indicum* 'indigo' (because of its early use denoting an indoxyl glucoside occurring in the leaves of indigo plants) + **-AN.**

in·di·cant /ˈindikənt/ ▶*n.* a thing that indicates something. ▷early 17th cent.: from Latin *indicant-* 'pointing out,' from the verb *indicare* (see **INDICATE**).

in·di·cate /ˈindiˌkāt/ [*trans.*] ▶*v.* **1** point out; show: *dotted lines indicate the text's margins.* ■ be a sign or symptom of; strongly imply: *sales indicate a growing market for such art* | [with *clause*] *his tone indicated that he didn't hold out much hope.* ■ admit to or state briefly: *the president indicated his willingness to use force against the rebels.* ■ (of a person) direct attention to (someone or something) by means of a gesture: *he indicated Cindy with a brief nod of the head.* ■ (of a gauge or meter) register a reading of (a quantity, dimension, etc.). **2** (usu. **be indicated**) suggest as a desirable or necessary course of action: *the treatment is likely to be indicated in severely depressed patients.* ▷early 17th cent.: from Latin *indicat-* 'pointed out,' from the verb *indicare*, from *in-* 'toward' + *dicare* 'make known.'

in·di·cat·ed horse·pow·er ▶*n.* the power produced in a reciprocating engine by the working of the cylinders.

in·di·ca·tion /ˌindiˈkāsʜən/ ▶*n.* a sign or piece of information that indicates something: *the visit was an* ***indication of*** *the improvement in relations between the countries.* See note at **SIGN.** ■ a reading given by a gauge or meter. ■ a symptom that suggests certain medical treatment is necessary: *heavy bleeding is a common* ***indication for*** *hysterectomy.*

in·dic·a·tive /inˈdikətiv/ ▶*adj.* **1** serving as a sign or indication of something: *having recurrent dreams is not necessarily* ***indicative of*** *any psychological problem.* **2** *Grammar* denoting a mood of verbs expressing simple statement of a fact. Compare with **SUBJUNCTIVE.**
▶*n. Grammar* a verb in the indicative mood. ■ (**the indicative**) the indicative mood. —**in·dic·a·tive·ly** *adv.*

in·di·ca·tor /ˈindiˌkātər/ ▶*n.* **1** a thing, esp. a trend or fact, that indicates the state or level of something: *car ownership is frequently used as an* ***indicator of*** *affluence.* **2** a device providing specific information on the state or condition of something, in particular: ■ [usu. with *adj.*] a gauge or meter of a specified kind: *a speed indicator.* ■ *Brit.* a turn signal. **3** *Chemistry* a compound that changes color at a specific pH value or in the presence of a particular substance and can be used to monitor acidity, alkalinity, or the progress of a reaction. **4** (also **indicator species**) an animal or plant species that can be used to infer conditions in a particular habitat.

in·di·ca·tor di·a·gram ▶*n.* a diagram of the variation of pressure and volume within a cylinder of a reciprocating engine.

in·dic·a·to·ry /inˈdikəˌtôrē/ ▶*adj.* rare term for **INDICATIVE.**

in·dic·a·trix /ˈindiˌkātriks; inˈdikə-/ (also **optical indicatrix**) ▶*n.* (*pl.* **-tri·ces** /-triˌsēz/) *Crystallography* an imaginary ellipsoidal surface whose axes represent the refractive indices of a crystal for light following different directions with respect to the crystal axes. ▷late 19th cent.: modern Latin, feminine of Latin *indicator* 'something that points out.'

in·di·ces /ˈindiˌsēz/ ▶ plural form of **INDEX.**

in·di·ci·a /inˈdisʜ(ē)ə/ ▶*plural n. formal* signs, indications, or distinguishing marks: *learned footnotes and other indicia of scholarship.* ■ markings used on address labels or bulk mail as a substitute for stamps. ▷early 17th cent.: plural of Latin *indicium*, from *index, indic-* 'informer, sign.'

in·dic·o·lite /inˈdikəˌlīt/ ▶*n.* an indigo-blue gem variety of lithium-bearing tourmaline. ▷early 19th cent.: from Latin *indicum* 'indigo' + **-LITE.**

in·dict /inˈdīt/ ▶*v.* [*trans.*] (usu. **be indicted**) formally accuse or charge (someone) with a serious crime: *his former manager was* ***indicted for*** *fraud.* ▷Middle English *endite, indite*, from Anglo-Norman French *enditer*, based on Latin *indicere* 'proclaim, appoint,' from *in-* 'toward' + *dicere* 'pronounce, utter.' —**in·dict·ee** /ˌindīˈtē/ *n.* —**in·dict·er** *n.*

in·dict·a·ble /inˈdītəbəl/ ▶*adj.* (of an offense) rendering the person who commits it liable to be charged with a serious crime that warrants a trial by jury. ■ (of a person) liable to be charged with a crime.

in·dic·tion /inˈdiksʜən/ ▶*n. historical* a fiscal period of fifteen years used as a means of dating events and transactions in the Roman Empire and in the papal and some royal courts. The system was instituted by the Emperor Constantine in AD 313 and was used until the 16th century in some places. ■ [with *numeral*] a particular year in such a period. ▷from Latin *indiction-*, from the verb *indicere* (see **INDICT**).

in·dict·ment /inˈdītmənt/ ▶*n.* **1** *Law* a formal charge or accusation of a serious crime: *an* ***indictment for*** *conspiracy.* ■ the action of indicting or being indicted: *the indictment of twelve people who had imported cocaine.* **2** a thing that serves to illustrate that a system or situation is bad and deserves to be condemned: *these rapidly escalating crime figures are an indictment of our society.* ▷Middle English *enditement, inditement*, from Anglo-Norman French *enditement*, from *enditer* (see **INDICT**).

in·die /ˈindē/ *informal* ▶*adj.* (of a record label or film company) not belonging to or affiliated with a major record or film company. ■ characteristic of the deliberately unpolished or uncommercialized style of such groups.
▶*n.* a pop group or record label of this type. ■ an independent film company. ▷1920s (first used with reference to film production): abbreviation of **INDEPENDENT.**

in·dif·fer·ence /inˈdif(ə)rəns/ ▶*n.* lack of interest, concern, or sympathy: *she shrugged, feigning indifference.* ■ unimportance: *it cannot be regarded as a matter of indifference.* ▷late Middle English (in the sense 'being neither good nor bad'): from Latin *indifferentia*, from *in-* 'not' + *different-* 'differing, deferring' (from the verb *differre*).

in·dif·fer·ence curve ▶*n. Economics* a curve on a graph (the axes of which represent quantities of two commodities) linking those combinations of quantities that the consumer regards as of equal value.

in·dif·fer·ent /inˈdif(ə)rənt/ ▶*adj.* **1** having no particular interest or sympathy; unconcerned: *they all seemed indifferent rather than angry* | *most workers were* ***indifferent to*** *foreign affairs.* **2** neither good nor bad; mediocre: *attempts to distinguish between good, bad, and indifferent work.* ■ not especially good; fairly bad: *a pair of indifferent watercolors.* **3** neutral in respect of some specified physical property. ■ *archaic Biology* not specialized; undifferentiated. ▷late Middle English (in the sense 'having no partiality for or against'): via Old French from Latin *indifferent-* 'not making any difference,' from *in-* 'not' + *different-* 'differing' (see **DIFFERENT**). —**in·dif·fer·ent·ly** *adv.*

in·dif·fer·ent·ism /inˈdif(ə)rənˌtizəm/ ▶*n.* the belief that differences of religious belief are of no importance. —**in·dif·fer·ent·ist** *n.*

in·di·gene /ˈindiˌjēn/ ▶*n.* an indigenous person. ▷late 16th cent.: from French *indigène*, from Latin *indigena*, from *indi-* (strengthened form of *in-* 'into') + an element related to *gignere* 'beget.'

in·dig·e·nize /inˈdijəˌnīz/ ▶*v.* [*trans.*] bring (something) under the control, dominance, or influence of native people: *English has been indigenized in different parts of the world.* —**in·dig·e·ni·za·tion** /-ˌdijəniˈzāsʜən/ *n.*

in·dig·e·nous /inˈdijənəs/ ▶*adj.* originating or occurring naturally in a particular place; native: *the indigenous peoples of Siberia* | *coriander is* ***indigenous to*** *southern Europe.* ▷mid 17th cent.: from Latin *indigena* 'a native' (see **INDIGENE**) + **-OUS.** —**in·dig·e·nous·ly** *adv.* —**in·dig·e·nous·ness** *n.*

in·di·gent /ˈindijənt/ ▶*adj.* poor; needy.
▶*n.* a needy person. ▷late Middle English: via Old French from late Latin *indigent-* 'lacking,' from the verb *indigere*, from *indi-* (strengthened form of *in-* 'into') + *egere* 'to need.' —**in·di·gence** *n.*

in·di·gest·i·ble /ˌindiˈjestəbəl/ ▶*adj.* (of food) difficult or impossible to digest. ■ *figurative* too complex or awkward to read or understand easily: *a turgid and indigestible book.* ▷late 15th cent.: via French from late Latin *indigestibilis*, from *in-* 'not' + *digestibilis* (see

DIGESTIBLE). **—in·di·gest·i·bil·i·ty** /-ˌjestəˈbilitē/ *n.* **—in·di·gest·i·bly** /-blē/ *adv.*

in·di·ges·tion /ˌindiˈjesCHən; -dī-/ ▸*n.* pain or discomfort in the stomach associated with difficulty in digesting food. ▷late Middle English: from late Latin *indigestio(n-)*, from *in-* (expressing negation) + *digestio* (see DIGESTION). **—in·di·ges·tive** /-tiv/ *adj.*

In·di·gir·ka /ˌindəˈgirkə/ a river in eastern Siberia in Russia that flows north for 1,112 miles (1,779 km) to the Arctic Ocean, where it forms a wide delta.

in·dig·nant /inˈdignənt/ ▸*adj.* feeling or showing anger or annoyance at what is perceived as unfair treatment: *he was indignant at being the object of suspicion.* ▷late 16th cent.: from Latin *indignant-* 'regarding as unworthy,' from the verb *indignari*, from *in-* 'not' + *dignus* 'worthy.' **—in·dig·nant·ly** *adv.*

in·dig·na·tion /ˌindigˈnāSHən/ ▸*n.* anger or annoyance provoked by what is perceived as unfair treatment: *the letter filled Lucy with indignation.* ▷late Middle English (also in the sense 'disdain, contempt'): from Latin *indignatio(n-)*, from *indignari* 'regard as unworthy.'

in·dig·ni·ty /inˈdignitē/ ▸*n.* (*pl.* **-ties**) treatment or circumstances that cause one to feel shame or to lose one's dignity: *the indignity of needing financial help | he was subjected to all manner of indignities.* ▷late 16th cent.: from French *indignité* or Latin *indignitas*, from *indignari* 'regard as unworthy.'

in·di·go /ˈindiˌgō/ ▸*n.* (*pl.* **-gos** or **-goes**) **1** a tropical plant of the pea family, which was formerly widely cultivated as a source of dark blue dye. • Genus *Indigofera*, family Leguminosae: several species, in particular *I. tinctoria.* **2** the dark blue dye obtained from this plant. ■ a color between blue and violet in the spectrum. ▷mid 16th cent.: from Portuguese *índigo*, via Latin from Greek *indikon*, from *indikos* 'Indian (dye)' (see INDIC).

in·di·go bunt·ing ▸*n.* see BUNTING[1].

in·di·goid /ˈindiˌgoid/ ▸*adj.* (of a dye) related to indigotin in molecular structure.

in·di·go snake ▸*n.* a large, harmless American snake that typically has bluish-black skin that may be patterned. Also called CRIBO. • *Drymarchon corais*, family Colubridae. Alternative name: **blue gopher snake.**

in·dig·o·tin /inˈdigətin; ˌindəˈgōtn/ ▸*n. Chemistry* a dark blue crystalline compound that is the main constituent of the dye indigo. • Chem. formula: $(C_8H_6NO)_2$. ▷mid 19th cent.: from INDIGO + *-t-* (for ease of pronunciation) + -IN[1].

In·dio[1] /ˈindēˌō/ a desert city in southern California, southeast of Palm Springs; pop. 36,793.

In·di·o[2] ▸*n.* (*pl.* **-os**) a member of any of the indigenous peoples of America or eastern Asia in areas formerly subject to Spain or Portugal. ▷mid 19th cent.: from Spanish and Portuguese, literally 'Indian.'

in·di·rect /ˌindəˈrekt/ ▸*adj.* **1** not directly caused by or resulting from something: *full employment would have an indirect effect on wage levels.* ■ not done directly; conducted through intermediaries: *the nature of the threat can be pieced together only from indirect evidence.* ■ (of costs) deriving from overhead charges or subsidiary work. ■ (of taxation) levied on goods and services rather than income or profits. **2** (of a route) not straight; not following the shortest way. ■ (of lighting) from a concealed source and diffusely reflected. ■ *Soccer* denoting a free kick from which a goal may not be scored directly. **3** avoiding direct mention or exposition of a subject: *an indirect attack on the Senator.* ▷late Middle English (in the sense 'not in full grammatical concord'): from medieval Latin *indirectus*, from *in-* 'not' + *directus* (see DIRECT). **—in·di·rect·ly** *adv.* **—in·di·rect·ness** *n.*

in·di·rec·tion /ˌindəˈrekSHən/ ▸*n.* indirectness or lack of straightforwardness in action, speech, or progression: *his love of intrigue and sly indirection.* ▷late 16th cent.: from INDIRECT, on the pattern of *direction.*

in·di·rect ob·ject ▸*n. Grammar* a noun phrase referring to someone or something that is affected by the action of a transitive verb (typically as a recipient), but is not the primary object (e.g., *him* in *give him the book*). Compare with DIRECT OBJECT.

in·di·rect ques·tion ▸*n. Grammar* a question in reported speech, e.g., *they asked who I was.*

in·di·rect rule ▸*n.* a system of government of one nation by another in which the governed people retain certain administrative, legal, and other powers.

in·di·rect speech ▸*n.* another term for REPORTED SPEECH.

in·dis·ci·pline /inˈdisəplin/ ▸*n.* lack of discipline.

in·dis·creet /ˌindiˈskrēt/ ▸*adj.* having, showing, or proceeding from too great a readiness to reveal things that should remain secret or private: *they have been embarrassed by indiscreet friends.* ▷late Middle English (originally as *indiscrete* in the sense 'lacking discernment or judgment'): from late Latin *indiscretus* 'not separate or distinguishable' (in medieval Latin 'careless, indiscreet'), from *in-* 'not' + *discretus* 'separate' (see DISCREET). Compare with INDISCRETE. **—in·dis·creet·ly** *adv.*

in·dis·crete /ˌindiˈskrēt/ ▸*adj. rare* not divided into distinct parts. ▷early 17th cent. (in the sense 'not separate or distinguishable'; originally as *indiscreet*): from Latin *indiscretus*, from *in-* 'not' + *discretus* 'separate' (see DISCREET). Compare with INDISCREET.

in·dis·cre·tion /ˌindiˈskreSHən/ ▸*n.* behavior or speech that is indiscreet or displays a lack of good judgment: *he knew himself all too prone to indiscretion | sexual indiscretions.* See note at SIN. ▷Middle English: from late Latin *indiscretio(n-)*, from *in-* (expressing negation) + *discretio* 'separation' (in late Latin 'discernment'), from *discernere* 'separate out, discern.'

in·dis·crim·i·nate /ˌindiˈskrimənit/ ▸*adj.* done at random or without careful judgment: *terrorist gunmen engaged in indiscriminate killing.* ■ (of a person) not using or exercising discrimination: *she was indiscriminate with her affections.* ▷late 16th cent. (in the sense 'haphazard, not selective'): from IN-[1] 'not' + Latin *discriminatus*, past participle of *discriminare* (see DISCRIMINATE). **—in·dis·crim·i·nate·ly** *adv.* **—in·dis·crim·i·nate·ness** *n.* **—in·dis·crim·i·na·tion** /-ˌskriməˈnāSHən/ *n.*

in·dis·crim·i·nat·ing /ˌindiˈskriməˌnātiNG/ ▸*adj.* making no distinctions; indiscriminate.

in·dis·pen·sa·ble /ˌindiˈspensəbəl/ ▸*adj.* absolutely necessary: *he made himself* **indispensable to** *the parish priest.* See note at NECESSARY. ▷mid 16th cent. (in the sense 'not to be allowed or provided for by ecclesiastical dispensation'): from medieval Latin *indispensabilis*, from *in-* 'not' + *dispensabilis* (see DISPENSABLE). **—in·dis·pen·sa·bil·i·ty** /-ˌspensəˈbilitē/ *n.* **—in·dis·pen·sa·ble·ness** *n.* **—in·dis·pen·sa·bly** /-blē/ *adv.*

in·dis·pose /ˌindiˈspōz/ ▸*v.* [*trans.*] *archaic* **1** make (someone) unfit for or unable to do something. **2** make (someone) averse to something: *the miseries of the revolution had totally indisposed the people toward any interference with politics.*

in·dis·posed /ˌindiˈspōzd/ ▸*adj.* **1** slightly unwell: *my mother is indisposed.* **2** averse; unwilling: *the potential audience seemed* **indisposed to** *attend.* ▷late Middle English: from IN-[1] 'not' + DISPOSED, or past participle of *indispose* 'make unwell or unwilling.' **—in·dis·po·si·tion** /ˌindispəˈziSHən/ *n.*

in·dis·sol·u·ble /ˌindiˈsälyəbəl/ ▸*adj.* unable to be destroyed; lasting: *an indissoluble friendship.* ▷late 15th cent.: from Latin *indissolubilis*, from *in-* 'not' + *dissolubilis* (see DISSOLUBLE). **—in·dis·sol·u·bil·i·ty** /-ˌsälyəˈbilitē/ *n.* **—in·dis·sol·u·bly** /-blē/ *adv.*

in·dite /inˈdīt/ ▸*v.* [*trans.*] *archaic* write; compose: *he indites the wondrous tale of Our Lord.* ▷Middle English *endite*, from Old French *enditier*, based on Latin *indicere* (see INDICT).

in·di·um /ˈindēəm/ ▸*n.* the chemical element of atomic number 49, a soft, silvery-white metal occurring naturally in association with zinc and some other metals. (Symbol: **In**) ▷mid 19th cent.: from INDIGO (because there are two characteristic indigo lines in its spectrum) + -IUM.

in·di·vid·u·al /ˌindəˈvijəwəl/ ▸*adj.* **1** [*attrib.*] single; separate: *individual tiny flowers.* **2** of or for a particular person: *the individual needs of the children.* ■ designed for use by one person: *individual serving dishes.* ■ characteristic of a particular person or thing: *individual traits of style.* ■ having a striking or unusual character; original: *she creates her own, highly individual, landscapes.*

▸*n.* a single human being as distinct from a group, class, or family: *boat trips for parties and individuals.* ■ a single member of a class: *they live in a group or as individuals, depending on the species.* ■ [with *adj.*] *informal* a person of a specified kind: *the most selfish, egotistical individual I have ever met.* ■ a distinctive or original person. ▷late Middle English (in the sense 'indivisible'): from medieval Latin *individualis*, from Latin *individuus*, from *in-* 'not' + *dividuus* 'divisible' (from *dividere* 'to divide').

in·di·vid·u·al·ism /ˌindəˈvijo͞oəˌlizəm/ ▸*n.* **1** the habit or principle of being independent and self-reliant. ■ self-centered feeling or conduct; egoism. **2** a social theory favoring freedom of action for individuals over collective or state control. **—in·di·vid·u·al·ist** *n.* & *adj.* **—in·di·vid·u·al·is·tic** /-ˌvijo͞oəˈlistik/ *adj.* **—in·di·vid·u·al·is·ti·cal·ly** *adv.*

in·di·vid·u·al·i·ty /ˌindəˌvijəˈwalitē/ ▸*n.* **1** the quality or character of a particular person or thing that distinguishes them from others of the same kind, esp. when strongly marked: *clothes with real style and individuality.* ■ (**individualities**) individual characteristics. **2** separate existence: *anything but individuality, anything but aloneness.* ▷early 17th cent.: in early use from medieval Latin *individualitas.*

in·di·vid·u·al·ize /ˌindəˈvijo͞oəˌlīz/ ▸*v.* [*trans.*] give an individual character to: *have your shirt individualized with your own club name.* ■ [usu. as *adj.*] (**individualized**) tailor (something) to suit the individual: *an individualized learning program.* **—in·di·vid·u·al·i·za·tion** /-ˌvijo͞oələˈzāSHən/ *n.*

in·di·vid·u·al·ly /ˌindəˈvijəwəlē/ ▸*adv.* **1** one by one; singly; separately: *individually wrapped cheeses.* ■ in a distinctive manner: *each sign is individually designed and crafted.* **2** personally; in an individual capacity: *partnerships and individually owned firms.*

in·di·vid·u·ate /ˌindəˈvijo͞oˌāt/ ▸*v.* [*trans.*] distinguish from others of the same kind; single out: *it is easy to individuate and enumerate the significant elements.* ▷early 17th cent.: from medieval Latin *individuat-* 'singled out,' from the verb *individuare*, from Latin *individuus*, from *in-* 'into' + *dividuus* 'divisible' (from *dividere* 'to divide'). **—in·di·vid·u·a·tion** /-ˌvijo͞oˈāSHən/ *n.*

indn. ▸*abbr.* indication.

Indo- /ˈindō/ ▸*comb. form* (used commonly in linguistic and ethnological terms) Indian; Indian and . . . : *Indo-Iranian.* ■ relating to India. ▷from Latin *Indus*, from Greek *Indos* 'Indian.'

In·do-Ar·y·an ▸*adj.* **1** relating to or denoting an Indo-European people who invaded northwestern India in the 2nd millennium BC. See ARYAN. **2** another term for INDIC.

In·do-Chi·na a peninsula in Southeast Asia that consists of Myanmar (Burma), Thailand, Malaya, Laos, Cambodia, and Vietnam; esp., the land that includes Laos, Cambodia, and Vietnam. **—In·do-Chi·nese** /CHīˈnēz; -ˈnēs/ *adj.* & *n.*

in·do·chin·ite /ˌindōˈCHīˌnīt/ ▸*n. Geology* a tektite from the strewn field in Indo-China. ▷1940s: from INDO-CHINA + -ITE[1].

in·doc·ile /inˈdäsəl/ ▸*adj.* difficult to teach or discipline; not submissive. ▷early 17th cent.: from French, or from Latin *indocilis*, from *in-* 'not' + *docilis* (see DOCILE). **—in·do·cil·i·ty** /ˌindäˈsilitē/ *n.*

in·doc·tri·nate /inˈdäktrəˌnāt/ ▸*v.* [*trans.*] teach (a person or group) to accept a set of beliefs uncritically: *broadcasting was a vehicle for indoctrinating the masses.* ■ *archaic* teach or instruct (someone): *he indoctrinated them in systematic theology.* ▷early 17th cent. (formerly also as *endoctrinate*): from EN-[1], IN-[2] 'into' + DOCTRINE + -ATE[3], or from obsolete *indoctrine* (verb), from French *endoctriner*, based on *doctrine* 'doctrine.' **—in·doc·tri·na·tion** /-ˌdäktrəˈnāSHən/ *n.* **—in·doc·tri·na·tor** /-ˌnātər/ *n.* **—in·doc·tri·na·to·ry** /-nəˌtôrē/ *adj.* .

In·do-Eu·ro·pe·an ▸*adj.* of or relating to the family of languages spoken over the greater part of Europe and Asia as far as northern India. ■ another term for PROTO-INDO-EUROPEAN.

The Indo-European languages have a history of over 3,000 years. Their unattested, reconstructed ancestor, Proto-Indo-European, is believed to have been spoken well before 4000 BC in a region somewhere to the north or south of the Black Sea. The family comprises twelve branches: Indic (including Sanskrit and its descendants), Iranian, Anatolian (an extinct group including Hittite and other languages), Armenian, Hellenic (Greek), Albanian (possibly descended from Illyrian), Italic (including Latin and the Romance languages), Celtic, Tocharian (an extinct group from central Asia), Germanic (including English, German, Dutch, Gothic, and the Scandinavian languages), Baltic, and Slavic (including Russian, Czech, Bulgarian, and Serbo-Croat).

▸*n.* **1** the ancestral Proto-Indo-European language. ■ the Indo-European family of languages. **2** a speaker of an Indo-European language, esp. Proto-Indo-European.

In·do-Ger·man·ic ▸*adj.* & *n.* former term for INDO-EUROPEAN.

In·do-I·ra·ni·an ▸*adj.* relating to or denoting a subfamily of Indo-European languages spoken in northern India and Iran.

▸*n.* the Indo-Iranian subfamily of languages, divided

into the Indic group and the Iranian group. Also called **Aryan**.

in·dole /ˈinˌdōl/ ▸*n. Chemistry* a crystalline organic compound with an unpleasant odor, present in coal tar and in feces. • A heteroaromatic compound with fused benzene and pyrrole rings; chem. formula: C_8H_7N. ▷mid 19th cent.: blend of **indigo** (because obtained artificially from indigo blue) and Latin *oleum* 'oil.'

in·dole·a·ce·tic ac·id /ˌindōləˈsētik; -ˈsetik/ ▸*n. Biochemistry* a compound that is an acetic acid derivative of indole, esp. one found as a natural growth hormone (auxin) in plants. • Chem. formula: $C_8H_6(CH_3COOH)N$; seven isomers; auxin is **indole-3-acetic acid**.

in·do·lent /ˈindələnt/ ▸*adj.* **1** wanting to avoid activity or exertion; lazy. **2** *Medicine* (of a disease condition) causing little or no pain. ■ (esp. of an ulcer) slow to develop, progress, or heal; persistent. ▷mid 17th cent.: from late Latin *indolent-*, from *in-* 'not' + *dolere* 'suffer or give pain.' The sense 'idle' arose in the early 18th cent. —**in·do·lence** *n.* —**in·do·lent·ly** *adv.*

In·dol·o·gy /inˈdäləjē/ ▸*n.* the study of Indian history, literature, philosophy, and culture. —**In·dol·o·gist** /-jist/ *n.*

In·do-Ma·lay·sian (also **In·do-Ma·lay·an**) ▸*adj.* of or relating to both India and Malaya, in particular: ■ denoting an ethnological region comprising Sri Lanka, the Malay peninsula, and the Malaysian islands. ■ (also **In·do-Ma·le·sian**) *Biology* denoting a major biogeographical region comprising the Indian subcontinent, Malesia, and East and Southeast Asia.

in·do·meth·a·cin /ˌindōˈmeTHəsin/ ▸*n. Medicine* a compound with anti-inflammatory, antipyretic, and analgesic properties, used chiefly to treat rheumatoid arthritis and gout. • Chem. formula: $C_{19}H_{16}NO_4Cl$. ▷1960s: from *indo(le)* + *meth(yl)* + *ac(etic)* + **-in**[1].

in·dom·i·ta·ble /inˈdämitəbəl/ ▸*adj.* impossible to subdue or defeat: *a woman of indomitable spirit.* ▷mid 17th cent. (in the sense 'untamable'): from late Latin *indomitabilis*, from *in-* 'not' + Latin *domitare* 'to tame.' —**in·dom·i·ta·bil·i·ty** /-ˌdämitəˈbilitē/ *n.* —**in·dom·i·ta·ble·ness** *n.* —**in·dom·i·ta·bly** /-blē/ *adv.*

In·do·ne·sia /ˌindəˈnēZHə/ a country in Southeast Asia that consists of many islands in the Malay Archipelago; pop. 238,452,000; capital, Djakarta (on Java); languages, Indonesian (official), Dutch, English, Malay, Balinese, Chinese, Javanese, and others. Former name (until 1949) **Dutch East Indies**. ▷from **Indo-** + Greek *nēsos* 'island.'

Indonesia consists of the territories of the former Dutch East Indies, of which the largest are Java, Sumatra, southern Borneo, western New Guinea, the Moluccas, and Sulawesi. The Dutch established control over the area in the 17th century. Independence was won in 1949, although Irian Jaya was not handed over until 1963; East Timor was annexed in 1976. An attempted communist coup was crushed by the army in 1965. The autocratic General Suharto was president 1967–98. Abdurrahman Wahid became Indonesia's first democratically elected president in 1999, serving until 2001.

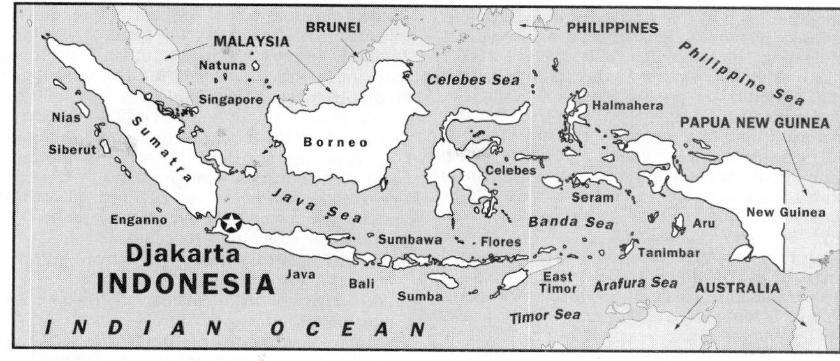

In·do·ne·sian /ˌindəˈnēZHən/ ▸*adj.* of or relating to Indonesia, Indonesians, or their languages.
▸*n.* **1** a native or national of Indonesia, or a person of Indonesian descent. **2** the group of Austronesian languages, closely related to Malay, that are spoken in Indonesia and neighboring islands. ■ another term for **Bahasa Indonesia**.

in·door /ˈinˌdôr/ ▸*adj.* [*attrib.*] situated, conducted, or used within a building or under cover: *indoor sports.* ■ of or relating to sports played indoors: *the national indoor champion.* ▷early 18th cent. (superseding earlier *within-door*): from **in** (as a preposition) + **door**. Compare with **indoors**.

in·doors /inˈdôrz/ ▸*adv.* into or within a building: *they went indoors and explored the building.*
▸*n.* the area or space inside a building: *the rain makes indoors feel so warm and safe.* ▷late 18th cent. (superseding earlier *within doors*): from **indoor**.

In·do-Pa·cif·ic ▸*adj.* of or relating to the Indian Ocean and the adjacent parts of the Pacific. ■ another term for **Austronesian**.
▸*n.* the Indo-Pacific seas or ocean.

In·dore /ˈinˌdôr/ a city in central India, in Madhya Pradesh; pop. 1,087,000.

in·dorse ▸*v.* variant spelling of **endorse**.

in·dorse·ment ▸*n.* variant spelling of **endorsement**.

in·dox·yl /inˈdäksəl/ ▸*n.* [as *adj.*] *Chemistry* of or denoting the radical $-ONC_8H_6$, derived from a hydroxy derivative of indole and present in indigotin.

In·dra /ˈindrə/ *Hinduism* the warrior king of the heavens, god of war and storm, to whom many of the prayers in the Rig Veda are addressed.

in·draft /ˈinˌdraft/ (*Brit.* **in·draught**) ▸*n.* the drawing in of something. ■ an inward flow or current, esp. of air.

in·drawn /ˈinˌdrôn/ ▸*adj.* **1** [*attrib.*] (of breath) taken in. **2** (of a person) shy and introspective.

in·dri /ˈindrē/ ▸*n.* (*pl.* **in·dris** /ˈindrēz/) a large, short-tailed Madagascan lemur that jumps from tree to tree in an upright position and rarely comes to the ground. • *Indri indri*, family Indriidae. ▷mid 19th cent.: from Malagasy *indry!* 'behold!' or *indry izy!* 'there he is!,' mistaken for its name. The Malagasy name is *babakoto*.

in·du·bi·ta·ble /inˈd(y)o͞obitəbəl/ ▸*adj.* impossible to doubt; unquestionable: *an indubitable truth.* ▷late Middle English: from Latin *indubitabilis*, from *in-* 'not' + *dubitabilis* (see **dubitable**). —**in·du·bi·ta·bly** /-blē/ *adv.* [*sentence adverb*] *indubitably, liberalism parades under many guises.*

in·duce /inˈd(y)o͞os/ ▸*v.* [*trans.*] **1** succeed in persuading or influencing (someone) to do something: *the pickets induced many workers to stay away.* **2** bring about or give rise to: *none of these measures induced a change of policy.* ■ produce (an electric charge or current or a magnetic state) by induction. ■ [usu. as *adj.*] (**induced**) *Physics* cause (radioactivity) by bombardment with radiation. **3** *Medicine* bring on (childbirth or abortion) artificially, typically by the use of drugs. ■ bring on childbirth in (a pregnant woman) in this way. ■ bring on the birth of (a baby) in this way. **4** *Logic* derive by inductive reasoning. ▷late Middle English (formerly also as *enduce*): from Latin *inducere* 'lead in,' from *in-* 'into' + *ducere* 'to lead,' or from French *enduire*. Compare with **endue**. —**in·duc·er** *n.* —**in·duc·i·ble** *adj.*

in·duced drag ▸*n. Aeronautics* that part of the drag on an airfoil that arises from the development of lift.

in·duce·ment /inˈd(y)o͞osmənt/ ▸*n.* a thing that persuades or influences someone to do something: *companies were prepared to build only in return for massive inducements* | [with *infinitive*] *there is no inducement to wait for payment.* ■ a bribe. ■ *Law* introductory statements in a pleading explaining the matter in dispute.

in·duct /inˈdəkt/ ▸*v.* [*trans.*] **1** admit (someone) formally to a position or organization: *each worker, if formally* ***inducted into*** *the Mafia, is known as a "soldier."* ■ formally introduce (a member of the clergy) into possession of a benefice. ■ enlist (someone) for military service. ■ (**induct someone in/into**) introduce someone to (a difficult or obscure subject): *my master inducted me into the skills of magic.* **2** *archaic* install in a seat or room. ▷late Middle English: from Latin *induct-* 'led into,' from the verb *inducere* (see **induce**). —**in·duc·tee** /ˌindəkˈtē/ *n.*

in·duc·tance /inˈdəktəns/ ▸*n. Physics* the property of an electric conductor or circuit that causes an electromotive force to be generated by a change in the current flowing: *the inductance of the winding* | *an inductance of 40 mH.* ■ a component with this property. ▷late 19th cent.: from **induction** + **-ance**.

in·duc·tion /inˈdəkSHən/ ▸*n.* **1** the action or process of inducting someone to a position or organization: *the league's* ***induction into*** *the Baseball Hall of Fame.* ■ [usu. as *adj.*] a formal introduction to a new job or position: *an induction course.* ■ enlistment into military service. **2** the process or action of bringing about or giving rise to something: *isolation, starvation, and other forms of stress induction.* ■ *Medicine* the process of bringing on childbirth or abortion by artificial means, typically by the use of drugs. **3** *Logic* the inference of a general law from particular instances. Often contrasted with **deduction**. ■ (**induction of**) the production of (facts) to prove a general statement. ■ (also **mathematical induction**) *Mathematics* a means of proving a theorem by showing that if it is true of any particular case, it is true of the next case in a series, and then showing that it is indeed true in one particular case. **4** *Physics* the production of an electric or magnetic state by the proximity (without contact) of an electrified or magnetized body. See also **magnetic induction**. ■ the production of an electric current in a conductor by varying the magnetic field applied to the conductor. **5** the stage of the working cycle of an internal combustion engine in which the fuel mixture is drawn into the cylinders. ▷late Middle English: from Latin *inductio(n-)*, from the verb *inducere* 'lead into' (see **induce**).

in·duc·tion coil ▸*n.* a coil for generating intermittent high voltage from a direct current.

in·duc·tion hard·en·ing ▸*n. Metallurgy* a process for hardening steel surfaces by induction heating followed by quenching.

in·duc·tion heat·ing ▸*n.* heating of a material by inducing an electric current within it.

in·duc·tion loop ▸*n.* a sound system in which a loop of wire around an area in a building, such as a theater, produces an electromagnetic signal received directly by hearing aids used by the partially deaf.

in·duc·tive /inˈdəktiv/ ▸*adj.* **1** characterized by the inference of general laws from particular instances: *instinct rather than inductive reasoning marked her approach to life.* **2** of, relating to, or caused by electric or magnetic induction. ■ possessing inductance. ▷late Middle English (in the sense 'leading to'): from Old French *inductif, -ive* or late Latin *inductivus* 'hypothetical' (later 'inducing, leading to'), from Latin *inducere* (see **induce**). Sense 1 dates from the mid 18th cent. —**in·duc·tive·ly** *adv.* —**in·duc·tive·ness** *n.*

in·duc·tiv·ism /inˈdəktəˌvizəm/ ▸*n.* the use of or preference for inductive methods of reasoning, esp. in science. —**in·duc·tiv·ist** *n.* & *adj.*

in·duc·tor /inˈdəktər/ ▸*n.* **1** a component in an electric or electronic circuit that possesses inductance. **2** a substance that promotes an equilibrium reaction by reacting with one of the substances produced. ▷mid 17th cent. (in the sense 'a person who inducts or initiates'): from late Latin, from Latin *inducere* (see **induce**), or from **induct** + **-or**[1]. Current senses date from the early 20th cent.

in·due ▸*v.* variant spelling of **endue**.

in·dulge /inˈdəlj/ ▸*v.* [*intrans.*] (**indulge in**) allow oneself to enjoy the pleasure of: *we indulged in some hot fudge sundaes.* ■ become involved in (an activity, typically one that is undesirable or disapproved of): *I don't indulge in idle gossip.* ■ *informal* allow oneself to enjoy a particular pleasure, esp. that of alcohol: *I only indulge on special occasions.* ■ [*trans.*] satisfy or yield freely to (a desire or interest): *she was able to indulge a growing passion for literature.* ■ [*trans.*] allow (someone) to enjoy a desired pleasure: *I spent time indulging myself with secret feasts.* ▷early 17th cent. (in the sense 'treat with excessive kindness'): from Latin *indulgere* 'give free rein to.' —**in·dulg·er** *n.*

in·dul·gence /inˈdəljəns/ ▸*n.* **1** the action or fact of indulging: *indulgence in self-pity.* ■ the state or attitude of being indulgent or tolerant: *she regarded his affairs with a casual, slightly amused indulgence.* ■ a thing that is indulged in; a luxury: *Claire collects shoes—it is her indulgence.* **2** *chiefly historical* (in the Roman Catholic Church) a grant by the pope of remission of the temporal punishment in purgatory still due for sins after absolution. The unrestricted sale of indulgences by pardoners was a widespread abuse during the later Middle Ages. **3** an extension of the time in which a bill or debt has to be paid. ▷late Middle English: via Old French from Latin *indulgentia*, from the verb *indulgere* (see **INDULGE**).

in·dul·gent /in'dəljənt/ ▶*adj.* having or indicating a readiness or overreadiness to be generous to or lenient with someone: *indulgent parents.* See note at **LENIENT.** ■ self-indulgent: *a slightly adolescent, indulgent account of a love affair.* ▷early 16th cent.: from French, or from Latin *indulgent-* 'giving free rein to,' from the verb *indulgere.* **—in·dul·gent·ly** *adv.*

in·du·line /'ind(y)ə,lēn; -lin/ ▶*n.* any of a group of insoluble blue azine dyes. ▷late 19th cent.: from *indo-* (denoting indigo) + **-ULE** + **-INE**[4].

in·dult /in'dəlt/ ▶*n.* (in the Roman Catholic Church) a license granted by the pope authorizing an act that the common law of the Church does not sanction. ▷late 15th cent.: from French, from late Latin *indultum* 'grant, concession,' neuter past participle of Latin *indulgere* 'indulge.'

in·du·men·tum /,ind(y)ə'mentəm/ ▶*n.* (*pl.* **-ta** /-tə/) *Botany & Zoology* a covering of hairs (or feathers) on an animal or plant. ▷mid 19th cent.: from Latin, literally 'garment,' from *induere* 'put on, don.'

in·du·rate /'ind(y)ə,rāt/ ▶*v.* [*trans.*] [usu. as *adj.*] (**indurated**) harden: *a bed of indurated clay.* ▷mid 16th cent.: from Latin *indurat-* 'made hard,' from the verb *indurare* (based on *durus* 'hard'). **—in·du·ra·tion** /,ind(y)ə'rāsʜən/ *n.* **—in·du·ra·tive** /-,rātiv/ *adj.*

In·dus[1] /'indəs/ a river in southern Asia, about 1,800 miles (2,900 km) long, that flows from Tibet through Kashmir and Pakistan to the Arabian Sea. Along its valley an early civilization, whose economic wealth was derived from sea and land trade with the rest of the Indian subcontinent, flourished from *c.*2600 to 1760 BC.

In·dus[2] /'indəs/ *Astronomy* an inconspicuous southern constellation (the Indian), between Capricornus and Pavo. ■ [as *genitive*] (**Indi** /-dī/) used with a preceding letter or numeral to designate a star in this constellation: *the star Alpha Indi.* ▷Latin.

indus. ▶*abbr.* ■ industrial or industry.

in·du·si·um /in'd(y)o͞ozʜēəm; -zēəm/ ▶*n.* (*pl.* **-si·a** /-zʜēə; -zēə/) *chiefly Botany* a thin membranous covering, esp. a shield covering a sorus on a fern frond. ▷early 18th cent.: from Latin, literally 'tunic,' from *induere* 'put on, don.'

in·dus·tri·al /in'dəstrēəl/ ▶*adj.* of, relating to, or characterized by industry: *a small industrial town.* ■ having highly developed industries: *the major industrial nations.* ■ designed or suitable for use in industry: *industrial heating oil.* ■ (of a disease or injury) contracted or sustained in the course of employment, esp. in a factory. ■ relating to or denoting a type of harsh, uncompromising rock music incorporating sounds resembling those produced by industrial machinery.
▶*n.* (**industrials**) shares in industrial companies. ▷late 15th cent.: from **INDUSTRY** + **-AL**; in later use influenced by French *industriel.* **—in·dus·tri·al·ly** *adv.*

in·dus·tri·al ar·chae·ol·o·gy ▶*n.* the study of equipment and buildings formerly used in industry.

in·dus·tri·al dia·mond ▶*n.* a small diamond, not of gem quality, used in abrasives and in cutting and drilling tools.

in·dus·tri·al es·pi·o·nage ▶*n.* spying directed toward discovering the secrets of a rival manufacturer or other industrial company.

in·dus·tri·al es·tate ▶*n.* British term for **INDUSTRIAL PARK.**

in·dus·tri·al·ism /in'dəstrēə,lizəm/ ▶*n.* a social or economic system built on manufacturing industries.

in·dus·tri·al·ist /in'dəstrēəlist/ ▶*n.* a person involved in the ownership and management of industry.

in·dus·tri·al·ize /in'dəstrēə,līz/ ▶*v.* [*trans.*] [often as *adj.*] (**industrialized**) develop industries in (a country or region) on a wide scale: *the industrialized nations.* ■ [*intrans.*] (of a country or region) build up a system of industries: *the country needs to industrialize to create both exports and jobs.* **—in·dus·tri·al·i·za·tion** /in-,dəstrēəli'zāsʜən/ *n.*

in·dus·tri·al mel·a·nism ▶*n. Zoology* the prevalence of dark-colored varieties of animals (esp. moths) in industrial areas where they are better camouflaged against predators than paler forms.

in·dus·tri·al park ▶*n.* an area of land developed as a site for factories and other industrial businesses.

in·dus·tri·al re·la·tions ▶*plural n.* the relations between management and workers in industry.

In·dus·tri·al Rev·o·lu·tion the rapid development of industry that occurred in Britain in the late 18th and 19th centuries, brought about by the introduction of machinery. It was characterized by the use of steam power, the growth of factories, and the mass production of manufactured goods.

in·dus·tri·al-strength ▶*adj.* very strong or powerful: *an industrial-strength cleaner.*

in·dus·tri·al un·ion /in'dəstrēəl 'yo͞onyən/ ▶*n.* see **VERTICAL UNION.**

In·dus·tri·al Work·ers of the World (abbr.: **IWW**) a radical U.S. labor movement, founded in Chicago in 1905 and, as part of the syndicalist movement, dedicated to the overthrow of capitalism. Its popularity declined after World War I, and by 1925 its membership was insignificant. Also called the **WOBBLIES.**

in·dus·tri·ous /in'dəstrēəs/ ▶*adj.* diligent and hardworking. See note at **BUSY.** ▷late 15th cent. (in the sense 'skillful, clever, ingenious'): from French *industrieux* or late Latin *industriosus*, from Latin *industria* 'diligence.' **—.in·dus·tri·ous·ly** *adv.* **—in·dus·tri·ous·ness** *n.*

in·dus·try /'indəstrē/ ▶*n.* (*pl.* **-tries**) **1** economic activity concerned with the processing of raw materials and manufacture of goods in factories: *the competitiveness of American industry.* ■ [with *adj.*] a particular form or branch of economic or commercial activity: *the car industry | the tourist industry.* ■ [with *adj.*] *informal* an activity or domain in which a great deal of time or effort is expended: *the Shakespeare industry.* **2** hard work: *the kitchen became **a hive of industry**.* ▷late Middle English (sense 2): from French *industrie* or Latin *industria* 'diligence.'

in·dwell /in'dwel/ ▶*v.* (*past* and *past part.* **-dwelt**) **1** [*trans.*] be permanently present in (someone's soul or mind); possess spiritually: *the Holy Spirit indwells God's people.* **2** [as *adj.*] (**indwelling**) *Medicine* (of a catheter, needle, etc.) fixed in a person's body for a long period of time. ▷late Middle English: originally translating Latin *inhabitare.* **—in·dwell·er** *n.*

In·dy /'indē/ ▶*n.* a form of auto racing in which specially constructed cars are driven around a banked, regular, typically oval circuit, which allows for exceptionally high speeds. ▷1950s: named after **INDIANAPOLIS**, where the principal Indy race is held.

In·dy car ▶*n.* a type of car used in Indy racing.
▶*adj.* of or relating to Indy or Indy cars.

-ine[1] ▶*suffix* **1** (forming adjectives) belonging to; resembling in nature: *Alpine | canine.* **2** forming adjectives from taxonomic names (such as *bovine* from the genus *Bos*). ▷from French *-in, -ine*, or from Latin *-inus.*

-ine[2] ▶*suffix* forming adjectives from the names of minerals, plants, etc.: *crystalline | hyacinthine.* ▷from Latin *-inus*, from Greek *-inos.*

-ine[3] ▶*suffix* forming feminine common nouns and proper names such as *heroine, Josephine.* ▷from French, via Latin *-ina* from Greek *-inē*, or from German *-in.*

-ine[4] ▶*suffix* **1** forming chiefly abstract nouns and diminutives such as *doctrine, medicine, figurine.* **2** *Chemistry* forming names of alkaloids, halogens, amines, amino acids, and other substances: *cocaine | chlorine | thymine.* ▷from French, from the Latin feminine form *-ina.*

in·e·bri·ant /i'nēbrēənt/ ▶*adj.* (of a substance) intoxicating: *beware of inebriant concoctions disguised as ordinary punch.*
▶*n.* an inebriating substance or agent; an intoxicant: *the seedpod is a powerful inebriant.*

in·e·bri·ate *formal or humorous* ▶*v.* /i'nēbrē,āt/ [*trans.*] [often as *adj.*] (**inebriated**) make drunk; intoxicate.
▶*n.* /-brē-it/ a drunkard.
▶*adj.* /-brē-it/ drunk; intoxicated. ▷late Middle English (as an adjective): from Latin *inebriatus*, past participle of *inebriare* 'intoxicate' (based on *ebrius* 'drunk'). **—in·e·bri·a·tion** /i,nēbrē'āsʜən/ *n.* **—in·e·bri·e·ty** /,ini'brī-itē/ *n.*

in·ed·it·ed /in'editid/ ▶*adj.* not edited or published. ■ published without editorial emendation.

in·ef·fa·ble /in'efəbəl/ ▶*adj.* too great or extreme to be expressed or described in words: *the ineffable natural beauty of the Everglades.* ■ not to be uttered: *the ineffable Hebrew name that gentiles write as Jehovah.* ▷late Middle English: from Old French, or from Latin *ineffabilis*, from *in-* 'not' + *effabilis* (see **EFFABLE**). **—in·ef·fa·bil·i·ty** /-efə'bilitē/ *n.* **—in·ef·fa·bly** /-blē/ *adv.*

in·ef·face·a·ble /,ini'fāsəbəl/ ▶*adj.* unable to be erased or forgotten. **—in·ef·face·a·bil·i·ty** /-,fāsə'bilitē/ *n.* **—in·ef·face·a·bly** /-blē/ *adv.*

in·ef·fec·tu·al /,ini'fekcʜo͞oəl/ ▶*adj.* not producing any or the desired effect: *an ineffectual campaign.* ■ (of a person) lacking the ability or qualities to cope with a role or situation: *she was neglectful and ineffectual as a parent.* ▷late Middle English: from medieval Latin *ineffectualis*, from *in-* 'not' + *effectualis*, from Latin *effectus* (see **EFFECT**); in later use from **IN-**[1] 'not' + **EFFECTUAL.** **—in·ef·fec·tu·al·i·ty** /-fekcʜo͞o'alitē/ *n.* **—in·ef·fec·tu·al·ly** *adv.* **—in·ef·fec·tu·al·ness** *n.*

in·ef·fi·cient /,ini'fisʜənt/ ▶*adj.* not achieving maximum productivity; wasting or failing to make the best use of time or resources: *an old, inefficient factory | the government was both inefficient and corrupt.* **—in·ef·fi·cien·cy** *n.* **—in·ef·fi·cient·ly** *adv.*

in·e·gal·i·tar·i·an /,ini,gali'te(ə)rēən/ ▶*adj.* characterized by or promoting inequality between people.

in·el·e·gant /in'eligənt/ ▶*adj.* having or showing a lack of physical grace, elegance, or refinement: *he came skidding to an inelegant halt | an inelegant bellow of laughter.* ■ unappealing through being unnecessarily complicated: *an inelegant and complex piece of legislation.* ▷early 16th cent.: from French *inélégant*, from Latin *inelegant-*, from *in-* 'not' + *elegant-* 'fastidious, refined' (see **ELEGANT**). **—in·el·e·gance** *n.* **—in·el·e·gant·ly** *adv.*

in·e·luc·ta·ble /,ini'ləktəbəl/ ▶*adj.* unable to be resisted or avoided; inescapable: *the ineluctable facts of history.* ▷early 17th cent.: from Latin *ineluctabilis*, from *in-* 'not' + *eluctari* 'struggle out.' **—in·e·luc·ta·bil·i·ty** /-,ləktə'bilitē/ *n.* **—in·e·luc·ta·bly** /-blē/ *adv.*

in·ept /i'nept/ ▶*adj.* having or showing no skill; clumsy: *the inept handling of the threat.* ▷mid 16th cent. (in the sense 'not apt, unsuitable'): from Latin *ineptus*, from *in-* 'not' + *aptus* (see **APT**). **—in·ept·i·tude** /-ti-,t(y)o͞od/ *n.* **—in·ept·ly** *adv.* **—in·ept·ness** *n.*

in·e·qual·i·ty /,ini'kwälitē/ ▶*n.* (*pl.* **-ties**) difference in size, degree, circumstances, etc.; lack of equality: *social inequality | the widening inequalities in income.* ■ *archaic* lack of smoothness or regularity in a surface: *the inequality of the ground hindered their footing.* ■ *Mathematics* the relation between two expressions that are not equal, employing a sign such as ≠ "not equal to," > "greater than," or < "less than." ■ *Mathematics* a symbolic expression of the fact that two quantities are not equal. ▷late Middle English: from Old French *inequalité*, or from Latin *inaequalitas*, from *in-* 'not' + *aequalis* (see **EQUAL**).

in·eq·ui·ta·ble /in'ekwitəbəl/ ▶*adj.* unfair; unjust: *the present taxes are inequitable.* **—in·eq·ui·ta·bly** /-blē/ *adv.*

in·eq·ui·ty /in'ekwitē/ ▶*n.* (*pl.* **-ties**) lack of fairness or justice: *policies aimed at redressing racial inequity | inequities in school financing.*

in·e·qui·valve /in'ēkwə,valv/ ▶*adj. Zoology* (of a bivalve shell) having the valves of different sizes.

in·e·rad·i·ca·ble /,inə'radikəbəl/ ▶*adj.* unable to be destroyed or removed: *ineradicable hostility.* **—in·e·rad·i·ca·bly** /-blē/ *adv.*

in·er·rant /in'erənt/ ▶*adj.* incapable of being wrong. ▷mid 19th cent.: from Latin *inerrant-* 'fixed,' from *in-* 'not' + *errant-* 'erring' (see **ERRANT**). **—in·er·ran·cy** *n.* **—in·er·ran·tist** /-tist/ *n.*

in·ert /i'nərt/ ▶*adj.* lacking the ability or strength to move: *she lay inert in her bed.* ■ lacking vigor: *an inert political system.* ■ chemically inactive. ▷mid 17th cent.: from Latin *iners, inert-* 'unskilled, inactive,' from *in-* (expressing negation) + *ars, art-* 'skill, art.' **—in·ert·ly** *adv.* **—in·ert·ness** *n.*

in·ert gas ▶*n.* another term for **NOBLE GAS.**

in·er·tia /i'nərsʜə/ ▶*n.* **1** a tendency to do nothing or to remain unchanged: *the bureaucratic inertia of government.* **2** *Physics* a property of matter by which it continues in its existing state of rest or uniform motion in a straight line, unless that state is changed by an external force. See also **MOMENT OF INERTIA.** ■ [with *adj.*] resistance to change in some other physical property: *the **thermal inertia** of the oceans will delay the full rise in temperature for a few decades.* ▷early 18th cent. (sense 2): from Latin, from *iners, inert-* (see **INERT**). **—in·er·tia·less** *adj.*

in·er·tial /i'nərsʜəl/ ▶*adj. chiefly Physics* of, relating to, or arising from inertia. ■ (of navigation or guidance) depending on internal instruments that measure a craft's acceleration and compare the calculated position with stored data. ■ (of a frame of reference) in which bodies continue at rest or in uniform straight motion unless acted on by a force.

in·er·tia reel ▸*n.* a reel device that allows a vehicle seat belt to unwind freely but locks under force of impact or rapid deceleration.

in·es·cap·a·ble /ˌiniˈskāpəbəl/ ▸*adj.* unable to be avoided or denied. —**in·es·cap·a·bil·i·ty** /-ˌskāpəˈbilitē/ *n.* —**in·es·cap·a·bly** /-blē/ *adv.*

in·es·cutch·eon /ˌineˈskəCHən/ ▸*n.* *Heraldry* a small shield placed within a larger one.

-iness ▸*suffix* forming nouns corresponding to adjectives ending in *-y* (such as *clumsiness* corresponding to *clumsy*). ▷see **-Y**[1], **-NESS**.

in es·se /in ˈesē; ˈese/ ▸*adv.* in actual existence. ▷late 16th cent.: Latin, literally 'in being'(the infinitive used as a noun in an oblique case).

in·es·sen·tial /ˌiniˈsenCHəl/ ▸*adj.* not absolutely necessary.
▸*n.* (usu. **inessentials**) a thing that is not absolutely necessary.

in·es·ti·ma·ble /inˈestəməbəl/ ▸*adj.* too great to calculate: *a treasure of inestimable value.* ▷late Middle English: via Old French from Latin *inaestimabilis*, from *in-* 'not' + *aestimabilis* (see **ESTIMABLE**). —**in·es·ti·ma·bly** /-blē/ *adv.*

in·ev·i·ta·ble /inˈevitəbəl/ ▸*adj.* certain to happen; unavoidable: *war was inevitable.* ■ *informal* so frequently experienced or seen that it is completely predictable: *the inevitable letter from the bank.*
▸*n.* (**the inevitable**) a situation that is unavoidable. ▷late Middle English: from Latin *inevitabilis*, from *in-* 'not' + *evitabilis* 'avoidable' (from *evitare* 'avoid'). —**in·ev·i·ta·bil·i·ty** /-ˌevitəˈbilitē/ *n.* —**in·ev·i·ta·bly** /-blē/ *adv.* [*sentence adverb*] *inevitably, she turned her experiences into a book.*

in·ex·cus·a·ble /ˌinikˈskyo͞ozəbəl/ ▸*adj.* too bad to be justified or tolerated: *Matt's behavior was inexcusable.* ▷late Middle English: from Latin *inexcusabilis*, from *in-* 'not' + *excusabilis* 'able to be excused' (see **EXCUSE**). —**in·ex·cus·a·bly** /-blē/ *adv.*

in·ex·haust·i·ble /ˌinigˈzôstəbəl/ ▸*adj.* (of an amount or supply of something) unable to be used up because existing in abundance: *his inexhaustible energy.* —**in·ex·haust·i·bil·i·ty** /-ˌzôstəˈbilitē/ *n.* —**in·ex·haust·i·bly** /-blē/ *adv.*

in·ex·o·ra·ble /inˈeksərəbəl/ ▸*adj.* impossible to stop or prevent: *the seemingly inexorable march of new technology.* ■ (of a person) impossible to persuade by request or entreaty: *the doctors were inexorable, and there was nothing to be done.* ▷mid 16th cent.: from French, or from Latin *inexorabilis*, from *in-* 'not' + *exorabilis* (from *exorare* 'entreat'). —**in·ex·o·ra·bil·i·ty** /-ˌeksərəˈbilitē/ *n.* —**in·ex·o·ra·bly** /-blē/ *adv.*

in·ex·pe·ri·ence /ˌinikˈspi(ə)rēəns/ ▸*n.* lack of experience, knowledge, or skill. ▷late 16th cent.: from French *inexpérience*, from late Latin *inexperientia*, from *in-* (expressing negation) + *experientia* 'experience.' —**in·ex·pe·ri·enced** *adj.*

in·ex·pert /inˈekspərt/ ▸*adj.* having or showing a lack of experience, skill, or knowledge: *an inexpert transcription from the real music.* ▷late Middle English (in the sense 'inexperienced'): via Old French from Latin *inexpertus*, from *in-* 'not' + *expertus* (see **EXPERT**). —**in·ex·pert·ly** *adv.*

in·ex·pi·a·ble /inˈekspēəbəl/ ▸*adj.* (of an offense or feeling) so bad as to be impossible to expiate. ▷late Middle English: from Latin *inexpiabilis*, from *in-* 'not' + *expiabilis* 'able to be appeased' (from *expiare* 'expiate'). —**in·ex·pi·a·bly** /-blē/ *adv.*

in·ex·pli·ca·ble /ˌinekˈsplikəbəl; inˈeksplikəbəl/ ▸*adj.* unable to be explained or accounted for: *for some inexplicable reason her mind went completely blank.* ▷late Middle English: from French, or from Latin *inexplicabilis* 'that cannot be unfolded,' from *in-* 'not' + *explicabilis* (see **EXPLICABLE**). —**in·ex·pli·ca·bil·i·ty** /ˈinek-ˌsplikəˈbilitē/ *n.* —**in·ex·pli·ca·bly** /-blē/ *adv.* [*sentence adverb*] *inexplicably, the pumps started to malfunction.*

in·ex·press·i·ble /ˌinikˈspresəbəl/ ▸*adj.* (of a feeling) too strong to be described or conveyed in words. *inexpressible joy.* —**in·ex·press·i·bly** /-blē/ *adv.*

in·ex·pres·sive /ˌinikˈspresiv/ ▸*adj.* showing no expression: *an inexpressive face.* —**in·ex·pres·sive·ly** /ˈˌinikˈspresəvlē; ˈˌinekˈspresəvlē/ *adv.* —**in·ex·pres·sive·ness** *n.*

in·ex·pug·na·ble /ˌinekˈspəgnəbəl; -ˈspyo͞onəbəl/ ▸*adj.* archaic term for **IMPREGNABLE**. ▷late Middle English: via Old French from Latin *inexpugnabilis*, from *in-* 'not' + *expugnabilis* 'able to be taken by assault.'

in ex·ten·so /ˌin əkˈstensō/ ▸*adv.* in full; at length: *the paper covered their speeches in extenso.* ▷Latin, from *in* 'in' + *extensus*, past participle of *extendere* 'stretch out.'

in·ex·tin·guish·a·ble /ˌinikˈstiNGgwiSHəbəl/ ▸*adj.* unable to be extinguished or quenched: *a small inextinguishable candle* | *figurative inextinguishable good humor.*

in ex·tre·mis /ˌin ekˈstrāmēs; ikˈstrēmis/ ▸*adv.* in an extremely difficult situation: *they suddenly find themselves in extremis 20 miles out to sea.* ■ at the point of death. ▷Latin, from *in* 'in' + *extremis*, ablative plural of *extremus* 'outermost.'

in·ex·tri·ca·ble /ˌinikˈstrikəbəl; inˈekstri-/ ▸*adj.* impossible to disentangle or separate: *the past and the present are inextricable.* ■ impossible to escape from: *an inextricable situation.* ▷mid 16th cent.: from Latin *inextricabilis*, from *in-* 'not' + *extricare* 'unravel' (see **EXTRICATE**). —**in·ex·tri·ca·bil·i·ty** /ˌinikˌstrikəˈbilitē/ *n.* —**in·ex·tri·ca·bly** /-blē/ *adv.*

INF ▸*abbr.* intermediate-range nuclear force(s).

inf. ▸*abbr.* ■ infantry. ■ inferior. ■ infield or infielder. ■ infinitive. ■ infinity. ■ infirmary. ■ information. ■ after; below. [from Latin *infra*] ■ (in prescriptions) infuse. ■ an infusion.

in·fall /ˈinˌfôl/ ▸*n.* *Astronomy* the falling of small objects or other matter onto or into a larger body.

in·fal·li·bil·i·ty /inˌfaləˈbilitē/ ▸*n.* the quality of being infallible; the inability to be wrong: *his judgment became impaired by faith in his own infallibility.* ■ (also **papal infallibility**) (in the Roman Catholic Church) the doctrine that in specified circumstances the pope is incapable of error in pronouncing dogma. ▷early 17th cent.: from obsolete French *infallibilité* or medieval Latin *infallibilitas* (based on Latin *fallere* 'deceive').

in·fal·li·ble /inˈfaləbəl/ ▸*adj.* incapable of making mistakes or being wrong: *doctors are not infallible.* ■ never failing; always effective: *infallible cures.* ■ (in the Roman Catholic Church) credited with papal infallibility: *for an encyclical to be infallible the pope must speak ex cathedra.* ▷late 15th cent.: from French *infaillible* or late Latin *infallibilis*, from *in-* 'not' + Latin *fallere* 'deceive.' —**in·fal·li·bly** /-blē/ *adv.*

in·fa·mous /ˈinfəməs/ ▸*adj.* well known for some bad quality or deed: *an infamous war criminal.* ■ wicked; abominable: *the medical council disqualified him for infamous misconduct.* ■ *historical Law* (of a person) deprived of all or some citizens' rights as a consequence of conviction for a serious crime. ▷late Middle English: from medieval Latin *infamosus*, from Latin *infamis* (based on *fama* 'fame'). —**in·fa·mous·ly** *adv.* —**in·fa·my** /-mē/ *n.* (*pl.* **-mies**).

in·fan·cy /ˈinfənsē/ ▸*n.* the state or period of early childhood or babyhood: *a son who died in infancy.* ■ the early stage in the development or growth of something: *opinion polls were **in their infancy**.* ■ *Law* the condition of being a minor. ▷late Middle English: from Latin *infantia* 'childhood, inability to speak,' from *infans, infant-* (see **INFANT**).

in·fang·thief /ˈinfaNGˌTHēf/ ▸*n.* *historical* the right of the lord of a manor to try and punish a thief caught within the limits of his demesne. ▷Old English *infangenthēof* 'thief seized within.'

in·fant /ˈinfənt/ ▸*n.* a very young child or baby. ■ [as *adj.*] denoting something in an early stage of its development: *the infant science of bioelectrical medicine.* ■ *Law* a person who has not attained legal majority. ▷late Middle English: from Old French *enfant*, from Latin *infant-* 'unable to speak,' from *in-* 'not' + *fant-* 'speaking' (from the verb *fari*).

in·fan·ta /inˈfantə/ ▸*n.* *historical* a daughter of the ruling monarch of Spain or Portugal, esp. the eldest daughter who was not heir to the throne. ▷late 16th cent.: Spanish and Portuguese, feminine of **INFANTE**.

in·fan·te /inˈfantā/ ▸*n.* *historical* the second son of the ruling monarch of Spain or Portugal. ▷mid 16th cent.: Spanish and Portuguese, from Latin *infans, infant-* (see **INFANT**).

in·fan·ti·cide /inˈfantiˌsīd/ ▸*n.* **1** the crime of a mother killing her child within a year of birth. ■ the practice in some societies of killing unwanted children soon after birth. **2** a person who kills an infant, esp. their own child. ▷mid 17th cent.: via French from late Latin *infanticidium*, from Latin *infant-* (see **INFANT**) + *-cidium* (see **-CIDE**). —**in·fan·ti·cid·al** /-ˌfantiˈsīdl/ *adj.*

in·fan·tile /ˈinfənˌtīl; ˈinfənt-il/ ▸*adj.* of or occurring among babies or very young children: *infantile colic.* ■ *derogatory* childish: *infantile jokes.* ▷late Middle English: from French, or from Latin *infantilis*, from *infans, infant-* (see **INFANT**). —**in·fan·til·i·ty** /ˌinfənˈtilitē/ *n.* (*pl.* **-ties**).

in·fan·tile pa·ral·y·sis ▸*n.* *dated* poliomyelitis.

in·fan·til·ism /ˈinfəntlˌizəm; inˈfan-/ ▸*n.* childish behavior. ■ *Psychology* the persistence of infantile characteristics or behavior in adult life.

in·fan·til·ize /ˈinfəntlˌīz; inˈfan-/ ▸*v.* [*trans.*] treat (someone) as a child or in a way that denies their maturity in age or experience: *seeing yourself as a victim infantilizes you.* —**in·fan·til·i·za·tion** /ˌinfəntl-iˈzāSHən; in ˌfan-/ *n.*

in·fan·tine /ˈinfənˌtīn; -ˌtēn/ ▸*adj.* archaic term for **INFANTILE**. ▷early 17th cent.: from obsolete French *infantin*, variant of Old French *enfantin*, from Latin *infans, infant-* (see **INFANT**).

in·fant mor·tal·i·ty ▸*n.* the death of children under the age of one year.

in·fan·try /ˈinfəntrē/ ▸*n.* soldiers marching or fighting on foot; foot soldiers collectively. ▷late 16th cent.: from French *infanterie*, from Italian *infanteria*, from *infante* 'youth, infantryman,' from Latin *infant-* (see **INFANT**).

in·fan·try·man /ˈinfəntrēmən/ ▸*n.* (*pl.* **-men**) a soldier belonging to an infantry unit.

in·farct /ˈinˌfärkt/ ▸*n.* *Medicine* a small localized area of dead tissue resulting from failure of blood supply. ▷late 19th cent.: from modern Latin *infarctus*, from *infarcire* 'stuff into or with,' from *in-* 'into' + Latin *farcire* 'to stuff.'

in·farc·tion /inˈfärkSHən/ ▸*n.* the obstruction of the blood supply to an organ or region of tissue, typically by a thrombus or embolus, causing local death of the tissue.

in·fat·u·ate /inˈfaCHo͞oˌāt/ ▸*v.* (**be infatuated with**) be inspired with an intense but short-lived passion or admiration for: *she is infatuated with a handsome police chief.* ▷mid 16th cent.: from Latin *infatuat-* 'made foolish,' from the verb *infatuare*, from *in-* 'into' + *fatuus* 'foolish.' —**in·fat·u·a·tion** /-ˌfaCHo͞oˈāSHən/ *n.*

in·fau·na /inˈfônə/ ▸*n.* *Ecology* the animals living in the sediments of the ocean floor or river or lake beds. Compare with **EPIFAUNA**. —**in·fau·nal** /-ˈfônl/ *adj.*

in·fect /inˈfekt/ ▸*v.* [*trans.*] affect (a person, organism, cell, etc.) with a disease-causing organism: *there is no evidence that the virus can infect humans.* ■ contaminate (air, water, etc.) with harmful organisms. ■ *Computing* affect with a virus. ■ *figurative* (of a negative feeling or idea) take hold of or be communicated to (someone): *the panic in his voice infected her.* ▷late Middle English: from Latin *infect-* 'tainted,' from the verb *inficere*, from *in-* 'into' + *facere* 'put, do.' —**in·fec·tor** /-ˈfektər/ *n.*

in·fec·tion /inˈfekSHən/ ▸*n.* the process of infecting or the state of being infected: *strict hygiene will limit the risk of infection.* ■ an infectious disease: *a chest infection.* ■ *Computing* the presence of a virus in, or its introduction into, a computer system. ▷late Middle English: from late Latin *infectio(n-)*, from Latin *inficere* 'dip in, taint' (see **INFECT**).

in·fec·tious /inˈfekSHəs/ ▸*adj.* (of a disease or disease-causing organism) likely to be transmitted to people, organisms, etc., through the environment. ■ likely to spread infection: *the dogs may still be infectious.* ■ likely to spread or influence others in a rapid manner: *her enthusiasm is infectious.* —**in·fec·tious·ly** *adv.* —**in·fec·tious·ness** *n.*

USAGE On the differences in meaning between **infectious** and **contagious**, see usage at **CONTAGIOUS**.

in·fec·tious mon·o·nu·cle·o·sis ▸*n.* an infectious viral disease characterized by swelling of the lymph glands and prolonged lassitude. Also called **glandular fever**.

in·fec·tive /inˈfektiv/ ▸*adj.* capable of causing infection. ■ *dated* infectious: *infective hepatitis.* ▷late Middle English: from Latin *infectivus*, from *inficere* 'to taint' (see **INFECT**). —**in·fec·tive·ness** *n.*

in·fe·cund /inˈfēkənd; -ˈfek-/ ▸*adj.* *Medicine & Zoology* (of a woman or female animal) having low or zero fecundity; unable to bear children or young. ▷late Middle English: from Latin *infecundus*, from *in-* 'not' + *fecundus* 'fecund.' —**in·fe·cun·di·ty** /ˌinfiˈkənditē/ *n.*

in·feed /ˈinˌfēd/ ▸*n.* the action or process of supplying material to a machine. ■ a mechanism that does this.

in·fe·lic·i·tous /ˌinfəˈlisitəs/ ▸*adj.* unfortunate; inappropriate: *his illustration is singularly infelicitous.* —**in·fe·lic·i·tous·ly** *adv.*

in·fe·lic·i·ty /ˌinfəˈlisitē/ ▸*n.* (*pl.* **-ties**) a thing that is inappropriate, esp. a remark or expression: *she winced at their infelicities and at the clumsy way they talked.*

Pronunciation Key ə *ago*; ər *over*; ˈə or ˌə *up*; ˈər or ˌər *fur*; a *hat*; ā *rate*; ä *car*; CH *chew*; e *let*; ē *see*; e(ə)r *air*; i *fit*; ī *by*; i(ə)r *ear*; NG *sing*; ō *go*; ô *for*; oi *boy*; o͝o *good*; o͞o *goo*; ou *out*; SH *she*; TH *thin*; TH *then*; (h)w *why*; ZH *vision*

I

■ *archaic* unhappiness; misfortune. ▷late Middle English (in the sense 'unhappiness'): from Latin *infelicitas*, from *infelix*, *infelic-* 'unhappy,' from *in-* 'not' + *felix* 'happy.'

in·fer /in'fər/ ▸*v.* (**-ferred**, **-fer·ring**) [*trans.*] deduce or conclude (information) from evidence and reasoning rather than from explicit statements: [with *clause*] *from these facts we can infer that crime has been increasing.* ▷late 15th cent. (in the sense 'bring about, inflict'): from Latin *inferre* 'bring in, bring about' (in medieval Latin 'deduce'), from *in-* 'into' + *ferre* 'bring.' —**in·fer·a·ble** (also **in·fer·ra·ble**) *adj.*

> ***USAGE*** There is a distinction in meaning between **infer** and **imply**. In the sentence *the speaker implied that the general had been a traitor*, the word **implied** means that something in the speaker's words 'suggested' that this man was a traitor (although nothing so explicit was actually stated). However, in *we* **inferred** *from his words that the general had been a traitor*, the word **inferred** means that something in the speaker's words enabled the listeners to 'deduce' that the man was a traitor. The two words **infer** and **imply** can describe the same event, but from different angles. Mistakes occur when **infer** is used to mean **imply**, as in *are you* **inferring** *that I'm a liar?* (instead of *are you* **implying** *that I'm a liar?*).

in·fer·ence /'inf(ə)rəns/ ▸*n.* a conclusion reached on the basis of evidence and reasoning. ■ the process of reaching such a conclusion: *his emphasis on order and health, and* **by inference** *cleanliness.* ▷late 16th cent.: from medieval Latin *inferentia*, from *inferent-* 'bringing in,' from the verb *inferre* (see **INFER**). —**in·fer·en·tial** /ˌinfə'renCHəl/ *adj.* —**in·fer·en·tial·ly** /ˌinfə'renCHəlē/ *adv.*

in·fe·ri·or /in'fi(ə)rēər/ ▸*adj.* **1** lower in rank, status, or quality: *schooling in inner-city areas was* **inferior to** *that in the rest of the country.* ■ of low standard or quality: *inferior goods.* ■ *Law* (of a court or tribunal) able to have its decisions overturned by a higher court. ■ *Economics* denoting goods or services that are in greater demand during a recession than in a boom, e.g., secondhand clothes. **2** *chiefly Anatomy* low or lower in position: *ulcers located in the inferior and posterior wall of the duodenum.* ■ (of a letter, figure, or symbol) written or printed below the line. ■ *Botany* (of the ovary of a flower) situated below the sepals and enclosed in the receptacle.
▸*n.* **1** a person lower than another in rank, status, or ability: *her social and intellectual inferiors.* **2** *Printing* an inferior letter, figure, or symbol. ▷late Middle English (sense 2): from Latin, comparative of *inferus* 'low.' —**in·fe·ri·or·ly** *adv.* (in sense 2 of the *adjective*).

in·fe·ri·or con·junc·tion ▸*n.* *Astronomy* a conjunction of Mercury or Venus with the sun, in which the planet and the earth are on the same side of the sun.

in·fe·ri·or·i·ty /inˌfi(ə)rē'ôritē; -'äritē/ ▸*n.* the condition of being lower in status or quality than another or others. ▷late 16th cent.: probably from medieval Latin *inferioritas*, from Latin *inferior* 'lower.'

in·fe·ri·or·i·ty com·plex ▸*n.* an unrealistic feeling of general inadequacy caused by actual or supposed inferiority in one sphere, sometimes marked by aggressive behavior in compensation.

in·fe·ri·or plan·et ▸*n.* *Astronomy* either of the two planets Mercury and Venus, whose orbits are closer to the sun than the earth's. Compare with **SUPERIOR PLANET**.

in·fer·nal /in'fərnl/ ▸*adj.* **1** of, relating to, or characteristic of hell or the underworld: *the infernal regions | the infernal heat of the forge.* **2** [*attrib.*] *informal* irritating and tiresome (used for emphasis): *you're an infernal nuisance.* ▷late Middle English: from Old French, from Christian Latin *infernalis*, from Latin *infernus* 'below, underground,' used by Christians to mean 'hell,' on the pattern of *inferni* (masculine plural) 'the shades' and *inferna* (neuter plural) 'the lower regions.' —**in·fer·nal·ly** *adv.*

in·fer·no /in'fərnō/ ▸*n.* (*pl.* **-nos**) **1** a large fire that is dangerously out of control. **2** (usu. **In·fer·no**) hell (with reference to Dante's *Divine Comedy*). ▷mid 19th cent.: from Italian, from Christian Latin *infernus* (see **INFERNAL**).

in·fer·tile /in'fərtl/ ▸*adj.* (of a person, animal, or plant) unable to reproduce. ■ (of land) unable to sustain crops or vegetation. ▷late 16th cent.: from French, or from late Latin *infertilis*, from *in-* 'not' + *fertilis* (see **FERTILE**). —**in·fer·til·i·ty** /ˌinfər'tilitē/ *n.*

in·fest /in'fest/ ▸*v.* [*trans.*] (usu. **be infested**) (of insects or animals) be present (in a place or site) in large numbers, typically so as to cause damage or disease: *the house is* **infested with** *cockroaches* | [as *adj.*, in *combination*] (**-infested**) *shark-infested waters* ▷late Middle English (in the sense 'torment, harass'): from French *infester* or Latin *infestare* 'assail,' from *infestus* 'hostile.' The current sense dates from the mid 16th cent. —**in·fes·ta·tion** /ˌinfe'stāSHən/ *n.*

in·feu·da·tion /ˌinfyo͞o'dāSHən/ ▸*n.* *historical* under the feudal system, the action of putting someone into possession of a fee or fief. ▷late 15th cent.: from medieval Latin *infeudatio(n-)*, from *infeudare* 'enfeoff' (based on *feudum* 'fee').

in·fib·u·late /in'fibyəˌlāt/ ▸*v.* [usu. as *adj.*] (**infibulated**) perform infibulation on (a girl or woman). ▷early 17th cent.: from Latin *infibulat-* 'fastened with a clasp,' from the verb *infibulare*, from *in-* 'into' + *fibula* 'brooch.'

in·fib·u·la·tion /inˌfibyə'lāSHən/ ▸*n.* the practice of excising the clitoris and labia of a girl or woman and stitching together the edges of the vulva to prevent sexual intercourse. It is traditional in some northeastern African cultures but is highly controversial.

in·fi·del /'infədl; -ˌdel/ ▸*n.* *chiefly archaic* a person who does not believe in religion or who adheres to a religion other than one's own: [as *plural n.*] (**the infidel**) *they wanted to secure the Holy Places from the infidel.*
▸*adj.* adhering to a religion other than one's own: *the infidel foe.* ▷late 15th cent.: from French *infidèle* or Latin *infidelis*, from *in-* 'not' + *fidelis* 'faithful' (from *fides* 'faith,' related to *fidere* 'to trust'). The word originally denoted a person of a religion other than one's own, specifically a Muslim (to a Christian), a Christian (to a Muslim), or a Gentile (to a Jew).

in·fi·del·i·ty /ˌinfi'delitē/ ▸*n.* (*pl.* **-ties**) **1** the action or state of being unfaithful to a spouse or other sexual partner: *her infidelity continued after her marriage | I ought not to have tolerated his infidelities.* **2** unbelief in a particular religion, esp. Christianity. ▷late Middle English (in the senses 'lack of faith' and 'disloyalty'): from Old French *infidelite* or Latin *infidelitas*, from *infidelis* 'not faithful' (see **INFIDEL**).

in·field /'inˌfēld/ ▸*n.* **1** the inner part of the field of play in various sports, in particular: ■ *Baseball* the area within and near the four bases. ■ *Cricket* the part of the field closer to the wicket. ■ the players stationed in the infield, collectively. **2** *Brit.* the land around or near a farmstead, esp. arable land.
▸*adv.* into or toward the inner part of the field of play. —**in·field·er** *n.* (in sense 1).

in·fight·ing /'inˌfītiNG/ ▸*n.* hidden conflict or competitiveness within an organization. ■ boxing closer to an opponent than at arm's length. —**in·fight·er** *n.*

in·fill /'inˌfil/ ▸*n.* material that fills or is used to fill a space or hole. ■ buildings constructed to occupy the space between existing ones.
▸*v.* [*trans.*] (often **be infilled**) fill or block up (a space or hole). ■ construct new buildings between (existing structures).

in·fil·trate /'infilˌtrāt; in'fil-/ ▸*v.* [*trans.*] **1** enter or gain access to (an organization, place, etc.) surreptitiously and gradually, esp. in order to acquire secret information: *other areas of the establishment were infiltrated by fascists.* ■ *figurative* permeate or become a part of (something) in this way: *computing has infiltrated most professions now.* ■ *Medicine* (of a tumor, cells, etc.) spread into or invade (a tissue or organ). **2** (of a liquid) permeate (something) by filtration: *virtually no water infiltrates deserts such as the Sahara.* ■ introduce (a liquid) into something in this way: *lignocaine was* **infiltrated into** *the wound.*
▸*n.* *Medicine* an infiltrating substance or a number of infiltrating cells. —**in·fil·tra·tion** /ˌinfil'trāSHən/ *n.* —**in·fil·tra·tor** /-ˌtrātər/ *n.*

infin. ▸*abbr.* infinitive.

in fine ▸*adv.* finally; in short; to sum up. ▷mid 16th cent.: Latin, literally 'in the end.'

in·fi·nite /'infənit/ ▸*adj.* **1** limitless or endless in space, extent, or size; impossible to measure or calculate: *the infinite mercy of God | the infinite number of stars in the universe.* ■ very great in amount or degree: *he bathed the wound with infinite care.* ■ *Mathematics* greater than any assignable quantity or countable number. ■ *Mathematics* (of a series) able to be continued indefinitely. **2** *Grammar* another term for **NONFINITE**.
▸*n.* (**the infinite**) a space or quantity that is infinite. ■ (**the Infinite**) God. ▷late Middle English: from Latin *infinitus*, from *in-* 'not' + *finitus* 'finished, finite' (see **FINITE**). —**in·fi·nite·ly** *adv.* [as *submodifier*] *the pay is infinitely better.* —**in·fi·nite·ness** *n.*

in·fi·nite re·gress ▸*n.* *chiefly Logic* a sequence of reasoning or justification that can never come to an end.

in·fin·i·tes·i·mal /ˌinfini'tes(ə)məl/ ▸*adj.* extremely small: *an infinitesimal pause.*
▸*n.* *Mathematics* an indefinitely small quantity; a value approaching zero. ▷mid 17th cent.: from modern Latin *infinitesimus*, from Latin *infinitus* (see **INFINITE**), on the pattern of *centesimal*. —**in·fin·i·tes·i·mal·ly** *adv.*

> ***USAGE*** Although this long word is commonly assumed to refer to large numbers, **infinitesimal** describes only very small size. While there may be an *infinite* number of grains of sand on the beach, a single grain may be said to be *infinitesimal*.

in·fin·i·tes·i·mal cal·cu·lus ▸*n.* see **CALCULUS** (sense 1).

in·fin·i·tive /in'finitiv/ ▸*n.* the basic form of a verb, without an inflection binding it to a particular subject or tense (e.g., *see* in *we came to see*, *let him see*).
▸*adj.* having or involving such a form. ▷late Middle English (as an adjective): from Latin *infinitivus*, from *infinitus* (see **INFINITE**). The noun dates from the mid 16th cent. —**in·fin·i·ti·val** /-ˌfini'tīvəl/ *adj.* —**in·fin·i·ti·val·ly** /-ˌfini'tīvəlē/ *adv.*

in·fin·i·tude /in'finiˌt(y)o͞od/ ▸*n.* the state or quality of being infinite or having no limit: *the infinitude of the universe.* ▷mid 17th cent.: from Latin *infinitus* (see **INFINITE**), on the pattern of *magnitude*.

in·fin·i·ty /in'finitē/ ▸*n.* (*pl.* **-ties**) the state or quality of being infinite: *the infinity of space.* ■ an infinite or very great number or amount: *an infinity of excuses.* ■ *Mathematics* a number greater than any assignable quantity or countable number (symbol ∞). ■ a point in space or time that is or seems infinitely distant: *the lawns stretched into infinity.* ▷late Middle English: from Old French *infinite* or Latin *infinitas*, from *infinitus* (see **INFINITE**).

in·firm /in'fərm/ ▸*adj.* not physically or mentally strong, esp. through age or illness. See note at **WEAK**. ■ *archaic* (of a person or their judgment) weak; irresolute: *he was infirm of purpose.* ▷late Middle English (in the general sense 'weak, frail'): from Latin *infirmus*, from *in-* 'not' + *firmus* 'firm.' —**in·firm·ly** *adv.*

in·fir·mar·er /in'fərmərər/ ▸*n.* *historical* a person in charge of the infirmary in a medieval monastery. ▷late Middle English: from Old French *enfermerier*, from *enfermerie* 'infirmary,' based on Latin *infirmus* (see **INFIRM**).

in·fir·ma·ry /in'fərm(ə)rē/ ▸*n.* (*pl.* **-ries**) a place in a large institution for the care of those who are ill: *the prison infirmary.* ■ a hospital. ▷late Middle English: from medieval Latin *infirmaria*, from Latin *infirmus* (see **INFIRM**).

in·fir·mi·ty /in'fərmitē/ ▸*n.* (*pl.* **-ties**) physical or mental weakness: *old age and infirmity come to men and women alike | the infirmities of old age.*

in·fix ▸*v.* /in'fiks/ [*trans.*] **1** implant or insert firmly in something. **2** *Grammar* insert (a formative element) into the body of a word.
▸*n.* /'inˌfiks/ *Grammar* a formative element inserted in a word. ▷early 16th cent.: from Latin *infix-* 'fixed in,' from the verb *infigere*, from *in-* 'into' + *figere* 'fasten,' reinforced by **IN-**[2] 'into' + **FIX**. The noun is on the pattern of *prefix* and *suffix*. —**in·fix·a·tion** /ˌinfik'sāSHən/ *n.* (in sense 2 of the *verb*).

infl. ▸*abbr.* ■ influence or influenced.

in fla·gran·te de·lic·to /ˌin flə'grāntā də'liktō; flə'grantē/ (also *informal* **in fla·gran·te**) ▸*adv.* in the very act of wrongdoing, esp. in an act of sexual misconduct: *he had been* **caught in flagrante** *with the wife of the association's treasurer.* ▷late 18th cent.: Latin, literally 'in blazing crime.'

in·flame /in'flām/ ▸*v.* [*trans.*] **1** provoke or intensify (strong feelings, esp. anger) in someone: *high fines further inflamed public feelings.* ■ provoke (someone) to strong feelings: *her sister was inflamed with jealousy.* ■ make (a situation) worse. **2** (usu. **be inflamed**) cause inflammation in (a part of the body): *the finger joints were inflamed with rheumatoid arthritis.* **3** *poetic/literary* light up with or as if with flames: *the torches inflame the night to the eastward.* ▷Middle English *enflaume*, *inflaume*, from Old French *enflammer*, from Latin *inflammare*, from *in-* 'into' + *flamma* 'flame.' —**in·flam·er** *n.*

in·flam·ma·ble /in'flaməbəl/ ▸*adj.* easily set on fire: *inflammable and poisonous gases.* ■ *figurative* likely to provoke strong feelings: *the most inflammable issue in U.S. politics today.* ▷early 17th cent.: from French, or from Latin *inflammare* (see **INFLAME**). —**in·flam·ma·bil·i·ty** /-ˌflamə'bilitē/ *n.* —**in·flam·ma·ble·ness** *n.* —**in·flam·ma·bly** /-blē/ *adv.*

USAGE Both **inflammable** and **flammable** mean 'easily set on fire.' The opposite is **nonflammable**. Where there is a danger that **inflammable** could be understood to mean its opposite, that is, 'not easily set on fire,' **flammable** should be used to avoid confusion. **Inflammable** is usually used figuratively or in nontechnical contexts (*his inflammable temper*).

in·flam·ma·tion /ˌinflə'māsʜən/ ▸*n.* a localized physical condition in which part of the body becomes reddened, swollen, hot, and often painful, esp. as a reaction to injury or infection: *chronic inflammation of the nasal cavities.* ▷late Middle English: from Latin *inflammatio(n-)*, from the verb *inflammare* (see INFLAME).

in·flam·ma·to·ry /in'flaməˌtôrē/ ▸*adj.* **1** relating to or causing inflammation of a part of the body. **2** (esp. of speech or writing) arousing or intended to arouse angry or violent feelings: *inflammatory slogans.*

in·flat·a·ble /in'flātəbəl/ ▸*adj.* capable of being filled with air: *an inflatable mattress.*
▸*n.* a plastic or rubber object that must be filled with air before use: *three sailors manned the inflatable.*

in·flate /in'flāt/ ▸*v.* [*trans.*] **1** fill (a balloon, tire, or other expandable structure) with air or gas so that it becomes distended. ■ [*intrans.*] become distended in this way. **2** increase (something) by a large or excessive amount: *objectives should be clearly set out so as not to duplicate work and inflate costs.* ■ [usu. as *adj.*] (**inflated**) exaggerate: *you have a very inflated opinion of your worth.* ■ bring about inflation of (a currency) or in (an economy). ▷late Middle English: from Latin *inflat-* 'blown into,' from the verb *inflare*, from *in-* 'into' + *flare* 'to blow.' —**in·flat·ed·ly** *adv.* —**in·fla·tor** /-'flātər/ (also **in·flat·er**) *n.*

in·fla·tion /in'flāsʜən/ ▸*n.* **1** the action of inflating something or the condition of being inflated: *the inflation of a balloon | the gross inflation of salaries.* ■ *Astronomy* (in some theories of cosmology) a very brief exponential expansion of the universe postulated to have interrupted the standard linear expansion shortly after the big bang. **2** *Economics* a general increase in prices and fall in the purchasing value of money: *policies aimed at controlling inflation* | [as *adj.*] *high inflation rates.* ▷Middle English (in the sense 'the condition of being inflated with a gas'): from Latin *inflatio(n-)*, from *inflare* 'blow in to' (see INFLATE). Sense 2 dates from the mid 19th cent. —**in·fla·tion·ism** /-ˌnizəm/ *n.* —**in·fla·tion·ist** /-nist/ *n.* & *adj.*

in·fla·tion·ar·y /in'flāsʜəˌnerē/ ▸*adj.* **1** of, characterized by, or tending to cause monetary inflation. **2** *Astronomy* of, relating to, or involving inflation.

in·flect /in'flekt/ ▸*v.* [*trans.*] (often **be inflected**) **1** *Grammar* change the form of (a word) to express a particular grammatical function or attribute, typically tense, mood, person, number, case, and gender. ■ [*intrans.*] (of a word or a language containing such words) undergo such change. **2** vary the intonation or pitch of (the voice), esp. to express mood or feeling. ■ influence or color (music or writing) in tone or style. ■ vary the pitch of (a musical note). **3** *technical* bend or deflect (something), esp. inward. ▷late Middle English (sense 3): from Latin *inflectere*, from *in-* 'into' + *flectere* 'to bend.' —**in·flec·tive** /-tiv/ *adj.*

in·flec·tion /in'fleksʜən/ (*chiefly Brit.* also **in·flex·ion**) ▸*n.* **1** *Grammar* a change in the form of a word (typically the ending) to express a grammatical function or attribute such as tense, mood, person, number, case, and gender. ■ the process or practice of inflecting words. **2** the modulation of intonation or pitch in the voice: *she spoke slowly and without inflection | the variety of his vocal inflections.* ■ the variation of the pitch of a musical note. **3** *chiefly Mathematics* a change of curvature from convex to concave at a particular point on a curve. ▷late Middle English (in the sense 'the action of bending inward'): from Latin *inflexio(n-)*, from the verb *inflectere* 'bend in, curve' (see INFLECT). —**in·flec·tion·al** /-sʜənl/ *adj.* —**in·flec·tion·al·ly** /-sʜənl-ē/ *adv.* —**in·flec·tion·less** *adj.*

in·flexed /in'flekst/ ▸*adj. technical* bent or curved inward.

in·flex·i·ble /in'fleksəbəl/ ▸*adj.* **1** unwilling to change or compromise: *once she had made up her mind, she was inflexible.* ■ not able to be changed or adapted to particular circumstances: *inflexible rules.* **2** not able to be bent; stiff: *the heavy inflexible armor of the beetles.* ▷late Middle English: from Latin *inflexibilis*, from *in-* 'not' + *flexibilis* 'flexible.' —**in·flex·i·bil·i·ty** /-ˌfleksə'bilitē/ *n.* —**in·flex·i·bly** /-blē/ *adv.*

in·flict /in'flikt/ ▸*v.* [*trans.*] cause (something unpleasant or painful) to be suffered by someone or something: *they **inflicted** serious injuries **on** three other men.* ■ (**inflict something on**) impose something unwelcome on: *she is wrong to inflict her beliefs on everyone else.* ▷mid 16th cent. (in the sense 'afflict, trouble'): from Latin *inflict-* 'struck against,' from the verb *infligere*, from *in-* 'into' + *fligere* 'to strike.' —**in·flict·a·ble** *adj.* —**in·flict·er** *n.*

in·flic·tion /in'fliksʜən/ ▸*n.* the action of inflicting something unpleasant or painful on someone or something: *the repeated infliction of pain.* ■ *informal, dated* a nuisance: *what an infliction he must be!*

in·flight /'inˌflīt/ ▸*adj.* occurring or provided during an aircraft flight: *inflight entertainment.*

in·flo·res·cence /ˌinflô'resəns; -flə-/ ▸*n. Botany* the complete flowerhead of a plant including stems, stalks, bracts, and flowers. ■ the arrangement of the flowers on a plant. ■ the process of flowering. ▷mid 18th cent. (denoting the arrangement of a plant's flowers): from modern Latin *inflorescentia*, from late Latin *inflorescere* 'come into flower,' from Latin *in-* 'into' + *florescere* 'begin to flower.'

in·flow /'inˌflō/ ▸*n.* a large amount of money, people, or water, that moves or is transferred into a place: *some enclosed seas are subject to large inflows of fresh water | the firm experienced two years of cash inflow.* —**in·flow·ing** *n.* & *adj.*

in·flu·ence /'inflo͝oəns/ ▸*n.* the capacity to have an effect on the character, development, or behavior of someone or something, or the effect itself: *the influence of television violence | I was still **under the influence of** my parents | their friends are having a bad **influence on** them.* ■ the power to shape policy or ensure favorable treatment from someone, esp. through status, contacts, or wealth: *the institute has considerable influence with teachers.* ■ a person or thing with such a capacity or power: *Frank was a good **influence on** her.* ■ *archaic Physics* electrical or magnetic induction.
▸*v.* [*trans.*] have an influence on: *social forces influencing criminal behavior.* ▷late Middle English: from Old French, or from medieval Latin *influentia* 'inflow,' from Latin *influere*, from *in-* 'into' + *fluere* 'to flow.' The word originally had the general sense 'an influx, flowing matter,' also specifically (in astrology) 'the flowing in of ethereal fluid (affecting human destiny).' The sense 'imperceptible or indirect action exerted to cause changes' was established in Scholastic Latin by the 13th cent., but not recorded in English until the late 16th cent. —**in·flu·ence·a·ble** *adj.* —**in·flu·enc·er** *n.*
▸*PHRASE* □ **under the influence** *informal* affected by alcoholic drink; drunk: *he was charged with driving under the influence.*

in·flu·ence ped·dling ▸*n.* the use of position or political influence on someone's behalf in exchange for money or favors. —**in·flu·ence ped·dler** *n.*

in·flu·ent /'inflo͝oənt/ ▸*adj.* flowing in: *the influent lines were relocated while waste water was still flowing.*
▸*n.* a stream, esp. a tributary, that flows into another stream or lake. ■ *Ecology* a nondominant organism that has a major effect on the balance of a plant or animal community. ▷late Middle English (as an adjective): from Latin *influent-* 'flowing in,' from *influere* (see INFLUENCE). The noun is recorded from the mid 19th cent.

in·flu·en·tial /ˌinflo͞o'encʜəl/ ▸*adj.* having great influence on someone or something: *her work is influential in feminist psychology.*
▸*n.* (usu. **influentials**) an influential person. ▷late 16th cent. (referring to astral influence): from medieval Latin *influentia* (see INFLUENCE). —**in·flu·en·tial·ly** *adv.*

in·flu·en·za /ˌinflo͞o'enzə/ ▸*n.* a highly contagious viral infection of the respiratory passages causing fever, severe aching, and catarrh, and often occurring in epidemics. Also called FLU. ▷mid 18th cent.: from Italian, literally 'influence,' from medieval Latin *influentia* (see INFLUENCE). The Italian word also has the sense 'an outbreak of an epidemic,' hence 'epidemic.' It was applied specifically to an influenza epidemic that began in Italy in 1743, later adopted in English as the name of the disease. —**in·flu·en·zal** *adj.*

in·flux /'inˌfləks/ ▸*n.* **1** an arrival or entry of large numbers of people or things: *a massive influx of refugees from front-line areas.* **2** an inflow of water into a river, lake, or the sea. ▷late 16th cent. (denoting an inflow of liquid, gas, or light): from late Latin *influxus*, from *influere* 'flow in' (see INFLUENCE).

in·fo /'infō/ ▸*n. informal* information. ▷early 20th cent.: abbreviation.

in·fo·bahn /'infōˌbän/ ▸*n. informal* a high-speed computer network, esp. the Internet. ▷1990s: blend of INFORMATION and AUTOBAHN.

in·fo·dem·ic /ˌinfə'demik/ ▸*n.* a surfeit of information about a problem that is viewed as being a detriment to its solution. ▷early 21st cent.: blend of *information* and *epidemic.*

in·fo·hol·ic /ˌinfə'hôlik; -'häl-/ ▸*n.* a person who feels compelled to search out news and information, especially online. ▷ from INFO, on the model of ALCOHOLIC.

in·fold /in'fōld/ ▸*v.* [*trans.*] **1** turn or fold inward; invaginate: [as *adj.*] (**infolded**) *an ovary formed from the infolded carpel.* **2** *dated* variant spelling of ENFOLD. —**in·fold·ing** *n. an infolding of mesodermal tissues.*

in·fo·me·di·ar·y /ˌinfō'mēdēˌerē/ ▸*n.* an Internet company that gathers and links information on particular subjects on behalf of commercial organizations and their potential customers. ▷1980s: from *info(rmation)* + *-mediary*, on the pattern of *intermediary.*

in·fo·mer·cial /'infōˌmərsʜəl/ ▸*n.* a television program that promotes a product in an informative and supposedly objective way. ▷1980s: blend of INFORMATION and COMMERCIAL.

in·fo·naut /'infōˌnôt/ ▸*n. informal* a frequent user of a high-speed computer network, in particular the Internet. ▷1990s: from INFORMATION, on the pattern of *astronaut.*

in·form /in'fôrm/ ▸*v.* **1** [*reporting verb*] give (someone) facts or information; tell: [*trans.*] *he wrote to her, informing her of the situation* | [*trans.*] *they were informed that no risk was involved* | [*intrans.*] *the role of television is to inform and entertain.* ■ [*intrans.*] give incriminating information about someone to the police or other authority: *surrendered terrorists began to **inform on** their former comrades.* **2** [*trans.*] give an essential or formative principle or quality to: *the relationship of the citizen to the state is informed by the democratic ideal.* ▷Middle English *enforme, informe* 'give form or shape to,' also 'form the mind of, teach,' from Old French *enfourmer*, from Latin *informare* 'shape, fashion, describe,' from *in-* 'into' + *forma* 'a form.'

in·for·mal /in'fôrməl/ ▸*adj.* having a relaxed, friendly, or unofficial style, manner, or nature: *an informal atmosphere | an informal agreement between the two companies.* ■ of or denoting a style of writing or conversational speech characterized by simple grammatical structures, familiar vocabulary, and use of idioms, e.g., *tu* in French. ■ (of dress) casual; suitable for everyday wear. —**in·for·mal·i·ty** /ˌinfôr'malitē/ *n.* —**in·for·mal·ly** *adv.*

in·form·ant /in'fôrmənt/ ▸*n.* a person who gives information to another. ■ another term for INFORMER. ■ a person from whom a linguist or anthropologist obtains information about language, dialect, or culture.

in·for·mat·ics /ˌinfər'matiks/ ▸*plural n.* [treated as *sing.*] *Computing* the science of processing data for storage and retrieval; information science. ▷1960s: from INFORMATION + -ICS, translating Russian *informatika.*

in·for·ma·tion /ˌinfər'māsʜən/ ▸*n.* **1** facts provided or learned about something or someone: *a vital piece of information.* See note at KNOWLEDGE. ■ *Law* a formal criminal charge lodged with a court or magistrate by a prosecutor without the aid of a grand jury: *the tenant may lay an information against his landlord.* **2** what is conveyed or represented by a particular arrangement or sequence of things: *genetically transmitted information.* ■ *Computing* data as processed, stored, or transmitted by a computer. ■ (in information theory) a mathematical quantity expressing the probability of occurrence of a particular sequence of symbols, impulses, etc., as contrasted with that of alternative sequences. ▷late Middle English (also in the sense 'formation of the mind, teaching'), via Old French from Latin *informatio(n-)*, from the verb *informare* (see INFORM). —**in·for·ma·tion·al** /-sʜənl/ *adj.* —**in·for·ma·tion·al·ly** /-sʜənl-ē/ *adv.*

in·for·ma·tion re·triev·al ▸*n. Computing* the tracing and recovery of specific information from stored data.

in·for·ma·tion rev·o·lu·tion ▸*n.* the proliferation of the availability of information and the accompanying changes in its storage and dissemination owing to the use of computers.

in·forma·tion scent ▸*n.* visual or textual cues provided on a Web site to suggest what information it or its links may contain. ■ the perceived usefulness of a page based on such information.

in·for·ma·tion sci·ence ▸*n. Computing* the study of processes for storing and retrieving information, esp. scientific or technical information.

in·for·ma·tion tech·nol·o·gy (abbr.: **IT**) ▸*n.* the study or use of systems (esp. computers and telecommunications) for storing, retrieving, and sending information.

in·for·ma·tion the·o·ry ▸*n.* the mathematical study of the coding of information in the form of sequences of symbols, impulses, etc., and of how rapidly such information can be transmitted, e.g., through computer circuits or telecommunications channels.

in·for·ma·tive /in'fôrmətiv/ ▸*adj.* providing useful or interesting information: *a thought-provoking, informative article.* ▷late Middle English (in the sense 'formative, giving life or shape'): from medieval Latin *informativus*, from Latin *informare* 'give form to, instruct' (see INFORM). **—in·for·ma·tive·ly** *adv.* **—in·for·ma·tive·ness** *n.*

in·for·ma·vore /in'fôrmə,vôr/ ▸*n. informal* a consumer of information: *we're all informavores now, hunting down and consuming data as our ancestors once sought woolly mammoths.* ▷from *informa(tion)* + *-vore* 'one who consumes or devours,' on the pattern of *carnivore, herbivore*.

in·formed /in'fôrmd/ ▸*adj.* having or showing knowledge of a particular subject or situation: *an informed readership.* ■ (of a decision or judgment) based on an understanding of the facts of the situation: *twenty-six young adults participated after giving* ***informed consent.*** **—in·form·ed·ly** /-m(i)dlē/ *adv.* **—in·form·ed·ness** /-m(i)dnis/ *n.*

in·form·er /in'fôrmər/ ▸*n.* a person who informs on another person to the police or other authority.

in·fo·tain·ment /,infō'tānmənt/ ▸*n.* broadcast material that is intended both to entertain and to inform. ▷1980s (originally U.S.): blend of INFORMATION and ENTERTAINMENT.

in·fo·tech /'infō,tek/ ▸*n.* short for INFORMATION TECHNOLOGY.

in·fo·war /'infō,wôr/ ▸*n.* **1** hostile actions against an enemy's information infrastructure: *an infowar against NATO's computer network.* **2** a propaganda war waged via electronic media. ▷blend of *information* and *war*.

in·fra /'infrə/ ▸*adv.* (in a written document) below; further on: *see note, infra.* ▷late 19th cent.: Latin, 'below.'

infra- ▸*prefix* below: *infrared* | *infrasonic.* ■ *Anatomy* below or under a part of the body: *infrarenal.* ▷from Latin *infra* 'below.'

in·fra·class /'infrə,klas/ ▸*n. Biology* a taxonomic category that ranks below a subclass.

in·frac·tion /in'fraksнən/ ▸*n.* a violation or infringement of a law, agreement, or set of rules. ▷late Middle English: from Latin *infractio(n-)*, from the verb *infringere* (see INFRINGE). **—in·frac·tor** /-tər/ *n.*

in·fra·di·an /in'frādēən/ ▸*adj. Physiology* (of a rhythm or cycle) having a period of recurrence longer than a day; occurring less than once a day. Compare with ULTRADIAN. ▷mid 20th cent.: from INFRA- 'below' (i.e., expressing a lower frequency), on the pattern of *circadian*.

in·fra dig ▸*adj.* [*predic.*] *informal* beneath one; demeaning: *it was somewhat infra dig for a man in his position to be found drinking.* ▷early 19th cent.: abbreviation of Latin *infra dignitatem* 'beneath (one's) dignity.'

in·fra·lap·sar·i·an /,infrəlap'se(ə)rēən/ *Theology* ▸*n.* a Calvinist holding the view that God's election of only some to everlasting life was not originally part of the divine plan, but a consequence of the Fall of Man.

▸*adj.* of or relating to the infralapsarians or their doctrine. ▷mid 18th cent.: from INFRA- 'below' + Latin *lapsus* 'fall' + -ARIAN.

in·fran·gi·ble /in'franjəbəl/ ▸*adj. formal* unbreakable; inviolable. ▷late 16th cent.: from French, or from medieval Latin *infrangibilis*, from *in-* 'not' + *frangibilis* (see FRANGIBLE). **—in·fran·gi·bil·i·ty** /-,franjə'bilitē/ *n.* **—in·fran·gi·bly** /-blē/ *adv.*

in·fra·or·der /'infrə,ôrdər/ ▸*n. Biology* a taxonomic category that ranks below a suborder.

in·fra·red /,infrə'red/ ▸*adj.* (of electromagnetic radiation) having a wavelength just greater than that of the red end of the visible light spectrum but less than that of microwaves. Infrared radiation has a wavelength from about 800 nm to 1 mm, and is emitted particularly by heated objects. ■ (of equipment or techniques) using or concerned with this radiation: *infrared cameras.*

▸*n.* the infrared region of the spectrum; infrared radiation.

in·fra·re·nal /,infrə'rēnl/ ▸*adj. Anatomy* below the kidney.

in·fra·son·ic /,infrə'sänik/ ▸*adj.* relating to or denoting sound waves with a frequency below the lower limit of human audibility.

in·fra·sound /'infrə,sound/ ▸*n.* sound waves with frequencies below the lower limit of human audibility.

in·fra·spe·cif·ic /,infrəspə'sifik/ ▸*adj. Biology* at a taxonomic level below that of species, e.g., subspecies, variety, cultivar, or form. In botany, Latin names at this level usually require the addition of a term denoting the rank. ■ occurring within a species: *infraspecific variation.*

in·fra·struc·ture /'infrə,strəkcнər/ ▸*n.* the basic physical and organizational structures and facilities (e.g., buildings, roads, and power supplies) needed for the operation of a society or enterprise. ▷early 20th cent.: from French (see INFRA-, STRUCTURE). **—in·fra·struc·tur·al** /,infrə'strəkcнərəl/ *adj.*

in·fre·quent /in'frēkwənt/ ▸*adj.* not occurring often; rare: *her visits were so infrequent.* ▷mid 16th cent. (in the sense 'little used, seldom done, uncommon'): from Latin *infrequent-*, from *in-* 'not' + *frequent-* 'frequent.' **—in·fre·quen·cy** *n.* **—in·fre·quent·ly** *adv.*

in·fringe /in'frinj/ ▸*v.* [*trans.*] actively break the terms of (a law, agreement, etc.): *making an unauthorized copy would infringe copyright.* ■ act so as to limit or undermine (something); encroach on: *his legal rights were being infringed* | [*intrans.*] *I wouldn't* ***infringe on*** *his privacy.* ▷mid 16th cent.: from Latin *infringere*, from *in-* 'into' + *frangere* 'to break.' **—in·fringe·ment** *n.* **—in·fring·er** *n.*

in·fruc·tes·cence /,infrək'tesəns/ ▸*n. Botany* an aggregate fruit. ▷late 19th cent.: from IN-² 'in' + Latin *fructus* 'fruit,' on the pattern of *inflorescence*.

in·fu·la /'infyələ/ ▸*n.* (*pl.* **-lae** /-lē/) (in the Christian Church) either of the two ribbons on a bishop's miter. ▷early 17th cent.: from Latin, denoting a woolen fillet worn by a priest or placed on the head of a sacrificial victim.

in·fun·dib·u·lum /,infən'dibyələm/ ▸*n.* (*pl.* **-la** /-lə/) *Anatomy & Zoology* a funnel-shaped cavity or structure. ■ the hollow stalk that connects the hypothalamus and the posterior pituitary gland. ▷mid 16th cent.: from Latin, 'funnel,' from *infundere* 'pour in.' **—in·fun·dib·u·lar** /-lər/ *adj.*

in·fu·ri·ate /in'fyŏŏrē,āt/ ▸*v.* [*trans.*] make (someone) extremely angry and impatient: *her silences infuriated him* | [as *adj.*] (**infuriating**) *that infuriating half-smile on his face.* ▷mid 17th cent.: from medieval Latin *infuriat-* 'made angry,' from the verb *infuriare*, from *in-* 'into' + Latin *furia* 'fury.' **—in·fu·ri·at·ing·ly** *adv.*

in·fuse /in'fyōōz/ ▸*v.* [*trans.*] **1** fill; pervade: *her work is* ***infused with*** *an anger born of pain and oppression.* ■ instill (a quality) in someone or something: *he did his best to* ***infuse*** *good humor* ***into*** *his voice.* ■ *Medicine* allow (a liquid) to flow into a patient, vein, etc.: *saline was* ***infused into*** *the aorta.* **2** soak (tea, herbs, etc.) in liquid to extract the flavor or healing properties: *infuse the dried flowers in boiling water.* ■ [*intrans.*] (of tea, herbs, etc.) be soaked in this way: *allow the mixture to infuse for 15 minutes.* ▷late Middle English: from Latin *infus-* 'poured in,' from the verb *infundere*, from *in-* 'into' + *fundere* 'pour.' **—in·fus·er** *n.*

in·fu·sion /in'fyōōzнən/ ▸*n.* **1** a drink, remedy, or extract prepared by soaking the leaves of a plant or herb in liquid. ■ the process of preparing such a drink, remedy, or extract. **2** the introduction of a new element or quality into something: *the infusion of $6.3 million for improvements* | *an infusion of youthful talent.* ■ *Medicine* the slow injection of a substance into a vein or tissue. ▷late Middle English (denoting the pouring in of a liquid): from Latin *infusio(n-)*, from the verb *infundere* (see INFUSE).

in·fu·so·ri·a /,infyə'zôrēə/ ▸*plural n. dated Zoology* single-celled organisms of the former group Infusoria, which consisted mainly of ciliate protozoans. ▷modern Latin, from Latin *infundere* (see INFUSE); so named because they were originally found in infusions of decaying organic matter.

-ing¹ /iNG/ ▸*suffix* **1** denoting a verbal action, an instance of this, or its result: *fighting* | *outing* | *building.* ■ denoting a verbal action relating to an occupation, skill, etc.: *banking* | *ice skating* | *welding.* **2** denoting material used for or associated with a process, etc.: *cladding* | *piping.* ■ denoting something involved in an action or process but with no corresponding verb: *scaffolding.* **3** forming the gerund of verbs (such as *painting* as in *I love painting*). ▷Old English *-ung, -ing*, of Germanic origin.

-ing² ▸*suffix* **1** forming the present participle of verbs: *doing* | *calling.* ■ forming present participles used as adjectives: *charming.* **2** forming adjectives from nouns: *hulking.* ▷Middle English: alteration of earlier *-ende*, later *-inde*.

-ing³ ▸*suffix* (used esp. in names of coins and fractional parts) a thing belonging to or having the quality of: *farthing* | *riding.* ▷Old English, of Germanic origin.

in·gath·er /'in,gaтнər/ ▸*v.* [*trans.*] *formal* gather (something) in or together: *it may not be possible to ingather that information within the time.*

Inge /iNG/, William (Motter) (1913–73) U.S. playwright. He wrote *Come Back, Little Sheba* (1950), *Picnic* (1953), *Bus Stop* (1955), and *The Dark at the Top of the Stairs* (1957).

in·gem·i·nate /in'jemə,nāt/ ▸*v.* [*trans.*] *archaic* repeat or reiterate (a word or statement), typically for emphasis. ▷late 16th cent. (originally as *engeminate*): from Latin *ingeminat-* 'redoubled,' from the verb *ingeminare*, from *in-* (expressing intensive force) + *geminare* (see GEMINATE).

Ing·en·housz /'iNGən,hous/, Jan (1730–99), Dutch scientist. He is noted for his work on photosynthesis, in which he discovered that green plants placed in sunlight produce oxygen.

in·gen·ious /in'jēnyəs/ ▸*adj.* (of a person) clever, original, and inventive: *he was ingenious enough to overcome the limited budget.* See note at CREATIVE. ■ (of a machine or idea) cleverly and originally devised and well suited to its purpose. ▷late Middle English: from French *ingénieux* or Latin *ingeniosus*, from *ingenium* 'mind, intellect'; compare with ENGINE. **—in·gen·ious·ly** *adv.* **—in·gen·ious·ness** *n.*

USAGE **Ingenious** and **ingenuous** are often confused. **Ingenious** means 'clever, skillful, resourceful' (*an ingenious device*), while **ingenuous** means 'artless, frank' (*charmed by the ingenuous honesty of the child*).

in·gé·nue /'anjə,nōō; 'änzн-/ ▸*n.* an innocent or unsophisticated young woman. ■ a part of this type in a play. ■ an actress who plays such a part. ▷French, feminine of *ingénu* 'ingenuous,' from Latin *ingenuus* (see INGENUOUS).

in·ge·nu·i·ty /,injə'n(y)ōōitē/ ▸*n.* the quality of being clever, original, and inventive. ▷late 16th cent. (also in the senses 'nobility' and 'ingenuousness'): from Latin *ingenuitas* 'ingenuousness,' from *ingenuus* 'inborn.' The current meaning arose by confusion of INGENUOUS with INGENIOUS.

in·gen·u·ous /in'jenyōōəs/ ▸*adj.* (of a person or action) innocent and unsuspecting. See note at GULLIBLE. ▷late 16th cent.: from Latin *ingenuus*, literally 'native, inborn,' from *in-* 'into' + an element related to *gignere* 'beget.' The original sense was 'noble, generous,' giving rise to 'honorably straightforward, frank,' hence 'innocently frank' (late 17th cent.). **—in·gen·u·ous·ly** *adv.* **—in·gen·u·ous·ness** *n.*

USAGE On the difference between **ingenuous** and **ingenious**, see **usage** at INGENIOUS.

in·gest /in'jest/ ▸*v.* [*trans.*] take (food, drink, or another substance) into the body by swallowing or absorbing it. ■ *figurative* absorb (information): *he spent his days ingesting the contents of the library.* ▷early 17th cent.: from Latin *ingest-* 'brought in,' from the verb *ingerere*, from *in-* 'into' + *gerere* 'carry.' **—in·ges·tion** /-'jescнən/ *n.* **—in·ges·tive** /-'jestiv/ *adj.*

in·ges·ta /in'jestə/ ▸*plural n. Medicine & Zoology* substances taken into the body as nourishment; food and drink. ▷early 18th cent.: from Latin, 'things brought in.'

-ing form ▸*n. Grammar* the form of an English verb ending in *-ing*, which can function as a noun, as an adjective, and in the formation of progressive tenses. See also PARTICIPLE, GERUND.

in·gle /'iNGgəl/ ▸*n. chiefly dialect* a domestic fire or fireplace. ■ an inglenook. ▷early 16th cent. (originally Scots): perhaps from Scottish Gaelic *aingeal* 'light, fire,' Irish *aingeal* 'live ember.'

in·gle·nook /'iNGgəl,nŏŏk/ ▸*n.* a space on either side of a large fireplace. ▷late 18th cent.: from Scots INGLE + NOOK.

in·glo·ri·ous /in'glôrēəs/ ▸*adj.* (of an action or situation) causing shame or a loss of honor: *the events are inglorious and culminate in a vicious gang crime.* ■ not famous or renowned. ▷mid 16th cent.: from Latin *inglorius* (from *in-* (expressing negation) + *gloria* 'glory') + -OUS. **—in·glo·ri·ous·ly** *adv.* **—in·glo·ri·ous·ness** *n.*

in·go·ing /ˈinˌgōiNG/ ▸*adj.* [*attrib.*] going into or toward a particular place: *the paths of ingoing and outgoing rays.*

in·got /ˈiNGgət/ ▸*n.* a block of steel, gold, silver, or other metal, typically oblong in shape. ▹late Middle English (denoting a mold in which metal is cast): perhaps from IN + Old English *goten*, past participle of *geotan* 'pour, cast.'

in·graft ▸*v.* variant spelling of ENGRAFT.

in·grain ▸*v.* /inˈgrān/ (also **en·grain**) [*trans.*] firmly fix or establish (a habit, belief, or attitude) in a person.
▸*adj.* /ˈinˌgrān/ (of a textile) composed of fibers that have been dyed different colors before being woven. ▹late Middle English (originally as *engrain* in the sense 'dye with cochineal or in fast colors'): from EN-[1], IN-[2] (as an intensifier) + the verb GRAIN. The adjective is from *in grain* 'fast-dyed,' from the old use of *grain* meaning 'kermes, cochineal.'

in·grain car·pet ▸*n.* a reversible carpet in which the pattern appears on both sides.

in·grained /inˈgrānd/ ▸*adj.* (also **en·grained**) **1** (of a habit, belief, or attitude) firmly fixed or established; difficult to change: *his deeply ingrained Catholic convictions.* See note at INHERENT. **2** (of dirt or a stain) deeply embedded and thus difficult to remove: *the ingrained dirt on the flaking paintwork.*

in·grate /ˈinˌgrāt/ ▸*n.* an ungrateful person.
▸*adj. poetic/literary* ungrateful. ▹late Middle English (as an adjective): from Latin *ingratus*, from *in-* 'not' + *gratus* 'grateful.'

in·gra·ti·ate /inˈgrāSHēˌāt/ ▸*v.* (**ingratiate oneself**) bring oneself into favor with someone by flattering or trying to please them: *a social climber who had tried to* ***ingratiate herself with*** *the city gentry.* ▹early 17th cent.: from Latin *in gratiam* 'into favor,' on the pattern of obsolete Italian *ingratiare*, earlier form of *ingraziare*. —**in·gra·ti·a·tion** /-ˌgrāSHēˈāSHən/ *n.*

in·gra·ti·at·ing /inˈgrāSHēˌātiNG/ ▸*adj.* intended to gain approval or favor; sycophantic: *an ingratiating manner.* —**in·gra·ti·at·ing·ly** *adv.*

in·grat·i·tude /inˈgratiˌt(y)o͞od/ ▸*n.* a discreditable lack of gratitude: *she returned her daughter's care with ingratitude and unkindness.* ▹Middle English: from Old French, or from late Latin *ingratitudo*, from Latin *ingratus* 'ungrateful' (see INGRATE).

in·gra·ves·cent /ˌingrəˈvesənt/ ▸*adj. rare Medicine* (of a condition or symptom) gradually increasing in severity. ▹early 19th cent.: from Latin *ingravescent-* 'growing heavy or worse,' from the verb *ingravescere* (based on *gravis* 'heavy'). —**in·gra·ves·cence** *n.*

in·gre·di·ent /inˈgrēdēənt; iNG-/ ▸*n.* any of the foods or substances that are combined to make a particular dish: *pork is an important ingredient in many stir-fried dishes.* ▪ a component part or element of something: *the affair contains all the ingredients of an insoluble mystery.* ▹late Middle English: from Latin *ingredient-* 'entering,' from the verb *ingredi*, from *in-* 'into' + *gradi* 'walk.'

In·gres /ˈaNGgrə/, Jean Auguste Dominique (1780–1867), French painter. He vigorously upheld neoclassicism in opposition to romanticism. Notable works: *Ambassadors of Agamemnon* (1801) and *The Bather* (1808).

in·gress /ˈinˌgres/ ▸*n.* **1** a place or means of access; an entrance. ▪ the action or fact of going in or entering. ▪ the capacity or right of entrance. ▪ *chiefly Brit.* the unwanted introduction of water, foreign bodies, contaminants, etc. into something. **2** *Astronomy & Astrology* the arrival of the sun, the moon, or a planet in a specified constellation or part of the sky. ▪ the beginning of a transit. ▹late Middle English (in the sense 'an entrance or beginning'): from Latin *ingressus*, from the verb *ingredi* 'enter.' —**in·gres·sion** /-ˈgresHən/ *n.*

in·gres·sive /inˈgresiv/ ▸*adj.* **1** of or relating to ingress; having the quality or character of entering. **2** *Phonetics* (of a speech sound) made with an intake of air rather than an exhalation. Compare with EGRESSIVE. ▪ (of an airflow) inward.
▸*n.* an ingressive sound, e.g., a click.

in-group ▸*n.* an exclusive, typically small, group of people with a shared interest or identity.

in·grow·ing /ˈinˌgrōiNG/ ▸*adj.* growing inward or within something, esp. (of a toenail) growing abnormally so as to press into the flesh.

in·grown /ˈinˌgrōn/ ▸*adj.* growing or having grown within a thing; innate: *as Greek instinct or ingrown habit would have dictated.* ▪ (of a toenail) having grown abnormally so as to press into the flesh. ▪ preoccupied with oneself; inward-looking: *direct mail is a clubby, ingrown world in which everybody knows everybody.* ▪ *Geology* (of an incised meander) asymmetric in cross section due to lateral erosion.

in·growth /ˈinˌgrōTH/ ▸*n.* a thing that has grown inward or within something. ▪ the action of growing inward: *blocked by tumor ingrowth.*

in·gui·nal /ˈiNGgwənəl/ ▸*adj.* [*attrib.*] *Anatomy* of the groin: *inguinal lymph nodes.* ▹late Middle English: from Latin *inguinalis*, from *inguen*, *inguin-* 'groin.' —**in·gui·nal·ly** *adv.*

in·gulf ▸*v.* archaic spelling of ENGULF.

in·gur·gi·tate /inˈgərjiˌtāt/ ▸*v.* [*trans.*] *poetic/literary* swallow (something) greedily. ▹late 16th cent.: from Latin *ingurgitat-* 'poured in, drenched,' from the verb *ingurgitare*, from *in-* 'into' + *gurges*, *gurgit-* 'whirlpool, gulf.' —**in·gur·gi·ta·tion** /-ˌgərjiˈtāSHən/ *n.*

In·gush /inˈgo͞osH/ ▸*n.* (*pl.* same or **-gush·es**) **1** a member of a people living mainly in the Ingushetiya in the central Caucasus, between Chechnya and North Ossetia. **2** the North Caucasian language of this people.
▸*adj.* of or relating to the Ingush or their language. ▹Russian.

INH ▸*abbr.* isonicotinic acid hydrazide.

in·hab·it /inˈhabit/ ▸*v.* (**-hab·it·ed**, **-hab·it·ing**) [*trans.*] (of a person, animal, or group) live in or occupy (a place or environment): *a bird that inhabits North America* | *urban centers inhabited by more than 10 million people* | [as *adj.*] (**inhabited**) *the loneliest inhabited place on Earth.* ▹late Middle English *inhabite*, *enhabite*, from Old French *enhabiter* or Latin *inhabitare*, from *in-* 'in' + *habitare* 'dwell' (from *habere* 'have'). —**in·hab·it·a·bil·i·ty** /-ˌhabitəˈbilitē/ *n.* —**in·hab·it·a·ble** *adj.* —**in·hab·i·ta·tion** /-ˌhabiˈtāSHən/ *n.*

in·hab·it·an·cy /inˈhabitn-sē/ (also **in·hab·it·ance**) ▸*n.* *archaic* living in a certain place as an inhabitant, esp. during a specified period so as to acquire certain rights.

in·hab·it·ant /inˈhabitnt/ ▸*n.* a person or animal that lives in or occupies a place. ▪ a person who fulfills the requirements for legal residency. ▹late Middle English: from Old French, from Latin *inhabitare* 'inhabit.'

in·hal·ant /inˈhālənt/ ▸*n.* a medicinal preparation for inhaling. ▪ a solvent or other material producing vapor inhaled by drug abusers.
▸*adj.* [*attrib.*] *chiefly Zoology* serving for inhalation: *inhalant canals.*

in·ha·la·tion /ˌinhəˈlāSHən/ ▸*n.* the action of inhaling or breathing in: *the inhalation of airborne particles* | *with every inhalation air passes over the vocal cords.* ▪ *Medicine* the inhaling of medicines or anesthetics in the form of a gas or vapor. ▪ *Medicine* a preparation to be inhaled in the form of a vapor or spray. ▹early 17th cent.: from medieval Latin *inhalatio(n-)*, from *inhalare* 'inhale.'

in·ha·la·tor /ˈinhəˌlātər/ ▸*n.* a device for inhaling something, esp. oxygen; a respirator; an inhaler.

in·hale /inˈhāl/ ▸*v.* breathe in (air, gas, smoke, etc.): [*trans.*] *they were taken to the hospital after inhaling fumes* | [*intrans.*] *she inhaled deeply on another cigarette.* ▪ [*trans.*] *informal* eat (food) greedily or rapidly: *later on I inhaled a box of chocolate cookies while watching cable TV.* ▹early 18th cent.: from Latin *inhalare* 'breathe in,' from *in-* 'in' + *halare* 'breathe.'

in·hal·er /inˈhālər/ ▸*n.* a portable device for administering a drug that is to be breathed in, used for relieving asthma and other bronchial or nasal congestion.

in·har·mon·ic /ˌinhärˈmänik/ ▸*adj.* *chiefly Music* not harmonic. —**in·har·mo·nic·i·ty** /-məˈnisitē/ *n.*

in·har·mo·ni·ous /ˌinhärˈmōnēəs/ ▸*adj.* not forming or contributing to a pleasing whole; discordant: *an inharmonious, negative state of mind.* —**in·har·mo·ni·ous·ly** *adv.*

in·here /inˈhi(ə)r/ ▸*v.* [*intrans.*] (**inhere in/within**) *formal* exist essentially or permanently in: *the potential for change that inheres within the adult education world.* ▪ *Law* (of rights, powers, etc.) be vested in a person or group or attached to the ownership of a property: *the rights inhering in the property they owned.* ▹mid 16th cent. (in the sense 'stick, cling to'): from Latin *inhaerere* 'stick to.'

in·her·ent /inˈhi(ə)rənt; -ˈher-/ ▸*adj.* existing in something as a permanent, essential, or characteristic attribute: *any form of mountaineering has its inherent dangers* | *the symbolism inherent in all folk tales.* ▪ *Law* vested in (someone) as a right or privilege: *the president's inherent foreign affairs power.* ▹late 16th cent.: from Latin *inhaerent-* 'sticking to,' from the verb *inhaerere*, from *in-* 'in, toward' + *haerere* 'to stick.' —**in·her·ence** *n.* —**in·her·ent·ly** *adv.*

THE RIGHT WORD **congenital, essential, inborn, ingrained, inherent, innate, intrinsic**

A quality that is **inherent** is a permanent part of a person's nature or essence (*an inherent tendency to fight back*).

If it is **ingrained**, it is deeply wrought into his or her substance or character (*ingrained prejudice against women*).

Inborn and **innate** are nearly synonymous, sharing the basic sense of existing at the time of birth, but *innate* is usually preferred in an abstract or philosophical context (*innate defects; innate ideas*), while *inborn* is reserved for human characteristics that are so deep-seated they seem to have been there from birth (*an inborn aptitude for the piano*).

Congenital also means from the time of one's birth, but it is primarily used in medical contexts and refers to problems or defects (*congenital color-blindness; a congenital tendency toward schizophrenia*).

Intrinsic and **essential** are broader terms that can apply to things as well as people. Something that is *essential* is part of the essence or constitution of something (*an essential ingredient; essential revisions in the text*), while an *intrinsic* quality is one that belongs naturally to a person or thing (*her intrinsic fairness; an intrinsic weakness in the design*).

in·her·it /inˈherit/ ▸*v.* (**-her·it·ed**, **-her·it·ing**) [*trans.*] receive (money, property, or a title) as an heir at the death of the previous holder: *she inherited a fortune from her father.* ▪ derive (a quality, characteristic, or predisposition) genetically from one's parents or ancestors: *she had inherited the beauty of her grandmother.* ▪ receive or be left with (a situation, object, etc.) from a predecessor or former owner: *spending commitments inherited from previous administrations.* ▪ come into possession of (belongings) from someone else: *she inherits all her clothes from her older sisters.* ▪ *archaic* come into possession of (something) as a right (esp. in biblical translations and allusions): *master, what must I do to inherit eternal life?* ▹Middle English *enherite* 'receive as a right,' from Old French *enheriter*, from late Latin *inhereditare* 'appoint as heir,' from Latin *in-* 'in' + *heres*, *hered-* 'heir.' —**in·her·i·tor** /-ˈheritər/ *n.*

in·her·it·a·ble /inˈheritəbəl/ ▸*adj.* capable of being inherited: *these characteristics are inheritable* | *inheritable property.* ▹late Middle English (formerly also as *enheritable*): from Anglo-Norman French *enheritable* 'able to be made heir,' from Old French *enheriter* (see INHERIT). —**in·her·it·a·bil·i·ty** /-ˌheritəˈbilitē/ *n.*

in·her·it·ance /inˈheritəns/ ▸*n.* a thing that is inherited: *he came into a comfortable inheritance.* ▪ the action of inheriting: *the inheritance of traits.* ▹late Middle English (formerly also as *enheritance*): from Anglo-Norman French *enheritaunce* 'being admitted as heir,' from Old French *enheriter* (see INHERIT).

in·her·it·ance tax ▸*n.* a tax imposed on someone who inherits property or money. Also called DEATH TAX.

in·he·sion /inˈhēZHən/ ▸*n.* *formal* the action or state of inhering in something. ▹mid 17th cent.: from late Latin *inhaesio(n-)*, from Latin *inhaerere* 'stick to.'

in·hib·in /inˈhibin/ ▸*n.* *Biochemistry* a gonadal hormone that inhibits the secretion of follicle-stimulating hormone, under consideration as a potential male contraceptive. ▹1930s: from Latin *inhibere* 'hinder' + -IN[1].

in·hib·it /inˈhibit/ ▸*v.* (**-hib·it·ed**, **-hib·it·ing**) [*trans.*] hinder, restrain, or prevent (an action or process): *cold inhibits plant growth.* See note at THWART. ▪ prevent or prohibit someone from doing something: *the earnings rule* ***inhibited*** *some retired people* ***from*** *working.* ▪ *Psychology* voluntarily or involuntarily restrain the direct expression of (an instinctive impulse). ▪ make (someone) self-conscious and unable to act in a relaxed and natural way: *his mother's strictures would always inhibit him.* ▪ *chiefly Physiology & Biochemistry* (chiefly of a drug or other substance) slow down or prevent (a process, reaction, or function) or reduce the activity of (an enzyme or other agent). ▪ (in ecclesiastical law) forbid (a member of the clergy) to exercise clerical functions. ▹late Middle English (in the sense 'forbid (a person) to do something'): from Latin *inhibere* 'hinder,' from *in-* 'in' + *habere* 'hold.' —**in·hib·i·tive** /-tiv/ *adj.* —**in·hib·i·to·ry** /-ˌtôrē/ *adj.*

in·hib·it·ed /inˈhibitid/ ▸*adj.* unable to act in a relaxed and natural way because of self-consciousness or mental restraint: *I could never appear nude, I'm far too inhibited.*

in·hi·bi·tion /ˌin(h)iˈbisʜən/ ▸*n.* a feeling that makes one self-conscious and unable to act in a relaxed and natural way: *the children, at first shy, soon lost their inhibitions | a powerful tranquilizer that causes lack of inhibition.* ■ *Psychology* a voluntary or involuntary restraint on the direct expression of an instinct. ■ the action of inhibiting, restricting, or hindering a process. ■ the slowing or prevention of a process, reaction, or function by a particular substance. ▷late Middle English (in the sense 'forbidding, a prohibition'): from Latin *inhibitio(n-)*, from the verb *inhibere* (see **INHIBIT**).

in·hib·i·tor /inˈhibitər/ ▸*n.* a thing that inhibits someone or something. ■ a substance that slows down or prevents a particular chemical reaction or other process, or that reduces the activity of a particular reactant, catalyst, or enzyme. ■ *Genetics* a gene whose presence prevents the expression of some other gene at a different locus.

in-home ▸*adj.* [*attrib.*] (of a service or activity) provided or taking place within a person's home: *the best in in-home entertainment.*

in·ho·mo·ge·ne·ous /inˌhōməˈjēnēəs; -ˌhämə-/ ▸*adj.* not uniform in character or content; diverse. ■ *Mathematics* consisting of terms that are not all of the same degree or dimensions. **—in·ho·mo·ge·ne·i·ty** /-ˌhōməjəˈnē-itē; -ˈnā-itē; -ˌhämə-/ *n.*

in·hos·pi·ta·ble /ˌinhäˈspitəbəl; inˈhäs-/ ▸*adj.* (of an environment) harsh and difficult to live in: *the inhospitable landscape.* ■ (of a person) unfriendly and unwelcoming toward people. ▷late 16th cent.: French, from *in-* 'not' + *hospitable* (see **HOSPITABLE**). **—in·hos·pi·ta·ble·ness** *n.* **—in·hos·pi·ta·bly** /-blē/ *adv.* **—in·hos·pi·tal·i·ty** /inˌhäspiˈtalitē; ˌinhäs-/ *n.*

in-house ▸*adj.* [*attrib.*] done or existing within an organization: *in-house publications.*
▸*adv.* without assistance from outside an organization; internally: *services previously provided in-house are being contracted out.*

in·hu·man /inˈ(h)yo͞omən/ ▸*adj.* **1** lacking human qualities of compassion and mercy; cruel and barbaric. **2** not human in nature or character: *the inhuman scale of the dinosaurs.* ▷late Middle English (originally as *inhumane*): from Latin *inhumanus*, from *in-* 'not' + *humanus* (see **HUMAN**). **—in·hu·man·ly** *adv.*

in·hu·man·i·ty /ˌin(h)yo͞oˈmanitē/ ▸*n.* (*pl.* **-ties**) extremely cruel and brutal behavior: *a justification for further cruelty and inhumanity.* ▷late 15th cent.: from Old French *inhumanite* or Latin *inhumanitas*, from *inhumanus* 'inhuman.'

in·hume /inˈ(h)yo͞om/ ▸*v.* [*trans.*] bury: *no hand his bones shall gather or inhume.* ▷early 17th cent.: from Latin *inhumare*, from *in-* 'into' + *humus* 'ground.' **—in·hu·ma·tion** /ˌin(h)yo͞oˈmāsʜən/ *n.*

in·im·i·cal /iˈnimikəl/ ▸*adj.* tending to obstruct or harm: *actions* **inimical to** *our interests.* ■ unfriendly; hostile: *an inimical alien power.* See note at **HOSTILE**. ▷early 16th cent.: from late Latin *inimicalis*, from Latin *inimicus* (see **ENEMY**). **—in·im·i·cal·ly** /-ik(ə)lē/ *adv.*

in·im·i·ta·ble /iˈnimitəbəl/ ▸*adj.* so good or unusual as to be impossible to copy; unique: *the inimitable ambience of Hawaii.* ▷late 15th cent.: from French, or from Latin *inimitabilis*, from *in-* 'not' + *imitabilis* (from *imitari* 'imitate'). **—in·im·i·ta·bil·i·ty** /iˌnimitəˈbilitē/ *n.* **—in·im·i·ta·bly** /-blē/ *adv.*

in·i·on /ˈinēən/ ▸*n.* *Anatomy* the projecting part of the occipital bone at the base of the skull. ▷early 19th cent.: from Greek, literally 'nape of the neck.'

in·iq·ui·ty /iˈnikwitē/ ▸*n.* (*pl.* **-ties**) immoral or grossly unfair behavior: *a den of iniquity | a liberal lawyer could uncover the iniquities committed on his own doorstep.* ▷Middle English: from Old French *iniquite*, from Latin *iniquitas*, from *iniquus*, from *in-* 'not' + *aequus* 'equal, just.' **—in·iq·ui·tous** /-witəs/ *adj.* **—in·iq·ui·tous·ly** /-witəslē/ *adv.* **—in·iq·ui·tous·ness** /-witəsnəs/ *n.*

in·i·tial /iˈnisʜəl/ ▸*adj.* [*attrib.*] existing or occurring at the beginning: *our initial impression was favorable.* ■ (of a letter) at the beginning of a word.
▸*n.* (usu. **initials**) the first letter of a name or word, typically a person's name or a word forming part of a phrase: *they carved their initials into the tree trunk.*
▸*v.* (**-tialed, -tial·ing**; *Brit.* **-tialled, -tial·ling**) [*trans.*] mark or sign (a document) with one's initials, esp. in order to authorize or validate it. ■ agree to or ratify (a treaty or contract) by signing it. ▷early 16th cent.: from Latin *initialis*, from *initium* 'beginning,' from *inire* 'go in,' from *in-* 'into' + *ire* 'go.'

in·i·tial·ese /iˌnisʜəˈlēz/ ▸*n.* *informal* the use of abbreviations formed by using initial letters.

in·i·tial·ism /iˈnisʜəˌlizəm/ ▸*n.* an abbreviation consisting of initial letters pronounced separately (e.g., *CPU*). ■ an acronym.

in·i·tial·ize /iˈnisʜəˌlīz/ ▸*v.* [*trans.*] *Computing* **1** (often **be initialized to**) set to the value or put in the condition appropriate to the start of an operation: *the counter is initialized to one.* **2** format (a computer disk). **—in·i·tial·i·za·tion** /iˌnisʜəliˈzāsʜən/ *n.*

in·i·tial·ly /iˈnisʜəlē/ ▸*adv.* [usu. *sentence adverb*] at first: *initially, he thought the new concept was nonsense.*

in·i·tial pub·lic of·fer·ing ▸*n.* a company's flotation on the stock exchange.

in·i·ti·and /iˈnisʜēˌand/ ▸*n.* a person about to be initiated. ▷early 20th cent.: from Latin *initiandus*, from *initiare* 'to initiate.'

in·i·ti·ate ▸*v.* /iˈnisʜēˌāt/ [*trans.*] **1** cause (a process or action) to begin: *he proposes to initiate discussions on planning procedures.* **2** admit (someone) into a secret or obscure society or group, typically with a ritual: *she had been formally* **initiated into** *the sorority.* ■ [as *plural n.*] (**the initiated**) *figurative* a small group of people who share obscure knowledge: *he flies over an airway marker beacon, known as a "fix" to the initiated.* ■ (**initiate someone in/into**) introduce someone to a particular activity or skill, esp. a difficult or obscure one: *they were initiated into the mysteries of trigonometry.*
▸*n.* /iˈnisʜēit/ a person who has been initiated into an organization or activity, typically recently: *initiates of the Shiva cult* | [as *adj.*] *the initiate Marines.* ▷mid 16th cent. (sense 2): from Latin *initiat-* 'begun,' from the verb *initiare*, from *initium* 'beginning.' **—in·i·ti·a·tion** /iˌnisʜēˈāsʜən/ *n.* **—in·i·ti·a·to·ry** /-əˌtôrē/ *adj.*

in·i·ti·a·tive /iˈnisʜ(ē)ətiv/ ▸*n.* **1** the ability to assess and initiate things independently: *use your initiative, imagination, and common sense.* **2** [in *sing.*] the power or opportunity to act or take charge before others do: *we have lost the initiative and allowed our opponents to dictate the subject.* **3** an act or strategy intended to resolve a difficulty or improve a situation; a fresh approach to something: *a new initiative against car crime.* ■ a proposal made by one nation to another in an attempt to improve relations: *diplomatic initiatives to end the war* | [with *adj.*] *a Middle East peace initiative.* **4** (**the initiative**) (esp. in some U.S. states and Switzerland) the right of citizens outside the legislature to originate legislation. ▷late 18th cent.: from French, from Latin *initiare*, from *initium* 'beginning.'
▸*PHRASES* □ **on one's own initiative** without being prompted by others. □ **take** (or **seize**) **the initiative** be the first to take action in a particular situation: *antihunting groups have seized the initiative in the dispute.*

in·i·ti·a·tor /iˈnisʜēˌātər/ ▸*n.* a person or thing that initiates someone or something. ■ *Chemistry* a substance that starts a chain reaction. ■ an explosive or device used to detonate a larger one.

inj. ▸*abbr.* injection.

in·ject /inˈjekt/ ▸*v.* [*trans.*] **1** drive or force (a liquid, esp. a drug or vaccine) into a person or animal's body with a syringe or similar device: *the doctor injected a painkilling drug.* ■ administer a drug or medicine to (a person or animal) in this way: *he* **injected** *himself* **with** *a drug overdose.* ■ [*intrans.*] inject oneself with a narcotic drug, esp. habitually: *people who want to stop injecting.* ■ introduce (something) into a passage, cavity, or solid material under pressure: *inject the foam and allow it to expand.* See note at **INSERT**. ■ *Physics* introduce or feed (a current, beam of particles, etc.) into a substance or device. ■ place (a spacecraft or other object) into an orbit or trajectory: *many meteoroids are* **injected into** *hyperbolic orbits.* **2** introduce (a new or different element) into something, esp. as a boost or interruption: *she tried to* **inject** *scorn* **into** *her tone.* ■ (**inject something with**) imbue something with (a new element): *he injected his voice with a confidence he didn't feel.* ▷late 16th cent. (in the sense 'throw or cast on something'): from Latin *inject-* 'thrown in,' from the verb *inicere*, from *in-* 'into' + *jacere* 'throw.' **—in·ject·a·ble** *adj.* & *n.*

in·jec·tion /inˈjeksʜən/ ▸*n.* **1** an instance of injecting or being injected: *painkilling injections | an injection of capital was needed.* ■ a thing that is injected: *a morphine injection.* ■ the action of injecting: *sometimes a polio vaccine is given by injection.* ■ short for **FUEL INJECTION**. **2** the entry or placing of a spacecraft or other object into an orbit or trajectory. ▷late Middle English: from Latin *injectio(n-)*, from the verb *inicere* (see **INJECT**).

in·jec·tion mold·ing ▸*n.* the shaping of rubber or plastic articles by injecting heated material into a mold. **—in·jec·tion-mold·ed** *adj.*

in·jec·tor /inˈjektər/ ▸*n.* a person or thing that injects something. ■ (also **fuel injector**) (in an internal combustion engine) the nozzle and valve through which fuel is sprayed into a combustion chamber. ■ (in a steam engine) a system of nozzles that uses steam to inject water into a pressurized boiler.

in·je·ra /inˈji(ə)rə/ ▸*n.* a white leavened Ethiopian bread made from teff flour, similar to a crepe. ▷Amharic.

in-joke ▸*n.* a joke that is shared exclusively by a small group of people.

In·jun /ˈinjən/ ▸*n.* *informal, offensive* an American Indian. ▷late 17th cent.: alteration of **INDIAN**.
▸*PHRASE* □ **honest Injun** *dated* honestly; really: *I won't run away, honest Injun.*

in·junc·tion /inˈjəNG(k)sʜən/ ▸*n.* an authoritative warning or order. ■ *Law* a judicial order that restrains a person from beginning or continuing an action threatening or invading the legal right of another, or that compels a person to carry out a certain act, e.g., to make restitution to an injured party. ▷late Middle English: from late Latin *injunctio(n-)*, from Latin *injungere* 'enjoin, impose.' **—in·junc·tive** /-ˈjəNG(k)tiv/ *adj.*

in·jure /ˈinjər/ ▸*v.* [*trans.*] do physical harm or damage to (someone): *the explosion injured several people.* ■ suffer physical harm or damage to (a part of one's body): *he injured his back.* ■ harm or impair (something): *a libel calculated to injure the company's reputation.* ■ *archaic* do injustice or wrong to (someone). ▷late Middle English: back-formation from **INJURY**. **—in·jur·er** *n.*

in·jured /ˈinjərd/ ▸*adj.* **1** harmed, damaged, or impaired: *a road accident left him severely injured.* **2** offended: *his injured pride.*

in·ju·ri·ous /inˈjo͝orēəs/ ▸*adj.* causing or likely to cause damage or harm: *high temperature is* **injurious to** *mangoes.* ■ (of language) maliciously insulting; libelous. ▷late Middle English: from French *injurieux* or Latin *injuriosus*, from *injuria* 'a wrong' (see **INJURY**). **—in·ju·ri·ous·ly** *adv.* **—in·ju·ri·ous·ness** *n.*

in·ju·ry /ˈinjərē/ ▸*n.* (*pl.* **-ries**) an instance of being injured: *she suffered an injury to her back | an ankle injury.* ■ the fact of being injured; harm or damage: *all escaped without serious injury.* ■ (**injury to**) offense to: *the possible injury to the feelings of others.* ▷late Middle English: from Anglo-Norman French *injurie*, from Latin *injuria* 'a wrong,' from *in-* (expressing negation) + *jus, jur-* 'right.'
▸*PHRASE* □ **do oneself an injury** *informal* suffer physical harm or damage.

in·ju·ry time ▸*n.* (in soccer and other sports) extra playing time allowed by a referee to compensate for time lost in dealing with injuries.

in·jus·tice /inˈjəstis/ ▸*n.* lack of fairness or justice: *the injustice of the death penalty.* ■ an unjust act or occurrence: *brooding over life's injustices.* ▷late Middle English: from Old French, from Latin *injustitia*, from *in-* 'not' + *justus* 'just, right.'
▸*PHRASE* □ **do someone an injustice** judge a person unfairly.

ink /iNGk/ ▸*n.* a colored fluid used for writing, drawing, printing, or duplicating: *the names are written in ink | a picture executed in colored inks.* ■ *informal* publicity: *cases in which prosecutors seek the death penalty are likely to be those that get lots of ink and air time.* ■ *Zoology* a black liquid ejected by a cuttlefish, octopus, or squid to confuse a predator.
▸*v.* **1** [*trans.*] mark (words or a design) with ink: *the cork has the name of the château inked onto the side.* ■ cover (type or a stamp) with ink before printing: *a raised image is inked to produce an impression.* ■ (**ink something in**) fill in writing or a design with ink: *she inked in a cloud of dust.* ■ (**ink something out**) obliterate something, esp. writing, with ink: *he carefully inked out each word.* **2** *informal* sign (a contract): *she's just inked a deal to host her own talk show.* ■ secure the services of (someone) with a contract: *he has been inked as host for next year's ceremony.* ▷Middle English *enke, inke*, from Old French *enque*, via late Latin from Greek *enkauston*, denoting the purple ink used by Roman emperors for signatures, from *enkaiein* 'burn in.' **—ink·er** *n.*

In·ka·tha /inˈkätə/ (in full **Inkatha Freedom Party**) (abbr.: **IFP**) a mainly Zulu political party and organization in South Africa, founded in 1928 and revived in 1975 by Chief Buthelezi. It has a professed aim of racial equality and universal franchise in South Africa, but progress toward political reform was obstructed by violent clashes between Inkatha factions and members of the rival ANC. ▷from Zulu *inkhata* 'crown of woven grass,' a tribal emblem symbolizing the force unifying the Zulu nation.

ink·ber·ry /ˈiNGkˌberē/ ▸*n.* (*pl.* **-ries**) **1** another term for **LOW GALLBERRY** (see **GALLBERRY**). **2** another term for **POKEWEED**.

ink·blot test /'iNGk,blät/ ▸*n.* another term for RORSCHACH TEST.

ink·horn /'iNGk,hôrn/ ▸*n. historical* a small portable container for ink. ■ [as *adj.*] denoting pedantic words or expressions used only in academic writing: *I will avoid many of the inkhorn terms coined by the narratologists.*

ink-jet print·er (also **ink·jet**) ▸*n.* a printer in which the characters are formed by minute jets of ink.

in·kle /'iNGkəl/ ▸*n.* a kind of linen tape formerly used to make laces, or the linen yarn from which this is manufactured. ▷mid 16th cent.: of unknown origin.

ink·ling /'iNGkliNG/ ▸*n.* a slight knowledge or suspicion; a hint: *the records give us an inkling of how people saw the world.* ▷late Middle English (in the sense 'a mention in an undertone, a hint'): from the rare verb *inkle* 'utter in an undertone,' of unknown origin.

ink pad ▸*n.* an ink-soaked pad in a shallow box, used for inking a rubber stamp or taking fingerprints.

ink·stand /'iNGk,stand/ ▸*n.* a stand for one or more ink bottles, typically incorporating a pen tray.

ink·well /'iNGk,wel/ ▸*n.* a container for ink typically housed in a hole in a desk.

ink·y /'iNGkē/ ▸*adj.* (**ink·i·er, ink·i·est**) **1** as dark as ink: *the cold inky blackness of a Mexican cave.* **2** stained with ink: *bureaucrats with inky fingers.* —**ink·i·ness** *n.*

ink·y cap ▸*n.* a widely distributed mushroom with a tall, narrow cap and slender white stem, turning into a black liquid after the spores are shed. • Genus *Coprinus*, family Coprinaceae, class Hymenomycetes: several species, including the **common ink cap** (*C. atramentarius*). See also SHAGGY MANE.

in·laid /'in,lād/ ▸ past and past participle of INLAY.

in·land /'in,land; -lənd/ ▸*adj.* situated in the interior of a country rather than on the coast: *the deserts of inland Australia.* ■ [*attrib.*] *chiefly Brit.* carried on within the limits of a country; domestic: *a network of waterways that allowed inland trade.*
▸*adv.* in or toward the interior of a country: *the path turned inland and met the road.*
▸*n.* (**the inland**) the parts of a country remote from the sea or borders; the interior. —**in·land·er** *n.*

in·land nav·i·ga·tion ▸*n.* transportation by canals, rivers, and lakes.

In·land Sea an almost landlocked arm of the Pacific Ocean that is surrounded by the Japanese islands of Honshu, Shikoku, and Kyushu. Its chief port is Hiroshima.

in·land sea ▸*n.* an entirely landlocked large body of salt or fresh water.

in-law ▸*n.* a relative by marriage.

in·lay ▸*v.* /,in'lā/ (*past* and *past part.* **-laid**) [*trans.*] (usu. **be inlaid**) ornament (an object) by embedding pieces of a different material in it, flush with its surface: *mahogany paneling **inlaid with** rosewood.* ■ embed (something) in an object in this way: *a small silver crown was inlaid in the wood.* ■ insert (a page, an illustration, etc.) in a space cut in a larger thicker page.
▸*n.* /'in,lā/ **1** a design, pattern, or piece of material inlaid in something: *ivory inlays that decorated wooden furnishings.* ■ a material or substance that is inlaid. ■ inlaid work: *the cathedral was decorated with mosaic and inlay.* ■ the technique of inlaying material. **2** a filling shaped to fit a tooth cavity. **3** *chiefly Brit.* a printed card or paper insert supplied with a CD, video, etc.: [as *adj.*] *an inlay card.* ▷mid 16th cent. (in the sense 'lay something in a place in order to hide or preserve it'): from IN-[2] 'into' + LAY[1]. —**in·lay·er** *n.*

in·let /'in,let; -lit/ ▸*n.* **1** a small arm of the sea, a lake, or a river. **2** a place or means of entry: *an air inlet.* **3** (chiefly in tailoring and dressmaking) an inserted piece of material. ▷Middle English (denoting admission): from IN + the verb LET[1].

in·li·er /'in,līər/ ▸*n. Geology* an older rock formation isolated among newer rocks. ▷mid 19th cent.: from IN, on the pattern of *outlier.*

in-line ▸*adj.* **1** having parts arranged in a line: *a 24-valve in-line 6-cylinder engine.* **2** constituting an integral part of a continuous sequence of operations or machines: *a two-stream in-line fuel-oil blender.* ■ constituting an integral part of a computer program: *the parameters can be set up as in-line code.*

in-lin·er ▸*n.* an in-line skater. ■ an in-line skate.

in-line skate ▸ *n.* a roller skate in which the wheels are fixed in a single line along the sole of the boot. —**in-line skat·er** *n.* —**in-line skat·ing** *n.*

in-line skate

in lo·co pa·ren·tis /in ,lōkō pə'rentis/ ▸*adv.* & *adj.* (of a teacher or other adult responsible for children) in the place of a parent: [as *adv.*] *he was used to **acting in loco parentis*** | [as *adj.*] *they adhered to an in loco parentis approach when dealing with students.* ▷early 19th cent.: Latin.

in·ly /'inlē/ ▸*adv. poetic/literary* inwardly: *inly stung with anger and disdain.* ▷Old English *innlīce* (see IN, -LY[2]).

In·man /'inmən/, Henry (1801–46) U.S. artist. A leading portraitist, he painted many well-known people of his time. He also helped to found the National Academy of Design 1826.

In·mar·sat /'inmär,sat/ an international organization founded in 1978 that provides telecommunication services, as well as distress and safety communication services, to the world's shipping, aviation, and offshore industries. ▷from initials of *International Maritime Satellite Organization.*

in·mate /'in,māt/ ▸*n.* a person confined to an institution such as a prison or hospital. ■ *archaic* one of several occupants of a house. ▷late 16th cent. (denoting a person who shared a house, specifically a lodger or subtenant): probably originally from INN + MATE[1], later associated with IN.

in me·di·as res /in 'mēdēəs 'res; 'mādē,äs/ ▸*adv.* into the middle of a narrative; without preamble: *having begun his story in medias res, he then interrupts it.* ■ into the midst of things. ▷late 18th cent.: Latin, literally 'into the middle of things.'

in me·mo·ri·am /,in mə'môrēəm/ ▸*n.* [often as *adj.*] an article written in memory of a dead person; an obituary: *in memoriam notices in the paper.*
▸*prep.* in memory of (a dead person): *an openly revolutionary work in memoriam Che Guevara.* ▷mid 19th cent.: Latin, literally 'to the memory (of).'

in·most /'in,mōst/ ▸*adj. poetic/literary* innermost. ▷Old English *innemest* (see IN, -MOST).

In·mut·too·yah·lat·lat /in,mōōtōōyä'lät,lät/ see JOSEPH[2].

inn /in/ ▸*n.* an establishment providing accommodations, food, and drink, esp. for travelers. ■ [usu. in *names*] a restaurant or bar, typically one in the country, in some cases providing accommodations: *the Waterside Inn.* ▷Old English (in the sense 'dwelling place, lodging'): of Germanic origin; related to IN. In Middle English the word was used to translate Latin *hospitium* (see HOSPICE), denoting a house of residence for students: this sense is preserved in the names of some buildings formerly used for this purpose, notably *Gray's Inn* and *Lincoln's Inn*, two of the INNS OF COURT. The current sense dates from late Middle English.

in·nards /'inərdz/ ▸*plural n. informal* entrails. ■ internal workings (of a device or machine). ▷early 19th cent.: representing a dialect pronunciation of INWARDS, used as a noun.

in·nate /i'nāt/ ▸*adj.* inborn; natural: *her innate capacity for organization.* See note at INHERENT. ■ *Philosophy* originating in the mind. ▷late Middle English: from Latin *innatus*, past participle of *innasci*, from *in-* 'into' + *nasci* 'be born.' —**in·nate·ly** *adv.* —**in·nate·ness** *n.*

in·ner /'inər/ ▸*adj.* [*attrib.*] **1** situated inside or further in; internal: *an inner courtyard | the inner thigh.* ■ close to the center: *the inner solar system.* ■ close to the center of power: *the inner cabinet.* **2** mental or spiritual: *a test of inner strength.* ■ (of thoughts or feelings) private and not expressed or discernible.
▸*n.* the inner part of something: *using his rock shoes as inners for his double boots.* ■ (in archery and shooting) a division of the target next to the bull's-eye. ■ a shot that strikes this. ▷Old English *innerra, innra*, comparative of IN. —**in·ner·ly** *adv.* (*poetic/literary*). —**in·ner·ness** *n.* (*poetic/literary*).

in·ner child ▸*n.* a person's supposed original or true self, esp. when regarded as damaged or concealed by negative childhood experiences.

in·ner cir·cle ▸*n.* an exclusive group close to the center of power of an organization or movement, regarded as elitist and secretive.

in·ner cit·y ▸*n.* the area near the center of a city, esp. when associated with social and economic problems: [as *adj.*] *beleaguered inner-city schools.*

in·ner-di·rect·ed ▸*adj. Psychology* (of a person or their behavior) governed by standards formed in childhood.

in·ner ear ▸*n.* the semicircular canals and cochlea, which form the organs of balance and hearing and are embedded in the temporal bone.

in·ner light ▸*n.* [in *sing.*] personal spiritual revelation; a source of enlightenment within oneself. ▷mid 19th cent.: originally in Quaker doctrine.

in·ner man ▸*n.* [in *sing.*] a man's soul or mind: *the complexities of the inner man.* ■ *humorous* a man's stomach: *the inner man was well catered for with pizza.*

In·ner Mon·go·li·a /mäNG'gōlēə/ an autonomous region in northern China, on the border with Mongolia; capital, Hohhot.

in·ner·most /'inər,mōst/ ▸*adj.* [*attrib.*] **1** (of thoughts or feelings) most private and deeply felt: *innermost beliefs and convictions.* **2** furthest in; closest to the center: *the innermost layer.*

in·ner plan·et ▸*n.* a planet whose orbit lies within the asteroid belt, i.e., Mercury, Venus, Earth, or Mars.

in·ner prod·uct ▸*n. Mathematics* a scalar function of two vectors, equal to the product of their magnitudes and the cosine of the angle between them. Also called DOT PRODUCT or SCALAR PRODUCT. Compare with VECTOR PRODUCT. • Written as **a.b** or **ab**.

in·ner sanc·tum ▸*n.* the most sacred place in a temple or church. ■ *figurative* a private or secret place to which few other people are admitted: *he walked into the inner sanctum of the editor's office.*

in·ner space ▸*n.* **1** the region between the earth and outer space. ■ the region below the surface of the sea. **2** the part of the mind not normally accessible to consciousness.

in·ner speech ▸*n.* the silent expression of conscious thought to oneself in a coherent linguistic form.

in·ner·spring /'inər,spriNG/ ▸*adj.* (of a mattress) with internal springs.

in·ner tube ▸*n.* a separate inflatable tube inside a pneumatic tire. ■ such a tube inflated and used for recreational purposes: *three men floating on inner tubes, making their third annual float trip downriver.*

in·ner·vate /i'nər,vāt; 'inər-/ ▸*v.* [*trans.*] *Anatomy & Zoology* supply (an organ or other body part) with nerves. ▷late 19th cent.: from IN-[2] 'into' + NERVE + -ATE[3]. —**in·ner·va·tion** /,inər'vāSHən/ *n.*

in·ner wom·an ▸*n.* [in *sing.*] a woman's soul or mind: *to behave as her inner woman prompts.* ■ *humorous* a woman's stomach: *after refreshing the inner woman, I was all for trying again.*

In·ness /'inis/, George (1825–94) U.S. artist. His early work, such as *Peace and Plenty* (1865), was related to the Hudson River School. Later, he painted in a more impressionistic style such as in *The Home of the Heron* (1893).

in·ning /'iniNG/ ▸*n. Baseball* a division of a game during which the two teams alternate as offense and defense and during which each team is allowed three outs while batting. ■ a single turn at bat for a team until three outs are made. ■ a similar division of play in other games, such as horseshoes. ■ a period during which a person or group can achieve something: *she thought that now her inning had come.* ▷Old English *innung* 'a putting or getting in,' related to IN. The current sense dates from the mid 19th cent.

in·nings /'iniNGz/ ▸*n.* (*pl.* same or *informal* **in·nings·es** /'iniNGziz/) **1** *Cricket* each of two or four divisions of a game during which one side has a turn at batting. ■ a player's turn at batting. ■ the score achieved during a player's turn at batting. **2** a period during which a person or group is active or effective.
▸PHRASE □ **someone had a good innings** *Brit., informal* someone had a long and fulfilling life or career (said at or before their death or retirement).

in·nit /'init/ *Brit., informal* ▸contraction of isn't it.

inn·keep·er /'in,kēpər/ ▸*n.* a person who runs an inn.

in·no·cence /'inəsəns/ ▸*n.* the state, quality, or fact of being innocent of a crime or offense: *they must prove their innocence.* ■ lack of guile or corruption; purity: *the healthy bloom in her cheeks gave her an aura of innocence.* ■ used euphemistically to refer to a person's virginity: *they'd avenge assaults on her innocence by others.* ▷Middle English: from Old French, from Latin *innocentia*, from *innocent-* 'not harming' (based on *nocere* 'injure'). —**in·no·cen·cy** *n.* (*archaic*).
▸PHRASE □ **in all innocence** without knowledge of something's significance or possible consequences: *she knew the gift had been chosen in all innocence.*

in·no·cent /'inəsənt/ ▸*adj.* **1** not guilty of a crime or offense: *the arbitrary execution of an innocent man | he was **innocent of** any fraud.* ■ [*predic.*] (**innocent of**) without; lacking: *a street quite innocent of bookstores.* ■ [*predic.*] (**innocent of**) without experience or knowledge of: *a man innocent of war's cruelties.*

2 [*attrib.*] not responsible for or directly involved in an event yet suffering its consequences: *an innocent bystander.* **3** free from moral wrong; not corrupted: *an innocent child.* ■ simple; naive: *she is a poor, innocent young creature.* **4** not intended to cause harm or offense; harmless: *an innocent mistake.*
▸*n.* an innocent person, in particular: ■ a pure, guileless, or naive person: *she was an innocent compared with this man.* ■ a person involved by chance in a situation, esp. a victim of crime or war: *they are prepared to kill or maim innocents in pursuit of a cause.* ■ (**the Innocents**) the young children killed by Herod after the birth of Jesus (Matt. 2:16). ▷Middle English: from Old French, or from Latin *innocent-* 'not harming,' from *in-* 'not' + *nocere* 'to hurt.' —**in·no·cent·ly** *adv.*

USAGE Innocent properly means 'harmless,' but it has long been extended in general language to mean 'not guilty.' The jury (or judge) in a criminal trial does not, strictly speaking, find a defendant 'innocent.' Rather, a defendant may be *guilty* or *not guilty* of the charges brought. In common use, however, owing perhaps to the concept of the *presumption of innocence*, which instructs a jury to consider a defendant free of wrongdoing until proven guilty on the basis of evidence, 'not guilty' and 'innocent' have come to be thought of as synonymous.
See also **usage** at **PLEAD**.

In·no·cen·tia /ˌinəˈsenCHə/, Sister Maria, see **HUMMEL**.

In·no·cents' Day (also **Holy Innocents' Day**) ▸*n.* a Christian festival commemorating the massacre of the Innocents, December 28.

in·noc·u·ous /iˈnäkyo͞oəs/ ▸*adj.* not harmful or offensive: *it was an innocuous question.* ▷late 16th cent.: from Latin *innocuus*, from *in-* 'not' + *nocuus* 'injurious' (see **NOCUOUS**). —**in·noc·u·ous·ly** *adv.* —**in·noc·u·ous·ness** *n.*

Inn of Court ▸*n.* (in the UK) each of the four legal societies having the exclusive right of admitting people to the English bar. ■ any of the sets of buildings in London occupied by these societies.

in·nom·i·nate /iˈnämənit/ ▸*adj.* not named or classified. ▷mid 17th cent.: from late Latin *innominatus*, from *in-* 'not' + *nominatus* 'named' (past participle of *nominare*).

in·nom·i·nate ar·ter·y ▸*n. Anatomy* a large artery that branches from the aortic arch and divides into the right common carotid and right subclavian arteries.

in·nom·i·nate bone ▸*n. Anatomy* the bone formed from the fusion of the ilium, ischium, and pubis; the hipbone.

in·nom·i·nate vein ▸*n. Anatomy* either of two large veins of the neck formed by the junction of the external jugular and subclavian veins.

in·no·vate /ˈinəˌvāt/ ▸*v.* [*intrans.*] make changes in something established, esp. by introducing new methods, ideas, or products: *the company's failure to diversify and innovate competitively.* ■ [*trans.*] introduce (something new, esp. a product): *innovating new products, developing existing ones.* ▷mid 16th cent.: from Latin *innovat-* 'renewed, altered,' from the verb *innovare*, from *in-* 'into' + *novare* 'make new' (from *novus* 'new'). —**in·no·va·tor** /-ˌvātər/ *n.* —**in·no·va·to·ry** /-vəˌtôrē/ *adj.*

in·no·va·tion /ˌinəˈvāSHən/ ▸*n.* the action or process of innovating. ■ a new method, idea, product, etc.: *technological innovations designed to save energy.* ▷late Middle English: from Latin *innovatio(n-)*, from the verb *innovare* (see **INNOVATE**). —**in·no·va·tion·al** /-SHənl/ *adj.*

in·no·va·tive /ˈinəˌvātiv/ ▸*adj.* (of a product, idea, etc.) featuring new methods; advanced and original: *innovative designs | innovative ways to help unemployed people.* ■ (of a person) introducing new ideas; original and creative in thinking: *an innovative thinker.*

Inn Riv·er /in/ a river in western Europe that rises in the Rhaetian Alps of Switzerland and flows for 320 miles (508 km) through the Austrian Tyrol past Innsbruck into southern Germany where it flows into the Danube River at Passau.

Inns·bruck /ˈinzˌbro͝ok/ a city in western Austria, capital of Tyrol; pop. 115,000. The Winter Olympic Games took place here in 1964 and 1976.

Inns of Court ▸*plural n.* see **INN OF COURT**.

in·nu·en·do /ˌinyo͞oˈendō/ ▸*n.* (*pl.* **-does** or **-dos**) an allusive or oblique remark or hint, typically a suggestive or disparaging one: *she's always making sly innuendoes | a constant torrent of innuendo, gossip, lies, and half-truths.* ▷mid 16th cent. (as an adverb in the sense 'that is to say, to wit,' used in legal documents to introduce an explanation): Latin, 'by nodding at, by pointing to,' ablative gerund of *innuere*, from *in-* 'toward' + *nuere* 'to nod.' The noun dates from the late 17th cent.

in·nu·mer·a·ble /iˈn(y)o͞omərəbəl/ ▸*adj.* too many to be counted (often used hyperbolically): *innumerable flags of all colors.* ▷Middle English: from Latin *innumerabilis*, from *in-* 'not' + *numerabilis* (see **NUMERABLE**). —**in·nu·mer·a·bil·i·ty** /iˌn(y)o͞oməraˈbilitē/ *n.* —**in·nu·mer·a·bly** /-blē/ *adv.*

in·nu·mer·ate /iˈn(y)o͞omərit/ ▸*adj.* without a basic knowledge of mathematics and arithmetic.
▸*n.* a person lacking such knowledge. —**in·nu·mer·a·cy** /-rəsē/ *n.*

in·nu·tri·tion /ˌi(n)n(y)o͞oˈtriSHən/ ▸*n. rare* lack of nourishment.

in·nu·tri·tious /ˌi(n)n(y)o͞oˈtriSHəs/ ▸*adj.* (of food) lacking in nutrients; not nourishing.

in·ob·serv·ance /ˌinəbˈzərvəns/ ▸*n. dated* failure to observe or notice; inattention. ■ failure to keep or observe a law, custom, promise, etc. ▷early 17th cent.: from French, or from Latin *inobservantia*, from *in-* (expressing negation) + *observantia* 'observance' (from *observare* 'observe').

in·oc·u·lant /iˈnäkyələnt/ ▸*n.* a substance suitable for inoculating.

in·oc·u·late /iˈnäkyəˌlāt/ ▸*v.* [*trans.*] treat (a person or animal) with a vaccine to produce immunity against a disease: *he **inoculated** his tenants **against** smallpox.* Compare with **VACCINATE**. ■ introduce (an infective agent) into an organism: *it can be **inoculated into** laboratory animals.* ■ introduce (cells or organisms) into a culture medium. ▷late Middle English (in the sense 'graft a bud or shoot into a plant of a different type'): from Latin *inoculat-* 'engrafted,' from the verb *inoculare*, from *in-* 'into' + *oculus* 'eye, bud.' The sense 'vaccinate' dates from the early 18th cent. —**in·oc·u·la·ble** /-ləbəl/ *adj.* —**in·oc·u·la·tion** /iˌnäkyəˈlāSHən/ *n.* —**in·oc·u·la·tor** /-ˌlātər/ *n.*

in·oc·u·lum /iˈnäkyələm/ ▸*n.* (*pl.* **-la** /-lə/) *Medicine* a substance used for inoculation. ▷early 20th cent.: modern Latin, from Latin *inoculare* (see **INOCULATE**), on the pattern of the pair *coagulate, coagulum*.

in·o·dor·ous /inˈōdərəs/ ▸*adj.* having no smell; odorless. ▷mid 17th cent.: from Latin *inodorus*, from *in-* 'not' + *odorus* 'odorous,' or from **IN-**[1] 'not' + **ODOROUS**.

in·of·fen·sive /ˌinəˈfensiv/ ▸*adj.* not objectionable or harmful: *the water ouzel is an agile, inoffensive creature | inoffensive wallpaper.* —**in·of·fen·sive·ly** *adv.* —**in·of·fen·sive·ness** *n.*

in·op·er·a·ble /inˈäp(ə)rəbəl/ ▸*adj.* **1** *Medicine* not able to be suitably operated on: *inoperable cancer of the pancreas.* **2** not able to be operated: *the airfield was bombed and made inoperable.* **3** impractical; unworkable: *the procedures were inoperable.* —**in·op·er·a·bil·i·ty** /-ˌäp(ə)rəˈbilitē/ *n.* —**in·op·er·a·bly** /-blē/ *adv.*

in·op·er·a·tive /inˈäp(ə)rətiv/ ▸*adj.* not working or taking effect: *the telescope is substantially inoperative due to an equipment failure.*

in·or·di·nate /iˈnôrdn-it/ ▸*adj.* unusually or disproportionately large; excessive: *a case that had taken up an inordinate amount of time.* ■ *archaic* (of a person) unrestrained in feelings or behavior; disorderly. ▷late Middle English: from Latin *inordinatus*, from *in-* 'not' + *ordinatus* 'arranged, set in order' (past participle of *ordinare*). —**in·or·di·nate·ly** *adv.* [as *submodifier*] *an inordinately expensive business.*

in·or·gan·ic /ˌinôrˈganik/ ▸*adj.* not arising from natural growth. ■ *Chemistry* of, relating to, or denoting compounds that are not organic (broadly, compounds not containing carbon). Compare with **ORGANIC**. ■ without organized physical structure. ■ *Linguistics* not explainable by the normal processes of etymology. —**in·or·gan·i·cal·ly** /-ik(ə)lē/ *adv.*

in·os·cu·late /inˈäskyəˌlāt/ ▸*v.* [*intrans.*] *formal* join by intertwining or fitting closely together. ▷late 17th cent.: from **IN-**[2] 'into' + Latin *osculare* 'provide with a mouth or outlet' (from *osculum*, diminutive of *os* 'mouth'), on the pattern of Greek *anastomoun*, in the same sense. —**in·os·cu·la·tion** /inˌäskyəˈlāSHən/ *n.*

in·o·sine /ˈinəˌsēn; -sin/ ▸*n. Biochemistry* a compound that is an intermediate in the metabolism of purine and is used in kidney transplantation to provide a temporary source of sugar. It is a nucleoside consisting of hypoxanthine linked to ribose. ▷early 20th cent.: from Greek *is, in-* 'fiber, muscle' + **-OSE**[2] + **-INE**[4].

in·o·si·tol /iˈnōsiˌtôl; -ˌtäl; īˈnō-/ ▸*n. Biochemistry* a simple carbohydrate that occurs in animal and plant tissue and is a vitamin of the B group. • Alternative name: **hexahydroxycyclohexane**; chem. formula: $C_6H_{12}O_6$. ▷late 19th cent.: from the earlier name *inosite* + **-OL**.

i·no·trop·ic /ˌēnəˈträpik; -ˈtrō-; ˌinə-/ ▸*adj. Physiology* modifying the force or speed of contraction of muscles.

INP ▸*abbr.* International News Photo.

in·pa·tient /ˈinˌpāSHənt/ ▸*n.* a patient who stays in a hospital while under treatment.

in per·so·nam /ˌin pərˈsōnəm/ ▸*adj.* & *adv. Law* made or availing against or affecting a specific person only; imposing a personal liability: [as *postpositive adj.*] *rights and duties in personam* | [as *adv.*] *the view that trusts operate in personam.* Compare with **IN REM**. ▷late 18th cent.: Latin, literally 'against a person.'

in-phase ▸*adj.* of or relating to electrical signals that are in phase.

in po·ten·ti·a /ˌin pōˈtensHēə/ ▸*adv.* as a possibility; potentially. ▷early 17th cent.: Latin, literally 'in potentiality.'

in·pour·ing /ˈinˌpôriNG/ ▸*n.* the action of pouring something in; an infusion: *vast inpouring of public money.*

in pro·pri·a per·so·na /ˌin ˈprōprēə pərˈsōnə/ ▸*adv.* in his or her own person: *many people find him, both in his verse and in propria persona, too loud and pushy.* ▷mid 17th cent.: Latin.

in·put /ˈinˌpo͝ot/ ▸*n.* **1** what is put in, taken in, or operated on by any process or system: *perceptions and sensory input.* ■ a contribution of work, information, or material: *there is little input from other professional members of the team.* ■ energy supplied to a device or system; an electrical signal: *the input is a low-frequency signal.* ■ the action or process of putting or feeding something in: *the input of data to the system.* ■ the information fed into a computer or computer program: *pen-based computers take input from a stylus.* **2** *Electronics* a place where, or a device through which, energy or information enters a system: *the signal being fed through the main input.*
▸*v.* (**-put·ting**; *past* and *past part.* **-put** or **-put·ted**) [*trans.*] put (data) into a computer. —**in·put·ter** /-ˌpo͝otər/ *n.*

in·put/out·put (abbr.: **I/O**) ▸*adj.* [*attrib.*] *Electronics* of, relating to, or for both input and output.

inq. ▸*abbr.* inquiry.

in·quest /ˈinˌkwest; ˈiNG-/ ▸*n. Law* a judicial inquiry to ascertain the facts relating to an incident, such as a death. ▷Middle English: from Old French *enqueste*, based on Latin *inquirere* (see **INQUIRE**).

in·qui·e·tude /inˈkwīəˌt(y)o͞od/ ▸*n.* physical or mental restlessness or disturbance. ▷late Middle English (in the sense 'disturbance of one's quietness or rest'): from Old French, or from late Latin *inquietudo*, from Latin *inquietus*, from *in-* 'not' + *quietus* 'quiet.'

in·qui·line /ˈinkwəˌlīn; -lin/ ▸*n. Zoology* an animal exploiting the living space of another, e.g., an insect that lays its eggs in a gall produced by another. ▷mid 17th cent.: from Latin *inquilinus* 'temporary resident,' from *in-* 'into' + *colere* 'dwell.'

in·quire /inˈkwīr; iNG-/ (also *chiefly Brit.* **en·quire**) ▸*v.* [*reporting verb*] ask for information from someone: [with *direct speech*] *"How well do you know Berlin?" he **inquired of** Hencke* | [with *clause*] *I inquired where he lived* | [*intrans.*] *he **inquired about** cottages for sale.* ■ [*intrans.*] (**inquire after**) ask about the health and well-being of (someone): *Annie inquired after her parents.* ■ [*intrans.*] (**inquire for**) ask to see or speak to (someone): *that was Mr. Paul inquiring for you—I told him he couldn't come in.* ■ [*intrans.*] (**inquire into**) investigate; look into: *the task of political sociology is to inquire into the causes of political events.* ▷Middle English *enquere* (later *inquere*), from Old French *enquerre*, from a variant of Latin *inquirere*, based on *quaerere* 'seek.' The spelling with *in-*, influenced by Latin, dates from the 15th cent. —**in·quir·er** *n.* —**in·quir·ing·ly** *adv.*

USAGE **Inquire** (and **inquiry**) are the usual U.S. spellings; **enquire** and **enquiry** are the standard forms in Britain. Some American speakers put the stress on the first syllable of the noun **inquiry**, but the dominant pronunciation stresses the second.

in·quir·ing /inˈkwīriNG; iNG-/ (also *chiefly Brit.* **en·quir·ing**) ▸*adj.* showing an interest in learning new things: *an open, inquiring mind.* ■ (of a look or expression) suggesting that information is sought: *he sent her an inquiring glance.* —**in·quir·ing·ly** *adv.*

in·quir·y /inˈkwī(ə)rē; ˈinˌkwī(ə)rē; ˈinkwərē; ˈiNG-/ (also *chiefly Brit.* **en·quir·y**) ▸*n.* (*pl.* **-quir·ies**) an act of asking for information: *the deluge of phone inquiries after a crash | they were following a definite line of inquiry.* ■ an official investigation.

USAGE See **usage** at **INQUIRE**.

in·qui·si·tion /ˌinkwiˈziSHən; ˌiNG-/ ▸*n.* **1** a period of prolonged and intensive questioning or investigation: *she relented in her determined inquisition and offered help.* ▪ *historical* a judicial or official inquiry. ▪ the verdict or finding of an official inquiry. **2** (**the Inquisition**) an ecclesiastical tribunal established by Pope Gregory IX *c.*1232 for the suppression of heresy. It was active chiefly in northern Italy and southern France, becoming notorious for the use of torture. In 1542 the papal Inquisition was reinstituted to combat Protestantism, eventually becoming an organ of papal government. See also **SPANISH INQUISITION**. ▷late Middle English (denoting a searching examination): via Old French from Latin *inquisitio(n-)* 'examination,' from the verb *inquirere* (see **INQUIRE**). **—in·qui·si·tion·al** /-SHənl/ *adj.*

in·quis·i·tive /inˈkwizitiv; iNG-/ ▸*adj.* curious or inquiring: *he was very chatty and inquisitive about everything.* ▪ unduly curious about the affairs of others; prying: *I didn't want to seem inquisitive.* ▷late Middle English: from Old French *inquisitif, -ive*, from late Latin *inquisitivus*, from the verb *inquirere* (see **INQUIRE**). **—in·quis·i·tive·ly** *adv.* **—in·quis·i·tive·ness** *n.*

in·quis·i·tor /inˈkwizitər/ ▸*n.* a person making an inquiry, esp. one seen to be excessively harsh or searching: *the professional inquisitors of the press.* ▪ *historical* an officer of the Inquisition. ▷late Middle English: from French *inquisiteur*, from Latin *inquisitor*, from the verb *inquirere* (see **INQUIRE**).

in·quis·i·tor-gen·er·al ▸*n.* the head of the Spanish Inquisition.

in·quis·i·to·ri·al /inˌkwiziˈtôrēəl/ ▸*adj.* of or like an inquisitor. ▪ offensively prying. ▪ *Law* (of a trial or legal procedure) in which the judge has an examining or inquiring role: *administration is accompanied by a form of inquisitorial justice.* Compare with **ACCUSATORIAL, ADVERSARIAL**. ▷mid 18th cent.: from medieval Latin *inquisitorius* (from Latin *inquisitor*, from *inquirere* 'inquire') + **-AL**. **—in·quis·i·to·ri·al·ly** *adv.*

in·quo·rate /inˈkwôˌrāt; -ˌrit/ ▸*adj. Brit.* (of an assembly) unable to proceed effectively because not enough members are present to make up a quorum: *they had boycotted the debate, leaving the house inquorate.*

in re /ˌin ˈrā/ ▸*prep.* in the legal case of; with regard to: *In re Mancet's Estate.* ▷early 17th cent.: Latin, 'in the matter of.'

in rem /ˌin ˈrem/ ▸*adj.* [often *postpositive*] *Law* made or availing against or affecting a thing, and therefore other people generally; imposing a general liability: *it confers a right in rem.* Compare with **IN PERSONAM**. ▷mid 18th cent.: Latin, 'against a thing.'

INRI ▸*abbr.* Jesus of Nazareth, King of the Jews (a traditional representation in art of the inscription over Christ's head at the Crucifixion). ▷from the initials of Latin *Iesus Nazarenus Rex Iudaeorum.*

in·ro /ˈinrō/ ▸*n.* (*pl.* same or **-ros**) an ornamental box with compartments for items such as seals and medicines, worn suspended from a waist sash as part of traditional Japanese dress. ▷early 17th cent.: from Japanese *inrō*, from *in* 'seal' + *rō* 'basket.'

in·road /ˈinˌrōd/ ▸*n.* **1** [usu. in *pl.*] progress; an advance: *an important way to* **make inroads in** *reducing spending.* ▪ an instance of something being affected, encroached on, or destroyed by something else: *serious* **inroads** *had now been* **made into** *my pitiful cash reserves.* **2** a hostile attack; a raid. ▷mid 16th cent. (sense 2): from **IN** + **ROAD** (from an early use in the sense 'riding').

in·rush /ˈinˌrəSH/ ▸*n.* [in *sing.*] the sudden arrival or entry of something: *a great inrush of water occurred.* **—in·rush·ing** *adj.* & *n.*

INS ▸*abbr.* Immigration and Naturalization Service.

in·sa·la·ta /ˌinsäˈlätə/ ▸*n.* an Italian-style salad: *insalata verde.* ▷Italian, 'salad.'

in·sa·lu·bri·ous /ˌinsəˈlo͞obrēəs/ ▸*adj. formal* (esp. of a climate or locality) not salubrious; unhealthy. ▷mid 17th cent.: from Latin *insalubris* (from *in-* 'not' + *salubris* 'salubrious') + **-OUS**. **—in·sa·lu·bri·ty** /-britē/ *n.*

in·sane /inˈsān/ ▸*adj.* in a state of mind that prevents normal perception, behavior, or social interaction; seriously mentally ill: *certifying patients as clinically insane | he had gone insane.* ▪ (of an action or quality) characterized or caused by madness: *charging headlong in an insane frenzy | his eyes glowing with insane fury.* ▪ in a state of extreme annoyance or distraction: *a fly whose buzzing had been driving me insane.* ▪ (of an action or policy) extremely foolish; irrational or illogical: *she had an insane desire to giggle.* ▷mid 16th cent.: from Latin *insanus*, from *in-* 'not' + *sanus* 'healthy.' **—in·sane·ly** *adv.*

in·san·i·tar·y /inˈsaniˌterē/ ▸*adj.* so dirty or ridden with germs as to be a danger to health: *insanitary conditions.*

in·san·i·ty /inˈsanitē/ ▸*n.* the state of being seriously mentally ill; madness: *he suffered from bouts of insanity* | [as *complement*] *he attempted to plead insanity.* ▪ extreme foolishness or irrationality: *it might be pure insanity to take this loan | the insanities of our time.* ▷late 16th cent.: from Latin *insanitas*, from *insanus* (see **INSANE**).

in·sa·tia·ble /inˈsāSHəbəl/ ▸*adj.* (of an appetite or desire) impossible to satisfy: *an insatiable hunger for success.* ▪ (of a person) having an insatiable appetite or desire for something, esp. sex. ▷late Middle English: from Old French *insaciable* or Latin *insatiabilis*, from *in-* 'not' + *satiare* 'fill, satisfy' (see **SATIATE**). **—in·sa·tia·bil·i·ty** /-ˌsāSHəˈbilitē/ *n.* **—in·sa·tia·bly** /-blē/ *adv.*

in·sa·ti·ate /inˈsāSHē-it/ ▸*adj. poetic/literary* never satisfied: *your strong desire is insatiate.* ▷late Middle English: from Latin *insatiatus*, from *in-* 'not' + *satiatus* 'filled, satisfied,' past participle of *satiare* (see **SATIATE**).

in·scape /ˈinˌskāp/ ▸*n. poetic/literary* the unique inner nature of a person or object as shown in a work of art, esp. a poem. ▷mid 19th cent. (originally in the poetic theory of Gerard Manley Hopkins): perhaps from **IN-**[2] 'within' + **-SCAPE**.

in-school ▸*adj.* [*attrib.*] denoting an activity or process that takes place during school hours or on school premises: *an in-school method of assessment.*

in·scribe /inˈskrīb/ ▸*v.* [*trans.*] (usu. **be inscribed**) **1** write or carve (words or symbols) on something, esp. as a formal or permanent record: *his name was inscribed on the new silver trophy.* ▪ mark (an object) with characters: *the memorial is* **inscribed with** *ten names* | [as *adj.*] (**inscribed**) *an inscribed watch.* ▪ write an informal dedication to someone in or on (a book): *he inscribed the first copy "To my dearest grandmother."* ▪ *archaic* enter the name of (someone) on a list or in a book; enroll. **2** *Geometry* draw (a figure) within another so that their boundaries touch but do not intersect: *a regular polygon inscribed in a circle.* Compare with **CIRCUMSCRIBE**. ▷late Middle English: from Latin *inscribere*, from *in-* 'into' + *scribere* 'write.' **—in·scrib·a·ble** *adj.* **—in·scrib·er** *n.*

in·scrip·tion /inˈskripSHən/ ▸*n.* words inscribed, as on a monument or in a book: *the inscription on her headstone.* ▪ the action of inscribing something: *the inscription of memorable utterances on durable materials.* ▷late Middle English (denoting a short descriptive or dedicatory passage at the beginning of a book): from Latin *inscriptio(n-)*, from the verb *inscribere* (see **INSCRIBE**). **—in·scrip·tion·al** /-SHənl/ *adj.* **—in·scrip·tive** /-ˈskriptiv/ *adj.*

in·scru·ta·ble /inˈskro͞otəbəl/ ▸*adj.* impossible to understand or interpret: *Guy looked blankly inscrutable.* ▷late Middle English: from ecclesiastical Latin *inscrutabilis*, from *in-* 'not' + *scrutari* 'to search' (see **SCRUTINY**). **—in·scru·ta·bil·i·ty** /-ˌskro͞otəˈbilitē/ *n.* **—in·scru·ta·bly** /-blē/ *adv.*

in·seam /ˈinˌsēm/ ▸*n.* the seam in a pair of pants from the crotch to the bottom of the leg, or the length of this.

in·sect /ˈinˌsekt/ ▸*n.* a small arthropod animal that has six legs and generally one or two pairs of wings. ▪ *informal* any small invertebrate animal, esp. one with several pairs of legs.

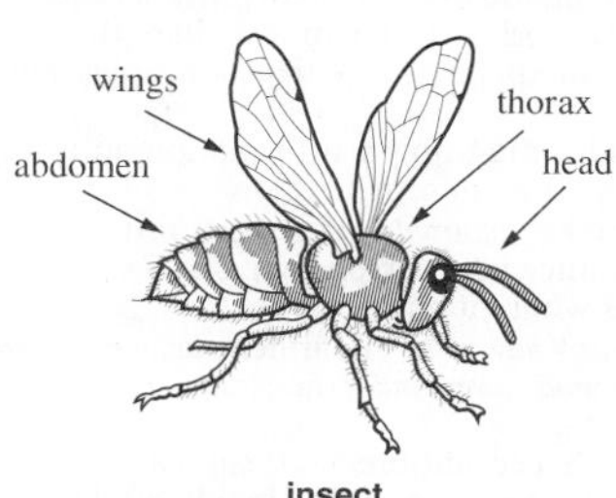

insect

Insects are usually placed in the class Insecta (see also **HEXAPODA**). The body of a typical adult insect is divided into head, thorax (bearing the legs and wings), and abdomen. The class includes many familiar forms, such as flies, bees, wasps, moths, beetles, grasshoppers, and cockroaches. Insects are the most numerous animals in both numbers of individuals and of different kinds, with more than a million species in all habitats except the sea, and they are of enormous economic importance as pests and carriers of disease, and also as pollinators.

▷early 17th cent. (originally denoting any small cold-blooded creature with a segmented body): from Latin *(animal) insectum* 'segmented (animal)' (translating Greek *zōion entomon*), from *insecare* 'cut up or into,' from *in-* 'into' + *secare* 'to cut.'

in·sec·tan /inˈsektən/ ▸*adj.* [*attrib.*] *Zoology* of or relating to insects: *the insectan orders.*

in·sec·tar·i·um /ˌinsekˈte(ə)rēəm/ (also **in·sec·tar·y** /ˈinsekˌterē; inˈsektə-/) ▸*n.* (*pl.* **in·sec·tar·i·ums** also **in·sec·tar·ies** /ˈinsekˌterēz/) a place where insects are kept, exhibited, and studied.

in·sec·ti·cide /inˈsektiˌsīd/ ▸*n.* a substance used for killing insects. **—in·sec·ti·cid·al** /-ˌsektiˈsīdl/ *adj.*

in·sec·tile /inˈsektl; -ˌtīl/ ▸*adj.* resembling or reminiscent of an insect or insects: *he folded his insectile hands.*

In·sec·tiv·o·ra /ˌinsekˈtivərə/ *Zoology* an order of mammals that comprises the shrews, moles, hedgehogs, tenrecs, moonrats, and solenodons. They are distinguished by mainly terrestrial habits and an insectivorous diet.

in·sec·ti·vore /inˈsektəˌvôr/ ▸*n.* an insectivorous animal or plant. ▪ *Zoology* a mammal of the order Insectivora. ▷mid 19th cent.: from modern Latin *insectivorus*, from *insectum* (see **INSECT**) + *-vorus* 'devouring,' on the pattern of Latin *carnivorus* 'carnivorous.'

in·sec·tiv·o·rous /ˌinˌsekˈtivərəs/ ▸*adj.* (of an animal) feeding on insects, worms, and other invertebrates. ▪ (of a plant such as the Venus flytrap) able to capture and digest insects.

in·se·cure /ˌinsiˈkyo͝or/ ▸*adj.* **1** (of a person) not confident or assured; uncertain and anxious: *a top model who is notoriously insecure about her looks | a rather gauche, insecure young man.* **2** (of a thing) not firm or set; unsafe. ▪ (of a job or position) from which removal or expulsion is always possible. ▪ not firmly fixed; liable to give way or break: *an insecure footbridge.* ▪ able to be broken into or illicitly accessed: *an insecure computer system.* ▷mid 17th cent.: from medieval Latin *insecurus* 'unsafe,' from *in-* 'not' + Latin *securus* 'free from care,' or from **IN-**[1] 'not' + **SECURE**. **—in·se·cure·ly** *adv.* **—in·se·cu·ri·ty** *n.*

in·sel·berg /ˈinsəlbərg/ ▸*n. Geology* an isolated hill or mountain rising abruptly from a plain. ▷early 20th cent.: from German, from *Insel* 'island' + *Berg* 'mountain.'

in·sem·i·nate /inˈseməˌnāt/ ▸*v.* [*trans.*] (often **be inseminated**) introduce semen into (a woman or a female animal) by natural or artificial means. ▷early 17th cent.: from Latin *inseminat-* 'sown,' from the verb *inseminare*, from *in-* 'into' + *seminare* 'plant, sow' (from *semen, semin-* 'seed, semen'). **—in·sem·i·na·tion** /-ˌseməˈnāSHən/ *n.*

in·sem·i·na·tor /inˈseməˌnātər/ ▸*n.* a man or male animal inseminating a female. ▪ a person who performs artificial insemination of farm animals.

in·sen·sate /inˈsenˌsāt; -sit/ ▸*adj.* lacking physical sensation: *a patient who was permanently unconscious and insensate.* ▪ lacking sympathy or compassion; unfeeling: *a positively insensate hatred.* ▪ completely lacking sense or reason: *insensate jabbering.* ▷late 15th cent.: from ecclesiastical Latin *insensatus*, from *in-* 'not' + *sensatus* 'having senses' (see **SENSATE**). **—in·sen·sate·ly** *adv.*

in·sen·si·bil·i·ty /inˌsensəˈbilitē/ ▸*n.* unconsciousness: *I flogged him into insensibility.* ▪ inability to feel something, esp. to be moved emotionally. ▪ lack of awareness or concern; indifference: *your* ***insensibility to*** *the extreme importance of the mission we are on.* ▷late Middle English: partly from Old French *insensibilite* or late Latin *insensibilitas* (from *in-* 'not' + Latin *sensibilis* 'sensible,' from *sensus* 'sense'), partly from **IN-**[1] 'without, lacking' + **SENSIBILITY**.

in·sen·si·ble /inˈsensəbəl/ ▸*adj.* **1** [usu. as *complement*] without one's mental faculties, typically a result of violence or intoxication; unconscious: *they knocked each other insensible with their fists | insensible with drink.* ▪ (esp. of a body or bodily extremity) numb; without feeling: *the horny and insensible tip of the beak.* **2** [*predic.*] (**insensible of/to**) unaware of; indifferent to: *they slept on, insensible to the headlight beams.* ▪ without emotion; callous. **3** too small or gradual to be perceived; inappreciable: *varying by*

Pronunciation Key ə ago; ər over; ˈə or ˌə up; ˈər or ˌər fur; a hat; ā rate; ä car; CH chew; e let; ē see; e(ə)r air; i fit; ī by; i(ə)r ear; NG sing; ō go; ô for; oi boy; o͝o good; o͞o goo; ou out; SH she; TH thin; T͟H then; (h)w why; ZH vision

insensible degrees. ▷late Middle English (also in the senses 'unable to be perceived' and 'incapable of physical sensation'): partly from Old French *insensible* (from Latin *insensibilis*, from *in-* 'not' + *sensibilis*, from *sensus* 'sense'), partly from IN-[1] 'not' + SENSIBLE. —**in·sen·si·bly** /-blē/ *adv.*

in·sen·si·tive /in'sensitiv/ ▸*adj.* showing or feeling no concern for others' feelings: *an insensitive remark.* ■ not sensitive to a physical sensation: *she was remarkably* ***insensitive to*** *pain.* ■ not aware of or able to respond to something: *both were in many ways* ***insensitive to*** *painting.* —**in·sen·si·tive·ly** *adv.* —**in·sen·si·tive·ness** *n.* —**in·sen·si·tiv·i·ty** /-,sensi'tivitē/ *n.*

in·sen·ti·ent /in'sensн(ē)ənt/ ▸*adj.* incapable of feeling or understanding things; inanimate: *it's arrogant to presume animals to be insentient.* —**in·sen·ti·ence** *n.*

in·sep·a·ra·ble /in'sep(ə)rəbəl/ ▸*adj.* unable to be separated or treated separately: *research and higher education seem inseparable.* ■ (of one or more people) unwilling to be separated; usually seen together: *they met 18 months ago and have been inseparable ever since.* ■ *Grammar* (of a prefix) not used as a separate word or (in German) not separated from the base verb when inflected.
▸*n.* a person or thing inseparable from another. ▷late Middle English: from Latin *inseparabilis*, from *in-* 'not' + *separabilis* (see SEPARABLE). —**in·sep·a·ra·bil·i·ty** /-,sep(ə)rə'bilitē/ *n.* —**in·sep·a·ra·bly** /-blē/ *adv.*

in·sert ▸*v.* /in'sərt/ [*trans.*] **1** place, fit, or thrust (something) into another thing, esp. with care: *a steel rod was* ***inserted into*** *the small hole | he pulled out a small cassette recorder and inserted a new tape.* ■ add (text) to a piece of writing: *he immediately inserted a clause into later contracts | the objection has been inserted in the minutes.* ■ place (a spacecraft or satellite) into an orbit or trajectory. ■ (usu. **be inserted**) *Biology* incorporate (a piece of genetic material) into a chromosome. **2** (**be inserted**) *Anatomy & Zoology* (of a muscle or other organ) be attached to a part, esp. that which is moved: *the muscle that raises the wing is* ***inserted on*** *the dorsal surface of the humerus.*
▸*n.* /'in,sərt/ a thing that has been inserted, in particular: ■ a loose page or section, typically one carrying an advertisement, in a magazine or other publication. ■ an ornamental section of cloth or needlework inserted into the plain material of a garment. ■ a shot inserted into a movie or video. ▷late 15th cent. (in the sense 'include (text) in a piece of writing'): from Latin *insert-* 'put in,' from the verb *inserere*, from *in-* 'into' + *serere* 'to join.' —**in·sert·a·ble** *adj.* —**in·sert·er** *n.*

THE RIGHT WORD **inject, insert, interject, interpolate, introduce, mediate**

If you want to put something in a fixed place between or among other things, you can **insert** it (*insert a new paragraph in an essay; insert photographs in the text of a book*).

If it's a liquid, you'll probably want to **inject** it (*inject the flu vaccine*), although to inject can also mean to add something new or different (*inject some humor into an otherwise dreary speech*).

If it's a person, you should **introduce** him or her, which suggests placing someone in the midst of a group so as to become part of it.

You can also introduce things (*introduce a new subject into the curriculum*), but if the thing you're introducing is extraneous or lacks authorization, you may have to **interpolate** it (*interpolate editorial comments*).

If you have remarks, statements, or questions to introduce in an abrupt or forced manner, you'll have to **interject** them (*in the midst of his speech, she interjected what she felt were important details*).

If you interject too often, however, you risk offending the speaker and may have to ask someone to **mediate**, which means to settle a dispute or bring about a compromise by taking a stand midway between extremes.

in·ser·tion /in'sərsнən/ ▸*n.* **1** the action of inserting something: *the insertion of a line or two into the script.* ■ the placing of a spacecraft or satellite into an orbit or trajectory. **2** a thing that is inserted, in particular: ■ an amendment or addition inserted in a text. ■ each appearance of an advertisement in a newspaper or periodical. ■ an ornamental section of cloth or needlework inserted into the plain material of a garment. **3** *Anatomy & Zoology* the manner or place of attachment of an organ: *close to the point of leaf insertion.* ■ the manner or place of attachment of a muscle to the part that it moves: *the names of the muscles and their* ***insertions on*** *the eyeball.* **4** *Biology* the addition of extra DNA or RNA into a section of genetic material. ▷mid 16th cent. (sense 2): from late Latin *insertio(n-)*, from Latin *inserere* (see INSERT).

in·serv·ice ▸*adj.* (of training) intended for those actively engaged in the profession or activity concerned: *in-service training of library staff.*

in·set ▸*n.* /'in,set/ a thing that is put in or inserted: *a pair of doors with their original stained-glass insets.* ■ a small picture or map inserted within the border of a larger one. ■ a section of fabric or needlework inserted into the material of a garment: *elastic insets in the waistband.* ■ an insert in a magazine or similar publication.
▸*v.* /in'set/ (**-set·ting**; *past* and *past part.* **-set** or **-set·ted**) (usu. **be inset**) put in (something, esp. a small picture or map) as an inset: *type in the text to be inset.* ■ decorate with an inset: *tables inset with ceramic tiles.* —**in·set·ter** *n.*

in·shal·lah /in'sнälə/ ▸*exclam.* if Allah wills it. ▷from Arabic *in šā'Allāh.*

in·shore /'in'sнôr/ ▸*adj.* at sea but close to the shore: *both mackerel and bluefish have returned to inshore waters by now.* ■ used at sea but close to the shore: *an inshore lifeboat.*
▸*adv.* toward or closer to the shore: *birds heading inshore to their breeding sites.*
▸*PHRASE* □ **inshore of** nearer to shore than.

in·side ▸*n.* /'in'sīd/ **1** [usu. in *sing.*] the inner side or surface of a thing: *she ran a finger around the inside of the bowl.* ■ the side of a bend or curve where the edge or surface is shorter: *the inside of the bend.* ■ the side of a racetrack nearer to the center, where the lanes are shorter: *he was blocked on the inside at the furlong marker.* **2** the inner part; the interior: *the inside of the car was like an oven | these boats are built of very thin cedar, with ribs* ***on the inside.*** ■ (usu. **insides**) *informal* the stomach and bowels: *my insides are out of order.* **3** (**the inside**) *informal* a position affording private information: *will you be my spy on the inside?*
▸*adj.* /,in'sīd; 'in,sīd/ [*attrib.*] situated on or in, or derived from, the inside: *an inside pocket.* ■ (in some team sports) denoting positions nearer to the center of the field: *possibly the best inside linebacker in the country.* ■ (in basketball) taking place within the perimeter of the defense: *he missed three consecutive inside shots.* ■ (of a pitch in baseball) passing between the batter and the strike zone: *an inside pitch to a right-handed hitter.*
▸*prep.* & *adv.* /,in'sīd/ **1** situated within the confines of (something): [as *prep.*] *a radio was playing inside the apartment | he fitted a light inside the cupboard |* [as *adv.*] *Mr. Jackson is waiting for you inside.* ■ moving so as to end up within (something): [as *prep.*] *Anatoly reached inside his shirt and brought out a map |* [as *adv.*] *we walked inside.* ■ [*adv.*] indoors: *they sat inside playing cards.* ■ within (the body or mind of a person), typically with reference to sensations of self-awareness: [as *prep.*] *she felt a stirring of life inside her | I just roll the phrases around inside my head |* [as *adv.*] *I was screaming inside.* ■ *informal* in prison: *sentenced to three years inside.* ■ *Baseball* close to the batter. ■ (in basketball, soccer, and other sports) closer to the center of the field than (another player): [as *prep.*] *he went inside Graves and scored near the post |* [as *adv.*] *he does an excellent job of getting the ball inside to Randall.* **2** [*prep.*] in less than (the period of time specified): *the oven will have paid for itself inside 18 months.* ▷late Middle English (denoting the interior of the body): from IN + SIDE.
▸*PHRASE* □ **inside of** *informal* within: *something inside of me wanted to believe him.* ■ in less than (the period of time specified): *rerigging a ship for a voyage inside of a week.*

in·side in·for·ma·tion ▸*n.* information only available to those within an organization.

in·side job ▸*n. informal* a crime committed by or with the assistance of a person living or working on the premises where it occurred.

in·side out ▸*adv.* with the inner surface turned outward: *we made a very quick change, and her dress was put on inside out.*
▸*adj.* in such a condition: *inside-out clothes.*
▸*PHRASES* □ **know something inside out** know something very thoroughly: *managers who know the business inside out.* □ **turn something inside out** turn the inner surface of something outward: *she played with her leather gloves, turning each finger inside out.* ■ change something utterly: *it is not so easy to turn your whole life inside out.* ■ *informal* cause utter confusion in; defeat totally: *he turned the defender inside out.*

In·side Pas·sage a water route from Seattle in Washington to Alaska that passes through islands in Washington, British Columbia, and southeastern Alaska.

in·sid·er /in'sīdər/ ▸*n.* a person within a group or organization, esp. someone privy to information unavailable to others: *political insiders.*

in·sid·er trad·ing (*Brit.* also **insider dealing**) ▸*n.* the illegal practice of trading on the stock exchange to one's own advantage through having access to confidential information.

in·side track ▸*n.* the inner, shorter track of a racecourse. ■ *figurative* a position of advantage: *he always had the inside track for the starring role.*

in·sid·i·ous /in'sidēəs/ ▸*adj.* proceeding in a gradual, subtle way, but with harmful effects: *sexually transmitted diseases can be insidious and sometimes without symptoms.* ■ treacherous; crafty: *tangible proof of an insidious alliance.* ▷mid 16th cent.: from Latin *insidiosus* 'cunning,' from *insidiae* 'an ambush or trick,' from *insidere* 'lie in wait for,' from *in-* 'on' + *sedere* 'sit.' —**in·sid·i·ous·ly** *adv.* —**in·sid·i·ous·ness** *n.*

in·sight /'in,sīt/ ▸*n.* the capacity to gain an accurate and deep intuitive understanding of a person or thing: *this paper is alive with sympathetic* ***insight into*** *Shakespeare.* ■ an understanding of this kind: *the signals would give marine biologists new insights into the behavior of whales.* ■ *Psychiatry* new understanding by a mentally ill person of the causes of their disorder. ▷Middle English (in the sense 'inner sight, mental vision, wisdom'): probably of Scandinavian and Low German origin and related to Swedish *insikt*, Danish *indsigt*, Dutch *inzicht*, and German *Einsicht*. —**in·sight·ful** /in'sītfəl/ *adj.* —**in·sight·ful·ly** /in'sītfəlē/ *adv.*

in·sight med·i·ta·tion ▸*n.* a form of Buddhist mediation that employs concentration sharply focused on bodily sensations and mental events, practiced with the intention of gaining insight into reality.

in·sig·ni·a /in'signēə/ ▸*n.* (*pl.* same or **-ni·as**) a badge or distinguishing mark of military rank, office, or membership of an organization; an official emblem: *a khaki uniform with colonel's insignia on the collar.* ■ *chiefly poetic/literary* a distinguishing mark or token of something: *they left eternally inert blooms, the insignia of melancholy.* ▷mid 17th cent.: from Latin, plural of *insigne* 'sign, badge of office,' neuter of *insignis* 'distinguished (as if by a mark),' from *in-* 'toward' + *signum* 'sign.'

USAGE **Insignia** is, in origin, a plural noun; its singular form is **insigne**, but this is rarely used. In modern use, **insignia** takes the plural **insignia** or, occasionally, **insignias**: both are acceptable.

in·sig·nif·i·cant /,insig'nifikənt/ ▸*adj.* too small or unimportant to be worth consideration: *the amount required was insignificant compared with military spending | no detail is insignificant.* ■ (of a person) without power or influence. ■ meaningless: *insignificant yet enchanting phrases.* —**in·sig·nif·i·cance** *n.* —**in·sig·nif·i·can·cy** *n.* —**in·sig·nif·i·cant·ly** *adv.*

in·sin·cere /,insin'si(ə)r/ ▸*adj.* not expressing genuine feelings: *she flashed him an insincere smile.* ▷mid 17th cent.: from Latin *insincerus*, from *in-* 'not' + *sincerus* 'sincere.' —**in·sin·cere·ly** *adv.* —**in·sin·cer·i·ty** /-'seritē/ *n.* (*pl.* **-ties**).

in·sin·u·ate /in'sinyə,wāt/ ▸*v.* [*trans.*] **1** suggest or hint (something bad or reprehensible) in an indirect and unpleasant way: [with *clause*] *he was insinuating that she had slept her way to the top.* **2** (**insinuate oneself into**) maneuver oneself into (a position of favor or office) by subtle manipulation: *she seemed to be taking over, insinuating herself into the family.* ■ [*trans.*] slide (oneself or a thing) slowly and smoothly into a position: *the bugs insinuate themselves between one's skin and clothes.* ▷early 16th cent. (used in legal contexts in the sense 'enter (a document) in the official register'): from Latin *insinuat-* 'introduced tortuously,' from the verb *insinuare*, from *in-* 'in' + *sinuare* 'to curve.' —**in·sin·u·at·ing·ly** *adv.* —**in·sin·u·a·tor** /-,wātər/ *n.*

in·sin·u·a·tion /in,sinyoo'āsнən/ ▸*n.* an unpleasant hint or suggestion of something bad: *I've done nothing to deserve all your vicious insinuations | a piece of filthy insinuation.* ▷mid 16th cent.: from Latin *insinuatio(n-)*, from *insinuare* (see INSINUATE).

in·sip·id /in'sipid/ ▸*adj.* lacking flavor: *mugs of insipid coffee.* ■ lacking vigor or interest: *many artists continued to churn out insipid, shallow works.* ▷early 17th cent.: from French *insipide* or late Latin *insipidus*, from *in-* 'not' + *sapidus* (see SAPID). —**in·si·pid·i·ty** /,insə'piditē/ *n.* —**in·sip·id·ly** *adv.* —**in·sip·id·ness** *n.*

in·sist /in'sist/ ▸*v.* [*intrans.*] demand something forcefully, not accepting refusal: *she* ***insisted on*** *carrying her own bag | I'll call him and cancel it, if you insist.*

■ **(insist on)** demand forcefully to have something: *he insisted on answers to his allegations.* ■ **(insist on)** persist in doing something even though it is annoying or odd: *the heavy studded boots she insisted on wearing.* ■ [*reporting verb*] maintain or put forward a statement positively and assertively: [with *clause*] *the chairman insisted that all was not doom and gloom* | [with *direct speech*] *"I really am all right now," Isabel insisted.* ▷late 16th cent. (in the sense 'persist, persevere'): from Latin *insistere* 'persist,' from *in-* 'upon' + *sistere* 'stand.'

in·sist·ence /in'sistəns/ ▸*n.* the fact or quality of insisting that something is the case or should be done: *his insistence on unilateral nuclear disarmament.* **—in·sis·ten·cy** *n.*

in·sist·ent /in'sistənt/ ▸*adj.* insisting or demanding something; not allowing refusal: *Tony's soft, insistent questioning* | [with *clause*] *she was very insistent that I call her.* ■ regular and repeated, and demanding attention: *a telephone started ringing, loud and insistent.* **—in·sis·tent·ly** *adv.*

in si·tu /,in 'sītoo; 'sē-/ ▸*adv.* & *adj.* in its original place: [as *adv.*] *mosaics and frescoes have been left in situ* | [as *adj.*] *a collection of in situ pumping engines.* ■ in position: [as *adv.*] *her guests were all in situ.* ▷mid 18th cent.: Latin.

in·so·bri·e·ty /,insə'brī-itē/ ▸*n.* drunkenness.

in·so·far /,insō'fär/ (also **in so far**) ▸*adv.* **(insofar as)** to the extent that: *he decided that philosophy spoke of personal problems only insofar as they illustrated general ones.*

insol. ▸*abbr.* insoluble.

in·so·la·tion /,insō'lāsHən/ ▸*n.* *technical* exposure to the sun's rays. ■ the amount of solar radiation reaching a given area. ▷early 17th cent.: from Latin *insolatio(n-)*, from the verb *insolare*, from *in-* 'toward' + *sol* 'sun.'

in·sole /'in,sōl/ ▸*n.* a removable sole worn in a shoe for warmth, as a deodorizer, or to improve the fit. ■ the fixed inner sole of a boot or shoe.

in·so·lent /'insələnt/ ▸*adj.* showing a rude and arrogant lack of respect: *she hated the insolent tone of his voice.* See note at **IMPERTINENT**. ▷late Middle English (also in the sense 'extravagant, going beyond acceptable limits'): from Latin *insolent-* 'immoderate, unaccustomed, arrogant,' from *in-* 'not' + *solent-* 'being accustomed' (from the verb *solere*). **—in·so·lence** *n.* **—in·so·lent·ly** *adv.*

in·sol·u·ble /in'sälyəbəl/ ▸*adj.* **1** impossible to solve: *the problem is not insoluble.* **2** (of a substance) incapable of being dissolved: *once dry, the paints become **insoluble in** water.* ▷late Middle English: from Old French, or from Latin *insolubilis*, from *in-* 'not' + *solubilis* (see **SOLUBLE**). **—in·sol·u·bil·i·ty** /-,sälyə'bilitē/ *n.* **—in·sol·u·bil·ize** /-,līz/ *v.* **—in·sol·u·bly** /-blē/ *adv.*

in·solv·a·ble /in'sälvəbəl/ ▸*adj.* rare term for **INSOLUBLE**.

in·sol·vent /in'sälvənt/ ▸*adj.* unable to pay debts owed: *the company became insolvent.* ■ relating to insolvency: *insolvent liquidation.*
▸*n.* an insolvent person. **—in·sol·ven·cy** *n.*

in·som·ni·a /in'sämnēə/ ▸*n.* habitual sleeplessness; inability to sleep. ▷early 17th cent.: from Latin, from *insomnis* 'sleepless,' from *in-* (expressing negation) + *somnus* 'sleep.' **—in·som·ni·ac** /-nē,ak/ *n.* & *adj.*

in·so·much /,insō'məcH/ ▸*adv.* **1** **(insomuch that)** to such an extent that: *self is the source of evil insomuch that the purity of the soul increases as it loses selfhood.* **2** **(insomuch as)** inasmuch as: *the artist touches on the Kurds only insomuch as they impact on his primary focus.* ▷late Middle English: originally as *in so much*, translating French *en tant (que)* 'in so much (as).'

in·sou·ci·ance /in'sōōsēəns; ,ansōō'syäNs/ ▸*n.* casual lack of concern; indifference: *an impression of boyish insouciance.* ▷late 18th cent.: French, from *insouciant*, from *in-* 'not' + *souciant* 'worrying' (present participle of *soucier*). **—in·sou·ci·ant** *adj.* **—in·sou·ci·ant·ly** *adv.*

in·sourc·ing /'in,sôrsiNG/ ▸*n.* the practice of using an organization's own personnel or other resources to accomplish a task: *offshore insourcing of expense reporting processing.* ■ the practice whereby an organization provides its own personnel to accomplish specialized tasks for a client, at the client's place of business. ▷on the pattern of *outsourcing*. **—in·source** *v.*

insp. ▸*abbr.* inspector.

in·span /in'span/ ▸*v.* **(-spanned, -span·ning)** [*trans.*] *S. African* yoke (draft animals, typically oxen) in a team to a vehicle. ▷early 19th cent.: from Dutch *inspannen* 'to stretch,' from *in-* 'in' + *spannen* 'to span.'

in·spect /in'spekt/ ▸*v.* [*trans.*] look at (someone or something) closely, typically to assess their condition or to discover any shortcomings: *they were inspecting my outside paintwork for cracks and flaws.* ■ examine (someone or something) to ensure that they reach an official standard: *customs officers came aboard to inspect our documents.* ▷early 17th cent.: from Latin *inspect-* 'looked into, examined,' from the verb *inspicere* (from *in-* 'in' + *specere* 'look at'), or from its frequentative, *inspectare*. **—in·spec·tion** /-'speksHən/ *n.*

in·spec·tor /in'spektər/ ▸*n.* **1** an official employed to ensure that official regulations are obeyed, esp. in public services: *a prison inspector.* ■ *Brit.* an official who examines bus or train tickets to check that they are valid. **2** a police officer ranking below a superintendent or police chief: [as *title*] *Inspector Simmons.* **—in·spec·to·ri·al** /,inspek'tôrēəl/ *adj.* **—in·spec·tor·ship** /-,sHip/ *n.*

in·spec·tor·ate /in'spektərit/ ▸*n.* a body that ensures that the official regulations applying to a particular type of institution or activity are obeyed: *the factory inspectorate.*

in·spec·tor gen·er·al (abbr.: **IG**) ▸*n.* (*pl.* **in·spec·tors gen·er·al**) an official in charge of inspecting a particular institution or activity: *a report by the Pentagon's inspector general.* ■ *Military* a staff officer responsible for conducting inspections and investigations.

in·spi·ra·tion /,inspə'rāsHən/ ▸*n.* **1** the process of being mentally stimulated to do or feel something, esp. to do something creative: *Helen had one of her flashes of inspiration* | *the history of fashion has provided designers with invaluable inspiration.* ■ the quality of having been so stimulated, esp. when evident in something: *a rare moment of inspiration in an otherwise dull display.* ■ a person or thing that stimulates in this way: *he is an inspiration to everyone.* ■ a sudden brilliant, creative, or timely idea: *then I had an inspiration.* ■ the divine influence believed to have led to the writing of the Bible. **2** the drawing in of breath; inhalation. ■ an act of breathing in; an inhalation. ▷Middle English (in the sense 'divine guidance'): via Old French from late Latin *inspiratio(n-)*, from the verb *inspirare* (see **INSPIRE**).

in·spi·ra·tion·al /,inspə'rāsHənl/ ▸*adj.* providing or showing creative or spiritual inspiration: *the team's inspirational captain.*

in·spir·a·to·ry /in'spīrə,tôrē/ ▸*adj.* *Physiology* relating to the act of breathing in.

in·spire /in'spīr/ ▸*v.* [*trans.*] **1** fill (someone) with the urge or ability to do or feel something, esp. to do something creative: [*trans.*] *his passion for romantic literature inspired him to begin writing* | [as *adj.*] **(inspiring)** *so far, the scenery is not very inspiring.* See note at **ENCOURAGE**. ■ create (a feeling, esp. a positive one) in a person: *their past record does not inspire confidence.* ■ **(inspire someone with)** animate someone with (such a feeling): *he inspired his students with a vision of freedom.* ■ give rise to: *the movie was successful enough to inspire a sequel.* **2** breathe in (air); inhale. ▷Middle English *enspire*, from Old French *inspirer*, from Latin *inspirare* 'breathe or blow into,' from *in-* 'into' + *spirare* 'breathe.' The word was originally used of a divine or supernatural being, in the sense 'impart a truth or idea to someone.' **—in·spir·er** *n.* **—in·spir·ing·ly** *adv.*

in·spired /in'spīrd/ ▸*adj.* **1** of extraordinary quality, as if arising from some external creative impulse: *they had to thank the goalie for some inspired saves.* ■ (of a person) exhibiting such a creative impulse in the activity specified: *she was an inspired gardener.* **2** (of air or another substance) that is breathed in: *inspired air must be humidified.* **—in·spir·ed·ly** *adv.*

in·spir·it /in'spirit/ ▸*v.* **(-spir·it·ed, -spir·it·ing)** [*trans.*] [usu. as *adj.*] **(inspiriting)** encourage and enliven (someone): *the inspiriting beauty of Gothic architecture.* **—in·spir·it·ing·ly** *adv.*

in·spis·sate /'inspi,sāt; in'spis,āt/ ▸*v.* [*trans.*] [usu. as *adj.*] **(inspissated)** thicken or congeal: *inspissated secretions.* ▷early 17th cent.: from late Latin *inspissat-* 'made thick,' from the verb *inspissare* (based on Latin *spissus* 'thick, dense'). **—in·spis·sa·tion** /,inspi'sāsHən/ *n.*

in·spis·sa·tor /'inspi,sātər; in'spis,ātər/ ▸*n.* a heating device for thickening or congealing a liquid.

inst. ▸*abbr.* ■ *dated* (in business letters) instant: *we are pleased to acknowledge receipt of your letter of 14 inst.* ■ institute; institution: *the Southwest Research Inst.*

in·sta·bil·i·ty /,instə'bilitē/ ▸*n.* (*pl.* **-ties**) lack of stability; the state of being unstable: *political and economic instability.* ■ tendency to unpredictable behavior or erratic changes of mood: *she showed increasing signs of mental instability.* ▷late Middle English: from French *instabilité*, from Latin *instabilitas*, from *instabilis*, from *in-* 'not' + *stabilis* (see **STABLE**[1]).

in·stall /in'stôl/ (*Brit.* also **in·stal**) ▸*v.* [*trans.*] **1** place or fix (equipment or machinery) in position ready for use: *we're planning to install a new shower.* **2** place (someone) in a new position of authority, esp. with ceremony: *he was installed as music director at the Cathedral of St. Barbara in Cracow.* ■ establish (someone) in a new place, condition, or role: *Ashley installed herself behind her table.* ▷late Middle English (sense 2): from medieval Latin *installare*, from *in-* 'into' + *stallum* 'place, stall.' Sense 1 dates from the mid 19th cent. **—in·stall·er** *n.*

in·stal·la·tion /,instə'lāsHən/ ▸*n.* **1** the action or process of installing someone or something, or of being installed: *the installation of a central air-conditioning system.* **2** a thing installed, in particular: ■ a large piece of equipment installed for use: *computer installations.* ■ a military or industrial establishment: *nuclear installations.* ■ an art exhibit constructed within a gallery: *a video installation.*

in·stall·ment /in'stôlmənt/ (*chiefly Brit.* **in·stal·ment**) ▸*n.* **1** a sum of money due as one of several equal payments for something, spread over an agreed period of time: *the first installment of a grant for housing* | *the purchase price is paid **in installments**.* **2** any of several parts of something that are published, broadcast, or made public in sequence at intervals: *filming the final installment in his Vietnam trilogy.* **3** the process of installing something; installation: *installment will begin early next year.* ▷mid 18th cent. (denoting the arrangement of payment by installments): alteration of obsolete *estalment* (probably by association with **INSTALLATION**), from Anglo-Norman French *estalement*, from Old French *estaler* 'to fix.'

in·stall·ment plan ▸*n.* an arrangement for payment by installments.

in·stance /'instəns/ ▸*n.* **1** an example or single occurrence of something: *a serious instance of corruption* | *the search finds every instance where the word appears.* ■ a particular case: *in this instance it mattered little.* **2** *rare Law* the institution of a legal suit.
▸*v.* [*trans.*] cite (a fact, case, etc.) as an instance or example: *here he instances in particular the work of Bach.* ▷Middle English: via Old French from Latin *instantia* 'presence, urgency,' from *instare* 'be present, press upon,' from *in-* 'upon' + *stare* 'to stand.' The original sense was 'urgency, urgent entreaty,' surviving in *at the instance of*. In the late 16th cent. the word denoted a particular case cited to disprove a general assertion, derived from medieval Latin *instantia* 'example to the contrary' (translating Greek *enstasis* 'objection'); hence the meaning 'single occurrence.'
▸*PHRASES* □ **at first instance** *Law* at the first court hearing concerning a case. □ **at the instance of** *formal* at the request or instigation of: *prosecution at the instance of the police.* □ **for instance** as an example: *take Canada, for instance.* □ **in the first** (or **second**, etc.) **instance** in the first (or second, etc.) place; at the first (or second, etc.) stage of a proceeding: *a tribunal should be formed, in the first instance to document these and other charges.*

in·stan·cy /'instənsē/ ▸*n.* *archaic* urgency: *he told his servants to press the message with greater instancy.* ▷early 16th cent.: from Latin *instantia* (see **INSTANCE**).

in·stant /'instənt/ ▸*adj.* **1** happening or coming immediately: *the offense justified instant dismissal.* ■ (of food) processed to allow quick preparation: *instant coffee.* ■ (of a person) becoming a specified thing immediately or very suddenly: *become an instant millionaire.* ■ prepared quickly and with little effort: *we can't promise instant solutions.* ■ producing immediate results: *an instant lottery ticket.* **2** urgent; pressing: *an instant desire to blame others when things go wrong.* **3** [*postpositive*] *dated* (in business letters) of the current month: *your letter of the 6th instant.* Compare with **PROXIMO**, **ULTIMO**. **4** *archaic* of the present moment.
▸*n.* **1** a precise moment of time: *come here this instant!* | *at that instant the sun came out.* **2** a very short space of time; a moment: *for an instant the moon disappeared.* **3** *informal* instant coffee. ▷late Middle English (in senses 2, 3, and 4 of the *adjective*): via Old French from Latin *instant-* 'being at hand,' from the verb *instare*, from *in-* 'in, at' + *stare* 'to stand.'

in·stan·ta·ne·ous /,instən'tānēəs/ ▸*adj.* **1** occurring or done in an instant or instantly: *her reaction was almost instantaneous.* ■ operating or providing something instantly: *modern methods of instantaneous communication.* **2** *Physics* existing or measured at a particular instant: *measurement of the instantaneous*

Pronunciation Key ə ago; ər over; 'ə or ,ə up; 'ər or ,ər fur; a hat; ā rate; ä car; cH chew; e let; ē see; e(ə)r air; i fit; ī by; i(ə)r ear; NG sing; ō go; ô for; oi boy; ŏŏ good; ōō goo; ou out; sH she; TH thin; TH then; (h)w why; ZH vision

velocity. ▷mid 17th cent.: from medieval Latin *instantaneus*, from Latin *instant-* 'being at hand' (from the verb *instare*), on the pattern of ecclesiastical Latin *momentaneus.* **—in·stan·ta·ne·i·ty** /in,stantn'ēitē/ *n.* **—in·stan·ta·ne·ous·ly** *adv.* **—in·stan·ta·ne·ous·ness** *n.*

in·stant cam·er·a ▶*n.* a camera of a type with internal processing that produces a finished print rapidly after each exposure.

in·stan·ter /in'stantər/ ▶*adv.* at once; immediately: *we sealed the bargain instanter.* ▷late 17th cent.: Latin.

in·stan·ti·ate /in'stanCHē,āt/ ▶*v.* [*trans.*] represent as or by an instance: *a study of two groups who seemed to instantiate productive aspects of this.* ■ **(be instantiated)** *Philosophy* (of a universal or abstract concept) have an instance; be represented by an actual example. ▷1940s: from Latin *instantia* (see **INSTANCE**) + **-ATE**[3]. **—in·stan·ti·a·tion** /-,stanCHē'āSHən/ *n.*

in·stant·ly /'instəntlē/ ▶*adv.* **1** at once; immediately: *she fell asleep almost instantly.* **2** *archaic* urgently or persistently.

in·stant mes·sag·ing (abbr.: **IM**) ▶*n. Computing* the exchange of typed messages between computer users in real time via the Internet. **—in·stant mes·sage** *n.*

in·stant re·play ▶*n.* an immediate playback of part of a television broadcast, typically one in slow motion showing an incident in a sports event.

in·star /'in,stär/ ▶*n. Zoology* a phase between two periods of molting in the development of an insect larva or other invertebrate animal. ▷late 19th cent.: from Latin, literally 'form, likeness.'

in·state /in'stāt/ ▶*v.* [*trans.*] (usu. **be instated**) set up in position; install or establish: *the restoration of those very authoritarian forms against which democracy had been instated.* ▷early 17th cent. (formerly also as *enstate*): from **EN-**[1], **IN-**[2] 'into' + the noun **STATE**. Compare with earlier **REINSTATE**.

in·stau·ra·tion /,instô'rāSHən/ ▶*n. formal* the action of restoring or renewing something. ▷early 17th cent.: from Latin *instauratio(n-)*, from *instaurare* 'renew,' from *in-* 'in, toward' + *staur-* (a stem also found in *restaurare* 'restore'). **—in·stau·ra·tor** /'instə,rātər/ *n.*

in·stead /in'sted/ ▶*adv.* as an alternative or substitute: *do not use lotions, but put on a clean dressing instead | she never married, preferring instead to remain single.* ■ **(instead of)** as a substitute or alternative to; in place of: *walk to work instead of going by car.* ▷Middle English (originally as two words): from **IN** + **STEAD**.

in·step /'in,step/ ▶*n.* the part of a person's foot between the ball and the ankle. ■ the part of a shoe that fits over or under this part of a foot. ■ a thing shaped like the inner arch of a foot. ▷late Middle English: of unknown origin; compare with West Frisian *ynstap* 'opening in a shoe for insertion of the foot.'

in·sti·gate /'insti,gāt/ ▶*v.* [*trans.*] bring about or initiate (an action or event): *they instigated a reign of terror | instigating legal proceedings.* ■ **(instigate someone to do something)** incite someone to do something, esp. something bad: *instigating men to refuse allegiance to the civil powers.* See notes at **ENCOURAGE, INCITE.** ▷mid 16th cent. (in the sense 'urge on'): from Latin *instigat-* 'urged, incited,' from the verb *instigare*, from *in-* 'toward' + *stigare* 'prick, incite.' **—in·sti·ga·tor** /-,gātər/ *n.*

in·sti·ga·tion /,insti'gāSHən/ ▶*n.* the action or process of instigating an action or event: *he was deported from Iran in 1891 for his instigation and support of the protest.* ▷late Middle English (in the sense 'incitement'): from Old French, or from Latin *instigatio(n-)*, from the verb *instigare* (see **INSTIGATION**).

in·still /in'stil/ (*Brit.* also **in·stil**) ▶*v.* [*trans.*] **1** gradually but firmly establish (an idea or attitude, esp. a desirable one) in a person's mind: *how do we **instill** a sense of rightness **in** today's youth?* **2** put (a substance) into something in the form of liquid drops: *she was told how to instill eye drops.* ▷late Middle English (sense 2): from Latin *instillare*, from *in-* 'into' + *stillare* 'to drop' (from *stilla* 'a drop'). **—in·stil·la·tion** /,instə'lāSHən/ *n.* **—in·still·ment** *n.*

in·stinct ▶*n.* /'in,stiNGkt/ an innate, typically fixed pattern of behavior in animals in response to certain stimuli: *birds have **an instinct to** build nests | maternal instincts.* ■ a natural or intuitive way of acting or thinking: *they retain their old authoritarian instincts.* ■ a natural propensity or skill of a specified kind: *his **instinct for** making the most of his chances.* ■ the fact or quality of possessing innate behavior patterns: *instinct told her not to ask the question.*

▶*adj.* /in'stiNGkt/ [*predic.*] **(instinct with)** *formal* imbued or filled with (a quality, esp. a desirable one): *these canvases are instinct with passion.* ▷late Middle English (also in the sense 'instigation, impulse'): from Latin *instinctus* 'impulse,' from the verb *instinguere*, from *in-* 'toward' + *stinguere* 'to prick.' **—in·stinc·tu·al** /in'stiNGkCHo͞oəl/ *adj.* **—in·stinc·tu·al·ly** *adv.*

USAGE See **usage** at **INSTINCTIVE.**

in·stinc·tive /in'stiNG(k)tiv/ ▶*adj.* relating to or prompted by instinct; apparently unconscious or automatic: *an instinctive distaste for conflict.* ■ (of a person) doing or being a specified thing apparently naturally or automatically: *an instinctive writer.* **—in·stinc·tive·ly** *adv.*

USAGE **Instinctive** and **instinctual** both mean 'relating to or prompted by instinct; unlearned, natural, automatic.' **Instinctual** (like *processual* and other similar formations) is a variant usually found in learned journals of the social sciences.

in·sti·tute /'insti,t(y)o͞ot/ ▶*n.* [usu. in *names*] **1** a society or organization having a particular object or common factor, esp. a scientific, educational, or social one: *the Institute for Advanced Studies | a research institute.* **2** (usu. **institutes**) *archaic* a commentary, treatise, or summary of principles, esp. concerning law.

▶*v.* [*trans.*] **1** set in motion or establish (something, esp. a program, system, or inquiry): *the Illinois Department of Conservation instituted a bowhunt to remove deer | the award was instituted in 1900.* ■ begin (legal proceedings) in a court. **2** (often **be instituted**) appoint (someone) to a position, esp. as a cleric: *his sons were **instituted to** his benefice in 1986 |* [with *complement*] *a testator who has instituted his daughter heir.* ▷Middle English (sense 2 of the *verb*): from Latin *institut-* 'established,' from the verb *instituere*, from *in-* 'in, toward' + *statuere* 'set up.' The noun is from Latin *institutum* 'something designed, precept,' neuter past participle of *instituere*; sense 1 dates from the early 19th cent.

in·sti·tu·tion /,insti't(y)o͞oSHən/ ▶*n.* **1** a society or organization founded for a religious, educational, social, or similar purpose: *a certificate from a professional institution.* ■ an organization providing residential care for people with special needs: *an institution for the severely handicapped.* ■ an established official organization having an important role in the life of a country, such as a bank, church, or legislature: *the institutions of democratic government.* ■ a large company or other organization involved in financial trading: *the interest rate financial institutions charge one another.* **2** an established law, practice, or custom: ***the institution of** marriage.* ■ *informal* a well-established and familiar person, custom, or object: *he soon became something of a national institution.* **3** the action of instituting something: *a delay in the institution of proceedings.* ▷late Middle English (in senses 2 and 3): via Old French from Latin *institutio(n-)*, from the verb *instituere* (see **INSTITUTE**). Sense 1 dates from the early 18th cent.

in·sti·tu·tion·al /,insti't(y)o͞oSHənl/ ▶*adj.* of, in, or like an institution or institutions: *institutional care | an institutional investor.* ■ unappealing or unimaginative: *institutional chocolate-colored paint.* ■ expressed or organized in the form of institutions: *institutional religion.* ■ (of advertising) intended to create prestige rather than immediate sales. **—in·sti·tu·tion·al·ism** /-,izəm/ *n.* **—in·sti·tu·tion·al·ly** *adv.*

in·sti·tu·tion·al in·ves·tor ▶*n. Finance* a large organization, such as a bank, pension fund, labor union, or insurance company, that makes substantial investments on the stock exchange.

in·sti·tu·tion·al·ize /,insti't(y)o͞oSHənl,īz/ ▶*v.* [*trans.*] **1** establish (something, typically a practice or activity) as a convention or norm in an organization or culture: *a system that institutionalizes bad behavior.* **2** (usu. **be institutionalized**) place or keep (someone) in a residential institution: *these adolescents had more contacts with the police and were charged and institutionalized more often.* **—in·sti·tu·tion·al·i·za·tion** /,insti,t(y)o͞oSHənl-i'zāSHən/ *n.*

in·sti·tu·tion·al·ized /,insti't(y)o͞oSHənl,īzd/ ▶*adj.* **1** established in practice or custom: *the danger of discrimination becoming institutionalized.* **2** established as part of an official organization: *one of the most insidious byproducts of the Cold War, institutionalized secrecy.* **3** (of a person, esp. a long-term patient or prisoner) made apathetic and dependent after a long period in an institution.

in-store ▶*adj.* & *adv.* within a store: [as *adj.*] *an in-store bakery |* [as *adv.*] *the goods are promoted in-store.*

instr. ▶*abbr.* ■ instructor. ■ instrument or instrumental.

in·struct /in'strəkt/ ▶*v.* **1** [*reporting verb*] direct or command someone to do something, esp. as an official order: [*trans.*] *she instructed him to wait |* [with *direct speech*] *"Look at me," he instructed |* [with *clause*] *I instructed that she be given hot, sweet tea.* **2** [*trans.*] teach (someone) a subject or skill: *he **instructed** them **in** the use of firearms |* [*trans.*] *instructing electors how to record their votes.* **3** [*trans.*] *Law* give a person direction, information, or authorization, in particular: ■ (of a judge) give information, esp. clarification of legal principles, to (a jury). ■ inform (someone) of a fact or situation: [with *clause*] *the bank was instructed that the money from the savings account was now held by the company.* ▷late Middle English (sense 2): from Latin *instruct-* 'constructed, equipped, taught,' from the verb *instruere*, from *in-* 'upon, toward' + *struere* 'pile up.'

in·struc·tion /in'strəkSHən/ ▶*n.* **1** (often **instructions**) a direction or order: *he issued instructions to the sheriff | he was acting on my instructions.* ■ **(instructions)** *Law* directions to a lawyer or to a jury. ■ *Computing* a code or sequence in a computer program that defines an operation and puts it into effect. **2** (**instructions**) detailed information telling how something should be done, operated, or assembled: *always study the instructions supplied.* **3** teaching; education: *the school offers personalized instruction in a variety of skills.* ▷late Middle English: via Old French from late Latin *instructio(n-)*, from the verb *instruere* (see **INSTRUCT**). **—in·struc·tion·al** /-SHənl/ *adj.*

in·struc·tion set ▶*n. Computing* the complete set of all the instructions in machine code that can be recognized and executed by a central processing unit.

in·struc·tive /in'strəktiv/ ▶*adj.* useful and informative: *it is instructive to compare the two projects.* **—in·struc·tive·ly** *adv.* **—in·struc·tive·ness** *n.*

in·struc·tor /in'strəktər/ ▶*n.* a person who teaches something: *a driving instructor.* ■ a college teacher ranking below assistant professor. **—in·struc·tor·ship** /-,SHip/ *n.*

in·stru·ment /'instrəmənt/ ▶*n.* **1** a tool or implement, esp. one for delicate or scientific work: *a surgical instrument | writing instruments.* See note at **TOOL**. ■ a thing used in pursuing an aim or policy; a means: *drama as an **instrument of** learning.* ■ a person who is exploited or made use of: *he was a mere instrument acting under coercion.* **2** a measuring device used to gauge the level, position, speed, etc., of something, esp. a motor vehicle or aircraft. **3** (also **musical instrument**) an object or device for producing musical sounds: *a percussion instrument.* **4** a formal document, esp. a legal one: *execution involves signature and unconditional delivery of the instrument.*

▶*v.* [*trans.*] equip (something) with measuring instruments. ▷Middle English: from Old French, or from Latin *instrumentum* 'equipment, implement,' from the verb *instruere* 'construct, equip.'

in·stru·men·tal /,instrə'mentl/ ▶*adj.* **1** serving as an instrument or means in pursuing an aim or policy: *the society was **instrumental in** bringing about legislation.* ■ relating to something's function as an instrument or means to an end: *a very instrumental view of education and how it relates to their needs.* **2** (of music) performed on instruments, not sung: *a largely instrumental piece.* ■ relating to musical instruments: *brilliance of instrumental color.* **3** of or relating to an implement or measuring device: *instrumental error | instrumental delivery of a baby.* **4** *Grammar* denoting or relating to a case of nouns and pronouns (and words in grammatical agreement with them) indicating a means or instrument.

▶*n.* **1** a piece of (usually nonclassical) music performed solely by instruments, with no vocals. **2** (**the instrumental**) *Grammar* the instrumental case. ■ a noun in the instrumental case. **—in·stru·men·tal·ly** *adv.*

in·stru·men·tal con·di·tion·ing ▶*n. Psychology* a learning process in which behavior is modified by the reinforcing or inhibiting effects of the resulting consequences.

in·stru·men·tal·ism /,instrə'mentl,izəm/ ▶*n.* **1** a pragmatic philosophical approach that regards an activity (such as science, law, or education) chiefly as an instrument or tool for some practical purpose, rather than in more absolute or ideal terms, in particular: ■ *Philosophy* the pragmatic philosophy of John Dewey that supposes that thought is an instrument for solving practical problems and that truth is not fixed but changes as the problems change. ■ (esp. in Marxist theory) the view that the state and social organizations are tools that are exploited by the ruling class or by individuals in their own interests. **2** *rare Music* instrumental technique.

in·stru·men·tal·ist /ˌinstrəˈmentl-ist/ ▸*n.* **1** a player of a musical instrument. **2** an adherent of instrumentalism.
▸*adj.* of or in terms of instrumentalism.

in·stru·men·tal·i·ty /ˌinstrəmenˈtalitē; -men-/ ▸*n.* (*pl.* **-ties**) the fact or quality of serving as an instrument or means to an end; agency: *a corporate body can act only through the instrumentality of human beings.* ■ a thing that serves as an instrument or means to an end.

in·stru·men·ta·tion /ˌinstrəmənˈtāsʜən; -men-/ ▸*n.* **1** the particular instruments used in a piece of music; the manner in which a piece is arranged for instruments: *Telemann's specified instrumentation of flute, violin, and continuo.* ■ the arrangement or composition of a piece of music for particular musical instruments: *an experiment in instrumentation.* **2** measuring instruments regarded collectively: *the controls and instrumentation of an aircraft.* ■ the design, provision, or use of measuring instruments.

in·stru·ment pan·el (also **instrument board**) ▸*n.* a surface in front of a driver's or pilot's seat, on which the vehicle's or aircraft's instruments are situated.

in·sub·or·di·nate /ˌinsəˈbôrdn-it/ ▸*adj.* defiant of authority; disobedient to orders: *an insubordinate attitude.* —**in·sub·or·di·nate·ly** *adv.* —**in·sub·or·di·na·tion** /-ˌbôrdnˈāsʜən/ *n.*

in·sub·stan·tial /ˌinsəbˈstancʜəl/ ▸*adj.* lacking strength and solidity: *the huts are relatively few and insubstantial | insubstantial evidence.* ■ not solid or real; imaginary: *the flickering light made her face seem insubstantial.* ▷early 17th cent.: from late Latin *insubstantialis*, from *in-* 'not' + *substantialis* (see SUBSTANTIAL). —**in·sub·stan·ti·al·i·ty** /-ˌstancʜēˈalitē/ *n.* —**in·sub·stan·tial·ly** *adv.*

in·suf·fer·a·ble /inˈsəf(ə)rəbəl/ ▸*adj.* too extreme to bear; intolerable: *the heat would be insufferable by July.* ■ having or showing unbearable arrogance or conceit: *an insufferable bully | insufferable French chauvinism.* ▷late Middle English: perhaps via French (now dialect) *insouffrable*, based on Latin *suffere* 'endure' (see SUFFER). —**in·suf·fer·a·ble·ness** *n.* —**in·suf·fer·a·bly** /-blē/ *adv.*

in·suf·fi·cien·cy /ˌinsəˈfisʜənsē/ ▸*n.* the condition of being insufficient: *insufficiency of adequate housing | there have been demands to redress such insufficiencies.* ■ *Medicine* the inability of an organ to perform its normal function: *renal insufficiency.* ▷early 16th cent. (in the sense 'incompetence, inability'): from late Latin *insufficientia*, from *in-* 'not' + Latin *sufficere* 'be sufficient.'

in·suf·flate /ˈinsəˌflāt/ ▸*v.* [*trans.*] **1** *Medicine* blow (air, gas, or powder) into a cavity of the body. ■ blow something into (a part of the body) in this way. **2** *Theology* blow or breathe on (someone) to symbolize spiritual influence. ▷late 17th cent.: from late Latin *insufflat-* 'blown into,' from the verb *insufflare*, from *in-* 'into' + *sufflare* 'blow' (from *sub-* 'from below' + *flare* 'to blow'). Sense 2 dates from the early 20th cent. —**in·suf·fla·tion** /ˌinsəˈflāsʜən/ *n.*

in·suf·fla·tor /ˈinsəˌflātər/ ▸*n.* **1** a device for blowing powder onto a surface in order to make fingerprints visible. **2** an instrument for medical insufflation.

in·su·la /ˈins(y)ələ/ ▸*n.* (*pl.* **-lae** /-ˌlē/) *Anatomy* a region of the brain deep in the cerebral cortex. ▷mid 19th cent.: Latin, literally 'island.'

in·su·lant /ˈins(y)ələnt/ ▸*n.* an insulating material.

in·su·lar /ˈins(y)ələr/ ▸*adj.* **1** ignorant of or uninterested in cultures, ideas, or peoples outside one's own experience: *a stubbornly insular farming people.* ■ lacking contact with other people: *people living restricted and sometimes insular existences.* **2** of, relating to, or from an island: *the movement of goods of insular origin.* ■ of or relating to the art and craftwork of Britain and Ireland in the early Middle Ages, esp. a form of Latin handwriting: *insular illumination of the 6th century.* ■ (of climate) equable because of the influence of the sea. **3** *Anatomy* of or relating to the insula of the brain. ▷mid 16th cent. (as a noun denoting an islander): from late Latin *insularis*, from *insula* 'island.' —**in·su·lar·i·ty** /ˌins(y)əˈlaritē; -ˈler-/ *n.* —**in·su·lar·ly** *adv.*

in·su·late /ˈins(y)əˌlāt/ ▸*v.* [*trans.*] (often **be insulated**) **1** protect (something) by interposing material that prevents the loss of heat or the intrusion of sound: *the room was heavily* ***insulated against*** *all outside noise.* ■ prevent the passage of electricity to or from (something) by covering it in nonconducting material: *the case is carefully insulated to prevent short circuits.* ■ *figurative* protect from the unpleasant effects or elements of something: *he claims that the service is complacent and* ***insulated from*** *outside pressures.* **2** *archaic* make (land) into an island: *the village was insulated by every flood of the river.* ▷mid 16th cent. (sense 2): from Latin *insula* 'island' + -ATE³.

in·su·lat·ing tape ▸*n.* another term for FRICTION TAPE.

in·su·la·tion /ˌins(y)əˈlāsʜən/ ▸*n.* the action of insulating something or someone: *keep your home warmer through insulation | heat insulation.* ■ the state of being insulated: *his comparative insulation from the world.* ■ material used to insulate something, esp. a building: *fit insulation to all exposed pipes.*

in·su·la·tor /ˈins(y)əˌlātər/ ▸*n.* a thing or substance used for insulation, in particular: ■ a substance that does not readily allow the passage of heat or sound: *cotton is a poor insulator.* ■ a substance or device that does not readily conduct electricity. ■ a block of material, typically glass or ceramic, enclosing a wire carrying an electric current where it crosses a support.

in·su·lin /ˈinsələn/ ▸*n.* *Biochemistry* a hormone produced in the pancreas by the islets of Langerhans that regulates the amount of glucose in the blood. The lack of insulin causes a form of diabetes. ■ an animal-derived or synthetic form of this substance used to treat diabetes. ▷early 20th cent.: from Latin *insula* 'island' + -IN¹.

in·su·lin shock ▸*n.* *Medicine* an acute physiological condition resulting from excess insulin in the blood, involving low blood sugar, weakness, convulsions, and potentially coma.

in·su·li·tis /ˌinsəˈlītis/ ▸*n.* *Medicine* disease of the pancreas caused by the infiltration of lymphocytes.

in·sult ▸*v.* /inˈsəlt/ [*trans.*] speak to or treat with disrespect or scornful abuse: *you're insulting the woman I love |* [as *adj.*] (**insulting**) *their language is crude and* ***insulting to*** *women.*
▸*n.* /ˈinˌsəlt/ **1** a disrespectful or scornfully abusive remark or action: *he hurled insults at us | he saw the book as a deliberate* ***insult to*** *the Church.* ■ a thing so worthless or contemptible as to be offensive: *the present offer is an absolute insult.* **2** *Medicine* an event or occurrence that causes damage to a tissue or organ: *the movement of the bone causes a severe tissue insult.* ▷mid 16th cent. (as a verb in the sense 'exult, act arrogantly'): from Latin *insultare* 'jump or trample on,' from *in-* 'on' + *saltare*, from *salire* 'to leap.' The noun (in the early 17th cent. denoting an attack) is from French *insulte* or ecclesiastical Latin *insultus*. The main current senses date from the 17th cent., the medical use dating from the early 20th cent. —**in·sult·er** *n.* —**in·sult·ing·ly** *adv.*
▸*PHRASE* □ **add insult to injury** act in a way that makes a bad or displeasing situation worse.

in·su·per·a·ble /inˈso͞op(ə)rəbəl/ ▸*adj.* (of a difficulty or obstacle) impossible to overcome: *insuperable financial problems.* ▷Middle English (in the general sense 'invincible'): from Old French, or from Latin *insuperabilis*, from *in-* 'not' + *superabilis* (from *superare* 'overcome'). —**in·su·per·a·bil·i·ty** /-ˌso͞op(ə)rəˈbilitē/ *n.* —**in·su·per·a·bly** /-blē/ *adv.*

in·sup·port·a·ble /ˌinsəˈpôrtəbəl/ ▸*adj.* **1** unable to be supported or justified: *he had arrived at a wholly insupportable conclusion.* **2** unable to be endured; intolerable: *the heat was insupportable.* ▷mid 16th cent.: from French, from *in-* 'not' + *supportable* (from *supporter* 'to support'). —**in·sup·port·a·bly** /-blē/ *adv.*

in·sur·ance /inˈsʜo͝orəns/ ▸*n.* **1** a practice or arrangement by which a company or government agency provides a guarantee of compensation for specified loss, damage, illness, or death in return for payment of a premium: *many new borrowers take out* ***insurance against*** *unemployment or sickness.* ■ the business of providing such an arrangement: *Howard is in insurance.* ■ money paid for this: *my insurance has gone up.* ■ money paid out as compensation under such an arrangement: *when will I be able to collect the insurance?* ■ an insurance policy. **2** a thing providing protection against a possible eventuality: *seeking closer ties with other oil-supplying nations as* ***insurance against*** *disruption of Middle East supplies | young people are not an insurance against loneliness in old age.* ▷late Middle English (originally as *ensurance* in the sense 'ensuring, assurance, a guarantee'): from Old French *enseurance*, from *enseurer* (see ENSURE). Sense 1 dates from the mid 17th cent.

in·sur·ance a·gent ▸*n.* a person employed to sell insurance policies.

in·sur·ance car·ri·er ▸*n.* an insurer; an insurance company.

in·sur·ance pol·i·cy ▸*n.* a document detailing the terms and conditions of a contract of insurance.

in·sure /inˈsʜo͝or/ ▸*v.* [*trans.*] arrange for compensation in the event of damage to or loss of (property), or injury to or the death of (someone), in exchange for regular advance payments to a company or government agency: *the table should be* ***insured for*** *$2,500 | the company had* ***insured*** *itself* ***against*** *a fall of the dollar |* [*intrans.*] *businesses can* ***insure against*** *exchange rate fluctuations.* ■ provide insurance coverage with respect to: *subsidiaries set up to insure the risks of a group of companies.* ■ (**insure someone against**) *figurative* secure or protect someone against (a possible contingency): *by appeasing Celia they might insure themselves against further misfortune |* [*intrans.*] *such changes could insure against further violence and unrest.* ▷late Middle English (in the sense 'assure someone of something'): alteration of ENSURE. —**in·sur·a·bil·i·ty** /-ˌsʜo͝orəˈbilitē/ *n.* —**in·sur·a·ble** *adj.*

USAGE There is considerable overlap between the meaning and use of **insure** and **ensure**. In both U.S. and British English, the primary meaning of **insure** is the commercial sense of providing financial compensation in the event of damage to property; **ensure** is not used at all in this sense. For the more general senses, **ensure** is more likely to be used, but **insure** and **ensure** are often interchangeable, particularly in U.S. English: *bail is posted to* ***insure*** *that the defendant appears for trial the system is run to* ***ensure*** *that a good quality of service is maintained.*

in·sured /inˈsʜo͝ord/ ▸*adj.* covered by insurance: *the insured car | a privately insured patient | an insured risk.*
▸*n.* (**the insured**) (*pl.* same) a person or organization covered by insurance.

in·sur·er /inˈsʜo͝orər/ ▸*n.* a person or company that underwrites an insurance risk; the party in an insurance contract undertaking to pay compensation.

in·sur·gent /inˈsərjənt/ ▸*adj.* [*attrib.*] rising in active revolt: *alleged links with insurgent groups.* See note at UPRISING. ■ of or relating to rebels: *a series of insurgent attacks.*
▸*n.* (usu. **insurgents**) a rebel or revolutionary: *an attack by armed insurgents.* ▷mid 18th cent. (as a noun): via French from Latin *insurgent-* 'arising,' from the verb *insurgere*, from *in-* 'into, toward' + *surgere* 'to rise.' —**in·sur·gence** *n.* —**in·sur·gen·cy** *n.* (*pl.* **-cies**).

in·sur·mount·a·ble /ˌinsərˈmountəbəl/ ▸*adj.* too great to be overcome: *an insurmountable problem.* —**in·sur·mount·a·bly** *adv.*

in·sur·rec·tion /ˌinsəˈreksʜən/ ▸*n.* a violent uprising against an authority or government: *the insurrection was savagely put down | opposition to the new regime led to armed insurrection.* See note at UPRISING. ▷late Middle English: via Old French from late Latin *insurrectio(n-)*, from *insurgere* 'rise up.' —**in·sur·rec·tion·ar·y** *adj.* —**in·sur·rec·tion·ist** *n.* & *adj.*

int. ▸*abbr.* ■ interior. ■ internal. ■ international.

in·tact /inˈtakt/ ▸*adj.* [often as *complement*] not damaged or impaired in any way; complete: *the church was almost in ruins, but its tower remained intact.* ▷late Middle English: from Latin *intactus*, from *in-* 'not' + *tactus* (past participle of *tangere* 'touch'). —**in·tact·ness** *n.*

in·tact fam·i·ly ▸*n.* a nuclear family in which membership has remained constant, in the absence of divorce or other divisive factors.

in·ta·gliat·ed /inˈtalēˌātid; -ˈtälē-/ ▸*adj.* *archaic* carved or engraved on the surface. ▷late 18th cent.: from Italian *intagliato* 'engraved,' past participle of *intagliare*, from *in-* 'into' + *tagliare* 'to cut.'

in·ta·glio /inˈtalyō; -ˈtäl-/ ▸*n.* (*pl.* **-glios**) a design incised or engraved into a material: *the dies bore a design* ***in intaglio.*** ■ a gem with an incised design. ■ any printing process in which the type or design is etched or engraved, such as photogravure or dry point.
▸*v.* (**-glioes, -glioed**) [*trans.*] [usu. as *adj.*] (**intaglioed**) engrave or represent by an engraving: *a carved box with little intaglioed pineapples on it.* ▷mid 17th cent.: Italian, from *intagliare* 'engrave.'

in·take /ˈinˌtāk/ ▸*n.* **1** an amount of food, air, or another substance taken into the body: *your daily intake of calories | his alcohol intake.* ■ an act of taking something into the body: *she heard his* ***sharp intake of breath*** *| a protective factor is the* ***intake of*** *cereal fiber.* **2** a location or structure through which something is taken in, e.g., water into a channel or pipe from a river, fuel or air into an engine or machine, commodities into a place, etc.: *cut rectangular holes for the air intake.* ■ the action of taking something in: *facilities for the* *intake of grain by road.* ▷Middle English (originally Scots and northern English): from IN + TAKE.

in·tan·gi·ble /inˈtanjəbəl/ ▶*adj.* unable to be touched or grasped; not having physical presence: *my companions do not care about cyberspace or anything else so intangible.* ■ difficult or impossible to define or understand; vague and abstract: *the rose symbolized something intangible about their relationship.* ■ (of an asset or benefit) not constituting or represented by a physical object and of a value not precisely measurable: *intangible business property like trademarks and patents.*

▶*n.* (usu. **intangibles**) an intangible thing: *intangibles like self-confidence and responsibility.* ▷early 17th cent. (as an adjective): from French, or from medieval Latin *intangibilis,* from *in-* 'not' + late Latin *tangibilis* (see TANGIBLE). —**in·tan·gi·bil·i·ty** /-ˌtanjəˈbilitē/ *n.* —**in·tan·gi·bly** /-blē/ *adv.*

in·tar·si·a /inˈtärsēə/ ▶*n.* [often as *adj.*] **1** a method of knitting with a number of colors, in which a separate length or ball of yarn is used for each area of color (as opposed to different yarns being carried at the back of the work): *an intarsia design.* **2** an elaborate form of marquetry using inlays in wood, esp. as practiced in 15th-century Italy. ■ similar inlaid work in stone, metal, or glass. ▷from Italian *intarsio;* in sense 2 superseding earlier *tarsia* (from Italian, 'marquetry'); the knitting term dates from the mid 19th cent.

in·te·ger /ˈintijər/ ▶*n.* **1** a whole number; a number that is not a fraction. **2** a thing complete in itself. ▷early 16th cent. (as an adjective meaning 'entire, whole'): from Latin, 'intact, whole,' from *in-* (expressing negation) + the root of *tangere* 'to touch.' Compare with ENTIRE, also with INTEGRAL, INTEGRATE, and INTEGRITY.

in·te·gral /ˈintigrəl; inˈteg-/ ▶*adj.* **1** necessary to make a whole complete; essential or fundamental: *games are an integral part of the school's curriculum | systematic training should be* ***integral to*** *library management.* ■ [*attrib.*] included as part of the whole rather than supplied separately: *the unit comes complete with integral pump and heater.* ■ [*attrib.*] having or containing all parts that are necessary to be complete: *the first integral recording of the ten Mahler symphonies.* **2** *Mathematics* of or denoted by an integer. ■ involving only integers, esp. as coefficients of a function.

▶*n. Mathematics* a function of which a given function is the derivative, i.e., which yields that function when differentiated, and which may express the area under the curve of a graph of the function. See also DEFINITE INTEGRAL, INDEFINITE INTEGRAL. ■ a function satisfying a given differential equation. ▷mid 16th cent.: from late Latin *integralis,* from *integer* 'whole' (see INTEGER). Compare with INTEGRATE and INTEGRITY. —**in·te·gral·i·ty** /ˌintiˈgralitē/ *n.* —**in·te·gral·ly** *adv.*

in·te·gral cal·cu·lus ▶*n.* a branch of mathematics concerned with the determination, properties, and application of integrals. Compare with DIFFERENTIAL CALCULUS.

in·te·grand /ˈintigrənd/ ▶*n. Mathematics* a function that is to be integrated. ▷late 19th cent.: from Latin *integrandus,* gerundive of *integrare* (see INTEGRATE).

in·te·grant /ˈintigrənt/ ▶*adj.* (of parts) making up or contributing to a whole; constituent.

▶*n.* a component. ▷mid 17th cent. (as an adjective): from French *intégrant,* from the verb *intégrer,* from Latin *integrare* (see INTEGRATE).

in·te·grate /ˈintiˌgrāt/ ▶*v.* [*trans.*] **1** combine (one thing) with another so that they become a whole: *transportation planning should be* ***integrated with*** *energy policy.* ■ combine (two things) so that they become a whole: *the problem of integrating the two approaches.* ■ [*intrans.*] (of a thing) combine with another to form a whole: *the stone will blend with the environment and* ***integrate into*** *the landscape.* **2** bring into equal participation in or membership of society or an institution or body: ***integrating*** *children with special needs* ***into*** *ordinary schools.* ■ [*intrans.*] come into equal participation in or membership of society or an institution or body: *she was anxious to* ***integrate*** *well* ***into*** *her husband's family.* **3** desegregate (a school, neighborhood, etc.), esp. racially: *there was a national campaign under way to integrate the lunch counters | [intrans.] cities' efforts to integrate across urban-suburban lines.* **4** *Mathematics* find the integral of. ▷mid 17th cent.: from Latin *integrat-* 'made whole,' from the verb *integrare,* from *integer* 'whole' (see INTEGER). Compare with INTEGRAL and INTEGRITY. —**in·te·gra·bil·i·ty** /ˌintigrəˈbilitē/ *n.* —**in·te·gra·ble** /-grəbəl/ *adj.*

in·te·grat·ed /ˈintiˌgrātid/ ▶*adj.* having been integrated, in particular: ■ (of an institution, body, etc.) desegregated, esp. racially: *integrated education.* ■ with various parts or aspects linked or coordinated: *an integrated and high-quality public transportation system.* ■ *chiefly Physics* indicating the mean value or total sum of (temperature, an area, etc.): *integrated electron density along the line of sight.*

in·te·grat·ed cir·cuit ▶*n.* an electronic circuit formed on a small piece of semiconducting material, performing the same function as a larger circuit made from discrete components.

in·te·grat·ed serv·ic·es dig·it·al net·work (abbr.: **ISDN**) ▶*n.* a telecommunications network through which sound, images, and data can be transmitted as digitized signals.

in·te·grat·ing /ˈintiˌgrātiNG/ ▶*adj.* (of an instrument) indicating the mean value or total sum of a measured quantity.

in·te·gra·tion /ˌintiˈgrāSHən/ ▶*n.* **1** the action or process of integrating: *economic and political integration |* ***integration*** *of individual countries* ***into*** *trading blocs.* ■ the intermixing of people or groups previously segregated: *integration is the best hope for both black and white Americans.* **2** *Mathematics* the finding of an integral or integrals: *integration of an ordinary differential equation | mathematical integrations.* **3** *Psychology* the coordination of processes in the nervous system, including diverse sensory information and motor impulses: *visuomotor integration.* ■ *Psychoanalysis* the process by which a well-balanced psyche becomes whole as the developing ego organizes the id, and the state that results or that treatment seeks to create or restore by countering the fragmenting effect of defense mechanisms. —**in·te·gra·tion·ist** /-nist/ *n.*

in·te·gra·tive /-ˌgrātiv/ ▶*adj.* serving or intending to unify separate things: *an integrative approach to learning.* ■ *Medicine* combining allopathic and complementary therapies: *a database for the integrative physician | integrative medicine.*

in·te·gra·tor /ˈintiˌgrātər/ ▶*n.* a person or thing that integrates, in particular: ■ (also **system integrator** or **systems integrator**) *Computing* a company that markets commercial integrated software and hardware systems. ■ *Electronics* a computer chip or circuit that performs mathematical integration. ■ an instrument for indicating or registering the total amount or mean value of some physical quality such as area or temperature.

in·teg·ri·ty /inˈtegritē/ ▶*n.* **1** the quality of being honest and having strong moral principles; moral uprightness: *he is known to be a man of integrity.* **2** the state of being whole and undivided: *upholding territorial integrity and national sovereignty.* ■ the condition of being unified, unimpaired, or sound in construction: *the structural integrity of the novel.* ■ internal consistency or lack of corruption in electronic data: [as *adj.*] *integrity checking.* ▷late Middle English (sense 2): from French *intégrité* or Latin *integritas,* from *integer* 'intact' (see INTEGER). Compare with ENTIRETY, INTEGRAL, and INTEGRATE.

in·teg·u·ment /inˈtegyəmənt/ ▶*n.* a tough outer protective layer, esp. that of an animal or plant. ▷early 17th cent. (denoting a covering or coating): from Latin *integumentum,* from the verb *integere,* from *in-* 'in' + *tegere* 'to cover.' —**in·teg·u·men·tal** /-ˌtegyəˈmentl/ *adj.* —**in·teg·u·men·ta·ry** /-ˌtegyəˈmentərē/ *adj.*

in·tel /ˈinˌtel/ ▶*n.* [often as *modifier*] *informal* military intelligence; information: *prewar intel.* ▷1980s: shortening.

in·tel·lect /ˈintlˌekt/ ▶*n.* the faculty of reasoning and understanding objectively, esp. with regard to abstract or academic matters: *he was a man of action rather than of intellect.* ■ the understanding or mental powers of a particular person: *his keen intellect.* ■ an intelligent or intellectual person: *sapping our country of some of its brightest intellects.* ▷late Middle English: from Latin *intellectus* 'understanding,' from *intellegere* 'understand' (see INTELLIGENT).

in·tel·lec·tion /ˌintlˈekSHən/ ▶*n.* the action or process of understanding, as opposed to imagination. —**in·tel·lec·tive** /-tiv/ *adj.*

in·tel·lec·tu·al /ˌintlˈekCHo͞oəl/ ▶*adj.* of or relating to the intellect: *children need intellectual stimulation.* ■ appealing to or requiring use of the intellect: *the movie wasn't very intellectual, but it caught the mood of the times.* ■ possessing a highly developed intellect: *you are an intellectual girl, like your mother.*

▶*n.* a person possessing a highly developed intellect. ▷late Middle English: from Latin *intellectualis,* from *intellectus* 'understanding,' from *intellegere* 'understand' (see INTELLIGENT). —**in·tel·lec·tu·al·i·ty** /ˌintlˌekCHo͞oˈalitē/ *n.* —**in·tel·lec·tu·al·ly** *adv.*

in·tel·lec·tu·al·ism /ˌintlˈekCHo͞oəˌlizəm/ ▶*n.* the exercise of the intellect at the expense of the emotions. ■ *Philosophy* the theory that knowledge is wholly or mainly derived from pure reason; rationalism. ▷early 19th cent. (as a term in philosophy): from INTELLECTUAL, on the pattern of German *Intellektualismus.* —**in·tel·lec·tu·al·ist** *n.*

in·tel·lec·tu·al·ize /ˌintlˈekCHo͞oəˌlīz/ ▶*v.* [*trans.*] **1** give an intellectual character to: *belief was a gut feeling—it couldn't be intellectualized.* **2** [*intrans.*] talk, write, or think intellectually: *people who* ***intellectualize about*** *fashion.* —**in·tel·lec·tu·al·i·za·tion** /-ˌekCHo͞oələˈzāSHən/ *n.*

in·tel·lec·tu·al prop·er·ty ▶*n. Law* a work or invention that is the result of creativity, such as a manuscript or a design, to which one has rights and for which one may apply for a patent, copyright, trademark, etc.

in·tel·li·gence /inˈtelijəns/ ▶*n.* **1** the ability to acquire and apply knowledge and skills: *an eminent man of great intelligence | they underestimated her intelligence.* ■ a person or being with this ability: *extraterrestrial intelligences.* **2** the collection of information of military or political value: *the chief of military intelligence |* [as *adj.*] *the intelligence department.* ■ people employed in this, regarded collectively: *French intelligence has been able to secure numerous local informers.* ■ information collected in this way: *the gathering of intelligence.* ■ *archaic* information in general; news. ▷late Middle English: via Old French from Latin *intelligentia,* from *intelligere* 'understand' (see INTELLIGENT). —**in·tel·li·gen·tial** /inˌteləˈjenCHəl/ *adj.* (*archaic*).

in·tel·li·gence quo·tient (abbr.: **IQ**) ▶*n.* a number representing a person's reasoning ability (measured using problem-solving tests) as compared to the statistical norm or average for their age, taken as 100.

in·tel·li·genc·er /inˈtelijənsər; -ˌjen-/ ▶*n. archaic* a person who gathers intelligence, esp. an informer, spy, or secret agent.

in·tel·li·gence test ▶*n.* a test designed to measure the ability to think and reason rather than acquired knowledge.

in·tel·li·gent /inˈtelijənt/ ▶*adj.* having or showing intelligence, esp. of a high level: *Annabelle is intelligent and hardworking | an intelligent guess.* ■ (of a device, machine, or building) able to vary its state or action in response to varying situations, varying requirements, and past experience. ■ (esp. of a computer terminal) incorporating a microprocessor and having its own processing capability. Often contrasted with DUMB. ▷early 16th cent.: from Latin *intelligent-* 'understanding,' from the verb *intelligere,* variant of *intellegere* 'understand,' from *inter* 'between' + *legere* 'choose.' —**in·tel·li·gent·ly** *adv.*

in·tel·li·gent de·sign ▶*n.* the theory that life, or the universe, cannot have arisen by chance and was designed and created by some intelligent entity.

in·tel·li·gent·si·a /inˌteliˈjentsēə/ ▶*n.* (usu. **the intelligentsia**) [treated as *sing.* or *pl.*] intellectuals or highly educated people as a group, esp. when regarded as possessing culture and political influence. ▷early 20th cent.: from Russian *intelligentsiya,* from Polish *inteligencja,* from Latin *intelligentia* (see INTELLIGENCE).

in·tel·li·gi·ble /inˈtelijəbəl/ ▶*adj.* able to be understood; comprehensible: *this would make the system more intelligible to the general public.* ■ *Philosophy* able to be understood only by the intellect, not by the senses. ▷late Middle English (also in the sense 'capable of understanding'): from Latin *intelligibilis,* from *intelligere* 'understand' (see INTELLIGENT). —**in·tel·li·gi·bil·i·ty** /-ˌtelijəˈbilitē/ *n.* —**in·tel·li·gi·bly** /-blē/ *adv.*

In·tel·sat /ˈintelˌsat/ an international organization of more than 100 countries, formed in 1964, that owns and operates the worldwide commercial communications satellite system. ▷from *In(ternational) Tel(ecommunications) Sat(ellite Consortium).*

in·tem·per·ate /inˈtemp(ə)rit/ ▶*adj.* having or showing a lack of self-control; immoderate: *intemperate outbursts concerning global conspiracies.* ■ given to or characterized by excessive indulgence, esp. in alcohol: *an intemperate social occasion.* ▷late Middle English (in the sense 'inclement'): from Latin *intemperatus,* from *in-* 'not' + *temperatus* (see TEMPERATE). —**in·tem·per·ance** /-rəns/ *n.* —**in·tem·per·ate·ly** *adv.* —**in·tem·per·ate·ness** *n.*

in·tend /inˈtend/ ▶*v.* [*trans.*] **1** have (a course of action) as one's purpose or objective; plan: [with *infinitive*] *the company intends to cut about 4,500 jobs |* [with *clause*] *it is intended that coverage shall be worldwide.* ■ plan that (something) function in a particular way: *a series of questions* ***intended as*** *a checklist.* ■ plan that speech should have (a particular meaning): *no offense was intended, I assure you.* **2** design or destine (someone or something) for a particular purpose or end: *pigs* ***intended for*** *human consumption* | [with *infinitive*] *a one-room cottage intended to accommodate a family.* ■ (**be intended for**) be meant or designed for (a particular person or group) to have or use: *this benefit is intended for people incapable of work.* ▷Middle English *entend* (in the sense 'direct the attention to'), from Old French *entendre,* from Latin *intendere* 'intend, extend, direct,' from *in-* 'toward' + *tendere* 'stretch, tend.' —**in·tend·er** *n.*

THE RIGHT WORD **aim, design, intend, mean, plan, propose, purpose**

If you **intend** to do something, you may or may not be serious about getting it done (*I intend to clean out the garage some day*), but at least you have a goal in mind.

Although **mean** can also imply either a firm resolve (*I mean to go, with or without her permission*) or a vague intention (*I've been meaning to write her for weeks*), it is a less formal word that usually connotes a certain lack of determination or a weak resolve.

Plan, like *mean* and *intend,* may imply a vague goal (*I plan to tour China some day*), but it is often used to suggest that you're taking active steps (*I plan to leave as soon as I finish packing*).

Aim indicates that you have an actual goal or purpose in mind and that you're putting some effort behind it (*I aim to be the first woman president*), without the hint of failure conveyed by *mean.*

If you **propose** to do something, you declare your intention ahead of time (*I propose that we set up a meeting next week*), and if you **purpose** to do it, you are even more determined to achieve your goal (*I purpose to write a three-volume history of baseball in America*).

Design suggests forethought in devising a plan (*design a strategy that will keep everyone happy*).

in·tend·ant /in'tendənt/ ▸*n.* **1** *chiefly historical* a title given to a high-ranking official or administrator, esp. in France, Spain, Portugal, or one of their colonies. **2** the administrator of an opera house or theater. ▷mid 17th cent.: from French, from Latin *intendere* 'to direct' (see **INTEND**). —**in·tend·an·cy** /-dənsē/ *n.*

in·tend·ed /in'tendid/ ▸*adj.* [*attrib.*] planned or meant: *the intended victim escaped.*

▸*n.* (**one's intended**) *informal* the person one intends to marry; one's fiancé or fiancée. —**in·tend·ed·ly** *adv.*

in·tend·ing /in'tendiNG/ ▸*adj.* [*attrib.*] (of a person) planning or meaning to do or be the specified thing: *an intending client.*

in·tend·ment /in'tendmənt/ ▸*n.* *Law* the sense in which the law understands or interprets something, such as the true intention of a piece of legislation. ▷late Middle English (denoting an intended meaning): from Old French *entendement,* from *entendre* 'intend.'

in·tense /in'tens/ ▸*adj.* **1** (of a condition, quality, feeling, etc.) existing in a high degree; forceful or extreme: *the job demands intense concentration* | *the heat was intense.* ■ (of an action) highly concentrated: *a phase of intense activity.* ■ (of a color) very strong or deep: *an intense blue.* **2** (of a person) feeling, or apt to feel, strong emotion; extremely earnest or serious: *an intense young woman, passionate about her art.* ■ expressing or marked by strong emotion: *a low, intense mutter.* ▷late Middle English: from Old French, or from Latin *intensus* 'stretched tightly, strained,' past participle of *intendere* (see **INTEND**). —**in·tense·ly** *adv.* —**in·tense·ness** *n.*

USAGE **Intense** and **intensive** are similar in meaning, but they differ in emphasis. **Intense** tends to relate to subjective responses—emotions and how we feel—while **intensive** tends to relate to objective descriptions. Thus *an* ***intensive*** *course* simply describes the type of course: one that is designed to cover a lot of ground in a short time (for example, by being full-time rather than part-time). On the other hand, in *the course was* ***intense,*** the word **intense** describes how someone felt about the course.

in·ten·si·fi·er /in'tensə,fīər/ ▸*n.* a person or thing that intensifies, in particular: ■ *Photography* a chemical used to intensify a negative. ■ *Grammar* an adverb used to give force or emphasis, for example, *really* in *my feet are really cold.* ■ short for **IMAGE INTENSIFIER.**

in·ten·si·fy /in'tensə,fī/ ▸*v.* (**-fies, -fied**) **1** become or make more intense: [*intrans.*] *the dispute began to intensify* | [*trans.*] *they had intensified their military campaign.* **2** [*trans.*] *Photography* increase the opacity of (a negative) using a chemical: *the negative may be intensified with bichloride.* ▷early 19th cent.: coined by Coleridge. —**in·ten·si·fi·ca·tion** /-,tensəfi'kāSHən/ *n.*

in·ten·sion /in'tenSHən/ ▸*n.* **1** *Logic* the internal content of a concept. Often contrasted with **EXTENSION** (sense 5). **2** *archaic* resolution or determination. ▷early 17th cent. (also in the sense 'straining, stretching'): from Latin *intensio(n-),* from *intendere* (see **INTEND**). Sense 1 dates from the mid 19th cent. —**in·ten·sion·al** /-SHənl/ *adj.* —**in·ten·sion·al·ly** /-SHənl-ē/ *adv.*

in·ten·si·ty /in'tensitē/ ▸*n.* (*pl.* **-ties**) **1** the quality of being intense: *gazing into her face with disconcerting intensity* | *the pain grew in intensity.* ■ an instance or degree of this: *an intensity that frightened her.* **2** *chiefly Physics* the measurable amount of a property, such as force, brightness, or a magnetic field: *hydrothermal processes of low intensity* | *different light intensities.*

in·ten·sive /in'tensiv/ ▸*adj.* **1** concentrated on a single area or subject or into a short time; very thorough or vigorous: *she undertook an intensive Arabic course* | *eight days of intensive arms talks.* ■ (of agriculture) aiming to achieve the highest possible level of production within a limited area, esp. by using chemical and technological aids: *intensive farming.* Often contrasted with **EXTENSIVE** (sense 2). ■ [usu. in *combination*] (typically in business and economics) concentrating on or making much use of a specified thing: *computer-intensive methods.* **2** *Grammar* (of an adjective, adverb, or particle) expressing intensity; giving force or emphasis. **3** denoting a property that is measured in terms of intensity (e.g., concentration) rather than of extent (e.g., volume), and so is not simply increased by addition of one thing to another.

▸*n.* *Grammar* an intensive adjective, adverb, or particle; an intensifier. ▷late Middle English (in the sense 'vehement, intense'): from French *intensif, -ive* or medieval Latin *intensivus,* from *intendere* (see **INTEND**). —**in·ten·sive·ly** *adv.* —**in·ten·sive·ness** *n.*

USAGE On the difference between **intensive** and **intense,** see usage at **INTENSE.**

in·ten·sive care ▸*n.* special medical treatment of a dangerously ill patient, with constant monitoring. ■ a unit or ward in a hospital devoted to such treatment: *she sat outside intensive care.*

in·tent /in'tent/ ▸*n.* intention or purpose: *with alarm she realized his intent* | *a real intent to cut back on social programs.*

▸*adj.* **1** [*predic.*] (**intent on/upon**) resolved or determined to do (something): *the administration was intent on achieving greater efficiency.* ■ attentively occupied with: *Jill was intent on her gardening magazine.* **2** (esp. of a look) showing earnest and eager attention: *a curiously intent look on her face.* ▷Middle English: from Old French *entent, entente,* based on Latin *intendere* (see **INTEND**). The adjective is from Latin *intentus,* past participle of *intendere.* —**in·tent·ly** *adv.* —**in·tent·ness** *n.*

▸*PHRASES* □ **to** (or **for**) **all intents and purposes** in all important respects: *a man who was to all intents and purposes illiterate.* □ **with intent** *Law* with the intention of committing a specified crime: *he denied arson with intent to endanger life* | *charges of wounding with intent.*

in·ten·tion /in'tenCHən/ ▸*n.* **1** a thing intended; an aim or plan: *she was full of good intentions* | [with *infinitive*] *the Ukraine and Kazakhstan have both declared their intention to be nuclear-free.* ■ the action or fact of intending: *intention is just one of the factors that will be considered.* ■ (**one's intentions**) a person's designs, esp. a man's, in respect to marriage: *if his intentions aren't honorable, I never want to see him again.* **2** *Medicine* the healing process of a wound. See **FIRST INTENTION, SECOND INTENTION.** ▷late Middle English: from Old French *entencion,* from Latin *intentio(n-)* 'stretching, purpose,' from *intendere* (see **INTEND**). —**in·ten·tioned** *adj.* [in *combination*] *a well-intentioned remark.*

in·ten·tion·al /in'tenCHənl/ ▸*adj.* done on purpose; deliberate: *intentional wrongdoing and harm.* ▷mid 16th cent. (in the sense 'existing only in intention'): from French *intentionnel* or medieval Latin *intentionalis,* from Latin *intentio(n-),* from *intendere* (see **INTEND**). —**in·ten·tion·al·ly** *adv.*

in·ten·tion·al fal·la·cy ▸*n.* (**the intentional fallacy**) (in literary theory) the fallacy of basing an assessment of a work on the author's intention rather than on one's response to the actual work.

in·ten·tion·al·ism /in'tenCHənl,izəm/ ▸*n.* the theory that a literary work should be judged in terms of the author's intentions.

in·ten·tion·al·i·ty /in,tenCHə'nalitē/ ▸*n.* the fact of being deliberate or purposive. ■ *Philosophy* the quality of mental states (e.g., thoughts, beliefs, desires, hopes) that consists in their being directed toward some object or state of affairs.

in·ten·tion trem·or ▸*n.* a trembling of a part of the body when attempting a precise movement, associated esp. with disease of the cerebellum.

in·ter /in'tər/ ▸*v.* (**-terred, -ter·ring**) [*trans.*] (usu. **be interred**) place (a corpse) in a grave or tomb, typically with funeral rites: *he was interred with the military honors due to him.* ▷Middle English: from Old French *enterrer,* based on Latin *in-* 'into' + *terra* 'earth.'

inter. ▸*abbr.* intermediate.

inter- ▸*prefix* **1** between; among: *interagency* | *interblend.* **2** mutually; reciprocally: *interactive.* ▷from Old French *entre-* or Latin *inter* 'between, among.'

in·ter·act /,intər'akt/ ▸*v.* [*intrans.*] act in such a way as to have an effect on another; act reciprocally: *all the stages in the process interact* | *the user* ***interacts*** *directly* ***with*** *the library.* —**in·ter·ac·tant** /-tənt/ *adj.* & *n.*

in·ter·ac·tion /,intər'akSHən/ ▸*n.* reciprocal action or influence: *ongoing* ***interaction between*** *the two languages.* ■ *Physics* a particular way in which matter, fields, and atomic and subatomic particles affect one another, e.g., through gravitation or electromagnetism. —**in·ter·ac·tion·al** /-SHənl/ *adj.*

in·ter·ac·tion·ism /,intər'akSHə,nizəm/ ▸*n.* *Philosophy* the theory that there are two entities, mind and body, each of which can have an effect on the other. —**in·ter·ac·tion·ist** *n.* & *adj.*

in·ter·ac·tive /,intər'aktiv/ ▸*adj.* (of two people or things) influencing or having an effect on each other: *fully sighted children in interactive play with others with defective vision.* ■ (of a computer or other electronic device) allowing a two-way flow of information between it and a user, responding to the user's input: *interactive video.* ▷mid 19th cent.: from **INTERACT,** on the pattern of *active.* —**in·ter·ac·tive·ly** *adv.* —**in·ter·ac·tiv·i·ty** /-ak'tivitē/ *n.*

in·ter·a·gen·cy /,intər'ājənsē/ ▸*adj.* taking place between different agencies: *yesterday's interagency decision.* ■ constituted from more than one agency: *an interagency crisis-management team.*

in·ter a·li·a /'intər 'ālēə; 'älēə/ ▸*adv.* among other things: *the study includes, inter alia, computers, aircraft, and pharmaceuticals.* ▷mid 17th cent.: Latin.

in·ter a·li·os /'intər 'ālē,ōs; 'älē,ōs/ ▸*adv.* among other people: *instruction to be given to them by, inter alios, a volunteer retired teacher.* ▷mid 17th cent.: Latin.

in·ter·al·lied /,intərə'līd/ ▸*adj.* [*attrib.*] of or relating to two or more states formally cooperating for military purposes.

In·ter-A·mer·i·can High·way the name for the section of the **PAN-AMERICAN HIGHWAY** between the U.S.-Mexico border at Nuevo Laredo in Mexico and Panama City in Panama.

in·ter·ar·tic·u·lar /,intərär'tikyələr/ ▸*adj.* *Anatomy* existing or acting between the adjacent surfaces of a joint.

in·ter·a·tom·ic /,intərə'tämik/ ▸*adj.* *Physics* existing or acting between atoms.

in·ter·bank /'intər,baNGk/ ▸*adj.* [*attrib.*] agreed, arranged, or operating between banks: *trading opportunities in the interbank market.*

in·ter·bed /'intər,bed/ ▸*v.* (**-bed·ded, -bed·ding**) (**be interbedded**) *Geology* (of a stratum) be embedded among or between others.

in·ter·breed /,intər'brēd/ ▸*v.* (*past* and *past part.* **-bred**) [*intrans.*] (of an animal) breed with another of a different race or species: *wolves and dogs can interbreed.* ■ (of an animal) inbreed: [as *n.*] (**interbreeding**) *their energy and physique had been sapped by interbreeding.* ■ [*trans.*] cause (an animal) to breed with another of a different race or species to produce a hybrid.

in·ter·ca·lar·y /in'tərkə,lerē; ,intər'kalərē/ ▸*adj.* **1** (of a day or a month) inserted in the calendar to harmonize it with the solar year, e.g., February 29 in leap years. ■ of the nature of an insertion: *elaborate intercalary notes and footnotes.* **2** *Botany* (of the meristem of a plant) located between its daughter cells, esp. (in a grass) at or near the base of a leaf. ▷early 17th cent.: from Latin *intercalarius,* from *intercalare* (see **INTERCALATE**).

Pronunciation Key ə *ago;* ər *over;* 'ə or ,ə *up;* 'ər or ,ər *fur;* a *hat;* ā *rate;* ä *car;* CH *chew;* e *let;* ē *see;* e(ə)r *air;* i *fit;* ī *by;* i(ə)r *ear;* NG *sing;* ō *go;* ô *for;* oi *boy;* o͝o *good;* o͞o *goo;* ou *out;* SH *she;* TH *thin;* T͟H *then;* (h)w *why;* ZH *vision*

in·ter·ca·late /inˈtərkəˌlāt/ ▸*v.* [*trans.*] **1** interpolate (an intercalary period) in a calendar. **2** (usu. **be intercalated**) insert (something) between layers in a crystal lattice, geological formation, or other structure. ▷early 17th cent.: from Latin *intercalat-* 'proclaimed as inserted in the calendar,' from the verb *intercalare*, from *inter-* 'between' + *calare* 'proclaim solemnly.' —**in·ter·ca·la·tion** /-ˌtərkəˈlāshən/ *n.*

in·ter·cede /ˌintərˈsēd/ [*intrans.*] ▸*v.* intervene on behalf of another: *I begged him to intercede for Theresa, but he never did a thing.* ▷late 16th cent.: from French *intercéder* or Latin *intercedere* 'intervene,' from *inter-* 'between' + *cedere* 'go.' —**in·ter·ced·er** *n.*

in·ter·cel·lu·lar /ˌintərˈselyələr/ ▸*adj. Biology* located or occurring between cells: *intercellular spaces.*

in·ter·cept /ˌintərˈsept/ ▸*v.* [*trans.*] obstruct (someone or something) so as to prevent them from continuing to a destination: *intelligence agencies intercepted a series of telephone calls | I intercepted Ed on his way to work.* ■ *chiefly Physics* cut off or deflect (light or other electromagnetic radiation). ■ *Mathematics* (of a line or surface) mark or cut off (part of a space, line, or surface).
▸*n.* an act or instance of intercepting something: *he read the file of radio intercepts.* ■ *Mathematics* the point at which a given line cuts a coordinate axis; the value of the coordinate at that point. ■ *Football* (of a defensive player) catch a forward pass. ▷late Middle English (in the senses 'contain between limits' and 'halt (an effect)'): from Latin *intercept-* 'caught between,' from the verb *intercipere*, from *inter-* 'between' + *capere* 'take.' —**in·ter·cep·tive** /-tiv/ *adj.*

in·ter·cep·tion /ˌintərˈsepshən/ ▸*n.* an act or instance of intercepting something, particularly: ■ *Football* an act of a defensive player catching a forward pass: *Oliver forced a fumble and had three interceptions, two of which were returned for touchdowns.* ■ an act or instance of receiving electronic transmissions before they reach the intended recipient: *designed for the clandestine interception of other people's telephone calls.*

in·ter·cep·tor /ˌintərˈseptər/ ▸*n.* a person or thing that stops or catches (someone or something) going from one place to another. ■ a fast aircraft for stopping or repelling hostile aircraft.

in·ter·ces·sion /ˌintərˈseshən/ ▸*n.* the action of intervening on behalf of another: *through the intercession of friends, I was able to obtain her a sinecure.* ■ the action of saying a prayer on behalf of another person: *prayers of intercession.* ▷late Middle English: from Latin *intercessio(n-)*, from the verb *intercedere* (see **INTERCEDE**). —**in·ter·ces·sor** /ˈintərˌsesər/ *n.* —**in·ter·ces·so·ry** /-ˈsesərē/ *adj.*

in·ter·chain /ˈintərˌchān/ ▸*adj. Chemistry* existing between different polymer chains: *interchain hydrogen bonds.*

in·ter·change ▸*v.* /ˌintərˈchānj/ [*trans.*] (of two or more people) exchange (things) with each other: *superior and subordinates freely interchange ideas and information.* ■ put each of (two things) in the other's place: *the terms are often interchanged.* ■ [*intrans.*] (of a thing) be able to be exchanged with another: *diesel units will* ***interchange with*** *the gasoline ones.*
▸*n.* /ˈintərˌchānj/ **1** the action of interchanging things, esp. information: *the interchange of ideas | a free-market interchange of goods and services.* ■ an exchange of words: *listening in shock to this venomous interchange.* **2** alternation: *the interchange of woods and meadows.* **3** a road junction designed on several levels so that traffic streams do not intersect. ▷late Middle English: from Old French *entrechangier*, from *entre-* 'between' + *changier* 'to change.' —**in·ter·change·a·bil·i·ty** /ˌintərˌchānjəˈbilitē/ *n.* —**in·ter·change·a·ble** *adj.* —**in·ter·change·a·ble·ness** *n.* —**in·ter·change·a·bly** /-blē/ *adv.*

in·ter·cit·y /ˈintərˌsitē/ ▸*adj.* [*attrib.*] existing or traveling between cities.

in·ter·class /ˌintərˈklas/ ▸*adj.* existing or conducted between different classes.

in·ter·col·le·giate /ˌintərkəˈlēj(ē)it/ ▸*adj.* existing or conducted between colleges or universities: *intercollegiate sports.*

in·ter·co·lum·ni·a·tion /ˌintərkəˌləmnēˈāshən/ ▸*n. Architecture* the distance between two adjacent columns. ■ the spacing of the columns of a building. —**in·ter·co·lum·nar** /-ˈləmnər/ *adj.*

in·ter·com /ˈintərˌkäm/ ▸*n.* an electrical device allowing one-way or two-way communication. ▷World War II: abbreviation of **INTERCOMMUNICATION**.

in·ter·com·mu·ni·cate /ˌintərkəˈmyo͞oniˌkāt/ ▸*v.* [*intrans.*] **1** engage in two-way communication: *Dr. Haber gazed at this while* ***intercommunicating with*** *his receptionist.* **2** (of two rooms) have a common connecting door: *there were two apartments on the next floor, intercommunicating.* ▷late 16th cent.: from Anglo-Latin *intercommunicat-* 'mutually communicated,' from the verb *intercommunicare.*

in·ter·com·mu·ni·ca·tion /ˌintərkəˌmyo͞oniˈkāshən/ ▸*n.* the action of engaging in two-way communication.

in·ter·com·mun·ion /ˌintərkəˈmyo͞onyən/ ▸*n.* participation in Holy Communion or other services by members of different religious denominations.

in·ter·con·nect /ˌintərkəˈnekt/ ▸*v.* [*intrans.*] connect with each other: *the way human activities* ***interconnect with*** *the environment | [trans.] a high-speed data service can interconnect the hundreds of thousands of host computers and workstations.*
▸*n.* a device used to connect two things together. —**in·ter·con·nec·tion** /-ˈnekshən/ *n.*

in·ter·con·ti·nen·tal /ˌintərˌkäntnˈentl/ ▸*adj.* relating to or traveling between continents: *an intercontinental flight | intercontinental ballistic missiles.* —**in·ter·con·ti·nen·tal·ly** *adv.*

in·ter·con·vert /ˌintərkənˈvərt/ ▸*v.* [*trans.*] (usu. **be interconverted**) cause (two things) to be converted into each other: *estrogens and androgens are easily interconverted in the laboratory.* —**in·ter·con·ver·sion** /-ˈvərzhən/ *n.* —**in·ter·con·vert·i·ble** *adj.*

in·ter·cool·er /ˌintərˈko͞olər/ ▸*n.* an apparatus for cooling gas between successive compressions, esp. in a supercharged vehicle engine. —**in·ter·cool** *v.*

in·ter·cor·re·la·tion /ˌintərˌkôrəˈlāshən/ ▸*n.* a mutual relationship or connection between two or more things: *analyses showing intercorrelations between sets of variables.* —**in·ter·cor·re·late** /-ˈkôrəˌlāt/ *v.*

in·ter·cos·tal /ˌintərˈkästəl/ *Anatomy* ▸*adj.* situated between the ribs: *the fifth left intercostal space.*
▸*n.* a muscle in this position. —**in·ter·cos·tal·ly** *adv.*

in·ter·course /ˈintərˌkôrs/ ▸*n.* communication or dealings between individuals or groups: *everyday social intercourse.* ■ short for **SEXUAL INTERCOURSE**. ▷late Middle English (denoting communication or dealings): from Old French *entrecours* 'exchange, commerce,' from Latin *intercursus*, from *intercurrere* 'intervene,' from *inter-* 'between' + *currere* 'run.' The specifically sexual use arose in the late 18th cent.

in·ter·crop ▸*v.* /ˌintərˈkräp/ (**-cropped**, **-crop·ping**) [*trans.*] [often as *n.*] (**intercropping**) grow (a crop) among plants of a different kind, usually in the space between rows: *lettuce is particularly good for intercropping among young Brussels sprouts.*
▸*n.* /ˈintərˌkräp/ a crop grown in such a way.

in·ter·cross /ˌintərˈkrôs/ ▸*v.* [*intrans.*] (of animals or plants of different breeds or varieties) interbreed. ■ [*trans.*] cause (animals or plants) to do this.
▸*n.* an instance of intercrossing of animals or plants. ■ an animal or plant resulting from this.

in·ter·cru·ral /ˌintərˈkro͞orəl/ ▸*adj.* between the legs.

in·ter·cur·rent /ˌintərˈkərənt; -ˈkə-rənt/ ▸*adj.* **1** *Medicine* (of a disease) occurring during the progress of another disease: *complicated by intercurrent infection with other microbes.* **2** *rare* (of a time or event) intervening. ▷early 17th cent.: from Latin *intercurrent-* 'intervening,' from the verb *intercurrere.*

in·ter·cut /ˌintərˈkət/ ▸*v.* (**-cut·ting**; *past* and *past part.* **-cut**) [*trans.*] alternate (scenes or shots) with contrasting scenes or shots to make one composite scene in a film: *pieces of archive film are* ***intercut with*** *brief interviews | [intrans.] the action intercuts between the time periods.*

in·ter·de·nom·i·na·tion·al /ˌintərdiˌnäməˈnāshənl/ ▸*adj.* of or relating to more than one religious denomination: *an interdenominational Thanksgiving service.* —**in·ter·de·nom·i·na·tion·al·ly** *adv.*

in·ter·den·tal /ˌintərˈdentl/ ▸*adj.* situated or placed between teeth or the teeth. ■ *Phonetics* (of a consonant) pronounced by placing the tip of the tongue between the teeth, such as the "th" sounds in the English words "thaw" and "though."
▸*n. Phonetics* a consonant pronounced in this way. —**in·ter·den·tal·ly** *adv.*

in·ter·de·part·men·tal /ˌintərdiˌpärtˈmentl; -ˌdēpärt-/ ▸*adj.* of or relating to more than one department. —**in·ter·de·part·men·tal·ly** *adv.*

in·ter·de·pend·ent /ˌintərdiˈpendənt/ ▸*adj.* (of two or more people or things) dependent on each other: *the increasingly global nature of human society, with interdependent economies.* —**in·ter·de·pend** *v.* —**in·ter·de·pend·ence** *n.* —**in·ter·de·pend·en·cy** *n.*

in·ter·dict ▸*n.* /ˈintərˌdikt/ an authoritative prohibition: *an interdict against marriage of those of close kin.* ■ (in the Roman Catholic Church) a sentence barring a person, or esp. a place, from ecclesiastical functions and privileges: *a papal interdict.*
▸*v.* /ˌintərˈdikt/ [*trans.*] **1** prohibit or forbid (something): *society will never interdict sex.* See note at **PROHIBIT**. ■ (**interdict someone from**) prohibit someone from (doing something): *I have not been interdicted from consuming or holding alcoholic beverages.* **2** intercept and prevent the movement of (a prohibited commodity or person): *the police established roadblocks throughout the country for interdicting drugs.* ■ *Military* impede (an enemy force), esp. by aerial bombing of lines of communication or supply. ▷Middle English *entredite* (in the ecclesiastical sense), from Old French *entredit*, from Latin *interdictum*, past participle of *interdicere* 'interpose, forbid by decree,' from *inter-* 'between' + *dicere* 'say.' The spelling change in the 16th cent. was due to association with the Latin form. —**in·ter·dic·tion** /ˌintərˈdikshən/ *n.*

in·ter·dic·tor /ˌintərˈdiktər/ ▸*n. Military* an aircraft designed to interrupt enemy supply operations by aerial bombing.

in·ter·dig·it·al /ˌintərˈdijitl/ ▸*adj.* between the fingers or toes.

in·ter·dig·i·tate /ˌintərˈdijiˌtāt/ ▸*v.* [*intrans.*] (of two or more things) interlock like the fingers of two clasped hands: [as *adj.*] (**interdigitating**) *interdigitating metal bars.* ▷mid 19th cent.: from **INTER-** 'between' + **DIGIT** + **-ATE**[3].

in·ter·dis·ci·pli·nar·y /ˌintərˈdisəpliˌnerē/ ▸*adj.* of or relating to more than one branch of knowledge: *an interdisciplinary research program.*

in·ter·est /ˈint(ə)rist/ ▸*n.* **1** the state of wanting to know or learn about something or someone: *she looked about her with interest.* ■ (**an interest in**) a feeling of wanting to know or learn about (something): *he developed an interest in art.* ■ the quality of exciting curiosity or holding the attention: *a tale full of interest.* ■ a subject about which one is concerned or enthusiastic: *my particular interest is twentieth-century poetry.* **2** money paid regularly at a particular rate for the use of money lent, or for delaying the repayment of a debt: *the monthly rate of interest* | [as *adj.*] *interest payments.* **3** the advantage or benefit of a person or group: *the merger is not contrary to the public interest | we are acting in the best interests of our customers.* ■ *archaic* the selfish pursuit of one's own welfare; self-interest. **4** a stake, share, or involvement in an undertaking, esp. a financial one: *holders of voting rights must disclose their interests | he must have no personal* ***interest in*** *the outcome of the case.* ■ a legal concern, title, or right in property: *third parties having an interest in a building.* **5** (usu. **interests**) a group or organization having a specified common concern, esp. in politics or business: *the regulation of national interests in India, Brazil, and Africa.*
▸*v.* [*trans.*] excite the curiosity or attention of (someone): *I thought the book might interest Eric.* ■ (**interest someone in**) cause someone to undertake or acquire (something): *efforts were made to interest her in a purchase.* ▷late Middle English (originally as *interess*): from Anglo-Norman French *interesse*, from Latin *interesse* 'differ, be important,' from *inter-* 'between' + *esse* 'be.' The *-t* was added partly by association with Old French *interest* 'damage, loss,' apparently from Latin *interest* 'it is important.' The original sense was 'the possession of a share in or a right to something'; hence sense 4. Sense 1 and the verb arose in the 18th cent. Sense 2 was influenced by medieval Latin *interesse* 'compensation for a debtor's defaulting.'
▸*PHRASES* □ **declare an** (or **one's**) **interest** make known one's financial interests in an undertaking before it is discussed. □ **in the interests** (or **interest**) **of something** for the benefit of: *in the interests of security we are keeping the information confidential.* □ **of interest** interesting: *much of it is of interest to historians.* □ **with interest** with interest charged or paid: *loans that must be paid back with interest.* ■ (of an action) reciprocated with more force or vigor than the original one: *he may have a reputation for getting even, with interest.*

in·ter·est·ed /ˈint(ə)ristid; ˈintəˌrestid/ ▸*adj.* **1** showing curiosity or concern about something or someone; having a feeling of interest: *I had always been* ***interested in*** *history.* **2** [*attrib.*] having an interest or involvement; not impartial or disinterested: *seeking views from all interested parties.* —**in·ter·est·ed·ly** *adv.* —**in·ter·est·ed·ness** *n.*

in·ter·est-free ▸*adj.* & *adv.* with no interest charged on money that has been borrowed: [as *adj.*] *interest-free credit* | [as *adv.*] *he lent the money interest-free.*

in·ter·est·ing /ˈint(ə)ristiNG; ˈintəˌrestiNG/ ▸*adj.* arousing curiosity or interest; holding or catching the attention: *an interesting debate | it will be very interesting to see what they come up with.* —**in·ter·est·ing·ly** *adv.* he *talked interestingly and learnedly* | [*sentence adverb*] *interestingly, the researchers did notice a link.* —**in·ter·est·ing·ness** *n.*

in·ter·face /ˈintərˌfās/ ▶*n.* **1** a point where two systems, subjects, organizations, etc., meet and interact: *the* ***interface between*** *accountancy and the law.* ■ *chiefly Physics* a surface forming a common boundary between two portions of matter or space, e.g., between two immiscible liquids: *the surface tension of a liquid at its air/liquid interface.* **2** *Computing* a device or program enabling a user to communicate with a computer. ■ a device or program for connecting two items of hardware or software so that they can be operated jointly or communicate with each other.
▶*v.* [*intrans.*] (**interface with**) **1** interact with (another system, person, organization, etc.): *his goal is to get people interfacing with each other.* **2** *Computing* connect with (another computer or piece of equipment) by an interface.

USAGE The word **interface** is a relatively new word, having been in the language (as a noun) since the 1880s. However, in the 1960s it became widespread in computer use and, by analogy, began to enjoy a vogue as both a noun and a verb in many other spheres. Traditionalists object to it on the grounds that there are plenty of other words that are more exact and sound less like trendy jargon.

in·ter·fa·cial /ˌintərˈfāsHəl/ ▶*adj.* **1** included between two faces of a crystal or other solid. **2** of, relating to, or forming a common boundary between two portions of matter or space.

in·ter·fac·ing /ˈintərˌfāsiNG/ ▶*n.* a moderately stiff material, esp. buckram, typically used between two layers of fabric in collars and facings.

in·ter·faith /ˈintərˈfāTH/ ▶*adj.* [*attrib.*] of, relating to, or between different religions or members of different religions: *action to encourage interfaith dialogue.*

in·ter·fere /ˌintərˈfi(ə)r/ ▶*v.* [*intrans.*] **1** (**interfere with**) prevent (a process or activity) from continuing or being carried out properly: *a job would interfere with his studies.* ■ (of a thing) strike against (something) when working; get in the way of: *the rotors are widely separated and do not interfere with one another.* ■ handle or adjust (something) without permission, esp. so as to cause damage: *he admitted interfering with a van.* ■ *Law* attempt to bribe or intimidate (a witness). **2** take part or intervene in an activity without invitation or necessity: *she tried not to* ***interfere in*** *her children's lives* | [as *adj.*] (**interfering**) *interfering busybodies.* **3** *Physics* (of light or other electromagnetic waveforms) mutually act upon each other and produce interference: *light pulses interfere constructively in a fiber to emit a pulse.* ■ cause interference to a broadcast radio signal. **4** (**interfere with**) *Brit.* sexually molest or assault (someone, esp. a child or young person) (used euphemistically). **5** (of a horse) knock one foot against the fetlock of another leg. ▷late Middle English: from Old French *s'entreferir* 'strike each other,' from *entre-* 'between' + *ferir* (from Latin *ferire* 'to strike'). —**in·ter·fer·er** *n.* —**in·ter·fer·ing·ly** *adv.*

in·ter·fer·ence /ˌintərˈfi(ə)rəns/ ▶*n.* **1** the action of interfering or the process of being interfered with: *he denied that there had been any* ***interference in*** *the country's internal affairs* | *an unwarranted* ***interference with*** *personal liberty.* ■ *Football* the action of illegally interfering with an opponent's ability to catch a passed or kicked ball. ■ *Football* the legal blocking of an opponent or opponents to clear a way for the ballcarrier. ■ *Baseball* any of various forms of hindering a player's ability to make a play, run, hit, etc. ■ (in ice hockey and other sports) the illegal hindering of an opponent not in possession of the puck or ball. **2** *Physics* the combination of two or more electromagnetic waveforms to form a resultant wave in which the displacement is either reinforced or canceled. ■ the fading or disturbance of received radio signals caused by unwanted signals from other sources, such as unshielded electrical equipment, or broadcasts from other stations or channels. ▷mid 18th cent.: from INTERFERE, on the pattern of words such as *difference.* —**in·ter·fe·ren·tial** /-fəˈrenCHəl/ *adj.*
▶*PHRASE* □ **run interference** *Football* move in such a way as to provide legal interference (see sense 1 above). ■ *informal* intervene on someone's behalf, typically so as to protect them from distraction or annoyance: *Elizabeth was quick to run interference and said that the professor would be very busy.*

in·ter·fer·ence fit ▶*n.* a fit between two parts in which the external dimension of one part slightly exceeds the internal dimension of the part into which it has to fit.

in·ter·fer·o·gram /ˌintərˈfi(ə)rəˌgram/ (*Brit.* also **in·ter·fer·o·gramme**) ▶*n.* *Physics* a pattern formed by wave interference, esp. one represented in a photograph or diagram.

in·ter·fer·om·e·ter /ˌintərfəˈrämitər/ ▶*n.* *Physics* an instrument in which wave interference is employed to make precise measurements of length of displacement in terms of the wavelength. —**in·ter·fer·o·met·ric** /-ˌfi(ə)rəˈmetrik/ *adj.* —**in·ter·fer·o·met·ri·cal·ly** *adv.* —**in·ter·fer·om·e·try** /-trē/ *n.*

in·ter·fer·on /ˌintərˈfi(ə)rˌän/ ▶*n.* *Biochemistry* a protein released by animal cells, usually in response to the entry of a virus, that has the property of inhibiting virus replication. ▷1950s: from INTERFERE + -ON.

in·ter·file /ˌintərˈfīl/ ▶*v.* [*trans.*] file (two or more sequences) together: *the index interfiles books and their authors in one alphabetical sequence.* ■ file (one or more items) into an existing sequence: *this index is* ***interfiled with*** *the main card catalog.*

in·ter·flow /ˌintərˈflō/ ▶*v.* [*intrans.*] *poetic/literary* mix or mingle: *the thousand varying shades interflowing.*

in·ter·fluve /ˈintərˌflo͞ov/ ▶*n.* *Geology* a region between the valleys of adjacent watercourses, esp. in a dissected upland. ▷early 20th cent.: back-formation from *interfluvial.* —**in·ter·flu·vi·al** /ˌintərˈflo͞ovēəl/ *adj.*

in·ter·fuse /ˌintərˈfyo͞oz/ ▶*v.* [*trans.*] *poetic/literary* join or mix (two or more things) together: *nowhere do art and life seem so interfused.* ▷late 16th cent.: from Latin *interfus-* 'poured among,' from the verb *interfundere,* from *inter-* 'between' + *fundere* 'pour.' —**in·ter·fu·sion** /-ˈfyo͞oZHən/ *n.*

in·ter·ga·lac·tic /ˌintərgəˈlaktik/ ▶*adj.* of, relating to, or situated between two or more galaxies: *intergalactic gas.* —**in·ter·ga·lac·ti·cal·ly** /-ik(ə)lē/ *adv.*

in·ter·ge·ner·ic /ˌintərjəˈnerik/ ▶*adj.* *Biology* existing between or obtained from different genera: *intergeneric differences* | *an intergeneric hybrid.*

in·ter·gla·cial /ˌintərˈglāSHəl/ *Geology* ▶*adj.* of or relating to a period of milder climate between two glacial periods. Compare with INTERSTADIAL.
▶*n.* an interglacial period.

in·ter·gov·ern·men·tal /ˌintərˌgəvər(n)ˈmentl/ ▶*adj.* of, relating to, or conducted between two or more governments: *an intergovernmental conference.* —**in·ter·gov·ern·men·tal·ly** *adv.*

in·ter·grade ▶*v.* /ˌintərˈgrād/ [*intrans.*] *Biology* pass into another form by a series of intervening forms: *they have several forms that intergrade with each other.*
▶*n.* /ˈintərˌgrād/ an intervening form of this kind. —**in·ter·gra·da·tion** /-grāˈdāSHən/ *n.*

in·ter·grow /ˌintərˈgrō/ ▶*v.* (*past* **-grew**; *past part.* **-grown**) [*intrans.*] [usu. as *adj.*] (**intergrown**) (chiefly of crystals) grow into each other: *finely intergrown siderite.*

in·ter·growth /ˈintərˌgrōTH/ ▶*n.* a thing produced by intergrowing, esp. of mineral crystals in rock.

in·ter·im /ˈintərəm/ ▶*n.* the intervening time: ***in the interim*** *I'll just keep my fingers crossed.*
▶*adj.* in or for the intervening period; provisional or temporary: *an interim arrangement.* ■ *chiefly Brit.* relating to less than a full year's business activity: *an interim dividend* | *interim profit.*
▶*adv. archaic* meanwhile. ▷mid 16th cent. (denoting a temporary or provisional arrangement, originally for the adjustment of religious differences between the German Protestants and the Roman Catholic Church): from Latin, 'meanwhile.'

in·te·ri·or /inˈti(ə)rēər/ ▶*adj.* **1** situated within or inside; relating to the inside; inner: *the interior lighting is not adequate.* ■ [*predic.*] (**interior to**) *chiefly technical* situated further in or within: *the layer immediately interior to the epidermis.* ■ drawn, photographed, etc., within a building: *a light that is ideal for every interior shot.* **2** [*attrib.*] remote from the coast or frontier; inland: *the interior jungle regions.* ■ relating to internal or domestic affairs: *the Interior Department.* **3** existing or taking place in the mind or soul; mental: *an interior monologue.*
▶*n.* (usu. **the interior**) **1** the inner or indoor part of something, esp. a building; the inside: *six men painting the outside of her house and three men painting the interior.* ■ an artistic representation of the inside of a building or room: *a few still lifes, interiors, and landscapes.* **2** the inland part of a country or region: *the plains of the interior.* ■ the internal affairs of a country: *the Department of the Interior.* ▷late 15th cent.: from Latin, 'inner,' comparative adjective from *inter* 'within.' —**in·te·ri·or·ize** /-ˌrīz/ *v.* —**in·te·ri·or·ly** *adv.*

in·te·ri·or an·gle ▶*n.* the angle between adjacent sides of a rectilinear figure.

in·te·ri·or dec·o·ra·tion (also **interior decorating**) ▶*n.* the decoration of the interior of a building or room, esp. with regard to color combination and artistic effect. —**in·te·ri·or dec·o·ra·tor** *n.*

in·te·ri·or de·sign ▶*n.* the art or process of designing the interior decoration of a room or building. —**in·te·ri·or de·sign·er** *n.*

in·te·ri·or·i·ty /inˌti(ə)rēˈôritē; -ˈär-/ ▶*n.* the quality of being interior or inward. ■ inner character or nature; subjectivity: *the profound interiority of faith.* ▷early 18th cent.: from medieval Latin *interioritas,* from Latin *interior* 'inner.'

in·te·ri·or mon·o·logue ▶*n.* a piece of writing expressing a character's inner thoughts.

interj. ▶*abbr.* interjection.

in·ter·ject /ˌintərˈjekt/ ▶*v.* [*trans.*] say (something) abruptly, esp. as an aside or interruption: *she interjected the odd question here and there* | [*intrans.*] *Christine felt bound to interject before there was open warfare.* See note at INSERT. ▷late 16th cent.: from Latin *interject-* 'interposed,' from the verb *interjicere,* from *inter-* 'between' + *jacere* 'to throw.' —**in·ter·jec·to·ry** /-t(ə)rē/ *adj.*

in·ter·jec·tion /ˌintərˈjekSHən/ ▶*n.* an abrupt remark, made esp. as an aside or interruption. ■ an exclamation, esp. as a part of speech, e.g., *ah!* or *dear me!* ▷late Middle English: via Old French from Latin *interjectio(n-),* from the verb *interjicere* (see INTERJECT). —**in·ter·jec·tion·al** /-SHənl/ *adj.*

in·ter·lace /ˌintərˈlās/ ▶*v.* [*trans.*] bind intricately together; interweave: *the trees interlaced their branches so that only tiny patches of sky were visible.* ■ (**interlace something with**) mingle or intersperse something with: *buttercups interlacing their gold with the silver of the daisies* | *discussion interlaced with esoteric mathematics.* ■ [*intrans.*] (of two or more things) cross each other intricately: [as *adj.*] (**interlacing**) *interlacing bundles of smooth muscle fibers.* ■ *Electronics* scan (a video image) in such a way that alternate lines form one sequence that is followed by the other lines in a second sequence: [as *adj.*] (**interlaced**) *interlaced displays.* ▷late Middle English: from Old French *entrelacier,* from *entre-* 'between' + *lacier* 'to lace.' —**in·ter·lace·ment** *n.*

in·ter·lan·guage /ˈintərˌlaNGgwij/ ▶*n.* a language or form of language having features of two others, typically a pidgin or a version produced by a foreign learner.

in·ter·lard /ˌintərˈlärd/ ▶*v.* [*trans.*] (**interlard something with**) intersperse or embellish speech or writing with different material: *a compendium of advertisements and reviews, interlarded with gossip.* ▷late Middle English (in the sense 'mix with alternate layers of fat'): from French *entrelarder,* from *entre-* 'between' + *larder* 'to lard.'

in·ter·lay ▶*v.* /ˌintərˈlā/ (*past* and *past part.* **-laid**) [*trans.*] lay between or among; interpose: *strips of granite are* ***interlaid with*** *creamy Sardinian sard.*
▶*n.* /ˈintərˌlā/ an inserted layer: *remember to use interlay under foam-backed carpets.* ■ *Printing* a sheet or piece of paper placed between a letterpress printing plate and its base to give increased pressure on certain areas.

in·ter·lay·er /ˈintərˌlāər/ ▶*n.* a layer sandwiched between two others.
▶*adj.* [*attrib.*] situated or occurring between two layers.

in·ter·leaf /ˈintərˌlēf/ ▶*n.* (*pl.* **-leaves**) an extra page, typically a blank one, between the leaves of a book.

in·ter·leave /ˌintərˈlēv/ ▶*v.* [*trans.*] insert pages, typically blank ones, between the pages of (a book): *books of maps* ***interleaved with*** *tracing paper.* ■ place something between the layers of (something): *pasta interleaved with strips of zucchini and carrot.* ■ *Telecommunications* mix (two or more digital signals) by alternating between them. ■ *Computing* divide (memory or processing power) between a number of tasks by allocating successive segments of it to each task in turn.

in·ter·leu·kin /ˈintərˌlo͞okin/ ▶*n.* *Biochemistry* any of a class of glycoproteins produced by leukocytes for regulating immune responses. ▷1970s: from INTER- 'occurring between' + *leukocyte* (variant of LEUKOCYTE) + -IN[1].

in·ter·li·brar·y loan /ˌintərˈlībrerē/ ▶*n.* a system in which one library borrows a book from another library for the use of an individual.

in·ter·line[1] /ˌintərˈlīn/ ▶*v.* [*trans.*] insert words between the lines of (a document or other text): *the writing was overwritten and interlined by many hands.* ■ insert (words) in this way. ▷late Middle English: from medieval Latin *interlineare*, from *inter-* 'between' + Latin *linea* 'line.'

in·ter·line[2] ▸*v.* [*trans.*] put an extra lining between the ordinary lining and the fabric of (a garment, curtain, etc.), typically to provide extra strength.

in·ter·lin·e·ar /ˌintərˈlinēər/ ▸*adj.* written or printed between the lines of a text: *interlinear glosses.* ■ (of a book) having the same text in different languages printed on alternate lines. ▷late Middle English: from medieval Latin *interlinearis*, from *inter-* 'between' + Latin *linearis* (from *linea* 'line').

in·ter·lin·e·ate /ˌintərˈlinēˌāt/ ▸*v.* another term for INTERLINE[1]. ▷late 17th cent.: from medieval Latin *interlineat-* 'interlined,' from the verb *interlineare.* —**in·ter·lin·e·a·tion** /-ˌlinēˈāsHən/ *n.*

in·ter·lin·gua /ˌintərˈliNGgwə/ ▸*n.* an artificial language, devised for machine translation, that makes explicit the distinctions necessary for successful translation into a target language even where they are not present in the source language. ■ (**Interlingua**) an artificial international language formed of elements common to the Romance languages, designed primarily for scientific and technical use. ▷early 20th cent.: from INTER- 'between' + Latin *lingua* 'tongue.'

in·ter·lin·gual /ˌintərˈliNGgwəl/ ▸*adj.* between or relating to two languages: *interlingual dictionaries.* ■ of or relating to an interlingua or artificial interlanguage.

in·ter·lin·ing /ˈintərˌlīniNG/ ▸*n.* material used as an extra lining between the ordinary lining and the fabric of a garment, curtain, etc.

in·ter·link /ˌintərˈliNGk/ ▸*v.* [*trans.*] join or connect (two or more things) together: *agreement has been reached to interlink the airport's two baggage systems.* —**in·ter·link·age** /-ˈliNGkij/ *n.*

in·ter·lob·u·lar /ˌintərˈläbyələr/ ▸*adj. Anatomy* situated between lobes (e.g., of the kidney or liver).

in·ter·lock ▸*v.* /ˌintərˈläk/ [*intrans.*] (of two or more things) engage with each other by overlapping or by the fitting together of projections and recesses: *their fingers interlocked.*

▸*n.* /ˈintərˌläk/ **1** a device or mechanism for connecting or coordinating the function of different components. **2** (also **interlock fabric**) a fabric knitted with closely interlocking stitches that allow it to stretch, typically used in underwear. —**in·ter·lock·er** *n.*

in·ter·loc·u·tor /ˌintərˈläkyətər/ ▸*n. formal* a person who takes part in a dialogue or conversation. ▷early 16th cent.: modern Latin, from Latin *interlocut-* 'interrupted (by speech),' from the verb *interloqui*, from *inter-* 'between' + *loqui* 'speak.' —**in·ter·lo·cu·tion** /-ləˈkyo͞osHən/ *n.*

in·ter·loc·u·to·ry /ˌintərˈläkyəˌtôrē/ ▸*adj.* **1** *Law* (of a decree or judgment) given provisionally during the course of a legal action. **2** *rare* of or relating to dialogue or conversation. ▷late 15th cent.: from medieval Latin *interlocutorius*, from Latin *interloqui* 'interrupt' (see INTERLOCUTOR).

in·ter·lop·er /ˈintərˌlōpər; ˌintərˈlōpər/ ▸*n.* a person who becomes involved in a place or situation where they are not wanted or are considered not to belong. ▷late 16th cent. (denoting an unauthorized trader trespassing on the rights of a trade monopoly): from INTER- 'amid' + *-loper* as in archaic *landloper* 'vagabond' (from Middle Dutch *landlooper*). —**in·ter·lope** /ˈintərˌlōp; ˌintərˈlōp/ *v.*

in·ter·lude /ˈintərˌlo͞od/ ▸*n.* **1** an intervening period of time: *enjoying a lunchtime interlude.* ■ a pause between the acts of a play. **2** something performed during a theater intermission: *an orchestral interlude.* ■ a piece of music played between other pieces or between the verses of a hymn. ■ a temporary amusement or source of entertainment that contrasts with what goes before or after: *the romantic interlude withered rapidly once he was back in town.* ▷Middle English (originally denoting a light dramatic entertainment): from medieval Latin *interludium*, from *inter-* 'between' + *ludus* 'play.'

in·ter·mar·riage /ˌintərˈmarij/ ▸*n.* marriage between people of different races, castes, or religions: *the main reason for the increase in intermarriage is probably greater religious and ethnic tolerance.* ■ marriage between close relations.

in·ter·mar·ry /ˌintərˈmarē/ ▸*v.* (**-ries, -ried**) [*intrans.*] (of people belonging to different races, castes, or religions) become connected by marriage: *over the centuries the Greeks* ***intermarried with*** *the natives.* ■ (of close relations) marry each other.

in·ter·me·di·ar·y /ˌintərˈmēdēˌerē/ ▸*n.* (*pl.* **-ar·ies**) a person who acts as a link between people in order to try to bring about an agreement or reconciliation; a mediator: ***intermediaries between*** *lenders and borrowers.*

▸*adj.* intermediate: *an intermediary stage.* ▷late 18th cent.: from French *intermédiaire*, from Italian *intermediario*, from Latin *intermedius* (see INTERMEDIATE).

in·ter·me·di·ate /ˌintərˈmēdē-it/ ▸*adj.* coming between two things in time, place, order, character, etc.: *an intermediate stage of development* | *a cooled liquid* ***intermediate between*** *liquid and solid.* ■ having more than a basic knowledge or level of skill but not yet advanced: *intermediate skiers.* ■ suitable for people of such a level: *an intermediate course.*

▸*n.* an intermediate thing. ■ a person at an intermediate level of knowledge or skill. ■ a chemical compound formed by one reaction and then taking part in another, esp. during synthesis.

▸*v.* [*intrans.*] act as intermediary; mediate: *the theory said that by intermediating between buyers and sellers, middlemen lower the costs of transactions.* ▷late Middle English: from medieval Latin *intermediatus*, from Latin *intermedius*, from *inter-* 'between' + *medius* 'middle.' —**in·ter·me·di·a·cy** /-əsē/ *n.* —**in·ter·me·di·ate·ly** *adv.* —**in·ter·me·di·ate·ness** *n.* —**in·ter·me·di·a·tion** /-ˌmēdēˈāsHən/ *n.* —**in·ter·me·di·a·tor** /-ˌātər/ *n.*

in·ter·me·di·ate fre·quen·cy ▸*n.* the frequency to which a radio signal is converted during heterodyne reception.

in·ter·me·di·ate host ▸*n. Biology* an organism that supports the immature or nonreproductive forms of a parasite. Compare with DEFINITIVE HOST.

in·ter·me·di·ate tech·nol·o·gy ▸*n.* technology suitable for use in developing countries, typically making use of locally available resources.

in·ter·me·din /ˌintərˈmēdn/ ▸*n. Physiology* another term for MELANOCYTE-STIMULATING HORMONE. ▷1930s: from modern Latin *(pars) intermedia* 'intermediate part (of the pituitary)' + -IN[1].

in·ter·me·di·um /ˌintərˈmēdēəm/ ▸*n.* (*pl.* **-di·a** /-dēə/) *Zoology* (in tetrapods) a carpal in the center of the wrist joint, or a tarsal in the center of the ankle joint. ▷late 16th cent. (denoting an intervening action or performance): from late Latin, neuter (used as a noun) of Latin *intermedius* 'intermediate.'

in·ter·ment /inˈtərmənt/ ▸*n.* the burial of a corpse in a grave or tomb, typically with funeral rites: *the day of interment* | *interments took place in the churchyard.*

USAGE **Interment**, which means 'burial,' should not be confused with **internment**, which means 'imprisonment.'

in·ter·mesh /ˌintərˈmesH/ ▸*v.* [*intrans.*] (of two or more things) mesh with one another.

in·ter·mez·zo /ˌintərˈmetsō/ ▸*n.* (*pl.* **-mez·zi** /-ˈmetsē/ or **-mez·zos**) a short connecting instrumental movement in an opera or other musical work. ■ a similar piece performed independently. ■ a short piece for a solo instrument. ■ a light dramatic, musical, or other performance inserted between the acts of a play. ▷late 18th cent.: from Italian, from Latin *intermedium* 'interval,' neuter of *intermedius* (see INTERMEDIATE).

in·ter·mi·na·ble /inˈtərmənəbəl/ ▸*adj.* endless (often used hyperbolically): *we got bogged down in interminable discussions.* See note at ETERNAL. ▷late Middle English: from Old French, or from late Latin *interminabilis*, from *in-* 'not' + *terminare* (see TERMINATE). —**in·ter·mi·na·bil·i·ty** /-ˌtərmənəˈbilitē/ *n.* —**in·ter·mi·na·ble·ness** *n.* —**in·ter·mi·na·bly** /-blē/ *adv.*

in·ter·min·gle /ˌintərˈmiNGgəl/ ▸*v.* mix or mingle together: [*intrans.*] *daisies* ***intermingled with*** *huge expanses of gorse and foxgloves* | [*trans.*] *Riesling grapes were always intermingled with other varieties.*

in·ter·mis·sion /ˌintərˈmisHən/ ▸*n.* a pause or break: *he was granted an intermission in his studies* | *the daily work goes on without intermission.* ■ an interval between parts of a play, movie, or concert. ▷late Middle English: from Latin *intermissio(n-)*, from the verb *intermittere* (see INTERMIT).

in·ter·mit /ˌintərˈmit/ ▸*v.* (**-mit·ted, -mit·ting**) [*trans.*] suspend or discontinue (an action or practice) for a time: *he was urged to intermit his application.* ■ [*intrans.*] (esp. of a fever or pulse) cease or stop for a time. ▷mid 16th cent.: from Latin *intermittere*, from *inter-* 'between' + *mittere* 'let go.'

in·ter·mit·tent /ˌintərˈmitnt/ ▸*adj.* occurring at irregular intervals; not continuous or steady: *intermittent rain.* ▷mid 16th cent.: from Latin *intermittent-* 'ceasing,' from the verb *intermittere* (see INTERMIT). —**in·ter·mit·tence** *n.* —**in·ter·mit·ten·cy** *n.* —**in·ter·mit·tent·ly** *adv.*

in·ter·mit·tent clau·di·ca·tion ▸*n.* see CLAUDICATION.

in·ter·mix /ˌintərˈmiks/ ▸*v.* mix together: [*trans.*] *the ore had to be handled so that it was not inadvertently* ***intermixed with*** *other material* | [*intrans.*] *along its southern edge low trees* ***intermix with*** *the shrubs.* ▷mid 16th cent. (originally as the past participle *intermixt*): from Latin *intermixtus*, past participle of *intermiscere* 'mix together,' from *inter-* 'between' + *miscere* 'to mix.' —**in·ter·mix·a·ble** *adj.* —**in·ter·mix·ture** /-ˈmiksCHər/ *n.*

in·ter·mod·al /ˌintərˈmōdl/ ▸*adj.* involving two or more different modes of transportation in conveying goods.

in·ter·mo·lec·u·lar /ˌintərməˈlekyələr/ ▸*adj.* existing or taking place between molecules.

In·ter·mon·tane Region /ˌintərˈmänˌtān/ (also **Intermountain Region**) a term for the mountain and basin regions lying between the Rocky Mountains and the mountains of the U.S. western coast.

in·tern ▸*n.* /ˈinˌtərn/ a recent medical graduate receiving supervised training in a hospital and acting as an assistant physician or surgeon. Compare with RESIDENT. ■ a student or trainee who works, sometimes without pay, at a trade or occupation in order to gain work experience.

▸*v.* /inˈtərn/ **1** [*trans.*] confine (someone) as a prisoner, esp. for political or military reasons. **2** [*intrans.*] serve as an intern. ▷early 16th cent. (as an adjective in the sense 'internal'): from French *interne* (adjective), *interner* (verb), from Latin *internus* 'inward, internal.' Current senses date from the 19th cent. —**in·tern·ment** *n.* —**in·tern·ship** /-ˌsHip/ *n.*

USAGE See usage at INTERMENT.

in·ter·nal /inˈtərnl/ ▸*adj.* of or situated on the inside: *the tube had an internal diameter of 1.1 mm.* ■ inside the body: *internal bleeding.* ■ existing or occurring within an organization: *an internal telephone system.* ■ relating to affairs and activities within a country rather than with other countries; domestic: *the government's internal policies* | *internal flights.* ■ experienced in one's mind; inner rather than expressed: *internal feelings.* ■ of the inner nature of a thing; intrinsic: *he creates a dialogue* ***internal to*** *his work.*

▸*plural n.* (**internals**) inner parts or features: *all the weapon's internals are well finished and highly polished.* ▷early 16th cent. (in the sense 'intrinsic'): from modern Latin *internalis*, from Latin *internus* 'inward, internal.' —**in·ter·nal·i·ty** /ˌintərˈnalitē/ *n.* —**in·ter·nal·ly** *adv.*

in·ter·nal clock ▸*n.* a person's innate sense of time. ■ another term for BIOLOGICAL CLOCK.

in·ter·nal com·bus·tion en·gine ▸*n.* an engine that generates motive power by the burning of gasoline, oil, or other fuel with air inside the engine, the hot gases produced being used to drive a piston or do other work as they expand.

in·ter·nal en·er·gy ▸*n. Physics* the energy in a system arising from the relative positions and interactions of its parts.

in·ter·nal ev·i·dence ▸*n.* evidence derived from the contents of the thing discussed.

in·ter·nal ex·ile ▸*n.* penal banishment from a part of one's own country.

in·ter·nal·ize /inˈtərnlˌīz/ ▸*v.* [*trans.*] **1** *Psychology* make (attitudes or behavior) part of one's nature by learning or unconscious assimilation. ■ acquire knowledge of (the rules of a language). **2** *Economics* incorporate (costs) as part of a pricing structure, esp. social costs resulting from the manufacture and use of a product. —**in·ter·nal·i·za·tion** /inˌtərnl-iˈzāsHən/ *n.*

in·ter·nal mar·ket ▸*n.* another term for SINGLE MARKET.

in·ter·nal rhyme ▸*n.* a rhyme involving a word in the middle of a line and another at the end of the line or in the middle of the next.

in·ter·na·tion·al /ˌintərˈnasHənl/ ▸*adj.* existing, occurring, or carried on between two or more nations: *international trade.* ■ agreed on by all or many nations: *a violation of international law.* ■ used by people of many nations: *large international hotels.*

▸*n.* **1** *Brit.* a game or contest between teams representing different countries in a sport. ■ a player who has taken part in such a game or contest. **2** (**International**) any of four associations founded (1864–1936) to promote socialist or communist action. ■ a member of any of these.

The First International was formed by Karl Marx in London in 1864 as an international working men's association. The Second International was formed in Paris in 1889 to celebrate the 100th anniversary of the French Revolution and still survives as a loose association of social democrats. The Third International, also known as the Comintern, was formed by the Bolsheviks in 1919 to further the cause of world revolution. It was abolished in 1943. The Fourth International, a body of Trotskyist organizations, was formed in 1938 in opposition to the policies of the Stalin-dominated Third International.

—**in·ter·na·tion·al·i·ty** /-ˌnashəˈnalitē/ *n.* —**in·ter·na·tion·al·ly** *adv.*

In·ter·na·tion·al A·tom·ic En·er·gy A·gen·cy (abbr.: **IAEA**) an international organization set up in 1957 to promote research into and the development of atomic energy for peaceful purposes.

In·ter·na·tion·al Bank for Re·con·struc·tion and De·vel·op·ment (abbr.: **IBRD**) an agency of the United Nations that constitutes the main part of the World Bank. It was established in 1945, and its headquarters are in Washington, DC. See also **World Bank**.

In·ter·na·tion·al Bri·gade a group of volunteers that was raised internationally by foreign communist parties and that fought on the Republican side in the Spanish Civil War.

in·ter·na·tion·al can·dle ▸*n.* see **candle**.

In·ter·na·tion·al Civ·il A·vi·a·tion Or·gan·i·za·tion an agency of the United Nations, founded in 1947 to study problems of international civil aviation and to establish standards and regulations. Its headquarters are in Montreal.

In·ter·na·tion·al Court of Jus·tice a judicial court of the United Nations, formed in 1945, that meets at The Hague.

In·ter·na·tion·al Date Line ▸*n.* see **Date Line**.

In·ter·na·tion·al De·vel·op·ment As·so·ci·a·tion (abbr.: **IDA**) an affiliate of the International Bank for Reconstruction and Development (World Bank) established in 1960 to provide assistance primarily in the poorer developing countries.

In·ter·na·tio·nale /ˌintərˌnashəˈnal; -ˈnäl/ **1** (**the Internationale**) a revolutionary song composed in France in the late 19th century. It was adopted by French socialists and subsequently by others, and was the official anthem of the USSR until 1944. **2** variant spelling of **international** (sense 2 of the *noun*). ▷French, feminine of *international* 'international.'

In·ter·na·tion·al En·er·gy A·gen·cy (abbr.: **IEA**) an agency founded in 1974, within the framework of the OECD, to coordinate energy supply and demand worldwide. Its headquarters are in Paris.

In·ter·na·tion·al Fi·nance Cor·po·ra·tion (abbr.: **IFC**) an affiliate of the International Bank for Reconstruction and Development (World Bank) established in 1956 to assist developing member countries by promoting the growth of the private sector of their economies.

In·ter·na·tion·al Fund for Ag·ri·cul·tur·al De·vel·op·ment (abbr.: **IFAD**) an agency of the United Nations whose purpose is to mobilize additional funds for agricultural and rural development in developing countries through programs that directly benefit the poorest rural populations. It began operations in 1977.

in·ter·na·tion·al·ism /ˌintərˈnashənlˌizəm/ ▸*n.* **1** the state or process of being international: *the internationalism of popular music.* ■ the advocacy of cooperation and understanding between nations. **2** (**Internationalism**) the principles of any of the four Internationals. —**in·ter·na·tion·al·ist** *n.*

in·ter·na·tion·al·ize /ˌintərˈnashənlˌīz/ ▸*v.* [*trans.*] **1** make (something) international. **2** bring (a place) under the protection or control of two or more nations: [as *adj.*] (**internationalized**) *an internationalized city.* —**in·ter·na·tion·al·i·za·tion** /-ˌnashənliˈzāshən/ *n.*

In·ter·na·tion·al La·bor Or·gan·i·za·tion (abbr.: **ILO**) an organization established in 1919 whose aim is to encourage lasting peace through social justice, awarded the Nobel Peace Prize in 1969.

in·ter·na·tion·al law ▸*n.* a body of rules established by custom or treaty and recognized by nations as binding in their relations with one another.

In·ter·na·tion·al Mon·e·tar·y Fund (abbr.: **IMF**) an international organization established in 1945 that aims to promote international trade and monetary cooperation and the stabilization of exchange rates. Member countries contribute in gold and in their own currencies to provide a reserve on which they may draw to meet foreign obligations during periods of deficit in their international balance of payments. Payments are usually made on the basis of the country's acceptance of stipulated measures for economic correction, which often entail cuts in public expenditure and an increased cost of living, and have frequently caused controversy. It is affiliated with the UN, with headquarters in Washington, DC.

In·ter·na·tion·al Or·gan·i·za·tion for Stand·ard·i·za·tion an organization founded in 1946 to standardize measurements for international industrial, commercial, and scientific purposes.

In·ter·na·tion·al Pho·net·ic Al·pha·bet (abbr.: **IPA**) an internationally recognized set of phonetic symbols developed in the late 19th century, based on the principle of strict one-to-one correspondence between sounds and symbols.

In·ter·na·tion·al So·ci·e·ty for Krish·na Con·scious·ness see **Hare Krishna**.

In·ter·na·tion·al Style ▸*n.* a functional style of 20th-century architecture, so called because it crossed national and cultural barriers. It is characterized by the use of steel and reinforced concrete, wide windows, uninterrupted interior spaces, simple lines, and strict geometric forms.

In·ter·na·tion·al Sys·tem of U·nits ▸*n.* a system of physical units (**SI Units**) based on the meter, kilogram, second, ampere, kelvin, candela, and mole, together with a set of prefixes to indicate multiplication or division by a power of ten. ▷translating French *Système International d'Unités.*

In·ter·na·tion·al Tel·e·com·mu·ni·ca·tions Un·ion (abbr.: **ITU**) an organization whose purpose is to promote international cooperation in the use and improvement of telecommunications of all kinds. Founded in Paris in 1865 as the International Telegraph Union, it became an agency of the United Nations in 1947.

in·ter·na·tion·al u·nit ▸*n.* a unit of activity or potency for vitamins, hormones, or other substances, defined individually for each substance in terms of the activity of a standard quantity or preparation.

In·ter·naut /ˈintərˌnôt/ ▸*n.* a user of the Internet, esp. a habitual or skilled one. ▷1990s: blend of **Internet** and **astronaut**.

in·terne ▸*n.* rare spelling of **intern**.

in·ter·ne·cine /ˌintərˈnesēn; -ˈnēsēn; -sin/ ▸*adj.* destructive to both sides in a conflict: *the region's history of savage internecine warfare.* ■ of or relating to conflict within a group or organization: *the party shrank from the trauma of more internecine strife.* ▷mid 17th cent. (in the sense 'deadly, characterized by great slaughter'): from Latin *internecinus*, based on *inter-* 'among' + *necare* 'to kill.'

in·tern·ee /ˌintərˈnē/ ▸*n.* a person who is confined as a prisoner, esp. for political or military reasons.

in·ter·neg·a·tive /ˌintərˈnegətiv/ ▸*n.* *Photography* a second negative of an image made from the original negative.

In·ter·net /ˈintərˌnet/ an international computer network providing e-mail and information from computers in educational institutions, government agencies, and industry, accessible to the general public via modem links. ▷late 20th cent.: from **inter-** 'reciprocal, mutual' + **network**.

in·ter·neu·ron /ˌintərˈn(y)o͝orˌän/ (*Brit.* also **in·ter·neu·rone** /-ˌrōn/) ▸*n.* *Anatomy & Physiology* a neuron that transmits impulses between other neurons, esp. as part of a reflex arc. ▷1930s: from **internuncial** + **neuron**. —**in·ter·neu·ro·nal** /-ˈn(y)o͝orənl; -n(y)o͝oˈrōnl/ *adj.*

in·tern·ist /inˈtərnist; ˈintər-/ ▸*n.* *Medicine* a specialist in internal medicine. ▷early 20th cent.: from **internal** + **-ist**.

in·ter·node /ˈintərˌnōd/ ▸*n.* a slender part between two nodes or joints, in particular: ■ *Botany* a part of a plant stem between two of the nodes from which leaves emerge. ■ *Anatomy* a stretch of a nerve cell axon sheathed in myelin, between two nodes of Ranvier. ▷mid 17th cent.: from Latin *internodium*, from *inter-* 'between' + *nodus* 'knot.'

in·ter·nu·cle·ar /ˌintərˈn(y)o͞oklēər/ ▸*adj.* between nuclei (esp. of atoms).

in·ter·nun·cial /ˌintərˈnənsēəl; -shəl/ ▸*adj.* [*attrib.*] *Anatomy & Physiology* (of neurons) forming connections between other neurons in the central nervous system. ▷mid 19th cent.: from Latin *internuntius* (from *inter-* 'between' + *nuntius* 'messenger') + **-al**.

in·ter·o·ce·an·ic /ˌintərˌōshēˈanik/ ▸*adj.* between or connecting two oceans.

in·ter·o·cep·tive /ˌintərōˈseptiv/ ▸*adj.* *Physiology* relating to stimuli produced within an organism, esp. in the gut and other internal organs. Compare with **exteroceptive**. ▷early 20th cent.: from **interior** + **receptive**.

in·ter·o·cep·tor /ˌintərōˈseptər/ ▸*n.* *Physiology* a sensory receptor that receives stimuli from within the body, esp. from the gut and other internal organs. Compare with **exteroceptor**.

in·ter·op·er·a·ble /ˌintərˈäp(ə)rəbəl/ ▸*adj.* (of computer systems or software) able to exchange and make use of information. —**in·ter·op·er·a·bil·i·ty** /-ˌäp(ə)rəˈbilitē/ *n.*

in·ter·os·se·ous /ˌintərˈäsēəs/ ▸*adj.* situated between bones, in particular: ■ of or denoting certain muscles of the hand and foot. ■ of or denoting certain arteries of the forearm.

interp. ▸*abbr.* interpreter.

in·ter·pel·late /ˌintərˈpelāt; inˈtərpəˌlāt/ ▸*v.* [*trans.*] **1** (in certain parliamentary systems) interrupt the order of the day by demanding an explanation from (the minister concerned). **2** *Philosophy* (of an ideology or discourse) bring into being or give identity to (an individual or category). [from the works of Althusser.] ▷late 16th cent. (in the sense 'interrupt'): from Latin *interpellat-* 'interrupted (by speech),' from the verb *interpellare*, from *inter-* 'between' + *pellere* 'to drive.' Sense 1 dates from the late 19th cent. —**in·ter·pel·la·tion** /ˌintərpəˈlāshən/ *n.* —**in·ter·pel·la·tor** /-ˌlātər/ *n.*

in·ter·pen·e·trate /ˌintərˈpeniˌtrāt/ ▸*v.* mix or merge together: [*intrans.*] *the two concepts interpenetrate in interesting ways* | [*trans.*] *fibers of meaning interpenetrate every strand of sound.* —**in·ter·pen·e·tra·tion** /-ˌpeniˈtrāshən/ *n.* —**in·ter·pen·e·tra·tive** /-ˌtrātiv/ *adj.*

in·ter·per·son·al /ˌintərˈpərsənəl/ ▸*adj.* [*attrib.*] of or relating to relationships or communication between people: *you will need good interpersonal skills.* —**in·ter·per·son·al·ly** *adv.*

in·ter·phase /ˈintərˌfāz/ ▸*n.* *Biology* the resting phase between successive mitotic divisions of a cell, or between the first and second divisions of meiosis.

in·ter·plan·e·tar·y /ˌintərˈplaniˌterē/ ▸*adj.* situated or traveling between planets: *interplanetary missions.*

in·ter·plant /ˌintərˈplant/ ▸*v.* [*trans.*] (usu. **be interplanted**) plant (a crop or plant) together with another crop or plant. ■ plant (land) with a mixture of crops or plants.

in·ter·play /ˈintərˌplā/ ▸*n.* the way in which two or more things have an effect on each other: *the* ***interplay between*** *inheritance and learning.*

in·ter·plead·er /ˌintərˈplēdər/ ▸*n.* *Law* a suit pleaded between two parties to determine a matter of claim or right to property held by a third party. ▷mid 16th cent.: from Anglo-Norman French *enterpleder*, from *enter-* 'between' + *pleder* 'to plead.'

In·ter·pol /ˈintərˌpôl; -ˌpäl/ an organization based in Paris that coordinates investigations made by the police forces of member countries into crimes with an international dimension. ▷originally the address for telegrams sent to the International Criminal Police Commission, founded in 1923; from *Inter(national) pol(ice).*

in·ter·po·late /inˈtərpəˌlāt/ ▸*v.* [*trans.*] insert (something) between fixed points: *illustrations were interpolated in the text.* See note at **insert**. ■ insert (words) in a book or other text, esp. in order to give a false impression as to its date. ■ make such insertions in (a book or text). ■ interject (a remark) in a conversation: [with *direct speech*] *"I dare say," interpolated her employer.* ■ *Mathematics* insert (an intermediate value or term) into a series by estimating or calculating it from surrounding known values. ▷early 17th cent.: from Latin *interpolat-* 'refurbished, altered,' from the verb *interpolare*, from *inter-* 'between' + *-polare* (related to *polire* 'to polish'). —**in·ter·po·la·tion** /-ˌtərpəˈlāshən/ *n.* —**in·ter·po·la·tive** /-ˌlātiv/ *adj.*

in·ter·po·la·tor /inˈtərpəˌlātər/ ▸*n.* a person who interpolates something. ■ a device or apparatus that guides a tool through a smooth curve when provided with a set of points defining the curve.

in·ter·pole /ˈintərˌpōl/ ▸*n.* an auxiliary pole of a commutator placed between the main poles to increase its efficiency.

in·ter·pose /ˌintərˈpōz/ ▸*v.* **1** [*trans.*] place or insert between one thing and another: *he* ***interposed*** *himself* ***between*** *her and the top of the stairs.* **2** [*intrans.*] intervene between parties: [with *infinitive*] *the legislature interposed to suppress these amusements.* ■ [*trans.*] say (words) as an interruption: *if I might interpose a personal remark here.* ■ [*trans.*] exercise or advance (a veto or objection) so as to interfere: *the memo interposes no objection to issuing a discharge.* ▷late 16th cent.: from French *interposer,* from Latin *interponere* 'put in' (from *inter-* 'between' + *ponere* 'put'), but influenced by *interpositus* 'inserted' and Old French *poser* 'to place.'

in·ter·po·si·tion /ˌintərpəˈzisʜən/ ▸*n.* the action of interposing someone or something: *the interposition of members between tiers of management.* ■ interference: *prevented from taking your life by the interposition of your wife.* ▷late Middle English: from Latin *interpositio(n-),* from the verb *interponere* (see **INTERPOSE**).

in·ter·pret /inˈtərprit/ ▸*v.* (**-pret·ed, -pret·ing**) [*trans.*] **1** explain the meaning of (information, words, or actions): *the evidence is difficult to interpret.* See note at **CLARIFY**. ■ [*intrans.*] translate orally the words of another person speaking a different language: *I agreed to interpret for Jean-Claude.* ■ perform (a dramatic role or piece of music) in a particular way that conveys one's understanding of the creator's ideas. **2** understand (an action, mood, or way of behaving) as having a particular meaning or significance: *her self-confidence was often* ***interpreted as*** *brashness.* ▷late Middle English: from Old French *interpreter* or Latin *interpretari* 'explain, translate,' from *interpres, interpret-* 'agent, translator, interpreter.' —**in·ter·pret·a·bil·i·ty** /-ˌtərpritəˈbilitē/ *n.* —**in·ter·pret·a·ble** *adj.* —**in·ter·pre·ta·tive** /-ˌtātiv/ *adj.* —**in·ter·pre·ta·tive·ly** /-ˌtātivlē/ *adv.* —**in·ter·pre·tive** /-ˈtərpritiv/ *adj.* —**in·ter·pre·tive·ly** /-ˈtərpritivlē/ *adv.*

USAGE Interpretative, which means 'serving to interpret or explain,' dates back to around 1560, but the shorter form **interpretive**, about a hundred years younger, is steadily pressing it out of employment. They mean the same thing, and both are correct. The traditional **interpretative** is still the preferred form in Britain, but in American usage, **interpretive** is far more common.

in·ter·pre·tant /inˈtərpritənt/ ▸*n.* (in Peirce's philosophy of language) the effect of a proposition or sign series on the person who interprets it.

in·ter·pre·ta·tion /inˌtərpriˈtāsʜən/ ▸*n.* the action of explaining the meaning of something: *the interpretation of data.* ■ an explanation or way of explaining: *this action is open to a number of interpretations.* ■ a stylistic representation of a creative work or dramatic role: *two differing interpretations, both bearing the distinctive hallmarks of each writer's perspective.* ▷late Middle English: from Old French *interpretation* or Latin *interpretatio(n-),* from the verb *interpretari* (see **INTERPRET**). —**in·ter·pre·ta·tion·al** /-sʜənl/ *adj.*

in·ter·pret·er /inˈtərpritər/ ▸*n.* a person who interprets, esp. one who translates speech orally. ■ *Computing* a program that can analyze and execute a program line by line. ▷late Middle English: from Old French *interpreteur,* from late Latin *interpretator,* from Latin *interpretari* (see **INTERPRET**).

in·ter·pro·vin·cial /ˌintərprəˈvinsʜəl/ ▸*adj.* existing or carried on between provinces of the same country. ▸*n.* (usu. **interprovincials**) a sports tournament between different provinces of the same country. ■ a member of a team competing in such a tournament.

in·ter·quar·tile /ˌintərˈkwôrˌtīl; -ˈkwôrtl/ ▸*adj. Statistics* situated between the first and third quartiles of a distribution.

in·ter·ra·cial /ˌintərˈrāsʜəl/ ▸*adj.* existing between or involving different races: *interracial conflict.* —**in·ter·ra·cial·ly** *adv.*

in·ter·reg·num /ˌintərˈregnəm/ ▸*n.* (*pl.* **-nums** or **-na** /-nə/) a period when normal government is suspended, esp. between successive reigns or regimes. ■ an interval or pause: *the interregnum between the discovery of radioactivity and its detailed understanding.* ▷late 16th cent. (denoting temporary rule between reigns or during suspension of normal government): from Latin, from *inter-* 'between' + *regnum* 'reign.'

in·ter·re·late /ˌintərəˈlāt/ ▸*v.* relate or connect to one another: [*intrans.*] *each component* ***interrelates with*** *all the others* | [*trans.*] *shared values and mechanisms that interrelate peoples in all corners of the world.* —**in·ter·re·lat·ed·ness** *n.*

in·ter·re·la·tion·ship /ˌintərəˈlāsʜənˌsʜip/ ▸*n.* the way in which each of two or more things is related to the other or others: *the* ***interrelationship between*** *the comprehension and production of early vocabulary.* —**in·ter·re·la·tion** *n.*

interrog. ▸*abbr.* interrogative.

in·ter·ro·gate /inˈterəˌgāt/ ▸*v.* [*trans.*] ask questions of (someone, esp. a suspect or a prisoner) closely, aggressively, or formally. ■ *Computing* obtain data from (a computer file, database, storage device, or terminal). ■ (of an electronic device) transmit a signal to (another device, esp. one on a vehicle) to obtain a response giving information about identity, condition, etc. ▷late 15th cent.: from Latin *interrogat-* 'questioned,' from the verb *interrogare,* from *inter-* 'between' + *rogare* 'ask.' —**in·ter·ro·ga·tor** /-ˌgātər/ *n.*

in·ter·ro·ga·tion /inˌterəˈgāsʜən/ ▸*n.* the action of interrogating or the process of being interrogated: *would he keep his mouth shut* ***under interrogation?*** | *he had conducted hundreds of criminal interrogations.* —**in·ter·ro·ga·tion·al** /-sʜənl/ *adj.*

in·ter·ro·ga·tion point (also **interrogation mark**) ▸*n.* another term for **QUESTION MARK**.

in·ter·rog·a·tive /ˌintəˈrägətiv/ ▸*adj.* having or conveying the force of a question: *a hard, interrogative stare.* ■ *Grammar* used in questions: *an interrogative adverb.* Contrasted with **AFFIRMATIVE** and **NEGATIVE**.
▸*n.* a word used in questions, such as *how* or *what.* ■ a construction that has the force of a question. ▷early 16th cent.: from late Latin *interrogativus,* from Latin *interrogare* (see **INTERROGATE**). —**in·ter·rog·a·tive·ly** *adv.*

in·ter·rog·a·to·ry /ˌintəˈrägəˌtôrē/ ▸*adj.* conveying the force of a question; questioning: *the guard moves away with an interrogatory stare.*
▸*n.* (*pl.* **-ries**) *Law* a written question that is formally put to one party in a case by another party and that must be answered. ▷mid 16th cent.: the noun from medieval Latin *interrogatoria,* plural of *interrogatorium;* the adjective from late Latin *interrogatorius,* based on Latin *interrogare* (see **INTERROGATE**).

in·ter·rupt /ˌintəˈrəpt/ ▸*v.* [*trans.*] **1** stop the continuous progress of (an activity or process): *the buzzer interrupted his thoughts.* ■ stop (someone speaking) by saying or doing something: *"Of course . . ." Shepherd began, but his son interrupted him* | [with *direct speech*] *"Hold on," he interrupted.* **2** break the continuity of (a line or surface): *the coastal plain is interrupted by chains of large lagoons.* ■ obstruct (something, esp. a view). ▷late Middle English: from Latin *interrupt-* 'broken, interrupted,' from the verb *interrumpere,* from *inter-* 'between' + *rumpere* 'to break.' —**in·ter·rupt·i·ble** *adj.* —**in·ter·rup·tion** /-sʜən/ *n.* —**in·ter·rup·tive** /-tiv/ *adj.*

in·ter·rupt·ed /ˌintəˈrəptid/ ▸*adj.* **1** *Botany* (of a compound leaf, inflorescence, or other plant organ) made discontinuous by smaller interposed leaflets or intervals of bare stem. **2** *Music* (of a cadence) having a penultimate dominant chord that is followed not by the expected tonic chord but by another chord, usually the submediant.

in·ter·rupt·er /ˌintəˈrəptər/ (also **in·ter·rup·tor**) ▸*n.* a person or thing that interrupts. ■ a device that automatically breaks an electric circuit if a fault develops.

in·ter se /ˈintər ˈsē; ˈsā/ ▸*adv.* between or among themselves: *agreements entered into by all the shareholders inter se.* ▷mid 19th cent.: Latin.

in·ter·sect /ˌintərˈsekt/ ▸*v.* [*trans.*] divide (something) by passing or lying across it: *occasionally the water table intersects the earth's surface, forming streams and lakes* | *the area is intersected only by minor roads.* ■ [*intrans.*] (of two or more things) pass or lie across each other: *lines of latitude and longitude intersect at right angles.* ▷early 17th cent.: from Latin *intersect-* 'cut, intersected,' from the verb *intersecare,* from *inter-* 'between' + *secare* 'to cut.'

in·ter·sec·tion /ˌintərˈseksʜən/ ▸*n.* a point or line common to lines or surfaces that intersect: *the intersection of a plane and a cone.* ■ a point at which two or more things intersect, esp. roads: *red and green lights at the nearby intersection.* ■ an action of intersecting: *his course is on a direct intersection with ours.* ▷mid 16th cent.: from Latin *intersectio(n-),* from *intersecare* (see **INTERSECT**). —**in·ter·sec·tion·al** /-sʜənl/ *adj.*

in·ter·seg·men·tal /ˌintərsegˈmentl/ ▸*adj. chiefly Zoology* situated or occurring between segments. —**in·ter·seg·men·tal·ly** *adv.*

in·ter·sep·tal /ˌintərˈseptl/ ▸*adj. Anatomy & Zoology* situated between septa or partitions.

in·ter·sex /ˈintərˌseks/ ▸*n.* the abnormal condition of being intermediate between male and female; hermaphroditism. ■ an individual in this condition; a hermaphrodite.

in·ter·sex·u·al /ˌintərˈseksʜo͞oəl/ ▸*adj.* **1** existing or occurring between the sexes: *intersexual selection, or mate choice, was, to Darwin, the job of females.* **2** relating to or having the condition of being intermediate between male and female. —**in·ter·sex·u·al·i·ty** /-ˌseksʜo͞oˈalitē/ *n.*

in·ter·space ▸*n.* /ˈintərˌspās/ a space between objects: *volcanic rock that has been crushed into fragments and the interspaces filled with turquoise and oxide of iron.*
▸*v.* /ˌintərˈspās/ [*trans.*] (usu. **be interspaced**) put or occupy a space between: *the great four-story houses were* ***interspaced with*** *the ramshackle cottages of the workmen.*

in·ter·spe·cif·ic /ˌintərspiˈsifik/ ▸*adj. Biology* existing or occurring between different species: *interspecific differences.* —**in·ter·spe·cif·i·cal·ly** /-ik(ə)lē/ *adv.*

in·ter·sperse /ˌintərˈspərs/ ▸*v.* [*trans.*] (often **be interspersed**) scatter among or between other things; place here and there: ***interspersed between*** *tragic stories are a few songs supplying comic relief.* ■ diversify (a thing or things) with other things at intervals: *a patchwork of open fields* ***interspersed with*** *copses of pine.* ▷mid 16th cent. (in the sense 'diversify (something) by introducing other things at intervals'): from Latin *interspers-* 'scattered between,' from *interspergere,* from *inter-* 'between' + *spargere* 'scatter.' —**in·ter·sper·sion** /-ˈsperzʜən/ *n.*

in·ter·spi·nal /ˌintərˈspīnl/ ▸*adj. Anatomy* situated between the spines or spinous protuberances of the vertebrae. —**in·ter·spi·nous** /-ˈspīnəs/ *adj.*

in·ter·sta·di·al /ˌintərˈstādēəl/ *Geology* ▸*adj.* of or relating to a minor period of less cold climate during a glacial period. Compare with **INTERGLACIAL**.
▸*n.* an interstadial period. ▷early 20th cent.: from **INTER-** 'between' + *stadial* from Latin *stadialis,* from *stadium* 'stage.'

in·ter·state /ˈintərˌstāt/ ▸*adj.* [*attrib.*] existing or carried on between states: *interstate travel.* ■ in a different state from one referred to or understood: *their interstate rivals.*
▸*n.* (also **interstate highway**) one of a system of expressways covering the 48 contiguous states: *a picnic area just off the interstate* | *Interstate 65 runs generally parallel to Route 31.*

in·ter·stel·lar /ˌintərˈstelər/ ▸*adj.* occurring or situated between stars: *interstellar travel.*

in·ter·stice /inˈtərstis/ ▸*n.* (usu. **interstices**) an intervening space, esp. a very small one: *sunshine filtered through the interstices of the arching trees.* ▷late Middle English: from Latin *interstitium,* from *intersistere* 'stand between,' from *inter-* 'between' + *sistere* 'to stand.'

in·ter·sti·tial /ˌintərˈstisʜəl/ ▸*adj.* of, forming, or occupying interstices: *the interstitial space.* ■ *Ecology* (of minute animals) living in the spaces between individual sand grains in the soil or aquatic sediments: *the interstitial fauna of marine sands.* —**in·ter·sti·tial·ly** *adv.*

in·ter·sub·jec·tive /ˌintərsəbˈjektiv/ ▸*adj. Philosophy* existing between conscious minds; shared by more than one conscious mind. —**in·ter·sub·jec·tive·ly** *adv.* —**in·ter·sub·jec·tiv·i·ty** /-ˌsəbjekˈtivitē/ *n.*

in·ter·tex·tu·al·i·ty /ˌintərˌteksʜo͞oˈalitē/ ▸*n.* the relationship between texts, esp. literary ones: *every text is a product of intertextuality.* —**in·ter·tex·tu·al** /-ˈteksʜo͞oəl/ *adj.* —**in·ter·tex·tu·al·ly** *adv.*

in·ter·ti·dal /ˌintərˈtīdl/ ▸*adj. Ecology* of or denoting the area of a seashore that is covered at high tide and uncovered at low tide.

in·ter·trib·al /ˌintərˈtrībəl/ ▸*adj.* existing or occurring between different tribes: *intertribal conflict.* ■ involving members of more than one tribe: *an intertribal group.*

in·ter·tri·go /ˌintərˈtrīgō/ ▸*n. Medicine* inflammation caused by the rubbing of one area of skin on another. ▷early 18th cent.: from Latin, 'a sore place caused by rubbing,' from *interterere* 'rub against each other.'

in·ter·trop·i·cal con·ver·gence zone /ˌintərˈträpikəl/ ▸*n.* a narrow zone near the equator where northern and southern air masses converge, typically producing low atmospheric pressure.

in·ter·twine /ˌintərˈtwīn/ ▸*v.* twist or twine together: [*trans.*] *a net made of cotton* ***intertwined with*** *other natural fibers* | [*intrans.*] *the coils* ***intertwine with*** *one another like strands of spaghetti.* ■ [*trans.*] *figurative* connect or link (two or more things) closely: *Dickens has been very clever to intertwine all these aspects and ideas.* —**in·ter·twine·ment** *n.*

in·ter·val /ˈintərvəl/ ▸*n.* **1** an intervening time or space: *after his departure, there was an interval of many years without any meetings the intervals between meals were very short.* **2** a pause; a break in activity: *an interval of mourning.* ■ *Brit.* an intermission separating parts of a theatrical or musical performance. ■ *Brit.* a break between the parts of an athletic contest: *leading 3-0 at the interval.* **3** a space between two things; a gap. ■ the difference in pitch between two musical sounds. ▷Middle English: from Old French *entrevalle,* based on Latin *intervallum* 'space between ramparts, interval,' from *inter-* 'between' + *vallum* 'rampart.' —**in·ter·val·lic** /ˌintərˈvalik/ *adj.*
▸*PHRASE* □ **at intervals 1** with time between, not

continuously: *the light flashed at intervals.* **2** with spaces between: *the path is marked with rocks at intervals.*

in·ter·val es·ti·mate ▶*n. Statistics* an interval within which the value of a parameter of a population has a stated probability of occurring. Compare with **POINT ESTIMATE.**

in·ter·val·om·e·ter /ˌintərvəˈlämitər/ ▶*n. Photography* an attachment or facility on a camera that operates the shutter regularly at set intervals over a period. On a movie camera the device is used for time-lapse photography.

in·ter·val train·ing ▶*n.* training in which a runner alternates between running and jogging over set distances. ■ training in which an athlete alternates between two activities, typically requiring different rates of speed, degrees of effort, etc.

in·ter·vene /ˌintərˈvēn/ ▶*v.* [*intrans.*] **1** come between so as to prevent or alter a result or course of events: *he acted outside his authority when he* ***intervened in*** *the dispute* | [with *infinitive*] *their forces intervened to halt the attack.* ■ (of an event or circumstance) occur as a delay or obstacle to something being done: *Christmas intervened, and the investigation was suspended.* ■ interrupt verbally: [with *direct speech*] *"It's true!" he intervened.* ■ *Law* interpose in a lawsuit as a third party. **2** [usu. as *adj.*] (**intervening**) occur in time between events: *to occupy the intervening months, she took a job in a hospital.* ■ be situated between things: *they heard the sound of distant gunfire, muffled by the intervening trees.* ▷late 16th cent. (in the sense 'come in as an extraneous factor or thing'): from Latin *intervenire,* from *inter-* 'between' + *venire* 'come.' —**in·ter·ven·er** *n.* —**in·ter·ven·ient** /-ˈvēnyənt/ *adj.* —**in·ter·ve·nor** /-ˈvēnər/ *n.*

in·ter·ven·tion /ˌintərˈvensHən/ ▶*n.* the action or process of intervening: *they are plants that grow naturally without human intervention.* ■ interference by a country in another's affairs: *the administration was reported to be considering military intervention.* ■ action taken to improve a situation, esp. a medical disorder: *two patients were referred for surgical intervention.* ▷late Middle English: from Latin *interventio(n-),* from the verb *intervenire* (see **INTERVENE**). —**in·ter·ven·tion·al** /-sHənl/ *adj.* (chiefly in the medical sense).

in·ter·ven·tion·ist /ˌintərˈvensHənist/ ▶*adj.* favoring intervention, esp. by a government in its domestic economy or by one country in the affairs of another. ▶*n.* a person who favors intervention of this kind. —**in·ter·ven·tion·ism** /-ˌnizəm/ *n.*

in·ter·ver·te·bral /ˌintərˈvərtəbrəl/ ▶*adj.* [*attrib.*] situated between vertebrae: *intervertebral joints.*

in·ter·ver·te·bral disk ▶*n.* see **DISK** (sense 3).

in·ter·view /ˈintərˌvyo͞o/ ▶*n.* a meeting of people face to face, esp. for consultation. ■ a conversation between a journalist or radio or television presenter and a person of public interest, used as the basis of a broadcast or publication. ■ an oral examination of an applicant for a job, college admission, etc.: *I am pleased to advise you that you have been selected for an interview.* ▶*v.* [*trans.*] (often **be interviewed**) hold an interview with (someone): *he arrived to be interviewed by a local TV station about the level of unemployment.* ■ question (someone) to discover their opinions or experience: *in a survey more than half the women interviewed hated the label "housewife."* ■ orally examine (an applicant for a job, college admission, etc.): *he came to be interviewed for a top job* | [*intrans.*] *I was interviewing all last week.* ■ [*intrans.*] perform (well or badly) at an interview. ▷early 16th cent. (formerly also as *enterview*): from French *entrevue,* from *s'entrevoir* 'see each other,' from *voir* 'to see,' on the pattern of *vue* 'a view.' —**in·ter·view·ee** /ˌintərˌvyo͞oˈē/ *n.* —**in·ter·view·er** *n.*

in·ter vi·vos /ˈintər ˈvēˌvōs; ˈvīˌvōs/ ▶*adv.* & *adj.* (esp. of a gift as opposed to a legacy) between living people: [as *adv.*] *gifts made inter vivos* | [as *postpositive adj.*] *a gift inter vivos.* ▷Latin.

in·ter·vo·cal·ic /ˌintərvōˈkalik/ ▶*adj. Phonetics* occurring between vowels: *in intervocalic position.* —**in·ter·vo·cal·i·cal·ly** /-ik(ə)lē/ *adv.*

in·ter·war /ˌintərˈwôr/ ▶*adj.* [*attrib.*] existing in the period between two wars, esp. the two world wars (i.e., between 1918 and 1939).

in·ter·weave /ˌintərˈwēv/ ▶*v.* (*past* **-wove**; *past part.* **-wov·en**) weave or become woven together: [*trans.*] *the rugs are made by tightly interweaving the warp and weft strands* | [*intrans.*] *the branches met and interwove above his head.* ■ [*trans.*] *figurative* blend closely: *Wordsworth's political ideas are often* ***interwoven with*** *his philosophical and religious beliefs.*

in·ter·wind /ˌintərˈwīnd/ ▶*v.* (*past* and *past part.* **-wound** /-ˈwound/) [*trans.*] [usu. as *adj.*] (**interwound**) wind together: *a transformer consists of two interwound coils.*

in·ter·work /ˌintərˈwərk/ ▶*v.* [*intrans.*] *Computing* (of items of hardware or software) be able to connect, communicate, or exchange data: *servers running new and old versions of the software will interwork.*

in·tes·tate /inˈtestāt; -tit/ ▶*adj.* [*predic.*] not having made a will before one dies: *he died intestate* | [*postpositive*] *in the event of his death intestate.* ■ [*attrib.*] of or relating to a person who dies without having made a will: *his brother's posthumous children are admissible as intestate heirs.* ▶*n.* a person who has died without having made a will. ▷late Middle English: from Latin *intestatus,* from *in-* 'not' + *testatus* 'testified, witness' (see **TESTATE**). —**in·tes·ta·cy** /-təsē/ *n.*

in·tes·ti·nal flo·ra /inˈtestənl ˈflôrə/ ▶*plural n.* [usu. treated as *sing.*] the symbiotic bacteria occurring naturally in the intestine.

in·tes·tine /inˈtestən/ (also **in·tes·tines**) ▶*n.* (in vertebrates) the lower part of the alimentary canal from the end of the stomach to the anus: *the contents of the intestine* | *loops of intestine.* See also **LARGE INTESTINE, SMALL INTESTINE.** ■ (esp. in invertebrates) the whole alimentary canal from the mouth downward. ▷late Middle English: from Latin *intestinum,* neuter of *intestinus,* from *intus* 'within.' —**in·tes·ti·nal** /-tənl/ *adj.*

in·thrall /inˈTHrôl/ ▶*v.* archaic spelling of **ENTHRALL.**

in·ti /ˈintē/ ▶*n.* (*pl.* same or **in·tis** /ˈintēz/) a former basic monetary unit of Peru, equal to 100 centimos.

in·ti·fa·da /ˌintəˈfädə/ ▶*n.* the Palestinian uprising against Israeli occupation of the West Bank and Gaza Strip, beginning in 1987. ▷from Arabic *intifāḍa* 'an uprising' (literally 'a jumping up as a reaction to something'), from *intifaḍa* 'be shaken, shake oneself.'

in·ti·ma /ˈintəmə/ ▶*n.* (*pl.* **-mae** /-ˌmē/) *Anatomy & Zoology* the innermost coating or membrane of a part or organ, esp. of a vein or artery. ▷late 19th cent.: shortening of modern Latin *tunica intima* 'innermost sheath.' —**in·ti·mal** /-məl/ *adj.*

in·ti·ma·cy /ˈintəməsē/ ▶*n.* (*pl.* **-cies**) close familiarity or friendship; closeness: *the* ***intimacy between*** *a husband and wife.* ■ a private cozy atmosphere: *the room had a peaceful sense of intimacy about it.* ■ an intimate act, esp. sexual intercourse. ■ an intimate remark: *here she was sitting swapping intimacies with a stranger.* ■ [in *sing.*] closeness of observation or knowledge of a subject: *he acquired an* ***intimacy with*** *Swahili literature.*

in·ti·mate[1] /ˈintəmit/ ▶*adj.* **1** closely acquainted; familiar, close: *intimate friends* | *they are on intimate terms.* ■ (of a place or setting) having or creating an informal friendly atmosphere: *an intimate little Italian restaurant.* ■ [*predic.*] used euphemistically to indicate that a couple is having a sexual relationship: *he was sickened by the thought of others having been* ***intimate with*** *her.* ■ involving very close connection: *their intimate involvement with their community.* **2** private and personal: *going into intimate details of his sexual encounters* | *intimate correspondence.* ■ used euphemistically to refer to a person's genitals: *touching her in the most intimate places.* **3** (of knowledge) detailed; thorough: *an intimate knowledge of the software.* ▶*n.* a very close friend: *his circle of intimates.* ▷early 17th cent. (as a noun): from late Latin *intimatus,* past participle of Latin *intimare* 'impress, make familiar,' from *intimus* 'inmost.' —**in·ti·mate·ly** *adv.*

in·ti·mate[2] /ˈintəˌmāt/ ▶*v.* [*trans.*] imply or hint: [with *clause*] *he had already intimated that he might not be able to continue.* ■ state or make known: *Mr. Hutchison has intimated his decision to retire.* ▷early 16th cent.: from late Latin *intimat-* 'made known,' from the verb *intimare* (see **INTIMATE**[1]). The noun *intimation* dates from late Middle English. —**in·ti·ma·tion** /ˌintəˈmāsHən/ *n.*

in·tim·i·date /inˈtimiˌdāt/ ▶*v.* frighten or overawe (someone), esp. in order to make them do what one wants: *he tries to intimidate his rivals* [as *adj.*] (**intimidating**) *the intimidating defense lawyer.* ▷mid 17th cent.: from medieval Latin *intimidat-* 'made timid,' from the verb *intimidare* (based on *timidus* 'timid'). —**in·tim·i·dat·ing·ly** *adv.* —**in·tim·i·da·tion** /-ˌtimiˈdāsHən/ *n.* —**in·tim·i·da·tor** /-ˌdātər/ *n.* —**in·tim·i·da·to·ry** /-dəˌtôrē/ *adj.*

In·tim·i·da·tor, the, see **EARNHARDT.**

in·ti·mism /ˈintəˌmizəm/ ▶*n.* a style of painting showing intimate views of domestic interiors using Impressionist techniques, used by artists such as Bonnard in the early 20th century. ▷early 20th cent.: from French *intimisme,* from Latin *intimus* 'innermost.' —**in·ti·mist** *adj.* & *n.*

in·tinc·tion /inˈtiNG(k)sHən/ ▶*n.* the action of dipping the bread in the wine at a Eucharist so that a communicant receives both together. ▷mid 16th cent.: from late Latin *intinctio(n-),* from Latin *intingere,* from *in-* 'into' + *tingere* 'dip.' The word originally denoted the general action of dipping, esp. into something colored; compare with **TINGE.** The current sense dates from the late 19th cent.

in·tit·ule /inˈtiCHo͝ol/ ▶*v.* [*trans.*] *Brit.* give a specified title to (a legislative act). ▷late 15th cent. (formerly also as *entitule*): from Old French *entituler, intituler* (see **ENTITLE**).

intl. ▶*abbr.* international.

in·to /ˈinto͞o/ ▶*prep.* **1** expressing movement or action with the result that someone or something becomes enclosed or surrounded by something else: *cover the bowl and put it into the fridge* | *Sara got into her car and shut the door* | *figurative he walked into a trap sprung by the opposition.* **2** expressing movement or action with the result that someone or something makes physical contact with something else: *he crashed into a parked car.* **3** indicating a route by which someone or something may arrive at a particular destination: *the narrow road that led down into the village.* **4** indicating the direction toward which someone or something is turned when confronting something else: *with the wind blowing into your face* | *sobbing into her skirt.* **5** indicating an object of attention or interest: *a clearer insight into what is involved* | *an inquiry into the squad's practices.* **6** expressing a change of state: *a peaceful protest which turned into a violent confrontation* | *the fruit can be made into jam.* **7** expressing the result of an action: *they forced the club into a humiliating and expensive special general meeting.* **8** expressing division: *three into twelve equals four.* **9** *informal* (of a person) taking a lively and active interest in (something): *he's into surfing.* ▷Old English *intō* (see **IN, TO**).

in·tol·er·a·ble /inˈtälərəbəl/ ▶*adj.* unable to be endured: *the intolerable pressures of his work.* ▷late Middle English: from Old French, or from Latin *intolerabilis,* from *in-* 'not' + *tolerabilis* (see **TOLERABLE**). —**in·tol·er·a·bil·i·ty** /-ˌtälərəˈbilitē/ *n.* —**in·tol·er·a·ble·ness** *n.* —**in·tol·er·a·bly** /-blē/ *adv.*

in·tol·er·ant /inˈtälərənt/ ▶*adj.* not tolerant of others' views, beliefs, or behavior that differ from one's own: *he was* ***intolerant of*** *ignorance.* ■ unable to be given (a medicine or other treatment) or to eat (a food) without adverse effects: *intolerant of aspirin* | [*postpositive*] *these patients were lactose intolerant.* ■ (of a plant or animal) unable to survive exposure to (physical influence). ▷mid 18th cent.: from Latin *intolerant-,* from *in-* 'not' + *tolerant-* 'enduring' (see **TOLERANT**). —**in·tol·er·ance** *n.* —**in·tol·er·ant·ly** *adv.*

in·to·nate /ˈintəˌnāt/ ▶*v.* intone. ▷late 18th cent.: from medieval Latin *intonat-* 'intoned,' from the verb *intonare* (see **INTONE**).

in·to·na·tion /ˌintəˈnāsHən; -tō-/ ▶*n.* **1** the rise and fall of the voice in speaking: *she spoke English with a German intonation.* ■ the action of intoning or reciting in a singing voice. **2** accuracy of pitch in playing or singing: *poor woodwind intonation at the opening.* **3** the opening phrase of a plainsong melody. ▷early 17th cent. (sense 3): from medieval Latin *intonatio(n-),* from *intonare* (see **INTONE**). —**in·to·na·tion·al** /-sHənl/ *adj.*

in·tone /inˈtōn/ ▶*v.* [*trans.*] say or recite with little rise and fall of the pitch of the voice: *he intoned a short Latin prayer* | [with *direct speech*] *"All rise," intoned the usher.* ▷late 15th cent. (originally as *entone*): from Old French *entoner* or medieval Latin *intonare,* from *in-* 'into' + Latin *tonus* 'tone.' —**in·ton·er** *n.*

in to·to /ˌin ˈtōtō/ ▶*adv.* as a whole: *such proposals should be subjected to specific criticism rather than rejected in toto.* ■ [*sentence adverb*] in all; overall: *there was, in toto, an increase in legal regulation and public surveillance.* ▷Latin.

in·tox·i·cant /inˈtäksikənt/ ▶*n.* an intoxicating substance.

in·tox·i·cate /inˈtäksikāt/ ▶*v.* [*trans.*] [usu. as *adj.*] (**intoxicated**) (of alcoholic drink or a drug) cause (someone) to lose control of their faculties or behavior. ■ poison. ■ *figurative* excite or exhilarate: *the team was intoxicated by the prospect of another victorious season.* ▷late Middle English (in the sense 'poison'): from medieval Latin *intoxicare,* from *in-* 'into' + *toxicare* 'to poison,' from Latin *toxicum* (see **TOXIC**). —**in·tox·i·ca·tion** /-ˌtäksiˈkāsHən/ *n.*

in·tox·i·cat·ing /inˈtäksikātiNG/ ▶*adj.* (of alcoholic

drink or a drug) liable to cause intoxication. ■ *figurative* exhilarating or exciting: *the intoxicating touch of freedom.* —**in·tox·i·cat·ing·ly** *adv.*

in·tox·im·e·ter /in'täksə,mētər/ ▸*n.* a nonportable instrument for measuring the alcohol content of a person's breath, esp. in cases of suspected drunk driving, usually sited at a police station. ▷1950s: from *intoxication* (see **INTOXICATE**) + **-METER**.

intr. ▸*abbr.* ■ intransitive. ■ introduce or introduced or introducing or introduction or introductory.

intra- ▸*prefix* (added to adjectives) on the inside; within: *intramural* | *intrauterine.* ▷from Latin *intra* 'inside.'

in·tra·cel·lu·lar /,intrə'selyələr/ ▸*adj. Biology* located or occurring within a cell or cells: *an increase in intracellular calcium.* —**in·tra·cel·lu·lar·ly** *adv.*

in·tra·cra·ni·al /,intrə'krānēəl/ ▸*adj.* within the skull: *intracranial hemorrhage.* —**in·tra·cra·ni·al·ly** *adv.*

in·trac·ta·ble /in'traktəbəl/ ▸*adj.* hard to control or deal with: *intractable economic problems* | *intractable pain.* ■ (of a person) difficult; stubborn. See note at **STUBBORN**. ▷late 15th cent.: from Latin *intractabilis*, from *in-* 'not' + *tractabilis* (see **TRACTABLE**). —**in·trac·ta·bil·i·ty** /-,traktə'bilitē/ *n.* —**in·trac·ta·ble·ness** *n.* —**in·trac·ta·bly** /-blē/ *adv.*

in·tra·day /'intrə,dā/ ▸*adj.* [*attrib.*] *Stock Market* occurring within one day: *the dollar slipped from an intraday high of 104.*

in·tra·dos /'intrə,däs; -,dōs; in'trā-/ ▸*n.* (*pl.* same or **-dos·es**) *Architecture* the lower or inner curve of an arch. Often contrasted with **EXTRADOS**. ▷late 18th cent.: from French, from *intra-* 'on the inside' + *dos* 'the back' (from Latin *dorsum*).

in·tra·mo·lec·u·lar /,intrəmə'lekyələr/ ▸*adj.* existing or taking place within a molecule. —**in·tra·mo·lec·u·lar·ly** *adv.*

in·tra·mu·ral /,intrə'myŏŏrəl/ ▸*adj.* situated or done within the walls of a building: *both intramural and churchyard graves.* ■ taking place within a single educational institution: *recreational intramural games.* ■ forming part of normal university or college studies. ■ *Medicine & Biology* situated within the wall of a hollow organ or a cell: *an intramural hematoma.* ■ situated or done within a community: *an intramural social symbol within the tribe.* ▷mid 19th cent.: from **INTRA-** 'within' + Latin *murus* 'wall' + **-AL**. —**in·tra·mu·ral·ly** *adv.*

in·tra·mus·cu·lar /,intrə'məskyələr/ ▸*adj.* situated or taking place within, or administered into, a muscle: *an intramuscular injection.* —**in·tra·mus·cu·lar·ly** *adv.*

in·tra·net /'intrə,net/ (also **In·tra·net**) ▸*n. Computing* a local or restricted communications network, esp. a private network created using World Wide Web software.

in·tran·si·gent /in'transijənt; -zi-/ ▸*adj.* unwilling or refusing to change one's views or to agree about something.

▸*n.* an intransigent person. ▷late 19th cent.: from French *intransigeant*, from Spanish *los intransigentes* (a name adopted by the extreme republicans in the Cortes, 1873–74); based on Latin *in-* 'not' + *transigere* 'come to an understanding.' —**in·tran·si·gence** *n.* —**in·tran·si·gen·cy** *n.* —**in·tran·si·gent·ly** *adv.*

in·tran·si·tive /in'transitiv; -zi-/ ▸*adj.* (of a verb or a sense or use of a verb) not taking a direct object, e.g., *look* in *look at the sky.* The opposite of **TRANSITIVE**.

▸*n.* an intransitive verb. ▷early 17th cent.: from late Latin *intransitivus* 'not passing over,' from *in-* 'not' + *transitivus* (see **TRANSITIVE**). —**in·tran·si·tive·ly** *adv.* —**in·tran·si·tiv·i·ty** /-,transi'tivitē; -zi-/ *n.*

in·tra·pre·neur /,intrəprə'nər; -'nŏŏr/ ▸*n.* a manager within a company who promotes innovative product development and marketing. ▷1970s (originally U.S.): from **INTRA-** 'within' + a shortened form of **ENTREPRENEUR**. —**in·tra·pre·neu·ri·al** /-ēəl/ *adj.*

in·tra·spe·cif·ic /,intrəspə'sifik/ ▸*adj. Biology* produced, occurring, or existing within a species or between individuals of a single species: *intraspecific competition.*

in·tra·the·cal /,intrə'THēkəl/ ▸*adj. Medicine* occurring within or administered into the spinal theca: *intrathecal injection.* —**in·tra·the·cal·ly** *adv.*

in·tra·u·ter·ine /,intrə'yōōtərin; -rīn/ ▸*adj.* within the uterus.

in·tra·u·ter·ine de·vice (abbr.: **IUD**) ▸*n.* a contraceptive device fitted inside the uterus and physically preventing the implantation of fertilized ova.

in·tra·vas·cu·lar /,intrə'vaskyələr/ ▸*adj. Medicine & Biology* situated or occurring within a vessel or vessels of an animal or plant, esp. within a blood vessel or blood vascular system. —**in·tra·vas·cu·lar·ly** *adv.*

in·tra·ve·nous /,intrə'vēnəs/ (abbr.: **IV**) ▸*adj.* existing or taking place within, or administered into, a vein or veins: *an intravenous drip.* —**in·tra·ve·nous·ly** *adv.*

in·tra·zon·al /,intrə'zōnl/ ▸*adj. Soil Science* (of a soil) having a well-developed structure different from that expected for its climatic and vegetational zone owing to the overriding influence of relief, parent material, or some other local factor.

in·trench ▸*v.* variant spelling of **ENTRENCH**.

in·trep·id /in'trepid/ ▸*adj.* fearless; adventurous (often used for rhetorical or humorous effect): *our intrepid reporter.* See note at **BOLD**. ▷late 17th cent.: from French *intrépide* or Latin *intrepidus*, from *in-* 'not' + *trepidus* 'alarmed.' —**in·tre·pid·i·ty** /,intrə'piditē/ *n.* —**in·trep·id·ly** *adv.* —**in·trep·id·ness** *n.*

in·tri·ca·cy /'intrikəsē/ ▸*n.* (*pl.* **-cies**) the quality of being intricate: *the exquisite intricacy of Indian silverwork.* ■ (**intricacies**) details, esp. of an involved or perplexing subject: *the intricacies of economic policymaking.*

in·tri·cate /'intrikit/ ▸*adj.* very complicated or detailed: *an intricate network of canals.* ▷late Middle English: from Latin *intricat-* 'entangled,' from the verb *intricare*, from *in-* 'into' + *tricae* 'tricks, perplexities.' —**in·tri·cate·ly** *adv.*

in·tri·gant /'intri,gənt; aNtrē'gäN/ (also **in·tri·guant**) ▸*n.* a person who makes secret plans to do something illicit or detrimental to someone else. ▷late 18th cent.: variant of French *intriguant*, from *intriguer* 'to intrigue.'

in·tri·gante /'intri,gənt; aNtrē'gäNt/ ▸*n.* a female intrigant. ▷early 19th cent.: variant of French *intriguante*, from *intriguer* 'to intrigue.'

in·trigue ▸*v.* /in'trēg/ (**-trigues**, **-trigued**, **-tri·guing**) **1** [*trans.*] arouse the curiosity or interest of; fascinate: *I was intrigued by your question* | [as *adj.*] (**intriguing**) *the food is an intriguing combination of German and French.* **2** [*intrans.*] make secret plans to do something illicit or detrimental to someone: *the delegates were intriguing for their own gains.*

▸*n.* /'in,trēg/ **1** the secret planning of something illicit or detrimental to someone: *the cabinet was a nest of intrigue* | *the intrigues of local government officials.* ■ a secret love affair. **2** a mysterious or fascinating quality: *within the region's borders is a wealth of interest and intrigue.* ▷early 17th cent. (in the sense 'deceive, cheat'): from French *intrigue* 'plot,' *intriguer* 'to tangle, to plot,' via Italian from Latin *intricare* (see **INTRICATE**). Sense 1 of the verb, which was influenced by a later French sense 'to puzzle, make curious,' arose in the late 19th cent. —**in·tri·guer** *n.* —**in·tri·guing·ly** *adv.: the album is intriguingly titled "The Revenge of the Goldfish."*

in·trin·sic /in'trinzik; -sik/ ▸*adj.* belonging naturally; essential: *access to the arts is* ***intrinsic to a high quality of*** *life.* See note at **INHERENT**. ■ (of a muscle) contained wholly within the organ on which it acts. ▷late 15th cent. (in the general sense 'interior, inner'): from French *intrinsèque*, from late Latin *intrinsecus*, from the earlier adverb *intrinsecus* 'inwardly, inward.' —**in·trin·si·cal·ly** /-ik(ə)lē/ *adv.*

in·trin·sic fac·tor ▸*n. Biochemistry* a substance secreted by the stomach that enables the body to absorb vitamin B_{12}. It is a glycoprotein.

in·tro /'intrō/ ▸*n.* (*pl.* **-tros**) *informal* an introduction. ▷early 19th cent.: abbreviation.

intro. ▸*abbr.* ■ introduce or introduced or introducing or introduction or introductory.

intro- ▸*prefix* into; inward: *introgression* | *introvert.* ▷from Latin *intro* 'to the inside.'

in·tro·duce /,intrə'd(y)ōōs/ ▸*v.* [*trans.*] **1** (often **be introduced**) bring (something, esp. a product, measure, or concept) into use or operation for the first time: *various new taxes were introduced* | [*trans.*] *measures were introduced to help families with children.* ■ (**introduce something to**) bring a subject to the attention of (someone) for the first time: *the program is a bid to introduce opera to the masses.* ■ present (a new piece of legislation) for debate in a legislative assembly. ■ bring (a new plant, animal, or disease) to a place and establish it there: *a cold-resistant strain of sugar cane was* ***introduced to*** *Louisiana.* **2** make (someone) known by name to another in person, esp. formally: *I hope to introduce Jenny to them very soon.* **3** insert or bring into something: *a device that introduces chlorine into the pool automatically.* See note at **INSERT**. **4** occur at the start of; open: *a longer, more lyrical opening that introduces her first solo.* ■ (of a person) provide an opening explanation or announcement for (a television or radio program, book, etc.). ▷late Middle English (in the sense 'bring (a person) into a place or group'): from Latin *introducere*, from *intro-* 'to the inside' + *ducere* 'to lead.' —**in·tro·duc·er** *n.*

in·tro·duc·tion /,intrə'dəksHən/ ▸*n.* **1** the bringing of a product, measure, concept, etc., into use or operation for the first time: *issues arising from the introduction of new technology.* ■ the action of bringing a new plant, animal, or disease to a place: *the introduction of muskrats into central Europe.* ■ a thing, such as a product, measure, plant, etc., newly brought in: *these grains are valuable introductions from Sweden.* **2** (often **introductions**) a formal presentation of one person to another, in which each is told the other's name: *he returned to his desk, leaving Michael to make the introductions* | *a letter of introduction.* **3** a thing preliminary to something else: *your talk will need an introduction that states clearly what you are talking about and why.* ■ an explanatory section at the beginning of a book, report, etc. ■ a preliminary section in a piece of music, often thematically different from the main section. ■ a book or course of study intended to introduce a subject to a person: *it is a simple introduction to Euclidean geometry.* ■ [in *sing.*] a person's first experience of a subject or thing: ***my introduction to*** *drama was through an amateur dramatic society.* ▷late Middle English: from Latin *introductio(n-)*, from the verb *introducere* (see **INTRODUCE**).

in·tro·duc·to·ry /,intrə'dəktərē/ ▸*adj.* serving as an introduction to a subject or topic; basic or preliminary: *an introductory course in Russian.* ■ intended to persuade someone to purchase something for the first time: *we are making a special introductory offer of a reduced subscription.* ▷late Middle English (as a noun denoting an introductory text): from late Latin *introductorius*, from Latin *introducere* (see **INTRODUCE**).

in·tro·gres·sion /,intrə'gresHən/ ▸*n. Biology* the transfer of genetic information from one species to another as a result of hybridization between them and repeated backcrossing. ▷mid 17th cent.: from Latin *introgredi* 'step in,' from *intro-* 'to the inside' + *gradi* 'proceed, walk,' on the pattern of *egression, ingression.* —**in·tro·gres·sive** /-'gresiv/ *adj.*

in·tro·it /'in,trō-it; -,troit/ ▸*n.* a psalm or antiphon sung or said while the priest approaches the altar for the Eucharist. ▷late Middle English (denoting an entrance or the action of going in): via Old French from Latin *introitus*, from *introire* 'enter,' from *intro-* 'to the inside' + *ire* 'go.'

in·tro·jec·tion /,intrə'jeksHən/ ▸*n. Psychoanalysis* the unconscious adoption of the ideas or attitudes of others. ▷mid 19th cent.: from **INTRO-** 'into,' on the pattern of *projection.* —**in·tro·ject** /-'jekt/ *v.*

in·tro·mis·sion /,intrə'misHən/ ▸*n.* the action or process of inserting the penis into the vagina in sexual intercourse.

in·tro·mit·tent or·gan /,intrə'mitnt/ ▸*n. Zoology* the male copulatory organ of an animal. ▷mid 19th cent.: *intromittent* from Latin *intromittent-* 'introducing,' from the verb *intromittere*, from *intro-* 'to the inside' + *mittere* 'send.'

in·tron /'in,trän/ ▸*n. Biochemistry* a segment of a DNA or RNA molecule that does not code for proteins and interrupts the sequence of genes. Compare with **EXON**[1]. ▷1970s: from **INTRA-** 'within' + **-GENIC** + **-ON**. —**in·tron·ic** /in'tränik/ *adj.*

in·trorse /'in,trôrs/ ▸*adj. Botany & Zoology* turned inward. The opposite of **EXTRORSE**. ■ (of anthers) releasing their pollen toward the center of the flower. ▷mid 19th cent.: from Latin *introrsus*, from *introversus* 'turned inward.' —**in·trorse·ly** *adv.*

in·tro·scan /'intrō,skan/ ▸*n.* a facility on some CD players that allows the first few seconds of each track to be played in turn in order to identify the required track.

in·tro·spect /,intrə'spekt/ ▸*v.* [*intrans.*] examine one's own thoughts or feelings: *what they don't do is introspect much about the reasons for their plight.* ▷late 17th cent.: from Latin *introspect-* 'looked into,' from the verb *introspicere*, or from *introspectare* 'keep looking into.'

in·tro·spec·tion /,intrə'speksHən/ ▸*n.* the examination or observation of one's own mental and emotional processes: *quiet introspection can be extremely valuable.* —**in·tro·spec·tive** /-'spektiv/ *adj.* —**in·tro·spec·tive·ly** /-'spektiv-lē/ *adv.* —**in·tro·spec·tive·ness** /-'spektivnis/ *n.*

in·tro·vert /'intrə,vərt/ ▸*n.* a shy, reticent, and typically self-centered person. ■ *Psychology* a person predominantly concerned with their own thoughts and feelings rather than with external things. Compare with **EXTROVERT**.

▸*adj.* another term for **INTROVERTED**. ▷mid 17th cent. (as a verb in the general sense 'turn one's thoughts inward [in spiritual contemplation]'): from modern Latin *introvertere*, from *intro-* 'to the inside' + *vertere*

I

'to turn.' Its use as a term in psychology dates from the early 20th cent. —**in·tro·ver·sion** /-ˌvərZHən/ *n.* —**in·tro·ver·sive** /-ˌvərsiv/ *adj.*

in·tro·vert·ed /'intrəˌvərtid/ ▶*adj.* **1** of, denoting, or typical of an introvert. ■ (of a community, company, or other group) concerned principally with its own affairs; inward-looking or parochial. **2** *Anatomy & Zoology* (of an organ or other body part) turned or pushed inward on itself.

in·trude /in'trōōd/ ▶*v.* **1** [*intrans.*] put oneself deliberately into a place or situation where one is unwelcome or uninvited: *he had no right to* **intrude into** *their lives | she felt awkward at* **intruding on** *private grief.* ■ enter with disruptive or adverse effect: *politics quickly* **intrude into** *the booklet.* ■ [*trans.*] introduce into a situation with disruptive or adverse effect: *to* **intrude** *political criteria* **into** *military decisions risks reducing efficiency.* **2** [*trans.*] *Geology* (of igneous rock) be forced or thrust into (a preexisting formation): *the granite may have intruded these rock layers.* ■ (usu. **be intruded**) force or thrust (igneous rock) into a preexisting formation. ▷mid 16th cent. (in the sense 'usurp an office or right'; originally as *entrude*): from Latin *intrudere*, from *in-* 'into' + *trudere* 'to thrust.'

in·trud·er /in'trōōdər/ ▶*n.* a person who intrudes, esp. into a building with criminal intent.

in·tru·sion /in'trōōZHən/ ▶*n.* **1** the action of intruding: *he was furious about this intrusion into his private life | unacceptable intrusions of privacy.* ■ a thing that intrudes: *they oppose the excavations as an intrusion on their heritage.* **2** *Geology* the action or process of forcing a body of igneous rock between or through existing formations, without reaching the surface. ■ a body of igneous rock that has intruded the surrounding strata. ▷late Middle English (in the sense 'invasion, usurpation'): from medieval Latin *intrusio(n-)*, from Latin *intrudere* 'thrust in' (see **INTRUDE**).

in·tru·sive /in'trōōsiv/ ▶*adj.* **1** making an unwelcome manifestation with disruptive or adverse effect: *that was an intrusive question | tourist attractions that are environmentally intrusive.* ■ (of a person) disturbing another by one's uninvited or unwelcome presence: *giving people information about their health without being too intrusive.* See note at **IMPERTINENT**. **2** *Phonetics* (of a sound) pronounced between words or syllables to facilitate pronunciation, such as an *r* in *saw a movie*, which occurs in the speech of some eastern New Englanders and metropolitan New Yorkers. **3** *Geology* of, relating to, or formed by intrusion. —**in·tru·sive·ly** *adv.* —**in·tru·sive·ness** *n.*

in·trust /in'trəst/ ▶*v.* archaic spelling of **ENTRUST**.

in·tu·bate /'int(y)ŏŏˌbāt/ ▶*v.* [*trans.*] *Medicine* insert a tube into (a person or a body part, esp. the trachea for ventilation). ▷late 19th cent.: from **IN-**[2] 'into' + Latin *tuba* 'tube' + **-ATE**[3]. —**in·tu·ba·tion** /ˌint(y)ŏŏ'bāSHən/ *n.*

in·tu·it /in't(y)ōō-it/ ▶*v.* [*trans.*] understand or work out by instinct: *I intuited his real identity.* ▷late 18th cent. (in the sense 'instruct, teach'): from Latin *intuit-* 'contemplated,' from the verb *intueri*, from *in-* 'upon' + *tueri* 'to look.' —**in·tu·it·a·ble** *adj.*

in·tu·i·tion /ˌint(y)ōō'iSHən/ ▶*n.* the ability to understand something immediately, without the need for conscious reasoning: *we shall allow our intuition to guide us.* ■ a thing that one knows or considers likely from instinctive feeling rather than conscious reasoning: *your insights and intuitions as a native speaker are positively sought.* ▷late Middle English (denoting spiritual insight or immediate spiritual communication): from late Latin *intuitio(n-)*, from Latin *intueri* 'consider' (see **INTUIT**). —**in·tu·i·tion·al** /-'iSHənl/ *adj.* —**in·tu·i·tion·al·ly** /-'iSHənl-ē/ *adv.*

in·tu·i·tion·ism /ˌint(y)ōō'iSHəˌnizəm/ (also **in·tu·i·tion·al·ism** /-'iSHənlˌizəm/) ▶*n.* *Philosophy* the theory that primary truths and principles (esp. those of ethics and metaphysics) are known directly by intuition. ■ the theory that mathematical knowledge is based on intuition and mental construction, rejecting certain modes of reasoning and the notion of independent mathematical objects. —**in·tu·i·tion·ist** *n.* & *adj.*

in·tu·i·tive /in't(y)ōōitiv/ ▶*adj.* using or based on what one feels to be true even without conscious reasoning; instinctive: *I had an intuitive conviction that there was something unsound in him.* ■ (chiefly of computer software) easy to use and understand. ▷late 15th cent. (originally used of sight, in the sense 'accurate, unerring'): from medieval Latin *intuitivus*, from Latin *intueri* (see **INTUIT**). —**in·tu·i·tive·ly** *adv.* —**in·tu·i·tive·ness** *n.*

in·tu·mesce /ˌint(y)ōō'mes/ ▶*v.* [*intrans.*] *rare* swell up. ▷late 18th cent.: from Latin *intumescere*, from *in-* 'into' + *tumescere* 'begin to swell' (from *tumere* 'swell'). —**in·tu·mes·cence** /-'mesəns/ *n.*

in·tu·mes·cent /ˌint(y)ōō'mesənt/ ▶*adj.* (of a coating or sealant) swelling up when heated, thus protecting the material underneath or sealing a gap in the event of a fire: *intumescent fire-retardant paints.*

in·tus·sus·cep·tion /ˌintəsə'sepSHən/ ▶*n.* **1** *Medicine* the inversion of one portion of the intestine within another. **2** *Botany* the growth of a cell wall by the deposition of cellulose: *the area of the surface increases uniformly by intussusception.* ▷early 18th cent. (in the sense 'absorption'): from modern Latin *intussusceptio(n-)*, from Latin *intus* 'within' + *susceptio(n-)* (from *suscipere* 'take up').

in·twine /in'twīn/ ▶*v.* archaic spelling of **ENTWINE**.

In·u·it /'in(y)ōō-it/ ▶*n.* **1** (*pl.* same or **-its**) a member of an indigenous people of northern Canada and parts of Greenland and Alaska. **2** the family of languages of this people, one of the three branches of the Eskimo-Aleut language family. It is also known, esp. to its speakers, as **Inuktitut**.
▶*adj.* of or relating to the Inuit or their language. ▷Inuit, plural of *inuk* 'person.'

USAGE The peoples inhabiting the regions from northwestern Canada to western Greenland speak **Inuit** languages (**Inuit** in Canada, **Greenlandic** in Greenland) and call themselves **Inuit** (not **Eskimo**), and **Inuit** now has official status in Canada. By analogy, **Inuit** is also used in the U.S., usually in an attempt to be politically correct, as a general synonym for **Eskimo**. This, however, is inaccurate because there are no **Inuit** in Alaska and **Inuit** therefore cannot include people from Alaska (who speak **Inupiaq**, which is closely related to **Inuit**, or **Yupik**, which is also spoken in Siberia). Since neither **Inupiaq** nor **Yupik** is in common U.S. usage, only **Eskimo** includes all of these peoples and their languages.
See also **usage at ESKIMO**.

I·nuk·ti·tut /i'n(y)ōōktiˌtōōt/ (also **I·nuk·ti·tuk** /-tōōk/) ▶*n.* the Inuit language spoken in the central and eastern Canadian arctic. ▷Inuit, literally 'the Inuk way,' used as the title of a periodical.

in·u·lin /'inyəlin/ ▶*n.* *Biochemistry* a complex of sugar present in the roots of various plants and used medically to test kidney function. It is a polysaccharide based on fructose. ▷early 19th cent.: from Latin *inula* (identified by medieval herbalists with elecampane) + **-IN**[1].

in·unc·tion /i'nəNG(k)SHən/ ▶*n.* chiefly *Medicine* the rubbing of ointment or oil into the skin. ▷late 15th cent.: from Latin *inunctio(n-)*, from *inunguere* 'smear on.'

in·un·date /'inənˌdāt/ ▶*v.* [*trans.*] (usu. **be inundated**) flood: *the islands may be the first to be inundated as sea levels rise.* ■ *figurative* overwhelm (someone) with things or people to be dealt with: *we've been* **inundated with** *complaints from listeners.* ▷late 16th cent.: from Latin *inundat-* 'flooded,' from the verb *inundare*, from *in-* 'into, upon' + *undare* 'to flow' (from *unda* 'a wave'). —**in·un·da·tion** /ˌinən'dāSHən/ *n.*

I·nu·pi·aq /i'n(y)ōōpēˌak/ (also **I·nu·pi·at** /-ˌat/, **I·nu·pik** /i'n(y)ōōpik/) ▶*n.* (*pl.* Inupiat) **1** a member of a group of the Eskimo people inhabiting northwestern Alaska. **2** the language of this people.
▶*adj.* of or relating to this people or their language. ▷Inupiaq, from *inuk* 'person' + *piaq* 'genuine.'

USAGE See **usage at INUIT**.

in·ure /i'n(y)ŏŏr/ (also **en·ure**) ▶*v.* **1** [*trans.*] (usu. **be inured to**) accustom (someone) to something, esp. something unpleasant: *these children have been inured to violence.* **2** [*intrans.*] (**enure for/to**) *Law* come into operation; take effect: *a release given to one of two joint contractors inures to the benefit of both.* ▷late Middle English *inure, enure*, from an Anglo-Norman French phrase meaning 'in use or practice,' from *en* 'in' + Old French *euvre* 'work' (from Latin *opera*). —**in·ure·ment** *n.*

in·urn /in'ərn/ (also **en·urn**) ▶*v.* [*trans.*] place or bury (something, esp. ashes after cremation) in an urn. —**in·urn·ment** *n.*

in u·ter·o /in 'yōōtərō/ ▶*adv.* & *adj.* in a woman's uterus; before birth: [as *adv.*] *this damage may occur in utero* | [as *adj.*] *the in utero development of the gastrointestinal tract.* ▷Latin.

in·u·tile /in'yōōtl; -'yōōˌtīl/ ▶*adj.* useless; pointless. ▷late Middle English: from Old French, from Latin *inutilis*, from *in-* 'not' + *utilis* 'useful.' —**in·u·til·i·ty** /ˌinyōō'tilitē/ *n.*

inv. ▶*abbr.* ■ invent or invented or invention or inventor. ■ inventory. ■ investment. ■ invoice.

in·vac·u·ate /in'vakyōōˌāt/ ▶*v.* [*trans.*] confine (people) to a space in an emergency: *these buildings can now invacuate tenants to safe havens within the building.* ▷on the pattern of *evacuate*. —**in·vac·u·a·tion** /inˌvakyōō'āSHən/ *n.*

in va·cu·o /in 'vakyəˌwō/ ▶*adv.* in a vacuum: *the hydrochloric acid was removed by evaporation in vacuo.* ■ away from or without the normal context or environment: *instead of dealing with individual aspects of lifestyle in vacuo, social factors are taken into account.* ▷Latin.

in·vade /in'vād/ ▶*v.* [*trans.*] (of an armed force or its commander) enter (a country or region) so as to subjugate or occupy it: *Iraq's intention to invade Kuwait* | [*intrans.*] *they would invade at dawn.* ■ enter (a place, situation, or sphere of activity) in large numbers, esp. with intrusive effect: *demonstrators invaded the presidential palace.* ■ (of a parasite or disease) spread into (an organism or bodily part). ■ (of a person or emotion) encroach or intrude on: *he felt his privacy was being invaded.* ▷late Middle English (in the sense 'attack or assault [a person]'): from Latin *invadere*, from *in-* 'into' + *vadere* 'go.' —**in·vad·er** *n.*

in·vag·i·nate /in'vajəˌnāt/ ▶*v.* (**be invaginated**) chiefly *Anatomy & Biology* be turned inside out or folded back on itself to form a cavity or pouch. ▷mid 17th cent.: back-formation from **INVAGINATION**.

in·vag·i·na·tion /inˌvajə'nāSHən/ ▶*n.* chiefly *Anatomy & Biology* the action or process of being turned inside out or folded back on itself to form a cavity or pouch. ■ a cavity or pouch so formed. ▷mid 17th cent.: from modern Latin *invaginatio(n-)*, based on **IN-**[2] 'into' + Latin *vagina* 'sheath.'

in·va·lid[1] /'invəlid/ ▶*n.* a person made weak or disabled by illness or injury: [as *adj.*] *an invalid husband.*
▶*v.* (**-lid·ed, -lid·ing**) [*trans.*] (usu. **be invalided**) remove (someone) from active service in the armed forces because of injury or illness: *he was badly wounded and* **invalided out** *of the infantry.* ■ disable (someone) by injury or illness. ▷mid 17th cent. (as an adjective in the sense 'infirm or disabled'): a special sense of **INVALID**[2], with a change of pronunciation. —**in·va·lid·ism** /-ˌizəm/ *n.*

in·val·id[2] /in'valid/ ▶*adj.* not valid, in particular: ■ (esp. of an official document or procedure) not legally recognized and therefore void because contravening a regulation or law: *the vote was declared invalid due to a technicality.* ■ (esp. of an argument, statement, or theory) not true because based on erroneous information or unsound reasoning: *a comparison is invalid if we are not comparing like with like.* ■ (of computer instructions, data, etc.) not conforming to the correct format or specifications. ▷mid 16th cent. (earlier than *valid*): from Latin *invalidus*, from *in-* 'not' + *validus* 'strong' (see **VALID**). —**in·val·id·ly** *adv.*

in·val·i·date /in'valiˌdāt/ ▶*v.* [*trans.*] **1** make (an argument, statement, or theory) unsound or erroneous. **2** deprive (an official document or procedure) of legal efficacy because of contravention of a regulation or law: *a technical flaw in her papers invalidated her nomination.* See note at **VOID**. ▷mid 17th cent.: from medieval Latin *invalidat-* 'annulled,' from the verb *invalidare* (based on Latin *validus* 'strong'). —**in·val·i·da·tion** /-ˌvali'dāSHən/ *n.* —**in·val·i·da·tor** /-ˌdātər/ *n.*

in·va·lid·i·ty /ˌinvə'liditē/ ▶*n.* **1** the fact of not being valid: *the invalidity of their independence declaration.* **2** chiefly *Brit.* the condition of being an invalid.

in·val·u·a·ble /in'valyōōəbəl/ ▶*adj.* extremely useful; indispensable: *an invaluable source of information.* —**in·val·u·a·ble·ness** *n.* —**in·val·u·a·bly** /-blē/ *adv.*

In·var /'inˌvär/ ▶*n.* *trademark* an alloy of iron and nickel with a negligible coefficient of expansion, used in the making of clocks and scientific instruments. ▷early 20th cent.: abbreviation of **INVARIABLE**.

in·var·i·a·ble /in've(ə)rēəbəl/ ▶*adj.* never changing: *disillusion was the almost invariable result.* ■ (of a noun in an inflected language) having the same form in both the singular and the plural, e.g., *sheep*. ■ *Mathematics* (of a quantity) constant. ▷late Middle English: from French, or from late Latin *invariabilis*, from *in-* 'not' + *variabilis* (see **VARIABLE**). —**in·var·i·a·bil·i·ty** /-ˌve(ə)rēə'bilitē/ *n.* —**in·var·i·a·ble·ness** *n.*

in·var·i·a·bly /in've(ə)rēəblē/ ▶*adv.* in every case or on every occasion; always: *the meals here are invariably big and hearty.*

in·var·i·ant /in've(ə)rēənt/ ▶*adj.* never changing: *the pattern of cell divisions was found to be invariant.*

▸*n.* *Mathematics* a function, quantity, or property that remains unchanged when a specified transformation is applied. —**in·var·i·ance** *n.*

in·va·sion /in'vāzhən/ ▸*n.* an instance of invading a country or region with an armed force: *the Soviet invasion of Czechoslovakia | in 1546 England had to be defended from invasion.* ■ an incursion by a large number of people or things into a place or sphere of activity: *stadium guards are preparing for another invasion of fans.* ■ an unwelcome intrusion into another's domain: *random drug testing of employees is an unwarranted invasion of privacy.* ■ the infestation of a body by harmful organisms: *a bacterial invasion.* ▷late Middle English: from late Latin *invasio(n-)*, from the verb *invadere* (see **INVADE**).

in·va·sive /in'vāsiv/ ▸*adj.* (esp. of plants or a disease) tending to spread prolifically and undesirably or harmfully. ■ (esp. of an action or sensation) tending to intrude on a person's thoughts or privacy: *the sound of the piano was invasive.* ■ (of medical procedures) involving the introduction of instruments or other objects into the body or body cavities: *minimally invasive surgery.* ▷late Middle English: from obsolete French *invasif, -ive* or medieval Latin *invasivus*, from Latin *invadere* (see **INVADE**).

in·vect·ed /in'vektid/ ▸*adj.* [usu. *postpositive*] *Heraldry* having convex semicircular projections along the edge. Compare with **ENGRAILED**.

in·vec·tive /in'vektiv/ ▸*n.* insulting, abusive, or highly critical language: *he let out a stream of invective.* ▷late Middle English (originally as an adjective meaning 'reviling, abusive'): from Old French *invectif, -ive*, from late Latin *invectivus* 'attacking,' from *invehere* (see **INVEIGH**). The noun is from late Latin *invectiva (oratio)* 'abusive or censorious (language).'

in·veigh /in'vā/ ▸*v.* [*intrans.*] (**inveigh against**) speak or write about (something) with great hostility: *Marx inveighed against the evils of the property-owning classes.* ▷late 15th cent. (in the sense 'carry in, introduce'; formerly also as *enveigh*): from Latin *invehere* 'carry in,' *invehi* 'be carried into, assail,' from *in-* 'into' + *vehere* 'carry.'

in·vei·gle /in'vāgəl/ ▸*v.* [*trans.*] persuade (someone) to do something by means of deception or flattery: *we cannot inveigle him into putting pen to paper.* See note at **TEMPT.** ■ (**inveigle oneself** or **one's way into**) gain entrance to (a place) by using such methods. ▷late 15th cent. (in the sense 'beguile, deceive'; formerly also as *enveigle*): from Anglo-Norman French *envegler*, alteration of Old French *aveugler* 'to blind,' from *aveugle* 'blind.' —**in·vei·gle·ment** *n.*

in·vent /in'vent/ ▸*v.* [*trans.*] create or design (something that has not existed before); be the originator of: *he invented an improved form of the steam engine.* ■ make up (an idea, name, story, etc.), esp. so as to deceive: *I did not have to invent any tales about my past.* ▷late 15th cent. (in the sense 'find out, discover'): from Latin *invent-* 'contrived, discovered,' from the verb *invenire*, from *in-* 'into' + *venire* 'come.'

in·ven·tion /in'venshən/ ▸*n.* the action of inventing something, typically a process or device: *the invention of printing in the 15th century.* ■ something, typically a process or device, that has been invented: *medieval inventions included spectacles for reading and the spinning wheel.* ■ creative ability: *his powers of invention were rather limited.* ■ something fabricated or made up: *you know my story is an invention.* ■ used as a title for a short piece of music: *Bach's two-part Inventions.* ▷Middle English (in the sense 'finding out, discovery'): from Latin *inventio(n-)*, from *invenire* 'discover' (see **INVENT**).

in·ven·tive /in'ventiv/ ▸*adj.* (of a person) having the ability to create or design new things or to think originally: *she is the most inventive painter around.* See note at **CREATIVE.** ■ (of a product, process, action, etc.) showing creativity or original thought: *methods of communication during the war were diverse and inventive.* ▷late Middle English: from French *inventif, -ive* or medieval Latin *inventivus*, from Latin *invenire* 'discover' (see **INVENT**). —**in·ven·tive·ly** *adv.* —**in·ven·tive·ness** *n.*

in·ven·tor /in'ventər/ ▸*n.* a person who invented a particular process or device or who invents things as an occupation.

in·ven·to·ry /'invən,tôrē/ ▸*n.* (*pl.* **-ries**) a complete list of items such as property, goods in stock, or the contents of a building. ■ a quantity of goods held in stock: *in our warehouse you'll find a large inventory of new and used bicycles.* ■ (in accounting) the entire stock of a business, including materials, components, work in progress, and finished products.
▸*v.* (**-ries, -ried**) [*trans.*] make a complete list of. ■ enter in a list: *about forty possible sites were inventoried.* ▷late Middle English: from medieval Latin *inventorium*, alteration of late Latin *inventarium*, literally 'a list of what is found,' from Latin *invenire* 'come upon.'

in·ve·rac·i·ty /,invə'rasitē/ ▸*n.* (*pl.* **-ties**) a lie. ■ untruthfulness.

In·ver·ness[1] /,invər'nes/ a city in Scotland, at the mouth of the Ness River; pop. 41,000.

In·ver·ness[2] ▸*n.* a sleeveless cloak with a removable cape.

Inverness[2]

in·verse /'invərs; in'vərs/ ▸*adj.* [*attrib.*] opposite or contrary in position, direction, order, or effect: *the well-observed inverse relationship between disability and social contact.* ■ *chiefly Mathematics* produced from or related to something else by a process of inversion.
▸*n.* [usu. in *sing.*] something that is the opposite or reverse of something else: *his approach is the inverse of most research on ethnic and racial groups.* ■ *Mathematics* a reciprocal quantity, mathematical expression, geometric figure, etc., that is the result of inversion. ■ *Mathematics* an element that, when combined with a given element in an operation, produces the identity element for that operation. ▷late Middle English: from Latin *inversus*, past participle of *invertere* (see **INVERT**). —**in·verse·ly** *adv.*

in·verse pro·por·tion (also **inverse ratio**) ▸*n.* a relation between two quantities such that one increases in proportion as the other decreases.

in·verse square law ▸*n.* *Physics* a law stating that the intensity of an effect such as illumination or gravitational force changes in inverse proportion to the square of the distance from the source.

in·ver·sion /in'vərzhən/ ▸*n.* **1** the action of inverting something or the state of being inverted: *the inversion of the normal domestic arrangement.* ■ reversal of the normal order of words, typically for rhetorical effect but also found in the regular formation of questions in English. ■ *Music* the process of inverting an interval, chord, or phrase. ■ *Music* an inverted interval, chord, or phrase. ■ *Physics* (also **population inversion**) a transposition in the relative numbers of atoms, molecules, etc., occupying particular energy levels. ■ *Chemistry* a reaction causing a change from one optically active configuration to the opposite configuration, esp. the hydrolysis of dextrose to give a levorotatory solution of fructose and glucose. ■ *Physics* the conversion of direct current into alternating current. **2** (also **temperature inversion** or **thermal inversion**) a reversal of the normal decrease of air temperature with altitude, or of water temperature with depth. ■ (also **inversion layer**) a layer of the atmosphere in which temperature increases with height. **3** *Mathematics* the process of finding a quantity, function, etc., from a given one such that the product of the two under a particular operation is the identity. ■ the interchanging of numerator and denominator of a fraction, or antecedent and consequent of a ratio. ■ the process of finding the expression that gives a given expression under a given transformation. ■ *Geometry* a transformation in which each point of a given figure is replaced by another point on the same straight line from a fixed point, esp. in such a way that the product of the distances of the two points from the center of inversion is constant. **4** (also **sexual inversion**) *dated Psychology,* the adoption of behavior typical of the opposite sex; homosexuality. ▷mid 16th cent. (as a term in rhetoric, denoting the turning of an argument against the person who put it forward): from Latin *inversio(n-)*, from the verb *invertere* (see **INVERT**). —**in·ver·sive** /-'vərsiv/ *adj.*

in·vert ▸*v.* /in'vərt/ [*trans.*] put upside down or in the opposite position, order, or arrangement: *invert the mousse onto a serving plate.* ■ *Music* modify (a phrase) by reversing the direction of pitch changes. ■ *Music* alter (an interval or triad) by changing the relative position of the notes in it. ■ *chiefly Mathematics* subject to inversion; transform into its inverse.
▸*n.* /'invərt/ **1** an arch constructed in an upside-down position to provide lateral support, e.g., in a tunnel. ■ the concave lower surface of a sewer or drain. **2** *dated Psychology,* a person showing sexual inversion; a homosexual. **3** *Philately* a postage stamp printed with an error such that part of its design is upside down. ▷mid 16th cent. (in the sense 'turn back to front'): from Latin *invertere*, literally 'turn inside out,' from *in-* 'into' + *vertere* 'to turn.' —**in·vert·i·bil·i·ty** /in,vərtə'bilitē/ *n.* —**in·vert·i·ble** *adj.*

in·vert·ase /in'vərtās; 'invər,tās; -,tāz/ ▸*n.* *Biochemistry* an enzyme produced by yeast that catalyzes the hydrolysis of sucrose, forming invert sugar. Also called **SUCRASE**.

in·ver·te·brate /in'vərtəbrit; -,brāt/ ▸*n.* an animal lacking a backbone, such as an arthropod, mollusk, annelid, coelenterate, etc. The invertebrates constitute an artificial division of the animal kingdom, comprising 95 percent of animal species and about 30 different phyla. Compare with **VERTEBRATE.**
▸*adj.* of, relating to, or belonging to this division of animals. ■ *humorous* irresolute; spineless: *so invertebrate is today's Congress regarding foreign policy responsibilities.* ▷early 19th cent. (as a noun): from modern Latin *invertebrata* (plural) 'the invertebrates' (former taxonomic group), from French *invertébrés*, from *in-* 'without' + Latin *vertebra* (see **VERTEBRA**).

in·vert·ed com·ma ▸*n.* *chiefly Brit.* another term for **QUOTATION MARK**.

in·vert·ed snob·ber·y ▸*n.* *derogatory* the attitude of seeming to despise anything associated with wealth or social status, while at the same time elevating those things associated with lack of wealth and social position. —**in·vert·ed snob** *n.*

in·vert·er /in'vərtər/ ▸*n.* **1** an apparatus that converts direct current into alternating current. **2** *Electronics* a device that converts either of the two binary digits or signals into the other.

in·vert sug·ar ▸*n.* a mixture of glucose and fructose obtained by the hydrolysis of sucrose. ▷late 19th cent.: *invert* from *inverted*, because of the reversal of optical activity involved in its formation (see the chemical sense of **INVERSION**.)

in·vest /in'vest/ ▸*v.* **1** [*intrans.*] expend money with the expectation of achieving a profit or material result by putting it into financial schemes, shares, or property, or by using it to develop a commercial venture: *getting workers to* ***invest in*** *private pension funds* | [*trans.*] *the company is to* ***invest*** *$12 million* ***in*** *its new manufacturing site.* ■ [*trans.*] devote (one's time, effort, or energy) to a particular undertaking with the expectation of a worthwhile result: *politicians who have* ***invested*** *so much time* ***in*** *the Constitution would be crestfallen.* ■ [*intrans.*] (**invest in**) *informal* buy (something) whose usefulness will repay the cost. **2** [*trans.*] (**invest someone/something with**) provide or endow someone or something with (a particular quality or attribute): *the passage of time has invested the words with an unintended humor.* ■ endow someone with (a rank or office). ■ (**invest something in**) establish a right or power in. **3** [*trans.*] *archaic* clothe or cover with a garment: *he stands before you* ***invested in*** *the full canonicals of his calling.* **4** [*trans.*] *archaic* surround (a place) in order to besiege or blockade it: *Fort Pulaski was invested and captured.* ▷mid 16th cent. (in the senses 'clothe,' 'clothe with the insignia of a rank,' and 'endow with authority'): from French *investir* or Latin *investire*, from *in-* 'into, upon' + *vestire* 'clothe' (from *vestis* 'clothing'). Sense 1 (early 17th cent.) is influenced by Italian *investire*. —**in·vest·a·ble** *adj.* —**in·vest·i·ble** *adj.* —**in·ves·tor** /-'vestər/ *n.*

in·ves·ti·ga·ble /in'vestigəbəl/ ▸*adj.* open to investigation, inquiry, or research. ▷late 16th cent.: from late Latin *investigabilis*, from *investigare* (see **INVESTIGATE**).

in·ves·ti·gate /in'vesti,gāt/ ▸*v.* [*trans.*] carry out a systematic or formal inquiry to discover and examine the facts of (an incident, allegation, etc.) so as to establish the truth: *police are investigating the alleged beating.* ■ carry out research or study into (a subject, typically one in a scientific or academic field) so as to discover facts or information: [with *clause*] *future studies will investigate whether long-term use of the drugs could prevent cancer.* ■ make inquiries as to the character, activities, or background of (someone): *everyone with a possible interest in your brother's death must be thoroughly investigated.* ■ [*intrans.*] make a check to find out something: *when you didn't turn up, I thought I'd better come back to investigate.* ▷early 16th cent.: from Latin *investigat-* 'traced out,' from the verb *investigare*, from *in-* 'into' + *vestigare* 'track, trace out.' —**in·ves·ti·ga·tor** /-,gātər/ *n.* —**in·ves·ti·ga·to·ry** /-gə,tôrē/ *adj.*

in·ves·ti·ga·tion /in,vesti'gāshən/ ▸*n.* the action of investigating something or someone; formal or systematic examination or research: *he is* ***under investigation*** *for receiving illicit funds.* ■ a formal inquiry or systematic study: *an* ***investigation*** *has been launched* ***into*** *the potential impact of the oil spill.* ▷late Middle English: from Latin *investigatio(n-)*, from the verb *investigare* (see INVESTIGATE). —**in·ves·ti·ga·tion·al** /-SHənl/ *adj.*

in·ves·ti·ga·tive /inˈvesti,gātiv/ (also **in·ves·ti·ga·to·ry** /-gə,tôrē/) ▶*adj.* of or concerned with investigating something: *a special investigative committee to look into the strikers' demands.* ■ (of journalism or a journalist) inquiring intensively into and seeking to expose malpractice, the miscarriage of justice, or other controversial issues.

in·ves·ti·ture /inˈvesticHər; -,cHŏŏr/ ▶*n.* **1** the action of formally investing a person with honors or rank: *the investiture of bishops.* ■ a ceremony at which honors or rank are formally conferred on a particular person. **2** the action of clothing or robing. ■ a thing that clothes or covers. ▷late Middle English: from medieval Latin *investitura*, from *investire* (see INVEST).

in·vest·ment /inˈves(t)mənt/ ▶*n.* **1** the action or process of investing money for profit or material result: *a debate over private* ***investment in*** *road-building | a total investment of $50,000.* ■ a thing that is worth buying because it may be profitable or useful in the future: *a used car is rarely a good investment.* ■ an act of devoting time, effort, or energy to a particular undertaking with the expectation of a worthwhile result: *the time spent in attending a one-day seminar is an investment in our professional futures.* **2** *archaic* the surrounding of a place by a hostile force in order to besiege or blockade it.

in·vest·ment bank ▶*n.* a bank that purchases large holdings of newly issued shares and resells them to investors. —**in·vest·ment bank·er** *n.* —**in·vest·ment bank·ing** *n.*

in·vest·ment cast·ing ▶*n. technical* a technique for making small, accurate castings in refractory alloys using a mold formed around a pattern of wax or similar material which is then removed by melting.

in·vest·ment grade ▶*n.* a level of credit rating for stocks regarded as carrying a minimal risk to investors.

in·vest·ment trust ▶*n.* a limited company whose business is the investment of shareholders' funds, the shares being traded like those of any other public company.

in·vet·er·ate /inˈvetərit/ ▶*adj.* [*attrib.*] having a particular habit, activity, or interest that is long-established and unlikely to change: *he was an inveterate gambler.* ■ (of a feeling or habit) long-established and unlikely to change. ▷late Middle English (referring to disease, in the sense 'of long standing, chronic'): from Latin *inveteratus* 'made old,' past participle of *inveterare* (based on *vetus, veter-* 'old'). —**in·vet·er·a·cy** /-rəsē/ *n.* —**in·vet·er·ate·ly** *adv.*

in·vid·i·ous /inˈvidēəs/ ▶*adj.* (of an action or situation) likely to arouse or incur resentment or anger in others: *she'd put herself in an invidious position.* ■ (of a comparison or distinction) unfairly discriminating; unjust: *it seems invidious to make special mention of one aspect of his work.* ▷early 17th cent.: from Latin *invidiosus*, from *invidia* (see ENVY). —**in·vid·i·ous·ly** *adv.* —**in·vid·i·ous·ness** *n.*

in·vig·i·late /inˈvijə,lāt/ ▶*v.* [*intrans.*] *Brit.* supervise candidates during an examination. ▷mid 16th cent. (in the general sense 'watch over, keep watch'): from Latin *invigilat-* 'watched over,' from the verb *invigilare*, from *in-* 'upon, toward' + *vigilare* 'watch' (from *vigil* 'watchful'). —**in·vig·i·la·tion** /-,vijəˈlāSHən/ *n.* —**in·vig·i·la·tor** /-,lātər/ *n.*

in·vig·or·ate /inˈvigə,rāt/ ▶*v.* [*trans.*] give strength or energy to: *the shower had invigorated her* | [as *adj.*] (**invigorating**) *a brisk, invigorating walk.* See note at QUICKEN. ▷mid 17th cent.: from medieval Latin *invigorat-* 'made strong,' from the verb *invigorare*, from *in-* 'toward' + Latin *vigorare* 'make strong' (from *vigor* 'vigor'). —**in·vig·or·at·ing·ly** *adv.* —**in·vig·or·a·tion** /-,vigəˈrāSHən/ *n.* —**in·vig·or·a·tor** /-,rātər/ *n.*

in·vin·ci·ble /inˈvinsəbəl/ ▶*adj.* too powerful to be defeated or overcome: *an invincible warrior.* ▷late Middle English (earlier than *vincible*): via Old French from Latin *invincibilis*, from *in-* 'not' + *vincibilis* (see VINCIBLE). —**in·vin·ci·bil·i·ty** /-,vinsəˈbilitē/ *n.* —**in·vin·ci·bly** /-blē/ *adv.*

in vi·no ve·ri·tas /in ˈvēnō ˈveri,täs; ˈvīnō ˈveri,tas/ ▶*exclam.* under the influence of alcohol, a person tells the truth. ▷Latin, literally 'truth in wine.'

in·vi·o·la·ble /inˈvīələbəl/ ▶*adj.* never to be broken, infringed, or dishonored: *an inviolable rule of chastity | the Polish–German border was inviolable.* ▷late Middle English: from French, or from Latin *inviolabilis*, from *in-* 'not' + *violabilis* 'able to be violated' (from the verb *violare*). —**in·vi·o·la·bil·i·ty** /-,vīələˈbilitē/ *n.* —**in·vi·o·la·bly** /-blē/ *adv.*

in·vi·o·late /inˈvīəlit/ ▶*adj.* free or safe from injury or violation: *an international memorial which must remain inviolate.* ▷late Middle English: from Latin *inviolatus*, from *in-* 'not' + *violare* 'violate.' —**in·vi·o·la·cy** /-ləsē/ *n.* —**in·vi·o·late·ly** *adv.*

in·vis·cid /inˈvisid/ ▶*adj. Physics* having no or negligible viscosity.

in·vis·i·ble /inˈvizəbəl/ ▶*adj.* unable to be seen; not visible to the eye: *this invisible gas is present to some extent in every home.* ■ concealed from sight; hidden: *he lounged in a doorway, invisible in the dark.* ■ *figurative* (of a person) treated as if unable to be seen; ignored or not taken into consideration: *before 1971, women artists were pretty well invisible.* ■ *Economics* relating to or denoting earnings that a country makes from the sale of services or other items not constituting tangible commodities: *tourism is the most important of our invisible exports.*
▶*n.* an invisible thing, person, or being: *religion is the attempt to eternalize* ***the invisible.*** ■ (**invisibles**) invisible exports and imports. ▷Middle English: from Old French, or from Latin *invisibilis*, from *in-* 'not' + *visibilis* (see VISIBLE). —**in·vis·i·bil·i·ty** /-,vizəˈbilitē/ *n.* —**in·vis·i·bly** /-blē/ *adv.*

in·vis·i·ble ink ▶*n.* a type of ink used to produce writing that cannot be seen until the paper is heated or otherwise treated.

in·vi·ta·tion /,inviˈtāSHən/ ▶*n.* a written or verbal request inviting someone to go somewhere or to do something: *a wedding invitation.* ■ the action of inviting someone to go somewhere or to do something: *a club with membership by invitation only | an herb garden where guests can go only* ***at the invitation of*** *the chef.* ■ [in *sing.*] a situation or action that tempts someone to do something or makes a particular outcome likely: *tactics like those of the colonel would have been an invitation to disaster.* ▷late Middle English: from French, or from Latin *invitatio(n-)*, from *invitare* (see INVITE).

in·vi·ta·tion·al /,inviˈtāSHənl/ ▶*adj.* (esp. of a competition) open only to those invited.
▶*n.* a competition of such a type.

in·vi·ta·to·ry /inˈvītə,tôrē/ ▶*adj.* containing or conveying an invitation. ■ (in the Christian Church) denoting a psalm or versicle acting as an invitation to worshipers, esp. Psalm 95. ▷Middle English: from late Latin *invitatorius*, from Latin *invitare* (see INVITE).

in·vite ▶*v.* /inˈvīt/ [*trans.*] make a polite, formal, or friendly request to (someone) to go somewhere or to do something: *we were* ***invited to*** *a dinner at the embassy* | [*trans.*] *she invited Patrick to sit down.* ■ make a formal or polite request for (something, esp. an application for a job or opinions on a particular topic) from someone. ■ (of an action or situation) tend to elicit (a particular reaction or response) or to tempt (someone) to do something: *his use of the word did little but invite criticism.*
▶*n.* /ˈin,vīt/ *informal* an invitation. ▷mid 16th cent.: from Old French *inviter*, or from Latin *invitare*. —**in·vi·tee** /,invīˈtē/ *n.* —**in·vit·er** /inˈvītər/ *n.*

in·vit·ing /inˈvītiNG/ ▶*adj.* offering the promise of an attractive or enjoyable experience: *the sea down there looks so inviting.* —**in·vit·ing·ly** *adv.*

in vi·tro /in ˈvē,trō/ ▶*adj.* & *adv. Biology* (of processes or reactions) taking place in a test tube, culture dish, or elsewhere outside a living organism: [as *adj.*] *in vitro fertilization.* The opposite of IN VIVO. ▷Latin, literally 'in glass.'

in vi·vo /in ˈvēvō/ ▶*adv.* & *adj. Biology* (of processes) taking place in a living organism. The opposite of IN VITRO. ▷Latin, 'in a living thing.'

in·vo·ca·tion /,invəˈkāSHən/ ▶*n.* the action of invoking something or someone for assistance or as an authority: *the invocation of new disciplines and methodologies.* ■ the summoning of a deity or the supernatural: *his invocation of the ancient mystical powers.* ■ an incantation used for this. ■ (in the Christian Church) a form of words such as "In the name of the Father" introducing a prayer, sermon, etc. ▷late Middle English: via Old French from Latin *invocatio(n-)*, from the verb *invocare* (see INVOKE). —**in·voc·a·to·ry** /inˈväkə,tôrē/ *adj.*

in·voice /ˈin,vois/ ▶*n.* a list of goods sent or services provided, with a statement of the sum due for these; a bill.
▶*v.* [*trans.*] send an invoice to (someone). ■ send an invoice for (goods or services provided). ▷mid 16th cent.: originally the plural of obsolete *invoy*, from obsolete French *envoy*, from *envoyer* 'send' (see ENVOY[1]).

in·voke /inˈvōk/ ▶*v.* [*trans.*] cite or appeal to (someone or something) as an authority for an action or in support of an argument: *the antiquated defense of insanity is rarely invoked today.* ■ call on (a deity or spirit) in prayer, as a witness, or for inspiration. ■ call earnestly for: *she invoked his help against this attack.* ■ summon (a spirit) by charms or incantation. ■ give rise to; evoke: *how could she explain how the accident happened without invoking his wrath?* ■ *Computing* cause (a procedure) to be carried out. ▷late 15th cent.: from French *invoquer*, from Latin *invocare*, from *in-* 'upon' + *vocare* 'to call.' —**in·vok·er** *n.*

in·vo·lu·cre /ˈinvə,lo͞okər/ (also **in·vo·lu·crum** /-krəm/) ▶*n. Botany* a whorl or rosette of bracts surrounding an inflorescence (esp. a capitulum) or at the base of an umbel. ▷late 16th cent.: from French, or from Latin *involucrum*, from *involvere* 'roll in, envelop' (see INVOLVE). —**in·vo·lu·cral** /,invəˈlo͞okrəl/ *adj.*

in·vol·un·tar·y /inˈvälən,terē/ ▶*adj.* **1** done without conscious control: *she gave an involuntary shudder.* ■ (esp. of muscles or nerves) concerned in bodily processes that are not under the control of the will. ■ caused unintentionally, esp. through negligence: *involuntary homicide.* **2** done against someone's will; compulsory: *a policy of involuntary repatriation.* —**in·vol·un·tar·i·ly** /in,välənˈte(ə)rəlē; -ˈvälən,ter-/ *adv.* —**in·vol·un·tar·i·ness** *n.*

in·vo·lute /ˈinvə,lo͞ot/ ▶*adj.* **1** *formal* involved; intricate: *the art novel has grown increasingly involute.* **2** *technical* curled spirally. ■ *Zoology* (of a shell) having the whorls wound closely around the axis. ■ *Botany* (of a leaf or the cap of a fungus) rolled inward at the edges.
▶*n. Geometry* the locus of a point considered as the end of a taut string being unwound from a given curve in the plane of that curve. Compare with EVOLUTE.
▶*v.* [*intrans.*] become involute; curl up. ▷mid 17th cent.: from Latin *involutus*, past participle of *involvere* (see INVOLVE).

in·vo·lut·ed /ˈinvə,lo͞otid/ ▶*adj.* complicated; abstruse: *his involuted prose.*

in·vo·lu·tion /,invəˈlo͞oSHən/ ▶*n.* **1** *Physiology* the shrinkage of an organ in old age or when inactive, e.g., of the uterus after childbirth. **2** *Mathematics* a function, transformation, or operator that is equal to its inverse, i.e., which gives the identity when applied to itself. **3** *formal* the process of involving or complicating, or the state of being involved or complicated: *periods of artistic involution.* ▷late Middle English (in the sense '[part] curling inward'): from Latin *involutio(n-)*, from *involvere* (see INVOLVE). —**in·vo·lu·tion·al** /-SHənl/ *adj.* —**in·vo·lu·tion·ar·y** /-,nerē/ *adj.*

in·volve /inˈvälv/ ▶*v.* [*trans.*] (of a situation or event) include (something) as a necessary part or result: *his transfer to another school would involve a lengthy assessment procedure.* ■ cause (a person or group) to experience or participate in an activity or situation: *what kind of organizations will be* ***involved in*** *setting up these projects?* ▷late Middle English (in the senses 'enfold' and 'entangle'; formerly also as *envolve*): from Latin *involvere*, from *in-* 'into' + *volvere* 'to roll.'

in·volved /inˈvälvd/ ▶*adj.* **1** [*predic.*] connected or concerned with someone or something, typically on an emotional or personal level: *Angela told me that she was* ***involved with*** *someone else.* **2** difficult to comprehend; complicated: *a long, involved conversation.*

in·volve·ment /inˈvälvmənt/ ▶*n.* the fact or condition of being involved with or participating in something: *he was imprisoned for his involvement in a plot to overthrow the government.* ■ emotional or personal association with someone.

in·vul·ner·a·ble /inˈvəlnərəbəl/ ▶*adj.* impossible to harm or damage. ▷late 16th cent. (earlier than *vulnerable*): from Latin *invulnerabilis*, from *in-* 'not' + *vulnerabilis* (see VULNERABLE). —**in·vul·ner·a·bil·i·ty** /-,vəlnərəˈbilitē/ *n.* —**in·vul·ner·a·bly** /-blē/ *adv.*

-in-wait·ing ▶*comb. form* **1** awaiting a turn, confirmation of a process, etc.: *a political administration-in-waiting.* ■ about to happen: *an explosion-in-waiting.* **2** denoting a position as attendant to a royal personage: *lady-in-waiting.*

in·wale /ˈin,wāl/ ▶*n.* a longitudinal structural piece on the inside of a boat; an internal gunwale.

in·ward /ˈinwərd/ ▶*adj.* [*attrib.*] directed or proceeding toward the inside; coming in from outside: *the* *inward rush of air* | *a graceful inward movement of her wrist.* ■ existing within the mind, soul, or spirit, and often not expressed: *she felt an inward sense of release.* ▸*adv.* (also **in·wards**) toward the inside: *the door began to swing inward.* ■ into or toward the mind, spirit, or soul: *people must look inward to gain insight into their own stress.* ▷Old English *inweard, inneweard, innanweard* (see **IN**, **-WARD**).

in·ward-look·ing ▸*adj.* not interested in or taking account of other people or groups: *inward-looking Christians who have lost their feeling for natural happiness.*

in·ward·ly /ˈinwərdlē/ ▸*adv.* (of a particular thought, feeling, or action) registered or existing in the mind but not expressed to others: *inwardly seething, he did as he was told.* ▷Old English *inweardlīce* (see **INWARD**, **-LY**2).

in·ward·ness /ˈinwərdnəs/ ▸*n.* preoccupation with one's inner self; concern with spiritual or philosophical matters rather than externalities.

in·wards /ˈinwərdz/ ▸*adv.* variant of **INWARD**.

in·wrought /inˈrôt/ ▸*adj. poetic/literary* (of a fabric or garment) intricately embroidered with a particular pattern or decoration: *robes inwrought with gold.*

In·yo Moun·tains /ˈinyō/ a range in east central California that includes Mount Whitney at 14,495 feet (4,418 m), the highest point in the U.S. outside Alaska.

in-your-face ▸*adj. informal* blatantly aggressive or provocative; impossible to ignore or avoid: *hard-boiled, in-your-face action thrillers.* ▷1970s: from *in your face*, used as a derisive insult.

I·o /ˈī-ō; ˈē-ō/ **1** *Greek Mythology* a priestess of Hera who was loved by Zeus. Trying to protect her from the jealousy of Hera, Zeus turned Io into a heifer. Hera sent a gadfly to torture the heifer, which then fled across the world and finally reached Egypt, where Zeus turned her back into human form. **2** *Astronomy* one of the Galilean moons of Jupiter, the fifth closest satellite to the planet. It is actively volcanic, colored red and yellow with sulfur compounds, and has a diameter of 2,526 miles (3,630 km).

I/O *Electronics* ▸*abbr.* input-output.

IOC ▸*abbr.* International Olympic Committee.

iod- ▸*comb. form* variant spelling of **IODO-** shortened before a vowel (as in *iodic*).

i·od·ic ac·id /īˈädik/ ▸*n. Chemistry* a crystalline acid with strong oxidizing properties, made by oxidation of iodine. • Chem. formula: HIO_3. —**i·o·date** /ˈīəˌdāt/ *n.*

i·o·dide /ˈīəˌdīd/ ▸*n. Chemistry* a compound of iodine with another element or group, esp. a salt of the anion I^-.

i·o·din·ate /ˈīədnˌāt/ ▸*v.* [*trans.*] [usu. as *adj.*] (**iodinated**) *Chemistry* introduce iodine into (a compound). —**i·o·din·a·tion** /ˌīədnˈāsʜən/ *n.*

i·o·dine /ˈīəˌdīn/ ▸*n.* the chemical element of atomic number 53, a nonmetallic element forming black crystals and a violet vapor. (Symbol: **I**) ■ a solution of this in alcohol, used as a mild antiseptic.

A member of the halogen group, iodine occurs chiefly as salts in seawater and brines. As a constituent of thyroid hormones, it is required in small amounts in the body, and deficiency can lead to goiter.

▷early 19th cent.: from French *iode* (from Greek *iōdēs* 'violet-colored,' from *ion* 'violet' + *-eidēs* 'like') + **-INE**4.

i·o·dism /ˈīəˌdizəm/ ▸*n. Medicine* iodine poisoning, causing thirst, diarrhea, weakness, and convulsions.

i·o·dize /ˈīəˌdīz/ ▸*v.* [*trans.*] [usu. as *adj.*] (**iodized**) treat or impregnate with iodine: *iodized salt.* —**i·o·di·za·tion** /ˌīədiˈzāsʜən/ *n.*

iodo- (usu. **iod-** before a vowel) ▸*comb. form Chemistry* representing **IODINE**.

i·o·do·form /īˈōdəˌfôrm; īˈädə-/ ▸*n.* a volatile pale yellow sweet-smelling crystalline organic compound of iodine, with antiseptic properties. • Alternative name: **triiodomethane**; chem. formula: CHI_3. ▷mid 19th cent.: from **IODINE**, on the pattern of *chloroform.*

i·o·dom·e·try /īəˈdämitrē/ ▸*n. Chemistry* the quantitative analysis of a solution of an oxidizing agent by adding an iodide that reacts to form iodine, which is then titrated. —**i·o·do·met·ric** /ˌīˌōdəˈmetrik/ *adj.*

i·o·do·phor /īˈōdəˌfôr/ ▸*n.* any of a group of disinfectants containing iodine in combination with a surfactant.

IOM ▸*abbr.* Isle of Man.

I·o moth ▸*n.* a large, mainly yellow North American moth of the silkworm moth family, with prominent eyespots on the hind wings. • *Automeris io*, family Saturniidae. ▷late 19th cent.: named after the Greek priestess **Io**.

Io moth

i·on /ˈīən; ˈīˌän/ ▸*n.* an atom or molecule with a net electric charge due to the loss or gain of one or more electrons. See also **CATION**, **ANION**. ▷mid 19th cent.: from Greek, neuter present participle of *ienai* 'go.'

Ion. ▸*abbr.* Ionic.

-ion ▸*suffix* forming nouns denoting verbal action: *communion.* ■ denoting an instance of this: *a rebellion.* ■ denoting a resulting state or product: *oblivion* | *opinion.* ▷via French from Latin *-ion-*.

USAGE The suffix **-ion** is usually found preceded by s (**-sion**), t (**-tion**), or x (**-xion**).

Io·na /īˈōnə/ a small island in the Inner Hebrides, off the western coast of Mull. It is the site of a monastery founded by St. Columba in about 563.

Io·nes·co /yôˈneskō; ˌēəˈneskō/, Eugène (1912–94), French playwright; born in Romania; a leading exponent of the theater of the absurd. Notable plays: *The Bald Soprano* (1949), *Rhinoceros* (1959), and *Exit the King* (1962).

i·on ex·change ▸*n.* the exchange of ions of the same charge between an insoluble solid and a solution in contact with it, used in water-softening and other purification and separation processes.

i·on ex·chang·er ▸*n.* a solid used in ion exchange, typically a special cross-linked synthetic resin or a zeolite.

I·o·nia /īˈōnēə/ in classical times, the central part of the west coast of Asia Minor, which had long been inhabited by Hellenic people (the Ionians) and was again colonized by Greeks from the mainland from about the 8th century BC.

I·o·ni·an /īˈōnēən/ ▸*n.* a member of an ancient Hellenic people inhabiting Attica, parts of western Asia Minor, and the Aegean islands in preclassical and classical times. They also colonized the islands that became known as the Ionian Islands. ■ a native or inhabitant of the Ionian Islands. ▸*adj.* of or relating to the Ionians, Ionia, or the Ionian Islands.

I·o·ni·an Is·lands a chain of about 40 Greek islands off the western coast of mainland Greece, in the Ionian Sea.

I·o·ni·an mode ▸*n. Music* the mode represented by the natural diatonic scale C–C (the major scale).

I·o·ni·an Sea the part of the Mediterranean Sea between western Greece and southern Italy, at the mouth of the Adriatic Sea.

I·on·ic /īˈänik/ ▸*adj.* **1** relating to or denoting a classical order of architecture characterized by a column with scroll shapes (volutes) on either side of the capital. **2** another term for **IONIAN**. ▸*n.* **1** the Ionic order of architecture. **2** the ancient Greek dialect used in Ionia. ▷late 16th cent.: via Latin from Greek *Iōnikos*, from *Iōnia* (see **IONIA**).

i·on·ic /īˈänik/ ▸*adj.* of, relating to, or using ions. ■ (of a chemical bond) formed by the electrostatic attraction of oppositely charged ions. Often contrasted with **COVALENT**. —**i·on·i·cal·ly** /-ik(ə)lē/ *adv.*

i·on·ic strength ▸*n. Chemistry* a quantity representing the strength of the electric field in a solution, equal to the sum of the molalities of each type of ion present multiplied by the square of their charges.

i·on·i·za·tion cham·ber /ˌīəniˈzāsʜən/ ▸*n.* an instrument for detecting ionizing radiation.

i·on·ize /ˈīəˌnīz/ ▸*v.* [*trans.*] (usu. **be ionized**) convert (an atom, molecule, or substance) into an ion or ions, typically by removing one or more electrons. ■ [*intrans.*] become converted into an ion or ions in this way. —**i·on·iz·a·ble** *adj.* —**i·on·i·za·tion** /ˌīəniˈzāsʜən/ *n.*

i·on·iz·er /ˈīəˌnīzər/ ▸*n.* a device that produces ionization, esp. one used to improve the quality of the air in a room.

i·on·iz·ing ra·di·a·tion ▸*n.* radiation consisting of particles, X-rays, or gamma rays with sufficient energy to cause ionization in the medium through which it passes.

i·on·o·mer /īˈänəmər/ ▸*n.* any of a class of polymer materials consisting of thermoplastic resins stabilized by ionic cross-linkages, used to make dental cement and sealants.

i·on·o·pause /īˈänəˌpôz/ ▸*n. Astronomy* the upper boundary of the ionosphere of a planet, comet, or other celestial object.

i·on·o·phore /īˈänəˌfôr/ ▸*n. Biochemistry* a substance that is able to transport particular ions across a lipid membrane in a cell.

i·on·o·sphere /īˈänəˌsfi(ə)r/ ▸*n.* the layer of the earth's atmosphere that contains a high concentration of ions and free electrons and is able to reflect radio waves. It lies above the mesosphere and extends from about 50 to 600 miles (80 to 1,000 km) above the earth's surface. ■ a similar region above the surface of another planet. —**i·on·o·spher·ic** /īˌänəˈsfi(ə)rik; -ˈsfer-/ *adj.*

i·on·to·pho·re·sis /īˌäntəfəˈrēsis/ ▸*n. Medicine* a technique of introducing ionic medicinal compounds into the body through the skin by applying a local electric current. ▷early 20th cent.: from **ION**, on the pattern of *electrophoresis.* —**i·on·to·pho·ret·ic** /-ˈretik/ *adj.* —**i·on·to·pho·ret·i·cal·ly** /-ˈretik(ə)lē/ *adv.*

IOOF ▸*abbr.* Independent Order of Odd Fellows.

-ior ▸*suffix* forming adjectives in the comparative degree: *anterior* | *junior* | *senior.* ▷from Latin.

i·o·ta /īˈōtə/ ▸*n.* **1** the ninth letter of the Greek alphabet (**Ι**, **ι**), transliterated as 'i.' ■ (**Iota**) [followed by Latin genitive] *Astronomy* the ninth star in a constellation: *Iota Piscium.* **2** [in *sing.*] [usu. with *negative*] an extremely small amount: *nothing she said seemed to make an iota of difference.* [iota being the smallest letter of the Greek alphabet. Compare with **JOT**.]

IOU ▸*n.* a signed document acknowledging a debt. ▷late 18th cent.: representing the pronunciation of *I owe you.*

-ious ▸*suffix* (forming adjectives) characterized by; full of: *cautious* | *vivacious.* ▷from French *-ieux*, from Latin *-iosus.*

I·o·wa /ˈīəwə/ a state in the northern central U.S., on the western banks of the Mississippi River; pop. 2,964,324; capital, Des Moines; statehood, Dec. 28, 1846 (29). It was acquired as part of the Louisiana Purchase in 1803. —**I·o·wan** *adj.* & *n.*

I·o·wa Cit·y a city in eastern Iowa, south of Cedar Rapids; pop. 62,220.

IP ▸*abbr. Computing* Internet protocol, the method by which information is sent between any two Internet computers on the Internet.

IPA ▸*abbr.* ■ India pale ale, a type of light-colored beer similar to bitter. [said to have been brewed originally for the British colonies.] ■ International Phonetic Alphabet.

IP ad·dress ▸*n. Computing* a unique string of numbers separated by periods that identifies each computer attached to the Internet. It also usually has a version containing words separated by periods.

ip·e·cac /ˈipikak/ (also **ip·e·cac·u·an·ha** /ˌipiˌkak(y)o͞oˈan(y)ə; ē,pākə-/) ▸*n.* **1** the dried rhizome of a South American shrub, or a drug prepared from this, used as an emetic and expectorant. **2** the shrub of the bedstraw family that produces this rhizome, native to Brazil and cultivated elsewhere. • *Cephaelis ipecacuanha*, family Rubiaceae. ■ used in names of other plants with similar uses, e.g., **American ipecac** (*Gillenia trifoliata*, family Rosaceae). ▷early 17th cent.: from Portuguese, from Tupi-Guarani *ipekaaguéne* 'emetic creeper,' from *ipe* 'small' + *kaa* 'leaves' + *guéne* 'vomit.'

Iph·i·ge·ni·a /ˌifijəˈnīə; -ˈnēə/ *Greek Mythology* the daughter of Agamemnon, who was obliged to offer her as a sacrifice to Artemis when the Greek fleet was becalmed at Aulis on its way to the Trojan War. In some versions of the story, Artemis saved her life and took her to Tauris in the Crimea, where she became a priestess until rescued by her brother Orestes.

I·pi·ros Greek name for **EPIRUS**.

ipm (also **i.p.m.**) ▸*abbr.* inches per minute.

IPO ▸*abbr.* initial public offering.

I·poh /ˈēpō/ a city in western Malaysia, the capital of the state of Perak; pop. 383,000.

ip·o·moe·a /ˌipəˈmēə/ ▸*n.* a plant of the genus *Ipomoea* in the family Convolvulaceae, esp. a morning glory. ▷modern Latin, from Greek *ips* 'worm' + *homoios* 'like.'

ip·pon /ˈipˌän/ ▸*n.* a full point scored in judo, karate, and other martial sports. ▷Japanese.

IPR ▸*abbr.* intellectual property rights.

i·pro·ni·a·zid /ˌīprōˈnīəˌzid/ ▸*n. Medicine* a synthetic compound used as a drug to treat depression. • A derivative of isoniazid; chem. formula: $(CH_3)_2CHNHNHCOC_5H_4N$. ▷mid 20th cent.: from *i(so)pro(pyl)* + *(iso)niazid*.

ip·se dix·it /ˈipsē ˈdiksit/ ▶*n.* a dogmatic and unproven statement. ▷Latin, literally 'he himself said it,' translating Greek *autos epha*, a phrase used of Pythagoras by his followers.

ip·si·lat·er·al /ˌipsəˈlatərəl/ ▶*adj.* belonging to or occurring on the same side of the body. ▷early 20th cent.: formed irregularly from Latin *ipse* 'self' + **LATERAL**. —**ip·si·lat·er·al·ly** *adv.*

ip·sis·si·ma ver·ba /ipˈsisəmə ˈvərbə/ ▶*plural n.* the precise words. ▷Latin.

ip·so fac·to /ˈipsō ˈfaktō/ ▶*adv.* by that very fact or act: *the enemy of one's enemy may be ipso facto a friend.* ▷Latin.

Ips·wich /ˈipswich/ a town in southeastern England, the county town of Suffolk, a port on the estuary of the Orwell River; pop. 116,000.

IQ ▶*abbr.* intelligence quotient.

i.q. ▶*abbr.* the same as. ▷from Latin *idem quod*.

Iq·bal /ˈikˌbäl/, Sir Muhammad (1875–1938), Indian poet and philosopher; generally regarded as the father of Pakistan.

-ique ▶*suffix* archaic spelling of **-IC**.

I·qui·tos /ēˈkētôs/ a city in northeastern Peru, a port on the west bank of the Amazon River; pop. 252,000.

IR ▶*abbr.* infrared.

Ir ▶*symbol* the chemical element iridium.

ir- ▶*prefix* variant spelling of **IN-**[1], **IN-**[2] assimilated before *r* (as in *irrelevant*, *irradiate*).

IRA ▶*abbr.* ■ (often /ˈīrə/) individual retirement account. ■ Irish Republican Army.

I·rá·kli·on /iˈräklēˌôn/ Greek name for **HERAKLION**.

I·ran /iˈrän; iˈran; īˈran/ a country in the Middle East, between the Caspian Sea and the Persian Gulf; pop. 69,018,000; capital, Tehran; languages, Farsi (Persian) (official), Turkish, Kurdish, Arabic, and others.

Previously known as Persia, the country adopted the name of Iran in 1935. Iran was a monarchy until 1979, when the shah was overthrown in a popular uprising that was headed by Ayatollah Khomeini. Soon after, Iran was established as an Islamic republic. From 1980 until 1988, it was at war with its neighbor Iraq.

See also **PERSIA**.

I·ran-Con·tra af·fair *n.* a political scandal of 1987 involving the covert sale by the U.S. of arms to Iran. The proceeds of the arms sales were used by officials to give arms to the anticommunist Contras in Nicaragua, despite congressional prohibition. Also called **IRANGATE**.

The sale occurred during the presidency of Ronald Reagan, at a time when official relations between the countries were suspended (and while Iran was at war with Iraq), and was followed by the release of American hostages held in the Middle East.

I·ran·gate /iˈranˌgāt; iˈrän-/ another term for the **IRAN-CONTRA AFFAIR**.

I·ra·ni·an /iˈrānēən; iˈrä-/ ▶*adj.* of or relating to Iran or its people. ■ relating to or denoting the group of Indo-European languages that includes Persian (Farsi), Pashto, Avestan, and Kurdish.

▶*n.* a native or national of Iran, or a person of Iranian descent.

I·ran–I·raq War the war of 1980–88 between Iran and Iraq in the general area of the Persian Gulf. It ended inconclusively after great hardship and loss of life on both sides. Also called **GULF WAR**.

I·raq /iˈräk; iˈrak; īˈrak/ a country in the Middle East, with an outlet on the Persian Gulf; pop. 25,374,000; capital, Baghdad; official language, Arabic.

Iraq is traversed by the Tigris and Euphrates rivers, whose valley was the site of the ancient civilizations of Mesopotamia. It was conquered by Arabia in the 7th century and from 1534 formed part of the Ottoman Empire. After World War I, a kingdom was established, although the country was under British administration until 1932. Saddam Hussein came to power as president in 1979. From 1980 to 1988, the country was at war with Iran, its eastern neighbor. In 1990, Iraq invaded Kuwait; it was driven back by an international coalition of forces in the Gulf War of 1991. The U.S. invaded Iraq in 2003 and captured Saddam Hussein. Sovereignty was transferred to an interim government June 28, 2004, but U.S. forces remained in Iraq amid rising chaos.

I·ra·qi /iˈräkē; iˈrakē/ ▶*adj.* of or relating to Iraq, its people, or their language.

▶*n.* (*pl.* **-qis**) **1** a native or national of Iraq, or a person of Iraqi descent. **2** the form of Arabic spoken in Iraq.

IRAS /ˈīˌras/ a satellite launched in 1983 to map the distribution of infrared radiation in the sky. ▷abbreviation of *Infrared Astronomical Satellite*.

i·ras·ci·ble /iˈrasəbəl/ ▶*adj.* (of a person) easily made angry. ■ characterized by or arising from anger: *their rebukes got progressively more irascible.* ▷late Middle English: via French from late Latin *irascibilis*, from Latin *irasci* 'grow angry,' from *ira* 'anger.' —**i·ras·ci·bil·i·ty** /iˌrasəˈbilitē/ *n.* —**i·ras·ci·bly** /-blē/ *adv.*

i·rate /īˈrāt/ ▶*adj.* feeling or characterized by great anger: *a barrage of irate letters.* ▷mid 19th cent.: from Latin *iratus*, from *ira* 'anger.' —**i·rate·ly** *adv.* —**i·rate·ness** *n.*

IRC ▶*abbr.* Internet Relay Chat, an area of the network where users can communicate interactively with each other.

ire /ī(ə)r/ ▶*n.* anger: *the plans provoked the ire of conservationists.* ▷Middle English: via Old French from Latin *ira*. —**ire·ful** /-fəl/ *adj.*

Ire·dell /ˈī(ə)rˌdel/, James (1751–99) U.S. Supreme Court associate justice 1790–99; born in England. Appointed to the Court by President Washington, he was a Federalist.

Ire·land /ˈīrlənd/ an island in the British Isles that lies west of Great Britain. Approximately four fifths of the area of Ireland constitutes the Republic of Ireland, with the remaining one fifth belonging to Northern Ireland. After an unsuccessful rebellion in 1798, union of Britain and Ireland followed in 1801. In 1921, Ireland was partitioned by the Anglo-Irish Treaty.

Ire·land, Republic of a country that comprises approximately four fifths of Ireland; pop. 3,523,400; capital, Dublin; languages, Irish (official) and English. Also called **IRISH REPUBLIC**.

The Anglo-Irish Treaty by which Ireland was partitioned in 1921 gave southern Ireland dominion status as the Irish Free State. The treaty was followed by civil war between the Free State government and the republicans, led by Eamon de Valera, who rejected partition. The war ended in victory for the government in 1923. A new constitution as a sovereign state (Eire) was adopted in 1937. Eire remained neutral during World War II; in 1949 it left the Commonwealth of Nations and became fully independent as the Republic of Ireland.

Ire·nae·us, St. /ˌīrəˈnēəs/ (*c.* AD 130–*c.*200), Greek theologian. He wrote *Against Heresies* (*c.*180), a detailed attack on Gnosticism. Feast day (Eastern Church) August 23; (Western Church) June 28.

i·ren·ic /īˈrenik; īˈrē-/ (also **ei·ren·ic**) ▶*adj. formal* aiming or aimed at peace.

▶*n.* (**irenics**) a part of Christian theology concerned with reconciling different denominations and sects. ▷mid 19th cent.: from Greek *eirēnikos*, from *eirēnē* 'peace.' —**i·ren·i·cal** *adj.* —**i·ren·i·cal·ly** /-ik(ə)lē/ *adv.* —**i·ren·i·cism** /-niˌsizəm/ *n.*

Ir·gun /irˈgo͞on/ a right-wing Zionist organization founded in 1931. During the period when it was active (1937–48), it carried out violent attacks on Arabs and Britons in its campaign to establish a Jewish state; it was disbanded after the creation of Israel in 1948. ▷from modern Hebrew *'irgūn (ṣĕḇā'ī lĕ'ummī)* '(national military) organization.'

I·ri·an Ja·ya /ˈirēˌän ˈjīə/ a province in eastern Indonesia that is on the western half of the island of New Guinea and the adjacent small islands; capital, Jayapura. Until its incorporation into Indonesia in 1963, it was known as Dutch New Guinea. Also called **WEST IRIAN**.

irid. ▶*abbr.* iridescent.

ir·i·da·ceous /ˌiriˈdāshəs/ ▶*adj. Botany* of, relating to, or denoting plants of the iris family (Iridaceae), which grow from bulbs, corms, or rhizomes. ▷mid 19th cent.: from modern Latin *Iridaceae* (plural), based on Greek *iris*, *irid-* 'rainbow,' + **-OUS**.

ir·i·dec·to·my /ˌiriˈdektəmē/ ▶*n.* (*pl.* **-mies**) a surgical procedure to remove part of the iris.

ir·i·des·cent /ˌiriˈdesənt/ ▶*adj.* showing luminous colors that seem to change when seen from different angles. ▷late 18th cent.: from Latin *iris*, *irid-* 'rainbow' + **-ESCENT**. —**ir·i·des·cence** *n.* —**ir·i·des·cent·ly** *adv.*

i·rid·i·um /iˈridēəm/ ▶*n.* the chemical element of atomic number 77, a hard, dense silvery-white metal. (Symbol: **Ir**) ▷early 19th cent.: modern Latin, from Latin *iris*, *irid-* 'rainbow' (so named because it forms compounds of various colors).

ir·i·dol·o·gy /ˌiriˈdäləjē/ ▶*n.* (in alternative medicine) diagnosis by examination of the iris of the eye. ▷early 20th cent.: from Greek *iris*, *irid-* 'iris' + **-LOGY**. —**ir·i·dol·o·gist** /-jist/ *n.*

i·rie /ˈīrē/ ▶*adj. black English* nice, good, or pleasing (used as a general term of approval): *the place is jumping with irie vibes | I'm feeling irie.*

▶*exclam.* used by Rastafarians as a friendly greeting. ▷perhaps representing a pronunciation of *all right*.

I·ris /ˈīris/ *Greek Mythology* the goddess of the rainbow, who acted as a messenger of the gods.

i·ris /ˈīris/ ▶*n.* **1** a flat, colored, ring-shaped membrane behind the cornea of the eye, with an adjustable circular opening (pupil) in the center. ■ (also **iris diaphragm**) an adjustable diaphragm of thin overlapping plates for regulating the size of a central hole, esp. for the admission of light to a lens. **2** a plant with sword-shaped leaves and showy flowers, typically purple, yellow, or white. Native to both Eurasia and North America, it is widely cultivated as an ornamental. • Genus *Iris*, family Iridaceae (the **iris family**): many species and numerous hybrids, including the **crested dwarf iris** (*I. cristata*) and the **sweet iris** (*I. pallida*). The iris family also includes the gladioli, crocuses, and freesias. **3** a rainbow or a rainbowlike appearance.

▶*v.* [*intrans.*] (of an aperture, typically that of a lens) open or close in the manner of an iris or iris diaphragm. ▷modern Latin, via Latin from Greek *iris* 'rainbow, iris.'

iris 2

Pronunciation Key ə *ago*; ər *over*; ˈə or ˌə *up*; ˈər or ˌər *fur*; a *hat*; ā *rate*; ä *car*; CH *chew*; e *let*; ē *see*; e(ə)r *air*; i *fit*; ī *by*; i(ə)r *ear*; NG *sing*; ō *go*; ô *for*; oi *boy*; o͝o *good*; o͞o *goo*; ou *out*; SH *she*; TH *thin*; T͟H *then*; (h)w *why*; ZH *vision*

I·rish /ˈīrisн/ ▸*adj.* of or relating to Ireland, its people, or the Goidelic language traditionally and historically spoken there.
▸*n.* **1** (also **Irish Gaelic**) the Goidelic language that is the first official language of the Republic of Ireland. **2** [as *plural n.*] (**the Irish**) the people of Ireland; Irish people collectively. ▷Middle English: from Old English *Īr-* (stem of *Īras* 'the Irish' and *Īrland* 'Ireland,' obscurely related to **Hibernian**) + **-ish**[1]. **—I·rish·ness** *n.*
▸*PHRASE* □ **get one's Irish up** cause one to become angry: *if someone tries to make me do something I don't want to do, it gets my Irish up.*

I·rish cof·fee ▸*n.* coffee mixed with a dash of Irish whiskey and served with cream on top.

I·rish elk ▸*n.* an extinct giant European and North African deer of the Pleistocene epoch, with massive antlers up to 10 feet (3 m) across. Also called **giant deer**. • *Megaloceros giganteus*, family Cervidae.

I·rish·man /ˈīrisнmən/ ▸*n.* (*pl.* **-men**) a native or national of Ireland, or a person of Irish descent, esp. a man.

I·rish moss ▸*n.* another term for **carrageen**.

I·rish Na·tion·al Lib·er·a·tion Ar·my (abbr.: **INLA**) a small paramilitary organization seeking union between Northern Ireland and the Republic of Ireland. It was formed in the early 1970s, probably as an offshoot of the Provisional IRA.

I·rish Re·pub·lic see **Ireland, Republic of**.

I·rish Re·pub·li·can Ar·my (abbr.: **IRA**) the military arm of Sinn Fein, aiming for union between the Republic of Ireland and Northern Ireland.

The IRA was formed during the struggle for independence from Britain in 1916–21; in 1969 it split into Official and Provisional wings. The Official IRA became virtually inactive, while the Provisional IRA stepped up the level of violence against military and civilian targets in Northern Ireland, Britain, and Europe. The IRA declared a cease-fire in 1994 and another in 1997.

I·rish Sea the sea that separates Ireland from England and Wales.

I·rish set·ter ▸*n.* a dog of a breed of setter with a long, silky dark red coat and a long feathered tail.

I·rish stew ▸*n.* a stew made with mutton or other meat, potatoes, and onions.

I·rish ter·ri·er ▸*n.* a terrier of a rough-haired light reddish-brown breed.

I·rish wolf·hound ▸*n.* a large, typically grayish hound of a rough-coated breed.

I·rish·wom·an /ˈīrisн,wŏŏmən/ ▸*n.* (*pl.* **-wom·en**) a female native or national of Ireland, or a woman of Irish descent.

i·ri·tis /īˈrītis/ ▸*n. Medicine* inflammation of the iris of the eye. **—i·rit·ic** /īˈritik/ *adj.*

irk /ərk/ ▸*v.* [*trans.*] irritate; annoy: **it irks** *her to think of the runaround she received.* ▷Middle English (in the sense 'be annoyed or disgusted'): perhaps from Old Norse *yrkja* 'to work.'

irk·some /ˈərksəm/ ▸*adj.* irritating; annoying. **—irk·some·ly** *adv.* **—irk·some·ness** *n.*

Ir·kutsk /irˈkŏŏtsk/ the chief city of Siberia in eastern Russia, on the western shore of Lake Baikal; pop. 635,000.

i·ron /ˈīərn/ ▸*n.* **1** a strong, hard magnetic silvery-gray metal, the chemical element of atomic number 26, much used as a material for construction and manufacturing, esp. in the form of steel. (Symbol: **Fe**) ■ compounds of this metal, esp. as a component of the diet: *serve liver as it's a good source of iron* | [as *adj.*] *how are your iron levels?* ■ used figuratively as a symbol or type of firmness, strength, or resistance: *her father had a will of iron* | [as *adj.*] *the iron grip of religion on minority cultures.*

Iron is widely distributed as ores such as hematite, magnetite, and siderite, and the earth's core is believed to consist largely of metallic iron and nickel. Besides steel, other important forms of the metal are cast iron and wrought iron. Chemically a transition element, iron is a constituent of some biological molecules, notably hemoglobin.

2 a tool or implement now or originally made of iron: *a caulking iron.* ■ (**irons**) fetters or handcuffs. ■ *informal* a handgun. **3** a hand-held implement with a flat steel base that is heated (typically with electricity) to smooth clothes, sheets, etc. **4** a golf club with a metal head (typically with a numeral indicating the degree to which the head is angled in order to loft the ball). **5** *Astronomy* (also **iron meteorite**) a meteorite containing a high proportion of iron.
▸*v.* [*trans.*] smooth (clothes, sheets, etc.) with an iron.
▸*phrasal v.* □ **iron something out** remove creases from clothes, sheets, etc., by ironing. ■ *figurative* solve or settle difficulties or problems: *they had ironed out their differences.* ▷Old English *īren, īsen, īsern*, of Germanic origin; related to Dutch *ijzer* and German *Eisen*, and probably ultimately from Celtic. **—i·ron·er** *n.* **—i·ron·like** /-,līk/ *adj.*
▸*PHRASES* □ **have many** (or **other**) **irons in the fire** have many (or a range of) options or courses of action available or be involved in many activities or commitments at the same time. □ **in irons 1** having the feet or hands fettered. **2** (of a sailing vessel) stalled head to wind and unable to come about or tack either way. □ **iron hand** (or **fist**) used to refer to firmness or ruthlessness of attitude or behavior: *Fascism's iron hand.* □ **an iron hand** (or **fist**) **in a velvet glove** firmness or ruthlessness cloaked in outward gentleness.

I·ron Age 1 a period that followed the Bronze Age, when weapons and tools came to be made of iron.

In Europe the Iron Age is conventionally taken as beginning in the early 1st millennium BC.

2 (in Greek and Roman mythology) the last and worst age of the world, a time of wickedness and oppression.

i·ron·bark /ˈīərn,bärk/ ▸*n.* an Australian eucalyptus tree with thick, solid bark and hard, dense, durable timber. • Genus *Eucalyptus*, family Myrtaceae: several species.

i·ron·bound /ˈīərnˈbound/ (also **i·ron-bound**) ▸*adj.* bound with iron: *a massive ironbound chest.* ■ rigorous; inflexible: *ironbound rules.* ■ *archaic* (of a coast) faced or enclosed with rocks.

I·ron Chan·cel·lor see **Bismarck**[2].

i·ron·clad /ˈīərn,klad/ ▸*adj.* covered or protected with iron. ■ impossible to contradict, weaken, or change: *an ironclad guarantee.*
▸*n. historical* a 19th-century warship with armor plating.

I·ron Cross ▸*n.* the highest German military decoration for bravery, instituted in 1813.

i·ron cur·tain ▸*n.* a notional barrier that prevents the passage of information or ideas between political entities, in particular: ■ (usu. **the Iron Curtain**) the notional barrier separating the former Soviet bloc and the West prior to the decline of communism that followed the political events in eastern Europe in 1989.

I·ron Duke see **Wellington**[2].

I·ron Gate a gorge through which a section of the Danube River flows and forms part of the boundary between Romania and Yugoslavia. Navigation was improved by means of a ship canal constructed through it in 1896. Romanian name **Porţile de Fier**, Serbo-Croat name **Gvozdena Vrata**.

i·ron gray ▸*n.* a dark gray color. ■ a horse of this color.

I·ron Guard a fascist Romanian political party that was founded in 1927 and ceased to exist after World War II.

i·ron horse ▸*n. poetic/literary* a steam locomotive. ■ (**Iron Horse**) see **Gehrig**.

i·ron·ic /īˈränik/ ▸*adj.* using or characterized by irony: *his mouth curved into an ironic smile.* ■ happening in the opposite way to what is expected, and typically causing wry amusement because of this: [with *clause*] *it was ironic that now that everybody had plenty of money for food, they couldn't obtain it because everything was rationed.* ▷mid 17th cent.: from French *ironique* or late Latin *ironicus*, from Greek *eirōnikos* 'dissembling, feigning ignorance,' from *eirōneia* (see **irony**[1]). **—i·ron·i·cal** *adj.*

i·ron·i·cal·ly /īˈränik(ə)lē/ ▸*adv.* in an ironic manner. ■ used to denote a paradoxical, unexpected, or coincidental situation: [*sentence adverb*] *ironically, the rescue craft that saved her was the boat she was helping to pay for.*

i·ron·ing /ˈīərniNG/ ▸*n.* the task of ironing clothes, sheets, etc. ■ clothes, sheets, etc., that need to be or have just been ironed.

i·ron·ing board ▸*n.* a long, narrow board covered with soft material and having folding legs, on which clothes, sheets, etc., are ironed.

i·ro·nist /ˈīrənist; ˈīərnist/ ▸*n.* a person who uses irony. ▷early 18th cent.: from Greek *eirōn* 'dissembler' + **-ist**.

i·ro·nize /ˈīrə,nīz; īərˈnīz/ ▸*v.* [*trans.*] use ironically: *this novel also follows and yet ironizes many of the conventions of the picaresque narrative.*

i·ron lung ▸*n.* a rigid case fitted over a patient's body, used for administering prolonged artificial respiration by means of mechanical pumps.

i·ron maid·en ▸*n.* (in historical contexts) an instrument of torture consisting of a coffin-shaped box lined with iron spikes.

I·ron Man see **Ripken**.

i·ron man (also **i·ron·man**) ▸*n.* (esp. in sporting contexts) an exceptionally strong or robust man. ■ [often as *adj.*] a multievent sporting contest demanding stamina, in particular a consecutive triathlon of swimming, cycling, and running.

i·ron mold ▸*n.* a spot caused by rust or an ink stain, esp. on fabric.

i·ron·mon·ger /ˈīərn,məNGgər; -,mäNGgər/ ▸*n. Brit.* a person or store selling hardware such as tools and household implements. **—i·ron·mon·ger·y** /-g(ə)rē/ *n.* (*pl.* **-ger·ies**).

i·ron-on ▸*adj.* [*attrib.*] able to be fixed to the surface of a fabric by ironing: *T-shirts with iron-on transfers.*

i·ron ore ▸*n.* a rock or mineral from which iron can be profitably extracted.

I·ron·sides /ˈīərn,sīdz/ ▸ **1** a nickname for Oliver Cromwell. **2** (**ironsides**) *historical* an ironclad.

i·ron·stone /ˈīərn,stōn/ ▸*n.* **1** sedimentary rock containing a substantial proportion of iron compounds. **2** [usu. as *adj.*] a kind of dense, opaque stoneware.

i·ron·ware /ˈīərn,wer/ ▸*n.* articles made of iron, typically domestic implements.

i·ron·wood /ˈīərn,wŏŏd/ ▸*n.* **1** any of a number of trees that produce very hard timber, in particular: • a southern African tree of the olive family (*Olea laurifolia*, family Oleaceae). • another term for the **American hornbeam** and the **Eastern hornbeam** (see **hornbeam**). **2** see **titi**[2].

i·ron·work /ˈīərn,wərk/ ▸*n.* things or parts made of iron.

i·ron·works /ˈīərn,wərks/ ▸*n.* [treated as *sing.* or *pl.*] a place where iron is smelted or iron goods are made.

i·ro·ny[1] /ˈīrənē; ˈīərnē/ ▸*n.* (*pl.* **-nies**) the expression of one's meaning by using language that normally signifies the opposite, typically for humorous or emphatic effect: *"Don't go overboard with the gratitude," he rejoined with heavy irony.* See note at **wit**. ■ a state of affairs or an event that seems deliberately contrary to what one expects and is often amusing as a result: [with *clause*] *the irony is that I thought he could help me.* ■ (also **dra·mat·ic** or **trag·ic i·ro·ny**) a literary technique, originally used in Greek tragedy, by which the full significance of a character's words or actions are clear to the audience or reader although unknown to the character. ▷early 16th cent. (also denoting Socratic irony): via Latin from Greek *eirōneia* 'simulated ignorance,' from *eirōn* 'dissembler.'

i·ro·ny[2] /ˈīərnē/ ▸*adj.* of or like iron: *an irony gray color.*

Ir·o·quoi·an /ˈirə,kwoiən/ ▸*n.* a language family of eastern North America, including the languages of the Five Nations, Tuscarora, Huron, Wyandot, and Cherokee. With the exception of Cherokee, all its members are extinct or nearly so.
▸*adj.* of or relating to the Iroquois people or the Iroquoian language family.

Ir·o·quois /ˈirə,kwoi/ ▸*n.* (*pl.* same) **1** a member of a former confederacy of North American Indian peoples originally comprising the Cayuga, Mohawk, Oneida, Onondaga, and Seneca peoples (known as the **Five Nations**), and later including also the Tuscarora (thus forming the **Six Nations**). **2** any of the Iroquoian languages.
▸*adj.* of or relating to the Iroquois or their languages. ▷mid 17th cent.: French, perhaps a term from a Basque-Algonquian pidgin *(h)irokoa* 'killer people,' from Basque *(h)ilo* 'kill'+ *koa* 'person.'

ir·ra·di·ance /iˈrādēəns/ ▸*n.* **1** *Physics* the flux of radiant energy per unit area (normal to the direction of flow of radiant energy through a medium). **2** *poetic/literary* the fact of shining brightly.

ir·ra·di·ant /iˈrādēənt/ ▸*adj. poetic/literary* shining brightly. ▷early 16th cent.: from Latin *irradiant-* 'shining upon,' from the verb *irradiare* (based on *radius* 'ray').

ir·ra·di·ate /iˈrādē,āt/ ▸*v.* [*trans.*] **1** (often **be irradiated**) expose to radiation. ■ expose (food) to gamma rays to kill microorganisms. **2** illuminate (something) by or as if by shining light on it: *sunlight streamed down through stained glass, irradiating the faces of family and friends.* ▷late 16th cent. (in the sense 'emit rays, shine upon'): from Latin *irradiat-* 'shone upon,' from the verb *irradiare*, from *in-* 'upon' +

radiare 'to shine' (from *radius* 'ray'). —**ir·ra·di·a·tor** /-ˌātər/ *n.*

ir·ra·di·a·tion /iˌrādēˈāshən/ ▸*n.* **1** the process or fact of irradiating or being irradiated. **2** *Optics* the apparent extension of the edges of an illuminated object seen against a dark background.

ir·ra·tion·al /iˈrashənl/ ▸*adj.* **1** not logical or reasonable. ■ not endowed with the power of reason. **2** *Mathematics* (of a number, quantity, or expression) not expressible as a ratio of two integers, and having an infinite and nonrecurring expansion when expressed as a decimal. Examples of irrational numbers are the number π and the square root of 2.
▸*n. Mathematics* an irrational number. ▷late Middle English: from Latin *irrationalis*, from *in-* 'not' + *rationalis* (see RATIONAL). —**ir·ra·tion·al·i·ty** /iˌrashəˈnalitē/ *n.* —**ir·ra·tion·al·ize** /-ˌīz/ *v.* —**ir·ra·tion·al·ly** *adv.*

ir·ra·tion·al·ism /iˈrashənlˌizəm/ ▸*n.* a system of belief or action that disregards or contradicts rational principles. —**ir·ra·tion·al·ist** *n.* & *adj.*

Ir·ra·wad·dy /ˌirəˈwädē/ the principal river of Myanmar (Burma), 1,300 miles (2,090 km) long. It flows through a large delta into the eastern part of the Bay of Bengal.

ir·re·claim·a·ble /ˌiriˈklāməbəl/ ▸*adj.* not able to be reclaimed or reformed. —**ir·re·claim·a·bly** /-blē/ *adv.*

ir·rec·on·cil·a·ble /iˌrekənˈsīləbəl; iˈrekənˌsī-/ ▸*adj.* (of ideas, facts, or statements) representing findings or points of view that are so different from each other that they cannot be made compatible: *these two views of the early medieval economy are irreconcilable.* ■ (of people) implacably hostile to each other.
▸*n.* (usu. **irreconcilables**) any of two or more ideas, facts, or statements that cannot be made compatible. —**ir·rec·on·cil·a·bil·i·ty** /-sīləˈbilitē/ *n.* —**ir·rec·on·cil·a·bly** /-blē/ *adv.*

ir·re·cov·er·a·ble /ˌiriˈkəvərəbəl/ ▸*adj.* not able to be recovered, regained, or remedied: *his liquid assets had to be written off as irrecoverable.* —**ir·re·cov·er·a·bly** /-blē/ *adv.*

ir·re·cu·per·a·ble /ˌiriˈk(y)o͞opərəbəl/ ▸*adj. rare* unable to be recovered from. ▷late Middle English: from Old French, from late Latin *irrecuperabilis*, from Latin *in-* 'not' + *recuperare* (see RECUPERATE).

ir·re·cu·sa·ble /ˌiriˈkyo͞ozəbəl/ ▸*adj. rare* (of evidence or a statement) not able to be challenged or rejected. ▷late 18th cent.: via French from late Latin *irrecusabilis*, from *in-* 'not' + *recusabilis* 'that should be refused' (from the verb *recusare*).

ir·re·deem·a·ble /ˌiriˈdēməbəl/ ▸*adj.* **1** not able to be saved, improved, or corrected: *so many irredeemable mistakes have been made.* **2** (of paper currency) for which the issuing authority does not undertake ever to pay coin. —**ir·re·deem·a·bil·i·ty** /-ˌdēməˈbilitē/ *n.* —**ir·re·deem·a·bly** /-blē/ *adv.*

ir·re·den·tist /ˌiriˈdentist/ ▸*n.* [usu. as *adj.*] a person advocating the restoration to their country of any territory formerly belonging to it. ■ *historical* (in 19th-century Italian politics) an advocate of the return to Italy of all Italian-speaking districts subject to other countries. ▷from Italian *irredentista*, from *(Italia) irredenta* 'unredeemed (Italy).' —**ir·re·den·tism** /-ˌtizəm/ *n.*

ir·re·duc·i·ble /ˌiriˈd(y)o͞osəbəl/ ▸*adj.* not able to be reduced or simplified. ■ not able to be brought to a certain form or condition: *the imagery remains irreducible to textual structures.* —**ir·re·duc·i·bil·i·ty** /-ˌd(y)o͞osəˈbilitē/ *n.* —**ir·re·duc·i·bly** /-blē/ *adv.*

ir·re·flex·ive /ˌirəˈfleksiv/ ▸*adj. Logic* denoting a relation that never holds between a term and itself.

ir·re·form·a·ble /ˌirəˈfôrməbəl/ ▸*adj.* (chiefly of religious dogma) unable to be revised or altered.

ir·ref·ra·ga·ble /iˈrefrəgəbəl/ ▸*adj.* not able to be refuted or disproved; indisputable. ▷mid 16th cent.: from late Latin *irrefragabilis*, from *in-* 'not' + *refragari* 'oppose.' —**ir·ref·ra·ga·bly** /-blē/ *adv.*

ir·ref·u·ta·ble /ˌirəˈfyo͞otəbəl; iˈrefyə-/ ▸*adj.* impossible to deny or disprove: *irrefutable evidence.* ▷early 17th cent.: from late Latin *irrefutabilis*, from *in-* 'not' + *refutabilis* (from *refutare* 'repel, rebut'). —**ir·ref·u·ta·bil·i·ty** /-ˌfyo͞otəˈbilitē; iˌrefyətə-/ *n.* —**ir·ref·u·ta·bly** /-blē/ *adv.*

irreg. ▸*abbr.* ■ irregular or irregularly.

ir·re·gard·less /ˌiriˈgärdlis/ ▸*adj.* & *adv. informal* regardless. ▷early 20th cent.: probably a blend of IRRESPECTIVE and REGARDLESS.

USAGE **Irregardless**, with its illogical negative prefix, is widely heard, perhaps arising under the influence of such perfectly correct forms as *irrespective*. **Irregardless** is avoided by careful users of English. Use **regardless** to mean 'without regard or consideration for' or 'nevertheless': *I go walking every day regardless of season or weather.*

ir·reg·u·lar /iˈregyələr/ ▸*adj.* **1** not even or balanced in shape or arrangement: *her features were too irregular.* ■ occurring at uneven or varying rates or intervals: *an irregular heartbeat.* ■ *Botany* (of a flower) having the petals differing in size and shape; zygomorphic. **2** contrary to the rules or to that which is normal or established: *they were questioned about their involvement in irregular financial dealings.* ■ [*attrib.*] (of troops) not belonging to regular or established army units. ■ *Grammar* (of a verb or other word) having inflections that do not conform to the usual rules.
▸*n.* (usu. **irregulars**) **1** a member of an irregular military force. **2** an imperfect piece of merchandise sold at a reduced price. ▷late Middle English (in the sense 'not conforming to rule [esp. that of the Church]'): via Old French from medieval Latin *irregularis*, from *in-* 'not' + *regularis* (see REGULAR). —**ir·reg·u·lar·ly** *adv.*

ir·reg·u·lar·i·ty /iˌregyəˈlaritē/ ▸*n.* (*pl.* **-ties**) the state or quality of being irregular: *there is evidence that fraud and irregularity continue on a large scale.* ■ mild recurring constipation. ■ (usu. **irregularities**) a thing that is irregular in form or nature: *irregularities of the heartbeat | financial irregularities.* ▷Middle English: from Old French *irregularite*, from late Latin *irregularitas*, from *irregularis* (see IRREGULAR).

ir·rel·a·tive /iˈrelətiv/ ▸*adj. rare* unconnected; unrelated. ■ irrelevant. —**ir·rel·a·tive·ly** *adv.*

ir·rel·e·vant /iˈreləvənt/ ▸*adj.* not connected with or relevant to something. —**ir·rel·e·vance** *n.* —**ir·rel·e·van·cy** *n.* (*pl.* **-cies**) —**ir·rel·e·vant·ly** *adv.*

USAGE See usage at IMMATERIAL.

ir·re·li·gious /ˌiriˈlijəs/ ▸*adj.* indifferent or hostile to religion: *an irreligious world.* ▷late Middle English: from Latin *irreligiosus*, from *in-* 'not' + *religiosus* (see RELIGIOUS). —**ir·re·li·gion** /-ˈlijən/ *n.* —**ir·re·li·gious·ly** *adv.* —**ir·re·li·gious·ness** *n.*

ir·re·me·di·a·ble /ˌiriˈmēdēəbəl/ ▸*adj.* impossible to cure or put right. ▷late Middle English: from Latin *irremediabilis*, from *in-* 'not' + *remediabilis* 'curable' (from *remedium* 'remedy'). —**ir·re·me·di·a·bly** /-blē/ *adv.*

ir·re·mis·si·ble /ˌiriˈmisəbəl/ ▸*adj.* **1** (of a crime) unpardonable. **2** (of an obligation or duty) binding. ▷late Middle English: from Old French, or from ecclesiastical Latin *irremissibilis*, from *in-* 'not' + *remissibilis* (from *remittere* 'remit').

ir·re·mov·a·ble /ˌiriˈmo͞ovəbəl/ ▸*adj.* incapable of being removed: *the irremovable taint of corruption.* ■ (of an official) unable to be displaced from office. —**ir·re·mov·a·bil·i·ty** /-ˌmo͞ovəˈbilitē/ *n.* —**ir·re·mov·a·bly** /-blē/ *adv.*

ir·rep·a·ra·ble /iˈrep(ə)rəbəl/ ▸*adj.* (of an injury or loss) impossible to rectify or repair: *they were doing irreparable damage to my heart and lungs.* ▷late Middle English: via Old French from Latin *irreparabilis*, from *in-* 'not' + *reparabilis* (see REPARABLE). —**ir·rep·a·ra·bil·i·ty** /iˌrep(ə)rəˈbilitē/ *n.* —**ir·rep·a·ra·bly** /-blē/ *adv.*

ir·re·place·a·ble /iriˈplāsəbəl/ ▸*adj.* impossible to replace if lost or damaged. —**ir·re·place·a·bly** /-blē/ *adv.*

ir·re·press·i·ble /ˌiriˈpresəbəl/ ▸*adj.* not able to be controlled or restrained: *a great shout of irrepressible laughter.* —**ir·re·press·i·bil·i·ty** /-ˌpresəˈbilitē/ *n.* —**ir·re·press·i·bly** /-blē/ *adv.*

ir·re·proach·a·ble /ˌiriˈprōchəbəl/ ▸*adj.* beyond criticism; faultless: *his private life was irreproachable.* ▷mid 17th cent.: from French *irréprochable*, from *in-* 'not' + *reprochable* (from *reprocher* 'to reproach'). —**ir·re·proach·a·bil·i·ty** /-ˌprōchəˈbilitē/ *n.* —**ir·re·proach·a·bly** /-blē/ *adv.*

ir·re·sist·i·ble /ˌiriˈzistəbəl/ ▸*adj.* too attractive and tempting to be resisted: *he found the delicious-looking cakes irresistible.* ■ too powerful or convincing to be resisted: *she felt an irresistible urge to object.* ▷late 16th cent.: from medieval Latin *irresistibilis*, from *in-* 'not' + *resistibilis* (from *resistere* 'resist'). —**ir·re·sist·i·bil·i·ty** /-ˌzistəˈbilitē/ *n.* —**ir·re·sist·i·bly** /-blē/ *adv.*

ir·res·o·lute /i(r)ˈrezəˌlo͞ot/ ▸*adj.* showing or feeling hesitancy; uncertain: *she stood irresolute outside his door.* ▷late 16th cent.: from Latin *irresolutus* 'not loosened,' or from IN-[1] 'not' + RESOLUTE. —**ir·res·o·lute·ly** *adv.* —**ir·res·o·lute·ness** *n.* —**ir·res·o·lu·tion** /-ˌrezəˈlo͞oshən/ *n.*

ir·re·solv·a·ble /ˌiriˈzälvəbəl/ ▸*adj.* (of a problem or dilemma) impossible to solve or settle.

ir·re·spec·tive /ˌiriˈspektiv/ ▸*adj.* [*predic.*] (**irrespective of**) not taking (something) into account; regardless of: *child benefit is paid irrespective of income levels.* —**ir·re·spec·tive·ly** *adv.*

ir·re·spon·si·ble /ˌiriˈspänsəbəl/ ▸*adj.* (of a person, attitude, or action) not showing a proper sense of responsibility: [with *infinitive*] *it would have been irresponsible just to drive on.*
▸*n.* an irresponsible person: *there will always be irresponsibles who take a risk.* —**ir·re·spon·si·bil·i·ty** /-ˌspänsəˈbilitē/ *n.* —**ir·re·spon·si·bly** /-blē/ *adv.*

ir·re·spon·sive /ˌiriˈspänsiv/ ▸*adj.* not responsive to someone or something. —**ir·re·spon·sive·ness** *n.*

ir·re·triev·a·ble /ˌiriˈtrēvəbəl/ ▸*adj.* not able to be retrieved or put right: *the irretrievable breakdown of their marriage.* —**ir·re·triev·a·bil·i·ty** /-ˌtrēvəˈbilitē/ *n.* —**ir·re·triev·a·bly** /-blē/ *adv.*

ir·rev·er·ent /iˈrev(ə)rənt/ ▸*adj.* showing a lack of respect for people or things that are generally taken seriously: *she is irreverent about the whole business of politics.* ▷late Middle English: from Latin *irreverent-* 'not revering,' from *in-* 'not' + *reverent-* 'revering' (see REVERENT). —**ir·rev·er·ence** *n.* —**ir·rev·er·en·tial** /iˌrevəˈrenshəl/ *adj.* —**ir·rev·er·ent·ly** *adv.*

ir·re·vers·i·ble /ˌiriˈvərsəbəl/ ▸*adj.* not able to be undone or altered: *she suffered irreversible damage to her health.* —**ir·re·vers·i·bil·i·ty** /-ˌvərsəˈbilitē/ *n.* —**ir·re·vers·i·bly** /-blē/ *adv.*

ir·re·vers·i·ble bi·no·mi·al ▸*n. Grammar* a noun phrase consisting of two nouns joined by a conjunction, in which the conventional order is fixed. Examples include *bread and butter* and *kith and kin.*

ir·rev·o·ca·ble /ˌiˈrevəkəbəl/ ▸*adj.* not able to be changed, reversed, or recovered; final: *an irrevocable step.* ▷late Middle English: from Old French, or from Latin *irrevocabilis*, from *in-* 'not' + *revocabilis* 'able to be revoked' (from the verb *revocare*). —**ir·rev·o·ca·bil·i·ty** /iˌrevəkəˈbilitē/ *n.* —**ir·rev·o·ca·bly** /-blē/ *adv.*

ir·ri·gate /ˈiriˌgāt/ ▸*v.* [*trans.*] supply water to (land or crops) to help growth, typically by means of channels. ■ (of a river or stream) supply (land) with water. ■ *Medicine* apply a continuous flow of water or liquid medication to (an organ or wound). ▷early 17th cent.: from Latin *irrigat-* 'moistened,' from the verb *irrigare*, from *in-* 'into' + *rigare* 'moisten, wet.' —**ir·ri·ga·ble** /-gəbəl/ *adj.* —**ir·ri·ga·tion** /ˌiriˈgāshən/ *n.* —**ir·ri·ga·tor** /-ˌgātər/ *n.*

ir·ri·ta·ble /ˈiritəbəl/ ▸*adj.* having or showing a tendency to be easily annoyed or made angry: *she was tired and irritable.* ■ *Medicine* (of a bodily part or organ) abnormally sensitive. ■ *Medicine* (of a condition) caused by such sensitivity. ■ *Biology* (of a living organism) having the property of responding actively to physical stimuli. ▷mid 17th cent.: from Latin *irritabilis*, from the verb *irritare* (see IRRITATE). —**ir·ri·ta·bil·i·ty** /ˌiritəˈbilitē/ *n.* —**ir·ri·ta·bly** /-blē/ *adv.*

ir·ri·ta·ble bow·el syn·drome (abbr.: **IBS**) ▸*n.* a widespread condition involving recurrent abdominal pain and diarrhea or constipation, often associated with stress, depression, anxiety, or previous intestinal infection.

ir·ri·tant /ˈiritənt/ ▸*n.* a substance that causes slight inflammation or other discomfort to the body. ■ *figurative* a thing that is continually annoying or distracting: *in 1966, Vietnam was becoming an irritant to the government.*
▸*adj.* causing slight inflammation or other discomfort to the body. —**ir·ri·tan·cy** *n.*

ir·ri·tate /ˈiriˌtāt/ ▸*v.* [*trans.*] make (someone) annoyed, impatient, or angry: *his tone irritated her* | [*intrans.*] *his voice tends to irritate* | [as *adj.*] (**irritating**) *highly irritating remarks.* ■ cause inflammation or other discomfort in (a part of the body). ■ *Biology* stimulate (an organism, cell, or organ) to produce an active response. ▷mid 16th cent. (in the sense 'excite, provoke'): from Latin *irritat-* 'irritated,' from the verb *irritare.* —**ir·ri·tat·ed·ly** *adv.* —**ir·ri·tat·ing·ly** *adv.* —**ir·ri·ta·tive** /-ˌtātiv/ *adj.* —**ir·ri·ta·tor** /-ˌtātər/ *n.*

ir·ri·ta·tion /ˌiriˈtāshən/ ▸*n.* the state of feeling annoyed, impatient, or angry. ■ a cause of this: *the minor irritations of life.* ■ the production of inflammation or other discomfort in a bodily part or organ. ■ *Biology* the stimulation of an organism, cell, or organ to produce an active response. ▷late Middle

Pronunciation Key ə ago; ər over; ˈə or ˌə up; ˈər or ˌər fur; a hat; ā rate; ä car; ch chew; e let; ē see; e(ə)r air; i fit; ī by; i(ə)r ear; ng sing; ō go; ô for; oi boy; o͝o good; o͞o goo; ou out; sh she; th thin; t͟h then; (h)w why; zh vision

I

English: from Latin *irritatio(n-)*, from the verb *irritare* (see IRRITATE).

ir·ro·ta·tion·al /irō'tāsHənl/ ▸*adj. Physics* (esp. of fluid motion) not rotational; having no rotation.

ir·rupt /i'rəpt/ ▸*v.* [*intrans.*] enter forcibly or suddenly: *the specter of social revolution once again* ***irrupted into*** *a confident capitalist world.* ■ (of a bird or other animal) migrate into an area in abnormally large numbers. ▷mid 19th cent.: from Latin *irrupt-* 'broken into,' from the verb *irrumpere*, from *in-* 'into' + *rumpere* 'break.' —**ir·rup·tion** /-sHən/ *n.* —**ir·rup·tive** /-tiv/ *adj.*

IRS ▸*abbr.* Internal Revenue Service.

Ir·tysh /ir'tisH; ər-/ a river in central Asia that rises in the Altai Mountains in northern China and flows west into northeastern Kazakhstan, where it turns northwest to join the Ob River near its mouth in Russia. Its length is 2,655 miles (4,248 km).

Ir·ving[1] /'ərviNG/ an industrial city in northeastern Texas, between Dallas and Fort Worth; pop. 191,615.

Ir·ving[2], John (Winslow) (1942–) U.S. writer and teacher. His works such as *The World According to Garp* (1978) combine tragedy with comedy He also wrote *The Hotel New Hampshire* (1981), *The Cider House Rules* (1985), and *A Widow for One Year* (1998).

Ir·ving[3], Washington (1783–1859), U.S. writer. He is best known for *The Sketch Book of Geoffrey Crayon, Gent.* (1819–20), which contains such tales as "Rip Van Winkle" and "The Legend of Sleepy Hollow."

Ir·ving·ton /'ərviNGtən/ an industrial and residential township in northeastern New Jersey, west of Newark; pop. 61,010.

is /iz/ ▸ third person singular present of BE.

Is. ▸*abbr.* ■ (also **Isa.**) *Bible* Isaiah. ■ Island(s). ■ Isle(s).

ISA ▸*abbr. Computing* industry standard architecture, a standard for connecting computers and their peripherals: [as *adj.*] *an ISA expansion slot.*

I·saac /'ī,zək/ (in the Bible) a Hebrew patriarch, son of Abraham and Sarah and father of Jacob and Esau.

Is·a·bel·la /,izə'belə/ ▸*n.* another term for FOX GRAPE. ■ a wine made from this grape.

Is·a·bel·la I (1451–1504), queen of Castile 1474–1504 and of Aragon 1479–1504. Her marriage in 1469 to Ferdinand of Aragon marked the beginning of the unification of Spain. They instituted the Spanish Inquisition in 1478 and supported the explorations of Christopher Columbus in 1492.

Is·a·bel·la of France (1292–1358), daughter of Philip IV of France and wife of Edward II of England 1308–27. She left England to return to France in 1325, where she and her lover, Roger de Mortimer, organized an invasion of England in 1326. They murdered Edward and replaced him with Isabella's son, Edward III.

i·sa·gog·ics /,īsə'gäjiks/ ▸*plural n.* [treated as *sing.*] introductory study, esp. of the literary and external history of the Bible prior to exegesis. ▷mid 19th cent.: plural of *isagogic*, via Latin from Greek *eisagōgikos*, from *eisagōgē* 'introduction,' from *eis* 'into' + *agein* 'to lead.' —**i·sa·gog·ic** /-jik/ *adj.*

I·sa·iah /ī'zāə/ a major Hebrew prophet of Judah in the 8th century BC, who taught the supremacy of the God of Israel and emphasized the moral demands on worshipers. ■ a book of the Bible containing his prophecies and, it is generally thought, those of at least one later prophet.

is·al·lo·bar /ī'salə,bär/ ▸*n. Meteorology* a line on a map connecting points at which the atmospheric pressure has changed by an equal amount during a specified time. ▷early 20th cent.: from ISO- 'equal' + ALLO- 'other' + BAR[2]. —**is·al·lo·bar·ic** /ī,salə'bärik/ *adj.*

i·sa·tin /'īsətin/ ▸*n. Chemistry* a red crystalline compound used in the manufacture of dyes. • An indole derivative; chem. formula: $C_8H_5NO_2$. ▷mid 19th cent.: from Latin *isatis* 'woad' (from Greek) + -IN[1].

ISBN ▸*abbr.* international standard book number, a ten-digit number assigned to every book before publication, recording such details as language, provenance, and publisher.

is·che·mi·a /is'kēmēə/ (*Brit.* **is·chae·mi·a**) ▸*n. Medicine* an inadequate blood supply to an organ or part of the body, esp. the heart muscles. ▷late 19th cent. (denoting the stanching of bleeding): modern Latin, from Greek *iskhaimos* 'stopping blood,' from *iskhein* 'keep back' + *haima* 'blood.' —**is·che·mic** /-mik/ *adj.*

Is·chi·a /'iskēə/ an island in the Tyrrhenian Sea off the western coast of Italy, about 16 miles (26 km) west of Naples.

is·chi·um /'iskēəm/ ▸*n.* (*pl.* **-chi·a** /-kēə/) the curved bone forming the base of each half of the pelvis. ▷early 17th cent.: from Latin, from Greek *iskhion* 'hip joint,' later 'ischium.' —**is·chi·ad·ic** /,iskē'adik/ *adj.* —**is·chi·al** /-kēəl/ *adj.*

ISDN ▸*abbr.* integrated services digital network.

Ise /'ēsā/ a city in Japan, on the central part of the island of Honshu, on Ise Bay; pop. 104,000. Former name (until 1956) UJIYAMADA.

-ise[1] ▸*suffix* variant spelling of -IZE.

> *USAGE* There are some verbs that must be spelled -ise and are not variants of the -ize ending. Most reflect a French influence: they include *advertise, televise, compromise, enterprise,* and *improvise.* For more details, see **usage** at -IZE.

-ise[2] ▸*suffix* forming nouns of quality, state, or function: *expertise* | *franchise* | *merchandise.* ▷from Old French *-ise*, from Latin *-itia, -itium.*

is·en·trop·ic /,īsən'träpik; -'trōpik/ ▸*adj. Physics* having equal entropy.

I·seult[1] /i'so͞olt; i'zo͞olt/ a princess in medieval legend; known as **Iseult the Fair**. She was the daughter of the king of Ireland. Tristram was sent to seek her hand on behalf of his uncle, King Mark of Cornwall. En route back to Cornwall Tristram and Iseult mistakenly drank the love potion intended for the wedding night of Iseult and Mark and fell hopelessly in love. Iseult was bound to marry King Mark, but she and Tristram continued their affair until Mark became suspicious and Tristram had to flee. The tragic story is part of the body of Arthurian literature. Versions of the legend were told by Thomas of Brittany (*fl.* 12th cent.), Gottfried von Strassburg (*fl.* 12th–13th cent.), Alfred, Lord Tennyson, and Richard Wagner in his opera *Tristan.* Also called ISOLDE.

I·seult[2] /i'so͞olt; i'zo͞olt/ ▸a princess in medieval legend; known as **Iseult of the White Hands.** She was the daughter of the king of Brittany and, in some versions of the legend, married Tristram after he was banished from Cornwall because of his love for Iseult the Fair.

Is·fa·han /,isfə'hän/ (also **Es·fa·han** /,esfə-/, **Is·pa·han** /,ispə-/) an industrial city in central Iran; pop. 1,127,000. It was the capital of Persia 1598–1722.

-ish[1] /isH/ ▸*suffix* forming adjectives: **1** (from nouns) having the qualities or characteristics of: *apish* | *girlish.* ■ of nationality or religious or ethnic group: *Swedish* | *Amish* | *Flemish.* **2** (from adjectives) somewhat: *yellowish.* ■ *informal* denoting an approximate age or time of day: *sixish.* ▷Old English *-isc*, of Germanic origin; related to Old Norse *-iskr*, German and Dutch *-isch*, also to Greek *-iskos* (suffix forming diminutive nouns).

-ish[2] ▸*suffix* forming verbs such as *abolish, establish.* ▷from French *-iss-* (from stems of verbs ending in *-ir*), from Latin *-isc-* (suffix forming inceptive verbs); compare with -ISH[1].

Ish·er·wood /'isHər,wo͝od/, Christopher (William Bradshaw) (1904–86), U.S. novelist; born in Britain. Notable works: *Mr. Norris Changes Trains* (1935) and *Goodbye to Berlin* (1939; movie, *Cabaret*, 1972).

Ishi·gu·ro /,isHi'go͞o,rō/, Kazuo (1954–), British novelist; born in Japan. Notable works: *An Artist of the Floating World* (1986) and *The Remains of the Day* (1989).

Ish·i·ha·ra test /,isHē'härə/ ▸*n.* a test for color-blindness in which the subject is asked to distinguish numbers or pathways printed in colored spots on a background of spots of a different color or colors. ▷early 20th cent.: named after Shinobu *Ishihara* (1879–1963), Japanese ophthalmologist.

Ish·ma·el /'isHmēəl; -mā-/ (in the Bible) a son of Abraham, by his wife Sarah's maid, Hagar, driven away with his mother after the birth of Sarah's son Isaac (Gen. 16:12). Ishmael (or Ismail) is also important in Islamic belief as the traditional ancestor of Muhammad and of the Arab peoples. —**Ish·ma·el·ite** /-,līt/ *n.*

Ish·tar /'isH,tär/ *Near Eastern Mythology* a Babylonian and Assyrian goddess of love and war whose name and functions correspond to those of the Phoenician goddess Astarte.

Is·i·dore of Se·ville, St. /'izə,dôr əv sə'vil/ (*c.*560–636), Spanish archbishop and doctor of the Church; also called *Isidorus Hispalensis.* He is noted for *Etymologies*, an encyclopedic work used by many medieval authors. Feast day, April 4.

i·sin·glass /'īzən,glas; 'īziNG-/ ▸*n.* a kind of gelatin obtained from fish, esp. sturgeon, and used in making jellies, glue, etc., and for clarifying ale. ■ mica or a similar material in thin transparent sheets. ▷mid 16th cent.: alteration (by association with GLASS) of obsolete Dutch *huysenblas* 'sturgeon's bladder,' from *huysen* 'sturgeon' + *blas* 'bladder.'

I·sis /'īsis/ *Egyptian Mythology* a goddess of fertility, wife of Osiris and mother of Horus. Her worship spread to western Asia, Greece, and Rome, where she was identified with various local goddesses.

Is·ken·de·run /is,kendə'ro͞on/ a port and naval base in southern Turkey, on the Mediterranean coast; pop. 159,000.

isl. (also **Isl.**) ▸*abbr.* ■ island or isle.

Is·lam /is'läm; iz-/ ▸*n.* the religion of the Muslims, a monotheistic faith regarded as revealed through Muhammad as the Prophet of Allah. ■ the Muslim world: *the most enormous complex of fortifications in all Islam.*

> Founded in the Arabian peninsula in the 7th century AD, Islam is now the professed faith of nearly a billion people worldwide, particularly in North Africa, the Middle East, and parts of Asia. The ritual observances and moral code of Islam were said to have been given to Muhammad as a series of revelations, which were codified in the Koran. Islam is regarded by its adherents as the last of the revealed religions, and Muhammad is seen as the last of the prophets, building on and perfecting the examples and teachings of Abraham, Moses, and Jesus. There are two major branches in Islam: Sunni and Shia.

▷from Arabic *'islām* 'submission,' from *'aslama* 'submit (to God).' —**Is·lam·ic** /-ik/ *adj.* —**Is·lam·i·ci·za·tion** /is,lämisi'zāsHən; iz-/ *n.* —**Is·lam·i·cize** /is'lämi,sīz; iz-/ *v.* —**Is·lam·ism** /'islə,mizəm; 'iz-/ *n.* —**Is·lam·ist** /-ist/ *n.* —**Is·lam·i·za·tion** /is,lämi'zāsHən; iz-/ *n.* —**Is·lam·ize** /'islə,mīz; 'iz-/ *v.*

Is·lam·a·bad /is'lämə,bäd; iz'lamə,bad/ the capital of Pakistan, a modern planned city in the north of the country; pop. 201,000. It replaced Rawalpindi as the capital in 1967.

Is·lam·ic Ji·had /is'lämik ji'had; -'häd; iz-/ (also **Je·had**) a Muslim fundamentalist terrorist group within the Shiite Hezbollah association.

Is·lam·o·pho·bi·a /is,lämə'fōbēə; iz-/ ▸*n.* a hatred or fear of Islam or Muslims, especially when feared as a political force. ▷from *Islam* + *-o-* + *phobia.*

Is·land /'ē,slän(t)/ Icelandic name for ICELAND.

is·land /'ilənd/ ▸*n.* a piece of land surrounded by water. ■ *figurative* a thing resembling an island, esp. in being isolated, detached, or surrounded in some way: *the university is the last island of democracy in this country.* ■ a freestanding kitchen cupboard unit with a countertop, allowing access from all sides. ■ *Anatomy* a detached portion of tissue or group of cells. Compare with ISLET.

▸*v.* [*trans.*] make into or like an island; place or enclose on or as on an island; isolate: *islanded among the new stores, these houses were valuable property* | *the house where she has been islanded.* ▷Old English *īegland*, from *īeg* 'island' (from a base meaning 'watery, watered') + LAND. The change in the spelling of the first syllable in the 16th cent. was due to association with the unrelated word ISLE.

is·land arc ▸*n. Geology* a curved chain of volcanic islands located at a tectonic plate margin, typically with a deep ocean trench on the convex side.

is·land·er /'iləndər/ ▸*n.* a native or inhabitant of an island.

is·land-hop ▸*v.* [*intrans.*] [usu. as *n.*] (**island-hopping**) travel from one island to another, esp. as a tourist in an area of small islands.

Is·lands of the Bless·ed (in classical mythology) a land, typically located near the place where the sun sets, to which the souls of the good were taken to enjoy a life of eternal bliss.

isle /īl/ ▸*n. chiefly poetic/literary* an island or peninsula, esp. a small one: *Crusoe's fabled isle* | [in *place names*] *the British Isles.* ▷Middle English *ile*, from Old French, from Latin *insula.* The spelling with *s* (also in 15th-cent. French) is influenced by Latin.

Isle of Man /man/ an island in the Irish Sea that is a British crown possession with home rule; pop. 70,000; capital, Douglas. Its ancient language, Manx, is still occasionally used for ceremonial purposes.

Isle of Wight /wīt/ an island in England, off the southern coast, a county since 1974; pop. 127,000; administrative center, Newport.

Isle Roy·ale /'roiəl/ an island in Michigan, in western Lake Superior, near Grand Portage in Minnesota. Part of a national park, it is noted for its wildlife.

is·let /'īlət/ ▸*n.* **1** a small island. **2** *Anatomy* a portion of tissue structurally distinct from surrounding tissues. ■ (**islets**) short for ISLETS OF LANGERHANS. ▷mid 16th cent.: from Old French, diminutive of *isle* (see ISLE).

is·lets of Lang·er·hans /ˈlaNGərˌhanz; ˈläNGərˌhäns/ (also **is·lands of Lang·er·hans**) ▸*plural n.* groups of pancreatic cells secreting insulin and glucagon. ▷late 19th cent.: named after Paul *Langerhans* (1847–88), the German anatomist who first described them.

Is·ley, Phyllis, see JONES[4].

ism /ˈizəm/ ▸*n. informal, chiefly derogatory* a distinctive practice, system, or philosophy, typically a political ideology or an artistic movement: *of all the isms, fascism is the most repressive.* ▷late 17th cent.: independent usage of **-ISM**. **—ist** *n.*

-ism ▸*suffix* forming nouns: **1** denoting an action or its result: *baptism* | *exorcism.* ■ denoting a state or quality: *barbarism.* **2** denoting a system, principle, or ideological movement: *Anglicanism* | *feminism* | *hedonism.* ■ denoting a basis for prejudice or discrimination: *racism.* **3** denoting a peculiarity in language: *colloquialism* | *Canadianism.* **4** denoting a pathological condition: *alcoholism.* ▷from French *-isme*, via Latin from Greek *-ismos*, *-isma*.

Is·ma·il /ˌismäˈēl/ Arabic spelling of **ISHMAEL**.

Is·ma·il·i /ˌismäˈēlē/ ▸*n.* (*pl.* **-il·is**) a member of a branch of Shiite Muslims that seceded from the main group in the 8th century because of their belief that Ismail, the son of the sixth Shiite imam, should have become the seventh imam.

Is·mail Sa·ma·ni Peak /ˈismīl səˈmänē/ one of the principal peaks in the Pamir Mountains of Tajikistan, rising to 24,590 feet (7,495 m). It was the highest mountain in the former Soviet Union. Former names: **Mount Garmo** (until 1933), **Stalin Peak** (1933–62), **Communism Peak** (1962–98). ▷named after the 9th-century founder of the Tajik nation.

is·n't /ˈizənt/ ▸*contraction of* is not.

ISO ▸*abbr.* International Organization for Standardization.

iso- ▸*comb. form* equal: *isochron* | *isosceles.* ■ *Chemistry* (chiefly of hydrocarbons) isomeric: *isooctane.* ▷from Greek *isos* 'equal.'

i·so·ag·glu·ti·na·tion /ˌīsōəglo͞otnˈāSHən/ ▸*n. Physiology* agglutination of sperms, erythrocytes, or other cells of an individual caused by a substance from another individual of the same species.

i·so·bar /ˈīsəˌbär/ ▸*n.* **1** *Meteorology* a line on a map connecting points having the same atmospheric pressure at a given time or on average over a given period. ■ *Physics* a curve or formula representing a physical system at constant pressure. **2** *Physics* each of two or more isotopes of different elements, with the same atomic weight. ▷mid 19th cent.: from Greek *isobaros* 'of equal weight,' from *isos* 'equal' + *baros* 'weight.' **—i·so·bar·ic** /ˌīsəˈbarik; -ˈbär-/ *adj.*

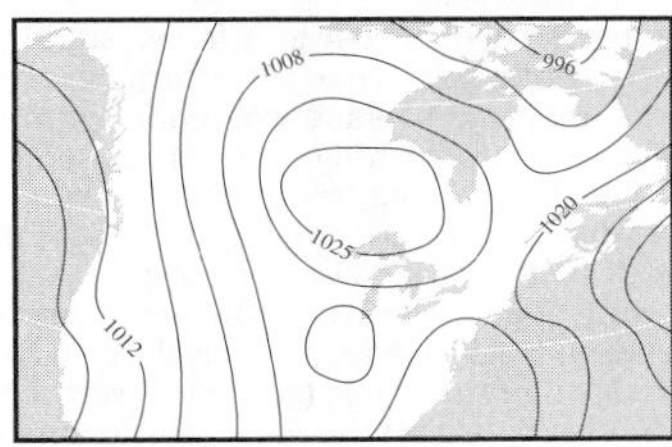

isobar 1

i·so·bu·tane /ˌīsəˈbyo͞otān; -byo͞oˈtān/ ▸*n. Chemistry* a gaseous hydrocarbon isomeric with butane. • Chem. formula: $CH_3CH(CH_3)_2$.

i·so·bu·tyl·ene /ˌīsəˈbyo͞otlˌēn/, ▸*n. Chemistry* an easily liquefied hydrocarbon gas, $(CH_3)_2C{=}CH_2$, used in the making of butyl rubber.

i·so·cheim /ˈīsəˌkīm/ ▸*n. Meteorology* a line on a map connecting points having the same average temperature in winter. ▷mid 19th cent.: from **ISO-** 'equal' + Greek *kheima* 'winter weather.'

i·so·chro·mat·ic /ˌīsəkrəˈmatik/ ▸*adj.* of a single color.

i·so·chron /ˈīsəˌkrän/ ▸*n. chiefly Geology* a line on a diagram or map connecting points relating to the same time or equal times. ▷late 17th cent. (as an adjective in the sense 'isochronous'): from Greek *isokhronos*, from *isos* 'equal' + *khronos* 'time.'

i·soch·ro·nous /īˈsäkrənəs/ ▸*adj.* occurring at the same time. ■ occupying equal time. ▷early 18th cent. (in the sense 'equal in duration or in frequency'): from modern Latin *isochronus* (from Greek *isokhronos*, from *isos* 'equal' + *khronos* 'time') + **-OUS**. **—i·soch·ro·nous·ly** *adv.*

i·so·cli·nal /ˌīsəˈklīnl/ ▸*adj. Geology* denoting a fold of strata so acute that the two limbs are parallel. ▷mid 19th cent. (denoting 'equal magnetic inclination'): from **ISO-** 'equal' + Greek *klinein* 'to lean, slope' + **-AL**.

i·so·cline /ˈīsəˌklīn/ ▸*n.* a line on a diagram or map connecting points of equal gradient or inclination. ▷late 19th cent. (denoting an isoclinal line or fold): from Greek *isoklinēs* 'equally balanced,' from *klinein* 'to lean, slope.' **—i·so·clin·ic** /ˌīsəˈklinik/ *adj.*

i·so·clin·ic line /ˌīsəˈklinik/ ▸*n.* a line on a map connecting points where the dip of the earth's magnetic field is the same.

i·so·crat·ic /ˌīsəˈkratik/ ▸*adj. Chemistry* (of a chromatographic method) involving a mobile phase whose composition is kept constant and uniform. ▷early 19th cent.: from Greek *isokratia* 'equality of power' (from *isos* 'equal' + *kratos* 'strength') + **-IC**.

i·so·di·a·met·ric /ˌīsōˌdīəˈmetrik/ ▸*adj. chiefly Botany* (of a cell, spore, etc.) roughly spherical or polyhedral.

i·so·dy·nam·ic /ˌīsədīˈnamik/ ▸*adj. Geography* indicating or connecting points on the earth's surface at which the intensity of the magnetic force is the same.

i·so·e·lec·tric /ˌīsō-iˈlektrik/ ▸*adj.* having or involving no net electric charge or difference in electrical potential.

i·so·e·lec·tric fo·cus·ing ▸*n. Biochemistry* a technique of electrophoresis in which the resolution is improved by maintaining a pH gradient between the electrodes.

i·so·e·lec·tron·ic /ˌīsō-ilekˈtränik; -ˌēlek-/ ▸*adj. Chemistry* having the same numbers of electrons or the same electronic structure.

i·so·en·zyme /ˌīsōˈenzīm/ ▸*n. Biochemistry* another term for **ISOZYME**.

i·sog·a·my /īˈsägəmē/ ▸*n. Biology* sexual reproduction by the fusion of similar gametes. Compare with **ANISOGAMY**. ▷late 19th cent.: from **ISO-** 'equal' + Greek *-gamia* (from *gamos* 'marriage'). **—i·so·gam·ete** /ˌīsēˈgamēt; īsōgəˈmēt/ *n.* **—i·sog·a·mous** /-məs/ *adj.*

i·so·gen·ic /ˌīsəˈjenik/ ▸*adj. Biology* (of organisms) having the same or closely similar genotypes.

i·so·ge·o·therm /ˌīsəˈjēəˌTHərm/ ▸*n. Geography* a line or plane on a diagram connecting points representing those in the interior of the earth having the same temperature. ▷mid 19th cent.: from **ISO-** 'equal' + **GEO-** 'earth' + Greek *thermē* 'heat.' **—i·so·ge·o·ther·mal** /-ˌjēəˈTHərməl/ *adj.*

i·so·gloss /ˈīsəˌglôs; -ˌgläs/ ▸*n. Linguistics* a line on a dialect map marking the boundary between linguistic features. ▷early 20th cent.: from **ISO-** 'equal' + Greek *glōssa* 'tongue, word.' **—i·so·glos·sal** /ˌīsəˈglôsəl; -ˈgläsəl/ *adj.*

i·so·gon·ic /ˌīsəˈgänik/ (also **i·sog·o·nal** /īˈsägənl/) ▸*adj. Geography* indicating or connecting points of the earth's surface at which the magnetic declination is the same. ▷mid 19th cent.: from Greek *isogōnios* 'equiangular' + **-IC**.

i·so·hel /ˈīsəˌhel/ ▸*n. Meteorology* a line on a map connecting points having the same duration of sunshine. ▷early 20th cent.: from **ISO-** 'equal' + Greek *hēlios* 'sun.'

i·so·hy·et /ˌīsəˈhī-it/ ▸*n. Meteorology* a line on a map connecting points having the same amount of rainfall in a given period. ▷late 19th cent.: from **ISO-** 'equal' + Greek *huetos* 'rain.'

i·so·ki·net·ic /ˌīsōkəˈnetik/ ▸*adj.* characterized by or producing a constant speed. ■ *Physiology* of or relating to muscular action with a constant rate of movement.

i·so·late ▸*v.* /ˈīsəˌlāt/ [*trans.*] cause (a person or place) to be or remain alone or apart from others: *a country that is* **isolated from** *the rest of the world.* ■ identify (something) and examine or deal with it separately: *you can't isolate stress from the management context.* ■ *Chemistry & Biology* obtain or extract (a compound, microorganism, etc.) in a pure form. ■ cut off the electrical or other connection to (something, esp. a part of a supply network). ■ place (a person or animal) in quarantine as a precaution against infectious or contagious disease.

▸*n.* /-lit/ a person or thing that has been or become isolated: *social isolates often become careless of their own welfare.* ■ *Biology* a culture of microorganisms isolated for study. ▷early 19th cent. (as a verb): back-formation from **ISOLATED**. **—i·so·la·ble** /-ləbəl/ *adj.* **—i·so·lat·a·ble** *adj.* **—i·so·la·tor** /-ˌlātər/ *n.*

i·so·lat·ed /ˈīsəˌlātid/ ▸*adj.* far away from other places, buildings, or people; remote: *isolated farms and villages.* ■ having minimal contact or little in common with others: *he lived a very isolated existence.* ■ single; exceptional: *they were isolated incidents.* ▷mid 18th cent.: from French *isolé*, from Italian *isolato*, from late Latin *insulatus* 'made into an island,' from Latin *insula* 'island.'

i·so·lat·ing /ˈīsəˌlātiNG/ ▸*adj.* (of a language) tending to have each element as an independent word without inflections.

i·so·la·tion /ˌīsəˈlāSHən/ ▸*n.* the process or fact of isolating or being isolated: *the isolation of older people.* ■ an instance of isolating something, esp. a compound or microorganism. ■ [as *adj.*] denoting a hospital or ward for patients with contagious or infectious diseases. ▷mid 19th cent.: from **ISOLATE**, partly on the pattern of French *isolation.*

▸*PHRASE* □ **in isolation** without relation to other people or things; separately: *environmental problems must not be seen* **in isolation from** *social ones.*

i·so·la·tion·ism /ˌīsəˈlāSHəˌnizəm/ ▸*n.* a policy of remaining apart from the affairs or interests of other groups, esp. the political affairs of other countries. **—i·so·la·tion·ist** *n.*

I·solde /iˈsōld; iˈsōldə; ēˈzôldə/ another name for **ISEULT**.

i·so·leu·cine /ˌīsəˈlo͞osēn; -sin/ ▸*n. Biochemistry* a hydrophobic amino acid that is a constituent of most proteins. It is an essential nutrient in the diet of vertebrates. • Chem. formula: $CH_3CH_2CH(CH_3)CH(NH_2)COOH$.

i·so·line /ˈīsəˌlīn/ ▸*n.* another term for **ISOPLETH**.

i·so·mer /ˈīsəmər/ ▸*n.* **1** *Chemistry* each of two or more compounds with the same formula but a different arrangement of atoms in the molecule and different properties. **2** *Physics* each of two or more atomic nuclei that have the same atomic number and the same mass number but different energy states. ▷mid 19th cent.: from Greek *isomerēs* 'sharing equally,' from *isos* 'equal' + *meros* 'a share.' **—i·so·mer·ic** /ˌīsəˈmerik/ *adj.* **—i·som·er·ism** /īˈsäməˌrizəm/ *n.* **—i·som·er·ize** /īˈsäməˌrīz/ *v.*

i·som·er·ase /īˈsäməˌrās; -ˌrāz/ ▸*n. Biochemistry* an enzyme that catalyzes the conversion of a specified compound to an isomer.

i·som·er·ous /īˈsämərəs/ ▸*adj. Biology* having or composed of parts that are similar in number or position. ▷mid 19th cent.: from Greek *isomerēs* (see **ISOMER**) + **-OUS**.

i·so·met·ric /ˌīsəˈmetrik/ ▸*adj.* **1** of or having equal dimensions. **2** *Physiology* of, relating to, or denoting muscular action in which tension is developed without contraction of the muscle. **3** (in technical or architectural drawing) incorporating a method of showing projection or perspective in which the three principal dimensions are represented by three axes 120° apart. **4** *Mathematics* (of a transformation) without change of shape or size. ▷mid 19th cent.: from Greek *isometria* 'equality of measure' (from *isos* 'equal' + *-metria* 'measuring') + **-IC**. **—i·so·met·ri·cal·ly** /-ik(ə)lē/ *adv.* **—i·som·e·try** /īˈsämitrē/ *n.* (in sense 4).

i·so·met·rics /ˌīsəˈmetriks/ ▸*plural n.* a system of physical exercises in which muscles are caused to act against each other or against a fixed object. Also called **isometric exercise**.

i·so·mor·phic /ˌīsəˈmôrfik/ (also **i·so·morph·ous** /-fəs/) ▸*adj.* corresponding or similar in form and relations. ■ having the same crystalline form. **—i·so·mor·phism** /-ˌfizəm/ *n.*

-ison ▸*suffix* (forming nouns) equivalent to **-ATION** (as in *comparison, jettison*). ▷from Old French *-aison*, *-eison*, etc., from Latin *-atio(n)-*.

i·so·ni·a·zid /ˌīsəˈnīəzid/ ▸*n. Medicine* a synthetic compound used as a bacteriostatic drug, chiefly to treat tuberculosis. • A derivative of nicotinic acid and hydrazine; chem. formula: $C_5H_5NCONHNH_2$. ▷1950s: from **ISO-** 'equal' + *ni(cotinic)* + *(hydr)azine* + **-IDE**.

i·so·oc·tane /ˌīsōˈäktān/ ▸*n. Chemistry* a liquid hydrocarbon present in petroleum. It serves as a standard in the system of octane numbers. • Chem. formula: $(CH_3)_3CCH_2CH(CH_3)CH_3$.

i·so·pach /ˈīsəˌpak/ ▸*n. Geology* a line on a map or diagram connecting points beneath which a particular stratum or group of strata has the same thickness. ▷early 20th cent.: from **ISO-** 'equal' + Greek *pakhus* 'thick.'

Pronunciation Key ə *ago*; ər *over*; ˈə *or* ˌə *up*; ˈər *or* ˌər *fur*; a *hat*; ā *rate*; ä *car*; CH *chew*; e *let*; ē *see*; e(ə)r *air*; i *fit*; ī *by*; i(ə)r *ear*; NG *sing*; ō *go*; ô *for*; oi *boy*; o͝o *good*; o͞o *goo*; ou *out*; SH *she*; TH *thin*; T͟H *then*; (h)w *why*; ZH *vision*

i·so·pleth /ˈīsəpleᴛʜ/ ▸*n. Meteorology* a line on a map connecting points having equal incidence of a specified meteorological feature. ▷early 20th cent.: from Greek *isoplēthēs* 'equal in quantity,' from *isos* 'equal' + *plēthos* 'multitude, quantity.'

I·sop·o·da /īˈsäpədə/ *Zoology* an order of crustaceans that includes the terrestrial wood lice and several marine and freshwater parasites. They have a flattened segmented body with seven similar pairs of legs. ▷modern Latin (plural), from Greek *isos* 'equal' + *pous, pod-* 'foot.' —**i·so·pod** /ˈīsəˌpäd/ *n.*

i·so·pre·na·line /ˌīsəˈprenl,ēn/ ▸*n.* another term for **ISOPROTERENOL**. ▷1950s: from elements of the systematic name *N-isopropylnoradrenaline*.

i·so·prene /ˈīsəˌprēn/ ▸*n. Chemistry* a volatile liquid hydrocarbon obtained from petroleum, whose molecule forms the basic structural unit of natural and synthetic rubbers. • Chem. formula: $CH_2{=}C(CH_3)CH{=}CH_2$. ▷mid 19th cent.: apparently from **ISO-** 'equal' + *pr(opyl)ene*.

i·so·pro·pa·nol /ˌīsəˈprōpəˌnôl; -ˌnäl/ ▸*n. Chemistry* a liquid alcohol, used as a solvent and in the industrial production of acetone. • Chem. formula: $CH_3CHOHCH_3$.

i·so·pro·pyl /ˌīsəˈprōpəl/ ▸*n.* [as *adj.*] *Chemistry* of or denoting the alkyl radical $-CH(CH_3)_2$, derived from propane by removal of a hydrogen atom from the middle carbon atom.

i·so·pro·pyl al·co·hol ▸*n. Chemistry* another term for **ISOPROPANOL**.

i·so·pro·ter·e·nol /ˌīsəprōˈterəˌnôl; -ˌnäl/ ▸*n. Medicine* a synthetic derivative of adrenalin, used for the relief of bronchial asthma and pulmonary emphysema. ▷1950s: from elements of the semisystematic name *N-isopropylarterenol*.

I·sop·te·ra /īˈsäptərə/ *Entomology* an order of insects that comprises the termites. ▷modern Latin (plural), from Greek *isos* 'equal' + *pteron* 'wing.' —**i·sop·te·ran** *n.* & *adj.*

i·so·pyc·nal /ˌīsəˈpiknl/ ▸*adj. Oceanography* (esp. of an imaginary line or surface on a map or chart) connecting points in the ocean where the water has the same density. ▷early 20th cent.: from **ISO-** 'equal' + Greek *puknos* 'dense' + **-AL**.

i·so·pyc·nic /ˌīsəˈpiknik/ ▸*adj. Biochemistry* of or denoting ultracentrifugal separation techniques making use of differences in density between the components of a mixture. ▷late 19th cent.: from **ISO-** 'equal' + Greek *puknos* 'dense' + **-IC**.

i·so·rhyth·mic /ˌīsəˈriᴛʜmik/ ▸*adj. Music* (of a composition or part) in which the rhythm is often repeated but the pitch of the notes is varied each time.

i·sos·bes·tic point /ˌīsəsˈbestik/ ▸*n. Chemistry* a wavelength at which the absorption of light by a mixed solution remains constant as the equilibrium between the components in the solution changes. ▷early 20th cent.: *isosbestic* from **ISO-** 'equal' + Greek *sbestos* 'extinguished' (from *sbennunai* 'quench') + **-IC**.

i·sos·ce·les /īˈsäsəˌlēz/ ▸*adj.* (of a triangle) having two sides of equal length. ▷mid 16th cent.: via late Latin from Greek *isoskelēs*, from *isos* 'equal' + *skelos* 'leg.'

i·so·seis·mal /ˌīsəˈsīzməl/ ▸*adj. Geology* relating to or denoting lines on a map connecting places where an earthquake was experienced with equal strength. —**i·so·seis·mic** /-mik/ *adj.*

i·sos·mot·ic /ˌīsäzˈmätik; -säs-/ ▸*adj. Biology* having the same osmotic pressure.

i·so·spin /ˈīsəˌspin/ ▸*n. Physics* a vector quantity or quantum number assigned to subatomic particles and atomic nuclei and having values such that similar particles differing only in charge-related properties (independent of the strong interaction between particles) can be treated as different states of a single particle. ▷1960s: contraction of *isotopic spin, isobaric spin*.

i·sos·ta·sy /īˈsästəsē/ ▸*n. Geology* the equilibrium that exists between parts of the earth's crust, which behaves as if it consists of blocks floating on the underlying mantle, rising if material (such as an ice cap) is removed and sinking if material is deposited. ▷late 19th cent.: from **ISO-** 'equal' + Greek *stasis* 'station.' —**i·so·stat·ic** /ˌīsəˈstatik/ *adj.*

i·so·tac·tic /ˌīsəˈtaktik/ ▸*adj. Chemistry* (of a polymer) in which all the repeating units have the same stereochemical configuration. ▷1950s: from **ISO-** 'equal' + Greek *taktos* 'arranged' + **-IC**.

i·so·there /ˈīsəˌᴛʜir/ ▸*n. Meteorology* a line on a map connecting points having the same average temperature in summer. ▷mid 19th cent.: from French *isothère*, from Greek *isos* 'equal' + *theros* 'summer.'

i·so·therm /ˈīsəˌᴛʜərm/ ▸*n.* a line on a map connecting points having the same temperature at a given time or on average over a given period. ■ *Physics* a curve on a diagram joining points representing states or conditions of equal temperature. ▷mid 19th cent.: from French *isotherme*, from Greek *isos* 'equal' + *thermē* 'heat.' —**i·so·ther·mal** /ˌīsəˈᴛʜərməl/ *adj.* & *n.* —**i·so·ther·mal·ly** /ˌīsəˈᴛʜərməlē/ *adv.*

i·so·thi·o·cy·a·nate /ˌīsōˌᴛʜī-ōˈsīənāt; -nit/ ▸*n.* a family of organic compounds found in tangy herbs such as horseradish, mustard, and onions. They have several patented applications including use as a pesticide, and their presence in the diet is thought to help prevent cancer in humans.

i·so·ton·ic /ˌīsəˈtänik/ ▸*adj. Physiology* **1** (of muscle action) taking place with normal contraction. **2** denoting or relating to a solution having the same osmotic pressure as some other solution, esp. one in a cell or a body fluid. ■ (of a drink) containing essential salts and minerals in the same concentration as in the body and intended to replace those lost as a result of sweating during vigorous exercise. ▷early 19th cent. (as a musical term designating a system of tuning, characterized by equal intervals): from Greek *isotonos*, from *isos* 'equal' + *tonos* 'tone.' —**i·so·ton·i·cal·ly** /-ik(ə)lē/ *adv.* —**i·so·to·nic·i·ty** /-təˈnisitē/ *n.*

i·so·tope /ˈīsəˌtōp/ ▸*n. Chemistry* each of two or more forms of the same element that contain equal numbers of protons but different numbers of neutrons in their nuclei, and hence differ in relative atomic mass but not in chemical properties; in particular, a radioactive form of an element. ▷1913: coined by F. Soddy, from **ISO-** 'equal' + Greek *topos* 'place' (because the isotopes occupy the same place in the periodic table of elements). —**i·so·top·ic** /ˌīsəˈtäpik/ *adj.* —**i·so·top·i·cal·ly** /ˌīsəˈtäpik(ə)lē/ *adv.* —**i·sot·o·py** /ˈīsəˌtōpē; īˈsätəpē/ *n.*

i·so·trop·ic /ˌīsəˈträpik; -ˈtrōpik/ ▸*adj. Physics* (of an object or substance) having a physical property that has the same value when measured in different directions. Often contrasted with **ANISOTROPIC**. ■ (of a property or phenomenon) not varying in magnitude according to the direction of measurement. ▷mid 19th cent.: from **ISO-** 'equal' + Greek *tropos* 'a turn' + **-IC**. —**i·so·trop·i·cal·ly** /-ik(ə)lē/ *adv.* —**i·sot·ro·py** /īˈsätrəpē/ *n.*

i·so·zyme /ˈīsəˌzīm/ ▸*n. Biochemistry* each of two or more enzymes with identical function but different structure.

ISP ▸*abbr.* Internet Service Provider.

Is·pa·han variant spelling of **ISFAHAN**.

I spy ▸*n.* a children's game in which one player specifies the first letter of an object they can see, the other players then having to guess the identity of this object.

Is·ra·el[1] /ˈizrēəl; ˈizˌrāl/ **1** (also **children of Israel**) the Hebrew nation or people. According to tradition, they are descended from the patriarch Jacob (also named Israel), whose twelve sons became founders of the twelve tribes of ancient Israel. See also **TRIBES OF ISRAEL**. **2** the northern kingdom of the Hebrews (*c.*930–721 BC), formed after the reign of Solomon, whose inhabitants were carried away to captivity in Babylon. See also **JUDAH** (sense 2). ▷from Hebrew *Yiśrā'ēl* 'he that strives with God' (see Gen. 32:28).

Is·ra·el[2] a country in the Middle East, on the Mediterranean Sea; pop. 6,199,000; capital (not recognized as such by the UN), Jerusalem; languages, Hebrew (official), English, and Arabic.

The modern state of Israel was established as a Jewish homeland in 1948, on land that was at that time part of the British mandated territory of Palestine. Israel has been in continual conflict with its Arab neighbors and today occupies territories taken in war, including the West Bank and Syrian Golan Heights. The violence intensified in 2000 and has continued. Irrigated agriculture, industry, tourism, and the support of Jews in the Diaspora are key to the well-being of Israel.

See also **PALESTINE**.

Is·rae·li /izˈrālē/ ▸*adj.* of or relating to the modern country of Israel.
▸*n.* (*pl.* **-lis**) a native or national of Israel, or a person of Israeli descent.

Is·ra·el·ite /ˈizrēəˌlīt/ ▸*n.* a member of the ancient Hebrew nation, esp. in the period from the Exodus to the Babylonian Captivity (*c.*12th to 6th centuries BC). ■ old-fashioned and sometimes offensive term for **JEW**.
▸*adj.* of or relating to the Israelites. ▷via late Latin from Greek *Israēlitēs*.

Is·ra·fil /ˈizrəˌfēl/ (in Muslim tradition) the angel of music, who will sound the trumpet on Judgment Day.

Is·sa /ēˈsä; iˈsä/ ▸*n.* (*pl.* same or **Is·sas**) a member of a Somali people living in Djibouti.
▸*adj.* of or relating to the Issa. ▷the name in Somali.

Is·sa·char /ˈisəˌkär/ (in the Bible) a Hebrew patriarch, son of Jacob and Leah (Gen. 30:18). ■ the tribe of Israel traditionally descended from him.

is·sei /ˈē(s)ˌsā/ ▸*n.* (*pl.* same) a Japanese immigrant to North America. Compare with **NISEI** and **SANSEI**. ▷Japanese, literally 'first generation.'

ISSN ▸*abbr.* international standard serial number, an eight-digit number assigned to many serial publications such as newspapers, magazines, annuals, and series of books.

is·su·ant /ˈisʜo͞oənt/ ▸*adj.* [*predic.* or *postpositive*] *Heraldry* (of the upper part of an animal) shown rising up or out from another bearing, esp. from the bottom of a chief or from behind a fess. ▷early 17th cent.: from **ISSUE** + **-ANT** (on the pattern of French present participles ending in *-ant*).

is·sue /ˈisʜo͞o/ ▸*n.* **1** an important topic or problem for debate or discussion: *the issue of global warming* | *money is not an issue.* ■ (**is·sues**) personal problems or difficulties: *a nice guy with a great sense of humor and not too many issues.* **2** the action of supplying or distributing an item for use, sale, or official purposes: *the issue of promissory notes by the bank.* ■ each of a regular series of publications: *the December issue of the magazine.* ■ a number or set of items distributed at one time: *a share issue has been launched.* **3** *formal* or *Law* children of one's own: *he died without male issue.* **4** the action of flowing or coming out: *the point of issue* | *an issue of blood.* **5** *dated* a result or outcome of something: *the chance of carrying such a scheme to a successful issue was small.*
▸*v.* (**is·sues, is·sued, is·su·ing**) **1** [*trans.*] supply or distribute (something): *licenses were* ***issued*** *indiscriminately to any company.* ■ (**issue someone with**) supply someone with (something). ■ formally send out or make known: *the minister issued a statement.* ■ put (something) on sale or into general use: *Christmas stamps to be issued in November.* **2** [*intrans.*] (**issue from**) come, go, or flow out from: *exotic smells issued from a nearby building.* ■ result or be derived from: *the struggles of history issue from the divided heart of humanity.* ▷Middle English (in the sense 'outflowing'): from Old French, based on Latin *exitus*, past part. of *exire* 'go out.' —**is·su·a·ble** *adj.* —**is·su·ance** /-əns/ *n.* —**is·sue·less** *adj.* —**is·su·er** *n.*
▸*PHRASES* □ **at issue** under discussion; in dispute. □ **make an issue of** treat too seriously or as a problem. □ **take issue with** disagree with; challenge: *she takes issue with the notion of crime as unique to contemporary society.*

IST ▸*abbr.* insulin shock therapy.

-ist /əst; ist/ ▸*suffix* forming personal nouns and some related adjectives: **1** denoting an adherent of a system of beliefs, principles, etc., expressed by nouns ending in *-ism*: *hedonist* | *Marxist*. See **-ISM** 2. ■ denoting a person who subscribes to a prejudice or practices discrimination: *sexist*. **2** denoting a member of a profession or business activity: *dentist* | *dramatist* | *florist*. ■ denoting a person who uses a thing: *flutist* | *motorist*. ■ denoting a person who does something expressed by a verb ending in *-ize*: *plagiarist*. ▷from Old French *-iste*, Latin *-ista*, from Greek *-istēs*.

-ista ▸*suffix informal* forming nouns denoting a person associated with a particular activity, often with a derogatory intent: *fashionista*. ▷from the Spanish suffix *-ista*, as in *Sandinista*.

Is·tan·bul /ˌistəmˈbo͞ol; -ˌtän-; -ˌtan-; -ˈbo͞ol/ a port in Turkey on the Bosporus that straddles Europe and Asia; pop. 7,309,000. Formerly the Roman city of Constantinople 330–1453, it was built on the site of the ancient Greek city of Byzantium. It was captured by the Ottoman Turks in 1453 and was the capital of Turkey from that time until 1923. ▷Turkish, from Greek *eis tēn polin* 'into the city.'

isth. (also **Isth.**) ▸*abbr.* isthmus.

isth·mi·an /ˈismēən/ ▸*adj.* of or relating to an isthmus. ■ (**Isthmian**) of or relating to the Isthmus of Corinth in southern Greece or the Isthmus of Panama.

isth·mus /ˈisməs/ ▸*n.* (*pl.* **-mus·es**) a narrow strip of land with sea on either side, forming a link between two larger areas of land. ■ (*pl.* **-mi** /-mī/) *Anatomy* a narrow organ, passage, or piece of tissue connecting two larger parts. ▷mid 16th cent.: via Latin from Greek *isthmos*.

is·tle /ˈis(t)lē/ ▸*n.* variant spelling of IXTLE.

ISV ▸*abbr.* ■ independent software vendor. ■ International Scientific Vocabulary.

IT ▸*abbr.* information technology.

it ▸*pron.* [*third person singular*] **1** used to refer to a thing previously mentioned or easily identified: *a room with two beds in it* | *this approach is refreshing because it breaks down barriers.* ■ referring to an animal or child of unspecified sex: *she was holding the baby, cradling it and smiling into its face.* ■ referring to a fact or situation previously mentioned, known, or happening: *stop it, you're hurting me.* **2** used to identify a person: *it's me* | *it's a boy!* **3** used in the normal subject position in statements about time, distance, or weather: *it's half past five* | *it was two miles to the island* | *it is raining.* **4** used in the normal subject or object position when a more specific subject or object is given later in the sentence: *it is impossible to assess the problem* | *she found it interesting to learn about their strategy.* **5** [with *clause*] used to emphasize a following part of a sentence: *it is the child who is the victim.* **6** the situation or circumstances; things in general: *no one can stay here—it's too dangerous now* | *he would like to see you right away if it's convenient.* **7** exactly what is needed or desired: *they thought they were it* | *you've either got it or you haven't.* **8** (usu. **"it"**) *informal* sex appeal: *he's still got "it."* ■ sexual intercourse. **9** (usu. **"it"**) (in children's games) the player who has to catch the others. ▷Old English *hit*, neuter of HE, of Germanic origin; related to Dutch *het*.

▸*PHRASES* □ **at it** see AT[1]. □ **that's it** **1** that is the main point or difficulty: *"Is she going?" "That's just it—she can't make up her mind."* **2** that is enough or the end: *okay, that's it, you've cried long enough.* □ **this is it** **1** the expected event is about to happen: *this is it—the big sale.* **2** this is enough or the end: *this is it, I'm going.* **3** this is the main point or difficulty.

ital. ▸*abbr.* italic (used as an instruction for a typesetter).

I·tal·ian /iˈtalyən/ ▸*adj.* of or relating to Italy, its people, or their language.
▸*n.* **1** a native or national of Italy, or a person of Italian descent. **2** the Romance language of Italy, also one of the official languages of Switzerland. ▷late Middle English: from Italian *italiano*, from *Italia* 'Italy.' —**I·tal·ian·ize** /-ˌnīz/ *v.*

I·tal·ian·ate /iˈtalyəˌnāt/ ▸*adj.* Italian in character or appearance: *an Italianate staircase with triple loggia.* ▷late 16th cent.: from Italian *italianato*, from *Italia* 'Italy.'

I·tal·ian·ism /iˈtalyəˌnizəm/ ▸*n.* **1** an Italian characteristic, expression, or custom. **2** attachment to Italy or Italian ideas or practices.

I·tal·ia·no /italˈyänō/, Anna Maria Luisa, see BANCROFT.

I·tal·ian pars·ley ▸*n.* another term for FLAT-LEAFED PARSLEY.

I·tal·ic /iˈtalik; īˈtal-/ ▸*adj.* relating to or denoting the branch of Indo-European languages that includes Latin, Oscan, Umbrian, and the Romance languages.
▸*n.* the Italic group of languages. ▷late 19th cent.: via Latin from Greek *Italikos*, from *Italia* 'Italy.'

i·tal·ic /iˈtalik; īˈtal-/ ▸*adj.* *Printing* of the sloping kind of typeface used esp. for emphasis or distinction and in foreign words. ■ (of handwriting) modeled on 16th-century Italian handwriting, typically cursive and sloping and with elliptical or pointed letters.
▸*n.* (also **i·tal·ics**) an italic typeface or letter: *the key words are **in italics**.* ▷late Middle English (in the general sense 'Italian'): via Latin from Greek *Italikos*, from *Italia* 'Italy.' Senses relating to writing date from the early 17th cent.

i·tal·i·cize /iˈtaliˌsīz; īˈtal-/ ▸*v.* [*trans.*] print (text) in italics: *she italicized the title* | [*intrans.*] *use this key to italicize.* —**i·tal·i·ci·za·tion** /iˌtalisiˈzāshən/ *n.*

Italo- ▸*comb. form* Italian; Italian and . . . : *Italophile* | *Italo-Grecian.* ■ relating to Italy.

It·a·ly /ˈitl-ē/ a country in southern Europe; pop. 58,057,000; capital, Rome; official language, Italian. Italian name ITALIA.

Successor to Rome, Italy achieved unification in the 19th century. It entered World War I on the Allied side in 1915. In 1922, the country was taken over by Fascist dictator Mussolini; participation in support of Germany during World War II resulted in defeat and Mussolini's downfall. Italy was a founding member of the EEC.

ITAR-Tass /ˈētär ˈtäs/ the official news agency of Russia, founded in 1925 in Leningrad as Tass, and renamed in 1992. ▷from the initials of Russian *Informatsionnoe telegrafnoe agentstvo Rossii* 'Information Telegraph Agency of Russia,' + TASS.

itch /icн/ ▸*n.* [usu. in *sing.*] an uncomfortable sensation on the skin that causes a desire to scratch. ■ *informal* a restless or strong desire: [with *infinitive*] *the itch to write fiction.* ■ [with *adj.*] a skin disease or condition of which itching is a symptom. ■ (**the itch**) *informal* scabies.
▸*v.* [*intrans.*] be the site of or cause an itch: *the bite itched like crazy.* ■ (of a person) experience an itch. ■ *informal* feel a restless or strong desire to do something: [with *infinitive*] *your hands itch to take the wheel.* ▷Old English *gycce* (noun), *gyccan* (verb); related to Dutch *jeuk* (noun) and Dutch *jeuken*, German *jucken* (verb).
▸*PHRASE* □ **an itchy** (or **itching**) **palm** *figurative* an avaricious nature.

itch mite ▸*n.* a parasitic mite that burrows under the skin, causing scabies in humans and sarcoptic mange in animals. • *Sarcoptes scabiei*, family Sarcoptidae.

itch·y /ˈicнē/ ▸*adj.* (**itch·i·er**, **itch·i·est**) having or causing an itch: *dry, itchy skin* | *an itchy rash.* —**itch·i·ness** *n.*
▸*PHRASE* □ **get** (or **have**) **itchy feet** *informal* have or develop a strong urge to travel or move from place to place.

it'd /ˈitid/ ▸*contraction of* ■ it had: *it'd been there for years.* ■ it would: *it'd be great to see you.*

-ite[1] ▸*suffix* **1** forming names denoting natives of a country: *Israelite* | *Samnite.* ■ *often derogatory* denoting followers of a movement, doctrine, etc.: *Luddite* | *Trotskyite.* **2** used in scientific and technical terms: ■ forming names of fossil organisms: *ammonite.* ■ forming names of minerals: *graphite.* ■ forming names of constituent parts of a body or organ: *somite.* ■ forming names of explosives and other commercial products: *dynamite* | *vulcanite.* ■ *Chemistry* forming names of salts or esters of acids ending in *-ous*: *sulfite.* ▷from French *-ite*, via Latin *-ita* from Greek *itēs*.

-ite[2] ▸*suffix* **1** forming adjectives such as *composite*, *erudite.* **2** forming nouns such as *appetite.* **3** forming verbs such as *unite.* ▷from Latin *-itus*, past participle of verbs ending in *-ere* and *-ire*.

i·tem /ˈītəm/ ▸*n.* an individual article or unit, esp. one that is part of a list, collection, or set: *the items on the agenda* | *an item of clothing.* ■ a piece of news or information. ■ an entry in an account.
▸*adv. archaic* used to introduce each item in a list: *item two statute books . . . item two drums.* ▷late Middle English (as an adverb): from Latin, 'in like manner, also.' The noun sense arose (late 16th cent.) from the use of the adverb to introduce each statement in a list.
▸*PHRASE* □ **be an item** *informal* (of a couple) be involved in an established romantic or sexual relationship.

i·tem·ize /ˈītəˌmīz/ ▸*v.* [*trans.*] present as a list of individual items: *I have itemized the morning's tasks.* ■ break down (a whole) into its constituent parts: [as *adj.*] (**itemized**) *an itemized bill.* ■ specify (an individual item or items). —**i·tem·i·za·tion** /ˌītəmiˈzāshən/ *n.* —**i·tem·iz·er** *n.*

it·er·ate /ˈitəˌrāt/ ▸*v.* [*trans.*] perform or utter repeatedly. ■ [*intrans.*] make repeated use of a mathematical or computational procedure, applying it each time to the result of the previous application; perform iteration.
▸*n.* *Mathematics* a quantity arrived at by iteration. ▷mid 16th cent.: from Latin *iterat-* 'repeated,' from the verb *iterare*, from *iterum* 'again.'

it·er·a·tion /ˌitəˈrāshən/ ▸*n.* the repetition of a process or utterance. ■ repetition of a mathematical or computational procedure applied to the result of a previous application, typically as a means of obtaining successively closer approximations to the solution of a problem. ■ a new version of a piece of computer hardware or software. ▷late Middle English: from Latin *iteratio(n-)*, from the verb *iterare* (see ITERATE).

it·er·a·tive /ˈitəˌrātiv; -rətiv/ ▸*adj.* relating to or involving iteration, esp. of a mathematical or computational process. ■ *Linguistics* denoting a grammatical rule that can be applied repeatedly. ■ *Grammar* another term for FREQUENTATIVE. ▷late 15th cent.: from French *itératif, -ive*, from Latin *iterare* 'to repeat'; the grammar term is from late Latin *iterativus*. —**it·er·a·tive·ly** *adv.*

it girl (also **It Girl**) ▸*n.* a young woman who has achieved celebrity, especially suddenly. ▷coined by American screenwriter Elinor Glyn (1864–1943), with reference to American actress and sex symbol Clara Bow (1905–65), who starred in Glyn's romantic comedy *It* (1927). The current usage dates from the 1960s.

Ith·a·ca /ˈithikə/ **1** an island off the western coast of Greece in the Ionian Sea, the legendary home of Odysseus. **2** an academic city in central New York, at the southern end of Cayuga Lake, home to Cornell University and Ithaca College; pop. 29,541.

I-Thou ▸*adj.* [*attrib.*] (of a personal relationship, esp. one with God) formed by personal encounter.

ith·y·phal·lic /ˌithəˈfalik/ ▸*adj.* (esp. of a statue of a deity or other carved figure) having an erect penis. ▷early 17th cent. (as a noun denoting a sexually explicit poem): via late Latin from Greek *ithuphallikos*, from *ithus* 'straight' + *phallos* 'phallus.'

-itic ▸*suffix* forming adjectives and nouns corresponding to nouns ending in *-ite* (such as *Semitic* corresponding to *Semite*). ■ corresponding to nouns ending in *-itis* (such as *arthritic* corresponding to *arthritis*). ■ from other bases: *syphilitic.* ▷from French *-itique*, via Latin *-iticus* from Greek *-itikos*.

i·tin·er·ant /īˈtinərənt; iˈtin-/ ▸*adj.* traveling from place to place: *itinerant traders.*
▸*n.* a person who travels from place to place. ▷late 16th cent. (used to describe a judge traveling on a circuit): from late Latin *itinerant-* 'traveling,' from the verb *itinerari*, from Latin *iter, itiner-* 'journey, road.' —**i·tin·er·a·cy** /-rəsē/ *n.* —**i·tin·er·an·cy** *n.* —**i·tin·er·ant·ly** *adv.*

i·tin·er·ar·y /īˈtinəˌrerē; iˈtin-/ ▸*n.* (*pl.* **-ar·ies**) a planned route or journey. ■ a travel document recording these. ▷late Middle English: from late Latin *itinerarium*, neuter of *itinerarius* 'of a journey or roads,' from Latin *iter, itiner-* 'journey, road.'

i·tin·er·ate /īˈtinəˌrāt; iˈtin-/ ▸*v.* [*intrans.*] (esp. of a church minister or a judge) travel from place to place to perform one's professional duty. ▷early 17th cent.: from late Latin *itinerat-* 'traveled,' from the verb *itinerari* (see ITINERANT). —**i·tin·er·a·tion** /īˌtinəˈrāshən; iˌtin-/ *n.*

-ition ▸*suffix* (forming nouns) equivalent to **-ATION** (as in *audition, rendition*). ▷from French, or from Latin *-itio(n)-*.

-itious[1] ▸*suffix* forming adjectives corresponding to nouns ending in *-ition* (such as *ambitious* corresponding to *ambition*). ▷from Latin *-itiosus*.

-itious[2] ▸*suffix* (forming adjectives) related to; having the nature of: *fictitious* | *suppositious.* ▷from late Latin *-itius*, alteration of Latin *-icius*.

-itis ▸*suffix* forming names of inflammatory diseases: *cystitis* | *hepatitis.* ■ *informal* used with reference to a tendency or state of mind that is compared to a disease: *creditcarditis.* ▷from Greek feminine form of adjectives ending in *-itēs* (combined with *nosos* 'disease' implied).

-itive ▶*suffix* (forming adjectives) equivalent to **-ATIVE** (as in *genitive, positive*). ▷from French *-itif, -itive* or Latin *-itivus* (from past participial stems ending in *-it*).

it'll /ˈitl/ ▶*contraction of* it shall; it will.

I·to /ˈētō/, Prince Hirobumi (1841–1909), Japanese statesman; premier 1885–88, 1892–96, 1898, 1900–01. He helped to draft the Japanese constitution 1889 and to establish a bicameral national diet 1890. He was assassinated by a member of the Korean independence movement.

-itous ▶*suffix* forming adjectives corresponding to nouns ending in *-ity* (such as *calamitous* corresponding to *calamity*). ▷from French *-iteux*, from Latin *-itosus*.

its /its/ ▶*possessive adj.* belonging to or associated with a thing previously mentioned or easily identified: *turn the camera on its side | he chose the area for its atmosphere.* ■ belonging to or associated with a child or animal of unspecified sex: *a baby in its mother's womb.*

USAGE Its is the possessive form of *it* (*the dog licked its paw*), while **it's** is the contraction of *it is* (*look, it's a dog licking its paw*) or *it has* (*It's been too long*). The apostrophe in **it's** never denotes a possessive. The confusion is at least partly understandable since other possessive forms (singular nouns) do take an apostrophe + **s**, as in *the girl's bike* or *the president's smile*.

it's /its/ ▶*contraction of* ■ it is: *it's my fault.* ■ it has: *it's been a hot day.*

USAGE See usage at **ITS**.

it·self /itˈself/ ▶*pron.* [*third person singular*] **1** [*reflexive*] used as the object of a verb or preposition to refer to a thing or animal previously mentioned as the subject of the clause: *his horse hurt itself | wisteria was tumbling over itself.* **2** [*emphatic*] used to emphasize a particular thing or animal mentioned: *the roots are several inches long, though the plant itself is only a foot tall.* ■ used after a quality to emphasize what a perfect example of that quality someone or something is: *Mrs. Vincent was kindness itself.* ▷Old English (see **IT**, **SELF**).

▶***PHRASES*** □ **by itself** see **BY ONESELF** at **BY**. □ **in itself** viewed in its essential qualities; considered separately from other things: *some would say bringing up a family was a full-time job in itself.*

it·ty-bit·ty /ˈitē ˈbitē/ (also **it·sy-bit·sy** /ˈitsē ˈbitsē/) ▶*adj. informal* very small; tiny. ▷1930s: from a child's form of **LITTLE** + **BITTY**.

ITU ▶*abbr.* International Telecommunication Union.

ITV (also **iTV**) ▶*abbr.* interactive television.

-ity ▶*suffix* forming nouns denoting quality or condition: *humility | probity.* ■ denoting an instance or degree of this: *a profanity.* ▷from French *-ité*, from Latin *-itas, -itatis*.

IU ▶*abbr.* international unit.

IUCN ▶*abbr.* International Union for the Conservation of Nature.

IUD ▶*abbr.* ■ intrauterine death (of the fetus before birth). ■ intrauterine device.

-ium ▶*suffix* **1** forming nouns adopted unchanged from Latin (such as *alluvium*) or based on Latin or Greek words (such as *euphonium*). **2** (also **-um**) forming names of metallic elements: *cadmium | magnesium.* **3** denoting a region of the body: *pericardium.* **4** denoting a biological structure: *mycelium.* ▷modern Latin in senses 2, 3, and 4, via Latin from Greek *-ion*.

IUPAC ▶*abbr.* International Union of Pure and Applied Chemistry.

IV ▶*abbr.* intravenous(ly).

▶*n.* an intravenous drip feed: *they put an IV in me.*

I·van /ˈīvən/ the name of six rulers of Russia: ■ **Ivan I** (*c.*1304–41), grand duke of Muscovy 1328–40. He strengthened and enlarged the duchy, making Moscow the ecclesiastical capital in 1326. ■ **Ivan II** (1326–59), grand duke of Muscovy 1353–59; known as **Ivan the Red**. ■ **Ivan III** (1440–1505), grand duke of Muscovy 1462–1505; known as **Ivan the Great**. He consolidated and enlarged his territory, defending it against a Tartar invasion in 1480. ■ **Ivan IV** (1530–84), grand duke of Muscovy 1533–47 and first tsar of Russia 1547–84; known as **Ivan the Terrible**. In 1581, Ivan killed his eldest son, Ivan, in a fit of rage; the succession passed to his mentally handicapped second son, Fyodor. ■ **Ivan V** (1666–96), nominal tsar of Russia 1682–96. ■ **Ivan VI** (1740–64), infant tsar of Russia 1740–41.

I·van·hoe /ˈīvənˌhō/, Burle Icle, see **IVES**[1].

I've /īv/ ▶*contraction of* I have.

-ive ▶*suffix* (forming adjectives, also nouns derived from them) tending to; having the nature of: *active | corrosive | palliative.* ▷from French *-if, -ive*, from Latin *-ivus*.

-ively ▶*suffix* forming adverbs corresponding to adjectives ending in *-ive* (such as *corrosively* corresponding to *corrosive*). ▷see **-IVE**, **-LY**.

-iveness ▶*suffix* forming nouns corresponding to adjectives ending in *-ive* (such as *corrosiveness* corresponding to *corrosive*). ▷see **-IVE**, **-NESS**.

i·ver·mec·tin /ˌīvərˈmektin/ ▶*n.* a compound used as an anthelmintic in veterinary medicine and as a treatment for river blindness.

Ives[1] /īvz/, Burl (1909–95) U.S. folk singer and actor; born *Burle Icle Ivanhoe*. He appeared in movies such as *East of Eden* (1955) and as the character Big Daddy in *Cat on a Hot Tin Roof* (1958).

Ives[2], Charles (Edward) (1874–1954), U.S. composer, noted for his use of polyrhythms, polytonality, quarter-tones, and aleatoric techniques. Notable works: *The Unanswered Question* (1906), *Three Places in New England* (1903–14), and *Concord* (1915).

Ives[3], James Merritt (1824–1907) U.S. publisher and artist who partnered with Nathaniel Currier to establish the company of Currier & Ives in 1857.

IVF ▶*abbr.* in vitro fertilization.

i·vied /ˈīvēd/ ▶*adj.* covered in ivy: *an ivied church.* ■ of or relating to the academic institutions of the Ivy League: *the ivied eastern schools and colleges.*

I·vo·ri·an /īˈvôrēən/ ▶*adj.* relating to the Ivory Coast or its people: *Ivorian protests.*

▶*n.* a native or inhabitant of the Ivory Coast: *a call for all Ivorians to participate.*

I·vo·ry /ˈīvərē/, James (1928–), U.S. movie director. He made a number of movies in partnership with producer Ismail Merchant, including *Heat and Dust* (1983), *A Room with a View* (1985), *Howards End* (1992), and *The Remains of the Day* (1993).

i·vo·ry /ˈīv(ə)rē/ ▶*n.* (*pl.* **-ries**) **1** a hard creamy-white substance composing the main part of the tusks of an elephant, walrus, or narwhal, often (esp. formerly) used to make ornaments and other articles: [as *adj.*] *a knife with an ivory handle.* ■ an object made of ivory. ■ (**the ivories**) *informal* the keys of a piano. ■ (**ivories**) *informal* a person's teeth. **2** a creamy-white color. ▷Middle English: from Anglo-Norman French *ivurie*, based on Latin *ebur*. —**i·vo·ried** /-rēd/ *adj.*

i·vo·ry black ▶*n.* a black carbon pigment made from charred ivory or (now usually) bone, used in drawing and painting.

I·vo·ry Coast See **CÔTE D'IVOIRE**.

i·vo·ry nut ▶*n.* the seed of a tropical American palm, which, when hardened, is a source of vegetable ivory. Also called **TAGUA NUT**. • The palm is *Phytelephas macrocarpa*, family Palmae.

i·vo·ry tow·er ▶*n.* a state of privileged seclusion or separation from the facts and practicalities of the real world: *the ivory tower of academia.* ▷early 20th cent.: translating French *tour d'ivoire*, used by the writer Sainte-Beuve (1804–69).

i·vy /ˈīvē/ ▶*n.* a woody evergreen Eurasian climbing plant, typically having shiny, dark green five-pointed leaves. • Genus *Hedera*, family Araliaceae: several species, in particular the common **English ivy** (*H. helix*), which is often seen climbing on tree trunks and walls. ■ used in names of similar climbing plants, e.g., **poison ivy**, **Boston ivy**. ▷Old English *īfig*, of Germanic origin; related to the first elements of Dutch *eiloof* and German *Efeu*.

English ivy

I·vy League ▶*n.* a group of long-established colleges and universities in the eastern U.S. having high academic and social prestige. It includes Harvard, Yale, Princeton, Columbia, Dartmouth, Cornell, Brown, and the University of Pennsylvania: [as *adj.*] *an Ivy League school.* ▷with reference to the ivy traditionally growing over the walls of these establishments. —**I·vy Lea·guer** *n.*

IW ▶*abbr.* ■ index word. ■ isotopic weight.

i.w. ▶*abbr.* ■ inside width. ■ isotopic weight.

IWC ▶*abbr.* International Whaling Commission.

I·wo Ji·ma /ˌēwə ˈjēmə; ˌēwō/ a small volcanic island, the largest of the Volcano Islands in the western Pacific Ocean, 760 miles (1,222 km) south of Tokyo. During World War II, it was a heavily fortified site of a Japanese airbase, and its attack and capture in 1944–45 was one of the severest U.S. campaigns. It was returned to Japan in 1968.

IWW ▶*abbr.* Industrial Workers of the World.

ix·i·a /ˈiksēə/ ▶*n.* a South African plant of the iris family that bears showy six-petaled starlike flowers on tall wiry stems and has sword-shaped leaves. • Genus *Ixia*, family Iridaceae: and many cultivars. ▷modern Latin, from Latin, denoting a kind of thistle, from Greek.

Ix·i·on /ikˈsīən; ˈiksēˌän/ *Greek Mythology* a king who, by Zeus's command, was pinned to a fiery wheel that revolved unceasingly through the underworld, as punishment for his alleged seduction of Hera.

ix·nay /ˈiksˌnā/ *informal* ▶*exclam.* (**ixnay on/to**) used in rejecting something specified: *a nice place to paddle, but ixnay on the swimming.*

▶*v.* [*trans.*] cancel or stop: *he ought to* **ixnay** *with the moral exhibitionism and get into the entertainment biz.* ▷1930s: pig Latin for *nix*.

ix·tle /ˈikstl-ē; ˈis(t)-/ (also **is·tle**) ▶*n.* (in Mexico and Central America) a plant fiber used for cordage, nets, and carpets. • This fiber is obtained chiefly from *Agave* species (family Agavaceae), in particular *A. funkiana* and *A. lecheguilla*. ▷late 19th cent.: via American Spanish from Nahuatl *ixtli*.

Iy·yar /ˈēˌyär; ēˈyär/ (also **I·yar**) ▶*n.* (in the Jewish calendar) the eighth month of the civil and second of the religious year, usually coinciding with parts of April and May. ▷from Hebrew *'iyyār*.

iz·ard /ˈizərd/ ▶*n.* (in the Pyrenees) a chamois. ▷late 18th cent.: from French *isard* or Gascon *isart*, of unknown origin.

-ization ▶*suffix* forming nouns corresponding to adjectives ending in *-ize* (such as *fossilization* corresponding to *fossilize*). ▷see **-IZE**, **-ATION**.

-ize ▶*suffix* forming verbs meaning: **1** make or become: *fossilize | privatize.* ■ cause to resemble: *Americanize.* **2** treat in a specified way: *pasteurize.* ■ treat or cause to combine with a specified substance: *carbonize | oxidize.* **3** follow a specified practice: *agonize | theorize.* ■ subject to a practice: *hospitalize.* ▷from French *-iser*, via late Latin *-izare* from Greek verbs ending in *-izein*.

USAGE 1 The form **-ize** has been in use in English since the 16th century. The alternative spelling **-ise** (reflecting a French influence) is in common use, esp. in British English. It is obligatory in certain cases: first, where it forms part of a larger word element, such as **-mise** (= sending) in **compromise**, and **-prise** (= taking) in **surprise**; and second, in verbs corresponding to nouns with **-s-** in the stem, such as **televise** (from *television*).

2 Adding **-ize** to a noun or adjective has been a standard way of forming new verbs for centuries, and verbs such as **characterize**, **terrorize**, and **sterilize** were all formed in this way hundreds of years ago. Some traditionalists object to recent formations of this type: during the 20th century, objections were raised against **prioritize**, **finalize**, and **hospitalize**, among others. There doesn't seem to be any coherent reason for this, except that verbs formed from nouns tend, inexplicably, to be criticized as vulgar formations. Despite objections, it is clear that **-ize** forms are an accepted part of the standard language.

-izer ▶*suffix* forming agent nouns corresponding to adjectives ending in *-ize* (such as *theorizer* corresponding to *theorize*). ▷see **-IZE**, **-ER**.

I·zhevsk /ˈēˌzhefsk/ an industrial city in central Russia, capital of the republic of Udmurtia; pop. 642,000. Former name (1984–87) **USTINOV**[1].

Iz·mir /izˈmi(ə)r/ a seaport and naval base in western Turkey, on an inlet of the Aegean Sea; pop. 1,757,000. Former name **SMYRNA**.

Iz·mit /izˈmit/ a city in northwestern Turkey, on the Gulf of Izmit; pop. 257,000.

Iz·ves·ti·a /izˈvestēə/ (also **Iz·ves·ti·ya**) a Russian daily newspaper founded in 1917 as the official organ of the Soviet government. It has continued to be published independently since the collapse of communist rule and the breakup of the Soviet Union. ▷from Russian *izvestiya* 'news.'

iz·zat /ˈizət/ ▶*n. Indian* honor, reputation, or prestige: *the izzat of the household was at stake.* ▷Persian and Urdu, from Arabic *'izza* 'glory.'

Jj

J[1] /jā/ (also **j**) ▸*n.* (*pl.* **Js** or **J's** /jāz/) **1** the tenth letter of the alphabet. ■ denoting the next after I (or H if I is omitted) in a set of items, categories, etc. **2** (**J**) a shape like that of a capital J. **3** *archaic* used instead of I as the Roman numeral for one in final position: *between ij and iij of the clock.*

J[2] ▸*abbr.* ■ jack (used in describing play in card games). ■ *Physics* joule(s). ■ (in titles) Journal (of): *J. Biol. Chem.* ■ Judge. ■ Justice.

j ▸*symbol* (*j*) (in electrical engineering and electronics) the imaginary quantity equal to the square root of minus one. Compare with **I**.

jab /jab/ ▸*v.* (**jabbed, jab·bing**) [*trans.*] poke (someone or something) roughly or quickly, esp. with something sharp or pointed: *she jabbed him in his ribs* | [*intrans.*] *he* ***jabbed at*** *the air with his finger.* ■ poke someone or something roughly or quickly with (a sharp or pointed object or a part of the body): *she jabbed the fork into the earth.*
▸*n.* a quick, sharp blow, esp. with the fist: *fast* ***jabs to*** *the face.* ■ *informal* a hypodermic injection, esp. a vaccination: *an anti-tetanus jab.* ■ a sharp painful sensation or feeling: *the jabs of pain up my spine* | *a jab of envy.* ▷early 19th cent. (originally Scots): variant of **JOB**[2].

Ja·bal·pur /ˈjəbəlˌpo͝or/ an industrial city and military post in central India, in Madhya Pradesh; pop. 760,000.

jab·ber /ˈjabər/ ▸*v.* [*intrans.*] talk rapidly and excitedly but with little sense: *he* ***jabbered away*** *to his friends.*
▸*n.* fast, excited talk that makes little sense: *stop your jabber.* ▷late 15th cent.: imitative.

jab·ber·wock·y /ˈjabərˌwäkē/ ▸*n.* (*pl.* **-wock·ies**) invented or meaningless language; nonsense. ▷early 20th cent.: from the title of a nonsense poem in Lewis Carroll's *Through the Looking Glass* (1871).

jab·i·ru /ˈjabəˌro͞o/ (also **jabiru stork**) ▸*n.* a large Central and South American stork with a black neck, mainly white plumage, and a large black upturned bill. • *Ephippiorhynchus mycteria*, family Ciconiidae. ■ either of two related storks found in Asia, Australasia, and Africa. ▷late 18th cent.: from Tupi-Guarani *jabirú*, from *j* 'that which has' + *abirú* 'swollen' (suggested by the bird's large neck).

Ja·bo·a·tão /ˌzhäbwäˈtoun/ a commercial city in northeastern Brazil, west of Recife; pop. 487,000.

jab·o·ran·di /ˌjabəˈrandē/ ▸*n.* **1** a drug made from the dried leaves of certain South American plants that contain the alkaloid pilocarpine and promote salivation when chewed. **2** any of the plants that yield this drug. • Several genera and species, in particular *Pilocarpus jaborandi* (family Rutaceae). ▷early 17th cent.: from Tupi-Guarani *jaburandi*, literally 'a person who spits.'

ja·bot /zhaˈbō; ja-/ ▸*n.* an ornamental frill or ruffle on the front of a shirt or blouse, typically made of lace. ▷early 19th cent. (denoting a frill on a man's shirt): French, originally 'crop of a bird.'

ja·cal /häˈkäl/ ▸*n.* (*pl.* **-ca·les** /-ˈkäläs/) (in Mexico and the southwestern U.S.) a thatched wattle-and-daub hut. ▷Mexican Spanish, from Nahuatl *xacalli*, contraction of *xamitl calli* 'adobe house.'

jac·a·mar /ˈjakəˌmär/ ▸*n.* an insectivorous bird of tropical American forests, with a long pointed bill, a long tail, and plumage that is typically iridescent green above. • Family Galbulidae: several genera and species. ▷early 19th cent.: from French, apparently from Tupi.

ja·ca·na /ˌzhäkəˈnä; ˌjä-/ (also **ja·ça·na** /ˌzhäsəˈnä; ˌjä-/) ▸*n.* a small tropical wading bird with greatly elongated toes and claws that enable it to walk on floating vegetation. Also called **LILY-TROTTER**. • Family Jacanidae: several genera and species. ▷mid 18th cent.: from Portuguese *jaçanã*, from Tupi-Guarani *jasanã*.

jac·a·ran·da /ˌjakəˈrandə/ ▸*n.* a tropical American tree that has blue trumpet-shaped flowers, fernlike leaves, and fragrant timber. • Genus *Jacaranda*, family Bignoniaceae. ▷mid 18th cent.: from Portuguese, from Tupi-Guarani *jakara'nda*.

ja·cinth /ˈjāsənth; ˈjas-/ ▸*n.* a reddish-orange gem variety of zircon. ▷Middle English: from Old French *iacinte* or medieval Latin *iacintus*, alteration of Latin *hyacinthus* (see **HYACINTH**).

jack[1] /jak/ ▸*n.* **1** a device for lifting heavy objects, esp. one for raising the axle of a motor vehicle off the ground so that a wheel can be changed or the underside inspected. **2** a playing card bearing a representation of a soldier, page, or knave, normally ranking next below a queen. **3** a socket with two or more pairs of terminals, designed to receive a jack plug. **4** (also **jack·stone**) a small round pebble or star-shaped piece of metal used in tossing and catching games. ■ (**jacks**) a game played by tossing and catching such pebbles or pieces of metal. **5** in lawn bowling, the small ball at which the players aim. **6** (**Jack**) *informal* used as a form of address to a man whose name is not known. [familiar form of the given name *John*.] ■ *informal* a lumberjack. ■ *archaic* a steeplejack. ■ the figure of a man striking the bell on a clock. **7** a small version of a national flag flown at the bow of a vessel in harbor to indicate its nationality. **8** *informal, dated* money. **9** a device for turning a spit. **10** a part of the mechanism in a spinet or harpsichord that connects a key to its corresponding string and causes the string to be plucked when the key is pressed down. **11** a marine fish that is typically laterally compressed with a row of large spiky scales along each side. Jacks are important in many places as food or game fish. Also called **POMPANO, SCAD.** [originally a West Indian term.] • Family Carangidae (the **jack family**): many genera and numerous species. The jack family also includes the horse mackerel, pilotfish, kingfishes, and trevallies. **12** the male of some animals, esp. a merlin or an ass. **13** used in names of animals that are smaller than similar kinds, e.g., **jacksnipe**. **14** short for **JACKRABBIT**. **15** *informal* short for **JACK SHIT**. ▷late Middle English: from *Jack*, nickname for the given name *John*. The term was used originally to denote an ordinary man (hence sense 6), also a youth (mid 16th cent.), hence the 'knave' in cards and 'male animal.' The word also denoted various devices saving human labor, as though one had a helper (senses 1, 3, 9, and 10, and in compounds such as **JACKHAMMER** and **JACKKNIFE**); the general sense 'laborer' arose in the early 18th cent. and survives in **CHEAPJACK, LUMBERJACK, STEEPLEJACK**, etc. Since the mid 16th cent. a notion of 'smallness' has arisen, hence senses 4, 5, 7, and 13.
▸*phrasal v.* □ **jack someone around** *informal* cause someone inconvenience or problems, esp. by acting unfairly or indecisively. □ **jack in** (or **into**) *informal* log into or connect up (a computer or electronic device). □ **jack off** *vulgar slang* masturbate. □ **jack up** *informal* inject oneself with a narcotic drug. □ **jack something up** raise something, esp. a vehicle, with a jack. ■ *informal* increase something by a considerable amount: *France jacked up its key bank interest rate.*
▸*PHRASES* □ **before one can say Jack Robinson** *informal* very quickly or suddenly. □ **every man jack** *informal, dated* each and every person (used for emphasis): *they're spies,* ***every man jack of them.*** □ **jack of all trades** (**and master of none**) a person who can do many different types of work but who is not necessarily very competent at any of them.

jack[2] ▸*n. historical* **1** another term for **BLACKJACK** (sense 4). **2** a sleeveless padded tunic worn by foot soldiers. [late Middle English: from Old French *jaque*; origin uncertain, perhaps based on Arabic.]

jack[3] /jak/ ▸*v.* [*trans.*] *informal* take (something) illicitly; steal: *his MO in the studio remains the same—jack other people's tracks and present them in a new context.* ■ rob (someone): *they jacked him for his car.* ▷1990s: from *hijack*.

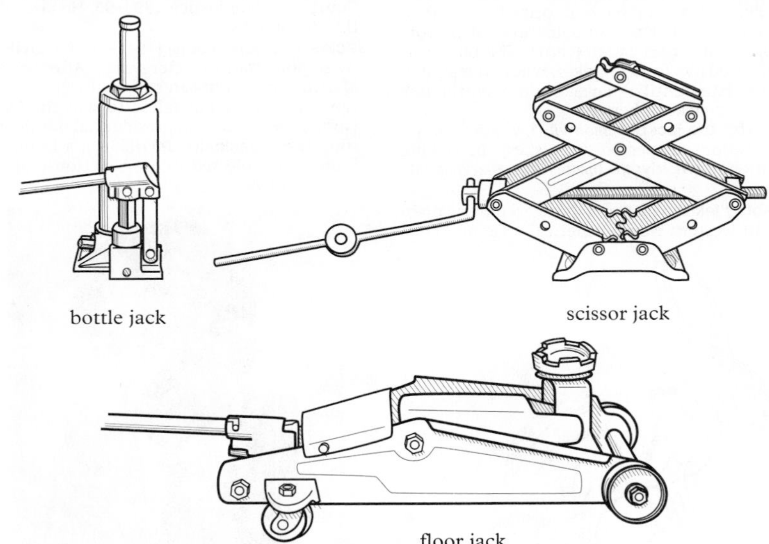

jack 1

Pronunciation Key ə *ago*; ər *over*; ˈə or ˌə *up*; ˈər or ˌər *fur*; a *hat*; ā *rate*; ä *car*; ch *chew*; e *let*; ē *see*; e(ə)r *air*; i *fit*; ī *by*; i(ə)r *ear*; ng *sing*; ō *go*; ô *for*; oi *boy*; o͝o *good*; o͞o *goo*; ou *out*; sh *she*; th *thin*; t͟h *then*; (h)w *why*; zh *vision*

J

jack·al /ˈjakəl/ ▶*n.* a slender, long-legged wild dog that feeds on carrion, game, and fruit and often hunts cooperatively, found in Africa and southern Asia. • Genus *Canis*, family Canidae: four species, including the **golden jackal** (*C. aureus*) and the **black-backed jackal** (*C. mesomelas*). ▷early 17th cent.: from Turkish *çakal*, from Persian *šagāl*. The change in the first syllable was due to association with JACK[1].

black-backed jackal

jack·a·napes /ˈjakəˌnāps/ ▶*n.* **1** *dated* an impertinent person. **2** *archaic* a tame monkey. ▷early 16th cent. (originally as *Jack Napes*): perhaps from a playful name for a tame ape, the initial *n-* by elision of *an ape* (compare with NEWT), and the final *-s* as in surnames such as *Hobbes*: hence applied to a person whose behavior resembled that of an ape.

jack arch ▶*n.* a small arch only one brick in thickness, esp. as used in numbers to support a floor.

jack·a·roo /ˌjakəˈro͞o/ ▶*n.* & *v.* variant spelling of JACKEROO.

jack·ass /ˈjakˌas/ ▶*n.* **1** a stupid person. **2** a male ass or donkey.

jack bean ▶*n.* a tropical American climbing plant of the pea family, which yields an edible bean and pod and is widely grown for fodder in tropical countries. • Genus *Canavalia*, family Leguminosae: in particular *C. ensiformis*. ■ the seed of this plant.

jack·boot /ˈjakˌbo͞ot/ ▶*n.* a large leather military boot reaching to the knee. ■ [in *sing.*] used as a symbol of cruel or authoritarian behavior or rule: *a country under the jackboot of colonialism.* —**jack·boot·ed** *adj.*

jack chain ▶*n.* a chain of unwelded links each consisting of a double loop of wire resembling a figure 8, but with the loops in planes at right angles to each other.

Jack cheese ▶*n.* another term for MONTEREY JACK.

jack·daw /ˈjakˌdô/ ▶*n.* a small, gray-headed crow that typically nests in tall buildings and chimneys, noted for its inquisitiveness. • Genus *Corvus*, family Corvidae: two species, in particular the Eurasian *C. monedula*.

jack·e·roo /ˌjakəˈro͞o/ (also **jack·a·roo**) *Austral., informal* ▶*n.* a young man working on a sheep or cattle station to gain experience.
▶*v.* [*intrans.*] work as a jackeroo. ▷late 19th cent.: alteration of an Aboriginal (Queensland) term *dhugaiiu* 'wandering white man,' by blending JACK[1] and KANGAROO.

jack·et /ˈjakit/ ▶*n.* an outer garment extending either to the waist or the hips, typically having sleeves and a fastening down the front. ■ an outer covering, esp. one placed around a tank or pipe to insulate it. ■ a metal casing for a bullet. ■ the skin of a potato: *potatoes cooked in their jackets.* ■ the dust jacket of a book. ■ a record sleeve. ■ a steel frame fixed to the seabed, forming the support structure of an oil production platform.
▶*v.* (**jack·et·ed, jack·et·ing**) [*trans.*] cover with a jacket. ▷late Middle English: from Old French *jaquet*, diminutive of *jaque* (see JACK[2]).

jack·et po·ta·to ▶*n. Brit.* a baked potato served with the skin on.

jack·fish /ˈjakˌfisʜ/ ▶*n.* (*pl.* same or **-fish·es**) a pike or sauger, esp. the northern pike.

Jack Frost ▶*n.* a personification of frost: *the seedlings battled with Jack Frost.*

jack·fruit /ˈjakˌfro͞ot/ ▶*n.* a fast-growing tropical Asian tree related to the breadfruit. • *Artocarpus heterophyllus*, family Moraceae. ■ the very large edible fruit of this tree, resembling a breadfruit and important as food in the tropics. ▷late 16th cent.: from Portuguese *jaca* (from Malayalam *chakka*) + FRUIT.

jack·ham·mer /ˈjakˌhamər/ ▶*n.* a portable pneumatic hammer or drill.
▶*v.* [*trans.*] beat or hammer heavily or loudly and repeatedly.

jack-in-the-box ▶*n.* a toy consisting of a box containing a figure on a spring that pops up when the lid is opened.

jack-in-the-pul·pit ▶*n.* any of several small plants of the arum family, in particular: • a North American arum with a green or purple-brown spathe. Genus *Arisaema*, family Araceae: three species, the **woodland jack-in-the-pulpit** (*A. atrorubens*), the **small** (or **swamp**) **jack-in-the-pulpit** (*A. triphyllum*), and the **northern jack-in-the-pulpit** (*A. stewardsonii*). • another term for CUCKOOPINT. ▷mid 19th cent.: so named because the erect spadix overarched by the spathe resembles a person in a pulpit.

woodland jack-in-the-pulpit

jack·knife /ˈjakˌnīf/ ▶*n.* (*pl.* **-knives**) **1** a knife with a folding blade. **2** a dive in which the body is first bent at the waist and then straightened. **3** *Statistics* a method of assessing the variability of data by repeating a calculation on the sets of data obtained by removing one value from the complete set.
▶*v.* (**-knifed, -knif·ing**) [*trans.*] move (one's body) into a bent or doubled-up position: *the Major jackknifed his thin body at the waist* | [*intrans.*] *she jackknifed into a sitting position.* ■ [*intrans.*] (of an articulated vehicle) bend into a V-shape in an uncontrolled skidding movement. ■ [*intrans.*] (of a diver) perform a jackknife.

jack·knife clam ▶*n.* another term for RAZOR CLAM.

jack·knife fish ▶*n.* a strikingly marked fish with a long, upright dorsal fin that lives among rocks and corals in the warm waters of the western Atlantic. • *Equetus lanceolatus*, family Sciaenidae.

jack·leg /ˈjakˌleg/ ▶*n. informal* an incompetent, unskillful, or dishonest person: [as *adj.*] *a jackleg carpenter.*

jack·light /ˈjakˌlīt/ ▶*n.* a portable light, esp. one used for fishing at night.

jack mack·er·el ▶*n.* a game fish of the jack family, occurring in the eastern Pacific. • *Trachurus symmetricus*, family Carangidae.

jack-o'-lan·tern /ˈjak ə ˌlantərn/ ▶*n.* **1** a lantern made from a hollowed-out pumpkin in which holes are cut to represent facial features, typically made at Halloween. **2** *archaic* an ignis fatuus.

jack pine ▶*n.* a small, hardy North American pine with very short needles, found chiefly in Canada. • *Pinus banksiana*, family Pinaceae.

jack plane ▶*n.* a medium-sized plane for use in carpentry.

jack plug ▶*n.* a plug consisting of a single shaft used to make a connection that transmits a signal, typically used in sound equipment.

jack·pot /ˈjakˌpät/ ▶*n.* a large cash prize in a game or lottery, esp. one that accumulates until it is won. ▷late 19th cent.: from JACK[1] + POT[1]. The term was originally used in a form of poker, where the pool or pot accumulated until a player could open the bidding with two jacks or better.
▶PHRASE □ **hit the jackpot** *informal* **1** win a jackpot. **2** have great or unexpected success, esp. in making a lot of money quickly: *the theater hit the jackpot with its first musical.*

jack·rab·bit /ˈjakˌrabət/ ▶*n.* a hare found in open country in western North America. • Genus *Lepus*, family Leporidae: several species, including the **blacktail jackrabbit** (*L. californicus*). ▷mid 19th cent.: abbreviation of *jackass-rabbit*, because of its long ears.

black-tailed jackrabbit

Jack Rus·sell /ˈrəsəl/ (also **Jack Russell terrier**) ▶*n.* a terrier of a small working breed with short legs. ▷early 20th cent.: named after John (*Jack*) *Russell* (1795–1883), an English clergyman famed in fox-hunting circles as a breeder of such terriers.

jack screw ▶*n.* a screw that can be turned to adjust the position of an object into which it fits. ■ a vehicle jack worked by a screw device. Also called SCREW JACK.

jack·shaft /ˈjakˌsʜaft/ ▶*n.* a small auxiliary or intermediate shaft in machinery.

jack shit ▶*n.* [usu. with *negative*] *vulgar slang* anything at all.

jack·snipe /ˈjakˌsnīp/ ▶*n.* a small dark Eurasian snipe. • *Lymnocryptes minima*, family Scolopacidae. ■ any similar wader, e.g., the pectoral sandpiper or the common snipe.

Jack·son[1] /ˈjaksən/ **1** an industrial city in south central Michigan; pop. 37,446. **2** the capital of Mississippi, an industrial and commercial city in the central part of the state, on the Pearl River; pop. 184,256. **3** a commercial city in western Tennessee; pop. 59,643.

Jack·son[2], Andrew (1767–1845) 7th president of the U.S. 1829–37; known as **Old Hickory**. A Tennessee Democrat, he served in the U.S. House of Representatives 1796–97 and as a U.S. Senator 1797–98, 1823–25. As a general in the U.S. Army during the War of 1812, he became known for his successful defense of New Orleans. As president, he vetoed the renewal of the charter of the Bank of the United States, opposed the nullification issue in South Carolina, and initiated the spoils system. During his administration, the national debt was paid off completely, the Wisconsin Territory was organized, Michigan was admitted as the 26th state, and the independence of Texas was recognized.

Andrew Jackson

Jack·son[3], Howell Edmunds (1832–95) U.S. Supreme Court associate justice 1893–95. He also served as a U.S. Senator 1881–86.

Jack·son[4], Jesse (Louis) (1941–), U.S. civil rights activist, politician, and clergyman. After working with Martin Luther King in the civil rights struggle, he campaigned for but failed to win the Democratic Party's 1984 and 1988 presidential nominations. His son, **Jesse Jackson, Jr.**(1965–), a Democrat from Illinois, was elected to the U.S. House of Representatives in 1995.

Jesse Jackson

J

Jack·son[5], Mahalia (1911–72) U.S. gospel singer and musician. She came into her own in the mid-1940s, when her recording of "Move Up a Little Higher" sold over a million copies. She was a featured performer at President Kennedy's inaugural ceremony.

Jack·son[6], Michael (1958–) U.S. singer, the top-selling pop artist of the 1980s. His hit albums include *Thriller* (1982), *Bad* (1987), *Dangerous* (1992), and *Blood on the Dance Floor* (1997).

Jack·son[7], Reggie (1946–) U.S. baseball player; full name *Reginald Martinez Jackson*; known as Mr. October. An outfielder, he played for the Kansas City A's (later Oakland Athletics) 1967–75, the Baltimore Orioles 1976, and the New York Yankees 1977–87. Baseball Hall of Fame (1993).

Jack·son[8], Robert Houghwout (1892–1954) U.S. Supreme Court associate justice 1941–54. He was the chief prosecutor for the U.S. at the Nuremberg war crimes tribunal 1945–46.

Jack·son[9], Thomas Jonathan (1824–63) American Confederate general; known as **Stonewall Jackson**. The commander of the Shenandoah campaign 1861–62, he was mortally wounded by one of his own sharpshooters at Chancellorsville in 1863.

Thomas "Stonewall" Jackson

Jack·son Heights a commercial and residential section of northern Queens in New York City.

Jack·son Hole a valley on the Snake River in northwestern Wyoming, partly in Grand Teton National Park, home to a fashionable resort.

Jack·so·ni·an /jak'sōnēən/ ▶*adj. Medicine* relating to or denoting a form of epilepsy in which seizures begin at one site (typically a digit or the angle of the mouth). ▷late 19th cent.: from the name of John H. *Jackson* (1835–1911), English physician and neurologist, + **-IAN**.

Jack·son·ville /'jaksən,vil/ **1** a city in central Arkansas, northeast of Little Rock; pop. 29,916. **2** an industrial city and port in northeastern Florida; pop. 735,617. **3** a city in southeastern North Carolina, a service town for nearby Camp Lejeune and other military facilities; pop. 66,715.

jack·staff /'jak,staf/ ▶*n.* a short flagpole at a ship's bow, on which a jack is flown.

jack·stay /'jak,stā/ ▶*n. Nautical* a rope, bar, or batten placed along a ship's yard to bend the head of a square sail to.

jack·stone /'jak,stōn/ ▶*n.* see **JACK**[1] (sense 4).

jack·straws /'jak,strôz/ ▶*plural n.* [*treated as sing.*] a game played with a heap of small rods of wood, bone, or plastic, in which players try to remove one at a time without disturbing the others.

Jack tar ▶*n. Brit., informal* or *dated* a sailor.

Jack-the-Lad ▶*n. Brit., informal* a brash, cocky young man. ▷nickname of *Jack Sheppard*, an 18th-cent. thief.

Jack the Rip·per an unidentified 19th-century English murderer. In 1888, at least six London prostitutes were brutally killed. Authorities received taunting notes from a person called Jack the Ripper, who claimed to be the murderer, but the cases remain unsolved.

jack-up (also **jack-up rig**) ▶*n.* an offshore drilling rig the legs of which are lowered to the seabed from the operating platform.

Jack·y liz·ard /'jakē/ ▶*n.* a brownish southeastern Australian lizard that becomes paler as the temperature rises. When threatened, it puffs itself up and opens its orange mouth. • *Amphibolus muricatus*, family Agamidae.

Jack·y Win·ter ▶*n.* an Australasian flycatcher that has a gray-brown back and whitish underside and constantly wags its white-edged tail. • *Microeca leucophaea*, family Eopsaltridae (or Muscicapidae). Alternative name: **Australian brown flycatcher**. ▷late 19th cent.: diminutive form of the nickname *Jack* (see **JACK**[1]) + *Winter* (imitative of the bird's cry).

Ja·cob /'jākəb/ (in the Bible) a Hebrew patriarch, the younger of the twin sons of Isaac and Rebecca, who persuaded his brother Esau to sell him his birthright and tricked him out of his father's blessing (Gen. 25, 27). Jacob's twelve sons became the founders of the twelve tribes of ancient Israel. See also **TRIBES OF ISRAEL**. ▷from Hebrew *ya'aqōb* 'following after, supplanter.'

Jac·o·be·an /,jakə'bēən/ ▶*adj.* of or relating to the reign of James I of England: *a Jacobean mansion.* ■ (of furniture) in the style prevalent during the reign of James I, esp. being the color of dark oak.
▶*n.* a person who lived during this period. ▷mid 19th cent. (in use earlier with reference to St. James): from modern Latin *Jacobaeus* (from ecclesiastical Latin *Jacobus* 'James,' from Greek *Iakōbos* 'Jacob') + **-AN**.

Jac·o·be·than /,jakə'bēTHən/ ▶*adj.* (esp. of architecture) displaying a combination of Elizabethan and Jacobean styles. ▷mid 20th cent.: blend of **JACOBEAN** and **ELIZABETHAN**.

Ja·co·bi /jə'kōbē/, Karl Gustav Jacob (1804–51), German mathematician. He worked on the theory of elliptic functions, in competition with Niels Abel.

Jac·o·bi·an /jə'kōbēən/ *Mathematics* ▶*adj.* of or relating to the work of the mathematician K. G. J. Jacobi.
▶*n.* a determinant whose constituents are the derivatives of a number of functions (*u*, *v*, *w*, . . .) with respect to each of the same number of variables (*x*, *y*, *z*, . . .).

Jac·o·bin /'jakəbən/ ▶*n.* **1** *historical* a member of a democratic club established in Paris in 1789. The Jacobins were the most radical and ruthless of the political groups formed in the wake of the French Revolution, and in association with Robespierre they instituted the Terror of 1793–4. ■ an extreme political radical. **2** *chiefly historical* a Dominican friar. **3** (**jacobin**) a pigeon of a breed with reversed feathers on the back of its neck like a cowl. **4** (**jacobin**) a mainly green Central and South American hummingbird, with blue feathers on the head. • *Florisuga mellivora* and *Melanotrichilus fuscus*, family Trochilidae. ▷Middle English (sense 2): from Old French, from medieval Latin *Jacobinus*, from ecclesiastical Latin *Jacobus* 'James.' The term was applied to the Dominicans in Old French from their church in Paris, St. Jacques, near which they built their first convent; the convent eventually became the headquarters of the French revolutionary group. —**Jac·o·bin·ic** /,jakə'binik/ *adj.* —**Jac·o·bin·i·cal** /,jakə'binikəl/ *adj.* —**Jac·o·bin·ism** /-,nizəm/ *n.*

Jac·o·bite[1] /'jakə,bīt/ ▶*n.* a supporter of the deposed James II and his descendants in their claim to the British throne after the Revolution of 1688. Drawing most of their support from Catholic clans of the Scottish Highlands, Jacobites made attempts to regain the throne in 1689–90, 1715, 1719, and 1745–46, finally being defeated at the Battle of Culloden. ▷from Latin *Jacobus* 'James' (see **JACOBEAN**) + **-ITE**[1]. —**Jac·o·bit·i·cal** /,jakə'bitikəl/ *adj.* —**Jac·o·bit·ism** /-bīt,izəm/ *n.*

Jac·o·bite[2] ▶*n.* a member of the Syrian Orthodox Church (Monophysite). ▷early 15th cent.: from medieval Latin *Jacobita*, from the name of *Jacobus* Baradaeus, a 6th-cent. Syrian monk.

Ja·cobs /'jākəbz/, Amos, see **THOMAS**[2].

Ja·cob's lad·der ▶*n.* **1** a plant of the northeastern U.S. with loose clusters of purplish-blue flowers and slender pointed leaves, rows of which are said to resemble a ladder. • *Polemonium van-bruntiae*, family Polemoniaceae. **2** a rope ladder with wooden rungs, esp. for access to a ship up the side. ▷mid 18th cent.: with biblical allusion to Jacob's dream of a ladder reaching to heaven (Gen. 28:12).

Ja·cob·son's or·gan /'jākəbsənz/ ▶*n. Zoology* a scent organ consisting of a pair of sacs or tubes typically in the roof of the mouth. Such organs are present in many vertebrates, notably snakes and lizards. ▷mid 19th cent.: named after Ludwig L. *Jacobson* (1783–1843), Dutch anatomist.

Ja·cob's staff ▶*n.* a rod with a sliding cursor formerly used for measuring distances and heights, esp. in navigation. ▷mid 16th cent. (denoting a pilgrim's staff): alluding to St. James (*Jacobus* in ecclesiastical Latin), whose symbols are a pilgrim's staff and a scallop shell.

jac·o·net /'jakə,net/ ▶*n.* a lightweight cotton cloth with a smooth and slightly stiff finish. ▷mid 18th cent.: from Hindi *Jagannāth(purī)* (now Puri) in India, its place of origin; see also **JUGGERNAUT**.

Ja·co·po del·la Quer·cia see **DELLA QUERCIA**.

jac·quard /'ja,kärd; jə'kärd/ ▶*n.* an apparatus with perforated cards, fitted to a loom to facilitate the weaving of figured and brocaded fabrics. ■ a fabric made on a loom with such a device, with an intricate variegated pattern. ▷early 19th cent.: named after Joseph M. *Jacquard* (1787–1834), French weaver and inventor.

jac·que·rie /zHäk'rē/ ▶*n.* a communal uprising or revolt. ▷early 16th cent. (referring to the 1357 peasants' revolt against the nobles in northern France): from Old French, literally 'villeins,' from *Jacques*, a given name used in the sense 'peasant.'

jac·ti·ta·tion /,jakti'tāsHən/ ▶*n. Medicine* the restless tossing of the body in illness. ■ the twitching of a limb or muscle. [expressive extension of *jactation* 'restless tossing,' from Latin *jactare* 'to throw.']
▶*PHRASE* □ **jactitation of marriage** *archaic* false declaration that one is married to a specified person. [*jactitation* in the sense 'public bragging,' from medieval Latin *jactitatio(n-)* 'false declaration,' from Latin *jactitare* 'to boast.']

ja·cuz·zi /jə'kōōzē/ ▶*n.* (*pl.* **-zis**) *trademark* a large bath with a system of underwater jets of water to massage the body. ▷1960s: named after Candido *Jacuzzi* (*c.*1903–86), Italian-born American inventor.

jade[1] /jād/ ▶*n.* a hard, typically green stone used for ornaments and implements and consisting of the minerals jadeite or nephrite. ■ an ornament made of this. ■ (also **jade green**) a light bluish-green: [as *adj.*] *a baggy jade T-shirt.* ▷late 16th cent.: from French *le jade* (earlier *l'ejade*), from Spanish *piedra de ijada* 'stone of the flank' (i.e., stone for colic, which it was believed to cure).

jade[2] ▶*n. archaic* **1** a bad-tempered or disreputable woman. **2** an inferior or worn-out horse. ▷late Middle English: of unknown origin.

jad·ed /'jādid/ ▶*adj.* tired, bored, or lacking enthusiasm, typically after having had too much of something: *meals to tempt the most jaded appetites.* ▷late 16th cent. (in the sense 'disreputable'): from **JADE**[2]. —**jad·ed·ly** *adv.* —**jad·ed·ness** *n.*

jade·ite /'jād,īt/ ▶*n.* a green, blue, or white mineral that is one of the forms of jade. It is a silicate of sodium, aluminum, and iron and belongs to the pyroxene group.

j'a·doube /zHa'dōōb/ ▶*exclam. Chess* a declaration by a player intending to adjust the placing of a chessman without making a move with it. ▷French, literally 'I adjust.'

jae·ger /'yāgər/ ▶*n.* any of the smaller kinds of Arctic-breeding skuas. • Genus *Stercorarius*, family Stercorariidae: three species, e.g., the **parasitic jaeger** or Arctic skua (*S. parasiticus*). ▷mid 19th cent. (applied to any predatory seabird): from German *Jäger* 'hunter,' from *jagen* 'to hunt.'

Jaf·fa /'jäfə; 'jafə/ a city and port on the Mediterranean coast of Israel, a southern suburb of Tel Aviv and since 1949 united with Tel Aviv; pop. (with Tel Aviv) 355,000. Hebrew name **YAFO**; biblical name **JOPPA**.

Jaff·na /'jäfnə/ a city and port on the Jaffna peninsula at the northern tip of Sri Lanka; pop. 129,000.

JAG ▶*abbr.* judge advocate general.

Jag /jag/ ▶*n. informal* a Jaguar car: *an E-type Jag.* ▷1950s: abbreviation.

jag[1] /jag/ ▶*n.* a sharp projection.
▶*v.* (**jagged** /'jagd/, **jag·ging**) [*trans.*] stab, pierce, or prick: *she jagged herself in the mouth.* ▷late Middle English (in the sense 'stab, pierce'): perhaps symbolic of sudden movement or unevenness (compare with **JAM**[1] and **RAG**[1]). —**jag·ger** *n.*

jag[2] ▶*n. informal* **1** a bout of unrestrained activity or emotion, esp. drinking, crying, or laughing: *an incredible crying jag.* **2** *dialect* a bundle: *a jag of hay.* ▷late 16th cent. (sense 2): of unknown origin. In the late 18th cent. the sense was 'portion, quantity,' later 'as much alcohol as one can hold,' hence 'a binge.' Sense 1 dates from the early 20th cent.

Jag·an·na·tha /,jəgə'nät-hə/ another name for **JUGGERNAUT**.

jag·ged /'jagid/ ▶*adj.* with rough, sharp points protruding: *the jagged edges gashed their fingers | figurative soothing her jagged nerves.* ▷late Middle English: from **JAG**[1]. —**jag·ged·ly** *adv.* —**jag·ged·ness** *n.*

Pronunciation Key ə *ago*; ər *over*; 'ə or ,ə *up*; 'ər or ,ər *fur*; a *hat*; ā *rate*; ä *car*; CH *chew*; e *let*; ē *see*; e(ə)r *air*; i *fit*; ī *by*; i(ə)r *ear*; NG *sing*; ō *go*; ô *for*; oi *boy*; ōō *good*; ōō *goo*; ou *out*; SH *she*; TH *thin*; TH *then*; (h)w *why*; ZH *vision*

Jag·ger /ˈjagər/, Mick (1943–), English rock singer and songwriter; full name *Michael Philip Jagger*. He formed the Rolling Stones *c.*1962 with guitarist Keith Richards (1943–), a childhood friend.

jag·ger·y /ˈjagərē/ ▸*n.* a coarse dark brown sugar made in India by evaporation of the sap of palm trees. ▷late 16th cent.: from Portuguese *xagara, jag(a)ra*, from Malayalam *cakkarā*, from Sanskrit *śarkarā* 'sugar.'

jag·gy /ˈjagē/ ▸*adj.* (**-gi·er, -gi·est**) jagged. ▸*n.* (*pl.* -ies) (usu. **jaggies**) *Computing informal* another term for ALIASING.

jag·uar /ˈjagˌwär/ ▸*n.* a large, heavily built cat that has a yellowish-brown coat with black spots, found mainly in the dense forests of Central and South America. • *Panthera onca*, family Felidae. ▷early 17th cent.: from Portuguese, from Tupi-Guarani *yaguára*.

jaguar

ja·gua·run·di /ˌjagwəˈrəndē/ ▸*n.* (*pl.* **-dis**) a small American wildcat with a uniform red or gray coat, slender body, and short legs, found from Arizona to Argentina. • *Felis yagouaroundi*, family Felidae. ▷mid 19th cent.: from Portuguese, from Tupi-Guarani, from *yaguára* 'jaguar' + *undi* 'dark.'

Jah /jä; yä/ ▸*n.* the Rastafarian name of God. ▷representing Hebrew *Yāh*, abbreviation of YAHWEH. The current use was popularized in the mid 20th cent.

jai a·lai /ˈhī (ə)ˌlī/ ▸*n.* a game like pelota played with large, curved wicker baskets. ▷Spanish, from Basque *jai* 'festival' + *alai* 'merry.'

jail /jāl/ (*Brit.* also **gaol**) ▸*n.* a place for the confinement of people accused or convicted of a crime: *he spent 15 years **in jail*** | [as *adj.*] *a jail sentence.* ■ confinement in a jail: *she was sentenced to three months' jail.* ▸*v.* [*trans.*] (usu. **be jailed**) put (someone) in jail: *the driver was jailed for two years.* ▷Middle English: based on Latin *cavea* (see CAGE). The word came into English in two forms, *jaiole* from Old French and *gayole* from Anglo-Norman French *gaole* (surviving in the spelling *gaol*), originally pronounced with a hard g, as in *gale*.

jail·bait /ˈjālˌbāt/ ▸*n.* [treated as *sing.* or *pl.*] *informal* a young woman, or young women collectively, considered in sexual terms but under the age of consent.

jail·bird /ˈjālˌbərd/ ▸*n.* *informal* a person who is or has been in prison, esp. a criminal who has been jailed repeatedly.

jail·break /ˈjālˌbrāk/ ▸*n.* an escape from jail.

jail·er /ˈjālər/ (also **jai·lor** or *Brit.* **gaol·er**) ▸*n.* a person in charge of a jail or of the prisoners in it.

jail·house /ˈjālˌhous/ ▸*n.* a prison.

Jain /jān/ ▸*n.* an adherent of Jainism. ▸*adj.* of or relating to Jainism. ▷via Hindi from Sanskrit *jaina* 'of or concerning a *Jina*' (a great Jain teacher or holy man, literally 'victor'), from *ji-* 'conquer' or *jyā-* 'overcome.'

Jain·ism /ˈjāˌnizəm/ ▸*n.* a nontheistic religion founded in India in the 6th century BC by the Jina Vardhamana Mahavira as a reaction against the teachings of orthodox Brahmanism, and still practiced there. The Jain religion teaches salvation by perfection through successive lives, and noninjury to living creatures, and is noted for its ascetics. See also SVETAMBARA and DIGAMBARA. —**Jain·ist** *n.*

Jai·pur /ˈjīˌpo͝or/ a city in western India, the capital of Rajasthan; pop. 1,455,000.

Ja·kar·ta /jəˈkärtə/ (also **Dja·kar·ta**) the capital of Indonesia, in northwestern Java; pop. 8,222,500. Former name (until 1949) BATAVIA.

jake /jāk/ ▸*adj.* [*predic.*] *informal* all right; satisfactory: *everything was jake again.* ▷early 20th cent.: of unknown origin.

jake brake ▸*n.* an engine brake for truck diesel engines that cuts off fuel flow and interrupts the transfer of mechanical energy to the drive mechanism. ▷1980s: from the *Jacobs* Company, who invented the most common implementation of the technology that the brake is based on.

jakes /jāks/ ▸*n.* a toilet, esp. an outdoor one. ▷mid 16th cent.: perhaps from the given name *Jacques*, or as the genitive of the nickname *Jack* (see JACK[1]).

Ja·kob·son /ˈyäkəbsən/, Roman (Osipovich) (1896–1982), U.S. linguist; born in Russia. He taught Slavic languages and literature and general linguistics at Harvard University from 1949 to 1967. His most influential work described universals in phonology.

Ja·lal ad-Din ar-Ru·mi /jəˈläl əˌdēn əˈro͞omē/ (1207–73), Persian poet and Sufi mystic; founder of the order of whirling dervishes; also called *Mawlana*.

jal·ap /ˈjäləp; ˈjal-/ ▸*n.* a purgative drug obtained chiefly from the tuberous roots of a Mexican climbing plant. • This drug is obtained from *Ipomoea purga*, family Convolvulaceae. ▷mid 17th cent.: from French, from Spanish *(purga de) Jalapa* (see JALAPA).

Ja·la·pa /häˈläpä/ a city in eastern central Mexico, capital of the state of Veracruz; pop. 288,000. Full name JALAPA ENRÍQUEZ.

ja·la·pe·ño /ˌhäləˈpänyō; -ˈpē-/ (also **ja·la·pe·ño pep·per**) ▸*n.* (*pl.* **-ños**) a very hot green chili pepper, used esp. in Mexican-style cooking. ▷1940s (originally U.S.): from Mexican Spanish *(chile) jalapeño*.

ja·le·o /häˈlā-ō/ ▸*n.* (*pl.* **-le·os**) a lively dance of Andalusian origin, or the music or handclapping that accompanies it. ■ a fast instrumental chorus in merengue music. ▷mid 19th cent.: Spanish, literally 'halloo.'

jal·fre·zi /jälˈfrāzē/ ▸*n.* (*pl.* **-zis**) a medium-hot Indian dish consisting of chicken or lamb with fresh chili peppers, tomatoes, and onions. ▷1980s: from Bengali *jalfrezi*, from *jal* 'hot.'

Ja·lis·co /häˈlēskō/ a state in western central Mexico, on the Pacific coast; capital, Guadalajara.

ja·lop·y /jəˈläpē/ ▸*n.* (*pl.* **-lop·ies**) *informal* an old car in a dilapidated condition. ▷1920s (originally U.S.): of unknown origin.

jal·ou·sie /ˈjaləˌsē/ ▸*n.* a blind or shutter made of a row of angled slats. ▷mid 18th cent.: French, literally 'jealousy,' from Italian *geloso* 'jealous,' also (by extension) 'screen,' associated with the screening of women from view in the Middle East.

jam[1] /jam/ ▸*v.* (**jammed, jam·ming**) **1** [*trans.*] squeeze or pack (someone or something) tightly into a specified space: *four of us were jammed in one compartment* | *people jammed their belongings into cars.* ■ push (something) roughly and forcibly into position or a space: *he jammed his hat on.* ■ [*trans.*] crowd onto (a road) so as to block it: *the roads were jammed with traffic.* ■ [*trans.*] cause (telephone lines) to be continuously busy with a large number of calls: *listeners jammed WBOQ's switchboard with calls.* ■ [*intrans.*] push or crowd into an area or space: *75,000 refugees jammed into a stadium today to denounce the accord.* **2** become or make unable to move or work due to a part seizing or becoming stuck: [*intrans.*] *the photocopier jammed* | [*trans.*] *the doors were jammed open.* ■ [*trans.*] make (a radio transmission) unintelligible by causing interference. **3** [*intrans.*] *informal* improvise with other musicians, esp. in jazz or blues: *the opportunity to jam with Atlanta blues musicians.* ▸*n.* **1** an instance of a machine or thing seizing or becoming stuck: *paper jams.* ■ *informal* an awkward situation or predicament: *I'm **in a jam**.* ■ short for TRAFFIC JAM. ■ [often with *adj.*] *Climbing* a handhold obtained by stuffing a part of the body such as a hand or foot into a crack in the rock. **2** (also **jam ses·sion**) an informal gathering of musicians improvising together, esp. in jazz or blues. ▷early 18th cent.: probably symbolic; compare with JAG[1] and CRAM.

▸*PHRASE* □ **jam on the brakes** operate the brakes of a vehicle suddenly and forcibly, typically in an emergency.

jam[2] ▸*n.* a sweet spread or preserve made from fruit and sugar boiled to a thick consistency. ▷mid 18th cent.: perhaps from JAM[1].

Jam. ▸*abbr.* ■ Jamaica. ■ *Bible* James.

Ja·mai·ca /jəˈmākə/ **1** an island country in the Caribbean Sea, southeast of Cuba; pop. 2,713,000; official capital, Kingston; language, English.

Visited by Columbus in 1494, Jamaica was colonized by the Spanish, who enslaved or killed the native people. Both the Spanish and the British, who took the island by force in 1655, imported slaves, mainly to work on sugar plantations. Self-government was achieved in 1944, and Jamaica became an independent Commonwealth of Nations state in 1962.

2 a commercial and residential section of east central Queens in New York City. —**Ja·mai·can** *adj.* & *n.*

Ja·mai·can sat·in·wood ▸*n.* see SATINWOOD.

jamb /jam/ ▸*n.* a side post or surface of a doorway, window, or fireplace. ■ a columnar mass or pillar in a mine or quarry. ▷Middle English: from Old French *jambe* 'leg, vertical support,' based on Greek *kampē* 'joint.'

jam·ba·lay·a /ˌjəmbəˈlīə/ ▸*n.* a Cajun dish of rice with shrimp, chicken, and vegetables. ▷Louisiana French, from Provenç al *jambalaia*.

jam·beau /ˈjambō/ ▸*n.* (*pl.* **-beaux** /-bōz/ or **-beaus**) *historical* a piece of armor for the leg. ▷late Middle English: apparently an Anglo-Norman French derivative of French *jambe* 'leg.'

Jam·bi /ˈjämbē/ (also **Djambi**) a commercial city in Indonesia, on southern Sumatra, on the Hari River; pop. 340,000.

jam·bo·ree /ˌjambəˈrē/ ▸*n.* a large celebration or party, typically a lavish and boisterous one: *the film industry's annual jamboree in Cannes.* ■ a large rally of Boy Scouts or Girl Scouts. ▷mid 19th cent. (originally U.S. slang): of unknown origin.

James[1] /jāmz/ the name of two kings of England: ■ James I (1566–1625), king of England and Ireland 1603–25; as **James VI**, king of Scotland (1567–1625). He was the son of Mary Stuart and the father of Charles I. A major accomplishment during his reign was the translation of the King James Bible (1611). ■ James II (1633–1701), king of England, Ireland, and Scotland (1685–88). The son of Charles I, he escaped to the Continent in 1648 and returned to England at the Restoration in 1660. He became king on the death of his brother Charles II in 1685, but his conversion to Catholicism made him extremely unpopular. William of Orange and his wife, Mary, James's daughter, were invited to England by Whig and Tory leaders in 1688, and James was allowed to escape to France.

James[2], Henry (1843–1916), U.S. novelist and critic, resident in England from 1896. Notable works: *Portrait of a Lady* (1881), *The Wings of the Dove* (1902), and *The Golden Bowl* (1904). He was the brother of William James.

James[3], Jesse Woodson (1847–82) U.S. outlaw. With brother **Frank** (1843–1915), he was a member of a notorious gang of train and bank robbers.

James[4], P. D., Baroness James of Holland Park (1920–), English detective novelist; full name *Phyllis Dorothy James*. Her novels feature the detective Adam Dalgliesh and include *An Unsuitable Job for a Woman* (1972), *A Certain Justice* (1997), and *Death in Holy Orders* (2001). Most of her novels have been filmed for television.

James[5], William (1842–1910), U.S. psychologist and philosopher who was a founder of pragmatism. He was the brother of William James. His works include *The Varieties of Religious Experience* (1902), *Pragmatism* (1907), and *Essays in Radical Empiricism* (1912).

James, St.[1] /jāmz/, an Apostle; son of Zebedee and brother of John; known as **St. James the Great**. He was put to death by Herod Agrippa I. Feast day, July 25.

James, St.[2], an Apostle; known as **St. James the Less**. Feast day (Eastern Church) October 9; (Western Church) May 1.

James, St.[3] leader of the early Christian Church at Jerusalem; known as **St. James the Just** or **the Lord's brother**. He was put to death by the Sanhedrin. Feast day, May 1. ■ the epistle of the New Testament traditionally ascribed to St. James.

James Bay a shallow southern arm of Hudson Bay, between Quebec and Ontario provinces in Canada. ▷named after Captain Thomas *James* (*c.*1593–*c.*1635), who explored the region in 1631.

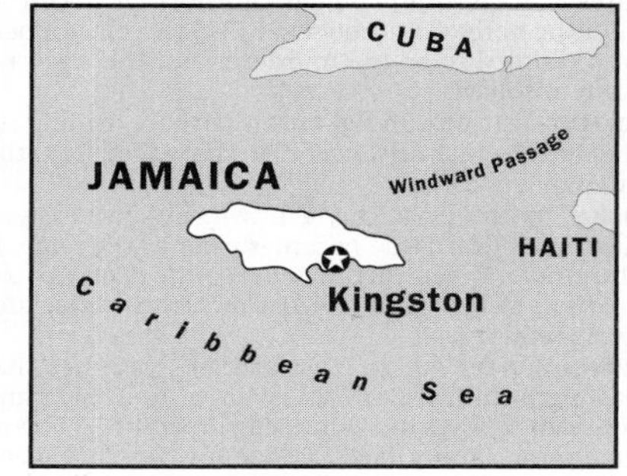

J

James Riv·er **1** a river that flows for 700 miles (1,100 km) from North Dakota through South Dakota into the Missouri River. Also called **DAKOTA RIVER**. **2** a river that flows for 340 miles (550 km) across eastern Virginia, past Richmond, and into the Tidewater region into Hampton Roads. Colonial Jamestown was on its estuary.

James·town /ˈjāmzˌtoun/ **1** a city in southwestern New York, on Lake Chautauqua; pop. 34,681. **2** a city in northeastern North Dakota; pop. 15,527. **3** a British settlement established on the James River in Virginia in 1607, abandoned when the colonial capital was moved to Williamsburg at the end of the 17th century.

jam·mer /ˈjamər/ ▸*n.* a transmitter used for jamming signals.

Jam·mu /ˈjəmo͞o/ a town in northwestern India; pop. 206,000. It is the winter capital of Jammu and Kashmir.

Jam·mu and Kash·mir /ˈkashˌmi(ə)r; ˈkazh-/ a mountainous state in northwestern India, at the western end of the Himalayas, formerly part of Kashmir; capitals, Srinagar (in summer) and Jammu (in winter).

jam·my /ˈjamē/ ▸*adj.* (**-mi·er, -mi·est**) covered with, filled with, or resembling jam: *a jammy doughnut.* ■ (of wine) having a strong fruity flavor or bouquet reminiscent of jam.

Jam·na·gar /jämˈnəgər/ a port and walled city in western India, in the state of Gujarat; pop. 325,000.

jam-packed ▸*adj. informal* extremely crowded or full to capacity: *rutabagas are **jam-packed with** nutrients.*

jam ses·sion ▸*n.* see **JAM**[1] (sense 2).

Jam·shed·pur /ˈjämshedˌpo͝or/ an industrial city in northeastern India, in the state of Bihar; pop. 461,000.

Jam·shid /jamˈshid/ a legendary early king of Persia, reputed inventor of the arts of medicine, navigation, and ironworking.

Jan. ▸*abbr.* January.

jane /jān/ ▸*n. informal* a woman. ▷early 20th cent.: from the given name *Jane.*

▸***PHRASE*** □ **plain Jane** an unattractive girl or woman.

Jane Doe /ˈjān ˈdō/ ▸*n. Law* an anonymous female party, typically the plaintiff, in a legal action. ■ *informal* a hypothetical average woman. See also **JOHN DOE**.

Janes·ville /ˈjānzˌvil/ an industrial city in southern Wisconsin, on the Rock River; pop. 59,498.

jan·gle /ˈjanggəl/ ▸*v.* make or cause to make a ringing metallic sound, typically a discordant one: [*intrans.*] *a bell jangled loudly* | [*trans.*] *Ryan stood on the terrace jangling his keys.* ■ [*trans.*] (with reference to nerves) set on edge: *a thirty-eight point game that jangled the nerves.*

▸*n.* [in *sing.*] a ringing metallic sound: *the jangle of a telephone.* ▷Middle English (in the sense 'talk excessively or noisily, squabble'): from Old French *jangler,* of unknown origin. —**jan·gly** *adj.*

jan·is·sar·y /ˈjaniˌserē/ (also **jan·i·zar·y** /-ˌzerē/) ▸*n.* (*pl.* **-sar·ies**) *historical* a member of the Turkish infantry forming the Sultan's guard between the 14th and 19th centuries. ■ a devoted follower or supporter. ▷early 16th cent.: from French *janissaire,* based on Turkish *yeniçeri,* from *yeni* 'new' + *çeri* 'troops.'

jan·i·tor /ˈjanitər/ ▸*n.* a person employed as a caretaker of a building; a custodian. ■ *archaic* a doorman or doorkeeper. ▷mid 16th cent.: from Latin, from *janua* 'door.' —**jan·i·to·ri·al** /ˌjaniˈtôrēəl/ *adj.*

Ja·nos /ˈyänōs; -nōsh/, James George, see **VENTURA**[2].

Jan·sen /ˈjansən; ˈyänsən/, Cornelius Otto (1585–1638), Flemish theologian; founder of Jansenism. A Roman Catholic, he strongly opposed the Jesuits and proposed reform of Christianity through a return to the teachings of St. Augustine.

Jan·sen·ism /ˈjansəˌnizəm/ ▸*n.* a Christian movement of the 17th and 18th centuries, based on Jansen's writings and characterized by moral rigor and asceticism. —**Jan·sen·ist** *n.*

Jan·sens /ˈyänsən/ (also **Jans·sen van Ceu·len** /vänˈkələn/) variant spelling of **JOHNSON**[4].

Jan·u·ar·y /ˈjanyo͞oˌerē/ ▸*n.* (*pl.* **-ar·ies**) the first month of the year, in the northern hemisphere usually considered the second month of winter: *Sophie was two in January* | [as *adj.*] *the January sales.* ▷Old English, from Latin *Januarius (mensis)* '(month) of *Janus*' (see **JANUS**), the Roman god who presided over doors and beginnings.

Ja·nus /ˈjānəs/ **1** *Roman Mythology* an ancient Italian deity, guardian of doorways and gates and protector of the state in time of war. He is usually represented with two faces, so that he looks both forward and backward. ■ [as *adj.*] two-faced; hypocritical; two-sided. **2** *Astronomy* a moon of Saturn, sixth closest to the planet, discovered in 1966, and having a diameter of 118 miles (190 km).

Jap /jap/ ▸*n. & adj. informal, offensive* short for **JAPANESE**.

Ja·pan /jəˈpan/ a country in eastern Asia that occupies a chain of islands in the Pacific Ocean roughly parallel with the eastern coast of the Asiatic mainland; pop. 127,333,000; capital, Tokyo; official language, Japanese. Japanese name **NIPPON**. ▷rendering of Chinese *Riben.*

From the late 19th century Japan began a modernizing process that eventually made it into a major world power. It fought wars against China 1894–95 and Russia 1904–05, and after World War I occupied Manchuria 1931 and invaded China 1937. Japan entered World War II on the Axis side with a surprise attack on Pearl Harbor in 1941. The country surrendered in 1945 after the U.S. dropped the atom bombs on Hiroshima and Nagasaki. Japan is now a highly industrialized country and the leading economic power in the region.

Ja·pan, Sea of the sea between Japan and mainland Asia.

ja·pan /jəˈpan/ ▸*n.* a hard, dark, enamellike varnish containing asphalt, used to give a black gloss to metal objects. ■ a kind of varnish in which pigments are ground, typically used to imitate lacquer on wood. ■ articles made in a Japanese style, esp. when decorated with lacquer or enamellike varnish.

▸*v.* (**-panned, -pan·ning**) [*trans.*] cover (something) with a hard black varnish: [as *adj.*] (**japanned**) *a japanned tin tray.* ▷late 17th cent.: from **JAPAN**.

Ja·pan Cur·rent another name for **KUROSHIO**.

Jap·a·nese /ˌjapəˈnēz; -ˈnēs/ ▸*adj.* of or relating to Japan or its language, culture, or people.

▸*n.* (*pl.* same) **1** a native or national of Japan, or a person of Japanese descent. **2** the language of Japan, spoken by almost all of its population.

Japanese is possibly related to Korean. It has many Chinese loanwords, and is usually written in vertical columns using Chinese characters (kanji) supplemented by two sets of syllabic characters (kana).

Jap·a·nese a·nem·o·ne ▸*n.* an autumn-flowering anemone with large pink or white flowers. It is native to China and naturalized in Japan, and several cultivars have been developed. • *Anemone hupehensis* var. *japonica,* family Ranunculaceae.

Jap·a·nese bee·tle ▸*n.* a metallic green and copper chafer that is a pest of fruit and foliage as an adult and of grass roots as a larva. It is native to Japan but has spread elsewhere. • *Popillia japonica,* family Scarabaeidae.

Jap·a·nese ce·dar ▸*n.* another term for **CRYPTOMERIA**.

Ja·pan·ese Cur·rent another name for **KUROSHIO**.

Jap·a·nese knot·weed ▸*n.* a tall fast-growing Japanese plant of the dock family, with bamboolike stems and small white flowers. It has been grown as an ornamental but tends to become an aggressive weed. Also called **MEXICAN BAMBOO**. • *Reynoutria japonica,* family Polygonaceae.

Jap·a·nese lan·tern ▸*n.* another term for **CHINESE LANTERN** (sense 1).

Jap·a·nese pa·per ▸*n.* paper of a kind traditionally handmade in Japan, typically from vegetable fibers such as mulberry bark and without being sized, used for art and craft work.

Jap·a·nese per·sim·mon ▸*n.* see **PERSIMMON**.

Jap·a·nese quince ▸*n.* another term for **FLOWERING QUINCE**.

Jap·a·nese stilt grass ▸*n.* an annual grass of Asian origin that is established as an invasive ecological threat in the eastern and southern U.S. • *Microstegium vimineum,* family Poaceae.

Jap·an·i·ma·tion /japˌanəˈmāshən/ ▸*n.* another term for **ANIME**. ▷1980s: blend of **JAPAN** and **ANIMATION**.

jape /jāp/ ▸*n.* a practical joke: *the childish jape of depositing a stink bomb in her locker.*

▸*v.* [*intrans.*] say or do something in jest or mockery. ▷Middle English: apparently combining the form of Old French *japer* 'to yelp, yap' with the sense of Old French *gaber* 'to mock.' —**jap·er·y** /ˈjāp(ə)rē/ *n.*

Ja·pheth /ˈjāfeth/ (in the Bible) a son of Noah (Gen. 10:1), traditional ancestor of the peoples living around the Mediterranean. His name is probably to be connected with that of Iapetus, a Titan in Greek mythology.

Jap·lish /ˈjaplish/ ▸*n. informal* a blend of Japanese and English, either Japanese speech that makes liberal use of English expressions or unidiomatic English spoken by a Japanese.

ja·pon·i·ca /jəˈpänikə/ ▸*n.* **1** another term for **COMMON CAMELLIA** (see **CAMELLIA**). **2** another term for **FLOWERING QUINCE**. ▷early 19th cent.: modern Latin, feminine of *japonicus* 'Japanese.'

Ja·pu·rá Riv·er /ˌzhäpo͞oˈrä/ (Colombian name Caquetá) a river that flows for 1,750 miles (2,815 km) from southwestern Colombia into Brazil to join the Amazon River.

Jaques-Dal·croze /ˌjäk dalˈkrōz/, Émile (1865–1950), Swiss music teacher and composer; born in Austria. He developed the eurhythmics method for teaching music and dance and established a school for eurhythmics instruction in 1910.

jar[1] /jär/ ▸*n.* a wide-mouthed, cylindrical container made of glass or pottery, esp. one used for storing food. ■ the contents of such a container: *jars of mustard.* ▷late 16th cent.: from French *jarre,* from Arabic *jarra.* —**jar·ful** /-ˌfo͝ol/ *n.* (*pl.* **-fuls**).

jar[2] ▸*v.* (**jarred, jar·ring**) **1** [*trans.*] send a painful or damaging shock through (something, esp. a part of the body): *he jarred his knee in training.* ■ [*intrans.*] strike against something with an unpleasant vibration or jolt: *the stick jarred on the bottom of the pond.* **2** [*intrans.*] have an unpleasant, annoying, or disturbing effect: *a laugh that **jarred on** the ears* | *the difference in their background began to jar.* ■ be incongruous in a striking or shocking way: *the play's symbolism **jarred with** the realism of its setting* | [as *adj.*] (**jarring**) *the only jarring note was the modern appearance of the customers.*

▸*n.* a physical shock or jolt. ■ *archaic* discord; disagreement. ▷late 15th cent. (as a noun in the sense 'disagreement, dispute'): probably imitative.

jar·di·niere /ˌjärdnˈi(ə)r; ˌzhärdnˈye(ə)r/ (also **jar·di·nière**) ▸*n.* **1** an ornamental pot or stand for the display of growing plants. **2** a garnish of mixed vegetables. ▷mid 19th cent.: from French *jardinière,* literally 'female gardener.'

jar·gon[1] /ˈjärgən/ ▸*n.* special words or expressions that are used by a particular profession or group and are difficult for others to understand: *legal jargon.* See note at **DIALECT**. ■ a form of language regarded as barbarous, debased, or hybrid. ▷late Middle English (originally in the sense 'twittering, chattering,' later 'gibberish'): from Old French *jargoun,* of unknown origin. The main modern sense dates from the mid 17th cent. —**jar·gon·is·tic** /ˌjärgəˈnistik/ *adj.* —**jar·gon·ize** /-ˌnīz/ *v.*

jar·gon[2] /ˈjärgän/ (also **jar·goon** /järˈgo͞on/) ▸*n.* a translucent, colorless, or smoky gem variety of zircon. ▷mid 18th cent.: from French, from Italian *giargone;* probably ultimately related to **ZIRCON**.

Jar·gon·elle /ˌjärgəˈnel/ ▸*n. Brit.* a pear of an early ripening variety. ▷late 17th cent.: from French, diminutive of **JARGON**[2] (with reference to the color).

jar·head /ˈjärˌhed/ ▸*n. military slang* a U.S. Marine.

jarl /yärl/ ▸*n. historical* a Norse or Danish chief. ▷Old Norse, literally 'man of noble birth'; related to **EARL**.

Jarls·berg /ˈyärlzbərg/ ▸*n. trademark* a kind of hard

J

yellow Norwegian cheese with many holes and a mild, nutty flavor. ▷named after the town of *Jarlsberg*, Norway.

jar·rah /ˈjarə/ ▸*n.* a eucalyptus tree native to western Australia, yielding durable timber. • *Eucalyptus marginata*, family Myrtaceae. ▷mid 19th cent.: from Nyungar *djarryl, jerrhyl.*

Jar·ry /zhäˈrē/, Alfred (1873–1907), French playwright. His satirical farce *Ubu Roi* (1896) anticipated surrealism and the Theater of the Absurd.

Ja·ru·zel·ski /ˌyärəˈzelskē/, Wojciech (1923–), Polish general and statesman; prime minister 1981–85; head of state 1985–89, and president 1989–90. Upon the rise of Solidarity, he imposed martial law and banned labor union activities; after Solidarity's victory in the 1989 elections, he supervised Poland's transition to a democracy.

Jar·vik /ˈjärvik/, Robert K. (1946–) U.S. biomedical research scientist. He patented an artificial heart driven by compressed air in 1979.

Jas. ▸*abbr.* James (in biblical references and generally).

jas·mine /ˈjazmən/ (also **jes·sa·mine** /ˈjesəmin/) ▸*n.* an Old World shrub or climbing plant that bears fragrant flowers that are used in perfumery or tea and is popular as an ornamental. • Genus *Jasminum*, family Oleaceae: many species, including the **winter jasmine**. ■ used in names of other shrubs or climbers with fragrant flowers, e.g., **Cape jasmine**, **yellow jasmine**. ▷mid 16th cent.: from French *jasmin* and obsolete French *jessemin*, from Arabic *yāsamīn*, from Persian *yāsamīn*.

jas·mine tea ▸*n.* a tea perfumed with dried jasmine blossoms.

Ja·son /ˈjāsən/ *Greek Mythology* the son of the king of Iolcos in Thessaly, and leader of the Argonauts in the quest for the Golden Fleece.

jas·pé /zhaˈspā/ ▸*adj.* randomly mottled or variegated, like jasper. ▷mid 19th cent.: French, past participle of *jasper* 'to marble,' from *jaspe* (see JASPER).

jas·per /ˈjaspər/ ▸*n.* **1** an opaque reddish-brown variety of chalcedony. **2** a kind of hard fine porcelain invented by Josiah Wedgwood and used for Wedgwood cameos and other delicate work. ▷Middle English (originally denoting any bright-colored chalcedony other than carnelian): from Old French *jasp(r)e*, from Latin *iaspis*, from Greek, of Asian origin.

Jas·sy /ˈyäsē/ German name for IAŞI.

Jat /jät/ ▸*n.* a member of a people widely scattered throughout the northwest of the Indian subcontinent. ▷from Hindi *Jāṭ*.

Ja·ta·ka /ˈjätəkə/ ▸*n.* any of the various stories of the former lives of the Buddha found in Buddhist literature. ▷from Sanskrit *jātaka* 'born under.'

ja·to /ˈjātō/ ▸*n.* (*pl.* **-tos**) *Aeronautics* jet-assisted takeoff. ■ an auxiliary power unit providing extra thrust at takeoff. ▷World War II (originally U.S.): acronym.

jaun·dice /ˈjôndis/ ▸*n.* a medical condition with yellowing of the skin or whites of the eyes, arising from excess of the pigment bilirubin and typically caused by obstruction of the bile duct, by liver disease, or by excessive breakdown of red blood cells. ■ bitterness, resentment, or envy. ▷Middle English *jaunes*, from Old French *jaunice* 'yellowness,' from *jaune* 'yellow.' The sense 'bitterness' (late 16th cent.) arose from the traditional association of the color yellow with jealousy.

jaun·diced /ˈjôndist/ ▸*adj.* having or affected by jaundice, in particular unnaturally yellow in complexion. ■ affected by bitterness, resentment, or envy: *they looked on politicians with a jaundiced eye.*

jaunt /jônt/ ▸*n.* a short excursion or journey for pleasure: *her little jaunt in France was over.* See note at JOURNEY.
▸*v.* [*intrans.*] make such an excursion or journey: *they went jaunting through Ireland.* ▷late 16th cent.: of unknown origin. Originally depreciatory, early senses included 'tire a horse out by riding it up and down,' 'traipse around,' and (as a noun) 'troublesome journey.' The current positive sense dates from the mid 17th cent.

jaunt·ing car ▸*n.* *historical* a light two-wheeled horse-drawn vehicle formerly used in Ireland.

jaun·ty /ˈjôntē/ ▸*adj.* (**-ti·er**, **-ti·est**) having or expressing a lively, cheerful, and self-confident manner: *there was no mistaking that jaunty walk.* ▷mid 17th cent. (in the sense 'well-bred, genteel'): from French *gentil* (see GENTLE, GENTEEL). —**jaun·ti·ly** /-tl-ē/ *adv.* —**jaun·ti·ness** *n.*

Jav. ▸*abbr.* Javanese.

Ja·va[1] /ˈjävə; ˈjavə/ a large island in the Malay Archipelago that forms part of Indonesia; pop. 112,160,000. —**Ja·van** *n.* & *adj.*

Ja·va[2] /ˈjävə/ ▸*n.* *trademark* a general-purpose computer programming language designed to produce programs that will run on any computer system.

ja·va /ˈjävə; ˈjavə/ ▸*n.* *informal* coffee. ▷mid 19th cent.: originally referring to coffee from JAVA[1].

Ja·va man ▸*n.* a fossil hominid of the middle Pleistocene epoch, whose remains were found in Java in 1891. • An early form of *Homo erectus* (formerly *Pithecanthropus*), family Hominidae.

Jav·a·nese /ˌjävəˈnēz; -ˈnēs/ ▸*n.* (*pl.* same) **1** a native or inhabitant of Java, or a person of Javanese descent. **2** the Indonesian language of central Java.
▸*adj.* of or relating to Java, its people, or their language.

Ja·van rhi·noc·er·os /ˈjävən/ ▸*n.* a rare, one-horned rhinoceros that is now confined to the lowland rain forests of Java. • *Rhinoceros sondaicus*, family Rhinocerotidae.

Ja·va·ri Riv·er /ˌzhäväˈrē/ (Peruvian name **Yavari**) a river that flows northeast for 500 miles (810 km) from eastern Peru, along the Peru-Brazil border, to the Amazon River.

Ja·va Sea a sea in the Malay Archipelago in southeastern Asia that is surrounded by the islands of Borneo, Java, and Sumatra.

Ja·va spar·row ▸*n.* a waxbill with a large red bill and black-and-white head, native to Java and Bali but introduced widely elsewhere and popular as a pet bird. • *Padda oryzivora*, family Estrildidae.

jave·lin /ˈjav(ə)lən/ ▸*n.* a light spear thrown in a competitive sport or as a weapon. ■ (**the javelin**) the athletic event or sport of throwing the javelin: *his nearest rival in the javelin.* ▷late Middle English: from Old French *javeline*, of Celtic origin.

ja·ve·li·na /ˌhävəˈlēnə/ ▸*n.* another term for PECCARY. ▷early 19th cent.: from Spanish *jabalina*, from the feminine form of *jabalí* 'wild boar,' from Arabic *jabali* 'mountaineer.'

jaw /jô/ ▸*n.* each of the upper and lower bony structures in vertebrates forming the framework of the mouth and containing the teeth. ■ the lower movable bone of such a structure or the part of the face containing it: *she suffered a broken jaw.* ■ (**jaws**) the mouth with its bones and teeth. ■ (**jaws**) the grasping, biting, or crushing mouthparts of an invertebrate. ■ (**jaws**) used to suggest the notion of being in danger from something such as death or defeat: *victory was snatched* ***from the jaws of*** *defeat.* ■ (usu. **jaws**) the gripping parts of a tool or machine, such as a wrench or vise. ■ (**jaws**) an opening likened to a mouth: *a passenger stepping from the jaws of a ferry.* ■ *informal* talk or gossip, esp. when lengthy or tedious: *committee work is just endless jaw | we ought to have a jaw.*
▸*v.* [*intrans.*] *informal* talk at length; chatter: *he could still hear men* ***jawing away about*** *the vacuum cleaners.* ▷late Middle English: from Old French *joe* 'cheek, jaw,' of unknown origin. —**jawed** *adj.* [in *combination*] *square-jawed young men.* —**jaw·less** *adj.*

jaw·bone /ˈjôˌbōn/ ▸*n.* a bone of the jaw, esp. that of the lower jaw (the mandible), or either half of this.
▸*v.* [*trans.*] attempt to persuade or pressure by the force of one's position of authority: *the Federal Reserve Board Vice Chairman jawboned the dollar higher by calling its recent steep decline a purely speculative phenomenon* | [*intrans.*] *an analyst jawboning about the industry.*

jaw·break·er /ˈjôˌbrākər/ ▸*n.* **1** *informal* a word that is very long or hard to pronounce. **2** a large, hard, spherical candy. **3** a machine with powerful jaws for crushing rock or ore.

jaw-drop·ping ▸*adj.* *informal* amazing: *jaw-dropping displays of genius.* —**jaw-drop·ping·ly** *adv.*

jaw·fish /ˈjôˌfish/ ▸*n.* (*pl.* same or **-fish·es**) a small fish with very large jaws that lives in shallow tropical seas. It often inhabits a burrow in the sand, the walls of which are lined with pieces of shell and stone. • Family Opistognathidae: several genera and species.

jaw·line /ˈjôˌlīn/ ▸*n.* the contour of the lower edge of a person's jaw: *he had a dark, unshaven jawline.*

Jaws of Life ▸*n.* *trademark* a hydraulic apparatus used to pry apart the wreckage of crashed vehicles in order to free people trapped inside.

Jay /jā/, John (1745–1829) U.S. chief justice 1789–95 and statesman. With James Madison and Alexander Hamilton, he was the author of the *Federalist* 1787–88. He served as the first chief justice of the U.S. and was responsible for Jay's Treaty 1794–95 that settled outstanding disputes with Britain.

jay /jā/ ▸*n.* **1** a bird of the crow family with boldly patterned plumage, typically having blue feathers in the wings or tail. • Family Corvidae: several genera and numerous species, in particular the Eurasian *Garrulus glandarius*, with a crest, mainly pinkish-brown plumage, and a harsh screech. **2** *archaic* a person who chatters impertinently. ▷late 15th cent.: via Old French from late Latin *gaius, gaia*, perhaps from the Latin given name *Gaius*.

Jay·cee /ˌjāˈsē/ ▸*n.* a member of a Junior Chamber of Commerce, a civic organization for business and community leaders. ▷1940s: representing the initials of *Junior Chamber*.

Jay·hawk State /ˈjāˌhôk/ a nickname for the state of KANSAS.

jay·walk /ˈjāˌwôk/ ▸*v.* [*intrans.*] cross or walk in the street or road unlawfully or without regard for approaching traffic. ▷early 20th cent.: from JAY in the colloquial sense 'silly person' + WALK. —**jay·walk·er** *n.*

jazz /jaz/ ▸*n.* a type of music of black American origin characterized by improvisation, syncopation, and usually a regular or forceful rhythm, emerging at the beginning of the 20th century. Brass and woodwind instruments and piano are particularly associated with jazz, although guitar and occasionally violin are also used; styles include Dixieland, swing, bebop, and free jazz. ■ *informal* enthusiastic or lively talk, esp. when considered exaggerated or insincere: *all this jazz about how they can't afford it is preposterous.*
▸*v.* [*intrans.*] *dated* play or dance to jazz music.
▸*phrasal v.* □ **jazz something up** make something more lively or cheerful: *jazz up an all-white kitchen with red tiles.* ▷early 20th cent.: of unknown origin. —**jazz·er** *n.*
▸*PHRASE* □ **and all that jazz** *informal* and such similar things: *oh, love, life, and all that jazz.*

Jazz Age the 1920s in the U.S. characterized as a period of carefree hedonism, wealth, freedom, and youthful exuberance, reflected in the novels of writers such as F. Scott Fitzgerald.

jazz·bo /ˈjazbō/ ▸*n.* (*pl.* **-bos**) *informal* **1** a jazz musician or jazz enthusiast. **2** *archaic* a person, esp. a black man. ▷early 20th cent.: of unknown origin.

jazz·er·cise /ˈjazərˌsīz/ ▸*n.* *trademark* a type of fitness training combining aerobic exercise and dancing to jazz music. ▷1970s: blend of JAZZ and EXERCISE.

jazz funk (also **jazz-funk**) ▸*n.* a style of popular dance music incorporating elements of jazz and funk: [*as modifier*] *a jazz-funk ensemble.*

jazz·man /ˈjazmən; -ˌman/ ▸*n.* (*pl.* **-men**) a male jazz musician.

jazz·y /ˈjazē/ ▸*adj.* (**jazz·i·er**, **jazz·i·est**) of, resembling, or in the style of jazz: *a jazzy piano solo.* ■ bright, colorful, and showy: *jazzy ties.* —**jazz·i·ly** /ˈjazəlē/ *adv.* —**jazz·i·ness** *n.*

JCD ▸*abbr.* ■ Doctor of Canon Law. [from modern Latin *Juris Canonici Doctor.*] ■ Doctor of Civil Law. [from Latin *Juris Civilis Doctor.*]

JCL ▸*abbr.* ■ *Computing* job control language. ■ Licentiate in Canon Law.

JCS ▸*abbr.* Joint Chiefs of Staff, the chief military advisory body to the president of the U.S.

jct. ▸*abbr.* junction.

JD ▸*abbr.* *informal* ■ juvenile delinquency. ■ juvenile delinquent. ■ Doctor of Law. [from Latin *juris doctor.*]

jeal·ous /ˈjeləs/ ▸*adj.* feeling or showing envy of someone or their achievements and advantages: *he grew* ***jealous of*** *her success.* ■ feeling or showing suspicion of someone's unfaithfulness in a relationship: *a jealous boyfriend.* ■ fiercely protective or vigilant of one's rights or possessions: *Howard is still a little* ***jealous of*** *his authority | they kept a jealous eye over their*

John Jay

interests. ■ (of God) demanding faithfulness and exclusive worship. ▷Middle English: from Old French *gelos*, from medieval Latin *zelosus* (see **ZEALOUS**). —**jeal·ous·ly** *adv.*

THE RIGHT WORD **covetous, envious, jealous,**

Envious implies wanting something that belongs to another and to which one has no particular right or claim (*envious of her good fortune*).

Jealous may refer to a strong feeling of envy (*it is hard not to be jealous of a man with a job like his*), or it may imply an intense effort to hold on to what one possesses (*jealous of what little time she has to herself*); it is often associated with distrust, suspicion, anger, and other negative emotions (*a jealous wife*).

Someone who is **covetous** has fallen prey to an inordinate or wrongful desire, usually for a person or thing that rightfully belongs to another.

In other words, a young man might be *jealous* of the other men who flirt with his girlfriend, while they might be *envious* of her obvious preference for him. But the young man had better not be *covetous* of his neighbor's wife.

jeal·ous·y /ˈjeləsē/ ▸*n.* (*pl.* **-ous·ies**) the state or feeling of being jealous: *a sharp pang of jealousy* | *resentments and jealousies festered.* ▷Middle English: from Old French *gelosie*, from *gelos* (see **JEALOUS**).

jean /jēn/ ▸*n.* heavy twilled cotton cloth, esp. denim: [as *adj.*] *a jean jacket.* ■ (in commercial use) a pair of jeans: *a button-fly jean.* ▷late 15th cent. (as an adjective): from Old French *Janne* (now *Gênes*), from medieval Latin *Janua* 'Genoa,' the place of original production. The noun sense comes from *jean fustian*, literally 'fustian from Genoa,' used in the 16th cent. to denote a heavy twilled cotton cloth.

jeans /jēnz/ ▸*plural n.* hard-wearing trousers made of denim or other cotton fabric, for informal wear. When blue, the typical color of jeans, they are also called **BLUE JEANS**. ▷mid 19th cent.: plural of **JEAN**.

jeb·el /ˈjebəl/ (also **djeb·el**) ▸*n.* (in the Middle East and North Africa) a mountain or hill, or a range of hills. ▷colloquial Arabic form of *jabal* 'mountain.'

Jed·dah /ˈjedə/ variant spelling of **JIDDAH**.

Jed·i /ˈjedˌī/ (also **Jed·i knight** or **Jed·i war·ri·or**) ▸*n.* (*pl.* same or **Jed·is**) a member of the mystical knightly order in the *Star Wars* films, trained to guard peace and justice in the universe. ■ anyone with special privileges or supernormal powers reminiscent of a Jedi: *these guys hang out in places mere mortal lobbyists who were not Jedi warriors cannot go.*

jeep /jēp/ ▸*n. trademark* a small, sturdy motor vehicle with four-wheel drive, esp. one used by the military. ▷World War II: from the initials *GP*, standing for *general purpose*, influenced by 'Eugene the Jeep,' a creature of great resourcefulness and power represented in the *Popeye* comic strip.

jee·pers /ˈjēpərz/ (also **jee·pers cree·pers**) ▸*exclam. informal* used to express surprise or alarm: *Jeepers! Do you think she saw?* ▷1920s: alteration of **JESUS**.

jeer /ji(ə)r/ ▸*v.* [*intrans.*] make rude and mocking remarks, typically in a loud voice: *some of the younger men jeered at him* | [as *adj.*] (**jeering**) *the jeering crowds.* ■ [*trans.*] shout such remarks at (someone): *the performers were jeered and heckled.*
▸*n.* a rude and mocking remark. ▷mid 16th cent.: of unknown origin. —**jeer·ing·ly** *adv.*

jeet kune do /ˈjēt ˌkōōn ˈdō/ ▸*n.* a modern martial art incorporating elements of kung fu, fencing, and boxing, devised by American actor Bruce Lee (1940–73). ▷1990s: from Cantonese, literally 'the way of the intercepting fist.'

Jeeves /jēvz/ the resourceful and influential valet of Bertie Wooster in the novels of P. G. Wodehouse.

jeez /jēz/ (also **geez**) ▸*exclam. informal* a mild expression used to show surprise or annoyance. ▷1920s: abbreviation of **JESUS**.

je·fe /ˈhefā/ ▸*n. informal* a boss or leader; a person in charge of something. ▷late 19th cent.: Spanish from French *chef* 'chief.'

Jef·fers /ˈjefərz/, (John) Robinson (1887–1962) U.S. poet. His poetry is collected in *Tamar and Other Poems* (1924), *The Women at Point Sur* (1927), and *Hungerfield and Other Poems* (1954).

Jef·fer·son /ˈjefərsən/, Thomas (1743–1826), 3rd president of the U.S. 1801–09. A Democratic Republican from Virginia, he played a key role in leadership during the American Revolution and was the principal drafter of the Declaration of Independence 1776. While president, he secured the Louisiana Purchase 1803 and authorized the Lewis-Clark expedition to explore this territory. Reelected to a second term, his poor handling of U.S. shipping and maritime policy made a third term impossible. He chartered the University of Virginia 1819 and served as its head. —**Jef·fer·so·ni·an** /ˌjefərˈsōnēən/ *adj.* & *n.*

Jef·fer·son Cit·y the capital of Missouri, in the central part of the state; pop. 39,636.

Jeff·er·son·town /ˈjefərsənˌtoun/ a city in north central Kentucky, an eastern suburb of Louisville; pop. 26,633.

je·had ▸*n.* variant spelling of **JIHAD**.

Je·hosh·a·phat /jəˈhäsнəˌfat; -ˈhäs-/ (also **Je·hos·a·phat**) a king of Judah in the mid 9th century BC. ■ [as *exclam.*] (also **jumping Jehoshaphat**) a mild expletive: *Jehoshaphat! That would be ghastly.* [probably a euphemism for **JESUS**.]

Je·ho·vah /jəˈhōvə/ ▸*n.* a form of the Hebrew name of God used in some translations of the Bible. ▷from medieval Latin *Iehouah, Iehoua*, from Hebrew *YHWH* or *JHVH*, the consonants of the name of God, with the inclusion of vowels taken from *ʾăḏōnāy* 'my lord'; see also **YAHWEH**.

Je·ho·vah's Wit·ness ▸*n.* a member of a Christian sect (the Watch Tower Bible and Tract Society) founded in the U.S. by Charles Taze Russell (1852–1916), denying many traditional Christian doctrines (including the divinity of Christ) but preaching the Second Coming of Christ, and refusing military service and blood transfusion on religious grounds.

Je·ho·vist /jəˈhōvist/ ▸*n.* another name for **YAHWIST**.

je·june /jiˈjōōn/ ▸*adj.* **1** naive, simplistic, and superficial: *their entirely predictable and usually jejune opinions.* **2** (of ideas or writings) dry and uninteresting: *the poem seems to me rather jejune.* ▷early 17th cent.: from Latin *jejunus* 'fasting, barren.' The original sense was 'without food,' hence 'not intellectually nourishing.' —**je·june·ly** *adv.* —**je·june·ness** *n.*

je·ju·noi·le·al /jiˌjōōnōˈilēəl/ ▸*adj. Medicine* of or involving the jejunum and the ileum, usually with reference to a bypass operation in which they are connected.

je·ju·num /jiˈjōōnəm/ ▸*n.* [in *sing.*] *Anatomy* the part of the small intestine between the duodenum and ileum. ▷mid 16th cent.: from medieval Latin, neuter of *jejunus* 'fasting' (because it is usually found to be empty after death). —**je·ju·nal** /ˈjōōnl/ *adj.*

Jek·yll /ˈjekəl/, Dr., the central character of Robert Louis Stevenson's story *The Strange Case of Dr. Jekyll and Mr. Hyde* (1886). He discovers a drug that creates a separate personality (appearing in the character of Mr. Hyde) into which Jekyll's evil impulses are channeled.
▸*PHRASE* □ **a Jekyll and Hyde** a person alternately displaying opposing good and evil personalities.

Je·li·nek /ˈyeləˌnek/, Elfriede (1946–), Austrian novelist, poet, and playwright. Her novels include *Women as Lovers* (1975), *Wonderful, Wonderful Times* (1980), *The Piano Teacher* (1983), and *Lust* (1989). Nobel Prize for Literature (2004).

jell /jel/ ▸*v.* [*intrans.*] (of jelly or a similar substance) set or become firmer: *the stew is jelling.* ■ (of a project or idea) take a definite shape; begin to work well: *everything seemed to jell for the magazine.* ■ (of people) relate well to one another: *it's gratifying seeing everybody jelling.* ▷mid 18th cent.: back-formation from **JELLY**.

jel·la·ba ▸*n.* variant spelling of **DJELLABA**.

jell·o /ˈjelō/ (also *trademark* **Jell-O**) ▸*n.* a fruit-flavored gelatin dessert made from a commercially prepared powder.

jel·ly /ˈjelē/ ▸*n.* (*pl.* **-lies**) a sweet, clear, semisolid, somewhat elastic spread or preserve made from fruit juice and sugar boiled to a thick consistency. ■ used figuratively and in similes to refer to sensations of fear or strong emotion: *her legs felt like jelly.* ■ a similar clear preparation made with fruit or other ingredients as a condiment: *roast pheasant with red currant jelly.* ■ a gelatinous savory preparation made by boiling meat and bones. ■ any substance of a gelatinous consistency: *spermicidal jellies* | *frogs lay eggs coated in jelly.* ■ *chiefly Brit.* a sweet, fruit-flavored gelatin dessert. ■ (**jellies**) jelly shoes.
▸*v.* (**-lies, -lied**) [*trans.*] [usu. as *adj.*] (**jellied**) set (food) as or in a jelly: *jellied cranberry sauce* | *jellied eels.* ▷late Middle English: from Old French *gelée* 'frost, jelly,' from Latin *gelata* 'frozen,' from *gelare* 'freeze,' from *gelu* 'frost.' —**jel·li·fi·ca·tion** /ˌjeləfiˈkāsнən/ *n.* —**jel·li·fy** /ˈjeləˌfī/ *v.* —**jel·ly·like** /-ˌlīk/ *adj.*

jel·ly bean (also **jel·ly·bean**) ▸*n.* a bean-shaped candy with a jellylike center and a firm sugar coating.

jel·ly·fish /ˈjelēˌfisн/ ▸*n.* (*pl.* same or **-fish·es**) **1** a free-swimming marine coelenterate with a jellylike bell- or saucer-shaped body that is typically transparent and has stinging tentacles around the edge. • Classes Scyphozoa and Cubozoa. **2** *informal* a feeble or weak-willed person.

jel·ly roll ▸*n.* a cylindrical cake with a spiral cross section, made from a flat sponge cake spread with a filling such as jam and rolled up. ■ *vulgar slang* a woman's genitals, or sexual intercourse.

jel·ly shoe ▸*n.* a sandal made from brightly colored or translucent molded plastic.

Je·mez Moun·tains /ˈhāmes/ a range in northern New Mexico, northwest of Santa Fe, the site of an enormous caldera called Valle Grande. Chicoma Peak (11,950 feet; 3,642 m) is the high point.

jem·my /ˈjemē/ ▸*n.* & *v.* British spelling of **JIMMY**.

Je·na /ˈyānə/ a university town in central Germany, in Thuringia; pop. 101,000.

je ne sais quoi /ˌzнə nə sā ˈkwä/ ▸*n.* a quality that cannot be described or named easily: *that je ne sais quoi that makes a professional.* ▷French, literally 'I do not know what.'

Jen·kins /ˈjeNGkinz/, Roy (Harris), Baron Jenkins of Hillhead (1920–), English politician and scholar. He was a member of Parliament 1948–76 and 1982–87 and then served as chancellor of Oxford University. Notable works: *Mr. Attlee* (1948), *Truman* (1986), and *Gladstone* (1995).

Jen·kins's Ear, War of a war between England and Spain (1739). It was precipitated by a British sea captain, Robert Jenkins, who appeared before Parliament to produce what he claimed was his ear, cut off by the Spanish while they were carrying out a search of his ship in the Caribbean.

Jen·ner /ˈjenər/, Edward (1749–1823), British physician; the pioneer of vaccination. He deliberately infected people with small amounts of cowpox because he believed it would protect them from catching the disease. The practice led to the widespread use of vaccination against disease.

jen·net /ˈjenit/ ▸*n.* **1** a female donkey. **2** (also **gen·et**) a small Spanish horse. ▷late Middle English: via French from Spanish *jinete* 'light horseman,' from Spanish Arabic *Zenāta*, the name of a Berber people famous for horsemanship.

Jen·nings[1] /ˈjeniNGz/, Peter (Charles) (1938–), Canadian television journalist. An award-winning reporter and correspondent for ABC from 1964, he became the anchor for ABC's "World News Tonight" in 1983.

Jen·nings[2], Waylon (Arnold) (1937–), U.S. country musician. He is noted for the songs "Mamas Don't Let Your Babies Grow Up to be Cowboys" (1978) and "The Eagle" (1991).

jen·ny /ˈjenē/ ▸*n.* (*pl.* **-nies**) **1** a female donkey or ass. **2** short for **SPINNING JENNY**. ▷early 17th cent. (used to denote a female mammal or bird): nickname for the given name *Janet* (compare with **JACK**[1]).

jen·ny wren ▸*n. Brit., informal* a wren.

jeon /ˈjēˌän/ ▸*n.* (*pl.* same) a monetary unit of South Korea, equal to one hundredth of a won. ▷Korean.

jeop·ard·ize /ˈjepərˌdīz/ ▸*v.* [*trans.*] put (someone or something) into a situation in which there is a danger of loss, harm, or failure: *a devaluation of the dollar would jeopardize New York's position as a financial center.*

jeop·ard·y /ˈjepərdē/ ▸*n.* danger of loss, harm, or failure: *Michael's job was not* **in jeopardy**. ■ *Law* danger arising from being on trial for a criminal offense. ▷Middle English *iuparti*, from Old French *ieu parti* '(evenly) divided game.' The term was originally used in chess and other games to denote a problem, or a position in which the chances of winning or losing were evenly balanced, hence 'a dangerous situation.'

Thomas Jefferson

J

Jeph·thah /ˈjefTHə; yifˈtäKH/ (in the Bible) a judge of Israel who sacrificed his daughter in consequence of a vow that if victorious in battle he would sacrifice the first living thing that met him on his return (Judges 11, 12).

je·quir·i·ty /jəˈkwiritē/ (also **jequirity bean**) ▶*n.* another term for ROSARY PEA. ▷late 19th cent.: from French *jéquirity*, from Tupi-Guarani *jekiriti*.

Jer. ▶*abbr. Bible* Jeremiah.

jer·bo·a /jərˈbōə/ ▶*n.* a desert-dwelling rodent with very long hind legs that enable it to walk upright and perform long jumps, found from North Africa to central Asia. • Family Dipodidae: several genera and species, including the **rough-legged** (or **northern three-toed**) **jerboa** (*Dipus sagitta*). ▷mid 17th cent.: modern Latin, from Arabic *yarbūʻ*.

rough-legged jerboa

jer·e·mi·ad /ˌjerəˈmīəd; -ˌad/ ▶*n.* a long, mournful complaint or lamentation; a list of woes. ▷late 18th cent.: from French *jérémiade*, from *Jérémie* 'Jeremiah,' from ecclesiastical Latin *Jeremias*, with reference to the Lamentations of Jeremiah in the Old Testament.

Jer·e·mi·ah /ˌjerəˈmīə/, (*c.*650–*c.*585 BC) a Hebrew prophet. He foresaw the fall of Assyria, the conquest of his country by Egypt and Babylon, and the destruction of Jerusalem. The biblical Lamentations are traditionally ascribed to Jeremiah. ■ a book of the Bible containing his prophecies. ■ [as *n.*] (**a Jeremiah**) a person who complains continually or foretells disaster.

Je·rez /hāˈres; -ˈreTH/ a town in southwestern Spain, in Andalusia; pop. 184,000. It is the center of a sherry-making industry. Full name JEREZ DE LA FRONTERA .

Jer·i·cho /ˈjeriˌkō/ a town in Palestine, on the West Bank, north of the Dead Sea. According to the Bible, Jericho was a Canaanite city destroyed by the Israelites after they crossed the Jordan River into the Promised Land. Occupied by the Israelis since the Six Day War of 1967, it was the first area given partial autonomy under the PLO–Israeli peace accord in 1994.

jerk[1] /jərk/ ▶*n.* **1** a quick, sharp, sudden movement: *he gave a sudden jerk of his head.* ■ a spasmodic muscular twitch. ■ [in *sing.*] *Weightlifting* the raising of a barbell above the head from shoulder level by an abrupt straightening of the arms and legs, typically as the second part of a clean and jerk. **2** *informal* a contemptibly obnoxious person.
▶*v.* [*trans.*] make (something) move with a jerk: *she jerked her chin up.* ■ [*intrans.*] move with a jerk: *his head jerked around | the van jerked forward.* ■ suddenly rouse or jolt (someone): *the thud jerked her back to reality.* ■ [*trans.*] *Weightlifting* raise (a weight) from shoulder level to above the head.
▶*phrasal v.* □ **jerk someone around** *informal* deal with someone dishonestly or unfairly. □ **jerk off** *vulgar slang* masturbate. ▷mid 16th cent. (denoting a stroke with a whip): probably imitative. **—jerk·er** *n.*

jerk[2] ▶*v.* [*trans.*] [usu. as *adj.*] (**jerked**) prepare (meat) by marinating it in spices and drying or barbecuing it over a wood fire: *jerked beef.*
▶*n.* meat cooked in this way: *fiery Jamaican jerk* | [as *adj.*] *jerk chicken.* ▷early 18th cent.: from Latin American Spanish *charquear*, from *charqui*, from Quechua *echarqui* 'dried flesh.'

jer·kin /ˈjərkin/ ▶*n.* a sleeveless jacket. ■ *historical* a man's close-fitting jacket, typically made of leather. ▷early 16th cent.: of unknown origin.

jerkin

jer·kin head ▶*n. Architecture* the end of a roof that is hipped for only part of its height, leaving a truncated gable. ▷mid 19th cent.: perhaps from an alteration of *jerking* (from the verb JERK[1]) + HEAD; compare also with earlier *kirkin-head* (apparently arbitrarily formed from KIRK) in the same sense.

jerk·wa·ter /ˈjərkˌwôtər; -ˌwätər/ ▶*adj.* [*attrib.*] *informal* of or associated with small, remote, and insignificant rural settlements: *some jerkwater town.* ▷mid 19th cent.: from JERK[1] + WATER, from the need for early railroad engines to be supplied with water in remote areas, by dipping a bucket into a stream and "jerking" it out by rope.

jerk·y[1] /ˈjərkē/ ▶*adj.* (**jerk·i·er**, **jerk·i·est**) **1** characterized by abrupt stops and starts: *shallow, jerky, irregular breathing.* **2** contemptibly foolish: *he makes mischief with his jerky pals.* **—jerk·i·ly** /-kəlē/ *adv.* **—jerk·i·ness** *n.*

jerk·y[2] ▶*n.* meat that has been cured by being cut into long, thin strips and dried: *beef jerky.* ▷mid 19th cent.: from American Spanish *charqui*, from Quechua.

jer·o·bo·am /ˌjerəˈbōəm/ ▶*n.* a wine bottle with a capacity four times larger than that of an ordinary bottle. ▷early 19th cent.: named after *Jeroboam*, a king of Israel, "who made Israel to sin" (1 Kings 11:28, 14:16).

Je·rome, St. /jəˈrōm/ (*c.*342–420), doctor of the Church. He is noted for his compilation of the Vulgate Bible. Feast day, September 30.

jer·ry-built ▶*adj.* badly or hastily built with materials of poor quality. ▷mid 19th cent.: origin unknown; sometimes said to be from the name of a firm of builders in Liverpool, or to allude to the walls of Jericho, which fell down at the sound of Joshua's trumpets (Josh. 6:20). **—jer·ry-build·er** *n.* **—jer·ry-build·ing** *n.*

jer·ry·can /ˈjerēˌkan/ (also **jer·ry can**, **jer·ri·can**) ▶*n.* a large, flat-sided metal container for storing or transporting liquids, typically gasoline or water. ▷World War II: from *Jerry* 'a German' (probably an alteration of GERMAN) + CAN[2], because such containers were first used in Germany.

Jer·sey /ˈjərzē/ the largest of the Channel Islands; pop. 83,000

jer·sey /ˈjərzē/ ▶*n.* (*pl.* **-seys**) **1** a knitted garment with long sleeves worn over the upper body. ■ a distinctive shirt worn by a player or competitor in certain sports. ■ a soft, fine knitted fabric. **2** (**Jersey**) an animal of a breed of light brown dairy cattle from Jersey. ▷late 16th cent. (denoting woolen worsted fabric made in Jersey): from JERSEY.

Jer·sey Cit·y an industrial city in northeastern New Jersey, on the Hudson River, opposite New York City; pop. 240,055.

Je·ru·sa·lem /jəˈro͞os(ə)ləm; -ˈro͞oz-/ the holy city of the Jews, sacred also to Christians and Muslims, that lies in the Judaean hills about 20 miles (32 km) from the Jordan River; pop. 562,000. From 1947, the city was divided between the states of Israel and Jordan until the Israelis occupied the whole city in June 1967 and proclaimed it the capital of Israel although it is not accepted as such by the United Nations. It is revered by Christians as the place of Christ's death and resurrection and by Muslims as the site of the Dome of the Rock.

Je·ru·sa·lem ar·ti·choke ▶*n.* **1** a knobby edible tuber with white flesh, eaten as a vegetable. **2** the tall North American plant, closely related to the sunflower, that produces this tuber. • *Helianthus tuberosus*, family Compositae. ▷early 17th cent.: *Jerusalem*, alteration of Italian *girasole* 'sunflower.'

Je·ru·sa·lem Bi·ble ▶*n.* a modern English translation of the Bible by mainly Roman Catholic scholars, published in 1966 and revised (as the **New Jerusalem Bible**) in 1985.

Je·ru·sa·lem cross ▶*n.* a cross with arms of equal length each ending in a bar; a cross potent.

Je·ru·sa·lem thorn ▶*n.* **1** a thorny tropical American tree of the pea family, grown as an ornamental. • *Parkinsonia aculeata*, family Leguminosae. **2** see CHRIST'S THORN.

Jer·vis /ˈjərvəs/, John, Earl St. Vincent (1735–1823), British admiral. In 1797, as commander of the British fleet, he defeated a Spanish fleet off the coast of Portugal.

Jer·vis Bay Ter·ri·to·ry /ˈjärvəs/ a territory on Jervis Bay on the southeastern coast of Australia.

Jes·per·sen /ˈyespərsən/ (Jens) Otto (Harry) (1860–1943), Danish philologist, grammarian, and educationist. He promoted the use of the "direct method" in language teaching. Notable works: *How to Teach a Foreign Language* (1904) and *Modern English Grammar* (1909–49).

jess /jes/ *Falconry* ▶*n.* (usu. **jesses**) a short leather strap that is fastened around each leg of a hawk, usually also having a ring or swivel to which a leash may be attached.
▶*v.* [*trans.*] put such straps on (a hawk). ▷Middle English: from Old French *ges*, based on Latin *jactus* 'a throw,' from *jacere* 'to throw.'

jes·sa·mine /ˈjesəmin/ ▶*n.* variant spelling of JASMINE.

Jes·se /ˈjesē/ (in the Bible) the father of David (1 Sam. 16), represented as the first in the genealogy of Jesus Christ.

Jes·sel /ˈjesəl/, George Albert (1898–1981) U.S. entertainer; known as America's "toastmaster general." He was best known as a master of ceremonies.

Jes·se tree ▶*n.* a representation usually in carving or stained glass of the genealogy of Jesus as a tree with Jesse at the base and intermediate descendants on branching scrolls of foliage.

Jes·se win·dow ▶*n.* a church window showing Jesus' descent from Jesse, typically in the form of a Jesse tree.

jest /jest/ ▶*n.* a thing said or done for amusement; a joke: *there are jests about administrative gaffes | it was said **in jest**.* ■ *archaic* an object of derision: *lowly virtue is the jest of fools.*
▶*v.* [*intrans.*] speak or act in a joking manner: *you jest, surely?* | [with *direct speech*] *"I don't know about maturing," jests William.* ▷late Middle English: from earlier *gest*, from Old French *geste*, from Latin *gesta* 'actions, exploits,' from *gerere* 'do.' The original sense was 'exploit, heroic deed,' hence 'a narrative of such deeds' (originally in verse); later the term denoted an idle tale, hence a joke (mid 16th cent.).

jest·er /ˈjestər/ ▶*n. historical* a professional joker or "fool" at a medieval court, typically wearing a cap with bells on it and carrying a mock scepter. ■ a person who habitually plays the fool.

Je·su /ˈjāzo͞o; ˈjē-; ˈyā-/ archaic form of JESUS. ▷Middle English: from Old French. *Jesus* became the usual spelling in the 16th cent., but *Jesu* was often retained in translations of the Bible, reflecting Latin vocative use.

Jes·u·it /ˈjeZHo͞oit; ˈjez(y)o͞o-/ ▶*n.* a member of the Society of Jesus, a Roman Catholic order of priests founded by St. Ignatius Loyola, St. Francis Xavier, and others in 1534, to do missionary work. The order was zealous in opposing the Reformation. Despite periodic persecution it has retained an important influence in Catholic thought and education. ▷from French *jésuite* or modern Latin *Jesuita*, from Christian Latin *Iesus* (see JESUS).

Jes·u·it·i·cal /ˌjeZHo͞oˈitikəl; ˌjez(y)o͞o-/ ▶*adj.* of or concerning the Jesuits. ■ dissembling or equivocating, in the manner associated with Jesuits. **—Jes·u·it·i·cal·ly** *adv.*

Jes·u·its' bark ▶*n. archaic* cinchona bark.

Je·sus /ˈjēzəs/ (also **Jesus Christ** or **Jesus of Nazareth**) the central figure of the Christian religion. Jesus conducted a mission of preaching and healing (with reported miracles) in Palestine in about AD 28–30, which is described in the Gospels. His followers considered him to be the Christ or Messiah and the Son of God, and belief in his resurrection from the dead is the central tenet of Christianity.

Je·sus freak ▶*n. informal, chiefly derogatory* a fervent evangelical Christian, esp. one who adopts a lifestyle like that of a hippie.

jet[1] /jet/ ▶*n.* **1** a rapid stream of liquid or gas forced out of a small opening: *a high-pressure shower with pulsating jets.* ■ a nozzle or narrow opening for sending out such a stream: *Agnes turned up the gas jet.* **2** an aircraft powered by one or more jet engines: *a private jet* | [as *adj.*] *a jet plane.* ■ a jet engine.
▶*v.* (**jet·ted**, **jet·ting**) [*intrans.*] **1** travel by jet aircraft: *the newlyweds jetted off for a honeymoon in New York.* **2** spurt out in jets: *blood jetted from his nostrils.* ▷late 16th cent. (as a verb meaning 'jut out'): from French *jeter* 'to throw,' based on Latin *jactare*, frequentative of *jacere* 'to throw.'

jet[2] ▶*n.* a hard black semiprecious variety of lignite, capable of being carved and highly polished. ■ a glossy black color: [as *adj.*] *the gloss of her jet hair jet black.* ▷Middle English: from Old French *jaiet*, from Latin *Gagates*, from Greek *gagatēs* 'from Gagai,' a town in Asia Minor.

je·té /ZHəˈtā/ ▶*n. Ballet* a jump in which a dancer springs from one foot to land on the other with one leg extended outward from the body while in the air. See also **GRAND JETÉ**, **PETIT JETÉ**. ▷French, past participle of *jeter* 'to throw.'

jet en·gine ▸*n.* an engine using jet propulsion for forward thrust, mainly used for aircraft.

jet·foil /ˈjetˌfoil/ ▸*n.* a type of passenger-carrying hydrofoil. ▷1970s: blend of **JET**[1] and **HYDROFOIL**.

jet lag ▸*n.* extreme tiredness and other physical effects felt by a person after a long flight across several time zones. —**jet-lagged** *adj.*

jet·lin·er /ˈjetˌlīnər/ ▸*n.* a large jet aircraft carrying passengers. ▷1940s: blend of **JET**[1] and **AIRLINER**.

jet pipe ▸*n.* the exhaust duct of a jet engine.

jet-pro·pelled ▸*adj.* moved by jet propulsion.

jet pro·pul·sion ▸*n.* propulsion by the backward ejection of a high-speed jet of gas or liquid.

jet·sam /ˈjetsəm/ ▸*n.* unwanted material or goods that have been thrown overboard from a ship and washed ashore, esp. material that has been discarded to lighten the vessel. Compare with **FLOTSAM**. ▷late 16th cent. (as *jetson*): contraction of **JETTISON**.

jet set ▸*n.* (**the jet set**) *informal* wealthy and fashionable people who travel widely and frequently for pleasure: [as *adj.*] *the jet-set lifestyle.* —**jet-set·ter** *n.* —**jet-set·ting** *adj.*

jet ski ▸*n. trademark* a small, jet-propelled vehicle that skims across the surface of water and typically is ridden like a a motorcycle.
▸*v.* (**jet-ski**) [*intrans.*] [often as *n.*] (**jet-skiing**) ride on such a vehicle. —**jet-ski·er** *n.*

jet stream ▸*n.* **1** a narrow, variable band of very strong, predominantly westerly air currents encircling the globe several miles above the earth. There are typically two or three jet streams in each of the northern and southern hemispheres. **2** a flow of exhaust gasses from a jet engine.

jet·ti·son /ˈjetisən; -zən/ ▸*v.* [*trans.*] throw or drop (something) from an aircraft or ship: *six aircraft jettisoned their loads in the sea.* ■ abandon or discard (someone or something that is no longer wanted): *he's ready to jettison communism.*
▸*n.* the action of jettisoning something. ▷late Middle English (as a noun denoting the throwing of goods overboard to lighten a ship in distress): from Old French *getaison*, from Latin *jactatio(n-)*, from *jactare* 'to throw' (see **JET**[1]). The verb dates from the mid 19th cent.

jet·ton /ˈjetn/ ▸*n. Brit.* a counter or token used as a gambling chip or to operate slot machines. ▷mid 18th cent.: from French *jeton*, from *jeter* 'throw, add up accounts' (see **JET**[1]); so named because the term was formerly used in accounting.

jet·ty /ˈjetē/ ▸*n.* (*pl.* **-ties**) a landing stage or small pier at which boats can dock or be moored. ■ a breakwater constructed to protect or defend a harbor, stretch of coast, or riverbank. ▷late Middle English: from Old French *jetee*, feminine past participle of *jeter* 'to throw' (see **JET**[1]).

jet·way /ˈjetˌwā/ ▸*n. trademark (in the UK)* a portable bridge put against an aircraft door to allow passengers to embark or disembark.

jeu d'es·prit /ˌZHə dəˈsprē; ˌZHœ/ ▸*n.* (*pl.* **jeux d'es·prit** *pronunc.* same) a lighthearted display of wit and cleverness, esp. in a work of literature. ▷French, literally 'game of the mind.'

jeu·nesse do·rée /ZHəˌnes dôˈrā/ ▸*n.* [treated as *sing.* or *pl.*] young people of wealth, fashion, and flair. ▷mid 19th cent.: French, literally 'gilded youth.'

Jew /jo͞o/ ▸*n.* a member of the people and cultural community whose traditional religion is Judaism and who trace their origins through the ancient Hebrew people of Israel to Abraham. ▷Middle English: from Old French *juiu*, via Latin from Greek *Ioudaios*, via Aramaic from Hebrew *yĕhûḏī*, from *yĕhûḏāh* 'Judah' (see **JUDAH**).
▸*PHRASE* □ **jew someone down** *offensive* bargain with someone in a miserly or petty way.

jew·el /ˈjo͞oəl/ ▸*n.* a precious stone, typically a single crystal or a piece of a hard lustrous or translucent mineral, cut into shape with flat facets or smoothed and polished for use as an ornament. ■ (usu. **jewels**) an ornament or piece of jewelry containing such a stone or stones. ■ a hard precious stone used as a bearing in a watch, compass, or other device. ■ a very pleasing or valued person or thing; a very fine example: *she was a jewel of a nurse.* ▷Middle English: from Old French *joel*, from *jeu* 'game, play,' from Latin *jocus* 'jest.'
▸*PHRASE* □ **the jewel in the** (or **one's**) **crown** the most valuable or successful part of something: *science is the brightest jewel in the crown of our civilization.*

jew·el bee·tle ▸*n.* a chiefly tropical beetle that has bold metallic colors and patterns. The larvae are mainly wood-borers and can be serious pests of timber. • Family Buprestidae: numerous genera.

jew·el box ▸*n.* a storage box for a compact disc.

jew·eled /ˈjo͞oəld/ (*Brit.* **jew·elled**) ▸*adj.* adorned, set with, or made from jewels: *a jeweled dagger.*

jew·el·er /ˈjo͞o(ə)lər/ (*Brit.* **jew·el·ler**) ▸*n.* a person or company that makes or sells jewels or jewelry. ▷Middle English: from Old French *juelier*, from *joel* (see **JEWEL**).

jew·el·er's rouge ▸*n.* finely ground ferric oxide, used as a polish for metal and optical glass.

jew·el·fish /ˈjo͞oəlˌfiSH/ ▸*n.* (*pl.* same or **-fish·es**) a scarlet and green tropical freshwater cichlid. • *Hemichromis bimaculatus*, family Cichlidae.

jew·el·ry /ˈjo͞o(ə)lrē/ (*Brit.* **jew·el·lery**) ▸*n.* personal ornaments, such as necklaces, rings, or bracelets, that are typically made from or contain jewels and precious metal. ▷late Middle English: from Old French *juelerie*, from *juelier* 'jeweler,' from *joel* (see **JEWEL**).

USAGE Avoid the pronunciation /ˈjo͞olərē/, widely regarded as uneducated.

jew·el·weed ▸another term for **TOUCH-ME-NOT**.

Jew·ess /ˈjo͞o-is/ ▸*n. often offensive* a Jewish woman or girl.

Jew·ett /ˈjo͞oət/, (Theodora) Sarah Orne (1849–1909) U.S. writer and poet; pen names **A. D. Eliot**, **Alice Eliot**, **Sarah C. Sweet**. Her works include *The King of Folly Island* (1888) and *The Country of the Pointed Firs* (1896).

jew·fish /ˈjo͞oˌfiSH/ ▸*n.* (*pl.* same or **-fish·es**) a large sporting or food fish of warm coastal waters: • a fish of the Atlantic and Pacific coasts of North America (*Epinephelus itajara*, family Serranidae). • a fish of the Indo-Pacific (family Sciaenidae: several species), in particular the mulloway.

Jew·ish /ˈjo͞o-iSH/ ▸*adj.* relating to, associated with, or denoting Jews or Judaism: *the Jewish people.* —**Jew·ish·ly** *adv.* —**Jew·ish·ness** *n.*

Jew·ish cal·en·dar ▸*n.* a complex ancient calendar in use among the Jews.

It is a lunar calendar adapted to the solar year, normally consisting of twelve months but having thirteen months in leap years, which occur seven times in every cycle of nineteen years. The years are reckoned from the Creation (which is placed at 3761 BC); the months are Nisan, Iyyar, Sivan, Thammuz, Ab, Elul, Tishri, Hesvan, Kislev, Tebet, Sebat, and Adar, with an intercalary month (First Adar) being added in leap years. The religious year begins with Nisan and ends with Adar; the civil year begins with Tishri and ends with Elul.

Jew·ish New Year ▸*n.* another term for **ROSH HASHANAH**.

Jew·i·son /ˈjo͞o-isən/, Norman (1926–), Canadian movie director and producer. He is known for the drama *In the Heat of the Night* (1967), which won five Academy Awards; the musical *Fiddler on the Roof* (1971); and the romantic comedy *Moonstruck* (1987).

Jew·ry /ˈjo͞orē/ ▸*n.* (*pl.* **-ries**) **1** Jews collectively. **2** *historical* a Jewish quarter in a town or city. ▷Middle English: from Old French *juierie*, from *juiu* (see **JEW**).

Jew's ear ▸*n.* a common fungus with a brown, rubbery, cup-shaped fruiting body, growing on dead or dying trees in both Eurasia and North America. • *Auricularia auricula-judae*, family Auriculariaceae, class Hymenomycetes. ▷mid 16th cent.: a mistranslation of medieval Latin *auricula Judae* 'Judas's ear,' from its shape, and because it grows on the elder, which was said to be the tree from which Judas Iscariot hanged himself.

Jew's harp ▸*n.* a small, lyre-shaped musical instrument held between the teeth and struck with a finger. It can produce only one note, but harmonics are sounded by the player altering the shape of the mouth cavity.

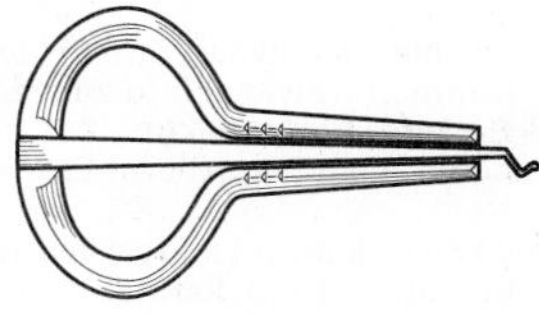

Jew's harp

Je·ze·bel /ˈjezəˌbel; -bəl/ (*fl.*9th century BC), a Phoenician princess, traditionally the great-aunt of Dido and in the Bible the wife of Ahab, king of Israel. She was denounced by Elijah for introducing the worship of Baal into Israel (1 Kings 16:31, 21:5–15, 2 Kings 9:30–7). ■ [as *n.*] (**a Jezebel**) a shameless or immoral woman.

jg ▸*abbr.* junior grade.

Jg. ▸*abbr. Bible* Judges.

Jhab·va·la /ˈjubwələ; -vələ/, Ruth Prawer (1923–), Indian screenwriter and novelist; born in Germany. Working with James Ivory and Ismail Merchant, she adapted for the screen *A Room with a View* (Academy Award, 1986), *Howards End* (Academy Award, 1992), and *The Remains of the Day* (1993).

Jhan·si /ˈjänsē/ a city in northern India, in the state of Uttar Pradesh; pop. 301,000.

Jhar·kand /ˈjärˌkand/ a state in northeastern India, formed in 2000 from the southern part of Bihar; capital, Ranchi.

Jhe·lum /ˈjäləm/ a river that rises in the Himalayas and flows through the Vale of Kashmir into Punjab, where it meets the Chenab River. About 450 miles (720 km) long, it is one of the five rivers that gave Punjab its name. In ancient times it was called the Hydaspes.

JHVH ▸*abbr.* **YHVH**.

Jia·mu·si /jēˈäˈmo͞oˈsē; ˈjyäˈmYˈsē/ a city in Heilongjiang province, in northeastern China, on the Sungari River, northeast of Harbin; pop. 493,000.

Jiang Jie Shi /ˌjäNG jē ˈSHē/ variant form of **CHIANG KAI-SHEK**.

Jiang·su /jēˈäNGˈso͞o/ (also **Kiang·su**) a province in eastern China; capital, Nanjing. It includes much of the Yangtze delta.

Jiang·xi /jēˈäNGˈSHē/ (also **Kiang·si**) a province in southeastern China; capital, Nanchang.

jiao /jyou/ ▸*n.* (*pl.* same) a monetary unit of China, equal to one tenth of a yuan. ▷from Chinese *jiǎo*.

Jia·xing /jēˈäˈSHiNG/ (formerly **Kashing**) a city in Zhejiang province, in eastern China, on the Grand Canal, southwest of Shanghai; pop. 697,000.

jib[1] /jib/ ▸*n.* **1** *Sailing* a triangular staysail set forward of the forwardmost mast. **2** the projecting arm of a crane. ▷mid 17th cent.: of unknown origin.

jib[2] ▸*v.* (**jibbed**, **jib·bing**) [*intrans.*] (of an animal, esp. a horse) stop and refuse to go on: *he jibbed at the final fence.* ■ (of a person) be unwilling to do or accept something: *he jibs at paying large bills.* ▷early 19th cent.: perhaps related to French *regimber* (earlier *regiber*) 'to buck, rear'; compare with **JIBE**[1]. —**jib·ber** *n.*

jib·ba /ˈjibə/ (also **jib·bah**, **djib·ba**, or **djib·bah**) ▸*n.* a long coat worn by Muslim men. ▷mid 19th cent.: Egyptian variant of Arabic *jubba*.

jib boom ▸*n. Sailing* a spar run out forward as an extension of the bowsprit.

jibe[1] /jīb/ ▸*n.* & *v.* variant spelling of **GIBE**.

jibe[2] (*Brit.* **gybe**) *Sailing* ▸*v.* [*intrans.*] change course by swinging a fore-and-aft sail across a following wind: *they jibed, and the boat turned over.* ■ [*trans.*] swing (a sail or boom) across the wind in such a way. ■ (of a sail or boom) swing or be swung across the wind: [as *adj.*] (**jibing**) *the skipper was hit by a jibing boom.*
▸*n.* an act or instance of jibing. ▷late 17th cent.: from obsolete Dutch *gijben*.

jibe[3] ▸*v.* [*intrans.*] *informal* be in accord; agree: *the verdict does not jibe with the medical evidence.* ▷early 19th cent.: of unknown origin.

jib sheet ▸*n. Sailing* a rope by which a jib is trimmed.

ji·ca·ma /ˈhikəmə; ˈhē-/ ▸*n.* the crisp, white-fleshed, edible tuber of a Central American climbing plant of the pea family (*Pachyrhizus erosus*, family Leguminosae), cultivated since pre-Columbian times and used esp. in Mexican cooking. ▷early 17th cent.: from Mexican Spanish *jícama*, from Nahuatl *xicama*.

Ji·ca·ril·la /ˌhēkəˈrēə; -ˈrēlyə/ ▸*n.* (*pl.* same or **-las**) **1** (also **Jicarilla Apache**) a member of an Apache people of northern New Mexico. **2** the Athabaskan language of this people.
▸*adj.* of or relating to this people or their language. ▷Mexican Spanish: probably diminutive of *jícara* 'chocolate-cup' (from the shape of a local hill); perhaps from Nahuatl *xicalli* 'drinking vessel, gourd'.

Ji·ca·ril·la Moun·tains /ˌhēkəˈrēə/ a range in south central New Mexico that reaches 8,200 feet (2,500 m) at Jicarilla Mountain.

Jid·dah /ˈjidə/ (also **Jid·da**, **Jed·dah**, or **Jed·da** /ˈjedə/)

J

a seaport on the Red Sea coast of Saudi Arabia, near Mecca; pop. 1,400,000.

jif·fy /ˈjifē/ (also **jiff**) ▸*n.* [in *sing.*] *informal* a moment: *we'll be back in a jiffy.* ▷late 18th cent.: of unknown origin.

jig /jig/ ▸*n.* **1** a lively dance with leaping movements. ■ a piece of music for such a dance, typically in compound time. **2** a device that holds a piece of work and guides the tools operating on it. **3** *Fishing* a type of artificial bait that is jerked up and down through the water.

▸*v.* (**jigged, jig·ging**) **1** [*intrans.*] dance a jig. ■ [with *adverbial*] move up and down with a quick jerky motion: *we were jigging about in our seats.* **2** [*trans.*] equip (a factory or workshop) with a jig or jigs. **3** [*intrans.*] fish with a jig: *a man* ***jigged for*** *squid.* ▷mid 16th cent.: of unknown origin.

▸*PHRASES* □ **in jig time** *informal* extremely quickly; in a very short time. □ **the jig is up** *informal* the scheme or deception is revealed or foiled.

jig·a·boo /ˈjigə,bo͞o/ ▸*n. informal, offensive* a black person. ▷early 20th cent.: related to slang *jig* (in the same sense); compare with the pair *bug, bugaboo.*

jig·ger[1] /ˈjigər/ ▸*n.* **1** a machine or vehicle with a part that rocks or moves back and forth, e.g., a jigsaw. **2** a person who dances a jig. **3** a small fore-and-aft sail set at the stern of a ship. ■ a small tackle consisting of a double and single block or two single blocks with a rope. **4** a measure or small glass of spirits or wine. **5** *dated Golf* a metal golf club with a narrow face. **6** used to refer to a thing whose name one does not know or does not wish to mention: *see them little jiggers?*

▸*v.* [*trans.*] *informal* rearrange or tamper with. ▷mid 16th cent. (originally a slang word for a door): from the verb JIG (the relationship with which is obscure in certain senses).

▸*PHRASE* □ **well, I'll be** (or **I'm**) **jiggered** used to express one's astonishment.

jig·ger[2] ▸*n.* variant spelling of CHIGGER.

jig·ger·y-pok·er·y /ˈjigərē ˈpōkərē/ ▸*n. informal, chiefly Brit.* deceitful or dishonest behavior. ▷late 19th cent.: probably a variant of Scots *joukery-pawkery*, from *jouk* 'dodge, skulk,' of unknown origin.

jig·gle /ˈjigəl/ ▸*v.* [*intrans.*] move about lightly and quickly from side to side or up and down: *his head jiggles up and down as he speaks.* ■ [*trans.*] shake (something) lightly up and down or from side to side: *he was jiggling his car keys in his hand.*

▸*n.* [in *sing.*] a quick light shake: *give that rack a jiggle.* ▷mid 19th cent.: partly an alteration of JOGGLE[1], reinforced by JIG. **—jig·gly** /ˈjig(ə)lē/ *adj.*

jig·gy /ˈjigē/ ▸*adj.* (**-gi·er, -gi·est**) *informal* **1** uninhibited, especially in a sexual manner: *the script required her to* ***get jiggy with*** *Leonardo.* **2** trembling or nervous, especially as the result of drug withdrawal. ▷1930s: from *jig* + *-y*.

jig·saw /ˈjig,sô/ ▸*n.* **1** (also **jigsaw puzzle**) a puzzle consisting of a picture printed on cardboard or wood and cut into various pieces of different shapes that have to be fitted together. ■ *figurative* a puzzle that can only be resolved by assembling various pieces of information: *help the police put all the pieces of the jigsaw together.* **2** a machine saw with a fine blade enabling it to cut curved lines in a sheet of wood, metal, or plastic.

ji·had /jiˈhäd/ ▸*n.* a holy war undertaken by Muslims against unbelievers. ■ *informal* a single-minded or obsessive campaign: *the quest for greater sales became a jihad.* ▷from Arabic *jihād*, literally 'effort,' expressing, in Muslim thought, struggle on behalf of God and Islam.

ji·had·i /jiˈhädē/ (also **je·had·i**) ▸*n.* (*pl.* **-is**) a person involved in a jihad; an Islamic militant. ▷from Arabic *jihādi*, from *jihād*.

ji·had·ist /jiˈhädist/ ▸*n.* a jihadi.

USAGE There doesn't seem to be a pressing need for this English-friendly form since the Arabic term for a holy warrior, *mujāhid*, has already made it into English in the plural forms (*mujahideen, mujahedin*), along with *jihadi*, a form more in keeping with Arabic morphology. *Jihadist*, however, is the preferred form for all writers who are vehemently anti-Arab or anti-Islam.

Ji·lin /ˈjēˈlin/ (also **Ki·rin**) a province in northeastern China; capital, Changchun. ■ an industrial city in Jilin province; pop. 2,252,000.

jill /jil/ ▸*n.* variant spelling of GILL[4].

jill·er·oo /ˈjilə,ro͞o/ (also **jill·ar·oo**) ▸*n. Austral., informal* a young woman working on a sheep or cattle station to gain experience. ▷1940s: from the given name *Jill*, on the pattern of *jackeroo*.

jil·lion /ˈjilyən/ ▸*cardinal number informal* an extremely large number: *they ran* ***jillions of*** *ads.* ▷1940s: fanciful formation on the pattern of *billion* and *million*.

jilt /jilt/ ▸*v.* [*trans.*] (often **be jilted**) suddenly reject or abandon (a lover): *she died of a broken heart after being jilted by her lover.*

▸*n. archaic* a person, esp. a woman, who capriciously rejects a lover. ▷mid 17th cent. (in the sense 'deceive, trick'): of unknown origin.

Jim Crow /ˈjim ˈkrō/ ▸*n.* **1** the former practice of segregating black people in the US: [as *adj.*] *Jim Crow laws.* ■ *offensive* a black person. **2** an implement for straightening steel bars or bending rails by screw pressure. ▷mid 19th cent.: the name of a black character in a 19th-cent. plantation song. **—Jim Crow·ism** /ˈkrō,izəm/ *n.*

jim-dan·dy /ˈjim ˈdandē/ *informal* ▸*adj.* fine, outstanding, or excellent.

▸*n.* an excellent or notable person or thing. ▷late 19th cent.: from the given name *Jim* (nickname for *James*) + DANDY.

Ji·mé·nez de Cis·ne·ros /hēˈmānəs dā sisˈnerōs/ (also **Xi·me·nes de Cis·ne·ros**), Francisco (1436–1517), Spanish cardinal and statesman; regent of Spain 1516–17. He was Grand Inquisitor for Castile and Léon from 1507 to 1517, during which time he undertook a massive campaign against heresy and had about 2,500 alleged heretics put to death.

jim·i·ny /ˈjimənē/ ▸*exclam.* used in phrases as an expression of surprise: ***by jiminy***, *she was right* | *jiminy cricket!* ▷early 19th cent.: alteration of GEMINI used as a mild oath in the mid 17th cent., a euphemistic form of *Jesus (Christ)*.

jim-jams /ˈjim ,jamz/ ▸*plural n. informal* a fit of depression or nervousness: *prerace jim-jams.* ▷mid 16th cent. (originally denoting a small article or knick-knack): fanciful reduplication. The current sense dates from the late 19th cent.

Jim·mu /ˈjēmo͞o/ the legendary first emperor of Japan (660 BC), descendant of the sun goddess Amaterasu and founder of the imperial dynasty.

jim·my /ˈjimē/ (*Brit.* **jem·my** /ˈjemē/) ▸*n.* (*pl.* **-mies**) a short crowbar used by a burglar to force open a window or door.

▸*v.* (**-mies, -mied**) [*trans.*] *informal* force open (a window or door) with a jimmy. ▷early 19th cent.: pet form of the given name *James* (compare with JACK[1]).

jim·son weed /ˈjimsən/ (also **jimp·son weed**) ▸*n.* a strong-smelling poisonous datura with large, trumpet-shaped white flowers and toothed leaves, which has become a weed of waste ground in many countries. • *Datura stramonium*, family Solanaceae. ■ the prickly fruit of this plant, which resembles that of a horse chestnut. ▷late 17th cent. (originally as *Jamestown weed*): named after JAMESTOWN in Virginia.

jimson weed

Jin /jin/ (also **Chin**) **1** a dynasty that ruled China AD 265–420, commonly divided into **Western Jin** (265–317) and **Eastern Jin** (317–420). **2** a dynasty that ruled Manchuria and northern China AD 1115–1234.

Ji·na /ˈjēnə/ ▸*n.* (in Jainism) a great teacher who has attained liberation from karma. ▷from Sanskrit (see also JAIN).

Ji·nan /ˈjēˈnän/ (also **Tsi·nan**) a city in eastern China, the capital of Shandong province; pop. 2,290,000.

jin·gle /ˈjiNGgəl/ ▸*n.* **1** [in *sing.*] a light ringing sound such as that made by metal objects being shaken together. **2** a short slogan, verse, or tune designed to be easily remembered, esp. as used in advertising. **3** (also **jingle shell**) a bivalve mollusk with a fragile, slightly translucent shell, the lower valve of which has a hole through which pass byssus threads for anchorage. • Family Anomidae: *Anomia* and other genera.

▸*v.* make or cause to make a light metallic ringing sound: [*intrans.*] *her bracelets were jingling* | [*trans.*] *he jingled the coins in his pocket.* ■ [*intrans.*] (of writing) be full of alliteration or rhymes. ▷late Middle English: imitative. **—jin·gler** *n.* **—jin·gly** /ˈjiNGg(ə)lē/ *adj.*

jin·go /ˈjiNGgō/ ▸*n.* (*pl.* **-goes**) *dated, chiefly derogatory* a vociferous supporter of policy favoring war, esp. in the name of patriotism. ▷late 17th cent. (originally a conjuror's word): *by jingo* (and the noun sense) come from a popular song adopted by those supporting the sending of a British fleet into Turkish waters to resist Russia in 1878. The chorus ran: "We don't want to fight, yet by Jingo! if we do, We've got the ships, we've got the men, and got the money too."

▸*PHRASE* □ **by jingo!** an exclamation of surprise.

jin·go·ism /ˈjiNGgō,izəm/ ▸*n. chiefly derogatory* extreme patriotism, esp. in the form of aggressive or warlike foreign policy. **—jin·go·ist** *n.* **—jin·go·is·tic** /,jiNGgōˈistik/ *adj.*

jink /jiNGk/ ▸*v.* [*intrans.*] change direction suddenly and nimbly, as when dodging a pursuer: *she was too quick for him and jinked away every time.*

▸*n.* a sudden quick change of direction. ▷late 17th cent. (originally Scots as *high jinks*, denoting antics at drinking parties): probably symbolic of nimble motion. Current senses date from the 18th cent.

jinn /jin/ (also **djinn** or **jin·ni** /jiˈnē; ˈjinē/) ▸*n.* (*pl.* same or **jinns**) (in Arabian and Muslim mythology) an intelligent spirit of lower rank than the angels, able to appear in human and animal forms and to possess humans. Compare with GENIE. ▷from Arabic *jinnī*, plural *jinn*.

Jin·nah /ˈjinə/, Muhammad Ali (1876–1948), Indian statesman and founder of Pakistan. He headed the Muslim League in its struggle with the Hindu-oriented Indian National Congress over Indian independence. In 1947, he became the first governor general and president of Pakistan.

jin·rik·i·sha /jinˈrikshô; -shä/ (also **jin·rick·sha**) ▸*n.* another term for RICKSHA. ▷Japanese, from *jin* 'man' + *riki* 'strength' + *sha* 'vehicle.'

jinx /jiNGks/ ▸*n.* a person or thing that brings bad luck.

▸*v.* [*trans.*] (usu. **be jinxed**) bring bad luck to; cast an evil spell on: *the play is jinxed.* ▷early 20th cent. (originally U.S.): probably a variant of *jynx* 'wryneck' (because the bird was used in witchcraft).

Jin·zhou /ˈjinˈjō/ a city in Liaoning province, in northeastern China, near the Gulf of Liaodong at the northern end of the Bo Hai; pop. 569,000.

jird /jərd/ ▸*n.* a long-tailed burrowing rodent related to the gerbils, found in deserts and steppes from North Africa to China. • Genus *Meriones*, family Muridae: several species, in particular *M. unguiculatus*, popular as a pet. ▷from Berber *(a)gherda*.

jir·ga /ˈjərgə/ ▸*n.* (in Afghanistan) a tribal council. A grand tribal council (**loya jirga**) presently has a legislative function in the country. ▷mid 19th cent.: Pashto, 'council, assembly.' *Loya jirga* is from Pashto, from *loya* 'great, grand' and *jirga*.

jism /ˈjizəm/ ▸*n. vulgar slang* semen. ▷mid 19th cent.: of unknown origin.

JIT ▸*abbr.* (of manufacturing systems) just-in-time.

jit·ney /ˈjitnē/ ▸*n.* (*pl.* **-neys**) *informal* a bus or other vehicle carrying passengers for a low fare. ▷early 20th cent. (originally denoting a five-cent piece): of unknown origin.

jit·ter /ˈjitər/ *informal* ▸*n.* **1** (**jitters**) feelings of extreme nervousness: *a bout of the jitters.* **2** slight irregular movement, variation, or unsteadiness, esp. in an electrical signal or electronic device.

▸*v.* [*intrans.*] act nervously: *an anxious student who jittered at any provocation.* ■ (of a signal or device) suffer from jitter. ▷1920s: of unknown origin. **—jit·ter·i·ness** /-rēnis/ *n.* **—jit·ter·y** *adj.*

jit·ter·bug /ˈjitər,bəg/ ▸*n.* **1** a fast dance popular in the 1940s, performed chiefly to swing music. ■ *dated* a person fond of dancing such a dance. **2** *informal, dated* a nervous person.

▸*v.* (**-bugged, -bug·ging**) [*intrans.*] dance the jitterbug. ▷1930s (originally U.S.): from the verb JITTER + BUG.

jiu·jit·su /,jo͞oˈjitso͞o/ ▸*n.* variant spelling of JUJITSU.

Ji·va·ro /ˈhēvə,rō/ ▶n. (pl. same or **-ros**) **1** a member of an indigenous people of the eastern slopes of the Andes in Ecuador and Peru. **2** any of the group of languages spoken by this people.
▶adj. of or relating to this people or their languages. ▷from Spanish *jíbaro*, probably from the local name *Shuara, Shiwora*. **—Ji·va·ro·an** /,hēvəˈrōən/ adj. & n. .

jive /jīv/ ▶n. **1** a lively style of dance popular esp. in the 1940s and 1950s, performed to swing music or rock and roll. ■ swing music. ■ a style of dance music popular in South Africa: *township jive.* **2** (also **jive talk**) a form of slang associated with black American jazz musicians. ■ *informal* a thing, esp. talk, that is deceptive or worthless: *a single image says more than any amount of blather and jive.*
▶v. *informal* **1** [*intrans.*] perform the jive or a similar dance to popular music: *people were jiving in the aisles.* **2** [*trans.*] *informal* taunt or sneer at: *Willy kept jiving him until Jimmy left.* ■ [*intrans.*] talk nonsense: *he wasn't jiving about that bartender.*
▶adj. *informal* deceitful or worthless. ▷1920s (originally U.S. denoting meaningless or misleading speech): of unknown origin; the later musical sense 'jazz' gave rise to 'dance performed to jazz' (1940s). **—jiv·er** n. **—jiv·ey** adj.

Ji·xi /ˈjēˈshē/ a city in Heilongjiang province, in northeastern China, on the Muling River, east of Harbin; pop. 684,000.

jizz /jiz/ ▶n. *Brit., informal* (among birdwatchers and naturalists) the characteristic impression given by a particular species of animal or plant. ▷1920s: of unknown origin.

JJ ▶abbr. ■ Judges. ■ Justices.

Jn ▶abbr. ■ *Bible* an epistle of John. ■ the Gospel of John.

Jnr ▶abbr. *chiefly Brit.* Junior (in names).

jnt. ▶abbr. joint.

Jo·a·chim /ˈjōəkim/ see **RITZ BROTHERS, THE.**

Jo·a·chim, St. /ˈyōəkim; ˈjō-/ (in Christian tradition) the husband of St. Anne and father of the Virgin Mary. He is first mentioned in an apocryphal work of the 2nd century, and then rarely referred to until much later in time.

Joan of Arc, St. /,jōn əv ˈärk/ (*c.*1412–31), French national heroine; known as **the Maid of Orleans**; French name **Jeanne d'Arc**. She led the French armies against the English in the Hundred Years War, relieving besieged Orleans in 1429 and ensuring that Charles VII could be crowned in Reims. Captured by the Burgundians in 1430, she was handed over to the English, convicted of heresy, and burned at the stake. Canonized in 1920, her feast day is May 30.

João Pes·soa /,zhwoun pesˈōə/ a city in northeastern Brazil, on the Atlantic coast, capital of the state of Paraíba; pop. 484,000.

Job /jōb/ (in the Bible) a prosperous man whose patience and piety were tried by undeserved misfortunes, and who, in spite of his bitter lamentations, remained confident in the goodness and justice of God. ■ a book of the Bible telling of Job.

job[1] /jäb/ ▶n. **1** a paid position of regular employment: *jobs are created in the private sector, not in Washington | a part-time job.* **2** a task or piece of work, esp. one that is paid: *she wants to be left alone to get on with the job | you* **did a good job of** *explaining.* ■ a responsibility or duty: *it's our job to find things out.* ■ [in *sing.*] *informal* a difficult task: *we thought you'd have a job getting there.* ■ [with *adj.*] *informal* a procedure to improve the appearance of something, esp. an operation involving plastic surgery: *she's had a nose job | someone had done a skillful paint job.* ■ [with *adj.*] *informal* a thing of a specified nature: *the car was a blue malevolent-looking job.* ■ *informal* a crime, esp. a robbery: *a series of daring bank jobs.* ■ *Computing* an operation or group of operations treated as a single and distinct unit.
▶v. (**jobbed, job·bing**) **1** [*intrans.*] [usu. as *adj.*] (**jobbing**) do casual or occasional work: *a jobbing builder.* **2** [*trans.*] buy and sell (stocks) as a broker-dealer, esp. on a small scale. **3** [*trans.*] *informal* cheat; betray. **4** [*intrans.*] *archaic* turn a public office or a position of trust to private advantage. ▷mid 16th cent. (sense 2 of the *noun*): of unknown origin.
▶PHRASES □ **do the job** *informal* achieve the required result: *a piece of board will do the job.* □ **do a job on someone** *informal* do something that harms or defeats an opponent: *I go out and do a job on anyone who is giving our top scorers a hard time.* □ **a good job** *informal, chiefly Brit.* a fortunate fact or circumstance: *it was a good job she hadn't brought the car.* □ **on the job** while working; at work. □ **out of a job** unemployed.

job[2] *archaic* ▶v. (**jobbed, job·bing**) [*trans.*] prod or stab: *he prepared to job the huge brute.* ■ thrust (something pointed) at or into something.
▶n. an act of prodding, thrusting, or wrenching. ▷late Middle English: apparently symbolic of a brief forceful action (compare with **JAB**).

job·ber /ˈjäbər/ ▶n. **1** a wholesaler. **2** a person who does casual or occasional work. **3** *historical* (in the UK) a principal or wholesaler who dealt only on the Stock Exchange with brokers, not directly with the public. ▷late 17th cent. (in the sense 'broker, middleman,' originally not derogatory): from **JOB**[1].

job·ber·y /ˈjäbərē/ ▶n. the practice of using a public office or position of trust for one's own gain or advantage.

job·bie /ˈjäbē/ ▶n. *informal* [with *adj.*] an object or product of a specified kind: *the room was a no-frills jobbie.*

job con·trol lan·guage ▶n. *Computing* a language enabling the user to define the tasks to be undertaken by the operating system.

job de·scrip·tion ▶n. a formal account of an employee's responsibilities.

job-hunt ▶v. [*intrans.*] [usu. as *n.*] (**job-hunting**) *informal* seek employment. **—job-hunt·er** n.

job·less /ˈjäbləs/ ▶adj. unemployed. **—job·less·ness** n.

job lot ▶n. a miscellaneous group of articles, esp. when sold or bought together: *a job lot of stuff I bought from a demolition firm.*

job ro·ta·tion ▶n. the practice of moving employees between different tasks to promote experience and variety.

Jobs /jäbz/, Steven (Paul) (1955–), U.S. computer entrepreneur. He set up the Apple computer company in 1976 with Steve Wozniak and served as chairman until 1985, returning in 1997 as CEO. He is also the CEO of the Pixar animation studio.

Job's com·fort·er /jōbz/ ▶n. a person who aggravates distress under the guise of giving comfort. ▷mid 18th cent.: alluding to the biblical story (Job 16:2) of **JOB**.

job-share ▶v. [*intrans.*] (of two part-time employees) jointly do a full-time job, sharing the remuneration.
▶n. an arrangement of such a kind. **—job-shar·er** n.

Job's tears /ˈjōbz ˈti(ə)rz/ ▶plural n. a widely cultivated Southeast Asian grass that bears its seeds inside hollow, pear-shaped receptacles, which are gray and shiny and sometimes used as beads. • *Coix lacryma-jobi*, family Gramineae. ▷late 16th cent.: named after the patriarch **JOB**.

Jo·burg /ˈjō,bərg/ a nickname for **JOHANNESBURG**.

Jo·cas·ta /jōˈkastə/ *Greek Mythology* a Theban woman, the wife of Laius and mother and later wife of Oedipus.

jock[1] /jäk/ ▶n. *informal* **1** a disc jockey. **2** an enthusiast or participant in a specified activity: *a computer jock.* ▷late 18th cent.: abbreviation.

jock[2] ▶n. *informal* another term for **JOCKSTRAP**. ■ an enthusiastic athlete or sports fan, esp. one with few other interests. ■ a slow-witted person of large size and great physical strength. **—jock·ish** adj.

jock[3] ▶n. *informal* a pilot or astronaut. ▷late 20th cent.: probably an abbreviation of **JOCKEY**, from its informal use in combinations such as *jet jockey, plow jockey*, where "operation" or "control" of equipment is involved.

jock·ey /ˈjäkē/ ▶n. (pl. **-eys**) a person who rides in horse races, esp. as a profession. ■ an enthusiast or participant in a specified activity: *a car jockey.*
▶v. (**-eys, -eyed**) [*intrans.*] struggle by every available means to gain or achieve something: *both men will be* **jockeying for** *the two top jobs.* ■ [*trans.*] handle or manipulate (someone or something) in a skillful manner: *Jason jockeyed his machine into a dive.* ▷late 16th cent.: diminutive of *Jock* 'ordinary man; a rustic,'Scots form of the given name *Jack*. The word came to mean 'mounted courier,' hence the current sense (late 17th cent.). Another early use 'horse dealer' (long a byword for dishonesty) probably gave rise to the verb sense 'manipulate,' whereas the main verb sense probably relates to the behavior of jockeys maneuvering for an advantageous position during a race. **—jock·ey·ship** /-,ship/ n.

jock·ey cap ▶n. a strengthened cap with a long visor of a kind worn by jockeys.

jock·ey shorts (also **Jock·ey shorts** or **Jock·eys**) ▶plural n. *trademark* men's close-fitting underpants with a short leg.

jock itch ▶n. *informal* a fungal infection of the groin area. ▷1970s: *jock* from **JOCKSTRAP**.

jocks /jäks/ ▶plural n. *informal* jockey shorts.

jock·strap /ˈjäk,strap/ ▶n. a support or protection for the male genitals, worn esp. by athletes. ▷late 19th cent.: from slang *jock* 'genitals' (of unknown origin) + **STRAP**.

jo·cose /jōˈkōs/ ▶adj. *formal* playful or humorous: *a jocose allusion.* ▷late 17th cent.: from Latin *jocosus*, from *jocus* (see **JOKE**). **—jo·cose·ly** adv. **—jo·cose·ness** n. **—jo·cos·i·ty** /-ˈkäsitē/ n. (pl. **-ties**).

joc·u·lar /ˈjäkyələr/ ▶adj. fond of or characterized by joking; humorous or playful: *she sounded in a jocular mood | his voice was jocular.* ▷early 17th cent.: from Latin *jocularis*, from *joculus*, diminutive of *jocus* (see **JOKE**). **—joc·u·lar·i·ty** /,jäkyəˈlaritē/ n. **—joc·u·lar·ly** adv.

joc·und /ˈjäkənd; ˈjō-/ ▶adj. *formal* cheerful and lighthearted: *a jocund wedding party.* ▷late Middle English: via Old French from Latin *jocundus*, variant (influenced by *jocus* 'joke') of *jucundus* 'pleasant, agreeable,' from *juvare* 'to delight.' **—jo·cun·di·ty** /jōˈkənditē/ n. (pl. **-ties**) **—joc·und·ly** adv.

Jodh·pur /ˈjädpər; -,pŏŏr/ **1** a city in western India, in Rajasthan; pop. 649,000. **2** a former princely state in India, now part of Rajasthan.

jodh·purs /ˈjädpərz/ ▶plural n. full-length trousers, worn for horseback riding, that are close-fitting below the knee and have reinforced patches on the inside of the leg. ▷late 19th cent.: named after **JODHPUR**, where similar garments are worn by Indian men as part of everyday dress.

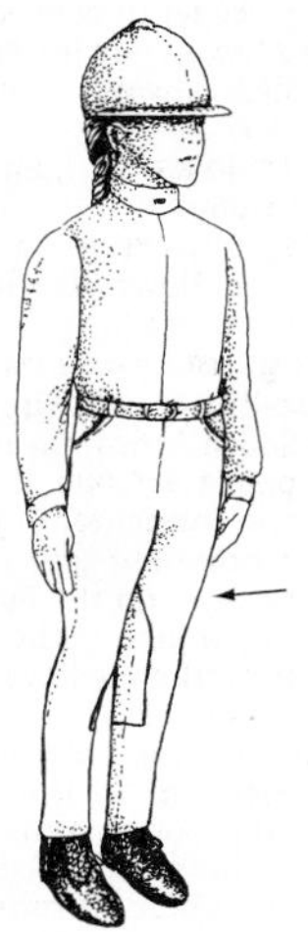
jodphurs

Jo·dy call ▶n. a song, refrain, or cadence sung in time to marching.

joe /jō/ ▶n. *informal* **1** coffee. [1940s: of unknown origin.] **2** an ordinary man: *the average joe.* [mid 19th cent.: nickname for the given name *Joseph*; compare with **JOE BLOW**.]

Joe Bloggs /blägz/ ▶n. British term for **JOE BLOW**.

Joe Blow /blō/ ▶n. *informal* a name for a hypothetical average man.

Jo·el[1] /jō(ə)l/ a Hebrew minor prophet of the 5th or possibly 9th century BC. ■ a book of the Bible containing his prophecies.

Joel[2], Billy (1949–), U.S. pop singer and songwriter; full name *William Martin Joel*. His many top ten hits include "Piano Man" (1973), "Just the Way You Are" (1977), "Tell Her About It" (1983), "We Didn't Start the Fire" (1989), and "The River of Dreams" (1993).

Joe Pub·lic ▶n. British term for **JOHN Q. PUBLIC**.

joe-pye weed /,jō ˈpī/ (also **joe pye weed**) ▶n. a tall North American perennial plant of the daisy family that bears clusters of small purple flowers. • Genus *Eupatorium*, family Compositae, several species, in particular **sweet joe-pye weed** *E. purpureum* and **spotted joe-pye weed** *E. maculatum*. ▷early 19th cent.: of unknown origin.

Joe Schmoe /shmō/ (also **Joe Schmo**) ▶n. (pl. **Joe Schmoes**) *informal* a hypothetical ordinary man: *a lot of Joe Schmoes make it to the big leagues.* ▷1940s: alteration of *schmuck*.

Joe Six·pack /ˈsiks,pak/ ▶n. a name for a hypothetical ordinary working man. ▷1970s: from *Joe*, familiar abbreviation of the given name *Joseph*, used to denote any ordinary man; see also **SIX-PACK**.

jo·ey[1] /ˈjō-ē/ ▶n. (pl. **-eys**) *Austral.* a young kangaroo, wallaby, or possum. ■ *informal* a baby or young child. ▷from Aboriginal *joè*.

jo·ey[2] ▶n. *Brit.* & *historical* a silver threepenny bit. ▷1930s: diminutive of the nickname *Joe*: the derivation remains unknown. The term (originally slang in London, England) denoted a fourpenny piece in the 19th cent.

Jof·fre /ˈjôfrə/, Joseph Jacques Césaire (1852–1931), French marshal; commander in chief of the French army on the western front during World War I.

Jof·frey /ˈjäfrē/, Robert (1930–88) U.S. ballet dancer and choreographer; born *Abdullah Jaffa Anver Bey Khan*. He founded the Joffrey Ballet in 1966.

jog /jäg/ ▶v. (**jogged, jog·ging**) **1** [*intrans.*] run at a

J

steady gentle pace, esp. on a regular basis as a form of physical exercise: *he began to jog along the road* | [as *n.*] (**jogging**) *try cycling or gentle jogging.* ■ (of a horse) move at a slow trot. ■ move in an unsteady way, typically slowly: *the bus jogged and jolted.* ■ (**jog along/on**) continue in a steady, uneventful way: *our marriage worked, and we jogged along.* **2** [*trans.*] nudge or knock slightly: *a hand jogged his elbow.*
▸*n.* **1** a spell of jogging: *his morning jog.* ■ [in *sing.*] a gentle running pace: *he set off along the bank at a jog.* **2** a slight push or nudge. ▷late Middle English (in the sense 'stab, pierce'): variant of JAG[1]. —**jog·ger** *n.*
▸*PHRASE* □ **jog someone's memory** cause someone to remember something suddenly.

jog·gle[1] /'jägəl/ ▸*v.* move or cause to move with repeated small bobs or jerks: [*intrans.*] *the car bounced and joggled on the rough road.*
▸*n.* a bobbing or jerking movement. ▷early 16th cent.: frequentative of JOG[1].

jog·gle[2] ▸*n.* a joint between two pieces of stone, concrete, or timber consisting of a projection in one of the pieces fitting into a notch in the other or a small piece let in between the two.
▸*v.* [*trans.*] join (pieces of stone, concrete, or timber) in such a way. ▷early 18th cent.: perhaps related to JAG[1].

Jog·ja·kar·ta /,jägjə'kärtə/ variant spelling of **Yogyakarta**.

jog·shut·tle ▸*n.* a facility on some video recorders that allows the speed at which the tape is played to be varied.

jog trot ▸*n.* *dated* a slow trot.

Jo·han·nes·burg /jō'hänəs,bərg; -'han-/ a city in South Africa, the capital of the province of Gauteng; pop. 1,916,000. It is the largest city in South Africa and the center of its gold-mining industry.

Jo·han·nine /jō'hanən; -īn/ ▸*adj.* relating to the Apostle St. John the Evangelist, or to the Gospel or epistles of John in the New Testament. ▷mid 19th cent.: from the medieval Latin given name *Johannes* 'John' + -INE[1].

Jo·han·nis·berg /jō'hanisbərg/ (also **Johannisberg Riesling**) ▸*n.* the chief variety of the Riesling wine grape, originating in Germany and widely grown in California and elsewhere. ■ a white wine made from this grape. ▷from the name of a castle and village on the Rhine, Germany, where it was originally produced.

Jo·han·nis·berg·er /jō'hanis,bərgər/ ▸*n.* variant of **Johannisberg**.

John[1] /jän/ (1165–1216), son of Henry II and Eleanor of Aquitaine; king of England 1199–1216; known as **John Lackland**. He lost most of his French possessions to Phillip II of France. In 1209, he was excommunicated for refusing to accept Stephen Langton as the archbishop of Canterbury. Forced to sign the Magna Carta by his barons in 1215, he ignored its provisions and civil war broke out.

John[2] the name of six kings of Portugal: ■ **John I** (1357–1433), reigned 1385–1433; known as **John the Great**. Reinforced by an English army, he defeated the Castilians at Aljubarrota in 1385 and won independence for Portugal. ■ **John II** (1455–95), reigned 1481–95. ■ **John III** (1502–57), reigned 1521–57. ■ **John IV** (1604–56), reigned 1640–56; known as **John the Fortunate**. The founder of the Braganza dynasty, he expelled a Spanish usurper and proclaimed himself king. ■ **John V** (1689–1750), reigned 1706–50. ■ **John VI** (1767–1826), reigned 1816–26.

John[3], Sir Elton (Hercules) (1947–), English singer, pianist, and songwriter; born *Reginald Kenneth Dwight*.His many hit songs include "Your Song" (1970), "Nikita" (1985), and "Don't Let the Sun Go Down on Me" (1991). His "Candle in the Wind" (1997) tribute to Diana, Princess of Wales, became the highest-selling single in history.

John, St. an Apostle; son of Zebedee and brother of James; known as **St. John the Evangelist** or **St. John the Divine**. He is traditionally credited with having written the fourth Gospel, Revelation, and three epistles of the New Testament. Feast day, December 27. ■ the fourth Gospel (see GOSPEL sense 2). ■ any of the three epistles of the New Testament attributed to St. John.

john /jän/ ▸*n.* *informal* **1** a toilet. **2** a prostitute's client. ▷early 20th cent. (sense 2): from the given name *John*, used from late Middle English as a form of address to a man, or to denote various occupations, including that of priest (late Middle English) and policeman (mid 17th cent.).

John III (1624–96), king of Poland 1674–96; known as **John Sobieski**. In 1683, he relieved Vienna when it was besieged by the Turks and became a hero in the Christian world.

John Bar·ley·corn /'bärlē,kôrn/ ▸*n.* a personification of barley, or of malt liquor.

john·boat /'jän,bōt/ ▸*n.* a small flat-bottomed boat with square ends, used chiefly on inland waterways.

John Bull ▸*n.* a personification of England or the typical Englishman, represented as a stout, red-faced farmer in a top hat and high boots. ▷late 18th cent.: from the name of a character representing the English nation in John Arbuthnot's satire *Law is a Bottomless Pit; or, the History of John Bull* (1712).

John Chrys·os·tom, St. see **Chrysostom, St. John**.

John Day Riv·er /'jän 'dā/ a river that flows for 280 miles (450 km) across northern Oregon to join the Columbia River east of The Dalles.

John Doe /dō/ ▸*n.* *Law* an anonymous party, typically the plaintiff, in a legal action. ■ *informal* a hypothetical average man. ▷mid 18th cent.: originally in legal use as a name of a fictitious plaintiff, corresponding to *Richard Roe*, used to represent the defendant.

John Do·ry /'dôrē/ ▸*n.* (*pl.* **-ries**) an edible dory (fish) of the eastern Atlantic and Mediterranean, with a black oval mark on each side. • *Zeus faber*, family Zeidae.

Joh·ne's dis·ease /'yōniz/ ▸*n.* a form of chronic enteritis in cattle and sheep, caused by a mycobacterium. ▷early 20th cent.: named after Heinrich A. *Johne* (1839–1910), German veterinary surgeon.

john·ny /'jänē/ ▸*n.* (*pl.* **-nies**) *informal* **1** a short gown fastened in the back, worn by hospital patients. **2** *Brit.* used as a name for an unknown man, often suggesting that he is unimportant or insignificant: *the security johnny insists that you sign the visitors' book.* ▷late 17th cent. (sense 2): nickname for the given name *John*.

john·ny·cake /'jänē,kāk/ ▸*n.* **1** cornbread typically baked or fried on a griddle. **2** (**johnny cake**) *Austral./NZ* a small, thin unleavened wheat loaf baked in wood ashes. ▷early 18th cent.: also referred to as *journey cake*, which may be the original form.

john·ny-come-late·ly ▸*n.* *informal* a newcomer to or late starter at a particular place or sphere of activity.

John·ny-on-the-spot ▸*n.* *informal, dated* a person who is at hand whenever needed.

John·ny Reb ▸*n.* another term for REB[2].

John of Da·mas·cus, St. (*c.*675–*c.*749), Syrian theologian and doctor of the Church. He wrote the influential encyclopedic work on Christian theology *The Fount of Wisdom*. Feast day, December 4.

John of Gaunt /gônt/ (1340–99), son of Edward III. He was the effective ruler of England during the final years of his father's reign and during the minority of Richard II. His son Henry Bolingbroke later became King Henry IV.

John of the Cross, St. (1542–91), Spanish mystic and poet; born *Juan de Yepis y Alvarez*. A Carmelite monk and priest, he cofounded, with St. Teresa of Ávila, the "discalced" Carmelite order in 1568. Feast day, December 14.

John Paul II (1920–), Polish cleric; pope 1978–; born *Karol Jozef Wojtyla*. The first non-Italian pope since 1522, he traveled abroad extensively during his papacy and upheld the Roman Catholic Church's traditional opposition to artificial contraception and abortion, homosexuality, the ordination of women, and the relaxation of the rule of celibacy for priests.

John Q. Pub·lic ▸*n.* *informal* a name for a hypothetical representative member of the general public, or the general public personified.

Johns /jänz/, Jasper (1930–), U.S. painter, sculptor, and printmaker. A key figure in the development of pop art, he depicted commonplace and universally recognized images. Notable works: *Flags, Targets* and *Numbers* (all series of the mid–1950s).

John·son[1] /'jänsən/, Andrew (1808–75), 17th president of the U.S. 1865–69. As vice president 1865, he succeeded to the presidency upon the assassination of President Lincoln. During his administration, Alaska was purchased from Russia. His lenient policy toward the Southern states after the Civil War and his refusal to cooperate with Congress led him to be the first president ever to be impeached. He was acquitted by one vote short of the two-thirds majority required.

John·son[2], Benj. F., see RILEY[3].

John·son [3], Caryn, see **Goldberg** [3].

John·son[4] (also **Jan·sens** or **Jans·sen van Ceu·len**), Cornelius (1593–*c.*1661), Dutch portrait painter; born in England. He painted for the court of Charles I; in 1643, after the outbreak of the English Civil War, he emigrated to Holland.

John·son[5], Earvin (1959–), U.S. basketball player; known as **Magic Johnson**. He played for the Los Angeles Lakers from 1979 to 1991. After being diagnosed HIV-positive, he played on the U.S. basketball team that won a gold medal at the 1992 Olympic games and then returned briefly to the Lakers.

John·son[6], Jack (1878–1946), U.S. boxer. He was the first black world heavyweight champion 1908–15.

John·son[7], James Weldon (1871–1938) U.S. writer, songwriter, and social activist. Originally a song lyricist and then a part of the U.S. consular service, he began writing and made many contributions to the Harlem Renaissance. He edited *The Book of American Negro Poetry* in 1922 and wrote his autobiography, *Along This Way*, in 1933.

John·son[8], Lyndon Baines (1908–73), 36th president of the U.S. 1963–69; known as **LBJ**. Before becoming vice president 1961–64, he was a U.S. senator 1949–61. He succeeded to the presidency upon the assassination of President Kennedy and was elected for four more years in 1964. His domestic programs, such as those for civil rights, were labeled the Great Society. During his administration, U.S. involvement in Vietnam increased, undermining his popularity, and he did not seek reelection.

Lyndon Baines Johnson

John·son[9], Philip Courtelyou (1906–) U.S. architect and writer. He designed many buildings in New York City, including Lincoln Center, the AT&T headquarters building (now the Sony building), and the Bobst Library at New York University. He coauthored *The International Style* (1932).

John·son[10], Robert (1911–38), U.S. blues singer and guitarist. Despite his mysterious early death, he was very influential on the 1960s blues movement. Notable songs: "I Was Standing at the Crossroads," "Love In Vain," and "I Believe I'll Dust My Broom."

John·son[11], Samuel (1709–84), British lexicographer, writer, critic, and conversationalist; known as **Dr. Johnson**. A leading figure in the literary London of his day, he is noted particularly for his *Dictionary of the English Language* (1755), his edition of Shakespeare (1765), and *The Lives of the English Poets* (1777). James Boswell's biography of Johnson records details of his life and conversation. —**John·so·ni·an** /jän'sōnēən/ *adj.*

John·son[12], Thomas (1732–1819) U.S. Supreme Court associate justice 1791–93. A chief judge in Maryland's court system, he was appointed to the Court by President Washington.

John·son[13], Walter Perry (1887–1946) U.S. baseball player; known as the Big Train. He pitched for the

Andrew Johnson

Washington Senators 1907–27 and had a record 113 career shutouts and led the American League in strikeouts for 12 seasons. Baseball Hall of Fame (1936).

John·son[14], William (1771–1834) U.S. Supreme Court associate justice 1804–34. A Democrat-Republican, he was appointed to the Court by President Jefferson.

John·son Cit·y an industrial city in northeastern Tennessee, part of a complex with Bristol and Kingsport; pop. 55,469.

John·ston[1] /ˈjänstən/ a town in northeastern Rhode Island, a southwestern suburb of Providence; pop. 28,195.

John·ston[2], Joseph Eggleston (1807–91), American Confederate officer and U.S. politician. A Confederate general, he was defeated by Grant at Vicksburg and surrendered to Sherman in 1865. From Virginia, he later served in the U.S. House of Representatives 1879–81.

John·ston Atoll /ˈjänstən/ an atoll in the central Pacific Ocean, southwest of Hawaii, that is controlled by the U.S. and used for military operations.

Johns·town /ˈjänz,toun/ an industrial city in southwestern Pennsylvania, southeast of Pittsburgh, noted as the site of a devastating flood in 1889; pop. 28,134.

John the Bap·tist, St., Jewish preacher and prophet; a contemporary of Jesus. In c.AD 27 he preached and baptized on the banks of the Jordan River. Among those whom he baptized was Jesus Christ. He was beheaded by Herod Antipas after denouncing the latter's marriage to Herodias, the wife of Herod's brother Philip (Matt. 14:1–12). Feast day, June 24.

John the E·van·ge·list, St. (also **John the Divine**) see JOHN, ST.

John the For·tu·nate, John IV of Portugal (see JOHN[2]).

John the Great, John I of Portugal (see JOHN[2]).

Jo·hor /jəˈhôr/ (also **Jo·hore**) a state in Malaysia, at the most southern point of mainland Asia, connected to Singapore by a causeway; capital, Johor Baharu.

Jo·hor Ba·ha·ru /bəˈhärōō/ a city in southwestern Malaysia, the capital of the state of Johor, opposite the island of Singapore; pop. 329,000.

joie de vi·vre /,zhwä də ˈvēvrə/ ▸*n.* exuberant enjoyment of life. ▷French, literally 'joy of living.'

join /join/ ▸*v.* [*trans.*] link; connect: *the tap was **joined to** a pipe* | *join the paragraphs **together**.* ■ become linked or connected to: *where the River Drave joins the Danube.* ■ connect (points) with a line: ***join up** the points in a different color.* ■ [*intrans.*] unite to form one entity or group: *they **joined up with** local environmentalists* | *countries **join together** to abolish restrictions on trade.* ■ become a member or employee of: *she joined the department last year.* ■ take part in: *I joined the demonstration* | [*intrans.*] *I **joined in** and sang along.* ■ [*intrans.*] (**join up**) become a member of the armed forces: *her brothers joined up in 1914.* ■ come into the company of: *after the show we were joined by Jessica's sister.* ■ support (someone) in an activity: *I am sure you will **join me in** wishing him every success.*
▸*n.* a place or line where two or more things are connected or fastened together. ▷Middle English: from Old French *joindre*, from Latin *jungere* 'to join.' **—join·a·ble** *adj.*
▸*PHRASES* □ **join battle** *formal* begin fighting. □ **join the club** see CLUB[1]. □ **join forces** combine efforts. □ **join hands** hold each other's hands. ■ *figurative* work together: *education has been shy to join hands with business.*

THE RIGHT WORD **combine, conjoin, connect, consolidate, join, unite**

It is possible for someone to **join** an investment club, to **consolidate** his or her financial resources, and to **combine** a background in economics with a strong interest in retirement planning. All of these words mean to bring together or to attach two or more things.

Join is the general term for bringing into contact or conjunction two discrete things (*join two pieces of wood; join one's friends in celebration*), while **conjoin** emphasizes both the separateness of the things that are joined and the unity that results (*her innate brilliance, conjoined with a genuine eagerness to learn, made her the ideal candidate for the job*).

In contrast, to *combine* is to mix or mingle things together, often to the point where they merge with one another (*combine the ingredients for a cake*).

Consolidate also implies a merger of distinct and separate elements, but the emphasis here is on achieving greater compactness, strength, or efficiency (*consolidate their furnishings and buy a new house together*).

Connect implies a loose or obvious attachment of things to each other, but with each thing's identity or physical separateness preserved (*the two families were connected by blood; she connected the computer to the printer*). In a physical context, it differs from *join* in that it implies an intervening element that permits movement; in other words, the bones are *connected* by ligaments, but bricks are *joined* by mortar.

When things are joined or combined so closely that they form a single thing, they are said to **unite** (*the parties were united in their support of the new law*).

join·der /ˈjoindər/ ▸*n.* *Law* the action of bringing parties together; union. ▷late Middle English: from Anglo-Norman French, from Old French *joindre* 'to join.'

joined-up ▸*adj.* *chiefly Brit.* (of handwriting) written with the characters joined; cursive. ■ (especially of a policy) characterized by coordination and coherence of thought; integrated: *a joined-up approach to rural poverty, public services, and employment.*

join·er /ˈjoinər/ ▸*n.* **1** a person who constructs the wooden components of a building, such as stairs, doors, and door and window frames. **2** *informal* a person who readily joins groups or campaigns: *a compulsive joiner of revolutionary movements.* ▷Middle English: from Old French *joigneor*, from *joindre* 'to join.'

join·er·y /ˈjoinərē/ ▸*n.* the wooden components of a building, such as stairs, doors, and door and window frames, viewed collectively.

joint /joint/ ▸*n.* **1** a point at which parts of an artificial structure are joined. ■ *Geology* a break or fracture in a mass of rock, with no relative displacement of the parts. ■ a piece of flexible material forming the hinge of a book cover. **2** a structure in the human or animal body at which two parts of the skeleton are fitted together. ■ each of the distinct sections of a body or limb between the places at which they are connected: *the top two joints of his index finger.* ■ *Brit.* a large piece of meat cooked whole or ready for cooking: *a **joint of** ham.* ■ the part of a stem of a plant from which a leaf or branch grows. ■ a section of a plant stem between such parts; an internode. **3** *informal* an establishment of a specified kind, esp. one where people meet for eating, drinking, or entertainment: *a burger joint.* ■ (**the joint**) prison. **4** *informal* a marijuana cigarette.
▸*adj.* [*attrib.*] shared, held, or made by two or more people or organizations together: *the companies issued a joint statement.* ■ shared, held, or made by both houses of a bicameral legislature: *a joint session of Congress* | *a joint congressional hearing.* ■ sharing in a position, achievement, or activity: *a joint winner.* ■ *Law* applied or regarded together. Often contrasted with SEVERAL.
▸*v.* [*trans.*] **1** provide or fasten (something) with joints: [as *adj.*] (**jointed**) *jointed lever arms.* ■ fill up the joints of (masonry or brickwork) with mortar; point. ■ prepare (a board) for being joined to another by planing its edge. **2** cut (the body of an animal) into joints. ▷Middle English: from Old French, past participle of *joindre* 'to join' (see JOIN). **—joint·less** *adj.* **—joint·ly** *adv.*
▸*PHRASE* □ **out of joint** (of a joint of the body) out of position; dislocated: *he put his hip out of joint.* ■ in a state of disorder or disorientation: *time was thrown completely out of joint.*

joint ac·count ▸*n.* a bank account held by more than one person, each individual having the right to deposit and withdraw funds.

joint and sev·er·al ▸*adj.* (of a legal obligation) undertaken by two or more people, each individual having liability for the whole.

Joint Chiefs of Staff ▸*n.* the chiefs of staff of the U.S. Army and Air Force, the commandant of the U.S. Marine Corps, and the chief of U.S. Naval Operations. This group's chairman, selected from one of the branches, is the highest-ranking military adviser to the president of the U.S.

joint·er /ˈjointər/ ▸*n.* a plane used for preparing a wooden edge for fixing or joining to another. ■ a tool used for pointing masonry and brickwork.

joint·ress /ˈjointrəs/ ▸*n.* *dated Law* a widow who holds a jointure. ▷early 17th cent.: feminine of obsolete *jointer* 'joint owner.'

joint-stock com·pa·ny ▸*n.* *Finance* a company whose stock is owned jointly by the shareholders.

joint ten·an·cy ▸*n.* the holding of an estate or property jointly by two or more parties, the share of each passing to the other or others on death. **—joint ten·ant** *n.*

join·ture /ˈjoinchər/ ▸*n.* *Law* an estate settled on a wife for the period during which she survives her husband, in lieu of a dower. ▷Middle English (in the sense 'junction, joint'): from Old French, from Latin *junctura* (see JUNCTURE). In late Middle English the term denoted the joint holding of property by a husband and wife for life, whence the current sense.

joint ven·ture ▸*n.* a commercial enterprise undertaken jointly by two or more parties that otherwise retain their distinct identities.

joist /joist/ ▸*n.* a length of timber or steel supporting part of the structure of a building, typically arranged in parallel series to support a floor or ceiling. ▷late Middle English *giste*, from Old French, 'beam supporting a bridge,' based on Latin *jacere* 'lie down.' **—joist·ed** *adj.*

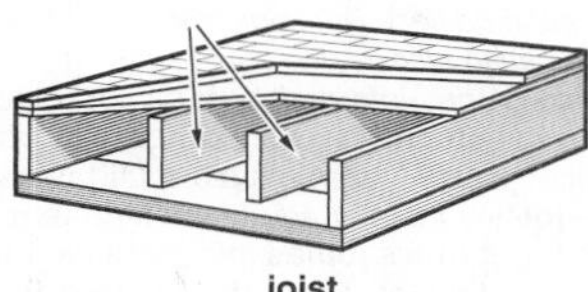

joist

jo·jo·ba /hōˈhōbə/ ▸*n.* **1** (also **jo·jo·ba oil**) an oil extracted from the seeds of an American shrub, widely used in cosmetics. **2** the leathery-leaved evergreen shrub or small tree that produces these seeds, native chiefly to the southwestern U.S. It is grown to prevent desertification as well as for its seeds. • *Simmondsia chinensis*, the only member of the family Simmondsiaceae. ▷early 20th cent.: from Mexican Spanish.

joke /jōk/ ▸*n.* a thing that someone says to cause amusement or laughter, esp. a story with a funny punchline: *she was in a mood to tell jokes.* ■ a trick played on someone for fun. ■ [in *sing.*] *informal* a person or thing that is ridiculously inadequate: *the transportation system is a joke.*
▸*v.* [*intrans.*] make jokes; talk humorously or flippantly: *she could laugh and **joke with** her colleagues* | [with *direct speech*] *"It's OK, we're not related," she joked.* ■ [*trans.*] *archaic* poke fun at: *he was pretending to joke his daughter.* ▷late 17th cent. (originally slang): perhaps from Latin *jocus* 'jest, wordplay.' **—jok·ey** (also **jok·y**) *adj.* **—jok·i·ly** /-kəlē/ *adv.* **—jok·i·ness** *n.* **—jok·ing·ly** *adv.*
▸*PHRASES* □ **be no joke** *informal* be a serious matter or difficult undertaking: *trying to shop with three children in tow is no joke.* □ **can** (or **can't**) **take a joke** be able (or unable) to receive humorous remarks or tricks in the spirit in which they are intended: *if you can't take a joke, you should never have joined.* □ **the joke is on someone** *informal* someone looks foolish, esp. after trying to make someone else look so. □ **make a joke of** laugh or be humorous about (something that is not funny in itself).

jok·er /ˈjōkər/ ▸*n.* **1** a person who is fond of joking. ■ *informal* a foolish or inept person: *a bunch of jokers.* **2** a playing card, typically bearing the figure of a jester, used in some games as a wild card. **3** a clause unobtrusively inserted in a bill or document and affecting its operation in a way not immediately apparent.
▸*PHRASE* □ **the joker in the pack** a person or factor likely to have an unpredictable effect on events.

jol·ie laide /ˈzhōlē ˈled/ ▸*n.* (*pl.* **jol·ies laides** *pronunc.* same) a woman whose face is attractive despite having ugly features. ▷French, from *jolie* 'pretty' and *laide* 'ugly,' feminine adjectives.

Jo·li·et /,jōlēˈet/ an industrial and commercial city in northeastern Illinois; pop. 106,221.

Jo·liot /ˈjōlyō/, Jean-Frédéric (1900–58), French nuclear physicist. As Marie Curie's assistant at the Radium Institute, he worked with her daughter **Irène** (1897–1956), whom he married (taking the name **Joliot-Curie**); together they discovered artificial radioactivity. Nobel Prize for Chemistry (1935, shared with his wife).

jo·li·o·ti·um /,jōlēˈōsh(ē)əm/ ▸*n.* the name proposed by IUPAC for the chemical element of atomic number

Pronunciation Key ə *ago;* ər *over;* ˈə *or* ,ə *up;* ˈər *or* ,ər *fur;* a *hat;* ā *rate;* ä *car;* ch *chew;* e *let;* ē *see;* e(ə)r *air;* i *fit;* ī *by;* i(ə)r *ear;* ng *sing;* ō *go;* ô *for;* oi *boy;* o͝o *good;* o͞o *goo;* ou *out;* sh *she;* th *thin;* t͟h *then;* (h)w *why;* zh *vision*

J

105, now called **dubnium**. ▷late 20th cent.: modern Latin, from the name of J. F. JOLIOT.

Jol·liet /zhôl'ye; zhōlē'et/, Louis (1645–1700) French-Canadian explorer. With Jacques Marquette, he explored the upper Mississippi River 1673–74.

jol·li·fi·ca·tion /ˌjäləfi'kāshən/ ▸*n.* lively celebration with others; merrymaking.

jol·li·ty /'jälitē/ ▸*n.* (*pl.* **-ties**) lively and cheerful activity or celebration: *a night of riotous jollity.* ■ the quality of being cheerful: *he was full of false jollity.* ▷Middle English: from Old French *jolite*, from *joli* (see JOLLY[1]).

jol·lof rice /'jäləf/ ▸*n.* a West African stew made with rice, chili peppers, and meat or fish. ▷*jollof*, variant of WOLOF.

jol·ly[1] /'jälē/ ▸*adj.* (**-li·er**, **-li·est**) happy and cheerful: *he was a jolly man full of jokes.* ■ *informal* or *dated* lively and entertaining: *we had a very jolly time.*
▸*v.* (**-lies**, **-lied**) [*trans.*] *informal* encourage (someone) in a friendly way: *he* **jollied** *people* **along** | *they were trying to jolly her out of her torpor.* ■ (**jolly someone/something up**) make someone or something more lively or cheerful: *ideas to jolly up a winter's party.*
▸*adv.* [as *submodifier*] *Brit.*, *informal* very; extremely: *that's a jolly good idea.*
▸*n.* (*pl.* **-lies**) *Brit.*, *informal* a party or celebration. ▷Middle English: from Old French *jolif*, an earlier form of *joli* 'pretty,' perhaps from Old Norse *jól* (see YULE). **—jol·li·ly** /'jäləlē/ *adv.* **—jol·li·ness** *n.*
▸*PHRASES* □ **get one's jollies** *informal* have fun or find pleasure. □ **jolly well** *Brit.*, *informal* used for emphasis, esp. when one is angry or irritated: *I'm going to keep on eating as much sugar as I jolly well like.*

jol·ly[2] (also **jol·ly boat**) ▸*n.* (*pl.* **-lies**) a lapstraked ship's boat that is smaller than a cutter, typically hoisted at the stern of the ship. ▷early 18th cent.: perhaps related to YAWL.

Jol·ly Rog·er /'jälē 'räjər/ ▸*n.* a pirate's flag with a white skull and crossbones on a black background. ▷late 18th cent.: of unknown origin.

Jolly Roger

Jol·son /'jōlsən/, Al (1886–1950), U.S. singer, movie actor, and comedian; born *Asa Yoelson* in Russia. He made the Gershwin song "Swanee" his trademark and appeared in the first full-length talking movie, *The Jazz Singer*, in 1927.

jolt /jōlt/ ▸*v.* [*trans.*] push or shake (someone or something) abruptly and roughly: *a surge in the crowd behind him jolted him forward.* ■ *figurative* give a surprise or shock to (someone) in order to make them act or change: *she tried to* **jolt** *him* **out of** *his depression.* ■ [*intrans.*] move with sudden lurches: *the train jolted into motion.*
▸*n.* an abrupt rough or violent movement. ■ a surprise or shock, esp. of an unpleasant kind and often manifested physically: *that information gave her a severe jolt.* ▷late 16th cent.: of unknown origin. **—jolt·y** *adj.*

Jon. ▸*abbr.* ■ *Bible* Jonah. ■ Jonathan.

Jon·a·gold /'jänəˌgōld/ ▸*n.* a dessert apple of a variety with greenish-gold skin and crisp flesh. ▷1960s: blend of JONATHAN[2] and GOLDEN DELICIOUS.

Jo·nah /'jōnə/ (in the Bible) a Hebrew minor prophet. He was called by God to preach in Nineveh, but disobeyed and attempted to escape by sea; in a storm he was thrown overboard as a bringer of bad luck and swallowed by a great fish, only to be saved and finally succeed in his mission. ■ a book of the Bible telling of Jonah.

J

Jon·a·than[1] /'jänəthən/ (in the Bible) a son of Saul, noted for his friendship with David (1 Sam. 18–20, 2 Sam. 1) and killed at the battle of Mount Gilboa (1 Sam. 31).

Jon·a·than[2] ▸*n.* a cooking apple of a red-skinned variety first grown in the U.S. ▷mid 19th cent.: named after *Jonathan* Hasbrouck (died 1846), American lawyer.

Jones[1] /jōnz/, Bobby (1902–71), U.S. golfer; full name *Robert Tyre Jones.* In a short competitive career 1923–30, and as an amateur, he won thirteen major competitions, including four U.S. and three British open championships.

Jones[2], Inigo (1573–1652), British architect and stage designer. He introduced the Palladian style to Britain in buildings such as the Queen's House at Greenwich (1616) and the Banqueting Hall at Whitehall (1619).

Jones[3], James (1921–77) U.S. writer. His novel *From Here to Eternity* (1951) was made into a movie in 1953. He also wrote *The Thin Red Line* (1962). *Whistle*, which he did not complete, was published posthumously in 1978.

Jones[4], James Earl (1931–), U.S. actor. He performed in numerous classical and contemporary plays, including *Othello* (1964) and *The Great White Hope* (Tony Award, 1969). He has appeared in more than fifty films, including *Dr. Strangelove* (1964) and *Field of Dreams* (1989); his distinctive resonant voice was heard in the roles of Darth Vader in *Star Wars* (1977) and King Mufasa in *The Lion King* (1994).

Jones[5], Jennifer (1919–) U.S. actress; born *Phyllis Isley.* She starred in *The Song of Bernadette* (Academy Award, 1943). Other movies in which she appeared include *Duel in the Sun* (1946), *Love Is a Many-Splendored Thing* (1955), *A Farewell to Arms* (1957, and *Tender Is the Night* (1961).

Jones[6], John Paul (1747–92), American naval officer; born *John Paul* in Scotland. Noted for his raids off the northern coasts of Britain during the American Revolution, he is said to have stated "I have not yet begun to fight!" after victory in a 1779 battle between the Americans and the British.

Jones[7], Quincy (Delight, Jr.) (1933–) U.S. composer, conductor, and jazz trumpeter. He founded his own recording label, Qwest Records, in 1975. He also wrote television scores, such as the theme for "The Bill Cosby Show," and movie scores, such as for *The Color Purple* (1985). In 1985, he also arranged and produced "We Are the World," a song that benefited world hunger.

Jones[8], Shirley (1934–) U.S. actress and singer. She starred in the movie musicals *Oklahoma!* (1955) and *Carousel* (1956), as well as in *Elmer Gantry* (Academy Award, 1960). She also played Shirley Partridge in television's "The Partridge Family" (1970–74).

Jones[9], Tom (1940–), Welsh pop singer; born *Thomas Jones Woodward.* Hits include "It's Not Unusual" (1965), "The Green, Green Grass of Home" (1966), and "Delilah" (1968).

jones /jōnz/ *informal* ▸*n.* a fixation on or compulsive desire for someone or something, typically a drug; an addiction: *a two-year amphetamine jones.*
▸*v.* [*intrans.*] (**jones on/for**) have a fixation on; be addicted to: *Palmer was jonesing for some coke again.* ▷1960s: said to come from *Jones* Alley, in Manhattan, associated with drug addicts.

Jones·bo·ro /'jōnzˌbərō/ a city in northeastern Arkansas; pop. 55,515.

Jones·es /'jōnziz/ (usu. **the Joneses**) ▸*n.* a person's neighbors or social equals. ▷late 19th cent.: from *Jones*, a commonly found British surname.
▸*PHRASE* □ **keep up with the Joneses** try to emulate or not be outdone by one's neighbors.

Jones·town /'jōnzˌtoun/ a former religious settlement in the jungle of Guyana, established by Reverend Jim Jones with about 1,000 followers, almost all of whom died in a mass suicide in late 1978.

Jong /'yông/, Erica (Mann) (1942–), U.S. novelist and poet. She is best known for her picaresque novels *Fear of Flying* (1973), recounting the sexual exploits of heroine Isadora Wing, and *Fanny* (1980), written in a pseudo-18th-century style.

jon·gleur /zhôn'glər; 'jängglər/ ▸*n.* *historical* an itinerant minstrel. ▷French, variant of *jougleur* 'juggler,' earlier *jogleor* 'pleasant, smiling,' from Latin *joculator* 'joker.'

Jön·kö·ping /'yœnˌchœping/ an industrial city in southern Sweden, at the southern end of Lake Vättern; pop. 111,000.

jon·quil /'jänkwəl/ ▸*n.* a widely cultivated narcissus with clusters of small fragrant yellow flowers and cylindrical leaves, native to southern Europe and northeastern Africa. • *Narcissus jonquilla*, family Liliaceae (or Amaryllidaceae). ▷early 17th cent.: from modern Latin *jonquilla* or French *jonquille*, from Spanish *junquillo*, diminutive of *junco*, from Latin *juncus* 'rush, reed.'

Jon·son /'jänsən/, Ben (1572–1637), British playwright and poet; full name *Benjamin Jonson.* With his play *Every Man in His Humour* (1598), he established his "comedy of humors," whereby each character is dominated by a particular obsession. Other notable works: *Volpone* (1606) and *Bartholomew Fair* (1614). **—Jon·so·ni·an** /jän'sōnēən/ *adj.*

jook /jo͝ok; jo͞ok/ ▸*n.* another term for JUKE JOINT.

Jop·lin[1] /'jäplin/ an industrial and commercial city in southwestern Missouri; pop. 45,504.

Jop·lin[2] /'jäplən/, Janis (1943–70), U.S. rock and blues singer. She became a vocalist with Big Brother and the Holding Company, and gave a raw, powerful performance at the Monterey pop festival in 1967. She died from a heroin overdose just before her most successful album, *Pearl*, and her number-one single "Me and Bobby McGee" were released in 1970.

Jop·lin[3], Scott (1868–1917), U.S. pianist and composer. He was the first of the creators of ragtime to write down his compositions. Notable works: "Maple Leaf Rag" (1899), "The Entertainer" (1902), and "Gladiolus Rag" (1907).

Jop·pa biblical name for JAFFA[1].

Jor·daens /'yôrˌdäns/, Jacob (1593–1678), Flemish painter. Influenced by Rubens, he is noted for his boisterous peasant scenes.

Jor·dan[1] /'jôrdən/ **1** a country in the Middle East, east of the Jordan River; pop. 5,611,000; capital, Amman; official language, Arabic. Official name HASHEMITE KINGDOM OF JORDAN.

Romans, Arabs, Crusaders, and Turks dominated the area successively until it was made a British protectorate in 1916 and achieved independence in 1946. During the war of 1948–49 that followed the establishment of the state of Israel, Jordan took over the area of the West Bank; this was recovered by Israel in the Six Day War of 1967, after which many Palestinian refugees entered the country. A peace treaty with Israel was signed in 1994, ending an official state of war between the two countries.

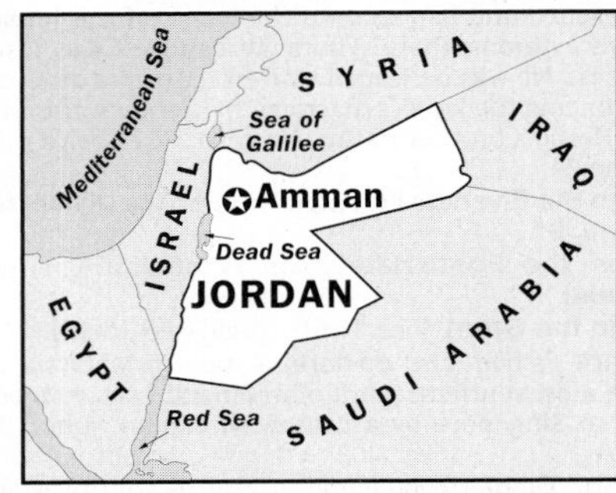

2 a river that flows south for 200 miles (320 km) from the Anti-Lebanon Mountains through the Sea of Galilee into the Dead Sea. John the Baptist baptized Jesus Christ in the Jordan River. It is regarded as sacred not only by Christians but also by Jews and Muslims. **—Jor·da·ni·an** /jôr'dānēən/ *adj.* & *n.*

Jor·dan[2], Barbara (Charline) (1936–96) U.S. lawyer, educator, and politician. She was a member of the Texas state senate 1967–72 before being elected to the U.S. House of Representatives 1973–79.

Jor·dan[3], Michael (Jeffrey) (1963–), U.S. basketball player. Playing for the Chicago Bulls 1984–93 and 1995–98, he led them to six titles and was the National Basketball Association's most valuable player five times. He retired in 1993 to play professional baseball, but returned to basketball in 1995, playing for the Bulls until 1999 and for the Washington Wizards 2001–03.

Michael Jordan

jor·dan al·mond /'jôrdn/ ▸*n.* a high-quality almond of a variety grown chiefly in southeastern Spain. ▷late Middle English: *jordan* apparently from French or Spanish *jardin* 'garden.'

Jor·na·da del Muer·to /hôr'nädə del 'mwertō/ a desert region in southern New Mexico, near White Sands, known as the "journey of death" for the difficulties early travelers endured.

jo·rum /'jôrəm/ ▸*n.* *historical* a large bowl or jug used for serving drinks such as tea or punch. ▷early 18th cent.: perhaps from *Joram* (2 Sam. 8:10), who "brought with him vessels of silver, and vessels of gold" to King David.

Jos. ▶*abbr.* ■ Joseph. ■ Josiah. ■ *Bible* Joshua.

Jo·seph1 /ˈjōzəf; -səf/ (in the Bible) a Hebrew patriarch, son of Jacob and oldest son of Rachel. He was given a coat of many colors by his father, but was then sold by his jealous brothers into captivity in Egypt, where he attained high office (Gen. 30–50).

Jo·seph2, Chief (c.1840–1904) American Indian chief; Indian name **Inmuttooyahlatlat**. As chief of the Nez Percé tribe, he defied the efforts of the U.S. government to move his people from Oregon until he was captured in 1877.

Chief Joseph

Jo·seph, St., husband of the Virgin Mary. A carpenter of Nazareth, he was betrothed to Mary at the time of the Annunciation. Feast day, March

Jo·se·phine /ˈjōzəˌfēn; ˌjōzəˈfēn/ (1763–181 em-press of France 1804–09; full name *Marie Jo hine Rose Tascher de la Pagerie*. She married Napole in 1796. Their marriage proved childless, and she as divorced by Napoleon in 1809.

Jo·seph of Ar·i·ma·the·a /ˌarəməˈTHēə/ a membe f the council at Jerusalem who, after the Crucifixi asked Pilate for Jesus' body, which he buried. He also known from the medieval story that he came England with the Holy Grail and built the fir church at Glastonbury.

Jo·seph·son junc·tion /ˈjōzəfsən; -səf-/ ▶*n. Physics* an electrical device in which two superconducting metals are separated by a thin layer of insulator, across which an electric current may flow in the absence of a potential difference. The current may be made to oscillate in proportion to an applied potential difference. ▷1960s: named after Brian D. *Josephson* (born 1940), British physicist.

Jo·se·phus /jōˈsēfəs/, Flavius (*c.*37–*c.*100), Jewish historian, general, and Pharisee; born *Joseph ben Matthias*. His *Jewish War* gives an eyewitness account of the events that led up to the Jewish revolt against the Romans in 66, in which he was a leader.

josh /jäsн/ *informal* ▶*v.* [*trans.*] tease (someone) in a playful way: *he loved to josh people.* ■ [*intrans.*] engage in joking or playful talk with others.
▶*n.* good-natured banter. ▷mid 19th cent. (as a verb): of unknown origin. —**josh·er** *n.*

Josh. ▶*abbr. Bible* Joshua.

Josh·u·a /ˈjäsнōōə/ (*fl. c.*13th century BC), Israelite leader who succeeded Moses and led his people into the Promised Land. ■ the sixth book of the Bible, telling of the conquest of Canaan and its division among the twelve tribes of Israel.

Josh·u·a tree ▶*n.* a yucca that grows as a tree and has clusters of spiky leaves, native to arid regions of southwestern North America. • *Yucca brevifolia*, family Agavaceae. ▷mid 19th cent.: apparently from JOSHUA (Josh. 8:18), the plant being likened to a man brandishing a spear.

Joshua tree

Josh·u·a Tree Na·tion·al Park /ˈjäsнōōə/ a national preserve in southern California, noted for its desert plant and animal life.

joss /jäs/ ▶*n.* a Chinese religious statue or idol. ▷early 18th cent.: from Javanese *dejos*, from obsolete Portuguese *deos*, from Latin *deus* 'god.'

jos·ser /ˈjäsər/ ▶*n. informal* **1** *Brit.* a man, typically an old man or one regarded with some contempt: *an old josser.* **2** *Austral.* a clergyman. ▷late 19th cent.: from JOSS + -ER1.

joss house ▶*n.* a Chinese temple.

joss stick ▶*n.* a thin stick consisting of a substance that burns slowly and with a fragrant smell, used as incense.

jos·tle /ˈjäsəl/ ▶*v.* [*trans.*] push, elbow, or bump against (someone) roughly, typically in a crowd: *passengers arriving and departing, jostling one another* | [*intrans.*] *people* **jostled against** *us.* ■ [*intrans.*] (**jostle for**) struggle or compete forcefully for: *a jumble of images jostled for attention.*
▶*n.* the action of jostling. ▷late Middle English *justle*, from *just*, an earlier form of JOUST. The original sense was 'have sexual intercourse with'; current senses date from the mid 16th cent.

jot /jät/ ▶*v.* (**jot·ted, jot·ting**) [*trans.*] write (something) quickly: *when you've found the answers,* **jot** *them* **down**.
▶*n.* [usu. with *negative*] a very small amount: *you didn't care a jot* | *I have yet to see* **one jot of** *evidence.* ▷late 15th cent. (as a noun): via Latin from Greek *iōta*, the smallest letter of the Greek alphabet (see IOTA).

jo·ta /ˈhōtə/ ▶*n.* a folk dance from northern Spain, danced in couples in fast triple time. ▷Spanish.

jot·ting /ˈjätiNG/ ▶*n.* (usu. **jottings**) a brief note.

Jo·tun /ˈyôtōōn/ ▶*n. Scandinavian Mythology* a member of the race of giants, enemies of the gods. ▷from Old Norse *jǫtunn*, related to Old English *eoten*, of Germanic origin.

jou·al /zнōōˈal; -ˈäl/ ▶*n.* a nonstandard form of popular Canadian French, influenced by English vocabulary and grammar. ▷Canadian French dialect, from French *cheval* 'horse,' apparently from the way *cheval* is pronounced in rural areas of Quebec.

jougs /jōōgz/ ▶*plural n. historical* a hinged iron collar chained to a wall or post, used in medieval Scotland as an instrument of punishment. ▷late 16th cent.: from French *joug* or Latin *jugum* 'yoke.'

jou·is·sance /zнwēˈsäNs/ ▶*n. formal* physical or intellectual pleasure, delight, or ecstasy. ▷French, from *jouir* 'enjoy.'

Joule /jōōl/, James Prescott (1818–89), British physicist. He established that all forms of energy were basically the same and interchangeable—the first law of thermodynamics. The Joule–Thomson effect, discovered with William Thomson (later Lord Kelvin) in 1852, led to the development of the refrigerator and to the science of cryogenics.

ɔule /jōōl; joul/ (abbr.: **J**) ▶*n.* the SI unit of work or en-ɛrgy, equal to the work done by a force of one new-ɔn when its point of application moves one meter the direction of action of the force, equivalent to e 3600th of a watt-hour. ▷late 19th cent.: named r J. P. JOULE.

J e ef·fect ▶*n. Physics* the heating that occurs h an electric current flows through a resistance.

Jo s law *Physics* a law stating that the heat produ by an electric current *i* flowing through a resis e *R* for a time *t* is proportional to i^2Rt.

Jou hom·son ef·fect ▶*n. Physics* the change of tem ture of a gas when it is allowed to expand with oing any external work. The gas becomes coole was initially below a certain temperature (the i sion temperature), or hotter if initially above

jounce s/ ▶*v.* jolt or bounce: [*intrans.*] *the car jounced* | [*trans.*] *the pilot jounced the plane through turbulenc* te Middle English: probably symbolic; compare BOUNCE.

jour. ▶*abbr* urnal. ■ journeyman.

jour·nal /ˈjə n. **1** a newspaper or magazine that deals with ticular subject or professional activity: *medical j ls* | [in *names*] *the* Wall Street Journal. **2** a dai ord of news and events of a personal nature iary. ■ *Nautical* a logbook. ■ (**the Journals**) a r of the daily proceedings in the British Houses arliament. ■ (in bookkeeping) a daily record of ness transactions with a statement of the acc to which each is to be debited and credited. **3** nics the part of a shaft or axle that rests on bea ▷late Middle English (originally denoting a containing the appointed times of daily pray rom Old French *jurnal*, from late Latin *diurnalis* URNAL).

jour·nal box ▶*n. Me* s a box that houses a journal and its bearing.

jour·nal·ese /ˌjərnlˈēz *informal, often derogatory* a hackneyed style of writing supposedly characteristic of newspapers and magazines.

jour·nal·ism /ˈjərnlˌizəm/ ▶*n.* the activity or profession of writing for newspapers or magazines or of broadcasting news on radio or television. ■ the product of such activity: *an art critic whose essays and journalism are never dull.*

jour·nal·ist /ˈjərnl-ist/ ▶*n.* a person who writes for newspapers or magazines or prepares news to be broadcast on radio or television. —**jour·nal·is·tic** /ˌjərnlˈistik/ *adj.* —**jour·nal·is·ti·cal·ly** /ˌjərnlˈistik(ə)lē/ *adv.*

jour·nal·ize /ˈjərnlˌīz/ ▶*v.* [*trans.*] *dated* enter (notes or information) in a journal or account book: *I would gladly journalize some of my proceedings.*

jour·ney /ˈjərnē/ ▶*n.* (*pl.* **-neys**) an act of traveling from one place to another: *she went on a long journey* | *figurative your journey through life.*
▶*v.* (**-neys, -neyed**) [*intrans.*] travel somewhere: *they journeyed south.* ▷Middle English: from Old French *jornee* 'day, a day's travel, a day's work' (the earliest senses in English), based on Latin *diurnum* 'daily portion,' from *diurnus* (see DIURNAL). —**jour·ney·er** *n.*

THE RIGHT WORD **excursion, expedition, jaunt, journey, pilgrimage, trip, voyage**

While all of these nouns refer to a course of travel to a particular place, usually for a specific purpose, there is a big difference between a **jaunt** to the nearest beach and an **expedition** to the rain forest.

While a **trip** may be either long or short, for business or pleasure, and taken at either a rushed or a leisurely pace (*a ski trip; a trip to Europe*), a **journey** suggests that a considerable amount of time and distance will be covered and that the travel will take place over land (*a journey into the Australian outback*).

A long trip by water or through air or space is a **voyage** (*a voyage to the Galapagos Islands; a voyage to Mars*), while a short, casual trip for pleasure or recreation is a *jaunt* (*a jaunt to the local shopping mall*).

Excursion also applies to a brief pleasure trip, usually no more than a day in length, that returns to the place where it began (*an afternoon excursion to the zoo*).

Unlike the rest of these nouns, *expedition* and **pilgrimage** apply to *journeys* that are undertaken for a specific purpose. An *expedition* is usually made by an organized group or company (*a scientific expedition; an expedition to locate new sources of oil*), while a *pilgrimage* is a journey to a place that has religious or emotional significance (*the Muslims' annual pilgrimage to Mecca; a pilgrimage to the place where her father died*).

jour·ney·man /ˈjərnēmən/ ▶*n.* (*pl.* **-men**) a trained worker who is employed by someone else. ■ a worker or sports player who is reliable but not outstanding: [as *adj.*] *a solid journeyman professional.* ▷late Middle English: from JOURNEY (in the obsolete sense 'day's work') + MAN; so named because the journeyman was no longer bound by indentures but was paid by the day.

jour·no /ˈjərnō/ ▶*n.* (*pl.* **-nos**) *informal* a journalist. ▷1960s (originally an Australian usage): abbreviation.

joust /joust/ ▶*v.* [*intrans.*] [often as *n.*] (**jousting**) *historical* (of a medieval knight) engage in a sports contest in which two opponents on horseback fight with lances. ■ *figurative* compete closely for superiority: *the guerrillas* **jousted for** *supremacy.*
▶*n.* a medieval sports contest in which two opponents on horseback fought with lances. ▷Middle English (originally in the sense 'join battle, engage'): from Old French *jouster* 'bring together,' based on Latin *juxta* 'near.' —**joust·er** *n.*

J'Ou·vert /zнōōˈver/ ▶*n.* (in the Caribbean) the official start of carnival, at dawn on the Monday preceding Lent. ▷French Creole, from French *jour ouvert* 'day opened.'

Jove /jōv/ another name for JUPITER. ▷from Latin *Jov-*, stem of Old Latin *Jovis*, replaced later by *Jupiter*. The exclamation *by Jove* dates from the late 16th cent.

▶*PHRASE* □ **by Jove** *dated* an exclamation indicating surprise or used for emphasis: *by Jove, that's a cold wind.*

jo·vi·al /ˈjōvēəl/ ▶*adj.* cheerful and friendly: *she was in a jovial mood.* ▷late 16th cent.: from French, from

J

late Latin *jovialis* 'of Jupiter' (see **JOVE**), with reference to the supposed influence of the planet Jupiter on those born under it. **—jo·vi·al·i·ty** /ˌjōvēˈalitē/ *n.* **—jo·vi·al·ly** *adv.*

Jo·vi·an /ˈjōvēən/ ▸*adj.* **1** (in Roman mythology) of or like the god Jove (or Jupiter). **2** of or relating to the planet Jupiter or the class of giant planets to which Jupiter belongs.
▸*n.* a hypothetical or fictional inhabitant of the planet Jupiter.

jowl /joul/ ▸*n.* (often **jowls**) the lower part of a person's or animal's cheek, esp. when it is fleshy or drooping: *she had a large nose and heavy jowls.* ■ the cheek of a pig used as meat. ■ the loose fleshy part of the neck of certain animals, such as the dewlap of cattle or the wattle of birds. ▷Old English *ceole* (related to German *Kehle* 'throat, gullet'), partly merged with Old English *ceafl* 'jaw' (related to Dutch *kevels* 'cheekbones'). **—jowled** *adj.* [in *combination*] *ruddy-jowled.* **—jowl·y** *adj.*

joy /joi/ ▸*n.* a feeling of great pleasure and happiness: *tears of joy | the joy of being alive.* ■ a thing that causes joy: *the joys of Manhattan.*
▸*v.* [*intrans.*] *poetic/literary* rejoice: *I felt shame that I had ever joyed in his discomfiture or pain.* ▷Middle English: from Old French *joie,* based on Latin *gaudium,* from *gaudere* 'rejoice.' **—joy·less** *adj.* **—joy·less·ly** *adv.*

Joyce /jois/, James (Augustine Aloysius) (1882–1941), Irish writer. An important writer of the modernist movement, he first became known for his short stories in *Dubliners* (1914). His novel *Ulysses* (1922) revolutionized the structure of the modern novel and developed the stream-of-consciousness technique. Other notable novels: *A Portrait of the Artist as a Young Man* (1914–15) and *Finnegans Wake* (1939). **—Joyc·e·an** /ˈjoisēən/ *adj.* & *n.*

joy·ful /ˈjoifəl/ ▸*adj.* feeling, expressing, or causing great pleasure and happiness: *joyful music.* **—joy·ful·ly** *adv.* **—joy·ful·ness** *n.*

Joy·ner–Ker·see /ˈjoinər ˈkərsē/, Jackie (1962–) U.S. track and field athlete. She won gold medals in the heptathlon in the 1988 and 1992 Olympic Games.

joy·ous /ˈjoiəs/ ▸*adj. chiefly poetic/literary* full of happiness and joy: *scenes of joyous celebration.* **—joy·ous·ly** *adv.* **—joy·ous·ness** *n.*

joy·pad /ˈjoiˌpad/ ▸*n.* an input device for a computer games console which uses buttons to control the motion of an image on the screen. ▷late 20th cent.: blend of **JOYSTICK** and **KEYPAD**.

joy·ride /ˈjoiˌrīd/ ▸*n. informal* a fast and dangerous ride, esp. one taken in a stolen vehicle: *kids stealing cars for a Saturday night joyride.*
▸*v.* [*intrans.*] go for a joyride. **—joy·rid·er** /-ˌrīdər/ *n.*

joy·rid·ing /ˈjoiˌrīdiNG/ ▸*n.* the action or practice of driving fast and dangerously in a stolen car for enjoyment.

joy·stick /ˈjoiˌstik/ ▸*n. informal* the control column of an aircraft. ■ a lever that can be moved in several directions to control the movement of an image on a computer or similar display screen.

JP ▸*abbr.* Justice of the Peace.

JPEG /ˈjāˌpeg/ ▸*n. Computing* a format for compressing images: [as *adj.*] *a JPEG image.* ▷1990s: abbreviation of *Joint Photographic Experts Group.*

Jr. ▸*abbr.* junior (in names): *John Smith Jr.*

JRC ▸*abbr.* Junior Red Cross.

JSD ▸*abbr.* Doctor of the Science of Law (Doctor of Juristic Science).

Juan Car·los /(h)wän ˈkärlōs/ (1938–), king of Spain 1975–; full name *Juan Carlos Víctor María de Borbón y Borbón*; grandson of Alfonso XIII. Franco's chosen successor, he became king after Franco's death. His reign has seen Spain's increasing liberalization and its entry into NATO and the European Community.

Juan de Fu·ca Strait /ˈ(h)wän də ˈfyōōkə/ an ocean passage between Vancouver Island in British Columbia and the Olympic Peninsula in Washington.

Juan Fer·nan·dez Is·lands /ˈ(h)wän fərˈnandəs/ a group of three almost uninhabited islands in the Pacific Ocean, 400 miles (640 km) west of Chile.

Juá·rez /(h)wäˈrez; ˈ(h)wärəs/, Benito Pablo (1806–72), Mexican statesman; president 1861–64 and 1867–72. Between 1864 and 1867, he was replaced as emperor by Maximilian, who was supported by the French.

Ju·ba /ˈjōōbə/ the capital of the southern region of Sudan, on the White Nile River; pop. 100,000.

ju·ba /ˈjōōbə/ ▸*n.* a dance originating among plantation slaves in the southern U.S., featuring rhythmic handclapping and slapping of the thighs. ▷late 19th cent.: of unknown origin.

Jub·ba /ˈjōōbə/ a river in East Africa that rises in the highlands of central Ethiopia and flows south for about 1,000 miles (1,600 km) through Somalia to the Indian Ocean.

ju·bi·lant /ˈjōōbələnt/ ▸*adj.* feeling or expressing great happiness and triumph. ▷mid 17th cent. (originally in the sense 'making a joyful noise'): from Latin *jubilant-* 'calling, hallooing,' from the verb *jubilare* (see **JUBILATE**). **—ju·bi·lance** *n.* **—ju·bi·lant·ly** *adv.*

Ju·bi·la·te /ˌjōōbəˈlātē; ˌyōōbəˈlätā/ ▸*n.* [in *sing.*] Psalm 100 (99 in the Vulgate), beginning *Jubilate deo* "rejoice in God," esp. as used as a canticle in the Anglican service of matins. ■ a musical setting of this. ▷Latin, 'shout for joy!,' imperative of *jubilare* (see **JUBILATE**).

ju·bi·late /ˈjōōbəˌlāt/ ▸*v.* [*intrans.*] *archaic* show great happiness; rejoice: *sing and jubilate aloud before God.* ▷mid 17th cent.: from Latin *jubilat-* 'called out,' from the verb *jubilare,* used by Christian writers to mean 'shout for joy.'

ju·bi·la·tion /ˌjōōbəˈlāSHən/ ▸*n.* a feeling of great happiness and triumph.

ju·bi·lee /ˈjōōbəˌlē; ˌjōōbəˈlē/ ▸*n.* a special anniversary of an event, esp. one celebrating twenty-five or fifty years of a reign or activity: [as *adj.*] *jubilee celebrations.* ■ *Judaism* (in Jewish history) a year of emancipation and restoration, celebrated every fifty years. ■ (in full **Jubilee Year**) a period of remission from the penal consequences of sin, granted by the Roman Catholic Church under certain conditions for a year, usually at intervals of twenty-five years.
▸*adj.* [*postpositive*] (of desserts) flambé: *cherries jubilee.* ▷late Middle English: from Old French *jubile,* from late Latin *jubilaeus (annus)* '(year) of jubilee,' based on Hebrew *yōḇēl,* originally 'ram's-horn trumpet,' with which the jubilee year was proclaimed.

Jud. ▸*abbr. Bible* ■ Judges. ■ Judith.

Ju·dae·a /jōōˈdēə; -ˈdāə/ the southern part of ancient Palestine that corresponds to the former kingdom of Judah. **—Ju·dae·an** *adj.*

Judaeo- ▸*comb. form chiefly Brit.* alternate spelling of **JUDEO-**.

Ju·dah /ˈjōōdə/ **1** (in the Bible) a Hebrew patriarch, the fourth son of Jacob and Leah. ■ the tribe of Israel traditionally descended from him, the most powerful of the twelve tribes of Israel. **2** the southern part of ancient Palestine, occupied by the tribe of Judah. After the reign of Solomon (*c.*930 BC) it formed a separate kingdom from Israel. Later known as **JUDAEA**.

Ju·da·ic /jōōˈdāik/ ▸*adj.* of or relating to Judaism or the ancient Jews: *tenets of Judaic law.* ▷early 17th cent.: from Latin *Judaicus,* from Greek *Ioudaïkos* from *Ioudaios* (see **JEW**).

Ju·da·ism /ˈjōōdēˌizəm; -dā-/ ▸*n.* the monotheistic religion of the Jews. ■ the Jews collectively.

For its origins Judaism looks to the bibl[...]e covenant made by God with Abraham, and to [...]h laws revealed to Moses and recorded in the T[...] (supplemented by the rabbinical Talmud), [...]ch established the Jewish people's special re[...]on-ship with God. Since the destruction of the [...]ple in Jerusalem in AD 70, the rituals of Judais[...]ave centered on the home and the synago[...] the chief day of worship being the Sabbath ([...]et on Friday to sunset on Saturday), and the a[...]al observances including Yom Kippur and Pa[...]er.

▷from late Latin *Judaismus,* from Greek [...] *daïsmos,* from *Ioudaios* (see **JEW**). **—Ju·da·ist** *n.*

Ju·da·ize /ˈjōōdēˌīz; -dā-/ ▸*v.* [*trans.*] mak[...]vish; convert to Judaism. ■ [*intrans.*] follow Jew[...]ustoms or religious rites. ▷late 16th cent.: f[...] Christian Latin *judaizare,* from Greek *ioudaize*[...]om *Ioudaios* (see **JEW**). **—Ju·da·i·za·tion** /ˌjōōdē-[...]Hən; -dā-/ *n.* **—Ju·da·iz·er** *n.*

Ju·das[1] /ˈjōōdəs/ an Apostle; full n[...] *Judas Iscariot.* He betrayed Jesus to the Jewish au[...]ities in return for thirty pieces of silver; the Go[...]s leave his motives uncertain. Overcome wit[...]morse, he later committed suicide. ■ [as *n.*] (us[...] **Judas**) a person who betrays a friend or comra[...]

Ju·das[2] see **JUDE, ST.**

ju·das /ˈjōōdəs/ (also **judas h**[...] *n.* a peephole in a door. ▷mid 19th cent.: fr[...] *Judas* Iscariot (see **JUDAS**[1]), because of his ass[...]on with betrayal.

Ju·das kiss ▸*n.* an act of be[...]l, esp. one disguised as a gesture of friendshi[...] ▷early 15th cent.: with biblical allusion (Matt. 26[...]o the betrayal of Jesus Christ by Judas Iscariot.

Ju·das Mac·ca·bae·us [...]əˈbēəs/ (died *c.*161 BC), Jewish leader. As the l[...] of a Jewish revolt in Judaea against Antioch[...] Epiphanes from around 167, he recovered J[...]em and rededicated the Temple. He is the hero of the two books of the Maccabees in the Apocrypha.

Ju·das tree ▸*n.* a Mediterranean tree of the pea family, with purple flowers that typically appear before the rounded leaves. • *Cercis siliquastrum,* family Leguminosae.

jud·der /ˈjədər/ ▸*v.* [*intrans.*] *chiefly Brit.* (esp. of something mechanical) shake and vibrate rapidly and with force: *the steering wheel juddered in his hand.*
▸*n.* an instance of rapid and forceful shaking and vibration: *the car gave a judder.* ▷1930s: imitative; compare with **SHUDDER**. **—jud·der·y** *adj.*

Jude, St. /jōōd/ an Apostle; supposedly the brother of James; also known as **Judas**. Thaddaeus is traditionally identified with him. According to tradition, he was martyred in Persia with St. Simon. Feast day (with St. Simon), October 28. ■ the last epistle of the New Testament, ascribed to St. Jude.

Ju·den·rat /ˈyōōdnˌrät/ ▸*n.* (*pl.* **-ra·te** /-ˌrätə/) a council representing a Jewish community, esp. in German-occupied territory during World War II. ▷German, 'Jewish council.'

ju·den·rein /ˈjōōdnˌrīn/ ▸*adj.* from which Jews are excluded (originally with reference to organizations in Nazi Germany). ▷German, 'free of Jews.'

Judeo- (also *chiefly Brit.* **Judaeo-**) ▸*comb. form* Jewish; Jewish and . . . : *Judaeo-Christian.* ■ relating to Judaea. ▷from Latin *Judaeus* 'Jewish.'

Ju·dez·mo /jōōˈdezmō/ ▸*n.* another term for **LADINO**.

Judg. ▸*abbr. Bible* Judges.

judge /j[...]/ ▸*n.* a public official appointed to decide cases in a law court. ■ a person who decides the results of a competition. ■ an official at a sports contest who watches for infractions of the rules. ■ a person able or qualified to give an opinion on something: *she was a* ***good judge of*** *character.* ■ a leader having temporary authority in ancient Israel in the period between Joshua and the kings. See also **JUDGES**.
▸*v.* [*trans.*] form an opinion or conclusion about: *scientists were judged according to competence* | [with *clause*] *it's hard to judge whether such opposition is justified* | [*intrans.*] ***judging from*** *his letters home, Monty was in good spirits.* ■ decide (a case) in a law court: *other cases were judged by tribunal.* ■ [*trans.*] give a verdict on (someone) in a law court: *she was judged innocent of murder.* ■ decide the results of (a competition). ▷Middle English: from Old French *juge* (noun), *juger* (verb), from Latin *judex, judic-,* from *jus* 'law' + *dicere* 'to say.' **—judge·ship** /-ˌSHip/ *n.*

judge ad·vo·cate ▸*n. Law* a lawyer who advises a court-martial on points of law and sums up the case.

judge ad·vo·cate gen·er·al ▸*n.* an officer in supreme control of the courts-martial of one of the armed forces.

judge-made ▸*adj. Law* constituted by judicial decisions rather than explicit legislation.

judge·ment ▸*n.* variant spelling of **JUDGMENT**.

judge·men·tal ▸*adj.* variant spelling of **JUDGMENTAL**.

Judg·es /ˈjəjiz/ the seventh book of the Bible, describing the conquest of Canaan under the leaders called "judges" in an account that is parallel to that of the Book of Joshua. The book includes the stories of Deborah, Gideon, Jephthah, and Samson.

judg·ment /ˈjəjmənt/ (also **judge·ment**) ▸*n.* **1** the ability to make considered decisions or come to sensible conclusions: *an error of judgment | that is not,* ***in my judgment,*** *the end of the matter.* ■ an opinion or conclusion: *they make subjective judgments about children's skills.* ■ a decision of a law court or judge. ■ a monetary or other obligation awarded by a court: *a lower court decision upholding the $100,000 judgment.* ■ the document recording this obligation. ■ short for **LAST JUDGMENT**. **2** a misfortune or calamity viewed as a divine punishment: *the crash had been a* ***judgment on*** *the parents for wickedness.* ▷Middle English: from Old French *jugement,* from *juger* 'to judge.'

▸*PHRASES* □ **against one's better judgment** contrary to what one believes to be wise or sensible. □ **pass judgment** (of a law court or judge) give a decision concerning a defendant or legal matter: *he* ***passed judgment on*** *the accused.* ■ criticize or condemn someone from a position of assumed moral superiority. □ **reserve judgment** delay the process of judging or giving one's opinion. □ **sit in judgment** assume the right to judge someone, esp. in a critical manner.

USAGE In British English, the normal spelling in general contexts is **judgement**. However, the spelling **judgment** is conventional in legal contexts, and standard in North American English.

J

judg·men·tal /jəj'mentl/ (also **judge·men·tal**) ▶*adj.* of or concerning the use of judgment: *judgmental errors.* ■ having or displaying an excessively critical point of view: *I don't like to sound judgmental, but it was a big mistake.* —**judg·men·tal·ly** *adv.*

Judg·ment Day ▶*n.* the time of the Last Judgment; the end of the world.

judg·ment in de·fault ▶*n. Law* judgment awarded to the plaintiff on the defendant's failure to plead.

Judg·ment of Sol·o·mon (in the Bible) the arbitration of King Solomon over a baby claimed by two women (1 Kings 3:16–28). He proposed cutting the baby in half, and then gave it to the woman who showed concern for its life.

ju·di·ca·ture /'jo͞odikə,cho͝or; -,kācHər/ ▶*n.* the administration of justice. ■ (**the judicature**) judges collectively; the judiciary. ▷mid 16th cent.: from medieval Latin *judicatura*, from Latin *judicare* 'to judge.' —**ju·di·ca·to·ry** /-kə,tôrē/ *adj.*

ju·di·cial /jo͞o'disHəl/ ▶*adj.* of, by, or appropriate to a law court or judge: *a judicial inquiry into the allegations | a judicial system.* ▷late Middle English: from Latin *judicialis*, from *judicium* 'judgment,' from *judex* (see JUDGE). —**ju·di·cial·ly** *adv.*

USAGE **Judicial** means 'relating to judgment and the administration of justice': *the judicial system; judicial robes.* Do not confuse it with **judicious**, which means 'prudent, reasonable': *getting off the highway the minute you felt tired was a judicious choice.* **Judiciary** refers to the judicial branch of government, the court system, or judges collectively.

ju·di·cial re·view ▶*n.* review by the U.S. Supreme Court of the constitutional validity of a legislative act. ■ (in the UK) a procedure by which a court can review an administrative action by a public body and (in England) secure a declaration, order, or award.

ju·di·cial sep·a·ra·tion ▶*n.* another term for LEGAL SEPARATION (sense 1).

ju·di·ci·ar·y /jo͞o'disHē,erē; -'disHərē/ ▶*n.* (*pl.* **-ar·ies**) (usu. **the judiciary**) the judicial authorities of a country; judges collectively. ▷early 19th cent.: from Latin *judiciarius*, from *judicium* 'judgment.'

USAGE See usage at JUDICIAL.

ju·di·cious /jo͞o'disHəs/ ▶*adj.* having, showing, or done with good judgment or sense: *the efficient and judicious use of pesticides.* ▷late 16th cent.: from French *judicieux*, from Latin *judicium* 'judgment' (see JUDICIAL). —**ju·di·cious·ly** *adv.* —**ju·di·cious·ness** *n.*

USAGE See usage at JUDICIAL.

Ju·dith /'jo͞odəTH/ (in the Apocrypha) a rich Israelite widow who saved the town of Bethulia from Nebuchadnezzar's army by seducing the besieging general Holofernes and cutting off his head while he slept. ■ a book of the Apocrypha recounting the story of Judith.

ju·do /'jo͞odō/ ▶*n.* a sport of unarmed combat derived from jujitsu and intended to train the body and mind. It involves using holds and leverage to unbalance the opponent. ▷late 19th cent.: Japanese, from *jū* 'gentle' + *dō* 'way.' —**ju·do·ist** /-ist/ *n.*

ju·do·ka /'jo͞odō,kä; ,jo͞odō'kä/ ▶*n.* a person who practices or is an expert in judo. ▷Japanese, from JUDO + *-ka* 'person, profession.'

Ju·dy /'jo͞odē/ ▶*n.* (*pl.* **-dies**) the wife of Punch in the Punch and Judy show. ▷early 19th cent.: nickname for the given name *Judith.*

jug /jəg/ ▶*n.* **1** a large container for liquids, with a narrow mouth and typically a stopper or cap. ■ the contents of such a container: *she gave us a big* **jug of** *water.* **2** (**the jug**) *informal* prison: *three months* **in the** *jug.* **3** (**jugs**) *vulgar slang* a woman's breasts. **4** (also **jug han·dle**) *Climbing* a secure hold that is cut into rock for climbing.

▶*v.* (**jugged, jug·ging**) [*trans.*] **1** [usu. as *adj.*] (**jugged**) stew or boil (a hare or rabbit) in a covered container: *jugged hare.* **2** *informal* prosecute and imprison (someone). ▷mid 16th cent.: perhaps from *Jug*, nickname for the given names *Joan, Joanna*, and *Jenny.* —**jug·ful** /-,fo͝ol/ *n.* (*pl.* **-fuls**).

ju·gal /'jo͞ogəl/ ▶*adj.* **1** *Anatomy* of or relating to the zygoma (the bony arch of the cheek). **2** *Entomology* of or relating to the jugum of an insect's forewing. ▷late 16th cent.: from Latin *jugalis*, from *jugum* 'yoke.'

jug band ▶*n.* a group of jazz, blues, or folk musicians using simple or improvised instruments such as jugs and washboards.

Ju·gend·stil /'yo͞ogənt,sHtēl/ ▶*n.* German term for ART NOUVEAU. ▷German, from *Jugend* 'youth' + *Stil* 'style.'

Jug·ger·naut /'jəgər,nôt/ *Hinduism* the form of Krishna worshiped in Puri, Orissa, where in the annual festival his image is dragged through the streets on a heavy chariot; devotees are said formerly to have thrown themselves under its wheels. Also called JAGANNATHA. ▷via Hindi from Sanskrit *Jagannātha* 'Lord of the world.'

jug·ger·naut /'jəgər,nôt/ ▶*n.* a huge, powerful, and overwhelming force or institution: *a juggernaut of secular and commercial culture.* ▷mid 19th cent.: extension of JUGGERNAUT.

jug·gle /'jəgəl/ ▶*v.* [*trans.*] continuously toss into the air and catch (a number of objects) so as to keep at least one in the air while handling the others, typically for the entertainment of others. ■ cope with by adroitly balancing: *she works full time,* **juggling** *her career* **with** *raising children.* ■ misrepresent (something) so as to deceive or cheat someone: *defense chiefs juggled the figures on bomb tests.*

▶*n.* [in *sing.*] an act of juggling. ▷late Middle English (in the sense 'entertain with jesting, tricks, etc.'): back-formation from *juggler*, or from Old French *jogler*, from Latin *joculari* 'to jest,' from *joculus*, diminutive of *jocus* 'jest.' Current senses date from the late 19th cent. —**jug·gler** /'jəg(ə)lər/ *n.* —**jug·gler·y** /'jəglərē/ *n.*

jug·u·lar /'jəgyələr/ ▶*adj.* **1** of the neck or throat. **2** *Zoology* (of fish's pelvic fins) located in front of the pectoral fins.

▶*n.* short for JUGULAR VEIN. ▷late 16th cent.: from late Latin *jugularis*, from Latin *jugulum* 'collarbone, throat,' diminutive of *jugum* 'yoke.'

▶*PHRASE* □ **go for the jugular** be aggressive or unrestrained in making an attack.

jug·u·lar vein ▶*n.* any of several large veins in the neck, carrying blood from the head and face.

jug·u·late /'jəgyə,lāt/ ▶*v.* [*trans.*] *archaic* kill (someone) by cutting the throat. ▷early 17th cent.: from Latin *jugulat-* 'slain by a cut to the throat,' from the verb *jugulare*, from *jugulum* 'throat' (see JUGULAR).

ju·gum /'jo͞ogəm/ ▶*n.* (*pl.* **-ga** /-gə/) *chiefly Zoology* a connecting ridge or projection. ■ *Entomology* a lobe on the forewing of some moths which interlocks with the hind wing in flight. ▷mid 19th cent.: from Latin, literally 'yoke.'

Ju·gur·tha /jo͞o'gərTHə/ (died 104 BC), joint king of Numidia *c.*118–104. His attacks on his royal partners prompted intervention by Rome and led to the outbreak of the Jugurthine War (112–105). Eventually captured by the Roman general Marius, he was executed in Rome. —**Ju·gur·thine** /-'gərTHən/ *adj.*

juice /jo͞os/ ▶*n.* the liquid obtained from or present in fruit or vegetables: *add the juice of a lemon.* ■ a drink made from such a liquid: *a carton of orange juice.* ■ (**juices**) fluid secreted by the body, esp. in the stomach to help digest food. ■ (**juices**) the liquid that comes from meat or other food when cooked. ■ *informal* electrical energy: *the batteries have run out of juice.* ■ *informal* gasoline: *he ran out of juice on the last lap.* ■ *informal* alcoholic drink. ■ (**juices**) a person's vitality or creative faculties: *it saps the creative juices.*

▶*v.* [*trans.*] **1** extract the juice from (fruit or vegetables): *juice one orange at a time.* **2** (**juice something up**) *informal* liven something up: *they juiced it up with some love interest.* **3** [as *adj.*] (**juiced**) *informal* drunk. ▷Middle English: via Old French from Latin *jus* 'broth, vegetable juice.' —**juice·less** *adj.*

juice box ▶*n.* a small disposable carton containing a single serving of fruit juice or fruit drink: *only juice boxes (no cans, no bottles) are allowed in the cafeteria.*

juic·er /'jo͞osər/ ▶*n.* **1** an appliance for extracting juice from fruit and vegetables. **2** *informal* a person who drinks alcoholic beverages excessively.

juic·y /'jo͞osē/ ▶*adj.* (**juic·i·er, juic·i·est**) (of food) full of juice; succulent: *a juicy apple | a juicy steak.* ■ *informal* interestingly scandalous: *juicy gossip.* ■ *informal* temptingly appealing: *the promise of juicy returns.* —**juic·i·ly** /-səlē/ *adv.* —**juic·i·ness** *n.*

Juil·li·ard /'jo͞olē,ärd/, Augustus D. (1840–1919), U.S. merchant and patron of music. In 1920 he founded the Juilliard Musical Foundation, which became the Juilliard School of Music in 1926.

ju·jit·su /,jo͞o'jitso͞o/ (also **jiu·jit·su** or **ju·jut·su** /,jo͞o'jət-/) ▶*n.* a Japanese system of unarmed combat and physical training. Compare with JUDO. ▷Japanese *jūjutsu*, from *jū* 'gentle' + *jutsu* 'skill.'

ju·ju[1] /'jo͞o,jo͞o/ ▶*n.* a style of music popular among the Yoruba in Nigeria and characterized by the use of guitars and variable-pitch drums. ▷perhaps from Yoruba *jo jo* 'dance.'

ju·ju[2] ▶*n.* a charm or fetish, esp. of a type used by some West African peoples. ■ supernatural power attributed to such a charm or fetish: *juju and witchcraft.* ▷early 17th cent.: of West African origin, perhaps from French *joujou* 'toy.'

ju·jube /'jo͞o,jo͞ob/ ▶*n.* **1** the edible berrylike fruit of a Eurasian plant, formerly taken as a cough cure. ■ a jujube-flavored lozenge or gumdrop. **2** (also **jujube bush**) the shrub or small tree that produces this fruit, native to the warmer regions of Eurasia. • *Ziziphus jujuba*, family Rhamnaceae. ▷late Middle English: from French, or from medieval Latin *jujuba*, based on Greek *zizuphos.*

juke /jo͞ok/ *informal* ▶*n.* **1** short for JUKE JOINT. **2** short for JUKEBOX.

▶*v.* [*intrans.*] **1** dance, especially to the music of a jukebox: *a middle-aged couple juked to the music.* **2** move in a zigzag fashion: *I juked down an alley.* ▷1930s: related to Gullah *juke* 'disorderly.'

juke·box /'jo͞ok,bäks/ ▶*n.* a machine that automatically plays a selected musical recording when a coin is inserted. ■ *Computing* a device that stores several computer disks in such a way that data can be read from any of them. ▷1930s: from *juke* 'roadhouse' (related to Gullah *juke* 'disorderly') + BOX[1].

juke joint ▶*n.* a bar featuring music on a jukebox and typically having an area for dancing: *she would slip out of the house with tall country boys . . . going out to good-time, finger popping juke joints.*

ju·ku /'jo͞oko͞o/ ▶*n.* (*pl.* same) (in Japan) a private school or college attended in addition to an ordinary educational institution. ▷Japanese.

Jul. ▶*abbr.* July.

ju·lep /'jo͞oləp/ ▶*n.* a sweet flavored drink made from a sugar syrup, sometimes containing alcohol or medication. ■ short for MINT JULEP. ▷late Middle English: from Old French, from medieval Latin *julapium*, via Arabic from Persian *gulāb*, from *gul* 'rose' + *āb* 'water.'

jul·ia /'jo͞olyə/ ▶*n.* an orange and black American butterfly with long narrow forewings, found chiefly in tropical regions. • *Dryas julia*, subfamily Heliconiinae, family Nymphalidae.

Jul·ian[1] /'jo͞olyən; -lēən/ ▶*adj.* of or associated with Julius Caesar. ▷from Latin *Julianus*, from the given name *Julius.*

Jul·ian[2] (*c.*AD 331–363), Roman emperor 360–363; nephew of Constantine; full name *Flavius Claudius Julianus*; known as **the Apostate**. He restored paganism as the state cult in place of Christianity, but this was reversed after his death.

Ju·li·an·a /jo͞olē'anə; -'änə/ (1909–2004), queen of the Netherlands 1948–80; full name *Juliana Louise Emma Marie Wilhelmina.* She was the daughter of Queen Wilhelmina and the mother of Queen Beatrix, in whose favor she abdicated.

Ju·lian Alps an Alpine range in western Slovenia and northeastern Italy. The highest peak is Triglav.

Jul·ian cal·en·dar ▶*n.* a calendar introduced by the authority of Julius Caesar in 46 BC, in which the year consisted of 365 days, every fourth year having 366 days. It was superseded by the Gregorian calendar though it is still used by some Orthodox Churches. Dates in the Julian calendar are sometimes designated "Old Style."

Jul·ian of Nor·wich (*c.*1342–*c.*1413), English mystic. She is said to have lived as a recluse outside St. Julian's Church in Norwich and is chiefly associated with the *Revelations of Divine Love* (*c.*1393), a description of a series of visions.

Jul·ia set /'jo͞olyə/ ▶*n. Mathematics* a set of complex numbers that do not converge to any limit when a given mapping is repeatedly applied to them. In some cases the result is a connected fractal set. ▷1970s: named after Gaston M. *Julia* (1893–1978), Algerian-born French mathematician.

ju·li·enne /,jo͞olē'en/ ▶*n.* a portion of food cut into short, thin strips: *a julienne of vegetables* | [as *adj.*] *julienne leeks.*

▶*v.* [*trans.*] cut (food) into short, thin strips. ▷early 18th cent. (originally as an adjective designating soup made of chopped vegetables, esp. carrots): French, from the male given names *Jules* or *Julien*, of obscure development.

Pronunciation Key ə *ago*; ər *over*; 'ə or ,ə *up*; 'ər or ,ər *fur*; a *hat*; ā *rate*; ä *car*; CH *chew*; e *let*; ē *see*; e(ə)r *air*; i *fit*; ī *by*; i(ə)r *ear*; NG *sing*; ō *go*; ô *for*; oi *boy*; o͝o *good*; o͞o *goo*; ou *out*; SH *she*; TH *thin*; TH *then*; (h)w *why*; ZH *vision*

J

Ju·li·et /ˌjo͞olēˈet; ˈjo͞olyət/ ▸*n.* a code word representing the letter J, used in radio communication.

Ju·li·et cap ▸*n.* a type of women's small ornamental cap, typically made of lace or net and often worn by brides. ▷early 20th cent.: so named because it forms part of the traditional costume of the heroine of Shakespeare's *Romeo and Juliet*.

Jul·ius Cae·sar /ˈjo͞olyəs/ see **CAESAR** [2].

Jul·lun·dur /ˈjələndər/ (also **Ja·lan·dhar**) a city in northwestern India, in Punjab; pop. 520,000.

Ju·ly /jo͝oˈlī/ ▸*n.* (*pl.* **Ju·lys**) the seventh month of the year, in the northern hemisphere usually considered the second month of summer: *I had a letter from him in July* | [as *adj.*] *one hot July afternoon in 1981.* ▷Middle English: from Latin *Julius (mensis)* '(month) of July,' named after Julius Caesar.

ju·mar /ˈjo͞omər; -ˌmär/ *Climbing* ▸*n.* a clamp that is attached to a fixed rope and automatically tightens when weight is applied and relaxes when it is removed.
▸*v.* (**-mared, -mar·ing**) [*intrans.*] climb with the aid of such a clamp. ▷1960s: originally in Swiss use, of unknown origin.

jum·bie /ˈjəmbē/ ▸*n.* *W. Indian* a spirit of a dead person, typically an evil one. ▷from Kikongo *zumbi* 'fetish.'

jum·bie bird ▸*n.* *W. Indian* a bird of ill omen, esp. a pygmy owl. • *Glaucidium brasilianum*, family Strigidae. Alternative name: **ferruginous pygmy owl**.

jum·ble /ˈjəmbəl/ ▸*n.* an untidy collection or pile of things: *the books were in a chaotic jumble.* ■ *Brit.* articles collected for a jumble sale.
▸*v.* [*trans.*] mix up in a confused or untidy way: *a drawer full of letters* ***jumbled together***. ▷early 16th cent.: probably symbolic.

THE RIGHT WORD **confusion, conglomeration, disarray, farrago, hodgepodge, jumble, mélange, muddle**

Confusion is a very broad term, applying to any indiscriminate mixing or mingling that makes it difficult to distinguish individual elements or parts (*a confusion of languages*).

The typical teenager's bedroom is usually a **jumble** of books, papers, clothing, CDs, and soda cans—the word suggests physical disorder and a mixture of dissimilar things.

If the disorder exists on a figurative level, it is usually called a **hodgepodge** (*a hodgepodge of ideas, opinions, and quotations, with a few facts thrown in for good measure*).

Conglomeration refers to a collection of dissimilar things, but with a suggestion that the collection is random or inappropriate (*a conglomeration of decorating styles*).

A **mélange** can be a mixture of foods (*add peppers or zucchini to the mélange*), but it can also be used in a derogatory way (*an error-filled mélange of pseudoscience, religion, and fanciful ideas*).

A **farrago** is an irrational or confused mixture of elements and is usually worse than a *conglomeration* (*a farrago of doubts, fears, hopes, and desires*), while a **muddle** is less serious and suggests confused thinking and lack of organization (*their bank records were in a complete muddle*).

Disarray implies disarrangement and is most appropriately used when order or discipline has been lost (*his unexpected appearance threw the meeting into disarray*).

J

jum·ble sale ▸*n.* *Brit.* a rummage sale.

jum·bo /ˈjəmbō/ *informal* ▸*n.* (*pl.* **-bos**) a very large person or thing. ■ (also **jum·bo jet**) a very large airliner (originally and specifically a Boeing 747).
▸*adj.* [*attrib.*] very large: *a jumbo pad.* ▷early 19th cent. (originally of a person): probably the second element of **MUMBO-JUMBO**. Originally denoting a large and clumsy person, the term was popularized as the name of an elephant at London Zoo, sold in 1882 to the Barnum and Bailey circus.

Jum·na /ˈjəmnə/ a river in northern India that rises in the Himalayas and flows more than 850 miles (1,370 km) in a large arc south and southeast, through Delhi, before joining the Ganges River below Allahabad. Its source (Yamunotri River) and its confluence with the Ganges River are both Hindu holy places. Hindi name **YAMUNA**.

jump /jəmp/ ▸*v.* **1** [*intrans.*] push oneself off a surface and into the air by using the muscles in one's legs and feet: *the cat jumped off his lap* | *he jumped twenty-five feet to the ground.* ■ [*trans.*] pass over (an obstacle or barrier) in such a way. ■ [with *adverbial*] (of an athlete or horse) perform in a competition involving such action: *his horse jumped well and won by five lengths.* ■ (esp. of prices or figures) rise suddenly and by a large amount: *exports jumped by 500 percent during the decade.* ■ *informal* (of a place) be full of lively activity: *the bar is jumping on Fridays and Saturdays.* ■ [*trans.*] *informal* (of driver or a vehicle) fail to stop at (a red traffic light). ■ [*trans.*] get on or off (a train or other vehicle) quickly, typically illegally or dangerously. ■ [*trans.*] take summary possession of (a mining concession or other piece of land) after alleged abandonment or forfeiture by the former occupant. **2** [*intrans.*] (of a person) move suddenly and quickly in a specified way: *Juliet* ***jumped to her feet*** | *they jumped back into the car and drove off.* ■ (of a person) make a sudden involuntary movement in reaction to something that causes surprise or shock: *an owl hooted nearby, making her jump.* ■ pass quickly or abruptly from one idea, subject, or state to another: *she jumped backward and forward in her narrative.* ■ [*trans.*] omit or skip over (part of something) and pass on to a further point or stage. ■ (of a machine or device) move or jerk suddenly and abruptly: *the vibration can cause the needle to jump.* ■ (of a person) make a sudden, impulsive rush to do something: *Gordon jumped to my defense.* ■ [*trans.*] (in checkers) capture (an opponent's piece) by jumping over it. ■ *Bridge* make a bid that is higher than necessary, in order to signal a strong hand: *East jumped to four spades.* ■ [*trans.*] *informal* attack (someone) suddenly and unexpectedly. ■ [*trans.*] *vulgar slang* have sexual intercourse with (someone). **3** [*trans.*] *informal* start (a vehicle) using jumper cables: *I jumped his Camry from my Civic.*
▸*phrasal v.* □ **jump at** accept (an opportunity or offer) eagerly: *he* ***jumped at the chance*** *to start his own company.* □ **jump off** (of a military campaign) begin: *the air-attack phase will continue before the ground attack jumps off.* □ **jump on** *informal* attack or take hold of (someone) suddenly.■ criticize (someone) suddenly and severely. ■ seize on (something) eagerly; give sudden (typically critical) attention to: *the paper jumped on the inconsistencies of his stories.* □ **jump out** have a strong visual or mental impact; be very striking: *advertising posters that really* ***jump out at*** *you.*
▸*n.* **1** an act of jumping from a surface by pushing upward with one's legs and feet: *in making the short jump across the gully he lost his balance.* ■ an obstacle to be jumped, esp. by a horse and rider in an equestrian competition. ■ an act of descending from an aircraft by parachute. ■ a sudden dramatic rise in amount, price, or value: *a 51 percent jump in annual profits.* ■ a large or sudden transition or change: *the jump from mass-market to luxury goods.* ■ (in checkers) the act of capturing an opponent's piece by jumping over it. ■ *Bridge* a bid that is higher than necessary, signaling strength. ■ *vulgar slang, dated* an act of sexual intercourse. **2** a sudden involuntary movement caused by shock or surprise: *I woke up with a jump.* ■ (**the jumps**) *informal* extreme nervousness or anxiety. ▷early 16th cent. (in the sense 'be moved or thrown with a sudden jerk'): probably imitative of the sound of feet coming into contact with the ground. —**jump·a·ble** *adj.*
▸*PHRASES* □ **be jumping up and down** *informal* be very angry, upset, or excited. □ **get** (or **have**) **the jump on someone** *informal* get (or have) an advantage over someone as a result of one's prompt action. □ **jump bail** see **BAIL**[1]. □ **jump someone's bones** *vulgar slang* have sexual intercourse with someone. □ **jump down someone's throat** *informal* respond to what someone has said in a sudden and angrily critical way. □ **jump for joy** be ecstatically happy: *I'm not exactly jumping for joy at the prospect.* □ **jump the gun** see **GUN**. □ **jump into bed with** *informal* engage readily in sexual intercourse with. □ **jump in with both feet** get started enthusiastically. □ **jump on the bandwagon** see **BANDWAGON**. □ **jump out of one's skin** *informal* be extremely startled. □ **jump the queue** *Brit.* cut in line. □ **jump rope** play or exercise using a jump rope. □ **jump ship** (of a sailor) leave the ship on which one is serving without having obtained permission to do so: *he jumped ship in Cape Town* | *figurative three producers jumped ship two weeks after the show's debut.* □ **jump through hoops** go through an elaborate or complicated procedure in order to achieve an objective. □ **jump** (or **leap**) **to conclusions** (or **the conclusion**) form an opinion hastily, before one has learned or considered all the facts. □ **jump to it!** *informal* used to exhort someone to prompt or immediate action. □ **jump the track** (of a train) become derailed. □ **one jump ahead** one step or stage ahead of someone else and so having the advantage over them: *the Americans were* ***one jump ahead of*** *the British in this.*

jump ball ▸*n.* *Basketball* a ball put in play by the referee, who throws it up between two opposing players.

jump blues ▸*n.* a style of popular music combining elements of swing and blues.

jump cut ▸*n.* (in film or television) an abrupt transition from one scene to another.
▸*v.* (**jump-cut**) [*intrans.*] make such a transition.

jumped-up ▸*adj.* *informal, chiefly Brit.* denoting someone who considers themselves to be more important than they really are, or who has suddenly and undeservedly risen in status: *she's not really a journalist, more a jumped-up PR woman.*

jump·er[1] /ˈjəmpər/ ▸*n.* **1** a collarless sleeveless dress, typically worn over a blouse. **2** *Brit.* a sweater. **3** *historical* a loose outer jacket worn by sailors. ▷mid 19th cent. (sense 3): probably from dialect *jump* 'short coat,' perhaps from Scots *jupe* 'a man's (later also a woman's) loose jacket or tunic,' via Old French from Arabic *jubba*. Compare with **JIBBA**.

jumper[1] 1

jump·er[2] ▸*n.* **1** a person or animal that jumps. **2** (also **jumper wire**) a short wire used to complete an electric circuit or bypass a break in a circuit. **3** *Basketball* another term for **JUMP SHOT**. **4** *Nautical* a rope made fast to keep a yard or mast from jumping. **5** a heavy chisel-ended steel bar for drilling blast holes.

jump·er ca·ble ▸*n.* each of a pair of thick electric cables fitted with clips at either end, used for starting a vehicle by connecting its dead battery to the battery of another vehicle.

jump·ing bean ▸*n.* a plant seed that jumps as a result of the movement of a moth larva that is developing inside it. • Affected seeds are found in several plants of the family Euphorbiaceae, in particular the Mexican plant *Sebastiana pavoniana*, the seeds of which can contain larvae of the moth *Cydia saltitans*.

jump·ing gene ▸*n.* informal term for **TRANSPOSON**.

jump·ing jack ▸*n.* **1** a calisthenic jump done from a standing position with legs together and arms at the sides to a position with the legs apart and the arms over the head. **2** a toy figure of a man, with movable limbs.

jump·ing Je·hosh·a·phat ▸*exclam.* see **JEHOSHAPHAT**.

jump·ing mouse ▸*n.* a mouselike rodent that has long back feet and typically moves in short hops, found in North America and China. • Family Zapodidae: three genera, in particular *Zapus*, and several species.

jump·ing-off place (also **jump·ing-off point**) ▸*n.* the point from which something is begun.

jump·ing spi·der ▸*n.* a large-eyed spider that hunts prey by stalking and pouncing on it. • Family Salticidae, order Araneae.

jump in·struc·tion ▸*n.* *Computing* an instruction in a computer program that causes processing to move to a different place in the program sequence.

jump jet ▸*n.* a jet aircraft that can take off and land vertically, without need of a runway.

jump lead /lēd/ ▸*n.* British term for **JUMPER CABLE**.

jump-off ▸*n.* a deciding round in a show-jumping competition.

jump ring ▸*n.* a wire ring made by bringing the two ends together without soldering or welding.

jump rope (also **jump·rope**) ▸*n.* a length of rope used for jumping by swinging it over the head and under the feet.

jump seat ▸*n.* an extra seat, esp. in a car or taxicab, that folds back when not in use.

jump shift ▸*n.* *Bridge* a bid that is both in a different suit from that bid by oneself or one's partner and at a higher level than necessary, typically indicating a strong hand.

jump shot ▸*n.* **1** *Basketball* a shot made while jumping. **2** *Billiards* a shot in which the cue ball is made to jump over another ball. —**jump shoot·er** *n.* (in sense 1).

jump-start ▸*v.* [*trans.*] start (a car with a dead battery) with jumper cables or by a sudden release of the clutch while it is being pushed. ■ *figurative* give an added impetus to (something that is proceeding slowly or is at a standstill): *she suggests ways to jump-start the sluggish educational system.*
▸*n.* an act of starting a car in such a way. ■ *figurative* an added impetus.

jump·sta·tion /ˈjəmp ˌstāSHən/ ▸*n. Computing* a site on the World Wide Web containing a collection of hypertext links, usually to pages on a particular topic.

jump·suit /ˈjəm(p)ˌso͞ot/ ▸*n.* a garment incorporating trousers and a sleeved top in one piece, worn as a fashion item, protective garment, or uniform. ▷1940s (originally U.S.): so named because it was first used to denote a parachutist's garment.

jump the shark /ˈjəmp T͟Hə ˈSHärk/ ▸*v. phr. informal* pass the peak of creativity, excellence, or inspiration, as evidenced by a decline in quality or performance: *He's like "The Simpson's." He's never jumped the shark.* ▷with allusion to an episode in 1977 of the television series *Happy Days,* in which a central character (the Fonz) jumps over a shark on water skis.

jump-up ▸*n.* **1** a jump in an upward direction. **2** an informal Caribbean dance or celebration.

jump·y /ˈjəmpē/ ▸*adj.* (**jump·i·er, jump·i·est**) *informal* (of a person) anxious and uneasy: *he was tired and jumpy.* ■ characterized by abrupt stops and starts or an irregular course: *a jumpy pulse.* **—jump·i·ly** /-pəlē/ *adv.* **—jump·i·ness** *n.*

jun /CHən/ ▸*n.* (*pl.* same) a monetary unit of North Korea, equal to one hundredth of a won. ▷Korean.

Jun. ▸*abbr.* ■ June. ■ Junior (in names): *John Smith Jun.*

junc. (also **Junc.**) ▸*abbr.* Junction.

jun·co /ˈjəNGkō/ ▸*n.* (*pl.* **-cos**) a North American songbird related to the buntings, with mainly gray and brown plumage. See also SNOWBIRD. • Genus *Junco,* family Emberizidae (subfamily Emberizinae): three or four species. ▷early 18th cent.: from Spanish, from Latin *juncus* 'rush, reed.'

junc·tion /ˈjəNGkSHən/ ▸*n.* **1** a point where two or more things are joined: *the junction of the two rivers.* ■ a place where two or more roads or railroad lines meet. **2** *Electronics* a region of transition in a semiconductor between a part where conduction is mainly by electrons and a part where it is mainly by holes. **3** the action or fact of joining or being joined. ▷early 18th cent. (sense 3): from Latin *junctio(n-),* from *jungere* 'to join.' **—junc·tion·al** /-SHənl/ *adj.*

junc·tion box ▸*n.* a box containing a junction of electric wires or cables.

junc·ture /ˈjəNGkCHər/ ▸*n.* a particular point in events or time: *it is difficult to say at this juncture whether this upturn can be sustained.* ■ a place where things join: *the plane crashed at the juncture of two mountains.* ■ *Phonetics* the set of features in speech that enable a hearer to detect a word or phrase boundary, e.g., distinguishing *I scream* from *ice cream.* ▷late Middle English (in the sense 'act of joining'): from Latin *junctura* 'joint,' from *jungere* 'to join.'

June /jo͞on/ ▸*n.* the sixth month of the year, in the northern hemisphere usually considered the first month of summer: *the roses flower in June* | [as *adj.*] *a June afternoon.* ▷Middle English: from Old French *juin,* from Latin *Junius (mensis)* '(month) of June,' variant of *Junonius* 'sacred to Juno.'

Ju·neau /ˈjo͞onō/ the capital of Alaska, a seaport on an inlet of the Pacific Ocean, in the southern part of the state; pop. 30,711. ▷named after Joseph *Juneau,* who discovered gold there in 1880.

june·ber·ry /ˈjo͞onˌberē/ (also **June·ber·ry**) ▸*n.* (*pl.* **-ries**) a North American shrub of the rose family, some kinds of which are grown for their showy white flowers and bright autumn colors. • Genus *Amelanchier,* family Rosaceae: many species, including the **smooth juneberry** (*A. laevis*) and the **inland juneberry** (*A. interior*). ■ the black edible berry of this plant.

June bug (also **June bee·tle**) ▸*n.* a large brown scarab beetle that appears in late spring and early summer. Also called MAY BEETLE. • Genus *Phyllophaga,* family Scarabaeidae: several species, esp. the **northern June bug** (*P. fusca*).

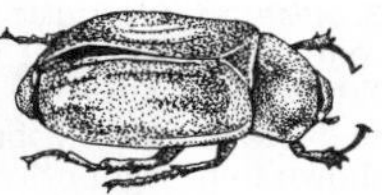
northern June bug

June·teenth /ˌjo͞onˈtēnTH/ ▸*n.* a festival held annually on the nineteenth of June by African Americans (especially in the southern states), to commemorate emancipation from slavery in Texas on that day in 1865. ▷1930s: blend of *June* and *(nine)teenth.*

June War Arab name for SIX-DAY WAR.

Jung /yo͝oNG/, Carl (Gustav) (1875–1961), Swiss psychologist. He originated the concept of introvert and extrovert personality and of the four psychological functions of sensation, intuition, thinking, and feeling. **—Jung·i·an** /ˈyo͝oNGgēən/ *adj.* & *n.*

jun·gle /ˈjəNGgəl/ ▸*n.* **1** an area of land overgrown with dense forest and tangled vegetation, typically in the tropics: *we set off into the jungle* | *the lakes are hidden in dense jungle.* ■ a wild tangled mass of vegetation or other things: *the garden was* ***a jungle of*** *bluebells.* ■ a situation or place of bewildering complexity or brutal competitiveness: *it's a jungle out there.* ■ (also **hobo jungle**) *informal* a hobo camp. **2** (also **jungle music**) a style of dance music incorporating elements of ragga, hip-hop, and hard core and consisting almost exclusively of very fast electronic drum tracks and slower synthesized bass lines, originating in Britain in the early 1990s. Compare with DRUM AND BASS. ▷late 18th cent.: via Hindi from Sanskrit *jāṅgala* 'rough and arid (terrain).' **—jun·gled** *adj.* **—jun·gly** *adj.*

▸*PHRASE* □ **the law of the jungle** the principle that those who are strong and apply ruthless self-interest will be most successful.

jun·gle cat ▸*n.* a small wildcat that has a yellowish or grayish coat with dark markings on the legs and tail, living in dry forests from Egypt to Southeast Asia. • *Felis chaus,* family Felidae.

jun·gle fe·ver ▸*n.* a severe form of malaria.

jun·gle fowl ▸*n.* (*pl.* same) a southern Asian game bird related to the domestic fowl, typically frequenting forested country. • Genus *Gallus,* family Phasianidae: four species, in particular the **red jungle fowl** (*G. gallus*), which is the ancestor of the domestic fowl.

jun·gle gym ▸*n.* a structure of joined bars or logs for children to climb on. ▷1920s: formerly a U.S. trademark.

jun·gle juice ▸*n. informal* powerful or roughly prepared alcoholic liquor.

jun·glist ▸*n.* a performer or enthusiast of jungle music: *M-Beat, junglists who recently had the genre's first chart hit.*

▸*adj.* of or relating to jungle music: *he's at the forefront of junglist innovation.*

jun·ior /ˈjo͞onyər/ ▸*adj.* **1** of, for, or denoting young or younger people: *junior tennis.* ■ of or for students in the third year of a course lasting four years in college or high school: *his junior year in college.* ■ (often **Junior**) [*postpositive*] [in *names*] denoting the younger of two who have the same name in a family, esp. a son as distinct from his father: *John F. Kennedy Junior.* ■ *Brit.* of, for, or denoting schoolchildren between the ages of 7 and 11. **2** low or lower in rank or status: *Virginia's junior senator* | *part of my function is to supervise those* ***junior to*** *me.*

▸*n.* **1** a person who is a specified number of years younger than someone else: *he's five years her junior.* ■ a student in the third year of college or high school. ■ (in sports) a young competitor, typically under sixteen or eighteen. ■ *informal* used as a nickname or form of address for one's son. **2** a person with low rank or status compared with others. **3** a size of clothing for teenagers or slender women. ▷Middle English (as an adjective following a family name): from Latin, comparative of *juvenis* 'young.' **—jun·ior·i·ty** /jo͞onˈyôritē; -ˈyär-/ *n.*

jun·ior bar·ris·ter ▸*n.* (in the UK) a barrister who has not taken silk, i.e., is not a Queen's (or King's) Counsel.

jun·ior col·lege ▸*n.* a college offering courses for two years beyond high school, either as a complete training or in preparation for completion at a four-year college.

jun·ior com·mon room ▸*n. Brit.* a room used for social purposes by the undergraduates of a college.

jun·ior high school ▸*n.* another term for MIDDLE SCHOOL.

jun·ior light·weight ▸*n.* a weight in professional boxing of 125–130 pounds (57.1–59 kg). ■ a professional boxer of this weight.

jun·ior mid·dle·weight ▸*n.* a weight in professional boxing of 146–154 pounds (66.7–69.8 kg). ■ a professional boxer of this weight.

jun·ior school ▸*n. Brit.* a school for children aged between about 7 and 11.

jun·ior wel·ter·weight ▸*n.* a weight in professional boxing of 135–140 pounds (61.2–63.5 kg). ■ a professional boxer of this weight.

ju·ni·per /ˈjo͞onəpər/ ▸*n.* an evergreen shrub or small tree that bears berrylike cones, widely distributed throughout Eurasia and North America. Many kinds have aromatic cones or foliage. • Genus *Juniperus,* family Cupressaceae: many species, including the shrubby **common juniper** (*J. communis*), the berries of which are used for flavoring gin. ▷late Middle English: from Latin *juniperus.*

junk[1] /jəNGk/ ▸*n.* **1** *informal* old or discarded articles that are considered useless or of little value. ■ worthless writing, talk, or ideas: *I can't write this kind of junk.* ■ *Finance* junk bonds. **2** *informal* heroin. **3** the lump of oily fibrous tissue in a sperm whale's head, containing spermaceti.

▸*v.* [*trans.*] *informal* discard or abandon unceremoniously: *sort out what could be sold off and junk the rest.* ▷late Middle English (denoting an old or inferior rope): of unknown origin. Sense 1 dates from the mid 19th cent.

junk[2] ▸*n.* a flat-bottomed sailing vessel typical in China and the East Indies, with a prominent stem, a high stern, and lugsails. ▷mid 16th cent.: from obsolete French *juncque* or Portuguese *junco,* from Malay *jong,* reinforced by Dutch *jonk.*

junk[2]

Junk·a·noo /ˈjəNGkəˌno͞o/ ▸*n.* (chiefly in Jamaica, Belize, and the Bahamas) a masquerade held at Christmas, consisting of a street procession of characters in traditional costumes and dancing to drums, bells, and whistles.

junk bond ▸*n.* a high-yield, high-risk security, typically issued by a company seeking to raise capital quickly in order to finance a takeover.

junk DNA ▸*n.* genomic DNA that does not encode proteins, and whose function, if it has one, is not well understood.

Jun·ker /ˈyo͝oNGkər/ (also **jun·ker**) ▸*n. historical* a German nobleman or aristocrat, esp. a member of the Prussian aristocracy. ▷German, earlier *Junkher,* from Middle High German *junc* 'young' + *herre* 'lord.' **—jun·ker·dom** /-dəm/ *n.* **—jun·ker·ism** /-ˌizəm/ *n.*

jun·ket /ˈjəNGkit/ ▸*n.* **1** a dish of sweetened and flavored curds of milk, often served with fruit. **2** *informal* an extravagant trip or celebration, in particular one enjoyed by a government official at public expense.

▸*v.* (**-ket·ed, -ket·ing**) [*intrans.*] [often as *n.*] (**junketing**) *informal* attend or go on such a trip or celebration. ▷late Middle English: from Old French *jonquette* 'rush basket,' from *jonc* 'rush,' from Latin *juncus.* Originally denoting a rush basket, esp. one for fish (remaining in dialect use), the term also denoted a cream cheese, formerly made in a rush basket or served on a rush mat. A later extended sense, 'feast, merrymaking,' gave rise to sense 2. **—jun·ke·teer** /ˌjəNGkiˈti(ə)r/ *n.*

junk food ▸*n.* food that has low nutritional value, typically produced in the form of packaged snacks needing little or no preparation.

junk·ie /ˈjəNGkē/ (also **junk·y**) ▸*n. informal* a drug addict. ■ [with *adj.*] a person with a compulsive habit or obsessive dependency on something: *power junkies.* ▷1920s (originally U.S.): from JUNK[1].

junk mail ▸*n. informal* unsolicited advertising or promotional material received through the mail and e-mail.

junk sci·ence ▸*n.* untested or unproven theories when presented as scientific fact, especially in a court of law.

junk shop ▸*n. informal* a shop selling secondhand goods or inexpensive antiques.

junk·y /ˈjəNGkē/ *informal* ▸*adj.* useless or of little value.
▸*n.* (*pl.* **junk·ies**) variant spelling of JUNKIE.

junk·yard /ˈjəNGkˌyärd/ ▸*n.* a place where scrap is collected before being discarded, reused, or recycled.

Ju·no /ˈjo͞oˌnō/ **1** *Roman Mythology* the most important goddess of the Roman state, wife of Jupiter. She was originally an ancient Italian goddess. Greek equivalent HERA. **2** *Astronomy* asteroid 3, discovered in 1804 (diameter 244 km).

J

Ju·no·esque /ˌjo͞onōˈesk/ ▶*adj.* (of a woman) imposingly tall and shapely. ▷mid 19th cent.: from **JUNO** + **-ESQUE.**

Junr ▶*abbr.* Junior (in names).

jun·ta /ˈho͝ontə; ˈjəntə/ ▶*n.* **1** a military or political group that rules a country after taking power by force: *the country's ruling military junta.* **2** *historical* a deliberative or administrative council in Spain or Portugal. ▷early 17th cent. (sense 2): from Spanish and Portuguese, from Latin *juncta,* feminine past participle of *jungere* 'to join.'

jun·to /ˈjəntō/ ▶*n.* (*pl.* **-tos**) *historical* a political grouping or faction, esp. in 17th- and 18th-century Britain. ▷alteration of **JUNTA**, on the pattern of Spanish nouns ending in *-o.*

Ju·pi·ter /ˈjo͞opitər/ **1** *Roman Mythology* the chief god of the Roman state religion, originally a sky god associated with thunder and lightning. His wife was Juno. Also called **JOVE**. Greek equivalent **ZEUS**. [Latin, from *Jovis pater,* literally 'Father Jove.'] **2** *Astronomy* the largest planet in the solar system, a gas giant that is the fifth in order from the sun and one of the brightest objects in the night sky.

Jupiter orbits between Mars and Saturn at an average distance of 778 million km from the sun. Although it has an equatorial diameter of 142,800 km, the planet rotates in less than ten hours. Its upper atmosphere consists mainly of hydrogen with swirling clouds of ammonia and methane, with a circulation system that results in a number of distinct latitudinal bands. There are at least sixteen satellites, four of which (the Galilean moons) are visible through binoculars, and a faint ring system.

Ju·ra[1] /ˈjo͝orə; ZHYˈrä/ a system of mountain ranges on the border of France and Switzerland. It has given its name to the Jurassic period, when most of its rocks were laid down.

Jura[2] an island of the Inner Hebrides, north of Islay and south of Mull, separated from the west coast of Scotland by the Sound of Jura.

ju·ral /ˈjo͝orəl/ ▶*adj. formal* of or relating to the law. ■ *Philosophy* of or relating to rights and obligations. ▷mid 17th cent.: from Latin *jus, jur-* 'law, right' + **-AL.**

Ju·ras·sic /jəˈrasik/ ▶*adj. Geology* of, relating to, or denoting the second period of the Mesozoic era, between the Triassic and Cretaceous periods. ■ [as *n.*] (**the Jurassic**) the Jurassic period or the system of rocks deposited during it.

The Jurassic lasted from about 208 million to 146 million years ago. Large reptiles, including the largest known dinosaurs, were dominant on both land and sea. Ammonites were abundant, and the first birds (including Archaeopteryx) appeared.

▷mid 19th cent.: from French *jurassique;* named after the *Jura* Mountains (see **JURA**[1]).

ju·rat /ˈjo͝orat/ ▶*n. Law* **1** *chiefly historical* a person who has taken an oath or who performs a duty on oath, e.g., a juror. **2** a statement on an affidavit of when, where, and before whom it was sworn. ▷late Middle English: based on Latin *juratus* 'sworn,' past participle of *jurare.*

ju·rid·i·cal /jo͝oˈridikəl/ ▶*adj. Law* of or relating to judicial proceedings and the administration of the law. ▷early 16th cent.: from Latin *juridicus* (from *jus, jur-* 'law' + *dicere* 'say') + **-AL.** —**ju·rid·i·cal·ly** *adv.*

ju·ris·con·sult /ˌjo͝orisˈkänˌsəlt; -kənˈsəlt/ ▶*n. Law, chiefly historical* an expert on law. ▷early 17th cent.: from Latin *jurisconsultus,* from *jus, jur-* 'law' + *consultus* 'skilled' (from *consulere* 'take counsel').

ju·ris·dic·tion /ˌjo͝orisˈdikSHən/ ▶*n.* the official power to make legal decisions and judgments: *federal courts had no* ***jurisdiction over*** *the case | the District of Columbia was placed under the* ***jurisdiction of*** *Congress.* ■ the extent of this power: *the claim will be* ***within the jurisdiction*** *of the industrial tribunal.* ■ a system of law courts; a judicature: *in some jurisdictions there is a mandatory death sentence for murder.* ■ the territory or sphere of activity over which the legal authority of a court or other institution extends: *several different tax jurisdictions.* ▷Middle English: from Old French *jurediction,* from Latin *jurisdictio(n-),* from *jus, jur-* 'law' + *dictio* 'saying' (from *dicere* 'say'). —**ju·ris·dic·tion·al** *adj.*

THE RIGHT WORD **authority, command, dominion, jurisdiction, power, sovereignty, sway**

The **authority** of our elected officials refers to their *power* (often conferred by rank or office) to give orders, require obedience, or make decisions.

Their authority is normally limited by their **jurisdiction**, which is a legally predetermined division of a larger whole, within which someone has a right to rule or decide (*the matter was beyond his jurisdiction*).

The president of the U.S. has more **power** than any other American official, which means that he has the ability to exert force or control over something. He does not, however, have the *authority* to make laws on his own.

As commander in chief, he does have **command** over the nation's armed forces, implying that he has the kind of authority that can enforce obedience.

Back in the days when Great Britain had **dominion**, or supreme authority, over the American colonies, it was the king of England who held **sway** over this country's economic and political life—an old-fashioned word that stresses the sweeping scope of one's power.

But his **sovereignty**, which emphasizes absolute or autonomous rule over something considered as a whole, was eventually challenged. The rest, as they say, is history.

ju·ris doc·tor /ˈjo͝oris ˈdäktər/ ▶*n. Law* see **JD.**

ju·ris·pru·dence /ˌjo͝orisˈpro͞odns/ ▶*n.* the theory or philosophy of law. ■ a legal system: *American jurisprudence.* ▷early 17th cent.: from late Latin *jurisprudentia,* from Latin *jus, jur-* 'law' + *prudentia* 'knowledge.' —**ju·ris·pru·dent** *adj.* & *n.* —**ju·ris·pru·den·tial** /-pro͞oˈdenCHəl/ *adj.*

ju·rist /ˈjo͝orist/ ▶*n.* an expert in or writer on law. ■ a lawyer or a judge. ▷late 15th cent. (in the sense 'lawyer'): from French *juriste,* medieval Latin *jurista,* from *jus, jur-* 'law.' —**ju·ris·tic** /jo͝oˈristik/ *adj.*

ju·ror /ˈjo͝orər; -ôr/ ▶*n.* a member of a jury. ■ *historical* a person taking an oath, esp. one of allegiance. Compare with **NONJUROR.** ▷late Middle English: from Old French *jureor,* from Latin *jurator,* from *jurare* 'swear,' from *jus, jur-* 'law.'

Ju·ruá Riv·er /ˌZHo͞orəˈä/ a river that flows for 1,500 miles (2,400 km) from eastern Peru through northwestern Brazil into the Amazon River.

ju·ry[1] /ˈjo͝orē/ ▶*n.* (*pl.* **-ries**) a body of people (typically twelve in number) sworn to give a verdict in a legal case on the basis of evidence submitted to them in court: *the jury returned unanimous guilty verdicts.* ■ a body of people selected to judge a competition.
▶*v.* (**-ries, -ried**) [*trans.*] (usu. **be juried**) judge (an art or craft exhibition or exhibit): *the exhibition was juried by a tapestry artist* | [as *adj.*] (**juried**) *the juried show.* ▷late Middle English: from Old French *juree* 'oath, inquiry,' from Latin *jurata,* feminine past participle of *jurare* 'swear' (see **JUROR**).
▶*PHRASE* □ **the jury is still out** a decision has not yet been reached on a controversial subject: *the jury is still out on whether self-regulation by doctors is adequate.*

ju·ry[2] ▶*adj.* [*attrib.*] *Nautical* (of a mast or other fitting) improvised or temporary: *we need to get that jury rudder fixed.* ▷early 19th cent.: independent usage of the first element of early 17th-cent. *jury-mast* 'temporary mast,' of uncertain origin (compare with **JURY-RIGGED**).

ju·ry box ▶*n.* a segregated area in which the jury sits in a court of law.

ju·ry-rigged ▶*adj.* (of a ship) having temporary makeshift rigging. ■ makeshift; improvised: *jury-rigged classrooms in gymnasiums.* ▷late 18th cent.: *jury* perhaps based on Old French *ajurie* 'aid.' —**ju·ry-rig** *v.*

jus /ZHo͞o(s); jo͞os/ ▶*n.* (esp. in French cuisine) a sauce: *chicken with a rich game jus.* ▷French.

jus co·gens /ˈjəs ˈkōjənz/ ▶*n. Law* the principles that form the norms of international law that cannot be set aside. ▷Latin, literally 'compelling law.'

jus gen·ti·um /ˈjəs ˈjenSHēəm/ ▶*n. Law* international law. ▷Latin, literally 'law of nations.'

Jus·sieu /jo͞oˈSHo͞o/, Antoine Laurent de (1748–1836), French botanist. He developed the system on which modern plant classification is based.

jus·sive /ˈjəsiv/ ▶*adj. Grammar* (of a form of a verb) expressing a command. ▷mid 19th cent.: from Latin *juss-* 'commanded' (from the verb *jubere*) + **-IVE.**

just /jəst/ ▶*adj.* based on or behaving according to what is morally right and fair: *a just and democratic society | fighting for a just cause.* ■ (of treatment) deserved or appropriate in the circumstances: *we all get our just deserts.* ■ (of an opinion or appraisal) well founded; justifiable: *these simplistic approaches have been the subject of just criticism.*
▶*adv.* **1** exactly: *that's just what I need | you're a human being, just like everyone else | conditions were* ***just as*** *bad | you can have it, but* ***not just yet.*** ■ exactly or almost exactly at this or that moment: *she's just coming | we were just finishing breakfast.* **2** very recently; in the immediate past: *I've just seen the local paper.* **3** barely; by a little: *I got here* ***just after*** *nine | inflation fell to* ***just over*** *4 percent | I* ***only just*** *caught the train.* **4** simply; only; no more than: *they were just interested in making money.* ■ really; absolutely (used for emphasis): *they're just great.* ■ used as a polite formula for giving permission or making a request: *just help yourselves.* ■ [with *modal*] possibly (used to indicate a slight chance of something happening or being true): *it might just help.* **5** *Brit.* expressing agreement: *"Simon really messed things up." "Didn't he just?"* ▷late Middle English: via Old French from Latin *justus,* from *jus* 'law, right.' —**just·ly** *adv.* —**just·ness** *n.*
▶*PHRASES* □ **just about** *informal* almost exactly; nearly: *he can do just about anything.* □ **just as well** a good or fortunate thing: *it was just as well I didn't know at the time.* □ **just in case** as a precaution. □ **just a minute, moment, second, etc.** used to ask someone to wait or pause for a short time.■ used to interrupt someone, esp. in protest or disagreement. □ **just now** **1** at this moment: *it's pretty hectic just now.* **2** a little time ago: *she was talking to me just now.* □ **just on** *Brit.* (with reference to time and numbers) exactly: *it was just on midnight.* □ **just the same** nevertheless: *I put on my raincoat and big straw hat. But we got soaked just the same.* □ **just so** **1** arranged or done very neatly and carefully: *polishing the furniture and making everything just so.* **2** *Brit., formal* used to express agreement.

juste mi·lieu /ˈZHYst mēˈlyə/ ▶*n.* the happy medium; judicious moderation. ▷French, literally 'correct mean.'

jus·tice /ˈjəstis/ ▶*n.* **1** just behavior or treatment: *a concern for justice, peace, and genuine respect for people.* ■ the quality of being fair and reasonable: *the justice of his case.* ■ the administration of the law or authority in maintaining this: *a tragic miscarriage of justice.* ■ (**Justice**) the personification of justice, usually a blindfolded woman holding scales and a sword. **2** a judge or magistrate, in particular a judge of the supreme court of a country or state. ▷late Old English *iustise* 'administration of the law,' via Old French from Latin *justitia,* from *justus* (see **JUST**). —**jus·tice·ship** /-ˌSHip/ *n.* (in sense 2).
▶*PHRASES* □ **bring someone to justice** arrest someone for a crime and ensure that they are tried in court. □ **do oneself justice** perform as well as one is able to. □ **do someone/something justice** (or **do justice to someone/something**) do, treat, or represent with due fairness or appreciation: *the brief menu does not do justice to the food.* □ **in justice to** out of fairness to: *I say this in justice to both of you.* □ **rough justice** see **ROUGH.**

jus·tice of the peace ▶*n.* a magistrate appointed to hear minor cases, perform marriages, grant licenses, etc., in a town, county, or other local district.

jus·ti·ci·a·ble /jəˈstiSH(ē)əbəl/ ▶*adj. Law* (of a state or action) subject to trial in a court of law. ▷late Middle English: from Old French, from *justicier* 'bring to trial,' from medieval Latin *justitiare,* from Latin *justitia* 'equity,' from *justus* (see **JUST**).

jus·ti·ci·ar /jəˈstiSH(ē)ər/ ▶*n. historical* an administrator of justice, in particular: ■ a regent and deputy presiding over the court of a Norman or early Plantagenet king of England. ■ either of two supreme judges in medieval Scotland. ▷late 15th cent.: from medieval Latin *justitiarius* (see **JUSTICIARY**).

jus·ti·ci·ar·y /ˌjəˈstiSHēˌerē/ ▶*n.* (*pl.* **-ar·ies**) the administration of justice: [as *adj.*] *justiciary cases.* ■ *chiefly Scottish* an administrator of justice. ▷mid 16th cent.: from medieval Latin *justitiarius,* from Latin *justitia,* from *justus* (see **JUST**).

jus·ti·fi·a·ble /ˈjəstəˌfīəbəl; ˌjəstəˈfī-/ ▶*adj.* able to be shown to be right or reasonable; defensible: *it is not financially justifiable | their justifiable fears.* ▷early 16th cent. (in the sense 'justiciable'): from French, from *justifier* 'to justify.' —**jus·ti·fi·a·bil·i·ty** /ˌjəstəˌfīəˈbilitē/ *n.* —**jus·ti·fi·a·ble·ness** *n.* —**jus·ti·fi·a·bly** /-blē/ *adv. he was justifiably angry.*

jus·ti·fi·a·ble hom·i·cide ▶*n.* the killing of a person in circumstances that allow the act to be regarded in law as without criminal guilt.

jus·ti·fied /ˈjəstəˌfīd/ ▶*adj.* **1** having, done for, or marked by a good or legitimate reason: *the doctors were* ***justified in*** *treating her.* **2** *Theology* declared or made righteous in the sight of God. **3** *Printing* having been adjusted so that the print fills a space evenly or forms a straight line at one or both margins: [in *combination*] *the output is left-justified.*

jus·ti·fy /ˈjəstəˌfī/ ▸*v.* (**-fies, -fied**) [*trans.*] **1** show or prove to be right or reasonable: *the person appointed has fully justified our confidence.* ■ be a good reason for: *the situation was grave enough to justify further investigation.* **2** *Theology* declare or make righteous in the sight of God. **3** *Printing* adjust (a line of type or piece of text) so that the print fills a space evenly or forms a straight edge at one or both margins. ▷Middle English (in the senses 'administer justice to' and 'inflict a judicial penalty on'): from Old French *justifier*, from Christian Latin *justificare* 'do justice to,' from Latin *justus* (see **JUST**). **—jus·ti·fi·ca·tion** /ˌjəstəfiˈkāSHən/ *n.* **—jus·tif·i·ca·to·ry** /jəˈstifəkəˌtôrē; ˌjəstəfiˈkātôrē/ *adj.* **—jus·ti·fi·er** *n.*

Jus·tin, St. /ˈjəstən/ (*c.*100–165), Christian philosopher; known as **St. Justin the Martyr**. According to tradition, he was martyred in Rome together with some of his followers. He is remembered for his *Apologia* (*c.*150). Feast day, June 1.

Jus·tin·i·an /jəˈstinēən/ (483–565), Byzantine emperor 527–565; Latin name *Flavius Petrus Sabbatius Justinianus.* He regained North Africa from the Vandals, Italy from the Ostrogoths, and Spain from the Visigoths. He codified Roman law 529.

just-in-time ▸*adj.* [*attrib.*] denoting a manufacturing system in which materials or components are delivered immediately before they are required in order to minimize inventory costs.

just war ▸*n.* a war that is deemed to be morally or theologically justifiable. ▷translation of Latin 'bellum justum.'

jut /jət/ ▸*v.* (**jut·ted, jut·ting**) [*intrans.*] extend out, over, or beyond the main body or line of something: *a rock jutted out from the side of the bank.* ■ [*trans.*] cause (something, such as one's chin) to protrude: *she put up her head and **jutted out** her chin with determination.*
▸*n.* a point that sticks out. ▷mid 16th cent.: variant of **JET**[1].

Jute /jo͞ot/ ▸*n.* a member of a Germanic people that may have come from Jutland and, according to the Venerable Bede, joined the Angles and Saxons in invading Britain in the 5th century, settling in a region including Kent and the Isle of Wight. ▷Old English *Eotas, Iotas*, influenced later in spelling by medieval Latin *Jutae, Juti.* **—Jut·ish** *adj.*

jute /jo͞ot/ ▸*n.* **1** rough fiber made from the stems of a tropical Old World plant, used for making twine and rope or woven into sacking or matting. **2** the herbaceous plant that is cultivated for this fiber, with edible young shoots. • Genus *Corchorus*, family Tiliaceae: several species, in particular *C. capsularis* of China and *C. olitorius* of India. ■ used in names of other plants that yield fiber, e.g., **Chinese jute**. ▷mid 18th cent.: from Bengali *jhūṭo*, from Prakrit *juṣṭi.*

Jut·land /ˈjətlənd/ a peninsula in northwestern Europe that includes the mainland of Denmark as well as the northern German state of Schleswig-Holstein. Danish name **JYLLAND**.

Jut·land, Bat·tle of a major naval battle in World War I, fought between the British Grand Fleet under Admiral Jellicoe and the German High Seas Fleet in the North Sea west of Jutland on May 31, 1916. Although the battle was indecisive, the German fleet never again sought a full-scale engagement, and the Allies retained control of the North Sea.

juv. ▸*abbr.* juvenile.

Ju·ve·nal /ˈjo͞ovənl/ (*c.*60–*c.*140), Roman satirist; Latin name *Decimus Junius Juvenalis.* He wrote 16-verse satires that savagely attacked the vices and follies of Roman society, chiefly during the reign of Domitian.

ju·ve·nes·cence /ˌjo͞ovəˈnesəns/ ▸*n. formal* the state or period of being young. ▷early 19th cent.: from Latin *juvenescent-* 'reaching the age of youth,' from the verb *juvenescere*, from *juvenis* 'young.' **—ju·ve·nes·cent** *adj.*

ju·ve·nile /ˈjo͞ovəˌnīl; -vənl/ ▸*adj.* of, for, or relating to young people: *juvenile crime.* See note at **YOUTHFUL**. ■ childish; immature: *she's bored with my juvenile conversation.* ■ of or denoting a theatrical or film role representing a young person: *the romantic juvenile lead.* ■ of or relating to young birds or other animals.
▸*n.* a young person. ■ *Law* a person below the age at which ordinary criminal prosecution is possible (18 in most countries). ■ a young bird or other animal. ■ an actor who plays juvenile roles. ▷early 17th cent.: from Latin *juvenilis*, from *juvenis* 'young, a young person.' **—ju·ve·nil·i·ty** /ˌjo͞ovəˈnilitē/ *n.*

ju·ve·nile court ▸*n.* a court of law responsible for the trial or legal supervision of children under a specified age (18 in most countries).

ju·ve·nile de·lin·quen·cy ▸*n.* the habitual committing of criminal acts or offenses by a young person, esp. one below the age at which ordinary criminal prosecution is possible. **—ju·ve·nile de·lin·quent** *n.*

ju·ve·nile hor·mone ▸*n. Entomology* any of a number of hormones regulating larval development in insects and inhibiting metamorphosis.

ju·ve·nile of·fend·er ▸*n.* a person below a specific age (18 in most countries) who has committed a crime.

ju·ve·nil·i·a /ˌjo͞ovəˈnilēə/ ▸*plural n.* works produced by an author or artist while still young. ▷early 17th cent.: from Latin, neuter plural of *juvenilis* (see **JUVENILE**).

ju·ve·nil·ize /ˈjo͞ovənlˌīz/ ▸*v.* [*trans.*] make or keep young or youthful; arrest the development of. ■ [as *adj.*] (**juvenilized**) *Entomology* (of an insect or part of one) having a juvenile appearance or physiology; showing arrested or reversed development.

Ju·ven·tud, Isla de la /ˈēslä dā lä ˌho͞ovānˈto͞od/ (English name **Isle of Youth**; formerly **Isle of Pines**) an island off southwestern Cuba, in the Caribbean Sea; pop. 71,000. Long a source of jurisdictional disputes between Cuba and the U.S., it has been a resort and a prison colony. Renamed in 1978, it has many facilities dedicated to youth.

ju·vie /ˈjo͞ovē/ ▸*n.* (*pl.* **-vies**) *informal* a juvenile delinquent. ▷1940s: abbreviation of **JUVENILE**.

jux·ta·glo·mer·u·lar /ˌjəkstəgləˈmeryələr; -glə-/ ▸*adj. Anatomy* denoting a group of structures secreting regulatory hormones into the arteriole that leads into a glomerulus in the kidney. ▷1930s: from Latin *juxta* 'near to' + *glomerular* (see **GLOMERULUS**).

jux·ta·pose /ˈjəkstəˌpōz; ˌjəkstəˈpōz/ ▸*v.* [*trans.*] place or deal with close together for contrasting effect: *black-and-white photos of slums were starkly **juxtaposed** with color images.* ▷mid 19th cent.: from French *juxtaposer*, from Latin *juxta* 'next' + French *poser* 'to place.' **—jux·ta·po·si·tion** /ˌjəkstəpəˈziSHən/ *n.* **—jux·ta·po·si·tion·al** /ˌjəkstəpəˈziSHənl/ *adj.*

JV ▸*abbr.* ■ joint venture. ■ junior varsity.

jwlr. ▸*abbr.* jeweler.

Jyl·land /ˈyo͞oˌlän/ Danish name for **JUTLAND**.

Kk

K¹ /kā/ (also **k**) ▸*n.* (*pl.* **Ks** or **K's**) the eleventh letter of the alphabet. ■ denoting the next after J in a set of items, categories, etc.

K² ▸*abbr.* ■ kelvin(s). ■ *Computing* kilobyte(s). ■ kilometer(s). ■ kindergarten. ■ king (used esp. in describing play in card games and recording moves in chess): *declarer overruffed with ♦K and led another spade | 18.Ke2.* ■ knit (as an instruction in knitting patterns): *K 42 rows.* ■ Köchel (catalog of Mozart's works): *the Sinfonia Concertante, K364.* ■ *informal* thousand (used chiefly in expressing salaries or other sums of money). [from KILO- 'thousand.'] ■ *Baseball* strikeout.

▸*symbol* the chemical element potassium. [from modern Latin *kalium*.]

k ▸*abbr.* ■ karat. ■ [in *combination*] (in units of measurement) kilo-: *a distance of 700 kpc.* ■ kopeck(s).

▸*symbol* a constant in a formula or equation. ■ *Chemistry* Boltzmann's constant.

K2 the highest mountain in the Karakoram range, on the border between Pakistan and China. The second highest peak in the world, it rises to 28,250 feet (8,611 m). It was discovered in 1856 and named K2 because it was the second peak to be surveyed in the Karakoram range. It was also formerly known as Mount Godwin-Austen after Col. H. H. Godwin-Austen (1834–1923), who first surveyed it. Also called **DAPSANG**.

Kaa·ba /ˈkäbə/ (also **Caa·ba**) a square stone building in the center of the Great Mosque at Mecca, the site most holy to Muslims and toward which they must face when praying. It stands on the site of a pre-Islamic shrine said to have been built by Abraham. ▷from Arabic *(al-)ka'ba*, literally '(the) square house.'

ka·ba·ka /kəˈbäkə/ ▸*n.* the traditional ruler of the Baganda people of Uganda. ▷a local title.

Ka·ba·le·ga Falls /ˌkäbəˈlāgə/ a waterfall on the lower Victoria Nile River near Lake Albert, in northwestern Uganda. Former name **MURCHISON FALLS**.

Kab·ar·di·no-Bal·kar·i·a /ˌkabərˈdēnō ˌbôlˈkarēə/ an autonomous republic in southwestern Russia, on the border with Georgia; pop. 768,000; capital, Nalchik. Also called **KABARDA-BALKAR REPUBLIC**.

Kab·ba·lah /ˈkabələ; kəˈbä-/ (also **Kab·ba·la**, **Ca·ba·la**, **Cab·ba·la**, or **Qa·ba·lah**) ▸*n.* the ancient Jewish tradition of mystical interpretation of the Bible, first transmitted orally and using esoteric methods (including ciphers). It reached the height of its influence in the later Middle Ages and remains significant in Hasidism. ▷from medieval Latin *cabala*, *cabbala*, from Rabbinical Hebrew *qabbālāh* 'tradition,' from *qibbēl* 'receive, accept.' **—Kab·ba·lism** /ˈkabəˌlizəm/ *n.* **—Kab·ba·list** /-list/ *n.* **—Kab·ba·lis·tic** /ˌkabəˈlistik/ *adj.*

Ka·bi·la /kəˈbēlə/, Laurent (1937–2001), African statesman; president of the Democratic Republic of the Congo (formerly Zaire) 1997–2001. His forces overthrew President Mobutu in 1997. He was assassinated in January 2001.

Ka·bi·nett /ˌkabiˈnet/ ▸*n.* a wine of German origin or style of superior or reserve quality, esp. one made from a specified quality of grape must, without added sugar. ▷from German *Kabinettwein*, literally 'chamber wine.'

ka·bloo·ey (also **ka·bloo·ie**) /kəˈblo͞oē/ ▸*adj. Informal* destroyed or ruined: *the amp will* **go kablooey** *since you will be sending an input signal far too strong for it.*

▸*exclam.* used to convey that something has happened in an abrupt way: *and, kablooey! The whole damn thing exploded!*

ka·bob ▸*n.* variant spelling of **KEBAB**.

ka·boo·dle ▸*n.* variant spelling of **CABOODLE**.

ka·boom /kəˈbo͞om/ ▸*exclam.* used to represent the sound of a loud explosion.

ka·bu·ki /kəˈbo͝okē/ ▸*n.* a form of traditional Japanese drama with highly stylized song, mime, and dance, now performed only by male actors, using exaggerated gestures and body movements to express emotions, and including historical plays, domestic dramas, and dance pieces. ▷Japanese, originally as a verb meaning 'act dissolutely,' later interpreted as if from *ka* 'song' + *bu* 'dance' + *ki* 'art.'

Ka·bul /ˈkäbəl; kəˈbo͞ol/ the capital of Afghanistan; pop. 700,000. It is situated in the northeastern part of the country, with a strategic position commanding the mountain passes through the Hindu Kush, esp. the Khyber Pass. Capital of the Mogul empire 1504–1738, it replaced Kandahar as capital of an independent Afghanistan in 1773.

Ka·bwe /ˈkäbwā/ a town in central Zambia, north of Lusaka; pop. 167,000. It is the site of a cave that has yielded human fossils associated with the Upper Pleistocene period. Former name (1904–65) **BROKEN HILL**.

Ka·byle /kəˈbīl/ ▸*n.* **1** a member of a Berber people inhabiting northern Algeria. **2** the Berber dialect of this people.

▸*adj.* of or relating to this people or their language. ▷probably from Arabic *ḳabā'il*, plural of *ḳabīla* 'tribe.'

Ka·chin /kəˈCHin/ ▸*n.* **1** a member of an indigenous people living in northern Myanmar (Burma) and adjacent parts of China and India. **2** the Tibeto-Burman language of this people.

▸*adj.* of or relating to this people or their language.

ka·chi·na /kəˈCHēnə/ (also **kat·si·na** /kətˈsēnə/) ▸*n.* (*pl.* **-nas**) a deified ancestral spirit in the mythology of Pueblo Indians. ■ (also **ka·chi·na danc·er**) a person who represents such a spirit in ceremonial dances. ■ (also **ka·chi·na doll**) a small carved figure representing such a spirit. ▷from Hopi *kacina* 'supernatural,' of Keres origin.

ka-ching /kəˈCHiNG/ (also **ker-ching** /kə(r)ˈCHiNG/) ▸*n.* used to represent the sound of a cash register, especially with reference to making money: *they likely have assets beyond the ka-ching of the cash register.* ▷early 1990s: imitative.

Ká·dár /ˈkäˌdär/, János (1912–89), Hungarian statesman; first secretary of the Hungarian Socialist Workers' Party 1956–88 and prime minister 1956–58 and 1961–65. After crushing the Hungarian uprising of 1956, he consistently supported the Soviet Union. His policy of "consumer socialism" made Hungary the most affluent state in Eastern Europe.

Kad·dish /ˈkädiSH/ ▸*n.* an ancient Jewish prayer sequence regularly recited in the synagogue service, including thanksgiving and praise and concluding with a prayer for universal peace. ■ a form of this prayer sequence recited for the dead. ▷from Aramaic *qaddīš* 'holy.'

ka·di ▸*n.* (*pl.* **ka·dis**) variant spelling of **CADI**.

Ka·di·köy /käˈdikœi; -koi/ Turkish name for **CHALCEDON**.

Kae·song /ˈkäˈsôNG/ a commercial and industrial city in southern North Korea, on the 38th Parallel (the South Korean border), the scene of armistice talks at the end of the Korean War; pop. 346,000.

kaf·fee·klatsch /ˈkäfēˌkläCH; -ˌklaCH; ˈkôfē-/ ▸*n.* an informal social gathering at which coffee is served. ■ talking or gossip at such gatherings. ▷German, from *Kaffee* 'coffee' + *Klatsch* 'gossip.'

Kaf·fir /ˈkafər/ ▸*n. chiefly S. African, offensive* an insulting and contemptuous term for a black African. ▷from Arabic *kāfir* 'infidel,' from *kafara* 'not believe.'

Kaf·fir lil·y ▸*n.* either of two South African plants with straplike leaves and stems bearing a number of red, pink, or orange flowers: • a plant with star-shaped flowers (*Schizostylis coccinea*, family Iridaceae). • another term for **CLIVIA**.

kaf·fir lime /ˈkafər/ ▸*n.* a citrus tree of southeast Asia with green fruit and aromatic leaves that are used in Thai and Indonesian cooking.

kaf·fi·yeh /kəˈfē(y)ə/ (also **kef·fi·yeh**) ▸*n.* a Bedouin Arab's kerchief worn as a headdress. ▷early 19th cent.: from Arabic *keffiyya*, *kūfiyya.*

kaffiyeh

Kaf·ir /ˈkafər/ ▸*n.* a member of a people of the Hindu Kush mountains of northeastern Afghanistan. ▷from Arabic *kāfir* (see **KAFFIR**). **—Kaf·i·ri** /ˈkafərē; kəˈfi(ə)rē/ *adj.* & *n.*

kaf·ir /ˈkafər/ ▸*n.* a person who is not a Muslim (used chiefly by Muslims). ▷from Arabic *kāfir* 'infidel, unbeliever.' Compare with **KAFFIR**.

Kaf·ka /ˈkäfkə/, Franz (1883–1924), Czech novelist, who wrote in German. His work is characterized by its portrayal of an enigmatic and nightmarish reality where the individual is perceived as lonely, perplexed, and threatened. Notable works: *The Metamorphosis* (1917), *The Trial* (1925), and *The Castle* (1926).

Kaf·ka·esque /ˌkäfkəˈesk/ ▸*adj.* characteristic or reminiscent of the oppressive or nightmarish qualities of Franz Kafka's fictional world.

kaf·tan /ˈkaftən; -ˌtan/ (also **caf·tan**) ▸*n.* a man's long belted tunic, worn in countries of the Near East. ■ a woman's long loose dress. ■ a loose shirt or top. ▷late 16th cent.: from Turkish, from Persian *ḳaftān*, partly influenced by French *cafetan.*

Ka·go·shi·ma /ˌkägəˈSHēmə; käˈgōSHēmə/ a city and port in Japan; pop. 537,000. Situated on the southern coast of Kyushu island, on the Satsuma Peninsula, it is noted for Satsuma ware, a type of porcelain.

Ka·ha·na·mo·ku /kəˌhänəˈmōko͞o/, Duke Paoa (1890–68) U.S. swimmer and surfer. The developer of the flutter kick, he won the 100-yard freestyle gold medals in the 1912 and 1920 Olympic Games, as well as the 800-meter relay gold medal in the 1920 games.

ka·hi·ka·te·a /ˌkīkəˈtēə/ ▸*n.* a tall coniferous New Zealand tree used for its timber and resin. Its seeds, which are borne on conspicuous red stems, were formerly eaten by the Maoris. Also called **WHITE PINE**. • *Podocarpus* (or **Dacrycarpus**) *dacrydioides*, family Podocarpaceae. ▷early 19th cent.: from Maori.

Kah·lú·a /kəˈlo͞oə/ ▸*n. trademark* a coffee-flavored liqueur.

Kahn /kän/, Abdullah Jaffa Anver Bey, see **JOFFREY**.

Ka·ho·o·la·we /käˌhō-ōˈläwā/ an island in Hawaii, southwest of Maui, formerly used as a military range.

Ka·hu·lu·i /ˌkäho͞oˈlo͞o-ē/ a city in Hawaii, on northern Maui Island; pop. 20,146.

ka·hu·na /kəˈho͞onə/ ▸*n.* (in Hawaii) a wise man or shaman. ■ *informal* an important person; the person in charge: *one big kahuna runs the whole show.* ■ *informal* (in surfing) a very large wave. ▷Hawaiian.

Kai·bab Plateau /ˈkīˌbab/ a highland region in northwestern Arizona, north of the Grand Canyon, that adjoins southern Utah.

Kai·feng /ˈkīˈfeNG/ a city in eastern China, in Henan province, on the Yellow River; pop. 693,100. Established in the 4th century BC, it is one of the oldest cities in China.

Kai·lua /kī'lo͞oə/ a community in southeastern Oahu on the island of Hawaii, in the Pacific Ocean, northeast of Honolulu; pop. 36,513.

kai·nic ac·id /'kīnik/ ▸*n. Medicine* an organic acid extracted from a red alga, used to kill intestinal worms. • Chem. formula: $C_{10}H_{15}NO_4$. ▷mid 20th cent.: *kainic* from Japanese *kainin* (from *kainin-sō*, name of the alga *Digenea simplex* from which it is extracted) + **-IC**.

kai·nite /'kī,nīt; 'kā-/ ▸*n.* a white mineral consisting of a double salt of hydrated magnesium sulfate and potassium chloride. ▷mid 19th cent.: from German *Kainit*, from Greek *kainos* 'new, recent,' because of the mineral's recent formation.

Kai·pa·ro·wits Plateau /kī'pärō-its/ a highland region in south central Utah, north of Lake Powell.

kai·ro·mone /'kīrə,mōn/ ▸*n. Biology* a chemical substance emitted by an organism and detected by another of a different species that gains advantage from this, e.g., a parasite seeking a host. ▷late 20th cent.: from Greek *kairos* 'advantage, opportunity,' on the pattern of *pheromone*.

kai·ros /'kīräs/ ▸*n.* [in *sing.*] *chiefly Theology* a propitious moment for decision or action. ▷mid 20th cent.: Greek, literally 'opportunity.'

Kair·ouan /ker'wän/ a city in northeastern Tunisia; pop. 72,250. It is a Muslim holy city and a place of pilgrimage.

Kai·ser /'kīzər/, Georg (1878–1945), German playwright. He is best known for his expressionist plays *The Burghers of Calais* (1914), *Gas I* (1918), and *Gas II* (1920); the last two provide a gruesome vision of futuristic science and end with the extinction of all life by poisonous gas.

kai·ser /'kīzər/ ▸*n.* **1** *historical* the German emperor, the emperor of Austria, or the head of the Holy Roman Empire: [as *title*] *Kaiser Wilhelm*. **2** see **KAISER ROLL**. ▷Middle English *cayser*, from Old Norse *keisari*, based on Latin *Caesar* (see **CAESAR**[3]), and later reinforced by Middle Dutch *keiser*. The modern English form (early 19th cent.) derives from German *Kaiser*. **—kai·ser·ship** /-,sHip/ *n.*

▸*PHRASE* □ **the Kai·ser's War** *dated* World War I.

ka·iser roll ▸*n.* a round, soft bread roll with a crisp crust, made by folding the corners of a square of dough into the center, resulting in a pinwheel shape when baked.

Kai·sers·lau·tern /,kīzərz'loutərn/ a city in western Germany, in Rhineland-Palatinate; pop. 100,540.

Kai·ser Wil·helm, Wilhelm II of Germany (see **WILHELM II**).

kai·zen /'kīzən/ ▸*n.* a Japanese business philosophy of continuous improvement of working practices, personal efficiency, etc. ▷Japanese, literally 'improvement.'

ka·ka /'käkə/ ▸*n.* a large New Zealand parrot with olive-brown and dull green upper parts and reddish underparts. • *Nestor meridionalis*, family Psittacidae. ▷late 18th cent.: from Maori.

ka·ka·po /'käkə,pō/ ▸*n.* (*pl.* **-pos**) a large flightless New Zealand parrot with greenish plumage. Now endangered, it is nocturnal and ground-dwelling. Also called **OWL PARROT**. • *Strigops habroptilus*, family Psittacidae. ▷mid 19th cent.: from Maori, literally 'night kaka.'

ka·ke·mo·no /,käkə'mōnō/ ▸*n.* (*pl.* **-nos**) a Japanese unframed painting made on paper or silk and displayed as a wall hanging. ▷late 19th cent.: Japanese, from *kake-* 'hang, suspend' + *mono* 'thing.'

ka·ki /'käkē/ ▸*n.* the Japanese persimmon. ▷early 18th cent.: from Japanese.

Ka·laal·lit Nu·naat /kä'lätlēt no͞o'nät; -'lälēt/ Inuit name for **GREENLAND**.

ka·la-a·zar /,kälə ə'zär/ ▸*n.* a form of the disease leishmaniasis marked by emaciation, anemia, fever, and enlargement of the liver and spleen. • This is caused by *Leishmania donovani*, phylum Kinetoplastida, kingdom Protista. ▷late 19th cent.: from Assamese, from *kālā* 'black' + *āzār* 'disease' (because of the bronzing of the skin often associated with it).

Ka·la·ha·ri Des·ert /,kälə'härē/ a high, vast, arid plateau in southern Africa north of the Orange River. It comprises most of Botswana with parts in Namibia and South Africa.

Kal·a·ma·zoo /,kaləmə'zo͞o/ an industrial and commercial city in southwestern Michigan; pop. 77,145.

kal·an·cho·e /,kalən'kō-ē; kə'lanGkō-ē/ ▸*n.* a tropical succulent plant with clusters of tubular flowers, sometimes producing miniature plants along the edges of the leaves and grown as an indoor or greenhouse plant. • Genus *Kalanchoe*, family Crassulaceae. ▷mid 19th cent.: modern Latin, from French, based on Chinese *gālāncài*.

Ka·lash·ni·kov /kə'läsHnə,kôf; -,kôv/ ▸*n.* a type of rifle or submachine gun made in Russia, esp. the AK-47 assault rifle. ▷1970s: named after Mikhail T. *Kalashnikov* (born 1919), the Russian designer of the weapons.

kale /kāl/ ▸*n.* **1** a hardy cabbage of a variety that produces erect stems with large leaves and no compact head. See also **CURLY KALE**. **2** *informal, dated* money. ▷Middle English: northern English form of **COLE**.

ka·lei·do·scope /kə'līdə,skōp/ ▸*n.* a toy consisting of a tube containing mirrors and pieces of colored glass or paper, whose reflections produce changing patterns that are visible through an eyehole when the tube is rotated. ■ [in *sing.*] a constantly changing pattern or sequence of objects or elements: *the dancers moved in a kaleidoscope of color.* ▷early 19th cent.: from Greek *kalos* 'beautiful' + *eidos* 'form' + **-SCOPE**. **—ka·lei·do·scop·ic** /-,līdə'skäpik/ *adj.* **—ka·lei·do·scop·i·cal·ly** /-,līdə'skäpik(ə)lē/ *adv.*

kal·ends ▸*plural n.* variant spelling of **CALENDS**.

Ka·le·va·la /,käli'välə/ a collection of Finnish legends transmitted orally until published in the 19th century, and now regarded as the Finnish national epic. ▷of Karelian origin.

Kale·yard School /'kāl,yärd/ a group of late 19th-century fiction writers, including J. M. Barrie, who described local town life in Scotland in a romantic vein and with much use of the vernacular. ▷from Scots *kaleyard*, literally 'kitchen garden.'

Kal·gan /'käl'gän; 'kal'gan/ Mongolian name for **ZHANGJIAKOU**.

Ka·li /'kälē/ *Hinduism* the most terrifying goddess, wife of Shiva, often identified with Durga, and in her benevolent aspect with Parvati. She is typically depicted as black, naked, old, and hideous. ▷from Sanskrit *Kālī* 'black.'

Ka·li·man·tan /,kälē'män,tän/ a region of Indonesia that is located on the southern part of the island of Borneo.

ka·lim·ba /kə'limbə/ ▸*n.* a type of African thumb piano. ▷1950s: a local word; related to **MARIMBA**.

Ka·li·nin[1] /kə'lēnən; kəl'yēnyən/ former name (1931–91) of **TVER**.

Ka·li·nin[2] /kə'lēnin/, Mikhail (Ivanovich) (1875–1946), Soviet statesman; head of state 1919–46. He founded the newspaper *Pravda* 1912.

Ka·li·nin·grad /kə'lēnin,grät; kəl'yēnyēn-/ **1** a port on the Baltic coast of eastern Europe, capital of the Russian region of Kaliningrad; pop. 406,000. It was known by its German name of Königsberg until 1946 when it was ceded to the Soviet Union under the Potsdam Agreement and renamed in honor of Kalinin. Its port is ice-free all year round and is an important naval base for the Russian fleet. **2** a region of Russia, an enclave situated on the Baltic coast of eastern Europe; capital, Kaliningrad.

Ka·lisz /'kälēsH/ a city in central Poland; pop. 106,150.

Kal·mar, Un·ion of the treaty that unified the crowns of Denmark, Sweden, and Norway in 1397, dissolved in 1523.

Kal·mar Sound /'kälmär/ a narrow strait between the mainland of southeastern Sweden and the island of Öland in the Baltic Sea.

kal·mi·a /'kalmēə/ ▸*n.* an evergreen leathery-leaved shrub of the heath family, bearing large clusters of pink, white, or red flowers. It is native to North America and Cuba and widely grown as an ornamental. • Genus *Kalmia*, family Ericaceae. ▷modern Latin, named after Pehr *Kalm* (1716–79), Swedish botanist.

Kal·muck /'kal,mək; kal'mək/ (also **Kal·myk**) ▸*n.* (*pl.* same or **-mucks** also **-myks** /-miks/) **1** a member of a mainly Buddhist people of Mongolian origin living chiefly in Kalmykia. **2** the Altaic language of this people.

▸*adj.* of or relating to this people or their language. ▷from Russian *kalmyk*.

Kal·myk·ia /kal'mikēə/ an autonomous republic in southwestern Russia, on the Caspian Sea; pop. 325,000; capital, Elista. Official name **REPUBLIC OF KALMYKIA-KHALMG TANGCH**.

ka·long /'kälônG; -läng/ ▸*n.* a flying fox found in Southeast Asia and Indonesia. • Genus *Pteropus*, family Pteropodidae, in particular the large flying fox (*P. vampyrus*). ▷early 19th cent.: from Javanese.

kal·so·mine ▸*n.* & *v.* variant spelling of **CALCIMINE**.

Ka·lu·ga /kə'lo͞ogə/ an industrial city and river port in Russia, on the Oka River, southwest of Moscow; pop. 314,000.

Kal·yan /kəl'yän/ a city on the west coast of India, in the state of Maharashtra, northeast of Bombay; pop. 1,014,000.

Ka·ma /'kämə/ *Hinduism* the god of love, typically represented as a youth with a bow of sugar cane, a bowstring of bees, and arrows of flowers.

kam·a·cite /'kamə,sīt/ ▸*n.* an alloy of iron and nickel occurring in some meteorites. ▷late 19th cent.: from Greek *kamax, kamak-* 'vine pole' (because of the occurrence of the alloy in bar-shaped masses) + **-ITE**[1].

Ka·ma Riv·er /'kämə/ a river in Russia that flows for 1,128 miles (1,805 km) from the central Ural Mountains to the Volga River near Kazan.

Ka·ma Su·tra /'kämə 'so͞otrə/ an ancient Sanskrit treatise on the art of love and sexual technique. ▷Sanskrit, from *kāma* 'love' + *sūtra* 'thread.'

Kam·ba /'kämbə/ ▸*n.* (*pl.* same, **Kam·bas**, or **Wa·kam·ba** /wä'kämbə/) **1** a member of a people of central Kenya, ethnically related to the Kikuyu. **2** the Bantu language of this people.

▸*adj.* of or relating to this people or their language. ▷a local name.

Kam·chat·ka /käm'cHätkə/ a mountainous peninsula on the northeast coast of Siberia in Russia that separates the Sea of Okhotsk from the Bering Sea; chief port, Petropavlovsk.

kame /kām/ ▸*n. Geology* a steep-sided mound of sand and gravel deposited by a melting ice sheet. ▷late 18th cent.: Scots form of **COMB**.

Ka·me·ha·me·ha I /kə,māə'māə/ (1758?–1819), king of the Hawaiian islands 1795–1819, known as *Kamehameha the Great*. He united all the islands under his rule.

Ka·men·sko·ye /'käminskəyə/ former name (until 1936) for **DNIPRODZERZHINSK**.

Ka·mensk-Ural·sky /'käminsk o͝or'älsk(y)ē/ an industrial city in central Russia, in the eastern foothills of the Urals; pop. 208,000.

Ka·mer·lingh On·nes /'kämərlinG 'ônəs/, Heike (1853–1926), Dutch physicist. During his studies of cryogenic phenomena, he succeeded in liquefying helium. He also discovered the phenomenon of superconductivity in 1911. Nobel Prize for Physics (1913).

ka·mi /'kämē/ ▸*n.* (*pl.* same) a divine being in the Shinto religion. ▷Japanese.

ka·mi·ka·ze /,kämi'käzē/ ▸*n.* (in World War II) a Japanese aircraft loaded with explosives and making a deliberate suicidal crash on an enemy target. ■ the pilot of such an aircraft.

▸*adj.* [*attrib.*] of or relating to such an attack or pilot. ■ reckless or potentially self-destructive: *he made a kamikaze run across three lanes of traffic.* ▷Japanese, from *kami* 'divinity' + *kaze* 'wind,' originally referring to the gale that, in Japanese tradition, destroyed the fleet of invading Mongols in 1281.

Ka·mi·la·roi /'kämē,läroi/ ▸*n.* (*pl.* same) **1** a member of a group of Australian Aboriginal peoples of northeastern New South Wales. **2** the language of these peoples, now extinct.

▸*adj.* of or relating to the Kamilaroi or their language. ▷the name in Kamilaroi.

Kam·pa·la /käm'pälə/ the capital of Uganda, in the southern part of the country on the northern shores of Lake Victoria; pop. 773,000. It replaced Entebbe as the capital when Uganda became independent in 1963.

kam·pong /'kämpônG; -päng/ ▸*n.* a Malaysian enclosure or village. ▷Malay; compare with **COMPOUND**[2].

Kam·pu·che·a /,kämpə'cHēə/ former name (1976–89) for **CAMBODIA**. **—Kam·pu·che·an** *n.* & *adj.*

Kan. ▸*abbr.* Kansas.

ka·na /'känə/ ▸*n.* the system of syllabic writing used for Japanese, having two forms, hiragana and katakana. Compare with **KANJI**. ▷Japanese.

ka·nak·a /kə'näkə/ ▸*n.* a native of Hawaii. ■ *historical* a Pacific Islander employed as an indentured laborer in Australia, esp. in the sugar and cotton plantations of Queensland. ▷Hawaiian, literally 'man.'

kan·al /'kanl/ ▸*n.* a land measure used in Pakistan, standardized under British rule to equal one-eighth acre: *seventeen kanals of agricultural land.*

kan·a·my·cin /,kanə'mīsin/ ▸*n. Medicine* a broad-spectrum antibiotic obtained from a strain of bacteria. ▷mid 20th cent.: from modern Latin *Streptomyces kanamyceticus*, the name of the source bacterium (see also **-MYCIN**).

Ka·nan·ga /kə'näNGgə/ (formerly **Luluabourg**) commercial city in south central Democratic Republic of the Congo (formerly Zaire), on the Lulua River; pop. 372,000.

Ka·na·rese /,känə'rēz; -'rēs/ ▸*n.* (*pl.* same) **1** a member of a people living mainly in Kanara, a district in southwestern India. **2** another term for **KANNADA**.
▸*adj.* of or relating to Kanara, its people, or their language.

Ka·na·wha Riv·er /kə'nô-wə; kə'noi/ a river in west central West Virginia that connects the New River with the Ohio River. Charleston and other industrial centers lie along it.

kan·ban /'kän,bän/ ▸*n.* (also **kanban system**) a Japanese manufacturing system in which the supply of components is regulated through the use of a card displaying a sequence of specifications and instructions, sent along the production line. ■ a card of this type. ▷late 20th cent.: Japanese, literally 'billboard, sign.'

Kan·chen·jun·ga /,kənCHən'jəNGgə; -'jŏŏNGgə/ (also **Kang·chen·jun·ga** or **Kin·chin·jun·ga**) a mountain in the Himalayas, on the border between Nepal and Sikkim. Rising to a height of 28,209 feet (8,598 m), it is the world's third highest mountain. ▷Tibetan, literally 'the five treasures of the snows,' referring to the five separate peaks of the summit.

Kan·da·har /,kəndə'här; 'kəndə,här/ a city in southern Afghanistan; pop. 225,500. It was Afghanistan's capital 1773–78.

Kan·din·sky /kən'dinskē/, Wassily (1866–1944), Russian painter and theorist. A pioneer of abstract art, he cofounded the Munich-based *Blaue Reiter* group of artists in 1911.

Kan·dy /'kandē/ a city in Sri Lanka; pop. 104,000. It contains one of the most sacred Buddhist shrines, the Dalada Maligava, which means Temple of the Tooth. **—Kan·dy·an** /-dēən/ *adj.*

Ka·ne·o·he /,känā'ōhā; ,känē'ō-ē/ a community on eastern Oahu Island in Hawaii, northeast of Honolulu; pop. 34,970.

kan·ga·roo /,kaNGgə'rōō/ ▸*n.* a large plant-eating marsupial with a long powerful tail and strongly developed hind limbs that enable it to travel by leaping, found only in Australia and New Guinea. • Genus *Macropus*, family Macropodidae: several species. ▷late 18th cent.: the name of a specific kind of kangaroo in an extinct Aboriginal language of northern Queensland, Australia.

kangaroo

kan·ga·roo care ▸*n.* a method of caring for premature babies in which the infants are held skin-to-skin with a parent, usually the mother, for as many hours as possible every day.

kan·ga·roo court ▸*n.* an unofficial court held by a group of people in order to try someone regarded, esp. without good evidence, as guilty of a crime or misdemeanor.

kan·ga·roo paw ▸*n.* an Australian plant that has long straplike leaves and tubular flowers with woolly outer surfaces. • Genera *Anigozanthos* and *Macropidia*, family Haemodoraceae: several species, in particular **Mangles' kangaroo paw** (*A. manglesii*), which is the floral emblem of Western Australia.

kan·ga·roo rat ▸*n.* a seed-eating hopping rodent with large cheek pouches and long hind legs, found from Canada to Mexico. • Genus *Dipodomys*, family Heteromyidae: several species.

Kang·chen·jun·ga /,käNGCHən'jŏŏNGgə/ variant spelling of **KANCHENJUNGA**.

Ka·nin /'känin/, Garson (1912–99) U.S. actor, director, and producer. He wrote stage plays, such as *Born Yesterday* (1946), and he directed stage productions, such as *The Diary of Anne Frank* (1955) and *Funny Girl* (1964). He also wrote screenplays for movies, including *Adam's Rib* (1949) and *Pat and Mike* (1952).

kan·ji /'känjē/ ▸*n.* a system of Japanese writing using Chinese characters. Compare with **KANA**. ▷Japanese, from *kan* 'Chinese' + *ji* 'character.'

Kan·ka·kee /,kaNGkə'kē/ a city in northeastern Illinois, on the Kankakee River; pop. 27,575.

Kan·na·da /'känədə/ ▸*n.* a Dravidian language related to Telugu and using a similar script. It is spoken by about 24 million people, mainly in Kanara and Karnataka in southwestern India. Also called **KANARESE**.
▸*adj.* of or relating to this language. ▷the name in Kannada.

Ka·no /'känō/ a city in northern Nigeria; pop. 553,000.

Kan·pur /'kän,pŏŏr/ (also **Cawn·pore**) a city in Uttar Pradesh, in northern India, on the Ganges River; pop. 2,100,000.

Kans. ▸*abbr.* Kansas.

Kan·sa /'kanzə; -sə/ ▸*n.* a North American people of eastern Kansas.■ the language of this people. Also called **KAW**.

Kan·sas /'kanzəs/ a state in the central U.S.; pop. 2,688,418; capital, Topeka; statehood, Jan. 29, 1861 (34). It was acquired by the U.S. as part of the Louisiana Purchase in 1803. **—Kan·san** /-zən/ *adj.* & *n.*

Kan·sas Cit·y each of two adjacent cities in the U.S., situated at the junction of the Missouri and Kansas rivers. One is in northeastern Kansas; pop. 146,866, and the other is in northwestern Missouri; pop. 441,545.

Kan·su /'kan,sōō; 'gän'sōō/ variant of **GANSU**.

Kant /känt/, Immanuel (1724–1804), German philosopher. In the *Critique of Pure Reason* (1781) he countered Hume's skeptical empiricism by arguing that any affirmation or denial regarding the ultimate nature of reality ("noumenon") makes no sense. His *Critique of Practical Reason* (1788) affirms the existence of an absolute moral law—the categorical imperative. **—Kant·i·an** /'käntēən/ *adj.* & *n.* **—Kant·i·an·ism** /-,nizəm/ *n.*

Kao·hsiung /'gouSHē'ŏŏNG; -'SHŏŏNG/ the chief port of Taiwan, on the southwestern coast; pop. 1,390,000.

kao·li·ang /,koulē'aNG/ ▸*n.* sorghum of a variety grown in China and used to make dough and alcoholic drinks. • *Sorghum bicolor* var. *nervosum*, family Gramineae. ▷early 20th cent.: from Chinese *gāoliang*, from *gāo* 'high' + *liáng* 'fine grain.'

ka·o·lin /'käəlin/ ▸*n.* a fine, soft white clay, resulting from the natural decomposition of other clays or feldspar. It is used for making porcelain and china, as a filler in paper and textiles, and in medicinal absorbents. Also called **CHINA CLAY**. ▷early 18th cent.: from French, from Chinese *gāolǐng*, literally 'high hill,' the name of a mountain in Jiangxi province where the clay is found. **—ka·o·lin·ize** /-,nīz/ *v.*

ka·o·lin·ite /'käələ,nīt/ ▸*n.* a white or gray clay mineral that is the chief constituent of kaolin.

ka·on /'kā,än/ ▸*n.* *Physics* a meson having a mass several times that of a pion. ▷1950s: from *ka* representing the letter *K* (as a symbol for the particle) + **-ON**.

ka·pell·meis·ter /kə'pel,mīstər/ ▸*n.* the leader or conductor of an orchestra or choir. ■ *historical* a leader of a chamber ensemble or orchestra attached to a German court. ▷mid 19th cent.: German, from *Kapelle* 'court orchestra' (from medieval Latin *capella* 'chapel') + *Meister* 'master.'

ka·pok /'kā,päk/ ▸*n.* a fine, fibrous cottonlike substance that grows around the seeds of the ceiba tree, used as stuffing for cushions, soft toys, etc. ■ (also **kapok tree**) another term for **CEIBA**. ▷mid 18th cent.: from Malay *kapuk*.

Ka·po·si's sar·co·ma /kə'pōsēz sär'kōmə; 'kapə,sēz; 'käpō,SHēz/ ▸*n.* *Medicine* a form of cancer involving multiple tumors of the lymph nodes or skin, occurring chiefly in people with depressed immune systems, e.g., as a result of AIDS. ▷late 19th cent.: named after Moritz K. *Kaposi* (1837–1902), Hungarian dermatologist.

kap·pa /'kapə/ ▸*n.* the tenth letter of the Greek alphabet (**K**, **κ**), transliterated in the traditional Latin style as 'c' (as in *Socrates* or *cyan*) or in the modern style as 'k' (as in *kyanite* and in the etymologies of this dictionary). ■ (**Kappa**) [followed by Latin genitive] *Astronomy* the tenth star in a constellation: *Kappa Orionis*. ■ [as *adj.*] *Biochemistry* denoting one of the two types of light polypeptide chain present in all immunoglobulin molecules (the other being lambda).

ka·pu /'käpō/ ▸*n.* (in Hawaiian traditional culture and religion) a set of rules and prohibitions for everyday life. ▷Hawaiian.

ka·put /kə'pŏŏt; kä-/ ▸*adj.* [*predic.*] *informal* broken and useless; no longer working or effective. ▷late 19th cent.: from German *kaputt*, from French (*être*) *capot* '(be) without tricks in a card game.'

kar·a·bi·ner ▸*n.* variant spelling of **CARABINER**.

Ka·ra·chai /,karə'CHī/ ▸*n.* **1** a member of an indigenous people living in Karachai-Cherkessia. **2** (also **Karachai-Balkar**) the Turkic language of this people.
▸*adj.* of or relating to this people or their language.

Ka·ra·chai-Cher·kes·sia /,karə'CHī CHir'kesēə/ an autonomous republic in the northern Caucasus, in southwestern Russia; pop. 436,000; capital, Cherkessk. Official name **KARACHAI-CHERKESS REPUBLIC**.

Ka·ra·chi /kə'räCHē/ a major city and port in Pakistan, capital of Sind province; pop. 6,700,000. Situated by the Arabian Sea, it was the capital of Pakistan 1947–59 before being replaced by Rawalpindi.

Ka·ra·gan·da /,kärə'gändə/ Russian name for **QARAGHANDY**.

Kar·a·ite /'karə,īt/ ▸*n.* a member of a Jewish sect founded in the 8th century and located chiefly in the Crimea and nearby areas, and in Israel, which rejects rabbinical interpretation in favor of a literal interpretation of the scriptures. ▷early 18th cent.: from Hebrew *Qārā'īm* 'Scripturalists' (from *qārā'* 'read') + **-ITE**[1].

Ka·raj /kä'räj/ a city in northern Iran, west of Tehran; pop. 442,000.

Ka·ra·jan /'kärə,yän/, Herbert von (1908–89), Austrian conductor. He was the principal conductor of the Berlin Philharmonic Orchestra 1955–89.

Ka·ra-Kal·pak /,kärə käl'päk; karə kal'pak; kə'rä kəl 'päk/ ▸*n.* **1** a member of an indigenous people living in the Kara-Kalpak Autonomous Republic of Russia, south of the Aral Sea. **2** the Turkic language of this people.
▸*adj.* of or relating to this people or their language.

Ka·ra·ko·ram /,karə'kôrəm/ a mountain system in central Asia that extends more than 300 miles (480 km) southeast from Afghanistan to Kashmir and that forms part of the borders of India and Pakistan with China. One of the highest mountain systems in the world, it consists of a group of parallel ranges that form a westward continuation of the Himalayas, with many peaks over 26,000 feet (7,900 m), the highest being K2.

kar·a·kul /'karəkəl/ (also **car·a·cul**) ▸*n.* a sheep of an Asian breed with a dark, curled fleece when young. ■ cloth or fur made from or resembling the fleece of such a sheep. ▷mid 19th cent.: from Russian, from the name of an oasis in Uzbekistan and of two lakes in Tadjikistan, based on Turkic.

Ka·ra Kum /,karə 'kōōm; ,kärə/ a desert in central Asia, east of the Caspian Sea, that covers much of Turkmenistan. Russian name **KARAKUMY**.

kar·a·o·ke /,karē'ōkē/ ▸*n.* a form of entertainment, offered typically by bars and clubs, in which people take turns singing popular songs into a microphone over prerecorded backing tracks. ▷1970s: from Japanese, literally 'empty orchestra.'

Ka·ra Sea /'karə; 'kärə/ an arm of the Arctic Ocean off the northern coast of Russia, bounded on the east by the islands of Severnaya Zemlya and on the west by those of Novaya Zemlya.

kar·at /'karət/ (*chiefly Brit.* also **car·at**) ▸*n.* a measure of the purity of gold, pure gold being 24 karats: *an ounce of 24-karat gold.*

ka·ra·te /kə'rätē/ ▸*n.* an Asian system of unarmed combat using the hands and feet to deliver and block blows, widely practiced as a sport. It was formalized in Okinawa in the 17th century and popularized via Japan after about 1920. Karate is performed barefoot in loose padded clothing, with a colored belt indicating the level of skill, and involves mental as well as physical training. ▷Japanese, from *kara* 'empty' + *te* 'hand.'

ka·ra·te chop ▸*n.* a sharp downward blow or movement executed with the side of the hand. **—ka·ra·te-chop** *v.*

ka·ra·te·ka /kə'rätē,kä/ ▸*n.* (*pl.* same or **-kas**) a practitioner of karate.

Kar·ba·la /'kärbələ/ a city in southern Iraq; pop. 185,000. A holy city for Shiite Muslims, it is the site of the tomb of Husayn, grandson of Muhammad, who was killed here in AD 680.

ka·rel·a /kəˈrelə/ ▸*n.* Indian name for **BITTER MELON.**

Ka·re·lia /kəˈrēlēə/ a region of northeastern Europe on the border between Russia and Finland. Following Finland's declaration of independence in 1917, part of Karelia became a region of Finland and part an autonomous republic of the Soviet Union. After the Russo-Finnish war of 1939–40, the greater part of Finnish Karelia was ceded to the Soviet Union. The remaining part of Karelia constitutes a province of eastern Finland. **—Ka·re·li·an** *adj.* & *n.*

Ka·ren /kəˈren/ ▸*n.* (*pl.* same or **-rens**) **1** a member of an indigenous people of eastern Myanmar (Burma) and western Thailand. **2** the language of this people, probably Sino-Tibetan.
▸*adj.* of or relating to this people or their language. ▹from Burmese *ka-reng* 'wild unclean man.'

Ka·ren State a state in southeastern Myanmar (Burma), on the border with Thailand; capital, Pa-an. Inaugurated in 1954 as an autonomous state of Burma, it was given the traditional Karen name of Kawthoolay in 1964, but reverted to Karen after the 1974 constitution limited its autonomy. The people are engaged in armed conflict with the Myanmar government in an attempt to gain independence. Also called **KAWTHOOLAY, KAWTHULEI.**

Ka·ri·ba, Lake /kəˈrēbə/ a large man-made lake on the Zambia–Zimbabwe border in central Africa. Created by damming the Zambezi River with the Kariba Dam, it is the chief source of hydroelectric power for Zimbabwe and Zambia.

Ka·ri·ba Dam a concrete arch dam on the Zambezi River on the Zambia-Zimbabwe border, 240 miles (385 km) downstream from Victoria Falls. Built in 1955–59, it created Lake Kariba and provided a bridge over the river between Zambia and Zimbabwe.

Karl XII variant spelling of **CHARLES XII.**

Karl-Marx-Stadt /kärl ˈmärks ˌsHtät/ former name (1953–90) for **CHEMNITZ.**

Kar·loff /ˈkärˌlôf/, Boris (1887–1969), U.S. actor, born in England; born *William Henry Pratt.* He appeared mostly in horror movies, such as *Frankenstein* (1931) and *The Body Snatcher* (1945).

Kar·lo·vy Va·ry /ˈkärlôvē ˈvärē/ a spa town in the western Czech Republic; pop. 56,290. It is noted for its alkaline thermal springs. German name **KARLSBAD.**

Karls·ru·he /ˈkärlzˌro͞oə/ an industrial town and port on the Rhine River in western Germany; pop. 279,000.

kar·ma /ˈkärmə/ ▸*n.* (in Hinduism and Buddhism) the sum of a person's actions in this and previous states of existence, viewed as deciding their fate in future existences. ■ *informal* destiny or fate, following as effect from cause. ▹from Sanskrit *karman* 'action, effect, fate.' **—kar·mic** /-mik/ *adj.* **—kar·mi·cal·ly** /-mik(ə)lē/ *adv.*

kar·ma yo·ga ▸*n. Hinduism* the discipline of selfless action as a way to perfection.

Kar·nak /ˈkärˌnak/ a village in Egypt on the Nile River, now largely amalgamated with Luxor. It is the site of the northern complex of monuments of ancient Thebes, including the great temple of Amun.

Kar·na·ta·ka /kärˈnätəkə/ a state in southwestern India; capital, Bangalore. Former name (until 1973) **MYSORE.**

Kar·naugh map /ˈkärˌnô/ (also **Karnaugh diagram**) ▸*n. Mathematics & Electronics* a diagram consisting of a rectangular array of squares, each representing a different combination of the variables of a Boolean function. ▹mid 20th cent.: named after U.S. physicist Maurice *Karnaugh* (1924–). **—Kar·naugh map·ping** *n.*

Kar·oo /kəˈro͞o/ (also **Kar·roo**) an elevated semidesert plateau in South Africa. ■ [as *n.*] (**a karoo**) *S. African* a tract of semidesert land. ▹from Khoikhoi, literally 'hard, dry.'

ka·ro·shi /käˈrōsHē; ˈkärˌō-/ ▸*n.* (in Japan) death caused by overwork or job-related exhaustion. ▹Japanese, from *ka* 'excess' + *rō* 'labor' + *shi* 'death.'

ka·ross /kəˈräs/ ▸*n. S. African* a rug or blanket of sewn animal skins, formerly worn as a garment by African people, now used as a bed or floor covering. ▹South African Dutch, from Khoikhoi *karos.*

Kar·pov /ˈkärˌpôf/, Anatoli (Yevgenevich) (1951–), Russian chess player. He was world champion from 1975 until defeated by Gary Kasparov in 1985.

kar·ri /ˈkarē/ ▸*n.* (*pl.* **-ris**) a tall Australian eucalyptus with hard red wood. • *Eucalyptus diversicolor*, family Myrtaceae. ▹late 19th cent.: from Nyungar.

Kar·roo variant spelling of **KAROO.**

karst /kärst/ ▸*n. Geology* landscape underlain by limestone that has been eroded by dissolution, producing ridges, towers, fissures, sinkholes, and other characteristic landforms: [as *adj.*] *karst topography* | *it was strange country, broken into hummocks and karsts and mesas.* ▹late 19th cent.: from German *der Karst*, the name of a limestone region in Slovenia. **—kars·tic** /ˈkärstik/ *adj.* **—kars·ti·fi·ca·tion** /ˌkärstəfiˈkāsHən/ *n.* **—kars·ti·fy** /ˈkärstəˌfī/ *v.* (**-fies, -fied**).

kart /kärt/ ▸*n.* a small unsprung racing vehicle typically having four wheels and consisting of a tubular frame with a rear-mounted engine. ▹mid 20th cent.: shortening of **GO-KART.** **—kart·ing** *n.*

Kart·ve·lian /kärtˈvēlēən/ ▸*adj.* another term for **SOUTH CAUCASIAN** (see **CAUCASIAN** sense 3). ▹from Georgian *Kartvelebi* 'Georgians' + **-IAN.**

karyo- ▸*comb. form Biology* denoting the nucleus of a cell: *karyotype.* ▹from Greek *karuon* 'kernel.'

kar·y·o·ki·ne·sis /ˌkarē-ōkəˈnēsis/ ▸*n. Biology* division of a cell nucleus during mitosis. ▹late 19th cent.: from **KARYO-** 'cell nucleus' + Greek *kinēsis* 'movement' (from *kinein* 'to move').

kar·y·ol·y·sis /ˌkarēˈäləsis/ ▸*n. Biology* dissolution of a cell nucleus, esp. during mitosis.

kar·y·o·type /ˈkarēəˌtīp/ ▸*n. Biology & Medicine* the number and visual appearance of the chromosomes in the cell nuclei of an organism or species. **—kar·y·o·typ·ic** /ˌkarēəˈtipik/ *adj.*

kar·y·o·typ·ing /ˈkarēəˌtīpiNG/ ▸*n. Biology & Medicine* the determination of a karyotype, e.g., to detect chromosomal abnormalities.

Ka·sai Riv·er /käˈsī/ (also **Cassai**) a river that flows for 1,100 miles (1,800 km) from central Angola through southern and central Democratic Republic of the Congo (formerly Zaire) into the Congo River. On its lower 500 miles (800 km), it is an important trade route.

kas·bah /ˈkäzbä/ ▸*n.* variant spelling of **CASBAH.**

Kash·a /ˈkasHə/ ▸*n. trademark* a soft, napped fabric of wool and hair. ■ a kind of cotton flannel used as a lining material. ▹early 20th cent.: of unknown origin.

ka·sha /ˈkäsHə/ ▸*n.* a soft food made from cooked buckwheat or similar grain. ■ uncooked buckwheat groats. ▹Russian.

Kash·mir /ˈkasHˌmi(ə)r; ˈkazH-/ a region on the northern border of India and in northeastern Pakistan. Formerly a state of India, it has been fought over by India and Pakistan since partition in 1947. The northwestern part is controlled by Pakistan, most of it forming the state of Azad Kashmir, while the remainder is incorporated into the Indian state of Jammu and Kashmir.

Kash·mir goat ▸*n.* a goat of a Himalayan breed, yielding fine, soft wool that is used to make cashmere.

Kash·mir·i /ˌkasHˈmi(ə)rē; ˌkazH-/ ▸*adj.* of or relating to Kashmir, its people, or their language.
▸*n.* **1** a native or inhabitant of Kashmir. **2** the Dardic language of Kashmir, written in both Devanagari and Arabic script.

kash·ruth /ˈkäsHrəTH; -ro͞ot; käsHˈro͞ot/ (also **kash·rut**) ▸*n.* the body of Jewish religious laws concerning the suitability of food, the fitness for use of ritual objects, etc. ■ the observance of these laws. ▹Hebrew, literally 'legitimacy (in religion)'; see also **KOSHER.**

Kas·pa·rov /ˈkäspəˌrôf; kəˈspäˌrôf/, Gary (1963–), Azerbaijani chess player; born *Gary Weinstein.* In 1985, at the age of 22, he defeated Anatoli Karpov to become the youngest-ever world chess champion. In 1997, he was beaten in a match with the IBM computer Deeper Blue, a loss that did not affect his world championship title.

Kas·se·baum /ˈkasəˌbôm; -ˌboum/, Nancy Landon (1932–) U.S. politician; the daughter of Alfred M. Landon. She was a U.S. senator from Kansas 1979–97 and in 1995 became the first female senator to head a major Senate committee–the Labor and Human Resources Committee.

Kas·sel /ˈkäsəl/ a city in central Germany, in Hesse; pop. 196,830. It was the capital of the kingdom of Westphalia 1807–13 and of the Prussian province of Hesse-Nassau 1866–1944.

Kas·ser·ine Pass /ˈkäsəˌrēn/ a historic site near the village of Al-Qasrayn in north central Tunisia. A gap in an extension of the Atlas Mountains, it was fought over by German and U.S. forces in 1943 during World War II.

Ka·sur /kəˈso͝or/ a city in northeastern Pakistan, in Punjab province; pop. 155,000.

ka·ta /ˈkätə/ ▸*n.* a system of individual training exercises for practitioners of karate and other martial arts. ■ (*pl.* same or **ka·tas**) an individual exercise of this kind. ▹Japanese.

kat·a·bat·ic /ˌkatəˈbatik/ ▸*adj. Meteorology* (of a wind) caused by local downward motion of cool air. Compare with **ANABATIC.** ▹late 19th cent.: from Greek *katabatikos*, from *katabainein* 'go down.'

Ka·tah·din, Mount /kəˈtädn/ (also **Ktaadn**) a peak in north central Maine, in Baxter State Park, 5,267 feet (1,606 m), the highest point in the state, site of the northern end of the Appalachian Trail.

ka·ta·ka·na /ˌkätəˈkänə/ ▸*n.* the more angular form of kana (syllabic writing) used in Japanese, primarily used for words of foreign origin. Compare with **HIRAGANA.** ▹early 18th cent.: Japanese, literally 'side kana.'

ka·ta·na /kəˈtänə/ ▸*n.* a long, single-edged sword used by Japanese samurai. ▹early 17th cent.: Japanese.

Ka·tan·ga /kəˈtäNGgə; -ˈtaNGgə/ former name (until 1972) for **SHABA.**

Kat·ang·ese /ˌkatäNGˈgēz; -ˈgēs; -aNG-/ ▸*n.* (*pl.* same) a native or inhabitant of Shaba (before 1972 called Katanga).
▸*adj.* of or relating to the Katangese.

ka·tha·re·vou·sa /ˌkäTHäˈrevo͞osä/ ▸*n.* the purist form of modern Greek used in traditional literary writing, as opposed to the form that is spoken and used in everyday writing (called demotic). ▹early 20th cent.: modern Greek, literally 'purifying,' feminine of *kathareuōn*, present active participle of Greek *kathareuein* 'be pure,' from *katharos* 'pure.'

Ka·thi·a·war /ˌkätēəˈwär/ a peninsula on the western coast of India, in the state of Gujarat, that separates the gulfs of Kutch and Cambay.

Kath·man·du /ˌkätmänˈdo͞o; ˌkatˌman-/ the capital of Nepal, in the east central part of the country; pop. 419,000. It is located in the Himalayas at an altitude of 4,450 feet (1,370 m).

Kat·mai Na·tion·al Park /ˈkatˌmī/ a national preserve in southwestern Alaska, on the Alaska Peninsula, noted for its volcanic activity and wildlife.

Ka·to·wi·ce /ˌkätəˈvētsə/ a city in southwestern Poland; pop. 349,000. It is the industrial center of the Silesian coal-mining region.

kat·si·na /kəˈCHēnə; kətˈsēnə/ ▸*n.* (*pl.* **-nam** /-nəm/ or **-nas**) variant of **KACHINA.**

kat·suo·bu·shi /ˌkätswōˈbo͝osHē; -ˈbo͞o-/ ▸*n.* dried fish prepared in hard blocks from the skipjack tuna and used in Japanese cooking. ▹Japanese.

kat·su·ra /ˈkätsərə/ ▸*n.* an ornamental eastern Asian tree that has leaves that resemble those of the Judas tree and light, fine-grained timber. • *Cercidiphyllum japonicum*, the only member of the family Cercidiphyllaceae. ▹early 20th cent.: from Japanese.

Kat·te·gat /ˈkätəˌgät; ˈkatəˌgat/ a strait, 140 miles (225 km) long, between Sweden and Denmark. It is linked to the North Sea by the Skagerrak and to the Baltic Sea by the Øresund.

ka·ty·did /ˈkātēˌdid/ ▸*n.* a large, typically green, long-horned grasshopper native to North America. The male makes a characteristic sound that resembles the name. • *Microcentrum* and other genera, family Tettigoniidae.

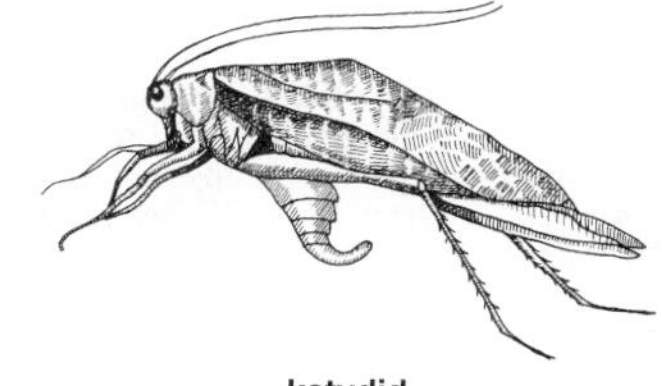

katydid

Katz /kats/, Jacob Ezra, see **KEATS**[1].

katz·en·jam·mer /ˈkatsənˌjamər/ ▸*n. informal, dated* confusion; uproar. ■ a hangover; a severe headache resulting from a hangover. ▹mid 19th cent.: from German *Katzen* (combining form of *Katze* 'cat') + *Jammer* 'distress'; popularized by the cartoon *Katzenjammer Kids*, drawn by Rudolf Dirks (1877–1968) in 1897 for the *New York Journal*, featuring two incorrigible children.

Kau·ai /ˈkou,ī/ an island in Hawaii, separated from Oahu by the Kauai Channel; chief town, Lihue.

Kauf·man /ˈkôfmən/, George S(imon) (1889–1961) U.S. journalist, playwright, and director. He collaborated with George Gershwin to write *Of Thee I Sing* (1931) and with Moss Hart to write *You Can't Take It with You* (1936) and *The Man Who Came to Dinner* (1939).

Kau·nas /ˈkounəs; -,näs/ an industrial city and river port in southern Lithuania, at the confluence of the Viliya and Neman rivers; pop. 430,000.

Ka·un·da /kəˈo͞ondə/, Kenneth (David) (1924–), Zambian statesman; first president of independent Zambia 1964–91.

kau·ri /ˈkourē/ ▸*n.* (*pl.* **-ris**) (also **kau·ri pine**) a tall coniferous forest tree that has broad leathery leaves and produces valuable timber and dammar resin. It grows in warm countries from Malaysia to New Zealand. • Genus *Agathis*, family Araucariaceae: several species, in particular *A. australis* of New Zealand. ▷early 19th cent.: from Maori.

kau·ri res·in (also **kauri gum**) ▸*n.* the resin of the kauri tree, used as a varnish, and often also found in fossilized form where the tree formerly grew.

ka·va /ˈkävə/ (also **ka·va-ka·va**) ▸*n.* **1** a narcotic sedative drink made in Polynesia from the crushed roots of a plant of the pepper family. **2** the Polynesian shrub from which this root is obtained. • *Piper methysticum*, family Piperaceae. ▷late 18th cent.: from Tongan.

Ka·ver·i variant spelling of **Cauvery**.

Kaw /käw/ ▸*n.* another name for **Kansa**.

Ka·wa·ba·ta /,käwəˈbätə/, Yasunari (1899–1972), Japanese novelist. At first an experimental writer, he reverted to traditional Japanese novel forms during the 1930s. Notable works: *The Izu Dancer* (1925) and *The Sound of the Mountain* (1949–54). Nobel Prize for Literature (1968).

Ka·wa·sa·ki /,käwəˈsäkē; ,kouə-/ an industrial city in eastern Japan, on the southeastern coast of the island of Honshu; pop. 1,174,000.

Ka·wa·sa·ki dis·ease ▸*n.* a disease of unknown cause, occurring primarily in young children and giving rise to a rash, glandular swelling, and sometimes damage to the heart. ▷1960s: named after Tomisaku *Kawasaki*, Japanese physician.

Kaw·thoo·lay /,kôᴛʜo͞oˈlā/ (also **Kaw·thu·lei**) former name (1964–74) for **Karen State**.

kay·ak /ˈkī,ak/ ▸*n.* a canoe of a type used originally by the Eskimo, made of a light frame with a watertight covering having a small opening in the top to sit in.
▸*v.* (**kay·aked, kay·ak·ing**) [*intrans.*] [usu. as *n.*] (**kayaking**) travel in or use a kayak. ▷mid 18th cent.: from Inuit *qayaq*. **—kay·ak·er** *n.*

kayak

Kay·an /ˈkīən/ ▸*n.* (*pl.* same or **-ans**) **1** a member of an indigenous people of Sarawak and Borneo. **2** the Indonesian language of this people.
▸*adj.* of or relating to this people or their language. ▷the name in Kayan.

Kaye /kā/, Danny (1913–87), U.S. actor and comedian; born *David Daniel Kominski*. He was noted for his mimicry, comic songs, and slapstick humor. Notable movies: *The Secret Life of Walter Mitty* (1947), *Hans Christian Andersen* (1952), and *The Court Jester* (1956).

kay·o /ˈkāˈō/ *informal Boxing* ▸*n.* (*pl.* **kay·os**) a knockout.
▸*v.* (**kay·oes, kay·oed**) [*trans.*] knock (someone) out. ▷1920s: representing the pronunciation of *KO*.

Kay·se·ri /,kīsəˈrē/ a city in central Turkey; pop. 421,000.

ka·za·choc /kəzäˈcʜôk/ ▸*n.* a Slavic dance with a fast and typically quickening tempo, featuring a step in which a squatting dancer kicks out each leg alternately to the front. ▷early 20th cent.: Russian, diminutive of *kazak* 'Cossack.'

Ka·zakh /kəˈzäk/ ▸*n.* **1** a member of a people living chiefly in Kazakhstan. Traditionally nomadic, Kazakhs are predominantly Sunni Muslims. **2** the Turkic language of this people.
▸*adj.* of or relating to this people or their language. ▷Russian, from Turkic; see **Cossack**.

Ka·zakh·stan /kəzäkˈstän; -zakˈstan/ a republic in central Asia, south of Russia, that extends east from the Caspian Sea to the Altai Mountains and China; population 15,143,000; capital, Astana; languages, Kazakh (official) and Russian.

The Turkic tribes of Kazakhstan were overrun by the Mongols in the 13th century, and the region was eventually absorbed into the Russian empire. Kazakhstan formed a constituent republic of the Soviet Union and became an independent republic within the Commonwealth of Independent States in 1991.

Ka·zan[1] /kəˈzän(yə)/ a port in western Russia, situated on the Volga River to the east of Nizhni Novgorod, capital of the autonomous republic of Tatarstan; pop. 1,103,000.

Ka·zan[2] /kəˈzan/, Elia (1909–2003), U.S. movie and theater director, born in Turkey; born *Elia Kazanjoglous*. In 1947, he cofounded the Actors' Studio, a leading center of method acting. He directed *A Streetcar Named Desire* (stage, 1947 and movie, 1953). Other notable movies: *On the Waterfront* (1954) and *East of Eden* (1955). He received an Academy Award for lifetime achievement in 1999.

ka·zil·lion /kəˈzilyən/ ▸*cardinal number informal* another term for **gazillion**.

ka·zoo /kəˈzo͞o/ ▸*n.* a small, simple musical instrument consisting of a hollow pipe with a hole in it, over which is a thin covering that vibrates and produces a buzzing sound when the player sings or hums into the pipe. ▷late 19th cent.: apparently imitative of the sound produced.

KB ▸*abbr.* ■ (also **Kb**) kilobyte(s). ■ (in the UK) King's Bench.

kb *Biochemistry* ▸*abbr.* kilobase(s).

Kbps ▸*abbr.* kilobits per second.

kbyte /ˈkā,bīt/ ▸*abbr.* kilobyte(s).

KC ▸*abbr.* ■ Kansas City. ■ (in the UK) King's Counsel.

kc ▸*abbr.* kilocycle(s).

kcal ▸*abbr.* kilocalorie(s).

kcl ▸*abbr.* kilocalorie.

kc/s ▸*abbr.* kilocycles per second.

KD ▸*abbr.* ■ kiln-dried. ■ knocked-down.

KE ▸*abbr.* kinetic energy.

ke·a /kēə/ ▸*n.* a New Zealand mountain parrot with a long, narrow bill and mainly olive-green plumage. • *Nestor notabilis*, family Psittacidae. ▷mid 19th cent.: from Maori, imitative of its call.

Kear·ney /ˈkärnē/ a city in southern Nebraska, on the north shore of the Platte River, southwest of Grand Island; pop. 27,431.

Kear·ny /ˈkärnē/ an industrial town in northeastern New Jersey, on Newark Bay, west of Jersey City; pop. 34,874.

Kea·ton[1] /ˈkētn/, Buster (1895–1966), U.S. actor and director; born *Joseph Francis Keaton*. Noted for his deadpan face and acrobatic skills, he starred in and directed films such as *The Navigator* (1924), and *The General* (1926).

Kea·ton[2], Diane (1946–) U.S. actress; born *Diane Hall*. She appeared in *Annie Hall* (Academy Award, 1977), *The Godfather* (1972, and its sequels 1974 and 1990), *The First Wives' Club* (1996), and *Something's Gotta Give* (2004).

Keats[1] /kēts/, Ezra Jack (1916–83) U.S. illustrator and author of children's books; born *Jacob Ezra Katz*. Some of his books in which the main character was a little boy named Peter included *The Snowy Day* (1962), *Whistle for Willie* (1964), *Goggles!* (1969), and *Pet Show* (1972).

Keats[2], John (1795–1821), English poet. A principal figure of the romantic movement, he wrote most of his best-known poems, including "La Belle Dame sans Merci," "Ode to a Nightingale," and "Ode on a Grecian Urn," in 1818; they were published in 1820. **—Keats·i·an** /ˈkētsēən/ *adj.*

ke·bab /kəˈbäb/ (also **ka·bob**) ▸*n.* a dish of pieces of meat roasted or grilled on a skewer or spit. ■ [usu. with *adj.*] a dish of any kind of food cooked in pieces in this way: *swordfish kebabs*. ▷late 17th cent.: from Arabic *kabāb*, partly via Urdu, Persian, and Turkish.

Ke·ble /ˈkēbəl/, John (1792–1866), English churchman; a founder of the Oxford Movement in 1833 with John Henry Newman and Edward Pusey.

keck /kek/ ▸*v.* [*intrans.*] *informal, chiefly Brit.* feel as if one is about to vomit: retch. ▷early 17th cent.: imitative.

kedge /kej/ ▸*v.* [*trans.*] move (a ship or boat) by hauling in a hawser attached to a small anchor dropped at some distance. ■ [*intrans.*] (of a ship or boat) move in such a way.
▸*n.* (also **kedge anchor**) a small anchor used for such a purpose. ▷late 15th cent.: perhaps a specific use of dialect *cadge* 'bind, tie.'

ked·ger·ee /ˈkejə,rē/ ▸*n.* **1** an Indian dish consisting chiefly of rice, lentils, onions, and eggs. **2** a European dish consisting chiefly of fish, rice, and hard-boiled eggs. ▷from Hindi *khichṛī*, from Sanskrit *khiccā*, a dish of rice and sesame.

keek /kēk/ *Scottish* ▸*v.* [*intrans.*] peep surreptitiously: *he keeked through the window*.
▸*n.* [in *sing.*] a surreptitious glance. ▷late Middle English: perhaps related to Dutch *kijken* 'have a look.'

keel[1] /kēl/ ▸*n.* the longitudinal structure along the centerline at the bottom of a vessel's hull, on which the rest of the hull is built, in some vessels extended downward as a blade or ridge to increase stability. ■ *Zoology* a ridge along the breastbone of many birds to which the flight muscles are attached; the carina. ■ *Botany* a prow-shaped pair of petals present in flowers of the pea family. ■ *poetic/literary* a ship.
▸*v.* [*intrans.*] (**keel over**) (of a boat or ship) turn over on its side; capsize. ■ *informal* (of a person or thing) fall over; collapse. ▷Middle English: from Old Norse *kjǫlr*, of Germanic origin. **—keeled** *adj.* [in *combination*] *a deep-keeled yacht*. **—keel·less** *adj.*

keel[2] ▸*n. Brit.* a flat-bottomed freight boat; a keelboat. ▷Middle English: from Middle Low German *kēl*, Middle Dutch *kiel* 'ship, boat.'

keel·boat /ˈkēl,bōt/ ▸*n.* **1** a yacht built with a permanent keel rather than a centerboard. **2** a large, flat freight boat used on rivers.

keel·haul /ˈkēl,hôl/ ▸*v.* [*trans.*] *historical* punish (someone) by dragging them through the water under the keel of a ship, either across the width or from bow to stern. ■ *often humorous* punish or reprimand severely. ▷mid 17th cent.: from Dutch *kielhalen*.

Kee·ling Is·lands /ˈkēliɴɢ/ another name for **Cocos Islands**.

keel·son /ˈkēlsən/ (also **kel·son**) ▸*n.* a centerline structure running the length of a ship and fastening the transverse members of the floor to the keel below. ▷Middle English *kelswayn*, related to Low German *kielswīn*, from *kiel* 'keel of a ship' + *swīn* 'swine' (used as the name of a timber).

Kee·lung /ˈkēˈlo͝oɴɢ/ see **Chilung**.

Kee·mun /ˈkēˈmo͞on; ˈkā-/ ▸*n.* a black tea grown in Keemun, China.

keen[1] /kēn/ ▸*adj.* **1** having or showing eagerness or enthusiasm: *keen believers in the monetary system* | *a keen desire to learn*. See note at **eager**. ■ [*predic.*] (**keen on**) interested in or attracted by (someone or something): *Bob makes it obvious he's keen on her*. **2** sharp or penetrating, in particular: ■ (of a sense) highly developed: *I have keen eyesight*. ■ (of mental faculties) quick to understand or function: *her keen intellect*. ■ (of the air or wind) extremely cold; biting. ■ (of the edge or point of a blade) sharp. ■ *poetic/literary* (of a smell, light, or sound) penetrating; clear. **3** [*predic.*] *informal & dated* excellent: *I would soon fly to distant stars—how keen!* **4** *Brit.* (of prices) very low; competitive. ▷Old English *cēne* 'wise, clever,' also 'brave, daring,' of Germanic origin; related to Dutch *koen* and German *kühn* 'bold, brave.' Current senses date from Middle English. **—keen·ly** *adv.* **—keen·ness** *n.*

THE RIGHT WORD **acute, astute, keen, penetrating, perspicacious, sharp, shrewd**

A knife can be **sharp**, even **keen**, but it can't be **astute**. While *keen* and *sharp* mean having a fine point or edge, they also pertain to mental agility and perceptiveness.

You might describe someone as having a *keen* mind, which suggests the ability to grapple with complex problems, or to observe details and see them as part of a larger pattern (*a keen appreciation of what victory would mean for the Democratic Party*) or a *keen* wit, which suggests an incisive or stimulating sense of humor.

Someone who is *sharp* has an alert and rational mind, but is not necessarily well grounded in a particular field and may in some cases be cunning or devious (*sharp enough to see how the situation might be turned to her advantage*).

An **astute** mind, in contrast, is one that has a thorough and profound understanding of a given subject or field (*an astute understanding of the legal principles involved*). Like *sharp*, **shrewd** implies both practicality and cleverness, but with an undercurrent of self-interest (*a shrewd salesperson*).

Acute is close in meaning to *keen*, but with more emphasis on sensitivity and the ability to make subtle distinctions (*an acute sense of smell*).

While a keen mind might see only superficial details, a **penetrating** mind would focus on underlying causes (*a penetrating analysis of the plan's feasibility*).

Perspicacious is the most formal of these terms, meaning both perceptive and discerning (*a perspicacious remark; perspicacious judgment*).

keen[2] ▶*v.* [*intrans.*] wail in grief for a dead person; sing a keen. ■ [usu. as *n.*] (**keening**) make an eerie wailing sound: *the keening of the cold night wind.*
▶*n.* an Irish funeral song accompanied by wailing in lamentation for the dead. ▷mid 19th cent.: from Irish *caoinim* 'I wail.' —**keen·er** *n.*

Keene /kēn/ a city in southwestern New Hampshire; pop. 22,563.

keep /kēp/ ▶*v.* (*past* **kept** /kept/) [*trans.*] **1** have or retain possession of: *my father would keep the best for himself* | *she had trouble keeping her balance.* ■ retain or reserve for use in the future: *return one copy to me, keeping the other for your files.* ■ put or store in a regular place: *the stand where her umbrella was kept.* ■ retain one's place in or on (a seat or saddle, the ground, etc.) against opposition or difficulty: *are you able to keep your saddle?* ■ delay or detain; cause to be late: *I won't keep you; I know you've got a busy evening.* **2** continue or cause to continue in a specified condition, position, course, etc.: [*intrans.*] *she could have had some boyfriend she kept quiet about* | *keep left along the wall* | [*trans.*] *she might be kept alive artificially by machinery.* ■ [*intrans.*] continue doing or do repeatedly or habitually: *he keeps going on about the murder.* ■ [*intrans.*] (of a perishable commodity) remain in good condition: *fresh ginger does not keep well.* ■ [*trans.*] make (someone) do something for a period of time: *I have kept her waiting too long.* ■ *archaic* continue to follow (a way, path, or course): *the friars and soldiers removed, keeping their course toward Jericho.* **3** provide for the sustenance of (someone): *he had to keep his large family in the manner he had chosen.* ■ provide (someone) with a regular supply of a commodity: *the money should* **keep** *him* **in** *cigarettes for a week.* ■ own and look after (an animal) for pleasure or profit. ■ own and manage (a shop or business). ■ guard; protect: *his only thought is to* **keep** *the boy* **from** *harm.* ■ support (someone, esp. a woman) financially in return for sexual favors: [as *adj.*] *a kept woman.* ■ [*intrans.*] act as a goalkeeper. **4** honor or fulfill (a commitment or undertaking): *I'll keep my promise, naturally.* ■ observe (a religious occasion) in the prescribed manner: *today's consumers do not keep the Sabbath.* ■ pay due regard to (a law or custom). **5** make written entries in (a diary) on a regular basis: *the master kept a weekly journal.* ■ write down as (a record): *keep a note of the whereabouts of each item.*
▶*phrasal v.* □ **keep someone after** make a student stay at school after normal hours as a punishment. □ **keep at** (or **keep someone at**) persist (or force someone to persist) with: *it was the best part of a day's work, but I kept at it.* □ **keep away** (or **keep someone away**) stay away (or make someone stay away): *keep away from the edge of the cliff.* □ **keep back** (or **keep someone/something back**) remain (or cause someone or something to remain) at a distance: *he had kept back from the river when he could.* □ **keep someone back** make a student repeat a year at school because of poor grades. □ **keep something back** retain or withhold something: *the father kept back $5 for himself.* ■ decline to disclose something. ■ prevent tears from flowing. □ **keep down** stay hidden by crouching or lying down: *Keep down! There's someone coming.* □ **keep someone down** hold someone in subjection: *but others doubted the injury would keep him down that long.* □ **keep something down** **1** cause something to remain at a low level: *the population of aphids is normally kept down by other animals.* **2** retain food or drink in one's stomach without vomiting. □ **keep from** (or **keep someone from**) avoid (or cause someone to avoid) doing something: *Dinah bit her lips to keep from screaming* | *he could hardly* **keep himself from** *laughing.* □ **keep something from** **1** cause something to remain a secret from (someone). **2** cause something to stay out of: *she could not keep the dismay from her voice.* □ **keep someone in** confine someone indoors or in a particular place: *he should be kept in overnight for a second operation.* □ **keep something in** restrain oneself from expressing a feeling: *he wanted to make me mad, but I kept it all in.* □ **keep off** **1** avoid encroaching on or touching. ■ avoid consuming or smoking: *the first thing was to keep off alcohol.* ■ avoid (a subject). **2** (of bad weather) fail to occur. □ **keep someone/something off** prevent someone or something from encroaching on or touching: *keep your hands off me.* □ **keep on** continue to do (something): *they would have preferred to keep on working.* □ **keep on about** speak about (something) repeatedly. □ **keep someone/something on** continue to use or employ someone or something. □ **keep out** (or **keep someone/something out**) remain (or cause someone or something to remain) outside: *cover with cheesecloth to keep out flies.* □ **keep to** avoid leaving (a path, road, or place). ■ adhere to (a schedule). ■ observe (a promise). ■ confine or restrict oneself to: *nothing is more irritating than people who do not keep to the point.* □ **keep someone under** hold a person or group in subjection: *the local people are kept under by the army.* □ **keep up** move or progress at the same rate as someone or something else: *often they had to pause to allow him to keep up.* ■ meet a commitment to pay or do something regularly: *if you do not* **keep up with** *the payments, the loan company can make you sell your home.* □ **keep up with** learn about or be aware of (current events or developments). ■ continue to be in contact with (someone). □ **keep someone up** prevent someone from going to bed or to sleep. □ **keep something up** maintain or preserve something in the existing state; continue a course of action: *keep up the good work.* ■ keep something in an efficient or proper state: *the new owners could not afford to keep up the grounds.* ■ make something remain at a high level: *he was whistling to keep up his spirits.*
▶*n.* **1** food, clothes, and other essentials for living: *working overtime to* **earn his keep**. ■ the cost of such items. **2** *archaic* charge; control: *if from shepherd's keep a lamb strayed far.* **3** the strongest or central tower of a castle, acting as a final refuge. ▷late Old English *cēpan* 'seize, take in,' also 'care for, attend to,' of unknown origin. —**keep·a·ble** *adj.*
▶*PHRASES* □ **you can't keep a good man** (or **woman**) **down** *informal* a competent person will always recover well from setbacks or problems. □ **for keeps** *informal* permanently; indefinitely. □ **keep one's feet** manage not to fall. □ **keep going** make an effort to live normally when in a difficult situation. □ **keep open house** provide general hospitality. □ **keep to oneself** avoid contact with others. □ **keep something to oneself** refuse to disclose or share something. □ **keep up with the Joneses** try to maintain the same social and material standards as one's friends or neighbors.

keep·er /'kēpər/ ▶*n.* **1** a person who manages or looks after something or someone, in particular: ■ a guard at a prison or a museum. ■ short for ZOOKEEPER. ■ short for GAMEKEEPER. ■ short for GOALKEEPER. ■ a person who is regarded as being in charge of someone else: *I would not stop him—I'm his wife, not his keeper.* **2** [with *adj.*] a food or drink that remains in a specified condition if stored: *hazelnuts are good keepers.* **3** *informal* a thing worth keeping: *they were deciding which drawings are questionable and which are keepers.* ■ a fish large enough to be kept when caught. **4** an object that keeps another in place, or protects something more fragile or valuable, in particular: ■ a ring worn to keep a more valuable one on the finger. ■ a bar of soft iron placed across the poles of a horseshoe magnet to maintain its strength. **5** *Football* a play in which the quarterback runs with the ball instead of handing it off or passing it. —**keep·er·ship** /-,SHip/ *n.*

keep·ing /'kēpiNG/ ▶*n.* the action of owning, maintaining, or protecting something: *the keeping of dogs* | [in *combination*] *careful record-keeping is needed.*
▶*PHRASES* □ **in someone's keeping** in someone's care or custody. □ **in** (or **out of**) **keeping with** in (or out of) harmony or conformity with: *the cuisine is in keeping with the hotel's Edwardian character.*

keep·sake /'kēp,sāk/ ▶*n.* a small item kept in memory of the person who gave it or originally owned it.

kees·hond /'kās,händ; -,hônt/ ▶*n.* a dog of a Dutch breed with long thick gray hair resembling a large Pomeranian. ▷1920s: Dutch, from *Kees* (nickname for the given name *Cornelius*) + *hond* 'dog.'

keeshond

kees·ter ▶*n.* variant spelling of KEISTER.

kef /kef/ (also **kif**) ▶*n.* a substance, esp. cannabis, smoked to produce a drowsy state. ▷early 19th cent.: from Arabic *kayf* 'enjoyment, well-being.'

Ke·fau·ver /'kē,fôvər/ (Carey) Estes (1903–63) U.S. politician. He was a member of the U.S. House of Representatives from Tennessee 1939–49, a member of the U.S. Senate 1949–63, and a Democratic vice presidential candidate 1956. As a senator, he conducted hearings 1950–51 to investigate organized crime in interstate commerce.

kef·fi·yeh ▶*n.* variant spelling of KAFFIYEH.

ke·fir /kə'fi(ə)r/ ▶*n.* a sour-tasting drink make from cow's milk fermented with certain bacteria. ▷from Russian.

Kef·la·vik /'keflə,vēk; 'kyeblə-/ a fishing port in southwestern Iceland; pop. 8,000. Iceland's international airport is located nearby.

kef·te·des /kef'tedēz; -'teTHes/ ▶*plural n.* (in Greek cooking) small meatballs made with herbs and onions. ▷from Greek *kephtedes*, plural of *kephtes*, via Turkish from Persian *koftah*.

keg /keg/ ▶*n.* **1** a small barrel, esp. one of less than 30 gallons or (in the UK) 10 gallons. **2** a unit of weight equal to 100 lb (45 kg), used for nails. ▷early 17th cent.: variant of Scots and U.S. dialect *cag*, from Old Norse *kaggi*.

Ke·gel ex·er·cise /'kēgəl; 'keg-/ ▶*n.* an exercise to strengthen the pelvic floor muscles, in which the levator muscles are squeezed and held for five seconds, then released for five seconds, for a number of repetitions. They are used to treat urinary incontinence, or to prepare for or recover from childbirth. ▷from California physician Dr. Arnold *Kegel*, who advocated such exercises from the late 1940s.

keg·ger /'kegər/ ▶*n. informal* (also **keg party**) a party at which beer is served, typically from kegs. ■ a keg of beer.

Keil·lor /'kēlər/, Garrison (Edward) (1942–), U.S. writer and radio entertainer. He created the radio program "A Prairie Home Companion" (1974–87, 1993–) and wrote fictional works such as *Happy to Be Here* (1982), *Lake Wobegon Days* (1985), and *Wobegon Boy* (1996). In 2004 he published *Homegrown Democrat: A Few Plain Thoughts from the Heart of America*.

kei·ret·su /kā'retsōō/ ▶*n.* (*pl.* same) (in Japan) a conglomeration of businesses linked together by cross-shareholdings to form a robust corporate structure. ▷Japanese, from *kei* 'systems' + *retsu* 'tier.'

keis·ter /'kēstər/ (also **kees·ter**) ▶*n.* **1** *informal* a person's buttocks. **2** *dated* a suitcase, bag, or box for carrying possessions or merchandise. ▷late 19th cent. (in the sense 'suitcase, bag'): of unknown origin.

Kei·zer /'kīzər/ a city in northwestern Oregon, a northern suburb of Salem; pop. 32,203.

Ke·ku·lé /'kekə,lā/, Friedrich August, (1829–96), German chemist; full name *Friedrich August Kekulé von Stradonitz*. One of the founders of structural organic chemistry, he is best known for discovering the ring structure of benzene.

Kel·ler /'kelər/, Helen (Adams) (1880–1968), U.S. writer, social reformer, and academic. Blind and deaf from an early age, she learned how to read, type, and speak with the help of her tutor, Anne Sullivan (1866–1936).

Kel·logg Pact /'kelôg; -âg/ (also **Kellogg–Briand Pact**) a treaty renouncing war as an instrument of national policy, signed in Paris in 1928 by representatives of fifteen nations. It grew out of a proposal made by the French Premier Aristide Briand (1862–1932) to Frank B. Kellogg (1856–1937), U.S. Secretary of State.

Kells, Book of /kelz/ an illuminated manuscript of the Gospels, perhaps made by Irish monks in Iona in the 8th or early 9th century, now kept at Trinity College, Dublin. ▷*Kells*, the name of a town in County Meath, Ireland, where the manuscript was formerly kept.

Kel·ly[1] /ˈkelē/, Emmett Lee (1898–1979), U.S. entertainer. He played Weary Willie, the mournful tramp clown, with Ringling Brothers and Barnum and Bailey Circus from 1942 until 1957.

Kel·ly[2], Gene (1912–96), U.S. dancer and choreographer; full name *Eugene Curran Kelly*. He performed in and choreographed many movie musicals, including *An American in Paris* (1951) and *Singin' in the Rain* (1952).

Kel·ly[3], Grace (Patricia) (1928–82), U.S. movie actress; also called (from 1956) **Princess Grace of Monaco**. She starred in *High Noon* (1952) and won an Academy Award for *The Country Girl* (1954). She retired from movies in 1956 to marry Prince Rainier III of Monaco. She died in an automobile accident.

Kel·ly[4], Ned (1855–80), Australian outlaw; full name *Edward Kelly*; leader of a band of horse and cattle thieves and bank robbers.

ke·loid /ˈkē,loid/ ▶*n. Medicine* an area of irregular fibrous tissue formed at the site of a scar or injury. ▷mid 19th cent.: via French from Greek *khēlē* 'crab's claw' + **-OID**.

kelp /kelp/ ▶*n.* a large brown seaweed that typically has a long, tough stalk with a broad frond divided into strips. Some kinds grow to a very large size and form underwater "forests" that support a large population of animals. • Family Laminariaceae, class Phaeophyceae, including the genera *Laminaria* (used in some areas as manure) and *Macrocystis* (harvested in the US as a source of algin). ■ the calcined ashes of seaweed, used as a source of various salts. ▷late Middle English: of unknown origin.

kelp·fish /ˈkelp,fisʜ/ ▶*n.* (*pl.* same or **-fish·es**) any of a number of fish that live among kelp or other marine algae, in particular: • a small fish with the dorsal fin running the length of the body, of the Pacific coast of North America (*Gibbonsia* and other genera, family Clinidae). • an Australian fish that lives among seagrass and algae (family Chironemidae: several genera).

kel·pie /ˈkelpē/ ▶*n.* **1** a water spirit of Scottish folklore, typically taking the form of a horse, reputed to delight in the drowning of travelers. **2** a sheepdog of an Australian breed with a smooth coat, originally bred from a Scottish collie. ▷late 17th cent.: perhaps from Scottish Gaelic *cailpeach, colpach* 'bullock, colt.' Sense 2 apparently comes from the name of a particular bitch, *King's Kelpie* (*c.*1879).

kel·son /ˈkelsən/ ▶*n.* variant spelling of **KEELSON**.

kelt /kelt/ ▶*n.* a salmon or sea trout after spawning and before returning to the sea. ▷Middle English: of unknown origin.

Kel·vin /ˈkelvən/, William Thomson, 1st Baron (1824–1907), British physicist and natural philosopher. He introduced the absolute scale of temperature and restated the second law of thermodynamics. He was involved in the laying of the first Atlantic cable, for which he invented several instruments.

kel·vin /ˈkelvən/ (abbr.: **K**) ▶*n.* the SI base unit of thermodynamic temperature, equal in magnitude to the degree Celsius. ▷late 19th cent.: named after Lord **KELVIN**.

Kel·vin scale ▶*n.* a scale of temperature with absolute zero as zero, and the triple point of water as exactly 273.16 degrees.

Ke·mal Pa·sha /keˈmäl ˈpäsʜə; kəˈmäl/ see **ATATÜRK**.

Kem·ble /ˈkembəl/, Fanny (1809–93), English actress; full name *Frances Anne Kemble*. She was a success in both Shakespearean comedy and tragedy, playing such parts as Portia, Beatrice, Juliet, and Lady Macbeth.

Ke·me·ro·vo /ˈkyemirəvə; -ə,vō/ an industrial city in south central Russia, to the east of Novosibirsk; pop. 521,000.

Kemp /kemp/, Jack (French) (1935–), U.S. politician. He was a professional football player 1957–69. A conservative Republican from New York State, he was a member of the U.S. House of Representatives 1971–89 and then served as secretary of Housing and Urban Development 1989–92. He was the Republican candidate for vice president in 1996.

kemp /kemp/ ▶*n.* a coarse hair or fiber in wool. ▷late Middle English (originally denoting a coarse human hair): from Old Norse *kampr* 'beard, whisker.' **—kemp·y** *adj.*

Kem·pis /ˈkempəs/, Thomas à, see **THOMAS À KEMPIS**.

kempt /kem(p)t/ ▶*adj. chiefly Brit.* (of a person or a place) maintained in a neat and clean condition; well cared for: *she was looking as thoroughly kempt as ever.* ▷Old English *cemd-*, past participle of *cemban* 'to comb,' of Germanic origin; related to **COMB**. The Middle English form *kemb* survives in dialect.

ken /ken/ ▶*n.* [in *sing.*] one's range of knowledge or sight: *such determination is **beyond my ken**.*
▶*v.* (**ken·ning**; *past* and *past part.* **kenned** or **kent** /kent/) [*trans.*] *Scottish & N. English* know: *d'ye ken anyone who can boast of that?* ■ recognize; identify: *that's him—d'ye ken him?* ▷Old English *cennan* 'tell, make known,' of Germanic origin; related to Dutch and German *kennen* 'know, be acquainted with,' from an Indo-European root shared by **CAN**[1] and **KNOW**. Current senses of the verb date from Middle English; the noun from the mid 16th cent.

ke·naf /kəˈnaf/ ▶*n.* a tropical plant of the mallow family that yields a jutelike fiber. • *Hibiscus cannabinus*, family Malvaceae. ■ the brown fiber of this plant, used to make paper, ropes, and coarse cloth. ▷late 19th cent.: from Persian, variant of *kanab* 'hemp.'

Ke·nai Peninsula /ˈkē,nī/ a region in southern Alaska, in the Gulf of Alaska, south of Anchorage.

Ken·dal Green /ˈkendl/ ▶*n.* a kind of rough green woolen cloth. ■ the green color of this cloth.

Ken·dall /ˈkendl/, Edward Calvin (1886–1972), U.S. biochemist. He isolated crystalline thyroxine from the thyroid gland, and he also discovered cortisone. Nobel Prize for Physiology or Medicine (1950, shared with Philip S. Hench 1896–1965 and Tadeus Reichstein 1897–1996).

ken·do /ˈken,dō/ ▶*n.* a Japanese form of fencing with two-handed bamboo swords, originally developed as a safe form of sword training for samurai. ▷Japanese, from *ken* 'sword' + *dō* 'way.' **—ken·do·ist** /-dōist/ *n.*

Ke·neal·ly /kəˈnēlē/, Thomas (Michael) (1935–), Australian novelist. He is best known for his novel *Schindler's List* (1982; movie, 1993), the true story of German industrialist Oskar Schindler, who helped more than 1,200 Jews escape death in Nazi concentration camps .

Ken·nan /ˈkenən/, George Frost (1904–) U.S. writer and diplomat. He held ambassadorships to the Soviet Union 1952 and to Yugoslavia 1961–63. He wrote *Russia Leaves the War* (1956), *Decision to Intervene* (1958), *Memoirs: 1925–1950* (1967), *Memoirs: 1950–1963* (1972), and *Cloud of Danger* (1977).

Ken·ne·bec Riv·er /ˈkenə,bek/ a river that flows for 150 miles (240 km) through west central Maine to the Atlantic Ocean. Waterville, Augusta, and Bath lie on it.

Ken·ne·dy[1] /ˈkenidē/ the name of a prominent U.S. political family: ■ **John Fitzgerald** (1917–63), 35th president of the U.S. 1961–63; known as **JFK**. The youngest person to be elected to the presidency, he was a popular advocate of civil rights. In foreign affairs he recovered from the Bay of Pigs fiasco to demand successfully the withdrawal of Soviet missiles from Cuba during the Cuban Missile Crisis, October 18–29, 1962. On November 22, 1963, he was assassinated while riding in a motorcade through Dallas, Texas. Lee Harvey Oswald was charged with his murder. ■ **Robert (Francis)** (1925–68), U.S. attorney general 1961–64; brother of John and Ted; known as **Bobby**. He closely assisted his brother John in domestic policy and was also a champion of the civil rights movement. He was assassinated during his campaign to become the 1968 Democratic presidential nominee. ■ **Edward** (1932–), U.S. senator 1962–; brother of John and Robert; known as **Ted**; full name *Edward Moore Kennedy*. His political career was overshadowed by his involvement in an automobile accident on Chappaquiddick Island in 1969, in which his assistant Mary Jo Kopechne (1940–69) drowned.

John F. Kennedy

Ken·ne·dy[2], Anthony McLeod (1935–) U.S. Supreme Court associate justice 1988– . Appointed to the Court by President Reagan, he maintained a generally conservative stance.

Ken·ne·dy[3], Joseph Patrick (1888–1969) U.S. businessman and diplomat; father of John Fitzgerald, Robert Francis, and Edward Moore Kennedy. He made his fortune in banking, the stock market, shipbuilding, and movies.

Ken·ne·dy[4], William (1928–) U.S. writer. His novels include *Ironweed* (1983), *Quinn's Book* (1988), *Very Old Bones* (1992), and *The Flaming Corsage* (1996).

Ken·ne·dy, Cape former name (1963–73) for **CANAVERAL, CAPE**.

ken·nel /ˈkenl/ ▶*n.* a small shelter for a dog or cat. ■ a boarding or breeding establishment for dogs or cats. ■ *figurative* a small or sordid dwelling.
▶*v.* (**-neled**, **-nel·ing**; *chiefly Brit.* **-nelled**, **-nel·ling**) [*trans.*] put (a dog or cat) in a kennel. ▷Middle English: from an Old Northern French variant of Old French *chenil*, from Latin *canis* 'dog.'

Ken·nel·ly /ˈkenələ/, Arthur Edwin (1861–1939), U.S. electrical engineer. He worked on the theory of alternating currents, and, independently of O. Heaviside, he also discovered the layer in the atmosphere responsible for reflecting radio waves back to the earth.

Ken·nel·ly lay·er (also **Ken·nel·ly–Heav·i·side lay·er** /ˈhevē,sīd/) ▶*n.* another name for **E LAYER**.

Ken·ner /ˈkenər/ a city in southeastern Louisiana, west of New Orleans; pop. 70,517.

Ken·neth I /ˈkenitʜ/ (d.858), king of Scotland *c.*844–858; known as **Kenneth MacAlpin**. He is traditionally viewed as the founder of the kingdom of Scotland, which was established following his defeat of the Picts in about 844.

Ken·ne·wick /ˈkenəwik/ a city in southeastern Washington, on the Columbia River; pop. 54,693.

ken·ning /ˈkeniɴɢ/ ▶*n.* a compound expression in Old English and Old Norse poetry with metaphorical meaning, e.g., *oar-steed* = ship. ▷late 19th cent.: from Old Norse, from *kenna* 'know, perceive'; related to **KEN**.

ke·no /ˈkēnō/ ▶*n.* a game of chance similar to lotto, based on the drawing of numbers that must correspond with selected numbers on cards. ▷early 19th cent.: from French *kine*, denoting a set of five winning lottery numbers.

Ke·no·sha /kəˈnōsʜə/ an industrial port city in southeastern Wisconsin, on Lake Michigan; pop. 90,352.

ke·no·sis /kəˈnōsis/ ▶*n.* (in Christian theology) the renunciation of the divine nature, at least in part, by Christ in the Incarnation. ▷late 19th cent.: from Greek *kenōsis* 'an emptying,' from *kenoun* 'to empty,' from *kenos* 'empty,' with biblical allusion (Phil. 2:7) to Greek *heauton ekenōse*, literally 'emptied himself.' **—ke·not·ic** /-ˈnätik/ *adj.*

Ken·sing·ton /ˈkenziɴɢtən/ a fashionable residential district in central London, England. Part of the borough of Kensington and Chelsea, it contains Kensington palace and gardens and the Victoria and Albert, Natural History, and Science museums.

ken·speck·le /ˈken,spekəl/ ▶*adj. Scottish* easily recognizable; conspicuous. ▷mid 16th cent.: of Scandinavian origin, probably based on Old Norse *kenna* 'know, perceive' and *spak-, spek-* 'wise or wisdom.'

Kent[1] /kent/ a county on the southeastern coast of England; county town, Maidstone. ▷from Latin *Cantium*, of Celtic origin. **—Kent·ish** *adj.*

Kent[2] **1** a city in northeastern Ohio, home to Kent State University; pop. 28,835. **2** a city in western Washington, on the Naches River, a southern suburb of Seattle; pop. 79,524.

kent /kent/ ▶ past and past participle of **KEN**.

ken·te /ˈkentə; -tē/ ▶*n.* a brightly colored, banded material made in Ghana. ■ a long garment made from this material, worn loosely around the shoulders and waist. ▷mid 20th cent.: from Twi, 'cloth.'

ken·ti·a palm /ˈkentēə/ (also **ken·ti·a**) ▶*n.* an Australasian palm tree that is popular as a houseplant while it is young. • *Howeia* (or **Howea**) *forsteriana* (formerly *Kentia forsteriana*), family Palmae. ▷late

19th cent.: modern Latin, named after William *Kent* (died 1828), botanical collector.

Ken·ton /'kentn/, Stan (1912–79), U.S. bandleader, composer, and arranger; born *Stanley Newcomb*. He formed his own orchestra in 1940 and is particularly associated with the big-band jazz style of the 1950s. Notable works: "Artistry in Rhythm" (1941) and "Eager Beaver" (1943).

Ken·tuck·y /kən'təkē/ a state in the southeastern U.S.; pop. 4,041,769; capital, Frankfort; statehood, June 1, 1792 (15). Ceded by the French to the British in 1763 and then to the U.S. in 1783 by the Treaty of Paris, it was explored by Daniel Boone. —**Ken·tuck·i·an** /-ēən/ *adj.*

Ken·tuck·y col·o·nel ▶*n.* an honorary commission given by the state of Kentucky to individuals noted for their public service and their work for the advancement of Kentucky.

Ken·tuck·y Der·by ▶*n.* an annual horse race for three-year-olds at Louisville, Kentucky. First held in 1875, it is the oldest horse race in the U.S. It is the first race of horse racing's Triple Crown.

Ken·ya /'kenyə; 'kēnyə/ a country in East Africa, on the Indian Ocean; pop. 32,021,000; capital, Nairobi; languages, Swahili (official), English (official), and Kikuyu. —**Ken·yan** *adj.* & *n.*

Populated largely by Bantu-speaking peoples, Kenya became a British Crown Colony in 1920. The demands made on land by European settlers led to the Mau Mau rebellion of the 1950s. Kenya became an independent state within the Commonwealth of Nations in 1963, and a republic was established the following year.

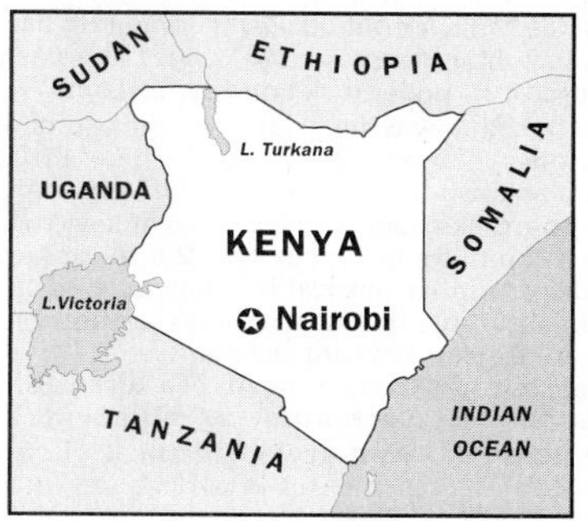

Ken·ya, Mount a mountain in central Kenya, just south of the equator, that rises to a height of 17,058 feet (5,200 m). The second highest mountain in Africa, it gave its name to the country of Kenya.

Ken·yat·ta /ken'yätə/, Jomo (*c.*1891–1978), Kenyan statesman; prime minister 1963 and president 1964–78.

kep·i /'kāpē; 'kepē/ ▶*n.* (*pl.* **kep·is**) a French military cap with a flat top and horizontal brim. ▷mid 19th cent.: from French *képi*, from Swiss German *Käppi*, diminutive of *Kappe* 'cap.'

kepi

Kep·ler /'keplər/, Johannes (1571–1630), German astronomer. He discovered the three laws that govern orbital motion. —**Kep·ler·i·an** /kep'li(ə)rēən/ *adj.*

Kep·ler's laws three theorems describing orbital motion. The first law states that planets move in elliptical orbits with the sun at one focus. The second states that the radius vector of a planet sweeps out equal areas in equal times. The third law relates the distances of the planets from the sun to their orbital periods.

kept /kept/ ▶ past and past participle of **KEEP**.

Ke·ra·la /'kerələ/ a state on the southwestern coast of India; capital, Trivandrum. It was created in 1956 from the former state of Travancore-Cochin and part of Madras. —**Ke·ra·lite** /-,līt/ *adj.* & *n.*

kerat- ▶*comb. form* variant spelling of **KERATO-** shortened before a vowel (as in *keratectomy*).

ker·a·tec·to·my /,kerə'tektəmē/ ▶*n.* surgical removal of a section or layer of the cornea, usually performed using a laser to correct myopia.

ker·a·tin /'kerətin/ ▶*n.* a fibrous protein forming the main structural constituent of hair, feathers, hoofs, claws, horns, etc. ▷mid 19th cent.: from Greek *keras, kerat-* 'horn' + **-IN**[1]. —**ke·rat·i·nous** /kə'ratn-əs/ *adj.*

ker·a·tin·ize /'kerətn,īz/ ▶*v. Biology* change or become changed into a form containing keratin: [*trans.*] *the products of the epidermal line are ultimately keratinized* | [*intrans.*] *the cells keratinize under estrogenic action.* ▷late 19th cent.: from Greek *keratinos* 'horny' + **-IZE**. —**ker·a·tin·i·za·tion** /,kerətn-i'zāshən/ *n.*

ker·a·tin·o·cyte /kə'ratn-ə,sīt/ ▶*n. Biology* an epidermal cell that produces keratin.

ker·a·ti·tis /,kerə'tītis/ ▶*n. Medicine* inflammation of the cornea of the eye.

kerato- ▶*comb. form* (also **kerat-**) **1** relating to keratin or horny tissue. **2** relating to the cornea. ▷from Greek *keras, kerat-* 'horn.'

ker·a·to·mi·leu·sis /,kerətōmī'lōōsis/ ▶*n.* the surgical reshaping of the cornea, carried out in order to correct a refractive error. ▷1990s: from *kerato-* 'of the cornea' + Greek *smileusis* 'carving.'

ker·a·to·plas·ty /'kerətə,plastē/ ▶*n.* surgery carried out on the cornea, esp. corneal transplantation.

ker·a·tose /'kerə,tōs/ ▶*adj. Zoology* (of certain sponges) composed of a horny substance. ▷mid 19th cent.: from Greek *keras, kerat-* 'horn' + **-OSE**[1].

ker·a·to·sis /,kerə'tōsis/ ▶*n.* (*pl.* **-ses** /-sēz/) *Medicine* a horny growth, esp. on the skin.

ker·a·tot·o·my /,kerə'tätəmē/ ▶*n.* a surgical operation involving cutting into the cornea of the eye. The most common form is **radial keratotomy**, performed to correct myopia.

kerb /kərb/ ▶*n.* British spelling of **CURB**.

Kerch /kerch/ a city in southern Ukraine, the chief port and industrial center of the Crimea, at the eastern end of the Kerch peninsula; pop. 176,000.

ker·chief /'kərchəf; -,chēf/ ▶*n.* a piece of fabric used to cover the head, or worn tied around the neck. ■ a handkerchief. ▷Middle English *kerchef*, from Old French *cuevrechief*, from *couvrir* 'to cover' + *chief* 'head.' —**ker·chiefed** *adj.*

Ke·res /'kā,rās/ ▶*n.* (*pl.* same) **1** a member of a Pueblo Indian people of New Mexico. **2** the language of this people, of unknown affinity.
▶*adj.* of or relating to this people or their language. ▷from American Spanish *Queres*, from American Indian. —**Ker·e·san** /'kerisən/ *adj.*

kerf /kərf/ ▶*n.* **1** a slit made by cutting, esp. with a saw. **2** the cut end of a felled tree. ▷Old English *cyrf* 'cutting, a cut'; related to **CARVE**. —**kerfed** *adj.*

ker·fuf·fle /kər'fəfəl/ ▶*n.* [in *sing.*] *informal, chiefly Brit.* a commotion or fuss, esp. one caused by conflicting views: *there was a kerfuffle over the chairmanship.* ▷early 19th cent.: perhaps from Scots *curfuffle* (probably from Scottish Gaelic *car* 'twist, bend' + imitative Scots *fuffle* 'to disorder'), or related to Irish *cior thual* 'confusion, disorder.'

Ker·guel·en Is·lands /'kərgələn; ,kərgə'len/ a group of islands in the southern Indian Ocean that comprise the island of Kerguelen and some 300 small islets, part of the French Southern and Antarctic Territories. The only settlement is a scientific base. ▷named after the Breton navigator Yves-Joseph de *Kerguélen*-Trémarec, who discovered the islands in 1772.

Kér·ki·ra /'kerki(ə)rə/ modern Greek name for **CORFU**.

Ker·mad·ec Is·lands /kər'madik/ a group of uninhabited islands in the western South Pacific Ocean, north of New Zealand, administered by New Zealand since 1887.

ker·mes /'kermēz/ ▶*n.* **1** a red dye used, esp. formerly, for coloring fabrics and manuscripts. ■ the dried bodies of a female scale insect, which are crushed to yield this dye. **2** (**oak kermes**) the scale insect that is used for this dye, forming berrylike galls on the kermes oak. • *Kermes ilicis*, family Eriococcidae, suborder Homoptera. ▷late 16th cent. (denoting the kermes oak): from French *kermès*, from Arabic *ḳirmiz*; related to **CRIMSON**.

ker·mes oak ▶*n.* a very small evergreen Mediterranean oak that sometimes remains a shrub. It has prickly hollylike leaves and was formerly prized as a host plant for the insect kermes. • *Quercus coccifera*, family Fagaceae.

ker·mis /'kərmis/ ▶*n.* a summer fair held in towns and villages in the Netherlands. ■ a fair or carnival, esp. one held to raise money for a charity. ▷late 16th cent.: Dutch, originally denoting a mass on the anniversary of the dedication of a church, when a fair was held, from *kerk* 'church' + *mis* 'Mass.'

Kern /kərn/, Jerome (David) (1885–1945), U.S. composer. A major influence in the development of the musical, he wrote several musical comedies, including *Showboat* (1927), which featured the song "Ol' Man River."

kern[1] /kərn/ *Printing* ▶*v.* [*trans.*] **1** [usu. as *n.*] (**kerning**) adjust the spacing between (letters or characters) in a piece of text to be printed. ■ make (letters) overlap. **2** design (metal type) with a projecting part beyond the body or shank.
▶*n.* the part of a metal type projecting beyond its body or shank. ▷late 17th cent.: perhaps from French *carne* 'corner,' from Latin *cardo, cardin-* 'hinge.'

kern[2] (also **kerne**) ▶*n.* **1** *historical* a light-armed Irish foot soldier. **2** *archaic* a peasant; a rustic. ▷late Middle English: from Irish *ceithearn*, from Old Irish *ceithern* 'band of foot soldiers.'

ker·nel /'kərnl/ ▶*n.* a softer, usually edible part of a nut, seed, or fruit stone contained within its hard shell. ■ the seed and hard husk of a cereal, esp. wheat. ■ [in *sing.*] the central or most important part of something: *this is the kernel of the argument.* ■ the most basic level or core of an operating system of a computer, responsible for resource allocation, file management, and security. ■ [as *adj.*] *Linguistics* denoting a basic unmarked linguistic string. ▷Old English *cyrnel*, diminutive of **CORN**[1].

kern·ite /'kərnīt/ ▶*n.* a transparent crystalline mineral that consists of hydrated sodium borate. ▷early 20th cent.: from *Kern* (the name of the California county where it was discovered) + **-ITE**[1].

ker·o·gen /'kerəjən/ ▶*n.* a complex fossilized organic material, found in oil shale and other sedimentary rock, that is insoluble in common organic solvents and yields petroleum products on distillation. ▷early 20th cent.: from Greek *kēros* 'wax' + **-GEN**.

ker·o·sene /'kerə,sēn; 'kar-; ,kerə'sēn; ,kar-/ (also *chiefly Brit.* **ker·o·sine**) ▶*n.* a light fuel oil obtained by distilling petroleum, used esp. in jet engines and domestic heaters and lamps and as a cleaning solvent. ▷mid 19th cent.: from Greek *kēros* 'wax' (because the solid form of paraffin is waxlike) + **-ENE**.

Ker·ou·ac /'kerōō,ak/, Jack (1922–69), U.S. novelist and poet; born *Jean-Louis Lebris de Kérouac*. A leading figure of the beat generation, he is best known for his semiautobiographical novel *On the Road* (1957). Other notable works: *Doctor Sax* (1959) and *Big Sur* (1962).

Kerr ef·fect /kər; kär/ ▶*n. Physics* **1** the rotation of the plane of polarization of light when reflected from a magnetized surface. **2** the production of double refraction in a substance by an electric field. ▷early 20th cent.: named after John *Kerr* (1824–1907), the Scottish physicist who studied these effects.

ker·ri·a /'kerēə/ ▶*n.* an eastern Asian shrub of the rose family, cultivated for its yellow flowers, esp. the double-flowered variety. • *Kerria japonica*, family Rosaceae. ▷early 19th cent.: modern Latin, named after William *Ker(r)* (died 1814), English botanical collector.

Ker·ri·gan /'kerigən/, Nancy (1969–) U.S. figure skater. She won a silver medal at the 1994 Olympic games despite a vicious assault planned by rival Tonya Harding (1970–) that injured her knee six weeks before the games.

Ker·ry[1] /'kerē/ a county of the Republic of Ireland, on the southwestern coast in the province of Munster; county town, Tralee.

Ker·ry[2], John Forbes (1943–), U.S. politician. A liberal Democrat from Massachusetts, he served in the U.S. Senate from 1985 and was the Democratic candidate for president in 2004. During his service in the U.S. Navy in Vietnam he received a Silver Star, a Bronze Star with Combat V, and three Purple

John F. Kerry

Pronunciation Key ə *ago*; ər *over*; 'ə or ,ə *up*; 'ər or ,ər *fur*; a *hat*; ā *rate*; ä *car*; ch *chew*; e *let*; ē *see*; e(ə)r *air*; i *fit*; ī *by*; i(ə)r *ear*; ng *sing*; ō *go*; ô *for*; oi *boy*; ŏŏ *good*; ōō *goo*; ou *out*; sh *she*; th *thin*; t͟h *then*; (h)w *why*; zh *vision*

Hearts. Upon returning from the war, he became a leader in Vietnam Veterans Against the War (VVAW) and gave powerful testimony before the Senate Foreign Relations Committee in 1971. He was a prosecutor in Massachusetts and then served as lieutenant governor 1982–1984.

Ker·ry blue (also **Kerry blue terrier**) ▶*n.* a terrier of a breed with a silky blue-gray coat.

ker·sey /ˈkərzē/ ▶*n.* a kind of coarse, ribbed cloth with a short nap, woven from short-stapled wool. ▷late Middle English: probably from *Kersey*, a town in Suffolk, England, where woolen cloth was made.

ker·sey·mere /ˈkərzē,mir/ ▶*n.* a fine twilled woolen cloth. ▷late 18th cent.: alteration of *cassimere*, variant of CASHMERE, changed by association with KERSEY.

Ker·u·len Riv·er /ˈkerə,len/ (also called **Herlen**) a river in northeastern Mongolia and northeastern China that rises in the Hentiyn Nuruu range northeast of Ulaanbaatar in Mongolia and flows south and east for 785 miles (1,263 km) to Hulun Lake in China's Heilongjiang Province.

Ke·sey /ˈkēzē/, Ken (Elton) (1935–2001), U.S. novelist. His best-known novel, *One Flew over the Cuckoo's Nest* (1962; film 1975), is based on his experiences as a ward attendant in a mental hospital.

kes·trel /ˈkestrəl/ ▶*n.* a small falcon that hovers with rapidly beating wings while searching for prey on the ground. • Genus *Falco*, family Falconidae: several species, in particular the **common kestrel** (*F. tinnunculus*) of Eurasia and Africa, and the **American kestrel** (*F. sparverius*). ▷late Middle English *castrel*, perhaps from *casserelle*, dialect variant of Old French *crecerelle*, perhaps imitative of its call.

ke·ta·mine /ˈketə,mēn; -min/ ▶*n.* a synthetic compound used as an anesthetic and analgesic drug and also (illicitly) as a hallucinogen. • Chem. formula: $C_{13}H_{16}NOCl$. ▷mid 20th cent.: blend of KETONE and AMINE.

ketch /keCH/ ▶*n.* a two-masted, fore-and-aft-rigged sailboat with a mizzenmast stepped forward of the rudder and smaller than the foremast. ▷mid 17th cent.: later form of obsolete *catch*, probably from CATCH.

Ketch·i·kan /ˈkeCHi,kan/ a city in southeastern Alaska, on Revillagigedo Island, in the Alexander Archipelago; pop. 7,922.

ketch·up /ˈkeCHəp/ (also **cat·sup** *pronunc.* same or /ˈkaCHəp; ˈkatsəp/) ▶*n.* a spicy sauce made chiefly from tomatoes and vinegar, used as a condiment. ▷late 17th cent.: perhaps from Chinese (Cantonese dialect) *k'ē chap* 'tomato juice.'

ke·tene /ˈkē,tēn/ ▶*n. Chemistry* a pungent colorless reactive gas, used as an intermediate in chemical synthesis. • Chem. formula: $CH_2{=}C{=}O$. ■ any substituted derivative of this. ▷early 20th cent.: from KETONE + -ENE.

ke·to ac·id /ˈkētō/ ▶*n. Chemistry* a compound whose molecule contains both a carboxyl group (−COOH) and a ketone group (−CO−).

ke·tone /ˈkē,tōn/ ▶*n. Chemistry* an organic compound containing a carbonyl group =C=O bonded to two alkyl groups, made by oxidizing secondary alcohols. The simplest such compound is acetone. ▷mid 19th cent.: from German *Keton*, alteration of *Aketon* 'acetone.' —**ke·ton·ic** /kēˈtänik/ *adj.*

ke·tone bod·y ▶*n. Biochemistry* any of three related compounds (acetone, acetoacetic acid, beta-hydroxybutyric acid) produced during the metabolism of fats.

ke·to·ne·mi·a /,kētəˈnēmēə/ (*Brit.* **ke·to·nae·mi·a**) ▶*n. Medicine* the presence of an abnormally high concentration of ketone bodies in the blood.

ke·to·nu·ri·a /,kētōˈn(y)o͝orēə/ ▶*n. Medicine* the excretion of abnormally large amounts of ketone bodies in the urine, characteristic of diabetes mellitus, starvation, or other medical conditions.

ke·to·sis /kēˈtōsis/ ▶*n. Medicine* a condition characterized by raised levels of ketone bodies in the body, associated with abnormal fat metabolism and diabetes mellitus. —**ke·tot·ic** /-ˈtätik/ *adj.*

Ket River /ˈket/ a river in Russia that flows west for 842 miles (1,355 km) from Krasnoyarsk into the Ob River at Kolpashevo.

Ket·ter·ing[1] /ˈketəriNG/ a city in southwestern Ohio, southeast of Dayton; pop. 57,502.

Ket·ter·ing[2], Charles Franklin (1876–1958), U.S. automobile engineer. He developed the electric starter in 1912 and went on to discover tetraethyl lead as an anti-knock agent and to define the octane rating of fuels.

ket·tle /ˈketl/ ▶*n.* a vessel, usually made of metal and with a handle, used for boiling liquids or cooking foods; a pot. ■ a teakettle. ▷Old English *cetel*, *cietel*, of Germanic origin, based on Latin *catillus*, diminutive of *catinus* 'deep container for cooking or serving food.' In Middle English the word's form was influenced by Old Norse *ketill*. —**ket·tle·ful** /-,fo͝ol/ *n.* (*pl.* **-fuls**).

▶*PHRASES* □ **a different kettle of fish** *informal* a completely different type of person or thing from the one previously mentioned: *the new office is a rather different kettle of fish.* □ **the pot calling the kettle black** see POT[1]. □ **a fine** (or **pretty**) **kettle of fish** *informal* an awkward state of affairs.

ket·tle corn ▶*n.* popcorn that is sweetened with sugar during cooking.

ket·tle·drum /ˈketl,drəm/ ▶*n.* a large drum shaped like a bowl, with a membrane adjustable for tension (and so pitch) stretched across. Also collectively called TIMPANI. —**ket·tle·drum·mer** *n.*

kettledrum

ket·tle hole ▶*n. Geology* a hollow, typically filled by a lake, resulting from the melting of a mass of ice trapped in glacial deposits.

keV ▶*abbr.* kiloelectronvolt(s).

Kev·lar /ˈkevlär/ ▶*n. trademark* a synthetic fiber of high tensile strength used esp. as a reinforcing agent in the manufacture of tires and other rubber products and protective gear such as helmets and vests.

Kew Gar·dens /kyo͞o/ the Royal Botanic Gardens at Kew, in Richmond, London. They were developed by the mother of George III with the aid of Sir Joseph Banks.

kew·pie /ˈkyo͞opē/ (also **kewpie doll**) ▶*n. trademark* a type of doll characterized by a large head, big eyes, chubby cheeks, and a curl or topknot on top of its head. ▷early 20th cent. (originally U.S.): from CUPID + -IE.

Key /kē/, Francis Scott (1779–1843) U.S. lawyer and poet. A witness to the successful U.S. defense against the British bombardment of Fort McHenry in Baltimore in September 1814, he wrote the poem "Defence of Fort M'Henry." The poem was later set to music, renamed "The Star-Spangled Banner," and, in 1931, adopted as the U.S. national anthem.

key[1] /kē/ ▶*n.* (*pl.* **keys**) **1** a small piece of shaped metal with incisions cut to fit the wards of a particular lock, and that is inserted into a lock and turned to open or close it. ■ a similar implement for operating a switch in the form of a lock, esp. one operating the ignition of a motor vehicle. ■ short for KEY CARD. ■ an instrument for grasping and turning a screw, peg, or nut, esp. one for winding a clock or turning a valve. ■ a pin, bolt, or wedge inserted between other pieces, or fitting into a hole or space designed for it, so as to lock parts together. **2** one of several buttons on a panel for operating a typewriter, word processor, or computer terminal. ■ a lever depressed by the finger in playing an instrument such as the organ, piano, flute, or concertina. ■ a lever operating a mechanical device for making or breaking an electric circuit, for example, in telegraphy. **3** a thing that provides a means of gaining access to or understanding something: *the* **key** *to Jack's behavior may lie submerged in his unhappy past.* ■ an explanatory list of symbols used in a map, table, etc. ■ a set of answers to exercises or problems. ■ a word or system for solving a cipher or code. ■ the first move in the solution of a chess problem. ■ *Computing* a field in a record that is used to identify that record uniquely. **4** *Music* a group of notes based on a particular note and comprising a scale, regarded as forming the tonal basis of a piece or passage of music: *the key of E minor.* ■ the tone or pitch of someone's voice: *his voice had changed to a lower key.* ■ *figurative* the prevailing tone or tenor of a piece of writing, situation, etc.: *it was like the sixties all over again, in a new, more austerely intellectual key.* ■ the prevailing range of tones or intensities in a painting: *these mauves, lime greens, and saffron yellows recall the high key of El Greco's palette.* **5** the dry winged fruit of an ash, maple, or sycamore maple, typically growing in bunches; a samara. **6** *Brit.* the part of a first coat of wall plaster that passes between the laths and so secures the rest. ■ [in *sing.*] the roughness of a surface, helping the adhesion of plaster or other material. **7** *Basketball* the keyhole-shaped area marked on the court near each basket, comprising the free-throw circle and the foul line.

▶*adj.* of paramount or crucial importance: *she became a key figure in the suffragette movement.*

▶*v.* (**keys**, **keyed** /kēd/) [*trans.*] **1** enter or operate on (data) by means of a computer keyboard: *she* **keyed in** *a series of commands* | [*intrans.*] *a hacker caused considerable disruption after* **keying into** *a vital database.* **2** [*trans.*] (usu. **be keyed**) fasten (something) in position with a pin, wedge, or bolt: *the coils may be keyed into the slots by fiber wedges.* ■ (**key something to**) make something fit in with or be linked to: *this optimism is keyed to the possibility that the U.S. might lead in the research field.* ■ (**key someone/something into/in with**) cause someone or something to be in harmony with: *to those who are keyed into his lunatic sense of humor, the arrival of any Bergman movie is a major comic event.* **3** *Brit.* roughen (a surface) to help the adhesion of plaster or other material. **4** word (an advertisement in a particular periodical), typically by varying the form of the address given, so as to identify the publication generating particular responses. **5** *informal* be the crucial factor in achieving: *Ewing keyed a 73–35 advantage on the boards with twenty rebounds.* **6** [*trans.*] vandalize a car by scraping the paint from it with a key: *somebody could key your car and not get punished.*

▶*phrasal v.* □ **key someone up** (usu. **be keyed up**) make someone nervous, tense, or excited, esp. before an important event. ▷Old English *cǣg*, *cǣge*, of unknown origin. —**keyed** *adj.* —**key·er** *n.* —**key·less** *adj.*

▶*PHRASES* □ **in** (or **out of**) **key** in (or out of) harmony: *this vaguely uplifting conclusion is out of key with the body of his book.* □ **under lock and key** see LOCK[1].

key[2] ▶*n.* a low-lying island or reef, esp. in the Caribbean. Compare with CAY. ▷late 17th cent.: from Spanish *cayo* 'shoal, reef,' influenced by QUAY.

key·board /ˈkē,bôrd/ ▶*n.* **1** a panel of keys that operate a computer or typewriter. **2** a set of keys on a piano or similar musical instrument. ■ an electronic musical instrument with keys arranged as on a piano: *she plays keyboard and guitar.*

▶*v.* [*trans.*] enter (data) by means of a keyboard. —**key·board·er** *n.* —**key·board·ist** /-ist/ *n.* (in sense 2).

key card (also **card key**) ▶*n.* a small plastic card, sometimes used instead of a door key in hotels, bearing magnetically encoded data that can be read and processed by an electronic device.

key·chain drive /ˈkē,CHān/ ▶*n. Computing* another term for USB FLASH DRIVE.

key grip ▶*n.* the person in a film crew who is in charge of the camera equipment.

key·hole /ˈkē,hōl/ ▶*n.* a hole in a lock into which the key is inserted. ■ a circle cut out of a garment as a decorative effect, typically at the front or back neckline of a dress.

key·hole saw ▶*n.* a saw with a long, narrow blade for cutting small holes such as keyholes.

key·hole sur·ger·y ▶*n. informal* minimally invasive surgery carried out through a very small incision, with special instruments and techniques including fiber optics.

Key Lar·go /ˈkē ˈlärgō/ a resort island off the southern coast of Florida, the northernmost and the longest of the Florida Keys.

key light ▶*n.* the main source of light in a photograph or film.

Key lime ▶*n.* a small yellowish lime with a sharp flavor. ▷named after the Florida *Keys*.

Key lime pie ▶*n.* a custard pie made with the juice of Key limes.

key mon·ey ▶*n. informal* money paid to a landlord as an inducement by a person wishing to rent a property.

Keynes /kānz/, John Maynard, 1st Baron (1883–1946), English economist. He laid the foundations of modern macroeconomics with *The General Theory of Employment, Interest and Money* (1936). —**Keynes·i·an** /ˈkānzēən/ *adj.* & *n.* —**Keynes·i·an·ism** /ˈkānzēə,nizəm/ *n.*

key·note /ˈkē,nōt/ ▶*n.* **1** a prevailing tone or central theme, typically one set or introduced at the start of a conference: *individuality is the keynote of the Nineties* | [*as adj.*] *he delivered the keynote address at the launch.* **2** *Music* the note on which a key is based. —**key·not·er** *n.*

key·pad /ˈkē,pad/ ▶*n.* a miniature keyboard or set of

buttons for operating a portable electronic device, telephone, or other equipment.

key·pal /ˈkē,pal/ ▸*n.* (especially among students) a person with whom one becomes friendly by exchanging e-mails. ▷1990s: from *key* + *pal*, by analogy with *pen pal*.

key·punch /ˈkē,pənCH/ ▸*n.* a device for transferring data by means of punching holes or notches on a series of cards or paper tape.
▸*v.* [*trans.*] put into the form of punched cards or paper tape by means of such a device. **—key·punch·er** *n.*

key ring ▸*n.* a metal ring onto which keys may be threaded in order to keep them together.

key sig·na·ture ▸*n.* *Music* any of several combinations of sharps or flats after the clef at the beginning of each stave indicating the key of a composition.

key·stone /ˈkē,stōn/ ▸*n.* a central stone at the summit of an arch, locking the whole together. ■ [usu. in *sing.*] the central principle or part of a policy, system, etc., on which all else depends: *cooperation remains the keystone of the government's security policy.*

keystone

Key·stone Kops /ˈkē,stōn käps/ a group of bumbling police characters featured in a number of the silent slapstick comedy films produced by Keystone Studios, which was founded by Mack Sennett in 1912.

key·stone spe·cies ▸*n.* (*pl.* same) a species on which other species in an ecosystem largely depend, such that if it were removed the ecosystem would change drastically.

Key·stone State a nickname for the state of **PENNSYLVANIA**.

key·stroke /ˈkē,strōk/ ▸*n.* a single depression of a key on a keyboard, esp. as a measure of work.

key·way /ˈkē,wā/ ▸*n.* a slot cut in a part of a machine or an electrical connector to ensure correct orientation with another part that is fitted with a key. ■ a keyhole for a flat key.

Key West a city in southern Florida, on Key West Island, at the southern tip of the Florida Keys; pop. 24,832. It is the southernmost city in the continental U.S.

key·word /ˈkē,wərd/ ▸*n.* a word or concept of great significance: *homes and jobs are the keywords in the campaign.* ■ a word that acts as the key to a cipher or code. ■ an informative word used in an information retrieval system to indicate the content of a document. ■ a significant word mentioned in an index.

KG ▸*abbr.* (in the UK) Knight of the Order of the Garter.

kg ▸*abbr.* ■ keg(s). ■ kilogram(s).

KGB the state security police (1954–91) of the former USSR with responsibility for external espionage, internal counterintelligence, and internal "crimes against the state." ▷Russian, abbreviation of *Komitet gosudarstvennoĭ bezopasnosti* 'Committee of State Security.'

kgf ▸*abbr.* kilogram force.

Kgs ▸*abbr.* *Bible* Kings.

Kha·ba·rovsk /KHəˈbärəfsk/ an administrative territory on the eastern coast of Siberia in Russia. ■ its capital, a city on the Amur River, on the Chinese border; pop. 608,000.

kha·di /ˈkädē/ (also **khad·dar** /ˈkädər/) ▸*n.* an Indian homespun cotton cloth. ▷from Punjabi, from Hindi *khādī*.

Kha·kas·sia /KHəˈkäsyə/ an autonomous republic in south central Russia; pop. 569,000; capital, Abakan.

khak·i /ˈkakē/ ▸*n.* (*pl.* **khak·is**) a textile fabric of a dull brownish-yellow color, in particular a strong cotton fabric used in military clothing. ■ a dull brownish-yellow color: [as *adj.*] *the pale khaki sand.* ■ (**khakis**) clothing, esp. pants, of this fabric and color. ▷mid 19th cent.: from Urdu *kākī* 'dust-colored,' from *kāk* 'dust,' from Persian.

Khak·i Camp·bell /ˈkakē ˈkambəl/ ▸*n.* a duck of a light brown breed, kept for egg laying.

Khalistan /,KHäliˈstän; ,käl-; -ˈstan/ the name given by Sikh nationalists to a proposed independent Sikh state. ▷compare with Arabic *khālsa* 'pure, real, proper.'

Khal·kha /ˈkalkə/ ▸*n.* **1** a member of a section of the Mongolian people, constituting the bulk of the population of Mongolia. **2** the language of these people, a demotic form of Mongolian adopted as the official language of Mongolia.
▸*adj.* of or relating to this people or their language. ▷of unknown origin.

Khal·sa /ˈkälsə/ ▸*n.* the body or company of fully initiated Sikhs, to which devout orthodox Sikhs are ritually admitted at puberty. The Khalsa was founded in 1699 by the last Guru (Gobind Singh). Members show their allegiance by five signs (called the five Ks): kangha (comb), kara (steel bangle), kesh (uncut hair, covered by a turban, and beard), kirpan (short sword), and kuccha (short trousers, originally for riding). ▷via Urdu from Persian, from the feminine form of Arabic *kāliṣ* 'pure, belonging to.'

Kha·ma /ˈkämə/, Sir Seretse (1921–80), Botswanan statesman; prime minister of Bechuanaland 1965 and first president of Botswana 1966–80.

Kham·bhat, Gulf of /ˈkəmbət/ (also **Gulf of Khambat**) another name for **CAMBAY, GULF OF**.

kham·sin /kämˈsēn/ ▸*n.* an oppressive, hot southerly or southeasterly wind blowing in Egypt in spring. ▷late 17th cent.: from Arabic *kamsīn*, from *kamsūn* 'fifty' (being the approximate duration in days).

Khan /kän/, Ayub, see **AYUB KHAN**.

khan[1] /kän/ ▸*n.* a title given to rulers and officials in central Asia, Afghanistan, and certain other Muslim countries. ■ any of the successors of Genghis Khan, supreme rulers of the Turkish, Tartar, and Mongol peoples and emperors of China in the Middle Ages. ▷late Middle English: from Old French *chan*, medieval Latin *canus*, *caanus*, from Turkic *kān* 'lord, prince.' **—khan·ate** /ˈkänāt/ *n.*

khan[2] ▸*n.* (in the Middle East) an inn for travelers, built around a central courtyard. ▷from Persian *kān*.

khan·sa·ma /ˈkänsə,mä/ ▸*n.* *Indian* a male cook, who often also assumes the role of house steward. ▷from Urdu and Persian *kānsāmān*, from *kān* 'master' + *sāmān* 'household goods.'

Kharg Is·land /kärg; KHärg/ a small island at the head of the Persian Gulf, site of Iran's principal deepwater oil terminal.

Khar·kiv /ˈKHärkif; ˈkär,kôf/ an industrial city in northeastern Ukraine, in the Donets basin; pop. 1,618,000. Russian name **KHARKOV**.

Khar·toum /kärˈto͞om/ the capital of Sudan, situated at the junction of the Blue Nile and the White Nile rivers; pop. 925,000. It was the capital of the Anglo-Egyptian government of Sudan until 1956, when it became the capital of the independent Republic of Sudan.

khat /kät/ ▸*n.* **1** the leaves of an Arabian shrub, which are chewed (or drunk as an infusion) as a stimulant. **2** the shrub that produces these leaves, growing in mountainous regions and often cultivated. • *Catha edulis*, family Celastraceae. ▷mid 19th cent.: from Arabic *kāt*.

Khay·lit·sa /kīˈlitsə/ a township 25 miles (40 km) southeast of Cape Town, South Africa; pop. 190,000. Designed to accommodate 250,000 people, it was built in 1983 for black Africans from the squatter camps of Crossroads, Langa, and KTC.

Kha·zar /kəˈzär/ ▸*n.* a member of a Turkic people who occupied a large part of southern Russia from the 6th to the 11th centuries and who converted to Judaism in the 8th century.
▸*adj.* of or relating to the Khazars. ▷of unknown origin.

khe·dive /kəˈdēv/ ▸*n.* the title of the viceroy of Egypt under Turkish rule (1867–1914). ▷via French from Ottoman Turkish *kediv*, from Persian *kadiw* 'prince' (variant of *kudaiw* 'minor god,' from *kudā* 'god'). **—Khe·div·al** /-ˈdēvəl/ *adj.* **—Khe·div·i·al** /-ˈdēvēəl/ *adj.*

Kher·son /KHerˈsôn; ker-/ a port on the coast of Ukraine, on the Dnieper estuary; pop. 361,000.

Khe Sanh /ˈkäˈsän/ a site in north central Vietnam of one of the costliest battles of the Vietnam War.

Khi·os /ˈKHē,ôs; ˈkē-/ Greek name for **CHIOS**.

Khi·tai /ˈkēˈtī/ variant of **CATHAY**.

Khmer /kəˈme(ə)r; kme(ə)r/ ▸*n.* **1** an ancient kingdom in Southeast Asia that reached the peak of its power in the 11th century, when it ruled the entire Mekong River valley from the capital at Angkor. It was destroyed by Thai conquests in the 12th and 14th centuries. **2** a native or inhabitant of the ancient Khmer kingdom. **3** a native or inhabitant of Cambodia. **4** the Mon-Khmer language that is the official language of Cambodia. Also called **CAMBODIAN**.
▸*adj.* of, relating to, or denoting the Khmers or their language. ▷the name in Khmer.

Khmer Re·pub·lic former official name (1970–75) for **CAMBODIA**.

Khmer Rouge /ˈro͞oZH/ a communist guerrilla organization that opposed the Cambodian government in the 1960s and waged a civil war from 1970, taking power in 1975. ▷from **KHMER** + French *rouge* 'red.'

Under Pol Pot the Khmer Rouge forced the reconstruction of Cambodian society with mass deportations from the towns to the countryside and mass executions. More than two million died before the regime was overthrown by the Vietnamese in 1979. Khmer Rouge forces have continued a program of guerrilla warfare from bases in Thailand.

Khoi·khoi /ˈkoi,koi/ (also **Khoi-khoin** / -,koi-in/, **Khoi**) ▸*n.* (*pl.* same) a member of a group of indigenous peoples of South Africa and Namibia, traditionally nomadic hunter-gatherers, including the Nama people and the ancestors of the Griquas.
▸*adj.* of or relating to this people or their languages. ▷Nama, literally 'men of men.'

Khoi·san /ˈkoi,sän/ ▸*n.* **1** [usu. treated as *pl.*] a collective term for the Khoikhoi (Hottentot) and San (Bushmen) peoples of southern Africa. **2** a language family of southern Africa, including the languages of the Khoikhoi and San, notable for the use of clicks as consonants.
▸*adj.* of or relating to these languages or their speakers. ▷blend of **KHOIKHOI** and **SAN**.

Kho·mei·ni /kōˈmānē; KHō-; ,KHōmāˈnē/, Ruhollah (1900–89), Iranian Shiite Muslim leader; known as **Ayatollah Khomeini**. He returned from exile in 1979 to lead an Islamic revolution that overthrew the shah. He established Iran as a fundamentalist Islamic republic and relentlessly pursued the Iran–Iraq War 1980–88.

Khon·su /ˈKHän,so͞o/ *Egyptian Mythology* a moon god worshiped esp. at Thebes, a member of a triad as the divine son of Amun and Mut.

Khor·ram·shahr /,KHôrəmˈSHähər; ,kôr-/ an oil port on the Shatt al-Arab waterway in western Iran. It was almost totally destroyed during the Iran–Iraq War of 1980–88. Former name (until 1924) **MOHAMMERAH**.

khoum /ko͞om; ko͝om/ ▸*n.* a monetary unit of Mauritania, equal to one fifth of an ouguiya. ▷from Arabic *kums* 'one fifth.'

Khru·shchev /ˈkro͞oSH,CHev; -,CHôf; KHro͞oSHˈCHyôf/, Nikita (Sergeevich) (1894–1971), Soviet statesman; premier 1958–64. He came close to war with the U.S. over the Cuban Missile Crisis in 1962 and also clashed with China, which led to his being ousted by Brezhnev and Kosygin. **—Khru·shchev·i·an** /kro͞oSHˈCHevēən/ *adj.*

Khu·fu /ˈko͞o,fo͞o/ see **CHEOPS**.

Khul·na /ˈko͝olnə/ an industrial city in southern Bangladesh, on the Ganges delta; pop. 601,000.

Khun·jer·ab Pass /ˈko͞onjə,räb/ a high-altitude pass through the Himalayas, on the Karakoram highway at a height of 16,088 feet (4,900 m), that links China and Pakistan.

khus-khus /ˈkəs kəs/ ▸*n.* another term for **VETIVER**. ▷early 19th cent.: from Urdu and Persian *kaskas*.

Khy·ber Pass /ˈkībər/ a mountain pass in the Hindu Kush, on the border between Pakistan and Afghanistan, at a height of 3,520 feet (1,067 m). It was for long of great commercial and strategic importance, the route by which successive invaders entered India, and it was garrisoned by the British intermittently between 1839 and 1947.

kHz ▸*abbr.* kilohertz.

ki ▸*n.* variant spelling of **QI**.

KIA (also **K.I.A.**) ▸*abbr.* killed in action.

ki·ang /kēˈäNG/ ▸*n.* an animal of a large race of the Asian wild ass with a thick furry coat, native to the Tibetan plateau. • *Equus hemionus kiang*, family Equidae; sometimes treated as a separate species. Compare with **ONAGER** . ▷mid 19th cent.: from Tibetan *kyang*.

Kiang·si /ˈkyaNGˈsē; ˈgyäNG-/ variant of **JIANGXI**.

Kiang·su /ˈkyaNGˈso͞o; ˈgyäNG-/ variant of **JIANGSU**.

Pronunciation Key ə *ago*; ər *over*; ˈə or ,ə *up*; ˈər or ,ər *fur*; a *hat*; ā *rate*; ä *car*; CH *chew*; e *let*; ē *see*; e(ə)r *air*; i *fit*; ī *by*; i(ə)r *ear*; NG *sing*; ō *go*; ô *for*; oi *boy*; o͝o *good*; o͞o *goo*; ou *out*; SH *she*; TH *thin*; T͟H *then*; (h)w *why*; ZH *vision*

K

ki·a·su /ˈkēə,so͞o/ ▸*n. SE Asian* a grasping, selfish attitude.
▸*adj.* (of a person) very anxious not to miss out on an opportunity; grasping. ▹from Chinese, 'scared to lose.'

kib·beh /ˈkibē/ ▸*n.* a Middle Eastern dish of ground lamb with bulgar wheat and seasonings, eaten cooked or raw. ▹from Arabic *kubbah.*

kib·ble[1] /ˈkibəl/ ▸*v.* [*trans.*] [usu. as *adj.*] (**kibbled**) grind or chop (beans, grain, etc.) coarsely.
▸*n.* ground meal shaped into pellets, esp. for pet food. ▹late 18th cent.: of unknown origin.

kib·ble[2] ▸*n. Brit.* an iron hoisting bucket used in mines. ▹late Middle English: from Middle High German *kübel,* from medieval Latin *cupellus* 'wheat measure, cask,' diminutive of *cuppa* 'cup.'

kib·butz /kiˈbo͝ots/ ▸*n.* (*pl.* **kib·but·zim** /ki,bo͝otˈsēm/) a communal settlement in Israel, typically a farm. ▹1930s: from modern Hebrew *qibbûṣ* 'gathering.'

kib·butz·nik /kiˈbo͝otsnik/ ▸*n.* a member of a kibbutz.

kibe /kīb/ ▸*n.* an ulcerated chilblain, esp. one on the heel. ▹late Middle English: of unknown origin.

kib·itz /ˈkibits/ ▸*v.* [*intrans.*] *informal* look on and offer unwelcome advice, esp. at a card game. ■ speak informally; chat: *she* **kibitzed with** *friends.* ▹1920s: Yiddish, from colloquial German, from German *Kiebitz* 'interfering onlooker' (literally 'lapwing'). **—kib·itz·er** *n.*

kib·lah ▸*n.* variant spelling of QIBLA.

ki·bosh /kəˈbäsʜ; ˈkī,bäsʜ/ ▸*n.* (in phrase **put the kibosh on**) *informal* put an end to; dispose of decisively: *he put the kibosh on the deal.* ▹mid 19th cent.: of unknown origin.

kick[1] /kik/ ▸*v.* **1** [*trans.*] strike or propel forcibly with the foot: *police* **kicked down** *the door* | [*trans.*] *he kicked the door open.* ■ [*intrans.*] strike out or flail with the foot or feet: *she* **kicked out at** *him* | [*trans.*] *he kicked his feet free of a vine.* ■ [*trans.*] (**kick oneself**) be annoyed with oneself for doing something foolish or missing an opportunity. ■ [*trans.*] (in football, rugby, etc) score (a goal) by a kick. ■ [*intrans.*] (of a gun) recoil when fired. **2** [*trans.*] *informal* succeed in giving up (a habit or addiction).
▸*phrasal v.* □ **kick against** express resentment at or frustration with (an institution or restriction). □ **kick around** (or **about**) (of a thing) lie unwanted or unexploited: *the idea has been kicking around for more than a year now.* ■ (of a person) drift idly from place to place: *I kicked around picking up odd jobs.* □ **kick someone around** (or **about**) treat someone roughly or without respect. □ **kick something around** (or **about**) discuss an idea casually or idly. □ **kick back** *informal* be at leisure; relax. □ **kick in** (esp. of a device or drug) become activated; come into effect. □ **kick something in** *informal* contribute something, esp. money: *if you subscribe now we'll kick in a bonus.* □ **kick off** (of a football game, soccer game, etc.) be started or resumed after a score by a player kicking the ball from a designated spot.■ (of a team or player) begin or resume a game in this way. ■ *informal* (of an event) begin. □ **kick something off 1** remove something, esp. shoes, by striking out vigorously with the foot or feet. **2** *informal* begin something: *the presidential primary kicks off the political year.* □ **kick someone out** *informal* expel or dismiss someone.
▸*n.* **1** a blow or forceful thrust with the foot: *a kick in the head.* ■ (in sports) an instance of striking the ball with the foot: *Ball blasted the kick wide.* ■ the recoil of a gun when discharged. ■ a sudden forceful jolt: *the shuttle accelerated with a kick.* **2** [in *sing.*] *informal* the sharp stimulant effect of something, esp. alcohol. ■ a thrill of pleasurable, often reckless excitement: *rich kids turning to crime just* **for kicks** | *I* **get** *such* **a kick out of** *driving a race car.* ■ [with *adj.*] a specified temporary interest or enthusiasm: *the jogging kick.* ▹late Middle English: of unknown origin. **—kick·a·ble** *adj.*
▸*PHRASES* □ **kick (some) ass** (or **butt**) *vulgar slang* act in a forceful or aggressive manner. □ **kick someone's ass** (or **butt**) *vulgar slang* beat, dominate, or defeat someone. □ **kick the bucket** *informal* die. □ **a kick in the pants** (or **up the backside**) *informal* an unwelcome surprise that prompts or forces fresh effort: *the competition will be healthy, but we needed a kick in the pants.* □ **a kick in the teeth** *informal* a grave setback or disappointment: *this broken promise is a kick in the teeth for football.* □ **kick someone in the teeth** *informal* cause someone a grave setback or disappointment. □ **kick someone when they are down** cause further misfortune to someone who is already in a difficult situation. □ **kick up a fuss** (or **a stink**) *informal* object loudly or publicly to something. □ **kick up one's heels** see HEEL[1]. □ **kick someone upstairs** *informal* remove someone from an influential position in a business by giving them an ostensible promotion.

kick[2] ▸*n. archaic* an indentation in the bottom of a glass bottle, diminishing the internal capacity. ▹mid 19th cent.: of unknown origin.

Kick·a·poo /ˈkikə,po͞o/ ▸*n.* (*pl.* same or **-poos**) **1** a member of an American Indian people formerly living in Wisconsin, and now in Kansas, Oklahoma, and north central Mexico. **2** the Algonquian language of this people.
▸*adj.* of or relating to this people or their language. ▹from Kickapoo *kiikaapoa.*

kick-ass ▸*adj.* [*attrib.*] *informal* forceful, vigorous, and aggressive: *he's a kick-ass guy who takes no prisoners* | *a kick-ass foreign policy.*

kick·back /ˈkik,bak/ ▸*n.* **1** a sudden forceful recoil: *the kickback from the gun punches your shoulder.* **2** *informal* a payment made to someone who has facilitated a transaction or appointment, esp. illicitly.

kick·ball /ˈkik,bôl/ ▸*n.* an informal game combining elements of baseball and soccer, in which an inflated ball is thrown to a person who kicks it and proceeds to run the bases.

kick·box·ing (also **kick-box·ing**) ▸*n.* a form of martial art that combines boxing with elements of karate, in particular kicking with bare feet. **—kick-box·er** *n.*

kick drum ▸*n. informal* a bass drum played using a pedal.

kick·er /ˈkikər/ ▸*n.* **1** a person or animal that kicks. ■ the player in a team who scores by kicking or who kicks to gain positional advantage. **2** *informal* an unexpected and often unpleasant discovery or turn of events: *the kicker was you couldn't get a permit.* ■ an extra clause in a contract: *Hale added a kicker to the mortgage.* **3** *informal* a small outboard motor. **4** (in poker) a high third card retained in the hand with a pair at the draw.

kick·ing /ˈkikiɴɢ/ ▸*n.* the action of striking or propelling someone or something with the foot: *games which involved the kicking of a ball.* ■ a punishment or assault in which the victim is kicked repeatedly: *they gave him a good kicking.*
▸*adj. informal* (esp. of music) lively and exciting: *their seriously kicking debut, "Paradise."*

kick·ing strap ▸*n.* a strap used to prevent a horse from kicking.

kick·off /ˈkik,ôf/ ▸*n.* the start or resumption of a football game, in which a player kicks the ball from the center of the field: *three minutes before kickoff.* ■ *informal* a start of an event or activity.

kick plate ▸*n.* a metal plate at the base of a door or panel to protect it from damage or wear.

kick pleat ▸*n.* an inverted pleat in a narrow skirt to allow freedom of movement.

kick pleat

kick·shaw /ˈkik,sʜô/ ▸*n. archaic* a fancy but insubstantial cooked dish, esp. one of foreign origin. ■ an elegant but insubstantial trinket. ▹late 16th cent.: from French *quelque chose* 'something.' The French spelling was common in the 17th cent.; the present form results from interpretation of *quelque chose* as plural.

kick·stand /ˈkik,stand/ ▸*n.* a metal rod attached to a bicycle or motorcycle, lying horizontally when not in use, that may be kicked into a vertical position to support the vehicle when it is stationary.

kick-start ▸*v.* [*trans.*] start (an engine on a motorcycle) with a downward thrust of a pedal. ■ *figurative* provide the initial impetus to: *they need to kick-start the economy.*
▸*n.* (also **kick start** or **kick starter**) a device to start an engine by the downward thrust of a pedal, as in older motorcycles. ■ an act of starting an engine in this way. ■ *figurative* an impetus given to get a process or thing started or restarted: *new investment will provide the kick-start needed to escape from recession.*

kick turn ▸*n. Skiing* a turn carried out while stationary by lifting first one and then the other ski through 180°. ■ (in skateboarding) a turn performed with the front wheels lifted off the ground. **—kick-turn** *v.*

kick·y /ˈkikē/ ▸*adj. informal* exciting or fashionable: *kicky high-heeled boots.*

kid[1] /kid/ ▸*n.* **1** *informal* a child or young person. ■ used as an informal form of address: *we'll be seeing ya, kid!* **2** a young goat. ■ leather made from a young goat's skin: [as *adj.*] *white kid gloves.*
▸*v.* (**kid·ded**, **kid·ding**) [*intrans.*] (of a goat) give birth. ▹Middle English (sense 2): from Old Norse *kith,* of Germanic origin; related to German *Kitze.*
▸*PHRASE* □ **kids'** (also **kid**) **stuff** *informal* a thing regarded as childishly simple or naive: *all this was kids' stuff though, compared to the directing.*

USAGE **Kid**, meaning 'child,' although widely seen in informal contexts, should, like its casual relatives *mom* and *dad,* be avoided in formal writing.

kid[2] ▸*v.* (**kid·ded**, **kid·ding**) [*trans.*] *informal* deceive (someone) in a playful or teasing way: *you're kidding me!* | [*intrans.*] *we were just* **kidding around.** ■ [*trans.*] deceive or fool (someone): *he likes to kid everyone he's the big macho tough guy* | *they* **kid themselves** *that it's still the same.* ▹early 19th cent.: perhaps from KID[1], expressing the notion 'make a child or goat of.' **—kid·der** *n.* **—kid·ding·ly** *adv.*
▸*PHRASE* □ **no kidding** used to emphasize the truth of a statement: *no kidding, she's gone.*

kid broth·er ▸*n. informal* a younger brother.

Kidd /kid/, William (1645–1701), Scottish pirate; known as **Captain Kidd**. In 1699, he went to Boston in the hope of obtaining a pardon, but was arrested and later hanged in London.

Kid·der·min·ster car·pet /ˈkidər,minstər/ ▸*n.* a reversible carpet made of two cloths of different colors woven together. ▹late 17th cent.: named after Kidderminster, England, a center of carpet-making.

kid·die /ˈkidē/ (also **kid·dy**) ▸*n.* (*pl.* **-dies**) *informal* a young child.

kid·do /ˈkidō/ ▸*n.* (*pl.* **-dos** or **-does**) *informal* used as a friendly or slightly condescending form of address.

kid·dush /ˈkidəsʜ; kēˈdo͝osʜ/ ▸*n.* [in *sing.*] a ceremony of prayer and blessing over wine, performed by the head of a Jewish household at the meal ushering in the Sabbath (on a Friday night) or a holy day, or at the lunch preceding it. ▹mid 18th cent.: from Hebrew *qiddûš* 'sanctification.'

kid gloves ▸*plural n.* gloves made of fine kid leather. ■ (also **kid-glove**) [as *adj.*] used in reference to careful and delicate treatment of a person or situation: *the star is getting kid-glove treatment.*
▸*PHRASE* □ **handle** (or **treat**) **someone or something with kid gloves** deal with someone or something very carefully or tactfully.

Kid·man /ˈkidmən/, Nicole (1967–), Australian actress; born in Hawaii. Notable films: *Eyes Wide Shut* (1999), *Moulin Rouge!* (2001), *The Hours* (Academy Award, 2002), and *Cold Mountain* (2003).

kid·nap /ˈkid,nap/ ▸*v.* (**-napped**, **-nap·ping**; also **-naped**, **-nap·ing**) [*trans.*] take (someone) away illegally by force, typically to obtain a ransom.
▸*n.* the action of kidnapping someone: *they were arrested for robbery and kidnap.* ▹late 17th cent.: back-formation from *kidnapper,* from KID[1] + slang *nap* 'nab, seize.' **—kid·nap·per** *n.*

kid·ney /ˈkidnē/ ▸*n.* (*pl.* **-neys**) each of a pair of organs in the abdominal cavity of mammals, birds, and reptiles, excreting urine. ■ the kidney of a sheep, ox, or pig as food. ■ temperament, nature, or kind: *I hoped that he would not prove of similar kidney.*

The kidneys' main function is to purify the blood by removing nitrogenous waste products and excreting them in the urine. They also control the fluid and ion levels in the body by excreting any excesses. The kidneys were anciently thought to control disposition and temperament.

▹Middle English: of obscure origin.

kid·ney bean ▸*n.* a kidney-shaped bean, esp. a dark red variety of the common bean plant *Phaseolus vulgaris.*

kid·ney di·al·y·sis ▸*n.* see DIALYSIS.

kid·ney stone ▸*n.* a hard mass formed in the kidneys, typically consisting of insoluble calcium compounds; a renal calculus.

kid·ney tu·bule ▸*n. Anatomy* each of the long, fine, convoluted tubules conveying urine from the glomeruli to the renal pelvis in the vertebrate kidney. Water and salts are reabsorbed into the blood along their length. Also called RENAL TUBULE, URINIFEROUS TUBULE.

kid sis·ter ▸*n. informal* a younger sister.

kid·skin /ˈkid,skin/ ▸*n.* another term for KID[1] (sense 2).

K

kid·ult /ki'dəlt; 'kid,əlt/ ▶*n.* *informal* an adult with childish tastes. ▷blend of *kid* and *adult.*

kid·vid /'kid,vid/ ▶*n.* *informal* children's television or video entertainment. ■ a children's program or videotape. ▷late 20th cent.: from *kids' video.*

Kiel /kēl/ a naval port in northern Germany, capital of Schleswig-Holstein, on the Baltic Sea coast at the eastern end of the Kiel Canal; pop. 247,000.

kiel·ba·sa /kil'bäsə; kēl-/ ▶*n.* a type of highly seasoned Polish sausage, typically containing garlic. ▷Polish, literally 'sausage.'

Kiel Ca·nal a man-made waterway, 61 miles (98 km) in length, in northwestern Germany, that runs westward from Kiel to Brunsbüttel at the mouth of the Elbe River. It connects the North Sea with the Baltic Sea and was constructed in 1895 to provide the German navy with a shorter route between these two seas.

Kiel·ce /'kyeltsə/ an industrial city in southern Poland; pop. 214,000.

kier /ki(ə)r/ ▶*n.* a vat. ▷late 16th cent.: from Old Norse *ker* 'container, tub.'

Kier·ke·gaard /'ki(ə)rki,gärd; -,gôr/, Søren (Aabye) (1813–55), Danish philosopher. A founder of existentialism, he affirmed the importance of individual experience and choice and believed that one could know God only through a "leap of faith," not through doctrine. **—Kier·ke·gaard·i·an** /,ki(ə)rki'gärdēən/ *adj.*

kie·sel·guhr /'kēzəlgər/ ▶*n.* a form of diatomaceous earth used in various manufacturing and laboratory processes, chiefly as a filter, filler, or insulator. ▷late 19th cent.: from German, from *Kiesel* 'gravel' + dialect *Guhr* (literally 'yeast') used to denote a loose earthy deposit, found in the cavities of rocks.

kie·ser·ite /'kēzə,rīt/ ▶*n.* a fine-grained white mineral consisting of hydrated magnesium sulfate, occurring often in salt mines in Europe and India. ▷mid 19th cent.: from the name of Dietrich G. *Kieser* (1779–1862), German physician, + **-ITE**[1].

Ki·ev /'kē,(y)ef; -,(y)ev/ the capital of Ukraine, an industrial city and port on the Dnieper River; pop. 2,616,000. Founded in the 8th century, it became capital of the Ukrainian Soviet Socialist Republic in 1934 and of independent Ukraine in 1991.

kif /kif/ ▶*n.* & *adj.* variant spelling of **KEF**.

Ki·ga·li /ki'gälē/ the capital of Rwanda, located in the central part of the country; pop. 234,000.

kike /kīk/ ▶*n.* *informal, offensive* a Jewish person. ▷early 20th cent.: of unknown origin.

Ki·klá·dhes /ki'kläTHis/ Greek name for **CYCLADES**.

ki·koi /ki'koi/ ▶*n.* (*pl.* **-kois**) a distinctive East African striped cloth with an end fringe. ■ a garment made of this cloth, worn around the waist. ▷mid 20th cent.: from Kiswahili.

Ki·kon·go /kē'käNGgō/ ▶*n.* either of two similar Bantu languages spoken in the Congo, the Republic of Congo, and adjacent areas.

▶*adj.* of or relating to this language. ▷the name in Kikongo.

Ki·ku·yu /ki'ko͞oyo͞o/ ▶*n.* (*pl.* same or **-yus**) **1** a member of the largest ethnic group in Kenya. **2** the Bantu language of this people. **3** (**ki·ku·yu**, **ki·ku·yu grass**) a creeping perennial grass native to Kenya and cultivated elsewhere as a lawn and fodder grass. • *Pennisetum clandestinum*, family Gramineae.

▶*adj.* of or relating to the Kikuyu people or their language. ▷a local name.

Ki·lau·ea /,kilə'wāə; ,kē,lou'āə/ an active volcano with a crater roughly 5 miles (8 km) long and 3 miles (5 km) wide on the island of Hawaii, situated on the eastern flank of Mauna Loa at an altitude of 4,090 feet (1,247 m).

Kil·dare /kil'de(ə)r/ a county in the Republic of Ireland, in the east, in the province of Leinster; county town, Naas.

kil·der·kin /'kildərkin/ ▶*n.* a cask for liquids or other substances, holding 16 or 18 gallons. ■ this amount as a unit of measurement. ▷late Middle English: from Middle Dutch *kinderkin*, variant of *kinerkijn*, diminutive of *kintal* (see **QUINTAL**).

ki·lim /kē'lēm; 'kiləm/ ▶*n.* a flat-woven carpet or rug made in Turkey, Kurdistan, and neighboring areas. ▷late 19th cent.: via Turkish from Persian *gelīm.*

Kil·i·man·ja·ro, Mount /,kilımən'järō/ an extinct volcano in northern Tanzania. It has twin peaks, the higher of which, Kibo (19,340 feet; 5,895 m), is the highest mountain in Africa.

Kil·ken·ny /kil'kenē/ a county of the Republic of Ireland, in the southeast, in the province of Leinster. ■ its county town; pop. 9,000.

kill[1] /kil/ ▶*v.* [*trans.*] **1** cause the death of (a person, animal, or other living thing): *her father was killed in a car crash* | [*intrans.*] *a robber armed with a shotgun who kills in cold blood.* ■ put an end to or cause the failure or defeat of (something): *the committee voted to kill the project.* ■ stop (a computer program or process). ■ *informal* switch off (a light or engine). ■ *informal* delete (a line, paragraph, or file) from a document or computer. ■ (in soccer or other ball games) make (the ball) stop. ■ (in tennis and similar games) hit (the ball) so forcefully that it cannot be returned. ■ neutralize or subdue (an effect or quality): *the sauce would kill the taste of the herbs.* ■ *informal* consume the entire contents of (a bottle containing an alcoholic drink). **2** *informal* overwhelm (someone) with an emotion: *the suspense is killing me.* ■ (**kill oneself**) overexert oneself: *I killed myself carrying those things home.* ■ used hyperbolically to indicate that someone is extremely angry with another person: *my parents will kill me if they catch me out here.* ■ cause pain or anguish to: *my feet are killing me.* **3** pass (time, or a specified amount of it), typically while waiting for a particular event: *when he reached the station, he found he actually had an hour to kill.*

▶*phrasal v.* □ **kill someone/something off** get rid of or destroy completely, esp. in large numbers: *there is every possibility all river life would be killed off for generations.* ■ (of a writer) bring about the "death" of a fictional character.

▶*n.* [usu. in *sing.*] an act of killing, esp. of one animal by another: *a lion has* **made a kill**. ■ an animal or animals killed, either by a hunter or by another animal: *the vulture is able to survey the land and locate a fresh kill.* ■ *informal* an act of destroying or disabling an enemy aircraft, submarine, tank, etc. ■ (in tennis and similar games) a very forceful shot that cannot be returned. ▷Middle English (in the sense 'strike, beat,' also 'put to death'): probably of Germanic origin and related to **QUELL**. The noun originally denoted a stroke or blow.

▶*PHRASES* □ **be in at the kill** be present at or benefit from the successful conclusion of an enterprise. □ **go** (or **move in** or **close in**) **for the kill** take decisive action, often ruthlessly, to turn a situation to one's advantage. □ **if it kills one** *informal* whatever the problems or difficulties involved: *we are going to smile and be pleasant if it kills us.* □ **kill oneself laughing** *informal* be overcome with laughter. □ **kill two birds with one stone** *proverb* achieve two aims at once. □ **kill with** (or **by**) **kindness** spoil with overindulgence.

THE RIGHT WORD **assassinate, dispatch, execute, kill, massacre, murder, slaughter, slay**

When it comes to depriving someone or something of life, the options are seemingly endless.

To **kill** is the most general term, meaning to cause the death of a person, animal, or plant, with no automatic implication of a method or cause (*killed in a car accident*). Even inanimate things may be killed (*Congress killed the project when they vetoed the bill*).

To **slay** is to kill deliberately and violently; it is used more often in written than in spoken English (*a novel about a presidential candidate who is slain by his opponent*).

Murder implies a malicious and premeditated killing of one person by another (*a gruesome murder carried out by the son-in-law*), while **assassinate** implies that a politically important person has been murdered, often by someone hired to do the job (*assassinate the head of the guerrilla forces*).

Someone who is put to death by a legal or military process is said to be **executed** (*execute by lethal injection*), but if someone is killed primarily to get rid of him or her, the appropriate verb is **dispatch**, which also suggests speed or promptness (*after delivering the secret documents, the informer was dispatched*).

While **slaughter** is usually associated with the killing of animals for food, it can also apply to a mass killing of humans (*the slaughter of innocent civilians provoked a worldwide outcry*).

Massacre also refers to the brutal murder of large numbers of people, but it is used more specifically to indicate the wholesale destruction of a relatively defenseless group of people (*the massacre of Bethlehem's male children by King Herod*).

kill[2] ▶*n.* [in *place names*] *chiefly New York State* a stream, creek, or tributary: *Kill Van Kull.* ▷mid 17th cent.: from Dutch *kil*, from Middle Dutch *kille* 'riverbed, channel.'

Kil·lar·ney /kil'ärnē/ a town in southwestern Republic of Ireland, in County Kerry, noted for the beauty of the nearby lakes and mountains; pop. 7,000.

kill·deer /'kil,di(ə)r/ (also **killdeer plover**) ▶*n.* a widespread American plover with a plaintive call that resembles its name. • *Charadrius vociferus*, family Charadriidae. ▷mid 18th cent.: imitative of its call.

killdeer

Kil·leen /ki'lēn/ a city in east central Texas, near Fort Hood; pop. 63,535.

kill·er /'kilər/ ▶*n.* a person, animal, or thing that kills: *police are still searching for the killer* | [as *adj.*] *a killer virus.* ■ *informal* a formidable or excellent person or thing: *that wind's a killer* | *they make a killer salsa.* ■ *informal* a hilarious joke.

kill·er app ▶*n.* *informal* a feature, function, or application of a new technology or product that is presented as virtually indispensable or much superior to rival products. ▷from *killer* and *app*, a shortening of *application.*

kill·er bee ▶*n.* *informal* an Africanized honeybee. See **AFRICANIZE** (sense 2).

kill·er cell ▶*n.* *Physiology* a white blood cell (a type of lymphocyte) that destroys infected or cancerous cells.

kill·er in·stinct ▶*n.* a ruthless determination to succeed or win.

kill·er whale ▶*n.* another term for **ORCA**.

kil·lick /'kilik/ ▶*n.* a heavy stone used by small craft as an anchor. ■ any anchor, esp. a small one. ▷mid 17th cent.: of unknown origin.

kil·li·fish /'kilē,fiSH/ ▶*n.* (*pl.* same or **-fish·es**) a small carplike fish of fresh, brackish, or salt water, typically brightly colored. They are mainly native to America and include many popular aquarium fishes. • Families Fundulidae and Cyprinodontidae, which include numerous genera of egg-laying killifishes. ▷early 19th cent.: apparently from **KILL**[2] and **FISH**[1].

kill·ing /'kiliNG/ ▶*n.* an act of causing death, esp. deliberately.

▶*adj.* causing death: [in *combination*] *weed-killing.* ■ *informal* exhausting; unbearable: *the suspense will be killing.* ■ *dated* overwhelmingly funny. **—kill·ing·ly** *adv.*

▶*PHRASE* □ **make a killing** have a great financial success: *they're a safe investment, you can make a killing overnight.*

kill·ing field ▶*n.* (usu. **killing fields**) a place where a heavy loss of life has occurred, typically as the result of massacre or genocide during a time of warfare or violent civil unrest.

kill·joy /'kil,joi/ ▶*n.* a person who deliberately spoils the enjoyment of others through resentful or overly sober behavior.

Kil·ly /'kēyē/, Jean-Claude (1943–) French alpine skier. He won three gold medals at the 1968 Olympic games and was a three-time world champion 1966, 1967, 1968; winner of the World Cup 1967, 1968; and professional world champion 1973.

kill zone (also **kill·ing zone**) ▶*n.* **1** the area of a military engagement with a high concentration of fatalities. **2** the area of the human body where entry of a projectile would kill, esp. as indicated on a target for shooting practice.

Kil·mer /'kilmər/, (Alfred) Joyce (1888–1918) U.S. poet. He was killed in action during World War I. His poetry is collected in *Summer of Love* (1911) and *Trees and Other Poems* (1914).

kiln /kiln; kil/ ▶*n.* a furnace or oven for burning, baking, or drying, esp. one for calcining lime or firing pottery.

▶*v.* [*trans.*] burn, bake, or dry in a kiln. ▷Old English *cylene*, from Latin *culina* 'kitchen, cooking stove.'

kiln-dry ▶*v.* [*trans.*] [usu. as *n.*] (**kiln-drying**) dry (a material such as wood or sand) in a kiln.

ki·lo /'kēlō/ ▶*n.* (*pl.* **ki·los**) **1** a kilogram. **2** *rare* a kilometer. **3** a code word representing the letter K, used in radio communication. ▷late 19th cent.: from French, abbreviation of *kilogramme, kilomètre*.

kilo- ▸*comb. form* (used commonly in units of measurement) denoting a factor of 1,000: *kilojoule | kiloliter*. ▷via French from Greek *khilioi* 'thousand.'

kil·o·base /ˈkiləˌbās/ (abbr.: **kb**) ▸*n. Biochemistry* (in expressing the lengths of nucleic acid molecules) 1,000 bases.

kil·o·bit /ˈkiləˌbit/ ▸*n.* a unit of computer memory or data equal to 1,024 (2^{10}) bits.

kil·o·byte /ˈkiləˌbīt/ (abbr.: **Kb** or **KB**) ▸*n. Computing* a unit of memory or data equal to 1,024 (2^{10}) bytes.

kil·o·cal·o·rie /ˈkiləˌkalərē/ ▸*n.* a unit of energy of 1,000 calories (equal to 1 large calorie).

kil·o·cy·cle /ˈkiləˌsīkəl/ (abbr.: **kc**) ▸*n.* a former measure of frequency, equivalent to 1 kilohertz.

kil·o·gram /ˈkiləˌgram/ (*Brit.* also **kil·o·gramme**) (abbr.: **kg**) ▸*n.* the SI unit of mass, equivalent to the international standard kept at Sèvres near Paris (approximately 2.205 lb). ▷late 18th cent.: from French *kilogramme* (see KILO-, GRAM[1]).

kil·o·hertz /ˈkiləˌhərts/ (abbr.: **kHz**) ▸*n.* a measure of frequency equivalent to 1,000 cycles per second.

kil·o·li·ter /ˈkiləˌlētər/ (*Brit.* **kil·o·li·tre**) (abbr.: **kl**) ▸*n.* 1,000 liters (equivalent to 220 imperial gallons).

kil·o·me·ter /kiˈlämitər; ˈkiləˌmētər/ (*Brit.* **kil·o·me·tre**) (abbr.: **km**) ▸*n.* a metric unit of measurement equal to 1,000 meters (approximately 0.62 miles). ▷late 18th cent.: from French *kilomètre* (see KILO-, METER[1]). —**kil·o·met·ric** /ˌkiləˈmetrik/ *adj.*

kil·o·ton /ˈkiləˌtən/ (*Brit.* also **kil·o·tonne**) ▸*n.* a unit of explosive power equivalent to 1,000 tons of TNT.

kil·o·volt /ˈkiləˌvōlt/ (abbr.: **kV**) ▸*n.* 1,000 volts.

kil·o·watt /ˈkiləˌwät/ (abbr.: **kW**) ▸*n.* a measure of 1,000 watts of electrical power.

kil·o·watt-hour (abbr.: **kWh**) ▸*n.* a measure of electrical energy equivalent to a power consumption of 1,000 watts for 1 hour.

Kil·roy /ˈkilˌroi/ a mythical person, popularized by American servicemen in World War II, who left such inscriptions as "Kilroy was here" on walls all over the world. ▷of the many unverifiable accounts of the source of the term, one claims that James J. *Kilroy* of Halifax, Massachusetts, a shipyard employee, wrote "Kilroy was here" on sections of warships after inspection; the phrase is said to have been reproduced by shipyard workers who entered the armed services.

kilt /kilt/ ▸*n.* a knee-length skirt of pleated tartan cloth, traditionally worn by men as part of Scottish Highland dress and now also worn by women and girls.
▸*v.* [*trans.*] gather (a garment or material) in vertical pleats: [as *adj.*] (**kilted**) *kilted skirts*. ▷Middle English (as a verb in the sense 'tuck up around the body'): of Scandinavian origin; compare with Danish *kilte (op)* 'tuck (up)' and Old Norse *kilting* 'a skirt.' The noun dates from the mid 18th cent. —**kilt·ed** *adj.*

kilt

kil·ter /ˈkiltər/ ▸*n.* (in phrase **out of kilter**) out of harmony or balance: *daylight savings throws everybody's body clock out of kilter*. ▷early 17th cent.: of unknown origin.

kilt·ie /ˈkiltē/ (also **kilt·y**) ▸*n.* **1** *informal* a person who wears a kilt (often used as a humorous or slightly derogatory term for a Scot). **2** a casual or sports shoe with a fringed tongue that covers the lacing: *a pair of suede kilties*. ■ the tongue of such a shoe: [as *adj.*] *oxfords with kiltie flaps*.

Kim·ber·ley /ˈkimbərlē/ **1** a city in South Africa, in the province of Northern Cape; pop. 167,000. It has been a diamond-mining center since the early 1870s. **2** (also **the Kimberleys**) a plateau region in the far north of Western Australia. A mining and cattle-rearing region, it was the scene of a gold rush in 1885.

kim·ber·lite /ˈkimbərˌlīt/ ▸*n. Geology* a rare, blue-tinged, coarse-grained intrusive igneous rock sometimes containing diamonds, found esp. in South Africa and Siberia. Also called BLUE GROUND. ▷late 19th cent.: from KIMBERLEY + -ITE[1].

Kim·bun·du /kimˈbo͝ondo͞o/ ▸ see MBUNDU.

Kim·chaek /ˈkēmˈCHak/ (formerly **Songjin**) an industrial port city in eastern North Korea, on the Sea of Japan; pop. 281,000.

kim·chi /ˈkimCHē/ (also **kim·chee**) ▸*n.* spicy pickled cabbage, the national dish of Korea. ▷Korean.

Kim Dae Jung /kim dī jo͝ong/ (1925–) Korean politician. Long a voice for democracy in Korea, he served as president of South Korea 1997–2003 and worked to reunify North and South Korea and to achieve peace in Asia. Nobel Peace Prize (2000).

Kim Il Sung /ˌkim ˌil ˈso͝ong; ˈsəNG/ (1912–94), Korean communist statesman; first premier of North Korea 1948–72 and president 1972–94; born *Kim Song Ju*. He precipitated the Korean War 1950–53. He maintained a one-party state and created a personality cult around himself and his family. He was succeeded by his son **Kim Jong Il** /ˈjôNG ˈil/ (1942–).

ki·mo·no /kəˈmōnō; -nə/ ▸*n.* (*pl.* **-nos**) a long, loose robe with wide sleeves and tied with a sash, originally worn as a formal garment in Japan and now also used elsewhere as a robe. ▷mid 17th cent.: Japanese, from *ki* 'wearing' + *mono* 'thing.' —**ki·mo·noed** /-nōd; -nəd/ *adj.*

kimono

kin /kin/ ▸*n.* [treated as *pl.*] one's family and relations: *he is expected to make a payment to his wife's kin*. ■ a natural class, group, or division of people, animals, plants, etc., with shared attributes or ancestry: *the area is frequented by crinoids, kin of sea urchins*.
▸*adj.* [*predic.*] related: *he was kin to the brothers*. See also AKIN. ▷Old English *cynn*, of Germanic origin; related to Dutch *kunne*, from an Indo-European root meaning 'give birth to,' shared by Greek *genos* and Latin *genus* 'race.' —**kin·less** *adj.*

-kin ▸*suffix* forming diminutive nouns such as *bumpkin, catkin*. ▷from Middle Dutch *-kijn, -ken*, Middle Low German *-kīn*.

ki·na ▸*n.* (*pl.* same) the basic monetary unit of Papua New Guinea, equal to 100 toea. ▷Papuan.

Ki·na·ba·lu, Mount /ˌkinəbəˈlo͞o/ a mountain in eastern Malaysia, on the northern coast of Borneo. Rising to 13,431 feet (4,094 m), it is the highest peak in Borneo and in Southeast Asia.

kin·aes·the·sia ▸*n.* British spelling of KINESTHESIA.

ki·nase /ˈkīˌnās; ˈkinās/ ▸*n.* [usu. with *adj.*] *Biochemistry* an enzyme that catalyzes the transfer of a phosphate group from ATP to a specified molecule. ▷early 20th cent.: from Greek *kinein* 'to move' + -ASE.

Kin·chin·jun·ga /ˌkinCHənˈjo͝oNGgə/ variant of KANCHENJUNGA.

kind[1] /kīnd/ ▸*n.* a group of people or things having similar characteristics: *all kinds of music | a new kind of education | more data of this kind would be valuable*. ■ character; nature: *the trials were different* ***in kind*** *from any that preceded them | true* ***to kind***. ■ each of the elements (bread and wine) of the Eucharist: *communion* ***in both kinds***. ▷Old English *cynd(e), gecynd(e)*, of Germanic origin; related to KIN. The original sense was 'nature, the natural order,' also 'innate character, form, or condition' (compare with KIND[2]); hence 'a class or race distinguished by innate characteristics.'
▸*PHRASES* □ **in kind** in the same way; with something similar: *if he responded positively, they would respond in kind*. ■ (of payment) in goods or services as opposed to money. □ **one's (own) kind** people with whom one has a great deal in common: *we stick with our own kind*. □ **someone's kind** used to express disapproval of a certain type of person: *I don't apologize to her kind ever*. □ **kind of** *informal* rather; to some extent (often expressing vagueness or used as a meaningless filler): *it got kind of cozy*. □ **a kind of** something resembling (used to express vagueness or moderate a statement): *teaching based on a kind of inspired guesswork*. □ **nothing of the kind** not at all like the thing in question: *my son had done nothing of the kind before*. ■ used to express an emphatic denial: *"He made you do that?" "He did nothing of the kind."* □ **of its kind** within the limitations of its class: *this new building was no doubt excellent of its kind*. □ **of a kind** used to indicate that something is not as good as it might be expected to be: *there is tribute, of a kind, in such popularity*. □ **one of a kind** unique. □ **something of the kind** something like the thing in question: *they had always suspected something of the kind*. □ **two** (or **three, four, etc.**) **of a kind** the same or very similar: *she and her sister were two of a kind*. ■ (of cards) having the same face value but of a different suit. ■ a hand consisting of such cards.

USAGE **1 Kind of** is sometimes used to be deliberately vague: *it was kind of a big evening; I was kind of hoping you'd call*. More often it reveals an inability to speak clearly: *he's kind of, like, inarticulate, you know?* Used precisely, it means 'sort' or 'type': *a maple is a kind of tree*.
2 The plural of **kind** often causes difficulty. With *this* or *that*, speaking of one kind, use a singular construction: *this kind of cake is my favorite; that kind of fabric doesn't need ironing*. With *these* or *those*, speaking of more than one kind, use a plural construction: *these kinds of guitars are very expensive; those kinds of animals ought to be left in the wild*. Although often encountered, sentences such as *I don't like these kind of things* are incorrect. The same recommendations apply to **sort** and **sorts**.

kind[2] ▸*adj.* having or showing a friendly, generous, and considerate nature: *she was a good, kind woman | he was very* ***kind to me***. ■ [*predic.*] used in a polite request: *would you be kind enough to repeat what you said?* ■ [*predic.*] (**kind to**) (of a consumer product) gentle on (a part of the body): *look for rollers that are kind to hair*. ■ *archaic* affectionate; loving. ▷Old English *gecynde* 'natural, native'; in Middle English the earliest sense is 'well born or well bred,' whence 'well disposed by nature, courteous, gentle, benevolent.'

kind·a /ˈkīndə/ *informal* ▸*contraction of* kind of: *I think it's kinda funny*. ▷early 20th cent. (originally U.S.): alteration.

kin·der·gar·ten /ˈkindərˌgärtn; -ˌgärdn/ ▸*n.* a school or class that prepares children for first grade. A child in kindergarten is typically 5 or 6 years old. ▷mid 19th cent.: from German, literally 'children's garden.' —**kin·der·gar·ten·er** /-ˌgärtnər; -ˌgärd-/ (also **kin·der·gart·ner**) *n.*

kind·heart·ed /ˈkīndˈhärtid/ ▸*adj.* having a kind and sympathetic nature. —**kind·heart·ed·ly** *adv.* —**kind·heart·ed·ness** *n.*

kin·dle[1] /ˈkindl/ ▸*v.* [*trans.*] light or set on fire. ■ arouse or inspire (an emotion or feeling): *a love of art was kindled in me*. ■ [*intrans.*] (of an emotion) be aroused: *she hesitated, suspicion kindling within her*. ■ [*intrans.*] become impassioned or excited: *the young man kindled at once*. ▷Middle English: based on Old Norse *kynda*, influenced by Old Norse *kindill* 'candle, torch.' —**kin·dler** *n.*

kin·dle[2] ▸*v.* [*intrans.*] (of a hare or rabbit) give birth. ▷Middle English: apparently a frequentative of KIND[1].

kin·dling /ˈkindliNG/ ▸*n.* **1** easily combustible small sticks or twigs used for starting a fire. **2** (in neurology) a process by which a seizure or other brain event is both initiated and its recurrence made more likely.

kind·ly /ˈkīn(d)lē/ ▸*adv.* in a kind manner: *"Never mind," she said kindly*. ■ please (used in a polite request or demand, often ironically): *will you kindly sign the enclosed copy of this letter*.
▸*adj.* (**-li·er, -li·est**) **1** kind; warmhearted; gentle: *he was a quiet, kindly man*. **2** *archaic* native-born. ▷Old English *gecyndelīce* 'naturally, characteristically' (see KIND[2], -LY[2]). —**kind·li·ness** *n.*
▸*PHRASES* □ **look kindly on** regard (someone or something) sympathetically. □ **not take kindly to** not welcome or be pleased by (someone or something). □ **take something kindly** like or be pleased by something. □ **thank someone kindly** thank someone very much.

kind·ness /ˈkīn(d)nis/ ▸*n.* the quality of being friendly, generous, and considerate. ■ a kind act: *it is a kindness I shall never forget*.

kin·dred /ˈkindrid/ ▸*n.* [treated as *pl.*] one's family and relations. ■ relationship by blood: *ties of kindred*.
▸*adj.* [*attrib.*] similar in kind; related: *books on kindred subjects*. ▷Middle English: from KIN + *-red* (from Old English *rǣden* 'condition'), with insertion of *-d-* in the modern spelling through phonetic development (as in *thunder*).

kin·dred spir·it ▸*n.* a person whose interests or attitudes are similar to one's own: *I longed to find a kindred spirit*.

kine /kīn/ ▸*plural n. archaic* cows collectively.

kin·e·mat·ics /ˌkinəˈmatiks/ ▸*plural n.* [usu. treated as *sing.*] the branch of mechanics concerned with the motion of objects without reference to the forces that cause the motion. Compare with DYNAMICS. ■ [usu. treated as *pl.*] the features or properties of motion in an object, regarded in such a way. ▷mid 19th cent.: from Greek *kinēma, kinēmat-* 'motion' (from *kinein* 'to move') + -ICS. —**kin·e·mat·ic** *adj.* —**kin·e·mat·i·cal·ly** /-ˈmatik(ə)lē/ *adv.*

kin·e·mat·o·graph /ˌkinəˈmatəˌgraf/ ▸*n.* variant spelling of **CINEMATOGRAPH.**

kin·e·scope /ˈkinəˌskōp/ ▸*n.* a television picture tube. ■ a film recording of a television broadcast. ▷mid 20th cent.: originally a proprietary name, from Greek *kinēsis* 'movement' + **-SCOPE.**

ki·ne·sics /kəˈnēsiks; -ziks/ ▸*plural n.* [usu. treated as *sing.*] the study of the way in which certain body movements and gestures serve as a form of nonverbal communication. ■ [usu. treated as *pl.*] certain body movements and gestures regarded in such a way. ▷1950s: from Greek *kinēsis* 'motion' (from *kinein* 'to move') + **-ICS.**

ki·ne·si·ol·o·gy /kəˌnēsēˈäləjē; -zē-/ ▸*n.* the study of the mechanics of body movements. ▷late 19th cent.: from Greek *kinēsis* 'movement' (from *kinein* 'to move') + **-LOGY.** —**ki·ne·si·o·log·i·cal** /-sēəˈläjikəl; -zēə-/ *adj.* —**ki·ne·si·ol·o·gist** /-jist/ *n.*

ki·ne·sis /kəˈnēsis/ ▸*n.* (*pl.* **-ses** /-ˌsēz/) movement; motion. ■ *Biology* an undirected movement of a cell, organism, or part in response to an external stimulus. Compare with **TAXIS.** ■ *Zoology* mobility of the bones of the skull, as in some birds and reptiles. ▷early 17th cent.: from Greek *kinēsis* 'movement,' from *kinein* 'to move.'

kin·es·the·sia /ˌkinəsˈTHēZHə/ (*Brit.* **kin·aes·the·sia**) ▸*n.* awareness of the position and movement of the parts of the body by means of sensory organs (proprioceptors) in the muscles and joints. ▷late 19th cent.: from Greek *kinein* 'to move' + *aisthēsis* 'sensation.' —**kin·es·thet·ic** /-ˈTHetik/ *adj.*

ki·net·ic /kəˈnetik/ ▸*adj.* of, relating to, or resulting from motion. ■ (of a work of art) depending on movement for its effect. ▷mid 19th cent.: from Greek *kinētikos*, from *kinein* 'to move.' —**ki·net·i·cal·ly** /-ik(ə)lē/ *adv.*

ki·net·ic art ▸*n.* a form of art that depends on movement for its effect. The term was coined by artists Naum Gabo (1890–1977) and his brother Antoine Pevsner (1886–1962) in 1920 and is associated with the mobiles of artist Alexander Calder.

ki·net·ic en·er·gy ▸*n.* *Physics* energy that a body possesses by virtue of being in motion. Compare with **POTENTIAL ENERGY.**

ki·net·ics /kəˈnetiks/ ▸*plural n.* [usu. treated as *sing.*] the branch of chemistry or biochemistry concerned with measuring and studying the rates of reactions. ■ [usu. treated as *pl.*] the rates of chemical or biochemical reaction. ■ *Physics* the study of forces acting on mechanisms.

ki·net·ic the·o·ry ▸*n.* the body of theory that explains the physical properties of matter in terms of the motions of its constituent particles.

ki·ne·tin /ˈkīnətin/ ▸*n.* *Biochemistry* & *Botany* a synthetic compound similar to kinin, used to stimulate cell division in plants. ▷1950s: from Greek *kinētos* 'movable' (from *kinein* 'to move') + **-IN**[1].

kineto- ▸*comb. form* relating to movement. ▷from Greek *kinētos* 'movable.'

ki·ne·to·chore /kəˈnetəˌkôr; -ˈnētə-/ ▸*n.* another term for **CENTROMERE.** ▷mid 20th cent.: from **KINETO-** 'of movement' + Greek *khōros* 'place.'

ki·ne·to·plast /kəˈnetəˌplast; -ˈnētə-/ ▸*n.* *Biology* a mass of mitochondrial DNA lying close to the nucleus in some flagellate protozoa.

ki·ne·to·scope /kəˈnetəˌskōp; -ˈnē-/ ▸*n.* an early motion-picture device in which the images were viewed through a peephole.

ki·ne·to·some /kəˈnetəˌsōm; -ˈnētə-; kī-/ ▸*n.* another term for **BASAL BODY.**

kin·folk /ˈkinˌfōk/ (also **kins·folk** /ˈkinz-/ or **kin·folks**) ▸*plural n.* (in anthropological or formal use) a person's blood relations, regarded collectively. ■ a group of people related by blood: *a set of kinfolk.*

King[1] /kiNG/, B. B. (1925–), U.S. blues singer and guitarist; born *Riley B. King.* An established blues performer, he came to the notice of a wider audience in the late 1960s, when his style of guitar playing was imitated by rock musicians.

King[2], Billie Jean (1943–), U.S. tennis player. She won a record 20 Wimbledon titles, including 6 singles titles (1966–68, 1972–73, and 1975), 10 doubles titles, and 4 mixed doubles titles. She retired in 1983.

King[3], Martin Luther, Jr. (1929–68), U.S. Baptist minister and civil rights leader. A noted orator, he opposed discrimination against blacks by organizing nonviolent resistance and peaceful mass demonstrations. He was assassinated in Memphis, Tennessee. Nobel Peace Prize (1964). His birthday, January 15, is a holiday.

King[4], Stephen (Edwin) (1947–) U.S. writer; pseudonym Richard Bachman. He is best known for his writings of horror and suspense, such as *Carrie* (1974, movie 1976); *The Shining* (1977, movie 1980); *The Green Mile* (1996, movie 1999); and *The Plant* (2000), a novel that he released several chapters of on the Internet.

King[5], William Lyon Mackenzie (1874–1950), Canadian statesman; prime minister 1921–26, 1926–30, and 1935–48.

king /kiNG/ ▸*n.* **1** the male ruler of an independent state, esp. one who inherits the position by right of birth: [as *title*] *King Henry VIII.* ■ a person or thing regarded as the finest or most important in its sphere or group: *a country where football is king | the king of rock.* ■ [*attrib.*] used in names of animals and plants that are particularly large, e.g., **king cobra.** ■ (**the King**) (in the UK) the national anthem when there is a male sovereign. **2** the most important chess piece, of which each player has one, which the opponent has to checkmate in order to win. The king can move in any direction, including diagonally, to any adjacent square that is not attacked by an opponent's piece or pawn. ■ a piece in the game of checkers with extra capacity for moving, made by crowning an ordinary piece that has reached the opponent's baseline. ■ a playing card bearing a representation of a king, normally ranking next below an ace.
▸*v.* [*trans.*] *archaic* make (someone) king. ■ (**king it**) *dated* act in an unpleasantly superior and domineering manner: *he* **kings it over** *the natives on his atoll.* ▷Old English *cyning, cyng*, of Germanic origin; related to Dutch *koning* and German *König*, also to **KIN.** —**king·hood** /-ˌho͝od/ *n.* —**king·less** *adj.* —**king·like** /-ˌlīk/ *adj.* —**king·li·ness** *n.* —**king·ly** *adj.* —**king·ship** /-ˌSHip/ *n.*
▸*PHRASES* □ **a king's ransom** see **RANSOM.** □ **live like a king** (or **queen**) live in great comfort and luxury.

king·bird /ˈkiNGˌbərd/ ▸*n.* a large American tyrant flycatcher, typically with a gray head and back and yellowish or white underparts. • Genus *Tyrannus*, family Tyrannidae: several species.

king bo·lete ▸*n.* another term for **CEP.**

king·bolt /ˈkiNGˌbōlt/ ▸*n.* a kingpin in a mechanical structure.

King Charles span·iel ▸*n.* a spaniel of a small breed, typically with a white, black, and tan coat.

king co·bra ▸*n.* a brownish cobra with an orange-cream throat patch, native to the Indian subcontinent. It is the largest of all venomous snakes. Also called **HAMADRYAD.** • *Ophiophagus hannah*, family Elapidae.

king crab ▸*n.* **1** an edible crab of the North Pacific, resembling a spider crab. • Genus *Paralithodes*, family Lithodidae. **2** another term for **HORSESHOE CRAB.**

king·craft /ˈkiNGˌkraft/ ▸*n.* *archaic* the art of ruling as a king, esp. with reference to the use of clever or crafty diplomacy in dealing with subjects.

king·cup /ˈkiNGˌkəp/ ▸*n.* British term for **MARSH MARIGOLD.**

king·dom /ˈkiNGdəm/ ▸*n.* **1** a country, state, or territory ruled by a king or queen: ■ a realm associated with or regarded as being under the control of a particular person or thing: *the kingdom of dreams.* **2** the spiritual reign or authority of God. ■ the rule of God or Christ in a future age. ■ heaven as the abode of God and of the faithful after death. **3** each of the three traditional divisions (animal, vegetable, and mineral) in which natural objects have conventionally been classified. ■ *Biology* the highest category in taxonomic classification. ▷Old English *cyningdōm* 'kingship' (see **KING, -DOM**).
▸*PHRASES* □ **come into** (or **to**) **one's kingdom** achieve recognition or supremacy. □ **till** (or **until**) **kingdom come** *informal* forever. □ **to kingdom come** *informal* into the next world: *the truck was blown to kingdom come.*

Martin Luther King, Jr.

king·fish /ˈkiNGˌfiSH/ ▸*n.* (*pl.* same or **-fish·es**) **1** any of a number of large sporting fish, many of which are edible: ■ a fish of the jack family (Carangidae), including the **yellowtail kingfish** (*Seriola grandis*) of the South Pacific. ■ (**northern kingfish**) a fish of the drum family (*Menticirrhus saxatilis*, family Sciaenidae), of the east coast of North America. ■ a western Atlantic fish of the mackerel family (*Scomberomorus cavalla*, family Scombridae). **2** *informal* a person regarded as an authority figure; an influential leader or boss.

king·fish·er /ˈkiNGˌfiSHər/ ▸*n.* an often brightly colored bird with a large head and long sharp beak, typically diving for fish from a perch. Many of the tropical kinds live in forests and feed on terrestrial prey such as insects and lizards. • Family Alcedinidae: many genera and numerous species, esp. the **belted kingfisher** (*Ceryle alcyon*), with blue-gray and white plumage and a shaggy crest, found throughout North America.

belted kingfisher

King James Bi·ble (also **King James Version**) ▸*n.* an English translation of the Bible made in 1611 at the order of King James I and still widely used. Also called **AUTHORIZED VERSION**, chiefly in the UK.

King Kong /ˈkiNG ˈkôNG; ˈkäNG/ a huge apelike monster featured in the film *King Kong* (1933).

king·let /ˈkiNGlit/ ▸*n.* **1** *chiefly derogatory* a minor king. **2** a very small greenish bird with a bright orange or yellow crown. • Genus *Regulus*, family Sylviidae: several species, e.g., the American **golden-crowned kinglet** (*R. satrapa*).

king·mak·er /ˈkiNGˌmākər/ ▸*n.* a person who brings leaders to power through the exercise of political influence. ▷used originally with reference to the Earl of Warwick (see **WARWICK**[2]).

king of beasts ▸*n.* *chiefly poetic/literary* the lion (used in reference to the animal's perceived grandeur).

King of Kings ▸*n.* used as a name or form of address for God. ■ (in the Christian Church) used as a name or form of address for Jesus Christ. ■ a title assumed by certain kings who rule over lesser kings.

king of the hill ▸*n.* a children's game in which the object is to beat one's rivals to the top of a mound or other high place, and to keep possession of the place. ■ one who is in command or successful: *your daddy brags about you—you're king of the hill with him.*

king pen·guin ▸*n.* a large penguin native to Antarctic islands as well as the Falklands and other subantarctic islands. • *Aptenodytes patagonica*, family Spheniscidae.

King Phil·ip's War (1675–77) the first large-scale military action in the American colonies, pitting various Indian tribes against New England colonists and their Indian allies. Marked by heavy slaughters on both sides (including killings of women and children), the war cost thousands of lives.

king·pin /ˈkiNGˌpin/ ▸*n.* a main or large bolt in a central position. ■ a vertical bolt used as a pivot. ■ a person or thing that is essential to the success of an organization or operation: *the kingpins of the television industry.*

king post ▸*n.* an upright post in the center of a roof truss, extending from the tie beam to the apex of the truss.

kin group ▸*n.* a group of people related by blood or marriage.

K

Kings /kiNGz/ the name of two books of the Bible, recording the history of Israel from the accession of Solomon to the destruction of the Temple in 586 BC.

King's Bench ▸*n.* (in the UK) in the reign of a king, the term for **QUEEN'S BENCH.**

Kings Can·yon Na·tion·al Park a national park in the Sierra Nevada, in south central California, north of Sequoia National Park. Established in 1940, it preserves groves of ancient sequoia trees, including some of the largest in the world.

King's Coun·sel (abbr.: **KC**) ▸*n.* (in the UK) in the reign of a king, the term for **QUEEN'S COUNSEL.**

King's Eng·lish ▸*n.* another term for **QUEEN'S ENGLISH.**

king's e·vil ▸*n.* (usu. **the king's evil**) *historical* scrofula, formerly held to be curable by the royal touch.

king·side /ˈkiNG,sīd/ ▸*n.* *Chess* the half of the board on which both kings stand at the start of a game (the right-hand side for White, left for Black).

king-sized (also **king-size**) ▸*adj.* (esp. of a commercial product) of a larger size than the standard; very large: *a king-sized bed.*

Kings·ley /ˈkiNGzlē/, Charles (1819–75), English novelist and clergyman. He is remembered for his historical novel *Westward Ho!* (1855) and for his classic children's story *The Water-Babies* (1863).

king snake ▸*n.* a large, smooth-scaled North American constrictor that typically has shiny dark brown or black skin with lighter markings. • Genus *Lampropeltis*, family Colubridae: several species, in particular *L. getulus*. Compare with **MILK SNAKE.**

king's pawn ▸*n.* *Chess* the pawn occupying the square immediately in front of each player's king at the start of a game.

Kings·port /ˈkiNGz,pôrt/ an industrial city in northeastern Tennessee, part of a complex with Johnson City and Bristol; pop. 44,905.

king's shil·ling ▸*n.* a shilling formerly given to a recruit when enlisting in the army during the reign of a king.

Kings·ton /ˈkiNGstən/ **1** a port in southeastern Canada, on Lake Ontario, at the head of the St. Lawrence River; pop. 56,597. **2** the capital and chief port of Jamaica; pop. 538,000. **3** a historic city in southeastern New York, on the Hudson River; pop. 23,095.

Kings·ton-up·on-Hull official name for **HULL.**

Kings·town /ˈkiNGz,toun/ the capital and chief port of St. Vincent and the Grenadines in the Caribbean; pop. 26,220.

ki·nin /ˈkīnin/ ▸*n.* **1** *Biochemistry* any of a group of substances formed in body tissue in response to injury. They are polypeptides and cause vasodilation and smooth muscle contraction. **2** *Botany* a compound that promotes cell division and inhibits aging in plants. Also called **CYTOKININ.** ▷1950s: from Greek *kinein* 'to move' + **-IN**[1].

kink /kiNGk/ ▸*n.* a sharp twist or curve in something that is otherwise straight: *a kink in the road.* ■ *figurative* a flaw or obstacle in a plan, operation, etc.: *though the system is making some headway, there are still some kinks to iron out.* ■ a stiffness in the neck, back, etc.; crick: *it takes the kinks out of stiff necks.* ■ *figurative* a quirk of character or behavior. ■ *informal* a person with unusual sexual preferences.
▸*v.* form or cause to form a sharp twist or curve: [*intrans.*] *the river kinks violently in a right angle* | [*trans.*] *when the spine gets kinked, the muscles react with pain.* ▷late 17th cent.: from Middle Low German *kinke*, probably from Dutch *kinken* 'to kink.'

kin·ka·jou /ˈkiNGkə,jo͞o/ ▸*n.* an arboreal nocturnal fruit-eating mammal with a prehensile tail and a long tongue, found in the tropical forests of Central and South America. • *Potos flavus*, family Procyonidae. ▷late 18th cent.: from French *quincajou*, alteration of **CARCAJOU.**

kink·y /ˈkiNGkē/ ▸*adj.* (**kink·i·er, kink·i·est**) **1** *informal,* involving or given to unusual sexual behavior. ■ (of clothing) sexually provocative in an unusual way: *kinky underwear.* **2** having kinks or twists: *long and kinky hair.* ▷mid 19th cent. (sense 2): from **KINK** + **-Y**[1].
—**kink·i·ly** /-kilē/ *adv.* —**kink·i·ness** *n.*

Kin·ner·et, Lake /kēˈneret/ another name for Sea of Galilee (see **GALILEE, SEA OF**).

kin·ni·kin·nick /,kinikiˈnik/ (also **kin·ni·kin·nic** or **kin·ni·kin·nik**) ▸*n.* a smoking mixture used by North American Indians as a substitute for tobacco or for mixing with it, typically consisting of dried sumac leaves and the inner bark of willow or dogwood. ■ the bearberry, which was also sometimes used in this mixture. ▷late 18th cent.: from a Delaware (Unami) word meaning 'mixture.'

ki·no /ˈkēnō/ ▸*n.* a gum obtained from certain tropical trees by tapping, used locally as an astringent in medicine and in tanning. • The trees belong to genera in various families, in particular *Pterocarpus* and *Butea* (family Leguminosae). ▷late 18th cent.: apparently from a West African language.

Kin·o·rhyn·cha /,kinəˈriNGkə; ,kē-/ *Zoology* a small phylum of minute marine invertebrates that have a spiny body and burrow in sand or mud. ▷modern Latin (plural), from Greek *kinein* 'set in motion' + *rhunkos* 'snout.' —**kin·o·rhynch** /ˈkinə,riNGk; ˈkē-/ *n.*

-kins ▸*suffix* equivalent to **-KIN**, often expressing endearment.

kin se·lec·tion ▸*n.* *Zoology* natural selection in favor of behavior by individuals that may decrease their chance of survival but increases that of their kin (who share a proportion of their genes).

Kin·sey /ˈkinzē/, Alfred Charles (1894–1956), U.S. zoologist and sex researcher. He carried out pioneering studies on sexual behavior by interviewing large numbers of people. His best-known work, *Sexual Behavior in the Human Male* (1948, also known as the *Kinsey Report*), was controversial but highly influential.

kins·folk /ˈkinz,fōk/ ▸*plural n.* another term for **KINFOLK.**

Kin·sha·sa /kinˈsHäsə/ the capital of the Democratic Republic of the Congo (formerly Zaire), a port on the Congo River, in the southwestern part of the country; pop. 3,804,000. Founded in 1881 by explorer Sir Henry Morton Stanley, it became capital of the Republic of Zaire in 1960. Former name (until 1966) **LÉOPOLDVILLE.**

kin·ship /ˈkin,sHip/ ▸*n.* blood relationship. ■ a sharing of characteristics or origins: *they felt a kinship with architects.*

kin·ship group ▸*n.* *Anthropology* a family, clan, or other group based on kinship.

kins·man /ˈkinzmən/ ▸*n.* (*pl.* **-men**) (in anthropological or formal use) one of a person's blood relations, esp. a male.

kins·wom·an /ˈkinz,wo͝omən/ ▸*n.* (*pl.* **-wom·en**) (in anthropological or formal use) one of a person's female blood relations.

ki·osk /ˈkē,äsk/ ▸*n.* a small open-fronted hut or cubicle from which newspapers, refreshments, tickets, etc., are sold. ■ (usu. **telephone kiosk**) *Brit.* a telephone booth. ■ *archaic* (in Turkey and Iran) a light open pavilion or summerhouse. ▷early 17th cent. (in the sense 'pavilion'): from French *kiosque*, from Turkish *köşk* 'pavilion,' from Persian *kuš*.

Ki·o·wa /ˈkīəwə/ ▸*n.* (*pl.* same or **-was**) **1** a member of an American Indian people of the southern plains of the U.S., now living mainly in Oklahoma. **2** the language of this people, related to the Tanoan group. **3** (in full **Kiowa Apache**) an Athabaskan (Apache) language of western Oklahoma and neighboring areas.
▸*adj.* of or relating to this people or these languages. ▷from American Spanish *Caygua*, perhaps from Caddoan *káhiwa'* 'Kiowa'.

kip[1] /kip/ ▸*n.* (in leather-making) the hide of a young or small animal. ■ a set or bundle of such hides. ▷late Middle English: perhaps related to Middle Dutch *kip, kijp* 'bundle (of hides).'

kip[2] ▸*n.* (*pl.* same or **kips**) the basic monetary unit of Laos, equal to 100 ats. ▷Thai.

kip[3] ▸*n.* a unit of weight equal to 1,000 lb (453.6 kg).

kip[4] *informal* ▸*n.* *Brit.* a sleep; a nap: *I might have a little kip* | *he was trying to get some kip.* ■ *chiefly Scottish* a bed.
▸*v.* (**kipped, kip·ping**) [*intrans.*] *Brit.* sleep: *they kipped down for the night.* ▷mid 18th cent. (in the sense 'brothel'): perhaps related to Danish *kippe* 'hovel, tavern.'

Kip·ling /ˈkipliNG/, (Joseph) Rudyard (1865–1936), British novelist, short-story writer, and poet, born in India. He is known for his poems, such as "If" and "Gunga Din," and for his children's tales, notably *The Jungle Book* (1894) and the *Just So Stories* (1902). Nobel Prize for Literature (1907). —**Kip·ling·esque** /,kipliNGˈesk/ *adj.*

kip·pa /kēˈpä/ (also **kip·pah**) ▸*n.* another term for **YARMULKE.** ▷mid 20th cent.: from modern Hebrew *kippāh*.

kip·per /ˈkipər/ ▸*n.* **1** a kippered fish, esp. a herring. **2** a male salmon in the spawning season.
▸*v.* [*trans.*] [usu. as *adj.*] (**kippered**) cure (a herring or other fish) by splitting it open and salting and drying it in the open air or in smoke. ▷Old English *cypera* (sense 2), of Germanic origin; related to Old Saxon *kupiro*, perhaps also to **COPPER**[1].

Kir /ki(ə)r/ (also **kir**) ▸*n.* *trademark* a drink made from dry white wine and crème de cassis. ▷1960s: named after Canon Félix *Kir* (1876–1968), a mayor of Dijon, France, who is said to have invented the recipe.

Kirch·hoff /ˈki(ə)r,KHôf/, Gustav Robert (1824–87), German physicist; a pioneer in spectroscopy. He developed the concept of black-body radiation and discovered the elements cesium and rubidium.

Kir·ghiz /ki(ə)rˈgēz/ (also **Kyr·gyz**) ▸*n.* (*pl.* same) **1** a member of an indigenous people of central Asia, living chiefly in Kyrgyzstan. **2** the Turkic language of this people.
▸*adj.* of or relating to this people or their language. ▷the name in Kirghiz.

Kir·ghi·zia /ki(ə)rˈgēzHə; -ˈgēzēə/ another name for **KYRGYZSTAN.**

Ki·ri·ba·ti /ˈki(ə)rə,bas/ a country in the southwestern Pacific Ocean that includes the Gilbert, Line, and Phoenix islands, as well as Banaba (Ocean Island); pop. 100,700,000; capital, Bairiki (on Tarawa); official languages, English and I-Kiribati (a local Austronesian language).

> Inhabited by Micronesian people, the islands were sighted by the Spaniards in the mid 16th century. Britain declared a protectorate over the Gilbert and Ellice Islands in 1892, and they became a colony in 1915. British links with the Ellice Islands (now Tuvalu) ended in 1975, and Kiribati became an independent republic within the Commonwealth of Nations in 1979.

Ki·rin /ˈkēˈrin/ variant of **JILIN.**

Ki·riti·mati /kəˈrisməs; ˈkris-/ an island in the Pacific Ocean, one of the Line Islands of Kiribati; pop. 3,000. The largest atoll in the world, it was discovered by Captain James Cook on Christmas Eve 1777 and was British until it became part of an independent Kiribati in 1979. Former name (until 1981) **CHRISTMAS ISLAND.**

kirk /kərk/ ▸*n.* *Scottish & N. English* **1** a church. **2** (**the Kirk** or **the Kirk of Scotland**) the Church of Scotland as distinct from the Church of England or from the Episcopal Church in Scotland. ▷Middle English: from Old Norse *kirkja*, from Old English *cirice* (see **CHURCH**).

Kirk·land /ˈkərklənd/ a city in west central Washington, northeast of Seattle; pop. 40,052.

Kirk·pat·rick /,kərkˈpatrik/, Jeane Jordan (1926–) U.S. educator and public official. A Democrat who switched to the Republican party in 1985, she

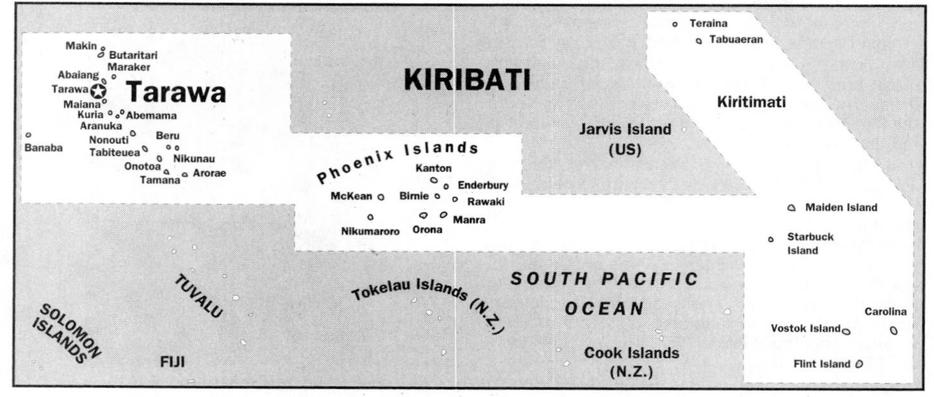

served as U.S. ambassador to the United Nations 1981–85 before returning to her teaching position at Georgetown University. She wrote *Political Women* (1974) and *The Withering Away of the Totalitarian State* (1990).

Kir·kuk /kir'ko͝ok/ an industrial city in northern Iraq, center of the oil industry in that region; pop. 208,000.

Kirk·wall /kər'kwôl/ a port in the Orkney Islands; pop. 6,000. Situated on Mainland, it is the chief town of the islands.

Kir·li·an pho·tog·ra·phy /'ki(ə)rlēən/ ▸*n.* a technique for recording photographic images of corona discharges and hence, supposedly, the auras of living creatures. ▷late 20th cent.: from the name of Semyon D. and Valentina K. *Kirlian*, Russian electricians.

Kir·man /kir'män/ ▸*n.* a carpet of a kind typically having soft, delicate coloring and naturalistic designs. ▷late 19th cent.: from *Kirman*, the name of a province and town in southeastern Iran.

Ki·rov /'ki(ə)r,ôf; -əf/ former name (1934–92) for **VYATKA**.

Ki·ro·va·bad /,kērəf'bät/ former name (1935–89) for **GÄNCÄ**.

kirsch /ki(ə)rsн/ (also **kirsch·wa·sser** /-,väsər/) ▸*n.* brandy distilled from the fermented juice of cherries. ▷German, abbreviation of *Kirschenwasser*, from *Kirsche* 'cherry' + *Wasser* 'water.'

kir·tle /'kərtl/ ▸*n. archaic* a woman's gown or outer petticoat. ■ a man's tunic or coat. ▷Old English *cyrtel*, of Germanic origin, probably based on Latin *curtus* 'short.'

ki·san /ki'sän/ ▸*n. Indian* an agricultural worker; a peasant. ▷1930s: Hindi *kisān*, from Sanskrit *kṛṣāṇa* 'person who plows.'

Ki·san·ga·ni /,kēsäng'gänē; kē'säng,gänē/ a city in northern Democratic Republic of the Congo (formerly Zaire), on the Congo River; pop. 373,000. Former name (until 1966) **STANLEYVILLE**.

Ki·shi·nev /'kisнə,nef; -,nev/ Russian name for **CHIŞINĂU**.

Ki·shi·nyov /'kisнə,nef; -,nev; kyisнə'nyôf/ Russian name for **CHIŞINĂU**.

kish·ke /'kisнkə/ ▸*n.* a beef intestine stuffed with a seasoned filling. ■ (usu. **kishkes**) *informal* a person's guts. ▷mid 20th cent.: Yiddish, from Polish *kiszka* or Ukrainian *kishka*.

kis·ka·dee /'kiskə,dē/ ▸*n.* a large tyrant flycatcher with a black-and-white-striped head and bright yellow breast, found mainly in tropical America. • The **greater kiskadee** (*Pitangus sulphuratus*) and the **lesser kiskadee** (*Philohydor lictor*), family Tyrannidae. ▷late 19th cent.: imitative of its call.

Kis·ka Is·land /'kiskə/ an island in the Aleutian Islands, in southwestern Alaska. It was occupied by the Japanese during World War II.

Kis·lev /'kisləv; kēs'lev/ ▸*n.* (in the Jewish calendar) the third month of the civil and ninth of the religious year, usually coinciding with parts of November and December. ▷from Hebrew *kislēw*.

kis·met /'kizmit; -,met/ ▸*n.* destiny; fate: *what chance did I stand against kismet?* ▷early 19th cent.: from Turkish, from Arabic *ḳismat* 'division, portion, lot,' from *ḳasama* 'to divide.'

kiss /kis/ ▸*v.* [*trans.*] touch with the lips as a sign of love, sexual desire, reverence, or greeting: *he kissed her on the lips* | [*trans.*] *she kissed the children goodnight* | [*intrans.*] *we started kissing.* ■ *Billiards* (of a ball) lightly touch (another ball) in passing.

▸*phrasal v.* □ **kiss someone/something off** *informal* dismiss someone rudely; end a relationship abruptly. □ **kiss up to** *informal* behave sycophantically or obsequiously toward (someone) in order to obtain something.

▸*n.* **1** a touch with the lips in kissing. ■ *Billiards* a slight touch of a ball against another ball. ■ used to express affection at the end of a letter (conventionally represented by the letter X): *she sent lots of love and a whole line of kisses.* **2** a small cake or cookie, typically a meringue. ■ a small candy, esp. one made of chocolate. ▷Old English *cyssan* (verb), of Germanic origin; related to Dutch *kussen* and German *küssen*. —**kiss·a·ble** *adj.*

▸*PHRASES* □ **kiss and make up** become reconciled. □ **kiss and tell** *chiefly derogatory* recount one's sexual exploits, esp. to the media concerning a famous person: [as *adj.*] *this isn't a kiss-and-tell book.* □ **kiss someone's ass** *vulgar slang* behave obsequiously toward someone. □ **kiss ass** *vulgar slang* behave in an obsequious or sycophantic way. □ **kiss something good-bye** (or **kiss good-bye to something**) *informal* accept the certain loss of something: *I could kiss my career good-bye.* □ **kiss something to make it better** *informal* comfort a sick or injured person, esp. a child, by kissing the sore or injured part of their body as a gesture of removing pain. □ **kiss of death** an action or event that causes certain failure for an enterprise: *it would be the kiss of death for the company if it could be proved that the food was unsafe.* □ **kiss of life** mouth-to-mouth resuscitation. ■ *figurative* an action or event that revives a failing enterprise: *good ratings gave the program the kiss of life.* □ **kiss of peace** a ceremonial kiss given or exchanged as a sign of unity, esp. during the Christian Eucharist. □ **kiss the rod** accept punishment submissively.

kiss-and-tell ▸*adj.* revealing private or confidential information: *a kiss-and-tell article by the actor's former girlfriend.*

kiss-ass ▸*adj. vulgar slang* having or showing an obsequious or sycophantic eagerness to please.

▸*n.* a person who behaves in such a way.

kiss-curl ▸*n.* British term for **SPIT CURL**.

kis·sel /'kisəl/ ▸*n.* a dessert made from fruit juice or purée, boiled with sugar and water and thickened with potato or cornstarch. ▷from Russian *kisel'*, from a base shared by *kislyĭ* 'sour.'

kiss·er /'kisər/ ▸*n.* **1** [usu. with *adj.*] a person who kisses someone: *he's a good kisser.* [mid 16th cent.: from the verb **KISS** + **-ER**[1].] **2** *informal* a person's mouth: *I belted him one, right on the kisser.* [mid 19th cent.: originally boxing slang.]

Kis·sim·mee /ki'simē/ a resort and agricultural city in central Florida; pop. 30,050.

kiss·ing bug ▸*n.* a bloodsucking North American assassin bug that can inflict a painful bite on humans and often attacks the face.

kiss·ing cous·in ▸*n.* a relative known well enough to be given a kiss in greeting.

kiss·ing dis·ease ▸*n. informal* a disease transmitted by contact with infected saliva, esp. infectious mononucleosis.

Kis·sin·ger /'kisənjər/, Henry (Alfred) (1923–), U.S. statesman and diplomat; born in Germany; secretary of state 1973–77. In 1973, he helped to negotiate the withdrawal of U.S. troops from South Vietnam. His numerous trips to foster Middle East negotiations led to the term "shuttle diplomacy." Nobel Peace Prize (1973).

kiss-off ▸*n. informal* a rude or abrupt dismissal, esp. from a job or romantic relationship.

kiss·o·gram /'kisə,gram/ ▸*n.* a novelty greeting or message delivered by a man or woman who accompanies it with a kiss, arranged as a humorous surprise for the recipient.

kiss·y /'kisē/ ▸*adj. informal* characterized by or given to kissing; amorous: *Dean and I were just getting kissy.*

kiss·y-face ▸*n. informal* a puckering of the lips as if to kiss someone: ***she made kissy-face*** *when she saw me.*

▸*PHRASE* □ **play kissy-face** (or **kissy-kissy**) engage in kissing or petting, esp. in public. ■ behave in an excessively friendly way in order to gain favor.

kist /kist/ ▸*n.* **1** variant spelling of **CIST**. **2** *chiefly Scottish* a chest used for storing clothes and linen.

Ki·swa·hi·li /,kiswä'hēlē/ ▸*n.* another term for **SWAHILI** (sense 1). ▷from the Bantu prefix *ki-* (used in names of languages) + **SWAHILI**.

kit[1] /kit/ ▸*n.* **1** a set of articles or equipment needed for a specific purpose: *a first-aid kit.* ■ a set of all the parts needed to assemble something: *an aircraft kit.* ■ *Brit.* the clothing and other items belonging to a soldier or used in an activity such as a sport: *boys in football kit.* **2** *chiefly Brit.* a large basket, box, or other container, esp. for fish.

▸*v.* [*trans.*] (**kit someone/something out/up**) (usu. **be kitted out/up**) *chiefly Brit.* provide someone or something with the appropriate clothing or equipment: *we were all kitted out in life jackets.* ▷Middle English: from Middle Dutch *kitte* 'wooden vessel,' of unknown origin. The original sense 'wooden tub' was later applied to other containers; the use denoting a soldier's equipment (late 18th cent.) probably arose from the idea of a set of articles packed in a container.

kit[2] ▸*n.* the young of certain animals, such as the beaver, fox, ferret, and mink. ■ informal term for **KITTEN**.

kit[3] ▸*n. historical* a small violin, esp. one used by a dancing master. ▷early 16th cent.: perhaps from Latin *cithara* (see **CITTERN**).

Ki·ta·kyu·shu /,kētä'kyo͞osнo͞o/ a port in southern Japan, on the northern coast of Kyushu island; pop. 1,026,000.

kit bag (also **kit·bag**) ▸*n.* a rectangular canvas bag, used esp. for carrying a soldier's clothes and personal possessions.

kitch·en /'kicнən/ ▸*n.* **1** a room or area where food is prepared and cooked. ■ a set of fixtures, cabinets, and appliances that are sold together and installed in such a room or area: *a complete kitchen at a bargain price.* ■ cuisine: *the dried shrimp pastes of the Thai kitchen.* **2** *informal* the percussion section of an orchestra. **3** [as *adj.*] (of a language) in an uneducated or domestic form: *kitchen Swahili.* ▷Old English *cycene*; related to Dutch *keuken* and German *Küche*, based on Latin *coquere* 'to cook.'

▸*PHRASE* □ **everything but the kitchen sink** *informal, humorous* everything imaginable.

kitch·en cab·i·net ▸*n.* a group of unofficial advisers to the holder of an elected office who are considered to be unduly influential.

Kitch·e·ner[1] /'kicн(ə)nər/ a city in Ontario, southern Canada; pop. 168,282. Settled as Dutch Sand Hills by German Mennonites in 1806, it was renamed Berlin in 1830 and Kitchener in 1916, in honor of Field Marshal Kitchener.

Kitch·e·ner[2], (Horatio) Herbert, 1st Earl Kitchener of Khartoum (1850–1916), British soldier and statesman, born in Ireland. He served as secretary of state for war during World War I.

kitch·en·ette /,kicнə'net/ ▸*n.* a small kitchen or part of a room equipped as a kitchen.

kitch·en gar·den ▸*n.* a garden or area where vegetables, fruit, or herbs are grown for domestic use.

kitch·en mid·den ▸*n.* a prehistoric refuse heap that marks an ancient settlement, chiefly containing bones, shells, and stone implements.

kitch·en po·lice (abbr.: **KP**) ▸*n.* [usu. treated as *pl.*] *military slang* enlisted personnel detailed to help the cook by washing dishes, peeling vegetables, and performing other kitchen duties. ■ the assigned duty of these personnel: *we were put* ***on KP*** *for four days.*

kitch·en-sink ▸*adj.* [*attrib.*] (in art forms) characterized by great realism in the depiction of drab or sordid subjects: *a kitchen-sink drama.*

kitch·en·ware /'kicнən,we(ə)r/ ▸*n.* the utensils used in a kitchen.

kite /kīt/ ▸*n.* **1** a toy consisting of a light frame with thin material stretched over it, flown in the wind at the end of a long string. ■ *informal Sailing* a spinnaker or other high, light sail. **2** a medium to large long-winged bird of prey that typically has a forked tail and frequently soars on updrafts of air. • *Ictinia, Elanoides*, and other genera, family Accipitridae: many species, including the **American swallow-tailed kite** (*E. forficatus*) and the **Mississippi kite** (*I. mississippiensis*). **3** *informal* a fraudulent check, bill, or receipt. ■ an illicit or surreptitious letter or note. ■ *archaic* a person who exploits or preys on others.

▸*v.* **1** [*intrans.*] [usu. as *n.*] (**kiting**) fly a kite. ■ [with *adverbial of direction*] fly; move quickly: *he kited into England on the Concorde.* **2** [*trans.*] *informal* write or use (a check, bill, or receipt) fraudulently. ▷Old English *cȳta* (as a noun in sense 2); probably of imitative origin and related to German *Kauz* 'screech owl.' The toy was so named because it hovers in the air like the bird.

▸*PHRASE* □ (**as**) **high as a kite** *informal* intoxicated with drugs or alcohol.

kite 2

kite·board·ing /'kīt,bôrding/ ▸*n.* another term for **KITESURFING**. —**kite·board·er** *n.*

kite-fly·ing ▸*n.* the action of flying a kite on a string. ■ the action of trying something out to test public opinion. ■ *informal* the fraudulent writing or using of a check, bill, or receipt.

kite·surf·ing /ˈkīt,sərfiNG/ ▸*n.* the sport or pastime of riding on a modified surfboard while holding on to a specially designed kite, using the wind for propulsion. Also called **KITEBOARDING**. **—kite·surf·er** *n.*

kit fox ▸*n.* a small nocturnal fox with a yellowish-gray back and large, close-set ears, found in the deserts and plains of the southwestern U.S. • *Vulpes macrotis*, family Canidae. ▷early 19th cent.: *kit* probably from **KIT**2 (because of its small size).

kith /kiTH/ ▸*n.* (in phrase **kith and kin** or **kith or kin**) one's friends, acquaintances, and relations: *a widow without kith or kin.* ▷Old English *cӯth*, of Germanic origin; related to **COUTH**. The original senses were 'knowledge,' 'one's native land,' and 'friends and neighbors.' The phrase *kith and kin* originally denoted one's country and relatives; later one's friends and relatives.

kith·a·ra /ˈkiTHərə/ ▸*n.* variant spelling of **CITHARA**.

kitsch /kiCH/ ▸*n.* art, objects, or design considered to be in poor taste because of excessive garishness or sentimentality, but sometimes appreciated in an ironic or knowing way: *the lava lamp is an example of sixties kitsch* | [as *adj.*] *kitsch decor.* ▷1920s: German. **—kitsch·i·ness** *n.* **—kitsch·y** *adj.*

kit·ten /ˈkitn/ ▸*n.* **1** a young cat. ■ the young of several other animals, such as the rabbit and beaver. **2** a stout furry gray and white moth, the caterpillar of which resembles that of the puss moth. • Genus *Furcula*, family Notodontidae.
▸*v.* [*intrans.*] (of a cat or certain other animals) give birth. ▷late Middle English *kitoun, ketoun*, from an Anglo-Norman French variant of Old French *chitoun*, diminutive of *chat* 'cat.'
▸PHRASE □ **have kittens** *informal* be extremely nervous or upset.

kit·ten heel ▸*n.* a type of curvy heel, typically between 1 and 2 inches in height.

kit·ten·ish /ˈkitn-iSH/ ▸*adj.* playful, lively, or flirtatious: *her voice had that kittenish quality.* **—kit·ten·ish·ly** *adv.* **—kit·ten·ish·ness** *n.*

kit·ti·wake /ˈkitē,wāk/ ▸*n.* a small gull that nests in colonies on sea cliffs, having a loud call that resembles its name. • Genus *Rissa*, family Laridae: two species, in particular the black-legged *Rissa tridactyla* of the North Atlantic and North Pacific. ▷early 17th cent. (originally Scots): imitative of its call.

kit·tle /ˈkitl/ ▸*adj. archaic* difficult to deal with; prone to erratic behavior. ▷mid 16th cent.: from *kittle* 'to tickle' (now Scots and dialect), probably from Old Norse *kitla*.

kit·ty1 /ˈkitē/ ▸*n.* (*pl.* **-ties**) a fund of money for communal use, made up of contributions from a group of people. ■ a pool of money in some gambling card games. ▷early 19th cent. (denoting a jail): of unknown origin.

kit·ty2 ▸*n.* (*pl.* **-ties**) a pet name or a child's name for a kitten or cat.

kit·ty-cor·ner ▸*adj.* & *adv.* another term for **CATER-CORNERED**.

Kit·ty Hawk /ˈkitē ,hôk/ a town on a narrow sand peninsula on the Atlantic Ocean coast of North Carolina. It was there that, in 1903, the Wright brothers made the first powered airplane flight.

Kit·we /ˈkē,twā/ a city in the Copperbelt mining region of northern Zambia; pop. 338,000.

ki·va /ˈkēvə/ ▸*n.* a chamber, built wholly or partly underground, used by male Pueblo Indians for religious rites. ▷late 19th cent.: from Hopi *kíva*.

Ki·vu, Lake /ˈkēvo͞o/ a lake in central Africa, on the Democratic Republic of the Congo (formerly Zaire)–Rwanda frontier.

Ki·wa·nis /kəˈwänis/ (in full **Kiwanis Club**) ▸*n.* a North American society of business and professional people formed to maintain commercial ethics and as a social and charitable organization. ▷early 20th cent.: of unknown origin. **—Ki·wa·ni·an** /-nēən/ *n.* & *adj.*

ki·wi /ˈkēwē/ ▸*n.* (*pl.* **ki·wis**) **1** a flightless New Zealand bird with hairlike feathers, having a long down-curved bill with sensitive nostrils at the tip. • Family Apterygidae and genus *Apteryx*: three species, including the **brown kiwi** (*A. australis*). **2** (**Kiwi**) *informal* a New Zealander, esp. a soldier or member of a national sports team. **3** short for **KIWI FRUIT**: *a bowl of cherries and kiwis.* ▷mid 19th cent.: from Maori.

brown kiwi

ki·wi fruit (also **ki·wi·fruit**) ▸*n.* (*pl.* same) a fruit with a thin hairy skin, green flesh, and black seeds. Also called **CHINESE GOOSEBERRY**. • This fruit is obtained from the eastern Asian climbing plant *Actinidia chinensis* (family Actinidiaceae).

Ki·zil Ir·mak /kiˈzil irˈmäk/ (ancient name **Halys**) the longest river in Turkey that flows for 715 miles (1,150 km) in a great curve through central Anatolia to the Black Sea.

kJ ▸*abbr.* kilojoule(s).

KJV ▸*abbr.* King James Version.

KKK ▸*abbr.* Ku Klux Klan.

Kkt ▸*abbr. Chess* king's knight.

KL *informal* ▸*abbr.* Kuala Lumpur.

kl ▸*abbr.* kiloliter(s).

Klai·pe·da /ˈklīpədə/ a city and port in Lithuania, on the Baltic Sea; pop. 206,000. Former name (1918–23 and 1941–44, when under German control) **MEMEL**.

Klam·ath /ˈklaməTH/ ▸*n.* (*pl.* same or **Klam·aths**) **1** a member of an American Indian people of southern Oregon and northern California. **2** the language of this people.
▸*adj.* of or relating to this people or their language. ▷from the Chinook name *łámał* 'those of the river'.

Klam·ath Moun·tains /ˈklaməTH/ a range in southwestern Oregon and northern California, through which the **Klamath River** flows to the Pacific Ocean.

Klan /klan/ ▸*n.* the Ku Klux Klan or a large organization within it. **—Klans·man** /ˈklanzmən/ *n.* (*pl.* **-men**). **—Klans·wom·an** /ˈklanz,wo͝omən/ *n.* (*pl.* **-wom·en**).

Klap·roth /ˈkläp,rōt/, Martin Heinrich (1743–1817), German chemist; one of the founders of analytical chemistry.

klatch /kläCH; klaCH/ (also **klatsch**) ▸*n.* a social gathering, esp. for coffee and conversation. ▷mid 20th cent.: from German *Klatsch* 'gossip.'

Klau·sen·burg /ˈklouzən,bo͝ork; -,bərg/ German name for **CLUJ–NAPOCA**.

klax·on /ˈklaksən/ ▸*n. trademark* an electric horn or a similar loud warning device. ▷early 20th cent.: from the name of the manufacturing company.

kleb·si·el·la /,klebzēˈelə; ,klepsē-/ ▸*n.* a bacterium that causes respiratory, urinary, and wound infections. • Genus *Klebsiella*; nonmotile Gram-negative rods. ▷modern Latin, from the name *Klebs*.

Klee /klā/, Paul (1879–1940), Swiss painter who lived in Germany from 1906. He joined the *Blaue Reiter* group in 1912 and later taught at the Bauhaus (1920–33).

Kleen·ex /ˈklē,neks/ ▸*n.* (*pl.* same or **Kleen·ex·es**) *trademark* an absorbent disposable paper tissue.

Klein1 /klīn/, Calvin (Richard) (1942–), U.S. fashion designer.

Klein2, Melanie (1882–1960), Austrian psychoanalyst. She was the first psychologist to specialize in the psychoanalysis of small children.

Klein bot·tle ▸*n. Mathematics* a closed surface with only one side, formed by passing one end of a tube through the side of the tube and joining it to the other end. ▷1940s.: named after Felix *Klein* (1849–1925), the German mathematician who first described it.

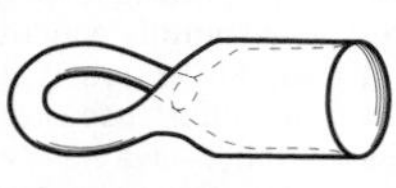
Klein bottle

Klem·per·er1 /ˈklempərər/, Otto (1885–1973), U.S. conductor and composer; born in Germany. He conducted the Los Angeles Symphony Orchestra 1933–39.

Klem·per·er2, Werner (1920–2000), U.S. actor; born in Germany. He was known for his portrayal of Colonel Klink on the 1960s television program "Hogan's Heroes" and also appeared on Broadway, in films, and as a narrator with symphony orchestras. He was the son of Otto Klemperer.

klepht /kleft/ ▸*n.* **1** a Greek independence fighter, esp. one who fought the Turks in the 15th century or during the war of independence (1821–28). **2** a Greek brigand or bandit. ▷from modern Greek *klephtēs*, from Greek *kleptēs* 'thief.' The original klephts led an outlaw existence in the mountains; those who maintained this after the war of independence became mere bandits.

klep·to·crat /ˈkleptə,krat/ ▸*n.* a ruler who uses political power to steal his or her country's resources. ▷1960s: from Greek *kleptēs* 'thief' + *-crat*. **—klep·toc·ra·cy** /klepˈtäkrəsē/ *n.* **—klep·to·crat·ic** /,kleptəˈkratik/ *adj.*

klep·to·ma·ni·a /,kleptəˈmānēə; -ˈmānyə/ ▸*n.* a recurrent urge to steal, typically without regard for need or profit. ▷mid 19th cent.: from Greek *kleptēs* 'thief' + **-MANIA**. **—klep·to·ma·ni·ac** /-ˈmānē,ak/ *n.* & *adj.*

klep·to·par·a·site /,kleptəˈparə,sīt/ ▸*n. Zoology* a bird, insect, or other animal that habitually robs animals of other species of food. ▷late 20th cent.: from Greek *kleptēs* 'thief' + **PARASITE**. **—klep·to·par·a·sit·ic** /-,parəˈsitik/ *adj.* **—klep·to·par·a·sit·ism** /-si,tizəm; -sī-/ *n.*

Klerk, F. W. de, see **DE KLERK**.

Klerks·dorp /ˈklerks,dôrp/ a city in South Africa, southwest of Johannesburg; pop. 238,865.

klez·mer /ˈklezmər/ ▸*n.* (*pl.* **klez·mo·rim** /klezˈmôrim; ,klezmə,rēm/) (also **klez·mer mu·sic**) traditional eastern European Jewish music. ■ a musician who plays this kind of music. ▷mid 20th cent.: Yiddish, contraction of Hebrew *kĕlē zemer* 'musical instruments.'

klick /klik/ (also **click**) ▸*n. informal* a kilometer: *about 200 klicks northwest of Moscow.* ▷mid 20th cent.: of unknown origin; the term was originally used in the Vietnam War.

klieg /klēg/ (usu. **klieg light**) ▸*n.* a powerful electric lamp used in filming. ▷1920s: named after the American brothers, Anton T. *Kliegl* (1872–1927) and John H. *Kliegl* (1869–1959), who invented it.

Klimt /klimt/, Gustav (1862–1918), Austrian painter and designer. Cofounder of the Vienna Secession (1897), he is known for his decorative and allegorical paintings and his portraits of women.

Kline·fel·ter's syn·drome /ˈklīn,feltərz/ ▸*n. Medicine* a syndrome affecting males in which the cells have an extra X chromosome (in addition to the normal XY), characterized by a tall thin physique, small infertile testes, and enlarged breasts. ▷mid 20th cent.: named after Harry F. *Klinefelter* (born 1912), American physician.

Kling·on /ˈkliNG,än/ ▸*n.* **1** a member of a warlike humanoid alien species in the television series *Star Trek* and its derivatives and sequels. **2** the language of the Klingons: *the site is also available in synthetic languages like Esperanto and Klingon.* ▷1960s: invented name.

klip·spring·er /ˈklip,spriNGər/ ▸*n.* a small rock-dwelling antelope with a yellowish-gray coat, an arched back, and a stiff bouncing gait, native to southern Africa. • *Oreotragus oreotragus*, family Bovidae. ▷late 18th cent.: from Afrikaans, from Dutch *klip* 'rock' + *springer* 'jumper.'

Klon·dike /ˈklän,dīk/ a tributary of the Yukon River, in Yukon Territory, northwestern Canada, that rises in the Ogilvie Mountains and flows west for 100 miles (160 km) to join the Yukon at Dawson. It gave its name to the surrounding region, which became famous when gold was found in nearby Bonanza Creek in 1896. ■ [as *n.*] *figurative* a source of valuable material. ■ [as *n.*] a form of the card game patience or solitaire.

klong /klông; kläNG/ ▸*n.* (in Thailand) a canal. ▷Thai.

kloof /klo͞of/ ▸*n. S. African* a steep-sided, wooded ravine or valley. ▷Afrikaans, from Middle Dutch *clove* 'cleft.'

kludge /klo͞oj/ (also **kluge**) *informal* ▸*n.* an ill-assorted collection of parts assembled to fulfill a particular purpose. ■ *Computing* a machine, system, or program that has been badly put together.
▸*v.* [*trans.*] use ill-assorted parts to make (something): *Hugh had to kludge something together.* ▷1960s (originally U.S.): invented word, perhaps symbolic. Compare with **FUDGE**.

klutz /kləts/ ▸*n. informal* a clumsy, awkward, or foolish person. ▷1960s: from Yiddish *klots* 'wooden block.' **—klutz·i·ness** *n.* **—klutz·y** *adj.*

Klux·er /ˈkləksər/ ▸*n. informal* a member of the Ku Klux Klan.

klys·tron /ˈklī,strän/ ▸*n. Physics* an electron tube that generates or amplifies microwaves by velocity modulation. ▷1930s: from Greek *kluzein, klus-* 'wash over' + **-TRON**.

km ▸*abbr.* kilometer(s).

K-me·son ▸*n.* another term for **KAON**. ▷1950s: from *K* (for **KAON**) + **MESON**.

kmph ▸*abbr.* kilometers per hour.

kmps ▸*abbr.* kilometers per second.

KN ▸*abbr. Chess* king's knight.

kn ▸*abbr.* knot(s).

knack /nak/ ▸*n.* [in *sing.*] an acquired or natural skill at performing a task: *she got the* ***knack of*** *it in the end.* ■ a tendency to do something: *the band has a* ***knack of*** *warping classic soul songs.* ▷late Middle English (originally denoting a clever or deceitful trick): probably related to obsolete *knack* 'sharp blow or sound,' of imitative origin (compare with Dutch *knak* 'crack, snap').

knack·er /ˈnakər/ *Brit.* ▸*n.* a person whose business is the disposal of dead or unwanted animals, esp. those whose flesh is not fit for human consumption.
▸*v.* [*trans.*] [often as *adj.*] (**knackered**) *informal* tire (someone) out; exhaust: *you look absolutely knackered.* ■ damage severely. ▷late 16th cent. (originally denoting a harness-maker, then a slaughterer of horses): possibly from obsolete *knack* 'trinket.' The word also had the sense 'old worn-out horse' (late 18th cent.). It is unclear whether the verb represents a figurative use of 'slaughter,' from the noun sense, or of 'castrate,' from a slang sense of the noun, 'testicles.'

knack·wurst /ˈnäk,wərst/ (also **knock·wurst**) ▸*n.* a type of short, fat, highly seasoned German sausage. ▷mid 20th cent.: from German *Knackwurst*, from *knacken* 'make a cracking noise' + *Wurst* 'sausage.'

knai·del /ˈk(ə)nädl/ (also **knei·del**) ▸*n.* (*pl.* **knai·dlach** /ˈk(ə)näd,läkʜ/) (usu. **knaidlach**) a type of dumpling eaten esp. in Jewish households during Passover. ▷from Yiddish *kneydel*.

knap[1] /nap/ ▸*n.* *archaic* the crest of a hill. ▷Old English *cnæpp, cnæp*.

knap[2] ▸*v.* (**knapped**, **knap·ping**) [*trans.*] *Architecture & Archaeology* shape (a piece of stone, typically flint) by striking it so as to make stone tools or weapons or to give a flat-faced stone for building walls: [as *adj.*] (**knapped**) *buildings made of knapped flint.* ■ *archaic* strike with a hard short sound; knock. ▷late Middle English (in the sense 'to knock, rap'): imitative; compare with Dutch and German *knappen* 'crack, crackle.' —**knap·per** *n.*

knap·sack /ˈnap,sak/ ▸*n.* a bag with shoulder straps, carried on the back, and typically made of canvas or other weatherproof material. ▷early 17th cent.: from Middle Low German, from Dutch *knapzack*, probably from German *knappen* 'to bite' + *zak* 'sack.'

knap·weed /ˈnap,wēd/ ▸*n.* a tough-stemmed plant of the daisy family that typically has purple thistlelike flowerheads, occurring typically in grassland and on roadsides. • Genus *Centaurea*, family Compositae: several species, including the widespread **black knapweed** (*C. nigra*) (also called **HARDHEADS**). ▷late Middle English (originally as *knopweed*): from **KNOP** (because of its hard rounded involucre or "head") + **WEED**.

knar /när/ ▸*n.* *archaic* a knot or protuberance on a tree trunk or root. ▷Middle English *knarre* (denoting a rugged rock or stone); related to Middle Low German *knarre* 'knobbly protuberance'; compare with **KNUR**.

knave /nāv/ ▸*n.* *archaic* a dishonest or unscrupulous man. ■ another term for **JACK**[1] in cards. ▷Old English *cnafa* 'boy, servant'; related to German *Knabe* 'boy.' —**knav·er·y** /-vərē/ *n.* (*pl.* **-er·ies**). —**knav·ish** *adj.* —**knav·ish·ly** *adv.* —**knav·ish·ness** *n.*

knawel /nôl/ ▸*n.* a low-growing inconspicuous plant of the pink family, growing in temperate regions of the northern hemisphere. • Genus *Scleranthus*, family Caryophyllaceae. ▷late 16th cent.: from German *Knauel*, *Knäuel* 'knotgrass.'

knead /nēd/ ▸*v.* [*trans.*] work (moistened flour or clay) into dough or paste with the hands. ■ make (bread or pottery) by such a process. ■ massage or squeeze with the hands: *she kneaded his back.* ▷Old English *cnedan*, of Germanic origin; related to Dutch *kneden* and German *kneten*. —**knead·a·ble** *adj.* —**knead·er** *n.*

knee /nē/ ▸*n.* the joint between the thigh and the lower leg in humans. ■ the corresponding or analogous joint in other animals. ■ the upper surface of someone's thigh when sitting; a person's lap: *they were eating their supper on their knees.* ■ the part of a garment covering the knee. ■ an angled piece of wood or metal frame used to connect and support the beams and timbers of a wooden vessel; a triangular plate serving the same purpose in a modern vessel. ■ an abrupt obtuse or approximately right-angled bend in a graph between parts where the slope varies smoothly.
▸*v.* (**knees**, **kneed**, **knee·ing**) [*trans.*] hit (someone) with one's knee: *she kneed him in the groin.* ▷Old English *cnēow, cnēo*, of Germanic origin; related to Dutch *knie* and German *Knie*, from an Indo-European root shared by Latin *genu* and Greek *gonu*.
▸*PHRASES* □ **at one's mother's** (or **father's**) **knee** at an early age. □ **bend** (or **bow**) **the** (or **one's**) **knee** (**to**) kneel in submission; submit. □ **bring someone/something to their/its knees** reduce someone or something to a state of weakness or submission. □ **fall** (or **drop**, **sink**, etc.) **to one's knees** assume a kneeling position. □ **on bended knee(s)** kneeling, esp. in entreaty or worship: *did he propose on bended knee?* □ **on one's knees** in a kneeling position. ■ *figurative* on the verge of collapse: *when they took over, the newspaper was on its knees.* □ **weak at the knees** overcome by a strong feeling, typically desire.

knee ac·tion ▸*n.* a form of independent front-wheel suspension in a motor vehicle: [as *adj.*] *knee-action wheels.*

knee bend ▸*n.* an act of bending the knee, esp. as a physical exercise in which the body is raised and lowered without the use of the hands.

knee·board /ˈnē,bôrd/ ▸*n.* a short board for surfing or waterskiing in a kneeling position. —**knee·board·er** *n.* —**knee·board·ing** *n.*

knee breech·es ▸*plural n.* *archaic* short trousers worn by men and fastened at or just below the knee.

knee·cap /ˈnē,kap/ ▸*n.* the convex bone in front of the knee joint; the patella.
▸*v.* (**-capped**, **-cap·ping**) [*trans.*] shoot (someone) in the knee or leg as a form of punishment: [as *n.*] (**kneecapping**) *petty crimes are punished by kneecapping.*

knee-deep ▸*adj.* immersed up to the knees: *we were knee-deep in snow.* ■ having more than one needs or wants of something: *we shall soon be knee-deep in conflicting legal views.* ■ so deep as to reach the knees: *the water was knee-deep on Main Street.*
▸*adv.* so as to be immersed up to the knees: *I plodded knee-deep through the mud.*

knee-high ▸*adj.* & *adv.* so high as to reach the knees: [as *adj.*] *knee-high boots* | [as *adv.*] *they were wading knee-high in the water.*
▸*n.* (usu. **knee-highs**) a sock or nylon stocking with an elasticized top that reaches to a person's knee.
▸*PHRASE* □ **knee-high to a grasshopper** *informal* very small or very young.

knee·hole /ˈnē,hōl/ ▸*n.* a space for the knees, esp. one under a desk: [as *adj.*] *a kneehole desk.*

knee-jerk ▸*n.* a sudden involuntary reflex kick caused by a blow on the tendon just below the knee.
▸*adj.* [*attrib.*] (of a response) automatic and unthinking: *a knee-jerk reaction.* ■ (of a person) responding in this way: *knee-jerk radicals.*

kneel /nēl/ ▸*v.* (*past* and *past part.* **knelt** /nelt/ also **kneeled**) [*intrans.*] (of a person) be in or assume a position in which the body is supported by a knee or the knees, typically as a sign of reverence or submission: *they **knelt down** and prayed.* ▷Old English *cnēowlian*, from *cnēow* (see **KNEE**).

kneel·er /ˈnēlər/ ▸*n.* a person who kneels, esp. in prayer. ■ a cushion or bench for kneeling on.

knee·pan /ˈnē,pan/ ▸*n.* old-fashioned term for **KNEECAP**.

knee-slap·per ▸*n.* *informal* an uproariously funny joke. —**knee-slap·ping** *adj.*

knees-up ▸*n.* [in *sing.*] *Brit., informal* a lively party or gathering: *we had a bit of a knees-up last night.*

knee-trem·bler ▸*n.* *informal* an act of sexual intercourse between people in a standing position.

knei·del /ˈk(ə)nädl/ ▸*n.* (*pl.* **knei·dlach** /ˈk(ə)näd,läkʜ/) variant spelling of **KNAIDEL**.

knell /nel/ *poetic/literary* ▸*n.* the sound of a bell, esp. when rung solemnly for a death or funeral. ■ *figurative* used with reference to an announcement, event, or sound that is regarded as a solemn warning of the end of something: *the decision will probably toll the knell for the facility.*
▸*v.* [*intrans.*] (of a bell) ring solemnly, esp. for a death or funeral. ■ [*trans.*] proclaim (something) by or as if by a knell. ▷Old English *cnyll* (noun), *cnyllan* (verb); related to Dutch *knal* (noun), *knallen* (verb) 'bang, pop, crack.' The current spelling (dating from the 16th cent.) is perhaps influenced by **BELL**[1].

knelt /nelt/ ▸ past and past participle of **KNEEL**.

Knes·set /k(ə)ˈneset/ the parliament of modern Israel, established in 1949. It consists of 120 members elected every four years. ▷Hebrew, literally 'gathering.'

knew /n(y)o͞o/ ▸ past of **KNOW**.

knick·er·bock·er /ˈnikər,bäkər/ ▸*n.* **1** (**knickerbockers**) see **KNICKERS**. **2** (**Knickerbocker**) a New Yorker. ■ a descendant of the original Dutch settlers in New York. ▷mid 19th cent. (originally in sense 2): named after Diedrich *Knickerbocker*, pretended author of W. Irving's *History of New York* (1809). Sense 1 is said to have arisen from the resemblance of knickerbockers to the breeches worn by Dutchmen in Cruikshank's illustrations in Irving's book. —**knick·er·bock·ered** *adj.*

knick·ers /ˈnikərz/ ▸*plural n.* **1** (also **knick·er·bock·ers**) loose-fitting trousers gathered at the knee or calf. **2** *Brit.* a woman's or girl's underpants. ▷late 19th cent. (in sense 1): abbreviation of *knickerbockers* (see **KNICKERBOCKER**). —**knick·ered** *adj.*
▸*PHRASE* □ **get one's knickers in a twist** *Brit., informal* become upset or angry.

knickers 1

knick·knack /ˈnik,nak/ (also **knick-knack**) ▸*n.* (usu. **knick-knacks**) a small worthless object, esp. a household ornament. ▷late 16th cent. (in the sense 'a petty trick'): reduplication of **KNACK**. —**knick·knack·er·y** /-,nakərē/ *n.*

knife /nīf/ ▸*n.* (*pl.* **knives** /nīvz/) a cutting instrument composed of a blade and a handle into which it is fixed, either rigidly or with a joint. ■ an instrument such as this used as a weapon. ■ a cutting blade forming part of a machine.
▸*v.* [*trans.*] stab (someone) with a knife. ■ [*intrans.*] cut like a knife: *a shard of steel knifed through the mainsail.* ▷late Old English *cnīf*, from Old Norse *knífr*, of Germanic origin. —**knife·like** /-,līk/ *adj.* —**knif·er** *n.*
▸*PHRASES* □ **before you can say knife** *informal* very quickly; almost instantaneously. □ (**so thick that**) **you could cut** (**it**) **with a knife** (of an accent, atmosphere, or sentiment) very obvious: *the patriotism was so thick that you could cut it with a knife* | *a southern accent you could cut with a knife.* □ **stick** (or **get**) **the knife into** (or **in**) **someone** *informal* do something hostile or aggressive to someone. □ **go** (or **be**) **under the knife** *informal* have surgery. □ **the knives are out** (**for someone**) *informal* there is open hostility (toward someone). □ **like a** (**hot**) **knife through butter** very easily; without any resistance or difficulty: *antiaircraft fire would slice through the car like a hot knife through butter.* □ **twist** (or **turn**) **the knife** (**in the wound**) deliberately make someone's sufferings worse.

knife block ▸*n.* a block of wood or other solid material, containing long grooves in which kitchen knives of various sizes can be inserted up to the handle.

knife edge ▸*n.* the edge of a knife. ■ [as *adj.*] (of creases or pleats in a garment) very fine: *knife-edge creases.* ■ [in *sing.*] a tense or uncertain situation, esp. one finely balanced between success and failure: *they have been living on a knife edge since his libel action.* ■ a steel wedge on which a pendulum or other device oscillates or is balanced. ■ a narrow, sharp ridge; an arête.

knife pleat ▸*n.* a sharp, narrow pleat on a skirt made in one direction and typically overlapping another.

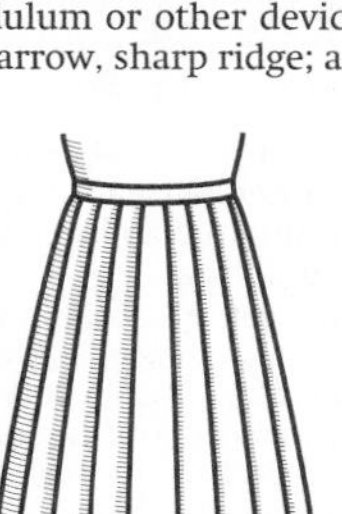

knife pleat

knife-point /ˈnīf,point/ ▸*n.* the pointed end of a knife.
▸*PHRASE* □ **at knifepoint** under threat of injury from a knife: *he was mugged at knifepoint.*

knife-throw·ing ▸*n.* a circus act or other entertainment in which knives are thrown at a target. —**knife-throw·er** *n.*

Knight[1] /nīt/, Bobby (1940–) U.S. basketball coach; full name *Robert Montgomery Knight*. The coach of the championship basketball team at Indiana University from 1971 until 2000, he also coached the 1984 gold medal Olympic team.

Knight[2], John Shively (1894–1981) U.S. newspaper publisher. He merged his newspapers in Detroit, Chicago, New York, and other large cities with the Ridder Publications chain in 1974 to form Knight–Ridder Newspapers, Inc.

knight /nīt/ ▸*n.* **1** (in the Middle Ages) a man who served his sovereign or lord as a mounted soldier in armor. ■ (in the Middle Ages) a man raised by a sovereign to honorable military rank after service as a page and squire. ■ *poetic/literary* a man devoted to

the service of a woman or a cause: *in all your quarrels I will be your knight.* ■ *dated* (in ancient Rome) a member of the class of equites. ■ (in ancient Greece) a citizen of the second class in Athens. **2** (in the UK) a man awarded a nonhereditary title by the sovereign in recognition of merit or service and entitled to use the honorific "Sir" in front of his name. **3** a chess piece, typically with its top shaped like a horse's head, that moves by jumping to the opposite corner of a rectangle two squares by three.
▸*v.* [*trans.*] (usu. **be knighted**) invest (someone) with the title of knight. ▷Old English *cniht* 'boy, youth, servant'; related to Dutch *knecht* and German *Knecht*. Sense 2 dates from the mid 16th cent.; the uses relating to Greek and Roman history derive from comparison with medieval knights. **—knight·li·ness** *n.* **—knight·ly** *adj.* & (*poetic/literary*) *adv.*
▸*PHRASES* □ **knight in shining armor** (or **knight on a white charger**) an idealized or chivalrous man who comes to the rescue of a woman in a difficult situation. □ **knight of the road** *informal* a man who frequents the roads, for example a traveling sales representative, tramp, or (formerly) a highwayman.

knight bach·e·lor ▸*n.* (*pl.* **knights bach·e·lor**) a knight not belonging to any particular order.

knight-er·rant (also **knight er·rant**) ▸*n.* (*pl.* **knights-er·rant**) a medieval knight wandering in search of chivalrous adventures. **—knight-er·rant·ry** *n.*

knight·hood /ˈnīt,ho͝od/ ▸*n.* the title, rank, or status of a knight: *he received a knighthood* | *the basis of feudal knighthood.*

Knights·bridge /ˈnīts,brij/ a district in the West End of London, to the south of Hyde Park, noted for its fashionable and expensive shops.

Knights Hos·pi·tal·lers a military and religious order founded as the Knights of the Order of the Hospital of St. John of Jerusalem in the 11th century.

Originally protectors of pilgrims, they also undertook the care of the sick. During the Middle Ages they became a powerful and wealthy military force, with foundations in various European countries. In England, the order was revived in 1831 and was responsible for the foundation of the St. John Ambulance Brigade in 1888.

Knights Tem·plars (also **Knights Tem·plar**) a religious and military order for the protection of pilgrims to the Holy Land, founded as the Poor Knights of Christ and of the Temple of Solomon in 1118.

The order became powerful and wealthy, but its members' arrogance toward rulers, together with their wealth and their rivalry with the Knights Hospitallers, led to their downfall; the order was suppressed in 1312, many of its possessions being given to the Hospitallers.

knish /k(ə)ˈnisн/ ▸*n.* a dumpling of dough that is stuffed with a filling and baked or fried. ▷Yiddish, from Russian *knish, knysh*, denoting a kind of bun or dumpling.

knit /nit/ ▸*v.* (**knit·ting**; *past* and *past part.* **knit·ted** or (esp. in sense 2) **knit**) **1** [*trans.*] make (a garment, blanket, etc.) by interlocking loops of wool or other yarn with knitting needles or on a machine. ■ make (a stitch or row of stitches) in such a way. ■ knit with a knit stitch: *knit one, purl one.* **2** [*intrans.*] become united: *disparate regions had begun to* ***knit together*** *under the king* | [as *adj.*, with *submodifier*] (**knit**) *a closely knit family.* ■ (of parts of a broken bone) become joined during healing. ■ [*trans.*] cause to unite or combine: *he* ***knitted together*** *a squad of players other clubs had disregarded.* **3** [*trans.*] tighten (one's brow or eyebrows) in a frown of concentration, disapproval, or anxiety. ■ [*intrans.*] (of someone's brow or eyebrows) tighten in such a frown.
▸*adj.* denoting or relating to a knitting stitch made by putting the needle through the front of the stitch from left to right. Compare with PURL[1].
▸*n.* a knitted fabric: *a machine-washable knit.* ■ a garment made of such fabric: *an array of casual knits.* ▷Old English *cnyttan*; related to German dialect *knütten*, also to KNOT[1]. The original sense was 'tie in or with a knot,' hence 'join, unite' (sense 2); an obsolete Middle English sense 'knot string to make a net' gave rise to sense 1. **—knit·ter** *n.*

knit·bone /ˈnit,bōn/ ▸*n.* another term for COMFREY.

knit·ting /ˈnitiNG/ ▸*n.* the craft or action of knitting. ■ material that is in the process of being knitted: *I put down my knitting.*
▸*PHRASE* □ **stick** (or **tend**) **to the** (or **one's**) **knitting** *informal* (of a person or an organization) concentrate on a familiar area of activity rather than diversify; mind one's own business.

knit·ting ma·chine ▸*n.* a machine with a bank of needles on which garments can be knitted.

knit·ting nee·dle ▸*n.* a long, thin, pointed rod used as part of a pair for knitting by hand.

knit·wear /ˈnit,we(ə)r/ ▸*n.* knitted garments.

knives /nīvz/ ▸ plural form of KNIFE.

knob /näb/ ▸*n.* a rounded lump or ball, esp. at the end or on the surface of something. ■ a handle on a door or drawer shaped like a ball. ■ a rounded button for adjusting or controlling a machine. ■ a small lump of a substance: *add* ***a knob of*** *butter or margarine.* ■ a prominent round hill. ■ *vulgar slang* a penis. ▷late Middle English: from Middle Low German *knobbe* 'knot, knob, bud.' **—knobbed** *adj.* **—knob·by** *adj.* **—knob·like** /-,līk/ *adj.*
▸*PHRASE* □ **with** (**brass**) **knobs on** *Brit.*, *informal* and something more: *it's evocative, with knobs on.* [with allusion to the addition of decorative knobs to an object as an embellishment.]

knob·bly /ˈnäblē/ ▸*adj.* (**-bli·er**, **-bli·est**) *chiefly Brit.* having lumps that give a misshapen appearance: *knobbly potatoes.*

knob·ker·rie /ˈnäb,kerē/ (also **knob·kie·rie**) ▸*n.* a short stick with a knobbed head, traditionally used as a weapon by the indigenous peoples of South Africa.
▸*v.* [*trans.*] beat with such a stick. ▷mid 19th cent.: from KNOB + *-kerrie* (from Nama *kieri* 'knobkerrie'), suggested by Afrikaans *knopkierie*.

knock /näk/ ▸*v.* **1** [*intrans.*] strike a surface noisily to attract attention, esp. when waiting to be let in through a door: *I* ***knocked on*** *the kitchen door.* ■ strike or thump together or against something: *my knees were knocking and my lips quivering.* ■ (of a motor or other engine) make a regular thumping or rattling noise because of improper ignition. **2** [*trans.*] collide with (someone or something), giving them a hard blow: *he deliberately ran into her, knocking her shoulder* | [*intrans.*] *he* ***knocked into*** *an elderly man.* ■ [*trans.*] force to move or fall with a deliberate or accidental blow or collision: *he'd* ***knocked over*** *a glass of water.* ■ injure or damage by striking: *she knocked her knee painfully on the table* | *figurative you have had a setback that has knocked your self-esteem.* ■ make (a hole or a dent) in something by striking it forcefully: *he suggests we knock a hole through the wall into the broom closet.* ■ demolish the barriers between (rooms or buildings): *two of the downstairs rooms had been* ***knocked into one.*** ■ *informal* talk disparagingly about; criticize.
▸*phrasal v.* □ **knock around** (or **about**) *informal* travel without a specific purpose: *for a couple of years she and I knocked around the Mediterranean.* ■ happen to be present: *it gets confusing when there are too many people knocking about.* ■ *chiefly Brit.* spend time with someone: *she* ***knocked around with*** *artists.* □ **knock someone/something about** (or **around**) injure or damage someone or something by rough treatment. □ **knock something back** *informal* consume a drink quickly and entirely: *we knocked back a few beers.* □ **knock someone down** (of a person or vehicle) strike or collide with someone so as to cause them to fall to the ground. □ **knock something down** **1** demolish a building.■ take machinery or furniture to pieces for transportation. **2** (at an auction) confirm the sale of an article to a bidder by a knock with a hammer.■ *informal* reduce the price of an article. **3** *informal* earn a specified sum as a wage. □ **knock off** *informal* stop work. □ **knock someone off** **1** *informal* kill someone. **2** *Brit.*, *vulgar slang* have sexual intercourse with a woman. □ **knock something off** **1** *informal* produce a piece of work quickly and easily, esp. to order. **2** *informal* deduct an amount from a total: *when the bill came, they knocked off $600 because of a little scratch.* **3** another way of saying KNOCK SOMETHING OVER. ■ *Brit.*, *informal* steal something. ■ *informal* make an illegal copy of a product. □ **knock someone out** make a person unconscious, typically with a blow to the head. ■ knock down (a boxer) for a count of ten, thereby winning the contest. ■ (**knock oneself out**) *informal* work so hard that one is exhausted. ■ *informal* astonish or greatly impress someone. □ **knock something out** **1** destroy a machine or damage it so that it stops working.■ destroy or disable enemy installations or equipment. **2** *informal* produce work at a steady fast rate: *if you knock out a thousand words a day you'll soon have it finished.* **3** empty a tobacco pipe by tapping it against a surface. □ **knock someone over** another way of saying KNOCK SOMEONE DOWN. □ **knock something over** *informal* rob a store or similar establishment: *they knocked over a liquor store.* □ **knock someone sideways** *informal* astonish someone. □ **knock something together** assemble something in a hasty and makeshift way. □ **knock someone up** **1** *vulgar slang* make a woman pregnant. **2** *Brit.* knock at someone's door.
▸*n.* **1** a sudden short sound caused by a blow, esp. on a door to attract attention or gain entry. ■ a continual thumping or rattling sound made by an engine because of improper ignition. **2** a blow or collision: *the casing is tough enough to withstand knocks.* ■ an injury caused by a blow or collision. ■ a discouraging experience; a setback: *the region's industries have taken a severe knock.* ■ *informal* a critical comment. ▷Old English *cnocian*, of imitative origin.
▸*PHRASES* □ **knock someone's block off** *informal* hit someone very hard in anger. □ **knock the bottom out of** see BOTTOM. □ **knock someone dead** *informal* greatly impress someone. □ **knock someone for a loop** see LOOP. □ **knock people's heads together** see BANG PEOPLE'S HEADS TOGETHER at BANG[1]. □ **knock something into a cocked hat** see COCKED HAT. □ **knock someone into the middle of next week** *informal* hit someone very hard. □ **knock someone/something into shape** see SHAPE. □ **knock it off** *informal* used to tell someone to stop doing something that one finds annoying or foolish. □ **knock someone on the head** stun or kill someone by a blow on the head. □ **knock on wood** see WOOD. □ **knock someone's socks off** see SOCK. □ **the school of hard knocks** painful or difficult experiences that are seen to be useful in teaching someone about life. □ **you could have knocked me** (or **her, him, etc.**) **down** (or **over**) **with a feather** *informal* used to express great surprise.

knock·a·bout /ˈnäkə,bout/ ▸*adj.* **1** denoting a rough, slapstick comic performance. **2** (of clothes) suitable for rough use.
▸*n.* **1** a rough, slapstick comic performance. **2** a tramp or vagrant. **3** a small yacht or dinghy.

knock·down /ˈnäk,doun/ (also **knock-down**) ▸*adj.* [*attrib.*] **1** *informal* (of a price) very low. [used earlier to refer to reserve prices set at an auction.] **2** capable of knocking down or overwhelming someone or something: *repeated knockdown blows.* ■ (of furniture) easily dismantled and reassembled.
▸*n.* *Boxing* an act of knocking an opponent down. ■ (also **knockdown pitch**) *Baseball* a pitch aimed so close to the body that the batter must drop to the ground to avoid being hit: *the catcher gave the sign for a knockdown pitch.* ■ *Sailing* an instance of a vessel being knocked on its side by the force of the wind.

knock-down-drag-out ▸*n.* *informal* a free-for-all fight: [as *adj.*] *knock-down-drag-out fights.*

knock·er /ˈnäkər/ ▸*n.* **1** short for DOOR KNOCKER. **2** *informal* a person who continually finds fault. **3** (**knockers**) *vulgar slang* a woman's breasts.

knock knees ▸*plural n.* a condition in which the legs curve inward so that the feet are apart when the knees are touching. **—knock-kneed** *adj.*

knock·off /ˈnäk,ôf/ (also **knock-off**) ▸*n.* *informal* a copy or imitation, esp. of an expensive or designer product: [as *adj.*] *knockoff merchandise.*

knock·out /ˈnäk,out/ ▸*n.* an act of knocking someone out, esp. in boxing: [as *adj.*] *a knockout blow.* ■ *informal* an extremely attractive or impressive person or thing: *he must have been a knockout when he was young.* ■ *Brit.* a tournament in which the loser in each round is eliminated.

knock·out drops ▸*plural n.* a drug in liquid form added to a drink to cause unconsciousness.

knock·out mouse ▸*n.* *Genetics* a mouse whose DNA has been genetically engineered so that it does not express particular proteins.

knock·wurst /ˈnäk,wərst/ ▸*n.* variant spelling of KNACKWURST.

Knole so·fa /nōl/ ▸*n.* a sofa with adjustable sides allowing conversion into a bed. ▷mid 20th cent.: named after *Knole* Park, Kent, England, site of the original sofa (*c.*1605–20) from which others were designed.

knoll[1] /nōl/ ▸*n.* a small hill or mound. ▷Old English *cnoll* 'hilltop,' of Germanic origin; related to German *Knolle* 'clod, lump, tuber' and Dutch *knol* 'tuber, turnip.'

knoll[2] ▸*v.* & *n.* archaic form of KNELL. ▷Middle English: probably an imitative alteration of KNELL.

knop /näp/ ▸*n.* a knob, esp. an ornamental one, for example in the stem of a wine glass. ■ an ornamental loop or tuft in yarn. ▷Middle English: from Middle Low German and Middle Dutch *knoppe*.

Knopf /(kə)ˈnäpf/, Alfred A. (1892–1984) U.S.

publisher. He founded Alfred A. Knopf, a publishing firm, in 1915.

Knos·sos /ˈnäsəs/ the principal city of Minoan Crete, the remains of which are situated on the northern coast of Crete.The city site was occupied from Neolithic times until *c.*1200 BC. Excavations by Sir Arthur Evans from 1899 revealed the remains of a luxurious palace, which he called the Palace of Minos.

knot[1] /nät/ ▸*n.* **1** a fastening made by tying a piece of string, rope, or something similar. ■ a particular method of tying a knot: *you need to master two knots, the clove hitch and the sheet bend.* ■ a tangled mass in something such as hair. ■ a complex and intractable problem: *a complicated knot of racial politics and pride.* ■ a tied or folded ribbon, worn as an ornament. **2** a knob, protuberance, or node in a stem, branch, or root. ■ a hard mass formed in a tree trunk at the intersection with a branch, resulting in a round cross-grained piece in timber when cut through. ■ a hard lump of tissue in an animal or human body. ■ a tense constricted feeling in the body: *the knot of tension at the back of her neck.* ■ a small tightly packed group of people: *the little* ***knot of*** *people clustered around the doorway.* **3** a unit of speed equivalent to one nautical mile per hour, used esp. of ships, aircraft, and winds. ■ *chiefly historical* a length marked by knots on a log line, as a measure of speed: *some days the vessel* ***logged 12 knots.***
▸*v.* (**knot·ted, knot·ting**) [*trans.*] **1** fasten with a knot: *the scarves were knotted loosely around their throats.* ■ make (a carpet or other decorative item) with knots. ■ make (something, esp. hair) tangled. **2** cause (a muscle) to become tense and hard. ■ [*intrans.*] (of the stomach) tighten as a result of nervousness or tension. ▷Old English *cnotta*; related to Dutch *knot*. **—knot·less** *adj.* **—knot·ter** *n.*
▸*PHRASES* □ **tie someone (up) in knots** *informal* make someone completely confused: *they* ***tied themselves in knots*** *over what to call the country.* □ **tie the knot** *informal* get married.

knot[2] ▸*n.* (*pl.* same or **knots**) a small, relatively short-billed sandpiper, with a reddish-brown or blackish breast in the breeding season. • Genus *Calidris*, family Scolopacidae: two species, in particular the **red knot** (*C. canutus*), which breeds in the Arctic and winters in the southern hemisphere. ▷late Middle English: of unknown origin.

knot gar·den ▸*n.* a formal garden laid out in an intricate design.

knot·grass /ˈnätˌgras/ ▸*n.* a common Eurasian plant of the dock family, with jointed creeping stems and small pink flowers. It is a serious weed in some areas. • Genus *Polygonum*, family Polygonaceae: several species, in particular *P. aviculare*. ■ any of a number of other plants, esp. grasses, with jointed stems.

knot·hole /ˈnätˌhōl/ ▸*n.* a hole in a piece of timber where a knot has fallen out, or in a tree trunk where a branch has decayed.

knot·ting /ˈnätiNG/ ▸*n.* the action or craft of tying knots in yarn or string to make carpets or other decorative items. ■ the knots tied in a carpet or other item.

knot·ty /ˈnätē/ ▸*adj.* (**knot·ti·er, knot·ti·est**) full of knots: *the room was paneled in knotty pine.* ■ (of a problem or matter) extremely difficult or intricate. **—knot·ti·ly** /ˈnätəlē/ *adv.* **—knot·ti·ness** *n.*

knot·weed /ˈnätˌwēd/ ▸*n.* a plant of the dock family that typically has sheaths where the leaves join the stems. It is often an invasive weed. • *Polygonum* and other genera, family Polygonaceae: several species, in particular **Japanese knotweed.** ■ knotgrass.

knout /nout/ ▸*n.* (in imperial Russia) a whip used to inflict punishment, often causing death.
▸*v.* [*trans.*] flog (someone) with such a whip. ▷mid 17th cent.: via French from Russian *knut*, from Old Norse *knútr*; related to KNOT[1].

know /nō/ ▸*v.* (*past* **knew** /n(y)o͞o/; *past part.* **known** /nōn/) **1** [with *clause*] be aware of through observation, inquiry, or information: *most people know that CFCs can damage the ozone layer | I know what I'm doing.* ■ [*trans.*] have knowledge or information concerning: *I would write to him if I knew his address* [*intrans.*] *I* ***know of*** *one local who shot himself.* ■ be absolutely certain or sure about something: *I just knew it was something I wanted to do* [*trans.*] *I knew it!* **2** [*trans.*] have developed a relationship with (someone) through meeting and spending time with them; be familiar or friendly with: *he knew and respected Laura.* ■ have a good command of (a subject or language). ■ recognize (someone or something): *Isabel couldn't hear the words clearly, but she knew the voice.* ■ be familiar or acquainted with (something): *a little restaurant she knew near Times Square.* ■ have personal experience of (an emotion or situation): *a man who had known better times.* ■ (usu. **be known as**) regard or perceive as having a specified characteristic: *he is also known as an amateur painter.* ■ (usu. **be known as**) give (someone or something) a particular name or title: *the doctor was universally known as "Hubert."* ■ (**know someone/something from**) be able to distinguish one person or thing from (another): *you are convinced you know your own baby from any other in the world.* **3** [*trans.*] *archaic* have sexual intercourse with (someone). [a Hebraism that has passed into modern languages; compare with German *erkennen*, French *connaître*.]. ▷Old English *cnāwan* (earlier *gecnāwan*) 'recognize, identify,' of Germanic origin; from an Indo-European root shared by Latin *(g)noscere*, Greek *gignōskein*, also by CAN[1] and KEN. **—know·a·ble** *adj.* **—know·er** *n.*
▸*PHRASES* □ **all one knows** used to emphasize the limited nature of one's knowledge concerning something: *all I knew was that she was a schoolteacher.* ■ used to emphasize the importance or significance of the following fact or facts: *all she knew was that she was cold and hungry and thirsty.* □ **and one knows it** said to emphasize that someone is well aware of a fact although they might pretend otherwise: *the senator's priorities do not add up and he knows it.* □ **—— as we know it** as is familiar or customary in the present: *by the year 2000 management as we know it will not exist.* □ **before one knows where one is** (or **before one knows it**) *informal* with baffling speed. □ **be in the know** be aware of something known only to a few people: *he had a tip from a friend in the know: the horse was a sure bet.* □ **be not to know** have no way of being aware of: *you weren't to know he was about to die.* □ **don't I know it!** *informal* used as an expression of rueful assent or agreement. □ **don't you know** *informal* used to emphasize what one has just said or is about to say: *I was, don't you know, a great automobile enthusiast in those days.* □ **for all someone knows** used to express the limited scope or extent of one's information: *she could be dead for all I know.* □ **God** (or **goodness** or **heaven**) **knows 1** used to emphasize that one does not know something: *God knows what else they might find.* **2** used to emphasize the truth of a statement: *God knows, we deserve a glass of bubbly after all these years.* □ **I know 1** I agree: *"It's not the same without Rosie." "I know."* **2** (also **I know what**) I have a new idea or suggestion: *I know what, let's do it now.* □ **know best** have better knowledge or more appropriate skills. □ **know better than** be wise or polite enough to avoid doing a particular thing: *you ought to know better than to ask that.* □ **know someone by sight** recognize someone by their appearance without knowing their name or being so well acquainted as to talk to them. □ **know different** (or **otherwise**) be aware of information or evidence to the contrary. □ **know something for a fact** be aware of something that is irrefutable or beyond doubt: *I know for a fact that he can't speak a word of Japanese.* □ **know someone in the biblical sense** *informal, humorous* have sexual intercourse with someone. □ **know no bounds** have no limits: *their courage knows no bounds.* □ **know one's own mind** be decisive and certain. □ **know one's way around** be familiar with (an area, procedure, or subject). □ **know the ropes** have experience of the appropriate procedures. [with reference to ropes used in sailing.] □ **know what's what** *informal* be experienced and competent in a particular area. □ **know who's who** be aware of the identity and status of each person. □ **let it be** (or **make something**) **known** ensure that people are informed about something, esp. via a third party: [with *clause*] *the commissioner let it be known that he was not seeking reappointment.* □ **not know from nothing** *informal* be totally ignorant, either generally or concerning something in particular: *she shakes her head while you talk, as if to say you don't know from nothing.* □ **not know the first thing about** have not the slightest idea about (something). □ **not know that** *informal* used to express one's doubts about one's ability to do something: *I don't know that I can sum up my meaning on paper.* □ **not know what to do with oneself** be at a loss as to know what to do, typically through boredom, embarrassment, or anxiety. □ **not know where** (or **which way**) **to look** feel great embarrassment and not know how to react. □ **not want to know** *informal* refuse to react or take notice: *they just didn't want to know when I gave my side of the story.* □ **what does —— know?** *informal* used to indicate that someone knows nothing about the subject in question: *what does he know about football, anyway?* □ **what do you know (about that)?** *informal* used as an expression of surprise. □ **wouldn't you like to know?** *informal* used to express the speaker's firm intention not to reveal something in spite of a questioner's curiosity: *"You're dating him, aren't you?" "Wouldn't you like to know?"* □ **you know** *informal* used to imply that what is being referred to is known to or understood by the listener: *when in Rome, you know.* ■ used as a gap-filler in conversation: *well, you know, I was wondering if you had any jobs for me.* □ **you know something** (or **what**)**?** *informal* used to indicate that one is going to say something interesting or surprising: *you know what? I believed her.* □ **you never know** *informal* you can never be certain; it's impossible to predict.

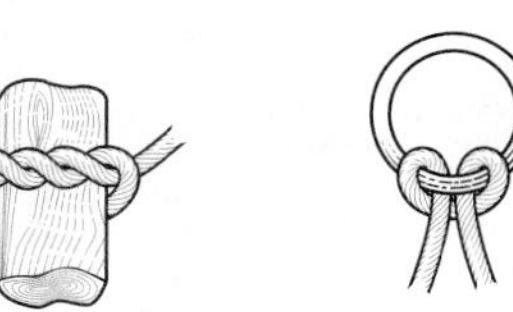
two half hitches

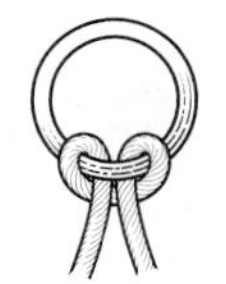
timber hitch

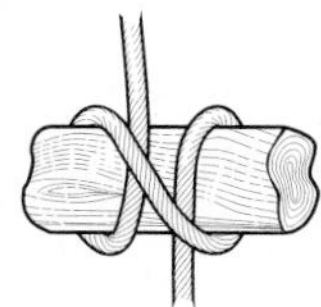
cow hitch

clove hitch

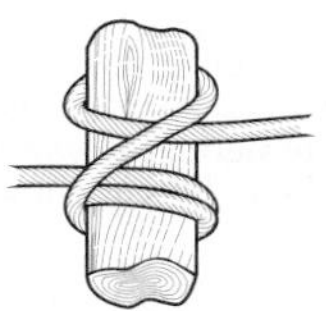
rolling hitch

slip knot

square knot

granny knot

bowline

overhand knot

figure-eight knot

barrel knot

knots

K

know·bot /ˈnō,bät/ ▸*n. Computing* a program on a network (esp. the Internet) that operates independently and has reasoning and decision-making capabilities. ▷late 20th cent.: from *knowledgeable robot.*

know-how ▸*n.* practical knowledge or skill; expertise: *technical know-how.*

know·ing /ˈnōiNG/ ▸*adj.* showing or suggesting that one has knowledge or awareness that is secret or known to only a few people: *a knowing smile.* ■ *chiefly derogatory* experienced or shrewd, esp. excessively or prematurely so: *today's society is too knowing, too corrupt.* ■ done in full awareness or consciousness: *a knowing breach of the order by the appellants.*
▸*n.* the state of being aware or informed. **—know·ing·ly** *adv.* **—know·ing·ness** *n.*
▸*PHRASE* □ **there is no knowing** no one can tell.

know-it-all ▸*n. informal* a person who behaves as if they know everything.

knowl·edge /ˈnälij/ ▸*n.* **1** facts, information, and skills acquired by a person through experience or education; the theoretical or practical understanding of a subject: *a thirst for knowledge | her considerable **knowledge of** antiques.* ■ what is known in a particular field or in total; facts and information: *the transmission of knowledge.* ■ *Philosophy* true, justified belief; certain understanding, as opposed to opinion. **2** awareness or familiarity gained by experience of a fact or situation: *the program had been developed **without his knowledge** | he denied all knowledge of the overnight incidents.*
▸*adj.* relating to organized information stored electronically or digitally: *the knowledge economy.* ▷Middle English (originally as a verb in the sense 'acknowledge, recognize,' later as a noun): from an Old English compound based on *cnāwan* (see KNOW).
▸*PHRASES* □ **come to one's knowledge** become known to one. □ **to (the best of) my knowledge** **1** so far as I know. **2** as I know for certain.

THE RIGHT WORD **erudition, information, knowledge, learning, pedantry, scholarship, wisdom**
How much do you know?
Knowledge applies to any body of facts gathered by study, observation, or experience, and to the ideas inferred from these facts (*an in-depth knowledge of particle physics; firsthand knowledge about the company*).
Information may be no more than a collection of data or facts (*information about vacation resorts*) gathered through observation, reading, or hearsay, with no guarantee of their validity (*false information that led to the arrest*).
Scholarship emphasizes academic knowledge or accomplishment (*a special award for scholarship*), while **learning** is knowledge gained not only by study in schools and universities but by individual research and investigation (*a man of great learning*), which puts it on a somewhat higher plane.
Erudition is on a higher plane still, implying bookish knowledge that is beyond the average person's comprehension (*exhibit extraordinary erudition in a doctoral dissertation*).
Pedantry, on the other hand, is a negative term for a slavish attention to obscure facts or details or an undue display of learning (*the pedantry of modern literary criticism*).
You can have extensive *knowledge* of a subject and even exhibit *erudition*, however, without attaining **wisdom**, the superior judgment and understanding that is based on both knowledge and experience.

knowl·edge·a·ble /ˈnäləjəbəl/ (also **knowl·edg·a·ble**) ▸*adj.* intelligent and well informed: *she is very knowledgeable about livestock and pedigrees.* **—knowl·edge·a·bil·i·ty** /,näləjəˈbilitē/ *n.* **—know·ledge·a·bly** /-blē/ *adv.*

knowl·edge base ▸*n.* **1** a store of information or data that is available to draw on. **2** the underlying set of facts, assumptions, and rules that a computer system has available to solve a problem.

knowl·edge man·age·ment /ˈnälij ,manijmənt/ ▸*n.* efficient handling of information and resources within a commercial organization.

knowl·edge work·er ▸*n. Computing* a person whose job involves handling or using information.

known /nōn/ ▸ past participle of KNOW.
▸*adj.* recognized, familiar, or within the scope of knowledge: *bivalved crustaceans little **known to** nonprofessionals | the known world.* ■ [*attrib.*] publicly acknowledged to be: *a known criminal.* ■ *Mathematics* (of a quantity or variable) having a value that can be stated.

know-noth·ing ▸*n.* **1** an ignorant person. **2** (**Know-Nothing**) *historical* a member of a political party in the U.S., prominent from 1853 to 1856, that was antagonistic toward Roman Catholics and recent immigrants and whose members preserved its secrecy by denying its existence. **—know-no·thing·ism** *n.*

Knox[1] /näks/, Henry (1750–1806) American military officer. He served in the American Revolution and then became the first U.S. secretary of war 1785–94.

Knox[2], John (*c.*1505–72), Scottish Protestant reformer. He played an important part in the establishment of the Church of Scotland within a Scottish Protestant state.

Knox·ville /ˈnäks,vil; -vəl/ a port on the Tennessee River, in eastern Tennessee; pop. 173,890. Twice the state capital (1796–1812 and 1817–19), it is now the headquarters of the Tennessee Valley Authority.

Knt. ▸*abbr.* Knight.

knuck·le /ˈnəkəl/ ▸*n.* a part of a finger at a joint where the bone is near the surface, esp. where the finger joins the hand: *Charlotte rapped on the window with her knuckles.* ■ a projection of the carpal or tarsal joint of a quadruped. ■ a cut of meat consisting of such a projection together with the adjoining parts: *a knuckle of pork.*
▸*v.* [*trans.*] rub or press (something, esp. the eyes) with the knuckles.
▸*phrasal v.* □ **knuckle down 1** apply oneself seriously to a task. **2** (also **knuckle under**) give in; submit. ▷Middle English *knokel* (originally denoting the rounded shape when a joint such as the elbow or knee is bent), from Middle Low German, Middle Dutch *knökel*, diminutive of *knoke* 'bone.' In the mid 18th cent. the verb *knuckle (down)* expressed setting the knuckles down to shoot the taw in a game of marbles, hence the notion of applying oneself with concentration. **—knuck·ly** *adj.*

knuck·le·ball /ˈnəkəl,bôl/ (also **knuck·ler**) ▸*n. Baseball* a slow pitch that has virtually no spin and moves erratically, typically made by releasing the ball from between the thumb and the knuckles of the first joints of the index and middle finger. **—knuck·le·ball·er** *n.*

knuck·le·bone /ˈnəkəl,bōn/ ▸*n.* **1** a bone forming or corresponding to a knuckle. ■ a knuckle of meat. **2** (**knucklebones**) animal knucklebones used in the game of jacks. ■ the game of jacks.

knuck·le·dust·er /ˈnəkəl,dəstər/ ▸*n.* a metal guard worn over the knuckles in fighting to increase the effect of blows.

knuck·le·head /ˈnəkəl,hed/ ▸*n. informal* a stupid person.

knuck·le joint ▸*n.* a joint connecting two parts of a mechanism, in which a projection in one fits into a recess in the other.

knuck·le sand·wich ▸*n. informal* a punch in the mouth.

knur /nər/ ▸*n.* a hard concretion. ■ a hard excrescence on the trunk of a tree. ▷late Middle English *knorre*, variant of *knarre* (see KNAR).

knurl /nərl/ ▸*n.* a small projecting knob or ridge, esp. in a series around the edge of something. ▷early 17th cent.: apparently a derivative of KNUR. **—knurled** *adj.*

Knut /kəˈnoot/ variant spelling of CANUTE.

KO /,kāˈō/ *informal Boxing* ▸*n.* a knockout in a boxing match. See also KAYO.
▸*v.* (**KO's, KO'd, KO'ing**) [*trans.*] knock (an opponent) out in a boxing match. ▷1920s: abbreviation.

ko·a /ˈkōə/ ▸*n.* a large Hawaiian forest tree that yields dark red timber. • *Acacia koa*, family Leguminosae. ▷early 19th cent.: from Hawaiian.

ko·a·la /kōˈälə/ ▸*n.* a bearlike arboreal Australian marsupial that has thick gray fur and feeds on eucalyptus leaves. Also called **native bear** in Australia. • *Phascolarctos cinereus*, the only member of the family Phascolarctidae. ▷early 19th cent.: from Dharuk.

koala

USAGE In general use, **koala bear** (as opposed to **koala**) is widely used. Zoologists, however, regard this form as incorrect on the grounds that, despite appearances, koalas are completely unrelated to bears.

ko·an /ˈkō,än/ ▸*n.* a paradoxical anecdote or riddle, used in Zen Buddhism to demonstrate the inadequacy of logical reasoning and to provoke enlightenment. ▷Japanese, literally 'matter for public thought,' from Chinese *gōngàn* 'official business.'

kob /käb; kōb/ ▸*n.* (*pl.* same) an antelope with a reddish coat and lyre-shaped horns, found on the savannas of southern Africa. • *Kobus kob*, family Bovidae. ▷late 18th cent.: from Wolof *kooba.*

Ko·be /ˈkōbā; -bē/ a port in central Japan, on the island of Honshu; pop. 1,477,000. The city was severely damaged by an earthquake in 1995.

Kø·ben·havn /,kœbənˈhoun/ Danish name for COPENHAGEN.

ko·bo /ˈkōbō/ ▸*n.* (*pl.* same) a monetary unit of Nigeria, equal to one hundredth of a naira. ▷corruption of COPPER[1].

ko·bold /ˈkō,bôld/ ▸*n. Germanic Mythology* **1** a familiar spirit that haunts houses; a brownie. **2** a gnome that haunts mines and other underground areas. ▷from German *Kobold.*

Koch /kôKH/, Robert (1843–1910), German bacteriologist. He identified the organisms that cause anthrax, tuberculosis, and cholera. Nobel Prize for Physiology or Medicine (1905).

Kö·chel num·ber /ˈkərsHəl; -kəl; ˈkœKHəl/ ▸*n. Music* a number given to each of Mozart's compositions in the complete catalog of his works compiled by the Austrian scientist Ludwig von Köchel (1800–77) and his successors.

ko·chi·a /ˈkōkēə/ ▸*n.* a shrubby Eurasian plant of the goosefoot family, grown for its decorative foliage, which turns deep fiery red in the autumn. Also called BURNING BUSH, SUMMER CYPRESS. • *Bassia* (formerly **Kochia**) *scoparia*, family Chenopodiaceae. ▷late 19th cent.: named after Wilhelm D. J. *Koch* (1771–1849), German botanist.

Ko·dá·ly /kōˈdī(yə); ˈkōdī/, Zoltán (1882–1967), Hungarian composer. He was deeply involved in the collection and publication of Hungarian folk songs. His works include *Psalmus Hungaricus* (1923) and the opera *Háry János* (1925–27).

Ko·di·ak bear /ˈkōdē,ak/ ▸*n.* an animal of a large race of the North American brown bear or grizzly, found on islands to the south of Alaska. • *Ursus arctos middendorffi*, family Ursidae. ▷late 19th cent.: named after *Kodiak* Island, Alaska.

Ko·di·ak Is·land /ˈkōdē,ak/ an island in the Gulf of Alaska, in southwestern Alaska, noted for its wildlife and sites of early European settlement.

ko·el /ˈkōəl/ ▸*n.* an Asian and Australasian cuckoo with a call that resembles its name, the male typically having all-black plumage. • Genus *Eudynamys*, family Cuculidae: one or two species, in particular *E. scolopacea.* ▷early 19th cent.: from Hindi *koēl*, from Sanskrit *kokila* in the same sense.

K of C ▸*abbr.* Knights of Columbus.

K of P ▸*abbr.* Knights of Pythias.

kof·ta /ˈkôftə/ ▸*n.* (*pl.* same or **-tas**) (in Middle Eastern and Indian cookery) a spiced meatball. ▷from Urdu and Persian, literally 'pounded meat.'

ko·hen /ˈkōhān; ˈkōən; kōˈhān/ (also **co·hen**) ▸*n.* (*pl.* **ko·ha·nim** /kōˈhänim; ,kôhäˈnēm/ or **co·hens**) *Judaism* a member of the priestly class, having certain rights and duties in the synagogue. ▷from Hebrew, literally 'priest.'

Ko·hi·ma /ˈkōhēmə/ a city in far northeastern India, capital of the state of Nagaland; pop. 53,000.

Koh-i-noor /ˈkō ə ,noor/ a famous Indian diamond that has a history going back to the 14th century. It passed into British possession on the annexation of Punjab in 1849 and was set in the queen's state crown for the coronation of George VI (1937). ▷from Persian *kōh-i nūr* 'mountain of light.'

Kohl /kōl/, Helmut (1930–), German statesman; chancellor of the Federal Republic of Germany 1982–90, and of Germany 1990–98. As chancellor, he showed a strong commitment to NATO and to closer ties within the EU.

kohl /kōl/ ▸*n.* a black powder, usually antimony sulfide or lead sulfide, used as eye makeup esp. in Eastern countries. ▷late 18th cent.: from Arabic *kuḥl.*

kohl·ra·bi /kōlˈräbē/ ▸*n.* (*pl.* **-bies**) a cabbage of a variety with an edible turniplike swollen stem. ▷early 19th cent.: via German from Italian *cavoli rape*, plural of *cavolo rapa*, from medieval Latin *caulorapa*, from Latin *caulis* (see COLE) + *rapum, rapa* 'turnip'; compare with French *chou-rave.*

kohlrabi

koi /koi/ (also **koi carp**) ▸*n.* (*pl.* same) a common carp of a large ornamental variety, originally bred in Japan. ▷early 18th cent.: from Japanese, 'carp.'

koi·ne /koi'nā; 'koinā/ ▸*n.* the common language of the Greeks from the close of the classical period to the Byzantine era. ■ a common language shared by various peoples; a lingua franca. ▷late 19th cent.: from Greek *koinē (dialektos)* 'common (language).'

koi·no·ni·a /ˌkoinə'nēə/ ▸*n. Theology* Christian fellowship or communion, with God or, more commonly, with fellow Christians. ▷early 20th cent.: from Greek *koinōnia* 'fellowship.'

ko·kan·ee /kō'kanē/ ▸*n.* (*pl.* same or **-ees**) a sockeye salmon of a dwarf variety that lives in landlocked lakes in western North America. ▷late 19th cent.: from Interior Salish.

Ko·ko·mo /'kōkəˌmō/ an industrial city in north central Indiana; pop. 46,113.

ko·la /'kōlə/ ▸*n.* variant spelling of **COLA** (sense 2).

Ko·la Pen·in·su·la /'kōlə/ a peninsula on the northwestern coast of Russia, that separates the White Sea from the Barents Sea. The port of Murmansk lies on its north coast.

Kol·ha·pur /'kōləˌpo͝or/ an industrial city in the state of Maharashtra, in western India; pop. 405,000.

ko·lin·sky /kə'linskē/ ▸*n.* (*pl.* **-skies**) a dark brown weasel with a bushy tail, found from Siberia to Japan. • *Mustela sibirica*, family Mustelidae. Alternative name: **Siberian weasel**. ■ the fur of this animal. ▷mid 19th cent.: from the place name *Kola*, a port in northwestern Russia, + the pseudo-Russian ending *-insky*.

Kol·ka·ta /käl'kätə; -'kətə/ official name (since 2000) for Calcutta, India.

Kol·khis /'kôlkēs/ Greek name for **COLCHIS**.

kol·khoz /kəl'kôz; -'ᴋʜôz/ ▸*n.* (*pl.* same or **-khoz·es** or **-kho·zy** /-'ᴋʜôzē/) a collective farm in the former USSR. ▷1920s: Russian, from *kol(lektivnoe) khoz(yaĭstvo)* 'collective farm.'

Köln /kœln/ German name for **COLOGNE**.

Kol Ni·dre /kōl 'nidrā; 'nidrə; ˌkôl nē'drā/ ▸*n.* an Aramaic prayer annulling vows made before God, sung by Jews at the opening of the Day of Atonement service on the eve of Yom Kippur. ▷from Aramaic *kol nidrē* 'all vows' (the opening words of the prayer).

ko·lo /'kōlō/ ▸*n.* (*pl.* **-los**) a Slavic dance performed in a circle. ▷late 18th cent.: Serbo-Croat, literally 'wheel.'

Ko·lozs·vár /'kōlōᴢʜˌvär/ Hungarian name for **CLUJ–NAPOCA**.

Ko·ly·ma /kə'lēmə/ a river in far eastern Siberia, which flows approximately 1,500 miles (2,415 km) north to the Arctic Ocean.

Ko·man·dor·ski Is·lands /ˌkəmən'dôrskyē/ an island group in extreme eastern Russia, off the eastern Kamchatka Peninsula. U.S. naval forces defeated the Japanese nearby in 1943.

ko·mat·ik /kō'matik/ ▸*n.* a sled drawn by dogs, used by the people of Labrador. ▷early 19th cent.: from Inuit *qamutik*.

Ko·ma·ti Riv·er /kə'mätē/ (also **Rio Incomati**) a river that flows for 500 miles (800 km) from the Drakensberg Range in South Africa, through Swaziland, South Africa, and Mozambique, to the Indian Ocean north of Maputo.

kom·bu·cha /kôm'bo͞ocʜə/ ▸*n.* a food supplement prepared from a symbiotic colony of yeast and bacteria that is added to tea for its alleged health benefits. ▷Japanese, 'tea sponge.'

Ko·mi /'kōmē/ an autonomous republic in northwestern Russia; pop. 1,265,000; capital, Syktyvkar.

Ko·mo·do /kə'mōdō/ a small island in Indonesia, in the Lesser Sunda Islands, situated between the islands of Sumbawa and Flores. It is home to the Komodo dragon.

Ko·mo·do drag·on ▸*n.* a heavily built monitor lizard that captures large prey such as pigs by ambush. Occurring only on Komodo and neighboring Indonesian islands, it is the largest living lizard. • *Varanus komodoensis*, family Varanidae.

Ko·mon·dor /'kōmənˌdôr; 'käm-/ ▸*n.* a powerful sheepdog of a white breed with a dense matted or corded coat. ▷Hungarian.

Komondor

Kom·so·mol /'kämsəˌmôl; ˌkəmsə'môl/ *historical* an organization for communist youth in the former USSR. ▷Russian, from *Kommunisticheskiĭ Soyuz Molodëzhi* 'Communist League of Youth.'

Kom·so·molsk /ˌkämsə'môlsk/ an industrial city in far eastern Russia, on the Amur River; pop. 318,000. It was built in 1932 by members of the Komsomol on the site of the village of Permskoe. Also called **Komsomolsk-on-Amur**.

Ko·na Coast /'kōnə/ the name for part of the southwestern coast of the island of Hawaii, noted for its resorts and coffee production.

Kon·go /'känɢgō/ ▸*n.* (*pl.* same or **-gos**) **1** a member of an indigenous people inhabiting the region of the Congo River in west central Africa. **2** the Bantu language of this people; Kikongo.
▸*adj.* of or relating to this people or their language. ▷the name in Kikongo.

kon·go·ni /käng'gōnē/ ▸*n.* (*pl.* same) a hartebeest, in particular one of a pale yellowish-brown race found in Kenya and Tanzania. • *Alcelaphus buselaphus cokii*, family Bovidae. ▷early 20th cent.: from Kiswahili.

Kö·nig·grätz /'kœnikʜˌgrets/ German name for **HRADEC KRÁLOVÉ**.

Kö·nigs·berg /'kœnikʜsˌberk/ German name for **KALININGRAD**.

ko·nim·e·ter /kō'nimitər/ ▸*n.* an instrument that measures the amount of dust in the air by directing a measured volume of air on to a greased slide to which any dust present will stick. ▷early 20th cent.: from Greek *konis* 'dust' + **-METER**.

Kon·ka·ni /'kôngkəˌnē; 'käng-/ ▸*n.* an Indic language that is the main language of Goa and adjacent parts of Maharashtra. Also called **GOANESE** (see **GOA**).
▸*adj.* of or relating to this language. ▷from Marathi and Hindi *koṅkaṇī*, from Sanskrit *koṅkaṇa* 'Konkan' (a coastal region of western India).

Kon-Ti·ki /kän 'tēkē/ the raft made of balsa logs in which Thor Heyerdahl sailed from the western coast of Peru to the islands of Polynesia in 1947. ▷named after an Inca god.

Kon·ya /'kônˌyä; kôn'yä/ a city in southwest central Turkey; pop. 513,350. An ancient Phrygian settlement, it became the capital of the Seljuk sultans toward the end of the 11th century.

kook /ko͞ok/ ▸*n. informal* a crazy or eccentric person. ▷1960s: probably from **CUCKOO**.

kook·a·bur·ra /'ko͝okəˌbərə/ ▸*n.* a very large Australasian kingfisher that feeds on terrestrial prey such as reptiles and birds. • Genus *Dacelo*, family Alcedinidae: two species, the **laughing kookaburra** (*D. gigas* or *D. novaeguineae*), which has a loud cackling call, and the **blue-winged kookaburra** (*D. leachii*). ▷late 19th cent.: from Wiradhuri *gugubarra*.

laughing kookaburra

kook·y /'ko͞okē/ ▸*adj.* (**kook·i·er**, **kook·i·est**) *informal* strange or eccentric: *I like kooky foreign films.* —**kook·i·ly** /-kəlē/ *adv.* —**kook·i·ness** *n.*

Koon·ing, Willem de, see **DE KOONING**.

Koop /ko͞op/, C(harles) Everett (1916–) U.S. physician and government official. As the U.S. surgeon general 1981–89, he campaigned vigorously against the tobacco industry and sought to impress upon the public the dangers of smoking.

Koo·te·nai Riv·er /'ko͞otn-ˌā/ (also **Kootneya**) a river that flows for 450 miles (720 km) from southeastern British Columbia into Montana and Idaho and then back into British Columbia, where it joins the Columbia River.

ko·pek /'kōpek/ (also **co·peck** or **ko·peck**) ▸*n.* a monetary unit of Russia and some other countries of the former USSR, equal to one hundredth of a ruble. ▷from Russian *kopeĭka*, diminutive of *kop'ë* 'lance' (from the figure on the coin (1535) of Tsar Ivan IV, bearing a lance instead of a sword).

ko·piy·ka /kô'pēkə/ ▸*n.* a monetary unit of Ukraine, equal to one-hundredth of a hryvna. ▷1990s: Ukrainian, from Russian *kopeĭka* 'kopek.'

kop·je /'käpē/ (also **kop·pie**) ▸*n. S. African* a small hill in a generally flat area. ▷from Afrikaans *koppie*, from Dutch *kopje*, diminutive of *kop* 'head.'

ko·ra /'kôrə/ ▸*n.* a West African musical instrument shaped like a lute, with 21 strings passing over a high bridge, and played like a harp. ▷late 18th cent.: a local word.

Ko·ran /kə'rän; kô-; 'kôrän/ (also **Qu·r'an** or **Qu·ran**) ▸*n.* the Islamic sacred book, believed to be the word of God as dictated to Muhammad by the archangel Gabriel and written down in Arabic. The Koran consists of 114 units of varying lengths, known as *suras*; the first sura is said as part of the ritual prayer. These touch upon all aspects of human existence, including matters of doctrine, social organization, and legislation. ▷from Arabic *ḳur'ān* 'recitation,' from *ḳara'a* 'read, recite.' —**Ko·ran·ic** /-'ränik/ *adj.*

Kor·but /'kôrbət/, Olga (1955–), Soviet gymnast, born in Belarus. She won two individual gold medals at the 1972 Olympic Games.

Kor·da /'kôrdə/, Sir Alexander (1893–1956), British movie producer and director, born in Hungary; born *Sándor Kellner*. Notable productions: *Things to Come* (1936) and *The Third Man* (1949).

ko·re /'kôrē; 'kôrā/ ▸*n.* (*pl.* **ko·rai** /'kôrī/) an archaic Greek statue of a young woman, standing and clothed in long loose robes. ▷from Greek *korē* 'maiden.'

Ko·re·a /kə'rēə/ a region in eastern Asia that forms a peninsula between the East Sea and the Yellow Sea, now divided into the countries of North Korea and South Korea. Ruled from the 14th century by the Korean Yi dynasty but more recently dominated by the Chinese and Japanese in turn, Korea was annexed by Japan in 1910. Following the Japanese surrender at the end of World War II, it was partitioned along the 38th parallel in 1948.

Ko·re·a, Dem·o·crat·ic Peo·ple's Re·pub·lic of official name for **NORTH KOREA**.

Ko·re·a, Re·pub·lic of official name for **SOUTH KOREA**.

Ko·re·an /kə'rēən; kô-/ ▸*adj.* of or relating to North or South Korea or its people or language.
▸*n.* **1** a native or national of North or South Korea, or a person of Korean descent. **2** the language of Korea, which has its own writing system and may be distantly related to Japanese.

Ko·re·an War the war of 1950–53 between North and South Korea.

UN troops, dominated by U.S. forces, countered the invasion of South Korea by North Korean forces by invading North Korea, while China intervened on the side of the North. Peace negotiations were begun in 1951, and the war ended two years later with the restoration of previous boundaries.

Kó·rin·thos /'kôrinˌᴛʜôs/ Greek name for **CORINTH**.

kor·ma /'kôrmə/ ▸*n.* a mildly spiced Indian curry dish of meat or fish marinated in yogurt or curds. ▷from Urdu *ḳormā*, from Turkish *kavurma*.

Kor·sa·koff's syn·drome /'kôrsəˌkôfs/ (also **Korsakoff's psychosis**) ▸*n. Psychiatry* a serious mental illness, typically the result of chronic alcoholism, characterized by disorientation and a tendency to invent explanations to cover a loss of memory of recent events. ▷early 20th cent.: named after Sergei S. *Korsakoff* (1854–1900), Russian psychiatrist.

ko·ru·na /'kôrənə/ ▸*n.* the basic monetary unit of Bohemia, Moravia, and Slovakia, equal to 100 haleru. ▷Czech, literally 'crown.'

Kos·ci·us·ko /ˌkäskē'əskō; ˌkäse-; kôsʜ'cʜo͞osʜkō/, Thaddeus (1746–1817), Polish soldier and patriot; Polish name *Tadeusz Andrzej Bonawentura Kościuszko*. After fighting for the Americans during the American Revolution, he led a nationalist uprising against Russia in Poland in 1794.

Kos·ci·us·ko, Mount /ˌkäzē'əskō/ a mountain in southeastern Australia, in the Great Dividing Range. Rising to a height of 7,234 feet (2,228 m), it is the highest mountain in Australia. ▷named by the explorer Sir Paul Edmund de Strzelecki (1797–1873) in honor of T. **KOSCIUSKO**.

ko·sher /'kōsʜər/ ▸*adj.* (of food, or premises in which food is sold, cooked, or eaten) satisfying the requirements of Jewish law: *a kosher kitchen.* ■ (of a person) observing Jewish food laws. ■ (of ritual objects) fit for use according to Jewish laws. ■ *figurative*

K

genuine and legitimate: *when he buys a record abroad, it is impossible to know whether it's kosher.*

Restrictions on the foods suitable for Jews are derived from rules in the books of Leviticus and Deuteronomy. Animals must be slaughtered and prepared in the prescribed way, in which the blood is drained from the body, while certain creatures, notably pigs and shellfish, are forbidden altogether. Meat and milk must not be cooked or consumed together, and separate utensils must be kept for each. Strict observance of these rules is today confined mainly to Orthodox Jews.

▸*v.* [*trans.*] prepare (food) according to the requirements of Jewish law. ■ *figurative* give (something) the appearance of being legitimate: *see them scramble to kosher illegal evidence.* ▷mid 19th cent.: from Hebrew *kāšēr* 'proper.'

▸**PHRASE** □ **keep** (or **eat**) **kosher** observe the Jewish food regulations (kashruth).

Ko·ši·ce /ˈkôsHētsə/ an industrial city in southern Slovakia; pop. 234,840.

Ko·sin·ski /kəˈzinskē/, Jerzy (Nikodem) (1933–91) U.S. writer; born in Poland. His many works include *Steps* (1968), *Being There* (1971), *The Devil Tree* (1973), *Blind Date* (1977), and *The Hermit of 69th Street* (1988).

Ko·so·vo /ˈkôsəˌvō; ˈkäs-/ an autonomous province of Serbia; capital, Priština. It borders on Albania and the majority of the people are of Albanian descent.

Ko·stro·ma /kəsträˈmä/ an industrial city in western Russia, situated on the Volga River, northwest of Nizhni Novgorod; pop. 280,000.

Ko·sty·ra /kôˈstirə/, Martha, see **STEWART**[4].

Ko·sy·gin /kəˈsēgin; -gyin/, Aleksei (Nikolaevich) (1904–80), Soviet statesman; premier 1964–80. He devoted most of his attention to internal economic affairs, being gradually eased out of the leadership by Brezhnev.

Ko·ta /ˈkōtə/ an industrial city in Rajasthan state, in northwestern India, on the Chambal River; pop. 536,000.

Ko·ta Ba·ha·ru /ˈkōtə ˈbähəˌro͞o/ a city in Malaysia, on the eastern coast of the Malay Peninsula; pop. 219,000.

Ko·ta Ki·na·ba·lu /ˈkōtə ˌkinəbəˈlo͞o/ a port in Malaysia, on the northern coast of Borneo; pop. 56,000.

ko·to /ˈkōtō/ ▸*n.* (*pl.* **-tos**) a Japanese zither about six feet long, with thirteen silk strings passed over small movable bridges. ▷late 18th cent.: Japanese.

Kou·fax /ˈkōfaks/, Sandy (1935–) U.S. baseball player; full name *Sanford Koufax.* A pitcher, he played for the Brooklyn (later Los Angeles) Dodgers 1955–66. His professional baseball career was cut short due to an arthritic elbow. Baseball Hall of Fame (1972).

kou·miss /ko͞oˈmis; ˈko͞omis/ (also **ku·miss** or **ku·mis**) ▸*n.* a drink made from fermented mare's milk, used also as a medicine by Asian nomads. ▷late 16th cent.: based on Tartar *kumiz.*

kou·ros /ˈko͞oräs/ ▸*n.* (*pl.* **kou·roi** /ˈko͞oroi/) an archaic Greek statue of a young man, standing and often naked. ▷Greek, Ionic form of *koros* 'boy.'

Kow·loon /ˈkouˈlo͞on/ a densely populated peninsula on the southeastern coast of China that forms part of Hong Kong. It is separated from Hong Kong Island by Hong Kong Harbor.

kow·tow /ˈkouˈtou/ ▸*v.* [*intrans.*] *historical* kneel and touch the ground with the forehead in worship or submission as part of Chinese custom. ■ *figurative* act in an excessively subservient manner: *she didn't have to* **kowtow** *to a boss.*

▸*n. historical* an act of kneeling and touching the ground with the forehead in such a way. ▷early 19th cent.: from Chinese *kētóu*, from *kē* 'knock' + *tóu* 'head.' —**kow·tow·er** *n.*

Ko·zhi·kode /ˈkōzHiˌkōd/ another name for **CALICUT**.

KP ▸*abbr.* kitchen police.

kph ▸*abbr.* kilometers per hour.

KR ▸*abbr. Chess* king's rook.

Kr ▸*symbol* the chemical element krypton.

kr. ▸*abbr.* ■ krona. ■ krone.

Kra, Isthmus of /krä/ the narrowest part of the Malay Peninsula, forming part of southern Thailand.

kraal /kräl/ *S. African* ▸*n.* a traditional African village of huts, typically enclosed by a fence. ■ another term for **HOMESTEAD** (sense 3). ■ an enclosure for cattle or sheep.

▸*v.* [*trans.*] drive (cattle or sheep) into an enclosure: *they kraal their sheep every night.* ■ *figurative* restrict or separate (people) to a particular area or into groups. ▷Dutch, from Portuguese *curral* (see **CORRAL**).

kraft /kraft/ (also **kraft paper**) ▸*n.* a kind of strong, smooth brown wrapping paper. ▷early 20th cent.: from Swedish, literally 'strength,' used to form the term *kraftpapper* 'kraft paper.'

Kra·gu·je·vac /ˈkrägo͞oyəˌväts/ a city in central Serbia; pop. 147,300. It was the capital of Serbia 1818–39.

krait /krīt/ ▸*n.* a highly venomous Asian snake of the cobra family. • Genus *Bungarus*, family Elapidae: several species, including the black and yellow **banded krait** (*B. fasciatus*). See also **SEA KRAIT**. ▷late 19th cent.: from Hindi *karait.*

Kra·ka·toa /ˌkrakəˈtōə; ˌkräk-/ a small volcanic island in Indonesia that lies between Java and Sumatra. It was the scene of a great eruption in 1883 that destroyed most of the island.

kra·ken /ˈkräkən/ ▸*n.* an enormous mythical sea monster said to appear off the coast of Norway. ▷Norwegian.

Kra·ków /ˈkräˌko͞of/ Polish name for **CRACOW**.

Kras·no·dar /ˌkräsnəˈdär/ an administrative territory in the northern Caucasus Mountains, on the Black Sea, in southern Russia. ■ its capital, a port on the lower Kuban River; pop. 627,000. Until 1922, it was known as Yekaterinodar (Ekaterinodar).

Kras·no·yarsk /ˌkräsnəˈyärsk/ an administrative territory in south central Russia. ■ its capital, a port on the Yenisei River; pop. 922,000.

kraut /krout/ ▸*n. informal* sauerkraut. ■ (also **Kraut**) *informal, offensive* a German. ▷World War I: shortening of **SAUERKRAUT**.

Kraut·rock /ˈkroutˌräk/ ▸*n.* an experimental style of rock music associated with German groups of the 1970s, characterized by improvisation and strong, hypnotic rhythms. —**Kraut·rock·er** *n.*

Krav Ma·ga /ˈkräv məˈgä/ ▸*n.* a form of self-defense and physical training, first developed by the Israeli army in the 1940s, based on the use of reflexive responses to threatening situations. ▷1990s: from Hebrew, 'contact combat.'

Krebs cy·cle /krebz/ ▸*n. Biochemistry* the sequence of reactions by which most living cells generate energy during the process of aerobic respiration. It takes place in the mitochondria, consuming oxygen, producing carbon dioxide and water as waste products, and converting ADP to energy-rich ATP. ▷1940s: named after Sir Hans A. *Krebs* (1900–81), German-born British biochemist.

Kre·feld /ˈkräˌfelt/ an industrial town and port on the Rhine River in western Germany, in North Rhine-Westphalia; pop. 245,000.

Kreis·ler /ˈkrislər/, Fritz (1875–1962), U.S. violinist and composer, born in Austria. In 1910, he gave the first performance of Elgar's violin concerto, which was dedicated to him.

Kre·men·chuk /ˌkriminˈCHo͞ok/ an industrial city in east central Ukraine, on the Dnieper River; pop. 238,000. Russian name **KREMENCHUG**.

krem·lin /ˈkremlin/ ▸*n.* a citadel within a Russian town. ■ (**the Kremlin**) the citadel in Moscow. ■ the Russian or (formerly) USSR government housed within this citadel. ▷mid 17th cent.: via French from Russian *kreml′* 'citadel.'

Krem·lin·ol·o·gy /ˌkremləˈnäləjē/ ▸*n.* the study and analysis of Soviet or Russian policies. —**Krem·lin·ol·o·gist** /-jist/ *n.*

krep·lach /ˈkrepläKH/ ▸*plural n.* (in Jewish cooking) triangular noodles filled with chopped meat or cheese and served with soup. ▷from Yiddish *kreplekh*, plural of *krepel*, from German dialect *Kräppel* 'fritter.'

krieg·spiel /ˈkrēgˌSHpēl; -ˌspēl/ ▸*n.* a war game in which blocks representing armies or other military units are moved about on maps. ■ a form of chess in which each player has a separate board and can only infer the position of the opponent's forces from limited information given by an umpire who disallows illegal moves. ▷late 19th cent.: from German, from *Krieg* 'war' + *Spiel* 'game.'

Kriem·hild /ˈkrēmhilt/ (in the Nibelungenlied) a Burgundian princess, wife of Siegfried and later of Etzel (Attila the Hun), whom she marries in order to be revenged on her brothers for Siegfried's murder.

krill /kril/ ▸*n.* a small shrimplike planktonic crustacean of the open seas. It is eaten by a number of larger animals, notably the baleen whales. • *Meganyctiphanes norvegica*, class Malacostraca. ▷early 20th cent.: from Norwegian *kril* 'young fry of fish.'

krim·mer /ˈkrimər/ ▸*n.* tightly curled gray or black fur made from the wool of young Crimean lambs. ▷mid 19th cent.: from German, from *Krim* 'Crimea.'

Krin·gle /ˈkriNGgəl/ ▸*n.*, Kris (or Kriss). Another name for **SANTA CLAUS**.

Kri·o /ˈkrēō/ ▸*n.* an English-based Creole language of Sierra Leone. It is the first language of about 350,000 people and is used as a lingua franca by over 3 million.

▸*adj.* of or relating to this language. ▷probably an alteration of **CREOLE**.

kris /krēs/ (also *archaic* **creese**) ▸*n.* a Malay or Indonesian dagger with a wavy blade. ▷late 16th cent.: based on Malay *keris.*

Krish·na /ˈkriSHnə/ *Hinduism* one of the most popular gods, the eighth and most important avatar or incarnation of Vishnu. ▷from Sanskrit *Kṛṣṇa*, literally 'black.'

He is worshiped in several forms: as the child god whose miracles and pranks are extolled in the Puranas; as the divine cowherd whose erotic exploits, esp. with his favorite, Radha, have produced both romantic and religious literature; and as the divine charioteer who preaches to Arjuna on the battlefield in the Bhagavadgita.

Krish·na Riv·er a river that rises in the Western Ghats of southern India and flows generally east for 805 miles (1,288 km) to the Bay of Bengal.

Kris·tall·nacht /ˈkristlˌnäkt; -ˌnäKHt/ the occasion of concerted violence by Nazis throughout Germany and Austria against Jews and their property on the night of November 9–10, 1938. ▷German, literally 'night of crystal,' referring to the broken glass produced by the smashing of store windows.

Kris·ti·an·i·a variant spelling of **CHRISTIANIA**.

Krí·ti /ˈkrētē/ Greek name for **CRETE**.

Kri·voi Rog /kriˈvoi ˈrōg; ˈrôk/ Russian name for **KRYVYY RIH**.

Kri·voy Rog /kriˈvoi ˈrôk/ Russian name for **KRYVY RIH**.

Kroc /kräk/, Ray(mond Albert) (1902–84) U.S. entrepreneur and philanthropist. In 1955, he founded the franchise empire of McDonald's fast-food restaurants.

Kroe·ber /ˈkrōbər/, Ursula, see **LE GUIN**.

kro·na /ˈkrōnə/ ▸*n.* **1** (*pl.* **-nor** /-nôr/) the basic monetary unit of Sweden, equal to 100 öre. [Swedish, 'crown.'] **2** (*pl.* **-nur** /-nər/) the basic monetary unit of Iceland, equal to 100 aurar. [from Old Norse *króna* 'crown.']

Kro·ne /ˈkrōnə/, Julie (1963–) U.S. jockey. She was the first woman to capture a Triple Crown horse-racing title 1993. She retired from racing in 1999.

kro·ne /ˈkrōnə/ ▸*n.* (*pl.* **-ner** /-nər/) the basic monetary unit of Denmark and Norway, equal to 100 øre. ▷Danish and Norwegian, literally 'crown.'

Kro·nos variant spelling of **CRONUS**.

Kron·stadt /ˈkränˌstät/ German name for **BRAŞOV**.

kroon /kro͞on/ ▸*n.* (*pl.* **kroons** or **kroo·ni** /ˈkro͞onē/) the basic monetary unit of Estonia, equal to 100 senti. ▷Estonian, literally 'crown'; compare with **KRONA**, **KRONE**.

Kru /kro͞o/ ▸*n.* (*pl.* same) **1** a member of a seafaring people of the coast of Liberia and Ivory Coast. **2** the Niger–Congo language of this people.

▸*adj.* of or relating to the Kru or their language. ▷from a West African language.

Kru Coast a section of the coast of Liberia to the northwest of Cape Palmas, inhabited by the Kru people.

Kru·ger /ˈkro͞ogər; ˈkryər/, Stephanus Johannes Paulus (1825–1904), South African soldier and statesman; president of Transvaal 1883–99. He led the Afrikaners to victory in the First Boer War in 1881.

Kru·ger·rand /ˈkro͞ogəˌrand/ (also **kru·ger·rand** or **Kru·ger**) ▸*n.* a South African gold coin with a portrait of President Kruger on the obverse. ▷1967: from the name of S. J. P. **KRUGER** + **RAND**[1].

krumm·holz /ˈkro͞omhōlts/ ▸*n.* stunted windblown trees growing near the tree line on mountains. ▷early 20th cent.: from German, literally 'crooked wood.'

krumm·horn /ˈkro͞omˌhôrn/ (also **crum·horn**) ▸*n.* a medieval wind instrument with an enclosed double reed and an upward-curving end, producing an even, nasal sound. ▷from German, from *krumm* 'crooked' + *Horn* 'horn.'

Kru·pa /ˈkro͞opə/, Gene (1909–73) U.S. jazz drummer and bandleader. He was the first major popular drum soloist.

Krupp /krəp; kro͞op/, Alfred (1812–87), German arms manufacturer. His company was a major arms producer for Germany from the 1840s through the end of World War II.

kryp·ton /ˈkripˌtän/ ▸*n.* the chemical element of atomic number 36, a member of the noble gas series. It is obtained by distillation of liquid air and is used in some kinds of electric light. (Symbol: **Kr**) ▷late 19th cent.: from Greek *krupton*, neuter of *kruptos* 'hidden.'

kry·tron /ˈkrīˌträn/ ▸*n. Physics* a high-speed solid-state switching device that is triggered by a pulse of coherent light and is used in the triggers of nuclear devices. ▷late 20th cent.: first element of obscure derivation + **-TRON**.

Kry·vyy Rih /kriˈvi ˈrikH/ an industrial city in southern Ukraine, at the center of an iron-ore mining region; pop. 717,000. Russian name **KRIVOI ROG**.

KS ▸*abbr.* ■ Kansas (in official postal use). ■ Kaposi's sarcoma.

Kshat·ri·ya /k(ə)ˈsHätrēə/ ▸*n.* a member of the second of the four great Hindu castes, the military caste. The traditional function of the Kshatriyas is to protect society by fighting in wartime and governing in peacetime. ▷late 18th cent.: from Sanskrit *kṣatriya*, from *kṣhatra* 'rule, authority.'

KT ▸*abbr.* ■ Knight Templar.

Kt ▸*abbr.* Knight.

kt. ▸*abbr.* ■ karat(s). ■ kiloton(s). ■ knot(s): *a cruising speed of 240 kt.*

K/T bound·a·ry short for **CRETACEOUS–TERTIARY BOUNDARY**. ▷late 20th cent.: *K/T*, from the symbols for *Cretaceous* and *Tertiary*.

Ku ▸*symbol* the chemical element kurchatovium.

Kua·la Lum·pur /ˌkwälə ˈlo͝omˌpo͝or; lo͝omˈpo͝or/ the capital of Malaysia, in the southwestern part of the Malay Peninsula; pop. 1,145,000.

Kua·la Treng·ga·nu /ˌkwälə treNGˈgäno͞o/ (also **Kua·la Te·reng·ga·nu** /ˌtereNG-/) a city in Malaysia, on the east coast of the Malay Peninsula at the mouth of the Trengganu River; pop. 229,000.

Kuan·tan /ˈkwänˌtän/ a city in Malaysia, on the east coast of the Malay Peninsula; pop. 199,000.

Ku-band /ˈkäˈyo͞o ˌband/ ▸*n.* a microwave frequency band used for satellite communication and broadcasting, using frequencies of about 12 gigahertz for terrestrial reception and 14 gigahertz for transmission. ▷1990s: from *Ku* (arbitrary serial designation) + *band*.

Ku·blai Khan /ˈko͞oblə ˈkän; ˈko͞oblī/ (1216–94), Mongol emperor of China; grandson of Genghis Khan. With his brother Mangu (then Mongol Khan), he conquered southern China (1252–59). After Mangu's death in 1259, he completed the conquest of China, founded the Yuan dynasty, and established his capital on the site of modern Beijing.

Küb·ler-Ross ▸, Elisabeth (1926–2004), U.S. psychiatrist, born in Switzerland. She was a pioneer in the field of palliative care and revolutionized attitudes toward treatment of the terminally ill. Among her many books was the influential *On Death and Dying* (1969).

Ku·brick /ˈko͞obrik/, Stanley (1928–99), U.S. movie director, producer, and writer. Notable movies: *Dr. Strangelove* (1964), *2001: A Space Odyssey* (1968) and *A Clockwork Orange* (1971).

ku·chen /ˈko͞okən; -kHən/ ▸*n.* (*pl.* same) a cake, esp. one eaten with coffee. ▷from German *Kuchen*.

Ku·ching /ˈko͞ocHiNG/ a port in Malaysia, on the Sarawak River near the northwestern coast of Borneo; pop. 148,000.

ku·dos /ˈk(y)o͞oˌdōs; -ˌdōz; -ˌdäs/ ▸*n.* praise and honor received for an achievement. ▷late 18th cent.: Greek.

> ***USAGE*** Kudos comes from Greek and means 'glory.' Despite appearances, it is not a plural form. This means that there is no singular form **kudo** and that use as a plural, as in the following sentence, is incorrect: *he received* **many** *kudos for his work* (correct use is *he received* **much** *kudos for his work*).

ku·du /ˈko͞odo͞o/ ▸*n.* (*pl.* same or **ku·dus**) an African antelope that has a grayish or brownish coat with white vertical stripes, and a short bushy tail. The male has long spirally curved horns. • Genus *Tragelaphus*, family Bovidae: the **greater kudu** (*T. strepsiceros*) and the **lesser kudu** (*T. imberbis*). ▷late 18th cent.: from Afrikaans *koedoe*, from Xhosa *i-qudu*.

kud·zu /ˈko͞odzo͞o/ (also **kud·zu vine**) ▸*n.* a quick-growing eastern Asian climbing plant with reddish-purple flowers, used as a fodder crop and for erosion control. It has become a terrible pest in the southeastern U.S. • *Pueraria lobata*, family Leguminosae. ▷late 19th cent.: from Japanese *kuzu*.

Ku·fic /ˈk(y)o͞ofik/ ▸*n.* an early angular form of the Arabic alphabet found chiefly in decorative inscriptions.
▸*adj.* of or in this type of script. ▷early 18th cent.: from the name *Kufa*, a city south of Baghdad, Iraq (because it was attributed to the city's scholars), + **-IC**.

ku·gel /ˈko͞ogəl; ˈko͞o-/ ▸*n.* (in Jewish cooking) a kind of sweet or savory pudding of noodles or potatoes. ▷Yiddish, literally 'ball'.

Kui·by·shev /ˈkwēbəˌsHef/ former name (1935–91) of **SAMARA**.

Kui·per belt /ˈkīpər ˌbelt/ ▸*n.* a region of the solar system beyond the orbit of Neptune, believed to contain many comets, asteroids, and other small bodies made largely of ice. ▷1990s: named after Gerard P. *Kuiper* (1905–73), Dutch-born U.S. astronomer.

Ku Klux Klan /ˈko͞o ˌkləks ˈklan/ (abbr.: **KKK**) an extremist right-wing secret society in the U.S. ▷perhaps from Greek *kuklos* 'circle' and **CLAN**. **—Ku Klux·er** *n.* **—Ku Klux Klans·man** /ˈklanzmən/ *n.* (*pl.* **-men**).

> The Ku Klux Klan was originally founded in the southern states after the Civil War to oppose social change and black emancipation by violence and terrorism. Although disbanded twice, it reemerged in the 1950s and 1960s and continues at a local level. Members disguise themselves in white robes and hoods and often use a burning cross as a symbol of their organization.

kuk·ri /ˈko͝okrē/ ▸*n.* (*pl.* **kuk·ris**) a curved knife broadening toward the point, used by Gurkhas. ▷early 19th cent.: from Nepalese *khukuri*.

ku·la /ˈko͞olə/ ▸*n.* (in some Pacific communities) an interisland system of ceremonial gift exchange as a prelude to or at the same time as regular trading. ▷Melanesian.

ku·lak /ko͞oˈlak; -ˈläk/ ▸*n. historical* a peasant in Russia wealthy enough to own a farm and hire labor. Emerging after the emancipation of serfs in the 19th century, the kulaks resisted Stalin's forced collectivization, but millions were arrested, exiled, or killed. ▷Russian, literally 'fist, tightfisted person,' from Turkic *kol* 'hand.'

kul·cha /ˈko͝olcHə/ ▸*n.* a small, round Indian bread made from flour, milk, and butter, typically stuffed with meat or vegetables. ▷from Persian *kulīca*.

kul·fi /ˈko͝olfē/ ▸*n.* a type of Indian ice cream, typically served in the shape of a cone. ▷from Hindi *kulfī*.

Kul·tur /ko͝olˈto͝or/ ▸*n.* German civilization and culture (sometimes used derogatorily to suggest elements of racism, authoritarianism, or militarism). ▷German, from Latin *cultura* or French *culture* (see **CULTURE**).

Kul·tur·kampf /ko͝olˈto͝orˌkäm(p)f/ a conflict from 1872 to 1887 between the German government (headed by Bismarck) and the papacy for the control of schools and Church appointments, in which Bismarck was forced to concede to the Catholic Church. ▷German, from **KULTUR** + *Kampf* 'struggle.'

Kum variant spelling of **QOM**.

Ku·ma·mo·to /ˌko͞oməˈmōtō/ a city in southern Japan, on the western coast of Kyushu Island; pop. 579,000.

Ku·ma·si /ko͞oˈmäsē; -ˈmasē/ a city in southern Ghana; pop. 376,250. It is the capital of the Ashanti region.

Ku·may·ri /ˈko͞oˌmīrē/ Russian name for **GYUMRI**.

Kumbh Me·la /ˈko͞om məˈlä/ ▸*n.* a Hindu festival and assembly, held once every twelve years at four locations in India, at which pilgrims bathe in the waters of the Ganges and Jumna rivers for the purification of sin. ▷from Sanskrit, literally 'pitcher festival,' from *kumbh* 'pitcher' + *melā* 'assembly.'

ku·mis (also **ku·miss**) ▸*n.* variant spelling of **KOUMISS**.

ku·mite /ˈko͞omiˌtā/ ▸*n.* (in martial arts) freestyle fighting. ▷Japanese, literally 'sparring.'

kum·kum /ˈko͞omˌko͞om/ ▸*n.* a red powder used ceremonially and cosmetically, esp. by Hindu women to make a small distinctive mark on the forehead. ▷mid 20th cent.: from Sanskrit *kuṅkuma* 'saffron.'

küm·mel /ˈkiməl/ ▸*n.* a sweet liqueur flavored with caraway and cumin seeds. ▷from German, from Old High German *kumil*, variant of *kumîn* (see **CUMIN**).

Ku·mon /ˈko͞omən; -män/ ▸*n. trademark* a tutoring program, originating in Japan, in which children improve their skills in a subject (esp. mathematics) by completing worksheets of increasing difficulty, led by a special instructor. ▷from the name of Tru *Kumon* (1914–95), the Japanese mathematics teacher who invented the method.

kum·quat /ˈkəmˌkwät/ (also **cumquat**) ▸*n.* **1** an orangelike fruit related to the citruses, with an edible sweet rind and acid pulp. It is eaten raw or used in preserves. **2** the eastern Asian shrub or small tree that yields this fruit and that hybridizes with citrus trees. • Genus *Fortunella*, family Rutaceae. ▷late 17th cent.: from Chinese (Cantonese dialect) *kam kwat* 'little orange.'

Ku·na /ˈko͞onə/ (also **Cu·na**) ▸*n.* (*pl.* same or **-nas**) **1** a member of an American Indian people of the isthmus of Panama. **2** the Chibchan language of this people.
▸*adj.* of or relating to the Kunas or their language. ▷the name in Kuna.

ku·na /ˈko͞onə/ ▸*n.* (*pl.* **-ne** /-nā/) the basic monetary unit of Croatia, equal to 100 lipa.

kun·da·li·ni /ˌko͝ondlˈēnē/ ▸*n.* (in yoga) latent female energy believed to lie coiled at the base of the spine. ■ (also **kundalini yoga**) a system of meditation directed toward the release of such energy. ▷Sanskrit, literally 'snake.'

Kun·de·ra /ˈko͝ondərə; ˌkənˈderə/, Milan (1929–), Czech novelist. He emigrated to France in 1975 after his books were condemned in Czechoslovakia following the Soviet military invasion of 1968. Notable works: *The Book of Laughter and Forgetting* (1979) and *The Unbearable Lightness of Being* (1984).

Kung /ko͝oNG/ ▸*n.* **1** (*pl.* same) a member of a San (Bushman) people of the Kalahari Desert in southern Africa. **2** the Khoisan language of this people.
▸*adj.* of or relating to the Kung or their language. ▷Khoikhoi *!Kung*, literally 'people.'

kung fu /ˈkəNG ˈfo͞o; ˈko͝oNG/ ▸*n.* a primarily unarmed Chinese martial art resembling karate. ▷from Chinese *gōngfū*, from *gōng* 'merit' + *fū* 'master.'

K'ung Fu-tzu /ˈko͝oNG ˈfo͞o ˈdzə/ see **CONFUCIUS**.

Ku·nitz /ˈko͞onits/, Stanley (Jasspon) (1905–) U.S. poet and editor. He is the author of *Selected Poems* (1958) and *Passing Through* (1995). In 2000, he was named U.S. poet laureate, a post he had held before 1974–76 when it was called consultant in poetry to the Library of Congress.

Kun·lun Shan /ˈko͞onˈlo͞on ˈsHän/ a range of mountains in western China, on the northern edge of the Tibetan plateau, that extends east for more than 1,000 miles (1,600 km) from the Pamir Mountains. The highest peak is Muztag, which rises to 25,338 feet (7,723 m).

Kun·ming /ˈko͞onˈmiNG/ a city in southwestern China, capital of Yunnan province; pop. 1,612,000.

kunz·ite /ˈko͝ontˌsīt/ ▸*n.* a lilac-colored gem variety of spodumene that fluoresces or changes color when irradiated. ▷early 20th cent.: from the name of George F. *Kunz* (1856–1932), American gemologist, + **-ITE**[1].

Kuo·min·tang /ˈkwōˈminˈtaNG; -ˈtäNG; ˈgwô-/ (also **Guo·min·dang** /ˈgwōˈminˈdäNG/) a nationalist party founded in China under Sun Yat-sen in 1912, and led by Chiang Kai-shek from 1925. It held power from 1928 until the Communist Party took power in October 1949, and it subsequently formed the central administration of Taiwan. ▷from Chinese, 'national people's party.'

Kupf·fer cell /ˈko͞opfər/ ▸*n. Anatomy* a phagocytic cell that forms the lining of the sinusoids of the liver and is involved in the breakdown of red blood cells. ▷early 20th cent.: named after Karl Wilhelm von *Kupffer* (1829–1902), Bavarian anatomist.

Ku·ra Riv·er /kəˈrä; ˈko͝orə/ a river that flows for 940 miles (1,510 km) from northeastern Turkey through Georgia and Azerbaijan into the Caspian Sea.

kur·cha·tov·i·um /ˌkərcHəˈtōvēəm/ ▸*n. historical* a name proposed in the former USSR for the artificial radioactive element of atomic number 104, now called **rutherfordium**. ▷1960s: named after Igor V. *Kurchatov* (1903–60), Russian nuclear physicist.

Kurd /kərd/ ▸*n.* a member of a mainly pastoral Islamic people living in Kurdistan. ▷the name in Kurdish.

Kurd·ish /ˈkərdisH/ ▸*adj.* of or relating to the Kurds or their language.
▸*n.* the Iranian language of the Kurds.

Kur·di·stan /ˌkərdəˈstän; ˌko͝or-; -ˈstan/ a region in the Middle East, south of the Caucasus Mountains, the traditional home of the Kurdish people. The area includes large parts of eastern Turkey, northern Iraq, western Iran, eastern Syria, Armenia, and Azerbaijan. Following persecution of the Kurds by Iraq in the aftermath of the Gulf War of 1991, certain areas designated safe havens were established for the Kurds in northern Iraq.

Ku·re /ˈko͝orä/ a city in southern Japan, on the southern coast of the island of Honshu, near Hiroshima; pop. 217,000.

Kur·gan /ko͝orˈgän/ a city in central Russia, commercial center for an agricultural region; pop. 360,000.

kur·gan /ko͝orˈgän; -ˈgan/ ▸*n.* *Archaeology* a prehistoric burial mound or barrow of a type found in southern Russia and Ukraine. ■ (**Kurgan**) a member of the ancient people who built such burial mounds.
▸*adj.* of or relating to the ancient Kurgans. ▷Russian, of Turkic origin; compare with Turkish *kurgan* 'castle.'

Ku·rile Is·lands /ˈk(y)o͝orˌēl; k(y)o͝oˈrēl/ (also **Ku·ril Is·lands** or **the Ku·rils**) a chain of 56 islands between the Sea of Okhotsk and the North Pacific Ocean, stretching from the southern tip of the Kamchatka peninsula to the northeastern corner of the Japanese island of Hokkaido. They are the subject of dispute between Russia and Japan.

Ku·ro·sa·wa /ˌko͝orəˈsäwə/, Akira (1910–98), Japanese movie director. Notable movies: *Rashomon* (1950) and *Ran* (1985).

Ku·ro·shi·o /ˌko͝orōˈshē-ō/ a warm current in the Pacific Ocean that flows northeast past Japan and toward Alaska. Also called **Japanese Current**, **Japan Current**. ▷late 19th cent.: Japanese, from *kuro* 'black' + *shio* 'tide.'

kur·ra·jong /ˈkərəˌjôNG; -ˌjäNG/ (also **cur·ra·jong**) ▸*n.* an Australian plant that produces useful tough fiber. • Several species, in particular a small tree with shiny pointed leaves and boat-shaped leathery seed cases (*Brachychiton populneus*, family Sterculiaceae). ▷early 19th cent.: from Dharuk *garrajung* 'fiber fishing line.'

Kursk /ko͝orsk/ an industrial city in southwestern Russia; pop. 430,000. It was the scene of an important Soviet victory in World War II.

kur·ta /ˈkərtə/ ▸*n.* a loose collarless shirt worn by people from the Indian subcontinent. ▷from Urdu and Persian *kurtah*.

kur·to·sis /kərˈtōsis/ ▸*n.* *Statistics* the sharpness of the peak of a frequency-distribution curve. ▷early 20th cent.: from Greek *kurtōsis* 'a bulging,' from *kurtos* 'bulging, convex.'

ku·ru /ˈko͝oro͞o/ ▸*n.* *Medicine* a fatal disease of the brain occurring in some peoples in New Guinea and thought to be caused by a viruslike agent such as a prion. ▷1950s: a local word.

ku·rus /kəˈro͞osh/ ▸*n.* (*pl.* same) a monetary unit of Turkey, equal to one hundredth of a Turkish lira. ▷from Turkish *kuruş*.

Ku·shan /ˈko͞oˌshän/ ▸*n.* (*pl.* same or **-shans**) a member of an Iranian dynasty that invaded the Indian subcontinent and established a powerful empire in the northwest between the 1st and 3rd centuries AD.
▸*adj.* of or relating to this people or their dynasty. ▷from Prakrit *kuṣāṇa* (adjective), from Iranian.

Ku·ta·i·si /ˌko͞otäˈēsē/ an industrial city in central Georgia; pop. 236,000. One of the oldest cities in Transcaucasia, it has been the capital of various kingdoms, including Colchis and Abkhazia.

Kutch, Gulf of /kəch/ an inlet of the Arabian Sea on the west coast of India.

Kutch, Rann of /ˈkəch, ˈrän əv/ a vast salt marsh in the northwestern part of the Indian subcontinent, on the shores of the Arabian Sea, that extends over the boundary between southeastern Pakistan and the state of Gujarat in northwestern India.

Ku·te·nai /ˈko͞otnˌā/ (also **Ku·te·nay**) ▸*n.* (*pl.* same or **-nais**) **1** a member of an American Indian people of the Rocky Mountains in British Columbia, Idaho, and Montana. **2** the language of this people, of unknown affinity.
▸*adj.* of or relating to the Kutenai or their language. ▷from Blackfoot *Kotonáai-*.

Ku·wait /kəˈwāt/ a country on the northwestern coast of the Persian Gulf; pop. 2,257,000; capital, Kuwait City; official language, Arabic. **—Ku·wai·ti** /-ˈwātē/ *adj.* & *n.*

With a history as a fishing and trading sheikhdom, Kuwait, since the 1930s, has become one of the world's leading oil producers. Iraqi claims on the area led to the 1990–91 occupation and resulting Gulf War.

Ku·wait Cit·y a port on the Persian Gulf, the capital city of Kuwait; pop. 150,000.

Kuz·bass /ko͞ozˈbäs/ another name for **Kuznets Basin**.

Kuz·nets Ba·sin /kəzˈnyets/ (also **Kuz·netsk** /-ˈnyetsk/) an industrial region in southern Russia, situated in the valley of the Tom River, between Tomsk and Novokuznetsk. It is rich in iron and coal deposits. Also called **Kuzbass**.

kV ▸*abbr.* kilovolt(s).

kvass /k(ə)ˈväs; kfäs/ ▸*n.* (esp. in Russia) a fermented drink, low in alcohol, made from rye flour or bread with malt. ▷from Russian *kvas*.

kvell /k(ə)vel/ ▸*v.* [*intrans.*] *informal* feel happy and proud: *my mom was kvelling—bursting with pride.* ▷1960s: from Yiddish *kveln*, from Middle High German, literally 'well up.'

kvetch /k(ə)vech; kfech/ *informal* ▸*n.* a person who complains a great deal. ■ a complaint.
▸*v.* [*intrans.*] complain. ▷1960s: from Yiddish *kvetsh* (noun), *kvetshn* (verb), from Middle High German *quetschen*, literally 'crush.'

kW ▸*abbr.* kilowatt(s).

Kwa /kwä/ ▸*n.* a major branch of the Niger–Congo family of languages, spoken from the Ivory Coast to Nigeria and including Ibo and Yoruba.
▸*adj.* of or relating to this group of languages. ▷the name in Kwa.

kwa·cha /ˈkwächə/ ▸*n.* the basic monetary unit of Zambia and Malawi, equal to 100 ngwee in Zambia and 100 tambala in Malawi. ▷previously used as a Zambian nationalist slogan calling for a new "dawn" of freedom, later applied to the currency of the newly independent state.

Kwa·ja·lein /ˈkwäjələn; -ˌlān/ the largest atoll in the Marshall Islands, in the west central Pacific Ocean, fought over by U.S. and Japanese forces during World War II.

Kwa·ki·u·tl /ˌkwäkēˈo͞otl/ ▸*n.* (*pl.* same or **-u·tls**) **1** a member of an American Indian people of the northwestern Pacific coast, living mainly on Vancouver Island. **2** the Wakashan language of this people.
▸*adj.* of or relating to the Kwakiutl or their language. ▷the name in Kwakiutl.

Kwang·chow /ˈkwäNGˈchō; ˈgwäNGˈjō/ variant of **Guangzhou**.

Kwang·ju /ˈgwôNGˈjo͞o/ a city in southwestern South Korea; pop. 1,145,000.

Kwang·si Chuang /ˈkwäNGˌsē ˈchwäNG; ˈgwäNGˌsē/ variant of **Guangxi Zhuang**.

Kwang·tung /ˈkwäNGˈto͝oNG; ˈgwäNGˈdo͝oNG/ variant of **Guangdong**.

kwan·za /ˈkwänzə/ ▸*n.* (*pl.* same or **-zas**) the basic monetary unit of Angola, equal to 100 lwei. ▷perhaps from a Swahili word meaning 'first.'

Kwan·zaa /ˈkwänzə/ ▸*n.* a secular festival observed by many African Americans from December 26 to January 1 as a celebration of their cultural heritage and traditional values. ▷from Kiswahili *matunda ya kwanza*, literally 'first fruits (of the harvest),' from *kwanza* 'first.'

kwash·i·or·kor /ˌkwäshēˈôrkôr; -kər/ ▸*n.* a form of malnutrition caused by protein deficiency in the diet, typically affecting young children in the tropics. ▷1930s: a local word in Ghana.

Kwa·Zu·lu-Na·tal /kwäˈzo͞olo͞o näˈtäl/ a province of eastern South Africa, on the Indian Ocean; capital, Pietermaritzburg. Formerly called Natal, it became one of the new provinces of South Africa following the democratic elections of 1994. See also **Natal**.

Kwei·chow /ˈkwāˈchou; -ˈchō; ˈgwāˈjō/ variant of **Guizhou**.

Kwei·lin /ˈkwāˈlin; ˈgwā-/ variant of **Guilin**.

Kwei·sui /ˈkwāˈswā; ˈgwā-/ former name (until 1954) of **Hohhot**.

Kwei·yang /ˈkwāˈyäNG; ˈgwā-/ variant of **Guiyang**.

kWh ▸*abbr.* kilowatt-hour(s).

kW-hr ▸*abbr.* kilowatt-hour.

KWIC /kwik/ ▸*n.* [as *adj.*] *Computing* keyword in context, denoting a database search in which the keyword is shown highlighted in the middle of the display, with the text forming its context on either side. ▷1950s: abbreviation.

KY ▸*abbr.* Kentucky (in official postal use).

Ky. ▸*abbr.* Kentucky.

ky·a·nite /ˈkīəˌnīt/ (also **cy·a·nite** /ˈsīə-/) ▸*n.* a blue or green crystalline mineral consisting of aluminum silicate, used in heat-resistant ceramics. ▷late 18th cent.: from Greek *kuanos*, *kuaneos* 'dark blue' + **-ite**[1]. **—ky·a·nit·ic** /ˌkīəˈnitik/ *adj.*

ky·an·ize /ˈkīəˌnīz/ ▸*v.* [*trans.*] treat (wood) with a solution of mercuric chloride to prevent decay. ▷mid 19th cent.: named after John H. *Kyan* (1774–1850), the Irish inventor who patented the process in 1832.

kyat /kēˈ(y)ät; kyät; chät/ ▸*n.* (*pl.* same or **kyats**) the basic monetary unit of Myanmar (Burma), equal to 100 pyas. ▷Burmese.

Kyd /kid/, Thomas (1558–94), English playwright. His anonymously published *The Spanish Tragedy* (1592), an early example of revenge tragedy, was very popular on the Elizabethan stage.

ky·lix /ˈkīliks; ˈkiliks/ ▸*n.* (*pl.* **ky·li·kes** /kīliˌkēz; kili-/ or **ky·lix·es**) an ancient Greek cup with a shallow bowl and a tall stem. ▷from Greek *kulix*.

ky·mo·graph /ˈkīməˌgraf/ ▸*n.* an instrument for recording variations in pressure, e.g., in sound waves or in blood within blood vessels, by the trace of a stylus on a rotating cylinder. ▷mid 19th cent.: from Greek *kuma* 'wave' + **-graph**. **—ky·mo·graph·ic** /ˌkīməˈgrafik/ *adj.*

Kyo·to /kēˈōtō/ an industrial city in central Japan, on the island of Honshu; pop. 1,461,000. Founded in the 8th century, it was the imperial capital from 794 until 1868.

ky·pho·sis /kīˈfōsis/ ▸*n.* *Medicine* excessive outward curvature of the spine, causing hunching of the back. Compare with **lordosis**. ▷mid 19th cent.: from Greek *kuphōsis*, from *kuphos* 'bent, hunchbacked.' **—ky·phot·ic** /-ˈfätik/ *adj.*

Kyr·gyz /kirˈgiz/ ▸*n.* & *adj.* variant spelling of **Kirghiz**.

Kyr·gyz·stan /ˌki(ə)rgiˈstän; -ˈstan; ˌkər-/ a mountainous country in central Asia, on the northwestern border of China; pop. 5,081,000; capital, Bishkek; official languages, Kyrgyz and Russian (since 2001). Also called **Kirghizia**; **Kyrgyz Republic**.

The region was annexed by Russia in 1864 and became a constituent republic of the Soviet Union. When the Soviet Union broke up in 1991, Kyrgyzstan became an independent republic within the Commonwealth of Independent States.

Kyr·i·e /ˈki(ə)rēˌā/ (also **Kyr·i·e e·le·i·son** /iˈlā-iˌsän; -sən/) ▸*n.* a short repeated invocation (in Greek or in translation) used in many Christian liturgies, esp. at the beginning of the Eucharist or as a response in a litany. ▷from Greek *Kurie eleēson* 'Lord, have mercy.'

Kyu·shu /kēˈo͞osho͞o/ the most southerly of the four main islands of Japan, constituting an administrative region; pop. 13,296,000; capital, Fukuoka.

Ky·zyl /kəˈzil/ a city in south central Russia, on the Yenisei River, capital of the republic of Tuva; pop. 80,000.

Ky·zyl Kum /kəˈzil ˈko͞om/ an arid desert region in central Asia that extends east from the Aral Sea to the Pamir Mountains and covers part of Uzbekistan and southern Kazakhstan.

Ll

L[1] /el/ (also **l**) ▶*n.* (*pl.* **Ls** or **L's**) **1** the twelfth letter of the alphabet. ■ denoting the next after K in a set of items, categories, etc. **2** (**L**) a shape like that of a capital L: [in *combination*] *a four-story **L-shaped** building.* **3** the Roman numeral for 50. [originally a symbol identified with the letter *L*, because of coincidence of form. In ancient Roman notation, *L* with a stroke above denoted 50,000.]

L[2] ▶*abbr.* ■ (in tables of sports results) games lost. ■ *Chemistry* levorotatory: *L-tryptophan.* ■ (**L.**) Lake, Loch, or Lough (chiefly on maps): *L. Ontario.* ■ large (as a clothes size). ■ Latin. ■ Liberal. ■ (**L.**) Linnaeus (as the source of names of animal and plant species): *Swallowtail Butterfly* Papilio machaon *(L., 1758).* ■ lire.
▶*symbol* ■ *Chemistry* Avogadro's number. ■ *Physics* inductance.

l ▶*abbr.* ■ (giving position or direction) left: *l to r: Gordon, Anthony, Jerry, and Mark.* ■ (chiefly in horse racing) length(s): *distances 5 l, 3 l.* ■ (**l.**) (in textual references) line: *l. 648.* ■ *Chemistry* liquid. ■ liter(s). ■ (**l.**) *archaic* pound(s): *a salary of 4l. a week.*
▶*symbol* (in mathematical formulas) length.

£ ▶*abbr.* (preceding a numeral) pound or pounds (of money). ▷the initial letter of Latin *libra* 'pound, balance,' written in copperplate with one or two crossbars: crossbars were formerly used to indicate an abbreviation.

LA ▶*abbr.* ■ Library Association. ■ Los Angeles. ■ Louisiana (in official postal use).

La ▶*abbr.* ■ (**La.**) Louisiana.
▶*symbol* ■ the chemical element lanthanum.

la /lä/ (*Brit.* also **lah**) ▶*n. Music* (in solmization) the sixth note of a major scale. ■ the note A in the fixed-do system. ▷Middle English: representing (as an arbitrary name for the note) the first syllable of Latin *labii*, taken from a Latin hymn (see **SOLMIZATION**).

laa·ger /ˈlägər/ *S. African* ▶*n. historical* a camp or encampment formed by a circle of wagons. ■ *figurative* an entrenched position or viewpoint that is defended against opponents: *an educational laager, isolated from the outside world.*
▶*v.* [*trans.*] *historical* form (vehicles) into a laager. ■ [*intrans.*] make camp. ▷South African Dutch, from Dutch *leger, lager* 'camp.' Compare with **LAGER** and **LAIR**.

Laa·youne variant spelling of **LA'YOUN**.

Lab /lab/ ▶*abbr.* a Labrador dog.

lab /lab/ ▶*n. informal* a laboratory: *a science lab.* ▷late 19th cent.: abbreviation.

La·ban /ˈläbən/, Rudolf von (1879–1958), Hungarian choreographer and dancer. In 1920, he published the first of several volumes outlining Labanotation, his system of dance notation.

la Bar·ca, Pe·dro Cal·de·rón de see **CALDERÓN DE LA BARCA**.

lab·a·rum /ˈlabərəm/ ▶*n. rare* a banner or flag bearing symbolic motifs. ■ *historical* Constantine the Great's imperial standard, which bore Christian symbolic imagery fused with the military symbols of the Roman Empire. ▷early 17th cent.: from late Latin, of unknown origin.

lab·da·num /ˈlabdənəm/ (also **la·da·num** /ˈlädn-əm; ˈladnəm/) ▶*n.* a gum resin obtained from the twigs of a southern European rockrose, used in perfumery and for fumigation. • The rockrose is usually *Cistus ladanifer*, family Cistaceae. ▷mid 16th cent.: via Latin from Greek *ladanon, lēdanon*, from *lēdon* 'mastic.'

La·bé /läˈbā/ a commercial town in west central Guinea, in the Fouta Djallon region, an Islamic center; pop. 110,000.

lab·e·fac·tion /ˌlabəˈfakshən/ ▶*n. archaic* deterioration or downfall. ▷early 17th cent.: from Latin *labefactio(n-)*, from *labefacere* 'weaken,' from *labi* 'to fall' + *facere* 'make.'

la·bel /ˈlābəl/ ▶*n.* **1** a small piece of paper, fabric, plastic, or similar material attached to an object and giving information about it. ■ a piece of fabric sewn inside a garment and bearing the brand name, size, or instructions for care. ■ the piece of paper in the center of a phonograph record giving the artist and title. ■ a company that produces recorded music: *independent labels.* ■ the name or trademark of a fashion company: *she plans to launch her own designer clothes label.* ■ a classifying phrase or name applied to a person or thing, esp. one that is inaccurate or restrictive: *my reluctance to stick a label on myself politically.* ■ (in a dictionary entry) a word or words used to specify the subject area, register, or geographical origin of the word being defined. ■ *Computing* a string of characters used to refer to a particular instruction in a program. ■ *Biology & Chemistry* a radioactive isotope, fluorescent dye, or enzyme used to make something identifiable for study. **2** *Heraldry* a narrow horizontal strip, typically with three downward projections, that is superimposed on a coat of arms by an eldest son during the life of his father. **3** *Architecture* another term for **DRIPSTONE**.
▶*v.* (**la·beled, la·bel·ing**; *Brit.* **la·belled, la·bel·ling**) [*trans.*] attach a label to (something): *she labeled the parcels neatly, writing the addresses in capital letters.* ■ assign to a category, esp. inaccurately or restrictively: *people who **were labeled as** "mentally handicapped"* | [*trans.*] *the critics labeled him a loser.* ■ give a name to (something): *she labeled his new Riviera a "Star Wars" car.* ■ *Biology & Chemistry* make (a substance, molecule, or cell) identifiable or traceable by replacing an atom with one of a distinctive radioactive isotope, or by attaching a fluorescent dye, enzyme, or other molecule. ▷Middle English (denoting a narrow strip or band): from Old French, 'ribbon,' probably of Germanic origin and related to **LAP**[1]. —**la·bel·er** *n.*

La Belle Prov·ince /lä ˌbel prəˈväns/ nickname for **QUEBEC**. ▷French, literally 'the Beautiful Province.'

la·bel·lum /ləˈbeləm/ ▶*n.* (*pl.* **-bel·la** /-ˈbelə/) **1** *Entomology* each of a pair of lobes at the tip of the proboscis in some insects. **2** *Botany* a central petal at the base of an orchid flower, typically larger than the other petals and of a different shape. ▷early 19th cent.: from Latin, diminutive of *labrum* 'lip.'

la·bi·a /ˈlābēə/ ▶*plural n.* **1** *Anatomy* the inner and outer folds of the vulva, at either side of the vagina. **2** plural form of **LABIUM**.

la·bi·al /ˈlābēəl/ ▶*adj.* **1** *chiefly Anatomy* of or relating to the lips. ■ *Dentistry* (of the surface of a tooth) adjacent to the lips. ■ *Zoology* of, resembling, or serving as a lip, liplike part, or labium. **2** *Phonetics* (of a consonant) requiring complete or partial closure of the lips (e.g., *p, b, f, v, m, w*), or (of a vowel) requiring rounded lips (e.g., *oo* in moon).
▶*n. Phonetics* a labial sound. ▷late 16th cent.: from medieval Latin *labialis*, from Latin *labium* 'lip.' —**la·bi·al·ize** /-ˌlīz/ *v.* (in sense 2). —**la·bi·al·ly** *adv.*

la·bi·a ma·jo·ra /məˈjôrə/ ▶*plural n. Anatomy* the larger outer folds of the vulva.

la·bi·a mi·no·ra /məˈnôrə/ ▶*plural n. Anatomy* the smaller inner folds of the vulva.

la·bi·ate /ˈlābē-it; -ˌāt/ ▶*n. Botany* a plant of the mint family (Labiatae) with a distinctive two-lobed flower.
▶*adj.* **1** *Botany* of, relating to, or denoting plants of the mint family. **2** *Botany & Zoology* resembling or possessing a lip or labium. ▷early 18th cent. (as an adjective in the sense 'two-lipped,' describing a corolla or calyx): from modern Latin *labiatus*, from *labium* 'lip.'

la·bile /ˈlāˌbīl; -bəl/ ▶*adj. technical* liable to change; easily altered. ■ of or characterized by emotions that are easily aroused or freely expressed, and that tend to alter quickly and spontaneously; emotionally unstable. ■ *Chemistry* easily broken down or displaced. ▷late Middle English (in the sense 'liable to err or sin'): from late Latin *labilis*, from *labi* 'to fall.' —**la·bil·i·ty** /lāˈbilətē; lə-/ *n.*

labio- /ˈlābēō/ ▶*comb. form* of or relating to the lips: *labiodental.* ▷from Latin *labium* 'lip.'

la·bi·o·den·tal /ˌlābēōˈdentl/ ▶*adj. Phonetics* (of a sound) made with the lips and teeth, for example *f* and *v*.
▶*n. Phonetics* a labiodental sound.

la·bi·o·ve·lar /ˌlābēōˈvēlər/ ▶*adj. Phonetics* (of a sound) made with the lips and soft palate, for example *w*.
▶*n. Phonetics* a labiovelar sound.

la·bi·um /ˈlābēəm/ ▶*n.* (*pl.* **-bi·a** /-bēə/) *Entomology* **1** a fused mouthpart that forms the floor of the mouth of an insect. ■ *Anatomy* a lip or liplike structure, esp. any of the four folds of skin on either side of the vulva. **2** *Botany* the lower lip of the flower of a plant of the mint family. ▷late 16th cent. (in the general sense 'lip, liplike structure'): from Latin, 'lip'; related to **LABRUM**.

lab·lab /ˈlabˌlab/ ▶*n.* another term for **HYACINTH BEAN**. ▷early 19th cent.: from Arabic *lablāb*.

la·bor /ˈlābər/ (*Brit.* **la·bour**) ▶*n.* **1** work, esp. hard physical work: *the price of repairs includes labor and parts* | *manual labor.* ■ workers, esp. manual workers, considered collectively: *nonunion casual labor.* ■ such workers considered as a social class or political force: [as *adj.*] *the labor movement.* ■ (**Labor**) a department of government concerned with a nation's workforce: *Secretary of Labor.* **2** the process of childbirth, esp. the period from the start of uterine contractions to delivery: *his wife is **in labor**.* **3** (**Labour**) [treated as *sing.* or *pl.*] (in the UK or Canada) the Labour Party.
▶*v.* [*intrans.*] work hard; make great effort: *they labored from dawn to dusk in two shifts* | *it now looks as if the reformers had labored in vain.* ■ work at an unskilled manual occupation: *he was eking out an existence by laboring.* ■ have difficulty in doing something despite working hard: *Coley labored against confident opponents.* ■ (of an engine) work noisily and with difficulty: *the wheels churned, the engine laboring.* ■ [with *adverbial of direction*] move or proceed with trouble or difficulty: *they **labored up** a steep, tortuous track.* ■ (of a ship) roll or pitch heavily. ■ [*trans.*] *archaic* till (the ground): *the land belonged to him who labored it.*
▶*phrasal v.* □ **labor under 1** carry (a heavy load or object) with difficulty. **2** be deceived or misled by (a mistaken belief): *you've been laboring under a misapprehension.* ▷Middle English *labo(u)r*, from Old French *labour* (noun), *labourer* (verb), both from Latin *labor* 'toil, trouble.'
▶***PHRASES*** □ **a labor of Hercules** see **HERCULES**. □ **a labor of love** a task done for pleasure, not reward. □ **labor the point** explain or discuss something at excessive or unnecessary length.

THE RIGHT WORD **drudgery, grind, labor, toil, travail, work**
Most people have to **work** for a living, meaning that they have to exert themselves mentally or physically in return for a paycheck. But *work* is not

L

Pronunciation Key ə *ago*; ər *over*; ˈə *or* ˌə *up*; ˈər *or* ˌər *fur*; a *hat*; ā *rate*; ä *car*; CH *chew*; e *let*; ē *see*; e(ə)r *air*; i *fit*; ī *by*; i(ə)r *ear*; NG *sing*; ō *go*; ô *for*; oi *boy*; o͝o *good*; o͞o *goo*; ou *out*; SH *she*; TH *thin*; TH *then*; (h)w *why*; ZH *vision*

always performed by humans (*a machine that works like a charm*).

Labor is not only human but usually physical work (*the labor required to build a stone wall*), although it can also apply to intellectual work of unusual difficulty (*the labor involved in writing a symphony*).

Anyone who has been forced to perform **drudgery** knows that it is the most unpleasant, uninspiring, and monotonous kind of labor (*a forklift that eliminates the drudgery of stacking boxes; the drudgery of compiling a phone book*).

A **grind** is even more intense and unrelenting than drudgery, emphasizing work that is performed under pressure in a dehumanizing way (*the daily grind of classroom teaching*).

Toil suggests labor that is prolonged and very tiring (*farmers who toil endlessly in the fields*), but not necessarily physical (*mothers who toil to teach their children manners*).

Those who **travail** endure pain, anguish, or suffering (*his hours of travail ended in heartbreak*).

lab·o·ra·to·ry /ˈlabrəˌtôrē/ ▸*n.* (*pl.* **-ries**) a room or building equipped for scientific experiments, research, or teaching, or for the manufacture of drugs or chemicals: *pepsin can be extracted in the laboratory* | [with *adj.*] *a film processing laboratory* | [as *adj.*] *a laboratory technician.* ■ [as *adj.*] (of an animal) bred for or used in experiments in laboratories: *studies on laboratory rats.* ▷early 17th cent.: from medieval Latin *laboratorium*, from Latin *laborare* 'to labor.'

la·bor camp ▸*n.* a prison camp in which a regime of hard labor is enforced.

La·bor Day ▸*n.* a public holiday or day of festivities held in honor of working people, in the U.S. and Canada on the first Monday in September, in many other countries on May 1.

la·bored /ˈlābərd/ (*Brit.* **la·boured**) ▸*adj.* done with great effort and difficulty: *his breathing was becoming less labored.* ■ (esp. of humor or a performance) not spontaneous or fluent: *one of Arthur's labored jokes.*

la·bor·er /ˈlāb(ə)rər/ (*Brit.* **la·bour·er**) ▸*n.* a person doing unskilled manual work for wages: *a farm laborer.*

la·bor force ▸*n.* all the members of a particular organization or population who are able to work, viewed collectively.

la·bor-in·ten·sive ▸*adj.* (of a form of work) needing a large workforce or a large amount of work in relation to output: *the labor-intensive task of tagging each item in the store.*

la·bo·ri·ous /ləˈbôrēəs/ ▸*adj.* (esp. of a task, process, or journey) requiring considerable effort and time: *years of laborious training* | *the work is very slow and laborious.* See note at **HARD.** ■ (esp. of speech or writing style) showing obvious signs of effort and lacking in fluency: *his slow, laborious style.* ▷late Middle English (also in the sense 'industrious, assiduous'): from Old French *laborieux*, from Latin *laboriosus*, from *labor* 'labor.' —**la·bo·ri·ous·ly** *adv.* —**la·bo·ri·ous·ness** *n.*

La·bor·ite /ˈlābəˌrīt/ (*Brit.* **La·bour·ite**) ▸*n.* a member or supporter of a labor party.

la·bor mar·ket ▸*n.* the supply of available workers in relation to available work: *a diverse workforce in a tight labor market.*

la·bor pain ▸*n.* [usu. in *pl.*] one of the recurrent pains felt by a woman during childbirth. Also called **BIRTH PANG.**

la·bor par·ty ▸*n.* a political party formed to represent the interests of ordinary working people. ■ (**the Labor Party**) a major party in Israel, Australia, and certain other countries. ■ variant spelling of **LABOUR PARTY.**

La·bor Par·ty, Aus·tral·ian see **AUSTRALIAN LABOR PARTY.**

la·bor-sav·ing ▸*adj.* [*attrib.*] (of an appliance) designed to reduce the amount of work needed to complete a task.

la·bor un·ion ▸*n.* an organized association of workers, often in a trade or profession, formed to protect and further their rights and interests.

la·bour, etc. ▸*n.* British spelling of **LABOR,** etc.

La·bour Par·ty ▸*n.* a major left-of-center British party that since World War II has been in power 1945–51, 1964–70, 1974–79, and since 1997. Arising from the trade union movement at the end of the 19th century, it replaced the Liberals as the country's second party after World War I.

la·bra /ˈlābrə; ˈlabrə/ ▸ plural form of **LABRUM.**

lab·ra·doo·dle /ˈlabrəˌdo͞odl/ ▸*n.* a dog resulting from a cross between a Labrador and a standard poodle.

Lab·ra·dor[1] /ˈlabrəˌdôr/ a coastal region of eastern Canada that forms the mainland part of the province of Newfoundland and Labrador.

Lab·ra·dor[2] (also **Labrador retriever**) ▸*n.* a retriever of a breed that predominantly has a black or yellow coat, widely used as a gun dog or as a guide for a blind person. ▷early 20th cent.: named after the **LABRADOR PENINSULA,** where the breed was developed. The name *Labrador dog* had been applied in the 19th cent. to a much larger breed, similar to the Newfoundland.

Labrador retriever

Lab·ra·dor Cur·rent a cold ocean current that flows south from the Arctic Ocean along the northeastern coast of North America. It meets the warm Gulf Stream in an area off the coast of Newfoundland that is noted for dense fogs.

lab·ra·dor·ite /ˈlabrədôˌrīt/ ▸*n.* a mineral of the plagioclase feldspar group, found in many igneous rocks. ▷early 19th cent.: from **LABRADOR PENINSULA,** where it was found, + **-ITE**[1].

Lab·ra·dor Pen·in·su·la a broad peninsula in eastern Canada, between Hudson Bay, the Atlantic Ocean, and the Gulf of St. Lawrence. Consisting of the Ungava Peninsula and Labrador, it contains most of Quebec and the mainland part of the province of Newfoundland and Labrador. Also called **LABRADOR-UNGAVA.**

Lab·ra·dor Sea a section of the Atlantic Ocean between Labrador and southern Greenland, noted for its icebergs.

Lab·ra·dor tea ▸*n.* a low-growing northern shrub of the heath family, with fragrant leathery evergreen leaves that are sometimes used as a tea substitute. • *Ledum groenlandicum*, family Ericaceae.

la·bret /ˈlābret; -brit/ ▸*n.* an object such as a small piece of shell, bone, or stone inserted into the lip as an ornament in some cultures. ▷mid 19th cent.: diminutive of **LABRUM.**

la·brum /ˈlābrəm; ˈlabrəm/ ▸*n.* (*pl.* **la·bra** /lābrə; ˈlabrə/) *Zoology* a structure corresponding to a lip, esp. the upper border of the mouthparts of a crustacean or insect. ▷early 18th cent.: from Latin, literally 'lip'; related to **LABIUM.** —**la·bral** /ˈlābrəl/ *adj.*

la·bru·sca /ləˈbrəskə/ ▸*n.* another term for **FOX GRAPE:** [as *adj.*] *labrusca grapes.* ■ a wine made from this grape. ▷from Latin *labrusca*, denoting a wild vine.

La·bu·an /ləˈbo͞oən/ a small Malaysian island off the northern coast of Borneo; pop. 26,000; capital, Victoria.

la·bur·num /ləˈbərnəm/ ▸*n.* a small European tree that has hanging clusters of yellow flowers succeeded by slender pods containing poisonous seeds. The hard timber is sometimes used as an ebony substitute. Native to Central and Southern Europe, laburnums have been widely planted as ornamentals. • Genus *Laburnum*, family Leguminosae. ▷modern Latin.

lab·y·rinth /ˈlab(ə)ˌrinTH/ ▸*n.* **1** a complicated irregular network of passages or paths in which it is difficult to find one's way; a maze: ***a labyrinth of*** *passages and secret chambers.* ■ *figurative* an intricate and confusing arrangement: ***a labyrinth of*** *conflicting laws and regulations.* **2** *Anatomy* a complex structure in the inner ear that contains the organs of hearing and balance. It consists of bony cavities (the **bony labyrinth**) filled with fluid and lined with sensitive membranes (the **membranous labyrinth**). ■ *Zoology* an organ of intricate structure, in particular the accessory respiratory organs of certain fishes. ▷late Middle English (referring to the maze constructed by Daedalus to house the Minotaur): from French *labyrinthe* or Latin *labyrinthus*, from Greek *laburinthos.* —**lab·y·rin·thi·an** /ˌlabəˈrinTHēən/ *adj.* —**lab·y·rin·thine** /ˌlabəˈrinˌTHēn; -ˈrinTHin; -ˈrinˌTHīn/ *adj.*

lab·y·rinth fish ▸*n.* a freshwater fish with poorly developed gills and a labyrinthine accessory breathing organ, native to Africa and Asia. • Suborder Anabantoidei: Belontiidae and related families, with many species, including such popular aquarium fishes as the gouramis and the fighting fish.

lab·y·rin·thi·tis /ˌlabərənˈTHītis/ ▸*n. Medicine* inflammation of the labyrinth or inner ear.

lab·y·rin·tho·dont /ˌlabəˈrinTHəˌdänt/ ▸*adj. Zoology* (of teeth) having the enamel deeply folded to form a labyrinthine structure. ■ *Paleontology* of or relating to a group of large fossil amphibians of the late Devonian to early Triassic periods having such teeth. ▸*n.* a labyrinthodont amphibian. • Former subclass Labyrinthodontia: several families, but no longer considered to be a single group. ▷mid 19th cent.: from modern Latin *Labyrinthodontia*, from Greek *laburinthos* 'labyrinth' + *odous, odont-* 'tooth.'

lac[1] /lak/ ▸*n.* a resinous substance secreted as a protective covering by the lac insect, used to make varnish, shellac, sealing wax, dyes, etc. ▷late Middle English: from medieval Latin *lac, lac(c)a*, from Portuguese *laca*, based on Hindi *lākh* or Persian *lāk*.

lac[2] ▸*adj.* [*attrib.*] *Biology* denoting the ability of normal strains of the bacterium *E. coli* to metabolize lactose, or the genetic factors involved in this ability (which is lost in some mutant strains). ▷1940s: abbreviation of **LACTOSE.**

lac[3] ▸*n.* variant spelling of **LAKH.**

La·can /läˈkäN/, Jacques (1901–81), French psychoanalyst and writer. A notable poststructuralist, he reinterpreted Freudian psychoanalysis, esp. the theory of the unconscious, in the light of structural linguistics and anthropology. —**La·can·i·an** /ləˈkānēən; -ˈkan-/ *adj.* & *n.* —**La·can·i·an·ism** /ləˈkānēəˌnizəm; -ˈkan-/ *n.*

Lac·ca·dive Is·lands /ˈlakəˌdīv/ one of the groups of islands that form the Indian Union Territory of Lakshadweep in the Indian Ocean.

lac·co·lith /ˈlakəˌliTH/ ▸*n. Geology* a mass of igneous rock, typically lens-shaped, that has been intruded between rock strata causing uplift in the shape of a dome. ▷late 19th cent.: from Greek *lakkos* 'reservoir' + **-LITH.**

lace /lās/ ▸*n.* **1** a fine open fabric, typically one of cotton or silk, made by looping, twisting, or knitting thread in patterns and used esp. for trimming garments. ■ braid used for trimming, esp. on military dress uniforms. **2** (usu. **laces**) a cord or leather strip passed through eyelets or hooks on opposite sides of a shoe or garment and then pulled tight and fastened.
▸*v.* [*trans.*] **1** fasten or tighten (a shoe or garment) by tying its laces: *he put the shoes on and* ***laced*** *them* ***up.*** ■ (**lace someone into**) fasten someone into (a garment) by tightening the laces: *Morris laced Bill and David into boxing gloves.* ■ (**lace something through**) pass a lace or cord through (a hole). ■ compress the waist of (someone) with a laced corset: *Rosina* ***laced*** *her* ***up*** *tight to show off her neat, pretty waist.* ■ [*intrans.*] (of a garment or shoe) be fastened by means of laces: *the shoes laced at the front.* **2** [*trans.*] entwine or tangle (things, esp. fingers) together: *he* ***laced*** *his fingers* ***together*** *and sat back.* **3** (often **be laced with**) add an ingredient, esp. alcohol, to (a drink or dish) to enhance its flavor or strength: *he gave us coffee laced with brandy* | *figurative his voice was laced with derision.* ■ streak with color or something of a contrasting appearance: *her brown hair was laced with gray.* **4** hit (something, esp. a baseball) hard: *he laced a double down the first-base line.*
▸*phrasal v.* □ **lace into** *informal* assail or tackle (something): *Marion laced into her opponent with a blistering criticism.* ▷Middle English: from Old French *laz, las* (noun), *lacier* (verb), based on Latin *laqueus* 'noose' (also an early sense in English). Compare with **LASSO.**

lace·bark /ˈlāsˌbärk/ ▸*n.* any of a number of trees or shrubs that possess a lacy bark or inner bark, in particular: • an evergreen Caribbean shrub with a lacy inner bark that is used ornamentally (*Lagetta lagetto*, family Thymelaeaceae). • a small ornamental New Zealand tree (genus *Hoheria*, family Malvaceae).

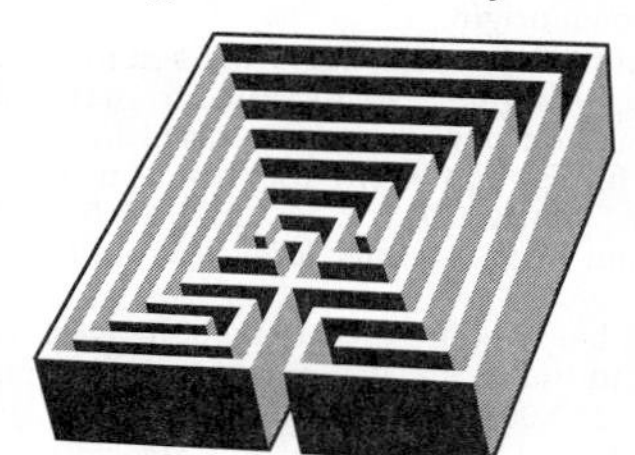

labyrinth 1

lace bug ▶*n.* a small plant-eating bug that has a raised netlike pattern on the wings and upper surface. • Family Tingidae, suborder Heteroptera: several genera.

lace-cur·tain ▶*adj. informal, often offensive* having social pretensions; self-consciously genteel: *the fancy sons of lace-curtain Boston lawyers.*

-laced /lāst/ ▶*adj.* [*in combination*] contaminated with a substance (usually harmful or toxic) present in small amounts: *dioxin-laced sludge | anthrax-laced letters.*

Lac·e·dae·mo·ni·an /ˌlasədəˈmōnēən/ ▶*n.* a native or inhabitant of Lacedaemon, an area of ancient Greece comprising the city of Sparta and its surroundings.
▶*adj.* of Lacedaemon or its inhabitants; Spartan.

lace·mak·ing /ˈlāsˌmākiNG/ ▶*n.* the activity of making lace. —**lace·mak·er** /-ˌmākər/ *n.*

lace pil·low ▶*n.* a hard cushion placed on the lap to provide support in lacemaking.

lac·er·ate /ˈlasəˌrāt/ ▶*v.* [*trans.*] tear or deeply cut (something, esp. flesh or skin): *the point had lacerated his neck |* [*as adj.*] (**lacerated**) *his badly lacerated hands and knees.* ■ *figurative* (of feelings or emotions) wound or injure: *an assertion calculated to lacerate nobody's feelings.* ▷late Middle English: from Latin *lacerat-* 'mangled,' from the verb *lacerare,* from *lacer* 'mangled, torn.' —**lac·er·a·tion** /ˌlasəˈrāSHən/ *n.*

La·cer·ta /ləˈsərtə/ *Astronomy* a small and inconspicuous northern constellation (the Lizard), on the edge of the Milky Way between Cygnus and Andromeda. ■ [*as genitive*] (**Lacertae** /-tē/) used with a preceding letter or numeral to designate a star in this constellation: *the star Alpha Lacertae.* ▷Latin.

la·cer·tid /ləˈsərtid/ ▶*n. Zoology* a lizard of a large family (Lacertidae) to which most European lizards belong. ▷late 19th cent.: from modern Latin *Lacertidae* (plural), from Latin *lacerta* 'lizard.'

Lac·er·til·i·a /ˌlasərˈtilēə; -ˈtilyə/ *Zoology* a group of reptiles that comprises the lizards. Also called **SAURIA**. • Suborder Lacertilia (or Sauria), order Squamata. ▷modern Latin (plural), from Latin *lacerta* 'lizard.' —**lac·er·til·i·an** /-ˈtilēən; -ˈtilyən/ *n. & adj.*

lace-up ▶*adj.* (of a shoe or garment) fastened with laces: *flat lace-up shoes.*
▶*n. chiefly Brit.* a shoe or boot that is fastened with laces: *brown leather lace-ups.*

lace·wing /ˈlāsˌwiNG/ ▶*n.* a slender, delicate insect with large clear membranous wings. Both the adults and larvae are typically predators of aphids. • Several families in the order Neuroptera, in particular Chrysopidae (the **green lacewings**).

lace·wood /ˈlāsˌwo͝od/ ▶*n.* the timber of the plane tree.

lace·work /ˈlāsˌwərk/ ▶*n.* lace fabric and other items made of lace viewed collectively. ■ the process of making lace.

lach·es /ˈlaCHiz/ ▶*n. Law* unreasonable delay in making an assertion or claim, such as asserting a right, claiming a privilege, or making an application for redress, which may result in refusal. ▷late Middle English (in the sense 'slackness, negligence'): from Old French *laschesse,* from *lasche* 'loose, lax,' based on Latin *laxus.* The current sense dates from the late 16th cent.

Lach·e·sis /ˈlakəsis/ *Greek Mythology* one of the three Fates. ▷Greek, literally 'obtaining by lot.'

Lach·lan /ˈläklən/ a river of New South Wales in Australia that rises in the Great Dividing Range and flows about 920 miles (1,472 km) northwest and then southwest to join the Murrumbidgee River near the border with Victoria. ▷named after *Lachlan* Macquarie (1761–1824), the governor of New South Wales 1809–21.

lach·ry·mal /ˈlakrəməl/ (also **lac·ri·mal** or **lac·ry·mal**) ▶*adj.* **1** *formal* or *poetic/literary* connected with weeping or tears. **2** (usu. **lacrimal**) *Physiology & Anatomy* concerned with the secretion of tears: *lacrimal cells.*
▶*n.* **1** (usu. **lacrimal** or **lacrimal bone**) *Anatomy* a small bone forming part of the eye socket. **2** short for **LACHRYMAL VASE**. ▷late Middle English (sense 2 of the *adjective*): from medieval Latin *lachrymalis,* from Latin *lacrima* 'tear.'

lach·ry·mal vase ▶*n. historical* a vial holding the tears of mourners at a funeral.

lach·ry·ma·tion /ˌlakrəˈmāSHən/ (also **lac·ri·ma·tion** or **lac·ry·ma·tion**) ▶*n. poetic/literary* or *Medicine* the flow of tears. ▷late 16th cent.: from Latin *lacrimatio(n-),* from *lacrimare* 'weep,' from *lacrima* 'tear.'

lach·ry·ma·tor /ˈlakrəˌmātər/ (also **lac·ri·ma·tor**) ▶*n. chiefly Medicine* a substance that irritates the eyes and causes tears to flow.

lach·ry·ma·to·ry /ˈlakrəməˌtôrē/ (also **lac·ri·ma·to·ry**) ▶*adj. technical* or *poetic/literary* relating to, tending to cause, or containing tears: *a lachrymatory secretion.*
▶*n.* (*pl.* **-ries**) a vial of a kind found in ancient Roman tombs and thought to be a lachrymal vase. ▷mid 17th cent. (as a noun denoting a vial): from Latin *lacrima,* on the pattern of *chrismatory.*

lach·ry·mose /ˈlakrəˌmōs; -ˌmōz/ ▶*adj. formal* or *poetic/literary* tearful or given to weeping: *she was pink-eyed and lachrymose.* ■ inducing tears; sad: *a lachrymose children's classic.* ▷mid 17th cent. (in the sense 'like tears; liable to exude in drops'): from Latin *lacrimosus,* from *lacrima* 'tear.' —**lach·ry·mose·ly** *adv.* —**lach·ry·mos·i·ty** /ˌlakrəˈmäsətē/ *n.*

lac·ing /ˈlāsiNG/ ▶*n.* **1** the laced fastening of a shoe or garment. ■ lace trimming, esp. on a uniform. **2** a dash of liquor added to a drink: *coffee to which he added a liberal* ***lacing of*** *brandy.*

la·cin·i·ate /ləˈsinēˌāt; -ē-it/ (also **la·cin·i·at·ed** /-ˌātid/) ▶*adj. Botany & Zoology* divided into deep narrow irregular segments. ▷mid 18th cent.: from Latin *lacinia* 'fringe, hem, flap of a garment' + **-ATE**[2].

lac in·sect /ˈlak ˈinˌsekt/ ▶*n.* an Asian scale insect that lives on trees and produces secretions that are used in the production of shellac. • *Laccifer lacca,* family Lacciferidae, suborder Homoptera.

lack /lak/ ▶*n.* the state of being without or not having enough of something: *the case was dismissed* ***for lack of*** *evidence | there is* ***no lack of*** *entertainment aboard ship |* [*in sing.*] *there is a lack of parking space in the town.*
▶*v.* [*trans.*] be without or deficient in: *the novel lacks imagination |* [*intrans.*] *she* ***lacks in*** *patience | Sam did not* ***lack for*** *friends.* ▷Middle English: corresponding to, and perhaps partly from, Middle Dutch and Middle Low German *lak* 'deficiency,' Middle Dutch *laken* 'lack, blame.'

THE RIGHT WORD **absence, dearth, lack, privation, shortage, want**

To suffer from a **lack** of food means to be partially or totally without it; to be in **want** of food also implies a *lack,* but with an emphasis on the essential or desirable nature of what is lacking; for example, you may experience a complete *lack* of pain following surgery, but you would be in *want* of medication if pain were suddenly to occur.

Absence, on the other hand, refers to the complete nonexistence of something or someone. A *lack* of dairy products in your diet implies that you're not getting enough; an *absence* of dairy products implies that you're not getting any at all.

If the scarcity or lack of something makes it costly, or if something is in distressingly low supply, the correct word is **dearth** (*a dearth of water in the desert; a dearth of nylon stockings during World War II*).

A **shortage** of something is a partial insufficiency of an established, required, or accustomed amount (*a shortage of fresh oranges after the late-season frost*), while **privation** is the negative state or absence of a corresponding positive (*they suffered from hunger, cold, and other privations*).

lack·a·dai·si·cal /ˌlakəˈdāzikəl/ ▶*adj.* lacking enthusiasm and determination; carelessly lazy: *a lackadaisical defense left the Spurs adrift in the second half.* ▷mid 18th cent. (also in the sense 'feebly sentimental'): from the archaic interjection *lackaday, lackadaisy* (see **ALACK**) + **-ICAL**. —**lack·a·dai·si·cal·ly** *adv.*

lack·a·day /ˈlakəˌdā/ ▶*exclam. archaic* an expression of surprise, regret, or grief. ▷late 17th cent.: shortening of *alack-a-day.*

Lack·a·wan·na /lakəˈwänə/ an industrial city in western New York, on Lake Erie, west of Buffalo; pop. 20,585.

lack·ey /ˈlakē/ ▶*n.* (*pl.* **-eys**) a servant, esp. a liveried footman or manservant. ■ *derogatory* a person who is obsequiously willing to obey or serve another person or group of people.
▶*v.* (also **lac·quey**) (**-queys, -queyed**) [*trans.*] *archaic* behave servilely to; wait upon as a lackey. ▷early 16th cent.: from French *laquais,* perhaps from Catalan *alacay,* from Arabic *al-ḳā'id* 'the chief.'

lack·ing /ˈlakiNG/ ▶*adj.* [*predic.*] not available or in short supply: *adequate resources and funds are both sadly lacking at present.* ■ (of a quality) missing or absent: *there was something lacking in our marriage.* ■ deficient or inadequate: *the students are not* ***lacking in*** *intellectual ability | workers were asked in what way they* ***found*** *their managers* ***lacking.***

lack·lus·ter /ˈlakˌləstər/ (*Brit.* **lack·lus·tre**) ▶*adj.* lacking in vitality, force, or conviction; uninspired or uninspiring: *no excuses were made for the team's lackluster performance.* ■ (of the hair or the eyes) not shining; dull.

Lac Lé·man /läk leˈmäN/ French name for Lake Geneva (see **GENEVA, LAKE**).

La·co·ni·a /ləˈkōnēə; -ˈkōnyə/ (also **La·ko·ni·a**) a modern department and an ancient region of Greece, in the southeastern Peloponnese. Throughout the classical period the region was dominated by its capital, Sparta. —**La·co·ni·an** *adj. & n.*

la·con·ic /ləˈkänik/ ▶*adj.* (of a person, speech, or style of writing) using very few words: *his laconic reply suggested a lack of interest in the topic.* See note at **TERSE**. ▷mid 16th cent. (in the sense 'Laconian'): via Latin from Greek *Lakōnikos,* from *Lakōn* 'Laconia, Sparta,' the Spartans being known for their terse speech. —**la·con·i·cal·ly** /-(ə)lē/ *adv.* —**la·con·i·cism** /ləˈkänəˌsizəm/ *n.* —**lac·o·nism** /ˈlakəˌnizəm/ *n.*

La Co·ru·ña /ˌlä kəˈro͞onyə/ Spanish name for **CORUNNA**.

lac·quer /ˈlakər/ ▶*n.* **1** a liquid made of shellac dissolved in alcohol, or of synthetic substances, that dries to form a hard protective coating for wood, metal, etc. ■ (also **hair lacquer**) British term for **HAIR SPRAY**. **2** the sap of the lacquer tree used to varnish wood or other materials. ■ decorative objects made of wood coated with lacquer: [*as adj.*] *a small lacquer box.*
▶*v.* [*trans.*] [often *as adj.*] (**lacquered**) coat with lacquer: *the lacquered Chinese table.* ▷late 16th cent. (denoting lac): from obsolete French *lacre* 'sealing wax,' from Portuguese *laca* (see **LAC**[1]). —**lac·quer·er** *n.*

lac·quer tree ▶*n.* an eastern Asian tree with white sap that turns dark on exposure to air, producing a hard-wearing varnish traditionally used in lacquerware. • *Rhus verniciflua,* family Anacardiaceae.

lac·quer·ware /ˈlakərˌwe(ə)r/ ▶*n.* articles that have a decorative lacquer coating, viewed collectively.

lac·quer·work /ˈlakərˌwərk/ ▶*n.* lacquerware. ■ the design, construction, or finish of lacquerware.

lac·quey ▶*n. & v.* archaic spelling of **LACKEY**.

lac·ri·mal ▶*adj. & n.* variant spelling of **LACHRYMAL**.

lac·ri·ma·tion ▶*n.* variant spelling of **LACHRYMATION**.

lac·ri·ma·tor ▶*n.* variant spelling of **LACHRYMATOR**.

lac·ri·ma·to·ry ▶*adj.* variant spelling of **LACHRYMATORY**.

La Crosse /lə ˈkrôs; ˈkräs/ an industrial and commercial city in western Wisconsin, on the Mississippi River; pop. 51,818.

la·crosse /ləˈkrôs; -ˈkräs/ ▶*n.* a team game, originally played by North American Indians, in which the ball is thrown, caught, and carried with a long-handled stick having a curved L-shaped or triangular frame at one end with a piece of shallow netting in the angle. ▷mid 19th cent.: from French *(le jeu de) la crosse* '(the game of) the hooked stick.' Compare with **CROSSE**.

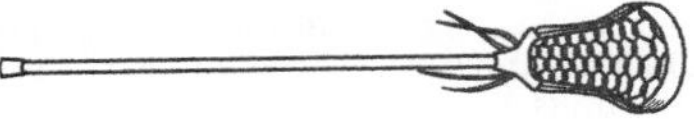

lacrosse stick

lac·ry·mal ▶*adj. & n.* variant spelling of **LACHRYMAL**.

lac·ry·ma·tion ▶*n.* variant spelling of **LACHRYMATION**.

lac·tal·bu·min /ˌlakˌtalˈbyo͞omin/ ▶*n. Biochemistry* a protein or mixture of similar proteins occurring in milk, obtained after the removal of casein and soluble in a salt solution. ▷late 19th cent.: from **LACTO-** 'of milk' + **ALBUMIN**.

lac·tam /ˈlakˌtam/ ▶*n. Chemistry* an organic compound containing an amide group −NHCO− as part of a ring. ▷late 19th cent.: blend of **LACTONE** and **AMIDE**.

lac·tar·i·us /lakˈte(ə)rēəs/ ▶*n.* a large woodland mushroom with a concave cap, the flesh exuding a white or colored milky fluid when cut. • Genus *Lactarius,* family Russulaceae, class Hymenomycetes: several species, including the edible **orange milk lactarius** (*L. deliciosus*).

lac·tase /ˈlakˌtās; -tāz/ ▶*n. Biochemistry* an enzyme that catalyzes the hydrolysis of lactose to glucose and galactose. ▷late 19th cent.: from **LACTOSE** + **-ASE**.

lac·tate[1] /ˈlakˌtāt/ ▶*v.* [*intrans.*] (of a female mammal) secrete milk. ▷late 19th cent.: back-formation from **LACTATION**.

lac·tate[2] ▸*n. Chemistry* a salt or ester of lactic acid. ▷late 18th cent.: from LACTIC + -ATE[1].

lac·ta·tion /lak'tāsHən/ ▸*n.* the secretion of milk by the mammary glands. ■ the suckling of young. ▷mid 17th cent.: from Latin *lactatio(n-)*, from *lactare* 'suckle,' from *lac, lact-* 'milk.' **—lac·ta·tion·al** /-'tāsHənl/ *adj.*

lac·te·al /'laktēəl/ ▸*adj.* of milk. ■ *Anatomy* (of a vessel) conveying chyle or other milky fluid.
▸*plural n.* (**lacteals**) *Anatomy* the lymphatic vessels of the small intestine that absorb digested fats. ▷mid 17th cent.: from Latin *lacteus* (from *lac, lact-* 'milk') + -AL.

lac·tes·cent /lak'tesənt/ ▸*adj.* milky in appearance. ■ *Botany* yielding a milky latex. ▷mid 17th cent.: from Latin *lactescent-* 'being milky,' from the verb *lactere*, from *lac, lact-* 'milk.'

lac·tic /'laktik/ ▸*adj.* of, relating to, or obtained from milk. ▷late 18th cent.: from Latin *lac, lact-* 'milk' + -IC.

lac·tic ac·id ▸*n. Biochemistry* a colorless syrupy organic acid formed in sour milk and produced in the muscle tissues during strenuous exercise. • Chem. formula: $CH_3CH(OH)COOH$.

lac·tif·er·ous /lak'tif(ə)rəs/ ▸*adj. chiefly Anatomy* forming or conveying milk or milky fluid: *lactiferous ducts.* ▷late 17th cent.: from Latin *lac, lact-* 'milk' + -FEROUS.

lacto- ▸*comb. form* **1** of or relating to milk: *lactometer.* **2** from or relating to lactic acid or lactose: *lactobacillus.* ▷from Latin *lac, lact-* 'milk.'

lac·to·ba·cil·lus /,laktōbə'siləs/ ▸*n.* (*pl.* **-cil·li** /-'si,lī; -'si,lē/) *Biology* a rod-shaped bacterium that produces lactic acid from the fermentation of carbohydrates. • Genus *Lactobacillus*; nonmotile Gram-postive bacteria.

lac·to·fer·rin /,laktō'ferin; -tə-/ ▸*n. Biochemistry* a protein present in milk and other secretions, with bactericidal and iron-binding properties.

lac·to·fla·vin /,laktō'flāvin; 'laktō,flāvin/ ▸*n. Brit.* another term for RIBOFLAVIN.

lac·to·gen·ic /,laktə'jenik/ ▸*adj. Physiology* (of a hormone or other substance) inducing the secretion of milk.

lac·to·glob·u·lin /,laktō'gläbyəlin/ ▸*n. Biochemistry* a protein or mixture of similar proteins occurring in milk, obtained after the removal of casein and precipitated in a salt solution.

lac·tom·e·ter /lak'tämətər/ ▸*n.* an instrument for measuring the density of milk.

lac·tone /'lak,tōn/ ▸*n. Chemistry* an organic compound containing an ester group —OCO— as part of a ring.

lac·to-o·vo-veg·e·tar·i·an /'laktō ,ōvō ,vejə'te(ə)rēən/ ▸*n.* a person who eats vegetables, eggs, and dairy products but who does not eat meat.

lac·to·pro·tein /,laktō'prō,tēn/ ▸*n.* the protein component of milk.

lac·tose /'lak,tōs; -,tōz/ ▸*n. Chemistry* a sugar present in milk. It is a disaccharide containing glucose and galactose units.

lac·to·veg·e·tar·i·an /'laktō,vejə'terēən/ ▸*n.* a person who abstains from eating meat and eggs, but who eats dairy products.

lac·tu·lose /'lakt(y)ə,lōs; -,lōz/ ▸*n. Chemistry* a synthetic sugar with laxative properties. It is a disaccharide consisting of glucose and fructose units. ▷1930s: from LACTO- 'of milk,' perhaps on the pattern of *cellulose*.

la·cu·na /lə'k(y)ōōnə/ ▸*n.* (*pl.* **-nae** /-nī; -nē/ or **-nas**) an unfilled space or interval; a gap: *the journal has filled a lacuna in Middle Eastern studies.* ■ a missing portion in a book or manuscript. ■ *Anatomy* a cavity or depression, esp. in bone. ▷mid 17th cent.: from Latin, 'pool,' from *lacus* 'lake.' **—la·cu·nal** /lə'k(y)ōōnl/ *adj.* **—lac·u·nar·y** /'lakyə,nerē; lə'k(y)ōōnərē/ *adj.* **—la·cu·nate** /-,nāt; -nit; 'lakyə,nāt/ *adj.* **—la·cu·nose** /'lakyə,nōs; -,nōz/ *adj.*

la·cu·nar[1] /lə'k(y)ōōnər/ ▸*adj.* of or relating to a lacuna.

la·cu·nar[2] ▸*n.* a vault or ceiling consisting of recessed panels. ■ a panel in such a vault or ceiling.

la·cus·trine /lə'kəstrin/ ▸*adj. technical* or *poetic/literary* of, relating to, or associated with lakes. ▷early 19th cent.: from Latin *lacus* 'lake' (the stem *lacustr-* influenced by Latin *palustris* 'marshy') + -INE[1].

lac·y /'lāsē/ ▸*adj.* (**lac·i·er, lac·i·est**) made of, resembling, or trimmed with lace: *a lacy petticoat.* **—lac·i·ly** /-səlē/ *adv.* **—lac·i·ness** *n.*

lad /lad/ ▸*n.* **1** *informal* a boy or young man (often as a form of address): *I read that book when I was a lad | come in, lad, and shut the door.* ■ (**lads**) *chiefly Brit.* a group of men sharing recreational, working, or other interests: *she wouldn't let him go out with the lads any more.* ■ *Brit.* a man who is boisterously macho in his behavior or actions, esp. one who is interested in sexual conquest: *Tony was **a bit of a lad**—always had an eye for the women.* **2** *Brit.* a stable worker (regardless of age or sex). ▷Middle English: of unknown origin.

La·dakh /lə'däk/ a high-altitude region in northwestern India, Pakistan, and China that contains the Ladakh and Karakoram mountain ranges and the upper Indus valley.

La·da·khi /lə'däkē/ ▸*n.* (*pl.* **-khis**) **1** a native or inhabitant of Ladakh. **2** the Tibetan dialect of this people.
▸*adj.* of or relating to Ladakh, the Ladakhis, or their language. ▷the name in Ladakhi.

lad·a·num /'lädn-əm; 'ladnəm/ ▸*n.* variant spelling of LABDANUM.

lad·der /'ladər/ ▸*n.* a structure consisting of a series of bars or steps between two upright lengths of wood, metal, or rope, used for climbing up or down something. ■ *figurative* a series of ascending stages by which someone or something may advance or progress: *employees on their way up the career ladder.* ■ *Brit.* (in tights or stockings) a run.
▸*v.* [*trans.*] *Brit.* cause (tights or stockings) to run. ■ [*intrans.*] (of tights or stockings) develop a run. ▷Old English *hlǣd(d)er*, of West Germanic origin; related to Dutch *leer* and German *Leiter*.

lad·der-back (also **ladder-back chair**) ▸*n.* an upright chair with a back resembling a ladder.

lad·der stitch ▸*n.* a stitch in embroidery consisting of transverse bars.

lad·der tour·na·ment ▸*n.* a sporting contest in which the participants are listed in ranking order and can move up by defeating the contestant above.

lad·die /'ladē/ ▸*n. informal, chiefly Scottish* a boy or young man (often as a form of address): *he's just a wee laddie.*

lad·dish /'ladisH/ ▸*adj. Brit.* characteristic of a young man who behaves in a boisterously macho manner. **—lad·dish·ness** *n.*

lad·du /'lədōō/ ▸*n.* (*pl.* **-dus**) an Indian confection, typically made from flour, sugar, and shortening, that is shaped into a ball. ▷from Hindi *laḍḍū*.

lade /lād/ ▸*v.* (*past part.* **lad·en** /'lādn/) [*trans.*] *archaic* load (a ship or other vessel). ■ ship (goods) as cargo. ■ [*intrans.*] (of a ship) take on cargo. ▷Old English *hladan*, of West Germanic origin; related to Dutch and German *laden* 'to load,' also to LADLE and perhaps to LATHE.

lad·en /'lādn/ ▸*adj.* heavily loaded or weighed down: *a tree **laden with** apples* | [in *combination*] *the moisture-laden air.* ▷late 16th cent.: past participle of LADE.

lad·ette /la'det/ ▸*n. Brit. informal* a young woman who behaves in a boisterously assertive or crude manner and engages in heavy drinking sessions. ▷1990s: from *lad* + *-ette*.

la-di-da /,lä dē 'dä/ (also **lah-di-dah** or **la-de-da**) *informal* ▸*adj.* pretentious or snobbish, esp. in manner or speech: *do I really look or sound like a la-di-da society lawyer?*
▸*exclam.* expressing derision at someone's pretentious manner or speech: *"La-di-da!" snapped Alison, as her sister sank into a curtsy.* ▷late 19th cent.: imitative of an affected manner of speech.

la·dies /'lādēz/ ▸ plural form of LADY.

la·dies chain ▸*n.* a figure in a square dance or other dance.

la·dies' man (also **la·dy's man**) ▸*n.* [in *sing.*] *informal* a man who enjoys spending time and flirting with women.

la·dies' night ▸*n.* a time at a bar or nightclub when women are charged less or admitted free. ■ a function at a men's institution or club to which women are invited.

la·dies' room ▸*n.* a restroom for women in a public or institutional building.

la·dies' tress·es (also **lady's tresses**) ▸*plural n.* [usu. treated as *sing.*] a short orchid with small white flowers arranged in a single or double spiral, growing chiefly in north temperate regions. • Genus *Spiranthes* (and *Goodyera*), family Orchidaceae: several species, including the **slender ladies' tresses** (*S. gracilis*) of North America.

La·din /lə'dēn/ ▸*n.* the Rhaeto-Romanic dialect of the Engadine in Switzerland. ▷mid 19th cent.: from Latin *Latinus* (see LATIN).

lad·ing /'lādiNG/ ▸*n. archaic* the action or process of loading a ship or other vessel with cargo. ■ a cargo.

La·di·no /lə'dēnō/ ▸*n.* (*pl.* **-nos**) **1** the language of some Sephardic Jews, esp. formerly in Mediterranean countries. It is based on medieval Spanish, with an admixture of Hebrew, Greek, and Turkish words, and is written in modified Hebrew characters. Also called JUDEZMO. **2** a mestizo or Spanish-speaking white person in Central America. ▷Spanish, from Latin *Latinus* (see LATIN).

la·di·no /lə'dīnō; -'dēnō/ ▸*n.* (*pl.* **-nos**) a white clover of a large variety native to Italy and cultivated for fodder in North America. ▷1920s: from Italian.

Lad·is·laus I /'lädis,lôs/ (*c.*1040–95), king of Hungary 1077–95; canonized as **St. Ladislaus.** He extended Hungarian power and advanced the spread of Christianity. Feast day, June 27.

Lad·is·laus II (*c.*1351–1434), king of Poland 1386–1434; Polish name **Władysław.** As grand duke of Lithuania, he came to the Polish throne upon his marriage to the Polish monarch, Queen Jadwiga, thus uniting Lithuania and Poland.

la·dle /'lādl/ ▸*n.* a large long-handled spoon with a cup-shaped bowl, used for serving soup, stew, or sauce. ■ a vessel for transporting molten metal in a foundry.
▸*v.* [*trans.*] serve (soup, stew, or sauce) with a ladle: *she **ladled out** onion soup figurative he was **ladling out** his personal philosophy of life.* ■ transfer (liquid) from one receptacle to another: *he ladled the water into an empty bucket.* ▷Old English *hlædel*, from *hladan* (see LADE). **—la·dle·ful** /-,fōōl/ *n.* (*pl.* **-fuls**) **—la·dler** *n.*

Lad·o·ga, Lake /'lädəgə; 'lad-/ a lake in northwestern Russia, northeast of St. Petersburg, near the border with Finland. It is the largest lake in Europe, with an area of 6,837 square miles (17,700 sq km).

lad's love ▸*n.* another term for SOUTHERNWOOD.

la·dy /'lādē/ ▸*n.* (*pl.* **-dies**) **1** a woman (used as a polite or old-fashioned form of reference): *I spoke to the lady at the travel agency* | [as *adj.*] *a lady doctor.* ■ (**the Ladies**) *Brit.* a women's public toilet. ■ an informal, often brusque, form of address to a woman: *I'm sorry, lady, but you have the wrong number.* **2** a woman of superior social position, esp. one of noble birth: *lords and ladies and royalty were once entertained at the house.* ■ a courteous, decorous, or genteel woman: *his wife was a real lady, with such nice manners.* ■ (**Lady**) (in the UK) a title used by peeresses, female relatives of peers, the wives and widows of knights, etc.: *Lady Caroline Lamb.* **3** (**one's lady**) *dated* a man's wife: *welcoming the vice president and his lady.* ■ (also **la·dy friend**) a woman with whom a man is romantically or sexually involved: *the young man bought a rose for his lady.* ■ *historical* a woman to whom a man, esp. a knight, is chivalrously devoted. ▷Old English *hlǣfdīge* (denoting a woman to whom homage or obedience is due, such as the wife of a lord or the mistress of a household, also specifically the Virgin Mary), from *hlāf* 'loaf' + a Germanic base meaning 'knead,' related to DOUGH; compare with LORD. In LADY DAY and other compounds where it signifies possession, it represents the Old English genitive *hlǣfdīgan* '(Our) Lady's.' **—la·dy·hood** /-,hōōd/ *n.*
▸*PHRASES* □ **it isn't over till the fat lady sings** used to convey that there is still time for a situation to change. [by association with the final aria in tragic opera.] □ **ladies who lunch** *informal* or *often derogatory* women with both the means and the free time to meet each other socially for lunch in expensive restaurants. □ **Lady Bountiful** a woman who engages in ostentatious acts of charity, more to impress others than out of a sense of concern for those in need. [early 19th cent.: from the name of a character in Farquhar's *The Beaux' Stratagem* (1707).] □ **Lady Luck** chance personified as a controlling power in human affairs: *it seemed Lady Luck was still smiling on them.* □ **Lady Muck** *Brit., informal* a haughty or pretentious woman (often as a mocking form of address). □ **lady of the house** a woman at the head of a household: *he always asked the lady of the house the shade of paint she would like.* □ **My Lady** a polite form of address to certain noblewomen.

la·dy·bird /'lādē,bərd/ ▸*n. chiefly Brit.* another term for LADYBUG.

la·dy·boy /'lādē,boi/ ▸*n.* (esp. in Thailand) a transvestite.

la·dy·bug /'lādē,bəg/ ▸*n.* a small beetle with a domed back, typically red or yellow with black spots. Both the adults and larvae are important predators of aphids. • Family Coccinellidae: several genera and

convergent ladybug

species, including the familiar **convergent ladybug** (*Hippodamia convergens*).

La·dy chap·el ▶*n.* a chapel in a church or cathedral dedicated to the Virgin Mary.

La·dy Day ▶*n.* March 25, the feast of the Annunciation. ▷with reference to *Our Lady*, the Virgin Mary.

la·dy fern ▶*n.* a tall, graceful fern of worldwide distribution that favors moist shady habitats. • *Athyrium* and other genera, family Woodsiaceae: several species, in particular *A. filix-femina*.

la·dy·fin·ger /ˈlādē,fiNGgər/ ▶*n.* a small finger-shaped sponge cake.

la·dy·fish /ˈlādē,fiSH/ ▶*n.* (*pl.* same or **-fish·es**) any of a number of marine fishes of warm, coastal waters, several of which are popular with anglers. ■ the tenpounder. ■ a bonefish.

la·dy-in-wait·ing ▶*n.* (*pl.* **la·dies-in-wait·ing**) a woman who attends a queen or princess.

la·dy·kill·er /ˈlādē,kilər/ ▶*n. informal* an attractive, charming man who is very attractive to women.

la·dy·like /ˈlādē,līk/ ▶*adj.* behaving or dressing in a way considered appropriate for or typical of a well-bred, decorous woman or girl. ■ (of an activity or occupation) considered suitable for such a woman or girl: *it wasn't ladylike to be too interested in men.* —**la·dy·like·ness** *n.*

la·dy·love /ˈlādē,ləv/ ▶*n. dated* a female lover or sweetheart: *he could not legally marry his ladylove.*

la·dy of the night ▶*n.* used euphemistically to refer to a prostitute.

la·dy·ship /ˈlādē,SHip/ ▶*n.* (**Her/Your Ladyship**) a respectful form of reference or address to a woman who has a title: *the car is outside, Your Ladyship.* ■ *ironic* a form of reference or address to a woman thought to be acting in a pretentious or snobbish way: *bow everyone, Her Ladyship's actually gracing us with her presence!*

la·dy's maid ▶*n. chiefly historical* a maid who attended to the personal needs of her mistress.

la·dy's man ▶*n.* variant spelling of LADIES' MAN.

la·dy's-slip·per (also **la·dy's slip·per**) ▶*n.* an orchid of north temperate regions, the flower of which has a lip that is a conspicuous slipper-shaped pouch. • Genus *Cypripedium*, family Orchidaceae: several species, in particular the large-pouched **showy lady's-slipper** (*C. reginae*), with bicolored (white and rose) flowers, and the **pink lady's-slipper** (*C. acaule*), with a deeply cleft dark pink or (rarely) white pouch.

showy lady's-slipper

la·dy's tress·es ▶*n.* variant spelling of LADIES' TRESSES.

Laen·nec's cir·rho·sis /lāˈneks/ ▶*n. Medicine* a type of cirrhosis of the liver characterized by a nodular appearance of the liver surface, associated with alcoholism. ▷early 19th cent.: named after René T. H. *Laënnec* (1781–1826), the French physician who described the condition.

La·e·trile /ˈlāə,tril; -trəl/ ▶*n. trademark* a compound extracted from amygdalin, formerly used controversially to treat cancer. ▷1950s: from a blend of *laevorotatory* (a variant of LEVOROTATORY) and NITRILE.

laevo- ▶*comb. form chiefly Brit.* alternate spelling of LEVO-. ▷from Latin *laevus* 'left.'

lae·vo·ro·ta·to·ry ▶*adj.* British spelling of LEVOROTATORY.

laev·u·lose ▶*n.* British spelling of LEVULOSE.

La Farge /lə ˈfärZH; ˈfärj/, John (1835–1910) U.S. artist. He was noted for his panels in St. Thomas' Church in New York City and for the stained glass at the Second Presbyterian Church in Chicago. His paintings include "Manua Our Boatman" (1891). He invented opaline glass.

La·fa·yette /,läfēˈet/ **1** an industrial and commercial city in northwestern Indiana; pop. 56,397. **2** a city in southern Louisiana, an oil industry center in Cajun country; pop. 110,257.

La·fa·yette /,lafēˈet; ,lafī-; ,läf-/ (also **La Fay·ette**), Marie Joseph Paul Yves Roch Gilbert du Motier, Marquis de (1757–1834), French soldier and statesman. He fought alongside the colonists in the American Revolution and commanded the French national guard 1789–91 in the French Revolution.

Laf·fer curve /ˈlafər/ ▶*n. Economics* a supposed relationship between economic activity and the rate of taxation that suggests the existence of an optimum tax rate that maximizes tax revenue. ▷1970s: named after Arthur *Laffer* (born 1942), American economist.

La Fol·lette /lə ˈfälit/, Robert (Marion, Sr.) (1855–1925), U.S. politician. He was a member of the U.S. House of Representatives from Wisconsin 1885–91 and served as governor of Wisconsin 1901–06. A U.S. senator 1906–25, he was a Progressive Party presidential candidate in 1924.

La Fon·taine /lä fänˈtān; fônˈten/, Jean de (1621–95), French poet. He is chiefly known for *Fables* (1668–94), drawn from oriental, classical, and contemporary sources.

lag[1] /lag/ ▶*v.* (**lagged, lag·ging**) [*intrans.*] **1** fall behind in movement, progress, or development; not keep pace with another or others: *they stopped to wait for one of the children who was* ***lagging behind***. See note at LOITER. **2** [*intrans.*] *Billiards* determine the order of play by striking the cue ball from balk to rebound off the top cushion, first stroke going to the player whose ball comes to rest nearer the bottom cushion.
▶*n.* **1** (also **time lag**) a period of time between one event or phenomenon and another: *there was a time lag between the commission of the crime and its reporting to the police.* **2** *Physics* a retardation in an electric current or movement. ▷early 16th cent. (as a noun in the sense 'hindmost person (in a game, race, etc.),' also 'dregs'): related to the dialect adjective *lag* (perhaps from a fanciful distortion of LAST[1], or of Scandinavian origin: compare with Norwegian dialect *lagga* 'go slowly'). —**lag·ger** *n.*

lag[2] ▶*v.* (**lagged, lag·ging**) [*trans.*] (usu. **be lagged**) enclose or cover (a boiler, pipes, etc.) with material that provides heat insulation: [as *adj.*] (**lagged**) *a lagged hot-water tank.*
▶*n.* the nonheat-conducting cover of a boiler, etc.; lagging. ■ a piece of this. ▷late 19th cent.: from earlier *lag* 'piece of insulating cover.' —**lag·ger** *n.*

lag[3] *chiefly Brit., informal* ▶*n.* a person who has been frequently convicted and sent to prison: *both* ***old lags*** *were sentenced to ten years' imprisonment.*
▶*v.* (**lagged, lag·ging**) [*trans.*] *archaic* arrest or send to prison. ▷late 16th cent. (as a verb in the sense 'carry off, steal'): of unknown origin. Current senses date from the 19th cent.

lag·an /ˈlagən/ ▶*n. archaic* (in legal contexts) goods or wreckage lying on the bed of the sea. ▷mid 16th cent.: from Old French, perhaps of Scandinavian origin and related to LAY[1].

la·gar /ləˈgär/ ▶*n.* (*pl.* **-ga·res** /-ˈgäräs/) (in Spain and Portugal) a large, typically stone trough in which grapes are trodden. ▷Spanish, from Latin *lacus*, denoting a vat for freshly pressed wine.

lag bolt ▶*n.* another term for LAG SCREW.

Lag b'O·mer /ˈläg bəˈōmər; ˈbōmər/ ▶*n.* a Jewish festival held on the 33rd day of the Omer (the period between Passover and Pentecost), traditionally regarded as celebrating the end of a plague in the 2nd century. ▷from Hebrew *lāg* (pronunciation of the letters L (*lamed*) and G (*gimel*) symbolizing 33) + *bā* 'in the' + *'ōmer* (see OMER).

la·ge·na /ləˈjēnə/ ▶*n.* (*pl.* **-ge·nae** /-ˈjē,nē/) *Zoology* an extension of the saccule of the ear in some vertebrates, corresponding to the cochlear duct in mammals. ▷late 19th cent.: from Latin, literally 'flagon,' from Greek *lagunos*.

la·ger /ˈlägər/ ▶*n.* a kind of beer, effervescent and light in color and body. ▷mid 19th cent.: from German *Lagerbier* 'beer brewed for keeping,' from *Lager* 'storehouse.' Compare with LAAGER and LAIR.

La·ger·löf /ˈlägər,ləv; -,lœf/, Selma (Ottiliana Lovisa) (1858–1940), Swedish novelist. She became known with the publication of *Gösta Berlings Saga* in 1891. Nobel Prize for Literature (1909).

la·ger lout ▶*n. Brit., informal* a young man who regularly behaves in an offensive way, typically as a result of excessive drinking.

lag·gard /ˈlagərd/ ▶*n.* a person who makes slow progress and falls behind others: *there was no time for laggards.*
▶*adj.* slower than desired or expected: *a bell to summon laggard children to school.* ▷early 18th cent. (as an adjective): from LAG[1]. —**lag·gard·ly** *adj.* & *adv.* —**lag·gard·ness** *n.*

lagged /lagd/ ▶*adj. Economics* showing a delayed effect: *a lagged measure of unemployment.*

lag·ging /ˈlagiNG/ ▶*n.* material providing heat insulation for a boiler, pipes, etc. ▷mid 19th cent.: from LAG[2].

La Gio·con·da /,lä jôˈkôndə; jōˈkändə/ another name for MONA LISA.

la·gniappe /,lanˈyap; ˈlan,yap/ ▶*n.* something given as a bonus or extra gift. ▷Louisiana French, from Spanish *la ñapa*.

Lag·o·mor·pha /,lagəˈmôrfə/ *Zoology* an order of mammals that comprises the hares, rabbits, and pikas. They are distinguished by the possession of double incisor teeth, and were formerly placed with the rodents. ▷modern Latin (plural), from Greek *lagōs* 'hare' + *morphē* 'form.' —**lag·o·morph** /ˈlagə,môrf/ *n.* & *adj.*

la·goon /ləˈgo͞on/ ▶*n.* a stretch of salt water separated from the sea by a low sandbank or coral reef. ■ the enclosed water of an atoll. ■ a small freshwater lake near a larger lake or river. ■ an artificial pool for the treatment of effluent or to accommodate surface water that overflows drains during heavy rain. ▷early 17th cent.: from Italian and Spanish *laguna*, from Latin *lacuna* (see LACUNA). —**la·goon·al** /-ˈgo͞onl/ *adj.*

La·gos /ˈlä,gōs; ˈlä,gäs; ˈlāgəs/ the chief city of Nigeria, a port on the Gulf of Guinea; pop. 1,347,000. Originally a slave trade center, it became capital of the newly independent Nigeria in 1960, but was replaced by Abuja in 1991.

La Grande Riv·er /lə ˈgräNd; ˈgrand/ a river that flows for 500 miles (800 km) across central Quebec to Hudson Bay.

La·grange /ləˈgrānj/, Joseph Louis, Comte de (1736–1813), French mathematician, born in Italy. He proved that every positive integer can be expressed as a sum of at most four square and worked on mechanics and its application to the description of planetary and lunar motion.

La·gran·gi·an point /ləˈgranjēən; -ˈgrän-/ ▶*n.* one of five points in the plane of orbit of one body around another (e.g., the moon around the earth) at which a small third body can remain stationary with respect to both.

lag screw ▶*n.* a heavy wood screw with a square or hexagonal head. Also called COACH SCREW, LAG BOLT.
▶ *v.* [*trans.*] (**lag-screw**) fasten with a lag screw.

La Guar·di·a /lə ˈgwärdēə/, Fiorello (Henry) (1882–1947) U.S. politician; nickname the **Little Flower**. He served in the U.S. House of Representatives from New York 1917–21 before he became a corruption-fighting mayor of New York City 1933–45.

La Ha·ba·na /,lä äˈbänä/ Spanish name for HAVANA[1].

La Ha·bra /lə ˈhäbrə/ a city in southwestern California, southeast of Los Angeles; pop. 51,266.

la·har /ˈlä,här/ ▶*n. Geology* a destructive mudflow on the slopes of a volcano. ▷1920s: from Javanese.

lah-di-dah ▶*n.* & *exclam.* variant spelling of LA-DI-DA.

Lahn·da /ˈländə/ ▶*n.* an Indic language of the western Punjab and adjacent areas of Pakistan, sometimes classified as a dialect of Punjabi.
▶*adj.* of or relating to this language. ▷early 20th cent.: from Punjabi *lahandā*, literally 'western.'

La·hore /ləˈhôr/ the capital of Punjab province and second largest city in Pakistan, situated near the border with India; pop. 3,200,000.

Lahr /lär/, Bert (1895–1967) U.S. comedian and actor; born *Irving Lahrheim*. He starred in *The Wizard of Oz* (1939) as the Cowardly Lion. His other movies include *Ship Ahoy* (1942) and *The Night They Raided Minsky's* (1968).

Lahr·heim /ˈlär,hīm/, Irving, see LAHR.

Lai·bach /ˈlī,bäk; -,bäKH/ German name for LJUBLJANA.

la·ic /ˈlāik/ *formal* ▶*adj.* nonclerical; lay.
▶*n.* a layperson; a noncleric. ▷mid 16th cent.: from late Latin *laicus* (see LAY[2]). —**la·i·cal** /-ikəl/ *adj.* —**la·i·cal·ly** /-ik(ə)lē/ *adv.*

la·ic·i·ty /lāˈisətē/ ▶*n. formal* the principles, status, or influence of the laity.

la·i·cize /ˈlāə,sīz/ ▶*v.* [*trans.*] *formal* withdraw clerical character, control, or status from (someone or something); secularize: *when his priestly vocation no longer satisfied him, he had asked to be laicized.* —**la·i·cism** /-,sizəm/ *n.* —**la·i·ci·za·tion** /,lāəsəˈzāSHən/ *n.*

laid /lād/ ▶ past and past participle of LAY[1].

laid-back ▶*adj. informal* relaxed and easygoing: *a shaggy dog with an engaging, laid-back temperament.*

laid pa·per ▶*n.* paper that has a finely ribbed appearance. Compare with WOVE PAPER.

lain /lān/ ▸ past participle of LIE[1].

Laing /laNG/, R. D. (1927–89), Scottish psychiatrist; full name *Ronald David Laing*. He was known for his controversial views on insanity and, in particular, on schizophrenia.

lair /le(ə)r/ ▸*n.* a wild animal's resting place, esp. one that is well hidden. ■ a secret or private place in which a person seeks concealment or seclusion. ▷Old English *leger* 'resting place, bed,' of Germanic origin; related to Dutch *leger* 'bed, camp' and German *Lager* 'storehouse,' also to LIE[1]. Compare with LAAGER and LAGER.

laird /le(ə)rd/ ▸*n.* (in Scotland) a person who owns a large estate. ▷late Middle English: Scots form of LORD. —**laird·ship** /-,SHip/ *n.*

lair·y /ˈle(ə)rē/ ▸*adj.* (**lair·i·er, lair·i·est**) *Brit. informal* **1** cunning or conceited. **2** ostentatiously attractive; flashy: *the former Hollywood bad girl is putting her lairy Tinseltown past behind her.* **3** aggressive or rowdy: *a couple of lairy people pushed me around.* ▷mid 19th cent. (originally Cockney slang): alteration of *leery*. Sense 2 was originally Australian slang and dates from the early 20th cent.

lais·sez-faire /,lesā ˈfe(ə)r; ,lezā/ ▸*n.* a policy or attitude of letting things take their own course, without interfering. ■ *Economics* abstention by governments from interfering in the workings of the free market: [as *adj.*] *laissez-faire capitalism.* ▷French, literally 'allow to do.' —**lais·sez-faire·ism** /ˈfe(ə)r,izəm/ *n.*

lais·sez-pas·ser /,lesā paˈsā; ,lezā/ ▸*n.* a document allowing the holder to pass; a permit. ▷French, literally 'allow to pass.'

la·i·ty /ˈlāətē/ ▸*n.* [usu. treated as *pl.*] (**the laity**) lay people, as distinct from the clergy. ■ ordinary people, as distinct from professionals or experts. ▷late Middle English: from LAY[2] + -ITY.

La·ius /ˈlāəs/ *Greek Mythology* a king of Thebes, the father of Oedipus and husband of Jocasta.

La Jol·la /ləˈhoiə/ a resort section of northern San Diego in California, on the Pacific Ocean. A number of well-known research institutions are in the area.

lake[1] /lāk/ ▸*n.* a large body of water surrounded by land: *boys were swimming in the lake* | [in names] *Lake Superior.* ■ a pool of liquid: *the fish was served in a bright lake of spicy carrot sauce.* ▷late Old English (denoting a pond or pool), from Old French *lac*, from Latin *lacus* 'basin, pool, lake.' —**lake·let** /-lit/ *n.*

lake[2] ▸*n.* [often with *adj.*] an insoluble pigment made by combining a soluble organic dye and an insoluble mordant. ■ a purplish-red pigment of this kind, originally one made with lac, used in dyes, inks, and paints. ▷early 17th cent.: variant of LAC[1].

Lake Al·bert, Lake Bai·kal, etc. see ALBERT, LAKE; BAIKAL, LAKE, etc.

lake·bed /ˈlāk,bed/ ▸*n.* the floor or bottom of a lake.

Lake Charles /CHärlz/ an industrial port city in southwestern Louisiana, on the Calcasieu River; pop. 71,757.

Lake Dis·trict a region of lakes and mountains in northwestern England, long associated with English poets, such as Wordsworth, Southey, and Coleridge.

lake dwell·ing ▸*n.* a prehistoric hut built on piles driven into the bed or shore of a lake. —**lake dwell·er** *n.*

lake ef·fect snow ▸*n.* snow falling on the lee side of a lake, generated by cold dry air passing over warmer water, especially in the Great Lakes region.

lake·front /ˈlāk,frənt/ ▸*n.* the land along the edge of a lake.
▸*adj.* located along the edge of a lake.

Lake Ha·va·su Cit·y /ˈhavə,so͞o/ a city in western Arizona, on the eastern shore of Lake Havasu; pop. 41,938. It is home to the reconstructed 19th-century London Bridge.

Lake·hurst /ˈlākhərst/ a borough in east central New Jersey, associated with the 1937 explosion and crash of the dirigible *Hindenburg*.

Lake·land /ˈlāklənd/ a city in central Florida, noted for its resorts and its citrus industry; pop. 70,576.

Lake·land ter·ri·er ▸*n.* a small, stocky terrier originating in the Lake District of England.

Lake Lou·ise /lo͞oˈēz/ a resort in southwestern Alberta, in the Rocky Mountains, noted for the beauty of the lake that gives it its name.

Lake of the O·zarks a lake in central Missouri, a well-known recreational area created by a dam built in 1931.

Lake of the Woods a lake on the border between Canada and the U.S., west of the Great Lakes.

Lake Os·we·go /äsˈwē,gō/ a city in northwestern Oregon, a southern suburb of Portland; pop. 35,278.

Lake Plac·id /ˈplasid/ a resort village in the Adirondack Mountains, in northeastern New York, site of Olympic competition in 1932 and 1980; pop. 2,485.

Lake Po·ets (also **Lake School**) the poets Samuel Taylor Coleridge, Robert Southey, and William Wordsworth, who lived in and were inspired by the Lake District.

lak·er /ˈlākər/ ▸*n. informal* **1** a lake trout. **2** a ship constructed for carrying cargo on the Great Lakes.

lake·shore /ˈlāk,SHôr/ ▸*n.* another term for LAKEFRONT.

lake·side /ˈlāk,sīd/ ▸*n.* the land adjacent to a lake: *this road hugs the flat land by the lakeside* | [as *adj.*] *beautiful lakeside cabins.*

lake trout ▸*n.* any of a number of fishes of the salmon family that live in large lakes and are highly prized as a game fish and as food: • a North American char (*Salvelinus namaycush*, family Salmonidae). • a European brown trout of a large race.

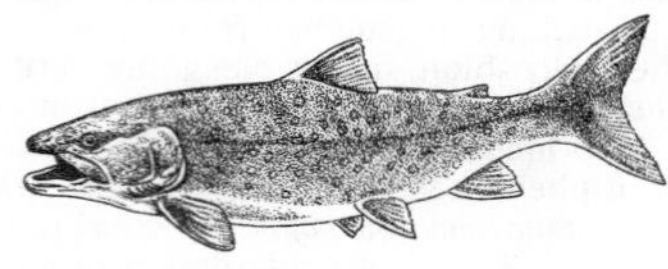

North American lake trout

Lake·wood /ˈlāk,wo͝od/ **1** a city in southwestern California, southeast of Los Angeles; pop. 73,557. **2** a city in north central Colorado, west of Denver; pop. 144,126. **3** a city in northeastern Ohio, west of Cleveland, on Lake Erie; pop. 56,646. **4** a city in northwestern Washington, a southwestern suburb of Tacoma; pop. 58,211.

lakh /läk; lak/ (also **lac**) ▸*n. Indian* a hundred thousand: *they fixed the price at five* **lakhs of** *rupees.* ▷via Hindi from Sanskrit *lakṣa*.

La·ko·ni·a variant spelling of LACONIA.

La·ko·ta /ləˈkōtə/ ▸*n.* (*pl.* same or **-tas**) **1** a member of an American Indian people of western South Dakota. Also called TETON SIOUX (see TETON). **2** the Siouan language of this people.
▸*adj.* of or relating to this people or their language. ▷the name in Lakota, related to the word DAKOTA[1].

lak·sa /ˈläksə/ ▸*n.* a Malaysian dish of Chinese origin, consisting of rice noodles served in a curry sauce or hot soup. ▷Malay.

Lak·shad·weep /ləkˈSHäd,wēp/ a Union Territory in India that consists of a group of islands off the Malabar Coast of southwestern India; pop. 51,680; capital, Kavaratti. The group consists of the Laccadive, Minicoy, and Amindivi Islands.

Laksh·mi /ˈləksHmē/ *Hinduism* the goddess of prosperity, consort of Vishnu. She assumes different forms (e.g., Radha, Sita) in order to accompany her husband in his various incarnations.

La La·gu·na /,lä läˈgo͞onə/ a university town and tourist center on Tenerife Island, in the Spanish Canary Islands; pop. 117,000.

la-la land /ˈlä ,lä/ ▸*n. informal* Los Angeles or Hollywood, esp. with regard to the lifestyle and attitudes of those living there or associated with it. ■ a fanciful state or dreamworld. ▷*la-la*, reduplication of LA (i.e., Los Angeles).

la·la·pa·loo·za ▸*n.* variant spelling of LOLLAPALOOZA.

La Le·che League /lə ,läˈCHā/ ▸*n.* an international nonprofit breastfeeding advocacy group. Local chapters hold meetings to provide breastfeeding information and support.

La·lique /läˈlēk/, René (1860–1945), French jeweler, known for his art nouveau brooches and combs and for his decorative glassware.

Lal·lans /ˈlalənz/ ▸*n.* a distinctive Scottish literary form of English, based on standard older Scots.
▸*adj.* of, in, or relating to this language. ▷early 18th cent. (also, as an adjective, *Lallan*): Scots variant of *Lowlands*, with reference to a central Lowlands dialect.

Lal·ly col·umn /ˈlälē/ ▸*n. trademark* a tubular steel column filled with concrete and used as a supporting member in a building.

lal·ly·gag ▸*v.* variant spelling of LOLLYGAG.

lam[1] /lam/ ▸*v.* (**lammed, lam·ming**) [*trans.*] *informal* hit (someone) hard: *I'll come over and lam you in the mouth in a minute.* ■ [*intrans.*] (**lam into**) attack: *they surged up and down in their riot gear, lamming into anyone in their path.* ▷late 16th cent.: perhaps of Scandinavian origin and related to Norwegian and Danish *lamme* 'paralyze.'

lam[2] *informal* ▸*n.* (in phrase **on the lam**) in flight, esp. from the police: *he* **went on the lam** *and is living under a false name.*
▸*v.* (**lammed, lam·ming**) [*intrans.*] escape; flee. ▷late 19th cent.: from LAM[1].

Lam. ▸*abbr. Bible* Lamentations.

la·ma /ˈlämə/ ▸*n.* **1** an honorific title applied to a spiritual leader in Tibetan Buddhism, whether a reincarnate lama (such as the Dalai Lama) or one who has earned the title in life. **2** a Tibetan or Mongolian Buddhist monk. ▷mid 17th cent.: from Tibetan *blama* (the initial *b* being silent), literally 'superior one.'

La·ma·ism /ˈlämə,izəm/ ▸*n.* the system of doctrine and observances inculcated and maintained by lamas; Tibetan Buddhism. —**La·ma·ist** *n.* & *adj.* —**La·ma·is·tic** /,läməˈistik/ *adj.*

La·mar[1] /ləˈmär/, Joseph Rucker (1857–1916) U.S. Supreme Court associate justice 1911–16. A former associate justice in Georgia's supreme court, he was appointed to the U.S. Supreme Court by President Taft.

La·mar[2], Lucius Quintus Cincinnatus (1825–93) U.S. Supreme Court associate justice 1888–93. A U.S. senator 1877–85 and secretary of the interior 1885–88, he was appointed to the Court by President Cleveland. During the Civil War, he served the Confederacy in various capacities.

La·marck /läˈmärk/, Jean Baptiste de (1744–1829), French naturalist. He was an early proponent of organic evolution, although his theory is not widely accepted today. —**La·marck·i·an** /ləˈmärkēən/ *n.* & *adj.* —**La·marck·ism** /ləˈmär,kizəm/ *n.*

La·mar·tine /lämärˈtēn/, Alphonse Marie Louis de (1790–1869), French poet, statesman, and historian. He served as minister of foreign affairs in the provisional government following the Revolution of 1848.

la·ma·ser·y /ˈlämə,serē/ ▸*n.* (*pl.* **-ser·ies**) a monastery of lamas.

La·maze /ləˈmäz/ ▸*adj.* [*attrib.*] relating to a method of childbirth involving exercises and breathing control to give pain relief without drugs. ▷1950s: from the name of Fernand *Lamaze* (1891–1957), French physician.

Lamb[1] /lam/, Charles (1775–1834), English essayist and critic. The author of *Essays of Elia* (1823), he wrote *Tales from Shakespeare* (1807) with his sister Mary (1764–1847).

Lamb[2], Wally (1950–) U.S. writer and teacher. His works include *She's Come Undone* (1992) and *I Know This Much Is True* (1998).

lamb /lam/ ▸*n.* a young sheep. ■ the flesh of such young sheep as food. ■ *figurative* used as the epitome of meekness, gentleness, or innocence: *to her amazement, he accepted her decision like a lamb.* ■ used to describe or address someone regarded with affection or pity, esp. a young child: *the poor lamb is very upset.* ■ (**the Lamb**) short for LAMB OF GOD.
▸*v.* [*intrans.*] (of a ewe) give birth to lambs. ■ [*trans.*] tend (ewes) at lambing time. ▷Old English, of Germanic origin; related to Dutch *lam* and German *Lamm*. —**lamb·er** *n.* —**lamb·like** /-,līk/ *adj.*
▸PHRASE □ **like a lamb to the slaughter** as a helpless victim.

lam·ba·da /lamˈbädə/ ▸*n.* a fast, erotic Brazilian dance that couples perform with their stomachs touching. ▷1980s: Portuguese, literally 'a beating,' from *lambar* 'to beat.'

lam·baste /lamˈbäst; -ˈbast/ (also **lam·bast** /-ˈbast/) ▸*v.* [*trans.*] criticize (someone or something) harshly: *they lambasted the report as a gross distortion of the truth.* ▷mid 17th cent. (in the sense 'beat, thrash'): from LAM[1] + BASTE[3]. The current sense dates from the late 19th cent.

lamb·da /ˈlamdə/ ▸*n.* the eleventh letter of the Greek alphabet (Λ, λ), transliterated as 'l.' ■ (**Lambda**) [followed by Latin genitive] *Astronomy* the eleventh star in a constellation: *Lambda Tauri.* ■ *Biology* a type of bacteriophage virus used in genetic research: [as *adj.*] *lambda phage.* ■ *Anatomy* the point at the back of the skull where the parietal bones and the occipital bone meet. ■ [as *adj.*] *Biochemistry* denoting one of the two types of light polypeptide chain present in all immunoglobulin molecules (the other being kappa).
▸*symbol* ■ (λ) wavelength. ■ (λ) *Astronomy* celestial longitude.

lamb·doid /ˈlam,doid/ ▸*adj.* resembling the Greek letter lambda in form. ■ *Anatomy* of or denoting the suture near the back of the skull that connects the parietal bones with the occipital. —**lamb·doi·dal** /lamˈdoidl/ *adj.*

lam·bent /ˈlambənt/ ▸*adj.* *poetic/literary* (of light or fire) glowing, gleaming, or flickering with a soft radiance: *the magical, lambent light of the north.* ■ (of wit, humor, etc.) lightly brilliant: *a touch of the lambent bitterness that sometimes surfaced in him.* ▷mid 17th cent.: from Latin *lambent-* 'licking,' from the verb *lambere.* **—lam·ben·cy** /-bənsē/ *n.* **—lam·bent·ly** *adv.*

Lam·ba·ré·né /ˌlämbəˈrānā/ a town in west central Gabon, on the Ogooué River, southeast of Libreville, a longtime base of missionary doctor Albert Schweitzer; pop. 15,000.

lam·bert /ˈlambərt/ ▸*n.* a former unit of luminance, equal to the emission or reflection of one lumen per square centimeter. ▷early 20th cent.: named after Johann H. *Lambert* (1728–77), German physicist.

Lam·beth /ˈlambəTH/ a borough of inner London, on the south bank of the Thames River; pop. 220,000.

Lam·beth Con·fer·ence ▸*n.* an assembly of bishops from the Anglican Communion, usually held every ten years (since 1867) at Lambeth Palace and presided over by the Archbishop of Canterbury.

Lam·beth Pal·ace a palace in the London borough of Lambeth, the residence of the Archbishop of Canterbury since 1197.

lamb·ing /ˈlamiNG/ ▸*n.* the birth of lambs on a farm: *lambing begins in mid-January.*

lamb·kin /ˈlamkin/ ▸*n.* a small or young lamb. ■ used as a term of endearment for a young child.

Lamb of God ▸*n.* a title of Jesus (see John 1:29). Compare with AGNUS DEI.

lam·bre·quin /ˈlambərkin; -brə-/ ▸*n.* **1** a short piece of decorative drapery hung over the top of a door or window or draped from a shelf or mantelpiece. **2** a piece of cloth covering the back of a medieval knight's helmet, represented in heraldry as the mantling. ▷early 18th cent. (sense 2): from French, from the Dutch diminutive of *lamper* 'veil.'

Lam·bru·sco /lamˈbrōōskō; -ˈbrōōs-/ ▸*n.* a variety of wine grape grown in the Emilia-Romagna region of northern Italy. ■ a sparkling red wine made from this grape. ■ a red or white wine of a similar kind produced elsewhere. ▷Italian, literally 'grape of the wild vine.'

lamb's ears ▸*plural n.* [usu. treated as *sing.*] a southwestern Asian plant of the mint family that has gray-green woolly leaves and is cultivated as an ornamental, particularly for ground cover. • *Stachys byzantina,* family Labiatae.

lamb·skin /ˈlamˌskin/ ▸*n.* prepared skin from a lamb, either with the wool on or as leather: [as *adj.*] *lambskin gloves.*

lamb's let·tuce ▸*n.* another term for CORN SALAD.

lamb's-quar·ters ▸*n.* a herbaceous plant with mealy, edible leaves, often considered to be a weed. Also called PIGWEED. • *Chenopodium album,* family Chenopodiaceae.

lamb's tongue ▸*n.* another term for LAMB'S EARS.

lambs·wool /ˈlamzˌwŏŏl/ ▸*n.* fine wool from a young sheep, used to make knitted garments, blankets, etc., with a soft texture.

lame /lām/ ▸*adj.* **1** (of a person or animal) unable to walk normally because of an injury or illness affecting the leg or foot: *his horse* **went lame**. ■ (of a leg or foot) affected in this way. **2** (of an explanation or excuse) unconvincingly feeble: *it was a lame statement and there was no excusing his behavior.* ■ (of something intended to be entertaining) uninspiring and dull. ■ (of a person) naive or inept, esp. socially: *anyone who doesn't know that is obviously lame.* ■ (of verse or metrical feet) halting; metrically defective.

▸*v.* [*trans.*] make (a person or animal) lame: *somebody lamed him with a stone.* ▷Old English *lama,* of Germanic origin, related to Dutch *lam* and German *lahm.* **—lame·ly** *adv.* **—lame·ness** *n.*

la·mé /laˈmā; lä-/ ▸*n.* fabric with interwoven gold or silver threads.

▸*adj.* (of fabric or a garment) having such threads. ▷1920s: French, from Latin *lamina* (see LAMINA).

lame·brain /ˈlāmˌbrān/ ▸*n.* *informal* a stupid person. **—lame·brained** *adj.*

lame duck ▸*n.* an official (esp. the president) in the final period of office, after the election of a successor: *as a lame duck, the president had nothing to lose by approving the deal* | [as *adj.*] *a lame-duck governor.* ■ an ineffectual or unsuccessful person or thing.

la·mel·la /ləˈmelə/ ▸*n.* (*pl.* **-mel·lae** /-ˈmelē; -ˈmelī/) a thin layer, membrane, scale, or platelike tissue or part, esp. in bone tissue. ■ *Botany* a membranous fold in a chloroplast. ▷late 17th cent.: from Latin, diminutive of *lamina* 'thin plate.' **—la·mel·lar** /-ˈmelər/ *adj.* **—la·mel·late** /ˈlaməlit; ləˈmelit; ˈlaməˌlāt/ *adj.* **—la·mel·li·form** /-ˈmeləˌfôrm/ *adj.* **—la·mel·lose** /-ˌlōs; -ˌlōz/ *adj.*

la·mel·li·branch /ləˈmeləˌbraNGk/ ▸*n.* another term for BIVALVE. ▷mid 19th cent.: from modern Latin *Lamellibranchia* (former class name), from Latin *lamella* (diminutive of *lamina* 'thin plate') + Greek *brankhia* 'gills.'

la·mel·li·corn /ləˈmeləˌkôrn/ ▸*n.* former term for SCARABAEOID. ▷mid 19th cent.: from modern Latin *Lamellicornia* (former taxonomic name), from Latin *lamella* 'thin plate' + *cornu* 'horn.'

la·mel·li·po·di·um /ləˌmeləˈpōdēəm/ ▸*n.* (*pl.* **-di·a** /-dēə/) *Zoology* a flattened extension of a cell, by which it moves over or adheres to a surface. ▷1970s: from LAMELLA, on the pattern of *pseudopodium.* **—la·mel·li·po·di·al** /-dēəl/ *adj.*

la·ment /ləˈment/ ▸*n.* a passionate expression of grief or sorrow: *his mother's night-long laments for his father* | *a song full of lament and sorrow.* ■ a song, piece of music, or poem expressing such emotions. ■ an expression of regret or disappointment; a complaint: *there were constant laments about the conditions of employment.*

▸*v.* [*trans.*] mourn (a person's loss or death): *he was lamenting the death of his infant daughter.* See note at MOURN. ■ [*intrans.*] (**lament for/over**) express one's deep grief about. ■ [*reporting verb*] express regret or disappointment over something considered unsatisfactory, unreasonable, or unfair: [*trans.*] *she lamented the lack of shops in the town* | [with *direct speech*] *Thomas Jefferson later lamented, "Heaven remained silent."* ▷late Middle English (as a verb): from French *lamenter* or Latin *lamentari,* from *lamenta* (plural) 'weeping, wailing.' **—lam·en·ta·tion** /ˌlamənˈtāSHən/ *n.* **—la·ment·er** *n.*

lam·en·ta·ble /ˈlaməntəbəl; ləˈmentəbəl/ ▸*adj.* **1** (of circumstances or conditions) deplorably bad or unsatisfactory: *the facilities provided were lamentable, not merely basic but squalid.* ■ (of an event, action, or attitude) unfortunate; regrettable: *her open prejudice showed lamentable immaturity.* **2** *archaic* full of or expressing sorrow or grief. ▷late Middle English (in the sense 'mournful,' also 'pitiable, regrettable'): from Old French, or from Latin *lamentabilis,* from the verb *lamentari* (see LAMENT). **—la·men·ta·bly** /-əblē/ *adv.* [as *submodifier*] *she was lamentably ignorant.*

Lam·en·ta·tions /ˌlamənˈtāSHənz/ (in full **the Lamentations of Jeremiah**) a book of the Bible telling of the desolation of Judah after the fall of Jerusalem in 586 BC.

la·ment·ed /ləˈmentid/ ▸*adj.* (often **the late lamented**) a conventional way of describing someone who has died or something that has been lost or that has ceased to exist: *the late and much lamented Leonard Bernstein.*

la·mi·a /ˈlāmēə/ ▸*n.* (*pl.* **-mi·as** or **-mi·ae** /-mēˌē/) a mythical monster, with the body of a woman or with the head and breasts of a woman and the body of a snake, said to prey on human beings and suck the blood of children. ▷via Latin from Greek, denoting a carnivorous fish or mythical monster.

lam·i·na /ˈlamənə/ ▸*n.* (*pl.* **-nae** /-ˌnē; -ˌnī/) *technical* a thin layer, plate, or scale of sedimentary rock, organic tissue, or other material. ▷mid 17th cent.: from Latin. **—lam·i·nose** /-ˌnōs; -ˌnōz/ *adj.*

lam·i·nal /ˈlamənl/ ▸*adj.* *Phonetics* (of a consonant) formed with the blade of the tongue touching the alveolar ridge (e.g., *n, s, t*).

▸*n.* *Phonetics* a laminal sound. ▷1950s: from LAMINA + -AL.

lam·i·na pro·pri·a /ˈprōprēə/ ▸*n.* technical term for BASEMENT MEMBRANE.

lam·i·nar /ˈlamənər/ ▸*adj.* **1** consisting of laminae. **2** *Physics* (of a flow) taking place along constant streamlines; not turbulent.

lam·i·nate ▸*v.* /ˈlaməˌnāt/ [*trans.*] [often as *adj.*] (**laminated**) overlay (a flat surface, esp. paper) with a layer of plastic or some other protective material. ■ manufacture by placing layer on layer. ■ split into layers or leaves. ■ beat or roll (metal) into thin plates.

▸*n.* /-nit; -ˌnāt/ a laminated structure or material, esp. one made of layers fixed together to form a hard, flat, or flexible material.

▸*adj.* /-nit; -ˌnāt/ in the form of a lamina or laminae. ▷mid 17th cent.: from LAMINA + -ATE[2]. **—lam·i·na·ble** /-nəbəl/ *adj.* **—lam·i·na·tion** /ˌlaməˈnāSHən/ *n.* **—lam·i·na·tor** /-ˌnātər/ *n.*

lam·i·nec·to·my /ˌlaməˈnektəmē/ ▸*n.* (*pl.* **-mies**) a surgical operation to remove the back of one or more vertebrae, usually to give access to the spinal cord or to relieve pressure on nerves.

lam·i·nin /ˈlamənin/ ▸*n.* *Biochemistry* a fibrous protein present in the basal lamina of the epithelia.

lam·i·ni·tis /ˌlaməˈnītis/ ▸*n.* inflammation of sensitive layers of tissue (laminae) inside the hoof in horses and other animals. It is particularly prevalent in ponies feeding on rich spring grass and can cause extreme lameness.

Lam·mas /ˈlaməs/ (also **Lammas Day**) ▸*n.* the first day of August, formerly observed in Britain as a harvest festival, during which bread baked from the first crop of wheat was blessed. ▷Old English *hlāfmæsse* (see LOAF[1], MASS), later interpreted as if it were from LAMB + MASS.

lam·mer·gei·er /ˈlamərˌgīər/ (also **lam·mer·gey·er**) ▸*n.* a large Old World vulture of mountainous country, with a wingspan of 10 feet (3 m) and dark beardlike feathers, noted for its habit of dropping bones from a height to break them. Also called BEARDED VULTURE. • *Gypaetus barbatus,* family Accipitridae. ▷early 19th cent.: from German *Lämmergeier,* from *Lämmer* (plural of *Lamm* 'lamb') + *Geier* 'vulture.'

lamp /lamp/ ▸*n.* a device for giving light, either one consisting of an electric bulb together with its holder and shade or cover, or one burning gas or a liquid fuel and consisting of a wick or mantle and a glass shade: *a table lamp.* ■ an electrical device producing ultraviolet, infrared, or other radiation, used for therapeutic purposes. ■ *poetic/literary* a source of spiritual or intellectual inspiration. ▷Middle English: via Old French from late Latin *lampada,* from Latin *lampas, lampad-* 'torch,' from Greek. **—lamp·er** *n.* **—lamp·less** *adj.*

lam·pas[1] /ˈlampəs/ (also **lam·pers** /-pərz/) ▸*n.* a condition of horses, in which there is swelling of the fleshy lining of the roof of the mouth behind the front teeth. ▷early 16th cent.: from French, probably via French dialect from the Germanic base of the verb LAP[3].

lam·pas[2] ▸*n.* a patterned drapery and upholstery fabric similar to brocade, made of silk, cotton, or rayon, originally imitating textiles from India and later imported from China, Iran, and France. ▷mid 19th cent.: from French *lampas, lampasse,* of unknown origin.

lamp·black /ˈlampˌblak/ ▸*n.* a black pigment made from soot.

lamp chim·ney ▸*n.* a glass cylinder positioned over the wick of an oil lamp or candlestick to encircle and provide a draft for the flame.

lamp·light /ˈlampˌlīt/ ▸*n.* the light cast from a lamp: *he was working in the stables by lamplight.* **—lamp·lit** /-ˌlit/ *adj.*

lamp·light·er /ˈlampˌlītər/ ▸*n.* *historical* a person employed to light street gaslights by hand.

lam·poon /lamˈpōōn/ ▸*v.* [*trans.*] publicly criticize (someone or something) by using ridicule, irony, or sarcasm: *the senator made himself famous as a pinch-penny watchdog of public spending, lampooning dubious federal projects.*

▸*n.* a speech or text criticizing someone or something in this way: *does this sound like a lampoon of student life?* See note at CARICATURE. ▷mid 17th cent.: from French *lampon,* said to be from *lampons* 'let us drink' (used as a refrain), from *lamper* 'gulp down,' nasalized form of *laper* 'to lap (liquid).' **—lam·poon·er** *n.* **—lam·poon·ist** /-ist/ *n.*

lamp·post /ˈlam(p)ˌpōst/ ▸*n.* a tall pole with a light at the top; a street light.

lam·prey /ˈlamprē/ ▸*n.* (*pl.* **-preys**) an eellike aquatic jawless vertebrate that has a sucker mouth with horny teeth and a rasping tongue. The adult is often parasitic, attaching itself to other fish and sucking their blood. • Family Petromyzonidae: several genera and species. ▷Middle English: from Old French *lampreie,* from medieval Latin *lampreda,* probably from Latin *lambere* 'to lick' + *petra* 'stone' (because the lamprey attaches itself to stones by its mouth).

lam·pro·phyre /ˈlamprəˌfīr/ ▸*n.* *Geology* a porphyritic igneous rock consisting of a fine-grained feldspathic groundmass with phenocrysts chiefly of biotite. ▷late 19th cent.: from Greek *lampros* 'bright, shining' + *porphureos* 'purple.'

lamp·shade /ˈlampˌSHād/ ▸*n.* a cover for a lamp, used to soften or direct its light.

lamp shell (also **lamp·shell**) ▸*n.* a marine invertebrate that superficially resembles a bivalve mollusk but has two or more arms of ciliated tentacles

L

(lophophores) that are extended for filter feeding. Lamp shells are common as fossils. Also called **BRACHIOPOD**. • Phylum Brachiopoda: numerous groups in the Paleozoic era but few surviving to the present day. ▷mid 19th cent.: from its resemblance to an ancient oil lamp.

LAN /lan/ ▸*abbr.* local area network.

La·nai /lə'nī/ an island in Hawaii, west of Maui, primarily agricultural, with some resorts.

la·na·i /lə'näē; lə'nī/ ▸*n.* (*pl.* **-na·is**) a porch or veranda. ▷Hawaiian.

Lan·cas·ter[1] /'laNG,kastər; -kəstər/ **1** a city in western England, north of Liverpool, on the estuary of the Lune River; pop. 44,000. **2** a city in southwestern California, northeast of Los Angeles, on the edge of the Mojave Desert; pop. 97,291. **3** a city in southeastern Pennsylvania, primarily a commercial center for the Pennsylvania Dutch Country; pop. 56,348.

Lan·cas·ter[2] /'lan,kastər; 'laNG-/, Burt (1913–94), U.S. movie actor; full name *Burton Stephen Lancaster*. He made his debut in *The Killers* (1946) and was often cast in "tough guy" roles. He starred in movies such as *From Here to Eternity* (1953); *Elmer Gantry* (1960), for which he won an Academy Award; and *Field of Dreams* (1989).

Lan·cas·ter, House of the English royal house descended from John of Gaunt, Duke of Lancaster, that ruled England from 1399 (Henry IV) until 1461 (the deposition of Henry VI) and again on Henry VI's brief restoration in 1470–71. With the red rose as its emblem, it fought the Wars of the Roses with the House of York; Lancaster's descendants, the Tudors, eventually prevailed through Henry VII's accession to the throne in 1485.

Lan·cas·ter House A·gree·ment an agreement that brought about the establishment of the independent state of Zimbabwe, reached in September 1979 at Lancaster House in London.

Lan·cas·tri·an /laNG'kastrēən/ ▸*n.* **1** a native of Lancashire or Lancaster in England. **2** *historical* a follower of the British House of Lancaster, esp. during the Wars of the Roses.
▸*adj.* of or relating to Lancashire or Lancaster, or the House of Lancaster.

lance /lans/ ▸*n. historical* a long weapon for thrusting, having a wooden shaft and a pointed steel head, used by a horseman in charging. ■ a similar weapon used in hunting fish or whales. ■ another term for **LANCER** (sense 1). ■ [usu. with *adj.*] a metal pipe supplying a jet of oxygen to a furnace or to a hot flame for cutting. ■ a rigid tube at the end of a hose for pumping or spraying liquid.
▸*v.* [*trans.*] *Medicine* prick or cut open with a lancet or other sharp instrument: *abscesses should not be lanced until there is a soft spot in the center* | *figurative the governor made it one of his priorities to* **lance the boil** *of corruption.* ■ pierce with or as if with a lance: *the teenager had been lanced by a wooden splinter* [*intrans.*] *figurative his eyes lanced right through her.* ■ [*intrans.*] move suddenly and quickly: *pain lanced through her.* ■ [*trans.*] *poetic/literary* fling; launch: *he affirms to have lanced darts at the sun.* ▷Middle English: from Old French *lance* (noun), *lancier* (verb), from Latin *lancea* (noun).

lance cor·po·ral ▸*n.* an enlisted person in the U.S. Marine Corps ranking above private first class and below corporal. ▷late 18th cent.: on the analogy of obsolete *lancepesade*, the lowest grade of noncommissioned officer, based on Italian *lancia spezzata* 'broken lance.'

lance·let /'lanslit/ ▸*n.* a small elongated marine invertebrate that resembles a fish but lacks jaws and obvious sense organs. Lancelets possess a notochord and are among the most primitive chordates. • Subphylum Cephalochordata, phylum Chordata: several species, including amphioxus. ▷mid 19th cent.: from the noun **LANCE** (because of its long narrow form) + **-LET**.

Lan·ce·lot /'lansə,lät; 'län-; -s(ə)lət/ (also **Laun·ce·lot**) (in Arthurian legend) the most famous of Arthur's knights, lover of Queen Guinevere and father of Galahad.

lan·ce·o·late /'lansēəlit; -,lāt/ ▸*adj. technical* shaped like the head of a lance; of a narrow oval shape tapering to a point at each end: *the leaves are lanceolate.* ▷mid 18th cent.: from late Latin *lanceolatus*, from Latin *lanceola*, diminutive of *lancea* 'a lance.'

lanc·er /'lansər/ ▸*n.* **1** *historical* a soldier of a cavalry regiment armed with lances. **2** (**lancers**) [treated as *sing.*] a quadrille for eight or sixteen pairs. ▷late 16th cent.: from French *lancier*, from *lance* 'a lance.'

lan·cet /'lansit/ ▸*n.* **1** a small, broad, two-edged surgical knife or blade with a sharp point. **2** a lancet arch or window. ■ [as *adj.*] shaped like a lancet arch: *a lancet clock.* ▷late Middle English (also denoting a small lance): from Old French *lancette*, diminutive of *lance* 'a lance.' **—lan·cet·ed** *adj.*

lan·cet arch ▸*n.* an arch with an acutely pointed head.

lan·cet win·dow ▸*n.* a high and narrow window with an acutely pointed head.

lance·wood /'lans,wo͝od/ ▸*n.* any of a number of hardwood trees with tough elastic timber, in particular: • a Caribbean tree (*Oxandra lanceolata*, family Annonaceae). • a New Zealand tree (*Pseudopanax crassifolius*, family Araliaceae). ■ the tough, elastic timber of any of these trees, used esp. where flexibility is required, such as in carriage shafts and fishing rods.

Lan·chow /,län'jō; 'län'cHou/ variant of **LANZHOU**.

Land[1] /länt; länd/ ▸*n.* (*pl.* **Länd·er** /'lendər/) in Germany or Austria, a province. ▷German, literally 'land.'

Land[2] /land/, Edwin (1909–91) U.S. inventor. He developed a new polarizing filter with wide use in optical instruments. In 1937, he founded the Polaroid Corporation and introduced the first Polaroid Land camera in 1947.

land /land/ ▸*n.* **1** the part of the earth's surface that is not covered by water, as opposed to the sea or the air: *the reptiles lay their eggs on land* | *after four weeks at sea we sighted land.* ■ [as *adj.*] living or traveling on land rather than in water or the air: *a land mammal.* ■ an expanse of land; an area of ground, esp. in terms of its ownership or use: *the land north of the village.* | (**lands**) *the Indians were wiped out as gold prospectors invaded their lands.* ■ (**the land**) ground or soil used as a basis for agriculture: *my family had worked the land for many years.* ■ property in the form of land: *she's trespassing on my land!* **2** a country: *the valley is one of the most beautiful in the land* | *the lands of the Middle East* | *America, the land of political equality.* ■ *figurative* a realm or domain: *you are living in a fantasy land.* **3** the space between the rifling grooves in a gun.
▸*v.* **1** [*trans.*] put ashore: *the lifeboat landed the survivors safely ashore.* ■ [*intrans.*] go ashore; disembark: *the marines landed at a small fishing jetty.* ■ unload (goods) from a ship: *the fishing boats landed their catch at the port.* ■ bring (a fish) to land, esp. with a net or hook: *I landed a scrappy three-pound walleye.* ■ *informal* succeed in obtaining or achieving (something desirable), esp. in the face of strong competition: *she landed the starring role in a new film.* **2** [*intrans.*] come down through the air and alight on the ground: *planes landing at the rate of two a minute.* ■ [*trans.*] bring (an aircraft or spacecraft) to the ground or the surface of water, esp. in a controlled way: *the copilot landed the plane.* ■ reach the ground after falling or jumping: *he leaped over the fence and landed nimbly on his feet.* ■ [with *adverbial of place*] (of an object) come to rest after falling or being thrown: *the plate landed in her lap.* ■ *informal* (of something unpleasant or unexpected) arrive suddenly: *there seemed to be more problems than ever landing on her desk this week.* **3** [*trans.*] (**land someone in**) *informal* cause someone to be in (a difficult or unwelcome situation): *his exploits always landed him in trouble.* ■ (**land someone with**) inflict (an unwelcome task or a difficult situation) on someone: *the mistake landed the company with a massive bill.* **4** [*trans.*] *informal* inflict (a blow) on someone: *I won the fight without landing a single punch* | [with *two objs.*] *I landed him one.*
▸*phrasal v.* □ **land up** reach a place or destination; end up: *I landed up in prison.* ▷Old English, of Germanic origin; related to Dutch *land* and German *Land*.
▸*PHRASES* □ **how the land lies** what the state of affairs is: *let's keep it to ourselves until we see how the land lies.* □ **in the land of the living** *humorous* alive or awake. □ **the land of Nod** *humorous* a state of sleep. [punningly, with biblical allusion to the place name *Nod* (Gen. 4:16).] □ **land on one's feet** have good luck or success: *after some ups and downs, he has finally landed on his feet.* □ **live off the land** live on whatever food one can obtain by hunting, gathering, or subsistence farming.

-land /land; lənd/ ▸*comb. form* forming nouns denoting a particular sphere of activity or group of people: *the blunt, charmless climate of technoland.*

Lan·dau /'lan,dou; lən'dou/, Lev (Davidovich) (1908–68), Soviet theoretical physicist. Active in many fields, Landau was noted for his work on the superfluidity and thermal conductivity of liquid helium. Nobel Prize for Physics (1962).

lan·dau /'lan,dou/ ▸*n.* a horse-drawn four-wheeled enclosed carriage with a removable front cover and a back cover that can be raised and lowered. ▷mid 18th cent.: named after *Landau*, near Karlsruhe in Germany, where it was first made.

landau

lan·dau·let /,landô'let/ ▸*n.* a small landau. ■ *chiefly historical* a car with a folding hood over the rear seats.

land bank ▸*n.* **1** a bank whose main function is to provide loans for land purchase, esp. by farmers. **2** a large body of land held by a public or private organization for future development or disposal.

land breeze ▸*n.* a breeze blowing toward the sea from the land, esp. at night, owing to the relative warmth of the sea. Compare with **SEA BREEZE**.

land bridge ▸*n.* a connection between two landmasses, esp. a prehistoric one that allowed humans and animals to colonize new territory before being cut off by the sea, as across the Bering Strait and the English Channel.

land crab ▸*n.* a crab that lives in burrows inland and migrates in large numbers to the sea to breed. • Family Gecarcinidae: *Cardisoma* and other genera.

land·ed /'landid/ ▸*adj.* [*attrib.*] owning much land, esp. through inheritance: *the landed aristocracy.* ■ consisting of, including, or relating to such land: *the decline of landed estates* | *landed income.*

Län·der /'lendər/ ▸ plural form of **LAND**[1].

land·er /'landər/ ▸*n.* a spacecraft designed to land on the surface of a planet or moon: *a lunar lander.* Compare with **ORBITER**.

Lan·ders /'landərz/, Ann (1918–2002), U.S. journalist; born Esther Pauline Friedman. Author of the "Ann Landers" advice column from 1955, she competed with her twin sister, Abigail Van Buren, who wrote a similar column.

land·fall /'lan(d),fôl/ ▸*n.* **1** an arrival at land on a sea or air journey. **2** a collapse of a mass of land, esp. one that blocks a route. **3** the contact of a hurricane with a landmass: *Javier* **made landfall** *at 10:46 this morning.* **—land·fall·ing** *adj.*

land·fill /'lan(d),fil/ ▸*n.* a place to dispose of refuse and other waste material by burying it and covering it over with soil, esp. as a method of filling in or extending usable land. ■ waste material used to reclaim ground in this way. ■ an area filled in by this process.
▸*v.* [*trans.*] bury in a landfill: *the Florida school intends to landfill its old computers* [as *adj.*] *landfilled waste.*

land·form /'lan(d),fôrm/ ▸*n.* a natural feature of the earth's surface.

land-grab·ber ▸*n.* a person who seizes and possesses land in an unfair or illegal manner. **—land-grab** *n.* **—land-grab·bing** *n.*

land grant ▸*n.* a grant of public land, esp. to an institution, organization, or to particular groups of people.

land·grave /'lan(d),grāv/ ▸*n. historical* a count having jurisdiction over a territory. ■ the title of certain German princes. ▷late Middle English: from Middle Low German, from *land* 'land' + *grave* 'count' (used as a title).

land·hold·er /'land,hōldər/ ▸*n.* a person who owns land, esp. one who either makes a living from it or rents it out to others.

land·hold·ing /'land,hōldiNG/ ▸*n.* a piece of land owned or rented. ■ possession or rental of land.

land·ing /'landiNG/ ▸*n.* **1** an instance of coming or bringing something to land, either from the air or from water: *we made a perfect landing at the airstrip.* ■ the action or process of doing this: *the landing of men on the moon.* ■ (also **landing place**) a place where people and goods can be landed from a boat or ship: *the ferry landing.* **2** a level area at the top of a staircase or between one flight of stairs and another.

land·ing craft ▸*n.* a boat specially designed for putting troops and military equipment ashore on a beach.

land·ing gear ▸*n.* the undercarriage of an aircraft, including the wheels or pontoons on which it rests while not in the air.

L

land·ing light ▸*n.* (usu. **landing lights**) a bright lamp on an aircraft that is switched on before landing. ■ a light of a kind that is arranged in rows along each side of an aircraft runway.

land·ing net ▸*n.* a net for landing a large fish that has been hooked.

land·ing pad ▸*n.* a small area designed for helicopters to land on and take off from.

land·ing stage ▸*n.* a platform, typically a floating one, onto which passengers from a boat or ship disembark or cargo is unloaded.

land·ing strip ▸*n.* an airstrip.

land·la·dy /ˈlan(d)ˌlādē/ ▸*n.* (*pl.* **-dies**) a woman who rents land, a building, or an apartment to a tenant. ■ a woman who owns or runs a boardinghouse, inn, or similar establishment.

länd·ler /ˈlendlər/ ▸*n.* an Austrian folk dance in triple time, a precursor of the waltz. ▷late 19th cent.: German, from *Landl* 'Upper Austria.'

land·less /ˈlan(d)lis/ ▸*adj.* (esp. of an agricultural worker) owning no land. —**land·less·ness** *n.*

land·line /ˈlan(d)ˌlīn/ ▸*n.* a conventional telecommunications connection by cable laid across land, typically either on poles or buried underground.

land·locked /ˈlan(d)ˌläkt/ ▸*adj.* (esp. of a country) almost or entirely surrounded by land; having no coastline or seaport: *a midget state landlocked in the mountains.* ■ (of a lake) enclosed by land and having no navigable route to the sea. ■ (of a fish, esp. a North American salmon) cut off from the sea in the past and now confined to fresh water.

land·lord /ˈlan(d)ˌlôrd/ ▸*n.* a person, esp. a man, who rents land, a building, or an apartment to a tenant. ■ a person who owns or runs a boardinghouse, inn, or similar establishment.

land·lord·ism /ˈlan(d)lôrˌdizəm/ ▸*n.* the system whereby land (or property) is owned by landlords to whom tenants pay a fixed rent.

land·lub·ber /ˈlan(d)ˌləbər/ ▸*n. informal* a person unfamiliar with the sea or sailing.

land·mark /ˈlan(d)ˌmärk/ ▸*n.* **1** an object or feature of a landscape or town that is easily seen and recognized from a distance, esp. one that enables someone to establish their location: *the spire was once a landmark for ships sailing up the river.* ■ *historical* the boundary of an area of land, or an object marking this. **2** an event, discovery, or change marking an important stage or turning point in something: *the birth of a child is an important landmark in the lives of all concerned* | [as *adj.*] *a landmark decision.*

land·mass /ˈlan(d)ˌmas/ (also **land mass**) ▸*n.* a continent or other large body of land.

land mine ▸*n.* an explosive mine laid on or just under the surface of the ground.

Land of En·chant·ment a nickname for the state of **New Mexico**.

land of·fice ▸*n.* a government office recording dealings in public land.
▸*PHRASE* □ **do a land-office business** *informal* do a lot of successful business: *the open-air air show did a land-office business.*

Land of Hi·a·wath·a a nickname for the **upper peninsula** of Michigan.

Land of Lin·coln a nickname for the state of **Illinois**.

Land of Op·por·tu·ni·ty a nickname for the state of **Arkansas**.

Land of Stead·y Hab·its a nickname for the state of **Connecticut**.

Land of the Da·ko·tas a nickname for the state of **North Dakota**.

Land of the Mid·night Sun a nickname for the state of **Alaska**.

Land of the Ris·ing Sun ▸*n.* a poetic name for Japan.

Lan·don /ˈlandən/, Alfred Mossman (1887–1987), U.S. politician. The governor of Kansas 1933–37, he was the unsuccessful Republican presidential candidate in 1936, losing to Franklin D. Roosevelt.

land·own·er /ˈlanˌdōnər/ ▸*n.* a person who owns land, esp. a large amount of land. —**land·own·er·ship** /-dōnərˌsʜip/ *n.* —**land·own·ing** /-dōniɴɢ/ *adj.* & *n.*

land·race /ˈlandˌrās/ ▸*n.* a local cultivar or animal breed that has been improved by traditional agricultural methods but has not been influenced by modern agricultural practices.

land rail ▸*n.* another term for **corn crake**.

land re·form ▸*n.* the statutory division of agricultural land and its reallocation to landless people.

Land·sat /ˈlan(d)ˌsat/ a series of artificial satellites that monitor the earth's resources by photographing the surface at different wavelengths. The resulting images provide information about agriculture, geology, ecological changes, etc.

land·scape /ˈlan(d)ˌskāp/ ▸*n.* **1** all the visible features of an area of countryside or land, often considered in terms of their aesthetic appeal: *the giant cacti that dominate this landscape* | *a bleak urban landscape.* ■ a picture representing an area of countryside: [as *adj.*] *a landscape painter.* ■ the genre of landscape painting. ■ *figurative* the distinctive features of a particular situation or intellectual activity: *the event transformed the political landscape.* **2** [as *adj.*] (of a page, book, or illustration, or the manner in which it is set or printed) wider than it is high. Compare with **portrait** (sense 2).
▸*v.* [*trans.*] (usu. **be landscaped**) improve the aesthetic appearance of (a piece of land) by changing its contours, adding ornamental features, or planting trees and shrubs: *the site has been tastefully landscaped* | [as *n.*] (**landscaping**) *the company spent $15,000 on landscaping.* ▷late 16th cent. (denoting a picture of natural scenery): from Middle Dutch *lantscap*, from *land* 'land' + *scap* (equivalent of **-ship**). —**land·scap·er** *n.* —**land·scap·ist** /-ˌskāpist/ *n.*

land·scape ar·chi·tec·ture ▸*n.* the art and practice of designing the outdoor environment, esp. designing parks or gardens together with buildings and roads. —**land·scape ar·chi·tect** *n.*

land·scape gar·den·ing ▸*n.* the art and practice of laying out grounds in a way that is ornamental or that imitates natural scenery. —**land·scape gar·den·er** *n.*

land scrip ▸*n.* see **scrip**[1] (sense 2).

Land's End a rocky promontory in southwestern Cornwall that is England's westernmost point.

lands·knecht /ˈläntsˌknekʜt/ ▸*n. historical* a member of a class of mercenary soldiers in the German and other continental armies in the 16th and 17th centuries. ▷from German *Landsknecht*, literally 'soldier of the land.'

land·slide /ˈlan(d)ˌslīd/ ▸*n.* **1** the sliding down of a mass of earth or rock from a mountain or cliff. **2** an overwhelming majority of votes for one party in an election: *winning the election **by a landslide*** | [as *adj.*] *a landslide victory.*

land·slip /ˈlan(d)ˌslip/ ▸*n. chiefly Brit.* another term for **landslide** (sense 1).

Lands·mål /ˈläntsˌmôl/ ▸*n.* another term for **Nynorsk**. ▷Norwegian, literally 'language of the land.'

lands·man /ˈlan(d)zmən/ ▸*n.* **1** (*pl.* **-men**) a person unfamiliar with the sea or sailing. **2** a fellow countryman.

Land·stei·ner /ˈlan(d)ˌstīnər; ˈläntˌsʜtīnər/, Karl (1868–1943), U.S. physician, born in Austria. In 1930, he devised the ABO system of classifying blood. He was also the first to describe the Rhesus factor in blood. Nobel Prize for Physiology or Medicine (1930).

land·ward /ˈlan(d)wərd/ ▸*adv.* (also **land·wards** /-wərdz/) toward land: *the ship turned landward.*
▸*adj.* facing toward land as opposed to sea: *the landward side of the road.*

land yacht ▸*n.* a wind-powered wheeled vehicle with sails, used for recreation and competition. ■ *informal* a large car: *the bechromed land yachts of the 1950s.*

lane /lān/ ▸*n.* **1** a narrow road, esp. in a rural area: *she drove along the winding lane.* ■ [in *place names*] a street in an urban area: *Park Lane.* ■ *Astronomy* a dark streak or band that shows up against a bright background, esp. in a spiral galaxy or emission nebula. **2** a division of a road marked off with painted lines and intended to separate single lines of traffic according to speed or direction: *the car accelerated and moved into the outside lane.* ■ each of a number of parallel strips of track or water for runners, rowers, or swimmers in a race: *she went into the final in lane three.* ■ a path or course prescribed for or regularly followed by ships or aircraft: *the shipping lanes of the South Atlantic.* ■ (in basketball) a 12-foot-wide area extending from the free-throw line to below the basket. ■ (in bowling) a long narrow strip of floor down which the ball is bowled. ■ *Biochemistry* each of a number of notional parallel strips in the gel of an electrophoresis plate, occupied by a single sample. ▷Old English, related to Dutch *laan*; of unknown ultimate origin.

Lang /laɴɢ/, Fritz (1890–1976), Austrian movie director, who worked in the U.S. from 1933. He made the transition from silent to sound movies in 1931 with the thriller *M*. Later works included *The Big Heat* (1953).

lang. ▸*abbr.* language.

Lange /laɴɢ/, Dorothea (1895–1965), U.S. photographer. She was known for her documentary photographs of the Great Depression, including "White Angel Breadline" (1932), and those of the Japanese-American concentration camps around 1942. Many of her later photoessays were published in *Life* magazine.

Lang·land /ˈlaɴɢlənd/, William (*c.*1330–*c.*1400), English poet. He is best known for *Piers Plowman* (*c.*1367–70), a long allegorical poem that is in the form of a spiritual pilgrimage.

lang·lauf /ˈläɴɢˌlouf/ ▸*n.* cross-country skiing: [as *adj.*] *langlauf skiers.* ▷1920s: from German, literally 'long run.'

Lang·ley[1] /ˈlaɴɢlē/ a community in northeastern Virginia, northwest of Washington, DC, home to the Central Intelligence Agency.

Lang·ley[2], Samuel Pierpoint (1834–1906), U.S. astronomer and aviation pioneer. He invented the bolometer (1879–81) and contributed to the design of early aircrafts.

Lang·muir /ˈlaɴɢˌmyo͝or/, Irving (1881–1957), U.S. chemist and physicist. His principal work was in surface chemistry, esp. applied to catalysis. He also worked on high-temperature electrical discharges in gases and studied atomic structure.

Lang·muir–Blod·gett film /ˈbläjit/ ▸*n. Chemistry* a monomolecular layer of an organic material that can be used to build extremely small electronic devices. ▷named after I. **Langmuir**, and Katherine B. *Blodgett* (1898–1979), American physicist and chemist.

lan·gos·ta /laɴɢˈgästə/ ▸*n.* another term for **langouste**. ▷Spanish.

lan·gouste /läɴɢˈgo͞ost/ ▸*n.* a spiny lobster, esp. in French cuisine; crawfish. ▷French, from Old Provençal *lagosta*, based on Latin *locusta* 'locust, crustacean.'

lan·gous·tine /ˈlaɴɢgəˌstēn/ ▸*n.* a large, commercially important prawn. • *Nephrops norvegicus*, class Malacostraca. ▷French, from *langouste* (see **langouste**).

lang syne /ˌlaɴɢ ˈzīn; ˈsīn/ *Scottish archaic* ▸*adv.* in the distant past; long ago: *we talked of races run lang syne.*
▸*n.* times gone by; the old days, esp. in the phrase, "auld lang syne.". ▷early 16th cent.: from *lang*, Scots variant of **long**[1] + **syne**.

Lang·ton /ˈlaɴɢtən/, Stephen (*c.*1150–1228), English prelate; archbishop of Canterbury 1207–15 and 1218–28. A champion of the English Church, he was involved in the negotiations leading to the signing of Magna Carta.

Lang·try /ˈlaɴɢtrē/, Lillie (1853–1929), British actress; born *Emilie Charlotte le Breton*. She was the mistress of the Prince of Wales, who later became Edward VII.

lan·guage /ˈlaɴɢgwij/ ▸*n.* **1** the method of human communication, either spoken or written, consisting of the use of words in a structured and conventional way: *a study of the way children learn language* | [as *adj.*] *language development.* ■ any nonverbal method of expression or communication: *a language of gesture and facial expression.* **2** the system of communication used by a particular community or country: *the book was translated into twenty-five languages.* ■ *Computing* a system of symbols and rules for writing programs or algorithms: *a new programming language.* **3** the manner or style of a piece of writing or speech: *he explained the procedure in simple, everyday language.* ■ the phraseology and vocabulary of a certain profession, domain, or group of people: *legal language.* ■ (usu. as **bad/strong language**) coarse, crude, or offensive language: *strong language.* ▷Middle English: from Old French *langage*, based on Latin *lingua* 'tongue.'
▸*PHRASE* □ **speak the same language** understand one another as a result of shared opinions or values.

lan·guage ar·e·a ▸*n.* **1** *Physiology* the area of the cerebral cortex thought to be particularly involved in the processing of language: *the language areas of the left cerebral hemisphere.* **2** a region where a particular language is spoken.

lan·guage arts ▸*n.* the study of grammar, composition, spelling, and (sometimes) public speaking, typically taught as a single subject in elementary and middle school.

L

lan·guage en·gi·neer·ing ▸*n.* any of a variety of computing procedures that use tools such as machine-readable dictionaries and sentence parsers in order to process natural languages for industrial applications such as speech recognition and speech synthesis.

lan·guage lab·o·ra·to·ry (also **language lab**) ▸*n.* a room equipped with audio and visual equipment, such as tape and video recorders, for learning a foreign language.

lan·guage of flow·ers ▸*n.* a set of symbolic meanings attached to different flowers when they are given or arranged.

langue /läNG(g)/ ▸*n.* (*pl.* same) *Linguistics* a language viewed as an abstract system used by a speech community, in contrast to the actual linguistic behavior of individuals. Contrasted with PAROLE. ▷1920s: French, from Latin *lingua* 'language, tongue.'

langued /laNGd/ ▸*adj. Heraldry* having the tongue of a specified tincture. ▷late Middle English: from French *langué* 'tongued' + -ED[2].

langue d'oc /ˌläNG(gə) 'dôk/ ▸*n.* the form of medieval French spoken south of the Loire, generally characterized by the use of *oc* to mean 'yes,' and forming the basis of modern Provençal. Compare with OCCITAN. ▷from Old French *langue* 'language' (from Latin *lingua* 'tongue'), *d'* (from *de* 'of'), and *oc* (from Latin *hoc*) 'yes.' Compare with LANGUE D'OÏL.

Langue·doc-Rous·sil·lon /ˌläNG'dôk ˌro͞osē'yôn/ a region of southern France, on the Mediterranean coast, extending from the Rhône delta to the border with Spain.

langue d'oïl /ˌläNG(gə) 'doi(l)/ ▸*n.* the form of medieval French spoken north of the Loire, generally characterized by the use of *oïl* to mean 'yes,' and forming the basis of modern French. ▷from Old French *langue* 'language' (from Latin *lingua* 'tongue'), *d'* (from *de* 'of'), and *oïl* (from Latin *hoc ille*) 'yes.' Compare with LANGUE D'OC.

lan·guid /'laNGgwid/ ▸*adj.* **1** (of a person, manner, or gesture) displaying or having a disinclination for physical exertion or effort; slow and relaxed: *they turned with languid movements from back to front so as to tan evenly.* ■ (of an occasion or period of time) pleasantly lazy and peaceful: *the terrace was perfect for languid days in the Italian sun.* **2** weak or faint from illness or fatigue: *she was pale, languid, and weak, as if she had delivered a child.* ▷late 16th cent. (sense 2): from French *languide* or Latin *languidus*, from *languere* (see LANGUISH). **—lan·guid·ly** *adv.* **—lan·guid·ness** *n.*

lan·guish /'laNGgwiSH/ ▸*v.* [*intrans.*] **1** (of a person or other living thing) lose or lack vitality; grow weak or feeble: *plants may appear to be languishing simply because they are dormant.* ■ fail to make progress or be successful: *many Japanese works still languish unrecognized in Europe.* ■ *archaic* pine with love or grief: *she still* **languished after** *Richard.* ■ *archaic* assume or display a sentimentally tender or melancholy expression or tone: *when a visitor comes in, she smiles and languishes.* **2** suffer from being forced to remain in an unpleasant place or situation: *he has been languishing in a Mexican jail since 1974.* ▷Middle English (in the sense 'become faint, feeble, or ill'): from Old French *languiss-*, lengthened stem of *languir* 'languish,' from a variant of Latin *languere*, related to *laxus* 'loose, lax.' **—lan·guish·er** *n.* **—lan·guish·ing·ly** *adv.* **—lan·guish·ment** *n.* (*archaic*).

lan·guor /'laNG(g)ər/ ▸*n.* **1** the state or feeling, often pleasant, of tiredness or inertia: *he remembered the languor and warm happiness of those golden afternoons.* **2** an oppressive stillness of the air: *the afternoon was hot, quiet, and heavy with languor.* ▷Middle English: via Old French from Latin, from *languere* (see LANGUISH). The original sense was 'illness, disease, distress,' later 'faintness, lassitude'; current senses date from the 18th cent., when such lassitude became associated with a sometimes rather self-indulgent romantic yearning. **—lan·guor·ous** /-g(ə)rəs; 'laNGərəs/ *adj.* **—lan·guor·ous·ly** /-g(ə)rəslē; 'laNGərəslē/ *adv.*

lan·gur /läNG'go͝or/ ▸*n.* a long-tailed arboreal Asian monkey with a characteristic loud call. • *Presbytis* and other genera, family Cercopithecidae: several species. Compare with LEAF MONKEY. ▷early 19th cent.: via Hindi from Sanskrit *lāṅgūla*.

La Ni·ña /lä 'nēnyə/ ▸*n.* a cooling of the water in the equatorial Pacific, which occurs at irregular intervals and is associated with widespread changes in weather patterns complementary to those of El Niño, but less extensive and damaging in their effects. ▷Spanish, literally 'the girl child,' after *El Niño*.

lank /laNGk/ ▸*adj.* (of hair) long, limp, and straight. ■ (of a person) lanky. ▷Old English *hlanc* 'thin, not filled out,' of Germanic origin; related to High German *lenken* 'to bend, turn,' also to FLINCH[1] and LINK[1]. **—lank·ly** *adv.* **—lank·ness** *n.*

lank·y /'laNGkē/ ▸*adj.* (**lank·i·er, lank·i·est**) (of a person) ungracefully thin and tall. **—lank·i·ly** /-kəlē/ *adv.* **—lank·i·ness** *n.*

lan·ner /'lanər/ (also **lanner falcon**) ▸*n.* a falcon with a dark brown back and buff cap, found in southeastern Europe, the Middle East, and Africa. • *Falco biarmicus*, family Falconidae. ▷late Middle English: from Old French *lanier*, perhaps a noun use of *lanier* 'cowardly,' from a derogatory use of *lanier* 'wool merchant,' from Latin *lanarius*, from *lana* 'wool.'

lan·o·lin /'lanl-in/ ▸*n.* a fatty substance found naturally on sheep's wool. It is extracted as a yellowish viscous mixture of esters and used as a base for ointments. ▷late 19th cent.: coined in German from Latin *lana* 'wool' + *oleum* 'oil' + -IN[1].

Lans·bur·y /'lanzˌberē/, Angela (Brigid) (1925–) U.S. actress; born in England. She appeared in movies such as *Gaslight* (1944) and *The Manchurian Candidate* (1963) and starred in the television series "Murder, She Wrote" 1984–96 and also the Broadway shows *Mame* (1966), *Gypsy* (1974), and *Sweeney Todd* (1979).

Lan·sing /'lansiNG/ the capital of Michigan, in the southern part of the state; pop. 119,128. First settled in 1847, it expanded rapidly after the establishment of the automobile industry there in 1887.

lans·que·net /ˌlanskə'net/ ▸*n.* **1** *historical* a gambling game of German origin involving betting on cards turned up by the dealer. **2** archaic variant of LANDSKNECHT. ▷early 17th cent. (sense 2): via French from German *Landsknecht* (see LANDSKNECHT).

lan·ta·na /lan'tanə; -'tänə/ ▸*n.* a tropical evergreen shrub of the verbena family, several kinds of which are cultivated as ornamentals. • Genus *Lantana*, family Verbenaceae: many species, in particular the South American scrambler *L. camara*, grown as an ornamental and sometimes becoming an invasive weed. ▷modern Latin, from the specific name of the wayfaring tree *Viburnum lantana*, which it resembles superficially.

Lan·tau /'län'dou/ an island of Hong Kong, situated to the west of Hong Kong Island and forming part of the New Territories. Chinese name TAI YUE SHAN.

lan·tern /'lantərn/ ▸*n.* **1** a lamp with a transparent case protecting the flame or electric bulb, and typically having a handle by which it can be carried or hung: *a paper lantern.* ■ the light chamber at the top of a lighthouse. ■ short for MAGIC LANTERN. **2** a square, curved, or polygonal structure on the top of a dome or a room, with the sides glazed or open, so as to admit light. ▷Middle English: from Old French *lanterne*, from Latin *lanterna*, from Greek *lamptēr* 'torch, lamp,' from *lampein* 'to shine.'

Lan·tern Fes·ti·val ▸*n.* another name for BON.

lan·tern fish ▸*n.* (*pl.* same or **fishe·s**) a deep-sea fish that has organs on its body that emit light, seen chiefly when it rises to the surface at night. • Family Myctophidae: several genera and species.

lan·tern jaw ▸*n.* a long, thin jaw and prominent chin. **—lan·tern-jawed** *adj.*

lan·tern slide ▸*n. historical* a mounted photographic transparency for projection by a magic lantern.

lan·tha·nide /'lanTHəˌnīd/ ▸*n. Chemistry* any of the series of fifteen metallic elements from lanthanum to lutetium in the periodic table. See also RARE EARTH. ▷1920s: from LANTHANUM + -IDE.

lan·tha·num /'lanTHənəm/ ▸*n.* the chemical element of atomic number 57, a silvery-white rare earth metal. (Symbol: **La**) ▷mid 19th cent.: from Greek *lanthanein* 'escape notice' (because it was long undetected in cerium oxide) + -UM.

la·nu·go /lə'n(y)o͞ogō/ ▸*n. Anatomy* fine, soft hair, esp. that which covers the body and limbs of a human fetus or newborn. ▷late 17th cent.: from Latin, 'down,' from *lana* 'wool.'

La·nús /lä'no͞os/ a city in eastern Argentina, south of Buenos Aires; pop. 467,000.

lan·yard /'lanyərd/ ▸*n.* a rope threaded through a pair of deadeyes, used to adjust the tension in the rigging of a sailing vessel. ■ a cord passed around the neck, shoulder, or wrist for holding a knife, whistle, or similar object. ■ a cord attached to a breech mechanism for firing a gun. ▷late Middle English *lanyer*, in the general sense 'a short length of rope or line for securing something,' from Old French *laniere*. The change in the ending in the 17th cent. was due to association with YARD[1].

Lan·za /'länzə/, Mario (1921–59) U.S. tenor; born *Alfredo Arnold Cocozza*. He became an international star as the portrayer of Enrico Caruso in the movies *The Great Caruso* (1951) and *The Seven Hills of Rome* (1958).

Lan·zhou /'länjō/ (also **Lan·chow**) a city in northern China, on the upper Yellow River, capital of Gansu province; pop. 1,480,000.

Lao /lou/ ▸*n.* (*pl.* same or **Laos** /louz/) **1** a member of an indigenous people of Laos and northeastern Thailand. **2** the Tai language of this people, closely related to Thai. Also called LAOTIAN.
▸*adj.* of or relating to the Lao or their language. ▷the name in Lao.

La·oc·o·on /lā'äkōˌän/ *Greek Mythology* a Trojan priest who, with his two sons, was crushed to death by two great sea serpents as a penalty for warning the Trojans against drawing the wooden horse of the Greeks into Troy.

La·od·i·ce·an /lāˌädə'sēən/ *archaic* ▸*adj.* lukewarm or halfhearted, esp. with respect to religion or politics.
▸*n.* a person with such an attitude. ▷early 17th cent.: from Latin *Laodicea* in Asia Minor, with reference to the early Christians there (Rev. 3:16), + -AN.

lao·gai /ˌlou'gī/ ▸*n.* (**the laogai**) (in China) a system of labor camps, many of whose inmates are political dissidents. ▷Chinese, 'reform through labor.'

Laois /lāSH; lēSH/ (also **Laoighis, Leix**) a county of the Republic of Ireland, in the province of Leinster; county town, Portlaoise. Former name QUEEN'S COUNTY.

Laos /'lä-ōs; lous; 'lāˌäs/ a landlocked country in Southeast Asia; pop. 6,068,000; capital, Vientiane; official language, Laotian. **—La·o·tian** /lā'ōSHən/ *adj.* & *n.*

Part of French Indo-China, Laos became independent in 1953, but for most of the next 25 years was torn by civil strife between the communist Pathet Lao movement and government supporters. In 1975, the Pathet Lao achieved total control, and a communist republic was established. The end of the 20th century saw a gradual return to free enterprise.

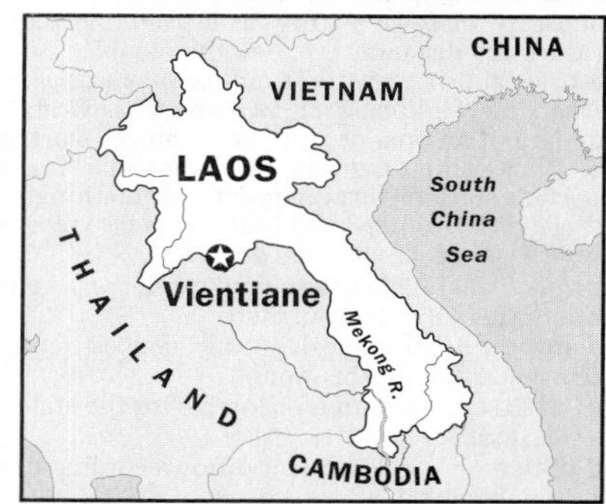

Lao-tzu /'lä-ō 'tso͞o; 'dzə/ (also **Lao·ze** /'tsä; 'dzä/) (*fl.* 6th century BC), Chinese philosopher traditionally regarded as the founder of Taoism and author of the Tao-te-Ching, its most sacred scripture. ▷Chinese, literally 'Lao the Master.'

lap[1] /lap/ ▸*n.* **1** (usu. **one's lap**) the flat area between the waist and knees of a seated person: *come and sit on my lap.* ■ the part of an item of clothing, esp. a skirt, covering the lap. **2** *archaic* a hanging flap on a garment or a saddle. ▷Old English *læppa*, of Germanic origin; related to Dutch *lap*, German *Lappen* 'piece of cloth.' The word originally denoted a fold or flap of a garment (compare with LAPEL), later specifically one that could be used as a pocket or pouch, or the front of a skirt when held up to catch or carry something (Middle English), hence the area between the waist and knees as a place where a child could be nursed or an object held. **—lap·ful** /-ˌfo͝ol/ *n.* (*pl.* **-fuls**).

▸*PHRASES* □ **fall** (or **drop**) **into someone's lap** (of something unexpected) come someone's way without any effort having been made: *not many reporters are lucky enough to have stories fall into their laps.* □ **in someone's lap** as someone's responsibility: *she dumped the problem in my lap.* □ **in the lap of luxury** in conditions of great comfort and wealth.

lap[2] ▸*n.* **1** one circuit of a track or racetrack. ■ a stage in a swim consisting of two lengths of a pool. ■ a section of a journey or other undertaking: *we caught a cab for the last lap of our journey.* **2** an overlapping or projecting part. ■ the amount by which one thing overlaps or covers a part of another. ■ *Metallurgy* a defect formed in rolling when a projecting part is accidentally folded over and pressed against the surface of the metal. ■ (in a steam engine) the distance by which the valve overlaps the steam port (or the exhaust port). **3** a single turn of rope, thread, or cable around a drum or reel. ■ a layer or sheet, typically wound on a roller, into which cotton or wool is formed during its manufacture. **4** (in a lapping machine) a rotating disk with a coating of fine abrasive for polishing. ■ a polishing tool of a special shape, coated or impregnated with an abrasive.

▶*v.* **(lapped, lap·ping)** [*trans.*] **1** overtake (a competitor in a race) to become one or more laps ahead: *she lapped all of her rivals in the 3,000 meters.* ■ [*intrans.*] (of a competitor or vehicle in a race) complete a lap, esp. in a specified time: *he lapped two tenths of a second faster than anyone else.* **2** [*trans.*] **(lap someone/something in)** *poetic/literary* enfold or swathe a person or thing, esp. a part of the body, in (something soft): *he was lapped in blankets | figurative I was accustomed to being lapped in luxury.* **3** [*intrans.*] project beyond or overlap something: *the blanket of snow* ***lapped over*** *the roofs of the house.* **4** [*trans.*] polish (a gem or a metal or glass surface) with a lapping machine. ▷Middle English (as a verb in the sense 'coil, fold, or wrap'): from LAP[1]. Sense 1 of the *noun* and *verb* date from the mid 19th cent.

lap[3] ▶*v.* **(lapped, lap·ping)** [*trans.*] **1** (of an animal) take up (liquid) with the tongue in order to drink: *the cat was* ***lapping up*** *a saucer of milk.* ■ **(lap something up)** accept something eagerly and with obvious pleasure: *she's lapping up the attention.* **2** (of water) wash against (something) with a gentle rippling sound: *the waves lapped the shore | [intrans.] the sound of the river lapping against the banks.*

▶*n.* [in *sing.*] the action of water washing gently against something: *listening to the comfortable lap of the waves against the shore.* ▷Old English *lapian*, of Germanic origin; related to Middle Low German and Middle Dutch *lapen*. **—lap·per** *n.*

lap·a·ros·co·py /ˌlapəˈräskəpē/ ▶*n.* (*pl.* **-pies**) a surgical procedure in which a fiber-optic instrument is inserted through the abdominal wall to view the organs in the abdomen or to permit a surgical procedure. ▷mid 19th cent.: from Greek *lapara* 'flank' + -SCOPY. **—lap·a·ro·scope** /ˈlap(ə)rəˌskōp/ *n.* **—lap·a·ro·scop·ic** /ˌlap(ə)rəˈskäpik/ *adj.* **—lap·a·ro·scop·i·cal·ly** *adv.*

lap·a·rot·o·my /ˌlapəˈrätəmē/ ▶*n.* (*pl.* **-mies**) a surgical incision into the abdominal cavity, for diagnosis or in preparation for surgery. ▷mid 19th cent.: from Greek *lapara* 'flank' + -TOMY.

La Paz /lä ˈpäz; ˈpäs/ **1** the capital of Bolivia, in the northwestern part of the country, near the border with Peru; pop. 711,000. Situated in the Andes at an altitude of 12,000 feet (3,660 m), it is the highest capital city in the world. **2** a city in Mexico, near the southern tip of the Baja California peninsula, capital of the state of Baja California Sur; pop. 100,000.

lap belt ▶*n.* a seat belt worn across the lap.

lap dance ▶*n.* an erotic dance or striptease performed close to, or sitting on the lap of, a paying customer. **—lap danc·er** *n.* **—lap danc·ing** *n.*

lap desk ▶*n.* a portable writing case or surface, esp. one for use on the lap.

lap dis·solve ▶*n.* a fade-out of a scene in a movie that overlaps with a fade-in of a new scene, so that one appears to dissolve into the other.

lap·dog /ˈlapˌdôg; -ˌdäg/ (also **lap dog**) ▶*n.* a small dog kept as a pet. ■ *figurative* a person or organization that is influenced or controlled by another: *the government and its media lapdogs.*

la·pel /ləˈpel/ ▶*n.* the part on each side of a coat or jacket immediately below the collar that is folded back on either side of the front opening. ▷mid 17th cent.: diminutive of LAP[1]. **—la·pelled** *adj.* [in *combination*] *a narrow-lapelled suit.*

lap·i·dar·y /ˈlapəˌderē/ ▶*adj.* (of language) engraved on or suitable for engraving on stone and therefore elegant and concise: *a lapidary statement.* ■ of or relating to stone and gems and the work involved in engraving, cutting, or polishing.

▶*n.* (*pl.* **-dar·ies**) a person who cuts, polishes, or engraves gems. ■ the art of cutting, polishing, or engraving gems. ▷Middle English (as a noun): from Latin *lapidarius* (in late Latin 'stonecutter'), from *lapis, lapid-* 'stone.' The adjective dates from the early 18th cent.

la·pil·li /ləˈpiˌlī/ ▶*plural n. Geology* rock fragments ejected from a volcano. ▷mid 18th cent. (in the general sense 'stones, pebbles'): via Italian from Latin, plural of *lapillus*, diminutive of *lapis* 'stone.'

lap·is laz·u·li /ˈlapis ˈlazyəˌlī; ˈlazʜəˌlī; ˈlazyəlē/ (also **lap·is**) ▶*n.* a bright blue metamorphic rock consisting largely of lazurite, used for decoration and in jewelry. ■ a bright blue pigment formerly made by crushing this, being the original ultramarine. ■ the color ultramarine. ▷late Middle English: from Latin *lapis* 'stone' and medieval Latin *lazuli*, genitive of *lazulum*, from Persian *lāžward* 'lapis lazuli.' Compare with AZURE.

Lap·ith /ˈlapiᴛʜ/ ▶*n. Greek Mythology* a member of a Thessalian people who fought and defeated the centaurs. ▷via Latin from Greek *Lapithai* (plural).

lap joint ▶*n.* a joint made with two pieces of metal, timber, etc., by halving the thickness of each member at the joint and fitting them together.

La·place /läˈpläs/, Pierre Simon, Marquis de (1749–1827), French applied mathematician and theoretical physicist. His treatise *Mécanique céleste* (1799–1825) is an extensive mathematical analysis of geophysical matters and of planetary and lunar motion.

Lap·land /ˈlapˌland; -lənd/ a region in northern Europe that extends from the Norwegian Sea to the White Sea and lies mainly within the Arctic Circle. It consists of the northern parts of Norway, Sweden, and Finland, as well as the Kola Peninsula of Russia. ▷late 16th cent.: from Swedish *Lappland*, from *Lapp* (see LAPP) + *land* 'land.' **—Lap·land·er** *n.*

La Pla·ta /lə ˈplätə; lä ˈplätä/ a port in Argentina, on the Plate River (Río de la Plata) southeast of Buenos Aires; pop. 640,000.

Lapp /lap/ ▶*n.* **1** a member of an indigenous people of far northern Scandinavia, traditionally associated with the herding of reindeer. **2** the Finno-Ugric language of this people, with nine distinct dialects.

▶*adj.* of or relating to the Lapps or their language. ▷Swedish, perhaps originally a term of contempt and related to Middle High German *lappe* 'simpleton.'

> ***USAGE*** Although the term **Lapp** is still widely used and is the most familiar term to many people, the people themselves prefer to be called **Sami**.

lap·pet /ˈlapit/ ▶*n.* **1** a small flap or fold, in particular: ■ a fold or hanging piece of flesh in some animals. ■ a loose or overlapping part of a garment. **2** (also **lappet moth**) a brownish moth, the hairy caterpillars of which have fleshy lappets along each side of the body. • Several species in the family Lasiocampidae: including *Phyllodesma americana.* ▷late Middle English (denoting a lobe of the ear, liver, etc.): diminutive of LAP[1]. **—lap·pet·ed** *adj.*

lap·ping ma·chine ▶*n.* a machine with a rotating abrasive disk for polishing gems, metal, and optical glass.

Lap·pish /ˈlapisʜ/ ▶*adj.* of or relating to the Lapps (Sami) or their language.

▶*n.* the Lapp language.

lap pool ▶*n.* a swimming pool specially designed or designated for swimming laps.

lap robe ▶*n.* a thick blanket or pelt used for warming the lap and legs while traveling or sitting outdoors.

lap·sang sou·chong /ˈlapˌsaɴɢ ˈsoōˌcʜäɴɢ; ˈläp ˌsäng; ˈsoōˌsʜäɴɢ/ ▶*n.* a variety of souchong tea with a smoky flavor. ▷late 19th cent.: from an invented first element + SOUCHONG.

lapse /laps/ ▶*n.* **1** a temporary failure of concentration, memory, or judgment: *a* ***lapse of*** *concentration in the second set cost her the match.* ■ a weak or careless decline from previously high standards: *tracing his* ***lapse into*** *petty crime.* ■ *Law* the termination of a right or privilege through disuse or failure to follow appropriate procedures. **2** an interval or passage of time: *there was a considerable* ***lapse of*** *time between the two events.*

▶*v.* [*intrans.*] **1** (of a right, privilege, or agreement) become invalid because it is not used, claimed, or renewed; expire: *my membership to the gym has lapsed.* ■ (of a state or activity) fail to be maintained; come to an end: *if your diet has lapsed it's time you revived it.* ■ (of an adherent to a particular religion or doctrine) cease to follow the rules and practices of that religion or doctrine: [as *adj.*] **(lapsed)** *a lapsed Catholic.* **2** **(lapse into)** pass gradually into (an inferior state or condition): *the country has lapsed into chaos.* ■ revert to (a previous or more familiar style of speaking or behavior): *the girls lapsed into French.* ▷late Middle English: from Latin *lapsus*, from *labi* 'to glide, slip, or fall'; the verb reinforced by Latin *lapsare* 'to slip or stumble.'

lapse rate ▶*n.* the rate at which air temperature falls with increasing altitude.

lap·strake /ˈlapˌstrāk/ ▶*n.* a clinker-built boat.

▶*adj.* (also **lap·straked**) clinker-built.

lap·sus ca·la·mi /ˈlapsəs ˈkaləˌmī; -ˌmē/ ▶*n.* (*pl.* same) *formal* a slip of the pen. ▷Latin.

lap·sus lin·guae /ˈläpsəs ˈliɴɢˌgwī; -ˌgwē/ ▶*n.* (*pl.* same) *formal* a slip of the tongue. ▷Latin.

Lap·tev Sea /ˈlapˌtev; -ˌtef/ a part of the Arctic Ocean that lies to the north of Russia between the Taimyr Peninsula and the New Siberian Islands.

lap·top /ˈlapˌtäp/ (also **laptop computer**) ▶*n.* a microcomputer that is portable and suitable for use while traveling.

lap-weld ▶*v.* [*trans.*] weld (something) with the edges overlapping.

▶*n.* **(lap weld)** a weld made in this way.

lap·wing /ˈlapˌwiɴɢ/ ▶*n.* a large plover, typically having a black and white head and underparts and a loud call. • Genus *Vanellus*, family Charadriidae: several species, in particular the **northern lapwing** (*V. vanellus*) of Eurasia (also called the GREEN PLOVER or PEWIT), which has a dark green back and a crest. ▷Old English *hlēapewince*, from *hlēapan* 'to leap' and a base meaning 'move from side to side' (whence also WINK); so named because of the way it flies. The spelling was changed in Middle English by association with LAP[2] and WING.

Lar·a·mie /ˈlarəmē/ a city in southeastern Wyoming; pop. 27,204. It was first settled in 1868 during the construction of the Union Pacific Railroad.

lar·board /ˈlärˌbôrd; -bərd/ ▶*n. Nautical* archaic term for PORT[3]. ▷Middle English *ladebord* (see LADE, BOARD), referring to the side on which cargo was put aboard. The change to *lar-* in the 16th cent. was due to association with STARBOARD.

lar·ce·ny /ˈlärs(ə)nē/ ▶*n.* (*pl.* **-nies**) theft of personal property. See also GRAND LARCENY, PETTY LARCENY. ▷late 15th cent.: from Old French *larcin*, from Latin *latrocinium*, from *latro(n-)* 'robber,' earlier 'mercenary soldier,' from Greek *latreus*. **—lar·ce·ner** /-nər/ *n.* (*archaic*) **—lar·ce·nist** /-nist/ *n.* **—lar·ce·nous** /-nəs/ *adj.*

larch /lärcʜ/ ▶*n.* a coniferous tree with bunches of deciduous bright green needles, found in cool regions of the northern hemisphere. It is grown for its tough timber and its resin (which yields turpentine). See also TAMARACK. • Genus *Larix*, family Pinaceae: several species, including the **common** (or **European**) **larch** (*L. decidua*). ▷mid 16th cent.: from Middle High German *larche*, based on Latin *larix*.

lard /lärd/ ▶*n.* fat from the abdomen of a pig that is rendered and clarified for use in cooking. ■ *informal* excess human fat that is seen as unhealthy and unattractive.

▶*v.* [*trans.*] **1** insert strips of fat or bacon in (meat) before cooking. ■ smear or cover (a foodstuff) with lard or fat, typically to prevent it from drying out during storage. **2** (usu. **be larded with**) embellish (talk or writing) with a variety of expressions: *his conversation is larded with quotations from Coleridge.* ■ cover or fill thickly or excessively: *the pages were larded with corrections and crossings-out.* ▷Middle English (also denoting fat bacon or pork): from Old French, 'bacon,' from Latin *lardum, laridum*, related to Greek *larinos* 'fat.' **—lard·y** *adj.*

lard·ass /ˈlärˌdas/ ▶*n. informal, derogatory* a fat person, esp. one with large buttocks or who is regarded as lazy.

lard·er /ˈlärdər/ ▶*n.* a room or large cupboard for storing food. ▷Middle English (denoting a store of meat): from Old French *lardier*, from medieval Latin *lardarium*, from *laridum* (see LARD).

lar·der bee·tle ▶*n.* a brownish scavenging beetle that is a pest of stored products, esp. meat and hides. • *Dermestes lardarius*, family Dermestidae.

Lard·ner /ˈlärdnər/, Ring(gold Wilmer) (1885–1933), U.S. writer and journalist. He wrote *You Know Me Al: A Busher's Letters* (1914), *Treat 'Em Rough* (1918), and *The Real Dope* (1919), all collections of his stories that featured his character, baseball pitcher Jack Keefe.

lar·don /ˈlärdn/ (also **lar·doon** /lärˈdoōn/) ▶*n.* a piece of bacon used to lard meat. ▷late Middle English: from French, from *lard* 'bacon' (see LARD).

La·re·do /ləˈrādō/ an industrial port city in southern Texas, across the Rio Grande from Nuevo Laredo in Mexico; pop. 176,576.

lar·es /ˈläˌrēz; ˈle(ə)rēz/ ▶*plural n.* gods of the household worshiped in ancient Rome. See also PENATES. ▷Latin.

▶***PHRASE*** □ **lares and penates** the home.

Pronunciation Key ə *ago*; ər *over*; ˈə or ˌə *up*; ˈər or ˌər *fur*; a *hat*; ā *rate*; ä *car*; cʜ *chew*; e *let*; ē *see*; e(ə)r *air*; i *fit*; ī *by*; i(ə)r *ear*; ɴɢ *sing*; ō *go*; ô *for*; oi *boy*; o͝o *good*; o͞o *goo*; ou *out*; sʜ *she*; ᴛʜ *thin*; T͟H *then*; (h)w *why*; zʜ *vision*

large /lärj/ ▸*adj.* **1** of considerable or relatively great size, extent, or capacity: *add a large clove of garlic | the concert attracted large crowds.* ■ of greater size than the ordinary, esp. with reference to a size of clothing or to the size of a packaged commodity: *the sweater comes in small, medium, and large sizes.* ■ pursuing an occupation or commercial activity on a significant scale: *many large investors are likely to take a different view.* **2** of wide range or scope: *we can afford to take a larger view of the situation.* **3** *Sailing* another term for FREE (sense 8).
▸*adv. Sailing* another term for FREE (sense 2). ▷Middle English (in the sense 'liberal in giving, lavish, ample in quantity'): via Old French from Latin *larga*, feminine of *largus* 'copious.' **—large·ness** *n.* **—larg·ish** /-jisH/ *adj.* (usu. in sense 1).
▸*PHRASES* □ **at large 1** (esp. of a criminal or dangerous animal) at liberty; escaped or not yet captured: *the fugitive was still at large.* **2** as a whole; in general: *there has been a loss of community values in society at large.* **3** (also **at-large**) in a general way; without particularizing: *the magazine's editor at large.* **4** *dated* at length; in great detail: *writing at large on the policies he wished to pursue.* □ **in large measure** (or **part**) to a great extent: *the success of the conference was due in large part to its organizers.* □ (**as**) **large as life** see LIFE. □ **larger than life** see LIFE.

large cal·o·rie ▸*n.* see CALORIE.

large-cap ▸*adj. Finance* denoting or relating to the stock of a company with a large capitalization.

large-heart·ed ▸*adj.* sympathetic and generous.

large in·tes·tine ▸*n. Anatomy* the cecum, colon, and rectum collectively.

large·ly /'lärjlē/ ▸*adv.* [*sentence adverb*] to a great extent; on the whole; mostly: *he was soon arrested, largely through the efforts of Tom Poole* | [as *submodifier*] *their efforts were largely unsuccessful.*

large-mind·ed ▸*adj.* open to and tolerant of other people's ideas; liberal.

large·mouth /'lärj,mouTH/ ▸*n.* the largemouth bass (see BLACK BASS).

large-scale ▸*adj.* **1** involving large numbers or a large area; extensive: *large-scale commercial farming.* **2** (of a map or model) made to a scale large enough to show certain features in detail.

lar·gesse /lär'zHes; -'jes/ (also **lar·gess**) ▸*n.* generosity in bestowing money or gifts upon others: *dispensing his money with such largesse.* ■ money or gifts given generously: *the distribution of largesse to the local population.* See note at PRESENT. ▷Middle English: from Old French, from Latin *largus* 'copious.'

lar·ghet·to /lär'getō/ *Music* ▸*adv.* & *adj.* (esp. as a direction) in a fairly slow tempo.
▸*n.* (*pl.* **-tos**) a passage or movement marked to be performed in this way. ▷Italian, diminutive of *largo* 'broad.'

lar gib·bon /'lär/ ▸*n.* another term for WHITE-HANDED GIBBON.

Lar·go /'lär,gō/ a resort city in west central Florida, southwest of Clearwater; pop. 65,674.

lar·go /'lärgō/ *Music* ▸*adv.* & *adj.* (esp. as a direction) in a slow tempo and dignified in style.
▸*n.* (often **Largo**) (*pl.* **-gos**) a passage, movement, or composition marked to be performed in this way. ▷Italian, from Latin *largus* 'copious, abundant.'

la·ri /'lärē/ ▸*n.* (*pl.* same or **la·ris**) a monetary unit of the Maldives, equal to one hundredth of a rufiyaa. ▷from Persian.

Lar·i·am /'larēəm/ ▸*n.* trademark for MEFLOQUINE. ▷1980s: probably from partial rearrangement of MALARIA.

lar·i·at /'larēət/ ▸*n.* a rope used as a lasso or for tethering. ▷mid 19th cent.: from Spanish *la reata*, from *la* 'the' and *reatar* 'tie again' (based on Latin *aptare* 'adjust,' from *aptus* 'apt, fitting').

La Rio·ja /lä rē'ōhä/ an autonomous region of northern Spain, in the wine-producing valley of the Ebro River; capital, Logroño.

La·ris·sa /lə'risə/ a city in east central Greece; pop. 113,000. Greek name LÁRISA .

lark[1] /lärk/ ▸*n.* a small ground-dwelling songbird, typically with brown streaky plumage, a crest, and elongated hind claws, and with a song that is delivered in flight. • Family Alaudidae: many genera and numerous species, e.g., the **skylark**. ■ used in names of similar birds of other families, e.g., the **meadowlark**. ▷Old English *lāferce*, *lǣwerce*; related to Dutch *leeuwerik* and German *Lerche*; of unknown ultimate origin.

lark[2] *informal* ▸*n.* something done for fun, esp. something mischievous or daring; an amusing adventure or escapade: *I only went along* ***for a lark.*** ■ [usu. with *adj.*] *Brit.* used to suggest that an activity is foolish or a waste of time: *he's serious about this music lark.*
▸*v.* [*intrans.*] enjoy oneself by behaving in a playful and mischievous way: *he jumped the fence to go larking the rest of the day.* ▷early 19th cent.: perhaps from dialect *lake* 'play,' from Old Norse *leika*, but compare with SKYLARK in the same sense, which is recorded earlier. **—lark·ish** *adj.* **—lark·y** *adj.*

lark·spur /'lärk,spər/ ▸*n.* an annual Mediterranean plant of the buttercup family that bears spikes of spurred flowers. It is closely related to the delphiniums, with which it has been bred to produce a number of cultivated hybrids. • Genus *Consolida* (formerly *Delphinium*), family Ranunculaceae.

larn /lärn/ ▸*v.* dialect form of LEARN.

La·rousse /lə'rōōs; lä-/, Pierre (1817–75), French lexicographer and encyclopedist. He edited the 15-volume *Grand dictionnaire universel du XIX*[e] *siècle* (1866–76) and cofounded the publishing house of Larousse in 1852.

lar·ri·kin /'larikin/ ▸*n. Austral.* a boisterous, often badly behaved young man. ■ a person with apparent disregard for convention; a maverick: [as *adj.*] *the larrikin trade union leader.* ▷mid 19th cent.: from English dialect, perhaps from the given name *Larry* (nickname for *Lawrence*) + -KIN.

lar·rup /'larəp/ ▸*v.* (**-ruped**, **-rup·ing**) [*trans.*] *informal* thrash or whip (someone). ▷early 19th cent. (originally dialect): perhaps related to LATHER or LEATHER.

Lar·son /'lärsən/, Gary (1950–), U.S. cartoonist and writer. His one-panel comic "The Far Side," which he began in 1984 and retired in 1995, was syndicated in more than 900 newspapers.

lar·va /'lärvə/ ▸*n.* (*pl.* **-vae** /-vē; -,vī/) the active immature form of an insect, esp. one that differs greatly from the adult and forms the stage between egg and pupa, e.g., a caterpillar or grub. Compare with NYMPH (sense 2). ■ an immature form of other animals that undergo some metamorphosis, e.g., a tadpole. ▷mid 17th cent. (denoting a disembodied spirit or ghost): from Latin, literally 'ghost, mask.' **—lar·val** /-vəl/ *adj.* **—lar·vi·cide** /-,sīd/ *n.*

Lar·va·ce·a /lär'vāsHēə/ *Zoology* a class of minute transparent planktonic animals related to the sea squirts. They have a tadpolelike body that is typically enclosed in a gelatinous "house" that is regularly shed and replaced. ▷modern Latin (plural), from LARVA. **—lar·va·ce·an** *adj.* & *n.*

la·ryn·ge·al /lə'rinj(ē)əl; ,larən'jēəl/ ▸*adj.* of or relating to the larynx: *the laryngeal artery.* ■ *Phonetics* (of a speech sound) made in the larynx with the vocal cords partly closed and partly vibrating (producing, in English, the so-called "creaky voice" sound): *laryngeal consonants.*
▸*n. Phonetics* a laryngeal sound. ▷late 18th cent.: from modern Latin *laryngeus* 'relating to the larynx' + -AL.

la·ryn·ges /lə'rin,jēz/ ▸ plural form of LARYNX.

lar·yn·gi·tis /,larən'jītis/ ▸*n.* inflammation of the larynx, typically resulting in huskiness or loss of the voice, harsh breathing, and a painful cough. **—lar·yn·git·ic** /-'jitik/ *adj.*

lar·yn·gol·o·gy /,larəNG'gäləjē/ ▸*n.* the branch of medicine that deals with the larynx and its diseases. **—lar·yn·gol·o·gist** /-jist/ *n.*

la·ryn·go·scope /lə'riNGgə,skōp; -'rinjə-/ ▸*n.* an instrument for examining the larynx, or for inserting a tube through it. **—lar·yn·gos·co·py** /,larən-'gäskəpē; ,larəNG'gä-/ *n.*

lar·yn·got·o·my /,larən'gätəmē; ,larəNG'gä-/ ▸*n.* surgical incision into the larynx, typically to provide an air passage when breathing is obstructed.

lar·ynx /'lariNGks; 'ler-/ ▸*n.* (*pl.* **la·ryn·ges** /lə'rin,jēz/ or **lar·ynx·es**) *Anatomy* the hollow muscular organ forming an air passage to the lungs and holding the vocal cords in humans and other mammals; the voice box. ▷late 16th cent.: modern Latin, from Greek *larunx*.

la·sa·gna /lə'zänyə/ (also **la·sa·gne**) ▸*n.* pasta in the form of wide strips. ■ a baked Italian dish consisting of this cooked and layered with meat or vegetables, cheese, and tomato sauce. ▷Italian, plural of *lasagna*, based on Latin *lasanum* 'chamber pot,' perhaps also 'cooking pot.'

La Salle /lə 'sal; lä 'säl/, René-Robert Cavelier, Sieur de (1643–87), French explorer. He sailed from Canada down the Ohio and Mississippi rivers to the Gulf of Mexico in 1682, naming the Mississippi basin Louisiana in honor of Louis XIV. In 1684, he led an expedition to establish a French colony on the Gulf of Mexico, but was murdered when his followers mutinied.

La Sca·la /lä 'skälə/ an opera house in Milan built 1776–78 on the site of the church of Santa Maria della Scala.

las·car /'laskər/ ▸*n. dated* a sailor from India or Southeast Asia. ▷early 17th cent.: from Portuguese *lascari*, from Urdu and Persian *laškarī* 'soldier,' from *laškar* 'army.'

Las·caux /läs'kō; las-/ the site of a cave in the Dordogne, France, which is richly decorated with Paleolithic wall paintings of animals dated to the Magdalenian period.

las·civ·i·ous /lə'sivēəs/ ▸*adj.* (of a person, manner, or gesture) feeling or revealing an overt and often offensive sexual desire: *he gave her a lascivious wink.* ▷late Middle English: from late Latin *lasciviosus*, from Latin *lascivia* 'lustfulness,' from *lascivus* 'lustful, wanton.' **—las·civ·i·ous·ly** *adv.* **—las·civ·i·ous·ness** *n.*

Las Cru·ces /läs'krōōsəs/ a city in southern New Mexico, on the Rio Grande; pop. 74,267.

lase /lāz/ ▸*v.* [*intrans.*] (of a substance, esp. a gas or crystal) undergo the physical processes employed in a laser; function as or in a laser. ▷1960s: back-formation from LASER, interpreted as an agent noun.

la·ser /'lāzər/ ▸*n.* a device that generates an intense beam of coherent monochromatic light (or other electromagnetic radiation) by stimulated emission of photons from excited atoms or molecules. Lasers are used in drilling and cutting, alignment and guidance, and in surgery; the optical properties are exploited in holography, reading bar codes, and in recording and playing compact discs. ▷1960s: acronym from *light amplification by stimulated emission of radiation*, on the pattern of *maser*.

la·ser·disc /'lāzər,disk/ (also **la·ser disc**) ▸*n.* a disk that resembles a compact disc and functions in a similar manner; an optical disc. It is used mainly for high-quality video and for interactive multimedia on computer.

la·ser gun ▸*n.* a hand-held device incorporating a laser beam, used typically for reading a bar code or for determining the distance or speed of an object. ■ (in science fiction) a weapon that uses a powerful laser beam.

la·ser point·er ▸*n.* a pen-shaped pointing device that contains a small diode laser that emits an intense beam of light, used to direct attention during presentations.

la·ser print·er ▸*n.* a printer linked to a computer producing good-quality printed material by using a laser to form a pattern of electrostatically charged dots on a light-sensitive drum, which attract toner (or dry ink powder). The toner is transferred to a piece of paper and fixed by a heating process.

la·ser tweez·ers ▸*plural n.* another term for OPTICAL TWEEZERS.

La·ser·Vi·sion /'lāzər'vizHən/ ▸*n. trademark* a system for the reproduction of video signals recorded on a laserdisc. ▷1980s: from LASER + VISION, on the pattern of *television*.

lash /lasH/ ▸*v.* [*trans.*] **1** strike (someone) with a whip or stick: *they lashed him repeatedly about the head.* ■ beat forcefully against (something): *waves lashed the coast* | [*intrans.*] *torrential rain was lashing down.* ■ (**lash someone into**) drive someone into (a particular state or condition): *fear lashed him into a frenzy.* **2** [*trans.*] (of an animal) move (a part of the body, esp. the tail) quickly and violently: *the cat was lashing its tail back and forth.* ■ [*intrans.*] (of a part of the body) move in this way. **3** [*trans.*] fasten (something) securely with a cord or rope: *the hatch was securely* ***lashed down*** | *he lashed the flag to the mast.*
▸*phrasal v.* □ **lash out 1** hit or kick out at someone or something: *sticks with which to lash out and strike the prisoner.* ■ *figurative* attack verbally: *he used his thank-you speech to lash out at critics.* **2** *Brit.* spend money extravagantly: *let's* ***lash out on*** *a taxi.*
▸*n.* **1** a sharp blow or stroke with a whip or rope, typically given as a form of punishment: *he was sentenced to fifty lashes for his crime* | *figurative she felt the lash of my tongue.* ■ the flexible leather part of a whip, used for administering such blows. ■ (**the lash**) punishment in the form of a beating with a whip or rope: *they were living under the threat of the lash.* **2** (usu. **lashes**) an eyelash: *she fluttered her long dark lashes.* ▷Middle English (in the sense 'make a sudden movement'): probably imitative. **—lashed** *adj.* [in *combination*] *long-lashed eyes.* **—lash·er** *n.* **—lash·less** *adj.*

lashed /lasHt/ ▸*adj. Brit., informal* very drunk: *all eager to get lashed and start their working week off with a hangover.*

lash·ing /ˈlaSHiNG/ ▸*n.* **1** an act or instance of whipping: *I threatened to give him a good lashing! figurative he was on the receiving end of a verbal lashing yesterday.* **2** (usu. **lashings**) a cord used to fasten something securely.

lash·ings /ˈlaSHiNGz/ ▸*plural n. Brit., informal* a copious amount of something, esp. food or drink: *chocolate cake with **lashings of** cream.*

lash-up ▸*n. chiefly Brit.* a makeshift, improvised structure or arrangement.

LASIK /ˈlāzik/ ▸*n.* eye surgery to correct vision in which a laser reshapes the inner cornea. ▷from L(aser) A(ssisted) I(n-)S(itu) K(eratomileusis).

Las Pal·mas /läs ˈpälməs/ a port and resort on the north coast of the island of Gran Canaria, capital of the Canary Islands; pop. 372,000. Full name **Las Palmas de Gran Canaria** .

La Spe·zia /lä ˈspetsēə/ an industrial port in northwestern Italy; pop. 103,000. From 1861, it was Italy's chief naval station.

lass /las/ ▸*n. chiefly Scottish & N. English* a girl or young woman: *he married a lass from Yorkshire.* ▷Middle English: based on Old Norse *laskura* (feminine adjective) 'unmarried.'

Las·sa fe·ver /ˈläsə; ˈlasə/ ▸*n.* an acute and often fatal viral disease, with fever, occurring chiefly in West Africa. It is usually acquired from infected rats. ▷1970s: named after the village of *Lassa*, in northwestern Nigeria, where it was first reported.

las·si /ˈlasē/ ▸*n.* a sweet or savory Indian drink made from a yogurt or buttermilk base with water. ▷from Hindi *lassī.*

las·sie /ˈlasē/ ▸*n. chiefly Scottish & N. English* another term for **lass**.

las·si·tude /ˈlasəˌt(y)o͞od/ ▸*n.* a state of physical or mental weariness; lack of energy: *she was overcome by lassitude and retired to bed | a patient complaining of lassitude and inability to concentrate.* ▷late Middle English: from French, from Latin *lassitudo*, from *lassus* 'tired.'

las·so /ˈlasō; ˈlaso͞o; laˈso͞o/ ▸*n.* (*pl.* **-sos** or **-soes**) a rope with a noose at one end, used esp. in North America for catching cattle or horses.
▸*v.* (**-soes, -soed**) [*trans.*] catch (an animal) with a lasso: *at last his father lassoed the horse.* ▷mid 18th cent.: representing a Spanish American pronunciation of Spanish *lazo*, based on Latin *laqueus* 'noose.' Compare with **lace**. **—las·so·er** *n.*

Las·sus /ˈläsəs/, Orlande de (*c.*1532–94), Flemish composer; Italian name *Orlando di Lasso.* He wrote over 2,000 secular and sacred works.

last¹ /last/ ▸*adj.* [*attrib.*] **1** coming after all others in time or order; final: *they caught the last bus.* ■ met with or encountered after any others: *the last house in the village.* ■ the lowest in importance or rank: *finishing in last place* | [as *complement*] *he **came last** in the race.* ■ (**the last**) the least likely or suitable: *addicts are often the last people to face up to their problems | **the last thing she needed** was a husband.* **2** most recent in time; latest: *last year* | [*postpositive*] *your letter of Sunday last.* ■ immediately preceding in order; previous in a sequence: *their last album.* ■ most recently mentioned or enumerated: *this last point is critical.* **3** only remaining: *it's our last hope.* **4** single; individual: *Holly was ceremoniously savoring **every last** crumb of her chocolate doughnut.*
▸*adv.* **1** on the last occasion before the present; previously: *he looked much older than when I'd last seen him.* **2** [*in combination*] after all others in order or sequence: *the two last-mentioned classes.* **3** (esp. in enumerating points) finally; in conclusion: *and last, I'd like to thank you all for coming.*
▸*n.* (*pl.* same) the last person or thing; the one occurring, mentioned, or acting after all others: *the last of their guests had gone | eating as if every mouthful were his last.* ■ (**the last of**) the only part of something that remains: *they drank the last of the wine.* ■ [in *sing.*] last position in a race, contest, or ranking: *he came from last in a slowly run race.* ■ (**the last**) the end or last moment, esp. death: *she did love me **to the last**.* ■ (**the last**) the last mention or sight of someone or something: *that was **the last we saw of** her.* ▷Old English *latost* (adverb) 'after all others in a series,' of Germanic origin; related to Dutch *laatst, lest* and German *letzt*, also to **late**.
▸**PHRASES** □ **at last** (or **at long last**) after much delay: *you've come back to me at last!* □ **as a last resort** see **resort**. □ **—— one's last** do something for the last time: *the dying embers sparked their last.* □ **last but not least** last in order of mention or occurrence but just as important. □ **last call** (in a bar) an expression used to inform customers that closing time is approaching and that any further drinks should be purchased immediately: *the hours were 11:00 last call and drink up by 11:15.* □ **last ditch** used to denote a final, often desperate, act to achieve something in the face of difficulty: [as *adj.*] *a last-ditch attempt to acquire some proper qualifications.* □ **one's** (or **the**) **last gasp** see **gasp**. □ **the last straw** see **straw**. □ **on one's last legs** see **leg**.

USAGE In precise usage, **latest** means 'most recent' (*my latest project is wallpapering my dining room*), and **last** means 'final' (*the last day of the school year will be June 18*). But *last* is often used in place of *latest*, esp. in informal contexts: *I read his last novel.*

last² ▸*v.* [*intrans.*] **1** [with *adverbial*] (of a process, activity, or state of things) continue for a specified period of time: *the guitar solo lasted for twenty minutes | childhood seems to last forever.* **2** continue to function well or to be in good condition for a considerable or specified length of time: *the car is built to last | a lip pencil lasts longer than lipstick.* ■ (of a person) manage to continue in a job or course of action: *how long does he think he'll last as manager?* ■ survive or endure: *his condition is so serious that he won't last the night.* ■ [*trans.*] (of provisions or resources) be adequate or sufficient for (someone), esp. for a specified length of time: *he filled the freezer with enough food to last him for three months.* ▷Old English *lǣstan*, of Germanic origin, related to German *leisten* 'afford, yield,' also to **last**³.

last³ ▸*n.* a shoemaker's model for shaping or repairing a shoe or boot. ▷Old English *lǣste*, of Germanic origin, from a base meaning 'follow'; related to Dutch *leest* and German *Leisten.*

last-born ▸*adj.* last in order of birth; youngest.
▸*n.* a youngest or last-born child.

Last Fron·tier a nickname for the state of **Alaska**.

last-gasp ▸*adj.* [*attrib.*] *informal* done at the last possible moment, typically in desperation: *GIs who turned back Hitler's last-gasp gamble.*

last hur·rah ▸*n.* a final act, performance, or effort: *"This is my last hurrah in newsprint," said Mr. Evans.*

last·ing /ˈlastiNG/ ▸*adj.* enduring or able to endure over a long period of time: *they left a lasting impression | a lasting, happy marriage.* **—last·ing·ly** *adv.* **—last·ing·ness** *n.*

Last Judg·ment ▸*n.* the judgment of humankind expected in some religious traditions to take place at the end of the world.

last·ly /ˈlastlē/ ▸*adv.* in the last place (used to introduce the last of a series of points or actions): *lastly, I would like to thank my parents.*

last min·ute (also **last moment**) ▸*n.* the latest possible time before an event: *the visit was canceled **at the last minute*** | [as *adj.*] *a last-minute change of plans.*

last name ▸*n.* one's surname.

last post ▸*n.* (in the British armed forces) the second of two bugle calls giving notice of the hour of retiring at night, played also at military funerals and acts of remembrance.

last rites ▸*plural n.* (in the Christian Church) rites administered to a person who is about to die.

Last Sup·per the supper eaten by Jesus and his disciples on the night before the Crucifixion, as recorded in the New Testament and commemorated by Christians in the Eucharist. ■ an artistic representation based on this event.

last trump ▸*n.* the trumpet blast that in some religious beliefs is thought will wake the dead on Judgment Day.

last word ▸*n.* **1** a final or definitive pronouncement on or decision about a subject: *he's always determined to **have the last word**.* **2** the finest or most modern, fashionable, or advanced example of something: *the spa **is the last word in** luxury and efficiency.*

Las Ve·gas /läs ˈvāgəs/ a city in southern Nevada; pop. 478,434. It is noted for its casinos and nightclubs.

lat¹ /lat; lät/ ▸*n.* (*pl.* **la·ti** /ˈlätē/ or **lats**) the basic monetary unit of Latvia, equal to 100 santims. ▷from the first syllable of *Latvija* 'Latvia.'

lat² /lat/ ▸*n.* (usu. **lats**) *informal* (in bodybuilding) a latissimus muscle. ▷mid 20th cent.: abbreviation.

lat. ▸*abbr.* latitude: *between approximately 40° and 50° S. lat.*

Lat·a·ki·a /ˌlatəˈkēə/ a seaport on the coast of western Syria, opposite the northeastern tip of Cyprus; pop. 293,000.

latch /laCH/ ▸*n.* a metal bar with a catch and lever used for fastening a door or gate. ■ a spring lock for an outer door that catches when the door is closed and can only be opened from the outside with a key. ■ *Electronics* a circuit that retains whatever output state results from a momentary input signal until reset by another signal. ■ the part of a knitting machine needle that closes or opens to hold or release the wool.
▸*v.* [*trans.*] fasten (a door or gate) with a latch: *she latched the door carefully.* ■ [*intrans.*] *Electronics* (of a device) become fixed in a particular state.
▸*phrasal v.* □ **latch onto** *informal* attach oneself to (someone) as a constant and usually unwelcome companion: *a knack for latching onto people with greater initiative and enterprise.* ■ take up (an idea or trend) enthusiastically: *the media have latched onto the snappy "Generation X" catchphrase.* ■ (of one substance) cohere with (another). ▷Old English *læccan* 'take hold of, grasp (physically or mentally),' of Germanic origin.

latch·et /ˈlaCHit/ ▸*n. archaic* a narrow thong or lace for fastening a shoe or sandal. ▷late Middle English: from Old French *lachet*, variant of *lacet*, from *laz* 'lace.'

latch·key /ˈlaCHˌkē/ ▸*n.* (*pl.* **-keys**) a key of an outer door of a house.

latch·key child (also *informal* **latch·key kid**) ▸*n.* a child who is at home without adult supervision for some part of the day, esp. after school until a parent returns from work.

late /lāt/ ▸*adj.* **1** doing something or taking place after the expected, proper, or usual time: *his late arrival | she was half an hour **late for** her lunch appointment.* **2** belonging or taking place near the end of a particular time or period: *they won the game with a late goal.* ■ [*attrib.*] denoting the advanced stage of a period: *the late 1960s | arriving in the late afternoon.* ■ far on into the day or night: *I'm sorry the call is so late | it's **too late for** lunch.* ■ originating at a point well into an artistic period or artist's life: *his highly abstracted late landscapes | late Gothic style.* ■ flowering or ripening toward the end of the season: *the last late chrysanthemums.* **3** (**the/one's late**) (of a specified person) no longer alive: *the late William Jennings Bryan | her late husband's grave.* ■ no longer having the specified status; former: *a late colleague of mine.* **4** (**latest**) of recent date: *the latest news.*
▸*adv.* **1** after the expected, proper, or usual time: *she arrived late.* **2** toward the end of a period: *it happened **late in** 1984.* ■ at or until a time far into the day or night: *now I'm old enough to stay up late.* ■ (**later**) at a time in the near future; afterward: *I'll see you later | **later on** it will be easier.* **3** (**late of**) formerly but not now living or working in a specified place or institution: *Captain Falconer, late of the British army.*
▸*n.* (**the latest**) the most recent news or fashion: *have you heard the latest?* ▷Old English *læt* (adjective; also in the sense 'slow, tardy'), *late* (adverb), of Germanic origin; related to German *lass*, from an Indo-European root shared by Latin *lassus* 'weary,' **let**¹, and **let**². **—late·ness** *n.*
▸**PHRASES** □ **at the latest** no later than the time specified: *all new cars will be required to meet this standard by 1997 at the latest.* □ **late in the game** (or **day**) at a late stage in proceedings, esp. too late to be useful. □ **of late** recently: *she'd been drinking too much of late.*

USAGE See usage at **last**¹.

late·com·er /ˈlātˌkəmər/ ▸*n.* a person who arrives late: *latecomers were not admitted before the intermission | figurative he was **a latecomer to** modernism.*

la·teen /ləˈtēn; la-/ ▸*n.* (also **lateen sail**) a triangular sail on a long yard at an angle of 45° to the mast. ■ a ship rigged with such a sail. ▷mid 16th cent.: from French *(voile) Latine* 'Latin (sail),' so named because it was common in the Mediterranean.

lateen

Pronunciation Key ə *ago*; ər *over*; ˈə or ˌə *up*; ˈər or ˌər *fur*; a *hat*; ā *rate*; ä *car*; CH *chew*; e *let*; ē *see*; e(ə)r *air*; i *fit*; ī *by*; i(ə)r *ear*; NG *sing*; ō *go*; ô *for*; oi *boy*; o͝o *good*; o͞o *goo*; ou *out*; SH *she*; TH *thin*; T͟H *then*; (h)w *why*; ZH *vision*

late-gla·cial (also **late gla·cial**) ▸*adj.* *Geology* of or relating to the later stages of the final glaciation, from the beginning of the rise in temperature about 15,000 years ago to about 10,000 years ago. Compare with **POSTGLACIAL.**

late Lat·in ▸*n.* Latin of about AD 200–600.

late·ly /ˈlātlē/ ▸*adv.* recently; not long ago: *she hasn't been looking too well lately.* ▷Old English *lǣtlīce* 'slowly, tardily' (see **LATE, -LY**[2]).

late-mod·el ▸*adj.* (esp. of a car) recently made or of a recent design.

la·ten·cy /ˈlātn-sē/ ▸*n.* another term for **LATENT PERIOD.**

La Tène /lə ˈten/ ▸*n.* [usu. as *adj.*] *Archaeology* the second cultural phase of the European Iron Age, following the Halstatt period (*c.*480 BC) and lasting until the coming of the Romans. This culture represents the height of Celtic power. ▷late 19th cent.: named after a district in Switzerland, where remains of the culture were first identified.

la·tent /ˈlātnt/ ▸*adj.* (of a quality or state) existing but not yet developed or manifest; hidden; concealed: *discovering her latent talent for diplomacy.* ■ *Biology* (of a bud, resting stage, etc.) lying dormant or hidden until circumstances are suitable for development or manifestation. ■ (of a disease) in which the usual symptoms are not yet manifest. ■ (of a microorganism, esp. a virus) present in the body without causing disease, but capable of doing so at a later stage or when transmitted to another body. ▷late Middle English: from Latin *latent-* 'being hidden,' from the verb *latere.* **—la·tent·ly** *adv.*

> ***THE RIGHT WORD*** **abeyant, dormant, latent, quiescent, potential**
>
> All of these words refer to what is not currently observable or showing signs of activity.
>
> A **latent** talent is one that has not yet manifested itself, while **potential** suggests a talent that exists in an undeveloped state (*a potential concert violinist*). A child may have certain *latent* qualities of which his or her parents are unaware; but teachers are usually quick to spot a *potential* artist or poet in the classroom.
>
> **Dormant** and **quiescent** are less frequently associated with people and more often associated with things. A volcano might be described as *dormant*, which applies to anything that is currently inactive but has been active in the past and is capable of becoming active again in the future. *Dormant* carries the connotation of sleeping (*plants that are dormant in the winter*), while *quiescent* means motionless (*a quiescent sea*), emphasizing inactivity without referring to past or future activity.
>
> **Abeyant**, like *dormant*, means suspended or temporarily inactive, but it is most commonly used in its noun form (*personal rights and privileges kept in abeyance until the danger had passed*).

la·tent heat ▸*n.* *Physics* the heat required to convert a solid into a liquid or vapor, or a liquid into a vapor, without change of temperature.

la·tent im·age ▸*n.* *Photography* an image on an exposed film or print that has not yet been made visible by developing.

la·tent pe·ri·od ▸*n.* **1** *Medicine* (also **la·ten·cy pe·ri·od**) the period between infection with a virus or other microorganism and the onset of symptoms, or between exposure to radiation and the appearance of a cancer. **2** *Physiology* (also **la·ten·cy**) the delay between the receipt of a stimulus by a sensory nerve and the response to it.

lat·er /ˈlātər/ ▸*adj.* & *adv.* comparative of **LATE.**
▸*exclam.* *informal* goodbye for the present; see you later.

-later ▸*comb. form* denoting a person who worships a specified thing: *idolater.* ▷from Greek *-latrēs* 'worshiper.'

lat·er·al /ˈlatərəl; ˈlatrəl/ ▸*adj.* of, at, toward, or from the side or sides: *the plant takes up water through its lateral roots.* ■ *Anatomy & Zoology* situated on one side or other of the body or of an organ, esp. in the region furthest from the median plane. The opposite of **MEDIAL.** ■ *Medicine* (of a disease or condition) affecting the side or sides of the body, or confined to one side of the body. ■ *Physics* acting or placed at right angles to the line of motion or of strain. ■ *Phonetics* (of a consonant, esp. *l*, or its articulation) formed by or involving partial closure of the air passage by the tongue, which is so placed as to allow the breath to flow on one or both sides of the point of contact.
▸*n.* **1** a side part of something, esp. a shoot or branch growing out from the side of a stem. **2** *Phonetics* a lateral consonant. **3** *Football* (also **lateral pass**) a pass thrown either sideways or backward from the position of the passer.
▸*v.* [*trans.*] throw (a football) in a sideways or backward direction: *he tried to lateral a kick return but fumbled.* ■ [*intrans.*] throw a lateral: *he got the ball back on a handoff and then lateraled to a halfback.* ▷late Middle English: from Latin *lateralis*, from *latus, later-* 'side.' **—lat·er·al·ly** *adv.*

lat·er·al bud ▸*n.* another term for **AXILLARY BUD.**

lat·er·al·i·ty /ˌlatəˈralətē/ ▸*n.* dominance of one side of the brain in controlling particular activities or functions, or of one of a pair of organs such as the eyes or hands.

lat·er·al·ize /ˈlatərəˌlīz; ˈlatrə-/ ▸*v.* (**be lateralized**) (of the brain) show laterality. ■ [with *adverbial*] (of an organ, function, or activity) be largely under the control of one side of the brain: *this is a function that is usually lateralized on the right.* ■ [with *adverbial*] *Medicine* (of a lesion or pathological process) be diagnosed as localized to one or the other side of the brain. **—lat·er·al·i·za·tion** /ˌlatərəliˈzāshən; ˌlatrə-; -ˌlīˈzā/ *n.*

lat·er·al line ▸*n.* *Zoology* a visible line along the side of a fish consisting of a series of sense organs that detect pressure and vibration.

lat·er·al ven·tri·cle ▸*n.* *Anatomy* each of the first and second ventricles in the center of each cerebral hemisphere of the brain.

Lat·er·an /ˈlatərən/ the site in Rome containing the cathedral church of Rome (a basilica dedicated to St. John the Baptist and St. John the Evangelist) and the Lateran Palace, where the popes resided until the 14th century.

Lat·er·an Coun·cil any of five general councils of the Western Church held in the Lateran Palace in 1123, 1139, 1179, 1215, and 1512–17. The council of 1215 condemned the Albigenses as heretical and clarified the Church doctrine on transubstantiation, the Trinity, and the Incarnation.

Lat·er·an Trea·ty a concordat signed in 1929 in the Lateran Palace between the kingdom of Italy (represented by Mussolini) and the Holy See (represented by Pope Pius XI), which recognized the papal state as fully sovereign and independent under the name Vatican City.

lat·er·ite /ˈlatəˌrīt/ ▸*n.* a reddish clayey material, hard when dry, forming a topsoil in some tropical or subtropical regions and sometimes used for building. ■ *Geology* a clayey soil horizon rich in iron and aluminum oxides, formed by weathering of igneous rocks in moist warm climates. ▷early 19th cent.: from Latin *later* 'brick' + **-ITE**[1]. **—lat·er·it·ic** /ˌlatəˈritik/ *adj.*

la·tex /ˈlāˌteks/ ▸*n.* (*pl.* **la·tex·es** or **lat·i·ces** /ˈlatəˌsēz/) a milky fluid found in many plants, such as poppies and spurges, that exudes when the plant is cut and coagulates on exposure to the air. The latex of the rubber tree is the chief source of natural rubber. ■ a synthetic product resembling this consisting of a dispersion in water of polymer particles, used to make paints, coatings, and other products. ▷mid 17th cent. (denoting various bodily fluids, esp. the watery part of blood): from Latin, literally 'liquid, fluid.'

lath /laTH/ ▸*n.* (*pl.* **laths** /la<u>TH</u>Z; laTHs/) a thin flat strip of wood, esp. one of a series forming a foundation for the plaster of a wall or the tiles of a roof, or made into a trellis or fence. ■ laths collectively as a building material, esp. as a foundation for supporting plaster.
▸*v.* [*trans.*] cover (a wall or ceiling) with laths. ▷Old English *lætt*, of Germanic origin; related to Dutch *lat* and German *Latte*, also to **LATTICE.**

lathe /lā<u>TH</u>/ ▸*n.* a machine for shaping wood, metal, or other material by means of a rotating drive that turns the piece being worked on against changeable cutting tools.

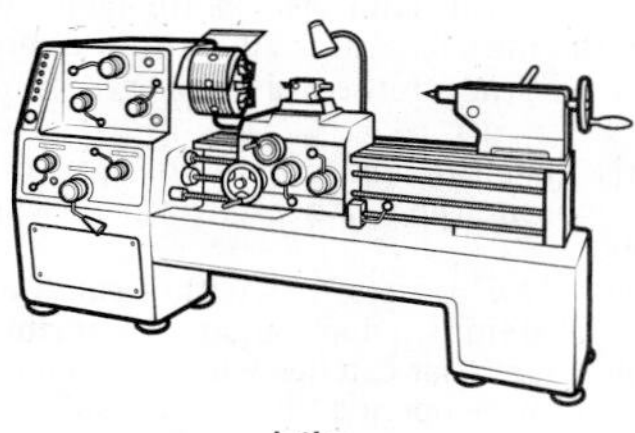

lathe

▸*v.* [*trans.*] shape with a lathe. ▷Middle English: probably from Old Danish *lad* 'structure, frame,' perhaps from Old Norse *hlath* 'pile, heap,' related to *hlatha* (see **LADE**).

lath·er /ˈla<u>TH</u>ər/ ▸*n.* a frothy white mass of bubbles produced by soap or a similar cleansing substance when mixed with water. ■ heavy sweat visible on a horse's coat as a white foam. ■ (**a lather**) *informal* a state of agitation or nervous excitement: *Larry was worked into a lather and shouted at the mayor.*
▸*v.* [*trans.*] **1** cause (soap) to form a frothy white mass of bubbles when mixed with water. ■ [*intrans.*] (of soap or a similar cleansing substance) form a frothy white mass of bubbles in such a way: *soap will not lather in hard water.* ■ rub soap onto (a part of the body) until a lather is produced: *she was lathering herself languidly beneath the shower* | [*intrans.*] *he lathered and started to shave.* ■ cause (a horse) to become covered with sweat: *his horse was* ***lathered up*** *by the end of the day.* ■ (**lather something with**) cover something liberally with (a substance): *she lathered a slice of toast with butter.* **2** *informal* thrash (someone). ▷Old English *lǣthor* (denoting washing soda or its froth), *lēthran* (verb), of Germanic origin; related to Old Norse *lauthr* (noun), from an Indo-European root shared by Greek *loutron* 'bath.' **—lath·er·y** *adj.*

lath·y·rism /ˈlaTHəˌrizəm/ ▸*n.* a tropical disease marked by tremors, muscular weakness, and paraplegia, esp. prevalent in the Indian subcontinent. It is commonly attributed to continued consumption of the seeds of the grass pea. ▷late 19th cent.: from modern Latin *Lathyrus* (genus name of various leguminous plants) + **-ISM.**

lat·i·ces /ˈlatəˌsēz/ ▸ plural form of **LATEX.**

la·tic·i·fer /lāˈtisəfər/ ▸*n.* *Botany* a cell, tissue, or vessel that contains or conducts latex. ▷mid 19th cent.: from Latin *latex, latic-* 'fluid' + *-fer* 'bearing.' **—lat·i·cif·er·ous** /ˌlatəˈsif(ə)rəs/ *adj.*

lat·i·fun·di·um /ˌlatəˈfəndēəm/ ▸*n.* (*pl.* **-di·a** /-dēə/) a large landed estate or ranch in ancient Rome or more recently in Spain or Latin America, typically worked by slaves. ▷mid 17th cent.: from Latin, from *latus* 'broad' + *fundus* 'landed estate,' partly via Spanish.

Lat·in /ˈlatn/ ▸*n.* **1** the language of ancient Rome and its empire, widely used historically as a language of scholarship and administration.

> Latin is a member of the Italic branch of the Indo-European family of languages. After the decline of the Roman Empire, it continued to be a medium of communication among educated people throughout the Middle Ages in Europe and remained the liturgical language of the Roman Catholic Church until the reforms of the Second Vatican Council (1962–65); it is still used for scientific names in biology and astronomy. The Romance languages are derived from it.

2 a native or inhabitant of a country whose language developed from Latin, esp. a Latin American. ■ music of a kind originating in Latin America, characterized by dance rhythms and extensive use of indigenous percussive instruments.
▸*adj.* of, relating to, or in the Latin language: *Latin poetry.* ■ of or relating to the countries or peoples using languages, esp. Spanish, that developed from Latin. ■ of, relating to, or characteristic of Latin American music or dance: *snapping his fingers to a Latin beat.* ■ of or relating to the Western or Roman Catholic Church (as historically using Latin for its rites): *the Latin patriarch of Antioch.* ■ *historical* of or relating to ancient Latium or its inhabitants. ▷from Latin *Latinus* 'of Latium' (see **LATIUM**). **—Lat·in·ism** /-ˌizəm/ *n.* **—Lat·in·ist** /-ist/ *n.*

La·ti·na /ləˈtēnə; la-/ ▸*n.* a female Latin American inhabitant of the United States.
▸*adj.* of or relating to these inhabitants. ▷Latin American Spanish, feminine of *Latino* (see **LATINO**).

Lat·in A·mer·i·ca the parts of the American continent where Spanish or Portuguese is the main national language (i.e., Mexico and, in effect, the whole of Central and South America including many of the Caribbean islands). **—Lat·in A·mer·i·can** *n.* & *adj.*

Lat·in·ate /ˈlatnˌāt/ ▸*adj.* (of language) having the character of Latin: *Latinate suffixes.*

Lat·in Church the Christian Church that originated in the Western Roman Empire, giving allegiance to the pope of Rome, and historically using Latin for the liturgy; the Roman Catholic Church as distinguished from Orthodox and Uniate Churches.

Lat·in cross ▸*n.* a plain cross in which the vertical

part below the horizontal is longer than the other three parts.

La·tin·i·ty /lə'tinətē; la-/ ▶*n.* the use of Latin style or words of Latin origin.

Lat·in·ize /'latn,īz/ ▶*v.* [*trans.*] **1** give a Latin or Latinate form to (a word): *his name was Latinized into Confucius.* ■ *archaic* translate into Latin. ■ [*intrans.*] *archaic* use Latin forms or idiom. **2** make (a people or culture) conform to the ideas and customs of the ancient Romans, the Latin peoples, or the Latin Church. ▷late 16th cent.: from late Latin *Latinizare*, from Latin *Latinus* (see **LATIN**). —**Lat·in·i·za·tion** /,latn-ə'zāSHən/ *n.* —**Lat·in·iz·er** *n.*

Lat·in lov·er ▶*n.* a Latin male popularly characterized as having a romantic, passionate temperament and great sexual prowess.

La·ti·no /lə'tēnō; la-/ ▶*n.* (*pl.* **-nos**) a Latin American inhabitant of the United States.
▶*adj.* of or relating to these inhabitants. ▷Latin American Spanish, probably a special use of Spanish *latino* (see **LATIN**).

Lat·in square ▶*n.* an arrangement of letters or symbols that each occur *n* times, in a square array of n^2 compartments so that no letter appears twice in the same row or column. ■ such an arrangement used as the basis of experimental procedures in which it is desired to control or allow for two sources of variability while investigating a third.

lat·ish /'lātiSH/ ▶*adj.* & *adv.* fairly late: [as *adv.*] *Margaret came in latish.*

la·tis·si·mus /lə'tisəməs/ (also **la·tis·si·mus dor·si** /'dôrsī/) ▶*n.* (*pl.* **-mi** /-,mī; -,mē/) *Anatomy* either of a pair of large, roughly triangular muscles covering the lower part of the back, extending from the sacral, lumbar, and lower thoracic vertebrae to the armpits. ▷early 17th cent.: modern Latin, from *musculus latissimus dorsi*, literally 'broadest muscle of the back.'

lat·i·tude /'latə,t(y)o͞od/ ▶*n.* **1** the angular distance of a place north or south of the earth's equator, or of a celestial object north or south of the celestial equator, usually expressed in degrees and minutes: *at a latitude of 51° N* | *lines of latitude.* ■ (**latitudes**) regions, esp. with reference to their temperature and distance from the equator: *temperate latitudes* | *northern latitudes.* ■ *Astronomy* see **CELESTIAL LATITUDE**. **2** scope for freedom of action or thought: *journalists have considerable latitude in criticizing public figures.* See note at **RANGE**. ■ *Photography* the range of exposures for which an emulsion or printing paper will give acceptable contrast: *a film with a latitude that is outstanding.* ▷late Middle English: from Latin *latitudo* 'breadth,' from *latus* 'broad.' —**lat·i·tu·di·nal** /,latə-'t(y)o͞odn-əl/ *adj.* —**lat·i·tu·di·nal·ly** /,latə't(y)o͞odn-əlē/ *adv.*

latitude 1

lat·i·tu·di·nar·i·an /,latə,t(y)o͞odn'erēən/ ▶*adj.* allowing latitude in religion; showing no preference among varying creeds and forms of worship.
▶*n.* a person with a latitudinarian attitude. ▷mid 17th cent.: from Latin *latitudo* 'breadth' (see **LATITUDE**) + **-ARIAN**. —**lat·i·tu·di·nar·i·an·ism** /-,nizəm/ *n.*

La·ti·um /'lāSH(ē)əm/ an ancient region in west central Italy, west of the Apennines and south of the Tiber River. Settled during the early part of the 1st millennium BC by a branch of the Indo-European people known as the Latini, it was dominated by Rome by the end of the 4th century BC.

lat·ke /'lätkə/ ▶*n.* (in Jewish cooking) a pancake, esp. one made with grated potato. ▷Yiddish.

La·to·na /lə'tōnə/ *Roman Mythology* Roman name for **LETO**.

la·tri·a /lə'trīə/ ▶*n.* (in the Roman Catholic Church) supreme worship allowed to God alone. Compare with **DULIA**. ▷early 16th cent.: from late Latin, from Greek *latreia* 'worship,' from *latreuein* 'serve.'

la·trine /lə'trēn/ ▶*n.* a toilet, esp. a communal one in a camp or barracks. ▷Middle English (rare before the mid 19th cent): via French from Latin *latrina*, contraction of *lavatrina*, from *lavare* 'to wash.'

La·trobe /lə'trōb/, Benjamin Henry (1764–1820) U.S. architect; born in England. He designed the south wing of the U.S. Capitol in Washington, DC, and rebuilt the Capitol after its destruction by the British in 1815–17.

-latry ▶*comb. form* denoting worship of a specified thing: *idolatry.* ▷from Greek *-latreia* 'worship.'

lat·te /'lä,tā/ ▶*n.* short for **CAFFÈ LATTE**.

lat·ten /'latn/ ▶*n. historical* an alloy of copper and zinc resembling brass, hammered into thin sheets and used to make monumental brasses and church ornaments. ▷Middle English: from Old French *laton*, of unknown origin.

lat·ter /'latər/ ▶*adj.* [*attrib.*] **1** situated or occurring nearer to the end of something than to the beginning: *the latter half of 1989.* ■ belonging to the final stages of something, esp. of a person's life: *heart disease dogged his latter years.* ■ recent: *the project had low cash flows in its latter years.* **2** (**the latter**) denoting the second or second mentioned of two people or things: *the Russians could advance into either Germany or Austria—they chose the latter option.* ▷Old English *lætra* 'slower,' comparative of *læt* (see **LATE**).

USAGE **Latter** means 'the second-mentioned of two.' Its use to mean 'the last-mentioned of three or more' is common, but is considered incorrect by some because **latter** means 'later' rather than 'latest.' *Last* or *last-mentioned* is preferred where three or more things are involved. See also **usage** at **FORMER**[1].

lat·ter-day ▶*adj.* [*attrib.*] modern or contemporary, esp. when mirroring some person or thing of the past: *the book is built around the story of the Flood and a latter-day Noah.*

Lat·ter-Day Saints (abbr.: **LDS**) ▶*plural n.* another name for the Mormons.

lat·ter·ly /'latərlē/ ▶*adv.* recently: *latterly, his painting has shown a new freedom of expression.* ■ in the later stages of a period of time, esp. of a person's life: *he worked on the paper for fifty years, latterly as its political editor.*

lat·tice /'latis/ ▶*n.* a structure consisting of strips of wood or metal crossed and fastened together with square or diamond-shaped spaces left between, used typically as a screen or fence or as a support for climbing plants. ■ an interlaced structure or pattern resembling this: *the lattice of branches above her.* ■ *Physics* a regular repeated three-dimensional arrangement of atoms, ions, or molecules in a metal or other crystalline solid. ▷Middle English: from Old French *lattis*, from *latte* 'lath,' of Germanic origin.

lattice

lat·ticed /'latist/ ▶*adj.* decorated with or in the form of a lattice: *a latticed screen.*

lat·tice en·er·gy ▶*n. Chemistry* a measure of the energy contained in the crystal lattice of a compound, equal to the energy that would be released if the component ions were brought together from infinity.

lat·tice frame (also **lattice girder**) ▶*n.* an iron or steel structure consisting of two horizontal beams connected by diagonal struts.

lat·tice win·dow ▶*n.* a window with small panes set in diagonally crossing strips of lead.

lat·tice·work /'latis,wərk/ ▶*n.* interlacing strips of wood, metal, or other material forming a lattice.

lat·ti·ci·nio /,lati'CHēnyō/ (also **lat·ti·ci·no** /-'CHēnō/) ▶*n.* an opaque white glass used in threads to decorate clear Venetian glass. ▷Italian, literally 'dairy produce,' from medieval Latin *lacticinium*.

Lat·via /'latvēə/ a country on the eastern shore of the Baltic Sea, between Estonia and Lithuania; pop. 2,306,000; capital, Riga; languages, Latvian (official), Russian, Lithuanian.

Latvia was annexed by Russia in the 18th century after periods of Polish and Swedish rule. It was proclaimed an independent republic in 1918, but in 1940 was annexed by the Soviet Union as a constituent republic. In 1991, on the breakup of the Soviet Union, Latvia became an independent republic once again. It joined both NATO and the EU in 2004.

Lat·vi·an /'latvēən/ ▶*adj.* of or relating to Latvia, its people, or its language.
▶*n.* **1** a native or citizen of Latvia, or a person of Latvian descent. **2** the Baltic language of Latvia.

lau·an /'lo͞o-än/ ▶*n.* another term for **PHILIPPINE MAHOGANY**.

Laud /'lôd/, William (1573–1645), English prelate; archbishop of Canterbury 1633–45. His attempts to restore pre-Reformation practices in England and Scotland contributed to the causes of the English Civil War. He was executed for treason.

laud /lôd/ ▶*v.* [*trans.*] *formal* praise (a person or their achievements) highly, esp. in a public context: *the obituary lauded him as a great statesman and soldier* | [as *adj.*, with *submodifier*] (**lauded**) *her much lauded rendering of Lady Macbeth.* See note at **PRAISE**.
▶*n. archaic* praise: *all glory, laud, and honor to Thee.* ▷late Middle English: the noun from Old French *laude*, the verb from Latin *laudare*, both from Latin *laus, laud-* 'praise' (see also **LAUDS**).

laud·a·ble /'lôdəbəl/ ▶*adj.* (of an action, idea, or goal) deserving praise and commendation: *laudable though the aim might be, the results have been criticized.* ▷late Middle English: from Latin *laudabilis*, from *laus, laud-* 'praise.' —**laud·a·bil·i·ty** /,lôdə'bilətē/ *n.* —**laud·a·bly** /-blē/ *adv.*

lau·da·num /'lôdn-əm; 'lôdnəm/ ▶*n.* an alcoholic solution containing morphine, prepared from opium and formerly used as a narcotic painkiller. ▷mid 16th cent. (applied to various preparations containing opium): modern Latin, the name given by Paracelsus to a costly medicament of which opium was believed to be the active ingredient; perhaps a variant of Latin *ladanum* (see **LABDANUM**).

lau·da·tion /lô'dāSHən/ ▶*n. formal* praise; commendation. ▷late Middle English: from Latin *laudatio(n-)*, from the verb *laudare* (see **LAUD**).

laud·a·to·ry /'lôdə,tôrē/ ▶*adj.* (of speech or writing) expressing praise and commendation. ▷mid 16th cent.: from late Latin *laudatorius*, from *laudat-* 'praised,' from the verb *laudare* (see **LAUD**).

lauds /lôdz/ ▶*n.* a service of morning prayer in the Divine Office of the Western Christian Church, traditionally said or chanted at daybreak, though historically it was often held with matins on the previous night. ▷Middle English: from the frequent use, in Psalms 148–150, of the Latin imperative *laudate!* 'praise ye!' (see also **LAUD**).

laugh /laf/ ▶*v.* [*intrans.*] make the spontaneous sounds and movements of the face and body that are the instinctive expressions of lively amusement and sometimes also of contempt or derision: *she couldn't help laughing at his jokes* | *he* **laughed out loud** | [with *direct speech*] *she laughed, "Not a chance."* ■ (**laugh at**) ridicule; scorn. ■ (**laugh something off**) dismiss something embarrassing, unfortunate, or potentially serious by treating it in a lighthearted way or making a joke of it. ■ (**be laughing**) *informal* be in a fortunate or successful position: *if next year's model is as successful, Ford will be laughing.*
▶*n.* **1** an act of laughing: *she gave a loud, silly laugh.* **2** (**a laugh**) *informal* a thing that causes laughter or derision: *that's a laugh, the idea of you cooking a meal!* ■ a

Pronunciation Key ə *ago*; ər *over*; 'ə or ,ə *up*; 'ər or ,ər *fur*; a *hat*; ā *rate*; ä *car*; CH *chew*; e *let*; ē *see*; e(ə)r *air*; i *fit*; ī *by*; i(ə)r *ear*; NG *sing*; ō *go*; ô *for*; oi *boy*; o͝o *good*; o͞o *goo*; ou *out*; SH *she*; TH *thin*; T͟H *then*; (h)w *why*; ZH *vision*

L

person who is good fun or amusing company: *I like Peter—he's **a good laugh**.* ■ a source of fun or amusement: *she decided to play along with him **for a laugh** | he knew his performance was **good for a laugh**.* ▷Old English *hlæhhan, hliehhan*, of Germanic origin; related to Dutch and German *lachen*, also to **LAUGHTER**.

▸*PHRASES* □ **be laughing all the way to the bank** *informal* be making a great deal of money very easily. □ **have the last laugh** be finally vindicated, thus confounding earlier skepticism. □ **laugh one's head off** laugh heartily or uncontrollably. □ **laugh in someone's face** show open contempt for someone by laughing rudely at them in their presence: *figurative vandals and muggers who laugh in the face of the law.* □ **the laugh is on me** (or **you**, **him**, etc.) the tables are turned and now the other person is the one who appears ridiculous: *all the critics had laughed at him—well, the laugh was on them now.* □ **laugh like a drain** *Brit., informal* laugh raucously. □ **a laugh a minute** very funny: *it's a laugh a minute when Lois gets together with her dad.* □ **laugh out of the other side of one's mouth** be discomfited after feeling satisfaction or confidence about something: *you'd be laughing out the other side of your mouth if we were sitting in jail right now.* □ **laugh someone/something out of court** dismiss with contempt as being obviously ridiculous. □ **laugh oneself silly** (or **sick**) laugh uncontrollably or for a long time. □ **laugh something to scorn** *dated* ridicule something. □ **laugh up one's sleeve** be secretly or inwardly amused. □ **no laughing matter** something serious that should not be joked about: *heavy snoring is no laughing matter.* □ **play something for laughs** (of a performer) try to arouse laughter in an audience, esp. in inappropriate circumstances.

laugh·a·ble /ˈlafəbəl/ ▸*adj.* so ludicrous as to be amusing: *if it didn't make me so angry it would be laughable.* **—laugh·a·bly** /-blē/ *adv.* [as *submodifier*] *his antics were laughably pretentious.*

laugh·er /ˈlafər/ ▸*n.* **1** a person who laughs. **2** *informal* a sports contest or other competition that is so easily won by one team or competitor that it seems absurd.

laugh·ing gas ▸*n.* nontechnical term for **NITROUS OXIDE**.

laugh·ing hy·e·na ▸*n.* another term for **SPOTTED HYENA**.

laugh·ing jack·ass ▸*n. Austral.* the laughing kookaburra. See **KOOKABURRA**.

laugh·ing·ly /ˈlafiNGlē/ ▸*adv.* with amused ridicule or ludicrous inappropriateness: *we finally reached what we laughingly called civilization.* ■ in an amused way; with laughter.

laugh·ing·stock /ˈlafiNG,stäk/ ▸*n.* [in *sing.*] a person subjected to general mockery or ridicule.

laugh·ing thrush ▸*n.* a gregarious thrushlike babbler of South and Southeast Asia, typically with dark gray or brown plumage and a boldly marked head, and having a cackling call. • Genus *Garrulax*, family Timaliidae: many species.

Laugh·lin /ˈläklən; ˈläflən/ a community in southern Arizona, across the Colorado River from Bullhead City; pop. 4,791.

laugh·ter /ˈlaftər/ ▸*n.* the action or sound of laughing: *he roared with laughter.* ▷Old English *hleahtor*, of Germanic origin; related to German *Gelächter*, also to **LAUGH**.

Laugh·ton /ˈlôtn/, Charles (1899–1962), U.S. actor, born in England. He is remembered for character roles such as Henry VIII (*The Private Life of Henry VIII*, 1933) and Captain Bligh (*Mutiny on the Bounty*, 1935); he also played Quasimodo in *The Hunchback of Notre Dame* (1939).

launce /lôns; läns/ ▸*n.* another term for **SAND EEL**. ▷early 17th cent.: early variant of **LANCE** (because of its shape).

Laun·ce·lot /ˈlônsə,lät; ˈlän-; -lət/ variant spelling of **LANCELOT**.

launch[1] /lônCH; länCH/ ▸*v.* [*trans.*] **1** set (a boat) in motion by pushing it or allowing it to roll into the water: *the town's lifeboat was launched to rescue the fishermen.* ■ set (a newly built ship or boat) afloat for the first time, typically as part of an official ceremony: *King Gustav II Adolph of Sweden launched a huge new warship.* ■ send (a missile, satellite, or spacecraft) on its course or into orbit: *they launched two Scud missiles.* ■ [*trans.*] hurl (something) forcefully: *she launched a tortoiseshell comb.* ■ [with *adverbial of direction*] (**launch oneself**) (of a person) make a sudden energetic movement: *I launched myself out of bed.* ■ utter (criticism or a threat) vehemently: *scores of customers launched a volley of complaints.* **2** start or set in motion (an activity or enterprise): *she was launching a campaign against ugly architecture.* ■ introduce (a new product or publication) to the public for the first time: *the company has launched a software package specifically for the legal sector.*

▸*phrasal v.* □ **launch into** begin (something) energetically and enthusiastically: *he launched into a two-hour sales pitch.* □ **launch out** make a start on a new and challenging enterprise: *she wasn't brave enough to launch out by herself.*

▸*n.* an act or an instance of launching something: *the launch of a new campaign against drinking and driving.* ■ an occasion at which a new product or publication is introduced to the public: *a book launch.* ▷Middle English (in the sense 'hurl a missile, discharge with force'): from Anglo-Norman French *launcher*, variant of Old French *lancier* (see **LANCE**).

launch[2] ▸*n.* a large motorboat, used esp. for short trips. Also called **MOTOR LAUNCH**. ■ *historical* the largest boat carried on a man-of-war. ▷late 17th cent. (denoting the longboat of a man-of-war): from Spanish *lancha* 'pinnace,' perhaps from Malay *lancharan*, from *lanchar* 'swift, nimble.'

launch·er /ˈlônCHər; ˈlän-/ ▸*n.* a structure that holds a rocket or missile during launching. ■ a rocket that is used to convey a satellite or spacecraft into orbit. ■ a catapult for aircraft. ■ an attachment to the muzzle of a rifle permitting the firing of grenades.

launch pad (also **launc·hing pad**) ▸*n.* the area on which a rocket stands for launching, typically consisting of a platform with a supporting structure.

launch ve·hi·cle ▸*n.* a rocket-powered vehicle used to send artificial satellites or spacecraft into space.

laun·der /ˈlôndər; ˈlän-/ ▸*v.* [*trans.*] wash, or wash and iron, (clothes or linens): *he wasn't used to laundering his own bed linens* | [as *adj.*, with *submodifier*] (**laundered**) *freshly laundered sheets.* ■ conceal the origins of (money obtained illegally) by transfers involving foreign banks or legitimate businesses. ■ alter (information) to make it appear more acceptable: *we began to notice attempts to launder the data retrospectively.*

▸*n.* a trough for holding or conveying water, esp. (in mining) one used for washing ore. ■ a channel for conveying molten metal from a furnace or container to a ladle or mold. ▷Middle English (as a noun denoting a person who washes linen): contraction of *lavender*, from Old French *lavandier*, based on Latin *lavanda* 'things to be washed,' from *lavare* 'to wash.' **—laun·der·er** *n.*

laun·der·ette /,lôndəˈret; ,län-/ (also **laun·drette**) ▸*n.* a laundromat.

laun·dress /ˈlôndrəs; ˈlän-/ ▸*n.* a woman who is employed to launder clothes and linens.

Laun·dro·mat /ˈlôndrə,mat; ˈlän-/ (also **laun·dro·mat**) ▸*n. trademark* an establishment with coin-operated washing machines and dryers for public use. ▷1940s (originally U.S., as the proprietary name of a washing machine): blend of **LAUNDER** and **AUTOMATIC**.

laun·dry /,lôndrē; ˈlän-/ ▸*n.* (*pl.* **-dries**) **1** clothes and linens that need to be washed or that have been newly washed: *piles of dirty laundry.* ■ the action or process of washing such items: *I talked her into letting me help Ben with the rest of the laundry.* **2** a room in a house, hotel, or institution where clothes and linens can be washed and ironed. ■ a business that washes and irons clothes and linens commercially. ▷early 16th cent.: contraction of Middle English *lavendry*, from Old French *lavanderie*, from *lavandier* 'person who washes linen' (see **LAUNDER**).

laun·dry list ▸*n.* a long or exhaustive list of people or things: *there's **a laundry list of** possible triggers for migraines.*

laun·dry·man /ˈlôndrēmən; ˈlän-/ ▸*n.* (*pl.* **-men**) a man who is employed to launder clothes and linens, or deliver them to customers.

Laur·a·sia /lôˈrāZHə/ a vast continental area believed to have existed in the northern hemisphere and to have resulted from the breakup of Pangaea in Mesozoic times. It comprised the present North America, Greenland, Europe, and most of Asia north of the Himalayas.

lau·re·ate /ˈlôrē-it; ˈlär-/ ▸*n.* a person who is honored with an award for outstanding creative or intellectual achievement: *a Nobel laureate.* ■ short for **POET LAUREATE**.

▸*adj. poetic/literary* wreathed with laurel as a mark of honor. ■ (of a crown or wreath) consisting of laurel. ▷late Middle English (as an adjective): from Latin *laureatus*, from *laurea* 'laurel wreath,' from *laurus* 'laurel.' **—lau·re·ate·ship** /-,SHip/ *n.*

Lau·rel /ˈlôrəl/ a city in central Maryland, between Washington, DC, and Baltimore; pop. 19,960.

lau·rel /ˈlôrəl;ˈlär-/ ▸*n.* **1** any of a number of shrubs and other plants with dark green glossy leaves, in particular: • short for **MOUNTAIN LAUREL**. • short for **CHERRY LAUREL**. • the bay tree. See **BAY**[2]. **2** an aromatic evergreen shrub related to the bay tree, several kinds of which form forests in tropical and warm countries. • Family Lauraceae: many genera and species. **3** (usu. **laurels**) the foliage of the bay tree woven into a wreath or crown and worn on the head as an emblem of victory or mark of honor in classical times. ■ *figurative* honor: *she has rightly won laurels for this brilliantly perceptive first novel.*

▸*v.* (**-reled**, **-rel·ing**; *Brit.* **-relled**, **-rel·ling**) [*trans.*] adorn with or as if with a laurel: *they banish our anger forever when they laurel the graves of our dead.* ▷Middle English *lorer*, from Old French *lorier*, from Provençal *laurier*, from earlier *laur*, from Latin *laurus*.

▸*PHRASES* □ **look to one's laurels** be careful not to lose one's superior position to a rival. □ **rest on one's laurels** be so satisfied with what one has already achieved that one makes no further effort.

Lau·rel and Har·dy /ˈlôrəl and ˈhärdē/ U.S. comedy duo that consisted of **Stan Laurel** (born *Arthur Stanley Jefferson*) (1890–1965) and **Oliver Hardy** (1892–1957). British-born Laurel played the scatterbrained and often tearful innocent; Hardy played his pompous, overbearing, and frequently exasperated friend. They brought their distinctive slapstick comedy to many movies from 1927.

Stan Laurel and Oliver Hardy

Lau·ren·tian Pla·teau /lôˈrenSHən/ another name for **CANADIAN SHIELD**. ▷*Laurentian* from Latin *Laurentius* 'Lawrence' (from St. *Lawrence* River) + **-AN**.

Lau·ri·er /ˈlôrē,ā; lôrˈyā/, Sir Wilfrid (1841–1919), Canadian statesman; prime minister 1896–1911. He was Canada's first French-Canadian and first Roman Catholic prime minister.

lau·rus·ti·nus /,lôrəˈstīnəs; ,lä-; -ˈstē-/ ▸*n.* an evergreen winter-flowering viburnum with dense glossy green leaves and white or pink flowers, native to the Mediterranean area and cultivated elsewhere. • *Viburnum tinus*, family Caprifoliaceae. ▷early 17th cent.: modern Latin, from Latin *laurus* 'laurel' + *tinus* 'wild laurel.'

Lau·sanne /lōˈzän/ a town in southwestern Switzerland, on the north shore of Lake Geneva; pop. 123,000.

Lau·sit·zer Neis·se /ˈlouzitsər ˈnīsə/ German name for **NEISSE** (sense 1).

lav /lav/ ▸*n. informal* a lavatory. ▷early 20th cent.: abbreviation.

la·va /ˈlävə; ˈlavə/ ▸*n.* hot molten or semifluid rock erupted from a volcano or fissure, or solid rock resulting from cooling of this. ▷mid 18th cent.: from Italian (Neapolitan dialect), denoting the lava stream from Vesuvius, but originally denoting a stream caused by sudden rain, from *lavare* 'to wash,' from Latin.

la·va·bo /ləˈväbō; -ˈvābō/ ▸*n.* (*pl.* **-boes**) (in the Roman Catholic Church) a towel or basin used for the ritual washing of the celebrant's hands at the offertory of the Mass. ■ ritual washing of this type. ■ *dated* a washbasin. ■ a washing trough in a monastery. ▷mid 18th cent.: from Latin, literally 'I will wash,' in *Lavabo inter innocentes manus meas* 'I will wash my hands among the innocent' (Ps. 26:6), which was recited at the washing of hands in the Roman rite.

la·va dome ▸*n.* a mound of viscous lava that has been extruded from a volcanic vent.

la·va flow ▸*n.* a mass of flowing or solidified lava.

la·vage /ləˈväZH; ˈlavij/ ▸*n. Medicine* washing out of a body cavity, such as the colon or stomach, with water or a medicated solution. ▷late 18th cent. (in the general sense 'washing, a wash'): from French, from *laver* 'to wash.'

la·va lamp ▸*n.* a transparent electric lamp containing a viscous liquid in which a brightly colored waxy substance is suspended, rising and falling in irregular and constantly changing shapes.

la·vash /lə'väsʜ/ ▸*n.* a Middle Eastern crisp flatbread. ▷Armenian, from Turkish.

lav·a·to·ri·al /ˌlavə'tôrēəl/ ▸*adj.* of or relating to lavatories, in particular: ■ (of conversation or humor) characterized by undue reference to toilets and their use: *the comic's lavatorial schoolboy humor.* ■ resembling the style or architecture supposed to typify public lavatories: *the lavatorial utility that was a feature of subway design.*

lav·a·to·ry /'lavəˌtôrē/ ▸*n.* (*pl.* **-ries**) a room or compartment with a toilet and washbasin; a bathroom. ■ a sink or washbasin in a bathroom. ■ *Brit.* a flush toilet. ▷late Middle English: from late Latin *lavatorium* 'place for washing,' from Latin *lavare* 'to wash.' The word originally denoted something in which to wash, such as a bath or piscina, later (mid 17th cent.) a room with washing facilities; the current sense dates from the 19th cent.

la·va tube ▸*n.* a natural tunnel within a solidified lava flow, formerly occupied by flowing molten lava.

lave /lāv/ ▸*v.* [*trans.*] *poetic/literary* wash: *she ran cold water in the basin, laving her face and hands.* ■ (of water) wash against or over (something): *the sea below laved the shore with small, agitated waves.* ▷Old English *lafian*, from Latin *lavare* 'to wash'; reinforced in Middle English by Old French *laver*. **—la·va·tion** /lə'vāsʜən/ *n.*

lav·en·der /'lavəndər/ ▸*n.* **1** a small aromatic evergreen shrub of the mint family, with narrow leaves and bluish-purple flowers. Lavender has been widely used in perfumery and medicine since ancient times. • Genus *Lavandula*, family Labiatae. ■ the flowers and stalks of such a shrub dried and used to give a pleasant smell to clothes and bed linens. ■ (also **lavender oil**) a scented oil distilled from lavender flowers. ■ *dated* used in reference to refinement or gentility: [as *adj.*] *she had a certain lavender charm.* **2** a pale blue color with a trace of mauve.
▸*v.* [*trans.*] perfume with lavender. ▷Middle English: from Anglo-Norman French *lavendre*, based on medieval Latin *lavandula*.

lav·en·der cot·ton (*chiefly Brit.* also **cotton lavender**) ▸*n.* a small aromatic shrubby plant of the daisy family, with silvery or greenish lavenderlike foliage and yellow button flowers. Native to the Mediterranean area, it has insecticidal properties and is widely cultivated for garden plantings. • Genus *Santolina*, family Compositae: several species, in particular *S. chamaecyparissus*.

lav·en·der wa·ter ▸*n.* a perfume made from distilled lavender, alcohol, and ambergris.

La·ver /'lāvər/, Rod (1938–), Australian tennis player; full name *Rodney George Laver*. In 1962, he won the four major singles championships (British, American, French, and Australian) in one year, called the "Grand Slam," a feat he repeated in 1969.

la·ver[1] /'lāvər; 'lävər/ (also **purple laver**) ▸*n.* an edible seaweed with thin sheetlike fronds of a reddish-purple and green color that becomes black when dry. Laver typically grows on exposed shores, but in Japan it is cultivated in estuaries. • *Porphyra umbilicaulis*, division Rhodophyta. ▷late Old English (as the name of a water plant mentioned by Pliny), from Latin. The current sense dates from the early 17th cent.

la·ver[2] /'lāvər/ ▸*n. archaic* or *poetic/literary* a basin or similar container used for washing oneself. ■ (in biblical use) a large brass bowl for the ritual ablutions of Jewish priests. ▷Middle English: from Old French *laveoir*, from late Latin *lavatorium* 'place for washing' (see LAVATORY).

lav·ish /'lavisʜ/ ▸*adj.* sumptuously rich, elaborate, or luxurious: *a lavish banquet.* ■ (of a person) very generous or extravagant: *he was lavish with his hospitality.* ■ spent or given in profusion: *lavish praise.* See note at PROFUSE.
▸*v.* [*trans.*] (**lavish something on**) bestow something in generous or extravagant quantities upon: *the media couldn't lavish enough praise on the film.* ■ (**lavish something with**) cover something thickly or liberally with: *she lavished our son with kisses.* ▷late Middle English (as a noun denoting profusion): from Old French *lavasse* 'deluge of rain,' from *laver* 'to wash,' from Latin *lavare*. **—lav·ish·ly** *adv.* **—lav·ish·ness** *n.*

La·voi·sier /lə'vwäzyā; lävwä'zyā/, Antoine Laurent (1743–94), French scientist. He is regarded as the father of modern chemistry.

law /lô/ ▸*n.* **1** (often **the law**) the system of rules that a particular country or community recognizes as regulating the actions of its members and may enforce by the imposition of penalties: *they were taken to court for **breaking the law** | a license is required **by law** |* [as *adj.*] *law enforcement.* ■ an individual rule as part of such a system: *an initiative to tighten up the laws on pornography.* ■ such systems as a subject of study or as the basis of the legal profession: *he was still practicing law |* [as *adj.*] *a law firm.* Compare with JURISPRUDENCE. ■ a thing regarded as having the binding force or effect of a formal system of rules: *what he said was law.* ■ (**the law**) *informal* the police: *he'd never been in trouble with the law in his life.* ■ statutory law and the common law. Compare with EQUITY. ■ a rule defining correct procedure or behavior in a sport: *the laws of the game.* **2** a statement of fact, deduced from observation, to the effect that a particular natural or scientific phenomenon always occurs if certain conditions are present: *the second law of thermodynamics.* ■ a generalization based on a fact or event perceived to be recurrent: *the first law of American corporate life is that dead wood floats.* **3** the body of divine commandments as expressed in the Bible or other religious texts. ■ (**the Law**) the Pentateuch as distinct from the other parts of the Hebrew Bible (the Prophets and the Writings). ■ (also **the Law of Moses**) the precepts of the Pentateuch. Compare with TORAH. ▷Old English *lagu*, from Old Norse *lag* 'something laid down or fixed,' of Germanic origin and related to LAY[1].
▸*PHRASES* □ **at** (or **in**) **law** according to or concerned with the laws of a country: *an agreement enforceable at law | an attorney-at-law.* □ **be a law unto oneself** behave in a manner that is not conventional or predictable. □ **go to law** resort to legal action in order to settle a matter. □ **law and order** a situation characterized by respect for and obedience to the rules of a society. □ **the law of the jungle** see JUNGLE. □ **lay down the law** issue instructions to other people in an authoritative or dogmatic way. □ **take the law into one's own hands** punish someone for an offense according to one's own ideas of justice, esp. in an illegal or violent way. □ **take someone to law** initiate legal proceedings against someone. □ **there's no law against it** *informal* used in spoken English to assert that one is doing nothing wrong, esp. in response to an actual or implied criticism: *I can laugh, can't I? There's no law against it.*

law-a·bid·ing ▸*adj.* obedient to the laws of society: *a law-abiding citizen.* **—law-a·bid·ing·ness** *n.*

law·break·er /'lôˌbrākər/ ▸*n.* a person who violates the law. **—law·break·ing** /-ˌbrākiɴɢ/ *n.* & *adj.*

law clerk ▸*n.* an assistant to an experienced attorney, typically a recent law-school graduate, whose function is to relieve the attorney of routine legal and administrative tasks.

law court ▸*n.* a court of law.

law·ful /'lôfəl/ ▸*adj.* conforming to, permitted by, or recognized by law or rules: *it is an offense to carry a weapon in public without lawful authority.* ■ *dated* (of a child) born within a lawful marriage. **—law·ful·ly** *adv.* **—law·ful·ness** *n.*

law·giv·er /'lôˌgivər/ ▸*n.* a person who draws up and enacts laws.

law·less /'lôləs/ ▸*adj.* not governed by or obedient to laws; characterized by a lack of civic order: *it was a lawless, anarchic city.* **—law·less·ly** *adv.* **—law·less·ness** *n.*

law·mak·er /'lôˌmākər/ ▸*n.* a legislator. **—law·mak·ing** /-ˌmākiɴɢ/ *adj.* & *n.*

law·man /'lôˌmən; -ˌman/ ▸*n.* (*pl.* **-men**) a law-enforcement officer, esp. a sheriff.

lawn[1] /lôn/ ▸*n.* an area of short, mown grass in a yard, garden, or park. ▷mid 16th cent.: alteration of dialect *laund* 'glade, pasture,' from Old French *launde* 'wooded district, heath,' of Celtic origin. The current sense dates from the mid 18th cent. **—lawned** *adj.*

lawn[2] ▸*n.* a fine linen or cotton fabric used for making clothes. ▷Middle English: probably from *Laon*, the name of a city in France important for linen manufacture. **—lawn·y** *adj.*

lawn bowl·ing (*Brit.* **bowls**) ▸*n.* a game played with heavy wooden balls, the object of which is to propel one's ball so that it comes to rest as close as possible to a previously bowled small ball (the jack) without touching it. Lawn bowling is played chiefly outdoors (though an indoor version is also popular in Britain) on a closely trimmed lawn called a green.

lawn chair ▸*n.* a folding chair for use outdoors.

lawn fla·min·go ▸*n.* a pink plastic flamingo, often with metal legs, used as a lawn decoration.

lawn mow·er ▸*n.* a machine for cutting the grass on a lawn.

lawn par·ty ▸*n.* a garden party.

lawn ten·nis ▸*n. dated* or *formal* the standard form of tennis, played with a soft ball on an open court. Compare with COURT TENNIS.

law of av·er·ag·es ▸*n.* the principle that supposes most future events are likely to balance any past deviation from a presumed average.

law of·fice ▸*n.* a lawyer's office.

law of mass ac·tion *Chemistry n.* the principle that the rate of a chemical reaction is proportional to the masses of the reacting substances.

law of na·tions ▸*n. Law* international law.

law of na·ture ▸*n.* **1** another term for NATURAL LAW. **2** *informal* a regularly occurring or apparently inevitable phenomenon observable in human society: *it's a law of nature—however much space you have, you fill it.*

law of par·si·mo·ny ▸*n.* see PARSIMONY.

law of suc·ces·sion ▸*n.* the law regulating the inheritance of property. ■ the law regulating the appointment of a new monarch or head of state.

Law·rence[1] /'lôrəns; 'lär-/ **1** a city in northeastern Kansas, home to the University of Kansas, the scene of fierce fighting before and during the Civil War; pop. 80,098. **2** a city in northeastern Massachusetts, northeast of Lowell; pop. 72,043.

Law·rence[2] /'lôrəns; 'lär-/, D. H. (1885–1930), English novelist, poet, and essayist; full name *David Herbert Lawrence*. His work is characterized by its condemnation of industrial society and its frank exploration of sexual relationships. Notable works: *The Rainbow* (1915), *Lady Chatterley's Lover* (1928), and *Sons and Lovers* (1913).

Law·rence[3], Ernest Orlando (1901–58), U.S. physicist. He developed the first circular particle accelerator, later called a cyclotron, and opened the way for high-energy physics. He also worked on providing fissionable material for the atom bomb. Nobel Prize for Physics (1939).

Law·rence[4], Jacob (1917–2000) U.S. artist and educator. He is noted for *Migration* (1941–42), a series of 60 murals that depict the migration of blacks northward in hopes of finding employment. He wrote *Harriet and the Promised Land* (1993) for children.

Law·rence[5], T. E. (1888–1935), British soldier and writer; full name *Thomas Edward Lawrence*; known as **Lawrence of Arabia**. From 1916 on, he helped to organize the Arab revolt against the Turks in the Middle East, contributing to General Allenby's eventual victory in Palestine in 1918. He described this in *The Seven Pillars of Wisdom* (1926).

Law·rence, St. (died 258), Roman martyr and deacon of Rome; Latin name *Laurentius*. According to tradition, when Lawrence offered the poor people of Rome as the treasure of the Church to the prefect of Rome, he was roasted to death on a gridiron. Feast day, August 10.

law·ren·ci·um /lô'rensēəm/ ▸*n.* the chemical element of atomic number 103, a radioactive metal of the actinide series. Lawrencium does not occur naturally and was first made by bombarding californium with boron nuclei. (Symbol: **Lr**) ▷1960s: modern Latin, named after E. O. *Lawrence* (see LAWRENCE[2]), who founded the laboratory in which it was produced.

laws of war ▸*plural n.* international rules and conventions that limit belligerents' action.

Law·son cy·press /'lôsən/ ▸*n.* another term for PORT ORFORD CEDAR. ▷mid 19th cent.: named after Peter *Lawson* (died 1820) and his son Charles (1794–1873), the Scottish nurserymen who first cultivated it.

law·suit /'lôˌso͞ot/ ▸*n.* a claim or dispute brought to a court of law for adjudication: *his lawyer **filed a lawsuit against** Los Angeles city.*

Law·ton /'lôtn/ a city in southwestern Oklahoma; pop. 92,757.

law·yer /'loi-ər; 'lôyər/ ▸*n.* a person who practices or studies law; an attorney or a counselor.
▸*v.* [*intrans.*] practice law; work as a lawyer: [as *n.*] (**lawyering**) *lawyering is a craft that takes a long time to become proficient at.* ■ [*trans.*] (of a lawyer) work on the legal aspects of (a contract, lawsuit, etc.): *there is always a danger that the deal will be lawyered to death.* **—law·yer·ly** *adj.*

L

law·yer·ing /ˈloi-əriNG; ˈlôyər-/ ▸*n.* the work of practicing law: *although he holds a law degree, he lets his hired guns do the real lawyering.*

lax /laks/ ▸*adj.* **1** not sufficiently strict or severe: *lax security arrangements at the airport | he'd been a bit lax about discipline in school lately.* See note at LENIENT. ■ careless: *why do software developers do little more than parrot their equally lax competitors?* **2** (of the limbs or muscles) relaxed. ■ (of the bowels) loose. ■ *Phonetics* (of a speech sound, esp. a vowel) pronounced with the vocal muscles relaxed. The opposite of TENSE[1]. ▷late Middle English (in the sense 'loose,' said of the bowels): from Latin *laxus.* —**lax·i·ty** /ˈlaksətē/ *n.* —**lax·ly** *adv.* —**lax·ness** *n.*

lax·a·tive /ˈlaksətiv/ ▸*adj.* (chiefly of a drug or medicine) tending to stimulate or facilitate evacuation of the bowels.
▸*n.* a medicine that has such an effect. ▷late Middle English: via Old French *laxatif, -ive* or late Latin *laxativus,* from Latin *laxare* 'loosen' (from *laxus* 'loose').

lay[1] /lā/ ▸*v.* (*past* **laid** /lād/) **1** [*trans.*] put down, esp. gently or carefully: *she laid the baby in his crib.* ■ [*trans.*] prevent (something) from rising off the ground: *there may have been the odd light shower just to lay the dust.* **2** [*trans.*] put down and set in position for use: *it is advisable to have your carpet laid by a professional | figurative the groundwork for change had been laid.* ■ set cutlery, crockery, and mats on (a table) in preparation for a meal: *she laid the table for the evening meal.* ■ (often **be laid with**) cover (a surface) with objects or a substance: *the floor was laid with tiles.* ■ make ready (a trap) for someone: *she wouldn't put it past him to lay a trap for her.* ■ put the material for (a fire) in place and arrange it. ■ work out (an idea or suggestion) in detail ready for use or presentation: *I'd like more time to lay my plans.* ■ (**lay something before**) present information or suggestions to be considered and acted upon by (someone): *he laid before the House proposals for the establishment of the committee.* ■ (usu. **be laid**) locate (an episode in a play, novel, etc.) in a certain place: *no one who knew the area could be in doubt where the scene was laid.* ■ *Nautical* follow (a specified course). ■ [*intrans.*] *Nautical* go or come: *they had to lay aloft.* ■ [*trans.*] stake (an amount of money) in a wager: *she suspected he was pulling her leg, but she wouldn't have laid money on it.* **3** [*trans.*] used with an abstract noun so that the phrase formed has the same meaning as the verb related to the noun used, e.g., "lay the blame on" means 'to blame': *she* **laid** *great* **stress** *on little courtesies.* ■ (**lay something on**) require (someone) to endure or deal with a responsibility or difficulty: *this is an absurdly heavy guilt trip to lay on anyone.* **4** [*trans.*] (of a female bird, insect, reptile, or amphibian) produce (an egg) from inside the body: *flamingos lay only one egg | [intrans.] the hens were laying at the same rate as usual.* **5** [*trans.*] *vulgar slang* have sexual intercourse with. ■ [*intrans.*] (**get laid**) have sexual intercourse.
▸*phrasal v.* □ **lay about (someone)** beat or attack (someone) violently: *they weren't against laying about you with sticks and stones.* ■ (**lay about one**) strike out wildly on all sides: *the mare laid about her with her front legs and teeth.* □ **lay something aside** put something to one side: *he laid aside his book.* ■ keep business to deal with later. ■ reserve money for the future or for a particular cause: *he begged them to lay something aside toward the cause.* ■ give up a practice or attitude: *the situation gave them a good reason to lay aside their differences.* □ **lay something down 1** put something that one has been holding on the ground or another surface: *she finished her eclair and laid down her fork.* ■ give up the use or enjoyment of something: *they renounced violence and laid down their arms.* ■ sacrifice one's life in a noble cause: *he laid down his life for his country.* **2** formulate and enforce or insist on a rule or principle: *stringent criteria have been laid down.* **3** set something in position for use on the ground or a surface: *the floors were constructed by laying down precast concrete blocks.* ■ establish something in or on the ground: *the ancient grid of streets was laid down by Roman planners.* ■ begin to construct a ship or railroad. ■ (usu. **be laid down**) build up a deposit of a substance: *these cells lay down new bone tissue.* **4** store wine in a cellar. **5** pay or wager money. **6** *informal* record a piece of music: *he was invited to the studio to lay down some backing vocals.* □ **lay something in/up** build up a stock of something in case of need. □ **lay into** *informal* attack violently with words or blows: *three youths laid into him.* □ **lay off** *informal* give up: *I laid off smoking for seven years.* ■ [usu. in *imperative*] used to advise someone to stop doing something: *lay off—he's not going to tell you.* □ **lay someone off** discharge a worker, esp. temporarily because of a shortage of work. □ **lay someone out 1** prepare someone for burial after death. **2** *informal* knock someone unconscious: *he was lucky that the punch didn't lay him out.* □ **lay something out 1** spread something out to its full extent, esp. so that it can be seen: *the police were insisting that suitcases should be opened and their contents laid out.* **2** construct or arrange buildings or gardens according to a plan: *they proceeded to lay out a new town.* ■ arrange and present material for printing and publication: *the brochure is beautifully laid out.* ■ explain something clearly and carefully: *we need a paper laying out our priorities.* **3** *informal* spend a sum of money: *look at the money I had to lay out for your uniform.* □ **lay up** *Golf* hit the ball deliberately to a lesser distance than possible, typically in order to avoid a hazard. □ **lay someone up** put someone out of action through illness or injury: *he was laid up with his familiar fever.* □ **lay something up 1** see LAY SOMETHING IN above. **2** take a ship or other vehicle out of service: *our boats were laid up during the winter months.* **3** assemble layers in the arrangement required for the manufacture of plywood or other laminated material.
▸*n.* **1** [in *sing.*] the general appearance of an area, including the direction of streams, hills, and similar features: *the lay of the surrounding countryside.* ■ the position or direction in which something lies: *roll the carpet against the lay of the nap.* ■ the direction or amount of twist in rope strands. **2** *vulgar slang* an act of sexual intercourse. ■ [with *adj.*] a person with a particular ability or availability as a sexual partner. **3** the laying of eggs or the period during which they are laid. ▷Old English *lecgan,* of Germanic origin; related to Dutch *leggen* and German *legen,* also to LIE[1].
▸PHRASES □ **lay something at someone's door** see DOOR. □ **lay something bare** bring something out of concealment; expose something: *the sad tale of failure was laid bare.* □ **lay a charge** make an accusation: *we could lay a charge of gross negligence.* □ **lay claim to something** assert that one has a right to something: *four men laid claim to the leadership.* ■ assert that one possesses a skill or quality: *she has never laid claim to medical knowledge.* □ **lay down the law** see LAW. □ **lay eyes on** see EYE. □ **lay a** (or **the**) **ghost** get rid of a distressing, frightening, or worrying memory or thought: *we need to lay the ghost of the past and move ahead.* □ **lay hands on 1** find and take possession of: *they huddled, trying to keep warm under anything they could lay hands on.* **2** place one's hands on or over, esp. in confirmation, ordination, or spiritual healing. □ **lay** (or **put**) **one's hands on** find and acquire: *I would read every book I could lay my hands on.* □ **lay hold of** (or **on**) catch at with one's hands: *he was afraid she might vanish if he did not lay hold of her.* ■ gain possession of: *the gun was the only one he had been able to lay hold of.* □ **lay it on the line** see LINE[1]. □ **the lay** (*Brit.* **lie**) **of the land** the way in which the features or characteristics of an area present themselves. ■ *figurative* the current situation or state of affairs: *she was beginning to see the lay of the land with her in-laws.* □ **lay someone low** (of an illness) reduce someone to inactivity. ■ bring to an end the high position or good fortune formerly enjoyed by someone: *she reflected on how quickly fate can lay a person low.* □ **lay something on the table** see TABLE. □ **lay something on thick** (or **with a trowel**) *informal* grossly exaggerate or overemphasize something. □ **lay someone open to** expose someone to the risk of (something): *his position could lay him open to accusations of favoritism.* □ **lay over** break one's journey: *Steven and I will lay over in New York, then fly to London.* □ **lay siege to** see SIEGE. □ **lay store by** see STORE. □ **lay someone/something to rest** bury a body in a grave. ■ soothe and dispel fear, anxiety, grief, or a similar unpleasant emotion: *suspicion will be laid to rest by fact rather than hearsay.* □ **lay something (to) waste** see WASTE.

USAGE The verb **lay** means, broadly, 'put something down': *they are going to* **lay** *the carpet.* The past tense and the past participle of **lay** is **laid**: *they* **laid** *the groundwork; she had* **laid** *careful plans.*
The verb **lie**, on the other hand, means 'assume a horizontal or resting position': *why don't you* **lie** *on the floor?* The past tense of **lie** is **lay**: *he* **lay** *on the floor earlier in the day.* The past participle of **lie** is **lain**: *she had* **lain** *on the bed for hours.*
In practice, many speakers inadvertently get the **lay** forms and the **lie** forms into a tangle of right and wrong usage. Here are some examples of typical incorrect usage: *have you been* **laying** *on the sofa all day?* (should be **lying**); *he* **lay** *the books on the table* (should be **laid**); *I had* **laid** *in this position so long, my arm was stiff* (should be **lain**).
See also **usage** at LIE[1].

lay[2] ▸*adj.* [*attrib.*] **1** not ordained into or belonging to the clergy: *a lay preacher.* **2** not having professional qualifications or expert knowledge, esp. in law or medicine: *lay and professional views of medicine.* ▷Middle English: from Old French *lai,* via late Latin from Greek *laïkos,* from *laos* 'people.' Compare with LAIC.

lay[3] ▸*n.* a short lyric or narrative poem meant to be sung. ■ *poetic/literary* a song: *on his lips there died the cheery lay.* ▷Middle English: from Old French *lai,* corresponding to Provençal *lais,* of unknown origin.

lay[4] ▸ past of LIE[1].

lay·a·bout /ˈlāə,bout/ ▸*n. derogatory* a person who habitually does little or no work.

lay·a·way /ˈlāə,wā/ ▸*n.* (also **layaway plan**) a system of paying a deposit to secure an item for later purchase: *she picked up a coat she had* **on layaway.**

lay·back /ˈlā,bak/ ▸*n. Climbing* a method of climbing a crack in rock by leaning back and pulling with the hands on one face, with the feet against the other face.

lay broth·er ▸*n.* a man who has taken the vows of a religious order but is not ordained or obliged to take part in the full cycle of liturgy and is employed in ancillary or manual work.

lay-by ▸*n.* (*pl.* **lay-bys**) an area at the side of a road where vehicles may pull off the road and stop. ■ a similar arrangement on a canal, or in a river or harbor.

lay·er /ˈlāər/ ▸*n.* **1** a sheet, quantity, or thickness of material, typically one of several, covering a surface or body: *bears depend on* **a layer of** *blubber to keep them warm in the water | figurative a larger missile would provide a layer of defense at higher altitudes.* ■ a level of seniority in the hierarchy of an organization: *a managerial layer.* **2** [in *combination*] a person or thing that lays something: *the worms are prolific egg-layers.* ■ a hen that lays eggs. **3** a shoot fastened down to take root while attached to the parent plant.
▸*v.* [*trans.*] [often as *adj.*] (**layered**) **1** arrange in a layer or layers: *the current trend for layered clothes.* ■ cut (hair) in overlapping layers: *her layered, shoulder-length hair.* **2** propagate (a plant) as a layer: *a layered shoot.* ▷Middle English (denoting a mason): from LAY[1] + -ER[1]. The sense 'stratum of material covering a surface' (early 17th cent.) may represent a respelling of an obsolete agricultural use of LAIR denoting quality of soil.

lay·er cake ▸*n.* a cake of two or more layers with icing or another filling between them.

lay·er·ing /ˈlāəriNG/ ▸*n.* **1** the action of arranging something in layers. ■ *Geology* the presence or formation of layers in sedimentary or igneous rock. **2** the method or activity of propagating a plant by producing layers.

lay·ette /lāˈet/ ▸*n.* a set of clothing, linens, and sometimes toiletries for a newborn child. ▷mid 19th cent.: from French, diminutive of Old French *laie* 'drawer,' from Middle Dutch *laege.*

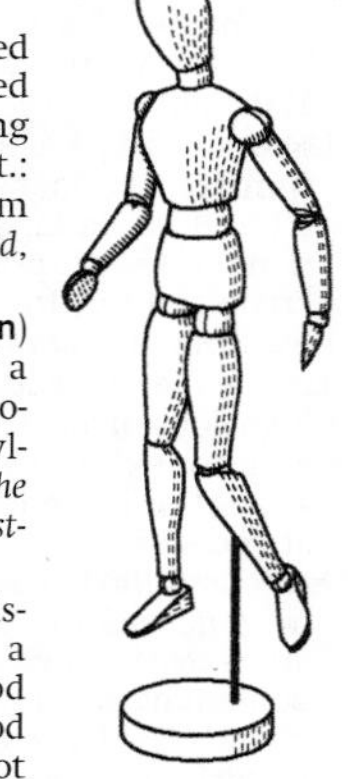
lay figure

lay fig·ure ▸*n.* a dummy or jointed manikin of a human body used by artists, esp. for arranging drapery on. ▷late 18th cent.: from obsolete *layman,* from Dutch *leeman,* from obsolete *led,* earlier form of *lid* 'joint.'

lay·man /ˈlāmən/ ▸*n.* (*pl.* **-men**) **1** a nonordained member of a church. **2** a person without professional or specialized knowledge in a particular subject: *the book seems well suited to the interested layman.*

lay·off /ˈlā,ôf; -,äf/ ▸*n.* **1** a discharge, esp. temporary, of a worker or workers. ■ a period when this is in force. **2** a period during which someone does not take part in a customary sport or other activity: *they needed to rehabilitate injuries or just brush up after long layoffs.*

La'youn /läˈyoon/ (also **Laa·youne**) the capital of Western Sahara; pop. 97,000. Arabic name EL AAIÚN.

lay·out /ˈlā,out/ ▸*n.* the way in which the parts of

something are arranged or laid out: *changing the layout of the ground floor.* | *elaborate HTML layouts.* ■ the way in which text or pictures are set out on a page: *the layout is uncluttered and the illustrations are helpful.* ■ the process of setting out material on a page or in a work: *doing layout for newspapers and magazines.* ■ a thing arranged or set out in a particular way: *a model railroad layout.* ■ *Diving, Gymnastics* a position in which the body is extended, the head upright, the legs held straight and together, and the arms held out to the sides.

lay·o·ver /ˈlāˌōvər/ ▸*n.* a period of rest or waiting before a further stage in a journey.

lay·per·son /ˈlāˌpərsən/ ▸*n.* (*pl.* **lay·peo·ple**) a nonordained member of a church. ■ a person without professional or specialized knowledge in a particular subject.

lay read·er ▸*n.* (in the Anglican Church) a layperson licensed to preach and to conduct some religious services, but not licensed to celebrate the Eucharist.

lay·shaft /ˈlāˌsнaft/ ▸*n. chiefly Brit.* a second or intermediate transmission shaft in a machine.

lay sis·ter ▸*n.* a woman who has taken the vows of a religious order but is not obliged to take part in the full cycle of liturgy and is employed in ancillary or manual work.

Lay·ton /ˈlātn/ a city in northern Utah, south of Ogden; pop. 58,474.

lay·up /ˈlāəp/ ▸*n.* **1** *Basketball* a one-handed shot made from near the basket, esp. one that rebounds off the backboard. **2** (also **lay-up**) the state or action of something, esp. a ship, being laid up.

lay·wom·an /ˈlāˌwo͝omən/ ▸*n.* (*pl.* **-wom·en**) a nonordained female member of a church.

laz·ar /ˈlazər; ˈlāzər/ ▸*n. archaic* a poor and diseased person, esp. one afflicted by a feared, contagious disease such as leprosy. ▷Middle English: from medieval Latin *lazarus,* with biblical allusion to *Lazarus,* the name of a beggar covered in sores (Luke 16:20).

laz·a·rette /ˌlazəˈret/ (also **laz·a·ret**) ▸*n.* **1** a small compartment below the deck in the after end of a vessel, used for stores. **2** a lazaretto. ▷early 17th cent. (denoting an isolation hospital): from French *lazaret,* from Italian *lazaretto* (see LAZARETTO).

laz·a·ret·to /ˌlazəˈretō/ ▸*n.* (*pl.* **-tos**) *chiefly historical* an isolation hospital for people with infectious diseases, esp. leprosy or plague. ■ a building (or ship) used for quarantine. ■ a military or prison hospital. ▷mid 16th cent.: from Italian, diminutive of *lazzaro* 'beggar,' from medieval Latin *lazarus* (see LAZAR).

Laz·a·rist /ˈlazərist/ ▸*n.* another name for VINCENTIAN. ▷from French *Lazariste,* from the biblical name *Lazarus* (see LAZAR).

Laz·a·rus /ˈlazərəs/, Emma (1849–87), U.S. poet. She is best known as the author of "The New Colossus" (1883), her sonnet to the Statue of Liberty that is carved on the pedestal of the statue.

laze /lāz/ ▸*v.* [*intrans.*] spend time in a relaxed, lazy manner: *she spent the day at home, reading the papers and generally* ***lazing around.*** ■ [*trans.*] (**laze something away**) pass time in such a way: *laze away a long summer day.*

▸*n.* [in *sing.*] a spell of acting in such a way. ▷late 16th cent.: back-formation from LAZY.

laz·u·li /ˈlaz(y)əˌlī; ˈlazнə-; -lē/ ▸*n.* short for LAPIS LAZULI.

laz·u·lite /ˈlazyo͞oˌlīt; ˈlazə-/ ▸*n.* an azure-blue mineral with a glasslike luster. • Chem. formula: $(FeMg)Al_2P_2O_8(OH)_2$

laz·u·rite /ˈlaz(y)əˌrīt; ˈlazнə-/ ▸*n.* a bright blue mineral that is the main constituent of lapis lazuli and consists chiefly of a silicate and sulfate of sodium and aluminum.

la·zy /ˈlāzē/ ▸*adj.* (**la·zi·er, la·zi·est**) **1** unwilling to work or use energy: *I'm very lazy by nature* | *he was too lazy to cook.* ■ characterized by lack of effort or activity: *lazy summer days.* ■ showing a lack of effort or care: *lazy writing.* ■ (of a river) slow-moving. **2** (of a livestock brand) placed on its side rather than upright: *a logo with a lazy E.* ▷mid 16th cent.: perhaps related to Low German *lasich* 'languid, idle.' —**la·zi·ly** /-zəlē/ *adv.* —**la·zi·ness** *n.*

la·zy·bones /ˈlāzēˌbōnz/ ▸*n.* (*pl.* same) *informal* a lazy person (often as a form of address).

la·zy dai·sy stitch ▸*n.* an embroidery stitch in the form of a flower petal.

la·zy eye ▸*n.* an eye with poor vision that is mainly caused by underuse, esp. the unused eye in strabismus.

la·zy Su·san /ˈso͞ozən/ ▸*n.* a revolving stand or tray on a table, used esp. for holding condiments.

la·zy tongs ▸*n.* a set of extending tongs for grasping objects at a distance, with several connected pairs of levers pivoted like scissors.

lb. ▸*abbr.* ■ pound(s) (in weight). [from Latin *libra.*]

LBO ▸*abbr.* leveraged buyout.

LC ▸*abbr.* ■ landing craft. ■ Library of Congress.

l.c. ▸*abbr.* ■ in the passage cited. [from Latin *loco citato.*] ■ letter of credit. ■ lowercase.

L/C (also **l.c.**) ▸*abbr.* letter of credit.

LCD ▸*abbr.* ■ *Electronics & Computing* liquid crystal display. ■ *Mathematics* lowest (or least) common denominator.

LCL ▸*abbr.* less-than-carload lot.

LCM *Mathematics* ▸*abbr.* lowest (or least) common multiple.

LCpl ▸*abbr.* lance corporal.

LCS ▸*abbr.* ■ landing craft support. ■ liquid crystal shutter.

LCT ▸*abbr.* ■ land conservation trust. ■ landing craft, tank. ■ local civil time.

LD ▸*abbr.* ■ learning disabled. ■ lethal dose (of a toxic compound, drug, or pathogen). It is usually written with a following numeral indicating the percentage of a group of animals or cultured cells or microorganisms killed by such a dose, typically standardized at 50 percent (**LD_{50}**).

Ld. ▸*abbr.* Lord: *Ld. Lothian.*

ld. ▸*abbr.* ■ lead. ■ load.

LDC ▸*abbr.* less-developed country.

LDL *Biochemistry* ▸*abbr.* low-density lipoprotein.

L-do·pa /ˌel ˈdōpə/ ▸*n. Biochemistry* the levorotatory form of dopa, used to treat Parkinson's disease. Also called LEVODOPA.

LDS ▸*abbr.* Latter-Day Saints.

LE ▸*abbr.* language engineering.

-le[1] ▸*suffix* **1** forming names of appliances or instruments: *bridle* | *thimble.* **2** forming names of animals and plants: *beetle.* ▷Old English, of Germanic origin.

-le[2] (also **-el**) ▸*suffix* forming nouns having or originally having a diminutive sense: *mantle* | *battle* | *castle.* ▷Middle English *-el, -elle,* partly from Old English and partly from Old French (based on Latin forms).

-le[3] ▸*suffix* (forming adjectives from an original verb) apt to; liable to: *brittle* | *nimble.* ▷Middle English: from earlier *-el,* of Germanic origin.

-le[4] ▸*suffix* forming verbs, chiefly those expressing repeated action or movement (as in *babble, dazzle*), or having diminutive sense (as in *nestle*). ▷Old English *-lian,* of Germanic origin.

lea /lē/ ▸*n. poetic/literary* an open area of grassy or arable land: *the lowing herd winds slowly o'er the lea.* ▷Old English *lēa(h),* of Germanic origin; related to Old High German *loh* 'grove,' from an Indo-European root shared by Sanskrit *lokás* 'open space,' Latin *lucus* 'grove,' and perhaps also LIGHT[1].

lea. ▸*abbr.* league.

leach /lēcн/ ▸*v.* [*trans.*] make (a soluble chemical or mineral) drain away from soil, ash, or similar material by the action of percolating liquid, esp. rainwater: *the nutrient is quickly leached away.* ■ [*intrans.*] (of a soluble chemical or mineral) drain away from soil, ash, etc., in this way: *coats of varnish prevent the dye leaching out.* ■ [*trans.*] subject (soil, ash, etc.) to this process. ▷Old English *leccan* 'to water,' of West Germanic origin. The current sense dates from the mid 19th cent.

leach·ate /ˈlēˌcнāt/ ▸*n. technical* water that has percolated through a solid and leached out some of the constituents.

Lea·cock /ˈlēˌkäk/, Stephen (Butler) (1869–1949), Canadian humorist and economist. He is known for his many humorous short stories, parodies, and essays. Notable works: *Sunshine Sketches of a Little Town* (1912) and *Arcadian Adventures with the Idle Rich* (1914).

lead[1] /lēd/ ▸*v.* (*past* and *past part.* **led** /led/) [*trans.*] **1** cause (a person or animal) to go with one by holding them by the hand, a halter, a rope, etc., while moving forward: *she emerged leading a bay horse.* ■ show (someone or something) the way to a destination by going in front of or beside them: *she stood up and led her friend to the door.* ■ be a reason or motive for (someone): *nothing that I have read about the case* ***leads*** *me* ***to*** *the conclusion that anything untoward happened* | *a fascination for art led him to start a collection of paintings.* ■ [*intrans.*] be a route or means of access to a particular place or in a particular direction: *a door leading to a better-lit corridor.* ■ [*intrans.*] (**lead to**) culminate in (a particular event): *closing the plant will lead to the loss of 300 jobs.* ■ [*intrans.*] (**lead on to**) form a stage in a process that leads probably or inevitably to (a particular end): *his work on digestion led on to study of proteins and fats.* ■ (**lead something through**) cause a liquid or easily moving matter to pass through (a channel). **2** [*trans.*] be in charge or command of: *a military delegation was led by the Chief of Staff.* ■ organize and direct: *the conference included sessions led by people with personal knowledge of the area.* ■ set (a process) in motion: *they are waiting for an expansion of world trade to lead a recovery.* ■ be the principal player of (a group of musicians): *since the forties he has led his own big bands.* ■ [*intrans.*] (**lead with**) assign the most important position to (a particular news item): *the news on the radio led with the murder.* **3** be superior to (competitors or colleagues): *there will be specific areas or skills in which other nations* ***lead the world.*** ■ have the first place in (a competition); be ahead of (competitors): *the veteran jockey was leading the field.* ■ [*intrans.*] have the advantage in a race or game: *Dallas was fortunate to lead 85-72.* **4** have or experience (a particular way of life): *she's led a completely sheltered life.* **5** initiate (action in a game or contest), in particular: ■ (in card games) play (the first card) in a trick or round of play. ■ [*intrans.*] (**lead with**) *Boxing* make an attack with (a particular punch or fist): *Adam led with a left.* ■ [*intrans.*] *Baseball* (of a base runner) advance one or more steps from the base one occupies while the pitcher has the ball: *the runner leads from first.*

▸*phrasal v.* □ **lead off 1** start: *the newsletter leads off with a report on tax bills.* ■ *Baseball* bat first in a game or inning. **2** (of a door, room, or path) provide access away from a central space: *a farm track led off to the left.* □ **lead someone on** mislead or deceive someone, esp. into believing that one is in love with or attracted to them. □ **lead up to** immediately precede: *the weeks leading up to the elections.* ■ result in: *fashioning a policy appropriate to the situation entails understanding the forces that led up to it.*

▸*n.* /lēd/ **1** the initiative in an action; an example for others to follow: *The U.S. is now* ***taking the*** *environmental* ***lead.*** ■ a clue to be followed in the resolution of a problem: *detectives investigating the murder are chasing new leads.* ■ (in card games) an act or right of playing first in a trick or round of play: *it's your lead.* ■ the card played first in a trick or round. **2** (**the lead**) a position of advantage in a contest; first place: *they were beaten 5-3 after twice being* ***in the lead.*** ■ an amount by which a competitor is ahead of the others: *the team held a slender one-goal lead.* ■ *Baseball* an advance of one or more steps taken by a base runner from the base they occupy while the pitcher has the ball. **3** the chief part in a play or film: *she had the lead in a new film* | [as *adj.*] *the lead role.* ■ the person playing the chief part: *he still looked like a romantic lead.* ■ [usu. as *adj.*] the chief performer or instrument of a specified type: *that girl will be your lead dancer.* ■ [often as *adj.*] the item of news given the greatest prominence in a newspaper or magazine: *the lead story.* **4** a leash for a dog or other animal. **5** a wire that conveys electric current from a source to an appliance, or that connects two points of a circuit together. **6** the distance advanced by a screw in one turn. **7** a channel, in particular: ■ an artificial watercourse leading to a mill. ■ a channel of water in an ice field. ▷Old English *lǣdan,* of Germanic origin; related to Dutch *leiden* and German *leiten,* also to LOAD and LODE.

▸*PHRASES* □ **lead someone astray** cause someone to act or think foolishly or wrongly. □ **lead someone by the nose** *informal* control someone totally, esp. by deceiving them. □ **lead someone a dance** see DANCE. □ **lead from the front** take an active role in what one is urging and directing others to do. □ **lead someone up** (or **down**) **the garden path** *informal* give someone misleading clues or signals. □ **lead the way** see WAY. □ **lead with one's chin** *informal* (of a boxer) leave one's chin unprotected. ■ *figurative* behave or speak incautiously.

lead[2] /led/ ▸*n.* **1** a heavy, bluish-gray, soft, ductile metal, the chemical element of atomic number 82. It has been used in roofing, plumbing, ammunition, storage batteries, radiation shields, etc., and its compounds have been used in crystal glass, as an antiknock agent in gasoline, and (formerly) in paints. (Symbol: **Pb**) **2** an item or implement made of lead, in particular: ■ *Nautical* a lead casting suspended on a line to determine the depth of water. ■ bullets. **3** graphite used as the part of a pencil that makes a mark. **4** *Printing* a blank space between lines of print. [originally with reference to

L

leaves

the metal strip used to create this space.] ▷Old English *lēad*, of West Germanic origin; related to Dutch *lood* 'lead' and German *Lot* 'plummet, solder.'
▸*PHRASE* □ **get the lead out** *informal* move or work more quickly.

lead-ac·id /led/ ▸*adj.* denoting a secondary cell or battery in which the electrodes are plates or grids of lead (or lead alloy) immersed in dilute sulfuric acid. The anode is coated with lead dioxide and the cathode with spongy lead.

lead ar·ti·cle /lēd/ ▸*n.* the principal article in a newspaper or magazine.

lead bal·loon /led/ ▸*n.* (in phrase **go over like a lead balloon**) (of something said or written) be poorly received: *Jenkins' book has gone over like a lead balloon.*

lead crys·tal /led/ ▸*n.* another term for LEAD GLASS.

lead·ed /ˈledid/ ▸*adj.* **1** (of windowpanes or a roof) framed, covered, or weighted with lead: *Georgian-style leaded windows.* **2** (of gasoline) containing tetraethyl lead: *leaded fuel.* **3** (of type) having the lines separated by leads.

lead·en /ˈledn/ ▸*adj.* dull, heavy, or slow: *his eyelids were leaden with sleep.* ■ of the color of lead; dull gray: *the snow fell from a leaden sky.* ■ *archaic* made of lead: *a leaden coffin.* ▷Old English *lēaden* (see LEAD[2], -EN[2]). **—lead·en·ly** *adv.* **—lead·en·ness** *n.*

lead·en seal ▸*n. chiefly historical* a seal made of lead, used esp. for papal documents.

lead·er /ˈlēdər/ ▸*n.* **1** the person who leads or commands a group, organization, or country: *the leader of a protest group.* ■ a person followed by others: *he is a leader among his classmates.* ■ an organization or company that is the most advanced or successful in a particular area: *a* **leader in** *the use of video conferencing.* ■ the horse placed at the front in a team or pair. ■ (also **Leader of the House**) *Brit.* a member of the government officially responsible for initiating business in Parliament. **2** the principal player in a music group. ■ a conductor of a band or small musical group. ■ *Brit.* the principal first violinist in an orchestra. **3** *Brit.* a leading article or editorial in a newspaper. **4** a short strip of nonfunctioning material at each end of a reel of film or recording tape for connection to the spool. ■ a length of filament attached to the end of a fishing line to carry the hook or fly. **5** a shoot of a plant at the apex of a stem or main branch. **6** (**leaders**) *Printing* a series of dots or dashes across the page to guide the eye, esp. in tabulated material. **—lead·er·less** *adj.*

lead·er board ▸*n.* a scoreboard showing the names and current scores of the leading competitors, esp. in a golf tournament.

lead·er·ship /ˈlēdərˌsʜɪp/ ▸*n.* the action of leading a group of people or an organization: *different styles of leadership.* ■ the state or position of being a leader: *the leadership of the party.* ■ [treated as *sing.* or *pl.*] the leaders of an organization, country, etc.: *a change of leadership had become desirable.* ■ the ability to lead skillfully: *they hailed DuPont's courage and leadership.*

lead foot /led/ ▸*n.* [in *sing.*] *informal* a tendency to drive fast: *she drives with a lead foot.*

lead-foot·ed /led/ ▸*adj. informal* **1** slow; clumsy: *the most lead-footed guy can try aerobic moves.* **2** tending to drive too quickly.

lead-free /led/ ▸*adj.* (of gasoline) unleaded. ■ not containing or covered with lead: *lead-free paint.*

lead glass /led/ ▸*n.* glass containing a substantial proportion of lead oxide, making it more refractive. Also called LEAD CRYSTAL.

lead-in /ˈlēd ˌin/ ▸*n.* **1** an introduction or preamble that allows one to move smoothly on to the next part of something: [as *adj.*] *the lead-in note.* **2** a wire leading in from outside, esp. from an antenna to a receiver or transmitter.

lead·ing[1] /ˈlēdiNG/ ▸*adj.* [*attrib.*] most important: *a number of leading politicians.*
▸*n.* guidance or leadership, esp. in a spiritual context. ■ an instance of such guidance: *the leadings of the Holy Spirit.*

lead·ing[2] /ˈlediNG/ ▸*n.* the amount of blank space between lines of print.

lead·ing ar·ti·cle /ˈlēdiNG/ ▸*n. Brit.* the chief editorial or article in a newspaper.

lead·ing ec·o·nom·ic in·di·ca·tor ▸*n.* a variable that reflects current economic conditions and can suggest future trends in the nation's economy.

lead·ing edge /ˈlēdiNG/ ▸*n.* the front edge of something, in particular: ■ *Aeronautics* the foremost edge of an airfoil, esp. a wing or propeller blade. ■ *Electronics* the part of a pulse in which the amplitude increases. ■ the forefront or vanguard, esp. of technological development: [as *adj.*] *leading-edge research.*

lead·ing la·dy /ˈlēdiNG/ ▸*n.* the actress playing the principal female part in a movie, play, or television show.

lead·ing light /ˈlēdiNG/ ▸*n.* a person who is prominent or influential in a particular field or organization: *Glass is one of the leading lights in modern music.*

lead·ing man /ˈlēdiNG/ ▸*n.* the actor playing the principal male part in a movie, play, or television show.

lead·ing note /ˈlēdiNG/ ▸*n. Music* another term for SUBTONIC.

lead·ing ques·tion /ˈlēdiNG/ ▸*n.* a question that prompts or encourages the desired answer.

lead·ing rein /ˈlēdiNG/ ▸*n.* a rein used to lead a horse along, esp. when ridden by an inexperienced rider.

lead·ing tone /ˈlēdiNG/ ▸*n. Music* another term for SUBTONIC.

lead-off /ˈlēd/ ▸*adj.* (of an action) beginning a series or a process: *the album's lead-off track.* ■ (**lead·off**) *Baseball* denoting the first batter in a lineup or of an inning.

lead pen·cil /led/ ▸*n.* a pencil of graphite enclosed in wood.

lead poi·son·ing /led/ ▸*n.* acute or chronic poisoning due to the absorption of lead into the body. Also called PLUMBISM.

lead shot /led/ ▸*n.* another term for SHOT[1] (sense 3).

lead tet·ra·eth·yl /led/ ▸*n. Chemistry* another term for TETRAETHYL LEAD.

lead time /lēd / ▸*n.* the time between the initiation and completion of a production process.

lead-up /lēd/ ▸*n.* [in *sing.*] an event, point, or sequence that leads up to something else: **the lead-up to** *the elections.*

Lead·ville /ˈledˌvil/ a historic mining city in central Colorado, the highest U.S. city at 10,190 feet (3,108 m); pop. 2,629.

lead·wort /ˈledˌwərt; -ˌwôrt/ ▸*n.* another term for PLUMBAGO (sense 2).

leaf /lēf/ ▸*n.* (*pl.* **leaves** /lēvz/) **1** a flattened structure of a higher plant, typically green and bladelike, that is attached to a stem directly or via a stalk. Leaves are the main organs of photosynthesis and transpiration. Compare with COMPOUND LEAF, LEAFLET. See also illustration at TREE. ■ any of a number of similar plant structures, e.g., bracts, sepals, and petals. ■ foliage regarded collectively. ■ the state of having leaves: *the trees are still* **in leaf**. ■ the leaves of tobacco or tea: [as *adj.*] *leaf tea.* **2** a thing that resembles a leaf in being flat and thin, typically something that is one of two or more similar items forming a set or stack. ■ a single thickness of paper, esp. in a book with each side forming a page. ■ [with *adj.*] gold, silver, or other specified metal in the form of very thin foil. ■ the hinged part or flap of a door, shutter, or table. ■ an extra section inserted to extend a table. ■ the inner or outer part of a cavity wall or double-glazed window. ■ any of the stacked metal strips that form a leaf spring.
▸*v.* [*intrans.*] **1** (of a plant, esp. a deciduous one in spring) put out new leaves. **2** (**leaf through**) turn over (the pages of a book or the papers in a pile), reading them quickly or casually: *he leafed through the stack of notes.* ▷Old English *lēaf*, of Germanic origin; related to Dutch *loof* and German *Laub*. **—leaf·age** /ˈlēfij/ *n.* **—leafed** *adj.* (see LEAVED). **—leaf·less** *adj.* **—leaf·like** /-ˌlīk/ *adj.*
▸*PHRASES* □ **shake** (or **tremble**) **like a leaf** (of a person) tremble greatly, esp. from fear. □ **take a leaf out of someone's book** see BOOK. □ **turn over a new leaf** see TURN.

leaf bee·tle ▸*n.* a small beetle that feeds chiefly on leaves and typically has bright metallic coloring. Some kinds are serious crop pests. • Family Chrysomelidae: numerous species.

leaf·bird /ˈlēfˌbərd/ ▸*n.* a tree-dwelling songbird of South and Southeast Asia with mainly green plumage and a black bill, the male typically having a black throat. • Genus *Chloropsis*, family Irenidae (or Chloropseidae): several species.

leaf curl ▸*n.* a plant condition distinguished by the presence of curling leaves, caused by environmental stress or disease.

leaf·cut·ter ant /ˈlēfˌkətər/ ▸*n.* a tropical ant that cuts pieces from leaves and carries them back to the nest for use as a culture medium for growing food fungi. • Genus *Atta*, family Formicidae.

leaf·cut·ter bee ▸*n.* a solitary bee that cuts pieces from leaves, typically of roses, and uses them to construct cells in its nest. • Genus *Megachile*, family Megachilidae.

leafed /ˈlēfd/ ▸*adj.* another term for LEAVED.

leaf fat ▸*n.* dense fat occurring in layers around the kidneys of some animals, esp. pigs.

leaf fish ▸*n.* a small, deep-bodied, predatory freshwater fish, with mottled brownish-green coloration that gives it a leaflike appearance. • Two species in the family Nandidae: *Monocirrhus polyacanthus* of South America, and *Polycentropsis abbreviata* of Africa.

leaf green ▸*n.* a bright, deep green color.

leaf·hop·per /ˈlēfˌhäpər/ ▸*n.* a small plant bug that is typically brightly colored and leaps when disturbed. It can be a serious crop pest in warm regions. • Family Cicadellidae, suborder Homoptera: numerous genera.

leaf in·sect ▸*n.* a large, slow-moving tropical insect related to the stick insects, with a flattened body that is leaflike in shape and color. • Family Phylliidae, order Phasmida: *Phyllium* and other genera.

leaf lard ▸*n.* lard prepared from the leaf fat of a hog.

leaf·let /ˈlēflit/ ▸*n.* **1** a printed sheet of paper, sometimes folded, containing information or advertising and usually distributed free. **2** *Botany* each of the leaflike structures that together make up a compound leaf, such as in the ash and horse chestnut. ■ (in general use) a young leaf.
▸*v.* (**-let·ed, -let·ing**) [*trans.*] distribute leaflets to (people or an area): *I won't be leafleting neighborhoods* | [*intrans.*] *the union has leafleted, protested, and staged petition drives.*

leaf lit·ter ▸*n.* see LITTER (sense 3).

leaf·love /ˈlēfˌləv/ ▸*n.* an African bulbul that frequents dense thickets, with mainly drab brown plumage and a loud bubbling call. • The **leaflove** (*Phyllastrephus scandens*) and the **yellow-throated leaflove** (*Chlorocichla flavicollis*), family Pycnonotidae.

leaf min·er ▸*n.* a small fly, moth, beetle, or sawfly whose larvae burrow between the two surfaces of a leaf.

leaf mold (also **leaf-mold**) ▸*n.* **1** soil consisting chiefly of decayed leaves. **2** a fungal disease of plants in which mold develops on the leaves. • The fungus is *Fulvia fulva* (formerly *Cladosporium fulvum*), subdivision Deuteromycotina.

leaf mon·key ▸*n.* a leaf-eating, arboreal Asian monkey that is related to the langurs. • Genus *Presbytis*, family Cercopithecidae: several species.

leaf-nosed bat ▸*n.* a bat with a leaflike appendage on the snout. • Families Hipposideridae (Old World) and Phyllostomatidae (New World): numerous species.

leaf-nosed bat

leaf spot ▸*n.* [usu. with *adj.*] any of a large number of fungal, bacterial, or viral plant diseases that cause leaves to develop discolored spots.

leaf spring ▸*n.* a spring made of a number of strips of metal curved slightly upward and clamped together one above the other.

leaf·stalk /ˈlēfˌstôk/ ▸*n.* a petiole.

leaf-tailed geck·o ▸*n.* a gecko with a wide, flat, leaf-shaped tail and skin color that blends with its surroundings. • Genus *Phyllurus* (four Australian species), family Pygopodidae, and *Uroplatus* (several Madagascarn species), family Gekkonidae.

leaf trace ▸*n. Botany* a strand of conducting vessels extending from the stem to the base of a leaf.

leaf war·bler ▸*n.* a small, slender Old World songbird with a brown or greenish back and whitish or yellowish underparts. • Genus *Phylloscopus*, family Sylviidae: many species, including the chiffchaff.

leaf·y /ˈlēfē/ ▸*adj.* (**leaf·i·er**, **leaf·i·est**) (of a plant) having many leaves. ■ having or characterized by much foliage because of an abundance of trees or bushes: *a remote, leafy glade.* ■ (of a plant) producing or grown for its broad-bladed leaves: *green leafy vegetables.* ■ resembling a leaf or leaves: *a three-pointed leafy bract.* **—leaf·i·ness** *n.*

leaf·y spurge ▸*n.* a perennial Eurasian herb that produces a flat-topped cluster of yellow bracts bearing small flowers. It is a noxious weed in prairie and grassland areas of the U.S., where it aggressively displaces native plants. • *Euphorbia esula*, family Euphorbiaceae.

league[1] /lēg/ ▸*n.* **1** a collection of people, countries, or groups that combine for a particular purpose, typically mutual protection or cooperation: *the League of Nations.* ■ an agreement to combine in this way. **2** a group of sports clubs that play each other over a period for a championship. ■ the contest for the championship of such a league: *the year we won the league.* **3** a class or category of quality or excellence: *the two men were **not in the same league** | Jack's in **a league of his own**.*
▸*v.* (**leagues**, **leagued**, **lea·guing**) [*intrans.*] join in a league or alliance: *Oscar had **leagued with** other construction firms.* ▹late Middle English (denoting a compact for mutual protection or advantage): via French from Italian *lega*, from *legare* 'to bind,' from Latin *ligare*.
▸*PHRASE* □ **in league** conspiring with another or others: *he is **in league with** the devil.*

league[2] ▸*n.* a former measure of distance by land, usually about three miles. ▹late Middle English: from late Latin *leuga*, *leuca*, late Greek *leugē*, or from Provençal *lega* (modern French *lieue*).

League of Na·tions an association of countries established in 1919 by the Treaty of Versailles to promote international cooperation and achieve international peace and security. It was powerless to stop Italian, German, and Japanese expansionism leading to World War II and was replaced by the United Nations in 1945.

lea·guer /ˈlēgər/ ▸*n.* [with *adj.*] a member of a particular league, esp. a sports player: *minor leaguers in spring training.*

leak /lēk/ ▸*v.* [*intrans.*] (of a container or covering) accidentally lose or admit contents, esp. liquid or gas, through a hole or crack: *the roof leaked* | [as *adj.*] (**leaking**) *a leaking gutter* | [*trans.*] *the drums were leaking an unidentified liquid.* ■ (of liquid, gas, etc.) pass in or out through a hole or crack in such a way: *water kept leaking in.* ■ *figurative* (of secret information) become known: *the news **leaked out**.* ■ [*trans.*] intentionally disclose (secret information): *who had a motive to leak the story?* | [as *adj.*] (**leaked**) *a leaked government document.*
▸*n.* a hole in a container or covering through which contents, esp. liquid or gas, may accidentally pass: *I checked all of the pipes for leaks.* ■ the action of leaking in such a way: *the leak of fluid may occur | a gas leak.* ■ a similar escape of electric charge or current. ■ an intentional disclosure of secret information: *one of the employees was responsible for the leak.* ▹late Middle English: probably of Low German or Dutch origin and related to LACK. **—leak·er** *n.*
▸*PHRASE* □ **take a leak** *informal* urinate.

leak·age /ˈlēkij/ ▸*n.* the accidental admission or escape of a fluid or gas through a hole or crack: *we're saving water by reducing leakage | there have been no leakages of radioactive material.* ■ *Physics* the gradual escape of an electric charge or current, or magnetic flux. ■ deliberate disclosure of confidential information.

Lea·key /ˈlēkē/ a family of Kenyan archaeologists and anthropologists. **Louis (Seymour Bazett)** (1903–72), born in Kenya of British parents, pioneered the investigation of human origins in East Africa. He began excavations at Olduvai Gorge and together with his wife discovered the remains of early hominids, including *Australopithecus* (or *Zinjanthropus*) *boisei*, and their implements in 1959. His wife **Mary (Douglas)** (1913–96), born in England, discovered *Homo habilis* and *Homo erectus* at Olduvai in 1960. Their son **Richard (Erskine)** (1944–), born in Kenya, was appointed director of the new Kenya Wildlife Service in 1989 and was a strong opponent of elephant poaching; he resigned in 1994 following a controversial political campaign to remove him. He was elected to an oppostion seat in the Kenyan parliament in 1997.

leak·proof /ˈlēkˌpro͞of/ ▸*adj.* designed or constructed to prevent leakage.

leak·y /ˈlēkē/ ▸*adj.* (**leak·i·er**, **leak·i·est**) having a leak or leaks: *a leaky roof.* **—leak·i·ness** *n.*

leal /lēl/ ▸*adj. Scottish archaic* loyal and honest: *his leal duty to the King.* ▹Middle English: from Old French *leel*, earlier form of *loial* (see LOYAL).

Lean /lēn/, Sir David (1908–91), English movie director. His many movies include *The Bridge on the River Kwai* (1957), *Lawrence of Arabia* (1962), *Doctor Zhivago* (1965), and *A Passage to India* (1984).

lean[1] /lēn/ ▸*v.* (*past and past part.* **leaned** /lēnd/ or *chiefly Brit.* **leant** /lent/) [*intrans.*] be in or move into a sloping position: *he leaned back in his chair.* ■ (**lean against/on**) incline from the perpendicular and rest for support on or against (something): *a man was leaning against the wall.* ■ [*trans.*] (**lean something against/on**) cause something to rest on or against: *he leaned his elbows on the table.*
▸*phrasal v.* □ **lean on** **1** rely on or derive support from: *they have learned to lean on each other for support.* **2** put pressure on (someone) to act in a certain way: *a determination not to allow the majority to lean on the minority.* □ **lean to/towards** incline or be partial to (a view or position): *I now lean toward sabotage as the cause of the crash.*
▸*n.* a deviation from the perpendicular; an inclination: *the vehicle has a definite lean to the left.* ▹Old English *hleonian*, *hlinian*, of Germanic origin; related to Dutch *leunen* and German *lehnen*, from an Indo-European root shared by Latin *inclinare* and Greek *klinein*.

lean[2] /lēn/ ▸*adj.* **1** (of a person or animal) thin, esp. healthily so; having no superfluous fat: *his lean, muscular body.* See note at THIN. ■ (of meat) containing little fat: *lean bacon.* ■ (of an industry or company) efficient and with no waste: *he made leaner government a campaign theme.* **2** (of an activity or a period of time) offering little reward, substance, or nourishment; meager: *the lean winter months | keep a small reserve to tide you over **the lean years**.* **3** (of a vaporized fuel mixture) having a high proportion of air: *lean air-to-fuel ratios.*
▸*n.* the lean part of meat. ▹Old English *hlǣne*, of Germanic origin. **—lean·ly** *adv.* **—lean·ness** *n.*

lean-burn ▸*adj.* of or relating to an internal combustion engine designed to run on a lean mixture to reduce pollution: *lean-burn technology.*

Le·an·der /lēˈandər/ *Greek Mythology* a young man, the lover of the priestess Hero. He was drowned swimming across the Hellespont to visit her.

lean·ing /ˈlēniNG/ ▸*n.* (often **leanings**) a tendency or partiality of a particular kind: *his early leanings toward socialism.*

lean-to ▸*n.* (*pl.* **-tos**) a building sharing one wall with a larger building, and having a roof that leans against that wall: [as *adj.*] *a lean-to garage.* ■ a temporary shelter, either supported or freestanding.

leap /lēp/ ▸*v.* (*past* or *past part.* **leaped** /lēpt/ or **leapt** /lept/) [*intrans.*] jump or spring a long way, to a great height, or with great force: *I leaped across the threshold | figurative Fabia's heart leapt excitedly.* ■ move quickly and suddenly: *Polly leapt to her feet.* ■ [*trans.*] jump across or over: *a coyote leaped the fence.* ■ make a sudden rush to do something; act eagerly and suddenly: *it was time for me to leap into action.* ■ (**leap at**) accept (an opportunity) eagerly: *they leapt at the opportunity to combine fun with fund-raising.* ■ (of a price or figure) increase dramatically: *sales leaped 40 percent during the Christmas season.* ■ (**leap out**) (esp. of writing) be conspicuous; stand out: *amid the notes, a couple of items leap out.*
▸*n.* a forceful jump or quick movement: *she came downstairs in a series of flying leaps.* ■ a dramatic increase in price, amount, etc.: *a leap of 75 percent in two years.* ■ a sudden, abrupt change or transition: *a leap of faith.* ■ [in *place names*] a thing to be leaped over or from: *Lover's Leap.* ▹Old English *hlēapan* (verb), *hlȳp* (noun), of Germanic origin; related to Dutch *lopen*, German *laufen* (verb), and Dutch *loop*, German *Lauf* (noun), all meaning 'run,' also to LOPE. **—leap·er** *n.*
▸*PHRASES* □ **a leap in the dark** a daring step or enterprise whose consequences are unpredictable. □ **by** (or **in**) **leaps and bounds** with startlingly rapid progress: *productivity improved in leaps and bounds.* □ **leap to the eye** (or **to mind**) be immediately apparent: *one dire question leaped to our minds.*

leap day ▸*n.* the intercalary day in a leap year; February 29.

leap·frog /ˈlēpˌfrôg; -ˌfräg/ ▸*n.* a game in which players in turn vault with parted legs over the backs of others who are bending down.
▸*v.* (**-frogged**, **-frog·ging**) [*intrans.*] perform such a vault: *they leapfrogged around the courtyard.* ■ (of a person or group) surpass or overtake another to move into a leading or dominant position: *she leapfrogged into a sales position.* ■ [*trans.*] pass over (a stage or obstacle): *attempts to leapfrog the barriers of class.*

leap sec·ond /ˈsekənd/ ▸*n.* a second that is occasionally inserted into the atomic scale of reckoning time in order to bring it into line with solar time. It is indicated by an additional beep in the time signal at the end of some years.

leap year ▸*n.* a year, occurring once every four years, that has 366 days including February 29 as an intercalary day. ▹late Middle English: probably from the fact that feast days after February in such a year fell two days later than in the previous year, rather than one day later as in other years, and could be said to have "leaped" a day.

Lear[1] /li(ə)r/ a legendary early king of Britain, the central figure in Shakespeare's tragedy *King Lear*. He is mentioned by the chronicler Geoffrey of Monmouth.

Lear[2], Edward (1812–88), English humorist and illustrator. He wrote *A Book of Nonsense* (1845) and *Laughable Lyrics* (1877). He published *Illustrations of the Family of the Psittacidae* (1832), as well as illustrated accounts of his travels around the Mediterranean.

learn /lərn/ ▸*v.* (*past* **learned** /lərnd/ or *chiefly Brit.* **learnt** /lərnt/) [*trans.*] **1** gain or acquire knowledge of or skill in (something) by study, experience, or being taught: *they'd started learning French* | [with *infinitive*] *she is learning to play the piano* | [*intrans.*] *we learn from experience.* ■ commit to memory: *I'd learned too many grim poems in school.* ■ become aware of (something) by information or from observation: [with *clause*] *I learned that they had eaten already* | [*intrans.*] *the military **learned of** a plot to attack the presidential compound.* **2** *archaic, informal* teach (someone): *"That'll learn you," he chuckled* | [*trans.*] *we'll have to learn you to milk cows.* ▹Old English *leornian* 'learn' (in Middle English also 'teach'), of West Germanic origin; related to German *lernen*, also to LORE[1]. **—learn·a·bil·i·ty** /ˌlərnəˈbilətē/ *n.* **—learn·a·ble** *adj.* **—learn·er** *n.*
▸*PHRASE* □ **learn one's lesson** see LESSON.

learn·ed /ˈlərnid/ ▸*adj.* (of a person) having much knowledge acquired by study. ■ showing, requiring, or characterized by learning; scholarly: *an article in a learned journal.* ▹Middle English: from LEARN, in the sense 'teach.' **—learn·ed·ly** /-nidlē/ *adv.* **—learn·ed·ness** /-nidnis/ *n.*

learned help·less·ness /lərnd/ ▸*n. Psychiatry* a condition in which a person suffers from a sense of powerlessness, arising from a traumatic event or persistent failure to succeed. It is thought to be one of the underlying causes of depression.

learn·fare /ˈlərnˌfe(ə)r/ ▸*n.* a public assistance program in which attendance at school, college, or a training program is necessary to receive benefits.

Pronunciation Key ə *ago*; ər *over*; ˈə or ˌə *up*; ˈər or ˌər *fur*; a *hat*; ā *rate*; ä *car*; CH *chew*; e *let*; ē *see*; e(ə)r *air*; i *fit*; ī *by*; i(ə)r *ear*; NG *sing*; ō *go*; ô *for*; oi *boy*; o͝o *good*; o͞o *goo*; ou *out*; SH *she*; TH *thin*; T͟H *then*; (h)w *why*; ZH *vision*

learn·ing /ˈlərniNG/ ▸*n.* the acquisition of knowledge or skills through experience, practice, or study, or by being taught: *these children experienced difficulties in learning* | [as *adj.*] *an important learning process.* ■ knowledge acquired in this way: *I liked to parade my learning in front of my sisters.* See note at KNOWLEDGE. ▷Old English *leornung* (see LEARN, -ING[1]).

learn·ing curve ▸*n.* the rate of a person's progress in gaining experience or new skills: *the latest software packages have a steep learning curve.*

learn·ing dis·a·bil·i·ty ▸*n.* a condition giving rise to difficulties in acquiring knowledge and skills to the level expected of those of the same age, esp. when not associated with a physical handicap. —**learn·ing-dis·a·bled** *adj.*

USAGE The phrase **learning disability** became prominent in the 1980s. It is broad in scope, covering general conditions such as Down syndrome as well as more specific cognitive or neurological conditions such as dyslexia and attention deficit disorder. In emphasizing the difficulty experienced rather than any perceived 'deficiency,' it is considered less discriminatory and more positive than other terms such as **mentally handicapped**, and is now the standard accepted term in official contexts.
See also **usage** at HANDICAPPED.

Leary /ˈli(ə)rē/, Timothy (Francis) (1920–96), U.S. psychologist. After experimenting with consciousness-altering drugs, including LSD, he was dismissed from his teaching job at Harvard University in 1963 and became a figurehead for the hippie drug culture.

lease /lēs/ ▸*n.* a contract by which one party conveys land, property, services, etc., to another for a specified time, usually in return for a periodic payment.
▸*v.* [*trans.*] grant (property) on lease; let: *she* **leased** *the site* **to** *a local company.* ■ take (property) on lease; rent: *land was* **leased from** *the city.* ▷late Middle English: from Old French *lais, leis,* from *lesser, laissier* 'let, leave,' from Latin *laxare* 'make loose,' from *laxus* 'loose, lax.' —**leas·a·ble** *adj.*
▸*PHRASE* □ **a new lease on life** a substantially improved chance to lead a happy or successful life.

lease·back /ˈlēs,bak/ ▸*n.* [often as *adj.*] the leasing of a property back to the vendor: *leaseback agreements.*

lease·hold /ˈlēs,hōld/ ▸*n.* the holding of property by lease: *a form of leasehold* | [as *adj.*] *leasehold premises.* Often contrasted with FREEHOLD. ■ a property held by lease. ▷early 18th cent.: from LEASE, on the pattern of *freehold.* —**lease·hold·er** *n.*

leash /lēsH/ ▸*n.* a strap or cord for restraining and guiding a dog or other animal. ■ *Falconry* a thong or string attached to the jesses of a hawk, used for tying it to a perch or a creance. ■ *figurative* a restraint: *her bristling temper was kept on a leash.*
▸*v.* [*trans.*] put a leash on (a dog). ■ *figurative* restrain: *his violence was barely leashed.* ▷Middle English: from Old French *lesse, laisse,* from *laissier* in the specific sense 'let run on a slack lead' (see LEASE).
▸*PHRASE* □ **strain at the leash** *figurative* be eager to begin or do something.

least /lēst/ ▸*adj.* & *pron.* (usu. **the least**) smallest in amount, extent, or significance: [as *adj.*] *who has the least money? he never had the least idea what to do about it* | [as *pron.*] *how others see me is* **the least of** *my worries* | *it's the least I can do.*
▸*adj.* used in names of very small animals and plants, e.g., **least shrew**.
▸*adv.* to the smallest extent or degree: *my best number was the one I had practiced* **the least** | *turning up when he was least expected* | *only the least expensive lot sold* | *I never hid the truth,* **least of all** *from you.* ▷Old English *lǣst, lǣsest,* of Germanic origin; related to LESS.
▸*PHRASES* □ **at least 1** not less than; at the minimum: *clean the windows at least once a week.* **2** if nothing else (used to add a positive comment about a generally negative situation): *the options aren't complete, but at least they're a start.* **3** anyway (used to modify something just stated): *they seldom complained—officially at least.* □ **at the least** (or **very least**) **1** (used after amounts) not less than; at the minimum: *stay ten days at the least.* **2** taking the most pessimistic or unfavorable view: *a program that is, at the very least, excellent PR for the hospital.* □ **least said, soonest mended** *proverb* a difficult situation will be resolved more quickly if there is no more discussion of it. □ **not in the least** not in the smallest degree; not at all: *he was not in the least taken aback.* □ **not least** in particular; notably: *there is a great deal at stake, not least in relation to the environment.* □ **to say the least** used as an understatement (implying the reality is more extreme, usually worse): *his performance was disappointing to say the least.*

USAGE On the punctuation of **least** in compound adjectives, see **usage** at WELL[1].

least com·mon de·nom·i·na·tor ▸*n.* another term for LOWEST COMMON DENOMINATOR.

least com·mon mul·ti·ple ▸*n.* another term for LOWEST COMMON MULTIPLE.

least sig·nif·i·cant bit (abbr.: **LSB**) ▸*n. Computing* the bit in a binary number that is of the lowest numerical value.

least squares ▸*n.* a method of estimating a quantity or fitting a graph to data so as to minimize the sum of the squares of the differences between the observed values and the estimated values.

least·ways /ˈlēst,wāz/ (also **least·wise** /-,wīz/) ▸*adv. dialect* or *informal* at least: *there is no place like our home, leastways not this side of hell.*

leath·er /ˈleTHər/ ▸*n.* **1** a material made from the skin of an animal by tanning or a similar process: [as *adj.*] *a leather jacket.* **2** a thing made of leather, in particular: ■ a piece of leather as a polishing cloth. ■ short for STIRRUP LEATHER. ■ (**leathers**) leather clothes, esp. those worn by a motorcyclist.
▸*adj. informal* of, relating to, or catering to people who wear leather clothing and accessories as a sign of rough masculinity, esp. homosexuals who practice sadomasochistic sex: *leather bar* | *leather queen.*
▸*v.* [*trans.*] **1** [usu. as *adj.*] (**leathered**) cover with leather: *dancers in leathered costumes.* **2** beat or thrash (someone): *he caught me and leathered me black and blue* | [as *n.*] (**leathering**) *go, before you get a leathering.* ▷Old English *lether,* of Germanic origin; related to Dutch *leer* and German *Leder,* from an Indo-European root shared by Irish *leathar* and Welsh *lledr.*

leath·er·back /ˈleTHər,bak/ (also **leatherback turtle**) ▸*n.* a very large black turtle with a thick leathery shell, living chiefly in tropical seas. • *Dermochelys coriacea,* the only member of the family Dermochelyidae.

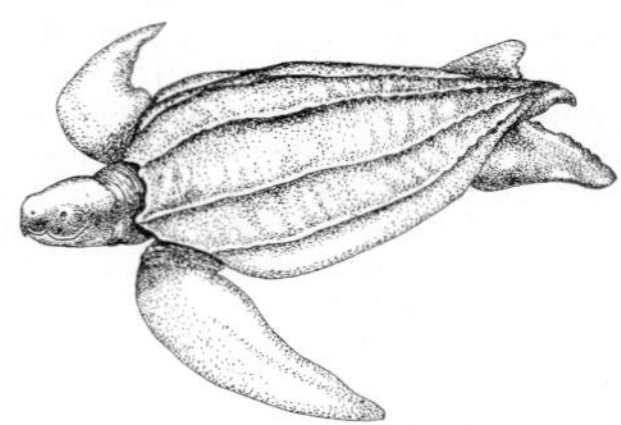

leatherback

leath·er·bound ▸*adj.* (esp. of a book) covered or held together by leather.

leath·er carp ▸*n.* a carp of a variety that lacks scales.

leath·er·ette /,leTHəˈret/ ▸*n.* imitation leather.

leath·er-hard ▸*adj.* (of unfired pottery) dried and hardened enough to be trimmed or decorated with slip but not hard enough to be fired.

leath·er·jack·et /ˈleTHər,jakit/ ▸*n.* **1** any of a number of tough-skinned marine fishes, in particular: • a fish of the jack family (Carangidae), in particular a slender fish of American coastal waters, with a greenish back and a bright yellow tail (*Oligoplites saurus*). • a filefish or triggerfish (family Balistidae). **2** *Brit.* the tough-skinned larva of a large crane fly. It lives in the soil, where it feeds on plant matter and can seriously damage the roots of grasses and crops. • Genus *Tipula,* family Tipulidae.

leath·er·leaf /ˈleTHər,lēf/ ▸*n.* a low-growing evergreen shrub of the heath family, found in north temperate regions. • *Chamaedaphne calyculata,* family Ericaceae.

leath·ern /ˈleTHərn/ ▸*adj. archaic* made of leather.

leath·er·neck /ˈleTHər,nek/ ▸*n. informal* a U.S. marine. ▷late 19th cent.: with allusion to the leather lining inside the collar of a marine's uniform.

leath·er·wear /ˈleTHər,wer/ ▸*n.* articles of clothing made of leather.

leath·er·wood /ˈleTHər,wo͝od/ ▸*n.* **1** see TITI[2]. **2** a North American shrub with yellow flowers and very short leafstalks. Its tough, pliant bark was formerly used by American Indians for making baskets, fishing lines, and bowstrings. • *Dirca palustris,* family Thymelaeaceae.

leath·er·work /ˈleTHər,wərk/ ▸*n.* work or decoration done in leather. ■ an article or articles made of leather.

leath·er·y /ˈleTH(ə)rē/ ▸*adj.* having a tough, hard texture: *brown, leathery skin.* —**leath·er·i·ness** *n.*

leave[1] /lēv/ ▸*v.* (*past* and *past part.* **left** /left/) **1** [*trans.*] go away from: *she left New York on June 6* | [*intrans.*] *we were almost the last to leave the Bruins* **left for** *Toronto on Monday.* ■ depart from permanently: *at the age of sixteen he left home.* ■ cease attending (a school or college) or working for (an organization): *she is leaving NBC after 20 years.* **2** [*trans.*] allow to remain: *the parts he disliked he would alter, and the parts he didn't dislike he'd leave.* ■ (**be left**) remain to be used or dealt with: *we've even got one of the plum puddings* **left over** *from last year* | *a retired person with no mortgage left to pay.* ■ go away from a place without taking (someone or something): *we had not* **left** *any of our belongings* **behind** | *figurative women had been* **left behind** *in the struggle for pay equality.* ■ abandon (a spouse or partner): *her boyfriend* **left** *her* **for** *another woman.* ■ have as (a surviving relative) after one's death: *he leaves a wife and three children.* ■ bequeath: *he left $500 to the Police Athletic League.* | *Harry had left her $5,000 a year for life.* **3** [*trans.*] cause (someone or something) to be in a particular state or position: *he'll leave you in no doubt about what he thinks* | *I'll leave the door open* | *the children were* **left with** *feelings of loss.* ■ let (someone) do or deal with something without offering help or assistance: *infected people are often rejected by family and friends, leaving them to face this chronic condition alone.* ■ cause to remain as a trace or record: *dark fruit that would leave purple stains on the table napkins* | *figurative they leave the impression that they can be bullied.* ■ deposit or entrust to be kept, collected, or attended to: *she left a note for me.* ■ [*trans.*] (**leave something to**) entrust a decision, choice, or action to (someone else, esp. someone considered better qualified): *the choice of which link to take is generally* **left up to** *the reader.*
▸*phrasal v.* □ **leave off** discontinue (an activity): *the dog left off chasing the sheep.* ■ come to an end: *he resumed the other story at the point where the previous author had left off.* □ **leave something off** omit to put on: *a bolt may have been left off the plane's forward door during production.* □ **leave someone/something out** fail to include: *it seemed unkind to leave Daisy out; so she was invited, too* | [as *adj.*] (**left out**) *Janet was feeling rather left out.*
▸*n.* (in pool, billiards, snooker, croquet, and other games) the position of the balls after a shot. ▷Old English *lǣfan* 'bequeath,' also 'allow to remain, leave in place,' of Germanic origin; related to German *bleiben* 'remain.' —**leav·er** *n.*
▸*PHRASES* □ **be left at the post** be beaten from the start of a race or competition. □ **be left for dead** be abandoned as being almost dead or certain to die. □ **be left to oneself** be allowed to do what one wants: *women, left to themselves, would make the world a beautiful place to live in.* ■ be in the position of being alone or solitary: *left to himself, he removed his shirt and tie.* □ **leave someone/something alone** see ALONE. □ **leave someone be** refrain from disturbing or interfering with someone. □ **leave someone cold** fail to interest someone: *the Romantic poets left him cold.* □ **leave hold of** cease holding. □ **leave it at that** abstain from further comment or action: *if you are not sure of the answers, say so, and leave it at that.* □ **leave much** (or **a lot**) **to be desired** be highly unsatisfactory.

leave[2] ▸*n.* **1** (also **leave of absence**) time when one has permission to be absent from work or from duty in the armed forces: *Joe was home* **on leave** | *he took a leave of absence last year.* **2** [often with *infinitive*] permission: *he is seeking leave to appeal the injunction.* ▷Old English *lēaf* 'permission'; related to LIEF and LOVE.
▸*PHRASES* □ **by** (or **with**) **your leave** with your permission: *with your leave, I will send him your address.* □ **take one's leave** *formal* say goodbye: *he went to* **take his leave of** *his hostess.* □ **take leave of one's senses** see SENSE.

leave[3] ▸*v.* put forth leaves.

leaved /lēvd/ (also **leafed**) ▸*adj.* [in *combination*] having a leaf or leaves of a particular kind or number: *broad-leaved evergreens* | *red-leafed lettuce.*

leav·en /ˈlevən/ ▸*n.* a substance, typically yeast, that is added to dough to make it ferment and rise. ■ dough that is reserved from an earlier batch in order to start a later one fermenting. ■ *figurative* a pervasive influence that modifies something or transforms it for the better: *they acted as an intellectual leaven to the warriors who dominated the city.*
▸*v.* [*trans.*] **1** [usu. as *adj.*] (**leavened**) cause (dough or bread) to ferment and rise by adding leaven: *leavened breads are forbidden during Passover.* **2** permeate and modify or transform (something) for the better: *the proceedings should be leavened by humor* | [as *n.*] (**leavening**) *companies of militia volunteers with a leavening of regular soldiers.* ▷Middle English: from Old French

levain, based on Latin *levamen* 'relief' (literally 'means of raising'), from *levare* 'to lift.'

Leav·en·worth /'levən,wərTH/ a city in northeastern Kansas, on the Missouri River, home to several prisons and also military facilities; pop. 35,420.

leave of ab·sence ▶*n.* see LEAVE[2] (sense 1).

leaves /lēvz/ ▶ plural form of LEAF.

leave-tak·ing ▶*n.* an act of saying goodbye: *the leave-taking was restrained, with none of her earlier displays of emotion.*

leav·ings /'lēviNGz/ ▶*plural n.* things that have been left as worthless: *she dropped her lunch leavings into the trash.*

Lea·wood /'lē,wo͝od/ a city in eastern Kansas, a southern suburb of Kansas City; pop. 27,656.

Leb·a·non /'lebə,nän; -,nən/ **1** a country in the Middle East, with a coastline on the Mediterranean Sea; pop. 3,777,000; capital, Beirut; official language, Arabic.

Part of the Ottoman Empire from the early 16th century, Lebanon became a French mandate after World War I and achieved independence in 1943. Until the mid 1970s the country prospered, but conflict between the Christian and Muslim communities, the influx of Palestinian refugees, and repeated Middle Eastern wars destabilized the country. The first general elections in 20 years were held in 1992.

2 an industrial city in southeastern Pennsylvania, in Pennsylvania Dutch country; pop. 24,800. **—Leb·a·nese** /,lebə'nēz; -'nēs/ *adj.* & *n.*

Leb·a·non Moun·tains a range of mountains in Lebanon that runs parallel to the Mediterranean coast. It rises to a height of 10,022 feet (3,087 m) at Qornet es Saouda and is separated from the Anti-Lebanon Mountains, on the border with Syria, by the Bekaa valley.

Le·bens·raum /'lābəns,roum; -bənz-/ ▶*n.* the territory that a state or nation believes is needed for its natural development, esp. associated with Nazi Germany. ▷German, literally 'living space' (originally with reference to Germany).

Le·blanc /lə'bläNGk; -'blän/, Nicolas (1742–1806), French surgeon and chemist. He developed a process for making soda ash (sodium carbonate) from common salt, which enabled the large-scale manufacture of glass, soap, paper, and other chemicals.

Le·brun /lə'brœn/, Charles (1619–90), French painter, designer, and decorator.

Le Car·ré /lə ka'rā/, John (1931–), English novelist; pseudonym of *David John Moore Cornwell*. His unromanticized and thoughtful spy novels, which often feature British agent George Smiley, include *The Spy Who Came in from the Cold* (1963) and *Tinker, Tailor, Soldier, Spy* (1974).

lech /leCH/ *informal, derogatory* ▶*n.* a lecher. ■ a lecherous urge or desire: *I think he has a kind of lech for you.* ▶*v.* [*intrans.*] act in a lecherous or lustful manner: *businessmen leching after bimbos.* ▷late 18th cent. (denoting a strong desire, particularly sexually): back-formation from LECHER.

Le Cha·te·lier's prin·ci·ple /lə 'shätl,yāz/ *Chemistry* a principle stating that if a constraint (such as a change in pressure, temperature, or concentration of a reactant) is applied to a system in equilibrium, the equilibrium will shift so as to tend to counteract the effect of the constraint. ▷early 20th cent.: named after Henry *le Chatelier* (1850–1936), French chemist.

lech·er /'leCHər/ ▶*n.* a lecherous man. ▷Middle English: from Old French *lichiere, lecheor*, from *lechier* 'live in debauchery or gluttony,' ultimately of West Germanic origin and related to LICK.

lech·er·ous /'leCH(ə)rəs/ ▶*adj.* having or showing excessive or offensive sexual desire: *she ignored his lecherous gaze.* ▷Middle English: from Old French *lecheros*, from *lecheor* (see LECHER). **—lech·er·ous·ly** *adv.* **—lech·er·ous·ness** *n.*

lech·er·y /'leCH(ə)rē/ ▶*n.* excessive or offensive sexual desire; lustfulness. ▷Middle English: from Old French *lecherie*, from *lecheor* (see LECHER).

lech·u·guil·la /,leCHə'gēə/ ▶*n.* a succulent desert plant (*Agave lecheguilla*) of Mexico, with pointed basal leaves and a tall flower spike. It is a principal source of ixtle.

le·chwe /'leCHwē; -,wā/ ▶*n.* (*pl.* same) a rough-coated grazing antelope with pointed hooves and long horns, found in swampy grassland in southern Africa and the Sudan. • Genus *Kobus*, family Bovidae: two species, in particular *K. leche*. ▷mid 19th cent.: from Setswana.

lec·i·thin /'lesəTHin/ ▶*n. Biochemistry* a substance widely distributed in animal tissues, egg yolk, and some higher plants, consisting of phospholipids linked to choline. ▷mid 19th cent.: from Greek *lekithos* 'egg yolk' + -IN[1].

lec·i·thin·ase /'lesəTHi,nās; -,nāz/ ▶*n. Biochemistry* another term for PHOSPHOLIPASE.

Le·clan·ché cell /lə'klänsHā/ ▶*n.* a primary electrochemical cell having a zinc cathode in contact with zinc chloride, ammonium chloride (as a solution or a paste) as the electrolyte, and a carbon anode in contact with a mixture of manganese dioxide and carbon powder. ▷late 19th cent.: named after Georges *Leclanché* (1839–82), French chemist.

Le Cor·bu·sier /lə ,kôrbə'zyā; -bY'zyā/ (1887–1965), French architect and city planner, born in Switzerland; born *Charles Édouard Jeanneret*. A pioneer of the international style, he developed theories on functionalism, the use of new materials and industrial techniques, and a modular system of standard-sized units (Modulor).

lect. ▶*abbr.* lecture.

lec·tern /'lektərn/ ▶*n.* a tall stand with a sloping top to hold a book or notes, and from which someone, typically a preacher or lecturer, can read while standing up. ▷Middle English: from Old French *letrun*, from medieval Latin *lectrum*, from *legere* 'to read.'

lectern

lec·tin /'lektin/ ▶*n. Biochemistry* any of a class of proteins, chiefly of plant origin, that bind specifically to certain sugars and so cause agglutination of particular cell types. ▷1950s: from Latin *lect-* 'chosen' (from the verb *legere*) + -IN[1].

lec·tion /'leksHən/ ▶*n. archaic* a reading of a text found in a particular copy or edition. ▷Middle English (in the sense 'election'): from Latin *lection-* 'choosing, reading,' from the verb *legere*. The current sense dates from the mid 17th cent.

lec·tion·ar·y /'leksHə,nerē/ ▶*n.* (*pl.* **-ar·ies**) a list or book of portions of the Bible appointed to be read at a church service. ▷late 18th cent.: from medieval Latin *lectionarium*, from Latin *lect-* 'chosen, read,' from the verb *legere*.

lec·tor /'lektər; -,tôr/ ▶*n.* **1** a reader, esp. someone who reads lessons in a church service. **2** a lecturer, esp. one employed in a foreign university to teach in their native language. ▷late Middle English: from Latin, from *lect-* 'read, chosen,' from the verb *legere*.

lectr. ▶*abbr.* lecturer.

lec·ture /'lekCHər/ ▶*n.* an educational talk to an audience, esp. to students in a university or college. ■ a long, serious speech, esp. one given as a scolding or reprimand: *the usual lecture on table manners.* ▶*v.* [*intrans.*] deliver an educational lecture or lectures: *she was lecturing to her class of eighty students.* ■ [*trans.*] give a lecture to (a class or other audience): *he was lecturing future generations of health-service professionals.* ■ [*trans.*] talk seriously or reprovingly to (someone): *don't lecture me!* ▷late Middle English (in the sense 'reading, a text to read'): from Old French, or from medieval Latin *lectura*, from Latin *lect-* 'read, chosen,' from the verb *legere*.

lec·tur·er /'lekCHərər/ ▶*n.* a person who gives lectures, esp. as an occupation at a university or college.

lec·ture·ship /'lekCHər,sHip/ ▶*n.* a post as a lecturer: *a three-year lectureship in English literature.*

LED ▶*abbr.* light-emitting diode, a semiconductor diode that glows when a voltage is applied.

led /led/ ▶ past and past participle of LEAD[1].

Le·da /'lēdə/ *Greek Mythology* the wife of Tyndareus, king of Sparta. She was loved by Zeus, who visited her in the form of a swan; among her children were the Dioscuri, Helen, and Clytemnestra.

Led·bet·ter /'led,betər/, Huddie (1885–1949) U.S. blues singer and composer; known as **Leadbelly**. His many recordings include "Good Morning, Blues" (1940) and his compositions include "Good Night, Irene" (1943).

le·der·ho·sen /'lādər,hōzən/ ▶*plural n.* leather shorts with H-shaped suspenders, traditionally worn by men in Alpine regions such as Bavaria. ▷from German, from *Leder* 'leather' + *Hosen* 'trousers.'

ledge /lej/ ▶*n.* **1** a narrow horizontal surface projecting from a wall, cliff, or other surface: *he heaved himself up over a ledge.* **2** an underwater ridge, esp. of rocks beneath the sea near the shore. **3** *Mining* a stratum of metal- or ore-bearing rock; a vein of quartz or other mineral. ▷Middle English (denoting a strip of wood or other material fixed across a door, gate, etc.): perhaps from an early form of LAY[1]. Sense 1 dates from the mid 16th cent. **—ledg·y** /'lejē/ *adj.*

ledg·er /'lejər/ ▶*n.* **1** a book or other collection of financial accounts of a particular type: *the total balance of the purchases ledger.* **2** a flat stone slab covering a grave. **3** a horizontal scaffolding pole, parallel to the face of the building. ▷late Middle English *legger, ligger* (denoting a large bible or breviary), probably from variants of LAY[1] and LIE[1], influenced by Dutch *legger* and *ligger*. Current senses date from the 16th cent., except the fishing senses, known from the 17th cent.

ledg·er line (also **leg·er line**) ▶*n. Music* a short line added for notes above or below the range of a staff.

Lee[1] /lē/, Ann (1736–84) U.S. religious leader; born in England; known as **Mother Ann**. A Shaker leader, she founded the first Shaker colony in the U.S. at Watervliet, NY 1776.

Lee[2], Bruce (1941–73), U.S. actor; born *Lee Yuen Kam*. An expert in kung fu, he starred in a number of martial arts movies, such as *Fists of Fury* (1972) and *Enter the Dragon* (1973).

Lee[3], Francis Lightfoot (1734–97) American statesman. He was a delegate to the Continental Congress 1775–79 and a signer of the Declaration of Independence in 1776.

Lee[4], Gypsy Rose (1914–70), U.S. striptease artist; born *Rose Louise Hovick*. In the 1930s, she became famous on Broadway for her sophisticated striptease act. Her autobiography, *Gypsy* (1957) was made into a movie in 1962.

Lee[5], (Nelle) Harper (1926–), U.S. novelist. She won a Pulitzer Prize for her only novel, *To Kill a Mockingbird* (1960), about the trial of a black man falsely charged with raping a white woman.

Lee[6], Henry (1756–1818) U.S. soldier and politician; known as **Light-Horse Harry**; father of Robert E. Lee. Noted as a brilliant cavalry commander in the American Revolution, he later became governor of Virginia 1792–95 and a member of the U.S. House of Representatives 1799–1801.

Lee[7], Robert E. (1807–70), Confederate general; full name *Robert Edward Lee*. He was the commander of the Confederate Army of Northern Virginia for most of the Civil War. A noted tactician and strategist, his invasion of the North was repulsed at the Battle of Gettysburg (1863), and he surrendered in 1865.

Robert E. Lee

Lee[8], Spike (1957–), U.S. movie director; born *Shelton Jackson Lee*. His movies express the richness of

Pronunciation Key ə *ago*; ər *over*; 'ə or ,ə *up*; 'ər or ,ər *fur*; a *hat*; ā *rate*; ä *car*; CH *chew*; e *let*; ē *see*; e(ə)r *air*; i *fit*; ī *by*; i(ə)r *ear*; NG *sing*; ō *go*; ô *for*; oi *boy*; o͝o *good*; o͞o *goo*; ou *out*; SH *she*; TH *thin*; TH *then*; (h)w *why*; ZH *vision*

L

black culture. He first won recognition for the comedy *She's Gotta Have It* (1986). Movies such as *Do the Right Thing* (1989) and *Malcolm X* (1992) sparked controversy with their treatment of racism.

lee /lē/ ▸*n.* shelter from wind or weather given by a neighboring object, esp. nearby land: *we pitch our tents in the lee of a rock.* ■ (also **lee side**) the sheltered side; the side away from the wind: *ducks were taking shelter on the lee of the island.* Contrasted with WEATHER. ▷Old English *hlēo, hlēow* 'shelter,' of Germanic origin; probably related to *luke-* in LUKEWARM.

lee·board /'lē,bôrd/ ▸*n.* a plate or board fixed to the side of a flat-bottomed boat and let down into the water to reduce drift to the leeward side.

leech[1] /lēCH/ ▸*n.* **1** an aquatic or terrestrial annelid worm with suckers at both ends. Many species are bloodsucking parasites, esp. of vertebrates, and others are predators. • Class Hirudinea: many species. See also MEDICINAL LEECH. **2** a person who extorts profit from or sponges on others: *they are leeches feeding off the hardworking majority.*
▸*v.* [*intrans.*] habitually exploit or rely on: *he's leeching off the kindness of others.* ▷Old English *lǣce, lȳce*; related to Middle Dutch *lake, lieke.*

leech[2] ▸*n. archaic* a doctor or healer. ▷Old English *lǣce*, of Germanic origin.

leech[3] ▸*n. Sailing* the after or leeward edge of a fore-and-aft sail, the leeward edge of a spinnaker, or a vertical edge of a square sail. ▷late 15th cent.: probably of Scandinavian origin and related to Swedish *lik*, Danish *lig*, denoting a rope sewn round the edge of a sail to stop the canvas from tearing.

leech·craft /'lēCH,kraft/ ▸*n. archaic* the art of healing. ▷Old English *lǣcecræft* (see LEECH[2], CRAFT).

Leeds /lēdz/ an industrial city in northern England; pop. 674,000. It developed as a wool town in the Middle Ages and became a clothing center during the Industrial Revolution.

Lee-En·field /'lē 'enfēld/ (also **Lee-Enfield rifle**) ▸*n.* a bolt-action rifle of a type formerly used by the British army.

lee helm ▸*n. Sailing* the tendency of a vessel to turn its bow to leeward.

leek /lēk/ ▸*n.* a plant related to the onion, with flat overlapping leaves forming an elongated cylindrical bulb that together with the leaf bases is eaten as a vegetable. It is used as a Welsh national emblem. • *Allium porrum*, family Liliaceae (or Alliaceae). ▷Old English *lēac*, of Germanic origin; related to Dutch *look* and German *Lauch.*

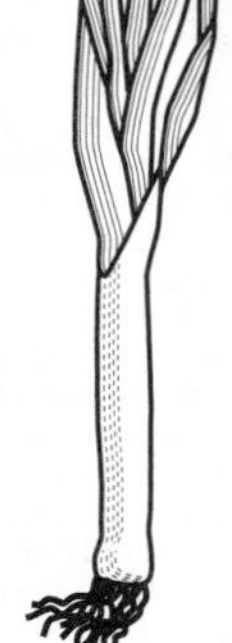
leek

leer /li(ə)r/ ▸*v.* [*intrans.*] look or gaze in an unpleasant, malicious, or lascivious way: *bystanders were leering at the nude painting* | [as *adj.*] (**leering**) *every leering eye in the room was on her.*
▸*n.* an unpleasant, malicious, or lascivious look. ▷mid 16th cent. (in the general sense 'look sideways or askance'): perhaps from obsolete *leer* 'cheek,' from Old English *hlēor*, as though the sense were 'to glance over one's cheek.' —**leer·ing·ly** *adv.*

leer·y /'li(ə)rē/ ▸*adj.* (**leer·i·er, leer·i·est**) cautious or wary due to realistic suspicions: *a city* **leery of** *gang violence.* ▷late 17th cent.: from obsolete *leer* 'looking askance,' from LEER + -Y[1]. —**leer·i·ness** *n.*

lees /lēz/ ▸*plural n.* the sediment of wine in the barrel. ■ *figurative* dregs; refuse: *the lees of the Venetian underworld.* ▷late Middle English: plural of obsolete *lee* in the same sense, from Old French *lie*, from medieval Latin *liae* (plural), of Gaulish origin.

lee shore ▸*n.* a shore lying on the leeward side of a ship (and onto which a ship could be blown in foul weather).

lee side ▸*n.* see LEE.

Lee's Summit /lēz/ an industrial city in northwestern Missouri, southeast of Kansas City; pop. 70,700.

leet /lēt/ ▸*n. historical* (in England) a yearly or half-yearly court of record that the lords of certain manors held. ■ the jurisdiction of such a court. ▷Middle English: from Anglo-Norman French *lete* or Anglo-Latin *leta*, of unknown origin.

Lee·u·wen·hoek /'lāvən,hōōk; 'lāvən-/, Antoni van (1632–1723), Dutch naturalist. He developed a lens for scientific purposes and was the first to observe bacteria, protozoa, and yeast. He accurately described red blood cells, capillaries, striated muscle fibers, spermatozoa, and the crystalline lens of the eye.

lee·ward /'lēwərd; 'lōōərd/ ▸*adj. & adv.* on or toward the side sheltered from the wind or toward which the wind is blowing; downwind: [as *adj.*] *the leeward side of the house* | [as *adv.*] *we pitched our tents* **leeward of** *a hill.* Contrasted with WINDWARD.
▸*n.* the side sheltered or away from the wind: *the ship was drifting* **to leeward.**

Lee·ward Is·lands /'lēwərd/ a group of islands in the Caribbean Sea that constitutes the northern part of the Lesser Antilles. The group includes Guadeloupe, Antigua, St. Kitts, and Montserrat. ▷*Leeward* with reference to the islands' situation further downwind (in terms of the prevailing southeasterly winds) than the Windward Islands.

lee wave ▸*n.* a standing atmospheric wave generated on the sheltered side of a mountain by an air current passing over or around it, and often made visible by the formation of clouds.

lee·way /'lē,wā/ ▸*n.* **1** the amount of freedom to move or act that is available: *the government had several months' leeway to introduce reforms.* ■ margin of safety: *there is little leeway if anything goes wrong.* **2** the sideways drift of a ship or an aircraft to leeward of the desired course: *the leeway is only about 2°.*

left[1] /left/ ▸*adj.* **1** on, toward, or relating to the side of a human body or of a thing that is to the west when the person or thing is facing north: *her left eye* | *the left side of the road.* ■ denoting the side of something that is in an analogous position: *the left edge of the text.* ■ on this side from the point of view of a spectator. **2** of or relating to a person or group favoring liberal, socialist, or radical views: *Left politics.* [see LEFT WING.]
▸*adv.* on or to the left side: *turn left here* | *keep left.*
▸*n.* **1** (**the left**) the left-hand part, side, or direction: *a turn to the left* | (**one's left**) *the general sat to his left.* ■ (in soccer or a similar sport) the left-hand half of the field when facing the opponents' goal: *a free kick from the left.* ■ (**left**) *Baseball* short for LEFT FIELD: *a sacrifice fly to left.* ■ the left wing of an army: *a token attack on the Russian left.* **2** (often **the Left**) [treated as *sing.* or *pl.*] a group or party favoring liberal, socialist, or radical views: *the Left is preparing to fight presidential elections.* ■ the section of a party or group holding such views more strongly: *he is on the left of the party.* **3** a thing on the left-hand side or done with the left hand, in particular: ■ a left turn: *take a left here.* ■ a road, entrance, etc., on the left: *my road's the first left.* ■ a person's left fist, esp. a boxer's: *a dazzler with the left.* ■ a blow given with this: *a left to the body.* ▷Old English *lyft, left* 'weak' (the left-hand side being regarded as the weaker side of the body). —**left·ish** *adj.*
▸*PHRASES* □ **have two left feet** be clumsy or awkward. □ **left, right, and center** (also **left and right** or **right and left**) on all sides: *deals were being done left, right, and center.*

left[2] ▸ past and past participle of LEAVE[1].

Left Bank a district of Paris, France, situated on the left bank of the Seine River, to the south of the river. It is an area noted for its intellectual and artistic life.

left bank ▸*n.* the bank of a river on the left as one faces downstream.

left brain ▸*n.* the left-hand side of the human brain, which is believed to be associated with linear and analytical thought. —**left-brained** /'left ,brānd/ *adj.*

left coast /'left 'kōst/ ▸*n.* the West Coast of the U.S., especially California: *America's left coast should be on everyone's vacation list.*

left face ▸*exclam.* (**left face!**) (in military contexts) a command to turn 90 degrees to the left.

left field ▸*n. Baseball* the part of the outfield to the left of center field from the perspective of home plate: *a high fly* **to left field.** ■ the position of the defensive player stationed in left field: *I played left field a lot against him.* ■ *figurative* a position or direction that is surprising or unconventional: *seldom do so many witty touches come* **out of left field.** ■ *figurative* a position of ignorance, error, or confusion: *he's so far* **out in left field** *that even his followers are embarrassed.* —**left field·er** *n.*

left-foot·ed ▸*adj.* (of a person) using one's left foot more naturally and effectively than the right. ■ (esp. of a kick) done with a person's left foot: *he drove a left-footed shot into the net.*

left hand ▸*n.* the hand of a person's left side. ■ the region or direction on the left side of a person or thing: *there was a vast forest on the left hand.*
▸*adj.* [*attrib.*] on or toward the left side of a person or thing: *his left-hand pocket.* ■ done with or using the left hand: *an excellent left-hand catch.*

left-hand·ed ▸*adj.* **1** (of a person) using the left hand more naturally than the right: *a left-handed batter.* ■ (of a tool or item of equipment) made to be used with the left hand: *left-handed golf clubs.* ■ made or performed with the left hand: *my left-handed scrawl.* **2** turning to the left; toward the left, in particular: ■ (of a screw) advanced by turning counterclockwise. ■ *Biology* (of a spiral shell or helix) sinistral. ■ (of a racecourse) turning counterclockwise. **3** perverse: *we take a left-handed pleasure in our errors.* ■ (esp. of a compliment) ambiguous.
▸*adv.* with the left hand: *a significant number play the game left-handed.* —**left-hand·ed·ly** *adv.* —**left-hand·ed·ness** *n.*

left-hand·er ▸*n.* a left-handed person, esp. a left-handed baseball pitcher. ■ a blow struck with a person's left hand.

left·ie ▸*n.* variant spelling of LEFTY.

left·ist /'leftist/ ▸*n.* a person who supports the political views or policies of the left.
▸*adj.* supportive of the political views or policies of the left: *leftist radicals.* —**left·ism** /-,tizəm/ *n.*

left-lean·ing ▸*adj.* sympathetic to or tending toward the left in politics: *a left-leaning professor.*

left·most /'lef(t),mōst/ ▸*adj.* [*attrib.*] farthest to the left: *the leftmost edge of the screen.*

left·o·ver /'left,ōvər/ ▸*n.* (usu. **leftovers**) something, esp. food, remaining after the rest has been used or consumed.
▸*adj.* [*attrib.*] remaining; surplus: *yesterday's leftover bread.*

left turn ▸*n.* a turn that brings a person's front to face the way their left side did before: *take a left turn onto Paramus Road.*

left·ward /'leftwərd/ ▸*adv.* (also **left·wards** /-wərdz/) toward the left.
▸*adj.* going toward or facing the left: *they moved their eyes in a leftward direction.*

left wing ▸*n.* (**the left wing**) **1** the liberal, socialist, or radical section of a political party or system. [with reference to the National Assembly in France (1789–91), where the nobles sat to the president's right and the commons to the left.] **2** the left side of a team on the field in soccer, rugby, and field hockey: *his usual position on the left wing.* ■ the left side of an army: *the Allied left wing.*
▸*adj.* liberal, socialist, or radical: *left-wing activists.* —**left-wing·er** *n.*

left·y /'leftē/ (also **left·ie**) ▸*n.* (*pl.* **left·ies**) *informal* **1** a left-handed person. **2** a leftist.

leg /leg/ ▸*n.* **1** each of the limbs on which a person or animal walks and stands: *Adams broke his leg* | *he was off* **as fast as his legs would carry him** | [as *adj.*] *a leg injury.* ■ a leg of an animal or bird as food: *a roast leg of lamb.* ■ a part of a garment covering a leg or part of a leg: *his trouser leg.* ■ (**legs**) *informal* used to refer to the sustained popularity or success of a product or idea: *some books have legs; others don't.* **2** each of the supports of a chair, table, or other piece of furniture: *table legs.* ■ a long, thin support or prop: *the house was set on legs.* **3** a section or stage of a journey or process: *the return leg of his journey.* ■ *Sailing* a run made on a single tack. ■ (in soccer and other sports) each of two games constituting a round of a competition. ■ a section of a relay or other race done in stages: *one leg of its race around the globe.* ■ a single game in a darts match. **4** a branch of a forked object. **5** (also **leg side**) *Cricket* the half of the field (as divided lengthways through the pitch) away from which the batsman's feet are pointed when standing to receive the ball. The opposite of OFF. **6** *archaic* an obeisance made by drawing back one leg and bending it while keeping the front leg straight.
▸*v.* (**legged** /'legd/, **leg·ging**) [*trans.*] **1** (**leg it**) *informal* travel by foot; walk. ■ run away: *he legged it after someone shouted at him.* **2** *chiefly historical* propel (a boat) through a tunnel on a canal by pushing with one's legs against the tunnel roof or sides. ▷Middle English (superseding SHANK): from Old Norse *leggr* (compare with Danish *læg* 'calf (of the leg)'), of Germanic origin. —**leg·ged** /'legid/ *adj.* [in *combination*] *a four-legged animal.* —**leg·ger** *n.* [in *combination*] *a three-legger.*
▸*PHRASES* □ **feel** (or **find**) **one's legs** become able to stand or walk. □ **leg up** help to mount a horse or high object: **give me a leg up** *over the wall.* ■ help to improve one's position: *the council is to provide a financial leg up for the club.* □ **not have** (**the**) **legs** (of a ball, esp. in golf) not have sufficient momentum to reach the desired point. □ **not have a leg to stand on** have no facts or sound reasons to support one's argument or justify one's actions. □ **on one's last**

legs near the end of life, usefulness, or existence: *the foundry business was on its last legs.*

leg. ▶*abbr.* ■ legal. ■ legate. ■ *Music* legato. ■ legend. ■ legislation or legislative or legislature.

leg·a·cy /ˈlegəsē/ ▶*n.* (*pl.* **-cies**) an amount of money or property left to someone in a will. ■ a thing handed down by a predecessor: *the* **legacy of** *centuries of neglect.*
▶*adj. Computing* denoting software or hardware that has been superseded but is difficult to replace because of its wide use. ▷late Middle English (also denoting the function or office of a deputy, esp. a papal legate): from Old French *legacie*, from medieval Latin *legatia* 'legateship,' from *legatus* 'person delegated' (see **LEGATE**).

le·gal /ˈlēgəl/ ▶*adj.* **1** [*attrib.*] of, based on, or concerned with the law: *the American legal system.* ■ appointed or required by the law: *a legal requirement.* ■ of or relating to theological legalism. ■ *Law* recognized by common or statutory law, as distinct from equity. ■ (of paper) measuring 8½ by 14 inches. **2** permitted by law: *he claimed that it had all been legal.* ▷late Middle English (in the sense 'to do with Mosaic law'): from French, or from Latin *legalis*, from *lex*, *leg-* 'law.' Compare with **LOYAL**. **—le·gal·ly** *adv.* [*sentence adverb*] *legally, we're still very much married.*

le·gal age ▶*n.* the age at which a person takes on the rights and responsibilities of an adult.

le·gal aid ▶*n.* free legal advice or representation for a person who cannot afford it.

le·gal ca·pac·i·ty ▶*n.* a person's authority under law to engage in a particular undertaking or maintain a particular status.

le·gal clin·ic ▶*n.* a place where one can obtain legal advice and assistance, paid for by legal aid.

le·gal ea·gle (also **le·gal bea·gle**) ▶*n. informal* a lawyer, esp. one who is keen and astute.

le·gal·ese /ˌlēgəˈlēz; -ˈlēs/ ▶*n. informal, often derogatory* the formal and technical language of legal documents that is often hard to understand.

le·gal fic·tion ▶*n.* an assertion accepted as true, though probably fictitious, to achieve a particular goal in a legal matter.

le·gal hol·i·day ▶*n.* a public holiday established by law.

le·gal·ism /ˈlēgəˌlizəm/ ▶*n.* excessive adherence to law or formula. ■ *Theology* dependence on moral law rather than on personal religious faith. **—le·gal·ist** *n.* & *adj.* **—le·gal·is·tic** /ˌlēgəˈlistik/ *adj.* **—le·gal·is·ti·cal·ly** /ˌlēgəˈlistik(ə)lē/ *adv.*

le·gal·i·ty /ləˈgalətē/ ▶*n.* (*pl.* **-ties**) the quality or state of being in accordance with the law: *documentation testifying to the legality of the arms sale.* ■ **(legalities)** obligations imposed by law. ▷late Middle English: from French *légalité* or medieval Latin *legalitas* 'relating to the law,' from Latin *legalis* (see **LEGAL**).

le·gal·ize /ˈlēgəˌlīz/ ▶*v.* [*trans.*] make (something that was previously illegal) permissible by law: *a measure legalizing gambling in Deadwood.* **—le·gal·i·za·tion** /-ˌlēgələˈzāsʜən; -ˌlīˈzā-/ *n.*

le·gal pad ▶*n.* a ruled writing tablet, often yellow, that measures 8 1/2 by 14 inches. ■ a ruled pad of paper: *premium legal pads with recycled paper, 5 x 8, white.*

le·gal per·son ▶*n. Law* an individual, company, or other entity that has legal rights and is subject to obligations.

le·gal sep·a·ra·tion ▶*n.* **1** an arrangement by which a husband or wife remain married but live apart, following a court order. Also called **JUDICIAL SEPARATION**. **2** an arrangement by which a child lives apart from a natural parent and with the other natural parent or a foster parent, following a court order.

le·gal-size ▶*adj.* (of paper) measuring 8½ by 14 inches. ■ designed to hold paper of this size.

le·gal ten·der ▶*n.* coins or banknotes that must be accepted if offered in payment of a debt.

leg·ate /ˈlegit/ ▶*n.* **1** a member of the clergy, esp. a cardinal, representing the pope. ■ *archaic* an ambassador or messenger. **2** a general or governor of an ancient Roman province, or their deputy: *the Roman legate of Syria.* ▷late Old English, from Old French *legat*, from Latin *legatus*, past participle of *legare* 'depute, delegate, bequeath.' **—leg·ate·ship** /-ˌsʜip/ *n.* **—leg·a·tine** /ˈlegəˌtēn; -ˌtīn/ *adj.*

le·gate a la·te·re /ˈlegit ä ˈlätəˌrā/ ▶*n.* a papal legate of the highest class, with full powers. ▷early 16th cent.: from **LEGATE** + Latin *a latere* 'from the (pope's) side.'

leg·a·tee /ˌlegəˈtē/ ▶*n.* a person who receives a legacy. ▷late 17th cent.: from 15th-cent. *legate* 'bequeath' (from Latin *legare* 'delegate, bequeath') + **-EE**.

le·ga·tion /liˈgāsʜən/ ▶*n.* **1** a diplomatic minister, esp. one below the rank of ambassador, and their staff. ■ the official residence of a diplomatic minister. **2** *archaic* the position or office of legate; a legateship. ■ the sending of a legate, esp. a papal legate, on a mission. ▷late Middle English (denoting the sending of a papal legate; also the mission itself): from Latin *legatio(n-)*, from *legare* 'depute, delegate, bequeath.'

le·ga·to /liˈgätō/ ▶*adv.* & *adj. Music* in a smooth, flowing manner, without breaks between notes. Compare with **STACCATO**.
▶*n.* performance in this manner. ▷Italian, literally 'bound.'

le·ga·tor /liˈgātər/ ▶*n. rare* a testator, esp. one who leaves a legacy. ▷mid 17th cent.: from Latin, from *legat-* 'deputed, delegated, bequeathed,' from the verb *legare*.

leg·end /ˈlejənd/ ▶*n.* **1** a traditional story sometimes popularly regarded as historical but unauthenticated: *the legend of King Arthur | according to legend he banished all the snakes from Ireland.* **2** an extremely famous or notorious person, esp. in a particular field: *the man was* **a living legend** *| a Wall Street legend.* **3** an inscription, esp. on a coin or medal. ■ a caption: *a picture of a tiger with the legend "Go ahead, make my day."* ■ the wording on a map or diagram explaining the symbols used: *see legend under Fig. 1.* **4** *historical* the story of a saint's life: *the mosaics illustrate the legends of the saints.*
▶*adj.* very well known: *his speed and ferocity in attack were legend.* ▷Middle English (sense 4): from Old French *legende*, from medieval Latin *legenda* 'things to be read,' from Latin *legere* 'read.' Sense 1 dates from the early 17th cent.

leg·end·ar·y /ˈlejənˌderē/ ▶*adj.* **1** of, described in, or based on legends: *a legendary British king of the 4th century.* **2** remarkable enough to be famous; very well known: *her wisdom in matters of childbirth was legendary.* ▷early 16th cent. (as a noun denoting a collection of legends, esp. of saints' lives): from medieval Latin *legendarius*, from *legenda* 'things to be read' (see **LEGEND**). **—leg·end·ar·i·ly** /-ˌderəlē; ˌlejənˈde(ə)r-/ *adv.*

Lé·ger /lāˈzʜā/, Fernand (1881–1955), French painter. His works include the *Contrast of Forms* series (1913).

leg·er·de·main /ˌlejərdəˈmān; ˈlejərdəˌmān/ ▶*n.* skillful use of one's hands when performing conjuring tricks. ■ deception; trickery. ▷late Middle English: from French *léger de main* 'dexterous,' literally 'light of hand.'

leg·er line /ˈlejər/ ▶*n. Music* variant spelling of **LEDGER LINE**. ▷late 19th cent.: *leger*, variant of **LEDGER**.

leg·gings /ˈlegiɴɢz/ ▶*plural n.* tight-fitting stretch pants worn by women and children. ■ protective coverings for the legs.

leg·gy /ˈlegē/ ▶*adj.* (**-gi·er**, **-gi·est**) **1** (of a woman) having attractively long legs: *a leggy redhead.* ■ long-legged: *a leggy type of collie.* **2** (of a plant) having an excessively long and straggly stem: *tulips may grow tall and leggy.* **—leg·gi·ness** *n.*

leg·hold trap /ˈlegˌhōld/ ▶*n.* a type of trap with a mechanism that catches and holds an animal by one of its legs.

Leg·horn /ˈlegˌhôrn/ another name for **LIVORNO**.

leg·horn /ˈlegˌhôrn; ˈlegərn/ ▶*n.* **1** fine plaited straw. ■ (also **leghorn hat**) a hat made of this. **2** (**Leg·horn** /ˈlegərn; -ˌhôrn/) a chicken of a small hardy breed. ▷mid 18th cent.: anglicized from the Italian name *Leghorno* (now **LIVORNO**), from where the straw and fowls were imported.

leg·i·ble /ˈlejəbəl/ ▶*adj.* (of handwriting or print) clear enough to read: *the original typescript is scarcely legible.* ▷late Middle English: from late Latin *legibilis*, from *legere* 'to read.' **—leg·i·bil·i·ty** /ˌlejəˈbilətē/ *n.* **—leg·i·bly** /-blē/ *adv.*

le·gion /ˈlējən/ ▶*n.* **1** a unit of 3,000–6,000 men in the ancient Roman army. ■ **(the Legion)** the Foreign Legion. ■ **(the Legion)** any of the national associations of former servicemen and servicewomen instituted after World War I, such as the American Legion. **2** (**a legion/legions of**) a vast host, multitude, or number of people or things: *legions of photographers and TV cameras.*
▶*adj.* great in number: *her fans are legion.* ▷Middle English: via Old French from Latin *legion-*, from *legere* 'choose, levy.' The adjective dates from the late 17th cent., in early use often in the phrase *my, their, etc., name is legion*, i.e., 'we, they, etc., are many' (Mark 5:9).

le·gion·ar·y /ˈlējəˌnerē/ ▶*n.* (*pl.* **-ar·ies**) a soldier in a Roman legion.
▶*adj.* [*attrib.*] of an ancient Roman legion: *the legionary fortress of Isca.* ▷late Middle English: from Latin *legionarius*, from *legio(n-)* (see **LEGION**).

le·gioned /ˈlējənd/ ▶*adj. poetic/literary* arrayed in legions.

le·gion·el·la /ˌlējəˈnelə/ ▶*n.* (*pl.* **le·gion·el·lae** /ˌlējəˈnelē; -ˈnelˌī/) the bacterium that causes legionnaires' disease, flourishing in air conditioning and central heating systems. • *Legionella pneumophila*, a motile, aerobic, rod-shaped (or filamentous) Gram-negative bacterium. ■ *informal* legionnaires' disease. ▷late 20th cent.: modern Latin, from **LEGION** + the diminutive suffix *-ella*.

le·gion·naire /ˌlējəˈner/ ▶*n.* a member of a legion, in particular an ancient Roman legion or the French Foreign Legion. ▷early 19th cent.: from French *légionnaire*, from *légion* 'legion,' from Latin *legio* (see **LEGION**).

le·gion·naires' dis·ease ▶*n.* a form of bacterial pneumonia first identified after an outbreak at an American Legion meeting in 1976. It is spread chiefly by water droplets through air conditioning and similar systems. See also **LEGIONELLA**.

Le·gion of Hon·or a French order of distinction founded in 1802. ▷translation of French *Légion d'honneur*.

Le·gion of Mer·it ▶(abbr.: **LM**) *n.* a U.S. military decoration, ranking below the Silver Star and above the Distinguished Flying Cross, awarded for exceptional performance of services to the U.S.

leg i·ron ▶*n.* (usu. **leg irons**) a metal band or chain placed around a prisoner's ankle as a restraint.

legis. ▶*abbr.* ■ legislation. ■ legislative. ■ legislature.

leg·is·late /ˈlejəˌslāt/ ▶*v.* [*intrans.*] make or enact laws: *he didn't want to name anyone to the Court who would legislate from the bench.* ■ [*trans.*] cover, affect, or create by making or enacting laws: *Congress must legislate strong new laws.* ▷early 18th cent.: back-formation from **LEGISLATION**.

leg·is·la·tion /ˌlejəˈslāsʜən/ ▶*n.* laws, considered collectively: *tax legislation.* ▷mid 17th cent. (denoting the enactment of laws): from late Latin *legis latio(n-)*, literally 'proposing of a law,' from *lex* 'law' and *latus* 'raised' (past participle of *tollere*).

leg·is·la·tive /ˈlejəˌslātiv/ ▶*adj.* having the power to make laws: *the country's supreme legislative body.* ■ of or relating to laws or the making of them: *legislative proposals.* Often contrasted with **EXECUTIVE**. ■ of or relating to a legislature: *legislative elections.* **—leg·is·la·tive·ly** *adv.*

leg·is·la·tor /ˈlejəˌslātər/ ▶*n.* a person who makes laws; a member of a legislative body. ▷late 15th cent.: from Latin *legis lator*, literally 'proposer of a law,' from *lex* 'law' and *lator* 'proposer, mover' (see also **LEGISLATION**).

leg·is·la·ture /ˈlejəˌslācʜər/ ▶*n.* the legislative body of a country or state. ▷late 17th cent.: from **LEGISLATION**, on the pattern of *judicature*.

le·git /liˈjit/ ▶*adj. informal* legal; conforming to the rules: *is this car legit?* ■ (of a person) not engaging in illegal activity or attempting to deceive; honest: *to see if he's legit, I call up the business.* ▷early 20th cent.: abbreviation of **LEGITIMATE**.
▶*PHRASE* □ **go legit** begin to behave honestly after a period of illegal activity.

le·git·i·mate ▶*adj.* /liˈjitəmit/ conforming to the law or to rules: *his claims to legitimate authority.* See note at **GENUINE**. ■ able to be defended with logic or justification: *a legitimate excuse for being late.* ■ (of a child) born of parents lawfully married to each other. ■ (of a sovereign) having a title based on strict hereditary right: *the last legitimate Anglo-Saxon king.* ■ constituting or relating to serious drama as distinct from musical comedy, revue, etc.: *the legitimate theater.*
▶*v.* /-ˌmāt/ [*trans.*] make legitimate; justify or make lawful: *the regime was not legitimated by popular support.* ▷late Middle English (in the sense 'born of parents lawfully married to each other'): from medieval Latin *legitimatus* 'made legal,' from the verb *legitimare*, from Latin *legitimus* 'lawful,' from *lex*, *leg-* 'law.' **—le·git·i·ma·cy** /-məsē/ *n.* **—le·git·i·mate·ly** /-mitlē/ *adv.* **—le·git·i·ma·tion** /liˌjitəˈmāsʜən/ *n.* **—le·git·i·ma·tize** /-məˌtīz/ *v.*

le·git·i·mism /liˈjitəˌmizəm/ ▶*n.* support for a ruler whose claim to a throne is based on direct descent.

▷late 19th cent.: from French *légitimisme*, from *légitime*, from Latin *legitimus* (see LEGITIMATE). **—le·git·i·mist** *n.* & *adj.*

le·git·i·mize /li'jitə,mīz/ ▶*v.* [*trans.*] make legitimate: *voters legitimize the government through the election of public officials.* **—le·git·i·mi·za·tion** /li,jitəmə'zāsʜən/ *n.*

leg·less liz·ard /'legləs/ ▶*n.* a lizard that lacks legs and has a snakelike or wormlike appearance, in particular: • an Australian lizard of a group that includes the scalyfoots (several genera in the family Pygopodidae). • a North American lizard of California and Baja California (genus *Anniella*, family Anniellidae).

leg·man /'leg,man/ ▶*n.* (*pl.* **-men**) a reporter whose job it is to gather information about news stories at the scene of the event or from an original source. ■ a person employed to do simple tasks such as running errands or collecting information from outside their workplace.

Le·go /'legō/ ▶*n. trademark* a construction toy consisting of interlocking plastic building blocks. ▷1950s: from Danish *leg godt* 'play well,' from *lege* 'to play.'

leg-of-mut·ton sleeve ▶*n.* a sleeve that is full and loose on the upper arm but close-fitting on the forearm and wrist.

leg-of-mutton sleeve

leg-pull ▶*n. informal* a trick or practical joke. **—leg-pull·er** *n.* **—leg-pull·ing** *n.*

leg rest ▶*n.* a support for a seated person's leg.

leg·room /'leg,ro͝om; -,ro͞om/ ▶*n.* space where a seated person can put their legs.

leg-rope /'leg ,rōp/ ▶*n.* **1** (in surfing) a rope attached to a surfboard and tied to the surfer's ankle to prevent the board being washed away by the surf. **2** a rope secured to a horse's leg, used to prepare the horse for a rider.

leg show ▶*n. informal, dated* a theatrical production in which dancing girls display their legs.

Le Guin /lə 'gwin/, Ursula (Kroeber) (1929–), U.S. writer. She wrote science fiction for children and adults, as well as novels and poetry. Her science fiction includes the *Earthsea* trilogy for children (1968–72) and the Hain novels that include *Rocannon's World* (1966) and *The Left Hand of Darkness* (1969).

leg·ume /'leg,yo͞om; lə'gyo͞om/ ▶*n.* a leguminous plant, esp. one grown as a crop. ■ a seed, pod, or other edible part of a leguminous plant used as food. ■ *Botany* the long seedpod of a leguminous plant. ▷mid 17th cent. (denoting the edible portion of the plant): from French *légume*, from Latin *legumen*, from *legere* 'to pick' (because the fruit may be picked by hand).

le·gu·mi·nous /li'gyo͞omənəs/ ▶*adj. Botany* of, relating to, or denoting plants of the pea family (Leguminosae). They have seeds in pods, distinctive flowers, and typically root nodules containing symbiotic bacteria able to fix nitrogen. Compare with PAPILIONACEOUS. ▷late Middle English (in the sense 'relating to pulses'): from medieval Latin *leguminosus*, from *legumen* (see LEGUME).

leg warm·ers ▶*n.* a pair of tubular knitted garments designed to cover the leg from ankle to knee or thigh, esp. worn by dancers during rehearsal.

leg·work /'leg,wərk/ ▶*n.* work that involves much traveling to collect information, esp. when such work is difficult but boring.

Le·hár /'lā,här/, Franz (Ferencz) (1870–1948), Hungarian composer. He is known for his operettas, of which the best-known is *The Merry Widow* (1905).

Le Ha·vre /lə 'häv(rə)/ a port in northern France, on the English Channel at the mouth of the Seine River; pop. 197,000.

Le·high Riv·er /'lē,hī/ a river that flows for 103 miles (166 km) through eastern Pennsylvania to the Delaware River. Bethlehem and Allentown are among its centers.

Leh·mann /'lāmən/, Lottie (1888–1976), U.S. lyric soprano; born in Germany. She was known for her interpretations of Strauss and other great composers.

Leh·rer /'le(ə)rər/, Jim (1934–), U.S. television journalist; full name *James Charles Lehrer*. With Robert MacNeil he coanchored the "MacNeil/Lehrer News Hour" from 1983 until 1995 and then continued as the anchor of the "News Hour with Jim Lehrer."

lei[1] /lā/ ▶*n.* a Polynesian garland of flowers. ▷Hawaiian.

lei[2] ▶ plural form of LEU.

Leib·niz /'līb,nits; 'līp-/, Gottfried Wilhelm (1646–1716), German rationalist philosopher, mathematician, and logician. He argued that the world is composed of single units (monads) and also devised a method of calculus independently of Newton. **—Leib·niz·i·an** /līb'nitsēən/ *adj.* & *n.*

Lei·bo·vitz /'lēbə,vits/, Annie (1950–), U.S. photographer. She was chief photographer of *Rolling Stone* magazine 1973–83 before moving to *Vanity Fair*. She produced portraits of many celebrities and had numerous exhibitions, including those at the Smithsonian National Portrait Gallery in Washington, DC, in 1991.

Leices·ter[1] /'lestər/ a city in central England, on the Soar River; pop. 271,000.

Leices·ter[2], Earl of, see DUDLEY[2].

Leices·ter[3] ▶*n.* **1** (also **Red Leicester**) a kind of mild, firm cheese, typically orange-colored and originally made in Leicestershire. **2** (also **Border Leicester**) a sheep of a breed often crossed with other breeds to produce lambs for the meat industry. **3** (also **Blue-faced Leicester**) a sheep of a breed similar to the Border Leicester, but with finer wool and a darker face.

Leices·ter·shire /'lestərsʜər; -,sʜi(ə)r/ a county in central England; county town, Leicester.

Lei·den /'līdn; 'lādn/ (also **Ley·den**) a city in the western Netherlands, 9 miles (15 km) northeast of The Hague; pop. 111,950.

Leif Er·ics·son /,lēf 'eriksən/ see ERICSSON[2].

Leigh[1] /lē/, Janet (1927–2004), U.S. actress. Best known for her role in Alfred Hitchcock's *Psycho* (1960), she appeared in more than fifty other films, including *Little Women* (1949) and *The Manchurian Candidate* (1962),

Leigh [2], Vivien (1913–67), British actress, born in India; born *Vivian Mary Hartley*. She won Academy Awards for her performances in *Gone with the Wind* (1939) and *A Streetcar Named Desire* (1951). She was married to Laurence Olivier from 1940 to 1961.

Lein·ster /'lenstər/ a province of the Republic of Ireland, in the southeastern part of the country.

lei·o·thrix /'lī-ō,тʜriks/ (also **red-billed leiothrix**) ▶*n.* an Asian bird of the babbler family, with orange-yellow underparts and a melodious song, popular as a pet bird. Also called PEKIN ROBIN. • *Leiothrix lutea*, family Timaliidae. ▷modern Latin, from Greek *leios* 'smooth' + *thrix* 'hair.'

Leip·zig /'līpsig; -sik/ an industrial city in east central Germany; pop. 503,000.

leish·man·i·a /lēsʜ'mānēə; -'manēə/ ▶*n.* (*pl.* same or **-ma·ni·as** or **-m·an·iae** /-'mānē-ē; -'man-; -ē,ī/) a single-celled parasitic protozoan that spends part of its life cycle in the gut of a sandfly and part in the blood and other tissues of a vertebrate. • Genus *Leishmania*, phylum Kinetoplastida, kingdom Protista. ▷modern Latin, from the name of William B. *Leishman* (1856–1926), British pathologist.

leish·man·i·a·sis /,lēsʜmə'nīəsəs/ ▶*n.* a tropical and subtropical disease caused by leishmania and transmitted by the bite of sandflies. It affects either the skin or the internal organs.

leis·ter /'lēstər/ ▶*n.* a pronged spear used for catching fish.

▶*v.* [*trans.*] spear (a fish) with a leister. ▷mid 16th cent.: from Old Norse *ljóstr*, from *ljósta* 'to strike.'

lei·sure /'lēzʜər; 'lezʜər/ ▶*n.* free time. ■ use of free time for enjoyment: *increased opportunities for leisure* | [*as adj.*] *leisure activities.* ■ (**leisure for/to do something**) opportunity afforded by free time to do something: *writers with enough leisure to practice their art.* ▷Middle English: from Old French *leisir*, based on Latin *licere* 'be allowed.'

▶*PHRASES* □ **at leisure 1** not occupied; free: *the rest of the day can be spent at leisure.* **2** in an unhurried manner: *the poems were left for others to read at leisure.* □ **at one's leisure** at one's ease or convenience. □ **lady** (or **man** or **gentleman**) **of leisure** a woman or man of independent means or whose time is free from obligations to others. □ **leisure class** a social class that is independently wealthy or has much leisure.

lei·sured /'lēzʜərd; 'lezʜərd/ ▶*adj.* having ample leisure, esp. through being rich: *the leisured classes.* ■ leisurely: *a new, more leisured lifestyle.*

lei·sure·ly /'lēzʜərlē; 'lezʜər-/ ▶*adj.* acting or done at leisure; unhurried or relaxed: *a leisurely breakfast at our hotel.*

▶*adv.* without hurry: *couples strolled leisurely along.* **—lei·sure·li·ness** *n.*

lei·sure suit ▶*n.* a man's casual suit, consisting of pants and a matching shirtlike jacket, often in pastel colors.

lei·sure·wear /'lēzʜər,we(ə)r; 'lezʜər-/ ▶*n.* casual clothes designed to be worn for leisure activities, particularly sweatsuits and other sportswear.

leit·mo·tif /'lītmō,tēf/ (also **leit·mo·tiv**) ▶*n.* a recurrent theme throughout a musical or literary composition, associated with a particular person, idea, or situation. ▷late 19th cent.: from German *Leitmotiv*, from *leit-* 'leading' (from *leiten* 'to lead') + *Motiv* 'motive.'

Lei·trim /'lētrəm/ a county of the Republic of Ireland, in the province of Connacht.

Leix variant spelling of LAOIS.

lek[1] /lek/ ▶*n.* the basic monetary unit of Albania, equal to 100 qintars. ▷Albanian.

lek[2] ▶*n.* a patch of ground used for communal display in the breeding season by the males of certain birds and mammals, esp. black grouse. Each male defends a small territory in order to attract females for mating.

▶*v.* [*intrans.*] [usu. as *adj.*] (**lekking**) take part in such a display: *antelopes mate in lekking grounds.* ▷late 19th cent.: perhaps from Swedish *leka* 'to play.'

LEM /lem/ *abbr.* lunar excursion module.

lem·an /'lemən/ ▶*n.* (*pl.* **lem·ans**) *archaic* a lover or sweetheart. ■ an illicit lover, esp. a mistress. ▷Middle English *lēofman*, from *lēof* (see LIEF) + MAN.

Le Mans /lə män/ an industrial town in northwestern France; pop. 148,000. It is the site of a race car track, on which a 24-hour endurance race, established in 1923, is held each summer.

Le May /lə 'mā/, Curtis Emerson (1906–90) U.S. air force officer; known as **Old Iron Pants**. After serving in World War II, he directed the Berlin Airlift in 1948. He was the commanding general of the U.S. Strategic Air Command 1948–57 and Air Force chief of staff 1961–65.

Lem·berg /'lembərg; -bərk/ German name for LVIV.

Le·mieux /lə'myo͞o; lə'myœ/, Mario (1965–) Canadian hockey player. He played for the Pittsburgh Penguins 1984–97. Hockey Hall of Fame (1997).

lem·ma[1] /'lemə/ ▶*n.* (*pl.* **lem·mas** or **lem·ma·ta** /'lemətə/) **1** a subsidiary or intermediate theorem in an argument or proof. **2** a heading indicating the subject or argument of a literary composition, an annotation, or a dictionary entry. ▷late 16th cent.: via Latin from Greek *lēmma* 'something assumed'; derived from *lambanein* 'take.'

lem·ma[2] ▶*n.* (*pl.* **lem·mas** or **lem·ma·ta** /'lemətə/) *Botany* the lower bract of the floret of a grass. Compare with PALEA. ▷mid 18th cent. (denoting the husk or shell of a fruit): from Greek, from *lepein* 'to peel.'

lem·ma·tize /'lemə,tīz/ ▶*v.* [*trans.*] sort words by grouping inflected or variant forms of the same word. **—lem·ma·ti·za·tion** /,lemətə'zāsʜən/ *n.*

lem·me /'lemē/ *informal* ▶*contraction of* let me: *lemme ask you something.*

lem·ming /'lemiɴɢ/ ▶*n.* a small, short-tailed, thickset rodent related to the voles, found in the Arctic tundra. • *Lemmus*, *Dicrostonyx*, and other genera, family Muridae: several species, in particular the **Norway lemming** (*L. lemmus*), which is noted for its fluctuating populations and periodic mass migrations. ■ a person who unthinkingly joins a mass movement, esp. a headlong rush to destruction: *the flailings of the lemmings on Wall Street.* ▷early 18th cent.: from Norwegian and Danish; related to Old Norse *lómundr*.

Lem·mon /'lemən/, Jack (1925–2001), U.S. actor; born *John Uhler Lemmon III*. He made his name in comedies, such as *Some Like It Hot* (1959) and in serious dramatic parts. He was awarded Academy Awards for *Mr. Roberts* (1955) and *Save the Tiger* (1973).

Lem·nitz·er /'lem,nitsər/, Lyman Louis (1899–1988) U.S. army officer. He played a key role in the Allied invasions of Africa in World War II and in the negotiated surrender of Italy. Later he served as commander of UN forces in Korea 1955–57, as chairman of the U.S. joint chiefs of staff 1960–62, and as supreme allied commander in Europe 1962–69.

Lem·nos /'lem,näs; 'lemnəs/ a Greek island in the northern Aegean Sea. Greek name LÍMNOS.

lem·on /'lemən/ ▶*n.* **1** a yellow, oval citrus fruit with thick skin and fragrant, acidic juice. ■ a drink made from or flavored with lemon juice: *a port and lemon* | [*as adj.*] *lemon tea.* **2** (also **lemon tree**) the evergreen citrus tree that produces this fruit, widely cultivated in warm climates. • *Citrus limon*, family Rutaceae. **3** a pale yellow color: [*as adj.*] *lemon yellow* | *a lemon T-shirt.* **4** *informal* a person or thing, esp. an automobile, regarded as unsatisfactory, disappointing, or feeble. ▷Middle English: via Old French *limon* (in modern French denoting a lime) from Arabic *līmūn* (a collective term for fruits of this kind); compare with LIME[2]. —**lem·on·y** *adj.*

lem·on·ade /ˌleməˈnād; ˈleməˌnād/ ▸*n.* a drink made from lemon juice and sweetened water. ▷mid 17th cent.: from French *limonade*, from *limon* 'lemon.'

lem·on balm ▸*n.* see BALM (sense 3).

lem·on curd ▸*n.* a preserve with a thick consistency made from lemons, butter, eggs, and sugar.

Le Mond /lə ˈmôn(d)/, Greg (1971–) U.S. cyclist. In 1986, he became the first American to win the Tour de France bicycle race, a feat he repeated in 1989 and 1990.

lem·on drop ▸*n.* a yellow, lemon-flavored hard candy.

lem·on ge·ra·ni·um ▸*n.* a pelargonium that contains aromatic oil that smells of lemon. • *Pelargonium crispum*, family Geraniaceae.

lem·on·grass (also **lem·on grass**) ▸*n.* a fragrant tropical grass that yields an oil that smells lemon. It is widely used in Asian cooking and in perfumery and medicine. • *Cymbopogon citratus*, family Gramineae.

lem·on sole ▸*n.* a common European flatfish of the plaice family. It is an important food fish. • *Microstomus kitt*, family Pleuronectidae. ▷mid 19th cent.: *lemon* from French *limande*, of unknown origin.

lem·on thyme ▸*n.* thyme of a hybrid variety having lemon-scented leaves. • *Thymus × citriodorus*, family Labiatae.

lem·on ver·be·na ▸*n.* a South American shrub of the verbena family, with lemon-scented leaves that are used as flavoring and to make a sedative tea. • *Aloysia triphylla*, family Verbenaceae.

lem·on·wood /ˈlemənˌwo͝od/ ▸*n.* the light-colored wood of any of several tropical American trees, esp. the Cuban *Calycophyllum candidissimum* of the madder family (Rubiaceae).

lem·pi·ra /lemˈpi(ə)rə/ ▸*n.* the basic monetary unit of Honduras, equal to 100 centavos. ▷named after *Lempira*, a 16th-cent. Indian chieftain who opposed the Spanish conquest of Honduras.

le·mur /ˈlēmər/ ▸*n.* an arboreal primate with a pointed snout and typically a long tail, found only in Madagascar. Compare with FLYING LEMUR. • Lemuridae and other families, suborder Prosimii; includes also the sifaka, indri, and aye-aye. ▷late 18th cent.: modern Latin, from Latin *lemures* (plural) 'spirits of the dead' (from its specterlike face).

lem·u·res /ˈleməˌrās; ˈlemyəˌrēz/ ▸*plural n.* the family spirits of the dead in ancient Rome, considered frightening or troublesome, that must be exorcised or appeased through certain household rituals.

Le·na /ˈlānə; ˈlē-/ a river in Siberia, Russia, that rises in the mountains on the western shore of Lake Baikal and flows for 2,750 miles (4,400 km) into the Laptev Sea. It is noted for the goldfields in its basin.

Len·a·pe ▸ *n.* see LENNI LENAPE.

lend /lend/ ▸*v.* (*past* and *past part.* **lent** /lent/) [*trans.*] **1** grant to (someone) the use of (something) on the understanding that it shall be returned: *Stewart asked me to lend him my car | the pictures were lent to each museum in turn.* ■ allow (a person or organization) the use of (a sum of money) under an agreement to pay it back later, typically with interest: *no one would lend him the money | [intrans.] the bank lends only to its current customers |* [as *n.*] (**lending**) *balance sheets weakened by unwise lending.* **2** contribute or add (something, esp. a quality) to: *the smile lent his face a boyish charm.* **3** (**lend oneself to**) accommodate or adapt oneself to: *John stiffly lent himself to her enthusiastic embraces.* ■ (**lend itself to**) (of a thing) be suitable for: *bay windows lend themselves to blinds.* ▷Old English *lǣnan*, of Germanic origin; related to Dutch *lenen*, also to LOAN[1]. The addition of the final *-d* in late Middle English was due to association with verbs such as *bend* and *send.* —**lend·a·ble** *adj.*

▸*PHRASES* □ **lend an ear** (or **one's ears**) listen sympathetically or attentively: *the Samaritans lend their ears to those in crisis.* □ **lend a hand** (or **a helping hand**) see GIVE A HAND at HAND. □ **lend one's name to** allow oneself to be publicly associated with: *he lent his name and prestige to the organizers of the project.*

USAGE See usage at LOAN.

lend·er /ˈlendər/ ▸*n.* an organization or person that lends money: *a mortgage lender.*

lend·ing li·brar·y ▸*n.* a public library from which books may be borrowed and taken away for a short time.

Len·dl /ˈlendl/, Ivan (1960–), U.S. tennis player, born in Czechoslovakia. He won many singles titles in the 1980s and early 1990s, including the U.S., Australian, and French championships.

Lend-Lease *historical* an arrangement made in 1941 whereby the U.S. supplied military equipment and armaments to the UK and its allies, originally as a loan in return for the use of British-owned military bases.

Le·nex·a /ləˈneksə/ a city in eastern Kansas, a southwestern suburb of Kansas City; pop. 40,238.

L'Enfant /länfäN/, Pierre Charles (1754–1825) U.S. architect and soldier; born in France. In 1791, he submitted plans that were followed in the design of the city of Washington, DC.

L'Engle /ˈleNGgəl/, Madeleine (Camp) (1918–) U.S. writer. She wrote mainly children's fiction, including *A Wrinkle in Time* (1962), the first of a quartet that also included *A Wind in the Door* (1973), *A Swiftly Tilting Planet* (1978), and *Many Waters* (1986).

length /leNG(k)TH; lenth/ ▸*n.* **1** the measurement or extent of something from end to end; the greater of two or the greatest of three dimensions of a body: *it can reach over two feet* ***in length*** *| the length of the airport terminal.* ■ the amount of time occupied by something: *delivery must be within a reasonable length of time.* ■ the quality of being long: *the length of the waiting list.* ■ the full distance that a thing extends for: *the muscles running* ***the length of*** *my spine.* ■ the extent of a garment in a vertical direction when worn: *the length of her skirt.* ■ *Prosody & Phonetics* the metrical quantity or duration of a vowel or syllable. **2** the extent of something, esp. as a unit of measurement, in particular: ■ the length of a swimming pool as a measure of the distance swum: *fifty lengths of the pool.* ■ the length of a horse, boat, etc., as a measure of the lead in a race: *the mare won the race last year by seven lengths.* ■ (**one's length**) the full extent of one's body: *he awkwardly lowered his length into the small car.* **3** (in bridge or whist) the number of cards of a suit held in one's hand, esp. when five or more. **4** a stretch or piece of something: *a stout* ***length of*** *wood.* **5** a degree or extreme to which a course of action is taken: *they* ***go to great lengths to*** *avoid the press.* ▷Old English *lengthu*, of Germanic origin; related to Dutch *lengte*, also to LONG[1].

▸*PHRASES* □ **at length** **1** in detail; fully: *these aspects have been discussed at length.* **2** after a long time: *at length she laid down the pencil.* □ **the length and breadth of** the whole extent of: *women from the length and breadth of Russia.*

-length ▸*comb. form* reaching up to or down to the place specified: *knee-length.* ■ of the size, duration, or extent specified: *full-length | medium-length | feature-length.*

length·en /ˈleNG(k)THən; ˈlen-/ ▸*v.* make or become longer: [*trans.*] *she lengthened her stride to catch up |* [*intrans.*] *in the spring when the days are lengthening |* [as *adj.*] (**lengthening**) *the lengthening shadows.* ■ [*trans.*] *Prosody & Phonetics* make (a vowel or syllable) long.

length·ways /ˈleNG(k)THˌwāz; ˈlenTH-/ ▸*adv.* lengthwise.

length·wise /ˈleNG(k)THˌwīz; ˈlenTH-/ ▸*adv.* in a direction parallel with a thing's length: *halve the potatoes lengthwise.*

▸*adj.* [*attrib.*] lying or moving lengthwise: *a lengthwise crack.*

length·y /ˈleNG(k)THē; ˈlen-/ ▸*adj.* (**length·i·er**, **length·i·est**) (esp. in reference to time) of considerable or unusual length, esp. so as to be tedious: *lengthy delays | a lengthy book.* —**length·i·ly** /-THəlē/ *adv.* —**length·i·ness** *n.*

le·ni·ent /ˈlēnēənt; ˈlēnyənt/ ▸*adj.* **1** (of punishment or a person in authority) permissive, merciful, or tolerant: *judges were far too lenient with petty criminals.* **2** *archaic* emollient. ▷mid 17th cent. (sense 2): from Latin *lenient-* 'soothing,' from the verb *lenire*, from *lenis* 'mild, gentle.' —**le·ni·ence** *n.* —**le·ni·en·cy** *n.* —**le·ni·ent·ly** *adv.*

THE RIGHT WORD **forbearing, indulgent, lax, lenient, merciful, permissive**

Not all parents approach discipline in the same way. Someone who is **lenient** is willing to lower his or her standards of strictness when it comes to imposing discipline (*the principal was lenient with the students who had been caught playing hooky*).

A parent who is **forbearing** struggles against giving in to negative feelings and is therefore able to abstain from hasty or ill-tempered actions, no matter what the provocation (*her father's forbearing attitude meant that she escaped with only a lecture*).

Indulgent goes beyond forbearing and suggests catering to someone's whims (*an indulgent parent who seldom denied her child anything*).

Lax is a negative kind of leniency involving laziness or indifference (*a lax mother who never imposed a curfew*), while **merciful** suggests a relaxing of standards on the basis of compassion (*a merciful mother who understood her daughter's anger*).

To be **permissive** is also to be extremely lenient—an approach that connotes tolerance to the point of passivity (*the children's utter disregard for the rules was the result of their permissive upbringing*).

Le·nin /ˈlenən; ˈlyenyin/, Vladimir Ilich (1870–1924), the principal figure in the Russian Revolution and first premier of the Soviet Union 1918–24; born *Vladimir Ilich Ulyanov*. He was the first political leader to attempt to put Marxist principles into practice. In 1917 he established Bolshevik control after the overthrow of the tsar and in 1918 became head of state.

Vladimir Lenin

Le·nin·a·kan /liˌnēnəˈkän/ former name (1924–91) for GYUMRI.

Len·in·grad /ˈlenənˌgrad/ former name (1924–91) for ST. PETERSBURG.

Le·nin·ism /ˈlenəˌnizəm/ ▸*n.* Marxism as interpreted and applied by Lenin. ▷early 20th cent.: named after LENIN. —**Le·nin·ist** *n.* & *adj.* —**Le·nin·ite** /-ˌnīt/ *n.* & *adj.*

le·nis /ˈlēnis; ˈlā-/ *Phonetics* ▸*adj.* (of a consonant, in particular a voiced consonant) weakly articulated, esp. denoting the less or least strongly articulated of two or more similar consonants. The opposite of FORTIS.

▸*n.* (*pl.* **-nes** /-nēz/) a consonant of this type. ▷early 20th cent.: from Latin, literally 'mild, gentle.'

le·nite /ˈlēˌnīt; liˈnīt/ ▸*v.* (**be lenited**) (of a consonant) be pronounced with lenition. ▷early 20th cent.: back-formation from LENITION.

le·ni·tion /liˈnisHən/ ▸*n.* the process or result of weakened articulation of a consonant, causing the consonant to become voiced, spirantized, or lost. ▷early 20th cent.: from Latin *lenis* 'soft' + -ITION, suggested by German *Lenierung*.

len·i·tive /ˈlenətiv/ *archaic Medicine* ▸*adj.* (of a medicine) laxative.

▸*n.* a medicine of this type. ▷late Middle English: from medieval Latin *lenitivus*, from *lenit-* 'softened,' from the verb *lenire*.

len·i·ty /ˈlenətē/ ▸*n.* *poetic/literary* kindness; gentleness. ▷late Middle English: from Old French *lenite*, or from Latin *lenitas*, from *lenis* 'gentle.'

Len·ni Len·a·pe /ˈlenē ˈlenəpē; ləˈnäpē/ ▸*n.* **1** a group of North American Indian peoples who formerly occupied the Delaware and Hudson River valleys, with existing populations in Oklahoma, Kansas, Wisconsin, and Ontario. ■ a member of one of the Delaware peoples. **2** the Eastern Algonquian language spoken by any of the Delaware peoples.

Len·non /ˈlenən/, John (1940–80), English pop and rock singer, guitarist, and songwriter. A founding member of the Beatles, he wrote most of their songs in collaboration with Paul McCartney. After the group broke up in 1970, he continued recording material, such as *Imagine* (1971), some with his

L

second wife, Yoko Ono. He was fatally shot by a mentally disturbed fan outside his home in New York City.

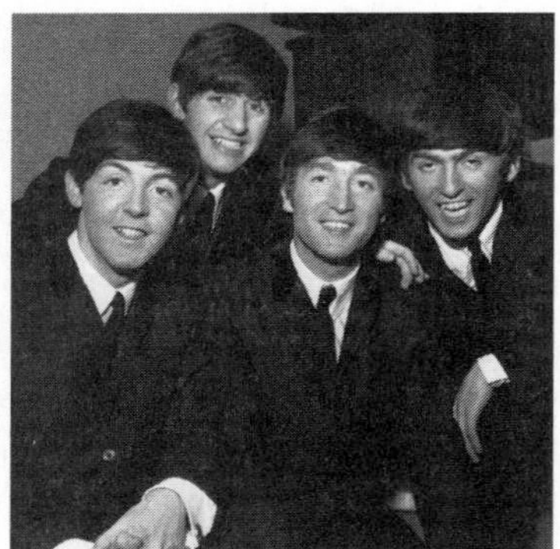

The Beatles

Le·no /ˈlenō/, Jay (1950–) U.S. comedian and talk show host; full name *James Douglas Muir Leno.* He replaced Johnny Carson as host of "The Tonight Show" in 1992.

le·no /ˈlēnō/ ▸*n.* (*pl.* **-nos**) an openwork fabric with the warp threads twisted in pairs before weaving. ▷late 18th cent.: from French *linon*, from *lin* 'flax,' from Latin *linum*. Compare with LINEN.

Le Nô·tre /lə ˈnôtrə/, André (1613–1700), French landscape gardener. He designed many formal gardens, including the parks of Vaux-le-Vicomte and Versailles.

Len·ox /ˈlenəks/ a resort town in western Massachusetts, in the Berkshire Hills, site of the summer music complex called Tanglewood; pop. 5,069.

lens /lenz/ ▸*n.* a piece of glass or other transparent substance with curved sides for concentrating or dispersing light rays, used singly (as in a magnifying glass) or with other lenses (as in a telescope). ■ the light-gathering device of a camera, typically containing a group of compound lenses. ■ *Physics* an object or device that focuses or otherwise modifies the direction of movement of light, sound, electrons, etc. ■ *Anatomy* short for CRYSTALLINE LENS. ■ short for CONTACT LENS. ▷late 17th cent.: from Latin, 'lentil' (because of the similarity in shape). **—lensed** *adj.* **—lens·less** *adj.*

lens hood ▸*n.* a tube or ring attached to the front of a camera lens to prevent unwanted light from reaching the film.

lens·man /ˈlenzmən; -ˌman/ ▸*n.* (*pl.* **-men**) a professional photographer or cameraman.

Lent /lent/ ▸*n.* the period preceding Easter that in the Christian Church is devoted to fasting, abstinence, and penitence in commemoration of Christ's fasting in the wilderness. In the Western Church it runs from Ash Wednesday to Holy Saturday and so includes forty weekdays. ▷Middle English: abbreviation of LENTEN.

lent /lent/ ▸ past and past participle of LEND.

-lent ▸*suffix* (forming adjectives) full of; characterized by: *pestilent* | *violent*. Compare with -ULENT.

len·tan·do /lenˈtändō/ ▸ *adv.* & *adj. Music* (as a direction) slowing gradually.

Lent·en /ˈlent(ə)n/ ▸*adj.* [*attrib.*] of, in, or appropriate to Lent: *Lenten food.* ▷Old English *lencten* 'spring, Lent,' of Germanic origin, related to LONG[1] (perhaps with reference to the lengthening of the day in spring); now interpreted as being from LENT + -EN[2].

len·tic /ˈlentik/ ▸*adj. Ecology* (of organisms or habitats) inhabiting or situated in still, fresh water. Compare with LOTIC. ▷mid 20th cent.: from Latin *lentus* 'calm, slow' + -IC.

len·ti·cel /ˈlentəˌsel/ ▸*n. Botany* one of many raised pores in the stem of a woody plant that allows gas exchange between the atmosphere and the internal tissues. ▷mid 19th cent.: from modern Latin *lenticella*, diminutive of Latin *lens, lent-* 'lentil.'

len·tic·u·lar /lenˈtikyələr/ ▸*adj.* **1** shaped like a lentil, esp. by being biconvex: *lenticular lenses.* **2** of or relating to the lens of the eye. ▷late Middle English: from Latin *lenticularis*, from *lenticula*, diminutive of *lens, lent-* 'lentil.'

len·ti·form nu·cle·us /ˈlentəˌfôrm/ ▸*n. Anatomy* the lower of the two gray nuclei of the corpus striatum. ▷early 18th cent.: *lentiform* from Latin *lens, lent-* 'lentil' + -IFORM.

len·ti·go /lenˈtīgō; -ˈtē-/ ▸*n.* (*pl.* **-tig·i·nes** /-ˈtijəˌnēz/) a condition marked by small brown patches on the skin, typically in elderly people. ▷late Middle English (denoting a freckle or pimple): from Latin, from *lens, lent-* 'lentil.'

len·til /ˈlent(ə)l/ ▸*n.* **1** a high-protein pulse that is dried and then soaked and cooked before eating. There are several varieties of lentils, including green ones and smaller orange ones, which are typically sold split. **2** the plant that yields this pulse, native to the Mediterranean and Africa and grown also for fodder. • *Lens culinaris*, family Leguminosae. ▷Middle English: from Old French *lentille*, from Latin *lenticula*, diminutive of *lens, lent-* 'lentil.'

len·tisk /ˈlenˌtisk/ (also **len·tisc**) ▸*n.* the mastic tree. ▷late Middle English: from Latin *lentiscus*.

len·tis·si·mo /lenˈtisiˌmō; -ˈtēsē-/ ▸*adj.* & *adv. Music* (as a direction) at a very slow tempo.

len·ti·vi·rus /ˈlentəˌvīrəs/ ▸*n. Medicine* any of a group of retroviruses producing illnesses characterized by a delay in the onset of symptoms after infection. ▷1970s: from Latin *lentus* 'slow' + VIRUS.

len·to /ˈlentō/ ▸*adv.* & *adj. Music* (esp. as a direction) slow or slowly.
▸*n.* (*pl.* **-tos**) a passage or movement marked to be performed in this way. ▷Italian.

len·toid /ˈlenˌtoid/ ▸*adj.* another term for LENTICULAR (sense 1). ▷late 19th cent.: from Latin *lens, lent-* 'lentil' + -OID.

Lent term ▸*n. Brit.* the university term in which Lent falls.

Lenz's law /ˈlentsiz; ˈlenziz/ *Physics* a law stating that the direction of an induced current is always such as to oppose the change in the circuit or the magnetic field that produces it. ▷mid 19th cent.: named after Heinrich F. E. *Lenz* (1804–65), German physicist.

Le·o[1] /ˈlēō/ the name of 13 popes, notably: ■ **Leo I** (died 461), pope from 440 and doctor of the Church; known as **Leo the Great**; canonized as **St. Leo I**. He defined the doctrine of the Incarnation at the Council of Chalcedon (451) and extended the power of the Roman see to Africa, Spain, and Gaul. Feast day (Eastern Church) February 18; (Western Church) April 11. ■ **Leo X** (1475–1521), pope from 1513; born *Giovanni de' Medici.* He excommunicated Martin Luther and bestowed the title of Defender of the Faith on Henry VIII of England. He was a noted patron of learning and of the arts.

Le·o[2] **1** *Astronomy* a large constellation (the Lion), said to represent the lion slain by Hercules. It contains the bright stars Regulus and Denebola and numerous galaxies. ■ [as *genitive*] (**Leonis** /lēˈōnis/) used with a preceding letter or numeral to designate a star in this constellation: *the star Omicron Leonis.* **2** *Astrology* the fifth sign of the zodiac, which the sun enters about July 23. ■ (**a Leo**) (*pl.* **Le·os**) a person born when the sun is in this sign. ▷Latin. **—Le·on·i·an** /lēˈōnēən/ *n.* & *adj.* (in sense 2).

Le·o III (c.680–741), Byzantine emperor 717–741. He repulsed several Muslim invasions and carried out an extensive series of reforms. In 726, he banned icons and other religious images; the resulting iconoclastic controversy led to more than a century of political and religious turmoil.

Le·o Mi·nor *Astronomy* a small and inconspicuous northern constellation (the Little Lion), immediately north of Leo. ■ [as *genitive*] (**Leonis Minoris** /lēˈōnis mīˈnôris/) used with a preceding letter or numeral to designate a star in this constellation: *the star Alpha Leonis Minoris.* ▷Latin.

Leom·in·ster /ˈlemənstər/ an industrial city in north central Massachusetts; pop. 38,145.

Le·ón /lāˈōn/ **1** an industrial city in central Mexico; pop. 872,000. **2** a city in western Nicaragua, the second largest city in the country; pop. 159,000. **3** a city in northern Spain; pop. 146,000. It is the capital of the province and former kingdom of León, now part of Castilla-León region.

Leon·ard[1] /ˈlenərd/, Elmore (John) (1925–), U.S. writer. After working as an advertising copywriter, he turned to writing screenplays and novels in 1967. Notable works: *Unknown Man No. 89* (1977), *Freaky Deaky* (1988), and *Get Shorty* (1990).

Leon·ard[2], Sugar Ray (1956–) U.S. boxer; full name *Ray Charles Leonard.* He won world championship titles in four different weight divisions: welterweight in 1979, middleweight in 1987, and super middleweight and light heavyweight in 1988.

Le·o·nar·do da Vin·ci /ˌlēəˈnärdō də ˈvinCHē; ˌlā-/ (1452–1519), Italian painter, scientist, and engineer. His paintings are notable for their use of the technique of *sfumato* and include *The Virgin of the Rocks* (1483–85), *The Last Supper* (1498), and the *Mona Lisa* (1504–05). He devoted himself to a wide range of other subjects, from anatomy and biology to mechanics and hydraulics: his 19 notebooks include studies of the human circulatory system and plans for a type of aircraft and a submarine.

Le·on·berg·er /ˈlēənˌbərgər/ ▸*n.* a large dog of a breed typically having a golden coat, produced by crossing a St. Bernard and a Newfoundland. ▷early 20th cent.: named after a town in southwestern Germany.

le·one /lēˈōn/ ▸*n.* the basic monetary unit of Sierra Leone, equal to 100 cents.

Le·o·nids /ˈlēənidz/ *Astronomy* an annual meteor shower with a radiant in the constellation Leo, reaching a peak about November 17. ▷late 19th cent.: from Latin *leo, leon-* (see LEO[2]) + -ID[3].

Le·o·nine ▸*adj.* **1** of or relating to one of the popes named Leo, esp. Leo IV and the part of Rome that he fortified. **2** *Prosody* (of medieval Latin verse) in hexameter or elegiac meter with internal rhyme. ■ (of English verse) with internal rhyme.
▸*plural n.* (**Leonines**) *Prosody* verse of this type. ▷late Middle English: from the name *Leo*, from Latin *leo* 'lion.' Sense 2 may be from the name of a medieval poet, but his identity is not known.

le·o·nine /ˈlēəˌnīn/ ▸*adj.* of or resembling a lion or lions: *a handsome, leonine profile.* ▷late Middle English: from Old French, or from Latin *leoninus*, from *leo, leon-* 'lion.'

Le·o·nine Cit·y /ˈlēəˌnīn/ the part of Rome in which the Vatican stands, walled and fortified by Pope Leo IV.

Le·on·ti·ef /lēˈ(y)ônˌtyef/, Wassily (1906–99), U.S. economist, educator, and writer; born in Russia. His most significant published work is *The Structure of the American Economy* (1919–29). Nobel Prize for Economics (1973).

leop·ard /ˈlepərd/ ▸*n.* a large, solitary cat that has a yellowish-brown or brown coat with black spots and usually hunts at night, widespread in the forests of Africa and southern Asia. Also called PANTHER. • *Panthera pardus*, family Felidae. See also BLACK PANTHER. ■ *Heraldry* the spotted leopard as a heraldic device; also, a lion passant guardant as in the arms of England. ■ [as *adj.*] spotted like a leopard: *a leopard-print outfit.* ▷Middle English: via Old French from late Latin *leopardus*, from late Greek *leopardos*, from *leōn* 'lion' + *pardos* (see PARD).
▸*PHRASE* □ **a leopard can't change his spots** *proverb* people can't change their basic nature.

leop·ard cat ▸*n.* a small eastern Asian wild cat that has a yellowish-brown coat with black spots and often lives near water. • *Felis bengalensis*, family Felidae.

leop·ard·ess /ˈlepərdis/ ▸*n.* a female leopard.

leop·ard frog ▸*n.* a common greenish-brown North American frog that has dark leopardlike spots with a pale border. • *Rana pipiens*, family Ranidae.

leop·ard lil·y /ˈlepərd ˌlilē/ ▸*n.* a lily resembling a tiger lily, native to the southwestern U.S. • *Lilium pardalinum*, family Liliaceae.

leop·ard moth ▸*n.* a large white European moth with black spots, the larvae of which tunnel into trees and can cause damage. • *Zeuzera pyrina*, family Cossidae.

leop·ard's bane ▸*n.* a herbaceous Eurasian plant of the daisy family, with large yellow flowers that typically bloom early in the spring. • Genus *Doronicum*, family Compositae.

leop·ard seal ▸*n.* a large, gray Antarctic seal that has leopardlike spots and preys on penguins and other seals. • *Hydrurga leptonyx*, family Phocidae.

leop·ard-skin ▸*adj.* (of a garment) made of a fabric resembling the spotted skin of a leopard: *leopard-skin pedal pushers.*

Le·o·pold I /ˈlēəˌpōld/ (1790–1865), first king of Belgium 1831–65. The fourth son of the Duke of Saxe-Coburg-Saalfield, he was an uncle of Britain's Queen Victoria.

Lé·o·pold·ville /ˈlēəˌpōldˌvil; ˈlā-/ former name (until 1966) of KINSHASA.

le·o·tard /ˈlēəˌtärd/ ▸*n.* a close-fitting one-piece garment, made of a stretchy fabric, which covers a person's body from the shoulders to the top of the thighs and typically the arms, worn by dancers or people exercising indoors. ■ (**leotards**) close-fitting leggings or tights, esp. those worn by dancers. ▷early 20th cent.: named after Jules *Léotard* (1839–70), French trapeze artist.

Le·o the Great Pope Leo I (see LEO[1]).

Le·pan·to, Bat·tle of /li'pantō; 'lepän,tō/ a naval battle fought in 1571 close to the port of Lepanto at the entrance to the Gulf of Corinth. The Christian forces of Rome, Venice, and Spain defeated a large Turkish fleet, ending for the time being Turkish naval domination in the eastern Mediterranean.

Le·pan·to, Gulf of /lə'päntō; -'pan-/ another name for the Gulf of Corinth (see CORINTH, GULF OF).

Lep·cha /'lepchə/ ▸*n.* **1** a member of a people living mainly in mountain valleys in the Indian state of Sikkim, western Bhutan, and parts of Nepal and West Bengal. **2** the Tibeto-Burman language of this people.
▸*adj.* of or relating to the Lepchas or their language. ▷from Nepali *lāpche.*

lep·er /'lepər/ ▸*n.* a person suffering from leprosy. ■ a person who is avoided or rejected by others for moral or social reasons: *the story made her out to be a social leper.* ▷late Middle English: probably from an attributive use of *leper* 'leprosy,' from Old French *lepre,* via Latin from Greek *lepra,* feminine of *lepros* 'scaly,' from *lepos, lepis* 'scale.'

lep·i·do·cro·cite /,lepədō'krō,sīt/ ▸*n.* a red to reddish-brown mineral consisting of ferric hydroxide, typically occurring as scaly or fibrous crystals.

le·pid·o·lite /li'pidl,īt/ ▸*n.* a mineral of the mica group containing lithium, typically gray or lilac in color. ▷late 18th cent.: from Greek *lepis, lepid-* 'scale' + -LITE.

Lep·i·dop·ter·a /,lepə'däptərə/ *Entomology* an order of insects that comprises the butterflies and moths. They have four large scale-covered wings that bear distinctive markings, and larvae that are caterpillars. ■ (**lepidoptera**) [as *plural n.*] insects of this order. ▷modern Latin (plural), from Greek *lepis, lepid-* 'scale' + *pteron* 'wing.' —**lep·i·dop·ter·an** *adj.* & *n.* —**lep·i·dop·ter·ous** /-tərəs/ *adj.*

lep·i·dop·ter·ist /,lepə'däptərist/ ▸*n.* a person who studies or collects butterflies and moths.

Lep·i·dus /'lepidəs/, Marcus Aemilius (died *c.*13 BC), Roman statesman and triumvir. A supporter of Julius Caesar in the civil war against Pompey, he was elected consul in 46 and was appointed one of the Second Triumvirate with Octavian and Antony in 43.

Le·pon·tic /lə'päntik/ ▸*n.* an ancient Celtic language, possibly a variant of Gaulish, spoken at one time in parts of Switzerland and northern Italy.

lep·o·rine /'lepə,rīn; -rin/ ▸*adj.* of or resembling a hare or hares. ▷mid 17th cent.: from Latin *leporinus,* from *lepus, lepor-* 'hare.'

lep·o·spon·dyl /,lepə'spändl/ ▸*n.* an extinct, early amphibian of the Carboniferous and Permian periods, distinguished by vertebrae shaped liked hourglasses. • Microsauria and related orders, formerly placed in the subclass Lepospondyli. ▷1930s: from modern Latin *Lepospondyli* (plural), from Greek *lepos* 'husk' + *spondulos* 'vertebra.'

lep·re·chaun /'leprə,kän; -,kôn/ ▸*n.* (in Irish folklore) a small, mischievous sprite. ▷early 17th cent.: from Irish *leipreachán,* based on Old Irish *luchorpán,* from *lu* 'small' + *corp* 'body.'

le·prom·a·tous /li'prämətəs; -'prōmə-/ ▸*adj. Medicine* relating to or denoting the more severe of the two principal forms of leprosy, marked by thickening of the skin and nerves, the formation of lumps on the skin, and often severe loss of feeling and paralysis leading to disfigurement. Compare with TUBERCULOID.

lep·ro·sar·i·um /,leprə'se(ə)rēəm/ ▸*n.* a hospital for people with leprosy. ▷mid 19th cent.: from late Latin *leprosus* 'leprous' + -ARIUM.

lep·ro·sy /'leprəsē/ ▸*n.* a contagious disease that affects the skin, mucous membranes, and nerves, causing discoloration and lumps on the skin and, in severe cases, disfigurement and deformities. Leprosy is now mainly confined to tropical Africa and Asia. Also called HANSEN'S DISEASE. • Leprosy is caused by the bacterium *Mycobacterium leprae,* which is Gram-positive, nonmotile, and acid-fast. ▷mid 16th cent. (superseding Middle English *lepry*): from LEPROUS + -Y[3].

lep·rous /'leprəs/ ▸*adj.* **1** suffering from leprosy. ■ relating to or resembling leprosy: *leprous growths.* **2** covered with scales; scaly. ▷Middle English: via Old French from late Latin *leprosus,* from Latin *lepra* 'scaly' (see LEPER).

lep·ta /'leptə/ ▸ plural form of LEPTON[1].

lep·tin /'leptin/ ▸*n. Biochemistry* a protein produced by fatty tissue and believed to regulate fat storage in the body. ▷1990s: from Greek *leptos* 'fine, thin' + -IN[1].

lepto- ▸*comb. form* small; narrow: *leptocephalic.* ▷from Greek *leptos* 'fine, thin, delicate.'

lep·to·kur·tic /,leptə'kərtik/ ▸*adj. Statistics* (of a frequency distribution or its graphical representation) having greater kurtosis than the normal distribution; more concentrated about the mean. Compare with PLATYKURTIC, MESOKURTIC. ▷early 20th cent.: from LEPTO- 'narrow' + Greek *kurtos* 'bulging' + -IC. —**lep·to·kur·to·sis** /-tō,kər'tōsis/ *n.*

lep·to·me·nin·ges /,leptōmə'nin,jēz/ ▸*plural n. Anatomy* the inner two meninges, the arachnoid and the pia mater, between which circulates the cerebrospinal fluid. —**lep·to·me·nin·ge·al** /-,menən'jēəl/ *adj.*

lep·ton[1] /'lep,tän/ ▸*n.* (*pl.* **-ta** /-tə/) a monetary unit of Greece until the introduction of the euro, worth one hundredth of a drachma (used only in calculations). ▷from Greek *lepton,* neuter of *leptos* 'small.'

lep·ton[2] ▸*n. Physics* a subatomic particle, such as an electron, muon, or neutrino, that does not take part in the strong interaction. ▷1940s: from Greek *leptos* 'small' + -ON. —**lep·ton·ic** /lep'tänik/ *adj.*

lep·ton num·ber ▸*n. Physics* a quantum number assigned to subatomic particles that is ±1 for leptons and 0 for other particles and is conserved in all known interactions.

lep·to·spi·ro·sis /,leptə,spī'rōsis/ ▸*n.* an infectious bacterial disease that occurs in rodents, dogs, and other mammals and can be transmitted to humans. See also WEIL'S DISEASE. • The bacterium is a spirochete of the genus *Leptospira.* ▷1920s: from LEPTO- 'narrow' + Greek *speira* 'coil' + -OSIS.

lep·to·tene /'leptə,tēn/ ▸*n. Biology* the first stage of the prophase of meiosis, during which each chromosome becomes visible as two fine threads (chromatids). ▷early 20th cent.: from LEPTO- 'narrow, fine' + Greek *tainia* 'band, ribbon.'

Lep·us /'lepəs; 'lēpəs/ *Astronomy* a small constellation (the Hare) at the foot of Orion, said to represent the hare pursued by him. ■ [as *genitive*] (**Leporis** /'lepəris/) used with a preceding letter or numeral to designate a star in this constellation: *the star R Leporis.* ▷Latin.

Ler·ner /'lərnər/, Alan J. (1918–86), U.S. lyricist and playwright; full name *Alan Jay Lerner.* He wrote a series of musicals with composer Frederick Loewe (1904–88) that were also made into movies, including *Paint Your Wagon* (1951; movie, 1969) and *My Fair Lady* (1956; movie, 1964). He won Academy Awards for the movies *An American in Paris* (1951) and *Gigi* (1958).

Ler·wick /'lərwik/ the capital of the Shetland Islands, on the island of Mainland; pop. 7,220. The most northerly town in the British Isles, it is a fishing center and a service port for the oil industry.

les /lez/ (also **lez**) ▸*n. informal, chiefly offensive* a lesbian.

Les·bi·an /'lezbēən/ ▸*adj.* from or relating to the island of Lesbos.

les·bi·an /'lezbēən/ ▸*n.* a homosexual woman.
▸*adj.* of or relating to homosexual women or to homosexuality in women: *a lesbian relationship.* ▷late 19th cent.: via Latin from Greek *Lesbios,* from LESBOS, home of Sappho, who expressed affection for women in her poetry, + -IAN. —**les·bi·an·ism** /-,nizəm/ *n.*

les·bi·gay /'lezbi'gā/ ▸*adj.* relating to lesbians and male homosexuals collectively: *a lesbigay walking, running, and social group.* ▷from LESBIAN + GAY; sometimes analyzed as LESBIAN + BISEXUAL + GAY.

les·bo /'lezbō/ ▸*n.* (*pl.* **-bos**) *informal, chiefly offensive* a lesbian. ▷1940s: abbreviation.

Les·bos /'lez,bäs; 'lezbəs/ a Greek island in the eastern Aegean Sea, off the coast of northwestern Turkey. Its artistic golden age of the late 7th and early 6th centuries BC produced the poets Alcaeus and Sappho. Greek name LÉSVOS.

Lesch–Ny·han syn·drome /'lesh 'nīən/ ▸*n.* a rare hereditary disease that affects young boys, usually causing early death. It is marked by compulsive self-mutilation of the head and hands, together with mental retardation and involuntary muscular movements. ▷1960s: named after Michael *Lesch* (1939–) and William L. *Nyhan* (1926–), U.S. physicians.

lèse-maj·es·té /,lez ,majə'stā; ,lēz; 'majəstē/ ▸*n.* the insulting of a monarch or other ruler; treason. ▷late Middle English: from French *lèse-majesté,* from Latin *laesa majestas* 'injured sovereignty.'

le·sion /'lēzhən/ ▸*n. chiefly Medicine* a region in an organ or tissue that has suffered damage through injury or disease, such as a wound, ulcer, abscess, tumor, etc. ▷late Middle English: via Old French from Latin *laesio(n-),* from *laedere* 'injure.'

Le·so·tho /lə'sōotōo; lə'sōtō/ a landlocked mountainous country that forms an enclave in South Africa; pop. 1,816,000; capital, Maseru; official languages, Sesotho and English.

The region was settled by the Sotho people in the 16th century and came under British rule (as Basutoland) in 1868. It became an independent kingdom within the Commonwealth of Nations in 1966, changing its name to Lesotho.

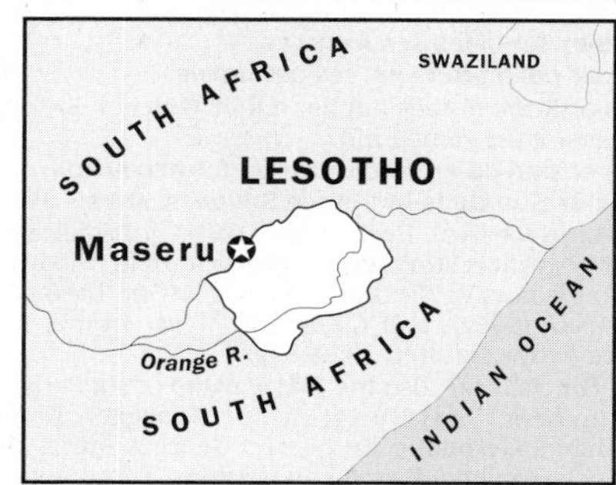

less /les/ ▸*adj.* & *pron.* a smaller amount of; not as much: [as *adj.*] *the less time spent there, the better* | [as *pron.*] *storage is* ***less of*** *a problem than it used to be* | *ready in* ***less than*** *an hour.* ■ fewer in number: [as *adj.*] *short hair presented less problems than long hair* | [as *pron.*] *a population of* ***less than*** *200,000.*
▸*adj. archaic* of lower rank or importance: *James the Less.*
▸*adv.* to a smaller extent; not so much: *he listened less to the answer than to Kate's voice* | *that this is a positive stereotype makes it* ***no less*** *a stereotype.* ■ (**less than**) far from; certainly not: *Mitch looked less than happy* | *the data was less than ideal.*
▸*prep.* before subtracting (something); minus: *$900,000 less tax.* ▷Old English *lǣssa,* of Germanic origin; related to Old Frisian *lēssa,* from an Indo-European root shared by Greek *loisthos* 'last.'
▸*PHRASES* □ **in less than no time** *informal* very quickly or soon. □ **less and less** at a continually decreasing rate. □ **much** (or **still**) **less** used to introduce something as being even less likely or suitable than something else already mentioned: *what woman would consider a date with him, much less a marriage?* □ **no less** used to suggest, often ironically, that something is surprising or impressive: *Peter cooked dinner—fillet steak and champagne, no less.* ■ (**no less than**) used to emphasize a surprisingly large amount.

USAGE In standard English, **less** should be used only with uncountable things (*less money; less time*). With countable things, it is incorrect to use **less**: thus, *less people* and *less words* should be corrected to *fewer people* and *fewer words.*
See also **usage** at FEW.

-less ▸*suffix* forming adjectives and adverbs: **1** (from nouns) not having; without; free from: *flavorless* | *skinless.* **2** (from verbs) not affected by or not carrying out the action of the verb: *fathomless* | *tireless.* ▷Old English *-lēas,* from *lēas* 'devoid of.'

less-de·vel·op·ed coun·try ▸*n.* a nonindustrialized or Third World country.

les·see /le'sē/ ▸*n.* a person who holds the lease of a property; a tenant. ▷late 15th cent.: from Old French *lesse,* past participle of *lesser* 'to let, leave,' + -EE. —**les·see·ship** /-,ship/ *n.*

less·en /'lesən/ ▸*v.* make or become less; diminish: [*trans.*] *the years have lessened the gap in age between us* | [*intrans.*] *the warmth of the afternoon lessened.*

Les·seps /'lesəps; lə'seps/, Ferdinand Marie, Vicomte de (1805–94), French diplomat. From 1854, while in the consular service in Egypt, he devoted himself to the Suez Canal project. In 1881, as the head of a private company, he embarked on the building of the Panama Canal, but the project was abandoned in 1889.

less·er /'lesər/ ▸*adj.* [*attrib.*] not so great or important as the other or the rest: *he was convicted of a lesser assault charge* | *they nest mostly in Alaska and* ***to a lesser ex-***

L

Pronunciation Key ə *ago;* ər *over;* 'ə or ,ə *up;* 'ər or ,ər *fur;* a *hat;* ā *rate;* ä *car;* CH *chew;* e *let;* ē *see;* e(ə)r *air;* i *fit;* ī *by;* i(ə)r *ear;* NG *sing;* ō *go;* ô *for;* oi *boy;* ŏŏ *good;* ōō *goo;* ou *out;* SH *she;* TH *thin;* TH *then;* (h)w *why;* ZH *vision*

tent in Siberia. ■ lower in terms of rank or quality: *the lesser aristocracy | you're looking down your nose at us lesser mortals.* ■ used in names of animals and plants that are smaller than similar kinds, e.g., **lesser spotted woodpecker, lesser celandine.** ▷Middle English: a double comparative, from LESS + -ER2.
▸*PHRASE* □ **the lesser evil** (or **the lesser of two evils**) the less harmful or unpleasant of two bad choices or possibilities: *authoritarianism may seem a lesser evil than abject poverty.*

USAGE On the punctuation of **lesser** in compound adjectives, see **usage** at WELL1.

Less·er An·til·les see ANTILLES.
less·er cel·an·dine ▸*n.* see CELANDINE.
less·er-known ▸*adj.* not as well or widely known as others of the same kind.
less·er pan·da ▸*n.* another term for RED PANDA.
Less·er Sun·da Is·lands see SUNDA ISLANDS.
Les·sing /ˈlesiNG/, Doris (May) (1919–), British novelist and short-story writer, brought up in Rhodesia. Notable novels: *The Grass is Singing* (1950), *The Golden Notebook* (1962), and *Canopus in Argus: Archives* (science-fiction quintet, 1979–83).
Les Six /lā ˈsēs/ (also **the Six**) a group of six Parisian composers (Louis Durey, Arthur Honegger, Darius Milhaud, Germaine Tailleferre, Georges Auric, and Francis Poulenc) formed after World War I, whose music represents a reaction against Romanticism and Impressionism. ▷French, literally 'the Six.'
-lessly ▸*suffix* forming adverbs corresponding to adjectives ending in *-less* (such as *flavorlessly* corresponding to *flavorless*). ▷see -LESS, -LY.
-lessness ▸*suffix* forming nouns corresponding to adjectives ending in *-less* (such as *flavorlessness* corresponding to *flavorless*). ▷see -LESS, -NESS.
les·son /ˈlesən/ ▸*n.* **1** an amount of teaching given at one time; a period of learning or teaching: *an advanced lesson in math | a driving lesson.* ■ a thing learned or to be learned by a student. ■ a thing learned by experience: *the tragedy is a* **lesson in** *disappointment.* ■ an occurrence, example, or punishment that serves or should serve to warn or encourage: *let that be a lesson to you!* **2** a passage from the Bible read aloud during a church service, esp. either of two readings at morning and evening prayer in the Anglican Church.
▸*v.* [*trans.*] *archaic* instruct or teach (someone). ■ admonish or rebuke (someone). ▷Middle English: from Old French *leçon*, from Latin *lectio* (see LECTION).
▸*PHRASES* □ **learn one's lesson** acquire a greater understanding of the world through a particular unpleasant or stressful experience. □ **teach someone a lesson** punish or hurt someone as a deterrent: *they were teaching me a lesson for daring to complain.*
les·sor /ˈlesˌôr; leˈsôr/ ▸*n.* a person who leases or lets a property to another; a landlord. ▷late Middle English: from Anglo-Norman French, from Old French *lesser* 'let, leave.'
lest /lest/ ▸*conj. formal* with the intention of preventing (something undesirable); to avoid the risk of: *he spent whole days in his room, headphones on lest he disturb anyone.* ■ (after a clause indicating fear) because of the possibility of something undesirable happening; in case: *she sat up late worrying lest he be held up on the way home.* ▷Old English *thȳ lǣs the* 'whereby less that,' later *the lǣste.*

USAGE There are very few contexts in English where the subjunctive mood is, strictly speaking, required: **lest** remains one of them. Thus the standard use is *she was worrying* **lest** *he* **be** *attacked* (not **lest** *he* **was** *attacked*), or *she is using headphones* **lest** *she* **disturb** *anyone* (not ... **lest** *she* **disturbs** *anyone*).
See also SUBJUNCTIVE.

Lés·vos /ˈlezˌvôs/ Greek name for LESBOS.
let1 /let/ ▸*v.* (**let·ting**; *past* **let**) **1** [*trans.*] not prevent or forbid; allow: *my boss let me leave early | you mustn't let yourself get so involved.* ■ [*trans.*] allow to pass in a particular direction: *could you let the dog out? | a tiny window that let in hardly any light.* **2** [*trans.*] used in the imperative to formulate various expressions: ■ (**let us** or **let's**) used as a polite way of making or responding to a suggestion, giving an instruction, or introducing a remark: *let's have a drink | "Shall we go?" "Yes, let's."* ■ (**let me** or **let us**) used to make a polite offer of help: *"Here, let me," offered Bruce.* ■ used to express one's strong desire for something to happen or be the case: *"Dear God," Jessica prayed, "let him be all right."* ■ used as a way of expressing defiance or challenge: *if he wants to walk out, well, let him!* ■ used to express an assumption upon which a theory or calculation is to be based: *let A and B stand for X and Y, respectively.* **3** [*trans.*] allow someone to have the use of (a room or property) in return for regular payments; rent: *homeowners will be able to let rooms to lodgers without having to pay tax | they've* **let out** *their apartment.* **4** [*trans.*] award (a contract for a particular project) to an applicant: *preliminary contracts were let and tunneling work started.*
▸*phrasal v.* □ **let down** (of an aircraft or a pilot) descend before making a landing. □ **let someone down** fail to support or help someone as they had hoped or expected. ■ (**let someone/something down**) have a detrimental effect on the overall quality or success of someone or something: *the whole machine is let down by the tacky keyboard.* □ **let something down 1** lower something slowly or in stages: *they let down a basket on a chain.* **2** make a garment longer, esp. by lowering the hem. □ **let oneself in for** *informal* involve oneself in (something likely to be difficult or unpleasant): *I didn't know what I was letting myself in for.* □ **let someone in on/into** allow someone to know or share (something secret or confidential): *I'll let you into a secret.* □ **let something into** set something back into (the surface to which it is fixed), so that it does not project from it: *the basin is partly let into the wall.* □ **let someone off 1** punish someone lightly or not at all for a misdemeanor or offense: *he was let off with a warning.* **2** excuse someone from a task or obligation: *he let me off work for the day.* □ **let something off** cause a gun, firework, or bomb to fire or explode. □ **let on** *informal* **1** reveal or divulge information to someone: *she knows a lot more than she lets on | [with clause] I never let on that he made me feel anxious.* **2** pretend: [with *clause*] *they all let on that they didn't hear me.* □ **let out** (of lessons at school, a meeting, or an entertainment) finish, so that those attending are able to leave: *his classes let out at noon.* □ **let someone out** release someone from obligation or suspicion: *they've started looking for motives—that lets me out.* □ **let something out 1** utter a sound or cry: *he let out a sigh of happiness.* **2** make a garment looser or larger, typically by adjusting a seam. **3** reveal a piece of information: [with *clause*] *she let out that he'd given her a ride home.* □ **let up** *informal* (of something undesirable) become less intense or severe: *the rain's letting up—it'll be clear soon.* ■ relax one's efforts: *she was so far ahead that she could afford to let up a bit.* ■ (**let up on**) *informal* treat or deal with in a more lenient manner: *she didn't let up on Cunningham.* ▷Old English *lǣtan* 'leave behind, leave out,' of Germanic origin; related to Dutch *laten* and German *lassen*, also to LATE.
▸*PHRASES* □ **let alone** used to indicate that something is far less likely, possible, or suitable than something else already mentioned: *he was incapable of leading a bowling team, let alone a country.* □ **let someone/something alone** see ALONE. □ **let someone/something be** stop disturbing or interfering with: *let him be—he knows what he wants.* □ **let someone down gently** seek to give someone bad news in a way that avoids causing them too much distress or humiliation. □ **let something drop** (or **fall**) casually reveal a piece of information: *from the things he let drop, I think there was a woman in his life.* □ **let fall** *Geometry* draw (a perpendicular) from an outside point to a line. □ **let fly** attack, either physically or verbally: *the troops let fly with tear gas.* □ **let oneself go 1** act in an unrestrained or uninhibited way: *you need to unwind and let yourself go.* **2** become careless or untidy in one's habits or appearance: *he's really let himself go since my mother died.* □ **let someone/something go 1** allow someone or something to escape or go free: *they let the hostages go.* ■ dismiss an employee. **2** (also **let go** or **let go of**) relinquish one's grip on someone or something: *Adam let go of the reins | figurative you must let the past go.* □ **let someone have it** *informal* attack someone physically or verbally: *I really let him have it for worrying me so much.* □ **let in** (or **out**) **the clutch** engage (or release) the clutch of a vehicle by releasing pressure on (or applying it to) the clutch pedal. □ **let it drop** (or **rest**) say or do no more about a matter or problem. □ **let it go** (or **pass**) choose not to react to an action or remark: *the decision worried us, but we let it go.* □ **let someone know** inform someone: *let me know what you think of him.* □ **let someone/something loose** release someone or something: *let the dog loose for a minute.* ■ allow someone freedom of action in a particular place or situation: *people are only* **let loose on** *the system once they have received sufficient training.* ■ suddenly utter a sound or remark: *he let loose a stream of abuse.* □ **let me see** (or **think**) used when one is pausing, trying to remember something, or considering one's next words: *now let me see, where did I put it?* □ **let me tell you** used to emphasize a statement: *let me tell you, I was very scared!* □ **let off steam** see STEAM. □ **let rip** see RIP1. □ **let's face it** (or **let's be honest**) *informal* used to convey that one must be realistic about an unwelcome fact or situation: *let's be honest, your taste in men is famously bad.* □ **let slip** see SLIP1. □ **let's pretend** a game or set of circumstances in which one behaves as though a fictional or unreal situation were a real one. □ **let's say** (or **let us say**) used as a way of introducing a hypothetical or possible situation: *let's say we agreed to go our separate ways.* □ **to let** *chiefly Brit.* (of a room or property) available for rent.
let2 ▸*n.* (in racket sports) a play that is nullified and has to be played again, esp. a when a served ball touches the top of the net.
▸*v.* (**let·ting**; *past* and *past part.* **let·ted** or **let**) [*trans.*] *archaic* hinder: *pray you let us not; we fain would greet our mother.* ▷Old English *lettan* 'hinder,' of Germanic origin; related to Dutch *letten*, also to LATE.
▸*PHRASES* □ **let or hindrance** *formal* obstruction or impediment: *the passport opened frontiers to the traveler* **without let or hindrance.** □ **play a let** (in tennis, squash, etc.) play a point again because the ball or one of the players has been obstructed.
-let ▸*suffix* **1** (forming nouns) denoting a smaller or lesser kind: *booklet | starlet.* **2** denoting articles of ornament or dress: *anklet | bracelet.* ▷originally corresponding to French *-ette* added to nouns ending in *-el.*
let·down /ˈletˌdoun/ ▸*n.* **1** a disappointment or a feeling of disappointment: *the election was a bit of a letdown.* ■ a decrease in size, volume, force: *letdowns in sales have been frequent and widespread.* **2** the release of milk in a nursing mother or lactating animal. **3** *Aeronautics* the descent of an aircraft or spacecraft before landing.
le·thal /ˈlēTHəl/ ▸*adj.* sufficient to cause death: *a lethal cocktail of alcohol and pills.* ■ harmful or destructive: *the Krakatoa eruption was the most lethal on record.* ▷late 16th cent. (in the sense 'causing spiritual death'): from Latin *lethalis*, from *lethum*, a variant (influenced by Greek *lēthē* 'forgetfulness') of *letum* 'death.' —**le·thal·i·ty** /lēˈTHalətē/ *n.* —**le·thal·ly** *adv.*
le·thal cham·ber ▸*n.* an enclosed space in which animals may be killed with gas.
le·thal gene ▸*n.* a gene that is capable of causing the death of an organism, usually during the development of the embryo. Also called **lethal factor, lethal mutation.**
le·thal in·jec·tion ▸*n.* an injection administered for the purposes of euthanasia or as a means of capital punishment.
le·thar·gic /ləˈTHärjik/ ▸*adj.* affected by lethargy; sluggish and apathetic: *I felt tired and a little lethargic.* ▷late Middle English: via Latin from Greek *lēthargikos*, from *lēthargos* 'forgetful.' —**le·thar·gi·cal·ly** /-jik(ə)lē/ *adv.*
leth·ar·gy /ˈleTHərjē/ ▸*n.* a lack of energy and enthusiasm: *periods of weakness and lethargy* | [in *sing.*] *she might have sunk into a lethargy.* ■ *Medicine* a pathological state of sleepiness or deep unresponsiveness and inactivity. ▷late Middle English: via Old French from late Latin *lethargia*, from Greek *lēthargia*, from *lēthargos* 'forgetful,' from the base of *lanthanesthai* 'forget.'
Le·the /ˈlēTHē; liˈTHē-/ *Greek Mythology* a river in Hades whose water when drunk made the souls of the dead forget their life on earth. ▷via Latin from Greek *lēthē* 'forgetfulness,' from the base of *lanthanesthai* 'forget.' —**Le·the·an** /ˈlēTHēən/ *adj.*
Le·to /ˈlētō/ *Greek Mythology* the daughter of a Titan, mother (by Zeus) of Artemis and Apollo. Roman name LATONA.
let's /lets/ ▸*contraction of* let us: *let's meet for a drink sometime.*
let·ter /ˈletər/ ▸*n.* **1** a character representing one or more of the sounds used in speech; any of the symbols of an alphabet: *a capital letter.* ■ a school or college initial as a mark of proficiency, esp. in sports: *I earned a varsity letter in tennis* | [as *adj.*] *a letter jacket.* **2** a written, typed, or printed communication, esp. one sent in an envelope by mail or messenger: *he sent a letter to Mrs. Falconer.* ■ (**letters**) a legal or formal document of this kind. **3** the precise terms of a statement or requirement; the strict verbal interpretation: *we must be seen to keep the spirit of the law as well as the letter.* **4** (**letters**) literature: *the world of letters.* ■ *archaic* scholarly knowledge; erudition. **5** *Printing* a style of typeface.
▸*v.* **1** [*trans.*] inscribe letters or writing on: *her name was lettered in gold.* ■ classify with letters: *he numbered and lettered the paragraphs.* **2** [*intrans.*] *informal* be

given a school or college initial as a mark of proficiency in sports: *juniors who lettered in soccer, basketball or softball.* ▷Middle English: from Old French *lettre*, from Latin *litera, littera* 'letter of the alphabet,' (plural) 'epistle, literature, culture.'

▸*PHRASE* □ **to the letter** with adherence to every detail: *the method was followed to the letter.*

let·ter bomb ▸*n.* an explosive device hidden in a small package and sent to someone with the intention of harming or killing them.

let·ter·box /ˈletər,bäks/ ▸*n. chiefly Brit.* a mailbox. ■ [usu. as *adj.*] a format for presenting wide-screen films on a standard television screen in which the image is displayed in approximately its original proportions across the middle of the screen, leaving horizontal black bands above and below: *this uncut version is presented in letterbox format.*

▸*v.* [*trans.*] record (a wide-screen film) onto video in letterbox format.

let·ter car·ri·er ▸*n.* a mail carrier.

let·tered /ˈletərd/ ▸*adj. dated* formally educated: *though not lettered, he read widely.*

let·ter·form /ˈletər,fôrm/ ▸*n.* the graphic form of a letter of the alphabet, either as written or in a particular type font.

let·ter·head /ˈletər,hed/ ▸*n.* a printed heading on stationery stating a person's or organization's name and address. ■ a sheet of paper with such a heading.

let·ter·ing /ˈletəriNG/ ▸*n.* the process of inscribing letters. ■ the letters inscribed on something, esp. decorative ones.

Let·ter·man /ˈletərmən/, David (1947–) U.S. comedian and talk show host. He hosted "The David Letterman Show" for about three months in 1980 and, after that, "Late Night with David Letterman."

let·ter·man /ˈletər,man; -mən/ ▸*n.* a high school or college student who has earned a letter in an interscholastic or intercollegiate activity, esp. a sport.

let·ter mis·sive (also **let·ters mis·sive**) ▸*n.* a letter from a superior to a group or an individual conveying a command, recommendation, permission, or an invitation. ■ in the Anglican church, a letter from a monarch to a dean and chapter nominating a person to be elected bishop.

let·ter of cred·it ▸*n.* a letter issued by a bank to another bank (typically in a different country) to serve as a guarantee for payments made to a specified person under specified conditions.

let·ter of in·tent ▸*n.* a document containing a declaration of the intentions of the writer.

let·ter of marque /märk/ ▸*n.* (usu. **letters of marque**) *historical* a license to fit out an armed vessel and use it in the capture of enemy merchant shipping and to commit acts which would otherwise have constituted piracy. ■ a ship carrying such a license. ▷late Middle English: Law French *marque*, from Old French *marque* 'right of reprisal.'

let·ter-per·fect ▸*adj.* (of an actor or speaker) knowing by heart the words for one's part or speech. ■ accurate to the smallest verbal detail: *when he delivered a manuscript, it was letter-perfect.*

let·ter·press /ˈletər,pres/ ▸*n.* **1** printing from a hard, raised image under pressure, using viscous ink. **2** *Brit.* printed text as opposed to illustrations.

let·ter-qual·i·ty ▸*adj.* (of a printer attached to a computer) producing print of a quality suitable for business letters. ■ (of a document) printed to such a standard.

let·ter·set /ˈletər,set/ ▸*n.* a method of printing in which ink is transferred from a raised surface to a blanket wrapped around a cylinder and from that to the paper. ▷1960s: blend of **LETTERPRESS** and **OFFSET**.

let·ters mis·sive ▸*n.* variant of **LETTER MISSIVE**.

let·ters of ad·min·is·tra·tion ▸*plural n. Law* authority to administer the estate of someone who has died without making a will.

let·ters pat·ent /ˈpatnt/ ▸*plural n.* an open document issued by a monarch or government conferring a patent or other right. ▷late Middle English: from medieval Latin *litterae patentes*, literally 'letters lying open.'

let·ters rog·a·to·ry /ˈrōgə,tôrē; ˈrägə-/ ▸*plural n. Law* documents making a request through a foreign court for the obtaining of information or evidence from a specified person within the jurisdiction of that court. ▷mid 19th cent.: *rogatory* from medieval Latin *rogatorius* 'interrogatory.'

let·ters tes·ta·men·ta·ry ▸*plural n. Law* a document issued by a court or public official authorizing the executor of a will to take control of a deceased person's estate.

let·tuce /ˈletis/ ▸*n.* **1** a cultivated plant of the daisy family, with edible leaves that are a usual ingredient of salads. Many varieties of lettuce have been developed with a range of form, texture, and color. • *Lactuca sativa*, family Compositae. ■ used in names of other plants with edible green leaves, e.g., **lamb's lettuce, sea lettuce. 2** *informal* paper money; greenbacks. ▷Middle English: from Old French *letues, laitues*, plural of *laitue*, from Latin *lactuca*, from *lac, lact-* 'milk' (because of its milky juice).

let·up /ˈlet,əp/ ▸*n.* [in *sing.*] *informal* a pause or reduction in the intensity of something dangerous, difficult, or tiring: *there had been no letup in the eruption.*

Letz·e·burg·esch /ˈletse,bŏŏrgəsh/ (also **Letz·e·buerg·esch**) ▸*n.* & *adj.* another term for **LUXEMBURGISH**. ▷from a local name for **LUXEMBOURG** + *-esch* (equivalent of **-ISH**[1]).

le·u /ˈlā(y)ōō/ ▸*n.* (*pl.* **lei** /lā/) the basic monetary unit of Romania, equal to 100 bani. ▷Romanian, literally 'lion.'

leu·cine /ˈlōō,sēn; -sin/ ▸*n. Biochemistry* a hydrophobic amino acid that is a constituent of most proteins. It is an essential nutrient in the diet of vertebrates. • Chem. formula: $(CH_3)_2CHCH_2CH(NH_2)COOH$. ▷early 19th cent.: coined in French from Greek *leukos* 'white' + **-INE**[4].

leu·cite /ˈlōō,sīt/ ▸*n.* a gray or white potassium aluminosilicate, typically found in alkali volcanic rocks. **—leu·cit·ic** /lōōˈsitik/ *adj.*

leuco- ▸*comb. form chiefly Brit.* variant spelling of **LEUKO-**. ▷from Greek *leukos* 'white.'

leu·co·der·ma /,lōōkəˈdərmə/ (also **leu·ko·der·ma**) ▸*n.* another term for **VITILIGO**.

leu·con /ˈlōō,kän/ ▸*n. Zoology* a sponge of the most complex structure, composed of a mass of flagellated chambers and water canals. Compare with **ASCON** and **SYCON**. **—leu·co·noid** /-kə,noid/ *adj.*

leu·co·plast /ˈlōōkə,plast/ ▸*n. Botany* a colorless organelle found in plant cells, used for the storage of starch or oil.

leu·ke·mi·a /lōōˈkēmēə/ (*Brit.* **leu·kae·m·ia**) ▸*n.* a malignant progressive disease in which the bone marrow and other blood-forming organs produce increased numbers of immature or abnormal leukocytes. These suppress the production of normal blood cells, leading to anemia and other symptoms. ▷mid 19th cent.: coined in German from Greek *leukos* 'white' + *haima* 'blood.' **—leu·ke·mic** /-ˈkēmik/ *adj.*

leu·ke·mo·gen·ic /lōō,kēməˈjenik/ (*Brit.* **leu·kae·mo·gen·ic**) ▸*adj. Medicine* relating to or promoting the development of leukemia. **—leu·ke·mo·gen** /-ˈkēməjən; -,jen/ *n.* **—leu·ke·mo·gen·e·sis** /-,kēməˈjenəsis/ *n.*

leuko- (also *chiefly Brit.* **leuco-**) ▸*comb. form* **1** white: *leukoma.* **2** representing **LEUKOCYTE**.

leu·ko·cyte /ˈlōōkə,sīt/ (*Brit.* also **leu·co·cyte**) ▸*n. Physiology* a colorless cell that circulates in the blood and body fluids and is involved in counteracting foreign substances and disease; a white (blood) cell. There are several types, all ameboid cells with a nucleus, including lymphocytes, granulocytes, monocytes, and macrophages. **—leu·ko·cyt·ic** /,lōōkəˈsitik/ *adj.*

leu·ko·cy·to·sis /,lōōkəsīˈtōsis; -kō-/ (*Brit.* also **leu·co·cy·to·sis**) ▸*n. Medicine* an increase in the number of white cells in the blood, esp. during an infection. **—leu·ko·cy·tot·ic** /-ˈtätik/ *adj.*

leu·ko·der·ma (also **leu·co·der·ma**) /,lōōkəˈdərmə/ ▸*n.* another term for **VITILIGO**.

leu·ko·ma /lōōˈkōmə/ ▸*n. Medicine* a white opacity in the cornea of the eye. ▷early 18th cent.: modern Latin, from Greek *leukōma.*

leu·ko·pe·ni·a /,lōōkəˈpēnēə/ (*Brit.* also **leu·co·pe·ni·a**) ▸*n. Medicine* a reduction in the number of white cells in the blood, typical of various diseases. ▷late 19th cent.: from Greek *leukos* 'white' + *penia* 'poverty.' **—leu·ko·pe·nic** /-nik/ *adj.*

leu·ko·pla·ki·a /,lōōkəˈplākēə/ ▸*n.* (*Brit.* also **leu·co·pla·ki·a**) a mucous membrane disorder characterized by white patches, esp. on the cheek, tongue, vulva, or penis. Also called **leukoplasia**.

leu·kor·rhe·a /,lōōkəˈrēə/ (also **leu·cor·rhe·a**, *Brit.* **leu·cor·rhoe·a**) ▸*n.* a whitish or yellowish discharge of mucus from the vagina.

leu·ko·sis /lōōˈkōsis/ (*Brit.* also **leu·co·sis**) ▸*n.* a leukemic disease of animals, esp. one of a group of malignant viral diseases of poultry or cattle. **—leu·kot·ic** /-ˈkätik/ *adj.*

leu·kot·o·my /lōōˈkätəmē/ ▸*n.* (*pl.* **-mies**) the surgical cutting of white nerve fibers within the brain, esp. prefrontal lobotomy, formerly used to treat mental illness.

leu·ko·tri·ene /,lōōkəˈtrī,ēn/ ▸*n. Biochemistry* any of a group of biologically active compounds, originally isolated from leukocytes. They are metabolites of arachidonic acid, containing three conjugated double bonds.

Lev. ▸*abbr. Bible* Leviticus.

lev /lev; lef/ ▸*n.* (*pl.* **lev·a** /ˈlevə/) the basic monetary unit of Bulgaria, equal to 100 stotinki. ▷Bulgarian, variant of *lăv* 'lion.'

Le·val·lois /lə,valˈwä; -ˈval,wä/ ▸*n.* [usu. as *adj.*] *Archaeology* a flint-working technique associated with the Mousterian culture of the Neanderthals, in which a flint is trimmed so that a flake of predetermined size and shape can be struck from it. ▷early 20th cent.: named after a suburb of northern Paris. **—Le·val·loi·si·an** /,levəˈloizēən; lə,valˈwäzēən/ *adj.*

le·va·mi·sole /ləˈvamə,sōl/ ▸*n. Medicine* a synthetic compound used as an anthelmintic drug (esp. in animals) and in cancer chemotherapy. • A polycyclic imidazole derivative; chem. formula: $C_{11}H_{12}N_2S$. ▷1960s: from **LEVO-** (it being a levorotatory isomer) + *(tetra)misole*, the name of an anthelmintic drug.

Le·vant /ləˈvant; ləˈvänt/ *archaic* the eastern part of the Mediterranean with its islands and neighboring countries. ▷late 15th cent.: from French, literally "rising," present participle of *lever* "to lift" used as a noun in the sense "point of sunrise, east."

le·vant /ləˈvant/ ▸*v.* [*intrans.*] *Brit., archaic* run away, typically leaving unpaid debts. ▷early 17th cent.: perhaps from **LEVANT**: compare with French *faire voile en Levant* 'be stolen or spirited away,' literally 'set sail for the Levant.'

le·vant·er[1] /ləˈvantər/ ▸*n.* a strong easterly wind in the Mediterranean region.

le·vant·er[2] /ləˈvantər/ ▸*n. archaic* a person who runs away leaving unpaid debts.

Le·van·tine /ˈlevən,tīn; -,tēn; ləˈvantin/ *chiefly archaic* ▸*adj.* of or trading to the Levant: *the Levantine coast.* ▸*n.* a person who lives in or comes from the Levant.

Le·vant mo·roc·co /ləˈvant/ (also **Le·vant**) ▸*n.* high-grade, large-grained morocco leather.

Le·vant worm·seed ▸*n.* see **WORMSEED**.

le·va·tor /ləˈvātər/ (also **levator muscle**) ▸*n. Anatomy* a muscle whose contraction causes the raising of a part of the body. ▷early 17th cent.: from Latin, literally 'a person who lifts,' from *levare* 'raise, lift.'

lev·ee[1] ▸*n.* an embankment built to prevent the overflow of a river. ■ a ridge of sediment deposited naturally alongside a river by overflowing water. ■ a landing place; a quay. ■ a ridge of earth surrounding a field to be irrigated. ▷early 18th cent. (originally U.S.): from French *levée*, feminine past participle of *lever* 'to lift.'

lev·ee[2] /ˈlevē/ ▸*n.* a reception or assembly of people, in particular: ■ a formal reception of visitors or guests. ■ *historical* an afternoon assembly for men held by the British monarch or their representative. ■ *archaic* a reception of visitors just after rising from bed. ▷late 17th cent. (denoting a reception of visitors after rising from bed): from French *levé*, variant of *lever* 'rising,' from the verb *lever.*

lev·el /ˈlevəl/ ▸*n.* **1** a position on a real or imaginary scale of amount, quantity, extent, or quality: *a high level of unemployment | debt rose to unprecedented levels.* ■ a social, moral, or intellectual standard: *at six he could play chess at an advanced level.* ■ a position in a real or notional hierarchy: *a fairly junior level of management.* **2** a height or distance from the ground or another stated or understood base: *storms caused river levels to rise.* **3** an instrument giving a line parallel to the plane of the horizon, for testing whether things are horizontal. ■ *Surveying* an instrument for giving a horizontal line of sight. **4** a flat tract of land: *flooded levels.*

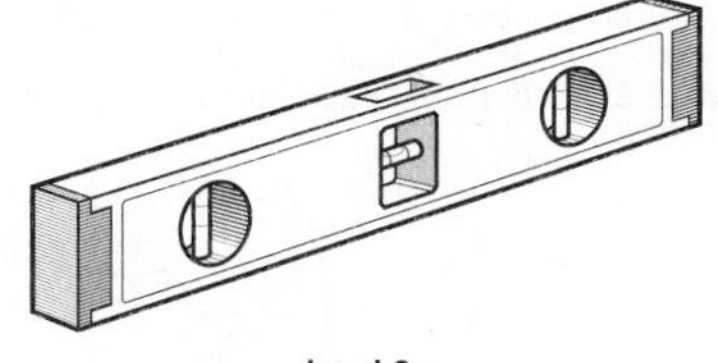

level 3

Pronunciation Key ə *ago;* ər *over;* ˈə or ,ə *up;* ˈər or ,ər *fur;* a *hat;* ā *rate;* ä *car;* CH *chew;* e *let;* ē *see;* e(ə)r *air;* i *fit;* ī *by;* i(ə)r *ear;* NG *sing;* ō *go;* ô *for;* oi *boy;* ŏŏ *good;* ōō *goo;* ou *out;* SH *she;* TH *thin;* T͟H *then;* (h)w *why;* ZH *vision*

▸*adj.* **1** having a flat and even surface without slopes or bumps: *we had reached level ground.* ■ horizontal: *a large paved double courtyard that was level, despite the steep gradient of the hill.* ■ at the same height as someone or something else: *his eyes were* **level with** *hers.* ■ having the same relative position; not in front of or behind: *the car braked suddenly, then backed rapidly until it was* **level with** *me.* ■ (of a quantity of a dry substance) with the contents not rising above the brim of the measure: *a level teaspoon of salt.* ■ unchanged; not having risen or fallen: *earnings were level at 57 cents a share.* **2** calm and steady: *"Adrian," she said in her most level voice.*

▸*v.* (**-eled**, **-el·ing**; also *chiefly Brit.* **-elled**, **-el·ling**) **1** [*trans.*] give a flat and even surface to: *contractors started leveling the ground for the new power station.* ■ *Surveying* ascertain differences in the height of (land). ■ demolish (a building or town): *bulldozers are now waiting to level their home.* **2** [*intrans.*] (**level off/out**) begin to fly horizontally after climbing or diving. ■ (of a path, road, or incline) cease to slope upward or downward: *the track leveled out, and there below us was the bay.* ■ cease to fall or rise in number, amount, or quantity: *inflation has leveled out at an acceptable rate.* ■ [*trans.*] (**level something up/down**) increase or reduce the amount, number, or quantity of something in order to remove a disparity. **3** [*trans.*] aim (a weapon): *he* **leveled** *a long-barreled pistol* **at** *us.* ■ direct (a criticism or accusation): *accusations of corruption had been* **leveled against** *him.* **4** [*intrans.*] (**level with**) *informal* be frank or honest with (someone): *when are you going to level with me?* ▷Middle English (denoting an instrument to determine whether a surface is horizontal): from Old French *livel*, based on Latin *libella*, diminutive of *libra* 'scales, balance.' **—lev·el·ly** *adv.* (in sense 2 of the *adjective*). **—lev·el·ness** *n.*

▸*PHRASES* □ **do one's level best** do one's utmost; make all possible efforts. □ **find its** (**own**) **level** (of a liquid) reach the same height in containers that are interconnected. ■ reach a stable level, value, or position without interference. □ **find one's** (**own**) **level** (of a person) reach a position or competency that seems appropriate and natural in relation to one's associates. □ **a level playing field** a situation in which everyone has a fair and equal chance of succeeding. □ **on the level** *informal* honest; truthful: *Eddie said my story was on the level.* □ **on a level with** in the same horizontal plane as. ■ equal with: *they were treated as menials, on a level with cooks.*

lev·el cross·ing ▸*n.* British term for **GRADE CROSSING**.

lev·el·er /'lev(ə)lər/ (*Brit.* **lev·el·ler**) ▸*n.* **1** a person who advocates the abolition of social distinctions. ■ (**Leveller**) an extreme radical dissenter in the English Civil War (1642–49), calling for the abolition of the monarchy, social and agrarian reforms, and religious freedom. **2** a person or thing that levels something.

lev·el·head·ed /'levəl'hedid/ ▸*adj.* calm and sensible. **—lev·el·head·ed·ly** *adv.* **—lev·el·head·ed·ness** *n.*

lev·el·ing rod ▸*n.* a graduated pole with a movable marker, held upright and used with a surveying instrument to measure differences in elevation. Also called **lev·el·ing pole**, **lev·el·ing staff**.

lev·el·ing screw ▸*n.* a screw for adjusting part of a machine or instrument to a precise level.

lev·er /'levər; 'lēvər/ ▸*n.* a rigid bar resting on a pivot, used to help move a heavy or firmly fixed load with one end when pressure is applied to the other. ■ a projecting arm or handle that is moved to operate a mechanism: *she pulled a lever at the base of the cage.* ■ *figurative* a means of exerting pressure on someone to act in a particular way: *rich countries increasingly use foreign aid as a lever to promote political pluralism.*

▸*v.* [*trans.*] lift or move with a lever: *she levered the lid off the pot with a screwdriver.* ■ move (someone or something) with a concerted physical effort: *she levered herself up against the pillows.* ■ [*intrans.*] use a lever: *the men got hold of the coffin and levered at it with crowbars.* ▷Middle English: from Old French *levier, leveor*, from *lever* 'to lift.'

fulcrum

lever

lev·er·age /'lev(ə)rij; 'lēv(ə)rij/ ▸*n.* **1** the exertion of force by means of a lever or an object used in the manner of a lever: *my spade hit something solid that wouldn't respond to leverage.* ■ mechanical advantage gained in this way: *use a metal bar to increase the leverage.* ■ *figurative* the power to influence a person or situation to achieve a particular outcome: *the right wing had lost much of its political leverage in the Assembly.* **2** *Finance* the ratio of a company's loan capital (debt) to the value of its common stock (equity).

▸*v.* [*trans.*] [usu. as *adj.*] (**leveraged**) use borrowed capital for (an investment), expecting the profits made to be greater than the interest payable: *a leveraged takeover bid.*

lev·er·aged buy·out ▸*n.* the purchase of a controlling share in a company by its management, using outside capital.

lev·er es·cape·ment ▸*n.* a mechanism in a watch connecting the escape wheel and the balance wheel with two levers.

lev·er·et /'lev(ə)rit/ ▸*n.* a young hare in its first year. ▷late Middle English: from Anglo-Norman French, diminutive of *levre*, from Latin *lepus, lepor-* 'hare.'

Le·ver·hulme /'levər,hyōōm/, 1st Viscount (1851–1925), English industrialist and philanthropist; born *William Hesketh Lever*. He and his brother founded Lever Bros., the company that later formed the basis of the international corporation Unilever. He founded the model village Port Sunlight for his company's workers.

Le·ver·ku·sen /'lāvər,kōōzən/ an industrial city in western Germany, in North Rhine-Westphalia, on the Rhine River north of Cologne; pop. 161,000.

Le Ver·ri·er /lə ver'yā/, Urbain (1811–77), French mathematician. His analysis of the motions of the planets suggested that an unknown body was disrupting the orbit of Uranus. Le Verrier prompted the German astronomer **Johann Galle** (1812–1910) to investigate, and the planet Neptune was discovered in 1846.

Le·vi[1] /'lē,vī/ (in the Bible) a Hebrew patriarch, third son of Jacob and Leah (Gen. 29:34). ■ the tribe of Israel traditionally descended from him.

Le·vi[2] /'levē/, Primo (1919–87), Italian novelist and poet. His experiences as a survivor of Auschwitz are recounted in his first book *If This Is a Man* (1947).

le·vi·a·than /lə'vīəTHən/ ▸*n.* (in biblical use) a sea monster, identified in different passages with the whale and the crocodile (e.g., Job 41, Ps. 74:14), and with the Devil (after Isa. 27:1). ■ a very large aquatic creature, esp. a whale: *the great leviathans of the deep.* ■ a thing that is very large or powerful, esp. a ship. ■ an autocratic monarch or state. [with allusion to Hobbes' *Leviathan* (1651).] ▷via late Latin from Hebrew *liwyāṯān*.

lev·i·gate /'levə,gāt/ ▸*v.* [*trans.*] reduce (a substance) to a fine powder or smooth paste. ▷mid 16th cent.: from Latin *levigat-* 'made smooth, polished,' from the verb *levigare*, from *levis* 'smooth.' **—lev·i·ga·tion** /,levə'gāSHən/ *n.*

lev·in /'levin/ ▸*n.* *archaic* lightning; thunderbolts. ▷Middle English: probably of Scandinavian origin.

lev·i·rate /'levərit; -,rāt/ ▸*n.* (usu. **the levirate**) a custom of the ancient Hebrews and other peoples by which a man may be obliged to marry his brother's widow: [as *adj.*] *levirate marriages.* ▷early 18th cent.: from Latin *levir* 'brother-in-law' + **-ATE**[1].

Le·vi's /'lē,vīz/ ▸*plural n. trademark* a type of denim jeans or overalls reinforced with rivets. ▷1920s: named after *Levi* Strauss, original U.S. manufacturer in the 1860s.

Lé·vi-Strauss /'lāvē 'strous/, Claude (1908–), French social anthropologist. He regarded language as an essential common denominator underlying cultural phenomena.

lev·i·tate /'levə,tāt/ ▸*v.* [*intrans.*] rise and hover in the air, esp. by means of supernatural or magical power: *he seems to levitate about three inches off the ground.* ■ [*trans.*] cause (something) to rise and hover in such a way. ▷late 17th cent.: from Latin *levis* 'light,' on the pattern of *gravitate*. **—lev·i·ta·tion** /,levə'tāSHən/ *n.* **—lev·i·ta·tor** /-,tātər/ *n.*

Le·vite /'lē,vīt/ ▸*n.* a member of the Hebrew tribe of Levi, esp. of that part of it that provided assistants to the priests in the worship in the Jewish temple. ▷Middle English: from late Latin *levita*, from Greek *leuitēs*, from Hebrew *Lēwī* 'Levi.'

Le·vit·i·cal /lə'vitikəl/ ▸*adj.* **1** of or relating to the Levites or the tribe of Levi: *a Levitical priest.* **2** *Judaism* (of rules concerning codes of conduct, temple rituals, etc.) derived from the biblical Book of Leviticus: *a Levitical edict.* ▷mid 16th cent.: via late Latin from Greek *levitikos*, from *Levi* (see **LEVITE**), + **-AL**.

Le·vit·i·cus /lə'vitikəs/ the third book of the Bible, containing details of law and ritual.

Lev·it·town /'levət,toun/ a village in central Long Island in New York, noted for its "cookie-cutter" houses, developed after World War II; pop. 53,286. There are also Levittowns in New Jersey, Pennsylvania, and Puerto Rico.

lev·i·ty /'levətē/ ▸*n.* humor or frivolity, esp. the treatment of a serious matter with humor or in a manner lacking due respect: *as an attempt to introduce a note of levity, the words were a disastrous flop.* ▷mid 16th cent.: from Latin *levitas*, from *levis* 'light.'

levo- (also *chiefly Brit.* **laevo-**) ▸*comb. form* on or to the left: *levorotatory*.

le·vo·do·pa /,levə'dōpə; ,lēvə/ (also **le·vo·do·pa·mine** /-'dōpəmēn/) ▸*n.* another term for **L-DOPA**.

le·vo·nor·ges·trel /,lēvənôr'jestrəl/ ▸*n.* *Biochemistry* a synthetic steroid hormone that has a similar effect to progesterone and is used in some contraceptive pills. ▷1970s: from **LEVO-** (it being a levorotatory isomer) + *norgestrel*, a synthetic steroid hormone.

le·vo·ro·ta·to·ry /,lēvə'rōtə,tôrē/ (*Brit.* **lae·vo·ro·ta·to·ry**) ▸*adj.* *Chemistry* (of a compound) having the property of rotating the plane of a polarized light ray to the left, i.e., counterclockwise facing the oncoming radiation. The opposite of **DEXTROROTATORY**. **—le·vo·ro·ta·tion** /-rō'tāSHən/ *n.*

lev·u·lose /'levyə,lōs; -,lōz/ (*Brit.* **laev·u·lose**) ▸*n.* *Chemistry* another term for **FRUCTOSE**.

le·vy /'levē/ ▸*v.* (**-vies**, **-vied**) [*trans.*] **1** (often **be levied**) impose (a tax, fee, or fine): *a new tax could be* **levied on** *industry to pay for cleaning up contaminated land.* ■ impose a tax, fee, or fine on: *there will be powers to levy the owner.* ■ [*intrans.*] (**levy on/upon**) seize (property) to satisfy a legal judgment: *there were no goods to levy upon.* **2** *archaic* enlist (someone) for military service: *he sought to levy one man from each parish for service.* ■ begin to wage (war).

▸*n.* (*pl.* **-vies**) **1** an act of levying a tax, fee, or fine: *union members were hit with a 2 percent* **levy on** *all pay.* ■ a tax so raised. ■ a sum collected for a specific purpose, esp. as a supplement to an existing subscription. ■ an item or set of items of property seized to satisfy a legal judgment. **2** *historical* an act of enlisting troops. ■ (usu. **levies**) a body of troops that have been enlisted: *lightly armed local levies.* ▷Middle English (as a noun): from Old French *levee*, feminine past participle of *lever* 'raise,' from Latin *levare*, from *levis* 'light.' **—lev·i·a·ble** *adj.*

lewd /lōōd/ ▸*adj.* crude and offensive in a sexual way: *she began to gyrate to the music and sing a lewd song.* ▷Old English *lǣwede*, of unknown origin. The original sense was 'belonging to the laity'; in Middle English, 'belonging to the common people, vulgar,' and later 'worthless, vile, evil,' leading to the current sense. **—lewd·ly** *adv.* **—lewd·ness** *n.*

Lew·is[1] /'lōō-is/, Cecil Day, see **DAY LEWIS**.

Lew·is[2], C. S. (1898–1963), British novelist, religious writer, and literary scholar; full name *Clive Staples Lewis*. He broadcast and wrote on religious and moral issues and created the imaginary land of Narnia for a series of children's books. Notable works: *The Screwtape Letters* (1942) and *The Lion, the Witch, and the Wardrobe* (1950).

Lew·is[3], Carl (1961–), U.S. track and field athlete; full name *Frederick Carleton Lewis*. He won Olympic gold medals in 1984, 1988, 1992, and 1996 (his ninth) for sprinting and the long jump and broke the world record for the 100 meters on several occasions.

Lew·is[4], Jerry (1926–), U.S. actor, comedian, and director; born *Joseph Levitch*. He was known initially for his act with Dean Martin 1946–1956 but then appeared on his own on the stage and in films and also worked as a director. Since 1966 he has hosted an annual telethon to fight muscular dystrophy.

Lew·is[5], Jerry Lee (1935–), U.S. rock-and-roll singer and pianist. In 1957, he had hits with "Whole Lotta Shakin' Going On" and "Great Balls of Fire." His career was interrupted when his marriage to his 14-year-old cousin caused a public outcry.

Lew·is[6], John Llewellyn (1880–1969) U.S. labor leader. He headed the United Mine Workers 1920–60 and organized the Committee for Industrial Organization 1935, which became the Congress of Industrial Organizations (CIO). He served as its president until 1940.

Lew·is[7], Meriwether (1774–1809), U.S. explorer. Together with William Clark, he led an expedition to explore the newly acquired Louisiana Purchase (1804–06). They traveled from St. Louis to the Pacific Northwest and back. He then served as governor of Louisiana Territory 1807–09.

Lew·is[8], (Harry) Sinclair (1885–1951), U.S. novelist, known for satirical works such as *Main Street* (1920), *Babbitt* (1922), and *Elmer Gantry* (1927). Nobel Prize for Literature (1930).

lew·is /ˈlo͞o-is/ ▸*n.* a steel device for gripping heavy blocks of stone or concrete for lifting, consisting of three pieces arranged to form a dovetail, the outside pieces being fixed in a dovetail mortise by the insertion of the middle piece. ▷late Middle English: probably from Old French *lous*, plural of *lou(p)* 'wolf,' the name of a kind of siege engine.

Lew·is ac·id ▸*n. Chemistry* a compound or ionic species that can accept an electron pair from a donor compound. ▷1940s: named after Gilbert N. *Lewis* (1875–1946), U.S. chemist.

Lew·is and Clark Trail /ˈlo͞oəs and ˈklärk/ the route of the Lewis and Clark expedition that explored the Louisiana Purchase from St. Louis in Missouri to the Pacific coast from 1803 until 1806. Official name **Lewis and Clark National Historic Trail**.

Lew·is base ▸*n. Chemistry* a compound or ionic species that can donate an electron pair to an acceptor compound. ▷1960s: named after G. N. *Lewis* (see LEWIS ACID).

Lew·is gun ▸*n. chiefly historical* a light, air-cooled machine gun with a magazine operated by gas from its own firing, used mainly in World War I. ▷early 20th cent.: named after its inventor, Isaac N. *Lewis* (1858–1931), a colonel in the U.S. Army.

lew·is·ite /ˈlo͞oəˌsīt/ ▸*n.* a dark, oily liquid producing an irritant gas that causes blisters, developed for use in chemical warfare. • An organic compound of arsenic; chem. formula: $ClCH=CHAsCl_2$. ▷1920s: named after Winford L. *Lewis* (1878–1943), U.S. chemist.

Lew·is·ton 1 an industrial city in northwestern Idaho, on the Snake River; pop. 30,904. **2** an industrial city in southwestern Maine, on the Androscoggin River, opposite Auburn; pop. 35,690.

lex /leks/ ▸*n.* (*pl.* **le·ges** /ˈlējēz; ˈlegēs/) LAW ▷Latin, literally 'law.'

lex. ▸*abbr.* ■ lexical. ■ lexicon.

Lex·an /ˈlekˌsan/ ▸*n. trademark* a transparent plastic (polycarbonate) of high impact strength, used for cockpit canopies, bulletproof screens, etc. ▷1950s: an invented name.

lex·eme /ˈlekˌsēm/ ▸*n. Linguistics* a basic lexical unit of a language, consisting of one word or several words, considered as an abstract unit, and applied to a family of words related by form or meaning. ▷1940s: from LEXICON + -EME.

lex fo·ri /ˈleks ˈfôrˌī; ˈfôrˌē/ ▸*n. Law* the law of the country in which an action is brought. ▷Latin, 'law of the court.'

lex·i·cal /ˈleksikəl/ ▸*adj.* of or relating to the words or vocabulary of a language: *lexical analysis*. ■ relating to or of the nature of a lexicon or dictionary: *a lexical entry*. ▷mid 19th cent.: from Greek *lexikos* 'of words' (from *lexis* 'word') + -AL. **—lex·i·cal·ly** /-ik(ə)lē/ *adv.*

lex·i·cal mean·ing ▸*n.* the meaning of a word considered in isolation from the sentence containing it and regardless of its grammatical context, e.g., of *love* in or as represented by *loves, loved, loving*, etc.

lex·i·cog·ra·pher /ˌleksəˈkägrəfər/ ▸*n.* a person who compiles dictionaries.

lex·i·cog·ra·phy /ˌleksəˈkägrəfē/ ▸*n.* the practice of compiling dictionaries. **—lex·i·co·graph·ic** /-kəˈgrafik/ *adj.* **—lex·i·co·graph·i·cal** /-kəˈgrafikəl/ *adj.* **—lex·i·co·graph·i·cal·ly** /-kəˈgrafik(ə)lē/ *adv.*

lex·i·col·o·gy /ˌleksəˈkäləjē/ ▸*n.* the study of the form, meaning, and use of words. **—lex·i·co·log·i·cal** /-kəˈläjikəl/ *adj.* **—lex·i·co·log·i·cal·ly** /-kəˈläjik(ə)lē/ *adv.*

lex·i·con /ˈleksiˌkän; -kən/ ▸*n.* (*pl.* **-cons** or **-ca** /-kə/) **1** the vocabulary of a person, language, or branch of knowledge: *the size of the English lexicon*. ■ a dictionary, esp. of Greek, Hebrew, Syriac, or Arabic: *a Greek–Latin lexicon*. **2** *Linguistics* the complete set of meaningful units in a language. ▷early 17th cent.: modern Latin, from Greek *lexikon (biblion)* '(book) of words,' from *lexis* 'word,' from *legein* 'speak.'

lex·i·gram /ˈleksiˌgram/ ▸*n.* a symbol representing a word, esp. one used in learning a language.

Lex·ing·ton /ˈleksiNGtən/ **1** a city in central Kentucky; pop. 260,512. It is a noted horse-breeding center. **2** a residential town in northeastern Massachusetts, northwest of Boston; pop. 28,970. In 1775, it was the scene of the first battle in the American Revolution.

lex·is /ˈleksis/ ▸*n.* the total stock of words in a language: *a notable loss of English lexis*. ■ the level of language consisting of vocabulary, as opposed to grammar or syntax. ▷1950s (denoting the wording, as opposed to other elements, in a piece of writing): from Greek, literally 'word' (see LEXICON).

lex lo·ci /ˈleks ˈlōsī; -ˌsē; -ˌkē; -ˌkī/ ▸*n. Law* the law of the country in which a transaction is performed, a tort is committed, or a property is situated. ▷Latin, 'law of the place.'

lex ta·li·o·nis /ˈleks ˌtalēˈōnis; ˌtalē-/ ▸*n.* the law of retaliation, whereby a punishment resembles the offense committed in kind and degree. ▷Latin, from *lex* 'law' and *talio(n-)* 'retaliation' (from *talis* 'such').

Ley·den /ˈlīdn/ variant spelling of LEIDEN.

Ley·den jar ▸*n.* an early form of capacitor consisting of a glass jar with layers of metal foil on the outside and inside. ▷mid 18th cent.: named after *Leyden* (see LEIDEN), where it was invented (1745).

Ley·land cy·press /ˈlālənd; ˈlē-/ ▸*n.* a fast-growing hybrid conifer that is narrowly conical with a dense growth of shoots bearing scalelike leaves, widely grown as a screening plant or for shelter. • × *Cupressocyparis leylandii*, family Cupressaceae; a hybrid between the Nootka cypress and the Monterey cypress (macrocarpa). ▷1930s: named after Christopher J. *Leyland* (1849–1926), British horticulturist.

Ley·te /ˈlāˌtē; -ˌtā/ an island in the central Philippines; pop. 1,362,050; chief town, Tacloban.

Ley·te Gulf /ˈlātē; ˈlātā/ an inlet of the Philippine Sea, in the eastern Philippines, between Leyte and Samar islands, scene of the destruction of a Japanese fleet in 1944, during World War II.

lez ▸*n.* variant spelling of LES.

lez·zy /ˈlezē/ ▸*n.* (*pl.* **-zies**) *informal, chiefly offensive* a lesbian.

LF ▸*abbr.* low frequency.

lg. ▸*abbr.* ■ large. ■ long.

lge. ▸*abbr.* large.

LH *Biochemistry* ▸*abbr.* luteinizing hormone.

l.h. ▸*abbr.* left hand.

Lha·sa /ˈläsə/ the capital of Tibet; pop. 140,000. It is situated in the northern Himalayas at an altitude of *c.*11,800 feet (3,600 m) on a tributary of the Brahmaputra River. Known as the Forbidden City until the 20th century because it was closed to foreign visitors, it was the seat of the Dalai Lama until 1959.

Lha·sa ap·so /ˈläsə ˈäpsō; ˈlasə; ˈap-/ ▸*n.* (*pl.* **ap·sos**) a dog of a small, long-coated breed, typically gold or gray and white, originating at Lhasa. ▷mid 20th cent.: from LHASA + Tibetan *a-sob*.

Lhasa apso

LHRH ▸*abbr.* luteinizing hormone-releasing hormone.

LI ▸*abbr.* ■ Long Island.

Li ▸*symbol* the chemical element lithium.

li /lē/ ▸*n.* (*pl.* same) a Chinese unit of distance, equal to about 0.6 km (0.4 mile).

li·a·bil·i·ty /ˌlīəˈbilətē/ ▸*n.* (*pl.* **-ties**) **1** the state of being responsible for something, esp. by law: *the partners accept unlimited* ***liability for*** *any risks they undertake*. ■ (usu. **liabilities**) a thing for which someone is responsible, esp. a debt or financial obligation: *valuing the company's liabilities and assets*. **2** [usu. in *sing.*] a person or thing whose presence or behavior is likely to cause embarrassment or put one at a disadvantage: *he has become a political liability*.

li·a·ble /ˈlī(ə)bəl/ ▸*adj.* **1** responsible by law; legally answerable: *the supplier of goods or services can become* ***liable for*** *breach of contract in a variety of ways*. See note at RESPONSIBLE. **2** likely to do or to be something: *patients were liable to faint if they stood up too suddenly*. ■ (**liable to**) likely to experience (something undesirable): *areas liable to flooding*. ▷late Middle English: perhaps from Anglo-Norman French, from French *lier* 'to bind,' from Latin *ligare*.

USAGE **Liable** is commonly used to mean 'likely (to do something undesirable)': *without his glasses, he's liable to run the car into a tree*. Precisely, however, **liable** means 'legally obligated': *he is liable for any damage his pets may have caused*.

li·aise /lēˈāz/ ▸*v.* [*intrans.*] establish a working relationship, typically in order to cooperate on a matter of mutual concern: *she will* ***liaise with*** *teachers across the country*. ▷1920s (originally British military slang): back-formation from LIAISON.

li·ai·son /ˈlēəˌzän; lēˈā-/ ▸*n.* **1** communication or cooperation that facilitates a close working relationship between people or organizations: *the head porter works in close* ***liaison with*** *the reception office*. ■ a person who acts as a link to assist communication or cooperation between groups of people: *he's our liaison with a number of interested parties*. ■ a sexual relationship, esp. one that is secret and involves unfaithfulness to a partner. **2** the binding or thickening agent of a sauce, often based on egg yolks. **3** *Phonetics* (in French and other languages) the sounding of a consonant that is normally silent at the end of a word because the next word begins with a vowel. ▷mid 17th cent. (as a culinary term): from French, from *lier* 'to bind.'

li·ai·son of·fi·cer ▸*n.* a person who is employed to form a working relationship between two organizations to their mutual benefit.

li·a·na /lēˈänə; -ˈanə/ (also **li·a·ne** /-ˈän; -ˈan/) ▸*n.* a woody climbing plant that hangs from trees, esp. in tropical rain forests. ■ the free-hanging stem of such a plant. ▷late 18th cent.: from French *liane* 'clematis, liana,' of unknown origin.

Liao[1] /lēˈou/ a river in northeastern China that rises in Inner Mongolia and flows about 900 miles (1,450 km) east and then south to the Gulf of Liaodong at the head of the Gulf of Bo Hai.

Liao[2] /liˈou/ a dynasty which ruled much of Manchuria and part of northeastern China AD 947–1125.

Liao·dong Pen·in·su·la /lēˈouˈdo͝oNG/ a peninsula in northeastern China that extends south into the Yellow Sea between Bo Hai and Korea Bay.

Liao·ning /lēˈouˈniNG/ a province in northeastern China, bordered on the east by North Korea; capital, Shenyang.

li·ar /ˈlīər/ ▸*n.* a person who tells lies. ▷Old English *lēogere* (see LIE[2], -AR[4]).

Li·ard Riv·er /ˈlēˌärd; lēˈärd/ a river that flows for 570 miles (920 km) from the Yukon Territory through British Columbia and the Northwest Territories to the Mackenzie River.

Li·as /ˈlīəs/ ▸*n.* (**the Lias**) *Geology* the earliest epoch of the Jurassic period, lasting from about 208 to 178 million years ago. ■ the system of rocks deposited during this epoch, consisting of shales and limestones rich in fossils. ▷late Middle English (denoting blue lias): from Old French *liais* 'hard limestone,' probably from *lie* (see LEES). **—li·as·sic** /līˈasik/ *adj.*

li·a·tris /līˈatris/ ▸*n.* (*pl.* same) a plant of a genus that includes the blazing stars of the daisy family. • Genus *Liatris*, family Compositae. ▷modern Latin, of unknown origin.

lib /lib/ ▸*n. informal* (in the names of political movements) liberation: *I'm all for* ***women's lib***. ▷1970s: abbreviation.

Lib. ▸*abbr.* Liberal.

li·ba·tion /līˈbāSHən/ ▸*n.* a drink poured out as an offering to a deity. ■ the pouring out of such a drink-offering: *gin was poured in libation*. ■ *humorous* a drink: *they steadily worked their way through free food and the occasional libation*. ▷late Middle English: from Latin *libatio(n-)*, from *libare* 'pour as an offering.'

lib·ber /ˈlibər/ ▸*n.* [usu. with *adj.*] *informal* a member or advocate of a movement calling for the liberation of people or animals: *a women's libber*.

li·bel /ˈlībəl/ ▸*n.* **1** *Law* a published false statement that is damaging to a person's reputation; a written defamation. Compare with SLANDER. ■ the action or crime of publishing such a statement: *a councilor who sued two national newspapers for libel* | [as *adj.*] *a libel action*. ■ a false and malicious statement about a person. ■ a thing or circumstance that brings undeserved discredit on a person by misrepresentation.

2 (in admiralty and ecclesiastical law) a plaintiff's written declaration.
▸*v.* (**-beled**, **-bel·ing**; *Brit.* **-belled**, **-bel·ling**) [*trans.*] **1** *Law* defame (someone) by publishing a libel: *she alleged the magazine had libeled her.* ■ make a false and malicious statement about. See note at MALIGN. **2** (in admiralty and ecclesiastical law) bring a suit against (someone). ▷Middle English (in the general sense 'a document, a written statement'): via Old French from Latin *libellus*, diminutive of *liber* 'book.' **—li·bel·er** *n.*

li·bel·ous /ˈlībələs/ (*Brit.* **li·bel·lous**) ▸*adj.* containing or constituting a libel: *a libelous newspaper story.* **—li·bel·ous·ly** *adv.*

Lib·e·ra·ce /ˌlibəˈräCHē/ (1919–87), U.S. pianist and entertainer; full name *Wladziu Valentino Liberace*. He was known for his romantic arrangements of popular piano classics and for his flamboyant costumes. He appeared on his own television show from 1952 to 1957.

lib·er·al /ˈlib(ə)rəl/ ▸*adj.* **1** open to new behavior or opinions and willing to discard traditional values: *they have more liberal views toward marriage and divorce than some people.* ■ favorable to or respectful of individual rights and freedoms: *liberal citizenship laws.* ■ (in a political context) favoring maximum individual liberty in political and social reform: *a liberal democratic state.* ■ (**Liberal**) of or characteristic of Liberals or a Liberal Party. ■ (**Liberal**) (in the UK) of or relating to the Liberal Democrat Party: *the Liberal leader.* ■ *Theology* regarding many traditional beliefs as dispensable, invalidated by modern thought, or liable to change. **2** [*attrib.*] (of education) concerned mainly with broadening a person's general knowledge and experience, rather than with technical or professional training. **3** (esp. of an interpretation of a law) broadly construed or understood; not strictly literal or exact: *they could have given the 1968 Act a more liberal interpretation.* **4** given, used, or occurring in generous amounts: *liberal amounts of wine had been consumed.* ■ (of a person) giving generously: *Sam was too **liberal with** the wine.*
▸*n.* a person of liberal views. ■ (**Liberal**) a supporter or member of a Liberal Party. ▷Middle English: via Old French from Latin *liberalis*, from *liber* 'free (man).' The original sense was 'suitable for a free man,' hence 'suitable for a gentleman' (one not tied to a trade), surviving in *liberal arts*. Another early sense 'generous' (compare with sense 4) gave rise to an obsolete meaning 'free from restraint,' leading to sense 1 (late 18th cent.). **—lib·er·al·ism** /-ˌlizəm/ *n.* **—lib·er·al·ist** /-rəlist/ *n.* **—lib·er·al·is·tic** /ˌlib(ə)rəˈlistik/ *adj.* **—lib·er·al·ly** *adv.* **—lib·er·al·ness** *n.*

lib·er·al arts ▸*plural n.* academic subjects such as literature, philosophy, mathematics, and social and physical sciences as distinct from professional and technical subjects. ■ *historical* the medieval trivium and quadrivium. ▷*liberal*, as distinct from *servile* or *mechanical* (i.e., involving manual labor) and originally referring to arts and sciences considered "worthy of a free man"; later the word related to general intellectual development rather than vocational training.

lib·er·al·i·ty /ˌlibəˈralətē/ ▸*n.* **1** the quality of giving or spending freely. **2** the quality of being open to new ideas and free from prejudice: *liberality toward bisexuality.* ▷Middle English: from Old French *liberalite*, or from Latin *liberalitas*, from *liberalis* (see LIBERAL).

lib·er·al·ize /ˈlib(ə)rəˌlīz/ ▸*v.* [*trans.*] remove or loosen restrictions on (something, typically an economic or political system): *several agreements to liberalize trade were signed.* **—lib·er·al·i·za·tion** /ˌlib(ə)rələˈzāSHən; -ˌlīˈzā-/ *n.* **—lib·er·al·iz·er** *n.*

Lib·er·al Par·ty ▸*n.* a political party advocating liberal policies, in particular a British party that emerged in the 1860s from the old Whig Party and until World War I was one of the two major parties in Britain. The name was discontinued in official use in 1988 when the party regrouped with elements of the Social Democratic Party to form the Social and Liberal Democrats, now known as the Liberal Democrats.

lib·er·ate /ˈlibəˌrāt/ ▸*v.* [*trans.*] (often **be liberated**) set (someone) free from a situation, esp. imprisonment or slavery, in which their liberty is severely restricted: *the serfs had been liberated.* ■ free (a country, city, or people) from enemy occupation: *twelve months earlier Paris had been liberated.* ■ release (someone) from a state or situation that limits freedom of thought or behavior: *the use of computers can **liberate** students **from** the constraints of disabilities* | [as *adj.*] (**liberating**) *the arts can have a liberating effect on people.* ■ free (someone) from rigid social conventions, esp. those concerned with accepted sexual roles: *ways of working politically that liberate women.* ■ *informal* steal (something): *the drummer's wearing a beret he's liberated from Lord knows where.* ■ *Chemistry & Physics* release (gas, energy, etc.) as a result of chemical reaction or physical decomposition: *energy liberated by the annihilation of matter.* ▷late 16th cent.: from Latin *liberat-* 'freed,' from the verb *liberare*, from *liber* 'free.' **—lib·er·a·tion** /ˌlibəˈrāSHən/ *n.* **—lib·er·a·tion·ist** /ˌlibəˈrāSHənist/ *n.* **—lib·er·a·tor** /-ˌrātər/ *n.*

lib·er·at·ed /ˈlibəˌrātid/ ▸*adj.* **1** (of a person) showing freedom from social conventions or traditional ideas, esp. with regard to sexual roles: *the modern image of the independent, liberated woman.* **2** (of a place or people) freed from enemy occupation: *liberated areas of the country.*

lib·er·a·tion the·ol·o·gy ▸*n.* a movement in Christian theology, developed mainly by Latin American Roman Catholics, that emphasizes liberation from social, political, and economic oppression as an anticipation of ultimate salvation.

Lib·er·a·tion Ti·gers of Tam·il Ee·lam /ˈtaməl ˈēˌlam/ another name for TAMIL TIGERS.

Li·be·ri·a /līˈbi(ə)rēə/ a country on the Atlantic coast of West Africa; pop. 3,390,000; capital, Monrovia; languages, English (official) and English-based pidgin. ▷from Latin *liber* 'free.' **—Li·be·ri·an** *adj. & n.*

Liberia was founded in 1822 as a settlement for freed slaves from the U.S. and was proclaimed independent in 1847. Indigenous peoples form the majority of the population. In 1980, the predominant Liberian-American elite was overthrown in a coup; a civil war, which ended with a cease-fire in 1996, began in 1990. After years of continuing unrest, a transitional government took control in 2003.

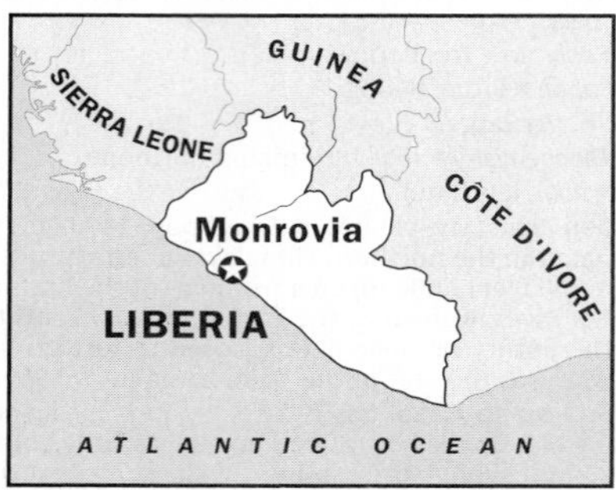

lib·er·tar·i·an /ˌlibərˈte(ə)rēən/ ▸*n.* **1** an adherent of libertarianism: [as *adj.*] *libertarian philosophy.* ■ a person who advocates civil liberty. **2** *Philosophy* a person who believes in the doctrine of free will. ▷late 18th cent. (sense 2): from LIBERTY, on the pattern of words such as *unitarian*.

lib·er·tar·i·an·ism /ˌlibərˈte(ə)rēəˌnizəm/ ▸*n.* an extreme laissez-faire political philosophy advocating only minimal state intervention in the lives of citizens.

The adherents of libertarianism believe that private morality is not the state's affair and that therefore activities such as drug use and prostitution, which arguably harm no one but the participants, should not be illegal. Libertarianism shares elements with anarchism, although it is generally associated more with the political right (chiefly in the U.S.). Unlike traditional liberalism, however, libertarianism lacks a concern with social justice.

lib·er·tine /ˈlibərˌtēn/ ▸*n.* **1** a person, esp. a man, who behaves without moral principles or a sense of responsibility, esp. in sexual matters. **2** a person who rejects accepted opinions in matters of religion; a freethinker.
▸*adj.* **1** characterized by a disregard of morality, esp. in sexual matters: *his more libertine impulses.* **2** freethinking in matters of religion. ▷late Middle English (denoting a freed slave or the son of one): from Latin *libertinus* 'freedman,' from *liber* 'free.' In the mid 16th cent., imitating French *libertin*, the term denoted a member of any of various antinomian sects in France; hence sense 2. **—lib·er·tin·age** /-ˌtēnij/ *n.* **—lib·er·tin·ism** /-ˌnizəm/ *n.*

Lib·er·ty, Statue of see STATUE OF LIBERTY.

lib·er·ty /ˈlibərtē/ ▸*n.* (*pl.* **-ties**) **1** the state of being free within society from oppressive restrictions imposed by authority on one's way of life, behavior, or political views: *compulsory retirement would interfere with individual liberty.* ■ (usu. **liberties**) an instance of this; a right or privilege, esp. a statutory one: *the Bill of Rights was intended to secure basic civil liberties.* ■ the state of not being imprisoned or enslaved: *people who have lost property or liberty without due process.* ■ (**Liberty**) the personification of liberty as a female figure. **2** the power or scope to act as one pleases: *individuals should enjoy the liberty to pursue their own interests and preferences.* ■ *Philosophy* a person's freedom from control by fate or necessity. ■ *informal* a presumptuous remark or action: *how did he know what she was thinking?—it was a liberty!* ■ *Nautical* shore leave granted to a sailor. ▷late Middle English: from Old French *liberte*, from Latin *libertas*, from *liber* 'free.'
▸*PHRASES* □ **at liberty 1** not imprisoned: *he was at liberty for three months before he was recaptured.* **2** allowed or entitled to do something: *competent adults are generally **at liberty to** refuse medical treatment.* □ **take liberties 1** behave in an unduly familiar manner toward a person: *you've **taken** too many **liberties with** me.* **2** treat something freely, without strict faithfulness to the facts or to an original: *the scriptwriter has **taken** few **liberties with** the original narrative.* □ **take the liberty** venture to do something without first asking permission: *I have **taken the liberty of** submitting an idea to several of their research departments.*

THE RIGHT WORD **freedom, independence, liberty, license, permission**

The Fourth of July is the day on which Americans commemorate their nation's **independence**, a word that implies the ability to stand alone, without being sustained by anything else.

While *independence* is usually associated with countries or nations, **freedom** and **liberty** more often apply to people. But unlike *freedom*, which implies an absence of restraint or compulsion (*the freedom to speak openly*), *liberty* implies the power to choose among alternatives rather than merely being unrestrained (*the liberty to select their own form of government*). *Freedom* can also apply to many different types of oppressive influences (*freedom from interruption; freedom to leave the room at any time*), while *liberty* often connotes deliverance or release (*he gave the slaves their liberty*).

License may imply the *liberty* to disobey rules or regulations imposed on others, especially when there is an advantage to be gained in doing so (*poetic license*). But more often it refers to an abuse of *liberty* or the power to do whatever one pleases (*a license to sell drugs*).

Permission is an even broader term than *license*, suggesting the capacity to act without interference or censure, usually with some degree of approval or authority (*permission to be absent from his post*).

Lib·er·ty Bell ▸*n.* a bell in Philadelphia first rung on July 8, 1776, to celebrate the first public reading of the Declaration of Independence. It bears the legend "Proclaim liberty throughout all the land unto all the inhabitants thereof" (Leviticus 25:10).

Liberty Bell

lib·er·ty cap ▸*n.* **1** a common small European toadstool that has a grayish-brown cap with a distinct boss and a long thin stem, containing the hallucinogen psilocybin. See also MAGIC MUSHROOM. • *Psilocybe semilanceata*, family Strophariaceae, class Hymenomycetes. **2** another term for CAP OF LIBERTY.

Lib·er·ty Is·land an island in New York Bay, off Jersey City in New Jersey, site (since 1885) of the Statue of Liberty.

Lib•er•ty ship ▶*n. historical* a prefabricated U.S.-built freighter of World War II.

li•bid•i•nous /lə'bidn-əs/ ▶*adj.* showing excessive sexual drive; lustful. ▷late Middle English: from Latin *libidinosus*, from *libido* 'desire, lust.' —**li•bid•i•nous•ly** *adv.* —**li•bid•i•nous•ness** *n.*

li•bi•do /lə'bēdō/ ▶*n.* (*pl.* **-dos**) sexual desire: *loss of libido | a deficient libido.* ■ *Psychoanalysis* the energy of the sexual drive as a component of the life instinct. ▷early 20th cent.: from Latin, literally 'desire, lust.' —**li•bid•i•nal** /-'bidn-əl/ *adj.* —**li•bid•i•nal•ly** /-'bidn-ələ/ *adv.*

Li Bo /'lē 'bō; 'bô/ variant of **Li Po**.

Li•bra /'lēbrə/ **1** *Astronomy* a small constellation (the Scales or Balance), said to represent the balance that is the symbol of justice. It contains no bright stars. ■ [as *genitive*] (**Librae** /-ˌbrī; -ˌbrē/) used with a preceding letter or numeral to designate a star in this constellation: *the star Alpha Librae.* **2** *Astrology* the seventh sign of the zodiac, which the sun enters at the northern autumnal equinox (about September 23). ■ (**a Libra**) a person born when the sun is in this sign. ▷Latin. —**Li•bran** *n.* & *adj.* (in sense 2).

li•bra /'lēbrə; 'lī-/ ▶*n.* (*pl.* **-brae** /-ˌbrī; -ˌbrē/) (in ancient Rome) a unit of weight, equivalent to 12 ounces (0.34 kg). It was the forerunner of the pound. ▷Latin, 'pound, balance.'

li•brar•i•an /lī'bre(ə)rēən/ ▶*n.* a person, typically with a degree in library science, who administers or assists in a library. ▷late 17th cent. (denoting a scribe or copyist): from Latin *librarius* 'relating to books,' (used as a noun) 'bookseller, scribe,' + **-AN**. —**li•brar•i•an•ship** /-ˌSHip/ *n.*

li•brar•y /'līˌbrerē; -brərē/ ▶*n.* (*pl.* **-brar•ies**) a building or room containing collections of books, periodicals, and sometimes films and recorded music for people to read, borrow, or refer to: *a school library* | [as *adj.*] *a library book.* ■ a collection of books and periodicals held in such a building or room: *the Institute houses an outstanding library of 35,000 volumes on the fine arts.* ■ a collection of films, recorded music, genetic material, etc., organized systematically and kept for research or borrowing: *a record library.* ■ a series of books, recordings, etc., issued by the same company and similar in appearance. ■ a room in a private house where books are kept. ■ (also **software library**) *Computing* a collection of programs and software packages made generally available, often loaded and stored on disk for immediate use. ▷late Middle English: via Old French from Latin *libraria* 'bookshop,' feminine (used as a noun) of *librarius* 'relating to books,' from *liber, libr-* 'book.'

li•brar•y e•di•tion ▶*n.* an edition of a book that is of large size and has good-quality print and binding, esp. the standard edition of a writer's works.

Li•brar•y of Con•gress the U.S. national library, in Washington, DC.

li•brar•y school ▶*n.* a graduate school of a university teaching library science.

li•brar•y sci•ence ▶*n.* the study of collecting, preserving, cataloging, and making available books and other documents in libraries.

li•bra•tion /lī'brāSHən/ ▶*n. Astronomy* an apparent or real oscillation of the moon, by which parts near the edge of the disc that are often not visible from the earth sometimes come into view. ▷early 17th cent. (denoting an oscillating motion, or equilibrium): from Latin *libratio(n-)*, from the verb *librare*, from *libra* 'a balance.' —**li•brate** /'lī,brāt/ *v.*

li•bret•to /lə'bretō/ ▶*n.* (*pl.* **-bret•ti** /-'bretē/ or **-bret•tos**) the text of an opera or other long vocal work. ▷mid 18th cent.: from Italian, diminutive of *libro* 'book,' from Latin *liber*. —**li•bret•tist** /-'bretist/ *n.*

Li•bre•ville /'lēbrəˌvil/ the capital of Gabon, a port on the Atlantic coast at the mouth of the Gabon River; pop. 352,000.

Lib•ri•um /'librēəm/ ▶*n.* trademark for **CHLORDIAZEPOXIDE**. ▷1960s: of unknown origin.

Lib•ya /'libēə/ a country in North Africa; in the Sahara Desert, with a coastline on the Mediterranean Sea; pop. 5,631,000; capital, Tripoli; official language, Arabic. ■ ancient northern Africa that lies west of Egypt. —**Lib•y•an** *adj.* & *n.*

The area came under Turkish domination in the 16th century, was annexed by Italy in 1912, and became an independent kingdom in 1951. The monarchy was overthrown in 1969, and the country emerged with a radical revolutionary leadership. In 2003 government announced it would cease its program to develop weapons of mass destruction. Libya has major oil deposits.

Lib•yan Des•ert the name for the northeastern Sahara Desert, west of the Nile in Egypt, Libya, and northwestern Sudan. In Egypt, it is also called the Western Desert.

lice /līs/ ▶ plural form of **LOUSE**.

li•cense /'līsəns/ ▶*n.* (*Brit.* **li•cence**) a permit from an authority to own or use something, do a particular thing, or carry on a trade (esp. in alcoholic beverages): *a gun license* | [as *adj.*] *vehicle license fees.* ■ formal or official permission to do something: *logging is permitted under license from the Forest Service.* ■ a writer's or artist's freedom to deviate from fact or from conventions such as grammar, meter, or perspective, for effect: *artistic license.* ■ freedom to behave as one wishes, esp. in a way that results in excessive or unacceptable behavior: *the government was criticized for giving the army too much license.* See note at **LIBERTY**. ■ (**a license to do something**) a reason or excuse to do something wrong or excessive: *police say that the lenient sentence is a license to assault.*
▶*v.* (*Brit.* also **li•cence**) [*trans.*] (often **be licensed**) grant a license to (someone or something) to permit the use of something or to allow an activity to take place: *brokers must be licensed to sell health-related insurance* | [*trans.*] *he ought not to have been licensed to fly a plane* | [as *adj.*] (**licensing**) *a licensing authority.* ■ authorize the use, performance, or release of (something): *the drug is already licensed for human use* | *he was required to delete certain scenes before the film could be licensed for showing.* ■ *dated* give permission to (someone) to do something: [*trans.*] *he was licensed to do no more than send a message.* ▷late Middle English: via Old French from Latin *licentia* 'freedom, licentiousness' (in medieval Latin 'authority, permission'), from *licere* 'be lawful or permitted.' —**li•cens•a•ble** *adj.* —**li•cens•er** *n.* —**li•cen•sor** /-sər; ˌlīsən'sôr/ *n.*
▶*PHRASE* □ **license to print money** a very lucrative commercial activity, typically one perceived as requiring little effort.

li•censed /'līsənst/ ▶*adj.* having an official license: *a licensed taxi operator.*

li•cen•see /ˌlīsən'sē/ ▶*n.* the holder of a license.

li•cense plate ▶*n.* a sign affixed to a vehicle displaying a series of letters or numbers indicating that the vehicle has been registered with the state.

li•cen•sure 'līsənSHər; -ˌSHŏŏr ▶*n.* the granting or regulation of licenses, as for professionals: *licensure for respiratory therapists.* ▷mid 19th cent.: from **LICENSE** + **-URE**.

li•cen•ti•ate /lī'sensH(ē)it/ ▶*n.* the holder of a certificate of competence to practice a certain profession. ■ (in certain universities, esp. in Europe) a degree between that of bachelor and master or doctor. ■ the holder of such a degree. ▷late 15th cent.: from medieval Latin, noun use of *licentiatus* 'having freedom,' based on *licentia* 'freedom.' —**li•cen•ti•ate•ship** /-ˌSHip/ *n.*

li•cen•tious /lī'sensHəs/ ▶*adj.* **1** promiscuous and unprincipled in sexual matters. **2** *archaic* disregarding accepted rules or conventions, esp. in grammar or literary style. ▷late Middle English: from Latin *licentiosus*, from *licentia* 'freedom.' —**li•cen•tious•ly** *adv.* —**li•cen•tious•ness** *n.*

li•chee ▶*n.* variant spelling of **LITCHI**.

li•chen /'līkən/ ▶*n.* **1** a simple slow-growing plant that typically forms a low crustlike, leaflike, or branching growth on rocks, walls, and trees.

Lichens are composite plants consisting of a fungus that contains photosynthetic algal cells. Their classification is based upon that of the fungal partner, which in most cases belongs to the subdivision Ascomycotina, and the algal partners are either green algae or cyanobacteria. Lichens obtain their water and nutrients from the atmosphere and can be sensitive indicators of atmospheric pollution.

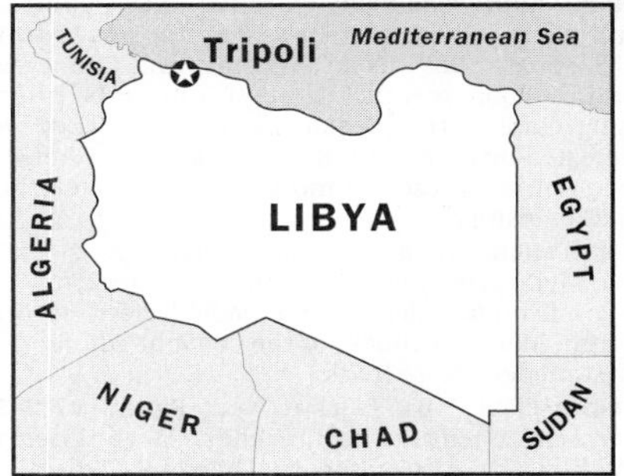

2 [usu. with *adj.*] a skin disease in which small pimples or bumps occur close together. ▷early 17th cent.: via Latin from Greek *leikhēn*. —**li•chened** *adj.* (in sense 1) —**li•chen•ol•o•gy** /ˌlīkə'näləjē/ *n.* (in sense 1) —**li•chen•ous** /-nəs/ *adj.* (in sense 2).

licht /liKHt/ ▶*n., adj.* & *v.* Scottish variant of **LIGHT**[1], **LIGHT**[2].

Lich•ten•stein /'liktənˌstēn/, Roy (1923–97), U.S. painter and sculptor. A leading exponent of pop art, he became known for paintings inspired by comic strips. Notable works: *Whaam!* (1963) and *Big Painting VI* (1965).

lic•it /'lisit/ ▶*adj.* not forbidden; lawful: *licit and illicit drugs.* ▷late 15th cent.: from Latin *licitus* 'allowed,' from the verb *licere*. —**lic•it•ly** *adv.*

lick /lik/ ▶*v.* [*trans.*] **1** pass the tongue over (something), typically in order to taste, moisten, or clean it: *he licked the stamp and stuck it on the envelope* | [*intrans.*] *he* **licked at** *his damaged hand with his tongue.* ■ [*intrans.*] *figurative* (of a flame, wave, or breeze) move lightly and quickly like a tongue: *the flames licked around the wood.* **2** *informal* defeat (someone) comprehensively: *all right Mary, I know when I'm licked.* ■ thrash: *she stands tall and could lick any man in the place.*
▶*n.* **1** an act of licking something with the tongue: *Sammy gave his fingers a long lick.* ■ *figurative* a movement of flame, water, etc., resembling this. **2** *informal* a small amount or quick application of something, esp. paint: *all she'd need to do to the kitchen was give it* **a lick of paint**. **3** (often **licks**) *informal* a short phrase or solo in jazz or popular music: *cool guitar licks.* **4** *informal* a smart blow: *his mother gave him several licks for daring to blaspheme.* ▷Old English *liccian*; related to Dutch *likken* and German *lecken*, from an Indo-European root shared by Greek *leikhein* and Latin *lingere*. —**lick•er** *n.* [usu. in *combination*] .
▶*PHRASES* □ **at a lick** *informal* at a fast pace; with considerable speed. □ **a lick and a promise** *informal* a hasty performance of a task, esp. of cleaning something. □ **lick someone's boots** (or *vulgar slang* **ass**) be excessively obsequious toward someone, esp. to gain favor from them. □ **lick someone/something into shape** see **SHAPE**. □ **lick one's lips** (or **chops**) look forward to something with eager anticipation. □ **lick one's wounds** retire to recover one's strength or confidence after a defeat or humiliating experience: *the political organization he worked for was licking its wounds after electoral defeat.*

lick•er•ish /'lik(ə)riSH/ ▶*adj.* lecherous: *a barrage of lickerish grins and dirty jokes.* ▷late 15th cent.: alteration of obsolete *lickerous*, in the same sense, from an Anglo-Norman French variant of Old French *lecheros* (see **LECHEROUS**). —**lick•er•ish•ly** *adv.*

lick•e•ty-split /'likətē 'split/ ▶*adv. informal* as quickly as possible; immediately: *I took off lickety-split across the lawn.* ▷early 19th cent. (in the phrase *as fast as lickety* 'at full speed'): from a fanciful extension of **LICK** + the verb **SPLIT**.

lick•ing /'likiNG/ ▶*n. informal* a severe defeat or beating.

lick•spit•tle /'likˌspitl/ ▶*n.* a person who behaves obsequiously to those in power.

lic•o•rice /'lik(ə)riSH; -ris/ (*Brit.* **liq•uo•rice**) ▶*n.* **1** a sweet, chewy, aromatic black substance made by evaporation from the juice of a root and used as a candy and in medicine. ■ a candy flavored with such a substance: [as *adj.*] *licorice gumdrops.* **2** the widely distributed plant of the pea family from which this product is obtained. • Genus *Glycyrrhiza*, family Leguminosae; many species are used locally to obtain licorice, the chief commercial source being the cultivated *G. glabra*. ▷Middle English: from Old French *licoresse*, from late Latin *liquiritia*, from Greek *glukurrhiza*, from *glukus* 'sweet' + *rhiza* 'root.'

lic•o•rice stick ▶*n.* a stick of licorice candy. ■ *dated, informal* a clarinet.

lic•tor /'liktər/ ▶*n.* (in ancient Rome) an officer attending the consul or other magistrate, bearing the fasces, and executing sentences on offenders. ▷Latin, perhaps related to *ligare* 'to bind.'

lid /lid/ ▶*n.* a removable or hinged cover for the top of a container: *a large frying pan with a lid* | *a garbage can lid.* ■ (usu. **lids**) an eyelid: *eyes now hooded beneath heavy lids.* ■ *Botany* the operculum of a moss capsule. ■ *informal* a hat. ▷Old English *hlid*, of Germanic origin, from a base meaning 'cover'; related to Dutch *lid*. —**lid•ded** *adj.* —**lid•less** *adj.*

Pronunciation Key ə *ago*; ər *over*; 'ə *or* ˌə *up*; 'ər *or* ˌər *fur*; a *hat*; ā *rate*; ä *car*; CH *chew*; e *let*; ē *see*; e(ə)r *air*; i *fit*; ī *by*; i(ə)r *ear*; NG *sing*; ō *go*; ô *for*; oi *boy*; ŏŏ *good*; ōō *goo*; ou *out*; SH *she*; TH *thin*; T͟H *then*; (h)w *why*; ZH *vision*

L

▸*PHRASES* □ **blow** (or **take**) **the lid off** *informal* reveal unwelcome secrets about: *prosecutors have taken the lid off a multimillion-dollar payoff scandal.* □ **keep a** (or **the**) **lid on** *informal* keep (an emotion or process) from going out of control: *she was no longer able to keep the lid on her simmering anger.* ■ keep secret: *she keeps a very tight lid on her own private life.* □ **put a** (or **the**) **lid on** *informal* put a stop to or be the culmination of: *it's time to put the lid on all the talk.*

li·dar /ˈlīdär/ ▸*n.* a detection system that works on the principle of radar, but uses light from a laser. ▷1960s: blend of LIGHT[1] and RADAR.

Lid·dell /ˈlidl; liˈdel/, Eric (Henry) (1902–45), British runner and missionary, born in China. In the 1924 Olympic Games, he won the 400 meters in world record time. His exploits were celebrated in the movie *Chariots of Fire* (1981).

Li·do /ˈlēdō/ an island reef off the coast of northeastern Italy, in the northern Adriatic. It separates the Lagoon of Venice from the Gulf of Venice. Full name **LIDO DI MALAMOCCO** .

li·do /ˈlēdō/ ▸*n.* (*pl.* **li·dos**) a public, open-air swimming pool or beach. ▷late 17th cent.: from Italian *Lido,* the name of a beach near Venice, from *lido* 'shore,' from Latin *litus.*

li·do·caine /ˈlīdəˌkān/ ▸*n.* *Medicine* a synthetic compound used as a local anesthetic, e.g., for dental surgery, and in treating abnormal heart rhythms. • An aromatic amide; chem. formula: $C_{14}H_{22}N_2O$. ▷1940s: from *(acetani)lid(e)* + *-caine* (from COCAINE).

Lie /lē/, Trygve Halvdan (1896–1968), Norwegian politician; first secretary-general of the UN 1946–53.

lie[1] /lī/ ▸*v.* (**ly·ing** /ˈlī-iNG/; *past* **lay** /lā/; *past part.* **lain** /lān/) [*intrans.*] **1** (of a person or animal) be in or assume a horizontal or resting position on a supporting surface: *the man lay face downward on the grass | I had to* **lie down** *for two hours because I was groggy | Lily lay back on the pillows and watched him.* ■ (of a thing) rest flat on a surface: *a book lay open on the table.* ■ (of a dead person) be buried in a particular place. **2** be, remain, or be kept in a specified state: *the church lies in ruins today | putting homeless families into apartments that would otherwise lie empty.* ■ (of something abstract) reside or be found: *the solution lies in a return to "traditional family values."* **3** (of a place) be situated in a specified position or direction: *the small town of Swampscott lies about ten miles north of Boston.* ■ (of a scene) extend from the observer's viewpoint in a specified direction: *stand here, and all of Amsterdam lies before you.* **4** *Law* (of an action, charge, or claim) be admissible or sustainable.

▸*phrasal v.* □ **lie ahead** be going to happen; be in store: *I'm excited by what lies ahead.* □ **lie around/about** (of an object) be left carelessly out of place: *there were pills and potions lying around in every corner of the house.* ■ (of a person) pass the time lazily or aimlessly: *you all just lay around all day on your backsides, didn't you?* □ **lie behind** be the real, often hidden, reason for (something): *a subtle strategy lies behind such silly claims.* □ **lie in** *Brit.* remain in bed after the normal time for getting up. ■ *archaic* (of a pregnant woman) go to bed to give birth. □ **lie off** *Nautical* (of a ship) stand some distance from shore or from another ship. □ **lie to** *Nautical* (of a ship) come almost to a stop with its head toward the wind. □ **lie with 1** (of a responsibility or problem) be attributable to (someone): *the ultimate responsibility for the violence lies with the country's president.* **2** *archaic* have sexual intercourse with.

▸*n.* (usu. **the lie**) the way, direction, or position in which something lies. ■ *Golf* the position in which a golf ball comes to rest, esp. as regards the ease of the next shot. ■ the lair or place of cover of an animal or a bird. ▷Old English *licgan,* of Germanic origin; related to Dutch *liggen* and German *liegen,* from an Indo-European root shared by Greek *lektron, lekhos* and Latin *lectus* 'bed.'

▸*PHRASES* □ **let something lie** take no action regarding a controversial or problematic matter. □ **lie heavy on one** cause one to feel troubled or uncomfortable. □ **lie in state** (of the corpse of a person of national importance) be laid in a public place of honor before burial. □ **lie in wait** conceal oneself, waiting to surprise, attack, or catch someone. □ **lie low** (esp. of a criminal) keep out of sight; avoid detection or attention: *at the time of the murder, he appears to have been lying low in a barn.* □ **take something lying down** [usu. with *negative*] accept an insult, setback, rebuke, etc., without reacting or protesting.

USAGE The verb **lie** ('assume a horizontal or resting position') is often confused with the verb **lay** ('put something down'), giving rise to incorrect uses such as *he is* **laying** *on the bed* (correct use is *he is* **lying** *on the bed*) or *why don't you* **lie** *the suitcase on the bed?* (correct use is *why don't you* **lay** *the suitcase on the bed?*). The confusion is only heightened by the fact that **lay** is not only the base form of **to lay**, but is also the past tense of **to lie**, so while *he is* **laying** *on the bed* is incorrect, *he* **lay** *on the bed yesterday* is quite correct.

For more discussion of these **lie** and **lay** verb forms, see **usage** at LAY[1].

lie[2] ▸*n.* an intentionally false statement: *Mungo felt a pang of shame at* **telling** *Alice* **a lie** *| the whole thing is* **a pack of lies.** ■ used with reference to a situation involving deception or founded on a mistaken impression: *all their married life she had been* **living a lie.**

▸*v.* (**lies, lied, ly·ing** /ˈlī-iNG/) [*intrans.*] tell a lie or lies: *why had Wesley lied about his visit to Philadelphia? |* [with *direct speech*] *"I am sixty-five," she lied.* ■ (**lie one's way into/out of**) get oneself into or out of a situation by lying: *you lied your way on to this voyage by implying you were an experienced sailor.* ■ (of a thing) present a false impression; be deceptive: *the camera cannot lie.* ▷Old English *lyge* (noun), *lēogan* (verb), of Germanic origin; related to Dutch *liegen* and German *lügen.*

▸*PHRASES* □ **give the lie to** serve to show that (something seemingly apparent or previously stated or believed) is not true: *these figures give the lie to the notion that Britain is excessively strike-ridden.* □ **I tell a lie** (or **that's a lie**) *informal* an expression used to correct oneself immediately when one realizes that one has made an incorrect remark: *I never used to dream—I tell a lie, I did dream when I was little.* □ **lie through one's teeth** *informal* tell an outright lie without remorse.

THE RIGHT WORD **equivocate, fabricate, fib, lie, prevaricate, rationalize**

If your spouse asks you whether you remembered to mail the tax forms and you say "Yes," even though you know they're still sitting on the passenger seat of your car, you're telling a **lie**, which is a deliberately false statement.

If you launch into a lengthy explanation of the day's frustrations and setbacks, the correct word would be **prevaricate**, which is to quibble, dodge the point, or confuse the issue so as to avoid telling the truth.

If you tell your spouse that you would have mailed the taxes, but then you started thinking about an important deduction you might be entitled to take and decided it would be unwise to mail them without looking into it, you're **rationalizing**, which is to come up with reasons that put your own behavior in the most favorable possible light.

If you say that there was an accident in front of the post office that prevented you from finding a parking space and there really wasn't, **fabricate** is the correct verb, meaning that you've invented a false story or excuse without the harsh connotations of *lie* (*she fabricated an elaborate story about how they got lost on their way home*).

Equivocate implies saying one thing and meaning another; it usually suggests the use of words that have more than one meaning, or whose ambiguity may be misleading. For example, if your spouse says, "Did you take care of the taxes today?" you might equivocate by saying "Yes," you took care of them—meaning that you finished completing the forms and sealing them in the envelope, but that you didn't actually get them to the post office.

To **fib** is to tell a falsehood about something unimportant; it is often used as a euphemism for *lie* (*a child who fibs about eating his vegetables*).

Lieb·chen /ˈlēbCHən; ˈlēp-; -SHən; -KHən/ ▸*n.* a person who is very dear to another (often used as a term of endearment). ▷German, diminutive of *lieb* 'dear.'

Lie·ber·man /ˈlēbərmən/, Joe (1942–) U.S. politician; full name *Joseph Isador Lieberman.* He served in the U.S. Senate 1989– as a Democrat from Connecticut and, in 2000, was picked by Al Gore to be his running mate in the presidential election. They were defeated by George W. Bush and Richard Cheney in one of the closest and most controversial elections in U.S. history.

Lieb·frau·milch /ˈlēbˌfrouˌmilCH; ˈlēp-; -ˌmilk; -ˌmilKH/ ▸*n.* a light white wine from the Rhine region. ▷German, from *lieb* 'dear' + *Frau* 'lady' (referring to the Virgin Mary, patroness of the convent where it was first made) + *Milch* 'milk.'

Lie·big /ˈlēbig; -biKH/, Justus von, Baron (1803–73), German chemist and teacher. With Friedrich Wöhler, he discovered the benzoyl radical and demonstrated that such radicals were groups of atoms that remained unchanged in many chemical reactions.

Liech·ten·stein /ˈliktənˌstīn; -ˌSHtīn/ a small independent principality in the Alps, between Switzerland and Austria; pop. 33,400; capital, Vaduz; official language, German. —**Lich·ten·stein·er** *n.*

The principality was created in 1719 within the Holy Roman Empire and became independent of the German confederation in 1866. Liechtenstein is economically integrated with Switzerland.

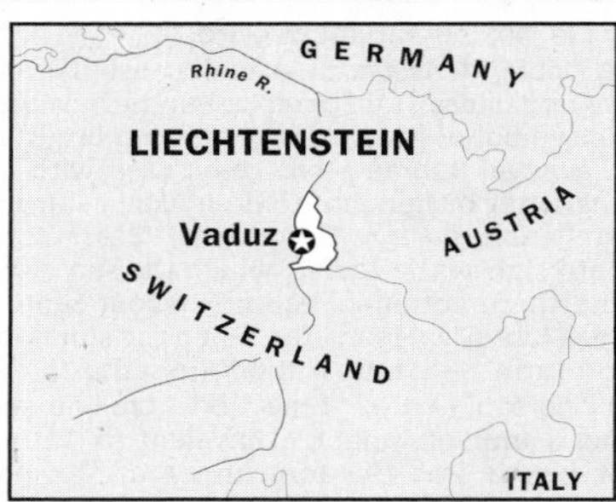

lied /lēd; lēt/ ▸*n.* (*pl.* **lie·der** /ˈlēdər/) a type of German song, esp. of the Romantic period, typically for solo voice with piano accompaniment. ▷from German *Lied.*

lie de·tec·tor ▸*n.* an instrument for determining whether a person is telling the truth by testing for physiological changes considered to be associated with lying. Compare with POLYGRAPH.

lief /lēf/ ▸*adv.* (**as lief**) *archaic* as happily; as gladly: *he would just as lief eat a pincushion.* ▷Old English *lēof* 'dear, pleasant,' of Germanic origin: related to LEAVE[2] and LOVE.

Liège /lēˈezH/ a province of eastern Belgium. Formerly ruled by independent prince-bishops, it became a part of the Netherlands in 1815 and of Belgium in 1830. Flemish name **LUIK.** ■ its capital city, situated at the junction of the Meuse and Ourthe rivers; pop. 195,000.

liege /lēj; lēzH/ *historical* ▸*adj.* [*attrib.*] concerned with or relating to the relationship between a feudal superior and a vassal: *an oath of fealty and* **liege homage.** ▸*n.* (also **liege lord**) a feudal superior or sovereign. ■ a vassal or subject: *the king's lieges.* ▷Middle English: via Old French *lige, liege* from medieval Latin *laeticus,* probably of Germanic origin.

liege·man /ˈlējˌman; -mən/ ▸*n.* (*pl.* **-men**) *historical* a vassal who owes feudal service or allegiance to a nobleman.

lien /ˈlē(ə)n/ ▸*n.* *Law* a right to keep possession of property belonging to another person until a debt owed by that person is discharged. ▷mid 16th cent.: from French, via Old French *loien* from Latin *ligamen* 'bond,' from *ligare* 'to bind.'

li·erne /lēˈərn/ ▸*n.* [usu. as *adj.*] *Architecture* (in vaulting) a short rib connecting the bosses and intersections of the principal ribs: *a fine lierne vault.* ▷late Middle English: from French, perhaps a transferred use of dialect *lierne* (standard French *liane*) 'clematis.'

lieu /lo͞o/ ▸*n.* (in phrase **in lieu**) instead: *the company issued additional shares to shareholders* **in lieu of** *a cash dividend.* ▷Middle English: via French from Latin *locus* 'place.'

Lieut. ▸*abbr.* lieutenant.

lieu·ten·ant /lo͞oˈtenənt/ ▸*n.* a deputy or substitute acting for a superior: *two of Lenin's leading lieutenants.* ■ see FIRST LIEUTENANT, SECOND LIEUTENANT. ■ a naval officer of a high rank, in particular a commissioned officer in the U.S. Navy or Coast Guard ranking above lieutenant junior grade and below lieutenant commander. ■ a police or fire department officer next in rank below captain. ▷late Middle English: from French (see LIEU, TENANT). —**lieu·ten·an·cy** /-ˈtenənsē/ *n.* (*pl.* **-cies**).

USAGE In the normal British pronunciation of **lieutenant**, the first syllable sounds like **lef**. In the standard U.S. pronunciation, the first syllable, in contrast, sounds like **loo**. It is difficult to explain where the **f** in the British pronunciation comes from. Probably, at some point before the 19th century, the **u** at the end of Old French **lieu** was read and pronounced as a **v**, and the **v** later became an **f**.

lieu·ten·ant col·o·nel ▸*n.* a commissioned officer in the U.S. Army, Air Force, or Marine Corps ranking above major and below colonel.

lieu·ten·ant com·man·der ▸*n.* a commissioned officer in the U.S. Navy or Coast Guard ranking above lieutenant and below commander.

lieu·ten·ant gen·er·al ▸*n.* a commissioned officer in the U.S. Army, Air Force, or Marine Corps ranking above major general and below general.

lieu·ten·ant gov·er·nor ▸*n.* the executive officer of a state who is next in rank to a governor and who takes the governor's place in case of disability or death. ■ the executive officer of a Canadian province, appointed by the governor general. **—lieu·ten·ant gov·er·nor·ship** *n.*

lieu·ten·ant jun·ior grade ▸*n.* a commissioned officer in the U.S. Navy or Coast Guard ranking above ensign and below lieutenant.

life /līf/ ▸*n.* (*pl.* **lives** /līvz/) **1** the condition that distinguishes animals and plants from inorganic matter, including the capacity for growth, reproduction, functional activity, and continual change preceding death: *the origins of life.* ■ living things and their activity: *some sort of life existed on Mars | lower forms of life | the ice-cream vendors were the only signs of life.* ■ the state of being alive as a human being: *she didn't want to die; she loved life | a superficial world where life revolved around the minutiae of outward appearance.* ■ [with *adj.*] a particular type or aspect of people's existence: *an experienced teacher will help you settle into school life | revelations about his private life.* ■ vitality, vigor, or energy: *she was beautiful and full of life.* **2** the existence of an individual human being or animal: *a disaster that claimed the lives of 266 Americans.* ■ [often with *adj.*] a way of living: *his father decided to start a new life in California.* ■ a biography: *a life of Shelley.* ■ either of the two states of a person's existence separated by death (as in Christianity and some other religious traditions): *too much happiness in this life could reduce the chances of salvation in the next.* ■ any of a number of successive existences in which a soul is held to be reincarnated (as in Hinduism and some other religious traditions). ■ a chance to live after narrowly escaping death (esp. with reference to the nine lives traditionally attributed to cats). **3** (usu. **one's life**) the period between the birth and death of a living thing, esp. a human being: *she has lived all her life in the country | I want to be with you for the rest of my life | they became friends* **for life**. ■ the period during which something inanimate or abstract continues to exist, function, or be valid: *underlay helps to prolong the life of a carpet.* ■ *informal* a sentence of imprisonment for life. **4** (in art) the depiction of a subject from a real model, rather than from an artist's imagination: *the pose and clothing were sketched* **from life** | [as *adj.*] *life drawing.* See also STILL LIFE. ▷Old English *līf*, of Germanic origin; related to Dutch *lijf*, German *Leib* 'body,' also to LIVE[1].

▸*PHRASES* □ **bring** (or **come**) **to life** regain or cause to regain consciousness or return as if from death: *all this was of great interest to her, as if she were coming to life after a long sleep.* ■ (with reference to a fictional character or inanimate object) cause or seem to be alive or real: *he brings the character of MacDonald to life with power and precision | all the puppets came to life again.* ■ make or become active, lively, or interesting: *soon, with the return of the peasants and fishermen, the village comes to life again | you can bring any room to life with these coordinating cushions.* □ **do anything for a quiet life** make any concession to avoid being disturbed. □ **for dear** (or **one's**) **life** as if or in order to escape death: *I clung to the tree for dear life | Sue struggled free and ran for her life.* □ **for the life of me** *informal* however hard I try; even if my life depended on it: *I can't for the life of me understand what it is you see in that place.* □ **frighten the life out of** terrify. □ **get a life** [often in *imperative*] *informal* start living a fuller or more interesting existence: *if he's a lout, then get yourself out of there and get a life.* □ **give one's life for** die for. □ (**as**) **large as life** *informal* used to emphasize that a person is conspicuously present: *he was standing nearby, large as life.* □ **larger than life** (of a person) attracting special attention because of unusual and flamboyant appearance or behavior. ■ (of a thing) seeming disproportionately important: *your problems seem larger than life at that time of night.* □ **life and limb** see LIMB[1]. □ **the life of the party** a vivacious and sociable person. □ **life in the fast lane** *informal* an exciting and eventful lifestyle, esp. one bringing wealth and success. □ **one's life's work** the work (esp. that of an academic or artistic nature) accomplished in or pursued throughout someone's lifetime. □ **lose one's life** be killed: *he lost his life in a car accident.* □ **a matter of life and death** a matter of vital importance. □ **not on your life** *informal* said to emphasize one's refusal to comply with a request: *"I want to see Clare alone." "Not on your life," said Buzz.* □ **save someone's** (or **one's own**) **life** prevent someone's (or one's own) death: *the driver of the truck managed to save his life by leaping out of the cab.* ■ *informal* provide much-needed relief from boredom or a difficult situation. □ **see life** gain a wide experience of the world, esp. its more pleasurable aspects. □ **take one's life in one's hands** risk being killed. □ **take someone's** (or **one's own**) **life** kill someone (or oneself). □ **that's life** an expression of one's acceptance of a situation, however difficult: *we'll miss each other, but still, that's life.* □ **this is the life** an expression of contentment with one's present circumstances: *Ice cubes clinked in crystal glasses. "This is the life," she said.* □ **to the life** exactly like the original: *there he was, Nathan to the life, sitting at a table.* □ **to save one's life** [with *modal* and *negative*] even if one's life were to depend on it: *she couldn't stop crying now to save her life.*

life-and-death ▸*adj.* deciding whether someone lives or dies; vitally important: *life-and-death decisions.*

life·belt /ˈlīfˌbelt/ ▸*n.* a life preserver in the shape of a belt.

life·blood /ˈlīfˌbləd/ ▸*n.* the blood, as being necessary to life. ■ *figurative* the indispensable factor or influence that gives something its strength and vitality: *my family was the lifeblood of the church.*

life·boat /ˈlīfˌbōt/ ▸*n.* a specially constructed boat launched from land to rescue people in distress at sea. ■ a small boat kept on a ship for use in emergency, typically one of a number on deck or suspended from davits. **—life·boat·man** /-mən/ *n.* (*pl.* **-men**).

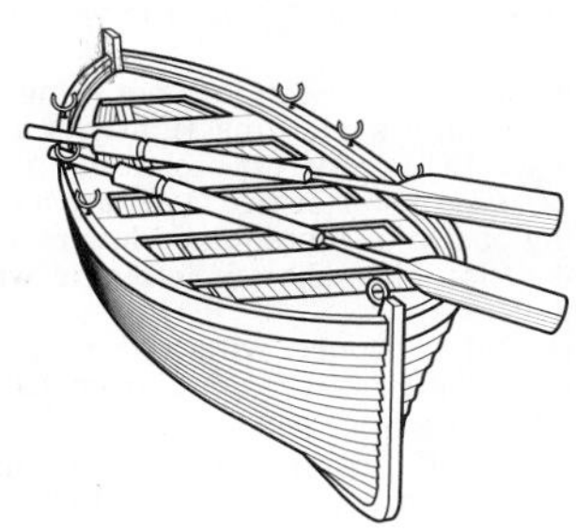

lifeboat

life·bu·oy /ˈlīfˌbo͞o-ē; -ˌboi/ ▸*n.* a life preserver, esp. one in the shape of a ring.

life coach /ˈlīf ˌkōch/ ▸*n.* a person who counsels and encourages clients on matters having to do with careers or personal challenges. **—life coach·ing** *n.*

life cy·cle ▸*n.* the series of changes in the life of an organism, including reproduction.

life ex·pec·tan·cy ▸*n.* the average period that a person may expect to live.

life force ▸*n.* the force or influence that gives something its vitality or strength: *the passionate life force of the symphony.* ■ the spirit or energy that animates living creatures; the soul.

life form ▸*n.* any living thing.

life-giv·ing ▸*adj.* sustaining or revitalizing life: *the life-giving water of baptism.*

life·guard /ˈlīfˌgärd/ ▸*n.* an expert swimmer employed to rescue bathers who get into difficulty in a swimming pool or at a beach.
▸*v.* [*intrans.*] work as a lifeguard.

Life Guards ▸*plural n.* (in the UK) a regiment of the Household Cavalry.

life his·to·ry ▸*n.* the series of changes undergone by an organism during its lifetime. ■ the story of a person's life, esp. when told at tedious length.

life in·stinct ▸*n.* *Psychoanalysis* an innate desire for self-preservation, manifest in hunger, self-defensive aggression, and the sexual instincts. Compare with DEATH INSTINCT.

life in·sur·ance ▸*n.* insurance that pays out a sum of money either on the death of the insured person or after a set period.

life in·ter·est ▸*n.* *Law* a right to property that a person holds for life but cannot dispose of further.

life jack·et ▸*n.* a sleeveless buoyant or inflatable jacket for keeping a person afloat in water.

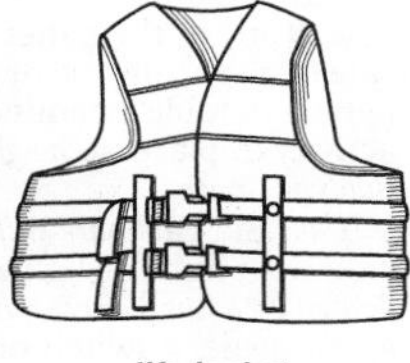

life jacket

life·less /ˈlīflis/ ▸*adj.* dead or apparently dead: *his lifeless body was taken from the river.* ■ lacking vigor, vitality, or excitement: *my hair always seems to look lifeless.* ■ devoid of living things: *the moon is lifeless.* ▷Old English *līflēas* (see LIFE, -LESS). **—life·less·ly** *adv.* **—life·less·ness** *n.*

life·like /ˈlīfˌlīk/ ▸*adj.* very similar to the person or thing represented: *the artist had etched a lifelike horse.* **—life·like·ness** *n.*

life·line /ˈlīfˌlīn/ ▸*n.* **1** a rope or line used for life-saving, typically one thrown to rescue someone in difficulties in water or one used by sailors to secure themselves to a boat. ■ a line used by a diver for sending signals to the surface. ■ *figurative* a thing that is essential for the continued existence of someone or something or that provides a means of escape from a difficult situation: *fertility treatment can seem like a lifeline to childless couples.* **2** (in palmistry) a line on the palm of a person's hand, regarded as indicating how long they will live.

▸*PHRASE* □ **throw a lifeline to** (or **throw someone a lifeline**) provide (someone) with a means of escaping from a difficult situation.

life list ▸*n.* *Ornithology* a list of all the kinds of birds observed by a person during his or her life.

life·long /ˈlīfˌlôNG; -ˌläNG/ ▸*adj.* lasting or remaining in a particular state throughout a person's life: *the two men were to remain lifelong friends | a lifelong conservative.*

life mem·ber ▸*n.* a person who has lifelong membership in a society. **—life mem·ber·ship** *n.*

life peer ▸*n.* (in the UK) a peer whose title cannot be inherited. **—life peer·age** *n.*

life peer·ess ▸*n.* (in the UK) a woman holding a life peerage.

life pre·serv·er ▸*n.* **1** a device made of buoyant or inflatable material, such as a life jacket or lifebelt, to keep someone afloat in water. **2** *Brit.* a short club with a heavily weighted end, used as a weapon; a blackjack.

lif·er /ˈlīfər/ ▸*n.* **1** *informal* a person serving a life sentence in prison. **2** a person who spends their life in a particular career, esp. in one of the armed forces.

life raft ▸*n.* a raft, typically inflatable, for use in an emergency at sea.

life·sav·er /ˈlīfˌsāvər/ ▸*n.* **1** *informal* a thing that saves one from serious difficulty: *a microwave oven could be a lifesaver this Christmas.* **2** a ring-shaped life preserver.

life sci·enc·es ▸*plural n.* the sciences concerned with the study of living organisms, including biology, botany, zoology, microbiology, physiology, biochemistry, and related subjects. Often contrasted with PHYSICAL SCIENCES. **—life sci·en·tist** *n.*

life sen·tence ▸*n.* a punishment for a felon of imprisonment for life.

life-size (also **life-sized**) ▸*adj.* of the same size as the person or thing represented: *a life-size statue of a discus-thrower.*

life·skill /ˈlīfˌskil/ ▸*n.* [often *plural*] a skill that is required to participate in everyday life: *drawing is an essential lifeskill enhancing children's powers of observation.*

life span (also **life·span**) ▸*n.* the length of time for which a person or animal lives or a thing functions: *the human life span.*

life·style /ˈlīfˌstīl/ ▸*n.* the way in which a person or group lives: *the benefits of a healthy lifestyle.* ■ [as *adj.*] denoting advertising or products designed to appeal to a consumer by association with a desirable lifestyle.

life·style drug ▸*n.* a drug used to improve the quality of one's life rather than alleviating pain or curing disease.

This term has been variously applied to drugs used for cosmetic reasons (e.g., for hair replacement), drugs used to enhance one's sex life (e.g., for erectile dysfunction), and drugs used to alleviate medical problems that are in some part attributable to lifestyle choices (e.g., for obesity). Some objections have been raised to the use of this term, as it may trivialize serious health problems.

life sup·port ▸*n.* *Medicine* maintenance of the vital functions of a critically ill or comatose person or a person undergoing surgery: [as *adj.*] *a life-support machine.* ■ *informal* equipment in a hospital used for this: *a patient on life support.*

Pronunciation Key ə *ago*; ər *over*; ˈə or ˌə *up*; ˈər or ˌər *fur*; a *hat*; ā *rate*; ä *car*; CH *chew*; e *let*; ē *see*; e(ə)r *air*; i *fit*; ī *by*; i(ə)r *ear*; NG *sing*; ō *go*; ô *for*; oi *boy*; o͝o *good*; o͞o *goo*; ou *out*; SH *she*; TH *thin*; T͟H *then*; (h)w *why*; ZH *vision*

life ta·ble ▸*n.* a table of statistics relating to life expectancy and mortality for a given category of people. ■ *Zoology* a similar table for a population of animals divided into cohorts of given age.

life·time /ˈlīfˌtīm/ ▸*n.* the duration of a person's life: *a reward for a lifetime's work.* ■ the duration of a thing's existence or usefulness: *a plan to extend the lifetime of satellites.* ■ *informal* used to express the view that a period is very long: *five weeks was a lifetime, and anything could have happened.*

▸*PHRASE* □ **of a lifetime** (of a chance or experience) such as does not occur more than once in a person's life: *because of Frankie she had rejected the opportunity of a lifetime.*

life·work /ˈlīfˈwərk/ ▸*n.* the entire or principal work, labor, or task of a person's lifetime.

life·world /ˈlīfˌwərld/ ▸*n. Philosophy* all the immediate experiences, activities, and contacts that make up the world of an individual or corporate life. ▷1940s: translating German *Lebenswelt.*

Lif·fey /ˈlifē/ a river in eastern Ireland that flows for 50 miles (80 km) from the Wicklow Mountains to Dublin Bay. The city of Dublin is situated at its mouth.

Lif·ford /ˈlifərd/ the county town of Donegal, in the Republic of Ireland; pop. 1,460 (1986).

LIFO /ˈlīfō/ ▸*abbr.* last in, first out (chiefly with reference to methods of stock valuation and data storage). Compare with **FIFO**.

lift /lift/ ▸*v.* [*trans.*] **1** raise to a higher position or level: *he lifted his trophy over his head.* ■ move (one's eyes or face) to face upward and look at someone or something: *he lifted his eyes from the paper for an instant.* ■ increase the volume or pitch of (one's voice): *Willie sang boldly, **lifting up** his voice.* ■ increase (a price or amount): *higher than expected oil prices lifted Oklahoma's revenue.* ■ transport by air: *a helicopter lifted 11 crew members to safety from the ship.* ■ hit or kick (a ball) high into the air. ■ [*intrans.*] move upward; be raised: *Thomas's eyelids drowsily lifted | their voices lifted in wails and cries.* ■ [*intrans.*] (of a cloud, fog, etc.) move upward or away: *the factory smoke hung low, never lifted | the gray weather lifted on the following Wednesday.* ■ perform cosmetic surgery on (esp. the face or breasts) to reduce sagging: *surgeons lift and remove excess skin from the face and neck.* **2** pick up and move to a different position: *he lifted her down from the pony's back.* ■ *figurative* enable (someone or something) to escape from a particular state of mind or situation, esp. an unpleasant one: *two billion barrels of oil that could **lift** this nation **out of** chronic poverty.* **3** raise (a person's spirits or confidence); encourage or cheer: *we heard inspiring talks that lifted our spirits.* ■ [*intrans.*] (of a person's mood) become happier: *suddenly his heart lifted, and he could have wept with relief.* **4** formally remove or end (a legal restriction, decision, or ban): *the European Community lifted its oil embargo against South Africa.* **5** *informal* steal (something, esp. a minor item of property): *the shirt she had lifted from a supermarket.* ■ use (a person's work or ideas) without permission or acknowledgment; plagiarize: *this is a hackneyed adventure lifted straight from a vintage Lassie episode.*

▸*phrasal v.* □ **lift off** (of an aircraft, spacecraft, or rocket) rise from the ground or a launch pad, esp. vertically.

▸*n.* **1** something that is used for lifting, in particular: ■ British term for **ELEVATOR**. ■ a device incorporating a moving cable for carrying people, typically skiers, up or down a mountain. ■ a built-up heel or device worn in a boot or shoe to make the wearer appear taller or to correct shortening of a leg. **2** an act of lifting: *weightlifters attempting a particularly heavy lift.* ■ a rise in price or amount: *the company has already produced a 10 percent lift in profits.* ■ an increase in volume or pitch of a person's speaking voice. ■ *informal* an instance of stealing or plagiarizing something. ■ an upward force that counteracts the force of gravity, produced by changing the direction and speed of a moving stream of air: *it had separate engines to provide lift and generate forward speed.* ■ the maximum weight that an aircraft can raise. **3** a free ride in another person's vehicle: *Miss Green is giving me a lift back to school.* **4** a feeling of encouragement or increased cheerfulness: *winning this game has **given** everyone on the team **a lift**.* ▷Middle English: from Old Norse *lypta,* of Germanic origin; related to **LOFT**. —**lift·a·ble** *adj.* —**lift·er** *n.*

▸*PHRASES* □ **lift a finger** (or **hand**) [usu. with *negative*] make the slightest effort to do something, esp. to help someone: *he never once lifted a finger to get Jimmy released from prison.* □ **lift his** (or **its**) **leg** *informal* (of a male dog) urinate.

lift-off /ˈliftˌôf; -ˌäf/ ▸*n.* takeoff, esp. the vertical takeoff of a rocket or helicopter.

lift pump ▸*n.* a simple pump consisting of a piston moving in a cylinder, both parts incorporating a valve.

lig·a·ment /ˈligəmənt/ ▸*n. Anatomy* a short band of tough, flexible, fibrous connective tissue that connects two bones or cartilages or holds together a joint. ■ a membranous fold that supports an organ and keeps it in position. ■ any similar connecting or binding structure. ■ *archaic* a bond of union. ▷late Middle English: from Latin *ligamentum* 'bond,' from *ligare* 'to bind.' —**lig·a·men·tal** /ˌligəˈmentl/ *adj.* —**lig·a·men·ta·ry** /ˌligəˈment(ə)rē/ *adj.* —**lig·a·men·tous** /ˌligəˈmentəs/ *adj.*

li·gand /ˈligənd; ˈlī-/ ▸*n. Chemistry* an ion or molecule attached to a metal atom by coordinate bonding. ■ *Biochemistry* a molecule that binds to another (usually larger) molecule. ▷1950s: from Latin *ligandus* 'that can be tied,' gerundive of *ligare* 'to bind.'

li·gase /ˈlīˌgās; -ˌgāz/ ▸*n. Biochemistry* an enzyme that brings about ligation of DNA or another substance. ▷1960s: from Latin *ligare* 'to bind' + **-ASE**.

li·gate /ˈlīˌgāt/ ▸*v.* [*trans.*] (usu. **be ligated**) *Surgery* tie up or otherwise close off (an artery or vessel). ▷late 16th cent.: from Latin *ligat-* 'tied,' from the verb *ligare.*

li·ga·tion /līˈgāsʜən/ ▸*n.* **1** the surgical procedure of closing off a blood vessel or other duct or tube in the body by means of a ligature or clip. **2** *Biochemistry* the joining of two DNA strands or other molecules by a phosphate ester linkage. ▷late Middle English: from late Latin *ligatio(n-),* from the verb *ligare* (see **LIGATE**).

lig·a·ture /ˈligəcʜər; -ˌcʜo͝or/ ▸*n.* **1** a thing used for tying or binding something tightly. ■ a cord or thread used in surgery, esp. to tie up a bleeding artery. **2** *Music* a slur or tie. **3** *Printing* a character consisting of two or more joined letters, e.g., *æ, fl.* ■ a stroke that joins adjacent letters in writing or printing.

▸*v.* [*trans.*] bind or connect with a ligature. ▷Middle English: via late Latin *ligatura* from Latin *ligat-* 'bound,' from the verb *ligare.*

li·ger /ˈlīgər/ ▸*n.* the hybrid offspring of a male lion and a tigress. Compare with **TIGON**. ▷1930s: blend of **LION** and **TIGER**.

light[1] /līt/ ▸*n.* **1** the natural agent that stimulates sight and makes things visible: *the light of the sun* | [in *sing.*] *the street lamps shed a faint light into the room.* ■ a source of illumination, esp. an electric lamp: *a light came on in his room.* ■ (**lights**) decorative illuminations: *Christmas lights.* ■ a traffic light: *turn right at the light.* ■ [in *sing.*] an expression in someone's eyes indicating a particular emotion or mood: *a shrewd light entered his eyes.* ■ the amount or quality of light in a place: *the plant requires good light | in some lights she could look beautiful.*

> Visible light is electromagnetic radiation whose wavelength falls within the range to which the human retina responds, i.e., between about 390 nm (violet light) and 740 nm (red). White light consists of a roughly equal mixture of all visible wavelengths, which can be separated to yield the colors of the spectrum, as was first demonstrated conclusively by Newton. In the 20th century it has become apparent that light consists of energy quanta called photons that behave partly like waves and partly like particles. The velocity of light in a vacuum is 299,792 km per second.

2 understanding of a problem or mystery; enlightenment: *she saw light dawn on the woman's face.* ■ spiritual illumination by divine truth. ■ (**lights**) a person's opinions, standards, and abilities: *leaving the police to do the job **according to their lights**.* **3** an area of something that is brighter or paler than its surroundings: *sunshine will brighten the natural lights in your hair.* **4** a match or lighter that produces a flame or spark. ■ the flame produced: *he asked me for a light.* **5** a window or opening in a wall to let light in. ■ any of the perpendicular divisions of a mullioned window. ■ any of the panes of glass forming the roof or side of a greenhouse or the top of a cold frame. **6** a person notable or eminent in a particular sphere of activity or place: *such lights of Liberalism as the historian Goldwin Smith.*

▸*v.* (*past* and *past part.* **lit** /lit/ or **light·ed**) [*trans.*] **1** provide with light or lighting; illuminate: *the room was lighted by a number of small lamps | lightning suddenly **lit up** the house.* ■ switch on (an electric light): *only one of the table lamps was lit.* ■ [*intrans.*] (**light up**) become illuminated: *the sign to fasten seat belts lit up.* **2** make (something) start burning; ignite: *Allen gathered sticks and lit a fire* | [as *adj.*] (**lighted** or **lit**) *a lighted cigarette.* ■ [*intrans.*] begin to burn; be ignited: *the gas wouldn't light properly.* ■ (**light something up**) ignite a cigarette, cigar, or pipe and begin to smoke it: *she lit up a cigarette and puffed on it serenely* | [*intrans.*] *workers who light up in prohibited areas face dismissal.*

▸*phrasal v.* □ **light up** (or **light something up**) (with reference to a person's face or eyes) suddenly become or cause to be animated with liveliness or joy: *his eyes lit up and he smiled | a smile of delight lit up her face.*

▸*adj.* **1** having a considerable or sufficient amount of natural light; not dark: *the bedrooms are light and airy | it was almost light outside.* **2** (of a color) pale: *her eyes were light blue.* ▷Old English *lēoht, līht* (noun and adjective), *līhtan* (verb), of Germanic origin; related to Dutch *licht* and German *Licht,* from an Indo-European root shared by Greek *leukos* 'white' and Latin *lux* 'light.' —**light·ish** *adj.* —**light·less** *adj.* —**light·ness** *n.*

▸*PHRASES* □ **bring** (or **come**) **to light** make (or become) widely known or evident: *an investigation to bring to light examples of extravagant expenditure.* □ **go out like a light** *informal* fall asleep or lose consciousness suddenly. □ **in a —— light** in the way specified; so as to give a specified impression: *the audit portrayed the company in a very favorable light.* □ **in** (**the**) **light of** drawing knowledge or information from; taking (something) into consideration: *the exorbitant prices are explainable in the light of the facts.* □ **light a fire under someone** see **FIRE**. □ **light at the end of the tunnel** a long-awaited indication that a period of hardship or adversity is nearing an end. □ **light the fuse** see **FUSE**[2]. □ **the light of day** daylight. ■ general public attention: *bringing old family secrets into the light of day.* □ **the light of someone's life** a much loved person. □ **lights out** bedtime in a school dormitory, military barracks, or other institution, when lights should be switched off. ■ a bell, bugle call, or other signal announcing this. □ **lit up** *informal, dated* drunk. □ **see the light** understand or realize something after prolonged thought or doubt. ■ undergo religious conversion. □ **see the light of day** be born. ■ *figurative* come into existence; be made public, visible, or available: *this software first saw the light of day back in 1993.* □ **shed** (or **throw** or **cast**) **light on** help to explain (something) by providing further information about it.

light[2] ▸*adj.* **1** of little weight; easy to lift: *they are very light and portable | you're **as light as a feather**.* ■ deficient in weight, esp. by a specified amount: *the sack of potatoes is 5 pounds light.* ■ not strongly or heavily built or constructed; small of its kind: *light, impractical clothes | light armor.* ■ carrying or suitable for small loads: *light commercial vehicles.* ■ carrying only light armaments: *light infantry.* ■ (of a vehicle, ship, or aircraft) traveling unladen or with less than a full load. ■ (of food or a meal) small in quantity and easy to digest: *a light supper.* ■ (of a foodstuff) low in fat, cholesterol, sugar, or other rich ingredients: *stick to a light diet.* ■ (of drink) not too sweet or rich in flavor or strongly alcoholic: *a glass of light Hungarian wine.* ■ (of food, esp. pastry or sponge cake) fluffy or well aerated during cooking. ■ (of soil) friable, porous, and workable. ■ (of an isotope) having not more than the usual mass; (of a compound) containing such an isotope. **2** relatively low in density, amount, or intensity: *passenger traffic was light | light summer breezes | trading was light for most of the day.* ■ (of sleep or a sleeper) easily disturbed. ■ easily borne or done: *he received a relatively light sentence | some light housework.* **3** gentle or delicate: *she planted a light kiss on his cheek | my breathing was steady and light.* ■ (of a building) having an appearance suggestive of lightness: *the building is lofty and light in its tall nave and choir.* ■ (of type) having thin strokes; not bold. **4** (of entertainment) requiring little mental effort; not profound or serious: *pop is thought of as light entertainment | some light reading.* ■ not serious or solemn: *his tone was light.* ■ free from worry or unhappiness; cheerful: *I left the island with a light heart.* **5** *archaic* (of a woman) unchaste; promiscuous. ▷Old English *lēocht, līht* (noun), *lēohte* (adverb), of Germanic origin; related to Dutch *licht* and German *leicht,* from an Indo-European root shared by **LUNG**. —**light·ish** *adj.* —**light·ly** *adv.* —**light·ness** *n.*

▸*PHRASES* □ **be light on** be rather short of: *light on hard news.* □ **be light on one's feet** (of a person) be quick or nimble. □ **a** (or **someone's**) **light touch** the ability to deal with something delicately, tactfully, or in an understated way: *a novel that handles its tricky subject with a light touch.* □ **make light of** treat as unimportant: *I didn't mean to make light of your problems.* □ **make light work of** accomplish (a task) quickly and easily. □ **travel light** travel with a minimum load or minimum luggage.

light[3] ▸*v.* (*past* and *past part.* **lit** /lit/ or **light·ed**) [*intrans.*] **1** (**light on/upon**) come upon or discover by chance: *he lit on a possible solution.* **2** *archaic* descend: *from the horse he lit down.* ■ (**light on**) fall and settle or land on (a surface): *a feather just lighted on the ground.*
▸*phrasal v.* □ **light into** *informal* criticize severely; attack: *he lit into him for his indiscretion.* □ **light out** *informal* depart hurriedly. ▷Old English *līhtan* (sense 2; also 'lessen the weight of'), from LIGHT[2]; compare with ALIGHT[1].

light air ▸*n.* a very light movement of the air. ■ a wind of force 1 on the Beaufort scale (1–3 knots or 1–3.5 mph).

light box ▸*n.* a flat box with a side of translucent glass or plastic and containing an electric light, so as to provide an evenly lighted flat surface or even illumination, such as in an art or photography studio.

light breeze ▸*n.* a wind of force 2 on the Beaufort scale (4–6 knots or 4.5-7 mph).

Light Bri·gade, Charge of the see CHARGE OF THE LIGHT BRIGADE.

light bulb (also **light·bulb**) ▸*n.* a glass bulb inserted into a lamp or a socket in a ceiling, that provides light by passing an electric current through a pocket of inert gas.

light chain ▸*n. Biochemistry* a protein subunit that, as one of a pair, forms part of the main antigen-binding region of an immunoglobulin molecule.

light cone ▸*n. Physics* a surface in space-time, represented as a cone in three dimensions, comprising all the points from which a light signal would reach a given point (at the apex) simultaneously, and that therefore appear simultaneous to an observer at the apex.

light curve ▸*n. Astronomy* a graph showing the variation in the light received over a period of time from a variable star or other varying celestial object.

light-emit·ting di·ode ▸*n.* see **LED**.

light·en[1] /ˈlītn/ ▸*v.* make or become lighter in weight, pressure, or severity: [*trans.*] *efforts to lighten the burden of regulation* | [*intrans.*] *the strain had lightened.* ■ make or become more cheerful or less serious: [*trans.*] *she attempted a joke to lighten the atmosphere* | [*intrans.*] *Robbie felt her spirits lighten a little.*

light·en[2] ▸*v.* **1** make or become lighter or brighter: [*intrans.*] *the sky began to lighten in the east* | [*trans.*] *she had lightened her hair.* ■ [*trans.*] *archaic* enlighten spiritually: *now the Lord lighten thee, thou art a great fool.* **2** [*intrans.*] (**it lightens, it is lightening,** etc.) *rare* emit flashes of lightning; flash with lightning: *it thundered and lightened.*

USAGE Years ago, the phrase **it is lightening** (as in 'thundering and lightening') was contracted to **it is light'ning**, which eventually became further shortened to **it is lightning**. In modern use, the word **lightning** stands on its own as a noun (*did you see that lightning?*) and a verb (*it looks as if it's going to start lightning*). Today, in the context of electrical storms, **lightening** would likely be considered a misspelling of **lightning**, rather than a variant spelling.

light en·gine ▸*n.* a railroad locomotive running with no vehicles attached.
▸*adv.* (of a locomotive) running with no vehicles attached: *75069 returned light engine.*

light·en·ing /ˈlītn-iNG; ˈlītniNG/ ▸*n.* a drop in the level of the uterus during the last weeks of pregnancy as the head of the fetus engages in the pelvis.

light·er[1] /ˈlītər/ ▸*n.* a device that produces a small flame, typically used to light cigarettes.

light·er[2] ▸*n.* a flat-bottomed barge or other unpowered boat used to transfer cargo to and from ships in harbor.
▸*v.* [*trans.*] transport (goods) in a lighter: *they lightered their cargo ashore.* ▷late Middle English: from LIGHT[2] (in the sense 'unload'), or from Middle Low German *luchter.* —**light·er·man** /-mən/ *n.* (*pl.* **-men**).

light·er·age /ˈlītərij/ ▸*n.* the transfer of cargo by means of a lighter; the charge levied for such transfer.

light·er-than-air ▸*adj.* [*attrib.*] relating to or denoting a balloon or other aircraft weighing less than the air it displaces, and so flying as a result of its own buoyancy.

light·face /ˈlītˌfās/ ▸*n.* typeface or font characterized by light, thin lines.

light·fast /ˈlītˌfast/ ▸*adj.* (of a dye or pigment) not prone to discolor when exposed to light. —**light·fast·ness** *n.*

light-fin·gered ▸*adj.* **1** prone to steal: *light-fingered shoplifters.* **2** having or showing delicate skill with the hands: *it is played with an irresistibly light-fingered spontaneity.*

light fly·weight ▸*n.* the lowest weight in amateur boxing, ranging up to 106 pounds (48 kg). ■ an amateur boxer of this weight.

light-foot·ed ▸*adj.* fast, nimble, or stealthy on one's feet: *a light-footed leap.* —**light-foot·ed·ly** *adv.*

light gun ▸*n. Computing* a hand-held gunlike photosensitive device used chiefly in computer games, held to the display screen for passing information to the computer.

light·head·ed /ˈlītˌhedid/ ▸*adj.* dizzy and slightly faint: *I was lightheaded from fear.* —**light·head·ed·ly** *adv.* —**light·head·ed·ness** *n.*

light·heart·ed /ˈlītˌhärtid/ ▸*adj.* cheerful and carefree: *excited, lighthearted chatter.* —**light·heart·ed·ly** *adv.* —**light·heart·ed·ness** *n.*

light heav·y·weight ▸*n.* a weight in boxing and other sports intermediate between middleweight and heavyweight. In the amateur boxing scale it ranges from 165 to 178 pounds (75 to 81 kg). ■ a boxer or other competitor of this weight.

Light-Horse Har·ry see LEE[6].

light·house /ˈlītˌhous/ ▸*n.* a tower or other structure containing a beacon light to warn or guide ships at sea.

lighthouse

light in·dus·try ▸*n.* the manufacture of small or light articles.

light·ing /ˈlītiNG/ ▸*n.* equipment in a home, workplace, studio, theater, or street for producing light: *the heartless glare of strip lighting.* ■ the arrangement or effect of lights: *the lighting was very flat.*

light·ing cam·er·a·man ▸*n.* (in films) a person in charge of the lighting of sets being filmed.

light ma·chine gun ▸*n.* any air-cooled machine gun with a caliber no greater than .30 inch (7.6 mm).

light me·ter ▸*n.* an instrument for measuring the intensity of light, used chiefly to show the correct exposure when taking a photograph. Also called EXPOSURE METER.

light mid·dle·weight ▸*n.* a weight in amateur boxing ranging from 148 to 156 pounds (67 to 71 kg). ■ an amateur boxer of this weight.

light·ning /ˈlītniNG/ ▸*n.* the occurrence of a natural electrical discharge of very short duration and high voltage between a cloud and the ground or within a cloud, accompanied by a bright flash and typically also thunder: *a tremendous flash of lightning.* ■ *poetic/literary* a flash or discharge of this kind: *the sky was a mass of black cloud out of which lightnings flashed.*
▸*v.* [*intrans.*] (of the sky) emit a flash or discharge of this kind: *what's a person supposed to do when it starts to lightning?*
▸*adj.* [*attrib.*] very quick: *a lightning cure for his hangover* | *galloping across the country at lightning speed.* ▷Middle English: special use of *lightening* (verbal noun from LIGHTEN[2]).
▸*PHRASES* □ **lightning never strikes twice in the same place** *proverb* an unusual situation or event is unlikely to happen again in exactly the same circumstances or to the same person. □ **like (greased) lightning** very quickly.

USAGE See usage at LIGHTEN[2].

light·ning bug ▸*n.* another term for FIREFLY.

light·ning rod ▸*n.* a metal rod or wire fixed to an exposed part of a building or other tall structure to divert lightning harmlessly into the ground. ■ *figurative* a person or thing that attracts a lot of criticism, esp. in order to divert attention from more serious issues or to allow a more important public figure to appear blameless.

Light on the Moun·tain a nickname for the state of IDAHO.

light op·er·a ▸*n.* another term for OPERETTA.

light pen ▸*n.* **1** *Computing* a hand-held, penlike photosensitive device held to the display screen of a computer terminal for passing information to the computer. **2** a hand-held, light-emitting device used for reading bar codes.

light pol·lu·tion ▸*n.* brightening of the night sky that inhibits the observation of stars and planets, caused by street lights and other man-made sources.

light·proof /ˈlītˌpro͞of/ ▸*adj.* able to block out light completely.

light rail·way ▸*n.* a railroad constructed for light traffic.

light re·ac·tion ▸*n.* **1** the reaction of something, esp. the iris of the eye, to different intensities of light. **2** (**the light reaction**) *Biochemistry* the reaction that occurs as the first phase of photosynthesis, in which energy in the form of light is absorbed and converted to chemical energy in the form of ATP.

lights /līts/ ▸*plural n.* the lungs of sheep or pigs used as food, esp. for pets. ▷Middle English: use of LIGHT[2] as a noun (so named because of their lightness). Compare with LUNG.

light-sen·si·tive ▸*adj.* (of a surface or substance) changing physically or chemically when exposed to light. ■ *Biology* (of a cell, organ, or tissue) able to detect the presence or intensity of light.

light·ship /ˈlītˌSHip/ ▸*n.* a moored or anchored vessel with a beacon light to warn or guide ships at sea.

light show ▸*n.* a spectacle of colored lights that move and change, esp. at a pop concert.

light·some /ˈlītsəm/ ▸*adj. chiefly poetic/literary* **1** merry and carefree. **2** gracefully nimble: *lightsome, high-flying dancers.* —**light·some·ly** *adv.* —**light·some·ness** *n.*

light ta·ble ▸*n.* a horizontal or tilted surface of translucent glass or plastic with a light behind it, used as a light box fordrawing or viewing transparencies or negatives.

light trap ▸*n.* **1** *Zoology* an illuminated trap for attracting and catching nocturnal animals, esp. moths and other flying insects. **2** *Photography* a device for excluding light from a darkroom without preventing entry into it.

light wa·ter ▸*n.* **1** water containing the normal proportion (or less) of deuterium oxide, i.e., about 0.02 percent, esp. to distinguish it from heavy water. **2** foam formed by water and a fluorocarbon surfactant, which floats on flammable liquids lighter than water and is used in firefighting.

light·weight /ˈlītˌwāt/ ▸*n.* **1** a weight in boxing and other sports intermediate between featherweight and welterweight. In the amateur boxing scale it ranges from 125 to 132 pounds (57 to 60 kg). ■ a boxer or other competitor of this weight. **2** a person or thing that is lightly built or constructed. ■ a person of little importance or influence, esp. in a particular sphere: *he was regarded as a political lightweight.*
▸*adj.* **1** of thin material or build and weighing less than average: *a lightweight gray suit.* **2** containing little serious matter: *the newspaper is lightweight and trivial.*

light well ▸*n.* an open area or vertical shaft in the center of a building, typically roofed with glass, bringing natural light to the lower floors or basement.

light wel·ter·weight ▸*n.* a weight in amateur boxing ranging from 132 to 140 pounds (60 to 63.5 kg). ■ an amateur boxer of this weight.

light·wood /ˈlītˌwo͝od/ ▸*n.* firewood that burns easily and with a bright flame, esp. dry, resinous pine.

light year ▸*n. Astronomy* a unit of astronomical distance equivalent to the distance that light travels in one year, which is 9.4607×10^{12} km (nearly 6 trillion miles). ■ (**light years**) *informal* a long distance or great amount: *the new range puts them* ***light years ahead*** *of the competition.*

lig·ne·ous /ˈlignēəs/ ▸*adj.* made, consisting of, or resembling wood; woody. ▷early 17th cent.: from Latin *ligneus* 'relating to wood' + -OUS.

ligni- ▸*comb. form* relating to wood: *lignify.* ▷from Latin *lignum* 'wood.'

lig·ni·fy /ˈlignəˌfī/ ▸*v.* (**-fies, -fied**) [*trans.*] [usu. as *adj.*] (**lignified**) *Botany* make rigid and woody by the deposition of lignin in cell walls. —**lig·ni·fi·ca·tion** /ˌlignəfəˈkāSHən/ *n.*

lig·nin /ˈlignin/ ▸*n. Botany* a complex organic polymer deposited in the cell walls of many plants, making them rigid and woody. ▷early 19th cent.: from LIGNI- 'of wood' + -IN[1].

L

lig·nite /ˈligˌnīt/ ▸*n.* a soft brownish coal showing traces of plant structure, intermediate between bituminous coal and peat. ▷early 19th cent.: coined in French from Latin *lignum* 'wood' + **-ITE**1. **—lig·nit·ic** /ligˈnitik/ *adj.*

ligno- ▸*comb. form* relating to wood: *lignotuber.* ■ representing **LIGNIN**: *lignocellulose.* ▷from Latin *lignum* 'wood.'

lig·no·caine /ˈlignəˌkān/ ▸*n.* another term for **LIDOCAINE**. ▷1950s: from **LIGNO-** (Latin equivalent of **XYLO-**, used in the earlier name *xylocaine* and reflecting chemical similarity to **XYLENE**) + *-caine* (from **COCAINE**).

lig·no·cel·lu·lose /ˌlignōˈselyəˌlōs; -ˌlōz/ ▸*n. Botany* a complex of lignin and cellulose present in the cell walls of woody plants.

lig·no·tu·ber /ˈlignōˌt(y)o͞obər/ ▸*n. Botany* a rounded woody growth at or below ground level on some shrubs and trees that grow in areas subject to fire or drought, containing a mass of buds and food reserves.

lig·num vi·tae /ˈlignəm ˈvīˌtē; ˈvēˌtī/ ▸*n.* another term for **GUAIACUM**. ▷Latin, 'wood of life.'

lig·ro·in /ˈligrō-in/ ▸*n. Chemistry* a volatile hydrocarbon mixture obtained from petroleum and used as a solvent. ▷late 19th cent.: of unknown origin.

lig·u·la /ˈligyələ/ ▸*n.* (*pl.* **-lae** /-ˌlē; -ˌlī/) *Entomology* the strap-shaped terminal part of an insect's labium, typically lobed. ▷mid 18th cent.: from Latin, 'strap.' **—lig·u·lar** *adj.*

lig·u·late /ˈligyəˌlāt; -lit/ ▸*adj. chiefly Botany* strap-shaped, such as the ray florets of plants of the daisy family. ■ (of a plant) having ray florets or ligules.

lig·ule /ˈligˌyo͞ol/ ▸*n. Botany* a narrow strap-shaped part of a plant, esp., in most grasses and sedges, a membranous scale on the inner side of the leaf sheath at its junction with the blade. ▷early 19th cent.: from Latin *ligula* 'strap.'

Li·gu·ri·a /liˈg(y)o͞orēə/ a coastal region of northwestern Italy that extends along the Mediterranean coast from Tuscany to the border with France; capital, Genoa. In ancient times, Liguria extended as far as the Atlantic Ocean. ▷from Latin *Ligur* 'Ligurian,' from Greek *Ligus.* **—Li·gu·ri·an** *adj.* & *n.*

Li·gu·ri·an Sea /liˈg(y)o͞orēən/ a part of the northern Mediterranean Sea, between Corsica and the northwestern coast of Italy.

li·gus·trum /liˈgəstrəm/ ▸*n.* a plant of a genus that comprises the privets. • Genus *Ligustrum*, family Oleaceae. ▷mid 17th cent.: from Latin.

lik·a·ble /ˈlīkəbəl/ (also **like·a·ble**) ▸*adj.* (esp. of a person) pleasant, friendly, and easy to like. **—lik·a·bil·i·ty** /ˌlīkəˈbilətē/ *n.* **—lik·a·ble·ness** *n.* **—lik·a·bly** /-blē/ *adv.*

like1 /līk/ ▸*prep.* **1** having the same characteristics or qualities as; similar to: *there were other suits like mine in the shop | they were like brothers | she looked nothing like Audrey Hepburn.* ■ in the manner of; in the same way or to the same degree as: *he was screaming like a banshee | you must run like the wind.* ■ in a way appropriate to: *students were angry at being treated like children.* ■ such as one might expect from; characteristic of: *just like you to put a damper on people's enjoyment.* ■ used in questions to ask about the characteristics or nature of someone or something: *What is it like to be a tuna fisherman? | What's she like?* **2** used to draw attention to the nature of an action or event: *I apologize for coming over unannounced like this | why are you talking about me like that?* **3** such as; for example: *the cautionary vision of works like* Animal Farm *and* 1984.
▸*conj. informal* **1** in the same way that; as: *people who change countries like they change clothes.* **2** as though; as if: *I felt like I'd been kicked by a camel.*
▸*n.* used with reference to a person or thing of the same kind as another: *the quotations could be arranged to put* **like with like** *| I know him—him and his like.* ■ (**the like**) a thing or things of the same kind (often used to express surprise or for emphasis): *did you ever hear the like? | a church interior* **the like of which** *he had never seen before.*
▸*adj.* (of a person or thing) having similar qualities or characteristics to another person or thing: *I responded in like manner | the grouping of children of like ability together.* ■ (of a portrait or other image) having a faithful resemblance to the original: *"Who painted the dog's picture? It's very like."*
▸*adv.* **1** *informal* used in speech as a meaningless filler or to signify the speaker's uncertainty about an expression just used: *there was this funny smell—sort of dusty like.* **2** *informal* used to convey a person's reported attitude or feelings in the form of direct speech (whether or not representing an actual quotation): *so she comes into the room and she's like "Where is everybody?"* **3** (**like as/to**) *archaic* in the manner of: *like as a ship with dreadful storm long tossed.* ▷Middle English: from Old Norse *líkr*; related to **ALIKE**.
▸*PHRASES* □ **and the like** and similar things; et cetera. □ **like anything** *informal* to a great degree: *they would probably worry like anything.* □ (**as**) **like as not** probably: *she would be in bed by now, like as not.* □ **like enough** (or **most like**) *archaic* probably: *he'll have lost a deal of blood, I dare say, and like enough he's still losing it.* □ **like ——, like ——** as —— is, so is ——: *like father, like son.* □ **like so** *informal* in this manner: *the votive candles are arranged like so.* □ **the likes of** *informal* used of someone or something regarded as a type: *she didn't want to associate with the likes of me.* □ **more like** *informal* nearer to (a specified number or description) than one previously given: *he believes the figure should be more like $10 million.* ■ (**more like it**) nearer to what is required or expected; more satisfactory. □ **of (a) like mind** (of a person) sharing the same opinions or tastes.

USAGE The use of **like** as a conjunction meaning 'as' or 'as if' (*I don't have a wealthy set of in-laws like you do; they sit up like they're begging for food*) is considered by many to be incorrect. Although **like** has been used as a conjunction in this way since the 15th century by many respected writers, it is still frowned upon and considered unacceptable in formal English. In more precise use, **like** is a preposition, used before nouns and pronouns: *to fly like a bird; a town like ours.*
See also **usage** at **GO**1.

like2 ▸*v.* [*trans.*] **1** find agreeable, enjoyable, or satisfactory: *I like all Angela Carter's stories | people who don't like reading books | I like to be the center of attention.* **2** wish for; want: *would you like a cup of coffee? | I'd like to rent a car | I'd like you to stay |* [*intrans.*] *we would* **like for** *you to work for us.* ■ (**would like to do something**) used as a polite formula: *we would like to apologize for the late running of this service.* ■ (**not like doing/to do something**) feel reluctant to do something: *I don't like leaving her on her own too long.* ■ choose to have (something); prefer: *how do you like your coffee?* ■ [*in questions*] feel about or regard (something): *how would you like it if it happened to you?*
▸*n.* (**likes**) the things one likes or prefers: *a wide variety of likes, dislikes, tastes, and income levels.* ▷Old English *līcian* 'be pleasing,' of Germanic origin; related to Dutch *lijken.*
▸*PHRASES* □ **if you like 1** if it suits or pleases you: *we could go riding if you like.* **2** used when expressing something in a new or unusual way: *it's a whole new branch of chemistry, a new science if you like.* □ **I like that!** used as an exclamation expressing affront. □ **like it or not** *informal* used to indicate that someone has no choice in a matter: *you're celebrating with us, like it or not.* □ **not like the look** (or **sound**) **of** find worrying or alarming: *I don't like the look of that head injury.*

-like ▸*comb. form* (added to nouns) similar to; characteristic of: *pealike | crustlike.*

like·a·ble ▸*adj.* variant spelling of **LIKABLE**.

like·li·hood /ˈlīklēˌho͝od/ ▸*n.* the state or fact of something's being likely; probability: *young people who can see no* **likelihood of** *finding employment |* [*in sing.*] *situations where there is* **a likelihood of** *violence.*
▸*PHRASE* □ **in all likelihood** very probably.

like·ly /ˈlīklē/ ▸*adj.* (**like·li·er**, **like·li·est**) **1** such as well might happen or be true; probable: *the likely effects of the drought on sugar beet yields |* **it was likely that** *he would make a televised statement | sales are likely to drop further.* **2** apparently suitable; promising: *a likely-looking spot.* ■ appearing to have vigor or ability: *likely lads.*
▸*adv.* probably: *we will most likely go to a bar.* ▷Middle English: from Old Norse *líkligr*, from *líkr* (see **LIKE**1). **—like·li·ness** *n.*
▸*PHRASES* □ **a likely story** used to express disbelief in an account or excuse: *Gone running, has he? A likely story!* □ **as likely as not** probably: *I won't take their pills because as likely as not they'd poison me.* □ **not likely!** *informal* certainly not; I refuse: *"Are you going home?" "Not likely!"*

USAGE In U.S. English, the adverb **likely** preceded by a submodifier (such as *very, most,* or *more*) is a common construction, but the use of **likely** without a submodifier is common as well, and not regarded as incorrect: *we will* **likely** *see him later.* In standard British English, however, **likely** must be preceded by a submodifier: *we will* **very likely** *see him later.*

like-mind·ed ▸*adj.* having similar tastes or opinions: *a small group of like-minded friends.* **—like-mind·ed·ness** *n.*

lik·en /ˈlīkən/ ▸*v.* [*trans.*] (**liken someone/something to**) point out the resemblance of someone or something to: *they likened the reigning emperor to a god.* ▷Middle English: from **LIKE**1 + **-EN**1.

like·ness /ˈlīknis/ ▸*n.* the fact or quality of being alike; resemblance: *her* **likeness to** *him was astonishing | a family likeness can be seen among all the boys.* ■ the semblance, guise, or outward appearance of: *humans are described as being made in God's likeness.* ■ a portrait or representation: *the only known likeness of Dorothy as a young woman.* ▷Old English *gelīknes* (see **ALIKE**, **-NESS**).

THE RIGHT WORD **affinity, analogy, likeness, resemblance, similarity, similitude**
Two sisters who are only a year apart in age and who are very similar to each other in terms of appearance and personality would be said to bear a **likeness** to one another.
Similarity applies to people or things that are merely somewhat alike (*there was a similarity between the two women, both of whom were raised in the Midwest*), while **resemblance** suggests a similarity only in appearance or in superficial or external ways (*with their short hair and blue eyes, they bore a strong resemblance to each other*).
Affinity adds to *resemblance* a natural kinship, temperamental sympathy, common experience, or some other relationship (*she has an affinity for young children*).
Similitude is a more literary word meaning *likeness* or *similarity* in reference to abstract things (*a similitude of the truth*).
An **analogy** is a comparison of things that are basically unlike but share certain attributes or circumstances (*he drew an analogy between the human heart and a bicycle pump*).

like·wise /ˈlīkˌwīz/ ▸*adv.* **1** in the same way; also: *the dream of young people is to grow old, and it is likewise the dream of their parents to relive youth.* ■ used to introduce a point similar or related to one just made: *you will forget the bad things that have happened in the past. Likewise, I will forget what you have done to me.* **2** in a like manner; similarly: *I stuck out my tongue and Frankie* **did likewise**. ▷late Middle English: from the phrase *in like wise.*

lik·ing /ˈlīkiNG/ ▸*n.* [in *sing.*] a feeling of regard or fondness: *Mrs. Parsons had* **a liking for** *gin and tonic she'd* **taken an** *instant* **liking to** *Arnie's new girlfriend.* ▷Old English *līcung* (see **LIKE**2, **-ING**1).
▸*PHRASES* □ **for one's liking** to suit one's taste or wishes: *he is a little too showy for my liking.* □ **to one's liking** to one's taste; pleasing: *his coffee was just to his liking.*

Li·kud /liˈko͞od; -ˈko͝od/ a coalition of right-wing Israeli political parties, formed in 1973. Likud returned to power in 1996 under Benjamin Netanyahu. ▷Hebrew, literally 'consolidation, unity.'

li·ku·ta /liˈko͞otə/ ▸*n.* (*pl.* **ma·ku·ta** /məˈko͞otə/) a monetary unit of the Democratic Republic of the Congo (formerly Zaire), equal to one hundredth of a zaire. ▷Kikongo.

li·lac /ˈlīˌläk; -ˌlak; -lək/ ▸*n.* a Eurasian shrub or small tree of the olive family, that has fragrant violet, pink, or white blossoms and is widely cultivated as an ornamental. • Genus *Syringa*, family Oleaceae; several species, in particular the **common lilac** (*S. vulgaris*), with many cultivars. ■ a pale pinkish-violet color.
▸*adj.* of a pale pinkish-violet color. ▷early 17th cent.: from obsolete French, via Spanish and Arabic from Persian *līlak*, variant of *nīlak* 'bluish,' from *nīl* 'blue.'

li·lan·ge·ni /ˌliläNGˈgenē/ ▸*n.* (*pl.* **e·ma·lan·ge·ni** /ˌeməläNGˈgenē/) the basic monetary unit of Swaziland, equal to 100 cents. ▷from the Bantu prefix *li-* (used to denote a singular) + *-langeni* 'member of a royal family.'

lil·i·a·ceous /ˌliléˈāsHəs/ ▸*adj. Botany* of, relating to, or denoting plants of the lily family (Liliaceae). These have elongated leaves that grow from a corm, bulb, or rhizome. ▷mid 18th cent.: from modern Latin *Liliaceae* (plural), based on Latin *lilium* 'lily,' + **-OUS**.

Lil·i·en·thal /ˈlilēənˌTHôl; -ˌtäl/, Otto (1848–96), German pioneer in the design and flying of gliders. Working with his brother, he made over 2,000 flights in various gliders before being killed in a crash.

Lil·ith /ˈliliTH/ a female demon of Jewish folklore, who tries to kill newborn children. In the Talmud she is the first wife of Adam, dispossessed by Eve.

Li·li·u·o·ka·la·ni /lĭ,lēə,wäkə'länē/ (1838–1917) Hawaiian queen; also known as **Lydia Paki Liliuokalani**. The last reigning queen of the Hawaiian Islands 1891–93, she ascended the throne in 1891. As queen, she fought for the independence of Hawaii. She was deposed by U.S. marines in 1893 and formally renounced her royal claim in 1895.

Lille /lēl/ an industrial city in northern France, near the border with Belgium; pop. 178,000.

Lil·le·ham·mer /'lilə,hämər/ a resort town and capital of Oppland county, in southern Norway, site of the 1994 Winter Olympics; pop. 23,000.

Lil·li·pu·tian /,lilə'pyo͞osHən/ ▸*adj.* trivial or very small: *America's banks no longer look Lilliputian in comparison with Japan's.*
▸*n.* a trivial or very small person or thing. ▷early 18th cent.: from the imaginary country of *Lilliput* in Swift's *Gulliver's Travels*, inhabited by people 6 inches (15 cm) high, + **-IAN**.

Li·lon·gwe /li'lôNGwā/ the capital of Malawi, founded in 1975; pop. 234,000.

lilt /lilt/ ▸*n.* a characteristic rising and falling of the voice when speaking; a pleasant gentle accent: *he spoke with a faint but recognizable Irish lilt.* ■ a pleasant, gently swinging rhythm in a song or tune: *the lilt of the Hawaiian music.* ■ *archaic, chiefly Scottish* a cheerful tune.
▸*v.* [*intrans.*] [often as *adj.*] (**lilting**) speak, sing, or sound with a lilt: *a lilting Welsh accent.* ▷late Middle English *lulte* (in the senses 'sound (an alarm)' or 'lift up (the voice)'), of unknown origin.

lil·y /'lilē/ ▸*n.* **1** a bulbous plant with large trumpet-shaped, typically fragrant, flowers on a tall, slender stem. Lilies have long been cultivated, some kinds being of symbolic importance and some used in perfumery. • Genus *Lilium*, family Liliaceae (the **lily family**). This family includes many flowering bulbs, such as bluebells, hyacinths, and tulips. Several plants are often placed in different families, esp. the Alliaceae (onions and their relatives), Aloaceae (aloes), and Amaryllidaceae (amaryllis, daffodils, jonquil), and as many as 38 families are sometimes recognized. ■ short for **WATER LILY**. ■ used in names of other plants with similar flowers or leaves, e.g., **arum lily**. **2** a heraldic fleur-de-lis. ▷Old English *lilie*, from Latin *lilium*, from Greek *leirion*. —**lil·ied** /'lilēd/ *adj.*

lil·y-liv·ered ▸*adj.* weak and cowardly.

lil·y-of-the-Nile ▸*n.* another term for **AGAPANTHUS**.

lil·y of the val·ley ▸*n.* a widely cultivated European plant of the lily family, with broad leaves and arching stems of fragrant, bell-shaped white flowers. • *Convallaria majalis*, family Liliaceae.

lily of the valley

lil·y pad ▸*n.* a round, floating leaf of a water lily.

lil·y-trot·ter ▸*n.* (esp. in Africa) a jacana.

lil·y-white ▸*adj.* pure or ideally white. ■ without fault or corruption; totally innocent or immaculate: *they want me to conform, to be lily-white.* ■ consisting only of white people and excluding nonwhite people: *lily-white suburban communities.*

lim. ▸*abbr.* limit.

Li·ma /'lēmə/ **1** the capital of Peru; pop. 5,706,000. Founded in 1535 by Francisco Pizarro, it was the capital of the Spanish colonies in South America until the 19th century. ■ a code word representing the letter L, used in radio communication. **2** an industrial city in northwestern Ohio, north of Dayton; pop. 45,549.

li·ma bean /'līmə/ ▸*n.* **1** an edible flat whitish bean. See also **BUTTER BEAN**. **2** the tropical American plant that yields this bean. • *Phaseolus lunatus* (or **limensis**) , family Leguminosae. ▷mid 18th cent.: *lima* from the name of the Peruvian capital **LIMA**.

Li·mas·sol /,lēmə'sôl/ a port on the south coast of Cyprus, on Akrotiri Bay; pop. 143,000.

limb[1] /lim/ ▸*n.* an arm or leg of a person or four-legged animal, or a bird's wing. ■ a large branch of a tree. ■ a projecting landform such as a spur of a mountain range, or each of two or more such projections as in a forked peninsula or archipelago. ■ a projecting section of a building. ■ a branch of a cross. ■ each half of an archery bow. ▷Old English *lim* (also in the sense 'organ or part of the body'), of Germanic origin. —**limbed** *adj.* [in *combination*] *long-limbed.* —**limb·less** *adj.*
▸*PHRASES* □ **life and limb** life and all bodily faculties: *a reckless disregard for life and limb.* □ **out on a limb** in or into a dangerous or uncompromising position, where one is not joined or supported by anyone else; vulnerable: *she's prepared to* **go out on a limb** *and do something different.* □ **tear someone limb from limb** violently dismember someone.

limb[2] ▸*n.* **1** *Astronomy* the edge of the disk of a celestial object, esp. the sun or moon. **2** *Botany* the blade or broad part of a leaf or petal. ■ the spreading upper part of a tube-shaped flower. **3** the graduated arc of a quadrant or other scientific instrument, used for measuring angles. ▷late Middle English: from French *limbe* or Latin *limbus* 'hem, border.'

Lim·ba /'limbə/ ▸*n.* (*pl.* same or **Lim·bas**) **1** a member of a people of Sierra Leone and Guinea. **2** the Niger–Congo language of this people.
▸*adj.* of or relating to the Limbas or their language. ▷the name in Limba.

lim·ber[1] /'limbər/ ▸*adj.* (of a person or body part) lithe; supple. See note at **FLEXIBLE**. ■ (of a thing) flexible: *limber graphite fishing rods.*
▸*v.* [*intrans.*] warm up in preparation for exercise or activity, esp. sports: *the acrobats were* **limbering up** *for the big show.* ■ [*trans.*] make (oneself or a body part) supple: *I limbered my fingers by playing a few scales.* ▷mid 16th cent. (as an adjective): perhaps from **LIMBER**[2] in the dialect sense 'cart shaft,' with allusion to a to-and-fro motion. —**lim·ber·ness** *n.*

lim·ber[2] ▸*n.* the detachable front part of a gun carriage, consisting of two wheels and an axle, a pole, and a frame holding one or more ammunition boxes.
▸*v.* [*trans.*] attach a limber to (a gun). ▷Middle English *lymour*, apparently related to medieval Latin *limonarius* from *limo, limon-* 'shaft.'

lim·ber·neck /'limbər,nek/ ▸*n.* a kind of botulism affecting poultry.

lim·ber pine ▸*n.* a small pine tree with tough pliant branches, native to the Rocky Mountains. • *Pinus flexilis*, family Pinaceae.

lim·bi /'lim,bī; -,bē/ ▸ plural form of **LIMBUS**.

lim·bic sys·tem /'limbik/ ▸*n.* a complex system of nerves and networks in the brain, involving several areas near the edge of the cortex concerned with instinct and mood. It controls the basic emotions (fear, pleasure, anger) and drives (hunger, sex, dominance, care of offspring). ▷late 19th cent.: *limbic* from French *limbique*, from Latin *limbus* 'edge.'

lim·bo[1] /'limbō/ ▸*n.* **1** (also **Limbo**) (in some Christian beliefs) the supposed abode of the souls of unbaptized infants, and of the just who died before Christ's coming. **2** an uncertain period of awaiting a decision or resolution; an intermediate state or condition: *the fate of the Contras is now* **in limbo**. ■ a state of neglect or oblivion: *children left in an emotional limbo.* ▷late Middle English: from the medieval Latin phrase *in limbo*, from *limbus* 'hem, border, limbo.'

lim·bo[2] ▸*n.* (*pl.* **-bos**) a West Indian dance in which the dancer bends backward to pass under a horizontal bar that is progressively lowered to a position just above the ground.
▸*v.* [*intrans.*] dance in such a way. ▷1950s: from **LIMBER**[1].

Lim·burg·er /'lim,bərgər/ ▸*n.* a soft white cheese with a characteristic strong smell, originally made in Limburg, a former duchy of Lorraine.

lim·bus /'limbəs/ ▸*n.* (*pl.* **-bi** /-,bī; -,bē/) *Anatomy* the border or margin of a structure, esp. the junction of the cornea and sclera in the eye. ▷late Middle English (denoting limbo): from Latin, 'edge, border.' The current sense dates from the late 17th cent.

lime[1] /līm/ ▸*n.* (also **quick·lime**) a white caustic alkaline substance consisting of calcium oxide, obtained by heating limestone. ■ (also **slaked lime**) a white alkaline substance consisting of calcium hydroxide, made by adding water to quicklime. ■ (in general use) any of a number of calcium compounds, esp. calcium hydroxide, used as an additive to soil or water. ■ *archaic* birdlime.
▸*v.* [*trans.*] **1** treat (soil or water) with lime to reduce acidity and improve fertility or oxygen levels. ■ [often as *adj.*] (**limed**) give (wood) a bleached appearance by treating it with lime: *limed oak dining furniture.* **2** *archaic* catch (a bird) with birdlime. ▷Old English *līm*, of Germanic origin; related to Dutch *lijm*, German *Leim*, also to **LOAM**. —**lim·y** /'līmē/ *adj.* (**lim·i·er, lim·i·est**).

lime[2] ▸*n.* **1** a rounded citrus fruit similar to a lemon but greener, smaller, and with a distinctive acid flavor. **2** (also **lime tree**) the evergreen citrus tree that produces this fruit, widely cultivated in warm climates. • *Citrus aurantifolia*, family Rutaceae. **3** a bright light green color like that of a lime: [as *adj.*] *day-glo orange, pink, or lime green.* ▷mid 17th cent.: from French, from modern Provençal *limo*, Spanish *lima*, from Arabic *līma*; compare with **LEMON**.

lime[3] (also **lime tree**) ▸*n.* another term for **LINDEN**, esp. the European linden. ▷early 17th cent.: alteration of obsolete *line*, from Old English *lind* (see **LINDEN**).

lime·ade /,līm'ād; 'līm,ād/ ▸*n.* a drink made from lime juice and water sweetened with sugar.

lime-burn·er ▸*n.* *historical* a person whose job was burning limestone in order to obtain lime.

lime·kiln /'līm,kil(n)/ ▸*n.* a kiln in which limestone is burned or calcined to produce quicklime.

lime·light /'līm,līt/ ▸*n.* intense white light obtained by heating a cylinder of lime in an oxyhydrogen flame, formerly used in theaters. ■ (**the limelight**) the focus of public attention: *the works that brought the artists into the limelight.*

li·men /'līmən/ ▸*n.* (*pl.* **li·mens** or **lim·i·na** /'limənə/) *Psychology* a threshold below which a stimulus is not perceived or is not distinguished from another. ▷mid 17th cent.: from Latin, 'threshold.'

lim·er·ence /'limərəns/ ▸n. *Psychology* the state of being infatuated or obsessed with another person, typically involuntary, and characterized by a strong desire for reciprocation of one's feelings but not primarily for a sexual relationship.

Lim·er·ick /'lim(ə)rik/ a county in the Republic of Ireland, in the western part of the province of Munster. ■ its county town, on the Shannon River; pop. 52,000.

lim·er·ick /'lim(ə)rik/ ▸*n.* a humorous, frequently bawdy, verse of three long and two short lines rhyming *aabba*, popularized by Edward Lear. ▷late 19th cent.: said to be from the chorus "Will you come up to Limerick?", sung between improvised verses at a gathering.

lime·scale /'līm,skāl/ ▸*n.* *chiefly Brit.* a whitish deposit on the inside of pipes, pots, and kettles, caused by minerals leeched from the water.

lime·stone /'līm,stōn/ ▸*n.* a hard sedimentary rock, composed mainly of calcium carbonate or dolomite, used as building material and in the making of cement.

lime sul·fur ▸*n.* an insecticide and fungicide containing calcium polysulfides, made by boiling lime and sulfur in water.

lime·wa·ter /'līm,wôtər; -,wätər/ ▸*n.* *Chemistry* a solution of calcium hydroxide in water, which is alkaline and turns milky in the presence of carbon dioxide.

Lim·ey /'līmē/ ▸*n.* (*pl.* **-eys**) *chiefly derogatory* a British person. ▷late 19th cent.: from **LIME**[2] + **-Y**[1], because of the former enforced consumption of lime juice to prevent scurvy in the British navy.

lim·i·na /'limənə/ ▸ plural form of **LIMEN**.

lim·i·nal /'limənl/ ▸*adj.* *technical* **1** of or relating to a transitional or initial stage of a process. **2** occupying a position at, or on both sides of, a boundary or threshold. ▷late 19th cent.: from Latin *limen, limin-* 'threshold' + **-AL**. —**lim·i·nal·i·ty** /,limə'nalətē/ *n.*

lim·it /'limit/ ▸*n.* **1** a point or level beyond which something does not or may not extend or pass: *the* **limits of** *presidential power | the 10-minute* **limit on** *speeches | there was no* **limit to** *his imagination.* ■ (often **limits**) the terminal point or boundary of an area or movement: *the city limits | the upper limit of the tidal reaches.* ■ the furthest extent of one's physical or mental endurance: *Mary Ann tried everyone's patience* **to the limit** *| other horses were reaching their limit.* **2** a restriction on the size or amount of something permissible or possible: *an age limit | a weight limit.* ■ a speed limit: *a 30 mph limit.* ■ (in card games) an agreed maximum stake or bet. ■ (also **legal limit**) the maximum concentration of alcohol in the blood that the law allows in the driver of a motor vehicle: *the risk of drinkers inadvertently going* **over the limit**. **3** *Mathematics* a point or value that a sequence, function, or sum of a series can be made to approach progressively, until it is as close to the point or value as desired.
▸*v.* (**lim·it·ed, lim·it·ing**) [*trans.*] set or serve as a limit

Pronunciation Key ə *ago*; ər *over*; 'ə or ,ə *up*; 'ər or ,ər *fur*; a *hat*; ā *rate*; ä *car*; CH *chew*; e *let*; ē *see*; e(ə)r *air*; i *fit*; ī *by*; i(ə)r *ear*; NG *sing*; ō *go*; ô *for*; oi *boy*; o͝o *good*; o͞o *goo*; ou *out*; SH *she*; TH *thin*; T͟H *then*; (h)w *why*; ZH *vision*

L

to: *try to limit the amount you drink* | *class sizes are* ***limited to*** *a maximum of 10* | [as *adj.*] **(limiting)** *a limiting factor.* ▷late Middle English: from Latin *limes, limit-* 'boundary, frontier.' The verb is from Latin *limitare,* from *limes.* **—lim·i·ta·tive** /ˈlimə,tātiv/ *adj.*

▸PHRASES □ **be the limit** *informal* be intolerably troublesome or irritating. □ **off limits** out of bounds: *they declared the site off limits* | *figurative there was no topic that was off limits for discussion.* □ **within limits** moderately; up to a point: □ **without limit** with no restriction.

lim·i·tar·y /ˈlimə,terē/ ▸*adj. rare* of, relating to, or subject to restriction.

lim·i·ta·tion /,liməˈtāsнən/ ▸*n.* **1** (often **limitations**) a limiting rule or circumstance; a restriction: *severe* ***limitations on*** *water use.* ■ a condition of limited ability; a defect or failing: *she knew her limitations better than she knew her worth.* ■ the action of limiting something: *the limitation of local authorities' powers.* **2** (also **limitation period**) *Law* a legally specified period beyond which an action may be defeated or a property right is not to continue. See also STATUTE OF LIMITATIONS. ▷late Middle English: from Latin *limitatio(n-),* from the verb *limitare* (see LIMIT).

lim·it bid ▸*n. Bridge* a bid showing that the value of the bidder's hand is within a narrow range, typically ten or eleven points.

lim·it·ed /ˈlimitid/ ▸*adj.* restricted in size, amount, or extent; few, small, or short: *a limited number of places are available* | *special offers available for a limited period* | *the legislation has had a limited effect.* ■ (of a monarchy or government) exercised under limitations of power prescribed by a constitution. ■ (of a person) not great in ability or talents: *I think he is a very limited man.* ■ (of a train or other vehicle of public transportation) making few intermediate stops; express. ■ **(Limited)** *Brit.* denoting a company whose owners are legally responsible for its debts only to the extent of the amount of capital they invested (used after a company name): *Times Newspapers Limited.* **—lim·it·ed·ness** *n.*

lim·it·ed ed·i·tion ▸*n.* an edition of a book, or reproduction of a print or object, limited to a specific number of copies.

lim·it·ed part·ner ▸*n.* a partner in a company or venture who receives limited profits from the business and whose liability toward its debts is legally limited to the extent of his or her investment. **—lim·it·ed part·ner·ship** *n.*

lim·it·ed war ▸*n.* a war in which the weapons used, the nations or territory involved, or the objectives pursued are restricted in some way, in particular one in which the use of nuclear weapons is avoided.

lim·it·er /ˈlimitər/ ▸*n.* a person or thing that limits something, in particular: ■ *Electronics* a circuit whose output is restricted to a certain range of values irrespective of the size of the input. Also called CLIPPER. ■ (also **speed limiter**) a device that prevents a vehicle from being driven above a specified speed.

lim·it·less /ˈlimitlis/ ▸*adj.* without end, limit, or boundary: *our resources are not limitless.* **—lim·it·less·ly** *adv.* **—lim·it·less·ness** *n.*

lim·it point ▸*n. Mathematics* a point for which every neighborhood contains at least one point belonging to a given set.

lim·it switch ▸*n.* a switch preventing the travel of an object in a mechanism past some predetermined point, mechanically operated by the motion of the object itself.

limn /lim/ ▸*v.* [*trans.*] *poetic/literary* depict or describe in painting or words. ■ suffuse or highlight (something) with a bright color or light: *a crescent moon limned each shred with white gold.* ▷late Middle English (in the sense 'illuminate a manuscript'): alteration of obsolete *lumine* 'illuminate,' via Old French *luminer* from Latin *luminare* 'make light.'

lim·ner /ˈlim(n)ər/ ▸*n. chiefly historical* a painter, esp. of portraits or miniatures.

lim·nol·o·gy /limˈnäləjē/ ▸*n.* the study of the biological, chemical, and physical features of lakes and other bodies of fresh water. ▷late 19th cent.: from Greek *limnē* 'lake' + -LOGY. **—lim·no·log·i·cal** /,limnəˈläjikəl/ *adj.* **—lim·nol·o·gist** /-jist/ *n.*

Lím·nos /ˈlim,nôs/ Greek name for LEMNOS.

lim·o /ˈlimō/ ▸*n.* (*pl.* **lim·os**) short for LIMOUSINE.

Li·moges /lēˈmōzн/ a city in west central France; pop. 136,000. Famous in the late Middle Ages for enamel work, it has been noted since the 18th century for the production of porcelain.

lim·o·nene /ˈlimə,nēn/ ▸*n. Chemistry* a colorless liquid hydrocarbon with a lemonlike scent, present in lemon oil, orange oil, and similar essential oils. • A terpene; chem. formula: $C_{10}H_{16}$.

li·mo·nite /ˈlīmə,nīt/ ▸*n.* an amorphous brownish secondary mineral consisting of a mixture of hydrous ferric oxides, important as an iron ore. ▷early 19th cent.: from German *Limonit,* probably from Greek *leimōn* 'meadow' (suggested by the earlier German name *Wiesenerz,* literally 'meadow ore'). **—li·mo·nit·ic** /,līməˈnitik/ *adj.*

lim·ou·sine /ˈlimə,zēn; ,liməˈzēn/ ▸*n.* a large, luxurious automobile, esp. one driven by a chauffeur who is separated from the passengers by a partition. ■ a similar vehicle hired to take passengers to a special event or destination. ■ a passenger vehicle carrying people to and from an airport. ▷early 20th cent.: from French, feminine adjective meaning 'of Limousin,' originally denoting a caped cloak worn in *Limousin:* the car originally had a roof that protected the outside driving seat.

lim·ou·sine lib·er·al ▸*n. derogatory* a wealthy liberal.

limp[1] /limp/ ▸*v.* [*intrans.*] walk with difficulty, typically because of a damaged or stiff leg or foot: *he limped off during Saturday's game.* ■ [with *adverbial of direction*] (of a damaged ship, aircraft, or vehicle) proceed with difficulty: *the badly damaged aircraft limped back to Sicily.*

▸*n.* a tendency to limp; a gait impeded by injury or stiffness: *he walked with a limp.* ▷late Middle English (in the sense 'fall short of'): related to obsolete *limphalt* 'lame,' and probably of Germanic origin.

limp[2] ▸*adj.* lacking internal strength or structure; not stiff or firm: *she let her whole body go limp* | *the flags hung limp and still.* ■ having or denoting a book cover that is not stiffened with board. ■ without energy or will: *he was feeling too limp to argue* | *a limp handshake.* ▷early 18th cent.: of unknown origin; perhaps related to LIMP[1], having the basic sense 'hanging loose.' **—limp·ly** *adv.* **—limp·ness** *n.*

lim·pet /ˈlimpit/ ▸*n.* a marine mollusk with a shallow conical shell and a broad muscular foot, noted for the way it clings tightly to rocks. • Patellidae, Fissurellidae (the keyhole limpets), and other families, class Gastropoda: numerous species, including the **common limpet** (*Patella vulgata*). ▷Old English *lempedu,* from medieval Latin *lampreda* 'limpet, lamprey.'

lim·pet mine ▸*n.* a mine designed to be attached magnetically to a ship's hull and set to explode after a certain time.

lim·pid /ˈlimpid/ ▸*adj.* (of a liquid) free of anything that darkens; completely clear. ■ (of a person's eyes) unclouded; clear. ■ (esp. of writing or music) clear and accessible or melodious: *the limpid notes of a recorder.* ▷late Middle English: from Latin *limpidus;* perhaps related to LYMPH. **—lim·pid·i·ty** /limˈpidətē/ *n.* **—lim·pid·ly** *adv.*

limp·kin /ˈlim(p)kin/ ▸*n.* a wading marsh bird related to the rails, with long legs and a long bill, found in the southeastern U.S. and tropical America. • *Aramus guarauna,* the only member of the family Aramidae. ▷late 19th cent.: from LIMP[1] (with reference to the bird's limping gait) + -KIN.

Lim·po·po /limˈpōpō/ a river in southeastern Africa. Rising as the Crocodile River near Johannesburg, it flows 1,100 miles (1,770 km) in a sweeping curve to the north and east to meet the Indian Ocean north of Maputo, Mozambique. For much of its course it forms South Africa's boundary with Botswana and Zimbabwe.

limp-wrist·ed ▸*adj. informal,* **1** weak; ineffectual. **2** *derogatory* (of a man, esp. a homosexual) effeminate.

lim·u·lus /ˈlimyələs/ ▸*n.* (*pl.* **-li** /-,lī; -,lē/) an arthropod of a genus that comprises the North American horseshoe crab and its extinct relatives. • Genus *Limulus,* class Merostomata. ▷modern Latin, from Latin *limulus* 'somewhat oblique,' from *limus* 'oblique.'

Lin /lin/, Maya (1959–) U.S. architect. She designed the Vietnam Veterans' Memorial in Washington, DC, which was dedicated in 1982, and the Civil Rights Memorial at the Southern Poverty Law Center in Montgomery, Alabama in 1989.

lin. ▸*abbr.* ■ lineal or linear. ■ liniment.

lin·ac /ˈlin,ak/ ▸*n.* short for LINEAR ACCELERATOR.

Lin·a·cre /ˈlinəkər/, Thomas (*c.*1460–1524), English physician and classical scholar. In 1518, he founded the College of Physicians in London and became its first president.

lin·age /ˈlīnij/ ▸*n.* the number of lines in printed or written matter, esp. when used to calculate payment.

Lin Biao /ˈlin ˈbyou/ (also **Lin Piao**) (1908–71), Chinese communist statesman and general. Having been nominated to become Mao's successor in 1969, he staged an unsuccessful coup in 1971 and was reported to have been killed in a plane crash while fleeing to the Soviet Union.

linch·pin /ˈlincн,pin/ (also **lynch·pin**) ▸*n.* **1** a pin passed through the end of an axle to keep a wheel in position. **2** a person or thing vital to an enterprise or organization: *regular brushing is the linchpin of all good dental hygiene.* ▷late Middle English: from Old English *lynis* (in the sense 'linchpin') + PIN.

Lin·coln[1] /ˈlingkən/ **1** the state capital of Nebraska; pop. 225,581. Founded as Lancaster in 1856, it was made the state capital in 1867 and renamed in honor of Abraham Lincoln. **2** a city in eastern England, the county town of Lincolnshire; pop. 82,000. It was founded by the Romans as Lindum Colonia.

Lin·coln[2], Abraham (1809–65), 16th president of the U.S. 1861–65. A Republican, his election to the presidency on an anti-slavery platform helped to precipitate the Civil War, which was fought during his administration. He was assassinated shortly after the war ended and before he could fulfill his campaign promise to reconcile the North and the South. He was noted for his succinct, eloquent speeches, including the Gettysburg Address of 1863. **—Lin·coln·esque** /,lingkəˈnesk/ *adj.*

Abraham Lincoln

Lin·coln green ▸*n. historical* bright green woolen cloth originally made at Lincoln, England.

Lin·coln Me·mo·ri·al a monument in Washington, DC, to Abraham Lincoln, designed by Henry Bacon (1866–1924). Built in the form of a Greek temple, the monument houses a large statue of Lincoln.

Lincoln Memorial

Lin·coln·shire /ˈlingkənsнər; -,sнi(ə)r/ a county on the eastern coast of England; county town, Lincoln.

Lin·coln's Inn one of the Inns of Court in London.

Lind[1] /lind/, James (1716–94), Scottish physician. He laid the foundations for the discovery of vitamins by performing experiments on scurvy in sailors. After his death, the Royal Navy officially adopted the practice of giving lime juice to sailors.

Lind[2], Jenny (1820–87), Swedish soprano; born *Johanna Maria Lind Goldschmidt.* She was known as "the Swedish nightingale" for the purity and agility of her voice.

lin·dane /ˈlin,dān/ ▸*n.* a synthetic organochlorine insecticide, now generally restricted in use due to its toxicity and persistence in the environment. Also called GAMMA-HCH. • An isomer of benzene hexachloride; chem. formula: $C_6H_{12}Cl_6$. ▷1940s: named after Teunis van der *Linden,* 20th-cent. Dutch chemist.

Lind·bergh[1] /ˈlin(d),bərg/, Anne Morrow (1906–2001), U.S. writer; the wife of Charles Lindbergh. Her writings, such as *North to the Orient* (1935), *Gift from the Sea* (1955), and *War Within and Without* (1980), told of her life experiences esp. those regarding aviation, the kidnapping and murder of her two-year-old son, the political climate of the times, and her general philosophy.

Lind·bergh[2], Charles (Augustus) (1902–74), U.S. aviator. In 1927, he made the first solo transatlantic flight in a single-engined monoplane, *Spirit of St. Louis*. Known thereafter as "Lucky Lindy," he moved to Europe with his wife, Anne Morrow Lindbergh, to escape the publicity surrounding the kidnapping and murder of their two-year-old son in 1932. He recounted his historic flight of 1927 in *The Spirit of St. Louis* (1953)

Lin·den /ˈlindən/ an industrial city in northeastern New Jersey, south of Elizabeth, noted for its oil refineries; pop. 36,701.

lin·den /ˈlindən/ ▸*n.* a deciduous tree with heart-shaped leaves and fragrant yellowish blossoms, native to north temperate regions. The pale soft timber is used for carving and furniture. See also BASSWOOD. • Genus *Tilia*, family Tiliaceae: many species, including the **American linden** (*T. americana*) and the **European linden** (*T. europaea*). ▷Old English (as an adjective in the sense 'made of wood from the lime tree'): from *lind* 'lime tree' (compare with LIME[3]) + -EN[3], reinforced by obsolete Dutch *lindenboom* and German *Lindenbaum*.

Lind·say /ˈlinzē/, (Nicholas) Vachel (1879–1931), U.S. poet. His works are collected in *General Booth Enters into Heaven and Other Poems* (1913), *The Congo and Other Poems* (1914), and *Every Soul Is a Circus* (1929).

line[1] /līn/ ▸*n.* **1** a long, narrow mark or band: *a row of closely spaced dots will look like a continuous line | I can't draw a straight line.* ■ *Mathematics* a straight or curved continuous extent of length without breadth. ■ a positioning or movement of a thing or things that creates or appears to follow such a line: *her mouth set in an angry line | the ball rose in a straight line.* ■ a furrow or wrinkle in the skin of the face or hands. ■ a contour or outline considered as a feature of design or composition: *crisp architectural lines | the artist's use of clean line and color.* ■ (on a map or graph) a curve connecting all points having a specified common property. ■ a line marking the starting or finishing point in a race. ■ a line marked on a field or court that relates to the rules of a game or sport. ■ *Football* the line of scrimmage. ■ (**the Line**) the equator. ■ a notional limit or boundary: *the issue of peace cut across class lines | television blurs the line between news and entertainment.* ■ each of the very narrow horizontal sections forming a television picture. ■ *Physics* a narrow range of the spectrum noticeably brighter or darker than the adjacent parts. ■ (**the line**) the level of the base of most letters, such as *h* and *x*, in printing and writing. ■ [as *adj.*] *Printing & Computing* denoting an illustration or graphic consisting of lines and solid areas, with no gradation of tone: *a line block | line art.* ■ each of (usually five) horizontal lines forming a stave in musical notation. ■ a sequence of notes or tones forming an instrumental or vocal melody: *a powerful melodic line.* ■ a dose of a powdered narcotic or hallucinatory drug, esp. cocaine or heroin, laid out in a line. **2** a length of cord, rope, wire, or other material serving a particular purpose: *wring the clothes and hang them on the line | a telephone line.* ■ one of a vessel's mooring ropes. ■ a telephone connection: *she had a crank **on the line**.* ■ a railroad track. ■ a branch or route of a railroad system: *the Philadelphia to Baltimore line.* ■ a company that provides ships, aircraft, or buses on particular routes on a regular basis: *a major shipping line.* **3** a horizontal row of written or printed words. ■ a part of a poem forming one such row: *each stanza has eight lines.* ■ (**lines**) the words of an actor's part in a play or film. ■ a particularly noteworthy written or spoken sentence: *his speech ended with a line about the failure of justice.* ■ (**lines**) *Brit.* an amount of text or number of repetitions of a sentence written out as a school punishment. **4** a row of people or things: *a line of acolytes proceeded down the aisle.* ■ a row or sequence of people or vehicles awaiting their turn to be attended to or to proceed. ■ a connected series of people following one another in time (used esp. of several generations of a family): *we follow the history of a family through the male line.* ■ (in football, hockey, etc.) a set of players in the forwardmost positions for offense or defense. ■ *Football* one of the positions on the line of scrimmage. ■ a series of related things: *the bill is the latest in a long line of measures to protect society from criminals.* ■ a range of commercial goods: *the company intends to hire more people and expand its product line.* ■ *informal* a false or exaggerated account or story: *he feeds me a line about this operation.* ■ the point spread for sports events on which bets may be made. **5** an area or branch of activity: *the stresses unique to their **line of work**.* ■ a direction, course, or channel: *lines of communication | he opened another line of attack.* ■ (**lines**) a manner of doing or thinking about something: *you can't run a business **on** these **lines** | the superintendent was thinking **along the same lines**.* ■ an agreed-upon approach; a policy: *the official line is that there were no chemical attacks on allied troops.* **6** a connected series of military fieldworks or defenses facing an enemy force: *raids behind enemy lines.* ■ an arrangement of soldiers or ships in a column or line formation; a line of battle. ■ (**the line**) regular army regiments (as opposed to auxiliary forces or household troops).

▸*v.* [*trans.*] **1** stand or be positioned at intervals along: *a processional route lined by people waving flags.* **2** [usu. as *adj.*] (**lined**) mark or cover with lines: *a thin woman with a lined face | lined paper.* **3** *Baseball* hit a line drive.

▸*phrasal v.* □ **line out** *Baseball* be put out by hitting a line drive that is caught. □ **line something out** transplant seedlings from beds into nursery lines, where they are grown before being moved to their permanent position. □ **line someone/something up 1** arrange a number of people or things in a straight row. ■ (**line up**) (of a number of people or things) be arranged in this way: *we would line up across the parade ground, shoulder to shoulder.* **2** have someone or something ready or prepared: *have you got any work lined up?* ▷Old English *līne* 'rope, series,' probably of Germanic origin, from Latin *linea (fibra)* 'flax (fiber),' from *linum* 'flax,' reinforced in Middle English by Old French *ligne*, based on Latin *linea*.

▸*PHRASES* □ **above the line 1** *Finance* denoting or relating to money spent on items of current expenditure. **2** *Bridge* denoting bonus points and penalty points, which do not count toward the game. □ **all (the way) down** (or **along**) **the line** at every point or stage: *the mistakes were caused by lack of care all down the line.* □ **along** (or **down**) **the line** at a further, later, or unspecified point: *I knew that somewhere down the line there would be an inquest.* □ **below the line 1** *Finance* denoting or relating to money spent on items of capital expenditure. **2** *Bridge* denoting points for tricks bid and won, which count toward the game. □ **bring someone/something into line** cause someone or something to conform: *the change in the law will **bring** Britain **into line with** Europe.* □ **come down to the line** (of a race) be closely fought right until the end. □ **come into line** conform: *Britain has **come into line with** other Western democracies in giving the vote to its citizens living abroad.* □ **the end of the line** the point at which further effort is unproductive or one can go no further. □ **get a line on** *informal* learn something about. □ **in line 1** under control: *that threat **kept** a lot of people **in line**.* **2** in a row waiting to proceed: *I always peer at other people's shopping carts as we **stand in line**.* □ **in line for** likely to receive: *she might be in line for a cabinet post.* □ **in the line of duty** while one is working (used mainly of police officers firefighters, or soldiers). □ **in** (or **out of**) **line with** in (or not in) alignment or accordance with: *remuneration is in line with comparable international organizations.* □ **lay** (or **put**) **it on the line** speak frankly. □ **(draw) a line in the sand** (state that one has reached) a point beyond which one will not go. □ **line of communications** see COMMUNICATION. □ **line of credit** an amount of credit extended to a borrower. □ **line of fire** the expected path of gunfire or a missile: *residents within line of fire were evacuated from their homes.* □ **line of flight** the route taken through the air. □ **line of force** an imaginary line that represents the strength and direction of a magnetic, gravitational, or electric field at any point. □ **the line of least resistance** see RESISTANCE. □ **line of march** the route taken in marching. □ **line of sight** a straight line along which an observer has unobstructed vision: *a building that obstructs our line of sight.* □ **line of vision** the straight line along which an observer looks: *Jimmy moved forward into Len's line of vision.* □ **on the line 1** at serious risk: *their careers were on the line.* **2** (of a picture in an exhibition) hung with its center about level with the spectator's eye. □ **out of line** *informal* behaving in a way that breaks the rules or is considered disreputable or inappropriate: *he had never **stepped out of line** with her before.*

line[2] ▸*v.* [*trans.*] cover the inside surface of (a container or garment) with a layer of different material: *a basket **lined with** polyethylene.* ■ form a layer on the inside surface of (an area); cover as if with a lining: *hundreds of telegrams lined the walls.* ▷late Middle English: from obsolete *line* 'flax,' with reference to the common use of linen for linings.

▸*PHRASE* □ **line one's pockets** make money, esp. by dishonest means.

lin·e·age /ˈlinē-ij/ ▸*n.* **1** lineal descent from an ancestor; ancestry or pedigree. ■ *Anthropology* a social group tracing its descent from a single ancestor. **2** *Biology* a sequence of species each of which is considered to have evolved from its predecessor: *the chimpanzee and gorilla lineages.* ■ a sequence of cells in the body that developed from a common ancestral cell: *the myeloid lineage.* ▷Middle English: from Old French *lignage*, from Latin *linea* 'a line' (see LINE[1]).

lin·e·al /ˈlinēəl/ ▸*adj.* **1** in a direct line of descent or ancestry: *a lineal descendant.* **2** of, relating to, or consisting of lines; linear. ▷late Middle English: via Old French from late Latin *linealis*, from *linea* 'a line' (see LINE[1]). —**lin·e·al·ly** *adv.*

lin·e·a·ment /ˈlin(ē)əmənt/ ▸*n.* **1** (usu. **lineaments**) *poetic/literary* a distinctive feature or characteristic, esp. of the face. **2** *Geology* a linear feature on the earth's surface, such as a fault. ▷late Middle English: from Latin *lineamentum*, from *lineare* 'make straight,' from *linea* 'a line' (see LINE[1]).

lin·e·ar /ˈlinēər/ ▸*adj.* **1** arranged in or extending along a straight or nearly straight line: *linear arrangements | linear in shape | linear movement.* ■ consisting of or predominantly formed using lines or outlines: *simple linear designs.* ■ involving one dimension only: *linear elasticity.* ■ *Mathematics* able to be represented by a straight line on a graph; involving or exhibiting directly proportional change in two related quantities: *linear functions | linear relationship.* **2** progressing from one stage to another in a single series of steps; sequential: *a linear narrative.* ▷mid 17th cent.: from Latin *linearis*, from *linea* 'a line' (see LINE[1]). —**lin·e·ar·i·ty** /ˌlinēˈaritē/ *n.* —**lin·e·ar·ly** *adv.*

Lin·e·ar A /ˌlinēər/ the earlier of two related forms of writing discovered at Knossos in Crete between 1894 and 1901, found on tablets and vases dating from *c.*1700 to 1450 BC and still largely unintelligible.

lin·e·ar ac·cel·er·a·tor ▸*n.* *Physics* an accelerator in which particles travel in straight lines, not in closed orbits.

Lin·e·ar B a form of Bronze Age writing discovered on tablets in Crete, dating from *c.*1400 to 1200 BC. In 1952 it was shown to be a syllabic script composed of linear signs, derived from Linear A and older Minoan scripts, representing a form of Mycenaean Greek.

lin·e·ar e·qua·tion ▸*n.* an equation between two variables that gives a straight line when plotted on a graph.

lin·e·ar·ize /ˈlinēəˌrīz/ ▸*v.* [*trans.*] *technical* make linear; represent in or transform into a linear form. —**lin·e·ar·i·za·tion** /ˌlinēərəˈzāshən/ *n.* —**lin·e·ar·iz·er** *n.*

lin·e·ar mo·tor ▸*n.* an electric induction motor that produces straight-line motion (as opposed to rotary motion) by means of a linear stator and rotor placed in parallel. It has been used to drive streetcars and monorails, where one part of the motor is on the underside of the vehicle and the other is in the track.

lin·e·ar per·spec·tive ▸*n.* a type of perspective used by artists in which the relative size, shape, and position of objects are determined by drawn or imagined lines converging at a point on the horizon.

lin·e·ar pro·gram·ming ▸*n.* a mathematical technique for maximizing or minimizing a linear function of several variables, such as output or cost.

lin·e·a·tion /ˌlinēˈāshən/ ▸*n.* the action or process of drawing lines or marking with lines. ■ a line or linear marking; an arrangement or group of lines: *magnetic lineations.* ■ a contour or outline. ■ the division of text into lines: *the punctuation and lineation are reproduced accurately.* ▷late Middle English: from Latin *lineatio(n-)*, from *lineare* 'make straight.'

line·back·er /ˈlīnˌbakər/ ▸*n.* *Football* a defensive player normally positioned behind the line of scrimmage, but in front of the safeties.

Pronunciation Key ə *ago*; ər *over*; ˈə or ˌə *up*; ˈər or ˌər *fur*; a *hat*; ā *rate*; ä *car*; CH *chew*; e *let*; ē *see*; e(ə)r *air*; i *fit*; ī *by*; i(ə)r *ear*; NG *sing*; ō *go*; ô *for*; oi *boy*; o͝o *good*; o͞o *goo*; ou *out*; SH *she*; TH *thin*; T͟H *then*; (h)w *why*; ZH *vision*

L

line breed·ing ▸*n.* the selective breeding of animals for a desired feature by mating them within a closely related line.

line cut ▸*n.* a photoengraving from a drawing consisting of solid blacks and whites, without gradations of color.

line danc·ing ▸*n.* a type of country and western dancing in which dancers line up in a row without partners and follow a choreographed pattern of steps to music. —**line dance** *n.* —**line-dance** *v.* —**line danc·er** *n.*

line draw·ing ▸*n.* a drawing done using only narrow lines, the variation of which, in width and density, produce such effects as tone and shading.

line drive ▸*n. Baseball* a powerfully hit ball that travels in the air and relatively close to and parallel with the ground.

line en·grav·ing ▸*n.* the art or technique of engraving by lines incised on the plate, as distinguished from etching and mezzotint. ■ an engraving executed in this manner. —**line-en·graved** *adj.* —**line en·grav·er** *n.*

line feed ▸*n.* the action of advancing paper in a printing machine by the space of one line. ■ *Computing* the analogous movement of text on a VDT screen.

line in·te·gral ▸*n. Mathematics* the integral, taken along a line, of any function that has a continuously varying value along that line.

Line Is·lands a group of 11 islands in the central Pacific Ocean that straddle the equator south of Hawaii. Eight of the islands, including Kiritimati (Christmas Island), form part of Kiribati; the remaining three are uninhabited dependencies of the U.S.

line i·tem ▸*n.* an entry that appears on a separate line in a bookkeeping ledger or a fiscal budget. ■ a single item in a legislative appropriations bill.

line-i·tem ve·to ▸*n.* (also **i·tem ve·to**) the power of a president, governor, or other elected executive to reject individual provisions of a bill.

line·man /ˈlīnmən/ ▸*n.* (*pl.* **-men**) **1** a person employed in laying and maintaining railroad track. ■ a person employed for the repair and maintenance of telephone or electricity power lines. **2** *Football* a player normally positioned on the line of scrimmage.

line man·ag·er ▸*n. chiefly Brit.* a person with direct managerial responsibility for a particular employee. —**line man·age·ment** *n.*

lin·en /ˈlinin/ ▸*n.* cloth woven from flax. ■ garments or other household articles such as sheets made, or originally made, of linen. ▷Old English *līnen* (as an adjective in the sense 'made of flax'); related to Dutch *linnen*, German *Leinen*, also to obsolete *line* 'flax.'

lin·en·fold /ˈlinin,fōld/ ▸*n.* carved or molded ornaments, esp. on a panel, representing folds or scrolls of linen.

line of bat·tle ▸*n.* a disposition of troops for action in battle. ■ *historical* a battle formation of warships in line ahead (one behind another).

line of scrim·mage ▸*n. Football* the imaginary line separating the teams at the beginning of a play.

line print·er ▸*n.* a machine that prints output from a computer a line at a time rather than character by character.

lin·er[1] /ˈlīnər/ ▸*n.* **1** (also **ocean liner**) a large luxurious passenger ship of a type formerly used on a regular line. **2** a fine paintbrush used for painting thin lines and for outlining. ■ a cosmetic used for outlining or accentuating a facial feature, or a brush or pencil for applying this. **3** *informal* another term for LINE DRIVE.

lin·er[2] ▸*n.* a lining in an appliance, device, or container, esp. a removable one, in particular: ■ the lining of a garment. ■ (also **cylinder liner**) a replaceable metal sleeve placed within the cylinder of an engine, forming a durable surface to withstand wear from the piston.

-liner ▸*comb. form informal* denoting a text of a specified number, usually a small number, of lines such as an advertisement or a spoken passage in a play, dialogue, etc.: *two-liner.*

lin·er note ▸*n.* (usu. **liner notes**) the text printed on a paper insert issued as part of the packaging of a compact disc or on the sleeve of a phonograph record.

line score ▸*n.* a summary of the scoring in a game displayed in a horizontal table, esp. an inning-by-inning record of the runs, hits, and errors in a baseball game.

lines·man /ˈlīnzmən/ ▸*n.* (*pl.* **-men**) (in games played on a field or court) an official who assists the referee or umpire from the sideline, esp. in deciding on whether the ball is out of play.

line spec·trum ▸*n. Physics* an emission spectrum consisting of separate isolated lines. ■ an emission (of light, sound, or other radiation) composed of a number of discrete frequencies or energies.

line squall ▸*n. Meteorology* a violent local storm occurring as one of a number along a cold front.

line-up /ˈlīn,əp/ ▸*n.* **1** a group of people or things brought together in a particular context, esp. the members of a sports team or a group of musicians or other entertainers: *a talented batting lineup.* ■ the schedule of television programs for a particular period: *NBC's Thursday lineup of hit comedies.* **2** a group of people including a suspect for a crime assembled for the purpose of having an eyewitness identify the suspect from among them. ■ a line or linelike arrangement of people or things.

line work ▸*n.* **1** drawings or designs carried out with a pen or pencil, as opposed to wash or similar techniques. **2** work on lines, esp. as a lineman or a production-line worker.

ling[1] /liNG/ ▸*n.* any of a number of long-bodied edible marine fishes: • a large eastern Atlantic fish related to the cod (genus *Molva*, family Gadidae), in particular *M. molva*, which is of commercial importance. • a related Australian fish (*Lotella callarias*, family Gadidae). • a similar but unrelated Australian fish (*Genypterus blacodes*, family Ophidiidae). ▷Middle English *lenge*, probably from Middle Dutch; related to LONG[1].

ling[2] ▸*n.* the common heather of Eurasia. ▷Middle English: from Old Norse *lyng*, of unknown origin.

ling. ▸*abbr.* linguistics.

-ling ▸*suffix* **1** forming nouns from nouns, adjectives, and verbs (such as *hireling, youngling*). **2** forming nouns from adjectives and adverbs (such as *darling, sibling, underling*). **3** forming diminutive words: *gosling | sapling.* ■ often with depreciatory reference: *princeling.* ▷Old English; sense 3 from Old Norse.

Lin·ga·la /liNGˈgälə/ ▸*n.* a Bantu language used by over 8 million people as a lingua franca in northern parts of Congo and the Democratic Republic of the Congo (formerly Zaire). ▷a local name.

lin·gam /ˈliNGgəm/ (also **lin·ga** /-gə/) ▸*n. Hinduism* a symbol of divine generative energy, esp. a phallus or phallic object worshiped as a symbol of Shiva. Compare with YONI. ▷from Sanskrit *liṅga*, literally 'mark, (sexual) characteristic.'

ling·cod /ˈliNG,käd/ ▸*n.* (*pl.* same) a large slender greenling that has large teeth and is greenish-brown with golden spots. It lives along the Pacific coast of North America, where it is a valuable commercial and sport fish. • *Ophiodon elongatus*, family Hexagrammidae.

lin·ger /ˈliNGgər/ ▸*v.* [*intrans.*] stay in a place longer than necessary, typically because of a reluctance to leave: *she lingered in the yard, enjoying the warm sunshine | she let her eyes linger on him suggestively.* ■ (**linger over**) spend a long time over (something): *she lingered over her meal.* ■ be slow to disappear or die: *the tradition seems to* ***linger on*** *| we are thankful that she didn't* ***linger on*** *and suffer.* ▷Middle English (in the sense 'dwell, abide'): frequentative of obsolete *leng* 'prolong,' of Germanic origin; related to German *längen* 'make long(er),' also to LONG[1]. —**lin·ger·er** *n.*

lin·ge·rie /,länzhəˈrā; -jə-/ ▸*n.* women's underwear and nightclothes. ▷mid 19th cent.: from French, from *linge* 'linen.'

lin·ger·ing /ˈliNGg(ə)riNG/ ▸*adj.* lasting for a long time or slow to end: *there are still some lingering doubts in my mind | a painful and lingering death.* —**lin·ger·ing·ly** *adv.*

lin·go /ˈliNGgō/ ▸*n.* (*pl.* **-gos** or **-goes**) *informal, often humorous* or *derogatory* a foreign language or local dialect: *they were unable to speak a word of the local lingo.* See note at DIALECT. ■ the vocabulary or jargon of a particular subject or group of people: *fat, known in medical lingo as adipose tissue.* ▷mid 17th cent.: probably via Portuguese *lingoa* from Latin *lingua* 'tongue.'

ling·on·ber·ry /ˈliNGən,berē/ ▸*n.* (*pl.* **-ries**) another term for the mountain cranberry, esp. in Scandinavia, where the berries are much used in cooking. ▷1950s: from Swedish *lingon* 'mountain cranberry' + BERRY.

lin·gua fran·ca /ˈliNGgwə ˈfraNGkə/ ▸*n.* (*pl.* **lin·gua fran·cas**) a language that is adopted as a common language between speakers whose native languages are different. ■ *historical* a mixture of Italian with French, Greek, Arabic, and Spanish, formerly used in the Levant. ▷late 17th cent.: from Italian, literally 'Frankish tongue.'

lin·gual /ˈliNGgwəl/ ▸*adj. technical* **1** of or relating to the tongue. ■ *Phonetics* (of a sound) formed by the tongue. ■ *Anatomy* near or on the side toward the tongue. **2** of or relating to speech or language: *his demonstrations of lingual dexterity.*
▸*n. Phonetics* a lingual sound. ▷mid 17th cent.: from medieval Latin *lingualis*, from Latin *lingua* 'tongue, language.' —**lin·gual·ly** *adv.*

lin·gui·ne /liNGˈgwēnē/ (also **lin·gui·ni**) ▸*n.* small pieces of pasta in the form of narrow ribbons. ▷Italian, plural of *linguina*, diminutive of *lingua* 'tongue.'

lin·guist /ˈliNGgwist/ ▸*n.* **1** a person skilled in foreign languages. **2** a person who studies linguistics. ▷late 16th cent.: from Latin *lingua* 'language' + -IST.

lin·guis·tic /liNGˈgwistik/ ▸*adj.* of or relating to language or linguistics. —**lin·guis·ti·cal·ly** /tik(ə)lē/ *adv.*

lin·guis·tic com·pe·tence ▸*n.* see COMPETENCE (sense 2).

lin·guis·tic per·for·mance ▸*n.* see PERFORMANCE (sense 2).

lin·guis·tic pro·fil·ing ▸*n.* the analysis of a person's speech or writing, especially to assist in identifying or characterizing an individual or particular subgroup: *linguistic profiling revealed that the bomber was probably an uneducated Southerner.*

lin·guis·tics /liNGˈgwistiks/ ▸*plural n.* [treated as *sing.*] the scientific study of language and its structure, including the study of morphology, syntax, phonetics, and semantics. Specific branches of linguistics include sociolinguistics, dialectology, psycholinguistics, computational linguistics, historical-comparative linguistics, and applied linguistics. —**lin·guis·ti·cian** /,liNGgwəˈstiSHən/ *n.*

lin·gu·late /ˈliNGgyə,lāt/ ▸*adj. Botany & Zoology* tongue-shaped. ■ *Zoology* denoting a type of burrowing brachiopod with an inarticulate shell and a long pedicle. ▷mid 19th cent.: from Latin *lingulatus*, based on *lingua* 'tongue,' from *lingere* 'to lick.'

lin·i·ment /ˈlinəmənt/ ▸*n.* a liquid or lotion, esp. one made with oil, for rubbing on the body to relieve pain. ▷late Middle English: from late Latin *linimentum*, from Latin *linire* 'to smear.'

lin·ing /ˈlīniNG/ ▸*n.* a layer of different material covering the inside surface of something: *a lining of fireproof insulation* | [as *adj.*] *lining paper.* ■ an additional layer of different material attached to the inside of a garment or curtain to make it warmer or hang better: *leather gloves with fur linings.*

link[1] /liNGk/ ▸*n.* **1** a relationship between two things or situations, esp. where one thing affects the other: *investigating a link between pollution and forest decline.* ■ a social or professional connection between people or organizations: *he retained strong links with the media.* ■ something that enables communication between people: *sign language interpreters represent a vital link between the deaf and hearing communities.* ■ a means of contact by radio, telephone, or computer between two points: *they set up a satellite link with Tokyo.* ■ a means of travel or transport between two places: *a rail link from Newark to Baltimore.* ■ *Computing* a code or instruction that connects one part of a program or an element in a list to another. **2** a ring or loop in a chain. ■ a unit of measurement of length equal to one hundredth of a surveying chain (7.92 inches).
▸*v.* make, form, or suggest a connection with or between: [*trans.*] *rumors that* ***linked*** *his name* ***with*** *Judith | foreign and domestic policy are linked |* [*intrans.*] *she was* ***linked up with*** *an artistic group.* ■ connect or join physically: [*trans.*] *a network of routes linking towns and villages | the cows are* ***linked up to*** *milking machines |* [*intrans.*] *three different groups, each* ***linking with*** *the other.* ■ [*trans.*] clasp; intertwine: *once outside he linked arms with her.* ▷late Middle English (denoting a loop; also as a verb in the sense 'connect physically'): from Old Norse *hlekkr*, of Germanic origin; related to German *Gelenk* 'joint.'

link[2] ▸*n. historical* a torch of pitch and tow for lighting the way in dark streets. ▷early 16th cent.: perhaps from medieval Latin *li(n)chinus* 'wick,' from Greek *lukhnos* 'light.'

link·age /ˈliNGkij/ ▸*n.* the action of linking or the state of being linked. ■ a system of links: *a complex linkage of nerves.* ■ the linking of different issues in political negotiations. ■ *Genetics* the tendency of groups of genes on the same chromosome to be inherited together.

linked list ▸*n. Computing* an ordered set of data elements, each containing a link to its successor (and sometimes its predecessor).

link·er /ˈliNGkər/ ▸*n.* a thing that links other things, in particular: ■ *Computing* a program used with a compiler or assembler to provide links to the libraries needed for an executable program. ■ an attachment on a knitting machine for linking two pieces of knitting.

link·ing /ˈlɪNGkɪNG/ ▶*adj.* connecting or joining something to something else. ■ *Phonetics* denoting a consonant that is sounded at a boundary between two words or morphemes where two vowels would otherwise be adjacent, as in *law(r) and order.* See also **LIAISON**.

Lin·kö·ping /ˈlin,CHœ̄piNG; -,CHœ-/ an industrial town in southeastern Sweden; pop. 122,000. It was a noted cultural and ecclesiastical center during the Middle Ages.

links /liNGks/ ▶*plural n.* (also **golf links**) [treated as *sing.* or *pl.*] a golf course. ▷Old English *hlinc* 'rising ground,' perhaps related to **LEAN**[1].

links·land /ˈliNGkslənd/ ▶*n. Scottish* level or undulating sandy ground covered by coarse grass and near the sea. ▷1920s: from Scots *links* 'rising ground' (see **LINKS**) + **LAND**.

link·up /ˈliNGk,əp/ (also **link-up**) ▶*n.* an instance of two or more people or things connecting or joining. ■ a connection enabling two or more people or machines to communicate with each other: *a live satellite linkup.*

link·work /ˈliNGk,wərk/ ▶*n.* something made of links, as a chain. ■ a kind of gearing that transmits motion by a series of links rather than by wheels or bands.

linn /lin/ ▶*n. Scottish archaic* a waterfall. ■ the pool below a waterfall. ■ a steep precipice. ▷early 16th cent.: from Scottish Gaelic *linne*, Irish *linn*, related to Welsh *llyn* 'lake.'

Lin·nae·us /liˈnēəs/, Carolus (1707–78), Swedish botanist; founder of modern systematic botany and zoology; Latinized name of *Carl von Linné*. He devised an authoritative classification system for flowering plants involving binomial Latin names (later superseded by that of Antoine Jussieu) and also a classification method for animals. **—Lin·nae·an** /-ˈnēən; -ˈnā-/ (also **Lin·ne·an**) *adj.* & *n.*

lin·net /ˈlinit/ ▶*n.* a mainly brown and gray finch with a reddish breast and forehead. • Genus *Acanthis*, family Fringillidae: three species, in particular the Eurasian *A. cannabina*. ▷early 16th cent.: from Old French *linette*, from *lin* 'flax' (because the bird feeds on flaxseeds).

li·no /ˈlīnō/ ▶*n.* (*pl.* **-nos**) *chiefly Brit.* informal term for **LINOLEUM**.

li·no·cut /ˈlīnō,kət/ ▶*n.* a design or form carved in relief on a block of linoleum. ■ a print made from such a block. **—li·no·cut·ting** *n.*

lin·o·le·ic ac·id /,linəˈlēik; -ˈlā-; ləˈnōlēik/ ▶*n. Chemistry* a polyunsaturated fatty acid present as a glyceride in linseed oil and other oils and essential in the human diet. • Chem. formula: $C_{17}H_{31}COOH$. ▷mid 19th cent.: from Latin *linum* 'flax' + **OLEIC ACID**. **—li·no·le·ate** /ləˈnōlē,āt/ *n.*

lin·o·le·nic ac·id /,linəˈlēnik; -ˈlenik/ ▶*n. Chemistry* a polyunsaturated fatty acid (with one more double bond than linoleic acid) present as a glyceride in linseed and other oils and essential in the human diet. • Chem. formula: $C_{17}H_{29}COOH$; several isomers, notably **gamma-linolenic acid**, present in evening primrose oil. ▷late 19th cent.: from German *Linolensaüre*, from *Linolsaüre* 'linoleic acid,' with the insertion of *-en-* (from **-ENE**). **—lin·o·le·nate** /-ˈlē,nāt; -ˈlen-,āt/ *n.*

li·no·le·um /ləˈnōlēəm/ ▶*n.* a material consisting of a canvas backing thickly coated with a preparation of linseed oil and powdered cork, used esp. as a floor covering. ▷late 19th cent.: from Latin *linum* 'flax' + *oleum* 'oil.' **—li·no·le·umed** *adj.*

Lin·o·type /ˈlīnə,tīp/ ▶*n. trademark Printing* a composing machine producing lines of words as single strips of metal, used chiefly for newspapers. It is now rarely used. ▷late 19th cent.: alteration of the phrase *line o' type.*

Lin Piao variant of **LIN BIAO**.

lin·sang /ˈlin,saNG/ ▶*n.* a small secretive relation of the civet, with a spotted or banded coat and a long tail, found in the forests of Southeast Asia and West Africa. • Family Viverridae: genera *Prionodon* (two Asian species) and *Poiana* (one African species). ▷early 19th cent.: via Javanese from Malay.

lin·seed /ˈlin,sēd/ ▶*n.* the seeds of the flax plant, which are the source of linseed oil and linseed cake. Also called **FLAXSEED**. ■ the flax plant, esp. when grown for linseed oil. ▷Old English *līnsǣd*, from *līn* 'flax' + *sǣd* 'seed.'

lin·seed oil ▶*n.* a pale yellow oil extracted from linseed, used esp. in paint and varnish.

lin·sey-wool·sey /ˈlinzē ˈwŏŏlzē/ ▶*n.* a strong, coarse fabric with a linen or cotton warp and a woolen weft. ▷late 15th cent.: from *linsey*, originally denoting a coarse linen fabric (probably from *Lindsey*, a village in Suffolk, England, where the material was first made) + **WOOL** + *-sey* as a rhyming suffix.

lin·stock /ˈlin,stäk/ ▶*n. historical* a long pole used to hold a match for firing a cannon. ▷late 16th cent.: from earlier *lintstock*, from Dutch *lontstok*, from *lont* 'match' + *stok* 'stick.' The change in the first syllable was due to association with **LINT**.

lint /lint/ ▶*n.* short, fine fibers that separate from the surface of cloth or yarn during processing. ■ a fabric, originally of linen, with a raised nap on one side, used for dressing wounds. ■ the fibrous material of a cotton boll. ■ *chiefly Scottish* flax fibers prepared for spinning. ▷late Middle English *lynnet* 'flax prepared for spinning,' perhaps from Old French *linette* 'linseed,' from *lin* 'flax.' **—lint·y** *adj.*

lin·tel /ˈlintl/ ▶*n.* a horizontal support of timber, stone, concrete, or steel across the top of a door or window. ▷Middle English: from Old French, based on late Latin *liminare*, from Latin *limen* 'threshold.' **—lin·teled** (*Brit.* **lin·telled**) *adj.*

lint·er /ˈlintər/ ▶*n.* a machine for removing the short fibers from cotton seeds after ginning. ■ (**linters**) fibers of this kind.

Lin·ux /ˈlinəks/ ▶*n. trademark* an open-source version of the UNIX operating system.

lin·y /ˈlīnē/ ▶*adj.* (**lin·i·er**, **lin·i·est**) *informal* marked with lines; wrinkled.

Linz /lin(t)s/ an industrial city in northern Austria, on the Danube River; pop. 203,000.

li·on /ˈlīən/ ▶*n.* a large tawny-colored cat that lives in prides, found in Africa and northwestern India. The male has a flowing shaggy mane and takes little part in hunting, which is done cooperatively by the females. • *Panthera leo*, family Felidae. ■ (**the Lion**) the zodiacal sign or constellation Leo. ■ *figurative* a brave or strong person. ■ an influential or celebrated person: *a literary lion.* ■ (**Lion**) a member of a Lions Club. ■ the lion as an emblem (e.g., of English or Scottish royalty) or as a charge in heraldry. ▷Middle English: from Anglo-Norman French *liun*, from Latin *leo, leon-*, from Greek *leōn, leont-*. **—li·on·like** /-,līk/ *adj.*

▶*PHRASE* □ **throw someone to the lions** cause someone to be in an extremely dangerous or unpleasant situation. [with reference to the throwing of Christians to the lions in Roman times.]

lion

li·on dance ▶*n.* a traditional Chinese dance in which the dancers are masked and costumed to resemble lions.

li·on·ess /ˈlīənəs/ ▶*n.* a female lion.

li·on·heart·ed /ˈlīən,härtid/ ▶*adj.* brave and determined.

li·on·ize /ˈlīə,nīz/ ▶*v.* [*trans.*] give a lot of public attention and approval to (someone); treat as a celebrity: *modern athletes are lionized.* **—li·on·i·za·tion** /,līənəˈzāSHən/ *n.* **—li·on·iz·er** *n.*

Li·ons Club ▶*n.* a worldwide charitable society devoted to social and international service, taking its membership primarily from business and professional groups.

li·on's paw ▶*n.* a large Caribbean bivalve mollusk with a thick reddish fan-shaped shell that bears coarse radial ribs. • *Chlamys nodosus*, family Pectinidae.

li·on's share ▶*n.* the biggest or greatest part: *William was appointed editor, which meant that he did the lion's share of the work.*

li·on tam·a·rin ▶*n.* a rare tamarin with a golden or black and golden coat and an erect mane, found only in Brazil. • Genus *Leontopithecus*, family Callitrichidae (or Callithricidae): the **golden lion tamarin** (*L. rosalia*), and three other species that have been recently recognized or discovered.

golden lion tamarin

lip /lip/ ▶*n.* **1** either of the two fleshy parts that form the upper and lower edges of the opening of the mouth: *he kissed her on the lips.* ■ (**lips**) used to refer to a person's speech or to current topics of conversation: *downsizing is **on everyone's lips** at the moment.* ■ another term for **LABIUM** (senses 1 and 2). ■ another term for **LABELLUM**. **2** the edge of a hollow container or an opening: *drawing her finger around the lip of the cup.* ■ a rounded, raised, or extended piece along an edge. **3** *informal* impudent talk: *don't give me any of your lip!*

▶*v.* (**lipped**, **lip·ping**) [*trans.*] (of water) lap against: *beaches lipped by the surf rimming the Pacific.* ■ *Golf* hit the rim of (a hole) but fail to go in. ▷Old English *lippa*, of Germanic origin; related to Dutch *lip* and German *Lippe*, from an Indo-European root shared by Latin *labia, labra* 'lips.' **—lip·less** *adj.* **—lip·like** /-līk/ *adj.* **—lipped** *adj. her pale-lipped mouth.*

▶*PHRASES* □ **bite one's lip** repress an emotion; stifle laughter or a retort: *she bit her lip to stop the rush of bitter words.* □ **curl one's lip** raise a corner of one's upper lip to show contempt; sneer. □ **lick** (or **smack**) **one's lips** look forward to something with relish; show one's satisfaction. □ **my** (or **his**, etc.) **lips are sealed** see **SEAL**[1]. □ **pass one's lips** be eaten, drunk, or spoken. □ **pay lip service to** express approval of or support for (something) without taking any significant action.

li·pa /ˈlē,pä; -pə/ ▶*n.* (*pl.* same or **li·pas**) a monetary unit of Croatia, equal to one hundredth of a kuna.

Lip·a·ri Is·lands /ˈlipərē/ a group of seven volcanic islands in the Tyrrhenian Sea, off the northeastern coast of Sicily, in Italian possession. Believed by the ancient Greeks to be the home of Aeolus, they were formerly known as the Aeolian Islands.

li·pase /ˈlip,ās; ˈlī,pās/ ▶*n. Biochemistry* a pancreatic enzyme that catalyzes the breakdown of fats to fatty acids and glycerol or other alcohols. ▷late 19th cent.: from Greek *lipos* 'fat' + **-ASE**.

lip balm ▶*n.* a preparation, typically in stick form, to prevent or relieve chapped lips.

Lip·chitz /ˈlipSHits/, Jacques (1891–1973), French sculptor, born in Lithuania; born *Chaim Jacob Lipchitz*. After producing cubist works such as *Sailor with a Guitar* (1914), he explored the interpenetration of solids and voids in his series of "transparent" sculptures of the 1920s.

lip·ec·to·my /liˈpektəmē; lī-/ ▶*n.* the surgical removal of fatty tissue, esp. from the abdomen in obese persons.

li·pe·mi·a /liˈpēmēə/ (also **li·pae·mi·a**) ▶*n. Medicine* the presence in the blood of an abnormally high concentration of emulsified fat. ▷late 19th cent.: from Greek *lipos* 'fat' + **-EMIA**.

Li·petsk /ˈlē,pitsk/ an industrial city in southwestern Russia, on the Voronezh River; pop. 455,000.

lip·gloss /ˈlip,gläs; -,glôs/ (also **lip gloss**) ▶*n.* a cosmetic applied to the lips to provide a glossy finish, often tinted.

lip·id /ˈlipid/ ▶*n. Chemistry* any of a class of organic compounds that are fatty acids or their derivatives and are insoluble in water but soluble in organic solvents. They include many natural oils, waxes, and steroids. ▷early 20th cent.: from French *lipide*, based on Greek *lipos* 'fat.'

li·pi·do·sis /,lipəˈdōsis/ ▶*n.* (*pl.* **-ses** /-,sēz/) *Medicine* a disorder of lipid metabolism in the body tissues.

Lip·iz·za·ner /ˈlipə,zänər; ,lipəˈtsänər/ (also **Lip·pi·za·ner**) ▶*n.* a horse of a fine white breed used esp. in displays of dressage. ▷early 20th cent.: from German, from *Lippiza*, site of the former Austrian Imperial stud near Trieste.

lip·lin·er /ˈlip,līnər/ ▶*n.* a cosmetic applied to the outline of the lips, mainly to prevent the unwanted spreading of lipstick or lipgloss.

Li Po /ˈlē ˈpō; ˈbō/ (also **Li Bo** /ˈlē ˈbō/ or **Li T'ai Po** /ˈlē ˈtī ˈbō/) (AD 701–62), Chinese poet.

lipo- ▶*comb. form* relating to fat or other lipids: *liposuction* | *lipoprotein.* ▷from Greek *lipos* 'fat.'

li·po·dys·tro·phy syn·drome /,lipəˈdistrəfē; ,lipə-/ ▶*n.* a metabolic disease in which fat distribution in the body becomes abnormal, often as a result of taking protease inhibitor drugs. Fat is lost from the face, arms, and legs, and is built up in other places, especially the breasts, abdomen, and back of the neck.

lip·o·gen·e·sis /ˌlipōˈjenəsis; ˌlī-/ ▸*n. Physiology* the metabolic formation of fat. —**lip·o·gen·ic** /-ˈjenik/ *adj.*

lip·o·gram /ˈlipəˌgram; ˈlī-/ ▸*n.* a composition from which the writer systematically omits a certain letter or certain letters of the alphabet. ▷early 18th cent.: back-formation from Greek *lipogrammatos* 'lacking a letter,' from *lip-* (stem of *leipein* 'to leave (out)') + *gramma* 'letter.' —**lip·o·gram·mat·ic** /ˌlipōgrəˈmatik; ˌlī-/ *adj.*

lip·oid /ˈlipˌoid; ˈlīˌpoid/ ▸*adj.* (also **lip·oid·al**) *Biochemistry* relating to or resembling fat.
▸*n.* a fatlike substance; a lipid. ▷late 19th cent.: from Greek *lipos* 'fat' + **-OID**.

li·pol·y·sis /liˈpäləsis; lī-/ ▸*n. Physiology* the breakdown of fats and other lipids by hydrolysis to release fatty acids. —**li·po·lyt·ic** /ˌlipəˈlitik; ˌlī-/ *adj.*

li·po·ma /liˈpōmə/ ▸*n.* (*pl.* **-mas** or **-ma·ta** /-mədə/) *Medicine* a benign tumor of fatty tissue. —**li·pom·a·tous** /-mətəs/ *adj.*

lip·o·phil·ic /ˌlipəˈfilik; ˌlī-/ ▸*adj. Biochemistry* tending to combine with or dissolve in lipids or fats.

lip·o·pol·y·sac·cha·ride /ˈlipōˌpälēˈsakəˌrīd; ˈlī-/ ▸*n. Biochemistry* a complex molecule containing both lipid and polysaccharide parts.

lip·o·pro·tein /ˌlipəˈprōˌtēn; ˌlī-/ ▸*n. Biochemistry* any of a group of soluble proteins that combine with and transport fat or other lipids in the blood plasma.

lip·o·some /ˈlipəˌsōm; ˈlī-/ ▸*n. Biochemistry* a minute spherical sac of phospholipid molecules enclosing a water droplet, esp. as formed artificially to carry drugs or other substances into the tissues.

lip·o·suc·tion /ˈlipōˌsəksHən; ˈlī-/ ▸*n.* a technique in cosmetic surgery for removing excess fat from under the skin by suction.

lip·o·tro·pin /ˌlipəˈtrōpin; ˌlīpə-/ (also **lip·o·tro·phin** /-ˈtrōfən/) ▸*n. Biochemistry* a hormone secreted by the anterior pituitary gland. It promotes the release of fat reserves from the liver into the bloodstream.

Lip·pes loop /ˈlipēz/ ▸*n.* a type of intrauterine contraceptive device made of inert plastic in a double S-shape, which can be left in place for long periods. ▷1960s: named after Jack *Lippes* (born 1924), American obstetrician.

Lip·pi·zan·er /ˈlipəˌzänər; ˌlipəˈtsänər/ ▸*n.* variant spelling of **LIPIZZANER**.

Lipp·mann1 /ˈlipmən/, Gabriel Jonas (1845–1921), French physicist. He is best known for his production of the first fully orthochromatic color photograph in 1893.

Lipp·mann2, Walter (1899–1974), U.S. journalist and essayist. He was a founder and associate editor of the *New Republic* (1914–17) and a columnist for the *New York Herald Tribune* 1931–67. Notable works: *A Preface to Morals* (1929), *The Good Society* (1937), and *Western Unity and the Common Market* (1962). His excellence in news analysis was recognized in 1958 by a Pulitzer Prize Special Citation.

lip·py /ˈlipē/ *informal* ▸*adj.* (**-pi·er, -pi·est**) **1** insolent; impertinent. **2** having prominent lips.

lip-read /ˌrēd/ (also **lip·read**) ▸*v.* [*intrans.*] (of a deaf person) understand speech from observing a speaker's lip movements. —**lip-read·er** *n.*

lip·stick /ˈlipˌstik/ ▸*n.* colored cosmetic applied to the lips from a small solid stick.

lip-sync /ˌsiNGk/ (also **lip-synch**) ▸*v.* [*trans.*] (of an actor or singer) move the lips silently in synchronization with (a recorded soundtrack).
▸*n.* the action of using such a technique. —**lip-sync·er** *n.*

Lip·ton /ˈliptən/, Sir Thomas Johnstone (1850–1931), Scottish merchant and yachtsman. He worked at a number of jobs in the U.S. before he developed a chain of food stores in Scotland. He then invested in tea and coffee and had some of it packed in the U.S. Also noted for his yachts, he entered five of them in the America's Cup races.

liq. ▸*abbr.* ■ liquid. ■ liquor. ■ (in prescriptions) solution. [from Latin *liquor*]

li·quate /ˈlīˌkwāt; ˈlikˌwāt/ ▸*v.* [*trans.*] *Metallurgy* separate or purify (a metal) by melting it. ▷mid 19th cent.: from Latin *liquat-* 'made liquid,' from the verb *liquare*; related to **LIQUOR**. —**li·qua·tion** /līˈkwāsHən; li-/ *n.*

liq·ue·fied pet·ro·le·um gas (abbr.: **LPG**) ▸*n.* a mixture of light gaseous hydrocarbons (ethane, propane, butane, etc.) made liquid by pressure and used as fuel.

liq·ue·fy /ˈlikwəˌfī/ (also **liq·ui·fy**) ▸*v.* (**-fies, -fied**) make or become liquid: [*trans.*] *the minimum pressure required to liquefy a gas* | [*intrans.*] *as the fungus ripens, the cap turns black and liquefies.* ■ convert (solid food) into a liquid or purée, typically by using a blender. ▷late Middle English: from French *liquéfier*, from Latin *liquefacere* 'make liquid,' from *liquere* 'be liquid.' —**liq·ue·fac·tion** /ˌlikwəˈfaksHən/ *n.* —**liq·ue·fac·tive** /ˌlikwəˈfaktiv/ *adj.* —**liq·ue·fi·a·ble** /ˌlikwəˈfīəbəl/ *adj.* —**liq·ue·fi·er** *n.*

li·ques·cent /liˈkwesənt/ ▸*adj. poetic/literary* becoming or apt to become liquid. ▷early 18th cent.: from Latin *liquescent-* 'becoming liquid,' from the verb *liquescere* (see **LIQUEFY**). —**li·ques·cence** *n.*

li·queur /liˈkər; -ˈk(y)o͝or/ ▸*n.* a strong, sweet flavored alcoholic liquor, usually drunk after a meal. ▷mid 18th cent.: from French, 'liquor.'

liq·uid /ˈlikwid/ ▸*adj.* **1** having a consistency like that of water or oil, i.e., flowing freely but of constant volume. ■ having the clear shimmer of water: *looking into those liquid dark eyes.* ■ denoting a substance normally a gas that has been liquefied by cold or pressure: *liquid oxygen.* ■ not fixed or stable; fluid. **2** (of a sound) clear, pure, and flowing; harmonious: *the liquid song of the birds.* **3** *Phonetics* (of a consonant) produced by allowing the airstream to flow over the sides of the tongue, typically *l* and *r*, and able to be prolonged like a vowel. **4** (of assets) held in cash or easily converted into cash. ■ having ready cash or liquid assets. ■ (of a market) having a high volume of activity.
▸*n.* **1** a liquid substance: *drink plenty of liquids.* **2** *Phonetics* a liquid consonant. ▷late Middle English: from Latin *liquidus*, from *liquere* 'be liquid.' —**liq·uid·ly** *adv.* —**liq·uid·ness** *n.*

liq·uid·am·bar /ˌlikwidˈambər/ ▸*n.* a deciduous North American and Asian tree with maplelike leaves and bright autumn colors, yielding aromatic resinous balsam. • Genus *Liquidambar*, family Hamamelidaceae: several species, including *L. orientalis* of Asia, which yields liquid storax, and the sweet gum of North America. ■ liquid balsam obtained chiefly from the Asian liquidambar tree, used medicinally and in perfume. Also called **STORAX**. ▷late 16th cent.: modern Latin, apparently formed irregularly from Latin *liquidus* 'liquid' + medieval Latin *ambar* 'amber.'

liq·ui·date /ˈlikwəˌdāt/ ▸*v.* [*trans.*] **1** wind up the affairs of (a company or firm) by ascertaining liabilities and apportioning assets. ■ [*intrans.*] (of a company) undergo such a process. ■ convert (assets) into cash: *a plan to liquidate $10,000,000 worth of property over seven years.* ■ pay off (a debt). **2** eliminate, typically by violent means; kill. ▷mid 16th cent. (in the sense 'set out (accounts) clearly'): from medieval Latin *liquidat-* 'made clear,' from the verb *liquidare*, from Latin *liquidus* (see **LIQUID**). Sense 1 was influenced by Italian *liquidare* and French *liquider*, sense 2 by Russian *likvidirovat'*. —**liq·ui·da·tion** /ˌlikwəˈdāsHən/ *n.*

liq·ui·da·tor /ˈlikwəˌdātər/ ▸*n.* a person appointed to wind up the affairs of a company or firm.

liq·uid crys·tal ▸*n.* a substance that flows like a liquid but has some degree of ordering in the arrangement of its molecules.

liq·uid crys·tal dis·play ▸*n.* a form of visual display used in electronic devices in which a layer of a liquid crystal is sandwiched between two transparent electrodes. The application of an electric current to a small area of the layer alters the alignment of its molecules, which affects its reflectivity or its transmission of polarized light and makes it opaque.

liq·uid·i·ty /liˈkwidətē/ ▸*n. Finance* the availability of liquid assets to a market or company. ■ liquid assets; cash. ■ a high volume of activity in a market. ▷early 17th cent.: from French *liquidité* or medieval Latin *liquiditas*, from Latin *liquidus* (see **LIQUID**).

li·quid·i·ty ra·tio ▸*n. Finance* the ratio between the liquid assets and the liabilities of a bank or other institution.

liq·uid·ize /ˈlikwəˌdīz/ ▸*v.* [*trans.*] *Brit.* another term for **LIQUEFY**. —**liq·uid·iz·er** *n.*

liq·uid lunch ▸*n. informal, humorous* a drinking session at lunchtime sometimes taking the place of a meal.

liq·uid meas·ure ▸*n.* a unit for measuring the volume of liquids.

liq·uid par·af·fin ▸*n. chiefly Brit.* a colorless, odorless oily liquid consisting of a mixture of hydrocarbons obtained from petroleum, used as a laxative.

liq·uid sto·rax ▸*n.* see **STORAX** (sense 1).

liq·ui·fy /ˈlikwəˌfī/ ▸*v.* variant spelling of **LIQUEFY**.

liq·uor /ˈlikər/ ▸*n.* **1** alcoholic drink, esp. distilled spirits. **2** a liquid produced or used in a process of some kind, in particular: ■ water used in brewing. ■ liquid in which something has been steeped or cooked. ■ liquid that drains from food during cooking. ■ the liquid from which a substance has been crystallized or extracted.
▸*phrasal v.* □ **liquor up** (or **liquor someone up**) *informal* get (or make someone) drunk. ▷Middle English (denoting liquid or something to drink): from Old French *lic(o)ur*, from Latin *liquor*; related to *liquare* 'liquefy,' *liquere* 'be fluid.'

liq·uo·rice /ˈlik(ə)risH; -ris/ ▸*n.* British spelling of **LICORICE**.

liq·uor·ish /ˈlik(ə)risH/ ▸*adj.* archaic form of **LICKERISH**. —**liq·uor·ish·ness** *n.*

li·ra /ˈli(ə)rə/ ▸*n.* (*pl.* **li·re** /ˈli(ə)rā; ˈli(ə)rə/) **1** the basic monetary unit of Italy (until replaced by the euro), notionally equal to 100 centesimos. **2** the basic monetary unit of Turkey, equal to 100 kurus. ▷Italian, from Provençal *liura*, from Latin *libra* 'pound.'

lir·i·o·den·dron /ˌli(ə)rēəˈdendrən/ ▸*n.* a tree of a small genus that includes the tulip tree. • Genus *Liriodendron*, family Magnoliaceae. ▷modern Latin, from Greek *leirion* 'lily' + *dendron* 'tree.'

lir·i·pipe /ˈli(ə)rəˌpīp/ ▸*n.* a long tail hanging from the back of a hood, esp. in medieval or academic dress. ▷early 17th cent.: from medieval Latin *liripipium* 'tippet of a hood, cord,' of unknown origin.

Lis·bon /ˈlizbən/ the capital and chief port of Portugal, on the Atlantic coast at the mouth of the Tagus River; pop. 678,000. Portuguese name **LISBOA** .

li·sen·te /liˈsentē/ ▸ plural form of **SENTE**.

lisle /līl/ (also **lisle thread**) ▸*n.* a fine, smooth cotton thread used esp. for hosiery. ▷mid 16th cent.: from *Lisle*, former spelling of **LILLE**, the original place of manufacture.

Lisp /lisp/ (also **LISP**) ▸*n.* a high-level computer programming language devised for list processing. ▷1950s: from *lis(t) p(rocessor)*.

lisp /lisp/ ▸*n.* a speech defect in which *s* is pronounced like *th* in *thick* and *z* is pronounced like *th* in *this*.
▸*v.* [*intrans.*] speak with a lisp. ▷Old English *wlispian* (recorded in *āwlyspian*), from *wlisp* (adjective) 'lisping,' of imitative origin; compare with Dutch *lispen* and German *lispeln*. —**lisp·er** *n.* —**lisp·ing·ly** *adv.*

lis pen·dens /ˈlis ˈpenˌdenz/ ▸*n. Law* a pending legal action. ■ a formal notice of this. ▷Latin.

Lis·sa·jous fig·ure /ˈlēsəˌzHo͞o; ˌlēsəˈzHo͞o/ ▸*n. Mathematics* any of a number of characteristic looped or curved figures traced out by a point undergoing two independent simple harmonic motions at right angles with frequencies in a simple ratio. ▷late 19th cent.: named after Jules A. *Lissajous* (1822–80), French physicist.

lis·some /ˈlisəm/ (also *chiefly Brit.* **lis·som**) ▸*adj.* (of a person or their body) thin, supple, and graceful. ▷late 18th cent.: contraction, from **LITHE** + **-SOME1**. —**lis·some·ness** *n.*

list1 /list/ ▸*n.* **1** a number of connected items or names written or printed consecutively, typically one below the other: *consult the list of drugs on page 326* | *writing a shopping list.* ■ a set of items considered as being in the same category or having a particular order of priority: *tourism is at the top of the list of potential job creators.* ■ *Computing* a formal structure analogous to a list by which items of data can be stored or processed in a definite order. [late 16th cent.: from French *liste*, of Germanic origin.] **2** (**lists**) *historical* barriers enclosing an area for a jousting tournament. ■ the scene of a contest or combat. [late Middle English: from Old French *lisse*.] **3** a selvage of a piece of fabric. [Middle English, from Old English *liste* 'border,' of Germanic origin; related to Dutch *lijst* and German *Leiste*.]
▸*v.* [*trans.*] **1** make a list of: *I have listed four reasons below.* ■ (often **be listed**) include or enter in a list: *93 men were still listed as missing.* ■ [*intrans.*] (**list at/for**) be on a list of products at (a specified price): *the bottom-of-the-line Mercedes lists for $52,050.* **2** *archaic* enlist for military service. —**list·a·ble** *adj.*
▸*PHRASE* □ **enter the lists** issue or accept a challenge.

list2 ▸*v.* [*intrans.*] (of a ship) lean to one side, typically because of a leak or unbalanced cargo. Compare with **HEEL2**.
▸*n.* an instance of a ship leaning over in such a way. ▷early 17th cent.: of unknown origin.

list3 *archaic* ▸*v.* [*intrans.*] want; like: *let them think what they list.*
▸*n.* desire; inclination: *I have little list to write.* ▷Old

English *lystan* (verb), of Germanic origin, from a base meaning 'pleasure.'

list·box /'lis(t),bäks/ ▶*n. Computing* a box on the screen that contains a list of options, only one of which can be selected.

list·ed /'listid/ ▶*adj.* **1** admitted for trading on a stock exchange: *listed securities.* **2** represented in a telephone directory.

lis·tel /'listəl/ ▶*n. Architecture* a narrow strip with a flat surface running between moldings. Also called FILLET. ▷late 16th cent.: from Italian *listello*, diminutive of *lista* 'strip, band.'

lis·ten /'lisən/ ▶*v.* [*intrans.*] give one's attention to a sound: *evidently he was not listening | sit and* **listen to** *the radio.* ■ take notice of and act on what someone says; respond to advice or a request: *I told her over and over again, but she wouldn't listen.* ■ make an effort to hear something; be alert and ready to hear something: *they* **listened for** *sounds from the baby's room.* ■ used to urge someone to pay attention to what one is going to say: *listen, I've got an idea.*
▶*phrasal v.* □ **listen in** listen to a private conversation, often secretly. ■ use a radio receiving set to listen to a broadcast or conversation.
▶*n.* [in *sing.*] an act of listening to something. ▷Old English *hlysnan* 'pay attention to,' of Germanic origin.

lis·ten·a·ble /'lisənəbəl/ ▶*adj.* easy or pleasant to listen to. —**lis·ten·a·bil·i·ty** /,lis(ə)nə'bilitē/ *n.*

lis·ten·er /'lis(ə)nər/ ▶*n.* a person who listens, esp. someone who does so in an attentive manner. ■ a person listening to a radio station or program.

lis·ten·ing post ▶*n.* a station for intercepting electronic communications. ■ a position from which to listen or gather information. ■ a point near an enemy's lines for detecting movements by sound.

Lis·ter /'listər/, Joseph, 1st Baron (1827–1912), English surgeon, inventor of antiseptic techniques in surgery. He realized the significance of Louis Pasteur's germ theory in connection with sepsis, and in 1865 he used carbolic acid dressings on patients who had undergone surgery.

list·er /'listər/ ▶*n.* a plow with a double moldboard. ▷late 19th cent.: from late 18th-cent. *list* 'prepare land for a crop' (see LIST[1], -ER[1]).

lis·te·ri·a /li'stirēə/ ▶*n.* a type of bacterium that infects humans and other warm-blooded animals through contaminated food. • *Listeria monocytogenes*; motile aerobic Gram-negative rods. ■ *informal* food poisoning or other disease caused by infection with listeria; listeriosis. ▷1940s: modern Latin, named after Joseph *Lister* (1827–1912), English surgeon.

lis·te·ri·o·sis /li,sti(ə)rē'ōsis/ ▶*n.* disease caused by infection with listeria.

list·ing /'listiNG/ ▶*n.* **1** a list or catalog. ■ the drawing up of a list. ■ an entry in a list or register. **2** a selvage of a piece of fabric.

list·less /'lis(t)lis/ ▶*adj.* (of a person or their manner) lacking energy or enthusiasm: *bouts of listless depression.* ▷Middle English: from obsolete *list* 'appetite, desire' + -LESS. —**list·less·ly** *adv.* —**list·less·ness** *n.*

Lis·ton /'listən/, Sonny (1932–70), U.S. heavyweight boxing champion; born *Charles Liston.* He defeated Floyd Patterson for the world heavyweight championship in 1962 but lost the title to Muhammad Ali (then Cassius Clay) in 1964.

list price ▶*n.* the price of an article as shown in a list issued by the manufacturer or by the general body of manufacturers of the particular class of goods.

list proc·ess·ing ▶*n. Computing* the manipulation of data organized as lists.

LISTSERV /'lis(t),sərv/ ▶*n. trademark* an electronic mailing list of people who wish to receive specified information from the Internet. ■ (also **listserv**) any similar application.

Liszt /list/, Franz (1811–86), Hungarian composer and pianist. He was a key figure in the romantic movement; many of his piano compositions combine lyricism with great technical complexity, while his 12 symphonic poems 1848–58 created a new musical form. —**Liszt·i·an** /-tēən/ *adj.* & *n.*

lit /lit/ ▶ past and past participle of LIGHT[1], LIGHT[3].

lit ▶*adj. Informal* drunk.

lit. ▶*abbr.* ■ liter or liters. ■ literal or literally. ■ literary or literature.

Li T'ai Po /'lē 'tī 'bō; 'pō/ variant of LI PO.

lit·a·ny /'litn-ē/ ▶*n.* (*pl.* **-nies**) a series of petitions for use in church services or processions, usually recited by the clergy and responded to in a recurring formula by the people. ■ a tedious recital or repetitive series: *a litany of complaints.* ▷Middle English: from Old French *letanie*, via ecclesiastical Latin from Greek *litaneia* 'prayer,' from *litē* 'supplication.'

li·tas /'lē,täs/ ▶*n.* (*pl.* same) the basic monetary unit of Lithuania, equal to 100 centas.

LitB ▶*abbr.* ■ Bachelor of Letters. ■ Bachelor of Literature. ▷from Latin, *Li(t)erārum Baccalaureus.*

li·tchi /'lēCHē/ (also **ly·chee** or **li·chee**) ▶*n.* **1** a small rounded fruit with sweet white scented flesh, a large central stone, and a thin rough skin. Also called **litchi nut** when dried. **2** the Chinese tree that bears this fruit. • *Nephelium litchi* (or *Litchi chinensis*), family Sapindaceae. ▷late 16th cent.: from Chinese *lìzhī.*

lit crit /'lit ,krit/ ▶*abbr.* literary criticism.

LitD ▶*abbr.* ■ Doctor of Letters. ■ Doctor of Literature. ▷from modern Latin, *Li(t)erārum Doctor.*

lite /līt/ ▶*adj.* of or relating to low-fat or low-sugar versions of manufactured food or drink products: *lite beer.* ■ *informal* lacking in substance; superficial.
▶*n.* **1** beer with relatively few calories. **2** *informal* used as a simplified spelling of LIGHT[1], esp. commercially. ▷1950s: a deliberate respelling of LIGHT[1], LIGHT[2].

-lite ▶*suffix* forming names of rocks, minerals, and fossils: *rhyolite | zeolite.* ▷from French, from Greek *lithos* 'stone.'

li·ter /'lētər/ (*Brit.* **li·tre**) (abbr.: **l**) ▶*n.* a metric unit of capacity, formerly defined as the volume of 1 kilogram of water under standard conditions, now equal to 1,000 cubic centimeters (about 1.75 pints). ▷late 18th cent.: from French *litre*, alteration of *litron* (an obsolete measure of capacity), via medieval Latin from Greek *litra*, a Sicilian monetary unit.

lit·er·a·cy /'litərəsē; 'litrə-/ ▶*n.* the ability to read and write. ■ competence or knowledge in a specified area: *wine literacy can't be taught in three hours.* ▷late 19th cent.: from LITERATE, on the pattern of *illiteracy.*

li·te·rae hu·ma·ni·o·res /'litə,rī hyōō,manē'ō,rāz; 'litərē; -'ôr,ēz/ ▶*plural n.* [treated as *sing.*] the honors course in classics, philosophy, and ancient history at Oxford University. ▷Latin, literally 'the more humane studies.'

lit·er·al /'litərəl; 'litrəl/ ▶*adj.* **1** taking words in their usual or most basic sense without metaphor or allegory: *dreadful in its literal sense, full of dread.* ■ free from exaggeration or distortion: *you shouldn't take this as a literal record of events.* ■ *informal* absolute (used to emphasize that a strong expression is deliberately chosen to convey one's feelings): *fifteen years of literal hell.* **2** (of a translation) representing the exact words of the original text. ■ (of a visual representation) exactly copied; realistic as opposed to abstract or impressionistic. **3** (also **literal-minded**) (of a person or performance) lacking imagination; prosaic. **4** of, in, or expressed by a letter or the letters of the alphabet: *literal mnemonics.*
▶*n. Brit. Printing* a misprint of a letter. ▷late Middle English: from Old French, or from late Latin *litteralis*, from Latin *littera* (see LETTER). —**lit·er·al·i·ty** /,litə'ralətē/ —**lit·er·al·ize** /-,līz/ *v.* —**lit·er·al·ness** *n.*

USAGE See usage at LITERALLY.

lit·er·al·ism /'litərə,lizəm; 'litrə-/ ▶*n.* the interpretation of words in their usual or most basic sense, without allowing for metaphor or exaggeration: *biblical literalism.* ■ literal or nonidealistic representation in literature or art. —**lit·er·al·ist** *n.* —**lit·er·al·is·tic** /,litərə'listik; ,litrə-/ *adj.*

lit·er·al·ly /'litərəlē; 'litrə-/ ▶*adv.* in a literal manner or sense; exactly: *the driver* **took it literally** *when asked to go straight across the traffic circle | tiramisu, literally translated "pick me up."* ■ *informal* used for emphasis or to express strong feeling while not being literally true: *I have received literally thousands of letters.*

USAGE In its standard use, **literally** means 'in a literal sense, as opposed to a nonliteral or exaggerated sense,': *I told him I never wanted to see him again, but I didn't expect him to take it* **literally.** In recent years, an extended use of **literally** (and also **literal**) has become very common, where **literally** (or **literal**) is used deliberately in nonliteral contexts, for added effect: *they bought the car and* **literally** *ran it into the ground.* This use can lead to unintentional humorous effects (*we were* **literally** *killing ourselves laughing*) and is not acceptable in formal English.

lit·er·ar·y /'litə,rerē/ ▶*adj.* **1** [*attrib.*] concerning the writing, study, or content of literature, esp. of the kind valued for quality of form: *the great literary works of the nineteenth century.* ■ concerned with literature as a profession: *it was signed by such literary figures as Maya Angelou.* **2** (of language) associated with literary works or other formal writing; having a marked style intended to create a particular emotional effect. ▷mid 17th cent. (in the sense 'relating to the letters of the alphabet'): from Latin *litterarius*, from *littera* (see LETTER). —**lit·er·ar·i·ly** /,litə're(ə)rəlē/ *adv.* —**lit·er·ar·i·ness** *n.*

lit·er·ar·y a·gent ▶*n.* a professional agent who acts on behalf of an author in dealing with publishers and others involved in promoting the author's work.

lit·er·ar·y crit·i·cism ▶*n.* the art or practice of judging and commenting on the qualities and character of literary works.

Modern critics tend to pass over the concerns of earlier centuries, such as formal categories or the place of moral or aesthetic value; some analyze texts as self-contained entities, in isolation from external factors, while others discuss them in terms of spheres such as biography, history, Marxism, or feminism. Since the 1950s, the concepts of meaning and authorship have been explored or questioned by structuralism, poststructuralism, postmodernism, and deconstruction.

—**lit·er·ar·y crit·ic** *n.*

lit·er·ar·y ex·ec·u·tor ▶*n.* a person entrusted with a dead writer's papers and copyrighted and unpublished works.

lit·er·ate /'litərit/ ▶*adj.* (of a person) able to read and write. ■ having or showing education or knowledge, typically in a specified area: *we need people who are economically and politically literate.*
▶*n.* a literate person. ▷late Middle English: from Latin *litteratus*, from *littera* (see LETTER). —**lit·er·ate·ly** *adv.*

lit·e·ra·ti /,litə'rätē/ ▶*plural n.* well-educated people who are interested in literature. ▷early 17th cent.: from Latin, plural of *literatus* 'acquainted with letters,' from *littera* (see LETTER).

lit·e·ra·tim /,litə'rātim; -'rät-/ ▶*adv. formal* (of the copying of a text) letter by letter. ▷from medieval Latin.

lit·er·a·ture /'lit(ə)rəCHər; -,CHŏŏr; -,t(y)ŏŏr/ ▶*n.* **1** written works, esp. those considered of superior or lasting artistic merit: *a great work of literature.* ■ books and writings published on a particular subject: *the* **literature on** *environmental epidemiology.* ■ the writings of a country or period: *early French literature.* ■ leaflets and other printed matter used to advertise products or give advice. **2** the production or profession of writing. ▷late Middle English (in the sense 'knowledge of books'): via French from Latin *litteratura*, from *littera* (see LETTER).

lith /liTH/ ▶*n.* photographic film with a very thin coat of emulsion, producing images of high contrast and density. ▷mid 20th cent.: abbreviation of LITHOGRAPHY, LITHOGRAPHIC.

-lith ▶*suffix* denoting types of stone: *laccolith | monolith.* ▷from Greek *lithos* 'stone.'

lith·arge /'liTH,ärj; li'THärj/ ▶*n.* lead monoxide, esp. a red form used as a pigment and in glass and ceramics. • Chem. formula: PbO. ▷Middle English: from Old French *litarge*, via Latin from Greek *litharguros*, from *lithos* 'stone' + *arguros* 'silver.'

lithe /līTH/ (also **lithe·some**) ▶*adj.* (esp. of a person's body) thin, supple, and graceful. ▷Old English *līthe* 'gentle, meek,' also 'mellow,' of Germanic origin; related to German *lind* 'soft, gentle.' —**lithe·ly** *adv.* —**lithe·ness** *n.*

lith·i·a /'liTHēə/ ▶*n. Chemistry* lithium oxide, a white alkaline solid. • Chem. formula: Li_2O. ▷early 19th cent.: modern Latin, alteration of earlier *lithion*, from Greek, neuter of *litheios*, from *lithos* 'stone,' on the pattern of words such as *soda.*

li·thi·a·sis /li'THīəsis/ ▶*n. Medicine* the formation of stony concretions (calculi) in the body, most often in the gallbladder or urinary system. ▷mid 17th cent.: from medieval Latin, based on Greek *lithos* 'stone.'

lith·ic /'liTHik/ ▶*adj. chiefly Archaeology & Geology* of the nature of or relating to stone. ■ *dated Medicine* relating to calculi. ▷late 18th cent.: from Greek *lithikos*, from *lithos* 'stone.'

lith·i·fy /'liTHə,fī/ ▶*v.* (**-fies, -fied**) [*trans.*] *chiefly Geology* transform (a sediment or other material) into stone. ▷late 19th cent.: from Greek *lithos* 'stone' + -FY. —**lith·i·fi·ca·tion** /,liTHəfi'kāSHən/ *n.*

lith·i·um /'liTHēəm/ ▶*n.* the chemical element of atomic number 3, a soft silver-white metal. It is the lightest of the alkali metals. (Symbol: **Li**) ■ lithium carbonate or another lithium salt, used as a mood-stabilizing drug. ▷early 19th cent.: from LITHIA + -IUM.

lith·o /ˈliTHō/ *informal* ▶*n.* (*pl.* **-os**) short for LITHOGRAPHY or LITHOGRAPH.
▶*adj.* short for LITHOGRAPHIC.
▶*v.* (**-oes, -oed**) short for LITHOGRAPH.

litho- ▶*comb. form* **1** of or relating to stone: *lithosol.* **2** relating to a calculus: *lithotomy.* ▷from Greek *lithos* 'stone.'

lithog. ▶*abbr.* ■ lithograph. ■ lithography.

lith·o·graph /ˈliTHəˌgraf/ ▶*n.* a lithographic print.
▶*v.* [*trans.*] print by lithography: [as *adj.*] (**lithographed**) *a set of lithographed drawings.* ▷early 19th cent.: back-formation from LITHOGRAPHY.

lith·o·graph·ic /ˌliTHəˈgrafik/ ▶*adj.* of, relating to, or produced by lithography: *lithographic prints.* **—lith·o·graph·i·cal·ly** /-ik(ə)lē/ *adv.*

li·thog·ra·phy /liˈTHägrəfē/ ▶*n.* the process of printing from a flat surface treated so as to repel the ink except where it is required for printing. ■ *Electronics* an analogous method for making printed circuits.

The earliest forms of lithography used greasy ink to form an image on a piece of limestone that was then etched with acid and treated with gum arabic. In a modern press, rollers transfer ink to a thin aluminum plate wrapped around a cylinder. In **offset lithography** the image is transferred to an intermediate rubber-covered cylinder before being printed.

▷early 19th cent.: from German *Lithographie* (see LITHO-, -GRAPHY). **—li·thog·ra·pher** /-fər/ *n.*

li·thol·o·gy /liˈTHäləjē/ ▶*n.* the study of the general physical characteristics of rocks. Compare with PETROLOGY. ■ the general physical characteristics of a rock or the rocks in a particular area: *the lithology of South Dakota.* **—lith·o·log·ic** /ˌliTHəˈläjik/ *adj.* **—lith·o·log·i·cal** /ˌliTHəˈläjikəl/ *adj.* **—lith·o·log·i·cal·ly** /ˌliTHəˈläjik(ə)lē/ *adv.*

lith·o·phyte /ˈliTHəˌfīt/ ▶*n.* **1** *Botany* a plant that grows on bare rock or stone. **2** *Zoology* a polyp with a calcareous skeleton; a stony coral. **—lith·o·phyt·ic** /ˌliTHəˈfitik/ *adj.*

lith·o·pone /ˈliTHəˌpōn/ ▶*n.* a white pigment made from zinc sulfide and barium sulfate. ▷late 19th cent.: from LITHO- 'stone, crystals' + Greek *ponos* '(thing) produced by work.'

lith·o·sphere /ˈliTHəˌsfi(ə)r/ ▶*n. Geology* the rigid outer part of the earth, consisting of the crust and upper mantle. **—lith·o·spher·ic** /ˌliTHəˈsferik; -ˈsfi(ə)r-/ *adj.*

li·thot·o·my /liˈTHätəmē/ ▶*n.* surgical removal of a calculus (stone) from the bladder, kidney, or urinary tract. ▷mid 17th cent.: via late Latin from Greek *lithotomia* (see LITHO-, -TOMY). **—li·thot·o·mist** /-mist/ *n.*

li·thot·o·my po·si·tion ▶*n.* a supine position of the body with the legs separated, flexed, and supported in raised stirrups, originally used for lithotomy and later also for childbirth.

lith·o·trip·sy /ˈliTHəˌtripsē/ ▶*n. Surgery* a treatment, typically using ultrasound shock waves, by which a kidney stone or other calculus is broken into small particles that can be passed out by the body. ▷mid 19th cent.: from LITHO- 'of stone' + Greek *tripsis* 'rubbing,' from *tribein* 'to rub.' **—lith·o·trip·ter** /-ˌtriptər/ *n.* **—lith·o·trip·tic** /ˌliTHəˈtriptik/ *adj.*

li·thot·ri·ty /liˈTHätrətē/ ▶*n. Surgery* a surgical procedure involving the mechanical breaking down of gallstones or other calculi. ▷early 19th cent.: from LITHO- 'of stone' + Latin *tritor* 'thing that rubs' + -Y[3].

Lith·u·a·ni·a /ˌliTHəˈwānēə; -nyə/ a country on the southeastern shore of the Baltic Sea; pop. 3,765,000; capital, Vilnius; languages, Lithuanian (official), Russian, Polish.

Lithuania was absorbed into the Russian empire in 1795, having been united with Poland from 1386. It was declared an independent republic in 1918, but in 1940 was annexed by the Soviet Union as a constituent republic. In 1991, on the breakup of the Soviet Union, Lithuania became an independent republic once again. In 2004 it joined both NATO and the EU.

Lith·u·a·ni·an /ˌliTHəˈwānēən/ ▶*adj.* of or relating to Lithuania or its people or language.
▶*n.* **1** a native or citizen of Lithuania, or a person of Lithuanian descent. **2** the Baltic language of Lithuania.

lit·i·gant /ˈlitəgənt/ ▶*n.* a person involved in a lawsuit.
▶*adj.* [*postpositive*] *archaic* involved in a lawsuit: *the parties litigant.* ▷mid 17th cent.: from French, from Latin *litigant-* 'carrying on a lawsuit,' from the verb *litigare* (see LITIGATE).

lit·i·gate /ˈlitəˌgāt/ ▶*v.* [*intrans.*] go to law; be a party to a lawsuit. ■ [*trans.*] take (a claim or a dispute) to a court of law. ▷early 17th cent.: from Latin *litigat-* 'disputed in a lawsuit,' from the verb *litigare,* from *lis, lit-* 'lawsuit.' **—lit·i·ga·tion** /ˌlitəˈgāSHən/ *n.* **—lit·i·ga·tive** /ˈlitəˌgātiv/ *adj.* **—lit·i·ga·tor** /-ˌgātər/ *n.*

li·ti·gious /ləˈtijəs/ ▶*adj.* concerned with lawsuits or litigation. ■ unreasonably prone to go to law to settle disputes. ■ suitable to become the subject of a lawsuit. ▷late Middle English: from Old French *litigieux* or Latin *litigiosus,* from *litigium* 'litigation,' from *lis, lit-* 'lawsuit.' **—li·ti·gious·ly** *adv.* **—li·ti·gious·ness** *n.*

lit·mus /ˈlitməs/ ▶*n.* a dye obtained from certain lichens that is red under acid conditions and blue under alkaline conditions. ▷Middle English: from Old Norse *lit-mosi,* from *litr* 'dye' + *mosi* 'moss.'

lit·mus pa·per ▶*n.* paper stained with litmus, used to indicate the acidity or alkalinity of a substance.

lit·mus test ▶*n. Chemistry* a test for acidity or alkalinity using litmus. ■ *figurative* a decisively indicative test: *opposition to the nomination became a litmus test for political support of candidates.*

li·top·tern /liˈtäpˌtərn/ ▶*n.* an extinct South American hoofed mammal resembling a horse or camel, found from the Paleocene to the Pleistocene epochs. • Order Litopterna: several families. ▷early 20th cent.: from modern Latin *Litopterna,* from Greek *litos* 'smooth' + *pternē* 'heel bone.'

li·to·tes /ˈlītəˌtēz; ˈlit-; līˈtōtēz/ ▶*n. Rhetoric* ironical understatement in which an affirmative is expressed by the negative of its contrary (e.g., *you won't be sorry,* meaning *you'll be glad*). ▷late 16th cent.: via late Latin from Greek *litotēs,* from *litos* 'plain, meager.'

li·tre ▶*n.* British spelling of LITER.

LittB ▶*abbr.* ■ Bachelor of Letters. ■ Bachelor of Literature. ▷from Latin, *Li(t)erārum Baccalaureus.*

LittD ▶*abbr.* ■ Doctor of Letters. ■ Doctor of Literature. ▷from Latin *Litterarum Doctor.*

lit·ter /ˈlitər/ ▶*n.* **1** trash, such as paper, cans, and bottles, that is left lying in an open or public place: *fines for dropping litter.* ■ [in *sing.*] an untidy collection of things lying about: *a litter of sleeping bags on the floor.* **2** the group of young animals born to an animal at one time: *a litter of five kittens.* **3** material forming a surface-covering layer, in particular: ■ (also **cat litter**) granular absorbent material lining a tray where a cat can urinate and defecate when indoors. ■ straw or other plant matter used as bedding for animals. ■ (also **leaf litter**) decomposing but recognizable leaves and other debris forming a layer on top of the soil, esp. in forests. **4** *historical* a vehicle containing a bed or seat enclosed by curtains and carried on men's shoulders or by animals. ■ a stretcher, for transporting the sick and wounded.
▶*v.* [*trans.*] **1** make (a place) untidy with rubbish or a large number of objects left lying about: *clothes and newspapers littered the floor.* ■ (usu. **be littered**) leave (rubbish or a number of objects) lying untidily in a place: *there was broken glass littered about.* ■ (usu. **be littered with**) *figurative* fill (a text, history, etc.) with examples of something unpleasant: *news pages have been littered with doom and gloom about company collapses.* **2** *archaic* provide (a horse or other animal) with litter as bedding. ▷Middle English (sense 4 of the *noun*): from Old French *litiere,* from medieval Latin *lectaria,* from Latin *lectus* 'bed.' Sense 1 dates from the mid 18th cent. **—lit·ter·er** *n.*

litter 4

lit·té·ra·teur /ˌlitərəˈtər/ ▶*n.* a person who is interested in and knowledgeable about literature. ▷early 19th cent.: French.

lit·ter box ▶*n.* a box or tray containing granular absorbent material into which a cat can urinate or defecate.

lit·ter·bug /ˈlitərˌbəg/ ▶*n. informal* a person who carelessly drops litter in a public place.

lit·ter·mate /ˈlitərˌmāt/ ▶*n.* one member of a pair or group of animals born in the same litter.

lit·tle /ˈlitl/ ▶*adj.* small in size, amount, or degree (often used to convey an appealing diminutiveness or express an affectionate or condescending attitude): *the plants will grow into little bushes | a little puppy dog | a boring little man | he's a good little worker.* See note at SMALL. ■ (of a person) young or younger: *my little brother | when she was little she was always getting into scrapes.* ■ denoting something, esp. a place, that is named after a similar larger one: *New York's Little Italy.* ■ used in names of animals and plants that are smaller than related kinds, e.g., **little grebe.** ■ of short distance or duration: *stay for a little while | we climbed up a little way.* ■ relatively unimportant; trivial (often used ironically): *we have a little problem | I can't remember every little detail.*
▶*adj.* & *pron.* **1** (**a little**) a small amount of: [as *adj.*] *we got a little help from my sister* | [as *pron.*] *you only see* ***a little of*** *what he can do.* ■ [*pron.*] a short time or distance: *after a little, the rain stopped.* **2** used to emphasize how small an amount is: [as *adj.*] *I have little doubt of their identity | there was very little time to be lost* | [as *pron.*] *he ate and drank very little | the ruble is worth so little these days.*
▶*adv.* (**less** /les/, **least** /lēst/) **1** (**a little**) to a small extent: *he reminded me a little of my parents | I was always a little afraid of her.* **2** (used for emphasis) only to a small extent; not much or often: *he was little known in this country | he had slept little these past weeks.* ■ hardly or not at all: ***little did he know*** *what wheels he was putting into motion.* ▷Old English *lȳtel,* of Germanic origin; related to Dutch *luttel,* German dialect *lützel.* **—lit·tle·ness** *n.*
▶*PHRASES* □ **in little** *archaic* on a small scale; in miniature. □ **little by little** by degrees; gradually: *little by little the money dried up.* □ **little or nothing** hardly anything. □ **make little of** treat as unimportant: *they made little of their royal connection.* □ **no little** considerable: *a factor of no little importance.* □ **not a little** a great deal (of); much: *not a little consternation was caused.* ■ very: *it was not a little puzzling.* □ **quite a little** a fairly large amount of: *some spoke quite a little English.* ■ a considerable: *it turned out to be quite a little bonanza.*

Lit·tle Ar·a·rat see ARARAT, MOUNT.

lit·tle auk ▶*n.* British term for DOVEKIE.

Lit·tle Bear the constellation Ursa Minor.

Lit·tle Big·horn, Bat·tle of a battle in which General George Custer and his forces were defeated by Sioux and Cheyenne warriors on June 25, 1876, popularly known as Custer's Last Stand. It took place in the valley of the Little Bighorn River in Montana.

Lit·tle Big·horn Riv·er /ˈbigˌhôrn/ a river in northern Wyoming and southeastern Montana, scene of the 1876 defeat of George Custer's cavalry by Cheyenne and Sioux warriors.

Lit·tle Cor·po·ral a nickname for Napoleon.

Lit·tle Dip·per ▶*n.* the seven bright stars of the constellation Ursa Minor.

Lit·tle Eng·land·er /ˈiNG(g)ləndər/ ▶*n.* a person who opposes an international role or policy for Britain. **—Lit·tle Eng·land·ism** /-ˌdizəm/ *n.*

lit·tle fin·ger ▶*n.* the smallest finger, at the outer end of the hand, farthest from the thumb.
▶*PHRASE* □ **twist** (or **wrap** or **wind**) **someone around one's little finger** have the ability to make someone do whatever one wants.

Lit·tle Flow·er see LA GUARDIA.

lit·tle grebe ▶*n.* a small, puffy-looking Old World grebe with a short neck and bill and a trilling call. • Genus *Tachybaptus,* family Podicipedidae: three species, in particular the widespread *T. ruficollis* (also called **DABCHICK**).

lit·tle hours ▶*plural n.* (in the Roman Catholic Church) the offices of prime, terce, sext, and none.

Lit·tle Ice Age ▶*n.* a comparatively cold period occurring between major glacial periods, in particular one such period that reached its peak during the 17th century.

Lit·tle League ▶*n.* youth baseball or softball under the auspices of an organization founded in 1939, for children up to age 12. **—Little Leaguer** *n.*

Lit·tle Lord Faunt·le·roy see **FAUNTLEROY**.

Lit·tle Mac see **MCCLELLAN**.

lit·tle man ▶*n.* a person who conducts business or life on a small or ordinary scale; an average person. ■ *dated* used as a form of address to a young boy.

Lit·tle Minch see **MINCH**.

Lit·tle Mis·sou·ri Riv·er a river that flows for 560 miles (900 km) from Wyoming, through Montana and the Dakotas, to the Missouri River.

Lit·tle Na·po·le·on see **MCGRAW, JOHN**.

Lit·tle Ouse another name for **OUSE** (sense 4).

lit·tle owl ▶*n.* a small owl with speckled plumage, native to Eurasia and Africa. • *Athene noctua*, family Strigidae.

lit·tle peo·ple ▶*plural n.* **1** the ordinary people in a country, organization, etc., who do not have much power. **2** people of small physical stature; midgets. ■ small supernatural creatures such as fairies and leprechauns.

Lit·tle Rhod·y a nickname for the state of **RHODE ISLAND**.

Lit·tle Rock the capital of Arkansas, located in the central part of the state, on the Arkansas River; pop. 183,133.

Lit·tle Rus·sian ▶*n.* & *adj.* former term for **UKRAINIAN**.

Lit·tle St. Ber·nard Pass see **ST. BERNARD PASS**.

lit·tle the·a·ter ▶*n.* a small independent theater used for experimental or avant-garde drama, or for community, noncommercial productions.

Lit·tle Ti·bet another name for **BALTISTAN**.

lit·tle toe ▶*n.* the smallest toe, on the outer side of the foot.

Lit·tle·ton /ˈlitl-tən/ an industrial city in north central Colorado, south of Denver, scene of a shooting at Columbine High School in April 1999 in which 15 (including the two student gunmen) died and 21 were wounded; pop. 40,340.

Lit·tle Tur·tle (c.1752–1812), chief of the Miami Indians. He led raids on settlers in the Northwest Territory and was successful until several defeats forced him to sign the Treaty of Greenville in 1795.

lit·to·ral /ˈlitərəl/ ▶*adj.* of, relating to, or situated on the shore of the sea or a lake: *the littoral states of the Indian Ocean.* ■ *Ecology* of, relating to, or denoting the zone of the seashore between high- and low-water marks, or the zone near a lake shore with rooted vegetation: *limpets and other littoral mollusks.*
▶*n.* a region lying along a shore: *irrigated regions of the Mediterranean littoral.* ■ *Ecology* the littoral zone. ▷mid 17th cent.: from Latin *littoralis*, from *litus, litor-* 'shore.'

Lit·tré /lēˈtrā/, Émile (1801–81), French lexicographer and philosopher. He was the author of the major *Dictionnaire de la langue française* (1863–77). A follower of Auguste Comte, he became the leading exponent of positivism after Comte's death.

li·tur·gi·cal /liˈtərjikəl/ ▶*adj.* of or related to liturgy or public worship. ▷mid 17th cent.: via medieval Latin from Greek *leitourgikos* (see **LITURGY**) + **-AL**. **—li·tur·gi·cal·ly** *adv.*

li·tur·gics /liˈtərjiks/ ▶*plural n.* [treated as *sing.*] the study of liturgies.

li·tur·gi·ol·o·gy /liˌtərjēˈäləjē/ ▶*n.* another term for **LITURGICS**. **—li·tur·gi·o·log·i·cal** /-jēəˈläjikəl/ *adj.* **—li·tur·gi·ol·o·gist** *n.*

lit·ur·gy /ˈlitərjē/ ▶*n.* (*pl.* **-gies**) **1** a form or formulary according to which public religious worship, esp. Christian worship, is conducted. ■ a religious service conducted according to such a form or formulary. ■ (**the Liturgy**) the Eucharistic service of the Eastern Orthodox Church. **2** (in ancient Athens) a public office or duty performed voluntarily by a rich Athenian. ▷mid 16th cent.: via French or late Latin from Greek *leitourgia* 'public service, worship of the gods,' from *leitourgos* 'minister,' from *lēitos* 'public' + *-ergos* 'working.' **—lit·ur·gist** *n.*

Liu·zhou /liˈyo͞oˈjō/ (also **Liu·chow** *pronunc.* same) an industrial city in southern China, in Guangxi Zhuang province, northeast of Nanning; pop. 740,000.

liv·a·ble /ˈlivəbəl/ (also **live·a·ble**) ▶*adj.* worth living; enjoyable: *fatherhood makes life more livable.* ■ (of an environment or climate) fit to live in: *one of the most livable cities in the world.* **—liv·a·bil·i·ty** /ˌlivəˈbilətē/ *n.*

live[1] /liv/ ▶*v.* **1** [*intrans.*] remain alive: *the doctors said she had only six months to live | both cats lived to a ripe age.* ■ be alive at a specified time: *he lived four centuries ago.* ■ spend one's life in a particular way or under particular circumstances: *people are living in fear in the wake of the shootings.* ■ [*trans.*] lead (one's life) in a particular way: *he was living a life of luxury in Australia.* ■ supply oneself with the means of subsistence: *they **live by** hunting and fishing.* ■ survive in someone's mind; be remembered: *only the name **lived on**.* ■ have an exciting or fulfilling life: *he couldn't wait to get out of school and really start living.* **2** [*intrans.*] make one's home in a particular place or with a particular person: *I've lived in New England all my life | they lived with his grandparents.*
▶*phrasal v.* □ **live something down** succeed in making others forget something embarrassing that has happened. □ **live for** regard as the purpose or most important aspect of one's life: *Tony lived for his painting.* □ **live in** (of an employee or student) reside at the place where one works or studies. □ **live off** (or **on**) depend on (someone or something) as a source of income or support: *if you think you're going to live off me for the rest of your life, you're mistaken.* ■ have (a particular amount of money) with which to buy food and other necessities. ■ subsist on (a particular type of food). ■ (of a person) eat, or seem to eat, only (a particular type of food): *she used to live on bacon and tomato sandwiches.* □ **live out** (of an employee or student) reside away from the place where one works or studies. □ **live something out 1** do in reality that which one has thought or dreamed about: *your wedding day is the one time that you can live out your most romantic fantasies.* **2** spend the rest of one's life in a particular place or particular circumstances: *he lived out his days as a happy family man.* □ **live through** survive (an unpleasant experience or period): *both men lived through the Depression.* □ **live together** (esp. of a couple not married to each other) share a home and have a sexual relationship. □ **live up to** fulfill (expectations). ■ fulfill (an undertaking): *the president lived up to his promise to set America swiftly on a new path.* □ **live with 1** share a home and have a sexual relationship with (someone to whom one is not married). **2** accept or tolerate (something unpleasant): *our marriage was a failure—you have to learn to live with that fact.* ▷Old English *libban, lifian*, of Germanic origin; related to Dutch *leven* and German *leben*, also to **LIFE** and **LEAVE**[1].
▶**PHRASES** □ **as I live and breathe** used, esp. in spoken English, to express one's surprise at coming across someone or something: *good Lord, Jack Stone, as I live and breathe!* □ **be living on borrowed time** see **BORROW**. □ **live and breathe something** be extremely interested in or enthusiastic about a particular subject or activity and so devote a great deal of one's time to it: *they live and breathe Italy and all things Italian.* □ **live and let live** *proverb* you should tolerate the opinions and behavior of others so that they will similarly tolerate your own. □ **live by one's wits** see **WIT**[1]. □ **live dangerously** do something risky, esp. on a habitual basis. □ **live for the moment** see **MOMENT**. □ **live in hope** be or remain optimistic about something. □ **live in the past** have old-fashioned or outdated ideas and attitudes. ■ dwell on or reminisce at length about past events. □ **live in sin** see **SIN**[1]. □ **live it up** *informal* spend one's time in an extremely enjoyable way, typically by spending a great deal of money or engaging in an exciting social life. □ **live off** (or **on**) **the fat of the land** see **FAT**. □ **live off the land** see **LAND**. □ **live out of a suitcase** live or stay somewhere on a temporary basis and with only a limited selection of one's belongings, typically because one's occupation requires a great deal of traveling. □ **live one's own life** follow one's own plans and principles independent of others. □ **live rough** live and sleep outdoors as a consequence of having no proper home. □ **live to fight another day** survive a particular experience or ordeal. □ **live to regret something** come to wish that one had not done something: *those who put work before their family life often live to regret it.* □ **live to tell the tale** survive a dangerous experience and be able to tell others about it. □ **live with oneself** be able to retain one's self-respect as a consequence of one's actions: *taking money from children—how can you live with yourself?* □ **long live ——!** said to express loyalty or support for a specified person or thing: *long live the Queen!* □ **where one lives** *informal* at, to, or in the right, vital, or most vulnerable spot: *it gets me where I live.* □ **you haven't lived** used, esp. in spoken English, as a way of enthusiastically recommending something to someone who has not experienced it: ***you haven't lived until** you've tasted their lobster ravioli.* □ **you** (or **we**) **live and learn** used, esp. in spoken English, to acknowledge that a fact is new to one.

live[2] /līv/ ▶*adj.* **1** not dead or inanimate; living: *live animals | the number of live births and deaths.* ■ (of a vaccine) containing viruses or bacteria that are living but of a mild or attenuated strain. ■ (of yogurt) containing the living microorganisms by which it is formed. **2** (of a musical performance) given in concert, not on a recording: *there is traditional live music played most nights.* ■ (of a broadcast) transmitted at the time of occurrence, not from a recording: *live coverage of the match.* ■ (of a musical recording) made during a concert, not in a studio: *a live album.* **3** (of a wire or device) connected to a source of electric current. ■ of, containing, or using undetonated explosive: *live ammunition.* ■ (of coals) burning; glowing. ■ (of a match) unused. ■ (of a wheel or axle in machinery) moving or imparting motion. ■ (of a ball in a game) in play, esp. in contrast to being foul or out of bounds. **4** (of a question or subject) of current or continuing interest and importance: *the future organization of Europe has become a live issue.*
▶*adv.* as or at an actual event or performance: *the match will be televised live.* ▷mid 16th cent.: shortening of **ALIVE**.
▶**PHRASE** □ **go live** *Computing* (of a system) become operational.

live·a·ble /ˈlivəbəl/ ▶*adj.* variant spelling of **LIVABLE**.

live ac·tion /līv/ ▶*n.* (in filmmaking) action involving real people or animals, as contrasted with animation or computer-generated effects: [as *adj.*] *a live-action version of the cartoon.*

live·bear·er /ˈlīvˌbe(ə)rər/ ▶*n.* a small, chiefly freshwater, carplike American fish that has internal fertilization and gives birth to live young. Many livebearers, including the guppy, swordtail, mollies, platyfish, and gambusias, are very popular in aquariums. • Family Poeciliidae: many genera and species.

live-bear·ing /ˈlīvˌbe(ə)riNG/ ▶*adj.* (of an animal) bearing live young rather than laying eggs; viviparous or ovoviviparous.

lived-in /ˈlivd ˌin/ ▶*adj.* (of a room or building) showing comforting signs of wear and habitation. ■ *informal* (of a person's face) marked by experience.

live-in /ˈliv ˌin/ ▶*adj.* (of a domestic employee) resident in an employer's house: *a live-in housekeeper.* ■ (of a person) living with another in a sexual relationship: *a live-in lover.* ■ residential: *a live-in treatment program.*
▶*n. informal* a person who shares another's living accommodations as a sexual partner or as an employee.

live·li·hood /ˈlīvlēˌho͝od/ ▶*n.* a means of securing the necessities of life: *people whose livelihoods depend on the rain forest.* ▷Old English *līflād* 'way of life,' from *līf* 'life' + *lād* 'course' (see **LODE**). The change in the word's form in the 16th cent. was due to association with **LIVELY** and **-HOOD**.

live load /līv/ ▶*n.* the weight of people or goods in a building or vehicle. Often contrasted with **DEAD LOAD**.

live·long /ˈlivˌlôNG; -ˌläNG/ ▶*adj. poetic/literary* (of a period of time) entire: *all this **livelong day** I lay in the sun.* ▷late Middle English *leve longe* 'dear long' (see **LIEF**, **LONG**[1]). The change in spelling of the first word was due to association with **LIVE**[1].

live·ly /ˈlīvlē/ ▶*adj.* (**live·li·er**, **live·li·est**) full of life and energy; active and outgoing: *she joined a lively team of reporters.* ■ (of a place or atmosphere) full of activity and excitement: *Barcelona's many lively bars.* ■ intellectually stimulating or perceptive: *a lively discussion | her lively mind.* ■ having a quick, bouncy tempo: *the violinist struck up a lively tune.* ■ (of a vessel) buoyant and responsive in a sea. ▷Old English *līflic* 'living, animate' (see **LIFE**, **-LY**[1]). **—live·li·ly** /-ləlē/ *adv.* **—live·li·ness** *n.*
▶**PHRASE** □ **look lively** (or **alive**) [usu. in *imperative*] *informal* move more quickly and energetically: *"Look lively, men!" Charlie shouted.*

liv·en /ˈlīvən/ ▶*v.* make or become more lively or interesting: [*trans.*] ***liven up** bland foods with a touch of*

Pronunciation Key ə *ago*; ər *over*; ˈə *or* ˌə *up*; ˈər *or* ˌər *fur*; a *hat*; ā *rate*; ä *car*; CH *chew*; e *let*; ē *see*; e(ə)r *air*; i *fit*; ī *by*; i(ə)r *ear*; NG *sing*; ō *go*; ô *for*; oi *boy*; o͝o *good*; o͞o *goo*; ou *out*; SH *she*; TH *thin*; TH *then*; (h)w *why*; ZH *vision*

mustard | [*intrans.*] *the match didn't* ***liven up*** *until the second half.*

live oak /līv/ ▸*n.* a large, spreading oak of the southern U.S. that has leathery, elliptical evergreen leaves. Live oaks typically support a large quantity of Spanish moss and other epiphytes. • *Quercus virginiana*, family Fagaceae.

liv·er[1] /ˈlivər/ ▸*n.* a large lobed glandular organ in the abdomen of vertebrates, involved in many metabolic processes. ■ a similar organ in other animals. ■ the flesh of an animal's liver as food: *slices of calf's liver* | [as *adj.*] *liver pâté* | *chicken livers.* ■ (also **liver color**) a dark reddish brown.

The liver's main role is in the processing of the products of digestion into substances useful to the body. It also neutralizes harmful substances in the blood, secretes bile for the digestion of fats, synthesizes plasma proteins, and stores glycogen and some minerals and vitamins. It was anciently supposed to be the seat of love and violent emotion.

▷Old English *lifer*, of Germanic origin; related to German *Leber*, Dutch *lever*.

liv·er[2] ▸*n.* [with *adj.*] a person who lives in a specified way: *a clean liver* | *high livers.*

liv·er chest·nut ▸*n.* a horse of a dark chestnut color.

liv·er fluke ▸*n.* a fluke that has a complex life cycle and is of medical and veterinary importance. The adult lives within the liver tissues of a vertebrate, and the larva within one or more secondary hosts such as a snail or fish. • Many species in the subclass Digenea, class Trematoda, including the **Chinese liver fluke** (*Opisthorchis sinensis*), which infests humans, and *Fasciola hepatica*, which infests sheep and cattle.

liv·er·ish /ˈliv(ə)risн/ ▸*adj.* slightly ill, as though having a disordered liver. ■ unhappy and bad-tempered. ■ resembling liver in color: *a liverish red.* **—liv·er·ish·ly** *adv.* **—liv·er·ish·ness** *n.*

Liv·er·more /ˈlivər,môr/ a city in north central California, east of Oakland; pop. 56,741.

Liv·er·pool[1] /ˈlivər,po͞ol/ a city and seaport in northwestern England, on the eastern side of the mouth of the Mersey River; pop. 448,000.

Liv·er·pool[2], Robert Banks Jenkinson, 2nd Earl of (1770–1828), British statesman; prime minister 1812–27.

Liv·er·pud·li·an /,livərˈpədlēən/ ▸*n.* a native of Liverpool. ■ the dialect or accent of people from Liverpool.
▸*adj.* of or relating to Liverpool. ▷mid 19th cent.: humorous formation from **LIVERPOOL**[1] + **PUDDLE**.

liv·er spot ▸*n.* a small brown spot on the skin, esp. as caused by a skin condition such as lentigo. **—liv·er-spot·ted** *adj.*

liv·er·wort /ˈlivər,wərt; -,wôrt/ ▸*n.* a small flowerless green plant with leaflike stems or lobed leaves, occurring in moist habitats. Liverworts lack true roots and reproduce by means of spores released from capsules. • Class Hepaticae, division Bryophyta. ▷late Old English, from **LIVER**[1] + **WORT**, translating medieval Latin *hepatica*.

liv·er·wurst /ˈlivər,wərst/ ▸*n.* a seasoned meat paste in the form of a sausage containing cooked liver, or a mixture of liver and pork. ▷mid 19th cent.: partial translation of German *Leberwurst* 'liver sausage.'

liv·er·y[1] /ˈliv(ə)rē/ ▸*n.* (*pl.* **-er·ies**) **1** special uniform worn by a servant or official. ■ a special design and color scheme used on the vehicles, aircraft, or products of a particular company. **2** short for **LIVERY STABLE**. **3** (in the UK) the members of a livery company collectively. **4** *historical* a provision of food or clothing for servants. ▷Middle English: from Old French *livree* 'delivered,' feminine past participle of *livrer*, from Latin *liberare* 'liberate' (in medieval Latin 'hand over'). The original sense was 'the dispensing of food, provisions, or clothing to servants'; hence sense 4, also 'allowance of provender for horses,' surviving in the phrase *at livery* and in **LIVERY STABLE**. Sense 1 arose because medieval nobles provided matching clothes to distinguish their servants from others'. **—liv·er·ied** /ˈliv(ə)rēd/ *adj.* (in sense 1).
▸*PHRASE* □ **at livery** (of a horse) kept for the owner and fed and cared for at a fixed charge.

liv·er·y[2] ▸*adj.* resembling liver in color or consistency: *he was short with livery lips.* ■ *informal* liverish: *port always makes you livery.*

liv·er·y com·pa·ny ▸*n.* (in the UK) any of a number of companies of the City of London descended from the medieval trade guilds. They are now largely social and charitable organizations. ▷mid 18th cent.: so named because of the distinctive costume formerly used for special occasions.

liv·er·y·man /ˈliv(ə)rēmən/ ▸*n.* (*pl.* **-men**) **1** an owner of or attendant in a livery stable. **2** (in the UK) a member of a livery company.

liv·er·y sta·ble (also **livery yard**) ▸*n.* a stable where horses are kept at livery or let out for hire.

lives /līvz/ ▸ plural form of **LIFE**.

live·stock /ˈlīv,stäk/ ▸*n.* farm animals regarded as an asset: *markets for the trading of livestock.*

live·ware /ˈlīv,we(ə)r/ ▸*n.* *informal* working personnel, esp. computer personnel, as distinct from the inanimate or abstract things they work with.

live weight /līv/ ▸*n.* the weight of an animal before it has been slaughtered and prepared as a carcass.

live wire /līv/ ▸*n.* *informal* an energetic and unpredictable person.

liv·id /ˈlivid/ ▸*adj.* **1** *informal* furiously angry: *he was livid at being left out.* **2** (of a color or the skin) having a dark inflamed tinge: *his face went livid, then purple.* See note at **PALE**. ■ of a bluish leaden color: *livid bruises.* ▷late Middle English (in the sense 'of a bluish leaden color'): from French *livide* or Latin *lividus*, from *livere* 'be bluish.' The sense 'furiously angry' dates from the early 20th cent. **—li·vid·i·ty** /ləˈvidətē/ *n.* **—liv·id·ly** *adv.* **—liv·id·ness** *n.*

liv·ing /ˈliviNG/ ▸*n.* **1** [usu. in *sing.*] an income sufficient to live on or the means of earning it: *she was struggling to* ***make a living*** *as a dancer* | *what does he* ***do for a living?*** ■ *Brit.* (in church use) a position as a vicar or rector with an income or property. **2** [with *adj.*] the pursuit of a lifestyle of the specified type: *the benefits of country living.*
▸*adj.* alive: *living creatures* | [as *plural n.*] (**the living**) *flowers were for the living.* See note at **ALIVE**. ■ (of a place) used for living rather than working in: *the living quarters of the ship.* ■ (of a language) still spoken and used. ■ *poetic/literary* (of water) perennially flowing: *streams of living water.*
▸*PHRASES* □ **be** (**the**) **living proof that** (or **of**) show by one's existence and qualities that something is the case: *she is living proof that hard work need not be aging.* □ **in** (or **within**) **living memory** within or during a time that is remembered by people still alive: *the worst recession in living memory.* □ **the living image of** an exact copy or likeness of.

liv·ing death ▸*n.* [in *sing.*] a state of existence that is very difficult; a life of hopeless and unbroken misery.

liv·ing rock ▸*n.* rock that is not detached but still forms part of the earth: *a chamber cut out of the living rock.*

liv·ing room ▸*n.* a room in a house for general and informal everyday use.

Liv·ing·ston /ˈliviNGstən/, Henry Brockholst (1757–1823), U.S. Supreme Court associate justice 1806–23. A Democrat-Republican, he was appointed to the Court by President Jefferson.

liv·ing stone ▸*n.* a small succulent southern African plant that resembles a pebble in appearance. It consists of two fleshy cushionlike leaves divided by a slit through which a daisylike flower emerges. • Genus *Lithops*, family Aizoaceae.

liv·ing wage ▸*n.* [in *sing.*] a wage that is high enough to maintain a normal standard of living.

liv·ing will ▸*n.* a written statement detailing a person's desires regarding their medical treatment in circumstances in which they are no longer able to express informed consent, esp. an advance directive.

Li·vo·nia /liˈvōnēə; -yə/ **1** a region on the eastern coast of the Baltic Sea, north of Lithuania, that comprises most of present-day Latvia and Estonia. German name **LIVLAND** . **2** an industrial city in southeastern Michigan, west of Detroit; pop. 100,545. **—Li·vo·ni·an** *adj.* & *n.*

Li·vor·no /lēˈvôrnō/ a port in northwestern Italy, in Tuscany, on the Ligurian Sea; pop. 171,265. Also called **LEGHORN**.

Liv·y /ˈlivē/ (59 BC–AD 17), Roman historian; Latin name *Titus Livius*. His history of Rome from its foundation to his own time filled 142 books, of which 35 survive.

lix·iv·i·ate /likˈsivē,āt/ ▸*v.* [*trans.*] *archaic Chemistry* separate (a substance) into soluble and insoluble constituents by the percolation of liquid. ▷mid 17th cent.: from modern Latin *lixiviat-* 'impregnated with lye,' from the verb *lixiviare*, from *lixivius* 'made into lye,' from *lix* 'lye.' **—lix·iv·i·a·tion** /-,sivēˈāsнən/ *n.*

Liz·ard /ˈlizərd/ a promontory in southwestern England, in Cornwall. Its southern tip, Lizard Point, is the southernmost point of the British mainland.

liz·ard /ˈlizərd/ ▸*n.* a reptile that typically has a long body and tail, four legs, movable eyelids, and a rough, scaly, or spiny skin. • Suborder Lacertilia (or Sauria), order Squamata: many families. ▷late Middle English: from Old French *lesard(e)*, from Latin *lacertus* 'lizard, sea fish,' also 'muscle.'

liz·ard·fish /ˈlizərd,fisн/ ▸*n.* (*pl.* same or **-fish·es**) a fish of lizardlike appearance with a broad bony head, pointed snout, and heavy shiny scales. It lives in warm shallow seas, where it often rests on the bottom propped up on its pelvic fins. • Family Synodontidae: several genera and species, including the widespread *Trachinocephalus myops* (also called **SNAKEFISH**).

liz·ard's tail ▸*n.* a North American bog plant with long tapering, drooping spikes of fragrant white flowers. • *Saururus cernuus*, family Saururaceae.

Lju·blja·na /lē,o͞oblēˈänə; lēˈo͞oblēə,nä/ the capital of Slovenia; pop. 267,000. It was founded as Emona by the Romans in 34 BC. German name **LAIBACH**.

Lk. ▸*abbr. Bible* the Gospel of Luke.

'll ▸*contraction of* shall; will: *I'll get the food on.*

ll. ▸*abbr.* (in textual references) lines.

lla·ma /ˈlämə/ ▸*n.* a domesticated pack animal of the camel family found in the Andes, valued for its soft woolly fleece. • *Lama glama*, family Camelidae, probably descended from the wild guanaco. ■ the wool of the llama. ■ cloth made from such wool. ▷early 17th cent.: from Spanish, probably from Quechua.

llama

lla·no /ˈlänō; ˈyä-/ ▸*n.* (*pl.* **-nos**) (in South America) a treeless grassy plain. ▷Spanish, from Latin *planum* 'plain.'

LLB ▸*abbr.* Bachelor of Laws. ▷from Latin *legum baccalaureus*.

LLD ▸*abbr.* Doctor of Laws. ▷from Latin *legum doctor*.

Llew·e·lyn /lo͝oˈ(w)elən/ (died 1282), prince of Gwynedd in North Wales; also known as **Llywelyn ap Gruffydd**. Proclaiming himself prince of all Wales in 1258, he was recognized by Henry III in 1265. His refusal to pay homage to Edward I led the latter to subjugate Wales 1277–84; Llewelyn died in an unsuccessful rebellion.

LLM ▸*abbr.* Master of Laws. ▷from Latin *legum magister*.

Llo·sa, Mario Vargas, see **VARGAS LLOSA**.

Lloyd /loid/, Harold (Clayton) (1893–1971), U.S. movie comedian. Performing his own hair-raising stunts, he used physical danger as a source of comedy in silent movies such as *High and Dizzy* (1920), *Safety Last* (1923), and *The Freshman* (1925). He received an honorary Academy Award in 1952.

Lloyd George, David, 1st Earl Lloyd George of Dwyfor (1863–1945), British statesman; prime minister 1916–22. His coalition government was threatened by economic problems and trouble in Ireland. He resigned when the Conservatives withdrew their support in 1922.

Lloyd's /loidz/ an incorporated society of insurance underwriters in London, made up of private syndicates. Founded in 1871, Lloyd's originally dealt only in marine insurance. ■ short for **LLOYD'S REGISTER**. ▷named after the coffeehouse of Edward *Lloyd* (*fl.* 1688–1726), in which underwriters and merchants congregated and where *Lloyd's List* was started in 1734.

Lloyd's Reg·is·ter (in full **Lloyd's Register of Shipping**) a classified list of merchant ships over a certain tonnage giving their seaworthiness classification and published annually in London. ■ the corporation that produces this list and lays down the specifications for ships on which it is based.

Lloyd Web·ber /ˈwebər/, Sir Andrew (1948–), English composer. His many musicals, several of them written in collaboration with lyricist Sir Tim Rice, include *Jesus Christ Superstar* (1970), *Cats* (1981), *The Phantom of the Opera* (1986), *Bombay Dreams* (2002), and *The Woman in White* (2004).

Lly·wel·yn ap Gruff·ydd /(h)lo͞oˈelin äp ˈgrifiтн/ see **LLEWELYN**.

LM ▸*abbr.* ■ long meter. ■ lunar module.

lm ▸*abbr.* lumen(s).

ln *Mathematics* ▸*abbr.* natural logarithm. ▷from modern Latin *logarithmus naturalis*.

LNB ▸*abbr.* low noise blocker, a circuit on a satellite dish that selects the required signal from the transmission.

LNG ▸*abbr.* liquefied natural gas.

lo /lō/ ▸*exclam. archaic* used to draw attention to an interesting or amazing event: *and lo, the star, which they saw in the east, went before them.* ▷natural exclamation: first recorded as *lā* in Old English; reinforced in Middle English by a shortened form of *loke* 'look!,' imperative of LOOK.

▸*PHRASE* □ **lo and behold** used to present a new scene, situation, or turn of events, often with the suggestion that though surprising, could in fact have been predicted: *you took me out and, lo and behold, I got home to find my house had been ransacked.*

lo·a /ˈlōä/ ▸*n.* (*pl.* same or **lo·as**) a god in the voodoo cult of Haiti. ▷Haitian Creole.

loach /lōCH/ ▸*n.* a small elongated bottom-dwelling freshwater fish with several barbels near the mouth, found in Eurasia and northwestern Africa. • Families Cobitidae and Homalopteridae (or Balitoridae): several genera and numerous species. ▷Middle English: from Old French *loche,* of unknown origin.

load /lōd/ ▸*n.* **1** a heavy or bulky thing that is being carried or is about to be carried: *in addition to their own food, they must carry a load of up to eighty pounds.* ■ the total number or amount that can be carried in something, esp. a vehicle of a specified type: ***a*** *tractor-trailer* ***load of*** *new appliances.* ■ the material carried along by a stream, glacier, ocean current, etc. ■ an amount of items washed or to be washed in a washing machine or dishwasher at one time: *I do at least six* ***loads of*** *washing a week.* **2** a weight or source of pressure borne by someone or something: *the increased* ***load on*** *the heart caused by a raised arterial pressure | the arch has hollow spandrels to lighten the* ***load on*** *the foundations.* ■ the amount of work to be done by a person or machine: *Arthur has a light teaching load.* ■ a burden of responsibility, worry, or grief: *consumers will find it difficult to service their heavy load of debt.* **3** (**a load of**) *informal* a lot of (often used to express one's disapproval or dislike of something): *she was talking* ***a load of garbage.*** ■ (**a load/loads**) *informal* plenty: *she spends* ***loads of*** *money on clothes | there's loads to see here, even when it rains.* **4** the amount of power supplied by a source; the resistance of moving parts to be overcome by a motor. ■ the amount of electricity supplied by a generating system at any given time. ■ *Electronics* an impedance or circuit that receives or develops the output of a transistor or other device. **5** *vulgar slang* semen.

▸*v.* [*trans.*] **1** put a load or large amount of something on or in (a vehicle, ship, container, etc.): *they* ***load up*** *their dugout canoes.* ■ (often **be loaded**) place (a load or large quantity of something) on or in a vehicle, ship, container, etc.: *stolen property from a burglary was* ***loaded into*** *a taxi.* ■ [*intrans.*] (of a ship or vehicle) take on a load: *when we came to the quay the ship was still loading.* **2** make (someone or something) carry or hold a large or excessive amount of heavy things: *Elaine was* ***loaded down with*** *bags full of shopping.* ■ (**load someone/something with**) *figurative* supply someone or something in overwhelming abundance or to excess with: *the King and Queen loaded Columbus with wealth and honors.* ■ (**load someone with**) *figurative* burden someone with (worries, responsibilities, etc.). ■ (usu. **be loaded**) bias toward a particular outcome: *the odds were loaded against them before the match.* **3** insert (something) into a device so that it will operate: *load the cassette into the camcorder.* ■ insert something into (a device) so that it can be operated. ■ charge (a firearm) with ammunition. ■ *Computing* transfer (a program or data) into memory, or into the central processor from storage. ■ *Computing* transfer programs into (a computer memory or processor). **4** add an extra charge to (an insurance premium) in the case of a poorer risk.

▸*phrasal v.* □ **load up on** consume a substantial amount of (food or beverage): *we were loading up on beer and raw oysters.* ▷Old English *lād* 'way, journey, conveyance,' of Germanic origin; related to German *Leite,* also to LEAD[1]; compare with LODE. The verb dates from the late 15th cent.

▸*PHRASES* □ **get a load of** *informal* used to draw attention to someone or something: *get a load of what we've just done.* □ **get** (or **have**) **a load on** *informal* become drunk. □ **load the bases** *Baseball* (of the team at bat) fill all three bases with runners; (of a pitcher) allow all three bases to be occupied by runners. □ **load the dice against/in favor of someone** put someone at a disadvantage or advantage. □ **take a** (or **the**) **load off one's feet** sit or lie down. □ **take a load off someone's mind** bring someone relief from anxiety.

load dis·place·ment ▸*n.* the weight of water displaced by a ship when laden.

load·ed /ˈlōdid/ ▸*adj.* **1** carrying or bearing a load, esp. a large one: *a heavily loaded freight train.* ■ (of a firearm) charged with ammunition: *a loaded gun.* ■ (**loaded with**) containing in abundance or to excess: *your average chocolate bar is loaded with fat.* ■ *informal* having a lot of money; wealthy: *she doesn't really have to work—they're loaded.* ■ *informal* having had too much alcohol; drunk: *man, did I* ***get loaded*** *after I left his house.* ■ *informal* (of a car) equipped with many optional extras; deluxe: *1989 Ford 250 LXT: low miles, loaded.* **2** weighted or biased toward a particular outcome: *a trick like the one with the loaded dice.* ■ (of a word, statement, or question) charged with an underlying meaning or implication: *avoid politically loaded terms like "nation" | the students fed him loaded questions on U.S. support of Cuba's dictator Batista.*

▸*PHRASE* □ **loaded for bear** see BEAR[2].

load·er /ˈlōdər/ ▸*n.* **1** a machine or person that loads something. ■ an attendant who loads guns at a shoot. **2** [in *combination*] a gun, machine, or truck that is loaded in a specified way: *a front-loader.*

load fac·tor ▸*n.* the ratio of the average or actual amount of some quantity and the maximum possible or permissible. ■ the ratio between the lift and the weight of an aircraft.

load·ing /ˈlōdiNG/ ▸*n.* **1** the application of a mechanical load or force to something. ■ the amount of electric current or power delivered to a device. ■ the maximum electric current or power taken by an appliance. ■ the provision of extra electrical inductance to improve the properties of a transmission wire or antenna. **2** the application of an extra amount of something to balance some other factor. ■ an increase in an insurance premium due to a factor increasing the risk involved.

▸*adj.* [in *combination*] (of a gun, machine, or truck) loaded in a specified way: *a front-loading dishwasher.*

load·ing coil ▸*n.* a coil used to provide additional inductance in an electric circuit in order to reduce distortion and attenuation of transmitted signals or to reduce the resonant frequency of an aerial.

load·ing dock ▸*n.* see DOCK[1].

load line ▸*n.* another term for PLIMSOLL LINE.

load·mas·ter /ˈlōdˌmastər/ ▸*n.* the member of an aircraft's crew responsible for the cargo.

load-shed·ding ▸*n.* action to reduce the load on something, esp. the interruption of an electricity supply to avoid excessive load on the generating plant.

load·space /ˈlōdˌspās/ ▸*n.* the space in a motor vehicle for carrying a load.

load·stone ▸*n.* archaic spelling of LODESTONE.

loaf[1] /lōf/ ▸*n.* (*pl.* **loaves** /lōvz/) bread that is shaped and baked in one piece and usually sliced before being eaten: ***a loaf of*** *bread | two loaves in the oven.* ■ food formed into a usu. oblong shape, and often sliced into portions. ▷Old English *hlāf,* of Germanic origin; related to German *Laib.*

▸*PHRASE* □ **half a loaf is better than none** *proverb* it is better to accept less than one wants or expects than to have nothing at all.

loaf[2] ▸*v.* [*intrans.*] idle one's time away, typically by aimless wandering or loitering: *don't let him see you* ***loafing around*** *with your hands in your pockets.* ▷mid 19th cent.: probably a back-formation from LOAFER.

loaf·er /ˈlōfər/ ▸*n.* **1** a person who idles time away. **2** *trademark* a leather shoe shaped like a moccasin, with a low flat heel. ▷mid 19th cent.: perhaps from German *Landläufer* 'tramp,' from *Land* 'land' + *laufen* (dialect *lofen*) 'to run.'

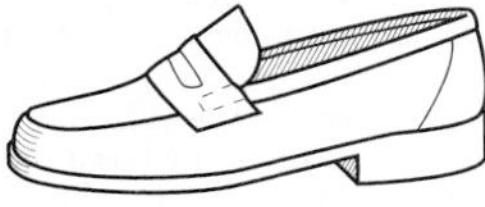

loafer 2

loam /lōm/ ▸*n.* a fertile soil of clay and sand containing humus. ■ *Geology* a soil with roughly equal proportions of sand, silt, and clay. ■ a paste of clay and water with sand, chopped straw, etc., used in making bricks and plastering walls. ▷Old English *lām* 'clay'; related to Dutch *leem* and German *Lehm,* also to LIME[1]. **—loam·i·ness** *n.* **—loamy** *adj.*

loan /lōn/ ▸*n.* a thing that is borrowed, esp. a sum of money that is expected to be paid back with interest: *borrowers can* ***take out a loan*** *for $84,000.* ■ an act of lending something to someone: *she offered to buy him dinner in return for the loan of the car.* ■ short for LOANWORD.

▸*v.* [*trans.*] (often **be loaned**) borrow (a sum of money or item of property): *the word processor was loaned to us by the theater | he knew Rob would not loan him money.* ▷Middle English (also denoting a gift from a superior): from Old Norse *lán,* of Germanic origin; related to Dutch *leen,* German *Lehn,* also to LEND. **—loan·a·ble** *adj.* **—loan·ee** /ˌlōˈnē/ *n.* **—loan·er** *n.*

▸*PHRASE* □ **on loan** (of a thing) being borrowed: *the painting is at present* ***on loan to*** *the gallery.* ■ (of a worker or sports player) released to another organization or team, typically for an agreed fixed period.

USAGE Traditionally, **loan** was a noun and **lend** was a verb: *I went to ask for a loan; can you lend me twenty dollars?* But **loan** is now widely used as a verb, esp. in financial contexts: *the banks were loaning money to speculators.*

loan shark ▸*n. informal,* often *derogatory* a moneylender who charges extremely high rates of interest, typically under illegal conditions. **—loan·shark·ing** /ˈlōnˌSHärkiNG/ *n.*

loan trans·la·tion ▸*n.* an expression adopted by one language from another in a more or less literally translated form. Also called CALQUE.

loan·word /ˈlōnˌwərd/ ▸*n.* a word adopted from a foreign language with little or no modification.

loath /lōTH; lōTH/ (also **loth**) ▸*adj.* reluctant; unwilling: *I was loath to leave.* ▷Old English *lāth* 'hostile, spiteful,' of Germanic origin; related to Dutch *leed,* German *Leid* 'sorrow.'

loathe /lōTH/ ▸*v.* [*trans.*] feel intense dislike or disgust for: *she loathed him on sight |* [as *n.*] (**loathing**) *the thought filled him with loathing.* See note at DESPISE. ▷Old English *lāthian,* of Germanic origin; related to LOATH. **—loath·er** *n.*

loath·some /ˈlōTHsəm; ˈlōTH-/ ▸*adj.* causing hatred or disgust; repulsive: *this loathsome little swine.* ▷Middle English: from archaic *loath* 'disgust, loathing' + -SOME[1]. **—loath·some·ly** *adv.* **—loath·some·ness** *n.*

loaves /lōvz/ ▸ plural form of LOAF[1].

lob /läb/ ▸*v.* (**lobbed, lob·bing**) [*trans.*] throw or hit (a ball or missile) in a high arc: *he lobbed the ball over their heads.* ■ (in tennis) hit the ball over (an opponent) in such a way.

▸*n.* (chiefly in tennis) a ball hit in a high arc over an opponent. ▷late 16th cent. (in the senses 'cause or allow to hang heavily' and 'behave like a lout'): from the archaic noun *lob* 'lout,' 'pendulous object,' probably from Low German or Dutch (compare with modern Dutch *lubbe* 'hanging lip'). The current sense dates from the mid 19th cent.

Lo·ba·chev·sky /ˌlōbəˈCHefskē; ləbəˈCHyefskyē/, Nikolai Ivanovich (1792–1856), Russian mathematician. At about the same time as Gauss and **János Bolyai** (1802–60), he independently discovered non-Euclidean geometry.

lo·bar /ˈlōˌbär; -bər/ ▸*adj. chiefly Anatomy & Medicine* of, relating to, or affecting a lobe, esp. a whole lobe of a lung.

lo·bate /ˈlōˌbāt/ ▸*adj. Biology* having a lobe or lobes: *lobate oak leaves.* **—lo·ba·tion** /lōˈbāSHən/ *n.*

lob·by /ˈläbē/ ▸*n.* (*pl.* **-bies**) **1** a room providing a space out of which one or more other rooms or corridors lead, typically one near the entrance of a public building. **2** a group of people seeking to influence politicians or public officials on a particular issue: *members of the anti-abortion lobby |* [as *adj.*] *lobby groups.* ■ [in *sing.*] an organized attempt by members of the public to influence politicians or public officials: *a recent* ***lobby of*** *Congress by retirees.*

▸*v.* (**-bies, -bied**) [*trans.*] seek to influence (a politician or public official) on an issue: *it is recommending that booksellers lobby their representatives |* [*intrans.*] *a group* ***lobbying for*** *better rail services.* ▷mid 16th cent. (in the sense 'monastic cloister'): from medieval Latin *lobia, lobium* 'covered walk, portico.' The verb sense derives from the practice of frequenting the lobby of a house of legislature to influence its members into supporting a cause. **—lob·by·ist** /-ist/ *n.*

lobe /lōb/ ▸*n.* a roundish and flattish part of something, typically each of two or more such parts divided by a fissure, and often projecting or hanging.

Pronunciation Key ə *ago;* ər *over;* ˈə or ˌə *up;* ˈər or ˌər *fur;* a *hat;* ā *rate;* ä *car;* CH *chew;* e *let;* ē *see;* e(ə)r *air;* i *fit;* ī *by;* i(ə)r *ear;* NG *sing;* ō *go;* ô *for;* oi *boy;* o͝o *good;* o͞o *goo;* ou *out;* SH *she;* TH *thin;* TH *then;* (h)w *why;* ZH *vision*

L

See also EARLOBE. ■ each of the parts of the cerebrum of the brain. ▷late Middle English: via late Latin from Greek *lobos* 'lobe, pod.' **—lobed** *adj.* **—lobe·less** *adj.*

lo·bec·to·my /lō'bektəmē/ ▶*n.* (*pl.* **-mies**) surgical removal of a lobe of an organ such as the thyroid gland, lung, or liver.

lobe-finned fish (also **lobe-fin**) ▶*n.* a fish of a largely extinct group having fleshy lobed fins, including the probable ancestors of the amphibians. Compare with RAY-FINNED FISH. • Subclass Crossopterygia (or Actinistia or Coelacanthimorpha): the only living representative is the coelacanth.

lo·bel·ia /lō'bēlēə; -'bēlyə/ ▶*n.* a chiefly tropical or subtropical plant of the bellflower family, in particular an annual widely grown as a bedding plant. Some kinds are aquatic, and some grow as thick-trunked shrubs or trees on African mountains. • Genus *Lobelia*, family Campanulaceae: many species, including the popular blue-flowered *L. erinus*. ▷modern Latin, named after Matthias de *Lobel* (1538–1616), Flemish botanist to James I.

Lo·bi·to /lō'bētō/ a seaport and natural harbor on the Atlantic coast of Angola; pop. 150,000.

lob·lol·ly /'läb,lälē/ ▶*n.* (*pl.* **-lies**) **1** (also **loblolly pine**) a pine tree of the southern U.S. that has very long slender needles and is an important source of timber. • *Pinus taeda*, family Pinaceae. **2** (also **loblolly bay**) a small evergreen tree of the tea family, with baylike leaves and white camelliailike flowers, native to the southeastern U.S. • *Gordonia lasianthus*, family Theaceae. **3** a marshy patch of ground. **4** *dated Cooking* a thick mush or gruel. ▷late 16th cent. (denoting thick gruel): the reason for the application of the word to the two plants, and the word's origin, are unknown.

lo·bo /'lōbō/ ▶*n.* (*pl.* **-bos**) (in the southwestern U.S. and Mexico) a timber wolf. ▷mid 19th cent.: from Spanish, from Latin *lupus* 'wolf.'

lo·bo·la /lōbələ/ (also **lo·bo·lo** /lə'bōlō/) ▶*n.* (among southern African peoples) a bride price, esp. one paid with cattle. ■ the practice of making such a payment. ▷Zulu and Xhosa.

lo·bo·pod /'lōbə,päd/ ▶*n.* *Zoology* the lobopodium of an onychophoran. ■ an onychophoran: [as *adj.*] *a lobopod animal.*

lo·bo·po·di·um /,lōbə'pōdēəm/ ▶*n.* (*pl.* **-di·a** /-dēə/) *Zoology* a blunt limb or organ resembling a limb, in particular: ■ the primitive leg of an onychophoran. ■ a lobelike pseudopodium in an ameba. ▷early 20th cent.: from modern Latin *lobosus* 'having many lobes, large-lobed' + PODIUM. **—lo·bo·po·di·al** /-dēəl/ *adj.*

lo·bot·o·mize /lə'bätə,mīz/ ▶*v.* [*trans.*] (often **be lobotomized**) *Surgery* perform a lobotomy on. ■ *informal* reduce the mental or emotional capacity or ability to function of: *couples we knew who had been lobotomized by the birth of their children.* **—lo·bot·o·mi·za·tion** /-,bätəmə'zāshən/ *n.*

lo·bot·o·my /lə'bätəmē/ ▶*n.* (*pl.* **-mies**) a surgical operation involving incision into the prefrontal lobe of the brain, formerly used to treat mental illness.

lob·scouse /'läb,skous/ ▶*n.* a stew formerly eaten by sailors, consisting of meat, vegetables, and hardtack. ▷early 18th cent.: of unknown origin; compare with Dutch *lapskous*, Danish and Norwegian *lapskaus*, and German *Lapskaus*.

lob·ster /'läbstər/ ▶*n.* a large marine crustacean with a cylindrical body, stalked eyes, and the first of its five pairs of limbs modified as pincers. • *Homarus* and other genera, class Malacostraca: several species, in particular the **American lobster** (*H. americanus*). ■ the flesh of this animal as food. ■ a deep red color typical of a cooked lobster. ■ any of various similar crustaceans, esp. certain crayfish whose claws are eaten as food.
▶*v.* [*intrans.*] catch lobsters. ▷Old English *lopustre*, alteration of Latin *locusta* 'crustacean, locust.'

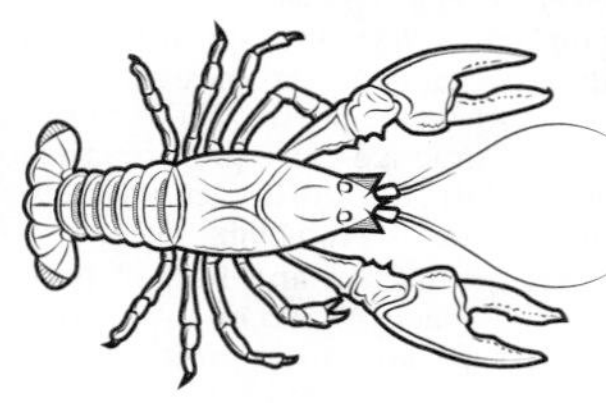

American lobster

lob·ster claw ▶*n.* a tropical American plant with brightly colored flowers that resemble a lobster claw, each being composed of boat-shaped bracts. • *Heliconia bihai*, family Heliconiaceae.

lob·ster·man /'läbstərmən/ ▶*n.* a person whose occupation is trapping lobsters.

lob·ster pot (also **lobster trap**) ▶*n.* a cratelike or basketlike trap in which lobsters are caught.

lob·ster ther·mi·dor /'THərmə,dôr/ ▶*n.* a dish of lobster cooked in a cream sauce, returned to its shell, sprinkled with cheese, and browned under the grill. ▷*thermidor* from THERMIDOR.

lob·ule /'läb,yōōl/ ▶*n.* *chiefly Anatomy* a small lobe. ▷late 17th cent.: from LOBE, on the pattern of words such as *globule*. **—lob·u·lar** /-yələr/ *adj.* **—lob·u·late** /-yə,lāt/ *adj.* **—lob·u·lat·ed** /-yə,lātid/ *adj.*

lob·worm /'läb,wərm/ ▶*n.* another term for LUGWORM. ▷mid 17th cent.: from LOB in the obsolete sense 'pendulous object.'

lo·cal /'lōkəl/ ▶*adj.* belonging or relating to a particular area or neighborhood, typically exclusively so: *researching local history | the local post office.* ■ denoting a telephone call made to a nearby place and charged at a relatively low rate. ■ denoting a train or bus serving a particular district, with frequent stops: *the town has an excellent local bus service.* Compare with EXPRESS². ■ (in technical use) relating to a particular region or part, or to each of any number of these: *a local infection | migration can regulate the local density of animals.* ■ *Computing* denoting a variable or other entity that is only available for use in one part of a program. ■ *Computing* denoting a device that can be accessed without the use of a network. Compare with REMOTE.
▶*n.* a local person or thing, in particular: ■ an inhabitant of a particular area or neighborhood: *the street was full of locals and tourists.* ■ *Brit., informal* a pub convenient to a person's home: *a pint in the local.* ■ a local train or bus service: *catch the local into New Delhi.* ■ a local branch of an organization, esp. a labor union. ■ short for LOCAL ANESTHESIA. ■ *Stock Exchange slang* a floor trader who trades on their own account, rather than on behalf of other investors. ▷late Middle English: from late Latin *localis*, from Latin *locus* 'place.' **—lo·cal·ly** *adv.* **—lo·cal·ness** *n.*

lo·cal an·es·the·sia ▶*n.* anesthesia that affects a restricted area of the body. Compare with GENERAL ANESTHESIA.

lo·cal ar·e·a net·work (abbr.: **LAN**) ▶*n.* a computer network that links devices within a building or group of adjacent buildings. Compare with WIDE AREA NETWORK.

lo·cal bus ▶*n.* *Computing* a high-speed data connection directly linking peripheral devices to the processor and memory, allowing activities that require high data transmission rates such as video display.

lo·cal col·or ▶*n.* **1** the customs, manner of speech, dress, or other typical features of a place or period that contribute to its particular character: *reporters in search of local color and gossip.* **2** *Art* the natural color of a thing in ordinary daylight, uninfluenced by the proximity of other colors.

lo·cale /lō'kal/ ▶*n.* a place where something happens or is set, or that has particular events associated with it: *her summers were spent in a variety of exotic locales.* ▷late 18th cent.: from French *local* (noun), respelled to indicate stress on the final syllable; compare with MORALE.

lo·cal gov·ern·ment ▶*n.* the administration of a particular, town, county or district, with representatives elected by those who live there.

Lo·cal Group *Astronomy* the cluster of galaxies of which the Milky Way is a member.

lo·cal·ism /'lōkə,lizəm/ ▶*n.* preference for a locality, particularly to one's own area or region. ■ *derogatory* the limitation of ideas and interests resulting from this. ■ a characteristic of a particular locality, such as a local idiom or custom. **—lo·cal·ist** *n.* & *adj.*

lo·cal·i·ty /lō'kalətē/ ▶*n.* (*pl.* **-ties**) the position or site of something: *the rock's size and locality.* ■ an area or neighborhood, esp. as regarded as a place occupied by certain people or as the scene of particular activities: *the results of other schools in the locality | a working-class locality.* ▷early 17th cent.: from French *localité* or late Latin *localitas*, from *localis* 'relating to a place' (see LOCAL).

lo·cal·ize /'lōkə,līz/ ▶*v.* [*trans.*] [often as *adj.*] (**localized**) restrict (something) to a particular place: *symptoms include localized pain and numbness.* ■ make (something) local in character: *there'd now be a more localized news service.* ■ assign (something) to a particular place: *most vertebrates localize sounds by orienting movements.* **—lo·cal·iz·a·ble** *adj.* **—lo·cal·i·za·tion** /,lōkələ'zāSHən/ *n.*

lo·cal op·tion ▶*n.* a choice available to a local administration to accept or reject national legislation (e.g., concerning the sale of alcoholic liquor).

lo·cal time ▶*n.* time as reckoned in a particular region or time zone. ■ time at a particular place as measured from the sun's transit over the meridian at that place, defined as noon.

lo·carb /'lō ,kärb/ ▶a variant spelling of LOW-CARB.

Lo·car·no /lō'kärnō/ a resort in southern Switzerland, at the northern end of Lake Maggiore; pop. 14,000.

lo·cate /'lō,kāt; lō'kāt/ ▶*v.* [*trans.*] discover the exact place or position of: *engineers were working to locate the fault.* ■ (usu. **be located**) situate in a particular place: *these popular apartments are centrally located.* ■ place within a particular context: *they locate their policies in terms of wealth creation.* ■ [*intrans.*] establish oneself or one's business in a specified place: *his marketing strategy has been to locate in small towns.* ▷early 16th cent.: from Latin *locat-* 'placed,' from the verb *locare*, from *locus* 'place.' The original sense was as a legal term meaning 'rent out,' later (late 16th cent.) 'assign to a particular place,' then 'establish in a place.' The sense 'discover the exact position of' dates from the late 19th cent. **—lo·cat·a·ble** /-,kātəbəl; lō'kāt-/ *adj.*

USAGE In formal English, one should avoid using **locate** to mean 'find (a missing object)': *he can't seem to locate his keys.* In precise usage, **locate** means 'discover the exact place or position of' or 'fix the position of, put in place': *the doctors hope to locate the source of the bleeding; the studio should be located on a north-facing slope.*

lo·ca·tion /lō'kāSHən/ ▶*n.* a particular place or position: *the property is set in a convenient location.* ■ an actual place or natural setting in which a film or broadcast is made, as distinct from a simulation in a studio: *the movie was filmed entirely **on location**.* ■ the action or process of placing someone or something in a particular position: *the location of new housing beyond the existing built-up areas.* ■ a position or address in computer memory. ▷late 16th cent.: from Latin *locatio(n-)*, from the verb *locare* (see LOCATE). **—lo·ca·tion·al** /-SHənl; -SHnəl/ *adj.*

loc·a·tive /'läkətiv/ *Grammar* ▶*adj.* relating to or denoting a case in some languages of nouns, pronouns, and adjectives, expressing location.
▶*n.* (**the locative**) the locative case. ■ a word in the locative case. ▷early 19th cent.: from LOCATE, on the pattern of *vocative*.

lo·ca·tor /'lō,kātər; lō'kā-/ ▶*n.* a device or system for locating something, typically by means of radio signals.

loc. cit. ▶*abbr.* in the passage already cited. ▷from Latin *loco citato*.

loch /läk; läKH/ ▶*n.* *Scottish* a lake. ■ (also **sea loch**) an arm of the sea, esp. when narrow or partially landlocked. ▷late Middle English: from Scottish Gaelic.

lo·chi·a /'lōkēə; 'läk-/ ▶*n.* *Medicine* the normal discharge from the uterus after childbirth. ▷late 17th cent.: modern Latin, from Greek *lokhia*, neuter plural (used as a noun) of *lokhios* 'of childbirth.' **—lo·chi·al** *adj.*

Loch Ness /läk 'nes; läKH/ a deep lake in northwestern Scotland, in the Great Glen. Forming part of the Caledonian Canal, it is 24 miles (38 km) long, with a maximum depth of 755 feet (230 m). The lake has long been rumored to be the home of the Loch Ness monster.

Loch Ness mon·ster a large creature alleged to live in the deep waters of Loch Ness. Reports of its existence date from the time of St. Columba (6th century); despite recent scientific expeditions, there is still no proof of its existence.

lo·ci /'lō,sī; -,sē; -,kē; -,kī/ ▶ plural form of LOCUS.

lo·ci clas·si·ci /'lō,sī 'klasə,sī; 'lō,sē 'klasə,sē; 'lō,kē 'klasi,kē; 'lō,kī 'klasi,kī/ ▶ plural form of LOCUS CLASSICUS.

lock¹ /läk/ ▶*n.* **1** a mechanism for keeping a door, lid, etc., fastened, typically operated only by a key of a particular form: *the key turned firmly in the lock.* ■ a similar device used to prevent the operation or movement of a vehicle or other machine: *a bicycle lock.* ■ (in wrestling and martial arts) a hold that prevents an opponent from moving a limb. ■ [in *sing.*] *archaic* a number of interlocked or jammed items: *a street closed by a lock of carriages.* **2** a short confined section of a canal or other waterway in which the water level can be changed by the use of gates and sluices, used for raising and lowering vessels between two gates. ■ an airlock. **3** (**a lock**) *informal* a person or thing that is certain to succeed; a certainty. **4** *archaic* a mechanism for exploding the charge of a gun.

▸*v.* **1** [*trans.*] fasten or secure (something) with a lock: *she closed and locked her desk* | [as *adj.*] (**locked**) *behind locked doors.* ■ (**lock something up**) shut and secure something, esp. a building, by fastening its doors with locks: *the diplomatic personnel locked up their building and walked off* | [*intrans.*] *you could lock up for me when you leave.* ■ enclose or shut in by locking or fastening a door, lid, etc.: *the prisoners are* **locked up** *overnight* | *Phil locked away the takings every night.* ■ (**lock someone up/away**) imprison someone. ■ (**lock something up/away**) invest money in something so that it is not easily accessible: *vast sums of money locked up in pension funds.* ■ (**lock someone down**) confine prisoners to their cells, esp. so as to gain control. ■ [*intrans.*] (of a door, window, box, etc.) become or be able to be secured through activation of a lock: *the door will automatically lock behind you.* **2** make or become rigidly fixed or immovable: [*trans.*] *he locked his hands behind her neck* | [*intrans.*] *their gaze locked for several long moments.* ■ (**lock someone/something in**) engage or entangle in (an embrace or struggle): *they were locked in a legal battle.* ■ trap or fix firmly or irrevocably. *this may tend to lock in many traders with their present holdings.* ■ (**lock someone/something into**) cause to become caught or involved in: *they were now locked into the system.* ■ (of land, hills, ice, etc.) enclose; surround: *the vessel was* **locked in** *ice.* **3** [*intrans.*] go through a lock on a canal: *we locked through at Moore Haven.*

▸*phrasal v.* □ **lock onto** locate (a target) by radar or similar means and then track. □ **lock someone out** **1** keep someone out of a room or building by locking the door. **2** (of an employer) subject employees to a lockout. □ **lock someone out of** exclude someone from: *those now locked out of the job market.* ▷Old English *loc*, of Germanic origin; related to German *Loch* 'hole.' —**lock·a·ble** *adj.* —**lock·less** *adj.*

▸*PHRASES* □ **have a lock on** *informal* have an unbreakable hold on or total control over. □ **lock horns** engage in conflict. □ **lock, stock, and barrel** including everything; completely: *the place is owned lock, stock, and barrel by an oil company.* [referring to the complete mechanism of a firearm.] □ **under lock and key** securely locked up.

lock[2] ▸*n.* a piece of a person's hair that coils or hangs together: *she pushed back* **a lock of** *hair.* ■ (**locks**) *chiefly poetic/literary* a person's hair: *flowing locks and a long white beard.* ■ a tuft of wool or cotton. ■ (**locks**) short for DREADLOCKS. ▷Old English *locc*, of Germanic origin; related to Dutch *lok*, German *Locke*, possibly also to LOCK[1]. —**locked** *adj. his curly-locked comrades.*

lock·age /ˈläkij/ ▸*n.* the construction or use of locks on waterways. ■ the amount of rise and fall of water levels resulting from the use of locks. ■ money paid as a toll for the use of a lock.

lock·box /ˈläk ˌbäks/ ▸*n.* **1** a box that locks, usually for storing money or valuables. **2** a service provided by a bank, whereby the bank receives, processes, and deposits all of a company's receivables. **3** any of various computerized devices or services intended to prevent the unauthorized distribution or copying of digitally stored or transmitted data.

lock·down /ˈläkˌdoun/ ▸*n.* the confining of prisoners to their cells, typically after an escape or to regain control during a riot.

Locke /läk/, John (1632–1704), English philosopher; a founder of empiricism and political liberalism. His *Two Treatises of Government* (1690) argues that the authority of rulers has a human origin and is limited. In *An Essay concerning Human Understanding* (1690) he argued that all knowledge is derived from sense-experience. —**Lock·e·an** /ˈläkēən/ *adj.*

lock·er /ˈläkər/ ▸*n.* **1** a small lockable closet or compartment, typically as one of a number placed together for public or general use, e.g., in schools, gymnasiums, or train stations. ■ a chest or compartment on a ship or boat for clothes, stores, equipment, or ammunition. **2** a device that locks something. ▷late Middle English: probably related to Flemish *loker*.

Lock·er·bie /ˈläkərbē/ a town in southwestern Scotland; pop. 4,000. In 1988, a U.S. airliner, destroyed by a terrorist bomb, crashed on the town and killed all those on board as well as 11 people on the ground.

lock·er room ▸*n.* a room containing lockers for the storage of personal belongings, esp. in schools or gymnasiums.

▸*adj.* regarded as characteristic of or suited to a men's locker room, esp. as being coarse or ribald: *locker-room humor.*

lock·et /ˈläkit/ ▸*n.* **1** a small ornamental case, typically made of gold or silver, worn around a person's neck on a chain and used to hold things of sentimental value, such as a photograph or lock of hair. **2** a metal plate or band on a scabbard. ▷late Middle English (sense 2): from Old French *locquet*, diminutive of *loc* 'latch, lock,' of Germanic origin; related to LOCK[1]. Sense 1 dates from the late 17th cent.

lock-in ▸*n.* the act or fact of locking in a person or thing. ■ an arrangement according to which a person or company is obliged to negotiate or trade only with a specific company. ■ a protest demonstration in which a group locks itself within an office, building, or factory.

lock·jaw /ˈläkˌjô/ ▸*n.* nontechnical term for TRISMUS.

lock-knit ▸*adj.* (of a fabric) knitted with an interlocking stitch.

lock·nut /ˈläkˌnət/ ▸*n.* a nut screwed down on another to keep it tight. ■ a nut designed so that, once tightened, it cannot be accidentally loosened.

lock·out /ˈläkˌout/ ▸*n.* **1** the exclusion of employees by their employer from their place of work until certain terms are agreed to. **2** a device used to ensure that machines remain inoperable while repairs or adjustments are made.

Lock·port /ˈläkˌpôrt/ a city in western New York, northeast of Buffalo, on the Erie Canal; pop. 24,426.

lock·set /ˈläkˌset/ ▸*n.* a complete locking system, including knobs, plates, and a locking mechanism, esp. for a door.

lock·smith /ˈläkˌsmiTH/ ▸*n.* a person who makes and repairs locks.

lock·step /ˈläkˌstep/ ▸*n.* a way of marching with each person as close as possible to the one in front: *the trio marched* **in lockstep** | [as *adv.*] *hundreds of shaven-headed youths march lockstep into the stadium.* ■ *figurative* close adherence to and emulation of another's actions: *they raised prices* **in lockstep with** *those of foreign competitors* | [as *adj.*] *the party touted a lockstep unity.*

lock·stitch ▸*n.* a stitch made by a sewing machine by firmly linking together two threads or stitches.

lock·up /ˈläkˌəp/ ▸*n.* **1** a jail, esp. a temporary one. **2** the locking up of premises for the night. ■ the time of doing this: *hurrying back to their dorms before lockup.* **3** the action of becoming fixed or immovable: *anti-lock braking helps prevent wheel lockup.* **4** an investment in assets that cannot readily be realized or sold in the short term.

Lock·yer /ˈläkyər/, Sir (Joseph) Norman (1836–1920), English astronomer. His spectroscopic analysis of the sun led to his discovery of a new element, which he named *helium*.

lo·co ▸*adj. informal* crazy. ▷late 19th cent.: from Spanish, 'insane.'

lo·co·mo·tion /ˌlōkəˈmōSHən/ ▸*n.* movement or the ability to move from one place to another: *the muscles that are concerned with locomotion* | *he preferred walking to other forms of locomotion.* ▷mid 17th cent.: from Latin *loco*, ablative of *locus* 'place' + *motio* (see MOTION).

lo·co·mo·tive /ˌlōkəˈmōtiv/ ▸*n.* a powered rail vehicle used for pulling trains: *a diesel locomotive.*

▸*adj.* of, relating to, or effecting locomotion: *locomotive power.* ■ *archaic* (of a machine, vehicle, or animal) having the power of progressive motion: *locomotive bivalves have the strongest hinges.* ▷early 17th cent. (as an adjective): from modern Latin *locomotivus*, from Latin *loco* (ablative of *locus* 'place') + late Latin *motivus* 'motive,' suggested by medieval Latin *in loco moveri* 'move by change of position.'

lo·co·mo·tor /ˌlōkəˈmōtər/ ▸*adj. chiefly Biology* of or relating to locomotion: *locomotor organs.* ▷early 19th cent.: from LOCOMOTION + MOTOR.

lo·co·mo·tor a·tax·i·a ▸*n.* another term for TABES DORSALIS.

lo·co·mo·to·ry /ˌlōkəˈmōtərē/ ▸*adj. chiefly Zoology* relating to or having the power of locomotion: *locomotory cilia.*

lo·co·weed /ˈlōkōˌwēd/ ▸*n.* **1** a widely distributed plant of the pea family that, if eaten by livestock, can cause a brain disorder, the symptoms of which include unpredictable behavior and loss of coordination. • Genus *Astragalus* (and *Oxytropis*), family Leguminosae. **2** *informal* cannabis.

Lo·cri·an mode /ˈlōkrēən; ˈläkrē-/ ▸*n. Music* the mode represented by the natural diatonic scale B–B (containing a minor 2nd, 3rd, 6th, and 7th, and a diminished 5th). ▷late 19th cent.: *Locrian* from Greek *Locris*, a division of ancient Greece, + -IAN; named after an ancient Greek mode but not identifiable with it.

loc·ule /ˈläkˌyo͞ol/ ▸*n. chiefly Botany* each of a number of small separate cavities, esp. in an ovary. —**loc·u·lar** /-yələr/ *adj.*

loc·u·lus /ˈläkyələs/ ▸*n.* (*pl.* **-li** /-ˌlī; -ˌlē/) another term for LOCULE. ▷mid 19th cent.: from Latin, 'compartment,' diminutive of *locus* 'place.'

lo·cum /ˈlōkəm/ ▸*n. informal, chiefly Brit.* short for LOCUM TENENS.

lo·cum te·nens /ˈlōkəm ˈtenənz; ˈtēˌnenz/ ▸*n.* (*pl.* **locum te·nen·tes** /təˈnentēz/) *chiefly Brit.* a person who stands in temporarily for someone else of the same profession, esp. a cleric or doctor. ▷mid 17th cent.: from medieval Latin, literally 'one holding a place' (see LOCUS, TENANT). —**lo·cum te·nen·cy** /ˈtenənsē; ˈtēnən-/ *n.*

lo·cus /ˈlōkəs/ ▸*n.* (*pl.* **lo·ci** /ˈlōˌsī; -ˌsē; -ˌkē; -ˌkī/) **1** *technical* a particular position, point, or place: *it is impossible to specify the exact locus in the brain of these neural events.* ■ the effective or perceived location of something abstract: *the real locus of power is the informal council.* ■ *Genetics* the position of a gene or mutation on a chromosome. **2** *Mathematics* a curve or other figure formed by all the points satisfying a particular equation of the relation between coordinates, or by a point, line, or surface moving according to mathematically defined conditions. ▷early 18th cent.: from Latin, 'place.'

lo·cus clas·si·cus /ˈlōkəs ˈklasikəs/ ▸*n.* (*pl.* **lo·ci clas·si·ci** /ˈlōˌsī ˈklasəˌsī; ˈlōˌsē ˈklasəˌsē; ˈlōˌkē ˈklasiˌkē; ˈlōˌkī ˈklasiˌkī/) a passage considered to be the best known or most authoritative on a particular subject. ▷Latin, literally 'classical place.'

lo·cust /ˈlōkəst/ ▸*n.* **1** a large and mainly tropical grasshopper with strong powers of flight. It is usually solitary, but from time to time there is a population explosion, and it migrates in vast swarms that cause extensive damage to crops. • Several species in the family Acrididae, including the **migratory locust** (*Locusta migratoria*), which is sometimes seen in Europe. ■ (also **seventeen-year locust**) the periodical cicada. **2** (also **locust bean**) the large edible pod of some plants of the pea family, in particular the carob bean, which is said to resemble a locust. **3** (also **locust tree**) any of a number of pod-bearing trees of the pea family, in particular the carob tree and the black locust. ▷Middle English: via Old French *locuste* from Latin *locusta* 'locust, crustacean.'

lo·cu·tion /lōˈkyo͞oSHən/ ▸*n.* **1** a word or phrase, esp. with regard to style or idiom. ■ a person's style of speech: *his impeccable locution.* **2** an utterance regarded in terms of its intrinsic meaning or reference, as distinct from its function or purpose in context. Compare with ILLOCUTION, PERLOCUTION. ■ language regarded in terms of locutionary rather than illocutionary or perlocutionary acts. ▷late Middle English: from Old French, or from Latin *locutio(n-)*, from *loqui* 'speak.' —**lo·cu·tion·ar·y** /-ˌnerē/ *adj.*

lode /lōd/ ▸*n.* a vein of metal ore in the earth. ■ [in *sing.*] *figurative* a rich source of something: *a rich lode of scandal and alleged crime.* ▷Old English *lād* 'way, course,' variant of LOAD. The term denoted a watercourse in late Middle English and a lodestone in the early 16th cent. The current sense dates from the early 17th cent.

lo·den /ˈlōdn/ ▸*n.* a thick waterproof woolen cloth. ■ the dark green color in which such cloth is often made. ▷early 20th cent.: from German *Loden*.

lode·star /ˈlōdˌstär/ ▸*n.* a star that is used to guide the course of a ship, esp. Polaris. ■ *figurative* a person or thing that serves as a guide: *she was his intellectual lodestar.* ▷Middle English: from LODE in the obsolete sense 'way, course' + STAR.

lode·stone /ˈlōdˌstōn/ ▸*n.* a piece of magnetite or other naturally magnetized mineral, able to be used as a magnet. ■ a mineral of this kind; magnetite. ■ *figurative* a thing that is the focus of attention or attraction.

Lodge[1] /läj/, David (John) (1935–), English novelist and academic. Notable works: *Changing Places* (1975), *Small World* (1984), and *Therapy* (1995).

Lodge[2], Henry Cabot (1850–1924), U.S. politician and writer. He was a member of the U.S. House Representatives 1887–93 and the U.S. Senate 1893–1924

Pronunciation Key ə *ago*; ər *over*; ˈə or ˌə *up*; ˈər or ˌər *fur*; a *hat*; ā *rate*; ä *car*; CH *chew*; e *let*; ē *see*; e(ə)r *air*; i *fit*; ī *by*; i(ə)r *ear*; NG *sing*; ō *go*; ô *for*; oi *boy*; o͝o *good*; o͞o *goo*; ou *out*; SH *she*; TH *thin*; TH *then*; (h)w *why*; ZH *vision*

as a Republican from Massachusetts. He opposed accepting the peace treaty that ended World War I and that was linked to the U.S. entry into the League of Nations. He was the grandfather of Henry Cabot Lodge.

Lodge[3], Henry Cabot (1902–85), U.S. politician and diplomat. He was a Republican vice presidential candidate in 1960 and served as ambassador to South Vietnam 1963–64, 1965–67. The grandson of Henry Cabot Lodge, he was the U.S. representative to the UN 1953–60.

lodge /läj/ ▸*n.* **1** a small house at the gates of a park or in the grounds of a large house, typically occupied by a gatekeeper, gardener, or other employee. ■ a small country house occupied in season for sports such as hunting, shooting, fishing, and skiing: *a hunting lodge.* ■ a large house or hotel: *Cumberland Lodge.* ■ a porter's quarters at the main entrance of a college or other large building. ■ the residence of a head of a college, esp. at Cambridge. ■ an American Indian hut. ■ a beaver's den. **2** a branch or meeting place of an organization such as the Freemasons. ■ the membership of such an organization.

▸*v.* **1** [*trans.*] present (a complaint, appeal, claim, etc.) formally to the proper authorities: *he has 28 days in which to lodge an appeal.* ■ (**lodge something in/with**) leave money or a valuable item in (a place) or with (someone) for safekeeping. **2** make or become firmly fixed or embedded in a particular place: [*trans.*] *they had to remove a bullet lodged near his spine* | [*intrans.*] *figurative the image had lodged in her mind.* **3** [*intrans.*] stay or sleep in another person's house, paying money for one's accommodations: *the man who lodged in the room next door.* ■ [*trans.*] provide (someone) with a place to sleep or stay in return for payment. **4** [*trans.*] (of wind or rain) flatten (a standing crop): [as *adj.*] (**lodged**) *rain that soaks standing or lodged crops.* ■ [*intrans.*] (of a crop) be flattened in such a way. ▷Middle English *loge,* via Old French *loge* 'arbor, hut' from medieval Latin *laubia, lobia* (see LOBBY), of Germanic origin; related to German *Laube* 'arbor.'

lodge·pole pine /ˈläjipōl/ ▸*n.* a straight-trunked pine tree that grows in the mountains of western North America, widely grown for timber and traditionally used by some American Indians in the construction of lodges. • *Pinus contorta* var. *latifolia,* family Pinaceae.

lodg·er /ˈläjər/ ▸*n.* a roomer.

lodg·ing /ˈläjiNG/ ▸*n.* a place in which someone lives or stays temporarily: *they found a cheap lodging in a backstreet* | *a fee for* **board and lodging.** ■ (**lodgings**) a room or rooms rented out to someone, usually in the same residence as the owner.

lodg·ing house ▸*n.* a rooming house.

lodg·ment /ˈläjmənt/ (also **lodge·ment**) ▸*n.* **1** *chiefly poetic/literary* a place in which a person or thing is located, deposited, or lodged: *they found a lodgment for the hook in the crumbling parapet.* **2** the depositing of money in a particular bank, account, etc. **3** *Military* a temporary defensive work made on a captured part of an enemy's fortifications to secure a position and provide protection. ▷late 16th cent.: from French *logement* 'dwelling,' from Old French *loge* 'arbor' (see LODGE).

Lo·di /ˈlō,dī/ a city in north central California, north of Stockton, in the San Joaquin Valley; pop. 51,874.

lod·i·cule /ˈlädə,kyoōl/ ▸*n. Botany* a small green or white scale below the ovary of a grass flower. ▷mid 19th cent.: from Latin *lodicula,* diminutive of *lodix* 'coverlet.'

Łódź /lädz; wōōCH/ an industrial city in central Poland, southwest of Warsaw, the second largest city in the country; pop. 842,000.

lo·ess /les; ləs; ˈlō,es/ ▸*n. Geology* a loosely compacted yellowish-gray deposit of windblown sediment of which extensive deposits occur, e.g., in eastern China and the American Midwest. ▷mid 19th cent.: from German *Löss,* from Swiss German *lösch* 'loose.' —**lo·ess·i·al** /ˈlesēəl; ˈlə-; lōˈes-/ *adj.* —**lo·ess·ic** /ˈlesik; ˈlə-; lōˈes-/ *adj.*

Loewe /lō/, Frederick (1901–88), U.S. composer; born in Austria. The collaboration he began with lyricist Alan Jay Lerner in 1942 became one of the most successful in the history of musical theater. He wrote the scores for *Brigadoon* (1947), *My Fair Lady* (1956), *Gigi* (1958), *Camelot* (1960), and *The Little Prince* (1974).

Loe·wi /ˈlō-ē/, Otto (1873–1961), U.S. pharmacologist and physiologist, born in Germany. He showed that a chemical neurotransmitter (acetylcholine) is produced at the junction of a parasympathetic nerve and a muscle. Nobel Prize for Physiology or Medicine (1936, shared with Sir Henry Dale).

lo-fi /ˈlō ˈfī/ (also **low-fi**) ▸*adj.* of or employing sound reproduction of a lower quality than hi-fi: *defiantly lo-fi recording techniques.* ■ (of popular music) recorded and produced with basic equipment and thus having a raw and unsophisticated sound.

▸*n.* sound reproduction or music of such a kind. ▷1950s: from an alteration of LOW[1] + *-fi* on the pattern of *hi-fi.*

Lo·fo·ten Is·lands /ˈlō,fōtn/ an island group off the northwestern coast of Norway. They are situated within the Arctic Circle in the Norwegian Sea.

loft /lôft; läft/ ▸*n.* **1** a room or space directly under the roof of a house or other building, which may be used for accommodations or storage. ■ a room or space over a stable or barn, used esp. for storing hay and straw: *the stable loft.* ■ a gallery in a church or hall: *a choir loft.* ■ short for ORGAN LOFT. ■ a large, open area over a shop, warehouse, or factory, sometimes converted into living space. ■ a pigeon house. **2** *Golf* upward inclination given to the ball in a stroke. ■ backward slope of the head of a club, designed to give upward inclination to the ball. **3** the thickness of insulating matter in an object such as a sleeping bag or a padded coat.

▸*v.* [*trans.*] kick, hit, or throw (a ball or missile) high up: *he lofted the ball over the infield.* ■ (**lofted**) give backward slope to the head of (a golf club): *a lofted metal club.* ▷late Old English, from Old Norse *lopt* 'air, sky, upper room,' of Germanic origin; related to Dutch *lucht* and German *Luft.*

loft·er /ˈlôftər; ˈläf-/ ▸*n. dated Golf* a nine-iron or similar lofted club. [late 19th cent.: from the verb LOFT.]

loft·y /ˈlôftē; ˈläf-/ ▸*adj.* (**loft·i·er, loft·i·est**) **1** of imposing height: *the elegant square was shaded by lofty palms.* ■ of a noble or exalted nature: *an extraordinary mixture of harsh reality and lofty ideals.* ■ proud, aloof, or self-important: *lofty intellectual disdain.* **2** (of wool and other textiles) thick and resilient. ▷Middle English: from LOFT, influenced by ALOFT. —**loft·i·ly** /-təlē/ *adv.* —**loft·i·ness** *n.*

log[1] /lôg; läg/ ▸*n.* **1** a part of the trunk or a large branch of a tree that has fallen or been cut off. **2** (also **log·book**) an official record of events during the voyage of a ship or aircraft: *a ship's log.* ■ a regular or systematic record of incidents or observations: *keep a detailed log of your activities.* **3** an apparatus for determining the speed of a ship, originally consisting of a float attached to a knotted line wound on a reel, the distance run out in a certain time being used as an estimate of the vessel's speed.

▸*v.* (**logged, log·ging**) [*trans.*] **1** enter (an incident or fact) in the log of a ship or aircraft or in another systematic record: *the incident has to be logged* | *the red book where we log our calls.* ■ (of a ship or aircraft) achieve (a certain distance or speed): *she had logged more than 12,000 miles since she had been launched.* ■ (of an aircraft pilot) attain (a certain amount of flying time). **2** cut down (an area of forest) in order to exploit the timber commercially.

▸*phrasal v.* □ **log in** (or **on**) go through the procedures to begin use of a computer system, which includes establishing the identity of the user. □ **log off** (or **out**) go through the procedures to conclude use of a computer system. ▷Middle English (in the sense 'bulky mass of wood'): of unknown origin; perhaps symbolic of the notion of heaviness. Sense 3 originally denoted a thin quadrant of wood loaded to float upright in the water, whence 'ship's journal' in which information from the log board was recorded.

▸*PHRASE* □ (**as**) **easy as falling off a log** *informal* very easy.

log[2] ▸*n.* short for LOGARITHM: [as *adj.*] *log tables* | [prefixed to a number or algebraic symbol] *log x.*

log. ▸*abbr.* logic.

-log ▸*comb. form* variant spelling of -LOGUE.

log$_e$ ▸*symbol* natural logarithm (a logarithm to the base *e.*

Lo·gan[1] /ˈlōgən/ a city in northern Utah; pop. 42,670.

Lo·gan[2] /ˈlōgən/, Joshua Lockwood, III (1908–88), U.S. director and playwright. He directed Broadway shows, including *Annie Get Your Gun* (1946), *Mister Roberts* (1948), *South Pacific* (1949) and *Fanny* (1954), as well as motion pictures, including *Picnic* (1955), *Bus Stop* (1956), *South Pacific* (1958), and *Camelot* (1967). He wrote or cowrote several of these and other titles, and in 1950 shared the Pulitzer Prize for Drama with his *South Pacific* cowriters Richard Rodgers and Oscar Hammerstein II.

Lo·gan, Mount /ˈlōgən/ a mountain in southwestern Yukon Territory, Canada, near the border with Alaska. Rising to 19,850 feet (6,054 m), it is the highest peak in Canada and the second-highest peak in North America.

lo·gan·ber·ry /ˈlōgən,berē/ ▸*n.* **1** an edible dull-red soft fruit, considered to be a hybrid of a raspberry and an American dewberry. **2** the scrambling blackberrylike plant that bears this fruit. • *Rubus loganobaccus,* family Rosaceae. ▷late 19th cent.: from the name of John H. *Logan* (1841–1928), American horticulturalist, + BERRY.

log·a·rithm /ˈlôgə,riTHəm; ˈlägə-/ (abbr.: **log**) ▸*n.* a quantity representing the power to which a fixed number (the base) must be raised to produce a given number.

> Logarithms can be used to simplify calculations because the addition and subtraction of logarithms is equivalent to multiplication and division, although the use of printed tables of logarithms for this has declined with the spread of electronic calculators. They also allow a geometric relationship to be represented conveniently by a straight line. The base of a **common logarithm** is 10, and that of a **natural logarithm** is the number *e* (2.71828 ...).

▷early 17th cent.: from modern Latin *logarithmus,* from Greek *logos* 'reckoning, ratio' + *arithmos* 'number.'

log·a·rith·mic /,lôgəˈriTHmik; ,lägə-/ ▸*adj.* of, relating to, or expressed in terms of logarithms. ■ (of a scale) constructed so that successive points along an axis, or graduations that are an equal distance apart, represent values that are in an equal ratio. ■ (of a curve) forming a straight line when plotted on a logarithmic scale; exponential. —**log·a·rith·mi·cal·ly** /-mik(ə)lē/ *adv.*

log·a·rith·mic spi·ral ▸*n. Geometry* a spiral such that the angle between the tangent and the radius vector is the same for all points of the spiral. Also called EQUIANGULAR SPIRAL.

log·book /ˈlôg,boŏk; ˈläg-/ ▸*n.* another term for LOG[1] (sense 2).

loge /lōZH/ ▸*n.* a private box or enclosure in a theater. ■ the front section of the first balcony in a theater. ■ a similar section in an arena or stadium. ▷mid 18th cent.: from French.

-loger ▸*comb. form* equivalent to -LOGIST. ▷on the pattern of words such as *(astro)loger.*

log·ger /ˈlôgər; ˈlägər/ ▸*n.* **1** a person who fells trees for timber; a lumberjack. **2** a device for making a systematic recording of events, observations, or measurements.

log·ger·head /ˈlôgər,hed; ˈlägər-/ ▸*n.* **1** (also **loggerhead turtle**) a reddish-brown turtle with a very large head, occurring chiefly in warm seas. • *Caretta caretta,* family Cheloniidae. **2** (also **loggerhead shrike**) a widespread North American shrike, having mainly gray plumage with a black eyestripe, wings, and tail. • *Lanius ludovicianus,* family Laniidae. **3** *archaic* a foolish person. ▷late 16th cent. (sense 3): from dialect *logger* 'block of wood for hobbling a horse' + HEAD.

▸*PHRASE* □ **at loggerheads** in stubborn dispute or disagreement: *council was* **at loggerheads with** *the government over the grant allocation.* [possibly a use of *loggerhead* in the late 17th-cent. sense 'long-handled iron instrument for heating liquids and tar,' perhaps wielded as a weapon.]

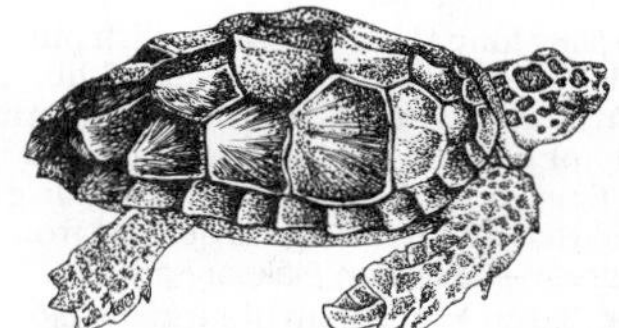

loggerhead turtle

log·gia /ˈlōj(ē)ə; ˈlô-/ ▸*n.* a gallery or room with one or more open sides, esp. one that forms part of a house and has one side open to the garden. ■ an open-sided extension to a house. ▷mid 18th cent.: from Italian, 'lodge.'

log·ging /ˈlôgiNG; ˈlägiNG/ ▸*n.* the activity or business of felling trees and cutting and preparing the timber.

lo·gi·a /ˈlōgēə; -jēə/ ▸ plural form of LOGION.

log·ic /ˈläjik/ ▸*n.* **1** reasoning conducted or assessed according to strict principles of validity: *experience is a better guide to this than deductive logic* | *he explains his* *move with simple logic | the logic of the argument is faulty.* ■ a particular system or codification of the principles of proof and inference: *Aristotelian logic.* ■ the systematic use of symbolic and mathematical techniques to determine the forms of valid deductive argument. ■ the quality of being justifiable by reason: *there's no logic in telling her not to hit people when that's what you're doing.* ■ (**logic of**) the course of action or line of reasoning suggested or made necessary by: *if the logic of capital is allowed to determine events.* **2** a system or set of principles underlying the arrangements of elements in a computer or electronic device so as to perform a specified task. ■ logical operations collectively. ▷late Middle English: via Old French *logique* and late Latin *logica* from Greek *logikē (tekhnē)* '(art) of reason,' from *logos* 'word, reason.' —**lo·gi·cian** /lə'jisHən; lō-/ *n.*

-logic ▸*comb. form* equivalent to **-LOGICAL** (as in *pharmacologic*). ▷from Greek *-logikos*.

log·i·cal /'läjikəl/ ▸*adj.* of or according to the rules of logic or formal argument: *a logical impossibility.* ■ characterized by clear, sound reasoning: *the information is displayed in a simple and logical fashion.* ■ (of an action, development, decision, etc.) natural or sensible given the circumstances: *it is a logical progression from the job before.* ■ capable of clear rational thinking: *her logical mind.* ▷late Middle English: from medieval Latin *logicalis*, from late Latin *logica* (see **LOGIC**). —**log·i·cal·i·ty** /ˌläjə'kalətē/ *n.* —**log·i·cal·ly** /-ik(ə)lē/ *adv. such a situation is logically impossible.*

-logical ▸*comb. form* in adjectives corresponding chiefly to nouns ending in *-logy* (such as *pharmacological* corresponding to *pharmacology*).

log·i·cal em·pir·i·cism ▸*n.* see **LOGICAL POSITIVISM**.

log·i·cal form ▸*n. Logic* the abstract form in which an argument or proposition may be expressed in logical terms, as distinct from its particular content.

log·i·cal ne·ces·si·ty ▸*n.* that state of things that obliges something to be as it is because no alternative is logically possible. ■ a thing that logically must be so.

log·i·cal op·er·a·tion ▸*n.* an operation of the kind used in logic, e.g., conjunction or negation. ■ *Computing* an operation that acts on binary numbers to produce a result according to the laws of Boolean logic (e.g., the AND, OR, and NOT functions).

log·i·cal op·er·a·tor ▸*n. Computing* a programming-language symbol that denotes a logical operation.

log·i·cal pos·i·tiv·ism ▸*n.* a form of positivism, developed by members of the Vienna Circle, that considers that the only meaningful philosophical problems are those that can be solved by logical analysis. Also called **LOGICAL EMPIRICISM**.

log·ic bomb ▸*n. Computing* a set of instructions secretly incorporated into a program so that if a particular condition is satisfied they will be carried out, usually with harmful effects.

log·ic cir·cuit ▸*n. Electronics* a circuit for performing logical operations on input signals.

log·in /'lôgˌin; 'läg-/ (also **log·on**) ▸*n.* an act of logging in to a computer system.

lo·gi·on /'lōgēˌän; -jē-/ ▸*n.* (*pl.* **-gi·a** /-gēə; -jēə/) a saying attributed to Jesus Christ, esp. one not recorded in the canonical Gospels. ▷late 19th cent.: from Greek, 'oracle,' from *logos* 'word.'

-logist ▸*comb. form* indicating a person skilled or involved in a branch of study denoted by a noun ending in *-logy* (such as *biologist* corresponding to *biology*).

lo·gis·tic /lə'jistik; lō-/ ▸*adj.* of or relating to logistics: *logistic problems.* —**lo·gis·ti·cal** /-tikəl/ *adj.* —**lo·gis·ti·cal·ly** /-tik(ə)lē/ *adv.*

lo·gis·tics /lə'jistiks; lō-/ ▸*plural n.* [treated as *sing.* or *pl.*] the detailed coordination of a complex operation involving many people, facilities, or supplies: *the logistics and costs of a vaccination campaign.* ■ *Military* the organization of moving, housing, and supplying troops and equipment. ■ the commercial activity of transporting goods to customers: [as *modifier*] *Germany's largest beverage logistics organization.* ▷late 19th cent. (in the sense 'movement and supplying of troops and equipment'): from French *logistique*, from *loger* 'lodge.'

log·jam /'lôgˌjam; 'läg-/ ▸*n.* a crowded mass of logs blocking a river. ■ a situation that seems irresolvable: *the president can use the power of the White House to* ***break the logjam*** *over this issue.* ■ a backlog: *keeping a diary may ease the logjam of work considerably.*

log-log ▸*adj. Mathematics* denoting a graph or graph paper having or using a logarithmic scale along both axes.

log-nor·mal ▸*adj. Statistics* of or denoting a set of data in which the logarithm of the variate is distributed according to a normal distribution. —**log-nor·mal·i·ty** *n.* —**log-nor·mal·ly** *adv.*

LOGO /'lōˌgō/ ▸*n. Computing* a high-level programming language used to teach computer programming to children. ▷from Greek *lógos*,'word,' spelled as if an acronym.

lo·go /'lōgō/ ▸*n.* (*pl.* **-gos**) a symbol or other small design adopted by an organization to identify its products, uniform, vehicles, etc.: *the Olympic logo was emblazoned across the tracksuits.* ▷1930s: abbreviation of **LOGOGRAM** or **LOGOTYPE**.

lo·go·cen·tric /ˌlôgə'sentrik; ˌlägə-/ ▸*adj.* regarding words and language as a fundamental expression of an external reality (esp. applied as a negative term to traditional Western thought by postmodernist critics). ▷1930s: from Greek *logos* 'word, reason' + **-CENTRIC**. —**logocentrism** /-ˌtrizəm/ *n.*

log·off /'lôgˌôf; 'läg-; -ˌäf/ ▸*n.* another term for **LOGOUT**.

log·o·gram /'lôgəˌgram; 'lägə-/ ▸*n.* a sign or character representing a word or phrase, such as those used in shorthand and some writing systems. ▷mid 19th cent.: from Greek *logos* 'word' + **-GRAM**[1].

log·o·graph /'lôgəˌgraf; 'lägə-/ ▸*n.* another term for **LOGOGRAM**. —**log·o·graph·ic** /ˌlôgə'grafik; ˌlägə-/ *adj.*

log·o·griph /'lôgəˌgrif; 'lägə-/ ▸*n.* a puzzle involving anagrams, esp. one in which a number of words that can be spelled using a group of letters are to be identified from their synonyms introduced into a set of verses. ▷late 16th cent.: from Greek *logos* 'word' + *griphos* 'fishing basket, riddle.'

lo·gom·a·chy /lō'gäməkē/ ▸*n.* (*pl.* **-chies**) *rare* an argument about words. ▷mid 16th cent.: from Greek *logomakhia*, from *logos* 'word' + *-makhia* 'fighting.'

log·on /'lôgˌän; 'läg-; -ˌôn/ ▸*n.* another term for **LOGIN**.

log·o·phile /'lôgəˌfil; 'lägə-/ ▸*n.* a lover of words.

log·or·rhe·a /ˌlôgə'rēə; ˌlägə-/ (*Brit.* **log·or·rhoe·a**) ▸*n.* a tendency to extreme loquacity. ▷early 20th cent.: from Greek *logos* 'word' + *rhoia* 'flow.' —**log·or·rhe·ic** /-'rēik/ *adj.*

Lo·gos /'lōˌgōs; -ˌgäs/ ▸*n. Theology* the Word of God, or principle of divine reason and creative order, identified in the Gospel of John with the second person of the Trinity incarnate in Jesus Christ. ■ (in Jungian psychology) the principle of reason and judgment, associated with the animus. Often contrasted with **EROS**. ▷Greek, 'word, reason.'

lo·go·type /'lôgəˌtip; 'lägə-/ ▸*n. Printing* a single piece of type that prints a word or group of separate letters. ■ a single piece of type that prints a logo or emblem. ■ a logo. ▷early 19th cent.: from Greek *logos* 'word' + **TYPE**.

log·out /'lôgˌout; 'läg-/ (also **log·off**) ▸*n.* an act of exiting a computer system or program.

log·roll·ing /'lôgˌrōliNG; 'läg-/ ▸*n.* **1** *informal* the practice of exchanging favors, esp. in politics by reciprocal voting for each other's proposed legislation. [from the phrase *you roll my log and I'll roll yours.*] **2** a sport in which two contestants stand on a floating log and try to knock each other off by spinning it with their feet. —**log·roll·er** /-lər/ *n.*

Lo·gro·ño /lə'grōnyō/ a market town in northern Spain, on the Ebro River; pop. 127,000.

-logue (also **-log**) ▸*comb. form* **1** denoting discourse of a specified type: *dialogue.* **2** denoting compilation: *catalogue.* **3** equivalent to **-LOGIST**. ▷from French *-logue*, from Greek *-logos*, *-logon*.

log·wood /'lôgˌwo͝od; 'läg-/ ▸*n.* a spiny Caribbean tree of the pea family, the dark heartwood of which yields hematoxylin and other dyes. • *Haematoxylon campechianum*, family Leguminosae.

lo·gy /'lōgē/ ▸*adj.* (**lo·gi·er**, **lo·gi·est**) dull and heavy in motion or thought; sluggish. ▷mid 19th cent.: of uncertain origin; compare with Dutch *log* 'heavy, dull.'

-logy ▸*comb. form* **1** (usu. as **-ology**) denoting a subject of study or interest: *psychology.* **2** denoting a characteristic of speech or language: *eulogy.* ■ denoting a type of discourse: *trilogy.* ▷from French *-logie* or medieval Latin *-logia*, from Greek.

Lo·hen·grin /'lōənˌgrin/ (in medieval French and German romances) the son of Perceval (Parsifal). He was summoned from the temple of the Holy Grail and taken in a boat to Antwerp, where he consented to marry Elsa of Brabant on condition that she not ask who he was. Elsa broke this condition, and he was carried away again in the boat.

lo·i·a·sis /lō'īəsis/ ▸*n.* a tropical African disease caused by infestation with eye worms that cause transient subcutaneous swellings, often accompanied by pain or fever. ▷early 20th cent.: modern Latin, from *loa* (a local Angolan word for the parasite) + **-IASIS**.

loin /loin/ ▸*n.* (usu. **loins**) the part of the body on both sides of the spine between the lowest (false) ribs and the hipbones. ■ (**loins**) *chiefly poetic/literary* the region of the sexual organs, esp. when regarded as the source of erotic or procreative power: *he felt a stirring in his loins at the thought.* ■ (**loin**) a large cut of meat that includes the vertebrae of the loins: ***loin of*** *pork with potatoes.* ▷Middle English: from Old French *loigne*, based on Latin *lumbus*.

▸*PHRASE* □ **gird (up) one's loins** see **GIRD**[1].

loin·cloth /'loinˌklôTH; -ˌkläTH/ ▸*n.* a single piece of cloth wrapped round the hips, typically worn by men in some hot countries as their only garment.

Loire /l(ə)'wär/ a river in west central France. The country's longest river, it rises in the Massif Central and flows 630 mi. (1,015 km.) north and west to the Atlantic Ocean at the town of Saint-Nazaire.

loi·ter /'loitər/ ▸*v.* [*intrans.*] stand or wait around idly or without apparent purpose: *she saw Mary loitering near the cloakrooms.* ■ travel indolently and with frequent pauses: *they loitered along in the sunshine, stopping at the least excuse.* ▷late Middle English: perhaps from Middle Dutch *loteren* 'wag around.' —**loi·ter·er** *n.*

THE RIGHT WORD **dally, dawdle, idle, lag, loiter**

Someone who hangs around downtown after the stores are closed and appears to be deliberately wasting time is said to **loiter**, a verb that connotes improper or sinister motives (*the police warned the boys not to loiter*).

To **dawdle** is to pass time leisurely or to pursue something halfheartedly (*dawdle in a stationery shop; dawdle over a sinkful of dishes*).

Someone who **dallies** dawdles in a particularly pleasurable and relaxed way, with connotations of amorous activity (*he dallied with his girlfriend when he should have been delivering papers*).

Idle suggests that the person makes a habit of avoiding work or activity (*idle away the hours of a hot summer day*), while **lag** suggests falling behind or failing to maintain a desirable rate of progress (*she lagged several yards behind her classmates as they walked to the museum*).

Lo·ki /'lōkē/ *Scandinavian Mythology* a mischievous and sometimes evil god who contrived the death of Balder and was punished by being bound to a rock.

Lok Sab·ha /'läk 'säbə; 'lōk/ ▸*n.* the lower house of the Indian Parliament. Compare with **RAJYA SABHA**. ▷from Hindi *lok* 'the public' and *sabhā* 'assembly.'

LOL ▸*abbr.* laughing (or laugh) out loud (used in e-mail).

Lo·li·ta /lō'lētə/ ▸*n.* a sexually precocious young girl. ▷from the name of a character in the novel *Lolita* (1958) by Vladimir Nabokov.

loll /läl/ ▸*v.* [*intrans.*] sit, lie, or stand in a lazy, relaxed way: *the two girls lolled in their chairs.* ■ hang loosely; droop: *he slumped against a tree trunk, his head lolling back | her tongue was* ***lolling out*** *between her teeth.* ■ [*trans.*] stick out (one's tongue) so that it hangs loosely out of the mouth: *the boy* ***lolled out*** *his tongue.* ▷late Middle English: probably symbolic of dangling.

lol·la·pa·loo·za /ˌläləpə'lo͞ozə/ (also **la·la·pa·loo·za** or **lol·la·pa·loo·sa**) ▸*n. informal* a person or thing that is particularly impressive or attractive: *it's a lollapalooza, just like your other books.* ▷late 19th cent.: of fanciful formation.

Lol·lard /'lälərd/ ▸*n.* a follower of John Wycliffe. The Lollards believed that the church should aid people to live a life of evangelical poverty and imitate Jesus Christ. Their ideas influenced the thought of John Huss, who in turn influenced Martin Luther. ▷originally a derogatory term, derived from a Dutch word meaning 'mumbler,' based on *lollen* 'to mumble.' —**Lol·lard·ism** /-ˌdizəm/ *n.* —**Lol·lard·y** *n.*

lol·li·pop /'lälēˌpäp/ ▸*n.* a flat, rounded candy on the end of a stick. ▷late 18th cent.: perhaps from dialect *lolly* 'tongue' + **POP**[1].

lol·lop /'läləp/ ▸*v.* (**-loped**, **-lop·ing**) [*intrans.*] move in an ungainly way in a series of clumsy paces or bounds: *the bear lolloped along the path.* ▷mid 18th cent.: probably from **LOLL**, associated with **TROLLOP**.

lol·ly /'lälē/ ▸*n.* (*pl.* **-lies**) *informal* **1** *chiefly Brit.* a lollipop. **2** *Brit.* money: *you've done brilliantly raising all that lovely lolly.* ▷mid 19th cent.: abbreviation. Sense 2 dates from the 1940s.

lol·ly·gag /ˈlälē,gag/ (also **lal·ly·gag**) ▸*v.* (**-gagged, -gag·ging**) [*intrans.*] *informal* spend time aimlessly; idle: *he sends her to Arizona every January to lollygag in the sun.* ■ dawdle: *we're lollygagging along.* ▷mid 19th cent.: of unknown origin.

lo·ma·ti·um /lōˈmāsʜ(ē)əm/ ▸*n.* a perennial herb of the parsley family, found throughout western North America It has various folk-medicine applications (mainly antibiotic) and is eaten as a survival food. • (genus *Lomatium*; numerous species).

Lomb /läm/, Henry (1828–1908) U.S. optician; born in Germany. He cofounded Bausch & Lomb Optical Company in 1853.

Lom·bard /ˈläm,bärd; -bərd/ ▸*n.* **1** a member of a Germanic people who invaded Italy in the 6th century. **2** a native of Lombardy in northern Italy. **3** the Italian dialect of Lombardy.
▸*adj.* of or relating to Lombardy, or to the Lombards or their language. ▷from Italian *lombardo*, representing late Latin *Langobardus*, of Germanic origin, from the base of LONG[1] + the ethnic name *Bardi*. **—Lom·bar·dic** /lämˈbärdik/ *adj.* (in sense 1).

Lom·bar·di /lämˈbärdē; ,ləm-/, Vince(nt Thomas) (1913–70) U.S. football coach. The legendary coach of the Green Bay Packers 1959–67, he led them to five NFL championships between 1961 and 1967 and two Super Bowl titles 1967, 1968. During 1969, he coached the Washington Redskins.

Lom·bar·do /lämˈbärdō; ,ləm-/, Guy (1902–77) U.S. band leader; born in Canada; full name *Gaetano Alberto Lombardo*. His dance band, formed in 1920 and named the Royal Canadians in 1927, played the "sweetest music this side of heaven," and his New Year's Eve broadcasts from New York City's Waldorf Astoria hotel became a national tradition.

Lom·bard Street /ˈläm,bärd; -bərd/ a street in the city of London that contains many of the principal London banks. ▷so named because formerly occupied by bankers from *Lombardy*.

Lom·bar·dy /ˈläm,bärdē; -bərdē/ a region of central northern Italy, between the Alps and the Po River; capital, Milan. Italian name LOMBARDIA .

Lom·bard·y pop·lar ▸*n.* a black poplar of a variety that has a distinctive tall, slender columnar form. It arose as a mutation in Italy and is widely cultivated. • *Populus nigra* var. *italica*, family Salicaceae.

Lom·bok /ˈläm,bäk/ a volcanic island of the Lesser Sunda group in Indonesia, between Bali and Sumbawa; pop. 2,500,000; chief town, Mataram.

Lo·mé /lōˈmā/ the capital and chief port of Togo, on the Gulf of Guinea; pop. 450,000.

lo·ment /ˈlōmənt; -,ment/ (also **lo·men·tum** /lōˈmentəm/) ▸*n.* *Botany* the pod of some leguminous plants, breaking up when mature into one-seeded joints. ▷mid 19th cent.: from Latin, literally 'bean meal' (originally used as a cosmetic), from *lavare* 'to wash.'

Lo·mond, Loch /ˈlōmənd/ a lake in west central Scotland, northwest of Glasgow. It is the largest freshwater lake in Scotland.

Lom·poc /ˈläm,päk/ a city in southwestern California, northwest of Santa Barbara; pop. 37,649.

Lon·don[1] /ˈləndən/ **1** the capital of the United Kingdom, in southeastern England on the Thames River; pop. 6,377,000. London, called Londinium, was settled as a river port and trading center shortly after the Roman invasion of AD 43 and has been a flourishing center since the Middle Ages.It is divided administratively into the City of London, which is the country's financial center, and 32 boroughs. **2** an industrial city in southeastern Ontario, Canada, north of Lake Erie; pop. 303,165. **—Lon·don·er** *n.*

Lon·don[2], Jack (1876-1916), U.S. novelist; pseudonym of *John Griffith Chaney*. The Klondike gold rush of 1897 provided the material for his works, which depict the struggle for survival. Notable works: *The Call of the Wild* (1903) and *White Fang* (1906).

Lon·don broil ▸*n.* a grilled steak served cut diagonally in thin slices.

Lon·don·der·ry /ˈləndən,derē; ,ləndənˈderē/ one of the six counties of Northern Ireland, formerly an administrative area. ■ its chief town, a city and port on the Foyle River near its outlet on the north coast; pop. 63,000. It was formerly called Derry, a name still used by many. In 1613 it was granted to the City of London for colonization and became known as Londonderry.

Lon·don pride ▸*n.* a European saxifrage with rosettes of fleshy leaves and stems of pink starlike flowers. • *Saxifraga × urbium*, family Saxifragaceae.

lone /lōn/ ▸*adj.* having no companions; solitary or single: *I approached a lone drinker across the bar | we sheltered under a lone tree.* ■ lacking the support of others; isolated: *I am by no means a lone voice.* ■ *poetic/literary* (of a place) unfrequented and remote: *houses in lone rural settings.* ▷late Middle English: shortening of ALONE.

lone hand ▸*n.* (in euchre or quadrille) a hand played against the rest, or a player playing such a hand.
▸*PHRASE* □ **play a lone hand** act on one's own without help.

lone·ly /ˈlōnlē/ ▸*adj.* (**-li·er, -li·est**) sad because one has no friends or company: *lonely old people whose families do not care for them.* ■ without companions; solitary: *passing long lonely hours looking onto the street.* ■ (of a place) unfrequented and remote: *a lonely stretch of country lane.* **—lone·li·ness** *n.*

lone·ly heart ▸*n.* [usu. as *adj.*] a person looking for a lover or friend by advertising in a newspaper: *a lonely hearts column.* **—lone·ly-heart·ed** *adj.*

lon·er /ˈlōnər/ ▸*n.* a person who prefers not to associate with others.

lone·some /ˈlōnsəm/ ▸*adj.* solitary or lonely: *she felt lonesome and out of things.* ■ remote and unfrequented: *a lonesome, unfriendly place.* **—lone·some·ness** *n.*
▸*PHRASE* □ **by one's lonesome** *informal* all alone.

Lone Star State a nickname for the state of TEXAS.

lone wolf ▸*n.* a person who prefers to act or be alone.

Long[1] /lôɴɢ/, Huey Pierce (1893–1935) U.S. politician; known as the **Kingfish**. A Democrat, he served as governor of Louisiana 1928–31 and as a U.S. senator 1932–35 and was known as a dictatorial demagogue with politically radical ideas, most notably his "Share the Wealth" program. Not long after he announced his plans to run for the U.S. presidency, he was assassinated.

Long[2], Stephen Harriman (1784–1864) U.S. Army officer and explorer. His expeditions included the upper Mississippi in 1817 and the Rocky Mountain region in 1820. Longs Peak in Colorado is named for him.

long[1] /lôɴɢ; läɴɢ/ ▸*adj.* (**long·er** /ˈlôɴɢgər; ˈläɴɢ-/, **long·est** /lôɴɢgist; ˈläɴɢ-/) **1** measuring a great distance from end to end: *a long corridor | long black hair | the line for tickets was long.* ■ (after a measurement and in questions) measuring a specified distance from end to end: *a boat 150 feet long | **how long** is the leash?* ■ (of a journey) covering a great distance: *I went for a long walk.* ■ (of a garment or sleeves on a garment) covering the whole of a person's legs or arms: *a sweater with long sleeves.* ■ of elongated shape: *shaped like a torpedo, long and thin.* ■ (of a ball in sports) traveling a great distance, or further than expected or intended: *he threw a long ball to the catcher.* ■ *informal* (of a person) tall. **2** lasting or taking a great amount of time: *a long and distinguished career | she took a long time to dress.* ■ (after a noun of duration and in questions) lasting or taking a specified amount of time: *the debates will be 90 minutes long.* ■ seeming to last more time than is the case; lengthy or tedious: *serving long hours on the committee.* ■ (of a person's memory) retaining things for a great amount of time. **3** relatively great in extent: *write a long report | a long list of candidates.* ■ (after a noun of extent and in questions) having a specified extent: *the statement was three pages long.* **4** *Phonetics* (of a vowel) categorized as long with regard to quality and length (e.g., in standard American English, the vowel in *food* is long, as distinct from the short vowel in *good*). ■ *Prosody* (of a vowel or syllable) having the greater of the two recognized durations. **5** (of odds or a chance) reflecting or representing a low level of probability: *winning against long odds | you're taking a long chance.* **6** *Finance* (of shares, bonds, or other assets) bought in advance, with the expectation of a rise in price. ■ (of a broker or their position in the market) buying or based on long stocks. ■ (of a security) maturing at a distant date. **7** (**long on**) *informal* well-supplied with: *an industry that seems long on ideas but short on cash.*
▸*n.* **1** a long interval or period: *see you **before long** | it will not be **for long**.* **2** a long sound such as a long signal in Morse code or a long vowel or syllable: *two longs and a short.* **3** (**longs**) *Finance* long-dated securities, esp. gilt-edged securities. ■ assets held in a long position.
▸*adv.* (**longer; longest**) **1** for a long time: *we hadn't known them long | an experience they will long remember | his long-awaited Grand Prix debut.* ■ in questions about a period of time: ***how long** have you been working?* ■ at a time distant from a specified event or point of time: *it was abandoned long ago | the work was compiled long after his death.* ■ after an implied point of time: *he could not wait any longer.* ■ (after a noun of duration) throughout a specified period of time: *it rained all day long.* **2** (with reference to the ball in sports) at, to, or over a great distance, or further than expected or intended: *the quarterback dropped back and threw the ball long.* ■ beyond the point aimed at; too far: *he threw the ball long.* ▷Old English *lang, long* (adjective), *lange, longe* (adverb), of Germanic origin; related to Dutch and German *lang*. **—long·ish** *adj.*
▸*PHRASES* □ **as** (or **so**) **long as 1** during the whole time that: *they have been there as long as anyone can remember.* **2** provided that: *as long as you fed him, he would be cooperative.* □ **be long** take a long time to happen or arrive: *it won't be long before you're hooked | sit down, tea won't be long.* □ **in the long run** over or after a long period of time; eventually: *it saves money in the long run.* □ **the long and the short of it** all that can or need be said: *the long and short of it is that he got himself mugged.* □ **long in the tooth** rather old. [originally said of horses, from the recession of the gums with age.] □ **long time no see** *informal* it's a long time since we last met (used as a greeting). [in humorous imitation of broken English spoken by an American Indian.] □ **not by a long shot** by no means: *we're not there yet, not by a long shot.* □ **take the long view** think beyond the current situation; plan for the future.

long[2] ▸*v.* [*intrans.*] have a strong wish or desire: *she **longed for** a little more excitement | [with infinitive] we are longing to see the new baby.* ▷Old English *langian* 'grow long, prolong,' also 'dwell in thought, yearn,' of Germanic origin; related to Dutch *langen* 'present, offer' and German *langen* 'reach, extend.'

long. ▸*abbr.* longitude.

-long ▸*comb. form* (added to nouns) for the duration of: *lifelong.*

lon·gan /ˈlôɴɢgən; ˈläɴɢ-/ ▸*n.* an edible juicy fruit from a plant related to the litchi, cultivated in Southeast Asia. • The plant is *Dimocarpus longan*, family Sapindaceae. ▷mid 18th cent.: from Chinese *lóngyǎn*, literally 'dragon's eye.'

Long Beach a port and resort in southwestern California, on the Pacific Ocean, south of Los Angeles; pop. 461,522.

long·board /ˈlôɴɢ,bôrd; ˈläɴɢ-/ ▸*n.* a type of long surfboard.

long·boat /ˈlôɴɢ,bōt; ˈläɴɢ-/ ▸*n.* a large boat that may be launched from a sailing ship. ■ another term for LONGSHIP.

long·bow /ˈlôɴɢ,bō; ˈläɴɢ-/ ▸*n.* a large bow drawn by hand and shooting a long feathered arrow. It was the chief weapon of English armies from the 14th century until the introduction of firearms.

Long Branch a city in east central New Jersey, on the Atlantic Ocean, long a noted summer resort; pop. 28,658.

long·case clock (also **long-case clock**) ▸*n.* another term for GRANDFATHER CLOCK.

long-day ▸*adj.* (of a plant) needing a long period of light each day to initiate flowering, which therefore happens naturally as the days lengthen in the spring.

long dis·tance ▸*adj.* (usu. **long-dis·tance**) traveling or operating between distant places: *a long-distance truck driver | long-distance phone calls.*
▸*adv.* between distant places: *traveling long distance.*
▸*n.* [often as *adj.*] *Track & Field* a race distance of 6 miles or 10,000 meters (6 miles 376 yds), or longer: *a long-distance runner.*

long di·vi·sion ▸*n.* arithmetical division in which the divisor has two or more figures, and a series of steps is made as successive groups of digits of the dividend are divided by the divisor, to avoid excessive mental calculation.

long·dog /ˈlôɴɢ,dôg; ˈläɴɢ,däg/ ▸*n.* *informal* a greyhound or other hound of similar body shape.

long doz·en ▸*n.* (**a long dozen**) thirteen.

long-drawn (often **long-drawn-out**) ▸*adj.* continuing for a long time, esp. for longer than is necessary: *long-drawn-out negotiations.*

longe /lənj/ (also **lunge**) ▸*n.* a long rein on which a horse is held and made to move in a circle around its trainer.
▸*v.* (**longe·ing**) [*trans.*] exercise (a horse or rider) on a longe. ▷early 18th cent.: French, from *allonge* 'lengthening out.'

long-eared bat ▸*n.* an insectivorous bat with ears that are very long in proportion to the body. • *Plecotus* and other genera, family Vespertilionidae: several species, in particular the **common** (or **brown**) **long-eared bat** (*P. auritus*) of Eurasia.

lon·ge·ron /ˈlänjərən; -ˌrän/ ▸*n.* a longitudinal structural component of an aircraft's fuselage. ▹early 20th cent.: from French, literally 'girder.'

lon·gev·i·ty /lônˈjevətē; län-/ ▸*n.* long life: *the greater longevity of women compared with men.* ■ long duration of service: *her longevity in office now appeared as a handicap to the party.* ▹early 17th cent.: from late Latin *longaevitas*, from Latin *longus* 'long' + *aevum* 'age.'

long face ▸*n.* an unhappy or disappointed expression. **—long-faced** *adj.*

Long·fel·low /ˈlôNGˌfelō/, Henry Wadsworth (1807–82), U.S. poet. He is known for "The Wreck of the Hesperus" and "The Village Blacksmith" (both 1841) and for narrative poems such as *Evangeline* (1847), *The Song of Hiawatha* (1855), and *Paul Revere's Ride* (1861).

long·hair /ˈlôNGˌhe(ə)r; ˈläNG-/ ▸*n.* **1** a person with long hair or characteristics associated with it, such as a hippie or intellectual. ■ a devotee of classical music. **2** a cat of a long-haired breed.

long·hand /ˈlôNGˌhand; ˈläNG-/ ▸*n.* ordinary handwriting (as opposed to shorthand, typing, or printing): *he wrote out the reply in longhand* | [as *adj.*] *a longhand draft.*

long haul ▸*n.* a long distance (in reference to the transport of freight or passengers): [as *adj.*] *a long-haul flight.* ■ a prolonged and difficult effort or task: *getting the proposal passed is likely to be a long haul* | *we're* ***in for the long haul.***

▸*PHRASE* □ **over the long haul** over an extended period of time.

long-head·ed ▸*adj.* **1** having a long head; dolichocephalic. **2** *dated* having or showing foresight and good judgment. **—long-head·ed·ness** *n.*

long·horn /ˈlôNGˌhôrn; ˈläNG-/ ▸*n.* **1** an animal of a breed of cattle with long horns. **2** (also **longhorn beetle**) an elongated beetle with long antennae, the larva of which typically bores in wood and can be a pest of timber. • Family Cerambycidae (formerly in the superfamily Longicornia).

long-horned grass·hop·per ▸*n.* an insect related to the grasshoppers, with very long antennae and a mainly carnivorous diet. Many kinds live among shrubby vegetation, active mainly at dusk and in the night. • Family Tettigoniidae: many genera.

long·house /ˈlôNGˌhous; ˈläNG-/ ▸*n.* a type of dwelling housing a family and animals under one roof. ■ *historical* the traditional dwelling of the Iroquois and other North American Indians. ■ a large communal village house in parts of Malaysia and Indonesia.

long hun·dred·weight ▸*n.* see HUNDREDWEIGHT.

lon·gi·corn /ˈlänjəˌkôrn/ ▸*n.* former term for LONGHORN (sense 2). ▹mid 19th cent.: from modern Latin *longicornis*, from Latin *longus* 'long' + *cornu* 'horn.'

long·ing /ˈlôNGiNG/ ▸*n.* a yearning desire: *Miranda felt a wistful* ***longing for*** *the old days* | [with *infinitive*] *a longing to be free* | *his tale of love and longing.*

▸*adj.* having or showing such desire: *her longing eyes.* **—long·ing·ly** *adv.*

Lon·gi·nus /länˈjīnəs/ (*fl.* 1st century AD), Greek scholar. He is the supposed author of a Greek literary treatise *On the Sublime*, concerned with the moral function of literature.

Long Is·land an island on the coast of New York State. Its western tip, comprising the New York boroughs of Brooklyn and Queens, is separated from Manhattan and the Bronx by the East River and is linked to Manhattan by several bridges.

Long Is·land Cit·y a section of Queens in New York City, across the East River from Manhattan.

lon·gi·tude /ˈlänjiˌt(y)o͞od; ˈlôn-/ ▸*n.* the angular distance of a place east or west of the meridian at Greenwich, England, or west of the standard meridian of a celestial object, usually expressed in degrees and minutes: *at a longitude of 2° W* | *lines of longitude.* ■ *Astronomy* see CELESTIAL LONGITUDE. ▹late Middle English (also denoting length and tallness): from Latin *longitudo*, from *longus* 'long.'

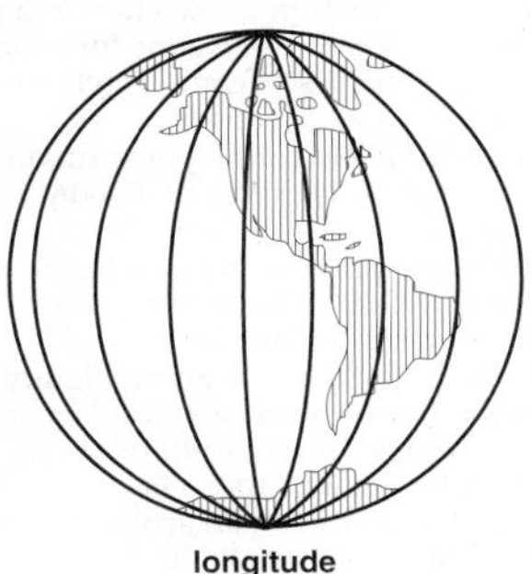

longitude

lon·gi·tu·di·nal /ˌlänjəˈt(y)o͞odn-əl; ˌlôn-; -ˈt(y)o͞odnəl/ ▸*adj.* **1** running lengthwise rather than across: *longitudinal muscles* | *longitudinal stripes* | *longitudinal extent.* ■ (of research or data) involving information about an individual or group gathered over a long period of time. **2** of or relating to longitude; measured from east to west: *longitudinal positions.* **—lon·gi·tu·di·nal·ly** *adv.*

lon·gi·tu·di·nal wave ▸*n.* *Physics* a wave vibrating in the direction of propagation.

long johns ▸*plural n.* *informal* underwear with closely fitted legs that extend to the wearer's ankles, often with a long-sleeved top.

long jump ▸*n.* (**the long jump**) an athletic event in which competitors jump as far as possible along the ground in one leap. **—long jump·er** *n.*

long·leaf pine /ˈlôNGˌlēf; ˈläNG-/ ▸*n.* a large pine tree of the southeastern U.S. with very long needles and cones. It was formerly an important source of turpentine. • *Pinus palustris*, family Pinaceae.

long·line /ˈlôNGˌlīn; ˈläNG-/ ▸*n.* a type of deep-sea fishing gear consisting of a long main line anchored to the bottom to which shorter lines with baited hooks are fastened at intervals: [as *adj.*] *a longline fishing boat.*

long·lin·er /ˈlôNGˌlīnər; ˈläNG-/ ▸*n.* a fishing vessel that uses longlines. ■ a fisherman who uses longlines.

long-lived /livd/ ▸*adj.* living or lasting a long time.

long-lost ▸*adj.* lost or absent for a long time: *a long-lost friend* | *his long-lost youth.*

Long March the epic withdrawal of the Chinese communists from southeastern to northwestern China in 1934–35, over a distance of 6,000 miles (9,600 km). 100,000 people, led by Mao Zedong, left the communist rural base after it was almost destroyed by the Kuomintang; 20,000 people survived the journey.

long me·ter (abbr.: **LM**) ▸*n.* (also **long measure**) **1** a metrical pattern for hymns in which the stanzas have four lines with eight syllables each. **2** *Prosody* a quatrain of iambic tetrameters with alternate lines rhyming.

Long·mont /ˈlôNGˌmänt/ a city in northern Colorado; pop. 71,093.

long·neck /ˈlôNGˌnek; ˈläNG-/ ▸*n.* *informal* a beer bottle with a long, narrow neck: *he smashed the bottom of his longneck on the bar.* ■ a bottle of beer: *drinking a cold longneck.*

Long Par·lia·ment the English Parliament that sat from November 1640 to March 1653, was restored for a short time in 1659, and finally voted its own dissolution in 1660. It was summoned by Charles I and sat through the English Civil War and on into the interregnum that followed.

long pig ▸*n.* a translation of a term formerly used in some Pacific Islands for human flesh as food.

long-play·ing ▸*adj.* (of a phonograph record) designed to be played at $33\frac{1}{3}$ revolutions per minute.

long-range ▸*adj.* **1** (esp. of vehicles or missiles) able to be used or be effective over long distances: *long-range bombers.* **2** relating to a period of time that extends far into the future: *long-range forecasts* | *long-range plans.*

long-run·ning ▸*adj.* continuing for a long time: *a long-running dispute* | *a long-running soap opera.*

long s ▸*n.* an obsolete form of lower-case s, written or printed as ſ. It was used in initial and medial but not final position in a word and was generally abandoned in English-language printing shortly before 1800.

long·ship /ˈlôNGˌSHip; ˈläNG-/ ▸*n.* a long, narrow warship, powered by both oar and sail, used by the Vikings and other northern European peoples.

longship

long·shore /ˈlôNGˌSHôr; ˈläNG-/ ▸*adj.* existing on, frequenting, or moving along the seashore: *longshore currents.* ▹early 19th cent.: from *along shore.*

long·shore drift ▸*n.* the movement of material along a coast by waves that approach at an angle to the shore but recede directly away from it.

long·shore·man /ˌlôNGˈSHôrmən; ˌläNG-/ ▸*n.* (*pl.* **-men**) a person employed in a port to load and unload ships.

long shot ▸*n.* a venture or guess that has only the slightest chance of succeeding or being accurate: *it's a long shot, but well worth trying.* ■ *Film* a shot including objects at a distance: *using a dummy in long shot* | *the film opened on a long lingering shot.*

▸*PHRASE* □ **(not) by a long shot** *informal* (not) by far or at all: *she had not told Tony everything, not by a long shot.*

long·sight·ed /ˈlôNGˌsītid; ˈläNG-/ ▸*adj.* British term for FARSIGHTED. **—long·sight·ed·ly** *adv.* **—long·sight·ed·ness** *n.*

long·spur /ˈlôNGˌspər; ˈläNG-/ ▸*n.* a mainly Canadian songbird related to the buntings, with brownish plumage and a boldly marked head in the male. • Genus *Calcarius*, family Emberizidae (subfamily Emberizinae): three or four species.

long-stand·ing (also **long·stand·ing**) ▸*adj.* having existed or continued for a long time: *a long-standing tradition.*

Long·street /ˈlôNGˌstrēt/, James (1821–1904) Confederate army officer. He was sometimes thought to be overcautious as a commander. He surrendered with Robert E. Lee at Appomattox and recounted his experiences in *From Manassas to Appomattox* (1896).

long-suf·fer·ing ▸*adj.* having or showing patience in spite of troubles, esp. those caused by other people: *his long-suffering wife.* **—long-suf·fer·ing·ly** *adv.*

long suit ▸*n.* (in bridge or whist) a holding of several cards of one suit in a hand, typically 5 or more out of the 13. ■ [usu. with *negative*] an outstanding personal quality or achievement: *tact was not his long suit.*

long-term ▸*adj.* occurring over or relating to a long period of time: *the long-term unemployed* | *the long-term effects of smoking.*

long·time /ˈlôNGˌtīm; ˈläNG-/ (also **long-time**) ▸*adj.* (esp. of a person) having had a specified role or identity for a long time: *his longtime friend and colleague.*

long tom ▸*n.* *informal, historical* **1** a large cannon with a long range. **2** a trough for washing gold-bearing deposits.

long ton ▸*n.* see TON[1].

lon·gueur /lôNGˈgər; läNG-/ ▸*n.* a tedious passage in a book or other work: *its brilliant comedy passages do not cancel out the occasional longueurs* | *the last act is sometimes marred by longueur.* ▹French, literally 'length.'

Long·view /ˈlôNGˌvyo͞o; ˈläNG-/ **1** a city in eastern Texas; pop. 70,311. **2** a port city in southwestern Washington, on the Cowlitz and Columbia rivers; pop. 31,499.

long waist ▸*n.* a low waist on a dress or a person's body. **—long-waist·ed** *adj.*

long wave ▸*n.* a radio wave of a wavelength above one kilometer (and a frequency below 300 kHz): [as *adj.*] *long-wave radio.* ■ broadcasting using radio waves of 1 to 10 km wavelength: *listening to news radio* ***on long wave.***

long-wind·ed /ˈwindid/ ▸*adj.* (of speech or writing) continuing at length and in a tedious way: *his good wishes were long-winded but sincere.* ■ *archaic* capable of doing something for a long time without needing a rest. **—long-wind·ed·ly** *adv.* **—long-wind·ed·ness** *n.*

long·wise /ˈlôNGˌwīz; ˈläNG-/ (also **long·ways** /-ˌwāz/) ▸*adv.* lengthwise: *it has been sliced longwise to show the internal structure.*

loo[1] /lo͞o/ ▸*n.* *Brit., informal* a toilet. ▹1940s: many theories have been put forward about the word's origin: one suggests the source is *Waterloo*, a trade name for iron cisterns in the early part of the century; the evidence remains inconclusive.

loo[2] ▸*n.* a gambling card game, popular from the 17th to the 19th centuries, in which a player who fails to win a trick must pay a sum to a pool. ▹late 17th cent.: abbreviation of obsolete *lanterloo*, from French *lanturlu*, a meaningless song refrain.

loo·ey /ˈlo͞o-ē/ (also **loo·ie**) ▸*n.* (*pl.* **loo·eys** or **loo·ies**) *military slang* short for LIEUTENANT.

loo·fah /ˈlo͞ofə/ (also **loo·fa**, **luf·fa**) ▸*n.* **1** a coarse, fibrous cylindrical object used like a bath sponge for washing. It consists of the dried fibrous matter of the fluid-transport system of a marrowlike fruit. **2** the tropical Old World climbing plant of the

Pronunciation Key ə *ago;* ər *over;* ˈə or ˌə *up;* ˈər or ˌər *fur;* a *hat;* ā *rate;* ä *car;* CH *chew;* e *let;* ē *see;* e(ə)r *air;* i *fit;* ī *by;* i(ə)r *ear;* NG *sing;* ō *go;* ô *for;* oi *boy;* o͝o *good;* o͞o *goo;* ou *out;* SH *she;* TH *thin;* T͟H *then;* (h)w *why;* ZH *vision*

gourd family that produces these fruits, which are also edible. • *Luffa cylindrica*, family Cucurbitaceae. ▷late 19th cent.: from Egyptian Arabic *lūfa*, denoting the plant.

look /lo͝ok/ ▶*v.* [*intrans.*] **1** direct one's gaze toward someone or something or in a specified direction: *people were **looking at** him | they looked up as he came quietly into the room.* ■ (of a building or room) have a view or outlook in a specified direction: *the principal rooms **look out over** Nahant Bay.* ■ (**look through**) ignore (someone) by pretending not to see them: *he glanced up once but looked right through me.* ■ [*trans.*] *dated* express or show (something) by one's gaze: *Poirot looked a question.* ■ (**look something over**) inspect something quickly with a view to establishing its merits: *they looked over a property on Ryer Avenue.* ■ (**look through**) peruse (a book or other written material): *we looked through all the books, and this was still the one we liked best.* ■ (**look round/around**) move around (a place or building) in order to view whatever it might contain that is of interest: *he spent the morning and afternoon looking around Cambridge.* ■ (**look at/on**) think of or regard in a specified way: *I look at tennis differently from some coaches.* ■ (**look at**) examine (a matter, esp. a problem) and consider what action to take: *a committee is looking at the financing of PBS.* ■ (**look into**) investigate: *the police looked into his business dealings.* ■ (**look for**) attempt to find: *Howard has been looking for you.* ■ [with *clause*] ascertain with a quick glance: *people finishing work don't **look where** they're going.* **2** have the appearance or give the impression of being: *her father looked unhappy | the home **looked like** a prison* | [as *adj.*, in *combination*] (**-looking**) *a funny-looking guy.* ■ (**look like**) *informal* show a likelihood of: *it doesn't look like you'll be moving to Brooklyn.* ■ (**look oneself**) appear one's normal, healthy self: *he just didn't look himself at all.* **3** (**look to**) rely on to do or provide something: *she will look to you for help.* ■ [with *infinitive*] hope or expect to do something: *universities are looking to expand their intakes.* ■ *archaic* take care; make sure: *Look ye obey the masters of the craft.*
▶*phrasal v.* □ **look after** take care of: *women who stay at home to look after children.* □ **look back 1** think of the past: *don't waste time **looking back on** things that have caused you distress.* **2** [with *negative*] suffer a setback or interrupted progress: *she launched her own company in 1981 and has never looked back.* □ **look down on** regard (someone) with a feeling of superiority. □ **look forward to** await eagerly: *we look forward to seeing you.* □ **look in** make a short visit or call: *I will **look in on** you tomorrow.* □ **look on** watch without getting involved: *Cameron was looking on and making no move to help.* □ **look out** [usu. in *imperative*] be vigilant and take notice: *"Look out!" warned Billie, seeing a movement from the room beyond | **look out for** the early warning signals.* □ **look something out** *Brit.* search for and produce something: *I've got a catalog somewhere and I'll look it out if you're interested.* □ **look up** (of a situation) improve: *things seemed to be looking up at last.* □ **look someone up** *informal* make social contact with someone. □ **look something up** search for and find a piece of information in a reference book. □ **look up to** have a great deal of respect for (someone): *he needed a model, someone to look up to.*
▶*n.* **1** an act of directing one's gaze in order to see someone or something: *let me get a closer look.* ■ an expression of a feeling or thought by such an act: *Brenton gave me a funny look.* ■ a scrutiny or examination: *the government should be **taking a look at** the amount of grant the council receives.* **2** the appearance of someone or something, esp. as expressing a particular quality: *the bedraggled look of the village.* ■ (**looks**) a person's facial appearance considered aesthetically: *he had charm, **good looks**, and an amusing insouciance.* ■ a style or fashion: *Italian designers unveiled their latest look.*
▶*exclam.* (also **look here!**) used to call attention to what one is going to say: *"Look, this is ridiculous."* ▷Old English *lōcian* (verb); related to German dialect *lugen.*
▶*PHRASES* □ **look one's age** appear to be as old as one really is. □ **look alive** see LIVELY. □ **look before you leap** *proverb* one shouldn't act without first considering the possible consequences or dangers. □ **look daggers at** see DAGGER. □ **look down one's nose at** another way of saying LOOK DOWN ON. □ **look for trouble** see TROUBLE. □ **look someone in the eye** (or **face**) look directly at someone without showing embarrassment, fear, or shame. □ **look lively** see LIVELY. □ **look the other way** deliberately ignore wrongdoing by others: *they do look the other way at corrupt practices here.* □ **look sharp** be quick. □ **look small** see SMALL. □ **look to the future** consider and plan for what is in the future, rather than worrying about the past or present. □ **look someone up and down** scrutinize someone carefully.

look-a-like (also **look·a·like**) ▶*n.* a person or thing that closely resembles another, esp. someone who looks very similar to a famous person: *an Elvis Presley look-alike.*

look-and-say ▶*n.* [as *adj.*] denoting a method of teaching reading based on the visual recognition of words rather than by the association of sounds and letters. Compare with PHONIC.

look·er /ˈlo͝okər/ ▶*n.* **1** a person who looks: *the percentage of lookers who actually buy is pretty low.* **2** [with *adj.*] a person with a specified appearance: *a tough looker is not necessarily a tough fighter.* ■ *informal* a very attractive person, esp. a woman: *he shook his head in admiration—she was some looker.*

look·er-on ▶*n.* (*pl.* **look·ers-on**) a person who is a spectator rather than a participant in a situation.

look-in ▶*n.* **1** an informal and brief visit. **2** *Football* a short pass pattern in which the receiver runs diagonally toward the center of the field. **3** [in *sing.*] *informal, Brit.* a chance to take part or succeed in something: *they didn't let the other side **get a look-in** in the semifinal.*

look·ing glass ▶*n.* a mirror: *she stared at her reflection in the looking glass.* ■ [as *adj.*] being or involving the opposite of what is normal or expected: *a looking-glass land | looking-glass logic.*

look·ism /ˈlo͝ok,izəm/ ▶*n.* construction of a standard for beauty and attractiveness, and judgments made about people on the basis of how well or poorly they meet the standard.

look·it /ˈlo͝okit/ *informal* ▶*v.* phonetic spelling of "look at": *Hey, lookit that!*
▶*exclam.* used to draw attention to what one is about to say: *lookit, Pete, this is serious.*

look·out /ˈlo͝ok,out/ ▶*n.* a place from which to keep watch or view landscape. ■ a person stationed to keep watch for danger or trouble: *they acted as lookouts at the post office.* ■ *archaic* a view over a landscape. ■ (**one's lookout**) *informal* a person's own concern: *everyone's life is his own lookout.* ■ [in *sing.*] *informal, chiefly Brit.* used to indicate whether a likely outcome is good or bad: *"What if he gets sick?" "It's a bad lookout in that case."*
▶*PHRASE* □ **be on the lookout** (or **keep a lookout**) **for** be alert to (danger or trouble): *he told them to be on the lookout for dangerous gas.* ■ keep searching for (something that is wanted): *we kept a sharp lookout for animals.*

Look·out Moun·tain /ˈlo͝ok,out/ an Appalachian ridge, on the Cumberland Plateau in Alabama, Georgia, and Tennessee, site near Chattanooga of a November 1863 Civil War battle.

look-see ▶*n.* *informal* a brief look or inspection: *we are just about to take a little look-see around the hotel.* ▷late 19th cent.: from, or in imitation of, pidgin English.

look·up /ˈlo͝ok,əp/ ▶*n.* [usually as *modifier*] the action of or a facility for systematic electronic information retrieval: *you need an online dictionary with fast phonetic lookup.*

look·y /ˈlo͝okē/ (also **look·ie**) ▶*exclam.* *informal* used to draw attention to what one is about to say: *Looky there! You've gone and broken it.*

loom[1] /lo͞om/ ▶*n.* an apparatus for making fabric by weaving yarn or thread. ▷Old English *gelōma* 'tool,' shortened to *lome* in Middle English.

loom[1]

loom[2] ▶*v.* [*intrans.*] appear as a shadowy form, esp. one that is large or threatening: *vehicles loomed out of the darkness.* ■ (of an event regarded as ominous or threatening) seem about to happen: *there is a crisis looming | higher mortgage rates **loomed large** last night.*
▶*n.* [in *sing.*] a vague and often exaggerated first appearance of an object seen in darkness or fog, esp. at sea: *the loom of the land ahead.* ■ the dim reflection by cloud or haze of a light that is not directly visible, e.g., from a lighthouse over the horizon. ▷mid 16th cent.: probably from Low German or Dutch; compare with East Frisian *lōmen* 'move slowly,' Middle High German *lüemen* 'be weary.'

loon[1] /lo͞on/ ▶*n.* *informal* a silly or foolish person. ▷late 19th cent.: from LOON[2] (referring to the bird's actions when escaping from danger), perhaps influenced by LOONY.

loon[2] ▶*n.* a large diving waterbird with a sleek black or gray head, a straight pointed bill, and short legs set far back under the body. Loons breed by lakes in northern latitudes and have wailing calls. • Family Gaviidae and genus *Gavia*: five species, including the **common loon** (*G. immer*) of both Canada and Eurasia. ▷mid 17th cent.: probably by alteration of Shetland dialect *loom*, denoting esp. a guillemot or a diver, from Old Norse.

loon[2]

loon·ie /ˈlo͞onē/ ▶*n.* (*pl.* **-ies**) *Canadian, informal* a Canadian one-dollar coin, introduced in 1987.

loon·y /ˈlo͞onē/ *informal* ▶*n.* (*pl.* **loon·ies**) a crazy or silly person: *she was working with a bunch of loonies.*
▶*adj.* (**loon·i·er**, **loon·i·est**) crazy or silly: *loony drivers.* ▷mid 19th cent.: abbreviation of LUNATIC. **—loon·i·ness** *n.*

loon·y bin ▶*n.* *informal, offensive* a home or hospital for the mentally ill.

loon·ey tunes (also **loon·y-tunes**) /ˈlo͞onē ,t(y)o͞onz/ *informal* ▶*adj.* (variously capitalized) crazy; deranged: *a Looney Tunes initiative for easing the parking problem.*
▶*pl. n.* crazy or deranged people. ▷1980s: from *Looney Tunes,* the name of an animated cartoon series that began in the 1930s, featuring Bugs Bunny and other characters.

loop /lo͞op/ ▶*n.* **1** a shape produced by a curve that bends around and crosses itself. ■ a length of thread, rope, or similar material, doubled or crossing itself, typically used as a fastening or handle. ■ a curved stroke forming part of a letter (e.g., *b, p*). ■ (also **loop-the-loop**) a maneuver in which an aircraft describes a vertical circle in the air. ■ *Skating* a maneuver describing a curve that crosses itself, made on a single edge. ■ (**the Loop**) informal name for the commercial district in downtown Chicago. **2** a structure, series, or process the end of which is connected to the beginning. ■ an endless strip of tape or film allowing continuous repetition. ■ a complete circuit for an electric current. ■ *Computing* a programmed sequence of instructions that is repeated until or while a particular condition is satisfied.
▶*v.* form (something) into a loop or loops; encircle: *she looped her arms around his neck.* ■ follow a course that forms a loop or loops: *the canal loops for two miles through the city.* ■ put into or execute a loop of tape, film, or computing instructions: *the program loops back on reaching a RETURN statement.* ■ (also **loop the loop**) circle an aircraft vertically in the air. ▷late Middle English: of unknown origin; compare with Scottish Gaelic *lùb* 'loop, bend.'
▶*PHRASES* □ **in** (or **out of**) **the loop** *informal* aware (or unaware) of information known to only a privileged few. □ **throw** (or **knock**) **someone for a loop** *informal* surprise or astonish someone; catch someone off guard.

loop di·u·ret·ic ▶*n.* *Medicine* a powerful diuretic that inhibits resorption of water and sodium from the loop of Henle.

loop·er /ˈlo͞opər/ ▶*n.* **1** another term for INCHWORM. **2** *Baseball* a fly ball that becomes a hit by dropping out of the reach of the infielders.

loop·hole /ˈlo͞op,(h)ōl/ ▶*n.* **1** an ambiguity or inadequacy in the law or a set of rules: *they exploited tax loopholes.* **2** *archaic* an arrow slit in a wall.
▶*v.* [*trans.*] make arrow slits in (a wall or building). ▷late 16th cent. (denoting an arrow slit): from obsolete *loop* 'embrasure' + HOLE.

loop of Hen·le /ˈhenlē/ ▸*n. Anatomy* the part of a kidney tubule that forms a long loop in the medulla of the kidney, from which water and salts are resorbed into the blood. ▷mid 19th cent.: named after Friedrich G. J. *Henle* (1809–85), German anatomist.

loop stitch ▸*n.* a method of sewing or knitting in which each stitch incorporates a free loop of thread for ornament or to give a thick pile. —**loop-stitched** *adj.* —**loop stitch·ing** *n.*

loop·y /ˈlo͞opē/ ▸*adj.* (**loop·i·er**, **loop·i·est**) **1** *informal* crazy or silly: *the author comes across as a bit loopy.* **2** having many loops: *a big, loopy signature.* —**loop·i·ness** *n.*

Loos /lo͞os/, Anita (1893–1981) U.S. writer. She wrote stories collected in *Gentlemen Prefer Blondes* (1925) that involved the character Lorelei Lee and that were later adapted for the stage and the screen.

loose /lo͞os/ ▸*adj.* **1** not firmly or tightly fixed in place: *a loose tooth* | *the truck's trailer came loose.* ■ detached or able to be detached: *a loose board.* ■ not held or tied together; not packaged or placed in a container: *wear your hair loose* | *pockets bulging with loose change.* ■ (of a person or animal) free from confinement; not bound or tethered: *the bull was loose with cattle in the field* | *the tethered horses* **broke loose**. ■ not strict or exact: *a loose interpretation.* ■ not close or compact in structure: *a loose weave* | *figurative a loose federation of political and industrial groups.* ■ typical of diarrhea: *many patients report loose bowel movements.* **2** (of a garment) not fitting tightly or closely: *she slipped into a loose T-shirt and shorts.* **3** relaxed; physically slack: *she swung back into her easy, loose stride* | *a loose-limbed walk.* ■ careless and indiscreet in what is said: *there is too much loose talk about the situation.* ■ *dated* promiscuous; immoral: *she ran the risk of being called a loose woman.* ■ (of the ball in a game) in play but not in any player's possession.
▸*v.* [*trans.*] set free; release: *the hounds have been loosed.* ■ untie; unfasten: *the ropes were loosed.* ■ relax (one's grip): *he loosed his grip suddenly.* ▷Middle English *loos* 'free from bonds,' from Old Norse *lauss*, of Germanic origin; related to Dutch and German *los*. —**loose·ly** *adv.* —**loose·ness** *n.*
▸*PHRASES* □ **hang** (or **stay**) **loose** [often as *imperative*] *informal* be relaxed; refrain from taking anything too seriously: *hang loose, baby!* □ **on the loose** having escaped from confinement: *a serial killer is on the loose.*

USAGE The adjective **loose**, meaning 'not tight,' should not be confused with the verb **loose**, which means 'let go': *they loosed the reins and let the horse gallop.* This verb in turn should not be confused with the verb **lose**, which means 'be deprived of, fail to keep': *I will lose my keys if I don't mend the hole in my pocket.*

loose can·non ▸*n.* an unpredictable or uncontrolled person who is likely to cause unintentional damage.

loose con·struc·tion ▸*n. Law* a broad interpretation of a statute or document by a court. —**loose con·struc·tion·ist** *n.*

loose end ▸*n.* a detail not yet settled or explained: *Mark arrived back at his office to tie up any loose ends.*
▸*PHRASE* □ **be at loose ends** have nothing specific to do: *he dropped out of school and found himself alone and at loose ends.*

loose-joint·ed ▸*adj.* having or characterized by easy, free movement; limber. ■ having loose joints. ■ loosely built, badly put together.

loose-knit ▸*adj.* knitted with large loose stitches: *she wears a large loose-knit sweater.* ■ connected in a tenuous or ill-defined way; not closely linked: *a loose-knit grouping of independent states.*

loose-leaf (also **loose·leaf**) ▸*adj.* **1** (of a notebook or folder) having each sheet of paper separate and removable. **2** (of lettuce) having leaves that overlap each other loosely rather than forming a compact head.

loos·en /ˈlo͞osən/ ▸*v.* [*trans.*] make (something tied, fastened, or fixed in place) less tight or firm: *loosen your collar and tie.* ■ make more lax: *his main mistake was to loosen monetary policy* | [as *n.*] (**loosening**) *a loosening of the benefit rules.* ■ relax (one's grip or muscles): *he loosened his hold so she could pull her arms free.* ■ [*intrans.*] become relaxed or less tight: *the stiffness in his shoulders had loosened.* ■ make (a connection or relationship) less strong: *he wanted to strengthen rather than loosen union links.* ■ (with reference to the bowels) make or become relaxed before excretion: [*intrans.*] *his bowels loosened in terror.*
▸*phrasal v.* □ **loosen up** warm up in preparation for an activity: *arrive early to loosen up and hit some practice shots.* ■ make or become relaxed: *they taught me to have fun at work and loosen up* | (**loosen someone up**) *the beer is loosening him up.* —**loos·en·er** *n.*
▸*PHRASE* □ **loosen someone's tongue** make someone talk freely.

loose·strife /ˈlo͞o(s),strīf/ ▸*n.* any of various tall plants that bear upright spikes of flowers: • several plants of the genus *Lythrum* (family Lythraceae), in particular the **purple loosestrife** (*L. salicaria*) of the Old World, now well established in North America. • several yellow-flowered plants of the genus *Lysimachia* (family Primulaceae), in particular the **garden loosestrife** (*L. vulgaris*) of Eurasia and North America. ▷mid 16th cent.: from LOOSE + STRIFE, taking the Greek name *lusimakheion* (actually from *Lusimakhos*, the name of its discoverer) to be directly from *luein* 'undo' + *makhē* 'battle.'

loos·ey-goos·ey /ˈlo͞osē ˈgo͞osē/ ▸*adj. informal* **1** not tense; relaxed and comfortable: *other guys can goof around, be all loosey-goosey before a game.* **2** undesirably lacking in definition, care, or precision: *a loosey-goosey interpretation of traditional doctrine.* ▷rhyming formation from the expression *loose as a goose*.

loot /lo͞ot/ ▸*n.* goods, esp. private property, taken from an enemy in war. ■ stolen money or valuables: *two men wearing stocking masks, each swinging a bag of loot.* ■ *informal* money; wealth: *the thief made off with $5 million in loot.*
▸*v.* [*trans.*] steal goods from (a place), typically during a war or riot: *police confronted the rioters who were looting shops.* ■ steal (goods) in such circumstances: *tons of food aid awaiting distribution had been looted.* ▷early 19th cent. (as a verb): from Hindi *lūṭ*, from Sanskrit *luṇṭh-* 'rob.' —**loot·er** *n.*

lop[1] /läp/ ▸*v.* (**lopped**, **lop·ping**) [*trans.*] cut off (a branch, limb, or other protrusion) from the main body of a tree: *they* **lopped off** *more branches to save the tree.* ■ *informal* remove (something regarded as unnecessary or burdensome): *it* **lops** *an hour* **off** *commuting time.* ■ remove branches from (a tree).
▸*n.* branches and twigs lopped off trees. ▷late Middle English (as a noun denoting branches and twigs of trees).

lop[2] ▸*v.* (**lopped**, **lop·ping**) [*intrans.*] hang loosely or limply; droop: *a stomach that lopped over his belt.* ■ move in a loping or slouching way: *he lopped toward the plane.* ■ *archaic* dawdle. ▷late 16th cent.: probably symbolic of limpness; compare with LOB.

lope /lōp/ ▸*v.* [*intrans.*] run or move with a long bounding stride: *the dog was loping along by his side* | [as *adj.*] (**loping**) *a loping stride.*
▸*n.* [in *sing.*] a long bounding stride: *they set off at a fast lope.* ▷Middle English: variant of Scots *loup*, from Old Norse *hlaupa* 'leap.'

lop-eared ▸*adj.* (of an animal) having ears that droop down by the sides of the head: *a lop-eared mule.*

lo·per·a·mide /lōˈperə,mīd/ ▸*n. Medicine* a synthetic drug of the opiate class that inhibits peristalsis and is used to treat diarrhea. ▷1970s: probably from *(ch)lo(ro-)* + *(pi)per(idine)* + AMIDE.

lopho- ▸*comb. form Zoology* crested: *lophodont.* ▷from Greek *lophos* 'crest.'

loph·o·dont /ˈläfə,dänt; ˈlōfə-/ ▸*adj. Zoology* (of molar teeth) having transverse ridges on the grinding surfaces, characteristic of some ungulates. ■ (of an ungulate) having such teeth. ▷late 19th cent.: from LOPHO- 'crest' + Greek *odous, odont-* 'tooth.'

lo·phoph·o·rate /ləˈfäfə,rāt; ,lōfəˈfôr,āt/ *Zoology* ▸*adj.* of or relating to small aquatic invertebrates belonging to a group of phyla characterized by the possession of lophophores. They include bryozoans, brachiopods, and phoronids.
▸*n.* a lophophorate animal.

loph·o·phore /ˈläfə,fôr; ˈlōfə-/ ▸*n. Zoology* a horseshoe-shaped structure bearing ciliated tentacles around the mouth in certain small marine invertebrates.

Lop Nor /lôp no͝or/ (also **Lop Nur**) a dried-up salt lake in the arid basin of the Tarim River in northwestern China, used since 1964 for nuclear testing.

lop·pers /ˈläpərz/ ▸*plural n.* a cutting tool, esp. for pruning trees: *a good pair of loppers.*

lop·sid·ed /ˈläp,sīdid/ ▸*adj.* with one side lower or smaller than the other: *a lopsided grin.* ▷early 18th cent.: from LOP[2] + SIDE + -ED[1]. —**lop·sid·ed·ly** *adv.* —**lop·sid·ed·ness** *n.*

loq. ▸*abbr. Latin* loquitur.

lo·qua·cious /lōˈkwāshəs/ ▸*adj.* talkative. See note at TALKATIVE. ▷mid 17th cent.: from Latin *loquax, loquac-* (from *loqui* 'talk') + -IOUS. —**lo·qua·cious·ly** *adv.* —**lo·qua·cious·ness** *n.* —**lo·quac·i·ty** /ˈkwasətē/ *n.*

lo·quat /ˈlō,kwät/ ▸*n.* **1** a small yellow egg-shaped acidic fruit. **2** the evergreen eastern Asian tree of the rose family that bears this fruit, cultivated in subtropical regions both for its fruit and as an ornamental. • *Eriobotrya japonica*, family Rosaceae. ▷early 19th cent.: from Chinese dialect *luh kwat* 'rush orange.'

lo·qui·tur /ˈläkwitər; ˈlōkwi-/ (abbr.: **loq.**) ▸*v.* (he or she) speaks (with the speaker's name following, as a stage direction or to inform the reader). ▷Latin, from *loqui* 'talk, speak.'

Lo·rain /lôˈrān/ a port city in north central Ohio, on Lake Erie, west of Cleveland; pop. 68,652.

lo·ran /ˈlôr,an/ (also **Lo·ran**) ▸*n.* a system of long-distance navigation in which position is determined from the intervals between signal pulses received from widely spaced radio transmitters. ▷1940s: from *lo(ng-)ra(nge) n(avigation).*

lor·az·e·pam /lôˈrazə,pam; -ˈrāzə-/ ▸*n. Medicine* a drug of the benzodiazepine group, used esp. to treat anxiety. ▷1960s: from *(ch)lor(o-)* (as in 'chlorine') + *-azepam*, on the pattern of words such as *diazepam*.

Lor·ca /ˈlôrkə/, Federico García (1898–1936), Spanish poet and playwright. His works include *Gypsy Ballads* (1928), *Blood Wedding* (1933), and *The House of Bernada Alba* (1936).

lord /lôrd/ ▸*n.* someone or something having power, authority, or influence: *lord of the sea* | *lords of the jungle.* ■ (in the UK) a man of noble rank or high office; a peer. ■ (**Lord**) (in the UK) a title given formally to a baron, and less formally to a marquess, earl, or viscount (prefixed to a family or territorial name): *Lord Derby.* ■ (**the Lords**) (in the UK) the House of Lords, or its members collectively. ■ (**Lord**) (in the UK) a courtesy title given to a younger son of a duke or marquess (prefixed to a Christian name): *Lord John Russell.* ■ (in the UK) in compound titles of other people of authority: *Lord High Executioner.* ■ *historical* a feudal superior, esp. the proprietor of a manor house. ■ a master or ruler: *our lord the king.* ■ (**Lord**) a name for God or Christ: *give thanks to the Lord.* ■ *dated Astrology* the ruling planet of a sign, house, or chart.
▸*exclam.* (**Lord**) used in exclamations expressing surprise or worry, or for emphasis: *Lord, I'm cold!*
▸*v.* **1** [*trans.*] *archaic* confer the title of Lord upon. **2** (**lord it over**) act in a superior and domineering manner toward (someone). ▷Old English *hlāford*, from *hlāfweard* 'bread-keeper,' from a Germanic base (see LOAF[1], WARD). Compare with LADY. —**lord·less** *adj.* —**lord·like** /-,līk/ *adj.*
▸*PHRASES* □ **live like a lord** live sumptuously. □ **Lord** (**God**) **of hosts** God as Lord over earthly or heavenly armies. □ **lord of the manor** the owner of a manor house (formerly the master of a feudal manor). □ **Lord of Misrule** *historical* a person presiding over Christmas games and revelry in a wealthy household. □ **the Lord's Day** Sunday. □ **the Lord's Prayer** the prayer taught by Jesus to his disciples, beginning "Our Father." □ **the Lord's Supper** the Eucharist; Holy Communion (esp. in Protestant use). □ **My Lord** (in the UK) a polite form of address to judges, bishops, and certain noblemen. □ **Our Lord** Christ.

Lord Chan·cel·lor (also **Lord High Chancellor**) ▸*n.* (in the UK) the highest officer of the Crown, who presides in the House of Lords, the Chancery Division, or the Court of Appeal. ■ *historical* an officer of state acting as head of the judiciary and administrator of the royal household.

Lord Faunt·le·roy see FAUNTLEROY.

Lord High Ad·mi·ral a title of the British monarch, originally the title of an officer who governed the Royal Navy and had jurisdiction over maritime causes.

lord·ling /ˈlôrdliNG/ ▸*n. archaic, chiefly derogatory* a minor lord.

lord·ly /ˈlôrdlē/ ▸*adj.* (**lord·li·er**, **lord·li·est**) of, characteristic of, or suitable for a lord: *lordly titles* | *they were putting on lordly airs.* ▷Old English *hlāfordlic* (see LORD, -LY[1]). —**lord·li·ness** *n.*

lord may·or ▸*n.* the title of the mayor in London and some other large British cities.

lor·do·sis /lôrˈdōsis/ ▸*n. Medicine* excessive inward curvature of the spine. Compare with KYPHOSIS. ■ a posture assumed by some female mammals during mating, in which the back is arched downward. ▷early 18th cent.: modern Latin, from Greek *lordōsis*, from *lordos* 'bent backward.' —**lor·dot·ic** /-ˈdätik/ *adj.*

Lord Pro·tec·tor ▸*n.* see PROTECTOR (sense 3).

lords-and-la·dies ▸*n.* another term for CUCKOOPINT.

lord·ship /ˈlôrd,SHip/ ▸*n.* **1** supreme power or rule: *his* ***lordship over*** *the other gods.* ■ *archaic* the authority or state of being a lord. ■ *historical* a piece of land or territory belonging to or under the jurisdiction of a lord: *lands including the lordship of Denbigh.* **2** (**His/ Your**, etc., **Lordship**) in the UK, a respectful form of reference or address to a judge, a bishop, or a man with a title: *if Your Lordship pleases.* ▷Old English *hlā-fordscipe* (see LORD, -SHIP).

Lords spir·it·u·al ▸*plural n.* the bishops in the House of Lords.

Lords tem·po·ral ▸*plural n.* the members of the House of Lords other than the bishops.

Lord·y /ˈlôrdē/ ▸*exclam. informal* used to express surprise or dismay: *Lordy! Whatever happened?*

lore[1] /lôr/ ▸*n.* a body of traditions and knowledge on a subject or held by a particular group, typically passed from person to person by word of mouth: *the jinns of Arabian lore | baseball lore.* ▷Old English *lār* 'instruction,' of Germanic origin: related to Dutch *leer*, German *Lehre*, also to LEARN.

lore[2] ▸*n. Zoology* the surface on each side of a bird's head between the eye and the upper base of the beak, or between the eye and nostril in snakes. ▷early 19th cent.: from Latin *lorum* 'strap.'

Lo·ren /ləˈren/, Sophia (1934–), Italian actress; born *Sofia Scicolone.* She starred in both Italian and U.S. movies, including *The Millionairess* (1960), *Marriage Italian Style* (1964), and *Two Women* (1961), for which she won an Academy Award. She also received an honorary Academy Award in 1991.

Lo·rentz /ˈlôrənts/, Hendrik Antoon (1853–1928), Dutch theoretical physicist. He worked on the forces affecting electrons and realized that electrons and cathode rays were the same thing. Nobel Prize for Physics (1902), shared with Pieter Zeeman (1865–1943).

Lo·rentz con·trac·tion ▸*n. Physics* the shortening of a moving body in the direction of its motion, esp. at speeds close to that of light.

Lo·rentz force ▸*n. Physics* the force that is exerted by a magnetic field on a moving electric charge.

Lo·rentz trans·for·ma·tion ▸*n. Physics* the set of equations that, in Einstein's special theory of relativity, relate the space and time coordinates of one frame of reference to those of another.

Lo·renz /ˈlôrənz; -rents/, Konrad (Zacharias) (1903–89), Austrian zoologist. He pioneered the science of ethology, emphasizing innate rather than learned behavior or conditioned reflexes. Notable works: *King Solomon's Ring* (1952) and *On Aggression* (1966). Nobel Prize for Physics (1973), shared with Karl von Frisch and Nikolaas Tinbergen.

Lo·renz at·trac·tor ▸*n. Mathematics* a strange attractor in the form of a two-lobed figure formed by a trajectory that spirals around the two lobes, passing randomly between them. ▷1970s: named after Edward N. *Lorenz* (born 1917), American meteorologist.

Lo·renz curve ▸*n. Economics* a graph on which the cumulative percentage of total national income (or some other variable) is plotted against the cumulative percentage of the corresponding population (ranked in increasing size of share). The extent to which the curve sags below a straight diagonal line indicates the degree of inequality of distribution. ▷early 20th cent.: named after Max O. *Lorenz* (born 1876), the American statistician who devised the curve.

Lo·ren·zo de' Me·di·ci /ləˈrenzō də ˈmedicHē; lôˈrentsō/ (1449–92), Italian statesman and scholar. A patron of the arts and humanist learning, he supported Botticelli, Leonardo da Vinci, and Michelangelo among others.

lo-res /ˈlō ˈrez/ ▸*adj.* variant spelling of LOW-RES.

lor·gnette /lôrnˈyet/ (also **lor·gnettes**) ▸*n.* a pair of glasses or opera glasses held in front of a person's eyes by a long handle at one side. ▷early 19th cent.: from French, from *lorgner* 'to squint.'

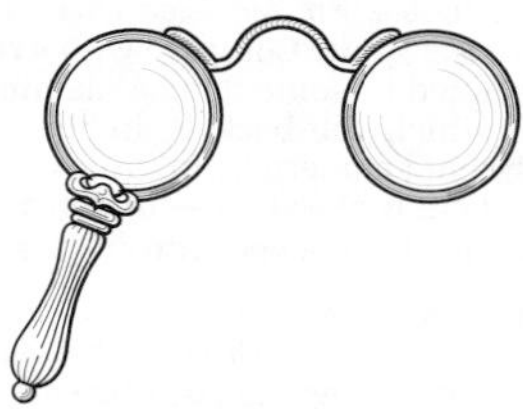

lorgnette

lo·ri·ca /ləˈrīkə/ ▸*n.* (*pl.* **-cae** /-,kē; -,sē/ or **-cas**) **1** *historical* a Roman corselet or cuirass of leather. **2** *Zoology* the rigid case or shell of some rotifers and protozoans. ▷Latin, literally 'breastplate.'

lor·i·cate /ˈlôrə,kāt/ ▸*adj. Zoology* (of an animal) having a protective covering of plates or scales. ■ having a lorica. ▷early 19th cent.: from Latin *loricatus*, from *lorica* 'breastplate,' from *lorum* 'strap.'

Lor·i·cif·er·a /,lôriˈsifərə/ *Zoology* a minor phylum of minute marine invertebrates (genus *Nanaloricus*), resembling rotifers and living in gravel. ▷modern Latin (plural), from Latin *lorica* 'breastplate' + *ferre* 'to bear.' —**lor·i·cif·er·an** *n.* & *adj.*

lor·i·keet /ˈlôrə,kēt; ˈlär-/ ▸*n.* a small bird of the lory family, found chiefly in New Guinea. • *Charmosyna* and other genera, family Loridae (or Psittacidae): several species. ▷late 18th cent.: diminutive of LORY, on the pattern of *parakeet*.

lo·ris /ˈlôris/ ▸*n.* (*pl.* **-ris·es**) a small, slow-moving nocturnal primate with a short or absent tail, living in dense vegetation in South Asia. • Genera *Loris* and *Nycticebus*, family Lorisidae, suborder Prosimii: the **slender loris** (*L. tardigradus*) of southern India and Sri Lanka, and the **slow loris** (genus *Nycticebus*, two species) of Southeast Asia. ▷late 18th cent.: from French, perhaps from obsolete Dutch *loeris* 'clown.'

lorn /lôrn/ ▸*adj. poetic/literary* lonely and abandoned; forlorn. ▷Middle English: past participle of obsolete *lese* from Old English *lēosan* 'lose.'

Lor·rain, Claude see CLAUDE LORRAINE.

Lor·raine /ləˈrān; lô-/ a region of northeastern France, between Champagne and the Vosges mountains. The modern region corresponds to the southern part of the medieval kingdom of Lorraine, which extended from the North Sea to Italy. ▷from Latin *Lotharingia*, from *Lothair*, the name of a king (825–869).

Lor·raine, Claude see CLAUDE LORRAINE.

Lor·raine cross ▸*n.* a cross with one vertical and two horizontal bars. It was the symbol of Joan of Arc, and in World War II it was adopted by the Free French forces of General de Gaulle.

Lor·re /ˈlôrē/, Peter (1904–64), U.S. actor, born in Hungary; born *Laszlo Lowenstein.* He was known for the sinister roles he played, as in *M* (1931), *The Maltese Falcon* (1941), and *The Raven* (1963). He also portrayed Mr. Moto, a Japanese detective, in eight movies (1937–39).

lor·ry /ˈlôrē; ˈlärē/ ▸*n.* (*pl.* **-ries**) *Brit.* a large, heavy motor vehicle for transporting goods or troops; a truck. ▷mid 19th cent.: perhaps from the given name *Laurie*.

lo·ry /ˈlôrē/ ▸*n.* (*pl.* **-ries**) a small Australasian and Southeast Asian parrot with a brush-tipped tongue for feeding on nectar and pollen, having mainly green plumage with patches of bright color. • Family Loridae (or Psittacidae): several genera and species, e.g., the brightly colored **rainbow lory** or **rainbow lorikeet** (*Trichoglossus haematodus*). ▷late 17th cent.: from Malay *lūri*.

LOS ▸*abbr.* ■ law of the sea. ■ length of stay. ■ line of scrimmage. ■ line of sight. ■ loss of signal.

Los Al·a·mos /lôs ˈalə,mōs; läs/ a town in northern New Mexico; pop. 11,455. It is a center for nuclear research.

Los An·ge·le·no /lôs ,anjəˈlēnō; läs/ ▸*n.* variant of ANGELENO.

Los An·ge·les /lôs ˈanjələs; läs; -,lēz/ a city on the Pacific coast of southern California; pop. 3,694,820. It is a major center of industry, filmmaking, and television.

lose /lo͞oz/ ▸*v.* (*past* and *past part.* **lost** /lôst; läst/) [*trans.*] **1** be deprived of or cease to have or retain (something): *I've lost my appetite | Linda was very upset about losing her job | the company may find itself losing customers to cheaper rivals.* ■ cause (someone) to fail to gain or retain (something): *you lost me my appointment at the university.* ■ be deprived of (a close relative or friend) through their death or as a result of the breaking off of a relationship: *she lost her husband in the fire.* ■ (of a pregnant woman) miscarry (a baby) or suffer the death of (a baby) during childbirth. ■ (**be lost**) be destroyed or killed, esp. through accident or as a result of military action: *a fishing disaster in which 19 local men were lost.* ■ decrease in (body weight); undergo a reduction of (a specified amount of weight): *she couldn't eat and began to lose weight.* ■ waste or fail to take advantage of (time or an opportunity): *they lost every chance to score in the first inning | he* ***lost no time in*** *attacking his opponent's tax proposals.* ■ (of a watch or clock) become slow by (a specified amount of time): *this clock will neither gain nor lose a second.* ■ (**lose it**) *informal* lose control of one's temper or emotions: *in the end I completely lost it—I was screaming at them.* **2** become unable to find (something or someone): *I've lost the car keys.* ■ cease or become unable to follow (the right route): *the clouds came down, and we lost the path.* ■ evade or shake off (a pursuer): *he came after me waving his revolver, but I easily lost him.* ■ *informal* get rid of (an undesirable person or thing): *lose that creep!* ■ *informal* cause (someone) to be unable to follow an argument or explanation: *sorry, Tim, you've lost me there.* ■ (**lose oneself in/be lost in**) be or become deeply absorbed in (something): *he had been lost in thought.* **3** fail to win (a game or contest): *the Bears lost the final game of the series |* [*intrans.*] *they lost by one vote |* [as *adj.*] (**losing**) *the losing side.* ■ cause (someone) to fail to win (a game or contest): *that shot lost him the championship.* **4** earn less (money) than one is spending or has spent: *the paper is losing $500,000 a month |* [*intrans.*] *he lost heavily on box-office flops.*

▸*phrasal v.* □ **lose out** be deprived of an opportunity to do or obtain something; be disadvantaged: *youngsters who were* ***losing out on*** *regular schooling.* ■ be beaten in competition or replaced by: *they were disappointed at losing out to Chicago in the playoffs.* ▷Old English *losian* 'perish, destroy,' also 'become unable to find,' from *los* 'loss.'

▸*PHRASES* □ **have nothing to lose** be in a situation that is so bad that even if an action or undertaking is unsuccessful, it cannot make it any worse. □ **lose face** come to be less highly respected: *he was trying to work out how he could go back home without losing face.* □ **lose heart** become discouraged. □ **lose one's heart to** see HEART. □ **lose height** (of an aircraft) descend to a lower level in flight. □ **lose one's mind** (or **one's marbles**) *informal* go insane. □ **lose sleep** [usu. with *negative*] worry about something: *no one is losing any sleep over what he thinks of us.* □ **lose one's** (or **the**) **way** become lost; fail to reach one's destination. ■ *figurative* no longer have a clear idea of one's purpose or motivation in an activity or business: *the company has lost its way and should pull out of general insurance.* □ **you can't lose** used to express the conviction that someone must inevitably profit from an action or undertaking: *we're offering them for only $5.00—you can't lose!*

USAGE See usage at LOOSE.

lo·sel /ˈlōzəl/ ▸*n. archaic* or *dialect* a worthless person. ▸*adj. archaic* or *dialect* good-for-nothing; worthless. ▷late Middle English: apparently from *los-*, stem of obsolete *lese* 'lose,' + -EL.

los·er /ˈlo͞ozər/ ▸*n.* a person or thing that loses or has lost something, esp. a game or contest. ■ a person who accepts defeat with good or bad grace, as specified: *we won fair and square—they should concede that and be good losers.* ■ a person or thing that is put at a disadvantage by a particular situation or course of action: *children are the losers when politicians keep fiddling around with education.* ■ *informal* a person who fails frequently or is generally unsuccessful in life: *a ragtag community of rejects and losers.* ■ *Bridge* a card that is expected to be part of a losing trick.

Los Gat·os /lôs ˈgatəs/ a city in north central California, southwest of San Jose; pop. 27,357.

los·ing bat·tle ▸*n.* [in *sing.*] a struggle that seems certain to end in failure: *the police force is fighting a losing battle against a rising tide of crime.*

los·ing·est /ˈlo͞oziNGist/ ▸*adj. informal* losing more often than others of its kind; least successful.

loss /lôs; läs/ ▸*n.* the fact or process of losing something or someone: *avoiding loss of time | funding cuts will lead to job losses | loss-making industries.* ■ the state or feeling of grief when deprived of someone or something of value: *I feel a terrible sense of loss.* ■ the detriment or disadvantage resulting from losing: *his fall from power was no loss to the world.* ■ [in *sing.*] a person or thing that is badly missed when lost: *he will be* ***a great loss to*** *many people.* ■ *Physics* a reduction of power within or among circuits, measured as a ratio of power input to power output. ▷Old English *los* 'destruction,' of Germanic origin; related to Old Norse *los* 'breaking up of the ranks of an army' and LOOSE; later probably a back-formation from *lost*, past participle of LOSE.

▸*PHRASE* □ **at a loss 1** puzzled or uncertain what to think, say, or do: [with *infinitive*] *she became popular, and was at a loss to know why he was* ***at a loss for*** *words.* **2** making less money than is spent buying, operating, or producing something: *a railroad running at a loss.*

loss-lead·er ▸*n.* a product sold at a loss to attract customers.

loss·less /'lôsləs; 'läs-/ ▸*adj.* having or involving no dissipation of electrical or electromagnetic energy. ■ *Computing* of or relating to data compression without loss of information.

loss ra·tio ▸*n.* the ratio of the claims paid by an insurer to the premiums earned, usually for a one-year period.

loss·y /'lôsē; 'läsē/ ▸*adj.* having or involving the dissipation of electrical or electromagnetic energy. ■ *Computing* of or relating to data compression in which unnecessary information is discarded.

lost /lôst; läst/ ▸ past and past participle of **LOSE**.
▸*adj.* **1** unable to find one's way; not knowing one's whereabouts: *Help! We're lost! | they* ***got lost*** *in the fog.* ■ unable to be found: *he turned up with my lost golf clubs.* ■ (of a person) very confused or insecure or in great difficulties: *she stood there clutching a drink, feeling completely lost | I'd* ***be lost without*** *her.* **2** denoting something that has been taken away or cannot be recovered: *if only one could recapture one's lost youth!* ■ (of time or an opportunity) not used advantageously; wasted: *the decision meant a lost opportunity to create 200 jobs.* ■ having perished or been destroyed: *a memorial to the lost crewmen.* **3** (of a game or contest) in which a defeat has been sustained: *the lost election of 1994.*
▸*PHRASES* □ **all is not lost** used to suggest that there is still some chance of success or recovery. □ **be lost for words** be so surprised, confused, or upset that one cannot think what to say. □ **be lost on** fail to influence or be noticed or appreciated by (someone): *the significance of his remarks was not lost on Scott.* □ **be lost to** be no longer affected by or accessible to: *once a vital member of the community, he is now lost to the world.* □ **get lost** [often in *imperative*] *informal* go away (used as an expression of anger or impatience): *Why don't you leave me alone? Go on, get lost!* □ **give someone up for lost** stop expecting that a missing person will be found alive. □ **make up for lost time** do something faster or more often in order to compensate for not having done it quickly or often enough before.

lost-and-found ▸*n.* a place where lost items are kept to await reclaiming by their owners.

lost cause ▸*n.* a person or thing that can no longer hope to succeed or be changed for the better.

lost gen·er·a·tion ▸*n.* the generation reaching maturity during and just after World War I, a high proportion of whose men were killed during those years. ■ an unfulfilled generation coming to maturity during a period of instability. ▷phrase applied by Gertrude Stein to disillusioned young American writers, such as Ernest Hemingway, F. Scott Fitzgerald, and Ezra Pound, who went to live in Paris in the 1920s.

Lost Tribes (also **Ten Lost Tribes of Israel**) the ten tribes of Israel taken away *c.*720 BC by Sargon II to captivity in Assyria (2 Kings 17:6), from which they are believed never to have returned while the tribes of Benjamin and Judah remained. See also **TRIBES OF ISRAEL**.

lost wax ▸*n.* a method of bronze casting using a clay core and a wax coating placed in a mold. The wax is melted in the mold and drained out, and bronze poured into the space left, producing a hollow bronze figure when the core is discarded. Also called **CIRE PERDUE**.

Lot[1] /lät/ a river in southern France that flows 300 miles (480 km) west to meet the Garonne River southeast of Bordeaux.

Lot[2] (in the Bible) the nephew of Abraham, who was allowed to escape from the destruction of Sodom (Gen. 19). His wife, who disobeyed orders and looked back, was turned into a pillar of salt.

lot /lät/ ▸*pron.* (**a lot** or **lots**) *informal* a large number or amount; a great deal: *there are* ***a lot of*** *actors in the cast | they took* ***a lot of*** *abuse | a lot can happen in eight months | we had* ***lots of*** *fun.* ■ (**the lot** or **the whole lot**) the whole number or quantity that is involved or implied: *you might as well take the whole lot.*
▸*adv.* (**a lot** or **lots**) *informal* a great deal; much: *my life is a lot better now | he played tennis a lot last year | thanks a lot | I feel* ***a whole lot*** *better.*
▸*n.* **1** [treated as *sing.* or *pl.*] *informal* a particular group, collection, or set of people or things: *it's just one lot of rich people stealing from another.* ■ *chiefly Brit.* a group or a person of a particular kind (generally used in a derogatory or dismissive way): *an inefficient lot, our town council | he was known as a bad lot |* ***you lot*** *think you're clever, don't you?* **2** an article or set of articles for sale at an auction: *nineteen lots failed to sell | the picture is lot 16.* **3** one of a set of objects such as straws, stones, or pieces of paper that are randomly selected as part of a decision-making process: *they* ***drew lots*** *to determine the order in which they asked questions.* ■ the making of a decision by such random selection: *officers were elected rather than selected* ***by lot.*** ■ [in *sing.*] the choice resulting from such a process: *eventually the lot fell on the king's daughter.* **4** [in *sing.*] a person's luck or condition in life, particularly as determined by fate or destiny: *plans to improve the lot of the disadvantaged.* **5** a plot of land assigned for sale or for a particular use: *a vacant lot | a fenced-off back lot.* ■ short for **PARKING LOT**. ■ an area of land near a television or movie studio where outside filming may be done. ■ the area at a car dealership where cars for sale are kept.
▸*v.* (**lot·ted**, **lot·ting**) [*trans.*] divide (items) into lots for sale at an auction: *the contents have already been lotted up, and the auction takes place on Monday.* ▷Old English *hlot* (noun), of Germanic origin; related to Dutch *lot*, German *Los*. The original meanings were sense 3 and (by extension) the sense 'a portion assigned to someone'; the latter gave rise to the other noun senses. The pronoun and adverb uses date from the early 19th cent.
▸*PHRASES* □ **all over the lot** *informal* in a state of confusion or disorganization. □ **fall to someone's lot** become someone's task or responsibility: *they accepted the burden of domestic responsibilities that fell to their lot.* □ **throw in one's lot with** decide to ally oneself closely with and share the fate of (a person or group).

USAGE 1 The expressions **a lot of** and **lots of** are used before nouns to mean 'a large number or amount of.' In common with other words denoting quantities, **lot** itself does not normally function as a head noun, meaning that it does not itself determine whether the following verb is singular or plural. Thus, although **lot** is singular in *a lot of people*, the verb that follows is not singular. In this case, the word **people** acts as the head noun and, being plural, ensures that the following verb is also plural: *a lot of people* ***were*** *assembled* (not *a lot of people* ***was*** *assembled*). See also **usage** at **NUMBER**.
2 **A lot of** and **lots of** are very common in speech and writing, but they still have a distinctly informal feel and are generally not considered acceptable for formal English, where alternatives such as **many** or **a large number** are used instead.
3 Written as one word, **alot** is incorrect, although not uncommon.

lo·ta /'lōtə/ ▸*n. Indian* a round water pot, typically of polished brass. ▷from Hindi *loṭā*.

lo-tech ▸*adj.* & *n.* variant spelling of **LOW-TECH**.

loth ▸*adj.* variant spelling of **LOATH**.

Lo·thar·i·o /lō'THe(ə)rē,ō; -'THär-/ ▸*n.* (*pl.* **-i·os**) a man who behaves selfishly and irresponsibly in his sexual relationships with women. ▷from a character in Rowe's *Fair Penitent* (1703).

lo·ti /'lōtē/ ▸*n.* (*pl.* **ma·lo·ti** /mə'lōtē/) the basic monetary unit of Lesotho, equal to 100 lisente. ▷Sesotho.

lo·tic /'lōtik/ ▸*adj. Ecology* (of organisms or habitats) inhabiting or situated in rapidly moving fresh water. Compare with **LENTIC**. ▷early 20th cent.: from Latin *lotus* 'washing' + **-IC**.

lo·tion /'lōSHən/ ▸*n.* a thick, smooth liquid preparation designed to be applied to the skin for medicinal or cosmetic purposes. ▷late Middle English: from Old French, or from Latin *lotio(n-)*, from *lot-* 'washed,' from the verb *lavare*.

lot·ta /'lätə/ (also **lot·sa** /'lätsə/) *informal* ▸*contraction of* lots of (representing nonstandard use): *I saw a lotta courage out there, and a lotta hard work.*

lot·ter·y /'lätərē/ ▸*n.* (*pl.* **-ter·ies**) a means of raising money by selling numbered tickets and giving prizes to the holders of numbers drawn at random. ■ [in *sing.*] a process or thing whose success or outcome is governed by chance: *the lottery of life.* ▷mid 16th cent.: probably from Dutch *loterij*, from *lot* 'lot.'

Lot·to /'lätō/, Lorenzo (*c.*1480–1556), Italian painter. He painted religious subjects as well as a number of notable portraits.

lot·to /'lätō/ ▸*n.* a lottery game similar to bingo. ▷late 18th cent.: from Italian.

lo·tus /'lōtəs/ ▸*n.* **1** any of a number of large water lilies, in particular: • (also **sacred lotus**) a lily of Asia and northern Australia, typically with dark pink or white-and-pink flowers (*Nelumbo nucifera*, family Nelumbonaceae). • (also **American lotus**) a yellow-flowered North American lily with bowl-shaped leaves (*Nelumbo lutea*, family Nelumbonaceae). • (also **Egyptian lotus**) a lily regarded as sacred in ancient Egypt (the white-flowered *Nymphaea lotus* and the blue-flowered *N. caerulea*, family Nymphaeaceae). **2** (in Greek mythology) a legendary plant whose fruit induces a dreamy forgetfulness and an unwillingness to depart. ■ the flower of the sacred lotus as a symbol in Asian art and religion. ■ short for **LOTUS POSITION**. ▷late 15th cent. (denoting a type of clover or trefoil, described by Homer as food for horses): via Latin from Greek *lōtos*, of Semitic origin. The term was used by classical writers to denote various trees and plants; the legendary plant (sense 2) mentioned by Homer, was thought by later Greek writers to be *Ziziphus lotus*, a relative of the jujube.

American lotus

lo·tus-eat·er ▸*n.* a person who spends time indulging in pleasure and luxury rather than dealing with practical concerns. ▷mid 19th cent.: from the people in Homer's *Odyssey* who lived on the fruit of the lotus, which was said to cause a dreamy forgetfulness in those who ate it. **—lo·tus-eat·ing** *adj.*

lo·tus·land /'lōtəs,land/ ▸*n.* a place or state concerned solely with, or providing, idle pleasure and luxury: *a lush lotusland where you can shed your inhibitions.*

lo·tus po·si·tion ▸*n.* a cross-legged position for meditation, with the feet resting on the thighs.

Lo·tus Su·tra /'lōtəs 'sŏŏtrə/ ▸*n. Buddhism* one of the most important texts in Mahayana Buddhism, significant particularly in China and Japan and given special veneration by the Nichiren sect.

Louang·phra·bang /lə'wäNGprə'bäNG/ variant spelling of **LUANG PRABANG**.

louche /lo͞osh/ ▸*adj.* disreputable or sordid in a rakish or appealing way: *the louche world of the theater.* ▷early 19th cent.: from French, literally 'squinting.'

loud /loud/ ▸*adj.* producing or capable of producing much noise; easily audible: *they were kept awake by loud music | she had a loud voice.* ■ strong or emphatic in expression: *there were loud protests from the lumber barons.* ■ vulgarly obtrusive; flashy: *a man in a loud checked suit.* ■ (of smell or flavor) powerful or offensive.
▸*adv.* with a great deal of volume: *they shouted as loud as they could.* ▷Old English *hlūd*; related to Dutch *luid*, German *laut*, from an Indo-European root meaning 'hear,' shared by Greek *kluein* 'hear,' *klutos* 'famous' and Latin *cluere* 'be famous.' **—loud·en** /'loudn/ *v.* **—loud·ly** *adv.* **—loud·ness** *n.*
▸*PHRASE* □ **out loud** aloud; audibly: *she laughed out loud.*

loud-hail·er (also **loud·hail·er**) ▸*n. chiefly Brit.* another term for **BULLHORN**

loud·mouth /'loud,mouTH/ ▸*n. informal* a person who tends to talk too much in an offensive or tactless way. **—loud-mouthed** /'loud,mou<u>TH</u>d; -,mouTHt/ (also **loud-mouthed**) *adj.*

loud·speak·er /'loud,spēkər/ ▸*n.* an apparatus that converts electrical impulses into sound, typically as part of a public address system or stereo equipment.

Lou·ga·nis /lo͞o'gānis/, Greg(ory) (1960–) U.S. diver. He won two gold medals each at the 1984 and 1988 Olympic Games.

Lou Gehr·ig's dis·ease /,lo͞o 'gerigz/ ▸*n.* another term for **AMYOTROPHIC LATERAL SCLEROSIS**. ▷1940s: named after H. L. **GEHRIG**, who died from it.

lough ▸*n.* Anglo-Irish spelling of **LOCH**. ▷Middle English: from Irish *loch*. The spelling *lough* survived in Ireland, but the pronunciation was replaced by that of the Irish word.

Lou·is[1] /'lo͞o-ē; lwē/ the name of 18 kings of France: ■ **Louis I** (778–840), son of Charlemagne; king of the West Franks and Holy Roman Emperor 814–40. ■ **Louis II** (846–879), reigned 877–879. ■ **Louis III** (863–882), son of Louis II; reigned 879–882. ■ **Louis IV** (921–954), reigned 936–954. ■ **Louis V** (967–987), reigned 979–987. ■ **Louis VI** (1081–1137), reigned 1108–37. ■ **Louis VII** (1120–80), reigned 1137–80. ■ **Louis VIII** (1187–1226), reigned 1223–26. ■ **Louis IX** (1214–70), son of Louis VIII; reigned 1226–70;

canonized as **St. Louis**. He conducted two unsuccessful crusades, dying of plague in Tunis during the second. Feast day, August 25. ■ **Louis X** (1289–1316), reigned 1314–16. ■ **Louis XI** (1423–83), son of Charles VII; reigned 1461–83. He continued his father's work in laying the foundations of a united France ruled by an absolute monarchy. ■ **Louis XII** (1462–1515), reigned 1498–1515. ■ **Louis XIII** (1601–43), son of Henry IV of France; reigned 1610–43. During his minority the country was ruled by his mother Marie de Médicis. From 1624, he was heavily influenced in policymaking by his chief minister Cardinal Richelieu. ■ **Louis XIV** (1638–1715), son of Louis XIII; reigned 1643–1715; known as **the Sun King**. His reign represented the high point of the Bourbon dynasty and of French power in Europe. His almost constant wars of expansion united Europe against him, however, and gravely weakened France's financial position. ■ **Louis XV** (1710–74), great-grandson and successor of Louis XIV; reigned 1715–74. He led France into the Seven Years' War (1756–63). ■ **Louis XVI** (1754–93), grandson and successor of Louis XV; reigned 1774–92. His minor concessions and reforms in the face of the emerging French Revolution proved disastrous. As the revolution became more extreme, he was executed with his wife, Marie Antoinette, and the monarchy was abolished. ■ **Louis XVII** (1785–95), son of Louis XVI; titular king who died in prison during the revolution. ■ **Louis XVIII** (1755–1824), brother of Louis XVI; reigned 1814–24. After his nephew Louis XVII's death, he became titular king in exile until the fall of Napoleon in 1814, when he returned to Paris on the summons of Talleyrand and was officially restored to the throne.

Lou·is[2] /ˈlo͞o-is/, Joe (1914–81), U.S. heavyweight boxing champion; born *Joseph Louis Barrow*; known as the **Brown Bomber**. He was heavyweight champion of the world 1937–49, defending his title 25 times during that period.

Lou·is, St., Louis IX of France (see LOUIS[1]).

lou·is /ˈlo͞o-ē/ (also **louis d'or** /dôr/) ▸*n.* (*pl.* same) a gold coin issued in France between 1640 and 1793. ■ another term for NAPOLEON (sense 2). ▷from *Louis*, the name of many kings of France.

Lou·is I /ˈlo͞o-is; ˈlo͞o-ē/ (1326–82), king of Hungary 1342–82 and of Poland 1370–82; known as **Louis the Great**. Under his rule, Hungary became a powerful state; he fought two successful wars against Venice (1357–58; 1378–81), and the rulers of Serbia, Wallachia, Moldavia, and Bulgaria became his vassals.

Lou·i·si·an·a /lo͞o,ēzēˈanə/ a state in the southern U.S., on the Gulf of Mexico; pop. 4,468,976; capital, Baton Rouge; statehood, Apr. 30, 1812 (18). It was sold by the French to the U.S. as part of the Louisiana Purchase in 1803. ▷named in honor of *Louis* XIV. **—Lou·i·si·an·an** (also **Lou·i·si·an·i·an** /-nēən/) *adj. & n.*

Lou·i·si·an·a French ▸*n.* French as spoken in Louisiana, esp. by the descendants of the original French settlers; Cajun.

Lou·i·si·an·a Pur·chase the territory sold by France to the U.S. in 1803, comprising the western part of the Mississippi valley and including the modern state of Louisiana. The area had been explored by France, ceded to Spain in 1762, and returned to France in 1800.

Lou·is Phi·lippe /ˈlo͞o-ē fēˈlēp/ (1773–1850), king of France 1830–48. After the restoration of the Bourbons, he was made king, replacing Charles X. His regime was eventually overthrown.

Lou·is the Great, Louis I of Hungary (see LOUIS I).

Lou·is·ville /ˈlo͞oē,vil; ˈlo͞owəvəl/ an industrial city and river port in northern Kentucky, on the Ohio River just south of the border with Indiana; pop. 256,231. It is the site of the annual Kentucky Derby.

lounge /lounj/ ▸*v.* [*intrans.*] lie, sit, or stand in a relaxed or lazy way: *several students were lounging about reading papers.*
▸*n.* **1** a public room, as in a hotel, theater, or club, in which to sit and relax. ■ a spacious area in an airport with seats for waiting passengers: *the departure lounge.* ■ short for COCKTAIL LOUNGE. **2** a couch or sofa, esp. a backless one having a headrest at one end. ▷early 16th cent. (in the sense 'move indolently'): perhaps symbolic of slow movement. Sense 1 of the *noun* dates from the late 19th cent.

lounge·core /ˈlounj,kôr/ ▸*n.* songs from the 1960s and 1970s, including easy listening music, orchestral versions of rock songs, and television or movie theme songs.

lounge liz·ard ▸*n. informal* an idle person, usually a man, who spends time in lounges and nightclubs.

loung·er /ˈlounjər/ ▸*n.* a person spending their time lazily or in a relaxed way. ■ *chiefly Brit.* another term for CHAISE LONGUE.

lounge suit ▸*n. chiefly Brit.* a man's business suit.

lounge·wear /ˈlounj,we(ə)r/ ▸*n.* clothing suitable for leisure activities.

loupe /lo͞op/ ▸*n.* a small magnifying glass used by jewelers and watchmakers. ▷late 19th cent.: from French.

lour ▸*v. & n.* variant spelling of LOWER[3].

Lourdes /lo͝ord(z)/ a town in southwestern France, at the foot of the Pyrenees; pop. 17,000. It has been a major place of Roman Catholic pilgrimage since 1858 when a young peasant girl, Marie Bernarde Soubirous (St. Bernadette), claimed to have had a series of visions of the Virgin Mary.

Lou·ren·ço Mar·ques /ləˈrensō ˌmärˈkes/ former name, until 1976, of MAPUTO.

louse ▸*n.* /lous/ **1** (*pl.* **lice** /līs/) a small, wingless, parasitic insect that lives on the skin of mammals and birds: • (**sucking louse**) an insect with piercing mouthparts, found only on mammals (order Anoplura or Siphunculata). See also BODY LOUSE, HEAD LOUSE. • (**biting louse**) an insect with a large head and jaws, found chiefly on birds (order Mallophaga). ■ used in names of small invertebrates that parasitize aquatic animals or infest plants, e.g., **fish louse**. **2** (*pl.* **lous·es**) *informal* a contemptible or unpleasant person.
▸*v.* /lous; louz/ [*trans.*] **1** (**louse something up**) *informal* spoil or ruin something: *he loused up my promotion chances.* **2** *archaic* remove lice from. ▷Old English *lūs*, (plural) *lȳs*, of Germanic origin; related to Dutch *luis*, German *Laus*.

louse fly ▸*n.* a flattened bloodsucking fly that may have reduced or absent wings and typically spends much of its life on one individual of the host species. • Family Hippoboscidae: several genera.

louse·wort /ˈlous,wərt; -,wôrt/ ▸*n.* a partially parasitic herbaceous plant of the figwort family, typically favoring damp habitats. It is native to both Eurasia and North America and was formerly reputed to harbor lice. • Genus *Pedicularis*, family Scrophulariaceae: several species, including **wood betony** (*P. canadensis*) and **swamp lousewort** (*P. lanceolata*).

lous·y /ˈlouzē/ ▸*adj.* (**lous·i·er**, **lous·i·est**) **1** *informal* very poor or bad; disgusting: *the service is usually lousy | lousy weather.* ■ ill; in poor physical condition: *she felt lousy.* **2** infested with lice. ■ [*predic.*] (**lousy with**) *informal* teeming with (something regarded as bad or undesirable): *the town is lousy with tourists.* **—lous·i·ly** /-zəlē/ *adv.* **—lous·i·ness** *n.*

lout /lout/ ▸*n.* an uncouth or aggressive man or boy: *drunken louts.* ▷mid 16th cent.: perhaps from archaic *lout* 'to bow down,' of Germanic origin. **—lout·ish** *adj.* **—lout·ish·ly** *adv.* **—lout·ish·ness** *n.*

Louth /lou<u>th</u>; louth/ a county of the Republic of Ireland, on the eastern coast in the province of Leinster; county town, Dundalk.

lou·var /ˈlo͞o,vär/ ▸*n.* a large, brightly colored fish with a distinctive high forehead. It lives in warm open seas, feeding on jellyfishes and comb jellies. • *Luvarus imperialis*, the only member of the family Luvaridae.

lou·ver /ˈlo͞ovər/ (also **lou·vre**) ▸*n.* **1** each of a set of angled slats or flat strips fixed or hung at regular intervals in a door, shutter, or screen to allow air or light to pass through. **2** a domed structure on a roof, with side openings for ventilation. ▷Middle English (sense 2): from Old French *lover*, *lovier* 'skylight,' probably of Germanic origin and related to LODGE. **—lou·vered** *adj.*

louver 1

Louvre /ˈlo͞ov(rə)/ the principal museum and art gallery of France, in Paris, housed in the former royal palace built by Francis I. The Louvre holds the Mona Lisa and the Venus de Milo.

lov·a·ble /ˈləvəbəl/ (also **love·a·ble**) ▸*adj.* inspiring or deserving love or affection. **—lov·a·bil·i·ty** /ˌləvəˈbilətē/ *n.* **—lov·a·ble·ness** *n.* **—lov·a·bly** /-blē/ *adv.*

lov·age /ˈləvij/ ▸*n.* a large, edible, white-flowered plant of the parsley family. • Several species in the family Umbelliferae, in particular a Mediterranean herb (*Levisticum officinale*), which is chiefly used for flavoring liqueurs. ▷Middle English *loveache*, alteration (as if from LOVE + obsolete *ache* 'parsley') of Old French *luvesche*, *levesche*, via late Latin *levisticum* from Latin *ligusticum*, neuter of *ligusticus* 'Ligurian.'

lov·at /ˈləvət/ ▸*n.* a muted green color used esp. in tweed and woolen garments. ▷early 20th cent.: from *Lovat*, a place name in Highland Scotland.

love /ləv/ ▸*n.* **1** an intense feeling of deep affection: *babies fill parents with intense feelings of love | their* **love** *for their country.* ■ a deep romantic or sexual attachment to someone: *it was love at first sight | they were both* **in love with** *her | we were slowly* **falling in love**. ■ (**Love**) a personified figure of love, often represented as Cupid. ■ a great interest and pleasure in something: *his* **love for** *football | we share a* **love of** *music.* ■ affectionate greetings conveyed to someone on one's behalf. ■ a formula for ending an affectionate letter: *take care, lots of love, Judy.* **2** a person or thing that one loves: *she was* **the love of his life** *| their two great loves are tobacco and whiskey.* ■ *Brit., informal* a friendly form of address: *it's all right, love.* ■ (**a love**) *Brit., informal* used to express affectionate approval for someone: *don't fret, there's a love.* **3** (in tennis, squash, and some other sports) a score of zero; nil: *love fifteen | he was down two sets to love.* [apparently from the phrase *play for love* (i.e., the love of the game, not for money); folk etymology has connected the word with French *l'oeuf* 'egg,' from the resemblance in shape between an egg and a zero.]
▸*v.* [*trans.*] feel a deep romantic or sexual attachment to (someone): *do you love me?* ■ like very much; find pleasure in: *I'd love a cup of tea, thanks | I just love dancing |* [as *adj.*, in *combination*] (**-loving**) *a fun-loving girl.* ▷Old English *lufu*, of Germanic origin; from an Indo-European root shared by Sanskrit *lubhyati* 'desires,' Latin *libet* 'it is pleasing,' *libido* 'desire,' also by LEAVE[2] and LIEF. **—love·less** *adj.* **—love·less·ly** *adv.* **—love·less·ness** *n.* **—love·wor·thy** /-,wər<u>th</u>ē/ *adj.*
▸*PHRASES* □ **for love** for pleasure not profit: *he played* **for the love of** *the game.* □ **for the love of God** used to express annoyance, surprise, or urgent pleading: *for the love of God, get me out of here!* □ **for the love of Mike** *informal* used to accompany an exasperated request or to express dismay. □ **love me, love my dog** *proverb* if you love someone, you must accept everything about them, even their faults or weaknesses. □ **make love** **1** have sexual intercourse. **2** (**make love to**) *dated* pay amorous attention to (someone). □ **not for love or money** *informal* not for any inducement or in any circumstances: *they'll not return for love or money.* □ **there's no** (or **little** or **not much**) **love lost between** there is mutual dislike between (two or more people mentioned).

love·a·ble /ˈləvəbəl/ ▸*adj.* variant spelling of LOVABLE.

love af·fair ▸*n.* a romantic or sexual relationship between two people, esp. one that is outside marriage. ■ an intense enthusiasm or liking for something: *the great American love affair with the automobile.*

love ap·ple ▸*n.* an old-fashioned term for a tomato.

love beads ▸*n.* a necklace of small beads, esp. as worn by hippies in the 1960s as a symbol of peace and goodwill.

love·bird /ˈləv,bərd/ ▸*n.* **1** a very small African and Madagascan parrot with mainly green plumage and typically a red or black face, noted for the affectionate behavior of mated birds. • Genus *Agapornis*, family Psittacidae: several species. **2** (**lovebirds**) *informal* an openly affectionate couple.

love bite ▸*n.* a temporary red mark on a person's skin caused by a lover biting or sucking it as a sexual act; a hickey.

Love Ca·nal /ˈləv/ a section of Niagara Falls in New York that was evacuated after 1970s exposure that chemical wastes were buried in its residential neighborhood. It has been partially reoccupied.

love child ▸*n.* a child born to parents who are not married to each other.

love feast ▸*n. historical* a feast in token of fellowship among early Christians; an agape. ■ a religious service or gathering imitating this, esp. among early Methodists.

love game ▸*n.* (in tennis and similar sports) a game in which the loser makes no score.

love han·dles ▸*plural n. informal* deposits of excess fat at the sides of a person's waistline.

love-hate ▸*adj.* (of a relationship) characterized by ambivalent feelings of love and hate felt by one or each of two or more parties.

love-in ▸*n. informal* a gathering or party at which people are encouraged to express feelings of friendship and physical attraction, associated with the hippies of the 1960s. ▷1960s: originally with reference to Californian hippie gatherings.

love-in-a-mist ▸*n.* a Mediterranean plant of the buttercup family that bears blue flowers surrounded by delicate threadlike green bracts, giving a hazy appearance to the flowers. • *Nigella damascena*, family Ranunculaceae.

love-in-i·dle·ness ▸*n.* another term for HEARTSEASE.

love in·ter·est ▸*n.* a theme or subsidiary plot in a story or film in which the main element is the affection of lovers. ■ an actor whose role is chiefly concerned with this.

Love·lace[1] /ˈləvləs/, Ada Augusta Byron King, Countess of (1815–52), English mathematician. The daughter of Lord Byron, she worked with Charles Babbage on his "analytical engine," a mechanical computer. The Ada standardized computer language was named for her in 1980.

Love·lace[2] /ˈləvlās/, Richard (1618–57), English poet. A Royalist, he was imprisoned in 1642, when he probably wrote "To Althea, from Prison."

Love·land /ˈləvlənd/ a city in north central Colorado, between Denver and Fort Collins; pop. 50,608.

love-lies-bleed·ing ▸*n.* a South American plant with long, drooping tassels of crimson flowers. Cultivated today as an ornamental, it was formerly an important cereal-type crop in the Andes. • *Amaranthus caudatus*, family Amaranthaceae.

love life ▸*n.* the area of a person's life concerning their relationships with lovers.

Love·lock /ˈləvläk; -lək/, James (Ephraim) (1919–), English scientist. He is best known for the Gaia hypothesis, first presented by him in 1972 and discussed in several popular books, including *Gaia* (1979).

love·lock /ˈləv,läk/ ▸*n. archaic* a curl of hair worn on the temple or forehead.

love·lorn /ˈləv,lôrn/ ▸*adj.* unhappy because of unrequited love.

love·ly /ˈləvlē/ ▸*adj.* (**-li·er**, **-li·est**) exquisitely beautiful: *you have lovely eyes* | *lovely views.* ■ *informal* very pleasant or enjoyable; delightful: *we've had a lovely day* | *she's a lovely person.*
▸*n.* (*pl.* **-lies**) *informal* a glamorous woman or girl: *a bevy of rock lovelies.* ▷Old English *luflic* (see LOVE, -LY[1]). —**love·li·ly** /-ləlē/ *adv.* —**love·li·ness** *n.*

love·mak·ing /ˈləv,mākiNG/ ▸*n.* sexual activity between lovers, esp. sexual intercourse. ■ *archaic* courtship.

love match ▸*n.* a marriage based on the mutual love of the couple rather than social or financial considerations.

love nest ▸*n. informal* a place where two lovers spend time together, esp. in secret.

lov·er /ˈləvər/ ▸*n.* a person having a sexual or romantic relationship with someone, often outside marriage. ■ a person who likes or enjoys something specified: *he was a great lover of cats* | *music lovers.* —**lov·er·less** *adj.*

love seat ▸*n.* a small sofa for two people. ■ a small sofa for two people, designed in an S-shape so that the couple can face each other

love·sick /ˈləv,sik/ ▸*adj.* in love, or missing the person one loves, so much that one is unable to act normally: *a lovesick teenager.* —**love·sick·ness** *n.*

love·some /ˈləvsəm/ ▸*adj. poetic/literary* lovely or lovable.

love vine ▸*n.* the dodder, which is sometimes used medicinally and as a love charm.

love·ware /ˈləv,we(ə)r/ ▸*n. informal* computer software that is distributed freely, with the developer asking for the users to think kindly of the developer or of a dedicatee in lieu of payment.

lov·ey /ˈləvē/ ▸*n.* (*pl.* **-eys**) *Brit., informal* used as an affectionate form of address: *Ruth, lovey, are you there?*
▸*adj. Brit., informal* short for LOVEY-DOVEY.

lov·ey-dov·ey /ˈləvē ˈdəvē/ ▸*adj. informal* very affectionate or romantic, esp. excessively so: *a lovey-dovey couple.*

lov·ing /ˈləviNG/ ▸*adj.* feeling or showing love or great care: *a kind and loving father.*
▸*n.* the demonstration of love or great care. —**lov·ing·ly** *adv.* —**lov·ing·ness** *n.*

lov·ing cup ▸*n.* a large two-handled cup, passed around at banquets for each guest to drink from in turn.

lov·ing·kind·ness /,ləviNGˈkīn(d)nis/ ▸*n.* tenderness and consideration toward others. ▷from usage in Coverdale's translation of the Psalms.

Low /lō/, Juliette Gordon (1860–1927) U.S. youth leader. She founded the Girl Scouts of America in 1912, first calling them Girl Guides as they were known in England.

low[1] /lō/ ▸*adj.* **1** of less than average height from top to bottom or to the top from the ground: *the school is a long, low building* | *a low table.* ■ situated not far above the ground, the horizon, or sea level: *the sun was low in the sky.* ■ located at or near the bottom of something: *low back pain* | *there were stunted trees **low down** on the ridge.* ■ *Baseball* (of a pitched ball) below a certain level, such as the batter's knees, as it comes across home plate, and thus outside the strike zone. ■ (of a river or lake) below the usual water level; shallow. ■ (of latitude) near the equator. ■ (of women's clothing) cut so as to reveal the neck and the upper part of the breasts: *the low neckline of her blouse* | [in *combination*] *a low-cut black dress.* ■ *Phonetics* (of a vowel) pronounced with the tongue held low in the mouth; open. ■ (of a sound or note) deep: *his low, husky voice.* **2** below average in amount, extent, or intensity; small: *bringing up children on a low income* | *shops with low levels of staff and service* | *cook over low heat.* ■ (of a substance or food) containing smaller quantities than usual of a specified ingredient: *vegetables are **low in** calories* | [in *combination*] *low-fat spreads.* ■ (of a supply) small or reduced in quantity: *food and ammunition were **running low**.* ■ having a small or reduced quantity of a supply: *they were **low on** fuel.* ■ (of a sound) not loud: *they were told to keep the volume very low.* **3** ranking below other people or things in importance or class: *jobs with low status* | *training will be given low priority.* ■ (of art or culture) considered to be inferior in quality and refinement: *the dual traditions of high and low art.* ■ less good than is expected or desired; inferior: *the standard of living is low.* ■ unscrupulous or dishonest: *practice a little low cunning* | *low tricks.* ■ (of an opinion) unfavorable: *he had a low opinion of himself.* **4** depressed or lacking in energy: *I was feeling low.*
▸*n.* a low point, level or figure: *his popularity ratings are at an all-time low.* ■ a particularly bad or difficult moment: *the highs and lows of an actor's life.* ■ *informal* a state of depression or low spirits. ■ an area of low atmospheric pressure; a depression.
▸*adv.* **1** in or into a low position or state: *she pressed on, bent low to protect her face.* **2** quietly: *we were talking low so we wouldn't wake Dean.* ■ at or to a low pitch: *the sopranos have to sing rather low.* ▷Middle English: from Old Norse *lágr*, of Germanic origin; related to Dutch *laag*, also to LIE[1]. —**low·ness** *n.*
▸*PHRASE* □ **the lowest of the low** the people regarded as the most immoral or socially inferior of all.

low[2] ▸*v.* [*intrans.*] (of a cow) make a characteristic deep sound: [as *n.*] (**lowing**) *the lowing of cattle.*
▸*n.* a sound made by cattle; a moo. ▷Old English *hlōwan*, of Germanic origin; related to Dutch *loeien*, from an Indo-European root shared by Latin *clamare* 'to shout.'

low·ball /ˈlō,bôl/ ▸*adj. informal* (of an estimate, bid, etc.) deceptively or unrealistically low.
▸*v.* [*trans.*] offer a deceptively or unrealistically low estimate, bid, etc.: *are you being lowballed by someone who hopes to make money on extras later?* —**low·ball·ing** *n.*

low beam ▸*n.* an automobile headlight providing short-range illumination, used on lit roads and when visible to oncoming traffic.

low blow ▸*n. Boxing* an illegal blow that strikes below an opponent's waist. ■ *figurative* an unfair or unsportsmanlike comment.

low-born ▸*adj.* born to a family that has a low social status.

low·boy /ˈlō,boi/ ▸*n.* a low chest or table with drawers and short legs. Compare with HIGHBOY.

low·bred /ˈlōˈbred/ ▸*adj.* characterized by coarse behavior or vulgar breeding.

low·brow /ˈlō,brou/ ▸*adj.* not highly intellectual or cultured: *lowbrow tabloids.*
▸*n.* a person of such a type.

low-carb (also **lo-carb**) ▸*adj.* low in carbohydrates.

Low Church ▸*adj.* of or adhering to a tradition within the Anglican Church (and some other denominations) that is Protestant in outlook and gives relatively little emphasis to ritual, sacraments, and the authority of the clergy. Compare with HIGH CHURCH, BROAD CHURCH.
▸*n.* [treated as *sing.* or *pl.*] the principles or adherents of this tradition. —**Low Church·man** *n.* (*pl.* **-men**).

low-class ▸*adj.* of a low or inferior standard, quality, or social class: *low-class places of amusement.*

low com·e·dy ▸*n.* comedy in which the subject and the treatment border on farce.

Low Coun·tries the region of northwestern Europe that includes the Netherlands, Belgium, and Luxembourg.

low-den·si·ty ▸*adj.* having a low concentration.

low-den·si·ty lip·o·pro·tein (abbr.: **LDL**) ▸*n.* the form of lipoprotein in which cholesterol is transported in the blood.

low-down /ˈlō,doun/ *informal* ▸*adj.* mean and unfair: *dirty lowdown tricks.*
▸*n.* (**the lowdown**) the true facts or relevant information about something: *get the lowdown on the sit-in.*

Low·ell[1] /ˈlōəl/ a city in northeastern Massachusetts, on the Concord and Merrimack rivers, developed after 1822 as a planned industrial community based on textile manufacturing; pop. 105,167.

Low·ell[2], Amy (Lawrence) (1874–1925), U.S. poet. She is known for her polyphonic prose and sensuous imagery. Notable works: *A Critical Fable* (1922) and *What's O'Clock* (1925).

Low·ell[3], James Russell (1819–91), U.S. poet and critic. His works include the satirical *Biglow Papers* (1848 and 1867) and volumes of essays including *Among My Books* (1870) and *My Study Window* (1871).

Low·ell[4], Percival (1855–1916), U.S. astronomer. He inferred the existence of a ninth planet beyond Neptune. When it was eventually discovered in 1930, it was given the name Pluto, with a symbol that also included his initials. He was the brother of poet Amy Lowell.

Low·ell[5], Robert (Traill Spence) (1917–77), U.S. poet. His poetry, often describing his manic depression, is notable for its intense confessional nature and for its complex imagery. Notable works: *Lord Weary's Castle* (1946), *Life Studies* (1959), and *The Dolphin* (1973).

low-end ▸*adj.* denoting the cheaper products of a range, esp. of audio or computer equipment.

low·er[1] /ˈlōər/ ▸*adj.* **1** comparative of LOW[1]. **2** less high: *the lower levels of the building* | *managers lower down the hierarchy.* ■ (of an animal or plant) showing relatively primitive or simple characteristics. ■ (often **Lower**) *Geology & Archaeology* denoting an older (and hence usually deeper) part of a stratigraphic division or archaeological deposit or the period in which it was formed or deposited: *Lower Cretaceous* | *Lower Paleolithic.* ■ *chiefly Brit.* (in names of grades in schools) denoting the first of two conventionally numbered grades through which students pass in successive years: *he left school in the lower sixth.* **3** [in *place names*] situated on less high land or to the south or toward the sea: *the sweatshops of the Lower East Side.*
▸*adv.* in or into a lower position: *the sun sank lower.* —**low·er·most** /-,mōst/ *adj.*

low·er[2] /ˈlōər/ ▸*v.* [*trans.*] move (someone or something) in a downward direction: *he watched the coffin being lowered into the ground.* ■ reduce the height, pitch, or elevation of: *she lowered her voice to a whisper.* ■ make or become less in amount, extent, or value: [*trans.*] *traffic speeds must be lowered* | [*intrans.*] *temperatures lowered.* ■ direct (one's eyes) downward. ■ (**lower oneself**) behave in a way that is perceived as unworthy or debased.
▸*PHRASE* □ **lower the boom on** *informal* treat or reprimand (someone) severely. ■ put a stop to (an activity): *let's lower the boom on high-level corruption.*

low·er[3] /ˈlou(ə)r/ (also **lour**) ▸*v.* [*intrans.*] look angry or sullen; frown: *the lofty statue lowers at patients in the infirmary.* ■ (of the sky, weather, or landscape) look dark and threatening: [as *adj.*] (**lowering**) *a day of lowering clouds.*
▸*n.* a scowl. ■ a dark and gloomy appearance of the sky, weather or landscape. ▷Middle English: of unknown origin. —**low·er·ing·ly** *adv.*

low·er an·i·mals /ˈlōər/ ▸*plural n.* animals of relatively simple or primitive characteristics as contrasted with humans or with more advanced animals such as mammals or vertebrates.

Low·er Cal·i·for·nia another name for BAJA CALIFORNIA.

Low·er Can·a·da the mainly French-speaking region of Canada around the lower St. Lawrence River, in what is now southern Quebec.

low·er·case /ˈlōər,kās/ (also **low·er case**) ▸*n.* small letters as opposed to capital letters (uppercase): *the* *name may be typed in lowercase* | [as *adj.*] *lowercase letters.* ▷referring originally to the lower of two cases of type positioned on an angled stand for use by a compositor (see UPPERCASE).

low·er cham·ber /ˈlōər/ ▶*n.* another term for LOWER HOUSE.

low·er class /ˈlōər/ ▶*n.* [treated as *sing.* or *pl.*] the social group that has the lowest status; the working class.
▶*adj.* of, relating to, or characteristic of people belonging to such a group: *a lower-class area.*

low·er court /ˈlōər/ ▶*n. Law* a court whose decisions may be overruled by another court on appeal.

low·er crit·i·cism /ˈlōər/ ▶*n. dated* another term for TEXTUAL CRITICISM (esp. as applied to the Bible, in contrast to HIGHER CRITICISM).

low·er deck /ˈlōər/ ▶*n.* the deck of a ship situated immediately above the hold.

Low·er East Side a district of southeastern Manhattan in New York City, noted as home to immigrants from the 1880s through the early 20th century.

Low·er Forty-eight (States) a term for the 48 contiguous U.S. states, excluding Alaska and Hawaii.

low·er house /ˈlōər/ ▶*n.* the larger of two sections of a bicameral legislature or parliament, typically with elected members and having the primary responsibility for legislation. ■ (**the Lower House**) (in the UK) the House of Commons.

Low·er Mer·i·on /ˈmerēən/ a township in southeastern Pennsylvania that contains many suburban communities northwest of Philadelphia; pop. 59,850.

low·er or·ders /ˈlōər/ ▶*plural n. dated* the lower classes of society.

low·er plants /ˈlōər/ ▶*plural n.* plants of relatively simple or primitive characteristics, esp. those that are not vascular plants, i.e., algae, mosses, liverworts, and sometimes fungi.

low·er re·gions /ˈlōər/ ▶*plural n. archaic* hell or the underworld.

Low·er Sax·o·ny a state of northwestern Germany; capital, Hanover. It corresponds to the northwestern part of the former kingdom of Saxony. German name NIEDERSACHSEN.

low·er school /ˈlōər/ ▶*n.* the section of a larger school that educates younger students, esp. those below the fifth grade.

low·est com·mon de·nom·i·na·tor ▶*n. Mathematics* the lowest common multiple of the denominators of several fractions. ■ *figurative* the broadest or most widely applicable requirement or circumstance. ■ *derogatory* the level of the least discriminating audience or consumer group: *they were accused of pandering to the lowest common denominator of public taste.*

low·est com·mon mul·ti·ple (abbr.: **LCM**) ▶*n. Mathematics* the lowest quantity that is a multiple of two or more given quantities (e.g., 12 is the lowest common multiple of 2, 3, and 4).

low-fi ▶*adj.* variant spelling of LO-FI.

low fre·quen·cy ▶*n.* (in radio) 30–300 kilohertz.

low gear ▶*n.* a gear that causes a wheeled vehicle to move slowly, because of a low ratio between the speed of the wheels and that of the mechanism driving them.

Low Ger·man ▶*n.* a vernacular language spoken in much of northern Germany, more closely related to Dutch than to standard German. Also called PLATTDEUTSCH.

low-grade ▶*adj.* of low quality or strength: *low-grade steel* | *low-grade fuels.* ■ at a low level in a salary or employment structure: *low-grade clerical jobs.* ■ (of a medical condition) of a less serious kind; minor: *a low-grade fever.*

low-hang·ing fruit /ˈlō ˌhaNGiNG ˈfro͞ot/ ▶*n. informal* a thing or person that can be won, obtained, or persuaded with little effort: *we know mining our own customer base is low-hanging fruit.* ▷because such fruit is easy to pick.

low-im·pact /ˈimˌpakt/ ▶*adj.* [*attrib.*] **1** denoting exercises, typically aerobics, designed to put little or no harmful stress on the body. **2** (of an activity, industry, or product) affecting or altering the environment as little as possible.

low-key ▶*adj.* not elaborate, showy, or intensive; modest or restrained: *their wedding was a very quiet, low-key affair.* ■ *Art & Photography* having a predominance of dark or muted tones.
▶*v.* [*trans.*] behave or speak with restraint: [as *adj.*] *a very simple, low-keyed style.*

low·land /ˈlōlənd; -ˌland/ ▶*n.* (also **lowlands**) low-lying country: *economic power gravitated toward the lowlands* | [as *adj.*] *lowland farming.* ■ (**the Lowlands**) the region of Scotland lying south and east of the Highlands. —**low·land·er** (also **Low·land·er**) *n.*

Low Lat·in ▶*n.* medieval and later forms of Latin.

low lat·i·tudes ▶*plural n.* regions near the equator.

low-lev·el ▶*adj.* situated relatively near or below ground level: *low-level flying was banned.* ■ of or showing a small degree of some measurable quantity, for example radioactivity: *the dumping of low-level waste.* ■ of relatively little importance, scope, or prominence; basic: *opportunities to progress beyond low-level jobs.* ■ *Computing* of or relating to programming languages or operations that are relatively close to machine code in form.

low·life /ˈlōˌlīf/ (also **low life**) ▶*n.* people or activities characterized as being disreputable and often criminal: *crackheads, loafers, and general Nineties low life.* —**low·lif·er** *n.*

low·light /ˈlōˌlīt/ ▶*n. informal* a particularly disappointing or dull event or feature. ▷early 20th cent.: from LOW[1], suggested by HIGHLIGHT.

low·ly /ˈlōlē/ ▶*adj.* (**low·li·er**, **low·li·est**) low in status or importance; humble: *she was too good for her lowly position.* ■ (of an organism) primitive or simple.
▶*adv.* to a low degree; in a low manner: *lowly paid workers.* —**low·li·ly** /ˈlōlə,lē/ *adv.* —**low·li·ness** *n.*

low-ly·ing ▶*adj.* at low altitude above sea level: *flooding problems in low-lying areas.*

low-main·te·nance /ˈlō ˈmānt(ə)nəns; ˈmāntn-əns/ ▶*adj.* requiring little work to keep in good condition: *low-maintenance lawns.* ■ *informal* (of living and abstract things) desirably trouble-free and undemanding: *the shift toward the low-maintenance small companion dog.*

Low Mass ▶*n.* (in the Roman Catholic Church) formerly, a Mass with no music and a minimum of ceremony.

low-mind·ed ▶*adj.* vulgar or sordid in mind or character. —**low-mind·ed·ness** *n.*

low-necked ▶*adj.* (of a dress or garment) cut so as to leave the neck and shoulders exposed; décolleté.

low·pass /ˈlōˌpas/ ▶*adj. Electronics* (of a filter) transmitting all frequencies below a certain value.

low-pitched ▶*adj.* **1** (of a sound or voice) deep or relatively quiet. **2** (of a roof) having only a slight slope.

low post ▶*n. Basketball* an offensive position on the court close to the basket.

low pro·file ▶*n.* [in *sing.*] a position of avoiding or not attracting much attention or publicity: *he's not the sort of politician to **keep a low profile**.*
▶*adj.* **1** avoiding attention or publicity: *a low-profile campaign.* **2** (of an object) lower or slimmer than is usual for objects of its type. ■ (of a motor vehicle tire) of smaller diameter and greater width than usual, for high-performance use.

low re·lief ▶*n. Sculpture* another term for BAS-RELIEF (see RELIEF sense 4).

low-res /ˈlō ˈrez/ ▶*adj. informal* (of a display or an image) showing a small amount of detail. ▷late 20th cent.: from *low-resolution.*

low-res·o·lu·tion ▶*adj. Computing* of or relating to a visual output device, such as a CRT or a printer, whose images are not sharply defined. ■ of or relating to an image that lacks sharp focus or fine detail.

low·rid·er /ˈlōˌrīdər/ ▶*n.* a customized vehicle with hydraulic jacks that allow the chassis to be lowered nearly to the road. —**low·rid·ing** /-ˌrīdiNG/ *n.*

low-rise ▶*adj.* (of a building) having few stories: *low-rise apartment blocks.*
▶*n.* a building having few stories.

low road ▶*n. informal* a behavior or approach that is unscrupulous or immoral.

low spir·its ▶*plural n.* a feeling of sadness and despondency: *he was **in low spirits**.* —**low-spir·it·ed** *adj.* —**low-spir·it·ed·ness** *n.*

Low Sun·day ▶*n.* the Sunday after Easter. ▷perhaps so named in contrast to the high days of Holy Week and Easter.

low-tech /ˈlō ˈtek/ (also **lo-tech**) ▶*adj.* involved in, employing, or requiring only low technology: *low-tech solar heating systems.*
▶*n.* (**low tech**) short for LOW TECHNOLOGY.

low tech·nol·o·gy ▶*n.* less advanced or relatively unsophisticated technological development or equipment.

low ten·sion (also **low voltage**) ▶*n.* an electrical potential not large enough to cause injury or damage if diverted.

low tide ▶*n.* the state of the tide when at its lowest level: *islets visible **at low tide**.*

low wa·ter ▶*n.* another term for LOW TIDE. ■ water in a stream or river at its lowest point.

low-wa·ter mark ▶*n.* the lowest level reached by the sea at low tide, or by a lake or river during a drought or dry season. ■ a minimum recorded level or value: *the market was approaching its low-water mark.*

Low Week ▶*n.* the week that begins with Low Sunday.

low-yield ▶*adj.* producing little; giving a low return: *low-yield investment.* ■ (of a nuclear weapon) having a relatively low explosive force.

lox[1] /läks/ (also **LOX**) ▶*n.* liquid oxygen. ▷early 20th cent.: acronym from *liquid oxygen explosive*, later interpreted as being from *liquid oxygen.*

lox[2] ▶*n.* smoked salmon. ▷1940s: from Yiddish *laks.*

lox·o·drome /ˈläksəˌdrōm/ ▶*n.* another term for RHUMB (sense 1).

Loy /loi/, Myrna (1905–93) U.S. actress; born Myrna Williams. She played Nora Charles in *The Thin Man* (1934) and in the five *Thin Man* movies that followed. She also starred in *The Best Years of Our Lives* (1946), *Mr. Blanding Builds His Dream House* (1948), and *Cheaper by the Dozen* (1950). She received a Lifetime Achievement Award at the 1991 Academy Award ceremonies.

loy·a jir·ga /ˈloiə/ ▶*n.* see JIRGA.

loy·al /ˈloiəl/ ▶*adj.* giving or showing firm and constant support or allegiance to a person or institution: *he remained **loyal to** the government* | *loyal service.* ▷mid 16th cent.: from French, via Old French *loial* from Latin *legalis* (see LEGAL). —**loy·al·ly** *adv.*

loy·al·ist /ˈloiəlist/ ▶*n.* a person who remains loyal to the established ruler or government, esp. in the face of a revolt. ■ (**Loyalist**) a colonist of the American revolutionary period who supported the British cause. ■ (**Loyalist**) a supporter of union between Great Britain and Northern Ireland. ■ (**Loyalist**) a supporter of the republic and opposer of Franco's revolt in the Spanish Civil War. —**loy·al·ism** /-ˌlizəm/ *n.*

loy·al·ty /ˈloiəltē/ ▶*n.* (*pl.* **-ties**) the quality of being loyal to someone or something: *her **loyalty to** her husband of 34 years.* ■ (often **loyalties**) a strong feeling of support or allegiance: *fights with in-laws are distressing because they cause **divided loyalties**.*

Loy·al·ty Is·lands a group of islands in the southwestern Pacific Ocean that forms part of the French overseas territory of New Caledonia; pop. 18,000.

loz·enge /ˈläzənj/ ▶*n.* a rhombus or diamond shape. ■ a small medicinal tablet, originally of this shape, taken for sore throats and dissolved in the mouth: *throat lozenges.* ■ *Heraldry* a charge in the shape of a solid diamond, in particular one on which the arms of an unmarried or widowed woman are displayed. ▷Middle English: from Old French *losenge*, probably derived from the base of Spanish *losa*, Portuguese *lousa* 'slab,' late Latin *lausiae (lapides)* 'stone slabs.'

LP ▶*abbr.* ■ long-playing (phonograph record): *two LP records* | *a collection of LPs.* ■ low pressure.

l.p. ▶*abbr.* low pressure.

LPG ▶*abbr.* liquefied petroleum gas.

LPGA ▶*abbr.* Ladies' Professional Golf Association.

LPM (also **lpm**) ▶*abbr.* lines per minute.

LPN ▶*abbr.* Licensed Practical Nurse. See PRACTICAL NURSE.

LR ▶*abbr.* ■ living room. ■ lower right. ■ low rate.

L/R ▶*abbr.* left/right.

Lr ▶*symbol* the chemical element lawrencium.

LRV ▶*abbr.* lunar roving vehicle.

LSAT ▶*abbr.* Law School Admission Test.

LSB *Computing* ▶*abbr.* least significant bit.

LSD ▶*n.* a synthetic crystalline compound, lysergic acid diethylamide, that is a potent hallucinogenic drug. • Chem. formula: $C_{20}H_{26}N_2O$. ▷mid 20th cent.: abbreviation.

LSI ▶*abbr.* large-scale integration.

Lt. ▶*abbr.* ■ lieutenant. ■ (also **lt**) light.

lt. ▶*abbr.* light.

l.t. ▶*abbr.* ■ *Football* left tackle. ■ local time. ■ long ton.

Lt. Col. (also **LTC**) ▶*abbr.* lieutenant colonel.

Lt. Comdr. (also **Lt. Com.**) ▶*abbr.* lieutenant commander.

Ltd. ▶*abbr.* (after a company name) Limited.

Lt. Gen. (also **LTG**) ▶*abbr.* lieutenant general.

Lt. Gov. ▶*abbr.* lieutenant governor.

LTJG ▶*abbr.* lieutenant junior grade.

LTP ▶*abbr.* long-term potentiation. See POTENTIATION.

LTR ▶*abbr.* (in personal ads) long-term relationship.

Lu ▶*symbol* the chemical element lutetium.

Lu·a·la·ba /ˌlo͞oəˈläbə/ a river in central Africa that

rises near the southern border of the Democratic Republic of the Congo (formerly Zaire) and flows north for about 400 miles (640 km) before it joins the Lomami River to form the Congo River.

Lu·an·da /lo͞o'ändə/ the capital of Angola, a port on the Atlantic coast; pop. 2,250,000.

Luang Pra·bang /lo͞o,äNG prə'bäNG/ (also **Louang·phra·bang**) a city in northwestern Laos, on the Mekong River; pop. 44,000. It was the royal residence and Buddhist religious center of Laos until the end of the monarchy in 1975.

lu·au /'lo͞o,ou/ ▸*n.* (*pl.* same or **lu·aus**) a Hawaiian party or feast, esp. one accompanied by entertainment. ▷from Hawaiian *lu'au.*

Lu·ba /'lo͞obə/ ▸*n.* (*pl.* same or **Lu·bas**) **1** a member of a people living mainly in southeastern Democratic Republic of the Congo (formerly Zaire). **2** the Bantu language of this people. Also called **CHILUBA.**
▸*adj.* of or relating to the Luba or their language. ▷a local name.

Lu·ba·vitch·er /'lo͞obə,viCHər; lo͞o'bäviCHər/ ▸*n.* a member of a Hasidic community founded in the 1700s by Rabbi Shneour Zalman.

lub·ber /'ləbər/ ▸*n.* **1** *archaic* or *dialect* a big, clumsy person. **2** short for **LANDLUBBER.** ▷late Middle English: perhaps via Old French *lobeor* 'swindler, parasite' from *lober* 'deceive.' **—lub·ber·like** /-,līk/ *adj.* **—lub·ber·ly** *adj.* & *adv.*

lub·ber's line (also **lub·ber line**) ▸*n.* a line marked on the compass in a ship or aircraft, showing the direction straight ahead.

Lub·bock /'ləbək/ a city in northwestern Texas; pop. 199,564.

lube /lo͞ob/ *informal* ▸*n.* a lubricant. ■ lubrication: [as *adj.*] *a lube job.*
▸*v.* [*trans.*] lubricate (something). ▷1930s: abbreviation.

Lü·beck /'lo͞o,bek; 'lY-/ a port in northern Germany, on the Baltic coast in Schleswig-Holstein, northeast of Hamburg; pop. 211,000. Between the 14th and 19th centuries it was an important city within the Hanseatic League.

Lu·bian·ka variant spelling of **LUBYANKA.**

Lub·lin /'lo͞oblən; 'lo͞o,blēn/ a manufacturing city in eastern Poland; pop. 351,000.

lu·bri·cant /'lo͞obrəkənt/ ▸*n.* a substance, such as oil or grease, used for minimizing friction, esp. in an engine or component.
▸*adj.* lubricating: *a thin lubricant film.* ▷early 19th cent.: from Latin *lubricant-* 'making slippery,' from the verb *lubricare* (see **LUBRICATE**).

lu·bri·cate /'lo͞obrə,kāt/ ▸*v.* [*trans.*] apply a substance such as oil or grease to (an engine or component) to minimize friction and allow smooth movement: *remove the nut and lubricate the thread* | [as *adj.*] (**lubricating**) *lubricating oils.* ■ make (something) slippery or smooth by applying an oily substance. ■ *figurative* make (a process) run smoothly: *the availability of credit lubricated the channels of trade.* ■ *figurative* make someone convivial, esp. with alcohol: *men lubricated with alcohol speak their true feelings.* ▷early 17th cent.: from Latin *lubricat-* 'made slippery,' from the verb *lubricare,* from *lubricus* 'slippery.' **—lu·bri·ca·tion** /,lo͞obrə'kāSHən/ *n.* **—lu·bri·ca·tor** /-,kātər/ *n.*

lu·bri·cious /lo͞o'briSHəs/ (also **lu·bri·cous** /'lo͞obrikəs/) ▸*adj.* **1** offensively displaying or intended to arouse sexual desire. **2** smooth and slippery with oil or a similar substance. ▷late 16th cent.: from Latin *lubricus* 'slippery' + **-IOUS.** **—lu·bri·cious·ly** *adv.* **—lu·bric·i·ty** /-'brisitē/ *n.*

Lu·bum·ba·shi /,lo͞obo͞om'bäSHē/ a city in southeastern Democratic Republic of the Congo (formerly Zaire), near the border with Zambia, capital of the region of Shaba; pop. 739,000. Former name (until 1966) **ELISABETHVILLE.**

Lu·byan·ka /lo͞o'byäNGkə/ (also **Lu·bian·ka**) a building in Moscow used as a prison and as the headquarters of the KGB and other Russian secret police organizations since the Russian Revolution.

Lucan[1] /'lo͝okən/ (AD 39–65), Roman poet, born in Spain; Latin name *Marcus Annaeus Lucanus.* He was forced to commit suicide after joining a conspiracy against Nero. His major work is *Pharsalia,* an epic in ten books dealing with the civil war between Julius Caesar and Pompey.

Lu·can[2] /'lo͞okən/ ▸*adj.* of or relating to St. Luke. ▷via ecclesiastical Latin from Greek *Loukas* 'Luke' + **-AN.**

Lu·cas /'lo͞okəs/, George (1944–), U.S. movie director, producer, and screenwriter. He wrote, directed, and produced the science-fiction movie *Star Wars* (1977) and then went on to write and produce *The Empire Strikes Back* (1980), *Return of the Jedi* (1983), and *Star Wars: Episode I: The Phantom Menace* (1999). He also wrote and produced the "Indiana Jones" series of movies (1981–89).

Luce[1] /lo͞os/, Clare Boothe (1903–87) U.S. playwright and public official; wife of Henry Robinson Luce. After a stint as managing editor of the magazine *Vanity Fair* 1929–34, she wrote the plays *The Women* (1936), *Kiss the Boys Goodbye* (1938), and *Margin for Error* (1939). She was a war correspondent during World War II, served in the U.S. House of Representatives 1943–46 as a Republican from Connecticut, and was U.S. ambassador to Italy 1953–57. Presidential Medal of Freedom (1983).

Luce[2], Henry Robinson (1898–1967) U.S. publisher and editor; born in China of U.S. parents; husband of Clare Boothe Luce. He cofounded *Time,* a weekly news magazine, in 1924. He later launched several other magazines: *Fortune* (1929), *Life* (1936), *House and Home* (1952), and *Sports Illustrated* (1954).

luce /lo͞os/ ▸*n.* (*pl.* same) a pike (fish), esp. when full-grown. ▷late Middle English: via Old French *lus, luis* from late Latin *lucius.*

lu·cent /'lo͞osənt/ ▸*adj. poetic/literary* glowing with or giving off light: *the moon was lucent in the background.* ▷late Middle English: from Latin *lucent-* 'shining,' from the verb *lucere* (see **LUCID**). **—lu·cen·cy** *n.*

Lu·cerne /lo͞o'sərn/ a resort on the western shore of Lake Lucerne, in central Switzerland; pop. 59,000. German name **LUZERN.**

Lu·cerne, Lake a lake in central Switzerland, surrounded by the four cantons of Lucerne, Nidwalden, Uri, and Schwyz. Also called **FOUR CANTONS, LAKE OF THE;** German name **VIERWALDSTÄTTERSEE.**

lu·cerne /lo͞o'sərn/ ▸*n. chiefly Brit.* another term for **ALFALFA.** ▷mid 17th cent.: from French *luzerne,* from modern Provençal *luzerno* 'glowworm' (with reference to its shiny seeds).

lu·cid /'lo͞osid/ ▸*adj.* **1** expressed clearly; easy to understand: *a lucid account* | *write in a clear and lucid style.* See note at **SENSIBLE.** ■ showing ability to think clearly, esp. in the intervals between periods of confusion or insanity: *he has a few lucid moments every now and then.* ■ *Psychology* (of a dream) experienced with the dreamer feeling awake, aware of dreaming, and able to control events consciously. **2** *poetic/literary* bright or luminous: *birds dipped their wings in the lucid flow of air.* ▷late 16th cent. (sense 2): from Latin *lucidus* (perhaps via French *lucide* or Italian *lucido*), from *lucere* 'shine,' from *lux, luc-* 'light.' **—lu·cid·i·ty** /lo͞o'sidətē/ *n.* **—lu·cid·ly** *adv.* **—lu·cid·ness** *n.*

Lu·ci·fer /'lo͞osəfər/ ▸*n.* **1** another name for **SATAN.** [by association with the 'son of the morning' (Isa. 14:12), believed by Christian interpreters to be a reference to Satan.] **2** *poetic/literary* the planet Venus when it rises in the morning. **3** (**lucifer**) *archaic* a match struck by rubbing it on a rough surface. ▷Old English, from Latin, 'light-bringing, morning star,' from *lux, luc-* 'light' + *-fer* 'bearing.'

lu·cif·u·gous /lo͞o'sifyəgəs/ ▸*adj. chiefly Zoology* shunning the light. ▷mid 17th cent.: from Latin *lucifugus* (from *lux, luc-* 'light' + *fugere* 'to fly') + **-OUS.**

lu·cine /'lo͞o,sīn/ ▸*n.* a bivalve mollusk that typically has a rounded white shell with radial and concentric ridges, found in tropical and temperate seas. • Family Lucinidae: *Lucina* and other genera.

Lu·cite /'lo͞o,sīt/ (also **lu·cite**) ▸*n. trademark* a solid transparent plastic made of polymethyl methacrylate (the same material as Perspex or Plexiglas). ▷1930s: from Latin *lux, luc-* 'light' + **-ITE**[1].

luck /lək/ ▸*n.* success or failure apparently brought by chance rather than through one's own actions: *it was just luck that the first kick went in* | *this charm was supposed to bring* ***good luck.*** ■ chance considered as a force that causes good or bad things to happen: *luck was with me.* ■ something regarded as bringing about or portending good or bad things: *I don't like Friday—it's* ***bad luck.***
▸*v.* [*intrans.*] (**luck into/onto**) *informal* chance to find or acquire: *he lucked into a disc-jockey job.* ■ (**luck out**) achieve success or advantage by good luck: *I lucked out and found a wonderful woman.* ▷late Middle English (as a verb): perhaps from Middle Low German or Middle Dutch *lucken.* The noun use (late 15th cent.) is from Middle Low German *lucke,* related to Dutch *geluk,* German *Glück,* of West Germanic origin and possibly related to **LOCK**[1].
▸*PHRASES* □ **as luck would have it** used to indicate the fortuitousness of a situation: *as luck would have it, his route took him very near where they lived.* □ **tough luck** *informal* used to express a lack of sympathy: *tough luck if they complain.* □ **be in** (or **out of**) **luck** be fortunate (or unfortunate). □ **for luck** to bring good fortune: *I wear this crystal under my costume for luck.* □ **good** (or **the best of**) **luck** used to express wishes for success: ***good luck*** *with your studies!* □ **the luck of the draw** the outcome of chance rather than something one can control: *quality of care depends largely on the luck of the draw.* □ **no such luck** *informal* used to express disappointment that something has not happened or is unlikely to happen. □ **try one's luck** do something that involves risk or luck, hoping to succeed: *he thought he'd* ***try his luck at*** *farming in Canada.* □ **with** (**any** or **a little** or **a bit of**) **luck** expressing the hope that something will happen in the way described: *with luck we should be there in time for breakfast.* □ **worse luck** *Brit., informal* used to express regret about something: *I have to go to secretarial school, worse luck.*

luck·i·ly /'ləkəlē/ ▸*adv.* [*sentence adverb*] it is fortunate that: *luckily they didn't recognize me* | ***luckily for*** *me it's worked out.*

luck·less /'ləkləs/ ▸*adj.* having bad luck; unfortunate. **—luck·less·ly** *adv.* **—luck·less·ness** *n.*

Luck·now /'lək,nou/ a city in northern India, capital of the state of Uttar Pradesh; pop. 1,592,000. In 1857, during the Indian Mutiny, its British residents were besieged by Indian insurgents twice.

luck·y /'ləkē/ ▸*adj.* (**luck·i·er, luck·i·est**) having, bringing, or resulting from good luck: *you had a very lucky escape* | *three's my lucky number.* **—luck·i·ness** *n.*
▸*PHRASES* □ **you, he,** etc., **should be so lucky** used to imply in an ironic or resigned way that someone's wishes or expectations are unlikely to be fulfilled: *"Moving in?" "You should be so lucky."* □ **lucky devil** (or **lucky you, her,** etc.) used to express envy at someone else's good fortune.

luck·y dip ▸*n.* British term for **GRAB BAG.**

lu·cra·tive /'lo͞okrətiv/ ▸*adj.* producing a great deal of profit: *a lucrative career as a stand-up comedian.* ▷late Middle English: from Latin *lucrativus,* from *lucrat-* 'gained,' from the verb *lucrari,* from *lucrum* (see **LUCRE**). **—lu·cra·tive·ly** *adv.* **—lu·cra·tive·ness** *n.*

lu·cre /'lo͞okər/ ▸*n.* money, esp. when regarded as sordid or distasteful or gained in a dishonorable way: *officials getting their hands grubby with* ***filthy lucre.*** ▷late Middle English: from French *lucre* or Latin *lucrum;* the phrase *filthy lucre* is with biblical allusion to Tit. 1:11.

Lu·cre·tia /lo͞o'krēSHə/ (in Roman legend) a woman who was raped by a son of Tarquinius Superbus and took her own life; this led to the expulsion of the Tarquins from Rome by a rebellion under Brutus.

Lu·cre·tius /lo͞o'krēSHəs/ (*c.*94–*c.*55 BC), Roman poet and philosopher; full name *Titus Lucretius Carus.* His didactic epic poem *On the Nature of Things* is an exposition of the materialist atomist physics of Epicurus.

lu·cu·brate /'lo͞ok(y)ə,brāt/ ▸*v.* [*intrans.*] *archaic* discourse learnedly in writing. ▷early 17th cent.: from Latin *lucubrat-* '(having) worked by lamplight,' from the verb *lucubrare.* **—lu·cu·bra·tor** /-,brātər/ *n.*

lu·cu·bra·tion /,lo͞ok(y)ə'brāSHən/ ▸*n. formal* study; meditation: *after sixteen years' lucubration he produced this account.* ■ (usu. **lucubrations**) a piece of writing, typically a pedantic or overelaborate one. ▷late 16th cent.: from Latin *lucubratio(n-),* from the verb *lucubrare* (see **LUCUBRATE**).

Lu·cul·lan /lo͞o'kələn/ ▸*adj.* (esp. of food) extremely luxurious: *Lucullan feasts.* ▷mid 19th cent.: from the name of Licinius *Lucullus,* Roman general of the 1st cent. BC, famous for giving lavish banquets, + **-AN.**

Lu·cy /'lo͞osē/ the nickname of a partial female skeleton of a fossil hominid found in Ethiopia in 1974, about 3.2 million years old and 4 feet (1.2 m) in height. • *Australopithecus afarensis,* family Hominidae. This species is regarded by many as the ancestor of all subsequent *Australopithecus* and *Homo* species.

Lu·da /'lo͞o'dä/ an industrial center and port in northeastern China, in the province of Liaoning at the southeastern tip of the Liaodong Peninsula; pop. 1,630,000. It consists of the cities of Lushun and Dalian.

Lud·dite /'ləd,īt/ ▸*n.* a member of any of the bands of English workers who destroyed machinery, esp. in cotton and woolen mills, that they believed was threatening their jobs (1811–16). ■ a person

L

opposed to increased industrialization or new technology: *a small-minded Luddite resisting progress.* ▷perhaps named after Ned *Lud*, a participant in the destruction of machinery, + -ITE[1]. —**Lud·dism** /-ˌizəm/ *n.* —**Lud·dit·ism** /-ˌitˌizəm/ *n.*

Lu·den·dorff /ˈlo͞odnˌdôrf/, Erich (1865–1937), German general; chief of staff to General von Hindenburg during World War I.

lu·der·ick /ˈlo͞od(ə)rik/ ▸*n.* (*pl.* same) an edible, herbivorous fish of Australasian coastal waters and estuaries. Also called BLACKFISH. • *Girella tricuspidata*, family Kyphosidae. ▷late 19th cent.: from Ganay (an Aboriginal language) *ludarag*.

Lu·dhi·a·na /ˌlo͞odēˈänə/ a city in northwestern India, in Punjab southeast of Amritsar; pop. 1,012,000.

lu·dic /ˈlo͞odik/ ▸*adj.* *formal* showing spontaneous and undirected playfulness. ▷1940s: from French *ludique*, from Latin *ludere* 'to play,' from *ludus* 'sport.'

lu·di·crous /ˈlo͞odəkrəs/ ▸*adj.* so foolish, unreasonable, or out of place as to be amusing; ridiculous: *it's ludicrous that I have been fined | every night he wore a ludicrous outfit.* See note at ABSURD. ▷early 17th cent. (in the sense 'sportive, intended as a jest'): from Latin *ludicrus* (probably from *ludicrum* 'stage play') + -OUS. —**lu·di·crous·ly** *adv.* *a ludicrously inadequate army.* —**lu·di·crous·ness** *n.*

Lud·lum /ˈlədləm/, Robert (1927–2001) U.S. writer; pen names **Jonathan Ryder, Michael Shepherd**. He wrote suspense novels, including *The Bourne Identity* (1980), *The Matarese Countdown* (1997), and *The Prometheus Deception* (2000).

Lud·wig /ˈlədwig; ˈlo͞od-; ˈlo͞otvikн/ the name of three kings of Bavaria: ■ **Ludwig I** (1786–1868), reigned 1825–48. He became unpopular due to his reactionary policies, lavish expenditures, and his domination by the dancer Lola Montez. He was forced to abdicate in favor of his son, Maximilian II. ■ **Ludwig II** (1845–86), reigned 1864–86. Son of Maximilian II and a patron of the arts, he became a recluse and built a series of elaborate castles. He was declared insane and deposed in 1886. ■ **Ludwig III** (1845–1921), reigned 1913–18. Succeeding his deposed cousin, Ludwig II, he became the last king of Bavaria.

Lud·wigs·ha·fen /ˌlo͞odviksˈhäfən/ an industrial river port in west central Germany, southwest of Mannheim, on the Rhine River in the state of Rhineland-Palatinate; pop. 165,000.

lu·es /ˈlo͞oˌēz/ (also **lu·es ve·ne·re·a** /vəˈni(ə)rēə/) ▸*n.* *dated* a serious infectious disease, particularly syphilis. ▷mid 17th cent.: from Latin *lues (venerea)*, literally '(venereal) plague.' —**lu·et·ic** /lo͞oˈetik/ *adj.*

luff /ləf/ *chiefly Sailing* ▸*n.* the edge of a fore-and-aft sail next to the mast or stay.

▸*v.* [*trans.*] **1** steer (a sailing vessel) nearer the wind to the point at which the sails just begin to flap: *I came aft and luffed her for the open sea.* ■ obstruct (an opponent in yacht racing) by sailing closer to the wind. **2** raise or lower (the jib of a crane or derrick). ▷Middle English: from Old French *lof*, probably from Low German.

luf·fa /ˈləfə; ˈlo͞ofə/ ▸*n.* variant spelling of LOOFAH.

Luft·waf·fe /ˈlo͞oftˌwäfə; -ˌväfə/ the German air force. ▷German, from *Luft* 'air' + *Waffe* 'weapon.'

lug[1] /ləg/ ▸*v.* (**lugged, lug·ging**) [*trans.*] carry or drag (a heavy or bulky object) with great effort: *she began to lug her suitcase down the stairs.* ■ *figurative* be encumbered with: *he had lugged his poor wife around for so long.*

▸*n.* a box or crate used for transporting fruit. ▷late Middle English: probably of Scandinavian origin: compare with Swedish *lugga* 'pull a person's hair' (from *lugg* 'forelock').

lug[2] ▸*n.* **1** a projection on an object by which it may be carried or fixed in place: *mount the fitting directly to the lugs at each side of the box.* **2** *informal* an uncouth, aggressive man: *a hood who, despite his fancy clothes, remains a lug.* [contemptuous use, perhaps from the 19th-cent. term denoting the lowest grade of tobacco.] **3** (usu. **lugs**) *Scottish* or *informal* a person's ear. ▷late 15th cent. (denoting the earflap of a hat): probably of Scandinavian origin: compare with Swedish *lugg* 'forelock, nap of cloth.'

lug[3] ▸*n.* short for LUGWORM.

lug[4] ▸*n.* short for LUGSAIL.

Lu·gan·da /lo͞oˈgändə; -ˈgan-/ ▸*n.* the Bantu language of the Baganda people, widely used in Uganda.

▸*adj.* of or relating to this language.

Lu·ga·no /lo͞oˈgänō/ a town in southern Switzerland, on the northern shore of Lake Lugano; pop. 26,000. It is a center of international finance and a health and recreational resort.

Lu·gansk /lo͞oˈgänsk/ Russian name for LUHANSK.

Lug·du·num /ləgˈdo͞onəm/ Roman name for LYONS.

luge /lo͞ozн/ ▸*n.* a light toboggan for one or two people, ridden in a sitting or supine position. ■ a sport in which competitors make a timed descent of a course riding such toboggans.

▸*v.* [*intrans.*] ride on a luge. ▷late 19th cent. (as a verb): from Swiss French.

Lu·ger /ˈlo͞ogər/ ▸*n.* *trademark* a type of German automatic pistol. ▷early 20th cent.: named after George *Luger* (1849–1923), German firearms expert.

lug·ga·ble /ˈləgəbəl/ ▸*adj.* (esp. of computer equipment) portable but only with difficulty.

lug·gage /ˈləgij/ ▸*n.* suitcases or other bags in which to pack personal belongings for traveling. ▷late 16th cent. (originally denoting inconveniently heavy baggage): from LUG[1] + -AGE.

lug·ger /ˈləgər/ ▸*n.* a small sailing ship with two or three masts and a lugsail on each. ▷mid 18th cent.: from LUGSAIL + -ER[1].

lug nut ▸*n.* a large rounded nut that fits over a heavy bolt, used esp. to attach the wheel of a vehicle to its axle.

Lu·go·si /ləˈgōsē/, Bela (born Béla Ferenc Blasko) (1884–1956), U.S. actor, born in Hungary. He was known for his roles in horror movies such as *Dracula* (1931), *Mark of the Vampire* (1935), and *The Wolf Man* (1940).

lug·sail /ˈləgsəl; -ˌsāl/ ▸*n.* an asymmetrical four-sided sail that is hoisted on a steeply inclined yard. ▷late 17th cent.: probably from LUG[2] + the noun SAIL.

lu·gu·bri·ous /ləˈg(y)o͞obrēəs/ ▸*adj.* looking or sounding sad and dismal. See note at GLUM. ▷early 17th cent.: from Latin *lugubris* (from *lugere* 'mourn') + -OUS. —**lu·gu·bri·ous·ly** *adv.* —**lu·gu·bri·ous·ness** *n.*

lug·worm /ˈləgˌwərm/ ▸*n.* a bristle worm that lives in muddy sand. It is widely used as bait for fishing. • Genus *Arenicola*, class Polychaeta: several species, including the **northern lugworm**, *A. marina*, which leaves characteristic worm casts on lower shores. ▷early 19th cent.: from earlier *lug* 'lugworm' (of unknown origin) + WORM.

Lu·hansk /lo͞oˈhänsk/ an industrial city in eastern Ukraine, in the Donets Basin; pop. 501,000. Former name VOROSHILOVGRAD (1935–58 and 1970–91). Russian name LUGANSK.

Luik /loik/ Flemish name for LIÈGE.

Luke, St. /lo͞ok/ an evangelist, closely associated with St. Paul and traditionally the author of the third Gospel and the Acts of the Apostles. Feast day, October 18. ■ the third Gospel (see GOSPEL sense 2).

luke·warm /ˈlo͞okˈwôrm/ ▸*adj.* (of liquid or food that should be hot) only moderately warm; tepid: *they drank bitter lukewarm coffee.* ■ (of a person, attitude, or action) unenthusiastic: *Israelis who had been lukewarm about the agreement.* ▷late Middle English: from dialect *luke* (probably from dialect *lew* 'lukewarm' and related to LEE) + WARM. —**luke·warm·ly** *adv.* —**luke·warm·ness** *n.*

lull /ləl/ ▸*v.* [*trans.*] calm or send to sleep, typically with soothing sounds or movements: *the rhythm of the boat lulled her to sleep.* ■ cause (someone) to feel deceptively secure or confident: *the rarity of earthquakes there has lulled people into a false sense of security.* ■ allay (a person's doubts, fears, or suspicions), typically by deception. ■ [*intrans.*] (of noise or a storm) abate or fall quiet: *conversation lulled for an hour.*

▸*n.* a temporary interval of quiet or lack of activity: *for two days there had been a* ***lull in*** *the fighting.* ▷Middle English: imitative of sounds used to calm a child; compare with Latin *lallare* 'sing to sleep,' Swedish *lulla* 'hum a lullaby,' and Dutch *lullen* 'talk nonsense.' The noun (first recorded in the sense 'soothing drink') dates from the mid 17th cent.

▸*PHRASE* □ **the lull before the storm** see STORM.

lull·a·by /ˈləlәˌbī/ ▸*n.* (*pl.* **-bies**) a quiet, gentle song sung to send a child to sleep.

▸*v.* (**-bies, -bied**) [*trans.*] *rare* sing to (someone) to get them to go to sleep: *she lullabied us, she fed us.* ▷mid 16th cent.: from LULL + *bye-bye*, a sound used as a refrain in lullabies.

Lul·ly /ˈlo͞olē; lʏˈlē/, Jean-Baptiste (1632–87), French composer, born in Italy; Italian name *Giovanni Battista Lulli*. His operas, which include *Alceste* (1674) and *Armide* (1686), mark the beginning of the French operatic tradition.

lu·lu /ˈlo͞oˌlo͞o/ ▸*n.* *informal* an outstanding example of a particular type of person or thing: *as far as nightmares went, this one was a lulu.* ▷late 19th cent.: perhaps from *Lulu*, nickname for the given name *Louise*.

lu·ma /ˈlo͞omə/ ▸*n.* (*pl.* same or **lu·mas**) a monetary unit of Armenia, equal to one hundredth of a dram.

lum·ba·go /ˌləmˈbāgō/ ▸*n.* pain in the muscles and joints of the lower back. ▷late 17th cent.: from Latin, from *lumbus* 'loin.'

lum·bar /ˈləmbər; -ˌbär/ ▸*adj.* relating to the lower part of the back: *backache in the lumbar region.* ▷mid 17th cent.: from medieval Latin *lumbaris*, from Latin *lumbus* 'loin.'

lum·bar punc·ture ▸*n.* *Medicine* the procedure of taking fluid from the spine in the lower back through a hollow needle, usually done for diagnostic purposes.

lum·ber[1] /ˈləmbər/ ▸*v.* [*intrans.*] move in a slow, heavy, awkward way: *a truck filled his mirror and lumbered past* | [as *adj.*] (**lumbering**) *Bob was the big, lumbering, gentle sort* | *figurative a lumbering bureaucracy.* ▷late Middle English *lomere*, perhaps symbolic of clumsy movement.

lum·ber[2] ▸*n.* **1** timber sawn into rough planks or otherwise partly prepared. **2** *chiefly Brit.* articles of furniture or other household items that are no longer useful and inconveniently take up storage space. [as *adj.*] *a lumber room.* ■ *figurative* a collection of beliefs or concepts that are regarded as no longer valid and encumber one's mental outlook.

▸*v.* **1** [*intrans.*] [usu. as *n.*] (**lumbering**) cut and prepare forest timber for transport and sale: *the traditional resource industries of the nation, chiefly fishing and lumbering.* **2** [*trans.*] (usu. **be lumbered with**) *Brit., informal* burden (someone) with an unwanted responsibility, task, or set of circumstances. ▷mid 16th cent.: perhaps from LUMBER[1]; later associated with obsolete *lumber* 'pawnbroker's shop.'

lum·ber·er /ˈləmbərər/ ▸*n.* a person engaged in the lumber trade, esp. a lumberjack.

lum·ber·jack /ˈləmbərˌjak/ ▸*n.* (a person who fells trees, cuts them into logs, or transports them to a sawmill. Also called LUMBERMAN.

lum·ber·jack·et /ˈləmbərˌjakit/ ▸*n.* a warm, thick jacket, typically in a bright color with a check pattern, of the kind worn by lumberjacks.

lum·ber·man /ˈləmbərˌmən/ ▸*n.* (*pl.* **-men** /-mən/) another term for LUMBERJACK.

lum·ber·yard /ˈləmbərˌyärd/ ▸*n.* a place that sells lumber and other building materials, usu. outdoors.

lu·men[1] /ˈlo͞omən/ (abbr.: **lm**) ▸*n.* *Physics* the SI unit of luminous flux, equal to the amount of light emitted per second in a unit solid angle of one steradian from a uniform source of one candela. ▷late 19th cent.: from Latin, literally 'light.'

lu·men[2] ▸*n.* (*pl.* **-mi·na** /-mənə/) *Anatomy* the central cavity of a tubular or other hollow structure in an organism or cell. ▷late 19th cent.: from Latin, literally 'opening.' —**lu·mi·nal** /-mənl/ *adj.*

Lu·mière /ˌlo͞omēˈe(ə)r; lʏmˈyer/, Auguste Marie Louis Nicholas (1862–1954) and Louis Jean (1864–1948), French inventors and movie pioneers. In 1895, the brothers patented their "Cinématographe," which combined a movie camera and projector. They also invented the improved "autochrome" process of color photography.

lu·mi·naire /ˌlo͞oməˈner/ ▸*n.* a complete electric light unit (used esp. in technical contexts). ▷early 20th cent.: from French.

lu·mi·nance /ˈlo͞omənəns/ ▸*n.* *Physics* the intensity of light emitted from a surface per unit area in a given direction. ■ the component of a television signal that carries information on the brightness of the image. ▷late 19th cent. (as a general term meaning 'light, brightness'): from Latin *luminant-* 'illuminating' (from the verb *luminare*) + -ANCE.

lu·mi·nar·i·a /ˌlo͞oməˈne(ə)rēə/ ▸*n.* **1** a Christmas lantern consisting of a votive candle set in a small paper bag weighted with sand and typically placed with others along a driveway, sidewalk, or rooftop as a holiday decoration. Also called FAROLITO. **2** (in New Mexico) a Christmas Eve bonfire.

lu·mi·nar·y /ˈlo͞oməˌnerē/ ▸*n.* (*pl.* **-nar·ies**) **1** a person who inspires or influences others, esp. one prominent in a particular sphere: *one of the luminaries of child psychiatry.* **2** an artificial light. ■ *poetic/literary* a natural light-giving body, esp. the sun or moon. ▷late Middle English: from Old French *luminarie* or late Latin *luminarium*, from Latin *lumen, lumin-* 'light.'

lu·mi·nesce /ˌlo͞oməˈnes/ ▸*v.* [*intrans.*] emit light by luminescence. ▷late 19th cent.: back-formation from LUMINESCENCE.

lu·mi·nes·cence /ˌlo͞oməˈnesəns/ ▸*n.* the emission of

L

light by a substance that has not been heated, as in fluorescence and phosphorescence. ▷late 19th cent.: from Latin *lumen, lumin-* 'light' + *-escence* (denoting a state). **—lu·mi·nes·cent** *adj.*

lu·mi·nif·er·ous /ˌlo͞oməˈnif(ə)rəs/ ▸*adj.* producing or transmitting light.

lu·mi·nos·i·ty /ˌlo͞oməˈnäsətē/ ▸*n.* (*pl.* **-ties**) luminous quality: *acrylic colors retain freshness and luminosity.* ■ *Astronomy* the intrinsic brightness of a celestial object (as distinct from its apparent brightness diminished by distance). ■ *Physics* the rate of emission of radiation, visible or otherwise.

lu·mi·nous /ˈlo͞omənəs/ ▸*adj.* full of or shedding light; bright or shining, esp. in the dark: *the luminous dial on his watch | a luminous glow.* See note at **BRIGHT**. ■ (of a person's complexion or eyes) glowing with health, vigor, or a particular emotion: *her eyes were* ***luminous with*** *joy.* ■ (of a color) very bright; harsh to the eye: *he wore luminous green socks.* ■ *Physics* relating to light as it is perceived by the eye, rather than in terms of its actual energy. ▷late Middle English: from Old French *lumineux* or Latin *luminosus*, from *lumen, lumin-* 'light.' **—lu·mi·nous·ly** *adv.* **—lu·mi·nous·ness** *n.*

lum·mox /ˈləməks/ ▸*n. informal* a clumsy, stupid person: *watch it, you great lummox!* ▷early 19th cent.: of unknown origin.

lump[1] /ləmp/ ▸*n.* a compact mass of a substance, esp. one without a definite or regular shape: *there was a* ***lump of*** *ice floating in the milk.* ■ a swelling under the skin, esp. one caused by injury or disease: *he was unhurt apart from a huge lump on his head.* ■ *informal* a heavy, ungainly, or slow-witted person: *I wouldn't stand a chance against a big lump like you.* ■ a small cube of sugar.

▸*v.* **1** [*trans.*] put in an indiscriminate mass or group; treat as alike without regard for particulars: *Hong Kong and Bangkok tend to* ***be lumped together*** *in travel brochures | he tends to be* ***lumped in*** *with the crowd of controversial businessmen.* ■ [*intrans.*] (in taxonomy) classify plants or animals in relatively inclusive groups, disregarding minor variations. **2** [*intrans.*] (**lump along**) proceed heavily or awkwardly: *I came lumping along behind him.* **3** [*intrans.*] concentrate or assemble together in an irregular mass: *we're lumped in a limo, bound for a Los Angeles medical center.* ▷Middle English: perhaps from a Germanic base meaning 'shapeless piece'; compare with Danish *lump* 'lump,' Norwegian and Swedish dialect *lump* 'block, log,' and Dutch *lomp* 'rag.'

▸*PHRASES* □ **a lump in the throat** a feeling of tightness or dryness in the throat caused by strong emotion, esp. sadness: *there was a lump in her throat as she gazed down at her uncle's gaunt features.* □ **take** (or **get**) **one's lumps** *informal* suffer punishment; be attacked or defeated.

lump[2] ▸*v.* [*trans.*] (**lump it**) *informal* accept or tolerate a disagreeable situation whether one likes it or not: *you can* ***like it or lump it*** *but I've got to work.* ▷late 16th cent. (in the sense 'look sulky'): symbolic of displeasure; compare with words such as *dump* and *grump*. The current sense dates from the early 19th cent.

lump·ec·to·my /ˌləmˈpektəmē/ ▸*n.* (*pl.* **-mies**) a surgical operation in which a lump is removed from the breast, typically when cancer is present but has not spread.

lum·pen /ˈləmpən; ˈlo͝om-/ ▸*adj.* (in Marxist contexts) uninterested in revolutionary advancement: *the lumpen public is enveloped in a culture of dependency.* ■ boorish and stupid: *growing ranks of lumpen, uninhibited, denim-clad youth.*

▸*plural n.* (**the lumpen**) the lumpenproletariat. ▷mid 20th cent.: back-formation from **LUMPENPROLETARIAT**.

lum·pen·pro·le·tar·i·at /ˈləmpənˌprōləˈte(ə)rēət; ˈlo͝om-/ ▸*n.* (esp. in Marxist terminology) the unorganized and unpolitical lower orders of society who are not interested in revolutionary advancement. ▷early 20th cent.: from German (a term originally used by Karl Marx), from *Lumpen* 'rag, rogue' + **PROLETARIAT**.

lump·er /ˈləmpər/ ▸*n.* **1** a laborer who unloads cargo. **2** a person (esp. a taxonomist) who attaches more importance to similarities than to differences in classification. Contrasted with **SPLITTER**.

lump·fish /ˈləmpˌfisH/ ▸*n.* (*pl.* same or **-fish·es**) a North Atlantic lumpsucker, the roe of which is sometimes used as a substitute for caviar. • *Cyclopterus lumpus*, family Cyclopteridae. ▷early 17th cent.: from Middle Low German *lumpen*, Middle Dutch *lompe* + **FISH**[1].

lump·ish /ˈləmpisH/ ▸*adj.* roughly or clumsily formed or shaped: *those large and lumpish hands could produce exquisitely fine work.* ■ (of a person) stupid and lethargic. **—lump·ish·ly** *adv.* **—lump·ish·ness** *n.*

lump·suck·er /ˈləmpˌsəkər/ ▸*n.* a globular fish of cooler northern waters, typically having a ventral sucker and spiny fins; a lumpfish. • Family Cyclopteridae: several genera and species.

lump sum ▸*n.* a single payment made at a particular time, as opposed to a number of smaller payments or installments.

lump·y /ˈləmpē/ ▸*adj.* (**lump·i·er, lump·i·est**) full of or covered with lumps: *he lay on the lumpy mattress.* ■ *Nautical* (of water) formed by the wind into small waves: *a large lumpy sea.* **—lump·i·ly** /-pəlē/ *adv.* **—lump·i·ness** *n.*

lump·y jaw ▸*n.* infection of the jaw with actinomycete bacteria, common in cattle.

Lu·na /ˈlo͞onə/ a series of Soviet moon probes launched in 1959–76. They made the first hard and soft landings on the moon (1959 and 1966).

lu·na·cy /ˈlo͞onəsē/ ▸*n.* (*pl.* **-cies**) the state of being a lunatic; insanity (not in technical use): *it has been suggested that originality demands a degree of lunacy.* ■ extreme folly or eccentricity: *such an economic policy would be sheer lunacy.* ▷mid 16th cent. (originally referring to insanity of an intermittent kind attributed to changes of the moon): from **LUNATIC** + **-ACY**.

lu·na moth /ˈlo͞onə/ ▸*n.* a very large North American moth that has pale green wings with long tails and transparent eyespots bearing crescent-shaped markings. • *Actias luna*, family Saturniidae. ▷late 19th cent.: *luna* from Latin *luna* 'moon' (from its markings).

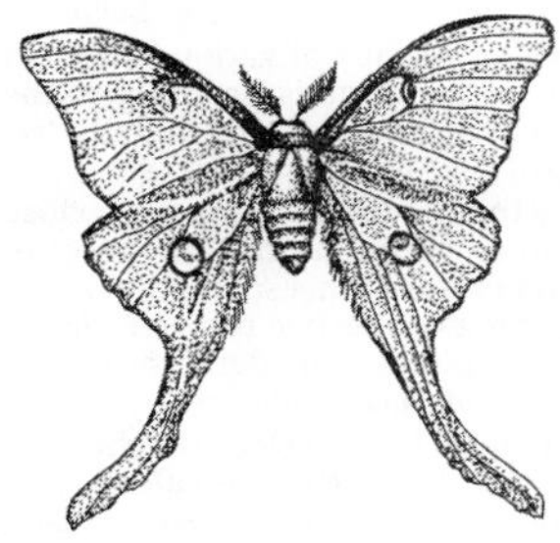

luna moth

lu·nar /ˈlo͞onər/ ▸*adj.* of, determined by, relating to, or resembling the moon: *a lunar landscape.* ▷late Middle English: from Latin *lunaris*, from *luna* 'moon.'

lu·nar caus·tic ▸*n. archaic Chemistry* silver nitrate, esp. fused in the form of a stick. ▷early 19th cent.: *lunar* in the sense 'containing silver.'

lu·nar cy·cle ▸*n.* another term for **METONIC CYCLE**.

lu·nar day ▸*n.* **1** the interval of time between two successive crossings of the earth's meridian by the moon (roughly 24 hours and 50 minutes). **2** *rare* the interval of time between two successive sunrises as seen from the moon.

lu·nar dis·tance ▸*n.* the angular distance of the moon from the sun, a planet, or a star, used in finding longitude at sea.

lu·nar e·clipse ▸*n.* an eclipse in which the moon appears darkened as it passes into the earth's shadow.

Lu·nar·i·an /lo͞oˈne(ə)rēən/ ▸*n.* (in science fiction) an imagined inhabitant of the moon.

lu·nar mod·ule (abbr.: **LM**) ▸*n.* a small craft used for traveling between the moon's surface and an orbiting spacecraft (formerly known as **lunar excursion module** or **LEM**).

lu·nar month ▸*n.* a month measured between successive new moons (roughly $29\frac{1}{2}$ days). ■ (in general use) a period of four weeks.

lu·nar node ▸*n. Astronomy* each of the two points at which the moon's orbit cuts the ecliptic.

lu·nar ob·ser·va·tion ▸*n.* **1** a measurement of the position of the moon in order to calculate longitude from lunar distance. **2** observational study of the moon.

lu·nar rov·ing ve·hi·cle (abbr.: **LRV**) (also **lu·nar ro·ver**) ▸*n.* a vehicle designed for use by astronauts on the moon's surface, used on the last three missions of the Apollo project. Also called **MOON BUGGY**.

lu·nar year ▸*n.* a period of twelve lunar months (approximately 354 days).

lu·nate /ˈlo͞oˌnāt/ ▸*adj.* crescent-shaped.

▸*n.* (also **lunate bone**) *Anatomy* a crescent-shaped carpal bone situated in the center of the wrist and articulating with the radius. ▷late 18th cent.: from Latin *lunatus*, from *luna* 'moon.'

lu·na·tic /ˈlo͞onəˌtik/ ▸*n.* a mentally ill person (not in technical use). ■ an extremely foolish or eccentric person: *this lunatic just accelerated out of the side of the road.*

▸*adj.* mentally ill (not in technical use). ■ extremely foolish, eccentric, or absurd: *he would be asked to acquiesce in some lunatic scheme.* ▷Middle English: from Old French *lunatique*, from late Latin *lunaticus*, from Latin *luna* 'moon' (from the belief that changes of the moon caused intermittent insanity).

lu·na·tic fringe ▸*n.* an extreme or eccentric minority within society or a group.

lu·na·tion /lo͞oˈnāsHən/ ▸*n. Astronomy* another term for **LUNAR MONTH**. ▷late Middle English: from medieval Latin *lunatio(n-)*, from Latin *luna* 'moon.'

lunch /lənCH/ ▸*n.* a meal eaten in the middle of the day, typically one that is lighter or less formal than an evening meal: *a vegetarian lunch | do join us for lunch.*

▸*v.* [*intrans.*] eat lunch: *he told his wife he was lunching with a client.* ■ [*trans.*] take (someone) out for lunch: *public relations people lunch their clients there.* ▷early 19th cent.: abbreviation of **LUNCHEON**. **—lunch·er** *n.*

▸*PHRASES* □ **do lunch** *informal* meet for lunch. □ **out to lunch** *informal* unaware of or inattentive to present conditions. □ **there's no such thing as a free lunch** *proverb* it isn't possible to get something for nothing.

lunch·box /ˈlənCHˌbäks/ ▸*n.* a container in which to carry a packed meal. Also called **LUNCH BUCKET, LUNCHPAIL**. ■ a portable computer slightly larger than a laptop.

lunch·eon /ˈlənCHən/ ▸*n.* a formal lunch, or a formal word for lunch. ▷late 16th cent. (in the sense 'thick piece, hunk'): possibly an extension of obsolete *lunch* 'thick piece, hunk,' from Spanish *lonja* 'slice.'

lunch·eon·ette /ˌlənCHəˈnet/ ▸*n.* a small, informal restaurant serving lunches.

lunch·meat /ˈlənCHˌmēt/ (also **lunch·eon meat**) ▸*n.* meat sold in slices for sandwiches; cold cuts.

lunch·pail /ˈlənCHˌpāl/ (also **lunch pail**) ▸*n.* another term for **LUNCHBOX**.

lunch·room /ˈlənCHˌro͞om; -ˌro͝om/ ▸*n.* a room or establishment in which lunch is served or in which it may be eaten; a school or office cafeteria.

lunch·time /ˈlənCHˌtīm/ ▸*n.* the time in the middle of day when lunch is eaten.

Lund /lo͝ond/ a city in southwestern Sweden, just northeast of Malmö; pop. 87,680 (1991). Its university was founded in 1666.

Lun·da /ˈlo͝ondə; ˈlo͞on-/ ▸*n.* (*pl.* same or **Ba·lun·da** /bə ˈlo͝ondə; -ˈlo͞on-/ or **Lun·das**) **1** a member of any of several peoples living mainly in northern Zambia and adjoining parts of the Democratic Republic of the Congo (formerly Zaire) and Angola. From the 16th to 19th centuries, they established a substantial empire in the region. **2** any of several Bantu languages of these peoples, esp. one spoken mainly in northwestern Zambia.

▸*adj.* of, relating to, or denoting this people or their language. ▷a local name.

Lun·dy /ˈləndē/ **1** a granite island in the Bristol Channel, off the coast of northern Devon. **2** a shipping forecast area covering the Bristol Channel and the eastern Celtic Sea.

lune /lo͞on/ ▸*n.* a crescent-shaped figure formed on a sphere or plane by two arcs intersecting at two points. ■ a filled pasta case made from a circle of pasta dough folded over. ▷early 18th cent.: from French, from Latin *luna* 'moon.'

lu·nette /lo͞oˈnet/ ▸*n.* something crescent-shaped, in particular: ■ an arched aperture or window, esp. one in a domed ceiling. ■ a crescent-shaped or semicircular alcove containing something such as a painting or statue. ■ a fortification with two faces forming a projecting angle, and two flanks. ■ *Christian Church* a holder for the consecrated host in a monstrance. ▷late 16th cent. (denoting a semicircular horseshoe): from French, diminutive of *lune* 'moon,' from Latin *luna*.

lung /ləNG/ ▸*n.* each of the pair of organs situated within the rib cage, consisting of elastic sacs with branching passages into which air is drawn, so that oxygen can pass into the blood and carbon dioxide be removed. Lungs are characteristic of vertebrates

Pronunciation Key ə *ago*; ər *over*; ˈə or ˌə *up*; ˈər or ˌər *fur*; a *hat*; ā *rate*; ä *car*; CH *chew*; e *let*; ē *see*; e(ə)r *air*; i *fit*; ī *by*; i(ə)r *ear*; NG *sing*; ō *go*; ô *for*; oi *boy*; o͝o *good*; o͞o *goo*; ou *out*; SH *she*; TH *thin*; T͟H *then*; (h)w *why*; ZH *vision*

other than fish, though similar structures are present in some other animal groups. ■ (usu. **lungs**) *Brit., figurative* the open spaces in a town or city, where its inhabitants can get fresher air. ▷Old English *lungen*, of Germanic origin; related to Dutch *long* and German *Lunge*, from an Indo-European root shared by **LIGHT**[2]; compare with **LIGHTS**. —**lunged** /ləNGd/ *adj.* [in *combination*] *strong-lunged*. —**lung·ful** /-,fo͝ol/ *n.* (*pl.* **-fuls**) —**lung·less** *adj.*

lunge[1] /lənj/ ▶*n.* a sudden forward thrust of the body, typically with an arm outstretched to attack someone or seize something: *he made a* **lunge at** *her.* ■ the basic attacking move in fencing, in which the leading foot is thrust forward with the knee bent while the back leg remains straightened. ■ an exercise or gymnastic movement resembling the lunge of a fencer.
▶*v.* (**lung·ing** or **lunge·ing**) [*intrans.*] make a lunge: *the sequined guests* **lunged at** *the food | John lunged forward and grabbed him by the throat.* ■ [*trans.*] make a sudden forward thrust with (a part of the body or a weapon): *Billy lunged his spear at the fish.* ▷mid 18th cent.: from earlier *allonge*, from French *allonger* 'lengthen.'

lunge[2] ▶*n.* variant of **LONGE**.

lunge[3] ▶*n.* short for **MUSKELLUNGE**.

lung·fish /'ləNG,fiSH/ ▶*n.* (*pl.* same or **-fish·es**) an elongated freshwater fish with one or two sacs that function as lungs, enabling it to breathe air. It lives in poorly oxygenated water and can estivate in mud for long periods to survive drought. • Subclass Dipnoi: families Ceratodontidae (one Australian species), Lepidosirenidae (one South American species), and Protopteridae (four African species).

lun·gi /'lo͞oNGgē/ ▶*n.* (*pl.* **lun·gis**) a length of cotton cloth worn as a loincloth in India or as a skirt in Myanmar (Burma), where it is the national dress for both sexes. ▷Urdu.

lunge·ing cav·es·son ▶*n.* another term for **CAVESSON**.

lung·worm /'ləNG,wərm/ ▶*n.* a parasitic nematode worm found in the lungs of mammals, esp. farm and domestic animals. • *Dictyocaulus* and other genera, class Phasmida.

lung·wort /'ləNG,wərt; -,wôrt/ ▶*n.* a bristly herbaceous European plant of the borage family, typically having white-spotted leaves and pink flowers that turn blue as they age. [so named because the leaves were said to have the appearance of a diseased lung.] • Genus *Pulmonaria*, family Boraginaceae: several species, in particular *P. officinalis*.

lu·ni·so·lar /,lo͞oni'sōlər/ ▶*adj.* of or concerning the combined motions or effects of the sun and moon. ■ of or employing a calendar year divided according to the phases of the moon, but adjusted in average length to fit the length of the solar cycle. ■ of or denoting a 532-year period over which both the lunar months and the days of the week return to the same point in relation to the solar year. ▷late 17th cent.: from Latin *luna* 'moon' + **SOLAR**[1].

lu·ni·tid·al /,lo͞oni'tīdl/ ▶*adj.* denoting the interval between the time at which the moon crosses a meridian and the time of high tide at that meridian.

lunk /ləNGk/ ▶*n.* short for **LUNKHEAD**.

lun·ker /'ləNGkər/ ▶*n.* *informal* an exceptionally large specimen of something, in particular (among anglers) a fish. ▷early 20th cent.: of unknown origin.

lunk·head /'ləNGk,(h)ed/ ▶*n.* *informal* a slow-witted person. ▷mid 19th cent.: probably from an alteration of **LUMP**[1] + **HEAD**. —**lunk·head·ed** *adj.*

Lunt /lənt/, Alfred (1892–1977), U.S. actor. See **FONTANNE**.

lu·nu·la /'lo͞onyələ/ ▶*n.* (*pl.* **-lae** /-,lē; -,lī/) a crescent-shaped object or mark, in particular: ■ the white area at the base of a fingernail. ■ *Printing* one of a pair of parentheses. ▷late 16th cent. (denoting a crescent-shaped geometric figure): from Latin, diminutive of *luna* 'moon.' —**lu·nu·lar** /-lər/ *adj.* —**lu·nu·late** /-,lāt; -lit/ *adj.*

lu·nule /'lo͞on,yo͞ol/ ▶*n.* a crescent-shaped or oval part or marking, in particular: ■ an oval depression in front of the beak on the outside of many clams. ■ a small area above the antennae on the front of some kinds of flies.

Lu·o /'lo͞o,ō/ ▶*n.* (*pl.* same or **Lu·os**) **1** a member of an East African people of Kenya and the upper Nile valley. **2** the Nilotic language of this people.
▶*adj.* of or relating to the Luo or their language. ▷the name in Luo.

Luo·yang /'lo͞o'yäNG/ an industrial city in east central China, in Henan province, on the Luo River; pop. 1,160,000. Between the 4th and 6th centuries AD, the construction of cave temples to the south of the city made it an important Buddhist center. Former name **HONAN**.

Lu·per·ca·li·a /,lo͞opər'kālēə; -'kālyə/ (also in *sing.* **Lu·per·cal** /'lo͞opər,kal/) ▶*plural n.* [usu. treated as *sing.*] an ancient Roman festival of purification and fertility, held annually on February 15. ▷Latin, neuter plural of *lupercalis* 'relating to *Lupercus*,' Roman equivalent of the Greek god Pan. —**Lu·per·ca·li·an** *adj.*

lu·pine[1] /'lo͞opin/ ▶*n.* a plant of the pea family, with deeply divided leaves and tall, colorful, tapering spikes of flowers. • Genus *Lupinus*, family Leguminosae: several species, in particular the popular cultivar **Russell lupine**. ▷late Middle English: from Latin *lupinus*.

lu·pine[2] /'lo͞o,pīn/ ▶*adj.* of, like, or relating to a wolf or wolves. ■ fierce or ravenous as a wolf. ▷mid 17th cent.: from Latin *lupinus*, from *lupus* 'wolf.'

Lu·pi·no /lə'pēnō; lo͞o-/, Ida (1918–95), U.S. actress and director; born in England. She starred in *They Drive by Night* (1940), *The Sea Wolf* (1936), and *The Big Knife* (1955). Movies that she both acted in and directed include *The Bigamist* (1953).

lu·pu·lin /'lo͞opyəlin/ ▶*n.* a bitter, yellowish powder found on glandular hairs beneath the scales of the flowers of the female hop plant. ▷early 19th cent.: from the modern Latin use as an epithet of Latin *lupulus* (as in *Humulus lupulus*), a plant mentioned by Pliny and perhaps denoting 'wild hops,' + **-IN**[1].

Lu·pus /'lo͞opəs/ *Astronomy* a southern constellation (the Wolf), lying partly in the Milky Way between Scorpius and Centaurus. ■ [as *genitive*] (**Lupi**) used with a preceding letter or numeral to designate a star in this constellation: *the star Delta Lupi.* ▷Latin.

lu·pus /'lo͞opəs/ ▶*n.* any of various ulcerous skin diseases, esp. lupus vulgaris or lupus erythematosus. ▷late 16th cent.: from Latin, literally 'wolf.' —**lu·poid** /-,poid/ *adj.* —**lu·pous** /-pəs/ *adj.*

lu·pus er·y·the·ma·to·sus /,erə,THēmə'tōsəs/ ▶*n.* an inflammatory autoimmune disease causing scaly red patches on the skin, esp. on the face, and sometimes affecting connective tissue in the internal organs. ▷from **LUPUS** + modern Latin *erythematosus*, from Greek *eruthēma* 'reddening.'

lu·pus vul·ga·ris /,vəl'ge(ə)ris/ ▶*n.* chronic direct infection of the skin with tuberculosis, causing dark red patches. ▷1940s: from **LUPUS** + Latin *vulgaris* 'common.'

lurch[1] /lərCH/ ▶*n.* [usu. in *sing.*] an abrupt uncontrolled movement, esp. an unsteady tilt or roll: *the boat* **gave a violent lurch**, *and he missed his footing.*
▶*v.* [*intrans.*] make an abrupt, unsteady, uncontrolled movement or series of movements; stagger: *the car lurched forward | Stuart lurched to his feet | figurative he was lurching from one crisis to the next.* ▷late 17th cent. (as a noun denoting the sudden leaning of a ship to one side): of unknown origin.

lurch[2] ▶*n.* (in phrase **leave someone in the lurch**) leave an associate or friend abruptly and without assistance or support in a difficult situation. ▷mid 16th cent. (denoting a state of discomfiture): from French *lourche*, the name of a game resembling backgammon, used in the phrase *demeurer lourche* 'be discomfited.'

lurch·er /'lərCHər/ ▶*n.* **1** a crossbred dog, typically a retriever, collie, or sheepdog crossed with a greyhound, of a kind originally used for hunting and by poachers for catching rabbits. **2** *archaic* a prowler, swindler, or petty thief. ▷early 16th cent. (sense 2): from obsolete *lurch* 'remain in a place furtively,' variant of **LURK**.

lur·dan /'lərdn/ (also **lur·dane**) *archaic* ▶*n.* an idle or incompetent person.
▶*adj.* lazy; good-for-nothing. ▷Middle English: from Old French *lourdin*, from *lourd* 'heavy,' *lort* 'foolish,' from Latin *luridus* 'lurid.'

lure /lo͝or/ ▶*v.* [*trans.*] tempt (a person or an animal) to do something or to go somewhere, esp. by offering some form of reward: *the child was lured into a car but managed to escape.* See note at **TEMPT**.
▶*n.* something that tempts or is used to tempt a person or animal to do something: *the film industry always has been a glamorous lure for young girls.* ■ the strongly attractive quality of a person or thing: *the lure of the exotic East.* ■ a type of bait used in fishing or hunting. ■ *Falconry* a bunch of feathers with a weighted object attached to a long string, swung around the head of the falconer to recall a hawk. ▷Middle English: from Old French *luere*, of Germanic origin; probably related to German *Luder* 'bait.'

Lur·ex /'lo͝or,eks/ (also **lur·ex**) ▶*n.* *trademark* a type of yarn or fabric that incorporates a glittering metallic thread. ▷1940s: of unknown origin.

lu·rid /'lo͝orid/ ▶*adj.* very vivid in color, esp. so as to create an unpleasantly harsh or unnatural effect: *lurid food colorings | a pair of lurid shorts.* ■ (of a description) presented in vividly shocking or sensational terms, esp. giving explicit details of crimes or sexual matters: *the more lurid details of the massacre were too frightening for the children.* ▷mid 17th cent. (in the sense 'pale and dismal in color'): from Latin *luridus*; related to *luror* 'wan or yellow color.' —**lu·rid·ly** *adv.* —**lu·rid·ness** *n.*

lurk /lərk/ ▶*v.* [*intrans.*] (of a person or animal) be or remain hidden so as to wait in ambush for someone or something: *a ruthless killer still lurked in the darkness.* ■ (of an unpleasant quality) be present in a latent or barely discernable state, although still presenting a threat: *fear lurks beneath the surface |* [as *adj.*] (**lurking**) *he lives with a lurking fear of exposure as a fraud.* ■ [*intrans.*] read communications on an electronic network without making one's presence known. ▷Middle English: perhaps from **LOUR** + the frequentative suffix *-k* (as in *talk*).

lurk·er /'lərkər/ ▶*n.* one who lurks, in particular a user of an Internet chat room or newsgroup who does not participate.

Lur·ton /'lərtn/, Horace Harmon (1844–1914), U.S. Supreme Court associate justice 1909–14. A judge in the U.S. Court of Appeals 1893–1909, he was appointed to the Court by President Taft.

Lu·sa·ka /lo͞o'säkə/ the capital of Zambia; pop. 982,000.

Lu·sa·tian /lo͞o'sāSHən/ ▶*adj.* & *n.* another term for **SORBIAN**.

lus·cious /'ləSHəs/ ▶*adj.* (of food or wine) having a pleasingly rich, sweet taste: *a luscious and fragrant dessert wine.* ■ richly verdant or opulent. ■ (of a woman) very sexually attractive. ▷late Middle English: perhaps an alteration of obsolete *licious*, shortened form of **DELICIOUS**. —**lus·cious·ly** *adv.* —**lus·cious·ness** *n.*

lush[1] /ləSH/ ▶*adj.* (of vegetation) growing luxuriantly: *lush greenery and cultivated fields.* See note at **PROFUSE**. ■ opulent and luxurious: *a hall of gleaming marble, as lush as a Byzantine church.* ■ (of color or music) very rich and providing great sensory pleasure: *lush orchestrations.* ■ (of a woman) very sexually attractive: *Marianne, with her lush body and provocative green eyes.* ▷late Middle English: perhaps an alteration of obsolete *lash* 'soft, lax,' from Old French *lasche* 'lax,' by association with **LUSCIOUS**. —**lush·ly** *adv.* —**lush·ness** *n.*

lush[2] *informal* ▶*n.* a heavy drinker, esp. a habitual one.
▶*v.* [*trans.*] *dated* make (someone) drunk: *Mr. Hobart* **got so lushed up** *he was spilling drinks down his shirt.* ▷late 18th cent.: perhaps a humorous use of **LUSH**[1].

Lu·shai /lo͞o'SHī; 'lo͞o,SHī/ ▶*n.* another name for **MIZO** (sense 2).

Lu·shun /'lo͞o'SHo͞on; 'lY-/ a port on the Liaodong Peninsula in northeastern China, now part of the urban complex of Luda. It was leased by Russia for use as a Pacific naval port 1898–1905, when it was known as Port Arthur.

Lu·si·ta·ni·a[1] /,lo͞osə'tānēə; -nyə/ an ancient Roman province on the Iberian peninsula that corresponds to modern Portugal. —**Lu·si·ta·ni·an** *adj.* & *n.*

Lu·si·ta·ni·a[2] a Cunard liner that was sunk by a German submarine in the Atlantic in May 1915 with the loss of over 1,000 lives.

lust /ləst/ ▶*n.* very strong sexual desire: *he knew that his* **lust for** *her had returned.* ■ [in *sing.*] a passionate desire for something: *a* **lust for** *power.* ■ (usu. **lusts**) *chiefly Theology* a sensual appetite regarded as sinful: *lusts of the flesh.*
▶*v.* [*intrans.*] have a very strong sexual desire for someone: *he really* **lusted after** *me in those days.* ■ feel a strong desire for something: *pregnant women* **lusting for** *pickles and ice cream.* ▷Old English (also in the sense 'pleasure, delight'), of Germanic origin; related to Dutch *lust* and German *Lust*. —**lust·ful** /-(t)fəl/ *adj.* —**lust·ful·ly** /-(t)fəlē/ *adv.* —**lust·ful·ness** /-(t)fəlnəs/ *n.*

lus·ter[1] /'ləstər/ (*Brit.* **lus·tre**) ▶*n.* **1** a gentle sheen or soft glow, esp. that of a partly reflective surface: *the luster of the Milky Way | she couldn't eat, and her hair lost its luster.* See note at **POLISH**. ■ *figurative* glory or distinction: *a celebrity player to* **add luster to** *the lineup.* ■ the manner in which the surface of a mineral reflects light. **2** a substance imparting or having a shine or glow, in particular: ■ a thin coating containing unoxidized metal that gives an iridescent glaze to ceramics. ■ ceramics with such a glaze; lusterware: [as *adj.*] *luster jugs.* ■ a type of finish on a photographic print, less reflective than a glossy finish. ■ a fabric or yarn with a sheen or gloss. ■ *Brit.* a thin dress material with a cotton warp, woolen weft, and a glossy surface. **3** a prismatic glass pendant on a chandelier or other ornament. ■ a cut-glass chandelier or candelabra. ▷early 16th cent.: from French *lustre*, from Italian *lustro*, from the verb *lustrare*, from Latin *lustrare* 'illuminate.' **—lus·ter·less** *adj.*

lus·ter[2] (*Brit.* **lus·tre**) ▸*n.* another term for LUSTRUM.

lus·tered /ˈləstərd/ ▸*adj.* (esp. of ceramics) having an iridescent surface; shining.

lus·ter·ware /ˈləstərˌwer/ (*Brit.* **lus·tre·ware**) ▸*n.* ceramic articles with an iridescent metallic glaze.

lus·tra /ˈləstrə/ ▸ plural form of LUSTRUM.

lus·tral /ˈləstrəl/ ▸*adj.* relating to or used in ceremonial purification. ▷mid 16th cent.: from Latin *lustralis*, from *lustrum* (see LUSTRUM).

lus·trate /ˈləsˌtrāt/ ▸*v.* [*trans.*] *rare* purify by expiatory sacrifice, ceremonial washing, or some other ritual action: *a soul lustrated in the baptismal waters.* ▷early 17th cent.: from Latin *lustrat-* 'purified by lustral rites,' from the verb *lustrare*, from *lustrum* (see LUSTRUM). **—lus·tra·tion** /ˌləsˈtrāSHən/ *n.*

lus·tre /ˈləstər/ ▸*n.* British spelling of LUSTER[1], LUSTER[2].

lus·tre·ware /ˈləstərˌwer/ ▸*n.* British spelling of LUSTERWARE.

lust·ring /ˈləstriNG/ ▸*n.* variant spelling of LUTESTRING.

lus·trous /ˈləstrəs/ ▸*adj.* having luster; shining: *large, lustrous eyes.* See note at BRIGHT. **—lus·trous·ly** *adv.* **—lus·trous·ness** *n.*

lus·trum /ˈləstrəm/ ▸*n.* (*pl.* **-tra** /-trə/ or **-trums**) *chiefly poetic/literary historical* a period of five years. ▷late 16th cent.: from Latin, originally denoting a purificatory sacrifice after a quinquennial census.

lust·y /ˈləstē/ ▸*adj.* (**lust·i·er**, **lust·i·est**) healthy and strong; full of vigor: *the other farms had lusty young sons to work the land | lusty singing.* ▷Middle English: from LUST (in the early sense 'vigor') + -Y[1]. **—lust·i·ly** /-tələ̄/ *adv.* **—lust·i·ness** *n.*

lu·sus na·tu·rae /ˈlo͞osəs nəˈt(y)o͝orˌē; -ˈt(y)o͝orˌī/ ▸*n.* (*pl.* same or **lu·sus·es na·tu·rae**) *rare* a freak of nature. ▷Latin, literally 'a sport of nature.'

lu·ta·nist ▸*n.* variant spelling of LUTENIST.

lute[1] /lo͞ot/ ▸*n.* a plucked stringed instrument with a long neck bearing frets and a rounded body with a flat front that is shaped like a halved egg. ▷Middle English: from Old French *lut*, *leut*, probably via Provençal from Arabic *al-ʿūd*.

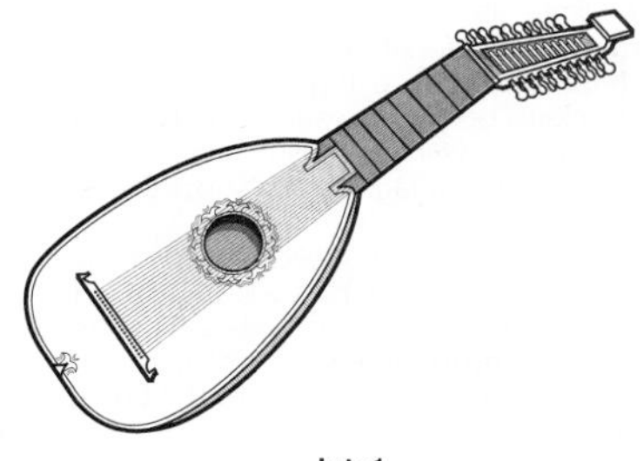

lute[1]

lute[2] ▸*n.* (also **lut·ing**) liquid clay or cement used to seal a joint, coat a crucible, or protect a graft.
▸*v.* [*trans.*] seal, join, or coat with lute. ▷late Middle English: from Old French *lut* or medieval Latin *lutum*, a special use of Latin *lutum* 'potter's clay.'

lu·te·al /ˈlo͞otēəl/ ▸*adj.* *Anatomy* of or relating to the corpus luteum.

lu·te·fisk /ˈlo͞otəˌfisk/ ▸*n.* a Scandinavian dish prepared by soaking dried cod in lye to tenderize it, then skinning, boning, and boiling the fish to a gelatinous consistency.

lu·te·in /ˈlo͞otēən; ˈlo͞oˌtēn/ ▸*n.* *Biochemistry* a deep yellow pigment of the xanthophyll class, found in the leaves of plants, in egg yolk, and in the corpus luteum. ▷mid 19th cent.: from Latin *luteum* 'yolk of egg' (neuter of *luteus* 'yellow') + -IN[1].

lu·te·in·iz·ing hor·mone /ˈlo͞otēəˌnīziNG; ˈlo͞otnˌīziNG/ ▸*n.* *Biochemistry* a hormone secreted by the anterior pituitary gland that stimulates ovulation in females and the synthesis of androgen in males.

lu·te·nist /ˈlo͞otn-ist; ˈlo͞otnist/ (also **lu·ta·nist**) ▸*n.* a lute player. ▷early 17th cent.: from medieval Latin *lutanista*, from *lutana* 'lute.'

luteo- ▸*comb. form* **1** orange-colored: *luteofulvous.* **2** relating to the corpus luteum: *luteotrophic.* ▷from Latin *luteus* (or neuter *luteum*) 'yellow.'

lu·te·o·trop·ic hor·mone /ˌlo͞otēəˈtrōpik; -ˈträpik/ (also **lu·te·o·troph·ic hormone** /-ˈträfik; -ˈtrō-/) ▸*n.* another term for PROLACTIN.

lute·string /ˈlo͞otˌstriNG/ (also **lus·trine** /ˈləstrēn/ or **lust·ring** /ˈləstriNG/) ▸*n.* *historical* a glossy silk fabric, or a satin-weave fabric resembling it. ▷late 17th cent.: from French *lustrine* or from Italian *lustrino*, from *lustro* 'luster.'

Lu·te·tia /lo͞oˈtēSH(ē)ə/ Roman name for PARIS[1].

lu·te·ti·um /lo͞oˈtēSH(ē)əm/ ▸*n.* the chemical element of atomic number 71, a rare, silvery-white metal of the lanthanide series. (Symbol: **Lu**) ▷early 20th cent.: from French *lutécium*, from Latin *Lutetia*, the ancient name of Paris, the home of its discoverer.

Lu·ther /ˈlo͞oTHər/, Martin (1483–1546), German theologian; the principal figure of the German Reformation. He preached the doctrine of justification by faith rather than by works and railed against the sale of indulgences and papal authority.

Martin Luther

Lu·ther·an /ˈlo͞oTH(ə)rən/ ▸*n.* a follower of Martin Luther. ■ a member of the Lutheran Church.
▸*adj.* of or characterized by the theology of Martin Luther. ■ of or relating to the Lutheran Church. **—Lu·ther·an·ism** /-ˌnizəm/ *n.* **—Lu·ther·an·ize** /-ˌnīz/ *v.*

Lu·ther·an Church the Protestant Church accepting the Augsburg Confession of 1530, with justification by faith alone as a cardinal doctrine. The Lutheran Church is the largest Protestant body worldwide, with substantial membership in Germany, Scandinavia, and the U.S.

lu·thern /ˈlo͞oTHərn/ ▸*n.* old-fashioned term for DORMER. ▷mid 17th cent.: perhaps an alteration of earlier *lucarne* 'skylight,' from Old French.

lu·thi·er /ˈlo͞otēər/ ▸*n.* a maker of stringed instruments such as violins or guitars. ▷late 19th cent.: from French, from *luth* 'lute.'

Lu·thu·li /lo͞oˈto͞olē/ (also **Lu·tu·li**), Albert John (*c.*1898–1967), South African political leader. His presidency of the African National Congress 1952–60 was marked by a program of civil disobedience. Nobel Peace Prize (1960).

lut·ing /ˈlo͞otiNG/ ▸*n.* see LUTE[2].

lu·ti·no /lo͞oˈtēnō/ ▸*n.* (*pl.* **-nos**) [often as *adj.*] a bird (esp. a bird of the parrot family that is often kept as a pet) with more yellow in the plumage than is usual for the species. ▷early 20th cent.: from Latin *luteus* 'yellow' + *-ino*, on the pattern of *albino.*

lut·ist /ˈlo͞otist/ ▸*n.* a lute player. ■ a maker of lutes; a luthier.

Lu·ton /ˈlo͞otn/ an industrial town northwest of London; pop. 167,000.

Lutsk /lo͞otsk/ (Polish name **Łuck**) a river port and industrial city in northwestern Ukraine, on the Styr River; pop. 210,000.

Lut·yens[1] /ˈlətyenz/, (Agnes) Elizabeth (1906–83), English composer; the daughter of Sir Edwin Lutyens. She was one of the first English composers to use the 12-note system.

Lut·yens[2], Sir Edwin (Landseer) (1869–1944), English architect. He is particularly known for his open garden-city layout in New Delhi in 1912 and for the Cenotaph in London (1919–21).

lutz /ləts; lo͞ots/ (also **Lutz**) ▸*n.* *Figure Skating* a jump with a backward takeoff from the backward outside edge of one skate to the backward outside edge of the other, with one or more full turns in the air. ▷1930s: probably from the name of Gustave *Lussi* (born 1898), who invented it.

luv /ləv/ ▸*n.* & *v.* nonstandard spelling of LOVE (representing informal or dialect use).

Lu·va·le /lo͞oˈvälā/ ▸*n.* (*pl.* same) **1** a member of a people living mainly in eastern Angola and western Democratic Republic of the Congo (formerly Zaire). **2** the Bantu language of this people, with around 600,000 speakers. Also called LWENA.
▸*adj.* of or relating to this people or their language.

luv·vy /ˈləvē/ (also **luv·vie**) ▸*n.* (*pl.* **-vies**) *Brit., informal, often derogatory* an actor or actress, esp. one who is particularly effusive or affected.

Lu·wi·an /ˈlo͞o-ēən/ (also **Lu·vi·an** /-vēən/) ▸*n.* an Anatolian language of the 2nd millennium BC. It is recorded in both cuneiform and hieroglyphic scripts and may have been the language spoken in Troy at the time of the Homeric war. ▷from *Luwia*, part of Asia Minor, + -AN.

lux /ləks/ (abbr.: **lx**) ▸*n.* (*pl.* same) the SI unit of illuminance, equal to one lumen per square meter. ▷late 19th cent.: from Latin, literally 'light.'

lux·ate /ˈləkˌsāt/ ▸*v.* [*trans.*] *Medicine* dislocate. ▷early 17th cent.: from Latin *luxat-* 'dislocated,' from the verb *luxare*, from *luxus* 'out of joint.' **—lux·a·tion** /ˌləkˈsāSHən/ *n.*

luxe /ləks; lo͝oks/ ▸*n.* luxury: [as *adj.*] *the luxe life.* ▷mid 16th cent.: from French, from Latin *luxus* 'abundance.'

Lux·em·bourg /ˈləksəmˌbərg; ˈlo͝oksəmˌbo͝ork/ a country in western Europe, between Belgium and Germany and north of France; pop. 462,000; capital, Luxembourg; official languages, Luxemburgish, French, and German. ■ the capital of the Grand Duchy of Luxembourg; pop. 76,000. It is the seat of the European Court of Justice. ■ a province in southeastern Belgium; capital, Arlon. **—Lux·em·bourg·er** *n.*

Annexed by France in 1795, Luxembourg became an independent grand duchy as a result of the Treaty of Vienna in 1815. It formed a customs union with Belgium in 1922, which was extended in 1948 into the Benelux Customs Union with the Netherlands. It was a founding member of the EEC in 1957.

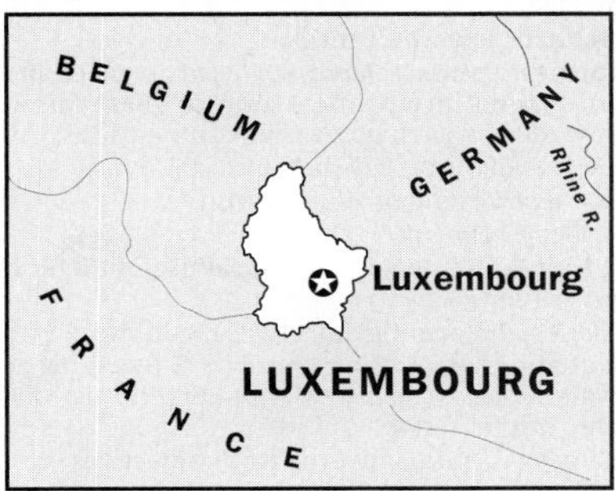

Lux·em·burg /ˈləksəmˌbərg; ˈlo͝oksəmˌbo͝ork/, Rosa (1871–1919), German revolutionary leader, born in Poland. Together with the German socialist **Karl Liebknecht** /ˈlēpknekHt/ (1871–1919), she founded the Spartacus League in 1916 and the German Communist Party in 1918.

Lux·em·burg·ish /ˈləksəmˌbərgiSH; ˈlo͝oksəmˌbo͝or-/ ▸*n.* the local language of Luxembourg, a form of German with a strong admixture of French. Also called LETZEBURGESCH.

Lux·or /ˈləkˌsôr; ˈlo͝ok-/ a city in eastern Egypt, on the eastern bank of the Nile River; pop. 142,000. The site of ancient Thebes, it contains the ruins of a temple built by Amenhotep III and of monuments erected by Ramses II. Arabic name **EL UQSUR**. ▷from Arabic *al-uqṣur* 'the castles.'

lux·u·ri·ant /ˌləgˈZHo͝orēənt; ˌləkˈSHo͝or-/ ▸*adj.* (of vegetation) rich and profuse in growth; lush: *forests of dark, luxuriant foliage | figurative luxuriant prose.* See note at PROFUSE. ■ (of hair) thick and healthy. ▷mid 16th cent.: from Latin *luxuriant-* 'growing rankly,' from the verb *luxuriare*, from *luxuria* 'luxury, rankness.' **—lux·u·ri·ance** *n.* **—lux·u·ri·ant·ly** *adv.*

USAGE See usage at LUXURIOUS.

lux·u·ri·ate /ˌləgˈZHo͝orēˌāt; ˌləkˈSHo͝or-/ ▸*v.* [*intrans.*] (often **luxuriate in**) enjoy oneself in a luxurious way;

L

Pronunciation Key ə *ago*; ər *over*; ˈə *or* ˌə *up*; ˈər *or* ˌər *fur*; a *hat*; ā *rate*; ä *car*; CH *chew*; e *let*; ē *see*; e(ə)r *air*; i *fit*; ī *by*; i(ə)r *ear*; NG *sing*; ō *go*; ô *for*; oi *boy*; o͝o *good*; o͞o *goo*; ou *out*; SH *she*; TH *thin*; T͟H *then*; (h)w *why*; ZH *vision*

take self-indulgent delight: *she was luxuriating in a long bath.* ▷early 17th cent.: from Latin *luxuriat-* 'grown in abundance,' from the verb *luxuriare.*

lux·u·ri·ous /ˌləgˈzHŏŏrēəs; ˌləkˈsHŏŏr-/ ▸*adj.* extremely comfortable, elegant, or enjoyable, esp. in a way that involves great expense: *the bedrooms have luxurious marble bathrooms | many of the leadership led relatively luxurious lives.* ■ giving self-indulgent or sensuous pleasure: *a luxurious wallow in a scented bath.* See note at **SENSUOUS.** ▷Middle English (in the sense 'lascivious'): from Old French *luxurios,* from Latin *luxuriosus,* from *luxuria* 'luxury.' —**lux·u·ri·ous·ly** *adv.* —**lux·u·ri·ous·ness** *n.*

USAGE **Luxuriant** and **luxurious** are sometimes confused. **Luxuriant** means 'lush, profuse, prolific': *forests of dark luxuriant foliage; luxuriant black eyelashes*). **Luxurious**, a much more common word, means 'supplied with luxuries, extremely comfortable': *a luxurious mansion.*

lux·u·ry /ˈləksH(ə)rē; ˈləgzH(ə)-/ ▸*n.* (*pl.* **-ries**) the state of great comfort and extravagant living: *he lived a life of luxury.* ■ an inessential, desirable item that is expensive or difficult to obtain: *luxuries like raspberry vinegar and state-of-the-art CD players | he considers bananas a luxury.*
▸*adj.* luxurious or of the nature of a luxury: *a luxury yacht | luxury goods.* ▷Middle English (denoting lechery): from Old French *luxurie, luxure,* from Latin *luxuria,* from *luxus* 'excess.' The earliest current sense dates from the mid 17th cent.

Lu·zon /lōōˈzän/ the largest and most northern island in the Philippines. Its chief towns are Quezon City and Manila, which is the country's capital.

lv. ▸*abbr.* ■ leave or leaves.

Lviv /ləˈvēf; ləˈvēōō/ an industrial city in western Ukraine, near the border with Poland; pop. 798,000. Russian name **Lvov**; Polish name **Lwów**; German name **LEMBERG.**

LVN ▸*abbr.* licensed vocational nurse.

lwei /ləˈwā/ ▸*n.* (*pl.* same) a monetary unit of Angola, equal to one hundredth of a kwanza. ▷a local word.

Lwe·na /ləˈwānə/ ▸*n.* another term for **LUVALE** (the language).

LWM ▸*abbr.* low-water mark.

L-word ▸*n. informal, humorous* used in place of the word "liberal" in a political context where this word is regarded as having negative connotations.

Lwów /ləˈvôf; -ˈvôv/ Polish name for **Lviv.**

LWV ▸*abbr.* League of Women Voters.

lx *Physics* ▸*abbr.* lux.

LXX ▸*symbol* Septuagint. ▷special use of the Roman numeral for 70.

-ly[1] /lē/ ▸*suffix* forming adjectives meaning: **1** having the qualities of: *brotherly | rascally.* **2** recurring at intervals of: *hourly | quarterly.* ▷Old English *-līc,* of Germanic origin; related to **LIKE**[1].

-ly[2] ▸*suffix* forming adverbs from adjectives, chiefly denoting manner or degree: *greatly | happily | pointedly.* ▷Old English *-līce,* of Germanic origin.

Lyall·pur /ˈlīl,pŏŏr/ former name (until 1979) for **FAISALABAD.**

ly·ase /ˈlī,ās; -,āz/ ▸*n. Biochemistry* an enzyme that catalyzes the joining of specified molecules or groups by a double bond.

ly·cae·nid /līˈsēnid/ ▸*n. Entomology* a small butterfly of a family (Lycaenidae) that includes the blues, coppers, hairstreaks, and arguses. ▷late 19th cent.: from modern Latin *Lycaenidae* (plural), from the genus name *Lycaena,* apparently from Greek *lukaina* 'she-wolf.'

ly·can·thrope /ˈlīkən,THrōp/ ▸*n.* a werewolf. ▷early 17th cent.: from modern Latin *lycanthropus,* from Greek *lukanthrōpos* 'wolf man' (see **LYCANTHROPY**).

ly·can·thro·py /līˈkanTHrəpē/ ▸*n.* the supernatural transformation of a person into a wolf, as recounted in folk tales. ■ *archaic* a form of madness involving the delusion of being an animal, usually a wolf, with correspondingly altered behavior. ▷late 16th cent. (as a supposed form of madness): from modern Latin *lycanthropia,* from Greek *lukanthrōpia,* from *lukos* 'wolf' + *anthrōpos* 'human being, man.' —**ly·can·throp·ic** /ˌlīkənˈTHräpik/ *adj.*

ly·cée /lēˈsā/ ▸*n.* (*pl. pronounced* same) a secondary school in France that is funded by the government. ▷French, from Latin *lyceum* (see **LYCEUM**).

Ly·ce·um /līˈsēəm/ the garden at Athens in which Aristotle taught philosophy. ■ (**the Lyceum**) Aristotelian philosophy and its followers. ■ (**a lyceum**) *archaic* a literary institution, lecture hall, or teaching place. ▷via Latin from Greek *Lukeion,* neuter of *Lukeios,* epithet of Apollo (from whose neighboring temple the Lyceum was named).

ly·chee /ˈlēCHē/ ▸*n.* variant spelling of **LITCHI.**

lych·gate /ˈliCH,gāt/ (also **lich·gate**) ▸*n.* a roofed gateway to a churchyard, formerly used during burials for sheltering a coffin until the clergyman's arrival. ▷late 15th cent.: from Old English *līc* 'body' + **GATE.**

lych·nis /ˈliknis/ ▸*n.* a plant of a genus that includes the campions and a number of cultivated ornamental flowers. • Genus *Lychnis,* family Caryophyllaceae. ▷modern Latin, via Latin from Greek *lukhnis,* denoting a red flower, from *lukhnos* 'lamp.'

Ly·cia /ˈlisH(ē)ə/ an ancient region on the coast of southwestern Asia Minor, between Caria and Pamphylia. —**Ly·ci·an** *adj. & n.*

Ly·ci·an /ˈlisH(ē)ən/ ▸*n.* **1** a native or inhabitant of ancient Lycia. **2** the Anatolian language of the Lycians.

ly·co·pene /ˈlīkə,pēn/ ▸*n. Biochemistry* a red carotenoid pigment present in tomatoes and many berries and fruits. ▷1930s: from the variant *lycopin* (from modern Latin *Lycopersicon,* a genus name including the tomato) + **-ENE.**

ly·co·pod /ˈlīkə,päd/ ▸*n. Botany* a club moss, esp. a lycopodium. Giant lycopods the size of trees were common in the Carboniferous period. • Class Lycopsida: several families. ▷mid 19th cent.: anglicized form of **LYCOPODIUM.**

ly·co·po·di·um /ˌlīkəˈpōdēəm/ ▸*n.* a plant of a genus that includes the common club mosses. • Genus *Lycopodium,* family Lycopodiaceae. ■ (usu. **lycopodium powder** or **lycopodium seed**) a fine, flammable powder consisting of club moss spores, formerly used as an absorbent in surgery, in experiments in the physical sciences, and in making fireworks. ▷modern Latin, from Greek *lukos* 'wolf' + *pous, pod-* 'foot' (because of the clawlike shape of the root).

Ly·cop·si·da /līˈkäpsədə/ *Botany* a class of pteridophyte plants that comprises the club mosses and their extinct relatives. ▷modern Latin (plural), from Greek *lukos* 'wolf' + *opsis* 'appearance.' —**ly·cop·sid** /-sid/ *n. & adj.*

Ly·cra /ˈlīkrə/ ▸*n. trademark* an elastic polyurethane fiber or fabric used esp. for close-fitting sports clothing.

Ly·cur·gus /līˈkərgəs/ (9th century BC), Spartan lawmaker. He is traditionally held to have been the founder of the constitution and military regime of ancient Sparta.

lydd·ite /ˈlid,īt/ ▸*n. chiefly historical* a high explosive containing picric acid, used chiefly by the British during World War I. ▷late 19th cent.: named after *Lydd,* a town in Kent, England, where the explosive was first tested, + **-ITE**[1].

Lyd·gate /ˈlid,gāt; -git/, John (*c.*1370–*c.*1450), English poet and monk.

Lyd·i·a /ˈlidēə/ an ancient region of western Asia Minor, south of Mysia and north of Caria. It became a powerful kingdom in the 7th century BC but in 546 Croesus, its last king, was defeated by Cyrus and it was absorbed into the Persian empire.

Lyd·i·an /ˈlidēən/ ▸*n.* **1** a native or inhabitant of Lydia. **2** the Anatolian language of the Lydians, of which some inscriptions and other texts have survived in a version of the Greek alphabet.
▸*adj.* of or relating to the Lydians or their language.

Lyd·i·an mode ▸*n. Music* the mode represented by the natural diatonic scale F–F (containing an augmented 4th).

lye /lī/ ▸*n.* a strongly alkaline solution, esp. of potassium hydroxide, used for washing or cleansing. ▷Old English *lēag,* of Germanic origin: related to Dutch *loog,* German *Lauge,* also to **LATHER.**

Ly·ell /ˈlī(ə)l/, Sir Charles (1797–1875), Scottish geologist. He held that the Earth's features were shaped over a long period of time by natural processes.

ly·ing[1] /ˈlī-iNG/ ▸ present participle of **LIE**[1].

ly·ing[2] ▸ present participle of **LIE**[2].
▸*adj.* not telling the truth: *he's a lying, cheating, snake in the grass.* —**ly·ing·ly** *adv.*

ly·ing-in ▸*n. archaic* seclusion before and after childbirth; confinement.

Ly·ly /ˈlilē/, John (*c.*1554–1606), English prose writer and playwright. His prose romance in two parts, *Euphues, The Anatomy of Wit* (1578) and *Euphues and His England* (1580), was written in a style that became known as *euphuism.*

Ly·man se·ries /ˈlīmən/ *Physics* a series of lines in the ultraviolet spectrum of atomic hydrogen, between 122 and 91 nanometers. ▷early 20th cent.: named after Theodore *Lyman* (1874–1954), American physicist.

Lyme /līm/ a town in southeastern Connecticut, on the Connecticut River, that gave its name to Lyme disease. Pop. 1,949.

Lyme dis·ease /līm/ ▸*n.* an inflammatory disease characterized at first by a rash, headache, fever, and chills, and later by possible arthritis and neurological and cardiac disorders, caused by bacteria that are transmitted by ticks. • Lyme disease is caused by the spirochete *Borrelia burgdorferi.* ▷1970s: named after *Lyme,* Connecticut, where an outbreak occurred.

lymph /limf/ ▸*n.* **1** *Physiology* a colorless fluid containing white blood cells, that bathes the tissues and drains through the lymphatic system into the bloodstream. ■ fluid exuding from a sore or inflamed tissue. **2** *poetic/literary* pure water. ▷late 16th cent. (sense 2): from French *lymphe* or Latin *lympha, limpa* 'water.' —**lymph·ous** /-fəs/ *adj.*

lymph- ▸*comb. form* variant spelling of **LYMPHO-** shortened before a vowel, as in *lymphangiography.*

lym·phad·e·ni·tis /ˌlim,fadnˈītis/ ▸*n. Medicine* inflammation of the lymph nodes.

lym·phad·e·nop·a·thy /ˌlim,fadnˈäpəTHē/ ▸*n. Medicine* a disease affecting the lymph nodes.

lym·phan·gi·og·ra·phy /ˌlim,fanjēˈägrəfē/ ▸*n. Medicine* X-ray examination of the vessels of the lymphatic system after injection of a substance opaque to X-rays. —**lym·phan·gi·o·gram** /limˈfanjēə,gram/ *n.* —**lym·phan·gi·o·graph·ic** /-jēəˈgrafik/ *adj.*

lym·phan·gi·tis /ˌlim,fanˈjītis/ ▸*n. Medicine* inflammation of the walls of the lymphatic vessels.

lym·phat·ic /limˈfatik/ ▸*adj.* **1** [*attrib.*] *Physiology* of or relating to lymph or its secretion: *lymphatic vessels | lymphatic drainage.* **2** *archaic* (of a person) pale, flabby, or sluggish.
▸*n. Anatomy* a veinlike vessel conveying lymph in the body. ▷mid 17th cent. (in the sense 'frenzied, mad'): from Latin *lymphaticus* 'mad,' from Greek *numpholēptos* 'seized by nymphs'; now associated with **LYMPH,** on the pattern of words such as *spermatic.*

lym·phat·ic sys·tem ▸*n.* the network of vessels through which lymph drains from the tissues into the blood.

lymph gland ▸*n.* less technical term for **LYMPH NODE.**

lymph node ▸*n. Physiology* each of a number of small swellings in the lymphatic system where lymph is filtered and lymphocytes are formed.

lympho- (also **lymph-** before a vowel) ▸*comb. form* representing **LYMPH:** *lymphocyte.*

lym·pho·blast /ˈlimfə,blast/ ▸*n. Medicine* an abnormal cell resembling a large lymphocyte, produced in large numbers in a form of leukemia. —**lym·pho·blas·tic** /ˌlimfəˈblastik/ *adj.*

lym·pho·cyte /ˈlimfə,sīt/ ▸*n. Physiology* a form of small leukocyte (white blood cell) with a single round nucleus, occurring esp. in the lymphatic system. —**lym·pho·cyt·ic** /ˌlimfəˈsitik/ *adj.*

lym·phog·ra·phy /limˈfägrəfē/ ▸*n.* short for **LYMPHANGIOGRAPHY.**

lym·phoid /ˈlim,foid/ ▸*adj. Anatomy & Medicine* of, relating to, or denoting the tissue responsible for producing lymphocytes and antibodies. This tissue occurs in the lymph nodes, thymus, tonsils, and spleen, and dispersed elsewhere in the body.

lym·pho·kine /ˈlimfə,kīn/ ▸*n. Physiology* a substance produced by lymphocytes, such as interferon, that acts upon other cells of the immune system, e.g., by activating macrophages. ▷1960s: from **LYMPHO-** + Greek *kinein* 'to move.'

lym·pho·ma /limˈfōmə/ ▸*n.* (*pl.* **-mas** or **-ma·ta** /-mətə/) *Medicine* cancer of the lymph nodes.

lym·pho·re·tic·u·lar /ˌlimfōriˈtikyələr/ ▸*adj.* another term for **RETICULOENDOTHELIAL.**

lym·pho·tox·in /ˌlimfəˈtäksin/ ▸*n. Immunology* a lymphokine that causes the destruction of certain cells, esp. tumor cells.

lynch /linCH/ ▸*v.* [*trans.*] (of a mob) kill (someone), esp. by hanging, for an alleged offense with or without a legal trial. ▷mid 19th cent.: from *Lynch's law,* early form of *lynch law* 'the practice of killing an alleged criminal by lynching,' named after Capt. William *Lynch,* head of a self-constituted judicial tribunal in Virginia *c.*1780. —**lynch·er** *n.*

Lynch·burg /ˈlinCH,bərg/ a city in west central Virginia, near the Blue Ridge Mountains; pop. 65,269.

lynch mob ▸*n.* a band of people intent on lynching someone.

lynch·pin /ˈlinCH,pin/ ▸*n.* variant spelling of **LINCHPIN.**

Lynn[1] /lin/ a city in northeastern Massachusetts, on Massachusetts Bay, northeast of Boston; pop. 89,050.

Lynn[2], Dame Vera (1917–), English singer; born *Vera Margaret Lewis.* She is known chiefly for her rendering of such songs as "We'll Meet Again" and "White Cliffs of Dover," which she sang to the troops during World War II.

Lynn[3], Loretta (1935–), U.S. country singer and songwriter; born Loretta Webb. She had hits with songs such as "Honky Tonk Girl" (1960), "Don't Come Home A-Drinkin' (With Loving on Your Mind)" (1966), and "Coal Miner's Daughter" (1970). Her life was recounted in the movie *Coal Miner's Daughter* (1980). Country Music Hall of Fame (1988).

Lynx /liNGks/ *Astronomy* an inconspicuous northern constellation (the Lynx), between Ursa Major and Gemini. ■ [as *genitive*] (**Lyncis**) used with a preceding letter or numeral to designate a star in this constellation: *the star Alpha Lyncis.* ▷via Latin from Greek *lunx.*

lynx /liNGks/ ▸*n.* a wild cat with yellowish-brown fur (sometimes spotted), a short tail, and tufted ears, found chiefly in the northern latitudes of North America and Eurasia. • Genus *Lynx*, family Felidae: the **Eurasian lynx** (*L. lynx*) and the **Canadian lynx** (*L. canadensis* or *L. lynx*). ■ the fur of the lynx. ■ (**African lynx**) see CARACAL. ▷Middle English: via Latin from Greek *lunx.*

Eurasian lynx

lynx-eyed ▸*adj.* keen-sighted.

ly·o·cell /ˈlīəˌsel/ ▸*n.* a strong synthetic fiber made from reconstituted cellulose, used in carpets and in apparel when blended with other fibers.

Ly·on /ˈlīən/, Mary Mason (1797–1849), U.S. educator. She founded Mount Holyoke Female Seminary (later Mount Holyoke College) in South Hadley, Massachusetts, in 1837 and served as its first president 1837–49.

ly·on·naise /ˌlīəˈnāz/ ▸*adj.* (of food, esp. sliced potatoes) cooked with onions or with a white wine and onion sauce. ▷French, 'characteristic of the city of Lyons.'

Ly·ons /lēˈôN; ˈlīənz/ an industrial city and river port in southeastern France, situated at the confluence of the Rhône and Saône rivers; pop. 422,000. Founded by the Romans in AD 43 as Lugdunum, it was an important city of Roman Gaul. French name **LYON.**

ly·o·phil·ic /ˌlīəˈfilik/ ▸*adj. Chemistry* (of a colloid) readily dispersed by a solvent and not easily precipitated. ▷early 20th cent.: from Greek *luein* 'loosen, dissolve' + *philos* 'loving.'

ly·oph·i·lize /līˈäfəˌlīz/ ▸*v.* [*trans.*] *technical* freeze-dry (a substance). **—ly·oph·i·li·za·tion** /-ˌäfələˈzāshən; -ˌlīˈzā-/ *n.*

ly·o·pho·bic /ˌlīəfōˈbik/ ▸*adj. Chemistry* (of a colloid) not lyophilic.

Lyo·tard /ˌlēəˈtär/, Jean-François (1924–1998), French philosopher and literary critic. He outlined his "philosophy of desire," based on the politics of Nietzsche, in *L'Économie libidinale* (1974). In later works, he adopted a postmodern quasi-Wittgensteinian linguistic philosophy.

lyr. ▸*abbr.* lyric.

Ly·ra /ˈlīrə/ *Astronomy* a small northern constellation (the Lyre), said to represent the lyre invented by Hermes. It contains the bright star Vega. ■ [as *genitive*] (**Lyrae**) used with a preceding letter or numeral to designate a star in this constellation: *the star Beta Lyrae.* ▷Latin.

lyre /līr/ ▸*n.* a stringed instrument like a small U-shaped harp with strings fixed to a crossbar, used esp. in ancient Greece. Modern instruments of this type are found mainly in East Africa. ▷Middle English: via Old French *lire* and Latin *lyra* from Greek *lura.*

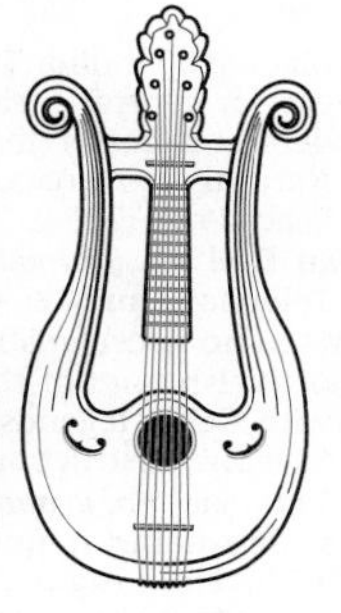

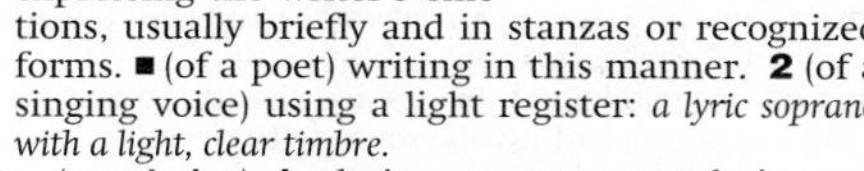

lyre

lyre·bird /ˈlīrˌbərd/ ▸*n.* a large Australian songbird, the male of which has a long, lyre-shaped tail and is noted for his remarkable song and display. • Family Menuridae and genus *Menura*: two species, in particular the **superb lyrebird** (*M. novaehollandiae*).

lyr·ic /ˈlirik/ ▸*adj.* **1** (of poetry) expressing the writer's emotions, usually briefly and in stanzas or recognized forms. ■ (of a poet) writing in this manner. **2** (of a singing voice) using a light register: *a lyric soprano with a light, clear timbre.*
▸*n.* (usu. **lyrics**) **1** a lyric poem or verse. ■ lyric poetry as a literary genre. **2** the words of a song: *she has published both music and lyrics for a number of songs.* ▷late 16th cent.: from French *lyrique* or Latin *lyricus*, from Greek *lurikos*, from *lura* 'lyre.'

lyr·i·cal /ˈlirikəl/ ▸*adj.* **1** (of literature, art, or music) expressing the writer's emotions in an imaginative and beautiful way: *the poet's combination of lyrical and descriptive power.* ■ (of poetry or a poet) lyric: *Wordsworth's Lyrical Ballads.* **2** of or relating to the words of a popular song: *the lyrical content of his songs.* **—lyr·i·cal·ly** /-ik(ə)lē/ *adv.*
▸*PHRASE* □ **wax lyrical** talk in a highly enthusiastic and effusive way: *waxing lyrical about his splendid son-in-law.*

lyr·i·cism /ˈlirəˌsizəm/ ▸*n.* an artist's expression of emotion in an imaginative and beautiful way; the quality of being lyrical.

lyr·i·cist /ˈlirəsist/ ▸*n.* a person who writes the words to a popular song or musical.

lyr·i·cize /ˈlirəˌsīz/ ▸*v.* [*intrans.*] *Music* write or sing lyrics. ■ to write in a lyric style. ■ [*trans.*] to treat in a lyric style or put into lyric form.

lyr·ist /ˈlīrist; ˈlirist/ ▸*n.* **1** a person who plays the lyre. **2** a lyric poet. ▷mid 17th cent.: from Latin *lyrista*, from Greek *luristēs*, from *lura* 'lyre.'

Ly·san·der /līˈsandər/ (died 395 BC) Spartan general. He defeated the Athenian navy in 405 and captured Athens in 404, bringing the Peloponnesian War to an end.

ly·sate /ˈlīˌsāt/ ▸*n. Biology* a preparation containing the products of lysis of cells.

lyse /līs; līz/ ▸*v. Biology* undergo or cause to undergo lysis. ▷early 20th cent.: back-formation from **LYSIS.**

Ly·sen·ko /līˈsenkō; liˈsyenkə/, Trofim Denisovich (1898–1976), Soviet biologist and geneticist. An adherent of Lamarck's theory of evolution by the inheritance of acquired characteristics, he dominated Soviet genetics for many years. **—Ly·sen·ko·ism** /-kōˌizəm/ *n.* **—Ly·sen·ko·ist** /-kōˌist/ *adj., n.*

ly·ser·gic ac·id /līˈsərjik; li-/ ▸*n. Chemistry* a crystalline compound prepared from natural ergot alkaloids or synthetically, from which the drug LSD (**lysergic acid diethylamide**) can be made. • A tetracyclic acid; chem. formula: $C_{16}H_{16}N_2O_2$. ▷1930s: *lysergic* from *(hydro)lys(is)* + *erg(ot)* + **-IC.**

ly·sin /ˈlīsin/ ▸*n. Biology* an antibody or other substance able to cause lysis of cells (esp. bacteria). ▷early 20th cent.: from German *Lysine.*

ly·sine /ˈlīˌsēn/ ▸*n. Biochemistry* a basic amino acid that is a constituent of most proteins. It is an essential nutrient in the diet of vertebrates. • Chem. formula: $NH_2(CH_2)_4CH(NH_2)COOH$. ▷late 19th cent.: from German *Lysin*, based on **LYSIS.**

ly·sis /ˈlīsis/ ▸*n.* **1** *Biology* the disintegration of a cell by rupture of the cell wall or membrane. **2** the gradual decline of disease symptoms. ▷early 19th cent.: from Latin, from Greek *lusis* 'loosening,' from *luein* 'loosen.'

-lysis ▸*comb. form* denoting disintegration or decomposition: ■ in nouns specifying an agent: *hydrolysis.* ■ in nouns specifying a reactant: *hemolysis.* ■ in nouns specifying the nature of the process: *autolysis.* ▷via Latin from Greek *lusis* 'loosening.'

ly·so·gen /ˈlīsəjən; -ˌjen/ ▸*n.* a lysogenic bacterium or bacterial strain.

Ly·sol /ˈlīˌsôl; -ˌsäl/ ▸*n. trademark* a disinfectant consisting of a mixture of cresols and soft soap. ▷late 19th cent.: from **LYSIS** + **-OL.**

ly·so·some /ˈlīsəˌsōm/ ▸*n. Biology* an organelle in the cytoplasm of eukaryotic cells containing degradative enzymes enclosed in a membrane. **—ly·so·so·mal** /ˌlīsəˈsōməl/ *adj.*

ly·so·zyme /ˈlīsəˌzīm/ ▸*n. Biochemistry* an enzyme that catalyzes the destruction of the cell walls of certain bacteria, occurring notably in tears and egg white. ▷early 20th cent.: from **LYSIS** + a shortened form of **ENZYME.**

lyt·ic /ˈlitik/ ▸*adj. Biology* of, relating to, or causing lysis: *the lytic activity of bile acids.* **—lyt·i·cal·ly** /ik(ə)lē/ *adv.*

-lytic ▸*comb. form* in adjectives corresponding to nouns ending in *-lysis* (such as *hydrolytic* corresponding to *hydrolysis*). ▷from Greek *-lutikos* 'able to loosen.'

Lyt·ton /ˈlitn/, Edward George Earle Lytton Bulwer-, 1st Baron Lytton of Knebworth (1803–73), British novelist, playwright, and statesman. He wrote *Pelham* (1828), a novel of fashionable society, and also wrote historical romances, such as *The Last Days of Pompeii* (1834), and plays. He served as viceroy of India from 1876 until 1880.

LZ ▸*abbr.* landing zone.

Mm

M¹ /em/ (also **m**) ▸*n.* (*pl.* **Ms** or **M's**) **1** the thirteenth letter of the alphabet. See also **EM**. ■ denoting the next after L in a set of items, categories, etc. **2** (**M**) a shape like that of a capital M. **3** the Roman numeral for 1,000. [from Latin *mille*.]

M² ▸*abbr.* ■ Majesty. ■ male. ■ Manitoba. ■ markka; markkas. ■ Marquis. ■ *Music* measure. ■ medicine. ■ medium (as a clothes size). ■ [in *combination*] (in units of measurement) mega-: *8 Mbytes of memory.* ■ meridian. ■ *Astronomy* Messier (catalog of nebulae): *the galaxy M33.* ■ *Chemistry* (with reference to solutions) molar: *0.15 M NaCl solution.* ■ Monday. ■ Monsieur: *M Chirac.* ■ money, when used with a following numeral in measures of money supply: *broad money, M3, grew by an annualized 9.7%.* ■ mountain. ■ noon. [from Latin *meridies*.]

M³ ▸*symb. Physics* mutual inductance.

m ▸*abbr.* ■ mare. ■ (in Germany) mark; marks. ■ married: *m twice; two d.* ■ masculine. ■ *Physics* mass. ■ (*m-*) [in *combination*] *Chemistry* meta-: *m-xylene.* ■ meter(s). ■ middle. ■ mile(s). ■ [in *combination*] (in units of measurement) milli-: *100 mA.* ■ million(s): *$5 m.* ■ minute(s). ■ (in prescriptions) mix. ■ modification of. ■ modulus. ■ molar. ■ month. ■ moon. ■ morning. ■ mouth. ■ noon. [from Latin *meridies*.]
▸*symbol Physics* mass: $E = mc^2$.

m' /m; mə/ ▸*possessive adj. Brit.* short for **MY** (representing the pronunciation used by lawyers in court to refer to or address the judge or a fellow barrister on the same side): *he can't hold the Bible, m'lud.*

'm¹ /m/ *informal* ▸*abbr.* am: *I'm a doctor.*

'm² ▸*n. informal* madam: *yes'm.*

M-1 ▸*n.* a .30-caliber semiautomatic clip-fed rifle capable of firing eight rounds before reloading, the standard rifle used by U.S. troops in World War II and the Korean War.

M-16 ▸*n.* a lightweight, fully automatic assault rifle that shoots small-caliber bullets at an extremely high velocity, used by U.S. troops after 1966.

MA ▸*abbr.* ■ Massachusetts (in official postal use). ■ Master of Arts: *David Jones, MA.* ■ *Psychology* mental age. ■ Military Academy.

Ma /mä/, Yo-Yo (1955–), U.S. cellist; born in France. He made his debut at New York City's Carnegie Hall at the age of nine and has performed throughout the world with major orchestras.

ma /mä/ ▸*n. informal* one's mother: *I didn't want to make trouble for my ma.* ▷early 19th cent.: abbreviation of **MAMA**.

ma'am /mam/ ▸*n.* a term of respectful or polite address used for a woman: *excuse me, ma'am.* ■ a term of address for a ranking female officer in the police or armed forces. ■ *Brit.* a term of address for female royalty. ▷mid 17th cent.: contraction of **MADAM**.

maar /mär/ ▸*n. Geology* a broad, shallow crater, typically filled by a lake, formed by a volcanic explosion with little lava. ▷early 19th cent.: from German dialect, originally denoting a kind of crater lake in the Eifel district of Germany.

Maas /mäs/ Dutch name for **MEUSE**.

Maa·sai ▸*n.* & *adj.* variant spelling of **MASAI**.

Maas·tricht /'mäs,trikt; -,trikʜt/ an industrial city in the Netherlands, situated on the Maas River near the Belgian and German borders; pop. 117,000. The treaty of the European Union was signed here in 1992.

Ma·at /mät/ *Egyptian Mythology* the goddess of truth, justice, and cosmic order, daughter of Ra. She is depicted as a young and beautiful woman, standing or seated, with a feather on her head.

Maa·thai /mə'tī/ Wangari (1940–), Kenyan environmentalist, human rights activist, and feminist. The founder of the Green Belt Movement, which has planted 30 million trees, she was the first woman in east or central Africa to earn a Ph.D. She became deputy minister in the Ministry of Environment, Natural Resources, and Wildlife in 2003. Nobel Peace Prize (2004).

Ma Bell ▸*n. informal* a nickname for the American Telephone and Telegraph Corporation.

Mab·i·no·gi·on /,mabə'nôgēən; -'nōgēən/ a collection of Welsh tales of the 11th–13th centuries, dealing with Celtic legends and mythology. ▷from Welsh *Mabinogi* 'instruction for young bards.'

Mac /mak/ ▸*n. informal* a form of address for a man whose name is unknown to the speaker. ▷early 17th cent. (originally a form of address to a Scotsman): from *Mac-*, a patronymic prefix in many Scots and Irish surnames.

mac /mak/ (also **mack**) ▸*n. informal, chiefly Brit.* a mackintosh. ▷early 20th cent.: abbreviation.

ma·ca·bre /mə'käbrə; -'käb/ ▸*adj.* disturbing and horrifying because of involvement with or depiction of death and injury: *a macabre series of murders.* ▷late 19th cent.: from French *macabre*, from *Danse Macabre* 'dance of death,' from Old French, perhaps from *Macabé* 'a Maccabee,' with reference to a miracle play depicting the slaughter of the Maccabees.

mac·ad·am /mə'kadəm/ ▸*n.* broken stone of even size used in successively compacted layers for surfacing roads and paths, and typically bound with tar or bitumen. ■ a stretch of road with such a surface. ▷early 19th cent.: named after John L. *McAdam* (1756–1836), the British surveyor who advocated using this material. **—mac·ad·amed** *adj.*

mac·a·da·mi·a /,makə'dāmēə/ ▸*n.* an Australian tree with slender, glossy evergreen leaves and globular edible nuts. • Genus *Macadamia*, family Proteaceae: several species, esp. *M. integrifolia* and *M. tetraphylla*, which are cultivated for their nuts. ■ (also **macadamia nut**) the edible nut of this tree. ▷modern Latin, named after John *Macadam* (1827–65), Australian chemist.

mac·ad·am·ize /mə'kadə,mīz/ ▸*v.* [*trans.*] make or cover with macadam: [as *adj.*] (**macadamized**) *macadamized roads.*

Mac·Al·pin /mə'kalpən/, Kenneth, see **KENNETH I**.

Ma·cao /mə'kou/ a Special Administrative Region (SAR) of the People's Republic, formerly a Portuguese dependency, on the southeastern coast of China, on the western side of the Pearl River estuary, opposite Hong Kong, comprising the Macao peninsula and the islands of Taipa and Cologne; pop. 467,000; capital, Macao City. Visited by Vasco da Gama in 1497, Macao was developed by the Portuguese as a trading post and became the chief center of trade between Europe and China in the 18th century. In 1999, Macao passed to China, as agreed upon in 1987. Portuguese name **MACAU**. **—Mac·a·nese** /,makə'nēz; -'nēs/ *adj.* & *n.*

Ma·ca·pá /,mäkə'pä/ a town in northern Brazil, on the Amazon delta; pop. 167,000.

ma·caque /mə'käk; -'kak/ ▸*n.* (also **macaque monkey**) a medium-sized, chiefly forest-dwelling Old World monkey that has a long face and cheek pouches for holding food. • Genus *Macaca*, family Cercopithecidae: several species, including the rhesus monkey and the Barbary ape. ▷late 17th cent.: via French and Portuguese; based on the Bantu morpheme *ma* (denoting a plural) + *kaku* 'monkey.'

Ma·ca·re·na /,mäkə'rānə/ ▸ *n.* a dance performed with hand and body language, including exaggerated hip motion, to 16 beats of music.

Mac·a·ro·ne·sia /,makərə'nēzʜə/ *Botany* a phytogeographical region comprising the Azores, Madeira, Canary Islands, and Cape Verde Islands in the eastern North Atlantic. ▷from Greek *makarōn nēsoi* 'islands of the Blessed' (mythical islands later associated with the Canaries). **—Mac·a·ro·ne·sian** /-'nēzʜēən/ *adj.*

mac·a·ro·ni /,makə'rōnē/ ▸*n.* (*pl.* **-nies**) **1** a variety of pasta formed in narrow tubes. **2** an 18th-century British dandy affecting Continental fashions. ▷late 16th cent.: from Italian *maccaroni* (now usually spelled *maccheroni*), plural of *maccarone*, from late Greek *makaria* 'food made from barley.'

mac·a·ron·ic /,makə'ränik/ ▸*adj.* denoting language, esp. burlesque verse, containing words or inflections from one language introduced into the context of another.
▸*n.* (usu. **macaronics**) macaronic verse, esp. that which mixes the vernacular with Latin. ▷early 17th cent. (in the sense 'characteristic of a jumble or medley'): from modern Latin *macaronicus*, from obsolete Italian *macaronico*, a humorous formation from *macaroni* (see **MACARONI**).

mac·a·ro·ni pen·guin ▸*n.* a penguin with an orange crest, breeding on islands in the Antarctic. • *Eudyptes chrysolophus*, family Spheniscidae. ▷early 19th cent.: so named because the orange crest was thought to resemble the hairstyle of dandies known as *macaronies* (see **MACARONI**).

mac·a·roon /,makə'rōōn/ ▸*n.* a light cookie made with egg white, sugar, and usually ground almonds or coconut. ▷late 16th cent.: from French *macaron*, from Italian *maccarone* (see **MACARONI**).

Mac·Ar·thur /mə'kärᴛʜər/, Douglas (1880–1964), U.S. general. Commander of U.S. (later Allied) forces in the southwestern Pacific during World War II, he accepted Japan's surrender in 1945 and administered the ensuing Allied occupation. He was in charge of UN forces in Korea 1950–51, before being forced to relinquish command by President Truman.

Ma·cas·sar /mə'kasər/ ▸*n.* **1** (also **Macassar oil**) a kind of oil formerly used, esp. by men, to make one's hair shine and lie flat. **2** variant spelling of **MAKASSAR**. ▷mid 17th cent.: earlier form of **MAKASSAR**. The oil was originally represented as consisting of ingredients from Makassar.

Ma·cau /mə'kou/ Portuguese name for **MACAO**.

Ma·cau·lay /mə'kôlē/, Thomas Babington, 1st Baron (1800–59), English historian, essayist, and philanthropist. Notable works: *The Lays of Ancient Rome* (1842) and *History of England* (1849–61).

ma·caw /mə'kô/ ▸*n.* a large long-tailed parrot with brightly colored plumage, native to Central and South America. • *Ara* and related genera, family Psittacidae: several species. ▷early 17th cent.: from Portuguese *macao*, of unknown origin.

Mac·beth /mək'beᴛʜ; ,mak-/ (*c.*1005–57), king of Scotland 1040–57. He came to the throne after killing his cousin Duncan I in battle and was himself defeated and killed by Malcolm III.

Macc. ▸*abbr.* Maccabees (Apocrypha) (in biblical references).

Mac·ca·bae·us, Judas, see **JUDAS MACCABAEUS**.

Mac·ca·bees /'makə,bēz/ ▸*plural n. historical* the members or followers of the family of the Jewish leader Judas Maccabaeus. ■ (in full **the Books of the Maccabees**) four books of Jewish history and theology, of which the first and second are in the Apocrypha and feature Judas Maccabaeus. ▷late Middle English: from Latin *Maccabaeus*, an epithet applied to Judas, perhaps from Hebrew *maqqeḇeṯ* 'hammer' (by association with the religious revolt led by Judas). **—Mac·ca·be·an** /,makə'bēən/ *adj.*

mac·chi·a·to /,mäkē'ätō/ ▸*n.* espresso coffee with a

M

dash of frothy steamed milk. ▷1970s: from Italian, literally 'stained, marked.'

Mac·don·ald /mək'dänəld/, Sir John Alexander (1815–91), Canadian statesman, born in Scotland; prime minister 1867–73 and 1878–91. He played a leading role in the confederation of the Canadian provinces and was appointed the first prime minister of the Dominion of Canada.

Mac·Don·ald, (James) Ramsay (1866–1937), British statesman, born in Scotland. He became Britain's first Labour prime minister in 1924 and headed the second Labour government 1929–31. When the cabinet split over proposed cuts in unemployment benefits, he led a coalition "National" government 1931–35.

Mac·Don·nel Rang·es /mək'dänl/ a series of mountain ranges extending west from Alice Springs in Northern Territory, Australia. The highest peak is Mount Ziel, which rises to a height of 5,023 feet (1,531 m).

Mace /mās/ ▸*n. trademark* an irritant chemical used in an aerosol to disable attackers.

▸*v.* (also **mace**) [*trans.*] spray (someone) with Mace. ▷1960s (originally U.S.): probably from MACE[1].

mace[1] /mās/ ▸*n.* **1** *historical* a heavy club, typically having a metal head and spikes. **2** a ceremonial staff of office. ▷Middle English: from Old French *masse* 'large hammer.'

mace[2] ▸*n.* the reddish fleshy outer covering of the nutmeg, dried as a spice. ▷Middle English *macis* (taken as plural), via Old French from Latin *macir*.

mac·é·doine /,mäsə'dwän/ ▸*n.* a mixture of vegetables or fruit cut into small pieces and served as a salad. ■ *figurative* a medley or jumble: *a macédoine of disjointed detail.* ▷French, literally 'Macedonia,' with reference to the mixture of peoples in the Macedonian Empire of Alexander the Great.

Mac·e·do·ni·a /,masə'dōnēə; -nyə/ **1** a landlocked republic in the Balkans; pop. 2,038,000; capital, Skopje; official language, Macedonian. Official name, **The Former Yugoslav Republic of Macedonia.**

Formerly a constituent republic of Yugoslavia, Macedonia became independent after a 1991 referendum.

2 (also **Mac·e·don** /'masədən; -,dän/) an ancient country in southeastern Europe, north of Greece. In classical times it was a kingdom that became a world power under Philip II and Alexander the Great. The region is now divided between Greece, Bulgaria, and the Republic of Macedonia. **3** a region in northeastern Greece; capital, Thessaloníki.

Mac·e·do·ni·an /,masə'dōnēən/ ▸*n.* **1** a native or inhabitant of the Former Yugoslav Republic of Macedonia. **2** a native of ancient Macedonia. ■ a native or inhabitant of the region of Macedonia in modern Greece. **3** the South Slavic language of the republic of Macedonia and adjacent parts of Bulgaria. **4** the language of ancient Macedonia, possibly a dialect of Greek.

▸*adj.* of or relating to Macedonia or Macedonian.

Mac·e·do·ni·an Wars a series of four wars between Rome and Macedonia in the 3rd and 2nd centuries BC, which ended in the defeat of Macedonia and its annexation as a Roman province (148 BC).

Ma·ceió /,mäsā'ō/ a port in eastern Brazil, on the Atlantic coast; pop. 700,000.

mac·er·ate /'masə,rāt/ ▸*v.* [*trans.*] **1** soften or break up (something, esp. food) by soaking in a liquid. ■ [*intrans.*] become softened or broken up by soaking. **2** *archaic* cause to grow thinner or waste away, esp. by fasting. ▷mid 16th cent.: from Latin *macerat-* 'made soft, soaked,' from the verb *macerare*. **—mac·er·a·tion** /,masə'rāsHən/ *n.* **—mac·er·a·tor** /-,rātər/ *n.*

Mach[1] /mäk; mäKH/, Ernst (1838–1916), Austrian physicist and philosopher of science. He did important work on aerodynamics.

Mach[2] (also **Mach number**) ▸*n.* the ratio of the speed of a body to the speed of sound in the surrounding medium. It is often used with a numeral (as **Mach 1**, **Mach 2**, etc.) to indicate the speed of sound, twice the speed of sound, etc.

mach. ▸*abbr.* ■ machine or machinery or machinist.

mache /mäsH/ (also **mâche**) ▸*n.* another term for CORN SALAD. ▷late 17th cent. (originally as the anglicized plural form *maches*): from French *mâche*.

mach·er /'mäKHər/ ▸*n. informal* a person who gets things done. ■ *derogatory* an overbearing person. ▷1930s: from Yiddish *makher*, from Middle High German *macher* 'doer, active person.'

ma·chet·e /mə'sHetē/ ▸*n.* a broad, heavy knife used as an implement or weapon, originating in Central America and the Caribbean. ▷late 16th cent.: from Spanish, from *macho* 'hammer.'

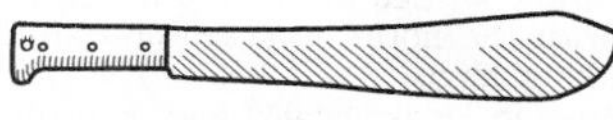

machete

Mach·i·a·vel /'makēə,vel; 'mäk-/ ▸*n. archaic* a person compared to Machiavelli for favoring expediency over morality.

Mach·i·a·vel·li /,mäkēə'velē; ,mak-/, Niccolò di Bernardo dei (1469–1527), Italian statesman and political philosopher. His *The Prince* (1532) advises rulers that the acquisition and effective use of power may necessitate unethical methods.

Mach·i·a·vel·li·an /,makēə'velēən; ,mäk-/ ▸*adj.* **1** cunning, scheming, and unscrupulous, esp. in politics or in advancing one's career. **2** of or relating to Niccolò Machiavelli.

▸*n.* a person who schemes in such a way. **—Mach·i·a·vel·li·an·ism** /-,nizəm/ *n.*

ma·chic·o·late /mə'CHikə,lāt/ ▸*v.* [*trans.*] [usu. as *adj.*] (**machicolated**) provide with machicolations: *a machicolated fortress.* ▷late 18th cent.: from Anglo-Latin *machicollare*, based on Provençal *machacol*, from *macar* 'to crush' + *col* 'neck.'

ma·chic·o·la·tion /mə,CHikə'lāsHən/ ▸*n.* (in medieval fortifications) an opening between the supporting corbels of a projecting parapet or the vault of a gate, through which stones or burning objects could be dropped on attackers. ■ a projecting structure containing a series of such openings.

ma·chin·a·ble /mə'sHēnəbəl/ ▸*adj.* (of a material) able to be worked by a machine tool. **—ma·chin·a·bil·i·ty** /mə,sHēnə'bilətē/ *n.*

mach·i·nate /'makə,nāt; 'masHə-/ ▸*v.* [*intrans.*] engage in plots and intrigues; scheme. ▷early 16th cent. (used transitively in the sense 'to plot (a malicious act)'): from Latin *machinat-* 'contrived,' from the verb *machinari*, from *machina* (see MACHINE). **—mach·i·na·tion** /,makə'näsHən; ,masHə-/ *n.* **—mach·i·na·tor** /-,nātər/ *n.*

ma·chine /mə'sHēn/ ▸*n.* an apparatus using or applying mechanical power and having several parts, each with a definite function and together performing a particular task: *a fax machine | a shredding machine.* ■ [usu. with *adj.*] a coin-operated dispenser: *a candy machine.* ■ *technical* any device that transmits a force or directs its application. ■ *figurative* an efficient and well-organized group of powerful people: *his campaign illustrated the continuing strength of a powerful political machine.* ■ *figurative* a person who acts with the mechanical efficiency of a machine: *comedians are more than just laugh machines.*

▸*v.* [*trans.*] (esp. in manufacturing) make or operate on with a machine: [as *adj.*] (**machined**) *a decoratively machined brass rod.* ▷mid 16th cent. (originally denoting a structure of any kind): from French, via Latin from Doric Greek *makhana* (Attic Greek *mēkhanē*, from *mēkhos* 'contrivance').

ma·chine code (also **machine language**) ▸*n.* a computer programming language consisting of binary or hexadecimal instructions that a computer can respond to directly.

ma·chine gun ▸*n.* an automatic gun that fires bullets in rapid succession for as long as the trigger is pressed.

▸*v.* (**ma·chine-gun**) [*trans.*] shoot with a machine gun. **—ma·chine-gun·ner** *n.*

ma·chine-read·a·ble ▸*adj.* (of data or text) in a form that a computer can process.

ma·chin·er·y /mə'sHēn(ə)rē/ ▸*n.* machines collectively: *farm machinery.* ■ the components of a machine: *the movement of the machinery.* ■ the organization or structure of something: *the machinery of democracy.* ■ the means devised or available to do something: *with the grievance machinery in place.*

ma·chine screw ▸*n.* a fastening device similar to a bolt but having a socket in its head that allows it to be turned with a screwdriver.

ma·chine tool ▸*n.* a nonportable power tool, such as a lathe or milling machine, used for cutting or shaping metal, wood, or other material. **—ma·chine-tooled** *adj.*

ma·chine trans·la·tion ▸*n.* translation carried out by a computer.

ma·chine wash·a·ble ▸*adj.* (of clothes or other fabric articles) able to be washed in a washing machine without damage.

ma·chin·ist /mə'sHēnist/ ▸*n.* a person who operates a machine, esp. a machine tool. ■ a person who makes or repairs machinery.

ma·chis·mo /mə'CHēzmō; -'kēz-/ ▸*n.* strong or aggressive masculine pride. ■ *figurative* daring or bravado: *the Japanese have taken culinary machismo to a new level.* ▷1940s: Mexican Spanish, from *macho* 'male' (see MACHO).

Mach·me·ter /'mäk,mētər/ ▸*n.* an instrument in an aircraft indicating airspeed as a Mach number.

Mach num·ber ▸*n.* see MACH[2].

MACHO /'mäCHō; 'maCHō/ ▸*n. Astronomy* a compact object, such as a brown dwarf, a low-mass star, or a black hole, of a kind that is thought by some to constitute part of the dark matter in galactic halos. ▷1990s: acronym from *Massive (Astrophysical) Compact Halo Object*.

ma·cho /'mäCHō/ ▸*adj.* showing aggressive pride in one's masculinity: *the big macho tough guy.*

▸*n.* (*pl.* **-chos**) a man who is aggressively proud of his masculinity. ■ machismo. ▷1920s: Mexican Spanish, 'masculine or vigorous,' from Latin *masculus*.

Mach's prin·ci·ple /mäks; mäKHs/ *Physics* the hypothesis that a body's inertial mass results from its interaction with the rest of the matter in the universe.

Ma·chu Pic·chu /,mäCHōō 'pi(k)CHōō/ a fortified Inca town in the Andes Mountains in Peru that the invading Spaniards never found. It is noted for its dramatic position, perched high on a steep-sided ridge.

Machu Picchu

mac·in·tosh ▸*n.* variant spelling of MACKINTOSH.

Mack /mak/, Connie (1862–1956), U.S. baseball player and manager; born *Cornelius Alexander McGillicuddy*. A catcher, he played with various teams from 1886 until 1896. In 1901, he became the manager of the Philadelphia Athletics, a job he held for 50 years. He led the team to nine American League pennants and five World Series championships. Baseball Hall of Fame (1937).

mack ▸*n.* variant spelling of MAC.

Mac·ken·zie[1] /mə'kenzē/, Sir Alexander (1764–1820), Scottish explorer in Canada. He discovered the Mackenzie River in 1789 and became the first European to reach the Pacific Ocean by land along a northern route in 1793.

Mac·ken·zie[2], William Lyon (1795–1861), Canadian politician and journalist, born in Scotland. He was involved with the movement for political reform in

Pronunciation Key ə *ago*; ər *over*; 'ə or ,ə *up*; 'ər or ,ər *fur*; a *hat*; ā *rate*; ä *car*; CH *chew*; e *let*; ē *see*; e(ə)r *air*; i *fit*; ī *by*; i(ə)r *ear*; NG *sing*; ō *go*; ô *for*; oi *boy*; ŏŏ *good*; ōō *goo*; ou *out*; SH *she*; TH *thin*; TH *then*; (h)w *why*; ZH *vision*

Canada. In 1837, he led an unsuccessful rebellion in Toronto and fled to New York.

Mac·ken·zie Riv·er /mə'kenzē/ a river that flows northwest for 1,060 miles (1,700 km) from Great Slave Lake to Beaufort Sea, which is a part of the Arctic Ocean. It is the longest river in Canada.

mack·er·el /'mak(ə)rəl/ ▸*n.* (*pl.* same or **-er·els**) a migratory surface-dwelling predatory fish, commercially important as a food fish. • *Scomber* and other genera, family Scombridae (the **mackerel family**): many species, in particular the **North Atlantic mackerel** (*S. scombrus*). The members of the mackerel family, which includes the tunas, are fast-moving marine predators and often popular as game fish. ▷Middle English: from Old French *maquerel*, of unknown origin.

mack·er·el shark ▸*n.* a shark of the family Lamnidae, esp. the porbeagle or the mako.

mack·er·el sky ▸*n.* a sky dappled with rows of small white fleecy clouds, typically cirrocumulus, like the pattern on a mackerel's back.

Mack·i·nac, Straits of / 'makə,nô/ a passage between lakes Huron and Michigan, crossed since 1957 by the Mackinac Bridge. The Upper Peninsula of Michigan lies to the north, and historic Mackinac Island lies just to the east.

mack·i·naw /'makə,nô/ (also **mackinaw coat** or **jacket**) ▸*n.* a short coat or jacket made of a thick, heavy woolen cloth, typically with a plaid design. ▷early 19th cent.: named after *Mackinaw* City, Michigan, formerly an important trading post.

Mack·in·tosh /'makən,täsн/, Charles Rennie (1868–1928), Scottish architect, designer, and painter. A leading exponent of art nouveau, he pioneered the new concept of functionalism in architecture and interior design.

mack·in·tosh /'makən,täsн/ (also **mac·in·tosh**) ▸*n. chiefly Brit.* a full-length waterproof coat. ■ [usu. as *adj.*] cloth waterproofed with rubber. ▷mid 19th cent.: named after Charles *Macintosh* (1766–1843), the Scottish inventor who originally patented the cloth.

mack·le /'makəl/ ▸*n.* a blurred impression in printing. ▷late 16th cent.: from French *macule*, from Latin *macula* 'stain.'

Mac·Laine /mə'klān/, Shirley (1934–), U.S. actress, dancer, and writer; born *Shirley MacLean Beaty*; the sister of actor Warren Beatty. She appeared in movies such as *Some Came Running* (1959), *The Apartment* (1960, *Irma la Douce* (1963), *The Turning Point* (1977), *Terms of Endearment* (Academy Award, 1983), and *Evening Star* (1996). She wrote *Don't Fall Off the Mountain* (1971).

ma·cle /'makəl/ ▸*n.* **1** a diamond or other crystal that is twinned. **2** another term for CHIASTOLITE. ▷early 19th cent.: from French, from Anglo-Latin *mascula* 'mesh.'

Mac·lean[1] /mə'klēn/, Alistair (1922–87), Scottish novelist. He wrote thrillers including *The Guns of Navarone* (1957; movie, 1961), *Where Eagles Dare* (1967; movie, 1969), and *Bear Island* (1971; movie, 1979).

Mac·lean[2], Donald (Duart) (1913–83), British foreign office official and Soviet spy. He fled to the Soviet Union with Guy Burgess in 1951.

Mac·Leish /mə'klēsн/, Archibald (1892–1982), U.S. poet. His award-winning works include *Conquistador* (1932), *Collected Poems* (1952), and *J.B.* (1958).

Mac·leod /mə'kloud/, John James Rickard (1876–1935), Scottish physiologist. He directed the research on pancreatic extracts by F. G. Banting and C. H. Best that led to the discovery and isolation of insulin. Nobel Prize for Physiology or Medicine (1923, shared with Banting).

Mac·mil·lan /mək'milən/, (Maurice) Harold, 1st Earl of Stockton (1894–1986), British statesman; prime minister 1957–63. During his term of office, the Test Ban Treaty (1963) with the U.S. and the Soviet Union was signed, and Britain granted independence to a number of its African colonies. Macmillan resigned on grounds of ill health shortly after the scandal surrounding John Profumo, a member of his government.

Mac·Neil /mək'nēl/, Robert (Breckenridge Ware) (1931–), U.S. broadcast journalist; born in Canada. With Jim Lehrer he coanchored the "MacNeil/Lehrer News Hour" (1983–95).

Ma·con /'mākən/ an industrial and commercial city in central Georgia, on the Ocmulgee River; pop. 97,255.

Mac·quar·ie Riv·er /mə'kwôrē; -'kwärē/ a river in New South Wales, Australia, that rises on the western slopes of the Great Dividing Range and flows northwest for 600 miles (960 km) to join the Darling River, of which it is a headwater.

mac·ra·mé /'makrə,mā/ ▸*n.* the art of knotting cord or string in patterns to make decorative articles. ■ [usu. as *adj.*] fabric or articles made in this way. ▷mid 19th cent.: French, from Turkish *makrama* 'tablecloth or towel,' from Arabic *miḳrama* 'bedspread.'

mac·ro /'makrō/ ▸*n.* (*pl.* **-ros**) **1** (also **macro instruction**) *Computing* a single instruction that expands automatically into a set of instructions to perform a particular task. **2** *Photography* short for MACRO LENS.
▸*adj.* **1** large-scale; overall: *the analysis of social events at the macro level.* Often contrasted with MICRO. **2** *Photography* relating to or used in macrophotography. ▷independent usage of MACRO-.

macro- ▸*comb. form* **1** long; over a long period: *macroevolution.* **2** large; large-scale: *macromolecule* | *macronutrient.* ■ (used in medical terms) large compared with the norm: *macrocephaly.* ▷from Greek *makros* 'long, large.'

mac·ro·bi·ot·ic /,makrōbī'ätik/ ▸*adj.* constituting, relating to, or following a diet of whole pure prepared foods that is based on Taoist principles of the balance of yin and yang.
▸*plural n.* (**macrobiotics**) [treated as *sing.*] the use or theory of such a diet.

mac·ro·car·pa /'makrə,kärpə/ ▸*n.* another term for MONTEREY CYPRESS. ▷early 20th cent.: modern Latin, from MACRO- 'large' + Greek *karpos* 'fruit.'

mac·ro·ce·phal·ic /,makrōsə'falik/ (also **mac·ro·ceph·a·lous** /-'sefələs/) ▸*adj. Anatomy* having an unusually large head. **—mac·ro·ceph·a·ly** /-'sefəlē/ *n.*

mac·ro·cosm /'makrə,käzəm/ (also **mac·ro·cos·mos** /-,käzməs; -mōs/) ▸*n.* the universe; the cosmos. ■ the whole of a complex structure, esp. as represented or epitomized in a small part of itself (a microcosm). **—mac·ro·cos·mic** /,makrə'käzmik/ *adj.* **—mac·ro·cos·mi·cal·ly** /,makrə'käzmik(ə)lē/ *adv.*

mac·ro·cy·clic /,makrō'siklik; -'sīklik/ ▸*adj. Chemistry* of, relating to, or denoting a ring composed of a relatively large number of atoms, such as occurs in heme, chlorophyll, and several natural antibiotics. **—mac·ro·cy·cle** /'makrō,sīkəl/ *n.*

mac·ro·ec·o·nom·ics /'makrō,ekə'nämiks; -,ēkə-/ ▸*plural n.* [treated as *sing.*] the part of economics concerned with large-scale or general economic factors, such as interest rates and national productivity. **—mac·ro·ec·o·nom·ic** *adj.* **—mac·ro·e·con·o·mist** /-i'känəmist/ *n.*

mac·ro·e·con·o·my /'makrō-i'känəmē/ ▸*n.* a large-scale economic system.

mac·ro·ev·o·lu·tion /,makrō-evə'lōōsнən; -,ēvə-/ ▸*n. Biology* major evolutionary change. The term applies mainly to the evolution of whole taxonomic groups over long periods of time. **—mac·ro·ev·o·lu·tion·ar·y** /-sнə,nerē; -,ēvə-/ *adj.*

mac·ro·gam·ete /,makrōgə'mēt; -'gam,ēt/ ▸*n. Biology* (esp. in protozoans) the larger of a pair of conjugating gametes, usually regarded as female.

mac·ro lens ▸*n. Photography* a lens suitable for taking photographs unusually close to the subject.

mac·ro·lep·i·dop·ter·a /'makrō,lepə'däptərə/ ▸*plural n. Entomology* the butterflies and larger moths, comprising those of interest to the general collector. Compare with MICROLEPIDOPTERA. ▷modern Latin (plural), from MACRO- 'large' + LEPIDOPTERA.

mac·ro·lide /'makrə,līd/ ▸*n.* any of a class of antibiotics containing a lactone ring, of which the first and best known is erythromycin. ▷mid 20th cent.: from *macro-* + *l(actone)* + *-ide.*

mac·ro·mol·e·cule /,makrō'mälə,kyōōl/ ▸*n. Chemistry* a molecule containing a very large number of atoms, such as a protein, nucleic acid, or synthetic polymer. **—mac·ro·mo·lec·u·lar** /-mə'lekyələr/ *adj.*

ma·cron /'mā,krän; 'mak-; 'mākrən/ ▸*n.* a written or printed mark (¯)used to indicate a long vowel in some languages and phonetic transcription systems, or a stressed vowel in verse. ▷mid 19th cent.: from Greek *makron*, neuter of *makros* 'long.'

mac·ro·nu·tri·ent /,makrō'nōōtrēənt/ ▸*n. Biology* a substance required in relatively large amounts by living organisms, in particular: ■ a type of food (e.g., fat, protein, carbohydrate) required in large amounts in the human diet. ■ a chemical element (e.g., potassium, magnesium, calcium) required in large amounts for plant growth and development.

mac·ro·phage /'makrə,fāj/ ▸*n. Physiology* a large phagocytic cell found in stationary form in the tissues or as a mobile white blood cell, esp. at sites of infection.

mac·ro·pho·tog·ra·phy /,makrōfə'tägrəfē/ ▸*n.* photography producing photographs of small items larger than life size.

mac·ro·phyte /'makrə,fīt/ ▸*n. Botany* a plant, esp. an aquatic plant, large enough to be seen by the naked eye.

mac·ro·pod /'makrə,päd/ ▸*n. Zoology* a plant-eating marsupial mammal of an Australasian family that comprises the kangaroos and wallabies. • Family Macropodidae: several genera, in particular *Macropus.* ▷late 19th cent.: from modern Latin *Macropodidae* (plural), from MACRO- 'large' + Greek *pous, pod-* 'foot.'

mac·ro·scop·ic /,makrə'skäpik/ ▸*adj.* visible to the naked eye; not microscopic. ■ of or relating to large-scale or general analysis. **—mac·ro·scop·i·cal·ly** /-ik(ə)lē/ *adv.*

Mac·ro-Siou·an /'makrō 'sōōən/ ▸*n.* a proposed phylum of North American languages including the Siouan, Iroquoian, and Caddoan families and some others.
▸*adj.* of or relating to this language phylum.

mac·ro·struc·ture /'makrō,strəkcнər/ ▸*n.* the large-scale or overall structure of something, e.g., an organism, a mechanical construction, or a written text. ■ a large-scale structure. **—mac·ro·struc·tur·al** /,makrō'strəkcнərəl/ *adj.*

ma·cru·ran /mə'krōōrən/ ▸*adj. Zoology* of, relating to, or denoting those decapod crustaceans (such as lobsters and crayfish) that have a relatively long abdomen. ▷mid 19th cent. (as a noun): from modern Latin *Macrura* (former suborder name), from Greek *makros* 'long' + *oura* 'tail,' + -AN. **—ma·cru·rous** *adj.*

mac·u·la /'makyələ/ ▸*n.* (*pl.* **-lae** /-,lē; -,lī/) a distinct spot, such as a discolored spot on the skin. Also called MACULE. ■ (also **mac·u·la lu·te·a**) /'lōōtēə/ (*pl.* **mac·u·lae lu·te·ae** /'lōōtē,ē; -tē,ī/) *Anatomy* an oval yellowish area surrounding the fovea near the center of the retina in the eye. It is the region of greatest visual acuity. ▷late Middle English: from Latin, 'spot.' **—mac·u·lar** /'makyələr/ *adj.*

mac·u·late /'makyə,lāt/ *poetic/literary* ▸*adj.* spotted or stained.
▸*v.* [*trans.*] mark with a spot or spots; stain. ▷late Middle English (as a verb): from Latin *maculat-* 'spotted,' from the verb *maculare*, from *macula* 'spot.' **—mac·u·la·tion** /,makyə'lāsнən/ *n.*

mac·ule /'mak,yōōl/ ▸*n.* another term for MACULA. ▷late 15th cent.: from French, or from Latin *macula* 'spot.'

ma·cum·ba /mə'kōōmbə/ ▸*n.* a black religious cult practiced in Brazil, using sorcery, ritual dance, and fetishes. ▷Portuguese.

MAD ▸*abbr.* mutual assured destruction.

mad /mad/ ▸*adj.* (**mad·der, mad·dest**) mentally ill; insane: *he felt as if he were* ***going mad.*** ■ (of a person, conduct, or an idea) extremely foolish or ill-advised: *they were all mad to go believing such a cock-and-bull story.* ■ in a frenzied mental or physical state: *she pictured loved ones* ***mad with*** *anxiety about her* | *it was a mad dash to get ready.* ■ *informal* enthusiastic about someone or something: *I wasn't* ***mad about*** *mountain bikes* | [in *combination*] *a sports-mad nation.* ■ *informal* very angry: *they were* ***mad at*** *each other.* ■ (of a dog) rabid. ■ *Brit., informal* very exciting.
▸*v.* (**mad·ded** /madəd/, **mad·ding**) [*trans.*] *archaic* make mad or insane. ▷Old English *gemǣd(e)d* 'maddened,' participial form related to *gemād* 'mad,' of Germanic origin.
▸*PHRASES* □ **like mad** *informal* with great intensity, energy, or enthusiasm: *I ran like mad.* □ **(as) mad as a hatter** *informal* completely crazy. [with reference to Lewis Carroll's character the Mad Hatter in *Alice's Adventures in Wonderland* (1865), the allusion being to the effects of mercury poisoning from the use of mercurous nitrate in the manufacture of felt hats.]

Mad·a·gas·car /,madə'gaskər/ an island country in the Indian Ocean, off the eastern coast of Africa; pop. 17,501,000; capital, Antananarivo; official languages, Malagasy and French. **—Mad·a·gas·can** /-'gaskən/ *adj.* & *n.*

Settled by peoples of mixed Indo-Melanesian and African descent, Madagascar was visited by the Portuguese in 1500 but resisted colonization until the French established control in 1896. It regained its independence as the Malagasy Republic in 1960 and changed its name back to Madagascar in 1975.

It is the fourth largest island in the world, and many of its plants and animals are unique to the island.

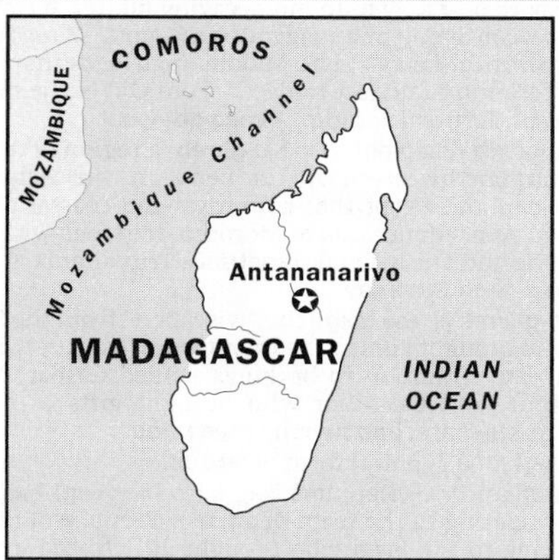

mad·am /ˈmadəm/ ▸*n.* used to address or refer to a woman in a polite or respectful way: *Can I help you, madam?* ■ (**Madam**) used to address a woman at the start of a formal or business letter: *Dear Madam, . . .* ■ (**Madam**) used before a title to address or refer to a female holder of that position: *Madam President.* ■ a woman who runs a brothel. ▷Middle English: from Old French *ma dame* 'my lady.'

Mad·ame /məˈdäm; -ˈdam/ ▸*n.* (*pl.* **Mes·dames** /mā ˈdäm; -ˈdam/) a title or form of address used of or to a French-speaking woman: *Madame Bovary.* ■ used as a title for women in artistic or exotic occupations, such as musicians or fortune-tellers. ▷French; compare with MADAM.

Mad An·tho·ny /ˈanTHənē/ see WAYNE[2].

mad·a·ro·sis /ˌmadəˈrōsis/ ▸*n. Medicine* absence or loss of the eyelashes (and sometimes the eyebrows), either as a congenital condition or as a result of an infection. ▷late 17th cent.: modern Latin, from Greek, 'baldness,' from *madaros* 'bald.'

mad·cap /ˈmadˌkap/ ▸*adj.* amusingly eccentric: *a surreal, madcap novel.* ■ done or thought up without considering the consequences; crazy or reckless: *some madcap money-making scheme.*
▸*n.* an eccentric person.

mad cow dis·ease ▸*n. informal* bovine spongiform encephalopathy. See **BSE**.

MADD /mad/ ▸*abbr.* Mothers Against Drunk Driving.

mad·den /ˈmadn/ ▸*v.* [*trans.*] make (someone) extremely irritated or annoyed: *the audacity of the convicts maddened the governor.* ■ [often as *adj.*] (**maddened**) drive (someone) insane: *a maddened crowd.*

mad·den·ing /ˈmadniNG; ˈmadn-iNG/ ▸*adj.* extremely annoying; infuriating: *his maddening stories.* —**mad·den·ing·ly** *adv.*

mad·der /ˈmadər/ ▸*n.* a scrambling or prostrate Eurasian plant of the bedstraw family, with whorls of four to six leaves. • Genera *Rubia* and *Sherardia*, family Rubiaceae: several species, in particular *R. tinctorum* of southern Europe and western Asia, formerly cultivated for its root, which yields a red dye, and the Eurasian **wild madder** (*R. peregrina*). ■ a red dye or pigment obtained from the root of this plant, or a synthetic dye resembling it. ▷Old English *mædere*, of Germanic origin; obscurely related to Dutch *mede*, in the same sense.

mad·ding /ˈmadiNG/ ▸*adj. poetic/literary* **1** acting madly; frenzied. **2** maddening.
▸*PHRASE* □ **far from the madding crowd** secluded or removed from public notice. [in allusion to use in Gray's *Elegy*, also to the title of one of Thomas Hardy's novels.]

made /mād/ ▸ past and past participle of MAKE.
▸*adj.* [usu. in *combination*] made or formed in a particular place or by a particular process: *a Japanese-made camera | handmade chocolates.*

Ma·dei·ra[1] /məˈdi(ə)rə; məˈde(ə)rə/ **1** an island in the Atlantic Ocean off the northwestern coast of Africa, the largest of the Madeiras, a group of islands that constitutes an autonomous region of Portugal; pop. 270,000; capital, Funchal. Encountered by the Portuguese in 1419, the islands were occupied by the Spanish 1580–1640 and the British 1807–14. **2** a river in northwestern Brazil that rises on the Bolivian border and flows about 900 miles (1,450 km) to meet the Amazon River east of Manaus. It is navigable to large oceangoing vessels as far as Pôrto Velho. ▷Portuguese, literally 'timber' (from Latin *materia* "substance"), because of the island's dense woods. —**Ma·dei·ran** *adj.* & *n.*

Ma·dei·ra[2] (also **Madeira wine**) ▸*n.* a fortified white wine from the island of Madeira.

mad·e·leine /ˈmadl-ən; ˌmadl-ˈān/ ▸*n.* a small rich cake, typically baked in a shell-shaped mold and often decorated with coconut and jam. ▷French, probably named after *Madeleine* Paulmier, 19th-cent. French pastry cook.

made man ▸*n.* a man whose success in life is assured.

Mad·e·moi·selle /ˌmad(ə)m(w)əˈzel; mamˈzel/ ▸*n.* (*pl.* **Mes·de·moi·selles** /ˌmād(ə)m(w)əˈzel(z)/) a title or form of address used of or to an unmarried French-speaking woman: *Mademoiselle Rossignol | thank you, Mademoiselle.* ■ (**mademoiselle**) a young Frenchwoman. ■ (**mademoiselle**) *dated* a French governess. ■ (**mademoiselle**) a female French teacher in an English-speaking school. ▷French, from *ma* 'my' + *demoiselle* 'damsel.'

mad·er·i·za·tion /ˌmadərəˈzāSHən/ ▸*n.* a form of oxidation that gives white wine a brownish color and caramelized flavor like that of Madeira. ▷1950s: from French *madérisation*, from *madériser*, from *Madère* 'Madeira.' —**mad·er·ized** /ˈmadəˌrīzd/ *adj.*

made to meas·ure ▸*adj. chiefly Brit.* specially made to fit a particular person or space: *bicycles are made to measure.* ■ *figurative* designed to fulfill a particular set of requirements: *amenities and attractions for a made-to-measure vacation.*

made to or·der ▸*adj.* specially made according to a customer's specifications: *the kitchen's made-to-order breads.* ■ *figurative* ideally suited to certain requirements: *a formalism seemingly made to order for the problem at hand.*

made-up ▸*adj.* **1** wearing makeup: *her immaculately made-up face.* **2** invented; not true: *a made-up story.*

mad·house /ˈmadˌhous/ ▸*n. historical* a mental institution. ■ *informal* a psychiatric hospital. ■ [in *sing.*] a scene of extreme confusion or uproar: *this place is a madhouse.*

Ma·dhya Pra·desh /ˈmädēə prəˈdesH/ a large state in central India, formed in 1956; capital, Bhopal.

Mad·i·son[1] /ˈmadəsən/ **1** a city in northern Alabama, southwest of Huntsville; pop. 29,329. **2** the capital of Wisconsin, situated in the central part of the state; pop. 208,054 (2000). ▷named after President James Madison (see MADISON[2]).

Mad·i·son[2], James (1751–1836), 4th president of the U.S. 1809–17. He played a major part in the drafting of the U.S. Constitution 1787, and he proposed the Bill of Rights 1791. A Democratic Republican, his presidency saw the U.S. emerge successfully from the War of 1812.

James Madison

Mad·i·son[3] ▸*n.* an energetic group dance popular in the 1960s. ▷of unknown origin.

Mad·i·son Av·e·nue /ˌmadəsən ˈavən(y)o͞o/ a street in New York City, center of the advertising business in the U.S. ■ used in allusion to the world of advertising: *Madison Avenue's youth-oriented approach.*

mad·ly /ˈmadlē/ ▸*adv.* in a manner suggesting or characteristic of insanity: *his eyes bulged madly.* ■ in a wild or uncontrolled manner: *her heart thudded madly against her ribs.* ■ *informal* with extreme intensity: *the boys are all* **madly in love with** *you.*

mad·man /ˈmadˌman; -mən/ ▸*n.* (*pl.* **-men**) a man who is mentally ill. ■ an extremely foolish or reckless person: *the car was out of control—some madman going too fast.* ■ used in similes to refer to a person who does something very fast, intensely, or violently: *I was working like a madman.*

mad·ness /ˈmadnəs/ ▸*n.* the state of being mentally ill, esp. severely. ■ extremely foolish behavior: *it is madness to allow children to roam around after dark.* ■ a state of frenzied or chaotic activity: *from about midnight to three in the morning it's absolute madness in here.*

Ma·don·na[1] /məˈdänə/ ▸*n.* (**the Madonna**) the Virgin Mary. ■ a picture, statue, or medallion of the Madonna, typically depicted seated and holding the infant Jesus. ■ (usu. **madonna**) an idealized virtuous and beautiful woman. ▷late 16th cent. (as a respectful form of address to an Italian woman): Italian, from *ma* (old form of *mia* 'my') + *donna* 'lady' (from Latin *domina*).

Ma·don·na[2] (1958–), U.S. pop singer and actress; born *Madonna Louise Ciccone*. Albums such as *Like a Virgin* (1984) and her image as a sex symbol brought her international stardom in the mid-1980s. Notable movies: *Desperately Seeking Susan* (1985), *A League of Their Own* (1992), and *Evita* (1996).

ma·don·na lil·y ▸*n.* a tall white-flowered lily with golden pollen. Native to Asia Minor, it is traditionally associated with purity and is often depicted in paintings of the Madonna. • *Lilium candidum*, family Liliaceae.

Ma·dras /məˈdras; məˈdräs/ **1** a seaport on the eastern coast of India, capital of Tamil Nadu; pop. 3,795,000 (1991). Official name (since 1995) CHENAI. **2** FORMER NAME (UNTIL 1968) OF THE INDIAN STATE OF TAMIL NADU.

mad·ras /ˈmadrəs; məˈdras/ ▸*n.* a strong, fine-textured cotton fabric, typically patterned with colorful stripes or checks. ▷mid 19th cent.: by association with MADRAS.

ma·dra·sa /məˈdrasə/ (also **ma·dra·sah** or **me·dre·se** /-ˈdresə/) ▸*n.* a college for Islamic instruction. ▷Arabic, from *darasa* 'to study.'

Mad·re·po·rar·i·a /ˌmadrəpəˈre(ə)rēə; məˌdrepə-/ *Zoology* another term for SCLERACTINIA. ▷modern Latin (plural), from *Madrepora* (genus name), from Italian, probably from *madre* 'mother,' with reference to the prolific growth of the coral. —**mad·re·po·rar·i·an** /-ˈre(ə)rēən/ *n.* & *adj.*

mad·re·pore /ˈmadrəˌpôr/ ▸*n.* **1** a stony coral of the genus *Madrepora*. **2** the polyp producing this. —**mad·re·por·ic** /ˌmadrəˈpôrik/ *adj.*

mad·re·por·ite /ˈmadrəˌpôˌrīt/ ▸*n. Zoology* a perforated plate by which the entry of seawater into the vascular system of an echinoderm is controlled. ▷early 19th cent.: from *madrepore* (see MADREPORARIA) + -ITE[1].

Ma·drid /məˈdrid/ the capital of Spain; pop. 2,985,000. Situated on a high plateau in the center of the country, it replaced Valladolid as capital in 1561.

mad·ri·gal /ˈmadrigəl/ ▸*n.* a part-song for several voices, esp. one of the Renaissance period, typically arranged in elaborate counterpoint and without instrumental accompaniment. Originally used of a genre of 14th-century Italian songs, the term now usually refers to English or Italian songs of the late 16th and early 17th c., in a free style strongly influenced by the text. ▷from Italian *madrigale* (from medieval Latin *carmen matricale* 'simple song'), from *matricalis* 'maternal or primitive,' from *matrix* 'womb.' —**mad·ri·gal·i·an** /ˌmadriˈgālēən/ *adj.* —**mad·ri·gal·ist** /-ist/ *n.*

mad·ri·lene /ˌmadrəˈlān; -ˈlen/ ▸*n.* a clear soup, usually served cold. ▷from French *(consommé à la) madrilène*, literally 'soup in the Madrid style.'

Mad·ri·le·nian /ˌmadrəˈlānēən/ ▸*adj.* of or relating to Madrid.
▸*n.* a native or inhabitant of Madrid. ▷from MADRILEÑO + -IAN.

Ma·dri·le·ño /ˌmädriˈlānyō/ ▸*n.* (*pl.* **-ños**) (*fem.* **Ma·dri·le·ña** /ˌmädriˈlānyə/) a native or inhabitant of Madrid. ▷Spanish.

ma·dro·ne /məˈdrōnə/ (also **ma·dro·ño** /-ˈdrōnyō/) ▸*n.* an evergreen tree of the heath family with white flowers, red berries, and glossy leaves, native to western North America. Typically, its smooth, thin red bark peels away to reveal a yellowish layer underneath. • Genus *Arbutus*, family Ericaceae: several species, in particular the **Pacific madrone** (*A. menziesii*). ▷mid 19th cent.: from Spanish.

mad·tom /ˈmadˈtäm/ ▸*n.* a small North American freshwater catfish that has a venom gland at the base of the pectoral fin spines, with which it can inflict a painful wound. • Genus *Noturus,* family Ictaluridae: numerous species, including the common **tadpole madtom** (*N. gyrinus*).

Ma·du·ra /mə'do͝orə/ an island of Indonesia, off the northeastern coast of Java.

Ma·du·rai /,mädə'rī/ a city in Tamil Nadu in southern India; pop. 952,000.

Mad·u·rese /,madyə'rēz; -'rēs/ ▸*n.* (*pl.* same) **1** a native or inhabitant of the island of Madura in Indonesia. **2** an Indonesian language spoken in Madura and nearby parts of Java.
▸*adj.* of or relating to the inhabitants of Madura or their language.

mad·wom·an /'mad,wo͝omən/ ▸*n.* (*pl.* **-wom·en**) a woman who is mentally ill. ▪ used in similes to refer to a woman who does something very fast, intensely, or violently: *she'd driven my father's convertible like a madwoman.*

MAE ▸*abbr.* ▪ Master of Aeronautical Engineering. ▪ Master of Art Education. ▪ Master of Arts in Education.

Mae·an·der /mē'andər/ ancient name of **Menderes**.

M.A.Ed. ▸*abbr.* Master of Arts in Education.

mael·strom /'māl,străm; -strəm/ ▸*n.* a powerful whirlpool in the sea or a river. ▪ *figurative* a scene or state of confused and violent movement or upheaval: *the train station was* ***a maelstrom of*** *crowds | a maelstrom of violence and recrimination.* ▷late 17th cent.: from early modern Dutch (denoting a mythical whirlpool supposed to exist in the Arctic Ocean, west of Norway), from *maalen* 'grind, whirl' + *stroom* 'stream.'

mae·nad /'mē,nad/ ▸*n.* (in ancient Greece) a female follower of Bacchus, traditionally associated with divine possession and frenzied rites. ▷late 16th cent.: via Latin from Greek *Mainas, Mainad-,* from *mainesthai* 'to rave.' **—mae·nad·ic** /mē'nadik/ *adj.*

ma·es·to·so /mī'stōsō; ,mīe-; -'stōzō/ *Music* ▸*adv.* & *adj.* (esp. as a direction) in a majestic manner.
▸*n.* (*pl.* **-sos**) a movement or passage marked to be performed in this way. ▷Italian, 'majestic,' based on Latin *majestas* 'majesty.'

maes·tro /'mīstrō/ ▸*n.* (*pl.* **maes·tri** /'mīstrē/ or **maes·tros**) a distinguished musician, esp. a conductor of classical music. ▪ a great or distinguished figure in any sphere: *a movie maestro.* ▷early 18th cent.: Italian, 'master,' from Latin *magister.*

Mae·ter·linck /'metər,liNGk/, Count Maurice (1862–1949), Belgian poet, playwright, and essayist. His prose dramas *La Princesse Maleine* (1889) and *Pelléas et Mélisande* (1892) established him as a leading figure in the symbolist movement. Nobel Prize for Literature (1911).

Mae West /'mā 'west/ ▸*n. informal, dated* an inflatable life jacket, originally as issued to pilots during World War II. ▷1940s: from the name of the U.S. movie actress *Mae West,* noted for her large bust.

Ma·fe·teng /'maf,teNG/ a town in western Lesotho, in an agricultural district, southwest of Maseru; pop. 206,000.

Ma·fi·a /'mäfēə/ ▸*n.* (**the Mafia**) [treated as *sing.* or *pl.*] an organized international body of criminals, operating originally in Sicily and now esp. in Italy and the U.S. and having a complex and ruthless behavioral code. ▪ (usu. **mafia**) any similar group using extortion and other criminal methods. ▪ (usu. **mafia**) a closed group of people in a particular field, having a controlling influence: *the conservative top tennis mafia.* ▷Italian (Sicilian dialect), originally in the sense 'bragging.'

maf·ic /'mafik/ ▸*adj. Geology* relating to, denoting, or containing a group of dark-colored, mainly ferromagnesian minerals such as pyroxene and olivine. Often contrasted with **felsic**. ▷early 20th cent.: blend of **magnesium** and a contracted form of **ferric**.

Ma·fi·o·so /,mäfē'ōsō; -zō/ (also **ma·fi·o·so**) ▸*n.* (*pl.* **-si** /-sē; -zē/) a member of the Mafia. ▷Italian.

mag /mag/ ▸*n. informal* **1** a magazine (periodical). **2** a magazine (of ammunition). **3** magnesium or magnesium alloy. **4** a magneto. **5** magnitude (of stars or other celestial objects).

Ma·ga·di, Lake /mə'gädē/ a salt lake in the Great Rift Valley, in southern Kenya, with extensive deposits of sodium carbonate and other minerals.

Mag·a·hi /'məgə,hē/ ▸*n.* a Bihari language spoken in central Bihar and West Bengal.
▸*adj.* of or relating to this language. ▷from Hindi *Magahī* 'of Magadha.'

mag·a·log /'magə,lôg; -,läg/ (also **mag·a·logue**) ▸*n.* a promotional catalog or sales brochure designed to resemble a high-quality magazine. ▷1970s: blend of **magazine** and **catalog**.

mag·a·zine /,magə'zēn; 'magə,zēn/ ▸*n.* **1** a periodical publication containing articles and illustrations, typically covering a particular subject or area of interest: *a car magazine | a women's magazine.* ▪ a regular television or radio program comprising a variety of topical news or entertainment items. **2** a chamber for holding a supply of cartridges to be fed automatically to the breech of a gun. ▪ a similar device feeding a camera, compact disc player, etc. **3** a store for arms, ammunition, explosives, and provisions for use in military operations. ▷late 16th cent.: from French *magasin,* from Italian *magazzino,* from Arabic *makzin, makzan* 'storehouse,' from *kazana* 'store up.' The term originally meant 'store' and was often used from the mid 17th cent. in the title of books providing information useful to particular groups of people, whence sense 1 (mid 18th cent.). Sense 3, a contemporary specialization of the original meaning, gave rise to sense 2 in the mid 18th cent.

Mag·da·le·na /,magdə'lānə; ,mäg-/ the principal river of Colombia, rising in the Andes and flowing north for about 1,000 miles (1,600 km) to enter the Caribbean Sea at Barranquilla.

mag·da·lene /'magdə,lēn; -,lin/ (also **mag·da·len**) ▸*n.* (**the Magdalene**) St. Mary Magdalene. ▪ *archaic* a reformed prostitute. ▪ *archaic* a home for reformed prostitutes. ▷late Middle English: via ecclesiastical Latin from Greek *(Maria hē) Magdalēnē* '(Mary of) *Magdala*' (to whom Jesus appeared after his resurrection; John 20:1–18), commonly identified (probably wrongly) with the sinner of Luke 8:37.

Mag·da·le·ni·an /,magdə'lēnēən/ ▸*adj. Archaeology* of, relating to, or denoting the final Paleolithic culture in Europe, following the Solutrean and dated to about 17,000–11,500 years ago. It is characterized by a range of bone and horn tools, and by highly developed cave art. ▪ [as *n.*] (**the Magdalenian**) the Magdalenian culture or period. ▷late 19th cent.: from French *Magdalénien* 'from La Madeleine,' a site in the Dordogne, France, where objects from this culture were found.

Mag·de·burg /'magdəbərg; 'mägdə,bo͝ork/ an industrial city in Germany, the capital of Saxony-Anhalt, situated on the Elbe River and linked to the Rhine and Ruhr rivers by the Mittelland Canal; pop. 290,000.

mage /māj/ ▸*n. archaic* or *poetic/literary* a magician or learned person. ▷late Middle English: anglicized form of Latin *magus* (see **magus**).

Ma·gel·lan[1] /mə'jelən/ an American space probe launched in 1989 to map the surface of Venus, using radar to penetrate the dense cloud cover. The probe was deliberately burned up in Venus's atmosphere in 1994.

Ma·gel·lan[2] Ferdinand (*c.*1480–1521), Portuguese explorer; Portuguese name *Fernão Magalhães.* In 1519, he sailed from Spain, rounding South America through the strait that now bears his name, and reached the Philippines in 1521. He was killed in a skirmish on Cebu; the survivors sailed back to Spain around Africa, completing the first circumnavigation of the globe in 1522.

Ma·gel·lan, Strait of a passage that separates Tierra del Fuego and other islands from mainland South America. It connects the Atlantic and Pacific oceans.

Mag·el·lan·ic Clouds /,majə'lanik/ *Astronomy* two diffuse luminous patches in the southern sky, now known to be small irregular galaxies that are the closest to our own. The **Large Magellanic Cloud** is about 169,000 light years away, and the **Small Magellanic Cloud** is about 210,000 light years away. ▷named after the Portuguese explorer *Magellan* (see **Magellan**[1]).

Ma·gen Da·vid /mä'gen dä'vēd; 'môgən 'dôvid/ ▸*n.* another name for **Star of David**. ▷early 20th cent.: Hebrew, literally 'shield of David,' with reference to David, King of Israel (see **David**[1]).

ma·gen·ta /mə'jentə/ ▸*n.* a light purplish red that is one of the primary subtractive colors, complementary to green. ▪ the dye fuchsin. ▷mid 19th cent.: named after *Magenta* in northern Italy, site of a battle (1859) fought shortly before the dye (of bloodlike color) was discovered.

mag·gid /'mägid; mä'gēd/ ▸*n.* (*pl.* **mag·gi·dim** /mä'gēdim; ,mäge'dēm/) an itinerant Jewish preacher. ▷late 19th cent.: from Hebrew *maggīd* 'narrator.'

Mag·gio·re, Lake /mä'jôrā/ the second largest of the lakes of northern Italy. It extends into southern Switzerland.

mag·got /'magət/ ▸*n.* **1** a soft-bodied legless larva, esp. that of a fly found in decaying matter. ▪ *Fishing* bait consisting of a maggot or maggots. **2** *archaic* a whimsical fancy. ▷late Middle English: perhaps an alteration of dialect *maddock,* from Old Norse *mathkr,* of Germanic origin. **—mag·got·y** *adj.*

Ma·ghrib /'məgrəb/ (also **Ma·ghreb**) a region of north and northwestern Africa between the Atlantic Ocean and Egypt that comprises the coastal plain and Atlas Mountains of Morocco, together with Algeria and Tunisia and sometimes Tripolitania. Compare with **Barbary**.

Ma·gi /'mā,jī/ (**the Magi**) the "wise men" from the East who brought gifts to the infant Jesus (Matt. 2:1), said in later tradition to be kings named Caspar, Melchior, and Balthasar who brought gifts of gold, frankincense, and myrrh. ▷see **magus**.

ma·gi /'mā,jī/ plural form of **magus**.

ma·gi·an /'māj(ē)ən; 'mā,jiən/ (also **Ma·gi·an**) ▸*adj.* of or relating to the magi of ancient Persia. ▪ of or relating to the Magi who brought gifts to the infant Jesus.
▸*n.* a magus or Magus.

mag·ic /'majik/ ▸*n.* the power of apparently influencing the course of events by using mysterious or supernatural forces: *do you believe in magic? | suddenly,* ***as if by magic,*** *the doors start to open.* ▪ mysterious tricks, such as making things disappear and appear again, performed as entertainment. ▪ a quality that makes something seem removed from everyday life, esp. in a way that gives delight: *the magic of the theater.* ▪ *informal* something that has such a quality: *their seaside town is pure magic.*
▸*adj.* **1** used in magic or working by magic; having or apparently having supernatural powers: *a magic wand.* ▪ [*attrib.*] very effective in producing results, esp. desired ones: *confidence is the magic ingredient needed to spark recovery.* **2** *informal* wonderful; exciting: *what a magic moment.*
▸*v.* (**mag·icked, mag·ick·ing**) [*trans.*] move, change, or create by or as if by magic: *he must have been magicked out of the car at the precise second it exploded.* ▷late Middle English (also in the sense 'a magical procedure'): from Old French *magique,* from Latin *magicus* (adjective), late Latin *magica* (noun), from Greek *magikē (tekhnē)* '(art of) a magus': magi were regarded as magicians.
▸*PHRASE* □ **like magic** remarkably effectively or rapidly: *it repels rain like magic.*

mag·i·cal /'majikəl/ ▸*adj.* **1** relating to or using magic: *a magical crystal ball.* ▪ resembling magic; produced or working as if by magic: *he had a gentle, magical touch with the child.* **2** beautiful or delightful in such a way as to seem removed from everyday life: *it was a magical evening of pure nostalgia.* **—mag·i·cal·ly** *adv.*

mag·i·cal re·al·ism ▸*n.* another term for **magic realism**.

mag·ic bul·let ▸*n. informal* a medicine or other remedy, esp. an undiscovered or hypothetical one, with wonderful or highly specific properties.

mag·ic eye ▸*n.* **1** *informal* a photoelectric cell or similar electrical device used for identification, detection, or measurement. **2** a small cathode-ray tube in some radio receivers that displays a pattern that enables the radio to be accurately tuned.

ma·gi·cian /mə'jisHən/ ▸*n.* a person with magical powers. ▪ a person who performs magic tricks for entertainment. ▪ *informal* a person with exceptional skill in a particular area: *he was the magician of the fan belt.* ▷late Middle English: from Old French *magicien,* from late Latin *magica* (see **magic**).

ma·gick ▸*n.* chiefly archaic spelling of **magic**. **—mag·i·ckal** *adj.*

mag·ic lan·tern ▸*n. historical* a simple form of image projector used for showing photographic slides.

Mag·ic Mark·er ▸*n. trademark* an indelible felt-tip marker, esp. one with a wide tip.

mag·ic mush·room ▸*n. informal* any toadstool with hallucinogenic properties, esp. the liberty cap and its relatives. • Genus *Psilocybe,* family Strophariaceae, class Hymenomycetes: several species, including *P. mexicana,* which is traditionally consumed by American Indians in Mexico.

mag·ic num·ber ▸*n.* a figure regarded as significant or momentous in a particular context. ▪ *chiefly Baseball* the number that, at a late stage in the season, signifies the combination of wins for the first-place team and losses for another team that will allow the former to end the season alone in first place.

mag·ic re·al·ism (also **mag·i·cal re·al·ism**) ▸*n.* a literary or artistic genre in which realistic narrative and naturalistic technique are combined with surreal elements of dream or fantasy. —**mag·ic re·al·ist** *n.*

mag·ic square ▸*n.* a square that is divided into smaller squares, each containing a number, such that the figures in each vertical, horizontal, and diagonal row add up to the same value.

8	18	16
22	14	6
12	10	20

magic square

Ma·gi·not Line /ˈmazнə ˌnō; ˈmaj-/ a line of defensive fortifications constructed by the French along their eastern border, extending from Switzerland to Luxembourg, between 1929 and 1936. In World War II, although the defenses held, the Germans outflanked them, going through Belgium to conquer France. ■ [as *n.*] (also **Maginot line**) an impressive but often ineffectual means of protection or defense: *the courts are our Maginot Line against industry.* ▹named after André *Maginot* (1877–1932), a French minister of war.

mag·is·ter /ˈmajəstər/ ▸*n. archaic* a title or form of address given to scholars, esp. those qualified to teach in a medieval university. ▹late Middle English: from Latin, 'master.'

mag·is·te·ri·al /ˌmajəˈsti(ə)rēəl/ ▸*adj.* **1** having or showing great authority: *a magisterial pronouncement.* ■ domineering; dictatorial: *he dropped his somewhat magisterial style of questioning.* **2** relating to or conducted by a magistrate. ■ (of a person) holding the office of a magistrate. ▹early 17th cent.: from medieval Latin *magisterialis*, from late Latin *magisterius*, from Latin *magister* 'master.' —**mag·is·te·ri·al·ly** *adv.*

mag·is·te·ri·um /ˌmajəˈsti(ə)rēəm/ ▸*n.* the teaching authority of the Roman Catholic Church, esp. as exercised by bishops or the pope. ■ the official and authoritative teaching of the Roman Catholic Church. ▹mid 19th cent.: Latin, 'the office of master,' from *magister* (see **MAGISTER**).

mag·is·tra·cy /ˈmajəstrəsē/ ▸*n.* (*pl.* **-cies**) the office or authority of a magistrate. ■ (**the magistracy**) magistrates collectively.

mag·is·tral /ˈmajəstrəl/ ▸*adj. formal* or *archaic* relating to a master or masters. ▹late 16th cent.: from French, or from Latin *magistralis*, from *magister* 'master.'

mag·is·trate /ˈmajəˌstrāt/ ▸*n.* a civil officer or lay judge who administers the law, esp. one who conducts a court that deals with minor offenses and holds preliminary hearings for more serious ones. ▹late Middle English: from Latin *magistratus* 'administrator,' from *magister* 'master.' —**mag·is·tra·ture** /-ˌstrācнər; -strəˌcнŏŏ(ə)r/ *n.*

mag·lev /ˈmagˌlev/ ▸*n.* [usu. as *adj.*] a transportation system in which trains glide above a track, supported by magnetic repulsion and propelled by a linear motor: *maglev trains.* ▹late 20th cent.: from *mag(netic) lev(itation).*

mag·ma /ˈmagmə/ ▸*n.* hot fluid or semifluid material below or within the earth's crust from which lava and other igneous rock is formed by cooling. ■ *dated* a fluid medicinal suspension of a solid. ▹late Middle English (in the sense 'residue of dregs after evaporation or pressing of a semiliquid substance'): via Latin from Greek *magma* (from *massein* 'knead'). —**mag·mat·ic** /magˈmatik/ *adj.*

mag·ma·tism /ˈmagməˌtizəm/ ▸*n. Geology* the motion or activity of magma.

Mag·na Car·ta /ˌmagnə ˈkärtə/ a charter of liberty and political rights obtained from King John of England by his rebellious barons at Runnymede in 1215, which came to be seen as the seminal document of English constitutional practice. ▹from medieval Latin, 'great charter.'

mag·na cum lau·de /ˌmagnə kŏŏm ˈloudə; ˌkəm ˈlôdə/ ▸*adv.* & *adj.* with great distinction (with reference to college degrees and diplomas). ▹Latin, literally 'with great praise.'

Mag·na Grae·ci·a /ˌmagnə ˈgrāsнə/ the ancient Greek cities of southern Italy, founded from *c.*750 BC onward by colonists from Euboea, Sparta, and elsewhere in Greece. ▹Latin, literally 'Great Greece.'

mag·nan·i·mous /magˈnanəməs/ ▸*adj.* very generous or forgiving, esp. toward a rival or someone less powerful than oneself. ▹mid 16th cent.: from Latin *magnanimus* (from *magnus* 'great' + *animus* 'soul') + -ous. —**mag·na·nim·i·ty** /ˌmagnəˈnimətē/ *n.* —**mag·nan·i·mous·ly** *adv.*

mag·nate /ˈmagˌnāt; ˈmagnət/ ▸*n.* a wealthy and influential person, esp. in business: *a media magnate.* ▹late Middle English: from late Latin *magnas, magnat-* 'great man,' from Latin *magnus* 'great.'

mag·ne·sia /magˈnēzнə; -ˈnēsнə/ ▸*n. Chemistry* magnesium oxide. • Chem. formula: MgO. ■ hydrated magnesium carbonate used as an antacid and laxative. ▹late Middle English (referring to a mineral said to be an ingredient of the philosopher's stone): via medieval Latin from Greek *Magnēsia*, denoting a mineral from Magnesia in Asia Minor.

mag·ne·sian /magˈnēzнən; -ˈnēsнən/ ▸*adj.* (chiefly of rocks and minerals) containing or relatively rich in magnesium.

mag·ne·site /ˈmagnəˌsīt/ ▸*n.* a whitish mineral consisting of magnesium carbonate, used as a heat-resistant lining in some furnaces.

mag·ne·si·um /magˈnēzēəm; -zнəm/ ▸*n.* the chemical element of atomic number 12, a silver-white metal of the alkaline earth series. It is used to make strong lightweight alloys, esp. for the aerospace industry, and is also used in flashbulbs and pyrotechnics because it burns with a brilliant white flame. (Symbol: **Mg**)

mag·ne·si·um flare (also **magnesium light**) ▸*n.* a brilliant white flare containing metallic magnesium wire or ribbon.

mag·net /ˈmagnət/ ▸*n.* a piece of iron (or an ore, alloy, or other material) that has its component atoms so ordered that the material exhibits properties of magnetism, such as attracting other iron-containing objects or aligning itself in an external magnetic field. ■ archaic term for **LODESTONE**. ■ *figurative* a person or thing that has a powerful attraction: *the beautiful stretch of white sand is **a magnet for** sun worshipers.* ▹late Middle English (denoting a lodestone): from Latin *magnes, magnet-*, from Greek *magnēs lithos* 'lodestone,' probably influenced by Anglo-Norman French *magnete* (from Latin *magnes, magnet-*).

mag·ne·tar /ˈmagniˌtär/ ▸*n. Astronomy* a neutron star with an extremely strong magnetic field. ▹1990s: from *magnetic* + *-ar*, on the pattern of *pulsar* and *quasar*.

mag·net·ic /magˈnetik/ ▸*adj.* **1** having the properties of a magnet; exhibiting magnetism: *the clock has a magnetic back to stick to the fridge.* ■ capable of being attracted by or acquiring the properties of a magnet: *steel is magnetic.* ■ relating to or involving magnetism: *an airborne magnetic survey.* ■ (of a bearing in navigation) measured relative to magnetic north. **2** very attractive or alluring: *his magnetic personality.* ▹early 17th cent.: from late Latin *magneticus*, from Latin *magneta* (see **MAGNET**). —**mag·net·i·cal·ly** /-ik(ə)lē/ *adv.*

mag·net·ic com·pass ▸*n.* another term for **COMPASS** (sense 1).

mag·net·ic disk ▸*n.* see **DISK** (sense 1).

mag·net·ic e·qua·tor ▸*n.* the irregular imaginary line, passing around the earth near the equator, on which a magnetic needle has no dip (see **DIP** sense 4).

mag·net·ic field ▸*n.* a region around a magnetic material or a moving electric charge within which the force of magnetism acts.

mag·net·ic in·cli·na·tion ▸*n.* another term for **DIP** (sense 4).

mag·net·ic in·duc·tion ▸*n.* **1** magnetic flux or flux density. **2** the process by which an object or material is magnetized by an external magnetic field.

mag·net·ic mine ▸*n.* a mine detonated by the proximity of a magnetized body such as a ship or tank.

mag·net·ic mo·ment ▸*n. Physics* the property of a magnet that interacts with an applied field to give a mechanical moment.

mag·net·ic nee·dle ▸*n.* a piece of magnetized steel used as an indicator on the dial of a compass and in magnetic and electrical apparatus.

mag·net·ic north ▸*n.* the direction in which the north end of a compass needle or other freely suspended magnet will point in response to the earth's magnetic field. It deviates from true north over time and from place to place because the earth's magnetic poles are not fixed in relation to its axis.

mag·net·ic pole ▸*n.* each of the points near the extremities of the axis of rotation of the earth or another celestial body where a magnetic needle dips vertically. ■ each of the two points or regions of an artificial or natural magnet to and from which the lines of magnetic force are directed.

mag·net·ic res·o·nance im·ag·ing (abbr.: **MRI**) ▸*n.* a form of medical imaging that measures the response of the atomic nuclei of body tissues to high-frequency radio waves when placed in a strong magnetic field, and that produces images of the internal organs.

mag·net·ic storm ▸*n.* a disturbance of the magnetic field of the earth (or other celestial body).

mag·net·ic tape ▸*n.* tape used in recording sound, pictures, or computer data.

mag·net·ic var·i·a·tion ▸*n.* see **VARIATION** (sense 1).

mag·net·ism /ˈmagnəˌtizəm/ ▸*n.* a physical phenomenon produced by the motion of electric charge, resulting in attractive and repulsive forces between objects. ■ the property of being magnetic. ■ *figurative* the ability to attract and charm people: *his personal magnetism attracted men to the brotherhood.*

All magnetism is due to circulating electric currents. In magnetic materials the magnetism is produced by electrons orbiting within the atoms; in most substances the magnetic effects of different electrons cancel each other out, but in some, such as iron, a net magnetic field can be induced by aligning the atoms.

▹early 17th cent.: from modern Latin *magnetismus*, from Latin *magneta* (see **MAGNET**).

mag·net·ite /ˈmagnəˌtīt/ ▸*n.* a gray-black magnetic mineral that consists of an oxide of iron and is an important form of iron ore. ▹mid 19th cent.: from **MAGNET** + **-ITE**[1].

mag·net·ize /ˈmagnəˌtīz/ ▸*v.* [*trans.*] give magnetic properties to; make magnetic. ■ *figurative* attract strongly as if by a magnet. —**mag·net·iz·a·ble** *adj.* —**mag·net·i·za·tion** /ˌmagnətəˈzāsнən/ *n.* —**mag·net·iz·er** *n.*

mag·ne·to /magˈnētō/ ▸*n.* (*pl.* **-tos**) a small electric generator containing a permanent magnet and used to provide high-voltage pulses, esp. (formerly) in the ignition systems of internal combustion engines. ▹late 19th cent.: abbreviation of **MAGNETO-ELECTRIC**.

magneto- ▸*comb. form* relating to a magnet or magnetism: *magneto-electric.*

mag·ne·to-e·lec·tric ▸*adj.* relating to the electric currents generated in a material by its motion in a magnetic field. ■ (of an electric generator) using permanent magnets. —**mag·ne·to-e·lec·tric·i·ty** *n.*

mag·ne·to·graph /magˈnētəˌgraf/ ▸*n.* an instrument for recording measurements of magnetic forces.

mag·ne·to·hy·dro·dy·nam·ics /magˌnētōˌhīdrəˌdīˈnamiks/ ▸*plural n.* [treated as *sing.*] the branch of physics that studies the behavior of an electrically conducting fluid such as a plasma or molten metal acted on by a magnetic field. —**mag·ne·to·hy·dro·dy·nam·ic** /-ˌhīdrōˌdīˈnamik/ *adj.*

mag·ne·tom·e·ter /ˌmagnəˈtämətər/ ▸*n.* an instrument used for measuring magnetic forces, esp. the earth's magnetism. —**mag·ne·tom·e·try** /-ətrē/ *n.*

mag·ne·to·mo·tive force /magˌnētōˈmōtiv/ ▸*n. Physics* a quantity representing the line integral of the magnetic intensity around a closed line (e.g., the sum of the magnetizing forces along a circuit).

mag·ne·ton /ˈmagnəˌtän/ ▸*n.* a unit of magnetic moment in atomic and nuclear physics. ▹early 20th cent.: from **MAGNETIC** + **-ON**.

mag·ne·to-op·ti·cal ▸*adj.* of, relating to, or employing both optical and magnetic phenomena or technology.

mag·ne·to·pause /magˈnētəˌpôz/ ▸*n.* the outer limit of a magnetosphere.

mag·ne·to·re·sist·ance /magˌnētəriˈzistəns/ ▸*n. Physics* the dependence of the electrical resistance of a body on an external magnetic field. —**mag·ne·to·re·sist·ive** /magˌnētəriˈzistiv/ *adj.*

mag·ne·to·sphere /magˈnētəˌsfir/ ▸*n.* the region surrounding the earth or another astronomical body in which its magnetic field is the predominant effective magnetic field. —**mag·ne·to·spher·ic** /ˌmag ˌnētəˈsfirik/ *adj.*

mag·ne·to·tail /magˈnētəˌtāl/ ▸*n. Astronomy* the broad elongated extension of a planet's magnetosphere on the side away from the sun.

mag·ne·tron /ˈmagnəˌträn/ ▸*n.* an electron tube for amplifying or generating microwaves, with the flow of electrons controlled by an external magnetic field. ▹early 20th cent.: from **MAGNETIC** + *-tron* from **ELECTRON**.

mag·net school ▸*n.* a public school offering special instruction and programs not available elsewhere, designed to attract a more diverse student body from throughout a school district.

Mag·nif·i·cat /mag'nifi,kät; män'yifi-/ ▸*n.* a canticle used in Christian liturgy, esp. at vespers and evensong, the text being the hymn of the Virgin Mary (Luke 1:46–55). ▷Middle English: Latin, literally 'magnifies' (from the opening words, which translate as 'my soul magnifies the Lord').

mag·ni·fi·ca·tion /,magnəfi'kāSHən/ ▸*n.* the action or process of magnifying something or being magnified, esp. visually: *visible under high magnification.* ■ the degree to which something is or can be magnified: *at this magnification the pixels making up the image become visible.* ■ the magnifying power of an instrument: *this microscope should give a magnification of about 100.* ■ a magnified reproduction of something.

mag·nif·i·cence /mag'nifəsəns/ ▸*n.* the quality of being magnificent. ■ (**His, Your**, etc., **Magnificence**) *chiefly historical* a title given to a monarch or other distinguished person, or used in addressing them.

mag·nif·i·cent /mag'nifəsənt/ ▸*adj.* **1** impressively beautiful, elaborate, or extravagant; striking: *a dramatic landscape of magnificent mountains | the interior layout is magnificent.* **2** very good; excellent: *she paid tribute to their magnificent efforts.* ▷late Middle English: via Old French from Latin *magnificent-* 'making great, serving to magnify,' based on *magnus* 'great.' **—mag·nif·i·cent·ly** *adv.*

mag·nif·i·co /mag'nifi,kō/ ▸*n.* (*pl.* **-coes**) *informal* an eminent, powerful, or illustrious person. ▷late 16th cent.: Italian, 'magnificent,' originally used to denote a Venetian magnate.

mag·ni·fy /'magnə,fī/ ▸*v.* (**-fies, -fied**) [*trans.*] **1** make (something) appear larger than it is, esp. with a lens or microscope: *the camera's zoom mode can magnify a certain area if required.* ■ [*intrans.*] be capable of increasing the size or apparent size of something: *a pair of binoculars that magnify about eight power.* ■ increase the volume of (a sound). ■ intensify: *the risk is magnified if there is any dirty material next to the skin.* ■ exaggerate the importance or effect of: *she tended to magnify the defects of those she disliked.* **2** *archaic* extol; glorify: *praise the Lord and magnify Him.* ▷late Middle English (in the senses 'show honor to (God)' and 'make greater in size or importance'): from Old French *magnifier* or Latin *magnificare*, based on Latin *magnus* 'great.' Sense 1 dates from the mid 17th cent. **—mag·ni·fi·er** /-,fīər/ *n.*

mag·ni·fy·ing glass ▸*n.* a lens that produces an enlarged image, typically set in a frame with a handle and used to examine small or finely detailed things such as fingerprints, stamps, and fine print.

mag·nil·o·quent /mag'niləkwənt/ ▸*adj.* using high-flown or bombastic language. ▷mid 17th cent.: from Latin *magniloquus* (from *magnus* 'great' + *-loquus* '-speaking') + **-ENT**. **—mag·nil·o·quence** *n.* **—mag·nil·o·quent·ly** *adv.*

Mag·ni·to·gorsk /məg,nētə'gôrsk/ an industrial city in southern Russia, on the Ural River close to the border with Kazakhstan; pop. 443,000.

mag·ni·tude /'magnə,t(y)o͞od/ ▸*n.* **1** the great size or extent of something: *they may feel discouraged at the magnitude of the task before them.* ■ great importance: *events of tragic magnitude.* **2** size: *electorates of less than average magnitude.* ■ a numerical quantity or value: *the magnitudes of all the economic variables could be determined.* **3** the degree of brightness of a star. The magnitude of an astronomical object is now reckoned as the negative logarithm of the brightness; a decrease of one magnitude represents an increase in brightness of 2.512 times. A star with an apparent magnitude of six is barely visible to the naked eye. See also **APPARENT MAGNITUDE, ABSOLUTE MAGNITUDE**. ■ the class into which a star falls by virtue of its brightness. ■ a difference of one on a scale of brightness, treated as a unit of measurement. ▷late Middle English (also in the sense 'greatness of character'): from Latin *magnitudo*, from *magnus* 'great.'
▸*PHRASE* □ **of the first magnitude** see **FIRST**.

mag·no·lia /mag'nōlyə/ ▸*n.* a tree or shrub with large, typically creamy-pink, waxy flowers. Magnolias are widely grown as ornamental trees. • Genus *Magnolia*, family Magnoliaceae: numerous species, including *M. campbellii*, native to the Himalayas and from which several varieties have been cultivated in North America. ▷modern Latin, named after Pierre *Magnol* (1638–1715), French botanist.

Mag·no·lia State a nickname for the state of **MISSISSIPPI**.

mag·no·lia vine ▸*n.* another term for **SCHIZANDRA**.

mag·num /'magnəm/ ▸*n.* (*pl.* **-nums**) a thing of a type that is larger than normal, in particular: ■ a wine bottle of twice the standard size, normally $1^1/_2$ liters. ■ (often **Magnum**) [often as *adj.*] *trademark* a gun designed to fire cartridges that are more powerful than its caliber would suggest: *his .357 Magnum pistol.* ▷late 18th cent.: from Latin, neuter (used as a noun) of *magnus* 'great.'

mag·num o·pus /'magnəm 'ōpəs/ ▸*n.* (*pl.* **mag·num o·pus·es** or **mag·na o·pe·ra** /'magnə 'ōpərə; 'äpərə/) a large and important work of art, music, or literature, esp. one regarded as the most important work of an artist or writer. ▷late 18th cent.: from Latin, 'great work.'

Mag·nus ef·fect /'magnəs / ▸*n.* *Physics* the force exerted on a rapidly spinning cylinder or sphere moving through air or another fluid in a direction at an angle to the axis of spin. This force is responsible for the swerving of balls when hit or thrown with spin. ▷1920s: named after Heinrich G. *Magnus* (1802–70), German scientist.

Ma·gog /mə'gäg/ see **GOG AND MAGOG**.

mag·pie /'mag,pī/ ▸*n.* **1** a long-tailed crow with boldly marked (or green) plumage and a raucous voice. • Family Corvidae: five genera and several species, in particular the black-and-white **black-billed magpie** (*Pica pica*) of Eurasia and North America. **2** used in similes or comparisons to refer to a person who collects things, esp. things of little use or value, or a person who chatters idly. ▷late 16th cent.: probably shortening of dialect *maggot the pie, maggoty-pie*, from *Magot* (Middle English nickname for the given name *Marguerite*) + **PIE**[2].

black-billed magpie

M.Agr. ▸*abbr.* Master of Agriculture.

Ma·gritte /mə'grēt; ma-/, René (François Ghislain) (1898–1967), Belgian surrealist painter. His paintings are startling or amusing juxtapositions of the ordinary, the strange, and the erotic, depicted in a realist manner.

ma·guey /mə'gā/ ▸*n.* an agave plant, esp. one yielding pulque. ▷mid 16th cent.: via Spanish from Taino.

ma·gus /'māgəs/ ▸*n.* (*pl.* **ma·gi** /'mā,jī/) a member of a priestly caste of ancient Persia. See also **MAGI**. ■ a sorcerer. ▷Middle English: via Latin and Greek from Old Persian *maguš*.

mag wheel /mag / ▸*n.* a motor-vehicle wheel made from lightweight magnesium steel, typically having a pattern of holes or spokes around the hub.

Mag·yar /'mag,yär/ ▸*n.* **1** a member of a people who originated in the Urals and migrated westward to settle in what is now Hungary in the 9th century AD. **2** the Uralic language of this people; Hungarian.
▸*adj.* of or relating to this people or language. ▷the name in Hungarian.

Ma·gyar·or·szág /'mädyär,ôr,säg/ Hungarian name for **HUNGARY**.

Mah·a·bad /,mähə'bäd/ a city in northwestern Iran, near the Iraqi border, with a chiefly Kurdish population; pop. 63,000 (1986).Between 1941 and 1946 it was the center of a Soviet-supported Kurdish republic.

Ma·ha·bha·ra·ta /,mähə'bärətə/ one of the two great Sanskrit epics of the Hindus, existing in its present form since *c.*AD 400.It describes the civil war waged between the five Pandava brothers and their 100 stepbrothers at Kuruksetra near modern Delhi. ▷Sanskrit, literally 'great Bharata,' i.e., the great epic of the Bharata dynasty.

magnolia

ma·hal /mə'häl/ ▸*n.* *Indian* **1** a mansion or palace (in names): *the Taj Mahal.* **2** living quarters set aside for a particular group of people: *the servant mahal.* ▷early 17th cent.: from Urdu and Persian *maḥal(l)*, from Arabic *maḥall*, from *ḥall*, 'stopping-place, abode.'

ma·hant /mə'hənt/ ▸*n.* *Hinduism* a chief priest of a temple or the head of a monastery. ▷Hindi.

ma·ha·ra·ja /,mähə'räjə; -'räZHə/ (also **ma·ha·ra·jah**) ▸*n.* *historical* an Indian prince. ▷from Hindi *mahārājā*, from Sanskrit *mahā* 'great' + *rājan* 'raja.'

ma·ha·ra·ni /,mähə'ränē/ (also **ma·ha·ra·nee**) ▸*n.* a maharaja's wife or widow. ▷from Hindi *mahārānī*, from Sanskrit *mahā* 'great' + *rājñī* 'ranee.'

Ma·ha·rash·tra /,mä(h)ə'räsHtrə/ a large state in western India that borders on the Arabian Sea, formed in 1960 from the southeastern part of the former state of Bombay; capital, Bombay. **—Ma·ha·rash·tri·an** /-trēən/ *adj.* & *n.*

Ma·ha·ri·shi /,mähə'rēSHē; mə'härəSHē/ ▸*n.* a great Hindu sage or spiritual leader. ▷alteration of Sanskrit *maharṣi*, from *mahā* 'great' + *ṛṣi* 'rishi.'

ma·hat·ma /mə'hätmə; -'hatmə/ ▸*n.* (in the Indian subcontinent) a person regarded with reverence or loving respect; a holy person or sage. ■ (**the Mahatma**) Mahatma Gandhi. ■ (in some forms of theosophy) a person in India or Tibet said to have supernatural powers. ▷from Sanskrit *mahātman*, from *mahā* 'great' + *ātman* 'soul.'

Ma·ha·we·li /,mähə'wālē/ the major river in Sri Lanka. Rising in the central highlands, it flows north for 206 miles (330 km) to the Bay of Bengal.

Ma·ha·ya·na /,mähə'yänə/ (also **Mahayana Buddhism**) ▸*n.* one of the two major traditions of Buddhism, now practiced in a variety of forms esp. in China, Tibet, Japan, and Korea. The tradition emerged around the 1st century AD and is typically concerned with altruistically oriented spiritual practice as embodied in the ideal of the bodhisattva. Compare with **THERAVADA**. ▷from Sanskrit, from *mahā* 'great' + *yāna* 'vehicle.'

Mah·di /'mädē/ ▸*n.* (*pl.* **Mah·dis**) (in popular Muslim belief) a spiritual and temporal leader who will rule before the end of the world and restore religion and justice. ■ a person claiming to be this leader, notably Muhammad Ahmad of Dongola in Sudan (1843–85), whose revolutionary movement captured Khartoum and overthrew the Egyptian regime. ■ (in Shiite belief) the twelfth imam, who is expected to return and triumph over injustice. ▷from Arabic *(al-)mahdī* 'he who is guided in the right way,' passive participle of *hadā* 'to guide.' **—Mah·dism** /'mä,dizəm/ *n.* **—Mah·dist** /'mädist/ *n.* & *adj.*

Mah·fouz /mä'fo͞oz/, Naguib (1911–), Egyptian novelist and short-story writer. Notable works: *Miramar* (1967) and *Wedding Song* (1981). Nobel Prize for Literature (1988).

Ma·hi·can /mə'hēkən/ (also **Mo·hi·can**) ▸*n.* **1** a member of an American Indian people formerly inhabiting the Upper Hudson Valley in New York. Compare with **MOHEGAN**. **2** the Algonquian language of this people.
▸*adj.* of or relating to the Mahicans or their language. ▷the name in Mahican, meaning 'people of the estuary'.

Ma·hi·lyow /məgil'yôf/ an industrial city and railroad center in eastern Belarus, on the Dnieper River; pop. 363,000. Russian name **MOGILYOV**.

ma·hi·ma·hi /,mähē'mähē/ ▸*n.* an edible marine fish of warm seas, with silver and bright blue or green coloration when alive. Also called **DOLPHIN** or **DORADO**. • Family Coryphaenidae and genus *Coryphaena*: two species, in particular the large *C. hippurus*. ▷1940s: from Hawaiian.

mah-jongg /mä 'ZHäNG; -ZHôNG/ (also **mah-jong** or **mah·jongg** or **mah·jong**) ▸*n.* a Chinese game played, usually by four people, with 136 or 144 rectangular pieces called tiles. The object is to collect winning sets of these tiles, as in card games such as gin rummy. ▷early 20th cent.: from Chinese dialect *ma tsiang*, literally 'sparrows.'

Mah·ler /'mälər/, Gustav (1860–1911), Austrian composer, conductor, and pianist. His works, which include symphonies and songes, form a link between romanticism and the experimentalism of Schoenberg. **—Mah·ler·i·an** /mä'le(ə)rēən/ *adj.*

mahl·stick /'môl,stik/ (also **maul·stick**) ▸*n.* a light stick with a padded leather ball at one end, held against work by a painter or signwriter to support and steady the brush hand. ▷mid 17th cent.: from Dutch *maalstok*, from *malen* 'to paint' + *stok* 'stick.'

ma·hoe[1] /mə'hō; 'mä,hō/ ▸*n.* a small bushy New Zealand tree of the violet family, with whitish bark and clusters of small greenish flowers. • *Melicytus ramiflorus*, family Violaceae. ▷early 19th cent.: from Maori.

ma·hoe[2] ▸*n. W. Indian* any of a number of tropical trees and shrubs yielding bast that is used to make cordage. • Several species, esp. of the genus *Hibiscus* (family Malvaceae), in particular the widespread *H. tiliaceus* and the Caribbean *H. elatus*. ▷from Arawak *maho*.

ma·hog·a·ny /mə'hägənē/ ▸*n.* **1** hard reddish-brown timber from a tropical tree, used for high-quality furniture. ■ a rich reddish-brown color like that of mahogany wood. **2** the tropical American tree that produces this timber, widely harvested from the wild. • Genus *Swietenia*, family Meliaceae: three species, esp. *S. mahagoni*. ■ used in names of trees that yield similar timber, e.g., **Philippine mahogany**. ▷mid 17th cent.: of unknown origin.

Ma·hon /mə'hōn; mä'ōn/ (also **Port Mahon**) the capital of the island of Minorca, a port on the southeastern coast; pop. 22,000. Spanish name **MAHÓN**.

Ma·ho·ney /mə'hōnē/, Sally, see **FIELD**[2].

ma·ho·ni·a /mə'hōnēə/ ▸*n.* an evergreen shrub of the barberry family that produces clusters of small fragrant yellow flowers followed by purple or black berries, native to eastern Asia and North and Central America. • Genus *Mahonia*, family Berberidaceae. ▷modern Latin, named after Bernard McMahon (*c.*1775–1816), American botanist.

Ma·hore /mə'hôr/ another name for **MAYOTTE**.

ma·hout /mə'hout/ ▸*n.* (in the Indian subcontinent and Southeast Asia) a person who works with, rides, and tends an elephant. ▷from Hindi *mahāvat*.

Mah·pi·ua Lu·ta /'mäkʜ'pēwä 'lo͞otä/ see **RED CLOUD**.

Mah·rat·ta /mə'rätə/ ▸*n.* variant spelling of **MARATHA**.

Mah·rat·ti /mə'rätē/ ▸*n.* variant spelling of **MARATHI**.

ma·hua /'mä,hwä; -ho͞oə/ (also **ma·hwa**) ▸*n.* an Indian tree that has fleshy edible flowers and yields oil-rich seeds. • *Madhuca latifolia*, family Sapotaceae. ■ an alcoholic drink produced from the nectar-rich flowers of this tree. ▷late 17th cent.: via Hindi from Sanskrit *madhūka*, from *madhu* 'sweet.'

Ma·ia[1] /'mīə/ *Greek Mythology* the daughter of Atlas and mother of Hermes.

Ma·ia[2] *Roman Mythology* a goddess associated with Vulcan and also (by confusion with **MAIA**[1]) with Mercury (Hermes). She was worshiped on May 1 and May 15; that month is named after her.

maid /mād/ ▸*n.* a female domestic servant. ■ *archaic* or *poetic/literary* a girl or young woman, esp. an unmarried one. ■ *archaic* or *poetic/literary* a virgin. ▷Middle English: abbreviation of **MAIDEN**.

mai·dan /mī'dän/ ▸*n.* (in the Indian subcontinent) an open space in or near a town, used as a parade ground or for events such as public meetings and polo matches. ▷from Urdu and Persian *maidān*, from Arabic *maydān*.

maid·en /'mādn/ ▸*n.* **1** *archaic* or *poetic/literary* a girl or young woman, esp. an unmarried one. ■ a virgin. **2** (also **maiden over**) *Cricket* an over in which no runs are scored.
▸*adj.* [*attrib.*] **1** (of a woman, esp. an older one) unmarried: *a maiden aunt.* ■ (of a female animal) unmated. **2** being or involving the first attempt or act of its kind: *the ship's maiden voyage.* ■ denoting a horse that has never won a race, or a race intended for such horses. ■ (of a tree or other fruiting plant) in its first year of growth. ▷Old English *mægden*, from a Germanic diminutive meaning 'maid, virgin'; related to German *Mädchen*, diminutive of *Magd* 'maid,' from an Indo-European root shared by Old Irish *mug* 'boy, servant.' **—maid·en·hood** /-,ho͝od/ *n.* **—maid·en·ish** *adj.* **—maid·en·like** /-,līk/ *adj.* **—maid·en·ly** *adj.*

maid·en·hair /'mādn,he(ə)r/ (also **maidenhair fern**) ▸*n.* a chiefly tropical fern of delicate appearance, having slender-stalked fronds with round or wedge-shaped divided lobes. • Genus *Adiantum*, family Adiantaceae: several species, in particular *A. capillus-veneris* of Eurasia and North America.

maid·en·hair tree ▸*n.* the ginkgo, whose leaves resemble those of the maidenhair fern.

maid·en·head /'mādn,hed/ ▸*n.* virginity. ■ *dated* the hymen.

maid·en name ▸*n.* the surname that a married woman used from birth, prior to its being legally changed at marriage.

maid·en o·ver ▸*n.* see **MAIDEN** (sense 2).

maid of hon·or ▸*n.* an unmarried woman acting as principal bridesmaid at a wedding. ■ an unmarried woman, typically of noble birth, attending a queen or princess.

maid·serv·ant /'mād,sərvənt/ ▸*n. dated* a female domestic servant.

Maid·stone /'mād,stōn/ a town in southeastern England, on the Medway River; pop. 133,000.

ma·ieu·tic /mä'yo͞otik/ ▸*adj.* of or denoting the Socratic mode of inquiry, which aims to bring a person's latent ideas into clear consciousness.
▸*plural n.* (**maieutics**) [treated as *sing.*] the maieutic method. ▷mid 17th cent.: from Greek *maieutikos*, from *maieuesthai* 'act as a midwife,' from *maia* 'midwife.'

Mai·kop /mī'käp/ a city in southwestern Russia, capital of the republic of Adygea; pop. 120,000.

mail[1] /māl/ ▸*n.* letters and packages conveyed by the postal system. ■ (also **the mails**) the postal system: *you can order* **by mail** | *the check is* **in the mail** | [as *adj.*] *a mail truck.* ■ [in *sing.*] a single delivery or collection of mail: *the new magazine that came in the mail today.* ■ *Computing* electronic mail. ■ *dated* a vehicle, such as a train, carrying mail. ■ *archaic* a bag of letters to be conveyed by the postal system.
▸*v.* [*trans.*] send (a letter or package) using the postal system: *if you will mail the coupon, we'll send you a free trial package.* ■ *Computing* send (someone) electronic mail. ▷Middle English (in the sense 'traveling bag'): from Old French *male* 'wallet,' of West Germanic origin. The notion 'by post' dates from the mid 17th cent. **—mail·a·ble** *adj.*

mail[2] ▸*n. historical* armor made of metal rings or plates, joined together flexibly. ■ the protective shell or scales of certain animals.
▸*v.* [*trans.*] clothe or cover with mail: [as *adj.*] (**mailed**) *a mailed gauntlet.* ▷Middle English (also denoting the individual metal elements composing mail armor): from Old French *maille*, from Latin *macula* 'spot or mesh.'
▸*PHRASE* □ **the mailed fist** the use of physical force to maintain control or impose one's will.

mail·bag /'māl,bag/ ▸*n.* a large sack or bag for carrying mail.

mail·boat /'māl,bōt/ (also **mail boat**) ▸*n. chiefly historical* a ship or boat that carries mail.

mail bomb ▸*n.* **1** another term for **LETTER BOMB**. **2** an overwhelmingly large quantity of e-mail messages sent to one e-mail address.
▸*v.* (**mail-bomb**) [*trans.*] send an overwhelmingly large quantity of e-mail messages to (someone).

mail·box /'māl,bäks/ ▸*n.* a public box with a slot into which mail is placed for collection by the post office. ■ a private box into which mail is delivered, esp. one mounted on a post at the entrance to a person's property. ■ a computer file in which e-mail messages received by a particular user are stored.

mail call ▸*n. Military* the distribution of mail to soldiers.

mail car·ri·er ▸*n.* a person who is employed to deliver and collect letters and parcels.

mail drop ▸*n.* **1** a receptacle for mail, esp. one in which mail is kept until the addressee collects it. **2** *Brit.* a delivery of mail, advertising leaflets, or other material.

Mail·er /'mālər/, Norman (1923–), U.S. novelist and essayist. His novels, in which he frequently deals with the effect of war and violence on human relationships, include *The Naked and the Dead* (1948) and *Ancient Evenings* (1983). His nonfiction works include the prize-winning *The Armies of the Night* (1968) and *The Executioner's Song* (1979).

mail·er /'mālər/ ▸*n.* **1** the sender of a letter or package by mail. ■ a person employed to dispatch newspapers or periodicals by mail. ■ a free advertising pamphlet, brochure, or catalog sent out by mail. ■ a container used for conveying items by mail, esp. a padded envelope or protective tube. **2** *Computing* a program that sends electronic mail messages.

mail·ing /'māliɴɢ/ ▸*n.* the action or process of sending something by mail. ■ something sent by mail, esp. a piece of mass advertising.

mail·ing list ▸*n.* a list of the names and addresses of people to whom material such as advertising matter, information, or a magazine may be mailed, esp. regularly.

mail·lot /mī'ō/ ▸*n.* (*pl.* same) **1** a pair of tights worn for dancing or gymnastics. ■ a woman's tight-fitting one-piece swimsuit. **2** a jersey or top, esp. one worn in sports such as cycling. ▷French.

Mail·man /'māl,man/, The, see **MALONE**.

mail·man /'māl,man/ ▸*n.* (*pl.* **-men**) a person who is employed to deliver and collect letters and parcels.

mail merge ▸*n. Computing* the automatic addition of names and addresses from a database to letters and envelopes in order to facilitate sending mail, esp. advertising, to many addresses.

mail or·der ▸*n.* the selling of goods to customers by mail, generally involving selection from a special catalog: *available by mail order only* | [as *adj.*] *a mail-order distributor of generic drugs.*

mail-out ▸*n. chiefly Brit.* an instance of sending out by mail a number of promotional brochures or other items at one time.

maim /mām/ ▸*v.* [*trans.*] wound or injure (someone) so that part of the body is permanently damaged: *100,000 soldiers were killed or maimed.* ▷Middle English: from Old French *mahaignier*, of unknown origin.

Mai·mon·i·des /mī'mänidēz/ (1135–1204), Jewish philosopher and rabbinic scholar, born in Spain; born *Moses ben Maimon*. His *Guide for the Perplexed* (1190) attempts to reconcile Talmudic scripture with the philosophy of Aristotle.

Main /mīn/ a river of southwestern Germany that rises in northern Bavaria and flows west for 310 miles (500 km), through Frankfurt to meet the Rhine River at Mainz.

main[1] /mān/ ▸*adj.* [*attrib.*] chief in size or importance: *a main road* | *the main problem is one of resources.* ■ denoting the center of a network, from which other parts branch out: *I am seldom at the main office.*
▸*n.* **1** a principal pipe carrying water or gas to buildings, or taking sewage from them: [with *adj.*] *a faulty gas main.* ■ *Brit.* a principal cable carrying electricity. **2** (**the main**) *archaic* or *poetic/literary* the open ocean. **3** *Nautical* short for **MAINSAIL** or **MAINMAST**. ▷Middle English: from Old English *mægen* 'physical force,' reinforced by Old Norse *meginn*, *megn* 'strong, powerful,' both from a Germanic base meaning 'have power.'
▸*PHRASES* □ **by main force** through sheer strength. □ **in the main** on the whole; chiefly.

main[2] ▸*n.* **1** *historical* a match between fighting cocks. **2** (in the game of hazard) a number (5, 6, 7, 8, or 9) called by a player before dice are thrown. ▷late 16th cent.: probably from the phrase *main chance*.

main brace ▸*n.* one of the braces attached to the main yard of a sailing ship.

main clause ▸*n. Grammar* a clause that can form a complete sentence standing alone, having a subject and a predicate. Contrasted with **SUBORDINATE CLAUSE**.

main course ▸*n.* **1** the most substantial course of a meal. **2** the mainsail of a square-rigged sailing ship.

main drag ▸*n.* (usu. **the main drag**) *informal* the main street of a town.

Maine /mān/ a state in the northeastern U.S., one of the six New England states, on the Atlantic coast, on the U.S.-Canada border; pop. 1,274,923; capital, Augusta; statehood, Mar. 15, 1820 (23). Visited by John Cabot in 1498 and colonized by England in the 1600s and 1700s, it was annexed to Massachusetts from 1652 until 1820. **—Main·er** *n.*

Maine coon (also **Maine coon cat**) ▸*n.* a large, powerful domestic cat of a long-haired breed, native to America. ▷1970s: so named because of partial resemblance to the raccoon.

Maine Coon

main·frame /'mān,frām/ ▸*n.* **1** a large high-speed computer, esp. one supporting numerous workstations or peripherals. **2** the central processing unit and primary memory of a computer.

Main·land /'mānlənd; -,land/ **1** the largest island in the Orkney Islands. **2** the largest island in the Shetland Islands.

main·land /ˈmānˌland; -lənd/ ▸*n.* a large continuous extent of land that includes the greater part of a country or territory, as opposed to offshore islands and detached territories. **—main·land·er** *n.*

Main Line a popular name for a series of affluent suburbs west of Philadelphia in Pennsylvania, along the old Pennsylvania Railroad main line.

main line ▸*n.* a chief railroad line: [as *adj.*] *a main-line station.* ■ a principal route, course, or connection: *the main line of evolution.* ■ a chief road or street. ■ *informal* a principal vein as a site for a drug injection.
▸*v.* (**main·line**) [*trans.*] *informal* inject (a drug) intravenously: *Mariella mainlines cocaine five to seven times a day.* **—main·lin·er** *n.*

main·ly /ˈmānlē/ ▸*adv.* more than anything else: *he is mainly concerned with fiction.* ■ for the most part: *the west will be mainly dry.*

main man ▸*n. informal* **1** a close and trusted male friend. **2** the most important man in a team, organization, or situation: *now their main man can give his loving fans a big present by helping his team go all the way.*

main·mast /ˈmānˌmast/ ▸*n.* the principal mast of a ship, typically the second mast in a sailing ship of three or more masts.

main·plane /ˈmānˌplān/ ▸*n.* a principal supporting surface of an aircraft (typically a wing), as opposed to a horizontal stabilizer.

main·sail /ˈmānsəl; -ˌsāl/ ▸*n.* the principal sail of a ship, esp. the lowest sail on the mainmast in a square-rigged vessel. ■ the sail set on the after side of the mainmast in a fore-and-aft-rigged vessel.

main se·quence ▸*n. Astronomy* a series of star types to which most stars belong, represented on a Hertzsprung–Russell diagram as a continuous band extending from the upper left (hot, bright stars) to the lower right (cool, dim stars).

main·sheet /ˈmānˌsʜēt/ ▸*n.* a sheet used for controlling the mainsail of a sailing vessel.

main·spring /ˈmānˌspriɴɢ/ ▸*n.* the principal spring in a watch, clock, or other mechanism. ■ *figurative* something that plays a principal part in motivating or maintaining a movement, process, or activity: *the mainspring of anticommunism.*

main·stay /ˈmānˌstā/ ▸*n.* a stay that extends from the maintop to the foot of the foremast of a sailing ship. ■ *figurative* a thing on which something else is based or depends: *whitefish are the mainstay of the local industry.*

main stor·age ▸*n. Computing* the total memory available to executing programs, equivalent to RAM on modern computers.

main·stream /ˈmānˌstrēm/ ▸*n.* (**the mainstream**) the ideas, attitudes, or activities that are regarded as normal or conventional; the dominant trend in opinion, fashion, or the arts: *companies that are bringing computers to the mainstream of American life.* ■ (also **mainstream jazz**) jazz that is neither traditional nor modern, based on the 1930s swing style and consisting esp. of solo improvisation on chord sequences.
▸*adj.* belonging to or characteristic of the mainstream: *mainstream politics* | *a mixture of mainstream and avant-garde artists.* ■ (of a school or class) for students without special needs: *children with minor handicaps would be able to attend mainstream schools.*
▸*v.* [*trans.*] (often **be mainstreamed**) bring (something) into the mainstream: *vegetarianism has been mainstreamed.* ■ place (a student with special needs) into a mainstream class or school: *students with serious disabilities who are fully mainstreamed into student life.*

main street ▸*n.* the principal street of a town. ■ (**Main Street**) used in reference to the materialism, mediocrity, or parochialism regarded as typical of small-town life. [from the title of a novel (1920) by Sinclair Lewis.]

main·tain /mānˈtān/ ▸*v.* [*trans.*] **1** cause or enable (a condition or state of affairs) to continue: *the need to maintain close links between industry and schools.* ■ keep (something) at the same level or rate: *agricultural prices will have to be maintained.* ■ keep (a building, machine, or road) in good condition or in working order by checking or repairing it regularly. ■ hold (a position) in the face of attack or competition: *the objective to maintain a competitive market position.* **2** provide with necessities for life or existence: *the allowance covers the basic costs of maintaining a child.* ■ keep (a military unit) supplied with equipment and other requirements. ■ *archaic* give one's support to; uphold: *the king swears he will maintain the laws of God.* **3** [*reporting verb*] state something strongly to be the case; assert: [*trans.*] *he has always maintained his innocence* | [with *clause*] *he had persistently maintained that he would not stand against his old friend* | [with *direct speech*] *"It was not an ideology at all," she maintained.* ▷Middle English (also in the sense 'practice (a good or bad action) habitually'): from Old French *maintenir*, from Latin *manu tenere* 'hold in the hand.' **—main·tain·a·bil·i·ty** /ˌmānˌtānəˈbilətē/ *n.* **—main·tain·a·ble** *adj.*

main·tain·er /mānˈtānər/ ▸*n.* a person or thing that maintains something, in particular computer software. ■ (also **main·tai·nor**) *historical Law* a person guilty of aiding a party in a legal action without lawful cause.

main·te·nance /ˈmānt(ə)nəns; ˈmāntn-əns/ ▸*n.* **1** the process of maintaining or preserving someone or something, or the state of being maintained: *crucial conditions for the maintenance of democratic government.* ■ the process of keeping something in good condition: *car maintenance* | [as *adj.*] *essential maintenance work.* **2** the provision of financial support for a person's living expenses, or the support so provided. ■ alimony or child support. ■ *historical Law* the former offense of aiding a party in a legal action without lawful cause. ▷Middle English (in the sense 'aiding a party in a legal action without lawful cause'): from Old French, from *maintenir* (see **MAINTAIN**).

Main·te·non /ˌmant(ə)ˈnôɴ/, Françoise d'Aubigné, Marquise de (1635–1719), mistress and later second wife of the French king Louis XIV.

main·top /ˈmānˌtäp/ ▸*n.* a platform around the head of the lower section of a sailing ship's mainmast.

main-top·mast ▸*n.* the second section of a sailing ship's mainmast.

main verb ▸*n. Grammar* **1** the verb in a main clause. **2** the head of a verb phrase, for example *eat* in *might have been going to eat it.*

Mainz /mīn(t)s/ a city in western Germany, capital of Rhineland-Palatinate, situated at the confluence of the Rhine and Main rivers; pop. 183,000.

ma·iol·i·ca /mīˈäləkə/ ▸*n.* fine earthenware with colored decoration on an opaque white tin glaze, originating in Italy during the Renaissance. ▷mid 16th cent.: Italian, from *Maiolica* 'Majorca.'

mai·son·ette /ˌmāzəˈnet/ ▸*n.* a set of rooms for living in, typically on two stories of a larger building and with its own entrance from outside. ▷late 18th cent.: from French *maisonnette*, diminutive of *maison* 'house.'

mai tai /ˈmī ˌtī/ ▸*n.* a cocktail based on light rum, curaçao, and fruit juices. ▷Polynesian.

Mai·thi·li /ˈmītilē/ ▸*n.* a Bihari language spoken in northern Bihar, elsewhere in India, and in Nepal. ▷Sanskrit (as an adjective), from *Mithilā*, a place in northern Bihar.

maî·tre d'hô·tel /ˌmātrə dōˈtel; ˌmetrə/ (also **maî·tre d'** /ˌmātrə ˈdē; ˌmātər/) ▸*n.* (*pl.* **maî·tres d'hô·tel** *pronunc.* same; also **maître d's**) the person in a restaurant who oversees the waitpersons and busboys, and who typically handles reservations. ■ the manager of a hotel. ▷mid 16th cent.: French, literally 'master of (the) house.'

Mai·tre·ya /mīˈtrāə/ *Buddhism* the Buddha who will appear in the future. ▷Sanskrit, from *mitra* 'friend or friendship.'

maize /māz/ ▸*n.* technical or chiefly British term for **CORN**[1]. ▷mid 16th cent.: from Spanish *maíz*, from Taino *mahiz*.

Maj. ▸*abbr.* Major.

ma·jes·tic /məˈjestik/ ▸*adj.* having or showing impressive beauty or dignity: *watching majestic eagles soar along the Mississippi.* **—ma·jes·ti·cal·ly** /-(ə)lē/ *adv.*

maj·es·ty /ˈmajəstē/ ▸*n.* (*pl.* **-ties**) **1** impressive stateliness, dignity, or beauty: *experience the majesty of the Rockies.* **2** royal power: *the majesty of the royal household.* ■ (**His**, **Your**, etc., **Majesty**) a title given to a sovereign or a sovereign's wife or widow: *Her Majesty the Queen.* ■ (**Her** or **His Majesty's**) *Brit.* used in the title of several state institutions: *Her Majesty's Inspectorate of Schools.* ▷Middle English (in the sense 'greatness of God'): from Old French *majeste*, from Latin *majestas*, from a variant of *majus*, *major-* (see **MAJOR**).

Maj. Gen. ▸*abbr.* Major General.

maj·lis /ˈmajlis; majˈlis/ ▸*n.* the parliament of various North African and Middle Eastern countries, esp. Iran. ▷Arabic, literally 'assembly.'

ma·jol·i·ca /məˈjälikə/ ▸*n.* a kind of earthenware made in imitation of Italian maiolica, esp. in England during the 19th century. ▷variant of **MAIOLICA**.

Ma·jor /ˈmājər/, John (1943–), British statesman; prime minister 1990–97. His premiership saw the negotiations leading to the Maastricht Treaty and progress toward peace in Northern Ireland.

ma·jor /ˈmājər/ ▸*adj.* **1** [*attrib.*] important, serious, or significant: *the use of drugs is a major problem.* ■ greater or more important; main: *he got the major share of the spoils.* ■ (of a surgical operation) serious or life-threatening: *he had to undergo major surgery.* **2** *Music* (of a scale) having an interval of a semitone between the third and fourth degrees and the seventh and eighth degrees. Contrasted with **MINOR**. ■ (of an interval) equivalent to that between the tonic and another note of a major scale, and greater by a semitone than the corresponding minor interval. ■ [*postpositive*] (of a key) based on a major scale, tending to produce a bright or joyful effect: *Prelude in G Major.* ■ (of a triad) having a major third as the bottom interval. **3** of full legal age. **4** *Logic* (of a term) occurring as the predicate in the conclusion of a categorical syllogism. ■ (of a premise) containing the major term in a categorical syllogism. **5** *Brit., dated* (appended to a surname in some schools) indicating the elder of two brothers.
▸*n.* **1** an army officer of high rank, in particular (in the U.S. Army, Air Force, and Marine Corps) an officer ranking above captain and below lieutenant colonel. [Shortening of **SERGEANT MAJOR**, formerly a high rank.] **2** *Music* a major key, interval, or scale. ■ (**Major**) *Bell-ringing* a system of change-ringing using eight bells. **3** a student's principal subject or course of study. ■ [often with *adj.*] a student specializing in a specified subject: *a math major.* **4** a major world organization, company, or competition: *it's not unreasonable to believe someone can win all four majors.* ■ (**the majors**) the major leagues. **5** a person of full legal age. **6** *Logic* a major term or premise. **7** *Bridge* short for **MAJOR SUIT**.
▸*v.* [*intrans.*] (**major in**) specialize in (a particular subject) at a college or university: *I was trying to decide if I should major in drama or English.* ▷Middle English: from Latin, comparative of *magnus* 'great'; perhaps influenced by French *majeur*.

ma·jor ar·ca·na ▸*n.* see **ARCANA**.

ma·jor ax·is ▸*n. Geometry* the longer axis of an ellipse, passing through its foci.

Ma·jor·ca /məˈjôrkə; mäˈyôrkə/ the largest of the Balearic Islands; pop. 614,000; capital, Palma. Spanish name **MALLORCA**. **—Ma·jor·can** *adj.* & *n.*

ma·jor-do·mo /ˌmājər ˈdōmō/ ▸*n.* (*pl.* **-do·mos**) the chief steward of a large household. ▷late 16th cent.: via Spanish and Italian from medieval Latin *major domus* 'highest official of the household.'

ma·jor·ette /ˌmājəˈret/ ▸*n.* short for **DRUM MAJORETTE**.

ma·jor gen·er·al ▸*n.* (*pl.* **ma·jor gen·er·als**) an officer in the U.S. Army, Air Force, and Marine Corps ranking above brigadier general and below lieutenant general. ▷mid 17th cent.: shortening of *sergeant major general*.

ma·jor his·to·com·pat·i·bil·i·ty com·plex (abbr.: **MHC**) ▸*n.* a genetic system that allows large proteins in immune system cells to identify compatible or foreign proteins. It allows the matching of potential organ or bone marrow donors with recipients.

ma·jor·i·tar·i·an /məˌjôriˈte(ə)rēən; -ˌjär-/ ▸*adj.* governed by or believing in decision by a majority.
▸*n.* a person who is governed by or believes in decision by a majority. **—ma·jor·i·tar·i·an·ism** /-ˌnizəm/ *n.*

ma·jor·i·ty /məˈjôrətē; -ˈjär-/ ▸*n.* (*pl.* **-ties**) **1** the greater number: *in* ***the majority of*** *cases all will go smoothly* | [as *adj.*] *it was a majority decision.* ■ the number by which votes for one candidate in an election are more than those for all other candidates combined. ■ *Brit.* the number by which the votes for one party or candidate exceed those of the next in rank. ■ a party or group receiving the greater number of votes. **2** the age when a person is legally considered a full adult, in most contexts either 18 or 21. **3** the rank or office of a major. ▷mid 16th cent. (denoting superiority): from French *majorité*, from medieval Latin *majoritas*, from Latin *major* (see **MAJOR**).
▸**PHRASE** □ **be in the majority** belong to or constitute the larger group or number: *publishing houses where women are in the majority.*

***USAGE* 1** Strictly speaking, **majority** should be used with countable nouns to mean 'the greater number': *the majority of cases.* The use of **majority** with uncountable nouns to mean 'the greatest part' (*I spent the majority of the day reading*), although common in informal contexts, is not considered good standard English.

2 **Majority** means more than half: *fifty-one out of a hundred is a majority.* A **plurality** is the largest number among three or more. Consider the following scenarios: If Anne received 50 votes, Barry received 30, and Carlos received 20, then Anne received a **plurality**, and no candidate won a **majority**. If Anne got 35 votes, Barry 14, and Carlos 51, then Carlos won both the **plurality** and the **majority**.

ma·jor·i·ty lead·er ▸*n.* the head of the majority party in a legislative body, esp. the U.S. Senate or House of Representatives.

ma·jor·i·ty rule ▸*n.* the principle that the greater number should exercise greater power.

ma·jor league ▸*n.* a professional baseball league of the highest level, in the U.S. either the American League or the National League: *my dream of pitching in the major leagues* | [as *adj.*] *future major-league ballplayers.* ■ the highest-level professional league or leagues in another sport. ■ *figurative* the highest attainable level in any endeavor or activity: [as *adj.*] *many of the nation's service companies are major-league corporations.* —**ma·jor-lea·guer** *n.*

ma·jor·ly /ˈmājərlē/ ▸*adv.* [as *submodifier*] *informal* very; extremely: *I'm majorly depressed.*

ma·jor med·i·cal ▸*n.* insurance designed to cover medical expenses due to severe or prolonged illness by paying all or most of the bills above a set amount.

ma·jor piece ▸*n. Chess* a rook or queen.

ma·jor plan·et ▸*n.* any of the nine planets of the solar system, as distinct from an asteroid or smaller body.

ma·jor proph·et ▸*n.* any of the prophets after whom the longer prophetic books of the Bible are named: Isaiah, Jeremiah, Ezekiel, or Daniel.

ma·jor suit ▸*n. Bridge* spades or hearts. ▷early 20th cent.: so named because of their higher scoring value.

ma·jor tran·quil·iz·er ▸*n.* a tranquilizer of the kind used to treat psychotic states.

ma·jus·cule /ˈmajəsˌkyo͞ol/ ▸*n.* large lettering, either capital or uncial, in which all the letters are usually the same height. ■ a large letter. ▷early 18th cent.: from French, from Latin *majuscula (littera)* 'somewhat greater (letter).' —**ma·jus·cu·lar** /məˈjəskyələr/ *adj.*

Ma·kar·i·os III /məˈkarēəs; -ˌōs; mäˈkärēˌôs/ (1913–77), Greek Cypriot archbishop and statesman; first president of the republic of Cyprus 1960–77; born *Mikhail Christodolou Mouskos.* He reorganized the movement for enosis (union of Cyprus with Greece) and was exiled 1956–59 by the British for allegedly supporting terrorism.

Ma·kas·sar·ese /məˌkasəˈrēz; -ˈrēs/ (also **Ma·kas·sar·ese**) ▸*n.* (*pl.* same) **1** a native or inhabitant of Makassar (now Ujung Pandang) in Indonesia. **2** the Indonesian language of this people.
▸*adj.* of or relating to this people or their language.

Ma·kas·sar /məˈkasər/ (also **Ma·cas·sar** or **Ma·kas·ar**) former name (until 1973) for **UJUNG PANDANG**.

Ma·kas·sar Strait /məˈkasər/ a stretch of water that separates the islands of Borneo and Sulawesi and links the Celebes Sea in the north with the Java Sea in the south.

make /māk/ ▸*v.* (*past* **made** /mād/) [*trans.*] **1** form (something) by putting parts together or combining substances; construct; create: *my grandmother made a dress for me* | *the body is* **made from** *four pieces of maple* | *baseball bats are* **made of** *ash.* ■ (**make something into**) alter something so that it forms or constitutes (something else): *buffalo's milk can be made into cheese.* ■ compose, prepare, or draw up (something written or abstract): *she made her will.* ■ prepare (a dish, drink, or meal) for consumption: *she was making lunch for Lucy and Francis* | [with *two objs.*] *I'll make us both a cup of tea.* ■ arrange bedclothes tidily on (a bed) ready for use. ■ arrange and light materials for (a fire). ■ *Electronics* complete or close (a circuit). **2** cause (something) to exist or come about; bring about: *the drips had made a pool on the floor.* ■ [*trans.* or *infinitive*] cause to become or seem: *decorative features make brickwork more interesting* | *the best way to disarm your critics is to make them laugh.* ■ carry out, perform, or produce (a specified action, movement, or sound): *Unger made a speech of forty minutes* | *anyone can make a mistake.* ■ communicate or express (an idea, request, or requirement): *I tend to* **make** *heavy* **demands on** *people* | [with *two objs.*] *make him an offer he can't refuse.* ■ undertake or agree to (an aim or purpose): *we made a deal.* ■ *chiefly archaic* enter into a contract of (marriage): *a marriage made in heaven.* ■ [*trans.*] appoint or designate (someone) to a position: *he was made a colonel in the Mexican army.* ■ [*trans.*] represent or cause to appear in a specified way: *the sale price and extended warranty make it an excellent value.* ■ cause or ensure the success or advancement of: *the work which really made Wordsworth's reputation.* **3** [*trans.*] compel (someone) to do something: *she bought me a brandy and made me drink it.* **4** constitute; amount to: *they made an unusual duo.* ■ serve as or become through development or adaptation: *this fern makes a good houseplant.* ■ consider to be; estimate as: *How many are there? I* **make it** *sixteen.* ■ agree or decide on (a specified arrangement), typically one concerning a time or place: *let's* **make it** *7:30.* **5** gain or earn (money or profit): *he'd made a lot of money out of hardware.* **6** arrive at (a place) within a specified time or in time for (a train or other transport): *we've got a lot to do if you're going to make the shuttle* | *they didn't always* **make it** *on time.* ■ (**make it**) succeed in something; become successful: *he waited confidently for his band to make it.* ■ achieve a place in: *these dogs seldom make the news* | *they* **made it to** *the semifinals.* ■ achieve the rank of: *he wasn't going to make captain.* **7** [*intrans.*] go or prepare to go in a particular direction: *he struggled to his feet and* **made toward** *the car.* ■ [with *infinitive*] act as if one is about to perform an action: *she* **made as if to** *leave the room.* **8** *informal* induce (someone) to have sexual intercourse with one: *he had been trying to make Cynthia for two years now* | *his alleged quest to* **make it with** *the world's most attractive women.* **9** (in bridge, whist, and similar games) win (a trick). ■ win a trick with (a card). ■ win the number of tricks that fulfills (a contract). ■ shuffle (a pack of cards) for dealing. **10** [*intrans.*] (of the tide) begin to flow or ebb.
▸*phrasal v.* □ **make after** *archaic* pursue (someone). □ **make away** another way of saying **MAKE OFF**. □ **make away with** another way of saying **MAKE OFF WITH**. ■ kill (someone) furtively and illicitly: *for all we know she could have been made away with.* □ **make for 1** move or head toward (a place): *I made for the life raft and hung on for dear life.* ■ approach (someone) to attack them. **2** tend to result in or be received as (a particular thing): *job descriptions never make for exciting reading.* **3** (**be made for**) be eminently suited for (a particular function): *a man made for action.* ■ form an ideal partnership; be ideally suited: *you two were just* **made for each other**. □ **make something of** give or ascribe a specified amount of attention or importance to: *oddly, he* **makes little of** *America's low investment rates.* ■ understand or derive advantage from: *they stared at the stone but could* **make nothing of** *it.* ■ [with *negative* or in *questions*] conclude to be the meaning or character of: *he wasn't sure what to make of Russell.* □ **make off** leave hurriedly, esp. in order to avoid duty or punishment: *they made off without paying.* □ **make off with** carry (something) away illicitly: *burglars made off with all their wedding presents.* □ **make out** *informal* **1** make progress; fare: *how are you making out, now that the summer's over?* **2** *informal* engage in sexual activity: *Ernie was* **making out with** *Bernice.* □ **make someone/something out 1** manage with some difficulty to see or hear something: *in the dim light it was difficult to make out the illustration.* ■ understand the character or motivation of someone: *I can't make her out—she's so inconsistent.* **2** [with *infinitive* or *clause*] assert; represent: *I'm not as bad as I'm* **made out to be**. ■ try to give a specified impression; pretend: *he made out he was leaving.* **3** draw up or write out a list or document, esp. an official one: *advice about making out a will* | *send a check* **made out to** *Trinity College.* □ **make something over 1** transfer the possession of something to someone: *if he dies childless he is to make over his share of the estate to his brother.* **2** completely transform or remodel something, esp. a person's hairstyle, makeup, or clothes. □ **make up** be reconciled after a quarrel: *let's kiss and make up.* □ **make someone up** apply cosmetics to oneself or another. □ **make something up 1** (also **make up for**) serve or act to compensate for something lost, missed, or deficient: *I'll make up the time tomorrow.* ■ (**make it up to**) compensate someone for negligent or unfair treatment: *I'll try to make it up to you in the future.* **2** (**make up**) (of parts) compose or constitute (a whole): *women make up 56 percent of the student body* | *the team is made up of three women and two men.* ■ complete an amount or group: *he brought along a girl to make up a foursome.* **3** put together or prepare something from parts or ingredients: *make up the mortar to a consistency that can be molded in the hands* ■ get an amount or group together: *he was trying to make up a party to go dancing.* ■ prepare a bed for use with fresh bedclothes. ■ *Printing* arrange type and illustrations into pages or arrange the type and illustrations on a page. **4** concoct or invent a story, lie, or plan: *she enjoyed making up tall tales.* □ **make up to** *informal* attempt to win the favor of (someone) by being pleasant: *you can't go on about morals when you're making up to Adam like that.* □ **make with** *informal* proceed to use or supply: *make with the feet, honey—we're late.*
▸*n.* **1** the manufacturer or trade name of a particular product: *the make, model, and year of his car.* ■ the structure or composition of something. **2** the making of electrical contact. ■ the position in which this is made. ▷Old English *macian*, from a base meaning 'fitting'; related to **MATCH**[1]. —**mak·a·ble** /-əbəl/ (also **make·a·ble**) *adj.*
▸*PHRASES* □ **be made of money** [often with *negative*] *informal* be very rich. □ **have (got) it made** *informal* be in a position where success is certain: *because your dad's a manager, he's got it made.* □ **make a day** (or **night**) **of it** devote a whole day (or night) to an activity, esp. an enjoyable one. □ **make someone's day** make an otherwise ordinary or dull day pleasingly memorable for someone. □ **make do** manage with the limited or inadequate means available: *Dad would have to* **make do with** *an old car.* □ **make like** *informal* pretend to be; imitate: *tell the whole group to make like a bird by putting their arms out.* □ **make or break** be the factor that decides whether (something) will succeed or fail. □ **make sail** *Sailing* spread a sail or sails. ■ start a voyage. □ **make time 1** find an occasion when time is available to do something: *the nurse should make time to talk to the patient.* **2** *informal* make sexual advances to someone: *I couldn't* **make time with** *Marilyn because she was already a senior.* □ **make up one's mind** make a decision; decide: *he made up his mind to attend the meeting.* □ **make way 1** allow room for someone or something else: *the land is due to be bulldozed to* **make way for** *a parking garage.* **2** *chiefly Nautical* make progress; travel. □ **on the make** *informal* intent on gain, typically in an unscrupulous way. ■ looking for a sexual partner. □ **put the make on** *informal* make sexual advances to (someone).

make-and-break ▸*adj.* denoting a switch or other device that alternately makes and breaks electrical contact.
▸*n.* a switch or other device in which electrical contact is automatically made and broken.

make-be·lieve ▸*n.* the action of pretending or imagining, typically that things are better than they really are: *she's living in a world of make-believe.*
▸*adj.* imitating something real; pretend: *he was firing a make-believe gun at the spy planes.*
▸*v.* pretend; imagine: [with *clause*] *Brenda rode along, make-believing she was a knight riding to the rescue.*

make-do ▸*adj.* [*attrib.*] makeshift, ad hoc, or temporary: *his make-do clothes and borrowed tie.*

make·o·ver /ˈmākˌōvər/ ▸*n.* a complete transformation or remodeling of something, esp. a person's hairstyle, makeup, or clothes.

mak·er /ˈmākər/ ▸*n.* **1** [usu. in *combination*] a person or thing that makes or produces something: *a cabinetmaker.* **2** (**our, the,** etc., **Maker**) God; the Creator.
▸*PHRASE* □ **meet one's Maker** *chiefly humorous* die.

make·read·y /ˈmākˌredē/ ▸*n.* (in letterpress printing) final adjustment of a form for printing, with overlays and underlays to achieve the correct pressure over the whole printing area.

make·shift /ˈmākˌshift/ ▸*adj.* serving as a temporary substitute; sufficient for the time being: *arranging a row of chairs to form a makeshift bed.*
▸*n.* a temporary substitute or device.

make·up /ˈmākˌəp/ (also **make-up**) ▸*n.* **1** cosmetics such as lipstick or powder applied to the face, used to enhance or alter the appearance. **2** the composition or constitution of something: *studying the makeup of ocean sediments.* ■ the combination of qualities that form a person's temperament: *a nastiness that had long been in his makeup.* **3** *Printing* the arrangement of type, illustrations, etc., on a printed page: *page makeup.* **4** a supplementary test or assignment given to a student who missed or failed the original one: [as *adj.*] *Tony has a makeup exam.*

make·weight /ˈmākˌwāt/ ▸*n.* something put on a scale to make up the required weight. ■ an extra person or thing needed to complete something; a filler: *use it for casserole toppings or makeweight in meatloaf.* ■ an unimportant point added to make an argument seem stronger: *this suggestion was thrown in as a makeweight.*

make-work ▸*adj.* denoting an activity that serves mainly to keep someone busy and is of little value in itself: *a make-work scheme for lawyers.*

▸*n.* work or activity of this kind.

Ma·khach·ka·la /mə,käCHkə'lä/ a port in southwestern Russia, on the Caspian Sea, capital of the autonomous republic of Dagestan; pop. 327,000. Former name (until 1922) **PORT PETROVSK**.

Makh·pi·ya-lu·ta /'mäKH'pēä 'lo͞otä/ see **RED CLOUD**.

mak·ing /'mākiNG/ ▸*n.* **1** the process of making or producing something: *the making of videos* | [in *combination*] *glassmaking.* **2** (**makings**) *informal* money made; earnings or profit. **3** (**makings**) essential qualities or ingredients needed for something: *a film with all the makings of a cinematic success.* ■ (**makings**) *informal* or *dated* paper and tobacco for rolling a cigarette.

▸*PHRASES* □ **be the making of someone** ensure someone's success or favorable development: *this place has been the making of me in many ways.* □ **in the making** in the process of developing or being made: *a campaign that's been two years in the making.* □ **of one's (own) making** (of a difficulty) caused by oneself.

ma·ki /'mäkē/ (also **ma·ki zu·shi** /'zo͞oSHē/) ▸*n.* a Japanese dish consisting of sushi and raw vegetables wrapped in seaweed. ▷1970s: Japanese, from *maki-* (combining form of *maku* 'roll up') + *-zushi*, *sushi.*

Mak·kah /'mak(k)ə; -kä/ Arabic name for **MECCA**.

ma·ko /'mākō; 'mäkō/ (also **ma·ko shark**) ▸*n.* (*pl.* **-kos**) a large fast-moving oceanic shark with a deep blue back and white underparts. • Genus *Isurus*, family Lamnidae: two species. ▷mid 19th cent.: from Maori.

Ma·kon·de /mə'kändā/ ▸*n.* (*pl.* same or **-des**) **1** a member of a people inhabiting southern Tanzania and northeastern Mozambique. **2** the Bantu language of this people.

▸*adj.* of or relating to this people or their language. ▷the name in Makonde.

Mak·su·tov tel·e·scope /'maksə,tôv; mäk'so͞ot,ôv/ ▸*n.* a type of catadioptric telescope having a deeply curved meniscus lens and a spheroidal primary mirror. A secondary mirror on the back of the lens brings the light to a focus just behind a hole in the primary mirror. ▷mid 20th cent.: named after Dmitri D. *Maksutov* (1896–1964), Soviet astronomer.

Ma·ku·a /'mako͞oə/ ▸*n.* (*pl.* same or **-ku·as**) **1** a member of a people inhabiting the border regions of Mozambique, Malawi, and Tanzania. **2** the Bantu language of this people. ▷a local name.

ma·ku·ta /mə'ko͞otə/ ▸ plural form of **LIKUTA**.

Mal. ▸*abbr. Bible* Malachi.

mal- ▸*comb. form* **1** in an unpleasant degree: *malodorous.* **2** in a faulty manner: *malfunction.* ■ in an improper manner: *malpractice.* ■ in an inadequate manner: *malnourishment.* **3** not: *maladroit.* ▷from French *mal*, from Latin *male* 'badly.'

Mal·a·bar Coast /'malə,bär/ the southern part of the western coast of India, including the coastal region of Karnataka and most of the state of Kerala. ▷*Malabar* from *Malabars*, the name of an ancient Dravidian people.

Ma·la·bo /mə'läbō/ the capital of Equatorial Guinea, on the island of Bioko; pop. 10,000.

mal·ab·sorp·tion /,maləb'sôrpSHən; -'zôrp-/ ▸*n.* imperfect absorption of food material by the small intestine.

Ma·lac·ca variant spelling of **MELAKA**.

Ma·lac·ca, Strait of /mə'läkə; -'lakə/ the channel between the Malay Peninsula and the Indonesian island of Sumatra, an important sea passage linking the Indian Ocean to the South China Sea. The ports of Melaka and Singapore lie on this strait.

ma·lac·ca /mə'lakə/ ▸*n.* brown cane that is widely used for walking sticks and umbrella handles. • The cane is obtained from the stem of a Malaysian climbing palm (*Calamus scipionum*, family Palmae). ■ a walking stick of malacca cane. ▷mid 19th cent.: from the place name **MALACCA**.

Mal·a·chi /'malə,kī/ a book of the Bible belonging to a period before Ezra and Nehemiah. ▷from Hebrew *mal'āḵī*, literally 'my messenger'; *Malachi* is probably not a personal name, though often taken as such.

mal·a·chite /'malə,kīt/ ▸*n.* a bright green mineral consisting of copper hydroxyl carbonate. It typically occurs in masses and fibrous aggregates with azurite and is capable of taking a high polish. ▷late Middle English: from Old French *melochite*, via Latin from Greek *molokhitis*, from *molokhē*, variant of *malakhē* 'mallow.'

malaco- ▸*comb. form* soft: *malacostracan.* ▷from Greek *malakos* 'soft.'

mal·a·col·o·gy /,malə'käləjē/ ▸*n.* the branch of zoology that deals with mollusks. Compare with **CONCHOLOGY**. —**mal·a·co·log·i·cal** /-kə'läjikəl/ *adj.* —**mal·a·col·o·gist** /-jist/ *n.*

Mal·a·cos·tra·ca /,malə'kästrəkə/ *Zoology* a large class of crustaceans that includes crabs, shrimps, lobsters, isopods, and amphipods. They have compound eyes, which are typically on stalks. ▷modern Latin (plural), from **MALACO-** 'soft' + Greek *ostrakon* 'shell.' —**mal·a·cos·tra·can** /-kən/ *adj.* & *n.*

mal·a·dap·tive /,malə'daptiv/ ▸*adj. technical* not providing adequate or appropriate adjustment to the environment or situation. —**mal·ad·ap·ta·tion** /-,adəp'tāSHən; -,ad,ap-/ *n.* —**mal·a·dap·ted** /-'daptəd/ *adj.*

mal·ad·just·ed /,malə'jəstid/ ▸*adj.* failing or unable to cope with the demands of a normal social environment: *maladjusted behavior.* —**mal·ad·just·ment** /-'jəstmənt/ *n.*

mal·ad·min·is·ter /,maləd'ministər/ ▸*v.* [*trans.*] *formal* manage or administer inefficiently, badly, or dishonestly. —**mal·ad·min·is·tra·tion** /-,minə'strāSHən/ *n.*

mal·a·droit /,malə'droit/ ▸*adj.* ineffective or bungling; clumsy. ▷late 17th cent.: French. —**mal·a·droit·ly** *adv.* —**mal·a·droit·ness** *n.*

mal·a·dy /'malədē/ ▸*n.* (*pl.* **-dies**) a disease or ailment: *an incurable malady* | *figurative the nation's maladies.* ▷Middle English: from Old French *maladie*, from *malade* 'sick,' based on Latin *male* 'ill' + *habitus* 'having (as a condition).'

ma·la fi·de /,malə 'fīdē; fīdə/ ▸*adj.* & *adv. chiefly Law* in bad faith; with intent to deceive: [as *adj.*] *a mala fide abuse of position.* ▷Latin, ablative of **MALA FIDES**.

ma·la fi·des /,malə 'fīdēz; 'fē,dāz/ ▸*n. chiefly Law* bad faith; intent to deceive. ▷Latin.

Mal·a·ga[1] /'maləgə; 'mälə,gä/ a seaport on the Andalusian coast of southern Spain; pop. 525,000. Spanish name **MÁLAGA** .

Mal·a·ga[2] ▸*n.* a sweet fortified wine from Malaga.

Mal·a·gas·y /,malə'gasē/ ▸*n.* (*pl.* same or **-gas·ies**) **1** a native or national of Madagascar. **2** the Austronesian language of Madagascar.

▸*adj.* of or relating to Madagascar or its people or language. ▷variant of **MADAGASCAR**; earlier forms included *Malegass*, *Madegass*, because of dialect division between the sounds *-l-* and *-d-*.

Mal·a·gas·y Re·pub·lic former name (1960–75) for **MADAGASCAR**.

ma·la·gue·ña /,mälə'g(w)ānyə; ,mal-/ ▸*n.* a Spanish dance similar to the fandango. ▷mid 19th cent.: Spanish.

ma·la·guet·ta /,malə'getə/ (also **malaguetta pepper**) ▸*n.* another term for **GRAINS OF PARADISE**. ▷mid 16th cent.: probably from French *malaguette*, perhaps based on a diminutive of Italian *melica* 'millet.'

ma·laise /mə'lāz; -'lez/ ▸*n.* a general feeling of discomfort, illness, or uneasiness whose exact cause is difficult to identify: *a society afflicted by a deep cultural malaise* | *a general air of malaise.* ▷mid 18th cent.: from French, from Old French *mal* 'bad' (from Latin *malus*) + *aise* 'ease.'

Mal·a·mud /'maləməd/, Bernard (1914–86), U.S. novelist and short-story writer. Notable works: *The Fixer* (1967), *Dubin's Lives* (1979), and *Stories of Bernard Malamud* (1983).

mal·a·mute /'malə,myo͞ot/ (also **mal·e·mute**) ▸*n.* see **ALASKAN MALAMUTE**.

ma·lan·ga /mə'laNGgə/ ▸*n.* see **YAUTIA**. ▷early 20th cent.: from American Spanish, probably from Kikongo, plural of *elanga* 'water lily.'

mal·a·pert /,malə'pərt/ *archaic* ▸*adj.* boldly disrespectful to a person of higher standing.

▸*n.* an impudent person. ▷Middle English: from **MAL-** 'improperly' + archaic *apert* 'insolent.'

mal·a·prop /'malə,präp/ (also **mal·a·prop·ism**) ▸*n.* the mistaken use of a word in place of a similar-sounding one, often with unintentionally amusing effect, as in, for example, "dance a *flamingo*" (instead of *flamenco*). ▷mid 19th cent.: from the name of the character Mrs. *Malaprop* in Sheridan's play *The Rivals* (1775) + **-ISM**.

mal·ap·ro·pos /,mal,aprə'pō/ *formal* ▸*adv.* inopportunely; inappropriately.

▸*adj.* inopportune; inappropriate: *these terms applied to him seem to me malapropos.*

▸*n.* (*pl.* same) something inappropriately said or done. ▷mid 17th cent.: from French *mal à propos*, from *mal* 'ill' + *à* 'to' + *propos* 'purpose.'

ma·lar /'mālər/ ▸*adj. Anatomy & Medicine* of or relating to the cheek: *a slight malar flush.*

▸*n.* (also **malar bone**) another term for **ZYGOMATIC BONE**. ▷late 18th cent.: from modern Latin *malaris*, from Latin *mala* 'jaw.'

Mä·lar·en /'mā,lär,ən/ a lake in southeastern Sweden, extending inland from the Baltic Sea. The city of Stockholm is situated at its outlet.

ma·lar·i·a /mə'le(ə)rēə/ ▸*n.* an intermittent and remittent fever caused by a protozoan parasite that invades the red blood cells. The parasite is transmitted by mosquitoes in many tropical and subtropical regions. • The parasite belongs to the genus *Plasmodium* (phylum Sporozoa) and is transmitted by female mosquitoes of the genus *Anopheles.* ▷mid 18th cent.: from Italian, from *mal'aria*, contracted form of *mala aria* 'bad air.' The term originally denoted the unwholesome atmosphere caused by the exhalations of marshes, to which the disease was formerly attributed. —**ma·lar·i·al** /-ēəl/ *adj.* —**ma·lar·i·an** /-ēən/ *adj.* —**ma·lar·i·ous** /-ēəs/ *adj.*

ma·lar·key /mə'lärkē/ ▸*n. informal* meaningless talk; nonsense: *don't give me that malarkey.* ▷1920s: of unknown origin.

mal·a·thi·on /,malə'THī,än/ ▸*n.* a synthetic organophosphorus compound that is used as an insecticide and is relatively harmless to plants and other animals. ▷1950s: from *(diethyl) mal(eate)* (see **MALEIC ACID**) + **THIO-** + **-ON**.

Ma·la·wi /mə'läwē/ a landlocked country in southern central Africa, in the Great Rift Valley, on the western shore of Lake Nyasa; pop. 11,906,000; capital, Lilongwe; official languages, English and Nyanja. —**Ma·la·wi·an** /-wēən/ *adj.* & *n.*

Malawi was a British protectorate called Nyasaland from 1891 and was a part of the Federation of Rhodesia and Nyasaland from 1891 until 1963. It became an independent Commonwealth state under Hastings Banda in 1964 and a republic in 1966.

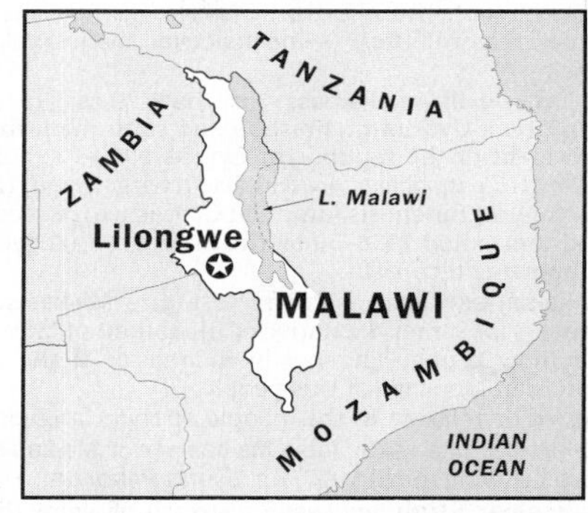

Ma·la·wi, Lake another name for Lake Nyasa (see **NYASA, LAKE**).

Ma·lay /mə'lā; 'mā,lā/ ▸*n.* **1** a member of a people inhabiting Malaysia and Indonesia. ■ a person of Malay descent. **2** the Austronesian language of the Malays, closely related to Indonesian, that is the official language of Malaysia.

▸*adj.* of or relating to this people or language. ▷from Malay *Malayu* (now *Melayu*).

Ma·la·ya /mə'lāə/ a former country in Southeast Asia that consists of the southern part of the Malay Peninsula and some adjacent islands (originally including Singapore) and that now forms the western part of the federation of Malaysia and is known as West Malaysia. The area was colonized by the Dutch, Portuguese, and the British, who eventually dominated; the several Malay states federated under British control in 1896.The country became independent in 1957, and the federation expanded and became Malaysia in 1963.

Mal·a·ya·lam /,malē'äləm/ ▸*n.* the Dravidian language of the Indian state of Kerala, closely related to Tamil.

▸*adj.* of or relating to this language or its speakers. ▷early 19th cent.: from Malayalam, from *mala* (Tamil *malai*) 'mountain' + *āḷ* 'man.'

Ma·lay·an /mə'lāən/ ▸*n.* another term for **MALAY**.

▸*adj.* of or relating to Malays, the Malay language, or Malaya (now part of Malaysia).

Ma·lay·an sun bear ▸*n.* see **SUN BEAR**.

M

Ma·lay Ar·chi·pel·a·go a very large group of islands, including Sumatra, Java, Borneo, the Philippines, and New Guinea, that lie between Southeast Asia and Australia. They constitute the bulk of the area formerly known as the East Indies.

Malayo- ▸*comb. form* Malay; Malay and . . . : *Malayo-Polynesian.*

Ma·lay·o-Pol·y·ne·sian /mə'lāō ˌpälə'nēzʜən/ ▸*n.* another term for **AUSTRONESIAN.**

Ma·lay Pen·in·su·la a peninsula in Southeast Asia that separates the Indian Ocean from the South China Sea. It extends approximately 700 miles (1,100 km) south from the Isthmus of Kra and comprises the southern part of Thailand and all of Malaya (West Malaysia).

Ma·lay·sia /mə'lāzʜə/ a country in Southeast Asia; pop. 23,522,000; capital, Kuala Lumpur; languages, Malay (official), English, Tamil, Chinese dialects. **—Ma·lay·sian** *adj.* & *n.*

Malaysia is a federation that consists of **East Malaysia** (the northern part of Borneo, including Sabah and Sarawak) and **West Malaysia** (the southern part of the Malay Peninsula, formerly Malaya). The two parts of Malaysia are separated from each other by 400 miles (650 km) of the South China Sea. Malaysia was federated as an independent Commonwealth of Nations state in 1963; Singapore, briefly a part of the federation, withdrew in 1965.

Mal·colm /'malkəm/ the name of four kings of Scotland: ▪ **Malcolm I** (died 954), reigned 943–954. ▪ **Malcolm II** (*c.*954–1034), reigned 1005–34. ▪ **Malcolm III** (*c.*1031–93), son of Duncan I; reigned 1058–93; known as **Malcolm Canmore** (from Gaelic *Ceann-mor* great head). He came to the throne after killing Macbeth in battle (1057) and was responsible for helping to form Scotland into an organized kingdom. ▪ **Malcolm IV** (1141–65), grandson of David I; reigned 1153–65; known as **Malcolm the Maiden.** His reign witnessed a progressive loss of power to Henry II of England.

Mal·colm X /'malkəm 'eks/ (1925–65), U.S. political activist; born *Malcolm Little.* He joined the Nation of Islam in 1946 and became a vigorous campaigner for black rights, initially advocating the use of violence. In 1964, he converted to orthodox Islam and moderated his views on black separatism; he was assassinated the following year.

Malcolm X

mal·con·tent /ˌmalkən'tent; 'malkənˌtent/ ▸*n.* a person who is dissatisfied and rebellious.
▸*adj.* dissatisfied and complaining or making trouble. ▷late 16th cent.: from French, from *mal* 'badly, ill' + *content* 'pleased.' **—mal·con·tent·ed** *adj.*

mal de mer /ˌmal də 'me(ə)r/ ▸*n.* seasickness. ▷French.

Mal·den[1] /'môldən/ a city in eastern Massachusetts, north of Boston; pop. 53,884.

Mal·den[2], Karl (1914–), U.S. actor; born Mladen Sekulovich. He appeared in the movies *A Streetcar Named Desire* (Academy Award, 1951) and *On the Waterfront* (1955) before starring in the television series "The Streets of San Francisco" (1972–77).

mal·de·vel·op·ment /ˌmaldi'veləpmənt/ ▸*n. chiefly Medicine & Biology* faulty or imperfect development.

mal·dis·tri·bu·tion /ˌmalˌdistrə'byo͞osʜən/ ▸*n.* uneven distribution of something, esp. when disadvantageous or unfair: *the maldistribution of wealth.* **—mal·dis·trib·ut·ed** /ˌmaldə'stribyətəd/ *adj.*

Mal·dives /'môlˌdēvz; -ˌdīvz; 'mäl-/ (also **Mal·dive Islands**) a country that consists of a chain of coral islands in the Indian Ocean, southwest of Sri Lanka; pop. 339,000; capital, Male; official language, Maldivian. **—Mal·div·i·an** /môl'divēən; mäl-/ *adj.* & *n.*

The islands were probably first settled from southern India and Sri Lanka, but later came under Arab influence. A British protectorate from 1887, the Maldives became independent within the Commonwealth of Nations under the rule of a sultan in 1965 and then as a republic in 1968.

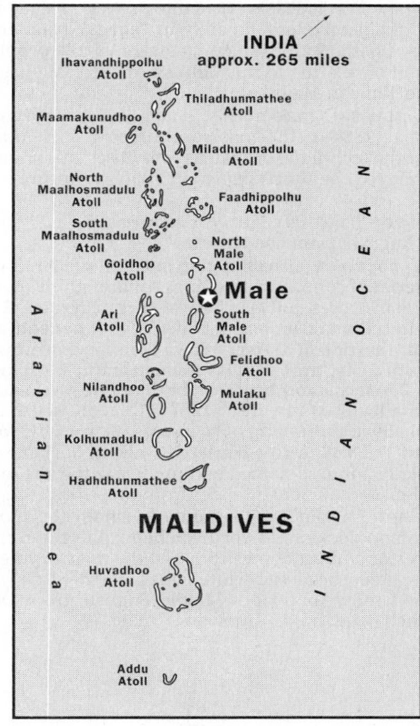

mal du siè·cle /ˌmal də sē'ek(lə)/ ▸*n.* world-weariness. ▷French, literally 'sickness of the century.'

Ma·le /'mälā/ the capital of the Maldives; pop. 55,000.

male /māl/ ▸*adj.* of or denoting the sex that produces small, typically motile gametes, esp. spermatozoa, with which a female may be fertilized or inseminated to produce offspring: *male children.* ▪ relating to or characteristic of men or male animals; masculine: *male unemployment | a deep male voice.* ▪ (of a plant or flower) bearing stamens but lacking functional pistils. ▪ (of parts of machinery, fittings, etc.) designed to enter, fill, or fit inside a corresponding female part.
▸*n.* a male person, plant, or animal: *the audience consisted of adult males | the male of the species.* ▷late Middle English: from Old French *masle,* from Latin *masculus,* from *mas* 'a male.' **—male·ness** *n.*

THE RIGHT WORD **male, manful, manly, mannish, masculine, virile**

We speak of a **male** ancestor, a **masculine** scent, and a **manly** activity, but only of women as **mannish.**

While all of these adjectives apply to what is characteristic of the male of the species (particularly the human species), *male* can refer to plants or animals as well as human beings and is used to describe whatever is biologically distinguished from the female sex (*an all-male choir; a male cat; a male holly bush*).

Masculine refers to the qualities, characteristics, and behaviors associated with or thought to be appropriate to men and boys (*a masculine handshake*).

Manly emphasizes the desirable qualities that a culture associates with a mature man, such as courage and independence (*the manly virtues; the manly sport of football*).

Manful differs from *manly* primarily in its emphasis on sturdiness and resoluteness (*a manful effort to hold back tears*).

Virile is a stronger word than *masculine* or *manly* and is applied only to mature men; it suggests the vigor, muscularity, and forcefulness—and especially the sexual potency—associated with mature manhood (*a virile man who looked like Charlton Heston in his youth*).

mal·e·dic·tion /ˌmalə'diksʜən/ ▸*n.* a magical word or phrase uttered with the intention of bringing about evil or destruction; a curse. ▷late Middle English: from Latin *maledictio(n-),* from *maledicere* 'speak evil of.' **—mal·e·dic·tive** /-'diktiv/ *adj.* **—mal·e·dic·to·ry** /-'diktərē/ *adj.*

mal·e·fac·tor /'maləˌfaktər/ ▸*n. formal* a person who commits a crime or some other wrong. ▷late Middle English: from Latin, from *malefact-* 'done wrong,' from the verb *malefacere,* from *male* 'ill' + *facere* 'do.' **—mal·e·fac·tion** /ˌmalə'faksʜən/ *n.*

male fern ▸*n.* a fern with brown scales on the stalks of the fronds, found in wooded areas of the northeastern U.S., but much more common in Eurasia. • Genus *Dryopteris,* family Dryopteridaceae: several species, in particular *D. filix-mas.*

ma·lef·ic /mə'lefik/ ▸*adj. poetic/literary* causing or capable of causing harm or destruction, esp. by supernatural means. ▪ *Astrology* relating to the planets Saturn and Mars, traditionally considered to have an unfavorable influence. ▷mid 17th cent.: from Latin *maleficus,* from *male* 'ill' + *-ficus* 'doing.' **—ma·lef·i·cence** /-'lefəsəns/ *n.* **—ma·lef·i·cent** /-'lefəsənt/ *adj.*

Ma·le·gaon /ˌmälə'goun/ a city in western India, in Maharashtra, northeast of Bombay; pop. 342,000.

ma·le·ic ac·id /mə'lēik; -'lā- / ▸*n. Chemistry* a crystalline acid made by distilling malic acid and used in making synthetic resins. • Alternative name: ***cis*-butenedioic acid**; chem. formula: HOOCCH=CHCOOH. ▷mid 19th cent.: *maleic* from French *maléique,* alteration of *malique* (see **MALIC ACID**). **—mal·e·ate** /mə'lēˌāt; -ət/ *n.*

male men·o·pause ▸*n.* a stage in a middle-aged man's life supposedly corresponding to the menopause of a woman, associated with the loss of sexual potency and a crisis of confidence and identity (not in technical use).

mal·e·mute /'maləˌmyo͞ot/ ▸*n.* variant spelling of **MALAMUTE.**

Ma·le·sia /mə'lēzʜə/ *Botany* a phytogeographical region comprising Malaysia, Indonesia, New Guinea, the Philippines, and Brunei. **—Ma·le·sian** *adj.*

Ma·le·vich /məl'yāvicʜ/, Kazimir (Severinovich) (1878–1935), Russian painter and designer. In his abstract works he used only basic geometric shapes and a severely restricted range of color.

ma·lev·o·lent /mə'levələnt/ ▸*adj.* having or showing a wish to do evil to others: *the glint of dark, malevolent eyes | some malevolent force of nature.* ▷early 16th cent.: from Latin *malevolent-* 'wishing evil,' from *male* 'ill' + *volent-* 'wishing' (from the verb *velle*). **—ma·lev·o·lence** *n.* **—ma·lev·o·lent·ly** *adv.*

mal·fat·ti /mäl'fätē/ ▸*plural n.* dumplings or gnocchi made with spinach and ricotta. ▷1980s: Italian, from *malfatto* 'badly made' (because they resemble ravioli without their pasta envelopes).

mal·fea·sance /mal'fēzəns/ ▸*n. Law* wrongdoing, esp. by a public official. ▷late 17th cent.: from Anglo-Norman French *malfaisance,* from *mal-* 'evil' + Old French *faisance* 'activity.' Compare with **MISFEASANCE.** **—mal·fea·sant** /-'fēzənt/ *n.* & *adj.*

mal·for·ma·tion /ˌmalfôr'māsʜən; -fər-/ ▸*n.* a deformity; an abnormally formed part of the body. ▪ the condition of being abnormal in shape or form: *malformation of one or both ears.* **—mal·formed** /mal'fôrmd/ *adj.*

mal·func·tion /mal'fəngksʜən/ ▸*v.* [*intrans.*] (of a piece of equipment or machinery) fail to function normally or satisfactorily: *the unit is clearly malfunctioning.*
▸*n.* a failure to function in a normal or satisfactory manner.

Pronunciation Key ə *ago;* ər *over;* 'ə *or* ˌə *up;* 'ər *or* ˌər *fur;* a *hat;* ā *rate;* ä *car;* cʜ *chew;* e *let;* ē *see;* e(ə)r *air;* i *fit;* ī *by;* i(ə)r *ear;* ɴɢ *sing;* ō *go;* ô *for;* oi *boy;* o͝o *good;* o͞o *goo;* ou *out;* sʜ *she;* tʜ *thin;* t͟ʜ *then;* (h)w *why;* zʜ *vision*

Ma·li /ˈmälē/ a landlocked country in West Africa, south of Algeria, in the Sahel except for desert in the north; pop. 11,900,000; capital, Bamako; languages, French (official) and others mainly of the Mande group. Former name (until 1958) **French Sudan.** —**Ma·li·an** /-ēən/ *adj.* & *n.*

Conquered by the French in the late 19th century, Mali became part of French West Africa. It was a partner with Senegal in the Federation of Mali in 1959 and achieved full independence a year later, when Senegal withdrew.

Mal·i·bu[1] /ˈmaləˌbo͞o/ a resort on the Pacific Ocean coast of southern California, west of Los Angeles. It is home to many movie stars.

Mal·i·bu[2] (also **Mal·i·bu board**) ▸*n.* (*pl.* **-bus**) a lightweight surfboard, typically relatively long with a rounded front end. ▷1960s: named after *Malibu* beach (see **Malibu**[1]).

mal·ic ac·id /ˈmalik/ ▸*n.* *Chemistry* a crystalline acid present in unripe apples and other fruits. • Chem. formula: $HOOCCH_2CH(OH)COOH$. ▷late 18th cent.: *malic* from French *malique*, from Latin *malum* 'apple.' —**mal·ate** /ˈmalˌāt; ˈmāˌlāt/ *n.*

mal·ice /ˈmaləs/ ▸*n.* the intention or desire to do evil; ill will: *I bear no malice toward anybody.* ■ *Law* wrongful intention, esp. as increasing the guilt of certain offenses. ▷Middle English: via Old French from Latin *malitia*, from *malus* 'bad.'

mal·ice a·fore·thought ▸*n.* *Law* the intention to kill or harm, which is held to distinguish unlawful killing from murder.

ma·li·cious /məˈlisHəs/ ▸*adj.* characterized by malice; intending or intended to do harm: *malicious destruction of property.* ▷Middle English (also in the sense 'wicked'): from Old French *malicios*, from Latin *malitiosus*, from *malitia* (see **malice**). —**ma·li·cious·ly** *adv.* —**ma·li·cious·ness** *n.*

ma·li·cious mis·chief ▸*n.* *Law* the willful destruction of another person's property for vicious, wanton, or mischievous purposes.

ma·lign /məˈlīn/ ▸*adj.* evil in nature or effect; malevolent: *she had a strong and malign influence.* ■ *archaic* (of a disease) malignant.
▸*v.* [*trans.*] speak about (someone) in a spitefully critical manner: *don't you dare malign her in my presence.* ▷Middle English: via Old French *maligne* (adjective), *malignier* (verb), based on Latin *malignus* 'tending to evil,' from *malus* 'bad.' —**ma·lign·er** *n.* —**ma·lig·ni·ty** /-ˈlignətē/ *n.* —**ma·lign·ly** *adv.*

THE RIGHT WORD **calumniate, defame, libel, malign, slander, vilify**

Do you want to ruin someone's life? You can **malign** someone, which is to say or write something evil without necessarily lying (*she was maligned for her past association with radical causes*).

To **calumniate** is to make false and malicious statements about someone; the word often implies that you have seriously damaged that person's good name (*after leaving his job, he spent most of his time calumniating and ridiculing his former boss*).

To **defame** is to cause actual injury to someone's good name or reputation (*he defamed her by accusing her of being a spy*).

If you don't mind risking a lawsuit, you can **libel** the person, which is to write or print something that defames him or her (*the tabloid libeled the celebrity and ended up paying the price*).

Slander, which is to defame someone orally, is seldom a basis for court action but can nevertheless cause injury to someone's reputation (*after a loud and very public argument, she accused him of slandering her*).

If all else fails, you can **vilify** the person, which is to engage in abusive name-calling (*even though he was found innocent by the jury, he was vilified by his neighbors*).

ma·lig·nan·cy /məˈlignənsē/ ▸*n.* (*pl.* **-cies**) **1** the state or presence of a malignant tumor; cancer: *after biopsy, evidence of malignancy was found.* ■ a cancerous growth. ■ a form of cancer: *diffuse malignancies such as leukemia.* **2** the quality of being malign or malevolent: *her eyes sparkled with renewed malignancy.*

ma·lig·nant /məˈlignənt/ ▸*adj.* **1** (of a disease) very virulent or infectious. ■ (of a tumor) tending to invade normal tissue or to recur after removal; cancerous. Contrasted with **benign. 2** malevolent: *in the hands of malignant fate.* ▷mid 16th cent. (also in the sense 'likely to rebel against God or authority'): from late Latin *malignant-* 'contriving maliciously,' from the verb *malignare*. The term was used in its early sense to describe those sympathetic to the royalist cause during the English Civil War (1642–49). —**ma·lig·nant·ly** *adv.*

ma·lin·ger /məˈliNGgər/ ▸*v.* [*intrans.*] exaggerate or feign illness in order to escape duty or work. ▷early 19th cent.: back-formation from *malingerer*, apparently from French *malingre*, perhaps formed as *mal-* 'wrongly, improperly' + *haingre* 'weak,' probably of Germanic origin. —**ma·lin·ger·er** *n.*

Ma·lin·ke /məˈliNGkā/ ▸*n.* (*pl.* same or **-kes**) **1** a member of a people living mainly in Senegal, Mali, and Ivory Coast. **2** the Mande language of this people.
▸*adj.* of or relating to the Malinke or their language. ▷the name in Malinke.

Ma·li·now·ski /ˌmaləˈnôfskē; -ˈnäf-; ˌmäl-/, Bronisław Kaspar (1884–1942), Polish anthropologist. He initiated the technique of "participant observation" and developed the functionalist approach to anthropology.

mal·i·son /ˈmaləsən; -zən/ ▸*n.* *archaic* a curse. ▷Middle English: from Old French.

mall /môl/ ▸*n.* **1** (also **shopping mall**) a large building or series of connected buildings containing a variety of retail stores and typically also restaurants. **2** a sheltered walk or promenade. ■ (also **pedestrian mall**) a section of a street, typically in the downtown area of a city, from which vehicular traffic is excluded. **3** *historical* another term for the game **pall-mall.** ■ an alley used for this. ▷mid 17th cent. (sense 3): probably a shortening of **pall-mall.** Sense 2 derives from *The Mall*, a tree-bordered walk in St. James's Park, London, so named because it was the site of a pall-mall alley. Sense 1 dates from the 1960s.

mal·lard /ˈmalərd/ ▸*n.* (*pl.* same or **-lards**) the most common duck of the northern hemisphere and the ancestor of most domestic ducks, the male having a dark green head and white collar. • *Anas platyrhynchos*, family Anatidae. ▷Middle English: from Old French 'wild drake,' from *masle* 'male.'

mallard

Malle /mäl/, Louis (1932–95), French movie director. His movies are seminal examples of the French *nouvelle vague*. Notable movies: *Les Amants* (1959), *Pretty Baby* (1978), and *Au Revoir les enfants* (1987).

mal·le·a·ble /ˈmalyəbəl; ˈmalēə-/ ▸*adj.* (of a metal or other material) able to be hammered or pressed permanently out of shape without breaking or cracking. ■ *figurative* easily influenced; pliable: *Anna was shaken enough to be malleable.* ▷late Middle English (in the sense 'able to be hammered'): via Old French from medieval Latin *malleabilis*, from Latin *malleus* 'a hammer.' —**mal·le·a·bil·i·ty** /ˌmalyəˈbilitē; ˌmalēə-/ *n.* —**mal·le·a·bly** /-blē/ *adv.*

mal·lee /ˈmalē/ ▸*n.* a low-growing bushy Australian eucalyptus that typically has several slender stems. • Genus *Eucalyptus*, family Myrtaceae: several species, in particular *E. dumosa*. ■ scrub that is dominated by mallee bushes, typical of some arid parts of Australia. ▷mid 19th cent.: from Wuywurung (an Aboriginal language).

mal·lee fowl ▸*n.* (*pl.* same) a megapode found in the mallee scrub of southern Australia, with pale patterned plumage. • *Leipoa ocellata*, family Megapodiidae.

mal·le·o·lus /məˈlēələs/ ▸*n.* (*pl.* **-li** /-ˌlī; -ˌlē/) *Anatomy* a bony projection with a shape likened to a hammer head, esp. each of those on either side of the ankle. ▷late 17th cent.: from Latin, diminutive of *malleus* 'hammer.' —**mal·le·o·lar** /məˈlēələr/ *adj.*

mal·let /ˈmalət/ ▸*n.* a hammer with a large wooden head, used esp. for hitting a chisel. ■ a long-handled wooden stick with a head like a hammer, used for hitting a croquet or polo ball. ■ *Music* a wooden or plastic stick with a rounded head, used to play certain percussion instruments such as xylophone and marimba. ▷late Middle English: from Old French *maillet*, from *mail* 'hammer,' from Latin *malleus*.

mallet

mal·le·us /ˈmalēəs/ ▸*n.* (*pl.* **mal·le·i** /ˈmalēˌī; -ēˌē/) *Anatomy* a small bone in the middle ear that transmits vibrations of the eardrum to the incus. ▷mid 17th cent.: from Latin, literally 'hammer.'

mall·ing /ˈmôliNG/ ▸*n.* **1** the development of shopping malls: *the malling of America.* **2** the action or activity of passing time in a shopping mall: *Jessie had time to go malling.*

Mal·lon /ˈmalən/, Mary (c.1870–1938) U.S. cook; born in Ireland; known as **Typhoid Mary**. Immune to typhoid herself, she spread the disease while working in New York City. She was institutionalized for life from 1914 to protect others.

Mal·loph·a·ga /məˈläfəgə/ *Entomology* an order of insects that comprises the biting lice. See also **Phthiraptera.** ▷modern Latin (plural), from Greek *mallos* 'lock of wool' + *-phagos* 'eating.' —**mal·loph·a·gan** /-gən/ *n.* & *adj.*

Mal·lor·ca /mäˈyôrkə/ Spanish name for **Majorca.**

mal·low /ˈmalō/ ▸*n.* a herbaceous plant with hairy stems, pink or purple flowers, and disk-shaped fruit. Several kinds are grown as ornamentals, and some are edible. • Genus *Malva*, family Malvaceae (the **mallow family**): many species. This family also includes the hollyhocks, hibiscus, and abutilon. See also **marsh mallow, rose mallow.** ▷Old English *meal(u)we*, from Latin *malva*; related to Greek *malakhē*; compare with **mauve.**

malm /mä(l)m/ ▸*n.* a soft, crumbly, chalky rock, or the fertile loamy soil produced as it weathers. ■ (also **malm brick**) a fine-quality brick made originally from malm, marl, or a similar chalky clay. ▷Old English *mealm-*, of Germanic origin; related to **meal**[2].

Malmö /ˈmälˌmo͞o; -ˌmœ/ a port and fortified city in southwestern Sweden, situated on the Øresund opposite Copenhagen; pop. 234,000.

malm·sey /ˈmä(l)mzē/ ▸*n.* a fortified Madeira wine of the sweetest type. ■ *historical* a strong, sweet white wine imported from Greece and the eastern Mediterranean islands. ▷late Middle English: from Middle Dutch *malemeseye*, via Old French from *Monemvasia*, the name of a port in southeastern mainland Greece. Compare with **malvoisie.**

mal·nour·ished /malˈnərisHt; -ˈnə-risHt/ ▸*adj.* suffering from malnutrition. —**mal·nourish·ment** /-ˈnərisHmənt/ *n.*

mal·nu·tri·tion /ˌmalno͞oˈtrisHən/ ▸*n.* lack of proper nutrition, caused by not having enough to eat, not eating enough of the right things, or being unable to use the food that one does eat.

mal·oc·clu·sion /ˌmaləˈklo͞ozHən/ ▸*n.* *Dentistry* imperfect positioning of the teeth when the jaws are closed.

mal·o·dor /malˈōdər/ ▸*n.* a very unpleasant smell.

mal·o·dor·ous /malˈōdərəs/ ▸*adj.* smelling very unpleasant.

ma·lo·lac·tic /ˌmaləˈlaktik; ˌmālə-/ ▸*adj.* of or denoting bacterial fermentation that converts malic acid to lactic acid, esp. as a secondary process used to reduce the acidity of some wines.
▸*n.* fermentation of this kind.

Ma·lone[1] /məˈlōn/, Karl (1963–), U.S. basketball player; nickname **The Mailman**. He played for the Utah Jazz 1985–2003 before joining the Los Angeles Lakers in 2004. He was a member of the 1992 and 1996 Olympic basketball teams.

Ma·lone[2], Moses (1955–), U.S. basketball player. In 1976, he joined the Buffalo Braves and then played for the Houston Rockets, the Philadelphia 76ers, the Washington Bullets, the Atlanta Hawks, the

Milwaukee Bucks, and the San Antonio Spurs until his retirement in 1995.

ma·lo·nic ac·id /mə'lōnik; -'län- / ▶*n. Chemistry* a crystalline acid obtained by the oxidation of malic acid. • Alternative name: **propane-1,3-dioic acid;** chem. formula: $HOOCCH_2COOH$. ▷mid 19th cent.: *malonic* from French *malonique*, alteration of *malique* 'malic.' **—mal·o·nate** /'malə,nāt; 'mā-/ *n.*

Mal·o·ry /'malərē/, Sir Thomas (died 1471), English writer. His major work, *Le Morte d'Arthur*, which was printed in 1483, is a prose translation of a collection of legends of King Arthur.

ma·lo·ti /mə'lōtē; -'lōōtē/ ▶ plural form of LOTI.

mal·per·for·mance /,malpər'fôrməns/ ▶*n.* faulty or inadequate performance of a task.

Mal·pi·ghi /mal'pigē; mäl-/, Marcello (*c.*1628–94), Italian microscopist. He discovered the alveoli and capillaries in the lungs and the fibers and red cells of clotted blood, and he demonstrated the pathway of blood from arteries to veins.

Mal·pigh·i·an lay·er /,mal'pigēən; -'pēgē- / ▶*n. Zoology & Anatomy* a layer in the epidermis in which skin cells are continually formed by division.

Mal·pigh·i·an tu·bule ▶*n. Zoology* a tubular excretory organ, numbers of which open into the gut in insects and some other arthropods.

mal·prac·tice /mal'praktəs/ ▶*n.* improper, illegal, or negligent professional activity or treatment, esp. by a medical practitioner, lawyer, or public official: *victims of medical malpractice | investigations into malpractices and abuses of power.*

mal·pres·en·ta·tion /,mal,prezən'tāsHən/ ▶*n. Medicine* abnormal positioning of a fetus at the time of delivery.

Mal·raux /mal'rō; mäl-/, André (1901–76), French novelist, politician, and art critic. Involved in the Chinese Communist uprising of 1927 and the Spanish Civil War, he was later appointed the first minister of cultural affairs 1959–69.

MALS ▶*abbr.* Master of Library Science.

malt /môlt/ ▶*n.* barley or other grain that has been steeped, germinated, and dried, used esp. for brewing or distilling and vinegar-making. ■ *chiefly Brit.* short for MALT WHISKEY. ■ short for MALTED MILK.
▶*v.* [*trans.*] convert (grain) into malt: [as *n.*] (**malting**) *barley is grown for malting.* ■ [*intrans.*] (of a seed) become malt when germination is checked by drought. ▷Old English *m(e)alt*, of Germanic origin; related to MELT. **—malt·i·ness** /-tēnis/ *n.* **—malt·y** *adj.*

Mal·ta /'môltə/ an island country in the central Mediterranean Sea, about 60 miles (100 km) south of Sicily; pop. 398,000; capital, Valletta; official languages, Maltese and English.

Historically of great strategic importance, the island has been held in turn by invaders that have included the Greeks, Arabs, Normans, and Knights Hospitallers. It was annexed by Britain in 1814 and was an important naval base until independence within the Commonwealth of Nations in 1964. Besides the island of Malta, the country includes the islands of Gozo and Comino.

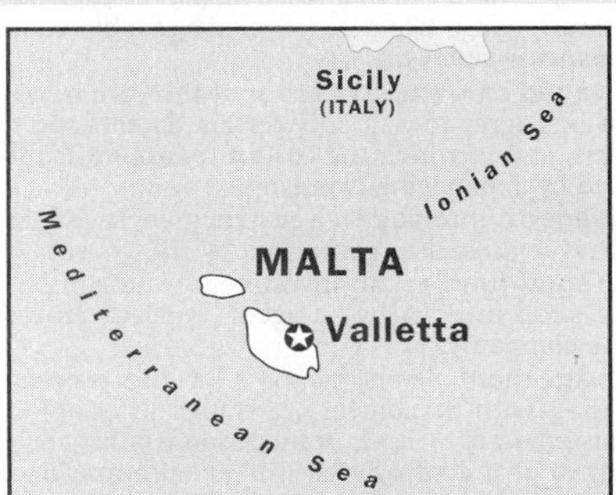

malt·ase /'môl,tās; -,tāz/ ▶*n. Biochemistry* an enzyme, present in saliva and pancreatic juice, that catalyzes the breakdown of maltose and similar sugars to form glucose.

malt·ed /môltid/ ▶*adj.* mixed with malt or a malt extract. ■ [as *n.*] malted milk: *they were sipping malteds at the drive-in.*

malt·ed milk ▶*n.* a drink combining milk, a malt preparation, and ice cream or flavoring. ■ the powdered mixture from which this drink is made.

Mal·tese[1] /môl'tēz/ ▶*n.* (*pl.* same) **1** a native or national of Malta or a person of Maltese descent. **2** the national language of Malta, a Semitic language derived from Arabic but much influenced by Italian, Spanish, and Norman French.
▶*adj.* of or relating to Malta, its people, or their language.

Mal·tese[2] (also **Maltese terrier**) ▶*n.* a dog of a very small long-haired breed, typically with white hair.

Maltese[2]

Mal·tese cross ▶*n.* **1** a cross with arms of equal length that broaden from the center and have their ends indented in a shallow V-shape. **2** a plant of the pink family (*Lychnis chalcedonica*), with small scarlet petals arranged in the shape of a Maltese cross. ▷so named because the cross was formerly worn by the Knights of Malta, a religious order.

malt·house /'môlt,hous/ ▶*n.* a building in which malt is prepared and stored.

Mal·thus /'malTHəs; 'môl-/, Thomas Robert (1766–1834), English economist and clergyman. In *Essay on Population* (1798) he argued that without the practice of "moral restraint" the population tends to increase at a greater rate than its means of subsistence, resulting in the population checks of war, famine, and epidemic. **—Mal·thu·sian** /mal'TH(y)ōōzHən; môl-/ *adj. & n.* **—Mal·thu·sian·ism** /mal'TH(y)ōōzHə,nizəm; môl-/ *n.*

malt liq·uor ▶*n.* alcoholic liquor made from malt by fermentation rather than distillation; beer with a relatively high alcohol content.

mal·to·dex·trin /,môltō'dekstrən/ ▶*n.* dextrin containing maltose, used as a food additive.

malt·ose /'môl,tōs; -,tōz/ ▶*n. Chemistry* a sugar produced by the breakdown of starch, e.g., by enzymes found in malt and saliva. It is a disaccharide consisting of two linked glucose units. ▷mid 19th cent.: from MALT + -OSE[2].

mal·treat /mal'trēt/ ▶*v.* [*trans.*] (often **be maltreated**) treat (a person or animal) cruelly or with violence. ▷early 18th cent.: from French *maltraiter*. **—mal·treat·er** *n.* **—mal·treat·ment** *n.*

malt whis·key ▶*n.* whiskey made only from malted barley and not blended with grain whiskey.

Ma·lu·ku Indonesian name for MOLUCCA ISLANDS.

mal·va·ceous /mal'vāsHəs/ ▶*adj. Botany* of, relating to, or denoting plants of the mallow family (Malvaceae). ▷late 17th cent.: from modern Latin *Malvaceae* (plural), based on Latin *malva* 'mallow,' + -OUS.

Mal·va·si·a /mal'vāzHə/ ▶*n.* a variety of grape used to make white and red wines, esp. in Italy. ▷Italian form of the place name *Monemvasia*, in the Peloponnese (see MALMSEY).

mal·ver·sa·tion /,malvər'sāsHən/ ▶*n. formal* corrupt behavior in a position of trust, esp. in public office: *ineptitude and malversation were major factors in the trouncing of the group's candidates.* ▷mid 16th cent.: from French, from *malverser*, from Latin *male* 'badly' + *versari* 'behave.'

Mal·vi·nas, Islas /môl'vēnəs/ the name by which the Falkland Islands are known in Argentina.

mal·voi·sie /,mal,vwä'zē; -,voi-/ ▶*n.* (in French-speaking regions) any of several grape varieties used to make full-flavored white wines. ▷from Old French *malvesie*, from the French form of *Monemvasia* (see MALMSEY).

mal·ware /'mal,we(ə)r/ ▶*n. Computing* software that is intended to damage or disable computers and computer systems: *protect your computer against viruses and other malware.* ▷blend of *malicious* and *software.*

mam /mäm/ ▶*n. informal* **1** *chiefly Brit.* one's mother: [as *name*] *it was better when Mam was alive.* [late 16th cent.: perhaps imitative of a child's first syllables (see MAMA).] **2** a term of respectful or polite address used for any woman: *"You all ride them horses down here?" "Yes, mam."* [variant of MA'AM.]

ma·ma /'mämə/ (also **mam·ma**) ▶*n.* **1** one's mother (esp. as a child's term): [as *name*] *come and meet Mama.* **2** *informal* a mature woman: *the ultimate tough blues mama.* ▷mid 16th cent.: imitative of a child's first syllables *ma, ma.*

ma·ma-san /'mämə ,sän/ ▶*n.* (in Japan and the Far East) a woman in a position of authority, esp. one in charge of a geisha house or bar. ▷Japanese, from *mama* 'mother' + *san*, an honorific title used as a mark of politeness.

ma·ma's boy ▶*n.* a boy or man who is excessively influenced by or attached to his mother.

mam·ba /'mämbə/ ▶*n.* a large, agile, highly venomous African snake. • Genus *Dendroaspis*, family Elapidae: three species. See also BLACK MAMBA. ▷mid 19th cent.: from Zulu *imamba.*

mam·bo /'mämbō/ ▶*n.* (*pl.* **-bos**) **1** a Latin American dance similar in rhythm to the rumba. **2** a voodoo priestess.
▶*v.* (**-boes, -boed**) [*intrans.*] dance the mambo. ▷1940s: from American Spanish, probably from Haitian Creole, from Yoruba, literally 'to talk.'

mam·ee /mäm'ē/ ▶*n.* variant spelling of MAMMEE.

Mam·e·luke /'mamə,lōōk/ ▶*n.* a member of a regime that formerly ruled parts of the Middle East. Descended from slaves, they ruled Syria (1260–1516) and Egypt (1250–1517), and continued as a ruling military caste in Ottoman Egypt until massacred by the viceroy Muhammad Ali in 1811. ▷from French *mameluk*, from Arabic *mamlūk* (passive participle used as a noun meaning 'slave'), from *malaka* 'possess.'

Mam·et /'mamit/, David (1947–), U.S. playwright, director, screenwriter, and novelist. Notable works: *Glengarry Glen Ross* (Pulitzer Prize, play, 1984) and *The Village* (novel, 1994).

ma·mey /mäm'ē/ ▶*n.* variant spelling of MAMMEE.

ma·mil·la /mam'ilə/ ▶*n.* variant spelling of MAMMILLA.

mam·ma[1] ▶*n.* variant spelling of MAMA.

mam·ma[2] /'mamə/ ▶*n.* (*pl.* **mam·mae** /'mamē; 'mam,ī/) a milk-secreting organ of female mammals (in humans, the breast). ■ a corresponding nonsecretory structure in male mammals. ▷Old English, from Latin, 'breast.' **—mam·mi·form** /'mamə,fôrm/ *adj.*

mam·mal /'maməl/ ▶*n.* a warm-blooded vertebrate animal of a class that is distinguished by the possession of hair or fur, the secretion of milk by females for the nourishment of the young, and (typically) the birth of live young.

The first small mammals evolved from reptiles about 200 million years ago, and the group diversified rapidly after the extinction of the dinosaurs to become the dominant form of land animal, with about 4,000 living species. Mammals belong to the class Mammalia, which contains the subclass Prototheria (monotremes) and the infraclasses Metatheria (marsupials) and Eutheria (placental mammals such as rodents, cats, whales, bats, and humans).

▷early 19th cent.: anglicized form (first used in the plural) of modern Latin *mammalia*, neuter plural of Latin *mammalis* (adjective), from *mamma* 'breast' (see MAMMA[2]). **—mam·ma·li·an** /mə'mālēən/ *adj.*

mam·ma·lif·er·ous /,mamə'lifərəs/ ▶*adj. Geology* containing mammalian fossil remains.

mam·mal-like rep·tile /'mamə(l),līk/ ▶*n.* another term for SYNAPSID.

mam·mal·o·gy /mə'maləjē/ ▶*n.* the branch of zoology concerned with mammals. **—mam·mal·o·gist** /-jist/ *n.*

mam·ma·ry /'mamərē/ ▶*adj.* [*attrib.*] denoting or relating to the human female breasts or the milk-secreting organs of other mammals: *mammary tumor viruses.*
▶*n.* (*pl.* **-ries**) *informal* a breast. ▷late 17th cent.: from MAMMA[2] + -ARY[1].

mam·ma·ry gland ▶*n.* the milk-producing gland of women or other female mammals.

mam·mee /mä'mā; -'mē/ (also **ma·mee, ma·mey**) ▶*n.* **1** (also **mammee apple**) a tropical American tree having large edible red fruit with red rind and sweet yellow flesh. • *Mammea americana*, family Guttiferae. **2** (also **mam·mee sa·po·te** /sə'pōtē; -tā/) a Central American tree having edible russet fruit with spicy red flesh. [*sapote* from Spanish *zapote* 'sapodilla.'] • *Pouteria sapota*, family Sapotaceae. ▷late 16th cent.: from Spanish *mamei*, from Taino.

mam·mil·la /mə'milə/ (also **ma·mil·la**) ▶*n.* (*pl.* **-mil·lae** /-'milē; -'mil,ī/) *Anatomy* the nipple of a woman's breast. ■ the corresponding organ in any mammal. ■ a nipple-shaped structure. ▷late 17th cent.: from Latin, diminutive of *mamma* 'breast' (see MAMMA²).

mam·mil·lar·y /ˈmaməˌlerē/ (also **mam·il·lar·y**) ▸*adj.* rounded like a breast or nipple, in particular: ■ (of minerals) having several smoothly rounded convex surfaces. ■ *Anatomy* denoting two rounded bodies in the floor of the hypothalamus in the brain. ▷early 17th cent.: from modern Latin *mamillaris*, from *mamilla* (see MAMILLA). The spelling variant of *-mm-* was due to association with MAMMARY.

mam·mil·lat·ed /ˈmaməˌlātid/ (also **mam·il·lat·ed**) ▸*adj. technical* covered with rounded mounds or lumps. ■ (of minerals) mammillary. ▷mid 18th cent.: from MAMILLA + the adjectival suffix *-ated*. **—mam·mil·late** /-ˌlāt/ *adj.*

mam·mo·gram /ˈmaməˌgram/ ▸*n.* an image obtained by mammography.

mam·mog·ra·phy /maˈmägrəfē/ ▸*n. Medicine* a technique using X-rays to diagnose and locate tumors of the breasts. ▷1930s: from MAMMA² + -GRAPHY.

mam·mon /ˈmamən/ (also **Mam·mon**) ▸*n.* wealth regarded as an evil influence or false object of worship and devotion. It was taken by medieval writers as the name of the devil of covetousness, and revived in this sense by Milton. ▷late Middle English: via late Latin from New Testament Greek *mamōnas* (see Matt. 6:24, Luke 16:9–13), from Aramaic *māmōn* 'riches.' **—mam·mon·ism** /-ˌizəm/ *n.* **—mam·mon·ist** /-ˌist/ *n.*

mam·moth /ˈmaməth/ ▸*n.* a large extinct elephant of the Pleistocene epoch, typically hairy with a sloping back and long curved tusks. • Genus *Mammuthus*, family Elephantidae: several species.

▸*adj.* huge: *a mammoth corporation.* ▷early 18th cent.: from Russian *mamo(n)t*, probably of Siberian origin.

Mam·moth Cave Na·tion·al Park a national park in west central Kentucky, site of the largest known cave system in the world. It consists of over 300 miles (480 km) of charted passageways and contains some spectacular rock formations.

mam·my /ˈmamē/ ▸*n.* (*pl.* **-mies**) *informal* one's mother (esp. as a child's word): *he was screaming for his mammy.* ■ *offensive* (formerly in the southern U.S.) a black nursemaid or nanny in charge of white children. ▷early 16th cent.: from MAM + -Y²; compare with MOMMY and MUMMY².

Ma·mout·zu /mäˈmo͞otso͞o/ the capital (since 1977) of Mayotte; pop. 12,000.

Mam'·selle /mamˈzel/ ▸*n.* short for MADEMOISELLE.

Man, Isle of see ISLE OF MAN.

man /man/ ▸*n.* (*pl.* **men** /men/) **1** an adult human male. ■ a male worker or employee: *more than 700 men were laid off | CNN's man in India.* ■ a male member of a sports team: *Johnson took the ball past three men and scored.* ■ (**men**) ordinary members of the armed forces as distinct from the officers: *he had a platoon of forty men to prepare for battle.* ■ a husband, boyfriend, or lover: *the two of them lived for a time as man and wife.* ■ [with *adj.*] a male person associated with a particular place, activity, or occupation: *a Harvard man | I'm a solid union man.* ■ a male pursued or sought by another, esp. in connection with a crime: *Inspector Bull was sure they would find their man.* ■ *dated* a manservant or valet: *get me a cocktail, my man.* ■ *historical* a vassal. **2** a human being of either sex; a person: *God cares for all races and all men.* ■ (also **Man**) [in *sing.*] human beings in general; the human race: *places untouched by the ravages of man.* ■ [in *sing.*] an individual; one: *a man could buy a lot with eighteen million dollars.* ■ a person with the qualities often associated with males such as bravery, spirit, or toughness: *she was more of a man than any of them.* ■ [in *sing.*] [with *adj.*] a type of prehistoric human named after the place where the remains were found: *Cro-Magnon man.* **3** (usu. **the Man**) *informal* a group or person in a position of authority over others, such as a corporate employer or the police: *it was a vicarious way of powerless people being able to stick it to the Man.* ■ *black slang* white people collectively regarded as the controlling group in society: *he urged that black college athletes boycott the Man's Rose Bowl.* **4** a figure or token used in playing a board game.

▸*v.* (**manned**, **man·ning**) [*trans.*] **1** (often **be manned**) provide (something, esp. a place or machine) with the personnel to run, operate, or defend it: *the firemen manned the pumps and fought the blaze.* ■ provide someone to fill (a post or office): *the chaplaincy was formerly manned by the cathedral.* **2** *archaic* fortify the spirits or courage of: *he manned himself with dauntless air.*

▸*exclam. informal* used, irrespective of the sex of the person addressed, to express surprise, admiration, delight, etc., or for emphasis: *man, what a show!* ▷Old English *man(n)*, (plural) *menn* (noun), *mannian* (verb), of Germanic origin; related to Dutch *man*, German *Mann*, and Sanskrit *manu* 'mankind.' **—man·less** *adj.*

▸*PHRASES* □ **as —— as the next man** as —— as the average person: *I'm as ambitious as the next man.* □ **as one man** with everyone acting together or in agreement: *the crowd rose to their feet as one man.* □ **be someone's man** be the person perfectly suited to a particular requirement or task: *for any coloring and perming services, David's your man.* □ **be man enough for** (or **to do**) be brave enough to do: *who's man enough for the job? | he has not been man enough to face up to his responsibilities.* □ **every man for himself** *proverb* everyone should (or does) look after their own interests rather than considering those of others: *when the bottom drops out of the market, it's every man for himself.* □ **make a man out of someone** (of an experience or person) turn a young man into a mature adult: *I make men out of them and teach them never to let anyone outsmart them.* □ **man about town** a fashionable male socialite. □ **man and boy** *dated* throughout life from youth: *the time when families worked in the fields man and boy.* □ **the man in the moon** the imagined likeness of a face seen on the surface of a full moon. ■ *figurative* used, esp. in comparisons, to refer to someone regarded as out of touch with real life: *a kid with no more idea of what to do than the man in the moon.* □ **the man in** (or **on**) **the street** an ordinary person, often with regard to their opinions, or as distinct from an expert: *it will be interesting to hear what the man in the street has to say about these latest tax cuts.* □ **man of action** see ACTION. □ **man of the cloth** a clergyman. □ **man of God** a clergyman. ■ a holy man or saint. □ **man of honor** a man who adheres to what is right or to a high standard of conduct. □ **man of the house** the male head of a household. □ **man of letters** a male scholar or author. □ **man of the moment** a man of importance at a particular time. □ **man of the world** see WORLD. □ **man's best friend** an affectionate or approving way of referring to the dog. □ **a man's man** a man whose personality is such that he is as popular and at ease, or more so, with other men than with women. □ **man to man** (or **man-to-man**) **1** in a direct and frank way between two men; openly and honestly: *he was able to talk man to man with the delegates | a man-to-man chat.* **2** denoting a defensive tactic in a sport such as football or basketball in which each player is responsible for defending against one opponent: *Washington's cornerbacks are fast enough to cover man-to-man.* □ **men in white coats** *humorous* psychiatrists or psychiatric workers (used to imply that someone is mad or mentally unbalanced): *I wondered how much more stupid I could get before the men in white coats would lead me away.* □ **separate** (or **sort out**) **the men from the boys** *informal* show or prove which people in a group are truly competent, brave, or mature. □ **to a man** without exception: *to a man, we have all taken a keen interest in the business.*

USAGE Traditionally, the word **man** has been used to refer not only to adult males but also to human beings in general, regardless of sex. There is a historical explanation for this: in Old English, the principal sense of **man** was 'a human being,' and the words **wer** and **wif** were used to refer specifically to 'a male person' and 'a female person,' respectively. Subsequently, **man** replaced **wer** as the normal term for 'a male person,' but at the same time the older sense 'a human being' remained in use.

In the second half of the 20th century, the generic use of **man** to refer to 'human beings in general' (*reptiles were here long before man appeared on the earth*) became problematic; the use is now often regarded as sexist or old-fashioned. In some contexts, terms such as **the human race** or **humankind** may be used instead of **man** or **mankind**. However, in other cases, particularly in compound forms, alternatives have not yet become established: there are no standard accepted alternatives for **manpower** or the verb **man**, for example.

Man. ▸*abbr.* Manitoba.

-man ▸*comb. form* in nouns denoting: ■ a male of a specified nationality or origin: *Frenchman | Yorkshireman.* ■ a man belonging to a distinct specified group: *layman.* ■ a person, esp. a male, having a specified occupation or role: *exciseman | chairman | oarsman.* ■ a ship of a specified kind: *merchantman.*

USAGE Traditionally, the form **-man** was combined with other words to create a term denoting an occupation or role, as in **fireman**, **layman**, **chairman**, and **mailman**. As the role of women in society has changed, with the result that women are now more likely to be in roles previously held exclusively by men, many of these terms ending in **-man** have been challenged as sexist and out of date. As a result, there has been a gradual shift away from **-man** compounds except where referring to a specific male person. Gender-neutral terms such as **firefighter** and **mail carrier** are widely accepted alternatives. And new terms such as **chairperson**, **layperson**, and **spokesperson**, which only a few decades ago seemed odd or awkward, are common today.

ma·na /ˈmänə/ ▸*n.* (esp. in Polynesian, Melanesian, and Maori belief) pervasive supernatural or magical power. ▷Maori.

man·a·cle /ˈmanikəl/ ▸*n.* (usu. **manacles**) a metal band, chain, or shackle for fastening someone's hands or ankles: *the practice of keeping prisoners in manacles.*

▸*v.* [*trans.*] (usu. **be manacled**) fetter (a person or a part of the body) with manacles: *his hands were manacled behind his back.* ▷Middle English: from Old French *manicle* 'handcuff,' from Latin *manicula*, diminutive of *manus* 'hand.'

man·age /ˈmanij/ ▸*v.* **1** [*trans.*] be in charge of (a company, establishment, or undertaking); administer; run: *their elder son managed the farm.* ■ administer and regulate (resources under one's control): *we manage our cash extremely well.* ■ have the position of supervising (staff) at work: *the skills needed to manage a young, dynamic team.* ■ be the manager of (a sports team or a performer): *he managed five or six bands in his career.* ■ maintain control or influence over (a person or animal): *she manages horses better than anyone I know.* ■ (often **be managed**) control the use or exploitation of (land): *the forest is managed to achieve maximum growth.* **2** [*intrans.*] succeed in surviving or in attaining one's aims, esp. against heavy odds; cope: *Catherine* **managed on** *five hours' sleep a night.* ■ [*trans.*] succeed in doing, achieving, or producing (something, esp. something difficult): *she managed a brave but unconvincing smile |* [with *infinitive*] *Beth finally managed to hail a cab | ironic one fund managed to lose money.* ■ [*trans.*] succeed in dealing with or withstanding (something): *there was more stress and anxiety than he could manage.* ■ [*trans.*] be free to attend on (a certain day) or at (a certain time): *he could not manage March 24 after all.* ▷mid 16th cent. (in the sense 'put (a horse) through the paces of the manège'): from Italian *maneggiare*, based on Latin *manus* 'hand.'

man·age·a·ble /ˈmanijəbəl/ ▸*adj.* able to be managed, controlled, or accomplished without great difficulty: *it leaves hair feeling soft and manageable | the situation was manageable, if a little nerve-racking.* **—man·age·a·bil·i·ty** /ˌmanijəˈbilətē/ *n.* **—man·age·a·ble·ness** *n.* **—man·age·a·bly** /-blē/ *adv.*

man·aged care ▸*n.* a system of health care in which patients agree to visit only certain doctors and hospitals, and in which the cost of treatment is monitored by a managing company.

man·aged cur·ren·cy ▸*n.* a currency whose exchange rate is regulated or controlled by the government.

man·aged fund ▸*n.* an investment fund run on behalf of an investor by an agent (typically an insurance company).

man·age·ment /ˈmanijmənt/ ▸*n.* **1** the process of dealing with or controlling things or people: *the management of elk herds.* ■ the responsibility for and control of a company or similar organization: *the management of a great metropolitan newspaper | a successful career in management.* ■ [treated as *sing.* or *pl.*] the people in charge of running a company or organization, regarded collectively: *management was extremely cooperative.* ■ *Medicine & Psychiatry* the treatment or control of diseases, injuries, or disorders, or the care of patients who suffer from them: *the use of combination chemotherapy in the management of breast cancer.* **2** *archaic* trickery; deceit: *if there has been any management in the business, it has been concealed from me.*

man·age·ment ac·count·ing ▸*n.* the provision of financial data and advice to a company for use in the organization and development of its business. **—man·age·ment ac·count·ant** *n.*

man·age·ment com·pa·ny ▸*n.* a company that is set up to manage a group of properties, a mutual fund, an investment fund, etc.

man·age·ment in·for·ma·tion sys·tem ▸(abbr. **MIS**) *n.* a computerized information-processing system designed to support the activities of company or organizational management.

man·ag·er /ˈmanijər/ ▸*n.* a person responsible for controlling or administering all or part of a company or similar organization: *the manager of a bar | the sales manager.* ■ a person who controls the activities, business dealings, and other aspects of the career of an entertainer, athlete, group of musicians, etc.: *she left it to her manager to deal with the canceled concerts.* ■ a person in charge of the activities, tactics, and training of a sports team: *Frank Robinson became baseball's first black manager.* ■ (in a high school or college) a student who assists the coach of an athletic team. ■ [with *adj.*] *Computing* a program or system that controls or organizes a peripheral device or process: *a file manager.* **—man·ag·er·ship** /-ˌSHip/ *n.*

man·ag·er·ess /ˈmanijərəs/ ▸*n. rare* a female manager.

man·a·ge·ri·al /ˌmanəˈji(ə)rēəl/ ▸*adj.* relating to management or managers, esp. of a company or similar organization: *I have a managerial role | managerial skills.* **—man·a·ge·ri·al·ly** *adv.*

man·a·ge·ri·al·ism /ˌmanəˈji(ə)rēəˌlizəm/ ▸*n.* belief in or reliance on the use of professional managers in administering or planning an activity. **—man·a·ge·ri·al·ist** *n.* & *adj.*

man·ag·ing /ˈmanijiNG/ ▸*adj.* [*attrib.*] having executive or supervisory control or authority: *a managing editor | the managing director.*

Ma·na·gua /məˈnägwə/ the capital of Nicaragua; pop 682,000. The city was almost completely destroyed by an earthquake in 1972.

man·a·kin /ˈmanəˌkin/ ▸*n.* a small tropical American bird with a large head and small bill, the male of which is typically brightly colored. Compare with MANNIKIN. • Family Pipridae (or Cotingidae, Tyrannidae): several genera and many species.

USAGE See usage at MANNEQUIN.

Ma·na·ma /məˈnämə/ a seaport and the capital of Bahrain; pop. 140,400.

ma·ña·na /mənˈyänə/ ▸*adv.* in the indefinite future (used to indicate procrastination): *the exhibition will be ready mañana.* ▷Spanish, literally 'tomorrow.'

Ma·nas·seh /məˈnasə/ (in the Bible) a Hebrew patriarch, son of Jacob and Rachel (Gen. 48:19). ■ the tribe of Israel traditionally descended from him.

ma·nat /ˈmanˌat/ ▸*n.* (*pl.* same) the basic monetary unit of Azerbaijan and Turkmenistan, equal to 100 gopik in Azerbaijan and 100 tenge in Turkmenistan.

man-at-arms ▸*n.* (*pl.* **men-at-arms**) *archaic* a soldier, esp. one heavily armed and mounted on horseback.

man·a·tee /ˈmanəˌtē/ ▸*n.* an aquatic mammal with a rounded tail flipper, living in shallow coastal waters and adjacent rivers of the tropical Atlantic. • Family Trichechidae and genus *Trichechus*: three species, all of which are endangered, including the **West Indian manatee** (*T. manatus*). ▷mid 16th cent.: from Spanish *manati*, from Carib *manáti*.

West indian manatee

Ma·naus /mäˈnous/ a city in northwestern Brazil; pop. 1,012,000. It is the principal commercial center of the upper Amazon region.

Man·ches·ter[1] /ˈmanˌCHestər; ˈmanCHi-/ **1** an industrial city in northwestern England; pop. 397,000. Founded in Roman times, it developed in the 18th and 19th centuries as a center of the English cotton industry. **2** a town in central Connecticut, east of Hartford; pop. 54,740. **3** the largest city in New Hampshire, on the Connecticut River, in the southern part of the state; pop. 107,006.

Man·ches·ter[2], William (1922–2004), U.S. historian and biographer. His works include *The Death of a President* (1967), *The Last Lion* (2 volumes, 1983, 1988), and *A World Lit Only by Fire* (1992).

Man·ches·ter ter·ri·er ▸*n.* a small terrier of a breed with a short black-and-tan coat.

man·chet /ˈmanCHət/ ▸*n. historical* a loaf of the finest kind of wheat bread. ▷late Middle English: perhaps from obsolete *maine* 'flour of the finest quality' + obsolete *cheat*, denoting a kind of wheaten bread.

man·chi·neel /ˌmanCHəˈnēl/ ▸*n.* a Caribbean tree that has acrid applelike fruit and poisonous milky sap that can cause temporary blindness. • *Hippomane mancinella*, family Euphorbiaceae. ▷mid 17th cent.: from French *mancenille*, from Spanish *manzanilla*, diminutive of *manzana* 'apple,' based on Latin *matiana (poma)* (neuter plural), denoting a kind of apple.

Man·chu /ˈmanˌCHo͞o; manˈCHo͞o/ ▸*n.* (*pl.* same or **-chus**) **1** a member of a people originally living in Manchuria who formed the last imperial dynasty of China (1644–1912). **2** the Tungusic language of the Manchus.
▸*adj.* of or relating to the Manchu people or their language. ▷the name in Manchu, literally 'pure.'

Man·chu·ri·a /manˈCHo͝orēə/ a mountainous region that forms the northeastern portion of China and comprises the provinces of Jilin, Liaoning, and Heilongjiang. In 1932, it was declared an independent state by Japan and renamed Manchukuo; it was restored to China in 1945.

Man·ci·ni /ˌmanˈsēnē/, Henry (1924–94), U.S. composer and conductor. He wrote many movie scores, including those for *The Pink Panther* (1964) and *Victor/Victoria* (1982). He also wrote "Moon River" for *Breakfast at Tiffany's* (1961).

man·ci·ple /ˈmansəpəl/ ▸*n. chiefly archaic* an officer who buys provisions for a college, monastery, or other institution. ▷Middle English: via Anglo-Norman French and Old French from Latin *mancipium* 'purchase,' from *manceps* 'buyer,' from *manus* 'hand' + *capere* 'take.'

Man·cu·ni·an /manˈkyo͞onēən/ ▸*n.* a native or inhabitant of Manchester, England.
▸*adj.* of or relating to Manchester, England. ▷early 20th cent.: from *Mancunium*, the Latin name of Manchester, + **-AN**.

-mancy ▸*comb. form* divination by a specified means: *geomancy.* ▷from Old French *-mancie*, via late Latin *-mantia* from Greek *manteia* 'divination.'

Man·dae·an /manˈdēən/ (also **Man·de·an**) ▸*n.* **1** a member of a Gnostic sect surviving in Iraq and southwestern Iran, who regard John the Baptist as the Messiah and stress salvation through knowledge of the divine origin of the soul. **2** the religious language of this sect, a form of Aramaic.
▸*adj.* of or relating to the Mandaeans or their language. ▷late 19th cent.: from Mandaean Aramaic *mandaia* 'Gnostics, those who have knowledge' (from *manda* 'knowledge') + **-AN**.

man·da·la /ˈmandələ; ˈmən-/ ▸*n.* a geometric figure representing the universe in Hindu and Buddhist symbolism. ■ *Psychoanalysis* such a symbol in a dream, representing the dreamer's search for completeness and self-unity. ▷from Sanskrit *maṇḍala* 'disk.' **—mandalic** /manˈdalik; ˌmən-/ *adj.*

Man·da·lay /ˌmandəˈlā/ a port on the Irrawaddy River in central Myanmar (Burma); pop. 533,000. Founded in 1857, it was the capital (until 1885) of the Burmese kingdom. It is an important Buddhist religious center.

man·da·mus /manˈdāməs/ ▸*n. Law* a judicial writ issued as a command to an inferior court or ordering a person to perform a public or statutory duty: *a writ of mandamus.* ▷mid 16th cent.: from Latin, literally 'we command.'

Man·dan[1] /ˈmandən/ a city in south central North Dakota, a northwestern suburb of Bismarck; pop. 16,718.

Man·dan[2] /ˈmandən; -ˌdan/ ▸*n.* (*pl.* same or **-dans**) **1** a member of an American Indian people formerly living on the upper Missouri River in North Dakota. **2** the Siouan language of this people, related to Winnebago.
▸*adj.* of or relating to this people or their language. ▷from Canadian French *Mandane*, probably from Dakota Sioux *mawátąna*.

man·da·rin[1] /ˈmandərən/ ▸*n.* **1** (**Mandarin**) the standard literary and official form of Chinese based on the Beijing dialect, spoken by over 730 million people: [as *adj.*] *Mandarin Chinese.* **2** an official in any of the nine top grades of the former imperial Chinese civil service. ■ [as *adj.*] (esp. of clothing) characteristic or supposedly characteristic of such officials: *a red-buttoned mandarin cap.* ■ an ornament consisting of a nodding figure in traditional Chinese dress, typically made of porcelain. ■ porcelain decorated with Chinese figures dressed as mandarins. ■ a powerful official or senior bureaucrat, esp. one perceived as reactionary and secretive: *a civil service mandarin.* ▷late 16th cent. (denoting a Chinese official): from Portuguese *mandarim*, via Malay from Hindi *mantrī* 'counselor.'

man·da·rin[2] (also **man·da·rine** /-dəˌrēn/, **man·da·rin or·ange**) ▸*n.* **1** a small flattish citrus fruit with a loose skin, esp. a variety with yellow-orange skin. Compare with TANGERINE. **2** the citrus tree that yields this fruit. • *Citrus reticulata*, family Rutaceae. ▷late 18th cent.: from French *mandarine*; perhaps related to MANDARIN[1], the color of the fruit being likened to the official's yellow robes.

man·da·rin col·lar ▸*n.* a small, close-fitting upright collar.

mandarin collar

man·da·rin duck ▸*n.* a small tree-nesting eastern Asian duck, the male of which has showy plumage with an orange ruff and orange saillike feathers on each side of the body. • *Aix galericulata*, family Anatidae.

man·da·rin jack·et ▸*n.* a plain jacket, typically of embroidered silk, with a mandarin collar.

man·da·tar·y /ˈmandəˌterē/ ▸*n.* (*pl.* **-tar·ies**) *historical* a person or country receiving a mandate. ▷late 15th cent. (denoting a person appointed by a papal mandate): from late Latin *mandatarius*, from *mandatum* (see MANDATE).

man·date /ˈmanˌdāt/ ▸*n.* **1** an official order or commission to do something: *a mandate to seek the release of political prisoners.* ■ *Law* a commission by which a party is entrusted to perform a service, esp. without payment and with indemnity against loss by that party. ■ *Law* an order from an appellate court to a lower court to take a specific action. ■ a written authority enabling someone to carry out transactions on another's bank account. ■ *historical* a commission from the League of Nations to a member state to administer a territory: *the British mandate in Palestine.* **2** the authority to carry out a policy or course of action, regarded as given by the electorate to a candidate or party that is victorious in an election: *a sick leader living beyond his mandate.* ■ *Canadian* a period during which a government is in power.
▸*v.* [*trans.*] **1** give (someone) authority to act in a certain way: *other colleges have mandated coed fraternities.* ■ require (something) to be done; make mandatory: *the government began mandating better car safety.* **2** *historical* assign (territory) under a mandate of the League of Nations: [as *adj.*] (**mandated**) *mandated territories.* ▷early 16th cent.: from Latin *mandatum* 'something commanded,' neuter past participle of *mandare*, from *manus* 'hand' + *dare* 'give.' Sense 2 of the *noun* has been influenced by French *mandat*.

man·da·to·ry /ˈmandəˌtôrē/ ▸*adj.* required by law or rules; compulsory: *wearing helmets was made mandatory for cyclists.* ■ of or conveying a command: *he did not want the guidelines to be mandatory.*
▸*n.* (*pl.* **-ries**) variant spelling of MANDATARY. ▷late 15th cent.: from late Latin *mandatorius*, from Latin *mandatum* 'something commanded.' **—man·da·to·ri·ly** /-ˌtôrəlē/ *adv.*

man-day ▸*n.* a day regarded in terms of the amount of work that can be done by one person within this period.

Man·de /ˈmänˌdā; mänˈdā/ ▸*n.* (*pl.* same or **-des**) **1** a member of any of a large group of peoples of West Africa. **2** any of the Niger–Congo languages or dialects spoken by these peoples, including Malinke, Mende, and Bambara.
▸*adj.* of or relating to these peoples or the Mande group of languages. ▷the name in Mande.

Man·de·an /manˈdēən/ ▸*n.* & *adj.* variant spelling of MANDAEAN.

Pronunciation Key ə *ago*; ər *over*; ˈə or ˌə *up*; ˈər or ˌər *fur*; a *hat*; ā *rate*; ä *car*; CH *chew*; e *let*; ē *see*; e(ə)r *air*; i *fit*; ī *by*; i(ə)r *ear*; NG *sing*; ō *go*; ô *for*; oi *boy*; o͝o *good*; o͞o *goo*; ou *out*; SH *she*; TH *thin*; T͟H *then*; (h)w *why*; ZH *vision*

M

Man·de·la /man'delə/, Nelson (Rolihlahla) (1918–), South African statesman, president 1994–99. He was sentenced to life imprisonment in 1964 as an activist for the African National Congress (ANC). Released in 1990, as leader of the ANC, he engaged in talks on the introduction of majority rule with President F. W. de Klerk. He became the country's first democratically elected president in 1994, serving until 1999. Nobel Peace Prize (1993, shared with de Klerk).

Nelson Mandela

Man·del·brot /'mandl,brät; -,brō; ,mändel'brô/, Benoit (1924–), French mathematician, born in Poland. He is known as the pioneer of fractal geometry.

Man·del·brot set ▸*n. Mathematics* a particular set of complex numbers that has a highly convoluted fractal boundary when plotted.

Man·del·stam /'mändl,stäm; məndyil'SHtäm/ (also **Man·del·shtam**), Osip (Emilevich) (1891–1938), Russian poet; a member of the Acmeist group. Sent into internal exile in 1934, he died in a prison camp. Notable works: *Stone* (1913) and *Tristia* (1922).

man·di·ble /'mandəbəl/ ▸*n. Anatomy & Zoology* the jaw or a jawbone, esp. the lower jawbone in mammals and fishes. ■ either of the upper and lower parts of a bird's beak. ■ either half of the crushing organ in an arthropod's mouthparts. ▷late Middle English: from Old French, or from late Latin *mandibula*, from *mandere* 'to chew.' —**man·dib·u·lar** /man'dibyələr/ *adj.* —**man·dib·u·late** /man'dibyə,lāt/ *adj.*

Man·ding /'mandiNG/ (also **Man·din·go** /man'diNGgō/) ▸*n. & adj.* another term for **MANDE**.

Man·din·ka /man'diNGkə/ ▸*n.* (*pl.* same or **-kas**) **1** a member of a people living mainly in Senegal, Gambia, and Sierra Leone. **2** the Mande language of this people.
▸*adj.* of or relating to the Mandinkas or their language. ▷the name in Mandinka.

man·do·la /man'dōlə/ ▸*n.* a large tenor or bass mandolin, used in ensembles and folk groups. ■ (also **man·do·ra** /-'dôrə/) *historical* an early stringed instrument of the mandolin or cittern type. ▷early 18th cent.: from Italian.

man·do·lin /,mandə'lin; 'mandələn/ ▸*n.* **1** a musical instrument resembling a lute, having paired metal strings plucked with a plectrum. It is played with a characteristic tremolo on long sustained notes. **2** variant spelling of **MANDOLINE**. ▷early 18th cent.: from French *mandoline*, from Italian *mandolino*, diminutive of *mandola* (see **MANDOLA**). —**man·do·lin·ist** /-'linist/ *n.*

mandolin 1

man·do·line /,mandə'lin; 'mandəlin/ (also **man·do·lin**) ▸*n.* a kitchen utensil consisting of a flat frame with adjustable cutting blades for slicing vegetables.

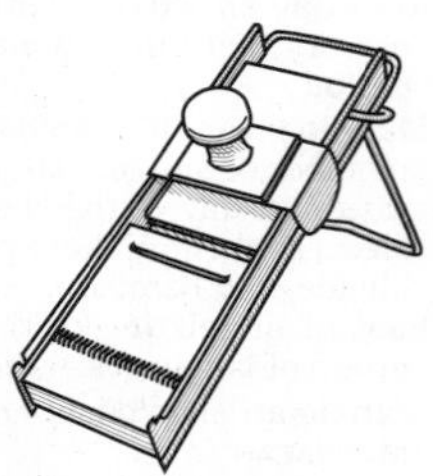

mandoline

man·dor·la /man'dôrlə/ (also **Man·dor·la**) ▸*n.* a pointed oval figure used as an architectural feature and as an aureole enclosing figures such as Jesus Christ or the Virgin Mary in medieval art. Also called **VESICA PISCIS**. ▷late 19th cent.: from Italian, literally 'almond.'

man·drag·o·ra /man'dragərə/ ▸*n. poetic/literary* the mandrake, esp. when used as a narcotic. ▷Old English, via medieval Latin from Latin and Greek *mandragoras*.

man·drake /'man,drāk/ ▸*n.* **1** a Mediterranean plant of the nightshade family, with white or purple flowers and large yellow berries. It has a forked fleshy root that supposedly resembles the human form and was formerly widely used in medicine and magic, allegedly shrieking when pulled from the ground. • *Mandragora officinarum*, family Solanaceae. **2** another term for **MAYAPPLE**. ▷Middle English *mandrag(g)e*, from Middle Dutch *mandrag(r)e*, from medieval Latin *mandragora*; associated with **MAN** (because of the shape of its root) + *drake* in the Old English sense 'dragon.'

Man·drax /'man,draks/ ▸*n. trademark* a sedative drug containing methaqualone and diphenhydramine hydrochloride. ▷1960s: of unknown origin.

man·drel /'mandrəl/ ▸*n.* **1** a shaft or spindle in a lathe to which work is fixed while being turned. **2** a cylindrical rod around which metal or other material is forged or shaped. ▷early 16th cent.: of unknown origin.

man·drill /'mandrəl/ ▸*n.* a large West African baboon with a brightly colored red and blue face, the male having a blue rump. • *Mandrillus sphinx*, family Cercopithecidae. ▷mid 18th cent.: probably from **MAN** + **DRILL**[3].

mandrill

man·du·cate /'manjə,kāt/ ▸*v.* [*trans.*] *formal* chew or eat. ▷early 17th cent.: from Latin *manducat-* 'chewed,' from the verb *manducare*, from *manduco* 'guzzler,' from *mandere* 'to chew.' —**man·du·ca·tion** /,manjə'kāSHən/ *n.* —**man·du·ca·to·ry** /-jəkə,tôrē/ *adj.*

mane /mān/ ▸*n.* a growth of long hair on the neck of a horse, lion, or other animal. ■ a person's long or thick hair: *he had a mane of white hair.* ▷Old English *manu*, of Germanic origin; related to Dutch *manen*. —**maned** *adj.* [in *combination*] *a black-maned lion.* —**mane·less** *adj.*

man-eat·er ▸*n.* **1** an animal that has a propensity for killing and eating humans. **2** *informal* a dominant woman who has many sexual partners. —**man-eat·ing** *adj.*

man·eb /'man,eb/ ▸*n.* a white compound used as a fungicidal powder on vegetables and fruit. • Alternative name: **manganese ethylene bisdithiocarbamate**; chem. formula: $C_4H_6N_2S_4Mn$.

maned wolf ▸*n.* a large, long-legged, endangered wild dog that has a reddish coat with black hair across the shoulders and large erect ears, native to the grasslands of South America. • *Chrysocyon brachyurus*, family Canidae.

ma·nège /ma'nezH; mə-/ ▸*n.* an arena or enclosed area in which horses and riders are trained. ■ the movements of a trained horse. ■ horsemanship. ▷mid 17th cent.: French, from Italian (see **MANAGE**).

ma·nes /'män,ās; 'mā,nēz/ ▸*plural n.* (in Roman mythology) the deified souls of dead ancestors. ▷Latin.

Ma·net /mä'nā/, Édouard (1832–83), French painter. He adopted a realist approach that greatly influenced the Impressionists, using pure color to give a direct unsentimental effect. Notable works: *Déjeuner sur l'herbe* (1863), *Olympia* (1865), and *A Bar at the Folies-Bergère* (1882).

Man·e·tho /'mani,THō/ (3rd century BC), Egyptian priest. He wrote a history of Egypt from mythical times to 323, in which he arbitrarily divided the succession of rulers known to him into 30 dynasties, an arrangement that is still followed.

ma·neu·ver /mə'nōōvər/ (*Brit.* **ma·noeu·vre**) ▸*n.* **1** a movement or series of moves requiring skill and care: *spectacular jumps and other daring maneuvers.* ■ a carefully planned scheme or action, esp. one involving deception: *shady financial maneuvers.* ■ the fact or process of taking such action: *the economic policy provided no* **room for maneuver**. **2** (**maneuvers**) a large-scale military exercise of troops, warships, and other forces: *the Russian vessel was* **on maneuvers**.
▸*v.* (**-vered, -ver·ing**) **1** perform or cause to perform a movement or series of moves requiring skill and care: [*intrans.*] *the truck was unable to maneuver comfortably in the narrow street* | | [*trans.*] *I'm maneuvering a loaded tray around the floor.* **2** [*trans.*] carefully guide or manipulate (someone or something) in order to achieve an end: *they were maneuvering him into a betrayal of his countryman.* ■ [*intrans.*] carefully manipulate a situation to achieve an end: [as *n.*] (**maneuvering**) *two decades of political maneuvering.* ▷mid 18th cent. (as a noun in the sense 'tactical movement'): from French *manœuvre* (noun), *manœuvrer* (verb), from medieval Latin *manuoperare*, from Latin *manus* 'hand' + *operari* 'to work.' —**ma·neu·ver·er** *n.*

ma·neu·ver·a·ble /mə'nōōvərəbəl/ (*Brit.* **ma·noeu·vra·ble**) ▸*adj.* (esp. of a craft or vessel) able to be maneuvered easily while in motion. —**ma·neu·ver·a·bil·i·ty** /mə,nōōvərə'bilətē/ *n.*

man Fri·day ▸*n.* a male helper or follower. ▷from *Friday*, the name of a character in Defoe's novel *Robinson Crusoe* (1719).

man·ful /'manfəl/ ▸*adj.* resolute or brave, esp. in the face of adversity: *a manful attempt to smile.* See note at **MALE**. —**man·ful·ly** *adv.* —**man·ful·ness** *n.*

man·ga /'mäNG,gä/ ▸*n.* a Japanese genre of cartoons, comic books, and animated films, typically having a science-fiction or fantasy theme and sometimes including violent or sexually explicit material. Compare with **ANIME**. ▷Japanese, from *man* 'indiscriminate' + *ga* 'picture.'

man·ga·bey /'maNGgə,bā/ ▸*n.* a medium-sized long-tailed monkey native to the forests of western and central Africa. • Genus *Cercocebus*, family Cercopithecidae: several species. ▷late 18th cent.: by erroneous association with *Mangabey*, a region of Madagascar.

man·ga·nate /'maNGgə,nāt/ ▸*n. Chemistry* a salt in which the anion contains both manganese and oxygen, esp. one of the anion MnO_4 II.

man·ga·nese /'maNGgə,nēz; -,nēs/ ▸*n.* the chemical element of atomic number 25, a hard gray metal of the transition series. Manganese is an important component of special steels and magnetic alloys. (Symbol: **Mn**) ■ the black dioxide of this as an industrial raw material or additive, esp. in glassmaking. ▷late 17th cent.: via French from Italian *manganese*, unexplained alteration of medieval Latin *magnesia* (see **MAGNESIA**).

man·ga·nese bronze ▸*n.* an alloy of copper and zinc with manganese.

man·ga·nese nod·ule ▸*n.* a small concretion consisting of manganese and iron oxides, occurring in large numbers in ocean-floor sediment.

man·gan·ic /man'ganik; maNG-/ ▸*adj. Chemistry* of manganese with a valence of three. Compare with **MANGANOUS**.

Man·ga·nin /'maNGgənin/ ▸*n. Brit., trademark* an alloy of copper, manganese, and nickel, used chiefly in electrical apparatus. ▷1920s: from **MANGANESE** + **-IN**[1].

man·ga·nite /'maNGgə,nīt/ ▸*n.* a mineral consisting of manganese oxyhydroxide, typically occurring as steel-gray or black prisms.

man·ga·nous /'maNGgənəs/ ▸*adj. Chemistry* of manganese with a valence of two. Compare with **MANGANIC**.

mange /mānj/ ▸*n.* a skin disease of mammals caused by parasitic mites and occasionally communicable to humans. It typically causes severe itching, hair loss, and the formation of scabs and lesions. See also **DEMODECTIC MANGE, SARCOPTIC MANGE**. ▷late Middle English: from Old French *mangeue*, from *mangier* 'eat,' from Latin *manducare* 'to chew.'

man·gel /'maNGgəl/ (also **man·gel-wur·zel**) ▸*n.* a beet of a variety with a large root, cultivated as feed for livestock. • *Beta vulgaris* subsp. *crassa*, family Chenopodiaceae. ▷mid 19th cent.: from German *Mangoldwurzel*, from *Mangold* 'beet' + *Wurzel* 'root.'

man·ger /'mānjər/ ▸*n.* a long open box or trough for horses or cattle to eat from. ▷Middle English: from Old French *mangeure*, based on Latin *manducat-* 'chewed' (see **MANDUCATE**).

man·ger scene ▸*n.* another term for **NATIVITY SCENE**.

man·gey /'mānjē/ ▸*adj.* variant spelling of **MANGY**.

man·gle[1] /'maNGgəl/ ▸*v.* [*trans.*] severely mutilate, disfigure, or damage by cutting, tearing, or crushing:

M

the car was mangled almost beyond recognition | figurative he was mangling Bach on the piano. ▷late Middle English: from Anglo-Norman French *mahangler*, apparently a frequentative of *mahaignier* 'maim.' —**man·gler** *n.*

man·gle[2] ▸*n.* a large machine for ironing sheets or other fabrics, usually when they are damp, using heated rollers. ■ *chiefly Brit.* a machine having two or more cylinders turned by a handle, between which wet laundry is squeezed (to remove excess moisture) and pressed.

▸*v.* [*trans.*] press or squeeze with a mangle. ▷late 17th cent.: from Dutch *mangel*, from *mangelen* 'to mangle,' from medieval Latin *mango, manga*, from Greek *manganon* 'axis, engine.'

man·go /ˈmaNGgō/ ▸*n.* (*pl.* **-goes** or **-gos**) **1** a fleshy yellowish-red tropical fruit that is eaten ripe or used green for pickles or chutneys. **2** (also **man·go tree**) the evergreen Indian tree of the cashew family that bears this fruit, widely cultivated in the tropics. • *Mangifera indica*, family Anacardiaceae; many local varieties. **3** a tropical American hummingbird that typically has green plumage with purple feathers on the wings, tail, or head. • Genus *Anthracothorax*, family Trochilidae: several species, e.g., the **Jamaican mango** (*A. mango*), which has a dark bronze-green back, purple head, and black underside. ▷late 16th cent.: from Portuguese *manga*, from a Dravidian language.

man·gold /ˈmaNGgōld/ ▸*n.* another term for MANGEL.

man·go·nel /ˈmaNGgəˌnel/ ▸*n. historical* a military device for throwing stones and other missiles. ▷Middle English: from Old French *mangonel(le)*, from medieval Latin *manganellus*, diminutive of late Latin *manganum*, from Greek *manganon* 'axis of a pulley.'

man·go·steen /ˈmaNGgəˌstēn/ ▸*n.* **1** a tropical fruit with sweet juicy white segments of flesh inside a thick reddish-brown rind. **2** the slow-growing Malaysian tree that bears this fruit. • *Garcinia mangostana*, family Guttiferae. ▷late 16th cent.: from Malay *manggustan*, dialect variant of *manggis*.

man·grove /ˈmanˌgrōv; ˈmaNG-/ ▸*n.* a tree or shrub that grows in muddy, chiefly tropical coastal swamps that are inundated at high tide. Mangroves typically have numerous tangled roots above ground and form dense thickets. • Genera in several families, in particular *Rhizophora* and related genera (family Rhizophoraceae), and *Avicennia* (family Verbenaceae or Avicenniaceae). ■ (also **mangrove swamp**) a tidal swamp that is dominated by mangroves and associated vegetation. ▷early 17th cent.: probably from Portuguese *mangue*, Spanish *mangle*, from Taino. The change in the ending was due to association with GROVE.

man·gy /ˈmānjē/ (also **man·gey**) ▸*adj.* (**-gi·er**, **-gi·est**) having mange. ■ in poor condition; shabby: *a girl in a mangy fur coat.* —**man·gi·ness** /-jēnis/ *n.*

man·han·dle /ˈmanˌhandl/ ▸*v.* [*trans.*] move (a heavy object) by hand with great effort: *seven guys had to manhandle the piano down the stairs.* ■ *informal* handle (someone) roughly by dragging or pushing: *a drunk had manhandled one of the deputies.*

Man·hat·tan /manˈhatn; mən-/ **1** a commercial city in northeastern Kansas; pop. 44,831. **2** an island near the mouth of the Hudson River that forms part of the city of New York. The site of the original Dutch settlement of New Amsterdam, it is now a borough containing the commercial and cultural center of New York City. ▷(in sense 2): named after the Algonquin tribe from whom the Dutch settlers claimed to have bought the island in 1626.

man·hat·tan /manˈhatn; mən-/ (also **Man·hat·tan**) ▸*n.* a cocktail made of whiskey and vermouth, sometimes with a dash of bitters.

Man·hat·tan clam chow·der ▸*n.* a chowder made with clams, vegetables, salt pork, and seasonings in a tomato-based broth.

Man·hat·tan Pro·ject the code name for the American project set up in 1942 to develop an atom bomb. The project culminated in 1945 with the detonation of the first nuclear weapon, at White Sands in New Mexico.

man·hole /ˈmanˌhōl/ ▸*n.* a small covered opening in a floor, pavement, or other surface to allow a person to enter, esp. an opening in a city street leading to a sewer.

man·hood /ˈmanˌhŏŏd/ ▸*n.* the state or period of being a man rather than a child: *boys in the process of growing to manhood.* ■ men, esp. those of a country, regarded collectively: *Germany had lost the best of her young manhood.* ■ qualities traditionally associated with men, such as courage, strength, and sexual potency: *we drank to prove our manhood.* ■ *archaic* the condition of being human: *the unity of Godhead and manhood in Christ.* ■ (**one's manhood**) *informal* used euphemistically to refer to a man's genitals.

man-hour ▸*n.* an hour regarded in terms of the amount of work that can be done by one person within this period.

man·hunt /ˈmanˌhənt/ ▸*n.* an organized search for a person, esp. a criminal.

ma·ni·a /ˈmānēə/ ▸*n.* mental illness marked by periods of great excitement, euphoria, delusions, and overactivity. ■ an excessive enthusiasm or desire; an obsession: *he had* ***a mania for*** *automobiles.* ▷late Middle English: via late Latin from Greek, literally 'madness,' from *mainesthai* 'be mad.'

-mania ▸*comb. form Psychology* denoting a specified type of mental abnormality or obsession: *kleptomania.* ■ denoting extreme enthusiasm or admiration: *Beatlemania.*

ma·ni·ac /ˈmānēˌak/ ▸*n. informal* a person exhibiting extreme symptoms of wild behavior, esp. when violent and dangerous: *a homicidal maniac.* ■ [with *adj.*] an obsessive enthusiast: *a gambling maniac.* ■ *archaic Psychiatry* a person suffering from mania. ▷early 16th cent. (as an adjective): via late Latin from late Greek *maniakos*, from *mania* (see MANIA). —**ma·ni·a·cal** /məˈnīəkəl/ *adj.* —**ma·ni·a·cal·ly** /məˈnīək(ə)lē/ *adv.*

-maniac ▸*comb. form Psychology* forming nouns corresponding to words ending in *-mania*: *kleptomaniac | Beatlemaniac.*

man·ic /ˈmanik/ ▸*adj.* showing wild and apparently deranged excitement and energy: *his manic enthusiasm | a manic grin.* ■ frenetically busy; frantic: *the pace is utterly manic.* ■ *Psychiatry* relating to or affected by mania: *the manic interludes in depression.* —**man·i·cal·ly** /-(ə)lē/ *adv.*

man·ic de·pres·sion ▸*n.* another term, esp. formerly, for BIPOLAR DISORDER. —**man·ic-de·pres·sive** *adj.* & *n.*

Man·i·chae·an /ˌmanəˈkēən/ (also **Man·i·che·an**) ▸*adj. chiefly historical* of or relating to Manichaeism. ■ of or characterized by dualistic contrast or conflict between opposites.

▸*n.* an adherent of Manichaeism. —**Man·i·chae·an·ism** /-ˈkēəˌnizəm/ *n.*

Man·i·chae·ism /ˈmanəˌkēizəm/ (also **Man·i·che·ism**) ▸*n.* a dualistic religious system with Christian, Gnostic, and pagan elements, founded in Persia in the 3rd century by Manes (*c.*216–*c.*276). The system was based on a supposed primeval conflict between light and darkness. It spread widely in the Roman Empire and in Asia, and survived in Chinese Turkestan until the 13th century. ■ religious or philosophical dualism. ▷early 17th cent.: from late Latin *Manichaeus* (from the name *Manes*: see above) + -ISM.

Man·i·chee /ˈmanəˌkē/ ▸*n.* & *adj.* archaic term for MANICHAEAN. ▷Middle English: from late Latin *Manichaei*, plural of *Manichaeus* (see MANICHAEISM).

ma·ni·cot·ti /ˌmanəˈkätē/ ▸*n.* pasta in the shape of large tubes. ■ [treated as *sing.*] an Italian dish consisting largely of these stuffed with cheese, typically with tomato sauce. ▷Italian, plural of *manicotto* 'muff.'

man·i·cure /ˈmaniˌkyŏŏr/ ▸*n.* a cosmetic treatment of the hands involving cutting, shaping, and often painting of the nails, removal of the cuticles, and softening of the skin.

▸*v.* [*trans.*] give a manicure to. ■ [usu. as *adj.*] (**manicured**) trim neatly: *manicured lawns.* ▷late 19th cent.: from French, from Latin *manus* 'hand' + *cura* 'care.'

man·i·cur·ist /ˈmaniˌkyŏŏrist/ ▸*n.* a person who performs manicures professionally.

man·i·fest[1] /ˈmanəˌfest/ ▸*adj.* clear or obvious to the eye or mind: *the system's manifest failings.*

▸*v.* [*trans.*] display or show (a quality or feeling) by one's acts or appearance; demonstrate: *Ray manifested signs of severe depression.* ■ (often **be manifested in**) be evidence of; prove: *bad industrial relations are often manifested in disputes and strikes.* ■ [*intrans.*] (of an ailment) become apparent through the appearance of symptoms: *a disorder that usually manifests in middle age.* ■ [*intrans.*] (of a ghost or spirit) appear: *one deity manifested in the form of a bird.* ▷late Middle English: via Old French from Latin *manifestus*. —**man·i·fest·ly** *adv.*

man·i·fest[2] ▸*n.* a document giving comprehensive details of a ship and its cargo and other contents, passengers, and crew for the use of customs officers. ■ a list of passengers or cargo in an aircraft. ■ a list of the cars forming a freight train.

▸*v.* [*trans.*] record in such a manifest: *every passenger is manifested at the point of departure.* ▷mid 16th cent. (denoting a manifestation): from Italian *manifesto* (see MANIFESTO). The current sense dates from the early 17th cent.

man·i·fes·ta·tion /ˌmanəfəˈstāSHən; -ˌfesˈtāSHən/ ▸*n.* an event, action, or object that clearly shows or embodies something, esp. a theory or an abstract idea: *the first obvious manifestations of global warming.* See note at SIGN. ■ the action or fact of showing something in such a way: *the manifestation of anxiety over the upcoming exams.* ■ a symptom or sign of an ailment: *a characteristic manifestation of Lyme disease.* ■ a version or incarnation of something or someone: *Purity and Innocence and Young Love in all their gentle manifestations.* ■ an appearance of a ghost or spirit. ▷late Middle English: from late Latin *manifestatio(n-)*, from the verb *manifestare* 'make public.'

Man·i·fest Des·ti·ny ▸*n.* the 19th-century doctrine or belief that the expansion of the U.S. throughout the American continents was both justified and inevitable.

man·i·fes·to /ˌmanəˈfestō/ ▸*n.* (*pl.* **-tos**) a public declaration of policy and aims, esp. one issued before an election by a political party or candidate. ▷mid 17th cent.: from Italian, from *manifestare*, from Latin, 'make public,' from *manifestus* 'obvious' (see MANIFEST[1]).

man·i·fold /ˈmanəˌfōld/ ▸*adj.* many and various: *the implications of this decision were manifold.* ■ having many different forms or elements: *the appeal of the crusade was manifold.*

▸*n.* **1** [often with *adj.*] a pipe or chamber branching into several openings: *the pipeline manifold.* ■ (in an internal combustion engine) the part conveying air and fuel from the carburetor to the cylinders or that leading from the cylinders to the exhaust pipe: *the exhaust manifold.* **2** *technical* something with many different parts or forms, in particular: ■ *Mathematics* a collection of points forming a certain kind of set, such as those of a topologically closed surface or an analog of this in three or more dimensions. ■ (in Kantian philosophy) the sum of the particulars furnished by sense before they have been unified by the synthesis of the understanding. ▷Old English *manigfeald*; current noun senses date from the mid 19th cent. —**man·i·fold·ly** *adv.* —**man·i·fold·ness** *n.*

man·i·kin /ˈmanikən/ (also **man·ni·kin**) ▸*n.* **1** a person who is very small, esp. one not otherwise abnormal or deformed. **2** a jointed model of the human body, used in anatomy or as an artist's lay figure. ▷mid 16th cent.: from Dutch *manneken* (Middle Dutch *mannekijn*), diminutive of *man* 'man.'

USAGE See usage at MANNEQUIN.

Ma·nil·a[1] /məˈnilə/ the capital and chief port of the Philippines, on the island of Luzon; pop. 1,599,000.

Ma·nil·a[2] (also **Ma·nil·la**) ▸*n.* **1** (also **Manila hemp**) the strong fiber of a Philippine plant, used for rope, matting, paper, etc.: [as *adj.*] *Manila rope.* See also ABACA. ■ (also **Manila paper**) strong brown paper, originally made from Manila hemp. **2** [often as *adj.*] a cigar or cheroot made in Manila. ▷late 17th cent. (as an adjective meaning 'from Manila'): from MANILA[1].

ma·nille /məˈnil/ ▸*n.* (in the card games ombre and quadrille) the second-best trump or honor. ▷late 17th cent.: from French (perhaps influenced by *main* 'hand'), from *malille*, also used as a term in card games, from Spanish *malilla*, diminutive of *mala*, feminine of *malo* 'bad.' Although "bad" because of its low value, the card acquires power when its suit is trumps.

man·i·oc /ˈmanēˌäk/ ▸*n.* another term for CASSAVA. ▷mid 16th cent.: from French, from Tupi *manioca*.

man·i·ple /ˈmanəpəl/ ▸*n.* **1** a subdivision of a Roman legion, containing either 120 or 60 men. **2** (in church use) a vestment formerly worn by a priest celebrating the Eucharist, consisting of a strip hanging from the left arm. ▷late Middle English (sense 2): from Old French *maniple*, from Latin *manipulus* 'handful, troop,' from *manus* 'hand' + the base of *plere* 'fill.' —**ma·nip·u·lar** /məˈnipyələr/ *adj.* (in sense 1).

ma·nip·u·late /məˈnipyəˌlāt/ ▸*v.* [*trans.*] **1** handle or control (a tool, mechanism, etc.), typically in a skillful manner: *he manipulated the dials of the set.* ■ alter, edit, or move (text or data) on a computer. ■ examine or treat (a part of the body) by feeling or moving it with the hand: *a system of healing based on manipulating the ligaments of the spine.* **2** control or influence (a person or situation) cleverly, unfairly, or unscrupulously: *the masses were deceived and manipulated by a tiny group.* ■ alter (data) or present (statistics) so as to mislead. ▷early 19th cent.: back-formation from earlier *manipulation*, from Latin *manipulus* 'handful.' **—ma·nip·u·la·bil·i·ty** /-ˌnipyələˈbilətē/ *n.* **—ma·nip·u·la·ble** /-ləbəl/ *adj.* **—ma·nip·u·lat·a·ble** /-ˌlātəbəl/ *adj.* **—ma·nip·u·la·tion** /məˌnipyəˈlāsʜən/ *n.* **—ma·nip·u·la·tor** /-ˌlātər/ *n.* **—ma·nip·u·la·to·ry** /-ləˌtôrē/ *adj.*

ma·nip·u·la·tive /məˈnipyələtiv; -ˌlātiv/ ▸*adj.* **1** characterized by unscrupulous control of a situation or person: *she was sly, selfish, and manipulative.* **2** of or relating to manipulation of an object or part of the body: *a manipulative skill.* **—ma·nip·u·la·tive·ly** *adv.* **—ma·nip·u·la·tive·ness** *n.*

Ma·ni·pur /ˈmanəˌpo͝or; ˌmənəˈpo͝or/ a small state in eastern India, east of Assam, on the border with Myanmar (Burma); capital, Imphal.

Man·i·pu·ri /ˌmanəˈpo͝orē/ ▸*n.* (*pl.* same or **-ris**) **1** a native or inhabitant of Manipur. **2** the official language of Manipur, belonging to the Tibeto-Burman family.
▸*adj.* of or relating to the people of Manipur or their language.

Manit. ▸*abbr.* Manitoba.

Man·i·to·ba /ˌmanəˈtōbə/ a province in central Canada, with a coastline on Hudson Bay; pop. 1,092,942; capital, Winnipeg. The area was part of Rupert's Land from 1670 until it was transferred to Canada by the Hudson's Bay Company and became a province in 1870. **—Man·i·to·ban** *adj.* & *n.*

man·i·tou /ˈmaniˌto͞o/ ▸*n.* (among certain Algonquian Indians) a good or evil spirit as an object of reverence. ▷late 17th cent.: via French from an Algonquian language.

Man·i·tou·lin Is·land /ˌmaniˈto͞olən/ an island in southern Canada, in the province of Ontario, in northern Lake Huron. At 1,068 square miles (2,766 sq km), it is the largest lake island in the world.

Man·ka·to /manˈkātō/ a city in south central Minnesota; pop. 31,477.

Man·kie·wicz /ˈmankəˌwits/, Joseph Leo (1909–93), U.S. movie director, producer, and screenwriter. He wrote and directed *A Letter to Three Wives* (Academy Award, 1949) and *All About Eve* (Academy Award, 1950).

Man·kil·ler /ˈmanˌkilər/, Wilma (Pearl) (1945–), U.S. Cherokee Nation tribal leader 1985–95 and historian. A women's rights activist, she wrote *Mankiller: A Chief and Her People* (1993).

man·kind /ˌmanˈkīnd; ˈmanˌkīnd/ ▸*n.* **1** human beings considered collectively; the human race: *research for the benefit of all mankind.* **2** /ˈmanˌkīnd/ *archaic* men, as distinct from women.

USAGE On the use of **mankind** versus that of **humankind** or **the human race**, see **usage** at MAN.

Man·ley /ˈmanlē/, Michael (Norman) (1923–97), Jamaican statesman; prime minister 1972–80 and 1989–92.

man·like /ˈmanˌlīk/ ▸*adj.* **1** resembling a human being: *a manlike creature.* **2** (of a woman) having an appearance or qualities associated with men.

man·ly /ˈmanlē/ ▸*adj.* (**-li·er**, **-li·est**) having or denoting those good qualities traditionally associated with men, such as courage and strength: *looking manly and capable in his tennis whites.* See note at MALE. ■ (of an activity) befitting a man, esp. in a traditional sense: *the manly art of knife-throwing.* **—man·li·ness** /-lēnis/ *n.*

man-made ▸*adj.* made or caused by human beings (as opposed to occurring or being made naturally); artificial: *a man-made lake.*

Mann[1] /man/, Horace (1796–1859), U.S. editor and politician. Considered the father of public education, he helped to establish the first state board of education while he was a representative to the Massachusetts state legislature 1827–37. He served as the board's president 1837–48.

Mann[2], Thomas (1875–1955), German novelist and essayist. The role and character of the artist in relation to society is a constant theme in his works. Notable works: *Buddenbrooks* (1901), *Death in Venice* (1912), *The Magic Mountain* (1924), and *Dr. Faustus* (1947). Nobel Prize for Literature (1929).

man·na /ˈmanə/ ▸*n.* (in the Bible) the substance miraculously supplied as food to the Israelites in the wilderness (Exod. 16). ■ an unexpected or gratuitous benefit: *the cakes were* **manna from heaven**. ■ (in Christian contexts) spiritual nourishment, esp. the Eucharist. ■ a sweet secretion from the manna ash or a similar plant, used as a mild laxative and as a principal source of mannitol. ▷Old English, via late Latin and Greek from Aramaic *mannā*, from Hebrew *mān*, corresponding to Arabic *mann*, denoting an exudation of the tamarisk *Tamarix mannifera*.

man·na ash ▸*n.* an ash tree that bears fragrant white flowers and exudes a sweet edible gum (manna) from its branches when they are damaged, native to southern Europe and southwestern Asia. • *Fraxinus ornus*, family Oleaceae.

Man·nar, Gulf of an inlet of the Indian Ocean that lies between northwestern Sri Lanka and the southern tip of India. It is south of Adam's Bridge, which separates it from the Palk Strait.

manned /mand/ ▸*adj.* (esp. of an aircraft or spacecraft) having a human crew: *a manned mission to Mars.*

man·ne·quin /ˈmanikən/ ▸*n.* a dummy used to display clothes in a store window. ■ *chiefly historical* a young woman or man employed to show clothes to customers. ▷mid 18th cent.: from French, from Dutch (see MANIKIN).

USAGE In English usage, the word **mannequin** occurs much more frequently than any of its relatives **manakin**, **manikin**, and **mannikin**. The source for all four words is the Middle Dutch *mannekijn* (modern Dutch *manneken*) 'little man,' 'little doll.'

Mannequin is the French spelling from this Dutch source. One of its French meanings, dating from about 1830, is 'a young woman hired to model clothes' (even though the word means 'little *man*'). This sense—still current, but rare in English—first appeared in 1902. The far more common sense of 'a life-size jointed figure or dummy used for displaying clothes' is first recorded in 1939.

Manikin has had the sense 'little man' (often contemptuous) since the mid 16th century, when it was sometimes spelled *manakin* (as it appeared in Shakespeare's *Twelfth Night*, as a term of abuse). **Manikin's** sense of 'an artist's lay figure' also dates from the mid 16th century (first recorded with the Dutch spelling *manneken*).

To confuse matters further, in modern usage the words **manakin** and **mannikin** refer to birds of two unrelated families. The history of these bird names is somewhat obscure. **Manakin** may have come from the Portuguese *manaquim* 'mannikin,' a variant of *manequim* 'mannequin.' **Mannikin** may have come directly from the source of the Portuguese words, the Middle Dutch *mannekijn*.

man·ner /ˈmanər/ ▸*n.* **1** a way in which a thing is done or happens: *taking notes in an unobtrusive manner.* ■ a style in literature or art: *a dramatic poem* **in the manner of** *Goethe.* ■ *Grammar* a semantic category of adverbs and adverbials that answer the question "how?": *an adverb of manner.* ■ (**manner of**) *chiefly poetic/literary* a kind or sort of: *what manner of man is he?* **2** a person's outward bearing or way of behaving toward others: *his arrogance and pompous manner | a shy and diffident manner.* **3** (**manners**) polite or well-bred social behavior: *didn't your mother teach you any manners?* ■ social behavior or habits: *Tim apologized for his son's bad manners.* ■ the way a motor vehicle handles or performs: *it impressed us with its distinctly unvanlike road manners.* ▷Middle English: from Old French *maniere*, based on Latin *manuarius* 'of the hand,' from *manus* 'hand.' **—man·ner·less** *adj.*
▸*PHRASES* □ **all manner of** many different kinds of: *they accuse me of all manner of evil things.* □ **by no** (or **any**) **manner of means** see MEANS. □ **in a manner of speaking** in some sense; so to speak. □ **to the manner born** naturally at ease in a specified job or situation: *she slipped into a more courtly role as if to the manner born.* [with allusion to Shakespeare's *Hamlet* I. iv. 17.] ■ destined by birth to follow a custom or way of life.

man·nered /ˈmanərd/ ▸*adj.* **1** [in *combination*] behaving in a specified way: *pleasant-mannered.* **2** (of a writer, artist, or artistic style) marked by idiosyncratic mannerisms; artificial, stilted, and overelaborate in delivery: *inane dialogue and mannered acting.*

man·ner·ism /ˈmanəˌrizəm/ ▸*n.* **1** a habitual gesture or way of speaking or behaving; an idiosyncrasy: *learning the great man's speeches and studying his mannerisms.* ■ *Psychiatry* an ordinary gesture or expression that becomes abnormal through exaggeration or repetition. **2** excessive or self-conscious use of a distinctive style in art, literature, or music: *he seemed deliberately to be stripping his art of mannerism.* **3** (**Mannerism**) a style of 16th-century Italian art preceding the Baroque, characterized by unusual effects of scale, lighting, and perspective, and the use of bright, often lurid colors. It is particularly associated with the work of Pontormo, Vasari,and the later Michelangelo. **—man·ner·ist** *n.* & *adj.* **—man·ner·is·tic** /ˌmanəˈristik/ *adj.*

man·ner·ly /ˈmanərlē/ ▸*adj.* well-mannered; polite. **—man·ner·li·ness** /-lēnis/ *n.*

Mann·heim /ˈmanˌhīm; ˈmän-/ an industrial port at the confluence of the Rhine and the Neckar rivers in Baden-Württemberg, in southwestern Germany; pop. 315,000.

man·ni·kin /ˈmanikən/ ▸*n.* **1** a small waxbill of the Old World tropics, typically having brown, black, and white plumage and popular as a pet bird. Compare with MANAKIN. • Genus *Lonchura*, family Estrildidae: many species. **2** variant spelling of MANIKIN.

USAGE See **usage** at MANNEQUIN.

man·nish /ˈmanisʜ/ ▸*adj.* *often derogatory* (of a woman) having characteristics that are stereotypically associated with men and can be considered unbecoming in a woman. See note at MALE. ▷Old English *mennisc* 'human' (see MAN, -ISH[1]). The current sense dates from late Middle English. **—man·nish·ly** *adv.* **—man·nish·ness** *n.*

man·ni·tol /ˈmanəˌtôl; -ˌtäl/ ▸*n.* *Chemistry* a colorless sweet-tasting crystalline compound that is found in many plants and is used in various foods and medical products. • An alcohol; chem. formula: $CH_2OH(CHOH)_4CH_2OH$. ▷late 19th cent.: from *mannite*, in the same sense, + -OL.

man·nose /ˈmanˌōs; -ˌōz/ ▸*n.* *Chemistry* a sugar of the hexose class that occurs as a component of many natural polysaccharides. ▷late 19th cent.: from *mannite* 'mannitol' + -OSE[2].

man·ny /ˈmanē/ ▸*n.* (*pl.* **-nies**) a male nanny: *my husband would like us to hire a manny for our two boys.* ▷1990s: blend of *man* and *nanny*.

Ma·no /ˈmänō/ a river of West Africa. It rises in northwestern Liberia and flows southwest to the Atlantic Ocean, forming for part of its length the boundary between Liberia and Sierra Leone.

ma·no a ma·no /ˌmänō ä ˈmänō/ (also **ma·no-a-ma·no**) *informal* ▸*adj.* (of combat or competition) hand-to-hand: *the exhilaration of the mano-a-mano battle.*
▸*adv.* in the manner of hand-to-hand combat or a duel: *they want to settle this mano a mano.*
▸*n.* (*pl.* **-nos**) an intense fight or contest between two adversaries; a duel: *a real courtroom mano-a-mano.* ▷Spanish, 'hand-to-hand.'

ma·noeu·vre ▸*n.* & *v.* British spelling of MANEUVER.

man-of-war (also **man-o'-war**) ▸*n.* (*pl.* **men-of-war** also **men-o'-war**) *historical* an armed sailing ship. ■ (also **man-o'-war bird**) another term for FRIGATE BIRD. ■ short for PORTUGUESE MAN-OF-WAR.

man-of-war fish ▸*n.* a fish (*Nomeus gronovii*, family Nomeidae) of tropical oceans that is often found among the tentacles of the Portuguese man-of-war, where it sometimes browses on the host's body and tentacles.

ma·nom·e·ter /məˈnämətər/ ▸*n.* an instrument for measuring the pressure acting on a column of fluid, esp. one with a U-shaped tube of liquid in which a difference in the pressures acting in the two arms of the tube causes the liquid to reach different heights in the two arms. ▷mid 18th cent.: from French *manomètre*, from Greek *manos* 'thin' + *-mètre* '(instrument) measuring.' **—man·o·met·ric** /ˌmanəˈmetrik/ *adj.* **—man·o·met·ri·cal·ly** /ˌmanəˈmetrik(ə)lē/ *adv.* **—ma·nom·e·try** /-trē/ *n.*

ma non trop·po /ˌmä ˌnôn ˈtrôpō/ ▸*adv.* see TROPPO[1].

man·or /ˈmanər/ ▸*n.* (also **manor house**) a large country house with lands; the principal house of a landed estate. ■ *chiefly historical* (esp. in England and Wales) a unit of land, originally a feudal lordship, consisting of a lord's demesne and lands rented to tenants. ■ *historical* (in North America) an estate or district leased to tenants, esp. one granted by royal charter in a British colony or by the Dutch governors of what is now New York. ▷Middle English: from Anglo-Norman French *maner* 'dwelling,' from Latin *manere* 'remain.' **—ma·no·ri·al** /məˈnôrēəl/ *adj.*

man page ▸*n.* *Computing* a document forming part of the online documentation of a computer system. ▷short for *manual page*.

man·pow·er /ˈmanˌpouər/ ▸*n.* the number of people working or available for work or service: *the police had only limited manpower.*

man·qué /mäNG'kā/ ▸*adj.* [*postpositive*] having failed to become what one might have been; unfulfilled: *a starlet manqué.* ▷late 18th cent.: French, past participle of *manquer* 'to lack.'

Man Ray see **RAY**[2].

man·rope /'man,rōp/ ▸*n.* a safety rope on a ship's deck, esp. a rope on the side of a ship's gangway or ladder for support in walking or climbing.

Mans, Le /'mäN, lə/ see **LE MANS**.

man·sard /'man,särd; -sərd/ ▸*n.* (also **mansard roof**) a roof that has four sloping sides, each of which becomes steeper halfway down. ■ a story or apartment under a mansard roof. ■ *Brit.* another term for **GAMBREL**. ▷mid 18th cent.: from French *mansarde,* named after F. **MANSART**.

Man·sart /män'sär(t)/, François (1598–1666), French architect. He rebuilt part of the château of Blois, which incorporated the type of roof now named after him.

manse /mans/ ▸*n.* the house occupied by a minister of a Presbyterian church. ■ a large stately house; a mansion. ▷late 15th cent. (denoting the principal house of an estate): from medieval Latin *mansus* 'house, dwelling,' from *manere* 'remain.'

man·serv·ant /'man,sərvənt/ ▸*n.* (*pl.* **men·ser·vants** /'men,sərvənts/) a male servant.

Mans·field[1] /'manz,fēld/ an industrial city in north central Ohio; pop. 50,627.

Mans·field[2], Katherine (1888–1923), New Zealand short-story writer; pseudonym of *Kathleen Mansfield Beauchamp Murray.* Her stories range from extended impressionistic evocations of family life to short sketches. Notable collections: *In a German Pension* (1911) and *Bliss* (1920).

-manship ▸*suffix* (forming nouns) denoting skill in a subject or activity: *marksmanship.*

man·sion /'manSHən/ ▸*n.* a large, impressive house. ■ a manor house (see **MANOR**). ■ [in *names*] *Brit.* a large building divided into apartments: *Carlyle Mansions.* ▷late Middle English (denoting the chief residence of a lord): via Old French from Latin *mansio(n-)* 'place where someone stays,' from *manere* 'remain.'

man-sized (also **man-size**) ▸*adj.* of the size of a human being: *man-sized plants.* ■ large enough to occupy, suit, or satisfy a man: *a man-sized breakfast.* ■ formidable: *a man-size job.*

man·slaugh·ter /'man,slôtər/ ▸*n.* the crime of killing a human being without malice aforethought, or otherwise in circumstances not amounting to murder: *the defendant was convicted of manslaughter.*

Man·son[1] /'mansən/, Charles (1934–), U.S. cult leader. He founded a commune based on free love and complete subordination to him. In 1969, its members carried out a series of murders, including that of actress Sharon Tate (1943–69), for which he and some followers received the death sentence, which was later commuted to life imprisonment.

Man·son[2], Sir Patrick (1844–1922), Scottish physician; pioneer of tropical medicine. He established that elephantiasis was spread by the bite of a mosquito and suggested a similar role for the mosquito in the spread of malaria.

man·sue·tude /'manswi,to͞od; man'so͞o-ə-/ ▸*n. archaic* meekness; gentleness. ▷late Middle English: from Old French, or from Latin *mansuetudo,* from *mansuetus* 'gentle, tame,' from *manus* 'hand' + *suetus* 'accustomed.'

man·ta /'mantə/ ▸*n.* **1** (also **manta ray**) a devil ray that occurs in all tropical seas and may reach very great size. It is sometimes seen leaping high out of the water. • *Manta birostris,* family Mobulidae. **2** a rough-textured cotton fabric made and used in Spanish America. ■ a shawl made of this fabric. ▷late 17th cent.: from Latin American Spanish, literally 'large blanket.'

man·teau /man'tō/ ▸*n.* (*pl.* **-teaus** or **-teaux** /-'tōz/) *historical* a loose gown or cloak worn by women. ▷late 17th cent.: from French; compare with **MANTUA**.

Man·te·ca /man'tēkə/ a city in central California, in the San Joaquin Valley; pop. 40,773.

Man·te·gna /män'tānyə/, Andrea (1431–1506), Italian painter and engraver, noted esp. for his frescoes.

man·tel /'mantl/ (also **man·tle**) ▸*n.* a mantelpiece or mantelshelf. ▷mid 16th cent.: specialized use of **MANTLE**[1].

man·te·let /'mantlət; 'mantl-ət/ (also **mant·let**) ▸*n.* **1** *historical* a woman's short, loose, sleeveless cloak or shawl. **2** a bulletproof screen for a soldier. ▷late Middle English: from Old French *mantelet,* diminutive of *mantel* 'mantle.'

man·tel·let·ta /,mantl'etə/ ▸*n.* (*pl.* **-tel·let·tas** or **-tel·let·te** /-tl'etā/) a sleeveless vestment reaching to the knees, worn by cardinals, bishops, and other high-ranking Roman Catholic ecclesiastics. ▷mid 19th cent.: from Italian, from a diminutive of Latin *mantellum* 'mantle.'

man·tel·piece /'mantl,pēs/ (also **man·tle·piece**) ▸*n.* a structure of wood, marble, or stone above and around a fireplace. ■ a mantelshelf.

man·tel·shelf /'mantl,SHelf/ (also **man·tle·shelf**) ▸*n.* a shelf above a fireplace. ■ *Climbing* a projecting shelf or ledge of rock. ■ *Climbing* a move for climbing on such a ledge from below by pressing down on it with the hands to raise the upper body, enabling a foot or knee to reach the ledge.
▸*v.* [*intrans.*] *Climbing* perform a mantelshelf move.

man·tel·tree /'mantl,trē/ (also **man·tle·tree**) ▸*n.* a beam or arch across the opening of a fireplace, supporting the masonry above.

man·tic /'mantik/ ▸*adj. formal* of or relating to divination or prophecy. ▷mid 19th cent.: from Greek *mantikos,* from *mantis* 'prophet.'

-mantic ▸*comb. form* in adjectives corresponding to nouns ending in *-mancy* (such as *geomantic* corresponding to *geomancy*).

man·ti·core /'manti,kôr/ ▸*n.* a mythical beast typically depicted as having the body of a lion, the face of a man, and the sting of a scorpion. ▷late Middle English: from Old French, via Latin from Greek *mantikhōras,* corrupt reading in Aristotle for *martikhoras,* from an Old Persian word meaning 'man-eater.'

man·tid /'mantid/ ▸*n.* another term for **MANTIS**.

man·til·la /man'tē(y)ə; -'tilə/ ▸*n.* a lace or silk scarf worn by women over the hair and shoulders, esp. in Spain. ▷Spanish, diminutive of *manta* 'mantle.'

mantilla

man·tis /'mantis/ (also **pray·ing man·tis**) ▸*n.* (*pl.* same or **-tis·es**) a slender predatory insect related to the cockroach. It waits motionless for prey with its large spiky forelegs folded like hands in prayer. • Suborder Mantodea, order Dictyoptera: Mantidae and other families, and many species, including *Mantis religiosa,* introduced to America from southern Europe and now found commonly in the northeastern U.S. ▷mid 17th cent.: modern Latin, from Greek, literally 'prophet.'

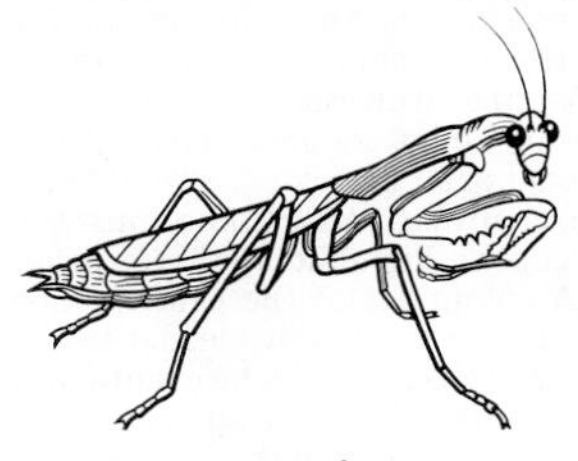
mantis

man·tis·sa /man'tisə/ ▸*n.* **1** *Mathematics* the part of a logarithm that follows the decimal point. **2** *Computing* the part of a floating-point number that represents the significant digits of that number, and that is multiplied by the base raised to the exponent to give the actual value of the number. ▷mid 17th cent.: from Latin, literally 'makeweight,' perhaps from Etruscan.

man·tis shrimp ▸*n.* a predatory marine crustacean with a pair of large spined front legs that resemble those of a mantis and are used for capturing prey. • Order Stomatopoda: many species, including the European *Squilla desmaresti.*

Man·tle /'mantl/, Mickey (Charles) (1931–95), U.S. baseball player. He played for the New York Yankees 1951–69. Baseball Hall of Fame (1974).

man·tle[1] /'mantl/ ▸*n.* **1** a loose sleeveless cloak or shawl, worn esp. by women. ■ *figurative* a covering of a specified sort: *the houses were covered with a thick mantle of snow.* ■ (also **gas mantle**) a fragile mesh cover fixed around a gas jet, kerosene wick, etc., to give an incandescent light when heated. ■ *Ornithology* a bird's back, scapulars, and wing coverts, esp. when of a distinctive color. ■ *Zoology* an outer or enclosing layer of tissue, esp. (in mollusks, cirripedes, and brachiopods) a fold of skin enclosing the viscera and secreting the substance that produces the shell. **2** an important role or responsibility that passes from one person to another: *the second son has now assumed his father's mantle.* [with allusion to the passing of Elijah's cloak (mantle) to Elisha (2 Kings 2:13).] **3** *Geology* the region of the earth's interior between the crust and the core, believed to consist of hot, dense silicate rocks (mainly peridotite). ■ the corresponding part of another planetary body: *the lunar mantle.*
▸*v.* **1** [*trans.*] *poetic/literary* clothe in or as if in a mantle; cloak or envelop: *heavy mists mantled the forested slopes.* ■ *archaic* (of blood) suffuse (the face): *a warm pink mounted to the girl's cheeks and mantled her brow.* ■ [*intrans.*] (of the face) glow with a blush: *her rich face mantling with emotion.* ■ [*intrans.*] *archaic* (of a liquid) become covered with a head or froth. **2** [*intrans.*] (of a bird of prey on the ground or on a perch) spread the wings and tail, esp. so as to cover captured prey. ▷Old English *mentel,* from Latin *mantellum* 'cloak'; reinforced in Middle English by Old French *mantel.*

man·tle[2] ▸*n.* variant spelling of **MANTEL**.

man·tle·piece ▸*n.* variant spelling of **MANTELPIECE**.

man·tle plume ▸*n.* see **PLUME**.

man·tle·shelf ▸*n.* variant spelling of **MANTELSHELF**.

mant·let /'mantlet/ ▸*n.* variant spelling of **MANTELET**.

man·tle·tree /'mantl,trē/ ▸*n.* variant spelling of **MANTELTREE**.

man·tling /'mantliNG; 'mantl-iNG/ ▸*n. Heraldry* a piece of ornamental drapery depicted issuing from a helmet and surrounding a shield. Compare with **LAMBREQUIN** (sense 2). ■ drapery of this kind. ▷late 16th cent.: from **MANTLE**[1] + **-ING**[1].

Man·toux test /man'to͞o / ▸*n. Medicine* a test for immunity to tuberculosis using intradermal injection of tuberculin. ▷1930s: named after Charles *Mantoux* (1877–1947), French physician.

man·tra /'mantrə; 'män-/ ▸*n.* (originally in Hinduism and Buddhism) a word or sound repeated to aid concentration in meditation. ■ a Vedic hymn. ■ a statement or slogan repeated frequently: *the environmental mantra that energy has for too long been too cheap.* ▷late 18th cent.: Sanskrit, literally 'instrument of thought,' from *man* 'think.' **—man·tric** /-trik/ *adj.*

man·trap /'man,trap/ ▸*n.* a trap for catching people, esp. trespassers or poachers.

man·tu·a /'manCHo͞oə/ ▸*n.* a woman's loose gown of a kind fashionable during the 17th and 18th centuries. ▷alteration of French *manteau.*

Man·u /'māno͞o; 'māno͞o/ the archetypal first man of Hindu mythology, survivor of the great flood and father of the human race.

man·u·al /'manyə(wə)l/ ▸*adj.* of or done with the hands: *manual dexterity | manual hauling of boats along the towpath.* ■ (of a machine or device) worked by hand, not automatically or electronically: *a manual typewriter.* ■ [*attrib.*] using or working with the hands: *a manual laborer.*
▸*n.* **1** a book of instructions, esp. for operating a machine or learning a subject; a handbook: *a computer manual | a training manual.* ■ a small book: *a pocket-sized manual of the artist's aphorisms.* ■ *historical* a book of the forms to be used by priests in the administration of the sacraments. **2** a thing operated or done by hand rather than automatically or electronically, in particular: ■ an organ keyboard played with the hands. ■ a vehicle with a manual transmission. ▷late Middle English: from Old French *manuel,* from (and later assimilated to) Latin *manualis,* from *manus* 'hand.' **—man·u·al·ly** *adv.*

man·u·al al·pha·bet ▸*n.* a set of sign-language symbols used in fingerspelling, in which different finger configurations correspond to letters of the alphabet.

man·u·al trans·mis·sion ▸*n.* an automotive transmission consisting of a system of interlocking gear wheels and a lever that enables the driver to shift gears manually.

ma·nu·bri·um /mə'n(y)o͞obrēəm/ ▸*n.* (*pl.* **-bri·a** /-brēə/ or **-bri·ums**) *Anatomy & Zoology* a handle-shaped projection or part, in particular: ■ the broad upper part of the sternum of mammals, with which the clavicles and first ribs articulate. ■ the tube that bears the mouth of a coelenterate. ▷mid 17th cent. (as a rare usage in the sense 'handle'): from Latin, 'haft.' **—ma·nu·bri·al** /-brēəl/ *adj.*

man·u·code /'manyə,kōd/ ▸*n.* a bird of paradise of which the male and female have similar blue-black plumage and breed as stable pairs. • Genus *Manucodia*, family Paradisaeidae: five species, in particular the **trumpet manucode** or trumpet bird (*M. keraudrenii*), the male of which has a loud trumpeting call. ▷mid 19th cent.: from French, from modern Latin *manucodiata* (used in the same sense from the mid 16th to 18th centuries), from Malay *manuk dewata* 'bird of the gods.'

Man·u·el·ine /man'wel,īn/ ▸*adj.* denoting a style of Portuguese architecture developed during the reign of Manuel I (1495–1521) and characterized by ornate elaborations of Gothic and Renaissance styles.

manuf. ▸*abbr.* ■ manufacture or manufacturer or manufacturing.

man·u·fac·to·ry /,manyə'fakt(ə)rē/ ▸*n.* (*pl.* **-ries**) *archaic* a factory. ▷early 17th cent. (denoting a manufactured article): from MANUFACTURE, on the pattern of *factory*.

man·u·fac·ture /,manyə'fakCHər/ ▸*n.* the making of articles on a large scale using machinery: *the manufacture of armored vehicles.* ■ [with *adj.*] a specified branch of industry: *the porcelain manufacture for which France became justly renowned.* ■ the production of a natural substance by a living thing: *the genetic blueprint for the manufacture of a protein.* ■ (**manufactures**) manufactured goods or articles: *exports and imports of manufactures.*
▸*v.* [*trans.*] **1** make (something) on a large scale using machinery: *a company that manufactured paint-by-number sets* | [as *adj.*] (**manufacturing**) *a manufacturing company.* ■ (of a living thing) produce (a substance) naturally. ■ make or produce (something abstract) in a merely mechanical way: [as *adj.*] (**manufactured**) *manufactured love songs.* **2** invent or fabricate (evidence or a story): *the tabloid industry that manufactures epochal discoveries out of thin air.* ▷mid 16th cent. (denoting something made by hand): from French (reformed by association with Latin *manu factum* 'made by hand'), from Italian *manifattura*. Sense 1 dates from the early 17th cent. **—man·u·fac·tur·a·bil·i·ty** /-,fakCHərə'bilətē/ *n.* **—man·u·fac·tur·a·ble** *adj.* **—man·u·fac·tur·er** *n.*

man·u·fac·tured home ▸*n.* (mainly in advertising) a mobile home.

man·u·fac·tured hous·ing ▸*n.* prefabricated houses that are constructed in a factory and then assembled at the building site in modular sections.

man·u·mat·ic /,manyə'matik/ ▸*n.* an automatic car transmission that enables the driver to shift through the gears manually. ▷1990s: blend of *manual* and *automatic*.

man·u·mit /,manyə'mit/ ▸*v.* (**-mit·ted, -mit·ting**) [*trans.*] *historical* release from slavery; set free. ▷late Middle English: from Latin *manumittere*, literally 'send forth from the hand,' from *manus* 'hand' + *mittere* 'send.' **—man·u·mis·sion** /-'misHən/ *n.* **—man·u·mit·ter** *n.*

ma·nure /mə'n(y)o͝or/ ▸*n.* animal dung used for fertilizing land. ■ any compost or artificial fertilizer.
▸*v.* [*trans.*] (often **be manured**) apply manure to (land): *the ground should be well dug and manured.* ▷late Middle English (as a verb in the sense 'cultivate (land)'): from Anglo-Norman French *mainoverer*, Old French *manouvrer* (see MANEUVER). The noun sense dates from the mid 16th cent.

ma·nus /'mānəs; 'mänəs/ ▸*n.* (*pl.* same) *chiefly Zoology* the terminal segment of a forelimb, corresponding to the hand and wrist in humans. ▷early 19th cent.: from Latin, 'hand.'

man·u·script /'manyə,skript/ ▸*n.* a book, document, or piece of music written by hand rather than typed or printed: *an illuminated manuscript.* ■ an author's text that has not yet been published: *preparing the final manuscript* | *her autobiography remained* **in manuscript**. ▷late 16th cent.: from medieval Latin *manuscriptus*, from *manu* 'by hand' + *scriptus* 'written' (past participle of *scribere*).

man·u·script pa·per ▸*n.* paper printed with staves for writing music on.

Ma·nu·ti·us, Aldus, see ALDUS MANUTIUS.

Manx /maNGks/ ▸*adj.* of or relating to the Isle of Man.
▸*n.* **1** the now extinct Goidelic language formerly spoken in the Isle of Man, still used for some ceremonial purposes. **2** (**the Manx**) the Manx people collectively. ▷from Old Norse, from Old Irish *Manu* 'Isle of Man' + *-skr* (equivalent of -ISH[1]). **—Manx·man** /-mən/ *n.* (*pl.* **-men**). **—Manx·wom·an** /-,wo͝omən/ *n.* (*pl.* **-wom·en**).

Manx cat ▸*n.* a cat of a breed having no tail or an extremely short one.

Manx shear·wa·ter ▸*n.* a dark-backed shearwater that nests on remote islands in the northeastern Atlantic, Mediterranean, and Hawaiian waters. • *Puffinus puffinus*, family Procellariidae.

man·y /'menē/ ▸*adj.* & *pron.* (**more** /môr/, **most** /mōst/) a large number of: [as *adj.*] *many people agreed with her* | [as *pron.*] *the solution to* **many of** *our problems* | *many think it is a new craze.*
▸*n.* [as *plural n.*] (**the many**) the majority of people: *music for the many.* ▷Old English *manig*, of Germanic origin; related to Dutch *menig* and German *manch*.
▸*PHRASES* □ **as many** the same number of: *changing his mind for the third time in as many months.* □ **a good** (or **great**) **many** a large number: *a good many of us.* □ **have one too many** *informal* become slightly drunk. □ **how many** used to ask what a particular quantity is: *how many books did you sell?* □ **many a** —— a large number of: *many a good man has been destroyed by booze.* □ **many's the** —— used to indicate that something happens often: *many's the night we've been wakened by that racket.*

man·y·fold /'menē,fōld/ ▸*adv.* by many times: *the problems would be multiplied manyfold.*
▸*adj.* involving multiplication by many times: *the manyfold increase in staffing levels.*

man·y-sid·ed ▸*adj.* having many sides or aspects: *the reasons for poor collaboration are complex and many-sided.* **—man·y-sid·ed·ness** *n.*

man·za·nil·la /,manzə'nē(y)ə/ ▸*n.* a pale, very dry Spanish sherry. ▷Spanish, literally 'chamomile' (because the flavor is said to be reminiscent of that of chamomile).

man·za·ni·ta /,manzə'nētə/ ▸*n.* an evergreen dwarf shrub related to the bearberry, native to California. • Genus *Arctostaphylos*, family Ericaceae: several species, in particular *A. manzanita*. ▷mid 19th cent.: from Spanish, diminutive of *manzana* 'apple.'

MAO ▸*Biochemistry abbr.* monoamine oxidase.

Mao /mou/ ▸*n.* [as *adj.*] denoting a jacket or suit of a plain style with a mandarin collar, associated with communist China: *dressed in a silver-gray Mao suit.* ▷1960s: by association with MAO ZEDONG.

MAOI ▸*abbr.* monoamine oxidase inhibitor.

Mao·ism /'mou,izəm/ ▸*n.* the communist doctrines of Mao Zedong as formerly practiced in China, having as a central idea permanent revolution and stressing the importance of the peasantry, of small-scale industry, and of agricultural collectivization. **—Mao·ist** *n.* & *adj.*

Ma·o·ri /'mourē/ ▸*n.* (*pl.* same or **-ris**) **1** a member of the aboriginal people of New Zealand. **2** the Polynesian language of this people.
▸*adj.* of or relating to the Maoris or their language. ▷the name in Maori.

mao-tai /'mou 'tī; 'dī/ ▸*n.* a strong sorghum-based liquor distilled in southwestern China. ▷named after a town in southwestern China.

Mao Ze·dong /'mou ,zə'dôNG/ (also **Mao Tse-tung** /,tsə 'to͝oNG; ,dzə 'do͝oNG/) (1893–1976), Chinese statesman; chairman of the Communist Party of the Chinese People's Republic 1949–76; head of state 1949–59. A cofounder of the Chinese Communist Party in 1921 and its effective leader from the time of the Long March (1934–35), he eventually defeated both the occupying Japanese and rival Kuomintang nationalist forces to create the People's Republic of China in 1949.

MAP ▸*abbr.* modified American plan (see AMERICAN PLAN).

map /map/ ▸*n.* **1** a diagrammatic representation of an area of land or sea showing physical features, cities, roads, etc.: *a street map* | *figurative expansion of the service sector is reshaping the map of employment.* ■ a two-dimensional representation of the positions of stars or other astronomical objects. ■ a diagram or collection of data showing the spatial arrangement or distribution of something over an area: *an electron density map.* ■ *Biology* a representation of the sequence of genes on a chromosome or of bases in a DNA or RNA molecule. ■ *Mathematics* another term for MAPPING. **2** *informal, dated* a person's face.
▸*v.* (**mapped, map·ping**) [*trans.*] represent (an area) on a map; make a map of: *inaccessible parts will be mapped from the air.* ■ record in detail the spatial distribution of (something): *the project to map the human genome.* ■ [*trans.*] associate (a group of elements or qualities) with an equivalent group, according to a particular formula or model: *the transformational rules map deep structures into surface structures.* ■ *Mathematics* associate each element of (a set) with an element of another set. ■ [*intrans.*] be associated or linked to something: *it is not obvious that the subprocesses of language will map onto individual brain areas.*
▸*phrasal v.* □ **map something out** plan a route or course of action in detail: *I mapped out a route over familiar country near home.* ▷early 16th cent.: from medieval Latin *mappa mundi*, literally 'sheet of the world,' from Latin *mappa* 'sheet, napkin' + *mundi* 'of the world' (genitive of *mundus*). **—map·less** *adj.* **—map·pa·ble** *adj.* **—map·per** *n.*
▸*PHRASES* □ **off the map** (of a place) very distant or remote: *just a hick town, right off the map.* □ **put something on the map** bring something to prominence: *the exhibition put Cubism on the map.* □ **wipe something off the map** obliterate something totally.

ma·ple /'māpəl/ ▸*n.* a tree or shrub with lobed leaves, winged fruits, and colorful autumn foliage, grown as an ornamental or for its timber or syrupy sap. • Genus *Acer*, family Aceraceae: many species, including the common European **field maple** (*A. campestre*), the North American **sugar maple** (*A. saccharum*), and the **Japanese maple** (*A. palmatum*), which has many cultivars. ■ the flavor of maple syrup or maple sugar. ▷Old English *mapel* (as the first element of *mapeltrēow*, *mapulder* 'maple tree'); used as an independent word from Middle English onward.

Ma·ple Grove a city in southeastern Minnesota, a northwestern suburb of Minneapolis; pop. 50,365.

ma·ple leaf ▸*n.* the leaf of the maple, used as an emblem of Canada.

ma·ple sug·ar ▸*n.* sugar produced by evaporating the sap of certain maples, esp. the sugar maple.

ma·ple syr·up ▸*n.* syrup produced from the sap of certain maples, esp. the sugar maple.

map·mak·er /'map,mākər/ ▸*n.* a cartographer. **—map·mak·ing** /-,mākiNG/ *n.*

Map·pa Mun·di /,mapə 'mo͝ondē/ a famous 13th-century map of the world, now in Hereford cathedral, England. The map is round and typical of similar maps of the time in that it depicts Jerusalem at its center. ▷from medieval Latin, literally 'sheet of the world.'

map·ping /'mapiNG/ ▸*n.* *Mathematics* & *Linguistics* an operation that associates each element of a given set (the domain) with one or more elements of a second set (the range).

map pro·jec·tion ▸*n.* see PROJECTION (sense 6).

map ref·er·ence ▸*n.* a set of numbers and letters specifying a location as represented on a map.

map tur·tle ▸*n.* a small North American freshwater turtle with bold patterns on the shell and head. • Genus *Graptemys*, family Emydidae: several species, in particular *G. geographica*.

Ma·pu·che /mə'po͝oCHē/ ▸*n.* (*pl.* same or **-ches**) **1** a member of an American Indian people of central Chile and adjacent parts of Argentina, noted for their resistance to colonial Spanish and later Chilean domination. **2** the Araucanian language of this people.
▸*adj.* relating to or denoting this people or their language. ▷the name in Mapuche, from *mapu* 'land' + *che* 'people.'

Ma·pu·to /mə'po͞otō/ the capital and chief port of Mozambique, on the Indian Ocean in the southern part of the country; pop. 1,098,000. Former name (until 1976) LOURENÇO MARQUES.

ma·quette /ma'ket/ ▸*n.* a sculptor's small preliminary model or sketch. ▷early 20th cent.: from French, from Italian *machietta*, diminutive of *macchia* 'spot.'

ma·qui·la /mə'kēlə/ ▸*n.* another term for MAQUILADORA.

ma·qui·la·do·ra /,makilə'dôrə/ ▸*n.* a factory in Mexico run by a foreign company and exporting its products to the country of that company. ▷Mexican Spanish, from *maquilar* 'assemble.'

ma·quil·lage /,mäkē'(y)äzH/ ▸*n.* makeup; cosmetics. ▷French, from *maquiller* 'to make up,' from Old French *masquiller* 'to stain.'

ma·quis /mä'kē/ ▸*n.* (*pl.* same) **1** (**the Maquis**) the French resistance movement during the German occupation (1940–45). ■ a member of this movement. **2** dense scrub vegetation consisting of hardy evergreen shrubs and small trees, characteristic of coastal regions in the Mediterranean. ▷early 19th cent. (sense 2): from French, 'brushwood,' from Corsican Italian *macchia*.

ma·qui·sard /,mäkē'zär/ ▸*n.* a member of the Maquis.

mar /mär/ ▸*v.* (**marred, mar·ring**) [*trans.*] impair the appearance of; disfigure: *no wrinkles marred her face.* ■ impair the quality of; spoil: *violence marred a number of New Year celebrations.* ▷Old English *merran* 'hinder, damage,' of Germanic origin; probably related to Dutch *marren* 'loiter.'

Mar. ▸*abbr.* March.

mar·a·bou /ˈmarəˌbo͞o/ ▸*n.* (also **marabou stork**) **1** a large African stork with a massive bill and large neck pouch, feeding mainly by scavenging. • *Leptoptilos crumeniferus*, family Ciconiidae. ■ down from the wing or tail of the marabou used as a trimming for hats or clothing, or on a fishing lure. **2** raw silk that can be dyed without being separated from the gum. ▷early 19th cent.: from French, from Arabic *murābiṭ* 'holy man' (see also MARABOUT), the stork being regarded as holy.

mar·a·bout /ˈmarəˌbo͞ot/ ▸*n.* **1** a Muslim hermit or monk, esp. in North Africa. ■ a shrine marking the burial place of a Muslim hermit or monk. **2** variant spelling of MARABOU. ▷early 17th cent.: via French and Portuguese from Arabic *murābiṭ* 'holy man.'

Mar·a·cai·bo /ˌmarəˈkībō/ a city and port in northwestern Venezuela, situated on the channel that links the Gulf of Venezuela with Lake Maracaibo; pop. 1,401,000.

Ma·ra·cai·bo, Lake a large lake in northwestern Venezuela, linked by a narrow channel to the Gulf of Venezuela and the Caribbean Sea.

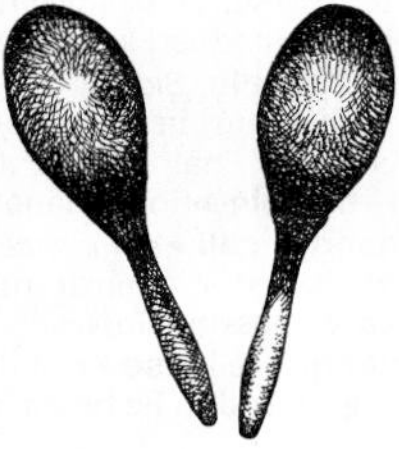
maracas

ma·rac·as /məˈräkəz/ ▸*plural n.* a pair of hollow clublike gourd or gourd-shaped containers filled with beans, pebbles, or similar objects, shaken as a percussion instrument. ▷early 17th cent.: from Portuguese *maracá*, from Tupi.

Ma·ra·do·na /ˌmärəˈdônə/, Diego (Armando) (1960–), Argentine soccer player. He captained the Argentine team that won the World Cup in 1986 and aroused controversy when his apparent handball scored a goal in the quarterfinal match against England.

mar·ag·ing steel /ˈmärˌājiNG/ ▸*n.* a steel alloy, containing up to 25 percent nickel and other metals, strengthened by a process of slow cooling and age hardening. ▷1960s: *maraging* from *mar-* (abbreviation of MARTENSITE, because the process involves conversion of austenite to martensite) + *aging* from the verb AGE.

Ma·ra·ñón /ˌmärəˈnyōn/ a river in northern Peru that rises in the Andes and forms one of the principal headwaters of the Amazon River.

ma·ran·ta /məˈrantə/ ▸*n.* a tropical American plant of a genus that includes the prayer plant and the arrowroot. • Genus *Maranta*, family Marantaceae. ■ a calathea. ▷modern Latin, named after Bartollomeo *Maranta*, 16th-cent. Italian herbalist.

mar·a·schi·no /ˌmarəˈSHēˌnō; -ˈskē-/ ▸*n.* (*pl.* **-nos**) a strong, sweet liqueur made from a variety of small bitter cherries. ■ a maraschino cherry. ▷Italian, from *marasca* (the name of the cherry), from *amaro* 'bitter,' from Latin *amarus*.

mar·a·schi·no cher·ry ▸*n.* a cherry preserved in maraschino or maraschino-flavored syrup.

ma·ras·mus /məˈrazməs/ ▸*n.* *Medicine* severe undernourishment causing an infant's or child's weight to be significantly low for their age (e.g., below 60 percent of normal). ▷mid 17th cent.: modern Latin, from Greek *marasmos* 'withering,' from *marainein* 'wither.' —**ma·ras·mic** /-mik/ *adj.*

Ma·rat /mäˈrä/, Jean Paul (1743–93), French revolutionary and journalist. A virulent critic of the moderate Girondists, he was instrumental (with Danton and Robespierre) in their fall from power in 1793. He was murdered in his bath by Girondin supporter Charlotte Corday

Ma·ra·tha /məˈrätə/ (also **Mah·rat·ta**) ▸*n.* a member of the princely and military castes of the former Hindu kingdom of Maharashtra in central India. ▷via Hindi from Sanskrit *Mahārāṣṭra* 'great kingdom.'

Ma·ra·thi /məˈrätē/ (also **Mah·rat·ti**) ▸*n.* the Indic language of the Marathas, spoken by about 60 million people in Maharashtra and elsewhere.

mar·a·thon /ˈmarəˌTHän/ ▸*n.* a long-distance running race, strictly one of 26 miles and 385 yards (42.195 km). ■ [usu. with *adj.*] a long-lasting or difficult task or operation of a specified kind: *the last leg of an interview marathon that began this summer.* ■ [as *adj.*] of great duration or distance; very long: *marathon workdays.* ▷late 19th cent.: from *Marathōn* in Greece, the scene of a victory over the Persians in 490 BC; the modern race is based on the tradition that a messenger ran from Marathon to Athens (22 miles) with the news. The original account by Herodotus told of the messenger Pheidippides running 150 miles from Athens to Sparta before the battle, seeking help. —**mar·a·thon·er** *n.*

ma·raud /məˈrôd/ ▸*v.* [*intrans.*] [often as *adj.*] (**marauding**) roam in search of things to steal or people to attack: *marauding gangs of looters.* ■ [*trans.*] raid and plunder (a place). ▷late 17th cent.: from French *marauder*, from *maraud* 'rogue.' —**ma·raud·er** *n.*

mar·a·ve·di /ˌmarəˈvādē/ ▸*n.* (*pl.* **-dis**) a medieval Spanish copper coin and monetary unit. ▷Spanish, from Arabic *murābiṭīn* 'holy men,' a name applied to the North African Berber rulers of Muslim Spain, from the late 11th cent. to 1145.

Mar·a·vich /ˈmarəˌviCH/, Pete (1947–88), U.S. basketball player; known as **Pistol Pete**. He played for the Atlanta Hawks 1970–74, the New Orleans Jazz (Utah Jazz from 1979) 1974–1980, and the Boston Celtics briefly in 1980. Basketball Hall of Fame (1987).

Mar·bel·la /märˈbāə/ a resort town on the Costa del Sol of southern Spain, in Andalusia; pop. 81,000.

mar·ble /ˈmärbəl/ ▸*n.* **1** a hard crystalline metamorphic form of limestone, typically white with mottlings or streaks of color, that is capable of taking a polish and is used in sculpture and architecture. ■ used in similes and comparisons with reference to the smoothness, hardness, or color of marble: *her shoulders were as white as marble.* ■ a marble sculpture. **2** a small ball of colored glass or similar material used as a toy. ■ (**marbles**) [treated as *sing.*] a game in which such balls are rolled along the ground. **3** (**one's marbles**) *informal* one's mental faculties: *I thought she'd **lost her marbles**, asking a question like that.*
▸*v.* [*trans.*] stain or streak (something) so that it looks like variegated marble: *the low stone walls were marbled with moss and lichen.* ▷Middle English: via Old French (variant of *marbre*) from Latin *marmor*, from Greek *marmaros* 'shining stone,' associated with *marmairein* 'to shine.' —**mar·bler** *n.* —**mar·bly** /-blē; -bəlē/ *adj.*
▸*PHRASE* □ **pick up one's marbles and go home** *informal* withdraw petulantly from an activity after having suffered a setback: *he doesn't have the guts to take a bad defeat, and is now picking up his marbles and going home.*

mar·ble cake ▸*n.* a cake with a streaked appearance, made of light and dark (esp. chocolate) batter.

mar·bled /ˈmärbəld/ ▸*adj.* having a streaked and patterned appearance like that of variegated marble. ■ (of meat) streaked with alternating layers or swirls of lean and fat.

Mar·ble·head /ˈmärbəlˌhed/ a coastal town in northeastern Massachusetts, a noted yachting and fishing port; pop. 19,971.

mar·ble·ize /ˈmärbəˌlīz/ ▸*v.* [*trans.*] give a marblelike variegated finish to (an object or material): [as *adj.*] (**marbleized**) *an old financial ledger with a marbleized cover.*

mar·bling /ˈmärbəliNG/ ▸*n.* coloring or marking that resembles variegated marble. ■ streaks of fat in lean meat.

Mar·burg /ˈmärˌbərg/ **1** a city in the state of Hesse in west central Germany; pop. 71,000. It was the scene in 1529 of a debate between German and Swiss theologians, notably Martin Luther and Ulrich Zwingli, on the doctrine of consubstantiation. **2** German name for MARIBOR.

Mar·burg dis·ease ▸*n.* an acute, often fatal, form of hemorrhagic fever. It is caused by a filovirus (**Marburg virus**) that normally lives in African monkeys. Also called GREEN MONKEY DISEASE.

marc /märk/ ▸*n.* the refuse of grapes or other fruit that has been pressed for winemaking. ■ an alcoholic spirit distilled from this. ▷early 17th cent.: from French, from *marcher* in the early sense 'to tread or trample.'

Mar·can /ˈmärkən/ (also **Mar·kan**) ▸*adj.* of or relating to St. Mark or the Gospel ascribed to him.

mar·ca·site /ˈmärkəˌsīt/ ▸*n.* a semiprecious stone consisting of pyrite. ■ a bronze-yellow mineral consisting of iron disulfide but differing from pyrite in typically forming aggregates of tabular crystals. ■ a piece of polished steel or a similar metal cut as a gem. ▷late Middle English: from medieval Latin *marcasita*, from Arabic *marḳašīṯa*, from Persian.

mar·ca·to /märˈkäˌtō/ ▸*adv.* & *adj.* *Music* (esp. as a direction) played with emphasis. ▷Italian, 'marked, accented,' of Germanic origin.

Mar·ceau /märˈsō/, Marcel (1923–), French mime artist. He is known for appearing as the white-faced Bip, a character he developed from the French Pierrot character.

mar·cel /märˈsel/ *dated* ▸*n.* (also **mar·cel wave**) a deep artificial wave in the hair.
▸*v.* (**-celled**, **-cel·ling**) [*trans.*] give such a wave to (hair). ▷late 19th cent.: named after *Marcel* Grateau (1852–1936), the Parisian hairdresser who invented it.

mar·ces·cent /märˈsesənt/ ▸*adj.* *Botany* (of leaves or fronds) withering but remaining attached to the stem. ▷early 18th cent.: from Latin *marcescent-* 'beginning to wither,' from *marcere* 'wither.' —**mar·ces·cence** *n.*

March[1] /märCH/ ▸*n.* the third month of the year, in the northern hemisphere usually considered the first month of spring: *the work was completed in March* | [as *adj.*] *the March issue of the magazine.* ▷Middle English: from an Old French dialect variant of *marz*, from Latin *Martius (mensis)* '(month) of Mars.'

March[2], Fredric (1897–1975), U.S. actor; born *Ernest Frederick McIntyre Bickel*. He starred in movies such as *Dr. Jekyll and Mr. Hyde* (Academy Award, 1932), *The Best Years of Our Lives* (Academy Award, 1946), *Inherit the Wind* (1960), and *Seven Days in May* (1964).

march[1] /märCH/ ▸*v.* [*intrans.*] walk in a military manner with a regular measured tread: *three companies of soldiers marched around the field.* ■ walk or proceed quickly and with determination: *without a word she marched from the room.* ■ [*trans.*] force (someone) to walk somewhere quickly: *she gripped Rachel's arm and marched her out through the doors.* ■ walk along public roads in an organized procession to protest about something: *antigovernment protesters marched today through major cities* | *they planned to **march on** Baton Rouge.* ■ *figurative* (of something abstract) proceed or advance inexorably: *time marches on.*
▸*n.* [usu. in *sing.*] an act or instance of marching: *the relieving force was more than a day's march away.* ■ a piece of music composed to accompany marching or with a rhythmic character suggestive of marching. ■ a procession as a protest or demonstration: *a protest march.* ■ *figurative* the progress or continuity of something abstract that is considered to be moving inexorably onward: *Marx's theory of the inevitable march of history.* ▷late Middle English: from French *marcher* 'to walk' (earlier 'to trample'), of uncertain origin.
▸*PHRASES* □ **march to (the beat of) a different drummer** *informal* consciously adopt a different approach or attitude from the majority of people; be unconventional. □ **on the march** marching: *the army was on the march at last.*

march[2] ▸*n.* (usu. **Marches**) a frontier or border area between two countries or territories, esp. between England and Wales or (formerly) England and Scotland: *the Welsh Marches.* ■ (**the Marches**) a region of east central Italy, between the Apennines and the Adriatic Sea; capital, Ancona. Italian name **MARCHE**.
▸*v.* [*intrans.*] (**march with**) *rare* (of a country, territory, or estate) have a common frontier with. ▷Middle English: from Old French *marche* (noun), *marchir* (verb), of Germanic origin; related to MARK[1].

Mar·chand /märˈSHänd/, Nancy (1928–2000), U.S. actress. She was noted for her role in the television drama "Marty" (1953) and for the parts she played on the television series "Lou Grant" (1977–82) and "The Sopranos" (1999–2000). She also appeared in movies.

mar·chands de vin /märˈSHän də ˈvaN/ ▸a French wine sauce sauce served hot or cold to accompany grilled or roasted meat. ▷French 'wine merchants.'

march·er[1] /ˈmärCHər/ ▸*n.* a person who marches, esp. one taking part in a protest march.

march·er[2] ▸*n.* *chiefly historical* an inhabitant of a frontier or border district.

mar·che·sa /märˈkāzə/ ▸*n.* (*pl.* **-che·se** /-ˈkāzā/) an Italian marchioness. ▷Italian, feminine of **MARCHESE**.

mar·che·se /märˈkāzā/ ▸*n.* (*pl.* **-che·si** /-ˈkāzē/) an Italian marquis. ▷Italian.

March hare ▸*n.* *informal* a brown hare in the breeding season, noted for its leaping, boxing, and chasing in circles.
▸*PHRASE* □ (**as**) **mad as a March hare** (of a person) completely mad or irrational; crazy.

march·ing or·der ▸*n.* *Military* equipment for marching: *they stood before their company commander dressed in full marching order.*

march·ing or·ders ▸*plural n.* instructions from a superior officer for troops to depart. ■ *informal* a

Pronunciation Key ə *ago*; ər *over*; ˈə or ˌə *up*; ˈər or ˌər *fur*; a *hat*; ā *rate*; ä *car*; CH *chew*; e *let*; ē *see*; e(ə)r *air*; i *fit*; ī *by*; i(ə)r *ear*; NG *sing*; ō *go*; ô *for*; oi *boy*; o͝o *good*; o͞o *goo*; ou *out*; SH *she*; TH *thin*; T͟H *then*; (h)w *why*; ZH *vision*

dismissal or sending off: *the ref called me over and gave me my marching orders.*

mar·chion·ess /ˈmärsH(ə)nəs/ ▸*n.* the wife or widow of a marquess. ■ a woman holding the rank of marquess in her own right. ▷late 16th cent.: from medieval Latin *marchionissa*, feminine of *marchio(n-)* 'ruler of a border territory,' from *marcha* 'march' (see MARCH2).

March Mad·ness ▸*n. informal* the time of the annual NCAA college basketball tournament, generally throughout the month of March.

march·pane /ˈmärcH,pān/ ▸*n.* archaic spelling of MARZIPAN.

Mar·ci·a·no /,märsēˈänō; -ˈanō/, Rocky (1923–69), U.S. heavyweight boxing champion; born *Rocco Francis Marchegiano*. He became world heavyweight champion in 1952 and successfully defended his title six times until he retired, undefeated, in 1956.

Mar·co·ni /märˈkōnē/, Guglielmo (1874–1937), Italian electrical engineer; the father of radio. In 1912, Marconi produced a continuously oscillating wave, essential for the transmission of sound. He went on to develop shortwave transmission over long distances. Nobel Prize for Physics (1909, shared with Carl Braun).

Mar·co Po·lo /ˈmärkō ˈpōlō/ (*c.*1254–*c.*1324), Italian traveler. With his father and uncle he traveled to China and the court of Kublai Khan via central Asia (1271–75). He eventually returned home (1292–95) via Sumatra, India, and Persia. His account of his travels spurred the European quest for the riches of the East.

Mar·cos /ˈmär,kōs/, Ferdinand (Edralin) (1917–89), president of the Philippines 1965–86. Amid charges of corruption and political intrigue he was unable to secure his 1986 reelection and was forced into exile after a government takeover in 1986 by a front led by Corazon Aquino, wife of Benigno Aquino (1932–83), who had been assassinated by Marcos forces.

Mar·cus Au·re·li·us /ˈmärkəs ôˈrēlēəs; ôˈrēlyəs/ see AURELIUS.

Mar·cu·se /märˈko͞ozə/, Herbert (1898–1979), U.S. philosopher, born in Germany. A member of the Frankfurt School, he argued in *Soviet Marxism* (1958) that revolutionary change can come only from alienated elites such as students.

Mar del Pla·ta /,mär dəl ˈplätə/ a fishing port and resort in Argentina, on the Atlantic coast south of Buenos Aires; pop. 520,000.

Mar·di Gras /ˈmärdē ,grä/ ▸*n.* a carnival held in some countries on Shrove Tuesday, most famously in New Orleans. ▷French, literally 'fat Tuesday,' alluding to the last day of feasting before the fast and penitence of Lent.

Mar·duk /ˈmär,do͝ok/ *Babylonian Mythology* the chief god of Babylon, who became lord of the gods of heaven and earth after conquering Tiamat, the monster of primeval chaos.

Mare, Walter de la, see DE LA MARE.

mare1 /me(ə)r/ ▸*n.* the female of a horse or other equine animal. ▷Old English *mearh* 'horse,' *mere* 'mare,' from a Germanic base with cognates in Celtic languages meaning 'stallion.' The sense 'male horse' died out at the end of the Middle English period.

ma·re2 /ˈmärā/ ▸*n.* (*pl.* **ma·ri·a** /ˈmärēə/) *Astronomy* a large, level basalt plain on the surface of the moon, appearing dark by contrast with highland areas: [in *names*] *Mare Imbrium.* ▷mid 19th cent.: special use of Latin *mare* 'sea'; these areas were once thought to be seas.

ma·re clau·sum /,märā ˈklousəm; ˈklô-/ ▸*n.* (*pl.* **ma·ri·a clau·sa** /,märēə ˈklousə; ˈklô-/) *Law* the sea under the jurisdiction of a particular country. ▷Latin, 'closed sea.'

Ma·rek's dis·ease /ˈmariks; ˈmär- / ▸*n.* an infectious disease of poultry caused by a herpesvirus that attacks nerves and causes paralysis or initiates widespread tumor formation. ▷1960s: named after Josef *Marek* (died 1952), Hungarian veterinary surgeon.

ma·re li·be·rum /,märā ˈlēbə,ro͝om/ ▸*n.* (*pl.* **ma·ri·a li·be·ra** /,märēə ˈlēbərə/) *Law* the sea open to all nations. ▷Latin, literally 'free sea.'

ma·rem·ma /məˈremə/ ▸*n.* (*pl.* **-rem·me** /-ˈremē/) (esp. in Italy) an area of low, marshy land near a seashore. ▷mid 19th cent.: Italian, from Latin *maritima*, feminine of *maritimus* (see MARITIME).

Ma·ren·go /məˈreNGgō/ ▸*adj.* [*postpositive*] (of chicken or veal) sautéed in oil, served with a tomato sauce, and traditionally garnished with eggs and crayfish: *chicken Marengo.* ▷named after the village of Marengo in northern Italy, scene of a battle in 1800 in which the French were victorious and after which the dish is said to have been served to Napoleon.

mare's nest ▸*n.* **1** a complex and difficult situation; a muddle: *your desk is usually a mare's nest.* **2** an illusory discovery: *the mare's nest of perfect safety.* ▷late 16th cent.: formerly in the phrase *to have found* (or *spied*) *a mare's nest* (i.e., something that does not exist), used in the sense 'to have discovered something amazing.'

mare's tail ▸*n.* **1** a widely distributed water plant with whorls of narrow leaves around a tall stout stem. • *Hippuris vulgaris*, family Haloragaceae. **2** (**mare's tails**) long straight streaks of cirrus cloud.

Mar·fan's syn·drome /ˈmärfənz; märˈfäNz / (also **Mar·fan syn·drome**) ▸*n. Medicine* a hereditary disorder of connective tissue, resulting in abnormally long and thin digits and also frequently in optical and cardiovascular defects. ▷1930s: named after Antonin B. J. *Marfan* (1858–1942), French pediatrician.

marg. ▸*abbr.* ■ margin or marginal.

Mar·ga·ret, Princess /ˈmärg(ə)rət/, Margaret Rose (1930–2002), member of the British royal family; the only sister of Elizabeth II.

Mar·ga·ret, St. (*c.*1046–93), Scottish queen; wife of Malcolm III. She exerted a strong influence over royal policy during her husband's reign and was instrumental in the reform of the Scottish Church. Feast day, November 16.

mar·ga·rine /ˈmärjərən/ ▸*n.* a butter substitute made from vegetable oils or animal fats. ▷late 19th cent.: from French, from Greek *margaron* 'pearl' (because of the luster of the crystals of margaric acid) + -INE4.

Mar·ga·ri·ta /,märgəˈrētə/ an island in the Caribbean Sea, off the coast of Venezuela. Visited by Columbus in 1498, it was used as a base by Simón Bolívar in 1816 during the struggle for independence from Spanish rule.

mar·ga·ri·ta /,märgəˈrētə/ ▸*n.* a cocktail made with tequila and citrus fruit juice. ▷from the Spanish given name equivalent to *Margaret.*

mar·gate /ˈmärgit; -,gāt/ ▸*n.* a deep-bodied grayish fish that typically occurs in small groups in warm waters of the western Atlantic. • Two species in the family Pomadasyidae: *Haemulon album*, a large grunt that is an important food fish, and the mainly nocturnal **black margate** (*Anisotremus surinamesis*). ▷mid 18th cent.: of unknown origin.

mar·gay /ˈmär,gā; märˈgā/ ▸*n.* a small South American wild cat with large eyes and a yellowish coat with black spots and stripes. • *Felis wiedii*, family Felidae. ▷late 18th cent.: via French from Tupi *marakaya.*

marge /märj/ ▸*n. poetic/literary* a margin or edge. ▷mid 16th cent.: from French, from Latin *margo* 'margin.'

mar·gin /ˈmärjən/ ▸*n.* **1** the edge or border of something: *the eastern margin of the Indian Ocean* | *figurative they were forced to live on the margins of society.* See note at BORDER. ■ the blank border on each side of the print on a page. ■ a line ruled on paper to mark off a margin. **2** an amount by which a thing is won or falls short: *they won by a convincing 17-point margin.* ■ an amount of something included so as to be sure of success or safety: *there was no* **margin for error**. ■ the lower limit of possibility, success, etc.: *the lighting is considerably brighter than before but is still at the margins of acceptability.* ■ a profit margin. ■ *Finance* a sum deposited with a broker to cover the risk of loss on a transaction or account.
▸*v.* (**-gined, -gin·ing**) [*trans.*] **1** provide with an edge or border: *its leaves are margined with yellow.* ■ *archaic* annotate or summarize (a text) in the margins. **2** deposit an amount of money with a broker as security for (an account or transaction): [as *adj.*] (**margined**) *a margined transaction.* ▷late Middle English: from Latin *margo, margin-* 'edge.' —**mar·gined** *adj.* [in *combination*] *a wide-margined volume.*
▸*PHRASE* □ **margin of error** an amount (usually small) that is allowed for in case of miscalculation or change of circumstances.

mar·gin·al /ˈmärjənl/ ▸*adj.* of, relating to, or situated at the edge or margin of something. ■ of secondary or minor importance; not central: *it seems likely to make only a marginal difference* | *a marginal criminal element.* ■ (of a decision or distinction) very narrow: *a marginal offside decision.* ■ of or written in the margin of a page: *marginal notes.* ■ of or relating to water adjacent to the land's edge or coast: *water lilies and marginal aquatics.* ■ (chiefly of costs or benefits) relating to or resulting from small or unit changes. ■ (of taxation) relating to increases in income. ■ *chiefly Brit.* (of a parliamentary seat) having a small majority and therefore at risk in an election. ■ close to the limit of profitability, esp. through difficulty of exploitation: *marginal farmland.*
▸*n.* a plant that grows in water adjacent to the edge of land. ▷late 16th cent.: from medieval Latin *marginalis*, from *margo, margin-* (see MARGIN). —**mar·gin·al·i·ty** /,märjəˈnalətē/ *n.*

mar·gin·al cost ▸*n. Economics* the cost added by producing one extra item of a product.

mar·gi·na·li·a /,märjəˈnālēə/ ▸*plural n.* marginal notes. ▷mid 19th cent.: from medieval Latin, neuter plural of *marginalis*, from *margo, margin-* (see MARGIN).

mar·gin·al·ize /ˈmärjənə,līz/ ▸*v.* [*trans.*] treat (a person, group, or concept) as insignificant or peripheral: *attempting to marginalize those who disagree* | [as *adj.*] (**marginalized**) *members of marginalized cultural groups.* —**mar·gin·al·i·za·tion** /,märjənələˈzāsHən/ *n.*

mar·gin·al·ly /ˈmärjənəlē/ ▸*adv.* to only a limited extent; slightly: *inflation is predicted to drop marginally* | [as *submodifier*] *he's marginally worse than he was.*

mar·gin·ate *Biology* ▸*v.* /ˈmärjə,nāt/ [*trans.*] provide with a margin or border; form a border to.
▸*adj.* /-nit; ,nāt/ having a distinct margin or border. —**mar·gin·a·tion** /,märjəˈnāsHən/ *n.*

mar·gin call ▸*n. Finance* a demand by a broker that an investor deposit further cash or securities to cover possible losses.

mar·gin re·lease ▸*n.* a device on a typewriter allowing a word to be typed beyond the margin normally set.

mar·go·sa /märˈgōsə/ ▸*n.* another term for NEEM. ▷Portuguese *amargosa*, feminine of *amargoso* 'bitter.'

mar·gra·vate /ˈmärgrə,vāt/ (also **mar·gra·vi·ate** /märˈgrāvē-it; -,āt/) ▸*n.* the territory ruled by a margrave.

mar·grave /ˈmär,grāv/ ▸*n. historical* the hereditary title of some princes of the Holy Roman Empire. ▷mid 16th cent., from Middle Dutch *markgrave* 'count of a border territory,' from *marke* 'boundary' + *grave* 'count' (used as a title).

mar·gra·vine /ˈmärgrə,vēn; ,märgrəˈvēn/ ▸*n. historical* the wife of a margrave. ▷late 17th cent.: from Dutch *markgravin*, feminine of *markgraaf*, earlier *markgrave* (see MARGRAVE).

Mar·gre·the II /märˈgrātə/ (1940–), queen of Denmark 1972– .

mar·gue·rite /,märg(y)əˈrēt/ ▸*n.* another term for OXEYE DAISY. ▷early 17th cent.: French equivalent of the given name Margaret.

Ma·ri /ˈmärē/ an ancient city on the western bank of the Euphrates River in Syria. Its period of greatest importance was late 19th–mid-18th centuries BC; the vast palace of the last king, Zimri-Lin, has yielded an archive of 25,000 cuneiform tablets, which are the principal source for the history of northern Syria and Mesopotamia at that time.

ma·ri·a /ˈmärēə/ ▸ plural form of MARE2.

ma·ri·a·chi /,märēˈäcHē/ ▸*n.* (*pl.* **-chis**) [as *adj.*] denoting a type of traditional Mexican folk music, typically performed by a small group of strolling musicians dressed in native costume. ■ a musician in such a group. ▷from Mexican Spanish *mariache, mariachi* 'street singer.'

Ma·ri·a de' Me·di·ci /mäˈrēä de ˈmedēcHē/ see MARIE DE MÉDICIS.

ma·riage blanc /märˈyäzH ˈbläN/ ▸*n.* (*pl.* **ma·riages blancs** *pronunc.* same) an unconsummated marriage. ▷French, literally 'white marriage.'

ma·riage de con·ve·nance /märˈyäzH də ,kônvəˈnäns/ ▸*n.* (*pl.* **ma·riages de con·ve·nance** *pronunc.* same) French term for MARRIAGE OF CONVENIENCE (see MARRIAGE).

Mar·i·an /ˈme(ə)rēən/ ▸*adj.* **1** of or relating to the Virgin Mary. **2** of or relating to Queen Mary I of England.

Ma·ri·an·a Is·lands /,me(ə)rēˈanə; ,marēˈänə/ (also **the Ma·ri·an·as**) a group of islands in the western Pacific comprising Guam and the Northern Marianas. In 1975, the Northern Marianas voted to establish a commonwealth in union with the U.S. and became self-governing three years later. ▷translating *Las Marianas*, the name given by Spanish colonists to the islands, in honor of *Maria Anna*, widow of Philip IV.

Ma·ri·an·a Trench an ocean trench to the southeast of the Mariana Islands in the western Pacific Ocean. Its greatest known ocean depth is 36,201 feet (11,034 m) at the Challenger Deep, which was discovered by HMS *Challenger II* in 1948.

Ma·ri·a The·re·sa /mə'rēə tə'räsə; -zə/ (1717–80), archduchess of Austria; queen of Hungary and Bohemia 1740–80. The daughter of Emperor Charles VI, she succeeded to the Habsburg dominions in 1740 by virtue of the Pragmatic Sanction. Her accession triggered the War of the Austrian Succession (1740–48), which led in turn to the Seven Years' War (1756–63).

Ma·ri Au·ton·o·mous Re·pub·lic another name for **Mari El**.

Ma·ri·bor /'märi,bôr/ an industrial city in northeastern Slovenia, on the Drava River near the border with Austria; pop. 104,000. German name **Marburg**.

Mar·i·co·pa Coun·ty /,mari'kōpə/ a county in south central Arizona that is home to more than half of all Arizonans. Its seat is Phoenix; pop. 3,072,149.

mar·i·cul·ture /'mari,kəlCHər/ ▸*n.* the cultivation of fish or other marine life for food. ▷early 20th cent.: from *mare, mari-* 'sea' + **culture**, on the pattern of words such as *agriculture*.

Ma·rie An·toi·nette /mə'rē ,ant(w)ə'net; ,äNtwä'net/ (1755–93), French queen; wife of Louis XVI. A daughter of Maria Theresa, she married the future Louis XVI of France in 1770. Her extravagant lifestyle led to widespread unpopularity and, like her husband, she was executed during the French Revolution.

Ma·rie Byrd Land /mə'rē bərd/ a region of Antarctica that borders on the Pacific Ocean, between Ellsworth Land and the Ross Sea. ▷named after the wife of Richard E. *Byrd*, the U.S. naval commander who explored the region in 1933–34.

Ma·rie Ce·leste /mə'rē sə'lest/ see **Mary Celeste**.

Ma·rie de Mé·di·cis /mä'rē də mādē'sēs/ (1573–1642), queen of France; Italian name *Maria de' Medici*. The second wife of Henry IV of France, she ruled as regent during the minority of her son Louis XIII (1610–17) and retained her influence after her son came to power.

Ma·ri El /'märē 'el/ an autonomous republic in European Russia, north of the Volga River; pop. 754,000; capital, Yoshkar-Ola. Also called **Mari Autonomous Republic**.

Mar·i·et·ta /,marē'etə/ a city in northwestern Georgia, a northwestern suburb of Atlanta; pop. 58,748.

mar·i·gold /'mari,gōld/ ▸*n.* a plant of the daisy family, typically with yellow, orange, or copper-brown flowers, that is widely cultivated as an ornamental. • Genera *Tagetes* (the **French** and **African marigolds**) and *Calendula* (the **common** (or **pot**) **marigold**), family Compositae. ■ used in names of other plants with yellow flowers, e.g., **corn marigold**, **marsh marigold**. ▷late Middle English: from the given name *Mary* (probably referring to the Virgin) + dialect *gold*, denoting the corn or garden marigold in Old English.

ma·ri·jua·na /,marə'(h)wänə/ (also **ma·ri·hua·na**) ▸*n.* cannabis, esp. as smoked in cigarettes. ▷late 19th cent.: from Latin American Spanish.

ma·rim·ba /mə'rimbə/ ▸*n.* a deep-toned xylophone of African origin. The modern form was developed in the U.S. *c.*1910. ▷early 18th cent.: from Kimbundu, perhaps via Portuguese.

ma·ri·na /mə'rēnə/ ▸*n.* a specially designed harbor with moorings for pleasure craft and small boats. ▷early 19th cent.: from Italian or Spanish, feminine of *marino*, from Latin *marinus* (see **marine**).

mar·i·nade /,marə'nād/ ▸*n.* a sauce, typically made of oil, vinegar, spices, and herbs, in which meat, fish, or other food is soaked before cooking in order to flavor or soften it. ■ [with *adj.*] a dish prepared using such a mixture: *a chicken marinade*.
▸*v.* also /'marə,nād/ another term for **marinate**. ▷late 17th cent. (as a verb): from French, from Spanish *marinada*, via *marinar* 'pickle in brine' from *marino* (see **marina**).

ma·ri·na·ra /,marə'narə; ,märə'närə/ ▸*n.* [usu. as *adj.*] (in Italian cooking) a sauce made from tomatoes, onions, and herbs, served esp. with pasta. ▷from the Italian phrase *alla marinara* 'sailor-style.'

mar·i·nate /'marə,nāt/ ▸*v.* [*trans.*] soak (meat, fish, or other food) in a marinade: *the beef was marinated in red wine vinegar.* ■ [*intrans.*] (of food) undergo such a process. ▷mid 17th cent.: from Italian *marinare* 'pickle in brine,' or from French *mariner* (from *marine* 'brine'). **—mar·i·na·tion** /,marə'nāSHən/ *n.*

Ma·rin Coun·ty /mə'rin/ a county that includes many affluent suburbs in northwestern California, across the Golden Gate from San Francisco; pop. 230,096.

ma·rine /mə'rēn/ ▸*adj.* of, found in, or produced by the sea: *marine plants | marine biology.* ■ of or relating to shipping or naval matters: *marine insurance.* ■ (of artists or painting) depicting scenes at sea: *marine painters.*
▸*n.* a member of a body of troops trained to serve on land or at sea, in particular a member of the U.S. Marine Corps. ▷Middle English (as a noun in the sense 'seashore'): from Old French *marin, marine*, from Latin *marinus*, from *mare* 'sea.'
▸*PHRASE* □ **tell that** (or **it**) **to the marines** a scornful expression of disbelief. [from the saying *that will do for the marines but the sailors won't believe it*, referring to the *horse marines*, an imaginary corps of cavalrymen employed to serve as marines (thus out of their element).]

Ma·rine Corps /mə'rēn kô(ə)rz/ a branch of the U.S. armed services (part of the U.S. Navy), founded in 1775 and trained to operate on land and at sea.

ma·rine i·gua·na ▸*n.* a large lizard with webbed feet that swims strongly and feeds on marine algae. It is native to the Galapagos Islands and is the only marine lizard. • *Amblyrhynchus cristatus*, family Iguanidae.

Ma·rine One ▸*n.* the helicopter used by the president of the U.S.

Mar·i·ner /'marənər/ a series of American space probes launched in 1962–77 to investigate the planets Venus, Mars, and Mercury.

mar·i·ner /'marənər/ ▸*n.* a sailor. ▷Middle English: from Old French *marinier*, from medieval Latin *marinarius*, from Latin *marinus* (see **marine**).

ma·rine toad ▸*n.* another term for **cane toad**.

Ma·ri·net·ti /,marə'netē; ,mär-/, Filippo Tommaso (1876–1944), Italian poet and playwright. He launched the futurist movement with a manifesto in 1909 that exalted technology, glorified war, and demanded revolution in the arts.

Ma·ri·no /mə'rēnō/, Dan(iel Constantine, Jr.) (1961–) U.S. football player. He was the quarterback for the Miami Dolphins 1983–2000.

Mar·i·ol·a·try /,me(ə)rē'älətrē/ ▸*n.* idolatrous worship of the Virgin Mary. ▷early 17th cent.: from *Maria* (Latin equivalent of 'Mary') + **-latry**, on the pattern of *idolatry*.

Mar·i·ol·o·gy /,me(ə)rē'äləjē/ ▸*n.* the part of Christian theology dealing with the Virgin Mary. **—Mar·i·o·log·i·cal** /,me(ə)rēə'läjikəl/ *adj.* **—Mar·i·ol·o·gist** /-jist/ *n.*

Mar·i·on[1] /'marēən; 'me(ə)r-/ **1** an industrial city in east central Indiana; pop. 32,618. **2** an industrial city in north central Ohio; pop. 34,075.

Mar·i·on[2], Francis (c.1732–1795), American Revolutionary commander; known as the **Swamp Fox**. He commanded militia troops in South Carolina and evaded the British by hiding in swamps and woods.

mar·i·on·ette /,marēə'net/ ▸*n.* a puppet worked from above by strings attached to its limbs. ▷early 17th cent.: from French *marionnette*, from *Marion*, diminutive of the given name *Marie*.

marionette

mar·i·po·sa lil·y /,marə'pōsə; -'pōzə/ (also **mariposa tulip**) ▸*n.* a plant of the lily family, with brightly colored cup-shaped flowers, native to Mexico and the western U.S. Closely related to the **sego**. • Genus *Calochortus*, family Liliaceae: several species. ▷mid 19th cent.: *mariposa* from Spanish, literally 'butterfly.'

Mar·is /'maris/, Roger (Eugene) (1934–85), U.S. baseball player. A New York Yankees right fielder, he broke Babe Ruth's record for most home runs in a season (60 in 1927) by hitting 61 in 1961. His record stood until 1998 when it was broken by Mark McGwire.

Mar·ist /'me(ə)rəst; 'mar-/ ▸*n.* **1** (also **Marist Father**) a member of the Society of Mary, a Roman Catholic missionary and teaching congregation. **2** (also **Marist Brother**) a member of the Little Brothers of Mary, a Roman Catholic teaching congregation. ▷late 19th cent.: from French *Mariste*, from the given name *Marie*, equivalent of *Mary*.

mar·i·tal /'maritl/ ▸*adj.* of or relating to marriage or the relations between husband and wife: *marital fidelity.* ▷early 16th cent.: from Latin *maritalis*, from *maritus* 'husband.' **—mar·i·tal·ly** *adv.*

mar·i·tal rape ▸*n.* sexual intercourse forced on a woman by her husband, knowingly against her will.

mar·i·tal sta·tus ▸*n.* a person's state of being single, married, separated, divorced, or widowed.

mar·i·time /'mari,tīm/ ▸*adj.* connected with the sea, esp. in relation to seafaring commercial or military activity: *a maritime museum | maritime law.* ■ living or found in or near the sea: *dolphins and other maritime mammals.* ■ bordering on the sea: *two species of Diptera occur in the maritime Antarctic.* ■ denoting a climate that is moist and temperate owing to the influence of the sea. ▷mid 16th cent.: from Latin *maritimus*, from *mare* 'sea.'

mar·i·time pine ▸*n.* a pine tree with long, thick needles and clustered cones, native to the coasts of the Mediterranean and Iberia. • *Pinus pinaster*, family Pinaceae.

Mar·i·time Prov·inc·es (also **the Mar·i·times**) the Canadian provinces of New Brunswick, Nova Scotia, and Prince Edward Island, with coastlines on the Gulf of St. Lawrence and the Atlantic Oceans. Compare with **Atlantic Provinces**.

Ma·ri·tsa /mə'rētsə/ a river in southern Europe that rises in southwestern Bulgaria and flows 300 miles (480 km) south to the Aegean Sea. It forms the border between Bulgaria and Greece and between Greece and Turkey. Its ancient name is the Hebros or Hebrus. Turkish name **Meriç**; Greek name **Évros**.

Ma·ri·u·pol /,märē'ōōpəl/ an industrial port on the southern coast of Ukraine, on the Sea of Azov; pop. 517,000. Former name (1948–89) **Zhdanov**.

Mar·i·us /'me(ə)rēəs; 'mar-/, Gaius (*c.*157–86 BC), Roman general and politician. Elected consul in 107 BC, he defeated Jugurtha and invading Germanic tribes. After a power struggle with Sulla he was expelled from Italy, but returned to take Rome by force in 87 BC.

mar·jo·ram /'märjərəm/ ▸*n.* (also **sweet marjoram**) an aromatic southern European plant of the mint family, the leaves of which are used as a culinary herb. • *Origanum majorana*, family Labiatae. ■ (also **wild marjoram**) another term for **oregano**. ▷late Middle English: from Old French *majorane*, from medieval Latin *majorana*, of unknown ultimate origin.

Mark, St. /märk/ an Apostle; companion of St. Peter and St. Paul; traditional author of the second Gospel. Feast day, April 25. ■ the second Gospel, the earliest in date (see **gospel** sense 2).

mark[1] /märk/ ▸*n.* **1** a small area on a surface having a different color from its surroundings, typically one caused by accident or damage: *the blow left a red mark down one side of her face.* ■ a spot, area, or feature on a person's or animal's body by which they may be identified or recognized: *he was five feet nine, with no distinguishing marks.* **2** a line, figure, or symbol made as an indication or record of something. ■ a written symbol made on a document in place of a signature by someone who cannot write. ■ a level or stage that is considered significant: *unemployment had passed the two million mark.* ■ a sign or indication of a quality or feeling: *the flag was at half-mast as a mark of respect.* ■ a characteristic property or feature: *it is the mark of a civilized society to treat its elderly members well.* ■ a competitor's starting point in a race. ■ *Nautical* a piece of material or a knot used to indicate a depth on a sounding line. ■ *Telecommunications* one of two possible states of a signal in certain systems. The opposite of **space**. **3** a point awarded for a correct answer or for proficiency in an examination or competition: *many candidates lose marks because they don't read the questions carefully | figurative full marks to them for highlighting the threat to the rain forest.* ■ a figure or letter representing the total of such points and signifying a person's score: *the highest mark was 98 percent.* ■ (esp. in track and field) a time or distance achieved by a competitor, esp. one which represents a record or personal best. **4** (followed by a numeral) a particular model or type of a vehicle, machine, or device: *a Mark 10 Jaguar.* **5** a target: *few bullets could have missed their mark.* ■ *informal* a person who is easily deceived or taken advantage of: *they figure I'm an easy mark.*
▸*v.* [*trans.*] **1** make (a visible impression or stain) on: *he fingered the photograph gently, careful not to mark it.*

■ [*intrans.*] become stained: *it is made from a sort of woven surface which doesn't mark or tear.* **2** write a word or symbol on (an object), typically for identification: *she marked all her possessions with her name* | [*trans.*] *an envelope marked "private and confidential."* ■ write (a word or figure) on an object: *she* **marked** *the date* **down** *on a card.* ■ (**mark something off**) put a line by or through something written or printed on paper to indicate that it has passed or been dealt with: *he marked off their names in a ledger.* **3** show the position of: *the top of the pass marks the border between Alaska and the Yukon.* ■ separate or delineate (a particular section or area of something): *you need to* **mark out** *the part of the garden where the sun lingers longest.* ■ (of a particular quality or feature) separate or distinguish (someone or something) from other people or things: *his sword* **marked** *him* **out** *as an officer.* ■ (**mark someone out for**) select or destine someone for (a particular role or condition): *the solicitor general marked him out for government office.* ■ (**mark someone down as**) judge someone to be (a particular type or class of person): *she had marked him down as a liberal.* ■ acknowledge, honor, or celebrate (an important event or occasion) with a particular action: *to mark its fiftieth anniversary, the group held a fashion show.* ■ be an indication of (a significant occasion, stage, or development): *a series of incidents which marked a new phase in the terrorist campaign.* ■ (usu. **be marked**) characterize as having a particular quality or feature: *the reaction to these developments has been marked by a note of hysteria.* ■ *chiefly Brit.* (of a clock or watch) show (a certain time): *his watch marked five past eight.* **4** (of a teacher or examiner) assess the standard of (a piece of written work) by assigning points for proficiency or correct answers: *the teachers are given adequate time to mark term papers.* ■ (**mark someone/something down**) reduce the number of marks awarded to a student, candidate, or their work: *I was marked down for having skipped the last essay question.* **5** notice or pay careful attention to: *he'll leave you,* **you mark my words!** **6** (of a player in a team game) stay close to (a particular opponent) in order to prevent them getting or passing the ball.

▸*phrasal v.* □ **mark something down** (of a retailer) reduce the indicated price of an item. □ **mark something up 1** (of a retailer) add a certain amount to the cost of goods to cover overhead and profit: *they mark up the price of imported wines by 66 percent.* **2** annotate or correct text for printing, keying, or typesetting. ▷Old English *mearc, gemerce* (noun), *mearcian* (verb), of Germanic origin; from an Indo-European root shared by Latin *margo* 'margin.'

▸*PHRASES* □ **be quick** (or **slow**) **off the mark** be fast (or slow) in responding to a situation or understanding something. □ **get off the mark** get started. □ **leave** (or **make**) **its** (or **one's** or **a**) **mark** have a lasting or significant effect: *she left her mark on the world of foreign policy.* □ **make one's mark** attain recognition or distinction. □ **mark time** (of troops) march on the spot without moving forward. ■ *figurative* pass one's time in routine activities until a more favorable or interesting opportunity presents itself. □ **mark you** *chiefly Brit.* used to emphasize or draw attention to a statement: *I was persuaded, against my better judgment, mark you, to vote for him.* □ **near** (or **close**) **to the mark** almost accurate: *to say he was their legal adviser would be nearer the mark.* □ **off** (or **wide of**) **the mark** incorrect or inaccurate: *his solutions are completely off the mark.* □ **of mark** *dated* having importance or distinction: *he had been a man of mark.* □ **on the mark** correct; accurate. □ **on your marks** used to instruct competitors in a race to prepare themselves in the correct starting position: *on your marks, get set, go!* □ **up to the mark** of the required standard. ■ [usu. with *negative*] (of a person) as healthy or in as good spirits as usual: *Johnny's not feeling up to the mark at the moment.*

mark[2] ▸*n.* **1** the basic monetary unit of Germany (until the introduction of the euro), equal to 100 pfennigs; a Deutschmark or, formerly, an Ostmark. **2** a former English and Scottish money of account, equal to thirteen shillings and four pence in the currency of the day. ■ a denomination of weight for gold and silver, formerly used throughout western Europe and typically equal to 8 ounces (226.8 grams). ▷Old English *marc*, from Old Norse *mǫrk*; probably related to **MARK**[1].

Mark An·to·ny see **ANTONY**.

mark·down /ˈmärk,doun/ ▸*n.* a reduction in price.

marked /märkt/ ▸*adj.* **1** having a visible mark: *plants with beautifully marked leaves.* ■ (of playing cards) having distinctive marks on their backs to assist cheating. ■ *Linguistics* (of words or forms) distinguished by a particular feature: *the word "drake" is semantically marked as masculine; the unmarked form is "duck."* **2** clearly noticeable; evident: *a marked increase in sales.* —**mark·ed·ly** /ˈmärkidlē/ *adv.* (in sense 2). —**mark·ed·ness** /ˈmärkidnis/ *n.*

marked man ▸*n.* a person who is singled out for special treatment, esp. to be harmed or killed.

mark·er /ˈmärkər/ ▸*n.* **1** an object used to indicate a position, place, or route: *they erected a granite marker at the crash site* | [as *adj.*] *marker posts* | *figurative the most portable marker of class privilege, the wearing of natural fibers.* ■ a thing serving as a standard of comparison or as an indication of what may be expected: *such studies may provide a unique marker in the quest to understand the brain.* ■ a radio beacon used to guide the pilot of an aircraft. ■ *informal* a promissory note; an IOU: *Phyllis owed a marker in the neighborhood of $100,000.* **2** a felt-tip pen with a broad tip. **3** (chiefly in soccer) a player who is assigned to mark a particular opponent. **4** *Brit.* a person who records the score in a game, esp. in snooker or billiards.

mar·ket /ˈmärkit/ ▸*n.* **1** a regular gathering of people for the purchase and sale of provisions, livestock, and other commodities: *farmers* **going to market**. ■ an open space or covered building where vendors convene to sell their goods. **2** an area or arena in which commercial dealings are conducted: *the sale of cruisers in the American market continues to plummet.* | *the labor market.* ■ a demand for a particular commodity or service: *there is* **a market for** *ornamental daggers.* ■ the state of trade at a particular time or in a particular context: *the bottom's fallen out of the market.* ■ the free market; the operation of supply and demand: *future development cannot simply be left to the market* | [as *adj.*] *a market economy.* ■ a stock market.
▸*v.* (**-ket·ed, -ket·ing**) [*trans.*] advertise or promote (something): *the product was marketed under the name "aspirin."* ■ offer for sale: *sheep farmers are still unable to market their lambs.* ■ [*intrans.*] buy or sell provisions in a market: [as *n.*] (**marketing**) *some people liked to do their marketing very early in the morning.* ▷Middle English, via Anglo-Norman French from Latin *mercatus*, from *mercari* 'buy' (see also **MERCHANT**). —**mar·ket·er** *n.*

▸*PHRASES* □ **be in the market for** wish to buy. □ **make a market** *Finance* take part in active dealing in particular shares or other assets. □ **on the market** available for sale: *he bought every new gadget as it* **came on the market**.

mar·ket·a·ble /ˈmärkitəbəl/ ▸*adj.* able or fit to be sold or marketed: *the fish are perfectly marketable.* ■ in demand: *marketable skills.* —**mar·ket·a·bil·i·ty** /,märkitəˈbilətē/ *n.*

mar·ket·eer /,märkəˈti(ə)r/ ▸*n.* a person who sells goods or services in a market: *a consumer-goods marketeer.* ■ [with *adj.*] a person who works in or advocates a particular type of market: *free-marketeers.*

mar·ket forc·es ▸*plural n.* the economic factors affecting the price, demand, and availability of a commodity: *leaving oil prices to be determined purely by market forces.*

mar·ket gar·den ▸*n.* British term for **TRUCK FARM**. —**mar·ket gar·den·er** *n.* —**mar·ket gar·den·ing** *n.*

mar·ket·ing /ˈmärkitiNG/ ▸*n.* the action or business of promoting and selling products or services, including market research and advertising.

mar·ket·ing mix ▸*n.* a combination of factors that can be controlled by a company to influence consumers to purchase its products.

mar·ket·i·za·tion /,märkitəˈzāSHən/ ▸*n.* the exposure of an industry or service to market forces. ■ the conversion of a national economy from a planned to a market economy: *the marketization of the Russian economy.* —**mar·ket·ize** /ˈmärkit,īz/ *v.*

mar·ket lead·er ▸*n.* the company selling the largest quantity of a particular type of product. ■ a product that outsells its competitors.

mar·ket mak·er (also **mar·ket-mak·er**) ▸*n.* a dealer in securities or other assets who undertakes to buy or sell at specified prices at all times.

mar·ket·place /ˈmärkət,plās/ ▸*n.* an open space where a market is or was formerly held in a town. ■ the arena of competitive or commercial dealings; the world of trade: *the changing demands of the global marketplace.*

mar·ket price ▸*n.* the price of a commodity when sold in a given market: *the world market price for nonfat dry milk.*

mar·ket re·search ▸*n.* the action or activity of gathering information about consumers' needs and preferences. —**mar·ket re·search·er** *n.*

mar·ket share ▸*n.* the portion of a market controlled by a particular company or product.

mar·ket tim·er ▸*n.* *Finance* a person or organization that makes decisions to buy or sell investments based on economic and other factors that might affect the direction of the market. —**mar·ket tim·ing** *n.*

mar·ket town /ˈmärkət ,tōn/ ▸*n.* a town of moderate size in a rural area, where a regular market is held.

mar·ket val·ue ▸*n.* the amount for which something can be sold on a given market. Often contrasted with **BOOK VALUE**.

mar·khor /ˈmär,kôr/ ▸*n.* a large wild goat with very long twisted horns, native to central Asia. • *Capra falconeri*, family Bovidae. ▷mid 19th cent.: from Persian *mār-ḵwār*, from *mār* 'serpent' + *ḵwār* '-eating.'

mark·ing /ˈmärkiNG/ ▸*n.* (usu. **markings**) an identification mark, esp. a mark or pattern of marks on an animal's fur, feathers, or skin: *the distinctive black-and-white markings on its head.* ■ *Music* a word or symbol on a score indicating the correct tempo, dynamic, or other aspect of performance.

mark·ka /ˈmär(k),kä/ ▸*n.* (*pl.* **-kaa** /-kä/) the basic monetary unit of Finland (until replaced by the euro), equal to 100 penniä. ▷Finnish.

Mar·ko·va /märˈkōvə/, Dame Alicia (1910–2004), British ballet dancer; born *Lilian Alicia Marks*. She made her debut with the Ballets Russes in 1924, established the Markova-Dolin Comapny in London with Anton Dolin (1904–83) in 1935, and was prima ballerina with the London Festival Ballet 1950–52. She directed the Metropolitan Opera Ballet 1963–69.

Mar·kov chain /ˈmär,kôf; -,kôv / (also **Markov model**) ▸*n.* *Statistics* a stochastic model describing a sequence of possible events in which the probability of each event depends only on the state attained in the previous event. ▷mid 20th cent.: named after Andrei A. *Markov* (1856–1922), Russian mathematician.

Marks /märks/, Simon, 1st Baron Marks of Broughton (1888–1964), English businessman. He developed a chain of retail stores called Marks & Spencer in 1926.

marks·man /ˈmärksmən/ ▸*n.* (*pl.* **-men**) a person skilled in shooting, esp. with a pistol or rifle: *a police marksman.* —**marks·man·ship** /-,SHip/ *n.*

marks·wom·an /ˈmärks,wo͝omən/ ▸*n.* (*pl.* **-wom·en**) a woman skilled in shooting, esp. with a pistol or rifle.

mark-to-mar·ket ▸*adj.* *Finance* denoting or relating to a system of valuing assets by the most recent market price.

mark·up /ˈmär,kəp/ ▸*n.* **1** the amount added to the cost price of goods to cover overhead and profit. **2** the process or result of correcting text in preparation for printing. ■ the process of making the final changes in a legislative bill: *the bill concerning acid rain is* **in markup**. **3** *Computing* a set of tags assigned to elements of a text to indicate their structural or logical relation to the rest of the text.

marl[1] /märl/ ▸*n.* an unconsolidated sedimentary rock or soil consisting of clay and lime, formerly used typically as fertilizer.
▸*v.* [*trans.*] (often **be marled**) apply marl to. ▷Middle English: from Old French *marle*, from medieval Latin *margila*, from Latin *marga*, of Celtic origin. —**marl·y** *adj.*

marl[2] ▸*v.* *Nautical* fasten with marline or other light rope; wind marline around (a rope), securing it with a half hitch at each turn.

Marl·bor·ough[1] /ˈmärl,bərō; -,bərə/ an industrial city in east central Massachusetts; pop. 31,813.

Marl·bor·ough[2], John Churchill, 1st Duke of (1650–1722), British general. He was commander of British and Dutch troops in the War of the Spanish Succession and won a series of victories (notably at Blenheim in 1704) over the French armies of Louis XIV.

Mar·ley /ˈmärlē/, Bob (1945–81), Jamaican reggae singer, guitarist, and songwriter; full name *Robert Nesta Marley*. Instrumental in popularizing reggae in the 1970s, his lyrics often reflected his commitment to Rastafarianism.

mar·lin /ˈmärlən/ ▸*n.* a large edible billfish of warm seas that is a highly prized game fish and typically reaches a great weight. • Genera *Makaira* and *Tetrapterus*, family Istiophoridae: several species, including the **striped marlin** (*T. audax*). ▷early 20th

M

cent.: from **MARLINSPIKE** (with reference to its pointed snout).

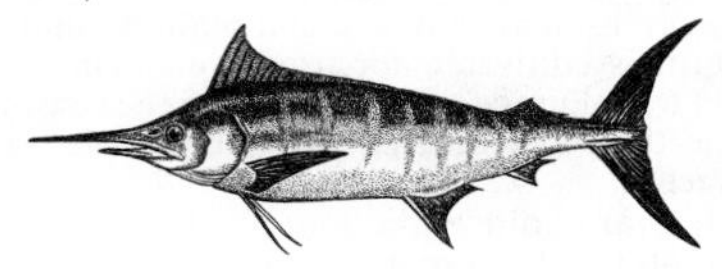

striped marlin

mar·line /'märlən/ ▸*n. Nautical* light two-stranded rope. ▷late Middle English: from Middle Low German *marling*, with the ending influenced by **LINE**[1].

mar·lin·spike /'märlən,spīk/ (also **mar·line·spike**) ▸*n.* a pointed metal tool used by sailors to separate strands of rope or wire, esp. in splicing. ▷early 17th cent. (originally as *marling spike*): from *marling*, present participle of *marl* 'fasten with marline' (from Dutch *marlen* 'keep binding') + **SPIKE**[1].

Mar·lowe /'märlō/, Christopher (1564–93), English playwright and poet whose work influenced Shakespeare's early historical plays. Notable plays: *Doctor Faustus* (*c.*1590) and *The Jew of Malta* (1592).

marm /märm/ ▸*n. dated* variant spelling of **MA'AM**.

mar·ma·lade /'märmə,lād/ ▸*n.* a preserve made from citrus fruit, esp. bitter oranges, prepared like jam. ▷late 15th cent.: from Portuguese *marmelada* 'quince jam,' from *marmelo* 'quince,' based on Greek *melimēlon* (from *meli* 'honey' + *mēlon* 'apple').

Mar·ma·ra, Sea of /'märmərə/ a small sea in northwestern Turkey. Connected by the Bosporus to the Black Sea and by the Dardanelles to the Aegean Sea, it separates European Turkey from Asian Turkey. In ancient times it was known as the Propontis.

mar·mite /'mär,mīt/ ▸*n.* an earthenware cooking container. ▷early 19th cent.: French, from Old French *marmite* 'hypocritical,' with reference to the hidden contents of the lidded pot, from *marmotter* 'to mutter' + *mite* 'cat.'

mar·mo·re·al /mär'môrēəl/ ▸*adj. poetic/literary* made of or likened to marble. ▷late 18th cent.: from Latin *marmoreus* (from *marmor* 'marble') + **-AL**. **—mar·mo·re·al·ly** *adv.*

mar·mo·set /'märmə,set; -,zet/ ▸*n.* a small Central and South American monkey with a silky coat and a long nonprehensile tail. • Family Callitrichidae (or Callithricidae): genus *Callithrix* (three species), and the **pygmy marmoset** (*Cebuella pygmaea*). ▷late Middle English (also in the sense 'grotesque figure'): from Old French *marmouset* 'grotesque image,' of unknown ultimate origin.

mar·mot /'märmət/ ▸*n.* a heavily built, gregarious, burrowing rodent of both Eurasia and North America, typically living in mountainous country. • Genus *Marmota*, family Sciuridae: several species. ▷early 17th cent.: from French *marmotte*, probably via Romansh *murmont* from late Latin *mus montanus* 'mountain mouse'; compare with French *marmotter* 'mutter through the teeth.'

Marne /märn/ a river in east central France that rises north of Dijon and flows 328 miles (525 km) north and then west to join the Seine River near Paris. Its valley was the scene of two World War I battles. The first (September 1914) halted and repelled the German advance on Paris; the second (July 1918) ended the final German offensive.

mar·o·cain /,märə'kān/ ▸*n.* a dress fabric of ribbed crepe, made of silk or wool or both. ▷1920s: from French, literally 'Moroccan,' from *Maroc* 'Morocco.'

Mar·o·nite /'me(ə)rə,nīt/ ▸*n.* a member of a Christian sect of Syrian origin that is in communion with the Roman Catholic Church and living chiefly in Lebanon.
▸*adj.* [*attrib.*] of or relating to the Maronites. ▷early 16th cent.: from medieval Latin *Maronita*, from the name of John *Maro*, a 7th-cent. Syrian religious leader, who may have been the first Maronite patriarch.

Ma·roon /mə'ro͞on/ ▸*n.* a member of a group of black people living in the mountains and forests of Suriname and the West Indies, descended from escaped slaves. ▷mid 17th cent.: from French *marron* 'feral,' from Spanish *cimarrón* 'wild,' (as a noun) 'escaped slave'; compare with **SEMINOLE**.

ma·roon[1] /mə'ro͞on/ ▸*adj.* of a brownish-crimson color.
▸*n.* **1** a brownish-crimson color. **2** *chiefly Brit.* a firework that makes a loud bang, used mainly as a signal or warning. [early 19th cent.: so named because the firework makes the noise of a chestnut (see below) bursting in the fire.] ▷late 17th cent. (in the sense 'chestnut'): from French *marron* 'chestnut,' via Italian from medieval Greek *maraon*. The sense relating to color dates from the late 18th cent.

ma·roon[2] ▸*v.* [*trans.*] (often **be marooned**) leave (someone) trapped and isolated in an inaccessible place, esp. an island: *a novel about schoolboys marooned on a desert island.* ▷early 18th cent.: from **MAROON**, originally in the form *marooned* 'lost in the wilds.'

Mar·quand /,mär'kwänd/, J(ohn) P(hillips) (1893–1960), U.S. writer. He created the character Mr. Moto, a Japanese detective featured in several of his novels, such as *Last Laugh, Mr. Moto* (1942). His other works include *The Late George Apley* (1937), *Point of No Return* (1949), and *Women and Thomas Harrow* (1958).

marque[1] /märk/ ▸*n.* a make of car, as distinct from a specific model. ▷early 20th cent.: from French, back-formation from *marquer* 'to brand,' of Scandinavian origin.

marque[2] ▸*n.* see **LETTER OF MARQUE**.

mar·quee /mär'kē/ ▸*n.* **1** a rooflike projection over the entrance to a theater, hotel, or other building. ■ [as *adj.*] leading; preeminent: *a marquee player.* [with allusion to the practice of billing the name of an entertainer on the *marquee* (i.e., awning) over the entrance to a theater.] **2** *chiefly Brit.* a large tent used for social or commercial functions. ▷late 17th cent.: from **MARQUISE**, taken as plural and assimilated to **-EE**.

mar·que·sa /mär'kāzə/ ▸*n.* a Spanish marchioness. ▷Spanish.

Mar·que·san /mär'kāzən/ ▸*n.* **1** a native or inhabitant of the Marquesas Islands, esp. a member of the aboriginal Polynesian inhabitants. **2** the Polynesian language of this people.
▸*adj.* of or relating to the Marquesans or their language.

Mar·que·sas Is·lands /'märkēsəz/ a group of volcanic islands in the South Pacific Ocean that forms part of French Polynesia; pop. 8,000. They were annexed by France in 1842. The largest island, Hiva Oa, is where painter Paul Gauguin spent the last two years of his life.

mar·quess /'märkwəs/ ▸*n.* a British nobleman ranking above an earl and below a duke. Compare with **MARQUIS**. ▷early 16th cent.: variant of **MARQUIS**.

mar·que·try /'märkətrē/ (also **mar·que·terie** or **mar·que·tery**) ▸*n.* inlaid work made from small pieces of variously colored wood or other materials, used chiefly for the decoration of furniture. ▷mid 16th cent.: from French *marqueterie*, from *marqueter* 'to variegate.'

Mar·quette[1] /mär'ket/ a port city in the Upper Peninsula in Michigan, on Lake Superior; pop. 21,977.

Mar·quette[2], Jacques (1637–75), French Jesuit missionary and explorer. Arriving in Canada in 1666, he played a prominent part in the attempt to Christianize the American Indians. He explored the Wisconsin, Mississippi, and Illinois rivers.

Már·quez, Gabriel García, see **GARCÍA MÁRQUEZ**.

mar·quis /mär'kē; 'märkwəs/ ▸*n.* (in some European countries) a nobleman ranking above a count and below a duke. Compare with **MARQUESS**. ■ another term for **MARQUESS**. ▷Middle English: from Old French *marchis*, reinforced by Old French *marquis*, both from the base of **MARCH**[2].

mar·quis·ate /'märkwəsət/ ▸*n.* the rank or dignity of a marquess or marquis. ■ the territorial lordship or possessions of a marquis or margrave. ▷early 16th cent.: from **MARQUIS**, on the pattern of words such as French *marquisat*, Italian *marchesato*.

Mar·quis de Sade /mär'kē də 'säd/ see **SADE**.

mar·quise /mär'kēz/ ▸*n.* **1** the wife or widow of a marquis. Compare with **MARCHIONESS**. ■ a woman holding the rank of marquis in her own right. **2** a finger ring set with a pointed oval gem or cluster of gems. **3** archaic term for **MARQUEE** (sense 2). **4** a chilled dessert similar to a chocolate mousse. ▷early 17th cent.: French, feminine of **MARQUIS**.

mar·qui·sette /,märk(w)ə'zet/ ▸*n.* a fine light cotton, rayon, or silk gauze fabric, now chiefly used for net curtains. ▷early 20th cent.: from French, diminutive of **MARQUISE**.

Mar·ra·kesh /,marə'kesh; 'marə,kesh; mə'rä-/ (also **Mar·ra·kech**) a city in western Morocco, in the foothills of the High Atlas Mountains; pop. 602,000. It was founded in 1062 as the capital of the Almoravids.

mar·ram grass /'marəm/ (also **mar·ram**) ▸*n.* a coarse grass of coastal sand dunes that binds the loose sand with its tough rhizomes, found in Europe, North America, and Australia. • *Ammophila arenaria*, family Gramineae. ▷mid 17th cent.: from Old Norse *marálmr*, from *marr* 'sea' + *hálmr* 'haulm.'

Mar·ra·no /mə'ränō/ ▸*n.* (*pl.* **-nos**) (in medieval Spain) a Christianized Jew or Moor, esp. one who merely professed conversion in order to avoid persecution. ▷Spanish, of unknown origin.

Mar·re·ner /'marənər/, Edythe, see **HAYWARD**[2].

mar·riage /'marij/ ▸*n.* **1** the formal union of a man and a woman, typically recognized by law, by which they become husband and wife. ■ a similar long-term relationship between partners of the same sex. ■ a relationship between married people or the period for which it lasts: *a happy marriage | the children from his first marriage.* ■ *figurative* a combination or mixture of two or more elements: *a marriage of jazz, pop, blues, and gospel.* **2** (in pinochle and other card games) a combination of a king and queen of the same suit. ▷Middle English: from Old French *mariage*, from *marier* 'marry.'
▸*PHRASES* □ **by marriage** as a result of a marriage: *a distant cousin by marriage.* □ **in marriage** as husband or wife: *he asked my father for my* ***hand in marriage.*** □ **marriage of convenience** a marriage concluded to achieve a practical purpose.

mar·riage·a·ble /'marijəbəl/ ▸*adj.* fit, suitable, or attractive for marriage, esp. in being of the right age. **—mar·riage·a·bil·i·ty** /,marijə'bilitē/ *n.*

mar·riage bro·ker ▸*n.* (in a culture where arranged marriages are customary) a person who arranges marriages for a fee.

mar·riage li·cense ▸*n.* a copy of the record of a legal marriage, with details of names, date, etc.

mar·riage por·tion ▸*n.* see **PORTION**.

mar·ried /'marēd/ ▸*adj.* (of two people) united in marriage: *a married couple.* ■ (of one person) having a husband or wife: *a happily married man.* ■ of or relating to marriage: *married life.* ■ *figurative* closely combined or linked: *in the seventeenth century, science was still* ***married to*** *religion.*
▸*n.* (usu. **marrieds**) a married person: *we were* ***young marrieds*** *during World War Two.*

Mar·ri·ott /'me(ə)rē,ät/, J(ohn) Willard (1900–1985), U.S. businessman. He founded the Marriott hotel chain, which began in 1927 with a Hot Shoppe in Washington, DC. Presidential Medal of Freedom (posthumously, 1988)

mar·ron gla·cé /ma'rôn glä'sā/ ▸*n.* (*pl.* **mar·rons gla·cés** *pronunc.* same) a chestnut preserved in and coated with sugar. ▷French, 'iced chestnut.'

mar·row /'marō/ ▸*n.* **1** (also **bone marrow**) a soft fatty substance in the cavities of bones, in which blood cells are produced (often taken as typifying strength and vitality). **2** (also **vegetable marrow**) *Brit.* a white-fleshed green-skinned gourd, which is eaten as a vegetable. ▷Old English *mearg, mærg*, denoting the plant that produces vegetable marrow, of Germanic origin; related to Dutch *merg* and German *Mark*. Sense 1 dates from the early 19th cent. **—mar·row·less** *adj.* **—mar·row·y** *adj.*
▸*PHRASE* □ **to the marrow** to one's innermost being: *a sight which chilled me to the marrow.*

mar·row·bone /'marō,bōn/ ▸*n.* a bone containing edible marrow. ■ (**marrowbones**) *dated, humorous* the knees.

mar·row·fat pea /'marō,fat/ ▸*n.* a pea of a large variety that is processed and sold in cans.

mar·ry[1] /'marē/ ▸*v.* (**-ries, -ried**) [*trans.*] **1** join in marriage: *I was married in church | the priest who married us | he was engaged to* ***get married to*** *Ginger.* ■ take (someone) as one's wife or husband in marriage: *Eric asked me to marry him.* ■ [*intrans.*] enter into marriage: *they had no plans to marry.* ■ [*intrans.*] (**marry into**) become a member of (a family) by marriage. ■ (of a parent or guardian) give (a son or daughter) in marriage, esp. for reasons of expediency: *her parents married her to a wealthy landowner.* **2** cause to meet or fit together; combine: *the two halves are trimmed and* ***married up*** *| the show* ***marries*** *poetry* ***with*** *art.* ■ [*intrans.*] meet or blend with something: *most Chardonnays don't* ***marry*** *well* ***with*** *salmon.* ■ *Nautical* splice (ropes) end to end without increasing their girth. ▷Middle English: from Old French *marier*, from Latin *maritare*, from *maritus*, literally 'married,' (as a noun) 'husband.'
▸*PHRASES* □ **marry in haste, repent at leisure** *proverb* those who rush impetuously into marriage may spend a long time regretting having done so. □ **marry money** *informal* marry a rich person.

mar·ry2 ▸*exclam. archaic* expressing surprise, indignation, or emphatic assertion. ▹late Middle English: variant of **Mary**1.

Mar·ry·at /ˈmarēət/, Frederick (1792–1848), English novelist and naval officer; known as **Captain Marryat**. Notable works: *Peter Simple* (1833), *Mr. Midshipman Easy* (1836), *The Children of the New Forest* (1847).

mar·ry·ing /ˈmarē-iNG/ ▸*adj.* [*attrib.*] likely or inclined to marry: *I'm not the marrying kind.*

Mars /märz/ **1** *Roman Mythology* the god of war and the most important Roman god after Jupiter.The month of March is named after him. Greek equivalent **Ares**. **2** *Astronomy* a small, reddish planet that is the fourth in order from the sun and is periodically visible to the naked eye.

Mars orbits between earth and Jupiter at an average distance of 141.6 million miles (228 million km) from the sun, and has an equatorial diameter of 4,208 miles (6,787 km). Its characteristic red color arises from the iron-rich minerals covering its surface. There is a tenuous atmosphere of carbon dioxide, and the seasonal polar caps are mainly of frozen carbon dioxide. Unambiguous evidence of life has yet to be found. There are two small satellites, Phobos and Deimos.

Mar·sa·la /märˈsälə/ ▸*n.* a dark, sweet, fortified dessert wine that resembles sherry, produced in Sicily.
▸*adj.* [*postpositive*] cooked or flavored with Marsala: *chicken Marsala.* ▹named after *Marsala*, a town in Sicily where it was originally made.

Mar·sal·is /märˈsalis/, Wynton (1961–) U.S. jazz trumpeter. He formed his own group in 1981 and was the first musician to win Grammy awards for both a jazz and a classical recording 1984. He cofounded Jazz at Lincoln Center and served as its artistic director from 1987. He is the brother of saxophonist Branford Marsalis (1960–).

Mar·sanne /märˈsän/ ▸*n.* a variety of white wine grape originating in the northern Rhône area of France. ▹from *Marsanne*, the name of a town in southern France.

Mar·seil·laise /ˌmärseˈyez/ the national anthem of France, written by Rouget de Lisle in 1792. ▹French, feminine of *Marseillais* 'of Marseilles.'

Mar·seilles /märˈsā/ a city and port on the Mediterranean coast of southern France; pop. 807,725. French name **Marseille** .

Mars Glob·al Sur·vey·or see **Global Surveyor**.

marsh /märsH/ ▸*n.* an area of low-lying land that is flooded in wet seasons or at high tide, and typically remains waterlogged at all times. ▹Old English *mer(i)sc* (perhaps influenced by late Latin *mariscus* 'marsh'), of West Germanic origin. **—marsh·i·ness** /ˈmärsHēnis/ *n.* **—marsh·y** *adj.*

mar·shal /ˈmärsHəl/ ▸*n.* **1** an officer of the highest rank in the armed forces of some countries, including France. ■ *chiefly historical* a high-ranking officer of state. **2** a federal or municipal law officer. ■ the head of a police department. ■ the head of a fire department. **3** an official responsible for supervising public events, esp. sports events or parades.
▸*v.* (**-shaled**, **-shal·ing**; *chiefly Brit.* **-shalled**, **-shal·ling**) [*trans.*] **1** arrange or assemble (a group of people, esp. soldiers) in order: *the general marshaled his troops* | *figurative he paused for a moment, as if marshaling his thoughts.* See note at **gather**. ■ [*trans.*] guide or usher (someone) ceremoniously: *guests were marshaled into position.* ■ [*trans.*] correctly position or arrange (rolling stock). ■ [*trans.*] guide or direct the movement of (an aircraft) on the ground at an airport. **2** *Heraldry* combine (coats of arms), typically to indicate marriage, descent, or the bearing of office. ▹Middle English (denoting a high-ranking officer of state): from Old French *mareschal* 'blacksmith, commander,' from late Latin *mariscalcus*, from Germanic elements meaning 'horse' (compare with **mare**1) and 'servant.' **—mar·shal·er** *n.* **—mar·shal·ship** /-ˌsHip/ *n.*

Mar·shall1 /ˈmärsHəl/, George C. (1880–1959), U.S. general and statesman; full name *George Catlett Marshall.* A career army officer, he served as chief of staff 1939–45 during World War II. As secretary of state 1947–49, he initiated the program of economic aid to European countries known as the Marshall Plan. Nobel Peace Prize (1953).

Mar·shall2, John (1755–1835), U.S. chief justice 1801–35. He is considered the father of the American system of constitutional law, esp. of the doctrine of judicial review.

Mar·shall3, Thurgood (1908–93), U.S. Supreme Court associate justice 1967–91. The first black justice appointed to the U.S. Supreme Court, he had previously won most of the cases he argued before the Court, including the landmark civil rights case *Brown v. Board of Education* in 1954. Known as a liberal, he championed individual rights and affirmative action.

Thurgood Marshall

Mar·shall·ese /ˌmärsHəˈlēz; -ˈlēs/ ▸*n.* (*pl.* same) **1** a native or inhabitant of the Marshall Islands. **2** the Micronesian language of the Marshall Islands.
▸*adj.* of or relating to the Marshall Islands, their inhabitants, or their language.

Mar·shall Is·lands (also **the Mar·shalls**) a country that consists of two chains of islands in the northwestern Pacific Ocean; pop. 57,700; capital, Majuro; languages, English (official) and local Austronesian languages. ▹named after John Marshall, an English adventurer who visited the islands in 1788.

The islands were made a German protectorate in 1885. After being under Japanese mandate following World War I, they were administered from 1947 until 1986 by the U.S. as part of the Pacific Islands Trust Territory and then became a republic in free association with the U.S.

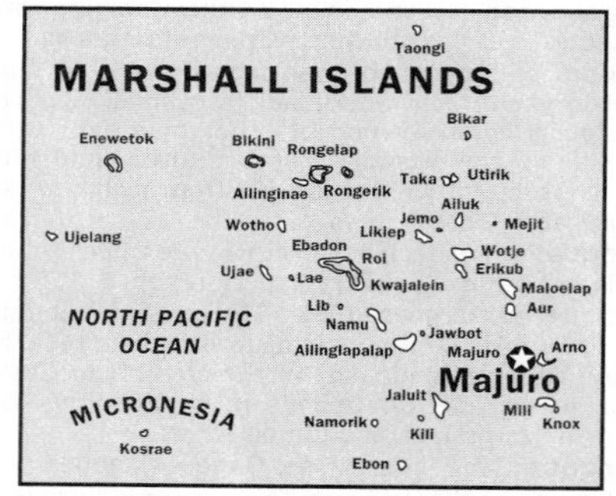

Mar·shall Plan /ˈmärsHəl ˈplan/ a program of financial aid and other initiatives, sponsored by the U.S., designed to boost the economies of western European countries after World War II. It was originally advocated by Secretary of State George C. Marshall and passed by Congress in 1948. Official name **European Recovery Program**.

mar·shal·sea /ˈmärsHəlsē/ ▸*n.* (in England) a court held before the marshal of the royal household. It was abolished in 1849. ■ (**the Marshalsea**) a former prison in London, used esp. to incarcerate debtors. It was abolished in 1842. ▹late Middle English (earlier *marchalcy*): from Anglo-Norman French *marschalcie*, from late Latin *mariscalcia*, from *mariscalcus* 'marshal.'

Marsh Ar·ab ▸*n.* a member of a seminomadic Arab people inhabiting marshland in southern Iraq, near the confluence of the Tigris and Euphrates rivers.

marsh fern ▸*n.* a tall, graceful fern that grows in moist meadows and marshes in North America and Eurasia. • *Thelypteris palustris*, family Thelypteridaceae.

marsh gas ▸*n.* methane, esp. as generated by decaying matter in marshes. Also called **swamp gas**.

marsh hawk ▸*n.* another term for **northern harrier**.

marsh·land /ˈmärsHˌland/ ▸*n.* (also **marshlands**) land consisting of marshes.

marsh·mal·low /ˈmärsHˌmelō; -ˌmalō/ ▸*n.* a spongy confection made from a soft mixture of sugar, albumen, and gelatin.

marsh mal·low ▸*n.* a tall pink-flowered plant that typically grows in brackish marshes. The roots were formerly used to make marshmallow, and it is sometimes cultivated for use in medicine. Introduced from Europe, it is found along the coast from Connecticut to Virginia. • *Althaea officinalis*, family Malvaceae.

marsh mar·i·gold ▸*n.* a plant of the buttercup family that has large yellow flowers and grows in damp ground and shallow water, native to north temperate regions. Also called **cowslip**. • *Caltha palustris*, family Ranunculaceae.

marsh marigold

marsh snail ▸*n.* any of a number of snails that live in marshy habitats or ponds, in particular: • an American salt-marsh snail (family Ellobiidae). • a European freshwater snail (*Galba* (or **Limnaea**) *palustris*, family Limnaeidae).

marsh tread·er /märsH ˈtredər/ ▸*n.* another term for **water measurer**.

Mars Path·find·er see **Pathfinder**.

Mars·ton Moor, Bat·tle of /ˈmärstən/ a battle of the English Civil War, fought in 1644 on Marston Moor near York, in which the Royalists were defeated, fatally weakening Charles I's cause.

mar·su·pi·al /märˈso͞opēəl/ *Zoology* ▸*n.* a mammal of an order whose members are born incompletely developed and are typically carried and suckled in a pouch on the mother's belly. Marsupials are found mainly in Australia and New Guinea, although three families, including the opossums, live in America. • Order Marsupialia and infraclass Metatheria, subclass Theria.
▸*adj.* of or relating to this order. ▹late 17th cent. (in the sense 'resembling a pouch'): from modern Latin *marsupialis*, via Latin from Greek *marsupion* 'pouch' (see **marsupium**).

mar·su·pi·um /märˈso͞opēəm/ ▸*n.* (*pl.* **-pi·a** /-pēə/) *Zoology* a pouch that protects eggs, offspring, or reproductive structures, esp. the pouch of a female marsupial mammal. ▹mid 17th cent.: via Latin from Greek *marsupion*, diminutive of *marsipos* 'purse.'

Mar·sy·as /ˈmärsēəs/ *Greek Mythology* a satyr who challenged Apollo to a contest in flute playing and was flayed alive when he lost.

mart /märt/ ▸*n.* [usu. with *adj.*] a trade center or market: *Atlanta's downtown apparel marts.* ▹late Middle English: from Middle Dutch *mart*, variant of *marct* 'market.'

Mar·ta·ban, Gulf of /ˌmärtəˈbän; -ˈban/ an inlet of the Andaman Sea, a part of the Indian Ocean, on the coast of southeastern Myanmar (Burma) east of Rangoon.

Mar·tel /märˈtel/, Charles, see **Charles Martel**.

Mar·tel·lo /märˈtelō/ (also **Mar·tel·lo tow·er**) ▸*n.* (*pl.* **-los**) any of numerous small circular forts that were erected for defense purposes along the southeast coasts of England during the Napoleonic Wars. ▹alteration (by association with Italian *martello* 'hammer') of Cape *Mortella* in Corsica, where such a tower proved difficult for the English to capture in 1794.

mar·ten /ˈmärtn/ ▸*n.* a chiefly arboreal weasellike mammal found in Eurasia and North America, hunted for its fur in many northern countries. • Genus *Martes*, family Mustelidae: several species. See **pine marten**, **stone marten**. ▹Middle English (frequently in the plural, denoting the fur): from Old French *(peau) martrine* 'marten (fur),' from *martre*, of West Germanic origin.

mar·tens·ite /ˈmärtnˌsīt/ ▸*n.* *Metallurgy* a hard and very brittle solid solution of carbon in iron that is the main constituent of hardened steel. ▹late 19th cent.: named after Adolf *Martens* (1850–1914), German metallurgist, + **-ite**1. **—mar·ten·sit·ic** /ˌmärtnˈsitik/ *adj.*

Mar·tha's Vine·yard /ˈmärTHəz/ an island off the coast of Massachusetts, to the south of Cape Cod. Settled by the English in 1642, it became an important center of fishing and whaling during the 18th and 19th centuries.

Mar·tial /ˈmärsHəl/ (*c.*40–*c.*AD 104), Roman epigrammatist, born in Spain; Latin name *Marcus Valerius Martialis.* His 15 books of epigrams, in a variety of meters, reflect all facets of Roman life.

mar·tial /ˈmärsHəl/ ▸*adj.* of or appropriate to war; warlike: *martial bravery.* ▷late Middle English: from Old French, or from Latin *martialis*, from *Mars, Mart-* (see **Mars**). —**mar·tial·ly** *adv.*

mar·tial arts ▸*plural n.* various sports or skills, mainly of Japanese origin, that originated as forms of self-defense or attack, such as judo, karate, and kendo. —**mar·tial art·ist** *n.*

mar·tial ea·gle ▸*n.* a brown eagle with a brown-spotted white belly. It is Africa's largest raptor. • *Polmaetus bellicosus*, family Accipitridae.

mar·tial law ▸*n.* military government involving the suspension of ordinary law.

Mar·tian /ˈmärsHən/ ▸*adj.* of or relating to the planet Mars or its supposed inhabitants.
▸*n.* a hypothetical or fictional inhabitant of Mars. ▷late Middle English (in the senses 'subject to Mars's influence' and 'martial'): from Latin *Mars, Mart-* (see **Mars**) + **-ian**.

Mar·tin[1] /ˈmärtn/, Dean (1917–95), U.S. singer and actor; born *Dino Paul Crocetti*. He became known originally for his comedy and singing act with Jerry Lewis from 1946 .He joined with Frank Sinatra and Sammy Davis, Jr. (1925–90) in a number of movies, including *Ocean's Eleven* (1960), and had his own television show 1965–73.

Mar·tin[2], Mary (1913–90), U.S. actress and singer. She starred in the Broadway musicals *South Pacific* (1949), *Peter Pan* (1954), and *The Sound of Music* (1959).

Mar·tin[3], Paul Edgar Philippe (1938–), Canadian statesman; prime minister of Canada from 2003.

Mar·tin[4], Steve (1945–), U.S. actor and comedian. He established his reputation in farcical movie comedies such as *The Jerk* (1979) and went on to make, among others, *Roxanne* (1987), *LA Story* (1991), and *Bowfinger* (1999).

Mar·tin, St. (died 397), French priest; bishop of Tours from 371; a patron saint of France. As he was giving half of his cloak to a beggar, he received a vision of Christ and was soon baptized. Feast day, November 11.

mar·tin /ˈmärtn/ ▸*n.* a swift-flying, insectivorous songbird of the swallow family, typically having a less strongly forked tail than a swallow. • Family Hirundinidae: several genera and numerous species, e.g., the **purple martin**. ▷late Middle English: probably a shortening of obsolete *martinet*, from French, probably from the name of St. *Martin* of Tours, celebrated at **Martinmas**.

mar·ti·net /ˌmärtnˈet/ ▸*n.* a strict disciplinarian, esp. in the armed forces. ▷late 17th cent. (denoting the drill system invented by Martinet): named after Jean *Martinet*, 17th-cent. French drillmaster. —**mar·ti·net·ish** (also **mar·ti·net·tish**) *adj.*

Mar·ti·nez /märˈtēnez/ an industrial port in north central California, on Suisun Bay, north of Oakland; pop. 31,808.

mar·tin·gale /ˈmärtn,gāl/ ▸*n.* **1** a strap, or set of straps, attached at one end to the noseband (**standing martingale**) or reins (**running martingale**) of a horse and at the other end to the girth. It is used to prevent the horse from raising its head too high. **2** a gambling system of continually doubling the stakes in the hope of an eventual win that must yield a net profit. ▷late 16th cent.: from French, from Spanish *almártaga*, from Arabic *al-marta'a* 'the fastening,' influenced by *martingale*, from Occitan *martegal* 'inhabitant of Martigues (in Provence).'

mar·ti·ni /märˈtēnē/ ▸*n.* a cocktail made from gin and dry vermouth. ▷named after *Martini* and Rossi, an Italian firm selling vermouth.

Mar·ti·nique /ˌmärtnˈēk/ a French island in the Caribbean Sea, in the Lesser Antilles group; pop. 360,000; capital, Fort-de-France. —**Mar·ti·niq·uan** /-ˈēkən/ *n.* & *adj.*

Mar·tin·ist /ˈmärtn-ist; märˈtan-/ ▸*n.* an adherent of a form of mystical pantheism developed by the French philosopher L. C. de Saint-Martin (1743–1803). —**Mar·tin·ism** /-izəm/ *n.*

Mar·tin·mas /ˈmärtnməs/ ▸*n.* St. Martin's Day, November 11.

mart·let /ˈmärtlət/ ▸*n.* *Heraldry* a bird like a swallow without feet, borne (typically with the wings closed) as a charge or a mark of cadency for a fourth son. ▷late Middle English (denoting a swift): from Old French *merlet*, influenced by *martinet* (see **martin**).

mar·tyr /ˈmärtər/ ▸*n.* a person who is killed because of their religious or other beliefs: *the first Christian martyr.* ■ a person who displays or exaggerates their discomfort or distress in order to obtain sympathy or admiration: *she wanted to play the martyr.* ■ (**martyr to**) a constant sufferer from (an ailment): *I'm a martyr to migraines!*
▸*v.* [*trans.*] (usu. **be martyred**) kill (someone) because of their beliefs: *she was martyred for her faith.* ■ cause great pain or distress to: *there was no need to martyr themselves again.* ▷Old English *martir*, via ecclesiastical Latin from Greek *martur* 'witness' (in Christian use, 'martyr'). —**mar·tyr·i·za·tion** /ˌmärtərəˈzāsHən/ *n.* —**mar·tyr·ize** /ˈmärtə,rīz/ *v.*

mar·tyr·dom /ˈmärtərdəm/ ▸*n.* the death or suffering of a martyr. ■ a display of feigned or exaggerated suffering to obtain sympathy or admiration. ▷Old English *martyrdōm* (see **martyr**, **-dom**).

mar·tyred /ˈmärtərd/ ▸*adj.* (of a person) having been martyred: *a martyred saint.* ■ (of an attitude or manner) showing feigned or exaggerated suffering to obtain sympathy or admiration: *he gave Mulder a brief, martyred look.*

mar·tyr·ol·o·gy /ˌmärtəˈräləjē/ ▸*n.* (*pl.* **-gies**) the branch of history or literature that deals with the lives of martyrs. ■ a list or register of martyrs. ▷late 16th cent.: via medieval Latin from ecclesiastical Greek *marturologion*, from *martur* 'martyr' + *logos* 'account.' —**mar·tyr·o·log·i·cal** /-rəˈläjikəl/ *adj.* —**mar·tyr·ol·o·gist** /-jist/ *n.*

mar·tyr·y /ˈmärtərē/ ▸*n.* (*pl.* **-tyr·ies**) a shrine or church erected in honor of a martyr. ▷Middle English (denoting martyrdom): via medieval Latin from Greek *marturion* 'martyrdom.'

Ma·ruts /ˈmərōōts/ *Hinduism* the sons of Rudra. In the Rig Veda they are the storm gods, Indra's helpers. Also called **Rudras**.

mar·vel /ˈmärvəl/ ▸*v.* (**-veled**, **-vel·ing**; *chiefly Brit.* **-velled**, **-vel·ling**) [*intrans.*] be filled with wonder or astonishment: *she* ***marveled at*** *Jeffrey's composure* | [with *direct speech*] *"Isn't this an evening," marveled John.*
▸*n.* a wonderful or astonishing person or thing: *the marvels of technology* | *Charlie, you're a marvel!* ▷Middle English (as a noun): from Old French *merveille*, from late Latin *mirabilia*, neuter plural of Latin *mirabilis* 'wonderful,' from *mirari* 'wonder at.' —**mar·vel·er** *n.*

Mar·vell /ˈmärvəl/, Andrew (1621–78), English metaphysical poet. Most of his poetry was published posthumously and was not recognized until the 20th century. Notable poems: "To his Coy Mistress" and "An Horatian Ode on Cromwell's Return from Ireland."

mar·vel of Pe·ru (also **mar·vel-of-Peru**) ▸*n.* another term for **four-o'clock**.

mar·vel·ous /ˈmärv(ə)ləs/ (*Brit.* **mar·vel·lous**) ▸*adj.* causing great wonder; extraordinary: *marvelous technological toys.* ■ extremely good or pleasing; splendid: *you have done a marvelous job* | *it's marvelous to see you.* ▷Middle English: from Old French *merveillus*, from *merveille* (see **marvel**). —**mar·vel·ous·ly** *adv.* —**mar·vel·ous·ness** *n.*

marv·y /ˈmärvē/ ▸*adj. informal* wonderful; marvelous.

Mar·wa·ri /mərˈwärē/ ▸*n.* an Indic language of Rajasthan in India.
▸*adj.* of or relating to this language. ▷from Hindi *Māṛvār*, from Sanskrit *maru* 'desert.'

Marx /märks/, Karl (Heinrich) (1818–83), German political philosopher and economist, resident of England from 1849. The founder of modern communism with Friedrich Engels, he collaborated with him in the writing of the *Communist Manifesto* (1848) and enlarged it into a series of books, most notably the three-volume *Das Kapital*.

Marx Broth·ers a family of U.S. comedians, consisting of brothers **Chico** (Leonard, 1886–1961), **Harpo** (Adolph Arthur, 1888–1964), **Groucho** (Julius Henry, 1890–1977), and **Zeppo** (Herbert, 1901–79). Their movies, which are characterized by their anarchic humor, include *Horse Feathers* (1932), *Duck Soup* (1933), and *A Night at the Opera* (1935).

Marx·ism /ˈmärk,sizəm/ ▸*n.* the political and economic theories of Karl Marx and Friedrich Engels, later developed by their followers to form the basis for the theory and practice of communism.

Central to Marxist theory is an explanation of social change in terms of economic factors, according to which the means of production provide the economic *base*, which influences or determines the political and ideological *superstructure*. Marx and Engels predicted the revolutionary overthrow of capitalism by the proletariat and the eventual attainment of a classless communist society.

—**Marx·i·an** /-sēən/ *adj.* —**Marx·ist** *n.* & *adj.*

Marx·ism–Le·nin·ism ▸*n.* the doctrines of Marx as interpreted and put into effect by Lenin in the Soviet Union and (at first) by Mao Zedong in China. —**Marx·ist–Le·nin·ist** *n.* & *adj.*

Mar·y[1] /ˈme(ə)rē/, mother of Jesus; known as **the (Blessed) Virgin Mary**, or **St. Mary**, or **Our Lady**. According to the Gospels, she was a virgin betrothed to Joseph and conceived Jesus by the power of the Holy Spirit. She has been venerated by Catholic and Orthodox Churches from earliest Christian times. Feast days, January 1 (Roman Catholic Church), March 25 (Annunciation), August 15 (Assumption), September 8 (Immaculate Conception).

Mar·y[2] the name of two queens of England: ■ **Mary I** (1516–58), daughter of Henry VIII and Catherine of Aragon; reigned 1553–58; known as **Mary Tudor** or **Bloody Mary**. In an attempt to reverse the country's turn toward Protestantism, she instigated the series of religious persecutions by which she earned her nickname. ■ **Mary II** (1662–94), daughter of James II; reigned 1689–94. Having been invited to replace her Catholic father on the throne after his deposition in 1689, she insisted that her husband, William of Orange, be crowned along with her.

Mar·y, St. see **Mary**[1].

Mar·y Ce·leste / səˈlest/ an American brig that was found adrift in the North Atlantic in December 1872 in perfect condition but abandoned. The fate of the crew and the reason for the abandonment of the ship remain a mystery. ■ [as *n.*] (also **Ma·rie Ce·leste**) a ship, building, or other thing that is deserted, esp. inexplicably. [The variant spelling 'Marie Celeste' was used by Sir Arthur Conan Doyle in his 1884 fictionalized account of the abandoned ship.]

Mar·y Jane /ˈme(ə)rē ˈjān/ ▸*n.* a flat, round-toed shoe for women and girls, with a single strap across the top. ▷1920s: from the female given name *Mary Jane*.

Mar·y·land /ˈmerələnd/ a state in the eastern U.S. that surrounds Chesapeake Bay, on the Atlantic coast; pop. 5,296,486; capital, Annapolis; statehood, Apr. 28, 1788 (7). Colonized by England in the 1600s, it was one of the original thirteen states. ▷named after Queen Henrietta *Maria* (1609–69), wife of Charles I. —**Mary·land·er** /-ˌlandər/ *n.*

Mar·y Mag·da·lene, St. /ˈmagdə,lēn; -lən/ (also **the Mag·da·len** /-lən/) (in the New Testament) a woman of Magdala in Galilee. She was a follower of Jesus, who cured her of evil spirits (Luke 8:2); she is also traditionally identified with the "sinner" of Luke 7:37. Feast day, July 22.

Mar·y, Queen of Scots (1542–87), daughter of James V; queen of Scotland 1542–67; queen consort of France 1559–60 as the wife of Francis II; known as **Mary Stuart**. A devout Catholic, she was unable to control her Protestant lords and fled from Scotland to England in 1567. She became the focus of several Catholic plots against Elizabeth I and was eventually beheaded. Her son James VI of Scotland became James I of England.

Mar·y Stu·art /ˈst(y)ōōərt/ see **Mary, Queen of Scots**.

Mar·y Tu·dor /ˈt(y)ōōdər/, Mary I of England (see **Mary**[2]).

mar·zi·pan /ˈmärzə,pan; ˈmärtsə-/ ▸*n.* a sweet, yellowish paste of ground almonds, sugar, and egg whites, often colored and used to make small cakes or confections or as an icing for larger cakes. Also called **almond paste**. ■ a confection or cake made of or based on marzipan. ▷late 15th cent. (as *marchpane*): from Italian *marzapane*, possibly from Arabic. The form *marchpane* (influenced by **March** and obsolete *pain* 'bread') was more usual until the late 19th cent., when *marzipan* (influenced by German, which has the same spelling) displaced it.

ma·sa /ˈmäsə; ˈmäsə/ ▸*n.* (in Latin American cuisine) dough made from corn flour and used to make tortillas, tamales, etc. ▷Spanish.

Ma·sac·cio /məˈsäcHē,ō/, (1401–28), Italian painter; born *Tommaso Giovanni di Simone Guidi*. The first artist to apply the laws of perspective to painting, he is known particularly for his frescoes in the Brancacci Chapel in Florence (1424–27).

Ma·sa·da /məˈsädə/ the site of the ruins of a palace and fortification built by Herod the Great on the southwestern shore of the Dead Sea in the 1st century BC.

Ma·sai /ˈmä,sī; mäˈsī/ (also **Maa·sai**) ▸*n.* (*pl.* same or **-sais**) **1** a member of a pastoral people living in Tanzania and Kenya. **2** the Nilotic language of the Masai.
▸*adj.* of or relating to the Masai or their language.

ma·sa·la /məˈsälə/ ▸*n.* any of a number of spice mixtures ground into a paste or powder for use in Indian cooking. ■ a dish flavored with this: *chicken masala.* ▹from Urdu *maṣālaḥ*, based on Arabic *maṣāliḥ* 'ingredients, materials.'

Ma·san /ˈmäˌsän/ a port city in southeastern South Korea, on an inlet of the Western Channel (the Korea Strait); pop. 497,000.

Ma·sa·ryk /ˈmäsəˌrik/, Tomáš (Garrigue) (1850–1937), Czech statesman; president 1918–35. He became Czechoslovakia's first president when independence was achieved in 1918.

Mas·ba·te /mäsˈbätē/ an island in the central Philippines; pop. 599,000.

masc. ▸*abbr.* masculine.

Mas·ca·gni /məˈskänē; mäˈskänyē/, Pietro (1863–1945), Italian composer and conductor. He is especially known for the opera *Cavalleria Rusticana* (1890).

mas·car·a /maˈskarə/ ▸*n.* a cosmetic for darkening and thickening the eyelashes. ▹late 19th cent.: from Italian, literally 'mask,' from Arabic *masḵara* 'buffoon.' **—mas·car·aed** /-ˈskarəd/ *adj.*

Mas·ca·rene Is·lands /ˌmaskəˈrēn/ (also **the Mas·ca·renes**) a group of three islands—Réunion, Mauritius, and Rodrigues—in the western Indian Ocean, east of Madagascar.

mas·car·po·ne /ˌmäskärˈpōn(e)/ ▸*n.* a soft, mild Italian cream cheese.

mas·cle /ˈmaskəl/ ▸*n. Heraldry* a lozenge voided, i.e., with a central lozenge-shaped aperture. ▹late Middle English: from Anglo-Norman French, from Anglo-Latin *mascula* 'mesh.'

mas·con /ˈmasˌkän/ ▸*n. Astronomy* a concentration of denser material below the surface of the moon or other body, causing a local increase in gravitational pull. ▹1960s: from *mas(s) con(centration).*

mas·cot /ˈmasˌkät; -kət/ ▸*n.* a person or thing that is supposed to bring good luck or that is used to symbolize a particular event or organization: *the squadron's mascot was a young lion cub.* ▹late 19th cent.: from French *mascotte*, from modern Provençal *mascotto*, feminine diminutive of *masco* 'witch.'

mas·cu·line /ˈmaskyələn/ ▸*adj.* **1** having qualities or appearance traditionally associated with men, esp. strength and aggressiveness: *he is outstandingly handsome and robust, very masculine.* ■ of or relating to men; male: *a masculine voice.* See note at **MALE**. **2** *Grammar* of or denoting a gender of nouns and adjectives, conventionally regarded as male. **3** *Music* (of a cadence) occurring on a metrically strong beat.
▸*n.* (**the masculine**) the male sex or gender: *the masculine as the norm.* ■ *Grammar* a masculine word or form. ▹late Middle English (in grammatical use): via Old French from Latin *masculinus*, from *masculus* 'male.' **—mas·cu·line·ly** *adv.* **—mas·cu·lin·i·ty** /ˌmaskyəˈlinitē/ *n.*

mas·cu·line rhyme ▸*n. Prosody* a rhyme of final stressed syllables (e.g., *blow/flow, confess/redress*). Compare with **FEMININE RHYME**.

mas·cu·lin·ist /ˈmaskyələˌnist/ (also **mas·cu·list** /-list/) ▸*adj.* characterized by or denoting attitudes or values held to be typical of men: *masculinist language.* ■ of or relating to the advocacy of the rights or needs of men.
▸*n.* an advocate of the rights or needs of men.

mas·cu·lin·ize /ˈmaskyələˌnīz/ ▸*v.* [*trans.*] induce male physiological characteristics in: *male sex steroids masculinize female hyenas.* ■ cause to appear or seem masculine: [as *adj.*] (**masculinized**) *a slightly masculinized swagger.* **—mas·cu·lin·i·za·tion** /ˌmaskyələnəˈzāshən/ *n.*

Mase·field /ˈmāsˌfēld/, John (Edward) (1878–1967), English poet and novelist. He was appointed poet laureate in 1930. Notable works: *Salt-Water Ballads* (1902) and *Reynard the Fox* (1919).

ma·ser /ˈmāzər/ ▸*n.* a device using the stimulated emission of radiation by excited atoms to amplify or generate coherent monochromatic electromagnetic radiation in the microwave range. ▹1950s: acronym from *microwave amplification by the stimulated emission of radiation.*

Ma·se·ru /ˈmäzəˌroo; ˈmaz-/ the capital of Lesotho, situated on the Caledon River near the border with the province of Free State in South Africa; pop. 367,000.

MASH /mash/ ▸*abbr.* mobile army surgical hospital.

mash /mash/ ▸*n.* a uniform mass made by crushing a substance into a soft pulp, sometimes with the addition of liquid: *pound the garlic to a mash.* ■ bran mixed with hot water given as a warm food to horses or other animals. ■ *Brit., informal* mashed potatoes. ■ (in brewing) a mixture of powdered malt and hot water, which is stood until the sugars dissolve to form the wort.
▸*v.* [*trans.*] **1** reduce (a food or other substance) to a uniform mass by crushing it: *mash the beans to a paste* | [as *adj.*] (**mashed**) *mashed bananas.* ■ crush or smash (something) to a pulp: *he almost had his head mashed by a slamming door.* ■ *informal* press forcefully on (something): *the worst thing you can do is mash the brake pedal.* **2** (in brewing) mix (powdered malt) with hot water to form wort. **3** *Brit., informal* infuse or brew (tea). ■ [*intrans.*] (of tea) draw; brew. ▹Old English *māsc* (used as a brewing term); perhaps ultimately related to **MIX**.

mashed po·ta·toes ▸*plural n.* a dish of potatoes that have been boiled and mashed, typically prepared with milk and butter.

mash·er /ˈmashər/ ▸*n.* **1** a utensil for mashing food: *a potato masher.* **2** *informal* a man who makes unwelcome sexual advances, often in public places and typically to women he does not know. [late 19th cent.: probably a derivative of slang *mash* 'attract sexually,' perhaps from Romany *masherava* 'allure.']

Mash·had /məˈshäd/ (also **Me·shed** /məˈshed/) a city in northeastern Iran, close to the border with Turkmenistan; pop. 1,463,000. The burial place in AD 809 of the Abbasid caliph Harun ar-Rashid and in 818 of the Shiite leader Ali ar-Rida, it is a holy city of the Shiite Muslims. It is the second largest city in Iran.

mash·ie /ˈmashē/ ▸*n. dated Golf* an iron used for lofting or for medium distances. ▹late 19th cent.: perhaps from French *massue* 'club.'

mash note ▸*n. informal* a letter that expresses infatuation with or gushing appreciation of someone. ▹late 19th cent.: from slang *mash* 'infatuation' + **NOTE**.

Ma·sho·na /məˈshōnə; -ˈshänə/ ▸*n.* the Shona people collectively.
▸*adj.* of or relating to the Shona people. ▹the name in Shona.

Ma·sho·na·land /məˈshōnəˌland; -ˈshänə-/ an area of northern Zimbabwe that is occupied by the Shona people. A former province of Southern Rhodesia, it is now divided into the three provinces of Mashonaland East, West, and Central.

mash-up ▸*n. informal* a recording created by digitally combining and synchronizing instrumental tracks with vocal tracks from two or more different songs: *a mash-up of Madonna's "Ray of Light" and the Sex Pistols.*

mas·jid /ˈməsjid; ˈmas-/ ▸*n.* Arabic word for a mosque.

mask /mask/ ▸*n.* **1** a covering for all or part of the face, in particular: ■ a covering worn as a disguise, or to amuse or terrify other people. ■ a covering made of fiber or gauze and fitting over the nose and mouth to protect against dust or air pollutants, or made of sterile gauze and worn to prevent infection of the wearer or (in surgery) of the patient. ■ a protective covering fitting over the whole face, worn in fencing, ice hockey, and other sports. ■ a respirator used to filter inhaled air or to supply gas for inhalation. ■ (also **masque**) a cosmetic preparation spread over the face and left for some time to cleanse and improve the skin. ■ *Entomology* the enlarged lower lip of a dragonfly larva, which can be extended to seize prey. **2** a likeness of a person's face in clay or wax, esp. one made by taking a mold from the face. ■ a person's face regarded as having set into a particular expression: *his face was a mask of rage.* ■ a hollow model of a human head worn by ancient Greek and Roman actors. ■ the face or head of an animal, esp. of a fox, as a hunting trophy. ■ *archaic* a masked person. **3** *figurative* a disguise or pretense: *she let her mask of moderate respectability slip.* **4** *Photography* a piece of something, such as a card, used to cover a part of an image that is not required when exposing a print. ■ *Electronics* a patterned metal film used in the manufacture of microcircuits to allow selective modification of the underlying material.
▸*v.* [*trans.*] cover (the face) with a mask. ■ conceal (something) from view: *the poplars masked a factory.* ■ disguise or hide (a sensation or quality): *brandy did not completely mask the bitter taste.* ■ cover (an object or surface) so as to protect it from a process, esp. painting: ***mask off** doors and cupboards with sheets of plastic.* ▹mid 16th cent.: from French *masque*, from Italian *maschera, mascara*, probably from medieval Latin *masca* 'witch, specter,' but influenced by Arabic *masḵara* 'buffoon.' **—masked** *adj.*

masked ball ▸*n.* a ball at which participants wear masks to conceal their faces.

mask·er /ˈmaskər/ ▸*n.* **1** a thing that masks or conceals something else. **2** a person taking part in a masquerade or masked ball.

mask·ing tape ▸*n.* adhesive tape used in painting to cover areas on which paint is not wanted.

mas·ki·nonge /ˈmaskəˌnänj/ ▸*n.* another term for **MUSKELLUNGE**.

Mas·low /ˈmazlō/, Abraham (Harold) (1908–70), U.S. psychologist. He was a leader of the humanistic school of psychology, and he postulated a "hierarchy of needs" to explain human motivation. He wrote *Motivation and Personality* (1954).

mas·och·ism /ˈmasəˌkizəm; ˈmaz-/ ▸*n.* the tendency to derive pleasure, esp. sexual gratification, from one's own pain or humiliation. ■ (in general use) the enjoyment of what appears to be painful or tiresome: *isn't there some masochism involved in taking on this kind of project?* ▹late 19th cent.: named after Leopold von Sacher-*Masoch* (1835–95), the Austrian novelist who described it, + **-ISM**. **—mas·och·ist** *n.* **—mas·och·is·tic** /ˌmasəˈkistik; ˌmaz-/ *adj.* **—mas·och·is·ti·cal·ly** /ˌmasəˈkistik(ə)lē; ˌmaz-/ *adv.*

Ma·son /ˈmāsən/, James (Neville) (1909–84), English actor. He acted in more than 100 movies, notably *A Star is Born* (1954), *Lolita* (1962), *Georgy Girl* (1966), and *The Verdict* (1982).

ma·son /ˈmāsən/ ▸*n.* **1** a builder and worker in stone. **2** (**Mason**) a Freemason.
▸*v.* [*trans.*] build from or strengthen with stone. ■ cut, hew, or dress (stone). ▹Middle English: from Old French *masson* (noun), *maçonner* (verb), probably of Germanic origin; perhaps related to **MAKE**.

ma·son bee ▸*n.* a solitary bee that nests in cavities within which it constructs cells of sand and other particles glued together with saliva. • *Osmia* and other genera, family Apidae.

Ma·son Cit·y /ˈmāsən/ an industrial city in northern central Iowa; pop. 29,172.

Ma·son–Dix·on line /ˈdiksən/ (also **Ma·son-Dix·on Line**) ▸*n.* (in the U.S.) the boundary between Maryland and Pennsylvania, taken as the northern limit of the slave-owning states before the abolition of slavery. ▹named after Charles *Mason* (1728–1786) and Jeremiah *Dixon* (1733–1779), the 18th-cent. English astronomers who surveyed it in 1763–67.

Ma·son·ic /məˈsänik/ ▸*adj.* of or relating to Freemasons: *a Masonic lodge.*

Ma·son·ite /ˈmāsəˌnīt/ ▸*n. trademark* a type of hardboard. ▹1920s: from the name of the *Mason* Fibre Co., Laurel, Mississippi, + **-ITE**[1].

ma·son jar (also **Ma·son jar**) ▸*n.* a wide-mouthed glass jar with an airtight screw top, used for preserving fruit and vegetables. ▹late 19th cent.: named after John L. *Mason* (died 1902), U.S. inventor.

ma·son·ry /ˈmāsənrē/ ▸*n.* **1** stonework. ■ the work of a mason. **2** (**Masonry**) Freemasonry.

ma·son wasp ▸*n.* a solitary wasp that nests in a cavity or in a hole in the ground, sealing the nest with mud or similar material. • Several genera in the family Eumenidae.

Ma·so·rah /məˈsôrə/ (also **Mas·so·rah**) ▸*n.* (**the Masorah**) the collection of information and comment on the text of the traditional Hebrew Bible by the Masoretes. ■ the Masoretic text of the Bible. ▹from Hebrew *māsōrāh*, based on *ʾāsar* 'to bind,' later interpreted in the sense 'tradition' (as if from *māsar* 'hand down').

Mas·o·rete /ˈmasəˌrēt/ (also **Mas·so·rete**) ▸*n.* any of the Jewish scholars of the 6th–10th centuries AD who contributed to the establishment of a recognized text of the Hebrew Bible, and to the compilation of the Masorah. ▹from French *Massoret* and modern Latin *Massoreta*, from Hebrew *māsōreṯ*; related to *māsōrāh* (see **MASORAH**). **—Mas·o·ret·ic** /ˌmasəˈretik/ *adj.*

masque /mask/ ▸*n.* **1** a form of amateur dramatic entertainment, popular among the nobility in 16th- and 17th-century England, which consisted of dancing and acting performed by masked players. ■ a masked ball. **2** variant spelling of **MASK** (sense 1). ▹early 16th cent. (in the sense 'masquerade or masked ball'): probably a back-formation (with spelling influenced by French *masque* 'mask') from *masker*, from Italian *mascar* 'person wearing a mask.' **—mas·quer** /ˈmaskər/ *n.*

mas·quer·ade /ˌmaskəˈrād/ ▸*n.* a false show or pretense: *his masquerade ended when he was arrested.* ■ the wearing of disguise: *dressing up, role-playing, and masquerade.* ■ a masked ball.
▸*v.* [*intrans.*] pretend to be someone one is not: *a journalist **masquerading as** a man in distress.* ■ be disguised or passed off as something else: *the idle gossip that*

masquerades as news in some local papers. ▷late 16th cent.: from French *mascarade*, from Italian *maschera-ta*, from *maschera* 'mask.' —**mas·quer·ad·er** *n.*

Mass /mas/ ▶*n.* the Christian Eucharist or Holy Communion, esp. in the Roman Catholic Church: *we went to Mass | the Latin Mass.* ■ a celebration of this: *there was a Mass and the whole family was supposed to go.* ■ a musical setting of parts of the liturgy used in the Mass. ▷Old English *mæsse*, from ecclesiastical Latin *missa*, from Latin *miss-* 'dismissed,' from *mittere*, perhaps from the last words of the service, *Ite, missa est* 'Go, it is the dismissal.'

mass /mas/ ▶*n.* **1** a coherent, typically large body of matter with no definite shape: ***a mass of*** *curly hair | from here the trees were a dark mass.* ■ a large number of people or objects crowded together: ***a mass of*** *cyclists.* ■ a large amount of material: ***a mass of*** *conflicting evidence.* ■ (**masses**) *informal* a large quantity or amount of something: *we get* ***masses of*** *homework.* ■ any of the main portions in a painting or drawing that each have some unity in color, lighting, or some other quality: *the masterly distribution of masses.* **2** (**the mass of**) the majority of: *the great mass of the population had little interest in the project.* ■ (**the masses**) the ordinary people. **3** *Physics* the quantity of matter that a body contains, as measured by its acceleration under a given force or by the force exerted on it by a gravitational field. ■ (in general use) weight.
▶*adj.* [*attrib.*] relating to, done by, or affecting large numbers of people or things: *the movie has mass appeal | a mass exodus of refugees.*
▶*v.* assemble or cause to assemble into a mass or as one body: [*trans.*] *both countries began massing troops in the region* | | [*intrans.*] *clouds massed heavily on the horizon.* ▷late Middle English: from Old French *masse*, from Latin *massa*, from Greek *maza* 'barley cake'; perhaps related to *massein* 'knead.' —**mass·less** *adj.*
▶*PHRASES* □ **be a mass of** be completely covered with: *his face was a mass of bruises.* □ **in the mass** as a whole: *her genuine affection for humanity in the mass.*

Mass. ▶*abbr.* Massachusetts.

mas·sa /ˈmasə/ ▶*n.* (in representations of black speech) master: *"Massa, I have some news for you, sah."*

Mas·sa·chu·sett /ˌmasəˈCHōōsit/ (**Mas·sa·chu·set**) ▶*n.* **1** (*pl.* same or **-setts**) a member of an extinct North American Indian people, formerly found in eastern Massachusetts. **2** the Algonquian language of this people.

Mas·sa·chu·setts /ˌmasəˈCHōōsits/ a state in the northeastern U.S., on the Atlantic coast, one of the six New England states; pop. 6,349,097; capital, Boston; statehood, Feb. 6, 1788 (6). Settled by the Pilgrims in 1620, it was a center of resistance to the British before becoming one of the original thirteen states.

Mas·sa·chu·setts Bay an inlet of the Atlantic Ocean between Cape Cod and Cape Ann, in eastern Massachusetts, of which Boston Harbor is an inlet.

Mas·sa·chu·setts In·sti·tute of Tech·nol·o·gy (abbr.: **MIT**) a U.S. institute of higher education, famous for scientific and technical research, founded in 1861 in Cambridge, Massachusetts.

mas·sa·cre /ˈmasikər/ ▶*n.* an indiscriminate and brutal slaughter of people: *the attack was described as a cold-blooded massacre | she says he is an accomplice to massacre.* ■ *informal* a heavy defeat of a sports team or contestant.
▶*v.* [*trans.*] deliberately and violently kill (a large number of people). See note at **KILL**. ■ *informal* inflict a heavy defeat on (a sports team or contestant). ▷late 16th cent.: from French, of unknown origin.

mas·sage /məˈsäZH; -ˈsäj/ ▶*n.* the rubbing and kneading of muscles and joints of the body with the hands, esp. to relieve tension or pain: *massage can ease tiredness and jet lag | a massage will help loosen you up.*
▶*v.* [*trans.*] **1** rub and knead (a person or part of the body) with the hands. ■ (**massage something in/into/onto**) rub a substance into (the skin or hair). ■ flatter (someone's ego): *I chose a man who massaged my bruised ego.* **2** manipulate (figures) to give a more acceptable result: *the accounts had been massaged and adjusted to suit the government.* ▷late 19th cent.: from French, from *masser* 'knead, treat with massage,' probably from Portuguese *amassar* 'knead,' from *massa* 'dough.' —**mas·sag·er** *n.*

mas·sage par·lor ▶*n.* an establishment providing massages. ■ such an establishment that is actually a front for prostitution.

mas·sa·sau·ga /ˌmasəˈsôgə/ ▶*n.* a small North American rattlesnake of variable color that favors damp habitats. • *Sistrurus catenatus*, family Viperidae. ▷mid 19th cent.: formed irregularly from **MISSISSAUGA**.

Mas·sa·soit /ˌmasəˈsoit/ (c.1580–1661), chief of the Wampanoag Indians; father of King Philip. He signed a peace treaty with the Pilgrims at Plymouth in 1621 and remained a friend to white settlers.

Mass card ▶*n.* (in the Roman Catholic Church) a card sent to the family of someone who has died, stating that the sender has arranged for a Mass to be said in memory of the deceased.

mass de·fect ▶*n. Physics* the difference between the mass of an isotope and its mass number.

mas·sé /maˈsā/ ▶*n.* [usu. as *adj.*] *Billiards* a stroke made with an inclined cue, imparting swerve to the ball: *a massé shot.* ▷late 19th cent.: French, past participle of *masser*, describing the action of making such a stroke.

mass en·er·gy ▶*n. Physics* mass and energy regarded as interconvertible manifestations of the same phenomenon, according to the laws of relativity. ■ the mass of a body regarded relativistically as energy.

mas·se·ter /məˈsētər; ma-/ (also **masseter muscle**) ▶*n. Anatomy* a muscle that runs through the rear part of the cheek from the temporal bone to the lower jaw on each side and closes the jaw in chewing. ▷late 16th cent.: from Greek *masētēr*, from *masasthai* 'to chew.'

mas·seur /maˈsər; mə-/ ▶*n.* a person, esp. a man, who provides massages professionally. ▷French, from *masser* 'to massage.'

mas·seuse /maˈsōōs; mə-; maˈsœz/ ▶*n.* a female masseur. ▷French.

Mas·sey /ˈmasē/, Raymond (Hart) (1896–1983), U.S. actor and producer; born in Canada. His movies include *Abe Lincoln in Illinois* (1940), *Arsenic and Old Lace* (1944) and *East of Eden* (1955). He also played Dr. Leonard Gillespie on the television series "Dr. Kildare" (1961–66).

mas·si·cot /ˈmasiˌkät/ ▶*n.* a yellow form of lead monoxide, used as a pigment. ▷late 15th cent.: from French (influenced by Italian *marzacotto* 'unguent'), ultimately from Arabic *martak*.

mas·sif /maˈsēf/ ▶*n.* a compact group of mountains, esp. one that is separate from other groups. ▷early 16th cent. (denoting a large building): French adjective meaning 'massive,' used as a noun. The current sense dates from the late 19th cent.

Mas·sif Cen·tral /mäˈsēf/ a mountainous plateau in south central France. It covers almost one sixth of the country and rises to a height of 6,188 feet (1,887 m) at Puy de Sancy, a mountain in the Auvergne region.

Mas·sil·lon /ˈmasələn/ a city in northeastern Ohio, south of Akron; pop. 31,007.

Mas·sine /mäˈsēn/, Léonide Fédorovitch (1895–1979), French choreographer and ballet dancer, born in Russia; born *Leonid Fyodorovich Myasin*. He was the originator of the symphonic ballet, and danced in and choreographed the movie *The Red Shoes* (1948).

mas·sive /ˈmasiv/ ▶*adj.* **1** large and heavy or solid: *a massive rampart of stone.* See note at **HEAVY**. **2** exceptionally large: *massive crowds are expected.* ■ very intense or severe: *a massive heart attack.* ■ *informal* particularly successful or influential: *the title song became a massive hit.* **3** *Geology* (of rocks or beds) having no discernible form or structure. ■ (of a mineral) not visibly crystalline. ▷late Middle English: from French *massif, -ive*, from Old Fre *massis*, based on Latin *massa* (see **MASS**). —**mas·sive·ly** *adv.* [as *submodifier*] *a massively complicated network.* —**mas·sive·ness** *n.*

mas·sive·ly par·al·lel ▶*adj.* (of a computer) consisting of many individual processing units, and thus able to carry out simultaneous calculations on a substantial scale: *a massively parallel computer with 168 processors.*

mass mar·ket ▶*n.* the market for goods that are produced in large quantities.
▶*v.* (**mass-mar·ket**) [*trans.*] market (a product) on a large scale.

mass me·di·a ▶*plural n.* (usu. **the mass media**) [treated as *sing.* or *pl.*] the media.

mass noun ▶*n. Grammar* **1** a noun denoting something that cannot be counted (e.g., a substance or quality), in English usually a noun that lacks a plural in ordinary usage and is not used with the indefinite article, e.g., *luggage, china, happiness.* Contrasted with **COUNT NOUN**. **2** a noun denoting something that normally cannot be counted but that may be countable when it refers to different units or types, e.g., *coffee, bread* (*drank some coffee, ordered two coffees; ate some bread, several different breads*).

mass num·ber ▶*n. Physics* the total number of protons and neutrons in a nucleus.

Mas·son /məˈsän; mäˈsôN/, André (1896–1987), French painter and graphic artist. He joined the surrealists in the mid 1920s and pioneered "automatic" drawing, a form of fluid, spontaneous composition intended to express images emerging from the unconscious.

Mas·so·rah /məˈsôrə/ ▶*n.* variant spelling of **MASORAH**.

Mas·so·rete /ˈmasəˌrēt/ ▶*n.* variant spelling of **MASORETE**.

mass-pro·duce /prəˈdōōs/ ▶*v.* [*trans.*] produce large quantities of (a standardized article) by an automated mechanical process: [as *adj.*] (**mass-produced**) *cheap mass-produced goods.* —**mass-pro·duc·er** *n.* —**mass pro·duc·tion** *n.*

mass spec·tro·graph ▶*n.* a mass spectrometer in which the particles are detected photographically.

mass spec·trom·e·ter ▶*n.* an apparatus for separating isotopes, molecules, and molecular fragments according to mass. The sample is vaporized and ionized, and the ions are accelerated in an electric field and deflected by a magnetic field into a curved trajectory that gives a distinctive mass spectrum.

mass spec·trum ▶*n.* a distribution of ions shown by the use of a mass spectrograph or mass spectrometer.

mass trans·it ▶*n.* public transportation, esp. in an urban area.

mass·y /ˈmasē/ ▶*adj. poetic/literary* or *archaic* consisting of a large mass; bulky; massive: *a round massy table.*

mast[1] /mast/ ▶*n.* **1** a tall upright post, spar, or other structure on a ship or boat, in sailing vessels generally carrying a sail or sails. ■ a similar structure on land, esp. a flagpole or a television or radio transmitter. **2** (in full **captain's mast**) (in the U.S. Navy) a session of court presided over by the captain of a ship, esp. to hear cases of minor offenses. ▷Old English *mæst*; related to Dutch *mast* and German *Mast*. —**mast·ed** *adj.* [in *combination*] *a single-masted fishing boat.*
▶*PHRASE* □ **before the mast** *historical* serving as an ordinary seaman in a sailing ship (quartered in the forecastle).

mast[1]

mast[2] ▶*n.* the fruit of beech, oak, chestnut, and other forest trees, esp. as food for pigs and wild animals. ▷Old English *mæst*; probably related to **MEAT**.

mas·ta·ba /ˈmastəbə/ (also **mas·ta·bah**) ▶*n.* **1** *Archaeology* an ancient Egyptian tomb rectangular in shape with sloping sides and a flat roof, standing to a height of 17–20 feet (5–6 m), consisting of an underground burial chamber with rooms above it (at ground level) in which to store offerings. **2** (in Islamic countries) a bench, typically of stone, attached to a house. ▷from Arabic *maṣṭaba*.

mast cell ▶*n.* a cell filled with basophil granules, found in numbers in connective tissue and releasing histamine and other substances during inflammatory and allergic reactions. ▷late 19th cent.: *mast* from German *Mast* 'fattening, feeding.'

mas·tec·to·my /maˈstektəmē/ ▶*n.* (*pl.* **-mies**) a surgical operation to remove a breast. ▷1920s: from Greek *mastos* 'breast' + **-ECTOMY**.

mas·ter[1] /ˈmastər/ ▶*n.* **1** *chiefly historical* a man who has people working for him, esp. servants or slaves: *he acceded to his master's wishes.* ■ a person who has dominance or control of something: *he was master of the situation.* ■ a machine or device directly controlling another: [as *adj.*] *a master cylinder.* Compare with **SLAVE**. ■ *dated* a male head of a household: *the master of the house.* ■ the owner of a dog, horse, or other domesticated animal. **2** a skilled practitioner of a particular art or activity: *I'm a master of disguise.* ■ a great artist, esp. one belonging to the accepted canon: *the* *work of the great masters is spread around the art galleries of the world.* ■ a very strong chess or bridge player, esp. one who has qualified for the title at international tournaments: *a chess master.* See also GRAND MASTER. ■ (**Masters**) [treated as *sing.*] (in some sports) a class for competitors over the usual age for the highest level of competition. **3** a person who holds a second or further degree from a university or other academic institution (only in titles and set expressions): *a master's degree* | *a Master of Arts.* **4** a man in charge of an organization or group, in particular: ■ *chiefly Brit.* a male schoolteacher, esp. at a public or prep school. ■ the head of a college or school. ■ the captain of a merchant ship. **5** used as a title prefixed to the name of a boy not old enough to be called "Mr.": *Master James Williams.* ■ *archaic* a title for a man of high rank or learning. ■ the title of the heir apparent of a Scottish viscount or baron. **6** an original movie, recording, or document from which copies can be made: [as *adj.*] *the master tape.*

▸*adj.* [*attrib.*] **1** having or showing very great skill or proficiency: *a master painter.* ■ denoting a person skilled in a particular trade and able to teach others: *a master bricklayer.* **2** main; principal: *the master bedroom.*

▸*v.* [*trans.*] **1** acquire complete knowledge or skill in (an accomplishment, technique, or art): *I never mastered Latin.* **2** gain control of; overcome: *I managed to master my fears.* **3** make a master copy of (a movie or record). ▷Old English *mæg(i)ster* (later reinforced by Old French *maistre*), from Latin *magister*; probably related to *magis* 'more' (i.e., 'more important'). —**mas·ter·dom** /-dəm/ *n.* —**mas·ter·hood** /-ˌho͝od/ *n.* —**mas·ter·less** *adj.* —**mas·ter·ship** /-ˌsʜip/ *n.*

mas·ter² ▸*n.* [*in combination*] a ship or boat with a specified number of masts: *a three-master.*

mas·ter-at-arms ▸*n.* (*pl.* **mas·ters-at-arms** /'mastərz ət 'ärmz/) a naval petty officer appointed to carry out or supervise police duties on board a ship.

mas·ter chief pet·ty of·fi·cer ▸*n.* a noncommissioned officer in the U.S. Navy or Coast Guard ranking above senior chief petty officer and below warrant officer.

mas·ter class (also **mas·ter·class**) ▸*n.* a class, esp. in music, given by an expert to highly talented students.

mas·ter·ful /'mastərfəl/ ▸*adj.* **1** powerful and able to control others: *behind the lace and ruffles was a masterful woman.* **2** performed or performing very skillfully: *a masterful assessment of the difficulties.* —**mas·ter·ful·ly** *adv.* —**mas·ter·ful·ness** *n.*

> *USAGE* **Masterful** and **masterly** overlap in meaning and are sometimes confused. **Masterful** can mean 'domineering,' but it also means 'very skillful, masterly.' Take note, however, that **masterful** used in this 'masterly' sense generally describes a person (*he has limited talent, but he's masterful at exploiting it*), while **masterly** usually describes an achievement or action (*that was a masterly response to our opponents' arguments*).

mas·ter gun·ner·y ser·geant ▸*n.* a noncommissioned officer in the U.S. Marine Corps ranking above master sergeant and below sergeant major.

mas·ter key ▸*n.* a key that opens several locks, each of which also has its own key: *the custodian has the master key to all the classrooms.*

mas·ter·ly /'mastərlē/ ▸*adj.* performed or performing in a very skillful and accomplished way: *his masterly account of rural France.*

> *USAGE* On the difference in use between **masterly** and **masterful**, see usage at MASTERFUL.

mas·ter ma·son ▸*n.* **1** a skilled mason, esp. one who employs other workers. **2** a fully qualified Freemason.

mas·ter·mind /'mastərˌmīnd/ ▸*n.* a person with an outstanding intellect: *an eminent musical mastermind.* ■ someone who plans and directs an ingenious and complex scheme or enterprise: *the mastermind behind the project.*

▸*v.* [*trans.*] plan and direct (an ingenious and complex scheme or enterprise): *he was accused of masterminding a gold-smuggling racket.*

mas·ter of cer·e·mo·nies ▸*n.* a person in charge of procedure at a state or public occasion. ■ a person who introduces speakers, players, or entertainers.

mas·ter·piece /'mastərˌpēs/ ▸*n.* a work of outstanding artistry, skill, or workmanship: *a great literary masterpiece* | *the car was a masterpiece of space-age technology.* ■ an artist's or craftsman's best piece of work: *the painting is arguably Picasso's masterpiece.* ■ *historical* a piece of work by a craftsman accepted as qualification for membership of a guild as an acknowledged master.

mas·ter plan ▸*n.* a comprehensive or far-reaching plan of action.

Mas·ters /'mastərz/, Edgar Lee (1869–1950), U.S. writer. His verse is collected in such works as *Spoon River Anthology* (1915), *Domesday Book* (1920), and *The New Spoon River* (1924). He also wrote biographies and novels.

mas·ter ser·geant ▸*n.* a noncommissioned officer in the U.S. armed forces of high rank, in particular (in the Army) an NCO above sergeant first class and below sergeant major, (in the Air Force) an NCO above technical sergeant and below senior master sergeant, or (in the Marine Corps) an NCO above gunnery sergeant and below master gunnery sergeant.

mas·ter·sing·er /'mastərˌsiɴɢər/ ▸*n.* another term for MEISTERSINGER.

Mas·ters Tour·na·ment /'mastərz / a prestigious U.S. golf competition, held in Augusta, Georgia, in which golfers (chiefly professionals) compete only by invitation on the basis of their past achievements.

mas·ter stroke ▸*n.* an outstandingly skillful and opportune act; a very clever move.

mas·ter switch ▸*n.* a switch controlling the supply of electricity or fuel to an entire system. ■ *Biology* a substance or gene that regulates gene expression or embryonic development, or initiates cancer.

mas·ter·work /'mastərˌwərk/ ▸*n.* a masterpiece.

mas·ter·y /'mast(ə)rē/ ▸*n.* **1** comprehensive knowledge or skill in a subject or accomplishment: *she played with some mastery.* ■ the action or process of mastering a subject or accomplishment: *a child's mastery of language.* **2** control or superiority over someone or something: *man's mastery over nature.* ▷Middle English: from Old French *maistrie*, from *maistre* 'master.'

mast·head /'mastˌhed/ ▸*n.* **1** the highest part of a ship's mast or of the lower section of a mast. **2** the title of a newspaper or magazine at the head of the front or editorial page. ■ the listed details in a newspaper or magazine referring to ownership, advertising rates, etc.

▸*v.* [*trans.*] **1** *historical* send (a sailor) to the masthead, esp. as a punishment. **2** raise (a flag or sail) to the masthead.

mas·tic /'mastik/ ▸*n.* **1** an aromatic gum or resin exuded from the bark of a Mediterranean tree, used in making varnish and chewing gum and as a flavoring. **2** (also **mastic tree**) the bushy evergreen Mediterranean tree of the cashew family that yields mastic and has aromatic leaves and fruit, closely related to the pistachio. • *Pistacia lentiscus*, family Anacardiaceae. **3** a puttylike waterproof filler and sealant used in building. ▷late Middle English: via Old French and Latin from Greek *mastikhē* (perhaps from *mastikhan* 'masticate').

mas·ti·cate /'mastiˌkāt/ ▸*v.* [*trans.*] chew (food). ▷mid 17th cent.: from late Latin *masticat-* 'chewed,' from the verb *masticare*, from Greek *mastikhan* 'gnash the teeth' (related to *masasthai* 'to chew'). —**mas·ti·ca·tion** /ˌmasti'kāsʜən/ *n.* —**mas·ti·ca·tor** /-ˌkātər/ *n.* —**mas·ti·ca·to·ry** /'mastikəˌtôrē/ *adj.*

mas·tiff /'mastif/ ▸*n.* a dog of a large, strong breed with drooping ears and pendulous lips. ▷Middle English: obscurely representing Old French *mastin*, based on Latin *mansuetus* 'tame.'

mastiff

mas·tiff bat ▸*n.* a heavily built, free-tailed bat with a broad muzzle, found mainly in America and Australasia. • *Eumops*, *Molossus*, and other genera, family Molossidae: several species, including the large **western mastiff bat** (*E. perotis*).

Mas·ti·goph·o·ra /ˌmasti'gäfərə/ *Zoology* a group of single-celled animals that includes the protozoal flagellates, which are now generally divided among several phyla of the kingdom Protista. • Subphylum (or superclass) Mastigophora. ▷modern Latin (plural), from Greek *mastigophoros*, from *mastix*, *mastig-* 'whip' + *-phoros* 'bearing.' —**mas·ti·goph·o·ran** /-'gäf(ə)rən/ *n.* & *adj.*

mas·ti·tis /ma'stītis/ ▸*n.* inflammation of the mammary gland in the breast or udder, typically due to bacterial infection via a damaged nipple or teat. ▷mid 19th cent.: from Greek *mastos* 'breast' + -ITIS.

mas·to·don /'mastəˌdän/ ▸*n.* a large, extinct, elephantlike mammal of the Miocene to Pleistocene epochs, having teeth of a relatively primitive form and number. • Mammutidae and other families, order Proboscidea: many species, including the **American mastodon** (*Mammut americanum*), which possibly survived to historical times in North America. ▷early 19th cent.: modern Latin, from Greek *mastos* 'breast' + *odous*, *odont-* 'tooth' (with reference to nipple-shaped tubercles on the crowns of its molar teeth).

mastodon

mas·toid /'masˌtoid/ ▸*adj.* *Anatomy* of or relating to the mastoid process: *mastoid disease.*

▸*n.* *Anatomy* the mastoid process. ■ (**mastoids**) [treated as *sing.*] *informal* mastoiditis. ▷mid 18th cent.: via French and modern Latin from Greek *mastoeidēs* 'breast-shaped,' from *mastos* 'breast.'

mas·toid·i·tis /ˌmasˌtoid'ītis/ ▸*n.* *Medicine* inflammation of the mastoid process.

mas·toid proc·ess ▸*n.* a conical prominence of the temporal bone behind the ear, to which neck muscles are attached, and which has air spaces linked to the middle ear.

mas·tur·bate /'mastərˌbāt/ ▸*v.* [*intrans.*] stimulate one's own genitals for sexual pleasure. ■ [*trans.*] stimulate the genitals of (someone) to give them sexual pleasure. ▷mid 19th cent.: from Latin *masturbat-* 'masturbated,' from the verb *masturbari*, of unknown ultimate origin. —**mas·tur·ba·tion** /ˌmastər'bāsʜən/ *n.* —**mas·tur·ba·tor** *n.* —**mas·tur·ba·to·ry** /-bəˌtôrē/ *adj.*

Ma·su·ri·a /mə'so͝orēə/ a low-lying forested lakeland region in northeastern Poland. Formerly part of East Prussia, it was assigned to Poland after World War II. Also called MASURIAN LAKES.

MAT¹ /mat/ ▸*n.* a technology that uses chemicals (usually petrolatum, dimethicone, and polyquaternium) to reduce the ability of bacteria to adhere to the skin: *the company is developing MAT-containing soaps.* ▷abbr. of *microbial anti-attachment technology.*

MAT² ▸*abbr.* Master of Arts in Teaching.

mat¹ /mat/ ▸*n.* **1** a piece of protective material placed on a floor, in particular: ■ a piece of coarse material placed on a floor for people to wipe their feet on. ■ a piece of resilient material for landing on in gymnastics, wrestling, or similar sports. ■ a small rug. ■ a piece of coarse material for lying on: *a beach mat.* **2** a small piece of cork, card, or similar material placed on a table or other surface to protect it from the heat or moisture of an object placed on it. **3** a thick, untidy layer of something hairy or woolly: *his chest was covered by a thick mat of soft fair hair.*

▸*v.* (**mat·ted**, **mat·ting**) [*trans.*] tangle (something, esp. hair) in a thick mass: *sweat matted his hair* | *the fur on its flank was matted with blood.* ■ [*intrans.*] become tangled. ▷Old English *m(e)att(e)*; related to Dutch *mat* and German *Matte*, from late Latin *matta*, from Phoenician.

▸**PHRASES** □ **go to the mat** *informal* vigorously engage in an argument or dispute, typically on behalf of a particular person or cause. □ **on the mat** *informal* being reprimanded by someone in authority. [with military reference to the orderly room mat, where an accused would stand before the commanding officer.]

mat² ▸*n.* short for MATRIX (sense 2).

mat³ ▸*adj.*, *n.*, & *v.* variant spelling of MATTE¹.

mat. ▸*abbr.* ■ matins. ■ maturity.

Mat·a·be·le /ˌmatə'bēlē/ ▸*n.* the Ndebele people collectively, particularly those of Zimbabwe. ▷from

Sotho *matebele*, singular *letebele*, the name given to this people.

mat·a·dor /ˈmatəˌdôr/ ▸*n.* **1** a bullfighter whose task is to kill the bull. **2** (in ombre, skat, and other card games) any of the highest trumps. **3** a domino game in which halves are matched so as to make a total of seven. ■ any of the dominoes that have seven spots altogether, together with the double blank. ▷Spanish, literally 'killer,' from *matar* 'to kill,' from Persian *māt* 'dead'; senses relating to games are extended uses, expressing a notion of dominance or control.

Mat·a·gor·da Bay /ˌmatəˈgôrdə/ an inlet of the Gulf of Mexico in southeastern Texas, at the mouth of the Colorado River.

Ma·ta Ha·ri /ˈmätə ˈhärē; ˈmatə ˈharē/ (1876–1917), Dutch dancer and secret agent; born *Margaretha Geertruida Zelle*. She probably worked for both French and German intelligence services before being executed by the French in 1917. ■ [as *n.*] (**a Mata Hari**) a beautiful and seductive female spy. ▷from Malay *mata* 'eye' and *hari* 'day,' as a compound meaning 'sun.'

ma·ta·ma·ta /ˌmatə məˈtä/ (also **ma·ta-ma·ta**) ▸*n.* a grotesque South American freshwater turtle that has a broad flat head and neck with irregular projections of skin resembling waterweed. • *Chelus fimbriatus*, family Chelidae. ▷mid 19th cent.: of unknown origin; probably from a South American Indian language.

Mat·a·nus·ka Val·ley /ˌmatəˈnōōskə/ an agricultural region in south central Alaska, northeast of Anchorage.

match[1] /mach/ ▸*n.* **1** a contest in which people or teams compete against each other in a particular sport: *a boxing match.* **2** a person or thing able to contend with another as an equal in quality or strength: *they were* **no match for** *the trained mercenaries.* **3** a person or thing that resembles or corresponds to another: *the child's identical twin would be a perfect match for organ donation.* ■ *Computing* a string that fulfills the specified conditions of a computer search. ■ a pair that corresponds or is very similar: *the headdresses and bouquet were a perfect match.* ■ the fact or appearance of corresponding: *stones of a perfect match and color.* **4** a person viewed in regard to their eligibility for marriage, esp. as regards class or wealth: *he was an unsuitable match for any of their girls.* ■ a marriage: *a dynastic match.*

▸*v.* [*trans.*] **1** correspond or cause to correspond in some essential respect; make or be harmonious: [*trans.*] *we bought green and blue curtains to match the bedspread* | *she* **matched** *her steps* **to** *his* | [*intrans.*] *the jacket and pants do not match* | [as *adj.*] (**matching**) *a set of matching coffee cups.* ■ team (someone or something) with someone or something else appropriate or harmonious: *they* **matched** *suitably qualified applicants* **with** *institutions that had vacancies* | *she was trying to* **match** *the draperies* **to** *the couch.* **2** be equal to (something) in quality or strength: *his anger matched her own.* ■ succeed in reaching or equaling (a standard or quality): *he tried to match her nonchalance.* ■ equalize (two coupled electrical impedances) so as to bring about the maximum transfer of power from one to the other. **3** place (a person or group) in contest or competition with another: *the big names were* **matched against** *nobodies* | [as *adj.*, with *submodifier*] (**matched**) *evenly matched teams.*

▸*phrasal v.* □ **match up to** be as good as or equal to: *she matches up to the challenges of the job.* □ **match someone with** *archaic* bring about the marriage of someone to: *try if you can to match her with a duke.* ▷Old English *gemæcca* 'mate, companion'; related to the base of **MAKE**. —**match·a·ble** *adj.*

▸*PHRASES* □ **make a match** form a partnership, esp. by getting married. □ **meet one's match** encounter one's equal in strength or ability: *Iris had met her match.* □ **to match** corresponding in some essential respect with something previously mentioned or chosen: *a new coat and a hat to match.*

match[2] ▸*n.* a short, thin piece of wood or cardboard used to light a fire, being tipped with a composition that ignites when rubbed against a rough surface. ■ *historical* a piece of wick or cord designed to burn at a uniform rate, used for firing a cannon or lighting gunpowder. ▷late Middle English (in the sense 'wick of a candle'): from Old French *meche*, perhaps from Latin *myxa* 'spout of a lamp,' later 'lamp wick.'

▸*PHRASE* □ **put a match to** set fire to.

match·board /ˈmachˌbôrd/ ▸*n.* any of a set of interlocking boards joined together by a tongue cut along the edge of one board and fitting into a groove along the edge of another. Also called **matched board**.

match·book /ˈmachˌbo͝ok/ ▸*n.* a small cardboard folder of matches with a striking surface on one side.

match·box /ˈmachˌbäks/ ▸*n.* a small box in which matches are sold. ■ [usu. as *adj.*] something very small, esp. a house, apartment, or room: *her new thimble-sized, matchbox apartment.*

match·less /ˈmachləs/ ▸*adj.* unable to be equaled; incomparable: *the Parthenon has a matchless beauty.* —**match·less·ly** *adv.*

match·lock /ˈmachˌläk/ ▸*n. historical* a type of gun with a lock in which a piece of wick or cord is placed for igniting the powder: [as *adj.*] *matchlock guns.* ■ a lock of this kind.

match·mak·er /ˈmachˌmākər/ ▸*n.* a person who arranges relationships and marriages between others, either informally or, in certain cultural communities, as a formal occupation. ■ *figurative* a person or company that brings parties together for commercial purposes. —**match·mak·ing** /-ˌmāking/ *n.*

match play ▸*n.* play in golf in which the score is reckoned by counting the holes won by each side, as opposed to the number of strokes taken. Compare with **STROKE PLAY**.

match point ▸*n.* **1** (in tennis and other sports) a point that if won by one contestant will also win the match. **2** (**matchpoint**) (in duplicate bridge) a unit of scoring in matches and tournaments: *a convincing margin of 54 matchpoints.*

match·stick /ˈmachˌstik/ ▸*n.* the stem of a match, esp. a wooden one. ■ something likened to a match in being long and thin: *cut the vegetables into matchsticks* | [as *adj.*] *matchstick legs.*

match·up /ˈmachəp/ (also **match-up**) ▸*n.* a contest between athletes or sports teams: *a matchup of two twenty-something pitchers wondering what it is like to win in the majors.* ■ *Basketball* another term for a man-to-man defense. See **MAN-TO-MAN** at **MAN**.

match·wood /ˈmachˌwo͝od/ ▸*n.* very small pieces or splinters of wood: *their boat was shattered into matchwood against the rocks.* ■ light wood suitable for making matches.

mate[1] /māt/ ▸*n.* **1** each of a pair of birds or other animals: *a male bird sings to court a mate.* ■ *informal* a person's husband, wife, or other sexual partner. ■ one of a matched pair: *a sock without its mate.* **2** [in *combination*] a fellow member or joint occupant of a specified thing: *his tablemates.* ■ *Brit., informal* used as a friendly form of address between men or boys: *"See you then, mate."* ■ *Brit., informal* a friend or companion: *I was with a mate* | *my best mate, Steve.* **3** an assistant or deputy, in particular: ■ an assistant to a skilled worker: *a plumber's mate.* ■ a deck officer on a merchant ship subordinate to the master. See also **FIRST MATE**.

▸*v.* **1** [*intrans.*] (of animals or birds) come together for breeding; copulate: *successful males may* **mate with** *many females* | [as *n.*] (**mating**) *ovulation occurs only if mating has taken place.* ■ [*trans.*] bring (animals or birds) together for breeding. ■ join in marriage or sexual partnership: *people tend to* **mate with** *others in their own social class.* **2** [*trans.*] join or connect mechanically: *a four-cylinder engine* **mated to** *a five-speed gearbox.* ■ [*intrans.*] be connected or joined. ▷late Middle English: from Middle Low German *māt(e)* 'comrade,' of West Germanic origin; related to **MEAT** (the underlying notion being that of eating together). —**mate·less** *adj.*

mate[2] ▸*n.* & *v. Chess* short for **CHECKMATE**. ▷Middle English: the noun from Anglo-Norman French *mat* (from the phrase *eschec mat* 'checkmate'); the verb from Anglo-Norman French *mater* 'to checkmate.'

ma·té /ˈmäˌtā/ (also **yer·ba ma·té**) ▸*n.* **1** (also **maté tea**) an infusion of the leaves of a South American shrub, which is high in caffeine and bitter. ■ the leaves of this shrub. **2** the South American shrub of the holly family that produces these leaves. • *Ilex paraguariensis*, family Aquifoliaceae. ▷early 18th cent.: from Spanish *mate*, from Quechua *mati*.

mat·e·las·sé /ˌmatl,äˈsā; ˌmätlä-/ ▸*adj.* (of a silk or wool fabric) having a raised design like quilting.

▸*n.* fabric of this type. ▷late 19th cent.: French, literally 'quilted,' past participle of *matelasser*, from *matelas* 'mattress.'

mate·lot /ˌmatlˈō; matˈlō/ ▸*n. Brit., informal* a sailor. ▷mid 19th cent. (nautical slang): from French, variant of *matenot*, from Middle Dutch *mattenoot* 'bed companion,' because sailors had to share hammocks in twos.

mat·e·lote /ˌmatlˈōt; matˈlōt/ ▸*n.* a dish of fish in a sauce of wine and onions. ▷French, from *à la matelote*, literally 'mariner-style,' from *matelot* 'sailor' (see **MATELOT**).

ma·ter /ˈmātər/ ▸*n. Brit., informal* or *dated* mother: *the mater has kept the house in London.* ▷Latin.

ma·ter do·lo·ro·sa /ˈmātər ˌdōləˈrōsə; ˈmätər; ˌdäl-/ the Virgin Mary sorrowing for the death of Jesus Christ, esp. as a representation in art. ▷from medieval Latin, 'sorrowful mother.'

ma·ter·fa·mil·i·as /ˌmātərfəˈmilēəs; ˌmätər-/ ▸*n.* (*pl.* **ma·tres·fa·mil·i·as** /ˌmāˌtrās-; ˌmätərz-/) the female head of a family or household. Compare with **PATERFAMILIAS**. ▷Latin, from *mater* 'mother' + *familias*, old genitive form of *familia* 'family.'

ma·te·ri·al /məˈti(ə)rēəl/ ▸*n.* **1** the matter from which a thing is or can be made: *goats can eat more or less any plant material* | *materials such as brass* | *highly flammable materials.* ■ (usu. **materials**) things needed for an activity: *cleaning materials.* ■ [with *adj.*] a person of a specified quality or suitability: *he's not really Olympic material.* **2** facts, information, or ideas for use in creating a book or other work: *there is much good material here for priests to use in sermons.* ■ items, esp. songs or jokes, comprising a performer's act: *a band playing original material.* **3** cloth or fabric: *a piece of dark material* | *dress materials.*

▸*adj.* **1** [*attrib.*] denoting or consisting of physical objects rather than the mind or spirit: *the material world* | *moral and material support.* ■ concerned with physical needs or desires: *material living standards have risen.* ■ concerned with the matter of reasoning, not its form: *political conflict lacks mathematical or material certitude.* **2** important; essential; relevant: *the insects did not do any material damage to the crop.* ■ *chiefly Law* (of evidence or a fact) significant, influential, or relevant, esp. to the extent of determining a cause or affecting a judgment: *information that could be* **material to** *a murder inquiry.* ▷late Middle English (in the sense 'relating to matter'): from late Latin *materialis*, adjective from Latin *materia* 'matter.'

ma·te·ri·al cause ▸*n. Philosophy* (in Aristotelian thought) the matter or substance that constitutes a thing.

ma·te·ri·al·ism /məˈti(ə)rēəˌlizəm/ ▸*n.* **1** a tendency to consider material possessions and physical comfort as more important than spiritual values. **2** *Philosophy* the doctrine that nothing exists except matter and its movements and modifications. ■ the doctrine that consciousness and will are wholly due to material agency. See also **DIALECTICAL MATERIALISM**. —**ma·te·ri·al·ist** *n.* & *adj.* —**ma·te·ri·al·is·tic** /məˌti(ə)rēəˈlistik/ *adj.* —**ma·te·ri·al·is·ti·cal·ly** *adv.*

ma·te·ri·al·i·ty /məˌti(ə)rēˈalitē/ ▸*n.* (*pl.* **-ties**) the quality or character of being material or composed of matter. ■ *chiefly Law* the quality of being relevant or significant: *the applicant must establish materiality on the balance of probabilities.*

ma·te·ri·al·ize /məˈti(ə)rēəˌlīz/ ▸*v.* [*intrans.*] **1** (of a ghost, spirit, or similar entity) appear in bodily form. ■ [*trans.*] cause to appear in bodily or physical form. ■ [*trans.*] *rare* represent or express in material form. **2** become actual fact; happen: *the assumed savings may not materialize.* ■ appear or be present: *the train didn't materialize.* —**ma·te·ri·al·i·za·tion** /məˌti(ə)rēələˈzāshən/ *n.*

ma·te·ri·al·ly /məˈti(ə)rēəlē/ ▸*adv.* **1** [often as *submodifier*] substantially; considerably: *materially different circumstances.* **2** in terms of wealth or material possessions: *a materially and culturally rich area.*

ma·te·ria med·i·ca /məˈti(ə)rēə ˈmedikə/ ▸*n.* the body of remedial substances used in the practice of medicine. ■ the study of the origin and properties of these substances. ▷late 17th cent.: modern Latin, translation of Greek *hulē iatrikē* 'healing material' (the title of a work by Dioscorides).

ma·te·ri·el /məˌti(ə)rēˈel/ (also **ma·té·ri·el**) ▸*n.* military materials and equipment. Often contrasted with **PERSONNEL**. ▷early 19th cent.: from French *matériel*, adjective (used as a noun).

ma·ter·nal /məˈtərnl/ ▸*adj.* of or relating to a mother, esp. during pregnancy or shortly after childbirth: *maternal age* | *maternal care.* ■ [*attrib.*] related through the mother's side of the family: *my maternal grandfather.* ■ denoting feelings associated with or typical of a mother; motherly: *maternal instincts.* ▷late 15th cent.: from French *maternel*, from Latin *maternus*, from *mater* 'mother.' —**ma·ter·nal·ism** /-ˌizəm/ *n.*

Pronunciation Key ə *ago*; ər *over*; ˈə or ˌə *up*; ˈər or ˌər *fur*; a *hat*; ā *rate*; ä *car*; CH *chew*; e *let*; ē *see*; e(ə)r *air*; i *fit*; ī *by*; i(ə)r *ear*; NG *sing*; ō *go*; ô *for*; oi *boy*; o͝o *good*; o͞o *goo*; ou *out*; SH *she*; TH *thin*; T͟H *then*; (h)w *why*; ZH *vision*

—**ma·ter·nal·ist** /-ist/ *adj.* —**ma·ter·nal·is·tic** /mə,tərnl'istik/ *adj.* —**ma·ter·nal·ly** *adv.*

ma·ter·ni·ty /mə'tərnətē/ ▸*n.* motherhood. ■ [usu. as *adj.*] the period during pregnancy and shortly after childbirth: *maternity leave | maternity clothes.* ■ a maternity ward in a hospital. ▷early 17th cent.: from French *maternité*, from Latin *maternus*, from *mater* 'mother.'

mate·y /'mātē/ *Brit., informal* ▸*n.* used as a familiar and sometimes hostile form of address, esp. to a stranger: *"Shove off, matey, she's mine."*
▸*adj.* (**mat·i·er, mat·i·est**) familiar and friendly; sociable: *a fixed, matey grin.*

math /maTH/ ▸*n. informal* mathematics: *she teaches math and science.* ▷mid 19th cent.: abbreviation.

math·e·mat·i·cal /,maTH(ə)'matikəl/ (also **math·e·mat·ic**) ▸*adj.* of or relating to mathematics: *mathematical equations.* ■ (of a proof or analysis) rigorously precise: *mathematical thinking | figurative he arranged the meal with mathematical precision on a plate.* ▷late Middle English: from Latin *mathematicalis*, from Greek *mathēmatikos*, from *mathēma*, *mathēmat-* 'science,' from the base of *manthanein* 'learn.' —**math·e·mat·i·cal·ly** /-ik(ə)lē/ *adv.*

math·e·mat·i·cal in·duc·tion ▸*n.* see INDUCTION (sense 3).

math·e·mat·i·cal log·ic ▸*n.* the part of mathematics concerned with the study of formal languages, formal reasoning, the nature of mathematical proof, provability of mathematical statements, computability, and other aspects of the foundations of mathematics.

math·e·ma·ti·cian /,maTH(ə)mə'tisHən/ ▸*n.* an expert in or student of mathematics. ▷late Middle English: from Old French *mathematicien*, from Latin *mathematicus* 'mathematical,' from Greek *mathēmatikos* (see MATHEMATICAL).

math·e·mat·ics /maTH(ə)'matiks/ ▸*plural n.* [usu. treated as *sing.*] the abstract science of number, quantity, and space. Mathematics may be studied in its own right (**pure mathematics**), or as it is applied to other disciplines such as physics and engineering (**applied mathematics**). ■ [often treated as *pl.*] the mathematical aspects of something: *the mathematics of general relativity.* ▷late 16th cent.: plural of obsolete *mathematic* 'mathematics,' from Old French *mathematique*, from Latin *(ars) mathematica* 'mathematical (art),' from Greek *mathēmatikē (tekhnē)*, from the base of *manthanein* 'learn.'

math·e·ma·tize /'maTH(ə)mə,tīz/ ▸*v.* [*trans.*] regard or treat (a subject or problem) in mathematical terms. —**math·e·ma·ti·za·tion** /,maTH(ə)mətə'zāsHən/ *n.*

Math·er[1] /'maTHər/, Cotton (1663–1728), American minister and writer; son of Increase Mather. Noted for his political writings, he sponsored the Massachusetts charter in 1691 and is thought to have influenced the events that led to the Salem witch trials in 1692.

Math·er[2], Increase (1639–1723), American minister; father of Cotton Mather. A Congregationalist, he was the pastor of North Church in Boston 1664–1723 and the president of Harvard College 1685–1701.

Math·ew·son /'maTHyōōsən/, Christy (1880–1925), U.S. baseball player; full name *Christopher Mathewson.* A pitcher for the New York Giants 1900–1916, he won 22 or more games per year for 12 straight years and pitched three shutouts in the 1905 World Series. He later managed the Cincinnati Reds 1916–18 and was president of the Boston Braves 1923–25. Baseball Hall of Fame (1936).

Ma·thi·as /mə'THīəs/, Bob (1930–), U.S. track and field athlete and politician; full name *Robert Bruce Mathias.* At 17, he was the youngest winner of the decathlon with a gold medal in the 1948 Olympic Games and another in the 1952 games. He later served as a member of the U.S. House of Representatives from California 1967–1975.

maths /maTHs/ ▸*plural n.* [treated as *sing.*] *Brit., informal* mathematics: [as *adj.*] *her mother was a maths teacher.* ▷early 20th cent.: abbreviation.

Ma·til·da[1] /mə'tildə/ (1102–67), English princess; daughter of Henry I and mother of Henry II; known as **the Empress Maud**. Henry's only legitimate child, she was named his heir, but her cousin Stephen seized the throne on Henry's death in 1135. She waged an unsuccessful civil war against Stephen until 1148.

Ma·til·da[2] ▸*n. Austral., informal* a bushman's bundle of possessions carried when traveling. ▷late 19th cent.: from the given name *Matilda.*
▸PHRASE □ **waltz** (or **walk**) **Matilda** carry such a bundle.

mat·in·al /'matn-l/ ▸*adj. rare* relating to or taking place in the morning. ▷early 19th cent.: from French, from *matin* 'morning.'

mat·i·nee /,matn'ā/ (also **mat·i·née**) ▸*n.* a performance in a theater or a showing of a movie that takes place in the daytime. ▷mid 19th cent.: from French *matinée*, literally 'morning (as a period of activity),' from *matin* 'morning.'

mat·i·nee i·dol ▸*n. informal, dated* a handsome actor admired chiefly by women.

mat·ins /'matnz/ (*Brit.* also **mat·tins**) ▸*n.* a service of morning prayer in various churches, esp. the Anglican Church. ■ a service forming part of the traditional Divine Office of the Western Christian Church, originally said (or chanted) at or after midnight, but historically often held with lauds on the previous evening. ■ (also **matin**) *poetic/literary* the morning song of birds. ▷Middle English: from Old French *matines*, plural (influenced by ecclesiastical Latin *matutinae* 'morning prayers') of *matin* 'morning,' from Latin *matutinum*, neuter of *matutinus* 'early in the morning,' from *Matuta*, the name of the dawn goddess.

Ma·tisse /mə'tēs; mä-/, Henri (Emile Benoît) (1869–1954), French painter and sculptor. His use of nonnaturalistic color led him to be considered a leader among the fauvists. His later paintings and sculptures display a trend toward formal simplification and abstraction.

Ma·to Gros·so /,mätə 'grōsōō/ a high plateau region in southwestern Brazil that forms a watershed between the Amazon and Plate river systems. ▷Portuguese, literally "dense forest."

ma·tri·arch /'mātrē,ärk/ ▸*n.* a woman who is the head of a family or tribe. ■ an older woman who is powerful within a family or organization: *a domineering matriarch.* ▷early 17th cent.: from Latin *mater* 'mother,' on the false analogy of *patriarch.* —**ma·tri·ar·chal** /,mātrē'ärkəl/ *adj.*

ma·tri·ar·chate /'mātrē,är,kāt; -,ärkət/ ▸*n.* a matriarchal form of social organization, esp. in a tribal society.

ma·tri·ar·chy /'mātrē,ärkē/ ▸*n.* (*pl.* **-chies**) a system of society or government ruled by a woman or women. ■ a form of social organization in which descent and relationship are reckoned through the female line. ■ the state of being an older, powerful woman in a family or group: *she cherished a dream of matriarchy—catered to by grandchildren.*

ma·tri·ces /'mātrə,sēz/ ▸ plural form of MATRIX.

mat·ri·cide /'matrə,sīd; 'mā-/ ▸*n.* the killing of one's mother: *a man suspected of matricide.* ■ a person who kills their mother. ▷late 16th cent.: from Latin *matricidium*, from *mater*, *matr-* 'mother' + *-cidium* (see -CIDE). —**mat·ri·cid·al** /,matrə'sīdl; ,mā-/ *adj.*

ma·tric·u·late /mə'trikyə,lāt/ ▸*v.* **1** [*intrans.*] be enrolled at a college or university: *he matriculated at the University of Vermont.* ■ [*trans.*] admit (a student) to a college or university. **2** [*trans.*] *Heraldry, chiefly Scottish* record (arms) in an official register.
▸*n.* a person who has been matriculated. ▷late 16th cent.: from medieval Latin *matriculat-* 'enrolled,' from the verb *matriculare*, from late Latin *matricula* 'register,' diminutive of Latin *matrix.* —**ma·tric·u·la·tion** /mə,trikyə'lāsHən/ *n.*

mat·ri·fo·cal /'matri,fōkəl; 'mā-/ ▸*adj.* (of a society, culture, etc.) based on the mother as the head of the family or household. ▷1950s: from Latin *mater*, *matr-* 'mother' + FOCAL.

mat·ri·lin·e·al /,matrə'linēəl; ,mā-/ ▸*adj.* of or based on kinship with the mother or the female line. ▷early 20th cent.: from Latin *mater*, *matr-* 'mother' + LINEAL. —**mat·ri·lin·e·al·ly** *adv.*

mat·ri·lo·cal /,matrə'lōkəl; 'mā-/ ▸*adj.* of or denoting a custom in marriage whereby the husband goes to live with the wife's community. ▷early 20th cent.: from Latin *mater*, *matr-* 'mother' + LOCAL. —**mat·ri·lo·cal·i·ty** /-lō'kalətē/ *n.*

mat·ri·mo·ni·al /,matrə'mōnēəl/ ▸*adj.* of or relating to marriage or married people: *matrimonial bonds.* ▷late Middle English: via Old French from Latin *matrimonialis*, from *matrimonium* (see MATRIMONY). —**mat·ri·mo·ni·al·ly** *adv.*

mat·ri·mo·ny /'matrə,mōnē/ ▸*n.* the state or ceremony of being married; marriage: *a couple joined in matrimony | the sacrament of holy matrimony.* ▷late Middle English: via Old French from Latin *matrimonium*, based on *mater*, *matr-* 'mother.'

ma·tri·osh·ka /,matrē'äsHkə/ ▸*n.* variant spelling of MATRYOSHKA.

ma·trix /'mātriks/ ▸*n.* (*pl.* **-tri·ces** /'mātrisēz/ or **-trix·es**) **1** an environment or material in which something develops; a surrounding medium or structure: *free choices become the matrix of human life.* ■ a mass of fine-grained rock in which gems, crystals, or fossils are embedded. ■ *Biology* the substance between cells or in which structures are embedded. ■ fine material: *the matrix of gravel paths is raked regularly.* **2** a mold in which something, such as printing type or a phonograph record, is cast or shaped. **3** *Mathematics* a rectangular array of quantities or expressions in rows and columns that is treated as a single entity and manipulated according to particular rules. ■ an organizational structure in which two or more lines of command, responsibility, or communication may run through the same individual. ▷late Middle English (in the sense 'womb'): from Latin, 'breeding female,' later 'womb,' from *mater*, *matr-* 'mother.'

ma·tron /'mātrən/ ▸*n.* **1** a woman in charge of domestic and medical arrangements at a boarding school or other establishment. ■ a female prison officer. **2** a married woman, esp. a dignified and sober middle-aged one. ▷late Middle English (sense 2): from Old French *matrone*, from Latin *matrona*, from *mater*, *matr-* 'mother.' —**ma·tron·hood** /-,ho͝od/ *n.*

ma·tron·ly /'mātrənlē/ ▸*adj.* like or characteristic of a matron, esp. in being dignified and staid and typically associated with having a large or plump build: *she was beginning to look matronly.*

ma·tron of hon·or ▸*n.* a married woman attending the bride at a wedding.

mat·ro·nym·ic /,matrə'nimik/ (also **met·ro·nym·ic** /,me-/) ▸*n.* a name derived from the name of a mother or female ancestor.
▸*adj.* (of a name) so derived. ▷late 18th cent.: from Latin *mater*, *matr-* 'mother,' on the pattern of *patronymic.*

ma·try·osh·ka /,matrē'äsHkə/ (also **ma·try·osh·ka doll**) ▸*n.* (*pl.* **-ki** /-kē/) each of a set of brightly painted hollow wooden dolls of varying sizes, designed to nest inside one another. Also called RUSSIAN DOLL. ▷1940s: from Russian *matrëshka.*

mat·su·ri /mat'so͝orē/ ▸*n.* a solemn festival celebrated periodically at Shinto shrines in Japan. ▷Japanese.

Ma·tsu·ya·ma /,mätsə'yämə/ a city in Japan, the capital and largest city of the island of Shikoku; pop. 443,000.

matt ▸*adj., n., & v.* variant spelling of MATTE[1].

Matt. ▸*abbr. Bible* Matthew.

matte[1] /mat/ (also **matt** or **mat**) ▸*adj.* (of a color, paint, or surface) dull and flat, without a shine: *matte black.*
▸*n.* **1** a matte color, paint, or finish: *the varnishes are available in gloss, satin, and matte.* **2** a sheet of cardboard placed on the back of a picture, either as a mount or to form a border around the picture.
▸*v.* (**mat·ted, mat·ting**) [*trans.*] (often **be matted**) give a matte appearance to (something). ▷early 17th cent. (as a verb): from French *mat.*

matte[2] ▸*n.* an impure product of the smelting of sulfide ores, esp. those of copper or nickel. ▷mid 19th cent.: from French (in Old French meaning 'curds'), feminine of *mat* (adjective) 'dull, matte,' used as a noun.

matte[3] ▸*n.* a mask used to obscure part of an image in a film and allow another image to be substituted, combining the two. ▷mid 19th cent.: from French, perhaps from *mat* (see MATT).

mat·ted /'matid/ ▸*adj.* **1** (esp. of hair or fur) tangled into a thick mass: *a cardigan of matted gray wool.* **2** covered or furnished with mats: *the matted floor.*

mat·ter /'matər/ ▸*n.* **1** physical substance in general, as distinct from mind and spirit; (in physics) that which occupies space and possesses rest mass, esp. as distinct from energy: *the structure and properties of matter.* ■ a substance or material: *organic matter | vegetable matter.* ■ a substance in or discharged from the body: *fecal matter | waste matter.* ■ written or printed material: *reading matter.* **2** an affair or situation under consideration; a topic: *a great deal of work was done on this matter | financial matters.* ■ *Law* something that is to be tried or proved in court; a case. ■ (**matters**) the present situation or state of affairs: *we can do nothing to change matters.* ■ (**a matter for/of**) something that evokes a specified feeling: *it's a matter of complete indifference to me.* ■ (**a matter for**) something that is the concern of a specified person or agency: *the evidence is a matter for the courts.* **3** [usu. with *negative* or in *questions*] (**the matter**) the reason for distress or a problem: *what's the matter? | pretend that nothing's the matter.* **4** the substance or content of a

M

text as distinct from its manner or form. ■ *Printing* the body of a printed work, as distinct from titles, headings, etc. ■ *Logic* the particular content of a proposition, as distinct from its form.

▸*v.* [*intrans.*] **1** [usu. with *negative* or in *questions*] be of importance; have significance: *it doesn't matter what the guests wear* | *what did it* **matter to** *them?* | *to him, animals mattered more than human beings.* ■ (of a person) be important or influential: *she was trying to get known by the people who matter.* **2** *rare* (of a wound) secrete or discharge pus. ▷Middle English: via Old French from Latin *materia* 'timber, substance,' also 'subject of discourse,' from *mater* 'mother.'

▸*PHRASES* □ **for that matter** used to indicate that a subject or category, though mentioned second, is as relevant or important as the first: *I am not sure what value it adds to determining public, or for that matter private, policy.* □ **in the matter of** as regards: *the British are given preeminence in the matter of tea.* □ **it is only a matter of time** there will not be long to wait: *it's only a matter of time before the general is removed.* □ **a matter of 1** no more than (a specified period of time): *they were shown the door in a matter of minutes.* **2** a thing that involves or depends on: *it's a matter of working out how to get something done.* □ **a matter of course** the natural or expected thing: *the reports are published as a matter of course.* □ **a matter of form** a point of correct procedure: *they must as a matter of proper form check to see that there is no tax liability.* □ **a matter of record** see **RECORD**. □ **no matter 1** [with *clause*] regardless of: **no matter what** *the government calls them, they are cuts.* **2** it is of no importance: *"No matter, I'll go myself."* □ **to make matters worse** with the result that a bad situation is made worse. □ **what matter?** *Brit., dated* why should that worry us?: *what matter if he was a Protestant or not?*

Mat·ter·horn /ˈmatərˌhôrn/ a mountain in the Alps that is 14,688 feet (4,477 m) high, on the border between Switzerland and Italy. French name **MONT CERVIN**; Italian name **MONTE CERVINO**.

Matterhorn

mat·ter of fact ▸*n.* something that belongs to the sphere of fact as distinct from opinion or conjecture: *it's a matter of fact that they had a relationship.* ■ *Law* the part of a judicial inquiry concerned with the truth of alleged facts. Often contrasted with **MATTER OF LAW**.

▸*adj.* (**matter-of-fact**) unemotional and practical: *he was characteristically calm and matter-of-fact.* ■ concerned only with factual content rather than style or expression: *the text is written in a breezy matter-of-fact manner.* —**mat·ter-of-fact·ly** *adv.* —**mat·ter-of-fact·ness** *n.*

▸*PHRASE* □ **as a matter of fact** in reality (used esp. to correct a falsehood or misunderstanding): *as a matter of fact, I was talking to him this afternoon.*

mat·ter of law ▸*n. Law* the part of a judicial inquiry concerned with the interpretation of the law. Often contrasted with **MATTER OF FACT**.

Mat·thau /ˈmaTHou/, Walter (1920–2000), U.S. actor; born *Walter Matasschanskayasky*; sometimes credited as *Walter Matuschanskayasky*. He starred in The *Odd Couple*, both on Broadway (1965) and in the movie (1968). Among his many other movies were *The Fortune Cookie* (Academy Award, 1966), *The Sunshine Boys* (1975), *Grumpy Old Men* (1993), and *Hanging Up* (2000).

Mat·thew, St. /ˈmaTHyo͞o/ an Apostle; a tax collector from Capernaum in Galilee; traditional author of the first Gospel. Feast day, September 21. ■ the first Gospel, written after AD 70 and based largely on that of St. Mark.

Mat·thew Par·is (*c.*1199–1259), English chronicler and Benedictine monk; noted for his *Chronica Majora*, a history of the world from the Creation to the mid 13th century.

Mat·thews /ˈmaT͟Hyo͞oz/, Stanley (1824–89), U.S. Supreme Court associate justice 1881–89. He was appointed to the Court by President Garfield. A previous nomination by President Hayes in 1880 had been rejected because it was felt that a conflict of interest existed.

Mat·thi·as, St. /məˈTHīəs/ an Apostle; chosen by lot after the Ascension to replace Judas. Feast day (Western Church) May 14; (Eastern Church) August 9.

Mat·thies·sen /ˈmaT͟H(y)əsən/, Peter (1927–), U.S. writer. He wrote fiction, including the novels *Far Tortuga* (1974) and *Killing Mr. Watson* (1990), as well as nonfiction, usually based on his travels, that included *The Snow Leopard* (1978) and *East of Lo Monthang* (1995).

mat·ting /ˈmatiNG/ ▸*n.* **1** material used for mats, esp. coarse fabric woven from a natural fiber: *rush matting.* **2** the process of becoming matted.

mat·tins /ˈmatnz/ ▸*n.* variant spelling of **MATINS**.

mat·tock /ˈmatək/ ▸*n.* an agricultural tool shaped like a pickax, with an adze and a chisel edge as the ends of the head. ▷Old English *mattuc*, of uncertain origin.

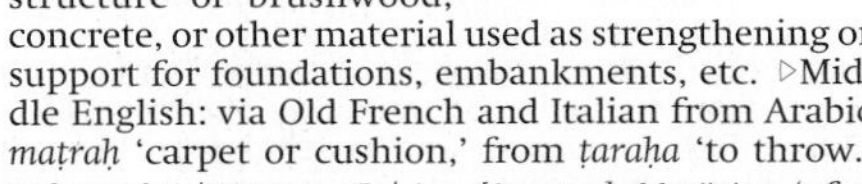

mattock

mat·tress /ˈmatrəs/ ▸*n.* a fabric case filled with deformable or resilient material, used for sleeping on. ■ *Engineering* a flat structure of brushwood, concrete, or other material used as strengthening or support for foundations, embankments, etc. ▷Middle English: via Old French and Italian from Arabic *maṭraḥ* 'carpet or cushion,' from *ṭaraḥa* 'to throw.'

mat·u·rate /ˈmaCHəˌrāt/ ▸*v.* [*intrans.*] *Medicine* (of a boil, abscess, etc.) form pus. ▷mid 16th cent.: from Latin *maturat-* 'ripened, hastened,' from the verb *maturare*, from *maturus* (see **MATURE**).

mat·u·ra·tion /ˌmaCHəˈrāSHən/ ▸*n.* the action or process of maturing: *sexual maturation.* ■ (of wine or other fermented drink) the process of becoming ready for drinking. ■ the ripening of fruit: *pod maturation.* ■ *Medicine* the development of functional ova or sperm cells. ■ the formation of pus in a boil, abscess, etc. ▷late Middle English (denoting the formation of pus): from medieval Latin *maturatio(n-)*, from Latin *maturare* (see **MATURE**). —**mat·u·ra·tion·al** *adj.* —**ma·tur·a·tive** /ˈmaCHəˌrātiv/ *adj.*

ma·ture /məˈCHo͝or; -ˈt(y)o͝or/ ▸*adj.* (**-tur·er**, **-tur·est**) **1** fully developed physically; full-grown: *she was now a mature woman* | *owls are sexually mature at one year.* ■ having reached an advanced stage of mental or emotional development characteristic of an adult: *a young man mature beyond his years.* ■ (of thought or planning) careful and thorough: *on mature reflection he decided they should not go.* ■ used euphemistically to describe someone as being middle-aged or old: *Miss Walker was a mature lady when she married.* ■ (of a style) fully developed: *Van Gogh's mature work.* ■ (of a plant or planted area) complete in natural development: *mature trees.* ■ (of certain foodstuffs or drinks) ready for consumption. **2** denoting an economy, industry, or market that has developed to a point where substantial expansion and investment no longer takes place. **3** (of a bill) due for payment.

▸*v.* [*intrans.*] **1** (of a person or animal) become physically mature: *children mature at different ages* | *she* **matured into** *a woman.* ■ develop fully: *the trees take at least thirty years to mature.* ■ (of a person) reach an advanced stage of mental or emotional development: *men mature as they grow older.* ■ (with reference to certain foodstuffs or drinks) become or cause to become ready for consumption: [*intrans.*] *leave the cheese to mature* | [*trans.*] *the Scotch is matured for a minimum of three years.* **2** (of an insurance policy, security, etc.) reach the end of its term and hence become payable. ▷late Middle English: from Latin *maturus* 'timely, ripe'; perhaps related to **MATINS**. —**ma·ture·ly** *adv.*

THE RIGHT WORD **age, develop, mature, mellow, ripen**

Most of us would prefer to **mature** rather than simply **age**. *Mature* implies gaining wisdom, experience, or sophistication as well as adulthood; when applied to other living things, it indicates fullness of growth and readiness for normal functioning (*a mature crop of strawberries*). To *age*, on the other hand, is to undergo the changes that result from the passage of time, often with an emphasis on the negative or destructive changes that accompany growing old (*the tragedy aged him five years*).

Develop is like *mature* in that it means to undergo a series of positive changes to attain perfection or effectiveness, but it can refer to a part as well as a whole organism (*the kitten's eyesight had begun to develop at three weeks*).

Ripen is a less formal word meaning to *mature*, but it usually applies to fruit (*the apples ripened in the sun*).

Mellow suggests the tempering or moderation of harshness that comes with time or experience. With its connotations of warmth, mildness, and sweetness, it is a more positive word than *mature* or *age* (*to mellow as one gets older*).

ma·tu·ri·ty /məˈCHo͝oritē; məˈt(y)o͝or-/ ▸*n.* the state, fact, or period of being mature: *their experience, maturity, and strong work ethic* | *the delicate style of his maturity.* ■ the time when an insurance policy, security, etc., matures. ■ an insurance policy, security, etc., having a fixed maturity date. ▷late Middle English: from Latin *maturitas*, from *maturus* (see **MATURE**).

Ma·tu·schan·ska·ya·sky /ˌmätəskänskäˈyäskē/, Walter, see **MATTHAU**.

ma·tu·ti·nal /məˈt(y)o͞otn-əl; ˌmaCHəˈtīnl/ ▸*adj. formal* of or occurring in the morning. ▷mid 16th cent.: from late Latin *matutinalis*, from Latin *matutinus* 'early.'

mat·zo (also **mat·zoh** or **mat·zah**) /ˈmätsə/ ▸*n.* (*pl.* **-zos** or **-zoth** /-ˌsōt; -ˌsōs/) a thin, crisp unleavened bread, traditionally eaten by Jews during Passover. ▷Yiddish, from Hebrew *maṣṣāh*.

mat·zo ball ▸*n.* a small dumpling made of seasoned matzo meal bound together with egg and chicken fat, typically served in chicken soup.

mat·zo meal ▸*n.* meal made from ground matzos.

maud /môd/ ▸*n.* a gray striped plaid cloak, formerly worn by shepherds in Scotland. ▷late 18th cent.: of unknown origin.

maud·lin /ˈmôdlin/ ▸*adj.* self-pityingly or tearfully sentimental, often through drunkenness: *the drink made her maudlin* | *a maudlin ballad.* See note at **SENTIMENTAL**. ▷late Middle English (as a noun denoting Mary Magdalen): from Old French *Madeleine*, from ecclesiastical Latin *Magdalena* (see **MAGDALENE**). The sense of the adjective derives from allusion to pictures of Mary Magdalen weeping.

Maugham /môm/, (William) Somerset (1874–1965), British novelist, short-story writer, and playwright, born in France. Notable novels: *Of Human Bondage* (1915), *The Moon and Sixpence* (1919), and *Cakes and Ale* (1930).

Mau·i /ˈmouē/ the second largest of the Hawaiian islands, northwest of the island of Hawaii.

maul /môl/ ▸*v.* [*trans.*] (of an animal) wound (a person or animal) by scratching and tearing: *the herdsmen were mauled by lions.* ■ treat (someone or something) roughly.

▸*n.* a tool with a heavy head and a handle, used for tasks such as ramming, crushing, and driving wedges; a beetle. ▷Middle English (in the sense 'hammer or wooden club,' also 'strike with a heavy weapon'): from Old French *mail*, from Latin *malleus* 'hammer.' —**maul·er** *n.*

maul·stick ▸*n.* variant of **MAHLSTICK**.

maul·vi ▸*n.* variant spelling of **MOULVI**.

Mau Mau /ˈmou ˌmou/ an African secret society originating among the Kikuyu that in the 1950s used violence and terror to try to expel European settlers and end British rule in Kenya. The British eventually subdued the organization, but Kenya gained independence in 1963. ■ (**mau-mau**) [as *v.*] [*trans.*] *informal* terrorize or threaten (someone). ▷Kikuyu.

Mau·na Kea /ˌmounə ˈkāə; ˌmônə/ an extinct volcano on the island of Hawaii, in the central Pacific. Rising to 13,796 feet (4,205 m), it is the highest peak in the Hawaiian islands. The summit area is the site of several large telescopes.

Mau·na Lo·a /ˈlōə; ˌmônə/ an active volcano on the island of Hawaii that is 13,678 feet (4,169 m) high, south of Mauna Kea.

maund /mônd/ ▸*n.* a varying unit of weight in some Asian countries, esp. an Indian unit of weight equal to 40 seers.

maun·der /ˈmôndər/ ▸*v.* [*intrans.*] talk in a rambling manner: *Dennis* **maundered on** *about the wine.* ■ [with *adverbial*] move or act in a dreamy or idle manner: *he maunders through the bank, composing his thoughts.* ▷early 17th cent.: perhaps from obsolete *maunder* 'to beg.'

Maun·der min·i·mum /ˈmôndər/ a prolonged minimum in sunspot activity on the sun between about 1645 and 1715, which coincided with the Little Ice Age in the northern hemisphere. ▷1970s: named after Edward W. *Maunder* (1851–1928), English astronomer.

Maun·dy Thurs·day /ˈmôndē/ ▸*n.* the Thursday before Easter, observed in the Christian Church as a commemoration of the Last Supper.

Mau·pas·sant /ˌmōpäˈsäɴ/, Guy de (1850–93), French novelist and short-story writer; full name *Henri René Albert Guy de Maupassant.* He wrote about 300 short stories and 6 novels in a simple, direct narrative style. Notable novels: *Une Vie* (1883) and *Bel-Ami* (1885).

Mau·re·ta·ni·a /ˌmôriˈtānēə; -ˈtānyə/ an ancient region of North Africa that corresponds to the northern part of Morocco and western and central Algeria. ▷based on Latin *Mauri* 'Moors,' by whom the region was originally occupied. **—Mau·re·ta·ni·an** *adj.* & *n.*

Mau·riac /ˌmôrˈyäk/, François (1885–1970), French novelist, playwright, and critic. His stories show the conflicts of convention, religion, and human passions suffered by prosperous bourgeoisie. Notable works: *Thérèse Desqueyroux* (novel, 1927) and *Asmodée* (play, 1938). Nobel Prize for Literature (1952).

Mau·ri·ta·ni·a /ˌmôriˈtānēə; -ˈtānyə/ a country in West Africa with a coastline on the Atlantic Ocean; pop. 2,900,000; capital, Nouakchott; languages, Arabic (official), Wolof (official), and French. **—Mau·ri·ta·ni·an** *adj.* & *n.*

Mauritania was a center of Berber power in the 11th and 12th centuries, at which time Islam was established in the region. Later, nomadic Arab tribes became dominant, while European nations, especially France, established trading posts on the coast. A French protectorate from 1902 and a colony from 1920, Mauritania achieved full independence in 1961.

Mau·ri·tius /môˈrisʜəs/ an island country in the Indian Ocean, about 550 miles (850 km) east of Madagascar; pop. 1,220,000; capital, Port Louis; languages, English (official), French (official), Creole, and Indian languages. The two main islands are Mauritius and Rodrigues. ▷named by the Dutch in honor of Prince *Maurice* of Nassau, a stadtholder of the United Provinces. **—Mau·ri·tian** /-ˈrisʜən/ *adj.* & *n.*

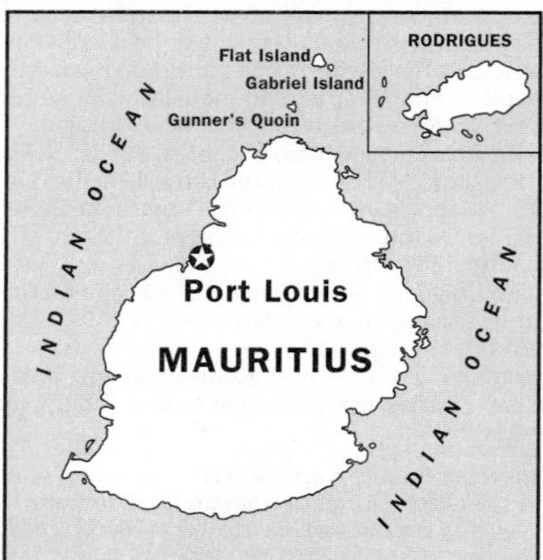

The Portuguese visited uninhabited Mauritius in the early 16th century. It was held by the Dutch 1598–1710 and then by the French until 1810, when it was ceded to Britain. Mauritius became independent as a member of the Commonwealth of Nations in 1968.

Mau·ry /ˈmôrē/, Matthew Fontaine (1806–73), U.S. oceanographer. He conducted the first systematic survey of oceanic winds and currents, and published charts of his findings.

Mau·ser /ˈmouzər/ ▸*n. trademark* a make of firearm, esp. a repeating rifle: [as *adj.*] *a Mauser rifle.* ▷late 19th cent.: named after Paul von *Mauser* (1838–1914), German inventor.

mau·so·le·um /ˌmôzəˈlēəm; ˌmôsə-/ ▸*n.* (*pl.* **-le·a** /-ˈlēə/ or **-le·ums**) a building, esp. a large and stately one, housing a tomb or tombs. ▷late 15th cent.: via Latin from Greek *Mausōleion*, from *Mausōlos*, the name of a king of Caria (4th cent. BC), to whose tomb in Halicarnassus the name was originally applied.

mauve /mōv; môv/ ▸*adj.* of a pale purple color.
▸*n.* **1** a pale purple color: *a few pale streaks of mauve were all that remained of the sunset | glowing with soft pastel mauves and pinks.* **2** *historical* a bright but delicate pale purple aniline dye prepared by William H. Perkin (1838–1907) in 1856. It was the first synthetic dyestuff. ▷mid 19th cent.: from French, literally 'mallow,' from Latin *malva*.

ma·ven /ˈmāvən/ ▸*n.* [often with *adj.*] *informal* an expert or connoisseur: *fashion mavens.* ▷1960s: Yiddish.

mav·er·ick /ˈmav(ə)rik/ ▸*n.* **1** an unorthodox or independent-minded person: *a free-thinking maverick.* ■ a person who refuses to conform to a particular party or group: *the maverick Connecticut Republican.* **2** an unbranded calf or yearling.
▸*adj.* unorthodox: *a maverick detective.* ▷mid 19th cent.: from the name of Samuel A. *Maverick* (1803–70), a Texas engineer and rancher who did not brand his cattle.

ma·vis /ˈmāvis/ ▸*n. poetic/literary* a song thrush. ▷late Middle English: from Old French *mauvis*, of unknown origin.

maw /mô/ ▸*n.* the jaws or throat of a voracious animal: *a gigantic wolfhound with a fearful, gaping maw.* ■ *informal* the mouth or gullet of a greedy person: *I was cramming large pieces of toast and cheese down my maw.* ▷Old English *maga* (in the sense 'stomach'), of Germanic origin; related to Dutch *maag* and German *Magen* 'stomach.'

mawk·ish /ˈmôkisʜ/ ▸*adj.* sentimental in a feeble or sickly way: *a mawkish poem.* See note at SENTIMENTAL. ■ *archaic* or *dialect* having a faint sickly flavor: *the mawkish smell of warm beer.* ▷mid 17th cent. (in the sense 'inclined to sickness'): from obsolete *mawk* 'maggot,' from Old Norse *mathkr*, of Germanic origin. **—mawk·ish·ly** *adv.* **—mawk·ish·ness** *n.*

Maw·la·na /mouˈlänä/ another name for JALAL AD-DIN AR-RUMI.

Max /maks/, Peter (1937–), U.S. artist; born in Germany. Noted for combining serious art with commercial outlets, his brightly colored works, begun as pop art in the 1960s, have included art for U.S. postage stamps, murals for border stations between the U.S. and Canada and the U.S. and Mexico, posters for Woodstock revivals and the Earth Summit, and an annual series of Statue of Liberty paintings.

max /maks/ ▸*abbr.* maximum.
▸*n. informal* a maximum amount or setting: *the sound is distorted* **to the max**.
▸*adv. informal* at the most: *our information can be in the commander's hand in half an hour, max.*
▸*v. informal* reach or cause to reach the limit of capacity or ability: *job growth in high technology will* **max out**.

max·i /ˈmaksē/ ▸*n.* (*pl.* **max·is**) a thing that is very large of its kind, in particular: ■ (also **max·i·skirt** or **max·i·coat**) a skirt or coat reaching to the ankle. ■ (also **max·i-yacht** or **max·i-boat**) a racing yacht of between approximately 15 and 20 meters in length. ▷1960s: abbreviation of MAXIMUM, on the pattern of *mini*.

max·il·la /makˈsilə/ ▸*n.* (*pl.* **max·il·lae** /makˈsilē; -ˈsilˌī/) *Anatomy & Zoology* the jaw or jawbone, specifically the upper jaw in most vertebrates. In humans it also forms part of the nose and eye socket. ■ (in many arthropods) each of a pair of mouthparts used in chewing. ▷late Middle English: from Latin, 'jaw.'

max·il·lar·y /ˈmaksəˌlerē/ ▸*adj. Anatomy & Zoology* of or attached to a jaw or jawbone, esp. the upper jaw: *a maxillary fracture | maxillary teeth.* ■ of or relating to the maxillae of an arthropod. ▷early 17th cent.: from MAXILLA, probably suggested by Latin *maxillaris*.

max·il·li·ped /makˈsiləˌped/ ▸*n. Zoology* (in crustaceans) an appendage modified for feeding, situated in pairs behind the maxillae. ▷mid 19th cent.: from MAXILLA + Latin *pes, ped-* 'foot.'

max·il·lo·fa·cial /makˌsilōˈfāsʜəl; maksəlō-/ ▸*n. Anatomy* of or relating to the jaws and face: *maxillofacial surgery.* ▷late 19th cent.: from *maxillo-* (combining form of Latin *maxilla* 'jaw') + FACIAL.

max·im /ˈmaksim/ ▸*n.* a short, pithy statement expressing a general truth or rule of conduct: *the maxim that actions speak louder than words.* See note at SAYING. ▷late Middle English (denoting an axiom): from French *maxime*, from medieval Latin *(propositio) maxima* 'largest or most important (proposition).'

max·i·ma /ˈmaksəmə/ ▸ plural form of MAXIMUM.

max·i·mal /ˈmaksəməl/ ▸*adj.* of or constituting a maximum; the highest or greatest possible: *the maximal speed.* **—max·i·mal·ly** *adv.*

max·i·mal·ist /ˈmaksəməlist/ ▸*n.* (esp. in politics) a person who holds extreme views and is not prepared to compromise.
▸*adj.* of or denoting an extreme opinion: *if we demand only maximalist ends, we will get nothing.* ▷early 20th cent.: from MAXIMAL, on the pattern of Russian *maksimalist*. **—max·i·mal·ism** /-ˌizəm/ *n.*

max·i·mand /ˈmaksəˌmand/ ▸*n. chiefly Economics* a quantity or thing that is to be maximized. ▷1950s: from MAXIMIZE + -AND.

Max·im gun /ˈmaksim / ▸*n.* the first fully automatic water-cooled machine gun, designed in Britain in 1884 and used esp. in World War I. ▷named after Sir Hiram S. *Maxim* (1840–1916), American-born British inventor.

Max·i·mil·ian /ˌmaksəˈmilyən/ (1832–67), Austrian emperor of Mexico 1864–67; full name *Ferdinand Maximilian Joseph.* The brother of Franz Josef, he became emperor of Mexico under French auspices in 1864. U.S. pressure forced Napoleon III to withdraw his support in 1867, and Maximilian was executed by a popular uprising led by Mexico's president Benito Juárez.

Max·i·mil·ian II ▸1811–64, king of Bavaria 1848–64. He became king upon the abdication of his father, Ludwig I. A patron of the arts and education, his liberal objectives went largely unrealized due to an adversarial political climate and his frequent bouts of ill health.

max·i·min /ˈmaksəˌmin; -sē-/ ▸*n. Mathematics* the largest of a series of minima. Compare with MINIMAX. ■ [as *adj.*] denoting a method or strategy in game theory that maximizes the smallest gain that can be relied on by a participant in a game or other situation of conflict. ▷1950s: blend of MAXIMUM and MINIMUM, on the pattern of *minimax*.

max·i·mize /ˈmaksəˌmīz/ ▸*v.* [*trans.*] make as large or great as possible: *the company was aiming to maximize profits.* ■ make the best use of: *a rider can maximize a young horse's athletic potential.* ▷early 19th cent.: from Latin *maximus* (see MAXIMUM) + -IZE. **—max·i·mi·za·tion** /ˌmaksəməˈzāsʜən/ *n.* **—max·i·miz·er** *n.*

max·i·mum /ˈmaksəməm/ ▸*adj.* [*attrib.*] as great, high, or intense as possible or permitted: *the vehicle's maximum speed | a maximum penalty of ten years' imprisonment.* ■ denoting the greatest or highest point or amount attained: *the maximum depth of the pool is 6 feet.*
▸*n.* (*pl.* **-ma** /-mə/ or **-mums**) the greatest or highest amount possible or attained: *the school takes a maximum of 32 students | production levels are near their maximum.* ■ a maximum permitted prison sentence for an offense: *an offense that carries a maximum of 14 years.*
▸*adv.* at the most: *it has a length of 4 feet maximum.* ▷mid 17th cent. (as a noun): from modern Latin, neuter (used as a noun) of the Latin adjective *maximus*, superlative of *magnus* 'great.' The adjective use dates from the early 19th cent.

max·i·mum sus·tain·a·ble yield (abbr.: **MSY**) ▸*n.* (esp. in forestry and fisheries) the maximum level at which a natural resource can be routinely exploited without long-term depletion. ■ *Ecology* the size of a natural population at which it produces a maximum rate of increase, typically at half the carrying capacity.

max·ixe /mäkˈsēks; mäkˈsʜēsʜə/ ▸*n.* a Brazilian dance for couples, resembling the polka and the local tango. ▷early 20th cent.: Portuguese.

Max·well[1] /ˈmaksˌwel/, Elsa (1883–1963), U.S. columnist and professional hostess. She was a legendary hostess for high society and royalty from the 1920s and began to write a syndicated gossip column during the 1940s.

Max·well[2], James Clerk (1831–79), Scottish physicist. He extended the ideas of Faraday and Kelvin with his equations of electromagnetism, and he succeeded in unifying electricity and magnetism, identifying the electromagnetic nature of light and postulating the existence of other electromagnetic radiation.

max·well /ˈmak,swel; -swəl/ (abbr.: **Mx**) ▸*n. Physics* a unit of magnetic flux in the centimeter-gram-second system, equal to that induced through one square centimeter by a perpendicular magnetic field of one gauss. ▷early 20th cent.: named after J. C. *Maxwell* (see **MAXWELL**[2]).

Max·well–Boltz·mann dis·tri·bu·tion /ˈmak,swel ˈbōltsmən; ˈmakswəl/ *Physics* a formula describing the statistical distribution of particles in a system among different energy levels. The number of particles in a given energy level is proportional to exp. $(-E/kT)$, where E is the energy of the level, k is Boltzmann's constant, and T is the absolute temperature. ▷1920s: named after J. C. *Maxwell* (see **MAXWELL**[2]) and L. **BOLTZMANN**.

Max·well's de·mon *Physics* a hypothetical being imagined as controlling a hole in a partition dividing a gas-filled container into two parts, and allowing only fast-moving molecules to pass in one direction, and slow-moving molecules in the other. This would result in one side of the container becoming warmer and the other cooler, in violation of the second law of thermodynamics. ▷late 19th cent.: named after J. C. *Maxwell* (see **MAXWELL**[2]).

Max·well's e·qua·tions *Physics* a set of four linear partial differential equations that summarize the classical properties of the electromagnetic field. ▷early 20th cent.: named after J. C. *Maxwell* (see **MAXWELL**[2]).

May /mā/ ▸*n.* the fifth month of the year, in the northern hemisphere usually considered the last month of spring: *the new model makes its showroom debut in May* | [as *adj.*] *a May morning.* ■ (usu. **one's May**) *poetic/literary* one's bloom or prime: *others murmured that their May was passing.* ▷late Old English, from Old French *mai*, from Latin *Maius (mensis)* '(month) of the goddess *Maia*.'

may[1] /mā/ ▸*modal verb* (*3rd sing. present* **may**; *past* **might** /mīt/) **1** expressing possibility: *that may be true* | *he may well win.* ■ used when admitting that something is so before making another, more important point: *they may have been old-fashioned, but they were excellent teachers.* **2** expressing permission: *you may use a sling if you wish* | *may I ask a few questions?* **3** expressing a wish or hope: *may she rest in peace.* ▷Old English *mæg*, of Germanic origin, from a base meaning 'have power'; related to Dutch *mogen* and German *mögen*, also to **MAIN**[1] and **MIGHT**[2].

▸*PHRASES* □ **be that as it may** despite that; nevertheless. □ **may as well** another way of saying **MIGHT AS WELL** (see **MIGHT**[1]).

USAGE Traditionalists insist that one should distinguish between **may** (present tense) and **might** (past tense) in expressing possibility: *I may have some dessert after dinner if I'm still hungry; I might have known that the highway would be closed because of the storm.* In casual use, though, **may** and **might** are generally interchangeable: *they might take a vacation next month; he may have called earlier, but the answering machine was broken.*

On the difference in use between **may** and **can**, see **usage** at **CAN**[1].

may[2] ▸*n.* the hawthorn or its blossom. ▷late Middle English: from **MAY**.

Ma·ya /ˈmīə/ ▸*n.* (*pl.* same or **Ma·yas**) **1** a member of a an American Indian people of Yucatán and adjacent areas. **2** the Mayan language of this people.

▸*adj.* of or relating to this people or their language.

The Maya civilization developed over an extensive area of southern Mexico, Guatemala, and Belize from the 2nd millennium BC, reaching its peak c.AD 300–c. 900. Its remains include stone temples built on pyramids and ornamented with sculptures. The Mayas had a system of pictorial writing and an extremely accurate calendar system.

▷the name in Maya.

ma·ya /ˈmīə; ˈmäyə/ ▸*n. Hinduism* the supernatural power wielded by gods and demons to produce illusions. ■ *Hinduism* the power by which the universe becomes manifest. ■ *Hinduism & Buddhism* the illusion or appearance of the phenomenal world. ▷from Sanskrit *māyā*, from *mā* 'create.'

Ma·ya·kov·sky /,mäyəˈkôfskē; -skyē/, Vladimir (Vladimirovich) (1893–1930), Soviet poet and playwright. A fervent futurist, he wrote in a declamatory, aggressive avant-garde style, which he altered to have a comic mass appeal after the Bolshevik revolution.

Ma·yan /ˈmīən/ ▸*n.* a large family of American Indian languages spoken in Central America, of which the chief members are Maya and Quiché.

▸*adj.* **1** denoting, relating to, or belonging to this family of languages. **2** relating to or denoting the Maya people.

may·ap·ple /ˈmā,apəl/ (also **May ap·ple**) ▸*n.* an American herbaceous plant of the barberry family with large, deeply divided leaves. The plant, which bears a yellow, egg-shaped edible fruit in May, has long been used medicinally. Also called **MANDRAKE**. • *Podophyllum peltatum*, family Berberidaceae.

may·be /ˈmābē/ ▸*adv.* perhaps; possibly: *maybe I won't go back* | *maybe she'd been wrong to accept this job.*

▸*n.* a mere possibility or probability: *no ifs, buts, or maybes.* ▷late Middle English: from the phrase *it may be (that).*

May bee·tle ▸*n.* another term for **JUNE BUG**.

May·day /ˈmā,dā/ (also **may·day**) ▸*exclam.* an international radio distress signal used by ships and aircraft.

▸*n.* a distress signal using the word "Mayday": *we sent out a Mayday* | [as *adj.*] *a Mayday call.* ▷1920s: representing a pronunciation of French *m'aider*, from *venez m'aider* 'come and help me.'

May Day ▸*n.* May 1, celebrated in many countries as a traditional springtime festival or as an international day honoring workers.

May·er /ˈmāər/, Louis B. (1885–1957), U.S. movie executive, born in Russia; full name *Louis Burt Mayer*; born *Eliezer Mayer*. In 1924, with Samuel Goldwyn, he formed Metro-Goldwyn-Mayer (MGM). He headed the company until 1951.

may·est /ˈmā-ist; māst/ ▸ archaic second person singular present of **MAY**[1].

May·fair /ˈmā,fe(ə)r/ a fashionable and opulent district in the West End of London. ▷originally the site of a fair held annually in May in the 17th and 18th cents.

May·flow·er /ˈmā,flou(-ə)r/ the ship in which the Pilgrims sailed from England to America in 1620.

may·flow·er /ˈmā,flou(-ə)r/ ▸*n.* a name given to several plants that bloom in May, esp. certain hepaticas and anemones and the trailing arbutus.

may·fly /ˈmā,flī/ ▸*n.* (*pl.* **-flies**) a short-lived, slender insect with delicate, transparent wings and two or three long filaments on the tail. It lives close to water, where the chiefly herbivorous aquatic larvae develop. • Order Ephemeroptera: several families and many species. ■ an artificial fishing fly that imitates such an insect.

may·hap /ˈmā,hap/ ▸*adv. archaic* perhaps; possibly. ▷mid 16th cent.: from *it may hap.*

may·hem /ˈmā,hem/ ▸*n.* violent or damaging disorder; chaos: *complete mayhem broke out.* ■ *Law, chiefly historical* the crime of maliciously injuring or maiming someone, originally so as to render the victim defenseless. ▷early 16th cent.: from Old French *mayhem* (see **MAIM**). The sense 'disorder, chaos' (originally U.S.) dates from the late 19th cent.

may·ing /ˈmā-iNG/ (also **May·ing**) ▸*n. archaic* celebration of May Day.

may·n't /ˈmā(ə)nt/ *rare* ▸*contraction of* may not.

Ma·yo[1] /ˈmā-ō/ a county in the Republic of Ireland, in the northwestern part of the province of Connacht; county town, Castlebar.

Ma·yo[2], William Worrall (1819–1911), U.S. physician; born in England. He helped the Sisters of St. Francis found St. Mary's Hospital in Rochester, Minnesota in 1899. His sons **William James** (1861–1939) and **Charles Horace** (1865–1939), both surgeons, developed the Mayo Clinic as a part of the hospital.

may·o /ˈmā-ō/ ▸*n. informal* short for **MAYONNAISE**.

may·on·naise /ˈmāə,nāz; ,māəˈnāz/ ▸*n.* a thick, creamy dressing consisting of egg yolks beaten with oil and vinegar and seasoned. ▷French, probably from the feminine of *mahonnais* 'of or from Port *Mahon*,' the capital of Minorca.

may·or /ˈmāər/ ▸*n.* the elected head of a city, town, or other municipality. ■ the titular head of a municipality that is administered by a city manager. ▷Middle English: from Old French *maire*, from the Latin adjective *major* 'greater,' used as a noun in late Latin. **—may·or·al** /māˈôrəl; ˈmāərəl/ *adj.* **—may·or·ship** /-,SHip/ *n.*

may·or·al·ty /ˈmāərəltē/ ▸*n.* (*pl.* **-ties**) the office of mayor: *the party failed to win the mayoralty.* ■ a mayor's period of office. ▷late Middle English: from Old French *mairalte*, from *maire* (see **MAYOR**).

may·or·ess /ˈmāərəs/ ▸*n.* **1** the wife of a mayor. **2** a woman holding the office of mayor.

Ma·yotte /mäˈyôt/ an island in the Indian Ocean, east of Comoros; pop. 94,000; capital, Mamoutzu. When the Comoros became independent in 1974, Mayotte remained an overseas territory of France. Also called **MAHORE**.

may·pole /ˈmā,pōl/ (also **May·pole**) ▸*n.* a pole painted and decorated with flowers, around which people traditionally dance on May Day, holding long ribbons that are attached to the top of the pole.

may·pop /ˈmā,päp/ ▸*n.* the yellow edible fruit of a North American passionflower. • The plant, grown chiefly in the southern U.S., is *Passiflora incarnata*, family Passifloraceae.

May queen ▸*n.* a girl or young woman chosen to be crowned in traditional celebrations of May Day.

Mayr /ˈmāər/, Ernst Walter (1904), U.S. zoologist, born in Germany. He argued for a neo-Darwinian approach to evolution in his classic *Animal Species and Evolution* (1963).

Mays /māz/, Willie (Howard, Jr.) (1931–), U.S. baseball player; known as the **Say Hey Kid**. A center fielder, he played for the New York (later San Francisco) Giants 1951–52, 1954–71 and the New York Mets 1971–72. Baseball Hall of Fame (1979).

Willie Mays

mayst /māst/ ▸ archaic second person singular present of **MAY**[1].

may·weed /ˈmā,wēd/ ▸*n.* a plant of the daisy family that typically grows as a weed of fields and waste ground. • Several species in the family Compositae, in particular **stinking mayweed** (*Anthemis cotula*). ▷mid 16th cent.: from *maythe(n)*, an earlier name for this plant (in Old English *mægethe, magothe*), + **WEED**.

Ma·zar-e-Sha·rif /məˈzär ē SHəˈrēf/ a city in northern Afghanistan; pop. 131,000. Its name means "tomb of the saint" and is the reputed burial place of Ali, son-in-law of Muhammad.

Maz·a·rin /ˈmäzərin; mäzäˈraN/, Jules (1602–61), French statesman, born in Italy; Italian name *Giulio Mazzarino*. Sent to Paris as the Italian papal legate (1634), he became a naturalized Frenchman and was made a cardinal in 1641 and then chief minister of Louis XIV in 1642.

Ma·za·tlán /,mäsätˈlän/ a seaport and resort in Mexico, on the Pacific coast in the state of Sinaloa; pop. 314,000. Founded in 1531, it developed as a center of trade with the Philippines.

Maz·da·ism /ˈmäzdə,izəm; maz-/ ▸*n.* another term for **ZOROASTRIANISM**. ▷late 19th cent.: from Avestan *mazdā* (short for **AHURA MAZDA**) + **-ISM**. **—Maz·da·ist** *n. & adj.*

maze /māz/ ▸*n.* a network of paths and hedges designed as a puzzle through which one has to find a way. ■ a complex network of paths or passages: *they were trapped in a menacing **maze** of corridors.* ■ a confusing mass of information: ***a maze of** petty regulations.*

▸*v.* (**be mazed**) *archaic* or *dialect* be dazed and confused: *she was still mazed with the drug she had taken.* ▷Middle English (denoting delirium or delusion):

probably from the base of **AMAZE**, of which the verb is a shortening.

ma·zel tov /ˈmäzəl ˌtôv; ˌtôf/ ▸*exclam.* a Jewish phrase expressing congratulations or wishing someone good luck. ▷from modern Hebrew *mazzāl ṭōḇ*, literally 'good star.'

ma·zer /ˈmāzər/ ▸*n. historical* a hardwood drinking bowl. ▷Middle English: from Old French *masere*, of Germanic origin.

ma·zu·ma /məˈzo͞omə/ ▸*n. informal* money; cash. ▷early 20th cent.: Yiddish, from Hebrew *mĕzummān*, from *zimmēn* 'prepare.'

ma·zur·ka /məˈzərkə; -ˈzo͝or-/ ▸*n.* a lively Polish dance in triple time. ▷early 19th cent.: via German from Polish *mazurka*, denoting a woman of the province Mazovia.

ma·zy /ˈmāzē/ ▸*adj.* (**ma·zi·er, ma·zi·est**) like a maze; labyrinthine: *the museum's mazy treasure house.*

maz·zard /ˈmazərd/ ▸*n.* (in full **mazzard cherry**) a cherry tree native to both Eurasia and North America, commercially important for both its fruit and wood. Also called **SWEET CHERRY**. • *Prunus avium*, family Rosaceae.

Maz·zi·ni /məˈzēnē; mädˈzēnē/, Giuseppe (1805–72), Italian nationalist leader. He founded the patriotic movement Young Italy (1831) and was a leader of the Risorgimento.

MB ▸*abbr.* ■ Bachelor of Medicine. [from Latin *Medicinae Baccalaureus*.] ■ Manitoba (in official postal use). ■ (also **Mb**) *Computing* megabyte: *a 800 MB hard disk.*

MBA ▸*abbr.* Master of Business Administration.

Mba·ba·ne /əmbäˈbänā/ the capital of Swaziland, in the northwestern part of the country; pop. 38,300.

mba·qan·ga /(ə)mbəˈkäNGgə/ ▸*n.* a rhythmical popular music style of southern Africa. ▷from Zulu *umbaqanga*, literally 'steamed cornbread,' used to express the combined notion of the homely cultural sustenance of the townships and the musicians' "daily bread" (coined in this sense by trumpeter Michael Xaba).

mbd ▸*abbr.* (of oil) million barrels per day.

mbi·ra /(ə)mˈbi(ə)rə/ ▸*n.* (esp. in southern Africa) another term for **THUMB PIANO**. ▷late 19th cent.: from Shona, probably an alteration of *rimba* 'a note.'

Mbps ▸*abbr. Computing* ■ millions of bits per second. ■ megabits per second. ■ (**MBps**) megabytes per second.

Mbun·du /(ə)mˈbo͝ondo͞o/ ▸*n.* (*pl.* same) **1** a member of either of two peoples of western Angola (sometimes distinguished as **Mbundu** and **Ovimbundu**). **2** either of the Bantu languages of these peoples, often distinguished as **Umbundu** (related to Herero) and **Kimbundu** (related to Kikongo).
▸*adj.* of or relating to these peoples or their languages.

Mbu·ti /(ə)mˈbo͞otē/ ▸*n.* (*pl.* same or **Mbu·tis**) a member of a pygmy people of western Uganda and adjacent areas of the Democratic Republic of the Congo (formerly Zaire).
▸*adj.* of or relating to this people. ▷the name in local languages.

Mbyte ▸*abbr.* megabyte(s).

MC ▸*abbr.* ■ Master of Ceremonies. ■ (in the U.S.) Member of Congress. ■ (in an astrological chart) the midheaven. [from Latin *Medium Coeli*.] ■ (in the UK) Military Cross. ■ music cassette (of prerecorded audiotape).

Mc ▸*abbr.* megacycle(s), a unit of frequency equal to one million cycles.

Mc·Al·len /miˈkalən/ a city in southern Texas, in the Rio Grande valley; pop. 84,021.

MCAT ▸*abbr.* Medical College Admissions Test.

MCB ▸*abbr.* miniature circuit-breaker.

Mc·Car·thy[1] /məˈkärTHē/, Joseph (Raymond) (1909–57), U.S. politician; a U.S. senator from Wisconsin 1947–57. Between 1950 and 1954, he was the instigator of widespread investigations into alleged communist infiltration in U.S. public life. Eventually discredited, he was censured by the Senate in 1954.

Mc·Car·thy[2], Mary (Therese) (1912–89), U.S. novelist and critic. Her novels are satirical social commentaries that draw on her experience with intellectual circles and academic life. Notable novels: *The Groves of Academe* (1952) and *The Group* (1963).

Mc·Car·thy·ism /məˈkärTHēˌizəm/ ▸*n.* a vociferous campaign against alleged communists in the U.S. government and other institutions carried out under Senator Joseph McCarthy in the period 1950–54. Many of the accused were blacklisted or lost their jobs, although most did not in fact belong to the Communist Party. ■ *figurative* any similar practice that endorses the use of unfair allegations and investigations: *he practiced McCarthyism long before there was a McCarthy.* —**Mc·Car·thy·ist** *adj.* & *n.* —**Mc·Car·thy·ite** /-THēˌīt/ *adj.* & *n.*

Mc·Cart·ney[1] /məˈkärtnē/, Linda (1941–98), U.S. photographer, entrepreneur, and musician; born Linda Eastman; wife of Paul McCartney. Well known for her photographs, esp. of musicians, she promoted vegetarianism and animal rights. She successfully started her own company that made prepackaged vegetarian meals.

Mc·Cart·ney[2], Sir (James) Paul (1942–), English pop and rock singer, songwriter, and bass guitarist. A founding member of the Beatles, he wrote most of their songs in collaboration with John Lennon. After the group broke up in 1970, he formed the band Wings. See photograph at **LENNON**.

Mc·Clel·lan /məˈklelən/, George Brinton (1826–85), U.S. army officer; known as **Little Mac**. He became general in chief of the U.S. Army 1861 during the Civil War. Although the victor at Antietam 1862, he was removed from command due to a lack of military aggressiveness. The Democratic presidential candidate in 1864, he was defeated by incumbent Abraham Lincoln. He later served as governor of New Jersey 1878–81.

Mc·Clin·tock /məˈklinˌtäk/, Barbara (1902–92), U.S. geneticist. The discovery of DNA vindicated her earlier findings of transposable genetic elements 1951. Nobel Prize for Physiology or Medicine (1983).

Barbara McClintock

Mc·Cor·mack /məˈkôrmək/, John (1884–1945), U.S. opera singer; born in Ireland. A tenor, he sang with various opera groups, including the Chicago and Metropolitan opera companies. He was also popular for his renderings of Irish folk songs.

Mc·Cor·mick /məˈkômək/, Cyrus Hall (1809–84), U.S. inventor and industrialist. His patented reaper 1834 was the cornerstone of his harvesting machinery company, and the innovative deferred-payment plans and guarantees that he offered customers became a model in U.S. consumerism.

Mc·Court /məˈkôrt/, Frank (1930–), U.S. writer. He wrote the award-winning *Angela's Ashes* (1996), a memoir about his impoverished childhood, some of which was spent in Ireland. Other works include *'Tis* (1999), also based on his past experiences.

Mc·Coy /məˈkoi/ ▸*n.* (in phrase **the real McCoy**) *informal* the real thing; the genuine article: *the apparent fake turned out to be the real McCoy.*

Mc·Cul·lers /məˈkələrz/, Carson (1917–67), U.S. writer; born *Lula Carson Smith*. Her work deals sensitively with loneliness and the plight of the eccentric. Notable works: *The Heart Is a Lonely Hunter* (1940), *The Member of the Wedding* (1946), and *The Ballad of the Sad Cafe* (1951).

Mc·Cul·lough /məˈkələ(k)/, Colleen (1937–), Australian writer. Her novels include *Tim* (1974), *The Thorn Birds* (1977) *The Song of Troy* (1998), and *Morgan's Run* (2000). She also wrote a series about ancient Rome.

Mc·En·roe /ˈmakənˌrō/, John (Patrick) (1959–), U.S. tennis player. A temperamental player, he dominated the game in the early 1980s. He won three Wimbledon singles titles 1981, 1983, and 1984 and four U.S. Open singles championships 1979, 1980, 1981, and 1984.

mcf (also **MCF** or **Mcf**) ▸*abbr.* one thousand cubic feet.

mcg ▸*abbr.* microgram.

Mc·Gil·li·cud·dy /məˈgiliˌkədē/, Cornelius Alexander see **MACK**.

Mc·Gov·ern /mə(k)ˈgəvərn/, George S(tanley) (1922–), U.S. politician. A Democrat from South Dakota, he was a member of the U.S. House of Representatives 1956–61 and of the U.S. Senate 1963–81. He was the Democratic presidential candidate in 1972.

Mc·Graw /mə(k)ˈgrô/, John (Joseph) (1873–1934), U.S. baseball player and manager; nickname **Little Napoleon**. He played for the Baltimore Orioles 1891–99 and then managed the New York Giants 1902–32. Baseball Hall of Fame (1937).

Mc·Guf·fey /mə(k)ˈgəfē/, William Holmes (1800–1873), U.S. public education reformer. He is best known for his series of *Eclectic Readers*, compiled between 1836 and 1857 and more commonly called *McGuffey Readers*.

Mc·Guf·fin /məˈgəfin/ ▸*n. chiefly Brit.* an object or device in a movie or a book that serves merely as a trigger for the plot. ▷late 20th cent.: a Scottish surname, said to have been borrowed by the English film director Alfred Hitchcock, from a humorous story involving such a pivotal factor.

Mc·Gwire /mə(k)ˈgwī(ə)r/, Mark (David) (1963–), U.S. baseball player. A first baseman, he played for the Oakland Athletics 1986–1997 and the St. Louis Cardinals 1997–2001. In 1998, he hit 70 home runs, breaking Roger Maris's record of 61 for the most home runs in a season.

mCi ▸*abbr.* millicurie(s), a quantity of a radioactive substance having one thousandth of a curie of radioactivity: *15 mCi of the radionuclide.*

Mc·In·tosh /ˈmakənˌtäSH/ (also **Mc·In·tosh red**) ▸*n.* a dessert apple of a variety native to North America, with deep red skin. ▷late 19th cent.: named after John *McIntosh* (1777–1845 or 1846), the American-born Canadian farmer on whose farm the apple was discovered as a wild variety.

Mc·Job /məkˈjäb/ ▸*n.* a low-paid job with few prospects, typically one taken by an overqualified person. ▷1980s: from *McDonald's*, a fast-food restaurant chain, + **JOB**.

Mc·Kees·port /miˈkēzˌpôrt/ a city in southwestern Pennsylvania, southeast of Pittsburgh; pop. 26,016.

Mc·Ken·na /məˈkenə/, Joseph (1843–1926), U.S. Supreme Court associate justice 1898–1925. He was the U.S. attorney general 1897–98 when he was appointed to the Court by President McKinley.

Mc·Kin·ley[1] /məˈkinlē/, John (1780–1852), U.S. Supreme Court associate justice 1837–52. A U.S. senator 1826–31, 1837 and a member of the U.S. House of Representatives 1833–35, he was appointed to the Court by President Van Buren.

Mc·Kin·ley[2], William (1843–1901), 25th president of the U.S. 1897–1901. A Republican, he favored big business and waged the Spanish–American War of 1898, which resulted in the acquisition of Puerto Rico, Cuba, and the Philippines, as well as the annexation of Hawaii, and brought the U.S. to the forefront of world power. He was assassinated by an anarchist while in Buffalo, New York.

William McKinley

Mc·Kin·ley, Mount /məˈkinlē/ a mountain in south central Alaska. Rising to 20,110 feet (6,194 m), it is the highest mountain in North America. Also called **DENALI**.

Mc·Ku·en /məˈkyo͞oən/, Rod (1933–), U.S. poet, writer, and composer. Some of his poetry is collected in *Stanyan Street and Other Sorrows* (1966) and *Listen to the Warm* (1967). He also wrote many songs and movie scores.

MCL ▸*abbr.* ■ Master of Civil Law. ■ Master of Comparative Law.

Mc·Lean /məˈklēn/, John (1785–1861), U.S. Supreme Court associate justice 1829–61. The U.S. postmaster general 1823–29, he was appointed to the Court by President Jackson.

Mc·Lu·han /mə'klo͞oən/, (Herbert) Marshall (1911–80), Canadian writer and thinker. He became known in the 1960s for his phrase "the medium is the message" and for his argument that it is the characteristics of a particular medium rather than the information it disseminates that influence and control society.

Mc·Man·sion /mək'mansʜən/ ▶*n.* a large modern house that is considered ostentatious and lacking in architectural integrity. ▷from *Mc-* + *mansion*, with reference to the name of a restaurant chain.

Mc·Minn·ville /mək'min,vil; -vəl/ a city in northwestern Oregon, northwest of Salem; pop. 26,499.

Mc·Mur·try /mək'mərtrē/, Larry (Jeff) (1936–), U.S. writer. Included in his works are *The Last Picture Show* (1966), *Terms of Endearment* (1975), *Lonesome Dove* (1985), and *Comanche Moon* (1997).

Mc·Na·mar·a /'maknə,marə/, Robert Strange (1916–), U.S. businessman and public official. He was secretary of the U.S. Department of Defense 1961–68 during the Kennedy and Johnson administrations and president of the World Bank 1968–81.

m-com·merce ▶*n.* electronic commerce conducted on cellular phones. ▷from *m(obile)* + *commerce*.

MCP *informal* ▶*abbr.* male chauvinist pig.

Mc·Phee /mək'fē/, John (Angus) (1931–), U.S. journalist and writer. He wrote for the *New Yorker* magazine from 1964 and also published such nonfiction works as *Coming into the Country* (1977) and *Basin and Range* (1981).

MCPO ▶*abbr.* master chief petty officer.

Mc·Rey·nolds /mək'renəl(d)z/, James Clark (1862–1946), U.S. Supreme Court associate justice 1914–41. The U.S. attorney general 1913–14, he was appointed to the Court by President Wilson.

Mc/s ▶*abbr.* megacycles per second, a unit of frequency equal to one million cycles per second.

MD ▶*abbr.* ■ Doctor of Medicine. [from Latin *Medicinae Doctor*.] ■ *Brit.* Managing Director. ■ Maryland (in official postal use). ■ *Medicine* mentally deficient. ■ musical director.

Md ▶*symbol* the chemical element mendelevium.

Md. ▶*abbr.* Maryland.

m/d (also **M/D**) ▶*abbr.* months after date.

MDF ▶*abbr.* medium density fiberboard.

M.Div. ▶*abbr.* Master of Divinity.

MDMA ▶*abbr.* methylenedioxymethamphetamine, the drug Ecstasy.

MDS ▶*abbr.* Master of Dental Science.

mdse. ▶*abbr.* merchandise.

MDT ▶*abbr.* Mountain Daylight Time (see **MOUNTAIN TIME**).

ME ▶*abbr.* ■ Maine (in official postal use). ■ medical examiner. ■ Middle English. ■ myalgic encephalitis.

Me ▶*abbr.* ■ Maine. ■ Maître (title of a French advocate).

me /mē/ ▶*pron.* [*first person singular*] **1** used by a speaker to refer to himself or herself as the object of a verb or preposition: *do you understand me?* | *wait for me!* Compare with **I**[2]. ■ used after the verb "to be" and after "than" or "as": *hi, it's me* | *you have more than me.* ■ *informal* to or for myself: *I've got me a job.* **2** *informal* used in exclamations: *dear me!* | *silly me!* ▷Old English *mē*, accusative and dative of **I**[2], of Germanic origin; related to Dutch *mij*, German *mir* (dative), from an Indo-European root shared by Latin *me*, Greek *(e)me*, and Sanskrit *mā*.

▶*PHRASE* □ **me and mine** /'mē ən 'mīn/ my relatives.

USAGE 1 Traditional grammar teaches that it is correct to say *between you and* **me** and incorrect to say *between you and* **I**. For details, see **usage** at **BETWEEN**. 2 Which of the following is correct: *you have more than* **me** or *you have more than* **I**? See **usage** at **PERSONAL PRONOUN**.

me·a cul·pa /,māə 'ko͝ol,pə; -,pä/ ▶*n.* an acknowledgment of one's fault or error: [as *exclam.*] *"Well, whose fault was that?" "Mea culpa!" Frank said.* ▷Latin, 'by my fault.'

Mead /mēd/, Margaret (1901–78), U.S. anthropologist and social psychologist. She worked in Samoa and the New Guinea area and wrote a number of studies of primitive cultures, including *Coming of Age in Samoa* (1928). Her writings made anthropology accessible to a wide readership and demonstrated its relevance to Western society.

Mead, Lake /mēd/ the largest U.S. reservoir, located in southeast Nevada, created after 1933 by the Hoover Dam on the Colorado River.

mead[1] /mēd/ ▶*n. chiefly historical* an alcoholic drink of fermented honey and water. ▷Old English *me(o)du*, of Germanic origin; related to Dutch *mee* and German *Met*, from an Indo-European root shared by Sanskrit *madhu* 'sweet drink, honey' and Greek *methu* 'wine.'

mead[2] ▶*n. poetic/literary* a meadow. ▷Old English *mǣd*, of Germanic origin; related to **MOW**[1].

Meade /mēd/, George Gordon (1815–72), U.S. army officer; born in Spain. The son of American parents, he was a graduate of West Point 1835 and commanded the Army of the Potomac 1863–65 during the Civil War. He is most noted for his victory at Gettysburg in 1863.

mead·ow /'medō/ ▶*n.* a piece of grassland, esp. one used for hay. ■ a piece of low ground near a river. ▷Old English *mǣdwe*, oblique case of *mǣd* (see **MEAD**[2]), from the Germanic base of **MOW**[2]. —**mead·ow·y** *adj.*

mead·ow fes·cue ▶*n.* a tall Eurasian fescue that is grown in North America as a pasture and hay grass. • *Festuca pratensis*, family Gramineae.

mead·ow grass ▶*n.* a perennial creeping grass that is widely used for fodder and lawns, and for sowing roadside borders. • Genus *Poa*, family Gramineae: many species, in particular **Kentucky bluegrass** (*P. pratensis*).

mead·ow·land /'medō,land; 'medə-/ ▶*n.* (also **meadowlands**) land used for the cultivation of grass, esp. for hay.

Mead·ow·lands /'medō,landz/ (**the Meadowlands**) an entertainment and sports complex in northeastern New Jersey, in the meadows of the Hackensack River, northwest of New York City.

mead·ow·lark /'medō,lärk; 'medə-/ ▶*n.* a ground-dwelling songbird of the American blackbird family, with a brown streaky back and typically yellow and black underparts. • Genus *Sturnella*, family Icteridae: five species, in particular the yellow-breasted **eastern meadowlark** (*S. magna*) and **western meadowlark** (*S. neglecta*).

eastern meadowlark

mead·ow mouse ▶*n.* another term for **MEADOW VOLE**.

mead·ow mush·room ▶*n.* another term for **CHAMPIGNON**.

mead·ow rue ▶*n.* a widely distributed plant of the buttercup family that typically has divided leaves and heads of small fluffy flowers or delicate drooping flowers. • Genus *Thalictrum*, family Ranunculaceae: many species, including the Eurasian **greater meadow rue** (*T. aquilegiifolium*) and the **early meadow rue** (*T. dioicum*) of North American woods.

mead·ow saf·fron ▶*n.* a poisonous autumn crocus that produces its flowers, usually lilac, in the autumn while leafless. Native to Europe and North Africa, it is a source of the drug colchicine. • *Colchicum autumnale*, family Liliaceae.

mead·ow·sweet /'medō,swēt; 'medə-/ ▶*n.* a tall plant of the rose family (Rosaceae) with clusters of sweet-smelling flowers: • *Spiraeae latifola* of North American meadows and roadsides, with white or pale pink flowers. • *Filipendula ulmaria*, native to Eurasia and naturalized in North America, with creamy white flowers and favoring damp meadows.

mead·ow vole ▶*n.* a burrowing vole that occurs in grassland and open country in Eurasia and North America. • Genus *Microtus*, family Muridae: numerous species, in particular *Microtus pennsylvanicus* of the northern U.S. and Canada.

mea·ger /'mēgər/ (*Brit.* **mea·gre**) ▶*adj.* (of something provided or available) lacking in quantity or quality: *they were forced to supplement their meager earnings.* ■ (of a person or animal) lean; thin. ▷Middle English (in the sense 'lean'): from Old French *maigre*, from Latin *macer*. —**mea·ger·ly** *adv.* —**mea·ger·ness** *n.*

meal[1] /mēl/ ▶*n.* any of the regular occasions in a day when a reasonably large amount of food is eaten, such as breakfast, lunch, or dinner. ■ the food eaten on such an occasion: *a perfectly cooked meal.* ▷Old English *mǣl* (also in the sense 'measure,' surviving in words such as *piecemeal* 'measure taken at one time'), of Germanic origin. The early sense of *meal* involved a notion of fixed time; compare with Dutch *maal* 'meal, (portion of) time' and German *Mal* 'time,' *Mahl* 'meal,' from an Indo-European root meaning 'to measure.'

▶*PHRASE* □ **meals on wheels** meals delivered to elderly people or invalids who are unable either to prepare meals or have meals otherwise provided.

meal[2] ▶*n.* the edible part of any grain or pulse ground to powder, such as cornmeal. ■ any powdery substance made by grinding: *herring meal.* ▷Old English *melu, meolo*, of Germanic origin; related to Dutch *meel* and German *Mehl*, from an Indo-European root shared by Latin *molere* 'to grind.'

meal·ie /'mēlē/ ▶*n.* (usu. **mealies**) *chiefly S. African* corn, esp. sweet corn. ■ corn kernels: [as *adj.*] *mealie pudding.* ■ an ear of corn. ▷early 19th cent.: from Afrikaans *mielie*, from Portuguese *milho* 'corn, millet' from Latin *milium*.

meal tick·et ▶*n.* a person or thing that is used as a source of regular income: *the violin was going to be my meal ticket.*

meal·time /'mēl,tīm/ ▶*n.* the time at which a meal is eaten: *fill up* **at mealtimes** *and get out of the habit of snacking* | *it must be mealtime soon.*

meal·worm /'mēl,wərm/ ▶*n.* the larva of a darkling beetle (genus *Tenebrio*), which is widely fed to captive birds and other insectivorous animals.

meal·y /'mēlē/ ▶*adj.* (**meal·i·er, meal·i·est**) of, like, or containing meal: *a mealy flavor* | *stomp along through deep, mealy sand.* ■ (of a person's complexion, an animal's muzzle, or a bird's plumage) pale. ■ (of part of a plant or fungus) covered with granules resembling meal. —**meal·i·ness** /-lēnis/ *n.*

meal·y·bug /'mēlē,bəg/ (also **meal·y bug**) ▶*n.* a small, sap-sucking scale insect that is coated with a white, powdery wax that resembles meal. It forms large colonies and can be a serious pest, esp. in greenhouses. • Family Pseudococcidae, suborder Homoptera: *Pseudococcus* and other genera.

meal·y-mouthed /'mēlē 'mouᴛʜd; -,mouᴛʜt/ (also **meal·y·mouthed**) ▶*adj.* afraid to speak frankly or straightforwardly: *mealy-mouthed excuses.*

mean[1] /mēn/ ▶*v.* (*past* and *past part.* **meant** /ment/) [*trans.*] **1** intend to convey, indicate, or refer to (a particular thing or notion); signify: *I don't know what you mean* | *he was asked to clarify what his remarks meant* | *I meant you, not Jones.* See note at **INTEND**. ■ (of a word) have (something) as its signification in the same language or its equivalent in another language: *its name means "painted rock" in Cherokee.* ■ genuinely intend to convey or express (something): *when she said that before, she meant it.* ■ (**mean something to**) be of some specified importance to (someone), esp. as a source of benefit or object of affection: *animals have always meant more to him than people.* **2** intend (something) to occur or be the case: *they mean no harm* | [with *infinitive*] *it was meant to be a secret.* ■ (**be meant to do something**) be supposed or intended to do something: *we were meant to go over yesterday.* ■ (often **be meant for**) design or destine for a particular purpose: *the jacket was meant for a much larger person.* ■ (**mean something by**) have as a motive or excuse in explanation: *what do you mean by leaving me out here in the cold?* **3** have as a consequence or result: *the proposals are likely to mean another hundred closures* | [with *clause*] *heavy rain meant that the ground was waterlogged.* ■ necessarily or usually entail or involve: *coal stoves mean a lot of smoke.* ▷Old English *mǣnan*; related to Dutch *meenen* and German *meinen*, from an Indo-European root shared by **MIND**.

▶*PHRASES* □ **I mean** used to clarify or correct a statement or to introduce a justification or explanation: *I mean, it's not as if I owned property.* □ **mean business** be in earnest. □ **mean to say** [usu. in *questions*] really admit or intend to say: *do you mean to say you've uncovered something new?* □ **mean well** have good intentions, but not always the ability to carry them out.

mean[2] ▶*adj.* **1** unwilling to give or share things, esp. money; not generous: *she felt mean not giving a tip* | *they're not* **mean with** *the garlic.* **2** unkind, spiteful, or unfair: *it was very* **mean of** *me* | *she is always* **mean to** *my little brother.* ■ vicious or aggressive in behavior: *the dogs were considered mean.* **3** (esp. of a place) poor in quality and appearance; shabby: *her home was mean and small.* ■ (of a person's mental capacity or understanding) inferior; poor: *it was obvious to even the meanest intelligence.* ■ *dated* of low birth or social class: *it was a hat like that worn by the meanest of people.* **4** *informal* excellent; very skillful or effective: *he's a* *mean cook | she dances a mean Charleston.* ▷Middle English, shortening of Old English *gemǣne*, of Germanic origin, from an Indo-European root shared by Latin *communis* 'common.' The original sense was 'common to two or more persons,' later 'inferior in rank,' leading to sense 3 and a sense 'ignoble, small-minded,' from which senses 1 and 2 (which became common in the 19th cent.) arose. **—mean·ly** *adv.* **—mean·ness** *n.*

▶*PHRASE* □ **no mean ——** denoting something very good of its kind: *it was no mean feat.*

mean[3] ▶*n.* **1** the quotient of the sum of several quantities and their number; an average: *acid output was calculated by taking the mean of all three samples.* See also ARITHMETIC MEAN, GEOMETRIC MEAN. ■ the term or one of the terms midway between the first and last terms of a progression. **2** a condition, quality, or course of action equally removed from two opposite (usually unsatisfactory) extremes: *the mean between two extremes.*

▶*adj.* [*attrib.*] **1** (of a quantity) calculated as a mean; average: *by 1989, the mean age at marriage stood at 24.8 for women and 26.9 for men.* **2** equally far from two extremes: *hope is the mean virtue between despair and presumption.* ▷Middle English: from Old French *meien*, from Latin *medianus* 'middle' (see MEDIAN).

mean a·nom·a·ly ▶*n. Astronomy* the angle in an imaginary circular orbit corresponding to a planet's eccentric anomaly.

me·an·der /mēˈandər/ ▶*v.* [*intrans.*] (of a river or road) follow a winding course: *a river that meandered gently through a meadow* | [as *adj.*] (**meandering**) *a meandering lane.* ■ (of a person) wander at random: *kids meandered in and out.* ■ [*intrans.*] (of a speaker or text) proceed aimlessly or with little purpose: *a stylish offbeat thriller which occasionally meanders.*

▶*n.* (usu. **meanders**) a winding curve or bend of a river or road: *the river flows in sweeping meanders.* ■ [in *sing.*] a circuitous journey, esp. an aimless one: *a leisurely meander around the twisting coastline road.* ■ an ornamental pattern of winding or interlocking lines, e.g., in a mosaic. ▷late 16th cent. (as a noun): from Latin *maeander*, from Greek *Maiandros*, the name of a river (see MENDERES).

mean free path ▶*n. Physics* the average distance traveled by a gas molecule or other particle between collisions with other particles.

mean·ie /ˈmēnē/ (also **mean·y**) ▶*n.* (*pl.* **mean·ies**) *informal* a mean or small-minded person.

mean·ing /ˈmēniNG/ ▶*n.* what is meant by a word, text, concept, or action: *the meaning of the word "supermarket" | it was as if time had lost all meaning.* ■ implied or explicit significance: *he gave me a look full of meaning.* ■ important or worthwhile quality; purpose: *this can lead to new meaning in the life of older people.*

▶*adj.* [*attrib.*] intended to communicate something that is not directly expressed: *she gave Gabriel a meaning look.* ▷late Middle English: verbal noun from MEAN[1]. **—mean·ing·ly** *adv.*

▶*PHRASE* □ **not know the meaning of the word** *informal* behave as if unaware of the concept referred to or implied: *"Humanity?" You don't know the meaning of the word!*

mean·ing·ful /ˈmēniNGfəl/ ▶*adj.* having meaning: *meaningful elements in a language | questions that are* **meaningful to** *students.* ■ having a serious, important, or useful quality or purpose: *making our lives rich and meaningful.* ■ communicating something that is not directly expressed: *meaningful glances and repressed passion.* ■ *Logic* having a recognizable function in a logical language or other sign system. **—mean·ing·ful·ly** *adv.* **—mean·ing·ful·ness** *n.*

mean·ing·less /ˈmēniNGlis/ ▶*adj.* having no meaning or significance: *the paragraph was a jumble of meaningless words.* ■ having no purpose or reason: *the Great War was an outstanding example of meaningless conflict | rules are* **meaningless to** *a child if they do not have a rationale.* **—mean·ing·less·ly** *adv.* **—mean·ing·less·ness** *n.*

means /mēnz/ ▶*plural n.* **1** [usu. treated as *sing.*] (often **means of something** or **means to do something**) an action or system by which a result is brought about; a method: *these pledges are a means to avoid prosecution | resolving disputes by peaceful means.* **2** money; financial resources: *a woman of modest but independent means | prospective students without the means to attend Cornell.* ■ resources; capability: *every country in the world has the means to make ethanol.* ■ wealth: *a man of means.* ▷late Middle English: plural of MEAN[3], the early sense being 'intermediary.'

▶*PHRASES* □ **beyond** (or **within**) **one's means** beyond (or within) one's budget or income: *the government is living beyond its means.* □ **by all means** of course; certainly (granting a permission): *"May I make a suggestion?" "By all means."* □ **by any means** (or **by any manner of means**) (following a negative) in any way; at all: *I'm not poor by any means.* □ **by means of** with the help or agency of: *supplying water to cities by means of aqueducts.* □ **by no means** (or **by no manner of means**) not at all; certainly not: *the outcome is by no means guaranteed.* □ **a means to an end** a thing that is not valued or important in itself but is useful in achieving an aim: *a computer is merely a means to an end.*

mean sea lev·el ▶*n.* the sea level halfway between the mean levels of high and low water.

means of production ▶*n.* (esp. in a political context) the facilities and resources for producing goods: *in this society, the means of production are communally owned.*

mean so·lar day ▶*n. Astronomy* the time between successive passages of the mean sun across the meridian.

mean so·lar time ▶*n. Astronomy* time as calculated by the motion of the mean sun. The time shown by an ordinary clock corresponds to mean solar time. Compare with APPARENT SOLAR TIME.

mean-spir·it·ed ▶*adj.* unkind and ungenerous; unwilling to help others: *the voice of an intolerant scold, narrow and shrill and mean-spirited.*

means test ▶*n.* an official investigation into someone's financial circumstances to determine whether they are eligible for a welfare payment or other public funds.

▶*v.* (**means-test**) [*trans.*] [usu. as *adj.*] (**means-tested**) make (a welfare payment, etc.) conditional on a means test: *means-tested benefits.* ■ subject (someone) to a means test.

mean streets ▶*plural n.* an area of a city where the poor or socially deprived live or work, or an area that is noted for violence and crime: *the mean streets of the South Bronx.*

mean sun ▶*n.* an imaginary sun conceived as moving through the sky throughout the year at a constant speed equal to the mean rate of the real sun, used in calculating mean solar time.

meant /ment/ ▶ past and past participle of MEAN[1].

mean·time /ˈmēnˌtīm/ ▶*adv.* (also **in the meantime**) meanwhile: *in the meantime, I'll make some inquiries of my own | South Korea, meantime, is stepping up imports of feed grains.* ▷Middle English (as a noun): from MEAN[3] + TIME.

mean time ▶*n.* another term for MEAN SOLAR TIME. See also GREENWICH MEAN TIME.

mean·while /ˈmēnˌ(h)wīl/ ▶*adv.* (also **in the meanwhile**) in the intervening period of time: *Julie has meanwhile found herself another dancing partner.* ■ at the same time: *steam for another five minutes; meanwhile, make a white sauce.* ▷late Middle English: from MEAN[3] + WHILE.

Mea·ny /ˈmēnē/, George (1894–1980), U.S. labor leader. He served as president of the AFL-CIO 1955–79.

mean·y /ˈmēnē/ ▶*n.* variant spelling of MEANIE.

meas. ▶*abbr.* ■ measurable or measured or measurement.

mea·sles /ˈmēzəlz/ ▶*plural n.* (often **the measles**) [treated as *sing.*] an infectious viral disease causing fever and a red rash on the skin, typically occurring in childhood. ■ a disease of pigs and other animals caused by the encysted larvae of the human tapeworm. ▷Middle English *maseles*, probably from Middle Dutch *masel* 'pustule' (compare with modern Dutch *mazelen* 'measles'). The spelling change was due to association with Middle English *mesel* 'leprous, leprosy.'

mea·sly /ˈmēzlē/ ▶*adj.* (**mea·sli·er, mea·sli·est**) *informal* contemptibly small or few: *three measly votes.* ▷late 16th cent. (describing a pig or pork infected with measles): from MEASLES + -Y[1]. The current sense dates from the mid 19th cent.

meas·ur·a·ble /ˈmezH(ə)rəbəl/ ▶*adj.* able to be measured: *objectives should be measurable and achievable.* ■ large enough to be measured; noticeable; definite: *a small but measurable improvement in behavior.* ▷Middle English (in the sense 'moderate'): from Old French *mesurable*, from late Latin *mensurabilis*, from Latin *mensurare* 'to measure.' **—meas·ur·a·bil·i·ty** /ˌmezH(ə)rəˈbilətē/ *n.* **—meas·ur·a·bly** *adv.* [as *submodifier*] *the company's performance was measurably better.*

meas·ure /ˈmezHər/ ▶*v.* [*trans.*] **1** ascertain the size, amount, or degree of (something) by using an instrument or device marked in standard units or by comparing it with an object of known size: *the amount of water collected is measured in pints | they will* **measure up** *the room and install the cabinets.* ■ be of (a specified size or degree): *the fabric measures 45 inches wide.* ■ ascertain the size and proportions of (someone) in order to make or provide clothes for them: *he will be measured for his tuxedo next week.* ■ (**measure something out**) take an exact quantity or fixed amount of something: *she helped to measure out the ingredients.* ■ estimate or assess the extent, quality, value, or effect of (something): *it is hard to measure teaching ability.* ■ (**measure someone/something against**) judge someone or something by comparison with (a certain standard): *she did not need to measure herself against some ideal.* ■ [*intrans.*] (**measure up**) reach the required or expected standard; fulfill expectations: *I'm afraid we didn't* **measure up to** *the standards they set.* ■ scrutinize (someone) keenly in order to form an assessment of them: *the two shook hands and silently* **measured** *each other* **up**. **2** consider (one's words or actions) carefully: *I had better measure my words so as not to embarrass anyone.* **3** *archaic* travel over (a certain distance or area): *we must measure twenty miles today.*

▶*n.* **1** a plan or course of action taken to achieve a particular purpose: *cost-cutting measures | children were evacuated as a precautionary measure.* ■ a legislative bill: *the Senate passed the measure by a 48–30 vote.* ■ *archaic* punishment or retribution imposed or inflicted on someone: *her husband had dealt out* **hard measure** *to her.* **2** a standard unit used to express the size, amount, or degree of something: *a furlong is an obsolete measure of length | tables of weights and measures.* ■ a system or scale of such units: *the original dimensions were in imperial measure.* ■ a container of standard capacity used for taking fixed amounts of a substance. ■ a particular amount of something: ***a measure of*** *egg white as a binding agent.* ■ a standard official amount of an alcoholic drink as served in a licensed establishment. ■ a graduated rod or tape used for ascertaining the size of something. ■ *Printing* the width of a full line of type or print, typically expressed in picas. ■ *Mathematics* a quantity contained in another an exact number of times; a divisor. **3** a certain quantity or degree of something: *the states retain a large measure of independence.* ■ an indication or means of assessing the degree, extent, or quality of something: *it was a measure of the team's problems that they were still working after 2 a.m.* **4** the rhythm of a piece of poetry or a piece of music. ■ a particular metrical unit or group: *measures of two or three syllables are more frequent in English prose.* ■ a bar of music or the time of a piece of music. ■ *archaic* a dance, typically one that is grave or stately: *now tread we a measure!* **5** (**measures**) [with *adj.*] a group of rock strata. ▷Middle English (as a noun in the senses 'moderation,' 'instrument for measuring,' 'unit of capacity'): from Old French *mesure*, from Latin *mensura*, from *mens-* 'measured,' from the verb *metiri*.

▶*PHRASES* □ **beyond measure** to a very great extent: *it irritates him beyond measure.* □ **for good measure** in addition to what has already been done, said, or given: *he added a couple of chili peppers for good measure.* □ **take** (or **get** or **have**) **the measure of** assess or have assessed the character, nature, or abilities of (someone or something): *he's got her measure—she won't fool him.* □ **in —— measure** to the degree specified: *his rapid promotion was due in some measure to his friendship with the CEO.*

meas·ured /ˈmezHərd/ ▶*adj.* having a slow, regular rhythm: *he walks with confident, measured steps.* ■ (of speech or writing) carefully considered; deliberate and restrained: *his measured prose.* **—meas·ured·ly** *adv.*

meas·ure·less /ˈmezHərlis/ ▶*adj.* having no bounds or limits; unlimited: *Otto had measureless charm.*

meas·ure·ment /ˈmezHərmənt/ ▶*n.* the action of measuring something: *accurate measurement is essential | a telescope with which precise measurements can be made.* ■ the size, length, or amount of something, as established by measuring: *his inseam measurement.* ■ a unit or system of measuring: *a hand is a measurement used for measuring horses.*

meas·ur·ing cup /ˈmezH(ə)riNG/ ▶*n.* a cup marked in graded amounts, used for measuring ingredients in cooking.

meas·ur·ing tape ▶*n.* another term for TAPE MEASURE.

meas·ur·ing worm ▶*n.* another term for INCHWORM.

meat /mēt/ ▸*n.* **1** the flesh of an animal (esp. a mammal) as food: *rabbit meat* | [as *adj.*] *meat sandwiches* | *assorted meats.* ■ the flesh of a person's body: *this'll put meat on your bones!* ■ the edible part of fruits or nuts. ■ (**the meat of**) the essence or chief part of something: *he did the meat of the climb on the first day.* **2** *archaic* food of any kind. ▷Old English *mete* 'food' or 'article of food' (as in *sweetmeat*), of Germanic origin. **—meat·less** *adj.*

▸*PHRASES* □ **be meat and drink to** *Brit.* **1** be a source of great pleasure to: *meat and drink to me, this life is!* **2** be a routine matter or task for: *he should be meat and drink to the English defense.* □ **meat and potatoes** ordinary but fundamental things; basic ingredients: *the club's meat and potatoes remains blues performers.* □ **one man's meat is another man's poison** *proverb* things liked or enjoyed by one person may be distasteful to another.

meat·ball /ˈmēt,bôl/ ▸*n.* a ball of ground or chopped meat, usually beef, with added seasonings. ■ *informal* a dull, stupid, or foolish person.

meat grind·er ▸*n. figurative* a destructive action or process: *trench warfare was the meat grinder that every soldier dreaded.*

Meath /mē<u>TH</u>; mēTH/ a county in the eastern part of the Republic of Ireland, in the province of Leinster; county town, Navan.

meat·head /ˈmēt,hed/ ▸*n. informal* a stupid person.

meat·hook /ˈmēt,ho͝ok/ ▸*n.* a sharp metal hook of a kind used to hang meat carcasses. ■ (**meathooks**) *informal* a person's hands or arms: *get your big meathooks out of those pies!*

meat loaf (also **meat·loaf**) ▸*n.* ground or chopped meat, usually beef, with added seasonings, molded into the shape of a loaf and baked.

meat mar·ket ▸*n. informal* a meeting place such as a bar or nightclub for people seeking sexual encounters.

meat·space /ˈmēt,spās/ ▸*n. informal* the physical world, as opposed to cyberspace or a virtual environment: *I'd like to know a little more before we talk about a get-together in meatspace.*

me·a·tus /mēˈātəs/ ▸*n.* (*pl.* same or **-tus·es**) *Anatomy* a passage or opening leading to the interior of the body: *the urethral meatus.* ■ (also **ex·ter·nal au·di·to·ry me·a·tus**) the passage leading into the ear. ▷late Middle English: from Latin, 'passage,' from *meare* 'to flow, run.'

meat wag·on ▸*n. informal* an ambulance or hearse.

meat·y /ˈmētē/ ▸*adj.* (**meat·i·er**, **meat·i·est**) consisting of or full of meat: *a meaty flavor.* ■ fleshy; brawny: *the tall, meaty young man.* ■ full of substance or interest; satisfying: *the ballet has stayed the course because of the meaty roles it offers.* **—meat·i·ly** /ˈmētl-ē/ *adv.* **—meat·i·ness** /ˈmētēnis/ *n.*

Mec·ca /ˈmekə/ a city in western Saudi Arabia, an oasis town in the Red Sea region of Hejaz, east of Jiddah, considered by Muslims to be the holiest city of Islam; pop. 618,000. The birthplace in AD 570 of the prophet Muhammad, it was the scene of his early teachings before his emigration to Medina in 622 (**THE HEGIRA**). On Muhammad's return to Mecca in 630 it became the center of the new Muslim faith. Arabic name **MAKKAH**. ■ [as *n.*] (**a Mecca**) a place that attracts people of a particular group or with a particular interest: *Holland is* **a Mecca for** *jazz enthusiasts.* **—Mec·can** *adj.* & *n.*

mech /mek/ ▸*n. informal* a mechanic. ▷mid 20th cent.: abbreviation.

me·chan·ic /məˈkanik/ ▸*n.* **1** a person who repairs and maintains machinery: *a car mechanic.* **2** *archaic* a manual laborer or artisan: *the Mechanics' Institute.* ▷late Middle English (as an adjective in the sense 'relating to manual labor'): via Old French or Latin from Greek *mēkhanikos*, from *mēkhanē* (see **MACHINE**).

me·chan·i·cal /məˈkanikəl/ ▸*adj.* **1** working or produced by machines or machinery: *a mechanical device.* ■ of or relating to machines or machinery: *a mechanical genius* | *mechanical failure.* **2** (of a person or action) not having or showing thought or spontaneity; automatic: *she stopped the mechanical brushing of her hair.* **3** relating to physical forces or motion; physical: *the smoothness was the result of mechanical abrasion.* ■ (of a theory) explaining phenomena in terms only of physical processes. ■ of or relating to mechanics as a science.

▸*n.* **1** (**mechanicals**) the working parts of a machine, esp. a car. **2** (usu. **mechanicals**) *archaic* (esp. with allusion to Shakespeare's *A Midsummer Night's Dream*) a manual worker: *rude mechanicals.* **3** *Printing* a completed assembly of artwork and copy, typically mounted on a sheet of stiff paper. ▷late Middle English (describing an art or occupation concerned with the design or construction of machines): via Latin from Greek *mēkhanikos* (see **MECHANIC**) + **-AL**. **—me·chan·i·cal·ly** *adv.* **—me·chan·i·cal·ness** *n.*

me·chan·i·cal ad·van·tage ▸*n.* the ratio of the force produced by a machine to the force applied to it, used in assessing the performance of a machine.

me·chan·i·cal draw·ing ▸*n.* a scale drawing of a mechanical or architectural structure done with precision instruments. ■ the action or process of making such drawings.

me·chan·i·cal en·gi·neer·ing ▸*n.* the branch of engineering dealing with the design, construction, and use of machines. **—me·chan·i·cal en·gi·neer** *n.*

me·chan·i·cal pen·cil ▸*n.* a pencil with a plastic or metal case and a thin replaceable lead that may be extended as the point is worn away by twisting the outer casing.

mech·a·ni·cian /,mekəˈnisHən/ ▸*n.* a person skilled in the design or construction of machinery.

me·chan·ics /məˈkaniks/ ▸*plural n.* **1** [treated as *sing.*] the branch of applied mathematics dealing with motion and forces producing motion. ■ machinery as a subject; engineering. **2** the machinery or working parts of something: *he looks at the mechanics of a car before the bodywork.* ■ the way in which something is done or operated; the practicalities or details of something: *the mechanics of cello playing.*

mech·an·ism /ˈmekə,nizəm/ ▸*n.* **1** a system of parts working together in a machine; a piece of machinery: *the gunner injured his arm in the turret mechanism.* **2** a natural or established process by which something takes place or is brought about: *we have no mechanism for assessing the success of forwarded inquiries* | *the mechanism by which genes build bodies.* ■ a contrivance in the plot of a literary work: *his* Irma La Douce *is a musical based on the farce mechanism.* **3** *Philosophy* the doctrine that all natural phenomena, including life and thought, allow mechanical explanation by physics and chemistry. ▷mid 17th cent.: from modern Latin *mechanismus*, from Greek *mēkhanē* (see **MACHINE**).

mech·a·nist /ˈmekənist/ ▸*n.* **1** *Philosophy* a person who believes in the doctrine of mechanism. **2** a person skilled in the design or construction of machinery.

mech·a·nis·tic /,mekəˈnistik/ ▸*adj.* of or relating to theories that explain phenomena in purely physical or deterministic terms: *a mechanistic interpretation of nature.* ■ determined by physical processes alone: *he insisted that animals were entirely mechanistic.* **—mech·a·nis·ti·cal·ly** /-(ə)lē/ *adv.*

mech·a·nize /ˈmekə,nīz/ ▸*v.* [*trans.*] (often **be mechanized**) introduce machines or automatic devices into (a process, activity, or place): *the farm was mechanized in the 1950s.* ■ equip (a military force) with modern weapons and vehicles: [as *adj.*] (**mechanized**) *the units comprised tanks and mechanized infantry.* ■ give a mechanical character to: *public virtue cannot be mechanized or formulated.* **—mech·a·ni·za·tion** /,mekənəˈzāsHən/ *n.* **—mech·a·niz·er** *n.*

mechano- ▸*comb. form* mechanical; relating to a mechanical source: *mechanoreceptor.* ▷from Greek *mēkhanē* 'machine.'

mech·a·no·re·cep·tor /,mekə,nōriˈseptər/ ▸*n. Zoology* a sense organ or cell that responds to mechanical stimuli such as touch or sound. **—mech·a·no·re·cep·tive** /-ˈseptiv/ *adj.*

mech·a·no·sen·sa·tion ▸*n.* the process by which mechanical stimuli are translated into neuronal impulses. It is the physiological basis for sense experiences such as touch, hearing, and balance.

mech·a·tron·ics /,mekəˈträniks/ ▸*plural n.* [treated as *sing.*] technology combining electronics and mechanical engineering. ▷1980s: blend of **MECHANICS** and **ELECTRONICS**. **—mech·a·tron·ic** *adj.*

Mech·lin /ˈmeklin/ (also **Mech·lin lace**) ▸*n.* lace made in the Belgian city of Mechelen (formerly known as Mechlin), characterized by patterns outlined in heavier thread.

Meck·len·burg-West Pom·er·a·ni·a /,päməˈrānēə/ a state in northeastern Germany, on the coast of the Baltic Sea; capital, Schwerin.

MEcon ▸*abbr.* Master of Economics.

me·co·ni·um /miˈkōnēəm/ ▸*n. Medicine* the dark green substance forming the first feces of a newborn infant. ▷early 18th cent.: from Latin, literally 'poppy juice,' from Greek *mēkōnion*, from *mēkōn* 'poppy.'

mec·o·nop·sis /,mēkəˈnäpsis; ,mek-/ ▸*n.* (*pl.* same or **-ses** /-sēz/) a Eurasian poppy that is sometimes grown as an ornamental. • Genus *Meconopsis*, family Papaveraceae: several species, in particular the blue-flowered *M. betonicifolia*. ▷modern Latin, from Greek *mēkōn* 'poppy' + *opsis* 'appearance.'

Me·cop·ter·a /miˈkäptərə/ *Entomology* an order of insects that comprises the scorpionflies. ▷modern Latin (plural), from Greek *mēkos* 'length' + *pteron* 'wing.' **—me·cop·ter·an** /-tərən/ *n.* & *adj.*

MEd ▸*abbr.* Master of Education.

Med /med/ ▸*n.* (**the Med**) *informal, chiefly Brit.* the Mediterranean Sea. ▷1940s: abbreviation.

med ▸*adj. informal* medical: *med school.*

med. ▸*abbr.* ■ medical. ■ medium.

mé·dail·lon /,mādīˈyôN/ ▸*n.* (*pl.* same) a small flat round or oval cut of meat or fish: *veal médaillons.* ▷French, literally 'medallion.'

me·da·ka /məˈdäkə/ (also **me·da·ka·fish** /məˈdäkə ,fisH/) ▸*n.* a small Japanese freshwater fish of variable color that is bred for aquariums and also extensively studied in the sciences. • *Oryzias latipes*, family Adrianichthyidae.

med·al /ˈmedl/ ▸*n.* a metal disk with an inscription or design, made to commemorate an event or awarded as a distinction to someone such as a soldier, athlete, or scholar.

▸*v.* (**med·aled**, **med·al·ing**; also *chiefly Brit.* **med·alled**, **med·al·ling**) [*intrans.*] earn a medal, esp. in an athletic contest: *Norwegian athletes medaled in 12 of the 14 events* | [as *adj.*] *the most medaled swimmer in Olympics history.* ▷late 16th cent.: from French *médaille*, from Italian *medaglia*, from medieval Latin *medalia* 'half a denarius,' from Latin *medialis* 'medial.' **—me·dal·lic** /məˈdalik/ *adj.*

med·al·ist /ˈmedl-ist/ (*Brit.* **med·al·list**) ▸*n.* **1** an athlete or other person awarded a medal: *an Olympic gold medalist.* **2** the lowest scorer in a qualifying round of a golf tournament. **3** an engraver or designer of medals.

me·dal·lion /məˈdalyən/ ▸*n.* a piece of jewelry in the shape of a medal, typically worn as a pendant. ■ an oval or circular painting, panel, or design used to decorate a building or textile. ■ another term for **MÉDAILLON**. ▷mid 17th cent.: from French *médaillon*, from Italian *medaglione*, augmentative of *medaglia* (see **MEDAL**).

Med·al of Hon·or (also **Congressional Medal of Honor**) ▸*n.* the highest U.S. military decoration, awarded by Congress to a member of the armed forces for gallantry and bravery in combat at the risk of life above and beyond the call of duty.

med·al play ▸*n. Golf* another term for **STROKE PLAY**.

Me·dan /māˈdän/ a city in Indonesia, in northeastern Sumatra near the Strait of Malacca; pop. 1,730,000. Established as a trading post by the Dutch in 1682, it became a leading commercial center.

Med·a·war /ˈmedəwər/, Sir Peter (Brian) (1915–87), English immunologist. He studied the biology of tissue transplantation and showed that the rejection of grafts was the result of an immune mechanism. Nobel Prize for Physiology or Medicine (1960).

med·dle /ˈmedl/ ▸*v.* [*intrans.*] interfere in or busy oneself unduly with something that is not one's concern: *I don't want him* ***meddling in*** *our affairs* | [as *n.*] (**meddling**) *bureaucratic meddling.* ■ (**meddle with**) touch or handle (something) without permission: *you have no right to come in here and meddle with my things.* ▷Middle English (in the sense 'mingle, mix'): from Old French *medler*, variant of *mesler*, based on Latin *miscere* 'to mix.' **—med·dler** /ˈmedlər; ˈmedl-ər/ *n.*

med·dle·some /ˈmedlsəm/ ▸*adj.* fond of meddling; interfering: *a gaggle of meddlesome politicians.* See note at **IMPERTINENT**. **—med·dle·some·ly** *adv.* **—med·dle·some·ness** *n.*

Mede /mēd/ ▸*n.* a member of an Iranian people who inhabited ancient Media, establishing an extensive empire during the 7th century BC, which was conquered by Cyrus the Great of Persia in 550 BC. ▷from Latin *Medi*, Greek *Mēdoi*, plural forms.

Me·de·a /miˈdēə/ *Greek Mythology* a sorceress, daughter of Aeetes king of Colchis, who helped Jason to obtain the Golden Fleece and married him. When Jason deserted her for Creusa, the daughter of King Creon of Corinth, she took revenge by killing Creon, Creusa, and her own children, and fled to Athens.

Me·del·lín /ˈmedə,yēn; ,medəˈyēn/ a city in eastern Colombia, the second largest city in the country;

pop. 1,581,000. A major center of coffee production, it has in recent years gained a reputation as the hub of the Colombian drug trade.

med·e·vac /ˈmedi,vak/ (also **med·i·vac**) ▸*n.* the evacuation of military or other casualties to the hospital in a helicopter or airplane.

▸*v.* (**-vacked**, **-vack·ing**) [*trans.*] transport (someone) to the hospital in this way: *the helicopter pilot who medevacked me the day I got shot.* ▷1960s: blend of MEDICAL and EVACUATION.

med·fly /ˈmed,flī/ ▸*n.* (*pl.* **-flies**) another term for MEDITERRANEAN FRUIT FLY.

Med·ford **1** a city in northeastern Massachusetts, northwest of Boston; pop. 57,407. **2** a commercial city in southwestern Oregon, in an agricultural area near the California border; pop. 63,154.

Med. Gr. ▸*abbr.* Medieval Greek.

Me·di·a /ˈmēdēə/ an ancient region of Asia, southwest of the Caspian Sea, corresponding approximately to present-day Azerbaijan, northwestern Iran, and northeastern Iraq. —**Me·di·an** *adj.*

me·di·a[1] /ˈmēdēə/ ▸*n.* **1** plural form of MEDIUM. **2** (usu. **the media**) [treated as *sing.* or *pl.*] the main means of mass communication (esp. television, radio, newspapers, and the Internet) regarded collectively: [as *adj.*] *the campaign won media attention.*

USAGE The word **media** comes from the Latin plural of **medium**. The traditional view is that it should therefore be treated as a plural noun in all its senses in English and be used with a plural rather than a singular verb: *the media **have** not followed the reports* (rather than ***has*** *not followed*). In practice, in the sense 'television, radio, the press, and the Internet, collectively,' **media** behaves as a collective noun (like *staff* or *clergy*, for example), which means that it is now acceptable in standard English for it to take either a singular or a plural verb.

me·di·a[2] ▸*n.* (*pl.* **-di·ae** /-dē,ē; -dē,ī/) **1** *Anatomy* an intermediate layer, esp. in the wall of a blood vessel. **2** *Phonetics* a voiced unaspirated stop; (in Greek) a voiced stop. [mid 19th cent.: from Latin, feminine of *medius* 'middle.'] ▷late 19th cent.: shortening of modern Latin *tunica* (or *membrana*) *media* 'middle sheath (or layer).'

me·di·a card ▸*n. Computing* a small cardlike information storage device that holds data in flash memory.

me·di·a·cy /ˈmēdēəsē/ ▸*n.* the quality of being mediate.

me·di·ae·val ▸*adj.* variant spelling of MEDIEVAL.

me·di·a e·vent ▸*n.* an event intended primarily to attract publicity: *a staged media event.*

me·di·a·gen·ic /,mēdēəˈjenik/ ▸*adj.* tending to convey a favorable impression when reported by the media, esp. by television: *the mediagenic politician.*

me·di·al /ˈmēdēəl/ ▸*adj. technical* situated in the middle, in particular: ■ *Anatomy & Zoology* situated near the median plane of the body or the midline of an organ. The opposite of LATERAL. ■ *Phonetics* (of a speech sound) in the middle of a word. ■ *Phonetics* (esp. of a vowel) pronounced in the middle of the mouth; central. ▷late 16th cent. (in the sense 'relating to the mean or average'): from late Latin *medialis*, from Latin *medius* 'middle.' —**me·di·al·ly** *adv.*

me·di·a mail ▸*n.* a class of mail for sending books, recordings, and computer media. It is cheaper and usually slower than first-class mail.

me·di·an /ˈmēdēən/ ▸*adj.* [*attrib.*] **1** denoting or relating to a value or quantity lying at the midpoint of a frequency distribution of observed values or quantities, such that there is an equal probability of falling above or below it: *the median duration of this treatment was four months.* ■ denoting the middle term of a series arranged in order of magnitude, or (if there is no middle term) the average of the middle two terms. For example, the median number of the series 55, 62, 76, 85, 93 is 76. **2** *technical, chiefly Anatomy* situated in the middle, esp. of the body: *the median part of the sternum.*

▸*n.* **1** the median value of a range of values: *acreages ranged from one to fifty-two with a median of twenty-four.* **2** (also **median strip**) the strip of land between the lanes of opposing traffic on a divided highway. **3** *Geometry* a straight line drawn from any vertex of a triangle to the middle of the opposite side. ▷late Middle English (denoting a median vein or nerve): from medieval Latin *medianus*, from *medius* 'middle, middle of.' —**me·di·an·ly** *adv.*

me·di·ant /ˈmēdēənt/ ▸*n. Music* the third note of the diatonic scale of any key. ▷mid 18th cent.: from French *médiante*, from Italian *mediante* 'coming between,' present participle of obsolete *mediare* 'come between,' from late Latin *mediare* 'be in the middle of.'

me·di·a·scape /ˈmēdēə,skāp/ ▸*n.* **1** communications media as a whole: *the rapidly changing mediascape in Belgium.* **2** the world as presented through, or perceived by, the mass media: *the vast, ubiquitous mediascape we inhabit today.*

me·di·as·ti·num /,mēdēəˈstīnəm/ ▸*n.* (*pl.* **-as·ti·na** /-əˈstīnə/) *Anatomy* a membranous partition between two body cavities or two parts of an organ, esp. that between the lungs. ▷late Middle English: neuter of medieval Latin *mediastinus* 'medial,' based on Latin *medius* 'middle.' —**me·di·as·ti·nal** /-ˈstīnl/ *adj.*

me·di·a stud·ies ▸*plural n.* [usu. treated as *sing.*] the study of the mass media, esp. as an academic subject.

me·di·ate ▸*v.* /ˈmēdē,āt/ **1** [*intrans.*] intervene between people in a dispute in order to bring about an agreement or reconciliation: *Wilson attempted to **mediate between** the powers to end the war.* See note at INSERT. ■ [*trans.*] intervene in (a dispute) to bring about an agreement. ■ [*trans.*] bring about (an agreement or solution) by intervening in a dispute: *efforts to mediate a peaceful resolution of the conflict.* **2** [*trans.*] *technical* bring about (a result such as a physiological effect): *the right hemisphere plays an important role in mediating tactile perception of direction.* ■ be a means of conveying: *this important ministry of mediating the power of the word.* ■ form a connecting link between: *structures that mediate gender divisions.*

▸*adj.* /ˈmēdēət/ connected indirectly through another person or thing; involving an intermediate agency: *public law institutions are a type of mediate state administration.* ▷late Middle English (as an adjective in the sense 'interposed'): from late Latin *mediatus* 'placed in the middle,' past participle of the verb *mediare*, from Latin *medius* 'middle.' —**me·di·ate·ly** /ˈmēdēətlē/ *adv.* —**me·di·a·tion** /,mēdēˈāsHən/ *n.* —**me·di·a·tor** /ˈmēdē,ātər/ *n.* —**me·di·a·to·ry** /ˈmēdēə,tôrē/ *adj.*

med·ic[1] /ˈmedik/ ▸*n. informal* a medical practitioner or student. ■ *Military* a medical corpsman who dispenses first aid at combat sites. ▷mid 17th cent.: from Latin *medicus* 'physician,' from *mederi* 'heal.'

med·ic[2] ▸*n.* variant spelling of MEDICK.

med·i·ca·ble /ˈmedikəbəl/ ▸*adj. rare* able to be treated or cured medically. ▷late 16th cent. (in the sense 'possessing medicinal properties'): from Latin *medicabilis*, from *medicari* 'administer remedies to' (see MEDICATE).

Med·i·caid /ˈmedi,kād/ a federal system of health insurance for those requiring financial assistance. ▷1960s: from MEDICAL + AID.

med·i·cal /ˈmedikəl/ ▸*adj.* of or relating to the science of medicine, or to the treatment of illness and injuries: *a medical center | the medical profession.* ■ of or relating to conditions requiring medical but not surgical treatment: *he was transferred for further treatment to a medical ward.* ▷mid 17th cent.: via French from medieval Latin *medicalis*, from Latin *medicus* 'physician.' —**med·i·cal·ly** *adv.*

med·i·cal·ize /ˈmedikə,līz/ ▸*v.* [*trans.*] view (something) in medical terms; treat as a medical problem, esp. unwarrantedly: *doctors tend to medicalize manifestations of distress, prescribing drugs such as sleeping tablets.* ▷1970s: from MEDICAL + -IZE. —**med·i·cal·i·za·tion** /,medikələˈzāsHən/ *n.*

med·i·cal ju·ris·pru·dence ▸*n.* the branch of law relating to medicine. ■ forensic medicine.

med·i·cal of·fi·cer ▸*n.* a doctor serving in the armed forces, in a prison, or in a public health service.

med·i·cal prac·ti·tion·er ▸*n.* a physician or surgeon.

me·dic·a·ment /məˈdikəmənt; ˈmedikə,ment/ ▸*n.* a substance used for medical treatment. ▷late Middle English: via French from Latin *medicamentum*, from *medicari* (see MEDICATE).

Med·i·care /ˈmedi,ke(ə)r/ a federal system of health insurance for people over 65 years of age and for certain younger people with disabilities. ▷1960s: from MEDICAL + CARE.

med·i·cate /ˈmedi,kāt/ ▸*v.* [*trans.*] (often **be medicated**) administer medicine or a drug to (someone): *both infants were heavily medicated to alleviate their seizures.* ■ treat (a condition) using medicine or a drug. ■ add a medicinal substance to (a dressing or product): [as *adj.*] (**medicated**) *medicated shampoo.* ▷early 17th cent.: from Latin *medicat-* 'treated,' from the verb *medicari* 'administer remedies to,' from *medicus* (see MEDIC[1]). —**med·i·ca·tive** /-,kātiv/ *adj.*

med·i·ca·tion /,medəˈkāsHən/ ▸*n.* a substance used for medical treatment, esp. a medicine or drug: *he'd been taking medication for depression | certain medications can cause dizziness.* ■ treatment using drugs: *chronic gastrointestinal symptoms which may require prolonged medication.*

Med·i·ce·an /,mediˈcHēən/ ▸*adj.* of or relating to the Medici family.

Med·i·ci /ˈmedicHē/ (also **de' Med·i·ci** /də/) a powerful Italian family of bankers and merchants whose members effectively ruled Florence for much of the 15th century and from 1569 were grand dukes of Tuscany. **Cosimo** and **Lorenzo de' Medici** were notable rulers and patrons of the arts in Florence; the family also provided four popes (including **Leo X**) and two queens of France (**Catherine de' Medici** and **Marie de Médicis**).

me·dic·i·nal /məˈdisənl/ ▸*adj.* (of a substance or plant) having healing properties: *medicinal herbs | humorous a large medicinal Scotch.* ■ relating to or involving medicines or drugs.

▸*n.* a medicinal substance. ▷late Middle English: from Latin *medicinalis*, from *medicina* (see MEDICINE). —**me·dic·i·nal·ly** *adv.*

me·dic·i·nal leech ▸*n.* a large European leech, introduced to North America, used in medicine for bloodletting. After biting, it secretes an anticoagulant to ensure the flow of blood. • *Hirudo medicinalis*, family Hirudidae.

med·i·cine /ˈmedisən/ ▸*n.* **1** the science or practice of the diagnosis, treatment, and prevention of disease (in technical use often taken to exclude surgery). **2** a compound or preparation used for the treatment or prevention of disease, esp. a drug or drugs taken by mouth: *give her some medicine | your doctor will be able to prescribe medicines.* ■ such substances collectively: *an aid convoy loaded with food and medicine.* **3** (among North American Indians and some other peoples) a spell, charm, or fetish believed to have healing, protective, or other power: *Fleur was murdering him by use of **bad medicine**.* ▷Middle English: via Old French from Latin *medicina*, from *medicus* 'physician.'

▸***PHRASES*** □ **give someone a dose** (or **taste**) **of their own medicine** give someone the same bad treatment that they have given to others: *tired of his humiliation of me, I decided to give him a taste of his own medicine.* □ **take one's medicine** submit to something disagreeable such as punishment.

med·i·cine ball ▸*n.* a large, heavy solid ball thrown and caught for exercise.

Med·i·cine Bow Moun·tains /ˈmedisin bō/ a range in the Rocky Mountains that extends the Front Range in Colorado into southern Wyoming.

med·i·cine cab·i·net (also **medicine chest**) ▸*n.* a box containing medicines and first-aid items, esp. one attached to a bathroom wall.

Med·i·cine Hat a commercial and industrial city in southeastern Alberta in Canada, on the South Saskatchewan River; pop. 43,625.

med·i·cine man ▸*n.* (among North American Indians and some other peoples) a person believed to have magical powers of healing and of seeing into the future; a shaman.

med·i·cine wheel ▸*n.* a stone circle built by North American Indians, believed to have religious, astronomical, territorial, or calendrical significance.

Mé·di·cis, Marie de, see MARIE DE MÉDICIS.

med·ick /ˈmedik/ ▸*n.* a plant of the pea family related to alfalfa, some kinds of which are grown for fodder or green manure and some kinds of which are troublesome weeds. • Genus *Medicago*, family Leguminosae: several species, including the prostrate **black medick** (*M. lupulina*). ▷late Middle English: from Latin *medica*, from Greek *Mēdikē* (*poa*) 'Median (grass).'

med·i·co /ˈmedi,kō/ ▸*n.* (*pl.* **-cos**) *informal* a medical practitioner or student. ▷late 17th cent.: via Italian from Latin *medicus* 'physician.'

medico- ▸*comb. form* relating to the field of medicine: *medico-social.* ▷from Latin *medicus* 'physician.'

me·di·e·val /,med(ē)ˈēvəl; ,mēd-; ,mid-/ (also **me·di·ae·val**) ▸*adj.* of or relating to the Middle Ages: *a medieval castle.* ■ *informal, derogatory* very old-fashioned or primitive: *the guerrillas' medieval behavior has become an embarrassment to their supporters.* ▷early 19th cent.: from modern Latin *medium aevum* 'middle age' + -AL. —**me·di·e·val·ism** /-,izəm/ *n.* —**me·di·e·val·ist** /-ist/ *n.* —**me·di·e·val·ize** /-,īz/ *v.* —**me·di·e·val·ly** *adv.*

me·di·e·val Lat·in ▸*n.* Latin of about AD 600–1500.

M

Me·di·na /mə'dīnə/ a city in western Saudi Arabia, around an oasis about 200 miles (320 km) north of Mecca; pop. 500,000. It is Muhammad's burial place and the site of the first Islamic mosque, which is constructed around his tomb. It is considered by Muslims to be the second most holy city after Mecca, and a visit to the prophet's tomb at Medina often forms a sequel to the formal pilgrimage to Mecca. Arabic name **AL MADINAH**.

me·di·na /mə'dēnə/ ▸*n.* the old Arab or non-European quarter of a North African town. ▷Arabic, literally 'town.'

me·di·oc·ra·cy /ˌmēdē'äkrəsē/ ▸*n.* (*pl.* **-cies**) a dominant class consisting of mediocre people, or a system in which mediocrity is rewarded.

me·di·o·cre /ˌmēdē'ōkər/ ▸*adj.* of only moderate quality; not very good: *a mediocre actor.* ▷late 16th cent.: from French *médiocre*, from Latin *mediocris* 'of middle height or degree,' literally 'somewhat rugged or mountainous,' from *medius* 'middle' + *ocris* 'rugged mountain.' **—me·di·o·cre·ly** *adv.*

me·di·oc·ri·ty /ˌmēdē'äkrətē/ ▸*n.* (*pl.* **-ties**) the quality or state of being mediocre: *heroes rising above the mediocrity that surrounds them.* ■ a person of mediocre ability.

med·i·tate /'medəˌtāt/ ▸*v.* [*intrans.*] think deeply or focus one's mind for a period of time, in silence or with the aid of chanting, for religious or spiritual purposes or as a method of relaxation. ■ (**meditate on/upon**) think deeply or carefully about (something): *he went off to meditate on the new idea.* ■ [*trans.*] plan mentally; consider: *they had suffered severely, and they began to meditate retreat.* ▷mid 16th cent.: from Latin *meditat-* 'contemplated,' from the verb *meditari*, from a base meaning 'measure'; related to **METE**[1]. **—med·i·ta·tor** /-ˌtātər/ *n.*

med·i·ta·tion /ˌmedə'tāsHən/ ▸*n.* the action or practice of meditating: *a life of meditation.* ■ a written or spoken discourse expressing considered thoughts on a subject: *his later letters are intense* ***meditations on*** *man's exploitation of his fellows.* ▷Middle English: from Old French, from Latin *meditatio(n-)*, from *meditari* (see **MEDITATE**).

med·i·ta·tive /'medəˌtātiv/ ▸*adj.* of, involving, or absorbed in meditation or considered thought: *meditative techniques.* ▷early 17th cent.: from **MEDITATE** + **-IVE**, reinforced by French *méditatif, -ive*. **—med·i·ta·tive·ly** *adv.* **—med·i·ta·tive·ness** *n.*

Med·i·ter·ra·ne·an /ˌmedətə'rānēən/ ▸*adj.* of or characteristic of the Mediterranean Sea, the countries bordering it, or their inhabitants: *a leisurely Mediterranean cruise | our temperatures are Mediterranean.* ■ (of a person's complexion) relatively dark, as is common in some Mediterranean countries.
▸*n.* **1** the Mediterranean Sea or the countries bordering it. **2** a native of a country bordering on the Mediterranean. ▷mid 16th cent.: from Latin *mediterraneus* 'inland' (from *medius* 'middle' + *terra* 'land') + **-AN**.

Med·i·ter·ra·ne·an cli·mate ▸*n.* a climate distinguished by warm, wet winters under prevailing westerly winds and calm, hot, dry summers, as is characteristic of the Mediterranean region and parts of California, Chile, South Africa, and southwestern Australia.

Med·i·ter·ra·ne·an fruit fly ▸*n.* a fruit fly whose larvae can be a serious pest of citrus and other fruits. Native to the Mediterranean region, it has spread to other regions including the U.S. Also called **MEDFLY**. • *Ceratitis capitata*, family Tephritidae.

Med·i·ter·ra·ne·an Sea an almost landlocked sea between southern Europe, the northern coast of Africa, and southwestern Asia. It is connected to the Atlantic Ocean by the Strait of Gibraltar, with the Red Sea by the Suez Canal and with the Black Sea by the Dardanelles, the Sea of Marmara, and the Bosporus.

me·di·um /'mēdēəm/ ▸*n.* (*pl.* **-di·a** /-dēə/ or **-di·ums**) **1** an agency or means of doing something: *using the latest technology as* ***a medium for*** *job creation | their primitive valuables acted as* ***a medium of*** *exchange.* ■ a means by which something is communicated or expressed: *here the Welsh language is the medium of instruction.* **2** the intervening substance through which impressions are conveyed to the senses or a force acts on objects at a distance: *radio communication needs no physical medium between the two stations | the medium between the cylinders is a vacuum.* ■ the substance in which an organism lives or is cultured: *grow bacteria in a nutrient-rich medium.* **3** a particular form of storage for digitized information, such as magnetic tape or discs: *moving or copying backed-up data through a hierarchy of different mediums.* **4** a liquid (e.g., oil or water) with which pigments are mixed to make paint. ■ the material or form used by an artist, composer, or writer: *oil paint is the most popular medium for glazing.* **5** (*pl.* **-di·ums**) a person claiming to be in contact with the spirits of the dead and to communicate between the dead and the living. **6** the middle quality or state between two extremes; a reasonable balance: *you have to* ***strike a happy medium between*** *looking like royalty and looking like a housewife.*
▸*adj.* about halfway between two extremes of size or another quality; average: *John is six feet tall, of medium build | medium-length hair.* ■ (of cooked meat) halfway between rare and well-done: *I wanted my burger to be medium.* ▷late 16th cent. (originally denoting something intermediate in nature or degree): from Latin, literally 'middle,' neuter of *medius*. **—me·di·um·ism** /-ˌmizəm/ *n.* (in sense 5). **—me·di·um·is·tic** /ˌmēdēə'mistik/ *adj.* (in sense 5). **—me·di·um·ship** /-ˌsHip/ *n.* (in sense 5).

me·di·um fre·quen·cy ▸*n.* a radio frequency between 300 kilohertz and 3 megahertz.

me·di·um-range ▸*adj.* (of an aircraft or missile) able to travel or operate over a medium distance: *medium-range nuclear missiles.*

med·i·vac ▸*n.* & *v.* variant spelling of **MEDEVAC**.

med·lar /'medlər/ ▸*n.* a small, bushy tree of the rose family that bears small, brown, applelike fruits. • *Mespilus germanica*, family Rosaceae. ■ the fruit of this tree, which is edible only after it has begun to decay. ▷late Middle English: from Old French *medler*, from *medle* 'medlar fruit,' from Latin *mespila*, from Greek *mespilē, mespilon*.

Med. Lat. ▸*abbr.* Medieval Latin.

med·ley /'medlē/ ▸*n.* (*pl.* **-leys**) a varied mixture of people or things; a miscellany: *an interesting medley of flavors.* ■ a collection of songs or other musical items performed as a continuous piece: *a medley of Beatles songs.* ■ a swimming race in which contestants swim sections in different strokes, either individually or in relay teams.
▸*adj. archaic* mixed; motley: *a medley range of vague and variable impressions.*
▸*v.* (*past* and *past part.* **-leyed** or **-lied**) [*trans.*] *archaic* make a medley of; intermix. ▷Middle English (denoting hand-to-hand combat, also cloth made of variegated wool): from Old French *medlee*, variant of *meslee* 'melee,' based on medieval Latin *misculare* 'to mix'; compare with **MEDDLE**.

Mé·doc /mā'dôk; -'däk/ ▸*n.* (*pl.* same) a red wine produced in Médoc, the area along the left bank of the Gironde estuary in southwestern France.

me·dre·se /mə'dresə/ ▸*n.* variant spelling of **MADRASA**.

me·dul·la /mə'dələ/ ▸*n. Anatomy* the inner region of an organ or tissue, esp. when it is distinguishable from the outer region or cortex (as in a kidney, an adrenal gland, or hair). ■ short for **MEDULLA OBLONGATA**. ■ *Botany* the soft internal tissue or pith of a plant. ▷late Middle English (in the sense 'bone marrow'): from Latin, 'pith or marrow.' **—med·ul·lar·y** /mə'dələrē; 'mejələrē/ *adj.*

me·dul·la ob·long·a·ta / äˌblônG'gätə/ ▸*n.* the continuation of the spinal cord within the skull, forming the lowest part of the brainstem and containing control centers for the heart and lungs. ▷late 17th cent.: modern Latin, literally 'elongated medulla.'

Me·du·sa /mə'd(y)ōōsə; -zə/ *Greek Mythology* the only mortal Gorgon, whom Perseus killed by cutting off her head.

me·du·sa /mə'dōōsə; -zə/ ▸*n.* (*pl.* **-sae** /-sē; -sī; -zē; -zī/ or **-sas**) *Zoology* a free-swimming sexual form of a coelenterate such as a jellyfish, typically having an umbrella-shaped body with stinging tentacles around the edge. In some species, medusae are a phase in the life cycle that alternates with a polypoid phase. Compare with **POLYP**. ■ a jellyfish. ▷mid 18th cent.: named by association with **MEDUSA**.

me·du·soid /mə'dōōˌsoid; -ˌzoid/ *Zoology* ▸*adj.* of, relating to, or resembling a medusa or jellyfish. ■ of, relating to, or denoting the medusa phase in the life cycle of a coelenterate. Compare with **POLYPOID** (sense 1).
▸*n.* a medusa or jellyfish. ■ a medusoid reproductive bud.

meed /mēd/ ▸*n. archaic* a deserved share or reward: *he must extract from her some meed of approbation.* ▷Old English *mēd*, of Germanic origin; from an Indo-European root shared by Greek *misthos* 'reward.'

meek /mēk/ ▸*adj.* quiet, gentle, and easily imposed on; submissive: *I used to call her Miss Mouse because she was so meek and mild | the meek compliance of our politicians.* ▷Middle English *me(o)c* (also in the sense 'courteous or indulgent'), from Old Norse *mjúkr* 'soft, gentle.' **—meek·ly** *adv.* **—meek·ness** *n.*

meer·kat /'mi(ə)rˌkat/ ▸*n.* a small southern African mongoose, esp. the suricate. • *Suricata* and other genera, family Herpestidae: three species. ▷early 18th cent.: from South African Dutch, from Dutch, 'long-tailed monkey,' apparently from *meer* 'sea' + *kat* 'cat,' but perhaps originally an alteration of an South Asian word; compare with Hindi *markaṭ* 'ape.'

meer·schaum /'mi(ə)rˌsHôm; -sHəm/ ▸*n.* a soft white claylike material consisting of hydrated magnesium silicate, found chiefly in Turkey. ■ (also **meerschaum pipe**) a tobacco pipe with the bowl made from this. ▷late 18th cent.: from German, literally 'sea-foam,' from *Meer* 'sea' + *Schaum* 'foam,' translation of Persian *kef-i-daryā* (alluding to the frothy appearance of the silicate).

Mee·rut /'mi(ə)rət/ a city in northern India, in Uttar Pradesh, northeast of Delhi; pop. 850,000. It was the scene in May 1857 of the first uprising against the British in the Indian Mutiny.

meet[1] /mēt/ ▸*v.* (*past* and *past part.* **met** /met/) [*trans.*] **1** come into the presence or company of (someone) by chance or arrangement: *a week later I met him in the street | [intrans.] we met for lunch | they arranged to* ***meet up*** *that afternoon.* ■ make the acquaintance of (someone) for the first time: *she took Paul to meet her parents [intrans.] we met at an office party.* ■ [*intrans.*] (of a group of people) assemble for a particular purpose: *the committee meets once a week.* ■ [*intrans.*] (**meet with**) have a meeting with (someone): *he met with the president on September 16.* ■ go to a place and wait there for (a person or their means of transport) to arrive: *I offered to meet their train.* ■ play or oppose in a contest: *in the final match, the U.S. will meet Brazil | [intrans.] the Twins and Mariners will not meet again until September.* ■ touch; join: *Harry's lips met hers | [intrans.] the curtains failed to meet in the middle | figurative our eyes met across the table.* ■ encounter or be faced with (a particular fate, situation, attitude, or reaction): *he met his death in 1946 | [intrans.] we* ***met with*** *a slight setback.* ■ (**meet something with**) have (a particular reaction) to: *the announcement was met with widespread protests.* ■ [*intrans.*] (**meet with**) receive (a particular reaction): *I'm sorry if it doesn't meet with your approval.* **2** fulfill or satisfy (a need, requirement, or condition): *this policy is doing nothing to meet the needs of women.* ■ deal with or respond to (a problem or challenge) satisfactorily: *they failed to meet the noon deadline.* ■ pay (a financial claim or obligation): *all your household expenses will still have to be met.*
▸*n.* an organized event at which a number of races or other sporting contests are held: *a swim meet.* ▷Old English *mētan* 'come upon, come across,' of Germanic origin; related to Dutch *moeten*, 'meet,'also to **MOOT**.
▸*PHRASES* □ **meet someone's eye** (or **eyes**) be visible: *the sight that met his eyes was truly amazing.* □ **meet someone's eye** (or **eyes** or **gaze**) look directly at someone: *for a moment, he refused to meet her eyes.* □ **meet someone halfway** make a compromise with someone: *I am prepared to meet him halfway by paying an additional $25,000.* □ **meet one's Maker** see **MAKER**. □ **meet one's match** see **MATCH**[1]. □ **there's more to someone/something than meets the eye** a person or situation is more complex or interesting than they appear.

meet[2] ▸*adj. archaic* suitable; fit; proper: *it is a theater* ***meet for*** *great events.* ▷Middle English (in the sense 'made to fit'): shortening of Old English *gemǣte*, of Germanic origin; related to **METE**[1]. **—meet·ly** *adv.* **—meet·ness** *n.*

meet·ing /'mētiNG/ ▸*n.* **1** an assembly of people, esp. the members of a society or committee, for discussion or entertainment: *the early-dismissal policy will be discussed at our next meeting.* ■ a gathering of people, esp. Quakers, for worship. **2** a coming together of two or more people, by chance or arrangement: *he intrigued her on their first meeting.*
▸*PHRASE* □ **a meeting of (the) minds** an understanding or agreement between people.

meet·ing·house /'mētiNGˌhous/ (also **meet·ing house**) ▸*n.* a Quaker place of worship. ■ *historical* a Protestant place of worship.

mef·lo·quine /'mefləˌkwēn; -ˌkwīn/ ▸*n. Medicine* an antimalarial drug consisting of a fluorinated

Pronunciation Key ə *ago*; ər *over*; 'ə or ˌə *up*; 'ər or ˌər *fur*; a *hat*; ā *rate*; ä *car*; CH *chew*; e *let*; ē *see*; e(ə)r *air*; i *fit*; ī *by*; i(ə)r *ear*; NG *sing*; ō *go*; ô *for*; oi *boy*; ŏŏ *good*; ōō *goo*; ou *out*; SH *she*; TH *thin*; TH *then*; (h)w *why*; ZH *vision*

M

derivative of quinoline. ▷1970s: from *me(thyl)* + *fl(uor)o* + *quin(olin)e*.

meg /meg/ ▸*n.* (*pl.* same or **megs**) short for MEGABYTE.

meg·a /'megə/ *informal* ▸*adj.* very large; huge: *a mega city.* ■ of great significance or importance: *it was one of the mega news stories of the century.*
▸*adv.* [as *submodifier*] extremely: *they are mega rich.* ▷1980s: independent usage of MEGA-.

mega- ▸*comb. form* **1** very large in size, extent, capacity, or amount: *megalith.* **2** (in units of measurement) denoting a factor of one million (10^6): *megahertz* | *megadeath.* **3** *Computing* denoting a factor of 2^{20}. ▷from Greek *megas* 'great.'

meg·a·bit /'megə,bit/ ▸*n. Computing* a unit of data size or (when expressed per second) network speed, equal to one million or (strictly) 1,048,576 bits.

meg·a·buck /'megə,bək/ ▸*n.* (usu. **megabucks**) *informal* a million dollars. ■ a huge sum of money: *he has been earning megabucks for decades* | [as *adj.*] *megabuck salaries.*

meg·a·byte /'megə,bīt/ (abbr.: **Mb** or **MB**) ▸*n. Computing* a unit of information equal to 2^{20} bytes or, loosely, one million bytes.

Meg·a·chi·rop·ter·a /,megə,kī'räptərə/ *Zoology* a division of bats that comprises the fruit bats and flying foxes. • Suborder Megachiroptera and family Pteropodidae, order Chiroptera. ▷modern Latin (plural), from MEGA- 'large' + CHIROPTERA. **—meg·a·chi·rop·ter·an** /-tərən/ *n.* & *adj.*

meg·a·death /'megə,deTH/ ▸*n.* a unit used in quantifying the casualties of nuclear war, equal to the deaths of one million people.

meg·a·dose /'megə,dōs/ ▸*n.* a dose many times larger than the usual, esp. of a vitamin or drug.

Me·gae·ra /mə'ji(ə)rə/ *Greek Mythology* one of the Furies.

meg·a·fau·na /'megə,fônə/ ▸*n. Zoology* the large mammals of a particular region, habitat, or geological period. ■ *Ecology* animals that are large enough to be seen with the naked eye. **—meg·a·fau·nal** /,megə'fônl/ *adj.*

meg·a·flop[1] /'megə,fläp/ ▸*n. Computing* a unit of computing speed equal to one million floating-point operations per second. ▷1970s: back-formation from *megaflops* (see MEGA-, -FLOP).

meg·a·flop[2] ▸*n. informal* a thing that is a complete failure. ▷late 20th cent.: a pun on MEGAFLOP[1].

meg·a·ga·mete /,megə'gam,ēt; ,megəgə'mēt/ ▸*n.* another term for MACROGAMETE.

meg·a·hertz /'megə,hərts/ (abbr.: **MHz**) ▸*n.* (*pl.* same) one million hertz, esp. as a measure of the frequency of radio transmissions or the clock speed of a computer.

meg·a·lith /'megə,liTH/ ▸*n. Archaeology* a large stone that forms a prehistoric monument (e.g., a menhir) or part of one (e.g., a stone circle or chamber tomb). ▷mid 19th cent.: back-formation from MEGALITHIC.

meg·a·lith·ic /,megə'liTHik/ ▸*adj. Archaeology* of, relating to, or denoting prehistoric monuments made of or containing megaliths. ■ (often **Megalithic**) of, relating to, or denoting prehistoric cultures characterized by the erection of megalithic monuments. ■ *figurative* massive or monolithic: *since June, the committee has become megalithic.* ▷mid 19th cent.: from MEGA- 'large' + Greek *lithos* 'stone' + -IC.

megalo- ▸*comb. form* abnormally large or great: *megaloblast* | *megalopolis.* ▷from Greek *megas, megal-* 'great.'

meg·a·lo·blast /'megələ,blast/ ▸*n. Medicine* a large, abnormally developed red blood cell typical of certain forms of anemia, associated with a deficiency of folic acid or of vitamin B_{12}. **—meg·a·lo·blas·tic** /,megəlō'blastik/ *adj.*

Meg·a·loc·er·os /,megə'läsərəs/ ▸*n.* a very large extinct deer of the Pleistocene epoch, of which the Irish elk was the main example. ▷modern Latin, from Greek *megas, megalo-* 'great' + *keras* 'horn.'

meg·a·lo·ma·ni·a /,megəlō'mānēə/ ▸*n.* obsession with the exercise of power, esp. in the domination of others. ■ delusion about one's own power or importance (typically as a symptom of manic or paranoid disorder). **—meg·a·lo·man·ic** /-'manik/ *adj.*

meg·a·lo·ma·ni·ac /,megəlō'mānē,ak/ ▸*n.* a person who is obsessed with their own power. ■ a person who suffers delusions of their own power or importance.
▸*adj.* exhibiting megalomania. **—meg·a·lo·ma·ni·a·cal** /-mə'nīəkəl/ *adj.*

meg·a·lop·o·lis /,megə'läpələs/ ▸*n.* a very large, heavily populated city or urban complex. ▷mid 19th cent.: from MEGALO- 'great' + Greek *polis* 'city.'

meg·a·lo·pol·i·tan /,megələ'pälətn/ ▸*adj.* of or denoting a very large city: *megalopolitan traffic.*
▸*n.* an inhabitant of a very large city. ▷mid 17th cent.: from MEGALO- 'great' + Greek *politēs* 'citizen' + -AN.

meg·a·lo·saur /,megələ'sôr/ (also **meg·a·lo·sau·rus** /-'sôrəs/) ▸*n.* a large carnivorous bipedal dinosaur of the mid Jurassic period, whose remains have been found only in England and France. • Genus *Megalosaurus*, suborder Theropoda, order Saurischia; the first dinosaur to be described and named (1824). ▷modern Latin, from MEGALO- 'great' + Greek *sauros* 'lizard.' **—meg·a·lo·sau·ri·an** /-'sôrēən/ *adj.*

meg·a·mouth /'megə,mouTH/ (also **megamouth shark**) ▸*n.* a shark with a very large wide mouth and tiny teeth, first captured in 1976 off the Hawaiian Islands. • *Megachasma pelagios*, the only member of the family Megachasmidae.

Meg·an's Law /'megənz; 'mā-/ ▸*n.* a law requiring authorities to notify communities of the whereabouts of convicted sex offenders. It was first enacted by New Jersey in 1995. ▷named after *Megan Kanka*, a 7-year-old New Jersey girl murdered by a neighbor who was a convicted sex offender.

meg·a·phone /'megə,fōn/ ▸*n.* a large funnel-shaped device for amplifying and directing the voice.
▸*v.* [*trans.*] utter through, or as if through, a megaphone: *the director stood around megaphoning orders* | [*intrans.*] *it was only their guides megaphoning to them.* **—meg·a·phon·ic** /,megə'fänik/ *adj.*

megaphone

meg·a·pix·el /'megə,piksəl/ ▸*n.* one million pixels, used as a measure of the resolution in digital cameras: [in *comb.*] *a 3.2-megapixel camera*

meg·a·pode /'megə,pōd/ ▸*n.* a large ground-dwelling Australasian and Southeast Asian bird that builds a large mound of debris to incubate its eggs by the heat of decomposition. Also called MOUND BUILDER. • Family Megapodiidae (the **megapode family**), which includes the brush turkeys and mallee fowl. ▷mid 19th cent.: from modern Latin *Megapodius* (genus name), from MEGA- 'large' + Greek *pous, pod-* 'foot.'

meg·a·spore /'megə,spôr/ ▸*n. Botany* the larger of the two kinds of spores produced by some ferns. Compare with MICROSPORE.

meg·a·star /'megə,stär/ ▸*n. informal* a very famous person, esp. in the world of entertainment. **—meg·a·star·dom** /,megə'stärdəm/ *n.*

meg·a·store /'megə,stôr/ ▸*n.* a very large store, typically one specializing in a particular type of product: *a computer megastore.*

meg·a·struc·ture /'megə,strəkCHər/ ▸*n.* a massive construction or structure, esp. a complex of many buildings.

meg·a·the·ri·um /,megə'THi(ə)rēəm/ ▸*n.* (*pl.* **-the·ri·ums** or **-the·ri·a** /-'THi(ə)rēə/) an extinct giant ground sloth of the Pliocene and Pleistocene epochs in America, reaching a height of 16 feet (5 m) when standing erect. • Genus *Megatherium*, family Megatheriidae. ▷modern Latin, from Greek *mega thērion* 'great animal.'

meg·a·ton /'megə,tən/ (abbr.: **MT**) ▸*n.* a unit of explosive power chiefly used for nuclear weapons, equivalent to one million tons of TNT: *H-bombs of fifteen megatons each.* **—meg·a·ton·nage** /,megə'tənij/ *n.*

meg·a·volt /'megə,vōlt/ (abbr.: **MV**) ▸*n.* a unit of electromotive force equal to one million volts.

meg·a·watt /'megə,wät/ (abbr.: **MW**) ▸*n.* a unit of power equal to one million watts, esp. as a measure of the output of a power station.

me gen·er·a·tion ▸*n.* a generation of people that are concerned chiefly with themselves, esp. in being selfishly materialistic.

Me·gha·la·ya /,māgə'lāə/ a small state in northeastern India, on the northern border of Bangladesh; capital, Shillong. It was created in 1970 from part of Assam.

Me·gid·do /mi'gidō/ an ancient city in northwestern Palestine, southeast of Haifa in present-day Israel. Its commanding location made the city the scene of many early battles, and the word *Armageddon* ("hill of Megiddo") is derived from its name. It was the scene in 1918 of the defeat of Turkish forces by the British under General Allenby.

Me·gil·lah /mə'gilə/ one of five books of the Hebrew scriptures (the Song of Solomon, Ruth, Lamentations, Ecclesiastes, and Esther) that are appointed to be read on certain Jewish notable days, esp. the Book of Esther, read at the festival of Purim. ■ [as *n.*] (**the whole megillah**) *informal* something in its entirety, esp. a complicated set of arrangements or a long-winded story. ▷from Hebrew *mĕgillāh*, literally 'scroll.'

me·gilp /mə'gilp/ ▸*n.* a mixture of mastic resin and linseed oil added to oil paints, widely used in the 19th century. ▷mid 18th cent.: of unknown origin.

meg·ohm /'meg,ōm/ ▸*n.* a unit of electrical resistance equal to one million ohms. ▷mid 19th cent.: from MEGA- (as a unit of measurement) + OHM.

me·grim /'mēgrim/ ▸*n. archaic* **1** (**megrims**) depression; low spirits: *fresh air and exercise, she generally found, could banish most megrims.* **2** a whim or fancy. **3** old-fashioned term for MIGRAINE. ▷late Middle English: variant of MIGRAINE.

Meh·ta /'mātä/, Zubin (1936–), U.S. symphony conductor; born in India. Often heading more than one orchestra at the same time, he was music director of the Los Angeles Philharmonic 1962–78, the Montreal Symphony Orchestra 1962–67, the New York Philharmonic 1978–91, and the Israel Philharmonic 1968. In 1998, he also became general music director of the Bavarian State Opera.

Mei·ji /'mājē/ ▸*n.* [usu. as *adj.*] the period when Japan was ruled by the emperor Meiji Tenno, marked by the modernization and westernization of the country. ▷Japanese, literally 'enlightened government.'

Mei·ji Ten·no /mā'jē 'te,nō/ (1852–1912), emperor of Japan 1868–1912; born *Mutsuhito*. He encouraged Japan's rapid modernization and political reform.

mei·o·fau·na /'mīə,fônə/ ▸*n. Ecology* minute interstitial animals living in soil and aquatic sediments. ▷1960s: from Greek *meiōn* 'less or smaller' + FAUNA.

mei·o·sis /mī'ōsəs/ ▸*n.* (*pl.* **-ses** /-sēz/) **1** *Biology* a type of cell division that results in two daughter cells each with half the chromosome number of the parent cell, as in the production of gametes. Compare with MITOSIS. **2** another term for LITOTES. ▷mid 16th cent. (sense 2): modern Latin, from Greek *meiōsis*, from *meioun* 'lessen,' from *meiōn* 'less.' Sense 1 dates from the early 20th cent. **—mei·ot·ic** /mī'ätik/ *adj.* **—mei·ot·i·cal·ly** /-ik(ə)lē/ *adv.*

Me·ir /mā'i(ə)r/, Golda (1898–1978), Israeli stateswoman, born in Ukraine; prime minister 1969–74; born *Goldie Mabovich*. She emigrated to the U.S. in 1907 and to Palestine in 1921. Following Israel's independence, she served in cabinet posts from 1949 to 1966 before being elected prime minister.

Golda Meir

Meis·sen /'mīsən/ ▸*n.* a fine hard-paste porcelain produced in Meissen since 1710. Often called DRESDEN CHINA. ▷named after the city of *Meissen* in eastern Germany.

Meiss·ner ef·fect /'mīsnər / ▸*n. Physics* the expulsion of magnetic flux when a material becomes superconducting in a magnetic field. If the magnetic field is applied after the material has become superconducting, the flux cannot penetrate it. ▷1930s; named after Fritz W. *Meissner* (1882–1974), German physicist.

Meiss·ner's cor·pus·cle ▸*n. Anatomy* a sensory nerve ending that is sensitive to mechanical stimuli, found in the dermis in various parts of the body. ▷late 19th cent.: named after Georg *Meissner* (1829–1905), German anatomist.

-meister ▸*comb. form* denoting a person regarded as skilled or prominent in a specified area of activity:

funk-meister | *gag-meister.* ▷from German *Meister* 'master.'

Mei·ster·sing·er /'mīstər,siNGər/ ▶*n.* (*pl.* same) a member of one of the guilds of German lyric poets and musicians that flourished from the 12th to 17th century. Their technique was elaborate and they were subject to rigid regulations. ▷German, from *Meister* 'master' + *Singer* 'singer.'

Meit·ner /'mītnər/, Lise (1878–1968), Austrian-born Swedish physicist. She worked in the field of radiochemistry with Otto Hahn, discovering the element protactinium with him in 1917. She also formulated the concept of nuclear fission with her nephew Otto Frisch.

meit·ner·i·um /mīt'ni(ə)rēəm/ ▶*n.* the chemical element of atomic number 109, a very unstable element made by high-energy atomic collisions. (Symbol: **Mt**) ▷modern Latin, from the name of L. MEITNER.

Mek·nès /mek'nes/ a city in northern Morocco, in the Middle Atlas Mountains, west of Fez; pop. 119,700.

Me·kong /'mā'kôNG; -'mē-/ a river in Southeast Asia that rises in Tibet and flows southeast and south for 2,600 miles (4,180 km) through southern China, Laos, Cambodia, and Vietnam to its extensive delta on the South China Sea. It forms the boundary between Laos, Myanmar (Burma), and Thailand.

me·la /'mālə/ ▶*n. Indian* a fair or Hindu festival. ▷from Sanskrit *melā* 'assembly.'

me·lae·na ▶*n.* British spelling of MELENA.

Me·la·ka /mə'läkə/ (also **Ma·lac·ca**) a state of Malaysia, on the southwestern coast of the Malay Peninsula, on the Strait of Malacca. ■ its capital and chief port; pop. 88,000. Conquered by the Portuguese in 1511, it played an important role in the development of trade between Europe and the East, esp. China.

mel·a·leu·ca /,melə'lo͝okə/ ▶*n.* an Australian shrub or tree that bears spikes of bottlebrushlike flowers. Some kinds are a source of timber or medicinal oil. • Genus *Melaleuca*, family Myrtaceae: many species, including the Australian paperbarks. ▷modern Latin: from Greek *melas* 'black' + *leukos* 'white' (because of the fire-blackened white bark of some Asian species).

mel·a·mine /'melə,mēn/ ▶*n.* **1** *Chemistry* a white crystalline compound made by heating cyanamide and used in making plastics. • A heterocyclic amine; chem. formula: $(CNH_2)_3N_3$. **2** (also **melamine resin**) a plastic used chiefly for laminated coatings, made by copolymerizing this compound with formaldehyde. ▷mid 19th cent.: from German *melam* (an arbitrary formation), denoting an insoluble amorphous organic substance, + AMINE.

mel·an·cho·li·a /,melən'kōlēə/ ▶*n.* deep sadness or gloom; melancholy: *rain slithered down the windows, encouraging a creeping melancholia.* ■ *dated* a mental condition marked by persistent depression and ill-founded fears. ▷late Middle English (denoting black bile): from late Latin (see MELANCHOLY). **—mel·an·cho·li·ac** /-'kōlē-ak/ *n.* & *adj.*

mel·an·chol·y /'melən,kälē/ ▶*n.* a deep, pensive, and long-lasting sadness. ■ another term for MELANCHOLIA (as a mental condition). ■ *historical* another term for BLACK BILE.

▶*adj.* sad, gloomy, or depressed: *she felt a little melancholy* | *the dog has a melancholy expression.* See note at GLUM. ■ causing or expressing sadness; depressing: *the study makes melancholy if instructive reading.* ▷Middle English: from Old French *melancolie*, via late Latin from Greek *melankholia*, from *melas, melan-* 'black' + *kholē* 'bile,' an excess of which was formerly believed to cause depression. **—mel·an·chol·ic** /,melən'kälik/ *adj.* **—mel·an·chol·i·cal·ly** /,melən'käləik(ə)lē/ *adv.*

Me·lanch·thon /mə'laNGkTHən; mā'länkHtôn/, Philipp (1497–1560), German reformer; born *Philipp Schwarzerd.* He succeeded Luther as leader of the Reformation movement in Germany in 1521 and drew up the Augsburg Confession in 1530.

Mel·a·ne·sia /,melə'nēZHə/ a region in the western Pacific Ocean, south of Micronesia and west of Polynesia. Its area includes the Bismarck Archipelago, the Solomon Islands, Vanuatu, New Caledonia, and Fiji. ▷from Greek *melas* 'black' + *nēsos* 'island.'

Mel·a·ne·sian /,melə'nēZHən/ ▶*adj.* of or relating to Melanesia, its peoples, or their languages.

▶*n.* **1** a native or inhabitant of any of the islands of Melanesia. **2** any of the languages of Melanesia, mostly Austronesian languages related to Malay but also including Neo-Melanesian (or Tok Pisin), an English-based pidgin.

mé·lange /mā'länj/ (also **me·lange**) ▶*n.* a mixture; a medley: *a mélange of tender vegetables and herbs.* See note at JUMBLE. ▷from French *mélange*, from *mêler* 'to mix.'

mel·a·nin /'melənin/ ▶*n.* a dark brown to black pigment occurring in the hair, skin, and iris of the eye in people and animals. It is responsible for tanning of skin exposed to sunlight. ▷mid 19th cent.: from Greek *melas, melan-* 'black' + -IN[1].

mel·a·nism /'melə,nizəm/ ▶*n. chiefly Zoology* unusual darkening of body tissues caused by excessive production of melanin, esp. as a form of color variation in animals. **—me·lan·ic** /mə'lanik/ *adj.* **—mel·a·nis·tic** /,melə'nistik/ *adj.*

mel·a·nite /'melə,nīt/ ▶*n.* a velvet-black variety of andradite (garnet). ▷early 19th cent.: from Greek *melas, melan-* 'black' + -ITE[1].

me·lan·o·cyte /'melənə,sīt; mə'lanō-/ ▶*n. Physiology* a mature melanin-forming cell, typically in the skin.

me·lan·o·cyte-stim·u·lat·ing hor·mone (abbr.: **MSH**) ▶*n. Physiology* a hormone secreted by the pituitary gland that is involved in pigmentation changes in some animals.

mel·a·noid /'melə,noid/ ▶*adj.* **1** resembling melanin. **2** resembling melanosis.

mel·a·no·ma /,melə'nōmə/ ▶*n.* (*pl.* **-no·mas** or **-no·ma·ta** /-'nōmətə/) *Medicine* a tumor of melanin-forming cells, typically a malignant tumor associated with skin cancer: *melanomas can appear anywhere on the body* | *the incidence of melanoma is rising steadily.* ▷mid 19th cent.: from Greek *melas, melan-* 'black' + -OMA.

mel·a·no·sis /,melə'nōsəs/ ▶*n. Medicine* a condition of abnormal or excessive production of melanin in the skin or other tissue. ▷early 19th cent.: modern Latin, from Greek *melas, melan-* 'black' + -OSIS. **—mel·a·not·ic** /-'nätik/ *adj.*

mel·a·to·nin /,melə'tōnin/ ▶*n. Biochemistry* a hormone secreted by the pineal gland that inhibits melanin formation and is thought to be concerned with regulating the reproductive cycle. ▷1950s: from Greek *melas* 'black' + *(sero)tonin.*

Mel·ba /'melbə/, Dame Nellie (1861–1931), Australian opera singer; born *Helen Porter Mitchell.* Born near Melbourne, she took her professional name from that of the city.

Mel·ba sauce ▶*n.* a sauce made from puréed raspberries thickened with powdered sugar.

Mel·ba toast ▶*n.* very thin crisp toast.

Mel·bourne[1] /'melbərn/ **1** the capital of Victoria, in southeastern Australia, on the Bass Strait, opposite Tasmania; pop. 2,762,000. A major port and the country's second-largest city, it was the capital of Australia 1901–27. **2** a resort city in east central Florida, south of Cape Canaveral; pop. 59,646.

Mel·bourne[2], William Lamb, 2nd Viscount (1779–1848), British statesman; prime minister 1834 and 1835–41. He became chief political adviser to Queen Victoria after her accession in 1837.

Mel·chi·or[1] /'melkē,ôr/ one of the three Magi, represented as a king of Nubia.

Mel·chi·or[2], Lauritz (Lebrecht Hommel) (1890–1973), U.S. tenor; born in Denmark. Considered the outstanding heldentenor of his day, he sang with the Metropolitan Opera 1926–50.

Mel·chiz·e·dek /mel'kizə,dek/ (in the Bible) a priest and king of Salem (which is usually identified with Jerusalem). He was revered by Abraham, who paid tithes to him (Gen. 14:18).

meld[1] /meld/ ▶*v.* blend; combine: [*trans.*] *Australia's winemakers have* ***melded*** *modern science* ***with*** *traditional art* | [*intrans.*] *the nylon bristles shrivel and* ***meld together.***

▶*n.* a thing formed by merging or blending: *a meld of many contributions.* ▷1930s: perhaps a blend of MELT and WELD[1].

meld[2] ▶*v.* [*trans.*] (in rummy, canasta, and other card games) lay down or declare (a combination of cards) in order to score points: *a player has melded four kings.*

▶*n.* a completed set or run of cards in any of these games. ▷late 19th cent. (originally U.S.): from German *melden* 'announce.'

me·lee /'mā,lā; mā'lā/ (also **mê·lée**) ▶*n.* a confused fight, skirmish, or scuffle: *several people were hurt in the melee.* ■ a confused mass of people: *the melee of people that was always thronging the streets.* ▷mid 17th cent.: from French *mêlée*, from an Old French variant of *meslee* (see MEDLEY).

me·le·na /mə'lēnə/ (*Brit.* **me·lae·na**) ▶*n. Medicine* dark sticky feces containing partly digested blood. ■ the production of such feces, following internal bleeding or the swallowing of blood. ▷early 19th cent.: modern Latin, from Greek *melaina*, feminine of *melas* 'black.'

mel·ic /'melik/ ▶*adj.* (of a poem, esp. an ancient Greek lyric) meant to be sung. ▷late 17th cent.: via Latin from Greek *melikos*, from *melos* 'song.'

Me·lil·la /mə'lēə/ a Spanish enclave on the Mediterranean coast of Morocco; pop. 57,000. It was occupied by Spain in 1497, and with Ceuta forms a community of Spain.

mel·i·lot /'melə,lät/ ▶*n.* a fragrant herbaceous plant of the pea family, native to Eurasia and north Africa, now widespread and sometimes grown as forage or green manure. Also called SWEET CLOVER. • Genus *Melilotus*, family Leguminosae: several species, esp. the **white sweet clover** (*M. alba*). ▷Middle English: from Old French, via Latin from Greek *melilōtos* 'honey lotus.'

mel·io·rate /'mēlēə,rāt/ ▶*v. formal* another term for AMELIORATE. ▷mid 16th cent.: from late Latin *meliorat-* 'improved,' from the verb *meliorare*, based on *melior* 'better.' **—mel·io·ra·tion** /,mēlēə'rāSHən/ *n.* **—mel·io·ra·tive** /-,rātiv/ *adj.*

mel·io·rism /'mēlēə,rizəm/ ▶*n. Philosophy* the belief that the world can be made better by human effort. ▷late 19th cent.: from Latin *melior* 'better' + -ISM. **—mel·io·rist** *n.* & *adj.* **—mel·io·ris·tic** /,melēə'ristik/ *adj.*

me·lis·ma /mə'lizmə/ ▶*n.* (*pl.* **-mas** or **-ma·ta** /-mətə/) *Music* a group of notes sung to one syllable of text. ▷late 19th cent.: from Greek, literally 'melody.' **—mel·is·mat·ic** /,meliz'matik/ *adj.*

Mel·kite /'mel,kīt/ ▶*n.* an Orthodox or Uniate Christian belonging to the patriarchate of Antioch, Jerusalem, or Alexandria. ■ *historical* an Eastern Christian adhering to the Orthodox faith as defined by the councils of Ephesus (AD 431) and Chalcedon (AD 451) and as accepted by the Byzantine emperor. ▷via ecclesiastical Latin from Byzantine Greek *Melkhitai*, representing Syriac *malkāyā* 'royalists' (i.e., expressing agreement with the Byzantine emperor), from *malkā* 'king.'

mel·lif·er·ous /mə'lifərəs/ ▶*adj.* yielding or producing honey. ▷mid 17th cent.: from Latin *mellifer* (from *mel* 'honey' + *-fer* 'bearing') + -OUS.

mel·lif·lu·ent /mə'liflo͞oənt/ ▶*adj.* another term for MELLIFLUOUS. ▷early 17th cent.: from late Latin *mellifluent-*, from Latin *mel, mell(i)-* 'honey' + *fluent-* 'flowing' (from the verb *fluere*). **—mel·lif·lu·ence** /-lo͞oəns/ *n.*

mel·lif·lu·ous /mə'liflo͞oəs/ ▶*adj.* (of a voice or words) sweet or musical; pleasant to hear: *the voice was mellifluous and smooth.* ▷late 15th cent.: from late Latin *mellifluus* (from *mel* 'honey' + *fluere* 'to flow') + -OUS. **—mel·lif·lu·ous·ly** *adv.* **—mel·lif·lu·ous·ness** *n.*

Mel·lon[1] /'melən/, Andrew (William) (1855–1937), U.S. financier and philanthropist; secretary of the treasury 1923–32. He donated his art collection and made gifts to establish the National Gallery of Art in Washington, DC, in 1941.

Mel·lon[2] /'melən/, Paul (1907–99), U.S. philanthropist; son of Andrew Mellon. He served as president of the Board of Trustees for the National Gallery 1938–39, 1963–78 and donated many works of art to the gallery.

mel·lo·phone /'melə,fōn/ ▶*n.* a brass instrument similar to the orchestral French horn, played mainly in military and concert bands. ▷1920s: from MELLOW + -PHONE.

mel·lo·tron /'melə,trän/ ▶*n.* an electronic keyboard instrument in which each key controls the playback of a single prerecorded musical sound. ▷1960s: from MELLOW + *-tron*, element of ELECTRONIC.

mel·low /'melō/ ▶*adj.* **1** (esp. of sound, taste, and color) pleasantly smooth or soft; free from harshness: *she was hypnotized by the mellow tone of his voice* | *slow cooking gives the dish a sweet, mellow flavor.* ■ *archaic* (of fruit) ripe, soft, sweet, and juicy: *a dish of mellow apples.* ■ (of wine) well-matured and smooth: *delicious, mellow, ripe, fruity wines.* **2** (of a person's character) softened or matured by age or experience: *a more mellow personality.* See note at MATURE. ■ relaxed and good-humored: *Jean was feeling mellow.* ■ *informal* relaxed and cheerful through being slightly drunk: *everybody got very mellow and slept well.* **3** (of earth) rich and loamy.

▶*v.* make or become mellow: [*trans.*] *getting older does mellow the hard edges around the anger* | [*intrans.*] *fuller-*

flavored whiskeys mellow with wood maturation informal I need to **mellow out**, *I need to calm down.* ▷late Middle English (in the sense '(of fruit) ripe, soft, sweet, and juicy'): perhaps from attributive use of Old English *melu, melw-* (see MEAL²). The verb dates from the late 16th cent. **—mel·low·ly** *adv.* **—mel·low·ness** *n.*

me·lo·de·on /mə'lōdēən/ (also **me·lo·di·on**) ▶*n.* **1** a small accordion of German origin, played esp. by folk musicians. [mid 19th cent.: probably from MELODY, on the pattern of *accordion.*] **2** a small organ popular in the 19th century, similar to the harmonium. [alteration of earlier *melodium.*]

me·lod·ic /mə'lädik/ ▶*adj.* of, having, or producing melody: *melodic and rhythmic patterns.* ■ pleasant-sounding; melodious: *his voice was deep and melodic.* ▷early 19th cent.: from French *mélodique*, via late Latin from Greek *melōidikos*, from *melōidia* 'melody.' **—me·lod·i·cal·ly** /-(ə)lē/ *adv.*

me·lod·i·ca /mə'lädikə/ ▶*n.* a wind instrument with a small keyboard controlling a row of reeds, and a mouthpiece at one end. ▷1960s: from MELODY, on the pattern of *harmonica.*

me·lod·ic mi·nor ▶*n.* *Music* a minor scale with the sixth and seventh degrees raised when ascending and lowered when descending.

me·lo·di·ous /mə'lōdēəs/ ▶*adj.* of, producing, or having a pleasant tune; tuneful: *the melodious chant of the monks.* ■ pleasant-sounding: *a melodious voice.* ▷late Middle English: from Old French *melodieus*, from *melodie* (see MELODY). **—me·lo·di·ous·ly** *adv.* **—me·lo·di·ous·ness** *n.*

mel·o·dist /'melədist/ ▶*n.* a composer of melodies. ■ a singer.

mel·o·dize /'melə,dīz/ ▶*v.* [*intrans.*] *rare* make or play music.

mel·o·dra·ma /'melə,drämə/ ▶*n.* **1** a sensational dramatic piece with exaggerated characters and exciting events intended to appeal to the emotions. ■ the genre of drama of this type. ■ language, behavior, or events that resemble drama of this kind: *what little is known of his early life is cloaked in melodrama.* **2** *historical* a play interspersed with songs and orchestral music accompanying the action. ▷early 19th cent.: from French *mélodrame*, from Greek *melos* 'music' + French *drame* 'drama.' **—mel·o·dram·a·tist** /,melə 'drämətist/ *n.* **—mel·o·dram·a·tize** /,melə'drämə,tīz/ *v.*

mel·o·dra·mat·ic /,melədrə'matik/ ▶*adj.* of or relating to melodrama. ■ characteristic of melodrama, esp. in being exaggerated, sensationalized, or overemotional: *he flung the door open with a melodramatic flourish.* **—mel·o·dra·mat·i·cal·ly** /-ik(ə)lē/ *adv.*

mel·o·dra·mat·ics /,melədrə'matiks/ ▶*plural n.* melodramatic behavior, action, or writing.

mel·o·dy /'melədē/ ▶*n.* (*pl.* **-dies**) a sequence of single notes that is musically satisfying: *he picked out an intricate melody on his guitar.* ■ such sequences of notes collectively: *his great gift was for melody.* ■ the principal part in harmonized music: *we have the melody and bass of a song composed by Strozzi.* ▷Middle English (also in the sense 'sweet music'): from Old French *melodie*, via late Latin from Greek *melōidia*, from *melos* 'song.'

mel·on /'melən/ ▶*n.* **1** the large round fruit of a plant of the gourd family, with sweet pulpy flesh and many seeds. ■ the edible flesh of such fruit: *a slice of melon.* **2** the Old World plant that yields this fruit. • *Cucumis melo* subsp. *melo*, family Cucurbitaceae: many varieties. **3** *Zoology* a mass of waxy material in the head of dolphins and other toothed whales, thought to focus acoustic signals. **4** *figurative* a large profit, esp. a stock dividend, to be divided among a number of people: *you can just see them sitting around the room* **cutting up the melon** *in advance.* ▷late Middle English: via Old French from late Latin *melo, melon-*, contraction of Latin *melopepo*, from Greek *mēlopepōn*, from *mēlon* 'apple' + *pepōn* 'gourd.'

Me·los /'mē,läs/ a Greek island in the Aegean Sea, in the southwest of the Cyclades group. The center of a flourishing civilization during the Bronze Age, it is the site of the discovery in 1820 of a Hellenistic marble statue of Aphrodite, the VENUS DE MILO. Greek name **MÍLOS**.

Mel·pom·e·ne /mel'pämənē/ *Greek & Roman Mythology* the Muse of tragedy. ▷Greek, literally 'singer.'

melt /melt/ ▶*v.* [*intrans.*] **1** become liquefied by heat: *place under the broiler until the cheese has melted | the icebergs were* **melting away.** ■ [*trans.*] change (something) to a liquid condition by heating it: *the hot metal melted the wax* | [as *adj.*] (**melted**) *asparagus with melted butter.* ■ [*trans.*] (**melt something down**) melt something, esp. a metal article, so that the material it is made of can be used again: *beautiful objects are being melted down and sold for scrap.* ■ dissolve in liquid: *add a cup of sugar and boil until the sugar melts.* **2** become more tender or loving: *she was so beautiful that I melted.* ■ [*trans.*] make (someone) more tender or loving: *Richard gave her a smile that* **melted her heart.** **3** [*intrans.*] leave or disappear unobtrusively: *the compromise was accepted and the opposition* **melted away** | *the figure melted into thin air.* ■ (of a feeling or state) disappear: *their original determination to exact vengeance* **melted away.** ■ (**melt into**) change or merge imperceptibly into (another form or state): *the cheers melted into gasps of admiration.*
▶*n.* an act of melting: *the precipitation falls as snow and is released during the spring melt.* ■ metal or other material in a melted condition. ■ an amount melted at any one time. ■ [with *adj.*] a sandwich, hamburger, or other dish containing or topped with melted cheese: *a tuna melt.* ▷Old English *meltan, mieltan*, of Germanic origin; related to Old Norse *melta* 'to malt, digest,' from an Indo-European root shared by Greek *meldein* 'to melt,' Latin *mollis* 'soft,' also by MALT. **—melt·a·ble** *adj.* **—melt·er** *n.* **—melt·ing·ly** *adv.*
▶*PHRASE* □ **melt in the** (or **your**) **mouth** (of food) be deliciously light or tender and need little or no chewing: *my shortbread melts in the mouth* | [as *adj.*] *melt-in-your-mouth chicken livers.*

melt·down /'melt,doun/ ▶*n.* an accident in a nuclear reactor in which the fuel overheats and melts the reactor core or shielding. ■ *figurative* a disastrous event, esp. a rapid fall in share prices: *the 1987 stock market meltdown.*

mel·te·mi /mel'temē/ (also **meltemi wind**) ▶*n.* a dry northwesterly wind that blows during the summer in the eastern Mediterranean. Also called ETESIAN WIND. ▷from modern Greek *meltémi*, Turkish *meltem.*

melt·ing point ▶*n.* the temperature at which a given solid will melt.

melt·ing pot ▶*n.* a pot in which metals or other materials are melted and mixed. ■ *figurative* a place where different peoples, styles, theories, etc., are mixed together: *a melting pot of disparate rhythms and cultures.*

mel·ton /'meltən/ ▶*n.* heavy woolen cloth with a close-cut nap, used for overcoats and jackets. ▷early 19th cent.: named after *Melton* Mowbray, a town in central England, formerly a center of manufacturing.

melt·wa·ter /'melt,wôtər; -,wätər/ ▶*n.* (also **melt·waters**) water formed by the melting of snow and ice, esp. from a glacier.

Mel·ville /'melvəl; -,vil/, Herman (1819–91), U.S. novelist and short-story writer. His experiences on a whaling ship formed the basis of several novels, notably *Moby Dick* (1851). Other notable works: *White-Jacket* (1850), *The Confidence Man* (1857), and *Billy Budd* (first published in 1924).

mem. ▶*abbr.* ■ member. ■ memoir. ■ memorandum. ■ memorial.

mem·an·tine /'memən,tēn/ ▶*n.* a prescription drug for the treatment of Alzheimer's disease. It protects the brain's nerve cells against glutamate, which is released in excess by Alzheimer's-damaged brain cells. Also called NAMENDA (*trademark*).

mem·ber /'membər/ ▶*n.* **1** an individual belonging to a group such as a society or team: *a member of the drama club | interest from members of the public.* ■ an animal or plant belonging to a taxonomic group: *a member of the lily family.* ■ (also **Member**) a person formally elected to take part in the proceedings of certain organizations: *members of Congress | Member of Parliament.* ■ a part or branch of a political body: [as *adj.*] *member countries of the Central African Customs Union.* **2** a constituent piece of a complex structure: *the main member that joins the front and rear axles.* ■ a part of a sentence, equation, group of figures, mathematical set, etc. **3** *archaic* a part or organ of the body, esp. a limb. ■ (also **male member**) the penis. Compare with MEMBRUM VIRILE. ■ *Botany* any part of a plant viewed with regard to its form and position, rather than to its function. ▷Middle English: via Old French from Latin *membrum* 'limb.' **—mem·bered** *adj.* [in *combination*] (*chiefly Chemistry*) *a six-membered oxygen-containing ring.*

mem·ber·ship /'membər,SHip/ ▶*n.* the fact of being a member of a group: *Taiwan has applied for membership in the World Trade Organization* | [as *adj.*] *a membership card.* ■ [in *sing.*] the number or body of members in a group: *our membership has grown by 600,000 in the past 18 months.*

mem·brane /'mem,brān/ ▶*n.* *Anatomy & Zoology* a pliable sheetlike structure acting as a boundary, lining, or partition in an organism. ■ a thin pliable sheet or skin of various kinds: *the concrete should include a membrane to prevent water seepage.* ■ *Biology* a microscopic double layer of lipids and proteins that bounds cells and organelles and forms structures within cells. ▷late Middle English: from Latin *membrana*, from *membrum* 'limb.' **—mem·bra·na·ceous** /,membrə'nāSHəs/ *adj.* **—mem·bra·ne·ous** /mem 'brānēəs/ *adj.* **—mem·bra·nous** /'membrənəs; mem 'brānəs/ *adj.*

mem·bra·nous lab·y·rinth /'membrənəs; mem 'brānəs / ▶*n.* see LABYRINTH.

mem·brum vir·ile /'membrəm 'virələ; vi'rīlē/ ▶*n.* *archaic* the penis. ▷Latin, literally 'male member.'

meme /mēm/ ▶*n.* *Biology* an element of a culture or system of behavior that may be considered to be passed from one individual to another by nongenetic means, esp. imitation. ▷1970s: from Greek *mimēma* 'that which is imitated,' on the pattern of *gene.* **—me·met·ic** /mē'metik; mə-/ *adj.*

Me·mel /'māməl/ **1** German name for **KLAIPEDA.** ■ a former district of East Prussia, centered on the city of Memel (Klaipeda). **2** the Neman River in its lower course (see **NEMAN**).

me·men·to /mə'men,tō/ ▶*n.* (*pl.* **-tos** or **-toes**) an object kept as a reminder or souvenir of a person or event: *you can purchase a memento of your visit.* ▷late Middle English (denoting a prayer of commemoration): from Latin, literally 'remember!,' imperative of *meminisse.*

me·men·to mo·ri /mə'men,tō 'môrē/ ▶*n.* (*pl.* same) an object serving as a warning or reminder of death, such as a skull. ▷Latin, literally 'remember (that you have) to die.'

mem·o /'memō/ ▶*n.* (*pl.* **mem·os**) *informal* a written message, esp. in business. ▷early 18th cent.: abbreviation of MEMORANDUM.

mem·oir /'mem,wär; -,wôr/ ▶*n.* **1** a historical account or biography written from personal knowledge or special sources: *in 1924 she published a short memoir of her husband.* ■ (**memoirs**) an autobiography or a written account of one's memory of certain events or people. **2** an essay on a learned subject: *an important memoir on Carboniferous crustacea.* ■ (**memoirs**) the proceedings or transactions of a learned society: *Memoirs of the Horticultural Society.* ▷late 15th cent. (denoting a memorandum or record): from French *mémoire* (masculine), a special use of *mémoire* (feminine) 'memory.' **—mem·oir·ist** /-ist/ *n.*

mem·o·ra·bil·i·a /,mem(ə)rə'bilēə/ ▶*plural n.* objects kept or collected because of their historical interest, esp. those associated with memorable people or events: *World Series memorabilia.* ■ *archaic* memorable or noteworthy things. ▷late 18th cent.: from Latin, neuter plural of *memorabilis* 'memorable.'

mem·o·ra·ble /'mem(ə)rəbəl/ ▶*adj.* worth remembering or easily remembered, esp. because of being special or unusual: *this victory was one of the most memorable of his career.* ▷late 15th cent.: from Latin *memorabilis*, from *memorare* 'bring to mind,' from *memor* 'mindful.' **—mem·o·ra·bil·i·ty** /,mem(ə)rə 'bilətē/ *n.* **—mem·o·ra·bly** /-blē/ *adv.*

mem·o·ran·dum /,memə'randəm/ ▶*n.* (*pl.* **-da** /-də/ or **-dums**) a note or record made for future use: *the two countries signed a memorandum of understanding on economic cooperation.* ■ a written message, esp. in business or diplomacy: *he told them of his decision in a memorandum.* ■ *Law* a document recording the terms of a contract or other legal details. ▷late Middle English: from Latin, literally 'something to be brought to mind,' gerundive of *memorare.* The original use was as an adjective, placed at the head of a note of something to be remembered or of a record made for future reference.

me·mo·ri·al /mə'môrēəl/ ▶*n.* **1** something, esp. a structure, established to remind people of a person or event: *a monument built as* **a memorial to** *those who fell in the Civil War.* ■ [as *adj.*] intended to commemorate someone or something: *a memorial service in the dead man's honor.* **2** *chiefly historical* a statement of facts, esp. as the basis of a petition: *the council sent a strongly worded memorial to the chancellor.* ■ a record or chronicle: *Mrs. Carlyle's Letters and Memorials.* ■ an informal diplomatic paper. ▷late Middle English: from late Latin *memoriale* 'record, memory, monument,' from Latin *memorialis* 'serving as a reminder,' from *memoria* 'memory.'

Me·mo·ri·al Day ▶*n.* a day on which those who died in active military service are remembered, traditionally observed on May 30 but now officially observed on the last Monday in May. Also called (esp. formerly) DECORATION DAY. ■ (also **Confederate Memorial Day**) (in the Southern states) any of various days (esp. the fourth Monday in April) on which similar remembrances are observed.

me·mo·ri·al·ist /mə'môrēəlist/ ▸*n.* a person who gives a memorial address or writes a memorial. ■ a writer of biographical or historical memorials; a memoirist.

me·mo·ri·al·ize /mə'môrēə,līz/ ▸*v.* [*trans.*] preserve the memory of; commemorate: *the novel memorialized their childhood summers.* **—me·mo·ri·al·i·za·tion** /mə ,môrēələ'zāsHən/ *n.* **—me·mo·ri·al·iz·er** *n.*

me·mo·ri·al park ▸*n.* a cemetery: *Pine View Memorial Park.* ■ a park designed for contemplation or recreation, commemorating the death of an individual or of many people through a natural or other disaster, or through military action: *Fort Griswold Memorial Park | Martin Luther King, Jr., Memorial Park.*

mem·o·rize /'memə,rīz/ ▸*v.* [*trans.*] commit to memory; learn by heart: *he memorized thousands of verses.* **—mem·o·riz·a·ble** /-,rīzəbəl/ *adj.* **—mem·o·ri·za·tion** /,memərə'zāsHən/ *n.* **—mem·o·riz·er** *n.*

mem·o·ry /'mem(ə)rē/ ▸*n.* (*pl.* **-ries**) **1** a person's power to remember things: *I've a great* ***memory for*** *faces | my grandmother is losing her memory.* ■ the power of the mind to remember things: *the brain regions responsible for memory.* ■ the mind regarded as a store of things remembered: *he searched his memory frantically for an answer.* ■ the capacity of a substance to return to a previous state or condition after having been altered or deformed. See also **SHAPE MEMORY**. **2** something remembered from the past; a recollection: *one of my earliest memories is of sitting on his knee | the mind can bury all memory of traumatic abuse.* ■ the remembering or recollection of a dead person, esp. one who was popular or respected: *clubs devoted to the memory of Sherlock Holmes.* ■ the length of time over which people continue to remember a person or event: *the worst slump in recent memory.* **3** the part of a computer in which data or program instructions can be stored for retrieval. ■ capacity for storing information in this way: *the module provides 16Mb of memory.* ▷Middle English: from Old French *memorie*, from Latin *memoria*, from *memor* 'mindful, remembering.'

▸*PHRASES* □ **from memory** without reading or referring to notes: *each child was required to recite a verse from memory.* □ **in memory of** intended to remind people of, esp. to honor a dead person. □ **take a trip** (or **walk**) **down memory lane** deliberately recall pleasant or sentimental memories.

mem·o·ry bank ▸*n.* the memory device of a computer or other device.

mem·o·ry board ▸*n. Computing* a detachable board containing memory chips, which can be connected to a computer.

mem·o·ry book ▸*n.* a scrapbook.

mem·o·ry cell ▸*n. Physiology* a long-lived lymphocyte capable of responding to a particular antigen on its reintroduction, long after the exposure that prompted its production.

mem·o·ry hole ▸*n.* an imaginary place where inconvenient or unpleasant information is put and quickly forgotten: *now that the trial's been postponed the whole case has dropped into the memory hole.* ▷a figurative extension of the same term in George Orwell's *1984*, which described a slot where historical documents could be disposed of to allow for manipulation of memories of the past.

mem·o·ry leak ▸*n.* a failure in a computer program to deallocate discarded memory, causing impaired performance or failure.

mem·o·ry map·ping ▸*n.* a technique in which a computer treats peripheral devices as if they were located in the main memory.

mem·o·ry trace ▸*n.* a hypothetical permanent change in the nervous system brought about by memorizing something; an engram.

Mem·phis /'memfəs/ **1** an ancient city in Egypt, whose ruins are situated on the Nile River about 10 miles (15 km) south of Cairo. It is the site of the pyramids of Saqqara and Giza and the Sphinx. **2** a river port on the Mississippi River in extreme southwestern Tennessee; pop. 650,100. Founded in 1819, it was the home of blues music in the late 19th century and the scene of the assassination of Martin Luther King in 1968. It is also the childhood home and burial place of Elvis Presley.

mem·sa·hib /'mem,sä(h)ib; -,säb/ ▸*n. Indian, dated* a married white or upper-class woman (often used as a respectful form of address by nonwhites). ▷from *mem* (representing an Indian pronunciation of **MA'AM**) + **SAHIB**.

men /men/ ▸ plural form of **MAN**.

men·ace /'menəs/ ▸*n.* a person or thing that is likely to cause harm; a threat or danger: *a new initiative aimed at beating the menace of drugs | the snakes are* ***a menace to*** *farm animals.* ■ a threatening quality, tone, or atmosphere: *he spoke the words with a hint of menace.* ■ *often humorous* a person or thing that causes trouble or annoyance: *his kid sister, that chatty little menace, had become the knockout of the neighborhood.*

▸*v.* [*trans.*] (often **be menaced**) threaten, esp. in a malignant or hostile manner: *Africa's elephants are still menaced by poaching* | [as *adj.*] (**menacing**) *a menacing tone of voice.* ▷Middle English: via Old French from late Latin *minacia*, from Latin *minax, minac-* 'threatening,' from *minae* 'threats.' **—men·ac·er** *n.* **—men·ac·ing** *adj.* **—men·ac·ing·ly** *adv.*

men·a·di·one /,menə'dī,ōn/ ▸*n. Medicine* a synthetic yellow compound related to menaquinone, used to treat hemorrhage. Also called **VITAMIN K**$_3$. • Alternative name: **2-methyl-1,4-naphthoquinone**; chem. formula: $C_{11}H_8O_2$. ▷1940s: from *me(thyl)* + *na(phthalene)* + the suffix *-dione*, used in names of compounds containing two carbonyl groups.

mé·nage /mā'näzH; mə-/ ▸*n.* the members of a household: *crisis had recently unsettled the Clelland ménage.* ■ the management of a household: *they were forced to conduct their ménage on a humbler scale than heretofore.* ▷Middle English: from Old French *menage*, from *mainer* 'to stay,' influenced by Old French *mesnie* 'household,' both ultimately based on Latin *manere* 'remain.'

mé·nage à trois /mā'näzH ä 't(r)wä; mə-/ ▸*n.* (*pl.* **mé·nages à trois** *pronunc.* same) an arrangement in which three people share a sexual relationship, typically a domestic situation involving a married couple and the lover of one of them. ▷French, 'household of three.'

me·nag·er·ie /mə'najərē; -'nazH-/ ▸*n.* a collection of wild animals kept in captivity for exhibition. ■ *figurative* a strange or diverse collection of people or things: *some other specimen in the television menagerie.* ▷late 17th cent.: from French *ménagerie*, from *ménage* (see **MÉNAGE**).

Men·ai Strait /'me,nī/ a channel that separates Anglesey from the mainland of northwestern Wales.

Me·nan·der /mə'nandər/ (*c.*342–292 BC), Greek playwright. His comic plays deal with domestic situations and capture colloquial speech patterns. The sole complete extant play is *Dyskolos*.

Men·ap·i·an /mə'napēən/ ▸*adj. Geology* of, relating to, or denoting a Middle Pleistocene glaciation in northern Europe, possibly corresponding to the Günz of the Alps. ■ [as *n.*] (**the Menapian**) the Menapian glaciation or the system of deposits laid down during it. ▷1950s: from Latin *Menapii*, a people of northern Gaul in Roman times, + **-IAN**.

men·a·qui·none /,menə'kwin,ōn; -'kwī,nōn/ ▸*n. Biochemistry* one of the K vitamins, a compound produced by bacteria in the large intestine and essential for the blood-clotting process. It is an isoprenoid derivative of menadione. Also called **VITAMIN K**$_2$. ▷1940s: from the chemical name *me(thyl)-na(phtho)quinone*.

men·ar·che /'men,ärkē/ ▸*n.* the first occurrence of menstruation. ▷late 19th cent.: modern Latin, from Greek *mēn* 'month' + *arkhē* 'beginning.' **—men·ar·che·al** /men'ärkēəl/ or **men·ar·chi·al** *adj.*

Men·ci·us /'mencHēəs/ (*c.*371–*c.*289 BC), Chinese philosopher; Latinized name of *Meng-tzu* or *Mengzi* ("Meng the Master"). Known as a developer of Confucianism, he believed that rulers should provide for the welfare of the people and that human nature is intrinsically good. ■ one of the Four Books of Confucianism, containing the teachings of Mencius.

Menck·en /'meNGkən/, H. L. (1880–1956), U.S. journalist and literary and social critic; full name *Henry Louis Mencken*. From 1908, he attacked the political and literary Establishment. In *The American Language* (1919) he opposed the dominance of European culture in the U.S., arguing for and establishing the study of American English in its own right.

mend /mend/ ▸*v.* [*trans.*] repair (something that is broken or damaged): *workmen were mending faulty cabling | a patch was used to mend the garment.* ■ [*intrans.*] return to health; heal: *foot injuries can take months to mend.* ■ improve (an unpleasant situation, esp. a disagreement): *quarrels could be mended by talking.*

▸*n.* a repair in a material: *the mends were so perfect you could not even tell the board had been damaged.* ▷Middle English: shortening of **AMEND**. **—mend·a·ble** *adj.* **—mend·er** *n.*

▸*PHRASES* □ **mend (one's) fences** make peace with a person: *is it too late to mend fences with your ex-wife?* □ **mend one's ways** improve one's habits or behavior. □ **on the mend** improving in health or condition; recovering: *on the mend after a stomach operation | the economy is on the mend.*

men·da·cious /men'dāsHəs/ ▸*adj.* not telling the truth; lying: *mendacious propaganda.* ▷early 17th cent.: from Latin *mendax, mendac-* 'lying' (related to *mendum* 'fault') + **-IOUS**. **—men·da·cious·ly** *adv.* **—men·da·cious·ness** *n.*

men·dac·i·ty /men'dasitē/ ▸*n.* untruthfulness: *people publicly castigated for past mendacity.* ▷mid 17th cent.: from ecclesiastical Latin *mendacitas*, from *mendax, mendac-* 'lying' (see **MENDACIOUS**).

Men·de /'mendē/ ▸*n.* (*pl.* same or **Men·des**) **1** a member of a people inhabiting Sierra Leone in West Africa. **2** the Mende language of this people.

▸*adj.* relating to or denoting this people or their language. ▷the name in Mende.

Men·del /'mendl/, Gregor Johann (1822–84), Moravian monk; the father of genetics. From systematically breeding peas, he demonstrated the transmission of characteristics in a predictable way by factors (genes) that remain intact and independent between generations and do not blend, although they may mask one another's effects.

Men·de·le·ev /,mendə'lāəf; myindi'leyef/, Dmitri (Ivanovich) (1834–1907), Russian chemist. He developed the periodic table.

men·de·le·vi·um /,mendə'lēvēəm; -'lā-/ ▸*n.* the chemical element of atomic number 101, a radioactive metal of the actinide series. It does not occur naturally and was first made in 1955 by bombarding einsteinium with helium ions. (Symbol: **Md**) ▷modern Latin, from the name of D. **MENDELEEV**.

Men·de·li·an /men'dēlēən/ ▸*adj. Biology* of or relating to Mendel's theory of heredity: *Mendelian genetics.*

▸*n.* a person who accepts or advocates Mendel's theory of heredity.

Men·del·ism /'mendl,izəm/ ▸*n. Biology* the theory of heredity as formulated by Mendel.

Men·dels·sohn /'mendl-sən/, Felix (1809–47), German composer and pianist; full name *Jakob Ludwig Felix Mendelssohn-Bartholdy*. His romantic music is elegant, light, and melodically inventive. Notable works: *Fingal's Cave* (1830–32), *Elijah* (1846), and eight volumes of *Lieder ohne Worte (Songs Without Words)* for piano.

Men·de·res /,mendə'res/ a river in southwestern Turkey. It rises in the Anatolian plateau and flows for about 240 miles (384 km) to the Aegean Sea south of the Greek island of Samos. Known in ancient times as the Maeander—and noted for its winding course—it gave its name to the verb *meander*.

men·di·cant /'mendikənt/ ▸*adj.* given to begging. ■ of or denoting one of the religious orders that originally relied solely on alms: *a mendicant friar.*

▸*n.* a beggar. ■ a member of a mendicant order. ▷late Middle English: from Latin *mendicant-* 'begging,' from the verb *mendicare*, from *mendicus* 'beggar,' from *mendum* 'fault.' **—men·di·can·cy** /-kənsē/ *n.*

men·dic·i·ty /men'disitē/ ▸*n.* the condition or activities of a beggar. ▷late Middle English: from Old French *mendicite*, from Latin *mendicitas*, from *mendicus* 'beggar.'

mend·ing /'mendiNG/ ▸*n.* things to be repaired by sewing or darning: *a muddle of books and mending.*

Men·do·ci·no /,mendə'sēnō/ a resort community in northwestern California, on the Pacific coast. **Cape Mendocino**, the most western point in the state, is farther to the north.

Men·do·za[1] /men'dōzə/ a city in western Argentina, located in the foothills of the Andes at the center of a wine-producing region; pop. 122,000.

Men·do·za[2], Antonio de (*c.*1490–1552), Spanish colonial administrator; first viceroy of New Spain (1535–50).

Men·e·la·us /,menə'lāəs/ *Greek Mythology* king of Sparta, husband of Helen and brother of Agamemnon. Helen was stolen from him by Paris, an event that provoked the Trojan War.

Me·nes /'mēnēz/, Egyptian pharaoh; reigned *c.*3100 BC. He founded the first dynasty that ruled Egypt.

men·folk /'men,fōk/ (also **men·folks**) ▸*plural n.* a group of men considered collectively, esp. the men of a particular family or community: *the menfolk of the village watch the goings-on.*

Meng-tzu /ˈmeNG ˈtsōō; dzə/ (also **Meng·zi** /-ˈzē/) Chinese name for MENCIUS.

men·ha·den /menˈhādn; mən-/ ▸*n.* a large deep-bodied fish of the herring family that occurs along the east coast of North America. The oil-rich flesh is used to make fish meal and fertilizer. • Genus *Brevoortia*, family Clupeidae: several species, in particular *B. tyrannus*. ▷late 18th cent.: from Algonquian.

men·hir /ˈmenˌhi(ə)r/ ▸*n. Archaeology* a tall upright stone of a kind erected in prehistoric times in western Europe. ▷mid 19th cent.: from Breton *men* 'stone' + *hir* 'long.'

me·ni·al /ˈmēnēəl/ ▸*adj.* (of work) not requiring much skill and lacking prestige: *menial factory jobs.* ■ [*attrib.*] *dated* (of a servant) domestic.
▸*n.* a person with a menial job. ■ *dated* a domestic servant. ▷late Middle English (in the sense 'domestic'): from Old French, from *mesnee* 'household.' —**me·ni·al·ly** *adv.*

Mé·nière's dis·ease /mānˈye(ə)rz/ (also **Ménière's syndrome**) ▸*n.* a disease of unknown cause affecting the membranous labyrinth of the ear, causing progressive deafness and attacks of tinnitus and vertigo. ▷late 19th cent.: named after Prosper *Ménière* (1799–1862), French physician.

me·nin·ges /məˈninjēz/ ▸*plural n.* (*sing.* **me·ninx** /ˈmēniNGks; ˈmeniNGks/) *Anatomy* the three membranes (the dura mater, arachnoid, and pia mater) that line the skull and vertebral canal and enclose the brain and spinal cord. ▷modern Latin, from Greek *mēninx*, *mēning-* 'membrane.' —**me·nin·ge·al** /məˈninjēəl/ *adj.*

me·nin·gi·o·ma /məˌninjēˈōmə/ ▸*n.* (*pl.* **-mas** or **-ma·ta** /-ˈōmətə/) *Medicine* a tumor, usually benign, arising from meningeal tissue of the brain.

men·in·gi·tis /ˌmenənˈjītis/ ▸*n.* inflammation of the meninges caused by viral or bacterial infection and marked by intense headache and fever, sensitivity to light, and muscular rigidity, leading (in severe cases) to convulsions, delirium, and death. —**men·in·git·ic** /-ˈjitik/ *adj.*

me·nin·go·cele /məˌniNGgōˈsēl/ ▸*n. Medicine* a protrusion of the meninges through a gap in the spine due to a congenital defect.

me·nin·go·coc·cus /məˌniNGgōˈkäkəs/ ▸*n.* (*pl.* **-coc·ci** /-ˈkäksī; -ˈkäksē/) a bacterium involved in some forms of meningitis and cerebrospinal infection. • *Neisseria meningitidis*, a nonmotile spherical Gram-negative bacterium. ▷late 19th cent.: from MENINGES + COCCUS. —**me·nin·go·coc·cal** /-ˈkäkəl/ *adj.*

me·nin·go·en·ceph·a·li·tis /məˌniNGgōinˌsefəˈlītis/ ▸*n. Medicine* inflammation of the membranes of the brain and the adjoining cerebral tissue.

me·ninx /ˈmēniNGks; ˈmen-/ ▸ singular form of MENINGES.

men·is·cec·to·my ▸*n.* surgical removal of a meniscus, esp. that of the knee.

me·nis·cus /məˈniskəs/ ▸*n.* (*pl.* **-ci** /-kē; -kī/ or **-cus·es**) *Physics* the curved upper surface of a liquid in a tube. ■ *Optics* [usu. as *adj.*] a lens that is convex on one side and concave on the other. ■ *Anatomy* a thin fibrous cartilage between the surfaces of some joints, e.g., the knee. ▷late 17th cent.: modern Latin, from Greek *mēniskos* 'crescent,' diminutive of *mēnē* 'moon.'

Men·lo Park **1** a city in north central California, south of San Francisco; pop. 28,040. **2** a historic community in central New Jersey, in the township of Edison, northeast of New Brunswick, the site of the laboratory of Thomas Edison.

Men·nin·ger /ˈmenənjər/, Karl Augustus (1893–1990), U.S. psychiatrist. He cofounded the Menninger Clinic 1920, where psychiatrists received training in psychoanalysis. In 1941, the Menninger Foundation, which he headed until 1990, was established.

Men·non·ite /ˈmenəˌnīt/ ▸*n.* (chiefly in the U.S. and Canada) a member of a Protestant sect originating in Friesland in the 16th century, emphasizing adult baptism and rejecting church organization, military service, and public office. ▷from the name of its founder, *Menno* Simons (1496–1561), + -ITE[1]. —**Men·no·nit·ism** /-izəm/ *n.*

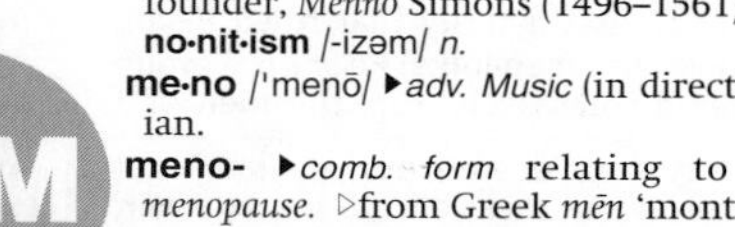

me·no /ˈmenō/ ▸*adv. Music* (in directions) less. ▷Italian.

meno- ▸*comb. form* relating to menstruation: *menopause.* ▷from Greek *mēn* 'month.'

me·nol·o·gy /məˈnäləjē/ ▸*n.* (*pl.* **-gies**) an ecclesiastical calendar of the months, esp. a calendar of the Greek Orthodox Church containing biographies of the saints in the order of the dates on which they are commemorated. ▷early 17th cent.: via modern Latin from ecclesiastical Greek *mēnologion*, from *mēn* 'month' + *logos* 'account.'

Me·nom·i·nee /məˈnämənē/ (also **Me·nom·i·ni**) ▸*n.* (*pl.* same or **-nees** or **-nis**) **1** a member of an American Indian people of northeastern Wisconsin. **2** the Algonquian language of this people.
▸*adj.* relating to or denoting this people or their language. ▷from Ojibwa *manōminī*, literally 'wild-rice person.'

me·no mos·so /ˈmenō ˈmäsō/ ▸*adv.* & *adj. Music* (esp. as a direction) less quickly. ▷Italian.

men·o·pause /ˈmenəˌpôz/ ▸*n.* the ceasing of menstruation. ■ the period in a woman's life (typically between 45 and 50 years of age) when this occurs. ▷late 19th cent.: from modern Latin *menopausis* (see MENO-, PAUSE). —**men·o·pau·sal** /ˌmenəˈpôzəl/ *adj.*

me·nor·ah /məˈnôrə/ ▸*n.* (**the Menorah**) a sacred candelabrum with seven branches used in the Temple in Jerusalem, originally that made by the craftsman Bezalel and placed in the sanctuary of the Tabernacle (Exod. 37:17–24). ■ a candelabrum used in Jewish worship, esp. one with eight branches and a central socket used at Hanukkah. ▷Hebrew.

menorah

men·or·rha·gi·a /ˌmenəˈrāj(ē)ə/ ▸*n. Medicine* abnormally heavy bleeding at menstruation. ▷late 18th cent.: modern Latin, from MENO- 'of menstruation' + *-rrhag-*, stem of Greek *rhēgnunai* 'to burst.'

men·or·rhe·a /ˌmenəˈrēə/ (also *chiefly Brit.* **men·or·rhoe·a**) ▸*n. Medicine* the flow of blood at menstruation. ▷mid 19th cent.: back-formation from AMENORRHEA.

Me·not·ti /məˈnätē/, Gian (1911–), U.S. composer; born in Italy. He wrote the operas *The Old Maid and the Thief* (1939), *The Consul* (1950), and *Amahl and the Night Visitors* (1951).

Men·sa[1] /ˈmensə/ *Astronomy* a small, faint southern constellation (the Table or Table Mountain), lying between Dorado and the south celestial pole. It contains part of the Large Magellanic Cloud. ■ [as *genitive*] (**Mensae** /-sē/) used with a preceding letter or numeral to designate a star in this constellation: *the star Alpha Mensae.* ▷Latin.

Men·sa[2] /ˈmensə/ an international organization founded in England in 1945 whose members must achieve very high scores in IQ tests to be admitted. ▷Latin, 'table,' with allusion to a round table at which all members have equal status.

mensch /menCH/ ▸*n.* (*pl.* **mensch·en** /ˈmenCHən/ or **mensch·es**) *informal* a person of integrity and honor. ▷1930s: Yiddish *mensh*, from German *Mensch*, literally 'person.'

men·ses /ˈmenˌsēz/ ▸*plural n.* blood and other matter discharged from the uterus at menstruation. ■ [treated as *sing.*] the time of menstruation: *a late menses.* ▷late 16th cent.: from Latin, plural of *mensis* 'month.'

Men·she·vik /ˈmenCHəˌvik/ ▸*n.* (*pl.* **Men·she·viks** /ˈmenCHəˌviks/ or **Men·she·vi·ki** /ˌmenCHəˈvikē/) *historical* a member of the non-Leninist wing of the Russian Social Democratic Workers' Party, opposed to the Bolsheviks and defeated by them after the overthrow of the tsar in 1917.
▸*adj.* of, relating to, or characteristic of Mensheviks or Menshevism. ▷from Russian *Men'shevik* 'a member of the minority,' from *men'she* 'less.' Lenin coined the name at a time when the party was (untypically) in the minority for a brief period. —**Men·she·vism** /-ˌvizəm/ *n.* —**Men·she·vist** /-vist/ *n.*

men's move·ment ▸*n.* a movement aimed at liberating men from traditional views about their character and role in society.

mens re·a /menz ˈrēə/ ▸*n. Law* the intention or knowledge of wrongdoing that constitutes part of a crime, as opposed to the action or conduct of the accused. Compare with ACTUS REUS. ▷mid 19th cent.: Latin, literally 'guilty mind.'

men's room ▸*n.* a restroom for men in a public or institutional building.

men·stru·al /ˈmenstr(ōō)əl/ ▸*adj.* of or relating to the menses or menstruation: *menstrual blood.* ▷late Middle English: from Latin *menstrualis*, from *menstruum* 'menses,' from *mensis* 'month.'

men·stru·al cy·cle ▸*n.* the process of ovulation and menstruation in women and other female primates.

men·stru·al per·i·od ▸*n.* see PERIOD (sense 4).

men·stru·ate /ˈmenstrəˌwāt; ˈmenˌstrāt/ ▸*v.* [*intrans.*] (of a woman) discharge blood and other material from the lining of the uterus as part of the menstrual cycle. ▷mid 17th cent.: from late Latin *menstruat-* 'menstruated,' from the verb *menstruare*, from Latin *menstrua* 'menses.'

men·stru·a·tion /ˌmenstrōōˈāSHən; menˈstrā-/ ▸*n.* the process in a woman of discharging blood and other materials from the lining of the uterus at intervals of about one lunar month from puberty until menopause, except during pregnancy.

men·stru·ous /ˈmenstr(ōō)əs/ ▸*adj.* of, relating to, or in the process of menstruation. ▷late Middle English: from Old French *menstrueus*, from late Latin *menstruosus*, from *menstrua* 'menses.'

men·stru·um /ˈmenstr(ōō)əm/ ▸*n.* (*pl.* **-stru·a** /-str(ōō)ə/) **1** menses. **2** (*pl.* also **-stru·ums**) *archaic* a solvent. ▷late Middle English (sense 1): from Latin, neuter of *menstruus* 'monthly,' from *mensis* 'month.' Sense 2 is by alchemical analogy of the supposed agency of a solvent in the transmutation of metals into gold with the supposed action of menses on the ovum.

men·sur·a·ble /ˈmenCHərəbəl; ˈmensər-/ ▸*adj.* able to be measured; having fixed limits. ■ *Music* another term for MENSURAL. ▷late Middle English (in the sense 'moderate'): from late Latin *mensurabilis*, from *mensurare* 'to measure,' from Latin *mensura* 'measure.' —**men·sur·a·bil·i·ty** /ˌmenCHərəˈbilətē; ˌmensər-/ *n.*

men·su·ral /ˈmenCHərəl; ˈmensərəl/ ▸*adj.* of or involving measuring: *mensural investigations.* ■ *Music* involving notes of definite duration and usually a regular meter. ▷late 16th cent.: from Latin *mensuralis*, from *mensura* 'measure.'

men·su·ra·tion /ˌmenCHəˈrāSHən; ˌmensə-/ ▸*n.* measuring. ■ *Mathematics* the measuring of geometric magnitudes, lengths, areas, and volumes. ▷late 16th cent. (denoting measurement in general): from late Latin *mensuratio(n-)*, from *mensurare* 'to measure.'

mens·wear /ˈmenzˌwe(ə)r/ (also **men's wear**) ▸*n.* clothes for men.

-ment /mənt/ ▸*suffix* **1** forming nouns expressing the means or result of an action: *curtailment* | *excitement* | *treatment.* **2** forming nouns from adjectives (such as *merriment* from *merry*). ▷from French, or from Latin *-mentum.*

men·tal /ˈmentl/ ▸*adj.* **1** of or relating to the mind: *mental faculties* | *mental phenomena.* ■ carried out by or taking place in the mind: *a quick mental calculation* | *I started my mental journey.* **2** of, relating to, or suffering from disorders or illnesses of the mind: *a mental hospital.* ■ [*predic.*] *informal* insane; crazy: *every time I'm five minutes late, they* **go mental**. ▷late Middle English: from late Latin *mentalis*, from Latin *mens, ment-* 'mind.' —**men·tal·ly** *adv.*

USAGE The use of **mental** in compounds such as **mental hospital** and **mental patient** is first recorded at the end of the 19th century and was the normal accepted term in the first half of the 20th century. It is still current and standard even though the term **psychiatric** has more recently come to be used in both general and official use.

men·tal age ▸*n.* a person's mental ability expressed as the age at which an average person reaches the same ability: *she was 65 but had a mental age of 2.*

men·tal block ▸*n.* an inability to recall some specific thing or perform some mental action.

men·tal cru·el·ty ▸*n.* conduct that makes another person suffer but does not involve physical assault.

men·tal·ism /ˈmentlˌizəm/ ▸*n. Philosophy* the theory that physical and psychological phenomena are ultimately explicable only in terms of a creative and interpretative mind. —**men·tal·ist** *n.* & *adj.* —**men·tal·is·tic** /ˌmentlˈistik/ *adj.*

men·tal·i·ty /menˈtalitē/ ▸*n.* (*pl.* **-ties**) **1** *often derogatory* the characteristic attitude of mind or way of thinking of a person or group: *the yuppie mentality of the eighties.* **2** the capacity for intelligent thought. ▷late 17th cent. (in the sense 'mental process'): from the adjective MENTAL + -ITY. Current senses date from the mid 19th cent.

men·tal·ly hand·i·capped /ˈmen(t)lē ˈhandēˌkapt/ ▸*adj.* (of a person) having very limited intellectual functions.

men·tal res·er·va·tion ▸*n.* a qualification tacitly added in making a statement, etc.; an unexpressed doubt or criticism.

men·ta·tion /men'tāsHən/ ▸*n. technical* mental activity. ▷mid 19th cent.: from Latin *mens, ment-* 'mind' + **-ATION.**

men·thol /'men,THôl; -,THäl/ ▸*n.* a crystalline compound with a cooling minty taste and odor, found in peppermint and other natural oils. It is used as a flavoring and in decongestants and analgesics. • An alcohol, **2-isopropyl-5-methylcyclohexanol**; chem. formula: $C_{10}H_{19}OH$. ▷late 19th cent.: from German, from Latin *mentha* 'mint' + **-OL.**

men·tho·lat·ed /'menTHə,lātid/ ▸*adj.* treated with or containing menthol: *mentholated shaving creams.*

men·tion /'mencHən/ ▸*v.* [*trans.*] refer to something briefly and without going into detail: *I haven't* ***mentioned it to*** *William yet* | [with *clause*] *I mentioned that my father was meeting me later.* ■ [*trans.*] (often **be mentioned**) make a reference to (someone) as being noteworthy, esp. as a potential candidate for a post: *he is still regularly* ***mentioned as*** *a possible secretary of state.*

▸*n.* a reference to someone or something: *their eyes light up at a mention of Sartre* | *she* ***made no mention of*** *her disastrous trip to Paris.* ■ a formal acknowledgment of something outstanding or noteworthy: *he received a special mention and a prize of $100* | *two other points are worthy of mention.* See also **HONORABLE MENTION.** ▷Middle English (originally in *make mention of*): via Old French from Latin *mentio(n-)*; related to **MIND.** **—men·tion·a·ble** *adj.*

▸*PHRASES* □ **don't mention it** a polite expression used to indicate that an apology or an expression of thanks is not necessary. □ **mention someone in one's will** leave a legacy to someone. □ **not to mention** used to introduce an additional fact or point that reinforces the point being made: *I'm amazed you find the time, not to mention the energy, to do any work at all.*

men·to /'mentō/ ▸*n.* (*pl.* **-tos**) a style of Jamaican folk music based on a traditional dance rhythm in duple time. ▷early 20th cent.: of unknown origin.

men·tor /'men,tôr; -tər/ ▸*n.* an experienced and trusted adviser: *he was her friend and mentor until his death in 1915.* ■ an experienced person in a company, college, or school who trains and counsels new employees or students.

▸*v.* [*trans.*] to advise or train (someone, esp. a younger colleague). ▷mid 18th cent.: via French and Latin from Greek *Mentōr*, the name of the adviser of the young Telemachus in Homer's *Odyssey*. **—men·tor·ship** /-,SHip/ *n.*

men·tum /'mentəm/ ▸*n. Entomology* a part of the base of the labium in some insects. ▷early 19th cent.: from Latin, literally 'chin.'

men·u /'menyoo/ ▸*n.* (*pl.* **men·us**) a list of dishes available in a restaurant: *the waiter handed her a menu* | *figurative politics and sport are on the menu tonight.* ■ the food available or to be served in a restaurant or at a meal: *a no-fuss dinner-party menu.* ■ *Computing* a list of commands or options, esp. one displayed on screen. ▷mid 19th cent.: from French, 'detailed list' (noun use of *menu* 'small, detailed'), from Latin *minutus* 'very small.'

men·u bar ▸*n. Computing* a horizontal bar, typically located at the top of the screen below the title bar, containing drop-down menus.

me·nu·do /mə'noodō/ ▸*n.* (*pl.* **-dos**) a spicy Mexican soup made from tripe. ▷noun use of a Mexican Spanish adjective meaning 'small.'

men·u-driv·en ▸*adj.* (of a program or computer) used by making selections from menus.

Men·u·hin /'menyooin/, Sir Yehudi (1916–99), British violinist; born in the U.S. In 1962, he founded a school of music, which is named after him, in Surrey, England.

Men·zies /'menzēz/, Sir Robert Gordon (1894–1978), Australian statesman; prime minister 1939–41 and 1949–66.

Me·o /mē'ō/ ▸*n.* (*pl.* same or **Me·os**) & *adj.* another term for **HMONG.**

me·ow /mē'ou/ (also **mi·aow**) ▸*n.* the characteristic crying sound of a cat.

▸*v.* [*intrans.*] (of a cat) make such a sound. ▷early 17th cent.: imitative.

mep·a·crine /'mepə,krin; -,krēn/ ▸*n.* another term for **QUINACRINE.** ▷1940s: from *me(thoxy-)* + *p(entane)* + *acr(id)ine.*

me·per·i·dine /mə'perə,dēn; -,din/ ▸*n. Medicine* a synthetic compound used as a painkilling drug, esp. for women in labor. ▷1940s: blend of **METHYL** and **PIPERIDINE.**

Meph·i·stoph·e·les /,mefə'stäfəlēz/ (also **Me·phis·to** /mə'fistō/) ▸*n.* an evil spirit to whom Faust, in the German legend, sold his soul. **—Meph·is·to·phe·le·an** /mə,fistə'fēlēən; ,mefəstə-/ (also **Meph·is·to·phe·li·an**) *adj.*

me·phit·ic /mə'fitik/ ▸*adj.* (esp. of a gas or vapor) foul-smelling; noxious. ▷early 17th cent.: from late Latin *mephiticus*, from *mephitis* 'noxious exhalation.'

me·phi·tis /mə'fītis/ ▸*n.* a noxious gas emanating from something, esp. from the earth. ■ a foul or poisonous stench. ▷early 18th cent.: from Latin.

me·pro·ba·mate /mə'prōbə,māt; ,meprō'ba-/ ▸*n.* a bitter-tasting addictive carbamate used, esp. before the 1970s, as a mild tranquilizer. • Chem. formula: $CH_3CH_2CH_2C(CH_2OCONH_2)_2CH_3$. ▷mid 20th cent.: from *me(thyl)* + *pro(pyl)* + *(car)bamate.*

mer. ▸*abbr.* ■ meridian.

-mer ▸*comb. form* denoting polymers and related kinds of molecule: *elastomer.* ▷from Greek *meros* 'part.'

mer·bro·min /,mər'brōmən/ ▸*n.* a greenish iridescent crystalline compound that dissolves in water to give a red solution used as an antiseptic. It is a fluorescein derivative containing bromine and mercury. ▷1940s: from **MERCURIC** + **BROMO-** + **-IN**[1].

mer·ca·do /mər'kädō/ ▸*n.* (*pl.* **-dos**) (in Spanish-speaking regions) a market. ▷Spanish, from Latin *mercatus* 'market.'

Mer·cal·li scale /mər'kalē/ a twelve-point scale for expressing the local intensity of an earthquake, ranging from I (virtually imperceptible) to XII (total destruction). ▷1920s: named after Giuseppe *Mercalli* (1850–1914), Italian geologist.

mer·can·tile /'mərkən,tēl; -,tīl/ ▸*adj.* of or relating to trade or commerce; commercial: *the shift of wealth to the mercantile classes.* ■ of or relating to mercantilism.

▸*n. dated* a general store: *we walked to the local mercantile.* ▷mid 17th cent.: from French, from Italian, from *mercante* 'merchant.'

mer·can·til·ism /'mərkənti,lizəm; -,tē-; -,tī-/ ▸*n.* belief in the benefits of profitable trading; commercialism. ■ *chiefly historical* the economic theory that trade generates wealth and is stimulated by the accumulation of profitable balances, which a government should encourage by means of protectionism. **—mer·can·til·ist** *n.* & *adj.* **—mer·can·til·is·tic** /,mərkənti'listik; -,tē-; -,tī-/ *adj.*

mer·cap·tan /mər'kap,tan/ ▸*n. Chemistry* another term for **THIOL.** ▷mid 19th cent.: from modern Latin *mer(curium) captan(s)*, literally 'capturing mercury.'

Mer·ca·tor /mər'kātər/, Gerardus (1512–94), Flemish geographer and cartographer, a resident in Germany from 1552; Latinized name of *Gerhard Kremer.* He invented the system of map projection that is named after him.

Mer·ca·tor pro·jec·tion /mər'kātər/ (also **Mer·ca·tor's pro·jec·tion**) ▸*n.* a projection of a map of the world onto a cylinder in such a way that all the parallels of latitude have the same length as the equator, used esp. for marine charts and certain climatological maps.

Mer·ced /mər'sed/ a city in central California, in the San Joaquin Valley; pop. 56,216.

mer·ce·nar·y /'mərsə,nerē/ ▸*adj. derogatory* (of a person or their behavior) primarily concerned with making money at the expense of ethics: *she's nothing but a mercenary little gold digger.*

▸*n.* (*pl.* **-nar·ies**) a professional soldier hired to serve in a foreign army. ■ a person primarily concerned with material reward at the expense of ethics: *the sport's most infamous mercenary.* ▷late Middle English (as a noun): from Latin *mercenarius* 'hireling,' from *merces, merced-* 'reward.' **—mer·ce·nar·i·ness** *n.*

Mer·cer /'mərsər/, Johnny (1909–76), U.S. songwriter; full name *John Herndon Mercer.* He wrote lyrics for hundreds of popular songs, including "Moon River" (1961) and "Days of Wine and Roses" (1962). His Broadway musicals include *Top Banana* (1951) and *Saratoga* (1959).

mer·cer /'mərsər/ ▸*n. Brit., chiefly historical* a dealer in textile fabrics, esp. silks, velvets, and other fine materials. ▷Middle English: from Old French *mercier*, based on Latin *merx, merc-* 'goods.' **—mer·cer·y** *n.*

mer·cer·ize /'mərsə,rīz/ ▸*v.* [*trans.*] [often as *adj.*] (**mercerized**) treat (cotton fabric or thread) under tension with caustic alkali to increase its strength and give it a shiny, silky appearance. ▷mid 19th cent.: from the name of John *Mercer* (died 1866), said to have invented the process, + **-IZE.**

mer·chan·dise ▸*n.* /'mərcHən,dīz; -,dīs/ goods to be bought and sold: *stores that offered an astonishing range of merchandise.* ■ products used to promote a particular movie, popular music group, etc., or linked to a particular fictional character; merchandising.

▸*v.* /'mərcHən,dīz/ (also **mer·chan·dize**) [*trans.*] promote the sale of (goods), esp. by their presentation in retail outlets: *a new breakfast food can easily be merchandised.* ■ advertise or publicize (an idea or person): *they are merchandising "niceness" to children.* ■ *archaic* trade or traffic in (something), esp. inappropriately. ■ [*intrans.*] *archaic* engage in the business of a merchant. ▷late Middle English: from Old French *marchandise*, from *marchand* 'merchant.' **—mer·chan·dis·a·ble** /-,dīzəbəl/ *adj.* **—mer·chan·dis·er** /-,dīzər/ *n.*

mer·chan·dis·ing /'mərcHən,dīziNG/ ▸*n.* the activity of promoting the sale of goods, esp. by their presentation in retail outlets: *problems rooted in overexpansion and poor merchandising.* ■ products used to promote a particular movie, popular music group, etc., or linked to a particular fictional character: *the characters are still popular and found on a wide variety of merchandising.*

Mer·chant /'mərcHənt/, Ismail (1936–), Indian movie producer. In 1961, he partnered with James Ivory to form Merchant Ivory Productions. Together, they have produced movies such as *Shakespeare Wallah* (1965), *The Bostonians* (1984), and *Howard's End* (1992).

mer·chant /'mərcHənt/ ▸*n.* **1** a person or company involved in wholesale trade, esp. one dealing with foreign countries or supplying merchandise to a particular trade: *the area's leading timber merchant* | *a tea merchant.* ■ a retail trader; a store owner: *the credit cards are accepted by 10 million merchants worldwide.* ■ (esp. in historical contexts) a person involved in trade or commerce: *prosperous merchants and clothiers had established a middle class.* **2** [usu. with *adj.*] *informal, chiefly derogatory* a person with a partiality or aptitude for a particular activity or viewpoint: *his driver was no speed merchant* | *a merchant of death.*

▸*adj.* [*attrib.*] of or relating to merchants, trade, or commerce: *the growth of the merchant classes.* ■ (of ships, sailors, or shipping activity) involved with commerce rather than military activity: *a merchant seaman.* ▷Middle English: from Old French *marchant*, based on Latin *mercari* 'to trade,' from *merx, merc-* 'merchandise.'

mer·chant·a·ble /'mərcHəntəbəl/ ▸*adj.* suitable for purchase or sale; marketable: *goods must be of merchantable quality.* ▷late 15th cent.: from the verb *merchant* 'haggle, trade as a merchant,' from Old French *marchander*, from *marchand* 'merchant.'

mer·chant ac·count ▸*n.* a bank account that enables the holder to accept credit cards for payment.

mer·chant·man /'mərcHəntmən/ ▸*n.* (*pl.* **-men**) a ship used in commerce; a vessel of the merchant marine.

mer·chant ma·rine ▸*n.* (often **the merchant marine**) a country's shipping that is involved in commerce and trade, as opposed to military activity.

mer·chant prince ▸*n.* a person involved in trade whose wealth is sufficient to confer political influence.

Mer·ci·a /'mərsH(ē)ə/ a former kingdom in central England. It was established by invading Angles in the 6th century in the border areas between the new Anglo-Saxon settlements in the east and the Celtic regions in the west. **—Mer·ci·an** *adj.* & *n.*

mer·ci·ful /'mərsifəl/ ▸*adj.* showing or exercising mercy: *it was the will of a merciful God that all should be saved.* See note at **LENIENT.** ■ (of an event) coming as a mercy; bringing someone relief from something unpleasant: *her death was a merciful release.* **—mer·ci·ful·ness** *n.*

mer·ci·ful·ly /'mərsif(ə)lē/ ▸*adv.* **1** in a merciful manner. **2** to one's great relief; fortunately: [*sentence adverb*] *mercifully, I was able to complete all I had to do within a few days.*

mer·ci·less /'mərsiləs/ ▸*adj.* showing no mercy or pity: *a merciless attack with a blunt instrument* | *figurative the merciless summer heat.* **—mer·ci·less·ly** *adv.* **—mer·ci·less·ness** *n.*

Merckx /mərks/, Eddy (1945–), Belgian cyclist. During his professional career he won the Tour de France five times (1969–72 and 1974).

Mer·cou·ri /mər'koorē/, Melina (1925–94), Greek actress and politician; born *Anna Amalia Mercouri.* Her movies include *Never on Sunday* (1960) and *Phaedra* (1962). Exiled for opposing the military junta that took power in Greece in 1967, she was elected to Parliament in 1978 and became minister of culture in 1985.

mer·cu·ri·al /mər,kyŏŏrēəl/ ▶*adj.* **1** (of a person) subject to sudden or unpredictable changes of mood or mind: *his mercurial temperament.* ■ (of a person) sprightly; lively. **2** of or containing the element mercury. **3** (**Mercurial**) of the planet Mercury.
▶*n.* (usu. **mercurials**) a drug or other compound containing mercury. ▷late Middle English (sense 3): from Latin *mercurialis* 'relating to the god Mercury,' from *Mercurius* 'Mercury.' Sense 1 dates from the mid 17th cent. **—mer·cu·ri·al·i·ty** /-,kyŏŏrē'alitē/ *n.* **—mer·cu·ri·al·ly** *adv.*

mer·cu·ric /mər,kyŏŏrik/ ▶*adj. Chemistry* of mercury with a valence of two; of mercury(II). Compare with MERCUROUS.

mer·cu·ric chlo·ride ▶*n.* a toxic white crystalline compound, used as a fungicide and antiseptic. • Chem. formula: $HgCl_2$.

Mer·cu·ro·chrome /mə(r)'kyŏŏrə,krōm/ (also **mer·cu·ro·chrome**) ▶*n.* trademark for MERBROMIN. ▷early 20th cent.: from MERCURY[1] + Greek *khrōma* 'color.'

mer·cu·rous /'mərkyərəs/ ▶*adj. Chemistry* of mercury with a valence of one; of mercury(I). Compare with MERCURIC.

mer·cu·rous chlor·ide ▶*n.* another term for CALOMEL.

Mer·cu·ry /'mərkyərē/ **1** *Roman Mythology* the Roman god of eloquence, skill, trading, and thieving, herald and messenger of the gods, who was identified with Hermes. [from Latin *Mercurius*, from *merx, merc-* 'merchandise.'] ■ used in names of newspapers and journals: *the San Jose Mercury News.* **2** *Astronomy* a small planet that is the closest to the sun in the solar system, sometimes visible to the naked eye just after sunset.

Mercury orbits within the orbit of Venus at an average distance of 36 million miles (57.9 million km) from the sun. With a diameter of 3,031 miles (4,878 km), it is only a third larger than earth's moon, which it resembles in having a heavily cratered surface. Its 'day' (equivalent to 58.65 Earth days) is precisely two thirds the length of its 'year' (87.97 Earth days). Daytime temperatures average 338°F (170°C). There is no atmosphere and the planet has no satellites.

3 a series of space missions, launched by the U.S. from 1958 to 1963, that achieved the first U.S. manned spaceflights. **—Mer·cu·ri·an** /mər'kyŏŏrēən/ *adj.*

mer·cu·ry[1] /'mərkyərē/ ▶*n.* the chemical element of atomic number 80, a heavy silvery-white metal that is liquid at ordinary temperatures. (Symbol: **Hg**) Also called QUICKSILVER. ■ the column of such metal in a thermometer or barometer, or its height as indicating atmospheric temperature or pressure: *the mercury rises, the skies steam, and the nights swelter.* ■ *historical* this metal or one of its compounds used medicinally, esp. to treat syphilis. ▷Middle English: from Latin *Mercurius* (see sense 1 of MERCURY).

mer·cu·ry[2] ▶*n.* a plant of the spurge family. • Genera *Mercurialis* and *Acalypha*, family Euphorbiaceae: several species, in particular the poisonous **dog's mercury** (*M. perennis*) of Eurasia and the **three-seeded mercury** (*A. virginica*) of North America. ▷mid 16th cent.: from Latin *mercurialis* 'of the god Mercury.'

mer·cu·ry switch ▶*n.* an electric switch in which the circuit is made by mercury flowing into a gap when the device tilts.

mer·cu·ry va·por lamp (also **mer·cu·ry-va·por lamp**) ▶*n.* a lamp in which light is produced by an electrical discharge through mercury vapor.

mer·cy /'mərsē/ ▶*n.* (*pl.* **-cies**) compassion or forgiveness shown toward someone whom it is within one's power to punish or harm: *the boy was screaming and begging for mercy | the mercies of God.* ■ an event to be grateful for, esp. because its occurrence prevents something unpleasant or provides relief from suffering: *his death was in a way a mercy.* ■ [as *adj.*] (esp. of a journey or mission) performed out of a desire to relieve suffering; motivated by compassion: *mercy missions to refugees caught up in the fighting.*
▶*exclam. archaic* used in expressions of surprise or fear: *"Mercy me!" uttered Mrs. Garfield.* ▷Middle English: from Old French *merci* 'pity' or 'thanks,' from Latin *merces, merced-* 'reward,' in Christian Latin 'pity, favor, heavenly reward.'
▶*PHRASES* □ **at the mercy of** completely in the power or under the control of: *consumers were at the mercy of every rogue in the marketplace.* □ **be thankful** (or **grateful**) **for small mercies** be relieved that an unpleasant situation is alleviated by minor advantages. □ **have mercy on** (or **upon**) show compassion or forgiveness to: *may the Lord have mercy on her soul.* □ **leave someone/something to the mercy of** expose someone or something to a situation of probable danger or harm: *the forest is left to the mercy of the loggers.* □ **throw oneself on someone's mercy** intentionally place oneself in someone's hands in the expectation that they will behave mercifully toward one.

THE RIGHT WORD **benevolence, charity, clemency, compassion, leniency, mercy**

If you want to win friends and influence people, it's best to start with **benevolence**, a general term for goodwill and kindness (*a grandfather's benevolence*).

Charity is even better, suggesting generous giving (*the baker gave him bread out of charity*) but also meaning tolerance and understanding of others (*she viewed his selfish behavior with charity*).

Compassion is a feeling of sympathy or sorrow for someone else's misfortune (*he has shown compassion for the homeless*), and often includes showing **mercy**.

Aside from its religious overtones, *mercy* means compassion or kindness in our treatment of others, especially those who have offended us or who deserve punishment (*mercy toward the pickpocket*).

Clemency is mercy shown by someone whose duty or function it is to administer justice or punish offenses (*the judge granted clemency*), while **leniency** emphasizes gentleness, softness, or lack of severity, even if it isn't quite deserved (*a father's leniency in punishing his young son*).

mer·cy kill·ing ▶*n.* the killing of a patient suffering from an incurable and painful disease, typically by the administration of large doses of painkilling drugs. See also EUTHANASIA. ■ the killing of an animal that is suffering from an incurable and painful disease or from extreme, life-threatening injuries.

merde /me(ə)rd/ ▶*exclam.* a French word for "shit," used as a mild, generally humorous exclamation in English: *Merde! What had she done!*

mere[1] /mi(ə)r/ ▶*adj.* [*attrib.*] that is solely or no more or better than what is specified: *it happened a mere decade ago | questions that cannot be answered by mere mortals.* ■ (**the merest**) the smallest or slightest: *the merest hint of makeup.* ▷late Middle English (in the senses 'pure' and 'sheer, downright'): from Latin *merus* 'undiluted.'

mere[2] ▶*n. chiefly poetic/literary* a lake, pond, or arm of the sea. ▷Old English, of Germanic origin; related to Dutch *meer* 'lake' and German *Meer* 'sea,' from an Indo-European root shared by Russian *more* and Latin *mare.*

Mer·e·dith /'merədiᴛʜ/, James Howard (1933–), U.S. civil rights activist. In 1962, he became the first African American to attend the University of Mississippi after 3,000 troops quelled riots. He wrote *Three Years in Mississippi* (1966) and *Mississippi: A Volume of Eleven Books* (1995).

mere·ly /'mi(ə)rlē/ ▶*adv.* just; only: *she seemed to him not merely an intelligent woman, but a kind of soul mate.*

me·ren·gue /mə'reɴɢgā/ ▶*n.* a Caribbean style of dance music typically in duple and triple time, chiefly associated with Dominica and Haiti. ■ a style of dancing associated with such music, with alternating long and short stiff-legged steps. ▷late 19th cent.: probably American Spanish; compare perhaps with the sense 'upheaval, disorder,' attested in Argentina, Paraguay, and Uruguay.

mer·e·tri·cious /merə'trisʜəs/ ▶*adj.* **1** apparently attractive but having in reality no value or integrity: *meretricious souvenirs for the tourist trade.* **2** *archaic* of, relating to, or characteristic of a prostitute. ▷early 17th cent.: from Latin *meretricius* (adjective from *meretrix, meretric-* 'prostitute,' from *mereri* 'be hired') + -OUS. **—mer·e·tri·cious·ly** *adv.* **—mer·e·tri·cious·ness** *n.*

mer·gan·ser /mər'gansər/ ▶*n.* a fish-eating diving duck with a long, thin serrated and hooked bill. Also called SAWBILL. • Genus *Mergus*, subfamily Merginae, family Anatidae: six species, including the conspicuously crested **red-breasted merganser** (*M. serrator*); **common merganser** (*M. merganser*), the male of which has a white body and dark green head; and smew. ▷mid 17th cent.: modern Latin, from Latin *mergus* 'diver' (from *mergere* 'to dive') + *anser* 'goose.'

merge /mərj/ ▶*v.* combine or cause to combine to form a single entity: [*intrans.*] *the utility companies are cutting costs and* **merging with** *other companies* | [*trans.*] *the company plans to merge its U.S. oil production operations* **with** *those of a London-based organization.* | *the files were merged using the patient identification code as the common variable.* ■ incorporate revisions to a document to supersede the original: [*trans.*] *if you answer "no" your changes will not be merged.* ■ [*intrans.*] blend or fade gradually into something else so as to become indistinguishable from it: *he crouched low and endeavored to merge into the darkness of the forest.* ■ [*trans.*] cause to blend or fade into something else in such a way. ▷mid 17th cent. (in the sense 'immerse (oneself)'): from Latin *mergere* 'to dip, plunge.' The use in legal contexts is from Anglo-Norman French *merger.*

merg·er /'mərjər/ ▶*n.* a combination of two things, esp. companies, into one: *a* **merger between** *two supermarket chains* | | *local companies ripe for merger or acquisition.* ▷early 18th cent.: from Anglo-Norman French *merger* (verb used as a noun): see MERGE.

Me·riç /mə'rēᴄʜ/ Turkish name for MARITSA.

Mé·ri·da /'meridə; 'mārē,dä/ a city in southeastern Mexico, capital of the state of Yucatán; pop. 557,000.

Mer·i·den /'merid(ə)n/ an industrial city in south central Connecticut; pop. 58,244.

Me·rid·i·an /mə'ridēən/ **1** a city in southwestern Idaho, west of Boise; pop. 34,919. **2** a city in eastern Mississippi; pop. 39,968.

me·rid·i·an /mə'ridēən/ ▶*n.* **1** a circle of constant longitude passing through a given place on the earth's surface and the terrestrial poles. ■ (also **celestial meridian**) *Astronomy* a circle passing through the celestial poles and the zenith of a given place on the earth's surface. **2** (in acupuncture and Chinese medicine) each of a set of pathways in the body along which vital energy is said to flow. There are twelve such pathways associated with specific organs.
▶*adj.* [*attrib.*] relating to or situated at a meridian: *the meridian moon.* ■ *poetic/literary* of noon. ■ *poetic/literary* of the period of greatest splendor, vigor, etc. ▷late Middle English: from Old French *meridien*, from Latin *meridianum* (neuter, used as a noun) 'noon,' from *medius* 'middle' + *dies* 'day.' The use in astronomy is due to the fact that the sun crosses a meridian at noon.

me·rid·i·an cir·cle ▶*n. Astronomy* a telescope mounted so as to move only on a north–south line, for observing the transit of celestial objects across the meridian.

me·rid·i·o·nal /mə'ridēənəl/ ▶*adj.* **1** of or in the south; southern: *the meridional leg of the journey.* ■ relating to or characteristic of the inhabitants of southern Europe, esp. the south of France: *she was meridional in temperament.* **2** of or relating to a meridian: *the meridional line of demarcation.* ■ *Meteorology* (chiefly of winds and air flow) aligned with lines of longitude.
▶*n.* a native or inhabitant of the south, esp. the south of France. ▷late Middle English: via Old French from late Latin *meridionalis*, formed irregularly from Latin *meridies* 'midday, south.'

me·ringue /mə'raɴɢ/ ▶*n.* an item of sweet food made from a mixture of well-beaten egg whites and sugar, baked until crisp and typically used as a topping for desserts, esp. pies. Individual meringues are often filled with fruit or whipped cream. ▷from French, of unknown origin.

me·ri·no /mə'rēnō/ ▶*n.* (*pl.* **-nos**) (also **me·ri·no sheep**) a sheep of a breed with long, fine wool. ■ a soft woolen or wool-and-cotton material resembling cashmere, originally of merino wool. ■ a fine woolen yarn. ▷late 18th cent.: from Spanish, of unknown origin.

mer·i·stem /'merə,stem/ ▶*n. Botany* a region of plant tissue, found chiefly at the growing tips of roots and shoots and in the cambium, consisting of actively dividing cells forming new tissue. ▷late 19th cent.: formed irregularly from Greek *meristos* 'divisible,' from *merizein* 'divide into parts,' from *meros* 'part.' The suffix *-em* is on the pattern of words such as *xylem.* **—mer·i·ste·mat·ic** /merəstə'matik/ *adj.*

mer·it /'merit/ ▶*n.* the quality of being particularly good or worthy, esp. so as to deserve praise or reward: *composers of outstanding merit.* ■ a feature or fact that deserves praise or reward: *the relative merits of both approaches have to be considered.* ■ *Brit.* a pass grade in an examination denoting above-average performance: *if you expect to pass, why not go for a merit or a distinction?* Compare with DISTINCTION. ■ (**merits**) *chiefly Law* the intrinsic rights and wrongs of a case,

M

outside of any other considerations: *a plaintiff who has a good arguable case* ***on the merits.*** ■ **(merits)** *Theology* good deeds regarded as entitling someone to a future reward from God.

▸*v.* **(mer·it·ed, mer·it·ing)** [*trans.*] deserve or be worthy of (something, esp. reward, punishment, or attention): *the results have been encouraging enough to merit further investigation.* ▷Middle English (originally in the sense 'deserved reward or punishment'): via Old French from Latin *meritum* 'due reward,' from *mereri* 'earn, deserve.'

▸*PHRASE* □ **judge** (or **consider**) **something on its merits** assess something solely with regard to its intrinsic quality rather than other external factors.

mer·i·toc·ra·cy /ˌmeriˈtäkrəsē/ ▸*n.* (*pl.* **-cies**) government or the holding of power by people selected on the basis of their ability. ■ a society governed by such people or in which such people hold power. ■ a ruling or influential class of educated or skilled people. **—mer·i·to·crat·ic** /ˌmeritəˈkratik/ *adj.*

mer·i·to·ri·ous /ˌmeriˈtôrēəs/ ▸*adj.* deserving reward or praise: *a medal for meritorious conduct.* ■ *Law* (of an action or claim) likely to succeed on the merits of the case. ▷late Middle English (in the sense 'entitling a person to reward'): from Latin *meritorius* (from *merit-* 'earned,' from the verb *mereri*) + **-OUS**. **—mer·i·to·ri·ous·ly** *adv.* **—mer·i·to·ri·ous·ness** *n.*

mer·kin /ˈmərkən/ ▸*n.* an artificial covering of hair for the pubic area. ▷early 17th cent.: apparently a variant of dialect *malkin*, diminutive of *Malde* (early form of the given name *Maud*).

merle /ˈmərl/ (also **merl**) ▸*n.* *Scottish* or *archaic* a blackbird. ▷late Middle English: via Old French from Latin *merula*.

Mer·lin /ˈmərlən/ (in Arthurian legend) a magician who aided and supported King Arthur.

mer·lin ▸*n.* a small dark falcon that hunts small birds, found throughout most of Eurasia and much of North America. Also called **PIGEON HAWK**. • *Falco columbarius*, family Falconidae. ▷late Middle English: from Anglo-Norman French *merilun*, from Old French *esmerillon*, augmentative of *esmeril*, of Germanic origin; related to German *Schmerl*.

mer·lon /ˈmərlən/ ▸*n.* the solid part of an embattled parapet between two embrasures. ▷early 18th cent.: from French, from Italian *merlone*, from *merlo* 'battlement.'

Mer·lot /mərˈlō/ (also **mer·lot**) ▸*n.* a variety of black wine grape originally from the Bordeaux region of France. ■ a red wine made from this grape. ▷French.

mer·maid /ˈmərˌmād/ ▸*n.* a fictitious or mythical half-human sea creature with the head and trunk of a woman and the tail of a fish, conventionally depicted as beautiful and with long flowing golden hair. ▷Middle English: from **MERE**[2] (in the obsolete sense 'sea') + **MAID**.

mer·maid's purse ▸*n.* the horny egg case of a skate, ray, or small shark.

Mer·man /ˈmərmən/, Ethel (1908–1984), U.S. singer and actress; born Ethel Zimmerman. The "queen of Broadway" for three decades, she performed in many plays and musicals, including *Annie Get Your Gun* (1946), *Call Me Madam* (1950), *Gypsy* (1959), and *Hello, Dolly!* (1970).

mer·man /ˈmərˌman; -mən/ ▸*n.* (*pl.* **-men**) the male equivalent of a mermaid.

mero- ▸*comb. form* partly; partial: *meronym*. Often contrasted with **HOMO-**. ▷from Greek *meros* 'part.'

Mer·oe /ˈmerōˌē/ an ancient city on the Nile River, in present-day Sudan northeast of Khartoum. Founded in *c.*750 BC, it was the capital of the ancient kingdom of Cush from *c.*590 BC until it fell to the invading Aksumites in the early 4th century AD. **—Mer·o·it·ic** /ˌmerōˈitik/ *adj.* & *n.*

mer·o·nym /ˈmerəˌnim/ ▸*n.* *Linguistics* a term that denotes part of something but which is used to refer to the whole of it, e.g., *faces* when used to mean *people* in *I see several familiar faces present.* ▷from Greek *meros* 'part' + *onuma* 'name.' **—meronymy** /məˈränəmē/ *n.*

-merous ▸*comb. form Biology* having a specified number of parts: *pentamerous.* ▷on the pattern of words such as *(di)merous* (see also **-MER**).

Mer·o·vin·gi·an /ˌmerəˈvinj(ē)ən/ ▸*adj.* of or relating to the Frankish dynasty founded by Clovis and reigning in Gaul and Germany *c.*500–750.

▸*n.* a member of this dynasty. ▷from French *mérovingien*, from medieval Latin *Merovingi* 'descendants of Merovich' (Clovis' grandfather, semilegendary 5th-cent. Frankish leader).

mer·ri·ly /ˈmerəlē/ ▸*adv.* **1** in a cheerful way. ■ in a brisk and lively way: *a fire burned merrily in the hearth.* **2** without consideration of possible problems or future implications: *no candidate can denounce high public spending while merrily buying local votes with the taxpayers' money.*

Mer·ri·mack /ˈmerəˌmak/ a town in southern New Hampshire; pop. 25,119.

Mer·ri·mack Riv·er a river that flows for 110 miles (180 km) from New Hampshire through eastern Massachusetts to the Atlantic Ocean.

mer·ri·ment /ˈmerēmənt/ ▸*n.* gaiety and fun: *her eyes sparkled with merriment.*

mer·ry /ˈmerē/ ▸*adj.* **(mer·ri·er, mer·ri·est)** cheerful and lively: *the narrow streets were dense with merry throngs of students* | *a merry grin.* ■ (of an occasion or season) characterized by festivity and rejoicing: *he wished me a merry Christmas.* ■ [*predic.*] *Brit., informal* slightly and good-humoredly drunk: *after the third bottle of beer he began to feel quite merry.* ▷Old English *myrige* 'pleasing, delightful,' of Germanic origin; related to **MIRTH**. **—mer·ri·ness** *n.*

▸*PHRASES* □ **go on one's merry way** *informal* carry on with a course of action regardless of the consequences. □ **make merry** enjoy oneself with others, esp. by dancing and drinking. □ **the more the merrier** the more people or things there are, the better or more enjoyable a situation will be.

mer·ry-an·drew /ˈanˌdro͞o/ ▸*n.* *archaic* a person who entertains others by means of comic antics; a clown.

mer·ry-go-round ▸*n.* a revolving machine with model horses or other animals on which people ride for amusement. ■ a large revolving device in a playground, for children to ride on. ■ *figurative* a continuous cycle of activities or events, esp. when perceived as having no purpose or producing no result: *the football management merry-go-round.*

mer·ry·mak·ing /ˈmerēˌmākiNG/ ▸*n.* the process of enjoying oneself with others, esp. by dancing and drinking. **—mer·ry·mak·er** /-ˌmākər/ *n.*

mer·ry·thought /ˈmerēˌTHôt/ ▸*n.* *dated, chiefly Brit.* the wishbone of a bird.

Mer·sa Ma·truh /ˈmərsə məˈtro͞o/ a town on the Mediterranean coast of Egypt, 156 miles (250 km) west of Alexandria; pop. 113,000.

Mer·senne num·ber /mərˈsen/ ▸*n.* *Mathematics* a number of the form $2^n - 1$, where *n* is a prime number. Such a number which is itself prime is also called a **Mersenne prime**. ▷late 19th cent.: named after Marin *Mersenne* (1588–1648), French mathematician.

Mer·sey /ˈmərzē/ a river in northwestern England that rises in the county of Derbyshire and flows 70 miles (112 km) to the Irish Sea near Liverpool.

Mer·sin /merˈsēn/ an industrial port in southern Turkey, on the Mediterranean Sea, southwest of Adana; pop. 422,000.

Mer·ton /ˈmərtn/, Thomas (James) (1915–68), U.S. Roman Catholic monk and writer; born in France. He was ordained 1949 as Father Louis in the Trappist order. His works include *The Seven Storey Mountain* (1948).

Me·sa /ˈmāsə/ a city in south central Arizona, east of Phoenix; pop. 396,375.

me·sa /ˈmāsə/ ▸*n.* an isolated flat-topped hill with steep sides, found in landscapes with horizontal strata. ▷mid 18th cent.: Spanish, literally 'table,' from Latin *mensa*.

Me·sa·bi Range /məˈsäbē/ low hills in northeastern Minnesota, site of one of the largest iron sources in the world.

mé·sal·li·ance /ˌmāzəˈlīəns; ˌmāˌzalˈyäNs/ ▸*n.* a marriage with a person thought to be unsuitable or of a lower social position. ▷French, from *més-* 'wrong, misdirected' + *alliance* (see **ALLIANCE**).

Me·sa Ver·de /ˈmāsə ˈvərdē/ a high plateau in southern Colorado, with the remains of many prehistoric Pueblo Indian dwellings. ▷Spanish, literally 'green table(land).'

mes·cal /meˈskal; mə-/ ▸*n.* **1** another term for **MAGUEY**. ■ an intoxicating liquor distilled from the sap of an agave. Compare with **TEQUILA, PULQUE**. **2** another term for **PEYOTE**. ▷early 18th cent.: from Spanish *mezcal*, from Nahuatl *mexcalli*.

mes·cal but·tons ▸*plural n.* another term for **PEYOTE BUTTONS**.

Mes·ca·le·ro /ˌmeskəˈle(ə)rō/ ▸*n.* (*pl.* same or **-ros**) **1** a member of an American Indian people of New Mexico. **2** the Athabaskan (Apache) language of this people.

▸*adj.* of or relating to this people or their language.

▷Spanish, literally 'people of the mescal,' with reference to their traditional use of the flesh of the mescal plant as part of their staple diet.

mes·ca·line /ˈmeskəlin; -ˌlēn/ ▸*n.* a hallucinogenic and intoxicating compound present in mescal buttons from the peyote cactus. • Alternative name: **3,4,5-trimethoxyphenethylamine**; chem. formula: $(CH_3O)_3C_6H_2CH_2CH_2NH_2$.

mes·clun /ˈmesklən/ (also **mesclun salad**) ▸*n.* a salad made from a selection of lettuces with other edible leaves such as dandelion greens, mustard greens, and radicchio. ▷Provençal, literally 'mixture,' from *mesclar* 'mix thoroughly.'

Mes·dames /māˈdäm/ ▸*plural n.* **1** plural form of **MADAME**. **2** *formal* used as a title to refer to more than one woman simultaneously: *prizes were won by Mesdames Carter, Roseby, and Barrington.*

Mes·de·moi·selles /ˈmādəm(w)əˌzel; ˈmādˌmwäˌzel/ ▸ plural form of **MADEMOISELLE**.

me·sem·bry·an·the·mum /məˌzembrēˈanTHəməm/ ▸*n.* a fleshy succulent plant of the carpetweed family, often with showy flowers. Several varieties are grown as ornamentals. • *Mesembryanthemum* and related genera (esp. *Carpobrotus*), family Aizoaceae. ▷modern Latin, based on Greek *mesēmbria* 'noon' + *anthemon* 'flower.'

mes·en·ceph·a·lon /ˌmezˌenˈsefəˌlän; ˌmes-; -lən/ ▸*n.* *Anatomy* another term for **MIDBRAIN**. ▷mid 19th cent.: from Greek *mesos* 'middle' + **ENCEPHALON**. **—mes·en·ce·phal·ic** /-ˌensəˈfalik/ *adj.*

mes·en·chyme /ˈmezənˌkīm; ˈmes-/ ▸*n.* *Embryology* a loosely organized, mainly mesodermal embryonic tissue that develops into connective and skeletal tissues, including blood and lymph. ▷late 19th cent.: from Greek *mesos* 'middle' + *enkhuma* 'infusion.' **—mes·en·chy·mal** /ˌmezˌenˈkīməl; ˌmes-/ *adj.*

mes·en·ter·on /meˈzenteˌrän; məˈsent-/ ▸*n.* *Zoology* the middle section of the intestine, esp. in an embryo or in an arthropod. ▷late 19th cent.: from Greek *mesos* 'middle' + *enteron* 'intestine.' **—mes·en·ter·on·ic** /-ˌzentəˈränik; -ˌsent-/ *adj.*

mes·en·ter·y /ˈmezənˌterē; ˈmes-/ ▸*n.* (*pl.* **-ter·ies**) *Anatomy* a fold of the peritoneum that attaches the stomach, small intestine, pancreas, spleen, and other organs to the posterior wall of the abdomen. ▷late Middle English: via medieval Latin from Greek *mesenterion*, from *mesos* 'middle' + *enteron* 'intestine.' **—mes·en·ter·ic** /ˌmezənˈterik; ˌmes-/ *adj.*

mesh /mesH/ ▸*n.* **1** material made of a network of wire or thread: *mesh for fishing nets* | *finer wire meshes are used for smaller particles.* ■ the spacing of the strands of such material: *if the mesh is too big, small rabbits can squeeze through.* **2** an interlaced structure: *cell fragments that agglutinate and form intricate meshes.* ■ [*in sing.*] *figurative* used with reference to a complex or constricting situation: *the raveled mesh of events and her own emotions.* ■ *Computing* a set of finite elements used to represent a geometric object for modeling or analysis. ■ *Computing* a computer network in which each computer or processor is connected to a number of others, esp. as an n-dimensional lattice.

▸*v.* **1** [*intrans.*] (of the teeth of a gearwheel) lock together or be engaged with another gearwheel: *one gear* ***meshes with*** *the input gear.* ■ make or become entangled or entwined: [*intrans.*] *their fingers meshed* | [*trans.*] *I don't want to get meshed in the weeds.* ■ *figurative* be in or bring into harmony: [*intrans.*] *her memory of events doesn't* ***mesh with*** *the world around her.* **2** [*trans.*] represent (a geometric object) as a set of finite elements for computational analysis or modeling. ▷late Middle English: probably from an unrecorded Old English word related to (and perhaps reinforced in Middle English by) Middle Dutch *maesche*, of Germanic origin. **—meshed** *adj.* **—mesh·y** *adj.*

▸*PHRASE* □ **in mesh** (of the teeth of gearwheels) engaged.

Me·shed variant of **MASHHAD**.

me·shu·ga /məˈSHo͝ogə/ (also **me·shug·ga** or **me·shu·gah**) ▸*adj.* *informal* (of a person) mad; idiotic: *either a miracle is taking place, or we're all meshuga.* ▷late 19th cent.: from Yiddish *meshuge*, from Hebrew.

me·shu·gaas /məSHo͝ogˈäs/ ▸*n.* *informal* mad or idiotic ideas or behavior: *there's method in this man's meshugaas.* ▷early 20th cent.: Yiddish, noun from **MESHUGA**.

me·shug·ga·na /məˈshoogənə/ (also **me·shug·ge·ner** or **me·shu·ge·nah**) ▶*n. informal* a mad or idiotic person. ▷early 20th cent.: variant of MESHUGA.

me·si·al /ˈmezēəl/ ▶*adj. Anatomy* of, in, or directed toward the middle line of a body. ▷early 19th cent.: formed irregularly from Greek *mesos* 'middle' + -IAL. **—me·si·al·ly** *adv.*

mes·ic[1] /ˈmezik; ˈmē-/ ▶*adj. Ecology* (of an environment or habitat) containing a moderate amount of moisture. Compare with HYDRIC and XERIC. ▷1920s: from Greek *mesos* 'middle' + -IC.

mes·ic[2] ▶*adj. Physics* of or relating to a meson. ■ denoting a system analogous to an atom in which a meson takes the place of either an orbital electron or the nucleus.

Mes·mer /ˈmesmər; ˈmez-/, Franz Anton (1734–1815), Austrian physician. He is noted for introducing a therapeutic technique involving hypnotism.

mes·mer·ic /mezˈmerik/ ▶*adj.* causing a person to become completely transfixed and unaware of anything else around them: *she found herself staring into his mesmeric gaze.* ■ *archaic* of, relating to, or produced by mesmerism. **—mes·mer·i·cal·ly** *adv.*

mes·mer·ism /ˈmezməˌrizəm/ ▶*n. historical* the therapeutic system of F. A. Mesmer. ■ (in general use) hypnotism. ▷late 18th cent.: named after F. A. MESMER. **—mes·mer·ist** /-ist/ *n.*

mes·mer·ize /ˈmezməˌrīz/ ▶*v.* [*trans.*] (often **be mesmerized**) hold the attention of (someone) to the exclusion of all else or so as to transfix them: *she was mesmerized by the blue eyes that stared so intently into her own* | [as *adj.*] (**mesmerizing**) *a mesmerizing stare.* ■ *archaic* hypnotize (someone). **—mes·mer·i·za·tion** /ˌmezmərəˈzāshən/ *n.* **—mes·mer·iz·er** *n.* **—mes·mer·iz·ing·ly** *adv.*

mesne /mēn/ ▶*adj. Law* intermediate. ▷late Middle English (as adverb and noun): from legal French, variant of Anglo-Norman French *meen* 'middle' (see MEAN[3]).

mesne prof·its ▶*plural n. Law* the profits of an estate received by a tenant in wrongful possession and recoverable by the landlord.

meso- ▶*comb. form* middle; intermediate: *mesomorph.* ▷from Greek *mesos* 'middle.'

Mes·o·A·mer·i·ca /ˈmezō; ˈmesō/ the central region of America, from central Mexico to Nicaragua, esp. as a region of ancient civilizations and native cultures before the arrival of the Spanish. **—Mes·o·A·mer·i·can** *adj.* & *n.*

mes·o·blast /ˈmezəˌblast; ˈmē-/ ▶*n. Embryology* the mesoderm of an embryo in its earliest stages. **—mes·o·blas·tic** /ˌmezəˈblastik; ˌmē-/ *adj.*

mes·o·carp /ˈmezəˌkärp; ˈmē-/ ▶*n. Botany* the middle layer of the pericarp of a fruit, between the endocarp and the exocarp.

mes·o·ce·phal·ic /ˈmezəsəˈfalik; ˌmē-/ ▶*adj. Anatomy* having a head of medium proportions, not markedly brachycephalic or dolichocephalic. **—mes·o·ceph·al·y** /-ˈsefəlē/ *n.*

mes·o·cy·clone /ˌmezəˈsīklōn; ˌmesə-; ˌmēzə-; ˌmēsə-/ ▶*Meteorology n.* a cyclonic air mass associated with a supercell; its presence is a condition for a tornado warning. ▷late 20th cent.

mes·o·derm /ˈmezəˌdərm; ˈmē-/ ▶*n. Embryology* the middle layer of an embryo in early development, between the endoderm and ectoderm. ▷late 19th cent.: from MESO- 'middle' + Greek *derma* 'skin.' **—mes·o·der·mal** /ˌmezəˈdəməl; mē-/ *adj.* **—mes·o·der·mic** /-ˈdərmik/ *adj.*

mes·o·gas·tri·um /ˌmezəˈgastrēəm; ˌmē-/ ▶*n.* (*pl.* **-tri·a** /-trēə/) *Anatomy* the middle region of the abdomen between the epigastrium and the hypogastrium. ▷mid 19th cent.: modern Latin, from MESO- 'middle' + Greek *gastēr, gastr-* 'stomach.' **—mes·o·gas·tric** /-trik/ *adj.*

mes·o·kur·tic /ˌmezəˈkərtik; ˌmē-/ ▶*adj. Statistics* (of a frequency distribution or its graphical representation) having the same kurtosis as the normal distribution. Compare with LEPTOKURTIC, PLATYKURTIC. ▷early 20th cent.: from MESO- 'middle' + Greek *kurtos* 'bulging' + -IC. **—mes·o·kur·to·sis** /ˌmezəkərˈtōsis; ˌmē-/ *n.*

mes·o·lect /ˈmezəˌlekt; ˈmesə-; ˈmēzə-; ˈmēsə-/ ▶*n.* (relative to the acrolect and the basilect) an intermediate dialect or variety of a particular language (used esp. in the study of Creoles). **—mes·o·lec·tal** /ˌmezəˈlektəl; ˌmesə-; ˌmēzə-; ˌmēsə-/ *adj.*

Mes·o·lith·ic /ˌmezəˈlithik; ˌmē-/ ▶*adj. Archaeology* of, relating to, or denoting the middle part of the Stone Age, between the Paleolithic and Neolithic. ■ [as *n.*] (**the Mesolithic**) the Mesolithic period. Also called MIDDLE STONE AGE.

In Europe, the Mesolithic falls between the end of the last glacial period (*c.*8500 BC) and the beginnings of agriculture. Mesolithic people lived by hunting, gathering, and fishing, and the period is characterized by the use of microliths and the first domestication of an animal (the dog).

▷mid 19th cent.: from MESO- 'middle' + Greek *lithos* 'stone' + -IC.

me·som·er·ism /məˈsäməˌrizəm; -ˈzä-/ ▶*n. Chemistry* old-fashioned term for RESONANCE. **—mes·o·mer·ic** /ˌmezəˈmerik; ˌmes-/ *adj.*

mes·o·morph /ˈmezəˌmôrf; ˈmē-/ ▶*n. Physiology* a person with a compact and muscular body build. Compare with ECTOMORPH and ENDOMORPH. ▷1920s: *meso-* from *mesodermal* (being the layer of the embryo giving rise to physical characteristics that predominate) + -MORPH. **—mes·o·mor·phic** /ˌmezəˈmôrfik; ˌmē-/ *adj.*

me·son /ˈmezˌän; ˈmāˌzän; ˈmēˌzän/ ▶*n. Physics* a subatomic particle that is intermediate in mass between an electron and a proton and transmits the strong interaction that binds nucleons together in the atomic nucleus. ▷1930s: from MESO- 'intermediate' + -ON. **—me·son·ic** /meˈzänik; mā-; mē-/ *adj.*

mes·o·pause /ˈmezəˌpôz; ˈmē-/ ▶*n.* the boundary in the earth's atmosphere between the mesosphere and the thermosphere, at which the temperature stops decreasing with increasing height and begins to increase.

mes·o·pe·lag·ic /ˌmezəpəˈlajik; ˌmē-/ ▶*adj. Biology* (of fish and other organisms) inhabiting the intermediate depths of the sea, approximately 650–3,300 feet (200–1,000 m) below the surface.

mes·o·phyll /ˈmezəˌfil; ˈmē-/ ▶*n. Botany* the inner tissue (parenchyma) of a leaf, containing many chloroplasts. ▷mid 19th cent.: from MESO- 'middle' + Greek *phullon* 'leaf.' **—mes·o·phyl·lic** /ˌmezəˈfilik; ˌmē-/ *adj.* **—mes·o·phyl·lous** /ˌmezəˈfiləs; ˌmē-/ *adj.*

mes·o·phyte /ˈmezəˌfīt; ˈmē-/ ▶*n. Botany* a plant needing only a moderate amount of water. **—mes·o·phyt·ic** /ˌmezəˈfitik; ˌmē-/ *adj.*

Mes·o·po·ta·mi·a /ˌmesəpəˈtāmēə/ an ancient region of southwestern Asia in present-day Iraq, lying between the Tigris and Euphrates rivers. Its alluvial plains were the site of the civilizations of Akkad, Sumer, Babylonia, and Assyria. ▷from Greek *mesos* "middle" + *potamos* "river." **—Mes·o·po·ta·mi·an** *adj.* & *n.*

mes·o·saur /ˈmezəˌsôr; ˈmē-/ (also **mes·o·sau·rus** /ˌmezəˈsôrəs/) ▶*n.* an extinct small aquatic reptile of the early Permian period, with an elongated body, flattened tail, and a long narrow snout with numerous needlelike teeth. • Genus *Mesosaurus*, order Mesosauria, subclass Anapsida. ▷1950s: modern Latin, from Greek *mesos* 'middle' + *sauros* 'lizard.' **—mes·o·sau·ri·an** *adj.*

mes·o·scale /ˈmezəˌskāl; ˈmē-/ ▶*n. chiefly Meteorology* an intermediate scale, esp. that between the scales of weather systems and of microclimates, on which storms and other phenomena occur.

mes·o·sphere /ˈmezəˌsfi(ə)r; ˈmē-/ ▶*n.* the region of the earth's atmosphere above the stratosphere and below the thermosphere, between about 30 and 50 miles (50 and 80 km) in altitude. **—mes·o·spher·ic** /ˌmezəˈsfi(ə)rik; ˌmē-/ *adj.*

mes·o·the·li·o·ma /ˈmezəˌthēlēˈōmə; ˌmē-/ ▶*n.* (*pl.* **-mas** or **-ma·ta**) *Medicine* a cancer of mesothelial tissue, associated esp. with exposure to asbestos.

mes·o·the·li·um /ˌmezəˈthēlēəm; ˌmē-/ ▶*n.* (*pl.* **-the·li·a** /-ˈthēlēə/) *Anatomy* the epithelium that lines the pleurae, peritoneum, and pericardium. ■ *Embryology* the surface layer of the embryonic mesoderm, from which this is derived. ▷late 19th cent.: from MESO- 'middle' + a shortened form of EPITHELIUM. **—mes·o·the·li·al** /-ˈthēlēəl/ *adj.*

mes·o·tho·rax /ˌmezəˈthôrˌaks/ ▶*n.* (*pl.* **-tho·rax·es** or **-tho·ra·ces** /-ˈthôrəˌsēz/) *Entomology* the middle segment of the thorax of an insect, bearing the forewings or elytra. **—mes·o·tho·rac·ic** /-thəˈrasik/ *adj.*

mes·o·zo·an /ˌmezəˈzōən; ˌmē-/ ▶*n. Zoology* a minute worm that is an internal parasite of marine invertebrates. It lacks any internal organs other than reproductive cells, and dissolved nutrients are absorbed directly from the host's tissues. • Phyla Orthonectida and Rhombozoa; formerly placed together in the phylum Mesozoa, which was thought to be intermediate between protozoans and metazoans. ▷early 20th cent.: from modern Latin *Mesozoa* (from *mesos* 'middle' + *zōion* 'animal') + -AN.

Mes·o·zo·ic /ˈmezəˈzōik; ˌmē-/ ▶*adj. Geology* of, relating to, or denoting the era between the Paleozoic and Cenozoic eras, comprising the Triassic, Jurassic, and Cretaceous periods. ■ [as *n.*] (**the Mesozoic**) the Mesozoic era or the system of rocks deposited during it.

The Mesozoic lasted from about 245 million to 65 million years ago. Large reptiles were dominant on land and sea throughout this time; vegetation had become abundant, and the first mammals, birds, and flowering plants appeared.

▷mid 19th cent.: from MESO- 'intermediate' + Greek *zōion* 'animal' (referring to the appearance of the first mammals) + -IC.

Mes·quite /məˈskēt/ a city in northeastern Texas, east of Dallas; pop. 101,484.

mes·quite /meˈskēt/ ▶*n.* a spiny tree or shrub of the pea family, native to arid regions of southwestern U.S. and Mexico. It yields useful timber, tanbark, medicinal products, and edible pods.The timber is used for fencing and flooring, and burned in barbecues as flavoring. • Genus *Prosopis*, family Leguminosae: several species, in particular *P. glandulosa*. ▷mid 18th cent.: from Mexican Spanish *mezquite*.

mes·quite bean ▶*n.* an edible pod from the mesquite that can be eaten whole, used to produce flour, or fed to animals.

mess /mes/ ▶*n.* [usu. in *sing.*] **1** a dirty or untidy state of things or of a place: *she made a mess of the kitchen* | *my hair was a mess.* ■ a thing or collection of things causing such a state: *she replaced the jug and mopped up the mess.* ■ a person who is dirty or untidy: *I look a mess.* ■ a portion of semisolid or pulpy food, esp. one that looks unappetizing: *a mess of mashed black beans and rice.* ■ [with *adj.*] used euphemistically to refer to the excrement of a domestic animal: *dog mess.* ■ *figurative* a situation or state of affairs that is confused or full of difficulties: *the economy is still in a terrible mess.* ■ *figurative* a person whose life or affairs are confused or troubled: *he needs treatment of some kind—he's a real mess.* **2** a building or room in which members of the armed forces take their meals; mess hall: *the sergeants' mess.* ■ a meal taken there.

▶*v.* **1** [*trans.*] make untidy or dirty: *you've **messed up** my beautiful carpet.* ■ [*intrans.*] (of a domestic animal) defecate: *they had some problems with dogs messing in the store.* ■ make dirty by defecating: *he feared he would mess the bed.* **2** [*intrans.*] take one's meals in a particular place or with a particular person, esp. in an armed forces' mess: *I messed at first with Harry, who was to become a lifelong friend* | *they messed together.*

▶*phrasal v.* □ **mess around/about** behave in a silly or playful way, esp. so as to cause irritation. ■ spend time doing something in a pleasantly desultory way, with no definite purpose or serious intent: *messing about in boats.* □ **mess around/about with** interfere with: *we don't want outsiders messing around with our schools.* ■ *informal* engage in a sexual relationship with (someone, esp. the partner of another person). □ **mess up** *informal* mishandle a situation: *he singled out the health care fiasco as an example of how the government has messed up.* □ **mess someone up** *informal* cause someone emotional or psychological problems: *I was unhappy and really messed up.* ■ inflict violence or injury on someone: *the wreck messed him up so much that he can't walk.* □ **mess something up** *informal* cause something to be spoiled by inept handling: *an error like that could easily mess up an entire day's work.* □ **mess with** *informal* meddle or interfere with so as to spoil or cause trouble: *stop messing with things you don't understand.* ▷Middle English: from Old French *mes* 'portion of food,' from late Latin *missum* 'something put on the table,' past participle of *mittere* 'send, put.' The original sense was 'a serving of food,' also 'a serving of liquid or pulpy food,' later 'liquid food for an animal'; this gave rise (early 19th cent.) to the senses 'unappetizing concoction' and 'predicament,' on which sense 1 is based. In late Middle English the term also denoted any of the small groups into which the company at a banquet was divided (who were served from the same dishes); hence, 'a group of people who regularly eat together' (recorded in military use from the mid 16th cent.).

▶PHRASE □ **mess with someone's head** *informal* cause someone to feel frustrated, anxious, or upset.

mes·sage /ˈmesij/ ▶*n.* **1** a verbal, written, or recorded communication sent to or left for a recipient who cannot be contacted directly: *if I'm not there, leave a*

M

message on the voice mail. ■ an official or formal communication, esp. a speech delivered by a head of state to a legislative assembly or the public: *the president's message to Congress.* ■ an item of electronic mail. ■ an electronic communication generated automatically by a computer program and displayed on a VDT: *an error message.* ■ a significant point or central theme, esp. one that has political, social, or moral importance: *a campaign to get the message about home security across.* ■ a divinely inspired communication from a prophet or preacher. ■ a television or radio commercial: *we will return after these messages.* **2** *chiefly Brit.* an errand: *all she did was make the tea and run messages.* ▷Middle English: from Old French, based on Latin *missus*, past participle of *mittere* 'send.'

▸*PHRASES* □ **get the message** *informal* infer an implication from a remark or action. □ **send a message** make a significant statement, either implicitly or by one's actions: *the elections sent a message to political quarters that the party was riding a wave of popularity.*

mes·sage board ▸*n. Computing* an Internet site where people can post and read messages, usually on a specific topic or area of interest. Compare with **BULLETIN BOARD.**

mes·sage box ▸*n. Computing* a small box that appears on a computer screen to inform the user of something, such as the occurrence of an error.

mes·sage switch·ing ▸*n. Computing & Telecommunications* a mode of data transmission in which a message is sent as a complete unit and routed via a number of intermediate nodes at which it is stored and then forwarded.

mes·sag·ing /ˈmesijiNG/ ▸*n.* the sending and processing of electronic mail by computer.

Mes·sei·gneurs /ˌmāsānˈyər(z)/ ▸ plural form of **MONSEIGNEUR.**

mes·sen·ger /ˈmesənjər/ ▸*n.* **1** a person who carries a message or is employed to carry messages. ■ *Biochemistry* a substance that conveys information or a stimulus within the body. **2** *Nautical* (also **messenger line**) an endless rope, cable, or chain used with a capstan to haul an anchor cable or to drive a powered winch. ■ a light line used to haul or support a larger cable.

▸*v.* [*trans.*] send (a document or package) by messenger: *could you have it messengered over to me?* ▷Middle English: from Old Northern French *messanger*, variant of Old French *messager*, from Latin *missus* (see **MESSAGE**).

▸*PHRASE* □ **shoot** (or **kill**) **the messenger** treat the bearer of bad news as if they were to blame for it.

mes·sen·ger RNA (abbr.: **mRNA**) ▸*n.* the form of RNA in which genetic information transcribed from DNA as a sequence of bases is transferred to a ribosome.

Mes·ser·schmidt /ˈmesərˌSHmit/, Willy (1898–1978), German aircraft designer and industrialist; full name *Wilhelm Emil Messerschmidt*. The Messerschmidt 109 became the standard fighter of the Luftwaffe during World War II.

mess hall ▸*n.* a room or building where groups of people, esp. soldiers, eat together.

Mes·siaen /mesˈyäN/, Olivier (Eugène Prosper Charles) (1908–92), French composer. His music was influenced by Greek and Hindu rhythms, birdsong, Stravinsky, Debussy, and his Roman Catholic faith.

mes·si·ah /məˈsīə/ ▸*n.* **1** (**the Messiah**) the promised deliverer of the Jewish nation prophesied in the Hebrew Bible. ■ Jesus regarded by Christians as the Messiah of the Hebrew prophecies and the savior of humankind. **2** a leader or savior of a particular group or cause: *to Germany, Hitler was more a messiah than a political leader.* ▷Old English *Messias*: via late Latin and Greek from Hebrew *māšîaḥ* 'anointed.' —**mes·si·ah·ship** /-ˌSHip/ *n.*

mes·si·an·ic /ˌmesēˈanik/ ▸*adj.* (also **Messianic**) of or relating to the Messiah: *the messianic role of Jesus.* ■ inspired by hope or belief in a messiah: *the messianic expectations of that time.* ■ fervent or passionate: *an admirable messianic zeal.* ▷mid 19th cent.: from French *messianique*, from *Messie* (see **MESSIAH**), on the pattern of *rabbinique* 'rabbinical.' —**mes·si·a·nism** /ˈmesēəˌnizəm; məˈsīə-/ *n.*

Mes·si·dor /ˌmesiˈdôr/ ▸*n.* the tenth month of the French Republican calendar (1793–1805), originally running from June 19 to July 18. ▷French, from Latin *messis* 'harvest' + Greek *dōron* 'gift.'

Mes·sier /ˈmesēˌā; mesˈyā/, Charles (1730–1817), French astronomer. He discovered a number of nebulae, galaxies, and star clusters, which he designated by M numbers.

Mes·sieurs /məsˈyœ(r)(z); mās-; məˈsi(ə)r(z)/ ▸ plural form of **MONSIEUR.**

Mes·si·na /məˈsēnə/ a city in northeastern Sicily, on the Strait of Messina; pop. 274,850.

Mes·si·na, Strait of a channel that separates the island of Sicily from the "toe" of Italy. It forms a link between the Tyrrhenian and Ionian seas. The strait, which is 20 miles (32 km) long, is noted for the strength of its currents.

mess jacket ▸*n.* a short jacket worn by a military officer on formal occasions. ■ a similar jacket worn as part of a waiter's or bellhop's uniform.

mess kit ▸*n.* a set of cooking and eating utensils, as used esp. by soldiers, scouts, or campers.

mess·mate /ˈmesˌmāt/ ▸*n.* a person with whom one takes meals, esp. in the armed forces.

Messrs. ▸*plural n. dated* or *chiefly Brit.* used as a title to refer formally to more than one man simultaneously, or in names of companies: *Messrs. Sotheby.* ▷late 18th cent.: abbreviation of **MESSIEURS.**

mes·suage /ˈmeswij/ ▸*n. Law* a dwelling house with outbuildings and land assigned to its use. ▷late Middle English: from Anglo-Norman French, based on Latin *manere* 'dwell.'

mess·y /ˈmesē/ ▸*adj.* (**mess·i·er**, **mess·i·est**) **1** untidy or dirty: *his messy hair.* ■ generating or involving mess or untidiness: *stripping wallpaper can be a messy job.* **2** (of a situation) confused and difficult to deal with: *a messy divorce.* —**mess·i·ly** /ˈmesəlē/ *adv.* —**mess·i·ness** *n.*

mes·ti·za /meˈstēzə/ ▸*n.* (in Latin America) a woman of mixed race, esp. the offspring of a Spaniard and an American Indian. ▷Spanish, feminine of *mestizo* (see **MESTIZO**).

mes·ti·zo /meˈstēzō/ ▸*n.* (*pl.* **-zos**) (in Latin America) a man of mixed race, esp. the offspring of a Spaniard and an American Indian. ▷Spanish, 'mixed,' based on Latin *mixtus*.

Met /met/ (**the Met**) *informal* ▸*abbr.* ■ the Metropolitan Opera House in New York City. ■ the Metropolitan Museum of Art in New York City.

met /met/ ▸ past and past participle of **MEET**[1].

met. ▸*abbr.* ■ metaphor. ■ metaphysics. ■ meteorology. ■ metropolitan.

met- ▸*comb. form* variant spelling of **META-** shortened before a vowel or *h* (as in *metonym*).

met·a /ˈmetə/ ▸*n.* short for **META KEY.**

▸*adj.* (of a creative work) referring to itself or to the conventions of its genre; self-referential. ▷1980s: from *meta-* in the sense 'beyond'.

meta- (also **met-** before a vowel or h) ▸*comb. form* **1** denoting a change of position or condition: *metamorphosis* | *metathesis.* **2** denoting position behind, after, or beyond: *metacarpus.* **3** denoting something of a higher or second-order kind: *metalanguage* | *metonym.* **4** *Chemistry* denoting substitution at two carbon atoms separated by one other in a benzene ring, e.g., in 1,3 positions: *metadichlorobenzene.* Compare with **ORTHO-** and **PARA-**[1]. **5** *Chemistry* denoting a compound formed by dehydration: *metaphosphoric acid.* ▷from Greek *meta* 'with, across, or after.'

met·a·bol·ic path·way /ˈmetəˈbälik/ ▸*n.* see **PATHWAY.**

me·tab·o·lism /məˈtabəˌlizəm/ ▸*n.* the chemical processes that occur within a living organism in order to maintain life.

Two kinds of metabolism are often distinguished: **constructive metabolism**, the synthesis of the proteins, carbohydrates, and fats that form tissue and store energy, and **destructive metabolism**, the breakdown of complex substances and the consequent production of energy and waste matter.

▷late 19th cent.: from Greek *metabolē* 'change' (from *metaballein* 'to change') + **-ISM.** —**met·a·bol·ic** /ˈmetəˈbälik/ *adj.* —**met·a·bol·i·cal·ly** /ˌmetəˈbälik(ə)lē/ *adv.*

me·tab·o·lite /məˈtabəˌlīt/ ▸*n. Biochemistry* a substance formed in or necessary for metabolism.

me·tab·o·lize /məˈtabəˌlīz/ ▸*v.* [*trans.*] (of a body or organ) process (a substance) by metabolism. ■ [*intrans.*] (of a substance) undergo processing by metabolism: *the refined foods soon metabolize.* —**me·tab·o·liz·a·ble** *adj.* —**me·tab·o·liz·er** *n.*

met·a·car·pal /ˈmetəˌkärpəl/ ▸*n.* any of the five bones of the hand. ■ any of the equivalent bones in an animal's forelimb.

▸*adj.* of or relating to these bones.

met·a·car·pus /ˈmetəˌkärpəs/ ▸*n.* (*pl.* **-pi** /-pē; -ˌpī/) the group of five bones of the hand between the wrist (carpus) and the fingers. ■ this part of the hand. ■ the equivalent group of bones in an animal's forelimb. ▷late Middle English: modern Latin, alteration of Greek *metakarpion*.

met·a·cen·ter /ˈmetəˌsentər/ (*Brit.* **met·a·cen·tre**) ▸*n.* the point of intersection between a vertical line through the center of buoyancy of a floating body such as a ship and a vertical line through the new center of buoyancy when the body is tilted, which must be above the center of gravity to ensure stability. ▷late 18th cent.: from French *métacentre* (see **META-**, **CENTER**). —**met·a·cen·tric** /ˌmetəˈsentrik/ *adj.*

met·a·chro·ma·sia /ˌmetəkrōˈmāZH(ē)ə/ (also **met·a·chro·ma·sy** /-ˈkrōməsē/) ▸*n. Biology* the property of certain biological materials of staining a different color from that of the stain used. ■ the property of certain stains of changing color in the presence of certain biological materials. ▷early 20th cent.: modern Latin, from **META-** (expressing change) + Greek *khrōma* 'color.' —**met·a·chro·mat·ic** /-krōˈmatik/ *adj.*

met·a·cog·ni·tion /ˌmetəˌkägˈniSHən/ ▸*n. Psychology* awareness and understanding of one's own thought processes. —**met·a·cog·ni·tive** /-ˈkägnətiv/ *adj.*

Met·a·com·et /ˌmetəˈkämit/ see **PHILIP**[4].

met·a·da·ta /ˈmetəˌdatə; -ˌdātə/ ▸*n.* a set of data that describes and gives information about other data.

met·a·fic·tion /ˈmetəˌfikSHən/ ▸*n.* fiction in which the author self-consciously alludes to the artificiality or literariness of a work by parodying or departing from novelistic conventions (esp. naturalism) and traditional narrative techniques. —**met·a·fic·tion·al** /ˌmetəˈfikSHənl/ *adj.*

met·a·file /ˈmetəˌfīl/ ▸*n. Computing* a piece of graphical information stored in a format that can be exchanged between different systems or software.

met·age /ˈmetij/ ▸*n.* the official weighing of loads of coal, grain, or other material. ■ the duty paid for this. ▷early 16th cent.: from **METE**[1] + **-AGE.**

met·a·gen·e·sis /ˌmetəˈjenəsis/ ▸*n. Biology* the alternation of generations between sexual and asexual reproduction. ▷late 19th cent.: modern Latin.

Met·air·ie /ˈmetərē/ a community in southeastern Louisiana, northwest of New Orleans; pop. 149,428.

met·a key ▸*n. Computing* a function key on a keyboard that is activated by simultaneously holding down a control key.

met·al /ˈmetl/ ▸*n.* **1** a solid material that is typically hard, shiny, malleable, fusible, and ductile, with good electrical and thermal conductivity (e.g., iron, gold, silver, copper, and aluminum, and alloys such as brass and steel): *vessels made of ceramics or metal* | *being a metal, aluminum readily conducts heat.* ■ *Heraldry* gold and silver (as tinctures in blazoning). **2** *Brit.* (also **road met·al**) broken stone for use in making roads. **3** molten glass before it is blown or cast. **4** heavy metal or similar rock music.

▸*v.* (**met·aled**, **met·al·ing**; *chiefly Brit.* **met·alled**, **met·al·ling**) [*trans.*] [usu. as *adj.*] (**metaled**) **1** make out of or coat with metal: *metaled key rings.* **2** *Brit.* make or mend (a road) with road metal: *follow the metalled road for about 200 yards.* ▷Middle English: from Old French *metal* or Latin *metallum*, from Greek *metallon* 'mine, quarry, or metal.'

metal. (also **metall.**) ▸*abbr.* ■ metallurgical or metallurgy.

met·a·lan·guage /ˈmetəˌlaNG(g)wij/ ▸*n.* a form of language or set of terms used for the description or analysis of another language. Compare with **OBJECT LANGUAGE** (sense 1). ■ *Logic* a system of propositions about propositions.

met·al de·tec·tor ▸*n.* an electronic device that gives an audible or other signal when it is close to metal, used for example to search for buried objects or to detect hidden weapons.

met·al·flake ▸*n.* [usu. as *adj.*] a metalized film added to paint to increase protection against rust. ▷1950s: from *Metalflake*, a trademark.

met·al·head /ˈmetlˌhed/ ▸*n. informal* another term for **HEADBANGER.**

met·a·lin·guis·tics /ˌmetəˌliNGˈgwistiks/ ▸*plural n.* [treated as *sing.*] the branch of linguistics that deals with metalanguages, self-reference in language, and the philosophy of science as it applies to linguistics. —**met·a·lin·guis·tic** *adj.*

met·al·ize /ˈmetlˌīz/ (also **met·al·lize**) ▸*v.* [*trans.*] coat with a thin layer of metal. ■ make metallic in form or appearance. —**met·al·i·za·tion** /ˌmetləˈzāSHən/ *n.*

metall. ▸*abbr.* variant spelling of **METAL.**

me·tal·lic /mə'talik/ ▸adj. of, relating to, or resembling metal or metals: *metallic alloys | a curious metallic taste.* ■ (of sound) resembling that produced by metal objects striking each other; sharp and ringing: *the terrifying, metallic clamor of the fire-engine bell.* ■ (of a person's voice); emanating or as if emanating via an electronic medium: *a metallic voice rasped tinnily from a concealed speaker.* ■ having the sheen or luster of metal: *a metallic green sports car.*
▸n. a paint, fiber, fabric, or color with a metallic sheen: *dresses that shine with sequins and metallics.* ▷late Middle English: via Latin from Greek *metallikos*, from *metallon* (see METAL). **—me·tal·li·cal·ly** /-ik(ə)lē/ adv.

met·al·lic·i·ty /,metl'isətē/ ▸n. (pl. **-ties**) the property of being metallic. ■ *Astronomy* the proportion of the material of a star or other celestial object that is in elements other than hydrogen or helium.

met·al·lif·er·ous /,metl'ifərəs/ ▸adj. (chiefly of deposits of minerals) containing or producing metal. ▷mid 17th cent.: from Latin *metallifer* 'metal-bearing' + -OUS.

met·al·line /'metl,īn/ ▸adj. *rare* metallic.

me·tal·lo·gen·ic /mə,talə'jenik/ ▸adj. *Geology* of or relating to the formation or occurrence of deposits of metals or their ores.

met·al·log·ra·phy /,metl'ägrəfē/ ▸n. the descriptive science of the structure and properties of metals. **—met·al·log·ra·pher** /-fər/ n. **—me·tal·lo·graph·ic** /'metl-ə'grafik/ adj. **—me·tal·lo·graph·i·cal** /,metl-ə'grafikəl/ adj. **—me·tal·lo·graph·i·cal·ly** /,metl-ə'grafik(ə)lē/ adv.

met·al·loid /'metl,oid/ ▸n. *Chemistry* an element (e.g., arsenic, antimony, or tin) whose properties are intermediate between those of metals and solid nonmetals or semiconductors.

met·al·lur·gy /'metl,ərjē/ ▸n. the branch of science and technology concerned with the properties of metals and their production and purification. ▷early 18th cent.: from Greek *metallon* 'metal' + *-ourgia* 'working.' **—met·al·lur·gic** /,metl'ərjik/ adj. **—met·al·lur·gi·cal** adj. **—met·al·lur·gi·cal·ly** adv. **—met·al·lur·gist** n.

met·al·mark /'metl,märk/ ▸n. a butterfly with brilliant metallic markings on the wings, found chiefly in tropical America. • Family Riodinidae: several genera.

met·al·ware /'metl,we(ə)r/ ▸n. utensils or other articles made of metal.

met·al·work /'metl,wərk/ ▸n. the art of making things out of metal. ■ metal objects collectively: *a wealth of fine metalwork, including a sword.* ■ the metal part of a construction: *engineers spotted cracks in the metalwork.* **—met·al·work·er** n. **—met·al·work·ing** n.

met·a·math·e·mat·ics /,metə,maTH(ə)'matiks/ ▸plural n. [usu. treated as *sing.*] the field of study that deals with the structure and formal properties of mathematics and similar formal systems. **—met·a·math·e·mat·i·cal** /-'matikəl/ adj. **—met·a·math·e·mat·i·cal·ly** /-'matik(ə)lē/ adv. **—met·a·math·e·ma·ti·cian** /-mə'tisHən/ n.

met·a·mere /'metəmir/ ▸n. *Zoology* another term for SOMITE. ▷late 19th cent.: from META- 'together with' + Greek *meros* 'part.'

met·a·mer·ic /,metə'merik/ ▸adj. **1** *Zoology* of, relating to, or consisting of several similar segments or somites. **2** *dated Chemistry* having the same proportional composition and molecular weight, but different functional groups and chemical properties; isomeric. **—met·a·mer** /'metəmər/ n. **—met·a·mer·i·cal·ly** adv. **—me·tam·er·ism** /mə'tamə,rizəm/ n.

met·a·mes·sage /'metə,mesij/ ▸n. an underlying meaning or implicit message, esp. in advertising.

met·a·mor·phic /'metə'môrfik/ ▸adj. **1** *Geology* denoting rock that has undergone transformation by heat, pressure, or other natural agencies, e.g., in the folding of strata or the nearby intrusion of igneous rocks. ■ of or relating to such rocks or metamorphism. **2** of or marked by metamorphosis: *the shift from dead stillness to hurricane-force winds was as metamorphic as Jekyll to Hyde.* ▷early 19th cent.: from META- (denoting a change of condition) + Greek *morphē* 'form' + -IC.

met·a·mor·phism /'metə'môr,fizəm/ ▸n. *Geology* alteration of the composition or structure of a rock by heat, pressure, or other natural agency.

met·a·mor·phose /,metə'môr,fōz; -,fōs/ ▸v. [*intrans.*] (of an insect or amphibian) undergo metamorphosis, esp. into the adult form: *feed the larvae to your fish before they* **metamorphose into** *adults.* ■ change completely in form or nature: *a father seeing his daughter metamorphosing from girl into woman.* ■ [*trans.*] cause (something) to change completely. ■ [*trans.*] *Geology* subject (rock) to metamorphism: [as *adj.*] (**metamorphosed**) *a metamorphosed sandstone.* ▷late 16th cent.: from French *métamorphoser*, from *métamorphose* (see METAMORPHOSIS).

met·a·mor·pho·sis /,metə'môrfəsəs/ ▸n. (pl. **-pho·ses** /-fə,sēz/) *Zoology* (in an insect or amphibian) the process of transformation from an immature form to an adult form in two or more distinct stages. ■ a change of the form or nature of a thing or person into a completely different one, by natural or supernatural means: *his metamorphosis from presidential candidate to talk-show host.* ▷late Middle English: via Latin from Greek *metamorphōsis*, from *metamorphoun* 'transform, change shape.'

met·a·noi·a /,metə'noiə/ ▸n. change in one's way of life resulting from penitence or spiritual conversion. ▷late 19th cent.: from Greek, from *metanoein* 'change one's mind.'

met·a·phase /'metə,fāz/ ▸n. *Biology* the second stage of cell division, between prophase and anaphase, during which the chromosomes become attached to the spindle fibers.

met·a·phor /'metə,fôr; -fər/ ▸n. a figure of speech in which a word or phrase is applied to an object or action to which it is not literally applicable: *"I had fallen through a trapdoor of depression," said Mark, who was fond of theatrical metaphors | her poetry depends on suggestion and metaphor.* ■ a thing regarded as representative or symbolic of something else, esp. something abstract: *the amounts of money being lost by the company were enough to make it a* **metaphor for** *an industry that was teetering.* ▷late 15th cent.: from French *métaphore*, via Latin from Greek *metaphora*, from *metapherein* 'to transfer.' **—met·a·phor·ic** /,metə'fôrik/ adj. **—met·a·phor·i·cal** /,metə'fôrikəl/ adj. **—met·a·phor·i·cal·ly** /,metə'fôrik(ə)lē/ adv.

met·a·phos·phor·ic ac·id /,metə,fäs'fôrik/ ▸n. *Chemistry* a glassy deliquescent solid obtained by heating orthophosphoric acid. • A polymer; chem. formula $(HPO_3)_n$. **—met·a·phos·phate** /-'fäs,fāt/ n.

met·a·phrase /'metə,frāz/ ▸n. a literal, word-for-word translation, as opposed to a paraphrase.
▸v. [*trans.*] alter the phrasing or language of. ▷early 17th cent. (denoting a metrical translation): from Greek *metaphrazein*, literally 'word differently.' **—met·a·phras·tic** /'metə'frastik/ adj.

met·a·phys·ic /,metə'fizik/ ▸n. a system of metaphysics.

met·a·phys·i·cal /,metə'fizikəl/ ▸adj. **1** of or relating to metaphysics: *the essentially metaphysical question of the nature of the mind.* ■ based on abstract (typically, excessively abstract) reasoning: *an empiricist rather than a metaphysical view of law.* ■ transcending physical matter or the laws of nature: *Good and Evil are inextricably linked in a metaphysical battle across space and time.* **2** of or characteristic of the metaphysical poets.
▸n. (**the Metaphysicals**) the metaphysical poets. **—met·a·phys·i·cal·ly** /-ik(ə)lē/ adv.

met·a·phys·i·cal po·ets a group of 17th-century poets whose work is characterized by the use of complex and elaborate images or conceits, typically using an intellectual form of argumentation to express emotional states. Members of the group include John Donne, George Herbert, Henry Vaughan, and Andrew Marvell.

met·a·phys·ics /,metə'fiziks/ ▸plural n. [usu. treated as *sing.*] the branch of philosophy that deals with the first principles of things, including abstract concepts such as being, knowing, substance, cause, identity, time, and space. ■ abstract theory or talk with no basis in reality: *his concept of society as an organic entity is, for market liberals, simply metaphysics.*

Metaphysics has two main strands: that which holds that what exists lies beyond experience (as argued by Plato), and that which holds that objects of experience constitute the only reality (as argued by Kant, the logical positivists, and Hume). Metaphysics has also concerned itself with a discussion of whether what exists is made of one substance or many, and whether what exists is inevitable or driven by chance.

▷mid 16th cent.: representing medieval Latin *metaphysica* (neuter plural), based on Greek *ta meta ta phusika* 'the things after the Physics,' referring to the sequence of Aristotle's works: the title came to denote the branch of study treated in the books, later interpreted as meaning 'the science of things transcending what is physical or natural.' **—met·a·phy·si·cian** /-fə'zisHən/ n.

met·a·pla·sia /,metə'plāzH(ē)ə/ ▸n. *Physiology* abnormal change in the nature of a tissue. ▷late 19th cent.: modern Latin, from German *Metaplase*, based on Greek *metaplassein* 'mold into a new form.' **—met·a·plas·tic** /-'plastik/ adj.

met·a·psy·chol·o·gy /'metə,sī'käləjē/ ▸n. speculation concerning mental processes and the mind–body relationship, beyond what can be studied experimentally. **—met·a·psy·cho·log·i·cal** /-,sīkə'läjikəl/ adj.

Me·ta Riv·er /'mātə/ a river that flows northeast for 650 miles (1,050 km) from central Colombia into the Orinoco River and that forms part of the Colombia-Venezuela boundary.

met·a·rule /'metə,rōōl/ ▸n. a rule governing the content, form, or application of other rules: *three particular metarules of international law provide especially weak support.*

met·a·se·quoi·a /,metəsi'kwoiə/ ▸n. another term for DAWN REDWOOD.

met·a·so·ma·tism /,metə'sōmə,tizəm/ ▸n. *Geology* change in the composition of a rock as a result of the introduction or removal of chemical constituents. ▷late 19th cent.: from META- (expressing change) + Greek *sōma, somat-* 'body' + -ISM. **—met·a·so·mat·ic** /-sə'matik/ adj. **—met·a·so·ma·tize** /-'sōmə,tīz/ v.

met·a·sta·ble /'metə,stābəl; ,metə'stābəl/ ▸adj. *Physics* (of a state of equilibrium) stable provided it is subjected to no more than small disturbances. ■ (of a substance or particle) theoretically unstable but so long-lived as to be stable for practical purposes. **—met·a·sta·bil·i·ty** /-stə'bilətē/ n.

me·tas·ta·sis /mə'tastəsəs/ ▸n. (pl. **-ses** /-,sēz/) *Medicine* the development of secondary malignant growths at a distance from a primary site of cancer. ■ a growth of this type. ▷late 16th cent. (as a rhetorical term, meaning 'rapid transition from one point to another'): from Greek, literally 'removal or change,' from *methistanai* 'to change.' **—met·a·stat·ic** /,metə'statik/ adj.

me·tas·ta·size /mə'tastə,sīz/ ▸v. [*intrans.*] *Medicine* (of a cancer) spread to other sites in the body by metastasis: *cancers that metastasize to the brain.* ■ (of a condition or circumstance) spread or grow, esp. unfavorably: *the capital gains form has metastasized from a 19-line form to a 54-step Rube Goldberg machine of higher mathematics.*

met·a·tar·sal /,metə'tärsəl/ ▸n. any of the bones of the foot (metatarsus). ■ any of the equivalent bones in an animal's hind limb.

met·a·tar·sus /,metə'tärsəs/ ▸n. (pl. **-si** /-sē; -,sī/) the group of bones in the foot, between the ankle and the toes. ■ this part of the foot. ■ the equivalent group of bones in an animal's hind limb. ▷late Middle English: modern Latin (see META-, TARSUS).

me·ta·te /mə'tätā/ (also **metate stone**) ▸n. (in Central America) a flat or slightly hollowed oblong stone on which materials such as grain and cocoa are ground using a smaller stone. ▷from American Spanish, from Nahuatl *métatl*.

Met·a·the·ri·a /,metə'THi(ə)rēə/ *Zoology* a group of mammals that comprises the marsupials. Compare with EUTHERIA. • Infraclass Metatheria, subclass Theria. ▷modern Latin (plural), from META- (expressing change) + Greek *thēria*, plural of *thērion* 'wild animal.' **—met·a·the·ri·an** n. & adj.

me·tath·e·sis /mə'taTHəsəs/ ▸n. (pl. **-ses** /-,sēz/) **1** *Grammar* the transposition of sounds or letters in a word. **2** (also **me·tath·e·sis re·ac·tion**) *Chemistry* a reaction in which two compounds exchange ions, typically with precipitation of an insoluble product. Also called DOUBLE DECOMPOSITION. ▷late 16th cent.: from Greek, from *metatithenai* 'transpose, change the position of.' **—met·a·thet·ic** /,metə'THetik/ adj. **—met·a·thet·i·cal** /,metəTHetikəl/ adj.

met·a·tho·rax /,metə'THôr,aks/ ▸n. (pl. **-tho·rax·es** or **-tho·ra·ces** /-'THôrə,sēz/) *Entomology* the posterior segment of the thorax of an insect, bearing the hind wings. **—met·a·tho·rac·ic** /-THə'rasik/ adj.

Met·a·zo·a /,metə'zōə/ *Zoology* a major division of the animal kingdom that comprises all animals other than protozoans and sponges. They are multicellular animals with differentiated tissues. • Subkingdom Metazoa, kingdom Animalia. ■ [as *plural n.*] (**metazoa**) animals of this division. ▷modern Latin (plural), from META- (expressing change) + *zōia* (plural of *zōion* 'animal'). **—met·a·zo·an** /-'zōən/ n. & adj.

mete[1] /mēt/ ▸v. [*trans.*] (**mete something out**) dispense or allot justice, a punishment, or harsh treatment:

M

he denounced the maltreatment meted out to minorities. ■ (in biblical use) measure out: *with what measure ye mete, it shall be measured to you again.* ▷Old English *metan* 'measure, determine the quantity of,' of Germanic origin; related to Dutch *meten* and German *messen* 'to measure,' from an Indo-European root shared by Latin *meditari* 'meditate,' Greek *medesthai* 'care for,' also by **MEET**2.

mete2 ▶*n.* (usu. **metes and bounds**) *chiefly historical* a boundary or boundary stone. ▷late Middle English: from Old French, from Latin *meta* 'boundary, goal.'

me·tem·psy·cho·sis /ˌmetəmˌsīˈkōsəs; məˌtemsiˈkōsəs/ ▶*n.* (*pl.* **-ses** /-sēz/) the supposed transmigration at death of the soul of a human being or animal into a new body of the same or a different species. ▷late 16th cent.: via late Latin from Greek *metempsukhōsis*, from *meta-* (expressing change) + *en* 'in' + *psukhē* 'soul.' **—me·tem·psy·chot·ic** /-ˈkätik/ *adj.* **—me·tem·psy·chot·i·cal·ly** /-ˈkätik(ə)lē/ *adv.* **—me·tem·psy·cho·sist** /-ˈkōsist/ *n.*

me·te·or /ˈmētēər; -ēˌôr/ ▶*n.* a small body of matter from outer space that enters the earth's atmosphere, becoming incandescent as a result of friction and appearing as a streak of light. ▷mid 16th cent. (denoting any atmospheric phenomenon): from modern Latin *meteorum*, from Greek *meteōron*, neuter (used as a noun) of *meteōros* 'lofty.'

meteor. ▶*abbr.* ■ meteorological. ■ meteorology.

me·te·or·ic /ˌmētēˈôrik/ ▶*adj.* **1** of or relating to meteors or meteorites: *meteoric iron.* ■ *figurative* (of the development of something, esp. a person's career) very rapid: *her* ***meteoric rise*** *to the top of her profession.* **2** *chiefly Geology* relating to or denoting water derived from the atmosphere by precipitation or condensation. **—me·te·or·i·cal·ly** /-ik(ə)lē/ *adv.*

me·te·or·ite /ˈmētēəˌrīt/ ▶*n.* a meteor that survives its passage through the earth's atmosphere such that part of it strikes the ground. More than 90 percent of meteorites are of rock, while the remainder consist wholly or partly of iron and nickel. **—me·te·or·it·ic** /ˈˌmētēəˈritik/ *adj.*

me·te·or·o·graph /ˌmētēˈôrəˌgraf/ ▶*n.* *archaic* an apparatus that records several meteorological phenomena at the same time. ▷late 18th cent.: from French *météorographe* (see **METEOR**, **-GRAPH**).

me·te·or·oid /ˈmētēəˌroid/ ▶*n.* *Astronomy* a small body moving in the solar system that would become a meteor if it entered the earth's atmosphere. **—me·te·o·roid·al** /ˌmētēəˈroidl/ *adj.*

me·te·or·ol·o·gy /ˌmētēəˈräləjē/ ▶*n.* the branch of science concerned with the processes and phenomena of the atmosphere, esp. as a means of forecasting the weather. ■ the climate and weather of a region. ▷early 17th cent.: from Greek *meteōrologia*, from *meteōron* 'of the atmosphere' (see **METEOR**). **—me·te·or·o·log·i·cal** /-rəˈläjikəl/ *adj.* **—me·te·or·o·log·i·cal·ly** /-rəˈläjik(ə)lē/ *adv.* **—me·te·or·ol·o·gist** /-rəˈläjist/ *n.*

me·te·or show·er ▶*n.* *Astronomy* a number of meteors that appear to radiate from one point in the sky at a particular date each year, due to the earth's regularly passing through a field of particles at that position in its orbit. Meteor showers are named after the constellation in which the radiant is situated, e.g., the Perseids.

me·ter1 /ˈmētər/ (*Brit.* **me·tre**) ▶*n.* the fundamental unit of length in the metric system, equal to 100 centimeters or approximately 39.37 inches. ■ (**—— meters**) a race over a specified number of meters: *he placed third in the 1,000 meters.* ▷late 18th cent.: from French *mètre*, from Greek *metron* 'measure.' **—me·ter·age** /-ij/ *n.*

me·ter2 (*Brit.* **me·tre**) ▶*n.* the rhythm of a piece of poetry, determined by the number and length of feet in a line: *the Horatian ode has an intricate governing meter | unexpected changes of stress and meter.* ■ the basic pulse and rhythm of a piece of music. ▷Old English, reinforced in Middle English by Old French *metre*, from Latin *metrum*, from Greek *metron* 'measure.'

me·ter3 ▶*n.* a device that measures and records the quantity, degree, or rate of something, esp. the amount of electricity, gas, or water used: *they read the meters once a month.* ■ *Philately* an imprint or label of specified value produced under government permit for the prepayment of postage.
▶*v.* [*trans.*] [often as *adj.*] (**metered**) measure by means of a meter: *a metered supply of water.* ▷Middle English (in the sense 'person who measures'): from **METE**1 + **-ER**1. The current sense dates from the 19th cent.

-meter ▶*comb. form* **1** in names of measuring instruments: *thermometer.* **2** *Prosody* in nouns denoting lines of poetry with a specified number of feet or measures: *hexameter.* ▷from Greek *metron* 'measure.'

me·ter-kil·o·gram-sec·ond (abbr.: **mks**) ▶*adj.* denoting a system of measure using the meter, kilogram, and second as the basic units of length, mass, and time.

meth /meTH/ ▶*n.* *informal* **1** (also **crystal meth**) the drug methamphetamine. **2** short for **METHADONE**.

meth·a·cryl·ic ac·id /ˌmeTHəˈkrilik/ ▶*n.* *Chemistry* a colorless, low-melting solid that polymerizes when distilled and is used in the manufacture of synthetic resins. • Alternative name: **1-methylacrylic acid**; chem. formula: $CH_2{=}C(CH_3)COOH$. **—meth·ac·ry·late** /meTHˈakrəˌlāt/ *n.*

meth·a·done /ˈmeTHəˌdōn/ ▶*n.* a synthetic analgesic drug that is similar to morphine in its effects but longer acting, used as a substitute drug in the treatment of morphine and heroin addiction. ▷1940s: from its chemical name, *(6-di)meth(yl)a(mino-4,4-)d(iphenyl-3-heptan)one.*

meth·am·phet·a·mine /ˌmeTHəmˈfetəˌmēn; -min/ ▶*n.* a synthetic drug with more rapid and lasting effects than amphetamine, used illegally as a stimulant and as a prescription drug to treat narcolepsy and maintain blood pressure. • A methyl derivative of amphetamine; chem. formula $C_6H_5CH_2CH(CH_3)NH(CH_3)$.

meth·a·nal /ˈmeTHəˌnal/ ▶*n.* systematic chemical name for **FORMALDEHYDE**. ▷late 19th cent.: blend of **METHANE** and **ALDEHYDE**.

meth·ane /ˈmeTHˌān/ ▶*n.* *Chemistry* a colorless, odorless flammable gas that is the main constituent of natural gas. It is the simplest member of the alkane series of hydrocarbons. • Chem. formula: CH_4. ▷mid 19th cent.: from **METHYL** + **-ANE**2.

meth·an·o·gen /ˈmeTHənəjən/ ▶*n.* *Biology* a methane-producing bacterium, esp. an archaean that reduces carbon dioxide to methane. **—meth·an·o·gen·ic** /ˌmeTHənəˈjenik/ *adj.*

meth·a·no·ic ac·id /ˌmeTHəˈnōik/ ▶*n.* systematic chemical name for **FORMIC ACID**. ▷late 19th cent.: *methanoic*, from **METHANE** + *-oic* (perhaps on the pattern of *benzoic*). **—me·than·o·ate** /məˈTHanōˌāt/ *n.*

meth·a·nol /ˈmeTHəˌnôl; -ˌnōl/ ▶*n.* *Chemistry* a toxic, colorless, volatile flammable liquid alcohol, originally made by distillation from wood and now chiefly by oxidizing methane. Also called **METHYL ALCOHOL**. • Chem. formula: CH_3OH. ▷late 19th cent.: from **METHANE** + **-OL**.

me·thaq·ua·lone /məˈTHakwəˌlōn/ ▶*n.* a sedative and sleep-inducing drug. Also called **QUAALUDE** (*trademark*). ▷1960s: from elements of its chemical name *meth- + -a- + qu(inine + a(zo- + -o)l + -one.*

meth·e·drine /ˈmeTHəˌdrēn; -drin/ (also **Meth·e·drine**) ▶*n.* *trademark* another term for **METHAMPHETAMINE**. ▷1930s: blend of **METHYL** and **BENZEDRINE**.

me·theg·lin /məˈTHeglən/ ▶*n.* *historical* a spiced or medicated variety of mead, associated particularly with Wales. ▷mid 16th cent.: from Welsh *meddyglyn*, from *meddyg* 'medicinal' (from Latin *medicus*) + *llyn* 'liquor.'

meth·e·mo·glo·bin /metˈhēməˌglōbən/ (*Brit.* **meth·ae·mo·glo·bin**) ▶*n.* *Biochemistry* a stable oxidized form of hemoglobin that is unable to release oxygen to the tissues, produced in some inherited abnormalities and by oxidizing drugs.

met·he·mo·glo·bi·ne·mi·a /ˌmetˌhēməˌglōbəˈnēmēə/ (*Brit.* **met·hae·mo·glo·bi·nae·mi·a**) ▶*n.* *Medicine* the presence of methemoglobin in the blood.

meth·i·cil·lin /ˌmeTHəˈsilən/ ▶*n.* *Medicine* a semisynthetic form of penicillin used against staphylococci that produce penicillinase. ▷1960s: from *meth(yl)* and *(pen)icillin.*

me·thinks /miˈTHiNGks/ ▶*v.* (*past* **me·thought** /miˈTHôt/) [*intrans.*] *archaic* or *humorous* it seems to me: *life has been rather hard on her, methinks* | [with *clause*] *methought you knew all about it.* ▷Old English *mē thyncth*, from *mē* 'to me' + *thyncth* 'it seems' (from *thyncan* 'seem,' related to, but distinct from, **THINK**).

me·thi·o·nine /məˈTHīəˌnēn/ ▶*n.* *Biochemistry* a sulfur-containing amino acid that is a constituent of most proteins. It is an essential nutrient in the diet of vertebrates. • Chem. formula: $CH_3S(CH_2)_2CH(NH_2)COOH$. ▷1920s: from **METHYL** + Greek *theion* 'sulfur.'

meth·od /ˈmeTHəd/ ▶*n.* (often **method for/of**) a particular form of procedure for accomplishing or approaching something, esp. a systematic or established one: *a method for software maintenance | labor-intensive production methods.* ■ orderliness of thought or behavior; systematic planning or action: *historical study is the rigorous combination of knowledge and method.* ■ (often **Method**) short for **METHOD ACTING**. ▷late Middle English (in the sense 'prescribed medical treatment for a disease'): via Latin from Greek *methodos* 'pursuit of knowledge,' from *meta-* (expressing development) + *hodos* 'way.'
▶***PHRASE*** □ **there is method in one's madness** there is a sensible foundation for what appears to be foolish or strange behavior. [from Shakespeare's *Hamlet* (II. ii. 211).]

meth·od act·ing ▶*n.* a technique of acting in which an actor aspires to complete emotional identification with a part, based on the system evolved by Stanislavsky and brought into prominence in the U.S. in the 1930s. Method acting was developed in institutions such as the Actors' Studio in New York City, notably by Elia Kazan and Lee Strasberg, and is particularly associated with actors such as Marlon Brando and Dustin Hoffman. **—meth·od ac·tor** *n.*

mé·thode cham·pen·oise /māˈtōd ˌSHäNpənˈwäz/ ▶*n.* [often as *adj.*] a method of making sparkling wine by allowing the last stage of fermentation to take place in the bottle. ■ sparkling wine made in this way, esp. a kind not made in the Champagne region of France. ▷French, literally 'champagne method.'

me·thod·i·cal /məˈTHädikəl/ ▶*adj.* done according to a systematic or established form of procedure: *a methodical approach to the evaluation of computer systems.* ■ (of a person) orderly or systematic in thought or behavior. ▷late 16th cent.: via late Latin from Greek *methodikos* (from *methodos*: see **METHOD**) + **-AL**. **—me·thod·ic** *adj.* **—me·thod·i·cal·ly** /-ik(ə)lē/ *adv.*

Meth·od·ist /ˈmeTHədəst/ ▶*n.* a member of a Christian Protestant denomination originating in the 18th-century evangelistic movement of Charles and John Wesley and George Whitefield.

> The Methodist Church grew out of a religious society established within the Church of England, from which it formally separated in 1791. It is particularly strong in the U.S. and now constitutes one of the largest Protestant denominations worldwide, with more than 30 million members. Methodism has a strong tradition of missionary work and concern with social welfare, and emphasizes the believer's personal relationship with God.

▶*adj.* of or relating to Methodists or Methodism: *a Methodist chapel.* ▷probably from the notion of following a specified "method" of Bible study. **—Meth·od·ism** /-ˌdizəm/ *n.* **—Meth·od·is·tic** /ˌmeTHəˈdistik/ *adj.* **—Meth·od·is·ti·cal** /ˌmeTHəˈdistikəl/ *adj.*

Me·tho·di·us, St. /məˈTHōdēəs/ the brother of St. Cyril (see **CYRIL, ST.**).

meth·od·ize /ˈmeTHəˌdīz/ ▶*v.* [*trans.*] *rare* arrange in an orderly or systematic manner. **—meth·od·iz·er** *n.*

meth·od·ol·o·gy /ˌmeTHəˈdäləjē/ ▶*n.* (*pl.* **-gies**) a system of methods used in a particular area of study or activity: *a methodology for investigating the concept of focal points | courses in research methodology and practice.* ▷early 19th cent.: from modern Latin *methodologia* or French *méthodologie*. **—meth·od·o·log·i·cal** /-dəˈläjikəl/ *adj.* **—meth·od·o·log·i·cal·ly** /dəˈläjik(ə)lē/ *adv.* **—meth·od·ol·o·gist** /-ˈdäləjist/ *n.*

meth·o·trex·ate /ˌmeTHəˈtrekˌsāt/ ▶*n.* *Medicine* a synthetic compound that interferes with cell growth and is used to treat leukemia and other forms of cancer. • Alternative name: **4-amino-10-methylfolic acid**; chem. formula: $C_{20}H_{22}N_8O_5$. ▷1950s: from *meth-* (denoting a substance containing methyl groups) + elements of unknown origin.

me·thought /miˈTHôt/ ▶ past of **METHINKS**.

Me·thu·se·lah /məˈTH(y)o͞oz(ə)lə/ (in the Bible) a patriarch, the grandfather of Noah, who is said to have lived for 969 years (Gen. 5:27). ■ used to refer to a very old person: *I'm feeling older than Methuselah.*

me·thu·se·lah ▶*n.* a wine bottle of eight times the standard size. ▷1930s: from **METHUSELAH**.

meth·yl /ˈmeTHəl/ ▶*n.* [as *adj.*] *Chemistry* of or denoting the alkyl radical $-CH_3$, derived from methane and present in many organic compounds: *methyl bromide.* ▷mid 19th cent.: from German *Methyl* or French *méthyle*, back-formations from German *Methylen* and French *méthylène* (see **METHYLENE**).

meth·yl al·co·hol ▶*n.* another term for **METHANOL**.

meth·yl·ate /ˈmeTHəˌlāt/ ▶*v.* [*trans.*] [often as *adj.*] (**methylated**) mix or impregnate with methanol or methylated spirit. ■ *Chemistry* introduce a methyl group into (a molecule or compound). **—meth·yl·a·tion** /ˌmeTHəˈlāSHən/ *n.*

meth·yl·at·ed spir·it (also **meth·yl·at·ed spir·its**) ▸*n.* alcohol for general use that has been made unfit for drinking by the addition of about 10 percent methanol and typically also some pyridine and a violet dye.

meth·yl·ben·zene /ˌmeTHəlˈbenˌzēn/ ▸*n.* systematic chemical name for **TOLUENE**.

meth·yl cy·a·nide ▸*n.* another term for **ACETONITRILE**.

meth·yl·ene /ˈmeTHəˌlēn/ ▸*n.* [as *adj.*] *Chemistry* the divalent radical or group $-CH_2-$, derived from methane by loss of two hydrogen atoms: *methylene chloride.* ▹mid 19th cent.: from French *méthylène* (formed irregularly from Greek *methu* 'wine' + *hulē* 'wood') + **-ENE**.

meth·yl·phen·i·date /ˌmeTHəlˈfenəˌdāt/ ▸*n.* *Medicine* a synthetic drug that stimulates the sympathetic and central nervous systems and is used to improve mental activity in attention deficit disorder and other conditions.

met·ic /ˈmetik/ ▸*n.* a foreigner living in an ancient Greek city who had some of the privileges of citizenship. ▹early 19th cent.: formed irregularly from Greek *metoikos*, from *meta-* (expressing change) + *oikos* 'dwelling.'

me·ti·cal /ˈmetikəl/ ▸*n.* (*pl.* **me·ti·cais** /metiˈkīSH/) the basic monetary unit of Mozambique, equal to 100 centavos. ▹Portuguese, based on Arabic *miṯkāl*, from *ṯaḳala* 'to weigh.'

me·tic·u·lous /məˈtikyələs/ ▸*adj.* showing great attention to detail; very careful and precise: *he had always been so meticulous about his appearance.* ▹mid 16th cent. (in the sense 'fearful or timid'): from Latin *meticulosus*, from *metus* 'fear.' The word came to mean 'overcareful about detail,' hence the current sense (early 19th cent.). **—me·tic·u·lous·ly** *adv.* **—me·tic·u·lous·ness** *n.*

mé·tier /meˈtyā; ˈmeˌtyā/ ▸*n.* a trade, profession, or occupation: *those who work honestly at their métier.* ■ an occupation or activity that one is good at: *she decided that her real métier was grand opera.* ■ an outstanding or advantageous characteristic: *subtlety is not his métier.* ▹late 18th cent.: French, based on Latin *ministerium* 'service.'

Mé·tis /mā'tēs/ (also **Me·tis**) ▸*n.* (*pl.* same) (esp. in western Canada) a person of mixed American Indian and Euro-American ancestry, in particular one of a group of such people who in the 19th century constituted the so-called **Métis nation** in the areas around the Red and Saskatchewan rivers.
▸*adj.* denoting or relating to such people. ▹from French, from Late Latin *mixticius*, from Latin *mixtus* 'mixed' (see also **MESTIZO**).

Me·tol /ˈmeˌtôl; -ˌtōl/ ▸*n.* *trademark* a soluble white compound used as a photographic developer. • A sulfate of 4-methylaminophenol (chem. formula: $CH_3NHC_6H_4OH$). ▹late 19th cent.: from German, arbitrarily named by the inventor.

Me·ton·ic cy·cle /meˈtänik/ ▸*n.* a period of 19 years (235 lunar months), after which the new and full moons return to the same days of the year. It was the basis of the ancient Greek calendar and is still used for calculating movable feasts such as Easter. ▹named after *Metōn*, an Athenian astronomer of the 5th cent. BC.

met·o·nym /ˈmetəˌnim/ ▸*n.* a word, name, or expression used as a substitute for something else with which it is closely associated. For example, *Washington* is a metonym for the federal government of the U.S. ▹mid 19th cent.: back-formation from **METONYMY**.

me·ton·y·my /məˈtänəmē/ ▸*n.* (*pl.* **-mies**) the substitution of the name of an attribute or adjunct for that of the thing meant, for example *suit* for *business executive*, or *the track* for *horse racing.* ▹mid 16th cent.: via Latin from Greek *metōnumia*, literally 'change of name.' **—met·o·nym·ic** /ˌmetəˈnimik/ *adj.* **—met·o·nym·i·cal** /ˌmetəˈnimikəl/ *adj.* **—met·o·nym·i·cal·ly** /ˌmetəˈnimik(ə)lē/ *adv.*

met·o·pe /ˈmetəpē/ ▸*n.* *Architecture* a square space between triglyphs in a Doric frieze. ▹mid 16th cent.: via Latin from Greek *metopē*, from *meta* 'between' + *opē* 'hole for a beam-end.'

met·o·pro·lol /məˈtäprəˌlôl; -ˌläl/ ▸*n.* *Medicine* a beta-blocking drug related to propranolol, used to treat hypertension and angina. ▹1970s: from *met-* (from **METHYL**) + *pro(prano)lol*.

M

me·tre ▸*n.* British spelling of **METER**[1], **METER**[2].

met·ric[1] /ˈmetrik/ ▸*adj.* **1** of or based on the meter as a unit of length; relating to the metric system: *all measurements are given in metric form.* ■ using the metric system: *we should have* **gone metric** *years ago.* **2** *Mathematics & Physics* relating to or denoting a metric.
▸*n.* **1** *technical* a system or standard of measurement. ■ *Mathematics & Physics* a binary function of a topological space that gives, for any two points of the space, a value equal to the distance between them, or to a value treated as analogous to distance for the purpose of analysis. **2** *informal* metric units, or the metric system: *it's easier to work in metric.* ▹mid 19th cent. (as an adjective relating to length): from French *métrique*, from *mètre* (see **METER**[1]).

met·ric[2] ▸*adj.* relating to or composed in a poetic meter.
▸*n.* (**metrics**) [treated as *sing.*] the meter of a poem. ▹late 15th cent. (denoting the branch of study dealing with meter): via Latin from Greek *metrikos*, from *metron* (see **METER**[2]).

-metric ▸*comb. form* in adjectives corresponding to nouns ending in *-meter* (such as *geometric* corresponding to *geometer* and *geometry*). ▹from French *-métrique*, from Latin (see **METRIC**[1]).

met·ri·cal /ˈmetrikəl/ ▸*adj.* **1** of, relating to, or composed in poetic meter: *metrical translations of the Psalms.* **2** of or involving measurement: *a metrical analysis of male and female scapulae.* ▹late Middle English: via Latin from Greek *metrikos* (from *metron*: see **METER**[2]) + **-AL**. **—met·ri·cal·ly** /-ik(ə)lē/ *adv.*

-metrical ▸*comb. form* equivalent to **-METRIC**.

-metrically ▸*comb. form* in adverbs corresponding to adjectives ending in *-meter* (such as *geometrically* corresponding to *geometric*).

met·ri·cate /ˈmetriˌkāt/ ▸*v.* [*trans.*] change or adapt to a metric system of measurement. **—met·ri·ca·tion** /ˌmetriˈkāSHən/ *n.*

met·ric hun·dred·weight ▸*n.* see **HUNDREDWEIGHT**.

met·ric mile ▸*n.* a distance of 1,500 meters, or a race over this distance.

met·rics /ˈmetriks/ ▸*n.* [treated as *sing.* or *pl.*] the use or study of poetic meters; prosody.

-met·rics ▸*comb. form* denoting the science of measuring as applied to a specific field of study: *econometrics.*

met·ric sys·tem ▸*n.* the decimal measuring system based on the meter, liter, and gram as units of length, capacity, and weight or mass. The system was first proposed by the French astronomer and mathematician Gabriel Mouton (1618–94) in 1670 and was standardized in France under the Republican government in the 1790s.

met·ric ton (also **tonne**) ▸*n.* a unit of weight equal to 1,000 kilograms (2,205 lb).

me·tri·tis /miˈtrītəs/ ▸*n.* *Medicine* inflammation of the uterus. ▹mid 19th cent.: from Greek *mētra* 'womb' + **-ITIS**.

met·ro /ˈmetrō/ ▸*n.* (*pl.* **-ros**) (also **Met·ro**) a subway system in a city, esp. Paris. ■ a subway train, esp. in Paris.
▸*adj.* [*attrib.*] metropolitan: *the Detroit metro area.* ▹early 20th cent.: from French *métro*, abbreviation of *métropolitain* (from *Chemin de Fer Métropolitain* 'Metropolitan Railroad').

me·trol·o·gy /meˈträləjē/ ▸*n.* the scientific study of measurement. ▹early 19th cent.: from Greek *metron* 'measure' + **-LOGY**. **—met·ro·log·i·cal** /ˌmetrəˈläjikəl/ *adj.* **—me·trol·o·gist** /-jist/ *n.*

met·ro·ni·da·zole /ˌmetrəˈnīdəˌzōl/ ▸*n.* *Medicine* a synthetic drug used to treat trichomoniasis and some similar infections. • A nitro-derivative of imidazole; chem. formula: $C_6H_9N_3O_3$. ▹mid 20th cent.: from *me(thyl)* + *(ni)tro-* + *(im)idazole*.

met·ro·nome /ˈmetrəˌnōm/ ▸*n.* a device used by musicians that marks time at a selected rate by giving a regular tick. ▹early 19th cent.: from Greek *metron* 'measure' + *nomos* 'law.' **—met·ro·nom·ic** /ˌmetrəˈnämik/ *adj.* **—met·ro·nom·i·cal·ly** /ˌmetrəˈnämik(ə)lē/ *adv.*

metronome

me·tro·nym·ic /ˌmetrəˈnimik/ ▸*adj.* & *n.* variant spelling of **MATRONYMIC**.

met·ro·plex /ˈmetrəˌpleks/ ▸*n.* a very large metropolitan area, esp. one that is an aggregation of two or more cities. ▹1960s: blend of **METROPOLITAN** and **COMPLEX**.

met·ro·pole /ˈmetrəˌpōl/ ▸*n.* the parent state of a colony. ▹late 15th cent.: from Old French *metropole*, based on Greek *mētēr*, *mētr-* 'mother' + *polis* 'city' (see **METROPOLIS**).

me·trop·o·lis /məˈträp(ə)ləs/ ▸*n.* the capital or chief city of a country or region. ■ a very large and densely populated industrial and commercial city. ▹late Middle English (denoting the see of a metropolitan bishop): via late Latin from Greek *mētropolis* 'mother state,' from *mētēr*, *mētr-* 'mother' + *polis* 'city.'

met·ro·pol·i·tan /ˌmetrəˈpälətn/ ▸*adj.* **1** of, relating to, or denoting a metropolis, often inclusive of its surrounding areas: *the Boston metropolitan area.* **2** of, relating to, or denoting the parent state of a colony or dependency: *metropolitan Spain.* **3** *Christian Church* of, relating to, or denoting a metropolitan or his see: *a metropolitan bishop.*
▸*n.* **1** *Christian Church* a bishop having authority over the bishops of a province, in particular (in many Orthodox Churches) one ranking above archbishop and below patriarch. **2** an inhabitant of a metropolis: *the sophisticated metropolitan.* ▹late Middle English (in the ecclesiastical sense): from late Latin *metropolitanus*, from Greek *mētropolitēs* 'citizen of a mother state,' from *mētropolis* (see **METROPOLIS**). **—met·ro·pol·i·tan·ate** /-ˈpälətnˌāt/ *n.* (in sense 1 of the *noun*). **—met·ro·pol·i·tan·ism** /-ˌpälətnˌizəm/ *n.*

Met·ro·pol·i·tan Mu·se·um of Art a major museum of art and archaeology in New York City, founded in 1870.

me·tror·rha·gi·a /ˌmētrəˈrāj(ē)ə; ˌmetrə-/ ▸*n.* abnormal bleeding from the uterus. ▹mid 19th cent.: modern Latin, from Greek *mētra* 'womb' + *-rrhag-*, stem of *rhēgnunai* 'to burst.'

met·ro·sex·u·al /ˌmetrōˈsekSHo͞oəl/ ▸*n.* a young, urban, heterosexual male with liberal political views, an interest in fashion, and a refined sense of taste. ▹from *metro-* + *(homo)sexual*. **—met·ro·sex·u·al·i·ty** /-ˌsekSHo͞oˈalitē/ *n.*

-metry ▸*comb. form* in nouns denoting procedures and systems corresponding to names of instruments ending in *-meter* (such as *calorimetry* corresponding to *calorimeter*). ▹from Greek *-metria*, from *-metrēs* 'measurer.'

Met·ter·nich /ˈmetərˌnik; -ˌniKH/, Klemens Wenzel Nepomuk Lothar, Prince of Metternich-Winneburg-Beilstein (1773–1859), Austrian statesman. As foreign minister (1809–48), he was one of the organizers of the Congress of Vienna (1814–15), which determined the settlement of Europe after the Napoleonic Wars.

met·tle /ˈmetl/ ▸*n.* a person's ability to cope well with difficulties or to face a demanding situation in a spirited and resilient way: *the team showed their true mettle in the second half.* ▹mid 16th cent.: specialized spelling (used for figurative senses) of **METAL**. **—met·tle·some** /-səm/ *adj.*
▸*PHRASES* □ **be on one's mettle** be ready or forced to prove one's ability to cope well with a demanding situation. □ **put someone on their mettle** (of a demanding situation) test someone's ability to face difficulties.

Metz /mets/ a city in Lorraine, in northeastern France, on the Moselle River; pop. 124,000.

meu·nière /mœnˈyer/ ▸*adj.* [usu. *postpositive*] (esp. of fish) cooked or served in lightly browned butter with lemon juice and parsley: *sole meunière.* ▹from French *(à la) meunière* '(in the manner of) a miller's wife.'

Meur·sault /mərˈsō; mœr-/ ▸*n.* (*pl.* same) a burgundy wine, typically white, produced near Beaune in eastern France. ▹named after a commune in the Côte d'Or region of France.

Meuse /myo͞oz; mo͞oz; mœz/ a river in western Europe that rises in northeastern France and flows 594 miles (950 km) through Belgium and the Netherlands to the North Sea south of Dordrecht. Flemish and Dutch name **Maas**.

MeV ▸*abbr.* mega-electronvolt(s).

mew[1] /myo͞o/ ▸*v.* [*intrans.*] (of a cat or some kinds of bird) make a characteristic high-pitched crying noise: *a throng of cats and kittens mewing to be fed* | [as *n.*] (**mewing**) *the mewing of gulls.*
▸*n.* the high-pitched crying noise made by a cat or bird: *a kitten's mew.* ▹Middle English: imitative.

mew[2] *Falconry* ▸*n.* (usu. **mews**) a cage or building for trained hawks, esp. while they are molting.
▸*v.* **1** [*intrans.*] (esp. of a trained hawk) molt. **2** [*trans.*] confine (a trained hawk) to a cage or building at the time of molting. ▹late Middle English: from Old French *mue*, from *muer* 'to molt,' from Latin *mutare* 'to change.'

mew gull ▸*n.* a migratory gull with greenish-gray legs, found locally in northern and eastern Eurasia and northwestern North America. • *Larus canus*, family Laridae. ▹mid 19th cent.: *mew* (in Old English *meau* 'mew gull'), of Germanic origin; related to Dutch *meeuw* and German *Möwe*.

mewl /myo͞ol/ ▸*v.* [*intrans.*] [often as *adj.*] (**mewling**) (esp. of a baby) cry feebly or querulously; whimper: *dozens of mewling babies.* ■ (of a cat or bird) mew: *the mewling cry of a hawk.* ▹late Middle English: imitative.

mews /myo͞oz/ ▸*n.* (*pl.* same) *chiefly Brit.* a row or street of houses or apartments that have been converted from stables or built to look like former stables. ■ a group of stables, typically with rooms above, built around a yard or along an alley. ▹late Middle English: plural of MEW[2], originally referring to the royal stables on the site of the hawk mews at Charing Cross, London. The sense 'converted dwellings' dates from the early 19th cent.

Mex ▸*adj.* & *n. informal* Mexican.

Mex·i·cal·i /ˌmeksəˈkalē/ the capital of the state of Baja California, in northwestern Mexico; pop. 602,000.

Mex·i·can bam·boo ▸*n.* another term for JAPANESE KNOTWEED.

Mex·i·can hair·less ▸*n.* a small dog of a breed lacking hair except for tufts on the head and tail.

Mex·i·can jump·ing bean ▸*n.* see JUMPING BEAN.

Mex·i·ca·no /ˌmeksiˈkänō; ˌmäkhē-/ ▸*n.* & *adj. informal* **1** the Nahuatl language. **2** a person of Mexican descent. ▹Spanish.

Mex·i·co /ˈmeksiˌkō; ˈmāhēkō/ a country in southwestern North America, with extensive coastlines on the Gulf of Mexico and the Pacific Ocean, bordered by the U.S. on the north; pop. 104,959,00; capital, Mexico City; language, Spanish (official). ■ a state in central Mexico, west of Mexico City; capital, Toluca de Lerdo. —**Mex·i·can** /ˈmeksəkən/ *adj.* & *n.*

The center of both Mayan and Aztec civilizations, Mexico was conquered and colonized by the Spanish in the early 16th century. It remained under Spanish rule until independence was achieved in 1821; a republic was established three years later. Texas rebelled and broke away in 1836, while all the remaining territory north of the Rio Grande was lost to the U.S. in the Mexican War of 1846–48.

Mex·i·co, Gulf of a large extension of the western Atlantic Ocean. Bounded in a sweeping curve by the U.S. on the north, by Mexico on the west and south, and by Cuba on the southeast, it is linked to the Atlantic Ocean by the Straits of Florida and to the Caribbean Sea by the Yucatán Channel.

Mex·i·co Cit·y the capital of Mexico; pop. 13,636,000. Founded about 1300 as the Aztec capital Tenochtitlán, it was destroyed in 1521 by the Spanish conquistador Cortés, who rebuilt it as the capital of New Spain.

Mey·er·beer /ˈmāərbi(ə)r; ˈmīərˌbe(ə)r/, Giacomo (1791–1864), German composer; born *Jakob Liebmann Beer*. After settling in Paris, he established himself as a leading exponent of French grand opera.

Mey·er·hof /ˈmīərˌhôf/, Otto Fritz (1884–1951), U.S. biochemist, born in Germany. He worked on the biochemical processes involved in muscle action and provided the basis for understanding the process by which glucose is broken down to provide energy. Nobel Prize for Physiology or Medicine (1922, shared with Archibald Hill [1886–1977]).

me·ze /meˈze/ (also **mez·ze**) ▸*n.* (*pl.* **me·ze·des** /meˈzeᴛʜəs/) in the Mediterranean, an appetizer. ▹Turkish and modern Greek.

me·ze·re·on /məˈzi(ə)rēən/ (also **me·ze·re·um** /-əm/) ▸*n.* a Eurasian shrub with fragrant purplish-red flowers and poisonous red berries, found chiefly in calcareous woodlands. • *Daphne mezereum*, family Thymelaeaceae. ▹late 15th cent.: from medieval Latin, from Arabic *māzaryūn*.

me·zu·zah /məˈzo͝ozə/ (also **me·zu·za**) ▸*n.* (*pl.* **me·zu·zahs** or **me·zu·zas** or **me·zu·zot** or **me·zu·zoth** /məˈzo͝ozōt/) a parchment inscribed with religious texts and attached in a case to the doorpost of a Jewish house as a sign of faith. ▹mid 17th cent.: from Hebrew *mĕzūzāh* 'doorpost.'

mez·za·lu·na /ˌmetsəˈlo͞onə/ ▸*n.* a utensil for chopping herbs, vegetables, etc., with a semicircular blade and a handle at each end. ▹1950s: from Italian, literally 'half moon.'

mez·za·nine /ˈmezəˌnēn; ˌmezəˈnēn/ ▸*n.* a low story between two others in a building, typically between the ground and first floors. ■ the lowest balcony of a theater, stadium, etc., or the front rows of the balcony.

▸*adj.* [*attrib.*] *Finance* relating to or denoting unsecured, higher-yielding loans that are subordinate to bank loans and secured loans but rank above equity. ▹early 18th cent.: from French, from Italian *mezzanino*, diminutive of *mezzano* 'middle,' from Latin *medianus* 'median.'

mez·za vo·ce /ˌmetsä ˈvōchā; ˌmedzä/ *Music* ▸*adv.* & *adj.* (esp. as a direction) using about half the singer's vocal power.

▸*n.* singing performed in this way. ▹Italian, literally 'half voice.'

mez·zo /ˈmetsō; ˈmedzō/ ▸*n.* (*pl.* **-zos**) (also **mez·zo-so·pra·no**) a female singer with a voice pitched between soprano and contralto. ■ a singing voice of this type, or a part written for one.

▸*adv.* half, moderately. ▹mid 18th cent.: Italian, from Latin *medius* 'middle.'

mez·zo for·te /ˌmetsō ˈfôrtā; ˌmedzō/ *Music* ▸*adv.* & *adj.* (esp. as a direction) moderately loud.

▸*n.* a moderately high volume of sound.

Mez·zo·gior·no /ˌmetsōˈjôrnō/ the southern part of Italy, including Sicily and Sardinia. ▹Italian, literally 'midday'; compare with MIDI.

mez·zo pi·a·no /ˌmetsō ˈpyänō; ˌmedzō/ *Music* ▸*adv.* & *adj.* (esp. as a direction) moderately soft.

▸*n.* a moderately low volume of sound.

mez·zo·tint /ˈmetsōˌtint; ˈmedzō-/ ▸*n.* a print made from an engraved copper or steel plate on which the surface has been partially roughened, for shading, and partially scraped smooth, giving light areas. The technique was much used in the 17th, 18th, and early 19th centuries for the reproduction of paintings. ■ the technique or process of making pictures in this way.

▸*v.* [*trans.*] engrave (a picture) in mezzotint. ▹from Italian *mezzotinto*, from *mezzo* 'half' + *tinto* 'tint.' —**mez·zo·tint·er** *n.*

MF ▸*abbr.* medium frequency.

mf ▸*abbr.* mezzo forte.

MFA ▸*abbr.* Master of Fine Arts.

mfd. ▸*abbr.* ■ manufactured. ■ microfarad.

mfg. ▸*abbr.* manufacturing.

MFH ▸*abbr.* Master of Foxhounds.

MFN ▸*abbr.* most favored nation.

MFP ▸*abbr. Physics* mean free path.

mfr. ▸*abbr.* ■ manufacture. ■ (*pl.* **mfrs.**) manufacturer.

MG ▸*abbr.* ■ machine gun. ■ *historical* Morris Garages.

mg ▸*symbol* the chemical element magnesium.

mg ▸*abbr.* milligram(s): *100 mg acetaminophen.*

mgd ▸*abbr.* millions of gallons per day.

MGM Metro-Goldwyn-Mayer, a movie company formed in 1924 by Samuel Goldwyn and Louis B. Mayer. The company released both *The Wizard of Oz* and *Gone With the Wind* in 1939, and also produced many famous musicals, including *Meet Me in St. Louis* (1944) and *An American in Paris* (1951).

mgmt. ▸*abbr.* management.

MGR *Brit.* ▸*abbr.* merry-go-round (train).

Mgr ▸*abbr.* ■ (**mgr**) manager. ■ Monseigneur. ■ Monsignor: *Mgr O'Flaherty.*

mgt. ▸*abbr.* management.

MGySgt ▸*abbr.* master gunnery sergeant.

MH ▸*abbr.* Medal of Honor.

mh (also **mH**) ▸*abbr.* millihenry or millihenries.

MHC ▸*abbr.* major histocompatibility complex.

MHD ▸*abbr. Physics* magnetohydrodynamics.

MHL ▸*abbr.* Master of Hebrew Literature.

mho /mō/ ▸*n.* (*pl.* **mhos**) the reciprocal of an ohm, a former unit of electrical conductance. ▹late 19th cent.: the word OHM reversed.

MHR ▸*abbr.* (in the U.S. and Australia) Member of the House of Representatives.

MHW (also **m.h.w.** or **M.H.W.**) ▸*abbr.* mean high water.

MHz ▸*abbr.* megahertz.

MI ▸*abbr.* ■ Michigan (in official postal use). ■ *Brit., historical* Military Intelligence: *MI5.*

mi /mē/ ▸*n. Music* (in solmization) the third note of a major scale. ■ the note E in the fixed-do system. ▹late Middle English *mi*, representing (as an arbitrary name for the note) the first syllable of *mira*, taken from a Latin hymn (see SOLMIZATION).

mi. ▸*abbr.* mile(s): *10 km/6 mi.*

MI5 (in the UK) the governmental agency responsible for dealing with internal security and counter-intelligence on British territory. Formed in 1909, the agency was officially named the Security Service in 1964, but the name MI5 remains in popular use. ▹from *Military Intelligence section 5.*

MI6 (in the UK) the governmental agency responsible for dealing with matters of internal security and counter-intelligence overseas. Formed in 1912, the agency was officially named the Secret Intelligence Service in 1964, but the name MI6 remains in popular use.

MIA ▸*abbr.* missing in action. ■ [as *n.*] a member of the armed forces who is missing in action.

Mi·am·i[1] /mīˈamē/ a city and port in southeastern Florida; pop. 362,470. Its subtropical climate and miles of beaches make this and the resort island of Miami Beach, separated from the mainland by Biscayne Bay, a year-round holiday resort.

Mi·am·i[2] ▸*n.* (*pl.* same or **Mi·am·is**) **1** a member of an American Indian people formerly living mainly in Illinois, Indiana, and Wisconsin and more recently

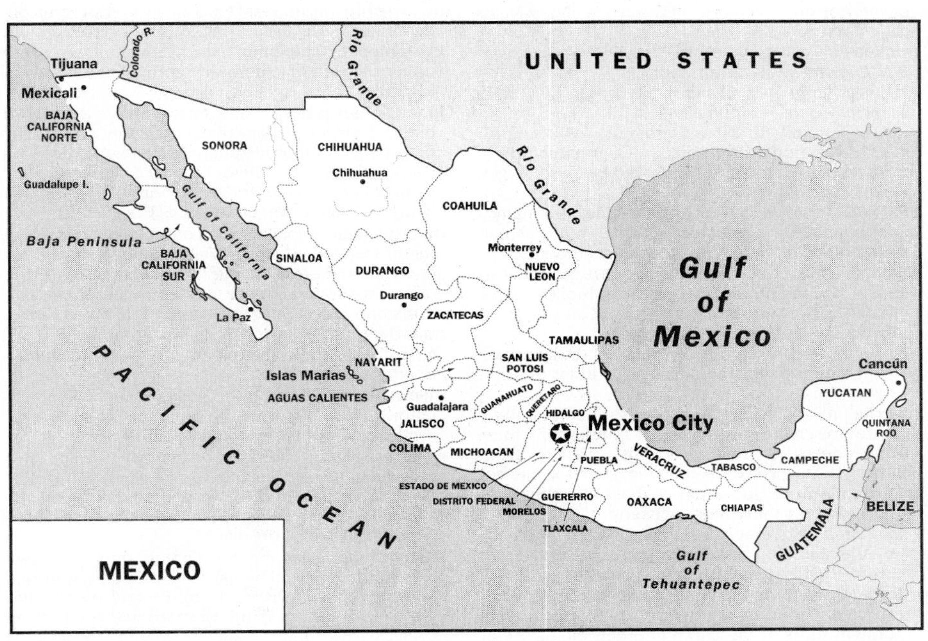

Pronunciation Key ə ago; ər over; ˈə or ˌə up; ˈər or ˌər fur; a hat; ā rate; ä car; ch chew; e let; ē see; e(ə)r air; i fit; ī by; i(ə)r ear; ng sing; ō go; ô for; oi boy; o͝o good; o͞o goo; ou out; sh she; th thin; t͟h then; (h)w why; zh vision

M

inhabiting areas of Ohio, Kansas, and Oklahoma. **2** the dialect of Illinois (an Algonquian language) of this people.

▸*adj.* of or relating to this people or their language. ▷French, from Illinois (an Algonquian language).

Mi·ami Beach a city in southeastern Florida, on the Atlantic Ocean, across Biscayne Bay from Miami; pop. 92,639.

Mi·ao /mē'ou/ ▸*n.* (*pl.* same) & *adj.* another term for **HMONG**. ▷from Chinese *Miáo*, literally 'tribes.'

mi·aow ▸*n.* & *v.* variant spelling of **MEOW**.

mi·asm /'mī,azəm; 'mē-/ ▸*n.* (in homeopathy) any of the three underlying chronic diseases that afflict humankind: sycosis, syphilis, and psora. ▷19th cent.: from Greek *miasma*, 'stain'.

mi·as·ma /mī'azmə; mē-/ ▸*n.* (*pl.* **-mas** or **-ma·ta** /-mətə/) *poetic/literary* a highly unpleasant or unhealthy smell or vapor: ***a miasma of*** *stale alcohol hung around him like marsh gas.* ■ *figurative* an oppressive or unpleasant atmosphere that surrounds or emanates from something: ***a miasma of*** *despair rose from the black workshops.* ▷mid 17th cent.: from Greek, literally 'defilement,' from *miainein* 'pollute.' **—mi·as·mal** *adj.* **—mi·as·mat·ic** /,mīəz'matik/ *adj.* **—mi·as·mic** /-mik/ *adj.* **—miasmically** /mik(ə)lē/ *adv.*

mic ▸*n.* short for **MICROPHONE**.

Mic. ▸*abbr. Bible* Micah.

mi·ca /'mīkə/ ▸*n.* a shiny silicate mineral with a layered structure, found as minute scales in granite and other rocks, or as crystals. It is used as a thermal or electrical insulator. ▷early 18th cent.: from Latin, literally 'crumb.' **—mi·ca·ceous** /mī'kāsʜəs/ *adj.*

Mi·cah /'mīkə/ (in the Bible) a Hebrew minor prophet. ■ a book of the Bible bearing his name, foretelling the destruction of Samaria and of Jerusalem.

mi·ca schist ▸*n.* a metamorphic rock that contains quartz and mica and resembles slate in being easily split.

mice /mīs/ ▸ plural form of **MOUSE**.

mi·celle /mī'sel/ ▸*n. Chemistry* an aggregate of molecules in a colloidal solution, such as those formed by detergents. ▷late 19th cent.: coined as a diminutive of Latin *mica* 'crumb.' **—mi·cel·lar** /mī'selər/ *adj.*

Mich. ▸*abbr.* Michigan.

Mi·chae·lis con·stant /mə'kālis/ ▸*n. Biochemistry* the concentration of a given enzyme that catalyzes the associated reaction at half the maximum rate. ▷1930s: named after Leonor *Michaelis* (1875–1949), German-born American chemist.

Mich·ael·mas /'mikəlməs/ ▸*n.* the feast of St. Michael, September 29. ▷Old English *Sanct Michaeles mæsse* 'Saint Michael's Mass,' referring to the Archangel.

Mich·ael·mas dai·sy ▸*n. chiefly Brit.* an aster, esp. *Aster novae-belgii*, a North American aster with numerous pinkish-lilac daisylike flowers that bloom around Michaelmas.

Mi·chel·an·ge·lo /,mikəl'anjəlō; ,mīkəl-; ,mēke'länjelō/ (1475–1564), Italian sculptor, painter, architect, and poet; full name *Michelangelo Buonarroti*. A leading figure of the High Renaissance, Michelangelo established his reputation with sculptures such as the *Pietà* (*c.*1497–1500) and *David* (1501–04). Under papal patronage he decorated the ceiling of the Sistine Chapel in Rome (1508–12) and painted the fresco *The Last Judgment* (1536–41), both important mannerist works. His architectural achievements include the completion of St. Peter's cathedral in Rome (1546–64).

Michelangelo

Mi·che·lin /'misʜələn/, André (1853–1931) and Édouard (1859–1940), French industrialists. They founded the Michelin Tire Company in 1888 and pioneered the use of pneumatic tires on automobiles.

Mi·che·loz·zo /,mēke'lôtsō/ (1396–1472), Italian architect and sculptor; full name *Michelozzo di Bartolommeo*. In partnership with Ghiberti and Donatello, he led a revival of interest in Roman architecture.

Mi·chel·son /'mīkəlsən/, Albert Abraham (1852–1931), U.S. physicist. He specialized in precision measurement in experimental physics. Nobel Prize for Physics (1907).

Mi·chel·son–Mor·ley ex·per·i·ment /,mīkəlsən 'môrlē/ *Physics* an experiment performed in 1887 that attempted to measure the relative motion of the earth and the ether by measuring the speed of light in directions parallel and perpendicular to the earth's motion. The result disproved the existence of the ether, which contradicted Newtonian physics but was explained by Einstein's special theory of relativity. ▷named after A. A. **MICHELSON** and E. W. **MORLEY**.

Miche·ner /'micʜ(ə)nər/, James (Albert) (1907–97), U.S. writer. He wrote *Tales of the South Pacific* (1947), which was made into the Broadway musical *South Pacific* (1949). He was also known for other fictionalized histories that included *Hawaii* (1959), *Chesapeake* (1978), *Texas* (1985), *Alaska* (1988), and *A Miracle in Seville* (1995).

Mich·i·gan /'misʜigən/ a state in the northern U.S., bordered on the west, north, and east by lakes Michigan, Superior, Huron, and Erie; pop. 9,938,444; capital, Lansing; statehood, Jan. 26, 1837 (26). It was acquired from Britain by the U.S. in 1783. **—Mich·i·gan·der** /-,gandər/ *n.*

Mich·i·gan·der /,misʜi'gandər/ ▸*n.* a native or inhabitant of Michigan.

Mich·i·gan, Lake one of the five Great Lakes. Bordered by Michigan, Wisconsin, Illinois, and Indiana, it is the only one of the Great Lakes to lie wholly within the U.S. The cities of Milwaukee and Chicago are on its shores.

Mi·cho·a·cán /,mēcʜō-ə'kän/ a state of western Mexico, on the Pacific coast; capital, Morelia.

Mick /mik/ ▸*n. informal, offensive* an Irishman. ▷mid 19th cent.: nickname for the given name *Michael*.

mick·ey /'mikē/ ▸*n.* **1** (also **Mickey**) short for **MICKEY FINN**: *I bet some guy* ***slipped me a mickey.*** **2** (in phrase **take the mickey**) *informal, chiefly Brit.* tease or ridicule someone. ▷1950s: of unknown origin.

Mick·ey Finn /'mikē 'fin/ ▸*n. informal* a surreptitiously drugged or doctored drink given to someone so as to make them drunk or insensible. ■ the substance used to adulterate such a drink. ▷1920s: of unknown origin; sometimes said to be the name of a notorious Chicago saloonkeeper (*c.*1896–1906).

Mick·ey Mouse /,mikē 'mous/ a Walt Disney cartoon character who first appeared as Mortimer Mouse in 1927, becoming Mickey in 1928. During the 1930s, he became established as the central Disney character. ■ [as *adj.*] (also **mickey mouse**) *informal* trivial or of inferior quality: *people think you're a Mickey Mouse outfit if you work from home.*

mick·le /'mikəl/ (also **muck·le** /'məkəl/) *archaic Scottish & N. English* ▸*n.* a large amount.

▸*adj.* very large: *she had a great big elephant ... that's one of those mickle beasts from Africa.*

▸*adj.* & *pron.* much; a large amount. ▷Old English *micel* 'great, numerous, much,' of Germanic origin; from an Indo-European root shared by Greek *megas, megal-*.

▸*PHRASE* □ **many a little makes a mickle** (also **many a mickle makes a muckle**) *proverb* many small amounts accumulate to make a large amount.

Mic·mac /'mik,mak/ (also **Mi'k·maq**) ▸*n.* (*pl.* same or **-macs**) **1** a member of an American Indian people inhabiting the Maritime Provinces of Canada. **2** the Algonquian language of this people.

▸*adj.* of or relating to this people or their language. ▷via French from the Micmac self-designation *mīkəmaw*.

mi·crite /'mik,rīt; 'mī,krīt/ ▸*n. Geology* microcrystalline calcite present in some types of limestone. ■ limestone consisting chiefly of this. ▷1950s: from *micr(ocrystalline)* + **-ITE**[1]. **—mi·crit·ic** /mi'kritik; mī-/ *adj.*

mi·cro /'mīkrō/ ▸*n.* (*pl.* **-cros**) **1** short for **MICROCOMPUTER**. **2** short for **MICROPROCESSOR**.

▸*adj.* [*attrib.*] extremely small: *a micro dining area.* ■ small-scale: *CO_2 emissions cannot be dealt with at the micro level.* Often contrasted with **MACRO**.

micro- ▸*comb. form* **1** small: *microcar.* ■ of reduced or restricted size: *microdot | microprocessor.* **2** (used commonly in units of measurement) denoting a factor of one millionth (10^{-6}): *microfarad.* ▷from Greek *mikros* 'small.'

mi·cro·a·nal·y·sis /,mīkrōə'naləsəs/ ▸*n.* the quantitative analysis of chemical compounds using a sample of a few milligrams. **—mi·cro·an·a·lyt·ic** /-,anl'itik/ *adj.* **—mi·cro·an·a·lyt·i·cal** /-,anl'itikəl/ *adj.*

mi·cro·an·a·lyz·er /,mīkrō'anl,īzər/ ▸*n.* another term for **MICROPROBE**.

mi·cro·ar·ray /'mīkrō-ə,rā/ ▸*n.* a grid of DNA segments of known sequence that is used to test and map DNA fragments, antibodies, or proteins.

mi·cro·bal·ance /,mīkrō'baləns/ ▸*n.* a balance for weighing masses of a fraction of a gram.

mi·crobe /'mī,krōb/ ▸*n.* a microorganism, esp. a bacterium causing disease or fermentation. ▷late 19th cent.: from French, from Greek *mikros* 'small' + *bios* 'life.' **—mi·cro·bi·al** /mī'krōbēəl/ *adj.* **—mi·cro·bic** /mī 'krōbik/ *adj.*

mi·cro·bi·ol·o·gy /,mīkrō,bī'äləjē/ ▸*n.* the branch of science that deals with microorganisms. **—mi·cro·bi·o·log·ic** /-,bīə'läjik/ *adj.* **—mi·cro·bi·o·log·i·cal** /-,bīə 'läjikəl/ *adj.* **—mi·cro·bi·o·log·i·cal·ly** /-,bīə'läjik(ə)lē/ *adv.* **—mi·cro·bi·ol·o·gist** /-jist/ *n.*

mi·cro·bi·o·ta /,mīkrō,bī'ōtə/ ▸*n.* the microorganisms of a particular site, habitat, or geological period.

mi·cro·brew /'mīkrə,brōō/ ▸*n.* a type of beer produced in a microbrewery.

▸*v.* [*trans.*] (usu. **be microbrewed**) produce (beer) in a microbrewery: *the beer is microbrewed in Racine* | [as *adj.*] (**microbrewed**) *microbrewed beer.* **—mi·cro·brew·er** *n.*

mi·cro·brew·er·y /,mīkrə'brōōərē/ ▸*n.* (*pl.* **-er·ies**) a limited-production brewery, typically producing specialty beers and often selling its products only locally.

mi·cro·brows·er /'mīkrō,brouzər/ ▸*n. Computing* a small Internet browser for use with cellular phones and other handheld devices.

mi·cro·burst /'mīkrō,bərst/ ▸*n.* a sudden, powerful, localized air current, esp. a downdraft.

mi·cro·cap·sule /,mīkrō'kapsəl; -sōōl/ ▸*n.* a small capsule used to contain drugs, dyes, or other substances and render them temporarily inactive.

mi·cro·car /'mīkrō,kär/ ▸*n.* a small and fuel-efficient car.

mi·cro·cel·lu·lar /,mīkrō'selyələr/ ▸*adj.* containing or made up of minute cells. ■ (of a mobile telephone system) having small cells, typically with a radius of less than half a mile.

mi·cro·ceph·a·ly /,mīkrō'sefəlē/ ▸*n. Medicine* abnormal smallness of the head, a congenital condition associated with incomplete brain development. **—mi·cro·ce·phal·ic** /-sə'falik/ *adj.* & *n.* **—mi·cro·ceph·a·lous** /-'sefələs/ *adj.*

mi·cro·chem·is·try /,mīkrō'keməstrē/ ▸*n.* the branch of chemistry concerned with the reactions and properties of substances in minute quantities, e.g., in living tissue.

mi·cro·chip /'mīkrō,cʜip/ ▸*n.* a tiny wafer of semiconducting material used to make an integrated circuit.

▸*v.* (**-chipped, -chip·ping**) [*trans.*] implant a microchip under the skin of (a domestic animal) as a means of identification.

Mi·cro·chi·rop·ter·a /,mīkrōkə'räptərə/ *Zoology* a major division of bats that comprises all but the fruit bats. • Suborder Microchiroptera, order Chiroptera: many families. ▷modern Latin (plural), from **MICRO-** 'small' + Greek *kheir* 'hand' + *pteron* 'wing.' **—mi·cro·chi·rop·ter·an** *n.* & *adj.*

mi·cro·cin·e·ma /'mīkrō,sinəmə/ ▸*n.* a genre consisting of low-budget alternative or independent films and videos: *she took a course in microcinema at the state college.* ■ a small room or theater used to show such films and videos: *the campus has three microcinemas.*

mi·cro·cir·cuit /'mīkrō,sərkət/ ▸*n.* a minute electric circuit, esp. an integrated circuit. **—mi·cro·cir·cuit·ry** /,mīkrō'sərkətrē/ *n.*

mi·cro·cir·cu·la·tion /,mīkrō,sərkyə'lāsʜən/ ▸*n.* circulation of the blood in the smallest blood vessels. **—mi·cro·cir·cu·la·to·ry** /-'sərkyələ,tôrē/ *adj.*

mi·cro·cli·mate /'mīkrō,klīmət/ ▸*n.* the climate of a very small or restricted area, esp. when this differs from the climate of the surrounding area. **—mi·cro·cli·mat·ic** /,mīkrō,klī'matik/ *adj.* **—mi·cro·cli·mat·i·cal·ly** /,mīkrō,klī'matik(ə)lē/ *adv.*

mi·cro·cline /'mīkrō,klīn/ ▸*n.* a green, pink, or brown crystalline mineral consisting of potassium-rich feldspar, characteristic of granite and pegmatites. ▷mid 19th cent.: from German *Mikroklin*, from Greek *mikros* 'small' + *klinein* 'to lean' (because its angle of cleavage differs only slightly from 90 degrees).

mi·cro·coc·cus /ˌmīkrōˈkäkəs/ ▸*n.* (*pl.* **-coc·ci** /-ˈkäk ˌ(s)ī; -ˈkäk(s)ē/) a spherical bacterium that is typically found on dead or decaying organic matter. Nonpathogenic forms are found on human and animal skin. • Family Micrococcaceae of Gram-positive nonmotile bacteria, in particular the genera *Micrococcus* and *Staphylococcus*. —**mi·cro·coc·cal** *adj.*

mi·cro·code /ˈmīkrəˌkōd/ ▸*n.* *Computing* a very low-level instruction set that is stored permanently in a computer or peripheral controller and controls the operation of the device.

mi·cro·com·pu·ter /ˈmīkrōkəmˌpyo͞otər/ ▸*n.* a small computer that contains a microprocessor as its central processor.

mi·cro·con·ti·nent /ˌmīkrōˈkäntn-ənt/ ▸*n.* *Geology* an isolated fragment of continental crust forming part of a small crust plate.

mi·cro·cop·y /ˈmīkrōˌkäpē/ ▸*n.* (*pl.* **-cop·ies**) a copy of printed matter that has been reduced in size by microphotography.
▸*v.* (**-cop·ies**, **-cop·ied**) [*trans.*] make a microcopy of.

mi·cro·cosm /ˈmīkrəˌkäzəm/ (also **mi·cro·cos·mos** /ˌmīkrəˈkäzməs; -mōs/) ▸*n.* a community, place, or situation regarded as encapsulating in miniature the characteristic qualities or features of something much larger: *Berlin is a microcosm of Germany, in unity as in division.* ▪ humankind regarded as the epitome of the universe. ▹Middle English: from Old French *microcosme* or medieval Latin *microcosmus*, from Greek *mikros kosmos* 'little world.' —**mi·cro·cos·mic** /ˌmīkrəˈkäzmik/ *adj.* —**mi·cro·cos·mi·cal·ly** /-ˈkäzmik(ə)lē/ *adv.*
▸*PHRASE* ▫ **in microcosm** in miniature.

mi·cro·cos·mic salt /ˌmīkrəˈkäzmik/ ▸*n.* *Chemistry* a white crystalline salt obtained from human urine. • Hydrated sodium ammonium hydrogen phosphate; chem. formula: $HNaNH_4PO_4{\cdot}4H_2O$. ▹late 18th cent.: translating Latin *sal microcosmicus*.

mi·cro·cred·it /ˈmīkrōˌkredit/ ▸*n.* the lending of small amounts of money at low interest to new businesses in the developing world. ▪ such a loan considered individually: *microcredits should not be considered a substitute for long-term investment in infrastructure.*

mi·cro·crys·tal·line /ˌmīkrōˈkristəlin; -ˌlīn; -ˌlēn/ ▸*adj.* (of a material) formed of microscopic crystals.

mi·cro·cyte /ˈmīkrəˌsīt/ ▸*n.* *Medicine* an unusually small red blood cell, associated with certain anemias. —**mi·cro·cyt·ic** /ˌmīkrəˈsitik/ *adj.*

mi·cro·den·si·tom·e·ter /ˌmīkrōˌdensəˈtämətər/ ▸*n.* a densitometer for measuring the density of very small areas of a photographic image.

mi·cro·derm·a·bra·sion /ˌmīkrōˌdərməˈbrāzhən/ ▸*n.* surgical removal of skin imperfections, especially wrinkles, by means of a vacuum containing mineral crystals.

mi·cro·dot /ˈmīkrəˌdät/ ▸*n.* **1** a microphotograph, esp. of a printed or written document, that is only about 0.04 inch (1 mm) across. ▪ [usu. as *adj.*] denoting a pattern of very small dots. **2** a tiny tablet or capsule (of LSD): *more than 1,000* **microdots** *of LSD.*

mi·cro·ec·o·nom·ics /ˌmīkrōˌekəˈnämiks; -ˌēkə-/ ▸*plural n.* [treated as *sing.*] the part of economics concerned with single factors and the effects of individual decisions. —**mi·cro·ec·o·nom·ic** *adj.*

mi·cro·e·lec·tro·me·chan·i·cal /ˌmīkrō-iˌlektrōməˈkanikəl/ ▸*adj.* denoting systems or components relating to microscopic electronic machines that are typically built on computer chips: *optical true-time delay devices with microelectromechanical mirror arrays.* —**mi·cro·e·lec·tro·me·chan·ics** *n.*

mi·cro·e·lec·tron·ics /ˌmīkrōiˌlekˈträniks/ ▸*plural n.* [usu. treated as *sing.*] the design, manufacture, and use of microchips and microcircuits. —**mi·cro·e·lec·tron·ic** *adj.*

mi·cro·en·vi·ron·ment /ˌmīkrōinˈvīrə(n)mənt; -ˈvī(ə)r(n)mənt/ ▸*n.* *Biology* the immediate small-scale environment of an organism or a part of an organism, esp. as a distinct part of a larger environment. —**mi·cro·en·vi·ron·men·tal** /-ˌvīrə(n)ˈmentl; -ˌvī(ə)r(n)-/ *adj.*

mi·cro·ev·o·lu·tion /ˌmīkrō-evəˈlo͞oshən; -ˌēvə-/ ▸*n.* *Biology* evolutionary change within a species or small group of organisms, esp. over a short period. —**mi·cro·ev·o·lu·tion·ar·y** /-ˈlo͞oshəˌnerē/ *adj.*

mi·cro·far·ad /ˈmīkrōˌfarəd; -ad/ ▸*n.* one millionth of a farad. Symbol μF.

mi·cro·fau·na /ˌmīkrōˈfônə; -ˈfänə/ ▸*n.* (*pl.* **-fau·nas** or **-fau·nae** /-ˈfônē; -ˈfänē/) *Biology* microscopic animals. ▪ *Ecology* the animals of a microhabitat. —**mi·cro·fau·nal** *adj.*

mi·cro·fi·ber /ˈmīkrōˌfībər/ ▸*n.* a very fine synthetic yarn.

mi·cro·fi·bril /ˌmīkrōˈfībrəl; -ˈfibrəl/ ▸*n.* *Biology* a small fibril in the cytoplasm or wall of a cell, visible only under an electron microscope, and typically aggregated into coarser fibrils or structures.

mi·cro·fiche /ˈmīkrəˌfēsh/ ▸*n.* (*pl.* same or **-fich·es**) a flat piece of film containing microphotographs of the pages of a newspaper, catalog, or other document: *this new journal is available as a microfiche | the index will be made available* **on microfiche**.
▸*v.* [*trans.*] make a microfiche of (a newspaper, catalog, or other document).

mi·cro·fil·a·ment /ˌmīkrōˈfiləmənt/ ▸*n.* *Biology* a small rodlike structure, about 4–7 nanometers in diameter, present in numbers in the cytoplasm of many eukaryotic cells.

mi·cro·fi·lar·i·a /ˌmīkrōfəˈle(ə)rēə/ ▸*n.* (*pl.* **-fi·lar·i·ae** /-fəˈle(ə)rēˌē; -ēˌī/) *Zoology* the minute larva of a filaria.

mi·cro·film /ˈmīkrəˌfilm/ ▸*n.* a length of film containing microphotographs of a newspaper, catalog, or other document: *all those forms go* **on microfilm** *| his vast hoard of microfilms.*
▸*v.* [*trans.*] make a microfilm of (a newspaper, catalog, or other document).

mi·cro·flo·ra /ˌmīkrōˈflôrə/ ▸*n.* (*pl.* **-flo·ras** or **-flo·rae** /-ˈflôrē/) *Biology* microscopic plants. ▪ *Ecology* the plants of a microhabitat. —**mi·cro·flo·ral** *adj.*

mi·cro·form /ˈmīkrəˌfôrm/ ▸*n.* microphotographic reproduction on film or paper of a manuscript, map, or other document.

mi·cro·fos·sil /ˈmīkrōˌfäsəl/ ▸*n.* a fossil or fossil fragment that can be seen only with a microscope.

mi·cro·fun·gus /ˌmīkrōˈfəNGgəs/ ▸*n.* (*pl.* **-fun·gi** /-ˈfənˌjī; -ˌgī; -ˌjē; -ˌgē/) *Biology* a fungus in which no sexual process has been observed or in which the reproductive organs are microscopic.

mi·cro·gam·ete /ˌmīkrōˈgamˌēt; -gəˈmēt/ ▸*n.* *Biology* (esp. in protozoans) the smaller of a pair of conjugating gametes, usually regarded as male.

mi·crog·li·a /ˌmīkrəˈglēə; ˈgliə/ ▸*plural n.* *Anatomy* glial cells derived from mesoderm that function as macrophages (scavengers) in the central nervous system and form part of the reticuloendothelial system. —**mi·crog·li·al** *adj.*

mi·cro·gram /ˈmīkrəˌgram/ ▸*n.* one millionth of a gram. (Symbol: μg)

mi·cro·graph /ˈmīkrəˌgraf/ ▸*n.* a photograph taken by means of a microscope. —**mi·cro·graph·ic** /ˌmīkrəˈgrafik/ *adj.* —**mi·cro·graph·ics** /ˌmīkrəˈgrafiks/ *n.* —**mi·crog·ra·phy** /mīˈkrägrəfē/ *n.*

mi·cro·grav·i·ty /ˌmīkrōˈgravətē/ ▸*n.* very weak gravity, as in an orbiting spacecraft.

mi·cro·groove /ˈmīkrəˌgro͞ov/ ▸*n.* the very narrow groove on a long-playing phonograph record.

mi·cro·hab·i·tat /ˌmīkrōˈhabəˌtat/ ▸*n.* *Ecology* a habitat that is of small or limited extent and which differs in character from some surrounding more extensive habitat.

mi·cro·in·ject /ˌmīkrō-inˈjekt/ ▸*v.* [*trans.*] *Biology* inject (something) into a microscopic object. —**mi·cro·in·jec·tion** /-ˈjekshən/ *n.*

mi·cro·in·struc·tion /ˌmīkrō-inˈstrəkshən/ ▸*n.* *Computing* a single instruction in microcode.

mi·cro·ker·nel /ˈmīkrōˌkərnl/ ▸*n.* *Computing* a small modular part of an operating system kernel that implements its basic features.

mi·cro·lep·i·dop·ter·a /ˌmīkrōˌlepəˈdäptərə/ ▸*plural n.* *Entomology* the numerous small moths. Compare with MACROLEPIDOPTERA. ▹modern Latin (plural), from MICRO- 'small' + LEPIDOPTERA.

mi·cro·li·ter /ˌmīkrōˈlētər/ (*Brit.* also **mi·cro·li·tre**) ▸*n.* one millionth of a liter. Symbol μl.

mi·cro·lith /ˈmīkrəˌliTH/ ▸*n.* *Archaeology* a minute shaped flint, typically part of a composite tool such as a spear. —**mi·cro·lith·ic** /ˌmīkrəˈliTHik/ *adj.*

mi·cro·man·age /ˌmīkrōˈmanij/ ▸*v.* [*trans.*] control every part, however small, of (an enterprise or activity). —**mi·cro·man·age·ment** /ˈmanijmənt/ *n.* —**mi·cro·man·ag·er** *n.*

mi·cro·me·te·or·ite /ˌmīkrōˈmēteəˌrīt/ ▸*n.* a micrometeoroid that has entered the earth's atmosphere.

mi·cro·me·te·or·oid /ˌmīkrōˈmēteəˌroid/ ▸*n.* a microscopic particle in space or of extraterrestrial origin that is small enough so that if it enters the earth's atmosphere, it will not burn up but drift to the earth's surface instead.

mi·cro·me·te·or·ol·o·gy /ˌmīkrōˌmētēəˈräləjē/ ▸*n.* the branch of meteorology concerned with small areas and with small-scale meteorological phenomena. —**mi·cro·me·te·or·o·log·i·cal** /-ˌmētēərəˈläjikəl/ *adj.*

mi·crom·e·ter[1] /mīˈkrämətər/ (also **micrometer caliper**) ▸*n.* a gauge that measures small distances or thicknesses between its two faces, one of which can be moved away from or toward the other by turning a screw with a fine thread. —**mi·crom·e·try** /-ətrē/ *n.*

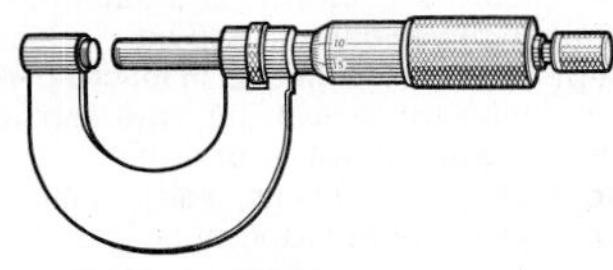

micrometer[1]

mi·cro·me·ter[2] /ˈmīkrōˈmētər/ (abbr.: μm) ▸*n.* one millionth of a meter.

mi·crom·e·tre ▸*n.* British spelling of MICROMETER[2].

mi·cro·min·i·a·tur·i·za·tion /ˌmīkrōˌminēəchəriˈzāshən; -ˌminichər-/ ▸*n.* the manufacture of extremely small versions of electronic devices. —**mi·cro·min·i·a·tur·ize** /-ˈminēəchəˌrīz; -ˌminichə-/ *v.*

mi·cron /ˈmīˌkrän/ ▸*n.* a unit of length equal to one millionth of a meter, used in many technological and scientific fields. ▹late 19th cent.: from Greek *mikron*, neuter of *mikros* 'small.'

Mi·cro·ne·sia /ˌmīkrəˈnēzhə/ **1** a region of the western Pacific Ocean, north of Melanesia and north and west of Polynesia. It includes the Mariana, Caroline, and Marshall island groups and Kiribati. **2** a group of associated island states that comprise the 600 islands of the Caroline Islands, in the western Pacific Ocean, north of the equator; pop. 108,000; capital, Palikir; languages, English (official) and Austronesian languages. Full name FEDERATED STATES OF MICRONESIA.

The group was administered by the U.S. as part of the Pacific Islands Trust Territory from 1947 and entered into free association with the U.S. as an independent state in 1986.

▹from Greek *mikros* 'small' + *nēsos* 'island.'

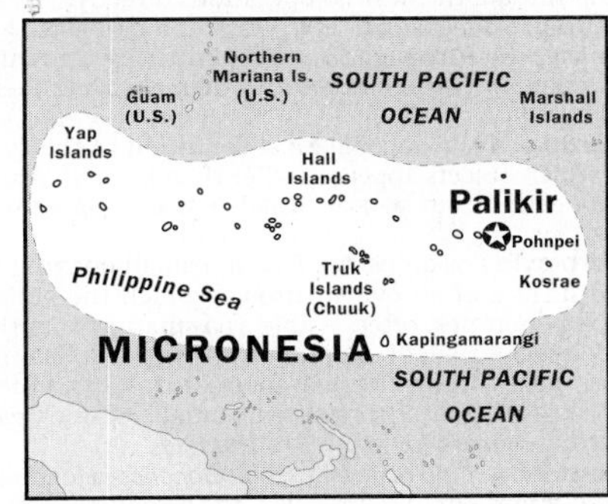

Mi·cro·ne·sian /ˌmīkrəˈnēzhən/ ▸*adj.* of or relating to Micronesia, its people, or their languages.
▸*n.* **1** a native of Micronesia. **2** the group of Austronesian languages spoken in Micronesia.

mi·cron·ize /ˈmīkrəˌnīz/ ▸*v.* [*trans.*] break (a substance) into very fine particles. —**mi·cron·i·za·tion** /ˌmīkrənəˈzāshən/ *n.* —**mi·cron·iz·er** *n.*

mi·cro·nu·tri·ent /ˌmīkrōˈn(y)o͞otrēənt/ ▸*n.* a chemical element or substance required in trace amounts for the normal growth and development of living organisms.

mi·cro·or·gan·ism /ˌmīkrōˈôrgəˌnizəm/ ▸*n.* a microscopic organism, esp. a bacterium, virus, or fungus.

mi·cro·pay·ment /ˈmīkrōˌpāmənt/ ▸*n.* a payment, typically via credit card, of a small amount of money.

mi·cro·phage /ˈmīkrōˌfāj/ ▸*n.* *Physiology* a small phagocytic blood cell, in particular a polymorphonuclear leukocyte.

mi·croph·a·gous /mīˈkräfəgəs/ ▸*adj.* *Zoology* (of an invertebrate) feeding on minute particles or microorganisms. —**mi·cro·phag·ic** /ˌmīkrəˈfājik; -ˈfajik/ *adj.*

mi·cro·phone /ˈmīkrəˌfōn/ ▸*n.* an instrument for converting sound waves into electrical energy variations, which may then be amplified, transmitted, or recorded. —**mi·cro·phon·ic** /ˌmīkrəˈfänik/ *adj.*

Pronunciation Key ə *ago*; ər *over*; ˈə or ˌə *up*; ˈər or ˌər *fur*; a *hat*; ā *rate*; ä *car*; CH *chew*; e *let*; ē *see*; e(ə)r *air*; i *fit*; ī *by*; i(ə)r *ear*; NG *sing*; ō *go*; ô *for*; oi *boy*; o͝o *good*; o͞o *goo*; ou *out*; SH *she*; TH *thin*; T͟H *then*; (h)w *why*; ZH *vision*

mi·cro·pho·to·graph /ˌmīkrəˈfōtəˌgraf/ ▸*n.* a photograph reduced to a very small size. ■ another term for **PHOTOMICROGRAPH.** —**mi·cro·pho·to·graph·ic** /-ˌfōtəˈgrafik/ *adj.* —**mi·cro·pho·tog·ra·phy** /-fəˈtägrəfē/ *n.*

mi·cro·phys·ics /ˌmīkrōˈfiziks/ ▸*plural n.* [treated as *sing.*] the branch of physics that deals with bodies and phenomena on a microscopic or smaller scale, esp. with molecules, atoms, and subatomic particles. —**mi·cro·phys·i·cal** /-ˈfizikəl/ *adj.*

mi·cro·pi·pette /ˌmīkrōˌpīˈpet/ (also **mi·cro·pi·pet**) ▸*n.* a very fine pipette for measuring, transferring, or injecting very small quantities of liquid.

mi·cro·pol·i·tan /ˌmīkrōˈpälətn/ ▸adj. relating to an urban area with a population of at least 10,000 but less than 50,000: *new, southern micropolitan areas have shown the greatest job growth in the last decade.*

mi·cro·pore /ˈmīkrəˌpôr/ ▸*n.* a very narrow pore, esp. in a material. —**mi·cro·po·ros·i·ty** /ˌmīkrōpəˈräsətē; -pôrˈäsətē/ *n.* —**mi·cro·po·rous** /ˌmīkrəˈpôrəs/ *adj.*

mi·cro·print /ˈmīkrəˌprint/ ▸*n.* printed text reduced by microphotography. —**mic·ro·print·ing** *n.*

mi·cro·probe /ˈmīkrəˌprōb/ ▸*n. Chemistry* an instrument in which a beam of electrons or other radiation is focused onto a minute area of a sample and the resulting secondary radiation (usually X-ray fluorescence) is analyzed to yield chemical information.

mi·cro·proc·es·sor /ˌmīkrəˈpräsesər; -ˈprōˌsesər/ ▸*n.* an integrated circuit that contains all the functions of a central processing unit of a computer. —**mi·cro·proc·ess·ing** *n.*

mi·cro·pro·gram /ˈmīkrəˌprōgrəm; -gram/ ▸*n.* a microinstruction program that controls the functions of a central processing unit or peripheral controller of a computer.
▸*v.* [*trans.*] use microprogramming with (a computer); bring about by means of a microprogram: *by 1980 virtually all computers were microprogrammed.* —**mi·cro·pro·gram·ma·ble** *adj.* —**mi·cro·pro·gram·mer** *n.*

mi·cro·pro·gram·ming /ˈmīkrəˌprōgrəmiNG; ˈmīkrəˌprōgramiNG/ ▸*n.* the technique of making machine instructions generate sequences of microinstructions in accordance with a microprogram rather than initiate the desired operations directly.

mi·cro·prop·a·ga·tion /ˌmīkrōˌpräpəˈgāSHən/ ▸*n. Botany* the propagation of plants by growing plantlets in tissue culture and then planting them out.

mi·crop·si·a /mīˈkräpsēə/ ▸*n.* a condition of the eyes in which objects appear smaller than normal. ▹mid 19th cent.: from **MICRO-** 'small' + Greek *-opsia* 'seeing.'

mi·cro·pyle /ˈmīkrəˌpīl/ ▸*n. Botany* a small opening in the surface of an ovule, through which the pollen tube penetrates, often visible as a small pore in the ripe seed. ■ a small opening in the egg of a fish, insect, etc., through which spermatozoa can enter. ▹early 19th cent.: from **MICRO-** 'small' + Greek *pulē* 'gate.' —**mi·cro·py·lar** /ˌmīkrəˈpīlər/ *adj.*

mi·cro·RNA /ˈmīkrōˌärenˈā/ ▸*n. Genetics* a cellular RNA fragment that prevents the production of a particular protein by binding to and destroying the messenger RNA that would have produced the protein.

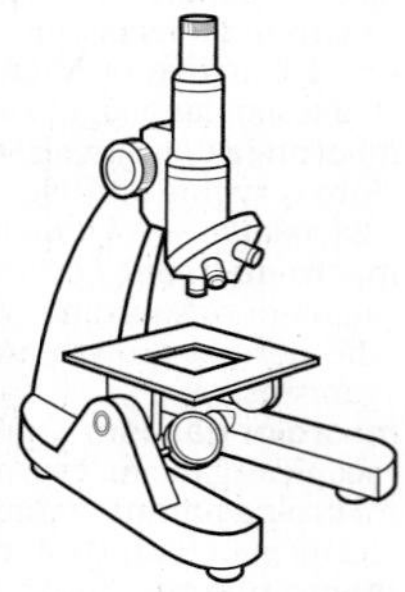

mi·cro·scope /ˈmīkrəˌskōp/ ▸*n.* an optical instrument used for viewing very small objects, such as mineral samples or animal or plant cells, typically magnified several hundred times. ▹mid 17th cent.: from modern Latin *microscopium* (see **MICRO-**, **-SCOPE**).
▸*PHRASE* □ **under the microscope** under critical examination.

microscope

mi·cro·scope slide ▸*n.* see **SLIDE** (sense 3).

mi·cro·scop·ic /ˌmīkrəˈskäpik/ ▸*adj.* **1** so small as to be visible only with a microscope: *microscopic algae.* ■ *informal* extremely small: *a microscopic skirt.* ■ concerned with minute detail: *such a vision is as microscopic as his is panoramic.* **2** of or relating to a microscope: *microscopic analysis of the soil.* —**mi·cro·scop·i·cal** *adj.* (in sense 2). —**mi·cro·scop·i·cal·ly** /-ik(ə)lē/ *adv.*

Mi·cro·sco·pi·um /ˌmīkrəˈskōpēəm/ *Astronomy* a small and inconspicuous southern constellation (the Microscope), between Piscis Austrinus and Sagittarius. ■ [as *genitive*] (**Microscopii**) used with a preceding letter or numeral to designate a star in this constellation: *the star Gamma Microscopii.* ▹modern Latin.

mi·cros·co·py /mīˈkräskəpē/ ▸*n.* the use of the microscope. —**mi·cros·co·pist** /-pist/ *n.*

mi·cro·sec·ond /ˈmīkrōˌsekənd/ (abbr.: **μs**) ▸*n.* one millionth of a second.

mi·cro·seism /ˈmīkrōˌsīzəm/ ▸*n. Geology* a very small earthquake, less than 2 on the Richter scale. —**mi·cro·seis·mic** /ˌmīkrōˈsīzmik/ *adj.*

mi·cro·site /ˈmīkrəˌsīt/ ▸*n.* **1** an auxiliary Web site with independent links and address that is accessed mainly from a larger site. **2** a small part of an ecosystem that differs markedly from its immediate surroundings.

mi·cro·some /ˈmīkrəˌsōm/ ▸*n. Biology* a fragment of endoplasmic reticulum and attached ribosomes obtained by the centrifugation of homogenized cells. —**mi·cro·so·mal** /ˌmīkrəˈsōməl/ *adj.*

mi·cro·sphere /ˈmīkrōˌsfir/ ▸*n.* a microscopic hollow sphere, esp. of a protein or synthetic polymer.

mi·cro·spo·ran·gi·um /ˌmīkrōspəˈranj(ē)əm/ ▸*n.* (*pl.* **-gi·a** /-j(ē)ə/) *Botany* a sporangium containing microspores.

mi·cro·spore /ˈmīkrəˌspôr/ ▸*n. Botany* the smaller of the two kinds of spore produced by some ferns. See also **MEGASPORE.**

mi·cro·struc·ture /ˌmīkrəˈstrəkCHər/ ▸*n.* the fine structure (in a metal or other material) that can be made visible and examined with a microscope.

mi·cro·suede /ˈmīkrəˌswād/ ▸*n.* a polyester microfiber fabric with a suedelike, water-repellent finished surface.

mi·cro·sur·ger·y /ˌmīkrōˈsərjərē/ ▸*n.* intricate surgery performed using miniaturized instruments and a microscope. —**mi·cro·sur·geon** /-ˈsərjən/ *n.* —**mi·cro·sur·gi·cal** /-ˈsərjikəl/ *adj.*

mi·cro·switch /ˈmīkrəˌswiCH/ ▸*n.* an electric switch that can be operated rapidly by a small movement.

mi·cro·tech·nol·o·gy /ˌmīkrōtekˈnäləjē/ ▸*n.* technology that uses microelectronics. —**mi·cro·tech·no·log·i·cal** /-nəˈläjikəl/ *adj.*

mi·cro·tome /ˈmīkrəˌtōm/ ▸*n. chiefly Biology* an instrument for cutting extremely thin sections of material for examination under a microscope.

mi·cro·tone /ˈmīkrəˌtōn/ ▸*n. Music* an interval smaller than a semitone. —**mi·cro·ton·al** /ˌmīkrəˈtōnl/ *adj.* —**mi·cro·to·nal·i·ty** /ˌmīkrətōˈnalətē/ *n.* —**mi·cro·ton·al·ly** /ˌmīkrəˈtōnl-ē/ *adv.*

mi·cro·tu·bule /ˌmīkrəˈt(y)o͞obyo͞ol/ ▸*n. Biology* a microscopic tubular structure present in numbers in the cytoplasm of cells, sometimes aggregating to form more complex structures.

mi·cro·vas·cu·lar /ˌmīkrōˈvaskyələr/ ▸*n.* of or relating to the smallest blood vessels.

mi·cro·vil·lus /ˌmīkrōˈviləs/ ▸*n.* (*pl.* **-vil·li** /-ˈvilˌī; -ˈvilē/) *Biology* each of a large number of minute projections from the surface of some cells. —**mi·cro·vil·lar** /-ˈvilər/ *adj.* —**mi·cro·vil·lous** /-ˈviləs/ *adj.*

mi·cro·wave /ˈmīkrəˌwāv/ ▸*n.* an electromagnetic wave with a wavelength in the range 0.001–0.3 m, shorter than that of a normal radio wave but longer than those of infrared radiation. Microwaves are used in radar, in communications, and for heating in microwave ovens and in various industrial processes. ■ short for **MICROWAVE OVEN.**
▸*v.* [*trans.*] cook (food) in a microwave oven. —**mi·cro·wave·a·ble** (also **mi·cro·wav·a·ble**) *adj.*

mi·cro·wave back·ground ▸*n. Astronomy* weak uniform microwave radiation that is detectable in nearly every direction of the sky. It is believed to be evidence of the big bang.

mi·cro·wave ov·en ▸*n.* an oven that uses microwaves to cook or heat food.

mic·tu·rate /ˈmikCHəˌrāt/ ▸*v.* [*intrans.*] *formal* urinate. ▹mid 19th cent.: back-formation from *micturition*, from Latin *micturit-* 'urinated,' from the verb *micturire.* —**mic·tu·ri·tion** /ˌmikCHəˈriSHən/ *n.*

mid[1] /mid/ ▸*adj.* [*attrib.*] of or in the middle part or position of a range: *the mid 17th century* | *in mid air.* ■ *Phonetics* (of a vowel) pronounced with the tongue neither high nor low: *a mid-central vowel.*

mid[2] ▸*prep. poetic/literary* in the middle of. ■ in the course of. ▹Shortening of **AMID.**

mid- ▸*comb. form* denoting the middle of: *midsection* | *mid-sentence.* ■ in the middle; medium; half: *midway.* ▹Old English *midd*, of Germanic origin; from an Indo-European root shared by Latin *medius* and Greek *mesos.*

mid·air /ˈmidˈe(ə)r/ (also **mid-air**) ▸*n.* a part or section of the air above ground level or above another surface: *he caught Murray's keys **in midair*** | [as *adj.*] *a midair collision.*

Mi·das /ˈmīdəs/ *Greek Mythology* a king of Phrygia, who, according to one story, was given by Dionysus the power of turning everything he touched into gold.
▸*PHRASE* □ **the Midas touch** the ability to make money out of anything one undertakes.

mid-At·lan·tic ▸*adj.* **1** situated or occurring in the middle of the Atlantic Ocean: *the mid-Atlantic fault line.* ■ having characteristics of both Britain and America, or designed to appeal to the people of both countries: *mid-Atlantic accents.* **2** of or relating to states on the middle Atlantic coast of the U.S., typically including New York, Pennsylvannia, New Jersey, West Virginia, Delaware, and Maryland.

Mid-At·lan·tic Ridge a submarine ridge system that extends the length of the Atlantic Ocean from the Arctic to the Antarctic. It is seismically and (in places) volcanically active; the islands of Iceland, the Azores, Ascension, St. Helena, and Tristan da Cunha are located on it.

Mid-At·lan·tic States term for the U.S. states between New England and the South that are on or near the Atlantic coast, usually including New York, New Jersey, and Pennsylvania, and sometimes also Delaware and Maryland.

mid·brain /ˈmidˌbrān/ ▸*n. Anatomy* a small central part of the brainstem, developing from the middle of the primitive or embryonic brain. Also called **MESENCEPHALON.**

mid·day /ˈmidˈdā/ ▸*n.* the middle of the day; noon: *he awoke **at midday.*** | [as *adj.*] *the midday sun.* ▹Old English *middæg* (see **MID-**, **DAY**).

mid·den /ˈmidn/ ▸*n.* a dunghill or refuse heap. ■ short for **KITCHEN MIDDEN.** ▹late Middle English *myddyng*, of Scandinavian origin; compare with Danish *møødding* 'dunghill.'

mid·dle /ˈmidl/ ▸*adj.* [*attrib.*] **1** at an equal distance from the extremities of something; central: *the early and middle part of life* | *middle and eastern Europe.* ■ (of a member of a group, series, or sequence) so placed as to have the same number of members on each side: *the woman was in her middle forties.* ■ intermediate in rank, quality, or ability: *there is a dearth of talent at the middle level.* ■ (of a language) of the period between the old and modern forms: *Middle High German.* **2** *Grammar* denoting a voice of verbs in some languages, such as Greek, that expresses reciprocal or reflexive action. ■ denoting a transitive or intransitive verb in English with a passive sense, e.g., *cuts* in *this meat cuts well.*
▸*n.* **1** [usu. in *sing.*] the point or position at an equal distance from the sides, edges, or ends of something: *she stood alone in the middle of the street.* ■ the point at or around the center of a process or activity, period of time, etc.: *we were married in the middle of December.* ■ *informal* a person's waist or waist and stomach: *he had a towel around his middle.* **2** *Grammar* the form or voice of a verb expressing reflexive or reciprocal action, or a passive sense for a transitive or intransitive verb. **3** short for **MIDDLE TERM.** ▹Old English *middel*; related to Dutch *middel* and German *Mittel*, also to **MID**[1].
▸*PHRASES* □ **down the middle** divided or dividing something equally into two parts. □ **in the middle of** engaged in or in the process of doing something. ■ involved in something, typically something unpleasant or dangerous: *he was caught in the middle of the emotional triangle.* □ **the middle of nowhere** *informal* a place that is remote and isolated. □ **steer** (or **take**) **a middle course** adopt a policy that avoids extremes.

mid·dle age ▸*n.* the period between early adulthood and old age, usually considered as the years from about 45 to 65. —**mid·dle-aged** (also **mid·dle-age**) *adj.*

Mid·dle Ag·es ▸*plural n.* the period of European history from the fall of the Roman Empire in the West (5th century) to the fall of Constantinople (1453), or, more narrowly, from *c.*1100 to 1453.

The earlier part of the period (*c.*500–*c.*1100) or *early Middle Ages* is sometimes distinguished as the Dark Ages, while the later part (*c.*1100–1453) or *high* or *late Middle Ages* is often thought of as the Middle Ages proper. The whole period is characterized by the emergence of separate kingdoms, the growth of trade and urban life, and the growth in power of monarchies and the Church. The growth of interest in classical models within art and scholarship in the 15th century is seen as marking the transition to the Renaissance period and the end of the Middle Ages.

mid·dle-age spread ▸*n.* the fat that may accumulate around the areas of the abdomen and buttocks during one's middle age.

Mid·dle A·mer·i·ca ▸*n.* **1** the middle class in the U.S., esp. when regarded as a conservative political force. ■ the Midwest of the U.S. **2** the North American region that includes Mexico and Central America, and often the West Indies. —**Mid·dle A·mer·i·can** *n.* —**Mid·dle-A·mer·i·can** *adj.*

Mid·dle At·lan·tic the region of the U.S. that generally includes New Jersey, Pennsylvania, and Delaware, and often also New York and Maryland.

mid·dle·brow /ˈmidlˈbrou/ *informal, chiefly derogatory* ▸*adj.* (of art or literature or a system of thought) demanding or involving only a moderate degree of intellectual application, typically as a result of not deviating from convention: *middlebrow fiction.*
▸*n.* a person who is capable of or enjoys only a moderate degree of intellectual effort.

mid·dle C ▸*n. Music* the C near the middle of the piano keyboard, written on the first ledger line below the treble staff or the first ledger line above the bass staff.

mid·dle class ▸*n.* [treated as *sing.* or *pl.*] the social group between the upper and working classes, including professional and business workers and their families.
▸*adj.* of, relating to, or characteristic of this section of society: *a middle-class suburb.* ■ attaching too much importance to convention, security, and material comfort: *the sterile goals of middle-class life.* —**mid·dle-class·ness** *n.*

mid·dle dis·tance ▸*n.* **1** (**the middle distance**) the part of a real or painted landscape between the foreground and the background. **2** [usu. as *adj.*] *Track & Field* a race distance of between 800 and 5,000 meters: *middle-distance runners.*

Mid·dle Dutch ▸*n.* the Dutch language from *c.*1100 to 1500.

mid·dle ear ▸*n.* the air-filled central cavity of the ear, behind the eardrum.

Mid·dle East an extensive area of southwestern Asia and northern Africa, stretching from the Mediterranean Sea to Pakistan and including the Arabian peninsula. —**Mid·dle East·ern** *adj.*

mid·dle eight (also **mid·dle-eight**) ▸*n.* a short section (typically of eight bars) in the middle of a conventionally structured popular song, generally of a different character from the other parts of the song.

Mid·dle Eng·lish ▸*n.* the English language from *c.*1150 to *c.*1470.

mid·dle fin·ger ▸*n.* the finger between the forefinger and the ring finger.

mid·dle game ▸*n.* the phase of a chess game after the opening, when all or most of the pieces and pawns remain on the board.

mid·dle ground ▸*n.* (usu. **the middle ground**) **1** an area of compromise or possible agreement between two extreme positions, esp. political ones: *each party wants to capture the votes of those perceived as* ***occupying the middle ground.*** **2** the middle distance of a painting or photograph.

Mid·dle High Ger·man ▸*n.* the language of southern Germany from *c.*1200 to 1500.

Mid·dle King·dom **1** a period of ancient Egyptian history (*c.*2040–1640 BC, 11th–14th dynasty). **2** *historical* China or its eighteen inner provinces.

Mid·dle Low Ger·man ▸*n.* the Low German language (spoken in northern Germany) from *c.*1200 to 1500.

mid·dle·man /ˈmidlˌman/ ▸*n.* (*pl.* **-men**) a person who buys goods from producers and sells them to retailers or consumers: *we aim to maintain value for money by* ***cutting out the middleman*** *and selling direct.* ■ a person who arranges business or political deals between other people.

mid·dle man·age·ment ▸*n.* the level in an organization just below that of senior administrators. ■ the managers at this level regarded collectively. —**mid·dle man·ag·er** *n.*

mid·dle name ▸*n.* a person's name (typically a personal name) placed after the first name and before the surname. ■ a quality for which a person is notable: *optimism is my middle name.*

mid·dle-of-the-road ▸*adj.* avoiding extremes; moderate: *the paper reflected the views of its middle-of-the-road readers.* ■ (of music) tuneful but somewhat bland and unadventurous. —**mid·dle-of-the-road·er** *n.*

mid·dle pas·sage ▸*n. historical* the sea journey undertaken by slave ships from West Africa to the West Indies.

Mid·dle Per·sian ▸*n.* the Persian language from *c.*300 BC to AD 800. See also PAHLAVI[2].

Mid·dles·brough /ˈmidlzbrə/ a port in northeastern England, on the estuary of the Tees River; pop. 141,100.

mid·dl·es·cent /ˌmidlˈesənt/ ▸*adj.* **1** middle-aged, but typically still maintaining the interests and activities of younger people. **2** (in technical use) people of age forty to sixty. ▷1960s: blend of *middle* + *adolescent.* —**mid·dl·es·cence** /ˌmidlˈesəns/ *n.*

mid·dle school ▸*n.* a school intermediate between an elementary school and a high school, typically for children in the sixth, seventh, and eighth grades.

mid·dle-sized ▸*adj.* of medium size: *a middle-sized farm.*

Mid·dle Stone Age the Mesolithic period.

mid·dle term ▸*n. Logic* the term common to both premises of a syllogism.

Mid·dle·ton /ˈmidltən/, Thomas (*c.*1570–1627), English playwright. Notable works: *The Changeling* (1622), written with playwright William Rowley, and *Women Beware Women* (1620–27).

Mid·dle·town /ˈmidlˌtoun/ **1** a commercial and industrial city in central Connecticut, on the Connecticut River, south of Hartford, home to Wesleyan University; pop. 42,762. **2** an industrial city in southwestern Ohio, between Cincinnati and Dayton; pop. 46,029.

mid·dle·ware /ˈmidlˌwe(ə)r/ ▸*n. Computing* software that occupies a position in a hierarchy between the operating system and the applications, whose task is to ensure that software from a variety of sources will work together correctly.

mid·dle watch ▸*n.* the period from midnight to 4 a.m. on board a ship.

mid·dle way ▸*n.* **1** a policy or course of action that avoids extremes: *there is no middle way between central planning and capitalism.* **2** (**the Middle Way**) the eightfold path of Buddhism between indulgence and asceticism.

mid·dle·weight /ˈmidlˌwāt/ ▸*n.* a weight in boxing and other sports intermediate between welterweight and light heavyweight. ■ a boxer or other competitor of this weight.

Middle West another term for MIDWEST. —**Mid·dle West·ern·er** *n.*

mid·dling /ˈmidliNG; ˈmidlin/ ▸*adj.* moderate or average in size, amount, or rank: *the village contained no poor households but a lot of middling ones.* ■ neither very good nor very bad: *he had had a* ***fair to middling*** *season.* ■ [*predic.*] *informal* (of a person) in reasonably good but not perfect health.
▸*n.* (**middlings**) bulk goods of medium grade, esp. flour of medium fineness.
▸*adv.* [as *submodifier*] *informal, dated* fairly or moderately: *middling rich.* ▷late Middle English (originally Scots): probably from MID- + the adverbial suffix *-ling.* —**mid·dling·ly** *adv.*

mid·dy /ˈmidē/ ▸*n.* (*pl.* **-dies**) **1** *informal* a midshipman. **2** (also **mid·dy blouse**) *chiefly historical* a woman's or child's loose blouse with a collar that is cut deep and square at the back and tapering to the front, resembling that worn by a sailor.

Mid·east U.S. term for MIDDLE EAST.

mid-en·gine (also **mid-en·gined**) ▸*adj.* (of a car) having the engine located centrally between the front and rear axles.

mid·field /ˈmidˌfēld; midˈfēld/ ▸*n.* (in football, soccer, etc.) the central part of the field. ■ *Soccer* the players on a team who play in a central position between attack and defense. —**mid·field·er** *n.*

Mid·gard /ˈmidˌgärd/ *Scandinavian Mythology* the region, encircled by the sea, in which human beings live; the earth.

midge /mij/ ▸*n.* **1** a small two-winged fly that is often seen in swarms near water or marshy areas where it breeds. • The families Chironomidae (the **nonbiting midges**), and Ceratopogonidae (see BITING MIDGE): numerous species. ■ [with *adj.*] any of a number of small flies whose larvae can be pests of plants, typically producing galls or damaging leaves. **2** *informal* a small person. ▷Old English *mycg(e),* of Germanic origin; related to Dutch *mug* and German *Mücke,* from an Indo-European root shared by Latin *musca* and Greek *muia* 'fly.'

mid·get /ˈmijit/ ▸*n. often offensive* an extremely or unusually small person.
▸*adj.* [*attrib.*] very small: *a midget submarine.* ▷mid 19th cent.: from MIDGE + -ET[1].

mid·gut /ˈmidˌgət/ ▸*n. Zoology* the middle part of the alimentary canal, including (in vertebrates) the small intestine.

mid·heav·en /ˈmidˌhevən/ ▸*n. Astrology* (on an astrological chart) the point where the ecliptic intersects the meridian.

MIDI /ˈmidē/ ▸*n.* [usu. as *adj.*] a widely used standard for interconnecting electronic musical instruments and computers: *a MIDI controller.* ▷1980s: acronym from *musical instrument digital interface.*

Mi·di /mēˈdē/ the south of France. ▷French, literally 'midday'; compare with MEZZOGIORNO.

mid·i /ˈmidē/ ▸*n.* (*pl.* **mid·is** /ˈmidēz/) short for **midiskirt**, a skirt that ends at the middle of the calf. ▷1960s: from MID[1], on the pattern of *maxi* and *mini.*

mid·i·nette /ˌmidnˈet; ˌmēdēˈnet/ ▸*n.* a seamstress or assistant in a Parisian fashion house. ▷French, from *midi* 'midday' + *dînette* 'light dinner' (because only a short break was taken at lunchtime).

Mi·di-Py·ré·nées /mēˈdē ˌpirəˈnā/ a region in southern France, between the Pyrenees and the Massif Central, centered on Toulouse.

mid·i·ron /ˈmidˌī(ə)rn/ ▸*n. Golf* an iron with a medium degree of loft, such as a four-, five-, or six-iron.

Mid·land /ˈmidlənd/ **1** a city in central Michigan; pop. 38,053. **2** a city in western Texas, an oil industry center in the Permian Basin; pop. 89,443.

mid·land /ˈmidlənd; -ˌland/ ▸*n.* the middle part of a country. ■ (**the Midlands**) the inland counties of central England. ■ (**Midland**) a part of the central U.S., roughly bounded by Illinois, South Carolina, and Delaware.
▸*adj.* of or in the middle part of a country. ■ (**Midland**) of or in the English Midlands. ■ (**Midland**) of or in the Midland of the U.S. —**mid·land·er** *n.*

mid·lat·i·tudes ▸*plural n.* areas lying between 35 and 55 (or more broadly, between 30 and 60) degrees north or south of the equator: *mesoscale convective systems in the tropics and midlatitudes.* —**mid·lat·i·tude** *adj.*

mid·life /midˈlīf/ (also **mid-life**) ▸*n.* the central period of a person's life, generally considered as the years from about 45 to 55: *a woman in midlife* | [as *adj.*] *your midlife financial review.*

mid·life cri·sis ▸*n.* an emotional crisis of identity and self-confidence that can occur in early middle age.

mid·line /ˈmidˌlīn/ ▸*n.* [often as *adj.*] a median line or plane of bilateral symmetry, esp. that of the body: *the abdomen was opened by a midline incision.*

mid·most /ˈmidˌmōst/ ▸*adj.* & *adv. poetic/literary* in the very middle or nearest the middle.

Midn. ▸*abbr.* Midshipman.

mid·night /ˈmidˌnīt/ ▸*n.* twelve o'clock at night: *I left* ***at midnight*** | [as *adj.*] *a midnight deadline.* ■ [often as *adj.*] the middle period of the night: *the midnight hours.* ▷Old English *midniht* (see MID-, NIGHT).

mid·night blue ▸*n.* a very dark blue.

mid·night sun ▸*n.* the sun when seen at midnight during the summer in either the Arctic or Antarctic Circle.

mid·o·cean ridge /midˈōSHən/ (also **mid-o·cean ridge**) ▸*n. Geology* a long, seismically active submarine ridge system situated in the middle of an ocean basin and marking the site of the upwelling of magma associated with seafloor spreading. An example is the Mid-Atlantic Ridge.

mid·point /ˈmidˌpoint/ ▸*n.* the exact middle point: *the midpoint of the line segment.* ■ a point somewhere in the middle: *he would have been at the midpoint in his career.*

mid·range /ˈmidˈrānj/ (also **mid-range**) ▸*n.* **1** *Statistics* the arithmetic mean of the largest and the smallest values in a sample or other group. **2** the middle part of the range of audible frequencies.
▸*adj.* (of a product) in the middle of a range of products with regard to size, quality, or price.

Mid·rash /ˈmidˌräSH/ (also **mid·rash**) ▸*n.* (*pl.* **Mid·ra·shim** /midˈräSHim/) an ancient commentary on part of the Hebrew scriptures, attached to the biblical text. The earliest Midrashim come from the 2nd century AD, although much of their content is older. ▷from Hebrew *miḏrāš* 'commentary,' from *dāraš* 'expound.' —**Mid·rash·ic** /midˈräSHik/ *adj.*

mid·rib /ˈmidˌrib/ ▸*n.* a large strengthened vein along the midline of a leaf.

Pronunciation Key ə *ago;* ər *over;* ˈə or ˌə *up;* ˈər or ˌər *fur;* a *hat;* ā *rate;* ä *car;* CH *chew;* e *let;* ē *see;* e(ə)r *air;* i *fit;* ī *by;* i(ə)r *ear;* NG *sing;* ō *go;* ô *for;* oi *boy;* o͝o *good;* o͞o *goo;* ou *out;* SH *she;* TH *thin;* T͟H *then;* (h)w *why;* ZH *vision*

M

mid·riff /ˈmidˌrif/ ▸*n.* the region of the front of the body between the chest and the waist. ■ *dated Anatomy* the diaphragm. ▷Old English *midhrif,* from MID[1] + *hrif* 'belly.'

mid·sec·tion /ˈmidˌsekSHən/ ▸*n.* the middle part of something. ■ the midriff.

mid·ses·sion /ˈmidˌseSHən; ˌmidˈseSH-/ ▸*n.* the middle of a session, particularly: ■ a period of active trading on a securities exchange: *the Mexico peso regained some lost ground to the U.S. dollar toward midsession Friday.* ■ a period of instruction: *both students and instructors can be called away in midsession to cope with emergencies.* ■ a legislative session.

mid·ship /ˈmidˌSHip/ ▸*n.* [usu. as *adj.*] the middle part of a ship or boat: *its powerful midship section.*

mid·ship·man /ˈmidˌSHipmən; midˈSHip-/ ▸*n.* (*pl.* **-men**) **1** a naval cadet in the U.S. Navy. ■ an officer in the Royal Navy ranking below sublieutenant. [early 17th cent.: so named because the officer was stationed amidships; he was, however, allowed to walk the quarterdeck, to which he aspired in promotion.] **2** an American toadfish with dorsal and anal fins that run most of the length of the body and rows of light organs on the underside. • Genus *Porichthys,* family *Batrachoididae*: two or three species.

mid·ships /ˈmidˌSHips/ ▸*adv.* & *adj.* another term for AMIDSHIPS.

mid·sole /ˈmidˌsōl/ ▸*n.* a layer of material between the inner and outer soles of a shoe, for absorbing shock.

midst /midst; mitst/ ▸*prep. archaic* or *poetic/literary* in the middle of.
▸*n. archaic* the middle point or part. ▷late Middle English: from *in middes* 'in the middle.'
▸*PHRASES* □ **in the midst of** in the middle of: *we were in the midst of a losing streak.* □ **in our** (or **your**, **their**, etc.) **midst** among us (or you or them).

mid·stream /ˈmidˈstrēm/ ▸*n.* the middle of a stream or river: *the ferry was moving out* **into midstream**.
▸*adj. Medicine* (of urine) passed in the middle part of an act of urinating.
▸*PHRASE* □ **in midstream** in the middle of a stream or river. ■ *figurative* (of an activity or process, esp. one that is interrupted) partway through its course: *our conversation was interrupted in midstream.*

mid·sum·mer /ˈmidˈsəmər/ ▸*n.* [often as *adj.*] the middle part of summer: *the midsummer heat.* ■ another term for SUMMER SOLSTICE. ▷Old English *midsumor* (see MID-, SUMMER[1]).

Mid·sum·mer Day (also **Mid·sum·mer's Day**) ▸*n.* (in England, Wales, and Ireland) June 24, originally coinciding with the summer solstice and in some countries marked by a summer festival.

mid·term /ˈmidˌtərm/ ▸*n.* the middle of a period of office, an academic term, or a pregnancy: *Nixon resigned* **in midterm** | [as *adj.*] *midterm elections.* ■ an exam in the middle of an academic term.

mid·town /ˈmidˌtoun/ ▸*n.* [usu. as *adj.*] the central part of a city between the downtown and uptown areas: *a huge midtown apartment.*

mid-Vic·to·ri·an ▸*adj.* of or relating to the middle of the Victorian era.

mid·wa·ter /ˈmidˌwôtər; -ˌwätər/ ▸*n.* the part of a body of water near neither the bottom nor the surface: *whales and seals feed in midwater or on the seabed* | [as *adj.*] *midwater fish.*

mid·way /ˈmidˌwā; -ˈwā/ ▸*adv.* & *adj.* in or toward the middle of something: [as *adv.*] *Father Peter came to a halt midway down the street* | [as *adj.*] *midway profits roared from $130 million to $160 million.* ■ having some of the characteristics of one thing and some of another: [as *adj.*] *a midway path is chosen between the diverging aspirations of the two factions* | [as *adv.*] *the leaves have a unique smell* **midway between** *eucalyptus and mint.*
▸*n.* an area of sideshows, games of chance or skill, or other amusements at a fair or exhibition: *the kids head straight for* **the midway**.

Mid·way Is·lands two small islands, in the central Pacific Ocean, in the western part of the Hawaiian chain, surrounded by a coral atoll. The islands were annexed by the U.S. in 1867 and remain a U.S. territory and naval base. They were the scene of the decisive Battle of Midway in 1942, in which Japanese expansion in the Pacific Ocean was ended.

mid·week /ˈmidˌwēk/ ▸*n.* the middle of the week, usually regarded as being from Tuesday to Thursday: *by midweek the strike could affect subways and buses.*
▸*adj.* & *adv.* in the middle of the week: [as *adj.*] *a special midweek reduction* | [as *adv.*] *we have opportunities to fish midweek.*

Mid·west /ˈmidˈwest/ the region of northern states of the U.S. from Ohio west to the Rocky Mountains. Formerly called FAR WEST. —**Mid·west·ern** /ˌmidˈwestərn/ *adj.*

Mid·west Cit·y /ˈmidˌwest/ a city in central Oklahoma, east of Oklahoma City; pop. 54,088.

mid·wife /ˈmidˌwīf/ ▸*n.* (*pl.* **-wives**) a person (typically a woman) trained to assist women in childbirth. ■ *figurative* a person or thing that helps to bring something into being or assists its development: *he survived to be one of the midwives of the Reformation.*
▸*v.* [*trans.*] assist (a woman) during childbirth. ■ *figurative* bring into being: *revolutions midwifed by new technologies of communication.* ▷Middle English: probably from the obsolete preposition *mid* 'with' + WIFE (in the archaic sense 'woman'), expressing the sense 'a woman who is with (the mother).' —**mid·wife·ry** /midˈwif(ə)rē; -ˈwīf(ə)rē/ *n.*

mid·wife toad ▸*n.* a European toad, the male of which has a distinctive piping call in spring and carries the developing eggs wrapped around his hind legs. • *Alytes obstetricans,* family Discoglossidae.

mid·win·ter /ˈmidˈwintər/ ▸*n.* the middle part of winter: **in midwinter** *the track became a muddy morass* | [as *adj.*] *the midwinter full moon.* ■ another term for WINTER SOLSTICE. ▷Old English (see MID-, WINTER).

mien /mēn/ ▸*n. poetic/literary* a person's look or manner, esp. one of a particular kind indicating their character or mood: *he has a cautious, academic mien.* ▷early 16th cent.: probably from French *mine* 'expression,' influenced by obsolete *demean* 'bearing, demeanor' (from DEMEAN[2]).

Mies van der Ro·he /ˈmēz van dər ˈrōə; ˈmēs vän/, Ludwig (1886–1969), German architect and designer. He designed the German pavilion at the 1929 International Exhibition at Barcelona and the Seagram Building in New York 1954–58 and was noted for his tubular steel furniture. Before emigrating to the U.S. in 1937, he served as director of the Bauhaus 1930–33. —**Mies·i·an** /ˈmēzēən/ *adj.*

mi·fep·ri·stone /ˌmifəˈprisˌtōn/ ▸*n. Medicine* a synthetic steroid that inhibits the action of progesterone, given orally in early pregnancy to induce abortion. Also called **RU-486** (*trademark*). ▷1980s: probably from Dutch *mifepriston,* from *mife-* (representing *aminophenol*) + *-pr-* (representing *propyl*) + *-ist-* (representing ESTRADIOL) + -ONE.

miff /mif/ ▸*v.* [*trans.*] (usu. **be miffed**) *informal* annoy: *she was slightly miffed at not being invited.*
▸*n. archaic* a petty quarrel or fit of pique. ▷early 17th cent.: perhaps imitative; compare with early modern German *muff,* an exclamation of disgust.

MiG /mig/ (also **Mig** or **MIG**) ▸*n.* a type of Russian fighter aircraft. ▷1940s: from the initial letters of the surnames of A. I. Mikoyan and M. I. Gurevich, linked by Russian *i* 'and.'

might[1] /mīt/ ▸*modal verb* (*3rd sing. present* **might**) **1** past of MAY[1], used esp.: ■ in reported speech, expressing possibility or permission: *he said he might be late.* ■ expressing a possibility based on a condition not fulfilled: *we might have won if we'd played better.* ■ expressing annoyance about something that someone has not done: *you might have told me!* ■ expressing purpose: *he avoided social engagements so that he might work.* **2** used in questions and requests: ■ tentatively asking permission: *might I ask one question?* ■ expressing a polite request: *you might just call me Jane, if you don't mind.* ■ asking for information, esp. condescendingly: *and who might you be?* **3** expressing possibility: *this might be true.* ■ making a suggestion: *you might try nonprescription pain relievers.*
▸*PHRASES* □ **might as well 1** used to make an unenthusiastic suggestion: *I might as well begin.* **2** used to indicate that a situation is the same as if the hypothetical thing stated were true: *for readers seeking illumination, this book might as well have been written in Serbo-Croatian.* □ **might have known** (or **guessed**) used to express one's lack of surprise about something: *I might have known it was you.*

USAGE On the difference in use between **might** and **may**, see **usage** at MAY[1].

might[2] ▸*n.* great and impressive power or strength, esp. of a nation, large organization, or natural force: *a convincing display of military might.* ▷Old English *miht, mieht,* of Germanic origin; related to MAY[1].
▸*PHRASES* □ **might is right** those who are powerful can do what they wish unchallenged, even if their action is in fact unjustified. □ **with all one's might** using all one's power or strength. □ **with might and main** with all one's strength or power.

might-have-been ▸*n. informal* a past possibility that no longer applies: *fretting about might-have-beens won't get us anywhere.*

might·n't /ˈmītnt/ ▸*contraction of* might not: *you mightn't believe it, but I saw him stop a fight.*

might·y /ˈmītē/ ▸*adj.* (**might·i·er**, **might·i·est**) possessing great and impressive power or strength, esp on account of size: *three mighty industrial countries* | *mighty beasts.* ■ (of an action) performed with or requiring great strength: *a mighty heave* | *figurative a mighty blow against racism.* ■ *informal* very large: *she gave a mighty hiccup.*
▸*adv.* [as *submodifier*] *informal* extremely: *this is mighty early to be planning a presidential campaign.* ▷Old English *mihtig* (see MIGHT[2], -Y[1]). —**might·i·ly** /ˈmītl-ē/ *adv.* —**might·i·ness** *n.*

mig·ma·tite /ˈmigməˌtīt/ ▸*n. Geology* a rock composed of two intermingled but distinguishable components, typically a granitic rock within a metamorphic host rock. ▷early 20th cent.: from Greek *migma, migmat-* 'mixture' + -ITE[1].

mi·gnon·ette /ˌminyəˈnet/ ▸*n.* a herbaceous plant with spikes of small fragrant greenish flowers. • Genus *Reseda,* family Resedaceae: several species, in particular the North African *R. odorata,* which is cultivated as an ornamental and for its essential oil, and the widespread **wild mignonette** (*R. alba*), originally a Mediterranean plant. ▷early 18th cent.: from French *mignonnette,* diminutive of *mignon* 'small and sweet.'

mi·graine /ˈmīˌgrān/ (also **migraine headache**) ▸*n.* a recurrent throbbing headache that typically affects one side of the head and is often accompanied by nausea and disturbed vision. ▷late Middle English: from French, via late Latin from Greek *hēmikrania,* from *hēmi-* 'half' + *kranion* 'skull.' —**mi·grain·ous** /-ˌgrānəs/ *adj.*

mi·grain·eur /ˌmēgrəˈnər; ˌmīgrā-/ ▸*n.* someone who suffers from migraine headaches.

mi·grant /ˈmīgrənt/ ▸*n.* an animal that migrates. ■ (also **migrant worker**) a worker who moves from place to place to do seasonal work.
▸*adj.* [*attrib.*] tending to migrate or having migrated: *migrant birds.*

mi·grate /ˈmīˌgrāt/ ▸*v.* [*intrans.*] (of an animal, typically a bird or fish) move from one region or habitat to another, esp. regularly according to the seasons: *as autumn arrives, the birds migrate south.* ■ (of a person) move from one area or country to settle in another, esp. in search of work: *rural populations have* **migrated to** *urban areas.* ■ move from one specific part of something to another: *cells that can form pigment migrate beneath the skin.* ■ *Computing* change or cause to change from using one system to another. ■ [*trans.*] *Computing* transfer (programs or hardware) from one system to another. ▷early 17th cent. (in the general sense 'move from one place to another'): from Latin *migrat-* 'moved, shifted,' from the verb *migrare.* —**mi·gra·tion** /mīˈgrāSHən/ *n.* —**mi·gra·tion·al** /mīˈgrāSHənl/ *adj.* —**mi·gra·tor** /-ˌgrātər/ *n.* —**mi·gra·to·ry** /ˈmīgrəˌtôrē/ *adj.*

mih·rab /ˈmi(ə)rəb/ ▸*n.* a niche in the wall of a mosque, at the point nearest to Mecca, toward which the congregation faces to pray. ▷from Arabic *miḥrāb* 'place for prayer.'

mi·ka·do /miˈkädō/ ▸*n. historical* a title given to the emperor of Japan. ▷Japanese, from *mi* 'august' + *kado* 'gate'; the title is a tranferred use of "gate (to the Imperial palace)," an ancient place of audience. Compare with PORTE.

mike[1] /mīk/ ▸*n.* a code word representing the letter M, used in radio communication.

mike[2] *informal* ▸*n.* a microphone.
▸*v.* [*trans.*] place a microphone close to (someone or something) or in (a place). ▷1920s: abbreviation.

Mi·ki·ta /miˈkētə/, Stanley (1940–), Canadian hockey player; born *Stanislav Gvoth*; born in Czechoslovakia. He played for the Chicago Blackhawks 1958–80 and led the National Hockey League in scoring four times 1964, 1965, 1967, 1968. Hockey Hall of Fame (1983).

Mi'k·maq /ˈmikˌmak/ ▸*n.* & *adj.* variant spelling of MICMAC.

Mí·ko·nos /ˈmēkəˌnôs/ Greek name for MYKONOS.

mik·veh /ˈmikvə/ (also **mik·va** or **mik·vah**) ▸*n.* (*pl.* **mik·vehs** or **mik·vahs** or **mik·voth** /mēkˈvōt/ or **mik·vot** /mēkˈvōt/ or **mik·vos** /mēkˈvəz; -ˈvōs/) a bath in which certain Jewish ritual purifications are performed. ■ the action of taking such a bath. ▷mid 19th cent.: from Yiddish *mikve,* from Hebrew *miqweh,* literally 'collection (usually of water).'

mil[1] /mil/ *informal* ▸*abbr.* ■ millimeters. ■ milliliters.

■ (used in sums of money) millions: *the insurance company coughed up five mil.*

mil[2] ▶*n.* one thousandth of an inch. ▷late 17th cent.: from Latin *millesimum* 'thousandth,' from *mille* 'thousand.'

mil. ▶*abbr.* ■ military. ■ militia.

mi·la·dy /mə'lādē; mī-/ ▶*n.* (*pl.* **-dies**) *historical* or *humorous* used to address or refer to an English noblewoman or great lady: *I went off to milady's boudoir.* ▷late 18th cent.: via French from English *my lady*; compare with MILORD.

mil·age ▶*n.* variant spelling of MILEAGE.

Mi·lan /mə'län; mə'lan/ an industrial city in northwestern Italy, the capital of Lombardy region; pop. 1,432,000. A powerful city, particularly from the 13th to the 15th centuries, Milan is today a leading financial and commercial center. Italian name MILANO. —**Mil·a·nese** /ˌmilə'nēz; -'nēs/ *adj.* & *n.*

mil·blog ▶*n.* a weblog dealing with military matters, or written by enlisted personnel.

milch /milk; milCH/ ▶*adj.* denoting a cow or other domestic mammal giving or kept for milk. ▷Middle English: from Old English *-milce*, only in *thrimilce* 'May' (when cows could be milked three times a day), from the Germanic base of MILK.

mild /mīld/ ▶*adj.* gentle and not easily provoked: *she was implacable, despite her mild exterior.* ■ (of a rule or punishment) of only moderate severity: *he received a mild sentence.* ■ not keenly felt or seriously intended: *she looked at him in mild surprise.* ■ (of an illness or pain) not serious or dangerous. ■ (of weather) moderately warm, esp. less cold than expected: *it is still mild enough to work outdoors.* ■ (of a medicine or cosmetic) acting gently and without causing harm. ■ (of food, drink, or tobacco) not sharp or strong in flavor: *a mild Italian cheese.* ▷Old English *milde* (originally in the sense 'gracious, not severe in command'), of Germanic origin; related to Dutch and German *mild*, from an Indo-European root shared by Latin *mollis* and Greek *malthakos* 'soft.' —**mild·ish** *adj.* —**mild·ness** *n.*

mil·dew /'milˌd(y)o͞o/ ▶*n.* a thin whitish coating consisting of minute fungal hyphae, growing on plants or damp organic material such as paper or leather. ▶*v.* affect or be affected with mildew. ▷Old English *mildēaw* 'honeydew,' of Germanic origin. The first element is related to Latin *mel* and Greek *meli* 'honey.' —**mil·dew·y** *adj.*

mild·ly /'mīldlē/ ▶*adv.* in a mild manner, in particular without anger or severity. ■ not seriously or dangerously: *he had suffered mildly from the illness since he was 23.* ■ [as *submodifier*] to a slight extent: *he kept his voice mildly curious.*

▶*PHRASE* □ **to put it mildly** (or **putting it mildly**) used to imply that the reality is more extreme, usually worse: *the proposals were, to put it mildly, unpopular.*

mild-man·nered ▶*adj.* (of a person) gentle and not given to extremes of emotion.

mild steel ▶*n.* steel containing a small percentage of carbon, strong and tough but not readily tempered.

mile /mīl/ ▶*n.* (also **statute mile**) a unit of linear measure equal to 5,280 feet, or 1,760 yards (approximately 1.609 kilometers). ■ *historical* (also **Roman mile**) a Roman measure of 1,000 paces (approximately 1,620 yards). ■ (usu. **miles**) *informal* a very long way or a very great amount: *vistas that stretch for miles.* ■ a race extending over a mile.

▶*adv.* [as *submodifier*] (**miles**) *informal* by a great amount or a long way: *the second tape is miles better.* ▷Old English *mīl*, based on Latin *mil(l)ia*, plural of *mille* 'thousand' (the original Roman unit of distance was *mille passus* 'a thousand paces').

▶*PHRASES* □ **be miles away** *informal* be lost in thought and consequently unaware of what is happening around one. □ **go the extra mile** be especially assiduous in one's attempt to achieve something. □ **a mile a minute** *informal* very quickly: *he talks a mile a minute.* □ **miles from anywhere** *informal* in a very isolated place. □ **see** (or **tell** or **spot**) **something a mile off** *informal* recognize something very easily: *the first-year campers can be spotted a mile off.* □ **stand** (or **stick**) **out a mile** *informal* be very obvious or incongruous.

mile·age /'mīlij/ (also **mil·age**) ▶*n.* **1** [usu. in *sing.*] a number of miles traveled or covered: *the car is in good condition, considering its mileage.* ■ [usu. as *adj.*] traveling expenses paid according to the number of miles traveled: *the mileage rate will be 34 cents per mile.* **2** *informal* the contribution made by something to one's aims or interests: *he was* **getting a lot of mileage out of** *the mix-up.* ■ the likely potential of someone or something: *there is bound to be a lot of mileage for the paperback.*

mile-a-min·ute weed ▶*n.* an invasive and noxious vine, native to Asia, that has downward-pointing barbs on the stem and the underside of leaves. It is considered an ecological threat in the eastern U.S. • *Polygonum perfoliatum*, family Polygonaceae.

mile·post /'mīlˌpōst/ ▶*n.* a marker set up to indicate how distant a particular place is. ■ another term for MILESTONE. ■ a post one mile from the finishing post of a race.

mil·er /'mīlər/ ▶*n.* *informal* a person or horse trained specially to run a mile. —**mil·ing** /'mīliNG/ *n.*

mi·les glo·ri·o·sus /'mēˌläs ˌglôrē'ōsəs/ ▶*n.* (*pl.* **mi·li·tes glo·ri·o·si** /'mēləˌtās ˌglôrē'ōsē/) (in literature) a boastful soldier as a stock figure. ▷Latin, from the title of a comedy by Plautus.

Mi·le·sian /mə'lēZHən; mī-/ ▶*n.* a native or inhabitant of ancient Miletus.

▶*adj.* of or relating to Miletus or its inhabitants. ▷mid 16th cent.: via Latin from Greek *Milēsios* + -AN.

mile·stone /'mīlˌstōn/ ▶*n.* a stone set up beside a road to mark the distance in miles to a particular place. ■ *figurative* an action or event marking a significant change or stage in development: *the speech is being hailed as a* **milestone in** *race relations.*

Mi·le·tus /mī'lētəs; mə-/ an ancient city of the Ionian Greeks in southwestern Asia Minor. In the 7th and 6th centuries BC it was a powerful port, from which more than 60 colonies were founded on the shores of the Black Sea and in Italy and Egypt.

mil·foil /'milˌfoil/ ▶*n.* **1** the common Eurasian yarrow. **2** (also **water milfoil**) a widely distributed and highly invasive aquatic plant with whorls of fine submerged leaves and wind-pollinated flowers. • Genus *Myriophyllum*, family Haloragaceae. ▷Middle English: via Old French from Latin *millefolium*, from *mille* 'thousand' + *folium* 'leaf.'

Mil·ford /ˌmilfərd/ a city in southwestern Connecticut, west of New Haven; pop. 49,938.

Mi·lhaud /mē'(y)ō/, Darius (1892–1974), French composer. A member of the group Les Six, he composed the music to Cocteau's ballet *Le Boeuf sur le toit* (1919). Much of his music was polytonal and influenced by jazz.

mil·i·a /'milēə/ ▶ plural form of MILIUM.

mil·i·ar·i·a /ˌmilē'e(ə)rēə/ ▶*n.* medical term for PRICKLY HEAT. ▷early 19th cent.: modern Latin, from Latin *miliarius* (see MILIARY).

mil·i·ar·y /'milēˌerē/ ▶*adj.* (of a disease) accompanied by a rash with lesions resembling millet seed: *miliary tuberculosis.* ▷late 17th cent.: from Latin *miliarius*, from *milium* 'millet.'

mi·lieu /mil'yo͞o; -'yə(r)/ ▶*n.* (*pl.* **mi·lieux** *pronunc.* same, or **mi·lieus**) a person's social environment: *he grew up in a military milieu.* ▷mid 19th cent.: French, from *mi* 'mid' + *lieu* 'place.'

mi·lieu ther·a·py ▶*n.* psychotherapy in which the patient's social environment is controlled or manipulated with a view to preventing self-destructive behavior.

Mi·li·la·ni Town /ˌmēlē'länē/ a planned community in Hawaii, on central Oahu Island, northwest of Honolulu; pop. 28,608.

mil·i·tant /'milətənt/ ▶*adj.* combative and aggressive in support of a political or social cause, and typically favoring extreme, violent, or confrontational methods: *an uprising by militant Islamic fundamentalists.*

▶*n.* a person who is active in this way. ▷late Middle English (in the sense 'engaged in warfare'): from Old French, or from Latin *militant-* 'serving as a soldier,' from the verb *militare* (see MILITATE). The current sense dates from the early 20th cent. —**mil·i·tan·cy** /-tənsē/ *n.* —**mil·i·tant·ly** *adv.*

mil·i·tar·i·a /ˌmili'te(ə)rēə/ ▶*plural n.* military articles of historical interest, such as weapons, uniforms, and equipment. ▷1960s: from MILITARY + -IA[2].

mil·i·ta·rism /'milətəˌrizəm/ ▶*n.* *chiefly derogatory* the belief or desire of a government or people that a country should maintain a strong military capability and be prepared to use it aggressively to defend or promote national interests. ▷mid 19th cent.: from French *militarisme*, from *militaire* (see MILITARY). —**mil·i·ta·rist** *n.* & *adj.* —**mil·i·ta·ris·tic** /ˌmilətə'ristik/ *adj.*

mil·i·ta·rize /'milətəˌrīz/ ▶*v.* [*trans.*] [often as *adj.*] (**militarized**) give (something, esp. an organization) a military character or style: *militarized police forces.* ■ equip or supply (a place) with soldiers and other military resources: *a militarized security zone.* —**mil·i·ta·ri·za·tion** /ˌmilətərə'zāSHən/ *n.*

mil·i·tar·y /'miləˌterē/ ▶*adj.* of, relating to, or characteristic of soldiers or armed forces: *both leaders condemned the buildup of military activity.*

▶*n.* (**the military**) the armed forces of a country. ▷late Middle English: from French *militaire* or Latin *militaris*, from *miles, milit-* 'soldier.' —**mil·i·tar·i·ly** /ˌmilə'te(ə)rəlē/ *adv.*

mil·i·tar·y at·ta·ché ▶*n.* an army officer serving with an embassy or attached as an observer to a foreign army.

mil·i·tar·y band ▶*n.* a group of musicians playing brass, woodwind, and percussion instruments, typically while marching.

mil·i·tar·y hon·ors ▶*plural n.* ceremonies performed by troops as a mark of respect at the burial of a member of the armed forces: *he was buried* **with full military honors.**

mil·i·tar·y-in·dus·tri·al com·plex ▶*n.* a country's military establishment and those industries producing arms or other military materials, regarded as a powerful vested interest.

mil·i·tar·y law ▶*n.* the law governing the armed forces.

mil·i·tar·y po·lice ▶*n.* [treated as *pl.*] the corps responsible for police and disciplinary duties in an army. —**mil·i·tar·y po·lice·man** *n.* —**mil·i·tar·y po·lice·wom·an** *n.*

mil·i·ta·ry sci·ence ▶*n.* the study of the causes and tactical principles of warfare.

mil·i·tar·y trib·une ▶*n.* see TRIBUNE[1].

mil·i·tate /'miləˌtāt/ ▶*v.* [*intrans.*] (**militate against**) (of a fact or circumstance) be a powerful or conclusive factor in preventing: *these fundamental differences will militate against the two communities coming together.* ▷late 16th cent.: from Latin *militat-* 'served as a soldier,' from the verb *militare*, from *miles, milit-* 'soldier.'

USAGE The verbs **militate** and **mitigate** are sometimes confused. See usage at MITIGATE.

mi·li·tes glo·ri·o·si /'mēləˌtās ˌglôrē'ōsē/ ▶ plural form of MILES GLORIOSUS.

mi·li·tia /mə'liSHə/ ▶*n.* a military force that is raised from the civil population to supplement a regular army in an emergency. ■ a military force that engages in rebel or terrorist activities, typically in opposition to a regular army. ■ all able-bodied civilians eligible by law for military service. ▷late 16th cent.: from Latin, literally 'military service,' from *miles, milit-* 'soldier.'

mi·li·tia·man /mə'liSHəmən/ ▶*n.* (*pl.* **-men**) a member of a militia.

mil·i·um /'milēəm/ ▶*n.* (*pl.* **mil·i·a** /'milēə/) *Medicine* a small, hard, pale keratinous nodule formed on the skin, typically by a blocked sebaceous gland. ▷mid 19th cent.: from Latin, literally 'millet' (because of a resemblance to a millet seed).

milk /milk/ ▶*n.* an opaque white fluid rich in fat and protein, secreted by female mammals for the nourishment of their young. ■ the milk of cows (or occasionally goats or ewes) as food for humans: *a glass of milk.* ■ the white juice of certain plants: *coconut milk.* ■ a creamy-textured liquid with a particular ingredient or use: *cleansing milk.*

▶*v.* [*trans.*] draw milk from (a cow or other animal), either by hand or mechanically. ■ [*intrans.*] (of an animal, esp. a cow) produce or yield milk: *the breed does seem to milk better in harder conditions.* ■ extract sap, venom, or other substances from. ■ *figurative* exploit or defraud (someone), typically by taking regular small amounts of money over a period of time: [with *complement*] *he had milked his grandmother dry of all her money.* ■ *figurative* get all possible advantage from (a situation): *the newspapers were milking the story for every possible drop of drama.* ■ *figurative* elicit a favorable reaction from (an audience) and prolong it for as long as possible: *he milked the crowd for every last drop of applause.* ▷Old English *milc, milcian*, of Germanic origin; related to Dutch *melk* and German *Milch*, from an Indo-European root shared by Latin *mulgere* and Greek *amelgein* 'to milk.'

▶*PHRASES* □ **in milk** (of an animal, esp. a cow) producing milk. □ **it's no use crying over spilt** (or **spilled**) **milk** *proverb* there is no point in regretting something that has already happened and cannot be changed or reversed. □ **milk and honey** prosperity and abundance. [with biblical allusion to the prosperity of the Promised Land (Exod. 3:8).] □ **milk** of human kindness care and compassion for others. [with allusion to Shakespeare's *Macbeth*.]

milk-and-wa·ter ▶*adj.* [*attrib.*] lacking the will or ability to act effectively: *a milk-and-water rebel.*

milk bar ▶*n. Brit.* a snack bar that sells milk drinks and other refreshments.

milk choc·o·late ▶*n.* solid chocolate made with the addition of milk.

milk·er /ˈmilkər/ ▶*n.* **1** a cow or other animal that is kept for milk, esp. one of a specified productivity: *the cows were no more than fair milkers.* **2** a person or contrivance that milks cows.

milk fe·ver ▶*n.* **1** an acute illness in female cows, goats, etc., that have just produced young, caused by calcium deficiency. **2** a fever in women caused by infection after childbirth, formerly supposed to be due to the swelling of the breasts with milk.

milk·fish /ˈmilkˌfisн/ ▶*n.* (*pl.* same or **-fish·es**) a large active silvery fish of the Indo-Pacific region, farmed for food in Southeast Asia and the Philippines. • *Chanos chanos*, the only member of the family Chanidae.

milk glass ▶*n.* semitranslucent glass, whitened by the addition of various ingredients: [as *adj.*] *milk-glass jars.* Also called **OPALINE**.

milk·ing par·lor ▶*n.* see **PARLOR** (sense 3).

milk·ing stool ▶*n.* a short three-legged stool, of a kind traditionally used while milking cows.

milk leg ▶*n.* painful swelling of the leg after giving birth, caused by thrombophlebitis in the femoral vein.

milk·maid /ˈmilkˌmād/ ▶*n. chiefly archaic* a girl or woman who milks cows or does other work in a dairy.

milk·man /ˈmilkmən; -ˌman/ ▶*n.* (*pl.* **-men**) a person who delivers and sells milk.

milk of mag·ne·sia ▶*n.* a white suspension of hydrated magnesium carbonate in water, used as an antacid or laxative. ▷from the trademark.

Milk Riv·er a river that flows for 625 miles (1,000 km) through northwestern Montana and southern Alberta, into the Missouri River. It is the most northwestern part of the Missouri-Mississippi river system.

milk run ▶*n.* a routine, uneventful journey, esp. by plane.

milk shake (also **milk·shake**) ▶*n.* a cold drink made of milk, a sweet flavoring such as fruit or chocolate, and typically ice cream, whisked until it is frothy.

milk sick·ness ▶*n.* a condition of cattle and sheep in the western U.S., caused by eating white snakeroot, which contains a toxic alcohol. It sometimes occurs in humans who have eaten meat or dairy products from affected animals.

milk snake ▶*n.* a harmless North American constrictor that is typically strongly marked with red and black on yellow or white. It was formerly supposed to suck milk from sleeping cows. • Genus *Lampropeltis*, family Colubridae: several species, in particular *L. triangulum*. Compare with **KING SNAKE**.

milk·sop /ˈmilkˌsäp/ ▶*n.* a person who is indecisive and lacks courage.

milk sug·ar ▶*n.* another term for **LACTOSE**.

milk this·tle ▶*n.* a European thistle with a solitary purple flower and glossy marbled leaves, naturalized in North America and used in herbal medicine. • *Silybum marianum*, family Compositae. ▪ another term for **SOW THISTLE**.

milk tooth ▶*n.* any of a set of early, temporary (deciduous) teeth in children or young mammals that fall out as the permanent teeth erupt (in children, between the ages of about 6 and 12).

milk vetch (also **milk-vetch**) ▶*n.* a plant of the pea family found throughout the temperate zone of the northern hemisphere, grown in several regions as a fodder plant. • Genus *Astragalus*, family Leguminosae: numerous species, including the widespread *A. canadensis*.

milk·weed /ˈmilkˌwēd/ ▶*n.* **1** a herbaceous American plant with milky sap. Some kinds attract butterflies, some yield a variety of useful products, and some are grown as ornamentals. • Genus *Asclepias*, family Asclepiadaceae: several species, in particular the **common milkweed** (*A. syriaca*). **2** (also **milkweed butterfly**) another term for **MONARCH BUTTERFLY**.

common milkweed

milk-white ▶*adj.* of the opaque white color of milk: *she had milk-white skin.*

milk·wort /ˈmilkˌwərt; -ˌwôrt/ ▶*n.* a small plant that was formerly believed to increase the milk yield of cows and nursing mothers. Its tiny flowers, which may be white, pink, yellow-orange, blue, or greenish, usually appear in cloverlike heads. • Genus *Polygala*, family Polygalaceae: several species, including the **cross-leaved milkwort** (*P. cruciata*) and the **yellow milkwort** (*P. lutea*).

milk·y /ˈmilkē/ ▶*adj.* (**milk·i·er, milk·i·est**) **1** containing or mixed with a large amount of milk: *a cup of sweet milky coffee.* ▪ (of a cow) producing a lot of milk. ▪ resembling milk, esp. in color: *not a blemish marred her milky skin.* ▪ (of something that is usually clear) cloudy: *the old man's milky, uncomprehending eyes.* **2** *informal, dated* weak and compliant: *they just talk that way to make you turn milky.* **—milk·i·ly** /-əlē/ *adv.* **—milk·i·ness** *n.*

milk·y spore ▶*n.* a bacterial disease of beetle larvae, including the Japanese beetle; the bacterium has been isolated and used in a commercial pesticide sold under the same name. • *Bacillus popilliae*, family Bacillaceae.

Milk·y Way a faint band of light crossing the sky, made up of vast numbers of faint stars. It corresponds to the plane of our Galaxy, in which most of its stars are located. ▪ the galaxy in which our sun is located.

Mill /mil/, John Stuart (1806–73), English philosopher and economist. He is best known for his political and moral works, esp. *On Liberty* (1859), which argued for the importance of individuality, and *Utilitarianism* (1861), which extensively developed Bentham's theory. **—Mill·i·an** /ˈmilēən/ *adj.*

mill[1] /mil/ ▶*n.* **1** a building equipped with machinery for grinding grain into flour. ▪ a piece of machinery of this type. ▪ a domestic device for grinding a solid substance to powder or pulp: *a coffee mill.* ▪ a building fitted with machinery for a manufacturing process: *a steel mill* | [as *adj.*] *a mill town.* ▪ a piece of manufacturing machinery. ▪ a place that processes things or people in a mechanical way: *a correspondence school that was just a diploma mill.* **2** *informal* an engine. **3** *informal, dated* a boxing match or a fistfight.

▶*v.* **1** [*trans.*] grind or crush (something) in a mill: *hard wheats are easily milled into white flour* | [as *adj.*, with *submodifier*] (**milled**) *freshly milled black pepper.* ▪ cut or shape (metal) with a rotating tool: [as *adj.*] (**milling**) *lathes and milling machines.* ▪ [usu. as *adj.*] (**milled**) produce regular ribbed markings on the edge of (a coin) as a protection against illegal clipping. **2** [*intrans.*] (**mill about/around**) (of people or animals) move around in a confused mass: *people milled about the room, shaking hands* | [as *adj.*] (**milling**) *the milling crowds of guests.* **3** [*trans.*] thicken (wool or another animal fiber) by fulling it. ▷Old English *mylen*, based on late Latin *molinum*, from Latin *mola* 'grindstone, mill,' from *molere* 'to grind.' **—mill·a·ble** *adj.*

▶*PHRASE* □ **go** (or **put someone**) **through the mill** undergo (or cause someone to undergo) an unpleasant experience.

mill[2] ▶*n.* a monetary unit used only in calculations, worth one thousandth of a dollar. ▷late 18th cent.: from Latin *millesimum* 'thousandth part'; compare with **CENT**.

Mil·lais /məˈlā/, Sir John Everett (1829–96), English painter. A founding member of the Pre-Raphaelite Brotherhood, he produced lavishly painted portraits and landscapes.

Mil·land /miˈland/, Ray (1907–86), U.S. actor; born in Wales; born *Reginald Alfred John-Truscott-Jones*. His many movies include *The Lost Weekend* (Academy Award, 1945), *A Life of Her Own* (1950), and *Dial M for Murder* (1954).

Mil·lay /miˈlā/, Edna St. Vincent (1892–1950), U.S. poet and writer; pen name **Nancy Boyd**. Much of her poetry is collected in *Renascence and Other Poems* (1917), *Collected Sonnets* (1941), and *Collected Lyrics* (1943).

mill·board /ˈmilˌbôrd/ ▶*n.* stiff gray pasteboard, used for the covers of books.

Mill·creek /ˈmilˌkrēk/ a township in northwestern Pennsylvania; pop. 52,129.

mill·dam /ˈmilˌdam/ ▶*n.* a dam built across a stream to raise the level of the water so that it will turn the wheel of a water mill.

Mille, Cecil B. de, see **DEMILLE**.

mille-feuille /ˌmēl fœy; fəˈwē/ ▶*n.* a rich dessert consisting of many very thin layers of puff pastry and such fillings as whipped cream, custard, fruit, etc. ▷French, literally 'thousand-leaf.'

mil·le·fi·o·ri /ˌmiləfēˈôrē/ ▶*n.* a kind of ornamental glass in which a number of glass rods of different sizes and colors are fused together and cut into sections that form various patterns, typically embedded in colorless transparent glass to make items such as paperweights. ▷mid 19th cent.: from Italian *millefiore*, literally 'a thousand flowers.'

mille·fleurs /mēlˈflər; -ˈflo͝or/ ▶*n.* a pattern of flowers and leaves used in tapestry, on porcelain, or in other decorative items. ▷mid 19th cent.: French, literally 'a thousand flowers.'

mil·le·nar·i·an /ˌmiləˈne(ə)rēən/ ▶*adj.* relating to or believing in Christian millenarianism. ▪ *figurative* believing in the imminence or inevitability of a golden age of peace, justice, and prosperity: *millenarian Marxists.* ▪ denoting a religious or political group seeking solutions to present crises through rapid and radical transformation of politics and society.

▶*n.* a person who believes in the doctrine of the millennium. ▷mid 17th cent.: from late Latin *millenarius* (see **MILLENARY**) + **-AN**.

mil·le·nar·i·an·ism /ˌmiləˈne(ə)rēəˌnizəm/ ▶*n.* the doctrine of or belief in a future (and typically imminent) thousand-year age of blessedness, beginning with or culminating in the Second Coming of Christ. It is central to the teaching of groups such as Plymouth Brethren, Adventists, Mormons, and Jehovah's Witnesses. ▪ belief in a future golden age of peace, justice, and prosperity. **—mil·le·nar·i·an·ist** *n.* & *adj.*

mil·le·nar·y /ˈmiləˌnerē/ ▶*n.* (*pl.* **-nar·ies**) a period of a thousand years. Compare with **MILLENNIUM**. ▪ a thousandth anniversary.

▶*adj.* consisting of a thousand people, years, etc. ▷mid 16th cent.: from late Latin *millenarius* 'containing a thousand,' based on Latin *mille* 'thousand.'

Mil·len·nial /miˈlenēəl/ ▶*n.* a member of the generation born from about 1980 onward.

mil·len·ni·al·ism /məˈlenēəˌlizəm/ ▶*n.* another term for **MILLENARIANISM**. **—mil·len·ni·al·ist** *n.* & *adj.*

mil·len·ni·um /məˈlenēəm/ ▶*n.* (*pl.* **-len·ni·a** /-ˈlenēə/ or **-len·ni·ums**) a period of a thousand years, esp. when calculated from the traditional date of the birth of Jesus Christ. ▪ an anniversary of a thousand years: *the millennium of the Russian Orthodox Church.* ▪ (**the millennium**) the point at which one period of a thousand years ends and another begins. ▪ (**the millennium**) *Christian Theology* the prophesied thousand-year reign of Christ at the end of the age (Rev. 20:1–5). ▪ (**the millennium**) *figurative* a utopian period of good government, great happiness, and prosperity. ▷mid 17th cent.: modern Latin, from Latin *mille* 'thousand,' on the pattern of *biennium*. **—mil·len·ni·al** /-ēəl/ *adj.*

> *USAGE* The spelling of **millennium** is less difficult if one remembers that it comes ultimately from two Latin words containing double letters: *mille*, 'thousand,' and *annum*, 'year.'

mil·le·pede /ˈmiləˌpēd/ ▶*n.* variant spelling of **MILLIPEDE**.

mil·le·pore /ˈmiləˌpôr/ ▶*n. Zoology* a fire coral. ▷mid 18th cent.: from French *millépore* or modern Latin *millepora*, from Latin *mille* 'thousand' + *porus* 'pore.'

Mill·er[1] /ˈmilər/, Arthur (1915–), U.S. playwright. He achieved success with *Death of a Salesman* (1949). *The Crucible* (1953) used the Salem witch trials of 1692 as an allegory for McCarthyism. He was married to Marilyn Monroe between 1955 and 1961. Other notable works: *All My Sons* (1947), *After the Fall* (1964), and *The Ryan Interview* (1995).

Mill·er[2], (Alton) Glenn (1904–44), U.S. jazz trombonist and bandleader. From 1938, he led his celebrated big band, with which he recorded his signature tune "Moonlight Serenade." He died when his airplane disappeared on a routine flight across the English Channel.

Mill·er[3], Henry (Valentine) (1891–1980), U.S. novelist. His autobiographical novels *Tropic of Cancer* (1934) and *Tropic of Capricorn* (1939) were banned in the U.S. until the 1960s because of frank depictions of sex and the use of obscenities.

Mil·ler[4], Samuel Freeman (1816–90), U.S. Supreme Court associate justice 1862–90. A strong advocate of individual rights, he was appointed to the Court by President Lincoln.

mill·er /ˈmilər/ ▶*n.* a person who owns or works in a grain mill.

M

mill·er·ite /ˈmiləˌrīt/ ▶*n.* a mineral consisting of nickel sulfide and typically occurring as slender needle-shaped bronze crystals. ▷mid 19th cent.: named after William H. *Miller* (1801–80), English scientist, + **-ITE**[1].

mill·er's thumb ▶*n.* a small European freshwater fish of the sculpin family, having a broad flattened head and most active at night. Also called **BULLHEAD**. • *Cottus gobio*, family Cottidae.

mil·les·i·mal /məˈlesəməl/ ▶*adj.* consisting of thousandth parts; thousandth.
▶*n.* a thousandth part. ▷early 18th cent.: from Latin *millesimus* (from *mille* 'thousand') + **-AL**. **—mil·les·i·mal·ly** *adv.*

Mil·let /mēˈye; -ˈle/, Jean (François) (1814–75), French painter. He was noted for the dignity he brought to the treatment of peasant subjects.

mil·let /ˈmilit/ ▶*n.* a fast-growing cereal plant that is widely grown in warm countries and regions with poor soils. The numerous small seeds are used to make flour or alcoholic drinks. • Several species in the family Gramineae, in particular **common millet** (*Panicum miliaceum*), of temperate regions, the tropical **finger millet** (*Eleusine caracana*), which is a staple in parts of Africa and India, and **PEARL MILLET**. ▷late Middle English: from French, diminutive of dialect *mil*, from Latin *milium*.

Mil·lett /ˈmilit/, Kate (1934–), U.S. feminist; full name *Katherine Millett*. She became involved in the civil rights movement of the 1960s and advocated a radical feminism in *Sexual Politics* (1970).

mill·hand /ˈmilˌhand/ ▶*n.* a worker in a mill or factory.

milli- ▶*comb. form* (used commonly in units of measurement) a thousand, chiefly denoting a factor of one thousandth: *milligram* | *millipede*. ▷from Latin *mille* 'thousand.'

mil·li·am·me·ter /ˌmilēˈa(m)ˌmētər/ ▶*n.* an instrument for measuring electric current in milliamperes.

mil·li·amp /ˈmilēˌamp/ ▶*n.* short for **MILLIAMPERE**.

mil·li·am·pere /ˌmilēˈamˌpir/ ▶*n.* one thousandth of an ampere, a measure for small electric currents.

mil·liard /ˈmilˌyärd; -yərd/ ▶*n. Brit.* one thousand million (a term now largely superseded by billion). ▷late 18th cent.: French, from *mille* 'thousand.'

mil·li·bar /ˈmiləˌbär/ ▶*n.* one thousandth of a bar, the cgs unit of atmospheric pressure equivalent to 100 pascals.

mil·lieme /mē(l)ˈyem/ ▶*n.* a monetary unit of Egypt, equal to one thousandth of a pound. ▷from French *millième* 'thousandth.'

mil·li·gram /ˈmiləˌgram/ (*Brit.* also **mil·li·gramme**) (abbr.: **mg**) ▶*n.* one thousandth of a gram.

Mil·li·kan /ˈmilikən/, Robert Andrews (1868–1953), U.S. physicist. He was the first to give an accurate figure for the electric charge on an electron. Nobel Prize for Physics (1923).

mil·li·li·ter /ˈmiləˌlētər/ (*Brit.* **mil·li·li·tre**) (abbr.: **ml**) ▶*n.* one thousandth of a liter (0.002 pint).

mil·li·me·ter /ˈmiləˌmētər/ (*Brit.* **mil·li·me·tre**) (abbr.: **mm**) ▶*n.* one thousandth of a meter (0.039 in.).

mil·li·ner /ˈmilənər/ ▶*n.* a person who makes or sells women's hats. ▷late Middle English (originally in the sense 'native of Milan,' later 'a vendor of fancy goods from Milan'): from **MILAN** + **-ER**[1].

mil·li·ner·y /ˈmiləˌnerē/ ▶*n.* (*pl.* **-ner·ies**) women's hats. ■ the trade or business of a milliner.

mil·lion /ˈmilyən/ ▶*cardinal number* (*pl.* **-lions** or (with numeral or quantifying word) same) **(a/one million)** the number equivalent to the product of a thousand and a thousand; 1,000,000 or 10^6: *a million people will benefit* | *a population of half a million* | *a cost of more than $20 million*. ■ **(millions)** the numbers from a million to a billion. ■ **(millions)** several million things or people: *millions of TV viewers*. ■ *informal* an unspecified but very large number or amount of something: *I've got millions of beer bottles in my cellar* | *you're **one in a million***. ■ **(the millions)** the bulk of the population: *movies for the millions*. ■ a million dollars: *the author is set to make millions*. ▷late Middle English: from Old French, probably from Italian *milione*, from *mille* 'thousand' + the augmentative suffix *-one*. **—mil·lion·fold** /-ˌfōld/ *adj.* & *adv.* **—mil·lionth** /-yənTH/ *ordinal number*.
▶PHRASE □ **look** (or **feel**) **(like) a million dollars** *informal* (of a person) look or feel extremely good.

mil·lion·aire /ˌmilyəˈne(ə)r; ˈmilyəˌner/ ▶*n.* a person whose assets are worth one million dollars or more. ▷early 19th cent.: from French *millionnaire*, from *million* (see **MILLION**).

mil·lion·air·ess /ˌmilyəˈne(ə)rəs/ ▶*n.* a female millionaire.

mil·li·pede /ˈmiləˌpēd/ (also **mil·le·pede**) ▶*n.* a myriapod invertebrate with an elongated body composed of many segments, most of which bear two pairs of legs. Most kinds are herbivorous and shun light, living in the soil or under stones and logs. • Class Diplopoda: several orders. ▷early 17th cent.: from Latin *millepeda* 'wood louse,' from *mille* 'thousand' + *pes, ped-* 'foot.'

mil·li·sec·ond /ˈmiləˌsekənd/ ▶*n.* one thousandth of a second.

mil·li·volt /ˈmiləˌvōlt/ ▶*n.* one thousandth of a volt.

mill·pond /ˈmilˌpänd/ (also **mill pond**) ▶*n.* the pool that is created by a milldam and provides the head of water that powers a water mill.

mill·race /ˈmilˌrās/ ▶*n.* the channel carrying the swift current of water that drives a mill wheel.

Mills /milz/, Sir John (Lewis Ernest Watts) (1908–), English actor. He is noted for his roles in war and adventure movies, such as *Scott of the Antarctic* (1948). He won an Academy Award for his portrayal of a village idiot in *Ryan's Daughter* (1971). His daughters **Juliet Mills** (1941–) and **Hayley Mills** (1946–) also have had acting careers.

mill·stone /ˈmilˌstōn/ ▶*n.* each of two circular stones used for grinding grain. ■ *figurative* a heavy and inescapable responsibility: *she threatened to become a millstone around his neck*.

mill·stream /ˈmilˌstrēm/ ▶*n.* the current of water in a millrace. ■ another term for **MILLRACE**.

Mill·ville /ˈmilˌvil/ a city in southern New Jersey, across the Maurice River from Vineland; pop. 25,992.

mill wheel ▶*n.* a wheel used to drive a water mill.

mill·work·er /ˈmilˌwərkər/ ▶*n.* a worker in a mill or factory.

mill·wright /ˈmilˌrīt/ ▶*n.* a person who designs or builds mills or who maintains mill machinery.

Milne /miln/, A. A. (1882–1956), English writer of stories and poems for children; full name *Alan Alexander Milne*. He created the character Winnie the Pooh for his son Christopher Robin. Notable works: *Winnie-the-Pooh* (1926) and *When We Were Very Young* (verse collection, 1924).

mi·lo /ˈmīlō/ ▶*n.* sorghum of a drought-resistant variety that is an important grain in the central U.S., Africa, and Asia. ▷late 19th cent.: from Sesotho *maili*.

mi·lord /məˈlôrd; mī-/ ▶*n. historical* or *humorous* used to address or refer to an English nobleman, esp. one traveling in Europe. ▷early 17th cent.: via French from English *my lord*; compare with **MILADY**.

Mí·los /ˈmēˌläs; -ˌlôs/ Greek name for **MELOS**.

Mi·losz /ˈmēlôSH/, Czeslaw (1911–2004), U.S. poet and writer; born in Lithuania. He wrote the political essay *The Captive Mind* (1953). His novels include *The Seizure of Power* (1953), and his poetry is collected in volumes such as *Bells in Winter* (1978) and *The Collected Poems, 1931–1987* (1988). Nobel Prize for Literature (1980).

milque·toast /ˈmilkˌtōst/ (also **Milque·toast**) ▶*n.* a person who is timid or submissive: [as *adj.*] *a soppy, milquetoast composer*. ▷1930s: from the name of a cartoon character, Caspar *Milquetoast*, created by H. T. Webster in 1924.

mil·reis /milˈrāSH; -ˈrās/ ▶*n.* (*pl.* same) a former monetary unit of Portugal and Brazil, equal to one thousand reis. ▷Portuguese, from *mil* 'thousand' + *reis*, plural of *real* (see **REAL**[2]).

milt /milt/ ▶*n.* the semen of a male fish. ■ a sperm-filled reproductive gland of a male fish. ▷Old English *milte* 'spleen,' of Germanic origin; perhaps related to **MELT**. The current sense dates from the late 15th cent.

Mil·ton /ˈmiltn/, John (1608–74), English poet. His three major works, *Paradise Lost* (1667; revised, 1674), *Paradise Regained* (1671), and *Samson Agonistes* (1671), which were completed after he had gone blind in 1652, show his mastery of blank verse. **—Mil·to·ni·an** /milˈtōnēən/ *adj.* **—Mil·ton·ic** /milˈtänik/ *adj.*

Mil·ton Keynes /ˌmiltn ˈkēnz/ a town in south central England; pop. 172,000.

Mil·wau·kee /milˈwôkē/ an industrial port and city in southeastern Wisconsin, on the western shore of Lake Michigan; pop. 596,974. It is noted for its brewing industry and is an important port on the St. Lawrence Seaway.

mim /mim/ ▶*adj. Scottish* affectedly modest or demure. ▷late 16th cent.: imitative of pursing the lips.

Mi·mas /ˈmīməs; ˈmē-/ *Astronomy* a satellite of Saturn, the seventh closest to the planet, discovered by W. Herschel in 1789. It has a diameter of 242 miles (390 km) and has many craters, one of which has a diameter of 80 miles (130 km), a third of the diameter of Mimas. ▷named after a giant in Greek mythology, killed by Ares.

mim·bar /ˈmimˌbär/ ▶*n.* variant spelling of **MINBAR**.

MIME /mīm; ˈem ˈī ˈem ˈē/ ▶*n. Computing* a standard for formatting files of different types, such as text, graphics, or audio, so they can be sent over the Internet and seen or played by a Web browser or e-mail application. ▷late 20th cent.: an acronym for *multipurpose Internet mail extensions*.

mime /mīm/ ▶*n.* **1** the theatrical technique of suggesting action, character, or emotion without words, using only gesture, expression, and movement. ■ a theatrical performance or part of a performance using such a technique. ■ an action or set of actions intended to convey the idea of another action or an idea or feeling: *he performed a brief mime of someone fencing*. ■ a practitioner of mime or a performer in a mime. **2** (in ancient Greece and Rome) a simple farcical drama including mimicry.
▶*v.* [*trans.*] use gesture and movement without words in the acting of (a play or role). ■ convey an impression of (an idea or feeling) by gesture and movement, without using words; mimic (an action or set of actions) in this way: *he stands up and mimes throwing a spear*. ▷early 17th cent. (also in the sense 'mimic or jester'): from Latin *mimus*, from Greek *mimos*. **—mim·er** *n.*

mim·e·o /ˈmimēˌō/ ▶*n.* short for **MIMEOGRAPH**.

mim·e·o·graph /ˈmimēəˌgraf/ ▶*n.* a duplicating machine that produces copies from a stencil, now superseded by the photocopier. ■ a copy produced on such a machine.
▶*v.* [*trans.*] make a copy of (a document) with such a machine. ▷late 19th cent.: formed irregularly from Greek *mimeomai* 'I imitate' + **-GRAPH**.

mi·me·sis /məˈmēsis; mī-/ ▶*n. formal* or *technical* imitation, in particular: ■ representation or imitation of the real world in art and literature. ■ the deliberate imitation of the behavior of one group of people by another as a factor in social change. ■ *Zoology* another term for **MIMICRY**. ▷mid 16th cent.: from Greek *mimēsis*, from *mimeisthai* 'to imitate.'

mi·met·ic /məˈmetik/ ▶*adj. formal* or *technical* relating to, constituting, or habitually practicing mimesis: *mimetic patterns in butterflies*. ▷mid 17th cent.: from Greek *mimētikos* 'imitation,' from *mimeisthai* 'to imitate.' **—mi·met·i·cal·ly** /-ik(ə)lē/ *adv.*

mim·e·tite /ˈmīməˌtīt; ˈmī-/ ▶*n.* a yellow or brown mineral consisting of a chloride and arsenate of lead, typically found as a crust or needlelike crystals in lead deposits. ▷mid 19th cent.: from Greek *mimētēs* 'imitator' + **-ITE**[1].

mim·ic /ˈmimik/ ▶*v.* (**mim·icked, mim·ick·ing**) [*trans.*] imitate (someone or their actions or words), typically in order to entertain or ridicule: *she mimicked Eileen's voice*. See note at **IMITATE**. ■ (of an animal or plant) resemble or imitate (another animal or plant), esp. to deter predators or for camouflage. ■ (of a drug) replicate the physiological effects of (another substance). ■ (of a disease) exhibit symptoms that bear a deceptive resemblance to those of (another disease).
▶*n.* a person skilled in imitating the voice, mannerisms, or movements of others in an entertaining way. ■ an animal or plant that exhibits mimicry.
▶*adj.* [*attrib.*] imitative of something, esp. for amusement: *they were waging mimic war*. ▷late 16th cent. (as noun and adjective): via Latin from Greek *mimikos*, from *mimos* 'mime.' **—mim·ick·er** *n.*

mim·ic·ry /ˈmimәkrē/ ▶*n.* (*pl.* **-ries**) the action or art of imitating someone or something, typically in order to entertain or ridicule: *the word was spoken with gently teasing mimicry* | *a playful mimicry of the techniques of realist writers*. See note at **CARICATURE**. ■ *Biology* the close external resemblance of an animal or plant (or part of one) to another animal, plant, or inanimate object. See also **BATESIAN MIMICRY, MÜLLERIAN MIMICRY**.

mi·mo·sa /miˈmōsə; mī-; -zə/ ▶*n.* **1** an Australian acacia tree with delicate fernlike leaves and yellow flowers that are used by florists. • *Acacia dealbata*, family Leguminosae. **2** another name for the **SILK**

TREE. **3** a plant of a genus that includes the sensitive plant. • Genus *Mimosa*, family Leguminosae. **4** a drink of champagne and orange juice. ▷modern Latin, apparently from Latin *mimus* 'mime' (because the plant seemingly mimics the sensitivity of an animal) + the feminine suffix *-osa*.

Min /min/ ▶*n.* a dialect of Chinese spoken by more than 50 million people, mainly in Fujian province, Hainan, and Taiwan. ▷Chinese.

min. ▶*abbr.* ■ minim (fluid measure). ■ minimum. ■ minute(s).

mi·na·cious /mə'nāsʜəs/ ▶*adj. rare* menacing; threatening. ▷mid 17th cent.: from Latin *minax, minac-* 'threatening' (from *minari* 'threaten') + **-ous**.

Mi·na·ma·ta dis·ease /ˌmēnə'mätə/ ▶*n.* chronic poisoning by alkyl mercury compounds from industrial waste, characterized by (usually permanent) impairment of brain functions such as speech, sight, and muscular coordination. ▷1950s: named after *Minamata*, a town in Japan.

Mi·nang·ka·bau /ˌmēˌnanɢkə'bou/ ▶*n.* an Indonesian language spoken by more than 6 million people in Sumatra and elsewhere. ▷Malay and Indonesian.

min·a·ret /ˌminə'ret/ ▶*n.* a tall slender tower, typically part of a mosque, with a balcony from which a muezzin calls Muslims to prayer. ▷late 17th cent.: from French, or from Spanish *minarete*, Italian *minaretto*, via Turkish from Arabic *manār(a)* 'lighthouse, minaret,' based on *nār* 'fire or light.' **—min·a·ret·ed** *adj.*

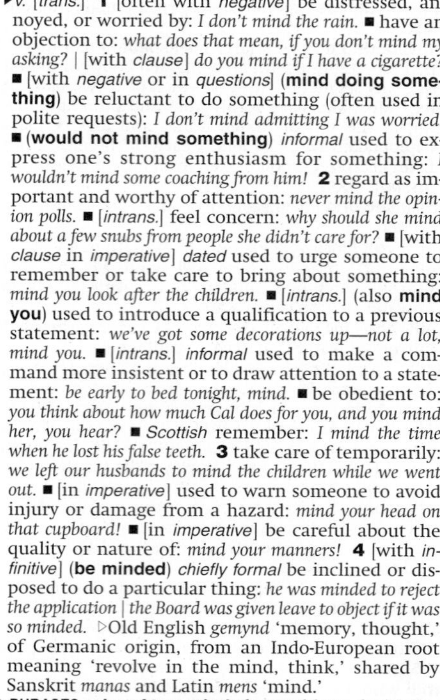
minaret

min·a·to·ry /'minəˌtôrē; 'mī-/ ▶*adj. formal* expressing or conveying a threat: *he is unlikely to be deterred by minatory finger-wagging.* ▷mid 16th cent.: from late Latin *minatorius*, from *minat-* 'threatened,' from the verb *minari*.

min·au·dière /ˌmēnōd'yer/ ▶*n.* a small, decorative handbag without handles or a strap. ▷French, literally 'coquettish woman,' from *minauder* 'simper.'

min·bar /'minˌbär/ (also **mim·bar** /'mim-/) ▶*n.* a short flight of steps used as a platform by a preacher in a mosque. ▷from Arabic *minbar*.

mince /mins/ ▶*v.* [*trans.*] **1** [often as *adj.*] (**minced**) cut up or grind (food, esp. meat) into very small pieces, typically in a machine with revolving blades: *minced beef.* **2** [*intrans.*] walk with an affected delicacy or fastidiousness, typically with short quick steps: *there were plenty of secretaries mincing about.*
▶*n.* something minced, esp. mincemeat: *put the mince on a dish.* ■ a quantity of something minced: *a mince of garlic.* ▷late Middle English: from Old French *mincier*, based on Latin *minutia* 'smallness.' **—minc·er** *n.* **—minc·ing·ly** *adv.* (in sense 2).
▶*PHRASE* □ **not mince words** (or **one's words**) speak candidly and directly, esp. when criticizing someone or something: *a gruff surgeon who does not mince words.*

mince·meat /'minsˌmēt/ ▶*n.* **1** a mixture of currants, raisins, sugar, apples, candied citrus peel, spices, and suet, typically baked in a pie. **2** minced meat.
▶*PHRASE* □ **make mincemeat of someone** *informal* defeat someone decisively or easily in a fight, contest, or argument.

mince pie ▶*n.* a small, round pie or tart containing sweet mincemeat, typically eaten at Christmas.

Minch /minch/ (**the Minch**) a channel in the Atlantic Ocean, between the mainland of Scotland and the Outer Hebrides. The northern stretch is called the **North Minch;** the southern stretch, northwest of Skye, is called the **Little Minch**. Also called **the Minches**.

mind /mīnd/ ▶*n.* **1** the element of a person that enables them to be aware of the world and their experiences, to think, and to feel; the faculty of consciousness and thought: *as the thoughts ran through his mind, he came to a conclusion | people have the price they are prepared to pay settled in their minds.* ■ a person's mental processes contrasted with physical action: *I wrote a letter in my mind.* **2** a person's intellect: *his keen mind.* ■ the state of normal mental functioning in a person: *the strain has affected his mind.* ■ a person's memory: *the company's name **slips** my **mind**.* ■ a person identified with their intellectual faculties: *he was one of the greatest minds of his time.* **3** a person's attention: *I expect my employees to keep their minds on the job.* ■ the will or determination to achieve something: *anyone can lose weight if they set their mind to it.*
▶*v.* [*trans.*] **1** [often with *negative*] be distressed, annoyed, or worried by: *I don't mind the rain.* ■ have an objection to: *what does that mean, if you don't mind my asking? |* [with *clause*] *do you mind if I have a cigarette?* ■ [with *negative* or in *questions*] (**mind doing something**) be reluctant to do something (often used in polite requests): *I don't mind admitting I was worried.* ■ (**would not mind something**) *informal* used to express one's strong enthusiasm for something: *I wouldn't mind some coaching from him!* **2** regard as important and worthy of attention: *never mind the opinion polls.* ■ [*intrans.*] feel concern: *why should she mind about a few snubs from people she didn't care for?* ■ [with *clause* in *imperative*] *dated* used to urge someone to remember or take care to bring about something: *mind you look after the children.* ■ [*intrans.*] (also **mind you**) used to introduce a qualification to a previous statement: *we've got some decorations up—not a lot, mind you.* ■ [*intrans.*] *informal* used to make a command more insistent or to draw attention to a statement: *be early to bed tonight, mind.* ■ be obedient to: *you think about how much Cal does for you, and you mind her, you hear?* ■ *Scottish* remember: *I mind the time when he lost his false teeth.* **3** take care of temporarily: *we left our husbands to mind the children while we went out.* ■ [in *imperative*] used to warn someone to avoid injury or damage from a hazard: *mind your head on that cupboard!* ■ [in *imperative*] be careful about the quality or nature of: *mind your manners!* **4** [with *infinitive*] (**be minded**) *chiefly formal* be inclined or disposed to do a particular thing: *he was minded to reject the application | the Board was given leave to object if it was so minded.* ▷Old English *gemynd* 'memory, thought,' of Germanic origin, from an Indo-European root meaning 'revolve in the mind, think,' shared by Sanskrit *manas* and Latin *mens* 'mind.'
▶*PHRASES* □ **be of two minds** be unable to decide between alternatives. □ **be of one** (or **a different**) **mind** share the same (or hold a different) opinion. □ **bear** (or **keep**) **in mind** remember and take into account: [with *clause*] *you need to bear in mind that the figures vary from place to place.* □ **close one's mind to** refuse to consider or acknowledge. □ **come** (or **spring**) **to mind** (of a thought or idea) occur to someone. □ **don't mind if I do** *informal* used to accept an invitation. □ **give someone a piece of one's mind** tell someone what one thinks of them, esp. in anger. □ **have a** (or **a good** or **half a**) **mind to do something** be very much inclined to do something: *I've a good mind to write to the manager to complain.* □ **have someone or something in mind** be thinking of. ■ intend: *I **had it in mind to** ask you to work for me.* □ **have a mind of one's own** be capable of independent opinion or action. ■ (of an inanimate object) seem capable of thought and intention, esp. by behaving contrary to the will of the person using it: *the shopping cart had a mind of its own.* □ **in one's mind's eye** in one's imagination or mental view. □ **mind over matter** the use of willpower to overcome physical problems. □ **mind one's own business** refrain from prying or interfering. □ **mind one's Ps & Qs** be careful to behave well and avoid giving offense. [of unknown origin; said by some to refer to the care a young student must take in differentiating the tailed letters *p* and *q*.] □ **mind the store** *informal* have charge of something temporarily. □ **never mind 1** used to urge someone not to feel anxiety or distress: *never mind—it's all right now.* ■ used to suggest that a problem or objection is not important: *that's getting off the subject, but never mind.* **2** (also **never you mind**) used in refusing to answer a question: *never mind where I'm going.* **3** used to indicate that what has been said of one thing applies even more to another: *he was so tired that he found it hard to think, never mind talk.* □ **not pay someone any mind** not pay someone any attention. □ **on someone's mind** preoccupying someone, esp. in a disquieting way: *new parents have many worries on their minds.* □ **an open mind** the readiness to consider something without prejudice. □ **open one's mind to** be receptive to: *he opened his mind to the ways of the rest of the world.* □ **out of one's mind** having lost control of one's mental faculties. ■ *informal* suffering from a particular condition to a very high degree: *she was bored out of her mind.* □ **put someone in mind of** resemble and so cause someone to think of or remember: *he was a small, well-dressed man who put her in mind of a jockey.* □ **put** (or **set**) **one's mind to** direct all one's attention to (achieving something): *she'd have made an excellent dancer, if she'd have put her mind to it.* □ **put someone/something out of one's mind** deliberately forget someone or something. □ **to my mind** in my opinion: *this story is, to my mind, a masterpiece.*

mind-al·ter·ing ▶*adj.* (of a hallucinogenic drug) producing mood changes or giving a sense of heightened awareness.

Min·da·na·o /ˌmində'näˌō; -'nou/ an island in southeastern Philippines, the country's second largest island. Its chief town is Davao.

mind-bend·ing ▶*adj. informal* (chiefly of a hallucinogenic drug) influencing or altering one's state of mind. **—mind-bend·er** *n.* **—mind-bend·ing·ly** *adv.*

mind-blow·ing ▶*adj. informal* overwhelmingly impressive: *for a kid, Chicago was really mind-blowing.* ■ (of a drug) inducing hallucinations. **—mind-blow·ing·ly** *adv.*

mind-bog·gling ▶*adj. informal* overwhelming; startling: *a chip that processes data at mind-boggling speed.* **—mind-bog·gling·ly** *adv.*

mind·ed /'mīndid/ ▶*adj.* [in *combination* or with *submodifier*] inclined to think in a particular way: *liberal-minded scholars | I'm not scientifically minded.* ■ [in *combination*] interested in or enthusiastic about the thing specified: *conservation-minded citizens.*

Min·del /'mindəl/ ▶*n.* [usu. as *adj.*] *Geology* a Pleistocene glaciation in the Alps preceding the Riss, possibly corresponding to the Elsterian of northern Europe. ■ the system of deposits laid down at this time. ▷early 20th cent.: from the name of a river in southern Germany.

mind·er /'mīndər/ ▶*n. chiefly Brit.* a person whose job it is to look after someone or something: [in *combination*] *their baby-minder is getting married.* ■ *informal* a bodyguard employed to protect a celebrity or criminal: *he was accompanied by his personal minder.* ■ an official whose job is to restrain access or the free flow of information, especially with an implied threat of force: *their dispatches were censored, delayed and sometimes blocked by military minders.*

mind-ex·pand·ing ▶*adj.* (esp. of a hallucinogenic drug) giving a sense of heightened or broader awareness.

mind·ful /'mīndfəl/ ▶*adj.* [*predic.*] conscious or aware of something: *we can be more **mindful of** the energy we use to heat our homes.* **—mind·ful·ly** *adv.* **—mind·ful·ness** *n.*

mind game ▶*n.* a series of deliberate actions or responses planned for psychological effect on another, typically for amusement or competitive advantage.

mind·less /'mīn(d)lis/ ▶*adj.* (of a person) acting without concern for the consequences: *a generation of mindless vandals.* ■ (esp. of harmful or evil behavior) done for no particular reason: *mindless violence.* ■ [*predic.*] (**mindless of**) not thinking of or concerned about: *mindless of the fact she was in her nightgown, she rushed to the door.* ■ (of an activity) so simple or repetitive as to be performed automatically without thought or skill: *the monotony of housework turns it into a mindless task.* **—mind·less·ly** *adv.* **—mind·less·ness** *n.*

mind-numb·ing ▶*adj.* so extreme or intense as to prevent normal thought: *the jury sat through hours of mind-numbing testimony.* **—mind-numb·ing·ly** *adv.*

Min·do·ro /min'dôrō/ an island in the Philippines, southwest of Luzon.

mind read·er (also **mind-read·er** or **mind·read·er**) ▶*n.* a person who can supposedly discern what another person is thinking. **—mind-read** /'mind ˌrēd/ *v.* **—mind-read·ing** *n.*

mind-set (also **mind·set**) ▶*n.* [usu. in *sing.*] the established set of attitudes held by someone: *the region seems stuck in a medieval mind-set.*

mind·share /'mīndˌsʜe(ə)r/ ▶*n.* relative public awareness of a phenomenon: *the need to compete for mindshare from an audience with a short attention span.*

mine[1] /mīn/ ▶*possessive pron.* used to refer to a thing or things belonging to or associated with the speaker: *you go your way and I'll go mine | some friends **of mine**.*
▶*possessive adj. archaic* (used before a vowel) my: *tears did fill mine eyes.* ▷Old English *mīn*, of Germanic origin; related to **ME**[1] and to Dutch *mijn* and German *mein*.

mine[2] ▶*n.* **1** an excavation in the earth for extracting coal or other minerals: *a copper mine.* ■ [in *sing.*] an abundant source of something: *the book contains **a mine of** information.* **2** a type of bomb placed on or just below the surface of the ground or in the water that detonates when disturbed by a person, vehicle, or ship. ■ *historical* a subterranean passage under the wall of a besieged fortress, esp. one in which explosives are put to blow up fortifications.
▶*v.* [*trans.*] (often **be mined**) **1** obtain (coal or other minerals) from a mine. ■ dig in (the earth) for coal

or other minerals: *the hills were **mined for** copper oxide* | [*intrans.*] *many financiers managed to obtain concessions to **mine for** silver.* ■ dig or burrow in (the earth). ■ *figurative* delve into (an abundant source) to extract something of value, esp. information or skill: *how do they manage to **mine** such **a rich vein of** talent?* **2** lay explosive mines on or just below the surface of (the ground or water): *the area was heavily mined.* ■ destroy by means of an explosive mine. ▷late Middle English: from Old French *mine* (noun), *miner* (verb), perhaps of Celtic origin; compare with Welsh *mwyn* 'ore,' earlier 'mine.' **—mine·a·ble** /ˈmīnəbəl/ (also **min·a·ble**) *adj.*

mine de·tec·tor ▶*n.* an instrument used for detecting explosive mines.

mine·field /ˈmīnˌfēld/ (also **mine field**) ▶*n.* an area planted with explosive mines. ■ *figurative* a subject or situation presenting unseen hazards: *a minefield of technical regulations.*

mine·lay·er /ˈmīnˌlāər/ ▶*n.* a warship, aircraft, or land vehicle from which explosive mines are laid. **—mine·lay·ing** /-ˌlāiNG/ *n.*

min·er /ˈmīnər/ ▶*n.* **1** a person who works in a mine. ■ a device used to mine ores, etc. ■ *historical* a person who digs tunnels in order to destroy an enemy position with explosives. **2** an Australian bird of the honeyeater family, having a loud call and typically nesting colonially. • Genus *Manorina*, family Meliphagidae: five species, including the **bell miner** or bellbird (*M. melanophrys*), with greenish plumage and a bell-like call. **3** a small South American bird of the ovenbird family that excavates a long burrow for breeding. • Genus *Geositta*, family Furnariidae: several species. **4** short for **LEAF MINER**. ▷Middle English: from Old French *minour*, from *miner* 'to mine' (see **MINE**[2]).

min·er·al /ˈmin(ə)rəl/ ▶*n.* **1** a solid inorganic substance of natural occurrence. ■ a substance obtained by mining. ■ an inorganic substance needed by the human body for good health. **2** (**minerals**) *Brit.* (in commercial use) effervescent soft drinks.
▶*adj.* of or denoting a mineral: *mineral ingredients such as zinc oxide.* ▷late Middle English: from medieval Latin *minerale*, neuter (used as a noun) of *mineralis*, from *minera* 'ore.'

min·er·al·ize /ˈmin(ə)rəˌlīz/ ▶*v.* [*trans.*] convert (organic matter) wholly or partly into a mineral or inorganic material or structure. ■ change (a metal) into an ore. ■ impregnate (water or another liquid) with a mineral substance. **—min·er·al·i·za·tion** /ˌmin(ə)rələˈzāSHən/ *n.*

min·er·al·o·cor·ti·coid /ˌmin(ə)rəˌlōˈkôrtiˌkoid/ ▶*n. Biochemistry* a corticosteroid, such as aldosterone, that is involved with maintaining the salt balance in the body.

min·er·al·o·gy /ˌminəˈräləjē; -ˈral-/ ▶*n.* the scientific study of minerals. **—min·er·al·og·i·cal** /ˌmin(ə)rəˈläjikəl/ *adj.* **—min·er·al·og·i·cal·ly** /ˌmin(ə)rəˈläjik(ə)lē/ *adv.* **—min·er·al·o·gist** /-jist/ *n.*

min·er·al oil ▶*n.* a distillation product of petroleum, esp. one used as a lubricant, moisturizer, or laxative.

min·er·al spir·its ▶*n.* a volatile, colorless liquid distilled from petroleum, used as a paint thinner and solvent.

min·er·al wa·ter ▶*n.* water found in nature with some dissolved salts present. ■ *chiefly Brit.* an artificial imitation of this, esp. soda water.

min·er·al wool ▶*n.* a substance resembling matted wool and made from inorganic mineral material, used chiefly for packing or insulation.

Mi·ner·va /məˈnərvə/ *Roman Mythology* the goddess of handicrafts, widely worshiped and regularly identified with the Greek goddess Athena, which led to her being regarded also as the goddess of war.

mine shaft (also **mine·shaft**) ▶*n.* a deep narrow vertical hole, or sometimes a horizontal tunnel, that gives access to a mine.

min·e·stro·ne /ˌminəˈstrōnē/ ▶*n.* a thick soup containing vegetables and pasta. ▷Italian.

mine·sweep·er /ˈmīnˌswēpər/ ▶*n.* a warship equipped for detecting and removing or destroying tethered explosive mines. **—mine·sweep·ing** /-ˌswēpiNG/ *n.*

Ming /miNG/ ▶*n.* the dynasty ruling China 1368–1644 founded by Zhu Yuanzhang (1328–98). ■ [usu. as *adj.*] Chinese porcelain made during the rule of the Ming dynasty, characterized by elaborate designs and vivid colors: *a priceless Ming vase.* ▷Chinese, literally 'clear or bright.'

ming·er /ˈmiNGər/ ▶*n. Brit. informal* an unattractive or unpleasant person or thing: *Why can't anyone see that Spencer is a complete minger?* ▷1990s: from **MINGING**.

ming·ing /ˈmiNGiNG/ ▶*adj. Brit. informal* foul-smelling. ■ very bad or unpleasant: *I'd really like to burn that minging beige jacket he has glued to him all the time.* ▷1970s: perhaps from Scots dialect *ming* 'excrement.'

min·gle /ˈmiNGgəl/ ▶*v.* mix or cause to mix together: [*intrans.*] *the sound of voices **mingled with** a scraping of chairs* | [*trans.*] *an expression that mingled compassion and bewilderment.* ■ [*intrans.*] move freely around a place or at a social function, associating with others: *over aperitifs, there was a chance to **mingle with** friends old and new.* ▷late Middle English: frequentative of obsolete *meng* 'mix or blend' (related to **AMONG**), perhaps influenced by Middle Dutch *mengelen*.

Min·gus /ˈmiNGgəs/, Charles (1922–79), U.S. jazz bassist and composer. A leading figure of the 1940s jazz scene, he experimented with atonality and was influenced by gospel and blues.

min·gy /ˈminjē/ ▶*adj.* (**-gi·er**, **-gi·est**) *informal* mean and stingy: *you've been too mingy with the sunscreen.* ■ unexpectedly or undesirably small: *a mingy kitchenette tucked in the corner.* ▷early 20th cent.: perhaps a blend of **MEAN**[2] and **STINGY**. **—ming·i·ly** /ˈminjəlē/ *adv.*

Mi·nho /ˈmēnyo͞o/ Portuguese name for **MIÑO**.

min·i /ˈminē/ ▶*adj.* [*attrib.*] denoting a miniature version of something: *a bouquet of mini carnations.*
▶*n.* (*pl.* **min·is**) **1** short for **MINISKIRT**. **2** short for **MINICOMPUTER**. ▷1960s: abbreviation.

mini- ▶*comb. form* very small or minor of its kind; miniature: *minicab* | *minicomputer.* ▷from **MINIATURE**, reinforced by **MINIMUM**.

min·i·a·ture /ˈmin(ē)əCHər; -ˌCHo͝or/ ▶*adj.* [*attrib.*] (esp. of a replica of something) of a much smaller size than normal; very small: *children dressed as miniature adults.* See note at **SMALL**.
▶*n.* a thing that is much smaller than normal, esp. a small replica or model. ■ a plant or animal that is a smaller version of an existing variety or breed. ■ a very small and highly detailed portrait or other painting. ■ a picture or decorated letter in an illuminated manuscript.
▶*v.* [*trans.*] *rare* represent on a smaller scale; reduce to miniature dimensions. ▷early 18th cent.: from Italian *miniatura*, via medieval Latin from Latin *miniare* 'rubricate, illuminate,' from *minium* 'red lead, vermilion' (used to mark particular words in manuscripts).
▶*PHRASE* □ **in miniature** on a small scale, but otherwise a replica: *a place that is Greece in miniature.*

min·i·a·ture golf ▶*n.* an informal version of golf played on a series of short constructed obstacle courses.

min·i·a·tur·ist /ˈmin(ē)əˌCHo͝orist; -CHərist/ ▶*n.* a painter of miniatures or an illuminator of manuscripts.

min·i·a·tur·ize /ˈmin(ē)əCHəˌrīz/ ▶*v.* [*trans.*] [usu. as *adj.*] (**miniaturized**) make on a smaller or miniature scale: *miniaturized computers.* **—min·i·a·tur·i·za·tion** /ˌmin(ē)əCHərəˈzāSHən/ *n.*

min·i·bar /ˈminēˌbär/ ▶*n.* a refrigerator in a hotel room containing a selection of refreshments that are charged for on the bill if used by the occupant.

min·i·bus /ˈminēˌbəs/ ▶*n.* a small bus for about ten to fifteen passengers.

min·i·cab /ˈminēˌkab/ ▶*n. Brit.* a car that is used as a taxi but that must be ordered in advance because it is not licensed to pick up passengers who hail it in the street.

min·i·cam /ˈminēˌkam/ ▶*n.* a hand-held video camera.

min·i·camp /ˈminēˌkamp/ ▶*n.* a session run by a professional sports team to train particular players, or to test potential new players, before the main preseason training.

min·i·car /ˈminēˌkär/ ▶*n.* a very small car, esp. a subcompact.

min·i·com·pu·ter /ˈminēkəmˌpyo͞otər/ ▶*n.* a computer of medium power, more than a microcomputer but less than a mainframe.

Min·i·coy Is·lands /ˈminəˌkoi/ one of the groups of islands forming the Indian Union Territory of Lakshadweep in the Indian Ocean.

min·i·disc /ˈminēˌdisk/ ▶*n.* a disc having a format similar to a small CD but able to record sound or data as well as play it back.

min·i·dress /ˈminēˌdres/ ▶*n.* a very short dress.

mini-golf ▶*n.* short for **MINIATURE GOLF**.

min·i·kin /ˈminikin/ ▶*adj. chiefly archaic* small; insignificant: *capable men devoting their lives to such minikin pursuits.*

min·im /ˈminim/ ▶*n.* **1** one sixtieth of a fluid dram, about one drop of liquid. **2** *Music* British term for **HALF NOTE**. **3** *Calligraphy* a short vertical stroke, as in the letters *i*, *m*, *n*, *u*. ▷late Middle English: from Latin *minima*, from *minimus* 'smallest.'

min·i·ma /ˈminəmə/ ▶ plural form of **MINIMUM**.

min·i·mal /ˈminəməl/ ▶*adj.* **1** of a minimum amount, quantity, or degree; negligible: *a minimal amount of information* | *production costs are minimal.* **2** *Art* characterized by the use of simple or primary forms or structures, esp. geometric or massive ones. ■ *Music* characterized by the repetition and gradual alteration of short phrases. **3** *Linguistics* (of a pair of forms) distinguished by only one feature: *"p" and "b" are a minimal pair, distinguished by the feature of voicing.* ▷mid 17th cent.: from Latin *minimus* 'smallest' + **-AL**. **—min·i·mal·ly** *adv.*

min·i·mal·ism /ˈminəməˌlizəm/ ▶*n.* **1** a trend in sculpture and painting that arose in the 1950s and used simple, typically massive, forms. **2** an avant-garde movement in music characterized by the repetition of very short phrases that change gradually, producing a hypnotic effect.

min·i·mal·ist /ˈminəməlist/ ▶*n.* **1** a person advocating minor or moderate reform in politics. **2** a person who advocates or practices minimalism in art or music.
▶*adj.* **1** advocating moderate political policies. **2** of or relating to minimalism in art or music. ▷early 20th cent.: first used with reference to the Russian Mensheviks. Usage in art and music dates from the 1960s.

min·i·mall ▶*n.* a shopping mall containing a relatively small number of retail outlets and with access to each shop from the outside rather than from an interior hallway.

min·i·mart /ˈminēˌmärt/ ▶*n.* a convenience store.

min·i·max /ˈminēˌmaks/ ▶*n. Mathematics* the lowest of a set of maximum values. Compare with **MAXIMIN**. ■ [as *adj.*] denoting a method or strategy in game theory that minimizes the greatest risk to a participant in a game or other situation of conflict. ■ [as *adj.*] denoting the theory that in a game with two players, a player's smallest possible maximum loss is equal to the same player's greatest possible minimum gain. ▷1940s: blend of **MINIMUM** and **MAXIMUM**.

min·i·mize /ˈminəˌmīz/ ▶*v.* [*trans.*] reduce (something, esp. something unwanted or unpleasant) to the smallest possible amount or degree: *the aim is to minimize costs.* ■ represent or estimate at less than the true value or importance: *they may minimize, or even overlook, the importance of such beliefs.* **—min·i·mi·za·tion** /ˌminəməˈzāSHən/ *n.* **—min·i·miz·er** *n.*

min·i·mum /ˈminəməm/ ▶*n.* (*pl.* **-ma** /-mə/ or **-mums**) [usu. in *sing.*] the least or smallest amount or quantity possible, attainable, or required: *technical difficulties have been **kept to a minimum*** | *they checked passports with **the minimum of** fuss.* ■ the lowest or smallest amount of a varying quantity (e.g., temperature) allowed, attained, or recorded: *clients with a minimum of $500,000 to invest* | *winter minima of -40 ° C have been recorded.* ■ *Mathematics* a point at which a continuously varying quantity ceases to decrease and begins to increase; the value of a quantity at such a point. ■ *Mathematics* the smallest element in a set.
▶*adj.* [*attrib.*] smallest or lowest: *this can be done with the minimum amount of effort.* ▷mid 17th cent.: from Latin, neuter of *minimus* 'least.'
▶*PHRASE* □ **at a** (or **the**) **minimum** at the very least: *we zipped along at a minimum of 55 mph.*

min·i·mum wage ▶*n.* the lowest wage permitted by law or by a special agreement (such as one with a labor union).

min·ing /ˈmīniNG/ ▶*n.* the process or industry of obtaining coal or other minerals from a mine.

min·ion /ˈminyən/ ▶*n.* a follower or underling of a powerful person, esp. a servile or unimportant one. ▷late 15th cent.: from French *mignon*, *mignonne*.

min·i·pill ▶*n.* a contraceptive pill containing progestin and not estrogen.

min·is·cule ▶*adj.* nonstandard spelling of **MINUSCULE**.

min·i·se·ries /ˈminēˌsi(ə)rēz/ ▶*n.* (*pl.* same) a television drama shown in a number of episodes.

min·i·skirt /ˈminēˌskərt/ ▶*n.* a very short skirt.

min·is·ter /ˈminəstər/ ▶*n.* **1** (also **minister of religion**) a member of the clergy, esp. in Protestant churches.

■ (also **minister general**) the superior of some religious orders. **2** (in certain countries) a head of a government department: *Britain's defense minister.* ■ a diplomatic agent, usually ranking below an ambassador, representing a state or sovereign in a foreign country. **3** *archaic* a person or thing used to achieve or convey something: *the Angels are ministers of the Divine Will.*
▸*v.* [*intrans.*] **1** (**minister to**) attend to the needs of (someone): *her doctor was busy ministering to the injured.* ■ [*trans.*] *archaic* provide (something necessary or helpful): *the story was able to minister true consolation.* **2** act as a minister of religion. ■ [*trans.*] administer (a sacrament). ▷Middle English (in noun senses 1 and 3): from Old French *ministre* (noun), *ministrer* (verb), from Latin *minister* 'servant,' from *minus* 'less.' **—min·is·ter·ship** /-,SHip/ *n.*

min·is·te·ri·al /,minə'sti(ə)rēəl/ ▸*adj.* **1** of or relating to a minister of religion. **2** of or relating to a government minister or ministers: *ministerial officials.* **3** *archaic* acting as an agent, instrument, or means in achieving a purpose: *those uses of conversation which are ministerial to intellectual culture.* ▷mid 16th cent.: from French *ministériel* or late Latin *ministerialis*, from Latin *ministerium* 'ministry.' **—min·is·te·ri·al·ly** *adv.*

min·is·tra·tion /,minə'strāSHən/ ▸*n.* (usu. **ministrations**) *chiefly formal* or *humorous* the provision of assistance or care: *a kitchen made spotless by the* ***ministrations of*** *a cleaning lady.* ■ the services of a minister of religion or of a religious institution. ■ the action of administering the sacrament. ▷late Middle English: from Latin *ministratio(n-)*, from *ministrare* 'wait upon,' from *minister* (see **MINISTER**). **—min·is·trant** /'minəstrənt/ *n.*

min·i·stroke /'minē,strōk/ ▸*n.* a temporary blockage of the blood supply to the brain, lasting only a few minutes and leaving no noticeable symptoms or deficits. Also called **TRANSIENT ISCHEMIC ATTACK**.

min·is·try /'minəstrē/ ▸*n.* (*pl.* **-tries**) **1** [usu. in *sing.*] the work or vocation of a minister of religion: *he is training for the ministry.* ■ the period of tenure of a minister of religion. ■ the spiritual work or service of any Christian or a group of Christians, esp. evangelism: *a ministry of Christian healing.* **2** (in certain countries) a government department headed by a minister of state: *the Ministry of Agriculture.* **3** (in certain countries) a period of government under one prime minister: *Gladstone's first ministry was outstanding.* **4** *rare* the action of ministering to someone: *the soldiers were no less in need of his ministry.* ▷Middle English (sense 1): from Latin *ministerium*, from *minister* (see **MINISTER**).

min·i·tow·er /'minē,tou-ər/ (or **min·i-tow·er**) ▸*n.* a small vertical case for a computer, or a computer mounted in such a case: *the desk has a compartment for a minitower* | [as *adj.*] *the minitower case is sturdy.*

min·i·van /'minē,van/ ▸*n.* a small van, typically one fitted with seats in the back for passengers.

min·i·ver /'minəvər/ ▸*n.* plain white fur used for lining or trimming clothes. ▷Middle English: from Old French *menu vair* 'little vair,' from *menu* 'little' + *vair* 'squirrel fur' (see **VAIR**).

mink /miNGk/ ▸*n.* (*pl.* same or **minks**) a small, semiaquatic, stoatlike carnivore native to North America and Eurasia. The American mink is widely farmed for its fur, resulting in its becoming naturalized in many parts of Europe. • Genus *Mustela*, family Mustelidae: the **American mink** (*M. vison*) and the smaller **European mink** (*M. lutreola*). ■ the thick brown fur of the mink. ■ a coat made of this. ▷late Middle English (denoting the animal's fur): from Swedish.

min·ke /'miNGkē/ (also **minke whale**) ▸*n.* a small rorqual whale with a dark gray back, white underparts, and pale markings on the fins and behind the head. • *Balaenoptera acutorostrata*, family Balaenopteridae. ▷1930s: probably from *Meincke*, the name of a Norwegian whaler.

Minn. ▸*abbr.* Minnesota.

Min·ne·ap·o·lis /,minē'apəlis/ an industrial city and port on the Mississippi River in southeastern Minnesota; pop. 382,618. It is a major agricultural center for the upper Midwest.

Min·nel·li[1] /mi'nelē/, Liza (May) (1946–), U.S. actress; daughter of Judy Garland and Vincente Minnelli. In 1965, at age 19, she won a Tony Award for her role in *Flora, the Red Menace* on Broadway. She also appeared in movies, including *The Sterile Cuckoo* (1969), *Cabaret* (Academy Award, 1972), *Arthur* (1981), and *Stepping Out* (1991).

Min·nel·li[2], Vincente (1910–86), U.S. movie director; husband of Judy Garland and father of Liza Minnelli. His movies include *The Clock* (1945), *Kismet* (1955), and *Gigi* (1958).

min·ne·o·la /,minē'ōlə/ ▸*n.* a deep reddish tangelo of a thin-skinned variety. ▷mid 20th cent.: named after a town in Florida.

min·ne·sing·er /'mini,siNGər; -ə,ziNGər/ ▸*n.* a German lyric poet and singer of the 12th–14th centuries who performed songs of courtly love. ▷early 19th cent.: from German *Minnesinger* 'love-singer.'

Min·ne·so·ta /,minə'sōtə/ a state in the northern central U.S., on the Canadian border; pop. 4,919,479; capital, St. Paul; statehood, May 11, 1858 (32). Part of it was ceded to Britain by the French in 1763 and then acquired by the U.S. in 1783. The remainder formed part of the Louisiana Purchase in 1803. **—Min·ne·so·tan** *n.* & *adj.*

Min·ne·so·ta Mul·ti·pha·sic Per·son·al·i·ty In·ven·to·ry (abbr.: **MMPI**) ▸*n.* a test consisting of hundreds of true-false questions, used as a diagnostic tool by psychologists.

Min·ne·so·ta Riv·er a river that flows for 320 miles (530 km) through Minnesota to join the Mississippi River just south of the Twin Cities of Minneapolis and St. Paul.

Min·ne·ton·ka /,minə'täNGkə/ a city in southeastern Minnesota, west of Minneapolis; pop. 51,301.

min·now /'minō/ ▸*n.* a small freshwater Eurasian cyprinoid fish that typically forms large shoals. • *Phoxinus phoxinus*, family Cyprinidae. ■ any fish of the family Cyprinidae, the largest family of fishes, which includes carps, shiners, spinefins, squawfishes, chubs, daces, and stonerollers. ■ used in names of similar small freshwater fishes, e.g., **mudminnow, topminnow**. ■ *Fishing* an artificial lure imitating a minnow. ■ a person or organization of relatively small size, power, or influence. ▷late Middle English: probably related to Dutch *meun* and German *Münne*, influenced by Anglo-Norman French *menu* 'small, minnow.'

Mi·ño /'mēnyō/ a river that rises in northwestern Spain and flows south to the Portuguese border, which it follows before entering the Atlantic Ocean north of Viana do Castelo. Portuguese name **MINHO**.

Mi·no·an /mə'nōən; mī-/ ▸*adj.* of, relating to, or denoting a Bronze Age civilization centered on Crete (*c.*3000–1050 BC), its people, or its language.
▸*n.* **1** an inhabitant of Minoan Crete or member of the Minoan people. **2** the language or scripts associated with the Minoans.

> The Minoan civilization had reached its zenith by the beginning of the late Bronze Age; impressive remains reveal the existence of large urban centers dominated by palaces. The civilization is also noted for its script (see **LINEAR A**) and distinctive art and architecture.

▷named after the legendary Cretan king **MINOS**, to whom a palace excavated at Knossos was attributed.

mi·nor /'mīnər/ ▸*adj.* **1** lesser in importance, seriousness, or significance: *she requested a number of minor alterations.* ■ (of a surgical operation) comparatively simple and not life-threatening. **2** *Music* (of a scale) having intervals of a semitone between the second and third degrees, and (usually) the fifth and sixth, and the seventh and eighth. Contrasted with **MAJOR**. ■ (of an interval) characteristic of a minor scale and less by a semitone than the equivalent major interval. Compare with **DIMINISHED**. ■ [usu. *postpositive*] (of a key or mode) based on a minor scale, tending to produce a sad or pensive effect: *Concerto in A minor.* **3** *Brit., dated* (following a surname in public schools) indicating the second or younger of two brothers or boys with the same family name: *Smith minor.* **4** *Logic* (of a term) occurring as the subject of the conclusion of a categorical syllogism. ■ (of a premise) containing the minor term in a categorical syllogism.
▸*n.* **1** a person under the age of full legal responsibility. **2** *Music* a minor key, interval, or scale. ■ (**Minor**) *Bell-ringing* a system of change-ringing using six bells. **3** (**the minors**) the minor leagues in a particular professional sport, esp. baseball: *he's been pitching in the minors for six years.* **4** a college student's subsidiary subject or area of concentration: *a minor in American Indian studies.* **5** *Logic* a minor term or premise. **6** *Bridge* short for **MINOR SUIT**. ▷Middle English: from Latin, 'smaller, less'; related to *minuere* 'lessen.' The term originally denoted a Franciscan friar, suggested by the Latin name *Fratres Minores* ('Lesser Brethren'), chosen by St. Francis for the order.
▸*phrasal v.* □ **minor in** study or qualify in as a subsidiary subject at a college or university.
▸*PHRASE* □ **in a minor key** (esp. of a literary work) understated.

mi·nor ar·ca·na ▸*n.* see **ARCANA**.

mi·nor ax·is ▸*n.* *Geometry* the shorter axis of an ellipse that is perpendicular to its major axis.

Mi·nor·ca /mə'nôrkə/ the most easterly and second largest of the Balearic Islands of Spain, in the western Mediterranean Sea; pop. 59,000; capital, Mahón. Spanish name **MENORCA**. **—Mi·nor·can** *adj.* & *n.*

Mi·nor·ite /'mīnə,rīt/ a Franciscan friar, or Friar Minor.

mi·nor·i·ty /mə'nôrətē/ ▸*n.* (*pl.* **-ties**) **1** the smaller number or part, esp. a number that is less than half the whole number: *harsher measures for* ***the minority*** *of really serious offenders* | [as *adj.*] *a minority party.* ■ the number of votes cast for or by the smaller party in a legislative assembly: *a blocking minority of 23 votes.* ■ a relatively small group of people, esp. one commonly discriminated against in a community, society, or nation, differing from others in race, religion, language, or political persuasion: *representatives of ethnic minorities* | [as *adj.*] *minority rights.* **2** the state or period of being under the age of full legal responsibility. ▷late 15th cent. (denoting the state of being a minor): from French *minorité* or medieval Latin *minoritas*, from Latin *minor* 'smaller' (see **MINOR**).
▸*PHRASES* □ **be** (or **find oneself**) **in a minority of one** *often humorous* be the sole person to be in favor of or against something. □ **in the minority** belonging to or constituting the smaller group or number: *those who acknowledge his influence are certainly in the minority.*

mi·nor·i·ty gov·ern·ment ▸*n.* a government in which the governing party has most seats but still less than half the total.

mi·nor·i·ty lead·er ▸*n.* the head of the minority party in a legislative body, esp. the U.S. Senate or House of Representatives.

mi·nor·i·ty re·port ▸*n.* a separate report presented by members of a committee or other group who disagree with the majority.

mi·nor league ▸*n.* a league below the level of the major league in a particular professional sport, esp. baseball: *he hit a lot of home runs in the minor leagues* | [as *adj*] *a minor-league outfielder.* ■ [as *adj.*] *figurative* of lesser power or significance: *a minor-league villain.* **—mi·nor-lea·guer** *n.*

mi·nor or·ders ▸*plural n. chiefly historical* the formal grades of Catholic or Orthodox clergy below the rank of deacon (most now discontinued).

mi·nor piece ▸*n.* *Chess* a bishop or knight. ▷early 19th cent.: named in contrast to the rook or queen.

mi·nor plan·et ▸*n.* an asteroid. Often contrasted with **MAJOR PLANET**.

mi·nor proph·et ▸*n.* any of the twelve prophets after whom the shorter prophetic books of the Bible, from Hosea to Malachi, are named.

mi·nor suit ▸*n.* *Bridge* diamonds or clubs. ▷early 20th cent.: so named because of their lower scoring value.

mi·nor tran·quil·iz·er ▸*n.* a tranquilizer of the kind used to treat anxiety states, esp. a benzodiazepine; an anxiolytic.

Mi·nos /'mī,näs; -nôs/ *Greek Mythology* a legendary king of Crete, son of Zeus and Europa. His wife Pasiphaë gave birth to the Minotaur; Minos later exacted tribute from Athens in the form of young people to be devoured by the monster.

Mi·not /'mīnät/ a commercial and industrial city in north central North Dakota; pop. 36,567.

Min·o·taur /'minə,tôr; 'mī-/ *Greek Mythology* a creature who was half man and half bull, the offspring of Pasiphaë and a bull with which she fell in love. Confined in Crete in a labyrinth made by Daedalus and fed on human flesh, it was eventually slain by Theseus. ▷from Old French, via Latin from Greek *Minōtauros*, from *Minōs* (see **MINOS**) + *tauros* 'bull.'

min·ox·i·dil /mə'näksə,dil/ ▸*n.* *Medicine* a synthetic drug that is used as a vasodilator in the treatment of hypertension, and is also used in lotions to promote hair growth. ▷1970s: from **AMINO** + **OXIDE** + *-dil* (perhaps representing **DILATE**).

Minsk /minsk/ the capital of Belarus, an industrial city in the central region of the country; pop. 1,613,000.

min·ster /'minstər/ ▸*n.* a large or important church, typically one of cathedral status in the north of England that was built as part of a monastery: *York Minster.* ▷Old English *mynster*, via ecclesiastical Latin from Greek *monastērion* (see **MONASTERY**).

min·strel /ˈminstrəl/ ▸*n.* a medieval singer or musician, esp. one who sang or recited lyric or heroic poetry to a musical accompaniment for the nobility. ■ a member of a band of entertainers with blackened faces who perform songs and music ostensibly of black American origin. ▷Middle English: from Old French *menestral* 'entertainer, servant,' via Provençal from late Latin *ministerialis* 'servant' (see MINISTERIAL).

min·strel show ▸*n.* a popular stage entertainment featuring songs, dances, and comic dialogue in highly conventionalized patterns, usually performed by white actors in blackface. It developed in the U.S. in the early and mid 19th century.

min·strel·sy /ˈminstrəlsē/ ▸*n.* the practice of performing as a minstrel: *a long tradition of minstrelsy.* ▷Middle English: from Old French *menestralsie,* from *menestrel* (see MINSTREL).

mint[1] /mint/ ▸*n.* **1** an aromatic plant native to temperate regions of the Old World, several kinds of which are used as culinary herbs. • Genus *Mentha,* family Labiatae (or Lamiaceae; the **mint family**): several species and hybrids, in particular the widely cultivated **common mint** or **spearmint** (*M. spicata*) and **peppermint** (*M.* × *piperita*). The mint family, the members of which have distinctive two-lobed flowers and square stems, includes numerous aromatic herbs, such as lavender, rosemary, sage, and thyme. ■ the flavor of mint, esp. peppermint. **2** a peppermint candy. ▷Old English *minte;* related to German *Minze,* ultimately via Latin from Greek *minthē.* —**mint·y** *adj.* (**mint·i·er, mint·i·est**).

mint[2] ▸*n.* a place where money is coined, esp. under state authority. ■ (**a mint**) *informal* a vast sum of money: *the car doesn't **cost a mint**.*
▸*adj.* (of an object) in pristine condition; as new: *a pair of speakers including stands, mint, $160.* [elliptically from *in mint condition.*]
▸*v.* [*trans.*] (often **be minted**) make (a coin) by stamping metal. ■ [usu. as *adj.,* with *submodifier*] (**minted**) produce for the first time: *an example of newly minted technology.* ▷Old English *mynet* 'coin'; related to Dutch *munt* and German *Münze,* from Latin *moneta* 'money.' —**mint·er** *n.*
▸*PHRASE* □ **in mint condition** (of an object) new or as if new.

mint·age /ˈmintij/ ▸*n.* the minting of coins. ■ the number of copies issued of a particular coin: *an estimated mintage of about 800.*

mint·ed /ˈmintid/ ▸*adj.* flavored or seasoned with mint: *grilled lamb chops with minted potatoes.*

mint ju·lep ▸*n.* a drink consisting of bourbon, crushed ice, sugar, and fresh mint, typically served in a tall frosted glass and associated chiefly with the southern U.S.

mint·mark (also **mint mark**) ▸*n.* a mark on a coin indicating the mint at which it was struck.

Min·ton /ˈmintn/, Sherman (1890–1965), U.S. Supreme Court associate justice 1949–56. A former U.S. senator 1935–41 and a U.S. circuit court of appeals judge 1941–49, he was appointed to the Court by President Truman.

mint par (also **mint par·i·ty**) ▸*n. Finance* the ratio between the gold equivalents of currency in two countries. ■ their rate of exchange based on such a ratio.

min·u·end /ˈminyəˌwend/ ▸*n. Mathematics* a quantity or number from which another is to be subtracted. ▷early 18th cent.: from Latin *minuendus,* gerundive of *minuere* 'diminish.'

min·u·et /ˌminyoo͞ˈet/ ▸*n.* a slow, stately ballroom dance for two in triple time, popular esp. in the 18th century. ■ a piece of music in triple time in the style of such a dance, typically as a movement in a suite, sonata, or symphony and frequently coupled with a trio.
▸*v.* (**-et·ed, -et·ing**) [*intrans.*] dance a minuet. ▷late 17th cent.: from French *menuet,* 'fine, delicate,' diminutive (used as a noun) of *menu* 'small.'

Min·u·it /ˈminyoo͞it/, Peter (1580–1638), Dutch colonial administrator. He was the first director general of the North American Dutch colony of New Netherland 1626–31. He purchased Manhattan Island from the Algonquin Indians in 1626 for 60 guilders ($24).

mi·nus /ˈmīnəs/ ▸*prep.* **1** with the subtraction of: *what's ninety-three minus seven?* ■ *informal* lacking; deprived of: *he was minus a finger on each hand.* **2** (of temperature) below zero: *minus 10° Fahrenheit.*
▸*adj.* **1** (before a number) below zero; negative: *minus five.* **2** (after a grade) slightly worse than: *my lowest grade was a B minus.* **3** having a negative electric charge.
▸*n.* **1** short for MINUS SIGN. ■ a mathematical operation of subtraction. **2** a disadvantage: *for every plus with this equipment there can be a minus.* ▷late 15th cent.: from Latin, neuter of *minor* 'less.'

mi·nus·cule /ˈminəˌskyoo͞l; minˈəsˌkyoo͞l/ ▸*adj.* **1** extremely small; tiny: *a minuscule fragment of DNA.* ■ *informal* so small as to be negligible or insufficient: *he believed the risk of infection was minuscule.* **2** of or in lowercase letters, as distinct from capitals or uncials. ■ of or in a small cursive script of the Roman alphabet, with ascenders and descenders, developed in the 7th century AD.
▸*n.* minuscule script. ■ a small or lowercase letter. ▷early 18th cent.: from French, from Latin *minuscula (littera)* 'somewhat smaller (letter).' —**mi·nus·cu·lar** /məˈnəskyələr/ *adj.*

USAGE The correct spelling is **minuscule** rather than **miniscule**. The latter is a common error, which has arisen by analogy with other words beginning with **mini-**, where the meaning is similarly 'very small.'

mi·nus sign ▸*n.* the symbol –, indicating subtraction or a negative value.

mi·nute[1] /ˈminit/ ▸*n.* **1** a period of time equal to sixty seconds or a sixtieth of an hour: *he stood in the shower for twenty minutes* | ***in ten minutes' time** he could be on his way.* ■ the distance covered in this length of time by someone driving or walking: *the hotel is situated just ten **minutes from** the center of the resort.* ■ *informal* a very short time: *come and sit down **for a minute**.* ■ an instant or a point of time: *she had been laughing **one minute** and crying **the next**.* **2** (also **arc minute** or **minute of arc**) a sixtieth of a degree of angular measurement (symbol: ′). ▷late Middle English: via Old French from late Latin *minuta,* feminine (used as a noun) of *minutus* 'made small.' The senses 'period of sixty seconds' and 'sixtieth of a degree' derive from medieval Latin *pars minuta prima* 'first minute part.'
▸*PHRASES* □ **any minute** (or **at any minute**) very soon. □ **by the minute** (esp. of the progress of a change) very rapidly: *matters grew worse by the minute.* □ **just** (or **wait**) **a minute 1** used as a request to delay an action, departure, or decision for a short time, usually to allow the speaker to do something: *wait a minute—I have to put my makeup on.* **2** as a prelude to a challenge, query, or objection: *just a minute—where do you think you're going?* □ **the minute** (or **the minute that**) as soon as: *let me know the minute he returns.* □ **not for a minute** not at all: *don't think for a minute that our pricing has affected our quality standards.* □ **this minute** (or **this very minute**) *informal* at once; immediately: *pull yourself together this minute.*

mi·nute[2] /mīˈn(y)oo͞t; mə-/ ▸*adj.* (**-nut·est**) extremely small: *a minute fraction of an inch.* See note at SMALL. ■ so small as to verge on insignificance: *he will have no more than a minute chance of exercising significant influence.* ■ (of an inquiry or investigation, or an account of one) taking the smallest points into consideration; precise and meticulous: *a minute examination of the islands.* ▷late Middle English (in the sense 'lesser,' with reference to a tithe or tax): from Latin *minutus* 'lessened,' past participle of *minuere.* —**mi·nute·ly** *adv.* —**mi·nute·ness** *n.*

mi·nute[3] /ˈminit/ ▸*n.* (**minutes**) a summarized record of the proceedings at a meeting. ■ an official memorandum authorizing or recommending a course of action.
▸*v.* [*trans.*] record or note (the proceedings of a meeting or a specified item among such proceedings): *the Secretary shall minute the proceedings of each meeting.* ▷late Middle English (in the singular in the sense 'note or memorandum'): from French *minute,* from the notion of a rough copy in "small writing" (Latin *scriptura minuta*) as distinct from the fair copy in book hand. The verb dates from the mid 16th cent.

mi·nute gun ▸*n.* a gun fired at intervals of a minute, esp. at a funeral.

min·ute hand ▸*n.* the hand on a watch or clock that indicates minutes.

min·ute·man /ˈminətˌman/ ▸*n.* (*pl.* **-men**) *historical* (in the period preceding and during the American Revolution) a member of a class of American militiamen who volunteered to be ready for service at a minute's notice. ■ (**Minuteman**) a type of three-stage intercontinental ballistic missile.

mi·nu·ti·ae /məˈn(y)oo͞shēˌē; -shēˌī/ (also **mi·nu·ti·a** /-shēˌə; -shə/) ▸*plural n.* the small, precise, or trivial details of something: *the minutiae of everyday life.* ▷mid 18th cent.: Latin, literally 'trifles,' from *minutia* 'smallness,' from *minutus* (see MINUTE[2]).

minx /mingks/ ▸*n. humorous* or *derogatory* an impudent, cunning, or boldly flirtatious girl or young woman. ▷mid 16th cent. (denoting a pet dog): of unknown origin. —**minx·ish** *adj.*

min·yan /ˈminyən/ ▸*n.* (*pl.* **min·ya·nim** /ˌminyəˈnēm/) a quorum of ten men (or in some synagogues, men and women) over the age of 13 required for traditional Jewish public worship. ■ a meeting of Jews for public worship. ▷mid 18th cent.: from Hebrew *minyān,* literally 'reckoning.'

Mi·o·cene /ˈmīəˌsēn/ ▸*adj. Geology* of, relating to, or denoting the fourth epoch of the Tertiary period, between the Oligocene and Pliocene epochs. ■ [as *n.*] (**the Miocene**) the Miocene epoch or the system of rocks deposited during it.

The Miocene epoch lasted from 23.3 million to 5.2 million years ago. During this time, the Alps and Himalayas were being formed and there was diversification of the primates, including the first apes.

▷mid 19th cent.: formed irregularly from Greek *meiōn* 'less' + *kainos* 'new.'

mi·o·sis /mīˈōsəs/ (also **my·o·sis**) ▸*n.* excessive constriction of the pupil of the eye. ▷early 19th cent.: from Greek *muein* 'shut the eyes' + -OSIS. —**mi·ot·ic** /mīˈätik/ *adj.*

MIP ▸*abbr.* monthly investment plan.

MIPS /mips/ ▸*n.* a unit of computing speed equivalent to a million instructions per second. ▷1970s: acronym.

Mique·lon /mēˈklôn/ see ST. PIERRE AND MIQUELON.

Mir /ˈmi(ə)r/ a Soviet space station, launched in 1986 and designed to be permanently manned.

Owing largely to its financial demands on an impoverished Russian government, the Mir program was terminated in March 2001, when the space station made its fiery reentry into the earth's atmosphere, splashing down in the South Pacific. During its 14 years in space, Mir (which means 'world' and 'peace' in Russian) housed a total of 104 astronauts from various nations.

Mi·ra /ˈmīrə/ *Astronomy* a star in the constellation Cetus, regarded as the prototype of long-period variable stars. ▷Latin, literally 'wonderful.'

Mi·ra·beau /ˌmi(ə)rəˈbō/, Honoré Gabriel Riqueti, Comte de (1749–91), French revolutionary politician. Prominent in the early days of the French Revolution, he pressed for a form of constitutional monarchy.

mir·a·belle /ˈmirəˌbel/ ▸*n.* a sweet yellow plumlike fruit that is a variety of the greengage. ■ the tree that bears such fruit. ■ a liqueur distilled from such fruit. ▷early 18th cent.: from French.

mi·ra·bi·le dic·tu /məˈräbəˌlā ˈdiktoo͞; məˈrabəlē/ ▸*adv.* wonderful to relate: *and for once, mirabile dictu, they all seem to be getting along.* ▷Latin.

mi·ra·cid·i·um /ˌmīrəˈsidēəm/ ▸*n.* (*pl.* **-cid·i·a** /-sidēə/) *Zoology* a free-swimming ciliated larval stage in which a parasitic fluke passes from the egg to its first host, typically a snail. ▷late 19th cent.: from Greek *meirakidion,* diminutive of *meirakion* 'boy, stripling.'

mir·a·cle /ˈmirikəl/ ▸*n.* a surprising and welcome event that is not explicable by natural or scientific laws and is therefore considered to be the work of a divine agency: *the miracle of rising from the grave.* ■ a highly improbable or extraordinary event, development, or accomplishment that brings very welcome consequences: *it was a miracle that more people hadn't been killed or injured* [as *adj.*] *a miracle drug.* ■ an amazing product or achievement, or an outstanding example of something: *a machine which was **a miracle of** design.* ▷Middle English: via Old French from Latin *miraculum* 'object of wonder,' from *mirari* 'to wonder,' from *mirus* 'wonderful.'

mir·a·cle play ▸*n.* a mystery play.

mi·rac·u·lous /məˈrakyələs/ ▸*adj.* occurring through divine or supernatural intervention, or manifesting such power: *a miraculous cure.* ■ highly improbable and extraordinary and bringing very welcome consequences: *I felt amazed and grateful for our **miraculous** escape.* ▷late Middle English: from French *miraculeux* or medieval Latin *miraculosus,* from Latin *miraculum* (see MIRACLE). —**mi·rac·u·lous·ly** *adv.* —**mi·rac·u·lous·ness** *n.*

mir·a·dor /ˈmirəˌdôr; ˌmirəˈdôr/ ▸*n.* a turret or tower attached to a building and providing an extensive view. ▷late 17th cent.: from Spanish, from *mirar* 'to look.'

mi·rage /mə'räzh/ ▶*n.* an optical illusion caused by atmospheric conditions, esp. the appearance of a sheet of water in a desert or on a hot road caused by the refraction of light from the sky by heated air. ■ something that appears real or possible but is not in fact so: *the notion that the public is pro-business is a mirage.* ▷early 19th cent.: from French, from *se mirer* 'be reflected,' from Latin *mirare* 'look at.'

Mi·ran·da[1] /mə'randə/ *Astronomy* a satellite of Uranus, the eleventh closest to the planet, with a diameter of 301 miles (485 km). Discovered in 1948, it is the innermost and smallest of the five major Uranian satellites and has a complex terrain of cratered areas and tracts of grooves and ridges. ▷named after the daughter of Prospero in Shakespeare's *The Tempest.*

Mi·ran·da[2] /mə'randə/ ▶*adj. Law* denoting or relating to the duty of the police to inform a person taken into custody of their right to legal counsel and the right to remain silent under questioning: *the patrolman read Lee his Miranda rights.* ▷mid 20th cent.: from *Miranda* v. Arizona (1966), the case that led to this ruling by the U.S. Supreme Court.

mire /mīr/ ▶*n.* a stretch of swampy or boggy ground. ■ soft and slushy mud or dirt. ■ *figurative* a situation or state of difficulty, distress, or embarrassment from which it is hard to extricate oneself: *he has been left to squirm in a mire of new allegations.* ■ *Ecology* a wetland area or ecosystem based on peat.
▶*v.* [*trans.*] (usu. **be mired**) cause to become stuck in mud: *sometimes a heavy truck gets* **mired down.** ■ cover or spatter with mud. ■ **(mire someone/something in)** *figurative* involve someone or something in (difficulties): *the economy is mired in its longest recession since World War II.* ▷Middle English: from Old Norse *mýrr,* of Germanic origin; related to **MOSS.**

mire·poix /mi(ə)r'pwä/ ▶*n.* a mixture of sautéed chopped vegetables used in various sauces. ▷French, named after the Duc de *Mirepoix* (1699–1757), French general.

mi·rex /'mī,reks/ ▶*n.* a synthetic insecticide of the organochlorine type used chiefly against ants. ▷1960s: of unknown origin.

mi·rid /'mīrid; 'mi(ə)r-/ ▶*n.* an active plant bug of a large family that includes numerous plant pests. Formerly called **CAPSID**[1]. • Family Miridae (formerly Capsidae), suborder Heteroptera. ▷1940s: from modern Latin *Miridae,* from *mirus* 'wonderful.'

mirk ▶*n.* & *adj.* archaic spelling of **MURK.**

mirk·y ▶*adj.* archaic spelling of **MURKY.**

mir·li·ton /'mərlə,tän/ ▶*n.* **1** a musical instrument with a nasal tone produced by a vibrating membrane, typically a toy instrument resembling a kazoo. **2** another term for **CHAYOTE** (sense 1). ▷early 19th cent.: from French, 'reed pipe,' of imitative origin.

Mi·ró /mi'rō/, Joan (1893–1983), Spanish painter. A prominent figure of surrealism, he painted a brightly colored fantasy world of variously spiky and amebic calligraphic forms against plain backgrounds.

mir·ror /'mirər/ ▶*n.* a reflective surface, now typically of glass coated with a metal amalgam, that reflects a clear image. ■ *figurative* something regarded as accurately representing something else: *the stage is supposed to be the mirror of life.* ■ (also **mirror site**) *Computing* a site on a network that stores some or all of the contents from another site.
▶*v.* [*trans.*] (of a reflective surface) show a reflection of: *the clear water mirrored the sky.* ■ *figurative* correspond to: *gradations of educational attainment that mirror differences in social background.* ■ *Computing* keep a copy of some or all of the contents of (a network site) at another site, typically in order to improve accessibility. ■ [usu. as *n.*] (**mirroring**) *Computing* store copies of data on (two or more hard disks) as a method of protecting it. ▷Middle English: from Old French *mirour,* based on Latin *mirare* 'look at.' Early senses also included 'a crystal used in magic' and 'a person deserving imitation.' —**mir·rored** *adj.*

mir·ror ball (also **mir·ror·ball**) ▶*n.* a revolving ball covered with small mirrored facets, used to provide lighting effects at discos or dances.

mir·ror carp ▶*n.* a common carp of an ornamental variety that has a row of large shiny platelike scales along each side. It has been naturalized in North America, Britain, and elsewhere.

mir·ror fin·ish ▶*n.* a very smooth reflective finish produced on the surface of a metal.

mir·ror glass ▶*n.* glass with a reflective metallic coating, as used for mirrors.

mir·ror im·age ▶*n.* an image or object that is identical in form to another, but with the structure reversed, as in a mirror. ■ a person or thing that closely resembles another: *the city was the mirror image of Algiers.*

mir·ror sym·me·try ▶*n.* symmetry about a plane, like that between an object and its reflection.

mir·ror writ·ing ▶*n.* reversed writing resembling ordinary writing reflected in a mirror.

mirth /mərth/ ▶*n.* amusement, esp. as expressed in laughter: *his six-foot frame shook with mirth.* ▷Old English *myrgth,* of Germanic origin; related to **MERRY.** —**mirth·ful** /-fəl/ *adj.* —**mirth·ful·ly** /-fəlē/ *adv.*

mirth·less /'mərthləs/ ▶*adj.* (of a smile or laugh) lacking real amusement and typically expressing irony: *he gave a short, mirthless laugh.* —**mirth·less·ly** *adv.* —**mirth·less·ness** *n.*

MIRV /mərv/ ▶*n.* a type of intercontinental nuclear missile carrying several independent warheads. ▷1960s: acronym from *Multiple Independently targeted Re-entry Vehicle.*

mir·y /'mīrē/ ▶*adj.* very muddy or boggy: *the roads were miry in winter.*

MIS *Computing* ▶*abbr.* management information system.

mis-[1] ▶*prefix* (added to verbs and their derivatives) wrongly: *misapply.* ■ badly: *mismanage.* ■ unsuitably: *misname.* ▷Old English, of Germanic origin.

mis-[2] ▶*prefix* occurring in a few words adopted from French expressing a sense with negative force: *misadventure* | *mischief.* ▷from Old French *mes-* (based on Latin *minus*), assimilated to **MIS-**[1].

mis·ad·ven·ture /,misəd'venchər/ ▶*n.* an unfortunate incident; a mishap: *an expensive misadventure in financial services.* ▷Middle English: from Old French *mesaventure,* from *mesavenir* 'turn out badly.'

mis·a·ligned /,misə'līnd/ ▶*adj.* having an incorrect position or alignment: *misaligned headlights.*

mis·a·lign·ment /,misə'līnmənt/ ▶*n.* the incorrect arrangement or position of something in relation to something else.

mis·al·li·ance /,misə'līəns/ ▶*n.* an unsuitable, unhappy, or unworkable alliance or marriage. ▷mid 18th cent.: from **MIS-**[1] 'awry' + **ALLIANCE,** on the pattern of French *mésalliance.*

mis·an·dry /mis'andrē/ ▶*n.* the hatred of men by women: *her brand of feminism is just poorly disguised misandry.* ▷1940s: from Greek *miso-* 'hating' + *anēr, andr-* 'man,' on the pattern of *misogyny.*

mis·an·thrope /'misən,thrōp; 'miz/ (also **mis·an·thro·pist** /mis'anthrəpist/) ▶*n.* a person who dislikes humankind and avoids human society. ▷mid 16th cent.: from Greek *misanthrōpos,* from *misein* 'to hate' + *anthrōpos* 'man.' —**mis·an·throp·ic** /,misən'thräpik/ *adj.* —**mis·an·throp·i·cal** /,misən'thräpikəl/ *adj.* —**mis·an·throp·i·cal·ly** /,misən'thräpik(ə)lē/ *adv.*

mis·an·thro·py /mis'anthrəpē/ ▶*n.* a dislike of humankind. ▷mid 17th cent.: from Greek *misanthrōpia,* from *miso-* 'hating' + *anthrōpos* 'man.'

mis·ap·ply /,misə'plī/ ▶*v.* (**-plies, -plied**) [*trans.*] (usu. **be misapplied**) use (something) for the wrong purpose or in the wrong way: *once new technology is adopted, it is often underused or misapplied.* —**mis·ap·pli·ca·tion** /-,aplə'kāshən/ *n.*

mis·ap·pre·hend /,mis,apri'hend/ ▶*v.* [*trans.*] misunderstand (words, a person, a situation, etc.).

mis·ap·pre·hen·sion /,mis,apri'henshən/ ▶*n.* a mistaken belief about or interpretation of something: *she must have been laboring* ***under the misapprehension that*** *you are nice.* —**mis·ap·pre·hen·sive** /-'hensiv/ *adj.*

mis·ap·pro·pri·ate /,misə'prōprē,āt/ ▶*v.* [*trans.*] (of a person) dishonestly or unfairly take (something, esp. money, belonging to another) for one's own use: *department officials had misappropriated funds.* —**mis·ap·pro·pri·a·tion** /-,prōprē'āshən/ *n.*

mis·be·got·ten /,misbə'gätn/ ▶*adj.* badly conceived, designed, or planned: *a misbegotten journey to Indianapolis.* ■ contemptible (used as a term of abuse): *you misbegotten hound!* ■ *archaic* (of a child) illegitimate.

mis·be·have /,misbi'hāv/ ▶*v.* [*intrans.*] (of a person, esp. a child) fail to conduct oneself in a way that is acceptable to others; behave badly. ■ (of a machine) fail to function correctly: *her regularly serviced car was misbehaving.* —**mis·be·hav·ior** /-'hāvyər/ *n.*

mis·be·lief /,misbə'lēf/ ▶*n.* a wrong or false belief or opinion: *the misbelief that alcohol problems require a specialist response.* ■ less common term for **DISBELIEF.** —**mis·be·liev·er** /-bəlēvər; -bē-/ *n.*

misc. ▶*abbr.* miscellaneous.

mis·cal·cu·late /mis'kalkyə,lāt/ ▶*v.* [*trans.*] calculate (an amount, distance, or measurement) wrongly. ■ assess (a situation) wrongly: *the government has seriously miscalculated the effect of privatization* | [*intrans.*] *you miscalculated if you imagined I'd fallen for your little scheme.* —**mis·cal·cu·la·tion** /,mis,kalkyə'lāshən/ *n.*

mis·call /mis'kôl/ ▶*v.* [*trans.*] call (something) by a wrong or inappropriate name: *the motile bacteria have been miscalled zoospores.*

mis·car·riage /mis'karij/ ▶*n.* **1** *also* 'mis,karij the expulsion of a fetus from the womb before it is able to survive independently, esp. spontaneously or as the result of accident: *his wife had a miscarriage* | *some pregnancies result in miscarriage.* **2** an unsuccessful outcome of something planned: *the miscarriage of the project.*

mis·car·riage of jus·tice ▶*n.* a failure of a court or judicial system to attain the ends of justice, esp. one that results in the conviction of an innocent person.

mis·car·ry /mis'karē; 'mis,karē/ ▶*v.* (**-ries, -ried**) [*intrans.*] **1** *also* 'mis,karē (of a pregnant woman) have a miscarriage: *Wendy conceived, but she miscarried after five weeks* | [*trans.*] *an ultrasound scan showed that she had miscarried her baby.* **2** (of something planned) fail to attain an intended or expected outcome: *such a rash crime, and one so very likely to miscarry!* ■ *dated* (of a letter) fail to reach its intended destination.

mis·cast /mis'kast/ ▶*v.* (*past* and *past part.* **-cast**) [*trans.*] (usu. **be miscast**) allot an unsuitable role to (a particular actor): *he is badly miscast in the romantic lead.* ■ allot the roles in (a play, movie, television show, etc.) to unsuitable actors.

mis·ceg·e·na·tion /mi,sejə'nāshən; ,misəjə-/ ▶*n.* the interbreeding of people considered to be of different racial types. ▷mid 19th cent.: formed irregularly from Latin *miscere* 'to mix' + *genus* 'race' + **-ATION.**

mis·cel·la·ne·a /,misə'lānēə/ ▶*plural n.* miscellaneous items, esp. literary compositions, that have been collected together. ▷late 16th cent.: from Latin, neuter plural of *miscellaneus* (see **MISCELLANEOUS**).

mis·cel·la·ne·ous /,misə'lānēəs/ ▶*adj.* (of items or people gathered or considered together) of various types or from different sources: *he picked up the miscellaneous papers.* ■ (of a collection or group) composed of members or elements of different kinds: *a miscellaneous collection of well-known ne'er-do-wells.* ▷early 17th cent.: from Latin *miscellaneus* (from *miscellus* 'mixed,' from *miscere* 'to mix') + **-OUS.** In earlier use the word also described a person as 'having various qualities.' —**mis·cel·la·ne·ous·ly** *adv.* —**mis·cel·la·ne·ous·ness** *n.*

mis·cel·la·ny /'misə,lānē; mi'selənē/ ▶*n.* (*pl.* **-nies**) a group or collection of different items; a mixture: *Talkeetna was a random* **miscellany of** *log cabins.* ■ a book containing a collection of pieces of writing by different authors. ▷late 16th cent.: from French *miscellanées* (feminine plural), from Latin *miscellanea* (see **MISCELLANEA**).

mis·chance /mis'chans/ ▶*n.* bad luck: *by pure mischance, the secret was revealed.* ■ an unlucky occurrence: *innumerable mischances might ruin the enterprise.* ▷Middle English: from Old French *mescheance,* from the verb *mescheoir,* from *mes-* 'adversely' + *cheoir* 'befall.'

mis·chief /'mischif/ ▶*n.* playful misbehavior or troublemaking, esp. in children: *she'll make sure Danny doesn't* **get into mischief.** ■ playfulness that is intended to tease, mock, or create trouble: *her eyes twinkled with irrepressible mischief.* ■ harm or trouble caused by someone or something: *she was bent on* ***making mischief.*** ■ *archaic* a person responsible for harm or annoyance. ▷late Middle English (denoting misfortune or distress): from Old French *meschief,* from the verb *meschever,* from *mes-* 'adversely' + *chever* 'come to an end' (from *chef* 'head').

mis·chief-mak·er ▶*n.* a person who deliberately creates trouble for others. —**mis·chief-mak·ing** *n.*

mis·chie·vous /'mischivəs/ ▶*adj.* (of a person, animal, or their behavior) causing or showing a fondness for causing trouble in a playful way: *two mischievous kittens had decorated the bed with shredded newspaper.* ■ (of an action or thing) causing or intended to cause harm or trouble: *a mischievous allegation for which there is not a shred of evidence.* ▷Middle English: from Anglo-Norman French *meschevous,* from Old French *meschever* 'come to an unfortunate end' (see **MISCHIEF**). The early sense was 'unfortunate or calamitous,' later 'having harmful effects'; the sense 'playfully troublesome' dates from the late 17th cent. —**mis·chie·vous·ly** *adv.* —**mis·chie·vous·ness** *n.*

USAGE Mischievous is a three-syllable word. Take care not to use this incorrect four-syllable pronunciation: /mis'CHēvēəs/.

misch met·al /misH/ ▶*n.* an alloy of cerium, lanthanum, and other rare earth metals, used as an additive in various alloys, e.g., in flints for cigarette lighters. ▷1920s: from German *Mischmetall*, from *mischen* 'to mix' + *Metall* 'metal.'

mis·ci·ble /'misəbəl/ ▶*adj.* (of liquids) forming a homogeneous mixture when added together: *sorbitol is* **miscible with** *glycerol.* ▷late 16th cent.: from medieval Latin *miscibilis*, from Latin *miscere* 'to mix.' **—mis·ci·bil·i·ty** /,misə'bilətē/ *n.*

mis·com·mu·ni·ca·tion /,miskə,myo͞onə'kāsHən/ ▶*n.* failure to communicate adequately.

mis·con·ceive /,miskən'sēv/ ▶*v.* [*trans.*] fail to understand correctly: *she was frustrated by professors who consistently misconceived her essays.* ■ (usu. **be misconceived**) judge or plan badly, typically on the basis of faulty understanding: *criticism of the trade surplus in Washington is misconceived* | [as *adj.*] (**misconceived**) *misconceived notions about gypsies.* **—mis·con·ceiv·er** *n.*

mis·con·cep·tion /,miskən'sepsHən/ ▶*n.* a view or opinion that is incorrect because it is based on faulty thinking or understanding: *public* **misconceptions about** *AIDS remain high.*

mis·con·duct ▶*n.* /mis'kän,dəkt/ **1** unacceptable or improper behavior, esp. by an employee or professional person: *she was found guilty of professional misconduct by a disciplinary tribunal.* ■ *Ice Hockey* a penalty assessed against a player for unsportsmanlike conduct. **2** mismanagement, esp. culpable neglect of duties.
▶*v.* /,miskən'dəkt/ **1** (**misconduct oneself**) behave in an improper or unprofessional manner. **2** [*trans.*] mismanage (duties or a project).

mis·con·fig·ure /,miskən'figyər/ ▶*v.* [*trans.*] *Computing* configure (a system or part of it) incorrectly: [often as *adj.*] (**misconfigured**) *misconfigured Windows systems.* **—mis·con·fig·u·ra·tion** /,miskən,figyə'rāsHən/ *n.*

mis·con·struct /,miskən'strəkt/ ▶*v.* [*trans.*] *rare* misconstrue (something). **—mis·con·struc·tion** /-'strəksHən/ *n.*

mis·con·strue /,miskən'stro͞o/ ▶*v.* (**-strues, -strued, -stru·ing**) [*trans.*] interpret (something, esp. a person's words or actions) wrongly: *my advice was deliberately misconstrued.* **—mis·con·struc·tion** /-'strəksHən/ *n.*

mis·count ▶*v.* /mis'kount/ [*trans.*] count (something) incorrectly.
▶*n.* /'mis,kount/ an incorrect reckoning of the total number of something: *a miscount necessitates a recount.*

mis·cre·ant /'miskrēənt/ ▶*n.* a person who behaves badly or in a way that breaks the law. ■ *archaic* a heretic.
▶*adj.* (of a person) behaving badly or in a way that breaks a law or rule: *her miscreant husband.* ■ *archaic* heretical. ▷Middle English (as an adjective in the sense 'disbelieving'): from Old French *mescreant*, present participle of *mescreire* 'disbelieve,' from *mes-* 'mis-' + *creire* 'believe' (from Latin *credere*).

mis·cue[1] /mis'kyo͞o/ ▶*n.* (in billiards) a shot in which the player fails to strike the ball properly with the cue. ■ (in other sports) a faulty strike, kick, or catch. ■ *figurative* a miscalculated action; a mistake: *political miscues that led to resignations.*
▶*v.* (**-cues, -cued, -cue·ing** or **-cu·ing**) [*trans.*] (in billiards and other games) fail to strike (the ball or a shot) properly.

mis·cue[2] ▶*n.* *Linguistics* an error in reading, esp. one caused by failure to respond correctly to a phonetic or contextual cue in the text.
▶*v.* [*intrans.*] (of a performer, esp. an actor on stage) miss one's cue, or answer to another's cue. ■ [*trans.*] give (a performer) the wrong cue.

mis·date /mis'dāt/ ▶*v.* [*trans.*] assign an incorrect date to (a document, event, or work of art).

mis·deal /mis'dēl/ ▶*v.* (*past* and *past part.* **-dealt**) [*intrans.*] make a mistake when dealing cards.
▶*n.* a hand dealt wrongly.

mis·deed /mis'dēd/ ▶*n.* a wicked or illegal act. ▷Old English *misdǣd* (see **MIS-**[1], **DEED**).

mis·de·mean·ant /,misdə'mēnənt/ ▶*n.* *formal* a person convicted of a misdemeanor or guilty of misconduct. ▷early 19th cent.: from archaic *misdemean* 'misbehave' + **-ANT**.

mis·de·mean·or /'misdi,mēnər/ (*Brit.* **mis·de·mean·our**) ▶*n.* a minor wrongdoing: *the player can expect a lengthy suspension for his latest misdemeanor.* ■ *Law* a nonindictable offense, regarded in the U.S. (and formerly in the UK) as less serious than a felony.

mis·de·scribe /,misdi'skrīb/ ▶*v.* [*trans.*] describe inaccurately or misleadingly: *he misdescribed the play as a tragedy.* **—mis·de·scrip·tion** /-'skripsHən/ *n.*

mis·di·ag·nose /mis'dī-ig,nōs; -,nōz/ ▶*v.* [*trans.*] make an incorrect diagnosis of (a particular illness). ■ make an incorrect diagnosis of the illness from which (someone) is suffering: *the consultant misdiagnosed her as having cancer.* **—mis·di·ag·no·sis** /,mis,dīig'nōsəs/ *n.*

mis·di·al /,mis'dī(ə)l/ ▶*v.* (**-di·aled, -di·al·ing**; *Brit.* **-di·alled, -di·al·ling**) [*intrans.*] dial a telephone number incorrectly.
▶*n.* an act of dialing a number incorrectly.

mis·di·rect /,misdə'rekt; -dī-/ ▶*v.* [*trans.*] (often **be misdirected**) send (someone or something) to the wrong place or in the wrong direction: *voters were misdirected to the wrong polling place.* ■ aim (something) in the wrong direction: *he misdirected a shot.* ■ (of a judge) instruct wrongly: *the appeals court was satisfied that the trial judge had misdirected the jury.* ■ use or apply (something) wrongly or inappropriately: *their efforts have been largely misdirected.* **—mis·di·rec·tion** /-'reksHən/ *n.*

mis·do·ing /mis'do͞oiNG/ ▶*n.* a misdeed.

mis·doubt /mis'dout/ ▶*v.* [*trans.*] *chiefly archaic* have doubts about the truth, reality, or existence of: *he was diffident and always misdoubted his own ability.* ■ fear or be suspicious about: *for I fear my father, and I misdoubt his hindrances.*

mis·ed·u·cate /mis'ejə,kāt/ ▶*v.* [*trans.*] educate, teach, or inform wrongly. **—mis·ed·u·ca·tion** /,mis,ejə'kāsHən/ *n.* **—mis·ed·u·ca·tive** /-'ejə,kātiv/ *adj.*

mise en scène /,mēz ,äN 'sen/ ▶*n.* [usu. in *sing.*] the arrangement of scenery and stage properties in a play. ■ the setting or surroundings of an event or action. ▷French, literally 'putting on stage.'

mis·em·ploy /,mis,im'ploi/ ▶*v.* [*trans.*] employ or use (something) wrongly or improperly. **—mis·em·ploy·ment** *n.*

mi·ser /'mīzər/ ▶*n.* a person who hoards wealth and spends as little money as possible. ▷late 15th cent. (as an adjective in the sense 'miserly'): from Latin, literally 'wretched.'

mis·er·a·ble /'miz(ə)rəbəl/ ▶*adj.* **1** (of a person) wretchedly unhappy or uncomfortable: *their happiness made Anne feel even more miserable.* ■ (of a situation or environment) causing someone to feel wretchedly unhappy or uncomfortable: *horribly wet and miserable conditions.* ■ (of a person) habitually morose: *a miserable man in his late sixties.* **2** pitiably small or inadequate: *all they pay me is a miserable $10,000 a year.* ■ [*attrib.*] contemptible (used as a term of abuse or for emphasis): *you miserable old creep!* ▷late Middle English: from French *misérable*, from Latin *miserabilis* 'pitiable,' from *miserari* 'to pity,' from *miser* 'wretched.' **—mis·er·a·ble·ness** *n.* **—mis·er·a·bly** /-blē/ *adv.*

mis·e·re·re /,mizə're(ə)rē; -'ri(ə)rē/ ▶*n.* **1** (also **Miserere**) a psalm in which mercy is sought, esp. Psalm 51 or the music written for it. ■ any prayer or cry for mercy. **2** another term for **MISERICORD** (sense 1). ▷Middle English: from Latin, 'have mercy!,' imperative of *misereri*, from *miser* 'wretched.'

mis·er·i·cord /mə'zeri,kôrd/ ▶*n.* **1** a ledge projecting from the underside of a hinged seat in a choir stall that, when the seat is turned up, gives support to someone standing. **2** *historical* an apartment in a monastery in which some relaxations of the monastic rule are permitted. **3** *historical* a small dagger used to deliver a death stroke to a wounded enemy. ▷Middle English (denoting pity): from Old French *misericorde*, from Latin *misericordia*, from *misericors* 'compassionate,' from the stem of *misereri* 'to pity' + *cor, cord-* 'heart.'

mi·ser·ly /'mīzərlē/ ▶*adj.* of, relating to, or characteristic of a miser: *his miserly great-uncle proved to be worth nearly $1 million.* ■ (of a quantity) pitiably small or inadequate: *last year's miserly growth in sales.* See note at **ECONOMICAL**. **—mi·ser·li·ness** *n.*

mis·er·y /'miz(ə)rē/ ▶*n.* (*pl.* **-er·ies**) a state or feeling of great distress or discomfort of mind or body: *she went upstairs and cried in misery* | *he wrote endlessly about his frustrations and miseries.* ■ (usu. **miseries**) a cause or source of great distress or discomfort: *the miseries of war.* ▷late Middle English: from Old French *miserie*, from Latin *miseria*, from *miser* 'wretched.'
▶*PHRASES* □ **make someone's life a misery** (or **make life a misery for someone**) cause someone severe distress by continued unpleasantness or harassment. □ **put someone/something out of their misery** end the suffering of a person or animal in pain by killing them. ■ *informal* release someone from suspense or anxiety by telling them something they are anxious to know.

mis·fea·sance /mis'fēzəns/ ▶*n.* *Law* a transgression, esp. the wrongful exercise of lawful authority. ▷early 17th cent.: from Old French *mesfaisance*, from *mesfaire*, from *mes-* 'wrongly' + *faire* 'do' (from Latin *facere*). Compare with **MALFEASANCE**.

mis·feed /mis'fēd; 'mis,fēd/ ▶*n.* an instance of faulty feeding of something (typically paper) through a machine.

mis·field /mis'fēld/ ▶*v.* [*trans.*] (in cricket and rugby) field (a ball) badly or clumsily.

mis·file /mis'fīl/ ▶*v.* [*trans.*] file wrongly.

mis·fire ▶*v.* /mis'fīr/ [*intrans.*] (of a gun or missile) fail to discharge or fire properly. ■ (of an internal combustion engine) undergo failure of the fuel to ignite correctly or at all: *the car would misfire occasionally from the cold.* ■ (esp. of a plan) fail to produce the intended result: *the killer didn't know that his plan had misfired.* ■ (of a nerve cell) fail to transmit an electrical impulse at an appropriate moment.
▶*n.* /'mis,fīr/ a failure of a gun or missile to fire correctly or of fuel in an internal combustion engine to ignite.

mis·fit /'mis,fit/ ▶*n.* a person whose behavior or attitude sets them apart from others in an uncomfortably conspicuous way: *a motley collection of social misfits.* ■ *archaic* something that does not fit or that fits badly.

mis·for·tune /mis'fôrCHən/ ▶*n.* bad luck: *the project was dogged by misfortune.* ■ an unfortunate condition or event: *never laugh at other people's misfortunes.*

mis·give /mis'giv/ ▶*v.* (*past* **-gave**; *past part.* **-giv·en**) [*trans.*] *poetic/literary* (of a person's mind or heart) fill (that person) with doubt, apprehension, or foreboding: *my heart misgave me when I saw him.*

mis·giv·ing /mis'giviNG/ ▶*n.* (usu. **misgivings**) a feeling of doubt or apprehension about the outcome or consequences of something: *we have* **misgivings about** *the way the campaign is being run* | *I felt a sense of misgiving at the prospect of retirement.* See note at **QUALM**.

mis·gov·ern /mis'gəvərn/ ▶*v.* [*trans.*] govern (a state or country) unfairly or inefficiently. **—mis·gov·ern·ment** /-'gəvər(n)mənt/ *n.*

mis·guide /mis'gīd/ ▶*v.* [*trans.*] *rare* mislead: *a long survey that can only baffle and misguide the general reader.* **—mis·guid·ance** /-gīdns/ *n.*

mis·guid·ed /mis'gīdid/ ▶*adj.* having or showing faulty judgment or reasoning: *misguided attempts to promote political correctness.* **—mis·guid·ed·ly** *adv.* **—mis·guid·ed·ness** *n.*

mis·han·dle /mis'handəl/ ▶*v.* [*trans.*] **1** manage or deal with (something) wrongly or ineffectively: *the officer had mishandled the situation.* **2** manipulate roughly or carelessly: *the equipment could be dangerous if mishandled.*

mis·hap /'mis,hap/ ▶*n.* an unlucky accident: *although there were a few minor mishaps, none of the pancakes stuck to the ceiling* | | *the event passed without mishap.*

Mi·sha·wa·ka /,misHə'wäkə; -'wôkə/ an industrial city in northeastern Indiana, east of South Bend; pop. 46,557.

mis·hear /mis'hi(ə)r/ ▶*v.* (*past* and *past part.* **-heard**) [*trans.*] fail to hear (a person or their words) correctly.

Mi·shi·ma /mi'sHēmə; 'mēsHē,mä/, Yukio (1925–70), Japanese writer; pseudonym of *Hiraoka Kimitake*. His books include the *The Sea of Fertility* (1965–70), which looks at reincarnation and the sterility of modern life. An avowed imperialist, he committed hara-kiri after failing to incite soldiers against the postwar regime.

mis·hit /,mis'hit/ ▶*v.* (**-hit·ting**; *past* and *past part.* **-hit**) [*trans.*] (in various sports) hit or kick (a ball) badly or in the wrong direction.
▶*n.* an instance of hitting or kicking a ball in such a way.

mish·mash /'misH,masH; -,mäsH/ ▶*n.* [in *sing.*] a confused mixture: *a mishmash of outmoded ideas.* ▷late 15th cent.: reduplication of **MASH**.

Mish·nah /'misHnə/ ▶*n.* (**the Mishnah**) an authoritative collection of exegetical material embodying the oral tradition of Jewish law and forming the first part of the Talmud. ▷from Hebrew *mišnāh* '(teaching by) repetition.' **—Mish·na·ic** /misH'nāik/ *adj.*

mi·shu·gas /məsʜŏŏ'gäs/ ▸*n.* variant spelling of MESHUGAAS.

mis·i·den·ti·fy /ˌmisī'dentəˌfī/ ▸*v.* (**-fies, -fied**) [*trans.*] identify (something or someone) incorrectly. —**mis·i·den·ti·fi·ca·tion** /-īˌdentəfə'kāsʜən/ *n.*

mis·in·form /ˌmisin'fôrm/ ▸*v.* [*trans.*] (often **be misinformed**) give (someone) false or inaccurate information.

mis·in·for·ma·tion /ˌmisinfər'māsʜən/ ▸*n.* false or inaccurate information, esp. that which is deliberately intended to deceive: *nuclear matters are often entangled in a web of secrecy and misinformation.*

mis·in·ter·pret /ˌmisin'tərprət/ ▸*v.* (**-pret·ed, -pret·ing**) [*trans.*] interpret (something or someone) wrongly. —**mis·in·ter·pre·ta·tion** /-inˌtərprə'tāsʜən/ *n.* —**mis·in·ter·pret·er** *n.*

mis·judge /ˌmis'jəj/ ▸*v.* [*trans.*] form a wrong opinion or conclusion about: *we misjudged the size of the surf.* ■ make an incorrect estimation or assessment of: *the horse misjudged the fence and Mrs. Weaver was thrown off.* —**mis·judg·ment** (also **mis·judge·ment**) *n.*

mis·key /mis'kē/ ▸*v.* (**-keys, -keyed**) [*trans.*] key (a word or piece of data) into a computer or other machine incorrectly.

Mis·ki·to /mə'skētō/ (also **Mos·qui·to**) ▸*n.* (*pl.* same or **-tos**) **1** a member of an American Indian people of the Atlantic coast of Nicaragua and Honduras. **2** the language of this people, possibly related to Chibchan.
▸*adj.* of or relating to the Miskito or their language. ▷the name in Miskito.

Mis·kolc /'misʜˌkōlts/ a city in northeastern Hungary; pop. 191,000.

mis·la·bel /mis'lābəl/ ▸*v.* (**-la·beled, -la·bel·ing**; *Brit.* **-la·belled, -la·bel·ling**) [*trans.*] label wrongly.

mis·lay /mis'lā/ ▸*v.* (*past* and *past part.* **-laid**) [*trans.*] unintentionally put (an object) where it cannot readily be found and so lose it temporarily: *I seem to have mislaid my car keys.*

mis·lead /mis'lēd/ ▸*v.* (*past* and *past part.* **-led**) [*trans.*] cause (someone) to have a wrong idea or impression about someone or something: *the government misled the public about the road's environmental impact.* —**mis·lead·er** *n.*

mis·lead·ing /mis'lēdiɴɢ/ ▸*adj.* giving the wrong idea or impression: *your article contains a number of misleading statements.* —**mis·lead·ing·ly** *adv.* —**mis·lead·ing·ness** *n.*

mis·like /mis'līk/ *archaic* ▸*v.* [*trans.*] consider to be unpleasant; dislike: *the pony snorted, misliking the smell of blood.*
▸*n.* distaste; dislike. ▷Old English *mislīcian* (see MIS-[1], LIKE[2]).

mis·man·age /mis'manij/ ▸*v.* [*trans.*] manage (something) badly or wrongly. —**mis·man·age·ment** *n.*

mis·match ▸*n.* /'misˌmacʜ/ a failure to correspond or match; a discrepancy: *a huge* **mismatch between** *supply and demand.*
▸*v.* /'ˌmis'macʜ/ [*trans.*] [usu. as *adj.*] (**mismatched**) match (people or things) unsuitably or incorrectly: *funky mismatched chairs and tables.*

mis·mat·ed /ˌmis'mātid/ ▸*adj.* badly matched or not matching.

mis·name /mis'nām/ ▸*v.* [*trans.*] give (something) a wrong or inappropriate name: *summer peas—misnamed, because they are beans—thrive in hot weather.*

mis·no·mer /mis'nōmər/ ▸*n.* a wrong or inaccurate name or designation: *"king crab" is a misnomer—these creatures are not crustaceans at all.* ■ a wrong or inaccurate use of a name or term: *to call this "neighborhood policing" would be a misnomer.* ▷late Middle English: from Anglo-Norman French, from the Old French verb *mesnommer*, from *mes-* 'wrongly' + *nommer* 'to name' (based on Latin *nomen* 'name').

mi·so /'mēsō/ ▸*n.* paste made from fermented soybeans and barley or rice malt, used in Japanese cooking. ▷Japanese.

mi·sog·a·my /mə'sägəmē/ ▸*n. rare* the hatred of marriage. ▷mid 17th cent.: from Greek *misos* 'hatred' + *gamos* 'marriage.' —**mi·sog·a·mist** /-mist/ *n.*

mi·sog·y·nist /mə'säjənist/ ▸*n.* a man who hates women.
▸*adj.* reflecting or inspired by a hatred of women: *a misogynist attitude.* —**mi·sog·y·nis·tic** /məˌsäjə'nistik/ *adj.*

mi·sog·y·ny /mə'säjənē/ ▸*n.* the hatred of women by men: *she felt she was struggling against thinly disguised misogyny.* ▷mid 17th cent.: from Greek *misos* 'hatred' + *gunē* 'woman.' —**mi·sog·y·nous** /-nəs/ *adj.*

mis·pick·el /'misˌpikəl/ ▸*n.* another term for ARSENOPYRITE. ▷late 17th cent.: from German.

mis·place /mis'plās/ ▸*v.* [*trans.*] (usu. **be misplaced**) put in the wrong place and lose temporarily because of this; mislay: *I'm sure the jewelry has just been misplaced, and not stolen.* —**mis·place·ment** *n.*

mis·placed /mis'plāst/ ▸*adj.* **1** incorrectly positioned: *a million dollars had been lost because of a misplaced comma.* ■ not appropriate or correct in the circumstances: *a telling sign of misplaced priorities.* ■ (of an emotion) directed unwisely or to an inappropriate object: *he began to wonder if his sympathy were misplaced.* **2** [*attrib.*] temporarily lost: *her misplaced keys.*

mis·placed mod·i·fi·er ▸*n. Grammar* a phrase or clause placed awkwardly in a sentence so that it appears to modify or refer to an unintended word. See also DANGLING PARTICIPLE.

USAGE See usage at MODIFIER.

mis·play ▸*v.* /mis'plā/ [*trans.*] play (a ball or card) wrongly, badly, or in contravention of the rules.
▸*n.* /'misˌplā/ an instance of playing a ball or card in such a way.

mis·print ▸*n.* /misˌprint/ an error in printed text: *Galway might be a misprint for Galloway.*
▸*v.* /'ˌmis'print/ [*trans.*] print (something) incorrectly.

mis·pri·sion[1] /mis'prizʜən/ (also **misprision of treason** or **felony**) ▸*n. Law, chiefly historical* the deliberate concealment of one's knowledge of a treasonable act or a felony. ▷late Middle English: from Old French *mesprision* 'error,' from *mesprendre*, from *mes-* 'wrongly' + *prendre* 'to take.'

mis·pri·sion[2] ▸*n. rare* erroneous judgment, esp. of the value or identity of something: *he despised himself for his misprision.* ▷late 16th cent.: from MISPRIZE, influenced by MISPRISION[1].

mis·prize /mis'prīz/ ▸*v.* [*trans.*] *rare* fail to appreciate the value of (something); undervalue. ▷late 15th cent.: from Old French *mesprisier*, from *mes-* 'wrongly' + *prisier* 'estimate the value of.'

mis·pro·nounce /ˌmisprə'nouns/ ▸*v.* [*trans.*] pronounce (a word) incorrectly: *she mispronounced my name.* —**mis·pro·nun·ci·a·tion** /-prəˌnənsē'āsʜən/ *n.*

mis·quote /mis'kwōt/ ▸*v.* [*trans.*] quote (a person or a piece of written or spoken text) inaccurately: *the foreign secretary had misquoted Qian.*
▸*n.* a passage or remark quoted inaccurately: *a misquote from a poem by Robert Burns.* —**mis·quo·ta·tion** /ˌmiskwō'tāsʜən/ *n.*

mis·read /mis'rēd/ ▸*v.* (*past* and *past part.* **-read** /-'red/) [*trans.*] read (a piece of text) wrongly. ■ judge or interpret (a situation or a person's manner or behavior) incorrectly: *had she been completely misreading his intentions?*

mis·re·mem·ber /ˌmisri'membər/ ▸*v.* [*trans.*] remember imperfectly or incorrectly.

mis·re·port /ˌmisri'pôrt/ ▸*v.* [*trans.*] give a false or inaccurate account of (something): *the press exaggerated and misreported the response to the book.*
▸*n.* a false or incorrect report.

mis·rep·re·sent /ˌmisˌrepri'zent/ ▸*v.* [*trans.*] give a false or misleading account of the nature of: *you are misrepresenting the views of the government.* —**mis·rep·re·sen·ta·tion** /-ˌzen'tāsʜən; -zən-/ *n.* —**mis·rep·re·sen·ta·tive** /-'zentətiv/ *adj.*

mis·rep·re·sen·ta·tion /misˌreprəzən'tāsʜən/ ▸*n. Law* a false or misleading statement: *persons who suffer from a realtor's misrepresentation may be able to recover their losses.* ■ the legal action to provide a remedy for a false or misleading statement.

mis·route /mis'rōōt; -'rout/ ▸*v.* [*trans.*] divert or direct to the wrong place or by the wrong route.

mis·rule /mis'rōōl/ ▸*n.* the unfair or inefficient conduct of the affairs of a country or state: *thirty years of misrule by the one-party socialist government.* ■ the disruption of peace; disorder: *there was a tradition of misrule before, during, and after games.*
▸*v.* [*trans.*] govern (a country or state) badly.

miss[1] /mis/ ▸*v.* [*trans.*] **1** fail to hit, reach, or come into contact with (something aimed at): *a laser-guided bomb had missed its target* | [*intrans.*] *he was given two free throws, but missed both times.* ■ pass by without touching; chance not to hit: *a piece of shrapnel missed him by inches.* ■ fail to catch (something thrown or dropped). ■ be too late to catch (a passenger vehicle, etc.): *we'll miss the train if he doesn't hurry.* ■ fail to notice, hear, or understand: *the villa is impossible to miss—it's right by the road.* ■ fail to attend, participate in, or watch (something one is expected to do or habitually does): *teachers were supposed to report those students who missed class that day.* ■ fail to see or have a meeting with (someone): *"Potter's been here this morning?" "You've just missed him."* ■ not be able to experience or fail to take advantage of (an opportunity or chance): *don't miss the chance to visit the breathtaking Dolomites* | [*intrans.*] *he failed to recover from a leg injury and* **missed out on** *a trip to Barcelona.* ■ avoid; escape: *smart Christmas shoppers go out early to miss the crowds.* ■ fail to include (someone or something); omit: *if we miss a few things in the first draft, we can add them later.* ■ (of a woman) fail to have (a monthly period). ■ [*intrans.*] (of an engine or motor vehicle) undergo failure of ignition in one or more cylinders. **2** notice the loss or absence of: *he's rich—he won't miss the money* | *she slipped away when she thought she wouldn't be missed.* ■ feel regret or sadness at no longer being able to enjoy the presence of: *she misses all her old friends.* ■ feel regret or sadness at no longer being able to go to, do, or have: *I still miss France and I wish I could go back.*
▸*n.* a failure to hit, catch, or reach something: *Elster's stunning catch in the third inning made up for his dreadful miss in the first.* ■ a failure, esp. an unsuccessful movie, television show, recording, etc.: *moviegoers will decide whether Brando's latest flick is a hit or a miss.* ▷Old English *missan*, of Germanic origin; related to Dutch and German *missen*. —**miss·a·ble** /'misəbəl/ *adj.*
▸*PHRASES* □ **give something a miss** *Brit., informal* decide not to do or have something: *we decided to give the popcorn a miss.* □ **miss a beat 1** (of the heart) temporarily fail or appear to fail to beat. **2** [usu. with *negative*] *informal* hesitate or falter, esp. in demanding circumstances or when making a transition from one activity to another: *his speech segued from child-care subsidies to nuclear disarmament, without missing a beat.* □ **miss the boat** (or **bus**) *informal* be too slow to take advantage of an opportunity: *the company missed the boat with its first attempt at a personal computer line five years ago.* □ **a miss is as good as a mile** *proverb* the fact of failure or escape is not affected by the narrowness of the margin. □ **not miss a trick** *informal* never fail to take advantage of a situation.

miss[2] ▸*n.* **1** (**Miss**) a title prefixed to the name of an unmarried woman or girl, or to that of a married woman retaining her maiden name for professional purposes: *Miss Hazel Armstrong.* ■ used in the title of the winner in a beauty contest: *Miss World.* ■ used as a polite form of address to a young woman or to a waitress, etc.: *where will you be staying in England, miss?* ■ *chiefly Brit.* used by children in addressing a female teacher: *please, Miss, can I be excused?* **2** *often derogatory* or *humorous* a girl or young woman, esp. one regarded as silly or headstrong: *there was none of the country bumpkin about this young miss.* **3** (**misses**) a range of standard sizes, usually 8 to 20, in women's clothing. ▷mid 17th cent.: abbreviation of MISTRESS.

Miss. ▸*abbr.* Mississippi.

mis·sal /'misəl/ ▸*n.* a book containing the texts used in the Catholic Mass throughout the year. ▷Middle English: from medieval Latin *missale*, neuter of ecclesiastical Latin *missalis* 'relating to the Mass,' from *missa* 'Mass.'

mis·sel thrush ▸*n.* variant spelling of MISTLE THRUSH.

mis·shape /mis'sʜāp/ ▸*v.* [*trans.*] *archaic* give a bad or ugly shape or form to; deform.

mis·shap·en /mis'sʜāpən/ ▸*adj.* not having the normal or natural shape or form: *misshapen fruit.* —**mis·shap·en·ly** *adv.* —**mis·shap·en·ness** *n.*

mis·sile /'misəl/ ▸*n.* an object that is forcibly propelled at a target, either by hand or from a mechanical weapon. ■ a weapon that is self-propelled or directed by remote control, carrying a conventional or nuclear explosive. ▷early 17th cent. (as an adjective in the sense 'suitable for throwing (at a target)'): from Latin *missile*, neuter (used as a noun) of *missilis*, from *miss-* 'sent,' from the verb *mittere*.

mis·sil·ery /'misəlrē/ ▸*n.* **1** the study of the use and characteristics of missiles. **2** missiles collectively.

miss·ing /'misiɴɢ/ ▸*adj.* (of a thing) not able to be found because it is not in its expected place: *a quantity of cash has* **gone missing**. ■ not present or included when expected or supposed to be: *passion was an element that had been* **missing from** *her life for too long* | *you can fill in the missing details later.* ■ (of a person) absent from a place, esp. home, and of unknown whereabouts: *she alerted police that her son was missing.* ■ (of a person) not yet traced or confirmed as alive, but not known to be dead, after an accident or during wartime: *servicemen listed as* **missing in action**.

miss·ing link ▸*n.* a thing that is needed in order to complete a series, provide continuity, or gain complete knowledge: *she is the missing link between the European ballad tradition and Anglo-American white soul.*

■ a hypothetical fossil form intermediate between two living forms, esp. between humans and apes.

mis·si·ol·o·gy /ˌmisēˈäləjē/ ▸*n.* the study of religious (typically Christian) missions and their methods and purposes. ▷1930s: formed irregularly from MISSION + -LOGY. —**mis·sio·log·i·cal** /ˌmisēəˈläjikəl/ *adj.*

mis·sion /ˈmisHən/ ▸*n.* an important assignment carried out for political, religious, or commercial purposes, typically involving travel: *a fact-finding* **mission** *to China.* ■ [treated as *sing.* or *pl.*] a group of people taking part in such an assignment: *by then, the mission had journeyed more than 3,500 miles.* ■ [in *sing.*] an organization or institution involved in a long-term assignment in a foreign country: *the majestic garden of the West German mission* | [as *adj.*] *the mission school.* ■ the vocation or calling of a religious organization, esp. a Christian one, to go out into the world and spread its faith: *the Christian mission* | *Gandhi's attitude to mission and conversion.* ■ a strongly felt aim, ambition, or calling: *his main mission in life has been to cut unemployment.* ■ an expedition into space. ■ an operation carried out by military aircraft at a time of conflict: *he was shot down on a supply mission.* ▷mid 16th cent. (denoting the sending of the Holy Spirit into the world): from Latin *missio(n-)*, from *mittere* 'send.'

mis·sion·ar·y /ˈmisHəˌnerē/ ▸*n.* (*pl.* **-ar·ies**) a person sent on a religious mission, esp. one sent to promote Christianity in a foreign country.
▸*adj.* of, relating to, or characteristic of a missionary or a religious mission: *missionary work* | *they have lost the missionary zeal they once had.* ▷mid 17th cent.: from modern Latin *missionarius*, from Latin *missio* (see MISSION).

mis·sion·ar·y po·si·tion ▸*n. informal* a position for sexual intercourse in which a couple lies face to face with the woman underneath the man. ▷said to be so named because early missionaries advocated the position as "proper" to primitive peoples, to whom the practice was unknown.

Mis·sion·ary Ridge /ˈmisHəˌnerē/ a historic site southeast of Chattanooga in Tennessee, on the Georgia border, scene of a November 1863 Civil War battle that followed that at nearby Lookout Mountain.

mis·sion creep ▸*n.* a gradual shift in objectives during the course of a military campaign, often resulting in an unplanned long-term commitment. ■ such a development in a nonmilitary context, resulting in undesirable policies or consequences: *the IMF's mission creep has been consistently endorsed by the Treasury Department as a way of furthering U.S. economic foreign policy.*

mis·sion-crit·i·cal ▸*adj. Computing* (of hardware or software) vital to the functioning of an organization.

mis·sion·er /ˈmisHənər/ ▸*n.* **1** a person in charge of a religious or charitable mission. **2** a missionary.

mis·sion state·ment ▸*n.* a formal summary of the aims and values of a company, organization, or individual.

mis·sis ▸*n.* variant spelling of MISSUS.

miss·ish /ˈmisisH/ ▸*adj.* affectedly demure, squeamish, or sentimental; prudish.

Mis·sis·sau·ga /ˌmisəˈsôgə/ a town in southern Ontario, on the western shores of Lake Ontario, a southern suburb of Toronto; pop. 463,388.

Mis·sis·sip·pi /ˌmisəˈsipē/ **1** a major river in North America that rises in Minnesota near the Canadian border and flows south to a delta on the Gulf of Mexico. With its chief tributary, the Missouri River, it is 3,710 miles (5,970 km) long. In the second half of the 17th century it provided a route south through the center of the continent for French explorers from Canada. From the 1830s, it was noted for the sternwheeler steamboats that plied between New Orleans and St. Louis and other northern cities. **2** a state in the southern U.S., on the Gulf of Mexico, bounded on the west by the lower Mississippi River; pop. 2,854,658; capital, Jackson; statehood, Dec. 10, 1817 (20). A French colony in the first half of the 18th century, it was ceded to Britain in 1763 and to the U.S. in 1783.

Mis·sis·sip·pi·an /ˌmisiˈsipēən/ ▸*adj.* **1** of or relating to the state of Mississippi. **2** *Geology* of, relating to, or denoting the early part of the Carboniferous period in North America from about 363 to 323 million years ago, following the Devonian and preceding the Pennsylvanian. ■ *Archaeology* of, relating to, or denoting a settled culture of the southeastern U.S., dated to about AD 800–1300.
▸*n.* **1** a native or inhabitant of Mississippi. **2** (**the Mississippian**) *Geology* the Mississippian period or the system of rocks deposited during it. ■ *Archaeology* the Mississippian culture or period.

Mis·sis·sip·pi mud pie ▸*n.* a type of rich, mousselike chocolate cake or pie.

mis·sive /ˈmisiv/ ▸*n.* a letter, esp. a long or official one: *he hastily banged out electronic missives.* ▷late Middle English (as an adjective, originally in the phrase LETTER MISSIVE): from medieval Latin *missivus*, from Latin *mittere* 'send.' The current sense dates from the early 16th cent.

Mis·sou·la /məˈzo͞olə/ a commercial city in western Montana, on the Clark Fork River; pop. 57,053.

Mis·sou·ri /məˈzo͝orē; -ˈzo͝orə/ **1** a major river in North America, one of the main tributaries of the Mississippi River. It rises in the Rocky Mountains in Montana and flows 2,315 miles (3,736 km) to meet the Mississippi River just north of St. Louis. **2** a state in the central part of the U.S., bounded on the east by the Mississippi River; pop. 5,595,211; capital, Jefferson City; statehood, Aug. 10, 1821 (24). It was acquired as part of the Louisiana Purchase in 1803 and admitted as a state as part of the Missouri Compromise. —**Mis·sour·i·an** /-ēən/ *n.* & *adj.*

mis·speak /misˈspēk/ ▸*v.* (*past* **-spoke**; *past part.* **-spok·en**) [*intrans.*] express oneself insufficiently clearly or accurately.

mis·spell /misˈspel/ ▸*v.* (*past* and *past part.* **-spelled** or **-spelt**) [*trans.*] spell (a word) incorrectly.

mis·spend /misˈspend/ ▸*v.* (*past* and *past part.* **-spent**) [*trans.*] [usu. as *adj.*] (**misspent**) spend (one's time or money) foolishly, wrongly, or wastefully: *perhaps I am atoning for my misspent youth.*

mis·state /misˈstāt/ ▸*v.* [*trans.*] make wrong or inaccurate statements about. —**mis·state·ment** *n.*

mis·step /misˈstep; ˈmisˌstep/ ▸*n.* a clumsy or badly judged step: *for a mountain goat, one misstep could be fatal.* ■ a mistake or blunder.

mis·sus /ˈmisəz; -əs/ (also **mis·sis**) ▸*n.* [in *sing.*] *informal* or *humorous* a man's wife: *I promised* **the missus** *I'd be home by eleven.* ■ *informal* used as a form of address to a woman whose name is not known: *sit down, missus.*

miss·y /ˈmisē/ ▸*n.* (*pl.* **miss·ies**) used as an affectionate or disparaging form of address to a young girl: *"Don't tell lies, missy," he said sternly.*
▸*adj.* of or relating to the misses range of garment sizes: *available in missy and petite sizes.*

mist /mist/ ▸*n.* a cloud of tiny water droplets suspended in the atmosphere at or near the earth's surface limiting visibility, but to a lesser extent than fog; strictly, with visibility remaining above 1.5 miles (1 km): *the peaks were shrouded in mist* | [in *sing.*] *a mist rose out of the river.* ■ [in *sing.*] a condensed vapor settling in fine droplets on a surface: *a breeze cooled the mist of perspiration that had dampened her temples.* ■ [in *sing.*] a haze or film over the eyes, esp. caused by tears, and resulting in blurred vision: *Ruth saw most of the scene through a mist of tears.* ■ used in reference to something that blurs one's perceptions or memory: *Sardinia's origins are lost in* **the mists of time.**
▸*v.* cover or become covered with mist: [*trans.*] *the windows were* **misted up** *with condensation* | [*intrans.*] *the glass was beginning to* **mist up.** ■ [*intrans.*] (of a person's eyes) become covered with a film of tears causing blurred vision: *her eyes misted at this heroic image.* ■ [*trans.*] spray (something, esp. a plant) with a fine cloud of water droplets. ▷Old English, of Germanic origin; from an Indo-European root shared by Greek *omikhlē* 'mist, fog.'

mis·take /məˈstāk/ ▸*n.* an action or judgment that is misguided or wrong: *coming here was a mistake* | *she* **made the mistake of** *thinking they were important.* ■ something, esp. a word, figure, or fact, that is not correct; an inaccuracy: *a couple of spelling mistakes.*
▸*v.* (*past* **-took**; *past part.* **-tak·en**) [*trans.*] be wrong about: *because I was inexperienced, I mistook the nature of our relationship.* ■ (**mistake someone/something for**) wrongly identify someone or something as: *she thought he'd mistaken her for someone else.* ▷late Middle English (as a verb): from Old Norse *mistaka* 'take in error,' probably influenced in sense by Old French *mesprendre.* —**mis·tak·a·ble** *adj.* —**mis·tak·a·bly** /-əblē/ *adv.*
▸*PHRASES* □ **and no mistake** *informal, dated* without any doubt: *it's a bad business and no mistake.* □ **by mistake** accidentally; in error: *she'd left her purse at home by mistake.* □ **make no mistake (about it)** *informal* do not be deceived into thinking otherwise. □ **there is no mistaking someone or something** it is impossible not to recognize someone or something: *there was no mistaking her sincerity.*

THE RIGHT WORD **blooper, blunder, error, faux pas, goof, mistake, slip**

It would be a **mistake** to argue with your boss the day before he or she evaluates your performance, but to forget an important step in an assigned task would be an **error**.

Although these nouns are used interchangeably in many contexts, a *mistake* is usually caused by poor judgment or a disregard of rules or principles (*it was a mistake not to tell the truth at the outset*), while an *error* implies an unintentional deviation from standards of accuracy or right conduct (*a mathematical error*).

A **blunder** is a careless, stupid, or blatant mistake involving behavior or judgment; it suggests awkwardness or ignorance on the part of the person who makes it (*his blunder that ruined the evening*).

A **slip** is a minor and usually accidental mistake that is the result of haste or carelessness (*her slip of the tongue spoiled the surprise*), while a **faux pas** (which means "false step" in French) is an embarrassing breach of etiquette (*it was a faux pas to have meat at the table when so many of the guests were vegetarians*).

Goofs and **bloopers** are humorous mistakes. A *blooper* is usually a mix-up in speech, while to *goof* is to make a careless error that is honestly admitted (*she shrugged her shoulders and said, "I goofed!"*)

mis·tak·en /məˈstākən/ ▸*adj.* [*predic.*] wrong in one's opinion or judgment: *she wondered whether she'd been mistaken about his intentions.* ■ [*attrib.*] (esp. of a belief) based on or resulting from a misunderstanding or faulty judgment: *don't buy a hard bed in the mistaken belief that it is good for you* | *an unfortunate case of mistaken identity.* —**mis·tak·en·ly** *adv.* —**mis·tak·en·ness** *n.*

mis·ter[1] /ˈmistər/ ▸*n.* variant form of MR., often used humorously or with offensive emphasis: *don't backtalk me, mister!* ■ *informal* used as a form of address to a man whose name is not known: *thanks, mister.* ■ *dialect* a woman's husband: *my thanks to you and the mister.* ▷mid 16th cent.: weakened form of MASTER[1] in unstressed use before a name.

mis·ter[2] ▸*n.* a device, such as a bottle, with a nozzle for spraying a mist of water, esp. on houseplants.

mis·time /misˈtīm/ ▸*v.* [*trans.*] choose a bad or inappropriate moment to do or say (something): *he lost $800 million by mistiming his withdrawal from the market.* ▷Old English *mistīmian* 'happen unfortunately' (see MIS-[1], TIME).

mis·tle thrush /ˈmisəl ˌTHrəsH/ (also **mis·sel thrush**) ▸*n.* a large Eurasian thrush with a spotted breast and harsh rattling call, with a fondness for mistletoe berries. • *Turdus viscivorus*, subfamily Turdinae, family Muscicapidae. ▷early 17th cent.: *mistle* from Old English *mistel* (see MISTLETOE).

mis·tle·toe /ˈmisəlˌtō/ ▸*n.* a leathery-leaved parasitic plant that grows on apple, oak, and other broadleaf trees and bears white glutinous berries in winter. • Several species in the family Viscaceae, in particular the Eurasian *Viscum album*, and in the family Loranthaceae, in particular the American *Phoradendron serotinum.* ▷Old English *misteltān*, from *mistel* 'mistletoe' (of Germanic origin, related to Dutch *mistel* and German *Mistel*) + *tān* 'twig.'

American mistletoe

mis·took /məˈsto͝ok/ ▸ past of MISTAKE.

mis·tral /ˈmistrəl; miˈsträl/ ▸*n.* a strong, cold northwesterly wind that blows through the Rhône valley and southern France into the Mediterranean, mainly in winter. ▷early 17th cent.: French, from Provençal, from Latin *magistralis (ventus)*, literally 'master wind.'

mis·trans·late /ˌmisˌtranzˈlāt; -ˌtransˈlāt/ ▸*v.* [*trans.*] translate (something) incorrectly. —**mis·trans·la·tion** /-ˈlāsHən/ *n.*

mis·treat /misˈtrēt/ ▸*v.* [*trans.*] treat (a person or animal) badly, cruelly, or unfairly. —**mis·treat·ment** *n.*

mis·tress /ˈmistris/ ▶*n.* **1** a woman in a position of authority or control: *she is always* ***mistress of*** *the situation, coolly self-possessed.* ■ a woman who is skilled in a particular subject or activity: *a* ***mistress of*** *the sound bite, she is famed for the acidity of her tongue.* ■ the female owner of a dog, cat, or other domesticated animal. ■ [with *adj.*] *chiefly Brit.* a female schoolteacher who teaches a particular subject: *a Geography mistress.* ■ *archaic* a female head of a household: *he asked for the mistress of the house.* ■ (esp. formerly) a female employer of domestic staff. **2** a woman having an extramarital sexual relationship, esp. with a married man: *Elsie knew her husband had a mistress tucked away somewhere.* ■ *archaic* or *poetic/literary* a woman loved and courted by a man. **3** (**Mistress**) *archaic* or *dialect* used as a title prefixed to the name of a married woman; Mrs. ▷Middle English: from Old French *maistresse*, from *maistre* 'master.'

mis·tri·al /ˈmisˌtrī(ə)l/ ▶*n.* a trial rendered invalid through an error in the proceedings. ■ an inconclusive trial, such as one in which the jury cannot agree on a verdict.

mis·trust /misˈtrəst/ ▶*v.* [*trans.*] be suspicious of; have no confidence in: *she had no cause to mistrust him.*
▶*n.* lack of trust: suspicion: *the public mistrust of government.*

mis·trust·ful /ˌmisˈtrəstfəl/ ▶*adj.* lacking in trust; suspicious: *he wondered if he had been unduly* ***mistrustful of*** *her.* —**mis·trust·ful·ly** *adv.* —**mis·trust·ful·ness** *n.*

mist·y /ˈmistē/ ▶*adj.* (**mist·i·er**, **mist·i·est**) full of, covered with, or accompanied by mist: *the evening was cold and misty | the misty air above the frozen river.* ■ (of a person's eyes) full of tears so as to blur the vision. ■ indistinct or dim in outline: *a misty out-of-focus silhouette | figurative a few misty memories.* ■ (of a color) not bright; soft: *a misty pink.* ▷Old English *mistig* (see MIST). —**mist·i·ly** /ˈmistəlē/ *adv.* —**mist·i·ness** *n.*

mis·type /misˈtīp/ ▶*v.* [*trans.*] **1** make a mistake in typing (a word or letter). **2** assign (someone or something) to an incorrect category: *I mistyped you—I didn't think you looked the hunting type.*

mis·un·der·stand /ˌmisˌəndərˈstand/ ▶*v.* (*past* and *past part.* **-stood**) [*trans.*] fail to interpret or understand (something) correctly: *he had misunderstood the policeman's hand signals | [intrans.] I must have misunderstood—I thought you were anxious to leave.* ■ fail to interpret or understand the words or actions of (someone) correctly: *don't misunderstand me—I'm not implying she should be working |* [as *adj.*] (**misunderstood**) *he is one of football's most misunderstood men.*

mis·un·der·stand·ing /ˌmisˌəndərˈstandiNG/ ▶*n.* a failure to understand something correctly: *a misunderstanding of the facts and the law | there must have been some kind of misunderstanding.* ■ a disagreement or quarrel: *he left the army after a slight misunderstanding with his commanding officer.*

mis·us·age /misˈyo͞osij/ ▶*n.* *archaic* unjust treatment: *they were determined to defend themselves from misusage.*

mis·use ▶*v.* /misˈyo͞oz; ˈmisˌyo͞oz/ [*trans.*] use (something) in the wrong way or for the wrong purpose: *he was found guilty of misusing public funds.* ■ treat (someone or something) badly or unfairly.
▶*n.* /ˌmisˈyo͞os; ˈmisˌyo͞os/ the wrong or improper use of something: *drugs of such potency that their misuse can have dire consequences | a misuse of power.* —**mis·us·er** /-ˈyo͞ozər/ *n.*

MIT ▶*abbr.* Massachusetts Institute of Technology.

Mi·tan·ni /məˈtanē/ an ancient kingdom which flourished in northern Mesopotamia in the 15th–14th centuries BC. —**Mi·tan·ni·an** /məˈtanēən/ *adj.* & *n.*

Mitch·ell[1] /ˈmicHəl/, Billy (1879–1936), U.S. army officer; full name *William Mitchell*; born in France. An outspoken advocate of air power, he was court-martialed in 1925 for his criticism of the war and navy departments. As a civilian, he continued to preach the importance of air power in warfare.

Mitch·ell[2], John (Newton) (1913–88), U.S. lawyer. He served as U.S. attorney general 1969–72 under President Nixon and was convicted in 1975 of conspiracy in the Watergate break-in and cover–up.

Mitch·ell[3], Joni (1943–), Canadian singer and songwriter; born *Roberta Joan Anderson*. She started to record in 1968 and gradually moved from folk to a fusion of folk, jazz, and rock. Notable albums: *Blue* (1971), *Hejira* (1976), and *Dog Eat Dog* (1986).

Mitch·ell[4], Margaret (1900–49), U.S. novelist. she wrote the best-selling and Pulitzer Prize–winning novel *Gone with the Wind* (1936; movie, 1939), set during the U.S. Civil War.

Mitch·ell[5], Maria (1818–89), U.S. astronomer. She established the orbit of a newly discovered comet in 1847 and became the first woman elected 1848 to the American Academy of Arts and Sciences. She taught astronomy at Vassar College 1865–88.

Mitch·um /ˈmicHəm/, Robert (1917–97), U.S. actor. He was a professional boxer before rising to stardom in movies such as *Out of the Past* (1947), *Night of the Hunter* (1955), *The Sundowners* (1960), and *Farewell My Lovely* (1975).

mite[1] /mīt/ ▶*n.* a minute arachnid that has four pairs of legs when adult, related to the ticks. Many kinds live in the soil and a number are parasitic on plants or animals. • Order (or subclass) Acari: numerous families. ▷Old English *mīte*, of Germanic origin.

mite[2] ▶*n.* **1** a small child or animal, esp. when regarded as an object of sympathy: *the* ***poor little mite*** *looks half-starved.* **2** a very small amount: *his teacher thought he needed* ***a mite of*** *discipline.* ■ *historical* a small coin, in particular a small Flemish copper coin of very low face value. See also WIDOW'S MITE.
▶*adv.* (**a mite**) *informal* a little; slightly: *all evening he's seemed a mite awkward.* ▷late Middle English (denoting a small Flemish copper coin): from Middle Dutch *mīte*; probably from the same Germanic word as MITE[1].

miter 1

mi·ter /ˈmītər/ (*Brit.* **mi·tre**) ▶*n.* **1** a tall headdress worn by bishops and senior abbots as a symbol of office, tapering to a point at front and back with a deep cleft between. ■ *historical* a headdress worn by a Jewish high priest. ■ *historical* a headband worn by women in ancient Greece. **2** (also **miter joint**) a joint made between two pieces of wood or other material at an angle of 90°, such that the line of junction bisects this angle. ■ a diagonal seam of two pieces of fabric that meet at a corner joining. **3** (also **miter shell**) a mollusk of warm seas that has a sharply pointed shell with a narrow aperture, supposedly resembling a bishop's miter. • Family Mitridae, class Gastropoda: *Mitra* and other genera.
▶*v.* [*trans.*] join by means of a miter. ▷late Middle English: from Old French, via Latin from Greek *mitra* 'belt or turban.'

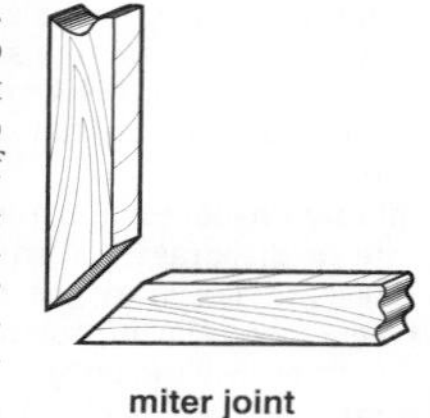
miter joint

mi·ter box ▶*n.* a guide to enable a saw to cut miter joints at the desired angle.

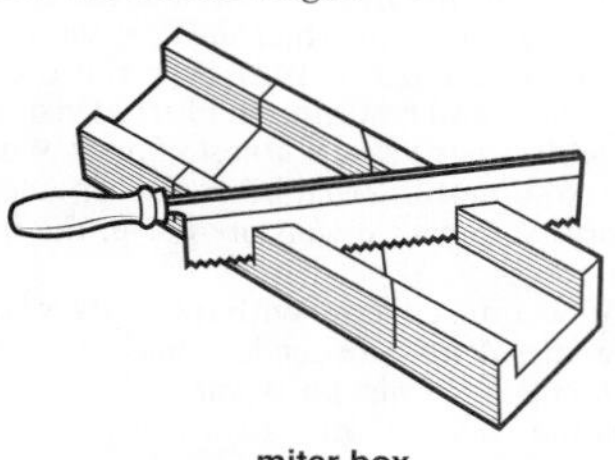
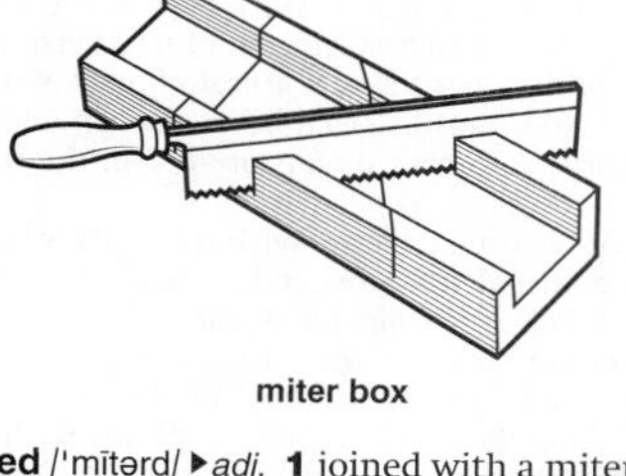
miter box

mi·tered /ˈmītərd/ ▶*adj.* **1** joined with a miter joint or seam: *complete the sides with mitered corners.* **2** bearing, wearing, or entitled to wear a miter: *the mitered bishop.*

Mit·ford /ˈmitfərd/, Nancy (Freeman) (1904–73) and her sister Jessica (Lucy) (1917–96), English writers. Nancy wrote comic novels, including *Love in a Cold Climate* (1949). Jessica became a U.S. citizen in 1944 and is best known for her works on American culture, notably *The American Way of Death* (1963).

Mith·ra·ism /ˈmiTHrəˌizəm/ ▶*n.* the cult of the god Mithras, which became popular among Roman soldiers of the later empire, and was the main rival to Christianity in the first three centuries AD. —**Mith·ra·ic** /miˈTHrā-ik/ *adj.* —**Mith·ra·ist** /miˈTHrā-ist/ *n.*

Mith·ras /ˈmiTHˌräs/ *Mythology* a god of light, truth, and honor, the central figure of the cult of Mithraism but probably of Persian origin. He was also associated with merchants and the protection of warriors.

Mith·ri·da·tes VI /ˌmiTHrəˈdātēz/ (also **Mith·ra·da·tes VI**) (*c.*132–63 BC), king of Pontus 120–163; known as **Mithridates the Great**. His expansionist policies led to three wars with Rome (88–85, 83–82, and 74–66). He was finally defeated by Pompey.

mith·ri·da·tize /ˌmiTHrəˈdātīz/ ▶*v.* [*trans.*] *rare* render immune against a poison by administering gradually increasing doses of the poison. ▷mid 19th cent.: from the name of *Mithridates* (see MITHRIDATES VI), who reputedly made himself immune to poisons by constantly taking antidotes, + -IZE.

mit·i·gate /ˈmitəˌgāt/ ▶*v.* [*trans.*] make less severe, serious, or painful: *he wanted to mitigate misery in the world.* See note at ALLEVIATE. ■ lessen the gravity of (an offense or mistake): [as *adj.*] (**mitigating**) *he would have faced a prison sentence but for* ***mitigating circumstances.*** ▷late Middle English: from Latin *mitigat-* 'softened, alleviated,' from the verb *mitigare*, from *mitis* 'mild.' —**mit·i·ga·ble** /-gibəl/ *adj.* —**mit·i·ga·tor** /-ˌgātər/ *n.* —**mit·i·ga·to·ry** /-gəˌtôrē/ *adj.*

USAGE The verbs **mitigate** and **militate** have a similarity in form but are quite different in meaning. **Mitigate** means 'make (something bad) less severe,' (*he wanted to* ***mitigate*** *misery in the world*), while **militate** is nearly always used in constructions with *against* to mean 'be a powerful factor in preventing' (*laws that* ***militate against*** *personal freedoms*).

mit·i·ga·tion /ˌmitəˈgāsHən/ ▶*n.* the action of reducing the severity, seriousness, or painfulness of something: *the emphasis is on the identification and mitigation of pollution.* ▷late Middle English: from Old French, or from Latin *mitigatio(n-)*, from the verb *mitigare* 'alleviate' (see MITIGATE).
▶*PHRASE* □ **in mitigation** so as to make something, esp. a crime, appear less serious and thus be punished more leniently: *in mitigation she said her client had been deeply depressed.*

mi·to·chon·dri·on /ˌmītəˈkändrēən/ ▶*n.* (*pl.* **-dri·a** /-drēə/) *Biology* an organelle found in large numbers in most cells, in which the biochemical processes of respiration and energy production occur. It has a double membrane, the inner layer being folded inward to form layers (cristae). ▷early 20th cent.: modern Latin, from Greek *mitos* 'thread' + *khondrion* (diminutive of *khondros* 'granule'). —**mi·to·chon·dri·al** /-drēəl/ *adj.*

mi·to·gen /ˈmītəjən/ ▶*n.* *Physiology* a substance that induces or stimulates mitosis. ▷1960s: from MITOSIS + -GEN. —**mi·to·gen·ic** /ˌmītəˈjenik/ *adj.*

mi·to·sis /mīˈtōsəs/ ▶*n.* (*pl.* **-ses** /-sēz/) *Biology* a type of cell division that results in two daughter cells each having the same number and kind of chromosomes as the parent nucleus, typical of ordinary tissue growth. Compare with MEIOSIS. ▷late 19th cent.: modern Latin, from Greek *mitos* 'thread.' —**mi·tot·ic** /mīˈtätik/ *adj.*

mi·tral /ˈmītrəl/ ▶*adj.* denoting or relating to the mitral valve. ▷early 17th cent.: from modern Latin *mitralis*, from Latin *mitra* 'belt or turban.'

mi·tral valve ▶*n.* *Anatomy* the valve between the left atrium and the left ventricle of the heart, consisting of two tapered cusps.

mi·tre ▶*n.* & *v.* British spelling of MITER.

mitt /mit/ ▶*n.* (usu. **mitts**) a mitten: *oven mitts.* ■ *Baseball* a mittenlike glove, worn by the catcher and first baseman. ■ a glove leaving the fingers and thumbtip exposed. ■ *informal* a person's hand. ▷mid 18th cent.: abbreviation of MITTEN.
▶*PHRASE* □ **keep one's mitts off** *informal* keep one's hands away from; not touch: *keep your mitts off the fan control!*

Mit·tel·land Ca·nal /ˈmitlˌländ/ a canal in northwestern Germany, part of an inland waterway network linking the Rhine and Elbe rivers, which was constructed between 1905 and 1930.

mit·ten /ˈmitn/ ▶*n.* (usu. **mittens**) a glove with two sections, one for the thumb and the other for all four fingers. ■ (**mittens**) *informal* boxing gloves. ▷Middle English: from Old French *mitaine*, perhaps from *mite*, pet name for a cat (because mittens were often made of fur). —**mit·tened** *adj.*

Mit·ter·rand /ˈmitəränd(d); mētˈräN/, François (Maurice Marie) (1916–96), French statesman; president 1981–95. As president, he initially moved to raise basic wages, increase social benefits, nationalize key industries, and decentralize government. When the Socialist Party lost its majority vote in the 1986 general election and right-wing Jacques Chirac became the prime minister, there was a reversal of some policies.

Mit·ty /ˈmitē/ see WALTER MITTY.

mitz·vah /ˈmitsvə/ ▶*n.* (*pl.* **mitz·voth** /ˈmitsˌvōt; -ˌvōs/) *Judaism* a precept or commandment. ■ a good deed done from religious duty. ▷mid 17th cent.: from Hebrew *miṣwāh* 'commandment.'

mix /miks/ ▸*v.* [*trans.*] combine or put together to form one substance or mass: *peppercorns are sometimes* **mixed with** *other spices for a table condiment | these two chemicals, when* **mixed together**, *literally explode.* ■ [*intrans.*] [often with *negative*] (of different substances) be able to be combined in this way: *oil and water don't mix.* ■ make or prepare by combining various ingredients: *mixing concrete is hard physical work.* ■ (esp. in sound recording) combine (two or more signals or soundtracks) into one: *up to eight tracks can be mixed simultaneously.* ■ produce (a sound signal or recording) by combining a number of separate signals or recorded soundtracks: *it took two years to mix his album.* ■ juxtapose or put together to form a whole whose constituent parts are still distinct: *he continues to* **mix** *an offhand sense of humor with a sharp insight.* ■ [*intrans.*] (of a person) associate with others socially: *the people he* **mixed with** *were nothing to do with show business.* ■ (**mix it** or **mix it up**) *informal* be belligerent verbally or physically, esp. with one's fists.
▸*phrasal v.* □ **mix something up** spoil the order or arrangement of a collection of things: *disconnect all the cables, mix them up, then try to reconnect them.* **mix someone/something up** ■ confuse someone or something with another person or thing: *I'd got her* **mixed up with** *her sister.*
▸*n.* [usu. in *sing.*] two or more different qualities, things, or people placed, combined, or considered together: *the decor is a mix of antique and modern.* ■ a group of people of different types within a particular society or community: *the school has a good social mix.* ■ [often with *adj.*] a commercially prepared mixture of ingredients for making a particular type of food or a product such as concrete: *cake mixes have made cooking easier.* ■ the proportion of different people or other constituents that make up a mixture: *arriving at the correct mix of full-time to part-time staff | pants made from a cotton and polyester mix.* ■ [often with *adj.*] a version of a recording in which the component tracks are mixed in a different way from the original: *a dance mix version of "This Charming Man."* ■ an image or sound produced by the combination of two separate images or sounds. ▷late Middle English: back-formation from MIXED (taken as a past participle). —**mix·a·ble** *adj.*
▸*PHRASES* □ **be** (or **get**) **mixed up in** be (or become) involved in (something regarded as dubious or dishonest): *Steve was mixed up in an insurance swindle.* □ **be** (or **get**) **mixed up with** be (or become) associated with (someone unsuitable or unreliable). □ **mix and match** select and combine different but complementary items, such as clothing or pieces of equipment, to form a coordinated set: *mix and match this season's colors for a combination that says winter |* [as *adj.*] *a mix-and-match menu.* □ **mix one's drinks** drink different kinds of alcohol in close succession.

Mix·co /'mēshkō/ a city in south central Guatemala, west of Guatemala City; pop. 413,000.

mixed /mikst/ ▸*adj.* consisting of different qualities or elements: *a varied, mixed diet | beaches with mixed sand and shingle.* ■ (of an assessment of, reaction to, or feeling about something) containing a mixture of both favorable and negative elements: *the movie opened last Friday to mixed reviews | I had* **mixed feelings** *about seeing Laura again.* ■ composed of different varieties of the same thing: *crab on a bed of mixed greens.* ■ involving or showing a mixture of races or social classes: *people of mixed race.* ■ (esp. of an educational establishment or a sports team or competition) of or for members of both sexes: *the college's mixed hockey team.* ▷late Middle English *mixt*: from Old French *mixte*, from Latin *mixtus*, past participle of *miscere* 'to mix.'

mixed bag ▸*n.* [in *sing.*] a diverse assortment of things or people: *a mixed bag of applause and catcalls.*

mixed bless·ing ▸*n.* a situation or thing that has disadvantages as well as advantages: *having children so early in their marriage was a mixed blessing.*

mixed com·pa·ny ▸*n.* a group of people consisting of members of both sexes: *such questions were not asked in mixed company.*

mixed dou·bles ▸*plural n.* [treated as *sing.*] (esp. in tennis and badminton) a game or competition involving teams, each consisting of a man and a woman.

mixed drink ▸*n.* an alcoholic drink consisting of liquor combined with fruit juice or other ingredients, usually shaken or stirred before serving.

mixed e·con·o·my ▸*n.* an economic system combining private and public enterprise.

mixed grill ▸*n.* a dish consisting of various items of grilled food, typically meats, tomatoes, and mushrooms.

mixed mar·riage ▸*n.* a marriage between people of different races or religions.

mixed me·di·a ▸*n.* the use of a variety of media in an entertainment or work of art.
▸*adj.* (**mixed-me·di·a**) another term for MULTIMEDIA.

mixed met·a·phor ▸*n.* a combination of two or more incompatible metaphors, which produces a ridiculous effect (e.g., *this tower of strength will forge ahead*).

mixed num·ber ▸*n.* a number consisting of an integer and a proper fraction.

mixed-up ▸*adj. informal* (of a person) suffering from psychological or emotional problems: *a lonely, mixed-up teenager.*

mix·er /'miksər/ ▸*n.* **1** [often with *adj.*] a machine or device for mixing things. esp. an electrical appliance for mixing foods: *a food mixer.* **2** [with *adj.*] a person considered in terms of their ability to mix socially with others: *media people need to be good mixers.* **3** a social gathering where people can make new acquaintances. **4** a soft drink that can be mixed with alcohol. **5** (in sound recording and cinematography) a device for merging input signals to produce a combined output in the form of sound or pictures. ■ [often with *adj.*] a person who operates such a device: *a sound mixer.*

Mix·mas·ter /'miks,mastər/ ▸*n. trademark* a type of electric food processor: *figurative he put together proposals, ideas, and advice in a kind of cerebral Mixmaster.* ■ (also **mixmaster**) *informal* a sound-recording engineer or disc jockey who is an accomplished mixer of music.

mix·ol·o·gist /mik'säləjist/ ▸*n. informal* a person who is skilled at mixing cocktails and other drinks. —**mix·ol·o·gy** /-əjē/ *n.*

Mix·o·lyd·i·an mode /,miksə'lidēən/ ▸*n. Music* the mode represented by the natural diatonic scale G–G (containing a minor 7th). ▷late 16th cent.: *Mixolydian* from Greek *mixo-ludios* 'half-Lydian' + -AN.

mixt /mikst/ ▸*v. archaic* past and past participle of MIX.

Mix·tec /'mēstek/ ▸*n.* (*pl.* same or **-tecs**) **1** a member of an American Indian people of southern Mexico, noted for their skill in pottery and metallurgy. **2** the Otomanguean language of this people.
▸*adj.* of or relating to the Mixtec or their language. ▷Spanish, from Nahuatl *mixtecah* 'person from a cloudy place.'

mix·ture /'mikschər/ ▸*n.* a substance made by mixing other substances together: *form the mixture into a manageable dough | shandy is* **a mixture of** *beer and lemonade.* ■ the process of mixing or being mixed. ■ (**a mixture of**) a combination of different qualities, things, or emotions in which the component elements are individually distinct: *she thumped the pillow with a mixture of anger and frustration | the old town is a mixture of narrow medieval streets and 18th-century architecture.* ■ a person regarded as a combination of qualities and attributes: *he was a curious mixture, an unpredictable man.* ■ *Chemistry* the product of the random distribution of one substance through another without any chemical reaction, as distinct from a compound. ■ the charge of gas or vapor mixed with air that is admitted to the cylinder of an internal combustion engine, esp. as regards the ratio of fuel to air: *newer pilots often leave their mixture rich during an entire flight.* ■ (also **mixture stop**) an organ stop in which each key sounds a group of small pipes of different pitches, giving a very bright tone. ▷late Middle English: from French *mixture* or Latin *mixtura* (see MIXED).

mix-up (also **mixup**) ▸*n. informal* a confusion of one thing with another, or a misunderstanding or mistake that results in confusion: *there's been a mix-up over the tickets.* ■ a combination of different things, esp. one whose effect is inharmonious: *a ghastly mix-up of furniture styles.*

Mi·zo /'mēzō/ ▸*n.* (*pl.* same or **-zos**) **1** a member of a people inhabiting Mizoram. **2** the Tibeto-Burman language of this people. Also called LUSHAI.
▸*adj.* of or relating to this people or their language. ▷the name in Mizo, literally 'highlander,' from *mi* 'person' + *zo* 'hill.'

Mi·zo·ram /mə'zôrəm/ a state in northeastern India that lies between Bangladesh and Myanmar (Burma); capital, Aizawl. Separated from Assam in 1972, it was administered as a Union Territory in India until 1986, when it became a state.

mi·zu·na /mə'zōōnə/ (also **mizuna greens**) ▸*n.* an oriental rape of a variety with finely cut leaves that are eaten as a salad vegetable. • *Brassica rapa* var. *nipposinica*, family Brassicaceae. ▷1990s: from Japanese.

miz·zen /'mizən/ (also **miz·en**) ▸*n.* **1** (also **miz·zen·mast**) the mast aft of a ship's mainmast. **2** (also **miz·zen·sail**) the lowest sail on a mizzenmast. ▷late Middle English: from Italian *mezzana* 'mizzensail,' feminine (used as a noun) of *mezzano* 'middle,' from Latin *medianus* (see MEDIAN).

miz·zle /'mizəl/ *chiefly dialect* ▸*n.* light rain; drizzle.
▸*v.* [*intrans.*] (**it mizzles, it is mizzling**, etc.) rain lightly: *it was mizzling steadily.* ▷late Middle English (as a verb): probably a frequentative from the base of MIST; compare with Low German *miseln* and Dutch dialect *miezelen.* —**miz·zly** /'mizlē/ *adj.*

Mk ▸*abbr.* ■ the German mark. ■ the Gospel of Mark (in biblical references). ■ (followed by a numeral) Mark, used to denote a design or model of car, aircraft, or other machine: *a VW Golf Mk III.*

mk. ▸*abbr.* ■ (*pl.* **mks.**) MARK[2] (sense 1). ■ markka.

mks ▸*abbr.* meter-kilogram-second.

mksA (also **MKSA** or **mksa**) ▸*abbr.* meter-kilogram-second-ampere.

mkt. ▸*abbr.* market.

mktg. ▸*abbr.* marketing.

ml ▸*abbr.* ■ mile(s). ■ milliliter(s).

MLA ▸*abbr.* ■ Member of the Legislative Assembly. ■ Modern Language Association (of America).

MLB ▸*abbr.* major league baseball.

MLC ▸*abbr.* Member of the Legislative Council.

MLD ▸*abbr.* ■ minimum lethal dose. ■ moderate learning difficulties: [as *adj.*] *a school for MLD pupils.*

MLF ▸*abbr.* multilateral nuclear force.

MLitt ▸*abbr.* Master of Letters: *Susan Williams, MLitt.* ▷from Latin *Magister Litterarum.*

Mlle (*pl.* **Mlles**) ▸*abbr.* Mademoiselle.

MLR ▸*abbr. Finance* minimum lending rate, influenced by the overnight rate established by the Federal Reserve.

MLS ▸*abbr.* ■ Master of Library Science. ■ Multiple Listing Service, an organization that holds computerized listings of U.S. real estate offered for sale. ■ Major League Soccer.

MLW ▸*abbr.* (of the tide) mean low water.

MM ▸*abbr.* Messieurs.

mm ▸*abbr.* millimeter(s).

Mme (*pl.* **Mmes**) ▸*abbr.* Madame.

m.m.f. ▸*abbr.* magnetomotive force.

MMPI ▸*abbr.* Minnesota Multiphasic Personality Inventory.

MMR ▸*abbr.* measles, mumps, and rubella, a vaccination given to small children.

MMus ▸*abbr.* Master of Music.

MN ▸*abbr.* ■ Minnesota (in official postal use).

Mn ▸*symbol* the chemical element manganese.

MNA ▸*abbr.* (in Canada) Member of the National Assembly (of Quebec).

mne·mon·ic /nə'mänik/ ▸*n.* a device such as a pattern of letters, ideas, or associations that assists in remembering something.
▸*adj.* aiding or designed to aid the memory. ■ of or relating to the power of memory. ▷mid 18th cent. (as an adjective): via medieval Latin from Greek *mnēmonikos*, from *mnēmōn* 'mindful.' —**mne·mon·i·cal·ly** /-ik(ə)lē/ *adv.*

mne·mon·ics /nə'mäniks/ ▸*plural n.* [usu. treated as *sing.*] the study and development of systems for improving and assisting the memory.

Mne·mos·y·ne /nə'mäsənē; -'mäz-/ *Greek Mythology* the Greek goddess of memory, and the mother of the Muses by Zeus. ▷from Greek *mnēmosunē*, literally 'memory.'

mngr. ▸*abbr.* manager.

MO ▸*abbr.* ■ *Computing* (of a disk or disk drive) magneto-optical. ■ Medical Officer. ■ Missouri (in official postal use). ■ modus operandi. ■ money order.

Mo ▸*symbol* the chemical element molybdenum.

mo /mō/ ▸*n.* [in *sing.*] *informal, chiefly Brit.* a short period of time: *hang on a mo!* ▷late 19th cent.: abbreviation of MOMENT.

mo. ▸*abbr.* month.

-mo ▸*suffix* forming nouns denoting a book size by the number of leaves into which a sheet of paper has been folded: *twelvemo.* ▷from the final syllable

of Latin ordinal numbers such as *duodecimo* (masculine ablative singular).

mo·a /ˈmōə/ ▸*n.* a large, extinct, flightless bird resembling the emu, formerly found in New Zealand. • Family Dinornithidae: several genera and species; *Dinornis maximus* was the tallest known bird, with a height of about 10 feet (3 m), but *Megalapteryx didinus*, which may have survived until the early 19th century, was much smaller. ▷mid 19th cent.: from Maori.

Mo·ab /ˈmō,ab/ the ancient kingdom of the Moabites, east of the Dead Sea.

Mo·ab·ite /ˈmōə,bīt/ ▸*n.* a member of a Semitic people living in Moab in biblical times, traditionally descended from Lot.
▸*adj.* of or relating to Moab or its people.

moan /mōn/ ▸*n.* a long, low sound made by a person expressing physical or mental suffering or sexual pleasure: *she gave a low moan of despair.* ■ a sound resembling this, esp. one made by the wind: *the moan of the wind in the chimneys.* ■ *informal* a complaint that is perceived as trivial and not taken seriously by others: *there were moans about the car's feeble ventilation.*
▸*v.* [*intrans.*] make a long, low sound expressing physical or mental suffering or sexual pleasure: *just then their patient moaned and opened his eyes* | [with *direct speech*] *"Oh God," I moaned.* ■ (of a thing) make a sound resembling this: *the foghorn moaned at intervals.* ■ [*reporting verb*] *informal* complain or grumble, typically about something trivial: [*intrans.*] *he joked and moaned about members of his family* | [with *clause*] *my husband moans that I'm not as slim as when we first met.* ■ *poetic/literary* lament. ▷Middle English (in the sense 'complaint or lamentation'): of unknown origin. **—moan·er** *n.* **—moan·ful** /-fəl/ *adj.*

moat /mōt/ ▸*n.* a deep, wide ditch surrounding a castle, fort, or town, typically filled with water and intended as a defense against attack.
▸*v.* [*trans.*] [often as *adj.*] (**moated**) surround (a place) with a moat: *a moated castle.* ▷late Middle English: from Old French *mote* 'mound.'

mob /mäb/ ▸*n.* a large crowd of people, esp. one that is disorderly and intent on causing trouble or violence: *a mob of protesters.* ■ (usu. **the Mob**) the Mafia or a similar criminal organization. ■ (**the mob**) the ordinary people: *the age-old fear that the mob may organize to destroy the last vestiges of civilized life.*
▸*v.* (**mobbed**, **mob·bing**) [*trans.*] (often **be mobbed**) crowd around (someone) in an unruly and excitable way in order to admire or attack them: *he was mobbed by autograph hunters.* ■ (of a group of birds or mammals) surround and attack (a predator or other source of threat) in order to drive it off. ■ crowd into (a building or place): *an unruly crowd mobbed the White House during an inaugural reception.* ▷late 17th cent.: abbreviation of archaic *mobile*, short for Latin *mobile vulgus* 'excitable crowd.' **—mob·ber** *n.*

mob·cap /ˈmäb,kap/ ▸*n.* a large soft hat covering all of the hair and typically having a decorative frill, worn indoors by women in the 18th and early 19th centuries. ▷mid 18th cent.: *mob*, variant of obsolete *mab* 'slut.' The word *mob* was first used in the sense 'prostitute' (mid to late 17th cent.), later denoting a negligee (mid 17th cent. to mid 18th cent.).

Mo·bile /mōˈbēl; ˈmō,bēl/ an industrial city and port on the coast of southern Alabama; pop. 198,915. It is situated at the head of Mobile Bay, an inlet of the Gulf of Mexico.

mo·bile ▸*adj.* /ˈmōbəl; -,bēl; -,bīl/ able to move or be moved freely or easily: *he has a major weight problem and is not very mobile* | *highly mobile international capital.* ■ (of the face or its features) indicating feelings with fluid and expressive movements: *her mobile features working overtime to register shock and disapproval.* ■ (of a store, library, or other service) accommodated in a vehicle so as to travel around and serve various places. ■ (of a military or police unit) equipped and prepared to move quickly to any place it is needed: *mobile army combat units.* ■ able or willing to move easily or freely between occupations, places of residence, or social classes: *an increasingly mobile and polarized society.*
▸*n.* /ˈmō,bēl/ a decorative structure that is suspended so as to turn freely in the air. ▷late 15th cent.: via French from Latin *mobilis*, from *movere* 'to move.' The noun dates from the 1940s.

mo·bile home ▸*n.* a large house trailer that is parked in one particular place and used as a permanent living accommodation.

mo·bile phone (also **mobile telephone**) ▸*n.* another term for CELLULAR PHONE.

mo·bile sculp·ture ▸*n.* a sculpture with moving parts.

mo·bil·i·ty /mōˈbilətē/ ▸*n.* the ability to move or be moved freely and easily: *this exercise helps retain mobility in the damaged joints.* ■ the ability to move between different levels in society or employment: *industrialization would open up increasing chances of social mobility.*

mo·bi·lize /ˈmōbə,līz/ ▸*v.* [*trans.*] **1** (of a country or its government) prepare and organize (troops) for active service: *the government mobilized regular forces, reservists, and militia* | [*intrans.*] *Russia is in no position to mobilize any time soon.* ■ organize and encourage (people) to act in a concerted way in order to bring about a particular political objective: *he used the press to mobilize support for his party.* ■ bring (resources) into use in order to achieve a particular goal: *at sea we will mobilize any amount of resources to undertake a rescue.* **2** make (something) movable or capable of movement: *doing yoga stretches to mobilize compacted joints.* ■ make (a substance) able to be transported by or as a liquid: *acid rain mobilizes the aluminum in forest soils.* ▷mid 19th cent.: from French *mobiliser*, from *mobile* (see MOBILE). **—mo·bi·liz·a·ble** *adj.* **—mo·bi·li·za·tion** /,mōbələˈzāshən/ *n.* **—mo·bi·liz·er** *n.*

Mö·bi·us strip /ˈmōbēəs/ ▸*n.* a surface with one continuous side formed by joining the ends of a rectangular strip after twisting one end through 180°. ▷early 20th cent.: named after August F. *Möbius* (1790–1868), German mathematician.

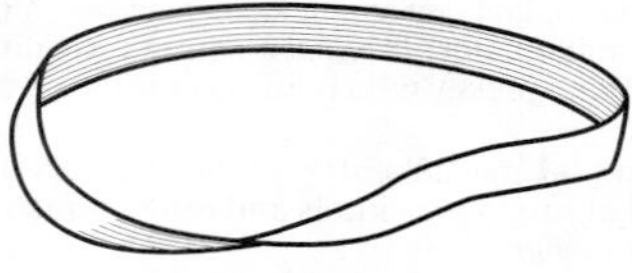
Möbius strip

mob·oc·ra·cy /mäbˈäkrəsē/ ▸*n.* (*pl.* **-cies**) rule or domination by the masses.

mob rule ▸*n.* control of a political situation by those outside the conventional or lawful realm, typically involving violence and intimidation.

mob·ster /ˈmäbstər/ ▸*n.* *informal* a member of a group of violent criminals; a gangster.

Mo·bu·tu /mōˈbōōtōō/, Sese Seko (1930–97), Zairean statesman; president 1965–97; born *Joseph-Désiré Mobutu*. Seizing power in a military coup in 1965, he retained control despite opposition until 1997, when he was finally forced to stand down.

Mobutu Se·se Se·ko, Lake Zairean name for Lake Albert (see ALBERT, LAKE).

moc /mäk/ ▸*n.* *informal* short for MOCCASIN.

mo·cap /ˈmō,kap/ ▸*n.* motion capture.

moc·ca·sin /ˈmäkəsən/ ▸*n.* **1** a soft leather slipper or shoe, strictly one without a separate heel, having the sole turned up on all sides and sewn to the upper in a simple gathered seam, in a style originating among North American Indians. **2** a venomous American pit viper. • Genus *Agkistrodon*, family Viperidae: several species, in particular the **water moccasin** (see COTTONMOUTH) and the **highland moccasin** (see COPPERHEAD.) ▷early 17th cent.: from Virginia Algonquian *mockasin*. The word is also found in other American Indian languages.

moc·ca·sin flow·er ▸*n.* another term for PINK LADY'S-SLIPPER (see LADY'S-SLIPPER).

moc·ca·sin tel·e·graph ▸*n.* Canadian term for BUSH TELEGRAPH.

mo·cha /ˈmōkə/ ▸*n.* **1** a fine-quality coffee. ■ a drink or flavoring made with or in imitation of this, typically with chocolate added. ■ a dark brown color. **2** a soft kind of leather made from sheepskin. ▷late 18th cent.: named after *Mocha*, a port on the Red Sea, from where the coffee and leather were first shipped.

mo·chac·ci·no /,mōkəˈchēnō/ ▸*n.* (*pl.* **-nos**) a cappuccino containing chocolate flavoring. ▷1990s: blend of *mocha* and *cappucino*.

Mo·che /ˈmōchā/ ▸*n.* *Archaeology* a pre-Inca culture that flourished on the coast of Peru in the 1st to 7th centuries AD. ▷from the name of an archaeological site on the northwest coast of Peru.

mo·chi /ˈmōchē/ ▸*n.* a short-grained, sweet, glutinous rice with a high starch content, used in Japanese cooking. ▷Japanese.

Mo·chi·ca /mōˈchēkə/ ▸*n.* (*pl.* same) **1** a member of the Moche people. **2** the language of this people.
▸*adj.* of or relating to this people or their language. ▷Spanish; compare with MOCHE.

mock /mäk/ ▸*v.* [*trans.*] tease or laugh at in a scornful or contemptuous manner: *he mocks them as Washington insiders* | [as *adj.*] (**mocking**) *the mocking hostility in his voice made her wince.* ■ make (something) seem laughably unreal or impossible: *at Christmas, arguments and friction mock our pretense of peace.* ■ mimic (someone or something) scornfully or contemptuously. See note at IMITATE.
▸*adj.* [*attrib.*] not authentic or real, but without the intention to deceive: *a mock-Georgian red brick house* | *Jim threw up his hands in mock horror.* ■ (of an examination, battle, etc.) arranged for training or practice, or performed as a demonstration: *Dukakis will have a mock debate with Barnett.*
▸*n.* *dated* an object of derision: *he has become the mock of all his contemporaries.* ▷late Middle English: from Old French *mocquer* 'deride.' **—mock·a·ble** *adj.* **—mock·er** *n.* **—mock·ing·ly** *adv.*

mock·er·y /ˈmäk(ə)rē/ ▸*n.* (*pl.* **-er·ies**) derision; ridicule: *stung by her mockery, Frankie hung his head.* ■ [in *sing.*] an absurd misrepresentation or imitation of something: *after **a mockery of** a trial in London, he was executed.* ■ *archaic* ludicrously futile action: *in her bitterness she felt that all rejoicing was mockery.* ▷late Middle English: from Old French *moquerie*, from *mocquer* 'to deride.'
▸*PHRASE* □ **make a mockery of** make (something) seem foolish or absurd: *the terrorists are making a mockery of security policy.*

mock-he·ro·ic ▸*adj.* (of a literary work or its style) imitating the style of heroic literature in order to satirize an unheroic subject.
▸*n.* (often as **mock heroics**) a burlesque imitation of the heroic character or literary style.

mock·ing·bird /ˈmäking,bərd/ ▸*n.* a long-tailed thrushlike songbird with grayish plumage, found mainly in tropical America and noted for its mimicry of the calls and songs of other birds. • Family Mimidae (the **mockingbird family**): three genera and several species, esp. the **northern mockingbird** (*Mimus polyglottos*) of North America. The mockingbird family also includes the catbirds, thrashers, and tremblers.

northern mockingbird

mock moon ▸*n.* informal term for PARASELENE.

mock or·ange ▸*n.* a bushy shrub of north temperate regions that is cultivated for its strongly scented white flowers whose perfume resembles orange blossom. • Genus *Philadelphus*, family Hydrangeaceae (formerly Philadelphaceae): several species and hybrids, in particular *P. coronarius*.

mock sun ▸*n.* informal term for PARHELION.

mock tur·tle·neck ▸*n.* a neck for a knit garment similar to a funnel neck but shorter and typically not as loose.

mock tur·tle soup ▸*n.* imitation turtle soup made from a calf's head.

mock·u·men·ta·ry (also **moc·u·men·ta·ry**) /,mäkyəˈment(ə)rē/ ▸*n.* (*pl.* **-ries**) a motion picture or television program that takes the form of a serious documentary in order to satirize its subject. ▷1960s: blend of *mock* and *(doc)umentary*. **—mock·u·men·tar·i·an** /,mäkyəmenˈte(ə)rēən/ *n.*

mock-up (also **mock·up**) ▸*n.* a model or replica of a machine or structure, used for instructional or experimental purposes. ■ an arrangement of text and pictures to be printed: *a mock-up of the following day's front page.*

mod[1] /mäd/ ▸*adj.* *informal* modern.
▸*n.* *Brit.* (esp. in the early 1960s) a young person of a subculture characterized by stylish dress, the riding of motor scooters, and a liking for soul music. ▷abbreviation of MODERN or MODERNIST.

mod[2] ▸*prep.* *Mathematics* another term for MODULO.

mod[3] *Computing* ▸*n.* (also **case mod**) a modification of a computer case, usually to add functions or accessories not intended or provided by the original manufacturer. ■ a modification of a computer by replacing the case with an unexpected type of container, often with windows to allow the electronic parts inside to be seen.
▸*v.* [*trans.*] modify a computer in this way. ▷from *modify*. **—mod·der** /ˈmädər/ *n.*

mod. ▸*abbr.* ■ moderate. ■ *Music* moderato. ■ modern.

mod·a·cryl·ic /,mädəˈkrilik/ ▸*adj.* of or denoting a synthetic textile fiber made from a polymer containing a high proportion of units derived from acrylonitrile.

▸*n.* a textile fiber of this kind. ▷1950s: from *modified* (past participle of **MODIFY**) + **ACRYLIC**.

mod·al /ˈmōdl/ ▸*adj.* **1** of or relating to mode or form as opposed to substance. **2** *Grammar* of or denoting the mood of a verb. ■ relating to a modal verb. **3** *Statistics* of or relating to a mode; occurring most frequently in a sample or population. **4** *Music* of or denoting music using melodies or harmonies based on modes other than the ordinary major and minor scales. **5** *Logic* (of a proposition) in which the predicate is affirmed of the subject with some qualification, or which involves the affirmation of possibility, impossibility, necessity, or contingency.

▸*n. Grammar* a modal word or construction. ▷mid 16th cent. (sense 5): from medieval Latin *modalis*, from Latin *modus* (see **MODE**). **—mod·al·ly** /ˈmōdl-ē/ *adv.*

mod·al·ism /ˈmodlˌizəm/ ▸*n.* **1** *Theology* the doctrine that the persons of the Trinity represent only three modes or aspects of the divine revelation, not distinct and coexisting persons in the divine nature. **2** *Music* the use of modal melodies and harmonies. **—mod·al·ist** *n.* & *adj.*

mo·dal·i·ty /mōˈdalitē/ ▸*n.* (*pl.* **-ties**) **1** modal quality: *the harmony had a touch of modality.* **2** a particular mode in which something exists or is experienced or expressed. ■ a particular method or procedure: *they addressed questions concerning the modalities of Soviet troop withdrawals.* ■ a particular form of sensory perception: *the visual and auditory modalities.* ■ (in medicine, particularly homeopathy) a symptom or pattern that aids in diagnosis: *The modality of "worse with activity" is associated with Rhus Tox.* ▷early 17th cent.: from medieval Latin *modalitas*, from *modalis* (see **MODAL**).

mod·al verb ▸*n. Grammar* an auxiliary verb that expresses necessity or possibility. English modal verbs include *must, shall, will, should, would, can, could, may,* and *might*. See also **AUXILIARY VERB**.

mode /mōd/ ▸*n.* **1** a way or manner in which something occurs or is experienced, expressed, or done: *his preferred mode of travel was a kayak | differences between language modes, namely speech and writing.* ■ an option allowing a change in the method of operation of a device, esp. a camera: *a camcorder* ***in automatic mode.*** ■ *Computing* a way of operating or using a system: *some computers provide several so-called processor modes.* ■ *Physics* any of the distinct kinds or patterns of vibration of an oscillating system. ■ *Logic* the character of a modal proposition (whether necessary, contingent, possible, or impossible). ■ *Logic & Grammar* another term for **MOOD**[2]. **2** a fashion or style in clothes, art, literature, etc.: *in the Seventies, the mode for activewear took hold.* **3** *Statistics* the value that occurs most frequently in a given set of data. **4** *Music* a set of musical notes forming a scale and from which melodies and harmonies are constructed.

The modes of plainsong and later Western music (including the usual major and minor scales) correspond to the diatonic scales played on the white notes of a piano. They are named arbitrarily after ancient Greek modes: Ionian (or major), Dorian, Phrygian, Lydian, Mixolydian, Aeolian, and Locrian.

5 (in full **mode beige**) a drab or light gray color. ▷late Middle English (in the musical and grammatical senses): from Latin *modus* 'measure,' from an Indo-European root shared by **METE**[1]; compare with **MOOD**[2].

mod·el /ˈmädl/ ▸*n.* **1** a three-dimensional representation of a person or thing or of a proposed structure, typically on a smaller scale than the original: *a model of St. Paul's Cathedral* | [as *adj.*] *a model airplane.* ■ (in sculpture) a figure or object made in clay or wax, to be reproduced in another more durable material. **2** a system or thing used as an example to follow or imitate: *the law became a model for dozens of laws banning nondegradable plastic products* | [as *adj.*] *a model farm.* ■ a simplified description, esp. a mathematical one, of a system or process, to assist calculations and predictions: *a statistical model used for predicting the survival rates of endangered species.* ■ (**model of**) a person or thing regarded as an excellent example of a specified quality: *as she grew older, she became a model of self-control* | [as *adj.*] *he was a model husband and father.* ■ (**model for**) an actual person or place on which a specified fictional character or location is based: *the author denied that Marilyn was the model for his tragic heroine.* **3** a person, typically a woman, employed to display clothes by wearing them: *a fashion model.* ■ a person employed to pose for an artist, photographer, or sculptor. **4** a particular design or version of a product: *trading your car in for a newer model.*

▸*v.* (**-eled, -el·ing**; *Brit.* **-elled, -el·ling**) [*trans.*] **1** fashion or shape (a three-dimensional figure or object) in a malleable material such as clay or wax: *use the icing to model a house.* ■ (in drawing or painting) represent so as to appear three-dimensional: *the body of the woman to the right is modeled in softer, riper forms.* ■ (**model something on/after**) use (esp. a system or procedure) as an example to follow or imitate: *the research method will be modeled on previous work.* ■ (**model oneself on**) take (someone admired or respected) as an example to copy: *he models himself on rock legend Elvis Presley.* ■ devise a representation, esp. a mathematical one, of (a phenomenon or system): *a computer program that can model how smoke behaves.* **2** display (clothes) by wearing them. ■ [*intrans.*] work as a model by displaying clothes or posing for an artist, photographer, or sculptor. ▷late 16th cent. (denoting a set of plans of a building): from French *modelle*, from Italian *modello*, from an alteration of Latin *modulus* (see **MODULUS**). **—mod·el·er** /ˈmädl-ər/ *n.*

THE RIGHT WORD **archetype, example, ideal, model, paradigm, pattern, prototype**

Most parents try to set a good **example** for their children, although they may end up setting a bad one. An *example*, in other words, is a precedent for imitation, either good or bad.

Most parents would do better to provide a **model** for their children, which refers to a person or thing that is to be followed or imitated because of its excellence in conduct or character. *Model* also connotes a physical shape to be copied closely (*a ship's model, a model airplane*).

Not all children regard their parents as an **ideal** to which they aspire, a word that suggests an imagined perfection or a standard based upon a set of desirable qualities (*the ideal gentleman; the ideal of what an artist should be*); but young people's lives often end up following the **pattern** established by their parents, meaning that their lives follow the same basic configuration or design.

While **prototype** and **archetype** are often used interchangeably, they really mean quite different things. An *archetype* is a perfect and unchanging form that existing things or people can approach but never duplicate (*the archetype of a mother*), while a *prototype* is an early, usually unrefined version of something that later versions reflect but may depart from (*a prototype for a hydrogen-fueled car*).

Paradigm can refer to an example that serves as a model, but today its use is primarily confined to a grammatical context, where it means a set giving all the various forms of a word, such as the conjugation of a verb.

mod·el home ▸*n.* a house in a newly built development that is furnished and decorated to be shown to prospective buyers.

mod·el·ing /ˈmädl-iNG/ (*Brit.* **mod·el·ling**) ▸*n.* **1** the work of a fashion model. **2** the art or activity of making three-dimensional models. ■ [often with *adj.*] the devising or use of abstract or mathematical models: *macroeconomic modeling and policy analysis.*

mo·dem /ˈmōdəm; ˈmōˌdem/ ▸*n.* a combined device for modulation and demodulation, for example, between the digital data of a computer and the analog signal of a telephone line.

▸*v.* [*trans.*] send (data) by modem. ▷mid 20th cent.: blend of *modulator* and *demodulator*.

Mo·de·na /ˈmôdnˌä; ˈmôdinə/ a city in northern Italy, northwest of Bologna; pop. 177,000.

mod·er·ate ▸*adj.* /ˈmäd(ə)rət/ average in amount, intensity, quality, or degree: *we walked at a moderate pace.* ■ (of a person, party, or policy); not radical or excessively right- or left-wing: *a moderate reform program.*

▸*n.* /ˈmäd(ə)rət/ a person who holds moderate views, esp. in politics.

▸*v.* /ˈmädəˌrāt/ **1** make or become less extreme, intense, rigorous, or violent: [*trans.*] *I shall not moderate my criticism* | [as *adj.*] (**moderating**) *his moderating influence in the army was now needed more than ever* | [*intrans.*] *the weather has moderated considerably.* **2** [*trans.*] (in academic and ecclesiastical contexts) preside over (a deliberative body) or at (a debate): *a panel moderated by a Harvard University law professor.* ■ [*intrans.*] preside; act as a moderator. **3** [*trans.*] *Physics* retard (neutrons) with a moderator. ▷late Middle English: from Latin *moderat-* 'reduced, controlled,' from the verb *moderare*; related to **MODEST**. **—mod·er·at·ism** /-ˌtizəm/ *n.*

mod·er·ate breeze ▸*n.* a wind of force 4 on the Beaufort scale (13–18 miles per hour, or 11–16 knots).

mod·er·ate gale ▸*n.* a wind of force 7 on the Beaufort scale (32–38 miles per hour, or 28–33 knots).

mod·er·ate·ly /ˈmäd(ə)rətlē/ ▸*adv.* [as *submodifier*] to a certain extent; quite; fairly: *these events were moderately successful | he answered all the questions moderately well.* ■ in a moderate manner: *growth continues moderately.* ■ within reasonable limits: *both hotels are moderately priced.*

mod·er·a·tion /ˌmädəˈrāSHən/ ▸*n.* **1** the avoidance of excess or extremes, esp. in one's behavior or political opinions: *he urged the police to show moderation.* See note at **ABSTINENCE**. ■ the action of making something less extreme, intense, or violent: *the union's approach was based on increased dialogue and* ***the moderation of*** *demands.* **2** *Physics* the retardation of neutrons by a moderator. ▷late Middle English: via Old French from Latin *moderatio(n-)*, from the verb *moderare* 'to control' (see **MODERATE**).

▸***PHRASE*** □ **in moderation** within reasonable limits; not to excess: *nuts can be eaten in moderation.*

mod·e·ra·to /ˌmädəˈrätō/ *Music* ▸*adv.* & *adj.* (esp. as a direction after a tempo marking) at a moderate pace: *allegro moderato.*

▸*n.* (*pl.* **-tos**) a passage marked to be performed in such a way. ▷Italian, literally 'moderate.'

mod·er·a·tor /ˈmädəˌrātər/ ▸*n.* **1** an arbitrator or mediator: *Egypt managed to assert its role as a regional moderator.* ■ a presiding officer, esp. a chairman of a debate. ■ a Presbyterian minister presiding over an ecclesiastical body. **2** *Physics* a substance used in a nuclear reactor to retard neutrons. **—mod·er·a·tor·ship** /-ˌSHip/ *n.*

mod·ern /ˈmädərn/ ▸*adj.* of or relating to the present or recent times as opposed to the remote past: *the pace of modern life | modern Chinese history.* ■ characterized by or using the most up-to-date techniques, ideas, or equipment: *they do not have modern weapons.* ■ [*attrib.*] denoting the form of a language that is currently used, as opposed to any earlier form: *modern German.* ■ [*attrib.*] denoting a current or recent style or trend in art, architecture, or other cultural activity marked by a significant departure from traditional styles and values: *Matisse's contribution to modern art.*

▸*n.* (usu. **moderns**) a person who advocates or practices a departure from traditional styles or values. ▷late Middle English: from late Latin *modernus*, from Latin *modo* 'just now.' **—mo·der·ni·ty** /məˈdərnitē; mə-; -ˈder-/ *n.* **—mod·ern·ly** *adv.* **—mod·ern·ness** *n.*

mod·ern dance ▸*n.* a free, expressive style of dancing started in the early 20th century as a reaction to classical ballet. In recent years it has included elements not usually associated with dance, such as speech and film.

mo·derne /mäˈdern; mə-/ ▸*adj.* of or relating to a popularization of the art deco style marked by bright colors and geometric shapes. ■ *often derogatory* denoting an ultramodern style. ▷mid 20th cent.: French, 'modern.'

mod·ern Eng·lish ▸*n.* the English language as it has been since about 1500.

Mod·ern Greats ▸*plural n.* (at Oxford University) the school of philosophy, politics, and economics.

mod·ern his·to·ry ▸*n.* history up to the present day, from some arbitrary point taken to represent the end of the Middle Ages. In some contexts it may be contrasted with "ancient" rather than "medieval" history, and start, e.g., from the fall of the Western Roman Empire.

mod·ern·ism /ˈmädərˌnizəm/ ▸*n.* modern character or quality of thought, expression, or technique: *when he waxes philosophical, he comes across as a strange mix of nostalgia and modernism.* ■ a style or movement in the arts that aims to break with classical and traditional forms. ■ a movement toward modifying traditional beliefs in accordance with modern ideas, esp. in the Roman Catholic Church in the late 19th and early 20th centuries.

mod·ern·ist /ˈmädərnist/ ▸*n.* a believer in or supporter of modernism, esp. in the arts.

▸*adj.* of or associated with modernism, esp. in the arts. **—mod·ern·is·tic** /ˌmädərˈnistik/ *adj.*

mod·ern·ize /ˈmädərˌnīz/ ▶*v.* [*trans.*] adapt (something) to modern needs or habits, typically by installing modern equipment or adopting modern ideas or methods: *a five-year plan to modernize Algerian agriculture.* —**mod·ern·i·za·tion** /ˌmädərnəˈzāsʜən/ *n.* —**mod·ern·iz·er** *n.*

mod·ern jazz ▶*n.* jazz as developed in the 1940s and 1950s, esp. bebop and the related music that followed it.

mod·ern lan·guages ▶*plural n.* European languages (esp. French and German) as a subject of study, as contrasted with classical Latin and Greek.

mod·ern Lat·in ▶*n.* Latin as developed since 1500, used esp. in scientific terminology.

mod·ern pen·tath·lon ▶*n.* see **PENTATHLON**.

mod·est /ˈmädəst/ ▶*adj.* **1** unassuming or moderate in the estimation of one's abilities or achievements: *he was a very modest man, refusing to take any credit for the enterprise.* **2** (of an amount, rate, or level of something) relatively moderate, limited, or small: *drink modest amounts of alcohol | employment growth was relatively modest.* ■ (of a place in which one lives, eats, or stays) not excessively large, elaborate, or expensive: *we had bought a modest house.* **3** (of a woman) dressing or behaving so as to avoid impropriety or indecency, esp. to avoid attracting sexual attention. ■ (of clothing) not revealing or emphasizing the figure: *modest dress means that hemlines must be below the knee.* ▷mid 16th cent.: from French *modeste*, from Latin *modestus* 'keeping due measure,' related to *modus* 'measure.' —**mod·est·ly** *adv.*

Mo·des·to /məˈdestō/ a city in north central California, in the San Joaquin Valley; pop. 164,730.

mod·es·ty /ˈmädəstē/ ▶*n.* the quality or state of being unassuming or moderate in the estimation of one's abilities: *with typical modesty he insisted on sharing the credit with others.* ■ the quality of being relatively moderate, limited, or small in amount, rate, or level: *the modesty of his political aspirations.* ■ behavior, manner, or appearance intended to avoid impropriety or indecency: *modesty forbade her to undress in front of so many people.*

mod·i·cum /ˈmädikəm; ˈmōd-/ ▶*n.* [in *sing.*] a small quantity of a particular thing, esp. something considered desirable or valuable: *his statement had more than* ***a modicum of*** *truth.* ▷late 15th cent.: from Latin, neuter of *modicus* 'moderate,' from *modus* 'measure.'

mod·i·fi·ca·tion /ˌmädəfəˈkāsʜən/ ▶*n.* the action of modifying something: *the parts supplied should fit with little or no modification.* ■ a change made: *there will be a number of modifications to the engines.* ▷late 15th cent. (in Scots law, denoting the assessment of a payment): from French, or from Latin *modificatio(n-)*, from *modificare* (see **MODIFY**).

mod·i·fi·er /ˈmädəˌfīər/ ▶*n.* a person or thing that makes partial or minor changes to something. ■ *Grammar* a word, esp. an adjective or noun used attributively, that restricts or adds to the sense of a head noun (e.g., *good* and *family* in *a good family house*). ■ *Genetics* a gene that modifies the phenotypic expression of a gene at another locus.

USAGE A **modifier** is said to be *misplaced* if it has no clear grammatical connection to another part of the sentence. Thus, in the sentence *having seen the movie, my views were offered*, the first phrase appears to modify *views* (that is, 'my views have seen the movie'). The sentence would be better worded, *having seen the movie, I offered my views.*

mod·i·fy /ˈmädəˌfī/ ▶*v.* (**-fies, -fied**) [*trans.*] make partial or minor changes to (something), typically so as to improve it or to make it less extreme: *she may be prepared to modify her views* | [as *adj.*] (**modified**) *a modified version of the aircraft.* ■ *Biology* transform (a structure) from its original anatomical form during development or evolution. ■ *Grammar* (esp. of an adjective) restrict or add to the sense of (a noun): *the target noun is modified by a "direction" word.* ■ *Phonetics* pronounce (a speech sound) in a way that is different from the norm for that sound. ▷late Middle English: from Old French *modifier*, from Latin *modificare*, from *modus* (see **MODE**). —**mod·i·fi·a·ble** *adj.* —**mod·i·fi·ca·to·ry** /ˈmädəfəkəˌtôrē; ˌmädəˈfikəˌtôrē/ *adj.*

Mo·di·glia·ni /ˌmōdēlˈyänē/, Amedeo (1884–1920), Italian painter and sculptor, resident in France from 1906. His portraits and nudes are noted for their elongated forms, linear qualities, and earthy colors.

mo·dil·lion /mōˈdilyən/ ▶*n.* *Architecture* a projecting bracket under the corona of a cornice in the Corinthian and other orders. ▷mid 16th cent.: from French *modillon*, from Italian *modiglione*, based on Latin *mutulus* 'mutule.'

mo·di·o·lus /məˈdīələs/ ▶*n.* (*pl.* **-li** /-ˌlī; -ˌlē/) *Anatomy* the conical central axis of the cochlea of the ear. ▷early 19th cent.: from Latin, literally 'nave of a wheel.'

mod·ish /ˈmōdisʜ/ ▶*adj.* *often derogatory* conforming to or following what is currently popular and fashionable: *it seems sad that such a scholar should feel compelled to use this modish jargon.* —**mod·ish·ly** *adv.* —**mod·ish·ness** *n.*

mo·diste /mōˈdēst/ ▶*n.* *dated* a fashionable milliner or dressmaker. ▷mid 19th cent.: French, from *mode* 'fashion.'

mod·u·lar /ˈmäjələr/ ▶*adj.* employing or involving a module or modules as the basis of design or construction: *modular housing units.* ■ *Mathematics* of or relating to a modulus. ▷late 18th cent.: from modern Latin *modularis*, from Latin *modulus* (see **MODULUS**). —**mod·u·lar·i·ty** /ˌmäjəˈle(ə)ritē/ *n.*

mod·u·late /ˈmäjəˌlāt/ ▶*v.* [*trans.*] exert a modifying or controlling influence on: *the state attempts to modulate private business's cash flow.* ■ vary the strength, tone, or pitch of (one's voice): *we all modulate our voice by hearing it.* ■ alter the amplitude or frequency of (an electromagnetic wave or other oscillation) in accordance with the variations of a second signal, typically one of a lower frequency: *radio waves are modulated to carry the analog information of the voice.* ■ [*intrans.*] *Music* change from one key to another: *the first half of the melody,* ***modulating from*** *E minor to G.* ■ [*intrans.*] (**modulate into**) change from one form or condition into (another): *ideals and opinions are not modulated into authoritative journalese.* ▷mid 16th cent. (in the sense 'intone [a song]'): from Latin *modulat-* 'measured, made melody,' from the verb *modulari*, from *modulus* 'measure' (see **MODULUS**). —**mod·u·la·tion** /ˌmäjəˈlāsʜən/ *n.* —**mod·u·la·tor** /-ˌlātər/ *n.*

mod·ule /ˈmäjo͞ol/ ▶*n.* each of a set of standardized parts or independent units that can be used to construct a more complex structure, such as an item of furniture or a building. ■ [usu. with *adj.*] an independent self-contained unit of a spacecraft. ■ *Computing* any of a number of distinct but interrelated units from which a program may be built up or into which a complex activity may be analyzed. ▷late 16th cent. (in the senses 'allotted scale' and 'plan, model'): from French, or from Latin *modulus* (see **MODULUS**). Current senses date from the 1950s.

mod·u·lo /ˈmäjəˌlō/ ▶*prep.* *Mathematics* (in number theory) with respect to or using a modulus of a specified number. Two numbers are congruent modulo a given number if they give the same remainder when divided by that number: *19 and 64 are congruent modulo 5.* ■ [as *adj.*] using moduli: *modulo operations.* ▷late 19th cent.: from Latin, ablative of *modulus* (see **MODULUS**).

mod·u·lus /ˈmäjələs/ *Mathematics* ▶*n.* (*pl.* **-li** /-ˌlī; -ˌlē/) **1** another term for **ABSOLUTE VALUE**. ■ the positive square root of the sum of the squares of the real and imaginary parts of a complex number. **2** a constant factor or ratio. ■ a constant indicating the relation between a physical effect and the force producing it. **3** a number used as a divisor for considering numbers in sets, numbers being considered congruent when giving the same remainder when divided by a particular modulus. ▷mid 16th cent. (denoting an architectural unit of length): from Latin, literally 'measure,' diminutive of *modus*.

mo·dus op·e·ran·di /ˈmōdəs ˌäpəˈrandē; -ˌdī/ ▶*n.* (*pl.* **mo·di op·e·ran·di** /ˈmōdē; ˈmōdī/) [usu. in *sing.*] a particular way or method of doing something, esp. one that is characteristic or well-established: *the volunteers were instructed to buy specific systems using our usual modus operandi—anonymously and with cash.* ■ the way something operates or works. ▷Latin, literally 'way of operating.'

mo·dus po·nens /ˈmōdəs ˈpōˌnenz/ ▶*n.* the rule of logic stating that if a conditional statement ("if *p* then *q*") is accepted, and the antecedent (*p*) holds, then the consequent (*q*) may be inferred. ■ an argument using this rule. ▷Latin, literally 'mood that affirms.'

mo·dus tol·lens /ˈmōdəs ˈtälˌenz/ ▶*n.* the rule of logic stating that if a conditional statement ("if *p* then *q*") is accepted, and the consequent does not hold (*not-q*), then the negation of the antecedent (*not-p*) can be inferred. ■ an argument using this rule. ▷Latin, literally 'mood that denies.'

mo·dus vi·ven·di /ˈmōdəs vəˈvendē; -ˌdī/ ▶*n.* (*pl.* **mo·di vi·ven·di** /ˈmōdē; ˈmōdī/) [usu. in *sing.*] an arrangement or agreement allowing conflicting parties to coexist peacefully, either indefinitely or until a final settlement is reached. ■ a way of living. ▷Latin, literally 'way of living.'

moe·ri·the·ri·um /ˌmirəˈᴛʜi(ə)rēəm/ ▶*n.* (*pl.* **-ri·a** /-rēə/) a medium-sized mammal of the late Eocene and Oligocene epochs with a long snout and short legs, related to modern elephants. • *Moeritherium trigodon.* ▷modern Latin, from the name of Lake *Moeris* in Egypt, where the first fossils were found + Greek *thērion* 'wild beast.'

mo·fette /mōˈfet/ ▶*n.* archaic term for **FUMAROLE**. ▷early 19th cent.: from French, from Neapolitan Italian *mofetta*.

mo·fo /ˈmōˌfō/ ▶*n.* *vulgar slang* short for **MOTHERFUCKER**.

Mo·ga·di·shu /ˌmôgəˈdisʜo͞o; ˌmägə-; -ˈdēsʜo͞o/ the capital of Somalia, a port on the Indian Ocean; pop. 377,000. Also called **MUQDISHO**; Italian name **MOGADISCIO**.

Mo·gi·lyov /ˌməgilˈyôf/ (also **Mo·gi·lev**) Russian name for **MAHILYOW**.

Mo·gul /ˈmōgəl/ (also **Mo·ghul** or **Mu·ghal**) ▶*n.* a member of the Muslim dynasty of Mongol origin founded by the successors of Tamerlane, which ruled much of India from the 16th to the 19th century: [as *adj.*] *Mogul architecture.* ■ (often **the Great Mogul**) *historical* the Mogul emperor of Delhi. ▷from Persian *muğul* 'Mongol.'

mo·gul[1] /ˈmōgəl/ ▶*n.* **1** *informal* an important or powerful person, esp. in the motion picture or media industry. **2** (**Mogul**) a steam locomotive with three pairs of driving wheels and one pair of smaller wheels in the front. ▷late 17th cent.: figurative use of **MOGUL**.

mo·gul[2] ▶*n.* a bump on a ski slope formed by the repeated turns of skiers over the same path: [as *adj.*] *a mogul field.* ▷1960s: probably from southern German dialect *Mugel, Mugl.*

MOH ▶*abbr.* ■ Medical Officer of Health (chief health executive of a local authority). ■ Ministry of Health.

mo·hair /ˈmōˌhe(ə)r/ ▶*n.* the long, silky hair of the angora goat. ■ a yarn or fabric made from this, typically mixed with wool: [as *adj.*] *a mohair sweater.* ▷late 16th cent.: from Arabic *mukayyar* 'cloth made of goat's hair' (literally 'choice, select'). The change in ending was due to association with **HAIR**.

Mo·ham·med ▶*n.* variant spelling of **MUHAMMAD**[1].

Mo·ham·me·dan /mo͞oˈhamid(ə)n; mo-/ ▶*n.* & *adj.* variant spelling of **MUHAMMADAN**.

Mo·ham·me·rah /məˈhämərə/ former name (until 1924) for **KHORRAMSHAHR**.

Mo·ha·ve Des·ert variant spelling of **MOJAVE DESERT**.

Mo·hawk /ˈmōˌhôk/ ▶*n.* (*pl.* same or **-hawks**) **1** a member of an American Indian people, one of the Five Nations, originally inhabiting parts of eastern New York. **2** the Iroquoian language of this people. **3** a hairstyle with the head shaved except for a strip of hair from the middle of the forehead to the back of the neck, typically stiffened to stand erect or in spikes. [erroneously associated with the Mohawk people (see **HURON**).] **4** *Figure Skating* a step from either edge of the skate to the same edge on the other foot in the opposite direction.
▶*adj.* of or relating to the Mohawks or their language. ▷from Narragansett *mohowawog*, literally 'maneaters.'

Mo·hawk Riv·er a river that flows across central New York for 140 miles (230 km) to join the Hudson River above Albany. The Mohawk Valley is the site of much of the Erie Canal.

Mo·he·gan /mōˈhēgən/ (also **Mo·hi·can** /-ˈhēkən/) ▶*n.* **1** a member of an American Indian people formerly inhabiting eastern Connecticut. Compare with **MAHICAN**. **2** the Algonquian language of this people, closely related to Pequot.
▶*adj.* of or relating to the Mohegans or their language. ▷from Mohegan, literally 'people of the tidal waters.'

mo·hel /moil; ˈmō(h)el/ ▶*n.* a person who performs the Jewish rite of circumcision. ▷mid 17th cent.: from Hebrew *mōhēl*.

Mo·hen·jo-Da·ro /mōˈhenjō ˈdärō/ an ancient city of the civilization of the Indus valley (*c.*2600–1700 BC), now a major archaeological site in Pakistan, southwest of Sukkur.

Mo·hi·can /mōˈhēkən/ ▶*adj.* & *n.* old-fashioned variant spelling of **MAHICAN** or **MOHEGAN**.

Mo·ho /ˈmōˌhō/ ▶*n.* *Geology* short for **MOHOROVIČIĆ DISCONTINUITY**.

Mo·holy-Nagy /məˈhōlē ˈnäj; ˈmôhoi ˈnädyə/, László

(1895–1946), U.S. painter, sculptor, and photographer; born in Hungary. He pioneered the experimental use of plastic materials, light, photography, and film.

Mo·ho·ro·vi·čić dis·con·ti·nu·i·ty /ˌmōhəˈrōviˌCHiCH/ ▸*n. Geology* the boundary surface between the earth's crust and the mantle, lying at a depth of about 6–7 miles (10–12 km) under the ocean bed and about 24–30 miles (40–50 km) under the continents. ▷1930s: named after Andrija *Mohorovičić;* (1857–1936), Yugoslav seismologist.

Mohs' scale /mōz; mōs; ˈmōsəz/ ▸*n.* a scale of hardness used in classifying minerals. It runs from 1 to 10 using a series of reference minerals, and a position on the scale depends on the ability to scratch minerals rated lower. ▷late 19th cent.: named after Friedrich *Mohs* (1773–1839), German mineralogist.

moi /mwä/ ▸*exclam.* (usu. **moi?**) *humorous* me? (used esp. when accused of something that one knows one is guilty of): *sarcastic, moi?* ▷French, 'me.'

moi·dore /ˈmoiˌdôr/ ▸*n.* a Portuguese gold coin, current in England in the early 18th century and then worth about 27 shillings. ▷from Portuguese *moeda d'ouro* 'money of gold.'

moi·e·ty /ˈmoiətē/ ▸*n.* (*pl.* **-ties**) *formal* or *technical* each of two parts into which a thing is or can be divided. ■ *Anthropology* each of two social or ritual groups into which a people is divided, esp. among Australian Aboriginals and some American Indians. ■ a part or portion, esp. a lesser share. ■ *Chemistry* a distinct part of a large molecule: *the enzyme removes the sulfate moiety.* ▷late Middle English: from Old French *moite,* from Latin *medietas* 'middle,' from *medius* 'mid, middle.'

moil /moil/ ▸*v.* [*intrans.*] work hard: *men who moiled for gold.* ■ [with *adverbial*] move around in confusion or agitation: *a crowd of men and women moiled in the smoky haze.*
▸*n.* hard work; drudgery. ■ turmoil; confusion: *the moil of his intimate thoughts.* ▷late Middle English (in the sense 'moisten or bedaub'): from Old French *moillier* 'paddle in mud, moisten,' based on Latin *mollis* 'soft.' The sense 'work' dates from the mid 16th cent., often in the phrase *toil and moil.*

Moi·rai /ˈmoiˌrī/ *Greek Mythology* the Fates.

moi·re /môˈrā; mwä-; mwär/ (also **moi·ré** /mwäˈrā; mô-/) ▸*n.* silk fabric that has been subjected to heat and pressure rollers after weaving to give it a rippled appearance.
▸*adj.* (of silk) having a rippled, lustrous finish. ■ denoting or showing a pattern of irregular wavy lines like that of such silk, produced by the superposition at a slight angle of two sets of closely spaced lines. ▷mid 17th cent.: French *moire* 'mohair' (the original fabric); the variant *moiré* 'given a watered appearance' (past participle of *moirer,* from *moire*).

Mois·san /mwäˈsäN/, Ferdinand Frédéric Henri (1852–1907), French chemist. In 1886 he succeeded in isolating the element fluorine. In 1892, he invented the electric-arc furnace that bears his name. Nobel Prize for Chemistry (1906).

moist /moist/ ▸*adj.* slightly wet; damp or humid: *the air was moist and heavy.* ■ (of the eyes) wet with tears: *her brother's eyes became moist.* ■ (of a climate) rainy. ■ *Medicine* marked by a fluid discharge. ▷late Middle English: from Old French *moiste,* based on Latin *mucidus* 'moldy' (influenced by *musteus* 'fresh,' from *mustum*: see **MUST**[2]). **—moist·ly** *adv.* **—moist·ness** *n.*

mois·ten /ˈmoisən/ ▸*v.* [*trans.*] wet slightly: *she moistened her lips with the tip of her tongue.* ■ [*intrans.*] (of the eyes) fill with tears: *her eyes moistened.*

mois·ture /ˈmoisCHər/ ▸*n.* water or other liquid diffused in a small quantity as vapor, within a solid, or condensed on a surface. ▷late Middle English (denoting moistness): from Old French *moistour,* from *moiste* (see **MOIST**). **—mois·ture·less** *adj.*

mois·tur·ize /ˈmoisCHəˌrīz/ ▸*v.* [*trans.*] make (something, esp. the skin) less dry.

mois·tur·iz·er /ˈmoisCHəˌrīzər/ ▸*n.* a lotion or cream used to prevent dryness in the skin.

mo·jar·ra /mōˈhärə/ ▸*n.* a small, typically silvery fish with a very protrusible mouth. It is particularly abundant in shallow coastal and brackish waters of tropical America. • Family Gerreidae: several genera and numerous species. ▷mid 19th cent.: from American Spanish.

Mo·ja·ve Des·ert /mōˈhävē/ (also **Mo·ha·ve**) a desert in southern California, southeast of the Sierra Nevada and north and east of Los Angeles.

mo·jo /ˈmōˌjō/ ▸*n.* (*pl.* **-jos**) a magic charm, talisman, or spell: *someone must have their mojo working over at the record company.* ■ magic power. ▷early 20th cent.: probably of African origin; compare with Gullah *moco* 'witchcraft.'

mo·jo /ˈmōˌjō; -ˌhō/, ▸*n.* a Cuban sauce or marinade containing garlic, olive oil, and sour oranges. ▷probably from Spanish *mojo* 'wet' from *mojar* 'make wet.'

moke /mōk/ ▸*n. Brit., informal* a donkey. ■ *Austral./NZ* a horse, typically one of inferior quality. ▷mid 19th cent.: of unknown origin.

mo·ksha /ˈmōksHə/ ▸*n.* (in Hinduism and Jainism) release from the cycle of rebirth impelled by the law of karma. ■ the transcendent state attained by this liberation. ▷from Sanskrit *mokṣa.*

MOL ▸*abbr.* Manned Orbital Laboratory.

mol /mōl/ *Chemistry* ▸*abbr.* **MOLE**[4].

mo·la /ˈmōlə/ ▸*n.* (*pl.* same or **mo·las**) another term for **SUNFISH** (sense 1). ▷late 16th cent.: from Latin, literally 'millstone,' with reference to the shape.

mo·lal /ˈmōləl/ ▸*adj. Chemistry* (of a solution) containing one mole of solute per kilogram of solvent. **—mo·lal·i·ty** /mōˈlalitē/ *n.*

mo·lar[1] /ˈmōlər/ ▸*n.* a grinding tooth at the back of a mammal's mouth. ▷late Middle English: from Latin *molaris,* from *mola* 'millstone.'

mo·lar[2] ▸*adj.* of or relating to mass; acting on or by means of large masses or units. ▷mid 19th cent.: from Latin *moles* 'mass' + **-AR**[1].

mo·lar[3] ▸*adj. Chemistry* of or relating to one mole of a substance. ■ (of a solution) containing one mole of solute per liter of solvent. **—mo·lar·i·ty** /mōˈle(ə)ritē/ *n.*

mo·las·ses /məˈlasəz/ ▸*n.* thick, dark brown, uncrystallized juice obtained from raw sugar during the refining process. ■ a paler, sweeter version of this used as a table syrup and in baking. ▷mid 16th cent.: from Portuguese *melaço,* from late Latin *mellacium* 'must,' based on *mel* 'honey.'

mold[1] /mōld/ (*Brit.* **mould**) ▸*n.* a hollow container used to give shape to molten or hot liquid material (such as wax or metal) when it cools and hardens. ■ something made in this way, esp. a gelatin dessert or a mousse: *lobster mold with a sauce of carrots and port.* ■ [in *sing.*] *figurative* a distinctive and typical style, form, or character: *he planned to conquer the world as a roving reporter* **in the mold of** *his hero | the latest policy document is still stuck in the old mold.* ■ a frame or template for producing moldings. ■ *archaic* the form or shape of something, esp. the features or physique of a person or the build of an animal.
▸*v.* [*trans.*] form (an object with a particular shape) out of easily manipulated material: *a Connecticut inventor molded a catamaran out of polystyrene foam.* ■ give a shape to (a malleable substance): *take the marzipan and* **mold** *it* **into** *a cone shape.* ■ influence the formation or development of: *the professionals who were helping to mold US policy.* ■ shape (clothing) to fit a particular part of the body: [as *adj.*] (**molded**) *a shoe with molded insole.* ■ [often as *adj.*] (**molded**) shape (a column, ceiling, or other part of a building) to a particular design, esp. a decorative molding: *a corridor with a molded cornice.* ▷Middle English: apparently from Old French *modle,* from Latin *modulus* (see **MODULUS**). **—mold·a·ble** *adj.* **—mold·er** *n.*
▸*PHRASE* □ **break the mold** put an end to a restrictive pattern of events or behavior by doing things in a markedly different way: *his work did much to break the mold of the old urban sociology.*

mold[2] (*Brit.* **mould**) ▸*n.* a furry growth of minute fungal hyphae occurring typically in moist warm conditions, esp. on food or other organic matter. • The fungi belong to the subdivision Deuteromycotina (or Ascomycotina). ▷late Middle English: probably from obsolete *mould,* past participle of *moul* 'grow moldy,' of Scandinavian origin; compare with Old Norse *mygla* 'grow moldy.'

mold[3] (*Brit.* **mould**) ▸*n.* soft loose earth. See also **LEAF MOLD.** ■ the upper soil of cultivated land, esp. when rich in organic matter. ▷Old English *molde,* from a Germanic base meaning 'pulverize or grind'; related to **MEAL**[2].

Mol·dau /ˈmôlˌdou/ German name for **VLTAVA.**

Mol·da·vi·a /mälˈdāvēə; môl-; -vyə/ **1** a former principality of southeastern Europe. Formerly a part of the Roman province of Dacia, it came under Turkish rule in the 16th century. In 1861, Moldavia united with Wallachia to form Romania. **2** another name for **MOLDOVA.**

Mol·da·vi·an /mälˈdāvēən; môl-/ ▸*n.* **1** a native or national of Moldavia. **2** the Romanian language as spoken and written (in the Cyrillic alphabet) in Moldavia.
▸*adj.* of or relating to Moldavia, its inhabitants, or their language.

mold·board /ˈmōldˌbôrd/ ▸*n.* a curved metal blade in a plow that turns the earth over: [as *adj.*] *moldboard plows.* ■ a similar device on the front of a snowplow or bulldozer, used for pushing snow or loose earth.

mold·er /ˈmōldər/ (*Brit.* **mould·er**) ▸*v.* [*intrans.*] [often as *adj.*] (**moldering**) slowly decay or disintegrate, esp. because of neglect: *there was a mushroomy smell of disuse and moldering books | figurative I couldn't permit someone of your abilities to* **molder away** *in a backwater.* ▷mid 16th cent.: perhaps from **MOLD**[3], but compare with Norwegian dialect *muldra* 'crumble.'

mold·ing /ˈmōldiNG/ (*Brit.* **mould·ing**) ▸*n.* an ornamentally shaped outline as an architectural feature, esp. in a cornice. ■ material such as wood, plastic, or stone shaped for use as a decorative or architectural feature.

Mol·do·va /məlˈdōvə/ a landlocked country in southeastern Europe, between Romania and Ukraine; pop. 4,384,000; capital, Chişinău; languages, Moldavian (official) and Russian;. Also called **MOLDAVIA.** **—Mol·do·van** *adj.* & *n.*

A former constituent republic of the USSR, Moldova was formed from territory ceded by Romania in 1940. It became independent as a member of the Commonwealth of Independent States in 1991.

mold·y /ˈmōldē/ (*Brit.* **mould·y**) ▸*adj.* (**mold·i·er, mold·i·est**) covered with a fungal growth that causes decay, due to age or damp conditions: *moldy bread.* ■ tediously old-fashioned: *moldy conventions.* ■ *informal, chiefly Brit.* dull or depressing: *evenings filled with moldy old shows.* **—mold·i·ness** *n.*

mole[1] /mōl/ ▸*n.* **1** a small burrowing insectivorous mammal with dark velvety fur, a long muzzle, and very small eyes. • Family Talpidae: several genera and species, including the **eastern mole** (*Scalopus aquaticus*) of North America. **2** a spy who achieves over a long period an important position within the security defenses of a country. ■ someone within an organization who anonymously betrays confidential information. ▷late Middle English: from the Germanic base of Middle Dutch and Middle Low German *mol.*

mole[1]

mole[2] /mōl/ ▸*n.* a small, often slightly raised blemish on the skin made dark by a high concentration of melanin. ▷Old English *māl* 'discolored spot,' of Germanic origin.

mole[3] /mōl/ ▸*n.* a large solid structure on a shore serving as a pier, breakwater, or causeway. ■ a harbor formed or protected by such a structure. ▷mid 16th cent.: from French *môle,* from Latin *moles* 'mass.'

mole[4] /mōl/ ▸*n. Chemistry* the SI unit of amount of substance, equal to the quantity containing as many elementary units as there are atoms in 0.012 kg of carbon-12. ▷early 20th cent.: from German *Mol*, from *Molekul*, from Latin (see **MOLECULE**).

mole[5] /mōl/ ▸*n. Medicine* an abnormal mass of tissue in the uterus. See also **HYDATIDIFORM MOLE.** ▷late Middle English: from French *môle*, from Latin *mola* in the sense 'false conception.'

mo·le[6] /ˈmōlā/ ▸*n.* a highly spiced Mexican sauce made chiefly from chili peppers and chocolate, served with meat. ▷Mexican Spanish, from Nahuatl *molli* 'sauce, stew.'

mole crick·et ▸*n.* a large burrowing nocturnal cricket with broad forelegs, the female of which lays her eggs in an underground nest and guards the young. • Family Gryllotalpidae, subfamily Gryllotalpinae: several genera.

mo·lec·u·lar /məˈlekyələr/ ▸*adj.* of, relating to, or consisting of molecules: *interactions between polymer and solvent at the molecular level | ozone is produced by dissociation of molecular oxygen.* **—mo·lec·u·lar·i·ty** /mə,lekyəˈle(ə)ritē/ *n.* **—mo·lec·u·lar·ly** *adv.*

mo·lec·u·lar bi·ol·o·gy ▸*n.* the branch of biology that deals with the structure and function of the macromolecules (e.g., proteins and nucleic acids) essential to life.

mo·lec·u·lar clock ▸*n. Genetics* the average rate at which a species' genome accumulates mutations, used to measure their evolutionary divergence and in other calculations.

mo·lec·u·lar e·lec·tron·ics ▸*plural n.* [treated as *singular*] a branch of electronics in which individual molecules perform the same function as microelectronic devices such as diodes. **—mo·lec·u·lar e·lec·tron·ic** *adj. molecular electronic materials and inorganic particles.*

mo·lec·u·lar for·mu·la ▸*n. Chemistry* a formula giving the number of atoms of each of the elements present in one molecule of a specific compound. Compare with **EMPIRICAL FORMULA, STRUCTURAL FORMULA.**

mo·lec·u·lar sieve ▸*n.* a crystalline substance (esp. a zeolite) with pores of molecular dimensions that permit the passage of molecules below a certain size.

mo·lec·u·lar weight ▸*n. Chemistry* the ratio of the average mass of one molecule of an element or compound to one twelfth of the mass of an atom of carbon-12.

mol·e·cule /ˈmälə,kyo͞ol/ ▸*n. Chemistry* a group of atoms bonded together, representing the smallest fundamental unit of a chemical compound that can take part in a chemical reaction. ▷late 18th cent.: from French *molécule*, from modern Latin *molecula*, diminutive of Latin *moles* 'mass.'

mole·hill /ˈmōl,hil/ ▸*n.* a small mound of earth thrown up by a mole burrowing near the surface.
▸*PHRASE* □ **make a mountain out of a molehill** exaggerate the importance of something trivial.

mole rat ▸*n.* a herbivorous, short-legged, ratlike rodent that typically lives permanently underground, with long incisors that protrude from the mouth and are used in digging. • Family Bathyergidae (African mole rats): several genera; also two subfamilies and three genera in the family Muridae (Eurasian blind mole rats and Asiatic mole rats).

mole sal·a·man·der ▸*n.* a stocky, broad-headed North American salamander that spends much of its life underground. • Family Ambystomatidae: several genera, in particular *Ambystoma*, and numerous species, including *A. talpoideum.*

mole·skin /ˈmōl,skin/ ▸*n.* **1** the skin of a mole used as fur. **2** a thick, strong cotton fabric with a shaved pile surface: [as *adj.*] *a moleskin coat.* ■ (**moleskins**) clothes, esp. trousers, made of such a fabric. ■ a soft fabric with adhesive backing used as a foot bandage.

mo·lest /məˈlest/ ▸*v.* [*trans.*] pester or harass (someone), typically in an aggressive or persistent manner: *the crowd was shouting abuse and molesting the two police officers.* See note at **ATTACK.** ■ assault or abuse (a person, esp. a woman or child) sexually. ▷late Middle English (in the sense 'cause trouble to, vex'): from Old French *molester* or Latin *molestare* 'annoy,' from *molestus* 'troublesome.' **—mo·les·ta·tion** /,mō,le-; ,mōləˈstāsʜən/ *n.* **—mo·lest·er** *n.*

mol·et·ron·ics /,mäliˈträniks/ ▸*plural n.* [treated as *singular*] short for **MOLECULAR ELECTRONICS.** **—mol·et·ron·ic** *adj.*

Mo·lière /mōlˈye(ə)r; mōlˈyer/ (1622–73), French playwright; pseudonym of *Jean-Baptiste Poquelin.* He wrote more than 20 comic plays about contemporary France, developing stock characters from Italian *commedia dell'arte.* Notable works: *Don Juan* (1665), *Le Misanthrope* (1666), and *Le Bourgeois gentilhomme* (1670).

Mo·li·na /məˈlēnə/, Alfred (1953–), British actor. Notable films include *Enchanted April* (1992), *Chocolat* (2000), and *Frida* (2002). He received a Tony nomination for his performance in *Fiddler on the Roof* (2004).

Mo·line /mōˈlēn/ a city on the Rock and Mississippi rivers in northwestern Illinois, one of the Quad Cities; pop. 43,202.

mo·line /məˈlēn; -ˈlīn/ ▸*adj.* [*postpositive*] *Heraldry* (of a cross) having each extremity broadened, split, and curved back. ▷mid 16th cent.: probably from Anglo-Norman French *moliné*, from *molin* 'mill,' because of a resemblance to the iron support of a millstone.

moll /mäl/ ▸*n. informal* **1** (also **gun moll**) a gangster's female companion. **2** a prostitute. ▷early 17th cent.: nickname for the given name *Mary.*

mol·li·fy /ˈmälə,fī/ ▸*v.* (**-fies, -fied**) [*trans.*] appease the anger or anxiety of (someone): *nature reserves were set up around the power stations to mollify local conservationists.* See note at **PACIFY.** ■ *rare* reduce the severity of (something); soften. ▷late Middle English (also in the sense 'make soft or supple'): from French *mollifier* or Latin *mollificare*, from *mollis* 'soft.' **—mol·li·fi·ca·tion** /,mäləfəˈkāsʜən/ *n.* **—mol·li·fi·er** *n.*

mol·li·sol /ˈmälə,säl; -,sôl/ ▸*n. Soil Science* a soil of an order comprising temperate grassland soils with a dark, humus-rich surface layer containing high concentrations of calcium and magnesium. ▷mid 20th cent.: from Latin *mollis* 'soft' + *solum* 'ground, soil.'

mol·lus·cum con·ta·gi·o·sum /mälˈəskəm kən,tājēˈōsəm/ ▸*n. Medicine* a chronic viral disorder of the skin characterized by groups of small, smooth, painless pinkish nodules with a central depression, that yield a milky fluid when squeezed. ▷early 19th cent.: from Latin *molluscum* (as a noun denoting a kind of fungus), neuter of *molluscus* + *contagiosum* (neuter of *contagiosus* 'contagious').

mol·lusk /ˈmäləsk/ (*chiefly Brit.* also **mollusc**) ▸*n.* an invertebrate of a large phylum that includes snails, slugs, mussels, and octopuses. They have a soft, unsegmented body and live in aquatic or damp habitats, and most kinds have an external calcareous shell. • Phylum Mollusca: several classes, in particular Gastropoda, Bivalvia, and Cephalopoda. ▷late 18th cent.: from modern Latin *mollusca*, neuter plural of Latin *molluscus*, from *mollis* 'soft.' **—mol·lus·kan** /məˈləs,kən/ (or **mol·lus·can**) *adj.*

Moll·wei·de pro·jec·tion /ˈmôl,vīdə; -wīdə/ ▸*n.* a projection of a map of the world onto an ellipse, with lines of latitude represented by straight lines (spaced more closely toward the poles) and meridians represented by equally spaced elliptical curves. This projection distorts shape but preserves relative area. ▷early 20th cent.: named after Karl B. *Mollweide* (died 1825), German mathematician and astronomer.

mol·ly /ˈmälē/ (also **mol·lie**) ▸*n.* a small, livebearing freshwater fish that is popular in aquariums and has been bred in many colors, esp. black. • Genus *Poecilia*, family Poeciliidae: several species, in particular *P. sphenops.* See also **SAILFIN MOLLY.** ▷1930s: from modern Latin *Mollienisia* (former genus name), from the name of Count *Mollien* (1758–1850), French statesman.

mol·ly·cod·dle /ˈmälē,kädl/ ▸*v.* [*trans.*] treat (someone) very indulgently or protectively.
▸*n.* an effeminate or ineffectual man or boy; a milksop. ▷mid 19th cent.: from *molly* 'girl or prostitute' (see **MOLL**) + **CODDLE.**

Mo·loch /ˈmälək; ˈmō,läk/ a Canaanite idol to whom children were sacrificed. ■ [as *n.*] (**a Moloch**) a tyrannical object of sacrifices. ▷via late Latin from Greek *Molokh*, from Hebrew *mōlek̲.*

mo·loch /ˈmälək; ˈmō,läk/ ▸*n.* a harmless spiny lizard of grotesque appearance that feeds chiefly on ants and is found in arid inland Australia. • *Moloch horridus*, family Agamidae.

Mo·lo·kai /,mäləˈkī; ,mō-/ an island in Hawaii, east of Oahu Island, site of numerous resorts.

Mo·lo·tov[1] /ˈmälə,tôf; -,tôv; ˈmōlə-/ former name (1940–57) for **PERM.**

Mo·lo·tov[2] /ˈmälə,tôf; -,täf; ˈmō-/, Vyacheslav (Mikhailovich) (1890–1986), Soviet statesman; born *Vyacheslav Mikhailovich Skryabin.* As commissar (later minister) for foreign affairs 1939–49 and 1953–56, he negotiated the nonaggression pact with Nazi Germany in 1939 and after 1945 represented the Soviet Union at the UN.

Mo·lo·tov cock·tail ▸*n.* a crude incendiary device typically consisting of a bottle filled with flammable liquid and with a means of ignition. The production of similar grenades was organized by Vyacheslav Molotov during World War II.

molt /mōlt/ (*Brit.* **moult**) ▸*v.* [*intrans.*] (of an animal) shed old feathers, hair, or skin, or an old shell, to make way for a new growth: *the adult birds were already molting into their winter shades of gray* | [*trans.*] *the snake molts its skin.* ■ (of hair or feathers) fall out to make way for new growth: *the last of his juvenile plumage had molted.*
▸*n.* a loss of plumage, skin, or hair, esp. as a regular feature of an animal's life cycle. ▷Middle English *moute*, from an Old English verb based on Latin *mutare* 'to change.' For the intrusive *-l-*, compare with words such as *fault.*

mol·ten /ˈmōltn/ ▸*adj.* (esp. of materials with a high melting point, such as metal and glass) liquefied by heat. ▷Middle English: archaic past participle of **MELT.**

mol·to /ˈmōl,tō; ˈmôl-/ ▸*adv. Music* (in directions) very: *molto maestoso | allegro molto.* ▷Italian, from Latin *multus* 'much.'

Mo·luc·ca Is·lands /məˈləkə/ an island group in Indonesia, between Sulawesi and New Guinea; capital, Amboina. Settled by the Portuguese in the early 16th century, the islands were captured a century later by the Dutch. They were formerly known as the Spice Islands. Indonesian name **MALUKU.** **—Mo·luc·can** *n.* & *adj.*

mol·vi /ˈmôlvē/ ▸*n.* variant spelling of **MOULVI.**

mol. wt. ▸*abbr.* molecular weight.

mol·y[1] /ˈmōlē/ ▸*n.* (*pl.* **mol·ies**) **1** a southern European plant related to the onions, with small yellow flowers. • *Allium moly*, family Liliaceae (or Alliaceae). **2** a mythical herb with white flowers and black roots, endowed with magic properties. ▷mid 16th cent. (sense 2): via Latin from Greek *mōlu.*

moly[2] ▸*n.* short for **MOLYBDENUM.** See also **CHROMEMOLY.**

mo·lyb·date /məˈlib,dāt/ ▸*n. Chemistry* a salt in which the anion contains both molybdenum and oxygen, esp. one of the anion MoO_4^{2-}. ▷late 18th cent.: from *molybdic (acid)*, a parent acid of molybdates, + **-ATE**[1].

mo·lyb·de·nite /məˈlibdə,nīt/ ▸*n.* a blue-gray mineral, typically occurring as hexagonal crystals. It consists of molybdenum disulfide and is the most common ore of molybdenum.

mo·lyb·de·num /məˈlibdənəm/ ▸*n.* the chemical element of atomic number 42, a brittle silver-gray metal of the transition series, used in some alloy steels. (Symbol: **Mo**) ▷early 19th cent.: modern Latin, earlier *molybdena* (originally denoting a salt of lead), from Greek *molubdaina* 'plummet,' from *molubdos* 'lead.'

mom /mäm/ ▸*n. informal* one's mother. ▷late 19th cent.: abbreviation of **MOMMA.**

mom-and-pop ▸*adj. informal* denoting a small store or business of a type often run by a married couple: *most of the town relies on a local mom-and-pop ISP for their e-mail.*

Mom·ba·sa /mämˈbäsə/ a seaport and industrial city in southeastern Kenya, on the Indian Ocean; pop. 465,000. It is the country's leading port and second largest city.

mo·ment /ˈmōmənt/ ▸*n.* **1** a very brief period of time: *she was silent* ***for a moment*** *before replying | a few moments later he returned to the office.* ■ an exact point in time: *she would always remember the moment they met.* ■ an appropriate time for doing something; an opportunity: *I was waiting for* ***the right moment.*** ■ a particular stage in something's development or in a course of events: *one of the great moments in aviation history.* **2** *formal* importance: *the issues were* ***of little moment*** *to the electorate.* **3** *Physics* a turning effect produced by a force acting at a distance on an object. ■ the magnitude of such an effect, expressed as the product of the force and the distance from its line of action to a given point. **4** *Statistics* a quantity that expresses the average or expected value of the first, second, third, or fourth power of the deviation of each component of a frequency distribution from some given value, typically mean or zero. The **first moment** is the mean, the **second moment** the variance, the **third moment** the skew, and the **fourth moment** the kurtosis. ▷late Middle English: from Latin *momentum* (see **MOMENTUM**).
▸*PHRASES* □ **any moment** (or **at any moment**) very soon. □ **at the** (or **this**) **moment** at the present time; now. □ **for the moment** for now. □ **have one's** (or **its**) **moments** have short periods that are better or more impressive than others: *thanks to his gently comic performance, the film has its moments.* □ **in a moment** **1** very soon: *I'll be back in a moment.* **2** instantly: *the*

M

fugitive was captured in a moment. □ **live for the moment** live or act without worrying about the future. □ **the moment** —— as soon as ——: *the heavens opened the moment we left the house.* □ **moment of truth** a time when a person or thing is tested, a decision has to be made, or a crisis has to be faced. [with allusion to the final sword-thrust in a bullfight.] □ **not a moment too soon** almost too late. □ **not for a** (or **one**) **moment** not at all; never. □ **of the moment** currently popular, famous, or important: *the buzzword of the moment.* □ **one moment** (or **just a moment**) a request for someone to wait for a short period of time, esp. to allow the speaker to do or say something.

mo·men·ta /mō'mentə; mə-/ ▸ plural form of MOMENTUM.

mo·men·tar·i·ly /ˌmōmən'te(ə)rəlē/ ▸*adv.* **1** for a very short time: *as he passed Jenny's door, he paused momentarily.* **2** at any moment; very soon: *my husband will be here to pick me up momentarily.*

mo·men·tar·y /'mōmənˌterē/ ▸*adj.* lasting for a very short time; brief: *a momentary lapse of concentration.* ▹late Middle English: from Latin *momentarius*, from *momentum* (see MOMENT). **—mo·men·tar·i·ness** *n.*

mo·ment·ly /'mōməntlē/ ▸*adv. archaic* or *poetic/literary* **1** from moment to moment; continually. **2** at any moment. **3** for a moment; briefly.

moment of in·er·tia ▸*n. Physics* a quantity expressing a body's tendency to resist angular acceleration. It is the sum of the products of the mass of each particle in the body with the square of its distance from the axis of rotation.

mo·men·tous /mō'men(t)əs; mə'-/ ▸*adj.* (of a decision, event, or change) of great importance or significance, esp. in its bearing on the future: *a period of momentous changes in East-West relations.* **—mo·men·tous·ly** *adv.* **—mo·men·tous·ness** *n.*

mo·men·tum /mō'mentəm; mə-/ ▸*n.* (*pl.* **-ta** /-tə/ or **-tums**) **1** *Physics* the quantity of motion of a moving body, measured as a product of its mass and velocity. **2** the impetus gained by a moving object: *the vehicle **gained momentum** as the road dipped.* ■ the impetus and driving force gained by the development of a process or course of events: *the investigation **gathered momentum** in the spring.* ▹late 17th cent.: from Latin, from *movimentum*, from *movere* 'to move.'

mom·ism /'mämˌizəm/ ▸*n. informal* excessive attachment to or domination by one's mother.

mom·ma ▸*n.* variant spelling of MAMA.

mom·my /'mämē/ ▸*n.* (*pl.* **-mies**) *informal* one's mother (chiefly as a child's term). ▹early 20th cent.: from MOMMA + -Y2.

mom·my track ▸*n. informal* a career path for women who opt to sacrifice promotions and pay raises in order to devote more time to raising their children. **—mom·my track·er** *n.* **—mom·my track·ing** *n.*

Mon /mōn/ ▸*n.* (*pl.* same or **Mons**) **1** a member of a people now inhabiting parts of southeastern Myanmar (Burma) and western Thailand but having their ancient capital at Pegu in southern Myanmar. **2** the language of this people, related to Khmer (Cambodian).

▸*adj.* of or relating to this people or their language. See also MON-KHMER. ▹the name in Mon.

Mon. ▸*abbr.* Monday.

mon- ▸*comb. form* variant spelling of MONO- shortened before a vowel (as in *monamine*).

Mon·a·co /'mänəkō/ a principality that forms an enclave within French territory, on the Mediterranean coast near the Italian frontier; pop. 32,000; language, French (official).

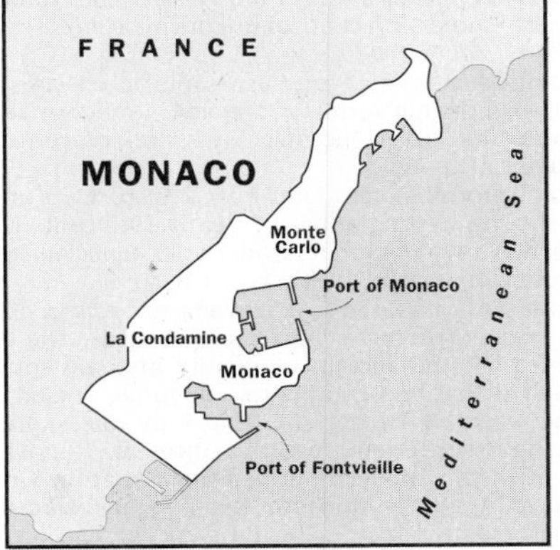

The smallest sovereign state in the world apart from the Vatican, Monaco was ruled by the Genoese from medieval times and by the Grimaldi family from 1297. It became a constitutional monarchy in 1911. Monaco includes the resort of Monte Carlo.

mon·ad /'mōˌnad/ ▸*n. technical* a single unit; the number one. ■ *Philosophy* (in the philosophy of Leibniz) an indivisible and hence ultimately simple entity, such as an atom or a person. ■ *dated Biology* a single-celled organism, esp. a flagellate protozoan, or a single cell. ▹early 17th cent.: via late Latin from Greek *monas, monad-* 'unit,' from *monos* 'alone.' **—mo·nad·ic** /mō'nadik; mə-/ *adj.* **—mon·ad·ism** /-ˌizəm/ *n.* (*Philosophy*).

mon·a·del·phous /ˌmänə'delfəs/ ▸*adj. Botany* (of stamens) united by their filaments so as to form one group. ▹early 19th cent.: from Greek *monos* 'one' + *adelphos* 'brother' + -OUS.

Mo·nad·nock, Mount /mə'nadˌnäk/ an isolated peak in southwestern New Hampshire whose name stands for any mountain of its type.

mo·nad·nock /mə'nadˌnäk/ ▸*n.* an isolated hill or ridge or erosion-resistant rock rising above a peneplain. ▹late 19th cent.: named after Mount *Monadnock* in New Hampshire.

Mon·a·ghan /'mänəˌhan; -hən/ a county of the Republic of Ireland, part of the old province of Ulster. ■ its county town; pop. 5,750.

Mo·na Li·sa /'mōnə 'lēsə; 'lēzə/ a painting (now in the Louvre in Paris) executed 1503–06 by Leonardo da Vinci. The sitter was the wife of Francesco del Giocondo; her enigmatic smile has become one of the most famous images in Western art. Also called LA GIOCONDA.

mon·amine /'mänəˌmēn/ ▸*n.* variant spelling of MONOAMINE.

mo·na mon·key /'mōnə/ ▸*n.* a West African guenon that has a bluish-gray face with a pink muzzle. The female has a distinctive moaning call. • *Cercopithecus mona*, family Cercopithecidae. ▹late 18th cent.: *mona* from Spanish and Portuguese *mona, mono*, Italian *monna.*

mo·nan·dry /'mänˌandrē; mə'nan/ ▸*n.* **1** the custom of having only one husband at a time. **2** *Botany* the state of having a single stamen. ▹mid 19th cent.: from MONO- 'single,' on the pattern of words such as *polyandry.* **—mo·nan·drous** /mə'nandrəs/ *adj.*

mon·arch /'mänərk; 'mänˌärk/ ▸*n.* **1** a sovereign head of state, esp. a king, queen, or emperor. **2** see MONARCH BUTTERFLY. ▹late Middle English: from late Latin *monarcha*, from Greek *monarkhēs*, from *monos* 'alone' + *arkhein* 'to rule.' **—mo·nar·chal** /mə'närkəl; mä-/ *adj.* **—mo·nar·chi·al** /mə'närkēəl; mä-/ *adj.* **—mo·nar·chic** /mə'närkik; mä-/ *adj.* **—mo·nar·chi·cal** /mə'närkikəl; mä-/ *adj.* **—mo·nar·chi·cal·ly** /mə'närkik(ə)lē; mä-/ *adv.*

mon·arch but·ter·fly (also **mon·arch**) ▸*n.* a large migratory orange and black butterfly that occurs mainly in North America. The caterpillar feeds on milkweed, using the toxins in the plant to render both itself and the adult unpalatable to predators. • *Danaus plexippus*, subfamily Danainae, family Nymphalidae.

monarch butterfly

Mo·nar·chi·an /mə'närkēən; mä-/ ▸*n.* a Christian heretic of the 2nd or 3rd century who denied the doctrine of the Trinity.

▸*adj.* of or relating to the Monarchians or their beliefs. ▹from late Latin *monarchiani* (plural), from *monarchia* (see MONARCHY).

mon·ar·chism /'mänərˌkizəm; 'mänˌär-/ ▸*n.* support for the principle of having monarchs. ▹mid 19th cent.: from French *monarchisme*. **—mon·ar·chist** *n.* & *adj.*

mon·ar·chy /'mänərkē; 'mänˌär-/ ▸*n.* (*pl.* **-chies**) a form of government with a monarch at the head. ■ a state that has a monarch. ■ (**the monarchy**) the monarch and royal family of a country: *the monarchy is the focus of loyalty and service.* ▹late Middle English: from Old French *monarchie*, via late Latin from Greek *monarkhia* 'the rule of one.'

mon·as·ter·y /'mänəˌsterē/ ▸*n.* (*pl.* **-ter·ies**) a community of persons, esp. monks or nuns, living under religious vows. ■ the place of residence occupied by such persons. ▹late Middle English: via ecclesiastical Latin from ecclesiastical Greek *monastērion*, from *monazein* 'live alone,' from *monos* 'alone.'

mo·nas·tic /mə'nastik/ ▸*adj.* of or relating to monks, nuns, or others living under religious vows, or the buildings in which they live: *a monastic order.* ■ resembling or suggestive of monks or their way of life, esp. in being austere, solitary, or celibate: *a monastic student bedroom.*

▸*n.* a monk or other follower of a monastic rule. ▹late Middle English (in the sense 'anchoritic'): from late Latin *monasticus*, from Greek *monastikos*, from *monazein* 'live alone.' **—mo·nas·ti·cal·ly** /-ik(ə)lē/ *adv.* **—mo·nas·ti·cism** /-təˌsizəm/ *n.*

mon·a·tom·ic /ˌmänə'tämik/ (also **mon·o·a·tom·ic** /ˌmonōə'tämik/) ▸*adj. Chemistry* consisting of one atom. ■ monovalent.

mon·au·ral /ˌmän'ôrəl/ ▸*adj.* of or involving one ear. ■ another term for MONOPHONIC (sense 1). **—mon·au·ral·ly** *adv.*

mon·a·zite /'mänəˌzīt/ ▸*n.* a brown crystalline mineral consisting of a phosphate of cerium, lanthanum, other rare earth elements, and thorium. ▹mid 19th cent.: from German *Monazit*, from Greek *monazein* 'live alone' (because of its rare occurrence).

Mön·chen·glad·bach /ˌmœ̄nkən'glädˌbäk; ˌmœn-KHən'glätˌbäKH/ a city in northwestern Germany; pop. 263,000. It is the site of NATO headquarters for northern Europe.

Monck /məNGk/, George, 1st Duke of Albemarle (1608–70), English general. Concerned at the growing unrest following Cromwell's death (1658), he negotiated the return of Charles II in 1660.

Mon·dale /'mänˌdāl/, Walter Frederick (1928–), U.S. vice president 1977–81. A Minnesota Democrat, he served in the U.S. Senate 1964–76. He ran for the U.S. vice presidency in 1980 and the U.S. presidency in 1984, losing both times to the Republican Reagan-Bush ticket. He was U.S. ambassador to Japan 1993–96.

Mon·day /'məndā/ ▸*n.* the day of the week before Tuesday and following Sunday: *I saw him **on Monday** | the Monday before last |* [as *adj.*] *Monday morning.*

▸*adv.* on Monday: *I'll call you Monday.* ■ (**Mondays**) on Mondays; each Monday: *the restaurant is closed Mondays.* ▹Old English *Mōnandæg* 'day of the moon,' translation of late Latin *lunae dies*; compare with Dutch *maandag* and German *Montag.*

Mon·day morn·ing quar·ter·back ▸*n. informal* a person who passes judgment on and criticizes something after the event. **—Mon·day morn·ing quar·ter·back·ing** *n.*

mon·do /'mändō/ ▸*adv.* & *adj. informal* used in reference to something very striking or remarkable of its kind (often in conjunction with a pseudo-Italian noun or adjective): [as *adv.*] *I think it's going to be mondo weirdo this year, Andy.* ▹from Italian *Mondo Cane*, literally 'dog's world,' the title of a film (1961) depicting bizarre behavior.

Mon·dri·an /'môndrēˌän/, Piet (1872–1944), Dutch painter; born *Pieter Cornelis Mondriaan.* He was a cofounder of the De Stijl movement and the originator of neo-plasticism, one of the earliest and strictest forms of geometric abstract painting.

Mon·é·gasque /ˌmänə'gäsk; -'gask/ ▸*n.* a native or national of Monaco.

▸*adj.* of or relating to Monaco or its inhabitants. ▹French.

Mo·nel /mō'nel/ (also **Monel metal**) ▸*n. trademark* a nickel-copper alloy with high tensile strength and resistance to corrosion. ▹early 20th cent.: named after Ambrose *Monell* (died 1921), U.S. businessman.

Mo·net /mō'nā/, Claude (1840–1926), French painter. A founding member of the Impressionists (his painting *Impression: Sunrise* [1872] gave the movement its name), his fascination with the play of light on objects led him to produce series of single subjects painted at different times of day and under different weather conditions, such as the *Haystacks* series (1890–91) and *Rouen Cathedral* (1892–95). Among his most famous paintings are the *Waterlilies* series, which he began in 1899 and which occupied him for the rest of his life.

mon·e·ta·rism /ˈmänitəˌrizəm; ˈmən-/ ▶*n.* the theory or practice of controlling the supply of money as the chief method of stabilizing the economy. **—mon·e·ta·rist** *n.* & *adj.*

mon·e·tar·y /ˈmänəˌterē; ˈmən-/ ▶*adj.* of or relating to money or currency: *documents with little or no monetary value.* See note at FINANCIAL. ▷early 19th cent.: from French *monétaire* or late Latin *monetarius*, from Latin *moneta* 'money.' **—mon·e·tar·i·ly** /-ˌte(ə)rəlē/ *adv.*

mon·e·tize /ˈmänəˌtīz/ ▶*v.* [*trans.*] convert into or express in the form of currency. ■ [usu. as *adj.*] (**monetized**) adapt (a society) to the use of money: *a fully monetized society.* ▷late 19th cent.: from French *monétiser*, from Latin *moneta* 'money.' **—mon·e·ti·za·tion** /ˌmänətəˈzāsнən; ˌmänəˌtīˈzāsнən/ *n.*

mon·ey /ˈmənē/ ▶*n.* a current medium of exchange in the form of coins and banknotes; coins and banknotes collectively: *I counted the money before putting it in my wallet | he borrowed money to modernize the store.* ■ (**moneys** or **monies**) *formal* sums of money: *a statement of all moneys paid into and out of the account.* ■ the assets, property, and resources owned by someone or something; wealth: *the college is very short of money.* ■ financial gain: *the main aim of a commercial organization is to **make money**.* ■ payment for work; wages: *she accepted the job at the public school since the money was better.* ■ a wealthy person or group: *her aunt had married money.* ▷Middle English: from Old French *moneie*, from Latin *moneta* 'mint, money,' originally a title of the goddess Juno, in whose temple in Rome money was minted. **—mon·ey·less** *adj.*

▶*PHRASES* □ **be in the money** *informal* have or win a lot of money. □ **for my money** in my opinion or judgment: *for my money, they're one of the best bands around.* □ (**the love of**) **money is the root of all evil** *proverb* greed gives rise to selfish or wicked actions. □ **money talks** *proverb* wealth gives power and influence to those who possess it. □ **one's money's worth** good value for one's money. □ **on the money** accurate; correct: *every criticism she made was **right on the money**.* □ **put money** (or **put one's money**) **on 1** place a bet on. **2** used to express one's confidence in the truth or success of something: *she won't have him back—I'd put money on it.* □ **put one's money where one's mouth is** *informal* take action to support one's statements or opinions. □ **see the color of someone's money** receive some proof that someone has enough money to pay for something. □ **throw one's money around** spend one's money extravagantly or carelessly. □ **throw money at something** try to solve a problem by recklessly spending money on it, without due consideration of what is required.

mon·ey-back ▶*adj.* denoting an agreement or guarantee that provides for the customer's money to be refunded if not satisfied.

mon·ey·bags /ˈmənēˌbagz/ ▶*plural n.* [usu. treated as *sing.*] *informal* a wealthy person.

mon·ey·chang·er (also **mon·ey-chang·er**) ▶*n.* a person whose business is the exchanging of one currency for another. **—mon·ey·chang·ing** (or **mon·ey-chang·ing** or **mon·ey chang·ing**) *n.*

mon·eyed /ˈmənēd/ ▶*adj.* having much money; affluent: *the industrial revolution created a new moneyed class.* ■ characterized by affluence: *a moneyed lifestyle.*

mon·ey·er /ˈmənēər/ ▶*n. archaic* a person who mints money.

mon·ey grab ▶*n. informal* an undignified or unprincipled acquisition of a large sum of money with little effort.

mon·ey-grub·bing ▶*adj. informal* overeager to make money; grasping: *money-grubbing speculators.* **—mon·ey-grub·ber** /-ˌgrəbər/ *n.*

mon·ey·lend·er /ˈmənēˌlendər/ (also **mon·ey-lend·er**) ▶*n.* a person whose business is lending money to others who pay interest. **—mon·ey·lend·ing** /-ˌlendiNG/ (or **mon·ey-lend·ing**) *n.* & *adj.*

mon·ey·mak·er /ˈmənēˌmākər/ (also **mon·ey-mak·er**) ▶*n.* a person or thing that earns a lot of money: *the movie became one of the year's top moneymakers.* **—mon·ey·mak·ing** /-ˌmākiNG/ (or **mon·ey-mak·ing**) *n.* & *adj.*

mon·ey mar·ket ▶*n.* the trade in short-term loans between banks and other financial institutions.

mon·ey of ac·count ▶*n.* a denomination of money used in reckoning, but not issued as actual coins or paper money.

mon·ey or·der ▶*n.* a printed order for payment of a specified sum, issued by a bank or post office.

mon·ey plant ▶*n.* another term for HONESTY (sense 2).

mon·ey-spin·ner ▶*n. chiefly Brit.* a thing that brings in a profit. **—mon·ey-spin·ning** /-ˌspiNiNG/ *adj.*

mon·ey sup·ply ▶*n.* the total amount of money in circulation or in existence in a country.

mon·ey tree ▶*n.* a source of easily obtained or unlimited money: *I knew how to **shake the money tree**.* ■ a real or artificial tree to which people attach paper money, esp. as a gift or donation.

mon·ey wag·es ▶*plural n.* income expressed in terms of its monetary value, with no account taken of its purchasing power.

mon·ey·wort /ˈmənēˌwərt; -ˌwôrt/ ▶*n.* a trailing evergreen plant with round glossy leaves and yellow flowers, growing in damp places and by water. Native to Europe, it is also common throughout the northeastern and north-central U.S. Also called CREEPING CHARLIE, CREEPING JENNY. • *Lysimachia nummularia*, family Primulaceae.

-monger ▶*comb. form* denoting a dealer or trader in a specified commodity: *fishmonger | cheesemonger.* ■ a person who promotes a specified activity, situation, or feeling, esp. one that is undesirable or discreditable: *rumormonger | warmonger.* ▷Old English *mangere*, from *mangian* 'to traffic,' of Germanic origin, based on Latin *mango* 'dealer.'

mon·go /ˈmäNGgō/ ▶*n.* (*pl.* same or **-gos**) a monetary unit of Mongolia, equal to one hundredth of a tugrik. ▷from Mongolian *möngö* 'silver.'

Mon·gol /ˈmäNGgəl/ ▶*adj.* **1** of or relating to the people of Mongolia or their language. **2** (**mongol**) *offensive* affected with Down syndrome.
▶*n.* **1** a native or national of Mongolia; a Mongolian. **2** the language of this people; Mongolian. **3** (**mongol**) *offensive* a person affected with Down syndrome. ▷Mongolian, perhaps from *mong* 'brave.'

USAGE See usage at MONGOLOID.

In the 13th century AD, the Mongol empire under Genghis Khan extended across central Asia from Manchuria in the east to European Russia in the west. Under Kublai Khan, China was conquered and the Mongol capital was moved to Khanbaliq (modern Beijing). The Mongol empire collapsed after a series of defeats culminating in the destruction of the Golden Horde by the Muscovites in 1380.

Mon·go·li·a /mäNGˈgōlēə/ a large and sparsely populated country in eastern Asia that includes the Gobi Desert, bordered by Siberia in Russia on the north and by China on the south; pop. 2,750,000; capital, Ulaanbaatar (Ulan Bator); language, Mongolian (official).

The center of the medieval Mongol empire, Mongolia subsequently became a Chinese province and achieved de facto independence in 1911. In 1924, it became a communist state patterned on the Soviet model; a new democratic constitution was introduced in 1992. It was formerly known as Outer Mongolia to distinguish it from Inner Mongolia, which remains a province of China.

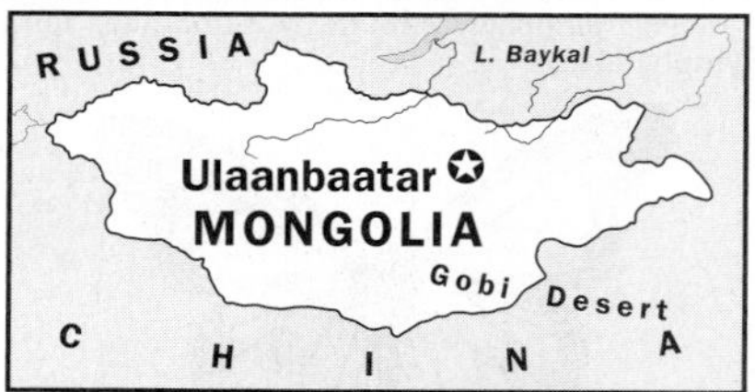

Mon·go·li·an /mänˈgōlēən; mäNG-/ ▶*adj.* of or relating to Mongolia, its people, or their language.
▶*n.* **1** a native or national of Mongolia. **2** the Altaic language of Mongolia, written in an unusual vertical cursive script; related forms are spoken in northern China.

mon·gol·ism /ˈmäNGgəˌlizəm/ ▶*n. offensive* another term for DOWN SYNDROME.

USAGE See usage at MONGOLOID.

Mon·gol·oid /ˈmäNGgəˌloid/ ▶*adj.* **1** *sometimes offensive* of or relating to the broad division of humankind including the indigenous peoples of eastern Asia, Southeast Asia, and the Arctic region of North America. **2** (**mongoloid**) *often offensive* affected with Down syndrome.
▶*n.* **1** *sometimes offensive* a person of a Mongoloid physical type. **2** *offensive* a person with Down syndrome.

USAGE 1 The terms **Mongoloid**, **Negroid**, **Caucasoid**, and **Australoid** were introduced by 19th-century anthropologists attempting to classify human racial types, but today they are recognized as having very limited validity as scientific categories. Although occasionally used when making broad generalizations about the world's populations, in most modern contexts they are potentially offensive, esp. when used of individuals. Instead, the names of specific peoples or nationalities should be used wherever possible.
2 The term **mongol**, or **Mongoloid**, was adopted in the late 19th century to refer to a person with **Down syndrome**, owing to the similarity of some of the physical symptoms of the disorder with the normal facial characteristics of eastern Asian people. The syndrome itself was thus called **mongolism**. In modern English, this use of **mongol** (and related forms) is unacceptable and is considered offensive. In scientific, as well as in most general contexts, **mongolism** has been replaced by the term **Down syndrome** (first recorded in the early 1960s).

mon·goose /ˈmänˌgo͞os; ˈmäNG-/ ▶*n.* (*pl.* **-goos·es**) a small carnivorous mammal with a long body and tail and a grizzled or banded coat, native to Africa and Asia. • Family Herpestidae (or Viverridae): several genera, in particular *Herpestes* and *Mungos*, and many species, including the **banded mongoose** (*M. mungo*). ▷late 17th cent.: from Marathi *mangūs*.

mongoose

mon·grel /ˈmäNGgrəl; ˈməNG-/ ▶*n.* a dog of no definable type or breed: [as *adj.*] *a mongrel bitch.* ■ any other animal resulting from the crossing of different breeds or types. ■ *offensive* a person of mixed descent. ▷late Middle English: of Germanic origin, apparently from a base meaning 'mix,' and related to MINGLE and AMONG. **—mon·grel·ism** /-grəˌlizəm/ *n.*

mon·grel·ize /ˈmäNGgrəˌlīz; ˈməNG-/ ▶*v.* [*trans.*] cause to become mixed in race, composition, or character: [as *adj.*] (**mongrelized**) *a patois of mongrelized French.* **—mon·grel·i·za·tion** /ˌmäNGgrələˈzāsнən; ˌməNG-/ *n.*

'mongst /ˈməNGst/ ▶*prep. poetic/literary* short for AMONGST (see AMONG).

mon·ic /ˈmänik/ ▶*adj. Mathematics* (of a polynomial) having the coefficient of the term of highest degree equal to one.

Mon·i·ca, St. /ˈmänikə/ (332–*c.*387), mother of St. Augustine of Hippo; often regarded as the model of Christian mothers for her patience with her son's spiritual crises. Feast day, August 27 (formerly May 4).

mon·ies /ˈmənēz/ ▶ plural form of MONEY, as used in financial contexts.

mon·i·ker /ˈmänikər/ (also **mon·ick·er**) ▶*n. informal* a name. ▷mid 19th cent.: of unknown origin. **—mon·i·kered** *adj.*

mo·nil·i·a /məˈnilēə/ ▶*n.* (*pl.* usu. same or **-nil·i·ae** /-ˈnilēˌē; -ēˌī/) former term for CANDIDA. ▷modern Latin, from Latin *monile* 'necklace' (with reference to the chains of spores).

mo·nil·i·form /məˈniləˌfôrm/ ▶*adj. Zoology* & *Botany* resembling a string of beads. ▷early 19th cent.: from French *moniliforme* or modern Latin *moniliformis*, from Latin *monile* 'necklace' + -IFORM.

mon·ism /ˈmänˌizəm; ˈmōˌnizəm/ ▶*n. Philosophy* & *Theology* a theory or doctrine that denies the existence of a distinction or duality in some sphere, such as that between matter and mind, or God and the world. ■ the doctrine that only one supreme being exists. Compare with PLURALISM. ▷mid 19th cent.: from modern Latin *monismus*, from Greek *monos* 'single.' **—mon·ist** *n.* & *adj.* **—mo·nis·tic** /mänˈistik; mōˈnistik/ *adj.*

mo·ni·tion /mə'nisHən/ ▸*n.* *rare* a warning of impending danger. ■ a formal notice from a bishop or ecclesiastical court admonishing a person not to do something specified. ▷late Middle English: via Old French from Latin *monitio(n-)*, from *monere* 'warn.'

mon·i·tor /'mänətər/ ▸*n.* **1** an instrument or device used for observing, checking, or keeping a continuous record of a process or quantity: *a heart monitor.* ■ a person operating such an instrument or device. ■ a person who observes a process or activity to check that it is carried out fairly or correctly, esp. in an official capacity: *the independent judicial monitor.* ■ a person who listens to and reports on foreign radio broadcasts and signals. ■ a jointed nozzle from which water streams in any desired direction, used in firefighting and hydraulic mining. ■ a raised section of roof running down the center of a railroad car, building, etc., providing light or ventilation; a clerestory. **2** a student with disciplinary or other special duties during school hours: *show the hall monitor your pass.* **3** a television receiver used in a studio to select or verify the picture being broadcast from a particular camera. ■ a television that displays an image generated by a computer. ■ a loudspeaker, esp. one used by performers on stage to hear themselves or in the studio to hear what has been recorded. **4** (also **monitor lizard**) a large tropical Old World lizard with a long neck, narrow head, forked tongue, strong claws, and a short body. Monitors were formerly believed to give warning of crocodiles. • Family Varanidae and genus *Varanus*: many species. See also **KOMODO DRAGON**. **5** *historical* a shallow-draft armored warship mounting one or two heavy guns for bombardment.
▸*v.* [*trans.*] observe and check the progress or quality of (something) over a period of time; keep under systematic review: *equipment was installed to monitor air quality.* ■ maintain regular surveillance over: *it was easy for the enemy to monitor his movements.* ■ listen to and report on (a foreign radio broadcast or a telephone conversation). ■ check or regulate the technical quality of (a radio transmission or television signal). ▷early 16th cent. (sense 2): from Latin, from *monit-* 'warned,' from the verb *monere*. Sense 1 dates from the 1930s. **—mon·i·to·ri·al** /ˌmänə'tôrēəl/ *adj.* **—mon·i·tor·ship** /-ˌsHip/ *n.*

mon·i·to·ry /'mänəˌtôrē/ ▸*adj.* *rare* giving or serving as a warning: *the monitory wail of an air-raid siren.*
▸*n.* (*pl.* **-ries**) (in church use) a letter of admonition from the pope or a bishop.

Monk /məNGk/, Thelonious (Sphere) (1917–82), U.S. jazz pianist and composer; a founder of the bebop style in the early 1940s. Notable compositions: "Round Midnight," "Straight, No Chaser," and "Well, You Needn't."

monk /məNGk/ ▸*n.* a member of a religious community of men typically living under vows of poverty, chastity, and obedience. ▷Old English *munuc*, based on Greek *monakhos* 'solitary,' from *monos* 'alone.' **—monk·ish** *adj.* **—monk·ish·ly** *adv.* **—monk·ish·ness** *n.*

monk·er·y /'məNGkərē/ ▸*n.* *derogatory* monasticism. ■ a monastery.

mon·key /'məNGkē/ ▸*n.* (*pl.* **-keys**) **1** a small to medium-sized primate that typically has a long tail, most kinds of which live in trees in tropical countries. • Families Cebidae and Callitrichidae (or Callithricidae) (**New World monkeys**, with prehensile tails), and Cercopithecidae (**Old World monkeys**, without prehensile tails). ■ (in general use) any primate. ■ a mischievous person, esp. a child: *where have you been, you little monkey!* ■ *figurative* a person who is dominated or controlled by another (with reference to the monkey traditionally kept by an organ grinder). **2** a pile-driving machine consisting of a heavy hammer or ram working vertically in a groove.
▸*v.* (**-keys, -keyed**) [*intrans.*] (**monkey around/about**) behave in a silly or playful way. ■ (**monkey with**) tamper with: *don't monkey with that lock!* ■ [*trans.*] *archaic* ape; mimic. ▷mid 16th cent.: of unknown origin, perhaps from Low German. **—mon·key·ish** *adj.*
▸*PHRASES* □ **make a monkey of** (or **out of**) **someone** humiliate someone by making them appear ridiculous. □ **a monkey on one's back** *informal* a burdensome problem. ■ a dependence on drugs.

mon·key bars ▸*plural n.* a piece of playground equipment consisting of a horizontally mounted overhead ladder, from which children may swing.

mon·key bread ▸*n.* the baobab tree or its fruit.

mon·key busi·ness ▸*n.* *informal* mischievous or deceitful behavior.

mon·key flow·er ▸*n.* a plant of boggy ground, having yellow or red tubular, often spotted flowers. • Genus *Mimulus*, family Scrophulariaceae: several species, in particular *M. guttatus.*

mon·key jack·et ▸*n.* a short, close-fitting jacket worn by sailors or waiters or by officers in their mess.

mon·key·pox /'məNGkēˌpäks/ ▸*n.* a viral disease of African origin, related to smallpox and transmitted to humans through fluid exchange by rodents and primates.

mon·key puz·zle (also **monkey puzzle tree**) ▸*n.* an evergreen coniferous tree with branches covered in spirals of tough, spiny, leaflike scales, native to Chile. • *Araucaria araucana*, family Araucariaceae. ▷mid 19th cent.: said to be so named in response to a remark that an attempt to climb the tree would puzzle a monkey.

mon·key·shines /'məNGkēˌsHīnz/ ▸*plural n.* *informal* mischievous behavior.

mon·key suit ▸*n.* *informal* a man's evening dress or formal suit.

mon·key wrench ▸*n.* an adjustable wrench with large jaws that has its adjusting screw contained in the handle.
▸*v.* (**mon·key·wrench**) [*trans.*] *informal* sabotage (something), esp. as a form of protest: [as *n.*] (**monkeywrenching**) *the five defendants who received jail sentences for monkeywrenching.* **—mon·key·wrench·er** *n.*
▸*PHRASE* □ **a monkey wrench in the works** (or **schedule, plan,** etc.) a person or thing that prevents the successful implementation of a plan: *even he couldn't throw a monkey wrench into the works | a cancellation can throw a real monkey wrench into the schedule.*

monk·fish /'məNGkˌfisH/ ▸*n.* (*pl.* same or **-fish·es**) a bottom-dwelling anglerfish of European waters. • *Lophius piscatorius*, family Lophiidae. ■ this fish as food. ■ another term for **GOOSEFISH**, esp. when referring to the fish as food.

Mon-Khmer /'mōn kə'me(ə)r; kme(ə)r/ ▸*n.* a family of languages spoken throughout Southeast Asia, of which the most important are Mon and Khmer. They are distantly related to Munda, with which they form the Austro-Asiatic phylum.
▸*adj.* relating to or denoting this group of languages.

monk seal ▸*n.* a seal with a dark back and pale underside, occurring in warm waters of the northern hemisphere. • Genus *Monachus*, family Phocidae: two or three species, including *M. tropicalis* of the Caribbean and the endangered *M. monachus* of the Mediterranean and adjacent seas.

monks·hood /'məNGksˌho͝od/ ▸*n.* an aconite with blue or purple flowers. The upper sepal of the flower covers the topmost petals, giving a hoodlike appearance. • Genus *Aconitum*, family Ranunculaceae: several species, including the North American *A. uncinatum* and the European *A. napellus.*

Mon·mouth /'mänməTH/, James Scott, Duke of (1649–85), English claimant to the throne of England. The illegitimate son of Charles II, he became the focus for Whig supporters of a Protestant succession. In 1685, he led a rebellion against the Catholic James II, but was defeated at the Battle of Sedgemoor and executed.

mon·o /'mänō/ ▸*adj.* **1** monophonic. **2** monochrome.
▸*n.* (*pl.* **-os**) **1** a monophonic recording. ■ monophonic reproduction. **2** a monochrome picture. ■ monochrome reproduction. **3** short for **INFECTIOUS MONONUCLEOSIS**. **4** short for **MONOFILAMENT**.

mono- (also **mon-** before a vowel) ▸*comb. form* **1** one; alone; single: *monorail.* ■ with an extreme, singular character to the point of dominance or exclusion: *monolithic | monomania | monopoly.* **2** *Chemistry* (forming names of compounds) containing one atom or group of a specified kind: *monoamine.* ▷from Greek *monos* 'alone.'

mon·o·a·mine /ˌmänōə'mēn; ˌmänō'amēn/ (also **mon·a·mine** /'mänəˌmēn/) ▸*n.* *Chemistry* a compound having a single amine group in its molecule, esp. one that is a neurotransmitter (e.g., serotonin, norepinephrine).

mon·o·a·mine ox·i·dase (abbr.: **MAO**) ▸*n.* *Biochemistry* an enzyme (present in most tissues) that catalyzes the oxidation and inactivation of monoamine neurotransmitters.

mon·o·a·mine ox·i·dase in·hib·i·tor ▸*n.* *Medicine* any of a group of antidepressant drugs that inhibit the activity of monoamine oxidase (so allowing accumulation of serotonin and norepinephrine in the brain).

mon·o·atom·ic ▸*n.* variant spelling of **MONATOMIC**.

mon·o·brow /'mänəˌbrou/ ▸*n.* *informal* another term for **UNIBROW**. **—mon·o·browed** *adj.*

mon·o·car·pic /ˌmänō'kärpik/ (also **mon·o·car·pous** /-pəs/) ▸*adj.* *Botany* (of a plant) flowering only once and then dying. ▷mid 19th cent.: from **MONO-** 'single' + Greek *karpos* 'fruit' + **-IC**.

mon·o·caus·al /ˌmänō'kôzəl/ ▸*adj.* in terms of a sole cause: *the pitfalls of monocausal explanations.*

Mo·noc·er·os /mə'näsərəs/ *Astronomy* an inconspicuous constellation (the Unicorn), lying on the celestial equator in the Milky Way between Canis Major and Canis Minor. ■ [as *genitive*] (**Monocerotis** /-ˌnäsə'rōtis/) used with a preceding letter or numeral to designate a star in this constellation: *the star Alpha Monocerotis.* ▷via Latin from Greek.

mon·o·cha·si·um /ˌmänō'kazH(ē)əm/ ▸*n.* (*pl.* **-si·a** /-zH(ē)ə/) *Botany* a cyme in which each flowering branch gives rise to one lateral branch, so that the inflorescence is helicoid or asymmetrical. ▷late 19th cent.: modern Latin, from **MONO-** 'one' + Greek *khasis* 'separation.'

mon·o·chord /'mänəˌkôrd/ ▸*n.* an instrument for comparing musical pitches mathematically, using a taut wire whose vibrating length can be adjusted with a movable bridge. ▷late Middle English: from Old French *monacorde*, via late Latin from Greek *monokhordon*, neuter (used as a noun) of *monokhordos* 'having a single string.'

mon·o·chro·mat·ic /ˌmänəkrō'matik/ ▸*adj.* containing or using only one color: *monochromatic light.* ■ *Physics* (of light or other radiation) of a single wavelength or frequency. ■ lacking in variety; monotonous: *her typically monochromatic acting style.* **—mon·o·chro·mat·i·cal·ly** /-ik(ə)lē/ *adv.*

mon·o·chro·ma·tism /ˌmänə'krōməˌtizəm/ ▸*n.* complete color-blindness in which all colors appear as shades of one color.

mon·o·chrome /'mänəˌkrōm/ ▸*n.* a photograph or picture developed or executed in black and white or in varying tones of only one color. ■ representation or reproduction in black and white or in varying tones of only one color.
▸*adj.* **1** (of a photograph or picture, or a television screen) consisting of or displaying images in black and white or in varying tones of only one color. **2** lacking variety and interest; insipid: *the monochrome circuit of traveling Broadway productions.* ▷mid 17th cent.: based on Greek *monokhrōmatos* 'of a single color.' **—mon·o·chro·mic** /ˌmänə'krōmik/ *adj.*

mon·o·cle /'mänikəl/ ▸*n.* a single eyeglass, kept in position by the muscles around the eye. ▷mid 19th cent.: from French (earlier in the sense 'one-eyed'), from late Latin *monoculus* 'one-eyed.' **—mon·o·cled** /-kəld/ *adj.*

mon·o·cline /'mänəˌklīn/ ▸*n.* *Geology* a bend in rock strata that are otherwise uniformly dipping or horizontal. ▷late 19th cent.: from **MONO-** 'single' + Greek *klinein* 'to lean.' **—mon·o·cli·nal** /ˌmänə'klīnl/ *adj.*

mon·o·clin·ic /ˌmänə'klinik/ ▸*adj.* of or denoting a crystal system or three-dimensional geometric arrangement having three unequal axes of which one is at right angles to the other two.

mon·o·clo·nal /ˌmänə'klōnl/ ▸*adj.* *Biology* forming a clone that is derived asexually from a single individual or cell.

mon·o·clo·nal an·ti·bod·y ▸*n.* an antibody produced by a single clone of cells or cell line and consisting of identical antibody molecules.

mon·o·coque /'mänəˌkōk; -ˌkäk/ ▸*n.* an aircraft or vehicle structure in which the chassis is integral with the body. ▷early 20th cent.: from French, from *mono-* 'single' + *coque* 'shell.'

mon·o·cot /'mänəˌkät/ ▸*n.* *Botany* short for **MONOCOTYLEDON**.

mon·o·cot·y·le·don /ˌmänəˌkätl'ēdn/ ▸*n.* *Botany* a flowering plant with an embryo that bears a single cotyledon (seed leaf). Monocotyledons constitute the smaller of the two great divisions of flowering plants, and typically have elongated stalkless leaves with parallel veins (e.g., grasses, lilies, palms). Compare with **DICOTYLEDON**. • Class Monocotyledoneae (or -donae, -dones; sometimes Liliopsida), subdivision Angiospermae. **—mon·o·cot·y·le·don·ous** /-'ēdn-əs/ *adj.*

mo·noc·ra·cy /mə'näkrəsē; mä-/ ▸*n.* (*pl.* **-cies**) a system of government by only one person. **—mon·o·crat** /'mänəˌkrat/ *n.* **—mon·o·crat·ic** /ˌmänə'kratik/ *adj.*

Pronunciation Key ə *ago*; ər *over*; 'ə or ˌə *up*; 'ər or ˌər *fur*; a *hat*; ā *rate*; ä *car*; CH *chew*; e *let*; ē *see*; e(ə)r *air*; i *fit*; ī *by*; i(ə)r *ear*; NG *sing*; ō *go*; ô *for*; oi *boy*; o͝o *good*; o͞o *goo*; ou *out*; SH *she*; TH *thin*; T͟H *then*; (h)w *why*; ZH *vision*

mo·noc·u·lar /mə'näkyələr; mä-/ ▸*adj.* with, for, or in one eye: *he had only monocular vision.*
▸*n.* an optical instrument for viewing distant objects with one eye, like one half of a pair of binoculars. ▷mid 17th cent.: from late Latin *monoculus* 'having one eye' + -AR[1]. **—mo·noc·u·lar·ly** *adv.*

mon·o·cul·ture /'mänə,kəlCHər/ ▸*n.* the cultivation of a single crop in a given area. **—mon·o·cul·tur·al** /,mänə'kəlCHərəl/ *adj.*

mon·o·cy·cle /'mänə,sīkəl/ ▸*n.* another term for UNICYCLE.

mon·o·cy·clic /,mänō'sīklik; -'sik-/ ▸*adj.* **1** *Chemistry* having one ring of atoms in its molecule. **2** *Botany* (of a set of floral parts such as sepals or stamens) forming a single whorl. **3** of or relating to a single cycle of activity.

mon·o·cyte /'mänə,sīt/ ▸*n. Physiology* a large phagocytic white blood cell with a simple oval nucleus and clear, grayish cytoplasm.

Mo·nod /mô'nō/, Jacques Lucien (1910–76), French biochemist. Together with fellow French biochemist François Jacob (1920–), he formulated a theory to explain how genes are activated, and, in 1961, he proposed the existence of messenger RNA. Nobel Prize for Physiology or Medicine (1965, shared with Jacob and André Lwoff 1902–94)

mon·o·dra·ma /'mänə,drämə; -,dramə/ ▸*n.* a dramatic piece for one performer.

mon·o·dy /'mänədē/ ▸*n.* (*pl.* **-dies**) **1** an ode sung by a single actor in a Greek tragedy. **2** a poem lamenting a person's death. **3** music with only one melodic line, esp. an early Baroque style with one singer and continuo accompaniment. ▷early 17th cent.: via late Latin from Greek *monōidia*, from *monōidos* 'singing alone.' **—mo·nod·ic** /mə'nädik/ *adj.* **—mon·o·dist** /-dist/ *n.*

mo·noe·cious /mə'nēsHəs/ ▸*adj. Biology* (of a plant or invertebrate animal) having both the male and female reproductive organs in the same individual; hermaphrodite. Compare with DIOECIOUS. ▷mid 18th cent.: from modern Latin *Monoecia* (denoting a class of such plants in Linnaeus's system), from Greek *monos* 'single' + *oikos* 'house.' **—mo·noe·cy** /'män,ēsē; 'mō-/ *n.*

mon·o·fil·a·ment /,mänə'filəmənt/ (also **mon·o·fil** /'mänə,fil/) ▸*n.* a single strand of man-made fiber. ■ a type of fishing line using such a strand.

mo·nog·a·my /mə'nägəmē/ ▸*n.* the practice or state of being married to one person at a time. ■ the practice or state of having a sexual relationship with only one partner. ■ *Zoology* the habit of having only one mate at a time. ▷early 17th cent.: from French *monogamie*, via ecclesiastical Latin from Greek *monogamia*, from *monos* 'single' + *gamos* 'marriage.' **—mo·nog·a·mist** /-mist/ *n.* **—mo·nog·a·mous** /-məs/ *adj.* **—mo·nog·a·mous·ly** /-məslē/ *adv.*

mon·o·ge·ne·an /,mänə'jēnēən/ *Zoology* ▸*adj.* of or relating to a group of flukes that are chiefly external or gill parasites of fish and only require a single host. Compare with DIGENEAN.
▸*n.* a monogenean fluke. • Class Monogenea, phylum Platyhelminthes; sometimes treated as a subclass of the class Trematoda. ▷1960s: from modern Latin *Monogenea* (from Greek *monos* 'single' + *genea* 'generation') + -AN.

mon·o·gen·e·sis /,mänə'jenəsəs/ ▸*n.* the theory that humans are all descended from a single pair of ancestors. Also called MONOGENY. ■ *Linguistics* the hypothetical origination of language or of a surname from a single source at a particular place and time. **—mon·o·ge·net·ic** /-jə'netik/ *adj.*

mon·o·gen·ic /,mänə'jenik/ ▸*adj. Genetics* involving or controlled by a single gene. **—mon·o·gen·i·cal·ly** /-ik(ə)lē/ *adv.*

mo·nog·e·ny /mə'näjənē/ ▸*n.* another term for MONOGENESIS. **—mo·nog·e·nism** /-,nizəm/ *n.* **—mo·nog·e·nist** /-jənist/ *n.*

mon·o·glot /'mänə,glät/ ▸*adj.* using or speaking only one language: *the moment when the monoglot heroine suddenly finds she can understand French.*
▸*n.* a person who speaks only one language. ▷mid 19th cent.: from Greek *monoglōttos*, from *monos* 'single' + *glōtta* 'tongue.'

mon·o·gram /'mänə,gram/ ▸*n.* a motif of two or more letters, typically a person's initials, usually interwoven or otherwise combined in a decorative design, used as a logo or to identify a personal possession.
▸*v.* [*trans.*] decorate with a monogram: [as *adj.*] (**monogrammed**) *monogrammed sheets.* ▷late 17th cent.: from French *monogramme*, from late Latin *monogramma*, from Greek. **—mon·o·gram·mat·ic** /,mänəgrə'matik/ *adj.*

mon·o·graph /'mänə,graf/ ▸*n.* a detailed written study of a single specialized subject or an aspect of it: *a series of monographs on music in late medieval and Renaissance cities.*
▸*v.* [*trans.*] write a monograph on; treat in a monograph. ▷early 19th cent. (earlier *monography*): from modern Latin *monographia*, from *monographus* 'writer on a single genus or species.' **—mo·nog·ra·pher** /mə'nägrəfər/ *n.* **—mo·nog·ra·phist** /mə'nägrəfist/ *n.*

mon·o·graph·ic /,mänə'grafik/ ▸*adj.* of or relating to a monograph. ■ (of an art gallery or exhibition) showing the works of a single artist.

mon·o·gyne /'mänə,jin/ ▸*adj. Entomology* (of a social insect) having only one egg-laying queen in each colony. ▷from MONO- 'one' + Greek *gunē* 'woman, wife.'

mo·nog·y·nous /mə'näjənəs/ ▸*adj. Botany* having only one pistil.

mo·nog·y·ny /mə'näjənē/ ▸*n.* the custom of having only one wife at a time. ■ *Entomology* the condition of having a single egg-laying queen in a colony of social insects. ▷late 19th cent.: from MONO- 'one' + Greek *gunē* 'woman, wife.'

mon·o·hull /'mänō,həl/ ▸*n.* a boat with only one hull, as opposed to a catamaran or multihull.

mon·o·hy·brid /,mänə'hībrid/ ▸*n. Genetics* a hybrid that is heterozygous with respect to a specified gene.

mon·o·hy·drate /,mänō'hī,drāt/ ▸*n. Chemistry* a hydrate containing one mole of water per mole of the compound.

mon·o·hy·dric /,mänō'hīdrik/ ▸*adj. Chemistry* (of an alcohol) containing one hydroxyl group.

mon·o·ki·ni /'mänə,kinē/ ▸*n.* a woman's one-piece beach garment equivalent to the lower half of a bikini. ▷1960s: from MONO- 'one' + a shortened form of BIKINI (the first syllable misinterpreted as *bi-* 'two').

Mo·no Lake /'mōnō/ a salt lake in east central California, near the Nevada border, noted for its rock exposed formations that occurred when local waters were diverted to the Los Angeles area.

mo·nol·a·try /mə'nälətrē/ ▸*n.* the worship of one god without denial of the existence of other gods. **—mo·nol·a·ter** /-tər/ *n.* **—mo·nol·a·trist** /-trist/ *n.* **—mo·nol·a·trous** /-trəs/ *adj.*

mon·o·lay·er /'mänə,lāər/ ▸*n. Chemistry* a layer one molecule thick. ■ *Biology & Medicine* a cell culture in a layer one cell thick.

mon·o·lin·gual /,mänə'liNGg(yə)wəl/ ▸*adj.* (of a person or society) speaking only one language: *monolingual families.* ■ (of a text, conversation, etc.) written or conducted in only one language: *monolingual and bilingual editions.*
▸*n.* a person who speaks only one language. **—mon·o·lin·gual·ism** /-,lizəm/ *n.*

mon·o·lith /'mänl-iTH/ ▸*n.* **1** a large single upright block of stone, esp. one shaped into or serving as a pillar or monument. ■ a very large and characterless building: *the 72-story monolith overlooking the waterfront.* ■ a large block of concrete sunk in water, e.g., in the building of a dock. **2** a large and impersonal political, corporate, or social structure regarded as intractably indivisible and uniform: *states struggling to break away from the Moscow-dominated communist monolith.* ▷mid 19th cent.: from French *monolithe*, from Greek *monolithos*, from *monos* 'single' + *lithos* 'stone.'

mon·o·lith·ic /,mänə'liTHik/ ▸*adj.* **1** formed of a single large block of stone. ■ (of a building) very large and characterless. **2** (of an organization or system) large, powerful, and intractably indivisible and uniform: *rejecting any move toward a monolithic European superstate.* **3** *Electronics* (of a solid-state circuit) composed of active and passive components formed in a single chip.

mon·o·logue /'mänl,ôg; -,äg/ ▸*n.* a long speech by one actor in a play or movie, or as part of a theatrical or broadcast program. ■ the form or style of such speeches: *the play oscillates between third-person narration and monologue.* ■ a long and typically tedious speech by one person during a conversation: *Fred carried on with his monologue as if I hadn't spoken.* ▷mid 17th cent.: from French, from Greek *monologos* 'speaking alone.' **—mon·o·log·ic** /,mänl'äjik/ *adj.* **—mon·o·log·i·cal** /,mänl'äjikəl/ *adj.* **—mon·o·log·ist** /mə'näləjist/ (also **-logu·ist**) *n.* **—mon·o·log·ize** /mə'nälə,jiz/ *v.*

mon·o·ma·ni·a /,mänə'mānēə/ ▸*n.* exaggerated or obsessive enthusiasm for or preoccupation with one thing. **—mon·o·ma·ni·ac** /-'mānē,ak/ *n.* & *adj.* **—mon·o·ma·ni·a·cal** /-mə'nīəkəl/ *adj.*

mon·o·mer /'mänəmər/ ▸*n. Chemistry* a molecule that can be bonded to other identical molecules to form a polymer. **—mon·o·mer·ic** /,mänə'merik/ *adj.*

mon·o·me·tal·lic /,mänōmə'talik/ ▸*adj.* consisting of one metal only. ■ of, involving, or using a standard of currency based on one metal. **—mon·o·met·al·lism** /-'metl,izəm/ *n.* **—mon·o·met·al·list** /-metlist/ *n.* & *adj.*

mo·no·mi·al /mə'nōmēəl; mä-/ *Mathematics* ▸*adj.* (of an algebraic expression) consisting of one term.
▸*n.* an algebraic expression of this type. ▷early 18th cent.: from MONO- 'one,' on the pattern of *binomial.*

mon·o·mo·lec·u·lar /,mänōmə'lekyələr/ ▸*adj. Chemistry* (of a layer) one molecule thick. ■ consisting of or involving one molecule.

mon·o·mor·phic /,mänə'môrfik/ ▸*adj.* chiefly *Biology* having or existing in only one form, in particular: ■ (of a species or population) showing little or no variation in morphology or phenotype. ■ (of an animal species) having sexes that are similar in size and appearance. ▷late 19th cent.: from MONO- 'single' + Greek *morphē* 'form.' **—mon·o·mor·phism** /-,fizəm/ *n.* **—mon·o·mor·phous** /-fəs/ *adj.*

Mo·non·ga·he·la Riv·er /mə,näNGgə'hēlə/ a river that flows for 128 miles (206 km) from West Virginia into western Pennsylvania to Pittsburgh where it joins the Allegheny River to form the Ohio River.

mon·o·nu·cle·ar /,mänō'n(y)o͞oklēər/ ▸*adj. Biology* (of a cell) having one nucleus.

mon·o·nu·cle·o·sis /,mänə,n(y)o͞oklē'ōsəs/ ▸*n. Medicine* an abnormally high proportion of monocytes in the blood. ■ short for INFECTIOUS MONONUCLEOSIS. Also called MONO.

mo·noph·a·gous /mə'näfəgəs/ ▸*adj. Zoology* (of an animal) eating only one kind of food.

mon·o·phon·ic /,mänə'fänik/ ▸*adj.* **1** *Music* consisting of a single musical line, without accompaniment: *the style of monophonic singing known as Gregorian chant.* **2** (of sound reproduction) using only one channel of transmission. Compare with STEREOPHONIC. ▷early 19th cent.: from MONO- 'one' + Greek *phōnē* 'sound' + -IC. **—mon·o·phon·i·cal·ly** /-ik(ə)lē/ *adv.* **—mo·noph·o·ny** /mə'näfənē/ *n.*

mon·oph·thong /'mänə(f),THôNG/ ▸*n. Phonetics* a vowel that has a single perceived auditory quality. Contrasted with DIPHTHONG, TRIPHTHONG. ▷early 17th cent.: from Greek *monophthongos*, from *monos* 'single' + *phthongos* 'sound.' **—mon·oph·thon·gal** /,mänə(f)'THôNG(g)əl/ *adj.*

mon·o·phy·let·ic /,mänōfī'letik/ ▸*adj. Biology* (of a group of organisms) descended from a common evolutionary ancestor or ancestral group, esp. one not shared with any other group.

Mo·noph·y·site /mə'näfə,sīt/ ▸*n. Christian Theology* a person who holds that in the person of Jesus Christ there is only one nature (wholly divine or only subordinately human), not two. ▷late 17th cent.: via ecclesiastical Latin from ecclesiastical Greek *monophusitēs*, from *monos* 'single' + *phusis* 'nature.' **—Mo·noph·y·sit·ism** /-,sīt,izəm/ *n.*

mon·o·plane /'mänə,plān/ ▸*n.* an airplane with one pair of wings. Often contrasted with BIPLANE, TRIPLANE.

mon·o·ple·gi·a /,mänō'plēj(ē)ə/ ▸*n.* paralysis restricted to one limb or region of the body. Compare with PARAPLEGIA. **—mon·o·ple·gic** /-'plējik/ *adj.*

mon·o·ploid /'mänə,ploid/ ▸*adj.* less common term for HAPLOID.

mon·o·pod /'mänə,päd/ ▸*n.* a one-legged support for a camera or fishing rod. ▷early 19th cent.: via Latin from Greek *monopodion*, from *monos* 'single' + *pous, pod-* 'foot.'

mon·o·po·di·um /,mänə'pōdēəm/ ▸*n.* (*pl.* **-po·di·a** /-'pōdēə/) *Botany* a single continuous growth axis that extends at its apex and produces successive lateral shoots. Compare with SYMPODIUM. **—mon·o·po·di·al** /-dēəl/ *adj.*

mon·o·pole /'mänə,pōl/ ▸*n.* **1** *Physics* a single electric charge or magnetic pole, esp. a hypothetical isolated magnetic pole. **2** a radio antenna or pylon consisting of a single pole or rod.

mo·nop·o·list /mə'näpəlist/ ▸*n.* a person or business that has a monopoly. **—mo·nop·o·lis·tic** /mə,näpə'listik/ *adj.* **—mo·nop·o·lis·ti·cal·ly** /mə,näpə'listik(ə)lē/ *adv.*

mo·nop·o·lize /mə'näpə,līz/ ▸*v.* [*trans.*] (of an organization or group) obtain exclusive possession or control of (a trade, commodity, or service). ■ have or take the greatest share of: *the bigger teams monopolize the most profitable sponsorships and TV deals.* ■ get or keep exclusively to oneself: *Sophie monopolized the guest of honor for most of the evening.* **—mo·nop·o·li·za·tion** /mə,näpələ'zāshən/ *n.* **—mo·nop·o·liz·er** *n.*

mo·nop·o·ly /mə'näpəlē/ ▸*n.* (*pl.* **-lies**) **1** the exclusive possession or control of the supply or trade in a commodity or service: *his likely motive was to protect his regional* ***monopoly on*** *furs.* ■ [usu. with *negative*] the exclusive possession, control, or exercise of something: *men don't have a* ***monopoly on*** *unrequited love.* ■ a company or group having exclusive control over a commodity or service: *areas where cable companies operate as monopolies.* ■ a commodity or service controlled in this way: *electricity, gas, and water were considered to be natural monopolies.* **2** (**Monopoly**) *trademark* a board game in which players engage in simulated property and financial dealings using imitation money. It was invented in the U.S. and the name was coined by Charles Darrow *c.*1935. ▷mid 16th cent.: via Latin from Greek *monopōlion*, from *monos* 'single' + *pōlein* 'sell.'

mo·nop·o·ly cap·i·tal·ism // ▸*n. Economics* a capitalist system typified by trade monopolies in the hands of a few people.

Mo·nop·o·ly mon·ey ▸*n.* imitation money used in the game of Monopoly. ■ *figurative* money having no real existence or value.

mon·o·pro·pel·lant /,mänōprə'pelənt/ ▸*n.* a substance used as rocket fuel without an additional oxidizing agent.
▸*adj.* using such a substance.

mo·nop·so·ny /mə'näpsənē/ ▸*n.* (*pl.* **-nies**) *Economics* a market situation in which there is only one buyer. ▷1930s: from **MONO-** 'one' + Greek *opsōnein* 'buy provisions' + **-Y**[3].

mon·o·pulse /'mänə,pəls/ ▸*adj.* denoting a system of radar in which the angular location of a target is determined by comparison of two or more simultaneously received signals.
▸*n.* a monopulse radar system or installation. ▷late 1950s: from *mono*, 'one' + *pulse*

mon·o·rail /'mänə,rāl/ ▸*n.* a railroad in which the track consists of a single rail, typically elevated, with the trains suspended from it or balancing on it.

mon·or·chid /mä'nôrkəd/ ▸*adj.* (of a person or animal) having only one testicle.
▸*n.* such a person or animal. ▷early 19th cent.: from modern Latin *monorchis*, *monorchid-*, from Greek *monos* 'single' + *orkhis* 'testicle.' **—mon·or·chid·ism** /mä'nôrki,dizəm/ *n.*

mon·o·sac·cha·ride /,mänə'sakə,rīd/ ▸*n. Chemistry* any of the class of sugars (e.g., glucose) that cannot be hydrolyzed to give a simpler sugar.

mon·o·se·my /'mänə,sēmē/ ▸*n. Linguistics* the property of having only one meaning. ▷1950s: from **MONO-** 'one' + Greek *sēma* 'sign' + **-Y**[3]. **—mon·o·se·mous** /,mänə'sēməs/ *adj.*

mon·o·ski /'mänə,skē/ ▸*n.* a single broad ski attached to both feet. **—mon·o·ski·er** /-,skēər/ *n.* **—mon·o·ski·ing** /-,skē-iNG/ *n.*

mon·o·so·di·um glu·ta·mate /,mänə,sōdēəm 'gloōtə,māt/ (abbr.: **MSG**) ▸*n.* a compound that occurs naturally as a breakdown product of proteins and is used as a flavor enhancer in food (although itself tasteless). A traditional ingredient in Asian cooking, it was originally obtained from seaweed but is now mainly made from bean and cereal protein. • Chem. formula: $HOOC(CH_2)_2(NH_2)COONa$.

mon·o·some /'mänə,sōm/ ▸*n. Biology* an unpaired (usually X) chromosome in a diploid chromosome complement.

mon·o·so·my /'mänə,sōmē/ ▸*n. Biology* the condition of having a diploid chromosome complement in which one (usually the X) chromosome lacks its homologous partner. **—mon·o·so·mic** /,mänə'sōmik/ *adj.*

mon·o·spe·cif·ic /,mänōspə'sifik/ ▸*adj. Biology* relating to or consisting of only one species. ■ (of an antibody) specific to one antigen.

mon·o·stroph·ic /,mänə'sträfik; -'strōfik/ ▸*adj. Prosody* consisting of repetitions of the same strophic arrangement.

mon·o·syl·lab·ic /,mänəsə'labik/ ▸*adj.* (of a word or utterance) consisting of one syllable. ■ (of a person) using brief words to signify reluctance to engage in conversation: *the nearer they came to Rome, the more quiet and monosyllabic Paul seemed to become.* **—mon·o·syl·lab·i·cal·ly** /-ik(ə)lē/ *adv.*

mon·o·syl·la·ble /,mänə'siləbəl; 'mänə,sil-/ ▸*n.* a word consisting of only one syllable. ■ (**monosyllables**) brief words, signifying reluctance to engage in conversation: *if she spoke at all it was* ***in monosyllables.***

mon·o·syn·ap·tic /,mänōsə'naptik/ ▸*adj. Physiology* (of a reflex pathway) involving a single synapse.

mon·o·the·ism /'mänə,thē,izəm/ ▸*n.* the doctrine or belief that there is only one God. ▷mid 17th cent.: from **MONO-** 'one' + Greek *theos* 'god' + **-ISM**. **—mon·o·the·ist** *n.* & *adj.* **—mon·o·the·is·tic** /,mänəthē'istik/ *adj.* **—mon·o·the·is·ti·cal·ly** /,mänəthē'istik(ə)lē/ *adv.*

Mo·noth·e·lite /mə'näthə,līt/ (also **Mo·noth·e·lete** /-,lēt/) ▸*n. Christian Theology* an adherent of the doctrine that Jesus had only one will, proposed in the 7th century to reconcile Monophysite and orthodox parties in the Byzantine Empire but condemned as heresy. ▷late Middle English: via ecclesiastical Latin from ecclesiastical Greek *monothelētēs*, from *monos* 'single' + *thelētēs* 'one that wills'(from *thelein* 'to will').

mon·o·tint /'mänə,tint/ ▸*n.* archaic term for **MONOCHROME**.

mon·o·tone /'mänə,tōn/ ▸*n.* [usu. in *sing.*] a continuing sound, esp. of someone's voice, that is unchanging in pitch and without intonation: *he sat and answered the questions* ***in a monotone.***
▸*adj.* (of a voice or other sound) unchanging in pitch; without intonation or expressiveness: *his monotone reading of the two-hour report.* ■ *figurative* without vividness or variety; dull: *the monotone housing developments of the big cities.* ■ of a single color: *this monotone effect is responsible for making the room seem larger than it is.* ▷mid 17th cent.: from modern Latin *monotonus*, from late Greek *monotonos*.

mon·o·ton·ic /,mänə'tänik/ ▸*adj.* **1** *Mathematics* (of a function or quantity) varying in such a way that it either never decreases or never increases. **2** speaking or uttered with an unchanging pitch or tone: *her dour, monotonic husband.* **—mon·o·ton·i·cal·ly** /-ik(ə)lē/ *adv.* **—mon·o·to·nic·i·ty** /,mänətn'isətē/ *n.*

mo·not·o·nous /mə'nätn-əs/ ▸*adj.* dull, tedious, and repetitious; lacking in variety and interest: *the statistics that he quotes with monotonous regularity.* ■ (of a sound or utterance) lacking in variation in tone or pitch: *soon we heard a low, monotonous wailing of many voices.* **—mo·not·o·nous·ly** *adv.*

mo·not·o·ny /mə'nätn-ē/ ▸*n.* lack of variety and interest; tedious repetition and routine: *you can become resigned to the* ***monotony of*** *captivity.* ■ sameness of pitch or tone in a sound or utterance: *depression flattens the voice almost to monotony.*

mon·o·treme /'mänə,trēm/ ▸*n. Zoology* a primitive mammal that lays large yolky eggs and has a common opening for the urogenital and digestive systems. Monotremes are now restricted to Australia and New Guinea, and comprise the platypus and the echidnas. • Order Monotremata and subclass Prototheria: two families. ▷mid 19th cent.: from **MONO-** 'single' + Greek *trēma* 'hole.'

mon·o·type /'mänə,tīp/ ▸*n.* **1** (**Monotype**) [usu. as *adj.*] *trademark Printing* a typesetting machine, now little used, that casts type in metal, one character at a time. **2** a single print taken from a design created in oil paint or printing ink on glass or metal. **3** *Biology* a monotypic genus or other taxon.

mon·o·typ·ic /,mänə'tipik/ ▸*adj. chiefly Biology* having only one type or representative, esp. (of a genus) containing only one species.

mon·o·un·sat·u·rat·ed /,mänō,ən'sachə,rātid/ ▸*adj. Chemistry* (of an organic compound, esp. a fat) saturated except for one multiple bond.

mon·o·va·lent /,mänə'vālənt/ ▸*adj. Chemistry* having a valence of one.

mon·ox·ide /mə'näk,sīd/ ▸*n. Chemistry* an oxide containing one atom of oxygen in its molecule or empirical formula.

mon·o·zy·got·ic /,mänō,zī'gätik/ (also **mon·o·zy·gous** /,mänə'zīgəs/) ▸*adj.* (of twins) derived from a single ovum, and so identical. ▷early 20th cent.: from **MONO-** 'single' + **ZYGOTE** + **-IC**. **—mon·o·zy·gos·ity** /-'gäsitē/ *n.*

Mon·roe[1] /mən'rō/ an industrial and commercial city in north central Louisiana, in a natural gas producing area; pop. 53,107.

Mon·roe[2], James (1758–1831), 5th president of the U.S. 1817–25. In 1803, while minister to France under President Jefferson, he negotiated and ratified the Louisiana Purchase. During his presidency, the Adams-Onis Treaty 1819, which allowed the U.S. to acquire Florida from Spain, was negotiated. A Democrat Republican, he is chiefly remembered, however, as the originator of the Monroe Doctrine.

Mon·roe[3], Marilyn (1926–62), U.S. actress; born *Norma Jean Mortenson*; later *Norma Jean Baker*. Her movie roles, largely in comedies, made her the definitive Hollywood sex symbol. Her husbands included Arthur Miller and Joe DiMaggio. She is thought to have died of an overdose of sleeping pills. Notable movies: *Gentlemen Prefer Blondes* (1953), *Some Like it Hot* (1959), and *The Misfits* (1961).

Marilyn Monroe

Mon·roe Doc·trine /mən'rō/ a principle of U.S. policy, originated by President James Monroe in 1823, that any intervention by external powers in the politics of the Americas is a potentially hostile act against the U.S.

Mon·ro·vi·a /mən'rōvēə/ **1** the capital and chief port of Liberia; pop. 500,000. Founded in 1822 for resettled U.S. slaves, it was later named for President James Monroe. **2** an industrial city in southwestern California, northeast of Los Angeles; pop. 35,761.

mons /mänz/ ▸*n.* short for **MONS PUBIS**.

Mon·sei·gneur /,mōnsān'yər/ ▸*n.* (*pl.* **Mes·sei·gneurs** /,māsān'yər(z)/) a title or form of address used of or to a French-speaking prince, cardinal, archbishop, or bishop. ▷French, from *mon* 'my' + *seigneur* 'lord.'

Mon·sieur /mə'syœ(r); mə'syər/ ▸*n.* (*pl.* **Mes·sieurs** /mə'syœ(r)(z); mā-; mə'syər(z)/) a title or form of address used of or to a French-speaking man, corresponding to *Mr.* or *sir*: *Monsieur Hulot | you are right, Monsieur.* ▷French, from *mon* 'my' + *sieur* 'lord.'

Mon·si·gnor /män'sēnyər; mən-/ ▸*n.* (*pl.* **Mon·si·gno·ri** /,mänsēn'yôrē/) the title of various senior Roman Catholic positions, such as a prelate or an officer of the papal court. ▷Italian, on the pattern of French *Monseigneur*.

mon·soon /män'soōn; 'män,soōn/ ▸*n.* a seasonal prevailing wind in the region of the Indian subcontinent and Southeast Asia, blowing from the southwest between May and September and bringing rain (the **wet monsoon**), or from the northeast between October and April (the **dry monsoon**). ■ the rainy season accompanying the wet monsoon. ▷late 16th cent.: from Portuguese *monção*, from Arabic *mawsim* 'season,' from *wasama* 'to mark, brand.' **—mon·soon·al** /män'soōnl/ *adj.*

mons pu·bis /'mänz 'pyoōbis/ ▸*n.* (*pl.* **mon·tes p·ubis** /'mäntēz/) the rounded mass of fatty tissue lying over the joint of the pubic bones, in women typically more prominent and also called the **mons veneris**. ▷late 19th cent.: Latin, 'mount of the pubes.'

James Monroe

Pronunciation Key ə *ago*; ər *over*; 'ə or ,ə *up*; 'ər or ,ər *fur*; a *hat*; ā *rate*; ä *car*; ch *chew*; e *let*; ē *see*; e(ə)r *air*; i *fit*; ī *by*; i(ə)r *ear*; ng *sing*; ō *go*; ô *for*; oi *boy*; oo *good*; oō *goo*; ou *out*; sh *she*; th *thin*; th *then*; (h)w *why*; zh *vision*

M

mon·ster /ˈmänstər/ ▸*n.* an imaginary creature that is typically large, ugly, and frightening. ■ an inhumanly cruel or wicked person: *he was an unfeeling, treacherous monster.* ■ *often humorous* a person, typically a child, who is rude or badly behaved: *Christopher is only a year old, but already he is a* **little monster**. ■ a thing or animal that is excessively or dauntingly large: *this is a* **monster of** *a book, almost 500 pages.* ■ a congenitally malformed or mutant animal or plant. ▸*adj.* [*attrib.*] *informal* of an extraordinary and daunting size or extent: *outfitted with a monster 120-mm gun.* ▸*v.* [*trans.*] *informal, chiefly Brit.* criticize or reprimand severely: *my mother used to monster me for coming home so late.* ▷late Middle English: from Old French *monstre*, from Latin *monstrum* 'portent or monster,' from *monere* 'warn.'

mon·ster·a /ˈmänstərə/ ▸*n.* a large tropical American climbing plant of the arum family that typically has divided or perforated leaves and corky aerial roots. Several kinds are cultivated as indoor plants when young. • Genus *Monstera*, family Araceae: several species, including the ceriman. ▷modern Latin, perhaps from Latin *monstrum* 'monster' (because of the unusual appearance of the leaves in some species).

mon·ster truck ▸*n.* an extremely large pickup truck, typically with greatly oversized tires. They are often raced across rough terrain or featured in exhibitions in which they drive over and demolish smaller automobiles.

mon·strance /ˈmänstrəns/ ▸*n.* (in the Roman Catholic Church) an open or transparent receptacle in which the consecrated Host is exposed for veneration. ▷late Middle English (also in the sense 'demonstration or proof'): from medieval Latin *monstrantia*, from Latin *monstrare* 'to show.'

mon·stros·i·ty /mänˈsträsətē/ ▸*n.* (*pl.* **-ties**) **1** something, esp. a building, that is very large and is considered unsightly: *the shopping center, a multistory monstrosity of raw concrete.* ■ something that is outrageously or offensively wrong: *he rebelled against Nazi monstrosities.* ■ a grossly malformed animal, plant, or person. **2** the state or fact of being monstrous. ▷mid 16th cent. (denoting an abnormality of growth): from late Latin *monstrositas*, from Latin *monstrosus* (see **MONSTROUS**).

mon·strous /ˈmänstrəs/ ▸*adj.* having the ugly or frightening appearance of a monster: *monstrous, bug-eyed fish.* ■ (of a person or an action) inhumanly or outrageously evil or wrong: *he wasn't lovable, he was monstrous and violent | it is a monstrous waste of money.* ■ extremely and dauntingly large: *the monstrous tidal wave swamped the surrounding countryside.* ▷late Middle English (in the sense 'strange or unnatural'): from Old French *monstreux* or Latin *monstrosus*, from *monstrum* (see **MONSTER**). Current senses date from the 16th cent. **—mon·strous·ly** *adv.* **—mon·strous·ness** *n.*

mons ve·ne·ris /ˈmänz ˈvenərəs/ ▸*n.* (*pl.* **mon·tes ve·ne·ris** /ˈmäntēz/) (in women) the mons pubis. ▷late 17th cent.: Latin, 'mount of Venus.'

Mont. ▸*abbr.* Montana.

mon·tage /mänˈtäzh; mōn-; mōn-/ ▸*n.* the process or technique of selecting, editing, and piecing together separate sections of film to form a continuous whole. ■ a sequence of film resulting from this: *a dazzling montage of the movie's central banquet scene.* ■ the technique of producing a new composite whole from fragments of pictures, text, or music: *the play often verged on montage.* ▷early 20th cent.: French, from *monter* 'to mount.'

Mon·ta·gnais /ˌmäntənˈyā/ ▸*n.* (*pl.* same) **1** a member of an American Indian people living in a vast area of Canada from north of the Gulf of St. Lawrence to the southern shores of Hudson Bay. **2** the Algonquian language of this people, closely related to Cree. ▸*adj.* of or relating to this people or their language. ▷from French, literally 'of the mountains.'

Mon·ta·gnard /ˌmäntənˈyärd/ ▸*n.* & *adj.* former term for **HMONG**. ▷French, from *montagne* 'mountain.'

Mon·taigne /mänˈtān; mônˈtenyə/, Michel (Eyquem) de (1533–92), French essayist. Widely regarded as the originator of the modern essay, he wrote about prominent personalities and ideas of his age in his skeptical *Essays* (1580 and 1588).

Mon·tan·a[1] /mänˈtanə/ a state in the western U.S., on the Canadian border, east of the Rocky Mountains; pop. 902,195; capital, Helena; statehood, Nov. 8, 1889 (41). Acquired from France as part of the Louisiana Purchase in 1803, it was explored by Lewis and Clark in 1805–06. **—Mon·tan·an** *adj.* & *n.*

Mon·tan·a[2] /mänˈtanə/, Joe (1956–), U.S. football player. He joined the San Francisco 49ers as quarterback in 1980 and played in four winning Super Bowls (1982, 1985, 1989, and 1990). He retired in 1995 after two seasons with the Kansas City Chiefs. Football Hall of Fame (2000).

mon·tane /mänˈtān; ˈmänˌtān/ ▸*adj.* [*attrib.*] of or inhabiting mountainous country: *montane grasslands.* ▷mid 19th cent.: from Latin *montanus*, from *mons*, *mont-* 'mountain.'

Mon·ta·nism /ˈmäntəˌnizəm/ ▸*n.* the tenets of a heretical millenarian and ascetic Christian sect that set great store by prophecy, founded in Phrygia by the priest Montanus in the middle of the 2nd century. **—Mon·ta·nist** *n.*

Mont Blanc /ˌmôn ˈbläNGk/ a mountain in the Alps on the border between France and Italy that is 15,771 feet (4,807 m) high. It is the highest peak in the Alps and in western Europe.

mont·bre·tia /mäntˈbrēsH(ē)ə/ ▸*n.* a plant of the iris family with bright orange-yellow trumpet-shaped flowers. • *Crocosmia × crocosmiflora*, family Iridaceae. ▷late 19th cent.: modern Latin, named after A. F. E. Coquebert de *Montbret* (1780–1801), French botanist.

Mont·calm /ˌmäntˈkäm/, Louis Joseph de Montcalm-Gozon, Marquis de (1712–59), French general. He defended Quebec against British troops, but was defeated and fatally wounded in the battle on the Plains of Abraham.

Mont Cer·vin /ˌmôn sərˈven/ French name for **MATTERHORN**.

Mont·clair /mäntˈkle(ə)r/ a township in northeastern New Jersey, northwest of Newark; pop. 37,729.

mon·te /ˈmäntē/ ▸*n.* **1** short for **THREE-CARD MONTE**. **2** a Spanish game of chance, played with forty-five cards. ▷early 19th cent.: Spanish, literally 'mountain,' also 'heap of cards left after dealing' (from an earlier game of chance played with forty-five cards).

Mon·te Al·bán /ˈmôntä älˈbän/ an ancient city, now in ruins, in Oaxaca, southern Mexico. Occupied from the 8th century BC, it was a center of the Zapotec culture from about the 1st century BC to the 8th century AD.

Mon·te Car·lo /ˌmäntē ˈkärlō/ a resort in Monaco that forms one of the four communes of the principality; pop. 12,000. It is famous as a gambling resort and as the terminus of the annual Monte Carlo automobile rally.

Mon·te Car·lo meth·od ▸*n.* *Statistics* a technique in which a large quantity of randomly generated numbers are studied using a probabilistic model to find an approximate solution to a numerical problem that would be difficult to solve by other methods. ▷1940s: named after *Monte Carlo* (see **MONTE CARLO**), a resort famous for its gambling casino.

Mon·te Cas·si·no /ˌmäntē kəˈsēnō/ a hill in central Italy near the town of Cassino, the site of the principal monastery of the Benedictines, founded by St. Benedict *c.*529. The monastery and the town were destroyed in 1944 during bitter fighting between Allied and German forces, but have since been restored.

Mon·te Cer·vi·no /ˌmôntä cHərˈvēnō/ Italian name for **MATTERHORN**.

Mon·te·go Bay /mənˈtēgō/ a free port and tourist resort on the northern coast of Jamaica; pop. 82,000.

Mon·te·ne·gro /ˌmäntəˈnegrō/ a mountainous, landlocked republic in the Balkans, formerly part of Yugoslavia; pop. 632,000; capital, Podgorica. Joined with Serbia before the Turkish conquest of 1355, Montenegro became independent in 1851. In 1918, it became part of the federation of Yugoslavia. Communism ended in 1991, Yugoslavia disintegrated along ethnic lines, and Serbia and Montenegro declared a new Federal Republic of Yugoslavia in April 1992. In February 2003, the two republics formed a loose federation called Serbia and Montenegro. **—Mon·te·ne·grin** /-ˈnegrən/ *adj.* & *n.*

Mon·te·rey /ˌmäntəˈrā; ˈmäntəˌrā/ a city and fishing port on the coast of California, founded by the Spanish in the 18th century; pop. 31,954.

Mon·te·rey cy·press ▸*n.* a cypress tree with a large spreading crown of horizontal branches and leaves that smell of lemon when crushed, native to a small area of California and widely planted in temperate climates worldwide. Also called **MACROCARPA**. • *Cupressus macrocarpa*, family Cupressaceae.

Mon·te·rey Jack (also **Monterey cheese** or **Jack cheese**) ▸*n.* a kind of cheese resembling cheddar. ▷from the name of *Monterey* County, California, where it was first made; the origin of *Jack* is unknown.

Mon·ter·rey /ˌmäntəˈrā/ an industrial city in northeastern Mexico, capital of the state of Nuevo León; pop. 2,522,000.

Mon·tes·pan /ˈmäntəˌspan; mônteˈspäN/, Françoise-Athénaïs de Rochechouart, Marquise de (1641–1707), French noblewoman. The mistress of Louis XIV from 1667 to 1679, she had seven children by him. She was replaced in the king's affections by Madame de Maintenon, the children's governess.

Mon·tes·quieu /ˌmäntiˈskyōō; mônteˈskyœ/, Charles Louis de Secondat, Baron de La Brède et de (1689–1755), French political philosopher. He is best known for *L'Esprit des lois* (1748), a comparative study of political systems in which he championed the separation of judicial, legislative, and executive powers as being most conducive to individual liberty.

Mon·tes·so·ri[1] /ˌmäntəˈsôrē/, Maria (1870–1952), Italian educator. In her book, *The Montessori Method* (1909), she advocated a child-centered approach to education, developed from her success with mentally handicapped children.

Mon·tes·so·ri[2] ▸*n.* [usu. as *adj.*] a system of education for young children that seeks to develop natural interests and activities rather than use formal teaching methods: *a Montessori school.* ▷early 20th cent.: named after M. *Montessori* (see **MONTESSORI**[1]).

Mon·te·ver·di /ˌmäntəˈverdē; ˌmonte-/, Claudio (1567–1643), Italian composer. He is noted for the use of harmonic dissonance in his madrigals. He wrote the opera *Orfeo* (1607) and *Vespers* (1610).

Mon·te·vi·de·o /ˌmäntəviˈdāō/ the capital and chief port of Uruguay, on the Plate River; pop. 1,360,000.

Mon·tez /ˈmäntez; mänˈtez/, Lola (1818–61), Irish dancer; born *Marie Dolores Eliza Rosanna Gilbert*. She became the mistress of Ludwig I of Bavaria in 1846 and exercised great influence over him until she was banished the following year.

Mon·te·zu·ma II /ˌmäntiˈzōōmə/ (1466–1520), Aztec emperor 1502–20. The last ruler of the Aztec empire in Mexico, he was defeated and imprisoned by the Spanish under Cortés in 1519.

Mon·te·zu·ma's re·venge ▸*n.* *informal* diarrhea suffered by travelers, esp. visitors to Mexico.

Mont·fort[1] /ˈmäntfərt; mônˈfôr/, Simon de (*c.*1165–1218), French soldier; father of Simon de Montfort, Earl of Leicester. From 1209, he led the Albigensian Crusade against the Cathars in southern France.

Mont·fort[2], Simon de, Earl of Leicester (*c.*1208–65), English soldier, born in Normandy. The son of Simon de Montfort, he led the baronial opposition to Henry III, defeating the king at Lewes in 1264 and summoning a Parliament in 1265.

Mont·gol·fi·er /mäntˈgälfēər; mônGôlˈfyā/, Joseph Michel (1740–1810) and Jacques Étienne (1745–99), French inventors and pioneers in hot-air ballooning.

Mont·gom·er·y[1] /məntˈgəm(ə)rē/ the state capital of Alabama; pop. 201,568. It served as the capital of the Confederate States of America from February until July during 1861.

Mont·gom·er·y[2], Bernard Law, 1st Viscount Montgomery of Alamein (1887–1976), British field marshal; known as **Monty**. His victory at El Alamein in 1942 was the first significant Allied success in World War II. He commanded the Allied ground forces in the invasion of Normandy in 1944 and accepted the German surrender on May 7, 1945.

Mont·gom·er·y[3], L. M. (1874–1942), Canadian novelist; full name *Lucy Maud Montgomery*. She is noted for *Anne of Green Gables* (1908) and its sequels, set on Prince Edward Island.

Mont·gom·ery Coun·ty a county in central Maryland that contains many suburbs north of Washington, DC; pop. 873,341.

month /mənTH/ ▸*n.* (also **calendar month**) each of the twelve named periods into which a year is divided: *the first six months of 1992 | it was the end of the month.* ■ a period of time between the same dates in successive calendar months: *the president's rule was extended for six more months from March 3.* ■ a period of 28 days or four weeks: *the fourth month of pregnancy.* ■ a lunar month. ▷Old English *mōnath*, of Germanic origin; related to Dutch *maand* and German *Monat*, also to **MOON**.

▸*PHRASE* □ **a month of Sundays** *informal* a very long, seemingly endless period of time: *no one will find them in a month of Sundays.*

month-long (also **month·long**) ▸*adj.* [*attrib.*] of a month's duration: *a month-long fishing trip.*

month·ly /ˈmənTHlē/ ▸*adj.* [*attrib.*] done, produced, or occurring once a month: *the council held monthly meetings.*

▸*adv.* once a month; every month; from month to month: *most of us get paid monthly.*
▸*n.* (*pl.* **-lies**) **1** a magazine that is published once a month. **2** (**monthlies**) *informal* a menstrual period.

Mon·ti·cel·lo /ˌmäntəˈselō/ a historic estate southeast of Charlottesville, in central Virginia, the home of Thomas Jefferson.

Monticello

mon·ti·cule /ˈmäntiˌkyo͞ol/ ▸*n.* a small hill. ■ a small mound caused by a volcanic eruption. ▷late 18th cent.: from French, from late Latin *monticulus,* diminutive of *mons, mont-* 'mountain.'

Mont·mar·tre /mônˈmärtrə/ a district in northern Paris, on a hill above the Seine River, much frequented by artists in the late 19th and early 20th centuries when it was a separate village.

mont·mo·ril·lon·ite /ˌmäntməˈriləˌnīt/ ▸*n.* an aluminum-rich clay mineral of the smectite group, containing some sodium and magnesium. ▷mid 19th cent.: from *Montmorillon,* the name of a town in France, + -ITE¹.

Mont·par·nasse /ˌmônpärˈnäs/ a district of Paris, on the left bank of the Seine River. Frequented in the late 19th century by writers and artists, it is traditionally associated with Parisian cultural life.

Mont·pe·lier /mäntˈpēlyər/ the capital of Vermont, in the north central part of the state, on the Winooski River; pop. 8,035.

Mont·pel·lier /ˌmônpelˈyā/ a city in southern France, near the Mediterranean coast, capital of Languedoc-Roussillon; pop. 211,000. A medical school and university, world famous in medieval times, was founded here in 1221.

Mon·tra·chet /ˌmōnträˈshe/ ▸*n.* a white wine produced in the Montrachet region of France.

Mont·re·al /ˌmäntrēˈôl/ a port on the St. Lawrence River in Quebec, southeastern Canada; pop. 1,017,666. Founded in 1642, it was under French rule until 1763; almost two thirds of its present-day population are French-speaking. French name **MONTRÉAL**.

Mont St. Mi·chel /ˈmôn san mēˈshel/, a rocky islet off the coast of Normandy, northwestern France. An island only at high tide, it is surrounded by sandbanks and linked to the mainland by a causeway. It is home to a medieval Benedictine abbey-fortress.

Mont·ser·rat /ˌmäntsəˈrät/ an island in the Caribbean, one of the Leeward Islands; pop. 12,000; capital, Plymouth. It was visited by Columbus in 1493 and named after a Benedictine monastery on the mountain of Montserrat in Catalonia, northeastern Spain. Colonized by Irish settlers in 1632 and now a British dependency, it has been severely affected by the ongoing eruption of the Soufrière Hills volcano since 1995. ▷visited by Columbus in 1493, the island was named after a Benedictine monastery on the mountain of *Montserrat* in Catalonia in northeastern Spain. **—Mont·ser·ra·ti·an** /-ˈrātēən/ *adj. & n.*

mon·tu·no /mänˈto͞onō/ ▸*n.* (*pl.* **-nos**) an improvised passage in a rumba. ▷mid 20th cent.: American Spanish, 'native to mountains, wild.'

mon·ty /ˈmäntē/ ▸*n.* (in phrase **the full monty**) *Brit., informal* the full amount expected, desired, or possible: *they'll do the full monty for a few thousand each.* ▷of unknown origin; the phrase is only recorded recently. Among various (unsubstantiated) theories, one cites the phrase *the full Montague Burton,* apparently meaning 'Sunday-best three-piece suit' (from the name of a tailor of made-to-measure clothing in the early 20th cent.); another recounts the possibility of a military usage, *the full monty* being 'the full cooked English breakfast' insisted upon by Field Marshal *Montgomery.*

mon·u·ment /ˈmänyəmənt/ ▸*n.* a statue, building, or other structure erected to commemorate a famous or notable person or event. ■ a statue or other structure placed by or over a grave in memory of the dead. ■ a building, structure, or site that is of historical importance or interest: *the amphitheater is one of the many Greek monuments in Sicily.* ■ *figurative* an outstanding, enduring, and memorable example of something: *recordings that are a* **monument to** *the art of playing the piano.* ■ a marker, typically of concrete or stone, placed at the boundary of a piece of property. ▷Middle English (denoting a burial place): via French from Latin *monumentum,* from *monere* 'remind.'

mon·u·men·tal /ˌmänyəˈmentl/ ▸*adj.* great in importance, extent, or size: *it's been a monumental effort.* ■ (of a work of art) great in ambition and scope: *the ballet came across as one of MacMillan's most monumental works.* ■ of or serving as a monument: *additional details are found in monumental inscriptions.* **—mon·u·men·tal·ism** *n.* **—mon·u·men·tal·i·ty** /ˌmänyəˌmenˈtalətē/ *n.* **—mon·u·men·tal·ly** /-ˈmentl-ē/ *adv.*

mon·u·men·tal·ize /ˌmänyəˈmentlˌīz/ ▸*v.* [*trans.*] make a permanent record of (something) by or as if by creating a monument: *a culture that too eagerly monumentalizes what it values.*

Mon·u·ment Val·ley a region in northeastern Arizona and southern Utah, west of the Four Corners, whose scenery has been the backdrop for many movies.

-mony ▸*suffix* forming nouns often denoting an action, state, or quality: *ceremony* | *harmony.* ▷from Latin *-monia, -monium.*

mon·zo·nite /ˈmänzəˌnīt/ ▸*n. Geology* a granular igneous rock with a composition intermediate between syenite and diorite, containing approximately equal amounts of orthoclase and plagioclase. ▷late 19th cent.: named after Mount *Monzoni* in the Tyrol, Italy, + -ITE¹. **—mon·zo·nit·ic** /ˌmänzəˈnitik/ *adj.*

moo /mo͞o/ ▸*v.* (**moos, mooed**) [*intrans.*] make the characteristic deep vocal sound of a cow.
▸*n.* (*pl.* **moos**) a sound of this kind. ▷mid 16th cent.: imitative.

mooch /mo͞och/ ▸*v. informal* **1** [*trans.*] ask for or obtain (something) without paying for it: *a bunch of your friends will show up, mooching food* | [*intrans.*] *I'm* **mooching off** *you all the time.* **2** [*intrans.*] (**mooch around/about**) loiter in a bored or listless manner: *he didn't want them mooching around all day.*
▸*n.* (also **mooch·er**) a beggar or scrounger: *the mooch who got everything from his dad.* ▷late Middle English (in the sense 'to hoard'): probably from Anglo-Norman French *muscher* 'hide, skulk.' A dialect sense 'play truant' dates from the early 16th cent.; current senses date from the mid 19th cent.

moo-cow ▸*n.* a child's name for a cow.

mood¹ /mo͞od/ ▸*n.* a temporary state of mind or feeling: *he appeared to be in a very good mood about something.* ■ an angry, irritable, or sullen state of mind: *he was obviously* **in a mood.** ■ the atmosphere or pervading tone of something, esp. a work of art: *Monet's "Mornings on the Seine" series, with their hushed and delicate mood.*
▸*adj.* [*attrib.*] (esp. of music) inducing or suggestive of a particular feeling or state of mind: *mood music* | *a Chekhov mood piece.* ▷Old English *mōd* (also in the senses 'mind' and 'fierce courage'), of Germanic origin; related to Dutch *moed* and German *Mut.*
▸*PHRASES* □ **in the mood for** (or **to do**) **something** feeling like doing or experiencing something: *if you're in the mood for an extra thrill, you can go paragliding.* □ **in no mood for** (or **to do**) **something** not wanting to do or experience something: *she was in no mood for sightseeing.*

mood² ▸*n.* **1** *Grammar* a category of verb use, typically expressing fact (indicative mood), command (imperative mood), question (interrogative mood), wish (optative mood), or conditionality (subjunctive mood). ■ a form or set of forms of a verb in an inflected language such as French, Latin, or Greek, serving to indicate whether it expresses fact, command, wish, or conditionality. **2** *Logic* any of the valid forms into which each of the figures of a categorical syllogism may occur. ▷mid 16th cent.: variant of MODE, influenced by MOOD¹.

mood-al·ter·ing ▸*adj.* (of a drug) capable of inducing changes of mood.

mood swing ▸*n.* an abrupt and apparently unaccountable change of mood.

Moo·dy /ˈmo͞odē/, William Henry (1853–1917), U.S. Supreme Court associate justice 1906–10. He was the U.S. attorney general 1904–06 before he was appointed to the Court by President Theodore Roosevelt.

mood·y /ˈmo͞odē/ ▸*adj.* (**mood·i·er, mood·i·est**) (of a person) given to unpredictable changes of mood, esp. sudden bouts of gloominess or sullenness: *she met his moody adolescent brother.* ■ giving an impression of melancholy or mystery: *grainy film that gives a soft, moody effect.* ▷Old English *mōdig* 'brave or willful' (see MOOD¹, -Y¹). **—mood·i·ly** /ˈmo͞odl-ē/ *adv.* **—mood·i·ness** *n.*

moo goo gai pan /ˈmo͞o ˈgo͞o ˈgī ˈpan/ ▸*n.* a Cantonese dish consisting of chicken sautéed with mushrooms, vegetables, and spices.

mook /mo͝ok/ ▸*n.* a perfect-bound pictorial publication issued in series, or based on an anime feature. ▷blend of *movie* or *magazine* and *book.*

moo·la /ˈmo͞oˌlä/ (also **moo·lah**) ▸*n. informal* money.

Moon /mo͞on/, Sun Myung (1920–), Korean industrialist and religious leader. In 1954, he founded the Holy Spirit Association for the Unification of World Christianity, which became known as the Unification Church. Disciples are called "Moonies."

moon /mo͞on/ ▸*n.* (also **Moon**) the natural satellite of the earth, visible (chiefly at night) by reflected light from the sun. ■ a natural satellite of any planet. ■ (**the moon**) *figurative* anything that one could desire: *you must know he'd give any of us the moon.* ■ a month, esp. a lunar month: *many moons had passed since he brought a prospective investor home.*

The earth's moon orbits the earth in a period of 29.5 days, going through a series of phases from new moon to full moon and back again during that time. Its average distance from the earth is some 239,000 miles (384,000 km) and it is 2,160 miles (3,476 km) in diameter. The bright and dark features that outline the face of "the man in the moon" are highland and lowland regions, the high regions being heavily pockmarked by craters due to the impact of meteorites. The moon has no atmosphere, and the same side is always presented to the earth.

▸*v.* **1** [*intrans.*] behave or move in a listless and aimless manner: *lying in bed eating candy, mooning around.* ■ act in a dreamily infatuated manner: *Timothy's* **mooning over** *her like a schoolboy.* **2** [*trans.*] *informal* expose one's buttocks to (someone) in order to insult or amuse them: *Dan had whipped around, bent over, and mooned the crowd.* ▷Old English *mōna,* of Germanic origin; related to Dutch *maan* and German *Mond,* also to MONTH, from an Indo-European root shared by Latin *mensis* and Greek *mēn* 'month,' and also Latin *metiri* 'to measure' (the moon being used to measure time). **—moon·less** *adj.* **—moon·like** /-ˌlīk/ *adj.*
▸*PHRASES* □ **many moons ago** *informal* a long time ago. □ **over the moon** *informal* extremely happy; delighted. [from *the cow jumped over the moon,* a line from a nursery rhyme.]

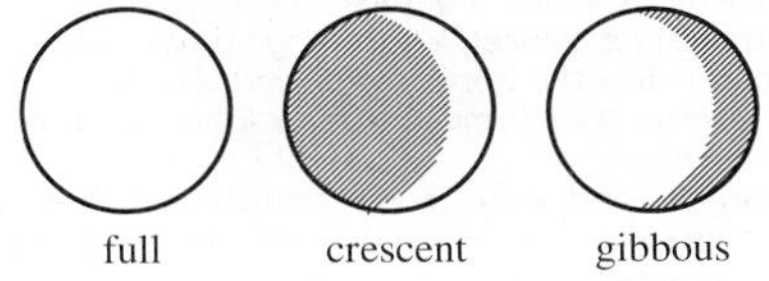

phases of the moon

moon·beam /ˈmo͞onˌbēm/ ▸*n.* a ray of moonlight.

moon blind·ness ▸*n.* (in horses) a recurrent inflammatory disease of the eyes, causing intermittent blindness. **—moon-blind** *adj.*

moon boot ▸*n.* a warm, thickly padded boot with an outer surface of fabric or plastic.

moon bug·gy ▸*n.* informal term for LUNAR ROVING VEHICLE.

moon·calf /ˈmo͞onˌkaf/ ▸*n.* (*pl.* **-calves**) a foolish person. ▷mid 16th cent.: from MOON + CALF¹, perhaps on the pattern of German *Mondkalb.* Originally in the sense 'shapeless mass in the womb,' thought to be produced by the influence of the moon.

moon child ▸*n.* a person born under the astrological sign of Cancer.

moon dog (also **moon·dog**) ▸*n.* informal term for PARASELENE.

moon·eye /ˈmo͞onˌī/ ▸*n.* a herringlike freshwater fish with large eyes, found exclusively in central and eastern North America. • Genus *Hiodon,* family Hiodontidae: two species, the **goldeye** (*H. alosoides*) and the larger-eyed **mooneye** (*H. tergisus*).

moon-faced ▸*adj.* having a round face.

Moon Fes·ti·val ▸*n.* a Chinese festival held in the middle of the autumn.

moon·fish /ˈmo͞onˌfisʜ/ ▸*n.* (*pl.* same or **-fish·es**) a deep-bodied laterally compressed marine fish, in particular: • a silvery fish of the jack family (Carangidae), including *Selene setapinnis* of the Atlantic. • an opah.

moon·flow·er /ˈmo͞onˌflou(-ə)r/ ▸*n.* a tropical American climbing plant of the morning glory family, with large, sweet-smelling white flowers that open at dusk and close at midday. • *Ipomoea alba*, family Convolvulaceae.

moon gate (also **moon·gate**) ▸*n.* (in China) a circular gateway in a wall.

Moon·ie /ˈmo͞onē/ ▸*n.* *often offensive* a member of the Unification Church. ▷1970s: from the name of its founder, Sun Myung *Moon*.

moon·let /ˈmo͞onlət/ ▸*n.* a small moon. ■ an artificial satellite.

moon·light /ˈmo͞onˌlīt/ ▸*n.* the light of the moon: *I wanted you to see the courtyard by moonlight.*
▸*adj.* [*attrib.*] illuminated or happening by the light of the moon: *a moonlight stroll.*
▸*v.* (*past* and *past part.* **-light·ed**) [*intrans.*] *informal* have a second job in addition to one's regular employment: *many instructors moonlight as professional consultants.* —**moon·light·er** *n.*

moon·lit /ˈmo͞onˌlit/ ▸*adj.* lit by the moon.

moon pool ▸*n.* a shaft through the bottom of a drilling ship, oil rig, etc., for lowering and raising equipment into or from the water.

moon·quake /ˈmo͞onˌkwāk/ ▸*n.* a tremor of the moon's surface.

moon·rat /ˈmo͞onˌrat/ ▸*n.* a shy insectivorous mammal of the hedgehog family, with a long snout and ratlike appearance, native to Southeast Asia and China. Also called **GYMNURE**. • Subfamily Galericinae, family Erinaceidae: several genera and species, in particular *Echinosorex gymnurus*.

moon·rise /ˈmo͞onˌrīz/ ▸*n.* [in *sing.*] the rising of the moon above the horizon. ■ the time of this: *it was actually about an hour after moonrise.*

moon·roof /ˈmo͞onˌro͞of; -ˌro͝of/ ▸*n.* a transparent section of the roof of an automobile, typically tinted and able to be opened.

moon·scape /ˈmo͞onˌskāp/ ▸*n.* a landscape having features characteristic of the surface of the moon, esp. in being rocky and barren: *regrowth on the once-barren moonscape around Mount St. Helens.* ■ the landscape of the moon.

moon·seed /ˈmo͞onˌsēd/ ▸*n.* a North American climbing plant with crescent-shaped seeds. • Genus *Menispermum*, family Menispermaceae: several species, in particular **Canada moonseed** (*M. canadense*).

moon·set /ˈmo͞onˌset/ ▸*n.* [in *sing.*] the setting of the moon below the horizon: *I'm greeted with a spectacular moonset.* ■ the time of this: *we left before moonset in the morning.*

moon-shaped ▸*adj.* **1** crescent-shaped: *blood cells that instead of being round are moon-shaped.* **2** round: *her moon-shaped face.*

moon·shine /ˈmo͞onˌsʜīn/ ▸*n.* **1** *informal* illicitly distilled or smuggled liquor. **2** foolish talk or ideas: *whatever I said, it was moonshine.* **3** another term for **MOONLIGHT**.

moon·shin·er /ˈmo͞onˌsʜīnər/ ▸*n.* *informal* an illicit distiller or smuggler of liquor.

moon shot (also **moon·shot**) ▸*n.* the launching of a spacecraft to the moon. ■ *figurative* a difficult or expensive task, the outcome of which is expected to have great significance: *it is said to be biology's moon shot.*

moon snail (also **moon shell**) ▸*n.* a marine mollusk with a shiny, almost spherical, shell and a large foot. • Family Naticidae, class Gastropoda: *Natica* and other genera.

moon·stone /ˈmo͞onˌstōn/ ▸*n.* a pearly white semiprecious stone consisting of alkali feldspar.

moon·struck /ˈmo͞onˌstrək/ ▸*adj.* unable to think or act normally, esp. because of being in love. ▷late 17th cent.: from **MOON** + *struck*, past participle of **STRIKE**; because it was believed that the moon could affect the mind.

moon·suit /ˈmo͞onˌso͞ot/ (also **moon suit**) ▸*n.* *informal* a protective coverall garment suitable for space travel. ■ a garment resembling this: *an emergency response team dressed in moonsuits.*

moon·walk /ˈmo͞onˌwôk/ ▸*n.* **1** an act of walking on the surface of the moon. **2** a dance step with a gliding motion, appearing as a forward step but in fact moving the dancer backward, resembling the characteristic weightless movement of walking on the moon.
▸*v.* [*intrans.*] **1** walk on the surface of the moon. **2** dance a moonwalk. —**moon·walk·er** *n.*

moon·wort /ˈmo͞onˌwərt; -ˌwôrt/ ▸*n.* a widely distributed fern with a single small frond of fan-shaped lobes and a separate spike bearing the spore-producing organs, growing typically in grassy uplands and old meadows. • Genus *Botrychium*, family Ophioglossaceae: several species, in particular the rare *B. lunaria*.

moon·y /ˈmo͞onē/ ▸*adj.* (**moon·i·er**, **moon·i·est**) **1** dreamy and unaware of one's surroundings, for example because one is in love: *she's not drunk, but still smiling in the same moony way | little girls go moony over horses.* **2** of or like the moon.

Moor /mo͝or/ ▸*n.* a member of a northwestern African Muslim people of mixed Berber and Arab descent. In the 8th century they conquered the Iberian peninsula, but were finally driven out of their last stronghold in Granada at the end of the 15th century. ▷from Old French *More*, via Latin from Greek *Mauros* 'inhabitant of Mauretania.' —**Moor·ish** *adj.*

moor[1] /mo͝or/ ▸*n.* a tract of open uncultivated upland; a heath. ■ a tract of such land preserved for shooting: [with *adj.*] *a grouse moor.* ■ a fen. ▷Old English *mōr*, of Germanic origin. —**moor·ish** *adj.* —**moor·y** *adj.*

moor[2] ▸*v.* [*trans.*] (often **be moored**) make fast (a vessel) to the shore or to an anchor: *twenty or so fishing boats were* **moored to** *the pier.* ■ [*intrans.*] (of a boat) be made fast somewhere in this way: *we moored alongside a jetty.* ▷late 15th cent.: probably from the Germanic base of Dutch *meren*. —**moor·age** /ˈmo͝orij/ *n.*

moor·cock /ˈmo͝orˌkäk/ ▸*n.* *Brit.* a male red grouse.

Moore[1] /mo͝or/ a city in central Oklahoma, a southern suburb of Oklahoma City; pop. 41,138.

Moore[2], Alfred (1755–1810), U.S. Supreme Court associate justice 1799–1804. A native of North Carolina, he was appointed to the Court by President John Adams.

Moore[3], Clement (Clarke) (1779–1863), U.S. writer. He is best known for his poem "A Visit from St. Nicholas" (1922), which was published anonymously.

Moore[4], Dudley (Stuart John) (1935–2002), English actor, comedian, and musician. His movies include *Arthur* (1981), *Arthur 2—On the Rocks* (1988), and *Crazy People* (1990).

Moore[5], G. E. (1873–1958), English moral philosopher and member of the Bloomsbury Group; full name *George Edward Moore*.

Moore[6], Henry (Spencer) (1898–1986), English sculptor and draftsman. His work is characterized by semiabstract reclining forms, large upright figures, and family groups, which Moore intended to be viewed in the open air.

Moore[7], Marianne (Craig) (1887–1972), U.S. poet. Her work is collected in *The Complete Poems of Marianne Moore* (1967).

Moore[8], Mary Tyler (1936–), U.S. actress. She starred in the television series "The Dick Van Dyke Show" 1961–66 as Laura Petrie and in "The Mary Tyler Moore Show" 1970–77 as Mary Richards. She also acted on Broadway and in movies such as *Ordinary People* (1980).

Moore[9], Thomas (1779–1852), Irish poet and musician. He wrote patriotic and nostalgic songs set to Irish tunes.

moor·fowl /ˈmo͝orˌfoul/ ▸*n.* (*pl.* same) *Brit.* another term for **RED GROUSE**.

Moor·head /ˈmo͝orˌhed/ a commercial city in western Minnesota, a transportation hub across the Red River of the North from Fargo in North Dakota; pop. 32,295.

moor·hen /ˈmo͝orˌhen/ ▸*n.* **1** a small aquatic rail with mainly blackish plumage. • Family Rallidae: two genera and four species, in particular the widespread common gallinule (*Gallinula chloropus*), with a red and yellow bill. **2** *Brit.* a female red grouse.

moor·ing /ˈmo͝oriɴɢ/ ▸*n.* (often **moorings**) a place where a boat or ship is moored: *the boat had been at its usual moorings immediately prior to the storm.* ■ the ropes, chains, or anchors by or to which a boat, ship, or buoy is moored: *the great ship* **slipped its moorings** *and slid out into the Atlantic.* ■ *figurative* the ideas, beliefs, or habits to which one is accustomed and from which one gains security or stability: *we can lose our spiritual moorings and drift into uncertain waters.*

moor·land /ˈmo͝o(ə)rlənd; -ˌland/ ▸*n.* (also **moorlands**) an extensive area of moor.

moose /mo͞os/ ▸*n.* (*pl.* same) a large deer with palmate antlers, a sloping back, and a growth of skin hanging from the neck. It is native to northern Eurasia and northern North America. Called **ELK** in Britain. • *Alces alces*, family Cervidae. ▷early 17th cent.: from an Eastern Algonquian language; compare Narragansett *moòs*.

moose

moose·burg·er /ˈmo͞osˌbərgər/ ▸*n.* a burger containing moose meat. ■ ground moose meat for use in burgers or other dishes.

Moose·head Lake /ˈmo͞osˌhed/ the largest lake in Maine, in the west central part of the state.

moose milk ▸*n.* *Canadian* an alcoholic drink consisting typically of rum, milk, and other ingredients such as eggs. ■ homemade liquor.

moose pas·ture ▸*n.* *Canadian* land of no value.

moose·wood /ˈmo͞osˌwo͝od/ ▸*n.* another term for **STRIPED MAPLE**.

moo shu pork /ˈmo͞o ˈsʜo͞o/ ▸*n.* a Chinese dish consisting of shredded pork with vegetables and seasonings, rolled in thin pancakes.

moot /mo͞ot/ ▸*adj.* subject to debate, dispute, or uncertainty, and typically not admitting of a final decision: *whether the temperature rise was mainly due to the greenhouse effect was* **a moot point**. ■ having no practical significance, typically because the subject is too uncertain to allow a decision: *it is moot whether this phrase should be treated as metaphor or not.*
▸*v.* [*trans.*] (usu. **be mooted**) raise (a question or topic) for discussion; suggest (an idea or possibility): *Sylvia needed a vacation, and a trip to Ireland had been mooted.*
▸*n.* **1** *Brit.* an assembly held for debate, esp. in Anglo-Saxon and medieval times. ■ a regular gathering of people having a common interest. **2** *Law* a mock trial set up to examine a hypothetical case as an academic exercise. ▷Old English *mōt* 'assembly or meeting' and *mōtian* 'to converse,' of Germanic origin; related to **MEET**[1]. The adjective (originally an attributive noun use: see **MOOT COURT**) dates from the mid 16th cent.; the current verb sense dates from the mid 17th cent.

moot court ▸*n.* a mock court at which law students argue imaginary cases for practice.

mop /mäp/ ▸*n.* an implement consisting of a sponge or a bundle of thick loose strings attached to a handle, used for wiping floors or other surfaces. ■ a thick mass of disordered hair: *her tousled mop of blonde hair.* ■ [in *sing.*] an act of wiping something clean, esp. a floor: *the kitchen needed a quick mop.*
▸*v.* (**mopped**, **mop·ping**) [*trans.*] clean or soak up (something) by wiping: *he was mopping his plate with a piece of bread.* ■ [*trans.*] wipe (something) away from a surface: *a barmaid rushed forward to* **mop up** *the spilled beer.* ■ wipe sweat or tears from (one's face or eyes): *he pulled a handkerchief from his pocket to* **mop his brow**.
▸*phrasal v.* □ **mop up** *informal* finish a task. □ **mop something up** *informal* put an end to or dispose of something: *he aims to mop up corruption.* ▷late 15th cent.: perhaps ultimately related to Latin *mappa* 'napkin.' —**mop·py** *adj.*

mop·board /ˈmäpˌbôrd/ ▸*n.* another term for **BASEBOARD**.

mope /mōp/ ▸*v.* [*intrans.*] be dejected and apathetic: *no use moping—things could be worse.* ■ (**mope around/about**) wander around listlessly and aimlessly because of unhappiness or boredom: *moping around at home won't get you anywhere.*
▸*n.* a person given to prolonged spells of low spirits: *they're just a bunch of mopes.* ■ (**mopes**) *dated* low spirits; depression. ▷mid 16th cent. (the early noun sense being 'fool or simpleton'): perhaps of Scandinavian origin; compare with Swedish dialect *mopa* 'to sulk.' —**mop·er** *n.* —**mop·ey** (also **mop·y**) *adj.* —**mop·i·ly** /ˈmōpəlē/ *adv.* —**mop·i·ness** /ˈmōpēnis/ *n.* —**mop·ish** *adj.*

mo·ped /ˈmōˌped/ ▸*n.* a low-power, lightweight motorized bicycle. ▷1950s: from Swedish, from *(trampcykel med) mo(tor och) ped(aler)* 'pedal cycle with motor and pedals.'

mop·er·y /ˈmōpərē/ ▸*n.* **1** *informal* the action of committing a minor or petty offense such as loitering: *we got guys doing stretches for passing bad checks and aggravated mopery.* **2** feelings of apathy and dejection.

mop·pet /ˈmäpət/ ▸*n. informal* a small endearingly sweet child. ▷early 17th cent.: from obsolete *moppe* 'baby or rag doll' + **-ET**[1].

mo·quette /mōˈket/ ▸*n.* a thick pile fabric used for carpets and upholstery. ▷1930s: from French, perhaps from obsolete Italian *mocaiardo* 'mohair.'

MOR ▸*abbr.* (of music) middle-of-the-road: *their music is too MOR for college radio.*

mor /môr/ ▸*n. Soil Science* humus formed under acid conditions. ▷1930s: from Danish.

Mo·rad·a·bad /məˈrädəbäd/ a city and railroad junction in northern India, in Uttar Pradesh; pop. 417,000.

mo·raine /məˈrān/ ▸*n. Geology* a mass of rocks and sediment carried down and deposited by a glacier, typically as ridges at its edges or extremity. ▷late 18th cent.: from French, from Italian dialect *morena*, from French dialect *morre* 'snout'; related to **MORION**[1]. —**mo·rain·al** /-ˈrānl/ *adj.* —**mo·rain·ic** /-ˈrānik/ *adj.*

mor·al /ˈmôrəl; ˈmär-/ ▸*adj.* concerned with the principles of right and wrong behavior and the goodness or badness of human character: *the moral dimensions of medical intervention* | *a moral judgment.* ■ concerned with or adhering to the code of interpersonal behavior that is considered right or acceptable in a particular society: *an individual's ambitions may get out of step with the general moral code.* ■ holding or manifesting high principles for proper conduct: *he is a caring, efficient, moral man.* ■ derived from or based on ethical principles or a sense of these: *the moral obligation of society to do something about the inner city's problems.* ■ [*attrib.*] examining the nature of ethics and the foundations of good and bad character and conduct: *moral philosophers.*

▸*n.* **1** a lesson, esp. one concerning what is right or prudent, that can be derived from a story, a piece of information, or an experience: ***the moral of this story*** *was that one must see the beauty in what one has.* **2** (**morals**) a person's standards of behavior or beliefs concerning what is and is not acceptable for them to do: *the corruption of public morals.* ■ standards of behavior that are considered good or acceptable: *they believe addicts have no morals and cannot be trusted.* ▷late Middle English: from Latin *moralis*, from *mos, mor-* 'custom,' (plural) *mores* 'morals.' As a noun the word was first used to translate Latin *Moralia*, the title of St. Gregory the Great's moral exposition of the Book of Job, and was subsequently applied to the works of various classical writers.

THE RIGHT WORD **ethical, honorable, moral, righteous, sanctimonious, virtuous**

You can be an **ethical** person without necessarily being a **moral** one, since *ethical* implies conformity with a code of fair and honest behavior, particularly in business or in a profession (*an ethical legislator who didn't believe in cutting deals*), while *moral* refers to generally accepted standards of goodness and rightness in character and conduct—especially sexual conduct (*the moral values she'd learned from her mother*).

In the same way, you can be **honorable** without necessarily being **virtuous**, since *honorable* suggests dealing with others in a decent and ethical manner, while *virtuous* implies the possession of moral excellence in character (*many honorable businesspeople fail to live a virtuous private life*).

Righteous is similar in meaning to **virtuous** but also implies freedom from guilt or blame (*righteous anger*); when the righteous person is also somewhat intolerant and narrow-minded, *self-righteous* might be a better adjective.

Someone who makes a hypocritical show of being righteous is often described as **sanctimonious**—in other words, acting like a saint without having a saintly character.

mor·al cer·tain·ty ▸*n.* probability so great as to allow no reasonable doubt: *it enjoys moral certainty and consequently has a normative role.*

mo·rale /məˈral/ ▸*n.* the confidence, enthusiasm, and discipline of a person or group at a particular time: *their morale was high.* ▷mid 18th cent.: from French *moral*, respelled to preserve the final stress in pronunciation.

mor·al haz·ard ▸*n. Economics* lack of incentive to guard against risk where one is protected from its consequences, e.g., by insurance.

mor·al·ism /ˈmôrəˌlizəm; ˈmär-/ ▸*n.* the practice of moralizing, esp. showing a tendency to make judgments about others' morality: *the patriotic moralism of many political leaders.*

mor·al·ist /ˈmôrəlist/ ▸*n.* a person who teaches or promotes morality. ■ a person given to moralizing. ■ a person who behaves in a morally commendable way. —**mor·al·is·tic** /ˌmôrəˈlistik/ *adj.* —**mor·al·is·ti·cal·ly** /ˌmôrəˈlistik(ə)lē/ *adv.*

mo·ral·i·ty /məˈralətē; mô-/ ▸*n.* (*pl.* **-ties**) principles concerning the distinction between right and wrong or good and bad behavior. ■ behavior as it is affected by the observation of these principles: *the past few years have seen a sharp decline in morality.* ■ a particular system of values and principles of conduct, esp. one held by a specified person or society: *a bourgeois morality.* ■ the extent to which an action is right or wrong: *behind all the arguments lies the issue of* ***the morality of*** *the possession of nuclear weapons.* ■ behavior or qualities judged to be good: *they saw the morality of equal pay.* See note at **GOODNESS**. ▷late Middle English: from Old French *moralite* or late Latin *moralitas*, from Latin *moralis* (see **MORAL**).

mo·ral·i·ty play ▸*n.* a kind of drama with personified abstract qualities as the main characters and presenting a lesson about good conduct and character, popular in the 15th and early 16th centuries.

mor·al·ize /ˈmôrəˌlīz; ˈmär-/ ▸*v.* [*intrans.*] [often as *n.*] (**moralizing**) comment on issues of right and wrong, typically with an unfounded air of superiority: *the self-righteous moralizing of his aunt was ringing in his ears.* ■ [*trans.*] interpret or explain as giving lessons on good and bad character and conduct: *mythographers normally moralize Narcissus as the man who wastes himself in pursuing worldly goods.* ■ [*trans.*] reform the character and conduct of: *he endeavored to moralize an immoral society.* ▷late Middle English (in the sense 'explain the moral meaning of'): from French *moraliser* or medieval Latin *moralizare*, from late Latin *moralis* (see **MORAL**). —**mor·al·i·za·tion** /ˌmôrələˈzāsHən; ˌmär-/ *n.* —**mor·al·iz·er** *n.* —**mor·al·iz·ing·ly** *adv.*

mor·al law ▸*n.* (in some systems of ethics) an absolute principle defining the criteria of right action (whether conceived as a divine ordinance or a truth of reason).

mor·al·ly /ˈmôrəlē/ ▸*adv.* **1** in relation to standards of good and bad character or conduct: *theories that assert that all inequality is morally wrong.* ■ in a way that conforms to standards of good behavior: *the task of education was to reinvigorate citizenship in order that students might act morally.* **2** [usu. as *submodifier*] on the basis of strong though not irresistible evidence or probability, esp. regarding a person's character: *I am* ***morally certain*** *that he is incapable of deliberately harming anyone.*

Mor·al Ma·jor·i·ty ▸*n.* a political action group formed in the 1970s to further a conservative and religious agenda, including the allowance of prayer in schools and strict laws against abortion. ■ (**moral majority**) [treated as *pl.*] the majority of people, regarded as favoring firm moral standards: *smokers are often made to feel like social outcasts by the moral majority.*

mor·al phi·los·o·phy ▸*n.* the branch of philosophy concerned with ethics.

Mor·al Re·ar·ma·ment an organization founded by the American Lutheran evangelist Frank Buchman (1878–1961) and first popularized in Oxford, England, in the 1920s (hence until about 1938 called the **Oxford Group Movement**). It emphasizes personal integrity and confession of faults, cooperation, and mutual respect, esp. as a basis for social transformation.

mor·al sci·ence ▸*n. dated* social sciences and/or philosophy.

mor·al sense ▸*n.* the ability to distinguish between right and wrong.

mor·al sup·port ▸*n.* support or help, the effect of which is psychological rather than physical.

mor·al vic·to·ry ▸*n.* a defeat that can be interpreted as a victory on moral terms, for example because the defeated party defended their principles.

Mor·ar, Loch /ˈmôrər, läk/ a lake in western Scotland. At 1,017 feet (310 m), it is Scotland's deepest lake.

mo·rass /məˈras; mô-/ ▸*n.* an area of muddy or boggy ground. ■ *figurative* a complicated or confused situation: *she would become lost in* ***a morass of*** *lies and explanations.* ▷late 15th cent.: from Dutch *moeras*, alteration (by assimilation to *moer* 'moor') of Middle Dutch *marasch*, from Old French *marais* 'marsh,' from medieval Latin *mariscus*.

mor·a·to·ri·um /ˌmôrəˈtôrēəm; ˌmär-/ ▸*n.* (*pl.* **-to·ri·ums** or **-to·ri·a** /-ˈtôrēə/) a temporary prohibition of an activity: *an indefinite* ***moratorium on*** *the use of drift nets.* ■ *Law* a legal authorization to debtors to postpone payment. ■ *Law* the period of this postponement. ▷late 19th cent.: modern Latin, neuter (used as a noun) of late Latin *moratorius* 'delaying,' from Latin *morat-* 'delayed,' from the verb *morari*, from *mora* 'delay.'

Mo·ra·vi·a /məˈrāvēə/ a region of the Czech Republic, located between Bohemia on the west and the Carpathians on the east; chief town, Brno. A province of Bohemia from the 11th century, it was made an Austrian province in 1848 and became a part of Czechoslovakia in 1918.

Mo·ra·vi·an /məˈrāvēən/ ▸*n.* a native of Moravia. ■ a member of a Protestant Church founded in Saxony by emigrants from Moravia holding views derived from the Hussites and accepting the Bible as the only source of faith.

▸*adj.* of or relating to Moravia or its people. ■ of or relating to the Moravian Church.

mo·ray /ˈmôrˌā; məˈrā/ (also **moray eel**) ▸*n.* a mainly nocturnal eellike predatory fish of warm seas that typically hides in crevices with just the head protruding. • Family Muraenidae: several genera and numerous species, including the **spotted moray** (*Gymnothorax moringa*) of the Gulf of Mexico and the southeastern U.S. Atlantic coast, and *Muraena helena* of the eastern Atlantic and Mediterranean. ▷early 17th cent.: from Portuguese *moréia*, via Latin from Greek *muraina*.

Mor·ay Firth a deep inlet of the North Sea on the northeastern coast of Scotland.

mor·bid /ˈmôrbəd/ ▸*adj.* **1** characterized by or appealing to an abnormal and unhealthy interest in disturbing and unpleasant subjects, esp. death and disease: *he had long held a morbid fascination with the horrors of contemporary warfare.* **2** *Medicine* of the nature of or indicative of disease: *the treatment of morbid obesity.* ▷mid 17th cent. (in the medical sense): from Latin *morbidus*, from *morbus* 'disease.' —**mor·bid·i·ty** /môrˈbidətē/ *n.* —**mor·bid·ly** *adv.* —**mor·bid·ness** *n.*

mor·bid a·nat·o·my ▸*n.* the anatomy of diseased organs and tissues.

mor·bif·ic /môrˈbifik/ ▸*adj. dated* causing disease: *in cholera the morbific matter is taken into the alimentary canal.* ▷mid 17th cent.: from French *morbifique* or modern Latin *morbificus*, from Latin *morbus* 'disease.'

mor·bil·li /môrˈbilˌī/ ▸*plural n.* technical term for **MEASLES**. ▷mid 16th cent.: Latin, plural of *morbillus* 'pustule,' from *morbus* 'disease.'

mor·bil·li·vi·rus /môrˈbiləˌvīrəs/ ▸*n. Medicine* any of a group of paramyxoviruses that cause measles, rinderpest, and canine distemper. ▷1970s: from Latin *morbilli* (plural of *morbillus* 'pustule,' from *morbus* 'disease') + **VIRUS**.

mor·ceau /môrˈsō/ ▸*n.* (*pl.* **-ceaux** /-ˈsō(z)/) a short literary or musical composition. ▷mid 18th cent.: French, literally 'morsel, piece.'

mor·da·cious /môrˈdāsHəs/ ▸*adj. formal* **1** denoting or using biting sarcasm or invective. **2** (of a person or animal) given to biting. ▷mid 17th cent.: from Latin *mordax, mordac-* 'biting' + **-IOUS**.

mor·dant /ˈmôrdnt/ ▸*adj.* (esp. of humor) having or showing a sharp or critical quality; biting: *a mordant sense of humor.*

▸*n.* a substance, typically an inorganic oxide, that combines with a dye or stain and thereby fixes it in a material. ■ an adhesive compound for fixing gold leaf. ■ a corrosive liquid used to etch the lines on a printing plate.

▸*v.* [*trans.*] impregnate or treat (a fabric) with a mordant. ▷late 15th cent.: from French, present participle of *mordre* 'to bite,' from Latin *mordere*. —**mor·dan·cy** /-dnsē/ *n.* —**mor·dant·ly** *adv.*

mor·dent /ˈmôrdnt/ ▸*n. Music* an ornament consisting of one rapid alternation of a written note with the note immediately below or above it in the scale (sometimes further distinguished as **lower mordent** and **upper mordent**). The term **inverted mordent**

usually refers to the **upper mordent**. ▷early 19th cent.: via German from Italian *mordente*, present participle of *mordere* 'to bite.'

Mor·dred /'môrdrəd/ (in Arthurian legend) the nephew of King Arthur who abducted Guinevere and raised a rebellion against Arthur.

Mord·vin·i·a /môrd'vinēə/ an autonomous republic in Russia, southeast of Nizhni Novgorod; pop. 964,000; capital, Saransk. Also called **MORDVINIAN AUTONOMOUS REPUBLIC**.

More /môr/, Sir Thomas (1478–1535), English scholar and statesman; lord chancellor 1529–32; canonized as **St. Thomas More**. His *Utopia* (1516), which described an ideal city-state, established him as a leading humanist of the Renaissance. He was imprisoned in 1534 after opposing Henry's marriage to Anne Boleyn and was beheaded for opposing the Act of Supremacy. Feast day, June 22.

more /môr/ ▸*adj.* & *pron.* **1** comparative of **MANY**, **MUCH**. **2** a greater or additional amount or degree: [as *adj.*] *I poured myself more coffee* | [as *pron.*] *tell me more* | *they proved* **more of** *a hindrance than a help.*
▸*adv.* **1** comparative of **MUCH**. **2** forming the comparative of adjectives and adverbs, esp. those of more than one syllable: *for them, enthusiasm is more important than talent.* **3** to a greater extent: *I like chicken* **more than** *turkey.* ■ **(more than)** extremely (used before an adjective conveying a positive feeling or attitude): *she is more than happy to oblige.* **4** again: *repeat* **once more**. **5** moreover: *he was rich, and more, he was handsome.* ▷Old English *māra*, of Germanic origin; related to Dutch *meer* and German *mehr*.
▸*PHRASES* □ **more and more** at a continually increasing rate: *vacancies were becoming more and more rare.* □ **more like it** see **LIKE**[1]. □ **more or less** speaking imprecisely; to a certain extent: *they are more or less a waste of time.* ■ approximately: *more or less symmetrical.* □ **more so** of the same kind to a greater degree: *the waiter found me delightful and my little sister even more so.* □ **no more 1** nothing further: *there was no more to be said about it.* **2** no further: *you must have some soup, but no more wine.* **3 (be no more)** exist no longer. **4** never again: *mention his name no more to me.* **5** neither: *I had no complaints and no more did Tom.*

Mo·reau /mô'rō/, Jeanne (1928–), French actress. Notable movies: *Les Liaisons dangereuses* (1959), *Jules et Jim* (1961), and *Nikita* (1990).

mo·reen /mô'rēn; mə-/ ▸*n.* a strong, ribbed cotton or wool fabric, used chiefly for curtains and upholstery. ▷mid 17th cent.: perhaps a fanciful formation from **MOIRE**.

mo·rel /mə'rel; mô-/ ▸*n.* a widely distributed edible fungus that has a brown oval or pointed fruiting body with an irregular honeycombed surface bearing the spores. • Genus *Morchella*, family Morchellaceae, subdivision Ascomycotina: several species, in particular the common *M. esculenta*. ▷late 17th cent.: from French *morille*, from Dutch *morilje*; related to German *Morchel* 'fungus.'

Mo·re·li·a /mə'rālyə/ a city in central Mexico, capital of the state of Michoacán; pop. 490,000. Founded in 1541, it was known as Valladolid until 1828. ▷renamed in honor of J. M. *Morelos y Pavón* (1765–1815), a key figure in Mexico's independence movement.

mo·rel·lo /mə'relō/ ▸*n.* (*pl.* **-los**) a dark cherry of a sour kind used in cooking: [as *adj.*] *morello cherries.* ▷mid 17th cent.: from Italian *morello* 'blackish,' from medieval Latin *morellus*, diminutive of Latin *Maurus* 'Moor.'

Mo·re·los /mə'rāləs/ a state in central Mexico, west of Mexico City; capital, Cuernavaca.

Mo·re·no Val·ley /mə'rānō/ a city in southwestern California, east of Riverside; pop. 118,779.

more·o·ver /môr'ōvər/ ▸*adv.* as a further matter; besides: *moreover, glass is electrically insulating.*

mo·res /'môr,āz/ ▸*plural n.* the essential or characteristic customs and conventions of a community: *an offense against social mores.* ▷late 19th cent.: from Latin, plural of *mos*, *mor-* 'custom.'

Mo·resque /mə'resk/ ▸*adj.* (of art or architecture) Moorish in style or design. ▷late Middle English (as a noun denoting arabesque ornament): from French, from Italian *moresco*, from *Moro* 'Moor.'

Mor·gan[1] /'môrgən/, J. P. (1837–1913), U.S. financier, philanthropist, and art collector; full name *John Pierpont Morgan*. He created General Electric in 1891 and the U.S. Steel Corporation in 1901. He bequeathed his large art collection to the Museum of Modern Art in New York City.

Mor·gan[2], Thomas Hunt (1866–1945), U.S. zoologist. His studies on inheritance using the fruit fly *Drosophila* showed that the genetic information is carried by genes arranged along the length of the chromosomes. Nobel Prize for Physiology or Medicine (1933).

Mor·gan[3] ▸*n.* a horse of a light thickset breed developed in New England. ▷mid 19th cent.: named after Justin *Morgan* (1747–98), U.S. teacher and owner of the original sire of the breed.

mor·ga·nat·ic /,môrgə'natik/ ▸*adj.* of or denoting a marriage in which neither the spouse of lower rank nor any children have any claim to the possessions or title of the spouse of higher rank. ▷early 18th cent.: from modern Latin *morganaticus*, from medieval Latin *matrimonium ad morganaticam* 'marriage with a morning gift' (because a morning gift, given by a husband to his wife on the morning after the marriage, was the wife's sole entitlement in a marriage of this kind). **—mor·ga·nat·i·cal·ly** /-ik(ə)lē/ *adv.*

mor·gan·ite /'môrgə,nīt/ ▸*n.* a pink transparent variety of beryl, used as a gemstone. ▷early 20th cent.: from the name of J. P. *Morgan* (see **MORGAN**[1]) + **-ITE**[1].

Mor·gan le Fay /'môrgən lə 'fā/ (in Arthurian legend) an enchantress, sister of King Arthur.

Mor·gan·town /'môrgən,toun/ a commercial city in northern West Virginia, home to West Virginia University; pop. 26,809.

mor·gen /'môrgən/ ▸*n.* a measure of land, in particular: ■ (in the Netherlands, South Africa, and parts of the U.S.) a measure of land equal to about 0.8 hectare or two acres. ■ (in Norway, Denmark, and Germany) a measure of land now equal to about 0.3 hectare or two thirds of an acre. ▷early 17th cent.: from Dutch, or from German *Morgen* 'morning,' apparently from the notion of "an area of land that can be plowed in a morning."

morgue /môrg/ ▸*n.* **1** a place where bodies are kept, esp. to be identified or claimed: *the cadavers were bagged and removed to the city morgue.* ■ used metaphorically to refer to a place that is quiet, gloomy, or cold: *she put us in that drafty morgue of a sitting room.* **2** *informal* in a newspaper office, a collection of old cuttings, photographs, and information: *conducting research in either a news morgue or a library.* ▷early 19th cent.: from French, originally the name of a building in Paris where bodies were kept until identified.

mor·i·bund /'môrə,bənd; 'mär-/ ▸*adj.* (of a person) at the point of death. ■ (of a thing) in terminal decline; lacking vitality or vigor: *the moribund commercial property market.* ▷early 18th cent.: from Latin *moribundus*, from *mori* 'to die.' **—mor·i·bun·di·ty** /,môrə'bəndətē; ,mär-/ *n.*

mo·ri·on[1] /'môrēən/ ▸*n.* a kind of helmet without beaver or visor, worn by soldiers in the 16th and 17th centuries. ▷French, from Spanish *morrión*, from *morro* 'round object.'

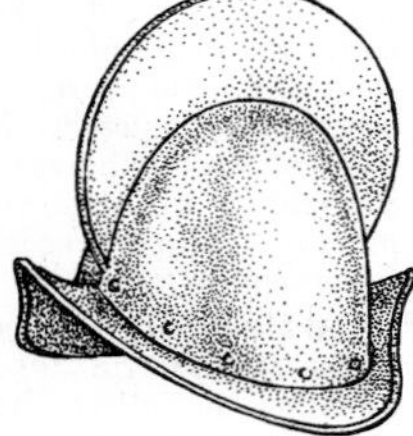
morian[1]

mo·ri·on[2] ▸*n.* a brown or black variety of quartz. ▷mid 18th cent.: from French, from Latin *morion*, a misreading (in Pliny) for *mormorion*.

Mo·ris·co /mə'riskō/ ▸*n.* (*pl.* **-cos** or **-coes**) *historical* a Moor in Spain, esp. one who had accepted Christian baptism. ▷Spanish, from *Moro* 'Moor.'

Mor·i·son /'môrəsən; 'mär-/, Samuel Eliot (1887–1976), U.S. historian and naval officer. He wrote *Oxford History of the United States* (1927), *Admiral of the Ocean Sea: A Life of Christopher Columbus* (1942), and *John Paul Jones* (1959).

Mo·ri·sot /môrē'sō; -'zō/, Berthe (Marie Pauline) (1841–95), French painter; the first woman to join the Impressionists. Her works typically depicted women and children and waterside scenes.

Mor·ley /'môrlē/, Edward Williams (1838–1923), U.S. chemist. In 1887, he collaborated with Albert Michelson in an experiment to determine the speed of light, the result of which disproved the existence of the ether. See also **MICHELSON–MORLEY EXPERIMENT**.

Mor·mon /'môrmən/ ▸*n.* a member of the Church of Jesus Christ of Latter-Day Saints, a religion founded in the U.S. in 1830 by Joseph Smith, Jr.

Smith claimed to have found and translated *The Book of Mormon* by divine revelation. It tells the story of a group of Hebrews who migrated to America *c.*600 BC and is taken as scriptural alongside the Bible. The Mormons came into conflict with the U.S. government over their practice of polygamy (officially abandoned in 1890) and moved their headquarters from Illinois to Salt Lake City, Utah, in 1847 under Smith's successor, Brigham Young. Mormon doctrine emphasizes tithing, missionary work, and the Second Coming of Christ.

▸*adj.* of or relating to the Church of Jesus Christ of Latter-Day Saints: *the leader of a Mormon congregation.* ▷the name of a prophet to whom Smith attributed *The Book of Mormon*. **—Mor·mon·ism** /-,nizəm/ *n.*

morn /môrn/ ▸*n. poetic/literary* term for **MORNING**. ▷Old English *morgen*, of Germanic origin.

mor·nay /môr'nā/ (also **Mor·nay**) ▸*adj.* denoting or served in a cheese-flavored white sauce: *mornay sauce* | [*postpositive*] *cauliflower mornay.* ▷named after *Mornay*, the French cook and eldest son of Joseph Voiron, chef of the restaurant Durand at the end of the 19th cent. and inventor of the sauce.

morn·ing /'môrniNG/ ▸*n.* the period of time between midnight and noon, esp. from sunrise to noon: *I toiled in the fields from morning till night* | *it was a little after eight* **in the morning**. ■ this time on a particular day, characterized by a specified type of activity or particular weather conditions: *it was a beautiful sunny morning.* ■ sunrise: *a hint of steely light showed that morning was on its way.*
▸*adv.* **(mornings)** *informal* every morning: *mornings, she'd sleep late.*
▸*exclam. informal* short for **GOOD MORNING**. ▷Middle English: from **MORN**, on the pattern of *evening*.
▸*PHRASE* □ **morning, noon, and night** all the time.

morn·ing af·ter ▸*n. informal* a morning on which a person has a hangover. ■ a hangover. ■ an unpleasant aftermath of imprudent behavior: *his first year of college was one long party—eventually he would have to face the morning after.*

morn·ing-af·ter pill ▸*n.* a contraceptive pill that is effective within about thirty-six hours after intercourse.

morn·ing coat ▸*n.* a man's formal coat with a cutaway.

morn·ing dress ▸*n.* a man's cutaway coat and striped pants, worn on formal occasions such as weddings, typically with a top hat.

morn·ing glo·ry ▸*n.* a climbing plant often cultivated for its showy trumpet-shaped flowers, which typically open in the early morning and wither by midday. • Genus *Ipomoea*, family Convolvulaceae: several species, in particular the **common morning glory** *I. purpurea*.

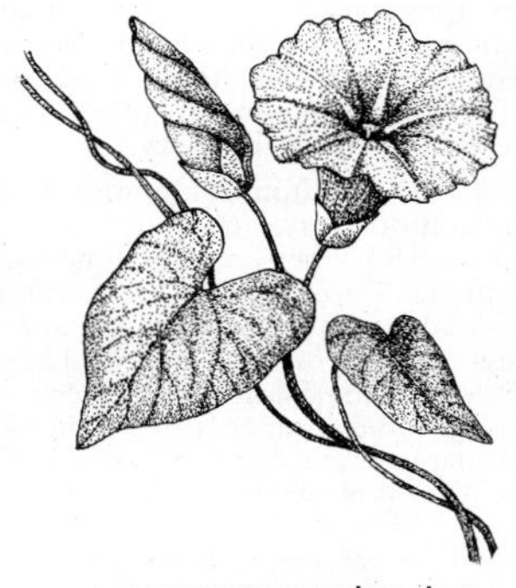
common morning glory

morn·ing prayer ▸*n.* (usu. **morning prayers**) a formal act of worship held in the morning, esp. regularly or by a group assembled for this purpose. ■ [in *sing.*] (in the Anglican Church) the service of matins.

morn·ing sick·ness ▸*n.* nausea in pregnancy, typically occurring in the first few months. Despite its name, the nausea can affect pregnant women at any time of day.

morn·ing star ▸*n.* **1 (the morning star)** a bright planet, esp. Venus, when visible in the east before sunrise. **2** *historical* a club with a heavy spiked head, sometimes attached to the handle by a chain. [translating German *Morgenstern*, comparing the weapon's spikes to rays of the star.]

morn·ing watch ▸*n.* the period from 4 to 8 a.m. on board a ship.

Mo·ro /'môrō/ ▸*n.* (*pl.* **-ros**) a Muslim inhabitant of the Philippines. ▷Spanish, literally 'Moor.'

Mo·roc·co /mə'räkō/ a country in northwestern Africa, with coastlines on the Mediterranean Sea and Atlantic Ocean; pop. 32,209,000; capital, Rabat; languages, Arabic (official) and Berber. **—Mo·roc·can** /-'räkən/ *adj.* & *n.*

Conquered by the Arabs in the 7th century, Morocco later fell under French and Spanish influence as each country established protectorates in the early 20th century. It became an independent monarchy after the withdrawal of the colonial powers in 1956 and the sultan became king. A bicameral legislature was established in 1997.

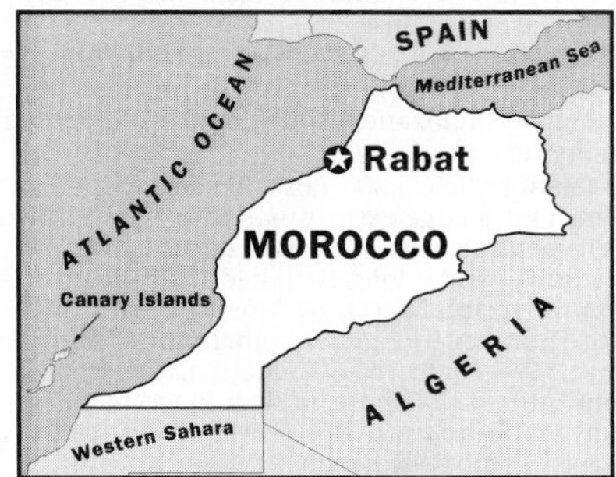

mo·roc·co /mə'räkō/ ▸*n.* (*pl.* **-cos**) fine flexible leather made (originally in Morocco) from goatskin tanned with sumac, used esp. for book covers and shoes: *a volume bound in red morocco* | [as *adj.*] *morocco leather.*

Mo·rón /mə'rōn/ a city in eastern Argentina, southwest of Buenos Aires; pop. 642,000.

mo·ron /'môr,än/ ▸*n. informal* a stupid person. ▷early 20th cent. (as a medical term denoting an adult with a mental age of about 8–12): from Greek *mōron,* neuter of *mōros* 'foolish.' **—mo·ron·ic** /mə'ränik; mô-/ *adj.* **—mo·ron·i·cal·ly** /mə'ränik(ə)lē; mô-/ *adv.*

Mo·ro·ni /mə'rōnē; mô-/ the capital of Comoros, on the island of Grande Comore; pop. 22,000.

mo·rose /mə'rōs; mô-/ ▸*adj.* sullen and ill-tempered. ▷mid 16th cent.: from Latin *morosus* 'peevish,' from *mos, mor-* 'manner.' **—mo·rose·ly** *adv.* **—mo·rose·ness** *n.*

morph[1] /môrf/ ▸*n.* an actual linguistic form: *the present participle in English is always the morph "-ing."* ▷1940s: from Greek *morphē* 'form.'

morph[2] ▸*n. Biology* each of several variant forms of an animal or plant. ▷1950s: from Greek *morphē* 'form.'

morph[3] ▸*v.* change or cause to change smoothly from one image to another by small gradual steps using computer animation techniques: *3-D objects can be morphed into other objects* | *you see her face morphing into the creature's face.*
▸*n.* an image that has been processed in this way. ■ an instance of changing an image in this way. ▷1990s: element from **METAMORPHOSIS**.

morph. ▸*abbr.* ■ morphological or morphology.

-morph ▸*comb. form* denoting something having a specified form or character: *endomorph* | *polymorph.* ▷from Greek *morphē* 'form.'

mor·phal·lax·is /,môrfə'laksəs/ ▸*n. Zoology* regeneration by the transformation of existing body tissues. ▷late 19th cent.: from Greek *morphē* 'form' + *allaxis* 'exchange.' **—mor·phal·lac·tic** /-'laktik/ *adj.*

mor·pheme /'môr,fēm/ ▸*n. Linguistics* a meaningful morphological unit of a language that cannot be further divided (e.g., *in, come, -ing,* forming *incoming*). ■ a morphological element considered with respect to its functional relations in a linguistic system. ▷late 19th cent.: from French *morphème,* from Greek *morphē* 'form,' on the pattern of French *phonème* 'phoneme.' **—mor·phe·mic** /môr'fēmik/ *adj.* **—mor·phe·mi·cal·ly** /môr'fēmik(ə)lē/ *adv.*

mor·phe·mics /môr'fēmiks/ ▸*plural n.* [treated as *sing.*] *Linguistics* the study of word structure in terms of minimal meaningful units.

Mor·phe·us /'môrfēəs; 'môwr,f(y)o͞os/ *Roman Mythology* the son of Somnus (god of sleep), the god of dreams and, in later writings, also god of sleep.

mor·phi·a /'môrfēə/ ▸*n.* old-fashioned term for **MORPHINE**.

mor·phic res·o·nance /'môrfik/ ▸*n.* (according to the theory developed by Rupert Sheldrake, British biologist 1942–) a paranormal influence by which a pattern of events or behavior can facilitate subsequent occurrences of similar patterns.

mor·phine /'môr,fēn/ ▸*n.* an analgesic and narcotic drug obtained from opium and used medicinally to relieve pain. • An alkaloid; chem. formula: $C_{17}H_{19}NO_3$. Compare with **HEROIN**. ▷early 19th cent.: from German *Morphin,* from the name of the Roman god *Morpheus* (see **MORPHEUS**).

mor·phin·ism /'môrfə,nizəm/ ▸*n. Medicine* dependence on or addiction to morphine.

mor·pho /'môrfō/ ▸*n.* (*pl.* **-phos**) a large tropical butterfly, the male of which has bright blue iridescent wings. Native to the Central and South American rain forests, they are caught in large numbers each year for use in the jewelry trade. • Genus *Morpho,* subfamily Morphinae, family Nymphalidae. ▷modern Latin, from Greek *Morphō,* an epithet of Aphrodite.

mor·pho·gen /'môrfəjən/ ▸*n. Biology* a chemical agent able to cause or determine morphogenesis.

mor·pho·gen·e·sis /,môrfə'jenəsəs/ ▸*n.* **1** *Biology* the origin and development of morphological characteristics. **2** *Geology* the formation of landforms or other structures. ▷late 19th cent.: modern Latin, from Greek *morphē* 'form' + **GENESIS**. **—mor·pho·ge·net·ic** /-jə'netik/ *adj.* **—mor·pho·gen·ic** /-'jenik/ *adj.*

mor·pho·line /'môrfə,lēn/ ▸*n. Chemistry* a synthetic compound used as a solvent for resins and dyes and (in the form of salts) as an ingredient of emulsifying soaps used in floor polishes. • A cyclic amine; chem. formula: C_4H_9NO. ▷late 19th cent.: from **MORPHINE**, with the insertion of the syllable *-ol-* (see **-OL**).

mor·phol·o·gy /môr'fäləjē/ ▸*n.* (*pl.* **-gies**) the study of the forms of things, in particular: ■ *Biology* the branch of biology that deals with the form of living organisms, and with relationships between their structures. ■ *Linguistics* the study of the forms of words. ▷mid 19th cent.: from Greek *morphē* 'form' + **-LOGY**. **—mor·pho·log·ic** /,môrfə'läjik/ *adj.* **—mor·pho·log·i·cal** /,môrfə'läjikəl/ *adj.* **—mor·pho·log·i·cal·ly** /,môrfə'läjik(ə)lē/ *adv.* **—mor·phol·o·gist** /-jist/ *n.*

mor·pho·met·rics /,môrfə'metriks/ ▸*plural n.* [usu. treated as *sing.*] *chiefly Biology* morphometry, esp. of living organisms.

mor·phom·e·try /môr'fämətrē/ ▸*n.* the process of measuring the external shape and dimensions of landforms, living organisms, or other objects. **—mor·pho·met·ric** /,môrfə'metrik/ *adj.* **—mor·pho·met·ri·cal·ly** /,môrfə'metrik(ə)lē/ *adv.*

mor·pho·pho·neme /,môrfə'fō,nēm/ ▸*n. Phonetics* any of the variant forms of a phoneme as determined by the context in which it is used. **—mor·pho·pho·ne·mic** /,môrfōfə'nēmik/ *adj.*

mor·pho·pho·ne·mics /,môrfōfə'nēmiks/ ▸*n.* another term for **MORPHOPHONOLOGY**.

mor·pho·pho·nol·o·gy /,môrfōfə'näləjē/ ▸*n.* the branch of linguistics that deals with the phonological representation of morphemes. **—mor·pho·phon·o·log·i·cal** /-,fänl'äjikəl/ *adj.* **—mor·pho·phon·o·log·i·cal·ly** /-,fänl'äjik(ə)lē/ *adv.*

mor·pho·syn·tac·tic /,môrfōsin'taktik/ ▸*adj. Linguistics* involving both morphology and syntax. **—mor·pho·syn·tac·ti·cal·ly** /-ik(ə)lē/ *adv.* **—mor·pho·syn·tax** /-'sin,taks/ *n.*

Mor·ris[1] /'môris; 'mär-/, Desmond John (1928–), British zoologist and writer. He studied animal behavior and the implications for the human condition. He put forth his findings in works such as *The Naked Ape* (1967) and *Animal-Watching* (1990).

Mor·ris[2], Gouverneur (1752–1816), U.S. politician. An active proponent of American independence, he represented New York as a member of the Continental Congress 1777–79, at the Constitutional Convention 1787, and in the U.S. Senate 1800–1803. It was while serving as Robert Morris's assistant superintendent of finance 1781–85 that he proposed the adoption of a decimal monetary system based on dollars and cents.

Mor·ris[3], Robert (1734–1806), U.S. politician and financier. He represented Pennsylvania at the Continental Congress 1775–78 and signed the Declaration of Independence in 1776. He provided extensive financial support for the colonial war effort and was later appointed superintendent of finance 1781–84 by the Continental Congress. After serving in the U.S. Senate 1789–95, he lost all his money in western land speculations and spent his final years in poverty.

Mor·ris[4], William (1834–96), English designer, craftsman, poet, and writer. He was a leading figure in the Arts and Crafts Movement.

Mor·ris[5], William Richard, see **NUFFIELD**.

Mor·ris chair /'môrəs; 'märəs/ ▸*n.* a type of armchair with open padded arms and an adjustable back. ▷late 19th cent.: named after William *Morris* (see **MORRIS**[4]).

mor·ris dance ▸*n.* a lively traditional English dance performed outdoors by groups known as "sides." Dancers wear distinctive costumes that are mainly black and white and have small bells attached, and often carry handkerchiefs or sticks. ▷late Middle English: *morris* from *morys,* variant of *Moorish* (see **MOOR**); the association with the Moors remains unexplained. **—mor·ris danc·er** *n.* **—mor·ris danc·ing** *n.*

Mor·ri·son[1] /'môrisən; 'mär-/, Jim (1943–71), U.S. rock singer; full name *James Douglas Morrison.* He was the lead singer of the Doors. He died in Paris of a heart attack in his bath.

Mor·ri·son[2], Toni (1931–), U.S. novelist; full name *Chloe Anthony Morrison.* Her novels depict the black American experience and heritage, often focusing on rural life in the South, as in *The Bluest Eye* (1970). Notable works: *Beloved* (1987), *Sula* (1973), *Tar Baby* (1981), and *Paradise* (1998). Nobel Prize for Literature (1993).

Toni Morrison

mor·row /'môrō; 'märō/ ▸*n.* (**the morrow**) *archaic* or *poetic/literary* the following day: *on the morrow, they attacked the city.* ■ the time following an event: *in the morrow of great victory, will they show some equanimity?* ■ the near future: *we have the religious enthusiast who takes no thought for the morrow.* ▷Middle English *morwe,* from Old English *morgen* (see **MORN**).

Morse code /'môrs/ ▸*n.* an alphabet or code in which letters are represented by combinations of long and short signals of light or sound.
▸*v.* [*trans.*] signal (something) using Morse code. ▷mid 19th cent.: named after Samuel F. B. *Morse* (1791–1872), U.S. inventor.

mor·sel /'môrsəl/ ▸*n.* a small piece or amount of food; a mouthful: *Julie pushed* **a** *last* **morsel of** *toast into her mouth* | *figurative real estate agents think the mansion will be a very tasty morsel for an international company.* ■ a small piece or amount: *reporters do their best to ferret out every morsel of information.* ▷Middle English: from Old French, diminutive of *mors* 'a bite,' from Latin *mors-* 'bitten,' from the verb *mordere.*

mort /môrt/ ▸*n. archaic Hunting* the note sounded on a horn when the quarry is killed. ▷Middle English: via Old French from Latin *mors, mort-* 'death.'

mor·ta·del·la /,môrtə'delə/ ▸*n.* a type of light pink, smooth-textured Italian sausage containing pieces of fat, typically served in slices. ▷Italian diminutive, formed irregularly from Latin *murtatum* '(sausage) seasoned with myrtle berries.'

mor·tal /'môrtl/ ▸*adj.* **1** (of a living human being, often in contrast to a divine being) subject to death: *all men are mortal.* ■ of or relating to humanity as subject to death: *the coffin held the mortal remains of her uncle.* ■ *informal* conceivable or imaginable: *punishment out of all mortal proportion to the offense.* **2** [*attrib.*] causing or liable to cause death; fatal: *a mortal disease* | *figurative the scandal appeared to have struck* **a mortal blow** *to the government.* ■ (of a battle) fought to the death: *from the outbuildings came the screams of men in* **mortal combat**. ■ (of an enemy or a state of hostility) admitting or allowing no reconciliation until death. ■ *Christian Theology* denoting a grave sin that is regarded as depriving the soul of divine grace. Often contrasted with **VENIAL**. ■ (of a feeling, esp. fear) very intense: *parents live in mortal fear of children's diseases.*

■ *informal* very great: *he was in a mortal hurry.* ■ *informal, dated* long and tedious: *for three mortal days it rained.*
▸*n.* a human being subject to death, often contrasted with a divine being. ■ *humorous* a person contrasted with others regarded as being of higher status or ability: *an ambassador had to live in a style that was not expected of* ***lesser mortals.*** ▷late Middle English: from Old French, or from Latin *mortalis,* from *mors, mort-* 'death.'

mor·tal·i·ty /môr'talətē/ ▸*n.* (*pl.* **-ties**) **1** the state of being subject to death: *the work is increasingly haunted by thoughts of mortality.* **2** death, esp. on a large scale: *the causes of mortality among infants and young children.* ■ (also **mortality rate**) the number of deaths in a given area or period, or from a particular cause: *postoperative mortality was 90 percent for some operations.* ▷late Middle English: via Old French from Latin *mortalitas,* from *mortalis* (see **MORTAL**).

mor·tal·ly /'môrtl-ē/ ▸*adv.* in such a manner as to cause death: *the gunner was mortally wounded.* ■ very intensely or seriously: *I expected him to be mortally offended.*

mor·tar[1] /'môrtər/ ▸*n.* **1** a cup-shaped receptacle made of hard material, in which ingredients are crushed or ground, used esp. in cooking or pharmacy: *a mortar and pestle.* **2** a short, smoothbore gun for firing shells (technically called bombs) at high angles. ■ a similar device used for firing a lifeline or firework.
▸*v.* [*trans.*] attack or bombard with shells fired from a mortar. ▷late Old English (sense 2), from Old French *mortier,* from Latin *mortarium* (to which the English spelling was later assimilated).

mortar[1] 1

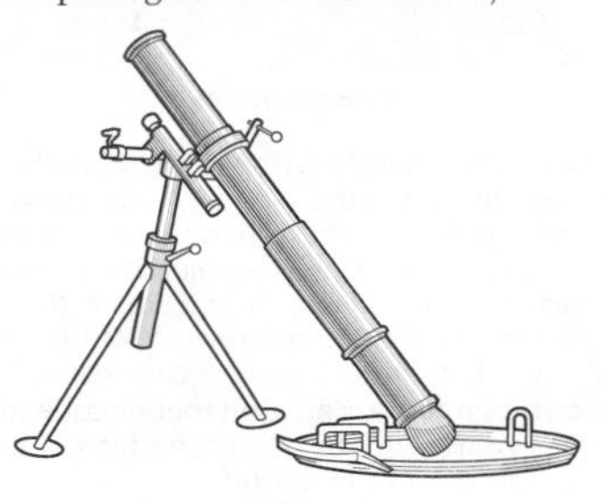
mortar[1] 2

mor·tar[2] ▸*n.* a mixture of lime with cement, sand, and water, used in building to bond bricks or stones.
▸*v.* [*trans.*] fix or join using mortar: *the pipe can be mortared in place.* ▷Middle English: from Old French *mortier,* from Latin *mortarium,* probably a transferred sense of the word denoting a container (see **MORTAR**[1]). **—mor·tar·less** *adj.* **—mor·tar·y** *adj.*

mor·tar·board /'môrtər,bôrd/ ▸*n.* **1** an academic cap with a stiff, flat, square top and a tassel. **2** a small square board with a handle on the underside, used by bricklayers for holding mortar.

mortarboard 1

mort·gage /'môrgij/ ▸*n.* the charging of real (or personal) property by a debtor to a creditor as security for a debt (esp. one incurred by the purchase of the property), on the condition that it shall be returned on payment of the debt within a certain period. ■ a deed effecting such a transaction. ■ a loan obtained through the conveyance of property as security: *I put down a hundred thousand in cash and took out a mortgage for the rest.*
▸*v.* [*trans.*] (often **be mortgaged**) convey (a property) to a creditor as security on a loan: *the estate was mortgaged up to the hilt.* ■ *figurative* expose to future risk or constraint for the sake of immediate advantage: *some people worry that selling off federal assets mortgages the country's future.* ▷late Middle English: from Old French, literally 'dead pledge,' from *mort* (from Latin *mortuus* 'dead') + *gage* 'pledge.' **—mort·gage·a·ble** *adj.*

mort·ga·gee /,môrgə'jē/ ▸*n.* the lender in a mortgage, typically a bank.

mort·gage rate ▸*n.* the rate of interest charged by a mortgage lender.

mort·ga·gor /,môrgi'jôr; 'môrgijər/ ▸*n.* the borrower in a mortgage, typically a homeowner.

mor·tice /'môrtəs/ ▸*n.* & *v.* variant spelling of **MORTISE.**

mor·ti·cian /môr'tisHən/ ▸*n.* an undertaker. ▷late 19th cent.: from Latin *mors, mort-* 'death' + **-ICIAN.**

mor·ti·fy /'môrtə,fī/ ▸*v.* (**-fies, -fied**) [*trans.*] **1** (often **be mortified**) cause (someone) to feel embarrassed, ashamed, or humiliated: [*trans.*] *she was mortified to see her wrinkles in the mirror* | [as *adj.*] (**mortifying**) *she refused to accept this mortifying disgrace.* **2** subdue (the body or its needs and desires) by self-denial or discipline: *return to heaven by* ***mortifying the flesh.*** **3** [*intrans.*] *archaic* (of flesh) be affected by gangrene or necrosis: *the cut in Henry's arm had mortified.* ▷late Middle English (in the senses 'put to death,' 'deaden,' and 'subdue by self-denial'): from Old French *mortifier,* from ecclesiastical Latin *mortificare* 'kill, subdue,' from *mors, mort-* 'death.' **—mor·ti·fi·ca·tion** /,môrtəfə'kāsHən/ *n.* **—mor·ti·fy·ing·ly** *adv.*

Mor·ti·mer /'môrtəmər/, Roger de, 8th Baron of Wigmore and 1st Earl of March (*c.*1287–1330), English noble. In 1326, he invaded England with his lover Isabella of France and replaced her husband Edward II with her son, the future Edward III. When Edward III assumed power in 1330, he had Mortimer executed.

mor·tise /'môrtis/ (also **mor·tice**) ▸*n.* a hole or recess cut into a part, designed to receive a corresponding projection (a tenon) on another part so as to join or lock the parts together.
▸*v.* [*trans.*] join securely by using a mortise and tenon. ■ [*trans.*] [often as *adj.*] (**mortised**) cut a mortise in or through: *the mortised ports.* ▷late Middle English: from Old French *mortaise.* **—mor·tis·er** *n.*

mor·tise lock ▸*n.* a lock that is set within the body of a door in a recess or mortise, as opposed to one attached to the door surface.

mort·main /'môrt,mān/ ▸*n. Law* the status of lands or tenements held inalienably by an ecclesiastical or other corporation. ▷late Middle English: from Anglo-Norman French, Old French *mortemain,* from medieval Latin *mortua manus* 'dead hand' (probably alluding to impersonal ownership).

Mor·ton[1] /'môrtn/, Jelly Roll (1885–1941), U.S. jazz pianist, composer, and bandleader; born *Ferdinand Joseph La Menthe Morton.* He was one of the principal links between ragtime and New Orleans jazz. He formed his band, the Red Hot Peppers, in 1926.

Mor·ton[2], John (*c.*1420–1500), English prelate and statesman. He was appointed archbishop of Canterbury in 1486 and chancellor under Henry VII a year later.

mor·tu·ar·y /'môrCHōō,erē/ ▸*n.* (*pl.* **-ar·ies**) a funeral home or morgue.
▸*adj.* [*attrib.*] of or relating to burial or tombs: *mortuary rituals* | *a mortuary temple.* ▷late Middle English (denoting a gift claimed by a parish priest from a deceased person's estate): from Latin *mortuarius,* from *mortuus* 'dead.' The current noun sense dates from the mid 19th cent.

mor·u·la /'môrələ; 'mär-/ ▸*n.* (*pl.* **-lae** /-lē/) *Embryology* a solid ball of cells resulting from division of a fertilized ovum, and from which a blastula is formed. ▷mid 19th cent.: modern Latin, diminutive of Latin *morum* 'mulberry.'

MOS ▸*abbr. Electronics* metal oxide semiconductor.

mos. ▸*abbr.* months.

Mo·sa·ic /mō'zā-ik/ ▸*adj.* of or associated with Moses. ▷mid 17th cent.: from French *mosaïque* or modern Latin *Mosaicus.*

mo·sa·ic /mō'zā-ik/ ▸*n.* **1** a picture or pattern produced by arranging together small colored pieces of hard material, such as stone, tile, or glass: *the mosaic shows the baptism of Christ* | [as *adj.*] *a mosaic floor.* ■ decorative work of this kind: *the walls and vaults are decorated by marble and mosaic.* ■ a colorful and variegated pattern: *the bird's plumage was* ***a mosaic of*** *slate-gray, blue, and brown.* ■ a combination of diverse elements forming a more or less coherent whole: *an incompetently constructed* ***mosaic of*** *competing interests.* ■ an arrangement of photosensitive elements in a television camera. **2** *Biology* an individual (esp. an animal) composed of cells of two genetically different types. **3** (also **mosaic disease**) a viral disease that results in leaf variegation in tobacco, corn, sugar cane, and other plants.
▸*v.* (**-sa·icked, -sa·ick·ing**) [*trans.*] decorate with a mosaic: [as *adj.*] (**mosaicked**) *the mosaicked swimming pool.* ■ combine (distinct or disparate elements) to form a picture or pattern: *the digital data were combined, or mosaicked, to delineate counties.* ▷late Middle English: from French *mosaïque,* based on Latin *musi(v)um* decoration with small square stones, perhaps ultimately from Greek *mousa* 'a muse.' **—mo·sa·i·cist** /mō'zāəsist/ *n.*

mo·sa·ic gold ▸*n.* an imitation gold pigment consisting of tin disulfide.

mo·sa·i·cism /mō'zāə,sizəm/ ▸*n. Biology* the property or state of being composed of cells of two genetically different types.

Mo·sa·ic Law ▸*n.* another term for **THE LAW OF MOSES** (see **LAW** sense 3).

Mo·san·der /mō'sändər/, Carl Gustaf (1797–1858), Swedish chemist. He discovered the elements lanthanum, erbium, and terbium, and the supposed element didymium.

mo·sa·saur /'mōsə,sôr/ (also **mo·sa·sau·rus** /,mōsə'sôrəs/) ▸*n.* a large extinct marine reptile of the late Cretaceous period, with large toothed jaws, paddle-like limbs, and a long flattened tail, related to the monitor lizards. • Family Mosasauridae, suborder Lacertilia: several genera, including *Mosasaurus.* ▷mid 19th cent.: from modern Latin *Mosasaurus,* from Latin *Mosa* 'Meuse' (a river in western Europe, near which it was first discovered) + Greek *sauros* 'lizard.' **—mo·sa·sau·ri·an** *adj.*

mos·ca·to /mas'kätō/ ▸*n.* a sweet Italian dessert wine. ▷Italian; related to **MUSCAT.**

Mos·cow /'mäs,kou; -kō/ **1** the capital of Russia, located at the center of European Russia, on the Moskva River; pop. 9,000,000. It became the capital when Ivan the Terrible proclaimed himself the first tsar in the 16th century. Peter the Great moved his capital to St. Petersburg in 1712, but, after the Bolshevik Revolution of 1917, Moscow was made the capital of the Soviet Union and seat of the new Soviet government, with its center in the Kremlin. Russian name **MOSKVA.** **2** a city in northwestern Idaho, home to the University of Idaho; pop. 21,291.

Mo·sel /mō'zel/ (also **Mo·selle**) a river of western Europe that rises in the Vosges mountains of northeastern France and flows northeast for 346 miles (550 km) through Luxembourg and Germany to meet the Rhine River at Koblenz.

Mose·ley /'mōzlē/, Henry Gwyn Jeffreys (1887–1915), English physicist. He determined the atomic numbers of elements from their X-ray spectra, demonstrated that an element's chemical properties are determined by this number, and showed that there are only 92 naturally occurring elements.

Mo·selle /mō'zel/ (also **Mo·sel**) ▸*n.* a light medium-dry white wine produced in the valley of the Moselle River (see **MOSEL**).

Mo·ses[1] /'mōzis; -zəz/ (*fl. c.*14th–13th centuries BC), Hebrew prophet and lawgiver; brother of Aaron. According to the biblical account, he was born in Egypt and led the Israelites across the desert toward the Promised Land. During the journey he was inspired by God on Mount Sinai to write down the Ten Commandments on tablets of stone (Exod. 20).

Mo·ses[2], Grandma (1860–1961), U.S. painter; full name *Anna Mary Robertson Moses.* She took up painting as a hobby when widowed in 1927 and produced more than a thousand paintings in a primitive style, mostly of rural life.

Grandma Moses

Mo·ses[3], Edwin (Corley) (1955–), U.S. track athlete. He won Olympic gold medals for the 400-meter

M

hurdles in 1976 and 1984. He also set successive world records in the event throughout these years.

Mo·ses of Her Peo·ple see **Tubman**.

mo·sey /ˈmōzē/ *informal* ▸*v.* (**-seys**, **-seyed**) [*intrans.*] walk or move in a leisurely manner: *we decided to mosey on up to Montgomery.*
▸*n. chiefly Brit.* a leisurely walk or drive. ▷early 19th cent.: of unknown origin. The original sense was 'go away quickly.'

MOSFET /ˈmäsˌfet/ ▸*n. Electronics* a field-effect transistor that has a thin layer of silicon oxide between the gate and the channel. ▷1960s: acronym from *metal oxide semiconductor field-effect transistor.*

mosh /mäsн/ ▸*v.* [*intrans.*] dance to rock music in a violent manner involving jumping up and down and deliberately colliding with other dancers. ▷1980s: perhaps from **mash** or **mush**[1].

mo·shav /mōˈsнäv/ ▸*n.* (*pl.* **mo·sha·vim** /ˌmōsнəˈvēm/) in Israel, a cooperative community of farmers. ▷from Hebrew *mōšāḇ*, literally 'dwelling.'

mosh pit ▸*n.* an area where moshing occurs, esp. in front of the stage at a rock concert.

Mos·kva /ˈmäskvä; ˈməsk-/ Russian name for **Moscow**.

Mos·lem /ˈmäzləm; ˈmäs-/ ▸*n.* & *adj.* variant spelling of **Muslim**.

USAGE See usage at **Muslim**.

Mo·so·tho /məˈsōōtōō/ ▸ singular form of **Basotho**.

mosque /mäsk/ ▸*n.* a Muslim place of worship.

Mosques consist of an area reserved for communal prayers, frequently in a domed building with a minaret, and with a niche (mihrab) or other structure indicating the direction of Mecca. There may also be a platform for preaching (minbar), and an adjacent courtyard in which water is provided for the obligatory ablutions before prayer.

▷late Middle English: from French *mosquée*, via Italian and Spanish from Egyptian Arabic *masgid*.

Mos·qui·to ▸*n.* (*pl.* **-tos**) & *adj.* variant spelling of **Miskito**.

mos·qui·to /məˈskētō/ ▸*n.* (*pl.* **-toes** or **-tos**) a slender long-legged fly with aquatic larvae. The bite of the bloodsucking female can transmit a number of serious diseases including malaria and encephalitis. • *Culex, Anopheles*, and other genera, family Culicidae. ▷late 16th cent.: from Spanish and Portuguese, diminutive of *mosca*, from Latin *musca* 'fly.' **—mos·qui·to·ey** /məˈskētəwē/ *adj.*

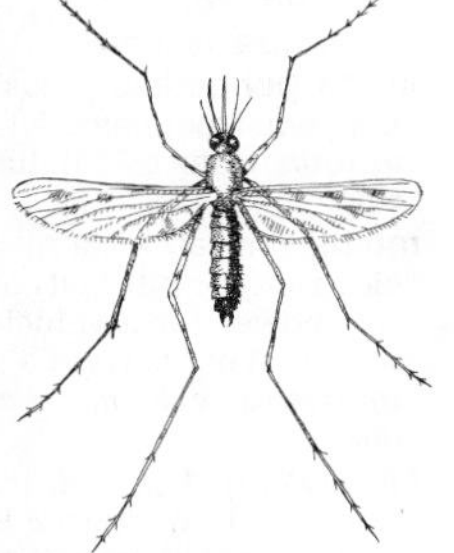
Anopheles mosquito

Mos·qui·to Coast /məˈskētō ˈkōst/ a sparsely populated coastal strip of swamp, lagoon, and tropical forest along the Caribbean coast of Nicaragua and northeastern Honduras, occupied by the Miskito people after whom it is named.

mos·qui·to coil ▸*n.* a spiral typically made from a dried paste of pyrethrum powder, which when lit burns slowly to produce a mosquito-repellent smoke.

mos·qui·to·fish /məˈskētōˌfisн/ (also **mos·qui·to fish**) ▸*n.* a small livebearing fish found chiefly in vegetated ponds and lakes and brackish waters of the U.S. and northern Mexico. Also called **gambusia**. • Genus *Gambusia*, family Poeciliidae: several species, in particular *G. affinis*, widely introduced for mosquito control. Its introduction has often resulted in the depletion of other fish populations.

mos·qui·to hawk ▸*n.* **1** a nighthawk. **2** a dragonfly.

mos·qui·to net·ting (also **mos·qui·to net**) ▸*n.* a fine net hung across a door or window or around a bed to keep mosquitoes away.

Moss /môs/, Stirling (1929–), English race car driver.

moss /môs/ ▸*n.* **1** a small flowerless green plant that lacks true roots, growing in low carpets or rounded cushions in damp habitats and reproducing by means of spores released from stalked capsules: *the trees are overgrown with vines and moss | the bog is home to rare mosses.* • Class Musci, division Bryophyta. ■ used in names of algae, lichens, and higher plants resembling moss, e.g., **reindeer moss**, **Ceylon moss**, **Spanish moss**. **2** *Scottish* & *N. English* a bog, esp. a peat bog.
▸*v.* [usu. as *adj.*] (**mossed**) cover with moss. ▷Old English *mos* 'bog or moss,' of Germanic origin; related to Dutch *mos* and German *Moos.* **—moss·like** /-ˌlīk/ *adj.*

Mos·sad /mäˈsäd; mə-/ **1** the Supreme Institution for Intelligence and Special Assignments, the principal secret intelligence service of the state of Israel, founded in 1951. **2** the Institution for the Second Immigration, an earlier organization formed in 1938 for the purpose of bringing Jews from Europe to Palestine. ▷from Hebrew *mōsāḏ* 'institution.'

moss ag·ate ▸*n.* agate with mosslike dendritic inclusions.

moss an·i·mal ▸*n.* a sedentary colonial aquatic animal found chiefly in the sea, either encrusting rocks, seaweeds, or other surfaces, or forming stalked fronds. Each minute zooid filter-feeds by means of a crown of ciliated tentacles (lophophore). • Phylum Bryozoa (or Polyzoa, Ectoprocta).

moss·back /ˈmôsˌbak/ ▸*n. informal* an old-fashioned or extremely conservative person. **—moss·backed** *adj.*

Möss·bau·er ef·fect /ˈməsˌbouər/ ▸*n. Chemistry* an effect in which certain atomic nuclei bound in a crystal emit gamma rays of sharply defined frequency, which can be used as a probe of energy levels in other nuclei. ▷1960s: named after Rudolf L. *Mössbauer* (1929–), German physicist.

moss cam·pi·on ▸*n.* an almost stemless campion with pink flowers, found on mountains and in arctic areas of both Eurasia and North America. • *Silene acaulis*, family Caryophyllaceae.

moss green ▸*n.* a bright green color like that of moss.

moss-grown ▸*adj.* overgrown with moss. ■ *figurative* old; antiquated: *the mystery of its moss-grown, cobwebby past.*

Mos·si /ˈmäsē/ ▸*n.* (*pl.* same or **Mos·sis**) a member of a people of Burkina Faso in West Africa.
▸*adj.* of or relating to this people. ▷the name in More.

moss·troop·er /ˈmôsˌtrōōpər/ ▸*n. historical* a person who lived by plundering property in the border region between England and Scotland during the 17th century.

moss·y /ˈmôsē/ ▸*adj.* (**moss·i·er**, **moss·i·est**) covered in or resembling moss: *mossy tree trunks.* ■ *informal* old-fashioned or extremely conservative. **—moss·i·ness** *n.*

moss·y·cup oak /ˈmôsēˌkəp/ ▸*n.* another term for **bur oak**.

moss·y rose gall ▸a reddish mosslike growth on rose bushes that forms in response to the developing larvae of a gall wasp. Also called **bedeguar**. • The wasp is *Diplolepis rosae*, family Cynipidae.

most /mōst/ ▸*adj.* & *pron.* **1** superlative of **many**, **much**. **2** greatest in amount or degree: [as *adj.*] *they've had the most success* | [as *pron.*] *they had the most to lose.* ■ the majority of; nearly all of: [as *adj.*] *most oranges are sweeter than these.* | [as *pron.*] *I spent* **most of** *the winter on the coast.*
▸*adv.* **1** superlative of **much**. **2** to the greatest extent: *the things he most enjoyed | what she wanted* **most of all.** ■ forming the superlative of adjectives and adverbs, esp. those of more than one syllable: *the most important event of my life | sandy plains where fire tends to spread most quickly.* **3** extremely; very: *it was most kind of you | that is most probably correct.* **4** *informal* almost: *most everyone understood.* ▷Old English *mǣst*, of Germanic origin; related to Dutch *meest* and German *meist.*
▸*PHRASES* □ **at (the) most** not more than: *the walk took four minutes at the most.* □ **be the most** *informal* be the best of all; be the ultimate. □ **for the most part** in most cases; usually: *the older members, for the most part, shun him.* □ **make the most of** use to the best advantage: *he was eager to make the most of his visit.* ■ represent at its best: *how to make the most of your features.*

-most ▸*suffix* forming superlative adjectives and adverbs from prepositions and other words indicating relative position: *innermost | uppermost.* ▷Old English *-mest*, assimilated to **most**.

Mo·star /ˈmōstär/ a city in southern Bosnia and Herzegovina, southwest of Sarajevo, the chief town of Herzegovina; pop. 126,000. Its chief landmark, an old Turkish bridge across the Neretva River, was destroyed during the siege of the city by Serbian forces in 1993. The majority of Mostar's inhabitants are Muslim.

most·est /ˈmōstəst/ ▸*pron. humorous* most: *the winner is the person who can get there quickest with the mostest.*

most fa·vored na·tion ▸*n.* a country that has been granted the most favorable trading terms available by another country.

Most High (**the Most High**) God.

most·ly /ˈmōstlē/ ▸*adv.* as regards the greater part or number: *I grow mostly annuals.* ■ usually: *weekends spent mostly alone.*

Most Rev·er·end ▸*n.* the title of an Anglican archbishop or an Irish Roman Catholic bishop.

most sig·nif·i·cant bit (abbr.: **MSB**) ▸*n. Computing* the bit in a binary number that is of the greatest numerical value.

Mo·sul /məˈsōōl; ˈmōˌsōōl/ a city in northern Iraq, on the Tigris River, opposite the ruins of Nineveh; pop. 571,000.

mot /mō/ ▸*n.* (*pl.* **mots** /mō(z)/) short for **bon mot**.

mote /mōt/ ▸*n.* a tiny piece of a substance: *the tiniest mote of dust.* ▷Old English *mot*, related to Dutch *mot* 'dust, sawdust.'
▸*PHRASE* □ **a mote in someone's eye** a fault in a person that is less serious than one in someone else who is being critical. [with biblical allusion to Matt. 7:3.]

mo·tel /mōˈtel/ ▸*n.* a roadside hotel designed primarily for motorists, typically having the rooms arranged in a low building with parking directly outside. ▷1920s: blend of **motor** and **hotel**.

mo·tet /mōˈtet/ ▸*n.* a short piece of sacred choral music, typically polyphonic and unaccompanied. ▷late Middle English: from Old French, diminutive of *mot* 'word.'

moth /môтн/ ▸*n.* (*pl.* **moths** /môт̲н̲z; môтнs/) a chiefly nocturnal insect related to the butterflies. It lacks the clubbed antennae of butterflies and typically has a stout body, drab coloration, and wings that fold flat when resting. • Most superfamilies of the order Lepidoptera. Formerly placed in a grouping known as the Heterocera. ■ *informal* short for **clothes moth**. ▷Old English *moththe*, of Germanic origin; related to Dutch *mot* and German *Motte.*
▸*PHRASE* □ **like a moth to the flame** with an irresistible attraction for someone or something: *wealthy amateurs who have been attracted like moths to the glittering flames of showbiz.*

moth·ball /ˈmôтнˌbôl/ ▸*n.* (usu. **mothballs**) a small pellet of a pungent substance, typically naphthalene, put among stored clothes to keep away moths.
▸*v.* [*trans.*] store (clothes) among or in mothballs. ■ stop using (a piece of equipment or a building) but keep it in good condition so that it can readily be used again. ■ cancel or postpone work on (a plan or project): *plans to invest in four superstores have been mothballed.*
▸*PHRASE* □ **in mothballs** unused but kept in good condition for future use.

moth-eat·en /ˈmôтн ˌētn/ ▸*adj.* damaged or destroyed by moths. ■ old-fashioned and no longer appropriate or useful.

moth·er /ˈməт̲н̲ər/ ▸*n.* **1** a woman in relation to a child or children to whom she has given birth. ■ a person who provides the care and affection normally associated with a female parent: *my adoptive mother.* ■ a female animal in relation to its offspring: [as *adj.*] *a mother penguin.* ■ *archaic* (esp. as a form of address) an elderly woman. ■ (**Mother**, **Mother Superior**, or **Reverend Mother**) (esp. as a title or form of address) the head of a female religious community. ■ [as *adj.*] denoting an institution or organization from which more recently founded institutions of the same type derive: *the mother church.* ■ *figurative* something that is the origin of or stimulus for something else: *the wish was* **the mother of** *the deed.* ■ *informal* an extreme example or very large specimen of something: *I got stuck in* **the mother of** *all traffic jams.* **2** *vulgar slang* short for **motherfucker**.
▸*v.* [*trans.*] **1** [often as *n.*] (**mothering**) bring up (a child) with care and affection: *the art of mothering.* ■ look after kindly and protectively, sometimes excessively so: *she felt mothered by her older sister.* **2** *dated* give birth to. ▷Old English *mōdor*, of Germanic origin; related to Dutch *moeder* and German *Mutter*, from an Indo-European root shared by Latin *mater* and Greek *mētēr.* **—moth·er·hood** /-ˌhŏŏd/ *n.* **—moth·er·less** *adj.* **—moth·er·less·ness** *n.* **—moth·er·like** /-ˌlīk/ *adj.* & *adv.*

Moth·er Ann see **Lee**[1].

moth·er·board /ˈməT͟Hər,bôrd/ ▸*n.* *Computing* a printed circuit board containing the principal components of a microcomputer or other device, with connectors into which other circuit boards can be slotted.

Moth·er Car·ey's chick·en /ˈke(ə)rēz/ ▸*n.* old-fashioned term for STORM PETREL. ▷mid 18th cent.: of unknown origin.

moth·er coun·try ▸*n.* (often **the mother country**) a country in relation to its colonies: *the bicentennial of our separation from the mother country.*

moth·er·craft /ˈməT͟Hər,kraft/ ▸*n.* *archaic* skill in or knowledge of looking after children as a mother.

Moth·er Earth ▸*n.* the earth considered as the source of all its living beings and inanimate things.

moth·er fig·ure ▸*n.* a woman who is regarded as a source of nurture and support: *a housekeeper named Evelyn became a mother figure to him.*

moth·er·fuck·er /ˈməT͟Hər,fəkər/ ▸*n.* *vulgar slang* a despicable or very unpleasant person or thing. **—moth·er·fuck·ing** /-,fəkiNG/ *adj.*

moth·er god·dess ▸*n.* a mother-figure deity, a central figure of many early nature cults in which maintenance of fertility was of prime religious importance. Examples of such goddesses include Isis, Astarte, Cybele, and Demeter. Also called GREAT MOTHER.

Moth·er Goose ▸*n.* the fictitious creator of a collection of nursery rhymes that was first published in London in the 1760s.

moth·er hen ▸*n.* a hen with chicks. ■ a person who sees to the needs of others, esp. in a fussy or interfering way.

moth·er·house /ˈməT͟Hər,hous/ ▸*n.* the founding house of a religious order.

Moth·er Hub·bard /ˈhəbərd/ ▸*n.* a long, loose-fitting, shapeless woman's dress or undergarment. ■ a kind of cloak. ▷so named from early illustrations of the nursery rhyme.

moth·er-in-law ▸*n.* (*pl.* **moth·ers-in-law**) the mother of one's husband or wife.

moth·er-in-law's tongue ▸*n.* a West African plant of the agave family, having long slender leaves with yellow marginal stripes, often grown as a houseplant. • *Sansevieria trifasciata*, family Agavaceae.

moth·er·land /ˈməT͟Hər,land/ ▸*n.* (often **the motherland**) one's native country.

moth·er lode ▸*n.* *Mining* a principal vein of an ore or mineral. ■ *figurative* a rich source of something: *your portfolio holds a mother lode of opportunities.*

moth·er·ly /ˈməT͟Hərlē/ ▸*adj.* of, resembling, or characteristic of a mother, esp. in being caring, protective, and kind: *she held both her arms wide in a gesture of motherly love.* ▷Old English *mōdorlic* (see MOTHER, -LY[1]). **—moth·er·li·ness** *n.*

moth·er-na·ked ▸*adj.* [*predic.*] wearing no clothes at all: *Dan was lying mother-naked.*

Moth·er Na·ture nature personified as a creative and controlling force: *Mother Nature has 80 percent control in putting out fires like this.*

Moth·er of God *Christian Church* a name given to the Virgin Mary (as mother of the divine Christ).

moth·er-of-pearl ▸*n.* a smooth shining iridescent substance forming the inner layer of the shell of some mollusks, esp. oysters and abalones, used in ornamentation.

Moth·er of Pres·i·dents a nickname for the state of VIRGINIA[1].

Moth·er of States a nickname for the state of VIRGINIA[1].

Moth·er of the West a nickname for the state of MISSOURI.

Moth·er's Day ▸*n.* a day of the year (in the U.S., the second Sunday in May) on which mothers are particularly honored by their children.

moth·er's help·er ▸*n.* a person who helps a mother, mainly by looking after her children.

moth·er ship ▸*n.* a large spacecraft or ship from which smaller craft are launched or maintained.

moth·er's milk ▸*n.* the milk of a particular child's own mother. ■ *figurative* something providing sustenance or regarded by a person as entirely appropriate to them: *the early work of Sturtevant and Morgan was mother's milk to geneticists.* ■ *informal* alcoholic liquor.

moth·er's son ▸*n.* *informal* a man: ***every mother's son*** *personally knew his friendly local CIA agent.*

Moth·er Su·pe·ri·or (also **mother superior**) ▸*n.* the head of a female religious community.

Moth·er Te·re·sa /təˈrēsə; təˈrāsə; təˈrēzə; təˈrāzə/ see TERESA, MOTHER.

moth·er-to-be ▸*n.* (*pl.* **moth·ers-to-be**) a woman who is expecting a baby.

moth·er tongue ▸*n.* the language that a person has grown up speaking from early childhood.

Moth·er·well /ˈməT͟Hər,wel/, Robert (1915–91), U.S. artist. He was a founder and leading exponent of the New York school of abstract expressionism. Many of his works, such as *Elegies to the Spanish Republic* (1948–68) were done in black and white oil paints.

moth·er wit ▸*n.* natural ability to cope with everyday matters; common sense.

moth·er·wort /ˈməT͟Hər,wərt; -,wôrt/ ▸*n.* a tall strong-smelling plant of the mint family, with purplish-pink lipped flowers clustering close to the axils. It is used in herbal medicine, esp. in the treatment of gynecological disorders. • *Leonurus cardiaca*, family Labiatae.

moth·proof /ˈmôTH,pro͞of/ ▸*adj.* (of clothes or fabrics) treated with a substance that repels moths.
▸*v.* [*trans.*] treat with a substance that repels moths.

moth·y /ˈmôTHē/ ▸*adj.* (**moth·i·er, moth·i·est**) infested with or damaged by moths: *tattered mothy curtains.*

mo·tif /mōˈtēf/ ▸*n.* a decorative design or pattern: *T-shirts featuring spiral motifs.* ■ a distinctive feature or dominant idea in an artistic or literary composition: *the nautical motif of his latest novel.* ■ *Music* a short succession of notes producing a single impression; a brief melodic or rhythmic formula out of which longer passages are developed: *the motif in the second violin is submerged by the first violin's countermelody.* ■ an ornament of lace, braid, etc., sewn separately on a garment. ■ *Biochemistry* a distinctive sequence on a protein or DNA, having a three-dimensional structure that allows binding interactions to occur. ▷mid 19th cent.: from French.

mo·tile /ˈmōtl; ˈmō,til/ ▸*adj.* **1** *Zoology & Botany* (of cells, gametes, and single-celled organisms) capable of motion. **2** *Psychology* of, relating to, or characterized by responses that involve muscular rather than audiovisual sensations. ▷mid 19th cent.: from Latin *motus* 'motion,' on the pattern of *mobile.* **—mo·til·i·ty** /mōˈtilətē/ *n.*

mo·tion /ˈmōSHən/ ▸*n.* **1** the action or process of moving or being moved: *the laws of planetary motion* | *a cushioned shoe that doesn't restrict motion.* ■ a gesture: *she made a motion with her free hand.* ■ a piece of moving mechanism. **2** a formal proposal put to a legislature or committee: *the head of our commission* ***made a motion*** *that we rewrite the constitution.* ■ *Law* an application for a rule or order of court. **3** *Music* the movement of a melodic line between successive pitches: *they rely heavily on repeated chord tones and much less often on conjunct melodic motion.*
▸*v.* [*trans.*] direct or command (someone) with a movement of the hand or head: *he motioned Dennis to a plush chair* | [*trans.*] *he motioned the young officer to sit down* | [*intrans.*] *he* ***motioned for*** *a time out.* ▷late Middle English: via Old French from Latin *motio(n-)*, from *movere* 'to move.' **—mo·tion·al** /-SHənl/ *adj.* **—mo·tion·less** *adj.* **—mo·tion·less·ly** *adv.*
▸*PHRASES* □ **go through the motions** do something perfunctorily, without any enthusiasm or commitment. ■ simulate an action: *a child goes through the motions of washing up.* □ **in motion** moving: *flowing blonde hair that was constantly in motion.* □ **set something in motion** start something moving or working. ■ start or trigger a process or series of events: *plunging oil prices set in motion an economic collapse.*

mo·tion cap·ture (also **mo·cap**) ▸*n.* a filmmaking technique in which actors wear special suits that allow computers to track their movements, to use as a basis for lifelike animated characters.

mo·tion pic·ture ▸*n.* another term for MOVIE: [as *adj.*] *the motion-picture industry.*

mo·tion sick·ness ▸*n.* nausea caused by motion, esp. by traveling in a vehicle.

mo·ti·vate /ˈmōtə,vāt/ ▸*v.* [*trans.*] provide (someone) with a motive for doing something: *he was primarily motivated by the desire for profit.* ■ stimulate (someone's) interest in or enthusiasm for doing something: *I'm going to motivate kids to study civics.* **—mo·ti·va·tor** /-,vātər/ *n.*

mo·ti·va·tion /,mōtəˈvāSHən/ ▸*n.* the reason or reasons one has for acting or behaving in a particular way: *escape can be a strong motivation for travel.* ■ the general desire or willingness of someone to do something: *keep staff up to date and maintain interest and motivation.* ▷late 19th cent.: from MOTIVE, reinforced by MOTIVATE. **—mo·ti·va·tion·al** /-SHənl/ *adj.* **—mo·ti·va·tion·al·ly** /-SHənl-ē/ *adv.*

mo·ti·va·tion re·search ▸*n.* the psychological or sociological investigation of motives, esp. those influencing the decisions of consumers.

mo·tive /ˈmōtiv/ ▸*n.* **1** a reason for doing something, esp. one that is hidden or not obvious: *a motive for his murder.* **2** (in art, literature, or music) a motif: *the entire work grows organically from the opening horn motive.*
▸*adj.* [*attrib.*] **1** producing physical or mechanical motion: *the charge of gas is the motive force for every piston stroke.* **2** causing or being the reason for something: *the motive principle of a writer's work.* ▷late Middle English: from Old French *motif* (adjective used as a noun), from late Latin *motivus*, from *movere* 'to move.' **—mo·tive·less** *adj.* **—mo·tive·less·ly** *adv.* **—mo·tive·less·ness** *n.*

mo·tive pow·er ▸*n.* the energy (in the form of steam, electricity, etc.) used to drive machinery. ■ the locomotive engines of a railroad system collectively.

mo·ti·vic /ˈmōtəvik/ ▸*adj.* *Music* of or relating to a motif or motifs.

mot juste /,mō ˈZHYST/ ▸*n.* (*pl.* **mots justes** *pronunc.* same) the exact, appropriate word.

mot·ley /ˈmätlē/ ▸*adj.* (**mot·li·er, mot·li·est**) incongruously varied in appearance or character; disparate: ***a motley crew*** *of discontents and zealots.*
▸*n.* **1** [usu. in *sing.*] an incongruous mixture: ***a motley of*** *interacting interest groups.* **2** *historical* the particolored costume of a jester: *life-size mannequins* ***in full motley.*** ▷late Middle English: of unknown origin; perhaps ultimately related to MOTE.

mot·mot /ˈmät,mät/ ▸*n.* a tree-dwelling tropical American bird with colorful plumage, typically having two long racketlike tail feathers. • Family Momotidae: several genera and species, in particular the widespread **blue-crowned motmot** (*Momotus momota*). ▷mid 19th cent.: from Latin American Spanish, of imitative origin.

mo·to·cross /ˈmōtō,krôs; -,kräs/ ▸*n.* cross-country racing on motorcycles. ▷late 20th cent.: abbreviation of MOTOR + CROSS. **—mo·to·cross·er** *n.*

mo·to·neu·ron /,mōtəˈn(y)o͝or,än/ ▸*n.* another term for MOTOR NEURON.

mo·to per·pet·u·o /ˈmōtō pərˈpetoo͞,ō/ ▸*n.* (*pl.* **mo·to per·pe·tu·i** /pərˈpetoo͞,ē/) *Music* another term for PERPETUUM MOBILE. ▷Italian, literally 'perpetual motion.'

mo·tor /ˈmōtər/ ▸*n.* a machine, esp. one powered by electricity or internal combustion, that supplies motive power for a vehicle or for some other device with moving parts. ■ a source of power, energy, or motive force: *hormones are the motor of the sexual functions.*
▸*adj.* [*attrib.*] **1** giving, imparting, or producing motion or action: *demand is the principle motor force governing economic activity.* ■ *Physiology* relating to muscular movement or the nerves activating it: *the motor functions of each hand.* **2** *chiefly Brit.* driven by a motor. ■ of or relating to motor vehicles: *a dominant figure in the world of motor sports.*
▸*v.* [*intrans.*] *informal* travel in a motor vehicle, typically a car or a boat: *we motored along a narrow road* | *we motored out of Breton Bay to begin our return trip down the Potomac.* ■ *informal* run or move as fast as possible: *he had motored along to second base on a passed ball.* ■ [*trans.*] *chiefly Brit.* convey (someone) somewhere in a motor vehicle: *he hired someone to motor him back.* ▷late Middle English (denoting a person who imparts motion): from Latin, literally 'mover,' based on *movere* 'to move.' The current sense of the noun dates from the mid 19th cent.

mo·tor ar·e·a ▸*n.* *Anatomy* a part of the central nervous system concerned with muscular action, esp. the motor cortex.

mo·tor·bike /ˈmōtər,bīk/ ▸*n.* a lightweight motorcycle. ■ a motorized bicycle.

mo·tor·boat /ˈmōtər,bōt/ ▸*n.* a boat powered by a motor, esp. a recreational boat.

mo·tor·bus /ˈmōtər,bəs/ ▸*n.* old-fashioned term for BUS (sense 1).

mo·tor·cade /ˈmōtər,kād/ ▸*n.* a procession of motor vehicles, typically carrying and escorting a prominent person. ▷early 20th cent.: from MOTOR, on the pattern of *cavalcade.*

mo·tor·car /ˈmōtər,kär/ ▸*n.* **1** *dated* or *Brit.* an automobile. **2** a self-propelled railroad vehicle used to carry railroad workers.

mo·tor coach ▸*n.* another term for COACH[1] (sense 3).

mo·tor cor·tex ▸*n.* *Anatomy* the part of the cerebral cortex in the brain where the nerve impulses originate that initiate voluntary muscular activity.

mo·tor·cy·cle /ˈmōtərˌsīkəl/ ▸*n.* a two-wheeled vehicle that is powered by a motor and has no pedals. **—mo·tor·cy·cling** /-ˌsīk(ə)liNG/ *n.* **—mo·tor·cy·clist** /-ˌsīk(ə)list/ *n.*

motorcycle

mo·tor drive ▸*n.* a mechanical system that includes an electric motor and drives a machine. ■ a battery-driven motor in a camera used to wind the film rapidly between exposures.

mo·tor gen·er·a·tor ▸*n.* a device consisting of a mechanically coupled electric motor and generator that may be used to control the voltage, frequency, or phase of an electrical supply.

mo·tor home ▸*n.* a motor vehicle equipped like a trailer for living in, with kitchen facilities, beds, etc.

mo·tor inn (also **motor hotel** or **motor lodge**) ▸*n.* a motel.

mo·tor·ist /ˈmōtərist/ ▸*n.* the driver of an automobile.

mo·tor·ize /ˈmōtəˌrīz/ ▸*v.* [*trans.*] [usu. as *adj.*] (**motorized**) equip (a vehicle or device) with a motor to operate or propel it: *a motorized wheelchair.* ■ equip (troops) with motor transportation: *three motorized divisions.* **—mo·tor·i·za·tion** /ˌmōtərəˈzāSHən / *n.*

mo·tor launch ▸*n.* see LAUNCH[2].

mo·tor·man /ˈmōtərˌmən/ ▸*n.* (*pl.* **-men**) the driver of an electric vehicle, esp. a streetcar or subway train.

mo·tor·mouth /ˈmōtərˌmouTH/ (also **mo·tor-mouth**) ▸*n. informal* a person who talks quickly and incessantly. **—mo·tor·mouthed** /-ˌmouT͟Hd; -ˌmouTHt/ (or **mo·tor-mouthed**) *adj.*

mo·tor nerve ▸*n.* a nerve carrying impulses from the brain or spinal cord to a muscle or gland.

mo·tor neu·ron ▸*n.* a nerve cell forming part of a pathway along which impulses pass from the brain or spinal cord to a muscle or gland.

mo·tor·sail·er /ˈmōtərˌsālər/ ▸*n.* a boat equipped with both sails and an engine.

mo·tor scoot·er ▸*n.* see SCOOTER.

mo·tor ve·hi·cle ▸*n.* a road vehicle powered by an internal combustion engine; an automobile.

mo·tor vo·ter law ▸*n.* another name for the National Voter Registration Act of 1993, designed to reverse declining voter registration by allowing voters to register at motor vehicle departments.

mo·tor·way /ˈmōtərˌwā/ ▸*n. Brit.* an expressway. ■ *informal* a wide, fast, easy ski run.

Mo·town /ˈmōˌtoun/ ▸*n.* **1** (also *trademark* **Tamla Motown**) music released on or reminiscent of the U.S. record label Tamla Motown. The first black-owned record company in the U.S., Tamla Motown was founded in Detroit in 1959 by Berry Gordy, and was important in popularizing soul music, producing artists such as the Supremes, Stevie Wonder, and Marvin Gaye. **2** informal name for DETROIT. ▷mid 20th cent.: shortening of *Motor Town*, by association with the car manufacturing industry of Detroit.

Mott /mät/, Lucretia (Coffin) (1793–1880), U.S. social reformer. A progressive Quaker minister, she was a highly motivated activist in the cause of abolition, women's rights, and freedom of religion. She wrote *Discourse on Women* (1850) and helped to form the Free Religious Association 1867.

motte /mät/ ▸*n.* **1** (also **mott**) a stand of trees, esp. in the southwestern U.S.; a grove. **2** *historical* a mound forming the site of a castle or camp. ▷late 19th cent.: from French, 'mound,' from Old French *mote* (see MOAT).

mot·tle /ˈmätl/ ▸*v.* [*trans.*] (usu. **be mottled**) mark with spots or smears of color: *the cow's coat was light red mottled with white* | [as *adj.*] (**mottled**) *a bird with mottled brown plumage.*

▸*n.* an irregular arrangement of spots or patches of color: *the ship was a mottle of khaki and black.* ■ (also **mottling**) a spot or patch forming part of such an arrangement: *the mottles on a trout* | *white marble with mottlings of black and gray.* ▷late 18th cent.: probably a back-formation from MOTLEY.

mot·to /ˈmätō/ ▸*n.* (*pl.* **-toes** or **-tos**) a short sentence or phrase chosen as encapsulating the beliefs or ideals guiding an individual, family, or institution: *the school motto, "Serve and obey"* | *he soon adopted the motto "work hard and play hard."* ■ *Music* a phrase that recurs throughout a musical work and has some symbolic significance. ▷late 16th cent.: from Italian, 'word.'

mo·tu pro·pri·o /ˈmōto͞o ˈprōprēˌō/ ▸*n.* (*pl.* **mo·tu pro·pri·os**) an edict issued by the pope personally to the Roman Catholic Church or to a part of it. ▷Latin, literally 'of one's own volition.'

moue /mo͞o/ ▸*n.* a pouting expression used to convey annoyance or distaste. ▷mid 19th cent.: French, earlier having the sense 'lip.'

mouf·lon /ˈmo͞ofˌlôn/ (also **mouf·flon**) ▸*n.* a small wild sheep with chestnut-brown wool, found in mountainous country from Iran to Asia Minor. It is the ancestor of the domestic sheep. • *Ovis orientalis*, family Bovidae. ▷late 18th cent.: from French, from Italian *muflone*.

mouil·lé /mo͞oˈyā/ ▸*adj. Phonetics* (of a consonant) palatalized. ▷French, 'wetted.'

mou·jik /mo͞oˈZHēk; -ˈZHik/ ▸*n.* variant spelling of MUZHIK.

mould /mōld/ ▸*n.* & *v.* British spelling of MOLD[1], MOLD[2], and MOLD[3].

mould·er /ˈmōldər/ ▸*v.* & *n.* British spelling of MOLDER.

mould·ing /ˈmōldiNG/ ▸*n.* British spelling of MOLDING.

mould·y /ˈmōldē/ ▸*adj.* British spelling of MOLDY.

mou·lin /mo͞oˈlan/ ▸*n.* a vertical or nearly vertical shaft in a glacier, formed by surface water percolating through a crack in the ice. ▷mid 19th cent.: French, literally 'mill.'

Mou·lin Rouge /mo͞oˈlan ˈro͞oZH/ a cabaret in Montmartre, Paris, a favorite resort of poets and artists around the end of the 19th century. Toulouse-Lautrec immortalized its dancers in his posters. ▷French, literally 'red windmill.'

Moul·mein /ˌmo͞olˈmān; ˌmōlˈmīn/ a port in southeastern Myanmar (Burma); pop. 220,000.

moult /mōlt/ ▸*v.* & *n.* British spelling of MOLT.

moul·vi /ˈmo͞olvē; ˈmôl-/ (also **maulvi, molvi**) ▸*n.* (*pl.* **-vis**) a Muslim doctor of law; an imam. ▷from Urdu *maulvī*, from Arabic *mawlawī* 'judicial' (adjective used as a noun), from *mawlā* 'mullah.'

mound[1] /mound/ ▸*n.* a rounded mass projecting above a surface. ■ a raised mass of earth, stones, or other compacted material, sometimes created artificially for purposes of defense or burial. ■ a small hill. ■ (**a mound of/mounds of**) a large pile or quantity of something: *burying potential problems under mounds of cash.* ■ *Baseball* (in full **pitcher's mound**) the elevated area from which the pitcher delivers the ball.

▸*v.* [*trans.*] heap up into a rounded pile: *mound the pie filling slightly in the center.* ■ *archaic* enclose, bound, or fortify with an embankment: *hills that mound the sea.* ▷early 16th cent. (as a verb in the sense 'enclose with a fence or hedge'): of obscure origin. An early sense of the noun was 'boundary hedge or fence.'

▸*PHRASE* □ **take the mound** *Baseball* (of a pitcher) have a turn at pitching: *Morris will take the mound Tuesday.*

mound[2] ▸*n. archaic* a ball representing the earth, used as part of royal regalia, e.g., on top of a crown, typically of gold and surmounted by a cross. ▷Middle English (denoting the world): from Old French *monde*, from Latin *mundus* 'world.'

mound build·er ▸*n.* another term for MEGAPODE.

Moun·dou /ˈmo͞ondo͞o/ a commercial city in southern Chad; pop. 281,000.

mounds·man /ˈmoun(d)zmən/ ▸*n.* (*pl.* **-men**) *Baseball* a pitcher.

mount[1] /mount/ ▸*v.* [*trans.*] **1** climb up (stairs, a hill, or other rising surface): *he mounted the steps to the front door.* ■ climb or move up on to (a raised surface): *the master of ceremonies mounted the platform.* ■ get up on (an animal or bicycle) in order to ride it. ■ (often **be mounted**) set (someone) on horseback; provide with a horse: *she was mounted on a white horse.* ■ (of a male mammal or bird) get on (a female) for the purpose of copulation. ■ [*intrans.*] (of the blood or its color) rise into the cheeks: *feeling the blush mount in her cheeks, she looked down quickly.* **2** organize and initiate (a campaign or other significant course of action): *the company had successfully mounted takeover bids.* ■ establish; set up: *security forces mounted checkpoints at every key road.* ■ produce (a play, exhibition, or other artistic event); present for public view or display. **3** [*intrans.*] grow larger or more numerous: *the costs* **mount up** *when you buy a home.* ■ (of a feeling) become stronger or more intense: *his anxiety mounted as messages were left unanswered.* **4** [*trans.*] place or fix (an object) on an elevated support: *fluorescent lights are* **mounted on** *the ceiling.* ■ fix (an object) in position: *the engine is mounted behind the rear seats.* ■ [*trans.*] place (a gun) on a fixed mounting. ■ [*trans.*] set in or attach to a backing or setting: *the photographs will be mounted and framed.* ■ [*trans.*] fix (an object for viewing) on a microscope slide. ■ [*trans.*] *Computing* make (a disk or disk drive) available for use.

▸*n.* **1** a backing or setting on which a photograph, gem, or work of art is set for display. ■ a glass microscope slide for securing a specimen to be viewed. ■ *Philately* a clear plastic or paper sleeve used to display a postage stamp. **2** a support for a gun, camera, or similar piece of equipment. **3** a horse being ridden or that is available for riding: *he hung on to his mount's bridle.* ■ an opportunity to ride a horse, esp. as a jockey: *the jockey's injuries forced him to give up the coveted mount on Cool Ground.* ▷Middle English: from Old French *munter*, based on Latin *mons, mont-* 'mountain.' **—mount·a·ble** *adj.* **—mount·er** *n.*

▸*PHRASE* □ **mount guard** keep watch, esp. for protection or to prevent escape.

mount[2] ▸*n.* a mountain or hill (archaic except in place names): *Mount Everest.* ■ any of several fleshy prominences on the palm of the hand regarded in palmistry as signifying the degree of influence of a particular planet: *mount of Mars.* ▷Old English *munt*, from Latin *mons, mont-* 'mountain,' reinforced in Middle English by Old French *mont*.

moun·tain /ˈmountn/ ▸*n.* a large natural elevation of the earth's surface rising abruptly from the surrounding level; a large steep hill: *the village is backed by awe-inspiring mountains* | *we set off down the mountain* | [as *adj.*] *the ice and snow of a mountain peak.* ■ (**mountains**) a region where there are many such features, characterized by remoteness and inaccessibility: *they sought refuge in the mountains* | [as *adj.*] (**mountain**) *his attempt to picture the mountain folk in ridiculous attire.* ■ (**a mountain/mountains of**) a large pile or quantity of something: *a mountain of paperwork.* ■ [usu. with *adj.*] a large surplus stock of a commodity: *this farming produced huge food mountains.* ▷Middle English: from Old French *montaigne*, based on Latin *mons, mont-* 'mountain.' **—moun·tain·y** *adj.*

▸*PHRASES* □ **make a mountain out of a molehill** see MOLEHILL. □ **move mountains 1** achieve spectacular and apparently impossible results. **2** make every possible effort: *his fans move mountains to catch as many of his performances as possible.*

moun·tain ash ▸*n.* **1** a small deciduous tree of the rose family, with compound leaves, white flowers, and red berries. Also called ROWAN. • Genus *Sorbus*, family Rosaceae: several species, in particular the North American *S. americana*. **2** *Austral.* a eucalyptus tree that is widely used for timber. • Genus *Eucalyptus*, family Myrtaceae: several species, in particular the very tall *E. regnans*.

moun·tain av·ens ▸*n.* a creeping arctic-alpine plant with white flowers and glossy leaves. See also DRYAS. • *Dryas octopetala*, family Rosaceae.

moun·tain bea·ver ▸*n.* a burrowing forest-dwelling rodent occurring only in western North America, from British Columbia to California. Also called SEWELLEL. • *Aplodontia rufa*, the only member of the family Aplodontidae.

moun·tain bike ▸*n.* a bicycle with a light sturdy frame, broad deep-treaded tires, and multiple gears, originally designed for riding on mountainous terrain. **—moun·tain bik·er** *n.* **—moun·tain bik·ing** *n.*

moun·tain·board·ing /ˈmountnˌbôrdiNG/ ▸*n.* the sport or recreational activity of riding a dirtboard down hills and mountains. **—moun·tain·board** *n.*

moun·tain chain ▸*n.* a connected series of mountains.

moun·tain cran·ber·ry ▸*n.* (*pl.* **-ries**) a low-growing evergreen dwarf shrub of the heath family that bears dark red berries and grows in upland habitats in the north. Also called COWBERRY, LINGONBERRY. • *Vaccinium vitis-idaea*, family Ericaceae. ■ the edible acid berry of this plant, which may be used as a cranberry substitute.

moun·tain dew ▸*n. informal* illicitly distilled liquor, esp. whiskey or rum; moonshine.

moun·tain dul·ci·mer ▸*n.* see DULCIMER.

moun·tain·eer /ˌmountn'i(ə)r/ ▸*n.* a person who takes part in mountaineering. ■ *rare* a person living in a mountainous area.

moun·tain·eer·ing /ˌmountn'i(ə)riNG/ ▸*n.* the sport or activity of climbing mountains.

moun·tain gem ▸*n.* a green hummingbird found in the upland forests of Central America. • Genus *Lampornis*, family Trochilidae: several species.

moun·tain goat ▸*n.* **1** (also **Rocky Mountain goat**) a goat-antelope with shaggy white hair and backward curving horns, living in the Rocky Mountains. • *Oreamnos americanus*, family Bovidae. **2** any goat that lives on mountains, proverbial for agility.

mountain goat

moun·tain lau·rel ▸*n.* a North American kalmia that bears clusters of white or pink flowers. • *Kalmia latifolia*, family Ericaceae.

moun·tain li·on ▸*n.* another term for COUGAR.

moun·tain·ous /'mountn-əs/ ▸*adj.* (of a region) having many mountains. ■ huge: *struggling under mountainous debts.*

moun·tain range ▸*n.* a line of mountains connected by high ground.

moun·tain sheep ▸*n.* another term for BIGHORN. ■ any sheep that lives on mountains.

moun·tain sick·ness ▸*n.* another term for ALTITUDE SICKNESS.

moun·tain·side /'mountnˌsīd/ ▸*n.* the sloping surface of a mountain.

Moun·tain State a nickname for the state of WEST VIRGINIA.

Moun·tain States the region of the U.S. that includes states that contain part of the Rocky Mountains. New Mexico, Colorado, Wyoming, Utah, Idaho, and Montana are generally considered Mountain States.

Moun·tain time the standard time in a zone including parts of the U.S. and Canada in or near the Rocky Mountains, specifically: • (**Mountain Standard Time** abbrev.: **MST**) standard time based on the mean solar time at the meridian 105° W., seven hours behind GMT. • (**Mountain Daylight Time** abbrev.: **MDT**) Mountain time during daylight saving time, six hours behind GMT.

Moun·tain View a city in north central California, near the southern end of San Francisco Bay, part of the Silicon Valley complex; pop. 67,460.

Mount Ar·a·rat, Mount Car·mel, etc. see ARARAT, MOUNT; CARMEL, MOUNT, etc.

Mount·bat·ten /ˌmoun(t)'batn/, Louis (Francis Albert Victor Nicholas), 1st Earl Mountbatten of Burma (1900–79), British admiral and administrator; his nephew was Britain's Prince Philip. He was supreme Allied commander in Southeast Asia 1943–45; after the war, he was the last viceroy 1947 and first governor general of India 1947–48. He was killed by an IRA bomb while on his yacht.

Mount Des·ert Is·land an island in the Atlantic Ocean, in southeastern Maine, site of Bar Harbor and other resorts. Most of the island is in Acadia National Park.

moun·te·bank /'mountiˌbaNGk/ ▸*n.* a person who deceives others, esp. in order to trick them out of their money; a charlatan. See note at QUACK. ■ *historical* a person who sold patent medicines in public places. ▷late 16th cent.: from Italian *montambanco*, from the imperative phrase *monta in banco!* 'climb on the bench!' (with allusion to the raised platform used to attract an audience). **—moun·te·bank·er·y** /-ˌbaNGkərē/ *n.*

mount·ed /'mountid/ ▸*adj.* [*attrib.*] riding an animal, typically a horse, esp. for military or other duty: *mounted police controlled the crowd.*

Moun·tie /'mountē/ ▸*n.* *informal* a member of the Royal Canadian Mounted Police.

mount·ing /'mountiNG/ ▸*n.* **1** a backing, setting, or support for something: *he pulled the curtain rod from its mounting.* **2** the action of mounting something: *the mounting of rapid-fire guns.*

Mount of Ol·ives the highest point in the range of hills to the east of Jerusalem. It is a holy place for both Judaism and Christianity and is frequently mentioned in the Bible. The Garden of Gethsemane is located nearby.

Mount Pleas·ant a town in southeastern South Carolina, a resort on the Atlantic Ocean, east of Charleston; pop. 47,609.

Mount Ver·non /'vərnən/ **1** a city in southeastern New York, north of the Bronx in New York City; pop. 68,381. **2** an estate in northeastern Virginia, about 15 miles (24 km) from Washington, DC, on a site overlooking the Potomac River. Built in 1743, it was the home of George Washington 1747–99.

mourn /môrn/ ▸*v.* [*trans.*] feel or show deep sorrow or regret for (someone or their death), typically by following conventions such as the wearing of black clothes: *Isabel mourned her husband* | [*intrans.*] *she had to* ***mourn for*** *her friends who died in the accident.* ■ feel regret or sadness about (the loss or disappearance of something): *publishers mourned declining sales of hardback fiction.* ▷Old English *murnan*, of Germanic origin.

THE RIGHT WORD **bemoan, grieve, lament, mourn, rue, sorrow**

Not everyone exhibits unhappiness in the same way. In this "unhappy" group of verbs, the stongest is **grieve**, implying deep mental anguish or suffering, often endured alone and in silence (*she grieved for years over the loss of her baby*).

Mourn is more formal and often more public; although it implies deep emotion felt over a period of time, that emotion may be more ceremonial than sincere (*the people mourned the loss of their leader*).

Lament comes from a Latin word meaning to wail or weep, and it therefore suggests a vocal or verbal expression of loss (*The shrieking women lamented their husbands' deaths*).

Bemoan also suggests suppressed or inarticulate sounds of *grief*, often expressing regret or disapproval (*to bemoan one's fate*).

Sorrow combines deep sadness with regret and often pertains to a less tragic loss than *grieve* or *mourn* (*sorrow over a lost love*), while **rue** has even stronger connotations of regret and repentance (*she rued the day she was born*).

mourn·er /'môrnər/ ▸*n.* **1** a person who attends a funeral as a relative or friend of the dead person. ■ *chiefly historical* a person hired to attend a funeral. **2** any of a number of drab-colored South American tyrant flycatchers and related birds. • Families Tyrannidae, Pipridae, and Cotingidae: four genera and several species; the classification is uncertain.

mourn·ful /'môrnfəl/ ▸*adj.* feeling or expressing sadness, regret, or grief: *the third boy stared fixedly at me with mournful, basset-hound eyes.* ■ suggestive of or inducing sadness, regret, or unhappiness: *his voice on one track, mournful piano on another.* **—mourn·ful·ly** *adv.* **—mourn·ful·ness** *n.*

mourn·ing /'môrniNG/ ▸*n.* the expression of deep sorrow for someone who has died, typically involving following certain conventions such as wearing black clothes: *she's still* ***in mourning*** *after the death of her husband.* ■ black clothes worn as an expression of grief when someone dies.

mourn·ing band ▸*n.* a strip of black material that is worn around a person's sleeve as a mark of respect for someone who has recently died.

mourn·ing cloak ▸*n.* a migratory butterfly with deep purple yellow-bordered wings. • *Nymphalis antiopa*, subfamily Nymphalinae, family Nymphalidae.

mourning cloak

mourn·ing dove ▸*n.* a North and Central American dove with a long tail, a gray-brown back, and a plaintive call. • *Zenaida macroura*, family Columbidae.

mourn·ing ring ▸*n.* *historical* a ring worn to remind the wearer of someone who has died.

mouse ▸*n.* /mous/ (*pl.* **mice** /mīs/) **1** a small rodent that typically has a pointed snout, relatively large ears and eyes, and a long tail. • Family Muridae: many genera and numerous species. Also, some species in the families Heteromyidae, Zapodidae, and Muscardinidae. ■ (in general use) any similar small mammal, such as a shrew or vole. ■ a shy, timid, and quiet person. **2** a dull light brown color reminiscent of a mouse's fur: *her blonde hair dulled to mouse.* **3** (*pl.* also **mous·es**) *Computing* a small handheld device that is dragged across a flat surface to move the cursor on a computer screen, typically having buttons that are pressed to control computer functions. **4** *informal* a lump or bruise, esp. one on or near the eye.
▸*v.* /mouz/ [*intrans.*] **1** (of a cat or an owl) hunt for or catch mice. ■ [with *adverbial*] prowl around as if searching: *he was mousing among the books of the old library.* **2** [with *adverbial of direction*] *informal Computing* use a mouse to move a cursor on a computer screen: *mouse over to the window and click on it.* ▷Old English *mūs*, (plural) *mȳs*, of Germanic origin; related to Dutch *muis* and German *Maus*, from an Indo-European root shared by Latin and Greek *mus.* **—mouse·like** *adj.*

mouse·bird /'mousˌbərd/ ▸*n.* a small gregarious African bird with mainly drab plumage, a crest, and a long tail. • Genera *Colius* and *Urocolius*, family Coliidae: six species.

mouse deer ▸*n.* another term for CHEVROTAIN.

mouse-ear chickweed ▸*n.* see CHICKWEED.

mouse-eared bat ▸*n.* another term for MYOTIS.

mouse le·mur ▸*n.* a small nocturnal Madagascan lemur with large ears, close-set eyes, and a long tail. • Genus *Microcebus*, family Cheirogaleidae: three species. See also DWARF LEMUR.

mouse mat (also **mouse·mat**) ▸*n.* British term for MOUSE PAD.

mouse o·pos·sum ▸*n.* a mouselike opossum with large ears and no marsupial pouch, native to Central and South America. • Genus *Marmosa*, family Didelphidae: several species.

mouse pad (also **mouse·pad**) ▸*n.* a piece of rigid or slightly resilient material on which a computer mouse is moved.

mouse po·ta·to ▸*n.* *informal* a person who spends large amounts of time operating a computer. ▷1990s: on the pattern of *couch potato.*

mous·er /'mousər; -zər/ ▸*n.* an animal that catches mice, esp. a cat.

mouse-tailed bat ▸*n.* an insectivorous bat with a long mouselike tail, native to Africa and Asia and often found in man-made structures. • Family Rhinopomatidae and genus *Rhinopoma*: three species.

mouse·trap /'mousˌtrap/ ▸*n.* a trap for catching and usually killing mice, esp. one with a spring bar that snaps down onto the mouse when it touches a piece of cheese or other bait attached to the mechanism.
▸*v.* (**-trapped, -trap·ping**) [*trans.*] *informal* induce (someone) to do something by means of a trick: *the editor mousetrapped her into giving him an article.* ■ (often as **mousetrapping**) block (a user's) efforts to exit from a Web site, usually one to which they have been redirected: *mousetrapping is a tactic commonly used by pornographic Web sites.*
▸*PHRASE* □ **better mousetrap** an improved version of a well-known item. [from Ralph Waldo Emerson's comment "all men have to do is to invent a better mousetrap."]

mous·ey ▸*adj.* variant spelling of MOUSY.

mous·sa·ka /mo͞o'säkə; ˌmo͞osə'kä/ ▸*n.* a Greek dish made of ground lamb, eggplant, and tomatoes, with cheese on top. ▷from Turkish *musakka*, based on Arabic.

mousse /mo͞os/ ▸*n.* a sweet or savory dish made as a smooth light mass with whipped cream and beaten egg white, flavored with chocolate, fish, etc., and typically served chilled: *roulade of sole with a lobster mousse* | *dark chocolate mousse.* ■ a soft, light, or aerated gel such as a soap preparation: *fragrant shower mousse.* ■ a frothy preparation that is applied to the hair, enabling it to be styled more easily. ■ (also **chocolate mousse**) a brown frothy emulsion of oil and seawater formed by weathering of an oil slick.
▸*v.* [*trans.*] style (hair) using mousse. ▷mid 19th cent.: from French, 'moss or froth.'

mousse·line /ˌmo͞osə'lēn; -'slēn/ ▸*n.* **1** a fine, semi-opaque fabric similar to muslin, typically made of silk, wool, or cotton. **2** a soft, light mousse. **3** (also **sauce mousseline**) hollandaise sauce that has been made frothy with whipped cream or egg white, served mainly with fish or asparagus. ▷late 17th cent.: from French (see MUSLIN).

mousse·ron /ˌmōōs(ə)'rôN/ ▸*n.* an edible mushroom with a flattish white cap, pink gills, and a mealy smell. • *Clitopilus prunulus*, family Agaricaceae, class Hymenomycetes.

mous·seux /mōō'sœ/ ▸*adj.* (of wine) sparkling: *vin mousseux.*

▸*n.* (*pl.* same) sparkling wine. ▷from French, from *mousse* 'froth.'

mous·tache ▸*n.* variant spelling of MUSTACHE.

Mous·te·ri·an /mōō'sti(ə)rēən/ ▸*adj. Archaeology* of, relating to, or denoting the main culture of the Middle Paleolithic period in Europe, between the Acheulian and Aurignacian periods (chiefly 80,000–35,000 years ago), and associated with Neanderthal peoples. ■ [as *n.*] (**the Mousterian**) the Mousterian culture or period. ▷late 19th cent.: from French *moustiérien*, from *Le Moustier*, a cave in southwestern France where objects from this culture were found.

mous·y /'mousē; -zē/ (also **mous·ey**) ▸*adj.* (**mous·i·er, mous·i·est**) of or like a mouse. ■ (of hair) of a dull light brown color. ■ (of a person) nervous, shy, or timid; lacking in presence or charisma: *his mousy sister had become a dynamic journalist.* —**mous·i·ness** *n.*

Mou·tan /'mōōˌtan/ (also **Moutan peony**) ▸*n.* a tall shrubby peony with pink or white mottled flowers, native to China and Tibet and the parent of many garden varieties. • *Paeonia suffruticosa*, family Paeoniaceae. ▷early 19th cent.: from Chinese *mudan.*

mouth ▸*n.* /mouTH/ (*pl.* **mouths** /mouT͟Hz; mouTHs/) **1** the opening in the lower part of the human face, surrounded by the lips, through which food is taken in and from which speech and other sounds are emitted. ■ the cavity behind this, containing the teeth and tongue. ■ the corresponding opening through which an animal takes in food (at the front of the head in vertebrates and many other creatures), or the cavity behind this. ■ [usu. with *adj.*] a horse's readiness to feel and obey the pressure of the bit in its mouth: *the horse had a **hard mouth.*** ■ the character or quality of a wine as judged by its feel or flavor in the mouth (rather than its aroma). ■ *informal* talkativeness; impudence: *you've got more mouth on you than anyone I've ever known.* **2** an opening or entrance to a structure that is hollow, concave, or almost completely enclosed: *standing before the mouth of a cave.* ■ the opening for filling or emptying something used as a container: *the mouth of the bottle.* ■ the muzzle of a gun. ■ the opening or entrance to a harbor or bay: *walking to the mouth of the bay to absorb the view.* ■ the place where a river enters the sea.

▸*v.* /mouT͟H; mouTH/ [*trans.*] **1** say (something dull or unoriginal), esp. in a pompous or affected way: *this clergyman mouths platitudes in breathy, soothing tones.* ■ utter very clearly and distinctly: *she would carefully mouth the right pronunciation.* ■ move the lips as if saying (something) or in a grimace: *she mouthed a silent farewell* | [with *direct speech*] *"Come on," he mouthed.* **2** take in or touch with the mouth: *puppies may mouth each other's collars during play.* ■ train the mouth of (a horse) so that it responds to a bit.

▸*phrasal v.* □ **mouth off** *informal* talk in an unpleasantly loud and boastful or opinionated way: *he was mouthing off about society in general.* ■ (**mouth off at**) loudly criticize or abuse. ▷Old English *mūth*, of Germanic origin; related to Dutch *mond* and German *Mund*, from an Indo-European root shared by Latin *mentum* 'chin.' —**mouthed** /mouT͟Hd; mouTHt/ *adj.* [in *combination*] *wide-mouthed.* —**mouth·er** /'mouT͟Hər/ *n.* —**mouth·less** /'mouTHləs/ *adj.*

▸*PHRASES* □ **a mouth to feed** a person, typically a child, who has to be looked after and fed: *how can they afford another mouth to feed?* □ **be all mouth** *informal* tend to talk boastfully without any intention of acting on one's words. □ **keep one's mouth shut** *informal* not say anything, esp. not reveal a secret: *would he keep his mouth shut under interrogation?* □ **open one's mouth** *informal* say something: *sorry, I'll never open my mouth about you again.* □ **watch one's mouth** *informal* be careful about what one says.

mouth·brood·er /'mouTHˌbrōōdər/ ▸*n.* a freshwater cichlid fish that protects its eggs (and in some cases its young) by carrying them in its mouth. • *Sarotherodon* and other genera, family Cichlidae.

mouth·feel /'mouTHˌfēl/ ▸*n.* the physical sensations in the mouth produced by a particular food: *this Cabernet has a dense, tightly woven mouthfeel, with complex, chewy, and velvety tannins.*

mouth·ful /'mouTHˌfŏŏl/ ▸*n.* (*pl.* **-fuls**) **1** a quantity of food or drink that fills or can be put into the mouth: *he took **a mouthful of** beer* | *savor the flavor of each mouthful.* **2** a long or complicated word or phrase that is difficult to say: *"Galinsoga" was too much of a mouthful for most nonbotanists.*

▸*PHRASES* □ **give someone a mouthful** *informal* talk to or shout at someone in an angry, abusive, or severely critical way. □ **say a mouthful** *informal* say something noteworthy.

mouth·guard /'mouTHˌgärd/ ▸*n.* a plastic shield held in the mouth by an athlete to protect the teeth and gums.

mouth or·gan ▸*n.* another term for HARMONICA.

mouth·part /'mouTHˌpärt/ ▸*n.* (usu. **mouthparts**) *Zoology* any of the appendages, typically found in pairs, surrounding the mouth of an insect or other arthropod and adapted for feeding.

mouth·piece /'mouTHˌpēs/ ▸*n.* **1** a thing designed to be put in or against the mouth: *the snorkel's mouthpiece.* ■ a part of a musical instrument placed between or against the lips. ■ the part of a telephone for speaking into. ■ the part of a tobacco pipe placed between the lips. ■ a mouthguard. **2** *chiefly derogatory* a person or organization that speaks on behalf of another person or organization: *they become nothing more than a mouthpiece for the company.* ■ *informal* a lawyer.

mouth-to-mouth ▸*adj.* denoting a method of artificial respiration in which a person breathes into an unconscious patient's lungs through the mouth: *mouth-to-mouth resuscitation.*

▸*n.* respiration of this kind.

mouth·wash /'mouTHˌwôsH; -ˌwäsH/ ▸*n.* a liquid used for rinsing the mouth or gargling with, typically containing an antiseptic.

mouth·wa·ter·ing /'mouTHˌwôtəriNG; -ˌwôtəriNG/ ▸*adj.* smelling, looking, or sounding delicious: *a small but mouthwatering collection of recipes.* ■ highly attractive or tempting: *investors expected the new boss to tie up some mouthwatering deals.*

mouth·y /'mouT͟Hē; 'mouTHē/ ▸*adj.* (**mouth·i·er, mouth·i·est**) *informal* inclined to talk a lot, esp. in an impudent way.

mou·ton /'mōōˌtän; mōō'tän/ ▸*n.* sheepskin cut and dyed to resemble beaver fur or sealskin. ▷mid 20th cent.: from French, literally 'sheep.'

mov·a·ble /'mōōvəbəl/ (also **move·a·ble**) ▸*adj.* **1** capable of being moved: *they stripped the town of all movable objects and fled.* ■ (of a feast or festival) variable in date from year to year. See also MOVABLE FEAST. **2** *Law* (of property) of the nature of a chattel, as distinct from land or buildings. Compare with HERITABLE.

▸*n.* (usu. **movables**) property or possessions not including land or buildings. ■ an article of furniture that may be removed from a house, as distinct from a fixture. ▷late Middle English: from Old French, from *moveir* 'to move.' —**mov·a·bil·i·ty** /ˌmōōvə'bilətē/ *n.* —**mov·a·bly** /-blē/ *adv.*

mov·a·ble-do /'mōōvəbəl 'dō/ (*Brit.* **mov·a·ble-doh**) ▸*adj.* [*attrib.*] *Music* denoting a system of solmization (such as tonic sol-fa) in which do is the keynote of any major scale. Compare with FIXED-DO.

mov·a·ble feast ▸*n.* a religious feast day that does not occur on the same calendar date each year. The term refers most often to Easter and other Christian holy days whose dates are related to it.

mov·ant /'mōōvənt/ ▸*n. Law* a person who applies to or petitions a court or judge for a ruling in his or her favor. ▷late 19th cent.: from MOVE + -ANT.

move /mōōv/ ▸*v.* **1** [*intrans.*] go in a specified direction or manner; change position: *she stood up and moved to the door* | *he let his eyes move across the rows of faces.* ■ [*trans.* often] change the place or position of: *she moved the tray to a side table.* ■ change one's place of residence or work: *his family moved to London when he was a child.* ■ [*trans.*] change the date or time of (an event). ■ (of a player) change the position of a piece in a board game: *White has forced his opponent to move* | [*trans.*] *if Black moves his bishop, he loses a pawn.* **2** change or cause to change from one state, opinion, sphere, or activity to another: [*intrans.*] *the school moved over to the new course in 1987* | [*trans.*] *she deftly moved the conversation to safer territory.* ■ [*trans.*] influence or prompt (someone) to do something: *his deep love of music moved him to take lessons with Dr. Hill.* ■ [*intrans.*] take action: *hard-liners may yet **move against** him, but their success might be limited.* ■ [*trans.*] (usu. **be moved**) provoke a strong feeling, esp. of sorrow or sympathy, in: *he was **moved to tears** by a get-well message from the president.* ■ [*trans.*] *archaic* stir up (an emotion) in someone: *he justly moves one's derision.* **3** [*intrans.*] make progress; develop in a particular manner or direction: *aircraft design had moved forward a long way* | *legislators are anxious to **get things moving** as soon as possible.* ■ [*intrans.*] *informal* depart; start off: *let's move—it's time we started shopping.* ■ [in *imperative*] (**move it**) *informal* used to urge or command someone to hurry up: *come on—move it!* ■ [*intrans.*] *informal* go quickly: *Kenny was really moving when he made contact with a tire at the hairpin and flipped over.* ■ [*intrans.*] (of merchandise) be sold: *despite the high prices, goods are moving.* ■ [*trans.*] sell (merchandise). **4** [*intrans.*] (**move in/within**) spend one's time or be socially active in (a particular sphere) or among (a particular group of people): *they moved in different circles of friends.* **5** [*trans.*] propose for discussion and resolution at a meeting or legislative assembly: *she intends to move an amendment to the bill* | [with *clause*] *I beg to move that this House deplores the current economic policies.* ■ make a formal request or application to (a court or assembly) for something: *his family **moved** the court **for** adequate "maintenance expenses" to run the household.* **6** [*trans.*] empty (one's bowels). ■ [*intrans.*] (of the bowels) be emptied.

▸*phrasal v.* □ **move along** [often in *imperative*] change to a new position, esp. to avoid causing an obstruction: *"Move along, move along," said the cop.* □ **move aside** see MOVE OVER below. □ **move in 1** take possession of a new house or business premises. ■ (**move in with**) start to share accommodations with (an existing resident). **2** intervene, esp. so as to take control of a situation: *this riot could have been avoided had the police moved in earlier.* □ **move in on** approach, esp. so as to take action: *the police moved in on him.* ■ become involved with so as to take control of or put pressure on: *the bank did not usually move in on doubtful institutions until they were almost bankrupt.* □ **move on** (or **move someone on**) go or cause to leave somewhere, esp. because one is causing an obstruction: *the Mounties briskly ordered them to move on.* ■ (**move on**) progress: *ballet has moved on, leaving Russia behind.* □ **move out** (or **move someone out**) leave or cause to leave one's place of residence or work. □ **move over** (or **aside**) adjust one's position to make room for someone else: *Jo motioned to the girls on the couch to move over.* ■ relinquish a job or leading position, typically because of being superseded by someone or something more competent or important: *it's time for the film establishment to move aside and make way for a new generation.* □ **move up** adjust one's position, either to be nearer or make room for someone else: *there'd be room for me if you'd just move up a bit.*

▸*n.* a change of place or position: *she made a sudden move toward me* | *his eyes followed her every move.* ■ a change of house or business premises. ■ a change of job, career, or business direction: *a career move.* ■ a change of state or opinion: *the country's move to independence.* ■ an action that initiates or advances a process or plan: *my next move is to talk to Matthew.* ■ a maneuver in a sport or game. ■ a change of position of a piece in a board game: *that move will put your king in check.* ■ a player's turn to make such a change: *it's your move.* ▷Middle English: from Old French *moveir*, from Latin *movere.*

▸*PHRASES* □ **get a move on** [often in *imperative*] *informal* hurry up. □ **get moving** [often in *imperative*] *informal* make a prompt start (on a journey or an undertaking): *you're here to work, so get moving.* □ **make a move** take action: *each army was waiting for the other side to make a move.* ■ *Brit.* set off; leave somewhere: *I think I'd better be making a move.* □ **make a move on** (or **put the moves on**) *informal* make a proposition to (someone), esp. of a sexual nature. □ **move the goalposts** see GOALPOST. □ **move heaven and earth** see HEAVEN. □ **move mountains** see MOUNTAIN. □ **move with the times** keep abreast of current thinking or developments. □ **not move a muscle** see MUSCLE. □ **on the move** in the process of moving from one place or job to another: *it's difficult to contact her because she's always on the move.* ■ making progress: *the economy appeared to be on the move.*

move·a·ble /'mōōvəbəl/ ▸*adj.* & *n.* variant spelling of MOVABLE.

move·less /'mōōvləs/ ▸*adj. chiefly poetic/literary* not moving or capable of moving or being moved.

move·ment /'mōōvmənt/ ▸*n.* **1** an act of changing physical location or position or of having this

Pronunciation Key ə *ago*; ər *over*; 'ə or ˌə *up*; 'ər or ˌər *fur*; a *hat*; ā *rate*; ä *car*; CH *chew*; e *let*; ē *see*; e(ə)r *air*; i *fit*; ī *by*; i(ə)r *ear*; NG *sing*; ō *go*; ô *for*; oi *boy*; ŏŏ *good*; ōō *goo*; ou *out*; SH *she*; TH *thin*; T͟H *then*; (h)w *why*; ZH *vision*

M

changed: *a slight movement of the upper body | the principle of the free movement of goods between member states.* ■ an arrival or departure of an aircraft. ■ (also **bowel movement**) an act of defecation. ■ (**movements**) the activities and whereabouts of someone, esp. during a particular period of time: *your movements and telephone conversations are recorded.* ■ the general activity or bustle of people or things in a particular place: *the scene was almost devoid of movement.* ■ the quality of suggesting motion in a work of art: *the painting was a busy landscape, full of detail and movement.* ■ the progressive development of a poem or story: *the novel shows minimal concern for narrative movement.* ■ a change or development in something: *movements in the underlying financial markets.* **2** [often with *adj.*] a group of people working together to advance their shared political, social, or artistic ideas: *the labor movement.* ■ [usu. in *sing.*] a campaign undertaken by such a group: *a* **movement to** *declare war on poverty.* ■ a change in policy or general attitudes seen as positive: *the* **movement toward** *greater sexual equality.* **3** *Music* a principal division of a longer musical work, self-sufficient in terms of key, tempo, and structure: *the slow movement of his violin concerto.* **4** the moving parts of a mechanism, esp. a clock or watch. ▷late Middle English: via Old French from medieval Latin *movimentum*, from Latin *movere* 'to move.'

mov·er /ˈmo͞ovər/ ▶*n.* **1** a person or thing in motion, esp. an animal: *this horse is a lovely mover and jumper.* ■ a person whose job is to remove and transport furniture from one building, esp. a house, to another: *he watched movers load the remaining boxes.* **2** a person who makes a formal proposal at a meeting or in an assembly: *movers and seconders rise and give speeches.* ■ a person who instigates or organizes something: *she was a key mover in making this successful conference happen.*

▶*PHRASE* □ **mover and shaker** a powerful person who initiates events and influences people. [from *movers and shakers*, a phrase from O'Shaughnessy's *Music & Moonlight* (1874).]

mov·ie /ˈmo͞ovē/ ▶*n.* a story or event recorded by a camera as a set of moving images and shown in a theater or on television; a motion picture. ■ (**the movies**) a movie theater: *we decided to go to the movies.* ■ motion pictures generally or the motion-picture industry: *a lifelong love of the movies.*

mov·ie·go·er /ˈmo͞ovē,gōər/ ▶*n.* a person who goes to the movies, esp. regularly. **—mov·ie·go·ing** /-,gōiNG/ *n.* & *adj.*

mov·ie·mak·er /ˈmo͞ovē,mākər/ ▶*n.* a person who makes motion pictures; filmmaker. **—mov·ie·mak·ing** /-,mākiNG/ *n.*

mov·ie·o·ke /,mo͞ovēˈōkē/ ▶a form of entertainment, offered typically by bars and clubs, in which people take turns speaking movie dialogue while a subtitled silent version plays in the background. ▷from MOVIE + KARAOKE.

mov·ie the·a·ter (also **movie house**) ▶*n.* a theater where movies are shown for public entertainment.

mov·ing /ˈmo͞oviNG/ ▶*adj.* **1** [often with *submodifier*] in motion: *a fast-moving river.* **2** producing strong emotion, esp. sadness or sympathy: *an unforgettable and moving book.* **3** relating to the process of changing one's residence: *moving expenses.* **4** [*attrib.*] involving a moving vehicle: *tickets for moving violations.* **—mov·ing·ly** *adv.* (in sense 2).

THE RIGHT WORD **affecting, moving, pathetic, poignant, touching**

A movie about the Holocaust might be described as **moving**, since it arouses emotions or strong feelings, particularly feelings of pathos.

A movie about a young girl's devotion to her dog might more accurately be described as **touching**, which means arousing tenderness or compassion, while a movie dealing with a young girl's first experience with love would be **poignant**, since it pierces one's heart or keenly affects one's sensibilities.

While *poignant* implies a bittersweet response that combines pity and longing or other contradictory emotions, **pathetic** means simply moving one to pity (*a pathetic scene in which the dog struggled to save his drowning mistress*).

Almost any well-made film can be **affecting**, a more general term that suggests moving one to tears or some other display of feeling (*the affecting story of a daughter's search for her birth mother*).

mov·ing av·er·age ▶*n.* *Statistics* a succession of averages derived from successive segments (typically of constant size and overlapping) of a series of values.

mov·ing-coil ▶*adj.* [*attrib.*] (of an electrical device such as a voltmeter or microphone) containing a wire coil suspended in a magnetic field, so that the coil either moves in response to a current or produces a current when it is made to move.

mov·ing pic·ture ▶*n.* *dated* a movie.

mov·ing side·walk (*Brit.* **moving pavement**) ▶*n.* a mechanism resembling a conveyor belt for pedestrians in a place such as an airport.

mov·ing stair·way ▶*n.* another term for ESCALATOR.

mov·i·o·la /,mo͞ovēˈōlə/ (also **Mov·i·o·la** or **mov·ie·o·la**) ▶*n.* *trademark* a device that reproduces the picture and sound of a movie on a small scale, to allow checking and editing. ▷1920s: from MOVIE + *-ola* (probably from PIANOLA).

mow[1] /mō/ ▶*v.* (*past part.* **mowed** or **mown** /mōn/) [*trans.*] cut down (an area of grass) with a machine: *Roger mowed the lawn* | [as *adj.*] (**mown**) *the smell of newly mown grass.* ■ *chiefly historical* cut down (grass or a cereal crop) with a scythe or a sickle.

▶*phrasal v.* □ **mow someone down** kill someone with a fusillade of bullets or other missiles. ■ recklessly knock someone down with a car or other vehicle. ▷Old English *māwan*, of Germanic origin; related to Dutch *maaien*, German *mähen* 'mow,' also to MEAD[2]. **—mow·er** *n.*

mow[2] /mou/ ▶*n.* [often with *adj.*] a stack of hay, grain, or other similar crop: *the hay mow.* ■ a place in a barn where such a stack is put. ▷Old English *mūga*; of unknown ultimate origin; compare with Swedish and Norwegian *muga* 'heap.'

mow·ing /ˈmō-iNG/ ▶*n.* the action of mowing. ■ (**mowings**) loose pieces of grass resulting from mowing. ■ a field of grass grown for hay.

MOX /mäks/ ▶*n.* a type of nuclear fuel designed for use in breeder reactors, consisting of a blend of uranium and plutonium oxides. ▷from *m(ixed) ox(ides)*.

mox·a /ˈmäksə/ ▶*n.* a downy substance obtained from the dried leaves of an Asian plant related to mugwort. It is burned on or near the skin in Eastern medicine as a counterirritant. • The plant is *Crossostephium artemisioides*, family Compositae. ▷late 17th cent.: from Japanese *mogusa*, from *moe kusa* 'burning herb.'

mox·i·bus·tion /,mäksəˈbəsCHən/ ▶*n.* (in Eastern medicine) the burning of moxa on or near a person's skin as a counterirritant.

mox·ie /ˈmäksē/ ▶*n.* *informal* force of character, determination, or nerve: *when you've got moxie, you need the clothes to match.* ▷mid 20th cent.: from *Moxie*, the proprietary name of a soft drink.

Moy·ga·shel /ˈmoigəSHəl/ ▶*n.* *trademark* a type of Irish linen. ▷1930s: named after a village in County Tyrone, Northern Ireland.

Moy·ni·han /ˈmoi-nə,han/, Daniel Patrick (1927–2003), U.S. politician and educator. He taught at various colleges before serving in the U.S. senate 1977–2001 as a Democrat from New York. He wrote *The Negro Family: The Case for National Action* (1965).

Mo·zam·bique /,mōzamˈbēk/ a country on the eastern coast of southern Africa; pop. 18,811,000; capital, Maputo; languages, Portuguese (official) and Bantu languages. **—Mo·zam·bi·can** /-ˈbēkən/ *adj.* & *n.*

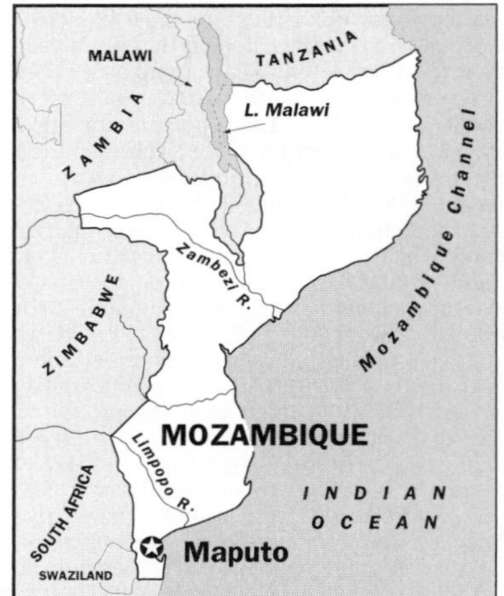

First visited by Vasco da Gama, Mozambique was colonized by the Portuguese in the early 16th century and became a center of the slave trade in the 17th and 18th centuries. It became an independent republic in 1975, after a ten-year armed struggle by the Frelimo liberation movement; civil war between the Frelimo government and the Renamo opposition followed until a peace agreement was signed in 1992.

Mo·zam·bique Chan·nel an arm of the Indian Ocean that separates the eastern coast of mainland Africa from the island of Madagascar.

Moz·ar·a·bic /mōˈzarəbik/ ▶*adj.* *historical* of or relating to the Christian inhabitants of Spain under the Muslim Moorish kings. ▷late 17th cent.: from Spanish *mozárabe* (from Arabic *mustaʿrib*, literally 'making oneself an Arab') + -IC. **—Moz·ar·ab** *n.*

Mo·zart /ˈmō,tsärt/, (Johann Chrysostom) Wolfgang Amadeus (1756–91), Austrian composer. A child prodigy, he came to epitomize classical music in its purity of form and melody. He wrote many symphonies, piano concertos, and string quartets, as well as operas, including *The Marriage of Figaro* (1786), *Don Giovanni* (1787), *Così fan tutte* (1790), and *The Magic Flute* (1791). **—Mo·zar·ti·an** /mōˈtsärtēən/ *adj.* & *n.*

mo·zo /ˈmōsō; -zō/ ▶*n.* (*pl.* **-zos**) (in Spanish-speaking regions) a male servant or attendant. ▷Spanish, literally 'boy.'

moz·za·rel·la /,mätsəˈrelə/ ▶*n.* a mild, semisoft white Italian cheese, often used in Italian cooking as a melted topping, esp. on pizzas. ▷Italian, diminutive of *mozza*, denoting a kind of cheese, from *mozzare* 'cut off.'

moz·zet·ta /mōtˈsetə; mōˈzetə/ (also **mo·zet·ta**) ▶*n.* (*pl.* **-zet·tas** or **-zet·te** /-ˈsetā; -ˈzetā/) a short cape with a hood, worn by the pope, cardinals, and some other ecclesiastics in the Roman Catholic Church. ▷late 18th cent.: Italian, shortened form of *almozzetta*, from medieval Latin *almucia* 'amice' + the diminutive suffix *-etta*.

MP ▶*abbr.* ■ Member of Parliament: *Robert Brown, MP.* ■ military police. ■ military policeman.

mp ▶*abbr.* mezzo piano.

m.p. ▶*abbr.* melting point.

MPA ▶*abbr.* ■ Master of Public Administration. ■ Master of Public Accounting.

MPC ▶*abbr.* multimedia personal computer.

MPD ▶*abbr.* multiple personality disorder.

MPE ▶*abbr.* Master of Public Education.

MPEG ▶*n.* *Computing* an international standard for encoding and compressing video images. ▷late 20th cent.: from *Motion Pictures Experts Group*.

mpg ▶*abbr.* miles per gallon (a measurement of a vehicle's rate of fuel consumption).

MPH ▶*abbr.* Master of Public Health.

mph ▶*abbr.* miles per hour.

MPhil ▶*abbr.* Master of Philosophy.

MPLA the Popular Movement for the Liberation of Angola, a Marxist organization founded in the 1950s that emerged as the ruling party in Angola after independence from Portugal in 1975. Once in power, the MPLA fought UNITA and other rival groups for many years. ▷abbreviation of Portuguese *Movimento Popular de Libertação de Angola*.

MPV ▶*abbr.* multipurpose vehicle, a large vanlike car.

Mr. /ˈmistər/ ▶*n.* a title used before a surname or full name to address or refer to a man without a higher or honorific or professional title: *Mr. Robert Smith.* ■ used before the name of an office to address a man who holds it: *yes, Mr. President.* ■ *humorous* used before an invented surname to imply that someone has a particular characteristic: *Mr. Big-Shot.* ■ (often as **Mister**) used in the armed forces to address a senior warrant officer, officer cadet, or junior naval officer. ▷late Middle English: originally an abbreviation of MASTER[1]; compare with MISTER[1].

MRA ▶*abbr.* Moral Rearmament.

MRBM ▶*abbr.* medium-range ballistic missile.

Mr. Clean ▶*n.* *informal* a man, esp. a public figure, who has an impeccable image, record, or reputation. Sometimes used with **Miss, Mrs.**, or **Ms.** when referring to a woman: *he comes up Mr. Clean on the sheets—not even a parking ticket.* ▷from the trademark *Mr. Clean*, a brand of household cleaner.

MRE ▶*abbr.* meal ready to eat (a precooked and prepackaged meal used by military personnel).

MRI ▶*abbr.* magnetic resonance imaging.

MRIA ▶*abbr.* Member of the Royal Irish Academy.

mri·dan·gam /mriˈdäNGgəm/ ▶*n.* a barrel-shaped double-headed drum with one head larger than the other, used in southern Indian music. ▷late 19th cent.: Tamil alteration of Sanskrit *mṛdaṅga*.

mRNA *Biology* ▸*abbr.* messenger RNA.

Mr. Right ▸*n. informal* the ideal future husband: *I expect you're waiting for Mr. Right.*

Mrs. /ˈmisəz; ˈmiz-; -əs/ ▸*n.* a title used before a surname or full name to address or refer to a married woman, or a woman who has been married, without a higher or honorific or professional title: *Mrs. Sally Jones.* ▹early 17th cent.: abbreviation of **MISTRESS**; compare with **MISSUS**.

Mrs. Grun·dy /ˈgrəndē/ ▸*n.* (*pl.* **Mrs. Grun·dys**) a person with conventional standards of propriety. ▹early 19th cent.: a person repeatedly mentioned in T. Morton's comedy *Speed the Plough* (1798), often in the phrase "What will Mrs. Grundy say?," which became a popular catchphrase.

MS ▸*abbr.* ■ (also **ms**) manuscript. ■ Master of Surgery. ■ Master of Science. ■ Mississippi (in official postal use). ■ motor ship. ■ multiple sclerosis.

Ms. /miz/ ▸*n.* a title used before the surname or full name of any woman regardless of her marital status (a neutral alternative to **Mrs.** or **Miss**): *Ms. Sarah Brown.* ■ *humorous* used before an invented surname to imply that someone has a particular characteristic: *Ms. Do-Right.* ▹1950s: combination of **Mrs.** and **MISS**[2].

MSB ▸*abbr.* most significant bit.

MSc ▸*abbr.* Master of Science.

MS-DOS /ˌem ˌes ˈdäs; dôs/ *trademark Computing* ▸*abbr.* Microsoft disk operating system.

msec. ▸*abbr.* millisecond or milliseconds.

Mses. ▸*abbr.* plural form of **Ms.**

MSG ▸*abbr.* monosodium glutamate.

msg. ▸*abbr.* message.

Msgr ▸*abbr.* ■ Monseigneur. ■ Monsignor.

MSgt (also **MSGT**) ▸*abbr.* master sergeant.

MSH ▸*abbr.* melanocyte-stimulating hormone.

MS in LS ▸*abbr.* Master of Science in Library Science.

m.s.l. (also **MSL**) ▸*abbr.* mean sea level.

MSN ▸*abbr.* Master of Science in Nursing.

MSS (also **mss**) ▸*abbr.* manuscripts.

MST ▸*abbr.* Mountain Standard Time (see **MOUNTAIN TIME**).

MSTS ▸*abbr.* Military Sea Transportation Service.

MSW ▸*abbr.* ■ Master of Social Welfare. ■ Master of Social Work.

MSY ▸*abbr.* maximum sustainable yield.

MT ▸*abbr.* ■ machine translation. ■ megaton. ■ (also **m.t.**) metric ton. ■ Montana (in official postal use).

Mt ▸*abbr.* ■ the Gospel of Matthew (in biblical references). ■ [in *place names*] (also **Mt.**) Mount: *Mt. Everest.*
▸*symbol* the chemical element meitnerium.

MTB ▸*abbr.* mountain bike.

MTBF ▸*abbr.* mean time between failures, a measure of the reliability of a device or system.

mtg. ▸*abbr.* ■ meeting. ■ mortgage.

mtge. ▸*abbr.* mortgage.

mtn. ▸*abbr.* mountain.

mts. (also **Mts.**) ▸*abbr.* mountains.

M2M ▸*abbr.* machine-to-machine, denoting technologies designed to facilitate communication between appliances and electronic controllers. ■ machine-to-mobile. ■ mobile-to-machine.

MTV *trademark* a cable and satellite television channel that broadcasts popular music and promotional music videos. ▹late 20th cent.: abbreviation of *music television*.

mu /m(y)o͞o/ ▸*n.* the twelfth letter of the Greek alphabet (**Μ, μ**), transliterated as 'm.' ■ (**Mu**) [followed by Latin genitive] *Astronomy* the twelfth star in a constellation: *Mu Cassiopeiae.* ■ [as *adj.*] *Physics* relating to muons: *mu particle.*
▸*symbol* ■ (μ) micron. ■ (μ) [in *combination*] "micro-" in symbols for units: *the recommended daily amount is 750μg.* ■ (μ) permeability.

Mu·ba·rak /mo͞oˈbärək/, (Muhammad) Hosni (Said) (1928–), Egyptian statesman; president 1981– . He did much to establish closer links among Egypt and other Arab nations, while opposing militant Islamic fundamentalism in Egypt.

much /məcн/ ▸*adj.* & *pron.* (**more** /môr/, **most** /mōst/) [often with *negative* or in *questions*] a large amount: [as *adj.*] *I did not get much sleep | I did* **so much** *shopping* | [as *pron.*] *he does not eat much | they must bear* **much of** *the blame.* ■ [as *pron.*] [with *negative*] used to refer disparagingly to someone or something as being a poor specimen: *I'm* **not much of a** *gardener.*
▸*adv.* to a great extent; a great deal: *did it hurt much? | thanks* **very much** *| they did not mind, much to my surprise* | [with *comparative*] *they look much better* | [with *superlative*] *Nicolai's English was much the worst.* ■ [usu. with *negative* or in *questions*] for a large part of one's time; often: *I'm not there much.* ▹Middle English: shortened from *muchel*, from Old English *micel* (see **MICKLE**). **—much·ly** *adv.* (*humorous*).
▸*PHRASES* □ **as much** the same: *I am sure she would do as much for me.* □ **a bit much** *informal* somewhat excessive or unreasonable: *his earnestness can be a bit much.* □ **how much** used to ask what a particular amount or cost is. □ **make much of** give or ascribe a significant amount of attention or importance to: *the island can make much of its history as a trading post between Europe and the Arab world.* □ (**as**) **much as** even though: *much as I had enjoyed my adventure, it was good to be back.* □ **much less** see **LESS**. □ **so much the better** (or **worse**) that is even better (or worse): *we want to hear what you have to say, but if you can make it short, so much the better.* □ **this much** the fact about to be stated: *I know this much, you would defy the world to get what you wanted.* □ **too much** an intolerable, impossible, or exhausting situation or experience: *the effort proved* **too much for** *her.*

mu·cha·cha /mo͞oˈcнäcнə/ ▸*n.* (in Spanish-speaking regions) a young woman. ▹Spanish, feminine of *muchacho* (see **MUCHACHO**).

mu·cha·cho /mo͞oˈcнäcнō/ ▸*n.* (*pl.* **-chos**) (in Spanish-speaking regions) a young man. ▹Spanish.

much·ness /ˈməcнnəs/ ▸*n.* [in *sing.*] greatness in quantity or degree: *this romantic muchness can be overlooked in a story that has a good deal to say.*
▸*PHRASE* □ (**much**) **of a muchness** *informal* very similar: *to the untrained eye, anything to do with railroad memorabilia seems much of a muchness.*

mu·cho /ˈmo͞ocнō/ *informal, humorous* ▸*adj.* much or many: *that caused me mucho problems.*
▸*adv.* [usu. as *submodifier*] very: *he was being mucho macho.* ▹Spanish.

mu·ci·lage /ˈmyo͞os(ə)lij/ ▸*n.* a viscous secretion or bodily fluid. ■ a polysaccharide substance extracted as a viscous or gelatinous solution from plant roots, seeds, etc., and used in medicines and adhesives. ■ an adhesive solution; gum or glue. ▹late Middle English: via French from late Latin *mucilago* 'musty juice,' from Latin *mucus* (see **MUCUS**). **—mu·ci·lag·i·nous** /ˌmyo͞osəˈlajənəs/ *adj.*

mu·cin /ˈmyo͞osən/ ▸*n. Biochemistry* a glycoprotein constituent of mucus. ▹mid 19th cent.: from **MUCUS** + **-IN**[1].

mu·ci·nous /ˈmyo͞osənəs/ ▸*adj.* of, relating to, or covered with mucus.

muck /mək/ ▸*n.* dirt, rubbish, or waste matter: *I'll just clean the muck off the windshield.* ■ farmyard manure, widely used as fertilizer. ■ *informal* something regarded as worthless, sordid, or corrupt: *the muck that passes for music in the pop charts.*
▸*v.* [*trans.*] **1** (**muck up**) *informal* mishandle (a job or situation); spoil (something): *she had mucked up her first few weeks at college.* **2** (**muck out**) *chiefly Brit.* remove (manure and other dirt) from a horse's stable or other animal's dwelling. **3** *rare* spread manure on (land).
▸*phrasal v.* □ **muck about/around** *chiefly Brit., informal* behave in a silly or aimless way, esp. by wasting time when serious activity is expected: *he spent his summers mucking about in boats.* ■ (**muck about/around with**) spoil (something) by interfering with it: *they did not want designers mucking about with their newspapers.* ▹Middle English *muk*, probably of Scandinavian origin: compare with Old Norse *myki* 'dung,' from a Germanic base meaning 'soft,' shared by **MEEK**.
▸*PHRASES* □ **as common as muck** *Brit., informal* of low social status. □ **make a muck of** *chiefly Brit., informal* handle incompetently: *it's useless now that they've made a muck of it.*

muck·er /ˈməkər/ ▸*n.* **1** *informal* or *dated* a rough or coarse person. [late 19th cent.: probably from German *Mucker* 'sulky person.'] **2** a person who removes dirt and waste, esp. from stables. [late 19th cent.: from **MUCK** + **-ER**[1].]

muck·et·y-muck /ˈməkətē ˌmək/ (also **muck·y-muck** /ˈməkē ˌmək/ or **muck-a-muck** /ˈmək ə ˌmək/) ▸*n. informal* a person of great importance or self-importance: *a big Hollywood muckety-muck.* ▹mid 19th cent.: from Chinook Jargon, shortening of **HIGH MUCK-A-MUCK**.

muck·le /ˈməkəl/ ▸*n., adj.* & *pron.* variant form of **MICKLE**.

muck·rak·ing /ˈməkˌrākiNG/ ▸*n.* the action of searching out and publicizing scandalous information about famous people in an underhanded way: *candidacy was threatened by her opponent's muckraking* | [as *adj.*] *a muckraking journalist.* ▹coined by President T. Roosevelt in a speech (1906) alluding to Bunyan's *Pilgrim's Progress* and the man with the *muck rake*. **—muck·rake** /-ˌrāk/ *v.* **—muck·rak·er** /-ˌrākər/ *n.*

muck sweat ▸*n. informal* a state of perspiring profusely: *I arrived in a muck sweat.*

muck·y /ˈməkē/ ▸*adj.* (**muck·i·er, muck·i·est**) covered with or consisting of dirt or filth: *guests carried their food on trays to mucky tables.* **—muck·i·ness** *n.*

muco- /ˈmyo͞okō/ ▸*comb. form Biochemistry* representing **MUCUS**.

mu·coid /ˈmyo͞oˌkoid/ ▸*adj.* of, involving, resembling, or of the nature of mucus.
▸*n.* a substance resembling mucin, esp. a proteoglycan.

mu·co·pol·y·sac·cha·ride /ˌmyo͞okōˌpälēˈsakəˌrīd/ ▸*n. Biochemistry* former term for **GLYCOSAMINOGLYCAN**.

mu·co·sa /myo͞oˈkōzə/ ▸*n.* (*pl.* **-sae** /-zē; -ˌzī/) a mucous membrane: *the intestinal mucosa.* ▹late 19th cent.: modern Latin, feminine of *mucosus* (see **MUCOUS**). **—mu·co·sal** *adj.*

mu·cous /ˈmyo͞okəs/ ▸*adj.* relating to, producing, covered with, or of the nature of mucus. ▹mid 17th cent.: from Latin *mucosus* (see **MUCUS**). **—mu·cos·i·ty** /ˌmyo͞oˈkäsətē/ *n.*

mu·cous mem·brane ▸*n.* an epithelial tissue that secretes mucus and that lines many body cavities and tubular organs including the gut and respiratory passages.

mu·cro /ˈmyo͞okrō/ ▸*n. Botany & Zoology* a short sharp point at the end of a part or organ. ▹mid 17th cent.: from Latin, 'sharp point.'

mu·cro·nate /ˈmyo͞okrəˌnāt/ ▸*adj. Botany & Zoology* ending abruptly in a short sharp point or mucro. ▹late 18th cent.: from Latin *mucronatus*, from *mucro*, *mucron-* 'point.'

mu·cus /ˈmyo͞okəs/ ▸*n.* a slimy substance, typically not miscible with water, secreted by mucous membranes and glands for lubrication, protection, etc. ■ a gummy substance found in plants; mucilage. ▹mid 17th cent.: from Latin.

MUD /məd/ ▸*n.* a computer-based text or virtual reality game that several players play at the same time, interacting with each other as well as with characters controlled by the computer. ▹late 20th cent.: from *multiuser dungeon* or *multiuser dimension*.

mud /məd/ ▸*n.* soft, sticky matter resulting from the mixing of earth and water. ■ *figurative* information or allegations regarded as damaging, typically concerned with corruption: *they are trying to* **sling mud** *at me to cover up their defeat.* ▹late Middle English: probably from Middle Low German *mudde*.
▸*PHRASES* □ **as clear as mud** *informal* not at all easy to understand. □ **drag someone through the mud** slander or denigrate someone publicly. □ **here's mud in your eye!** *chiefly Brit., informal* used to express friendly feelings toward one's companions before drinking. □ **one's name is mud** *informal* one is in disgrace or unpopular: *if you forget their birthdays, your name is mud.*

Mu·dan·jiang /ˈmo͞oˈdänˈjyäNG/ a city in Heilongjiang province, in northeastern China, on the Mudan River, southeast of Harbin; pop. 572,000.

mud·bank /ˈmədˌbaNGk/ ▸*n.* a bank of mud on the bed of a river or the bottom of the sea.

mud bath ▸*n.* a bath in the mud of mineral springs, taken esp. for therapeutic purposes, such as to relieve rheumatic ailments, or as part of a beauty treatment. ■ a muddy place.

mud brick ▸*n.* a brick made from baked mud: [as *adj.*] *mud-brick houses.*

mud·bug /ˈmədˌbəg/ ▸*n. informal* a freshwater crayfish.

mud daub·er ▸*n.* a solitary wasp that builds a mud nest typically consisting of a series of tubelike cells on an exposed surface. • Several genera in the family Sphecidae.

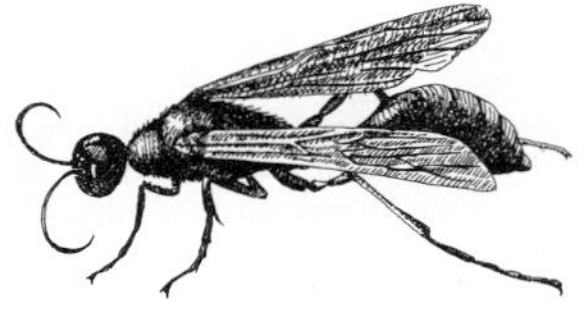

blue mud dauber

Pronunciation Key ə ago; ər over; ˈə or ˌə up; ˈər or ˌər fur; a hat; ā rate; ä car; CH chew; e let; ē see; e(ə)r air; i fit; ī by; i(ə)r ear; NG sing; ō go; ô for; oi boy; o͝o good; o͞o goo; ou out; SH she; TH thin; T͟H then; (h)w why; ZH vision

mud·dle /ˈmədl/ ▸*v.* [*trans.*] bring into a disordered or confusing state: *they were* ***muddling up*** *the cards.* ■ confuse (a person or their thoughts): *I do not wish to muddle him by making him read more books.* ■ [*intrans.*] busy oneself in a confused and ineffective way: *he was muddling about in the kitchen.* ■ mix (a drink) or stir (an ingredient) into a drink.
▸*phrasal v.* □ **muddle through** cope more or less satisfactorily despite lack of expertise, planning, or equipment: *we don't have an ultimate ambition; we just muddle through.* □ **muddle something up** confuse two or more things with each other: *at the time, archaeology was commonly muddled up with paleontology.*
▸*n.* [usu. in *sing.*] an untidy and disorganized state or collection: *a muddle of French, English, Ojibwa, and a dash of Gaelic | the finances were* ***in a muddle*** *| an admirable chairman, she cut through the confusion and muddle.* See note at JUMBLE. ■ a mistake arising from or resulting in confusion: *a bureaucratic muddle.* ▷late Middle English (in the sense 'wallow in mud'): perhaps from Middle Dutch *moddelen*, frequentative of *modden* 'dabble in mud'; compare with MUD. The sense 'confuse' was initially associated with alcoholic drink (late 17th cent.), giving rise to 'busy oneself in a confused way' and 'jumble up' (mid 19th cent.). **—mud·dling·ly** /ˈmədliNGlē; ˈmədl-iNGlē/ *adv.* **—mud·dly** /ˈmədlē; ˈmədl-ē/ *adj.*

mud·dled /ˈmədld/ ▸*adj.* in a state of bewildered or bewildering confusion or disorder: *misplaced suggestions and muddled thinking.*

mud·dle-head·ed (also **mud·dle·head·ed**) ▸*adj.* mentally disorganized or confused: *a muddle-headed idealist with utopian views.* **—mud·dle-head·ed·ness** (or **mud·dle·head·ed·ness**) *n.*

mud·dler /ˈmədlər; ˈmədl-ər/ ▸*n.* **1** a person who creates muddles, esp. because of a disorganized method of thinking or working. **2** (also **muddler minnow**) a type of fly used in trout fishing. **3** a stick used to stir mixed drinks.

mud·dy /ˈmədē/ ▸*adj.* (**-di·er**, **-di·est**) covered in or full of mud: *they changed their muddy boots | it was very muddy underfoot.* ■ (of a liquid) discolored and made cloudy by mud. ■ (of a color) dull and dirty-looking: *the original colors were blurred into muddy pink and yellow.* ■ (of a sound, esp. in music) not clearly defined: *an awful muddy sound that renders his vocal incoherent.* ■ confused, vague, or illogical: *some sentences are so muddy that their meaning can only be guessed.*
▸*v.* (**-dies**, **-died**) [*trans.*] cause to become covered in or full of mud: *the linoleum floor was muddied |* [as *adj.*] (**muddied**) *cold, muddied feet.* ■ make (something) hard to perceive or understand: *the first year's results muddy rather than clarify the situation.* **—mud·di·ly** /ˈmədl-ē/ *adv.* **—mud·di·ness** *n.*
▸*PHRASE* □ **muddy the waters** make an issue or a situation more confusing by introducing complications.

Mu·dé·jar /mo͞oˈT͟Heˌhär/ ▸*adj.* of or denoting a partly Gothic, partly Islamic style of architecture and art prevalent in Spain in the 12th to 15th centuries. ■ of or relating to Muslim subjects of Christian monarchs during the reconquest of the Iberian peninsula from the Moors (11th–15th centuries).
▸*n.* (*pl.* **-ja·res** /-häräs/) a subject Muslim during the Christian reconquest of the Iberian peninsula from the Moors who, until 1492, was allowed to retain Islamic laws and religion in return for loyalty to a Christian monarch. ▷via Spanish from Arabic *mudajjan* 'allowed to stay.'

mud·fish /ˈmədˌfiSH/ ▸*n.* (*pl.* same or **-fish·es**) **1** any of a number of elongated fish that are able to survive long periods of drought by burrowing in the mud: • a New Zealand fish (genus *Neochanna*, family Galaxiidae). • an African lungfish (*Protopterus annectens*, family Protopteridae). **2** another term for BOWFIN.

mud flap (also **mud·flap**) ▸*n.* a flap that hangs behind the wheel of a vehicle and is designed to prevent water, mud, and stones thrown up from the road from hitting the bodywork of the vehicle or any following vehicles.

mud·flat /ˈmədˌflat/ (also **mud flat**) ▸*n.* (usu. **mudflats**) a stretch of muddy land left uncovered at low tide.

mud·flow /ˈmədˌflō/ ▸*n.* a fluid or hardened stream or avalanche of mud.

mud·guard /ˈmədˌgärd/ ▸*n.* a curved strip or cover over a wheel of a vehicle, esp. a bicycle or motorcycle, designed to the protect the vehicle and rider from water and dirt thrown up from the road.

mud·lark /ˈmədˌlärk/ (also **mud·lark·er**) ▸*n.* a person who scavenges in river mud for objects of value. ■ *historical* a street urchin.

mud·min·now /ˈmədˌminō/ ▸*n.* a small stout-bodied freshwater fish of both Eurasia and North America, able to survive low concentrations of oxygen and very low temperatures. • Genus *Umbra*, family Umbridae: several species.

mud·pack /ˈmədˌpak/ ▸*n.* a paste of fuller's earth or a similar substance, applied thickly to the face to improve the condition of the skin.

mud pie (also **mud·pie**) ▸*n.* **1** mud made into a pie shape by a child. **2** short for MISSISSIPPI MUD PIE. ■ any of a variety of similar desserts, typically with a chocolate cookie crust, an ice cream filling and a chocolate sauce topping.

mud·pup·py ▸*n.* a large aquatic salamander of the eastern U.S., reaching sexual maturity while retaining an immature body form with feathery external gills. • *Necturus maculosus*, family Proteidae. Compare with WATERDOG.

mu·dra /məˈdrä/ ▸*n.* a symbolic hand gesture used in Hindu and Buddhist ceremonies and statuary, and in Indian dance. ■ a movement or pose in yoga. ▷from Sanskrit *mudrā* 'sign or token.'

mud·skip·per /ˈmədˌskipər/ ▸*n.* a goby (fish) with its eyes on raised bumps on top of the head, found in mangrove swamps from East Africa to Australia. It moves around on land with great agility, often basking on mud or mangrove roots. • *Periopthalmodon* and related genera, family Gobiidae: several species, including the common and widespread *P. schlosseri* (or *barbarus*).

mud·slide /ˈmədˌslīd/ ▸*n.* a mass of mud and other earthy material that is falling or has fallen down a hillside or other slope.

mud·sling·ing /ˈmədˌsliNGiNG/ (also **mud-sling·ing**) ▸*n. informal* the use of insults and accusations, esp. unjust ones, with the aim of damaging the reputation of an opponent. **—mud·sling** (also **mud-sling**) *v.* **—mud·sling·er** /-ˌsliNGər/ (also **mud-sling·er**) *n.*

mud·stone /ˈmədˌstōn/ ▸*n.* a dark sedimentary rock formed from consolidated mud and lacking the laminations of shale.

mud tur·tle ▸*n.* any of a number of drab-colored freshwater turtles that often crawl onto mudbanks, in particular: • an American turtle with scent glands that produce an unpleasant odor (genus *Kinosternon*, family Kinosternidae). • an African side-necked turtle (genus *Pelusios*, family Pelomedusidae). • an Asian soft-shell (genera *Lissemys* and *Pelochelys*, family Trionychidae).

Mud·ville /ˈmədvil/ ▸*n. informal* the world of baseball: *the Astros aren't exactly the Yankees, and the unbridled joy here in Mudville South was short-lived.* ▷from the fictional locality in the 1888 poem *Casey at the Bat*, written by Ernest L. Thayer (1863–1940).

mud vol·ca·no ▸*n.* a small vent or fissure in the ground discharging hot mud.

Muen·ster /ˈmənstər; ˈmo͝on-/ (also **muen·ster**, **Mun·ster**, or **mun·ster**) ▸ *n.* a mild, semisoft cheese made from whole milk . ▷for *Munster*, a town in the Alsace region of France.

mues·li /ˈm(y)o͞ozlē/ ▸*n.* (*pl.* **mues·lis**) a mixture of cereals (esp. rolled oats), dried fruit, and nuts, typically eaten with milk at breakfast. ▷Swiss German.

mu·ez·zin /m(y)o͞oˈezən; ˈmo͞oəzən/ ▸*n.* a man who calls Muslims to prayer from the minaret of a mosque. ▷late 16th cent.: dialect variant of Arabic *mu'aḏḏin*, active participle of *'aḏḏana* 'proclaim.'

muff[1] /məf/ ▸*n.* **1** a tube made of fur or other warm material into which the hands are placed for warmth. ■ a warm or protective covering for other parts of the body. **2** *vulgar slang* a woman's genitals. ▷mid 16th cent.: from Dutch *mof*, Middle Dutch *muffel*, from medieval Latin *muff(u)la*, of unknown ultimate origin.

muff[2] *informal* ▸*v.* [*trans.*] handle (a situation, task, or opportunity) clumsily or badly: *the administration muffed several of its biggest projects.* ■ fail to catch or receive (a ball) or to hit (a shot or a target): *the catcher muffed a perfect throw home.* ■ speak (lines from a theatrical part) badly: *he was starting to muff his lines.*
▸*n.* a mistake or failure, esp. a failure to catch or receive a ball cleanly. ■ *dated, chiefly Brit.* a person who is awkward or stupid, esp. in relation to a sport or manual skill. ▷early 19th cent.: of unknown origin.

muff div·er ▸*n. vulgar slang* a person who performs cunnilingus. **—muff-div·ing** *n.*

muf·fin /ˈməfən/ ▸*n.* a small domed cake or quick bread made from batter or dough: *blueberry muffins.* ■ short for ENGLISH MUFFIN. ▷early 18th cent.: of unknown origin.

muf·fin pan ▸*n.* a pan with cylindrical indentations used for baking cupcakes or muffins.

muf·fle /ˈməfəl/ ▸*v.* [*trans.*] (often **be muffled**) wrap or cover for warmth: *on a chair by the far wall, muffled in an absurd overcoat.* ■ cover or wrap up (a source of sound) to reduce its loudness: [as *adj.*] (**muffled**) *the soft beat of a muffled drum.* ■ make (a sound) quieter or less distinct: *his voice was muffled.* ■ restrain or conceal (someone) with wrappings: *the boy was bound and muffled.*
▸*n.* [usu. as *adj.*] a receptacle in a furnace or kiln in which things can be heated without contact with combustion products. ▷late Middle English (as a verb): perhaps a shortening of Old French *enmoufler*; the noun (mid 17th cent.) from Old French *moufle* 'thick glove.'

muf·fler /ˈməf(ə)lər/ ▸*n.* **1** a scarf or wrap worn around the neck and face for warmth. **2** a part of a motor vehicle's exhaust system, serving to muffle the sound of the vehicle. ■ a device used to deaden the sound of a drum, bell, piano, or other instrument.

muf·ti[1] /ˈməftē/ ▸*n.* (*pl.* **muf·tis**) a Muslim legal expert who is empowered to give rulings on religious matters. ▷late 16th cent.: from Arabic *muftī*, active participle of *'aftā* 'decide a point of law.'

muf·ti[2] ▸*n.* plain clothes worn by a person who wears a uniform for their job, such as a soldier or police officer: *I was a flying officer* ***in mufti.*** ▷early 19th cent.: perhaps humorously from MUFTI[1].

mug[1] /məg/ ▸*n.* **1** a large cup, typically cylindrical and with a handle and used without a saucer. ■ the contents of such a cup: *a large* ***mug of*** *tea vanished in a single gulp.* **2** *informal* a person's face. **3** *informal* a hoodlum or thug. **4** *Brit., informal* a stupid or gullible person.
▸*v.* (**mugged**, **mug·ging**) *informal* **1** [*trans.*] (often **be mugged**) attack and rob (someone) in a public place: *he was mugged by three men who stole his bike |* [as *n.*] (**mugging**) *a brutal mugging.* ■ *dated* fight or hit (someone). **2** [*intrans.*] make faces, esp. silly or exaggerated ones, before an audience or a camera: *he mugged for the camera.* ▷early 16th cent. (originally Scots and northern English, denoting an earthenware bowl): probably of Scandinavian origin; compare with Norwegian *mugge*, Swedish *mugg* 'pitcher with a handle.' **—mug·ful** /ˈməgˌfo͝ol/ *n.* (*pl.* **-fuls**).
▸*PHRASE* □ **a mug's game** *informal* an activity in which it is foolish to engage because it is likely to be unsuccessful or dangerous: *playing with drugs is a mug's game.*

mug[2] ▸*v.* (**mugged**, **mug·ging**) [*trans.*] (**mug something up**) *Brit., informal* learn or review a subject as much as possible in a short time; cram: *I'm constantly having to mug up things ahead of teaching them |* [*intrans.*] *we had* ***mugged up on*** *all things Venetian before the start of the course.* ▷mid 19th cent.: of unknown origin.

Mu·ga·be /mo͞oˈgäbē/, Robert (Gabriel) (1924–), Zimbabwean statesman; prime minister 1980–87 and president 1987– .

Mu·gan·da /mo͞oˈgändə/ ▸*n.* singular form of BAGANDA.

mug·ger[1] /ˈməgər/ ▸*n.* a person who attacks and robs another in a public place.

mug·ger[2] ▸*n.* a large short-snouted Indian crocodile, venerated by many Hindus. • *Crocodylus palustris*, family Crocodylidae. ▷mid 19th cent.: from Hindi *magar*.

mug·gins /ˈməginz/ ▸*n.* (*pl.* same or **mug·gins·es**) *Brit., informal* a foolish and gullible person. ■ *humorous* used to refer to oneself in order to suggest that one has been stupid, esp. in allowing oneself to be exploited: *muggins has volunteered to do the catering.* ▷mid 19th cent.: perhaps a use of the surname *Muggins*, with allusion to MUG[1].

mug·gle /ˈməgəl/ (also **Mug·gle**) ▸*n. informal* an unimaginative or boring person: *this video game won't appeal to muggles.* ▷with allusion to the meaning 'nonwizard' (that is, 'ordinary human') in J. K. Rowling's *Harry Potter* books.

Mug·gle·to·nian /ˌməgəlˈtōnēən/ ▸*n.* a member of a small Christian sect founded in England *c.*1651 by Lodowicke Muggleton (1609–98) and John Reeve (1608–58), who claimed to be the two witnesses mentioned in the book of Revelation (Rev. 11:3–6). Despite many eccentric doctrines, the sect survived into the late 19th century.
▸*adj.* of or relating to this sect.

mug·gy /ˈməgē/ ▸*adj.* (**-gi·er**, **-gi·est**) (of the weather) unpleasantly warm and humid. ▷mid 18th cent.: from dialect *mug* 'mist, drizzle,' from Old Norse *mugga*. **—mug·gi·ness** *n.*

M

Mu·ghal /ˈmo͞ogəl/ ▶ variant spelling of MOGUL.

mug shot (also **mug·shot**) ▶*n. informal* a photograph of a person's face made for an official purpose, esp. police records. ■ *humorous* any photograph of a person's face.

mug·wort /ˈməgˌwərt; -ˌwôrt/ ▶*n.* a plant of the daisy family, with aromatic divided leaves that are dark green above and whitish below, native to north temperate regions. • Genus *Artemisia*, family Compositae: several species, in particular the common *A. vulgaris*, which has long been connected with magic and superstition. ▷Old English *mucgwyrt* (see MIDGE, WORT).

mug·wump /ˈməgˌwəmp/ ▶*n.* a person who remains aloof or independent, esp. from party politics. ■ a Republican who in 1884 refused to support James G. Blaine, the Republican nominee for president. ▷mid 19th cent.: from Algonquian *mugquomp* 'great chief.'

Mu·ham·mad[1] /mo͞oˈhäməd; -ˈham-; -ˈkʜäm-; mō-/ (also **Mo·ham·med**) (*c.*570–632), Arab prophet and founder of Islam. In *c.*610, in Mecca, he received the first of a series of revelations that, as the Koran, became the doctrinal and legislative basis of Islam. In the face of opposition to his preaching, he and his small group of supporters were forced to flee to Medina in 622 (the Hegira). Muhammad led his followers into a series of battles against the Meccans. In 630, Mecca capitulated and by his death Muhammad had united most of Arabia.

Mu·ham·mad[2] /məˈhäməd/, Elijah (1897–1975), U.S. activist; born *Elijah Poole*. He directed the growth of the Black Muslim movement from 1934 and advocated black separatism.

Mu·ham·mad Ah·mad /ˈaməd; ˈäm-/ see MAHDI.

Mu·ham·mad A·li[1] /mōˈhäməd äˈlē; -ˈham-/ (1769–1849), Ottoman viceroy and pasha of Egypt 1805–49. He modernized Egypt's infrastructure, making it a leading power and established a dynasty that survived until 1952.

Mu·ham·mad A·li[2] see ALI[2].

Mu·ham·mad·an /mōˈhämədən; mə-; ˈham-/ (also **Mo·ham·med·an**) ▶*n.* & *adj.* archaic term for MUSLIM (not favored by Muslims). ▷late 17th cent.: from the name of the prophet *Muhammad* (see MUHAMMAD[1], + -AN. —**Mu·ham·mad·an·ism** /-ˌizəm/ *n.*

USAGE See usage at MUSLIM.

Mu·har·ram /mo͞oˈhärəm/ ▶*n.* the first month of the year in the Islamic calendar. ■ an annual celebration in this month commemorating the death of Husayn, grandson of Muhammad, and his retinue. ▷from Arabic *muḥarram* 'inviolable.'

Mühl·hau·sen /ˈmyo͞olˌhoizən; ˈmʏl-/ German name for MULHOUSE.

mu·ja·hi·deen /ˌmo͞ojəhiˈdēn/ (also **mu·ja·he·din, mu·ja·hi·din,** or **mu·ja·hed·din**) ▶*plural n.* guerrilla fighters in Islamic countries, esp. those who are Islamic fundamentalists. ▷from Persian and Arabic *mujāhidīn*, colloquial plural of *mujāhid*, denoting a person who fights a jihad.

Mu·ji·bur Rah·man /ˈmo͞ojiˌbo͝or ˈräkʜmən; ˈräkʜˌmän/ (1920–75), Bangladeshi statesman; first prime minister of independent Bangladesh 1972–75 and president 1975; known as **Sheikh Mujib**. After failing to establish parliamentary democracy as prime minister, he assumed dictatorial powers in 1975. He and his family were assassinated in a military coup.

muj·ta·hid /mo͞ojˈtähid/ ▶*n.* (*pl.* **-ta·hids** or **-ta·hi·dūn** /-ˈtähiˌdo͞on/) *Islam* a person accepted as an original authority in Islamic law. Such authorities continue to be recognized in the Shia tradition, but Sunni Muslims accord this status only to the great lawmakers of early Islam. ▷Persian, from Arabic, active participle of *ijtahada* 'strive.'

Mu·kal·la /mo͞oˈkalə/ a port on the southern coast of Yemen, in the Gulf of Aden; pop. 154,000.

Muk·den /ˈmo͝okdən/ former name for SHENYANG.

mukh·tar /mo͝okˈtär/ ▶*n.* (in Turkey and some Arab countries) the head of local government of a town or village. ▷from Arabic *muḵtār*, passive participle of *iḵtāra* 'choose.'

muk·luk /ˈməkˌlək/ ▶*n.* a high, soft boot that is worn in the American Arctic and is traditionally made from sealskin. ▷mid 19th cent.: from Yupik *maklak* 'bearded seal.'

muk·tuk /ˈməkˌtək/ ▶*n.* the skin and blubber of a whale, typically the narwhal or the beluga, used as food by the Inuit. ▷from Inuit *maktak*.

mu·lat·to /m(y)o͞oˈlätō; -ˈlatō/ *dated* ▶*n.* (*pl.* **-toes** or **-tos**) a person of mixed white and black ancestry, esp. a person with one white and one black parent. ▶*adj.* relating to or denoting a mulatto or mulattoes. ▷late 16th cent.: from Spanish *mulato*, from Arabic *muwallad* 'person of mixed race.'

mul·ber·ry /ˈməlˌberē/ ▶*n.* **1** (also **mulberry tree** or **bush**) a small deciduous tree with broad leaves, native to the Far East and long cultivated elsewhere. • Genus *Morus*, family Moraceae, in particular the **white mulberry** (*M. alba*), originally grown for feeding silkworms, and the **black** (or **common**) **mulberry** (*M. nigra*), grown for its fruit. See also PAPER MULBERRY. ■ the dark red or white loganberrylike fruit of this tree. **2** a dark red or purple color: [as *adj.*] *a mulberry carpet*. ▷Old English *mōrberie*, from Latin *morum* + BERRY; related to Dutch *moerbezie* and German *Maulbeere*.

mulch /məlcʜ/ ▶*n.* a material (such as decaying leaves, bark, or compost) spread around or over a plant to enrich or insulate the soil. ■ an application of such a material: *regular mulches keep down annual weeds*. ■ a formless mass or pulp: *a mulch of sodden brown stems*.
▶*v.* [*intrans.*] apply a mulch. ■ [*trans.*] treat or cover with mulch. ▷mid 17th cent.: probably from dialect *mulch* 'soft' used as a noun, from Old English *melsc, mylsc*.

mulct /məlkt/ *formal* ▶*v.* [*trans.*] extract money from (someone) by fine or taxation: *no government dared propose to mulct the taxpayer for such a purpose*. ■ (**mulct someone of**) deprive someone of (money or possessions) by fraudulent means: *he mulcted Shelly of $75,000*.
▶*n.* a fine or compulsory payment. ▷late 15th cent.: from Latin *mulctare, multare*, from *mulcta* 'a fine.'

Mul·doon /məlˈdo͞on/, Sir Robert (David) (1921–92), New Zealand statesman; prime minister 1975–84. His premiership was marked by domestic measures to tackle low economic growth and high inflation.

mule[1] /myo͞ol/ ▶*n.* **1** the offspring of a donkey and a horse (strictly, a male donkey and a female horse), typically sterile and used as a beast of burden. Compare with HINNY[1]. ■ a person compared to a mule, esp. in being stubborn or obstinate. ■ *informal* a courier for illegal drugs. ■ a small tractor or locomotive, typically one that is electrically powered. **2** a hybrid plant or animal, esp. a sterile one. ■ any of several standard crossbred varieties of sheep. **3** (also **spinning mule**) a kind of spinning machine producing yarn on spindles, invented by Samuel Crompton (1753–1827) in 1779. **4** a coin with the obverse and reverse of designs not originally intended to be used together. ▷Old English *mūl*, probably of Germanic origin, from Latin *mulus, mula*; reinforced in Middle English by Old French *mule*.

mule[2] ▶*n.* a slipper or light shoe without a back. ▷mid 16th cent.: from French, 'slipper.'

mule[2]

mule deer ▶*n.* a western North American deer with large ears. The mule deer of the Rocky Mountains has a black tipped tail; the subspecies of the northwest Pacific coast (**blacktail deer**) has a tail with a blackish upper side. • *Odocoileus hemionus*, family Cervidae.

mule ears ▶*plural n.* [usu. treated as *sing.*] a sunflowerlike composite plant of the western U.S., with large oval leaves. • Genus *Wyethia*, family Compositae: several species, including the yellow-flowered **gray mule ears** (*W. helenioides*), with gray-haired leaves and very large bracts, and the white-flowered **white mule ears** (*W. helianthoides*).

gray mule ears

mu·le·ta /myo͞oˈlātə/ ▶*n.* a small red cape fixed to a stick, employed by a matador to guide the bull during a bullfight. ▷Spanish.

mu·le·teer /ˌmyo͞oləˈtir/ ▶*n.* a person who drives mules. ▷mid 16th cent.: from French *muletier*, from *mulet*, diminutive of Old French *mul* 'mule.'

mul·ey[1] /ˈmyo͞olē/ ▶*adj.* (of cattle) hornless.
▶*n. informal* a cow, esp. a hornless one. ▷late 16th cent. (as noun): perhaps from Irish *maol* or Welsh *moel*, literally 'bald,' used in the sense 'hornless cow.' The adjective dates from the mid 19th cent.

mul·ey[2] (also **mul·ie**) ▶*n.* (*pl.* **mul·eys** or **mul·ies**) *informal* a mule deer.

mul·ga /ˈməlgə/ ▶*n.* (also **mulga tree** or **bush**) a small Australian acacia tree or shrub with grayish foliage, forming dense scrubby growth and yielding brown and yellow timber. • *Acacia aneura*, family Leguminosae. ■ an area of scrub or bush dominated by this plant. ■ (**the mulga**) *Austral., informal* the outback. ▷mid 19th cent.: from Yuwaalaraay (an Aboriginal language of New South Wales).

Mül·heim /ˈmyo͞olˌhim; ˈmʏl-/ an industrial city in western Germany, in North Rhine-Westphalia, southwest of Essen; pop. 177,000. Full name MÜLHEIM AN DER RUHR.

Mul·house /məˈlo͞oz; mʏ-/ an industrial city in northeastern France, in Alsace; pop. 110,000. It was a free imperial city until it joined the French Republic in 1798. In 1871, after the Franco-Prussian War, the city became part of the German Empire until it was reunited with France in 1918. German name MÜHLHAUSEN.

mu·li·eb·ri·ty /ˌmyo͞olēˈebrətē/ ▶*n. poetic/literary* womanly qualities; womanhood. ▷late 16th cent.: from late Latin *muliebritas*, from Latin *mulier* 'woman.'

mul·ish /ˈmyo͞olisʜ/ ▶*adj.* resembling or likened to a mule in being stubborn: *Belinda's face took on a mulish expression*. —**mul·ish·ly** *adv.* —**mul·ish·ness** *n.*

Mull /məl/ a large island of the Inner Hebrides; chief town, Tobermory.

mull[1] /məl/ ▶*v.* [*trans.*] think about (a fact, proposal, or request) deeply and at length: *she began to* ***mull over*** *the various possibilities*. ▷mid 19th cent.: of uncertain origin.

mull[2] ▶*v.* [*trans.*] [usu. as *adj.*] (**mulled**) warm (a beverage, esp. wine, beer, or cider) and add spices and sweetening to it: *a tankard of mulled ale*. ▷early 17th cent.: of unknown origin.

mull[3] ▶*n. Soil Science* humus formed under nonacid conditions. ▷1920s: from Danish *muld* 'soil.'

mull[4] ▶*n.* thin, soft, plain muslin, used in bookbinding for joining the spine of a book to its cover. ▷late 17th cent.: abbreviation, from Hindi *malmal*.

mul·lah /ˈmo͝olə; ˈmo͞olə/ (also **mul·la**) ▶*n.* a Muslim learned in Islamic theology and sacred law. ▷early 17th cent.: from Persian, Turkish, and Urdu *mullā*, from Arabic *mawlā*.

mul·lein /ˈmələn/ ▶*n.* a herbaceous plant of the figwort family with woolly leaves and tall spikes of yellow flowers, native to Eurasia but now widely and commonly distributed. • Genus *Verbascum*, family Scrophulariaceae: several species, in particular the widespread **common** (or **great**) **mullein** (*V. thapsus*). ▷late Middle English: from Old French *moleine*, of Celtic origin; compare with the Breton *melen*, Cornish and Welsh *melyn* 'yellow.'

common mullein

Mul·ler /ˈmələr; ˈmyo͞o-/, Hermann Joseph (1890–1967), U.S. geneticist. He discovered that X-rays induce mutations in the genetic material of the fruit fly *Drosophila* and thus recognized the danger of X-radiation to living things. Nobel Prize for Physiology or Medicine (1946).

Mül·ler[1] /ˈm(y)o͞olər/, Johannes Peter (1801–58), German anatomist and zoologist. He was a pioneer of comparative and microscopical methods in biology. His investigations included the physiology of respiration, the nervous and sensory systems, and the glandular system, as well as a method for the classification of marine animals.

Mül·ler[2], Paul Hermann (1899–1965), Swiss chemist. He synthesized DDT in 1939 and patented it as an insecticide. It was immediately successful, but was withdrawn by most countries in the 1970s when its environmental persistence and toxicity in higher animals was realized. Nobel Prize for Physiology and Medicine (1948).

mull·er /ˈmələr/ ▶*n.* a stone or other heavy weight used for grinding artists' pigments or other material on a slab. ▷late Middle English: perhaps from Anglo-Norman French *moldre* 'to grind.'

Mül·le·ri·an mim·ic·ry /myo͞oˈli(ə)rēən; milˈi(ə)r-/ ▶*n. Zoology* a form of mimicry in which two or more noxious animals develop similar appearances as a shared protective device, the theory being that if a predator learns to avoid one of the noxious species, it will avoid the mimic species as well. Compare with **BATESIAN MIMICRY**. ▷late 19th cent.: named after Johann F. T. *Müller* (1821–97), German zoologist.

mul·let[1] /ˈmələt/ ▶*n.* **1** a chiefly marine fish that is widely caught for food. • Families Mullidae (see **RED MULLET**) and Mugilidae (see **GRAY MULLET**). **2** a hairstyle in which the hair is cut short at the front and sides and left long in back. ▷late Middle English: from Old French *mulet*, diminutive of Latin *mullus* 'red mullet,' from Greek *mullos*. The origin of sense two is unknown but may be related to the fish.

mul·let[2] ▶*n. Heraldry* a star with five (or more) straight-edged points or rays, as a charge or a mark of cadency for a third son. ▷late Middle English: from Old French *molette* 'rowel,' diminutive of *meule* 'millstone,' from Latin *mola* 'grindstone.'

Mul·li·gan /ˈməligən/, Gerry (1927–96), U.S. jazz baritone saxophonist and songwriter; full name *Gerald Joseph Mulligan*. He is most often identified with cool jazz.

mul·li·gan /ˈməligən/ ▶*n. informal* **1** (also **mulligan stew**) a stew made from odds and ends of food. **2** (in informal golf) an extra stroke allowed after a poor shot, not counted on the scorecard. ▷early 20th cent.: apparently from the surname *Mulligan*.

mul·li·ga·taw·ny /ˌməligəˈtônē; -ˈtänē/ (also **mulligatawny soup**) ▶*n.* a spicy meat or chicken soup originally made in India. ▷from Tamil *miḷaku-taṇṇi* 'pepper-water.'

mul·lion /ˈməlyən/ ▶*n.* a vertical bar between the panes of glass in a window. Compare with **TRANSOM**. ▷mid 16th cent. **—mul·lioned** *adj.*

mullion

mul·lo·way /ˈmələˌwā/ ▶*n.* a large edible fast-swimming predatory fish of Australian coastal waters, popular with anglers. Also called **JEWFISH**. • *Johnius antarctica*, family Sciaenidae. ▷mid 19th cent.: from Yaralde (an Aboriginal language of South Australia).

Mul·ro·ney /məlˈrōnē; -ˈro͞o-/, (Martin) Brian (1939–), Canadian statesman; prime minister 1984–93.

Mul·tan /mo͝olˈtän/ a commercial city in Punjab province, in east central Pakistan; pop. 980,000.

mul·tan·gu·lar /ˌməlˈtaNGgyələr/ ▶*adj. rare* (of a polygon) having many angles. ▷late 17th cent.: from medieval Latin *multangularis*.

multi- ▶*comb. form* more than one; many, esp. variegated: *multicolor* | *multicultural*. ▷from Latin *multus* 'much, many.'

mul·ti·ac·cess /ˌməltēˈakˌses; ˌməlˌtī-/ ▶*adj.* (of a computer system) allowing the simultaneous connection of a number of terminals.

mul·ti·a·gen·cy /ˌməltēˈājənsē; ˌməlˌtī-/ ▶*adj.* involving cooperation among several organizations, esp. in crime prevention, social welfare programs, or research: *a multiagency team has been working to nurture community support.*

mul·ti·cast /ˈməltiˌkast; ˌməltiˈkast/ ▶*v.* (*past* and *past part.* **-cast**) [*trans.*] send (data) across a computer network to several users at the same time.
▶*n.* a set of data sent across a computer network to many users at the same time.

mul·ti·cel·lu·lar /ˌməltiˈselyələr; ˌməltī-/ ▶*adj. Biology* (of an organism or part) having or consisting of many cells. **—mul·ti·cel·lu·lar·i·ty** /-ˌselyəˈlerətē/ *n.*

mul·ti·chan·nel /ˈməltiˌCHanl; ˈməlˌtī-/ ▶*adj.* employing or possessing many television or communications channels.

mul·ti·col·ored /ˌməltiˈkələrd; ˌməlˌtī-/ (also **mul·ti·col·or**) ▶*adj.* having many colors.

mul·ti·cul·ti /ˌməltēˈkəltē; ˌməltī-/ *informal* ▶*adj. informal* multicultural: *the author's multiculti persona comes through, or it may just be sloppy editing.*
▶*n.* **1** popular music incorporating ethnically disparate elements. **2** one who is literate or comfortable in more than one culture: *the multiculti* ▷1990s: rhyming alteration of *multicultural*.

mul·ti·cul·tur·al /ˌməltēˈkəlCH(ə)rəl; ˌməlˌtī-/ ▶*adj.* of, relating to, or constituting several cultural or ethnic groups within a society: *multicultural education.* **—mul·ti·cul·tur·al·ism** *n.* **—mul·ti·cul·tur·al·ist** *n.* & *adj.* **—mul·ti·cul·tur·al·ly** *adv.*

mul·ti·di·men·sion·al /ˌməltidəˈmenCHənl; ˌməlˌtī-/ ▶*adj.* of or involving several dimensions or aspects: *multidimensional space* | *a novel that lends itself to multidimensional readings.* **—mul·ti·di·men·sion·al·i·ty** /-də ˌmenCHəˈnalətē/ *n.* **—mul·ti·di·men·sion·al·ly** /-də ˈmenCHənl-ē/ *adv.*

mul·ti·di·rec·tion·al /ˌməltidəˈrekSHənl/ ▶*adj.* of, involving, or operating in several directions: *a multidirectional antenna.*

mul·ti·dis·ci·pli·nar·y /ˌməltiˈdisəpliˈnerē; ˌməlˌtī-/ ▶*adj.* combining or involving several academic disciplines or professional specializations in an approach to a topic or problem.

mul·ti·eth·nic /ˌməltēˈeTHnik; ˌməlˌtī-/ ▶*adj.* of, relating to, or constituting several ethnic groups: *she teaches science in a multiethnic secondary school.*

mul·ti·fac·et·ed /ˌməltiˈfasətəd; ˌməlˌtī-/ ▶*adj.* having many facets: *the play of light on the diamond's multifaceted surface* | *figurative this is a multifaceted subject.*

mul·ti·fac·to·ri·al /ˌməltiˌfakˈtôrēəl; ˌməlˌtī-/ ▶*adj.* involving or dependent on a number of factors or causes.

mul·ti·far·i·ous /ˌməlt(ə)ˈfe(ə)rēəs/ ▶*adj.* many and of various types: *multifarious activities.* ■ having many varied parts or aspects: *a vast multifarious organization.* ▷late 16th cent.: from Latin *multifarius* + **-OUS**. **—mul·ti·far·i·ous·ly** *adv.* **—mul·ti·far·i·ous·ness** *n.*

mul·ti·fe·tal /ˌməltēˈfētl; ˌməltī-/ ▶*adj.* involving two or more fetuses: *multifetal pregnancy.*

mul·ti·fid /ˈməltiˌfid; ˈməltə-; ˈməlˌtī-/ ▶*adj. Botany* & *Zoology* divided into several or many parts by deep clefts or notches. ▷mid 18th cent.: from Latin *multifidus*, from *multus* 'much, many' + *-fid* from *fidus* 'cleft, split.'

mul·ti·fil·a·ment /ˌməltiˈfiləmənt; ˌməlˌtī-/ ▶*adj.* denoting a cord or yarn composed of a number of strands or filaments wound together.

mul·ti·flo·ra /ˈməltiˌflôrə/ (also **multiflora rose**) ▶*n.* an eastern Asian shrubby or climbing rose that bears clusters of small single pink or white flowers. • *Rosa multiflora*, family Rosaceae. ▷early 19th cent.: from late Latin, feminine of *multiflorus* 'multiflorous.'

mul·ti·fo·cal /ˌməltiˈfōkəl; ˌməlˈtī-/ ▶*adj. chiefly Medicine* & *Optics* having more than one focus.

mul·ti·fold /ˈməltiˌfōld/ ▶*adj.* manifold.

mul·ti·form /ˈməltiˌfôrm/ ▶*adj.* existing in many forms or kinds: *a complex, multiform illness like cancer.* **—mul·ti·for·mi·ty** /-ˈfôrmətē/ *n.*

mul·ti·func·tion·al /ˌməltiˈfəNGkSHənl; ˌməltī-/ (also **mul·ti·func·tion** /-SHən/) ▶*adj.* having or fulfilling several functions: *a multifunctional analog meter.*

mul·ti·gen·er·a·tion·al /ˌməltiˌjenəˈrāSHənl; ˌməlˌtī-/ ▶*adj.* of or relating to several generations: *multigenerational families.*

mul·ti·grade /ˈməltiˌgrād; ˈməltə-; ˈməlˌtī-/ ▶*n.* **1** an engine oil meeting the requirements of several standard grades. **2** (**Multigrade**) *trademark* a kind of photographic paper made with two emulsions of different sensitivities, from which prints with different levels of contrast can be made using color filters: [as *adj.*] *Multigrade paper.*

mul·ti·grain /ˈməltiˌgrān; ˈməlˌtī-/ ▶*adj.* (of bread) made from more than one kind of grain.

mul·ti·grav·i·da /ˌməltiˈgravədə/ ▶*n.* (*pl.* **-grav·id·ae** /-ˈgravəˌdē; -ˌdī/) *Medicine* & *Zoology* a woman (or female animal) who is or has been pregnant for at least a second time. ▷late 19th cent.: from **MULTI-** 'many,' on the pattern of *primigravida*.

mul·ti·hull /ˈməltiˌhəl; ˈməlˌtī-/ ▶*n.* a boat with two or more hulls, esp. three.

mul·ti·lat·er·al /ˌməltiˈlatərəl/ ▶*adj.* agreed upon or participated in by three or more parties, esp. the governments of different countries: *multilateral negotiations* | *multilateral nuclear disarmament.* ■ having members or contributors from several groups, esp. several different countries: *multilateral aid agencies.* **—mul·ti·lat·er·al·ism** /-ˌlizəm/ *n.* **—mul·ti·lat·er·al·ist** /-list/ *adj.* & *n.* **—mul·ti·lat·er·al·ly** *adv.*

mul·ti·lay·er /ˈməltiˈlāər; ˈməlˌtī-/ *chiefly technical* ▶*adj.* relating to or consisting of several or many layers: *a multilayer circuit board.*
▶*n.* a coating or deposit consisting of several or many layers.

mul·ti·lay·ered /ˈməltiˈlāərd; ˈməlˌtī-/ ▶*adj.* having or involving several or many layers.

mul·ti·lev·el /ˈməltēˈlevəl; ˈˌməlˌtī-/ ▶*adj.* of, relating to, or involving many levels.

mul·ti·lin·gual /ˌməltēˈliNGg(yə)wəl; ˌməlˌtī-/ ▶*adj.* in or using several languages: *a multilingual dictionary.* **—mul·ti·lin·gual·ism** /-ˌlizəm/ *n.* **—mul·ti·lin·gual·ly** *adv.*

mul·ti·me·di·a /ˈməltiˈmēdēə; ˈməlˌtī-/ ▶*adj.* (of art, education, etc.) using more than one medium of expression or communication: *a multimedia art form that is a mélange of film, ballet, drama, mime, acrobatics, and stage effects.*
▶*n.* an extension of hypertext allowing the provision of audio and video material cross-referenced to a computer text.

mul·tim·e·ter /ˈməltiˌmētər; ˌməlˈtimətər/ ▶*n.* an instrument designed to measure electric current, voltage, and usually resistance, typically over several ranges of value.

mul·ti·mil·lion /ˈməltiˈmilyən; ˈməlˌtī-/ ▶*adj.* [*attrib.*] costing or involving several million units of a currency: [*in combination*] *a multimillion-dollar advertising campaign.*

mul·ti·mil·lion·aire /ˌməltiˌmilyəˈner; ˌməlˌtī-/ ▶*n.* a person with assets worth several million dollars.

mul·ti·mod·al /ˈməltiˌmōd; ˈməlˌtī-/ (also **mul·ti·mode**) ▶*adj.* characterized by several different modes of activity or occurrence. ■ *Statistics* (of a frequency curve or distribution) having several modes or maxima. ■ *Statistics* (of a property) occurring with such a distribution.

mul·ti·na·tion·al /ˌməltiˈnaSHənl; ˌməlˌtī-/ ▶*adj.* including or involving several countries or individuals of several nationalities: *1,500 troops were sent to join the multinational force.* ■ (of a business organization) operating in several countries: *multinational corporations.*
▶*n.* a company operating in several countries. **—mul·ti·na·tion·al·ly** *adv.*

mul·ti·no·mi·al /ˌməltiˈnōmēəl; ˌməlˌtī-/ ▶*adj.* & *n. rare Mathematics* another term for **POLYNOMIAL**. ▷early 17th cent.: from **MULTI-** 'many,' on the pattern of *binomial*.

mul·ti·pack /ˈməltiˌpak; ˈməlˌtī-/ ▶*n.* a package containing a number of similar or identical products sold at a discount compared to the price when bought separately.

mul·tip·a·ra /məlˈtipərə/ ▶*n.* (*pl.* **-rae** /-ˌrē; -ˌrī/) *Medicine* & *Zoology* a woman (or female animal) who has had more than one pregnancy resulting in viable offspring. ▷mid 19th cent.: modern Latin, feminine of *multiparus* 'multiparous.'

mul·tip·a·rous /ˌməlˈtipərəs/ ▶*adj. Medicine* (of a woman) having borne more than one child. ■ *chiefly Zoology* producing more than one young at a birth.

mul·ti·par·tite /ˌməltiˈpärˌtīt/ ▶*adj.* having several or many parts or divisions. ■ *Biology* (of a virus) existing as two or more separate but incomplete particles. ■ another term for **MULTIPARTY**.

mul·ti·par·ty /ˈməltiˈpärtē; ˈməlˌtī-/ ▶*adj.* of or involving several political parties: *multiparty elections.*

mul·ti·phase /ˈməltēˌfāz/ ▶*adj.* in, of, or relating to more than one phase. ■ (of an electrical device or circuit) polyphase.

mul·ti·play /ˈməltiˌplā; ˈməlˌtī-/ ▶*adj.* denoting a compact disc player that can be stacked with a number of discs before needing to be reloaded.

mul·ti·play·er /ˈməltiˌplāər; ˈməlˌtī-/ ▶*n.* a multimedia computer and home entertainment system that integrates a number of conventional and interactive audio and video functions with those of a personal computer.
▶*adj.* denoting a computer game designed for or involving several players.

mul·ti·ple /ˈməltəpəl/ ▶*adj.* having or involving several parts, elements, or members: *multiple occupancy* | *a multiple birth.* ■ numerous and often varied: *words with multiple meanings.* ■ (of a disease, injury, or disability) complex in its nature or effects, or affecting several parts of the body: *a multiple fracture of the femur.* ■ of or designating electrical circuits arranged in parallel. ■ of or designating an electrical circuit that has several points at which connection can occur.

▸*n.* **1** a number that can be divided by another number without a remainder: *15, 20, or any other* ***multiple*** *of five.* **2** an arrangement of terminals that allows connection with an electrical circuit at any one of several points. ▷mid 17th cent.: from French, from late Latin *multiplus*, alteration of Latin *multiplex* (see **MULTIPLEX**).

mul·ti·ple-choice ▸*adj.* (of a question on a test) accompanied by several possible answers from which the candidate must try to choose the correct one.

mul·ti·ple fruit ▸*n. Botany* a fruit formed from carpels derived from several flowers, such as a pineapple.

mul·ti·ple per·son·al·i·ty ▸*n.* [often as *adj.*] *Psychology* a rare dissociative disorder in which two or more personalities with distinct memories and behavior patterns apparently exist in one individual: *multiple-personality disorder.*

mul·ti·ple scle·ro·sis ▸*n.* a chronic, typically progressive disease involving damage to the sheaths of nerve cells in the brain and spinal cord, whose symptoms may include numbness, impairment of speech and of muscular coordination, blurred vision, and severe fatigue.

mul·ti·ple star ▸*n.* a group of stars very close together as seen from the earth, esp. one whose members are in fact close together and rotate around a common center.

mul·ti·plet /ˈməltəplət/ ▸*n. Physics* a group of closely associated things, esp. closely spaced spectral lines or atomic energy levels, or subatomic particles differing only in a single property (e.g., charge or strangeness). ▷1920s: from **MULTIPLE**, on the pattern of words such as *doublet* and *triplet*.

mul·ti·plex /ˈməltiˌpleks/ ▸*adj.* consisting of many elements in a complex relationship: *multiplex ties of work and friendship.* ■ involving simultaneous transmission of several messages along a single channel of communication. ■ (of a movie theater) having several separate screens within one building.

▸*n.* **1** a system or signal involving simultaneous transmission of several messages along a single channel of communication. Compare with **DUPLEX**, **SIMPLEX**. **2** a movie theater with several separate screens.

▸*v.* [*trans.*] incorporate into a multiplex signal or system. ▷late Middle English in the mathematical sense 'multiple': from Latin. —**mul·ti·plex·er** (also **mul·ti·plex·or**) *n.*

mul·ti·pli·a·ble /ˈməltəˌplīəbəl; ˌməltəˈplīəbəl/ (also **mul·ti·plic·a·ble** /ˌməltəˈplikəbəl; ˌməltēˈplikəbəl/) ▸*adj.* able to be multiplied.

mul·ti·pli·cand /ˌməltəpliˈkand/ ▸*n.* a quantity that is to be multiplied by another (the multiplier). ▷late 16th cent.: from medieval Latin *multiplicandus* 'to be multiplied,' gerundive of Latin *multiplicare* (see **MULTIPLY**[1]).

mul·ti·pli·ca·tion /ˌməltəpliˈkāSHən/ ▸*n.* the process or skill of multiplying: *we need to use both multiplication and division to find the answers | the rapid multiplication of abnormal white blood cells.* ■ *Mathematics* the process of combining matrices, vectors, or other quantities under specific rules to obtain their product. ▷late Middle English: from Old French, or from Latin *multiplicatio(n-)*, from *multiplicare* (see **MULTIPLY**[1]).

mul·ti·pli·ca·tion sign ▸*n.* a sign, esp. ×, used to indicate that one quantity is to be multiplied by another, as in *2×3=6*.

mul·ti·pli·ca·tion ta·ble ▸*n.* a table of the products of two factors, esp. the integers 1 to 12.

mul·ti·pli·ca·tive /ˌməltəˈplikətiv; ˈməltəpləˌkātiv/ ▸*n.* subject to or of the nature of multiplication: *coronary risk factors are multiplicative.*

mul·ti·plic·i·ty /ˌməltəˈplisətē/ ▸*n.* (*pl.* **-ties**) a large number: *his climbing record lists a multiplicity of ascents.* ■ a large variety: *the rain forests and the multiplicity of species that they harbor.* ▷late Middle English: from late Latin *multiplicitas*, from Latin *multiplex* (see **MULTIPLEX**).

mul·ti·pli·er /ˈməltəˌplīər/ ▸*n.* a person or thing that multiplies. ■ a quantity by which a given number (the multiplicand) is to be multiplied. ■ *Economics* a factor by which an increment of income exceeds the resulting increment of savings or investment. ■ a device for increasing by repetition the intensity of an electric current, force, etc., to a measurable level.

mul·ti·ply[1] /ˈməltəˌplī/ ▸*v.* (**-plies, -plied**) [*trans.*] obtain from (a number) another that contains the first number a specified number of times: *I asked you to* ***multiply*** *fourteen* ***by*** *nineteen* | [*intrans.*] *we all know how to multiply by ten.* ■ increase or cause to increase greatly in number or quantity: [*intrans.*] *ever since I became a landlord my troubles have multiplied tenfold* | [*trans.*] *cigarette smoking combines with other factors to multiply the risks of atherosclerosis.* ■ [*intrans.*] (of an animal or other organism) increase in number by reproducing. ■ propagate (plants). ▷Middle English: from Old French *multiplier*, from Latin *multiplicare*.

mul·ti·ply[2] /ˈməltəplē/ ▸*adv.* [often as *submodifier*] in several different ways or respects: *multiply injured patients.*

mul·ti·po·lar /ˌməltiˈpōlər; ˌməltī-/ ▸*adj.* **1** having many poles or extremities. **2** polarized in several ways or directions. —**mul·ti·po·lar·i·ty** /-pōˈlaritē; -pə-/ *n.* —**mul·ti·pole** /ˈməltiˌpōl; ˈməltī-/ *n.*

mul·ti·proc·ess·ing /ˌməltiˈpräˌsesiNG; ˌməlˌtī-; -ˈpräsəsiNG/ (also **mul·ti·pro·gram·ming**) ▸*n. Computing* the running of two or more programs or sequences of instructions simultaneously by a computer with more than one central processor.

mul·ti·proc·es·sor /ˌməltiˈpräˌsesər; -ˈpräsəsər/ ▸*n.* a computer with more than one central processor.

mul·ti·pur·pose /ˌməltēˈpərpəs; ˌməlˌtī-/ ▸*adj.* having several purposes or functions: *a seven-acre multipurpose civic center.*

mul·ti·ra·cial /ˌməltiˈrāSHəl; ˌməlˌtī-/ ▸*adj.* made up of or relating to people of several or many races: *multiracial education.* —**mul·ti·ra·cial·ism** /-ˌlizəm/ *n.* —**mul·ti·ra·cial·ist** /-list/ *adj.* & *n.* —**mul·ti·ra·cial·ly** *adv.*

mul·ti·role /ˈməltiˌrōl; ˈməlˌtī-/ ▸*adj.* [*attrib.*] (chiefly of an aircraft) capable of performing several roles.

mul·ti·ses·sion /ˈməltiˌseSHən; ˈməlˌtī-/ ▸*adj. Computing* denoting a format for recording digital information onto a CD-ROM disc over two or more separate sessions.

mul·ti·slack·ing /ˌməltēˈslakiNG; ˌməltī-/ ▸*n. informal* the practice of using a computer at work for tasks or activities that are not related to one's job: *most employers tolerate a certain amount of multislacking.* ▷*multi-* + *slacking* 'working slowly or lazily,' on the pattern of *multitasking*. —**mul·ti·slack·er** *n.*

mul·ti·spec·tral /ˌməltiˈspektrəl; ˌməlˌtī-/ ▸*adj.* operating in or involving several regions of the electromagnetic spectrum: *multispectral images from satellites.*

mul·ti·stage /ˈməltiˈstāj; ˌməlˌtī-/ ▸*adj.* [*attrib.*] consisting of or relating to several stages or processes: *a multistage decision-making process.* ■ (of a rocket) having at least two sections, each of which contains its own motor and is jettisoned as its fuel runs out. ■ (of a pump, turbine, or similar device) having more than one rotor.

mul·ti·sto·ry /ˈməltiˌstôrē; ˈməlˌtī-/ (also **mul·ti·sto·ried**) ▸*adj.* [*attrib.*] (of a building) having several stories.

mul·ti·task·ing /ˌməltiˈtaskiNG; ˌməlˌtī-/ ▸*n. Computing* the simultaneous execution of more than one program or task by a single computer processor. —**mul·ti·task** /ˈməltiˌtask; ˈməlˌtī-/ *v.*

mul·ti·thread·ing /ˈməltiˈTHrediNG; ˈməlˌtī-/ ▸*n. Computing* a technique by which a single set of code can be used by several processors at different stages of execution. —**mul·ti·thread·ed** /-ˈTHredəd/ *adj.*

mul·ti·track /ˈməltiˌtrak; ˈməlˌtī-/ ▸*adj.* relating to or made by the mixing of several separately recorded tracks of sound: *a digital multitrack recorder.*

▸*n.* a recording made from the mixing of several separately recorded tracks.

▸*v.* [*trans.*] record using multitrack recording: [as *adj.*] (**multitracked**) *multitracked vocals.*

mul·ti·tu·ber·cu·late /ˌməltit(y)əˈbərkyələt/ ▸*n.* a small primitive extinct mammal of a mainly Cretaceous and Paleocene order, distinguished by having molar teeth with several cusps arranged in two or three rows. • Order Multituberculata, subclass Allotheria. ▷late 19th cent.: from modern Latin *Multituberculata*, from **MULTI-** 'many' + Latin *tuberculum* 'tubercle.'

mul·ti·tude /ˈməltəˌt(y)o͞od/ ▸*n.* a large number: ***a multitude of*** *medical conditions are due to being overweight.* ■ (**the multitudes**) large numbers of people: *the multitudes using the roads.* ■ (**the multitude**) a large gathering of people: *Father Peter addressed the multitude.* ■ (**the multitude**) the mass of ordinary people without power or influence: *placing ultimate political power in the hands of the multitude.* ■ *archaic* the state of being numerous: *they would swarm over the river in their multitude.* ▷Middle English: via Old French from Latin *multitudo*, from *multus* 'many.'

▸*PHRASE* □ **cover a multitude of sins** see **COVER**.

mul·ti·tu·di·nous /ˌməltəˈt(y)o͞odn-əs/ ▸*adj.* very numerous: *the tinkling of multitudinous bells from the herd.* ■ consisting of or containing many individuals or elements: *the multitudinous array of chemical substances that exist in the natural world.* ■ *poetic/literary* (of a body of water) vast. ▷early 17th cent.: from Latin *multitudo* (see **MULTITUDE**) + **-OUS**. —**mul·ti·tu·di·nous·ly** *adv.* —**mul·ti·tu·di·nous·ness** *n.*

mul·ti·us·er /ˈməltēˈyo͞ozər; ˈməlˌtī-/ ▸*adj.* [*attrib.*] (of a computer system) able to be used by a number of people simultaneously. ■ denoting a computer game in which several players interact simultaneously using the Internet or other communications.

mul·ti·va·lent /ˌməltiˈvālənt; ˌməlˌtī-/ ▸*adj.* **1** having or susceptible to many applications, interpretations, meanings, or values: *visually complex and multivalent work.* **2** *Medicine* (of an antigen or antibody) having several sites at which attachment to an antibody or antigen can occur: *a multivalent antiserum.* Compare with **POLYVALENT**. **3** *Chemistry* another term for **POLYVALENT**. —**mul·ti·va·lence** *n.* —**mul·ti·va·len·cy** *n. Brit.*

mul·ti·valve /ˌməltiˈvalv; ˌməlˌtī-/ ▸*adj.* [*attrib.*] **1** *Zoology* (of a shell, etc.) having several valves. **2** (of an internal combustion engine) having more than two valves per cylinder, typically four (two inlet and two exhaust).

▸*n.* a multivalve shell, or an animal having such a shell, as a chiton.

mul·ti·var·i·ate /ˌməltiˈve(ə)rēət; ˌməltī-/ ▸*adj. Statistics* involving two or more variable quantities.

mul·ti·ven·dor /məltiˈvendər/ ▸*adj.* [*attrib.*] denoting or relating to computer hardware or software products or network services from more than one supplier.

mul·ti·verse /ˈməltiˌvərs/ ▸*n.* an infinite realm of being or potential being of which the universe is regarded as a part or instance.

mul·ti·ver·si·ty /ˌməltiˈvərsətē/ ▸*n.* (*pl.* **-ties**) a large university with many different departments. ▷mid 20th cent.: from **MULTI-** + a shortened form of **UNIVERSITY**.

mul·ti·vi·bra·tor /ˌməltiˈvīˌbrātər/ ▸*n. Electronics* a device consisting of two amplifying transistors or valves, each with its output connected to the input of the other, producing an oscillatory signal.

mul·ti·vi·ta·min /ˌməltiˈvītəmən/ ▸*adj.* [*attrib.*] containing a combination of vitamins: *a daily multivitamin supplement.*

▸*n.* a pill containing a combination of vitamins.

mul·ti·way /ˈməltiˌwā; ˈməlˌtī-/ ▸*adj.* having several paths, routes, or channels: *a multiway switch.*

mul·tum in par·vo /ˈmo͝oltəm in ˈpärvō; -ˈpärwō/ ▸*n.* a great deal in a small space. ▷Latin, literally 'much in little.'

mul·ture /ˈməlCHər/ ▸*n. historical* a toll of grain or flour due to a miller in return for grinding grain. ■ the right to collect this. ▷Middle English: from Old French *moulture*, from medieval Latin *molitura*, from *molit-* 'ground,' from the verb *molere*.

mum[1] /məm/ ▸*adj.* silent. ▷late Middle English: imitative of a sound made with closed lips.

▸*PHRASES* □ **keep mum** *informal* remain silent, esp. so as not to reveal a secret: *he was keeping mum about a possible move to Canada.* □ **mum's the word** *informal* (as a request or warning) say nothing; don't reveal a secret.

mum[2] ▸*v.* (**mummed, mum·ming**) [*intrans.*] act in a traditional masked mime or a mummers' play. ▷late Middle English: compare with **MUM**[1] and Middle Low German *mummen*.

mum[3] ▸*n. informal* a cultivated chrysanthemum. ▷abbreviation of **CHRYSANTHEMUM**.

mum[4] ▸*n.* British term for **MOM**. ▷mid 17th cent.: abbreviation of **MUMMY**[2].

Mum·bai /ˈməmˌbī/ official name (from 1995) for **BOMBAY**. —**Mum·bai·kar** /ˌməmbīˈkär/ *n.* & *adj.*

mum·ble /ˈməmbəl/ ▸*v.* **1** [*reporting verb*] say something indistinctly and quietly, making it difficult for others to hear: [*trans.*] *he mumbled something she didn't catch* | [with *direct speech*] *"Sorry," she mumbled.* **2** [*trans.*] bite or chew with toothless gums or eat without making much use of the teeth.

▸*n.* [usu. in *sing.*] a quiet and indistinct utterance: *Rosie had replied in a mumble.* ▷Middle English: frequentative of **MUM**[1]. —**mum·bler** /ˈməmb(ə)lər/ *n.* —**mum·bling·ly** /ˈməmb(ə)liNGlē/ *adv.*

mum·ble·ty-peg /ˈməmbəltē ˌpeg/ (also **mum·ble·ty·peg**) ▸*n.* a game in which each player in turn throws a knife or pointed stick from a series of positions, continuing until it fails to stick in the ground.

▷early 17th cent.: also in the form *mumble the peg*, from *mumble* in the late 16th-cent. sense 'bite as if with toothless gums,' from the requirement of the game that an unsuccessful player withdraw a peg from the ground using the mouth.

mum·bo-jum·bo /ˈməmbō ˈjəmbō/ (also **mum·bo· jum·bo**) ▸*n. informal* language or ritual causing or intended to cause confusion or bewilderment: *a maze of legal mumbo jumbo.* ▷mid 18th cent. (as *Mumbo Jumbo*, denoting a supposed African idol): of unknown origin; the current sense dates from the late 19th cent.

mu me·son /myo͞o/ ▸*n.* another term for MUON.

Mum·ford /ˈməmfərd/, Lewis (1895–1990), U.S. social philosopher. He was an expert on regional and city planning and wrote *The Renewal of Life* in four volumes (1934–51), *The Culture of Cities* (1938), *The City in History* (1961), and *The Myth of the Machine* (1967).

mum·mer /ˈməmər/ ▸*n.* an actor in a traditional masked mime, esp. of a type associated with Christmas and popular in England in the 18th and early 19th centuries. ■ a pantomimist. ■ *archaic* or *derogatory* an actor in the theater. ▷late Middle English: from Old French *momeur*, from *momer* 'act in a mime'; perhaps of Germanic origin.

mum·mer·y /ˈməmərē/ ▸*n.* (*pl.* **-mer·ies**) a performance by mummers. ■ ridiculous ceremonial, esp. of a religious nature: *that's all it is, mere mummery.* ▷mid 16th cent.: from Old French *momerie*, from *momer* (see MUMMER).

mum·mi·chog /ˈməmiˌCHôg; -ˌCHäg/ ▸*n.* a small marine killifish that lives along the sheltered shores and estuaries of eastern North America. It is widely kept in aquariums and is also used as bait and for biological research. • *Fundulus heteroclitus*, family Fundulidae (or Cyprinodontidae). ▷late 18th cent.: from Narragansett *moamitteaug*.

mum·mi·fy /ˈməməˌfī/ ▸*v.* (**-fies, -fied**) [*trans.*] [usu. as *adj.*] (**mummified**) (esp. in ancient Egypt) preserve (a body) by embalming it and wrapping it in cloth: *the mummified bodies entombed in the pyramids of Egypt.* See also MUMMY[1]. ■ shrivel or dry up (a body or a thing), thus preserving it: *the wind must have dehydrated and mummified the body.* —**mum·mi·fi·ca·tion** /ˌməməfiˈkāSHən/ *n.*

mum·my[1] /ˈməmē/ ▸*n.* (*pl.* **-mies**) **1** (esp. in ancient Egypt) a body of a human being or animal that has been ceremonially preserved by removal of the internal organs, treatment with natron and resin, and wrapping in bandages. **2** a well-preserved, desiccated body. ▷late Middle English (denoting a substance taken from embalmed bodies and used in medicines): from French *momie*, from medieval Latin *mumia* and Arabic *mūmiyā* 'embalmed body,' perhaps from Persian *mūm* 'wax.'

mum·my[2] ▸*n.* (*pl.* **-mies**) British term for MOMMY. ▷late 18th cent.: perhaps an alteration of earlier MAMMY.

mump·ish /ˈməmpiSH/ ▸*adj. informal, dated* sullen or sulky. ▷early 18th cent.: from obsolete *mump* 'grimace, have a miserable expression' + -ISH[1].

mumps /məmps/ ▸*plural n.* [treated as *sing.*] a contagious and infectious viral disease causing swelling of the parotid salivary glands in the face, and a risk of sterility in adult males. ▷late 16th cent.: from obsolete *mump* 'grimace, have a miserable expression.'

mump·si·mus /ˈməmpsiməs/ ▸*n.* (*pl.* **-mus·es**) a traditional custom or notion adhered to although shown to be unreasonable. ■ a person who obstinately adheres to such a custom or notion. ▷mid 16th cent.: erroneously for Latin *sumpsimus* in *quod in ore sumpsimus* 'which we have taken into the mouth' (Eucharist), in a story of an illiterate priest who, when corrected, replied "I will not change my old mumpsimus for your new sumpsimus."

Munch /məNGk; mo͝oNGk/, Edvard (1863–1944), Norwegian painter and engraver. He infused his subjects with an intense emotionalism, exploring the use of vivid color and linear distortion to express feelings about life and death. His works include the painting *The Scream* (1893).

munch /mənCH/ ▸*v.* [*trans.*] eat (something) with a continuous and often audible action of the jaws: *he munched a chicken wing* | [*intrans.*] *popcorn to* **munch on** *while watching the movie.* ▷late Middle English: imitative; compare with CRUNCH. —**munch·er** *n.*

Mun·chau·sen, Ba·ron /ˈmo͞onˌCHouzən; ˈmən-/ the hero of a book of fantastic travelers' tales (1785) written in English by a German, Rudolph Erich Raspe. The original Baron Munchausen is said to have lived 1720–97, to have served in the Russian army against the Turks, and to have related extravagant tales of his prowess.

Mun·chau·sen's syn·drome ▸*n. Psychiatry* a mental disorder in which a person repeatedly feigns severe illness so as to obtain hospital treatment. ■ (**Munchausen's syndrome by proxy**) a mental disorder in which a person seeks attention by inducing or feigning illness in another person, typically a child.

Mün·chen /ˈminCHən; ˈmYnKHən/ German name for MUNICH.

munch·ie /ˈmənCHē/ ▸*n.* (*pl.* **munch·ies**) (usu. **munchies**) *informal* a snack or small item of food. ■ (**the munchies**) a sudden strong desire for food: *these camping trips always give me the munchies.*

munch·kin /ˈmənCHkin/ ▸*n. informal* a child. ▷from the *Munchkins*, depicted as a race of small childlike creatures, in L. Frank Baum's *The Wonderful Wizard of Oz* (1900).

Mun·cie /ˈmənsē/ an industrial city in east central Indiana, noted as the 'Middletown' of sociological literature; pop. 67,430.

Mun·da /ˈmo͝ondə/ ▸*n.* (*pl.* same or **-das**) **1** a member of a group of indigenous peoples living scattered in a region from east central India to Nepal and Bangladesh. **2** a family of languages spoken by these peoples, distantly related to the Mon-Khmer family, with which they are sometimes classified as Austro-Asiatic. ■ any language of this family.
▸*adj.* relating to or denoting the Munda or their languages. ▷the name in Munda.

mun·dane /ˌmənˈdān/ ▸*adj.* **1** lacking interest or excitement; dull: *seeking a way out of his mundane, humdrum existence.* **2** of this earthly world rather than a heavenly or spiritual one: *according to the Shinto doctrine, spirits of the dead can act upon the mundane world.* ■ of, relating to, or denoting the branch of astrology that deals with political, social, economic, and geophysical events and processes. ▷late Middle English (sense 2): from Old French *mondain*, from late Latin *mundanus*, from Latin *mundus* 'world.' Sense 1 dates from the late 19th cent. —**mun·dane·ly** *adv.* —**mun·dane·ness** *n.* —**mun·dan·i·ty** /-ˈdānətē/ *n.* (*pl.* **-ties**).

mung /məNG/ (also **mung bean**) ▸*n.* **1** a small round green bean. **2** the tropical Old World plant that yields these beans, commonly grown as a source of bean sprouts. • *Vigna radiata* (or *Phaseolus aureus*), family Leguminosae. ▷early 19th cent.: from Hindi *mūng*.

mun·go /ˈməNGgō/ ▸*n.* cloth made from recycled woven or felted material. ▷mid 19th cent.: of unknown origin.

mu·ni[1] /ˈmyo͞onē/ ▸*n.* (*pl.* **mu·nis**) short for MUNICIPAL BOND.

mu·ni[2] /ˈmo͞onē/ ▸*n.* (*pl.* **mu·nis**) (in India) an inspired holy person; an ascetic, hermit, or sage. ▷from Sanskrit, literally 'silent,' from *man* 'think.'

Mu·nich /ˈmyo͞onik; -niKH/ a city in southeastern Germany, capital of Bavaria; pop. 1,229,000. German name MÜNCHEN.

Mu·nich Pact (also **Munich Agreement**) an agreement between Britain, France, Germany, and Italy, signed at Munich on September 29, 1938, under which the Sudetenland was ceded to Nazi Germany, often cited as an example of misjudged or dishonorable appeasement.

mu·nic·i·pal /myo͞oˈnisəpəl; myə-/ ▸*adj.* of or relating to a city or town or its governing body: *national and municipal elections* | *municipal offices.* ▷mid 16th cent. (originally relating to the internal affairs of a state as distinct from its foreign relations): from Latin *municipalis*, from *municipium* 'free city,' from *municeps*, *municip-* 'citizen with privileges,' from *munia* 'civic offices' + *capere* 'take.' —**mu·nic·i·pal·ly** *adv.*

mu·nic·i·pal bond ▸*n.* a security issued by or on behalf of a local authority.

mu·nic·i·pal·i·ty /myo͞oˌnisəˈpalətē; myə-/ ▸*n.* (*pl.* **-ties**) a city or town that has corporate status and local government. ■ the governing body of such an area. ▷late 18th cent.: from French *municipalité*, from *municipal* (see MUNICIPAL).

mu·nic·i·pal·ize /myo͞oˈnisəpəˌlīz; myə-/ ▸*v.* [*trans.*] bring under the control or ownership of the authorities of a city or town: *an expensive commitment to municipalize rented housing.* —**mu·nic·i·pal·i·za·tion** /-ˌnisəpələˈzāSHən/ *n.*

mu·nif·i·cent /myo͞oˈnifəsənt; myə-/ ▸*adj.* (of a gift or sum of money) larger or more generous than is usual or necessary: *a munificent gesture.* ■ (of a person) very generous. ▷late 16th cent.: from Latin *munificent-*, stem of *munificentior*, comparative of *munificus* 'bountiful,' from *munus* 'gift.' —**mu·nif·i·cence** *n.* —**mu·nif·i·cent·ly** *adv.*

mu·ni·ment /ˈmyo͞onəmənt/ ▸*n.* (usu. **muniments**) a document or record, esp. one kept in an archive. ▷late Middle English: via Old French from Latin *munimentum* 'defense' (in medieval Latin 'title deed'), from *munire* 'fortify.'

mu·ni·tion /myo͞oˈniSHən; myə-/ ▸*plural n.* (**munitions**) military weapons, ammunition, equipment, and stores: *reserves of nuclear, chemical, and conventional munitions* | [as *adj.*] *a munitions expert* | [as *adj.*] (**munition**) *munition factories.*
▸*v.* [*trans.*] supply with munitions. ▷late Middle English (denoting a granted right or privilege): from French, from Latin *munitio(n-)* 'fortification,' from *munire* 'fortify or secure.' —**mu·ni·tion·er** *n.* (*rare*).

Mun·ro[1] /mənˈrō/, Alice (1931–), Canadian writer. Many of her short stories are collected in *Dance of the Happy Shades* (1968), *The Progress of Love* (1987), *Open Secrets* (1995), and *The Love of a Good Woman* (1998). Her novels include *Lives of Girls and Women* (1971).

Mun·ro[2], H. H., see SAKI.

Mun·si /ˈmo͝onsē/ ▸*n.* see DELAWARE[2] (sense 2). ▷the name in Munsi.

Mun·ster /ˈmənstər/ a province of the Republic of Ireland, in the southwestern part of the country.

Mün·ster /ˈminstər; ˈmYn-/ a city in northwestern Germany; pop. 250,000. It was formerly the capital of Westphalia; the Treaty of Westphalia, which ended the Thirty Years War, was signed simultaneously here and at Osnabrück in 1648.

mun·tin /ˈməntn/ ▸*n.* a bar or rigid supporting strip between adjacent panes of glass. ▷early 17th cent.: variant of obsolete *montant* (from French, literally 'rising'). —**mun·tined** /ˈməntnd/ *adj.*

munt·jac /ˈməntˌjak/ ▸*n.* a small Southeast Asian deer, the male of which has tusks, small antlers, and a doglike bark. Also called BARKING DEER. • Genus *Muntiacus*, family Cervidae: several species, including the **Chinese muntjac** (*M. reevesi*), which is naturalized in England and France. ▷late 18th cent.: from Sundanese *minchek*.

mu·on /ˈmyo͞oˌän/ ▸*n. Physics* an unstable subatomic particle of the same class as an electron (a lepton), but with a mass around 200 times greater. Muons make up much of the cosmic radiation reaching the earth's surface. ▷1950s: contraction of MU MESON; the particle, however, is no longer regarded as a meson. —**mu·on·ic** /myo͞oˈänik/ *adj.*

Muq·di·sho /mo͞okˈdiSHō/ another name for MOGADISHU.

mu·ral /ˈmyo͝orəl/ ▸*n.* a painting or other work of art executed directly on a wall.
▸*adj.* [*attrib.*] of, like, or relating to a wall: *a mural escarpment.* ■ *Medicine* of, relating to, or occurring in the wall of a body cavity or blood vessel: *mural thrombosis.* ▷late Middle English: from French, from Latin *muralis*, from *murus* 'wall.' The adjective was first used in MURAL CROWN; later (mid 16th cent.) the sense 'placed or executed on a wall' arose, reflected in the current noun use (dating from the early 20th cent.). —**mu·ral·ist** *n.*

mu·ral crown ▸*n.* **1** *Heraldry* a representation of a city wall in the form of a crown, borne above the shield in the arms of distinguished soldiers and of some civic authorities. **2** (in ancient Roman times) a crown or garland given to the soldier who was first to scale the wall of a besieged town.

Mu·ra·no glass /myo͝oˈränō/ ▸*n.* another term for VENETIAN GLASS.

Mu·rat /m(y)o͞oˈrä(t); mYˈrä/, Joachim (*c.*1767–1815), French general, king of Naples 1808–15. A cavalry commander in Napoleon's Italian campaign 1800, he was made king of Naples. His attempt to become king of all Italy in 1815 failed, and he was captured in Calabria and executed.

Mur·chi·son Falls /ˈmərCHəsən/ former name for KABALEGA FALLS.

Mur·cia /ˈmərSH(ē)ə; ˈmo͝orsēə/ an autonomous region in southeastern Spain. In the Middle Ages, along with Albacete, it formed an ancient Moorish kingdom. ■ its capital city; pop. 329,000.

mur·der /ˈmərdər/ ▸*n.* the unlawful premeditated killing of one human being by another: *the stabbing murder of an off-Broadway producer* | *he was put on trial for attempted murder.* See note at KILL. ■ *informal* a very difficult or unpleasant task or experience: *my first job at the steel mill was murder.* ■ *informal* something causing great discomfort to a part of the body: *that exercise is* **murder on** *the lumbar regions.*
▸*v.* [*trans.*] kill (someone) unlawfully and with premeditation: *somebody tried to murder Joe.* ■ *informal* punish severely or be very angry with: *my father will murder me if I'm home late.* ■ *informal* conclusively

M

defeat (an opponent) in a game or sport. ■ spoil by lack of skill or knowledge: *the only thing he had murdered was the English language.* ▷Old English *morthor,* of Germanic origin; related to Dutch *moord* and German *Mord,* from an Indo-European root shared by Sanskrit *mará* 'death' and Latin *mors;* reinforced in Middle English by Old French *murdre.* **—mur·der·er** *n.* **—mur·der·ess** /'mərdərəs/ *n.*

▶*PHRASES* □ **get away with murder** *informal* succeed in doing whatever one chooses without being punished or suffering any disadvantage. □ **murder one** (or **two**) *informal* first-degree (or second-degree) murder. □ **murder will out** murder cannot remain undetected. □ **scream** (or **yell**) **bloody** (or *Brit.* **blue**) **murder** *informal* scream loudly due to pain or fright; make an extravagant and noisy protest: *she had tripped and was screaming bloody murder.*

mur·der·ous /'mərdərəs/ ▶*adj.* capable of or intending to murder; dangerously violent: *a brutal and murderous despot | her estranged husband was seized with murderous jealousy.* ■ (of an action, event, or plan) involving murder or extreme violence: *murderous acts of terrorism.* ■ *informal* extremely arduous or unpleasant: *the team had a murderous schedule of four games in ten days.* ■ *informal* (of a person or their expression) extremely angry: *Mary emerged from the locker room, looking murderous.* **—mur·der·ous·ly** *adv.* **—mur·der·ous·ness** *n.*

Mur·doch[1] /'mərdäk; -dək/, Dame (Jean) Iris (1919–99), British novelist and philosopher, born in Ireland. She is primarily known for her novels, many of which explore complex sexual relationships and spiritual life. Notable novels: *The Sandcastle* (1957), *The Sea, The Sea* (1978), and *The Philosopher's Pupil* (1983).

Mur·doch[2], (Keith) Rupert (1931–), U.S. publisher and media entrepreneur, born in Australia. As the founder and head of the News International Communications empire, he owned major newspapers in Australia, Britain, and the U.S., together with movie and television companies and HarperCollins, a publisher.

mure /'myo͝or/ ▶*v.* [*trans.*] *archaic* shut up in an enclosed space; immure. ▷late Middle English: from Old French *murer,* from Latin *murare,* from *murus* 'wall.'

mu·rex /'myo͝or,eks/ ▶*n.* (*pl.* **-ri·ces** /-rə,sēz/ or **-rex·es**) a predatory tropical marine mollusk, the shell of which bears spines and forms a long narrow canal extending downward from the aperture. • Genus *Murex,* family Muricidae, class Gastropoda. ▷late 16th cent.: from Latin; perhaps related to Greek *muax* 'sea mussel.'

Mur·frees·boro /'mərfrēz,bərō; -,bərə/ a commercial city in central Tennessee, southeast of Nashville; pop. 68,816. A Civil War battle fought near here in January 1863 is also called the Battle of Stones River.

mu·ri·at·ic ac·id /,myo͝orē'atik/ ▶*n.* archaic term for **HYDROCHLORIC ACID.** ▷late 17th cent.: *muriatic* from Latin *muriaticus,* from *muria* 'brine.' **—mu·ri·ate** /'myo͝orē,āt/ *n.*

mu·ri·cate /'myo͝ori,kāt; -kit/ (also **mu·ri·cat·ed**) ▶*adj. Botany & Zoology* studded with short rough points. ▷mid 17th cent.: from Latin *muricatus* 'shaped like a murex.'

mu·rid[1] /'myo͝orid/ ▶*n. Zoology* a rodent of a very large family (Muridae) that includes most kinds of rats, mice, and voles. ▷early 20th cent.: from modern Latin *Muridae* (plural), based on Latin *mus, mur-* 'mouse.'

mu·rid[2] ▶*n.* a follower of a Muslim holy man, esp. a Sufi disciple. ■ (**Murid**) a member of any of several Muslim movements, esp. one that advocated rebellion against the Russians in the Caucasus in the late 19th century. ▷from Arabic *murīd,* literally 'he who desires.'

Mu·ril·lo /m(y)o͝o'rilō; mo͝o'rēyō/, Bartolomé Esteban (*c.*1618–82), Spanish painter. He is noted for his genre scenes of urchins and peasants and for his devotional pictures.

mu·rine /'myo͝or,īn/ ▶*adj. Zoology* of, relating to, or affecting mice or related rodents. • Murine rodents belong to the family Muridae, in particular the subfamily Murinae of the Old World. ▷early 17th cent.: from Latin *murinus,* from *mus, mur-* 'mouse.'

murk /mərk/ ▶*n.* darkness or thick mist that makes it difficult to see: *my eyes were straining to see through the murk of the rainy evening.*
▶*adj. archaic* murky; gloomy. ▷Old English *mirce,* of Germanic origin; reinforced in Middle English by Old Norse *myrkr.*

murk·y /'mərkē/ ▶*adj.* (**murk·i·er, murk·i·est**) dark and gloomy, esp. due to thick mist: *the sky was murky and a thin drizzle was falling.* ■ (of liquid) dark and dirty; not clear: *the murky silt of a muddy pond.* ■ not fully explained or understood, esp. with concealed dishonesty or immorality: *the murky world of espionage.* **—murk·i·ly** *adv.* **—murk·i·ness** *n.*

Mur·mansk /mo͝or'mansk; -'mänsk/ a port in northwestern Russia, on the northern coast of the Kola Peninsula, in the Barents Sea; pop. 472,000. It is the largest city located north of the Arctic Circle. Its port is ice-free throughout the year.

mur·mur /'mərmər/ ▶*n.* a soft, indistinct sound made by a person or group of people speaking quietly or at a distance: *his voice was little more than a murmur.* ■ a softly spoken or almost inaudible utterance: *she accepted his offer with a quiet murmur of thanks.* ■ the quiet or subdued expression of a particular feeling by a group of people: *there was a murmur of approval from the crowd.* ■ a rumor: *he had heard hints only, murmurs.* ■ a low continuous sound: *the murmur of bees in the rhododendrons.* ■ *Medicine* a recurring sound heard in the heart through a stethoscope that is usually a sign of disease or damage. ■ *informal* a condition in which the heart produces or is apt to produce such a sound: *she had been born with a heart murmur.*
▶*v.* [*reporting verb*] say something in a low, soft, or indistinct voice: [*trans.*] *Nina murmured an excuse and hurried away* | [with *direct speech*] *"How interesting," he murmured quietly.* ■ [*intrans.*] make a low continuous sound: *the wind was murmuring through the trees.* ■ say something cautiously and discreetly: [*intrans.*] *they began to murmur of an uprising.* ■ [*intrans.*] (**murmur against**) *archaic* express one's discontent about (someone or something) in a subdued manner. ▷late Middle English: from Old French *murmure,* from *murmurer* 'to murmur,' from Latin *murmurare,* from *murmur* 'a murmur.' **—mur·mur·er** *n.* **—mur·mur·ous** /-mərəs/ *adj.*

▶*PHRASE* □ **without a murmur** without complaining.

mur·mur·a·tion /,mərmə'rāsʜən/ ▶*n. poetic/literary* **1** the action of murmuring: *the murmuration of a flock of warblers.* **2** *rare* a flock of starlings. ▷late Middle English: from French, from Latin *murmuratio(n-),* from *murmurare* 'to murmur.' The usage as a collective noun dates from the late 15th cent.

mur·mur·ing /'mərmərɪɴɢ/ ▶*n.* a soft, low, or indistinct sound produced by a person or group of people speaking quietly or at a distance. ■ (usu. **murmurings**) a subdued or private expression of discontent or dissatisfaction: *murmurings of discontent from the fans.* ■ (usu. **murmurings**) an insinuation: *his father's life had been ruined by the murmurings and innuendoes of lesser men.* ■ a low continuous sound: *the murmuring of the wind.* **—mur·mur·ing·ly** *adv.*

Mur·phy[1] /'mərfē/, Audie (1924–71), U.S. soldier and actor. The most decorated combat soldier of World War II, he appeared in war adventure movies such as *Beyond Glory* (1948) and *To Hell and Back* (1955), the latter being a movie version of his autobiography.

Mur·phy[2], Frank (1890–1949), U.S. Supreme Court associate justice 1940–49. Governor-general of the Philippines 1933–35 and the governor of Michigan 1937–38, he was appointed to the Court by President Franklin D. Roosevelt.

mur·phy /'mərfē/ ▶*n.* (*pl.* **-phies**) *informal* a potato. ▷early 19th cent.: from *Murphy,* an Irish surname.

Mur·phy's Law /'mərfēz/ a supposed law of nature, expressed in various humorous popular sayings, to the effect that anything that can go wrong will go wrong.

mur·rain /'mərən/ ▶*n.* **1** an infectious disease, esp. babesiosis, affecting cattle or other animals. **2** *archaic* or *humorous* a plague, epidemic, or crop blight. ▷late Middle English: from Old French *morine,* based on Latin *mori* 'to die.'

Mur·ray[1] /'mərē; mə-rē/ a city in northern Utah, a southern suburb of Salt Lake City; pop. 34,024.

Mur·ray[2], (George) Gilbert (Aimé) (1866–1957), British classical scholar, born in Australia. His translations of Greek dramatists helped to revive interest in Greek drama. He was also a founder of the League of Nations and later a joint president of the UN.

Mur·ray[3], Sir James (Augustus Henry) (1837–1915), Scottish lexicographer. He was chief editor of the *Oxford English Dictionary,* but did not live to see the work completed.

Mur·ray Riv·er the principal river of Australia. It rises in the Great Dividing Range in New South Wales and flows 1,610 miles (2,590 km) generally northwest, forming part of the border between the states of Victoria and New South Wales, before turning south in South Australia to empty into the Indian Ocean southeast of Adelaide.

murre /mər/ ▶*n.* a white-breasted North American auk. • Genus *Uria,* family Alcidae: two species, the **thick-billed** (or **Brunnich's**) **murre** (*U. lomvia*) and the **thin-billed** (or **common**) **murre** (*U. aalge*). ▷late 16th cent.: of unknown origin.

murre·let /'mərlit/ ▶*n.* a small North Pacific auk, typically having a gray back and white underparts. • Genera *Brachyramphus* and *Synthliboramphus,* family Alcidae: six species.

mur·rey /'mərē/ ▶*n. archaic* a deep purple-red cloth. ■ the deep purple-red color of a mulberry. ■ *Heraldry* another term for **SANGUINE.** ▷late Middle English: via Old French from medieval Latin *moratus,* from *morum* 'mulberry.'

Mur·row /'mərō; 'mə-rō/, Edward R. (1908–65), U.S. journalist; born *Egbert Roscoe Murrow.* He broadcast from bomb-ridden London during World War II, ending each program with "Good night, and good luck." He produced and narrated the radio series "Hear It Now" (1950–51) and the television series "See It Now" (1951–58). He was also well known for his television series "Person to Person" (1953–59).

Edward R. Murrow

Mur·rum·bidg·ee /,mərəm'bijē/ a river in southeastern Australia, in New South Wales. Rising in the Great Dividing Range, it flows west for 1,099 miles (1,759 km) to join the Murray River, of which it is a major tributary.

mur·ther /'mərт͟ʜər/ ▶*n.* & *v.* archaic spelling of **MURDER.**

mus. ▶*abbr.* ■ museum. ■ music or musical or musician.

MusB (also **Mus Bac**) ▶*abbr.* Bachelor of Music. ▷from Latin *Musicae Baccalaureus.*

Mus·ca /'məskə/ *Astronomy* a small southern constellation (the Fly), lying in the Milky Way between the Southern Cross and the south celestial pole. ■ [as *genitive*] (**Muscae** /-kē/) used with a preceding letter or numeral to designate a star in this constellation: *the star Beta Muscae.* ▷Latin.

mus·ca·del /,məskə'del/ ▶*n.* variant spelling of **MUSCATEL.**

Mus·ca·det /,məskə'dā; -'de/ ▶*n.* a dry white wine from the part of the Loire region in France nearest the west coast. ▷French, from *muscade* 'nutmeg,' from *musc* 'musk.'

mus·ca·dine /'məskə,dīn/ ▶*n.* any of a group of species and varieties of wine grape native to Mexico and the southeastern U.S., typically having thick skins and a musky flavor. • Genus *Vitis* (section *Muscadinia*): several species, in particular *V. rotundifolia.* ▷probably an alteration of **MUSCATEL.**

mus·cae vol·i·tan·tes /'məskē ,välə'tan,tēz/ ▶*plural n. Medicine* dark specks appearing to float before the eyes, generally caused by particles in the vitreous humor of the eye. ▷mid 18th cent.: Latin, literally 'flying flies.'

mus·ca·rine /'məskə,rēn/ ▶*n. Chemistry* a poisonous compound present in certain fungi, including the fly agaric. • An alkaloid; chem. formula: $C_9H_{21}NO_3$. ▷late 19th cent.: based on Latin *musca* 'fly.'

Mus·cat /'mə,skät/ the capital of Oman, a port in the northeastern part of the country on the southeastern coast of the Arabian peninsula; pop. 41,000.

mus·cat /'məs,kat; -kət/ ▶*n.* [often as *adj.*] a variety of white, red, or black grape with a musky scent, grown in warm climates for wine or raisins or as

Pronunciation Key ə *ago*; ər *over*; 'ə *or* ,ə *up*; 'ər *or* ,ər *fur*; a *hat*; ā *rate*; ä *car*; ᴄʜ *chew*; e *let*; ē *see*; e(ə)r *air*; i *fit*; ī *by*; i(ə)r *ear*; ɴɢ *sing*; ō *go*; ô *for*; oi *boy*; o͝o *good*; o͞o *goo*; ou *out*; sʜ *she*; тʜ *thin*; т͟ʜ *then*; (h)w *why*; ᴢʜ *vision*

table grapes. ■ a wine made from a muscat grape, esp. a sweet or fortified white wine. ▷French, from Provençal, from *musc* 'musk.'

Mus·cat and O·man former name (until 1970) for **OMAN**.

mus·ca·tel /ˌməskəˈtel/ (also **mus·ca·del** /-ˈdel/) ▶*n.* a muscat grape, esp. as grown for drying to make raisins. ■ a raisin made from such a grape. ■ a wine made from such a grape. ▷via Old French from Provençal, diminutive of *muscat* (see **MUSCAT**).

mu·schel·kalk /ˈmo͝osHəlˌkälk/ ▶*n. Geology* a limestone or chalk deposit from the Middle Triassic in Europe, esp. in Germany. ▷mid 19th cent.: from German, literally 'mussel chalk.'

mus·cid /ˈməsid/ ▶*n. Entomology* an insect of the housefly family (Muscidae). ▷late 19th cent.: from modern Latin *Muscidae* (plural), from Latin *musca* 'fly.'

mus·cle /ˈməsəl/ ▶*n.* **1** a band or bundle of fibrous tissue in a human or animal body that has the ability to contract, producing movement in or maintaining the position of parts of the body: *the calf muscle | the sheet of muscle between the abdomen and chest.* ■ such a band or bundle of tissue when well developed or prominently visible under the skin: *showing off our muscles to prove how strong we were.*

Muscles are formed of bands, sheets, or columns of elongated cells (or fibers) containing interlocking parallel arrays of the proteins actin and myosin. Projections on the myosin molecules respond to chemical signals by forming and reforming chemical bonds to the actin, so that the filaments move past each other and interlock more deeply. This converts chemical energy into the mechanical force of contraction, and also generates heat.

2 physical power; strength: *he had muscle but no brains.* ■ *informal* a person or persons exhibiting such power or strength: *an ex-marine of enormous proportions who'd been brought along as muscle.* ■ power or influence, esp. in a commercial or political context: *he had enough muscle and resources to hold his position on the council.*

▶*v.* [*trans.*] *informal* move (an object) in a particular direction by using one's physical strength: *they were muscling baggage into the hold of the plane.* ■ *informal* coerce by violence or by economic or political pressure: *he was eventually muscled out of business.*

▶*phrasal v.* □ **muscle in/into** *informal* force one's way into (something), typically in order to gain an advantage: ***muscling his way into** meetings and important conferences | he was determined to **muscle in on** the union's affairs.* □ **muscle up** *informal* build up one's muscles. ▷late Middle English: from French, from Latin *musculus*, diminutive of *mus* 'mouse' (some muscles being thought to be mouselike in form). **—mus·cled** /ˈməsəld/ *adj.* [in *combination*] *hard-muscled.* **—mus·cle·less** *adj.*

▶*PHRASES* □ **flex one's muscles** give a show of strength or power. □ **not move a muscle** be completely motionless.

mus·cle-bound ▶*adj.* having well-developed or overdeveloped muscles: *the muscle-bound bartender.*

mus·cle dys·mor·phi·a ▶*n.* a psychological disorder marked by a negative body image and an obsessive desire to have a muscular physique.

mus·cle·man /ˈməsəlˌman/ ▶*n.* (*pl.* **-men**) a large, strong man, esp. one employed to protect someone or to intimidate people.

mus·cle tone ▶*n.* see **TONE** (sense 6).

mus·cly /ˈməs(ə)lē/ ▶*adj.* muscular: *his muscly forearms.*

mus·co·va·do /ˌməskəˈvādō; -ˈvādō/ (also **muscovado sugar**) ▶*n.* unrefined sugar made from the juice of sugar cane by evaporating it and draining off the molasses. ▷early 17th cent.: from Portuguese *mascabado (açúcar)* '(sugar) of the lowest quality.'

Mus·co·vite /ˈməskəˌvīt/ ▶*n.* a native or citizen of Moscow. ■ *archaic* a Russian.

▶*adj.* of or relating to Moscow. ■ *archaic* of or relating to Russia. ▷from modern Latin *Muscovita*, from *Muscovia* (see **MUSCOVY**).

mus·co·vite /ˈməskəˌvīt/ ▶*n.* a silver-gray form of mica occurring in many igneous and metamorphic rocks. ▷mid 19th cent.: from obsolete *Muscovy glass* (in the same sense) + **-ITE**[1].

Mus·co·vy /ˈməskəvē/ a medieval principality in west central Russia, centered around Moscow, that formed the nucleus of modern Russia. As Muscovy expanded, princes of Muscovy became the rulers of Russia; in 1472 Ivan III, grand duke of Muscovy, completed the unification of the country, and in 1547 Ivan the Terrible became the first tsar of Russia. ■ archaic name for Russia. ▷from obsolete French *Muscovie*, from modern Latin *Moscovia*, from Russian *Moskva* 'Moscow.'

Mus·co·vy duck /ˈməskəvē; -ˌkōvē/ ▶*n.* a large tropical American tree-nesting duck, having glossy greenish-black plumage in the wild but bred in a variety of colors as a domestic bird. • *Cairina moschata*, family Anatidae.

mus·cu·lar /ˈməskyələr/ ▶*adj.* of or affecting the muscles: *energy is needed for muscular activity | muscular tension.* ■ having well-developed muscles: *her legs were strong and muscular.* ■ *figurative* vigorously robust: *a muscular economy.* ▷late 17th cent.: alteration of earlier *musculous*, in the same sense. **—mus·cu·lar·i·ty** /ˌməskyəˈle(ə)ritē/ *n.* **—mus·cu·lar·ly** *adv.*

mus·cu·lar Chris·ti·an·i·ty ▶*n.* a Christian life of brave and cheerful physical activity, esp. as popularly associated with the writings of Charles Kingsley and with boys' prep schools of the Victorian British Empire.

mus·cu·lar dys·tro·phy ▶*n.* a hereditary condition marked by progressive weakening and wasting of the muscles.

mus·cu·la·ture /ˈməskyələCHər; -ˌCHo͝or/ ▶*n.* the system or arrangement of muscles in a body, a part of the body, or an organ. ▷late 19th cent.: from French, from Latin *musculus* (see **MUSCLE**).

mus·cu·lo·skel·e·tal /ˌməskyəlōˈskelətl/ ▶*adj.* relating to or denoting the musculature and skeleton together.

MusD (also **Mus Doc**) ▶*abbr.* Doctor of Music. ▷from Latin *Musicae Doctor.*

Mus.Dr. (also **Mus.D.** or **Mus.Doc.**) ▶*abbr.* Doctor of Music. ▷from modern Latin *Mūsicae Doctor.*

Muse /myo͞oz/ ▶*n.* (in Greek and Roman mythology) each of nine goddesses, the daughters of Zeus and Mnemosyne, who preside over the arts and sciences. ■ (**muse**) a woman, or a force personified as a woman, who is the source of inspiration for a creative artist.

The Muses are generally listed as Calliope (epic poetry), Clio (history), Euterpe (flute playing and lyric poetry), Terpsichore (choral dancing and song), Erato (lyre playing and lyric poetry), Melpomene (tragedy), Thalia (comedy and light verse), Polyhymnia (hymns, and later mime), and Urania (astronomy).

▷late Middle English: from Old French, or from Latin *musa*, from Greek *mousa.*

muse /myo͞oz/ ▶*v.* [*intrans.*] be absorbed in thought: *he was **musing on** the problems he faced.* ■ [with *direct speech*] say to oneself in a thoughtful manner: *"I think I've seen him somewhere before," mused Rachel.* ■ (**muse on**) gaze thoughtfully at.

▶*n. dated* an instance or period of reflection. ▷Middle English: from Old French *muser* 'meditate, waste time,' perhaps from medieval Latin *musum* 'muzzle.' **—mus·ing·ly** *adv.*

muse·og·ra·phy /ˌmyo͞ozēˈägrəfē/ ▶*n.* another term for **MUSEOLOGY**. ■ *rare* the systematic description of objects in museums. **—museographic** /ˌmyo͞ozēəˈgrafik/ *adj.* **—museographical** /ˌmyo͞ozēəˈgrafikəl/ *adj.*

mu·se·ol·o·gy /ˌmyo͞ozēˈäləjē/ ▶*n.* the science or practice of organizing, arranging, and managing museums. **—mu·se·o·log·i·cal** /-zēəˈläjikəl/ *adj.* **—mu·se·ol·o·gist** /-jist/ *n.*

mu·sette /myo͞oˈzet/ ▶*n.* **1** a kind of small bagpipe played with bellows, common in the French court in the 17th–18th centuries and in later folk music. ■ a tune or piece of music imitating the sound of this, typically with a drone. ■ a dance to such a tune, esp. in the 18th-century French court. ■ a small simple variety of oboe, used chiefly in 19th-century France. **2** (also **musette bag**) a small knapsack. ▷late Middle English: from Old French, diminutive of *muse* 'bagpipe.'

mu·se·um /myo͞oˈzēəm/ ▶*n.* a building in which objects of historical, scientific, artistic, or cultural interest are stored and exhibited. ▷early 17th cent. (denoting a university building, specifically one erected at Alexandria by Ptolemy Soter): via Latin from Greek *mouseion* 'seat of the Muses,' based on *mousa* 'muse.'

mu·se·um piece ▶*n.* an object that is worthy of display in a museum. ■ a person or object regarded as old-fashioned, irrelevant, or useless: *we're nothing but museum pieces—machines can do everything that we can do.*

Mu·se·ve·ni /ˌmo͞osəˈvānē/, Yoweri (Kaguta) (1944–), Ugandan statesman; president 1986– . After ousting Milton Obote, he brought some stability to a country that had suffered under the dictatorial Obote and Idi Amin.

mush[1] /məsH/ ▶*n.* **1** a soft, wet, pulpy mass: *she trudged through the mush of fallen leaves.* ■ *figurative* feeble or cloying sentimentality: *the film's not just romantic mush.* **2** thick porridge, esp. made of cornmeal. **3** *Brit., informal* a person's mouth or face.

▶*v.* [*trans.*] [usu. as *adj.*] (**mushed**) reduce (a substance) to a soft, wet, pulpy mass: *simmer until the apples and potatoes are tender but not mushed.* ▷late 17th cent. (sense 2): apparently a variant of **MASH**.

mush[2] ▶*v.* [*intrans.*] go on a journey across snow with a dogsled: *by the end of winter he will have snowshoed up to 700 miles and mushed about the same.* ■ [*trans.*] urge on (the dogs) during such a journey.

▶*exclam.* a command urging on dogs during such a journey.

▶*n.* a journey across snow with a dogsled: *a twelve-day mush.* ▷mid 19th cent.: probably an alteration of French *marchez!* or *marchons!*, imperatives of *marcher* 'to advance.'

Mu·shar·raf /mo͞oˈsHärəf/, Pervez (1943–), Pakistani general and statesman; president of Pakistan from 2001. He became head of state in 1999 following a bloodless coup d'état.

mush·er /ˈməsHər/ ▶*n.* the driver of a dogsled.

Mu·shin /ˈmo͞osHin/ an industrial city in southwestern Nigeria, northeast of Lagos; pop. 294,000.

mush·rat /ˈməsHˌrat/ ▶*n.* another term for **MUSKRAT**.

mush·room /ˈməsHˌro͞om; -ˌro͝om/ ▶*n.* a fungal growth that typically takes the form of a domed cap on a stalk, often with gills on the underside of the cap.

Mushrooms are fruiting bodies that produce spores, growing from the hyphae of fungi concealed in soil or wood. They are proverbial for rapid growth. Toadstools are often called mushrooms, esp. when they are considered to be edible. Numerous varieties are poisonous.

■ a thing resembling a mushroom in shape: *a mushroom of smoke and flames.* ■ a pale pinkish-brown color: [as *adj.*] *a mushroom leather bag.* ■ *figurative* a person or thing that appears or develops suddenly or is ephemeral: *he was one of those showbiz mushrooms who spring up overnight.*

▶*v.* [*intrans.*] **1** increase, spread, or develop rapidly: *environmental concern mushroomed in the 1960s.* **2** (of the smoke, fire, or flames produced by an explosion) spread into the air in a shape resembling that of a mushroom: *the grenade mushroomed into red fire as it hit the hillside.* ■ (of a bullet) expand and flatten on reaching its target. **3** [usu. as *n.*] (**mushrooming**) (of a person) gather mushrooms. ▷late Middle English (originally denoting any fungus having a fleshy fruiting body): from Old French *mousseron*, from late Latin *mussirio(n-)*. **—mush·room·y** *adj.*

mush·room an·chor ▶*n.* an anchor whose shape resembles that of a mushroom.

mush·room cloud ▶*n.* a mushroom-shaped cloud of dust and debris formed after a nuclear explosion.

mush·y /ˈməsHē/ ▶*adj.* (**mush·i·er**, **mush·i·est**) soft and pulpy: *cook until the fruit is mushy | mushy vegetables.* ■ (of a motor vehicle's brakes) lacking firmness; spongy. ■ *figurative* excessively sentimental: *he gets as mushy as a Hallmark valentine.* See note at **SENTIMENTAL**. **—mush·i·ly** /ˈməsHəlē/ *adv.* **—mush·i·ness** *n.*

Mu·si·al /ˈmyo͞ozēəl/, Stan (1920–), U.S. baseball player; full name *Stanley Frank Musial*; known as **Stan the Man**. A first baseman and an outfielder, he played for the St. Louis Cardinals 1941–63 and led the National League in batting seven times. Baseball Hall of Fame (1969).

mu·sic /ˈmyo͞ozik/ ▶*n.* **1** the art or science of combining vocal or instrumental sounds (or both) to produce beauty of form, harmony, and expression of emotion: *he devoted his life to music.* ■ the vocal or instrumental sound produced in this way: *couples were dancing to the music | baroque music.* ■ a sound perceived as pleasingly harmonious: *the background music of softly lapping water.* **2** the written or printed signs representing such sound: *Tony learned to **read music**.* ■ the score or scores of a musical composition or compositions: *the music was open on a stand.* ▷Middle English: from Old French *musique*, via Latin from Greek *mousikē (tekhnē)* '(art) of the Muses,' from *mousa* 'muse.'

▶*PHRASES* □ **face the music** see **FACE**. □ **music of the spheres** see **SPHERE**. □ **music to one's ears** something that is pleasant or gratifying to hear or discover: *the commission's report was music to the ears of the administration.*

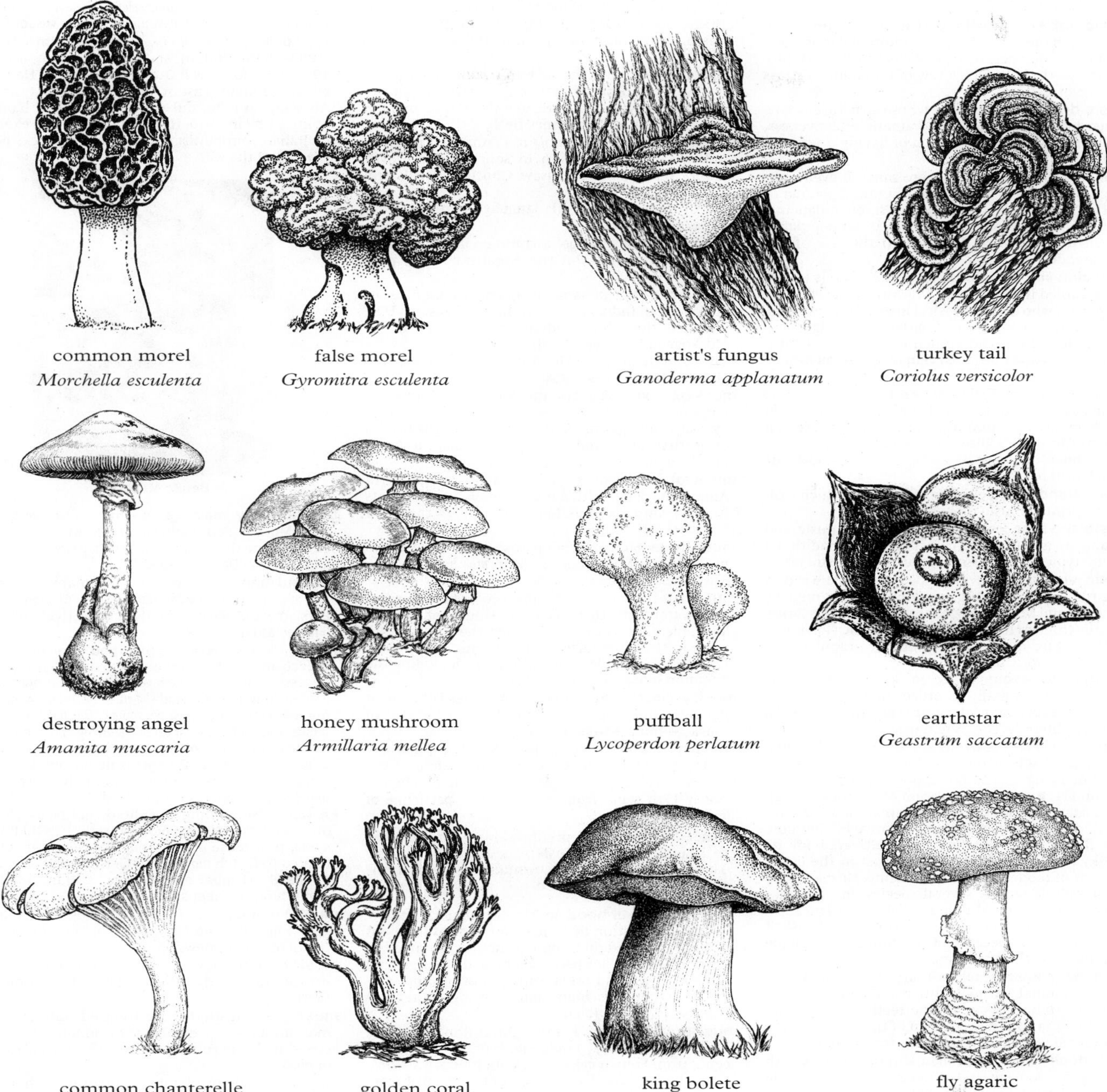

mushrooms and related fungi

mu·si·ca fic·ta /ˈmyo͞ozikə ˈfiktə/ ▸*n. Music* (in early contrapuntal music) the introduction by a performer of sharps, flats, or other accidentals to avoid unacceptable intervals. ▷early 19th cent.: Latin, literally 'feigned music.'

mu·si·cal /ˈmyo͞ozikəl/ ▸*adj.* **1** of or relating to music: *they shared similar musical tastes.* ■ set to or accompanied by music: *an evening of musical entertainment.* ■ fond of or skilled in music: *Henry was very musical, but his wife was tone-deaf.* **2** having a pleasant sound; melodious; tuneful: *they burst out into rich, musical laughter.*
▸*n.* a play or movie in which singing and dancing play an essential part. Musicals developed from light opera in the early 20th century. ▷late Middle English: from Old French, from medieval Latin *musicalis*, from Latin *musica* (see MUSIC). —**mu·si·cal·ly** /-ik(ə)lē/ *adv.*

mu·si·cal chairs ▸*n.* a party game in which players compete for a decreasing number of chairs, the losers in successive rounds being those unable to find a chair to sit on when the accompanying music is abruptly stopped. ■ a series of changes or exchanges of position, esp. in a political or commercial organization: *the appointment of the chief executive comes after a prolonged period of musical chairs involving top management.*

mu·si·cal com·e·dy ▸*n.* a light play or movie with songs, dialogue, and dancing, connected by a plot.

mu·si·cal di·rec·tor ▸*n.* the person responsible for the musical aspects of a performance, production, or organization, typically the conductor or leader of a music group: *in 1991 the New York Philharmonic hired a new musical director.*

mu·si·cale /ˌmyo͞oziˈkal/ ▸*n.* a musical gathering or concert, typically small and informal. ▷late 19th cent.: French, from *soirée musicale* 'evening of music.'

mu·si·cal glass·es ▸*plural n.* a series of drinking glasses or bowls filled with varying amounts of water and played as a musical instrument by rubbing the rims with the fingers. See also GLASS HARMONICA.

mu·si·cal in·stru·ment ▸*n.* see INSTRUMENT (sense 3).

mu·si·cal·i·ty /ˌmyo͞oziˈkalətē/ ▸*n.* tastefulness and accomplishment in music: *she sings with unfailing musicality.* ■ the quality of being melodious and tuneful: *his speaking voice hinted at musicality.* ■ awareness of music and rhythm, esp. in dance: *the audition panel was looking for coordination, musicality, and flexibility.*

mu·si·cal·ize /ˈmyo͞ozikəˌlīz/ ▸*v.* [*trans.*] set (a text or play) to music: *a problem inherent in any attempt to musicalize science fiction.*

mu·si·cal saw ▸*n.* a saw used as a musical instrument, typically held between the knees and played

Pronunciation Key ə *ago*; ər *over*; ˈə *or* ˌə *up*; ˈər *or* ˌər *fur*; a *hat*; ā *rate*; ä *car*; CH *chew*; e *let*; ē *see*; e(ə)r *air*; i *fit*; ī *by*; i(ə)r *ear*; NG *sing*; ō *go*; ô *for*; oi *boy*; o͝o *good*; o͞o *goo*; ou *out*; SH *she*; TH *thin*; T͟H *then*; (h)w *why*; ZH *vision*

with a bow like a cello, the note varying with the degree of bending of the blade.

mu·sic box ▸*n.* a small box that plays a tune, typically when the lid is opened. A traditional music box contains a cylinder, turned by clockwork, with projecting teeth that pluck a row of tuned metal strips as it revolves.

mu·sic dra·ma ▸*n.* an opera whose structure is governed by considerations of dramatic effectiveness, rather than by the convention of having a series of formal arias.

mu·sic hall ▸*n.* a theater where musical events are staged. ■ a form of variety entertainment popular in Britain from *c.*1850, consisting of singing, dancing, comedy, acrobatics, and novelty acts. Its popularity declined after World War I with the rise of the movie industry.

mu·si·cian /myo͞oˈzisHən/ ▸*n.* a person who is talented or skilled in music: *your father was a fine musician.* ■ a person who plays a musical instrument, esp. professionally: *aspiring rock and pop musicians.* ▷late Middle English: from Old French *musicien,* from Latin *musica* (see MUSIC). **—mu·si·cian·ly** *adj.* **—mu·si·cian·ship** /-ˌSHip/ *n.*

mu·si·col·o·gy /ˌmyo͞oziˈkäləjē/ ▸*n.* the study of music as an academic subject, as distinct from training in performance or composition; scholarly research into music. ▷early 20th cent.: from French *musicologie.* **—mu·si·co·log·i·cal** /-kəˈläjikəl/ *adj.* **—mu·si·col·o·gist** /-jist/ *n.*

mu·sic stand ▸*n.* a rack or light frame on which written or printed music is supported.

mu·sic the·a·ter ▸*n.* a combination of music and drama in modern form distinct from traditional opera, typically for a small group of performers.

mu·sic vid·e·o ▸*n.* a videotaped performance of a recorded popular song, usually accompanied by dancing and visual images interpreting the lyrics. Usually three to five minutes long, music videos typically feature quick cuts, computer graphics, and fanciful or erotic imagery.

mu·sique con·crète /m(y)o͞oˈzēk kôNˈkret/ ▸*n.* music constructed by mixing recorded sounds, first developed by experimental composers in the 1940s. ▷French, literally 'concrete music.'

musk /məsk/ ▸*n.* **1** a strong-smelling reddish-brown substance that is secreted by the male musk deer for scent-marking and is an important ingredient in perfumery. ■ a similar secretion of another animal: *civets habitually deposit tiny amounts of musk.* **2** (also **musk plant** or **musk flower**) a relative of the monkey flower that was formerly cultivated for its musky perfume, which has been lost in the development of modern varieties. • Genus *Mimulus,* family Scrophulariaceae: several species, in particular *M. moschatus.* ▷late Middle English: from late Latin *muscus,* from Persian *mušk,* perhaps from Sanskrit *muṣka* 'scrotum' (because of the similarity in shape of a musk deer's musk bag).

musk deer ▸*n.* a small solitary deerlike eastern Asian mammal without antlers, the male having long protruding upper canine teeth. Musk is produced in a sac on the abdomen of the male. • Family Moschidae and genus *Moschus*: several species.

musk duck ▸*n.* an Australian stiff-tailed duck with dark gray plumage and a musky smell, the male having a large black lobe of skin hanging below the bill. • *Biziura lobata,* family Anatidae.

mus·keg /ˈməsˌkeg/ ▸*n.* a North American swamp or bog consisting of a mixture of water and partly dead vegetation, frequently covered by a layer of sphagnum or other mosses. ▷early 19th cent.: from Cree.

Mus·ke·gon /məsˈkēgən/ an industrial port in western Michigan, on Lake Michigan; pop. 40,283.

mus·kel·lunge /ˈməskəˌlənj/ ▸*n.* a large pike that occurs only in the Great Lakes region. Also called MASKINONGE or MUSKIE. • *Esox masquinongy,* family Esocidae. ▷late 18th cent.: from Canadian French *maskinongé,* from Ojibwa *māskinōšē.*

mus·ket /ˈməskit/ ▸*n. historical* an infantryman's light gun with a long barrel, typically smooth-bored, muzzleloading, and fired from the shoulder. ▷late 16th cent.: from French *mousquet,* from Italian *moschetto* 'crossbow bolt,' from *mosca* 'a fly.'

mus·ket·eer /ˌməskəˈtir/ ▸*n. historical* a soldier armed with a musket.

mus·ket·ry /ˈməskətrē/ ▸*n.* musket fire: *a terrible explosion of musketry.* ■ soldiers armed with muskets: *the Prussian musketry.* ■ the art or technique of handling a musket.

Mus·kie /ˈməskē/, Edmund (Sixtus) (1914–96), U.S. lawyer and politician. He served as governor of Maine 1955–59, as a member of the U.S. Senate 1959–80, and as U.S. secretary of state 1980–81. He was a Democratic vice presidential candidate in 1968.

musk·mel·on /ˈməskˌmelən/ ▸*n.* an edible melon of a type that has a raised network of markings on the skin. Its many varieties include those with orange, yellow, green, or white juicy flesh.

Mus·ko·ge·an /məˈskōgēən/ ▸*n.* a family of American Indian languages spoken in southeastern North America, including Chikasaw, Choctaw, Creek, and Seminole.
▸*adj.* of or relating to this language family. ▷from MUSKOGEE + -AN.

Mus·ko·gee[1] /ˌməˈskōgē/ a commercial city in east central Oklahoma, on the Arkansas River; pop. 38,310.

Mus·ko·gee[2] ▸*n.* (*pl.* same or **-gees**) **1** a member of an American Indian people of the southeastern U.S., who led the Creek Indian confederacy. **2** the Muskogean language of this people.
▸*adj.* of or relating to the Muskogees or their language. ▷from Creek *ma:skó:ki.*

musk·ox /ˈməskˌäks/ (also **musk ox**) ▸*n.* (*pl.* **-ox·en**) a large heavily built goat-antelope with a thick shaggy coat and large curved horns, native to the tundra of North America and Greenland. • *Ovibos moschatus,* family Bovidae.

musk·rat /ˈməˌskrat/ ▸*n.* a large semiaquatic North American rodent with a musky smell, valued for its fur. • *Ondatra zibethicus,* family Muridae. ■ the fur of the muskrat.

musk rose ▸*n.* a rambling rose with large white musk-scented flowers. • *Rosa moschata,* family Rosaceae.

musk tur·tle ▸*n.* a small drab-colored American freshwater turtle that has scent glands that produce an unpleasant musky odor when the turtle is disturbed. Also called STINKPOT. • Genus *Sternotherus,* family Kinosternidae: several species, including the **common musk turtle** (*S. odoratus*).

musk·y /ˈməskē/ ▸*adj.* (**musk·i·er**, **musk·i·est**) of or having a smell or taste of musk, or suggestive of musk. **—musk·i·ness** *n.*

Mus·lim /ˈməzləm; ˈmo͝oz-/ (also **Mos·lem** /ˈmäzləm; ˈmäs-/) ▸*n.* a follower of the religion of Islam.
▸*adj.* of or relating to the Muslims or their religion. ▷early 17th cent.: from Arabic, active participle of *'aslama* (see ISLAM).

USAGE **Muslim** is the preferred term for 'follower of Islam,' although **Moslem** is also widely used. The archaic term **Muhammadan** (or **Mohammedan**) should be avoided.

Mus·lim Broth·er·hood an Islamic religious and political organization dedicated to the establishment of a nation based on Islamic principles. Founded in Egypt in 1928, it has become a radical underground force in Egypt and other Sunni countries, promoting strict moral discipline and opposing Western influence, often by violence.

mus·lin /ˈməzlən/ ▸*n.* lightweight cotton cloth in a plain weave: [as *adj.*] *a white muslin dress.* ▷early 17th cent.: from French *mousseline,* from Italian *mussolina,* from *Mussolo* 'Mosul' (the name of the place of manufacture in Iraq). **—mus·lined** /ˈməzlənd/ *adj.*

Mus.M. ▸*abbr.* Master of Music. ▷from modern Latin *Mūsicae Magister.*

mu·so /ˈmyo͞ozō/ ▸*n.* (*pl.* **-sos**) *Brit., informal* a musician, esp. one overly concerned with technique. ■ an avid music fan, esp. one who has expensive stereo equipment. ▷1960s: abbreviation.

mus·quash /ˈməˌskwäsH; ˈməˌskwôsH/ ▸*n.* archaic term for MUSKRAT. ■ *Brit.* the fur of the muskrat. ▷early 17th cent.: from Abnaki *mòskwas.*

muss /məs/ *informal* ▸*v.* [*trans.*] make (someone's hair or clothes) untidy or messy: *she sat down carefully so she wouldn't muss her clothes.*
▸*n.* [usu. in *sing.*] a state of disorder. ▷mid 19th cent. (also as a noun in the sense 'disturbance or row'): apparently a variant of MESS. **—muss·y** /ˈməsē/ *adj.* (*dated*).

mus·sel /ˈməsəl/ ▸*n.* any of a number of bivalve mollusks with a brown or purplish-black shell: • a marine bivalve that uses byssus threads to anchor to a firm surface (family Mytilidae, order Mytiloidea), including the **edible mussel** (*Mytilus edulis*). • a freshwater bivalve that typically lies on the bed of a river, some species forming small pearls (family Unionidae, order Unionoida). ▷Old English *mus(c)le,* superseded by forms from Middle Low German *mussel,* Middle Dutch *mosscele*; ultimately from late Latin *muscula,* from Latin *musculus* (see MUSCLE).

Mus·so·li·ni /ˌmo͞osəˈlēnē/, Benito (Amilcaro Andrea) (1883–1945), Italian statesman; prime minister 1922–43; known as **Il Duce** ('the leader'). He founded the Italian Fascist Party in 1919, annexed Abyssinia in 1936, and entered World War II on Germany's side in 1940. He was captured and executed by Italian communist partisans a few weeks before the end of the war.

Benito Mussolini

Mus·sorg·sky /məˈsôrgskē; -ˈzôrg-/ (also **Mous·sorg·sky**), Modest (Petrovich) (1839–81), Russian composer. He wrote the opera *Boris Godunov* (1874) and *Songs and Dances of Death* (1875–77).

Mus·sul·man /ˈməsəlmən/ ▸*n.* (*pl.* **-mans** or **-men**) & *adj.* archaic term for MUSLIM. ▷late 16th cent.: from Persian *musulmān* (originally an adjective), from *muslim* (see MUSLIM).

must[1] /məst/ ▸*modal verb* (*past* **had to** or in reported speech **must**) **1** be obliged to; should (expressing necessity): *you must show your ID card | it must not be over 2,000 words | she said she must be going.* ■ expressing insistence: *you must try some of this fish | if you must smoke, you could at least go in the living room.* ■ used in ironic questions expressing irritation: *must you look so utterly suburban?* **2** expressing an opinion about something that is logically very likely: *there must be something wrong | you must be tired.*
▸*n. informal* something that should not be overlooked or missed: *this video is a must for parents.* ▷Old English *mōste,* past tense of *mōt* 'may,' of Germanic origin; related to Dutch *moeten* and German *müssen.*
▸*PHRASES* □ **I must say** see SAY. □ **must needs do something** see NEEDS.

must[2] ▸*n.* grape juice before or during fermentation. ▷Old English, from Latin *mustum,* neuter (used as a noun) of *mustus* 'new.'

must[3] ▸*n.* mustiness, dampness, or mold: *a pervasive smell of must.* ▷early 17th cent.: back-formation from MUSTY.

must[4] (also **musth**) ▸*n.* the frenzied state of certain male animals, esp. elephants or camels, that is associated with the rutting season: *a big old bull elephant in must.*
▸*adj.* (of a male elephant or camel) in such a state. ▷late 19th cent.: via Urdu from Persian *mast* 'intoxicated.'

mus·tache /ˈməsˌtasH; məˈstasH/ (also **mous·tache**) ▸*n.* a strip of hair left to grow above the upper lip. ■ (**mustaches**) a long mustache. ■ a similar growth, or a marking that resembles it, around the mouth of some animals. ▷late 16th cent.: from French, from Italian *mostaccio,* from Greek *mustax, mustak-.* **—mus·tached** *adj.*

mus·tache cup ▸*n.* a cup with a partial cover that protects the mustache of the person drinking from it.

mus·ta·chios /məˈstasHēˌōz/ ▸*plural n.* a long or elaborate mustache. ▷mid 16th cent.: from Spanish *mostacho* (singular), from Italian *mostaccio* (see MUSTACHE). **—mus·ta·chioed** /-ˌōd/ *adj.*

mus·tang /ˈməsˌtaNG/ ▸*n.* an American feral horse, typically small and lightly built. ▷early 19th cent.: from a blend of Spanish *mestengo* (from *mesta* 'company of graziers') and *mostrenco,* both meaning 'wild or masterless cattle.'

mus·tard /ˈməstərd/ ▸*n.* **1** a pungent-tasting yellow or brown paste made from the crushed seeds of certain plants, typically eaten with meat or used as a cooking ingredient. **2** the yellow-flowered Eurasian

M

plant of the cabbage family whose seeds are used to make this paste. • Genera *Brassica* and *Sinapis*, family Brassicaceae: several species, in particular **black mustard** (*B. nigra*) and **white mustard** (*S. alba*). ■ used in names of related plants, only some of which are used to produce mustard for the table, e.g., **hedge mustard. 3** a dark yellow color. ▷Middle English: from Old French *moustarde*, from Latin *mustum* 'must' (the condiment being originally prepared with 'must'). **—mus·tard·y** *adj.*

▸*PHRASE* □ **cut the mustard** see CUT.

mus·tard gas ▸*n.* a colorless oily liquid whose vapor is a powerful irritant and vesicant, used in chemical weapons. • Chem. formula: $(ClCH_2CH_2)_2S$.

mus·tard greens ▸*plural n.* the leaves of the mustard plant used in salads.

mus·tard plas·ter ▸*n.* a poultice made with mustard.

mus·te·lid /ˈməstəlid/ ▸*n. Zoology* a mammal of the weasel family (Mustelidae), distinguished by having a long body, short legs, and musky scent glands under the tail. ▷early 20th cent.: from modern Latin *Mustelidae* (plural), from Latin *mustela* 'weasel.'

mus·ter /ˈməstər/ ▸*v.* [*trans.*] **1** assemble (troops), esp. for inspection or in preparation for battle. ■ [*intrans.*] (of troops) come together in this way: *the cavalrymen mustered beside the other regiments.* ■ [*intrans.*] (of a group of people) gather together: *reporters mustered outside her house.* **2** collect or assemble (a number or amount): *he could fail to muster a majority.* ■ summon up (a particular feeling, attitude, or response): *he replied with as much dignity as he could muster.* See note at GATHER.

▸*phrasal v.* □ **muster someone in** (or **out**) enroll someone into (or discharge someone from) military service.

▸*n.* a formal gathering of troops, esp. for inspection, display, or exercise. ■ short for MUSTER ROLL. ▷late Middle English: from Old French *moustrer* (verb), *moustre* (noun), from Latin *monstrare* 'to show.'

▸*PHRASE* □ **pass muster** be accepted as adequate or satisfactory: *a treaty that might pass muster with the voters.*

mus·ter roll ▸*n.* an official list of officers and men in a military unit or ship's company.

musth /ˈməst/ ▸*n.* variant spelling of MUST[4].

must-have ▸*adj.* essential or highly desirable: *the must-have blouse of the season.*

▸*n.* an essential or highly desirable item: *this season's must-have is an ostrich bowling bag.*

must·n't /ˈməsənt/ ▸*contraction of* must not.

must-read /rēd/ ▸*n. informal* a piece of writing that should or must be read: *it's a must-read for anyone interested in the geologic history recorded in the landscape.*

must-see ▸*n. informal* something that should or must be seen, esp. a remarkable sight or entertainment: *this sassy and superior suspense thriller is a must-see.*

mus·ty /ˈməstē/ ▸*adj.* (**mus·ti·er, mus·ti·est**) having a stale, moldy, or damp smell: *a dark musty library filled with old books.* ■ having a stale taste: *the beer tasted sour, thin, and musty.* ■ *figurative* lacking originality or interest: *when I read it again, the play seemed musty.* ▷early 16th cent.: perhaps an alteration of *moisty* 'moist,' influenced by MUST[2]. **—mus·ti·ly** /-təlē/ *adv.* **—mus·ti·ness** *n.*

Mut /mo͞ot/ *Egyptian Mythology* a goddess who was the wife of Amun and mother of Khonsu.

mu·ta·ble /ˈmyo͞otəbəl/ ▸*adj.* liable to change: *the mutable nature of fashion.* ■ *poetic/literary* inconstant in one's affections: *youth is said to be fickle and mutable.* ▷late Middle English: from Latin *mutabilis*, from *mutare* 'to change.' **—mu·ta·bil·i·ty** /ˌmyo͞otəˈbilətē/ *n.*

mu·ta·gen /ˈmyo͞otəjən/ ▸*n.* an agent, such as radiation or a chemical substance, that causes genetic mutation. ▷1940s: from MUTATION + -GEN. **—mu·ta·gen·e·sis** /ˌmyo͞otəˈjenəsəs/ *n.* **—mu·ta·gen·ic** /ˌmyo͞otəˈjenik/ *adj.*

mu·ta·gen·ize /ˈmyo͞otəjəˌnīz/ ▸*v.* [*trans.*] [usu. as *adj.*] (**mutagenized**) *Biology* treat (a cell, organism, etc.) with mutagenic agents: *mutagenized DNA.*

mu·tant /ˈmyo͞otnt/ ▸*adj.* resulting from or showing the effect of mutation: *a mutant gene.*

▸*n.* a mutant form. ▷early 20th cent.: from Latin *mutant-* 'changing,' from the verb *mutare.*

Mu·ta·re /mo͞oˈtärā/ an industrial town in the eastern highlands of Zimbabwe; pop. 70,000. Former name (until 1982) **UMTALI.**

mu·tate /ˈmyo͞oˌtāt/ ▸*v.* change or cause to change in form or nature: [*intrans.*] *technology continues to mutate at an alarming rate* | [*trans.*] *the quick-dry solution really worked, even if it did mutate the skin on her fingers to reptilian scales.* ■ *Biology* (with reference to a cell, DNA molecule, etc.) undergo or cause to undergo change in a gene or genes: [*intrans.*] *the virus is able to* **mutate into** *new forms that are immune to the vaccine* | [*trans.*] *certain nucleotides were mutated.* ▷early 19th cent.: back-formation from MUTATION. **—mu·ta·tor** /-ˌtātər/ *n.*

mu·ta·tion /myo͞oˈtāshən/ ▸*n.* **1** the action or process of mutating: *the mutation of ethnic politics into nationalist politics* | *his first novel went through several mutations.* **2** the changing of the structure of a gene, resulting in a variant form that may be transmitted to subsequent generations, caused by the alteration of single base units in DNA, or the deletion, insertion, or rearrangement of larger sections of genes or chromosomes. ■ a distinct form resulting from such a change. **3** *Linguistics* regular change of a sound when it occurs adjacent to another, in particular: ■ (in Germanic languages) the process by which the quality of a vowel was altered in certain phonetic contexts; umlaut. ■ (in Celtic languages) change of an initial consonant in a word caused (historically) by the preceding word. See also LENITION. ▷late Middle English: from Latin *mutatio(n-)*, from *mutare* 'to change.' **—mu·ta·tion·al** /-shənl/ *adj.* **—mu·ta·tion·al·ly** /-shənl-ē/ *adv.* **—mu·ta·tive** /ˈmyo͞otətiv/ *adj.*

mu·ta·tis mu·tan·dis /m(y)o͞oˈtätəs m(y)o͞oˈtändəs; -ˈtātəs; -ˈtandəs/ ▸*adv.* (used when comparing two or more cases or situations) making necessary alterations while not affecting the main point at issue: *what is true of undergraduate teaching in England is equally true, mutatis mutandis, of American graduate schools.* ▷Latin, literally 'things being changed that have to be changed.'

mutch·kin /ˈməchkin/ ▸*n.* a Scottish unit of capacity equal to a little less than a pint, or roughly three quarters of an imperial pint (0.43 liters). ▷late Middle English: from early modern Dutch *mudsekin*, diminutive of *mud* 'hectoliter.'

mute /myo͞ot/ ▸*adj.* **1** refraining from speech or temporarily speechless: *Irene, the talkative one, was now mute.* ■ not expressed in speech: *she gazed at him in mute appeal.* ■ characterized by an absence of sound; quiet: *the great church was mute and dark.* ■ *dated, chiefly offensive* (of a person) without the power of speech. **2** (of a letter) not pronounced: *mute e is generally dropped before suffixes beginning with a vowel.*

▸*n.* **1** *date, usu. offensive* a person without the power of speech. ■ *historical* (in some Asian countries) a servant who was deprived of the power of speech. ■ *historical* an actor in a dumbshow. ■ *historical* a professional attendant or mourner at a funeral. **2** a device that softens the sound (and typically alters the tone) of a musical instrument, in particular: ■ a clamp placed over the bridge of a stringed instrument to deaden the resonance without affecting the vibration of the strings. ■ a pad or cone placed in the opening of a brass or other wind instrument. **3** a device on a television, telephone, or other appliance that temporarily turns off the sound: *she put the remote on mute.*

▸*v.* [*trans.*] **1** (often **be muted**) deaden, muffle, or soften the sound of: *her footsteps were muted by the thick carpet.* ■ muffle the sound of (a musical instrument), esp. by the use of a mute. ■ *figurative* reduce the strength or intensity of: *his professional contentment was muted by personal sadness.* **2** turn off (the sound on a television, telephone, or other appliance) by activating the mute: *he turns the set on, mutes the sound, but flicks through the channels.* ▷Middle English: from Old French *muet*, diminutive of *mu*, from Latin *mutus.* **—mute·ly** *adv.* **—mute·ness** *n.*

USAGE To describe a person without the power of speech as **mute** (esp. as in **deaf-mute**) is today likely to cause offense. Nevertheless, there are no accepted alternative terms in general use, aside from the possibly imprecise euphemism *speech-impaired.* See also **usage** at DEAF-MUTE.

mute but·ton ▸*n.* a button that can be pressed to temporarily halt the sound on a television, telephone, remote, or other apparatus.

mut·ed /ˈmyo͞otid/ ▸*adj.* (of a sound or voice) quiet and soft: *they discussed the accident in muted voices.* ■ (of a musical instrument) having a muffled sound as a result of being fitted with a mute. ■ *figurative* not expressed strongly or openly: *muted anger.* ■ (of color or lighting) not bright; subdued: *a dress in muted tones of powder blue and dusty pink.*

mute swan ▸*n.* the most common Eurasian swan, having white plumage and an orange-red bill with a black knob at the base. Introduced to the northeastern U.S., its range is expanding along the Atlantic coast and the Great Lakes region. • *Cygnus olor*, family Anatidae.

muth·a /ˈmət͟hə/ ▸*n.* variant spelling of MOTHER (esp. sense 2).

mu·ti·late /ˈmyo͞otlˌāt/ ▸*v.* [*trans.*] (usu. **be mutilated**) inflict a violent and disfiguring injury on: *the leg was badly mutilated* | [as *adj.*] (**mutilated**) *mutilated bodies.* ■ inflict serious damage on: *the 14th-century church had been partly mutilated in the 18th century.* ▷early 16th cent.: from Latin *mutilat-* 'maimed, mutilated, lopped off,' from the verb *mutilare*, from *mutilus* 'maimed.' **—mu·ti·la·tion** /ˌmyo͞otlˈāshən/ *n.* **—mu·ti·la·tor** /-ˌātər/ *n.*

mu·ti·neer /ˌmyo͞otnˈi(ə)r/ ▸*n.* a person, esp. a soldier or sailor, who rebels or refuses to obey the orders of a person in authority. ▷early 17th cent.: from French *mutinier*, from *mutin* 'rebellious,' from *muete* 'movement,' based on Latin *movere* 'to move.'

mu·ti·nous /ˈmyo͞otn-əs/ ▸*adj.* (of a soldier or sailor) refusing to obey the orders of a person in authority. ■ willful or disobedient: *Antoinette looked mutinous, but she obeyed.* ▷late 16th cent.: from obsolete *mutine* 'rebellion' (see MUTINY) + -OUS. **—mu·ti·nous·ly** *adv.*

mu·ti·ny /ˈmyo͞otn-ē/ ▸*n.* (*pl.* **-nies**) an open rebellion against the proper authorities, esp. by soldiers or sailors against their officers: *a mutiny by those manning the weapons could trigger a global war* | *mutiny at sea.* See note at UPRISING.

▸*v.* (**-nies, -nied**) [*intrans.*] refuse to obey the orders of a person in authority. ▷mid 16th cent.: from obsolete *mutine* 'rebellion,' from French *mutin* 'mutineer,' based on Latin *movere* 'to move.'

mut·ism /ˈmyo͞otˌizəm/ ▸*n.* inability to speak, typically as a result of congenital deafness or brain damage. ■ (in full **elective mutism**) unwillingness or refusal to speak, arising from psychological causes such as depression or trauma. ▷early 19th cent.: from French *mutisme*, from Latin *mutus* 'mute.'

mu·ton /ˈmyo͞oˌtän; ˈmyo͞otn/ ▸*n. Biology* the smallest element of genetic material capable of undergoing a distinct mutation, usually identified as a single pair of nucleotides.

Mu·tsu·hi·to /ˌmo͞otso͞oˈhētō/ see MEIJI TENNO.

mutt /mət/ ▸*n. informal* **1** *humorous* or *derogatory* a dog, esp. a mongrel: *a long-haired mutt of doubtful pedigree.* **2** a person regarded as stupid or incompetent: *"Do not give me orders, mutt."* ▷late 19th cent.: abbreviation of MUTTONHEAD.

mut·ter /ˈmətər/ ▸*v.* [*reporting verb*] say something in a low or barely audible voice, esp. in dissatisfaction or irritation: [*trans.*] *he muttered something under his breath* | [with *direct speech*] *"I knew she was a troublemaker," Rebecca muttered* | [*intrans.*] *she muttered in annoyance as the keys slid from her fingers.* ■ [*intrans.*] speak privately or unofficially about someone or something; spread rumors: *when he disappeared, people began to mutter.*

▸*n.* a barely audible utterance, esp. a dissatisfied or irritated one: *a little mutter of disgust.* ▷late Middle English: imitative; compare with German dialect *muttern.* **—mut·ter·er** *n.* **—mut·ter·ing·ly** *adv.*

mut·ton /ˈmətn/ ▸*n.* the flesh of sheep, esp. mature sheep, used as food: *roast mutton.* ▷Middle English: from Old French *moton*, from medieval Latin *multo(n-)*, probably of Celtic origin; compare with Scottish Gaelic *mult*, Welsh *mollt*, and Breton *maout.* **—mut·ton·y** *adj.*

mut·ton·chops /ˈmətnˌchäps/ (also **mut·ton·chop whis·kers**) ▸*n.* the whiskers on a man's cheek when shaped like a meat chop, narrow at the top and broad and rounded at the bottom.

muttonchops

mute swan

Pronunciation Key ə ago; ər over; ˈə or ˌə up; ˈər or ˌər fur; a hat; ā rate; ä car; ch chew; e let; ē see; e(ə)r air; i fit; ī by; i(ə)r ear; ng sing; ō go; ô for; oi boy; o͝o good; o͞o goo; ou out; sh she; th thin; t͟h then; (h)w why; zh vision

M

mut·ton·head /ˈmətn,hed/ ▸*n. informal* or *dated* a dull or stupid person (often used as a general term of abuse). —**mut·ton·head·ed** *adj.*

mu·tu·al /ˈmyo͞ocho͞oəl/ ▸*adj.* **1** (of a feeling or action) experienced or done by each of two or more parties toward the other or others: *a partnership based on mutual respect and understanding | my father hated him from the start, and the feeling was mutual.* ■ (of two or more people) having the same specified relationship to each other: *they were mutual beneficiaries of the settlement.* **2** held in common by two or more parties: *we were introduced by a mutual friend.* ■ denoting an insurance company or other corporate organization owned by its members and dividing some or all of its profits between them. ▷late 15th cent.: from Old French *mutuel*, from Latin *mutuus* 'mutual, borrowed'; related to *mutare* 'to change.'

USAGE Traditionalists consider using **mutual** to mean 'common to two or more people' (*a mutual friend; a mutual interest*) to be incorrect, holding that the sense of reciprocity is necessary (*mutual respect; mutual need*). However, both senses are well established and acceptable in standard English.

mu·tu·al fund ▸*n.* an investment program funded by shareholders that trades in diversified holdings and is professionally managed.

mu·tu·al in·duct·ance ▸*n. Physics* a measure or coefficient of mutual induction, usually expressed in henries. ■ the property of a circuit that permits mutual induction.

mu·tu·al in·duc·tion ▸*n. Physics* the production of an electromotive force in a circuit by a change in the current in an adjacent circuit that is linked to the first by the flux lines of a magnetic field.

mu·tu·al in·sur·ance ▸*n.* insurance in which some or all of the profits are divided among the policyholders.

mu·tu·al·ism /ˈmyo͞ocho͞oə,lizəm/ ▸*n.* the doctrine that mutual dependence is necessary to social well-being. ■ *Biology* symbiosis that is beneficial to both organisms involved. —**mu·tu·al·ist** *n.* & *adj.* —**mu·tu·al·is·tic** /,myo͞ocho͞oəˈlistik/ *adj.* —**mu·tu·al·is·ti·cal·ly** /,myo͞ocho͞oəˈlistik(ə)lē/ *adv.*

mu·tu·al·i·ty /,myo͞ocho͞oˈalitē/ ▸*n.* mutual character, quality, or activity: *a high degree of mutuality of respect for each other's expertise.*

mu·tu·al·ize /ˈmyo͞ocho͞oə,līz/ ▸*v.* [*trans.*] organize (a company or business) on mutual principles. ■ divide (something, esp. insurance losses) between involved parties.

mu·tu·al·ly /ˈmyo͞ocho͞oəlē/ ▸*adv.* with mutual action; in a mutual relationship: [as *submodifier*] *adoption and fostering are not necessarily mutually exclusive alternatives.*

mu·tu·el /ˈmyo͞ocho͞oəl/ ▸*n.* (in betting) a pari-mutuel. ▷early 20th cent.: shortening of **PARI-MUTUEL**.

mu·tule /ˈmyo͞o,cho͞ol/ ▸*n. Architecture* a stone block projecting under a cornice in the Doric order. ▷mid 17th cent.: from French, from Latin *mutulus*.

muu·muu /ˈmo͞o,mo͞o/ ▸*n.* a woman's loose, brightly colored dress, esp. one traditionally worn in Hawaii. ▷early 20th cent.: from Hawaiian *mu'u mu'u*, literally 'cut off.'

mux /məks/ ▸*n.* a multiplexer.
▸*v.* short for **MULTIPLEX**.

Mu·zak /ˈmyo͞o,zak/ ▸*n. trademark* recorded light background music played through speakers in public places. ▷1930s: alteration of **MUSIC**.

mu·zhik /mo͞oˈzhēk; -ˈzhik/ (also **mou·jik**) ▸*n. historical* a Russian peasant. ▷Russian.

Muz·tag /mo͞osˈtäg/ a mountain in western China, on the northern Tibetan border close to the Karamiran Shankou pass. Rising to 25,338 feet (7,723 m), it is the highest peak in the Kunlun Shan range.

muzz /məz/ ▸*n. informal* a muddle or blur: *in the echoey hall, every other word is lost in the muzz.* ▷mid 18th cent. (as a verb in the sense 'study intently'): of unknown origin; based partly perhaps on an alteration of **MUSE**.

muz·zle /ˈməzəl/ ▸*n.* **1** the projecting part of the face, including the nose and mouth, of an animal such as a dog or horse. ■ a guard, typically made of straps or wire, fitted over this part of an animal's face to stop it from biting or feeding. ■ *informal* the part of a person's face including the nose, mouth, and chin. ■ *figurative* any restraint on free speech: *the muzzle the prime minister put on foreign journalists.* **2** the open end of the barrel of a firearm.
▸*v.* [*trans.*] put a muzzle on (an animal). ■ *figurative* prevent (a person or an institution, esp. the press) from expressing their opinions freely: *the politicians want to muzzle us and control what we write.* ▷late Middle English: from Old French *musel*, diminutive of medieval Latin *musum*, of unknown ultimate origin.

muz·zle·load·er /ˈməzəl,lōdər/ (also **muz·zle-load·er**) ▸*n. historical* a gun that is loaded through its muzzle. —**muz·zle·load·ing** /-,lōdiNG/ (also **muz·zle-load·ing**) *adj.*

muz·zle ve·loc·i·ty ▸*n.* the velocity with which a bullet or shell leaves the muzzle of a gun.

muz·zy /ˈməzē/ ▸*adj.* (**muz·zi·er**, **muz·zi·est**) **1** unable to think clearly; confused: *she was shivering and her head felt muzzy from sleep.* ■ not thought out clearly; vague: *society's muzzy notion of tolerance.* **2** (of a person's eyes or a visual image) blurred: *a slightly muzzy picture.* ■ (of a sound) indistinct: *the bass and drums are, even on CD, appallingly muzzy.* ▷early 18th cent.: of unknown origin. —**muz·zi·ly** /ˈməzəlē/ *adv.* —**muz·zi·ness** *n.*

MV ▸*abbr.* ■ megavolt(s). ■ motor vessel: *on board the MV Alcinous.* ■ muzzle velocity.

MVD the Ministry of Internal Affairs, the secret police of the former USSR from 1946 to 1953. ▷abbreviation of Russian *Ministerstvo vnutrennikh del.*

MVP ▸*abbr.* most valuable player (an award given in various sports to the best player on a team or in a league): *Bill Walton was named NBA MVP in 1978* | [as *adj.*] *he earned MVP honors in the All-Star Game.*

MW ▸*abbr.* ■ megawatt(s).

mW ▸*abbr.* milliwatt(s).

MX ▸*abbr.* missile experimental (a U.S. intercontinental ten-warhead ballistic missile).

Mx ▸*abbr.* maxwell(s).

mxd. ▸*abbr.* mixed.

my /mī/ ▸*possessive adj.* **1** belonging to or associated with the speaker: *my name is John | my friend.* ■ *informal* used with a name to refer to a member of the speaker's family: *my Francine won top honors in the science fair.* ■ used with forms of address in affectionate, sympathetic, humorous, or patronizing contexts: *my dear boy | my poor baby.* **2** used in various expressions of surprise: *my goodness! | oh my!* ▷Middle English *mi* (originally before words beginning with any consonant except *h*-), reduced from *min*, from Old English *mīn* (see **MINE**[1]).
▸*PHRASE* □ **My Lady** (or **Lord**) a polite form of address to certain titled people.

m.y. ▸*abbr.* million years.

my- ▸*comb. form* variant spelling of **MYO-** shortened before a vowel (as in *myalgia*).

my·al·gi·a /mīˈalj(ē)ə/ ▸*n.* pain in a muscle or group of muscles. ▷mid 19th cent.: modern Latin, from Greek *mus* 'muscle' + **-ALGIA**. —**my·al·gic** /-jik/ *adj.*

my·al·gic en·ceph·a·li·tis ▸*n.* clinical term for chronic fatigue syndrome.

My·an·mar /myänˈmär; ,mī,änˈmär/ a country in Southeast Asia, on the Bay of Bengal; pop. 42,528,000; capital, Rangoon; official language, Burmese. Official name (since 1989) **UNION OF MYANMAR**; also called **BURMA**.

Annexed by the British during the 19th century, the country was occupied by the Japanese from 1942 to 1945 and became an independent republic in 1948. In 1962, an army coup led by Ne Win overthrew the government and established an authoritarian state. The National League for Democracy (NLD) won the election held in May 1990, even though its leader Aung San Suu Kyi was under house arrest; however, the military regime did not relinquish power.

USAGE The military authorities in Burma have promoted the name Myanmar as the official name for their state since 1989; Burma is often preferred by people who oppose the current government of Myanmar. Inhabitants of the country are referred to as *Burmese*.

my·as·the·ni·a /,mīəsˈTHēnēə/ ▸*n.* a condition causing abnormal weakness of certain muscles. ■ (in full **myasthenia gravis** /ˈgravis/) a rare chronic autoimmune disease marked by muscular weakness without atrophy, and caused by a defect in the action of acetylcholine at neuromuscular junctions. ▷mid 19th cent.: modern Latin, from Greek *mus* 'muscle' + **ASTHENIA**.

my·ce·li·um /mīˈsēlēəm/ ▸*n.* (*pl.* **-li·a** /-lēə/) *Botany* the vegetative part of a fungus, consisting of a network of fine white filaments (hyphae). ▷mid 19th cent.: modern Latin, from Greek *mukēs* 'fungus,' on the pattern of *epithelium*. —**my·ce·li·al** /-lēəl/ *adj.*

My·ce·nae /mīˈsēnē/ an ancient city in Greece, situated near the coast in the northeastern Peloponnese, the center of the late Bronze Age Mycenaean civilization. The capital of King Agamemnon, it was at its most prosperous *c.*1400–1200 BC; systematic excavation of the site began in 1840.

My·ce·nae·an /mīˈsēnēən/ (also **My·ce·ne·an**) *Archaeology* ▸*adj.* of, relating to, or denoting a late Bronze Age civilization in Greece represented by finds at Mycenae and other ancient cities of Peloponnesus.
▸*n.* an inhabitant of Mycenae or member of the Mycenaean people.

The Mycenaeans controlled the Aegean after the fall of the Minoan civilization *c.*1400 BC, and built fortified citadels and impressive palaces. They spoke a form of Greek, written in a distinctive script (see **LINEAR B**), and their culture is identified with that portrayed in the Homeric poems. Their power declined during widespread upheavals at the end of the Mediterranean Bronze Age, around 1100 BC.

my·ce·to·ma /,mīsəˈtōmə/ ▸*n. Medicine* chronic inflammation of the tissues caused by infection with a fungus or with certain bacteria. ▷late 19th cent.: modern Latin, from Greek *mukēs*, *mukēt-* 'fungus' + **-OMA**.

-mycin ▸*comb. form* in names of antibiotic compounds derived from fungi: *streptomycin.* ▷based on **MYCO-**.

myco- ▸*comb. form* relating to fungi: *mycoprotein.* ▷formed irregularly from Greek *mukēs* 'fungus, mushroom.'

my·co·bac·te·ri·um /,mīkōbakˈti(ə)rēəm/ ▸*n.* (*pl.* **-te·ri·a** /-ˈti(ə)rēə/) a bacterium of a group that includes the causative agents of leprosy and tuberculosis. • Genus *Mycobacterium*, family Mycobacteriaceae. —**my·co·bac·te·ri·al** /-ˈti(ə)rēəl/ *adj.*

mycol. ▸*abbr.* ■ mycological or mycology.

my·col·o·gy /mīˈkäləjē/ ▸*n.* the scientific study of fungi. —**my·co·log·i·cal** /,mīkəˈläjikəl/ *adj.* —**my·co·log·i·cal·ly** /,mīkəˈläjik(ə)lē/ *adv.* —**my·col·o·gist** /-jist/ *n.*

my·co·plas·ma /,mīkōˈplazmə/ ▸*n.* (*pl.* **-mas** or **-ma·ta** /-mətə/) any of a group of small typically parasitic bacteria that lack cell walls and sometimes cause diseases. • Class Mollicutes and order Mycoplasmatales.

my·co·plas·ma pneu·mo·nia ▸*n.* technical term for **WALKING PNEUMONIA**.

my·cor·rhi·za /,mīkəˈrīzə/ ▸*n.* (*pl.* **-rhi·zae** /-ˈrīzē/) *Botany* a fungus that grows in association with the roots of a plant in a symbiotic or mildly pathogenic relationship. ▷late 19th cent.: modern Latin, from **MYCO-** 'of fungi' + Greek *rhiza* 'root.' —**my·cor·rhi·zal** *adj.*

my·co·sis /mīˈkōsəs/ ▸*n.* (*pl.* **-ses** /-sēz/) a disease caused by infection with a fungus, such as ringworm or thrush. —**my·cot·ic** /-ˈkätik/ *adj.*

my·co·tox·in /,mīkəˈtäksən/ ▸*n.* any toxic substance produced by a fungus.

my·co·troph·ic /ˌmīkəˈträfik/ ▸*adj.* *Botany* (of a plant) living in association with a mycorrhiza or another fungus that appears to improve the uptake of nutrients. ▷1920s: from **MYCO-** 'of fungi' + Greek *trophē* 'nourishment.' —**my·cot·ro·phy** /mīˈkätrəfē/ *n.*

my·dri·a·sis /məˈdrīəsəs/ ▸*n.* *Medicine* dilation of the pupil of the eye. ▷early 19th cent.: via Latin from Greek *mudriasis.*

my·e·lin /ˈmīələn/ ▸*n.* *Anatomy & Physiology* a mixture of proteins and phospholipids forming a whitish insulating sheath around many nerve fibers, increasing the speed at which impulses are conducted. ▷late 19th cent.: from Greek *muelos* 'marrow' + **-IN**[1]. —**my·e·li·nat·ed** /-ləˌnātəd/ *adj.* —**my·e·li·na·tion** /ˌmīələˈnāSHən/ *n.*

my·e·li·tis /ˌmīəˈlītəs/ ▸*n.* *Medicine* inflammation of the spinal cord. ▷mid 19th cent.: modern Latin, from Greek *muelos* 'marrow' + **-ITIS.**

my·e·loid /ˈmīəˌloid/ ▸*adj.* **1** of or relating to bone marrow. ■ (of leukemia) characterized by the proliferation of cells originating in the bone marrow. **2** of or relating to the spinal cord. ▷mid 19th cent.: from Greek *muelos* 'marrow' + **-OID.**

my·e·lo·ma /ˌmīəˈlōmə/ ▸*n.* (*pl.* **-mas** or **-ma·ta** /-mətə/) *Medicine* a malignant tumor of the bone marrow. ▷mid 19th cent.: modern Latin, from Greek *muelos* 'marrow' + **-OMA.**

my·e·lop·a·thy /ˌmīəˈläpəTHē/ ▸*n.* *Medicine* disease of the spinal cord.

my·en·ter·ic /ˌmīenˈterik/ ▸*adj.* *Anatomy* relating to or denoting a plexus of nerves of the sympathetic and parasympathetic systems situated between and supplying the two layers of muscle in the small intestine.

myg·a·lo·morph /ˈmigələˌmôrf/ ▸*n.* *Zoology* a large spider of a group that includes the tarantulas and funnel-web spiders. Mygalomorphs have several primitive features, including fangs that stab downward rather than toward one another. • Suborder Mygalomorphae, order Araneae. ▷1920s: from modern Latin *Mygalomorphae*, from Greek *mugalē* 'shrew' + *morphē* 'form.'

My·ko·la·yiv /ˌmēkəˈlīəf/ an industrial city in southern Ukraine, on the Southern Bug River near the northern tip of the Black Sea; pop. 508,000. Russian name **NIKOLAEV.**

Myk·o·nos /ˈmēkəˌnôs; ˈmikəˌnäs/ a Greek island in the Aegean Sea, one of the Cyclades. Greek name **MÍKONOS.**

My Lai /ˈmēˈlī/ a village in Son My district, in central Vietnam, south of Quang Ngai, site of a 1968 massacre of Vietnamese civilians by U.S. troops during the Vietnam War.

My·lar /ˈmīˌlär/ ▸*n.* *trademark* a form of polyester resin used to make heat-resistant plastic films and sheets. ▷1950s: an arbitrary formation.

my·lo·don /ˈmīləˌdän/ ▸*n.* an extinct giant ground sloth found in deposits formed during the ice age of the Pleistocene epoch in South America. It died out only 11,000 years ago. • Genus *Glossotherium* (formerly *Mylodon*), family Mylodontidae. ▷mid 19th cent.: modern Latin, from Greek *mulē* 'mill, molar' + *odous, odont-* 'tooth.'

my·lo·nite /ˈmīləˌnīt; ˈmil-/ ▸*n.* *Geology* a fine-grained metamorphic rock, typically banded, resulting from the grinding or crushing of other rocks. ▷late 19th cent.: from Greek *mulōn* 'mill' + **-ITE**[1].

My·men·singh /ˈmīmənˌsiNG/ a port on the Brahmaputra River in central Bangladesh; pop. 186,000.

my·nah /ˈmīnə/ (also **my·na** or **my·nah bird**) ▸*n.* an Asian and Australasian starling that typically has dark plumage, gregarious behavior, and a loud call. • Family Sturnidae: several genera and species, in particular the **hill mynah** (*Gracula religiosa*), which is popular as a pet bird because of its ability to mimic the human voice. ▷mid 18th cent.: from Hindi *mainā.*

hill mynah

myo- (also **my-** before a vowel) ▸*comb. form* of muscle; relating to muscles: *myocardium* | *myometrium.* ▷from Greek *mus, mu-* 'mouse or muscle.'

my·o·car·di·al in·farc·tion ˌmīəˈkärdēəl ▸*n.* another term for **HEART ATTACK.**

my·o·car·di·tis /ˌmīəˌkärˈdītəs/ ▸*n.* *Medicine* inflammation of the heart muscle.

my·o·car·di·um /ˌmīəˈkärdēəm/ ▸*n.* *Anatomy* the muscular tissue of the heart. ▷late 19th cent.: modern Latin, from **MYO-** 'muscle' + Greek *kardia* 'heart.' —**my·o·car·di·al** /-dēəl/ *adj.*

my·oc·lo·nus /mīˈäklənəs/ ▸*n.* *Medicine* spasmodic jerky contraction of groups of muscles. —**my·o·clon·ic** /ˌmīəˈklänik/ *adj.*

my·o·fi·bril /ˌmīōˈfībrəl; -ˈfib-/ ▸*n.* any of the elongated contractile threads found in striated muscle cells.

my·o·gen·ic /ˌmīəˈjenik/ ▸*adj.* *Physiology* originating in muscle tissue (rather than from nerve impulses).

my·o·glo·bin /ˌmīəˈglōbən; ˈmīəˌglōbən/ ▸*n.* *Biochemistry* a red protein containing heme that carries and stores oxygen in muscle cells. It is structurally similar to a subunit of hemoglobin.

my·ol·o·gy /mīˈäləjē/ ▸*n.* the study of the structure, arrangement, and action of muscles. —**my·o·log·i·cal** /ˌmīəˈläjikəl/ *adj.* —**my·ol·o·gist** /-jist/ *n.*

my·o·mere /ˈmīəˌmir/ ▸*n.* another term for **MYOTOME.**

my·o·me·tri·um /ˌmīəˈmētrēəm/ ▸*n.* *Anatomy* the smooth muscle tissue of the uterus. ▷early 20th cent.: modern Latin, from **MYO-** 'muscle' + Greek *mētra* 'womb.'

My·o·mor·pha /ˌmīəˈmôrfə/ *Zoology* a major division of the rodents that includes the rats, mice, voles, hamsters, and their relatives. • Suborder Myomorpha, order Rodentia. ▷modern Latin (plural), from Greek *mus, mu-* 'mouse' + *morphē* 'form.' —**my·o·morph** /ˈmīəˌmôrf/ *n.* & *adj.*

my·op·a·thy /mīˈäpəTHē/ ▸*n.* (*pl.* **-thies**) *Medicine* a disease of muscle tissue. —**my·o·path·ic** /ˌmīəˈpaTHik/ *adj.*

my·ope /ˈmīˌōp/ ▸*n.* a nearsighted person. ▷early 18th cent.: from French, via late Latin from Greek *muōps*, from *muein* 'to shut' + *ōps* 'eye.'

my·o·pi·a /mīˈōpēə/ ▸*n.* nearsightedness. ■ lack of imagination, foresight, or intellectual insight: *historians have been censured for their myopia in treating modern science as a western phenomenon.* ▷early 18th cent.: modern Latin, from late Greek *muōpia*, from Greek *muōps* (see **MYOPE**). —**my·op·ic** /mīˈäpik/ *adj.* —**my·op·i·cal·ly** /mīˈäpik(ə)lē/ *adv.*

my·o·sin /ˈmīəsən/ ▸*n.* *Biochemistry* a fibrous protein that forms (together with actin) the contractile filaments of muscle cells and is also involved in motion in other types of cells.

my·o·sis /mīˈōsəs/ ▸*n.* variant spelling of **MIOSIS.**

my·o·si·tis /mīōˈsītəs/ ▸*n.* *Medicine* inflammation and degeneration of muscle tissue. ▷early 19th cent.: formed irregularly from Greek *mus, mu-* 'muscle' + **-ITIS.**

my·o·so·tis /ˌmīəˈsōtəs/ ▸*n.* a plant of a genus that includes the forget-me-nots. • Genus *Myosotis*, family Boraginaceae. ▷modern Latin, from Greek *muosōtis*, from *mus, mu-* 'mouse' + *ous, ōt-* 'ear.'

my·o·tis /mīˈōtəs/ ▸*n.* an insectivorous bat with mouselike ears, a slender muzzle, and a flight membrane that extends between the hind legs and the tip of the tail. Also called **MOUSE-EARED BAT.** • Genus *Myotis*, family Vespertilionidae: numerous species, including the **little brown myotis** (*M. lucifugus*), one of the most common and widespread bats in the U.S. and Canada. ▷modern Latin, based on Greek *mus, mu-* 'mouse.'

my·o·tome /ˈmīəˌtōm/ ▸*n.* *Embryology* the dorsal part of each somite in a vertebrate embryo, giving rise to the skeletal musculature. Compare with **DERMATOME, SCLEROTOME.** ■ each of the muscle blocks along either side of the spine in vertebrates (esp. fish and amphibians). Also called **MYOMERE.**

my·o·to·ni·a /ˌmīəˈtōnēə/ ▸*n.* inability to relax voluntary muscle after vigorous effort. ▷late 19th cent.: from **MYO-** 'muscle' + Greek *tonos* 'tone.' —**my·o·ton·ic** /-ˈtänik/ *adj.*

my·o·ton·ic dys·tro·phy /ˌmīəˈtänik/ ▸*n.* *Medicine* a form of muscular dystrophy accompanied by myotonia.

Myr·dal[1] /ˈmi(ə)rˌdäl/, Alva (Reimer) (1902–86), Swedish diplomat and peace activist; wife of Gunnar Myrdal. She served the United Nations as director of social welfare 1949–50 and was Swedish ambassador to India 1955–61. An advocate of disarmament, she wrote *The Game of Disarmament* (1976). Nobel Peace Prize (1982, shared with Alfonso Garcia Robles (1911–91)).

Myr·dal[2] (Karl) Gunnar (1898–1987), Swedish economist and writer; husband of Alva Myrdal. His works include *An American Dilemma* (1944) and *The Challenge of Affluence* (1963). Nobel Prize for Economics (1974, shared with Hayek).

myr·i·ad /ˈmirēəd/ *poetic/literary* ▸*n.* **1** a countless or extremely great number: *networks connecting **a myriad of** computers.* **2** (chiefly in classical history) a unit of ten thousand.
▸*adj.* countless or extremely great in number: *the myriad lights of the city.* ■ having countless or very many elements or aspects: *the myriad political scene.* ▷mid 16th cent. (sense 2 of the *noun*): via late Latin from Greek *murias, muriad-*, from *murioi* '10,000.'

USAGE **Myriad** is derived from a Greek noun and adjective meaning 'ten thousand'. It was first used in English as a noun in reference to a great but indefinite number. The adjectival sense of 'countless, innumerable' appeared much later. In modern English, use of **myriad** as a noun and adjective are equally standard and correct, despite the fact that some traditionalists consider the adjective as the only acceptable use of the word.

myr·i·a·pod /ˈmirēəˌpäd/ ▸*n.* *Zoology* an arthropod of a group that includes the centipedes, millipedes, and related animals. Myriapods have elongated bodies with numerous leg-bearing segments. • Classes Chilopoda, Diplopoda, Pauropoda, and Symphyla; formerly placed together in the class Myriapoda.
▸*adj.* (also **myriapodous**) of or belonging to the myriapods. ▷early 19th cent.: from modern Latin *Myriapoda*, from Greek *murias* (see **MYRIAD**) + *pous, pod-* 'foot.'

myr·in·got·o·my /ˌmirənˈgätəmē/ ▸*n.* surgical incision into the eardrum, to relieve pressure or drain fluid. ▷late 19th cent.: from modern Latin *myringa* 'eardrum' + **-TOMY.**

myr·me·col·o·gy /ˌmərməˈkäləjē/ ▸*n.* the branch of entomology that deals with ants. ▷late 19th cent.: from Greek *murmēx, murmēk-* 'ant' + **-LOGY.** —**myr·me·co·log·i·cal** /-kəˈläjikəl/ *adj.* —**myr·me·col·o·gist** /-jist/ *n.*

myr·me·co·phile /ˈmərmikōˌfīl/ ▸*n.* *Biology* an invertebrate or plant that has a symbiotic relationship with ants, such as being tended and protected by ants or living inside an ants' nest. ▷late 19th cent.: from Greek *murmēx, murmēk-* 'ant' + **-PHILE.** —**myr·me·coph·i·lous** /ˌmərməˈkäfələs/ *adj.* —**myr·me·coph·i·ly** /ˌmərməˈkäfəlē/ *n.*

Myr·mi·don /ˈmərməˌdän; -mədən/ ▸*n.* a member of a warlike Thessalian people led by Achilles at the siege of Troy. ■ (usu. **myrmidon**) a hired ruffian or unscrupulous subordinate: *he wrote to one of Hitler's myrmidons.* ▷late Middle English: from Latin *Myrmidones* (plural), from Greek *Murmidones.*

my·rob·a·lan /mīˈräbələn; mə-/ ▸*n.* **1** (also **myrobalan plum**) another term for **PURPLE LEAF PLUM.** **2** a tropical tree of a characteristic pagoda shape that yields a number of useful items including dye, timber, and medicinal products. • Genus *Terminalia*, family Combretaceae: several species, in particular *T. chebula.* ■ (also **myrobalan nut**) the fruit of this tree, used esp. for tanning leather. ▷late Middle English: from French *myrobolan* or Latin *myrobalanum*, from Greek *murobalanos*, from *muron* 'unguent' + *balanos* 'acorn.'

myrrh[1] /mər/ ▸*n.* a fragrant gum resin obtained from certain trees and used, esp. in the Near East, in perfumery, medicines, and incense. • The trees belong to the genus *Commiphora*, family Burseraceae, in particular *C. myrrha.* ▷Old English *myrra, myrre*, via Latin from Greek *murra*, of Semitic origin; compare with Arabic *murr* 'bitter.' —**myrrh·y** *adj.*

myrrh[2] ▸*n.* another term for **CICELY.** ▷late 16th cent.: from Latin *myrris*, from Greek *murris.*

myr·tle /ˈmərtl/ ▸*n.* **1** an evergreen shrub that has glossy aromatic foliage and white flowers followed by purple-black oval berries. • *Myrtus communis*, family Myrtaceae (the **myrtle family**). This family also includes several aromatic plants (clove, allspice) and many characteristic Australian plants (eucalyptus trees, bottlebrushes). **2** the lesser periwinkle. • *Vinca minor*, family Apocynaceae. See **PERIWINKLE**[1]. ▷late Middle English: from medieval Latin *myrtilla, myrtillus*, diminutive of Latin *myrta, myrtus*, from Greek *murtos.*

Myr·tle Beach /ˈmərtl/ a resort city in northeastern South Carolina, the hub of the part of the Atlantic coast that is called the Grand Strand; pop. 22,759.

Pronunciation Key ə *ago*; ər *over*; ˈə or ˌə *up*; ˈər or ˌər *fur*; a *hat*; ā *rate*; ä *car*; CH *chew*; e *let*; ē *see*; e(ə)r *air*; i *fit*; ī *by*; i(ə)r *ear*; NG *sing*; ō *go*; ô *for*; oi *boy*; o͝o *good*; o͞o *goo*; ou *out*; SH *she*; TH *thin*; T͟H *then*; (h)w *why*; ZH *vision*

my·self /mī'self; mə-/ ▸*pron.* [*first person singular*] **1** [*reflexive*] used by a speaker to refer to himself or herself as the object of a verb or preposition when he or she is the subject of the clause: *I hurt myself by accident* | *I strolled around, muttering to myself.* **2** [*emphatic*] I or me personally (used to emphasize the speaker): *I myself am unsure how this problem should be handled* | *I wrote it myself.* **3** poetic/literary term for **I**[2] : *myself presented to him a bronze sword.* ▷Old English *me self,* from **ME**[1] + **SELF** (used adjectivally); the change of *me* to *my* occurred in Middle English.

▸*PHRASES* □ **(not) be myself** see **BE ONESELF, NOT BE ONESELF** at **BE.** □ **by myself** see **BY ONESELF** at **BY.**

My·sia /'misHēə/ an ancient region in northwestern Asia Minor, on the Mediterranean coast south of the Sea of Marmara. —**My·si·an** *adj. & n.*

my·sid /'mīsid/ ▸*n. Zoology* a crustacean of an order that comprises the opossum shrimps. • Order Mysidacea, class Malacostraca. ▷mid 20th cent.: from modern Latin *Mysis* (genus name) + **-ID**[3].

My·sore /mī'sôr/ **1** a city in the Indian state of Karnataka; pop. 480,000. **2** former name (until 1973) for **KARNATAKA.**

mys·ta·gogue /'mistə,gäg/ ▸*n.* a teacher or propounder of mystical doctrines. ▷mid 16th cent.: from French, or via Latin from Greek *mustagōgos,* from *mustēs* 'initiated person' + *agōgos* 'leading.' —**mys·ta·go·gy** /-,gōjē/ *n.*

mys·te·ri·ous /mə'sti(ə)rēəs/ ▸*adj.* **1** difficult or impossible to understand, explain, or identify: *his colleague had vanished in mysterious circumstances* | *a mysterious benefactor provided the money.* ■ (of a location) having an atmosphere of strangeness or secrecy: *a dark, mysterious, windowless building.* **2** (of a person) deliberately enigmatic: *she was mysterious about herself but said plenty about her husband.* ▷late 16th cent.: from French *mystérieux,* from *mystère* 'mystery.' —**mys·te·ri·ous·ly** *adv.* —**mys·te·ri·ous·ness** *n.*

mys·ter·y[1] /'mist(ə)rē/ ▸*n.* (*pl.* **-ter·ies**) **1** something that is difficult or impossible to understand or explain: *the mysteries of outer space* | *hoping that the inquest would solve the mystery.* See note at **RIDDLE.** ■ the condition or quality of being secret, strange, or difficult to explain: *much of her past is shrouded in mystery.* ■ a person or thing whose identity or nature is puzzling or unknown: *"He's a bit of a mystery," said Nina* | [as *adj.*] *a mystery guest.* **2** a novel, play, or movie dealing with a puzzling crime, esp. a murder. **3** (**mysteries**) the secret rites of Greek and Roman pagan religion, or of any ancient or tribal religion, to which only initiates are admitted. ■ the practices, skills, or lore peculiar to a particular trade or activity and regarded as baffling to those without specialized knowledge: *the mysteries of analytical psychology.* ■ the Christian Eucharist. **4** *chiefly Christian Theology* a religious belief based on divine revelation, esp. one regarded as beyond human understanding: *the mystery of Christ.* ■ an incident in the life of Jesus or of a saint as a focus of devotion in the Roman Catholic Church, esp. each of those commemorated during recitation of successive decades of the rosary. ▷Middle English (in the sense 'mystic presence, hidden religious symbolism'): from Old French *mistere* or Latin *mysterium,* from Greek *mustērion*; related to **MYSTIC.**

mys·ter·y[2] ▸*n.* (*pl.* **-ter·ies**) *archaic* a handicraft or trade. ▷late Middle English: from medieval Latin *misterium,* contraction of *ministerium* 'ministry,' by association with *mysterium* (see **MYSTERY**[1]).

mys·ter·y play ▸*n.* a popular medieval play based on biblical stories or the lives of the saints. Also called **MIRACLE PLAY.**

Mystery plays were performed by members of trade guilds in Europe from the 13th century, in churches or later on wagons or temporary stages along a route, frequently introducing apocryphal and satirical elements. Several cycles of plays survive in association with particular English cities and towns.

mys·ter·y re·li·gion ▸*n.* a religion centered on secret or mystical rites for initiates, esp. any of a number of cults popular during the late Roman Empire.

mys·ter·y shop·per ▸*n.* another term for **SECRET SHOPPER.**

mys·tic /'mistik/ ▸*n.* a person who seeks by contemplation and self-surrender to obtain unity with or absorption into the Deity or the absolute, or who believes in the spiritual apprehension of truths that are beyond the intellect.

▸*adj.* another term for **MYSTICAL.** ▷Middle English (in the sense 'mystical meaning'): from Old French *mystique,* or via Latin from Greek *mustikos,* from *mustēs* 'initiated person,' from *muein* 'close the eyes or lips,' also 'initiate.' The current sense of the noun dates from the late 17th cent.

mys·ti·cal /'mistikəl/ ▸*adj.* **1** of or relating to mystics or religious mysticism: *the mystical experience.* ■ spiritually allegorical or symbolic; transcending human understanding: *the mystical body of Christ.* ■ of or relating to ancient religious mysteries or other occult or esoteric rites: *the mystical practices of the Pythagoreans.* ■ of hidden or esoteric meaning: *a geometric figure of mystical significance.* **2** inspiring a sense of spiritual mystery, awe, and fascination: *the mystical forces of nature.* ■ concerned with the soul or the spirit, rather than with material things: *the beliefs of a more mystical age.* —**mys·ti·cal·ly** /-ik(ə)lē/ *adv.*

Mys·ti·ce·ti /,mistə'sē,tī/ *Zoology* a division of the whales that comprises the baleen whales. • Suborder Mysticeti, order Cetacea. ▷modern Latin (plural), from Greek *mustikētos* representing (in old editions of Aristotle) the phrase *ho mus to kētos* 'the mouse, the whale so called.' —**mys·ti·cete** /'mistə,sēt/ *n. & adj.*

mys·ti·cism /'mistə,sizəm/ ▸*n.* **1** belief that union with or absorption into the Deity or the absolute, or the spiritual apprehension of knowledge inaccessible to the intellect, may be attained through contemplation and self-surrender. **2** belief characterized by self-delusion or dreamy confusion of thought, esp. when based on the assumption of occult qualities or mysterious agencies.

mys·ti·fy /'mistə,fī/ ▸*v.* (**-fies, -fied**) [*trans.*] utterly bewilder or perplex (someone): *maladies that have mystified and alarmed researchers for over a decade* | [as *adj.*] (**mystifying**) *a mystifying phenomenon.* ■ *dated* take advantage of the credulity of; hoax: *he took a childlike delight in mystifying his officials.* ■ make obscure or mysterious: *lawyers who mystify the legal system so that laymen find it unintelligible.* ▷early 19th cent.: from French *mystifier,* formed irregularly from *mystique* 'mystic' or from *mystère* 'mystery.' —**mys·ti·fi·ca·tion** /,mistəfi'kāsHən/ *n.* —**mys·ti·fi·er** *n.* —**mys·ti·fy·ing·ly** *adv.*

mys·tique /mis'tēk/ ▸*n.* a fascinating aura of mystery, awe, and power surrounding someone or something: *the West is lately rethinking its cowboy mystique* | *the tiger has a mystique that man has always respected and revered.* ■ an air of secrecy surrounding a particular activity or subject that makes it impressive or baffling to those without specialized knowledge: *eliminating the mystique normally associated with computers.* ▷late 19th cent.: from French, from Old French (see **MYSTIC**).

myth /miTH/ ▸*n.* **1** a traditional story, esp. one concerning the early history of a people or explaining some natural or social phenomenon, and typically involving supernatural beings or events. ■ such stories collectively: *the heroes of Greek myth.* **2** a widely held but false belief or idea: *he wants to dispel the myth that sea kayaking is too risky or too strenuous* | *there is a popular myth that corporations are big people with lots of money.* ■ a misrepresentation of the truth: *attacking the party's irresponsible myths about privatization.* ■ a fictitious or imaginary person or thing. ■ an exaggerated or idealized conception of a person or thing: *the book is a scholarly study of the Churchill myth.* ▷mid 19th cent.: from modern Latin *mythus,* via late Latin from Greek *muthos.*

myth. ▸*abbr.* ■ mythological or mythology.

myth·ic /'miTHik/ ▸*adj.* of, relating to, or resembling myth: *we explain spiritual forces in mythic language.* ■ exaggerated or idealized: *he was a national hero of mythic proportions.* ■ fictitious: *a mythic land of plenty.* ▷mid 17th cent.: via late Latin from Greek *muthikos,* from *muthos* 'myth.'

myth·i·cal /'miTHikəl/ ▸*adj.* occurring in or characteristic of myths or folk tales: *one of Denmark's greatest mythical heroes.* ■ idealized, esp. with reference to the past: *a mythical age of contentment and social order.* ■ fictitious: *a mythical customer whose name appears in brochures.* —**myth·i·cal·ly** /-ik(ə)lē/ *adv.*

myth·i·cize /'miTHə,sīz/ ▸*v.* [*trans.*] turn into myth; interpret mythically. —**myth·i·cism** /-,sizəm/ *n.* —**myth·i·cist** /-sist/ *n.*

myth·i·fy /'miTHə,fī/ ▸*v.* (**-fies, -fied**) [*trans.*] mythicize: *as success mythified their reputation, the stormtroopers grew in distinctiveness.* ▷early 20th cent.: from *myth* + *-fy.* —**myth·i·fi·ca·tion** /,miTHəfi'kāsHən/ *n.*

mytho- ▸*comb. form* of or relating to myth: *mythography.* ▷from Greek *muthos,* or from **MYTH.**

my·thog·ra·pher /mə'THägrəfər/ ▸*n.* a writer or collector of myths.

my·thog·ra·phy /mə'THägrəfē/ ▸*n.* **1** the representation of myths, esp. in the plastic arts. **2** the creation or collection of myths.

mythol. ▸*abbr.* ■ mythological or mythology.

my·thol·o·gize /mə'THälə,jīz/ ▸*v.* [*trans.*] convert into myth or mythology; make the subject of a myth: *there is a grave danger of mythologizing the past.* —**my·thol·o·giz·er** *n.*

my·thol·o·gy /mə'THäləjē/ ▸*n.* (*pl.* **-gies**) **1** a collection of myths, esp. one belonging to a particular religious or cultural tradition: *Ganesa was the god of wisdom and success in Hindu mythology* | *a book discussing Jewish and Christian mythologies.* ■ a set of stories or beliefs about a particular person, institution, or situation, esp. when exaggerated or fictitious: *in popular mythology, truckers are kings of the road.* **2** the study of myths. ▷late Middle English: from French *mythologie,* or via late Latin from Greek *muthologia,* from *muthos* 'myth' + *-logia* (see **-LOGY**). —**my·thol·o·ger** /-jər/ *n.* —**myth·o·log·ic** /,miTHə'läjik/ *adj.* —**myth·o·log·i·cal** /,miTHə'läjikəl/ *adj.* —**myth·o·log·i·cal·ly** /,miTHə'läjik(ə)lē/ *adv.* —**my·thol·o·gist** /-jist/ *n.*

myth·o·ma·ni·a /,miTHə'mānēə/ ▸*n.* an abnormal or pathological tendency to exaggerate or tell lies. —**myth·o·ma·ni·ac** /-'mānē,ak/ *n. & adj.*

myth·o·poe·ia /,miTHə'pēə/ ▸*n.* the making of a myth or myths. ▷1950s: from Greek *muthopoiia,* from *muthos* 'myth' + *poiein* 'make.' —**myth·o·poe·ic** /-'pēik/ *adj.*

myth·o·po·et·ic /,miTHəpō'etik/ ▸*adj.* of or relating to the making of a myth or myths. ■ relating to or denoting a movement for men that uses activities such as storytelling and poetry reading as a means of self-understanding.

myth·os /'miTHōs; -äs/ ▸*n.* (*pl.* **myth·oi** /'miTHoi/) *chiefly technical* a myth or mythology. ■ (in literature) a traditional or recurrent narrative theme or plot structure. ■ a set of beliefs or assumptions about something: *the rhetoric and mythos of science create the comforting image of linear progression toward truth.* ▷mid 18th cent.: from Greek.

myx·e·de·ma /,miksə'dēmə/ (*Brit.* **myx·oe·de·ma**) ▸*n. Medicine* swelling of the skin and underlying tissues giving a waxy consistency, typical of patients with underactive thyroid glands. ■ the more general condition associated with hypothyroidism, including weight gain, mental dullness, and sensitivity to cold.

myxo- (also **myx-**) ▸*comb. form* relating to mucus: *myxovirus* | *myxedema.* ▷from Greek *muxa* 'slime, mucus.'

myx·o·ma /mik'sōmə/ ▸*n.* (*pl.* **-mas** or **-ma·ta** /-mətə/) *Medicine* a benign tumor of connective tissue containing mucous or gelatinous material. —**myx·om·a·tous** /-mətəs/ *adj.*

myx·o·ma·to·sis /mik,sōmə'tōsəs/ ▸*n.* a highly infectious and usually fatal viral disease of rabbits, causing swelling of the mucous membranes and inflammation and discharge around the eyes.

myx·o·my·cete /,miksə'mī,sēt/ ▸*n. Biology* a slime mold, esp. an acellular one whose vegetative stage is a multinucleate plasmodium. • Division Myxomycota, kingdom Fungi, in particular the class Myxomycetes; also treated as protozoan (phylum Gymnomyxa, kingdom Protista). ▷late 19th cent.: from modern Latin *Myxomycetes,* from **MYXO-** 'slime' + Greek *mukētes* 'fungi.'

myx·o·vi·rus /'miksə,vīrəs/ ▸*n.* any of a group of RNA viruses, including the influenza virus.

M

N

Nn

N[1] /en/ (also **n**) ▸*n.* (*pl.* **Ns** or **N's**) the fourteenth letter of the alphabet. See also **EN**. ■ denoting the next after M in a set of items, categories, etc.

N[2] ▸*abbr.* ■ (used in recording moves in chess) knight: *17.Na4?* [N represents *knight*, since the initial letter *k-* represents 'king.'] ■ Nationalist. ■ (on a gear lever) neutral. ■ (chiefly in place names) New: *N Zealand.* ■ *Physics* newton(s). ■ Noon. ■ *Chemistry* (with reference to solutions) normal: *the pH was adjusted to 7.0 with 1 N HCl.* ■ Norse. ■ North or Northern: *78° N | N Ireland.* ■ *Finance* note. ■ nuclear: *the N bomb.*
▸*symbol* the chemical element nitrogen.

n ▸*abbr.* ■ name. ■ [in *combination*] (in units of measurement) nano- (10^{-9}): *the plates were coated with 500 ng of protein in sodium carbonate buffer.* ■ born. [from Latin *nātus.*] ■ nephew. ■ net. ■ *Grammar* neuter. ■ new. ■ nominative. ■ noon. ■ (**n-**) [in *combination*] *Chemistry* normal (denoting straight-chain hydrocarbons): n-*hexane.* ■ north or northern. ■ note (used in a book's index to refer to a footnote): *450n.* ■ *Finance* note. ■ *Grammar* noun. ■ number.
▸*symbol* an unspecified or variable number: *at the limit where n equals infinity.* See also **NTH**.

'n' /ən/ ▸*contraction of* and (conventionally used in informal contexts to coordinate two closely connected elements): *rock 'n' roll.*

-n[1] ▸*suffix* variant spelling of **-EN**[2].

-n[2] ▸*suffix* variant spelling of **-EN**[3].

NA ▸*abbr.* ■ National Army. ■ North America. ■ not applicable. ■ numerical aperture.

Na ▸*symbol* the chemical element sodium. ▷from modern Latin *natrium.*

na /nə/ ▸*adv.* Scottish form of **NOT**, used after an auxiliary verb: *I couldna sleep nights.*

n/a ▸*abbr.* ■ not applicable. ■ not available.

NAACP /'en dəbəl ā sē 'pē/ ▸*abbr.* National Association for the Advancement of Colored People.

naan ▸*n.* variant spelling of **NAN**.

NAB ▸*abbr.* ■ National Association of Broadcasters. ■ New American Bible.

nab /nab/ ▸*v.* (**nabbed, nab·bing**) [*trans.*] *informal* catch (someone) doing something wrong: *Olympic drug tests nabbed another athlete yesterday.* ■ take or grab (something): *Dan nabbed the seat next to mine.* ■ steal: *the raider nabbed $215.* ▷late 17th cent. (also as *napp*; compare with **KIDNAP**): of unknown origin.

Nab·a·tae·an /ˌnabə'tēən/ (also **Nab·a·te·an**) ▸*n.* **1** a member of an ancient Arabian people who from 312 BC formed an independent kingdom with its capital at Petra (now in Jordan). **2** the Aramaic dialect of this people, strongly influenced by Arabic.
▸*adj.* of or relating to the Nabataeans or their language. ▷from Latin *Nabat(h)aeus*, Greek *Nabat(h)aios* (compare with the Arabic adjective *Nabaṭī* 'relating to the Nabataeans)' + **-AN**.

nabe /nāb/ ▸*n. informal* a neighborhood. ■ a local movie theater. ■ a neighbor.

Na·bi Group /'näbē/ a group of late 19th-century French painters, largely symbolist in their approach and heavily indebted to Gauguin. Members of the group included Maurice Denis, Pierre Bonnard, and Edouard Vuillard. ▷*Nabi* from Hebrew *nāḇī* 'prophet.'

Nab·lus /'näbləs; 'na-/ a town in the West Bank; pop. 120,000.

na·bob /'nābäb/ ▸*n. historical* a Muslim official or governor under the Mogul empire. ■ a person of conspicuous wealth or high status. ■ *chiefly historical* a person who returned from India to Europe with a fortune. ▷from Portuguese *nababo* or Spanish *nabab*, from Urdu; see also **NAWAB**.

Na·bo·kov /'näbəˌkôf; nə'bôˌkôf/, Vladimir (Vladimorovich) (1899–1977), U.S. novelist and poet, born in Russia. His most notable novel is *Lolita* (1958), about a middle-aged man's obsession with a 12-year-old girl. Other notable works: *The Real Life of Sebastian Knight* (1941), *Pale Fire* (1962), and *Ada: A Family Chronicle* (1969).

Nacala /nə'kälə/ a deep-water port on the eastern coast of Mozambique; pop. 104,000. It is linked by rail with landlocked Malawi.

na·celle /nə'sel/ ▸*n.* a streamlined housing or tank for something on the outside of an aircraft or motor vehicle. ■ the outer casing of an aircraft engine. ■ *chiefly historical* the car of an airship. ▷early 20th cent. (originally denoting the car of an airship): from French, from late Latin *navicella*, diminutive of Latin *navis* 'ship.'

nach·es /'näkHəs/ (also **nach·as** pronunc. same) ▸*n.* pride or gratification, esp. at the achievements of one's children. ■ congratulations: *naches to Miriam Goldstein on her acceptance into rabbinic school.* ▷early 20th cent.: from Yiddish *nakhes*, from Hebrew *naḥaṯ* 'contentment.'

na·cho /'näCHō/ ▸*n.* (*pl.* **-chos**) a small piece of a crisp tortilla, typically topped with melted cheese and spices. ▷perhaps from Mexican Spanish *Nacho*, nickname for *Ignacio*, given name of the chef credited with creation of the dish. An alternative derivation is from Spanish *nacho* 'flat-nosed.'

Nac·o·do·ches /ˌnakə'dōCHəz/ a historic city in eastern Texas, on the Angelina River; pop. 30,872.

na·cre /'nākər/ ▸*n.* mother-of-pearl. ▷late 16th cent.: from French, of unknown origin. **—na·cre·ous** /-krēəs/ *adj.*

NACU ▸*abbr.* National Association of Colleges and Universities.

NAD *Biochemistry* ▸*abbr.* nicotinamide adenine dinucleotide, a coenzyme important in many biological oxidation reactions.

nad ▸*abbr.* **1** nothing abnormal detected. **2** no appreciable response.

na·da /'nädə/ ▸*pron. informal* nothing. ▷Spanish.

Na-De·ne /ˌnä dā'nā; nä 'dānē/ ▸*adj.* denoting or belonging to a postulated phylum of North American Indian languages including the Athabaskan family, Tlingit, and (in some classifications) Haida.
▸*n.* this language group. ▷early 20th cent.: from Tlingit *naa* 'tribe' (related to Haida *náa* 'dwell') + North Athabaskan *dene* 'tribe.'

Na·der /'nādər/, Ralph (1934–), U.S. consumer-rights advocate and lawyer. He campaigned on behalf of public safety and gave impetus to the consumer rights movement from the 1960s. He prompted legislation concerning car design, radiation hazards, food packaging, and insecticides. In 2000, Nader was the unsuccessful presidential candidate for the Green Party, and he was on the ballot as an Independent in some states in 2004.

Ralph Nader

NADH ▸*abbr.* nicotinamide adenine dinucleotide.

na·dir /'nādər; 'nādi(ə)r/ ▸*n.* [in *sing.*] the lowest point in the fortunes of a person or organization: *they had reached the nadir of their sufferings.* ■ *Astronomy* the point on the celestial sphere directly below an observer. The opposite of **ZENITH**. ▷late Middle English (in the astronomical sense): via French from Arabic *naẓīr (as-samt)* 'opposite (to the zenith).'

NADP ▸*abbr.* nicotinamide adenine dinucleotide phosphate.

NADPH ▸*abbr.* nicotinamide adenine dinucleotide phosphate.

nae /nā/ ▸*adj., exclam., adv., & n.* Scottish form of **NO**.
▸*adv. & n.* Scottish form of **NOT**.

nae·vus ▸*n.* (*pl.* **nae·vi**) British spelling of **NEVUS**.

naff[1] /naf/ ▸*v.* [*intrans.*] (**naff off**) *Brit., informal* go away: *she told press photographers to naff off.* ▷1950s: euphemism for **FUCK**; compare with **EFF**.

naff[2] ▸*adj. Brit., informal* lacking taste or style. ▷1960s: of unknown origin. **—naff·ness** *n.*

NAFTA /'naftə/ (also **Nafta**) ▸*abbr.* North American Free Trade Agreement.

nag[1] /nag/ ▸*v.* (**nagged, nag·ging**) [*trans.*] annoy or irritate (a person) with persistent fault-finding or continuous urging: *she constantly* **nags** *her daughter* **about** *getting married* | [with *infinitive*] *she nagged him to do the housework* | [*intrans.*] *he's always* **nagging at** *her for staying out late.* ■ [often as *adj.*] (**nagging**) be persistently painful, troublesome, or worrying to: *there was a nagging pain in his chest* | [*intrans.*] *something nagged at the back of his mind.*
▸*n.* a person who nags someone. ■ a persistent feeling of anxiety: *he felt once again that little nag of doubt.* ▷early 19th cent. (originally dialect in the sense 'gnaw'): perhaps of Scandinavian or Low German origin; compare with Norwegian and Swedish *nagga* 'gnaw, irritate' and Low German *(g)naggen* 'provoke.' **—nag·ger** *n.* **—nag·ging·ly** *adv.* **—nag·gy** *adj.*

nag[2] ▸*n. informal, often derogatory* a horse, esp. one that is old or in poor health. ■ *archaic* a horse suitable for riding as opposed to a draft animal. ▷Middle English: of unknown origin.

Na·ga /'nägə/ ▸*n.* **1** a member of a group of peoples living in or near the Naga Hills of Myanmar (Burma) and northeastern India. **2** any of the Tibeto-Burman languages of these peoples.
▸*adj.* of or relating to the Nagas or their language. ▷perhaps from Sanskrit *nagna* 'naked' or *naga* 'mountain.'

na·ga /'nägə/ ▸*n.* (in Indian mythology) a member of a semidivine race, part human and part cobra in form, associated with water and sometimes with mystical initiation. ▷from Sanskrit *nāga* 'serpent.'

Na·ga·land /'nägəˌland; nə'gäland/ a state in northeast India, on the border with Myanmar (Burma); capital, Kohima. It was created in 1962 from parts of Assam.

na·ga·na /nə'gänə/ ▸*n.* a disease of cattle, antelope, and other livestock in southern Africa, characterized by fever, lethargy, and edema, and caused by trypanosome parasites transmitted by the tsetse fly. ▷late 19th cent.: from Zulu *nakane.*

Na·ga·no /nä'gänō/ a commercial and industrial city in central Japan, on central Honshu Island, site of a

Pronunciation Key ə *ago*; ər *over*; 'ə or ˌə *up*; 'ər or ˌər *fur*; a *hat*; ā *rate*; ä *car*; CH *chew*; e *let*; ē *see*; e(ə)r *air*; i *fit*; ī *by*; i(ə)r *ear*; NG *sing*; ō *go*; ô *for*; oi *boy*; o͝o *good*; o͞o *goo*; ou *out*; SH *she*; TH *thin*; TH *then*; (h)w *why*; ZH *vision*

major Buddhist shrine and of the 1998 Winter Olympic games; pop. 347,000.

Na·ga·sa·ki /ˌnägəˈsäkē/ a city and port in southwestern Japan, on the western coast of Kyushu island; pop. 445,000. On August 9, 1945, it became the target of the second atom bomb dropped by the U.S.

nage /näzʜ/ ▸*n.* an aromatic court bouillon or stock, used for cooking shellfish. ▷from French.

Na·gor·no-Ka·ra·bakh /nəˈgôrnō ˌkarəˈbäk; -ˈbäкʜ/ a region of Azerbaijan in the southern foothills of the Caucasus; pop. 192,000; capital, Xankändi. Fighting between Azerbaijan and Armenia began in 1985, with the majority of the Armenian population desiring to be separated from Muslim Azerbaijan and united with Armenia; the region declared unilateral independence in 1991. A cease-fire was signed in 1994.

Na·go·ya /nəˈgoiə; ˈnägōyä/ a city in central Japan, on the southern coast of the island of Honshu; pop. 2,155,000.

Nag·pur /ˈnägˌpo͝or/ a city in central India, in the state of Maharashtra; pop. 1,622,000.

Nags Head /ˈnagz/ a resort town in eastern North Carolina, in the Outer Banks; pop. 1,838.

nag·ware /ˈnagˌwe(ə)r/ ▸*n. informal* computer software that is free for a trial period during which the user is frequently reminded on screen to register and pay for the program in order to continue using it when the trial period is over.

Nagy /näj; ˈnädyə/, Imre (1896–1958), Hungarian communist statesman, prime minister 1953–55 and 1956. In 1956, seeking neutral status for his country, he withdrew Hungary from the Warsaw Pact. He was executed after the Red Army crushed the uprising.

nah /nä/ ▸*exclam.* variant spelling of NO, used to answer a question: *"Want a lift?" "Nah, that's okay."*

Nah. ▸*abbr. Bible* Nahum.

Na·ha /ˈnähä/ a port in southern Japan, capital of Okinawa island; pop. 305,000.

Na·hua·tl /ˈnäˌwätl/ ▸*n.* (*pl.* same) **1** a member of a group of peoples native to southern Mexico and Central America, including the Aztecs. **2** the Uto-Aztecan language of these peoples.
▸*adj.* of or relating to these peoples or their language. ▷via Spanish from Nahuatl *náhuatl* 'what pleases the ear.'

Na·hum /ˈnāhəm/ (in the Bible) a Hebrew minor prophet. ■ a book of the Bible containing his prophecy of the fall of Nineveh (early 7th century BC).

NAIA ▸*abbr.* National Association of Intercollegiate Athletics.

nai·ad /ˈnāad; -əd; nī-/ ▸*n.* (*pl.* **-ads** or **-ades** /-əˌdēz/) **1** (also **Naiad**) (in classical mythology) a water nymph said to inhabit a river, spring, or waterfall. **2** the aquatic larva or nymph of a dragonfly, mayfly, or stonefly. **3** a submerged aquatic plant with narrow leaves and minute flowers. • Genus *Najas*, family Najadaceae. ▷via Latin from Greek *Naias, Naiad-*, from *naein* 'to flow.' Use as a term in entomology and botany dates from the early 20th cent.

na·iant /ˈnāənt/ ▸*adj.* [*postpositive*] *Heraldry* (of a fish or marine creature) swimming horizontally. ▷mid 16th cent.: from Anglo-Norman French, variant of Old French *noiant* 'swimming,' present participle of *noier*, from Latin *natare* 'to swim.'

na·if /nīˈēf/ (also **na·ïf**) ▸*adj.* naive or ingenuous.
▸*n.* a naive or ingenuous person. ▷from French *naïf.*

nail /nāl/ ▸*n.* **1** a small metal spike with a broadened flat head, driven typically into wood with a hammer to join things together or to serve as a peg or hook. **2** a horny covering on the upper surface of the tip of the finger and toe in humans and other primates. ■ an animal's claw. ■ a hard growth on the upper mandible of some soft-billed birds. **3** *historical* a medieval unit of measurement: ■ a measure of length for cloth, equal to $2^1/_4$ inches. ■ a measure of wool, beef, or other commodity, roughly equal to 7 or 8 pounds.
▸*v.* [*trans.*] **1** [*trans.*] fasten to a surface or to something else with a nail or nails: *nail the edge framing to the wall | the teacher was nailing up the lists.* **2** *informal* expose (someone) as deceitful or criminal; catch or arrest: *have you nailed the killer?* ■ expose (a lie or other instance of deception). **3** *informal Football* tackle the quarterback or ballcarrier, esp. at or behind the line of scrimmage. ■ *Baseball* (of a fielder) put (a runner) out by throwing to a base: *he dropped a perfect throw home that should have nailed Joe by yards.* ■ (of a player) defeat or outwit (an opponent): *Navratilova tried to nail her on the backhand side.* ■ (of a player) secure (esp. a victory) conclusively: *there's no doubt I had chances to nail it in the last set.* **4** *vulgar slang* (of a man) have sexual intercourse with (someone).
▸*phrasal v.* □ **nail someone down** elicit a firm promise or commitment from someone: *I can't nail her down to a specific date.* □ **nail something down 1** fasten something securely with nails. **2** identify something precisely: *something seems unexpected—I can't nail it down, but it makes me uneasy.* **3** secure something, esp. an agreement: *the company has finally nailed down the agreement with its distributors.* ▷Old English *nægel* (noun), *næglan* (verb), of Germanic origin; related to Dutch *nagel* and German *Nagel*, from an Indo-European root shared by Latin *unguis* and Greek *onux*. **—nailed** *adj.* [in *combination*] *dirty-nailed fingers.* **—nail·less** *adj.*
▸*PHRASES* □ **fight tooth and nail** see TOOTH. □ **hard as nails** (of a person) very tough; completely callous or unfeeling. □ **a nail in the coffin** an action or event regarded as likely to have a detrimental or destructive effect on a situation, enterprise, or person: *this was going to put the final nail in the coffin of his career.* □ **on the nail** *Brit.* (of payment) without delay.

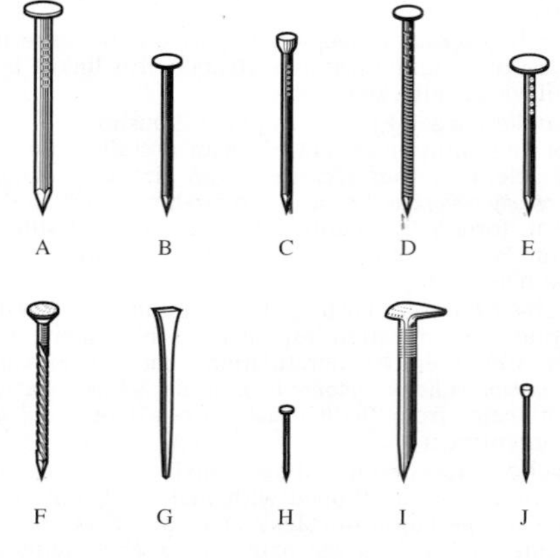

A common nail
B box nail
C finish *or* finishing nail
D ring *or* anchor nail
E roofing nail
F screw nail
G cut *or* flooring nail
H wire nail
I wrought nail
J brad

nail 1

nail bed ▸*n.* the formative layer of cells underlying the fingernail or toenail.

nail-bit·er (also **nail bit·er**) ▸*n.* a situation causing great anxiety or tension: *a nail-biter of a victory.* **—nail-bit·ing** *adj.*

nail brush ▸*n.* a small brush designed for cleaning the fingernails and toenails.

nail e·nam·el ▸*n.* nail polish.

nail·er /ˈnālər/ ▸*n.* **1** *chiefly historical* a maker of nails. **2** a power tool for inserting nails. **—nail·er·y** *n.*

nail file ▸*n.* a strip of roughened metal or an emery board used for smoothing and shaping the fingernails and toenails.

nail gall ▸*n.* a small, conical, nail-shaped gall that forms on the leaves of lime trees in response to the presence of mites. • The mite is *Eriophyes tiliae*, family Eriophyidae.

nail·head /ˈnālˌhed/ ▸*n.* the rounded head of a nail. ■ an ornament like the head of a nail, used chiefly in architecture and on clothing.

nail pol·ish ▸*n.* varnish applied to the fingernails or toenails to color them or make them shiny.

nail scis·sors ▸*plural n.* small scissors with curved blades for cutting the fingernails or toenails.

nail set (also **nail punch**) ▸*n.* a tool hit with a hammer to sink the head of a nail below a surface.

nail sick·ness ▸*n.* the condition of a structure that is held together with corroded nails.

nail var·nish ▸*n. Brit.* nail polish.

nail wrap ▸*n.* a type of beauty treatment, in which a nail strengthener, usu. containing fibers, is either brushed on or applied with adhesive.

nain·sook /ˈnānˌso͝ok/ ▸*n.* a fine, soft cotton fabric, originally from the Indian subcontinent. ▷late 18th cent.: from Hindi *nainsukh*, from *nain* 'eye' + *sukh* 'pleasure.'

Nai·paul /ˈnīpôl; nīˈpôl/, V. S. (1932–), Trinidadian writer, resident in Britain from 1950; full name *Sir Vidiadhar Surajprasad Naipaul*. He is best known for his satirical novels, such as *A House for Mr. Biswas* (1961) and *In a Free State* (1971). Other notable works: *A Way in the World* (1994) and *Beyond Belief: Islamic Excursions among the Converted People* (1998). Nobel Prize for Literature (2001).

nai·ra /ˈnīrə/ ▸*n.* the basic monetary unit of Nigeria, equal to 100 kobo. ▷contraction of NIGERIA.

Nai·ro·bi /nīˈrōbē/ the capital of Kenya; pop. 1,346,000. It is situated on the central Kenyan plateau at an altitude of 5,500 feet (1,680 m).

Nai·smith /ˈnāˌsmiтʜ/, James A. (1861–1939), Canadian physical education teacher. He invented the game of basketball in 1891, while teaching at the Young Men's Christian Association Training School in Springfield, Massachusetts. Basketball Hall of Fame (1959).

nais·sant /ˈnāsənt/ ▸*adj. Heraldry* (of a charge, esp. an animal) issuing from the middle of an ordinary, esp. a fess. ▷late 16th cent.: from French, literally 'being born,' present participle of *naître*, from Latin *nasci* 'be born.'

na·ive /nīˈēv/ (also **na·ïve**) ▸*adj.* (of a person or action) showing a lack of experience, wisdom, or judgment: *the rather naive young man had been totally misled.* ■ (of a person) natural and unaffected; innocent: *Andy had a sweet, naive look when he smiled.* ■ of or denoting art produced in a straightforward style that deliberately rejects sophisticated artistic techniques and has a bold directness resembling a child's work, typically in bright colors with little or no perspective. ▷mid 17th cent.: from French *naïve*, feminine of *naïf*, from Latin *nativus* 'native, natural.' **—na·ive·ly** *adv.* **—na·ive·ness** *n.*

na·ive·té /ˌnīˌēv(ə)ˈtā; nīˈēv(ə)ˌtā/ (also **na·ïve·té**, *Brit.* **na·ive·ty**) ▸*n.* lack of experience, wisdom, or judgment: *the administration's naiveté and inexperience in foreign policy.* ■ innocence or unsophistication: *they took advantage of his naiveté and deep pockets.* ▷late 17th cent.: from French *naïveté*, from *naïf*, *-ive* (see NAIVE).

Na·jaf /ˈnäjəf/ (also **An Na·jaf** /än ˈnäjəf/) a city in southern Iraq, on the Euphrates River; pop. 243,000. It contains the shrine of Ali, the prophet Muhammad's son-in-law, and is a holy city for the Shiite Muslims.

na·ked /ˈnākid/ ▸*adj.* (of a person or part of the body) without clothes: *he'd never seen a naked woman before | he was stripped naked.* ■ (of an object) without the usual covering or protection: *her room was lit by a single naked bulb.* ■ (of a tree, plant, or animal) without leaves, hairs, scales, shell, etc.: *the twisted trunks and naked branches of the trees.* ■ *figurative* exposed to harm; unprotected or vulnerable: *John looked naked and defenseless without his glasses.* ■ [*attrib.*] (of something such as feelings or behavior) undisguised; blatant: *naked, unprovoked aggression | the naked truth.* ▷Old English *nacod*, of Germanic origin; related to Dutch *naakt* and German *nackt*, from an Indo-European root shared by Latin *nudus* and Sanskrit *nagna*. **—na·ked·ly** *adv.* **—na·ked·ness** *n.*

THE RIGHT WORD **bald, bare, barren, naked, nude**
Someone who isn't wearing any clothes is **naked**; this adjective is usually associated with revealing a part or all of the body (*her naked shoulder; a naked man ran from the burning building*).
A *naked* person who appears in a painting or photograph is called a **nude**, a euphemistic but more socially acceptable term referring to the unclothed human body.
Bare can describe the branches of a tree as well as human limbs; it implies the absence of the conventional or appropriate covering (*a bare wooden floor; bare legs; four bare walls*).
Bald also suggests a lack of covering, but it refers particularly to a lack of natural covering, especially hair (*a bald head*).
Barren implies a lack of vegetation, and it also connotes destitution and fruitlessness (*a barren wasteland devoid of life*).
A *bald* artist might paint a *nude* woman whose *bare* arms are extended against a *barren* winter landscape.

na·ked eye ▸*n.* (usu. **the naked eye**) unassisted vision, without a telescope, microscope, or other device: *threadworm eggs are so small that they cannot be seen with the naked eye.*

na·ked mole rat ▸*n.* a blind and hairless mole rat living in large underground colonies in eastern Africa.

The colony structure is similar to that of social insects, with only one pair breeding and most other individuals acting as workers. • *Heterocephalus glaber*, family Bathyergidae.

na·ker /ˈnākər/ ▸*n. historical* a kettledrum. ▹late Middle English: from Old French *nacaire*, from Arabic *naḳḳāra* 'drum.'

nak·fa /ˈnäkfə/ ▸*n.* (*pl.* same or **-fas**) the basic monetary unit of Eritrea, equal to 100 cents. ▹1990s: from *Nakfa*, the name of the town where the country's armed struggle against the Ethiopian regime was launched.

Na·khi·che·van /ˌnäkicнəˈvän/ Russian name for **Naxçivan**.

Na·ku·ru /nəˈko͞oro͞o/ an industrial city in western Kenya; pop. 162,800. Nearby is Lake Nakuru, noted for its spectacular flocks of flamingos.

Nal·chik /ˈnälcнik/ a city in the Caucasus, in southwestern Russia, capital of the republic of Kabardino-Balkaria; pop. 237,000.

na·li·dix·ic ac·id /ˌnäliˈdiksik/ ▸*n. Medicine* a synthetic compound that inhibits the multiplication of bacteria, used chiefly to treat urinary infections. • A heterocyclic compound; chem. formula: $C_{12}H_{12}N_2O_3$. ▹1960s: *nalidixic* by rearrangement of elements from **naphthalene**, *carboxylic*, and **di-**[1] (forming the systematic name).

nal·ox·one /nəˈläksōn/ ▸*n. Medicine* a synthetic drug, similar to morphine, that blocks opiate receptors in the nervous system. ▹1960s: contraction of *N-allylnoroxymorphone*.

nal·trex·one /nalˈtreksōn/ ▸*n. Medicine* a synthetic drug, similar to morphine, that blocks opiate receptors in the nervous system and is used chiefly in the treatment of heroin addiction. ▹1970s: from a contraction of *N-al(lylnoroxymorph)one* (see **naloxone**), with the insertion of the arbitrary element *-trex-*.

NAM ▸*abbr.* National Association of Manufacturers.

Nam /näm; nam/ (also **'Nam**) informal name for **Vietnam** in the context of the Vietnam War.

Na·ma /ˈnämä/ ▸*n.* (*pl.* same or **Na·mas**) **1** a member of one of the Khoikhoi peoples of South Africa and southwestern Namibia. **2** the Khoisan language of this people.
▸*adj.* of or relating to this people or their language. ▹the name in Nama.

Na·man·gan /ˌnämənɢˈgän/ a city in eastern Uzbekistan, near the border with Kyrgyzstan; pop. 312,000.

Na·ma·qua·land /nəˈmäkwəˌland/ a region of southwestern Africa, the homeland of the Nama people. **Little Namaqualand** lies immediately to the south of the Orange River in South Africa, while **Great Namaqualand** lies to the north of the river in Namibia.

nam·as·kar /ˌnäməsˈkär/ ▸*n.* a traditional Indian greeting or gesture of respect, made by bringing the palms together before the face or chest and bowing. ▹via Hindi from Sanskrit *namaskāra*, from *namas* 'bowing' + *kāra* 'action.'

na·ma·ste /ˈnäməˌstā/ ▸*exclam.* a respectful greeting said when giving a namaskar.
▸*n.* another term for **namaskar**. ▹via Hindi from Sanskrit *namas* 'bowing' + *te* 'to you.'

Na·math /ˈnāməтн/, Joe (1943–), U.S. football player; nickname **Broadway Joe**. A quarterback with the New York Jets 1965–76, he led them to a 1969 Super Bowl title. He also played for the Los Angeles Rams 1977–78. Football Hall of Fame (1985).

nam·by-pam·by /ˈnambē ˈpambē/ ▸*adj. derogatory* lacking energy, strength, or courage; feeble or effeminate in behavior or expression: *these weren't namby-pamby fights, but brutal affairs where heads hit the sidewalk.*
▸*n.* (*pl.* **-bies**) a feeble or effeminate person. ▹mid 18th cent.: fanciful formation based on the given name of *Ambrose* Philips (died 1749), an English writer whose pastorals were ridiculed by the writers Henry Carey (1687?–1743) and Alexander Pope (1688–1744).

name /nām/ ▸*n.* **1** a word or set of words by which a person, animal, place, or thing is known, addressed, or referred to: *my name is Parsons, John Parsons | Köln is the German* **name for** *Cologne.* ■ someone or something regarded as existing merely as a word and lacking substance or reality: *he was still simply a name in a gossip column.* **2** a famous person: *as usual, the big race will lure the top names.* ■ [in *sing.*] a reputation, esp. a good one: *he set up a school that gained a name for excellence.*
▸*v.* [*trans.*] give a name to: *hundreds of diseases had not yet been isolated or named | [trans.] she named the child Edward.* ■ identify by name; give the correct name for: *the dead man has been* **named as** *John Mackintosh.* ■ give a particular title or epithet to: *she was named "Artist of the Decade."* ■ appoint (someone) to a particular position or task: *he was named to head a joint UN–OAS diplomatic effort.* ■ mention or cite by name: *the sea is as crystal clear as any spot in the Caribbean you might care to name.* ■ specify (an amount, time, or place) as something desired, suggested, or decided on: *he showed them the picture and named a price.*
▸*phrasal v.* □ **name someone/something after** (also **for**) call someone or something by the same name as: *Nathaniel* **was named after** *his maternal grandfather | Ricksburg, Idaho,* **named for** *one Thomas Ricks.*
▸*adj.* [*attrib.*] (of a person or commercial product) having a name that is widely known: *countless specialized* **name brands** *geared to niche markets.* ▹Old English *nama, noma* (noun), *(ge)namian* (verb), of Germanic origin; related to Dutch *naam* and German *Name*, from a root shared by Latin *nomen* and Greek *onoma*. **—name·a·ble** /ˈnāməbəl/ *adj.* **—nam·er** *n.*
▸*PHRASES* □ **by name** using the name of someone or something: *ask for the street by name.* □ **by the name of** called: *a woman by the name of Smith.* □ **call someone names** insult someone verbally. □ **give one's name to** invent, discover, found, or be closely associated with something that then becomes known by one's name: *Lou Gehrig gave his name to the disease that claimed his life.* □ **something has someone's name on it** a person is destined or particularly suited to receive or experience a specified thing: *he feared the next bullet would have his name on it.* □ **have to one's name** [often with *negative*] have in one's possession: *I had a child on the way and hardly a penny to my name.* □ **in all but name** existing in a particular state but not formally recognized as such: *these new punks are hippies in all but name.* □ **in someone's name 1** formally registered as belonging to or reserved for someone: *the house was in her name.* **2** on behalf of someone: *he began to question what had been done in his name.* □ **in the name of** bearing or using the name of a specified person or organization: *a driver's license in the name of William Sanders.* ■ for the sake of: *he withdrew his candidacy in the name of party unity.* ■ by the authority of: *crimes committed in the name of religion.* ■ (**in the name of Christ/God/Allah/heaven**, etc.) used for emphasis: *what in the name of God do you think you're doing?* □ **in name only** by description but not in reality: *a college in name only.* □ **make a name for oneself** become well known: *by the time he was thirty-five, he had made a name for himself as a contractor.* □ **name the day** arrange a date for a specific occasion, esp. a wedding. □ **one's name is mud** see **mud**. □ **name names** mention specific names, esp. of people involved in something wrong or illegal: *if you're convinced my staff is part of this operation, then name names.* □ **the name of the game** *informal* the main purpose or most important aspect of a situation: *the name of the game is short-term gain.* □ **put down** (or **enter**) **one's** (or **someone's**) **name** apply to enter an educational institution, course, competition, etc.: *I* **put my name down for** *the course.* □ **put a name to** remember or report what someone or something is called: *viewers were asked if they could put a name to the voice of the kidnapper.* □ **take someone's name in vain** see **vain**. □ **to name (but) a few** giving only these as examples, even though more could be cited: *the ingredients used are drawn from nature—avocado, lemongrass, and chamomile to name a few.* □ **under the name ——** using a name that is not one's real name, esp. for professional purposes: *that mad doctor who, under the name Céline, produced some of the greatest fiction in Western literature.* ■ (of a product, company, or organization) sold, doing business as, or known by a particular name: *a synthetic version is sold in the U.S.* **under the name of** *Actigall.* □ **what's in a name?** names are arbitrary labels: *What's in a name? If you know her by Elizabeth or Lizzie, she's still the same person.* □ **you name it** *informal* whatever you can think of (used to express the extent or variety of something): *easy-to-assemble kits of trains, cars, trucks, ships . . . you name it.*

name-call·ing ▸*n.* abusive language or insults. **—name-call·er** *n.*

name-check /ˈnāmˌcнek/ (also **name·check**) ▸*n.* a public mention or listing of the name of a person or thing such as a product, esp. in acknowledgment or for publicity purposes.
▸*v.* [*trans.*] publicly mention or list the name of: *he name-checks a legion of producers and DJs.*

name day ▸*n.* the feast day of a saint after whom a person is named.

name-drop·ping ▸*n.* the practice of casually mentioning the names of famous people one knows or claims to know in order to impress others. **—name-drop** *v.* **—name-drop·per** *n.*

name·less /ˈnāmlis/ ▸*adj.* **1** having no name or no known name. ■ deliberately not identified; anonymous: *the director of a voluntary organization which shall remain nameless.* ■ *archaic* (of a child) illegitimate. **2** (esp. of an emotion) not easy to describe; indefinable: *a nameless yearning for transcendence.* ■ too loathsome or horrific to be described: *the myths talk about nameless horrors infesting our universe.* **—name·less·ly** *adv.* **—name·less·ness** *n.*

name·ly /ˈnāmlē/ ▸*adv.* that is to say; to be specific (used to introduce detailed information or a specific example): *to me there is only one kind of rock, namely, loud rock.*

Na·men /ˈnämən/ Flemish name for **Namur**.

Na·men·da /nəˈmendə/ ▸*n.* trademark for **memantine**.

name·plate /ˈnāmˌplāt/ ▸*n.* a plate or sign, typically made of metal, displaying the name of someone, such as the person working in a building or the builder of a ship. ■ a brand of a product, esp. a maker of automobiles: *Honda is busiest among the import nameplates, with three new cars and a sport utility vehicle.*

name·sake /ˈnāmˌsāk/ ▸*n.* a person or thing that has the same name as another: *Hugh Capet paved the way for his son and namesake to be crowned king of France.* ▹mid 17th cent.: from the phrase *for the name's sake*.

name·tape /ˈnāmˌtāp/ ▸*n.* a piece of cloth tape bearing the name of a person, fixed to a garment of theirs to identify it.

Na·mib Des·ert /ˈnämib/ a desert in southwestern Africa. It extends for 1,200 miles (1,900 km) along the Atlantic coast from the Curoca River in southwestern Angola through Namibia to the border between Namibia and South Africa.

Na·mib·i·a /nəˈmibēə/ a country in southwestern Africa, largely desert, with a coastline on the Atlantic Ocean; pop. 1,834,000; capital, Windhoek; languages, English (official), Afrikaans, and various Bantu and Khoisan languages . **—Na·mib·i·an** *adj.* & *n.*

Namibia was made the protectorate of German South West Africa in 1884. In 1920, it was mandated to South Africa by the League of Nations and became known as South West Africa. Despite international pressure, South Africa continued to administer the country after the ending of the UN mandate in 1964 and agreed to withdraw only after several years of fighting by SWAPO guerrillas. Namibia became fully independent in 1990.

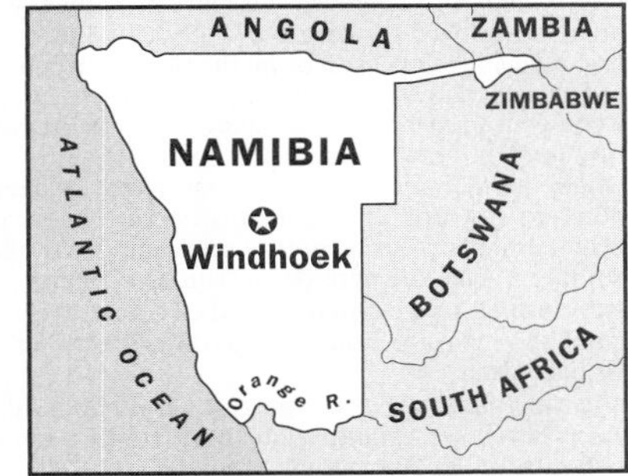

Nam·pa /ˈnampə/ a city in southwestern Idaho, southwest of Boise; pop. 51,867.

nam pla /ˌnäm ˈplä/ ▸*n.* Thai term for **fish sauce**.

Nam·po /ˈnämˈpō/ (also **Chinnampo**) an industrial city in western North Korea, southwest of Pyongyang, for which it is the port; pop. 691,000.

Na·mur /nəˈmo͝or/ a province in central Belgium. It was the scene of the last German offensive in the Ardennes in 1945. Flemish name **Namen**. ■ the capital of this province, at the junction of the Meuse and Sambre rivers; pop. 103,000.

nan /nän/ (also **naan**) ▸*n.* (in Indian cooking) a type of leavened bread, typically of teardrop shape and traditionally cooked in a clay oven. ▹from Urdu and Persian *nān*.

nan·a /ˈnanə/ ▸*n. informal* one's grandmother. ▹mid 19th cent.: child's pronunciation of **nanny** or **gran**.

Na·nak /ˈnänək/ (1469–1539), Indian religious leader

and founder of Sikhism; known as **Guru Nanak**. He preached that spiritual liberation could be achieved through meditating on the name of God. His teachings are contained in a number of hymns that form part of the Adi Granth.

nance /nans/ ▸*n.* another term for NANCY.

Nan·chang /ˈnänˈCHäNG/ a city in southeastern China, capital of Jiangxi province; pop. 1,330,000.

Nan·cy /näNˈsē/ a city in northeastern France, chief town of Lorraine; pop. 102,000.

nan·cy /ˈnansē/ ▸*n.* (*pl.* **-cies**) (also **nancy boy**) *offensive chiefly Brit.* an effeminate or homosexual man. ▸*adj.* effeminate. ▷early 20th cent.: nickname for the given name *Ann*.

NAND /nand/ ▸*n. Electronics* a Boolean operator that gives the value zero if and only if all the operands have a value of one, and otherwise has a value of one (equivalent to NOT AND). ■ (also **NAND gate**) a circuit that produces an output signal until there are signals on all of its inputs.

Nan·di /ˈnändē/ *Hinduism* a bull that serves as the mount of Shiva and symbolizes fertility. ▷Sanskrit.

nan·di·na /nanˈdēnə/ ▸*n.* an evergreen eastern Asian shrub that resembles bamboo and is cultivated for its foliage, which turns red or bronze in autumn. Also called CELESTIAL BAMBOO. • *Nandina domestica*, family Berberidaceae. ▷mid 19th cent.: modern Latin (genus name), adapted from Japanese *nanten*.

nan·dro·lone /ˈnandrəˌlōn/ ▸*n.* an anabolic steroid with tissue-building properties, used unlawfully to enhance performance in sports. ▷1950s: shortened form of its chemical name *norandrostenolone*.

Nan·ga Par·bat /ˌnəNGgə ˈpərbət/ a mountain in northern Pakistan, in the western Himalayas. It is 26,660 feet (8,126 m) high.

Nan·jing /ˈnänˈjiNG/ (also **Nan·king** /ˈnanˈkiNG/) a city in eastern China, on the Yangtze River, capital of Jiangsu province; pop. 3,682,000.

nan·keen /nanˈkēn/ ▸*n.* a yellowish cotton cloth. ■ (**nankeens**) *historical* pants made of this cloth. ■ the characteristic yellowish-buff color of this cloth. ▸*adj.* of this color. ▷mid 18th cent.: from the name of the city of *Nanking* (see NANJING), where it was first made.

Nan·ning /ˈnäˈniNG/ the capital of Guangxi Zhuang, an autonomous region in southern China; pop. 1,070,000.

nan·no·fos·sil /ˌnanəˈfäsəl/ (also **nan·o·fos·sil**) ▸*n.* the fossil of a minute planktonic organism, esp. a calcareous unicellular alga. ▷1960s: *nanno-* from *nannoplankton* (variant of NANOPLANKTON) + FOSSIL.

nan·ny /ˈnanē/ ▸*n.* (*pl.* **-nies**) **1** a person, typically a woman, employed to care for a child in its own home. ■ *figurative* a person or institution regarded as interfering and overprotective: [as *adj.*] *a precarious path between freedom and the nanny state.* **2** (in full **nanny goat**) a female goat. ▸*v.* (**-nies, -nied**) [*trans.*] [usu. as *n.*] (**nannying**) be overprotective toward: *his well-intentioned nannying.* ▷early 18th cent. (as a noun): nickname for the given name *Ann*. The verb dates from the 1950s.

nan·ny cam ▸*n.* a webcam or closed-circuit television camera in a private home for parents to monitor their babysitter.

nan·ny·gai /ˈnanēˌgī/ ▸*n.* (*pl.* **-gais**) the redfish of Australia (*Centroberyx affinis*). ▷late 19th cent.: from a New South Wales Aboriginal language.

na·no /ˈnanō/ ▸*n. informal* short for NANOTECHNOLOGY.

nano- ▸*comb. form* denoting a factor of 10^{-9} (used commonly in units of measurement): *nanosecond.* ■ denoting a very small item: *nanoplankton.* ▷via Latin from Greek *nanos* 'dwarf.'

nan·o·bac·te·ri·um /ˌnanōbakˈti(ə)rēəm; ˌnā-/ ▸*n.* (*pl.* **-te·ri·a** /-ˈti(ə)rēə/) a microorganism about a tenth the size of the smallest normal bacteria, claimed to have been discovered in living tissue and in rock.

nan·obe /ˈnanˌōb; ˈnāˌnōb/ ▸ another term for NANOBACTERIUM. ▷by shortening and alteration.

nan·o·me·ter /ˈnanəˌmētər/ (*Brit.* **nan·o·me·tre**) (abbr.: **nm**) ▸*n.* one billionth of a meter.

nan·o·plank·ton /ˌnanəˈplaNGktən/ ▸*n. Biology* very small unicellular plankton, at the limits of resolution of light microscopy. ▷early 20th cent.: from German, from Greek *nanos* 'dwarf' + PLANKTON.

nan·o·ro·bot /ˈnanəˌrōbät; -bət; ˈnā-/ ▸*n.* a machine made from individual atoms or molecules that is designed to perform a small and specific job.

nan·o·scale /ˈnanəˌskāl, ˈnā-/ ▸*adj.* of a size measurable in nanometers or microns: *the use of viruses as nanoscale building tools.*

nan·o·struc·ture /ˈnanəˌstrəkCHər; ˈnā-/ ▸*n.* a nanoscale object: *tightly bound micelle nanostructures.*

nan·o·sec·ond /ˈnanəˌsekənd/ (abbr.: **ns**) ▸*n.* one billionth of a second.

nan·o·tech·nol·o·gy /ˌnanəˌtekˈnäləjē; ˌnanō-/ ▸*n.* the branch of technology that deals with dimensions and tolerances of less than 100 nanometers, esp. the manipulation of individual atoms and molecules. —**nan·o·tech·no·log·i·cal** /ˌteknəˈläjikəl/ *adj.* —**nan·o·tech·nol·o·gist** /-jist/ *n.*

nan·o·tube /ˈnanəˌt(y)o͞ob/ ▸*n. Chemistry* a cylindrical molecule of a fullerene.

nan·o·wire /ˈnanəˌwī(ə)r; ˈnā-/ ▸*n.* a nanoscale rod made of semiconducting material, used in miniature transistors and some laser applications.

Nan·sen /ˈnansən; ˈnän-/, Fridtjof (1861–1930), Norwegian Arctic explorer. In 1888, he led the first expedition to cross the Greenland ice fields, and, five years later, on board the *Fram*, he sailed from Siberia for the North Pole, which he failed to reach. He later organized relief work among the victims of famine in Russia. Nobel Peace Prize (1922).

Nan·sen pass·port ▸*n. historical* a document of identification issued to stateless people after World War I.

Nantes /näNt/ a city in western France, on the Loire River; pop. 252,000.

Nantes, E·dict of an edict of 1598 signed by Henry IV of France granting toleration to Protestants and ending the French Wars of Religion. It was revoked by Louis XIV in 1685.

Nan·tuck·et /nanˈtəkit/ an island off the coast of Massachusetts, south of Cape Cod and east of Martha's Vineyard. Now a popular resort, it was an important whaling center during the 18th and 19th centuries.

nap[1] /nap/ ▸*v.* (**napped, nap·ping**) [*intrans.*] sleep lightly or briefly, esp. during the day. ▸*n.* a short sleep, esp. during the day: *excuse me, I'll just take a little nap.* ▷Old English *hnappian*, probably of Germanic origin.

▸PHRASE □ **catch someone napping** *informal* (of a person, action, or event) find someone off guard and unprepared to respond: *he caught the runner napping off second base and tagged him out.*

nap[2] ▸*n.* [in *sing.*] the raised hairs, threads, or similar small projections on the surface of fabric or suede (used esp. with reference to the direction in which they naturally lie): *carefully machine the seam, following the direction of the nap.* ▷late Middle English *noppe*, from Middle Dutch, Middle Low German *noppe* 'nap,' *noppen* 'trim the nap from.' —**nap·less** *adj.*

nap[3] ▸*n.* a card game resembling whist in which players declare the number of tricks they expect to take, up to five. ▷early 19th cent.: abbreviation of NAPOLEON, the original name of the card game.

nap[4] ▸*v.* (**napped, nap·ping**) [*intrans.*] (of a horse) refuse, esp. habitually, to go on at the rider's instruction; jib. ▷1950s: back-formation from *nappy*, an adjective first used to describe heady beer (late Middle English), later used in the sense 'intoxicated by drink' (early 18th cent.), and since the 1920s used to describe a disobedient horse. —**nap·py** /ˈnapē/ *adj.*

NAPA ▸*abbr.* National Association of Performing Artists.

Na·pa /ˈnapə/ a commercial city in north central California, hub of the wine-making Napa Valley; pop. 61,842.

na·pa ▸*n.* variant spelling of NAPPA.

na·pa cab·bage /ˈnapə; ˈnä-/ ▸*n.* a cabbagelike Chinese plant whose long, white leaves are used in salads and cooking. ▷*napa*, of unknown origin.

na·palm /ˈnāpä(l)m/ ▸*n.* a highly flammable sticky jelly used in incendiary bombs and flamethrowers, consisting of gasoline thickened with special soaps. ▸*v.* [*trans.*] attack with bombs containing napalm. ▷1940s: from *na(phthenic)* and *palm(itic acid)*.

nape /nāp/ ▸*n.* (also **nape of the neck**) the back of a person's neck. ▷Middle English: of unknown origin.

Na·per·ville /ˈnāpərˌvil/ a city in northeastern Illinois, west of Chicago; pop. 128,358.

na·per·y /ˈnāpərē/ ▸*n.* household linen, esp. tablecloths and napkins. ▷Middle English: from Old French *naperie*, from *nape* 'tablecloth.'

Naph·ta·li /ˈnaftəˌlī/ (in the Bible) a Hebrew patriarch, second son of Jacob and Bilhah (Gen. 30:7–8). ■ the tribe of Israel traditionally descended from him.

naph·tha /ˈnafTHə; ˈnap-/ ▸*n. Chemistry* a flammable oil containing various hydrocarbons, obtained by the dry distillation of organic substances such as coal, shale, or petroleum. ▷late Middle English *napte*, from Latin *naphtha*, from Greek, of Asian origin; the Latin spelling was introduced in the late 16th cent.

naph·tha·lene /ˈnafTHəˌlēn; ˈnap-/ ▸*n. Chemistry* a volatile white crystalline compound produced by the distillation of coal tar, used in mothballs and as a raw material for chemical manufacture. • A bicyclic aromatic hydrocarbon; chem. formula: $C_{10}H_8$. ▷early 19th cent.: from NAPHTHA + -ENE, with the insertion of *-l-* for ease of pronunciation. —**naph·thal·ic** /nafˈTHalik; nap-/ *adj.*

naph·thene /ˈnafTHēn; nap-/ ▸*n. Chemistry* any of a group of cyclic aliphatic hydrocarbons (e.g., cyclohexane) obtained from petroleum. —**naph·the·nic** /nafˈTHēnik; nap-; -THenik/ *adj.*

naph·thol /ˈnafTHôl; ˈnap-; -THäl/ ▸*n. Chemistry* a crystalline solid derived from naphthalene, used to make antiseptics and dyes. • Chem. formula: $C_{10}H_7OH$; two isomers, esp. naphthalen-2-ol (**β-naphthol**).

Na·pi·er /ˈnāpēər; nəˈpi(ə)r/, John (1550–1617), Scottish mathematician. He invented the logarithm.

na·pi·er grass /ˈnāpēər/ ▸*n.* another term for ELEPHANT GRASS.

Na·pier·i·an log·a·rithm /nāˈpi(ə)rēən; nə-/ ▸*n.* another term for NATURAL LOGARITHM. ▷early 19th cent.: named after J. NAPIER.

Na·pier's bones ▸*plural n. Mathematics* slips of ivory or other material divided into sections marked with digits, devised by John Napier and formerly used to facilitate multiplication and division.

nap·kin /ˈnapkin/ ▸*n.* **1** (also **table napkin**) a square piece of cloth or paper used at a meal to wipe the fingers or lips and to protect garments, or to serve food on. **2** another term for SANITARY NAPKIN. **3** *Brit., dated* a baby's diaper. ▷late Middle English: from Old French *nappe* 'tablecloth' (from Latin *mappa*: see MAP) + -KIN.

nap·kin ring ▸*n.* a ring used to hold (and distinguish) a person's table napkin when not in use.

Na·ples /ˈnāpəlz/ **1** a city and port on the western coast of Italy; pop. 1,206,000. It was formerly the capital of the kingdom of Naples and Sicily (1816–60). Italian name NAPOLI. **2** a resort city in southwestern Florida, on the Gulf of Mexico; pop. 19,505. ▷from Latin *Neapolis*, from Greek *neos* 'new' + *polis* 'city.'

Na·ples yel·low ▸*n.* a pale yellow pigment containing lead and antimony oxides. ■ the pale yellow color of this pigment, now commonly produced using cadmium, zinc, or iron-based substitutes. ▷mid 18th cent.: named after NAPLES, the city where such a pigment was originally made.

Na·po·le·on /nəˈpōlēən; -yən/ the name of three rulers of France: ■ **Napoleon I** (1769–1821), emperor 1804–14 and 1815; full name *Napoleon Bonaparte*; known as **Napoleon**. In 1799, he joined a conspiracy that overthrew the Directory, becoming the supreme ruler of France. He declared himself emperor in 1804 and established an empire stretching from Spain to Poland. After defeats at Trafalgar in 1805 and in Russia in 1812, he abdicated and was exiled to the island of Elba in 1814. He returned to power in 1815, but was defeated at Waterloo and exiled to the island of St. Helena. ■ **Napoleon II** (1811–1832), son of Napoleon I and Empress Marie-Louise; full name *Napoleon François Charles Joseph Bonaparte*. ■ **Napoleon III** (1808–73), emperor 1852–70; full name *Charles Louis Napoleon Bonaparte*; known as **Louis-Napoleon**. A nephew of Napoleon I, Napoleon III was elected president of the Second Republic in 1848 and staged a coup in 1851.

na·po·le·on /nəˈpōlēən/ ▸*n.* **1** a flaky rectangular pastry with a sweet filling. **2** *historical* a gold twenty-franc French coin minted during the reign of Napoleon I. **3** (also **napoleon boot**) *historical* a 19th-century man's boot reaching above the knee in front and with a piece cut out behind, originally worn by cavalrymen.

Na·po·le·on·ic Wars /nəˌpōlēˈänik/ a series of campaigns (1800–15) of French armies under Napoleon against Austria, Russia, Great Britain, Portugal, Prussia, and other European powers. They ended with Napoleon's defeat at the Battle of Waterloo.

Na·po·li /ˈnäpəlē/ Italian name for NAPLES.

nap·pa /ˈnapə/ (also **nap·a**) ▸*n.* a soft leather made by a special tawing process from the skin of sheep or goats. ▷late 19th cent.: from *Napa*, the name of a valley in California.

nappe /nap/ ▸*n. Geology* a sheet of rock that has moved sideways over neighboring strata as a result of an overthrust or folding. ▷late 19th cent.: from French *nappe* 'tablecloth.'

napped[1] /napt/ ▸*adj.* [usu. in *combination*] (of a textile) having a nap, usually of a specified kind: *a long-napped paint roller.*

napped[2] ▸*adj.* (of food) served in a sauce or other liquid: *mushrooms* **napped with** *melted butter.* ▷1970s: from French *napper* 'coat with (a sauce),' from *nappe* 'cloth,' figuratively 'pool of liquid,' + -ED[2].

nap·py[1] /ˈnapē/ ▸*n.* (*pl.* **-pies**) *Brit.* a baby's diaper. ▷early 20th cent.: abbreviation of NAPKIN.

nap·py[2] ▸*adj. informal* (of a black person's hair) frizzy. ▷late 15th cent. (in the sense 'shaggy'): from Middle Dutch *noppigh*, Middle Low German *noppich*, from *noppe* (see NAP[2]). The current sense dates from the early 20th cent.

na·prox·en /nəˈpräksən/ ▸*n. Medicine* a synthetic compound used as an anti-inflammatory drug, esp. in the treatment of headache and arthritis. • Chem. formula: $C_{14}H_{14}O_3$. ▷1970s: from *na(phthyl)* + *pr(opionic)* + *ox(y-)*, + *-en* on the pattern of words such as *tamoxifen.*

Na·ra /ˈnäˈrä/ a city in central Japan, on the island of Honshu; pop. 349,000. It was the first capital of Japan (710–784) and an important center of Japanese Buddhism.

Na·ra·yan /nəˈrīən/, R. K. (1906–2001), Indian novelist and short-story writer; full name *Rasipuram Krishnaswamy Narayan.* Many of his novels are set in Malgudi, an imaginary small Indian town. Notable works: *Swami and Friends* (1935), *The Man-Eater of Malgudi* (1961), and *The Painter of Signs* (1977).

Na·ra·yan·ganj /nəˈrāyəNG,gənj/ a river port in Bangladesh, on the Ganges delta southeast of Dhaka; pop. 406,000.

narc /närk/ (also **nark**) ▸*n. informal* a federal agent or police officer who enforces the laws regarding illicit sale or use of drugs and narcotics. ▷1960s: abbreviation of NARCOTIC.

nar·cis·sism /ˈnärsə,sizəm/ ▸*n.* excessive or erotic interest in oneself and one's physical appearance. ■ *Psychology* extreme selfishness, with a grandiose view of one's own talents and a craving for admiration, as characterizing a personality type. See note at EGOTISM. ■ *Psychoanalysis* self-centeredness arising from failure to distinguish the self from external objects, either in very young babies or as a feature of mental disorder. ▷early 19th cent.: via Latin from the Greek name *Narkissos* (see NARCISSUS) + -ISM. —**nar·cis·sist** /ˈnärsəsəst/ *n.* —**nar·cis·sis·tic** /,närsəˈsistik/ *adj.* —**nar·cis·sis·ti·cal·ly** /,närsəˈsistik(ə)lē/ *adv.*

Nar·cis·sus /närˈsisəs/ *Greek Mythology* a beautiful youth who rejected the nymph Echo and fell in love with his own reflection in a pool. He pined away and was changed into the flower that bears his name.

nar·cis·sus /närˈsisəs/ ▸*n.* (*pl.* same, **-cis·si** /-ˈsisī; -sē/, or **-cissuses**) a bulbous Eurasian plant of a genus that includes the daffodil, esp. (in gardening) one with flowers that have white or pale outer petals and a shallow orange or yellow cup in the center. • Genus *Narcissus*, family Liliaceae (or Amaryllidaceae): many species and varieties, in particular *N. poeticus.* ▷via Latin from Greek *narkissos*, perhaps from *narkē* 'numbness,' with reference to its narcotic effects.

nar·co /ˈnärkō/ ▸*n.* (*pl.* **-cos**) *informal* short for NARCOTIC. ■ a dealer in drugs. ■ a narcotics officer.

narco- ▸*comb. form* relating to a state of insensibility: *narcolepsy.* ■ relating to narcotic drugs or their use: *narcoterrorism.* ▷from Greek *narkē* 'numbness.'

nar·co·lep·sy /ˈnärkə,lepsē/ ▸*n. Medicine* a condition characterized by an extreme tendency to fall asleep whenever in relaxing surroundings. ▷late 19th cent.: from Greek *narkē* 'numbness,' on the pattern of *epilepsy.* —**nar·co·lep·tic** /,närkəˈleptik/ *adj.* & *n.*

nar·co·sis /närˈkōsis/ ▸*n. Medicine* a state of stupor, drowsiness, or unconsciousness produced by drugs. See also NITROGEN NARCOSIS. ▷late 17th cent.: from Greek *narkōsis*, from *narkoun* 'make numb.'

nar·co·ter·ror·ism /,närkōˈterə,rizəm/ ▸*n.* terrorism associated with trade in illicit drugs. ▷1980s: from NARCO- 'relating to illegal narcotics' + *terrorism* (see TERRORIST). —**nar·co·ter·ror·ist** *n.*

nar·cot·ic /närˈkätik/ ▸*n.* a drug or other substance affecting mood or behavior and sold for nonmedical purposes, esp. an illegal one. ■ *Medicine* a drug that relieves pain and induces drowsiness, stupor, or insensibility.

▸*adj.* relating to or denoting narcotics or their effects or use: *the substance has a mild narcotic effect.* ▷late Middle English: from Old French *narcotique*, via medieval Latin from Greek *narkōtikos*, from *narkoun* 'make numb.' —**nar·cot·i·cal·ly** /-tik(ə)lē/ *adv.* —**nar·co·tism** /ˈnärkə,tizəm/ *n.*

nar·co·tize /ˈnärkə,tīz/ ▸*v.* [*trans.*] stupefy with or as if with a drug. ■ make (something) have a soporific or narcotic effect: *the essence of apple blossom narcotizes the air.* —**nar·co·ti·za·tion** /,närkətiˈzāSHən/ *n.*

nard /närd/ ▸*n.* the Himalayan spikenard. ▷late Old English, via Latin from Greek *nardos*; related to Sanskrit *nalada, narada.*

nar·es /ˈne(ə)rēz/ ▸*plural n.* (*sing.* **nar·is** /ˈne(ə)ris/) *Anatomy & Zoology* the nostrils. ▷late 17th cent.: plural of Latin *naris* 'nostril, nose.' —**nar·i·al** /-ēəl/ *adj.*

nar·ghi·le /ˈnärgəlē/ (also **nar·gi·leh**) ▸*n.* an oriental tobacco pipe with a long tube that draws the smoke through water; a hookah. ▷mid 18th cent.: from Persian *nārgīl* 'coconut, hookah,' from Sanskrit *nārikela* 'coconut.'

nar·is /ˈne(ə)ris/ ▸ singular form of NARES.

nark /närk/ *informal* ▸*n.* **1** variant spelling of NARC. **2** *chiefly Brit.* a police informer. **3** *Austral./NZ* an annoying person or thing.

▸*v.* [*trans.*] (usu. **be narked**) *chiefly Brit.* annoy or exasperate: *I was narked at being pushed around.* ▷mid 19th cent.: from Romany *nāk* 'nose.'

▸*PHRASE* □ *chiefly Brit.* **nark it!** stop that!

Nar·ma·da /nərˈmədə/ a river that rises in Madhya Pradesh, central India, and flows west for 778 miles (1,245 km) to the Gulf of Cambay. Hindus consider it a sacred river.

Nar·ra·gan·sett /,narəˈgansit/ (also **Nar·ra·gan·set**) ▸*n.* (*pl.* same or **-setts**) **1** a member of an American Indian people originally of Rhode Island. They came into conflict with the New England colonists in the 17th century, and few now remain. **2** the Algonquian language of this people. ▷the name in Narragansett, literally 'people of the promontory.'

Nar·ra·gan·sett Bay an inlet of the Atlantic Ocean in southeastern Rhode Island.

nar·rate /ˈnar,āt/ ▸*v.* [*trans.*] (often **be narrated**) give a spoken or written account of: *the voyages, festivities, and intrigues are narrated with unflagging gusto* | *the tough-but-sensitive former bouncer narrates much of the story.* ■ provide a spoken commentary to accompany (a movie, broadcast, piece of music, etc.). ▷mid 17th cent.: from Latin *narrat-* 'related, told,' from the verb *narrare* (from *gnarus* 'knowing'). —**nar·rat·a·ble** *adj.* —**nar·ra·tion** /naˈrāSHən/ *n.*

nar·ra·tive /ˈnarətiv/ ▸*n.* a spoken or written account of connected events; a story: *the hero of his modest narrative.* ■ the narrated part or parts of a literary work, as distinct from dialogue. ■ the practice or art of narration: *traditions of oral narrative.*

▸*adj.* in the form of or concerned with narration: *a narrative poem* | *narrative technique.* ▷late Middle English (as an adjective): from French *narratif, -ive*, from late Latin *narrativus* 'telling a story,' from the verb *narrare* (see NARRATE). —**nar·ra·tive·ly** *adv.*

nar·ra·tiv·i·ty /,narəˈtivətē/ ▸*n.* the quality or condition of presenting a narrative: *music has developed a narrativity that lends it the character of language.* ▷1970s: from French *narrativité.*

nar·ra·tiv·ize /ˈnarəti,vīz/ ▸*v.* [*trans.*] present or interpret (something such as experience or theory) in the form of a story or narrative.

nar·ra·tol·o·gy /,narəˈtäləjē/ ▸*n.* the branch of knowledge or literary criticism that deals with the structure and function of narrative and its themes, conventions, and symbols. —**nar·ra·to·log·i·cal** /,narətlˈäjikəl/ *adj.* —**nar·ra·tol·o·gist** /-jist/ *n.*

nar·ra·tor /ˈnarātər/ ▸*n.* a person who narrates something, esp. a character who recounts the events of a novel or narrative poem. ■ a person who delivers a commentary accompanying a movie, broadcast, piece of music, etc. —**nar·ra·to·ri·al** /,narəˈtôrēəl/ *adj.*

nar·row /ˈnarō/ ▸*adj.* (**-row·er**, **-row·est**) **1** (esp. of something that is considerably longer or higher than it is wide) of small width: *he made his way down the narrow road.* **2** limited in extent, amount, or scope; restricted: *his ability to get good results within narrow constraints of money and manpower.* ■ (of a person's attitude or beliefs) limited in range and lacking willingness or ability to appreciate alternative views: *companies fail through their narrow view of what contributes to profit.* ■ precise or strict in meaning: *some of the narrower definitions of democracy.* ■ (of a phonetic transcription) showing fine details of accent. ■ *Phonetics* denoting a vowel pronounced with the root of the tongue drawn back so as to narrow the pharynx. **3** (esp. of a victory, defeat, or escape) with only a small margin; barely achieved.

▸*v.* **1** become or make less wide: [*intrans.*] *the road narrowed and crossed an old bridge* | [*trans.*] *the embankment was built to narrow the river.* ■ [*intrans.*] (of a person's eyes) almost closed so as to focus on something or someone, or to indicate anger, suspicion, or other emotion: *Jake's eyes had* **narrowed to** *pinpoints.* ■ [*trans.*] (of a person) cause (one's eyes) to do this: *she narrowed her eyes at him suspiciously.* **2** become or make more limited or restricted in extent or scope: [*intrans.*] *their trade surplus* **narrowed to** *$70 million in January* | [*trans.*] *New England had narrowed Denver's lead from 13 points to 4.*

▸*phrasal v.* □ **narrow something down** reduce the number of possibilities or options of something: *the company has narrowed down the candidates for the job to two.*

▸*n.* (**narrows**) a narrow channel connecting two larger areas of water: *a basaltic fang rising from the narrows of the Upper Missouri.* ▷Old English *nearu*, of Germanic origin; related to Dutch *naar* 'dismal, unpleasant' and German *Narbe* 'scar.' Early senses in English included 'constricted' and 'miserly.' —**nar·row·ish** *adj.* —**nar·row·ness** *n.*

▸*PHRASE* □ **narrow circumstances** poverty.

nar·row·band /ˈnarō,band/ ▸*adj.* of or involving signals over a narrow range of frequencies.

nar·row·boat /ˈnarō,bōt/ ▸*n. Brit.* a canal boat less than 7 feet (2.1 m) wide with a maximum length of 70 feet (21.3 m) and steered with a tiller rather than a wheel.

nar·row·cast /ˈnarō,kast/ ▸*v.* (*past* and *past part.* **-cast** or **-cast·ed**) [*intrans.*] transmit a television program, esp. by cable, or otherwise disseminate information, to a comparatively small audience defined by special interest or geographical location: *the channel is licensed to narrowcast only to nondomestic outlets* | [as *n.*] (**narrowcasting**) *one journal has avoided the narrowcasting that seems to enslave so many mainstream magazines.*

▸*n.* transmission or dissemination in this way: *Colorado women's volleyball narrowcasts* | [as *adj.*] *narrowcast specialty channels.* ▷1930s: back-formation from *narrowcasting*, on the pattern of *broadcasting.* —**nar·row·cast·er** *n.*

nar·row gauge ▸*n.* a railroad gauge that is narrower than the standard gauge of 56.5 inches (143.5 c m).

nar·row·ly /ˈnerōlē/ ▸*adv.* **1** by only a small margin; barely: *he narrowly defeated Anderson to win a 12th term in office.* **2** closely or carefully: *he was looking at her narrowly.* **3** in a limited or restricted way: *narrowly defined tasks.*

nar·row-mind·ed ▸*adj.* not willing to listen to or tolerate other people's views; prejudiced. —**nar·row-mind·ed·ly** *adv.* —**nar·row-mind·ed·ness** *n.*

nar·row mon·ey ▸*n. Economics* money in forms that can be used as a medium of exchange, generally banknotes, coins, and certain balances held by banks.

Nar·rows /ˈnarōz/ (**the Narrows**) a strait about 2 miles (3.2 km) long connecting upper and lower New York Bay, between Staten Island and Brooklyn.

nar·thex /ˈnärTHeks/ ▸*n.* an antechamber, porch, or distinct area at the western entrance of some early Christian churches, separated off by a railing and used by catechumens, penitents, etc. ■ an antechamber or large porch in a modern church. ▷late 17th cent.: via Latin from Greek *narthēx.*

nar·whal /ˈnärwəl/ ▸*n.* a small Arctic whale, the male of which has a long forward-pointing spirally twisted tusk developed from one of its teeth. See WHALE[1]. • *Monodon monoceros*, family Monodontidae. ▷mid 17th cent.: from Dutch *narwal*, Danish *narhval*, based on Old Norse *nár* 'corpse,' with reference to skin color.

nar·y /ˈne(ə)rē/ ▸*adj.* informal or dialect form of NOT: *nary a murmur or complaint.* ▷mid 18th cent.: from the phrase *ne'er a.*

NASA /ˈnasə/ ▸*abbr.* National Aeronautics and Space Administration.

na·sal /ˈnāzəl/ ▸*adj.* **1** of, for, or relating to the nose: *the nasal passages* | *a nasal spray.* **2** (of a speech sound) pronounced by the voice resonating in the nose, e.g., *m, n, ng.* Compare with ORAL (sense 2). ■ (of the voice or speech) produced or characterized by resonating in the nose as well as the mouth.

Pronunciation Key ə *ago*; ər *over*; ˈə or ,ə *up*; ˈər or ,ər *fur*; a *hat*; ā *rate*; ä *car*; CH *chew*; e *let*; ē *see*; e(ə)r *air*; i *fit*; ī *by*; i(ə)r *ear*; NG *sing*; ō *go*; ô *for*; oi *boy*; o͝o *good*; o͞o *goo*; ou *out*; SH *she*; TH *thin*; T͟H *then*; (h)w *why*; ZH *vision*

N

▸*n.* **1** a nasal speech sound. **2** *historical* a nosepiece on a helmet. ▷Middle English (sense 2 of the *noun*): from medieval Latin *nasalis*, from Latin *nasus* 'nose.' **—na·sal·i·ty** /nā'zalitē/ *n.* **—na·sal·ly** *adv.*

na·sal con·cha ▸*n.* see CONCHA.

na·sal·ize /'nāzə,līz/ ▸*v.* [*trans.*] pronounce or utter (a speech sound) with the breath resonating in the nose: [as *adj.*] (**nasalized**) *a nasalized vowel.* **—na·sal·i·za·tion** /,nāzəli'zāSHən/ *n.*

NASCAR /'nas,kär/ ▸*abbr.* National Association for Stock Car Auto Racing.

nas·cent /'nāsənt; 'nasənt/ ▸*adj.* (esp. of a process or organization) just coming into existence and beginning to display signs of future potential: *the nascent space industry.* ■ *Chemistry* (chiefly of hydrogen) freshly generated in a reactive form. ▷early 17th cent.: from Latin *nascent-* 'being born,' from the verb *nasci.* **—nas·cence** *n.* **—nas·cen·cy** *n.*

NASD ▸*abbr.* National Association of Securities Dealers.

NASDAQ /'nazdak/ ▸*abbr.* National Association of Securities Dealers Automated Quotations, a computerized system for trading in securities.

Nase·by, Bat·tle of /'nāzbē/ a major battle of the English Civil War that took place in 1645 near the village of Naseby in Northamptonshire. The Royalist army of Prince Rupert and King Charles I was decisively defeated by the New Model Army under General Thomas Fairfax (1612–71) and Oliver Cromwell.

Nash[1] /naSH/, (Frederic) Ogden (1902–71), U.S. poet. His sophisticated light verse comprised puns, epigrams, and other verbal eccentricities and appeared in many collections from 1931.

Nash[2], John (1752–1835), English town planner and architect. He planned the layout of Regent's Park 1811–25 and Trafalgar Square 1826–*c.*1835, and designed the Marble Arch.

Nashe /naSH/, Thomas (1567–1601), English pamphleteer, prose writer, and playwright.

Nash e·qui·lib·ri·um ▸*n.* (in economics and game theory) a stable state of a system involving the interaction of different participants, in which no participant can gain by a unilateral change of strategy if the strategies of the others remain unchanged.

na·shi /'näSHē/ (also **nashi pear**) ▸*n.* another term for ASIAN PEAR. ▷1960s: from Japanese, literally 'pear.'

Nash·ua /'naSHo͞oə/ an industrial city on the Merrimack River in southern New Hampshire; pop. 86,605.

Nash·ville /'naSH,vil; -vəl/ the capital of Tennessee, in the north central part of the state, on the Cumberland River; pop. 569,891. It is noted for its music industry and for the Country Music Hall of Fame.

Na·sik /'näsik/ a city in western India, in Maharashtra, on the Godavari River, northeast of Bombay; pop. 647,000.

naso- ▸*comb. form* relating to the nose: *nasogastric.* ▷from Latin *nasus* 'nose.'

na·so·gas·tric /,nāzō'gastrik/ ▸*adj.* reaching or supplying the stomach via the nose: *she had to be fed by a nasogastric tube.*

na·so·phar·ynx /,nāzō'fariNGks/ ▸*n.* *Anatomy* the upper part of the pharynx, connecting with the nasal cavity above the soft palate. **—na·so·pha·ryn·ge·al** /-fə'rinj(ē)əl; -,farin'jēəl/ *adj.*

Nass /näs; nas/ ▸*n.* another name for NISHGA. ▷from the name of a river in British Colombia, Canada.

Nas·sau[1] /'na,sô/ **1** a former duchy of western Germany from which the House of Orange arose. **2** a port on the island of New Providence, capital of The Bahamas; pop. 172,000.

Nas·sau[2] ▸*n.* *Golf* an eighteen-hole match in which the players bet on the first nine holes, the second nine holes, and the entire round.

Nas·sau Coun·ty / 'nas,ô/ a county in central Long Island in New York, immediately east of Queens and home to many New York suburbs; pop. 1,334,544.

Nas·ser /'nasər; 'nä-/, Gamal Abdel (1918–70), Egyptian colonel and statesman; prime minister 1954–56 and president 1956–70. He deposed King Farouk in 1952 and President Muhammad Neguib in 1954. His nationalization of the Suez Canal brought war with Britain, France, and Israel in 1956; he also waged two unsuccessful wars against Israel (1956 and 1967).

Nas·ser, Lake a lake in southeastern Egypt that was created in the 1960s by building two dams on the Nile River at Aswan.

Nast /nast/, Thomas (1840–1902), U.S. political cartoonist; born in Germany. He was a staff artist at *Harper's Weekly* 1861–86 and creator of the Republican elephant and the Democratic donkey symbols as well as of the U.S. image of Santa Claus.

nas·tic /'nastik/ ▸*adj.* *Botany* (of the movement of plant parts) caused by an external stimulus but unaffected in direction by it. ▷early 20th cent.: from Greek *nastos* 'squeezed together' (from *nassein* 'to press') + -IC.

nas·tur·tium /na'stərSHəm; nə-/ ▸*n.* a South American trailing plant with round leaves and bright orange, yellow, or red edible flowers that is widely grown as an ornamental. • *Tropaeolum majus*, family Tropaeolaceae. ▷Old English, from Latin, apparently from *naris* 'nose' + *torquere* 'to twist.'

nas·ty /'nastē/ ▸*adj.* (**-ti·er**, **-ti·est**) **1** highly unpleasant, esp. to the senses; physically nauseating: *plastic bags burn with a nasty, acrid smell.* ■ (of the weather) unpleasantly cold or wet: *a cold, nasty day.* ■ repugnant to the mind; morally bad: *her stories are very nasty, full of murder and violence.* **2** (of a person or animal) behaving in an unpleasant or spiteful way: *Harry was a nasty, foul-mouthed old devil* | *when she confronted him, he turned nasty.* ■ annoying or unwelcome: *life has a nasty habit of repeating itself.* **3** physically or mentally damaging or harmful: *a nasty, vicious-looking hatchet.* ■ (of an injury, illness, or accident) having caused harm; severe: *a nasty bang on the head.*

▸*n.* (*pl.* **-ties**) (often **nasties**) *informal* an unpleasant or harmful person or thing: *bacteria and other nasties.* ■ *chiefly Brit.* a horror video or movie. ▷late Middle English: of unknown origin. **—nas·ti·ly** /-təlē/ *adv.* **—nas·ti·ness** *n.*

nas·ty·gram /'nastē,gram/ ▸*n.* *Computing* a particularly offensive electronic mail message.

nat. ▸*abbr.* ■ national. ■ nationalist. ■ native. ■ natural.

Na·tal /nə'täl/ **1** a province on the eastern coast of South Africa that was renamed KwaZulu-Natal in 1994. **2** a port on the Atlantic coast of northeastern Brazil; pop. 606,000.

na·tal[1] /'nātl/ ▸*adj.* of or relating to the place or time of one's birth: *after puberty a Hindu girl does not stay long in her natal home.* ▷late Middle English: from Latin *natalis*, from *nat-* 'born,' from the verb *nasci.*

na·tal[2] ▸*adj.* *Anatomy* of or relating to the buttocks: *the natal cleft.* ▷late 19th cent.: from NATES + -AL.

na·tal·i·ty /nā'talitē; nə-/ ▸*n.* the ratio of the number of births to the size of the population; birth rate: *in spite of falling natality, the population as a whole went up.* ▷late 19th cent.: from French *natalité*, from *nat-* 'born,' from the verb *nasci.*

na·tant /'nātnt/ ▸*adj.* *formal, rare* swimming or floating. ▷mid 18th cent.: from Latin *natant-* 'swimming,' from the verb *natare.*

na·ta·tion /nā'tāSHən; na-/ ▸*n.* *technical* or *poetic/literary* swimming. ▷mid 16th cent.: from Latin *natatio(n-)*, from *natare* 'to swim.' **—na·ta·to·ri·al** /,nātə'tôrēəl; ,na-/ *adj.* **—na·ta·to·ry** /'nātə,tôrē; 'na-/ *adj.*

na·ta·to·ri·um /,nātə'tôrēəm; ,na-/ ▸*n.* a swimming pool, esp. one that is indoors. ▷late 19th cent.: from late Latin, neuter (used as a noun) of *natatorius* 'relating to a swimmer,' from *natare* 'to swim.'

natch /naCH/ ▸*adv.* informal term for NATURALLY.

Natch·ez /'naCHiz/ a historic port city on the Mississippi River in southwestern Mississippi; pop. 19,460. The **Natchez Trace**, which leads from here to Nashville in Tennessee, was a 19th-century route for riverboatmen returning north from trips to New Orleans.

NATE ▸*abbr.* National Association of Teachers of English.

na·tes /'nā,tēz/ ▸*plural n.* *Anatomy* the buttocks. ▷late 17th cent.: Latin, plural of *natis* 'buttock, rump.'

nathe·less /'nāTHlis; 'na-/ (also **nath·less**) ▸*adv.* *archaic* nevertheless. ▷Old English.

Na·tion /'nāSHən/, Carrie Amelia (Moore) (1846–1911), U.S. temperance reformer. Her prohibitionist activism was characterized by scenes of hatchet-wielding saloon smashing, primarily in Kansas.

na·tion /'nāSHən/ ▸*n.* a large aggregate of people united by common descent, history, culture, or language, inhabiting a particular country or territory: *leading industrialized nations.* ■ a North American Indian people or confederation of peoples. ▷Middle English: via Old French from Latin *natio(n-)*, from *nat-* 'born,' from the verb *nasci.* **—na·tion·hood** /-,ho͝od/ *n.*

na·tion·al /'naSHənəl/ ▸*adj.* of or relating to a nation; common to or characteristic of a whole nation: *this policy may have been in the national interest* | *a national newspaper.* ■ owned, controlled, or financially supported by the federal government: *plans for a national art library.*

▸*n.* **1** a citizen of a particular country, typically entitled to hold that country's passport: *a German national* | *the new law on foreign nationals.* **2** (usu. **nationals**) a nationwide competition or tournament: *she finished 16th at the nationals that year.* ▷late 16th cent.: from French, from Latin *natio(n-)* 'birth, race of people' (see NATION). **—na·tion·al·ly** *adv.* [*sentence adverb*] *nationally, there has been a 2.5% drop in car crime.*

na·tion·al an·them ▸*n.* see ANTHEM (sense 1).

Na·tion·al As·sem·bly ▸*n.* an elected legislature in various countries. ■ *historical* the elected legislature in France during the first part of the French Revolution, 1789–91.

Na·tion·al As·so·ci·a·tion for the Ad·vance·ment of Col·ored Peo·ple (abbr.: **NAACP**) a U.S. civil rights organization set up in 1909 to oppose racial segregation and discrimination by nonviolent means.

na·tion·al bank ▸*n.* another term for CENTRAL BANK. ■ a commercial bank that is chartered under the federal government and is a member of the Federal Reserve System.

Na·tion·al Cit·y a city in southwestern California, south of San Diego, site of numerous naval facilities; pop. 54,249.

na·tion·al con·ven·tion ▸*n.* a convention of a major political party, esp. one that nominates a candidate for the presidency.

na·tion·al debt ▸*n.* the total amount of money that a country's government has borrowed, by various means.

Na·tion·al Foot·ball League (abbr. **NFL**) ▸*n.* the major professional football league in the U.S., consisting of the National and American football conferences and totaling thirty-one teams.

na·tion·al for·est ▸*n.* a large expanse of forest that is owned, maintained, and preserved by the federal government.

Na·tion·al Guard ▸*n.* **1** (in the U.S.) the primary reserve military force, partly maintained by the states but also available for federal use. ■ the primary military force of some other countries. **2** an armed force existing in France at various times between 1789 and 1871, first commanded by the Marquis de Lafayette. ■ a member of this force. **—Na·tion·al Guards·man** *n.*

na·tion·al in·come ▸*n.* the total amount of money earned within a country.

na·tion·al·ism /'naSHənə,lizəm/ ▸*n.* patriotic feeling, principles, or efforts. ■ an extreme form of this, esp. marked by a feeling of superiority over other countries. ■ advocacy of political independence for a particular country: *Palestinian nationalism.*

na·tion·al·ist /'naSHənəlist/ ▸*n.* a person who advocates political independence for a country: *a Scottish nationalist.* ■ a person with strong patriotic feelings, esp. one who believes in the superiority of their country over others.

▸*adj.* of or relating to nationalists or nationalism: *a nationalist movement.* **—na·tion·al·is·tic** /,naSHənə'listik/ *adj.* **—na·tion·al·is·ti·cal·ly** /,naSHənə'listik(ə)lē/ *adv.*

na·tion·al·i·ty /,naSHə'nalitē/ ▸*n.* (*pl.* **-ties**) **1** the status of belonging to a particular nation: *they changed their nationality and became Lebanese.* ■ distinctive national or ethnic character: *the change of a name does not discard nationality.* ■ patriotic sentiment; nationalism. **2** an ethnic group forming a part of one or more political nations: *all the main nationalities of Ethiopia.*

na·tion·al·ize /'naSHənə,līz/ ▸*v.* [*trans.*] **1** transfer (a major branch of industry or commerce) from private to state ownership or control. **2** make distinctively national; give a national character to: *in the 13th and 14th centuries church designs were further nationalized.* **3** [usu. as *adj.*] (**nationalized**) naturalize (a foreigner): *he is now a nationalized Frenchman.* **—na·tion·al·i·za·tion** /,naSHənəli'zāSHən/ *n.* **—na·tion·al·iz·er** *n.*

Na·tion·al League ▸*n.* one of the two major leagues in American professional baseball.

na·tion·al mon·u·ment ▸*n.* a historic site or geographical area set aside by a national government and maintained for public use.

na·tion·al park ▸*n.* a scenic or historically important area of countryside protected by the federal government for the enjoyment of the general public or the preservation of wildlife.

Na·tio·nal Ri·fle As·so·ci·a·tion (abbr. **NRA**) ▸*n.* a national organization founded in 1871 that promotes the legal use of guns and gun safety in the U.S. and defends a U.S. citizen's constitutional right to own and bear arms.

N

Na·tion·al Road a historic highway that in the early 19th century led from Maryland through the Appalachian Mountains to St. Louis in Missouri. It was once the major route for western expansion.

na·tion·al sea·shore ▸*n.* an expanse of coast protected and maintained by the federal government for the study of wildlife and for recreational use by the public.

Na·tion·al Se·cu·ri·ty A·gen·cy (abbr.: **NSA**) a secret body established in the U.S. after World War II to gather intelligence, deal with coded communications from around the world, and safeguard U.S. transmissions.

Na·tion·al Se·cu·ri·ty Coun·cil (abbr.: **NSC**) a body created in the U.S. by Congress after World War II to advise the president (who chairs it) on issues relating to national security in domestic, foreign, and military policy.

na·tion·al serv·ice ▸*n.* a period of compulsory service in the armed forces of some countries during peacetime. ■ a federal program that enables young people to pay back government loans through community work.

Na·tion·al So·cial·ism ▸*n. historical* the political doctrine of the Nazi Party of Germany. See NAZI. —**Na·tion·al So·cial·ist** *n.*

Na·tion·al Trust a trust for the preservation of places of historic interest or natural beauty in Britain.

Na·tion of Is·lam an exclusively black Islamic sect proposing a separate black nation, founded in Detroit *c.*1930. It was led from 1934 by Elijah Muhammad (1897–1975) and came to prominence under the influence of Malcolm X. Its current leader is Louis Farrakhan.

na·tion-state ▸*n.* a sovereign state whose citizens or subjects are relatively homogeneous in factors such as language or common descent.

na·tion·wide /ˈnāSHənˈwīd/ ▸*adj.* extending or reaching throughout the whole nation: *a nationwide hunt.*
▸*adv.* throughout a whole nation: *it employs 6,000 people nationwide.*

na·tive /ˈnātiv/ ▸*n.* a person born in a specified place or associated with a place by birth, whether subsequently resident there or not: *a* ***native of*** *Montreal | an eighteen-year-old Brooklyn native.* ■ a local inhabitant: *New York in the summer was too hot even for the natives.* ■ *dated, often offensive* one of the original inhabitants of a country, esp. a nonwhite as regarded by European colonists or travelers. ■ an animal or plant indigenous to a place: *the marigold is* ***a native of*** *southern Europe.*
▸*adj.* **1** associated with the country, region, or circumstances of a person's birth: *he's a native New Yorker | her native country.* ■ of the indigenous inhabitants of a place: *a ceremonial native dance from Fiji.* **2** (of a plant or animal) of indigenous origin or growth: *pigs are* ***native to*** *China | America's native black bear.* **3** (of a quality) belonging to a person's character from birth rather than acquired; innate: *some last vestige of native wit prompted Guy to say nothing | a jealousy and rage* ***native to*** *him.* ■ *Computing* designed for or built into a given system, esp. denoting the language associated with a given processor, computer, or compiler, and programs written in it. **4** (of a metal or other mineral) found in a pure or uncombined state. ▷late Middle English: from Latin *nativus*, from *nat-* 'born,' from the verb *nasci.* —**na·tive·ly** *adv.* —**na·tive·ness** *n.*
▸**PHRASE** □ **go native** *humorous* or *derogatory* (of a person living away from their own country or region) abandon one's own culture, customs, or way of life and adopt those of the country or region one is living in.

USAGE In contexts such as *a* ***native*** *of Boston*, the use of the noun **native** is quite acceptable. But when used as a noun without qualification, as in *this dance is a favorite with the* ***natives***, it is more problematic. In modern use, it is used humorously to refer to the local inhabitants of a particular place: *that bar is no longer popular with the* ***natives***. In other contexts, it has an old-fashioned feel and, because of being closely associated with a colonial European outlook on nonwhite peoples living in remote places, it may cause offense.

THE RIGHT WORD **aboriginal, endemic, indigenous, native**

A **native** New Yorker is probably not **indigenous**, although both words apply to persons or things that belong to or are associated with a particular place by birth or origin.

Native means born or produced in a specific region or country (*native plants; native dances*), but it can also apply to persons or things that were introduced from elsewhere some time ago—which is the case with most New Yorkers who consider themselves natives.

Indigenous, on the other hand, is more restricted in meaning; it applies only to someone or something that is not only native but was not introduced from elsewhere (*the pumpkin is indigenous to North America*). Generally speaking, *native* applies to individual organisms, while *indigenous* applies to races or species.

Something that is **endemic** is prevalent in a particular region because of special conditions there that favor its growth or existence (*heather is endemic in the Scottish Highlands; malaria is endemic in Central America*).

There are no longer any **aboriginal** New Yorkers, a word that refers to the earliest known inhabitants of a place or to ancient peoples who have no known ancestors and have inhabited a region since its earliest historical time. Australia is known for its *aboriginal* culture, which was preserved for centuries through geographical isolation.

Na·tive A·mer·i·can ▸*n.* a member of any of the indigenous peoples of the Americas.
▸*adj.* of or relating to these peoples.

USAGE **Native American** is now an accepted term in many contexts. The term **American Indian** is also used widely and acceptably.
See also **usage** at AMERICAN INDIAN.

na·tive speak·er ▸*n.* a person who has spoken the language in question from earliest childhood: *native speakers of English.*

na·tiv·ism /ˈnātiˌvizəm/ ▸*n.* **1** the policy of protecting the interests of native-born or established inhabitants against those of immigrants: *a deep vein of xenophobia and nativism.* **2** a return to or emphasis on traditional or local customs, in opposition to outside influences. **3** the theory or doctrine that concepts, mental capacities, and mental structures are innate rather than acquired or learned. —**na·tiv·ist** *n. & adj.* —**na·tiv·is·tic** /ˌnātiˈvistik/ *adj.*

na·tiv·i·ty /nəˈtivitē; nā-/ ▸*n.* (*pl.* **-ties**) the occasion of a person's birth: *the place of my nativity.* ■ (usu. **the Nativity**) the birth of Jesus Christ. ■ a picture, carving, or model representing Jesus Christ's birth. ■ a nativity play. ■ the Christian festival of Christ's birth; Christmas. ■ *dated Astrology* a horoscope relating to the time of birth; a birth chart. ▷Middle English: from Old French *nativite*, from late Latin *nativitas*, from Latin *nativus* 'arisen by birth' (see NATIVE).

na·tiv·i·ty play ▸*n.* a play, typically performed by children at Christmas, based on the events surrounding the birth of Jesus Christ.

na·tiv·i·ty scene ▸*n.* another term for CRÈCHE (sense 1).

natl. ▸*abbr.* national.

NATO /ˈnātō/ ▸*abbr.* North Atlantic Treaty Organization.

na·tri·u·re·sis /ˌnātrəyo͝oˈrēsis/ ▸*n. Physiology* excretion of sodium in the urine. ▷1950s: from NATRON + Greek *ourēsis* 'urination.' —**na·tri·u·ret·ic** /-ˈretik/ *adj.*

Na·tron, Lake /ˈnātrən/ a lake in northern Tanzania, on the border with Kenya, containing large deposits of salt and soda.

na·tron /ˈnāträn; -trən/ ▸*n.* a mineral salt found in dried lake beds, consisting of hydrated sodium carbonate. ▷late 17th cent.: from French, from Spanish *natrón*, via Arabic from Greek *nitron* (see NITER).

nat·ter /ˈnatər/ *informal* ▸*v.* [*intrans.*] talk casually, esp. about unimportant matters; chatter: *they* ***nattered away*** *for hours.*
▸*n.* [in *sing.*] a casual and leisurely conversation: *I could do with a drink and a natter.* ▷early 19th cent. (in the dialect sense 'grumble, fret'): imitative. —**nat·ter·er** *n.*

nat·ter·jack /ˈnatərˌjak/ (also **natterjack toad**) ▸*n.* a small European toad that has a bright yellow stripe down its back and runs in short bursts. • *Bufo calamita*, family Bufonidae. ▷mid 18th cent.: perhaps from NATTER (because of its loud croak) + JACK[1].

nat·ty[1] /ˈnatē/ ▸*adj.* (**-ti·er**, **-ti·est**) *informal* (esp. of a person or an article of clothing) smart and fashionable: *a natty blue blazer and designer jeans.* ▷late 18th cent. (originally slang): perhaps related to NEAT[1]. —**nat·ti·ly** /-təlē/ *adv.* —**nat·ti·ness** *n.*

nat·ty[2] ▸*adj.* [*attrib.*] (among Rastafarians) denoting hair that is unstraightened, uncombed, or matted, as in dreadlocks. ▷variant of KNOTTY.

Na·tu·fi·an /nəˈto͞ofēən/ ▸*adj. Archaeology* of, relating to, or denoting a late Mesolithic culture of the Middle East, dated to about 12,500–10,000 years ago. It provides evidence for the first settled villages. ■ [as *n.*] (**the Natufian**) the Natufian culture or period. ▷1930s: from Wadi *an-Natuf*, the type site (a cave northwest of Jerusalem), + -IAN.

nat·u·ral /ˈnaCHərəl/ ▸*adj.* **1** existing in or caused by nature; not made or caused by humankind: *carrots contain a natural antiseptic that fights bacteria | natural disasters such as earthquakes.* ■ (of fabric) having a color characteristic of the unbleached and undyed state; off-white. **2** of or in agreement with the character or makeup of, or circumstances surrounding, someone or something: *sharks have no natural enemies.* ■ [*attrib.*] (of a person) born with a particular skill, quality, or ability: *he was a natural entertainer.* ■ (of a skill, quality, or ability) coming instinctively to a person; innate: *writing appears to demand muscular movements that are not* ***natural to*** *children.* See note at NORMAL. ■ (of a person or their behavior) relaxed and unaffected; spontaneous: *he replied with too much nonchalance to sound natural.* ■ occurring as a matter of course and without debate; inevitable: *Ken was a natural choice for coach.* ■ [*attrib.*] (of law or justice) based on innate moral sense; instinctively felt to be right and fair. See also NATURAL LAW. ■ *Bridge* (of a bid) straightforwardly reflecting one's holding of cards. Often contrasted with CONVENTIONAL or ARTIFICIAL. **3** [*attrib.*] (of a parent or child) related by blood: *such adopted children always knew who their natural parents were.* ■ *chiefly archaic* illegitimate: *the Baron left a natural son by his mistress.* **4** *Music* (of a note) not sharped or flatted: [*postpositive*, in *combination*] *the bassoon plays G-natural instead of A-flat.* ■ (of a brass instrument) having no valves and able to play only the notes of the harmonic series above a fundamental note. ■ of or relating to the notes and intervals of the harmonic series. **5** *Christian Theology* relating to earthly or unredeemed human or physical nature as distinct from the spiritual or supernatural realm.
▸*n.* **1** a person regarded as having an innate gift or talent for a particular task or activity: *she was* ***a natural for*** *the sort of television work required of her.* ■ a thing that is particularly suited for something: *perky musical accompaniment would seem* ***a natural for*** *this series.* **2** *Music* a sign (♮) denoting a natural note when a previous sign or the key signature would otherwise demand a sharp or a flat. ■ a natural note. ■ any of the longer keys on a keyboard instrument that are normally white. **3** a creamy beige color. **4** a hand of cards, throw of dice, or other result that wins immediately, in particular: ■ a hand of two cards making 21 in the first deal in blackjack and similar games. ■ a first throw of 7 or 11 at craps. **5** *Fishing* an insect or other small creature used as bait, rather than an artificial imitation. **6** *dated, offensive* a person mentally handicapped from birth.
▸*adv. informal* or *dialect* naturally: *keep walking—just act natural.* ▷Middle English (in the sense 'having a certain status by birth'): from Old French, from Latin *naturalis*, from *natura* 'birth, nature, quality' (see NATURE). —**nat·u·ral·ness** *n.*

nat·u·ral-born ▸*adj.* having a specified innate characteristic or ability: *Glen was a natural-born sailor.* ■ *archaic* having a position by birth.

nat·u·ral child·birth ▸*n.* childbirth with minimal medical or technological intervention, usually involving special breathing and relaxation techniques.

nat·u·ral clas·si·fi·ca·tion ▸*n.* a scientific classification according to features that are held to be objectively significant, rather than being selected for convenience.

nat·u·ral fam·i·ly plan·ning ▸*n.* another term for RHYTHM METHOD.

nat·u·ral food ▸*n.* food that has undergone a minimum of processing or treatment with preservatives.

nat·u·ral fre·quen·cy ▸*n. Physics* the frequency at which a system oscillates when not subjected to a continuous or repeated external force.

nat·u·ral gas ▸*n.* flammable gas, consisting largely of methane and other hydrocarbons, occurring naturally underground (often in association with petroleum) and used as fuel.

nat·u·ral his·to·ry ▸*n.* **1** the scientific study of animals or plants, esp. as concerned with observation

rather than experiment, and presented in popular rather than academic form. ■ the study of the whole natural world, including mineralogy and paleontology. **2** *Medicine* the usual course of development of a disease or condition, esp. in the absence of treatment: *the natural history of cancerous tumors.* —**nat·u·ral his·to·ri·an** *n.*

nat·u·ral·ism /ˈnaCHərəˌlizəm/ ▶*n.* **1** (in art and literature) a style and theory of representation based on the accurate depiction of detail.

The name "Naturalism" was given to a 19th-century artistic and literary movement, influenced by contemporary ideas of science and society, that rejected the idealization of experience and adopted an objective and often uncompromisingly realistic approach to art. Notable figures include the novelist Zola and the painter Théodore Rousseau.

2 a philosophical viewpoint according to which everything arises from natural properties and causes, and supernatural or spiritual explanations are excluded or discounted. [translating French *naturalisme*.] ■ (in moral philosophy) the theory that ethical statements can be derived from nonethical ones. ■ another term for NATURAL RELIGION.

nat·u·ral·ist /ˈnaCHərəlist/ ▶*n.* **1** an expert in or student of natural history. **2** a person who practices naturalism in art or literature. ■ a person who adopts philosophical naturalism.
▶*adj.* another term for NATURALISTIC.

nat·u·ral·is·tic /ˌnaCHərəˈlistik/ ▶*adj.* **1** derived from real life or nature, or imitating it very closely: *verbatim records of children's speech in naturalistic settings.* **2** based on the theory of naturalism in art or literature: *naturalistic paintings of the city.* ■ of or according to the philosophy of naturalism: *phenomena once considered supernatural have yielded to naturalistic explanation.* —**nat·u·ral·is·ti·cal·ly** *adv.*

nat·u·ral·ize /ˈnaCHərəˌlīz/ ▶*v.* [*trans.*] **1** (often **be/become naturalized**) admit (a foreigner) to the citizenship of a country: *he was born in a foreign country and had never been naturalized* | [as *adj.*] (**naturalized**) *a naturalized U.S. citizen born in Germany.* ■ [*intrans.*] (of a foreigner) be admitted to the citizenship of a country: *the opportunity to naturalize as American.* ■ alter (an adopted foreign word) so that it conforms more closely to the phonology or orthography of the adopting language: *the* stoccafisso *of Liguria was naturalized in Nice as* stocaficada. **2** [usu. as *adj.*] (**naturalized**) *Biology* establish (a plant or animal) so that it lives wild in a region where it is not indigenous: *native and naturalized species* | *black mustard has become naturalized in America.* ■ establish (a cultivated plant) in a natural situation: *this species of crocus* **naturalizes itself** *very easily.* ■ [*intrans.*] (of a cultivated plant) become established in a natural situation: *these perennials should be planted where they can naturalize.* **3** regard as or cause to appear natural: *although women do more child care than men, feminists should beware of naturalizing that fact.* ■ explain (a phenomenon) in a naturalistic way. ▷mid 16th cent.: from French *naturaliser*, from Old French *natural* (see NATURAL). —**nat·u·ral·i·za·tion** /ˌnaCHərəliˈzāSHən/ *n.*

nat·u·ral kill·er cell ▶*n.* *Medicine* a lymphocyte able to bind to certain tumor cells and virus-infected cells without the stimulation of antigens, and kill them by the insertion of granules containing perforin.

nat·u·ral lan·guage ▶*n.* a language that has developed naturally in use (as contrasted with an artificial language or computer code).

nat·u·ral law ▶*n.* **1** a body of unchanging moral principles regarded as a basis for all human conduct. **2** an observable law relating to natural phenomena: *the natural laws of perspective.* ■ such laws collectively.

nat·u·ral life ▶*n.* the expected span of a person's life or a thing's existence under normal circumstances: *a man sentenced to spend the rest of his natural life in prison.*

nat·u·ral log·a·rithm (abbr.: **ln** or **log$_e$**) ▶*n.* *Mathematics* a logarithm to the base *e* (2.71828 . . .).

nat·u·ral·ly /ˈnaCHərəlē/ ▶*adv.* **1** in a natural manner, in particular: ■ in a normal manner; without distortion or exaggeration: *act naturally.* ■ as a natural result: *one leads naturally into the other.* ■ without special help or intervention: *naturally curly hair.* **2** [*sentence adverb*] as may be expected; of course: *naturally, I hoped for the best.*

nat·u·ral mag·ic ▶*n.* (in the Middle Ages) magic practiced for beneficial purposes, involving the making of images, healing, and the use of herbs.

nat·u·ral num·bers ▶*plural n.* the positive integers (whole numbers) 1, 2, 3, etc., and sometimes zero as well.

nat·u·ral phi·los·o·phy ▶*n.* *archaic* natural science, esp. physical science. —**nat·u·ral phi·los·o·pher** *n.*

nat·u·ral re·li·gion ▶*n.* religion, esp. deism, based on reason rather than divine revelation.

nat·u·ral re·sources ▶*plural n.* materials or substances such as minerals, forests, water, and fertile land that occur in nature and can be used for economic gain.

nat·u·ral sci·ence ▶*n.* (usu. **natural sciences**) a branch of science that deals with the physical world, e.g., physics, chemistry, geology, and biology. ■ the branch of knowledge that deals with the study of the physical world. —**nat·u·ral sci·en·tist** *n.*

nat·u·ral se·lec·tion ▶*n.* *Biology* the process whereby organisms better adapted to their environment tend to survive and produce more offspring. The theory of its action was first fully expounded by Charles Darwin and is now believed to be the main process that brings about evolution. Compare with SURVIVAL OF THE FITTEST (see SURVIVAL).

nat·u·ral the·ol·o·gy ▶*n.* theology or knowledge of God based on observed facts and experience apart from divine revelation.

nat·u·ral vir·tue ▶*n.* any of the traditional chief moral virtues, esp. the cardinal virtues.

na·ture /ˈnāCHər/ ▶*n.* **1** the phenomena of the physical world collectively, including plants, animals, the landscape, and other features and products of the earth, as opposed to humans or human creations: *the breathtaking beauty of nature.* ■ the physical force regarded as causing and regulating these phenomena: *it is impossible to change the laws of nature.* See also MOTHER NATURE. ■ the countryside, esp. when picturesque. ■ *archaic* a living thing's vital functions or needs. **2** [in *sing.*] the basic or inherent features of something, esp. when seen as characteristic of it: *helping them to realize the nature of their problems* | *there are a lot of other documents* **of that nature.** ■ the innate or essential qualities or character of a person or animal: *it's not in her nature to listen to advice* | *I'm not violent* **by nature.** See also HUMAN NATURE. ■ inborn or hereditary characteristics as an influence on or determinant of personality. Often contrasted with NURTURE. ■ [with *adj.*] *archaic* a person of a specified character: *Emerson was so much more luminous a nature.* ▷Middle English (denoting the physical power of a person): from Old French, from Latin *natura* 'birth, nature, quality,' from *nat-* 'born,' from the verb *nasci*.
▶*PHRASES* □ **against nature** unnatural or immoral. □ **someone's better nature** the good side of a person's character; their capacity for tolerance, generosity, or sympathy: *Charlotte planned to appeal to his better nature.* □ **call of nature** used euphemistically to refer to a need to urinate or defecate. □ **from nature** (in art) using natural scenes or objects as models: *I wanted to paint landscape directly from nature.* □ **get** (or **go**) **back to nature** return to the type of life (regarded as being more in tune with nature) that existed before the development of complex industrial societies. □ **in the nature of** similar in type to or having the characteristics of: *the promise was in the nature of a check that bounced.* □ **in the nature of things** **1** inevitable: *it is in the nature of things that the majority of music prizes get set up for performers rather than composers.* **2** inevitably: *in the nature of things, old people spend much more time indoors.* □ **in a state of nature** **1** in an uncivilized or uncultivated state. **2** totally naked. **3** *Christian Theology* in a morally unregenerate condition, unredeemed by divine grace. □ **the nature of the beast** *informal* the inherent or essential quality or character of something, which cannot be changed.

na·tured /ˈnāCHərd/ ▶*adj.* [in *combination*] having a nature or disposition of a specified kind: *a good-natured man.*

na·ture print·ing ▶*n.* a method of producing a print of a natural object (such as a leaf) or a textile (such as lace) by making an impression of it directly onto a soft metal printing plate under great pressure and then taking an inked impression on paper.

na·ture re·serve (also **nature preserve**) ▶*n.* a tract of land managed so as to preserve its flora, fauna, and physical features.

na·ture stud·y ▶*n.* the practical study of plants, animals, and natural phenomena, esp. as a school subject.

na·ture trail ▶*n.* a path through a forest or countryside designed to draw attention to natural features.

na·tur·ism /ˈnāCHəˌrizəm/ ▶*n.* **1** the practice of wearing no clothes in a vacation camp or for other leisure activities; nudism. **2** the worship of nature or natural objects. —**na·tur·ist** *n.* & *adj.*

na·tur·op·a·thy /ˌnāCHəˈräpəTHē; ˌna-/ ▶*n.* a system of alternative medicine based on the theory that diseases can be successfully treated or prevented without the use of drugs, by techniques such as control of diet, exercise, and massage. —**na·tur·o·path** /ˈnāCHərəˌpaTH; ˈna-/ *n.* —**na·tur·o·path·ic** /ˌnāCHərəˈpaTHik; ˌna-/ *adj.*

Nau·cal·pan de Jua·rez /nouˈkälpän dā ˈhwäres/ an industrial city in central Mexico, northwest of Mexico City; pop. 773,000.

Nau·ga·hyde /ˈnôgəˌhīd/ ▶*n.* *trademark* an artificial material designed to resemble leather, made from fabric coated with rubber or vinyl resin. ▷mid 20th cent.: from *Nauga(tuck)*, the name of a town in Connecticut, where rubber is manufactured, + *-hyde* (alteration of HIDE[2]).

Nau·ga·tuck /ˈnôgəˌtək/ an industrial borough in southwestern Connecticut, on the Naugatuck River next to Waterbury; pop. 30,625.

naught /nôt/ ▶*n.* the digit 0; zero.
▶*pron.* *archaic* nothing: *he's naught but a worthless fool.* ▷Old English *nāwiht, -wuht*, from *nā* 'no' + *wiht* 'thing' (see WIGHT).
▶*PHRASES* □ **bring to naught** *archaic* ruin; foil. □ **come to naught** be ruined or foiled. □ **set at naught** *archaic* disregard; despise.

naugh·ty /ˈnôtē/ ▶*adj.* (**-ti·er, -ti·est**) **1** (esp. of children) disobedient; badly behaved: *you've been a really naughty boy.* **2** *informal* mildly rude or indecent, typically because related to sex: *naughty drawings* | *naughty goings-on.* **3** *archaic* wicked. ▷late Middle English: from NAUGHT + -Y[1]. The earliest recorded sense was 'possessing nothing'; the sense 'wicked' also dates from late Middle English, and gave rise to the current senses. —**naugh·ti·ly** /-təlē/ *adv.* —**naugh·ti·ness** *n.*

naugh·ty bits ▶*plural n.* *Brit., informal, humorous* the parts of a person's body connected with sexual activity or attraction, esp. the genitals.

nau·pli·us /ˈnôplēəs/ ▶*n.* (*pl.* **-pli·i** /-plēˌī/) *Zoology* the first larval stage of many crustaceans, having an unsegmented body and a single eye. ▷mid 19th cent.: from Latin, denoting a kind of shellfish, or from the Greek name *Nauplios*, the son of Poseidon.

Na·u·ru /näˈo͞oro͞o/ an island country in the southwestern Pacific Ocean, near the equator; pop. 12,800; no official capital but government is in Yaren District; official languages, Nauruan (an Austronesian language) and English. —**Na·u·ru·an** /-ro͞owən/ *adj.* & *n.*

Since 1968 it has been an independent republic with a limited form of membership of the Commonwealth of Nations. The world's smallest independent republic, Nauru joined the UN in 1999. It has the world's richest deposits of phosphates.

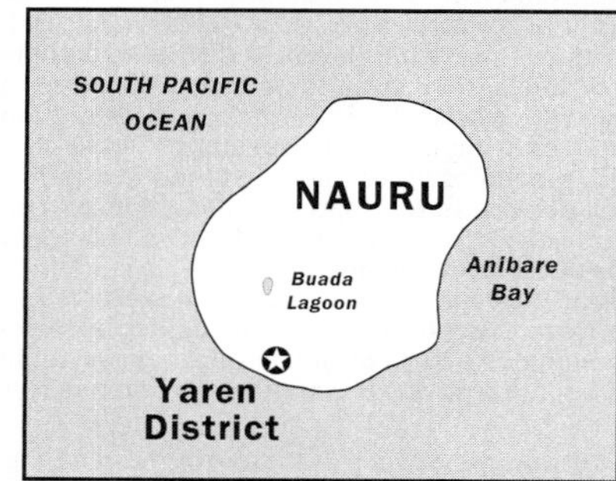

nau·se·a /ˈnôzēə; -ZHə/ ▶*n.* a feeling of sickness with an inclination to vomit. ■ loathing; revulsion: *intended to induce a feeling of nostalgia, it only induces in me a feeling of nausea.* ▷late Middle English: via Latin from Greek *nausia*, from *naus* 'ship.'

nau·se·ate /ˈnôzēˌāt; -ZHēˌāt/ ▶*v.* [*trans.*] make (someone) feel sick; affect with nausea: *the thought of food nauseated her* | [as *adj.*] (**nauseating**) *the stench became nauseating.* ■ fill (someone) with revulsion; disgust: *I was nauseated by the vicious comment.* ▷mid 17th cent.: from Latin *nauseat-* 'made to feel sick,' from the verb *nauseare*, from *nausea* (see NAUSEA). —**nau·se·at·ing·ly** *adv.*

USAGE A distinction has traditionally been drawn between **nauseated**, meaning 'affected with nausea,' and **nauseous**, meaning 'causing nausea.'

Today, however, the use of **nauseous** to mean 'affected with nausea' is so common that it is generally considered to be standard.

nau·seous /ˈnôshəs; -zhəs; -ēəs/ ▶*adj.* **1** affected with nausea; inclined to vomit: *a rancid, cloying odor that made him nauseous.* **2** causing nausea; offensive to the taste or smell: *the smell was nauseous.* ■ disgusting, repellent, or offensive: *this nauseous account of a court case.* ▷early 17th cent.: from Latin *nauseosus* (from *nausea* 'seasickness'). **—nau·seous·ly** *adv.* **—nau·seous·ness** *n.*

USAGE See usage at **NAUSEATE**.

naut. ▶*abbr.* nautical.

nautch /nôch/ ▶*n.* (in the Indian subcontinent) a traditional dance performed by professional dancing girls. ▷from Hindi *nāc*, from Prakrit *nachcha*, from Sanskrit *nṛtya* 'dancing.'

nau·ti·cal /ˈnôtikəl/ ▶*adj.* of or concerning sailors or navigation; maritime: *nautical charts.* ▷mid 16th cent.: from French *nautique*, or via Latin from Greek *nautikos*, from *nautēs* 'sailor,' from *naus* 'ship.' **—nau·ti·cal·ly** /-ik(ə)lē/ *adv.*

nau·ti·cal al·ma·nac ▶*n.* a yearbook containing astronomical and sometimes also tidal and other information for navigators.

nau·ti·cal mile ▶*n.* a unit used in measuring distances at sea, equal to approximately 2,025 yards (1,852 m). Compare with **SEA MILE**.

nau·ti·loid /ˈnôtl,oid/ ▶*n.* *Zoology* a mollusk of a group of mainly extinct marine mollusks that includes the pearly nautilus. • Subclass Nautiloidea, class Cephalopoda: *Nautilus* is the only surviving genus. ▷mid 19th cent.: from the modern Latin genus name *Nautilus* (from Greek *nautilos* 'sailor') + **-OID**.

Nau·ti·lus /ˈnôtl-əs/ the first nuclear-powered submarine, launched in 1954. This U.S. Navy vessel made a historic journey (August 1–5, 1958) under the ice of the North Pole. ■ *trademark* an exercise machine that matches resistance with output of force. ▷a name previously given to Robert Fulton's "diving boat" (1800), also to the fictitious submarine in Jules Verne's *Twenty Thousand Leagues under the Sea*.

nau·ti·lus /ˈnôtl-əs/ ▶*n.* (*pl.* **nau·ti·lus·es** or **nau·ti·li** /ˈnôtl-ī/) **1** a cephalopod mollusk with a light external spiral shell and numerous short tentacles around the mouth. Nautiluses swim with the buoyant gas-filled shell upright and descend to greater depths during the day. • Genus *Nautilus*, the only surviving genus of the subclass Nautiloidea: several species, in particular the common **chambered nautilus** (*Nautilus pompilius*) of the Indo-Pacific, with a shell that is white with brownish bands on the outside and lined with mother-of-pearl on the inside. **2** (also **paper nautilus**) another term for **ARGONAUT**. ▷modern Latin, from Latin, from Greek *nautilos*, literally 'sailor.'

chambered nautilus

NAV ▶*abbr.* net asset value.

nav /nav/ ▶*n.* *informal* short for **NAVIGATION**. ■ short for **NAVIGATOR**.

nav·aid /ˈnav,ād/ ▶*n.* a navigational device in an aircraft, ship, or other vehicle. ▷1950s: from *navigational aid*.

Nav·a·jo /ˈnavə,hō; ˈnä-/ (also **Nav·a·ho**) ▶*n.* (*pl.* same or **-jos**) **1** a member of an American Indian people of New Mexico and Arizona. **2** the Athabaskan language of this people.
▶*adj.* of or relating to this people or their language. ▷from Spanish *(Apaches de) Navajó* '(Apaches from) Navajo,' from Tewa *navahu:* 'fields adjoining an arroyo.'

na·val /ˈnāvəl/ ▶*adj.* of, in, or relating to a navy or navies: *a naval officer | naval operations.* ▷late Middle English: from Latin *navalis*, from *navis* 'ship.'

na·val a·cad·e·my ▶*n.* a college where naval officers are trained.

na·val ar·chi·tec·ture ▶*n.* the designing of ships. **—na·val ar·chi·tect** *n.*

na·val stores ▶*plural n.* articles or materials used in shipping.

Na·va·ra·tri /,nəvəˈrätrē/ (also **Na·va·ra·tra**) /-trə/ ▶*n.* a Hindu autumn festival extending over nine nights. It is associated with many local observances, esp. the Bengali festival of Durga. ▷Sanskrit, literally 'nine nights.'

na·va·rin /ˈnavərin/ ▶*n.* a stew of lamb or mutton with vegetables. ▷French.

Nav·a·ri·no, Bat·tle of /,navəˈrēnō/ a decisive naval battle in the Greek struggle for independence from the Ottoman Empire, fought in 1827 in the Bay of Navarino off Pylos in Peloponnesus. Britain, Russia, and France sent a combined fleet that destroyed the Egyptian and Turkish fleet.

Na·varre /nəˈvär/ an autonomous region of northern Spain, on the border with France; capital, Pamplona. It represents the southern part of the former kingdom of Navarre. Spanish name **NAVARRA** .

nave[1] /nāv/ ▶*n.* the central part of a church building, intended to accommodate most of the congregation. In traditional Western churches it is rectangular, separated from the chancel by a step or rail, and from adjacent aisles by pillars. ▷late 17th cent.: from Latin *navis* 'ship.'

nave[2] ▶*n.* the hub of a wheel. ▷Old English *nafu*, *nafa*, of Germanic origin; related to Dutch *naaf* and German *Nabe*, from an Indo-European root shared by Sanskrit *nābhis* 'nave, navel.' Compare with **NAVEL**.

na·vel /ˈnāvəl/ ▶*n.* a rounded, knotty depression in the center of a person's belly caused by the detachment of the umbilical cord after birth; the umbilicus. ■ *figurative* the central point of a place: *the Incas saw Cuzco as the navel of the world.* ▷Old English *nafela*, of Germanic origin; related to Dutch *navel* and German *Nabel*, from an Indo-European root shared by Latin *umbo* 'boss of a shield,' *umbilicus* 'navel,' and Greek *omphalos* 'boss, navel.' Compare with **NAVE**[2].
▶*PHRASE* □ **contemplate one's navel** spend time complacently considering oneself or one's own interests; concentrate on one issue at the expense of a wider view.

na·vel-gaz·ing ▶*n.* complacent self-absorption; concentration on a single issue at the expense of a wider view.

na·vel or·ange ▶*n.* a large, seedless orange that has a navellike depression at the top and contains a small secondary fruit underneath it.

na·vel·wort /ˈnāvəl,wərt; -,wôrt/ ▶*n.* a low plant of the borage family that resembles the forget-me-not and is cultivated for ground cover and rock gardens. • Genus *Omphalodes*, family Boraginaceae: several species, including *O. cappadocica*, widely introduced from Turkey.

na·vic·u·lar /nəˈvikyələr/ ▶*adj.* *chiefly archaic* boat-shaped.
▶*n.* **1** (also **navicular bone**) a boat-shaped bone in the ankle or wrist, esp. that in the ankle between the talus and the cuneiform bones. **2** (also **navicular disease** or **navicular syndrome**) a chronic disorder of the navicular bone in horses, causing lameness in the front feet. ▷late Middle English: from French *naviculaire* or late Latin *navicularis*, from Latin *navicula* 'little ship,' diminutive of *navis*.

nav·i·ga·ble /ˈnavigəbəl/ ▶*adj.* **1** (of a waterway or sea) able to be sailed on by ships or boats. ■ (of a track or road) suitable for transportation; passable: *those minor roads would be navigable in emergencies.* ■ (esp. of a Web site) easy to get around in; maneuverable: *a navigable Web browser.* **2** (of a vessel) properly equipped, maintained, and operated. ▷early 16th cent.: from French *navigable* or Latin *navigabilis*, from the verb *navigare* 'to sail' (see **NAVIGATE**). **—nav·i·ga·bil·i·ty** /,navəgəˈbilitē/ *n.*

nav·i·gate /ˈnavi,gāt/ ▶*v.* **1** [*intrans.*] plan and direct the route or course of a ship, aircraft, or other form of transportation, esp. by using instruments or maps: *they* **navigated by** *the stars.* ■ [*intrans.*, *with adverbial of direction*] travel on a desired course after planning a route: *he taught them how to navigate across the oceans.* ■ (of an animal or bird) find its way, esp. over a long distance: *whales use their own inbuilt sonar system to navigate.* ■ (of a passenger in a vehicle) assist the driver by reading the map and planning a route: *we'll go in my car—you can navigate.* ■ (of a ship or boat) sail; proceed: [with *adverbial of direction*] *we sailed out surrounded by loose ice while navigating around larger grounded icebergs.* **2** [*trans.*] sail or travel over (a stretch of water or terrain), esp. carefully or with difficulty: *ships had been lost while navigating the narrows.* ■ guide (a vessel or vehicle) over a specified route or terrain: *she navigated the car safely through the traffic.* ■ make one's way with difficulty over (a route or terrain): *the drivers skillfully navigated a twisting and muddy course.* ■ *Computing* [*intrans.*] move from one accessible page, section, or view of a file or Web site to another: *the new layout makes it easier to navigate through their atlas of world maps.* ▷late 16th cent. (in the sense 'travel in a ship'): from Latin *navigat-* 'sailed,' from the verb *navigare*, from *navis* 'ship' + *agere* 'drive.'

nav·i·ga·tion /,naviˈgāshən/ ▶*n.* **1** the process or activity of accurately ascertaining one's position and planning and following a route. **2** the passage of ships: *bridges to span rivers without hindering navigation.* ▷early 16th cent. (denoting the action of traveling on water): from French, or from Latin *navigatio(n-)*, from the verb *navigare* (see **NAVIGATE**). **—nav·i·ga·tion·al** /-nəl/ *adj.*

nav·i·ga·tion lights ▶*plural n.* a set of lights shown by a ship or aircraft at night to indicate its position and orientation, esp. with respect to other vessels or aircraft.

nav·i·ga·tor /ˈnavi,gātər/ ▶*n.* a person who directs the route or course of a ship, aircraft, or other form of transportation, esp. by using instruments and maps. ■ an instrument or device that assists in directing the course of a vessel or aircraft. ■ *Computing* a browser program for retrieving data on the World Wide Web or another information system. ■ *historical* a person who explores by sea.

Nav·ra·til·o·va /,navrətəˈlōvə; ,näv-/, Martina (1956–), U.S. tennis player, born in Czechoslovakia. She dominated women's tennis throughout the 1980s and won nine Wimbledon singles titles 1978–79, 1982–87, and 1990.

NAVSTAR ▶*abbr.* Navigation Satellite Timing and Ranging.

nav·vy /ˈnavē/ ▶*n.* (*pl.* **-vies**) *Brit.*, *dated* a laborer employed in the excavation and construction of a road, railroad, or canal. ▷early 19th cent.: abbreviation of **NAVIGATOR**.

na·vy /ˈnāvē/ ▶*n.* (*pl.* **-vies**) **1** (often **the navy** or **the Navy**) the branch of a nation's armed services that conducts military operations at sea. ■ the ships of a navy: *a 600-ship navy | we built their navy.* ■ *poetic/literary* a fleet of ships. **2** (also **navy blue**) a dark blue color: [as *adj.*] *a navy-blue suit.* ▷late Middle English (in the sense 'ships collectively, fleet'): from Old French *navie* 'ship, fleet,' from popular Latin *navia* 'ship,' from Latin *navis* 'ship.'

na·vy bean ▶*n.* a small white type of kidney bean.

Na·vy Cross ▶*n.* a decoration bestowed by the U.S. Navy upon individuals who have shown exceptional heroism, esp. in enemy combat.

na·vy yard ▶*n.* a shipyard for the construction, repair, and equipping of naval vessels.

naw /nô/ ▶*exclam.* *informal* variant spelling of **NO**, used to answer a question: *"Want some toast?" "Naw."*

na·wab /nəˈwäb/ ▶*n.* *Indian, historical* a native governor during the time of the Mogul empire: [as *title*] *Nawab Haider Beg.* ■ a Muslim nobleman or person of high status. ▷from Urdu *nawwāb*, variant of Arabic *nuwwāb*, plural (used as singular) of *nā'ib* 'deputy'; compare with **NABOB**.

Nax·al·ite /ˈnaksəlīt/ ▶*n.* (in the Indian subcontinent) a member of an armed revolutionary group advocating Maoist communism. ▷1960s: from *Naxal(bari)*, a place name in West Bengal, India, + **-ITE**[1].

Nax·çi·van /,nəkēchiˈvän/ an Azerbaijani autonomous republic, predominantly Muslim, that is located on the borders of Turkey and northern Iran and is separated from the rest of Azerbaijan by a narrow strip of Armenia; pop. 300,000. In 1990, it was the first Soviet territory to declare unilateral independence. It has a predominantly Azerbaijani population and, along with Nagorno-Karabakh, is a point of conflict between Armenia and Azerbaijan. Russian name **NAKHICHEVAN**. ■ the capital city of this republic; pop. 51,000.

Nax·os /ˈnäk,sôs; ˈnaksəs/ a Greek island in the southern Aegean Sea, the largest of the Cyclades.

nay /nā/ ▶*adv.* **1** or rather; and more than that (used to emphasize a more appropriate word than one just used): *it will take months, nay years.* **2** *archaic* or *dialect* no: *nay, I must not think thus.*
▶*n.* a negative answer or vote: *the cabinet sits to give the final yea or nay to policies.* ▷Middle English (sense 2): from Old Norse *nei*, from *ne* 'not' + *ei* 'ever' (compare with **AYE**[2]).

Na·ya·rit /näyäˈrēt/ a state in western Mexico, on the Pacific coast; capital, Tepic.

nay·say /ˈnā,sā/ ▶*v.* (*past* and *past part.* **-said**) [*trans.*] say no to; deny or oppose: *I'm not going to naysay anything he does.* **—nay·say·er** *n.*

Naz·a·rene /ˈnazəˌrēn/ ▶*n.* **1** a native or inhabitant of Nazareth. ■ (**the Nazarene**) Jesus Christ. ■ (chiefly in Jewish or Muslim use) a Christian. ■ a member of an early sect or faction of Jewish Christians, esp. one in 4th-century Syria using an Aramaic version of the Gospels and observing much of the Jewish law. ■ a member of the Church of the Nazarene, a Christian Protestant denomination originating in the American holiness movement. **2** a member of a group of German painters working mainly in Rome who from 1809 sought to revive the art and techniques of medieval Germany and early Renaissance Italy.
▶*adj.* of or relating to Nazareth or Nazarenes. ▷via late Latin from Greek *Nazarēnos*, from *Nazaret* 'Nazareth.'

Naz·a·reth /ˈnaz(ə)rəTH/ a historic town in lower Galilee, in present-day northern Israel; pop. 39,000. Mentioned in the Gospels as the home of Mary and Joseph, it is closely associated with the childhood of Jesus Christ and is a center of Christian pilgrimage.

Na·zi /ˈnätsē/ ▶*n.* (*pl.* **Na·zis**) *historical* a member of the National Socialist German Workers' Party. ■ a member of an organization with similar ideology. ■ *derogatory* a person who holds and acts brutally in accordance with extreme racist or authoritarian views.

The Nazi Party was formed in Munich after World War I. It advocated right-wing authoritarian nationalist government and developed a racist ideology based on anti-Semitism and a belief in the superiority of "Aryan" Germans. Its charismatic leader, Adolf Hitler, who was elected Chancellor in 1933, established a totalitarian dictatorship, rearmed Germany in support of expansionist foreign policies in central Europe, and thus precipitated World War II. The Nazi Party collapsed at the end of the war and was outlawed in Germany.

▶*adj.* of or concerning the Nazis or Nazism. ▷German, abbreviation representing the pronunciation of *Nati-* in *Nationalsozialist* 'national socialist.' —**Na·zi·dom** /-dəm/ *n.* —**Na·zi·fy** /ˈnätsiˌfī/ *v.* (**-fies**, **-fied**). —**Na·zi·ism** /-ˌizəm/ *n.* —**Na·zism** /ˈnätˌsizəm/ *n.*

Naz·i·rite /ˈnazəˌrīt/ (also **Naz·a·rite**) ▶*n. historical* an Israelite consecrated to the service of God, under vows to abstain from alcohol, let the hair grow, and avoid defilement by contact with corpses (Num. 6). ▷from Hebrew *nāzîr* 'consecrated one,' from *nāzar* 'to separate or consecrate oneself,' + -ITE[1].

Na·zi sa·lute ▶*n.* a gesture or salute in which the right arm is straightened and inclined upward, with the hand open and palm down.

NB ▶*abbr.* ■ New Brunswick (in official postal use). ■ nota bene; take special note (used to precede a written note). [Latin.]

Nb ▶*symbol* the chemical element niobium.

NBA ▶*abbr.* ■ (in North America) National Basketball Association. ■ (in the U.S.) National Boxing Association.

NBC ▶*abbr.* ■ (in the U.S.) National Broadcasting Company. ■ (of weapons or warfare) nuclear, biological, and chemical.

NbE ▶*abbr.* north by east.

NbW ▶*abbr.* north by west.

NC ▶*abbr.* ■ network computer, a personal computer with reduced functionality intended to be used to access services on a network. ■ North Carolina (in official postal use).

NC-17 ▶*symbol* no one 17 and under admitted, a rating in the Voluntary Movie Rating System forbidding admission to children 17 years old and under. ▷representing *no children (under) 17*.

NCAA ▶*abbr.* National Collegiate Athletic Association.

NCLB ▶*abbr.* No Child Left Behind (Act), a 2001 federal law that revised and upgraded standards for public elementary education.

NCO ▶*abbr.* noncommissioned officer.

NCTE ▶*abbr.* National Council of Teachers of English.

NCTM ▶*abbr.* National Council of Teachers of Mathematics.

ND ▶*abbr.* North Dakota (in official postal use).

Nd ▶*symbol* the chemical element neodymium.

n.d. ▶*abbr.* no date (used esp. in bibliographies).

-nd ▶*suffix* variant spelling of -AND, -END.

N.Dak. ▶*abbr.* North Dakota.

NDEA ▶*abbr.* National Defense Education Act.

Nde·be·le /ˌəndəˈbelā; -ˈbēlē/ ▶*n.* (*pl.* same or **-les**) **1** a member of a Bantu people of Zimbabwe and northeastern South Africa. See also MATABELE. **2** the Nguni language of this people.
▶*adj.* of or relating to this people or their language. ▷the name in the Nguni languages.

N'Dja·me·na /ənjəˈmā/ the capital of Chad; pop. 531,000. Former name (1900–73) FORT LAMY.

Ndo·la /ənˈdōlə/ a city in central Zambia; pop. 376,000.

NE ▶*abbr.* ■ Nebraska (in official postal use). ■ New England. ■ northeast or northeastern.

Ne ▶*symbol* the chemical element neon.

né /nā/ ▶*adj.* originally called; born (used before the name by which a man was originally known): *Al Kelly, né Kabish.* ▷1930s: French, literally 'born,' masculine past participle of *naître*; compare with NÉE.

NEA ▶*abbr.* ■ National Education Association. ■ National Endowment for the Arts. ■ Nuclear Energy Agency.

Neagh, Lough /nā/ a shallow lake in Northern Ireland, the largest freshwater lake in the British Isles.

Neal /nēl/, Patricia (1926–), U.S. stage and movie actress; born *Patsy Louise Neal*. She was an award-winning actress when she suffered several massive strokes in 1965. Her long, hard recovery was remarkable, and she returned to acting in 1968. Among the many movies in which she appeared were *Hud* (Academy Award, 1963), *The Subject Was Roses* (1968), and *Cookie's Fortune* (1999).

Ne·an·der·thal /nēˈandərTHôl/ ▶*n.* (also **Neanderthal man**) an extinct species of human that was widely distributed in ice-age Europe between *c.*120,000–35,000 years ago, with a receding forehead and prominent brow ridges. The Neanderthals were associated with the Mousterian flint industry of the Middle Paleolithic. • *Homo neanderthalensis*; now usually regarded as a separate species from *H. sapiens* and probably at the end of a different evolutionary line. ■ *figurative* an uncivilized, unintelligent, or uncouth person, esp. a man: *the stereotype of the mechanic as a macho Neanderthal.*
▶*adj.* of or relating to this extinct human species. ■ *figurative* (esp. of a man) uncivilized, unintelligent, or uncouth: *your attitude to women is Neanderthal.* ▷mid 19th cent.: from *Neanderthal*, the name of a region in Germany, where remains of Neanderthal man were found.

neap /nēp/ ▶*n.* (usu. **neap tide**) a tide just after the first or third quarters of the moon when there is the least difference between high and low water.
▶*v.* (**be neaped**) (of a boat) be kept aground or in harbor by a neap tide. ■ [*intrans.*] *archaic* (of a tide) tend toward or reach the highest point of a neap tide. ▷late Middle English, originally an adjective from Old English *nēp*, first element of *nēpflōd* 'neap flood,' of unknown origin.

Ne·a·pol·i·tan /ˌnēəˈpälitn/ ▶*n.* a native or citizen of Naples.
▶*adj.* of or relating to Naples. ▷from Latin *Neapolitanus*, from Latin *Neapolis* 'Naples,' from Greek *neos* 'new' + *polis* 'city.'

Ne·a·pol·i·tan ice cream ▶*n.* ice cream made in layers of different colors, typically including chocolate, vanilla, and strawberry.

near /ni(ə)r/ ▶*adv.* **1** at or to a short distance away; nearby: *a bomb exploding somewhere near* | [*comparative*] *she took a step nearer.* **2** a short time away in the future: *the time for his retirement was drawing near.* **3** [as *submodifier*] almost: *a near perfect fit.* **4** *archaic* or *dialect* almost: *I near fell out of the chair.*
▶*prep.* (also **near to**) **1** at or to a short distance away from (a place): *the parking lot near the sawmill* | *do you live near here?* | [*superlative*] *the table nearest the door.* **2** a short period of time from: *near the end of the war* | [*comparative*] *details will be given nearer the date.* **3** close to (a state); verging on: *she gave a tiny smile, brave but near tears* | *she was near death.* ■ (used before an amount) a small amount below (something); approaching: *temperatures near 2 million degrees K.* **4** similar to: *a shape near to the original.*
▶*adj.* **1** located a short distance away: *a big house* **in the near distance** | [*superlative*] *I was fifteen miles from the nearest town.* **2** only a short time ahead: *the conflict is unlikely to be resolved* **in the near future**. **3** similar: [*superlative*] *walking in these shoes is the nearest thing to floating on air.* ■ [*attrib.*] close to being (the thing mentioned): *his state of near despair* | *a near disaster.* ■ [*attrib.*] having a close family connection: *the loss of a child or other near relative.* **4** [*attrib.*] located on the side of a vehicle that is normally closest to the curb: *the near right-hand end window of the trailer.* Compare with OFF (sense 3). **5** *archaic* (of a person) stingy; miserly.
▶*v.* [*trans.*] come near to (someone or something); approach: *soon the cab would be nearing State Street* | [*intrans.*] *lunchtime neared.* ▷Middle English: from Old Norse *nær* 'nearer,' comparative of *ná*, corresponding to Old English *nēah* 'nigh.' —**near·ish** *adj.* —**near·ness** *n.*
▶PHRASES □ **near at hand** within easy reach. ■ about to happen or come about: *an all-electric future was near at hand.* □ **near enough** sufficiently close to being the case for all practical purposes: *this price was near enough the going rate for rent.* □ **one's nearest and dearest** one's close friends and relatives. □ **so near and yet so far** a rueful comment on someone's narrow failure to achieve an aim.

near·by ▶*adj.* /ˈni(ə)rˌbī/ close at hand; not far away: *he slung his jacket over a nearby chair.*
▶*adv.* /ˌni(ə)rˈbī/ (*Brit.* also **near by**) close by; very near: *his four sisters live nearby.*

Ne·arc·tic /nēˈärktik; -ˈärtik/ ▶*adj. Zoology* of, relating to, or denoting a zoogeographical region comprising North America as far south as northern Mexico, together with Greenland. The fauna is closely related to that of the Palearctic region. Compare with HOLARCTIC. ■ [as *n.*] (**the Nearctic**) the Nearctic region. ▷mid 19th cent.: from NEO- 'new' + ARCTIC.

near-death ex·pe·ri·ence ▶*n.* an unusual experience taking place on the brink of death and recounted by a person after recovery, typically an out-of-body experience or a vision of a tunnel of light.

Near East (**the Near East**) a term originally applied to the Balkan states of southeastern Europe, but now generally applied to the countries of southwestern Asia between the Mediterranean Sea and India (including the Middle East), esp. in historical contexts. —**Near East·ern** *adj.*

near gale ▶*n.* another term for MODERATE GALE.

near-in·fra·red ▶*adj.* pertaining to or being in the infrared spectrum that is closest to visible light; it is used for studying red dwarfs, red giants, and other celestial objects.

Near Is·lands an island group at the western end of the Aleutian Islands, in southwestern Alaska. Attu is one of the Near Islands.

near·ly /ˈni(ə)rlē/ ▶*adv.* **1** very close to; almost: *David was nearly asleep* | *a rise of nearly 25 percent.* **2** closely: *in the absence of anyone more nearly related, I had been designated next of kin.*
▶PHRASE □ **not nearly** nothing like; far from: *you're not nearly as clever as you think you are.*

near miss ▶*n.* **1** a narrowly avoided collision, esp. between two aircraft. ■ something narrowly avoided; a lucky escape: *she had a near miss when her horse was nearly sucked into a dike.* **2** a bomb or shot that just misses its target. ■ something almost achieved: *a victory in Houston and a near miss in the semifinals of the French Open.*

near mon·ey ▶*n. Finance* assets that can readily be converted into cash, such as government bonds.

near rhyme ▶*n.* rhyming in which the words sound the same but do not rhyme perfectly. Also called OFF RHYME.

near·shore /ˈni(ə)rˌSHôr/ ▶*adj.* [*attrib.*] relating to or denoting the region of the sea or seabed relatively close to a shore.

near·sight·ed /ˈnirˌsītid/ ▶*adj.* unable to see things clearly unless they are relatively close to the eyes, owing to the focusing of rays of light by the eye at a point in front of the retina; myopic. —**near·sight·ed·ly** *adv.* —**near·sight·ed·ness** *n.*

near-term ▶*adj.* short-term. ■ (of a pregnant female or a fetus) close to the time of birth: *near-term sheep fetuses.*

neat[1] /nēt/ ▶*adj.* **1** (of a place or thing) arranged in an orderly, tidy way: *the books had been stacked up in neat piles.* ■ (of a person) habitually tidy, well groomed, or well organized: *her daughter was always neat and clean.* ■ having a pleasing shape or appearance; well formed or regular: *Alan noted down the orders in his neat, precise script.* ■ *informal* very good or pleasant; excellent: *I've been taking lessons in tracking from this really neat Indian guide.* **2** done with or demonstrating skill or efficiency: *Howard's neat, precise tackling.* ■ tending to disregard specifics for the sake of convenience; slick or facile: *this neat division does not take into account a host of associated factors.* **3** (of liquid, esp. liquor) not diluted or mixed with anything else: *he drank neat Scotch.* ▷late 15th cent. (in the sense 'clean, free from impurities'): from French *net*, from Latin *nitidus* 'shining,' from *nitere* 'to shine'; related to NET[2]. The sense 'bright' (now obsolete) was recorded in English in the late 16th cent. —**neat·ly** *adv.* —**neat·ness** *n.*

neat[2] ▶*n. archaic* a bovine animal. ■ cattle. ▷Old

English, of Germanic origin; related to Dutch *noot,* also to the base of dialect *nait* meaning 'companion.'

neat·en /'nētn/ ▸v. [*trans.*] make neat; arrange in an orderly, tidy way: *she made an attempt to neaten her hair.*

'neath /nēTH/ (also **neath**) ▸*prep. chiefly poetic/literary* beneath: *'neath the trees.*

neat's-foot oil ▸*n.* oil obtained by boiling the feet of cattle, used to dress leather.

NEB ▸*abbr.* ■ (in the UK) National Enterprise Board. ■ New English Bible.

neb /neb/ ▸*n. Scottish & N. English* a projecting part of something, in particular: ■ a nose or snout. ■ a bird's beak or bill. ■ the brim of a cap. ▷Old English *nebb,* of Germanic origin; related to Dutch *neb(be);* compare with NIB.

Neb. ▸*abbr.* Nebraska.

Neb·bi·o·lo /ˌnebē'ōlō/ ▸*n.* a variety of black wine grape grown in Piedmont in northern Italy. ■ a red wine made from this. ▷Italian, from *nebbia* 'mist' (because the grape ripens in the autumn).

neb·bish /'nebiSH/ ▸*n. informal* a person, esp. a man, who is regarded as pitifully ineffectual, timid, or submissive. ▷late 19th cent.: from Yiddish *nebekh* 'poor thing.' **—neb·bish·y** *adj.*

NEbE ▸*abbr.* northeast by east.

NEbN ▸*abbr.* northeast by north.

Nebr. ▸*abbr.* Nebraska.

Ne·bras·ka /nə'braskə/ a state in the central U.S., west of the Missouri River; pop. 1,711,263; capital, Lincoln; statehood, Mar. 1, 1867 (37). It was acquired as part of the Louisiana Purchase in 1803. **—Ne·bras·kan** *adj. & n.*

Neb·u·chad·nez·zar /ˌneb(y)əkə(d)'nezər/ ▸*n.* a very large wine bottle, equivalent in capacity to about twenty regular bottles. ▷early 20th cent.: from *Nebuchadnezzar* (see NEBUCHADNEZZAR II).

Neb·u·chad·nez·zar II /ˌneb(y)əkəd'nezər/ (*c.*630–562 BC), king of Babylon 605–562 BC. He rebuilt the city with massive walls, a huge temple, and a ziggurat, and extended his rule over neighboring countries. In 586 BC, he captured and destroyed Jerusalem and deported many Israelites in what is known as the Babylonian Captivity.

neb·u·la /'nebyələ/ ▸*n.* (*pl.* **-lae** /-lē/ or **-las**) **1** *Astronomy* a cloud of gas and dust in outer space, visible in the night sky either as an indistinct bright patch or as a dark silhouette against other luminous matter. ■ (in general use) any indistinct bright area in the night sky, for example, a distant galaxy. **2** *Medicine* a clouded spot on the cornea causing defective vision. ▷mid 17th cent. (as a medical term): from Latin, literally 'mist.'

neb·u·lar /'nebyələr/ ▸*adj.* of, relating to, or denoting a nebula or nebulae: *a vast nebular cloud.*

neb·u·lar hy·poth·e·sis (also **nebular theory**) ▸*n.* the theory that the solar and stellar systems were developed from a primeval nebula.

ne·bu·li·um /nə'byoolēəm/ ▸*n. historical Chemistry* a hypothetical chemical element proposed in the 1860s to explain certain lines in the spectra of nebulae, later discovered to arise from forbidden transitions in oxygen and nitrogen ions: [as *adj.*] *nebulium lines.*

neb·u·liz·er /'nebyəˌlīzər/ ▸*n.* a device for producing a fine spray of liquid, used for example for inhaling a medicinal drug. ▷late 19th cent.: from Latin *nebula* 'mist' + *-izer* (see -IZE). **—neb·u·lize** *v.*

neb·u·lous /'nebyələs/ ▸*adj.* in the form of a cloud or haze; hazy: *a giant nebulous glow.* ■ (of a concept or idea) unclear, vague, or ill-defined: *nebulous concepts like quality of life.* ■ another term for NEBULAR. ▷late Middle English (in the sense 'cloudy'): from French *nébuleux* or Latin *nebulosus,* from *nebula* 'mist.' The sense 'cloudlike, vague' dates from the early 19th cent. **—neb·u·los·i·ty** /ˌnebyə'läsitē/ *n.* **—neb·u·lous·ly** *adv.* **—neb·u·lous·ness** *n.*

neb·u·lous star ▸*n. Astronomy* a small cluster of indistinct stars, or a star in a luminous haze.

neb·u·ly /'nebyəlē/ ▸*adj. Heraldry* divided or edged with a line formed of deeply interlocking curves. ▷mid 16th cent.: from French *nébulé,* from medieval Latin *nebulatus* 'clouded' (the curves being thought of as representing clouds), from Latin *nebula* 'mist.'

NEC ▸*abbr.* ■ National Executive Committee. ■ (in the UK) National Exhibition Centre.

nec·es·sar·i·an /ˌnesə'se(ə)rēən/ ▸*n. & adj. Philosophy* another term for DETERMINIST (see DETERMINISM). **—nec·es·sar·i·an·ism** /-ˌnizəm/ *n.*

nec·es·sar·i·ly /ˌnesə'se(ə)rəlē/ ▸*adv.* as a necessary result; inevitably: *the prognosis can necessarily be only an educated guess.*

▸*PHRASE* □ **not necessarily** (as a response) what has been said or suggested may not be true or unavoidable.

nec·es·sar·y /'nesəˌserē/ ▸*adj.* **1** required to be done, achieved, or present; needed; essential: *members are admitted only after they have gained the necessary experience | it's not* **necessary for** *you to be here.* **2** determined, existing, or happening by natural laws or predestination; inevitable: *a necessary consequence.* ■ *Philosophy* (of a concept, statement, judgment, etc.) inevitably resulting from or produced by the nature of things, so that the contrary is impossible. ■ *Philosophy* (of an agent) having no independent volition.

▸*n.* (usu. **necessaries**) (also **necessaries of life**) the basic requirements of life, such as food and warmth. ■ small items required for a particular journey or purpose: *I hastily threw a few necessaries into a kit bag.* ▷late Middle English: from Latin *necessarius,* from *necesse* 'needful.'

▸*PHRASE* □ **a necessary evil** something that is undesirable but must be accepted.

THE RIGHT WORD **essential, indispensable, necessary, requisite**

Food is **essential** to human life, which means that we must have it to survive. *Essential* can also apply to something that makes up the *essence,* or necessary qualities or attributes, of a thing (*a good safecracker is essential to our plan*).

Clothing is **indispensable** in northern climates, which means that it cannot be done without if the specified or implied purpose—in this case, survival—is to be achieved.

Necessary applies to something without which a condition cannot be fulfilled (*cooperation was necessary to gather the harvest*), although it generally implies a pressing need rather than absolute indispensability.

Requisite refers to that which is required by the circumstances (*the requisite skills for a botanist*) and generally describes a requirement that is imposed from the outside rather than an inherent need.

ne·ces·si·tar·i·an /nəˌsesə'te(ə)rēən/ ▸*n. & adj. Philosophy* another term for DETERMINIST (see DETERMINISM). **—ne·ces·si·tar·i·an·ism** /-ˌnizəm/ *n.*

ne·ces·si·tate /nə'sesəˌtāt/ ▸*v.* [*trans.*] make (something) necessary as a result or consequence: *the severe arthritis eventually necessitated a total hip replacement.* ■ [*trans.*] force or compel (someone) to do something: *the late arrival had necessitated her getting out of bed.* See note at COMPEL. ▷early 17th cent.: from medieval Latin *necessitat-* 'compelled,' from the verb *necessitare,* based on Latin *necesse* 'needful.'

ne·ces·si·tous /nə'sesitəs/ ▸*adj.* (of a person) lacking the necessities of life; needy. ▷early 17th cent.: from French *nécessiteux,* or from NECESSITY + -OUS.

ne·ces·si·ty /nə'sesətē/ ▸*n.* (*pl.* **-ties**) **1** the fact of being required or indispensable: *the* **necessity of** *providing parental guidance should be apparent | the* **necessity for** *law and order.* ■ unavoidability: *the* **necessity of** *growing old.* ■ a state of things or circumstances enforcing a certain course: *created more by necessity than design.* **2** an indispensable thing: *a good book is a necessity when traveling.* **3** *Philosophy* the principle according to which something must be so, by virtue either of logic or of natural law. ■ a condition that cannot be otherwise, or a statement asserting this. ▷late Middle English: from Old French *necessite,* from Latin *necessitas,* from *necesse* 'needful.'

▸*PHRASES* □ **necessity is the mother of invention** *proverb* when the need for something becomes imperative, you are forced to find ways of getting or achieving it. □ **of necessity** unavoidably: *to alleviate labor shortages employers will, of necessity, offer better deals for part-timers.*

neck /nek/ ▸*n.* **1** the part of a person's or animal's body connecting the head to the rest of the body: *she is wearing a silk scarf around her neck |* [as *adj.*] *the neck muscles.* ■ the part of a shirt, dress, or other garment that is around or close to the neck: *her dress had three buttons at the neck undone | a polo neck.* ■ meat from an animal's neck: *neck of lamb made an excellent stew.* ■ *figurative* a person's neck regarded as bearing a burden of responsibility or guilt for something: *he'll be stuck with a loan* **around his neck.** **2** a narrow part of something, resembling a neck in shape or position: ■ the part of a bottle or other container near the mouth. ■ a narrow piece of terrain or sea, such as an isthmus, channel, or pass. ■ *Anatomy* a narrow part near one end of an organ such as the uterus. ■ the part of a violin, guitar, or other similar instrument that bears the fingerboard. ■ *Architecture* another term for NECKING. ■ (often **volcanic neck**) *Geology* a column of solidified lava or igneous rock formed in a volcanic vent, esp. when exposed by erosion. ■ *Botany* a narrow supporting part in a plant, esp. the terminal part of the fruiting body in a fern, bryophyte, or fungus. **3** the length of a horse's head and neck as a measure of its lead in a race: *the colt won the 122nd running of the Midsummer Derby by a neck.*

▸*v.* **1** [*intrans.*] *informal* (of two people) kiss and caress amorously: *we started necking on the sofa.* **2** [*intrans.*] form a narrowed part at a particular point when subjected to tension: *the nylon filament* **necks down** *to a fraction of its original diameter.* **3** [*trans.*] *Brit., informal* swallow (something, esp. a drink): *after necking some beers, we left the bar.* ▷Old English *hnecca* 'back of the neck,' of Germanic origin; related to Dutch *nek* 'neck' and German *Nacken* 'nape.' **—necked** *adj.* [in *combination*] *an open-necked shirt.* **—neck·er** *n.* **—neck·less** *adj.*

▸*PHRASES* □ **break one's neck 1** dislocate or seriously damage a vertebra or the spinal cord in one's neck. **2** (**break one's neck to do something**) *informal* exert oneself to the utmost to achieve something. □ **get** (or **catch**) **it in the neck** *informal* be severely criticized or punished. □ **neck and neck** even in a race, competition, or comparison: *we have six contestants who are neck and neck.* □ **neck of the woods** *informal* a particular area or locality: *imagine seeing her in this neck of the woods.* □ **save someone's neck** see SAVE[1]. □ **up to one's neck in** *informal* heavily burdened by or busily involved in: *they were up to their necks in debt | I'm up to my neck in rearranging the tournament.*

Neck·ar /'nekər/ a river in western Germany that rises in the Black Forest and flows 228 miles (367 km) north and then west through Stuttgart to meet the Rhine River at Mannheim.

neck·band /'nekˌband/ ▸*n.* a strip of material around the neck of a garment.

neck·cloth /'nekˌklôTH/ ▸*n.* a cravat.

Nec·ker /'nekər; ne'ker/, Jacques (1732–1804), Swiss-born banker and director general of French finances (1777–81; 1788–89). In 1789 he recommended summoning the States General and was dismissed, this being one of the factors that resulted in the storming of the Bastille.

neck·er·chief /'nekərˌCHif; -ˌCHēf/ ▸*n.* a square of cloth worn around the neck.

Neck·er cube ▸*n.* a line drawing of a transparent cube in which the lines of opposite sides are drawn parallel, so that the perspective is ambiguous and the orientation of the cube appears to alternate. ▷early 20th cent.: named after L. A. Necker (1786–1861), Swiss naturalist.

Necker cube

neck·ing /'nekiNG/ ▸*n.* **1** the action of two people kissing and caressing each other amorously. **2** *Architecture* a short, plain, concave section between the capital and the shaft of a classical Doric or Tuscan column.

neck·lace /'neklis/ ▸*n.* **1** an ornamental chain or string of beads, jewels, or links worn around the neck. **2** (chiefly in South Africa) a tire doused or filled with gasoline, placed around a victim's neck, and set on fire.

▸*v.* [*trans.*] (chiefly in South Africa) kill (someone) with a tire necklace.

neck·let /'neklit/ ▸*n.* a fairly close-fitting and typically rigid ornament worn around the neck.

neck·line /'nekˌlīn/ ▸*n.* the edge of a woman's garment at or below the neck, used with reference to its height or shape: *a sundress with a square neckline.*

neck·tie /'nekˌtī/ ▸*n.* another term for TIE (sense 2).

neck·tie par·ty ▸*n. informal* a lynching or hanging.

neck·wear /'nekˌwe(ə)r/ ▸*n.* items worn around the neck, such as ties or scarves, collectively.

necro- ▸*comb. form* relating to a corpse or death: *necromancy.* ▷from Greek *nekros* 'corpse.'

nec·ro·bi·o·sis /ˌnekrōbī'ōsis/ ▸*n. Medicine* gradual degeneration and death of cells in the body tissues. **—nec·ro·bi·ot·ic** /-ˌbī'ätik/ *adj.*

ne·crol·o·gist /ne'kräləjist/ ▸*n.* the author of an obituary notice.

N

ne·crol·o·gy /neˈkräləjē/ ▸*n.* (*pl.* **-gies**) *formal* **1** an obituary notice. **2** a list of deaths. **—ne·cro·log·i·cal** /ˌnekrəˈläjikəl/ *adj.*

nec·ro·man·cy /ˈnekrəˌmansē/ ▸*n.* the supposed practice of communicating with the dead, esp. in order to predict the future. ■ witchcraft, sorcery, or black magic in general. ▷Middle English *nigromancie*, via Old French from medieval Latin *nigromantia*, changed (by association with Latin *niger, nigr-* 'black') from late Latin *necromantia*, from Greek (see **NECRO-**, **-MANCY**). The spelling was changed in the 16th cent. to conform with the late Latin form. **—nec·ro·man·cer** /-sər/ *n.* **—nec·ro·man·tic** /ˌnekrəˈmantik/ *adj.*

nec·ro·phil·i·a /ˌnekrəˈfilēə/ ▸*n.* a morbid and esp. erotic attraction toward corpses. ■ sexual intercourse with a corpse. **—nec·ro·phile** /ˈnekrəˌfil/ *n.* **—nec·ro·phil·i·ac** /-ˈfilēˌak/ *n.* **—nec·ro·phil·ic** /-ˈfilik/ *adj.* **—ne·croph·i·lism** /neˈkräfəˌlizəm/ *n.* **—ne·croph·i·list** /neˈkräfəlist/ *n.*

nec·ro·pho·bi·a /ˌnekrəˈfōbēə/ ▸*n.* extreme or irrational fear of death or dead bodies.

ne·crop·o·lis /neˈkräpəlis/ ▸*n.* a cemetery, esp. a large one belonging to an ancient city. ▷early 19th cent.: from Greek, from *nekros* 'dead person' + *polis* 'city.'

nec·rop·sy /ˈnekräpsē/ ▸*n.* (*pl.* **-sies**) another term for **AUTOPSY**.

ne·cro·sis /neˈkrōsis/ ▸*n.* *Medicine* the death of most or all of the cells in an organ or tissue due to disease, injury, or failure of the blood supply. ▷mid 17th cent.: modern Latin, from Greek *nekrōsis* (see **NECRO-**, **-OSIS**). **—ne·crot·ic** /-ˈkrätik/ *adj.*

nec·ro·tiz·ing /ˈnekrəˌtīziNG/ ▸*adj.* [*attrib.*] causing or accompanied by necrosis. **—nec·ro·tized** /-ˌtīzd/ *adj.*

nec·ro·tiz·ing fas·ci·i·tis /ˌfasHēˈītis/ ▸*n.* *Medicine* an acute disease in which inflammation of the fasciae of muscles or other organs results in rapid destruction of overlying tissues. • This disease is caused by the bacterium *Streptococcus pyogenes*.

nec·tar /ˈnektər/ ▸*n.* **1** a sugary fluid secreted by plants, esp. within flowers to encourage pollination by insects and other animals. It is collected by bees to make into honey. **2** (in Greek and Roman mythology) the drink of the gods. ■ a delicious drink: *the cold beer at the pub was nectar.* ■ a thick fruit juice: *peach nectar.* ▷mid 16th cent. (sense 2): via Latin from Greek *nektar*. **—nec·tar·e·an** /nekˈte(ə)rēən/ *adj.* **—nec·tar·e·ous** /nekˈte(ə)rēəs/ *adj.* **—nec·tar·ous** /-əs/ *adj.*

nec·tar·if·er·ous /ˌnektəˈrifərəs/ ▸*adj.* *Botany* (of a flower) producing nectar.

nec·tar·ine /ˌnektəˈrēn/ ▸*n.* a peach of a variety with smooth, thin, brightly colored skin and rich firm flesh. ■ the tree bearing this fruit. ▷early 17th cent. (also used as an adjective meaning 'nectarlike'): from **NECTAR** + **-INE**[4].

nec·tar·iv·o·rous /ˌnektəˈrivərəs/ ▸*adj.* *Zoology* (of an animal) feeding on nectar.

nec·ta·ry /ˈnektərē/ ▸*n.* (*pl.* **-ries**) *Botany* a nectar-secreting glandular organ in a flower (floral) or on a leaf or stem (extrafloral). ▷mid 18th cent.: from modern Latin *nectarium*, from *nectar* (see **NECTAR**).

Ne·der·land /ˈnādərˌlänt/ Dutch name for **NETHERLANDS**.

née /nā/ ▸*adj.* originally called; born (used esp. in adding a woman's maiden name after her married name): *Mary Toogood, née Johnson.* ▷mid 18th cent.: French, literally 'born,' feminine past participle of *naître*; compare with **NÉ**.

need /nēd/ ▸*v.* [*trans.*] **1** require (something) because it is essential or very important: *I need help now* | [with *present participle*] *this shirt needs washing* | [with *infinitive*] *they need to win tomorrow.* ■ (**not need something**) not want to be subjected to something: *I don't need your sarcasm.* **2** [as *modal verb*] [with *negative* or in *questions*] expressing necessity or obligation: *need I say more?* | *I* **need not have** *worried.* **3** [*intrans.*] *archaic* be necessary: *lest you, even more than needs, embitter our parting.*

▸*n.* **1** circumstances in which something is necessary, or that require some course of action; necessity: *the basic human* **need for** *food* | [with *infinitive*] *there's no need to cry.* **2** (often **needs**) a thing that is wanted or required: *his day-to-day needs.* **3** the state of lacking basic necessities such as food or money: *a family whose need was particularly pressing.* ■ the state of requiring help or support: *help us in our* **hour of need**. ▷Old English *nēodian* (verb), *nēod, nēd* (noun), of Germanic origin; related to Dutch *nood* and German *Not* 'danger.'

▸*PHRASES* □ **at need** *archaic* when needed; in an emergency: *men whose experience could be called upon at need.* □ **had need** *archaic* ought to: *you had need hire men to chip it all over artistically.* □ **have need of** *formal* need: *Alida had need of company* □ **if need be** if necessary. □ **in need** requiring help: *children in need.* □ **in need of** requiring or needing (something): *he was in desperate need of medical care.*

need-blind /ˈnēd ˌblīnd/ ▸*adj.* of or denoting a college admissions policy in which applicants are judged solely on their merits, irrespective of their ability to pay for tuition.

need·ful /ˈnēdfəl/ ▸*adj.* **1** *formal* necessary; requisite: *a further word was needful.* **2** needy: *she gave her money away to needful people.* **—need·ful·ly** *adv.* **—need·ful·ness** *n.*

nee·dle /ˈnēdl/ ▸*n.* **1** a very fine slender piece of polished metal with a point at one end and a hole or eye for thread at the other, used in sewing. **2** something resembling a sewing needle in use, shape, or appearance, esp.: ■ such an instrument used in crafts such as crochet, knitting, and lacemaking. ■ the pointed hollow end of a hypodermic syringe. ■ a very fine metal spike used in acupuncture. ■ a thin, typically metal pointer on a dial, compass, or other instrument. ■ an etching tool. ■ the sharp, stiff, slender leaf of a fir or pine tree. ■ a pointed rock or peak. ■ a stylus used to play phonograph records. ■ an obelisk: *Cleopatra's Needle.* ■ a steel pin that explodes the cartridge of a breech-loading gun. ■ *Building* a beam used as a temporary support during underpinning.

▸*v.* [*trans.*] **1** prick or pierce (something) with or as if with a needle: *dust needled his eyes.* **2** *informal* provoke or annoy (someone), esp. by continual criticism or questioning: *I just said that to Charlie to needle him.* ▷Old English *nǣdl*, of Germanic origin; related to Dutch *naald* and German *Nadel*, from an Indo-European root shared by Latin *nere* 'to spin' and Greek *nēma* 'thread.'

▸*PHRASES* □ **the eye of a needle** a tiny aperture or opening through which it would seem impossible to pass (esp. with reference to Matt. 19:24). □ **give someone the needle** *informal* provoke or annoy someone: *Lady gives him the needle because she knows it isn't true.* □ **a needle in a haystack** something that is almost impossible to find because it is hidden among so many other things.

nee·dle·cord /ˈnēdlˌkôrd/ ▸*n.* *Brit.* fine-ribbed corduroy fabric.

nee·dle·craft /ˈnēdlˌkraft/ ▸*n.* needlework.

nee·dle·fish /ˈnēdlˌfisH/ ▸*n.* (*pl.* same or **-fish·es**) another term for **GARFISH**.

nee·dle·lace /ˈnēdlˌlās/ ▸*n.* another term for **NEEDLEPOINT** (sense 2).

nee·dle·point /ˈnēdlˌpoint/ ▸*n.* **1** embroidery worked over canvas, typically in a diagonal stitch covering the entire surface of the fabric. **2** (also **needlepoint lace**) lace made by hand using a needle rather than bobbins.

▸*v.* [*trans.*] embroider in needlepoint.

nee·dler /ˈnēdl-ər; -lər/ ▸*n.* **1** a person who annoys or antagonizes another. **2** (in science fiction) a weapon that fires needlelike projectiles.

need·less /ˈnēdlis/ ▸*adj.* (of something bad) unnecessary; avoidable: *I deplore needless waste.* **—need·less·ly** *adv.* **—need·less·ness** *n.*

▸*PHRASE* □ **needless to say** of course.

nee·dle valve ▸*n.* a valve closed by a thin tapering part.

nee·dle·wom·an /ˈnēdlˌwoŏmən/ ▸*n.* (*pl.* **-wom·en**) a woman or girl who has particular sewing skills or who sews for a living.

nee·dle·work /ˈnēdlˌwərk/ ▸*n.* the art or practice of sewing or embroidery: *Mrs. Zurndorfer specializes in needlework.* ■ sewn or embroidered items collectively: *exhibits include European and Eastern needlework.* **—nee·dle·work·er** *n.*

need·n't /ˈnēdnt/ ▸*contraction of* need not.

needs /nēdz/ ▸*adv.* (in phrase **must needs** (or **needs must**) **do something**) *archaic* cannot avoid or help doing something: *they must needs depart.* ▷Old English *nēdes* (see **NEED**, **-S**[3]).

need·y /ˈnēdē/ ▸*adj.* (**need·i·er**, **need·i·est**) (of a person) lacking the necessities of life; very poor: *needy and elderly people.* ■ (of circumstances) characterized by poverty: *those from needy backgrounds.* **—need·i·ness** *n.*

neem /nēm/ ▸*n.* a tropical Old World tree that yields mahoganylike timber, oil, medicinal products, and insecticide. • *Azadirachta indica*, family Meliaceae. Also called **margosa**. ▷early 19th cent.: via Hindi from Sanskrit *nimba*.

Nee·nah /ˈnēnə/ a city in eastern Wisconsin, on the Fox River; pop. 23,219.

neep /nēp/ ▸*n.* *Scottish* & *N. English* a turnip. ▷Old English *nǣp*, from Latin *napus*.

ne'er /ne(ə)r/ ▸*poetic/literary* or *dialect contraction of* never.

ne'er-do-well /ˈne(ə)r do͞o ˌwel/ ▸*n.* a person who is lazy and irresponsible.

▸*adj.* [*attrib.*] lazy and irresponsible.

nef /nef/ ▸*n.* an elaborate table decoration in the shape of a ship for holding such things as table napkins and condiments. ▷mid 19th cent.: from French, literally 'ship' (see **NAVE**[1]).

ne·far·i·ous /niˈfe(ə)rēəs/ ▸*adj.* (typically of an action or activity) wicked or criminal: *the nefarious activities of the organized-crime syndicates.* ▷early 17th cent.: from Latin *nefarius*, from *nefas, nefar-* 'wrong' (from *ne-* 'not' + *fas* 'divine law') + **-OUS**. **—ne·far·i·ous·ly** *adv.* **—ne·far·i·ous·ness** *n.*

Nef·er·ti·ti /ˌnefərˈtētē/ (also **Nof·re·te·te** /ˌnäfriˈtētē/) (*fl.* 14th century BC), Egyptian queen; wife of Akhenaten and half-sister of Tutankhamen.

Nefertiti

neg /neg/ ▸*n.* *informal* a photographic negative. ▷late 19th cent.: abbreviation.

neg. ▸*abbr.* negative: *HIV neg.*

nega- ▸*comb. form* denoting the negative counterpart of a unit of measurement, in particular a unit of energy saved as a result of conservation measures. ▷abbreviation of **NEGATIVE**.

ne·gate /nəˈgāt/ ▸*v.* [*trans.*] **1** nullify; make ineffective: *alcohol negates the effects of the drug.* See note at **VOID**. **2** . *Logic* & *Grammar* make (a clause, sentence, or proposition) negative in meaning. **3** deny the existence of (something): *negating the political nature of education.* ▷early 17th cent. (in senses 1 and 3): from Latin *negat-* 'denied,' from the verb *negare*.

ne·ga·tion /nəˈgāsHən/ ▸*n.* **1** the contradiction or denial of something: *there should be confirmation—or negation—of the findings.* ■ *Grammar* denial of the truth of a clause or sentence, typically involving the use of a negative word (e.g., *not, no, never*) or a word or affix with negative force (e.g., *nothing, non-*). ■ *Logic* a proposition whose assertion specifically denies the truth of another proposition: *the negation of A is, briefly, "not A."* ■ *Mathematics* inversion: *these formulae and their negations.* **2** the absence or opposite of something actual or positive: *evil is not merely the negation of goodness.* ▷late Middle English: from Latin *negatio(n-)*, from the verb *negare* 'deny' (see **NEGATE**). **—neg·a·to·ry** /ˈnegəˌtôrē/ *adj.*

neg·a·tive /ˈnegətiv/ ▸*adj.* **1** consisting in or characterized by the absence rather than the presence of distinguishing features. ■ (of a statement or decision) expressing or implying denial, disagreement, or refusal: *that, I take it, was a negative answer.* ■ (of the results of a test or experiment) indicating that a certain substance is not present or a certain condition does not exist: *so far all the patients have tested negative for TB.* ■ [*in combination*] (of a person or their blood) not having a specified substance or condition: *HIV-negative.* ■ (of a person, attitude, or situation) not optimistic; harmful or unwelcome: *the new tax was having a very negative effect on car sales* | *not all the news is negative.* ■ *informal* denoting a complete lack of something: *they were described as having negative vulnerability to water entry.* ■ *Grammar* & *Logic* (of a word, clause, or proposition) expressing denial, negation, or refutation; stating or asserting that something is not the case. Contrasted with **AFFIRMATIVE** and

INTERROGATIVE. **2** (of a quantity) less than zero; to be subtracted from others or from zero. ■ denoting a direction of decrease or reversal: *the industry suffered negative growth in 1992.* **3** of, containing, producing, or denoting the kind of electric charge carried by electrons. **4** (of a photographic image) showing light and shade or colors reversed from those of the original. **5** *Astrology* relating to or denoting any of the earth or water signs, considered passive in nature.
▸*n.* **1** a word or statement that expresses denial, disagreement, or refusal: *she replied **in the negative**.* ■ (often **the negative**) a bad, unwelcome, or unpleasant quality, characteristic, or aspect of a situation or person: *confidence will not be instilled by harping solely on the negative | the bus trip and the positive media have not had time to turn his significant negatives around.* ■ *Grammar* a word, affix, or phrase expressing negation. ■ *Logic* another term for NEGATION. **2** a photographic image made on film or specially prepared glass that shows the light and shade or color values reversed from the original, and from which positive prints can be made. **3** a result of a test or experiment indicating that a certain substance is not present or a certain condition does not exist: *the percentage of false negatives generated by a cancer test was of great concern.* **4** the part of an electric circuit that is at a lower electrical potential than another part designated as having zero electrical potential. **5** a number less than zero.
▸*exclam.* no (usually used in a military context): *"Any snags, Captain?" "Negative, she's running like clockwork."*
▸*v.* [*trans.*] **1** reject; refuse to accept; veto: *the bill was negatived by 130 votes to 129.* ■ disprove; contradict: *the insurer's main arguments were negatived by Lawrence.* **2** render ineffective; neutralize: *should criminal law allow consent to negative what would otherwise be a crime?* ▷late Middle English: from late Latin *negativus*, from *negare* 'deny' (see NEGATE). **—neg·a·tive·ly** *adv.* **—neg·a·tive·ness** *n.* **—neg·a·tiv·i·ty** /ˌnegəˈtivitē/ *n.*

neg·a·tive eq·ui·ty ▸*n. Brit.* potential indebtedness arising when the market value of a property falls below the outstanding amount of a mortgage secured on it.

neg·a·tive ev·i·dence ▸*n.* evidence for a theory provided by the nonoccurrence or absence of something.

neg·a·tive feed·back ▸*n. chiefly Biology* the diminution or counteraction of an effect by its own influence on the process giving rise to it, as when a high level of a particular hormone in the blood may inhibit further secretion of that hormone, or where the result of a certain action may inhibit further performance of that action. ■ *Electronics* the return of part of an output signal to the input, which is out of phase with it, so that amplifier gain is reduced and the output is improved.

neg·a·tive in·come tax ▸*n.* money credited as allowances to a taxed income, and paid as a benefit when it exceeds debited tax.

neg·a·tive in·stance ▸*n.* a piece of negative evidence.

neg·a·tive pole ▸*n.* the south-seeking pole of a magnet. ■ a cathode.

neg·a·tive sign ▸*n.* another term for MINUS SIGN.

neg·a·tiv·ism /ˈnegətivˌizəm/ ▸*n.* the practice of being or tendency to be negative or skeptical in attitude while failing to offer positive suggestions or views. **—neg·a·tiv·ist** *n.* & *adj.* **—neg·a·tiv·is·tic** /ˌnegətivˈistik/ *adj.*

ne·ga·tor /nəˈgātər/ ▸*n. Grammar* a word expressing negation, esp. (in English) the word *not.*

neg·en·trop·ic /ˌnegənˈträpik/ ▸*adj. Physics* of or characterized by a reduction in entropy (and corresponding increase in order). ▷mid 20th cent.: from NEGATIVE + *entropic* (see ENTROPY). **—neg·en·tro·py** /negˈentrəpē/ *n.*

Neg·ev /ˈneˌgev/ (**the Negev**) an arid region that forms most of southern Israel, between Beersheba and the Gulf of Aqaba, on the Egyptian border. Large areas are irrigated for agriculture and many Israeli communities have been established here.

ne·glect /niˈglekt/ ▸*v.* [*trans.*] fail to care for properly: *the old churchyard has been sadly neglected* | [as *adj.*] (**neglected**) *some severely neglected children.* ■ not pay proper attention to; disregard: *you neglect our advice at your peril.* ■ [with *infinitive*] fail to do something: *he neglected to write to her.*
▸*n.* the state or fact of being uncared for: *animals dying through disease or neglect.* ■ the action of not taking proper care of someone or something: *she was accused of child neglect.* ■ failure to do something: *he was reported for **neglect of** duty.* ▷early 16th cent.: from Latin *neglect-* 'disregarded,' from the verb *neglegere*, from *neg-* 'not' + *legere* 'choose, pick up.' **—ne·glect·ful** /-fəl/ *adj.* **—ne·glect·ful·ly** /-fəlē/ *adv.* **—ne·glect·ful·ness** /-fəlnəs/ *n.*

THE RIGHT WORD **disregard, ignore, neglect, overlook, slight**

One of the most common reasons why people fail to arrive at work on time is that they **neglect** to set their alarm clocks, a verb that implies a failure to carry out some expected or required action, either intentionally or through carelessness.

Some people, of course, choose to **disregard** their employer's rules pertaining to tardiness, which implies a voluntary, and sometimes deliberate, inattention.

Others hear the alarm go off and simply **ignore** it, which suggests not only a deliberate decision to *disregard* something but a stubborn refusal to face the facts.

No doubt they hope their employers will **overlook** their frequent late arrivals, which implies a failure to see or to take action, which can be either intentional or due to haste or lack of care (*to overlook minor errors*).

But they also hope no one will **slight** them for their conduct when it comes to handing out raises and promotions, which means to *disregard* or *neglect* in a disdainful way.

neg·li·gee /ˈnegləˌzhā/ ▸*n.* a woman's light dressing gown, typically made of a filmy, soft fabric. ▷mid 18th cent. (denoting a kind of loose gown worn by women in the 18th cent.): from French, literally 'given little thought or attention,' feminine past participle of *négliger* 'to neglect.'

neg·li·gence /ˈnegləjəns/ ▸*n.* failure to take proper care in doing something: *some of these accidents are due to negligence.* ■ *Law* failure to use reasonable care, resulting in damage or injury to another.

neg·li·gent /ˈnegləjənt/ ▸*adj.* failing to take proper care in doing something: *directors have been negligent in the performance of their duties.* ▷late Middle English: from Old French, or from Latin *negligent-* 'disregarding,' from the verb *negligere* (variant of *neglegere* 'disregard, slight': see NEGLECT). **—neg·li·gent·ly** *adv.*

neg·li·gi·ble /ˈneglijəbəl/ ▸*adj.* so small or unimportant as to be not worth considering; insignificant: *sound could at last be recorded with incredible ease and at negligible cost.* ▷early 19th cent.: from obsolete French, from *négliger* 'to neglect.' **—neg·li·gi·bil·i·ty** /ˌneglijəˈbilitē/ *n.* **—neg·li·gi·bly** /-blē/ *adv.*

ne·go·ti·a·ble /nəˈgōshəbəl/ ▸*adj.* open to discussion or modification: *the price was not negotiable.* ■ (of a document) able to be transferred or assigned to the legal ownership of another person. ■ (of an obstacle or pathway) able to be traversed; passable: *such walkways must be accessible and negotiable for all users.* **—ne·go·ti·a·bil·i·ty** /nəˌgōshəˈbilitē/ *n.*

ne·go·ti·ate /nəˈgōshēˌāt/ ▸*v.* **1** [*intrans.*] try to reach an agreement or compromise by discussion with others: *his government's willingness to negotiate.* ■ [*trans.*] obtain or bring about by negotiating: *he negotiated a new contract with the sellers.* **2** [*trans.*] find a way over or through (an obstacle or difficult path): *there was a puddle to be negotiated.* **3** [*trans.*] transfer (a check, bill, or other document) to the legal ownership of another person. ■ convert (a check) into cash. ▷early 17th cent.: from Latin *negotiat-* 'done in the course of business,' from the verb *negotiari*, from *negotium* 'business,' from *neg-* 'not' + *otium* 'leisure.' **—ne·go·ti·ant** /-sh(ē)ənt/ *n.* (*archaic*). **—ne·go·ti·a·tor** /-ˌātər/ *n.*

ne·go·ti·a·tion /nəˌgōshēˈāshən/ ▸*n.* (also **negotiations**) discussion aimed at reaching an agreement: *a worldwide ban is currently **under negotiation** | **negotiations between** unions and employers.* ■ the action or process of negotiating: *negotiation of the deals.* ■ the action or process of transferring ownership of a document. ▷late 15th cent. (denoting an act of dealing with another person): from Latin *negotiatio(n-)*, from the verb *negotiari* (see NEGOTIATE).

Ne·gress /ˈnēgris/ ▸*n. dated, often offensive* a woman or girl of black African origin. ▷late 18th cent.: from French *négresse*, feminine of *nègre* 'negro.'

USAGE See usage at NEGRO.

Ne·gril·lo /nəˈgrilō/ ▸*n.* (*pl.* **-los**) a member of a black people of short stature native to central and southern Africa. ▷Spanish, diminutive of *negro* 'black' (see NEGRO); compare with NEGRITO.

Ne·gri·to /nəˈgrētō/ ▸*n.* (*pl.* **-tos**) a member of a black people of short stature native to the Austronesian region. ▷Spanish, diminutive of *negro* 'black' (see NEGRO); compare with NEGRILLO.

ne·gri·tude /ˈnegriˌt(y)o͞od; ˈnē-/ (also **Ne·gri·tude**) ▸*n.* the quality or fact of being of black African origin. ■ the affirmation or consciousness of the value of black or African culture, heritage, and identity: *Negritude helped to guide Senegal into independence with pride.* ▷1950s: from French *négritude* 'blackness.'

Ne·gro /ˈnēgrō/ ▸*n.* (*pl.* **-groes**) *dated, often offensive* a member of a dark-skinned group of peoples originally native to Africa south of the Sahara.
▸*adj. dated, often offensive* of or relating to such people. ▷via Spanish and Portuguese from Latin *niger*, *nigr-* 'black.'

USAGE The word **Negro** was adopted from Spanish and Portuguese and first recorded from the mid 16th century. It remained the standard term throughout the 17th–19th centuries and was used by such prominent black American campaigners as W.E.B. DuBois and Booker T. Washington in the early 20th century. Since the Black Power movement of the 1960s, however, when the term **black** was favored as the term to express racial pride, **Negro** has dropped out of favor and now seems out of date or even offensive in both U.S. and British English.
See also **usage** at BLACK.

Ne·groid /ˈnēgroid/ ▸*adj. often offensive* of or relating to the division of humankind represented by the indigenous peoples of central and southern Africa.

USAGE The term **Negroid** belongs to a set of terms introduced by 19th-century anthropologists attempting to categorize human races. Such terms are associated with outdated notions of racial types, and so are now potentially offensive and best avoided.
See also **usage** at MONGOLOID.

Ne·gro Leagues ▸*n.* associations of professional baseball teams made up of African-American players, esp. active from the 1920s through the 1940s.

ne·gro·ni /nəˈgrōnē/ (also **Ne·gro·ni**) ▸*n.* a cocktail made from gin, vermouth, and Campari. ▷Italian.

Ne·gro·pho·bi·a /ˌnēgrəˈfōbēə/ ▸*n.* intense or irrational dislike or fear of black people. **—Ne·gro·phobe** /ˈnēgrəˌfōb/ *n.*

Ne·gros /ˈnāgrōs; ˈne-/ the fourth largest of the Philippine islands; pop. 3,182,000; chief city, Bacolod.

Ne·gro spir·it·u·al ▸*n.* see SPIRITUAL.

Ne·gus /ˈnēgəs/ ▸*n. historical* a ruler, or the supreme ruler, of Ethiopia. ▷from Amharic *n'gus* 'king.'

ne·gus /ˈnēgəs/ ▸*n. historical* a hot drink of port, sugar, lemon, and spices. ▷named after Colonel Francis *Negus* (died 1732), who created it.

Neh. ▸*abbr. Bible* Nehemiah.

Ne·he·mi·ah /ˌnēəˈmīə/ (5th century BC) a Hebrew leader who supervised the rebuilding of the walls of Jerusalem (*c.*444) and introduced moral and religious reforms (*c.*432). ■ a book of the Bible telling of this rebuilding and of the reforms.

Neh·ru /ˈnāˌro͞o; ˈne(ə)rˌo͞o/, Jawaharlal (1889–1964), Indian statesman; prime minister 1947–64; known as **Pandit Nehru**; father of Indira Gandhi. Nehru was elected leader of the Indian National Congress in 1929. Imprisoned nine times by the British for his nationalist campaigns, he went on to become the first prime minister of independent India.

Jawaharlal Nehru

Pronunciation Key ə *ago;* ər *over;* ˈə *or* ˌə *up;* ˈər *or* ˌər *fur;* a *hat;* ā *rate;* ä *car;* CH *chew;* e *let;* ē *see;* e(ə)r *air;* i *fit;* ī *by;* i(ə)r *ear;* NG *sing;* ō *go;* ô *for;* oi *boy;* o͝o *good;* o͞o *goo;* ou *out;* SH *she;* TH *thin;* <u>TH</u> *then;* (h)w *why;* ZH *vision*

neigh /nā/ ▸*n.* a characteristic high-pitched sound uttered by a horse.
▸*v.* [*intrans.*] (of a horse) make such a sound; utter a neigh. ■ (of a person) make a similar sound: *they neighed dutifully at jokes they did not understand.* ▷Old English *hnǣgan* (verb), of imitative origin; compare with Dutch dialect *neijen.*

neigh·bor /ˈnābər/ (*Brit.* **neigh·bour**) ▸*n.* a person living near or next door to the speaker or person referred to: *our garden was the envy of the neighbors.* ■ a person or place in relation to others near or next to it: *I chatted with my neighbor on the flight to New York | matching our investment levels with those of our North American neighbors.* ■ any person in need of one's help or kindness (after biblical use): *love thy neighbor as thyself.*
▸*v.* [*trans.*] (of a place or thing) be situated next to or very near (another): *the square neighbors the old quarter of the town* | [as *adj.*] (**neighboring**) *a couple at a neighboring table.* ▷Old English *nēahgebūr,* from *nēah* 'nigh, near' + *gebūr* 'inhabitant, peasant, farmer' (compare with BOOR). —**neigh·bor·less** *adj.*

neigh·bor·hood /ˈnābərˌho͝od/ (*Brit.* **neigh·bour·hood**) ▸*n.* a district, esp. one forming a community within a town or city: *she lived in a wealthy neighborhood of Boston.* ■ the people of such a district: *the party disturbed the whole neighborhood.* ■ neighborly feeling or conduct: *the importance of neighborhood to old people.* ■ the area surrounding a particular place, person, or object: *he was reluctant to leave the neighborhood of Butte.* ■ *Mathematics* the set of points whose distance from a given point is less than (or less than or equal to) some value.
▸*PHRASE* □ **in the neighborhood of** approximately; about: *the cost would be in the neighborhood of three billion.*

neigh·bor·hood watch ▸*n.* a program of systematic local vigilance by residents of a neighborhood to discourage crime, esp. burglary.

neigh·bor·ly /ˈnābərlē/ (*Brit.* **neigh·bour·ly**) ▸*adj.* characteristic of a good neighbor, esp. helpful, friendly, or kind. —**neigh·bor·li·ness** *n.*

Neis·se /ˈnīsə/ **1** a river in central Europe that rises in the north of the Czech Republic and flows over 140 miles (225 km) north, forming the southern part of the border between Germany and Poland (the Oder–Neisse Line) and joining the Oder River northeast of Cottbus. German name **LAUSITZER NEISSE**; Polish name **NYSA**. **2** a river in southern Poland that rises near the border with the Czech Republic and flows 120 miles (195 km) northeast, through the town of Nysa, and joins the Oder River southeast of Wrocław. German name **GLATZER NEISSE**.

nei·ther /ˈnē*th*ər; ˈnī-/ ▸*adj.* & *pron.* not the one nor the other of two people or things; not either: [as *adj.*] *neither side of the brain is dominant over the other* | [as *pron.*] ***neither of** us believes it.*
▸*adv.* **1** used before the first of two (or occasionally more) alternatives that are being specified (the others being introduced by "nor") to indicate that they are each untrue or each do not happen: *I am neither a liberal nor a conservative.* **2** used to introduce a further negative statement: *he didn't remember, and neither did I.* ▷Middle English: alteration (by association with EITHER) of Old English *nawther,* contraction of *nāhwæther* (from *nā* 'no' + *hwæther* 'whether').
▸*PHRASE* □ **neither here nor there** see HERE.

USAGE 1 The use of **neither** with another negative, as in *I **don't** like him **neither** or **not** much good at reading **neither*** is recorded from the 16th century onward, but is not thought to be good English. This is because it is an example of a **double negative**, which, though standard in some other languages such as Spanish and found in many dialects of English, is not acceptable in standard English. In the sentences above, **either** should be used instead. For more information, see **usage** at DOUBLE NEGATIVE.
2 When **neither** is followed by **nor**, it is important in good English style that the two halves of the structure mirror each other: *she saw herself as **neither** wife **nor** mother* rather than *she **neither** saw herself as wife **nor** mother.* For more details, see **usage** at EITHER.

Nejd /nejd/ an arid plateau region in central Saudi Arabia, north of the Rub' al Khali desert, at an altitude of about 5,000 feet (1,500 m).

nek·ton /ˈnektən; -tän/ ▸*n. Zoology* aquatic animals that are able to swim and move independently of water currents. Often contrasted with PLANKTON. ▷late 19th cent.: via German from Greek *nēkton,* neuter of *nēktos* 'swimming,' from *nēkhein* 'to swim.' —**nek·ton·ic** /nekˈtänik/ *adj.*

Nel·lore /neˈlôr/ a city and river port in southeastern India, in Andhra Pradesh, on the Penner River; pop. 316,000.

nel·ly /ˈnelē/ ▸*n.* (*pl.* **-lies**) *informal* **1** a silly person. **2** *offensive* an effeminate homosexual man. ▷mid 20th cent.: from the given name *Nelly.*
▸*PHRASE* □ **not on your nelly** *Brit.* certainly not. [originally as *not on your Nelly Duff,* rhyming slang for 'puff' (i.e., breath of life); modeled on the phrase *not on your life.*]

Nel·son[1] /ˈnelsən/, (John) Byron (1912–), U.S. golfer. He set the all-time PGA stroke average with 68.33 strokes per round over 120 rounds in 1945. PGA Hall of Fame (1953).

Nel·son[2], Horatio, Viscount Nelson, Duke of Bronte (1758–1805), British admiral. He became a national hero as a result of his victories at sea in the Napoleonic Wars, esp. at the Battle of Trafalgar, in which he was mortally wounded.

Nel·son[3], Samuel (1792–1873), U.S. Supreme Court associate justice 1845–72. Chief justice of New York state 1837–45, he was appointed to the U.S. Supreme Court by President Tyler.

Nel·son[4], Willie (1933–), U.S. country singer and songwriter. He is noted for hits such as "A Good Hearted Woman" (1976) and for his albums, such as *Red Haired Stranger* (1975) and *Teatro* (1998).

nel·son /ˈnelsən/ ▸*n.* a wrestling hold in which one arm is passed under the opponent's arm from behind and the hand is applied to the neck (**half nelson**), or both arms and hands are applied (**full nelson**). ▷late 19th cent.: apparently from the surname *Nelson,* but the reference is unknown.

Nel·son Riv·er /ˈnelsən/ a river that flows for 400 miles (640 km) across eastern Manitoba, to Hudson Bay, once a fur trade route.

ne·lum·bo /nəˈləmbō/ ▸*n.* (*pl.* **-bos**) a lotus with huge leaves and solitary large flowers that grow on stalks that can extend 6 feet (2 m) above the surface of the water. • Genus *Nelumbo,* family Nelumbonaceae: two species, the **American lotus** and the **sacred lotus** (see LOTUS). ▷modern Latin, from Sinhalese *neḷum̆ba.*

Ne·man /ˈnemən/ a river in eastern Europe that rises south of Minsk in Belarus and flows 597 miles (955 km) west and then north to the Baltic Sea. Its lower course, which forms the boundary between Lithuania and the Russian enclave of Kaliningrad, is called the Memel. Lithuanian name **NEMUNAS**, Belorussian name **NYOMAN**.

ne·mat·ic /niˈmatik/ ▸*adj.* relating to or denoting a state of a liquid crystal in which the molecules are oriented in parallel but not arranged in well-defined planes. Compare with SMECTIC.
▸*n.* a nematic substance. ▷early 20th cent.: from Greek *nēma, nēmat-* 'thread' + -IC.

nemato- (also **nemat-** before a vowel) ▸*comb. form* denoting something threadlike in shape: *nematocyst.* ■ relating to Nematoda: *nematocide.* ▷from Greek *nēma, nēmat-* 'thread.'

nem·a·to·cide /niˈmatəˌsīd; ˈnemətə-/ (also **nem·a·ti·cide**) ▸*n.* a substance used to kill nematode worms. ▷late 19th cent.: from NEMATO- 'of nematode worms' + -CIDE. —**nem·a·to·cid·al** /ˌnematəˈsīdl/ *adj.*

nem·a·to·cyst /ˈnemətəˌsist; niˈmatə-/ ▸*n. Zoology* a specialized cell in the tentacles of a jellyfish or other coelenterate, containing a barbed or venomous coiled thread that can be projected in self-defense or to capture prey. ▷late 19th cent.: from NEMATO- 'of threadlike shape' + CYST.

Nem·a·to·da /ˌnēməˈtōdə/ *Zoology* a large phylum of worms with slender, unsegmented, cylindrical bodies, including the roundworms, threadworms, and eelworms. They are found abundantly in soil and water, and many are parasites. ▷modern Latin (plural), from Greek *nēma, nēmat-* 'thread.' —**nem·a·tode** /ˈnēməˌtōd/ *n.*

nem·a·tol·o·gy /ˌneməˈtäləjē/ ▸*n.* the scientific study of nematode worms. —**nem·a·tol·o·gist** /-jist/ *n.*

Nem·a·to·mor·pha /ˌnemətəˈmôrfə; nəˌmatə-/ *Zoology* a small phylum that comprises the horsehair worms. ▷modern Latin (plural), from Greek *nēma, nēmat-* 'thread' + *morphē* 'form.' —**nem·a·to·morph** /ˈnemətəˌmôrf; nəˈmatə-/ *n.*

Nem·bu·tal /ˈnembyəˌtäl/ ▸*n. trademark* the drug pentobarbital sodium (see PENTOBARBITAL). ▷mid 20th cent.: from *N(a)* (symbol for sodium) + *e(thyl), m(ethyl), but(yl),* elements of the systematic name, + -AL.

nem. con. ▸*abbr.* nemine contradicente, with no one dissenting; unanimously: *the motions were carried nem. con.* ▷Latin.

Ne·mer·te·a /niˈmərtēə/ *Zoology* a small phylum that comprises the ribbon worms. ▷modern Latin (plural), from Greek *Nēmertēs,* the name of a sea nymph. —**ne·mer·te·an** *adj.* & *n.* —**ne·mer·tine** /ˈnemərˌtēn/ *adj.* & *n.*

ne·me·sia /nəˈmēzнə/ ▸*n.* a plant related to the snapdragon that is cultivated for its colorful, obliquely funnel-shaped flowers. • Genus *Nemesia,* family Scrophulariaceae: several species, in particular *N. strumosa* and its hybrids. ▷modern Latin, from Greek *nemesion,* denoting various similar plants.

Nem·e·sis /ˈneməsis/ *Greek Mythology* a goddess usually portrayed as the agent of divine punishment for wrongdoing or presumption (hubris).

nem·e·sis /ˈneməsis/ ▸*n.* (*pl.* **-ses** /-ˌsēz/) (usu. **one's nemesis**) the inescapable or implacable agent of someone's or something's downfall: *the balance beam was the team's nemesis, as two gymnasts fell from the apparatus.* ■ a downfall caused by such an agent: *one risks nemesis by uttering such words.* ■ (often **Nemesis**) retributive justice: *nemesis is notoriously slow.* ▷late 16th cent.: Greek, literally 'retribution,' from *nemein* 'give what is due.'

ne·mo dat /ˈnāmō ˈdat; ˈnēmō; ˈdät/ (in full **nemo dat quod non habet**) ▸*n. Law* the basic principle that a person who does not own property, esp. a thief, cannot confer it on another except with the true owner's authority. ▷Latin, literally 'no one gives (what he or she does not have).'

ne·ne /ˈnānā/ (also **ne-ne**) ▸*n.* (*pl.* same or **ne·nes**) another term for HAWAIIAN GOOSE. ▷early 20th cent.: from Hawaiian.

Nen·ets /ˈnenets/ ▸*n.* (*pl.* same or **Nen·tsy** /ˈnentsē/ or **Nen·tsi** /ˈnentsē/) **1** a member of a nomadic people of Siberia, whose main traditional occupation is reindeer herding. **2** the Samoyedic language of this people. ▷the name in Russian.

neo- ▸*comb. form* **1** new: *neonate.* **2** a new or revived form of: *neo-Georgian.* ▷from Greek *neos* 'new.'

ne·o·clas·si·cal /ˌnēōˈklasikəl/ (also **ne·o·clas·sic** /-ˈklasik/) ▸*adj.* of or relating to neoclassicism.

ne·o·clas·si·cism /ˌnēōˈklasiˌsizəm/ ▸*n.* the revival of a classical style or treatment in art, literature, architecture, or music.

As an aesthetic and artistic style this originated in Rome in the mid 18th century, combining a reaction against the late baroque and rococo with a new interest in antiquity. In music, the term refers to a return by composers of the early 20th century to the forms and styles of the 17th and 18th centuries, as a reaction against 19th-century romanticism.

—**ne·o·clas·si·cist** *n.* & *adj.*

ne·o·co·lo·ni·al·ism /ˌnēōkəˈlōnēəˌlizəm/ ▸*n.* the use of economic, political, cultural, or other pressures to control or influence other countries, esp. former dependencies. —**ne·o·co·lo·ni·al** *adj.* —**ne·o·co·lo·ni·al·ist** *n.* & *adj.*

ne·o·con /ˌnēōˈkän/ ▸*adj.* neoconservative, esp. in advocating democratic capitalism.
▸*n.* a neoconservative.

ne·o-Con·fu·cian·ism /ˌnēō kənˈfyo͞osнənizəm/ ▸*n.* a movement in religious philosophy derived from Confucianism in China around AD 1000 in response to the ideas of Taoism and Buddhism. —**ne·o-Con·fu·cian** *adj.*

ne·o·con·serv·a·tive /ˌnēōkənˈsərvətiv/ ▸*adj.* of or relating to an approach to politics, literary criticism, theology, history, or any other branch of thought, that represents a return to a modified form of a traditional viewpoint, in contrast to more radical or liberal schools of thought.
▸*n.* a person with neoconservative views. —**ne·o·con·serv·a·tism** /-tizəm/ *n.*

ne·o·cor·tex /ˌnēōˈkôrteks/ ▸*n.* (*pl.* **-cor·ti·ces** /-ˈkôrtiˌsēz/) *Anatomy* a part of the cerebral cortex concerned with sight and hearing in mammals, regarded as the most recently evolved part of the cortex. —**ne·o·cor·ti·cal** /-ˈkôrtikəl/ *adj.*

ne·o-Dar·win·i·an /ˌnēō därˈwinēən/ ▸*adj. Biology* of or relating to the modern version of Darwin's theory of evolution by natural selection, incorporating the findings of genetics. —**ne·o-Dar·win·ism** /ˈdärwiˌnizəm/ *n.* —**ne·o-Dar·win·ist** /ˈdärwinist/ *n.*

ne·o·dym·i·um /ˌnēōˈdimēəm/ ▸*n.* the chemical element of atomic number 60, a silvery-white metal of the lanthanide series. Neodymium is a component of misch metal and some other alloys, and its compounds are used in coloring glass and ceramics. (Symbol: **Nd**) ▷late 19th cent.: from **NEO-** 'new' + a shortened form of **DIDYMIUM**.

ne·o·fas·cist /ˌnēōˈfaSHist/ (also **ne·o-Fas·cist**) ▶*n.* a member of an organization similar to the Italian Fascist movement of the early 20th century.
▶*adj.* of or relating to neofascists or neofascism.
—**ne·o·fas·cism** *n.*

Ne·o·gae·a /ˌnēəˈjēə/ (also **Ne·o·ge·a**) *Zoology* a zoogeographical area comprising the Neotropical region. ▷modern Latin, from Greek *neos* 'new' + *gaia* 'earth.' —**Ne·o·gae·an** *adj.*

Ne·o·gene /ˈnēəˌjēn/ ▶*adj. Geology* of, relating to, or denoting the later division of the Tertiary period, comprising the Miocene and Pliocene epochs. ■ [as *n.*] (**the Neogene**) the Neogene subperiod or the system of rocks deposited during it.

The Neogene lasted from about 23 million to 1.6 million years ago. The mammals continued to evolve during this time, developing into the forms that are familiar today.

▷late 19th cent.: from **NEO-** 'new' + Greek *-genēs* 'born, of a specified kind' (see **-GEN**).

ne·o-Geor·gian ▶*adj.* of, relating to, or imitative of a revival of a Georgian style in architecture.

ne·o-Goth·ic ▶*adj.* of or in an artistic style that originated in the 19th century, characterized by the revival of Gothic and other medieval forms. In architecture it is manifested in pointed arches, vaulted ceilings, and mock fortifications.
▶*n.* the neo-Gothic style.

Ne·o·gram·mar·i·an /ˌnēōgrəˈmerēən/ ▶*n.* any of a group of 19th-century German scholars who, having noticed that sound changes in language are regular and that therefore lost word forms can be reconstructed, postulated the forms of entire lost languages such as Proto-Indo-European by the comparison of related forms in existing languages. They also believed that phonetic laws had no exceptions. ▷translation of German *Junggrammatiker*.

ne·o-Im·pres·sion·ism (also **Ne·o-Im·pres·sion·ism**) ▶*n.* a late 19th-century movement in French painting that sought to improve on Impressionism through a systematic approach to form and color, particularly using pointillist technique. The movement's leading figures included Georges Seurat, Paul Signac, and Camille Pissarro. —**ne·o-Im·pres·sion·ist** *adj.* & *n.*

Ne·o-Lat·in ▶*n.* another term for **MODERN LATIN**.

ne·o·lib·er·al /ˌnēōˈlibərəl/ ▶*adj.* relating to or denoting a modified form of liberalism tending to favor free-market capitalism.
▶*n.* a person holding such views. —**ne·o·lib·er·al·ism** /-ˌlizəm/ *n.*

ne·o·lith /ˈnēəˌliTH/ ▶*n.* a stone implement used during the Neolithic Period.

Ne·o·lith·ic /ˌnēəˈliTHik/ ▶*adj. Archaeology* of, relating to, or denoting the later part of the Stone Age, when ground or polished stone weapons and implements prevailed. ■ [as *n.*] (**the Neolithic**) the Neolithic period. Also called **NEW STONE AGE**.

In the Neolithic period farm animals were first domesticated, and agriculture was introduced. It began in the Near East by the 8th millennium BC and spread to northern Europe by the 4th millennium BC. Neolithic societies in northwestern Europe left such monuments as henges, long barrows, chamber tombs, and settlements inside concentric ditches spanned by causeways.

▷mid 19th cent.: from **NEO-** 'new' + Greek *lithos* 'stone' + **-IC**.

ne·ol·o·gism /nēˈäləˌjizəm/ ▶*n.* a newly coined word or expression. ■ the coining or use of new words. ▷early 19th cent.: from French *néologisme*. —**ne·ol·o·gist** /-jist/ *n.* —**ne·ol·o·gize** /-ˌjīz/ *v.*

ne·o-Mal·thu·sian·ism /ˌnēō malˈTHōōZHəˌnizəm/ ▶*n.* the view that the rate of increase of a population should be controlled. —**ne·o-Mal·thu·sian** *adj.* & *n.*

ne·o-Marx·ist /ˌnēō ˈmärksist/ ▶*adj.* of or relating to forms of political philosophy that arise from the adaptation of Marxist thought to accommodate or confront modern issues such as the global economy, the capitalist welfare state, and the stability of liberal democracies.
▶*n.* a person with neo-Marxist views. —**ne·o-Marx·ism** /-ˌizəm/ *n.*

Ne·o-Mel·a·ne·sian /ˌnēō ˌmeləˈnēZHən/ ▶*n.* another term for **TOK PISIN**.

ne·o·my·cin /ˌnēōˈmīsin/ ▶*n. Medicine* an antibiotic related to streptomycin, active against a wide variety of bacterial infections. • This antibiotic is obtained from the bacterium *Streptomyces fradiae*.

ne·on /ˈnēän/ ▶*n.* the chemical element of atomic number 10, an inert gaseous element of the noble gas group. It is obtained by the distillation of liquid air and is used in fluorescent lamps and advertising signs. (Symbol: **Ne**) ■ fluorescent lighting or signs (whether containing neon or some other gas): *the lobby of the hotel was bright with neon.* ■ a small lamp containing neon. ■ short for **NEON TETRA**. ■ a very bright or fluorescent color: *a denim cap outlined in neon* | [as *adj.*] *we bought ourselves neon bandannas.* ▷late 19th cent.: from Greek, literally 'something new,' neuter of the adjective *neos*.

ne·o·na·tal /ˌnēōˈnātl/ ▶*adj.* of or relating to newborn children (or mammals). —**ne·o·na·tol·o·gist** /-nāˈtäləjist/ *n.* —**ne·o·na·tol·o·gy** /-nāˈtäləjē/ *n.*

ne·o·nate /ˈnēəˌnāt/ ▶*n.* a newborn child or mammal. ■ *Medicine* an infant less than four weeks old. ▷1930s: from modern Latin *neonatus*, from Greek *neos* 'new' + Latin *nat-* 'born' (from the verb *nasci*).

ne·o-Na·zi ▶*n.* (*pl.* **ne·o-Na·zis**) a member of an organization similar to the German Nazi Party. ■ a person of extreme racist or nationalist views.
▶*adj.* of or relating to neo-Nazis or neo-Nazism.
—**ne·o-Na·zism** *n.*

ne·on tet·ra ▶*n.* a small Amazonian characin (fish) with a shining blue-green stripe along each side and a red band near the tail, popular in aquariums. • *Paracheirodon innesi*, family Characidae.

ne·on·tol·o·gy /ˌnēänˈtäləjē/ ▶*n.* the branch of zoology dealing with living forms as distinct from fossils. Often contrasted with **PALEONTOLOGY**. ▷late 19th cent.: from **NEO-** 'new,' on the pattern of *paleontology*. —**ne·on·to·log·i·cal** /-təˈläjikəl/ *adj.*

ne·o·pa·gan·ism /ˌnēōˈpāgiˌnizəm; -gə-/ ▶*n.* a modern religious movement that seeks to incorporate beliefs or ritual practices from traditions outside the main world religions, esp. those of pre-Christian Europe and North America.

Neopaganism is a highly varied mixture of ancient and modern elements, in which nature worship (influenced by modern environmentalism) often plays a major role. Other influences include shamanism, magical and occult traditions, and radical feminist critiques of Christianity.

—**ne·o·pa·gan** *n.* & *adj.*

ne·o·pho·bi·a /ˌnēōˈfōbēə/ ▶*n.* extreme or irrational fear or dislike of anything new, novel, or unfamiliar. —**ne·o·pho·bic** /-bik/ *adj.*

ne·o·phyte /ˈnēəˌfīt/ ▶*n.* a person who is new to a subject, skill, or belief: *four-day cooking classes are offered to neophytes and experts.* See note at **NOVICE**. ■ a new convert to a religion. ■ a novice in a religious order, or a newly ordained priest. ▷late Middle English: via ecclesiastical Latin from Greek *neophutos*, literally 'newly planted' but first used in the sense 'new convert' by St. Paul (1 Tim. 3:6), from *neos* 'new' + *phuton* 'plant.'

ne·o·pla·sia /ˌnēōˈplāZHə/ ▶*n. Medicine* the formation or presence of a new, abnormal growth of tissue.

ne·o·plasm /ˈnēəˌplazəm/ ▶*n.* a new and abnormal growth of tissue in some part of the body, esp. as a characteristic of cancer. ▷mid 19th cent.: from **NEO-** 'new' + Greek *plasma* 'formation' (see **PLASMA**).

ne·o·plas·tic[1] /ˌnēəˈplastik/ ▶*adj. Medicine* of or relating to a neoplasm or neoplasia.

ne·o·plas·tic[2] ▶*adj. Art* of or relating to neoplasticism. ▷1930s: back-formation from **NEOPLASTICISM**.

ne·o·plas·ti·cism /ˌnēōˈplastiˌsizəm/ ▶*n.* a style of abstract painting developed by Piet Mondrian, using only vertical and horizontal lines and rectangular shapes in black, white, gray, and primary colors. ▷1920s: coined by Piet Mondrian.

Ne·o·pla·to·nism /ˌnēōˈplātnˌizəm/ a philosophical and religious system developed by the followers of Plotinus in the 3rd century AD. —**Ne·o·pla·ton·ic** /-pləˈtänik/ *adj.* —**Ne·o·pla·to·nist** *n.*

Neoplatonism combined ideas from Plato, Aristotle, Pythagoras, and the Stoics with oriental mysticism. Predominant in pagan Europe until the early 6th century, it was a major influence on early Christian writers, on later medieval and Renaissance thought, and on Islamic philosophy. It envisages the human soul rising above the imperfect material world through virtue and contemplation toward knowledge of the transcendent One.

ne·o·prene /ˈnēəˌprēn/ ▶*n.* a synthetic polymer resembling rubber, resistant to oil, heat, and weathering. ▷1930s: from **NEO-** 'new' + *prene* (perhaps from **PROPYL** + **-ENE**), on the pattern of words such as *chloroprene*.

Ne·op·tol·e·mus /ˌnēäpˈtäləməs/ *Greek Mythology* the son of Achilles and killer of Priam after the fall of Troy.

ne·o-re·al·ism (also **ne·o·re·al·ism**) ▶*n.* a movement or school in art or philosophy representing a modified form of realism. ■ a naturalistic movement in Italian literature and cinema that emerged in the 1940s. Important exponents include the writer Italo Calvino and the film director Federico Fellini. —**ne·o·re·al·ist** *n.* & *adj.*

Ne·o·sho Riv·er /nēˈōSHō; -SHə/ (also **Grand River**) a river that flows for 460 miles (740 km) from central Kansas through northeastern Oklahoma, into the Arkansas River.

ne·o·stig·mine /ˌnēōˈstigmēn/ ▶*n. Medicine* a synthetic compound that inhibits cholinesterase and is used to treat ileus, glaucoma, and myasthenia gravis. ▷1940s: from **NEO-** 'new,' on the pattern of *physostigmine*.

ne·ot·e·ny /nēˈätn-ē/ ▶*n. Zoology* the retention of juvenile features in the adult animal. Also called **PEDOMORPHOSIS**. ■ the sexual maturity of an animal while it is still in a mainly larval state, as in the axolotl. Also called **PEDOGENESIS**. ▷late 19th cent.: coined in German as *Neotenie*, from Greek *neos* 'new' (in the sense 'juvenile') + *teinein* 'extend.' —**ne·o·te·nic** /ˌnēōˈtenik; -ˈtēnik/ *adj.* —**ne·o·te·nous** /nēˈätn-əs/ *adj.*

ne·o·ter·ic /ˌnēəˈterik/ ▶*adj.* recent; new; modern: *another effort by the White House to display its neoteric wizardry went awry.*
▶*n.* a modern person; a person who advocates new ideas. ▷late 16th cent.: via late Latin from Greek *neōterikos*, from *neōteros* 'newer,' comparative of *neos*.

Ne·o·trop·i·cal /ˌnēōˈträpikəl/ (also **ne·o·trop·i·cal**) ▶*adj. Zoology* of, relating to, or denoting a zoogeographical region comprising Central and South America, including the tropical southern part of Mexico and the Caribbean. Distinctive animals include edentates, opossums, marmosets, and tamarins. Compare with **NEOGAEA**. ■ *Botany* of, relating to, or denoting a phytogeographical kingdom comprising Central and South America but excluding the southern parts of Chile and Argentina. —**Ne·o·trop·ics** /-piks/ *plural n.*

NEP ▶*abbr.* ■ New Economic Policy, a program instituted by Lenin in 1921 in the Soviet Union. ■ non-English proficient.

Ne·pal /nəˈpäl; -ˈpôl/ a mountainous landlocked country in southern Asia, in the Himalayas (including Mount Everest); pop. 27,000,000; capital, Kathmandu; language, Nepali (official). —**Nep·a·lese** /ˌnepəˈlēz; -ˈlēs/ *adj.* & *n.*

Conquered by the Gurkhas in the 18th century, Nepal maintained its independence despite border defeats by the British in the 19th century. It was for long an absolute monarchy, but in 1990 democratic elections were held under a new constitutional monarchy. In 2001 the crown prince killed ten members of the royal family and took his own life. The following year, the new king dismissed the prime minister and his cabinet after they dissolved the parliament; the king and his appointed cabinet are governing and have negotiated a cease-fire with Maoist insurgents.

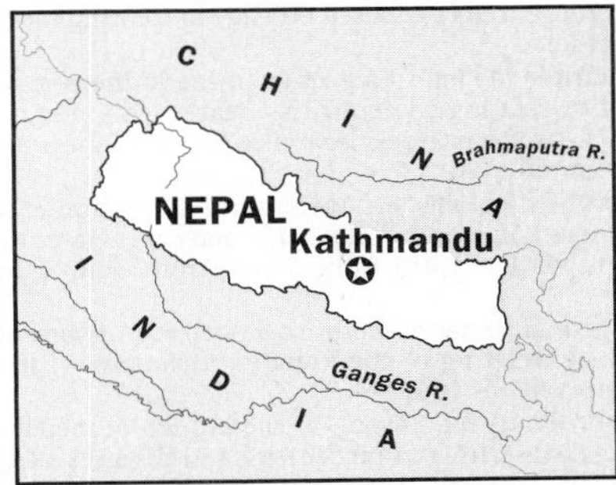

Ne·pal·i /nəˈpôlē; -ˈpälē/ ▶*n.* (*pl.* same or **-pal·is**) a native or national of Nepal. ■ the Indic language that

Pronunciation Key ə *ago*; ər *over*; ˈə *or* ˌə *up*; ˈər *or* ˌər *fur*; a *hat*; ā *rate*; ä *car*; CH *chew*; e *let*; ē *see*; e(ə)r *air*; i *fit*; ī *by*; i(ə)r *ear*; NG *sing*; ō *go*; ô *for*; oi *boy*; ŏŏ *good*; ōō *goo*; ou *out*; SH *she*; TH *thin*; TH *then*; (h)w *why*; ZH *vision*

is the official language of Nepal; also used in the Indian state of Sikkim.
▸*adj.* of or relating to Nepal or its language or people.

ne·pen·thes /nəˈpenTHēz/ ▸*n.* **1** (also **ne·pen·the**) /-THē/ *poetic/literary* a drug described in Homer's *Odyssey* as banishing grief or trouble from a person's mind. ■ any drug or potion bringing welcome forgetfulness. [via Latin from Greek *nēpenthes* 'dispelling pain,' from *nē-* 'not' + *penthos* 'grief.'] **2** a plant of a genus that comprises the Old World pitcher plants. [modern Latin.] • Genus *Nepenthes* and family Nepenthaceae.

ne·per /ˈnēpər; ˈnā-/ ▸*n.* *Physics* a unit used in comparing voltages, currents, and power levels, esp. in communications circuits. The difference between two values in nepers is equal to the natural logarithm of their ratio for voltages and currents or to half of this for power differences. ▷early 20th cent.: from *Neperus,* Latinized form of *Napier* (see **NAPIER**).

nep·e·ta /nəˈpētə/ ▸*n.* a plant of a genus that includes catnip and several kinds cultivated for their spikes of blue or violet flowers. • Genus *Nepeta,* family Labiatae. ▷modern Latin, from Latin *nepeta* 'calamint' (formerly in this genus).

neph·e·line /ˈnefəlin/ ▸*n.* a colorless, greenish, or brownish mineral consisting of an aluminosilicate of sodium (often with potassium) and occurring as crystals and grains in igneous rocks. ▷early 19th cent.: from French *néphéline,* from Greek *nephelē* 'cloud' (because its fragments are made cloudy on immersion in nitric acid) + **-INE**2.

neph·e·line-sy·e·nite ▸*n.* *Geology* a plutonic rock resembling syenite but containing nepheline and lacking quartz.

neph·e·lin·ite /ˈnefələˌnīt/ ▸*n.* *Geology* a fine-grained basaltic rock containing nepheline in place of plagioclase feldspar.

neph·e·lom·e·ter /ˌnefəˈlämitər/ ▸*n.* an instrument for measuring the size and concentration of particles suspended in a liquid or gas, esp. by means of the light they scatter. ▷late 19th cent.: from Greek *nephelē* 'cloud' + **-METER**.

neph·ew /ˈnefyo͞o/ ▸*n.* a son of one's brother or sister, or of one's brother-in-law or sister-in-law. ▷Middle English: from Old French *neveu,* from Latin *nepos* 'grandson, nephew,' from an Indo-European root shared by Dutch *neef* and German *Neffe.*

ne·phol·o·gy /nəˈfäləjē/ ▸*n.* the study or contemplation of clouds. ▷late 19th cent.: from Greek *nephos* 'cloud' + **-LOGY**.

nephr- ▸*comb. form* variant spelling of **NEPHRO-** shortened before a vowel (as in *nephrectomy*).

ne·phrec·to·my /nəˈfrektəmē/ ▸*n.* (*pl.* **-mies**) surgical removal of one or both of the kidneys.

ne·phrid·io·pore /nəˈfridēəˌpôr/ ▸*n.* *Zoology* the external opening of a nephridium.

ne·phrid·i·um /nəˈfridēəm/ ▸*n.* (*pl.* **-phrid·i·a** /-ˈfridēə/) *Zoology* (in many invertebrate animals) a tubule open to the exterior that acts as an organ of excretion or osmoregulation. It typically has ciliated or flagellated cells and absorptive walls. ▷late 19th cent.: modern Latin, from Greek *nephrion* (diminutive of *nephros* 'kidney') + the diminutive ending *-idium.* **—ne·phrid·i·al** /-ēəl/ *adj.*

neph·rite /ˈnefrīt/ ▸*n.* a hard pale green or white mineral that is one of the forms of jade. It is a silicate of calcium and magnesium. ▷late 18th cent.: from German *Nephrit,* from Greek *nephros* 'kidney' (with reference to its supposed efficacy in treating kidney disease).

ne·phrit·ic /nəˈfritik/ ▸*adj.* of or in the kidneys; renal. ■ of or relating to nephritis. ▷early 19th cent.: via late Latin from Greek *nephritikos* 'of the kidneys' (see **NEPHRITIS**).

ne·phri·tis /nəˈfrītis/ ▸*n.* *Medicine* inflammation of the kidneys. Also called **BRIGHT'S DISEASE**. ▷late 16th cent.: via late Latin from Greek, from *nephros* 'kidney.'

nephro- (also **nephr-** before a vowel) ▸*comb. form* of a kidney; relating to the kidneys: *nephrotoxic.* ▷from Greek *nephros* 'kidney.'

ne·phrol·o·gy /nəˈfräləjē/ ▸*n.* the branch of medicine that deals with the physiology and diseases of the kidneys. **—neph·ro·log·i·cal** /ˌnefrəˈläjikəl/ *adj.* **—ne·phrol·o·gist** /-jist/ *n.*

neph·ron /ˈnefrän/ ▸*n.* *Anatomy* each of the functional units in the kidney, consisting of a glomerulus and its associated tubule, through which the glomerular filtrate passes before emerging as urine. ▷1930s: via German from Greek *nephros* 'kidney.'

ne·phro·sis /nəˈfrōsis/ ▸*n.* kidney disease, esp. when characterized by edema and the loss of protein from the plasma into the urine due to increased glomerular permeability (also called **nephrotic syndrome**). **—ne·phrot·ic** /nəˈfrätik/ *adj.*

neph·ro·tox·ic /ˌnefrəˈtäksik/ ▸*adj.* damaging or destructive to the kidneys. **—neph·ro·tox·ic·i·ty** /-täkˈsisitē/ *n.* **—neph·ro·tox·in** /-sin/ *n.*

ne plus ul·tra /ˈnē ˌpləs ˈəltrə; ˈnā ˌplo͞os ˈo͝oltrə/ ▸*n.* the perfect or most extreme example of its kind; the ultimate: *he became* ***the ne plus ultra of*** *bebop trombonists.* ▷Latin, literally 'not further beyond,' the supposed inscription on the Pillars of Hercules prohibiting passage by ships.

nep·o·tism /ˈnepəˌtizəm/ ▸*n.* the practice among those with power or influence of favoring relatives or friends, esp. by giving them jobs. ▷mid 17th cent.: from French *népotisme,* from Italian *nepotismo,* from *nipote* 'nephew' (with reference to privileges bestowed on the "nephews" of popes, who were in many cases their illegitimate sons). **—nep·o·tist** *n.* **—nep·o·tis·tic** /ˌnepəˈtistik/ *adj.*

Nep·tune /ˈnept(y)o͞on/ **1** *Roman Mythology* the god of water and of the sea. Greek equivalent **POSEIDON**. [from Latin *Neptunus.*] **2** *Astronomy* a distant planet of the solar system, eighth in order from the sun, discovered in 1846.

> Neptune orbits between Uranus and Pluto at an average distance of 2,794 million miles (4,497 million km) from the sun (but temporarily outside the orbit of Pluto 1979–99). It is the fourth largest planet, with an equatorial diameter of 30,200 miles (48,600 km), and the most remote of the gas giants.The planet is predominantly blue, with an upper atmosphere mainly of hydrogen and helium with some methane. It has at least eight satellites, the largest of which is Triton, and a faint ring system.

Nep·tu·ni·an /nepˈt(y)o͞onēən/ ▸*adj.* **1** of or relating to the Roman sea god Neptune or to the sea. **2** of or relating to the planet Neptune. **3** *historical Geology* advocating Neptunism.

nep·tu·ni·an dike ▸*n.* *Geology* a deposit of sand cutting through sedimentary strata in the manner of an igneous dike, formed by the filling of an underwater fissure.

Nep·tun·ism /ˈnept(y)o͞oˌnizəm/ ▸*n.* *historical Geology* the erroneous theory that rocks such as granite were formed by crystallization from the waters of a primeval ocean. The chief advocate of this theory was Abraham Gottlob Werner (1749–1817). Compare with **PLUTONISM**. **—Nep·tun·ist** *n.* & *adj.*

nep·tu·ni·um /nepˈt(y)o͞onēəm/ ▸*n.* the chemical element of atomic number 93, a radioactive metal of the actinide series. Neptunium was discovered as a product of the bombardment of uranium with neutrons, and occurs only in trace amounts in nature. (Symbol: **Np**) ▷late 19th cent.: from **NEPTUNE**, on the pattern of *uranium* (Neptune being the next planet beyond Uranus).

nerd /nərd/ ▸*n.* *informal* a foolish or contemptible person who lacks social skills or is boringly studious: *one of those nerds who never asked a girl to dance.* ■ an intelligent, single-minded expert in a particular technical discipline or profession: *he single-handedly changed the Zero image of the computer nerd into one of savvy Hero.* ▷1950s: of unknown origin. **—nerd·ish** *adj.* **—nerd·ish·ness** *n.* **—nerd·y** *adj.*

Ne·re·id /ˈni(ə)rēid/ **1** (also **nereid**) *Greek Mythology* any of the sea nymphs, daughters of Nereus. They include Thetis, mother of Achilles. **2** *Astronomy* a satellite of Neptune, the farthest from the planet, discovered in 1949. It has an irregular shape, a diameter of 211 miles (340 km), and an eccentric orbit.

ne·re·id /ˈni(ə)rēid/ ▸*n.* *Zoology* a bristle worm of the polychaete family (Nereidae). ▷mid 19th cent.: from modern Latin *Nereidae,* from the Greek name *Nēreus* (see **NEREID**).

Ne·re·us /ˈni(ə)rēəs/ *Greek Mythology* an old sea god, the father of the Nereids. Like Proteus, he had the power of assuming various forms.

ne·ri·ne /nəˈrīnē/ ▸*n.* a bulbous South African plant with narrow, strap-shaped petals that are typically crimped and twisted and appear when there are no leaves. • Genus *Nerine,* family Liliaceae (or Amaryllidaceae). ▷modern Latin, derivative of Greek *Nērēis,* the name of a water nymph.

ner·ite /ˈni(ə)rˌīt/ ▸*n.* a chiefly tropical mollusk with a somewhat globe-shaped and brightly marked shell, typically found in water. • Superfamily Neritacea, class Gastropoda: several genera and species, including the European freshwater snail *Theodoxus fluviatilis.* ▷early 18th cent.: from Latin *nerita,* from Greek *nēritēs* 'sea mussel,' from the name of the sea god **NEREUS**.

ne·rit·ic /nəˈritik/ ▸*adj.* *Biology* & *Geology* of, relating to, or denoting the shallow part of the sea near a coast and overlying the continental shelf. ▷late 19th cent.: from **NERITE** + **-IC**.

Nernst /nərnst; nernst/, Hermann Walther (1864–1941), German physical chemist. He is noted for his discovery of the third law of thermodynamics (also known as **Nernst's heat theorem**). Nobel Prize for Chemistry (1920).

Ne·ro /ˈni(ə)rō/ (AD 37–68), Roman emperor 54–68; full name *Nero Claudius Caesar Augustus Germanicus.* Infamous for his cruelty, he ordered the murder of his mother Agrippina in 59 and wantonly executed leading Romans. His reign witnessed a fire that destroyed half of Rome in 64. A wave of uprisings in 68 led to his flight from Rome and his eventual suicide.

ner·o·li /ˈnerəlē/ (also **neroli oil**) ▸*n.* an essential oil distilled from the flowers of the Seville orange, used in perfumery. ▷late 17th cent.: via French from Italian *neroli,* said to be from the name of an Italian princess.

Ne·ru·da /nəˈro͞odə; neˈro͞odä/, Pablo (1904–73), Chilean poet and diplomat; born *Ricardo Eliezer Neftalí Reyes.* His *Canto General,* which he completed in 1950, is an epic covering the history of the Americas. Nobel Prize for Literature (1971).

Ner·va /ˈnərvə/, Marcus Cocceius (*c.* AD 30–98), Roman emperor 96–98. He returned to a liberal and constitutional form of rule after the autocracy of his predecessor, Domitian.

ner·va·tion /ˌnərˈvāSHən/ ▸*n.* *Botany* the arrangement of nerves in a leaf. ▷early 18th cent.: from French, based on *nerf* 'nerve.'

nerve /nərv/ ▸*n.* **1** (in the body) a whitish fiber or bundle of fibers that transmits impulses of sensation to the brain or spinal cord, and impulses from these to the muscles and organs: *the optic nerve.* **2** (**nerves**) a person's mental state, in particular the extent to which they are agitated or worried: *an amazing journey that tested her nerves to the full.* ■ nervousness or anxiety: *his first-night nerves soon disappeared.* **3** (often **one's nerve**) a person's steadiness, courage, and sense of purpose when facing a demanding situation: *the army's commanders were beginning to* ***lose their nerve*** | *I* ***got up the nerve*** *to ask Miss Kinnian to have dinner with me.* See note at **COURAGE**. ■ *informal* impudence or audacity: *he* ***had the nerve*** *to insult my cooking* | ***she's got nerve*** *wearing that short skirt with those legs.* **4** *Botany* a prominent unbranched rib in a leaf, esp. in the midrib of the leaf of a moss.
▸*v.* (**nerve oneself**) brace oneself mentally to face a demanding situation: *she nerved herself to enter the room.* ▷late Middle English (also in the sense 'tendon, sinew'): from Latin *nervus;* related to Greek *neuron* 'nerve' (see **NEURON**). **—nerved** *adj.* [usu. in *combination*] *she was still raw-nerved from reliving the past.*
▸*PHRASES* □ **a bundle of nerves** *informal* someone who is extremely timid or tense. □ **get on someone's nerves** *informal* irritate or annoy someone. □ **have nerves of steel** not be easily upset or frightened. □ **strain every nerve** make every possible effort. [from the earlier sense of *nerve* as 'tendon, sinew.'] □ **touch** (or **hit** or **strike**) **a nerve** (or **a raw nerve**) provoke a reaction by referring to a sensitive topic: *there are signs that some comments strike a raw nerve.* □ **war of nerves** a struggle in which opponents try to wear each other down by psychological means.

nerve block ▸*n.* *Medicine* the production of insensibility in a part of the body by injecting an anesthetic close to the nerves that supply it.

nerve cell ▸*n.* a neuron.

nerve cen·ter ▸*n.* a group of closely connected nerve cells that perform a particular function in the body; a ganglion. ■ the control center of an organization or operation: *Frankfurt is the economic nerve center of Germany.*

nerve cord ▸*n.* *Zoology* the major cord of nerve fibers running the length of an animal's body, esp. a ventral cord in invertebrates that connects segmental nerve ganglia.

nerve fi·ber ▸*n.* the axon of a neuron. A nerve is formed of a bundle of many such fibers, with their sheaths.

nerve gas ▸*n.* a poisonous vapor that rapidly disables or kills by disrupting the transmission of nerve impulses.

nerve im·pulse ▸*n.* a signal transmitted along a

nerve fiber. It consists of a wave of electrical depolarization that reverses the potential difference across the nerve cell membranes.

nerve·less /ˈnərvlis/ ▸*adj.* **1** inert; lacking vigor or feeling: *the knife dropped from Grant's nerveless fingers.* ■ (of literary or artistic style) diffuse or insipid: *Wilde and his art are described as "nerveless and effeminate."* **2** confident; not nervous: *with nerveless panache.* **3** *Anatomy & Biology* lacking nerves or nervures. **—nerve·less·ly** *adv.* **—nerve·less·ness** *n.*

nerve net ▸*n. Zoology* (in invertebrates such as coelenterates and flatworms) a diffuse network of neurons that conducts impulses in all directions from a point of stimulus.

nerve-rack·ing (also **nerve-wrack·ing**) ▸*adj.* causing stress or anxiety: *his driving test was a nerve-racking ordeal.*

nerve trunk ▸*n. Anatomy* the main stem of a nerve.

Ner·vi /ˈnərvē; ˈner-/, Pier Luigi (1891–1979), Italian engineer and architect. A pioneer of reinforced concrete, he helped to design the UNESCO building in Paris (1953) and designed the Pirelli skyscraper in Milan (1958) and Saint Mary's Cathedral in San Francisco (1970).

nerv·ine /ˈnərvēn/ ▸*adj.* (of a medicine) used to calm the nerves.
▸*n.* a medicine of this kind. ▷mid 17th cent.: from medieval Latin *nervinus* 'of the nerves or sinews,' or suggested by French *nervin.*

nerv·ous /ˈnərvəs/ ▸*adj.* **1** easily agitated or alarmed; tending to be anxious; highly strung: *a sensitive, nervous person | these quick, nervous birds.* ■ anxious or apprehensive: *staying in the house on her own made her nervous | I was nervous about my new job.* ■ (of a feeling or reaction) resulting from anxiety or anticipation: *nervous energy.* **2** relating to or affecting the nerves: *a nervous disorder.* ▷late Middle English (in the senses 'containing nerves' and 'relating to the nerves'): from Latin *nervosus* 'sinewy, vigorous,' from *nervus* 'sinew' (see NERVE). Sense 1 dates from the mid 18th cent. **—ner·vous·ly** *adv.* **—ner·vous·ness** *n.*

nerv·ous break·down ▸*n.* a period of mental illness resulting from severe depression, stress, or anxiety.

nerv·ous sys·tem ▸*n.* the network of nerve cells and fibers that transmits nerve impulses between parts of the body. See also AUTONOMIC NERVOUS SYSTEM, CENTRAL NERVOUS SYSTEM, PERIPHERAL NERVOUS SYSTEM.

nerv·ous wreck ▸*n. informal* a person suffering from stress or emotional exhaustion: *by the end of the day I was a nervous wreck.*

ner·vure /ˈnərvyo͝or/ ▸*n. Entomology* each of the hollow veins that form the framework of an insect's wing. ■ *Botany* the principal vein of a leaf. ▷early 19th cent.: from French, from *nerf* 'nerve.'

nerv·y /ˈnərvē/ ▸*adj.* (**nerv·i·er**, **nerv·i·est**) **1** *informal* bold or impudent: *it was kind of nervy for Billy to be telling him how to play.* **2** *chiefly Brit.* easily agitated or alarmed; nervous: *he was nervy and on edge.* ■ characterized or produced by apprehension or uncertainty: *they made a nervy start.* **3** *archaic* or *poetic/literary* sinewy or strong. **—nerv·i·ly** /ˈnərvəlē/ *adv.* **—nerv·i·ness** *n.*

n.e.s. (also **N.E.S.**) ▸*abbr.* not elsewhere specified.

Nes·bit /ˈnezbit/, E. (1858–1924), English novelist; full name *Edith Nesbit.* Noted for her children's books, which include *Five Children and It* (1902) and *The Railway Children* (1906).

nes·cient /ˈnesH(ē)ənt/ ▸*adj. poetic/literary* lacking knowledge; ignorant: *I ventured into the new Korean restaurant with some equally nescient companions.* ▷late Middle English: from Latin *nescient-* 'not knowing,' from the verb *nescire,* from *ne-* 'not' + *scire* 'know.' **—nesc·ience** *n.*

Ness, Loch see LOCH NESS.

ness /nes/ ▸*n.* [usu. in *place names*] a headland or promontory: *Orford Ness.* ▷Old English *næs,* perhaps reinforced in Middle English by Old Norse *nes;* related to Old English *nasu* 'nose.'

-ness /nəs; nis/ ▸forming nouns chiefly from adjectives: *suffix* **1** denoting a state or condition: *liveliness | sadness.* ■ an instance of this: *a kindness.* **2** something in a certain state: *wilderness.* ▷Old English *-nes, -ness,* of Germanic origin.

Nes·sie /ˈnesē/ informal name for LOCH NESS MONSTER.

Nes·sus /ˈnesəs/ *Greek and Roman Mythology* a centaur who was killed by Hercules, but whose blood soaked Hercules's tunic and consumed him in fire.
▸*PHRASE* □ **Nessus shirt** (or **shirt of Nessus**) used to refer to a destructive or expurgatory force or influence: *after the lost election of 1979 he found himself wearing this shirt of Nessus.*

nest /nest/ ▸*n.* **1** a structure or place made or chosen by a bird for laying eggs and sheltering its young. ■ a place where an animal or insect breeds or shelters: *an ants' nest.* ■ a person's snug or secluded retreat or shelter. ■ a bowl-shaped object likened to a bird's nest: *arrange in nests of lettuce leaves.* ■ a place filled with or frequented by undesirable people or things: ***a nest of spies.*** **2** a set of similar objects of graduated sizes, made so that each smaller one fits into the next in size for storage: ***a nest of tables.***
▸*v.* **1** [*intrans.*] (of a bird or other animal) use or build a nest: *the owls often nest in barns |* [as *adj.*] (**nesting**) *do not disturb nesting birds.* **2** [*trans.*] (often **be nested**) fit (an object or objects) inside a larger one: *the town is nested inside a large crater on the flanks of a volcano.* ■ [*intrans.*] (of a set of objects) fit inside one another: *Russian dolls that nest inside one another.* ■ (esp. in computing and linguistics) place (an object or element) in a hierarchical arrangement, typically in a subordinate position: [as *adj.*] (**nested**) *organisms classified in a series of nested sets | a nested relative clause.* ▷Old English *nest,* of Germanic origin; related to Latin *nidus,* from the Indo-European bases of NETHER (meaning 'down') and SIT. **—nest·ful** /-ˌfo͝ol/ *n.* (*pl.* **-fuls**). **—nest·like** /-ˌlīk/ *adj.*

nest box (also **nest·ing box**) ▸*n.* a box provided for a bird to make its nest in.

nest egg ▸*n.* **1** a sum of money saved for the future: *I worked hard to build up a nice little nest egg.* **2** a real or artificial egg left in a nest to induce hens to lay eggs there.

nest·er /ˈnestər/ ▸*n.* **1** [usu. with *adj.*] a bird that nests in a specified manner or place: *redstarts are nesters here | hole-nesters.* See also EMPTY NESTER. **2** a squatter who occupies rangeland in the U.S. West.

nes·tle /ˈnesəl/ ▸*v.* [*intrans.*] settle or lie comfortably within or against something: *the baby deer nestled in her arms |* [*trans.*] *she nestled her head against his shoulder.* ■ (of a place) lie or be situated in a half-hidden or obscured position: *picturesque villages nestle in the wooded hills |* (**be nestled**) *the hotel is nestled between two headlands.* ▷Old English *nestlian,* from NEST; compare with Dutch *nestelen.*

nest·ling /ˈnes(t)liNG/ ▸*n.* a bird that is too young to leave its nest.

Nes·tor /ˈnestər/ *Greek Mythology* a king of Pylos in Peloponnesus, who in old age led his subjects to the Trojan War. His wisdom and eloquence were proverbial.

Nes·to·ri·an·ism /nesˈtôrēəˌnizəm/ ▸*n. Theology* the doctrine that there were two separate persons, one human and one divine, in the incarnate Christ. It is named after Nestorius, patriarch of Constantinople (428–31), and was maintained by some ancient churches of the Middle East. A small Nestorian Church still exists in Iraq. **—Nes·to·ri·an** *adj.* & *n.*

net[1] /net/ ▸*n.* **1** a length of open-meshed material made of twine, cord, rope, or something similar, used typically for catching fish or other animals. ■ a piece of such material supported by a frame at the end of a handle, used typically for catching fish or other aquatic animals or insects. ■ a length of such material supported on a frame and forming part of the goal in various games such as soccer and hockey: *he turned Wilson's cross into the net.* ■ a length of such material supported on a cord between two posts to divide the playing area in various games such as tennis, badminton, and volleyball. ■ a safety net: *he felt like a tightrope-walker without a net.* ■ a hairnet. **2** a fine fabric with a very open weave: [as *adj.*] *net curtains.* **3** *figurative* a system or procedure for catching or entrapping someone; a trap: *the search was delayed, allowing the murderers to escape the net.* ■ a system or procedure for selecting or recruiting someone: *he spread his net far and wide in his search for success.* **4** a network, in particular: ■ a communications or broadcasting network: *the radio net was brought to life with a mayday.* ■ a network of interconnected computers: *a computer news net.* ■ (**the Net**) the Internet.
▸*v.* (**net·ted**, **net·ting**) [*trans.*] **1** catch or land (a fish or other animal) with a net. ■ fish with nets in (a river): *he has netted the creeks and found them clogged with fish.* ■ *figurative* acquire or obtain as if with a net: *customs officials have netted large caches of drugs.* **2** (in sports) hit or kick (a ball or puck) into the net; score (a goal): *in six years Wright has netted 177 goals |* [*intrans.*] *Aldridge netted twice.* **3** cover with a net: *we fenced off a rabbit-proof area for vegetables and netted the top.* ▷Old English *net, nett,* of Germanic origin; related to Dutch *net* and German *Netz.* **—net·ful** /-ˌfo͝ol/ *n.* (*pl.* **-fuls**). **—net·like** /-ˌlīk/ *adj.*

net[2] ▸*adj.* **1** (of an amount, value, or price) remaining after a deduction, such as tax or a discount, has been made: *net earnings per share rose | the net worth of the business.* Often contrasted with GROSS (sense 2). ■ (of a price) to be paid in full; not reducible. ■ (of a weight) excluding that of the packaging or container. ■ (of a score in golf) adjusted to take account of a player's handicap. **2** (of an effect or result) final or overall: *the net result is the same.*
▸*v.* (**net·ted**, **net·ting**) [*trans.*] acquire or obtain (a sum of money) as clear profit: *they sold their 20% stake, netting a huge profit in the process.* ■ [with *two objs.*] return (profit or income) for (someone): *the land netted its owner a turnover of $800,000.* ■ (**net something down/off/out**) exclude a nonnet amount, such as tax, when making a calculation, in order to reduce the amount left to a net sum: *the scrap or salvage value should be netted off against the original purchase price.* ■ get; obtain: *the Bills netted 5,276 yards of offense.* ▷Middle English (in the senses 'clean' and 'smart'): from French *net* 'neat'; see NEAT[1]. The sense 'free from deductions' is first recorded in late Middle English commercial documents.

Net·an·ya·hu /ˌnetänˈyäho͞o/, Benjamin (1949–), Israeli statesman; prime minister 1996–99. As the leader of the right-wing Likud coalition, he narrowly defeated Shimon Peres in the elections of 1996.

net as·set val·ue ▸*n.* the value of a mutual fund that is reached by deducting the fund's liabilities from the market value of all of its shares and then dividing by the number of issued shares.

net·ball /ˈnetˌbôl/ ▸*n. chiefly Brit.* a game with seven players on a side, similar to basketball except that a player receiving the ball must stand still until they have passed it to another player. ■ the ball used in this game.

net book val·ue ▸*n. Finance* the value of an asset as recorded in the accounts of its owner.

neth·er /ˈneTHər/ ▸*adj.* lower in position: *the ballast is suspended from its nether end.* ▷Old English *nithera, neothera,* of Germanic origin; related to Dutch *neder-* (found in compounds), *neer,* and German *nieder,* from an Indo-European root meaning 'down.' **—neth·er·most** /-ˌmōst/ *adj.*

Neth·er·lands /ˈneTHərlən(d)z/ a country in western Europe, on the North Sea; pop. 16,318,000; capital, Amsterdam; seat of government, The Hague; language, Dutch. Dutch name **NEDERLAND**. Also called **HOLLAND**. ■ *historical* the Low Countries. **—Neth·er·land·er** /-ˌlandər/ *n.* **—Neth·er·land·ish** /-ˌlandisH/ *adj.*

Following a struggle against the Spanish Habsburg empire, the northern (Dutch) part of the Low Countries won full independence in 1648 and became a leading imperial power. In 1814, north and south were united under a monarchy, but the south revolted in 1830 and, by 1839, had become the independent kingdom of Belgium. In 1948, the Netherlands formed the Benelux Customs Union with Belgium and Luxembourg. It became a founding member of the EEC in 1957. The name **Holland** strictly refers to the western coastal provinces of the country.

Neth·er·lands An·til·les two widely separated groups of Dutch islands in the Caribbean Sea, in the Lesser Antilles; capital, Willemstad, on Curaçao; pop. 189,000. The southernmost group, situated just off the north coast of Venezuela, consists of the islands of Bonaire and Curaçao. The northern group

N

comprises the islands of St. Eustatius, St. Martin, and Saba. In 1954, the islands were granted self-government and became an autonomous region of the Netherlands.

Neth·er·lands Re·formed Church the largest Protestant church in the Netherlands, established in 1816 as the successor to the Dutch Reformed Church.

neth·er re·gions ▸*plural n.* the lowest or furthest parts of a place, esp. with allusion to hell or the underworld: *rumors of strange creatures hauting the lake's bottomless nether regions.* ■ (**one's nether regions**) used euphemistically to refer to a person's genitals and buttocks.

neth·er·world /ˈneT͟Hər,wərld/ ▸*n.* (**the netherworld**) the underworld of the dead; hell. ■ a hidden underworld or ill-defined area: *the narcotic netherworld thriving in postwar America.*

net·i·quette /ˈnetəkit; -ˌket/ ▸*n.* the correct or acceptable way of communicating on the Internet. ▷1990s: blend of NET[1] and ETIQUETTE.

net·i·zen /ˈnetəzən/ ▸*n.* a user of the Internet, esp. a habitual or avid one. ▷1990s: blend of NET[1] (sense 4) and CITIZEN.

net·keep·er /ˈnet,kēpər/ ▸*n.* another term for GOALKEEPER.

net me·ter·ing ▸*n.* a system in which solar panels or other renewable energy generators are connected to a public-utility power grid and surplus power is transferred onto the grid, allowing customers to offset the cost of power drawn from the utility. ▷surplus energy, measured by an electric meter, is netted from the amount passing from the utility to the customer.

net na·tion·al prod·uct (abbr.: **NNP**) ▸*n.* the total value of goods produced and services provided in a country during one year, after depreciation of capital goods has been allowed for.

net pres·ent val·ue ▸*n.* see PRESENT VALUE.

net prof·it ▸*n.* the actual profit after working expenses not included in the calculation of gross profit have been paid.

ne·tsu·ke /ˈnetsəkē/ ▸*n.* (*pl.* same or **-kes** /-kēz/) a carved buttonlike ornament, esp. of ivory or wood, formerly worn in Japan to suspend articles from the sash of a kimono. ▷late 19th cent.: from Japanese.

net·ter /ˈnetər/ ▸*n.* **1** a fisherman who uses nets to catch fish: *because of the ban on gill nets, Louisianans fear an influx of jobless Florida netters.* ■ [usu. in *combination*] someone who uses a net of a specified type: *drift-netters.* **2** (also **Netter**) a person who uses the Internet.

net·ting /ˈnetiNG/ ▸*n.* open-meshed material made by knotting together twine, wire, rope, or thread.

net·tle /ˈnetl/ ▸*n.* a herbaceous plant that has jagged leaves covered with stinging hairs. • Genus *Urtica*, family Urticaceae: several species, in particular the Eurasian **stinging nettle** (*U. dioica*). ■ used in names of other plants of a similar appearance or properties, e.g., **dead-nettle**.
▸*v.* [*trans.*] **1** irritate or annoy (someone): *I was nettled by Alene's tone of superiority.* **2** *archaic* beat or sting (someone) with nettles. ▷Old English *netle, netele*, of Germanic origin; related to Dutch *netel* and German *Nessel*. The verb dates from late Middle English.

net·tle·rash /ˈnetl,rasH/ ▸*n.* another term for URTICARIA (from its resemblance to the sting of a nettle).

net·tle·some /ˈnetlsəm/ ▸*adj.* causing annoyance or difficulty: *complicated and nettlesome regional disputes.*

net·tle tree ▸*n.* an Old World tree related to the hackberries, with a straight, silvery-gray trunk and rough, toothed, nettlelike leaves. • Genus *Celtis*, family Ulmaceae: several species, in particular *C. australis*, which is a popular street and shade tree in Mediterranean countries.

net ton /tən/ ▸*n.* another term for TON[1] (sense 1).

net·work /ˈnet,wərk/ ▸*n.* **1** an arrangement of intersecting horizontal and vertical lines. ■ a complex system of roads, railroads, or other transportation routes: *a network of railroads.* **2** a group or system of interconnected people or things: *a trade network.* ■ a group of people who exchange information, contacts, and experience for professional or social purposes: *a support network.* ■ a group of broadcasting stations that connect for the simultaneous broadcast of a program: *the introduction of a second TV network* | [as *adj.*] *network television.* ■ a number of interconnected computers, machines, or operations: *specialized computers that manage multiple outside connections to a network* | *a local cellular phone network.* ■ a system of connected electrical conductors.
▸*v.* [*trans.*] connect as or operate with a network: *the stock exchanges have proven to be resourceful in networking these deals.* ■ link (machines, esp. computers) to operate interactively: [as *adj.*] (**networked**) *networked workstations.* ■ [*intrans.*] [often as *n.*] (**networking**) interact with other people to exchange information and develop contacts, esp. to further one's career: *the skills of networking, bargaining, and negotiation.* —**net·work·a·ble** *adj.*

net·work a·nal·y·sis ▸*n.* the mathematical analysis of complex working procedures in terms of a network of related activities. ■ calculation of the electric currents flowing in the various meshes of a network, often carried out by a device used to model the network.

net·work ap·pli·ance ▸*n.* a relatively low-cost computer designed chiefly to provide Internet access without the full capabilities of a standard personal computer.

net·work·er /ˈnet,wərkər/ ▸*n.* **1** *Computing* a person who operates from home or from an external office via a computer network. **2** a person who interacts or exchanges information with others working in a similar field, esp. to further their career.

Neu·châ·tel, Lake /ˌnōōsHäˈtel; nœ-/ the largest lake that lies wholly within Switzerland, located at the foot of the Jura Mountains in western Switzerland.

Neue Sach·lich·keit /ˈnoiə ˈzäKHlisHkīt/ a movement in the visual arts, music, and literature that developed in Germany during the 1920s and was characterized by realism and a deliberate rejection of romantic attitudes. ▷German, literally 'new objectivity.'

Neuf·châ·tel /ˌnōōsHəˈtel; ˌnœsHä-/ ▸*n.* a creamy white cheese made from whole or partly skimmed milk in Neufchâtel, France.

Neu·haus /ˈn(y)ōō,hous/, Solomon, see **NEWHOUSE**.

Neu·mann /ˈn(y)ōōmən; ˈnoimän/, John von (1903–57), U.S. mathematician and computer pioneer, born in Hungary. He pioneered game theory and the design and operation of electronic computers.

neume /n(y)ōōm/ ▸*n. Music* (in plainsong) a note or group of notes to be sung to a single syllable. ■ a sign indicating this. ▷late Middle English: from Old French *neume*, from medieval Latin *neu(p)ma*, from Greek *pneuma* 'breath.'

neur. ▸*abbr.* ■ neurological or neurology.

neu·ral /ˈn(y)ŏŏrəl/ ▸*adj.* of or relating to a nerve or the nervous system: *patterns of neural activity.* ▷mid 19th cent.: from Greek *neuron* in the sense 'nerve' + -AL. —**neu·ral·ly** *adv.*

neu·ral arch ▸*n. Anatomy* the curved rear (dorsal) section of a vertebra, enclosing the canal through which the spinal cord passes.

neu·ral com·pu·ter ▸*n.* a computer that uses neural networks based on the human brain. Also called NEUROCOMPUTER. —**neu·ral com·put·ing** *n.*

neu·ral·gia /n(y)ŏŏˈraljə/ ▸*n.* intense, typically intermittent pain along the course of a nerve, esp. in the head or face. —**neu·ral·gic** /-jik/ *adj.*

neu·ral net·work (also **neu·ral net**) ▸*n.* a computer system modeled on the human brain and nervous system.

neu·ral tube ▸*n. Zoology & Medicine* (in an embryo) a hollow structure from which the brain and spinal cord form. Defects in its development can result in congenital abnormalities such as spina bifida.

neu·ra·min·ic ac·id /ˌn(y)ŏŏrəˈminik/ ▸*n. Biochemistry* a crystalline compound of which derivatives occur in many animal substances, chiefly as sialic acids. • A sugar with amino and acid groups; chem. formula: $C_9H_{17}NO_8$. ▷mid 20th cent.: *neuraminic* from NEURO- (because it was originally isolated from brain tissue) + AMINE + -IC.

neu·ra·min·i·dase /ˌn(y)ŏŏrəˈminə,dās/ ▸*n. Biochemistry* an enzyme, present in many pathogenic or symbiotic microorganisms, that catalyzes the breakdown of glycosides containing neuraminic acid.

neur·as·the·ni·a /ˌn(y)ŏŏrəsˈTHēnēə/ ▸*n.* an ill-defined medical condition characterized by lassitude, fatigue, headache, and irritability, associated chiefly with emotional disturbance. —**neur·as·then·ic** /-ˈTHenik/ *adj.* & *n.*

neu·rec·to·my /n(y)ŏŏˈrektəmē/ ▸*n. Medicine* surgical removal of all or part of a nerve.

neu·ri·lem·ma /ˌn(y)ŏŏrəˈlemə/ ▸*n.* (*pl.* **-lem·mas** or **-lem·ma·ta** /-liˈmätə/) *Anatomy* the thin sheath around a nerve axon (including myelin where this is present). —**neu·ri·lem·mal** *adj.*

neu·ri·tis /n(y)ŏŏˈrītis/ ▸*n. Medicine* inflammation of a peripheral nerve or nerves, usually causing pain and loss of function. ■ (in general use) neuropathy. —**neu·rit·ic** /-ˈritik/ *adj.*

neuro- ▸*comb. form* relating to nerves or the nervous system: *neuroanatomy* | *neurohormone.* ▷from Greek *neuron* 'nerve, sinew, tendon.'

neu·ro·a·nat·o·my /ˌn(y)ŏŏrōəˈnatəmē/ ▸*n.* the anatomy of the nervous system. —**neu·ro·an·a·tom·i·cal** /-ˌanəˈtämikəl/ *adj.* —**neu·ro·a·nat·o·mist** /-mist/ *n.*

neu·ro·bics /n(y)ŏŏˈrōbiks/ ▸*n.* mental exercises designed to create new neural pathways in the brain by using the senses in unconventional ways.

neu·ro·bi·ol·o·gy /ˌn(y)ŏŏrōbīˈäləjē/ ▸*n.* the biology of the nervous system. —**neu·ro·bi·o·log·i·cal** /-bīəˈläjikəl/ *adj.* —**neu·ro·bi·ol·o·gist** /-jist/ *n.*

neu·ro·blast /ˈn(y)ŏŏrə,blast/ ▸*n. Embryology* an embryonic cell from which nerve fibers originate.

neu·ro·blas·to·ma /ˌn(y)ŏŏrōblaˈstōmə/ ▸*n. Medicine* a malignant tumor composed of neuroblasts, most commonly in the adrenal gland.

neu·ro·com·pu·ter /ˈn(y)ŏŏrōkəm,pyōōtər/ ▸ another term for NEURAL COMPUTER.

neu·ro·en·do·crine /ˌn(y)ŏŏrōˈendəkrin/ ▸*adj. Physiology* relating to or involving both nervous stimulation and endocrine secretion. —**neu·ro·en·do·cri·nol·o·gy** /-ˌendōkrəˈnäləjē/ *n.*

neu·ro·ep·i·the·li·um /ˌn(y)ŏŏrō,epiˈTHēlēəm/ ▸*n.* *Anatomy* **1** a type of epithelium containing sensory nerve endings and found in certain sense organs (e.g., the retina, the inner ear, the nasal membranes, and the taste buds). **2** (in embryology) ectoderm that develops into nerve tissue. —**neu·ro·ep·i·the·li·al** /-lēəl/ *adj.*

neu·ro·fi·bril /ˌn(y)ŏŏrəˈfībrəl; -ˈfib-/ ▸*n. Anatomy* a fibril in the cytoplasm of a nerve cell, visible by light microscopy. —**neu·ro·fi·bril·lar·y** /-ˈfibrə,lerē/ *adj.*

neu·ro·fi·bro·ma /ˌn(y)ŏŏrōfīˈbrōmə/ ▸*n.* (*pl.* **-mas** or **-ma·ta** /-mətə/) *Medicine* a tumor formed on a nerve cell sheath, frequently symptomless but occasionally malignant.

neu·ro·fi·bro·ma·to·sis /ˌn(y)ŏŏrō,fībrəməˈtōsis/ ▸*n.* *Medicine* a disease in which neurofibromas form throughout the body. Also called VON RECKLINGHAUSEN'S DISEASE.

neu·ro·gen·e·sis /ˌn(y)ŏŏrəˈjenəsis/ ▸*n. Physiology* the growth and development of nervous tissue.

neu·ro·gen·ic /ˌn(y)ŏŏrəˈjenik/ ▸*adj. Physiology* caused by, controlled by, or arising in the nervous system.

neu·rog·li·a /n(y)ŏŏˈräglēə/ ▸*n.* another term for GLIA. ▷mid 19th cent.: from NEURO- 'of nerves' + Greek *glia* 'glue.'

neu·ro·hor·mone /ˌn(y)ŏŏrōˈhôr,mōn/ ▸*n. Physiology* a hormone (such as vasopressin or norepinephrine) produced by nerve cells and secreted into the circulation. —**neu·ro·hor·mo·nal** /-hôrˈmōnəl/ *adj.*

neu·ro·hy·poph·y·sis /ˌn(y)ŏŏrōhīˈpäfəsis/ ▸*n.* (*pl.* **-ses** /-ˌsēz/) *Anatomy* the posterior lobe of the hypophysis (pituitary gland), which stores and releases oxytocin and vasopressin produced in the hypothalamus. —**neu·ro·hy·po·phys·e·al** /-ˌpäfəˈsēəl/ *adj.*

neu·ro·lep·tic /ˌn(y)ŏŏrəˈleptik/ *Medicine* ▸*adj.* (chiefly of a drug) tending to reduce nervous tension by depressing nerve functions.
▸*n.* a drug of this kind; a major tranquilizer. ▷mid 20th cent.: from NEURO- 'relating to nerves,' on the pattern of *psycholeptic*.

neu·ro·lin·guis·tic pro·gram·ming /ˌn(y)ŏŏrō,liNGˈgwistik/ (abbr.: **NLP**) ▸*n.* a system of alternative therapy intended to educate people in self-awareness and effective communication, and to model and change their patterns of mental and emotional behavior.

neu·ro·lin·guis·tics /ˌn(y)ŏŏrō,liNGˈgwistiks/ ▸*plural n.* [treated as *sing.*] the branch of linguistics dealing with the relationship between language and the structure and functioning of the brain. —**neu·ro·lin·guis·tic** *adj.*

neu·rol·o·gy /n(y)ŏŏˈräləjē/ ▸*n.* the branch of medicine or biology that deals with the anatomy, functions, and organic disorders of nerves and the nervous system. ▷late 17th cent.: from modern Latin *neurologia*, from NEURO- + -LOGY. —**neu·rolog·i·cal** /-rəˈläjikəl/ *adj.* —**neu·ro·log·i·cal·ly** *adv.* —**neu·rol·o·gist** *n.*

neu·ro·ma /n(y)ŏŏˈrōmə/ ▸*n.* (*pl.* **-mas** or **-ma·ta** /-mətə/) another term for NEUROFIBROMA.

neu·ro·mast /ˈn(y)ŏŏrə,mast/ ▸*n. Zoology* a sensory organ of fishes and larval or aquatic amphibians, typically forming part of the lateral line system. ▷early 20th cent.: from NEURO- 'of nerves' + Greek *mastos* 'breast.'

neu·ro·mus·cu·lar /ˌn(y)ŏŏrōˈməskyələr/ ▸*adj.* of or relating to nerves and muscles.

neu·ron /ˈn(y)o͝orän/ (*chiefly Brit.* also **neu·rone** /-rōn/) ▸*n.* a specialized cell transmitting nerve impulses; a nerve cell. ▷late 19th cent.: from Greek *neuron*, special use of the literal sense 'sinew, tendon.' See NERVE. **—neu·ron·al** /ˈn(y)o͝orənl; n(y)o͝oˈrōnl/ *adj.* **—neu·ron·ic** /n(y)o͝oˈränik/ *adj.*

neu·ro·path /ˈn(y)o͝orəˌpaTH/ ▸*n. dated* a person affected by nervous disease, or with an abnormally sensitive nervous system.

neu·ro·pa·thol·o·gy /ˌn(y)o͝orōpəˈTHäləjē/ ▸*n.* the branch of medicine concerned with diseases of the nervous system. **—neu·ro·path·o·log·i·cal** /-ˌpaTHəˈläjikəl/ *adj.* **—neu·ro·pa·thol·o·gist** *n.*

neu·rop·a·thy /n(y)o͝oˈräpəTHē/ ▸*n. Medicine* disease or dysfunction of one or more peripheral nerves, typically causing numbness or weakness. **—neu·ro·path·ic** /ˌn(y)o͝orəˈpaTHik/ *adj.*

neu·ro·pep·tide /ˌn(y)o͝orōˈpeptīd/ ▸*n. Biochemistry* any of a group of compounds that act as neurotransmitters and are short-chain polypeptides.

neu·ro·phar·ma·col·o·gy /ˌn(y)o͝orōˌfärməˈkäləjē/ ▸*n.* the branch of pharmacology that deals with the action of drugs on the nervous system. **—neu·ro·phar·ma·co·log·ic** /-kəˈläjik/ *adj.* **—neu·ro·phar·ma·co·log·i·cal** *adj.* **—neu·ro·phar·ma·col·o·gist** *n.*

neu·ro·phys·i·ol·o·gy /ˌn(y)o͝orōˌfizēˈäləjē/ ▸*n.* the physiology of the nervous system. **—neu·ro·phys·i·o·log·i·cal** /-ˌfizēəˈläjikəl/ *adj.* **—neu·ro·phys·i·ol·o·gist** *n.*

neu·ro·pil /ˈn(y)o͝orəˌpil/ ▸*n. Anatomy & Zoology* a dense network of interwoven unmyelinated nerve fibers and their branches and synapses, together with glial filaments. ▷late 19th cent.: probably an abbreviation of obsolete *neuropilema*, from Greek *neuron* 'nerve' + *pilēma* 'felt.'

neu·ro·psy·chi·a·try /ˌn(y)o͝orōsəˈkīətrē; -sīˈkī-/ ▸*n.* psychiatry relating mental or emotional disturbance to disordered brain function. **—neu·ro·psy·chi·at·ric** /-ˌsīkēˈatrik/ *adj.* **—neu·ro·psy·chi·a·trist** *n.*

neu·ro·psy·chol·o·gy /ˌn(y)o͝orōsīˈkäləjē/ ▸*n.* the study of the relationship between behavior, emotion, and cognition on the one hand, and brain function on the other. **—neu·ro·psy·cho·log·i·cal** /-ˌsīkəˈläjikəl/ *adj.* **—neu·ro·psy·chol·o·gist** *n.*

Neu·rop·ter·a /n(y)o͝oˈräptərə/ *Entomology* an order of predatory flying insects that includes the lacewings, snake flies, and ant lions. They have four finely veined membranous wings. ■ **(neuroptera)** [as *plural n.*] insects of this order. ▷modern Latin (plural), from NEURO- in the sense 'veined' + Greek *pteron* 'wing.' **—neu·rop·ter·an** *n. & adj.* **—neu·rop·ter·ous** /-rəs/ *adj.*

neu·ro·sci·ence /ˌn(y)o͝orōˈsīəns/ ▸*n.* any of the sciences, such as neurochemistry and experimental psychology, that deal with the structure or function of the nervous system and brain. ■ such sciences collectively. **—neu·ro·sci·en·tist** /-ˈsīəntist/ *n.*

neu·ro·sis /n(y)o͝oˈrōsis/ ▸*n.* (*pl.* **-ses** /-ˌsēz/) *Medicine* a relatively mild mental illness that is not caused by organic disease, involving symptoms of stress (depression, anxiety, obsessive behavior, hypochondria) but not a radical loss of touch with reality. Compare with PSYCHOSIS. ■ (in nontechnical use) excessive and irrational anxiety or obsession: *apprehension over mounting debt has created a collective neurosis in the business world.* ▷mid 18th cent.: modern Latin, from NEURO- 'of nerves' + -OSIS.

neu·ro·sur·ger·y /ˌn(y)o͝orōˈsərjərē/ ▸*n.* surgery performed on the nervous system, esp. the brain and spinal cord. **—neu·ro·sur·geon** /ˈn(y)ərōˌsərjən/ *n.* **—neu·ro·sur·gi·cal** /-jikəl/ *adj.*

neu·ro·syph·i·lis /ˌn(y)o͝orōˈsifəlis/ ▸*n.* syphilis that involves the central nervous system. **—neu·ro·syph·i·lit·ic** /-sifəˈlitik/ *adj. & n.*

neu·rot·ic /n(y)o͝oˈrätik/ ▸*adj. Medicine* suffering from, caused by, or relating to neurosis. ■ abnormally sensitive, obsessive, or tense and anxious: *everyone was neurotic about burglars | a neurotic obsession with neat handwriting.*
▸*n.* a neurotic person. **—neu·rot·ic·al·ly** *adv.* **—neu·rot·i·cism** /-ˈrätəˌsizəm/ *n.*

neu·rot·o·my /n(y)o͝oˈrätəmē/ ▸*n.* the surgical cutting of a nerve to produce sensory loss and relief of pain or to suppress involuntary movements.

neu·ro·tox·in /ˈn(y)o͝orōˌtäksin/ ▸*n.* a poison that acts on the nervous system. **—neu·ro·tox·ic** /ˌn(y)o͝orōˈtäksik/ *adj.* **—neu·ro·tox·ic·i·ty** /ˌn(y)o͝orōtäkˈsisitē/ *n.* **—neu·ro·tox·i·col·o·gy** /ˌn(y)o͝orōˌtäksiˈkäləjē/ *n.*

neu·ro·trans·mit·ter /ˌn(y)o͝orōˈtranzmitər/ ▸*n. Physiology* a chemical substance that is released at the end of a nerve fiber by the arrival of a nerve impulse and, by diffusing across the synapse or junction, causes the transfer of the impulse to another nerve fiber, a muscle fiber, or some other structure. **—neu·ro·trans·mis·sion** /-ˌtranzˈmiSHən/ *n.*

neu·ro·troph·ic /ˌn(y)o͝orəˈträfik; -ˈtrō-/ ▸*adj. Physiology* of or relating to the growth of nervous tissue.

neu·ro·trop·ic /ˌn(y)o͝orəˈträpik; -ˈtrō-/ ▸*adj. Medicine* (of a virus, toxin, or chemical) tending to attack or affect the nervous system preferentially. **—neu·rot·ro·pism** /n(y)o͝oˈrätrəˌpizəm/ *n.*

neus·ton /ˈn(y)o͞ostän/ ▸*n. Biology* small aquatic organisms inhabiting the surface layer or moving on the surface film of water. ▷early 20th cent.: via German from Greek, neuter of *neustos* 'swimming,' on the pattern of *plankton.* **—neus·ton·ic** /n(y)o͞oˈstänik/ *adj.*

neut. ▸*abbr.* ■ neuter. ■ neutral.

neu·ter /ˈn(y)o͞otər/ ▸*adj.* **1** of or denoting a gender of nouns in some languages, typically contrasting with masculine and feminine or common: *it is a neuter word in Greek.* **2** (of an animal) lacking developed sexual organs, or having had them removed. ■ (of a plant or flower) having neither functional pistils nor functional stamens. ■ (of a person) apparently having no sexual characteristics; asexual.
▸*n.* **1** *Grammar* a neuter word. ■ **(the neuter)** the neuter gender. **2** a nonfertile caste of social insect, esp. a worker bee or ant. ■ a castrated or spayed domestic animal. ■ a person who appears to lack sexual characteristics.
▸*v.* [*trans.*] castrate or spay (a domestic animal): [as *adj.*] **(neutered)** *a neutered tomcat.* ■ render ineffective; deprive of vigor or force: *disarmament negotiations that will neuter their military power.* ▷late Middle English: via Old French from Latin *neuter* 'neither,' from *ne-* 'not' + *uter* 'either.'

neu·tral /ˈn(y)o͞otrəl/ ▸*adj.* **1** not helping or supporting either of two opposing sides, esp. countries at war; impartial: *during the Second World War Portugal was neutral.* ■ belonging to an impartial party, country, or group: *on neutral ground.* ■ unbiased; disinterested: *neutral, expert scientific advice.* **2** having no strongly marked or positive characteristics or features: *the tone was neutral, devoid of sentiment | a fairly neutral background will make any small splash of color stand out.* ■ *Chemistry* neither acid nor alkaline; having a pH of about 7. ■ electrically neither positive nor negative.
▸*n.* **1** an impartial and uninvolved country or person: *he acted as a neutral between the parties | Sweden and its fellow neutrals.* ■ an unbiased person. **2** a neutral color or shade, esp. light gray or beige. **3** a disengaged position of gears in which the engine is disconnected from the driven parts: *she slipped the gear into neutral.* **4** an electrically neutral point, terminal, conductor, or wire. ▷late Middle English (as a noun): from Latin *neutralis* 'of neuter gender,' from *neuter* (see NEUTER). **—neu·tral·i·ty** /n(y)o͞oˈtralitē/ *n.* **—neu·tral·ly** *adv.*

neu·tral ax·is ▸*n. Engineering* a line or plane through a beam or plate connecting points at which no extension or compression occurs when the beam or plate is bent.

neu·tral cor·ner ▸*n. Boxing* either of the two corners of a boxing ring not used by the boxers and their handlers between rounds.

neu·tral den·si·ty fil·ter ▸*n.* a photographic or optical filter that absorbs light of all wavelengths to the same extent, causing overall dimming but no change in color.

neu·tral·ism /ˈn(y)o͞otrəˌlizəm/ ▸*n.* a policy of political neutrality. **—neu·tral·ist** *n.*

neu·tral·ize /ˈn(y)o͞otrəˌlīz/ ▸*v.* [*trans.*] render (something) ineffective or harmless by applying an opposite force or effect: *impatience at his frailty began to neutralize her fear.* ■ make (an acidic or alkaline substance) chemically neutral. ■ disarm (a bomb or similar weapon). ■ a euphemistic way of saying kill or destroy, esp. in a covert or military operation. ▷mid 17th cent.: from French *neutraliser*, from medieval Latin *neutralizare*, from Latin *neutralis* (see NEUTRAL). **—neu·tral·i·za·tion** /ˌn(y)o͞otrəliˈzāSHən/ *n.* **—neu·tral·iz·er** *n.*

neu·tral zone ▸*n.* **1** the central area of a hockey rink, lying between the two blue lines. **2** *Football* (before the start of a play) the imaginary zone running sideline to sideline from the front to the back point of the football.

neu·tri·no /n(y)o͞oˈtrēnō/ ▸*n.* (*pl.* **-nos**) a neutral subatomic particle with a mass close to zero and half-integral spin, rarely reacting with normal matter. Three kinds of neutrinos are known, associated with the electron, muon, and tau particle. ▷mid 20th cent.: from Italian, diminutive of *neutro* 'neutral.'

neu·tron /ˈn(y)o͞oträn/ ▸*n.* a subatomic particle of about the same mass as a proton but without an electric charge, present in all atomic nuclei except those of ordinary hydrogen. ▷early 20th cent.: from NEUTRAL + -ON.

neu·tron bomb ▸*n.* a nuclear weapon that produces large numbers of neutrons rather than heat or blast like conventional nuclear weapons.

neu·tron star ▸*n. Astronomy* a celestial object of very small radius (typically 18 miles/30 km) and very high density, composed predominantly of closely packed neutrons. Neutron stars are thought to form by the gravitational collapse of the remnant of a massive star after a supernova explosion, provided that the star is insufficiently massive to produce a black hole.

neu·tro·pe·ni·a /ˌn(y)o͞otrəˈpēnēə/ ▸*n. Medicine* the presence of abnormally few neutrophils in the blood, leading to increased susceptibility to infection. It is an undesirable side effect of some cancer treatments. ▷1930s: from *neutral* + Greek, *penia* 'poverty, lack.' **—neu·tro·pe·nic** /ˌn(y)o͞otrəˈpēnik; -ˈpenik/ *adj.*

neu·tro·phil /ˈn(y)o͞otrəfil/ ▸*n. Physiology* a neutrophilic white blood cell.

neu·tro·phil·ic /ˌn(y)o͞otrəˈfilik/ ▸*adj. Physiology* (of a cell or its contents) readily stained only by neutral dyes. ▷late 19th cent.: from NEUTRAL + *-philic* (see -PHILIA).

Nev. ▸*abbr.* Nevada.

Ne·va /ˈnēvə; ˈnā-/ a river in northwestern Russia that flows 46 miles (74 km) west from Lake Ladoga to the Gulf of Finland, passing through St. Petersburg.

Ne·va·da /nəˈvadə; -ˈvädə/ a state in the western U.S., on an arid plateau, almost totally in the Great Basin area; pop. 1,998,257; capital, Carson City; statehood, Oct. 31, 1864 (36). It was acquired from Mexico in 1848. An abundance of gold and silver ore (called the Comstock Lode) was discovered in 1859 near Virginia City. **—Ne·vad·an** *adj. & n.*

né·vé /nāˈvā/ ▸*n.* another term for FIRN. ▷mid 19th cent.: from Swiss French, literally 'glacier,' based on Latin *nix, niv-* 'snow.'

nev·er /ˈnevər/ ▸*adv.* **1** at no time in the past or future; on no occasion; not ever: *they had never been camping in their lives | I will* **never ever** *forget it.* **2** not at all: *he never turned up.* ▷Old English *nǣfre*, from *ne* 'not' + *ǣfre* 'ever.'
▸*PHRASES* □ **never fear** see FEAR. □ **never mind** see MIND. □ **never say die** see DIE[1]. □ **well I never!** *informal* expressing great surprise or indignation: *Well I never—that's not like you!*

nev·er-end·ing ▸*adj.* (esp. of something unpleasant) having or seeming to have no end. See note at ETERNAL.

nev·er·more /ˌnevərˈmôr/ ▸*adv. poetic/literary* at no future time; never again: *I order you gone, nevermore to return.*

nev·er-nev·er land ▸*n.* an imaginary utopian place or situation: *a never-never land of unreal prices and easy bank loans.* ▷often with allusion to the ideal country in J. M. Barrie's *Peter Pan.*

nev·er·the·less /ˌnevər<u>TH</u>əˈles/ ▸*adv.* in spite of that; notwithstanding; all the same: *statements which, although literally true, are nevertheless misleading.*

Nev·ille /ˈnevəl/, Richard, see WARWICK[2].

Ne·vis /ˈnēvəs/ one of the Leeward Islands in the Caribbean Sea, part of St. Kitts and Nevis; capital, Charlestown. **—Nevisian** /ˌnevəˈsēən/ *n. & adj.*

Nev·sky, Alexander, see ALEXANDER NEVSKY, ST.

ne·vus /ˈnēvəs/ (*Brit.* **nae·vus**) ▸*n.* (*pl.* **-vi** /-ˌvī/) a birthmark or a mole on the skin, esp. a birthmark in the form of a raised red patch. ▷mid 19th cent.: from Latin.

new /n(y)o͞o/ ▸*adj.* **1** not existing before; made, introduced, or discovered recently or now for the first time: *new crop varieties | this tendency is not new |* [as *n.*] **(the new)** *a fascinating mix of the old and the new.* ■ in original condition; not worn or used: *check that the wiring is new and in good condition.* ■ not previously used or owned: *a secondhand bus cost a fraction of a new one.* ■ of recent origin or arrival: *a new baby.* ■ (of food or drink) freshly or recently produced. ■ (of vegetables) dug or harvested early in the season: *new*

N

potatoes. **2** already existing but seen, experienced, or acquired recently or now for the first time: *her new bike.* ■ [*predic.*] (**new to**) unfamiliar or strange to (someone): *a way of living that was new to me.* ■ [*predic.*] (**new to/at**) (of a person) inexperienced at or unaccustomed to doing (something): *I'm quite new to gardening.* ■ different from a recent previous one: *I have a new assistant | this would be her new home.* ■ in addition to another or others already existing: *recruiting new pilots overseas.* ■ [in *place names*] discovered or founded later than and named after: *New York.* **3** just beginning and regarded as better than what went before: *starting a new life.* ■ (of a person) reinvigorated or restored: *a bottle of pills would make him a new man.* ■ (**the new**) renewed or reformed: *the new South Africa.* ■ superseding another or others of the same kind, and advanced in method or theory: *the new architecture.* ■ reviving another or others of the same kind: *the New Bohemians.* ■ recently affected or produced by social change: *the new rich.*

▸*adv.* [usu. in *combination*] newly; recently: *new-mown hay | new-fallen snow.* ▷Old English *nīwe, nēowe*, of Germanic origin; related to Dutch *nieuw* and German *neu*, from an Indo-European root shared by Sanskrit *nava*, Latin *novus*, and Greek *neos* 'new.' **—new·ish** *adj.* **—new·ness** *n.*

▸*PHRASES* □ **a new one** *informal* an account, idea, or joke not previously encountered by someone: *I've heard of lazy, but somebody being too lazy to talk—that's* ***a new one on me.*** □ **what's new? 1** (said on greeting someone) what's going on? how are you? **2** (also **what else is new?**) that is the usual situation: *she and I squabbled—so what's new? | men like to see women's legs. So what else is new?*

New Age ▸*n.* a broad movement characterized by alternative approaches to traditional Western culture, with an interest in spirituality, mysticism, holism, and environmentalism: [as *adj.*] *the New Age movement.* **—New Ag·er** *n.* **—New Agey** *adj.*

New Age mus·ic ▸*n.* a style of chiefly instrumental music characterized by light melodic harmonies, improvisation, and sounds reproduced from the natural world, intended to promote serenity.

New Al·ba·ny an industrial city in southern Indiana, across the Ohio River from Louisville in Kentucky; pop. 36,322.

New Am·ster·dam former name for the city of **New York.**

New·ark /ˈn(y)o͞owərk/ **1** a city in northwestern Delaware, home to the University of Delaware; pop. 28,547. **2** an industrial city in New Jersey; pop. 273,546. **3** an industrial and commercial city in central Ohio; pop. 44,389.

New Bed·ford an industrial port city in southeastern Massachusetts, on Buzzards Bay, a noted 19th-century whaling center; pop. 93,768.

New Bern a historic commercial city in eastern North Carolina; pop. 17,363.

new·bie /ˈn(y)o͞obē/ ▸*n.* (*pl.* **-bies**) an inexperienced newcomer, esp. in computing.

new·born /ˈn(y)o͞oˌbôrn/ ▸*adj.* (of a child or animal) recently or just born: *newborn babies | figurative a newborn star.*

▸*n.* a recently born child or animal.

New Braun·fels /ˈbrounfəlz/ a city in south central Texas; pop. 27,334.

New Brit·ain 1 a mountainous island in the South Pacific Ocean, part of Papua New Guinea, that lies off the northeastern coast of New Guinea; pop. 312,000; capital, Rabaul. **2** an industrial city in central Connecticut, noted for its hardware manufacturing; pop. 71,538.

New Bruns·wick 1 a maritime province on the southeastern coast of Canada; pop. 726,900; capital, Fredericton. It was first settled by the French and was ceded to Britain in 1713. It became one of the original four provinces in the Dominion of Canada in 1867. **2** a city in central New Jersey, on the Raritan River; pop. 41,711.

New·burgh /ˈn(y)o͞oˌbərg/ a historic industrial city in southeastern New York, on the Hudson River; pop. 26,454.

New·bury·port /ˈn(y)o͞obərēˌpôrt; -ˌberē-/ a historic port city, now chiefly residential, in northeastern Massachusetts, at the mouth of the Merrimack River; pop. 16,317.

New Cal·e·do·ni·a /ˌkaləˈdōnēə/ an island in the South Pacific, east of Australia; pop. 178,000; capital, Nouméa. Since 1946 it has formed, with its dependencies, a French overseas territory. French name **Nouvelle-Calédonie.** ▷named, by Captain Cook in 1774, after the Roman name *Caledonia* 'Scotland.' **—New Cal·e·do·ni·an** *n.* & *adj.*

New·cas·tle[1] /ˈn(y)o͞oˌkasəl/ **1** an industrial city in northeastern England, a port on the Tyne River; pop. 263,000. Full name **Newcastle-upon-Tyne. 2** an industrial town in west central England, southwest of Stoke-on-Trent; pop. 117,000. Full name **Newcastle-under-Lyme. 3** an industrial port on the southeastern coast of Australia, in New South Wales; pop. 262,000.

New·cas·tle[2], Thomas Pelham-Holles, 1st Duke of (1693–1768), British statesman; prime minister 1754–56 and 1757–62. During his second term in office, he headed a coalition with William Pitt the Elder until 1761.

New·cas·tle dis·ease ▸*n.* an acute infectious viral fever affecting birds, esp. poultry. Also called **fowl pest.** ▷1920s: so named because it was first recorded near Newcastle upon Tyne, England, in 1927.

New·combe /ˈn(y)o͞okəm/, John (1944–), Australian tennis player. He won Wimbledon three times (1967, 1970, 1971), as well as the U.S. singles championships in 1967 and 1973 and the Australian in 1973 and 1975.

New·com·en /n(y)o͞oˈkəmən/, Thomas (1663–1729), English engineer; developer of the first practical steam engine—an engine that operated a pump for the removal of water from mines—in 1712.

new·com·er /ˈn(y)o͞oˌkəmər/ ▸*n.* a person or thing that has recently arrived in a place or joined a group. ■ a novice in a particular activity or situation.

New Crit·i·cism an influential movement in literary criticism in the mid 20th century that stressed the importance of focusing on the text itself rather than being concerned with external biographical or social considerations. Associated with the movement were John Crowe Ransom (who first used the term in 1941), I. A. Richards, and Cleanth Brooks.

New Deal the economic measures introduced by President Franklin D. Roosevelt in 1933 to counteract the effects of the Great Depression. It involved a massive public works program, complemented by the large-scale granting of loans, and succeeded in reducing unemployment by between 7 and 10 million. **—New Deal·er** *n.*

New Del·hi see **Delhi.**

new e·con·o·my ▸*n.* new industries, such as biotechnology or the Internet, that are characterized by cutting-edge technology and high growth.

newel post

new·el /ˈn(y)o͞owəl/ ▸*n.* the central supporting pillar of a spiral or winding staircase. ■ (also **newel post**) a post at the head or foot of a flight of stairs, supporting a handrail. ▷late Middle English: from Old French *nouel* 'knob,' from medieval Latin *nodellus*, diminutive of Latin *nodus* 'knot.'

New Eng·land an area on the northeastern coast of the U.S. that consists of the states of Maine, New Hampshire, Vermont, Massachusetts, Rhode Island, and Connecticut. **—New Eng·land·er** *n.*

New Eng·land boiled din·ner ▸*n.* a dish of meat (often corned beef), cabbage or other vegetables, and potatoes, prepared by simmering in water.

New Eng·land clam chow·der ▸*n.* a thick chowder made with clams, onions, potatoes, salt pork, and milk or cream.

New Eng·lish Bi·ble (abbr.: **NEB**) ▸*n.* a modern English translation of the Bible, published in the UK in 1961–70 and revised (as the **Revised English Bible**) in 1989.

new·fan·gled /ˈn(y)o͞oˈfaNGgəld; -ˌfaNG-/ (also **new-fan·gled**) ▸*adj. derogatory* different from what one is used to; objectionably new: *I've no time for such newfangled nonsense.* ▷Middle English: from *newfangle* (now dialect) 'liking what is new,' from the adverb **new** + a second element related to an Old English word meaning 'to take.'

new-fash·ioned ▸*adj.* of a new type or style; up to date: *selling your product the new-fashioned way.*

New·fie /ˈn(y)o͞ofē/ *informal* ▸*n.* (*pl.* **-fies**) a Newfoundlander.

▸*adj.* coming from or associated with Newfoundland.

new·found /ˈn(y)o͞oˌfound/ (*Brit.* **new-found**) ▸*adj.* recently found or discovered: *armed with this newfound political consciousness, he sells his condo and quits his job.*

New·found·land[1] /ˌn(y)o͞ofəndˈland; ˈn(y)o͞ofəndlənd; -ˌland/ a large island off the eastern coast of Canada, at the mouth of the St. Lawrence River. It was united with Labrador (as Newfoundland and Labrador) in 1949 to form a province of Canada. **—New·found·land·er** *n.*

New·found·land[2] (in full **Newfoundland dog**) ▸*n.* a dog of a very large breed with a thick, coarse coat.

Newfoundland[2]

New·found·land and Lab·ra·dor a province of Canada that consists of the island of Newfoundland and the Labrador coast of eastern Canada; pop. 568,474; capital, St. John's. It joined the confederation of Canada in 1949.

New·gate /ˈn(y)o͞oˌgāt/ a former London prison whose unsanitary conditions became notorious in the 18th century before the building was burned down in 1780.

New Geor·gia a volcanic island group in the west central Solomon Islands, northwest of Guadalcanal. **New Georgia Sound,** along the N side, was called "the Slot" by Americans during World War II, when the area saw heavy fighting with Japanese forces. ■ the largest of these islands.

New Guin·ea an island in the western South Pacific Ocean, off the northern coast of Australia, the world's second largest island. It is divided into two parts; the western half is part of Irian Jaya, an Indonesian province; the eastern half forms part of Papua New Guinea. **—New Guin·e·an** /ˈginēən/ *n.* & *adj.*

New Hamp·shire /ˈhampSHər/ a state in the northeastern U.S., with a short border on the Atlantic coast, one of the six New England states; pop. 1,235,786; capital, Concord; statehood, June 21, 1788 (9). It was the first colony to declare independence from Britain in 1776 and then became one of the original thirteen states.

New·hart /ˈn(y)o͞oˌhärt/, Bob (1929–), U.S. comedian and actor; full name *George Robert Newhart.* His career as a comedian took off with a best-selling record album *The Button-Down Mind of Bob Newhart* (1959). His most successful television shows were "The Bob Newhart Show" (1972–78) and "Newhart" (1982–90).

New Ha·ven /ˌn(y)o͞o ˈhāvən/ an industrial city in south central Connecticut, on Long Island Sound, home to Yale University; pop. 123,626.

New Heb·ri·des former name (until 1980) for **Vanuatu.**

New Hope a borough in southeastern Pennsylvania, on the Delaware River, a well-known tourist destination and artists' colony; pop. 1,400.

New·house /ˈn(y)o͞oˌhous/, Samuel I(rving, Jr.) (1895–1979), U.S. publisher and philanthropist; born *Solomon Neuhaus.* Besides owning a large chain of newspapers and radio and television stations, he served as the chairman of Condé Nast Publications, Inc., from 1959.

New I·be·ri·a a city in southern Louisiana, on the Bayou Teche in Cajun Country; pop. 32,623.

Ne Win /ˌne ˈwin/ (1911–2002), Burmese general and socialist statesman; prime minister 1958–60; head of state 1962–74; president 1974–81. After a military coup in 1962, he established a military dictatorship and formed a one-party state.

New In·ter·na·tion·al Ver·sion (abbr.: **NIV**) ▸*n.* a modern English translation of the Bible published in 1973–78.

New Ire·land an island in the South Pacific Ocean, part of Papua New Guinea, that lies north of New Britain; pop. 87,000; capital, Kavieng.

New Jer·sey a state in the northeastern U.S., on the Atlantic coast; pop. 8,414,350; capital, Trenton; statehood, Dec. 18, 1787 (3). Colonized by Dutch settlers and ceded to Britain in 1664, it became one of the original thirteen states. **—New Jer·sey·an** /-zēən/ *n.* & *adj.*

New Je·ru·sa·lem *Theology* the abode of the blessed in heaven (with reference to Rev. 21:2). ■ [as *n.*] (**a New Jerusalem**) an ideal place or situation.

New Je·ru·sa·lem Church a Christian sect instituted by followers of Emanuel Swedenborg. It was founded in London in 1787.

New Lat·in ▸*n.* another term for MODERN LATIN.

New·ley /ˈn(y)o͞olē/, Anthony (1931–99), British composer, singer, and actor. He played the Artful Dodger in the movie version of *Oliver Twist* (1948) and cowrote and starred in the Broadway musicals *Stop the World—I Want to Get Off* (1961) and *The Roar of the Greasepaint—The Smell of the Crowd* (1965).

New Lon·don an industrial port city in southeastern Connecticut, across the Thames River from Groton, on Long Island Sound; pop. 28,540.

New Look a style of women's clothing introduced in 1947 by Christian Dior, featuring calf-length full skirts and a generous use of material in contrast to wartime austerity.

new·ly /ˈn(y)o͞olē/ ▸*adv.* **1** recently: *a newly acquired skill.* **2** again; afresh: *social confidence for the newly single.* ■ in a new or different manner: *we have to make ourselves newly aware of each text.*

new·ly·wed /ˈn(y)o͞olē,wed/ ▸*n.* (usu. **newlyweds**) a recently married person.

New·man1 /ˈn(y)o͞omən/, Barnett (1905–70), U.S. painter. A seminal figure in color-field painting, he juxtaposed large blocks of uniform color with narrow marginal strips of contrasting colors, such as in *Who's Afraid of Red, Yellow, and Blue III* (1966–67).

New·man2, John Henry (1801–90), English prelate and theologian; a founder of the Oxford Movement. He turned to Roman Catholicism in 1845 and became a cardinal in 1879.

New·man3, Paul (1925–), U.S. actor and movie director. Among his many movies are *Butch Cassidy and the Sundance Kid* (1969), *The Sting* (1973), *The Color of Money* (Academy Award 1987), and *Message in a Bottle* (1999). He directed his wife, Joanne Woodward, in *Rachel, Rachel* (1968). He is also known for his philanthropic activities.

Paul Newman

new man ▸*n.* a man who rejects sexist attitudes and the traditional male role, esp. in the context of domestic responsibilities and child care.

New·man–Keuls test /ˈn(y)o͞omən kəlz/ ▸*n. Statistics* a test for assessing the significance of differences between all possible pairs of different sets of observations, with a fixed error rate for the whole set of comparisons. ▹mid 20th cent.: named after D. *Newman* (*fl.* 1939), English statistician, and M. *Keuls* (*fl.* 1952), Dutch horticulturalist.

New·mar·ket /ˈn(y)o͞o,märkət/ ▸*n.* **1** a card game in which the players put down cards in sequence, hoping to be the first to play all their cards and also to play certain special cards on which bets have been placed. **2** (also **Newmarket coat**) a close-fitting overcoat of a style originally worn for riding.

new math (*Brit.* **new maths**) ▸*n.* a system of teaching mathematics to younger children, with emphasis on investigation and discovery and on set theory.

New Mex·i·co a state in the southwestern U.S., on the border with Mexico; pop. 1,819,046; capital, Santa Fe; statehood, Jan. 6, 1912 (47). It was obtained from Mexico in 1845 (annexation of Texas), 1848 (Treaty of Guadalupe Hidalgo that ended the Mexican-American War), and 1853 (Gadsden Purchase). —**New Mex·i·can** /-kən/ *adj.* & *n.*

new mon·ey ▸*n.* a fortune recently acquired; funds recently raised. ■ those whose wealth is recently acquired rather than inherited; the nouveau riche.

new moon ▸*n.* the phase of the moon when it is in conjunction with the sun and invisible from earth, or shortly thereafter when it appears as a slender crescent. ■ the time when this occurs.

new or·der ▸*n.* a new system, regime, or government: *a new economic order.* ■ (**New Order**) Hitler's planned reorganization of Europe under Nazi rule.

New Or·le·ans /ˈôrlinz; ôrˈlēnz/ a city and port in southeastern Louisiana, on the Mississippi River; pop. 484,674. Founded by the French in 1718, it was named after the Duc d'Orléans, regent of France. It is known for its annual Mardi Gras celebrations and for its association with the development of blues and jazz.

New·port /ˈn(y)o͞o,pôrt/ **1** an industrial town and port in southern Wales, on the Bristol Channel; pop. 130,000. Welsh name CASNEWYDD. **2** a historic port city in southern Rhode Island, on the island of Rhode Island. Home to naval facilities, it became known in the 19th century as a fashionable resort where the wealthy built opulent "cottages"; pop. 26,475.

New·port Beach a resort, residential, and industrial city in southwestern California, southeast of Los Angeles; pop. 66,643.

New·port News a city in southeastern Virginia, at the mouth of the James River on the Hampton Roads estuary; pop. 180,150.

New Prov·i·dence an island in the central Bahamas, home to most of the people in the Bahamas and to the capital (Nassau); pop. 172,000.

New Red Sand·stone ▸*n. Geology* a series of sedimentary rocks, chiefly soft red sandstones, belonging to the Permo-Triassic system of northwestern Europe.

New Re·vised Stand·ard Ver·sion (abbr.: **NRSV**) ▸*n.* a modern English translation of the Bible, based on the Revised Standard Version and published in 1990.

New River a river that flows for 320 miles (515 km) from North Carolina through Virginia and into West Virginia, where it enters the Kanawha River.

New Ro·chelle /rəˈshel; rō-/ a city in southeastern New York, northeast of New York City, on Long Island Sound; pop. 72,182.

New Ro·man·tic ▸*adj.* denoting a style of popular music and fashion popular in Britain in the early 1980s in which both men and women wore makeup and dressed in flamboyant clothes.
▸*n.* a performer or enthusiast of New Romantic music.

news /n(y)o͞oz/ ▸*n.* newly received or noteworthy information, esp. about recent or important events: *I've got some good news for you.* ■ (**the news**) a broadcast or published report of news: *he was back **in the news** again.* ■ (**news to**) *informal* information not previously known to someone: *this was hardly news to her.* ■ a person or thing considered interesting enough to be reported in the news: *Chanel became the hottest news in fashion.* ▹late Middle English: plural of NEW, translating Old French *noveles* or medieval Latin *nova* 'new things.'
▸*PHRASES* □ **make news** become a story in the news: *stolen babies make news.* □ **no news is good news** *proverb* without information to the contrary you can assume that all is well.

news a·gen·cy ▸*n.* an organization that collects news items and distributes them to newspapers or broadcasters.

news·a·gent /ˈn(y)o͞oz,ājənt/ ▸*n. Brit.* a person or a shop selling newspapers and magazines.

news·boy /ˈn(y)o͞oz,boi/ ▸*n.* a boy who sells or delivers newspapers.

news brief ▸*n.* a brief item of print or broadcast news.

news bul·le·tin ▸*n. Brit.* a short radio or television broadcast of news reports.

news·cast /ˈn(y)o͞oz,kast/ ▸*n.* a radio or television broadcast of news reports.

news·cast·er /ˈn(y)o͞oz,kastər/ ▸*n.* a person who reads broadcast news stories.

news con·fer·ence ▸*n.* a press conference.

news desk ▸*n.* the department of a broadcasting organization or newspaper responsible for collecting and reporting the news.

news·feed /ˈn(y)o͞oz,fēd/ ▸*n.* an electronic transmission of news, as from a broadcaster or an Internet newsgroup.

news flash ▸*n.* a single item of important news that is broadcast separately and often interrupts other programs.

news·gath·er·ing (also **news gath·er·ing**) ▸*n.* the process of researching news items, esp. those for broadcast or publication. —**news·gath·er·er** /-(ə)rər/ *n.*

news·group /ˈn(y)o͞oz,gro͞op/ ▸*n.* a group of Internet users who exchange e-mail messages on a topic of mutual interest.

news·hound /ˈn(y)o͞oz,hound/ ▸*n. informal* a newspaper reporter.

news·ie /ˈn(y)o͞ozē/ ▸*n.* (also **news·y**) (*pl.* **-ies**) *informal* a reporter. ■ *informal* a person who sells or delivers newspapers.

news·let·ter /ˈn(y)o͞oz,letər/ ▸*n.* a bulletin issued periodically to the members of a society, business, or organization.

news·mag·a·zine /ˈn(y)o͞oz,magə,zēn/ ▸*n.* a periodical, usually published weekly, that reports and comments on current events. ■ a regularly scheduled television news program consisting of short segments on a variety of subjects and featuring a varied format combining interviews, commentary, and entertainment.

news·man /ˈn(y)o͞oz,man/ ▸*n.* (*pl.* **-men**) a reporter or journalist.

news·mon·ger /ˈn(y)o͞oz,mäNGgər/ ▸*n.* a gossip.

New South Wales a state of southeastern Australia; pop. 5,827,000; capital, Sydney. First colonized by Britain in 1788, it was federated with the other states of Australia in 1901.

New Spain a former Spanish viceroyalty established in Central and North America in 1535 that was centered around present-day Mexico City. It was comprised of all the land under Spanish control north of the Isthmus of Panama and included parts of the southern U.S. It also came to include the Spanish possessions in the Caribbean and the Philippines. The viceroyalty was abolished in 1821, when Mexico achieved independence.

news·pa·per /ˈn(y)o͞oz,pāpər/ ▸*n.* a printed publication (usually issued daily or weekly) consisting of folded unstapled sheets and containing news, feature articles, advertisements, and correspondence. ■ the organization responsible for producing a particular newspaper. ■ another term for NEWSPRINT.

news·pa·per·man /ˈn(y)o͞oz,pāpər,man; -mən/ ▸*n.* (*pl.* **-men**) a male newspaper journalist.

news·pa·per·wom·an /ˈn(y)o͞oz,pāpər,wo͝omən/ ▸*n.* (*pl.* **-wom·en**) a female newspaper journalist.

new·speak /ˈn(y)o͞o,spēk/ ▸*n.* ambiguous euphemistic language used chiefly in political propaganda. ▹1949: the name of an artificial official language in George Orwell's *Nineteen Eighty-Four.*

news peg ▸*n.* an aspect or angle of a story that makes it newsworthy: *Talese further expanded traditional journalistic practice by delaying a story's news peg until as late in a story as he could manage.*

news·peo·ple /ˈn(y)o͞oz,pēpəl/ ▸*plural n.* professional reporters or journalists: *there's nothing wrong with docudrama so long as newspeople don't do it.*

news·print /ˈn(y)o͞oz,print/ ▸*n.* cheap, low-quality, absorbent printing paper made from coarse wood pulp and used chiefly for newspapers.

news·read·er /ˈn(y)o͞oz,rēdər/ ▸*n.* **1** *Computing* a computer program for reading e-mail messages posted to newsgroups. **2** *Brit.* a newscaster.

news·reel /ˈn(y)o͞oz,rēl/ ▸*n.* a short film of news and current affairs, formerly made for showing as part of the program in a movie theater.

news·room /ˈn(y)o͞oz,ro͞om; -,ro͝om/ ▸*n.* the area in a newspaper or broadcasting office where news is written and edited.

news·serv·er /n(y)o͞oz,sərvər/ ▸*n.* an Internet-connected server that receives and disseminates messages for a newsgroup.

news-sheet ▸*n.* a simple form of newspaper; a newsletter.

news·stand /ˈn(y)o͞oz,stand/ ▸*n.* a stand or stall for the sale of newspapers.

new star ▸*n.* a nova.

New Stone Age the Neolithic period.

New Style (abbr.: **NS**) ▸*n.* the method of calculating dates using the Gregorian calendar. It superseded the use of the Julian calendar in Scotland in England in 1752.

new-style ▸*adj.* [*attrib.*] having a new style; different from and usually better than a previous version: *a new-style retail and entertainment mix.*

Pronunciation Key ə ago; ər over; ˈə or ˌə up; ˈər or ˌər fur; a hat; ā rate; ä car; CH chew; e let; ē see; e(ə)r air; i fit; ī by; i(ə)r ear; NG sing; ō go; ô for; oi boy; o͝o good; o͞o goo; ou out; SH she; TH thin; T͟H then; (h)w why; ZH vision

N

news·week·ly /ˈn(y)o͞oz,wēklē/ (pl. **-lies**) ▸*n.* a newspaper or newsmagazine published on a weekly basis.

news wire ▸*n.* an electronically transmitted service providing up-to-the-minute news stories, financial market updates, and other information.

news·wor·thy /ˈn(y)o͞oz,wərT͟Hē/ ▸*adj.* noteworthy as news; topical: *you had to cover a lot of ground to find anything newsworthy.* —**news·wor·thi·ness** *n.*

news·y ▸*adj.* (**news·i·er, news·i·est**) *informal* full of news, esp. of a personal kind: *short, newsy letters.*
▸*n.* variant spelling of NEWSIE.

newt /n(y)o͞ot/ ▸*n.* a small, slender-bodied amphibian with lungs and a well-developed tail, typically spending its adult life on land and returning to water to breed. • *Notophthalmus, Taricha,* and other genera, family Salamandridae: numerous species, including the **red-spotted newt** (*N. viridescens viridescens*) of eastern North America and the **rough-skinned newt** (*T. granulosa*) of the Pacific coast from southern Alaska to northern California. ▷late Middle English: from *an ewt* (*ewt* from Old English *efeta*: see EFT), interpreted (by wrong division) as *a newt.*

rough-skinned newt

New Ter·ri·to·ries the part of Hong Kong on the southern coast of mainland China that lies north of the Kowloon peninsula and includes the islands of Lantau, Tsing Yi, and Lamma.

New Tes·ta·ment ▸*n.* the second part of the Christian Bible, written originally in Greek and recording the life and teachings of Jesus and his earliest followers. It includes the four Gospels, the Acts of the Apostles, twenty-one epistles by St. Paul and others, and the book of Revelation.

New·ton[1] /ˈn(y)o͞otn/ a city in eastern Massachusetts, on the Charles River, west of Boston; pop. 83,829.

New·ton[2], Sir Isaac (1642–1727), English mathematician and physicist, considered the greatest single influence on theoretical physics until Einstein. In *Principia Mathematica* (1687), he gave a mathematical description of the laws of mechanics and gravitation and applied these to planetary motion. *Opticks* (1704) records his optical experiments and theories, including the discovery that white light is made up of a mixture of colors. His work in mathematics included the binomial theorem and differential calculus.

new·ton /ˈn(y)o͞otn/ (abbr.: **N**) ▸*n. Physics* the SI unit of force. It is equal to the force that would give a mass of one kilogram an acceleration of one meter per second per second, and is equivalent to 100,000 dynes. ▷early 20th cent.: named after Sir Isaac NEWTON.

New·to·ni·an /n(y)o͞oˈtōnēən/ ▸*adj.* relating to or arising from the work of Sir Isaac Newton. ■ formulated or behaving according to the principles of classical physics.

New·to·ni·an me·chan·ics ▸*plural n.* [usu. treated as *sing.*] the system of mechanics that relies on Newton's laws of motion concerning the relations between forces acting and motions occurring.

New·to·ni·an tel·e·scope ▸*n. Astronomy* a reflecting telescope in which the light from the main mirror is deflected by a small, flat secondary mirror set at 45°, sending it to a magnifying eyepiece in the side of the telescope.

New·ton's laws of mo·tion *Physics* three fundamental laws of classical physics. The first states that a body continues in a state of rest or uniform motion in a straight line unless it is acted on by an external force. The second states that the rate of change of momentum of a moving body is proportional to the force acting to produce the change. The third states that if one body exerts a force on another, there is an equal and opposite force (or reaction) exerted by the second body on the first.

New·ton's rings ▸*plural n. Optics* a set of concentric circular fringes seen around the point of contact when a convex lens is placed on a plane surface or on another lens, caused by interference between light reflected from the upper and lower surfaces.

new town ▸*n.* a planned urban center created in an undeveloped or rural area, esp. with government sponsorship.

new wave ▸*n.* **1** another term for NOUVELLE VAGUE. **2** a style of rock music popular in the 1970s and 1980s, deriving from punk but generally more pop in sound and less aggressive in performance.

New World North and South America regarded collectively in relation to Europe, esp. after the early voyages of European explorers.

new year ▸*n.* the calendar year just begun or about to begin: *we're looking ahead to a profitable start to the new year | Happy New Year!* ■ the first few days or weeks of a year: *interest rates may climb **in the new year.*** ■ (usu. **New Year**) the period immediately before and after December 31: *the facilities are closed over Christmas and New Year.*
▸PHRASES □ **New Year's** *informal* New Year's Eve or New Year's Day. □ **ring in** (or **out**) **the new year** see RING[2].

New Year's Day ▸*n.* the first day of the year; in the modern Western calendar, January 1.

New Year's Eve ▸*n.* the last day of the year; in the modern Western calendar, December 31. ■ the evening of this day, typically marked with a celebration.

New York 1 a state in the northeastern U.S., on the Canadian border and Lake Ontario in the northwest, as well as on the Atlantic coast in the southeast; pop. 18,976,457; capital, Albany; statehood, July 26, 1788 (11). Originally settled by the Dutch, it was surrendered to the British in 1664. New York was one of the original thirteen states. **2** a major city and port in southeastern New York, situated on the Atlantic coast at the mouth of the Hudson River; pop. 7,322,564. It is situated mainly on islands, linked by bridges, and consists of five boroughs: Manhattan, Brooklyn, the Bronx, Queens, and Staten Island. Manhattan is the economic and cultural heart of the city, containing the stock exchange on Wall Street and the headquarters of the United Nations. Former name (until 1664) NEW AMSTERDAM. —**New York·er** *n.*

New York min·ute ▸*n. informal* a very short time; a moment: *you mention that price and she'll be out of here in a New York minute.* ▷with reference to the hectic pace of life in New York City.

New Zea·land /ˈzēlənd/ an island country in the South Pacific Ocean about 1,200 miles (1,900 km) east of Australia; pop. 3,990,000; capital, Wellington; languages, English (official) and Maori. Maori name AOTEAROA. —**New Zea·land·er** *n.*

New Zealand consists of two major islands (North and South Islands), separated by Cook Strait, and several smaller ones. The first European to sight New Zealand was Dutch navigator Abel Tasman in 1642; the islands were circumnavigated by Captain James Cook in 1769–70 and came under British sovereignty in 1840. Full dominion status was granted in 1907, and independence within the Commonwealth of Nations came in 1931 .

NEX ▸*abbr.* Navy exchange.

NEXRAD /ˈneks,rad/ ▸*n.* a system of Doppler radars across the U.S. that is used to track the location and movement of storm systems. ▷1990s: acronym from *NEXt generation weather RADar*

next /nekst/ ▸*adj.* **1** (of a time or season) coming immediately after the time of writing or speaking: *we'll go next year | next week's parade.* ■ (of a day of the week) nearest (or the nearest but one) after the present: *not this Wednesday, next Wednesday |* [*postpositive*] *on Monday next.* ■ (of an event or occasion) occurring directly in time after the present or most recent one, without anything of the same kind intervening: *the next election | next time I'll bring a hat.* **2** coming immediately after the present one in order or space: *the woman in the next room | the next chapter | who's next?* ■ coming immediately after the present one in rank: *building materials were next in importance.*
▸*adv.* on the first or soonest occasion after the present; immediately afterward: *wondering what would happen next | next, I heard the sound of voices.* ■ [with *superlative*] following in the specified order: *Joe was the next oldest after Martin.*
▸*n.* the next person or thing: *one moment he wasn't there, the next he was | the week **after next.***
▸*prep. archaic* next to: *he plodded along next him.* ▷Old English *nēhsta* 'nearest,' superlative of *nēah* 'nigh'; compare with Dutch *naast* and German *nächste.*
▸PHRASES □ **next in line** immediately below the present holder of a position in order of succession: *he is **next in line to** the throne.* □ **next to 1** in or into a position immediately to one side of; beside: *we sat next to each other.* **2** following in order or importance: *next to buying a whole new wardrobe, nothing lifts the spirits quite like a new hairdo!* **3** almost: *Charles knew **next to nothing** about farming.* **4** in comparison with: *next to her I felt like a fraud.* □ **the next world** (according to some religious beliefs) the place where one goes after death. □ **what next** an expression of surprise or amazement.

next best ▸*adj.* [*attrib.*] second in order of preference; to be preferred if one's first choice is not available: ***the next best thing** to flying is gliding.*

next door ▸*adv.* in or to the next house or room: *the caretaker lives next door.*
▸*adj.* (**next-door**) living or situated next door: *next-door neighbors.*
▸*n.* the building, room, or people next door: *a bleary-eyed man emerged from next door.*
▸PHRASES □ **the boy** (or **girl**) **next door** a person or type of person perceived as familiar, approachable, and dependable, typically in the context of a romantic partnership. □ **next door to** in the next house or room to: *the Old Executive Office Building next door to the White House.* ■ nearly; almost; near to: *it is next door to impossible.*

next of kin ▸*n.* [treated as *sing.* or *pl.*] a person's closest living relative or relatives.

nex·us /ˈneksəs/ ▸*n.* (*pl.* same or **-us·es**) a connection or series of connections linking two or more things: *the nexus between industry and political power.* ■ a connected group or series: *a nexus of ideas.* ■ the central and most important point or place: *the nexus of all this activity was the disco.* ▷mid 17th cent.: from Latin, 'a binding together,' from *nex-* 'bound,' from the verb *nectere.*

Nez Per·cé /,nez ˈpərs; pərˈsā/ ▸*n.* (*pl.* same or **Nez Per·cés**) **1** a member of an American Indian people of central Idaho, northeastern Oregon, and southeastern Washington. **2** the Sahaptian language of this people.
▸*adj.* of or relating to this people or their language. ▷French, literally 'pierced nose.'

NF ▸*abbr.* ■ Newfoundland (in official postal use).

n/f (also **N/F**) ▸*abbr.* no funds.

NFC ▸*abbr.* ■ National Finance Center. ■ National Football Conference.

NFL ▸*abbr.* National Football League.

Nfld ▸*abbr.* Newfoundland.

NFZ ▸*abbr.* no-fly zone.

NG ▸*abbr.* ■ National Guard. ■ natural gas. ■ newsgroup. ■ no good. ■ *Football* nose guard.

ng ▸*abbr.* nanogram.

Nga·li·e·ma, Mount /əNG,gālēˈāmə/ Zairean name for Mount Stanley (see STANLEY, MOUNT).

NGF ▸*abbr.* ■ National Golf Foundation. ■ nerve growth factor.

NGO ▸*abbr.* nongovernmental organization.

ngo·ma /əNGˈgōmə/ ▸*n.* (in East Africa) a dance; a night of dancing and music. ▷Kiswahili, literally 'drum, dance, music.'

Ngo·ni /əNGˈgōnē/ ▸*n.* (*pl.* same or **-nis**) **1** a member of a people now living chiefly in Malawi. **2** (**ngo·ni**) a kind of traditional African drum.
▸*adj.* of or relating to the Ngoni. ▷a local name.

Ngo·ron·go·ro /əNG,gôrôNGˈgōrō/ an extinct volcanic crater in the Great Rift Valley in northeastern Tanzania, 126 sq. mi. (326 sq. km.) in area.

NGU ▸*abbr.* nongonococcal urethritis.

ngul·trum /əNGˈgəltrəm/ ▸*n.* (*pl.* same) the basic monetary unit of Bhutan, equal to 100 chetrum. ▷Dzongkha.

Ngu·ni /əNGˈgo͞onē/ ▸*n.* (*pl.* same) **1** a member of a group of peoples living mainly in southern Africa. **2** the group of closely related Bantu languages,

including Ndebele, Swazi, Xhosa, and Zulu, spoken by these peoples.
▸*adj.* of or relating to this group of peoples or their languages. ▷from Zulu.

ngwee /əNG'gwē/ ▸*n.* (*pl.* same) a monetary unit of Zambia, equal to one hundredth of a kwacha. ▷a local word.

NH ▸*abbr.* New Hampshire (in official postal use).

NHL ▸*abbr.* National Hockey League.

Ni ▸*symbol* the chemical element nickel.

ni·a·cin /'nīəsin/ ▸*n.* another term for NICOTINIC ACID.

Ni·ag·a·ra Falls /nī'ag(ə)rə/ waterfalls on the Niagara River that consist of two principal parts separated by Goat Island: the Horseshoe Falls adjoin the western (Canadian) bank and fall 158 feet (47 m); the American Falls adjoin the eastern (U.S.) bank and fall 167 feet (50 m). ■ a city in upper New York located on the right bank of the Niagara River beside Niagara Falls; pop. 55,593. ■ a city in Canada, in southern Ontario, situated on the left bank of the Niagara River beside Niagara Falls, opposite the city of Niagara Falls, U.S., to which it is linked by bridges; pop. 75,399.

Niagara Falls

Ni·ag·a·ra Riv·er a river in North America that flows north for 35 miles (56 km) from Lake Erie to Lake Ontario and forms part of the border between Canada and the U.S.

Nia·mey /nē'ämā/ the capital of Niger, a port on the Niger River; pop. 410,000.

nib /nib/ ▸*n.* **1** the pointed end part of a pen, which distributes the ink on the writing surface. ■ a pointed or projecting part of an object. **2** (**nibs**) shelled and crushed coffee or cocoa beans. ■ small pieces of caramel, licorice, or other sweets. ▷late 16th cent. (in the sense 'beak, nose'): probably from Middle Dutch *nib* or Middle Low German *nibbe*, variant of *nebbe* 'beak' (see NEB).

nib·ble /'nibəl/ ▸*v.* take small bites out of: [*trans.*] *he sat nibbling a cookie* | [*intrans.*] *she* ***nibbled at*** *her food.* ■ [*intrans.*] eat in small amounts, esp. between meals. ■ gently bite at (a part of the body), esp. amorously or nervously: [*trans.*] *Tamar nibbled her bottom lip* | [*intrans.*] *he* ***nibbled at*** *her earlobe.* ■ *figurative* gradually erode or eat away: [*intrans.*] *inflation was* ***nibbling away at*** *spending power.* ■ [*intrans.*] *figurative* show cautious interest in a project or proposal: *there's a New York agent nibbling.*
▸*n.* [in *sing.*] an instance of nibbling something. ■ a small piece of food bitten off. ■ (**nibbles**) *informal* small savory snacks, typically eaten before a meal or with drinks. ■ an expression of cautious interest in a project or proposal: *now and then she gets a nibble, but no one will commit to an interview.* ▷late 15th cent.: probably of Low German or Dutch origin; compare with Low German *nibbeln* 'gnaw.'

nib·bler /'nib(ə)lər/ ▸*n.* **1** a person who habitually nibbles at food. **2** a cutting tool in which a rapidly reciprocating punch knocks out a line of overlapping small holes from a metal sheet.

Ni·be·lung /'nēbə,lo͝oNG/ ▸*n.* (*pl.* **-lungs** or **-lung·en** /-,lo͝oNGgən/) *Germanic Mythology* **1** a member of a Scandinavian race of dwarfs, owners of a hoard of gold and magic treasures, who were ruled by Nibelung, king of Nibelheim (land of mist). **2** (in the *Nibelungenlied*) a supporter of Siegfried or one of the Burgundians who stole the hoard from him. ▷from Old High German, from *nibel* 'mist' + the patronymic ending *-ung*.

Ni·be·lung·en·lied /,nēbə'lo͝oNGgən,lēd/ a 13th-century German poem, embodying a story found in the (Poetic) Edda, telling of the life and death of Siegfried, a prince of the Netherlands. There have been many adaptations of the story, including Wagner's epic music drama *Der Ring des Nibelungen* (1847–74). ▷German, from the name NIBELUNG + *Lied* 'song.'

nib·let /'niblit/ ▸*n.* a small piece of food. ▷late 19th cent.: from NIBBLE + -LET.

nib·lick /'niblik/ ▸*n.* *dated Golf* an iron with a heavy, lofted head, such as a nine-iron, used esp. for playing out of bunkers. ▷mid 19th cent.: of unknown origin.

nibs /nibz/ ▸*n.* (**his nibs**) *informal* a mock title used to refer to a self-important man, esp. one in authority. ▷early 19th cent.: of unknown origin; compare with earlier *nabs*, used similarly with a possessive adjective as in *his nabs*, on the pattern of references to the aristocracy such as *his lordship*.

NIC ▸*abbr.* ■ newly industrialized country.

ni·Cad /'nī,kad/ (also *trademark* **Ni·cad**) ▸*n.* [usu. as *adj.*] a battery or cell with a nickel anode, a cadmium cathode, and a potassium hydroxide electrolyte. NiCads are used chiefly as a rechargeable power source for portable equipment. ▷1950s: blend of NICKEL and CADMIUM.

Ni·cae·a /nī'sēə/ an ancient city in Asia Minor, on the site of modern Iznik in Turkey. Two ecumenical councils of the early Christian Church were held here in 325 and 787. See also NICENE CREED.

Nic·a·ra·gua /nikə'rägwə/ a country, the largest, in Central America, with a coastline on both the Atlantic and the Pacific oceans; pop. 5,359,000; capital, Managua; official language, Spanish. —**Nic·a·ra·guan** *adj.* & *n.*

Colonized by the Spaniards, Nicaragua broke away from Spain in 1821 and became an independent republic in 1838. In 1979, the dictator Anastasio Somoza was overthrown by a popular revolution; the new left-wing Sandinista regime then faced a counterrevolutionary guerrilla campaign by the U.S.-backed Contras. The Sandinistas lost power to an opposition coalition in the 1990 election and were defeated again in 1996 and 2001.

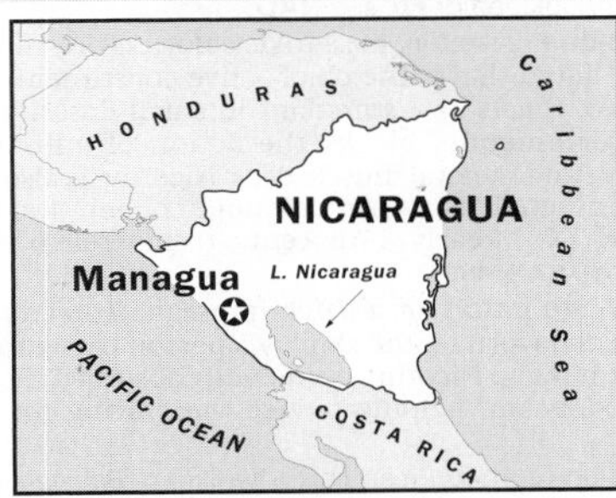

Nic·a·ra·gua, Lake a lake near the western coast of Nicaragua, the largest lake in Central America.

Nice /nēs/ a resort city on the French Riviera, near the border with Italy; pop. 346,000.

nice /nīs/ ▸*adj.* **1** pleasant; agreeable; satisfactory: *we had a nice time* | *that wasn't very* ***nice of*** *him* | *Jeremy had been very* ***nice to*** *her.* ■ (of a person) pleasant in manner; good-natured; kind: *he's a really nice guy.* **2** fine or subtle: *a nice distinction.* ■ requiring careful thought or attention: *a nice point.* **3** *archaic* fastidious; scrupulous. ▷Middle English (in the sense 'stupid'): from Old French, from Latin *nescius* 'ignorant,' from *nescire* 'not know.' Other early senses included 'coy, reserved,' giving rise to 'fastidious, scrupulous': this led both to the sense 'fine, subtle' (regarded by some as the "correct" sense), and to the main current senses. —**nice·ness** *n.*
▸*PHRASES* □ **make nice** (or **nice-nice**) *informal* be pleasant or polite to someone, typically in a hypocritical way: *the seat next to him was empty, so he wasn't required to make nice with a stranger.* □ **nice and —** — satisfactorily or adequately in terms of the quality described: *it's nice and warm in here.* □ **nice one** *informal* expressing approval or commendation. ■ used sarcastically to comment on an inept act: *oh, nice one, she put her finger up to her eye and tugged at the skin.* □ **nice to meet you** a polite formula used on being introduced to someone. □ **nice work** *informal* expressing approval of a task well done. □ **nice work if you can get it** *informal* used to express envy of what is perceived to be another person's more favorable situation, esp. if they seem to have reached it with little effort.

USAGE Nice originally had a number of meanings, including 'fine, subtle, discriminating' (*they are not very nice in regard to the company they keep*); 'refined in taste, hard to please, fastidious' (*for company so nice, the finest caterers would be engaged*); and 'precise, strict' (*she has a nice sense of decorum*). The popular overuse of **nice** to mean 'pleasant, agreeable, satisfactory' has rendered the word trite: *we had a very nice time; this is a nice room; he's a nice boy.*

nice·ly /'nīslē/ ▸*adv.* in a pleasant, agreeable, or attractive manner: *nicely dressed in flowered cotton.* ■ satisfactorily; perfectly well: *we're doing very nicely now.*

Ni·cene Creed /'nīsēn; nī'sēn/ a formal statement of Christian belief that is widely used in Christian liturgies, based on that adopted at the first Council of Nicaea in 325.

ni·ce·ty /'nīsitē/ ▸*n.* (*pl.* **-ties**) (usu. **niceties**) a fine detail or distinction, esp. one regarded as intricate and fussy: *she was never interested in the niceties of Greek and Latin.* ■ accuracy or precision: *she prided herself on her nicety of pronunciation.* ■ a minor aspect of polite social behavior; a detail of etiquette: *we were brought up to observe the niceties.* ▷Middle English (in the sense 'folly, foolish conduct'): from Old French *nicete*, based on Latin *nescius* 'ignorant' (see NICE).
▸*PHRASE* □ **to a nicety** precisely.

niche /niCH/ ▸*n.* a shallow recess, esp. one in a wall to display a statue or other ornament. ■ (**one's niche**) a comfortable or suitable position in life or employment: *he is now a partner at a leading law firm and feels he has found his niche.* ■ a specialized but profitable corner of the market: [as *adj.*] *important new niche markets.* ■ *Ecology* a position or role taken by a kind of organism within its community. Such a position may be occupied by different organisms in different localities, e.g., antelopes in Africa and kangaroos in Australia.
▸*v.* [*trans.*] place or position (something) in a niche. ▷early 17th cent.: from French, literally 'recess,' from *nicher* 'make a nest,' based on Latin *nidus* 'nest.'

Ni·chi·ren /'niCHərən/ (also **Nichiren Buddhism**) ▸*n.* a Japanese Buddhist sect founded by the religious teacher Nichiren (1222–82) with the Lotus Sutra as its central scripture. See also SOKA GAKKAI.

Nich·o·las /'nik(ə)ləs/ the name of two tsars of Russia: ■ **Nicholas I** (1796–1855), brother of Alexander I; reigned 1825–55. At home he pursued rigidly conservative policies, while his expansionism in the Near East led to the Crimean War. ■ **Nicholas II** (1868–1918), son of Alexander III; reigned 1894–1917. Forced to abdicate after the Russian Revolution in 1917, he was shot along with his family a year later.

Nich·o·las, St. (4th century), Christian prelate. Said to have been bishop of Myra in Lycia, he is the patron saint of children, sailors, Greece, and Russia. The cult of Santa Claus (a corruption of his name) comes from the Dutch custom of giving gifts to children on his feast day. Feast day December 6.

Nich·ols /'nikəlz/, Mike (1931–), U.S. director; born in Germany; born *Michael Igor Peschowsky*. He directed *Barefoot in the Park* (1963), *The Odd Couple* (1965), and *Annie* (1977) on Broadway. Movies he directed include *Who's Afraid of Virginia Woolf* (1966), *The Graduate* (Academy Award, 1967), *The Birdcage* (1996), *Primary Colors* (1998), and *What Planet Are You From?* (2000). In 2003 he directed the Emmy Award–winning *Angels in America* on HBO.

Nich·ol·son[1] /'nikəlsən/, Ben (1894–1982), English painter; full name *Benjamin Lauder Nicholson*. A pioneer of British abstract art, he was noted for his painted reliefs with circular and rectangular motifs.

Nich·ol·son[2], Jack (1937–), U.S. actor; full name *John Joseph Nicholson*. He gained wide recognition with his appearance in *Easy Rider* (1969) and won Academy Awards for *One Flew Over the Cuckoo's Nest* (1975), *Terms of Endearment* (1983), and *As Good as It Gets*

Jack Nicholson

(1997). Other movies include *About Schmidt* (2002) and *Something's Gotta Give* (2003).

ni·chrome /ˈnīˌkrōm/ (also **Ni·chrome**) ▶*n. trademark* an alloy of nickel with chromium (10 to 20 percent) and sometimes iron (up to 25 percent), used chiefly in high-temperature applications such as electrical heating elements. ▷early 20th cent.: blend of NICKEL and CHROME.

nick /nik/ ▶*n.* **1** a small cut or notch. **2** (**the nick**) *Brit., informal* prison. ■ a police station. **3** the junction between the floor and sidewalls in a court for playing tennis or squash.
▶*v.* [*trans.*] **1** make a nick or nicks in: *he had nicked himself while shaving.* **2** (**nick someone for**) *informal* cheat someone of (something, typically a sum of money): *he nicked me for fifteen hundred dollars.* **3** *Brit., informal* steal: *he'd had his car nicked by joyriders.* ■ arrest or apprehend (someone): *I got* **nicked for** *burglary.* ▷late Middle English: of unknown origin.
▶PHRASE □ **in the nick of time** only just in time.

nick·el /ˈnikəl/ ▶*n.* **1** a silvery-white metal, the chemical element of atomic number 28. (Symbol: **Ni**)

Nickel occurs naturally in various minerals, and the earth's core is believed to consist largely of metallic iron and nickel. The chief use of nickel is in alloys, esp. with iron, to which it imparts strength and resistance to corrosion, and with copper for coinage.

2 *informal* a five-cent coin; five cents.
▶*v.* (**-eled, -el·ing**; *Brit.* **-elled, -el·ling**) [*trans.*] coat with nickel. ▷mid 18th cent.: shortening of German *Kupfernickel*, the copper-colored ore from which nickel was first obtained, from *Kupfer* 'copper' + *Nickel* 'demon' (with reference to the ore's failure to yield copper).

nick·el-and-dime ▶*v.* [*trans.*] put a financial strain on (someone) by charging small amounts for many minor services: *we don't nickel-and-dime our customers like some vendors that charge extra for every little utility.*
▶*adj.* [*attrib.*] of little importance; petty: *the only games this weekend are nickel-and-dime stuff.* ▷1970s: originally designating a store selling articles costing five or ten cents.

nick·el brass ▶*n.* an alloy of copper, zinc, and a small amount of nickel.

nick·el-cad·mi·um bat·ter·y ▶*n.* a storage battery with a negative electrode made of cadmium, a positive electrode of nickel oxide, and a solution of potassium hydroxide as the electrolyte. Nickel-cadmium batteries have the advantage of an airtight battery container, which prevents the corrosive electrolyte from leaking.

nick·el·o·de·on /ˌnikəˈlōdēən/ ▶*n.* **1** *informal, dated* a jukebox, originally one operated by the insertion of a nickel coin. **2** *historical* a movie theater with an admission fee of one nickel. ▷early 20th cent.: from NICKEL in the sense 'five-cent coin' + a shortened form of MELODEON.

nick·el sil·ver ▶*n.* another term for GERMAN SILVER.

nick·el steel ▶*n.* a type of stainless steel containing chromium and nickel.

nick·er[1] /ˈnikər/ ▶*v.* [*intrans.*] (of a horse) give a soft, low whinny.
▶*n.* a sound of this kind. ▷late 16th cent.: imitative.

nick·er[2] ▶*n.* (*pl.* same) *Brit., informal* a pound sterling. ▷early 20th cent.: of unknown origin.

Nick·laus /ˈnikləs/, Jack William (1940–), U.S. golfer. He won more than eighty tournaments during his professional career, including the Masters (1963, 1965, 1966, 1972, 1975, 1986), the PGA (1963, 1971, 1973, 1975, 1980), the U.S. Open (1962, 1967, 1972, 1980), and the British Open (1966, 1970, 1978).

nick·nack /ˈnikˌnak/ (also **nick-nack**) ▶*n.* variant spelling of KNICKKNACK.

nick·name /ˈnikˌnām/ ▶*n.* a familiar or humorous name given to a person or thing instead of or as well as the real name.
▶*v.* [*trans.*] give a nickname to; call by a nickname: *his fraternity brothers nicknamed him "The Bird" because of his skydiving skills.* ▷late Middle English: from *an ekename* (*eke* meaning 'addition': see EKE[2]), misinterpreted, by wrong division, as *a neke name.*

Nic·o·bar·ese /ˌnikəbäˈrēz; -ˈrēs/ ▶*n.* (*pl.* same) **1** a native or inhabitant of the Nicobar Islands. **2** an ancient language spoken in the Nicobar Islands, distantly related to the Mon-Khmer and Munda families.
▶*adj.* of or relating to the Nicobar Islands, their inhabitants, or their language.

Nic·o·bar Is·lands /ˈnikəˌbär/ see ANDAMAN AND NICOBAR ISLANDS.

Ni·çois /nēˈswä/ ▶*n.* (*fem.* **Ni·çoise** /nēˈswäz/) a native or inhabitant of the city of Nice, France.
▶*adj.* of, relating to, or characteristic of Nice or its inhabitants: *the Niçois dialect.* ■ [*postpositive*] denoting food that is characteristic of Nice or the surrounding region, typically garnished with tomatoes, capers, and anchovies: *salade Niçoise.* ▷French.

Ni·col·let /ˌnikəˈlet/, Joseph Nicolas (1786–1843), U.S. explorer; born in France. With John Frémont as his assistant, he led a government surveying expedition that mapped the region between the upper Mississippi and Missouri rivers 1838–39.

Nic·ol prism /ˈnikəl/ ▶*n.* a device for producing plane-polarized light, consisting of two pieces of optically clear calcite or Iceland spar cemented together with Canada balsam in the shape of a prism. ▷mid 19th cent.: named after William *Nicol* (died 1851), the Scottish physicist who invented it.

Nic·o·sia /ˌnikəˈsēə/ the capital of Cyprus; pop. 186,000. Since 1974 it has been divided into Greek and Turkish sectors.

ni·co·ti·a·na /niˌkōshēˈänə; -ˈanə/ ▶*n.* an ornamental plant related to tobacco, with tubular flowers that are particularly fragrant at night. Also called TOBACCO PLANT. • Genus *Nicotiana*, family Solanaceae: several species, in particular *N. alata.* ▷from modern Latin *nicotiana (herba)* 'tobacco (plant),' named after Jean *Nicot*, a 16th-cent. French diplomat who introduced tobacco to France in 1560.

nic·o·tin·a·mide /ˌnikəˈtinəˌmīd; -ˈtēn-/ ▶*n. Biochemistry* a compound that is the form in which nicotinic acid often occurs in nature. • The amide of nicotinic acid; chem. formula: $(C_5H_4N)CONH_2$.

nic·o·tin·a·mide ad·e·nine di·nu·cle·o·tide /ˈadn-in dīˈn(y)o͞oklēəˌtīd/ ▶*n.* see **NAD**.

nic·o·tine /ˈnikəˌtēn/ ▶*n.* a toxic colorless or yellowish oily liquid that is the chief active constituent of tobacco. It acts as a stimulant in small doses, but in larger amounts blocks the action of autonomic nerve and skeletal muscle cells. Nicotine is also used in insecticides. • An alkaloid; chem. formula: $C_{10}H_{14}N_2$. ▷early 19th cent.: from French, from NICOTIANA + -INE[4].

nic·o·tine patch ▶*n.* a patch impregnated with nicotine and worn on the skin by a person trying to give up smoking. Nicotine is gradually absorbed into the bloodstream, helping reduce the craving for cigarettes.

nic·o·tin·ic ac·id /ˌnikəˈtinik; -ˈtēnik/ ▶*n. Biochemistry* a vitamin of the B complex that is widely distributed in foods such as milk, wheat germ, and meat, and can be synthesized in the body from tryptophan. Its deficiency causes pellagra. • Alternative name: **3-pyridinecarboxylic acid**; chem. formula: $(C_5H_4N)COOH$. —**nic·o·tin·ate** /-ˈtēˌnāt/ *n.*

nic·tate /ˈnikˌtāt/ (also **nic·ti·tate** /ˈniktiˌtāt/) ▶*v.* [*intrans.*] *technical* (esp. of the eyelid) blink. ▷late 17th cent.: from Latin *nictat-* 'blinked,' from the verb *nictare.* The variant *nictitate* is from the medieval Latin frequentative of *nictare.*

nic·ta·tion /nikˈtāshən/ ▶*n. technical* the action or process of blinking. ▷late 18th cent.: from Latin *nictatio(n-)*, from the verb *nictare* 'to blink.'

nic·ti·tat·ing mem·brane /ˈniktiˌtātiNG/ ▶*n. Zoology* a whitish or translucent membrane that forms an inner eyelid in birds, reptiles, and some mammals. It can be drawn across the eye to protect it from dust and keep it moist. Also called THIRD EYELID. ▷early 18th cent.: *nictitating* based on medieval Latin *nictitat-* 'blinked,' frequentative of *nictare.*

ni·da·tion /nīˈdāshən/ ▶*n.* another term for IMPLANTATION. ▷late 19th cent.: from Latin *nidus* 'nest' + -ATION.

nide /nīd/ ▶*n. archaic* a brood or nest of pheasants. ▷late 17th cent.: from French *nid* or Latin *nidus* 'nest.'

ni·dic·o·lous /nīˈdikələs/ ▶*adj.* another term for ALTRICIAL. ▷early 20th cent.: from Latin *nidus* 'nest' + *-colus* 'inhabiting' (from the verb *colere* 'live in, cultivate').

nid·i·fi·ca·tion /ˌnidəfiˈkāshən/ ▶*n. Zoology* nest-building. ▷mid 17th cent.: from Latin *nidificat-* 'made into a nest' (from the verb *nidificare*, from *nidus* 'nest') + -ATION.

ni·dif·u·gous /nīˈdifyəgəs/ ▶*adj.* another term for PRECOCIAL. ▷early 20th cent.: from Latin *nidus* 'nest' + *fugere* 'flee' + -OUS.

ni·dus /ˈnīdəs/ ▶*n.* (*pl.* **-di** /-ˌdī/ or **-dus·es**) a place in which something is formed or deposited; a site of origin. ■ *Medicine* a place in which bacteria have multiplied or may multiply; a focus of infection. ▷early 18th cent. (in the medical sense 'focus of infection'): from Latin, literally 'nest.'

Nie·buhr /ˈnēˌbo͝or/, Reinhold (1892–1971), U.S. theologian and political activist. Professor of Christian ethics at Union Theological Seminary 1928–60, he wrote *Moral Man and Immoral Society* (1932) and *The Irony of American History* (1952).

niece /nēs/ ▶*n.* a daughter of one's brother or sister, or of one's brother-in-law or sister-in-law. ▷Middle English: from Old French, based on Latin *neptis* 'granddaughter,' feminine of *nepos* 'nephew, grandson' (see NEPHEW), from an Indo-European root shared by Dutch *nicht*, German *Nichte.*

Nie·der·sach·sen /ˈnēdərˌsäksən/ German name for LOWER SAXONY.

ni·el·lo /nēˈelō/ ▶*n.* a black compound of sulfur with silver, lead, or copper, used for filling in engraved designs in silver or other metals. ■ objects decorated with this. ▷early 19th cent.: from Italian, from Latin *nigellus*, diminutive of *niger* 'black.' —**ni·el·loed** *adj.*

niels·bohr·i·um /ˌnēlzˈbôrēəm/ ▶*n.* a name proposed by the American Chemical Society for the chemical element of atomic number 107, now called **bohrium**. ▷modern Latin, from the name of the scientist *Niels Bohr* (see BOHR). The term was originally proposed (*c.*1971) by Soviet scientists for element 105 (hahnium).

Niel·sen /ˈnēlsən/, Carl August (1865–1931), Danish composer. He is best known for his six symphonies (1890–1925).

Nie·mey·er /ˈnēˌmīər/, Oscar (1907–), Brazilian architect. An early exponent of modernist architecture in Latin America, he designed the main public buildings of Brasilia, 1950–60.

ni·en·te /nēˈentā/ ▶*adv.* & *adj. Music* (esp. as a direction) with a soft sound or tone gradually fading to nothing. ▷Italian, literally 'nothing.'

Nier·stein·er /ˈni(ə)rˌstīnər; -ˌSHtīn-/ ▶*n.* a white Rhine wine produced in the region around Nierstein, a town in Germany.

Nietz·sche /ˈnēCHə/, Friedrich Wilhelm (1844–1900), German philosopher. He is known for repudiating Christianity's compassion for the weak, exalting the "will to power," and formulating the idea of the *Übermensch* (superman), who can rise above the restrictions of ordinary morality. —**Nietz·sche·an** /-CHēən/ *adj.* & *n.* —**Nietz·sche·an·ism** /ˈnēCHēəˌnizəm/ *n.*

ni·fed·i·pine /nīˈfedəpēn/ ▶*n. Medicine* a synthetic compound that acts as a calcium antagonist and is used as a coronary vasodilator in the treatment of cardiac and circulatory disorders. ▷1970s: from *ni(tro-)* + *fe* (alteration of PHENYL) + DI-[1] + *p(yrid)ine*, elements of the systematic name.

Ni·fl·heim /ˈnivəlˌhām/ *Scandinavian Mythology* an underworld of eternal cold, darkness, and mist inhabited by those who died of old age or illness. ▷from Old Norse *Niflheimr*, literally 'world of mist.'

nif·ty /ˈniftē/ ▶*adj.* (**-ti·er, -ti·est**) *informal* particularly good, skillful, or effective: *nifty footwork.* ■ fashionable; stylish: *a nifty black shirt.* ▷mid 19th cent.: of unknown origin. —**nif·ti·ly** /-təlē/ *adv.* —**nif·ti·ness** *n.*

ni·gel·la /nīˈjelə/ ▶*n.* a plant of a genus that includes love-in-a-mist. • Genus *Nigella*, family Ranunculaceae. ▷modern Latin, feminine of Latin *nigellus*, diminutive of *niger* 'black.'

Ni·ger /ˈnījər/ **1** a river in northwestern Africa that rises on the northeastern border of Sierra Leone and flows northeast and then southeast in a great arc for 2,550 miles (4,100 km) to Mali and through western Niger and Nigeria before turning south into the Gulf of Guinea. **2** a landlocked country in West Africa, on the southern edge of the Sahara Desert; pop. 11,360,000; capital, Niamey;

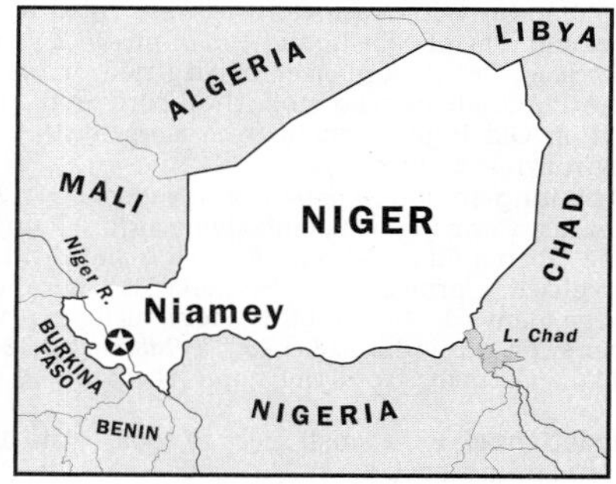

languages, French (official), Hausa, and other West African languages.

Part of French West Africa from 1922, it became an autonomous republic within the French Community in 1958 and fully independent in 1960. Niger's first free elections were held in 1993.

Ni·ger–Con·go ▸*adj.* denoting or belonging to a large phylum of languages in Africa, named after the rivers Niger and Congo. It comprises most of the languages spoken by the indigenous peoples of Africa south of the Sahara and includes the Bantu, Mande, Gur, and Kwa families.

Ni·ge·ri·a /nīˈji(ə)rēə/ a country on the coast of West Africa, bordered by the Niger River on the north; pop. 137,253,000; capital, Abuja; languages, English (official), Hausa, Ibo, Yoruba, and others. —**Ni·ge·ri·an** *adj.* & *n.*

The site of highly developed kingdoms in the Middle Ages, the area came under British influence during the 19th century and was consolidated into a single colony in 1914. Independence came in 1960, and it became a federal republic in 1963, while remaining a member of the Commonwealth of Nations. Oil was discovered in the 1960s and 1970s; since then, Nigeria has emerged as one of the world's major exporters.

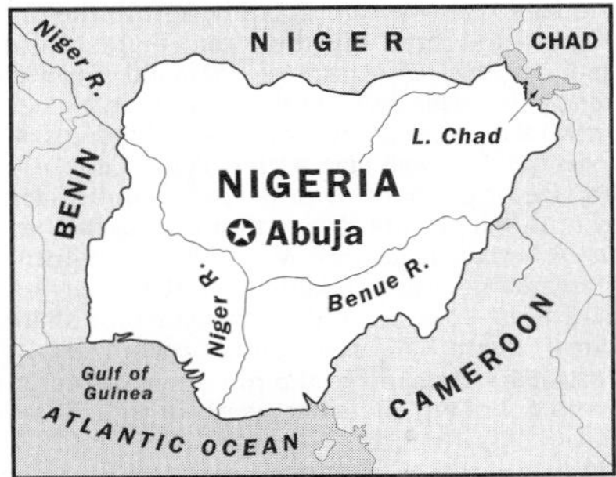

Ni·ge·ri·an let·ter ▸*n.* an e-mail whose sender promises to greatly enrich the recipient in exchange for personal information, such as bank account details. ▷early 2000s: from the fact that many such e-mails originally came from Nigerians.

nig·gard /ˈnigərd/ ▸*n. often offensive* a stingy or ungenerous person.
▸*adj. often offensive* archaic term for **NIGGARDLY**. ▷late Middle English: alteration of earlier *nigon*.

USAGE This word, along with its adverbial form **niggardly**, should be used with caution. Owing to the sound similarity to the highly inflammatory racial epithet **nigger**, these words can cause unnecessary confusion and unintentional offense.

nig·gard·ly /ˈnigərdlē/ ▸*adj. often offensive* not generous; stingy: *serving out the rations with a niggardly hand.* ■ meager; scanty: *their share is a niggardly 2.7 percent.*
▸*adv. archaic, often offensive* in a stingy or meager manner. —**nig·gard·li·ness** *n.*

USAGE See **usage** at **NIGGARD**.

nig·ger /ˈnigər/ ▸*n. offensive* a contemptuous term for a black or dark-skinned person. ▷late 17th cent. (as an adjective): from earlier *neger*, from French *nègre*, from Spanish *negro* 'black' (see **NEGRO**).

USAGE The word **nigger** was used as an adjective denoting a black person as early as the 17th century and has long had strong offensive connotations. Today it remains one of the most racially offensive words in the language. Also referred to as 'the n-word,' **nigger** is sometimes used by black people in reference to other black people in a jocular or disparaging manner, or some variant in between (in somewhat the same way that *queer* has been adopted by some gay and lesbian people as a term of self-reference, acceptable only when used by those within the community).

nig·gle /ˈnigəl/ ▸*v.* [*intrans.*] cause slight but persistent annoyance, discomfort, or anxiety: *a suspicion niggled at the back of her mind* | [as *adj.*] (**niggling**) *niggling aches and pains.* ■ [*trans.*] find fault with (someone) in a petty way: *colleagues say he loved to niggle and criticize people.*
▸*n.* a trifling complaint, dispute, or criticism. ▷early 17th cent. (in the sense 'do something in a fiddling or ineffectual way'): apparently of Scandinavian origin; compare with Norwegian *nigla*. Current senses date from the late 18th cent. —**nig·gling·ly** *adv.*

nigh /nī/ ▸*adv., prep.,* & *adj.* near: [as *adj.*] *departure time was drawing nigh* | [as *adv.*] *they drew nigh unto the city.* ■ almost: [as *adv.*] *a car weighing* **nigh on** *two tons* | *recovery will be* **well nigh** *impossible.* ▷Old English *nēh*, *nēah*, of Germanic origin; related to Dutch *na*, German *nah*. Compare with **NEAR**.

night /nīt/ ▸*n.* **1** the period of darkness in each twenty-four hours; the time from sunset to sunrise: *a moonless night* | *the office door is always locked* **at night**. ■ this as the interval between two days: *a two-bedroom cabin costs $90 per night* | *somebody put him up for the night.* ■ the darkness of night: *a line of watch-fires stretched away into the night.* ■ *poetic/literary* nightfall. **2** the period of time between afternoon and bedtime; an evening: *he was not allowed to go out on weekday nights.* ■ [with *adj.*] an evening appointed for some activity, or spent or regarded in a certain way: *wasn't it a great* **night out**?
▸*exclam. informal* short for **GOOD NIGHT**. ▷Old English *neaht*, *niht*, of Germanic origin; related to Dutch *nacht* and German *Nacht*, from an Indo-European root shared by Latin *nox* and Greek *nux*. —**night·less** *adj.*
▸***PHRASE*** □ **night and day** all the time; constantly: *she studied night and day.*

night ad·der ▸*n.* a venomous nocturnal African viper. • Genus *Causus*, family Viperidae: several species, in particular the gray and black *C. rhombeatus*, common in southern Africa.

night·bird /ˈnīt,bərd/ ▸*n.* another term for **NIGHT OWL**.

night blind·ness ▸*n.* less technical term for **NYCTALOPIA**.

night-bloom·ing ce·re·us ▸*n.* a tropical climbing cactus with aerial roots and heavily scented flowers that open only at night and are typically pollinated by bats. • Genera *Hylocereus* and *Selenicereus*, family Cactaceae: several species, in particular *H. undatus*.

night·cap /ˈnīt,kap/ ▸*n.* **1** *historical* a cap worn in bed. **2** an alcoholic or hot drink taken at the end of the day or before going to bed. **3** *Baseball* the second game of a doubleheader: *he pitched a four-hit shutout in the nightcap.*

night·clothes /ˈnīt,klō(T͟H)z/ ▸*plural n.* clothes worn to bed.

night·club /ˈnīt,kləb/ ▸*n.* an establishment for nighttime entertainment, typically serving drinks and offering music, dancing, etc. —**night·club·ber** *n.* —**night·club·bing** *n.*

night court ▸*n.* a criminal court that holds sessions at night for granting bail and quickly disposing of charges.

night crawl·er (also **night·crawl·er**) ▸*n.* an earthworm, in particular one that comes to the surface at night and is collected for use as fishing bait. ■ *informal* a person who is socially active at night: *the bar and nightclub are hot items with chic night crawlers.*

night·dress /ˈnīt,dres/ ▸*n.* another term for **NIGHTGOWN**.

night·fall /ˈnīt,fôl/ ▸*n.* the onset of night; dusk.

night·gown /ˈnīt,goun/ ▸*n.* **1** a light, loose garment worn by a woman or child in bed. **2** *historical* a dressing gown.

night·hawk /ˈnīt,hôk/ ▸*n.* **1** an American nightjar with sharply pointed wings. • Family Caprimulgidae: four genera and several species, in particular the **common nighthawk** (*Chordeiles minor*). **2** another term for **NIGHT OWL**.

night her·on ▸*n.* a small short-necked heron that is active mainly at night. • Genus *Nycticorax*, family Ardeidae: several species.

night·ie /ˈnītē/ ▸*n. informal* a nightgown.

Night·in·gale /ˈnītn,gāl; ˈnītiNG-/, Florence (1820–1910), English nurse and medical reformer. In 1854, during the Crimean War, she improved sanitation and medical procedures at the army hospital at Scutari, achieving a dramatic reduction in the mortality rate. She became known as the "Lady of the Lamp" for her nightly rounds.

night·in·gale /ˈnītn,gāl; ˈnītiNG-/ ▸*n.* a small European thrush with drab brownish plumage, noted for the rich melodious song of the male, heard esp. at night in breeding season. • *Luscinia megarhynchos*, subfamily Turdinae, family Muscicapidae. ▷Old English *nihtegala*, of Germanic origin; related to Dutch *nachtegaal* and German *Nachtigall*, from the base of **NIGHT** and a base meaning 'sing.'

night·jar /ˈnīt,jär/ ▸*n.* a nocturnal insectivorous bird with gray-brown camouflaged plumage, large eyes and gape, and a distinctive call. Also called **GOATSUCKER**. • Family Caprimulgidae (the **nightjar family**): several genera, esp. *Caprimulgus*, and many species, including the **European nightjar** (*C. europaeus*), which has a chirring call. The nightjar family also includes the nighthawks, pauraques, poorwills, whippoorwills, and chuck-will's-widow.

Night Jour·ney (in Muslim tradition) the journey through the air made by Muhammad, guided by the archangel Gabriel. They flew first to Jerusalem, where Muhammad prayed with earlier prophets, including Abraham, Moses, and Jesus, before entering the presence of Allah in heaven.

night·life /ˈnīt,līf/ ▸*n.* social activities or entertainment available at night in a town or city.

night·light /ˈnīt ,līt/ (also **night-light** or **night light**) ▸*n.* a small lamp, typically attached directly to an electrical outlet, providing a dim light during the night.

night liz·ard ▸*n.* a small dull-colored nocturnal lizard with large scales or bony plates on the head, occurring from the southwestern U.S. to Central America. • Family Xantusiidae: several genera and species, including the **desert night lizard** (*Xantusia vigilis*).

night·long /ˈnīt,lôNG/ ▸*adj.* lasting throughout the night: *a nightlong blizzard.*

night·ly /ˈnītlē/ ▸*adj.* **1** happening or done every night: *his prime-time, nightly TV talk show.* **2** happening, done, or existing in the night.
▸*adv.* every night: *the hotel features live music nightly.*

night·mare /ˈnīt,me(ə)r/ ▸*n.* a frightening or unpleasant dream: *I had nightmares after watching the horror movie.* ■ a terrifying or very unpleasant experience or prospect: *the nightmare of racial hatred* | *an astronaut's* **worst nightmare** *is getting detached during an extravehicle activity.* ■ a person, thing, or situation that is very difficult to deal with: *buying wine can be a nightmare if you don't know enough about it.* ▷Middle English (denoting a female evil spirit thought to lie upon and suffocate sleepers): from **NIGHT** + Old English *mære* 'incubus.' —**night·mar·ish** *adj.* —**night·mar·ish·ly** *adv.*

night mon·key ▸*n.* another term for **DOUROUCOULI**.

night owl ▸*n. informal* a person who is habitually active or wakeful at night.

night·rid·er /ˈnīt,rīdər/ ▸*n.* a member of a secret band of mounted men who committed nocturnal acts of violence and intimidation against blacks in the southern U.S. during Reconstruction.

nights /nīts/ ▸*adv. informal* during the night; at night: *investments that won't keep us awake nights with worry.*

night school ▸*n.* an institution providing evening classes for those working during the day.

night·shade /ˈnīt,SHād/ ▸*n.* a plant related to the potato, typically having poisonous black or red berries. Several kinds of nightshade have been used in the production of herbal medicines. • *Solanum* and other genera, family Solanaceae (the **nightshade family**): several species, including the European **woody nightshade** (*S. dulcamara*), a climber with purple flowers and red berries. The nightshade family includes many commercially important plants (potato, tomato, capsicum peppers, tobacco) as well as a number of highly poisonous ones (henbane, jimson weed). See also **DEADLY NIGHTSHADE**. ▷Old English *nihtscada*, apparently from **NIGHT** + **SHADE**, probably with reference to the dark color and poisonous properties of the berries. Compare with German *Nachtschatten*.

night shift ▸*n.* the period of time scheduled for work at night, as in a factory or other institution. ■ the group of people working during this period.

night·shirt /ˈnīt,SHərt/ ▸*n.* a long, loose shirt worn to bed.

night·side /ˈnīt,sīd/ ▸*n.* **1** *Astronomy* the side of a planet or moon that is facing away from the sun and is therefore in darkness. **2** the world at night; activities that take place during the night: *nightside was the province of the professional criminals.*

nightingale

Pronunciation Key ə *ago*; ər *over*; ˈə or ˌə *up*; ˈər or ˌər *fur*; a *hat*; ā *rate*; ä *car*; CH *chew*; e *let*; ē *see*; e(ə)r *air*; i *fit*; ī *by*; i(ə)r *ear*; NG *sing*; ō *go*; ô *for*; oi *boy*; o͝o *good*; o͞o *goo*; ou *out*; SH *she*; TH *thin*; T͟H *then*; (h)w *why*; ZH *vision*

N

night soil ▸*n.* human excrement collected at night from buckets, cesspools, and outhouses and sometimes used as manure.

night·spot /ˈnīt,spät/ ▸*n. informal* a nightclub.

night·stand /ˈnīt,stand/ (also **night table**) ▸*n.* a small low bedside table, typically having drawers.

night·stick /ˈnīt,stik/ ▸*n.* a police officer's club or billy.

night ter·rors ▸*plural n.* feelings of great fear experienced on suddenly waking in the night.

night·time /ˈnīt,tīm/ ▸*n.* the time between evening and morning; the time of darkness: *slipping away over the river in the nighttime* | [as *adj.*] *the government imposed a nighttime curfew.*

night vi·sion ▸*n.* the faculty of seeing in very low light, esp. after the eyes have become adapted.
▸*adj.* (**night-vi·sion**) denoting devices that enhance nighttime vision: *night-vision goggles.*

night watch·man ▸*n.* (*pl.* **-men**) a person whose job is to guard a building at night.

night·wear /ˈnīt,we(ə)r/ ▸*n.* clothing suitable for wearing to bed.

ni·gi·ri·zu·shi /ˈnigərē ˈzo͞osHē/ ▸*n.* sushi consisting of a small ball of rice, smeared with wasabi sauce and topped with raw fish or other seafood. ▷1990s: Japanese, from *nigiri-* (combining form of *nigiru*, 'clasp, clench, roll in the hands') + *zushi* 'sushi.'

ni·gres·cent /nīˈgresənt/ ▸*adj. rare* blackish. ▷mid 18th cent.: from Latin *nigrescent-* 'growing black,' from the verb *nigrescere*, from *niger, nigr-* 'black.' **—ni·gres·cence** *n.*

nig·ri·tude /ˈnigri,t(y)o͞od/ ▸*n. rare* blackness. ▷mid 17th cent.: from Latin *nigritudo* 'blackness,' from *niger, nigr-* 'black.'

NIH ▸*abbr.* National Institutes of Health.

ni·hil·ism /ˈnīə,lizəm; ˈnē-/ ▸*n.* the rejection of all religious and moral principles, often in the belief that life is meaningless. ■ *Philosophy* extreme skepticism maintaining that nothing in the world has a real existence. ■ *historical* the doctrine of an extreme Russian revolutionary party *c.*1900, which found nothing to approve of in the established social order. ▷early 19th cent.: from Latin *nihil* 'nothing' + **-ISM**. **—ni·hil·ist** *n.* **—ni·hil·is·tic** /,nīəˈlistik; ,nēə-/ *adj.*

ni·hil·i·ty /nīˈhilitē; ˈnē-/ ▸*n. rare* nonexistence; nothingness. ▷late 17th cent.: from medieval Latin *nihilitas*, from Latin *nihil* 'nothing.'

ni·hil ob·stat /ˈnīhil ˈäbstat/ ▸*n.* (in the Roman Catholic Church) a certification by an official censor that a book is not objectionable on doctrinal or moral grounds. ▷Latin, literally 'nothing hinders.'

Ni·i·ga·ta /nē-ēˈgätə/ an industrial port in central Japan, on the northwestern coast of Honshu; pop. 486,000.

Ni·i·hau /ˈnē-ē,hou/ an island in Hawaii, southwest of Kauai. Its residents are all native Hawaiians.

Ni·jin·sky /nəˈzHinskē; -ˈjin-; nyi-/, Vaslav (Fomich) (1890–1950), Russian ballet dancer and choreographer. The leading dancer with Diaghilev's Ballets Russes from 1909, he also choreographed Debussy's *L'Après-midi d'un faune* (1912) and Stravinsky's *The Rite of Spring* (1913).

Nij·me·gen /ˈnī,māgən/ an industrial town in the eastern Netherlands, south of Arnhem; pop. 146,000.

-nik ▸*suffix* (forming nouns) denoting a person associated with a specified thing or quality: *beatnik* | *refusenik.* ▷from Russian (on the pattern of *(sput)nik*) and Yiddish.

ni·kah /niˈkä/ ▸*n.* a Muslim marriage ceremony. ▷Urdu and Arabic.

Ni·ke /ˈnīkē/ *Greek Mythology* the goddess of victory. ▷Greek, literally 'victory.'

Nik·kei in·dex /ˈnēkā/ a figure indicating the relative price of representative shares on the Tokyo Stock Exchange. Also called **Nikkei average**. ▷1970s: *Nikkei*, abbreviation of *Ni(hon) Kei(zai Shimbun)* 'Japanese Economic Journal.'

Ni·ko·la·ev /,nēkəˈlīəf/ Russian name for **MYKOLAYIV**.

nil /nil/ ▸*n.* zero, esp. as a score in certain games: *they beat us three-nil.*
▸*adj.* nonexistent: *his chances for survival were slim, almost nil.* ▷mid 19th cent.: from Latin, contraction of *nihil* 'nothing.'

nil de·spe·ran·dum /ˈnil ,despəˈrändəm/ ▸*exclam.* do not despair; never despair. ▷from Latin *nil desperandum Teucro duce* 'no need to despair with Teucer as your leader,' from Horace's *Odes* 1.vii.27.

Nile /nīl/ a river in eastern Africa, the longest river in the world, that rises in east central Africa near Lake Victoria and flows 4,160 miles (6,695 km) north through Uganda, Sudan, and Egypt to empty through a large delta into the Mediterranean Sea. See also **BLUE NILE**, **ALBERT NILE**, **VICTORIA NILE**, **WHITE NILE**.

Nile blue ▸*n.* a pale greenish blue. ▷late 19th cent.: suggested by French *eau de Nil.*

Nile croc·o·dile ▸*n.* a large crocodile with a long narrow head, native to Africa and Madagascar. • *Crocodilus niloticus*, family Crocodylidae.

Nile green ▸*n.* a pale bluish green.

Nile mon·i·tor ▸*n.* a large heavily built African lizard that has grayish-olive skin with yellow markings and is semiaquatic. • *Varanus niloticus*, family Varanidae.

Nile perch ▸*n.* a large predatory fish found in lakes and rivers in northeastern and central Africa, widely caught for food or sport. • *Lates niloticus*, family Centropomidae.

nil·gai /ˈnilgī/ ▸*n.* a large Indian antelope, the male of which has a blue-gray coat and short horns, and the female a tawny coat and no horns. • *Boselaphus tragocamelus*, family Bovidae. ▷late 18th cent.: from Hindi *nīlgāī*, from *nīl* 'blue' + *gāī* 'cow.'

Nil·gi·ri Hills /ˈnilgərē/ a range of hills in southern India, in western Tamil Nadu. They are a branch of the Western Ghats.

Ni·lom·e·ter /nīˈlämətər/ ▸*n.* a graduated pillar or other vertical surface, serving to indicate the height to which the Nile rises during its annual floods. **—Ni·lo·met·ric** /,nīləˈmetrik/ *adj.*

Ni·lo-Sa·har·an /,nīlō səˈharən; -ˈhär-/ ▸*adj.* denoting or belonging to a phylum of languages that includes the Nilotic family together with certain other languages of northern and eastern Africa.
▸*n.* this phylum of languages.

Ni·lot·ic /nīˈlätik/ ▸*adj.* **1** of or relating to the Nile River or to the Nile region of Africa. **2** denoting or belonging to a subgroup of Nilo-Saharan languages spoken in Egypt, Sudan, Kenya, and Tanzania. The western group includes Luo and Dinka; the eastern group includes Masai and Turkana. ▷via Latin from Greek *Neilōtikos*, from *Neilos* 'Nile.'

nil·po·tent /nilˈpōtnt/ ▸*adj. Mathematics* equal to zero when raised to a positive integral power. ▷late 19th cent.: from **NIL** + Latin *potens, potent-* 'power.'

Nils·son /ˈnēlsən/, (Märta) Birgit (1918–), Swedish opera singer. A soprano, she gained international success in the 1950s, being particularly noted for her interpretation of Wagnerian roles.

nim /nim/ ▸*n.* a game in which two players alternately take one or more objects from one of a number of heaps, each trying to take, or to compel the other to take, the last remaining object. ▷early 20th cent.: apparently from archaic *nim* 'to take' or from German *nimm!* 'take!,' imperative of *nehmen.*

nim·ble /ˈnimbəl/ ▸*adj.* (**-bler**, **-blest**) quick and light in movement or action; agile: *with a deft motion of her nimble fingers.* ■ (of the mind) quick to comprehend: *she is well-read and intellectually nimble.* ▷Old English *næmel* 'quick to seize or comprehend,' related to *niman* 'take,' of Germanic origin. The *-b-* was added for ease of pronunciation. **—nim·ble·ness** *n.* **—nim·bly** /-blē/ *adv.*

nim·bo·stra·tus /,nimbōˈstratəs; -ˈstrā-/ ▸*n.* a type of cloud forming a thick uniform gray layer at low altitude, from which rain or snow often falls (without any lightning or thunder). ▷late 19th cent.: modern Latin, from **NIMBUS** + **STRATUS**.

nim·bus /ˈnimbəs/ ▸*n.* (*pl.* **-bi** /-,bī/ or **-bus·es**) **1** a luminous cloud or a halo surrounding a supernatural being or a saint. ■ a light, aura, color, etc., that surrounds someone or something. **2** a large gray rain cloud: [as *adj.*] *nimbus clouds.* ▷early 17th cent.: from Latin, literally 'cloud, aureole.'

NIMBY /ˈnimbē/ (also **Nimby**) ▸*n.* (*pl.* **NIMBYs**) acronym for *not in my backyard*, referring to those who object to the siting of something perceived as unpleasant or potentially dangerous in their own neighborhood, such as a landfill or hazardous waste facility. ▷1980s **—Nim·by·ism** /-izəm/ *n.*

Nîmes /nēm/ a city in southern France; pop. 134,000. It is noted for its well-preserved Roman remains.

nim·i·ny-pim·i·ny /ˈnimənē ˈpimənē/ ▸*adj.* affectedly prim or refined: *she had a niminy-piminy ladylike air.* ▷late 18th cent.: fanciful coinage; compare with **NAMBY-PAMBY**.

Nimitz /ˈnimits/, Chester William (1885–1966), U.S. naval officer. Chief of the Bureau of Navigation (1939–41), he became commander in chief of the Pacific Fleet after the Japanese attack on Pearl Harbor in 1941. A noted strategist, he introduced the practice of island hopping, which contributed to many victories. Nimitz accepted the Japanese surrender for the U.S. in 1945 aboard his flagship, the U.S.S. *Missouri*, and after World War II served as chief of naval operations 1945–47.

nim·rod /ˈnimräd/ ▸*n. chiefly humorous* a skillful hunter. ▷late 16th cent.: from Hebrew *Nimrōd*, the name of the great-grandson of Noah, reputed for his skill as a hunter (see Gen. 10:8-9).

Nim·rud /ˈnim,ro͞od/ modern name of an ancient Mesopotamian city on the east bank of the Tigris south of Nineveh, near the modern city of Mosul. It was the capital of Assyria 879–722 BC. The city was known in biblical times as Calah (Gen. 10:11); the modern name arose through association in Islamic mythology with the biblical figure of Nimrod.

Nin /nin; nēn/, Anaïs (1903–77), U.S. writer. She published her first novel *House of Incest* in 1936 and went on to produce collections of short stories, essays, diaries, and erotica. She is especially noted for her ceaselessly introspective *Diaries* (1966–81).

Ni·ña, La ▸see **LA NIÑA**.

nin·com·poop /ˈninkəm,po͞op; ˈniNG-/ ▸*n.* a foolish or stupid person. ▷late 17th cent.: perhaps from the given name *Nicholas* or from *Nicodemus* (by association with the Pharisee of this name, and his naive questioning of Jesus Christ; compare with French *nicodème* 'simpleton').

nine /nīn/ ▸*cardinal number* equivalent to the product of three and three; one more than eight, or one less than ten; 9: *all nine justices agreed that the law could not stand* | *nine of the twelve members.* (Roman numeral: **ix** or **IX**.) ■ a group or unit of nine individuals. ■ nine years old: *I was only nine.* ■ nine o'clock: *it's ten to nine.* ■ a size of garment or other merchandise denoted by nine. ■ a playing card with nine pips. ■ (**the Nine**) *Greek Mythology* the nine Muses. ▷Old English *nigon*, of Germanic origin; related to Dutch *negen* and German *neun*, from an Indo-European root shared by Sanskrit *nava*, Latin *novem*, and Greek *ennea*.
▸*PHRASES* □ **dressed to the nines** see **DRESS**. □ **nine times out of ten** on nearly every occasion; almost always.

9/11 /ˈnīn iˈlevən/ (also **September 11th**) *n.* September 11, 2001. On this date, two hijacked commercial airliners were flown into the World Trade Center in lower Manhattan. A third hijacked airliner was crashed into the Pentagon, and a fourth went down in a field in Pennsylvania: *the shroud of 9/11 will be draped over the nation's heart forever.*

nine·fold /ˈnīn,fōld/ ▸*adj.* nine times as great or as numerous: *a ninefold increase in the amount of traffic.* ■ having nine parts or elements.
▸*adv.* by nine times; to nine times the number or amount: *consumption increased ninefold.*

nine·pins /ˈnīn,pinz/ ▸*plural n.* [usu. treated as *sing.*] a British game similar to bowling, using nine wooden pins and played in an alley; the traditional form of skittles. ■ [treated as *pl.*] the pins used in this game.
▸*PHRASE* □ **go down** (or **drop** or **fall**) **like ninepins** *Brit.* succumb in large numbers or without much opposition.

nine·teen /nīnˈtēn; ˈnīn,tēn/ ▸*cardinal number* one more than eighteen; nine more than ten; 19: *nineteen of the interviewees had never worked.* (Roman numeral: **xix** or **XIX**.) ■ nineteen years old: *she married at nineteen.* ▷Old English *nigontȳne*. **—nine·teenth** /nīnˈtēnTH; ˈnīn,tēnTH/ *ordinal number.*

nine·teenth hole ▸*n. informal* the bar in a golf clubhouse, as reached after a standard round of eighteen holes.

nine-to-five ▸*adj.* used in reference to typical hours of work in an office, often to express an idea of routine or predictability: *a nine-to-five job.*
▸*n.* an occupation involving such hours. **—nine-to-fiv·er** *n.*

nine·ty /ˈnīntē/ ▸*n.* (*pl.* **-ties**) equivalent to the product of nine and ten; ten less than one hundred; 90: *ninety acres of soybeans will be harvested.* (Roman numeral: **xc** or **XC**.) ■ (**nineties**) the numbers from 90 to 99, esp. the years of a century or of a person's life: *art in the nineties.* ■ ninety years old: *she is nearly ninety.* ■ ninety miles an hour: *we passed the junction doing about ninety.* ▷Old English *nigontig*. **—nine·ti·eth** /-tēiTH/ *ordinal number.* **—nine·ty·fold** /-,fōld/ *adj.* & *adv.*

Nin·e·veh /ˈninəvə/ an ancient city located on the eastern bank of the Tigris River, opposite the modern city of Mosul. It was the oldest city of the ancient Assyrian empire and its capital until it was destroyed by a coalition of Babylonians and Medes in 612 BC.

Ning·xia /ˈniNGˈSHä/ (also **Ning·sia**) an autonomous region of north central China; capital, Yinchuan.

nin·hy·drin /ninˈhīdrin/ ▸*n. Chemistry* a synthetic crystalline compound that forms deeply colored products with primary amines and is used in analytical tests for amino acids. • A ketone derivative of indene; chem. formula: $C_9H_6O_4$. ▷early 20th cent.: from *nin-* (of unknown origin) + HYDRO- + -IN[1].

nin·ja /ˈninjə/ ▸*n.* a person skilled in ninjutsu. ▷Japanese, literally 'spy.'

nin·jut·su /ninˈjōōtsōō/ ▸*n.* the traditional Japanese technique of espionage, characterized by stealthy movement and camouflage. It was developed in feudal times for military purposes and subsequently used in the training of samurai. ▷Japanese, from *nin* 'stealth' + *jutsu* 'art, science.'

nin·ny /ˈninē/ ▸*n.* (*pl.* **-nies**) *informal* a foolish person. ▷late 16th cent.: perhaps from INNOCENT.

Ni·ño, El ▸see EL NIÑO.

ni·non /ˈnēnän/ ▸*n.* a lightweight sheer or silk fabric used for curtains and women's garments. ▷early 20th cent.: from French.

ninth /ninTH/ ▸*ordinal number* constituting number nine in a sequence; 9th: *the ninth century | the ninth of March.* ■ (**a ninth/one ninth**) each of nine equal parts into which something is or may be divided. ■ the ninth finisher or position in a race or competition: *he came in ninth.* ■ the ninth and final inning of a regulation baseball game: *he was rocked for five runs in the ninth.* ■ the ninth grade of a school. ■ *Music* an interval spanning nine consecutive notes in a diatonic scale. ■ *Music* the note that is higher by this interval than the tonic of a diatonic scale or root of a chord. ■ *Music* a chord in which the ninth note above the root forms an important component. —**ninth·ly** *adv.*

Ni·o·be /ˈnīəbē/ *Greek Mythology* the daughter of Tantalus. Apollo and Artemis, enraged because Niobe boasted herself superior to their mother Leto, slew her children and turned her into a stone.

ni·o·bi·um /nīˈōbēəm/ ▸*n.* the chemical element of atomic number 41, a silver-gray metal of the transition series, used in superconducting alloys. (Symbol: **Nb**) ▷mid 19th cent.: modern Latin, from NIOBE, by association with her father Tantalus (so named because the element was first found in TANTALITE).

Nip /nip/ ▸*n. informal, offensive* a Japanese person. ▷mid 20th cent.: abbreviation of the synonym *Nipponese*, from *Nippon* (see NIPPON).

nip[1] /nip/ ▸*v.* (**nipped**, **nip·ping**) **1** [*trans.*] pinch, squeeze, or bite sharply: *the dog nipped him on the leg.* ■ (of the cold or frost) cause sharp pain or harm to: *the vegetable garden, nipped now by frost.* ■ (**nip something off**) remove something by pinching or squeezing sharply. **2** *informal* defeat by a narrow margin. **3** [*trans.*] *informal* steal or snatch (something): *if I nipped a five-dollar bill I could slip it back the next day.*
▸*n.* a sharp pinch, squeeze, or bite. ■ a feeling of biting cold: *there was a real winter **nip in the air**.* ▷late Middle English: probably of Low German or Dutch origin.
▸*PHRASE* □ **nip something in the bud** suppress or destroy something, esp. at an early stage: *the idea has been nipped in the bud at the local level.*

nip[2] ▸*n.* a small quantity or sip of liquor.
▸*v.* (**nipped**, **nip·ping**) [*intrans.*] take a sip or sips of liquor: *the men nipped from the bottle.* ▷late 18th cent. (originally denoting a half-pint of ale): probably an abbreviation of the rare term *nipperkin* 'small measure'; compare with Low German and Dutch *nippen* 'to sip.'

ni·pa /ˈnēpə/ (also **nipa palm**) ▸*n.* a palm tree with creeping roots, characteristic of mangrove swamps in India and the Pacific islands. • *Nypa fruticans*, family Palmae. ▷late 16th cent. (denoting an alcoholic drink made from the sap of the tree): via Spanish or Portuguese from Malay *nipah*.

nip and tuck ▸*adv. & adj.* neck and neck; closely contested: [as *adv.*] *it was nip and tuck until the Tigers took the lead.*
▸*n. informal* a cosmetic surgical operation.

nip·per /ˈnipər/ ▸*n.* **1** *informal* a child, esp. a small boy. **2** (**nippers**) pliers, pincers, forceps, or a similar tool for gripping or cutting. **3** an insect or other creature that nips or bites. ■ (usu. **nippers**) the grasping claw of a crab or lobster.

nip·ple /ˈnipəl/ ▸*n.* **1** the small projection of a woman's or girl's breast in which the mammary ducts terminate and from which milk can be secreted. ■ the corresponding vestigial structure in a male. ■ the teat of a female animal. ■ the flexible tip of a baby's pacifier or feeding bottle. **2** a small projection on a device or machine, esp. one from which oil, grease, or other fluid is dispensed in small amounts. ■ a short section of pipe with a screw thread at each end for coupling.
▸*v.* [*trans.*] (usu. **be nippled**) provide (something) with a projection like a nipple: *rocks nippled with limpets.* ▷mid 16th cent. (also as *neble*, *nible*): perhaps a diminutive of NEB.

nip·ple·wort /ˈnipəlˌwərt; -ˌwôrt/ ▸*n.* a yellow-flowered plant of the daisy family, growing in woods and empty lots. • *Lapsana communis*, family Compositae.

Nip·pon /niˈpän/ Japanese name for JAPAN. ▷literally 'land where the sun rises or originates.' —**Nip·pon·ese** /ˌnipəˈnēz; -ˈnēs/ *n.* (*dated, offensive*) & *adj.*

nip·py /ˈnipē/ ▸*adj.* (**-pi·er**, **-pi·est**) *informal* **1** (of the weather) rather cold; chilly: *it's a bit nippy this morning.* **2** inclined to nip or bite: *macaws can sometimes be nippy and unpredictable.* **3** *chiefly Brit.* quick; nimble. —**nip·pi·ly** /ˈnipəlē/ *adv.*

Ni·ro, Robert De, see DE NIRO.

nir·va·na /nərˈvänə; nir-/ ▸*n. Buddhism* a transcendent state in which there is neither suffering, desire, nor sense of self, and the subject is released from the effects of karma and samsara. It represents the final goal of Buddhism. ■ *Hinduism* liberation of the soul from the effects of karma and from bodily existence. ■ a state of perfect happiness; an ideal or idyllic place: *Hollywood's dearest dream of small-town nirvana.* ▷from Sanskrit *nirvāṇa*, from *nirvā* 'be extinguished,' from *nis* 'out' + *vā-* 'to blow.'

Niš /nēSH/ (also **Nish**) a historically dominant industrial city in southeastern Serbia, in eastern Yugoslavia, on the Nišava River near its confluence with the Morava River; pop. 175,000.

Ni·san /ˈnisən; nēˈsän/ ▸*n.* (in the Jewish calendar) the seventh month of the civil and first of the religious year, usually coinciding with parts of March and April. ▷from Hebrew *nīsān*.

ni·sei /nēˈsā; ˈnēsā/ (also **Ni·sei**) ▸*n.* (*pl.* same or **-seis**) a person born in the U.S. or Canada whose parents were immigrants from Japan. Compare with ISSEI and SANSEI. ▷1940s: from Japanese, literally 'second generation.'

Nish·ga /ˈnisHgə/ (also **Nis·ka** /ˈniskə/) ▸*n.* (*pl.* same) **1** a member of a branch of the Tsimshian people of British Columbia inhabiting the Nass river basin. **2** the dialect of Tsimshian spoken by this people.
▸*adj.* of or relating to this people or their language. ▷the name in Nishga *nisqá'a*.

ni·si /ˈnīsī/ ▸*adj.* [*postpositive*] *Law* (of a decree, order, or rule) taking effect or having validity only after certain specified conditions are met. ▷mid 19th cent.: from Latin, literally 'unless.'

ni·sin /ˈnīsin/ ▸*n.* an antibiotic substance that is a mixture of related polypeptides and is used in some countries as a food preservative. • This substance is produced by the bacterium *Streptococcus lactis.* ▷1940s: from *(Group) N i(nhibitory) s(ubstance)* + -IN[1].

Nis·sen hut /ˈnisən/ ▸*n. chiefly Brit.* a hut made of corrugated iron with a concrete floor, similar to a Quonset hut. ▷early 20th cent.: named after Peter N. *Nissen* (1871–1930), the British engineer who invented it.

nit /nit/ ▸*n.* the egg or young form of a louse or other parasitic insect, esp. the egg of a head louse attached to a human hair. ▷Old English *hnitu*; related to Dutch *neet* and German *Nisse*. —**nit·ty** *adj.*
▸*PHRASE* □ **pick nits** look for and criticize small or insignificant faults or errors; nitpick.

nite /nīt/ ▸*n. informal* simplified spelling of NIGHT: *grist for a million late-nite TV jokes.*

ni·ter /ˈnītər/ (*Brit.* **ni·tre**) ▸*n.* another term for POTASSIUM NITRATE. ▷late Middle English: from Old French, from Latin *nitrum*, from Greek *nitron*.

Ni·te·rói /ˌnētəˈroi/ an industrial port on the coast of southeastern Brazil, on Guanabara Bay opposite Rio de Janeiro; pop. 455,000.

nit·er·y /ˈnītərē/ ▸*n. informal* (*pl.* **-er·ies**) a nightclub.

ni·ti·nol /ˈnitn-äl; -ôl/ ▸*n.* an alloy of nickel and titanium. ▷1960s: from the chemical symbols NI and TI + the initial letters of *Naval Ordnance Laboratory* (in Silver Spring, Maryland, where it was first produced).

nit·pick·ing /ˈnitˌpikiNG/ *informal* ▸*adj.* looking for small or unimportant errors or faults, esp. in order to criticize unnecessarily: *a nitpicking legalistic exercise.*
▸*n.* such fault-finding: *nitpicking over tiny details.* —**nit·pick** *v.* —**nit·pick·er** /-ˌpikər/ *n.*

ni·trate /ˈnītrāt/ ▸*n. Chemistry* a salt or ester of nitric acid, containing the anion NO_3^- or the group $-NO_3$. ■ sodium nitrate, potassium nitrate, or ammonium nitrate, used as fertilizer: *the fertilizer is usually a basic nitrate.*
▸*v.* [*trans.*] treat (a substance) with nitric acid (typically a concentrated mixture of nitric and sulfuric acids), esp. so as to introduce nitro groups. ▷late 18th cent.: from French (see NITER, -ATE[1]). —**ni·tra·tion** /nīˈtrāSHən/ *n.*

ni·traz·e·pam /nīˈtrazəˌpam/ ▸*n. Medicine* a short-acting hypnotic drug of the benzodiazepine group, used to treat insomnia, myoclonic seizures, and infantile spasms. ▷1960s: from *nitr(o)* + *az(o-)* + *ep(ine)* + *am(ide)*.

ni·tre ▸*n.* British spelling of NITER.

ni·tric /ˈnītrik/ ▸*adj. Chemistry* of or containing nitrogen with a higher valence, often five. Compare with NITROUS. ▷late 18th cent.: from French *(acide) nitrique* (see NITER, -IC).

ni·tric ac·id ▸*n. Chemistry* a colorless or pale yellow liquid acid that is corrosive and poisonous and has strong oxidizing properties, made in the laboratory by distilling nitrates with sulfuric acid. • Chem. formula: HNO_3. ▷late 18th cent.: from French *acide nitrique*.

ni·tric ox·ide ▸*n. Chemistry* a colorless toxic gas formed in many reactions in which nitric acid is reduced, as in reaction with copper. It reacts immediately with oxygen to form nitrogen dioxide. • Chem. formula: NO. Also called NITROGEN MONOXIDE.

ni·tride /ˈnītrīd/ ▸*n. Chemistry* a binary compound of nitrogen with a more electropositive element.
▸*v.* [*trans.*] [usu. as *n.*] (**nitriding**) *Metallurgy* heat steel in the presence of ammonia or other nitrogenous material so as to increase hardness and corrosion resistance. ▷mid 19th cent.: from *nitr-* (from NITER) + -IDE.

ni·tri·fy /ˈnītrəˌfī/ ▸*v.* **1** (**-fies**, **-fied**) [*trans.*] *Chemistry* convert (ammonia or another nitrogen compound) into nitrites or nitrates. **2** impregnate with nitrogen or nitrogen compounds. ▷early 19th cent.: from French *nitrifier*. —**ni·tri·fi·ca·tion** /ˌnītrəfiˈkāSHən/ *n.*

ni·trile /ˈnītril; -trīl/ ▸*n. Chemistry* an organic compound containing a cyanide group −CN bound to an alkyl group. ▷mid 19th cent.: from *nitr-* (from NITER) + *-ile* (alteration of -YL).

ni·trite /ˈnītrīt/ ▸*n. Chemistry* a salt or ester of nitrous acid, containing the anion NO_2^- or the group $-NO_2$. ▷early 19th cent.: from *nitr-* (from NITER) + -ITE[1].

ni·tro /ˈnītrō/ ▸*n.* short for NITROGLYCERIN.
▸*adj. Chemistry* containing the NITRO GROUP.

nitro- ▸*comb. form* of or containing nitric acid, nitrates, or nitrogen: *nitrogenous.* ■ *Chemistry* containing a nitro group: *nitromethane.* ▷from NITER or NITROGEN.

ni·tro·ben·zene /ˌnītrōˈbenzēn/ ▸*n. Chemistry* a yellow oily liquid made by nitrating benzene, used in chemical synthesis. • Chem. formula: $C_6H_5NO_2$.

ni·tro·blue tet·ra·zo·li·um /ˈnītrōˌblōō/ ▸*n.* see TETRAZOLIUM.

ni·tro·cel·lu·lose /ˌnītrōˈselyəˌlōs/ ▸*n. Chemistry* a highly flammable material made by treating cellulose with concentrated nitric acid, used to make explosives and celluloid. Also called CELLULOSE NITRATE.

ni·tro·fur·an·to·in /ˌnītrōˌfyōōˈrantōin/ ▸*n. Medicine* a synthetic compound with antibacterial properties, used to treat infections of the urinary tract. • A bicyclic furan derivative; chem. formula: $C_8H_6N_4O_5$.

ni·tro·gen /ˈnītrəjən/ ▸*n.* the chemical element of atomic number 7, a colorless, odorless unreactive gas that forms about 78 percent of the earth's atmosphere. Liquid nitrogen (made by distilling liquid air) boils at 77.4 kelvins (−195.8°C) and is used as a coolant. (Symbol: **N**) ▷late 18th cent.: from French *nitrogène* (see NITRO-, -GEN).

ni·tro·gen cy·cle ▸*n. Ecology* the series of processes by which nitrogen and its compounds are interconverted in the environment and in living organisms, including nitrogen fixation and decomposition.

ni·tro·gen di·ox·ide ▸*n. Chemistry* a reddish-brown poisonous gas used in the manufacture of nitric acid. It is also an air pollutant, a constituent of untreated automobile exhaust. • Chem. formula: NO_2. It usually exists in equilibrium with **dinitrogen tetroxide**, N_2O_4.

ni·tro·gen fix·a·tion ▸*n. Biology* the chemical processes by which atmospheric nitrogen is assimilated

N

into organic compounds, esp. by certain microorganisms as part of the nitrogen cycle.

ni·tro·gen mon·ox·ide ▸*n.* another term for **NITRIC OXIDE.**

ni·tro·gen mus·tard ▸*n. Chemistry* any of a group of organic compounds containing the group $-N(CH_2CH_2Cl)_2$. They are powerful cytotoxic alkylating agents and some are used in chemotherapy to treat cancer. ▷1940s: *mustard* denoting a substance chemically similar to **MUSTARD GAS.**

ni·tro·gen nar·co·sis ▸*n. Medicine* a drowsy state induced by breathing air under higher than atmospheric pressure, for example, in deep-sea diving.

ni·trog·e·nous /nīˈträjənəs/ ▸*adj.* containing nitrogen in chemical combination.

ni·tro·glyc·er·in /ˌnītrōˈglisərin/ (also **ni·tro·gly·ce·rine**) ▸*n. Chemistry* an explosive yellow liquid made by nitrating glycerol, used in explosives such as dynamite. It is also used in medicine as a vasodilator in the treatment of angina pectoris. • Alternative name: **glyceryl trinitrate**; chem. formula: $CH_2(NO_3)CH(NO_3)CH_2(NO_3)$.

ni·tro group ▸*n. Chemistry* a group, $-NO_2$, attached to an organic group in a molecule.

ni·tro·meth·ane /ˌnītrōˈmeTHān/ ▸*n. Chemistry* an oily liquid used as a solvent and as a rocket fuel. • Chem. formula: CH_3NO_2.

ni·troph·i·lous /nīˈträfələs/ ▸*adj. Botany* (of a plant) preferring soils rich in nitrogen.

ni·tros·a·mine /nīˈtrōsəmēn/ ▸*n. Chemistry* a compound containing the group =NNO attached to two organic groups. Compounds of this kind are generally carcinogenic. ▷late 19th cent.: from *nitroso-* (relating to nitric oxide in combination) + **AMINE.**

ni·trous /ˈnītrəs/ ▸*adj.* **1** *Chemistry* of or containing nitrogen with a lower valence, often three. Compare with **NITRIC. 2** of nitrogen; nitrogenous: *the effect of nitrous emissions on acid rain.* ▷early 17th cent.: from Latin *nitrosus* 'nitrous.'

ni·trous ac·id ▸*n. Chemistry* an unstable and weak acid, existing only in solution and in the gas phase, made by the action of acids on nitrites. • Chem. formula: HNO_2.

ni·trous ox·ide ▸*n. Chemistry* a colorless gas with a sweetish odor, prepared by heating ammonium nitrate. It produces exhilaration or anesthesia when inhaled and is used as an anesthetic and as an aerosol propellant. Also called **LAUGHING GAS.** • Chem. formula: N_2O.

nit·ty-grit·ty /ˈnitē ˈgritē/ ▸*n.* (**the nitty-gritty**) *informal* the most important aspects or practical details of a subject or situation: *let's **get down to the nitty-gritty** of finding a job* | [as *adj.*] *the nitty-gritty details.* ▷1960s: of unknown origin.

nit·wit /ˈnitˌwit/ ▸*n. informal* a silly or foolish person (often as a general term of abuse). ▷early 20th cent.: apparently from **NIT** + **WIT**[1]. **—nit·wit·ted** *adj.* **—nit·wit·ted·ness** *n.*

Ni·ue /nēˈōō/ an island territory in the South Pacific Ocean east of Tonga; pop. 2,239; capital, Alofi. Annexed by New Zealand in 1901, the island achieved self-government in free association with New Zealand in 1974. Niue is the world's largest coral island.

NIV ▸*abbr.* New International Version (of the Bible)

ni·val /ˈnīvəl/ ▸*adj.* of, relating to, or characteristic of a region of perpetual snow. ▷mid 17th cent.: from Latin *nivalis*, from *nix*, *niv-* 'snow.'

ni·va·tion /nīˈvāSHən/ ▸*n. Geography* erosion of the ground beneath and at the sides of a snowbank, mainly as a result of alternate freezing and thawing. ▷early 20th cent.: from Latin *nix*, *niv-* 'snow' + **-ATION.**

Niv·en /ˈnivən/, David (1909–83), British actor. His movies include *Around the World in 80 Days* (1956) and *Separate Tables* (Academy Award, 1958).

niv·e·ous /ˈnivēəs/ ▸*adj. poetic/literary* snowy or resembling snow. ▷early 17th cent.: from Latin *niveus* (from *nix*, *niv-* 'snow') + **-OUS.**

Ni·vose /nēˈvōz/ (also **Ni·vôse**) ▸*n.* the fourth month of the French Republican calendar (1793–1805), originally running from December 21 to January 19. ▷French *Nivôse*, from Latin *nivosus* 'snowy,' from *nix*, *niv-* 'snow.'

nix[1] /niks/ *informal* ▸*n.* nothing: *apart from that, nix.*
▸*exclam.* expressing denial or refusal: *"I owe you some money." "Nix, nix."*
▸*v.* [*trans.*] put an end to; cancel: *he nixed the deal just before it was to be signed.* ▷late 18th cent. (as a noun): from German, colloquial variant of *nichts* 'nothing.'

nix[2] ▸*n.* (*fem.* **nix·ie** /ˈniksē/) (in Germanic mythology) a water sprite. ▷mid 19th cent.: from German; related to the archaic English word *nicker*, denoting a water demon believed to live in the sea.

Nix·on /ˈniksən/, Richard Milhous (1913–94), 37th president of the U.S. 1969–74. His period of office was overshadowed by the Vietnam War. A Republican, he restored Sino-American diplomatic relations by his visit to China in 1972 and successfully ended the Vietnam War when peace negotiations were concluded by his secretary of state, Henry Kissinger, in 1973. Although he was reelected in 1972, he became the first president to resign from office, owing to his involvement in the Watergate scandal.

Richard M. Nixon

Ni·zam /niˈzäm; -ˈzam/ ▸*n. historical* **1** the title of the hereditary ruler of Hyderabad. [abbreviation of Urdu *nizām-al-mulk* 'administrator of the realm.'] **2** (**the nizam**) the Turkish regular army. [abbreviation of Turkish *nizām askeri* 'regular soldier.']

Ni·za·ri /niˈzärē/ ▸*n.* a member of a Muslim sect that split from the Ismaili branch in 1094 over disagreement about the succession to the caliphate. The majority of Nizaris now live in the Indian subcontinent; their leader is the Aga Khan.

Nizh·ni Nov·go·rod /ˈnizHnē ˈnôvgərəd/ a river port in western Russia on the Volga River; pop. 1,443,000. From 1932 to 1991, it was named Gorky after writer Maxim Gorky, who was born there.

Nizh·ni Ta·gil /ˈnizHnē təˈgil/ an industrial and metal-mining city in central Russia, in the Ural Mountains north of Ekaterinburg; pop. 440,000.

NJ ▸*abbr.* New Jersey (in official postal use).

NK cell ▸*abbr.* natural killer cell.

Nko·mo /(ə)NGˈkōmō/, Joshua (Mqabuko Nyongolo) (1917–99), Zimbabwean statesman; leader of the Zimbabwe African People's Union (ZAPU).

Nkru·mah /(ə)NGˈkrōōmə/, Kwame (1909–72), Ghanaian statesman; prime minister 1957–60; president 1960–66. The first prime minister after independence, he became increasingly dictatorial and was finally overthrown in a military coup.

NKVD the secret police agency in the former USSR that absorbed the functions of the former OGPU in 1934. It merged with the MVD in 1946. ▷abbreviation of Russian *Narodnyĭ komissariat vnutrennikh del* 'People's Commissariat of Internal Affairs.'

NL ▸*abbr. Baseball* National League.

NLF ▸*abbr.* National Liberation Front.

NLP ▸*abbr.* ■ natural language processing. ■ neurolinguistic programming.

NLRB ▸*abbr.* National Labor Relations Board.

NLT ▸*abbr.* night letter.

NM ▸*abbr.* New Mexico (in official postal use).

nm ▸*abbr.* ■ nanometer. ■ nautical mile.

n.m. ▸*abbr.* nautical mile.

N.Mex. ▸*abbr.* New Mexico.

NMI ▸*abbr.* no middle initial.

NMR *Physics* ▸*abbr.* nuclear magnetic resonance.

NNE ▸*abbr.* north-northeast.

NNP ▸*abbr.* net national product.

NNW ▸*abbr.* north-northwest.

No[1] ▸*symbol* the chemical element nobelium.

No[2] ▸*n.* variant spelling of **NOH.**

no /nō/ ▸*adj.* **1** not any: *there is no excuse* | *no two plants are alike.* **2** used to indicate that something is quite the opposite of what is being specified: *it was no easy task persuading her* | *Toby is no fool.* **3** hardly any: *you'll be back in no time.* **4** used in notices or slogans forbidding or rejecting something specified: *"No Smoking" signs* | *no nukes.*
▸*exclam.* used to give a negative response: *"Is anything wrong?" "No."* ■ expressing disagreement or contradiction: *"This is boring." "No, it's not!"* ■ expressing agreement with or affirmation of a negative statement: *they would never cause a fuss, oh no.* ■ expressing shock or disappointment at something one has heard or discovered: ***oh no**, look at this!*
▸*adv.* [with *comparative*] not at all; to no extent: *they were no more able to perform the task than I was.*
▸*n.* (*pl.* **noes**) a negative answer or decision, as in voting: *he was unable to change his automatic yes to a no.* ▷Old English *nō, nā* (adverb), from *ne* 'not' + *ō, ā* 'ever.' The determiner arose in Middle English (originally before words beginning with any consonant except *h-*), reduced from *non*, from Old English *nān* (see **NONE**[1]).
▸*PHRASES* □ **no can do** *informal* I am unable to do it. □ **the noes have it** the negative votes are in the majority. □ **no less** see **LESS.** □ **no longer** not now as formerly: *they no longer live here.* □ **no more** see **MORE.** □ **no place** nowhere. □ **no sooner —— than** see **SOON.** □ **not take no for an answer** persist in spite of refusals. □ **no two ways about it** used to convey that there can be no doubt about something. □ **no way** *informal* under no circumstances; not at all: *You think she's alone? No way.* □ **or no** or not: *she'd have ridden there, winter or no.* □ **—— or no ——** regardless of the specified thing: *recession or no recession there is always going to be a shortage of good people.*

No. ▸*abbr.* ■ North. ■ (also **no.**) number: *No. 27.* [from Latin *numero*, ablative of *numerus* 'number.']

NOAA ▸*abbr.* National Oceanic and Atmospheric Administration.

no-ac·count *informal* ▸*adj.* of little or no importance, value, or use; worthless: *a series of no-account boyfriends.*
▸*n.* such a person: *I do not intend to let some no-account get his hands on my money.*

No·a·chi·an /nōˈākēən/ ▸*adj.* **1** of or relating to the biblical patriarch Noah or his time. **2** *Astronomy* of, relating to, or denoting an early geological period on the planet Mars.

No·ah /ˈnōə/ (in the Bible) a patriarch represented as tenth in descent from Adam. According to a story in Genesis, he made the ark that saved his family and specimens of every animal from the Flood.

No·ah's ark ▸*n.* **1** the ship in which Noah, his family, and the animals were saved from the Flood, according to the biblical account (Genesis 6–8). **2** a small bivalve mollusk with a boat-shaped shell, found in the Mediterranean and off the Atlantic coasts of Africa and southern Europe. • *Arca noae*, family Arcidae. See also **ARK SHELL** at **ARK.**

nob[1] /näb/ ▸*n. Brit., informal* a person of wealth or high social position. ▷late 17th cent. (originally Scots as *knab*): of unknown origin. **—nob·by** *adj.*

nob[2] ▸*n. informal* a person's head. ▷late 17th cent.: apparently a variant of **KNOB.**
▸*PHRASE* □ **one for his nob** *Cribbage* a bonus point scored for holding the jack of the same suit as the card turned up by the dealer.

nob·ble /ˈnäbəl/ ▸*v.* [*trans.*] *Brit., informal* **1** try to influence or thwart (someone or something) by underhanded or unfair methods: *an attempt to nobble the jury.* ■ accost (someone), esp. in order to persuade them to do something: *people always tried to nobble her at parties.* ■ tamper with (a racehorse or greyhound) to prevent it from winning a race, esp. by giving it a drug. **2** obtain dishonestly; steal: *he intended to nobble Rose's money.* ■ seize: *they nobbled him and threw him onto the train.* ▷mid 19th cent.: probably a variant of dialect *knobble*, *knubble* 'knock, strike with the knuckles.' **—nob·bler** *n.*

No·bel /nōˈbel/, Alfred Bernhard (1833–96), Swedish chemist, engineer, and philanthropist. He invented dynamite in 1866, making a large fortune that enabled him to endow the prizes that bear his name.

No·bel·ist /nōˈbelist/ ▸*n.* a winner of a Nobel Prize.

no·bel·i·um /nōˈbelēəm/ ▸*n.* the chemical element of atomic number 102, a radioactive metal of the actinide series. Nobelium does not occur naturally and was first produced by bombarding curium with carbon nuclei. (Symbol: **No**) ▷1950s: modern Latin, from the name **NOBEL** + **-IUM.**

No·bel Prize /ˈnōbel/ ▸*n.* any of six international prizes awarded annually for outstanding work in physics, chemistry, physiology or medicine, literature, economics (since 1969), and the promotion of peace. The Nobel Prizes, first awarded in 1901, were established by the will of Alfred Nobel and are traditionally awarded on December 10, the anniversary of his death. The awards are decided by boards of deputies appointed by Swedish learned societies and, in the case of the peace prize, by the Norwegian Parliament. —**No·bel Prize win·ner** *n.*

Nob Hill /näb/ a commercial district of northern San Francisco in California, long noted for the homes of the wealthy ("nobs").

no·bil·i·ar·y /nō'bilē,erē; -'bilyərē/ ▸*adj. rare* of or relating to the nobility. ▷mid 18th cent.: from French *nobiliaire*, based on Latin *nobilis* (see **NOBLE**).

no·bil·i·ty /nō'bilitē/ ▸*n.* (*pl.* **-ties**) **1** the quality of being noble in character, mind, birth, or rank. **2** (usu. **the nobility**) the group of people belonging to the noble class in a country, esp. those with a hereditary or honorary title: *a member of the English nobility.* ▷late Middle English: from Old French *nobilite* or Latin *nobilitas*, from *nobilis* 'noted, highborn' (see **NOBLE**).

no·ble /'nōbəl/ ▸*adj.* (**-bler, -blest**) **1** belonging to a hereditary class with high social or political status; aristocratic: *the Duchess of Kent and other noble ladies.* **2** having or showing fine personal qualities or high moral principles and ideals: *the promotion of human rights was a noble aspiration.* ■ of imposing or magnificent size or appearance: *entering the building with its noble arches and massive granite columns.* ■ of excellent or superior quality.
▸*n.* **1** (esp. in former times) a person of noble rank or birth. **2** *historical* a former English gold coin. ▷Middle English: from Old French, from Latin *(g)nobilis* 'noted, highborn,' from an Indo-European root shared by **KNOW**. —**no·ble·ness** *n.* —**no·bly** /-blē/ *adv.*

no·ble gas ▸*n. Chemistry* any of the gaseous elements helium, neon, argon, krypton, xenon, and radon, occupying Group 0 (18) of the periodic table. They were long believed to be totally unreactive but compounds of xenon, krypton, and radon are now known.

no·ble·man /'nōbəlmən/ ▸*n.* (*pl.* **-men**) a man who belongs to the noble class.

no·ble met·al ▸*n. Chemistry* a metal (e.g., gold, silver, or platinum) that resists chemical action, does not corrode, and is not easily attacked by acids.

no·ble rot ▸*n.* a gray mold that is deliberately cultivated on grapes to enhance the making of certain sweet wines. • The fungus is *Botrytis cinerea*, subdivision Deuteromycotina. ▷1930s: translation of French *pourriture noble*.

no·ble sav·age ▸*n.* (usu. **the noble savage**) a representative of primitive humankind as idealized in Romantic literature, symbolizing the innate goodness of humanity when free from the corrupting influence of civilization.

no·blesse /nō'bles/ ▸*n.* the nobility. ▷French, literally 'nobility.'
▸*PHRASE* □ **noblesse oblige** /nō'bles ō'blēzH/ the inferred responsibility of privileged people to act with generosity and nobility toward those less privileged: *there was to being a celebrity a certain element of noblesse oblige.*

no·ble·wom·an /'nōbəl,wo͝omən/ ▸*n.* (*pl.* **-wom·en**) a woman who belongs to the noble class.

no·bod·y /'nō,bädē; -bədē/ ▸*pron.* no person; no one: *nobody was at home | nobody could predict how it might end.*
▸*n.* (*pl.* **-bod·ies**) a person of no importance or authority: *they went from nobodies to superstars.* ▷Middle English: originally as *no body*.
▸*PHRASES* □ **be nobody's fool** see **FOOL**[1]. □ **like nobody's business** see **BUSINESS**.

no-brain·er ▸*n. informal* something that requires or involves little or no mental effort.

no·ce·bo /nə'sēbō/ ▸*n.* (*pl.* **-bos**) a psychological or psychosomatic factor that engenders or exacerbates an illness. ▷1960s: from Latin, literally 'I shall cause harm,' from *nocere*, 'to harm,' on the pattern of *placebo*.
▸*PHRASE* □ **nocebo effect** a detrimental effect on health produced by psychological or psychosomatic factors such as negative expectations of treatment or prognosis, cultural beliefs about illness, personality traits, etc. In particular, the term is associated with adverse effects reported after the administration of a placebo.

no·ci·cep·tive /,nōsi'septiv/ ▸*adj. Physiology* of, relating to, or denoting pain arising from the stimulation of nerve cells (often as distinct from that arising from damage or disease in the nerves themselves). ▷early 20th cent.: from Latin *nocere* 'to harm' + **RECEPTIVE**.

no·ci·cep·tor /,nōsi'septər/ ▸*n. Physiology* a sensory receptor for painful stimuli. ▷early 20th cent.: from Latin *nocere* 'to harm' + **RECEPTOR**.

nock /näk/ ▸*n. Archery* a notch at either end of a bow for holding the string. ■ a notch at the back end of an arrow into which the bowstring fits.
▸*v.* [*trans.*] fit (an arrow) to the bowstring to ready it for shooting. ▷late Middle English: perhaps from Middle Dutch *nocke* 'point, tip.'

no-'count (also **no-count**) ▸*adj.* informal term for **NO-ACCOUNT**.

noc·tam·bu·list /näk'tambyəlist/ ▸*n. rare* a sleepwalker. ▷mid 18th cent.: from Latin *nox, noct-* 'night' + *ambulare* 'walk' + **-IST**. —**noc·tam·bu·lism** /-,lizəm/ *n.*

noc·ti·lu·ca /,näktə'lo͞okə/ ▸*n.* (*pl.* **-lu·cae** /-'lo͞o,sē/) a roughly spherical marine dinoflagellate that is strongly phosphorescent, esp. when disturbed. • Genus *Noctiluca*, division (or phylum) Dinophyta. ▷modern Latin, from Latin, literally 'night light, lantern.'

noc·ti·lu·cent cloud /,näktə'lo͞osənt/ ▸*n.* a high-altitude cloud that is luminous at night, esp. in summer in high latitudes. ▷late 19th cent.: from Latin *nox, noct-* 'night' + *lucere* 'to shine' + **-ENT**.

noc·tu·id /'näkCHo͞owid/ ▸*n. Entomology* a moth of a large family (Noctuidae) whose members typically have dull forewings and pale or colorful hind wings. Also called **OWLET**. ▷late 19th cent.: from modern Latin *Noctuidae* (plural), based on Latin *noctua* 'owl.'

noc·tule /'näkCHo͞ol/ ▸*n.* a large golden-brown bat native to Eurasia and North Africa with long slender wings, rounded ears, and a short muzzle. • *Nyctalus noctula*, family Vespertilionidae. ▷late 18th cent.: from French, from Italian *nottola* 'bat,' literally 'small night creature.'

noc·turn /'näktərn/ ▸*n.* (in the Roman Catholic Church) a part of matins originally said at night. ▷Middle English: from Old French *nocturne* or ecclesiastical Latin *nocturnum*, neuter of Latin *nocturnus* 'of the night.'

noc·tur·nal /näk'tərnl/ ▸*adj.* done, occurring, or active at night: *most owls are nocturnal.* ▷late 15th cent.: from late Latin *nocturnalis*, from Latin *nocturnus* 'of the night,' from *nox, noct-* 'night.' —**noc·tur·nal·ly** *adv.*

noc·tur·nal e·mis·sion ▸*n.* an involuntary ejaculation of semen during sleep.

noc·turne /'näk,tərn/ ▸*n.* **1** *Music* a short composition of a romantic or dreamy character suggestive of night, typically for piano. **2** *Art* a picture of a night scene. ▷mid 19th cent.: French, from Latin *nocturnus* 'of the night.'

noc·u·ous /'näkyo͞owəs/ ▸*adj. poetic/literary* noxious, harmful, or poisonous. ▷mid 17th cent.: from Latin *nocuus* (from *nocere* 'to hurt') + **-OUS**.

nod /näd/ ▸*v.* (**nod·ded, nod·ding**) **1** [*intrans.*] lower and raise one's head slightly and briefly, esp. in greeting, assent, or understanding, or to give someone a signal: *he nodded to Monica to unlock the door | [trans.] she nodded her head in agreement.* ■ [*trans.*] signify or express (greeting, assent, or understanding) in this way: *he nodded his consent.* ■ [*intrans.*] draw or direct attention to someone or something by moving one's head: *he nodded toward the corner of the room.* ■ move one's head up and down repeatedly: *he shut his eyes, nodding to the beat | figurative foxgloves nodding by the path.* **2** [*intrans.*] have one's head fall forward when drowsy or asleep: *Anna nodded over her book.*
▸*phrasal v.* □ **nod off** *informal* fall asleep, esp. briefly or unintentionally: *some of the congregation nodded off during the sermon.* □ **nod out** *informal* fall asleep, esp. from the effects of a drug: *they go to a coffee shop, get stoned, go to a club at 11, and nod out at midnight.*
▸*n.* an act of nodding the head: *at a nod from his father, he left the room.* ■ *figurative* a gesture of acknowledgement or concession: *a feel-good musical with **a nod to** pantomime.* ▷late Middle English (as a verb): perhaps of Low German origin; compare with Middle High German *notten* 'move around, shake.' The noun dates from the mid 16th cent.
▸*PHRASES* □ **a nodding acquaintance** a slight acquaintance with a person or cursory knowledge of a subject: *students will need **a nodding acquaintance with** three other languages.* □ **even Homer nods** *proverb* even the best person sometimes makes a mistake due to a momentary lack of alertness or attention. [with allusion to Latin *dormitat Homerus* (Horace *Ars Poetica* 359).] □ **get the nod** **1** be selected or approved. **2** receive a signal or information. □ **give someone/something the nod** **1** select or approve someone or something: *they banned one book but gave the other the nod.* **2** give someone a signal. □ **on the nod** □ *Brit., informal* **1** by general agreement and without discussion: *parliamentary approval of the treaty went through on the nod.* **2** *dated* on credit. **3** *informal* alternating wakefulness and sleepiness, due to heroin use.

nod·dle /'nädl/ ▸*n. informal, dated* a person's head. ▷late Middle English (denoting the back of the head): of unknown origin.

nod·dy /'nädē/ ▸*n.* (*pl.* **-dies**) **1** *dated* a silly or foolish person (esp. as a general term of abuse). [perhaps from the verb **NOD** + **-Y**[1].] **2** a tropical tern with mainly dark-colored plumage. [perhaps from the nodding behavior of the birds during courtship.] • Genera *Anous* and *Procelsterna*, family Sternidae (or Laridae): four species.

node /nōd/ ▸*n.* **1** a point at which lines or pathways intersect or branch; a central or connecting point. ■ *Computing* a piece of equipment, such as a PC or peripheral, attached to a network. ■ *Mathematics* a point at which a curve intersects itself. ■ *Astronomy* either of the two points at which a planet's orbit intersects the plane of the ecliptic or the celestial equator. ■ (in generative grammar) a vertex or endpoint in a tree diagram. **2** *Botany* the part of a plant stem from which one or more leaves emerge, often forming a slight swelling or knob. **3** *Anatomy* a lymph node or other structure consisting of a small mass of differentiated tissue. **4** *Physics & Mathematics* a point at which the amplitude of vibration in a standing wave system is zero. ■ a point at which a harmonic function has the value zero, esp. a point of zero electron density in an orbital. ■ a point of zero current or voltage. ▷late Middle English (denoting a knotty swelling or a protuberance): from Latin *nodus* 'knot.' —**nod·al** /'nōdl/ *adj.*

node of Ran·vier / 'ränvyā/ (also **Ranvier's node**) ▸*n. Anatomy* a gap in the myelin sheath of a nerve, between adjacent Schwann cells. ▷late 19th cent.: named after Louis Antoine *Ranvier* (1835–1922), French histologist.

nod·i·cal /'nōdikəl; 'nä-/ ▸*adj. Astronomy* of or relating to a node or the nodes of an orbit.

no·dose /'nōdōs/ ▸*adj. technical* having or characterized by hard or tight lumps; knotty. ▷early 18th cent.: from Latin *nodosus*, from *nodus* 'knot.' —**no·dos·i·ty** /nō'däsitē/ *n.*

nod·ule /'näjo͞ol/ ▸*n.* **1** a small swelling or aggregation of cells in the body, esp. an abnormal one. ■ (usu. **root nodule**) a swelling on a root of a leguminous plant, containing nitrogen-fixing bacteria. **2** a small rounded lump of matter distinct from its surroundings, for example, of flint in chalk, carbon in cast iron, or a mineral on the seabed. ▷late Middle English: from Latin *nodulus*, diminutive of *nodus* 'knot.' —**nod·u·lar** /-jələr/ *adj.* —**nod·u·lat·ed** /-jə,lātid/ *adj.* —**nod·u·la·tion** /,näjə'lāSHən/ *n.* —**nod·u·lose** /-jəlōs/ *adj.* —**nod·u·lous** /-jələs/ *adj.*

no·dus /'nōdəs/ ▸*n.* (*pl.* **-di** /-dī/) *rare* a problem, difficulty, or complication. ▷late Middle English (denoting a knotty swelling): from Latin, literally 'knot.'

NOED ▸*abbr.* *New Oxford English Dictionary.*

No·el /nō'el/ ▸*n.* Christmas, esp. as a refrain in carols and on Christmas cards. ▷early 19th cent.: French *Noël* 'Christmas.'

no·et·ic /nō'etik/ ▸*adj.* of or relating to mental activity or the intellect. ▷mid 17th cent.: from Greek *noētikos*, from *noētos* 'intellectual,' from *noein* 'perceive.'

no-fault ▸*adj.* [*attrib.*] not assigning fault or blame, in particular: ■ denoting an insurance policy that is valid regardless of whether the policyholder was at fault: *no-fault automobile insurance.* ■ denoting an insurance or compensation plan (esp. one covering medical or industrial accidents) whereby a claimant need not legally prove negligence against any party. ■ of or denoting a form of divorce granted without requiring one party to prove that the other is to blame for the breakdown of the marriage.

no-fly ▸*adj.* designating a list, person, or category of persons prevented from flying for security reasons.

no-fly zone ▸*n.* a designated area over which aircraft may not fly without risk of interception, esp. during a conflict.

no-frills ▸*adj.* [*attrib.*] without unnecessary extras, esp. ones for decoration or additional comfort: *cheap fast food in no-frills surroundings.*

nog[1] /näg/ ▸*n. archaic* a small block or peg of wood. ▷early 17th cent.: of unknown origin.

Pronunciation Key ə *ago*; ər *over*; 'ə or ,ə *up*; 'ər or ,ər *fur*; a *hat*; ā *rate*; ä *car*; CH *chew*; e *let*; ē *see*; e(ə)r *air*; i *fit*; ī *by*; i(ə)r *ear*; NG *sing*; ō *go*; ô *for*; oi *boy*; o͝o *good*; o͞o *goo*; ou *out*; SH *she*; TH *thin*; TH *then*; (h)w *why*; ZH *vision*

N

nog[2] ▸*n.* short for **EGGNOG**. ▷late 17th cent.: of unknown origin.

No·gal·es /nōˈgaləs; -ˈgäles/ a commercial city in northwestern Mexico, in Sonora state, on the U.S. border across from Nogales in Arizona; pop. 106,000.

nog·gin /ˈnägin/ ▸*n. informal* **1** a person's head. **2** a small quantity of liquor, typically a quarter of a pint. ▷mid 17th cent. (in the sense 'small drinking cup'): of unknown origin.

nog·ging /ˈnägiNG/ ▸*n. Building* brickwork that fills the spaces between studs or framing members. ■ a horizontal piece of wood fixed to a framework to strengthen it. ▷early 19th cent.: from **NOG**[1] + **-ING**[1].

no-go ▸*adj. informal* not ready or not functioning properly. ■ impossible, hopeless, or forbidden: *no-go zones for cars | some bad news: no-go response to my fax.* ▸*n.* a negative response; no.

no-go ar·e·a ▸*n.* an area that is dangerous or impossible to enter or to which entry is restricted or forbidden.

no-good ▸*adj.* [*attrib.*] *informal* (of a person) contemptible; worthless: *a no-good layabout.* ▸*n.* a worthless or contemptible person.

No·gu·chi /nōˈgo͞ocHē/, Isamu (1904–88), U.S. sculptor and designer. He created two bridges for Peace Park in Hiroshima, Japan, in 1951, as well as the Billy Rose Sculpture Garden at the Israeli Museum in Jerusalem between 1960 and 1965 and a sculpture called "Red Cube" at the Marine Midland building in New York City in 1968.

Noh /nō/ (also **No** or **Nō**) ▸*n.* traditional Japanese masked drama with dance and song, evolved from Shinto rites.

Noh dates from the 14th and 15th centuries, and its subject matter is taken mainly from Japan's classical literature. Traditionally the players were all male, with the chorus playing a passive narrative role.

▷Japanese.

no-hit·ter ▸*n. Baseball* a complete game in which a pitcher yields no hits to the opposing team.

no-hop·er ▸*n. informal* a person who is not expected to be successful.

no·how /ˈnō,hou/ ▸*adv.* **1** used, esp. in jocular or dialectal speech, to emphasize a negative: *the records simply don't exist—never, nowhere, and nohow.* **2** *archaic* not attractive, well, or in good order.

noil /noil/ ▸*n.* (usu. **noils**) short strands and knots combed out of wool fiber before spinning. ▷early 17th cent.: probably from Old French *noel*, from medieval Latin *nodellus*, diminutive of Latin *nodus* 'knot.'

no-i·ron ▸*adj.* (of clothes or fabric) wrinkle-resistant, and so not needing to be ironed after washing.

noise /noiz/ ▸*n.* **1** a sound, esp. one that is loud or unpleasant or that causes disturbance: *making a noise like a pig in a trough | what's that rustling noise outside the door?* ■ a series or combination of loud, confused sounds, esp. when causing disturbance: *dazed with the heat and noise | vibration and noise from traffic.* ■ (**noises**) conventional remarks or other sounds that suggest some emotion or quality: *Clarissa made encouraging noises.* **2** *technical* irregular fluctuations that accompany a transmitted electrical signal but are not part of it and tend to obscure it. ■ random fluctuations that obscure or do not contain meaningful data or other information: *over half the magnitude of the differences came from noise in the data.* ▸*v.* [*trans.*] (usu. **be noised about**) *dated* talk about or make known publicly: *you've discovered something that should not be noised about.* ■ [*intrans.*] *poetic/literary* make much noise. ▷Middle English (also in the sense 'quarreling'): from Old French, from Latin *nausea* 'seasickness' (see **NAUSEA**).

noise·core /ˈnoiz,kôr/ ▸a type of popular music derived from hardcore punk music, characterized by the use of dissonance, esp. loud distorted guitar, amplifier noise, and feedback: *a '90s noisecore quartet whose songs all kinda sounded alike.*

noise·less /ˈnoizlis/ ▸*adj.* silent; quiet: *the bicycle is a benign form of transportation, being noiseless and nonpolluting.* ■ *technical* accompanied by or introducing no random fluctuations that would obscure the real signal or data. —**noise·less·ly** *adv.* —**noise·less·ness** *n.*

noise·mak·er /ˈnoiz,mākər/ ▸*n.* a device for making a loud noise, as at a party or sporting event.

noise pol·lu·tion ▸*n.* harmful or annoying levels of noise, as from airplanes, industry, etc.

nois·es off ▸*plural n.* sounds made offstage to be heard by the audience of a play. ■ distracting or intrusive background noise.

noi·sette /nwäˈzet/ ▸*n.* **1** a small round piece of lean meat, esp. lamb. [French, diminutive of *noix* 'nut.'] **2** a chocolate made with hazelnuts. [French, in the sense 'hazelnut.']

noi·some /ˈnoisəm/ ▸*adj. poetic/literary* having an extremely offensive smell: *noisome vapors from the smoldering waste.* ■ disagreeable; unpleasant: *involved in noisome scandals.* ■ harmful, noxious. ▷late Middle English: from obsolete *noy* (shortened form of **ANNOY**) + **-SOME**[1]. —**noi·some·ness** *n.*

USAGE Noisome means 'bad-smelling.' It has no relation to the word *noise*; it is related to the word *annoy*.

nois·y /ˈnoizē/ ▸*adj.* (**nois·i·er**, **nois·i·est**) **1** making or given to making a lot of noise: *a noisy, giggling group of children | diesel cars can be very noisy.* ■ (of a person or group of people) stridently seeking to attract attention to their views. ■ (of a color or item of clothing) so gaudy as to attract attention: *wearing a noisy T-shirt.* **2** full of or characterized by noise: *noisy scenes outside the court building | the bar was crowded and noisy.* ■ *technical* accompanied by or introducing random fluctuations that obscure the real signal or data. —**nois·i·ly** /-əlē/ *adv.* —**nois·i·ness** *n.*

no-kill (also **no kill**) ▸*n.* a policy or an animal shelter in which abandoned, neglected, or lost animals are not put to sleep even if no home can be found for them: *there are thousands of no-kills that rescue pets.* ▸*adj.* opposed to or not killing animals that live in shelters: *find out if the organization has a no-kill policy.*

no-knock ▸*adj.* denoting or relating to a search or raid by the police made without warning or identification: *during a no-knock raid.*

No·lan /ˈnōlən/, Sir Sidney Robert (1917–93), Australian painter. He was known for his paintings of famous characters and events from Australian history.

no·lens vo·lens /ˈnōlənz ˈvōlənz/ ▸*adv. formal* whether a person wants or likes something or not. ▷Latin, from *nolens* 'not willing' and *volens* 'willing.'

no·li me tan·ge·re /ˈnōlē ,mā ˈtäNGgə,rā/ ▸*n.* **1** a warning or prohibition against meddling or interference. ■ a painting representing the appearance of Jesus to Mary Magdalen at the sepulcher (John 20:17). **2** another term for **TOUCH-ME-NOT**. ▷Latin, literally 'do not touch me.'

nol·le pros /,nôl ˈpräs/ (also **nol-pros**) (abbr.: **nol. pros.**) ▸*v.* (**prossed**, **pros·sing**) [*trans.*] *Law* abandon or dismiss (a suit) by issuing a nolle prosequi.

nol·le pros·e·qui /,nälē ˈpräsi,kwē/ ▸*n. Law* a formal notice of abandonment by a plaintiff or prosecutor of all or part of a suit or action. ■ the entry of this in a court record. ▷late 17th cent.: Latin, literally 'be unwilling to pursue.'

no-load ▸*adj.* (of shares in a mutual fund) sold without a commission being charged at the time of sale.

no·lo con·ten·de·re /,nōlō kənˈtendərē/ ▸*n.* (also **no·lo**) *Law* a plea by which a defendant in a criminal prosecution accepts conviction as though a guilty plea had been entered but does not admit guilt. ▷Latin, literally 'I do not wish to contend.'

nom. ▸*abbr.* nominal.

no·mad /ˈnō,mad/ ▸*n.* a member of a people having no permanent abode, and who travel from place to place to find fresh pasture for their livestock. ■ a person who does not stay long in the same place; a wanderer. ▸*adj.* relating to or characteristic of nomads. ▷late 16th cent.: from French *nomade*, via Latin from Greek *nomas, nomad-* 'roaming in search of pasture,' from the base of *nemein* 'to pasture.' —**no·mad·ic** /nōˈmadik/ *adj.* —**no·mad·i·cal·ly** /nōˈmadiklē/ *adv.* —**no·mad·ism** /ˈnōma,dizəm/ *n.*

no man's land ▸*n.* disputed ground, as between the front lines or trenches of two opposing armies: *enemy soldiers facing you across no man's land | figurative an unmapped no man's land between the traditional command economy and the market.* ■ land or area that is unowned, uninhabited, or undesirable. ▷Middle English: originally the name of a plot of ground lying outside the north wall of the city of London, the site of a place of execution.

nom·ar·chy /ˈnämärkē/ ▸*n.* (*pl.* **-chies**) formerly a province, now a smaller administrative division, of modern Greece. ▷mid 17th cent.: from Greek *nomarkhia*, from *nomos* 'nome' + *arkhē* 'government.'

nom·bril /ˈnämbrəl/ ▸*n. Heraldry* the point halfway between fess point and the base of the shield. ▷mid 16th cent.: from French, literally 'navel.'

nom de guerre /,näm də ˈger/ ▸*n.* (*pl.* **noms de guerre** *pronunc.* same) an assumed name under which a person engages in combat or some other activity or enterprise. ▷French, literally 'war name.'

nom de plume /,näm də ˈplo͞om/ ▸*n.* (*pl.* **noms de plume** *pronunc.* same) a pen name. ▷early 19th cent.: formed in English from French words, to render the sense 'pen name,' on the pattern of *nom de guerre*.

Nome /nōm/ a city in western Alaska, on the southern coast of the Seward Peninsula; pop. 3,500. Founded in 1896 as a gold-mining camp, it became a center of the Alaskan gold rush several years later.

nome /nōm/ ▸*n.* **1** one of the thirty-six territorial divisions of ancient Egypt. **2** an administrative division of modern Greece. ▷early 18th cent.: from Greek *nomos* 'division,' from *nemein* 'to divide.'

no·men /ˈnōmen/ ▸*n. Roman History* the second personal name of a citizen of ancient Rome, indicating the gens to which he belonged, for example, Marcus *Tullius* Cicero. ▷Latin, literally 'name.'

no·men·cla·ture /ˈnōmən,klācHər/ ▸*n.* the devising or choosing of names for things, esp. in a science or other discipline. ■ the body or system of such names in a particular field: *the nomenclature of chemical compounds.* ■ *formal* the term or terms applied to someone or something: *"customers" was preferred to the original nomenclature "passengers."* ▷early 17th cent.: from French, from Latin *nomenclatura*, from *nomen* 'name' + *clatura* 'calling, summoning' (from *calare* 'to call'). —**no·men·cla·tur·al** /,nōmənˈklācHərəl/ *adj.*

no·men·kla·tu·ra /,nōmənkləˈt(y)o͝orə/ ▸*n.* (in the former Soviet Union) a list of influential posts in government and industry to be filled by Communist Party appointees. ■ the holders of such posts collectively. ▷Russian, from Latin *nomenclatura* (see **NOMENCLATURE**).

nom·i·nal /ˈnäminəl/ ▸*adj.* **1** (of a role or status) existing in name only: *Thailand retained nominal independence under Japanese military occupation.* ■ of, relating to, or consisting of names. ■ *Grammar* relating to, headed by, or having the function of a noun. **2** (of a price or amount of money) very small; far below the real value or cost: *some firms charge only a nominal fee for the service.* **3** (of a quantity or dimension, esp. of manufactured articles) stated or expressed but not necessarily corresponding exactly to the real value: *legislation allowed variation around the nominal weight (that printed on each packet).* ■ *Economics* (of a rate or other figure) expressed in terms of a certain amount, without making allowance for changes in real value over time: *the nominal exchange rate.* **4** *informal* (chiefly in the context of space travel) functioning normally or acceptably. ▷late 15th cent. (as a term in grammar): from Latin *nominalis*, from *nomen, nomin-* 'name.' —**nom·i·nal·ly** *adv.*

nom·i·nal ac·count ▸*n. Finance* an account recording the financial transactions of a business in a particular category, rather than with a person or other organization.

nom·i·nal def·i·ni·tion ▸*n. Logic* a definition that describes something in terms of its properties, in order to distinguish it from other things, but without describing its underlying structure or essence.

nom·i·nal·ism /ˈnäminə,lizəm/ ▸*n. Philosophy* the doctrine that universals or general ideas are mere names without any corresponding reality, and that only particular objects exist; properties, numbers, and sets are thought of as merely features of the way of considering the things that exist. Important in medieval scholastic thought, nominalism is associated particularly with William of Occam. Often contrasted with **REALISM** (sense 3). ▷mid 19th cent.: from French *nominalisme*, from *nominal* 'relating to names' (see **NOMINAL**). —**nom·i·nal·ist** *n.* —**nom·i·nal·is·tic** /,nämənəˈlistik/ *adj.*

nom·i·nal·ize /ˈnäminə,līz/ ▸*v.* [*trans.*] *Grammar* convert (a word or phrase, as a verb or adjective) into a noun, for example, *output* from *put out*; *the poor* from *poor*. —**nom·i·nal·i·za·tion** /,näminəlˈzāsHən/ *n.*

nom·i·nal ledg·er ▸*n. Finance* a ledger containing nominal accounts, or one containing both nominal and real accounts.

nom·i·nal val·ue ▸*n. Economics* the value that is stated on currency; face value. ■ the price of a share, bond, or security when it was issued, rather than its current market value.

nom·i·nate ▸*v.* /ˈnämə,nāt/ [*trans.*] **1** propose or formally enter as a candidate for election or for an honor or award: *the film was **nominated for** several*

non·a·bra·sive *adj.*
non·ab·sor·bent *adj.*
non·ab·sorb·en·cy *n.*
non·a·bu·sive *adj.*
non·a·bu·sive·ly *adv.*
non·a·bu·sive·ness *n.*
non·ac·cep·tance *n.*
non·a·chiev·er *n.*
non·ac·tive *adj.*
non·ac·tion *n.*
non·ad·dic·tive *adj.*
non·ad·he·sive *adj.*
non·ad·he·sive·ness *n.*
non·ad·just·a·ble *adj.*
non·ad·just·a·bil·i·ty *n.*
non·al·ler·gen·ic *adj.*
non·al·ler·gic *adj.*
non·am·big·u·ous *adj.*
non-A·mer·i·can *adj. & n.*
non-Ar·y·an *adj. & n.*
non·as·so·ci·a·tive *adj.*
non·at·tached *adj.*
non·at·trib·ut·a·ble *adj.*
non·at·trib·ut·a·bly *adv.*
non·bel·lig·er·ent *adj. & n.*
non·bel·lig·er·ence *n.*
non·bi·o·de·grad·a·ble *adj.*
non·break·a·ble *adj.*
non·can·cer·ous *adj.*
non-Cath·o·lic *adj. & n.*
non-Chris·tian *adj. & n.*
non·cler·i·cal *adj. & n.*
non·clin·i·cal *adj.*
non·col·le·giate *adj.*
non·com·bus·ti·ble *adj.*
non·com·bus·ti·bil·i·ty *n.*
non·com·mu·ni·cat·ing *adj.*
non·com·mu·nist *adj. & n.* (also **non-Communist**)
non·com·pet·i·tive *adj.*
non·con·fi·den·tial *adj.*
non·con·fi·den·tial·ly *adv.*
non·con·struc·tive *adj.*
non·con·struc·tive·ly *adv.*
non·con·struc·tive·ness *n.*
non·con·ta·gious *adj.*
non·con·ten·tious *adj.*
non·con·tro·ver·sial *adj.*
non·de·duct·i·ble *adj.*
non·de·duct·i·bil·i·ty *n.*
non·de·grad·a·ble *adj.*
non·dis·clo·sure *n.*
non·dry·ing *adj.*
non·earn·ing *adj.*
non·ef·fec·tive *adj.*
non·emp·ty *adj.*
non-Eu·ro·pe·an *adj. & n.*
non·ex·ec·u·tive *adj. & n.*
non·ex·plo·sive *adj. & n.*
non·fat·ten·ing *adj.*
non·greas·y *adj.*
non·haz·ard·ous *adj.*
non·he·red·i·tar·y *adj.*
non·his·tor·i·cal *adj.*
non·i·den·ti·cal *adj.*
non·in·clu·sive *adj.*
non·in·fec·tious *adj.*
non·in·flam·ma·to·ry *adj.*
non·in·fla·tion·ar·y *adj.*
non·in·flect·ed *adj.*
non·in·te·grat·ed *adj.*
non·in·ter·change·a·ble *adj.*
non·in·ter·fer·ence *n.*
non·in·tox·i·cat·ing *adj.*
non·ir·ri·tat·ing *adj.*
non-Jew·ish *adj.*
non·liq·uid *n. & adj.*
non·lit·er·ar·y *adj.*
non·liv·ing *adj.*
non·mag·net·ic *adj.*
non·ma·lig·nant *adj.*
non·mi·gra·to·ry *adj.*
non·mil·i·tant *adj.*
non·mil·i·tar·y *adj.*
non·min·is·te·ri·al *adj.*
non·nar·cot·ic *adj. & n.*
non·ob·lig·a·to·ry *adj.*
non·ob·serv·ance *n.*
non·ob·serv·ant *adj.*
non·oc·cur·rence *n.*
non·of·fi·cial *adj.*
non·op·er·a·tion·al *adj.*
non·pay·ing *adj.*
non·per·ish·a·ble *adj.*
non·per·son·al *adj.*
non·phy·si·cal *adj.*
non·phys·i·cal·ly *adv.*
non·play·ing *adj.*
non·poi·son·ous *adj.*
non·po·lit·i·cal *adj.*
non·pol·lut·ing *adj.*
non·po·rous *adj.*
non·prac·tic·ing *adj.*
non·prof·it·a·ble *adj.*
non·pub·lic *adj.*
non·ran·dom *adj.*
non·ra·tion·al *adj.*
non·re·ac·tive *adj.*
non·re·cip·ro·cal *adj. & n.*
non·re·cip·ro·cat·ing *adj.*
non·re·cur·ring *adj.*
non·re·deem·a·ble *adj.*
non·re·fill·a·ble *adj.*
non·re·new·a·ble *adj.*
non·rep·re·sen·ta·tion·al *adj.*
non·re·sis·tant *adj.*
non·rhyth·mic *adj.*
non·sal·a·ried *adj.*
non·sci·en·tif·ic *adj.*
non·sci·en·tist *n.*
non·sea·son·al *adj.*
non·sex·ist *adj.*
non·sex·u·al *adj.*
non·smok·er *n.*
non·sol·u·ble *adj.*
non·speak·ing *adj.*
non·spe·cial·ist *n.*
non·stain·ing *adj.*
non·sub·scrib·er *adj.*
non·swim·mer *n.*
non·tar·nish·ing *adj.*
non·tax·a·ble *adj.*
non·think·ing *adj.*
non·threat·en·ing *adj.*
non·tra·di·tion·al *adj.*
non·trans·fer·a·ble *adj.*
non·u·ni·form *adj.*
non·u·ni·form·i·ty *n.*
non·u·ni·form·ly *adv.*
non·use *n.*
non·us·er *n.*
non·ven·om·ous *adj.*
non·vi·a·ble *adj.*
non·vir·u·lent *adj.*
non·vo·cal *adj.*
non·vot·ing *adj.*
non·vo t·er *n.*
non·work·ing *adj.*

Oscars. ■ appoint to a job or position: *the company* **nominated** *her* **as** *a delegate to the convention.* **2** specify (something) formally, typically the date or place for an event: *a day was nominated for the exchange of contracts.*

▸*adj.* /-nit/ *Zoology & Botany* denoting a race or subspecies that is given the same epithet as the species to which it belongs, for example, *Homo sapiens sapiens.* ▷late Middle English (as an adjective in the sense 'named'): from Latin *nominat-* 'named,' from the verb *nominare,* from *nomen, nomin-* 'a name.' The verb senses are first found in English in the 16th cent. —**nom·i·na·tor** /-ˌnātər/ *n.*

nom·i·na·tion /ˌnäməˈnāSHən/ ▸*n.* the action of nominating or state of being nominated: *women's groups opposed the nomination of the judge | the film received five nominations.* ■ a person or thing nominated: *send your nominations in by November 30th.*

nom·i·na·tive /ˈnämənətiv/ ▸*adj.* **1** *Grammar* relating to or denoting a case of nouns, pronouns, and adjectives (as in Latin and other inflected languages) used for the subject of a verb. **2** /-ˌnātiv/ of or appointed by nomination as distinct from election.
▸*n. Grammar* a word in the nominative case. ■ (**the nominative**) the nominative case. ▷late Middle English: from Latin *nominativus* 'relating to naming,' translation of Greek *onomastikē (ptōsis)* 'naming (case).'

nom·i·nee /ˌnäməˈnē/ ▸*n.* **1** a person who is proposed or formally entered as a candidate for an office or as the recipient of a grant or award: *the party's presidential nominee | an Oscar nominee.* **2** a person or company whose name is given as having title to a stock, real estate, etc., but who is not the actual owner. ▷mid 17th cent.: from **NOMINATE** + **-EE**.

nom·o·gram /ˈnäməˌgram/ (also **nom·o·graph** /-ˌgraf/) ▸*n.* a diagram representing the relations between three or more variable quantities by means of a number of scales, so arranged that the value of one variable can be found by a simple geometric construction, for example, by drawing a straight line intersecting the other scales at the appropriate values. ▷early 20th cent.: from Greek *nomos* 'law' + **-GRAM**[1]. —**nom·o·graph·ic** /ˌnäməˈgrafik; ˌnō-/ *adj.* —**nom·o·graph·i·cal·ly** /ˌnäməˈgrafik(ə)lē; ˌnō-/ *adv.* —**no·mog·ra·phy** /nəˈmägrəfē/ *n.*

nom·o·log·i·cal /ˌnäməˈläjikəl/ ▸*adj.* relating to or denoting certain principles, such as laws of nature, that are neither logically necessary nor theoretically explicable, but are simply taken as true. ■ another term for **NOMOTHETIC**. ▷mid 19th cent.: from Greek *nomos* 'law' + *-logical* (see **-LOGY**). —**nom·o·log·i·cal·ly** /-ik(ə)lē/ *adv.*

nom·o·thet·ic /ˌnäməˈTHetik/ ▸*adj.* of or relating to the study or discovery of general scientific laws. Often contrasted with **IDIOGRAPHIC**. ▷mid 17th cent.: from obsolete *nomothete* 'legislator' (from Greek *nomothetēs*) + **-IC**.

-nomy ▸*comb. form* denoting a specified area of knowledge or the laws governing it: *astronomy | gastronomy.* ▷from Greek *-nomia;* related to *nomos* 'law' and *nemein* 'distribute.'

non- ▸*prefix* **1** not doing; not involved with: *nonaggression | nonrecognition.* **2** not of the kind or class described: *nonbeliever | nonconformist.* ■ also forming nouns used attributively (such as *nonunion* in *nonunion miners*). **3** not of the importance implied: *nonissue.* **4** a lack of: *nonsense.* **5** (added to adverbs) not in the way described: *nonuniformly.* **6** (added to verbs to form adjectives) not causing or requiring: *nonskid | noniron.* **7** expressing a neutral negative sense when a corresponding form beginning with *in-* or *un-* has a special connotation (such as *nonhuman* compared with *inhuman*). ▷from Latin *non* 'not.'

USAGE The prefixes **non-** and **un-** both have the meaning 'not,' but tend to be used with a difference of emphasis. See **usage** at **UN-**[1].

nona- ▸*comb. form* nine; having nine: *nonagon.* ▷from Latin *nonus* 'ninth.'

non·age /ˈnänij; ˈnō-/ ▸*n.* [in *sing.*] *formal* the period of immaturity or youth. ▷late Middle English: from Old French *nonage,* from *non-* 'non-' + *age* 'age.'

non·a·ge·nar·i·an /ˌnänəjəˈne(ə)rēən; ˌnōnə-/ ▸*n.* a person who is from 90 to 99 years old. ▷early 19th cent.: from Latin *nonagenarius* (based on *nonaginta* 'ninety') + **-AN**.

non·ag·gres·sion /ˌnänəˈgreSHən/ ▸*n.* absence of the desire or intention to be aggressive, esp. on the part of nations or governments: *a treaty of nonaggression and friendship | [as adj.] a nonaggression pact.*

non·a·gon /ˈnänəˌgän/ ▸*n.* a plane figure with nine straight sides and nine angles. ▷mid 17th cent.: formed irregularly from Latin *nonus* 'ninth,' on the pattern of words such as *hexagon.* —**non·ag·o·nal** /nänˈagənəl/ *adj.*

non·al·co·hol·ic /ˌnänˌalkəˈhôlik; -ˈhälik/ ▸*adj.* (of a drink) not containing alcohol.

non·a·ligned /ˌnänəˈlīnd/ ▸*adj.* not aligned with something else. ■ (of countries) not aligned with a major power, esp. the former USSR or the U.S. —**non·a·lign·ment** /-ˈlīnmənt/ *n.*

no-name ▸*adj.* (of a product) having no brand name: *cheap, no-name cigarettes.* ■ (of a person) unknown, esp. in a particular profession: *no-name, no-frills chefs.*
▸*n.* such a person.

no·nane /ˈnōnān/ ▸*n. Chemistry* a colorless liquid hydrocarbon of the alkane series, present in petroleum spirit. • Chem. formula: C_9H_{20}; many isomers, esp. the straight-chain isomer (***n*-nonane**). ▷mid 19th cent.: from **NONA-** (denoting nine carbon atoms) + **-ANE**[2].

non·ap·pear·ance /ˌnänəˈpi(ə)rəns/ ▸*n.* failure to appear or be present, esp. at a gathering or engagement. ■ *Law* failure to appear or be present in a court of law, esp. as a witness, defendant, or plaintiff.

non·art /ˈnänˈärt/ ▸*n.* something that is not art or that rejects the conventional forms or methods of art.

no·na·ry /ˈnōnərē/ ▸*adj. rare* relating to or based on the number nine. ▷mid 17th cent. (as a noun): from Latin *nonus* 'ninth,' on the pattern of words such as *denary.*

non·at·ten·dance /ˌnänəˈtendəns/ ▸*n.* failure to attend or be present at a place where you are expected to be: *students' nonattendance at school.*

non·a·vail·a·bil·i·ty /ˌnänəˌvāləˈbilitē/ ▸*n.* the state of not being available, free, or able to be used.

non·bank /ˈnänˈbaNGk/ ▸*adj.* [*attrib.*] not relating to, connected with, or transacted by a bank.
▸*n.* a financial institution that is not a bank.

non·be·ing /nänˈbēiNG/ ▸*n.* the state of not being; nonexistence.

non·be·liev·er /ˌnänbəˈlēvər/ ▸*n.* a person who does not believe in something, esp. one who has no religious faith.

non·bi·o·log·i·cal /ˌnänbīəˈläjikəl/ ▸*adj.* not involving, relating to, or derived from biology or living organisms. ■ (of a detergent) not containing enzymes.

non·black ▸*adj.* (of a person) not black. ■ of or relating to people who are not black.
▸*n.* a person who is not black.

non·call·a·ble /nänˈkôləbəl/ ▸*adj.* (of stocks and bonds) not subject to redemption before a certain date or until maturity.

non·cap·i·tal /nänˈkapitl/ ▸*adj. Law* (of an offense) not punishable by death.

nonce[1] /näns/ ▸*adj.* (of a word or expression) coined for or used on one occasion: *a nonce usage.* ▷Middle English: from *then anes* 'the one (purpose)' (from *then,* obsolete oblique form of **THE** + *ane* 'one' + **-S**[3]), altered by misdivision; compare with **NEWT** and **NICKNAME**.
▸*PHRASE* □ **for the nonce** for the present; temporarily: *the room had been converted for the nonce into a nursery.*

nonce[2] ▶*n. Brit., informal* a person convicted of a sexual offense, esp. child molesting. ▷1970s: of unknown origin.

non·cha·lant /ˌnänsHə'länt/ ▶*adj.* (of a person or manner) feeling or appearing casually calm and relaxed; not displaying anxiety, interest, or enthusiasm: *she gave a nonchalant shrug.* ▷mid 18th cent.: from French, literally 'not being concerned,' from the verb *nonchaloir.* **—non·cha·lance** *n.* **—non·cha·lant·ly** *adv.*

non·cit·i·zen /nän'sitizən/ ▶*n.* a person who is not an inhabitant or national of a particular country or town.

non·clas·si·fied /nän'klasəfīd/ ▶*adj.* (of information or documents) not designated as officially secret; freely available (tending to be less forceful in meaning than **unclassified**).

non·cod·ing /nän'kōdiNG/ ▶*adj. Biology* (of a section of a nucleic acid molecule) not directing the production of a peptide sequence.

non·com /'nän,käm/ ▶*n. informal Military* a noncommissioned officer.

non·com·bat·ant /ˌnänkəm'batnt/ ▶*n.* a person who is not engaged in fighting during a war, esp. a civilian, chaplain, or medical practitioner.

non·com·e·do·gen·ic /ˌnän,kämədō'jenik/ ▶*adj.* denoting a skin-care product or cosmetic that is specially formulated so as not to cause blocked pores.

non·com·mis·sioned /ˌnankə'misHənd/ ▶*adj. Military* (of an officer in the armed forces) ranking below warrant officer, as sergeant or petty officer.

non·com·mit·tal /ˌnänkə'mitl/ ▶*adj.* (of a person or a person's behavior or manner) not expressing or revealing commitment to a definite opinion or course of action: *her tone was noncommittal, and her face gave nothing away.* **—non·com·mit·tal·ly** *adv.*

non·com·mu·ni·cant /ˌnänkə'myōōnikənt/ ▶*n.* (in church use) a person who does not receive Holy Communion, esp. regularly or at a particular service.

non·com·pli·ance /ˌnänkəm'plīəns/ ▶*n.* failure to act in accordance with a wish or command.

non com·pos men·tis /ˌnän 'kämpəs 'mentis/ (also **non com·pos**) ▶*adj.* not sane or in one's right mind. ▷Latin, literally 'not having control of one's mind.'

non·con·duc·tor /ˌnänkən'dəktər/ ▶*n.* a substance that does not conduct heat or electricity. **—non·con·duct·ing** /-'dəktiNG/ *adj.*

non·con·form·ist /ˌnänkən'fôrmist/ ▶*n.* **1** a person whose behavior or views do not conform to prevailing ideas or practices. **2** (**Nonconformist**) a member of a Protestant church in England that dissents from the established Anglican Church.
▶*adj.* **1** of or characterized by behavior or views that do not conform to prevailing ideas or practices. **2** (**Nonconformist**) of or relating to Nonconformists or their principles and practices. **—non·con·form·ism** /-ˌmizəm/ *n.*

non·con·form·i·ty /ˌnänkən'fôrmitē/ ▶*n.* **1** failure or refusal to conform to a prevailing rule or practice. ■ lack of similarity in form or type. **2** (**Nonconformity**) Nonconformists as a body, esp. Protestants in England dissenting from the Anglican Church. ■ the principles or practice of Nonconformists, esp. Protestant dissent.

non·con·tra·dic·tion /ˌnänkäntrə'diksHən/ ▶*n.* a lack or absence of contradiction, esp. as a principle of logic that a proposition and its opposite cannot both be true. **—non·con·tra·dic·to·ry** /-'diktərē/ *adj.*

non·con·trib·u·to·ry /ˌnänkən'tribyəˌtôrē/ ▶*adj.* **1** not playing a part in bringing something about. **2** (of a pension or pension plan) funded by regular payments by the employer, not the employee.

non·co·op·er·a·tion /ˌnänkō,äpə'rāsHən/ ▶*n.* failure or refusal to cooperate, esp. as a form of protest.

non·core /'non,kôr/ ▶*adj.* not considered to be essential; expendable: *substantial expenditure cuts in noncore service areas.*

non·count /'nän,kount/ ▶*adj. Grammar* (of a noun) not countable.

non·cus·to·di·al /ˌnän,kə'stōdēəl/ ▶*adj. Law* not having custody of one's children after a divorce: *the relationship between the children and their noncustodial father was virtually destroyed.*

non·dair·y /nän'de(ə)rē/ ▶*adj.* containing no milk or milk products: *a nondairy creamer.*

non·de·liv·er·y /ˌnändə'livərē/ ▶*n. chiefly Law* failure to provide or deliver goods.

non·de·nom·i·na·tion·al /ˌnändəˌnämə'nāsHənəl/ ▶*adj.* open or acceptable to people of any Christian denomination.

non·de·script /ˌnändə'skript/ ▶*adj.* lacking distinctive or interesting features or characteristics: *she lived in a nondescript suburban apartment block.*
▶*n.* a nondescript person or thing. ▷late 17th cent. (in the sense 'not previously described or identified scientifically'): from NON- + obsolete *descript* 'described, engraved' (from Latin *descriptus*). **—non·de·script·ly** *adv.* **—non·de·script·ness** /-'skrip(t)nis/ *n.*

non·de·struc·tive /ˌnändə'strəktiv/ ▶*adj. technical* not involving damage or destruction, esp. of an object or material that is being tested: *instruments subjected to nondestructive analysis by X-ray fluorescence.*

non·dig·i·tal /nän'dijitl/ ▶*adj.* **1** not represented by numbers, especially binary codes; not digitized: *nondigital items have only their location information (catalog records) in the digital library, as it happens in a traditional automated library situation.* **2** not using the Internet or computers: *nondigital submissions will be accepted only until February 1st.*

non·di·rec·tion·al /ˌnändə'reksHənəl/ ▶*adj.* lacking directional properties. ■ (of sound, light, radio waves, etc.) equally sensitive, intense, etc., in every direction.

non·dis·junc·tion /ˌnändis'jəNGksHən/ ▶*n. Genetics* the failure of one or more pairs of homologous chromosomes or sister chromatids to separate normally during nuclear division, usually resulting in an abnormal distribution of chromosomes in the daughter nuclei.

non·drink·er /nän'driNGkər/ ▶*n.* a person who does not drink alcohol.

non·drip /ˌnän'drip/ ▶*adj.* (of paint) specially formulated so that it does not drip or run when wet.

non·driv·er /'nän'drīvər/ ▶*n.* a person who does not or cannot drive a motor vehicle.

none[1] /nən/ ▶*pron.* not any: **none of** *you want to work* | *don't use any more water, or there'll be none left for me.* ■ no person; no one: *none could match her looks.*
▶*adv.* (**none the**) [with *comparative*] by no amount; not at all: *it is made none the easier by the differences in approach.* ▷Old English *nān,* from *ne* 'not' + *ān* 'one,' of Germanic origin; compare with German *nein* 'no!'
▶*PHRASES* □ **none the less** see NONETHELESS. □ **none other than** used to emphasize the surprising identity of a person or thing: *her first customer was none other than Henry du Pont.* □ **be none the wiser** see WISE[1]. □ **none the worse for** see WORSE. □ **none too** see TOO. □ **want** (or **will have**) **none of** (esp. with reference to behavior) refuse to accept (something): *Danny offered to wait below, but Peter would have none of it.*

USAGE It is sometimes held that **none** can take only a singular verb, never a plural verb: *none of them* **is** *coming tonight,* rather than *none of them* **are** *coming tonight.* There is little justification, historical or grammatical, for this view. **None** is descended from Old English **nān,** meaning 'not one,' and has been used for around a thousand years with both a singular and a plural verb, depending on the context and the emphasis needed.

none[2] (also **nones**) ▶*n.* a service forming part of the Divine Office of the Western Christian Church, traditionally said (or chanted) at the ninth hour of the day (3 p.m.). ▷mid 19th cent.: from French, from Latin *nona,* feminine singular of *nonus* 'ninth.' Compare with NOON.

non·en·ti·ty /nän'entitē/ ▶*n.* (*pl.* **-ties**) **1** a person or thing with no special or interesting qualities; an unimportant person or thing: *a political nonentity.* **2** nonexistence: *asserting the nonentity of evil.* ▷late 16th cent.: from medieval Latin *nonentitas* 'nonexistence.'

nones /nōnz/ ▶*plural n.* **1** in the ancient Roman calendar, the ninth day before the ides by inclusive reckoning, that is, the 7th day of March, May, July, and October, or the 5th of other months. **2** another term for NONE[2]. ▷via Old French from Latin *nonas,* feminine accusative plural of *nonus* 'ninth.'

non·es·sen·tial /ˌnänə'sencHəl/ ▶*adj.* not absolutely necessary: *during the strike nonessential hospital services were halted.*
▶*n.* (usu. **nonessentials**) a nonessential thing.

non est fac·tum /ˌnōn ˌest 'faktəm/ ▶*n. Law* a plea that a written agreement is invalid because the defendant was mistaken about its character when signing it. ▷Latin, literally 'it was not done.'

none·such /'nən,səcH/ (also **non·such**) ▶*n.* **1** a person or thing that is regarded as perfect or excellent. **2** another term for BLACK MEDICK (see MEDICK). ▷early 17th cent.: coined on the pattern of *nonpareil.*

no·net /nō'net/ ▶*n.* a group of nine people or things, esp. musicians. ■ a musical composition for nine voices or instruments. ▷mid 19th cent.: from Italian *nonetto,* from *nono* 'ninth,' from Latin *nonus.*

none·the·less /ˌnənTHə'les/ (also **none the less**) ▶*adv.* in spite of that; nevertheless: *it was the barest of welcomes, but it was a welcome nonetheless.*

non-Eu·clid·e·an /ˌnän yōō'klidēən/ ▶*adj. Geometry* denying or going beyond Euclidean principles in geometry, esp. in contravening the postulate that only one line through a given point can be parallel to a given line.

non·e·vent /ˌnänē'vent/ ▶*n.* a disappointing or insignificant event or occasion, esp. one that was expected or intended to be exciting or interesting. ■ a scheduled event that did not happen.

non·ex·ist·ent /ˌnänig'zistənt/ ▶*adj.* not existing, or not real or present: *she pretended to tie a nonexistent shoelace.* **—non·ex·ist·ence** *n.*

non·fac·tive /nän'faktiv/ ▶*adj. Linguistics* denoting a verb that takes a clausal object that may or may not designate a true fact, for example, *believe* as opposed to *know.* Contrasted with CONTRAFACTIVE, FACTIVE.

non·fat /'nän'fat/ ▶*adj.* (of a food) containing no fat; with all fat solids removed: *nonfat buttermilk.*

non·fea·sance /nän'fēzəns/ ▶*n. Law* failure to perform an act that is required by law.

non·fer·rous /nän'ferəs/ ▶*adj.* relating to or denoting a metal other than iron or steel.

non·fic·tion /nän'fiksHən/ ▶*n.* prose writing that is based on facts, real events, and real people, such as biography or history. **—non·fic·tion·al** /-nəl/ *adj.*

non·fig·ur·a·tive ▶*adj.* not figurative. ■ (of an artist or work of art) abstract.

non·fi·nite /nän'fīnīt/ ▶*adj.* not finite. ■ *Grammar* (of a verb form) not limited by tense, person, or number. Contrasted with FINITE.

non·flam·ma·ble /nän'flaməbəl/ ▶*adj.* not catching fire easily; not flammable.

USAGE See usage at INFLAMMABLE.

non·ful·fill·ment /ˌnänfōōl'filmənt/ ▶*n.* failure to fulfill or carry out something desired, planned, or promised.

non·func·tion·al /nän'fəNGksHənəl/ ▶*adj.* not having any particular purpose or function. ■ not operating or in working order.

non·gov·ern·men·tal /ˌnängəvər(n)'mentl/ ▶*adj.* (esp. of an organization) not belonging to or associated with any government.

non-Hodg·kin's lym·pho·ma ▶*n. Medicine* a form of malignant lymphoma distinguished from Hodgkin's disease only by the absence of binucleate giant cells.

non·hu·man /nän'(h)yōōmən/ ▶*adj.* of, relating to, or characteristic of a creature or thing that is not a human being: *ascribing human characteristics to nonhuman animals.*
▶*n.* a creature that is not a human being.

no·ni /'nōnē/ ▶*n.* any of various evergreen trees or shrubs of the madder family (Genus *Morinda*) native to the South Pacific. Various preparations, mainly for the treatment of pain, are made from their leaves, roots, and fruit. ▷Tahitian.

non·in·flam·ma·ble /ˌnänin'flaməbəl/ ▶*adj.* not catching fire easily; not flammable.

USAGE Technically, there is no difference between **nonflammable** and **noninflammable,** but the preferred, less confusing choice is **nonflammable.** See also **usage** at INFLAMMABLE.

non·in·her·ent /ˌnänin'herənt/ ▶*adj.* (of an adjective) having the relevant meaning only when used attributively with reference to a particular individual; for example, *poor* and *old* in *the poor old fellow,* which is not equivalent to *the fellow was poor and old.* Contrasted with INHERENT.

non·in·su·lin-de·pend·ent /'nän'insəlin/ ▶*adj. Medicine* relating to or denoting a type of diabetes in which there is some insulin secretion. Such diabetes typically develops in adulthood and can frequently be managed by diet and hypoglycemic agents.

non·in·ter·laced /ˌnänintər'lāst/ ▶*adj.* (of a monitor) denoting, relating to, or capable of graphic display in which adjacent lines or picture elements are displayed in succession, so as to form a single scanning sequence.

non·in·ter·ven·tion /ˌnänintər'vensHən/ ▶*n.* the principle or practice of not becoming involved in the affairs of others. ■ such a policy adopted by a country in its international relations. **—non·in·ter·ven·tion·ism** /-ˌnizəm/ *n.* **—non·in·ter·ven·tion·ist** /-nist/ *adj.* & *n.*

non·in·va·sive /ˌnänin'vāsiv/ ▶*adj.* **1** (of medical procedures) not requiring the introduction of instruments into the body: *noninvasive techniques such as ultrasound.* **2** (of a cancerous disease) not tending to spread. ■ (of plants) not tending to spread undesirably.

non·i·on·ic /ˌnäni'änik/ ▶*adj. Chemistry* not ionic. ■ (of a detergent) not dissociating into ions in aqueous solution.

non·ism /'nänizəm/ ▶*n.* general abstention from activities and substances regarded as damaging to one's health or well-being.

non·is·sue /'nän'isHo͞o/ ▶*n.* a topic of little or no importance.

non·judg·men·tal /ˌnänjəj'mentl/ (also **non·judge·men·tal**) ▶*adj.* not judgmental; avoiding moral judgments.

non·ju·di·cial /ˌnänjo͞o'disHəl/ ▶*adj.* **1** not resulting from a court ruling or judgment: *nonjudicial punishment.* **2** not involving courts or judges: *nonjudicial appointments.*

Non·ju·ror /nän'jo͝orər/ ▶*n.* a member of the English clergy who refused to take the oath of allegiance to William and Mary in 1689.

non·ju·ry /nän'jo͝orē/ ▶*adj. Law* denoting a trial or legal action not having or requiring a jury.

non li·cet /'nän 'lisit/ ▶*adj.* not allowed; unlawful. ▷Latin.

non·lin·e·ar /nän'linēər/ ▶*adj.* **1** not denoting, involving, or arranged in a straight line. ■ *Mathematics* designating or involving an equation whose terms are not of the first degree. ■ *Physics* involving a lack of linearity between two related qualities such as input and output. ■ *Mathematics* involving measurement in more than one dimension. ■ not linear, sequential, or straightforward; random: *Joyce's stream-of-consciousness, nonlinear narrative.* **2** of or denoting digital editing whereby a sequence of edits is stored on computer as opposed to videotape, thus facilitating further editing. **—non·lin·e·ar·i·ty** /ˌnänlinē'aritē/ *n.* **—non·line·ar·ly** *adv.*

▶*PHRASE* □ **go nonlinear** *informal* become excited or angry, esp. about a particular obsession.

non·log·i·cal /nän'läjikəl/ ▶*adj.* not derived from or according to the rules of logic or formal argument (less forceful in meaning than **illogical**). **—non·log·i·cal·ly** /-ik(ə)lē/ *adv.*

non·mem·ber /'nänˌmembər/ ▶*n.* a person, body, or country that is not a member of a particular organization. **—non·mem·ber·ship** /nän'membərˌsHip/ *n.*

non·met·al /ˌnän'metl/ ▶*n.* an element or substance that is not a metal. **—non·me·tal·lic** /ˌnänmə'talik/ *adj.*

non·mor·al /nän'môrəl/ ▶*adj.* not holding or manifesting moral principles: *nonmoral value judgments.*

non·na·tive /'nänˌnātiv/ ▶*adj.* (of a person, plant, or animal) not indigenous or native to a particular place. ■ (of a speaker) not having spoken the language in question from earliest childhood.

non·nat·u·ral /nän'nacHərəl/ ▶*adj.* not involving or manifesting natural means or processes. ■ *Philosophy* existing but not part of the natural world (a term used by G.E. Moore of ethical properties).

non·neg·a·tive /nän'negətiv/ ▶*adj.* not negative. ■ *Mathematics* either positive or equal to zero.

non·ne·go·ti·a·ble /ˌnä(n)nə'gōsHəbəl/ ▶*adj.* not open to discussion or modification. ■ (of a document) not able to be transferred or assigned to the legal ownership of another person.

non-net /nän'net/ ▶*adj.* (of an amount) including tax and other sums in addition to the net amount.

non·nu·cle·ar /nän'n(y)o͞oklēər/ ▶*adj.* **1** not involving or relating to nuclear energy or nuclear weapons. ■ (of a country) not possessing nuclear weapons. **2** *Physics* not involving, relating to, or forming part of a nucleus or nuclei.

no-no ▶*n.* (*pl.* **-nos**) *informal* a thing that is not possible or acceptable: *perming highlighted hair used to be **a** definite **no-no**, but it's now possible.*

non·ob·jec·tive /ˌnänəb'jektiv/ ▶*adj.* **1** (of a person or their judgment) influenced by personal feeling or opinions in considering and representing facts. **2** of or relating to abstract art.

no-non·sense ▶*adj.* simple and straightforward; sensible.

non·or·gan·ic /ˌnänôr'ganik/ ▶*adj.* not organic, in particular: ■ not relating to or derived from living matter: *nonorganic archaeological finds.* ■ (esp. of food or farming methods) not involving or relating to production by organic methods: *nonorganic hens' eggs | nonorganic pesticides.*

non·pa·ra·met·ric /ˌnänparə'metrik/ ▶*adj. Statistics* not involving any assumptions as to the form or parameters of a frequency distribution.

non·pa·reil /ˌnänpə'rel/ ▶*adj.* having no match or equal; unrivaled: *he is a nonpareil storyteller* | [*postpositive*] *a film critic nonpareil.*

▶*n.* **1** an unrivaled or matchless person or thing. **2** a flat round candy made of chocolate covered with white sugar sprinkles. **3** *Printing* an old type size equal to six points (larger than ruby or agate, smaller than emerald or minion). ▷late Middle English: from French, from *non-* 'not' + *pareil* 'equal' (from popular Latin *pariculus*, diminutive of Latin *par* 'equal').

non·par·tic·i·pat·ing /ˌnänpər'tisəˌpātiNG/ ▶*adj.* **1** not involved or taking part in an activity. **2** (of an insurance policy) not allowing the holder a share of the profits, typically in the form of a bonus, made by the company.

non·par·ti·san /nän'pärtizən/ ▶*adj.* not biased or partisan, esp. toward any particular political group.

non·par·ty ▶*adj.* independent of any political party.

non·past /'nänˌpast/ ▶*n. Grammar* a tense not expressing a past action or state.

non·pay·ment ▶*n.* failure to pay an amount of money that is owed: *homes repossessed for nonpayment of mortgages.*

non·pen·e·tra·tive ▶*adj.* (of sexual activity) in which penetration by the penis does not take place.

non·per·for·mance /ˌnänpər'fôrməns/ ▶*n.* failure or refusal to perform or fulfill a condition, promise, etc.: *the vendor will be sued by the customer for nonperformance.* ■ the state of not being performed: *plays developed in nonperformance workshops.*

non·per·son /ˌnän'pərsən/ ▶*n.* a person regarded as nonexistent or unimportant, or as having no rights; an ignored or forgotten person: *these players were famous within their own communities, but nonpersons outside them.* Compare with **UNPERSON**.

non pla·cet /ˌnän 'plāsit/ ▶*n.* a negative vote in a church or college assembly. ▷Latin, literally 'it does not please.'

non·plus /nän'pləs/ ▶*v.* (**-plussed**, **-plus·sing**) [*trans.*] (usu. **be nonplussed**) surprise and confuse (someone) so much that they are unsure how to react: *Diane was nonplussed by such an odd question.*

▶*n.* a state of being surprised and confused in this way. ▷late 16th cent.: from Latin *non plus* 'not more.' The noun originally meant 'a state in which no more can be said or done.'

non·plussed /nän'pləst/ (also **non·plused**) ▶*adj.* **1** (of a person) surprised and confused so much that they are unsure how to react: *he would be completely nonplussed and embarrassed at the idea.* **2** *informal* (of a person) not disconcerted; unperturbed.

USAGE In standard use, **nonplussed** means 'surprised and confused': *the hostility of the new neighbor's refusal left Mrs. Walker nonplussed.* In North American English, a new use has developed in recent years, meaning 'unperturbed'—more or less the opposite of its traditional meaning: *hoping to disguise his confusion, he tried to appear **nonplussed**.* This new use probably arose on the assumption that **non-** was the normal negative prefix and must therefore have a negative meaning. Although the use is common, it is not yet considered standard. The preferred spelling is **nonplussed**.

non·point source /nän'point/ ▶*n.* a source of pollution that issues from widely distributed or pervasive environmental elements: *cattle are the leading nonpoint source of pollution in Canada today.*

non pos·su·mus /ˌnän 'päs(y)əməs/ ▶*n.* used as a statement expressing inability to act in a matter. ▷Latin, literally 'we cannot.'

non·pre·scrip·tion /ˌnänprə'skripsHən/ ▶*adj.* (of a medicine) available for sale without a prescription. ■ denoting such sale or purchase.

non·pro·duc·tive /ˌnänprə'dəktiv/ ▶*adj.* not producing or able to produce goods, crops, or economic benefit (tending to be less forceful in meaning than **unproductive**). ■ achieving little. **—non·pro·duc·tive·ly** *adv.*

non·pro·fes·sion·al /ˌnänprə'fesHənəl/ ▶*adj.* relating to or engaged in a paid occupation that does not require advanced education or training: *nonprofessional grades of staff.* ■ relating to or engaged in an activity (esp. an interest or hobby) that is not a person's main paid occupation: *nonprofessional actors.*

▶*n.* a nonprofessional person.

non·prof·it /'nän'präfit/ ▶*adj.* [*attrib.*] not making or conducted primarily to make a profit: *charities and other nonprofit organizations.*

non·pro·lif·er·a·tion /ˌnänprəˌlifə'rāsHən/ ▶*n.* the prevention of an increase or spread of something, esp. the number of countries possessing nuclear weapons: [as *adj.*] *a nuclear nonproliferation treaty.*

non·pro·pri·e·tar·y /ˌnänprə'prīəˌterē/ ▶*adj.* (esp. of computer hardware or software) conforming to standards that are in the public domain or are widely licensed, and so not restricted to one manufacturer. ■ not registered or protected as a trademark or brand name; generic.

non-pros (abbr.: **non pros.**) /nän'präs/ ▶*v.* [*trans.*] *Law* adjudge (a plaintiff) in default.

non·ra·cial /nän'rāsHəl/ ▶*adj.* not involving racial factors or racial discrimination.

non·read·er /'nän'rēdər/ ▶*n.* a person who cannot or does not read.

non·res·i·dent /nän'rezidənt/ ▶*adj.* not living in a particular place, esp. a country or a place of work: *the building had a nonresident, part-time caretaker.* ■ (of a job or program of study) not requiring the holder or participant to reside at the place of work or instruction. ■ *Computing* (of software) not kept permanently in memory but available to be loaded from a backing store or external device: *if you want to use a nonresident font, you can manually download it.*

▶*n.* a person not living in a particular place: *parking permits are available for Richmond residents and nonresidents.* **—non·res·i·dence** *n.*

non·res·i·den·tial /ˌnänrezə'dencHəl/ ▶*adj.* not requiring or providing facilities for people to live on the premises: *two-day nonresidential workshops.* ■ (of property or land) containing or suitable for commercial premises rather than private houses.

non·re·sis·tance /ˌnänri'zistəns/ ▶*n.* the practice or principle of not resisting authority, even when it is unjustly exercised.

non·re·stric·tive /ˌnänri'striktiv/ ▶*adj.* **1** not involving restrictions or limitations. **2** *Grammar* (of a relative clause or descriptive phrase) giving additional information about a noun phrase whose particular reference has already been specified.

USAGE On the use of **restrictive** and **nonrestrictive** relative clauses, see **usage** at **RESTRICTIVE**, **THAT**, and **WHICH**.

non-re·turn /ˌnän ri'tərn/ ▶*adj. Brit.* permitting the flow of air or liquid in one direction only: *a nonreturn valve.*

non·re·turn·a·ble /ˌnänri'tərnəbəl/ ▶*adj.* (esp. of a deposit paid) not repayable in any circumstances. ■ (of bottles or other containers) not intended to be returned empty to the suppliers.

non·rho·tic /nän'rōtik/ ▶*n. Phonetics* relating to or denoting a dialect of English in which *r* is pronounced in prevocalic position only, common in eastern New England, New York City, and Britain.

non·rig·id /nän'rijid/ ▶*adj.* (esp. of materials) not rigid. ■ denoting an airship whose shape is maintained solely by the pressure of the gas inside.

non-scene /nän 'sēn/ ▶*adj. informal, chiefly Brit.* (of a homosexual) not inclined to participate in the social environment frequented predominantly by other homosexuals.

non·sched·uled /'nän'skejəld; -jo͞old/ ▶*adj.* denoting or relating to an airline that operates without fixed or published flying schedules: *measures for nonscheduled sites are being considered.*

non·sec·tar·i·an /ˌnänsek'te(ə)rēən/ ▶*adj.* not involving or relating to a specific religious sect or political group.

non·sense /'nänˌsens/ ▶*n.* **1** spoken or written words that have no meaning or make no sense: *he was talking absolute nonsense.* ■ [as *exclam.*] used to show strong disagreement: *"Nonsense! No one can do that."* ■ [as *adj.*] denoting verse or other writing intended to be amusing by virtue of its absurd or whimsical language: *nonsense poetry.* **2** foolish or unacceptable behavior: *put a stop to that nonsense, will you?* ■ something that one disagrees with or disapproves of: *the idea that the gut is full of toxins that have to be flushed away is dismissed as nonsense by gastroenterologists.* **—non·sen·si·cal** /nän'sensikəl/ *adj.* **—non·sen·si·cal·i·ty** /ˌnänsensə'kalitē/ *n.* **—non·sen·si·cal·ly** /nän'sensik(ə)lē/ *adv.*

N

THE RIGHT WORD **bull, bunk, drivel, nonsense, poppycock, twaddle**

If you write or speak in an obscure, senseless, or unintelligible manner, you'll probably be accused of producing **nonsense**. It is the most general of these nouns and may refer to behavior as well as to what is said (*the demonstrators were told in no uncertain terms to stop this nonsense or leave the room*).

Twaddle refers to silly, empty utterances from people who know nothing about a subject but who write or talk about it anyway (*I was sick of her twaddle about the dangers of electromagnetic fields*).

Bunk (short for bunkum) applies to an utterance that strikes the popular fancy even though it is lacking in worth or substance (*the speech, which received enthusiastic applause, was pure bunk*).

Poppycock applies to nonsense that is full of complex, confused, or clichéd ideas (*the report was a strange combination of logical thinking and outright poppycock*).

Bull is a slang term for deceitful and often boastful writing or speech (*he gave them a line of bull*).

Perhaps the most insulting of these terms is **drivel**, which implies a steady flow of inane, idle, or nonsensical speech or writing similar to what might be expected from a very young child or an idiot (*his first novel was full of romantic drivel*).

non·sense syl·la·ble ▶*n.* an arbitrarily formed syllable with no meaning, esp. in songs or as used in memory experiments and tests.

non·sense word ▶*n.* a word having no conventionally accepted meaning.

non se·qui·tur /ˌnän 'sekwitər/ ▶*n.* a conclusion or statement that does not logically follow from the previous argument or statement. ▷Latin, literally 'it does not follow.'

non·skid /ˌnän'skid/ ▶*adj.* designed to prevent sliding or skidding: *nonskid tires.*

non·slip ▶*adj.* designed to prevent slipping: *a nonslip bath mat.*

non·smok·ing /nän'smōkiNG/ ▶*adj.* denoting a place where smoking tobacco is forbidden: *a window seat in the nonsmoking section.* ■ denoting a person who does not smoke: *nonsmoking mothers.*
▶*n.* the practice or habit of not smoking.

non·so·lid col·or /nän'sälid/ ▶*n.* *Computing* a color simulated by a pattern of dots of other colors, extending the range of colors available.

non·spe·cif·ic /ˌnänspə'sifik/ ▶*adj.* not detailed or exact; general. ■ *Medicine* not assignable to a particular cause, condition, or category.

non·spe·cif·ic u·re·thri·tis /ˌyo͝orə'THrītis/ (abbr.: **NSU**) ▶*n.* *Medicine* inflammation of the urethra due to infection by chlamydiae or other organisms (other than gonococci).

non·stand·ard /'nän'standərd/ ▶*adj.* not average, normal, or usual: *people working nonstandard hours.* ■ (of language) not of the form that is accepted as standard.

non·start·er /'nän'stärtər/ ▶*n.* a person or animal that fails to take part in a race. ■ *informal* a person, plan, or idea that has no chance of succeeding or being effective.

non·stick /'nän'stik/ ▶*adj.* (of a pan or surface) covered with a substance that prevents food from sticking to it during cooking: *a nonstick frying pan.*

non·stoi·chi·o·met·ric /ˌnänˌstoikēō'metrik/ ▶*adj.* *Chemistry* relating to or denoting quantities of reactants that are not in a simple integral ratio or are not in the ratio expected from an ideal formula or equation.

non·stop /'nän'stäp/ ▶*adj.* continuing without stopping or pausing: *we had two days of almost nonstop rain.* ■ (of a passenger vehicle or journey) not having or making stops at intermediate places on the way to its destination: *a nonstop flight to Los Angeles.* ■ oppressively constant; relentless: *the show was axed after nonstop criticism.*
▶*adv.* without stopping or pausing: *Stephen had been working nonstop.*
▶*n.* a nonstop flight or train: *seven nonstops to New York every business day.*

non·struck /nän'strək/ ▶*adj.* **1** not having been the subject of a labor strike: *nonstruck Association members.* **2** not having been stricken: *occupants of the nonstruck side of the vehicle.* **3** not having been eliminated: *nonstruck jurors.*

non·such ▶*n.* variant spelling of **NONESUCH**.

non·suit /nän'so͞ot/ *Law* ▶*v.* [*trans.*] (of a judge or court) subject (a plaintiff) to the stoppage of their suit on the grounds of failure to make a legal case or bring sufficient evidence.
▶*n.* the stoppage of a suit on such grounds. ▷late Middle English (as a noun): from Anglo-Norman French, literally 'not pursuing' (see **NON-**, **SUIT**).

non·sup·port /ˌnänsə'pôrt/ ▶*n.* *Law* failure to provide for the maintenance of a child, spouse, or other dependent as required by law.

non·tech·ni·cal /nän'teknikəl/ ▶*adj.* not relating to or involving science or technology: *a simple, nontechnical procedure.* ■ without specialized or technical knowledge: *a nontechnical background.* ■ not using technical terms or requiring specialized knowledge.

non·tox·ic /nän'täksik/ ▶*adj.* not poisonous or toxic: *nontoxic waste.*

non·triv·i·al /nän'trivēəl/ ▶*adj.* not trivial; significant. ■ *Mathematics* having some variables or terms that are not equal to zero or an identity.

non·trop·i·cal sprue /nän'träpikəl 'spro͞o/ ▶*n.* see **SPRUE**[2].

non-U /nän 'yo͞o/ ▶*adj.* *informal, chiefly Brit.* (of language or social behavior) not characteristic of the upper social classes; not socially acceptable to certain people. ▷1950s: from **NON-** + **U**[3].

non·un·ion /nän'yo͞onyən/ ▶*adj.* not belonging to or relating to a labor union: *nonunion farm workers | nonunion agreements.* ■ (of a company) not having labor union members: *a high proportion of newly established firms are nonunion.* ■ not done or produced by members of a labor union: *he sells nonunion doughnuts.*

non·ver·bal /nän'vərbəl/ ▶*adj.* not involving or using words or speech: *forms of nonverbal communication.* —**non·ver·bal·ly** *adv.*

non·vin·tage /nän'vintij/ ▶*adj.* denoting a wine that is not made from the crop of a single identified district in a good year.

non·vi·o·lence /nän'vīələns/ ▶*n.* the use of peaceful means, not force, to bring about political or social change.

non·vi·o·lent /ˌnän'vīələnt/ ▶*adj.* (esp. of political action or resistance) characterized by nonviolence. ■ (esp. of a person) not using violence. —**non·vi·o·lent·ly** *adv.*

non·vol·a·tile /nän'välətl/ ▶*adj.* not volatile. ■ *Computing* (of a computer's memory) retaining data even if there is a break in the power supply.

non·white /ˌnän'(h)wīt/ ▶*adj.* denoting or relating to a person whose origin is not predominantly European.
▶*n.* a person whose origin is not predominantly European.

USAGE The term **nonwhite** has been objected to as politically incorrect on the grounds that it assumes that the norm is white. However, although alternatives such as **person of color** have been put forward in recent years, they have not yet become widespread. **Nonwhite** continues to be broadly accepted where a collective term is required to show a distinction, as in statistical or demographic categories.

See also **usage** at **PERSON OF COLOR**.

non·word /'nän'wərd/ ▶*n.* a group of letters or speech sounds that looks or sounds like a word but is not accepted as such by native speakers.

non·yl /'nänil; 'nō-/ ▶*n.* [as *adj.*] *Chemistry* of or denoting an alkyl radical $-C_9H_{19}$, derived from nonane.

non·ze·ro /nän'zērō/ ▶*adj.* having a positive or negative value; not equal to zero.

noo·dle[1] /'no͞odl/ ▶*n.* (usu. **noodles**) a strip, ring, or tube of pasta or a similar dough, typically made with egg and usually eaten with a sauce or in a soup. ▷late 18th cent.: from German *Nudel*, of unknown origin.

noo·dle[2] ▶*n.* *informal* a stupid or silly person. ■ a person's head. ▷mid 18th cent.: of unknown origin. The sense 'head' dates from the early 20th cent.

noo·dle[3] /'no͞odl/ ▶*v.* [*intrans.*] *informal* improvise or play casually on a musical instrument: *tapes of him noodling on his guitar* | [as *noun*] (**noodling**) *ambient synthesizer noodling.* ▷mid 19th cent.: of unknown origin.

noog·ie /'no͝ogē/ ▶*n.* a hard poke or grind with the knuckles, esp. on a person's head: *maybe he would just grab the little guy and plant a friendly noogie on his head.*

nook /no͝ok/ ▶*n.* a corner or recess, esp. one offering seclusion or security: *the nook beside the fire.* ▷Middle English (denoting a corner or fragment): of unknown origin.
▶*PHRASE* □ **every nook and cranny** every part or aspect of something: *the party reached into every nook and cranny of people's lives.*

nook·y /'no͝okē/ (also **nook·ie**) ▶*n.* *vulgar slang* sexual activity or intercourse. ▷early 20th cent.: perhaps from **NOOK**.

noon /no͞on/ ▶*n.* twelve o'clock in the day; midday: *his classes let out at noon | the service starts at* **twelve noon**. ▷Old English *nōn* 'the ninth hour from sunrise, i.e., approximately 3 p.m.,' from Latin *nona (hora)* 'ninth hour'; compare with **NONE**[2].

noon·day /'no͞onˌdā/ ▶*n.* the middle of the day: [as *adj.*] *the blinds were lowered to keep out the noonday sun.*

no one ▶*pron.* no person; not a single person: *no one came | she told no one she was going.*

noon·er /'no͞onər/ ▶*n.* *informal* an event that occurs in the middle of the day, esp. an act of sexual intercourse.

noon·ing /'no͞oniNG/ ▶*n.* *dialect* a rest or meal at midday.

noon·tide /'no͞onˌtīd/ (also **noon·time** /-ˌtīm/) ▶*n.* *poetic/literary* noon.

noose /no͞os/ ▶*n.* a loop with a running knot, tightening as the rope or wire is pulled and typically used to hang people or trap animals. ■ (**the noose**) death by hanging. ■ (**the noose**) *figurative* a difficult situation regarded as a restraint or bond: *the West is exploring ways to* **tighten the** *economic* **noose**.
▶*v.* [*trans.*] put a noose on (someone): *she was noosed and hooded, then strangled by the executioner.* ■ catch (an animal) with a noose. ■ form (a rope) into a noose. ▷late Middle English: probably via Old French *no(u)s* from Latin *nodus* 'knot.'
▶*PHRASE* □ **put one's head in a noose** bring about one's own downfall.

no·o·sphere /'nōəˌsfir/ ▶*n.* a postulated sphere or stage of evolutionary development dominated by consciousness, the mind, and interpersonal relationships (frequently with reference to the writings of Teilhard de Chardin). ▷1940s: from French *noösphere*, based on Greek *noos* 'mind.'

Noot·ka /'no͞otkə; 'no͝ot-/ ▶*n.* (*pl.* same or **-kas**) **1** a member of an American Indian people of Vancouver Island, Canada. **2** the Wakashan language of this people.
▶*adj.* of or relating to this people or their language. ▷named after *Nootka* Sound, an inlet on the coast of Vancouver Island.

Noot·ka cy·press ▶*n.* a conical cypress whose foliage has a turpentine smell when crushed. Native to western North America and typically growing at high altitudes, it is one of the parent species of the Leyland cypress. Also called **ALASKA CEDAR**. • *Chamaecyparis nootkatensis*, family Cupressaceae.

no·o·trop·ic /ˌnōə'träpik/ ▶*adj.* (of a drug) used to enhance memory or other cognitive functions.
▶*n.* a drug of this kind. ▷1970s: from French *nootrope* (from Greek *noos* 'mind' + *tropē* 'turning') + **-IC**.

n.o.p. (also **NOP**) ▶*abbr.* not our publication.

no·pal /'nōpəl; nō'päl/ ▶*n.* (*pl.* **-pa·les** /-'päles/) a cactus that is a major food plant of the bugs from which cochineal is obtained. • Genus *Nopalea*, family Cactaceae: several species, in particular *N. cochinellifera*. ■ (**nopales**) the edible fleshy pads of this cactus, used as a staple in Mexican cuisine. ■ the prickly pear cactus, when used in food supplements and herbal preparations. ▷mid 18th cent.: via French and Spanish from Nahuatl *nopalli* 'cactus.'

no·pal·es /nō'päles/ ▶ *n.* the fleshy leaves of a prickly pear cactus, used as an ingredient in Mexican cuisine.

nope /nōp/ ▶*exclam.* informal variant of **NO**.

nor /nôr/ ▶*conj.* & *adv.* **1** used before the second or further of two or more alternatives (the first being introduced by a negative such as "neither" or "not") to indicate that they are each untrue or each do not happen: *they were neither cheap nor convenient | the sheets were never washed, nor the towels, nor his shirts.* ■ [as *adv.*] poetic/literary term for **NEITHER**: *nor God nor demon can undo the done.* **2** used to introduce a further negative statement: *the struggle did not end, nor was it any less diminished.* **3** [*conj.* or *prep.*] *archaic* or *dialect* than: *she thinks she knows better nor me.*
▶*n.* (usu. **NOR**) *Electronics* a Boolean operator that gives the value one if and only if all operands have a value of zero and otherwise has a value of zero. ■ (also **NOR gate**) a circuit that produces an output signal only when there are no signals on any of the input connections. ▷Middle English: contraction of Old English *nother* 'neither.'

USAGE On the use of **neither ... nor**, see **usage** at **NEITHER**.

nor' /nôr/ ▶*abbr.* (esp. in compounds) north: *seek shelter from a raging nor'easter.*

nor- ▸*prefix Chemistry* denoting an organic compound derived from another, in particular by the shortening of a chain or ring by the removal of one methylene group or by the replacement of one or more methyl side chains by hydrogen atoms: *norepinephrine.* ▹from *nor(mal).*

NORAD /ˈnôr,ad/ ▸*abbr.* North American Aerospace Defense Command.

nor·a·dren·a·line /,nôrəˈdrenəlin/ (also **nor·a·dren·a·lin**) ▸*n.* another term for NOREPINEPHRINE. ▹1930s: from NOR- + ADRENALINE.

Nor·dic /ˈnôrdik/ ▸*adj.* of or relating to Scandinavia, Finland, Iceland, and the Faroe Islands. ■ relating to or denoting a physical type of northern European peoples characterized by tall stature, a bony frame, light coloring, and a dolichocephalic head. ■ *Skiing* relating to or denoting the disciplines of cross-country skiing or ski jumping. Often contrasted with ALPINE.
▸*n.* a native of Scandinavia, Finland, or Iceland. ▹from French *nordique*, from *nord* 'north.'

Nord·kapp /ˈno͝or,käp/ Norwegian name for NORTH CAPE.

Nord·kyn /ˈno͝orkin; -,kʏn/ a promontory on the northern coast of Norway, to the east of North Cape, the northernmost point on the European mainland.

Nord-Pas-de-Ca·lais /nôr ,pä də käˈlā/ a region of northern France, on the border with Belgium.

Nord·rhein-West·fa·len /ˈnôrt,rīn vestˈfälən/ German name for NORTH RHINE-WESTPHALIA.

nor·ep·i·neph·rine /,nôrepəˈnefrin/ ▸*n. Biochemistry* a hormone that is released by the adrenal medulla and by the sympathetic nerves and functions as a neurotransmitter. It is also used as a drug to raise blood pressure. Also called NORADRENALINE. • Chem. formula: $(HO)_2C_6H_3CHOHCH_2NH_2$. ▹1940s: from NOR- + EPINEPHRINE.

Nor·folk /ˈnôrfək/ **1** a county on the eastern coast of England, east of an inlet of the North Sea called the Wash; county town, Norwich. **2** a city in northeastern Nebraska, northwest of Omaha; pop. 23,516. **3** an industrial and naval port city in southeastern Virginia, on Hampton Roads; pop. 234,403.

Nor·folk Is·land an island in the Pacific Ocean, off the eastern coast of Australia, administered since 1913 as an external territory of Australia; pop. 1,912.

Nor·folk Is·land pine (also **Norfolk pine**) ▸*n.* an evergreen tree having horizontal branches with upswept shoots bearing small scalelike leaves. Native to Norfolk Island, it is widely grown as a houseplant. • *Araucaria heterophylla*, family Araucariaceae.

Nor·folk jack·et ▸*n.* a loose belted jacket with box pleats, typically made of tweed.

Nor·folk ter·ri·er ▸*n.* a small thickset terrier of a breed with a rough red or black-and-tan coat and drop ears.

Nor·ge /ˈnôrgə/ Norwegian name for NORWAY.

no·ri /ˈnôrē/ ▸*n.* an edible seaweed, eaten either fresh or dried in sheets, esp. by the Japanese. ▹Japanese.

no·ri·a /ˈnôrēə/ ▸*n.* a device for raising water from a stream or river, consisting of a chain of pots or buckets revolving around a wheel driven by the water current. ▹via Spanish from Arabic *nāʿūra.*

No·ri·e·ga /,nôrēˈāgə/, Manuel (Antonio Morena) (1940–), Panamanian statesman and general; head of state 1983–89. Charged with drug trafficking by a U.S. grand jury in 1988, he eventually surrendered to U.S. troops sent into Panama to capture him; he was brought to trial and convicted in 1992.

nor·ite /ˈnôrīt/ ▸*n. Geology* a coarse-grained plutonic rock similar to gabbro but containing hypersthene. ▹late 19th cent.: from NORWAY + -ITE[1].

norm /nôrm/ ▸*n.* **1** (**the norm**) something that is usual, typical, or standard: *this system has been the norm in Germany for decades.* ■ (usu. **norms**) a standard or pattern, esp. of social behavior, that is typical or expected of a group: *the norms of good behavior in the civil service.* ■ a required standard; a level to be complied with or reached: [with *adj.*] *the 7% pay norm had been breached again.* **2** *Mathematics* the product of a complex number and its conjugate, equal to the sum of the squares of its real and imaginary components, or the positive square root of this sum. ■ an analogous quantity used to represent the magnitude of a vector. ▹early 19th cent.: from Latin *norma* 'precept, rule, carpenter's square.'

norm. ▸*abbr.* normal.

Nor·ma /ˈnôrmə/ *Astronomy* a small and inconspicuous southern constellation (the Rule), lying partly in the Milky Way between Lupus and Ara. ■ [as *genitive*] (**Nor·mae** /-mē/) used with a preceding letter or numeral to designate a star in this constellation: *the star Gamma Normae.* ▹Latin, 'carpenter's square.'

Nor·mal /ˈnôrməl/ a town in central Illinois, home to Illinois State University (originally a *normal*, or teachers, school); pop. 40,023.

nor·mal /ˈnôrməl/ ▸*adj.* **1** conforming to a standard; usual, typical, or expected: *it's quite* **normal for** *puppies to bolt their food* | *normal working hours.* ■ (of a person) free from physical or mental disorders. **2** *technical* (of a line, ray, or other linear feature) intersecting a given line or surface at right angles. **3** *Medicine* (of a salt solution) containing the same salt concentration as the blood. ■ *dated Chemistry* (of a solution) containing one gram-equivalent of solute per liter. **4** *Geology* denoting a fault or faulting in which a relative downward movement occurred in the strata situated on the upper side of the fault plane.
▸*n.* **1** the usual, average, or typical state or condition: *her temperature was* **above normal** | *the service will be* **back to normal** *next week.* ■ a person who is physically or mentally healthy. **2** *technical* a line at right angles to a given line or surface. ▹mid 17th cent. (in the sense 'right-angled'): from Latin *normalis*, from *norma* 'carpenter's square' (see NORM). Current senses date from the early 19th cent. **—nor·mal·cy** /-məlsē/ *n.* **—nor·mal·i·ty** /nôrˈmalitē/ *n.*

USAGE **Normalcy** has been criticized as an uneducated alternative to **normality**, but actually is a common American usage and can be taken as standard: *we are anticipating a return to* **normalcy**.

THE RIGHT WORD **average, natural, normal, ordinary, regular, typical, usual**

Most people want to be regarded as **normal**, an adjective that implies conformity with established norms or standards and is the opposite of abnormal (*a normal body temperature; normal intelligence*).

Regular, like *normal*, is usually preferred to its opposite (irregular) and implies conformity to prescribed standards or established patterns (*their regular monthly meeting; a regular guy*), but *normal* carries stronger connotations of conformity within prescribed limits and sometimes allows for a wider range of differences.

Few of us think of ourselves as **ordinary**, a term used to describe what is commonplace or unexceptional (*an ordinary person wearing ordinary clothes*), although many people are ordinary in some ways and extraordinary in others.

Average also implies conformity with what is regarded as *normal* or *ordinary* (*a woman of average height*), although it tends to emphasize the middle ground and to exclude both positive and negative extremes.

Typical applies to persons or things possessing the representative characteristics of a type or class (*a typical teenager*).

Someone or something described as **natural** behaves or operates in accordance with an inherent nature or character (*his fears were natural for one so young*), while **usual** applies to that which conforms to common or ordinary use or occurrence (*we paid the usual price*).

nor·mal dis·tri·bu·tion ▸*n. Statistics* a function that represents the distribution of many random variables as a symmetrical bell-shaped graph.

nor·mal form ▸*n.* **1** *Computing* a defined standard structure for relational databases in which a relation may not be nested within another relation. **2** *Philosophy* a standard structure or format in which all propositions in a (usually symbolic) language can be expressed.

nor·mal·ize /ˈnôrmə,līz/ ▸*v.* **1** [*trans.*] bring or return to a normal condition or state: *Vietnam and China agreed to normalize diplomatic relations in 1991* | [*intrans.*] *the situation had normalized.* **2** [*trans.*] (often **be normalized**) *Mathematics* multiply (a series, function, or item of data) by a factor that makes the norm or some associated quantity such as an integral equal to a desired value (usually 1). ■ *Computing* (in floating-point representation) express (a number) in the standard form with regard to the position of the radix point, usually immediately preceding the first nonzero digit. **—nor·mal·i·za·tion** /,nôrmələˈzāSHən/ *n.* **—nor·mal·iz·er** *n.*

nor·mal·ly /ˈnôrməlē/ ▸*adv.* **1** [*sentence adverb*] under normal or usual conditions; as a rule: *normally, it takes three or four years to complete the training.* **2** in a normal manner; in the usual way: *try to breathe normally.* **3** *technical* at right angles to a given line or surface.

nor·mal·ly as·pi·rat·ed ▸*adj.* (of an engine) not turbocharged or supercharged.

nor·mal school ▸*n.* formerly, a school or college for the training of teachers.

Nor·man[1] /ˈnôrmən/ a city in central Oklahoma, south of Oklahoma City, home to the University of Oklahoma; pop. 95,694.

Nor·man[2] ▸*n.* **1** a member of a people of mixed Frankish and Scandinavian origin who settled in Normandy from about AD 912 and became a dominant military power in western Europe and the Mediterranean in the 11th century. ■ in particular, any of the Normans who conquered England in 1066 or their descendants. ■ a native or inhabitant of modern Normandy. ■ any of the English kings from William I to Stephen. **2** the form of French spoken by the Normans.
▸*adj.* of, relating to, or denoting the Normans. ■ denoting, relating to, or built in the style of Romanesque architecture used in Britain under the Normans. ■ of or relating to modern Normandy. ▹Middle English: from Old French *Normans*, plural of *Normant*, from Old Norse *Northmathr* 'Northman.' **—Nor·man·esque** /,nôrməˈnesk/ *adj.* **—Nor·man·ism** /-,nizəm/ *n.* **—Nor·man·ize** /-,nīz/ *v.*

Nor·man[3], Greg (1955–), Australian golfer; full name *Gregory John Norman*; called **Great White Shark**. He won the Australian Open in 1980, 1985, 1987, and 1995 and the British Open in 1986 and 1993.

Nor·man[4], Jessye (1945–), U.S. opera singer. She is noted for her interpretations of the works of Wagner, Schubert, and Mahler.

Nor·man Con·quest the conquest of England by William of Normandy (William the Conqueror) after the Battle of Hastings in 1066.

Nor·man·dy /ˈnôrməndē/ a former province of northwestern France with a coastline on the English Channel, now divided into the two regions of Lower Normandy (Basse-Normandie) and Upper Normandy (Haute-Normandie); chief town, Rouen.

Nor·man French ▸*n.* the northern form of Old French spoken by the Normans. ■ the variety of this used in English law courts from the 11th to 13th centuries; Anglo-Norman French. ■ the French dialect of modern Normandy.

nor·ma·tive /ˈnôrmətiv/ ▸*adj. formal* establishing, relating to, or deriving from a standard or norm, esp. of behavior: *negative sanctions to enforce normative behavior.* ▹late 19th cent.: from French *normatif, -ive*, from Latin *norma* 'carpenter's square' (see NORM). **—nor·ma·tive·ly** *adv.* **—nor·ma·tive·ness** *n.*

nor·mo·gly·ce·mi·a /,nôrmō,glīˈsēmēə/ (*Brit.* **nor·mo·gly·cae·mi·a**) ▸*n. Medicine* a normal concentration of sugar in the blood (as contrasted with hyper- or hypoglycemia). **—nor·mo·gly·ce·mic** /-ˈsēmik/ *adj.*

nor·mo·ten·sive /,nôrmōˈtensiv/ ▸*adj. Medicine* having or denoting a normal blood pressure.

Norn /nôrn/ ▸*n.* a form of Norse formerly spoken in the Orkney and Shetland Islands and some other parts of northern Scotland but largely extinct by the 19th century.
▸*adj.* of or relating to this language. ▹from Old Norse *norrœn* 'Norn, northern,' from *northr* 'north.'

Norns /nôrnz/ *Scandinavian Mythology* the three virgin goddesses of destiny (Urd or Urdar, Verdandi, and Skuld), who sit by the well of fate at the base of the ash tree Yggdrasil and spin the web of fate. ▹from Old Norse, of unknown origin.

No·ro·vi·rus /ˈnôrə,vīrəs/ ▸*n.* any of various single-stranded RNA nonenveloped viruses that can cause acute gastroenteritis in humans. • genus *Norovirus*, family Caliciviridae.

Nor·plant /ˈnôr,plant/ ▸*n. trademark* a contraceptive for women consisting of small rods implanted under the skin that gradually release the hormone levonorgestrel over a number of years. ▹1980s: from *(levo)nor(gestrel) (im)plant.*

Nor·ris /ˈnôris/, Frank (1870–1902), U.S. journalist and writer; full name *Benjamin Franklin Norris, Jr.* His fiction includes *McTeague: A Story of San Francisco* (1899) and *The Octopus* (1901). His unfinished trilogy *Epic of Wheat* documents the history of muckraking.

Norr·kö·ping /ˈnôr,SHəpiNG; -,SHœ-/ an industrial city

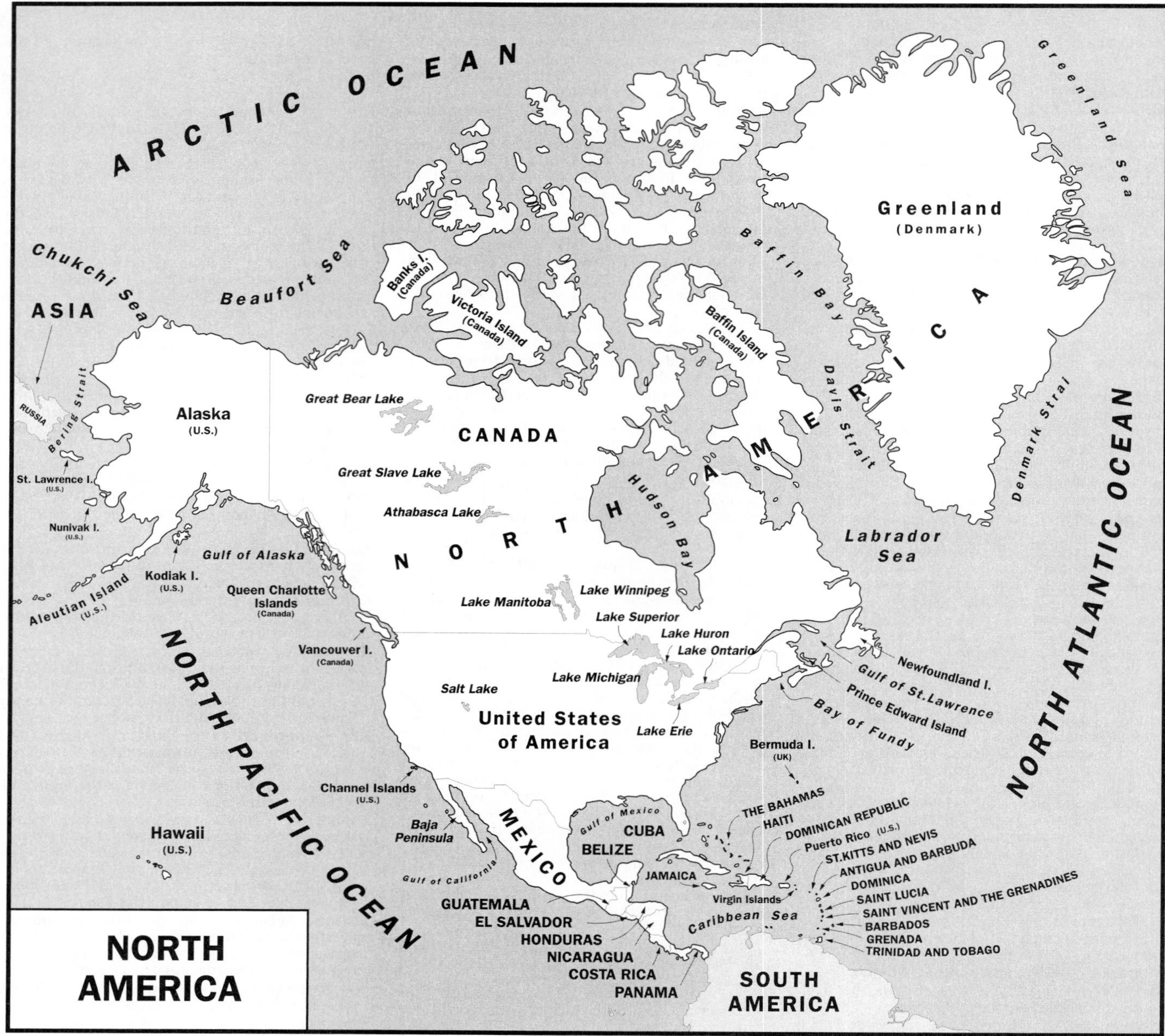

and port on an inlet of the Baltic Sea in southeastern Sweden; pop. 121,000.

Norse /nôrs/ ▸*n.* **1** the Norwegian language, esp. in its medieval form. ■ the Scandinavian language group. **2** [treated as *pl.*] Norwegians or Scandinavians, esp. in medieval times.

▸*adj.* of or relating to medieval Norway or Scandinavia, or their inhabitants or language. ▷from Dutch *noor(d)sch*, from *noord* 'north'; compare with Swedish, Danish, and Norwegian *Norsk*. **—Norse·man** /ˈnôrsmən/ *n.* (*pl.* **-men**).

nor·te·ño /nôrˈtānyō/ ▸*n.* **1** (*pl.* **-ños**) an inhabitant or native of northern Mexico. **2** (also **nor·te·ña** /nôrˈtānyə/) a style of folk music, associated particularly with northern Mexico and Texas, typically featuring an accordion and using polkas and other rhythms found in the music of central European immigrants. ▷Spanish, literally 'northerner.'

North[1] /nôrTH/, Frederick, Lord (1732–92), British statesman; prime minister 1770–82. He sought to avoid the American Revolution but was regarded as responsible for the loss of the American colonies.

North[2], Oliver (1943–), U.S. soldier. In 1986, he provided testimony to Congress on the Iran-Contra affair, saying that he believed that all of his activities as chief negotiator were authorized by his superiors. Three years later, he was found guilty on three of the twelve charges against him and was given a suspended jail sentence and fined $150,000. A conservative Republican, he ran unsuccessfully for the Senate from Virginia in 1994.

north /nôrTH/ ▸*n.* (usu. **the north**) **1** the direction in which a compass needle normally points, toward the horizon on the left side of a person facing east, or the part of the horizon lying in this direction: *a bitter wind blew from the north* | *Mount Kenya is* **to the north of** *Nairobi.* ■ the compass point corresponding to this. ■ a direction in space parallel to the earth's axis of rotation and toward the point on the celestial sphere around which the stars appear to turn counterclockwise. **2** the northern part of the world or of a specified country, region, or town: *cuisine from the north of Spain* | *limber pine in the central Rockies, and whitebark pine and alpine larch in the north.* ■ (usu. **the North**) the northern part of the U.S., esp. the northeastern states that fought to preserve the Union during the Civil War: *delegates from Virginia voted to join the North.* **3** (**North**) [as *name*] *Bridge* the player occupying a designated position at the table, sitting opposite and partnering South.

▸*adj.* [*attrib.*] **1** lying toward, near, or facing the north: *the north bank of the river* | *the north door.* ■ (of a wind) blowing from the north. **2** of or denoting the northern part of a specified area, city, or country or its inhabitants: *North African.*

▸*adv.* to or toward the north: *the landscape became more dramatic as we drove north* | *a north-facing wall.* ▷Old English, of Germanic origin; related to Dutch *noord* and German *nord.*

▸*PHRASES* □ **north by east** (or **west**) between north and north-northeast (or north-northwest). □ **up north** *informal* to or in the north of a country: *he's taken a teaching job up north.*

North Af·ri·ca the northern part of the African continent, esp. the countries bordering the Mediterranean and the Red Sea.

North A·mer·i·ca a continent comprising the northern half of the American landmass, connected to South America by the Isthmus of Panama. It contains Canada, the U.S., Mexico, the countries of Central America, and usually Greenland.

North A·mer·i·can ▸*adj.* of or relating to North America.

▸*n.* a native or inhabitant of North America, esp. a citizen of the U.S. or Canada.

North A·mer·i·can Free Trade A·gree·ment (abbr.: **NAFTA**) an agreement that came into effect in January 1994 between the U.S., Canada, and Mexico to remove barriers to trade between the three countries over a ten-year period.

North·amp·ton /nôrˈTHamptən/ **1** a town in southeast central England, on the Nene River; pop. 178,000. **2** an industrial and commercial city in west central Massachusetts, home to Smith College; pop. 29,289.

North At·lan·tic Drift a continuation of the Gulf Stream across the Atlantic Ocean and along the coast of northwestern Europe, where it has a significant warming effect on the climate.

North At·lan·tic O·cean see **ATLANTIC OCEAN**.

North At·lan·tic Trea·ty Or·gan·i·za·tion (abbr.: **NATO**) an association of European and North American countries, formed in 1949 for the defense of Europe and the North Atlantic against the perceived threat of Soviet aggression. By 2005, the alliance consisted of 26 countries, including several eastern European nations. NATO's purpose is to safeguard member countries by political and military means.

north·bound /ˈnôrTH,bound/ ▶*adj.* traveling or leading toward the north: *they slowly drove back along the shoulder of the northbound lane | northbound traffic.*

North Ca·na·di·an Riv·er (also **Beaver River**) a river that flows for 800 miles (1,300 km) from northeastern New Mexico, through Texas and Oklahoma, to the Canadian River.

North Cape a promontory on Magerøya, an island off the northern coast of Norway. North Cape is the northernmost point of the world accessible by road. Norwegian name **NORDKAPP**.

North Car·o·li·na a state in the eastern central U.S., on the Atlantic coast; pop. 8,049,313; capital, Raleigh; statehood, Nov. 21, 1789 (12). First settled by the English in the late 1600s, it was one of the original thirteen states. ▷*Carolina* from *Carolus*, the Latin name for Charles I and Charles II. **—North Car·o·lin·i·an** *n.* & *adj.*

North Chan·nel the stretch of sea that separates southwestern Scotland from Northern Ireland and connects the Irish Sea to the Atlantic Ocean.

North Charles·ton a city in southeastern South Carolina, a residential suburb with naval facilities; pop. 79,641.

North Chi·ca·go an industrial city in northeastern Illinois, on Lake Michigan, south of Waukegan; pop. 34,978.

North Coun·try in New York state, areas north of the Mohawk and Hudson rivers that extend to the St. Lawrence Valley and Lake Ontario.

North Da·ko·ta an agricultural state in the northern central U.S., on the border with Canada; pop. 642,200; capital, Bismarck; statehood, Nov. 2, 1889 (39). Its territory was acquired partly by the Louisiana Purchase in 1803 and partly from Britain by a treaty in 1818. The geographical center of North America lies within its boundaries. **—North Da·ko·tan** *n.* & *adj.*

North·east /,nôrTHˈēst/ a region of the U.S., usually thought to include the six New England states, New Jersey, and the eastern portions of New York state and Pennsylvania.

north·east /,nôrTHˈēst/ ▶*n.* **1** (usu. **the northeast**) the point of the horizon midway between north and east: *I pointed to the northeast.* ■ the compass point corresponding to this. ■ the direction in which this lies: *the entrance was through a small door to the northeast.* **2** the northeastern part of a country, region, or town: *people from the predominantly Russian towns in the northeast | the northeast of Brazil.*
▶*adj.* **1** lying toward, near, or facing the northeast. ■ (of a wind) coming from the northeast: *there was a strong northeast wind.* **2** of or denoting the northeastern part of a specified country, region, or town, or its inhabitants: *northeast Baltimore.*
▶*adv.* to or toward the northeast: *the ship sailed northeast | the northeast-facing slopes.* **—north·east·ern** /-ˈēstərn/ *adj.*

north·east·er /,nôrTHˈēstər/ (also **nor'east·er** /,nôrˈēstər/) ▶*n.* a wind blowing from the northeast. ■ a strong storm from the northeast, esp. in New England.

north·east·er·ly /,nôrTHˈēstərlē/ ▶*adj.* & *adv.* another term for **NORTHEAST**.
▶*n.* another term for **NORTHEASTER**.

North·east King·dom a nickname for the region that includes the three northernmost counties of Vermont.

Northeast Pas·sage a passage for ships along the northern coast of Europe and Asia, from the Atlantic Ocean to the Pacific Ocean via the Arctic Ocean, sought for many years as a possible trade route to the East. It was first navigated in 1878–79 by Swedish Arctic explorer Baron Nordenskjöld (1832–1901).

north·east·ward /,nôrTHˈēstwərd/ ▶*adv.* toward the northeast; in a northeast direction.
▶*adj.* situated in, directed toward, or facing the northeast.

North E·qua·to·ri·al Cur·rent an ocean current that flows west across the Pacific Ocean just north of the equator.

north·er /ˈnôrT͟Hər/ ▶*n.* a strong cold north wind blowing in autumn and winter over Texas, Florida, and the Gulf of Mexico.

north·er·ly /ˈnôrT͟Hərlē/ ▶*adj.* & *adv.* in a northward position or direction: [as *adj.*] *he set off in a northerly direction.* ■ (of wind) blowing from the north: [as *adj.*] *it will feel cold in the fresh northerly wind* | [as *adv.*] *the wind was gusting northerly.*
▶*n.* (often **northerlies**) a wind blowing from the north.

north·ern /ˈnôrT͟Hərn/ ▶*adj.* **1** [*attrib.*] situated in the north, or directed toward or facing the north: *the northern slopes | northern Europe.* ■ (of a wind) blowing from the north. **2** living in or originating from the north: *northern breeds of cattle.* ■ of, relating to, or characteristic of the north or its inhabitants: *an unmistakable northern accent.* ▷Old English *northerne* (see **NORTH, -ERN**). **—north·ern·most** /-,mōst/ *adj.*

North·ern blot ▶*n. Biology* an adaptation of the Southern blot procedure used to detect specific sequences of RNA by hybridization with complementary DNA.

North·ern·er /ˈnôrT͟Hərnər/ (also **north·ern·er**) ▶*n.* a native or inhabitant of the north, esp. of the northern U.S.

north·ern har·ri·er ▶*n.* a widespread harrier of open country, the male of which is mainly pale gray and the female brown. Also called **MARSH HAWK**. • *Circus cyaneus*, family Accipitridae.

north·ern hem·i·sphere the half of the earth that is north of the equator.

North·ern Ire·land a province of the United Kingdom that occupies the northeastern part of Ireland, comprised of six counties of Ulster; pop. 1,570,000; capital, Belfast. It was established as a self-governing province in 1920, after refusing to be part of the Irish Free State. Domination by the Protestant majority and discrimination against the Roman Catholic minority led to violent conflicts and, from 1969, British army units were present in an attempt to keep the peace.

north·ern lights another name for the aurora borealis. See **AURORA**.

North·ern Mar·i·an·as /,me(ə)rēˈanəz; ,mar-; -ˈänəz/ a self-governing territory in the western Pacific, comprising the Mariana Islands with the exception of Guam; pop. 78,200; capital, Chalan Kanoa (on Saipan). The Northern Marianas are constituted as a self-governing commonwealth in union with the U.S.

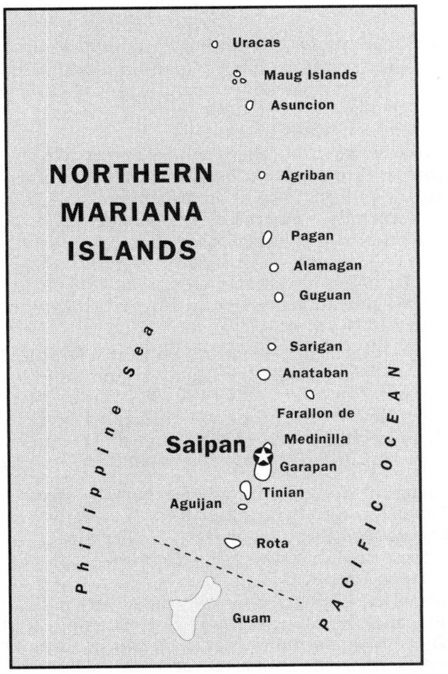

North·ern Neck a region in eastern Virginia between the Potomac and Rappahannock rivers, a tidewater peninsula.

North·ern Rho·de·sia /rōˈdēZHə/ former name (until 1964) of **ZAMBIA**.

north·ern snake·head ▶*n.* an Asian food fish of the carp family that is also a voracious predator. It is able to survive adverse conditions and has been inadvertently released into the wild in the U.S. • *Channa argus*, family Channidae.

North·ern Ter·ri·to·ry a state in northern central Australia; pop. 158,000; capital town, Darwin. The territory was annexed by the state of South Australia in 1863 and administered by the Commonwealth of Australia from 1911. It became a self-governing territory in 1978 and a full state in 1995.

North Fri·sian Is·lands see **FRISIAN ISLANDS**.

North Ger·man·ic ▶*n.* the northern branch of the Germanic languages, descended from Old Norse and comprising Danish, Norwegian, Swedish, Icelandic, and Faeroese.
▶*adj.* of or relating to North Germanic.

north·ing /ˈnôrTHiNG; -T͟HiNG/ ▶*n.* distance traveled or measured northward, esp. at sea: *we should have to make 300 miles of northing.* ■ a figure or line representing northward distance on a map (expressed by convention as the second part of a grid reference, after easting).

North Is·land the most northern of the two main islands of New Zealand, separated from South Island by Cook Strait.

North Kings·town /ˈkiNGstən; ˈkiNGz,toun/ a town in south central Rhode Island, on the western banks of Narragansett Bay; pop. 26,326.

North Ko·re·a a country in the Far East that occupies the northern part of the peninsula of Korea; pop. 22,227,000; capital, Pyongyang; official language, Korean. Official name **KOREA, DEMOCRATIC PEOPLE'S REPUBLIC OF**. **—North Ko·re·an** *adj.* & *n.*

North Korea was formed in 1948 when Korea was partitioned along the 38th parallel. In 1950, North Korean forces invaded the south, but in the war that followed were forced back to more or less the previous border (see **KOREAN WAR**). A communist state, which was long dominated by the personality of its leader Kim Il Sung from 1948 until 1994, North Korea has always sought Korean reunification.

north·land /ˈnôrTHlənd; -,land/ ▶*n.* (also **northlands**) *poetic/literary* the northern part of a country or region. ▷Old English (see **NORTH, LAND**).

North Las Ve·gas a city in southeastern Nevada, a northeastern suburb of Las Vegas; pop. 115,488.

north light ▶*n.* good natural light without direct sun, esp. as desired by artists.

North Lit·tle Rock a city in central Arkansas, an industrial center across the Arkansas River from Little Rock; pop. 60,433.

North·man /ˈnôrTHmən/ ▶*n.* (*pl.* **-men**) *archaic* a native or inhabitant of Scandinavia, esp. of Norway. ▷Old English (see **NORTH, MAN**).

North Minch see **MINCH**.

north-north·east ▶*n.* the compass point or direction midway between north and northeast.

north-north·west ▶*n.* the compass point or direction midway between north and northwest.

North Os·se·tia an autonomous republic of Russia, in the Caucasus, on the border with Georgia; pop. 638,000; capital, Vladikavkaz. Since 1994 it has been called Alania. See also **OSSETIA**.

North Platte /plat/ a city in central Nebraska, where the North and South Platte rivers meet; pop. 23,878.

North Platte Riv·er a river that flows for 620 miles (960 km) from northern Colorado, across Wyoming and Nebraska, to the Platte River. Its valley was part of the Oregon Trail.

North Pole ▸*n.* see **POLE**².

North Prov·i·dence /ˈprävidəns; -ˌdens/ a town in northeastern Rhode Island, a northwestern suburb of Providence; pop. 32,411.

North Rhine-West·pha·lia a state in west central Germany; capital, Düsseldorf. German name **NORDRHEIN-WESTFALEN**.

North Sea an arm of the Atlantic Ocean that lies between the mainland of Europe and the coast of Britain, important for its oil and gas deposits.

North Slope a name for regions of Alaska that lie north of the Brooks Range and extend to the Arctic Ocean. Sparsely populated, it is a site of much oil exploration and extraction.

North Star *Astronomy* another term for **POLARIS**.

North Star State a nickname for the state of **MINNESOTA**.

North Ton·a·wan·da /ˌtänəˈwändə/ an industrial city in western New York, on the Niagara River, north of Buffalo, at the western end of the historic Erie Canal; pop. 34,989.

North Uist see **UIST**.

Northumb. ▸*abbr.* Northumberland.

North·um·ber·land /nôrˈᴛʜəmbərlənd/ a county in northeastern England, on the Scottish border.

North·um·ber·land Strait /nôrˈᴛʜəmbərlənd/ an ocean passage in the Gulf of St. Lawrence that separates Prince Edward Island from New Brunswick and Nova Scotia.

North·um·bri·a /nôrˈᴛʜəmbrēə/ an area of northeastern England. ■ an ancient Anglo-Saxon kingdom in northeastern England that extends from the Humber Estuary to the Forth River. ▷from obsolete *Northumber*, denoting a person living beyond the Humber. **—North·um·bri·an** *adj.* & *n.*

North Vi·et·nam a former communist republic in Southeast Asia, in the northern part of Vietnam, created in 1954 when Vietnam was partitioned. After defeating noncommunist South Vietnam in the Vietnam War, it declared a reunited, socialist republic (1976).

north·ward /ˈnôrᴛʜwərd/ ▸*adj.* in a northerly direction.
▸*adv.* (also **northwards**) toward the north.
▸*n.* (**the northward**) the direction or region to the north. **—north·ward·ly** *adj.* & *adv.*

north·west /ˌnôrᴛʜˈwest/ ▸*n.* (usu. **the northwest**) **1** the point of the horizon midway between north and west: *he pointed to the northwest.* ■ the compass point corresponding to this. ■ the direction in which this lies. **2** the northwestern part of a country, region, or town: *they had originally come from someplace in the northwest of Mexico.*
▸*adj.* **1** lying toward, near, or facing the northwest: *the northwest corner of the square.* ■ (of a wind) blowing from the northwest. **2** of or denoting the northwestern part of a country, region, or town, or its inhabitants: *northwest Europe.*
▸*adv.* to or toward the northwest: *he turned onto the highway and headed northwest.* **—north·west·ern** /-ˈwestərn/ *adj.*

North·west An·gle a forested region in northern Minnesota that is separated from the rest of the state and the U.S. by Lake of the Woods. It is the most northern part of the contiguous U.S.

north·west·er /ˌnôrᴛʜˈwestər/ ▸*n.* a wind or storm blowing from the northwest.

north·west·er·ly /ˌnôrᴛʜˈwestərlē/ ▸*adj.* & *adv.* another term for **NORTHWEST**.
▸*n.* another term for **NORTHWESTER**.

North-West Fron·tier Prov·ince a province of northwestern Pakistan, on the border with Afghanistan; capital, Peshawar.

Northwest Pas·sage a sea passage along the northern coast of the North American continent, through the Canadian Arctic from the Atlantic Ocean to the Pacific Ocean. It was sought for many years as a possible trade route by explorers that included Sebastian Cabot, Sir Francis Drake, and Martin Frobisher; it was first navigated 1903-06 by Roald Amundsen.

North·west Ter·ri·to·ries a territory of northern Canada, between Yukon Territory and Nunavut; capital: Yellowknife. Much of it consists of sparsely inhabited forests and tundra. The Northwest Territories, then including the land that is now Nunavut, was ceded by Britain to Canada in 1870. Nunavut became a separate territory in 1999.

North·west Ter·ri·to·ry a region and former territory of the U.S. that lies between the Mississippi and Ohio rivers and the Great Lakes. It was acquired in 1783 after the American Revolution and now forms the states of Indiana, Ohio, Michigan, Illinois, and Wisconsin.

north·west·ward /ˌnôrᴛʜˈwestwərd/ ▸*adv.* (also **north·west·wards**) toward the northwest; in a northwest direction.
▸*adj.* situated in, directed toward, or facing the northwest.

Nor·walk /ˈnôrˌwôk/ **1** a city in southwestern California, southeast of Los Angeles; pop. 94,279. **2** an industrial city in southwestern Connecticut, on Long Island Sound; pop. 82,951.

Nor·walk vi·rus ▸*n.* a virus that can cause epidemics of severe gastroenteritis. It has been subsumed under the genus *Norovirus*. ▷1970s: from *Norwalk*, a town in Ohio where an outbreak of gastroenteritis occurred from which the virus was isolated.

Nor·way /ˈnôrˌwā/ a mountainous European country on the northern and western coastline of Scandinavia, on the Norwegian Sea and the Arctic Ocean; pop. 4,574,000; capital, Oslo; language, Norwegian (official). Norwegian name **NORGE**.

Norway was united with Denmark and Sweden by the Union of Kalmar in 1397, but after Sweden's withdrawal in 1523 became subject to Denmark. Ceded to Sweden in 1814, Norway emerged as an independent kingdom in 1905. An invitation to join the EC was rejected after a referendum in 1972; an application to join the European Union twenty years later was accepted by the European Parliament but failed to win approval in a 1994 referendum.

Nor·way lob·ster ▸*n.* another term for **LANGOUSTINE**.

Nor·way ma·ple ▸*n.* a large Eurasian maple with yellow flowers that appear before the lobed leaves, widely planted as an ornamental shade tree. • *Acer platanoides*, family Aceraceae.

Nor·way rat ▸*n.* another term for **BROWN RAT**.

Nor·way spruce ▸*n.* a long-coned European spruce that is widely grown as an ornamental and for timber and pulp. • *Picea abies*, family Pinaceae.

Nor·we·gian /nôrˈwējən/ ▸*adj.* of or relating to Norway or its people or language.
▸*n.* **1** a native or national of Norway, or a person of Norwegian descent. **2** the North Germanic language of Norway.

Norwegian today exists in two forms, *Bokmål*, the more widely used, a modified form of Danish, and *Nynorsk* ('new Norwegian'), a 19th-century literary form devised from the country dialects most closely descended from Old Norse and considered to be a purer form of the language than *Bokmål*.

▷from medieval Latin *Norvegia* 'Norway' (from Old Norse *Norvegr*, literally 'north way') + **-AN**.

Nor·we·gian Sea a sea that lies between Iceland and Norway and links the Arctic Ocean with the northeastern Atlantic Ocean.

Nor·wich **1** /ˈnôr(w)icʜ; ˈnôrij; ˈnär-/ a city in eastern England, the county town of Norfolk; pop. 121,000. **2** /ˈnôrwicʜ/ an industrial city in southeastern Connecticut, on the Thames River; pop. 37,391.

Nor·wich ter·ri·er ▸*n.* a small thickset terrier of a breed with a rough red or black-and-tan coat and pricked ears.

nos ▸*abbr.* numbers. ▷plural of **No.**

n.o.s. ▸*abbr.* not otherwise specified.

nose /nōz/ ▸*n.* **1** the part projecting above the mouth on the face of a person or animal, containing the nostrils and used for breathing and smelling. ■ [in *sing.*] the sense of smell, esp. a dog's ability to track something by its scent: *a dog with a keen nose.* ■ [in *sing.*] *figurative* an instinctive talent for detecting something: *he has **a nose for** a good script.* ■ the aroma of a particular substance, esp. wine. **2** the front end of an aircraft, car, or other vehicle. ■ a projecting part of something: *the nose of the saddle.* **3** [in *sing.*] a look, esp. out of curiosity: *she wanted a good **nose around** the house.* ■ *informal* a police informer.
▸*v.* **1** [*intrans.*] (of an animal) thrust its nose against or into something, esp. in order to smell it: *the pony nosed at the straw.* ■ [*trans.*] smell or sniff (something). **2** [*intrans.*] investigate or pry into something: *I was anxious to get inside and **nose around** her house | she's always **nosing into** my business.* ■ [*trans.*] detect in such a way. **3** [*intrans.*] (of a vehicle or its driver) make one's way cautiously forward: *he turned left and nosed into an empty parking space.* ■ (of a competitor) manage to achieve a winning or leading position, esp. by a small margin: *they nosed ahead by one point.* ▷Old English *nosu*; related to Dutch *neus*, and more remotely to German *Nase*, Latin *nasus*, and Sanskrit *nāsā*; also to **NESS**. **—nosed** *adj.* [in *combination*] *snub-nosed.* **—nose·less** *adj.*
▸*PHRASES* □ **by a nose** (of a victory) by a very narrow margin. □ **count noses** count people, typically in order to determine the numbers in a vote. □ **cut off one's nose to spite one's face** hurt oneself in the course of trying to hurt another. □ **give someone a bloody nose** inflict a resounding defeat on someone. □ **have one's nose in a book** be reading studiously or intently. □ **keep one's nose clean** *informal* stay out of trouble. □ **keep one's nose out of** refrain from interfering in (someone else's affairs). □ **keep one's nose to the grindstone** see **GRINDSTONE**. □ **nose to tail** (of vehicles) moving or standing close behind one another, esp. in heavy traffic. □ **not see further than one's** (or **the end of one's**) **nose** be unwilling or fail to consider different possibilities or to foresee the consequences of one's actions. □ **on the nose** **1** to a person's sense of smell: *the wine is pungently smoky and peppery on the nose.* **2** *informal* precisely: *at ten on the nose the van pulled up.* **3** *informal* (of betting) on a horse to win (as opposed to being placed). □ **put someone's nose out of joint** *informal* upset or annoy someone. □ **speak through one's nose** pronounce words with a nasal twang. □ **turn one's nose up at something** *informal* show distaste or contempt for something: *he turned his nose up at the job.* □ **under someone's nose** *informal* directly in front of someone: *he thrust the paper under the inspector's nose.* ■ (of an action) committed openly and boldly, but without someone noticing or noticing in time to prevent it. □ **with one's nose in the air** haughtily: *she walked past the cars with her nose in the air.*

nose·bag /ˈnōzˌbag/ ▸*n.* a strong canvas or leather bag containing grain, fastened over a horse's muzzle for feeding.

nose·band /ˈnōzˌband/ ▸*n.* the strap of a bridle or halter that passes over the horse's nose and under its chin.

nose·bleed /ˈnōzˌblēd/ ▸*n.* an instance of bleeding from the nose. ■ [as *adj.*] *informal* denoting cheap seating located in an extremely high position in a sports stadium, large theater, or concert hall: *he declined an offer of $2,200 for his game ticket in the **nosebleed section**.*

nose can·dy ▸*n.* *informal* an illegal drug that is inhaled, esp. cocaine.

nose cone ▸*n.* the cone-shaped nose of a rocket or aircraft.

nose·dive /ˈnōzˌdīv/ ▸*n.* a steep downward plunge by an aircraft. ■ *figurative* a sudden dramatic deterioration: *the player's fortunes **took a nosedive**.*
▸*v.* [*intrans.*] (of an aircraft) make a nosedive. ■ *figurative* deteriorate suddenly and dramatically: *massive strikes caused the economy to nosedive.*

no-see-um /nō ˈsē ˌəm/ ▸*n.* a minute bloodsucking insect, esp. a biting midge.

nose flute ▸*n.* a musical instrument of the flute type played by blowing through the nose rather than the mouth, associated esp. with Southeast Asia and the Pacific islands.

nose·gay /ˈnōzˌgā/ ▸*n.* a small bunch of flowers, typically one that is sweet-scented. ▷late Middle

English: from **NOSE** + **GAY** in the obsolete sense 'ornament.'

nose guard ▸*n.* another term for **NOSE TACKLE**.

nose job ▸*n. informal* an operation involving rhinoplasty or cosmetic surgery on a person's nose.

nose leaf ▸*n.* a fleshy leaf-shaped structure on the nose of many bats, used for echolocation.

no·se·ma /nō'sēmə/ ▸*n.* a spore-forming parasitic protozoan that chiefly affects insects. • Genus *Nosema*, phylum Microspora, kingdom Protista: several species, in particular *N. apis*, which causes infectious dysentery (**nosema disease**) in honeybees. ▷modern Latin, from Greek *nosēma* 'disease.'

nose·piece /'nōz,pēs/ ▸*n.* **1** the part of a helmet or headdress that protects a person's nose. ■ another term for **NOSEBAND**. ■ the central part of a pair of glasses that fits over the bridge of the nose. **2** the part of a microscope to which the objective lenses are attached.

nose ring ▸*n.* a ring fixed in the nose of an animal, typically a bull, for leading it. ■ a ring worn in a person's nose as a piece of jewelry.

nose tack·le ▸*n. Football* a defensive lineman positioned opposite the center.

nose wheel ▸*n.* a landing wheel under the nose of an aircraft.

nos·ey /'nōzē/ ▸*adj.* & *v.* variant spelling of **NOSY**.

nos·ey Par·ker ▸*n.* variant spelling of **NOSY PARKER**.

nosh /näsʜ/ *informal* ▸*n.* food: *filling the freezer with all kinds of nosh.* ■ a small item of food: *have plenty of noshes and nibbles conveniently placed.* ■ a light meal; a snack: *in between noshes we explored the city.*
▸*v.* [*intrans.*] eat food enthusiastically or greedily: *there are several restaurants, so you can nosh to your heart's content* | [*trans.*] *there I sat, noshing my favorite food.* ■ eat between meals: *today's grazing is different from what we used to call noshing or snacking.* ▷early 20th cent. (denoting a snack bar): Yiddish.

nosh·er·y /'näsʜərē/ ▸*n.* (*pl.* **-er·ies**) *informal* a restaurant or snack bar.

no-show ▸*n.* a person who has made a reservation, booking, or appointment but neither keeps nor cancels it.

nos·ing /'nōziNG/ ▸*n.* a rounded edge of a step or molding. ■ a metal shield for such an edge.

nos·o·co·mi·al /,näsə'kōmēəl/ ▸*adj. Medicine* (of a disease) originating in a hospital. ▷mid 19th cent.: from Greek *nosokomos* 'person who tends the sick' + **-IAL**.

nos·ode /'näs,ōd/ ▸*n.* (in homeopathy) a preparation of substances secreted in the course of a disease, used in the treatment of that disease. ▷late 19th cent.: from Greek *nosos* 'disease' + **-ODE**[1].

no·sog·ra·phy /nō'sägrəfē/ ▸*n.* the systematic description of diseases. ▷mid 17th cent.: from Greek *nosos* 'disease' + **-GRAPHY**. **—no·so·graph·ic** /,nōsə'grafik; ,nä-/ *adj.*

no·sol·o·gy /nō'säləjē/ ▸*n.* the branch of medical science dealing with the classification of diseases. ▷early 18th cent.: from Greek *nosos* 'disease' + **-LOGY**. **—nos·o·log·i·cal** /,näsə'läjikəl/ *adj.* **—no·sol·o·gist** /-jist/ *n.*

nos·tal·gia /nä'staljə; nə-/ ▸*n.* a sentimental longing or wistful affection for the past, typically for a period or place with happy personal associations: *I was overcome with acute nostalgia for my days in college.* ■ the evocation of these feelings or tendencies, esp. in commercialized form: *an evening of TV nostalgia.* ▷late 18th cent. (in the sense 'acute homesickness'): modern Latin (translating German *Heimweh* 'homesickness'), from Greek *nostos* 'return home' + *algos* 'pain.' **—nos·tal·gist** /-jist/ *n.*

nos·tal·gic /nä'staljik; nə-/ ▸*adj.* characterized by or exhibiting feelings of nostalgia.
▸*n.* a nostalgic person. *to see classmates' E-mail addresses, nostalgics pay $36 a year.* **—nos·tal·gi·cal·ly** /nä'staljik(ə)lē; nə-/ *adv.*

nos·tal·gie de la boue /,nôstäl'zʜēd lä 'bo͞o/ ▸*n.* a desire for degradation and depravity. ▷French, literally 'nostalgia for mud.'

nos·toc /'nästäk/ ▸*n. Biology* a microorganism composed of beaded filaments that aggregate to form a gelatinous mass, growing in water and damp places and able to fix nitrogen from the atmosphere. • Genus *Nostoc*, division Cyanobacteria. ▷name invented by Paracelsus.

nos·tos /'nästōs/ ▸*n.* (*pl.* **-toi** /-,toi/) *poetic/literary* a homecoming. ▷Greek.

Nos·tra·da·mus /,nôstrə'däməs; ,nästrə'dāməs/ (1503–66), French astrologer and physician; Latinized name of *Michel de Nostredame*. His cryptic and apocalyptic predictions in rhyming quatrains appeared in two collections, in 1555 and 1558, and their interpretation continues to be the subject of controversy.

Nos·trat·ic /nä'stratik/ ▸*n.* a hypothetical phylum of languages of which the principal members are the Indo-European, Semitic, Altaic, and Dravidian families.
▸*adj.* of or relating to this language phylum. ▷1960s: from German *nostratisch*, based on Latin *nostras*, *nostrat-* 'of our country.'

nos·tril /'nästrəl/ ▸*n.* either of two external openings of the nasal cavity in vertebrates that admit air to the lungs and smells to the olfactory nerves. ▷Old English *nosterl*, *nosthyrl*, from *nosu* 'nose' + *thȳr(e)l* 'hole.' **—nos·trilled** *adj.* [in *combination*] .

nos·trum /'nästrəm/ ▸*n.* a medicine, esp. one that is not considered effective, prepared by an unqualified person. ■ a pet scheme or favorite remedy, esp. one for bringing about some social or political reform or improvement.

nos·y /'nōzē/ (also **nos·ey**) *informal* ▸*adj.* (**nos·i·er**, **nos·i·est**) (of a person or their behavior) showing too much curiosity about other people's affairs: *he had to whisper to avoid being overheard by their nosy neighbors.*
▸*v.* [*intrans.*] pry into something: *they don't nosy into your business like some people.* **—nos·i·ly** /-zəlē/ *adv.* **—nos·i·ness** *n.*

Nos·y Par·ker (also **nos·y Park·er**) ▸*n. informal* an overly inquisitive person. ▷early 20th cent.: from the picture postcard caption, "The adventures of Nosey Parker," referring to a peeping Tom in Hyde Park, London.

not /nät/ ▸*adv.* **1** (also **n't** joined to a preceding verb) used with an auxiliary verb or "be" to form the negative: *he would not say* | *she isn't there* | *didn't you tell me?* ■ used in some constructions with other verbs: [with *infinitive*] *he has been warned not to touch* | *the pain of not knowing* | *she* **not only** *wrote the text* **but also** *researched the photographs.* **2** used as a short substitute for a negative clause: *maybe I'll regret it, but I hope not* | *"Don't you keep in touch?" "I'm afraid not."* | *they wouldn't know if I was telling the truth* **or not**. **3** used to express the negative of other words: *not a single attempt was made* | *treating the symptoms and not the cause* | *"How was it?" "Not so bad."* ■ used with a quantifier to exclude a person or part of a group: *not all the poems are serious.* ■ less than (used to indicate a surprisingly small quantity): *the brakes went on not ten feet from him.* **4** used in understatements to suggest that the opposite of a following word or phrase is true: *the not too distant future* | *not a million miles away.* ■ *informal, humorous* following and emphatically negating a statement: *that sounds like quality entertainment—not.* [a usage popularized by the film *Wayne's World*.]
▸*n.* (often **NOT**) *Electronics* a Boolean operator with only one variable that has the value one when the variable is zero and vice versa. ■ (also **not gate**) a circuit that produces an output signal only when there is not a signal on its input.
▸*adj.* (often **Not**) *Art* (of paper) not hot-pressed, and having a slightly textured surface. ▷Middle English: contraction of the adverb **NOUGHT**.
▸*PHRASES* □ **not at all 1** used as a polite response to thanks. **2** definitely not: *"You don't mind?" "Not at all."* □ **not but what** *archaic* nevertheless: *not but what the picture has its darker side.* □ **not half** see **HALF**. □ **not least** see **LEAST**. □ **not quite** see **QUITE**. □ **not that** it is not to be inferred that: *I'll never be allowed back—not that I'd want to go back.* □ **not a thing** nothing at all. □ **not very** see **VERY**.

no·ta be·ne /'nōtə 'benē/ (abbr.:**n.b.** or **N.B.**) ▸*v.* [in *imperative*] *formal* observe carefully or take special notice (used in written text to draw attention to what follows). ▷Latin, literally 'note well!'

no·ta·bil·i·ty /,nōtə'bilitē/ ▸*n.* (*pl.* **-ties**) a famous or important person: *I have met a number of new notabilities including Henry Moore, the sculptor.*

no·ta·ble /'nōtəbəl/ ▸*adj.* worthy of attention or notice; remarkable: *the gardens are* **notable for** *their collection of magnolias and camellias* | *the results, with one notable exception, have been superb.*
▸*n.* (usu. **notables**) a famous or important person: *businessmen and local notables.* ▷Middle English: from Old French, from Latin *notabilis* 'worthy of note,' from the verb *notare* 'to note, mark.'

no·ta·bly /'nōtəblē/ ▸*adv.* especially; in particular: *a diet low in animal fat protects against potentially fatal diseases, notably diabetes.* ■ in a way that is striking or remarkable: [as *submodifier*] *such a statement is notably absent from the administration's proposals.*

no·tam /'nōtəm/ (also **No·tam**) ▸*n.* a written notification issued to pilots before a flight, advising them of circumstances relating to the state of flying. ▷1940s: from *no(tice) t(o) a(ir)m(en)*.

no·taph·i·ly /nō'tafəlē/ ▸*n.* the collecting of banknotes as a hobby. **—no·ta·phil·ic** /,nōtə'filik/ *adj.* **—no·taph·i·list** /-list/ *n.*

no·ta·rize /'nōtə,rīz/ ▸*v.* [*trans.*] have (a document) legalized by a notary.

no·ta·ry /'nōtərē/ (in full **notary public**) ▸*n.* (*pl.* **-ries**) a person authorized to perform certain legal formalities, esp. to draw up or certify contracts, deeds, and other documents for use in other jurisdictions. ▷Middle English (in the sense 'clerk or secretary'): from Latin *notarius* 'secretary,' from *nota* 'mark.' **—no·tar·i·al** /nō'terēəl/ *adj.*

no·tate /'nō,tāt/ ▸*v.* [*trans.*] write (something, typically music) in notation. ▷early 20th cent.: back-formation from **NOTATION**. **—no·ta·tor** /-,tātər/ *n.*

no·ta·tion /nō'tāsʜən/ ▸*n.* **1** a series or system of written symbols used to represent numbers, amounts, or elements in something such as music or mathematics: *algebraic notation.* **2** a note or annotation: *he noticed the notations in the margin.* **3** short for **SCALE OF NOTATION** (see **SCALE**[3] sense 2). ▷late 16th cent.: from Latin *notatio(n-)*, from the verb *notare*, from *nota* 'mark.' **—no·ta·tion·al** /-nəl/ *adj.*

not-be·ing ▸*n.* nonexistence.

notch /näcʜ/ ▸*n.* **1** an indentation or incision on an edge or surface: *there was a notch in the end of the arrow for the bowstring.* ■ each of a series of holes for the tongue of a buckle: *he tightened his belt an extra notch.* ■ a nick made on something in order to keep a score or record: *he had a six-gun with four notches in it for guys he had killed.* ■ a point or degree in a scale: *her opinion of Nicole dropped a few notches.* **2** a deep, narrow mountain pass.
▸*v.* [*trans.*] **1** make notches in: [as *adj.*] (**notched**) *notched bamboo sticks.* ■ secure or insert by means of notches: *she notched her belt tighter.* **2** score or achieve (something): *she notched her second major championship.* ▷mid 16th cent.: probably from Anglo-Norman French *noche*, variant of Old French *osche*, of unknown origin. **—notch·er** *n.*

notch·back /'näcʜ,bak/ ▸*n.* a car with a back that extends approximately horizontally from the bottom of the rear window so as to make a distinct angle with it.

notch fil·ter ▸*n. Electronics* a filter that attenuates signals within a very narrow band of frequencies.

notch·y /'näcʜē/ ▸*adj.* (**notch·i·er**, **notch·i·est**) *Brit.* (of a manual gear-changing mechanism) difficult to use because the lever has to be moved accurately (as if into a narrow notch).

note /nōt/ ▸*n.* **1** a brief record of facts, topics, or thoughts, written down as an aid to memory: *I'll* **make a note** *in my diary* | *Robyn arranged her notes on the lectern.* ■ a short comment on or explanation of a word or passage in a book or article; an annotation: *see note iv above.* **2** a short informal letter or written message: *I left her a note explaining where I was going.* ■ an official letter sent from the representative of one government to another. ■ [usu. with *adj.*] a short official document that certifies a particular thing: *you need a sick note from your doctor.* **3** *Brit.* a banknote: *a ten-pound note.* **4** a single tone of definite pitch made by a musical instrument or the human voice: *the last notes of the symphony died away.* ■ a written sign representing the pitch and duration of such a sound. ■ a key of a piano or similar instrument: *black notes* | *white notes.* ■ a bird's song or call, or a single tone in this: *the tawny owl has a harsh flight note.* **5** [in *sing.*] a particular quality or tone that reflects or expresses a mood or attitude: *there was a note of scorn in her voice* | *the decade could have ended on an optimistic note.* ■ any of the basic components of fragrance or flavor: *the fresh note of bergamot.*
▸*v.* [*trans.*] **1** notice or pay particular attention to (something): *noting his mother's unusual gaiety* | [with *clause*] *please note that you will not receive a reminder that final payment is due.* ■ remark upon (something), typically in order to draw someone's attention to it: *we noted earlier the difficulties inherent in this strategy.* **2** record (something) in writing: *he* **noted down** *her address on a piece of paper.* ▷Middle English (sense 4 of the *noun* and sense 1 of the *verb*): from Old French *note* (noun), *noter* (verb), from Latin *nota* 'a mark,' *notare* 'to mark.'

Pronunciation Key ə *ago*; ər *over*; 'ə or ,ə *up*; 'ər or ,ər *fur*; a *hat*; ā *rate*; ä *car*; cʜ *chew*; e *let*; ē *see*; e(ə)r *air*; i *fit*; ī *by*; i(ə)r *ear*; NG *sing*; ō *go*; ô *for*; oi *boy*; o͝o *good*; o͞o *goo*; ou *out*; sʜ *she*; tʜ *thin*; T͟H *then*; (h)w *why*; zʜ *vision*

N

▸PHRASES □ **hit** (or **strike**) **the right** (or **wrong**) **note** say or do something in exactly the right (or wrong) way. □ **of note 1** worth paying attention to: *many of his comments are worthy of note.* **2** important; distinguished: *Roman historians of note include Livy, Tacitus, and Sallust.* □ **strike a false note** appear insincere or inappropriate: *she greeted him gushingly, and that struck a false note.* □ **strike** (or **sound**) **a note of** express (a particular feeling or view) about something: *he sounded a note of caution about the trend toward health foods.* □ **take note** pay attention: *employers should* **take note of** *the needs of disabled people.*

note·book /ˈnōtˌbo͝ok/ ▸*n.* a small book with blank or ruled pages for writing notes in. ■ a portable computer that is smaller than a laptop.

note·card /ˈnōtˌkärd/ (also **note card**) ▸*n.* a decorative card with a blank space for a short message.

note·case /ˈnōtˌkās/ ▸*n. Brit., dated* a small billfold or wallet.

note clus·ter ▸*n. Music* a chord containing a number of closely adjacent notes. Also called TONE CLUSTER.

not·ed /ˈnōtid/ ▸*adj.* well known; famous: *the restaurant is* **noted for** *its high standards of cuisine* | *a noted patron of the arts.*

note·pad /ˈnōtˌpad/ ▸*n.* a pad of blank or ruled pages for writing notes on. ■ (also **notepad computer**) a pocket-sized personal computer that has a stylus with which the user writes on the screen to input text.

note·pa·per /ˈnōtˌpāpər/ ▸*n.* paper for writing letters on.

note·wor·thy /ˈnōtˌwərT͟Hē/ ▸*adj.* interesting, significant, or unusual: [with *clause*] *it is noteworthy that no one at the bank has accepted responsibility for the failure.* **—note·wor·thi·ness** *n.*

not-for-prof·it ▸*adj.* another term for NONPROFIT.

'noth·er /ˈnəT͟Hər/ ▸*adj.* & *pron. informal* nonstandard spelling of ANOTHER, used to represent informal speech: *'nother thing just occurred to me.*

noth·ing /ˈnəTHiNG/ ▸*pron.* not anything; no single thing: *I said nothing* | *there's nothing you can do* | *they found nothing wrong.* ■ something of no importance or concern: *"What are you laughing at?" "Oh, nothing, sir."* | *they are nothing to him* | [as *n.*] *no longer could we be treated as nothings.* ■ (in calculations) no amount; zero.
▸*adj.* [*attrib.*] *informal* having no prospect of progress; of no value: *he had a series of nothing jobs.*
▸*adv.* not at all: *she cares nothing for others* | *he looks* **nothing like** *the others.* ■ [*postpositive*] *informal* used to contradict something emphatically: *"This is a surprise." "Surprise nothing."* ▷Old English *nān thing* (see NO, THING).
▸PHRASES □ **be nothing to do with** see DO[1]. □ **for nothing 1** at no cost; without payment: *working for nothing.* **2** to no purpose: *he died anyway; so it had all been for nothing.* □ **have nothing on someone** see HAVE. □ **have nothing to do with** see DO[1]. □ **no nothing** *informal* (concluding a list of negatives) nothing at all: *how could you solve it with no clues, no witnesses, no nothing?* □ **not for nothing** for a very good reason: *not for nothing have I got a brother-in-law who cooks professionally.* □ **nothing but** only: *nothing but the best will do.* □ **nothing daunted** see DAUNT. □ **nothing doing** *informal* **1** there is no prospect of success or agreement: *He wants to marry her. Nothing doing!* **2** nothing is happening: *there's nothing doing, and I've been waiting for weeks.* □ **nothing** (or **nothing else**) **for it** *Brit.* no alternative: *there was* **nothing for it but to** *follow.* □ **nothing less than** used to emphasize how extreme something is: *it was nothing less than sexual harassment.* □ **nothing loath** quite willing. □ **nothing much** not a great amount; nothing of importance. □ **there is nothing to it** there is no difficulty involved. □ **stop at nothing** see STOP. □ **sweet nothings** words of affection exchanged by lovers: *whispering sweet nothings in her ear.* □ **think nothing of it** do not apologize or feel bound to show gratitude (used as a polite response). □ **you ain't seen nothing yet** *informal* used to indicate that although something may be considered extreme or impressive, there is something even more extreme or impressive in store: *if you think that was muddy, you ain't seen nothing yet.*

noth·ing·ness /ˈnəTHiNGnis/ ▸*n.* the absence or cessation of life or existence: *the fear of the total nothingness of death.* ■ worthlessness; insignificance; unimportance: *the nothingness of it all overwhelmed him.*

noth·o·saur /ˈnōTHəˌsôr/ (also **noth·o·sau·rus** /ˌnōTHəˈsôrəs/) ▸*n.* an extinct semiaquatic carnivorous reptile of the Triassic period, having a slender body and long neck, related to the plesiosaurs. • Infraorder Nothosauria, superorder Sauropterygia. ▷1930s: from modern Latin *Nothosauria*, from Greek *nothos* 'false' + *sauros* 'lizard.' **—noth·o·sau·ri·an** *adj.*

no·tice /ˈnōtis/ ▸*n.* **1** attention; observation: *their silence did not escape my notice* | *it has* **come to our notice** *that you have been missing school.* **2** notification or warning of something, esp. to allow preparations to be made: *interest rates are subject to fluctuation without notice.* ■ a formal declaration of one's intention to end an agreement, typically one concerning employment or tenancy, at a specified time: *she handed in her notice.* **3** a displayed sheet or placard giving news or information: *the jobs were advertised in a notice posted in the common room.* ■ a small advertisement or announcement in a newspaper or magazine: *an obituary notice.* ■ (usu. **notices**) a short published review or comment about a new film, play, or book: *she had good notices in her first film.*
▸*v.* [*trans.*] become aware of: *he noticed the youths behaving suspiciously* | [with *clause*] *I noticed that she was looking tired* | [*intrans.*] *they were too drunk to notice.* ■ (usu. **be noticed**) treat (someone) with some degree of attention or recognition: *it was only last year that the singer really began to be noticed.* ■ *archaic* remark upon: *she looked so much better that Sir Charles noticed it to Lady Harriet.* ▷late Middle English (sense 2): from Old French, from Latin *notitia* 'being known,' from *notus* 'known' (see NOTION).
▸PHRASES □ **at short** (or **a moment's**) **notice** with little warning or time for preparation: *tours may be canceled at short notice.* □ **put someone on notice** (or **serve notice**) warn someone of something about or likely to occur, esp. in a formal or threatening manner: *we're going to put foreign governments on notice that we want a change of trade policy.* □ **take no notice** pay no attention to someone or something. □ **take notice** pay attention; show signs of interest.

no·tice·a·ble /ˈnōtisəbəl/ ▸*adj.* easily seen or noticed; clear or apparent: *a noticeable increase in staff motivation.* ■ noteworthy: *a noticeable new phenomenon.* **—no·tice·a·bly** /-blē/ *adv.*

THE RIGHT WORD **conspicuous, noticeable, outstanding, prominent, remarkable, striking**

A scratch on someone's face might be **noticeable**, while a scar that runs from cheekbone to chin would be **conspicuous**. When it comes to describing the things that attract our attention, *noticeable* means readily noticed or unlikely to escape observation (*a noticeable facial tic; a noticeable aversion to cocktail parties*), while *conspicuous* implies that the eye (or mind) cannot miss it (*her absence was conspicuous*).

Use **prominent** when you want to describe something that literally or figuratively stands out from its background (*a prominent nose; a prominent position on the committee*). It can also apply to persons or things that stand out so clearly they are generally known or recognized (| *a prominent citizen*).

Someone or something that is **outstanding** rises above or beyond others and is usually superior to them (*an outstanding student*).

Remarkable applies to anything that is noticeable because it is extraordinary or exceptional (*remarkable blue eyes*).

Striking is an even stronger word, used to describe something so out of the ordinary that it makes a deep and powerful impression on the observer's mind or vision (*a striking young woman over six feet tall*).

no·ti·fi·a·ble /ˌnōtəˈfīəbəl/ ▸*adj.* denoting something, typically a serious infectious disease, that must be reported to the appropriate authorities.

no·ti·fy /ˈnōtəˌfī/ ▸*v.* (**-fies, -fied**) [*trans.*] inform (someone) of something, typically in a formal or official manner: *you will be* **notified of** *our decision as soon as possible* | [*trans.*] *they were notified that John had been taken prisoner.* ■ *chiefly Brit.* give notice of or report (something) formally or officially: *if he does not notify the occurrences, he may be guilty of nondisclosure.* ▷late Middle English: from Old French *notifier*, from Latin *notificare* 'make known,' from *notus* 'known' (see NOTION) + *facere* 'make.' **—no·ti·fi·ca·tion** /ˌnōtəfiˈkāSHən/ *n.*

no-till·age (also **no-till**) ▸*adj.* designating a method of planting in which soil is not tilled but instead is planted by insertion of seeds in small slits, weeds being controlled by other means: *a no-tillage tomato production system using hairy vetch and subterranean clover mulches.*

no·tion /ˈnōSHən/ ▸*n.* **1** a conception of or belief about something: *children have different notions about the rôles of their parents.* See note at IDEA. ■ a vague awareness or understanding of the nature of something: *I had no notion of what her words meant.* **2** an impulse or desire, esp. one of a whimsical kind: *she had a notion to call her friend at work.* **3** (**notions**) items used in sewing, such as buttons, pins, and hooks. ▷late Middle English: from Latin *notio(n-)* 'idea,' from *notus* 'known,' past participle of *noscere*.

no·tion·al /ˈnōSHənəl/ ▸*adj.* **1** existing only in theory or as a suggestion or idea: *notional budgets for hospital and community health services.* ■ existing only in the imagination: *Lizzie seemed to vanish into thin air, as if her presence were merely notional.* **2** *Linguistics* denoting or relating to an approach to grammar that is dependent on the definition of terminology (e.g., "a verb is an action word") as opposed to identification of structures and processes. **3** (in language teaching) denoting or relating to a syllabus that aims to develop communicative competence. ▷late Middle English (in the Latin sense): from obsolete French, or from medieval Latin *notionalis* 'relating to an idea,' from *notion-* 'idea' (see NOTION). **—no·tion·al·ly** *adv.*

no·to·chord /ˈnōtəˌkôrd/ ▸*n. Zoology* a cartilaginous skeletal rod supporting the body in all embryonic and some adult chordate animals. ▷mid 19th cent.: from Greek *nōton* 'back' + CHORD[2].

No·to·gae·a /ˌnōtəˈjēə/ (also **No·to·ge·a**) *Zoology* a zoogeographical area comprising the Australian region. ▷mid 19th cent.: modern Latin, from Greek *notos* 'south wind' + *gaia* 'earth.' **—No·to·gae·an** *adj.*

no·to·ri·ous /nəˈtôrēəs; nō-/ ▸*adj.* famous or well known, typically for some bad quality or deed: *Los Angeles is* **notorious for** *its smog* | *he was a notorious drinker and womanizer.* ▷late 15th cent. (in the sense 'generally known'): from medieval Latin *notorius* (from Latin *notus* 'known') + -OUS. **—no·to·ri·e·ty** /ˌnōtəˈrīətē/ *n.* **—no·to·ri·ous·ly** *adv.*

no·tor·nis /nōˈtôrnis/ ▸*n.* another term for TAKAHE. ▷mid 19th cent.: from Greek *notos* 'south' + *ornis* 'bird.'

no·to·un·gu·late /ˌnōtōˈəNGgyəlit/ ▸*n.* an extinct hoofed mammal of a large and varied group that lived in South America throughout the Tertiary period, finally dying out in the Pleistocene. • Order Notoungulata: many families. ▷late 20th cent.: from modern Latin *Notoungulata*, from Greek *notos* 'south' + Latin *ungula* 'nail.'

not-out *Cricket* ▸*adj.* denoting a batsman who is not out when the team's innings ends, or a score or innings made by such a batsman.
▸*n.* a not-out score or innings.

No·tre Dame /ˌnōtrə ˈdām/ a Gothic cathedral in Paris, dedicated to the Virgin Mary, on the Île de la Cité (an island in the Seine). It was built between 1163 and 1250 and is especially noted for its innovative flying buttresses and sculptured facade. ▷French, literally 'our lady.'

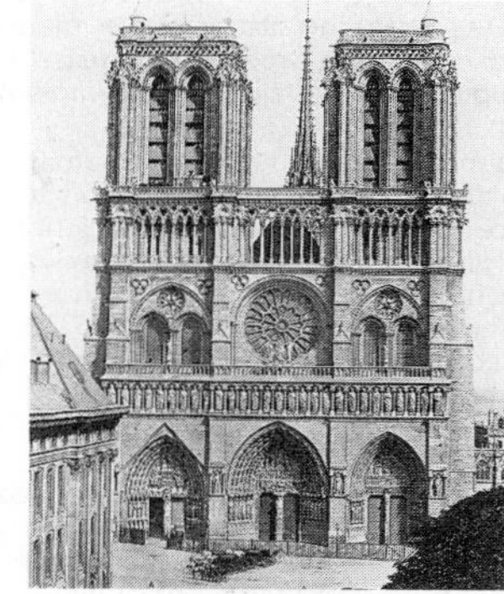

Notre Dame

no-trump ▸*n. Bridge* a situation in which no suit is designated as trump: *she reached three no-trump after her partner had opened with a weak two bid* | [as *adj.*] *a no-trump contract.*

Not·ting·ham /ˈnätiNGəm/ a city in east central England, the county town of Nottinghamshire; pop. 261,000.

Not·ting·ham lace /ˈnätiNGəm; -ˌham/ ▸*n.* a type of machine-made flat lace.

Not·ting·ham·shire /ˈnätiNGəmSHər; -ˌSHi(ə)r/ a county in central England; county town, Nottingham.

Notts. ▸*abbr.* Nottinghamshire.

no·tum /ˈnōtəm/ ▸*n.* (*pl.* **-ta** /-tə/) *Entomology* the dorsal exoskeleton of the thorax of an insect. ▷late 19th cent.: from Greek *nōton* 'back.' **—no·tal** /ˈnōtl/ *adj.*

not·with·stand·ing /ˌnätwiTHˈstandiNG; -wiTH-/ ▶*prep.* in spite of: *notwithstanding the evidence, the consensus is that the jury will not reach a verdict* | [*postpositive*] *this small contretemps notwithstanding, they both had a good time.*
▶*adv.* nevertheless; in spite of this: *she tells us she is an intellectual; notwithstanding, she faces the future as unprovided for as a beauty queen.*
▶*conj.* although; in spite of the fact that: ***notwithstanding that** the hall was packed with bullies, our champion played on steadily and patiently.* ▷late Middle English: from **NOT** + *withstanding*, present participle of **WITHSTAND**, on the pattern of Old French *non obstant* 'not providing an obstacle to.'

Nouak·chott /nəˈwäk,SHät/ the capital of Mauritania, situated on the Atlantic coast; pop. 850,000.

nou·gat /ˈnoōgit/ ▶*n.* a candy made from sugar or honey, nuts, and egg white. ▷early 19th cent.: from French, from Provençal *nogat*, from *noga* 'nut.'

nou·ga·tine /ˌnoōgəˈtēn/ ▶*n.* nougat covered with chocolate. ▷late 19th cent.: from **NOUGAT** + *-ine* 'resembling' (see **-INE**[1]).

nought ▶*n.* & *pron.* variant spelling of **NAUGHT**.

nought·ies /ˈnôtēz/ ▶*plural n. chiefly Brit.* the decade from 2000 to 2009: [as *modifier*] *the eighties hero will be duly updated for a noughties incarnation.* ▷1990s: from *nought* 'zero', on the pattern of *twenties, thirties*, etc.

noughts and cross·es ▶*plural n.* British term for **TIC-TAC-TOE**.

Nou·mé·a /noōˈmāə/ the capital of the island of New Caledonia; pop. 65,000. Former name **PORT DE FRANCE**.

nou·me·non /ˈnoōmə,nän/ ▶*n.* (*pl.* **-na** /-nə/) (in Kantian philosophy) a thing as it is in itself, as distinct from a thing as it is knowable by the senses through phenomenal attributes. ▷late 18th cent.: via German from Greek, literally '(something) conceived,' from *noien* 'conceive, apprehend.' **—nou·me·nal** /-nəl/ *adj.*

noun /noun/ ▶*n. Grammar* a word (other than a pronoun) used to identify any of a class of people, places, or things (**common noun**), or to name a particular one of these (**proper noun**). ▷late Middle English: from Anglo-Norman French, from Latin *nomen* 'name.' **—noun·al** /ˈnounəl/ *adj.*

noun phrase ▶*n. Grammar* a word or group of words that functions in a sentence as subject, object, or prepositional object.

nour·ish /ˈnəriSH; ˈnə-riSH/ ▶*v.* [*trans.*] **1** provide with the food or other substances necessary for growth, health, and good condition: *I was doing everything I could to nourish and protect the baby* | *figurative spiritual resources that nourished her in her darkest hours.* ■ enhance the fertility of (soil): *a clay base nourished with plant detritus.* **2** keep (a feeling or belief) in one's mind, typically for a long time: *he has long nourished an ambition to bring the show to Broadway.* ▷Middle English: from Old French *noriss-*, lengthened stem of *norir*, from Latin *nutrire* 'feed, cherish.' **—nour·ish·er** *n.*

nour·ish·ing /ˈnəriSHiNG; ˈnə-ri-/ ▶*adj.* (of food) containing substances necessary for growth, health, and good condition: *a simple but nourishing meal.* **—nour·ish·ing·ly** *adv.*

nour·ish·ment /ˈnəriSHmənt; ˈnə-riSH-/ ▶*n.* the substances necessary for growth, health, and good condition: *tubers from which plants obtain nourishment.* ■ food: *they often go days with little or no nourishment.* ■ the action of nourishing someone or something: *they suck out the sap and eliminate from it a sweet liquid for the nourishment of their young.*

nous /noōs; nous/ ▶*n.* **1** *Philosophy* the mind or intellect. **2** *informal, chiefly Brit.* common sense; practical intelligence: *if he had any nous at all, he'd sell the movie rights.* ▷late 17th cent. (sense 1): from Greek, 'mind, intelligence, intuitive apprehension.'

nou·veau /ˈnoōvō; noōˈvō/ ▶*adj. informal* **1** short for **NOUVEAU RICHE**. **2** modern; up to date.

nou·veau riche /ˈnoōvō ˈrēSH/ ▶*n.* [treated as *pl.*] (usu. **the nouveau riche**) people who have recently acquired wealth, typically those perceived as ostentatious or lacking in good taste.
▶*adj.* of, relating to, or characteristic of such people: *nouveau-riche social climbers.* ▷French, literally 'new rich.'

nou·veau ro·man /ˌnoōvō rōˈmän/ ▶*n.* a style of avant-garde French novel that came to prominence in the 1950s. It rejected the plot, characters, and omniscient narrator central to the traditional novel in an attempt to reflect more faithfully the sometimes random nature of experience. ▷French, literally 'new novel.'

nou·velle /noōˈvel/ ▶*adj.* of, relating to, or specializing in nouvelle cuisine: *nouvelle bistros.*

Nou·velle-Ca·lé·do·nie /noōˈvel ˌkälədôˈnē/ French name for **NEW CALEDONIA**.

nou·velle cui·sine /noōˈvel kwiˈzēn/ ▶*n.* a modern style of cooking that avoids rich, heavy foods and emphasizes the freshness of the ingredients and the presentation of the dishes. ▷French, literally 'new cooking.'

nou·velle vague /noōˈvel ˌväg/ ▶*n.* a grouping of French movie directors in the late 1950s and 1960s who reacted against established French cinema and sought to make more individualistic and stylistically innovative films. Exponents included Claude Chabrol, Jean-Luc Godard, Alain Resnais, and François Truffaut. ▷French, literally 'new wave.'

Nov. ▶*abbr.* November.

no·va /ˈnōvə/ ▶*n.* (*pl.* **-vae** /-vē; -ˌvī/ or **-vas**) *Astronomy* a star showing a sudden large increase in brightness and then slowly returning to its original state over a few months. See also **SUPERNOVA**. ▷late 19th cent.: from Latin, feminine of *novus* 'new' (because such stars were thought to be newly formed).

no·vac·u·lite /nōˈvakyə,līt/ ▶*n. Geology* a hard, dense, fine-grained siliceous rock resembling chert, with a high content of microcrystalline quartz. ▷late 18th cent.: from Latin *novacula* 'razor' + **-ITE**[1].

No·va Lis·bo·a /ˈnōvə lēZHˈbōə; ˌnôvə lēZHˈvōə/ former name (until 1978) for **HUAMBO**.

No·va Sco·tia /ˈnōvə ˈskōSHə/ **1** a peninsula on the southeastern coast of Canada that projects into the Atlantic Ocean and separates the Bay of Fundy from the Gulf of St. Lawrence. **2** a province in eastern Canada that consists of the Nova Scotia peninsula and adjoining Cape Breton Island; pop. 899,942; capital, Halifax. Settled as Acadia by the French in the early 18th century, it changed hands several times before being awarded to Britain in 1713. It became one of the original four provinces in the Dominion of Canada in 1867. **—No·va Sco·tian** *adj.* & *n.*

no·va·tion /nōˈvāSHən/ ▶*n. Law* the substitution of a new contract in place of an old one. ▷early 16th cent.: from late Latin *novatio(n-)*, from the verb *novare* 'make new.' **—no·vate** /ˈnōvāt; nōˈvāt/ *v.*

No·va·to /nəˈvätō/ a city in northwestern California, north of San Francisco; pop. 47,585.

No·va·ya Zem·lya /ˈnôvəyə ˌzemlēˈä; zimlēˈä/ two large uninhabited islands in the Arctic Ocean off the northern coast of Siberian Russia. The name means "new land."

nov·el[1] /ˈnävəl/ ▶*n.* a fictitious prose narrative of book length, typically representing character and action with some degree of realism: *the novels of Jane Austen.* ■ a book containing such a narrative: *she was reading a paperback novel.* ■ (**the novel**) the literary genre represented or exemplified by such works: *the novel is the most adaptable of all literary forms.* ▷mid 16th cent.: from Italian *novella (storia)* 'new (story),' feminine of *novello* 'new,' from Latin *novellus*, from *novus* 'new.' The word is also found from late Middle English until the 18th cent. in the sense 'a novelty, a piece of news,' from Old French *novelle* (see **NOVEL**[2]).

nov·el[2] ▶*adj.* new or unusual in an interesting way: *he hit on a novel idea to solve his financial problems.* ▷late Middle English (in the sense 'recent'): from Old French, from Latin *novellus*, from *novus* 'new.' **—nov·el·ly** *adv.*

no·vel·a /nōˈvelə/ ▶another term for **TELENOVELA**.

nov·el·ette /ˌnävəˈlet/ ▶*n. chiefly derogatory* a short novel, typically one that is light and romantic or sentimental in character. **—nov·el·et·tish** *adj.*

nov·el·ist /ˈnävəlist/ ▶*n.* a writer of novels.

nov·el·is·tic /ˌnävəˈlistik/ ▶*adj.* characteristic of or used in novels: *the novelistic detail of his film.*

nov·el·ize /ˈnävə,līz/ ▶*v.* [*trans.*] [usu. as *adj.*] (**novelized**) convert (a story, typically one in the form of a movie or screenplay) into a novel. **—nov·el·i·za·tion** /ˌnävəliˈzāSHən/ *n.*

no·vel·la /nōˈvelə/ ▶*n.* a short novel or long short story. ▷early 20th cent.: from Italian, 'novel.'

No·vel·lo /nəˈvelō/, Ivor (1893–1951), Welsh composer, songwriter, actor, and dramatist; born *David Ivor Davies*. He wrote "Keep the Home Fires Burning" (1914).

nov·el·ty /ˈnävəltē/ ▶*n.* (*pl.* **-ties**) **1** the quality of being new, original, or unusual: *the novelty of being a married woman wore off.* ■ a new or unfamiliar thing or experience: *in 1914 air travel was still a novelty.* ■ [as *adj.*] denoting something intended to be amusing as a result of its new or unusual quality: *a novelty teapot.* **2** a small and inexpensive toy or ornament: *he bought chocolate novelties to decorate the Christmas tree.* ▷late Middle English: from Old French *novelte*, from *novel* 'new, fresh' (see **NOVEL**[2]).

No·vem·ber /nōˈvembər; nə-/ ▶*n.* **1** the eleventh month of the year, in the northern hemisphere usually considered the last month of autumn: *the store opened in November* | [as *adj.*] *November days.* **2** a code word representing the letter N, used in radio communication. ▷Old English, from Latin, from *novem* 'nine' (being originally the ninth month of the Roman year).

no·ve·na /nōˈvēnə/ ▶*n.* (in the Roman Catholic Church) a form of worship consisting of special prayers or services on nine successive days. ▷mid 19th cent.: from medieval Latin, from Latin *novem* 'nine.'

No·verre /nōˈver/, Jean-Georges (1727–1810), French choreographer and dance theorist. He stressed the importance of dramatic motivation, as opposed to technical virtuosity, in ballet.

Nov·go·rod /ˈnôvgərət; ˈnävgə,räd/ a city in northwestern Russia, on the Volkhov River at the northern tip of Lake Ilmen; pop. 232,000. Russia's oldest city, it was settled by Varangian chief Rurik in 862 and ruled by Alexander Nevsky 1238–63, when it was an important center of medieval eastern Europe.

nov·ice /ˈnävəs/ ▶*n.* a person new to or inexperienced in a field or situation: *he was a complete novice in foreign affairs.* ■ a person who has entered a religious order and is under probation, before taking vows. ■ an animal, esp. a racehorse, that has not yet won a major prize or reached a level of performance to qualify for important events. ▷Middle English: from Old French, from late Latin *novicius*, from *novus* 'new.'

THE RIGHT WORD **apprentice, beginner, neophyte, novice, probationer**

All of these nouns are used to describe someone who has not yet acquired the skills and experience needed to qualify for a trade, a career, a profession, or a sphere of life.

Beginner is the most general and informal term, used to describe someone who has begun to acquire the necessary skills but has not yet mastered them (*violin lessons for beginners*).

An **apprentice** is also a beginner, usually a young person, who is serving under a more experienced master or teacher to learn the skills of a trade or profession (*an apprentice to one of the great Renaissance painters*). In a broad sense, *apprentice* refers to any beginner whose efforts are unpolished.

Novice implies that the person lacks training and experience (*a novice when it came to writing fiction*), while **neophyte** is a less negative term, suggesting that the person is eagerly learning the ways, methods, or principles of something (*he was a neophyte at this type of sailing*).

A **probationer** is a beginner who is undergoing a trial period, during which he or she must prove an aptitude for a certain type of work or life (*she was a lowly probationer, with no privileges or status*).

No·vi Sad /ˌnōvē ˈsäd/ an industrial city in Serbia in Yugoslavia, on the Danube River, capital of the autonomous province of Vojvodina; pop. 179,000.

no·vi·ti·ate /nōˈviSH(ē)ət; nə-/ (also **no·vi·ci·ate**) ▶*n.* the period or state of being a novice, esp. in a religious order. ■ a place housing religious novices. ■ a novice, esp. in a religious order. ▷early 17th cent.: from ecclesiastical Latin *noviciatus*, from Latin *novicius* 'new' (see **NOVICE**).

no·vo·caine /ˈnōvə,kān/ (also *trademark* **No·vo·cain**) ▶*n.* another term for **PROCAINE**. ▷early 20th cent.: from Latin *novus* 'new' + *-caine* (from **COCAINE**).

No·vo·kuz·netsk /ˌnōvəkoōzˈn(y)etsk/ an industrial city in Russia, in central Siberia, in the Kuznets Basin; pop. 601,000.

No·vo·si·birsk /ˌnōvəsiˈbirsk/ a city in Russia, in central Siberia, west of the Kuznets Basin, on the Ob River; pop. 1,443,000.

N

No·vot·ný /ˈnôvôt,nē/, Antonín (1904–75), Czech statesman; president 1957–68. A founding member of the Czechoslovak Communist Party in 1921, he played a major part in the communist seizure of power in 1948. He was ousted by the reform movement in 1968.

NOW ▸*abbr.* National Organization for Women.

now /nou/ ▸*adv.* **1** at the present time or moment: *where are you living now? | it's the most popular style of jazz* **right now** *| not now, I'm late |* [after *prep.*] *they should be back* **by now**. ■ at the time directly following the present moment; immediately: *if we leave now, we can be home by ten | I'd rather do it now than leave it till later.* ■ under the present circumstances; as a result of something that has recently happened: *it is now clear that we should not pursue this policy | I didn't receive the letter, but it hardly matters now.* ■ on this further occasion, typically as the latest in a series of annoying situations or events: *what do you want now?* ■ used to emphasize a particular length of time: *they've been married four years now.* ■ (in a narrative or account of past events) at the time spoken of or referred to: *it had happened three times now | she was nineteen now, and she was alone.* **2** used, esp. in conversation, to draw attention to a particular statement or point in a narrative: *now, my first impulse was to run away | I don't like Scotch. Now, if it had been Irish Whiskey you'd offered me.* ■ used when turning to a different subject or activity: *and* **now for** *something completely different* **3** used in or as a request, instruction, or question, typically to give a slight emphasis to one's words: *now, if you'll excuse me? | we can hardly send her back, now can we? | run along now.* ■ used when pausing or considering one's next words: *let me see now; oh yes, I remember.* **4** used at the end of an ironic question echoing a previous statement: *"Mom says for you to give me some of your stamps." "Does she now?"*

▸*conj.* as a consequence of the fact: *they spent a lot of time together* **now that** *he had retired |* **now that** *you mention it, I haven't seen her around for ages.*

▸*adj. informal* fashionable; up to date: *seventies disco dancing—very now.* ▷Old English *nū*, of Germanic origin; related to Dutch *nu*, German *nun*, from an Indo-European root shared by Latin *nunc* and Greek *nun*. **—now·ness** *n.*

▸***PHRASES*** □ **for now** until a later time: *that's all the news there is for now.* □ **now and again** (or **then**) from time to time. □ **now now** used as an expression of mild remonstrance: *now now, that's not the way to behave.* □ **now ——, now ——** at one moment ——, at the next ——: *a wind whipped about the house, now this way, now that.* □ **now or never** used to convey urgency: *it was now or never—I had to move fast.* □ **now then 1** used to get someone's attention or to invite a response: *now then, who's for a coffee?* **2** used as an expression of mild remonstrance or warning: *now then, Emily, I think Sarah has suffered enough.* □ **now you're talking** used to express one's enthusiastic agreement with or approval of a statement or suggestion: *The Beatles! Now you're talking.*

now·a·days /ˈnouə,dāz/ ▸*adv.* at the present time, in contrast with the past: *the sort of clothes worn by almost all young people nowadays |* [*sentence adverb*] *nowadays, many people condemn hunting.*

no·way /ˈnō,wā/ (also **noways**) ▸*adv.* another term for **NOWISE**. See also **NO WAY** at **NO**.

now·cast /ˈnou,kast/ ▸*n.* a description of present weather conditions and forecast of those immediately expected. **—now·cast·er** *n.* **—now·cast·ing** *n.*

nowed /noud/ ▸*adj.* [often *postpositive*] *Heraldry* knotted; (of a snake) depicted interlaced in a knot. ▷late 16th cent.: from French *noué* 'knotted.'

no·where /ˈnō,(h)we(ə)r/ ▸*adv.* not in or to any place; not anywhere: *plants and animals found nowhere else in the world | Andrea is nowhere to be found.*

▸*pron.* **1** no place: *there was nowhere for her to sit | there's nowhere better to experience the wonders of the Rockies.* **2** a place that is remote, uninteresting, or nondescript: *a stretch of road between nowhere and nowhere |* [as *n.*] *the town is a particularly American nowhere.*

▸*adj.* [*attrib.*] *informal* having no prospect of progress or success: *she's involved in a nowhere affair with a married executive.* ▷Old English *nāhwǣr* (see **NO, WHERE**).

▸***PHRASES*** □ **from** (or **out of**) **nowhere** appearing or happening suddenly and unexpectedly: *he materialized a taxi out of nowhere.* □ **get** (or **go**) **nowhere** make no progress: *I'm getting nowhere—maybe I should give up | the project was* **going nowhere fast**. □ **get someone nowhere** be of no use or benefit to someone: *being angry would get her nowhere.* □ **nowhere near** not nearly: *he's* **nowhere near as** *popular as he used to be.* □ **a road to nowhere** a situation or course of action offering no prospects of progress or advancement.

no·wheres /ˈnō,(h)werz/ *informal* ▸*adv.* nowhere: *that boat was going nowheres.*

no·wheres·ville /ˈnō(h)werz,vil/ (also **No·wheres·ville**) ▸*n. informal* **1** a remote town or village: *some American village that might justifiably lay claim to the title "Nowheresville."* **2** a job or position that lacks prestige, recognition, or the opportunity for advancement: *unless they were among the big boys, they were on the way to nowheresville.* **3** anything that is impractical, unrealistic, or fruitless: *we do okay on some things, then on others it's practically nowheresville.*

no-win ▸*adj.* of or denoting a situation in which success or a favorable outcome is impossible.

no·wise /ˈnō,wīz/ ▸*adv. archaic* in no way or manner; not at all: *I can nowise accept the accusation.*

nowt /nout/ ▸*pron.* & *adv. N. English* nothing: *it's nowt to do with me.*

NOx ▸*n.* oxides of nitrogen, esp. as atmospheric pollutants.

nox·ious /ˈnäksHəs/ ▸*adj.* harmful, poisonous, or very unpleasant: *they were overcome by the noxious fumes.* ▷late 15th cent.: from Latin *noxius* (from *noxa* 'harm') + **-OUS**. **—nox·ious·ly** *adv.* **—nox·ious·ness** *n.*

nox·ious weed ▸*n.* a plant considered harmful to animals or the environment.

no·yade /nwäˈyäd/ ▸*n. historical* an execution carried out by drowning. ▷early 19th cent. (referring esp. to a mass execution by drowning, carried out in France in 1794): from French, literally 'drowning,' from the verb *noyer*, from Latin *necare* 'kill without use of a weapon,' later 'drown.'

no·yau /nwäˈyō; ˈnwä,yō/ ▸*n.* (*pl.* **-yaux** /-ˈyō(z); -,yō(z)/) a liqueur made of brandy flavored with fruit kernels. ▷French, literally 'kernel,' based on Latin *nux*, *nuc-* 'nut.'

noz·zle /ˈnäzəl/ ▸*n.* a cylindrical or round spout at the end of a pipe, hose, or tube, used to control a jet of gas or liquid. ▷early 17th cent.: from **NOSE** + **-LE**[2].

NP ▸*abbr.* notary public.

Np ▸*symbol* the chemical element neptunium.

n.p. ▸*abbr.* ■ new paragraph. ■ no place of publication (used esp. in book classification).

NPN ▸*adj. Electronics* denoting a semiconductor device in which a *p*-type region is sandwiched between two *n*-type regions.

NPR ▸*abbr.* National Public Radio.

NPV ▸*abbr.* net present value. See **PRESENT VALUE**.

nr ▸*abbr.* near.

NRA ▸*abbr.* ■ National Rifle Association.

NRC ▸*abbr.* ■ National Research Council. ■ National Response Center. ■ Nuclear Regulatory Commission.

NRSV ▸*abbr.* New Revised Standard Version (of the Bible).

NS ▸*abbr.* ■ New Style. ■ Nova Scotia (in official postal use).

ns ▸*abbr.* nanosecond.

n/s ▸*abbr.* nonsmoker; nonsmoking (used in personal advertisements).

NSA ▸*abbr.* National Security Agency.

NSAID /ˈen,sed/ ▸*abbr.* nonsteroidal anti-inflammatory drug, of which aspirin is the archetype.

NSC ▸*abbr.* National Security Council.

NSE ▸*abbr.* National Stock Exchange.

nsec ▸*abbr.* nanosecond.

NSF ▸*abbr.* National Science Foundation.

n.s.f. ▸*abbr.* not sufficient funds.

NSPCA ▸*abbr.* National Society for the Prevention of Cruelty to Animals.

NSU *Medicine* ▸*abbr.* nonspecific urethritis.

NSW ▸*abbr.* New South Wales.

NT ▸*abbr.* ■ New Testament. ■ Northern Territory. ■ Northwest Territories (in official postal use). ■ *Bridge* no-trump.

n't ▸*contraction of* not, used with auxiliary verbs (e.g., *can't, won't, didn't*, and *isn't*).

Nth ▸*abbr.* North.

nth /enTH/ ▸*adj. Mathematics* denoting an unspecified member of a series of numbers or enumerated items: *systematic sampling by taking every nth name from the list.* ■ (in general use) denoting an unspecified item or instance in a series, typically the last or latest in a long series: *for the nth time that day they were forced to relate the whole story.*

▸***PHRASE*** □ **to the nth degree** to the utmost: *the gullibility of the electorate was tested to the nth degree by such promises.*

NTP *Chemistry* ▸*abbr.* normal temperature and pressure.

NTSB ▸*abbr.* National Transportation Safety Board.

NTSC ▸*n.* the television broadcasting system used in North America and Japan. ▷1950s: acronym from *National Television Standards Committee.*

n-tu·ple ▸*n. Mathematics* an ordered set with *n* elements.

nt. wt. ▸*abbr.* net weight.

n-type ▸*adj. Electronics* denoting a region in a semiconductor in which electrical conduction is due chiefly to the movement of electrons. Often contrasted with **P-TYPE**.

NU ▸*abbr.* Nunavut (in official postal use).

nu /n(y)o͞o/ ▸*n.* the thirteenth letter of the Greek alphabet (Ν, ν), transliterated as 'n.' ■ (**Nu**) [followed by Latin genitive] *Astronomy* the thirteenth star in a constellation: *Nu Draconis.*

▸*symbol* (ν) frequency.

nu- /n(y)o͞o/ ▸*comb. form* informal respelling of 'new,' used especially in names of new or revived genres of popular music: *nu-metal bands | nu-disco.*

nu·ance /ˈn(y)o͞o,äns/ ▸*n.* a subtle difference in or shade of meaning, expression, or sound: *the nuances of facial expression and body language.*

▸*v.* [*trans.*] (usu. **be nuanced**) give nuances to: *the effect of the music is nuanced by the social situation of listeners.* ▷late 18th cent.: from French, 'shade, subtlety,' from *nuer* 'to shade,' based on Latin *nubes* 'cloud.'

nub /nəb/ ▸*n.* **1** (**the nub**) the crux or central point of a matter: *the nub of the problem lies elsewhere.* **2** a small lump or protuberance: *he pressed down on the two nubs on top of the phone.* ■ a small chunk or nugget of metal or rock: *a nub of gold.* ▷late 17th cent.: apparently a variant of dialect *knub* 'protuberance,' from Middle Low German *knubbe, knobbe* 'knob.'

Nu·ba /ˈno͞obə/ ▸*n.* (*pl.* same or **-bas**) a member of a Nilotic people inhabiting southern Kordofan, a region in Sudan.

▸*adj.* of or relating to this people. ▷from Latin *Nubae* 'Nubians.'

nub·bin /ˈnəbən/ ▸*n.* a small lump or residual part: *nubbins of bone or cartilage.* ▷late 17th cent.: diminutive of **NUB**.

nub·by /ˈnəbē/ (also **nub·bly** /ˈnəblē/) ▸*adj.* (of fabric) coarse or knobbly in texture: *upholstered in nubby blue cotton.* ■ stubby; lumpy: *the nubby points of the new leaves.* ▷early 19th cent. (as *nubbly*): derivative of *nubble* 'small lump.'

Nu·bi·a /ˈn(y)o͞obēə/ an ancient region of southern Egypt and northern Sudan, including the Nile valley between Aswan and Khartoum and the surrounding area. Much of Nubia is now drowned by the waters of Lake Nasser, formed by the building of the two dams at Aswan. Nubians constitute an ethnic minority group in Egypt.

Nu·bi·an /ˈn(y)o͞obēən/ ▸*adj.* of or relating to Nubia, its people, or their language.

▸*n.* **1** a native or inhabitant of Nubia. **2** the Nilo-Saharan language of the Nubians. **3** a goat of a short-haired breed with long pendant ears and long legs, originally from Africa. ▷from medieval Latin *Nubianus*, from *Nubia* 'Nubia,' from Latin *Nubae* 'Nubians.'

nu·bile /ˈn(y)o͞o,bīl; -bəl/ ▸*adj.* (of a girl or young woman) sexually mature; suitable for marriage. ■ (of a girl or young woman) sexually attractive: *he employed a procession of nubile young secretaries.* ▷mid 17th cent.: from Latin *nubilis* 'marriageable,' from *nubere* 'cover or veil oneself for a bridegroom' (from *nubes* 'cloud'). **—nu·bil·i·ty** /n(y)o͞oˈbilitē/ *n.*

Nu·buck /ˈn(y)o͞o,bək/ ▸*n. trademark* cowhide leather that has been rubbed on the flesh side to give it a feel like that of suede.

nu·cel·lus /n(y)o͞oˈseləs/ ▸*n.* (*pl.* **-cel·li** /-ˈsel,ī; -ˈselē/) *Botany* the central part of an ovule, containing the embryo sac. ▷late 19th cent.: modern Latin, apparently an irregular diminutive of **NUCLEUS**. **—nu·cel·lar** /-ˈselər/ *adj.*

nu·chal /ˈn(y)o͞okəl/ ▸*adj. Anatomy* of or relating to the nape of the neck. ▷mid 19th cent.: from obsolete *nucha* 'nape' (from medieval Latin *nucha* 'medulla oblongata,' from Arabic *nuḵā'* 'spinal marrow') + **-AL**.

nuci- ▸*comb. form* of a nut or nuts. ▷from Latin *nux*, *nuc-* 'nut.'

nu·cle·ar /ˈn(y)o͞oklēər; -kl(ə)r/ ▸*adj.* **1** of or relating to the nucleus of an atom. ■ denoting, relating to, or powered by the energy released in nuclear fission or fusion: *nuclear energy | nuclear submarines.* ■ denoting, possessing, or involving weapons using this energy:

a nuclear bomb | nuclear nations. **2** *Biology* of or relating to the nucleus of a cell: *nuclear DNA.* ▷mid 19th cent.: from NUCLEUS + -AR[1].

USAGE A variant pronunciation, /ˈn(y)o͞okyələr/, has been used by many, but is widely regarded as unacceptable.

nu·cle·ar age ▸*n.* the period in history usu. considered to have begun with the first use of the atomic bomb (1945). It is characterized by nuclear energy as a military, industrial, and sociopolitical factor. Also called ATOMIC AGE.

nu·cle·ar club ▸*n.* the nations possessing nuclear weapons.

nu·cle·ar fam·i·ly ▸*n.* a couple and their dependent children, regarded as a basic social unit.

nu·cle·ar fis·sion ▸*n.* a nuclear reaction in which a heavy nucleus splits spontaneously or on impact with another particle, with the release of energy.

nu·cle·ar force ▸*n. Physics* a strong attractive force between nucleons in the atomic nucleus that holds the nucleus together.

nu·cle·ar-free ▸*adj.* (of a country or region) not having or allowing any nuclear weapons, materials, or power: *a nuclear-free zone.*

nu·cle·ar fuel ▸*n.* a substance that will sustain a fission chain reaction so that it can be used as a source of nuclear energy.

nu·cle·ar fu·sion ▸*n.* a nuclear reaction in which atomic nuclei of low atomic number fuse to form a heavier nucleus with the release of energy.

nu·cle·ar mag·net·ic res·o·nance (abbr.: **NMR**) ▸*n.* the absorption of electromagnetic radiation by a nucleus having a magnetic moment when in an external magnetic field, used mainly as an analytical technique and in diagnostic body imaging.

nu·cle·ar med·i·cine ▸*n.* the branch of medicine that deals with the use of radioactive substances in research, diagnosis, and treatment.

nu·cle·ar phys·ics ▸*plural n.* [treated as *sing.*] the physics of atomic nuclei and their interactions, esp. in the generation of nuclear energy.

nu·cle·ar pow·er ▸*n.* **1** electric or motive power generated by a nuclear reactor. **2** a country that has nuclear weapons. —**nu·cle·ar-pow·ered** *adj.*

nu·cle·ar re·ac·tion ▸*n. Physics* a change in the identity or characteristics of an atomic nucleus that results when it is bombarded with an energetic particle, as in fission, fusion, or radioactive decay.

nu·cle·ar re·ac·tor ▸*n.* see REACTOR.

nu·cle·ar thresh·old ▸*n.* a point in a conflict at which nuclear weapons are or would be brought into use.

nu·cle·ar um·brel·la ▸*n.* the supposed protection gained from an alliance with a country possessing nuclear weapons.

nu·cle·ar waste ▸*n.* radioactive waste material, for example from the use or reprocessing of nuclear fuel.

nu·cle·ar win·ter ▸*n.* a period of abnormal cold and darkness predicted to follow a nuclear war, caused by a layer of smoke and dust in the atmosphere blocking the sun's rays.

nu·cle·ase /ˈn(y)o͞oklēˌās; -ˌāz/ ▸*n. Biochemistry* an enzyme that cleaves the chains of nucleotides in nucleic acids into smaller units.

nu·cle·ate ▸*adj.* /ˈn(y)o͞oklēət; -ˌāt/ *chiefly Biology* having a nucleus.

▸*v.* /ˈn(y)o͞okléˌāt/ [*intrans.*] [usu. as *adj.*] (**nucleated**) form a nucleus. ■ form around a central area: *a nucleated village.* —**nu·cle·a·tion** /ˌn(y)o͞ookléˈāsʜən/ *n.*

nu·cle·i /ˈn(y)o͞ookléˌī/ ▸ plural form of NUCLEUS.

nu·cle·ic ac·id /n(y)o͞oˈklē-ik/ ▸*n. Biochemistry* a complex organic substance present in living cells, esp. DNA or RNA, whose molecules consist of many nucleotides linked in a long chain.

nucleo- ▸*comb. form* representing NUCLEUS, NUCLEAR, or NUCLEIC ACID.

nu·cle·o·cap·sid /ˌn(y)o͞oklē-ōˈkapsid/ ▸*n. Biology* the capsid of a virus with the enclosed nucleic acid.

nu·cle·o·lus /n(y)o͞oˈklēələs/ ▸*n.* (*pl.* **-li** /-ˌlī; -ˌlē/) *Biology* a small dense spherical structure in the nucleus of a cell during interphase. ▷mid 19th cent.: from late Latin, diminutive of Latin *nucleus* 'inner part, kernel' (see NUCLEUS). —**nu·cle·o·lar** /-lər/ *adj.*

nu·cle·on /ˈn(y)o͞ookléˌän/ ▸*n. Physics* a proton or neutron.

nu·cle·on·ics /ˌn(y)o͞ooklēˈäniks/ ▸*plural n.* [treated as *sing.*] the branch of science and technology concerned with atomic nuclei and nucleons, esp. the exploitation of nuclear power. ▷1940s: from NUCLEAR, on the pattern of *electronics.* —**nu·cle·on·ic** *adj.*

nu·cle·o·phil·ic /ˌn(y)o͞oklē-ōˈfilik/ ▸*adj. Chemistry* (of a molecule or group) having a tendency to donate electrons or react at electron-poor sites such as protons. Often contrasted with ELECTROPHILIC. —**nu·cle·o·phile** /ˈn(y)o͞ooklēəˌfil/ *n.*

nu·cle·o·plasm /ˈn(y)o͞ooklēəˌplazəm/ ▸*n. Biology* the substance of a cell nucleus, esp. that not forming part of a nucleolus.

nu·cle·o·pro·tein /ˌn(y)o͞ooklē-ōˈprōˌtēn/ ▸*n. Biochemistry* a complex consisting of a nucleic acid bonded to a protein.

nu·cle·o·side /ˈn(y)o͞ooklēəˌsīd/ ▸*n. Biochemistry* a compound (e.g., adenosine or cytidine) commonly found in DNA or RNA, consisting of a purine or pyrimidine base linked to a sugar.

nu·cle·o·some /ˈn(y)o͞ooklēəˌsōm/ ▸*n. Biology* a structural unit of a eukaryotic chromosome, consisting of a length of DNA coiled around a core of histones. —**nu·cle·o·so·mal** /ˌn(y)o͞ooklēəˈsōməl/ *adj.*

nu·cle·o·syn·the·sis /ˌn(y)o͞ooklē-ōˈsinтʜəsis/ ▸*n. Astronomy* the cosmic formation of atoms more complex than the hydrogen atom. —**nu·cle·o·syn·thet·ic** /-sinˈт̲ʜetik/ *adj.*

nu·cle·o·tide /ˈn(y)o͞ooklēəˌtīd/ ▸*n. Biochemistry* a compound consisting of a nucleoside linked to a phosphate group. Nucleotides form the basic structural unit of nucleic acids such as DNA.

nu·cle·us /ˈn(y)o͞ooklēəs/ ▸*n.* (*pl.* **-cle·i** /-klēˌī/) the central and most important part of an object, movement, or group, forming the basis for its activity and growth: *the nucleus of a film-producing industry.* ■ *Physics* the positively charged central core of an atom, containing most of its mass. ■ *Biology* a dense organelle present in most eukaryotic cells, typically a single rounded structure bounded by a double membrane, containing the genetic material. ■ *Astronomy* the solid part of the head of a comet. ■ *Anatomy* a discrete mass of gray matter in the central nervous system. ▷early 18th cent.: from Latin, literally 'kernel, inner part,' diminutive of *nux, nuc-* 'nut.'

nu·clide /ˈn(y)o͞oˌklīd/ ▸*n. Physics* a distinct kind of atom or nucleus characterized by a specific number of protons and neutrons. ▷1940s: from NUCLEUS + *-ide* (from Greek *eidos* 'form'). —**nu·clid·ic** /n(y)o͞oˈklidik/ *adj.*

nude /n(y)o͞od/ ▸*adj.* wearing no clothes; naked: *a painting of a nude model.* See note at NAKED. ■ [*attrib.*] depicting or performed by naked people: *he was asked to act in a frank nude scene.* ■ (esp. of hosiery) flesh-colored: *black shoes with beige or nude stockings.*

▸*n.* a naked human figure, typically as the subject of a painting, sculpture, or photograph: *a study of a kneeling nude.* ■ (**the nude**) the representation of the naked human figure as a genre in art: *the nude was regarded as the ultimate test of artistic skill.* ■ flesh color. ▷late Middle English (in the sense 'plain, explicit'): from Latin *nudus.* The current sense is first found in noun use in the early 18th cent.

▸*PHRASE* □ **in the nude** in an unclothed state: *I like to swim in the nude.*

nudge /nəj/ ▸*v.* [*trans.*] prod (someone) gently, typically with one's elbow, in order to draw their attention to something: *people were nudging each other and pointing at me.* ■ touch or push (something) gently or gradually: *the canoe nudged a bank of reeds.* ■ *figurative* coax or gently encourage (someone) to do something: *we have to* **nudge** *the politicians* **in the right direction.** ■ approach (an age, figure, or level) very closely: *both men were nudging fifty.*

▸*n.* a light touch or push: *he gave her shoulder a nudge | figurative she appreciated the nudge to her memory.* ▷late 17th cent. (as a verb): of unknown origin; compare with Norwegian dialect *nugga, nyggja* 'to push, rub.' —**nudg·er** *n.*

▸*PHRASE* □ **nudge nudge** (**wink wink**) used to draw attention to a sexual innuendo in the previous statement: *haven't seen much of the beach—we've been catching up on our sleep (nudge nudge).* [a catch phrase from *Monty Python's Flying Circus*, a British television comedy program.]

Nu·di·bran·chi·a /ˌn(y)o͞odəˈbrangkēə/ *Zoology* an order of shell-less marine mollusks that comprises the sea slugs. • Order Nudibranchia, class Gastropoda. ▷modern Latin (plural), from Latin *nudus* 'nude' + BRANCHIA. —**nu·di·branch** /ˈn(y)o͞odəˌbrangk/ *n.*

nud·ie /ˈn(y)o͞odē/ ▸*n.* (*pl.* **-ies**) *informal* a publication, entertainment, or venue featuring nude performers or models: *the magazine says the editor was fired, and for reasons unrelated to nudies of the star.*

▸*adj.* portraying, featuring, or including peo[...] nude: *a nudie bar.*

nud·ist /ˈn(y)o͞odist/ ▸*n.* a person who engage[...] practice of going naked wherever possible: *a* [...] *to encourage more public places to allow nudists* | [a[...] *a nudist beach.* —**nud·ism** /-ˌdizəm/ *n.*

nu·di·ty /ˈn(y)o͞odətē/ ▸*n.* the state or fact of b[...] naked: *scenes of full frontal nudity.*

nud·nik /ˈno͝odˌnik/ (also **nud·nick**) ▸*n. informal* a p[...]tering, nagging, or irritating person; a bore. ▷m[...] 20th cent.: Yiddish, from Russian *nudnyĭ* 'tedious[...]

Nu·e·ces Riv·er /n(y)o͞oˈāsəs/ a river that flows fo[...] 315 miles (515 km) from central Texas, past Corpus Christi, into the Gulf of Mexico at Nueces Bay.

nu·ée ar·dente /n(y)o͞oˈā ärˈdänt/ ▸*n. Geology* an incandescent cloud of gas, ash, and lava fragments ejected from a volcano, typically as part of a pyroclastic flow. ▷French, literally 'burning cloud.'

Nu·er /ˈno͞oər/ ▸*n.* (*pl.* same or **Nu·ers**) **1** a member of an African people of southeastern Sudan and Ethiopia, traditionally rearers of cattle. **2** the Nilotic language of this people.

▸*adj.* of or relating to this people or their language. ▷the name in Dinka.

Nue·vo La·re·do /ˈnwāvō ləˈrādō/ a commercial city in eastern Mexico, in Tamaulipas state, across the Rio Grande from Laredo in Texas; pop. 218,000.

Nue·vo Le·ón /ˌnwāvō lāˈōn; lēˈōn/ a state in northeastern Mexico, on the border with the U.S.; capital, Monterrey.

nue·vo sol /ˌnwāvō ˈsōl/ ▸*n.* another term for SOL[3]. ▷Spanish, 'new sol.'

nuff /nəf/ (also **'nuff**) ▸*adj., pron.,* & *adv.* nonstandard spelling of ENOUGH, representing informal speech: *The pen is mightier than the sword. Nuff said.* ■ [as *adj.*] *black English* much: *nuff respect goes out to Galliano.*

Nuf·field /ˈnəfˌēld/, William Richard Morris, 1st Viscount (1877–1963), British automobile manufacturer and philanthropist who opened the first Morris automobile factory in Oxford in 1912.

nu·gac·i·ty /n(y)o͞oˈgasitē/ ▸*n.* (*pl.* **-ties**) *rare* triviality; frivolity. ■ a trivial or frivolous thing or idea. ▷late 16th cent.: from late Latin *nugacitas*, from Latin *nugax, nugac-* 'trifling, frivolous.'

nu·ga·to·ry /ˈn(y)o͞ogəˌtôrē/ ▸*adj.* of no value or importance: *a nugatory and pointless observation.* ■ useless; futile: *the teacher shortages will render nugatory the hopes of implementing the new curriculum.* ▷early 17th cent.: from Latin *nugatorius*, from *nugari* 'to trifle,' from *nugae* 'jests.'

nug·get /ˈnəgət/ ▸*n.* a small lump of gold or other precious metal found ready-formed in the earth. ■ a small chunk or lump of another substance: *tiny nuggets of chicken and shrimp.* ■ a valuable idea or fact: *nuggets of information.* ▷mid 19th cent.: apparently from dialect *nug* 'lump,' of unknown origin. —**nug·get·y** *adj.*

nui·sance /ˈn(y)o͞osəns/ ▸*n.* a person, thing, or circumstance causing inconvenience or annoyance: *an unreasonable landlord could become a nuisance | I hope you're not going to make a nuisance of yourself.* ■ (also **private nuisance**) *Law* an unlawful interference with the use and enjoyment of a person's land. ■ *Law* see PUBLIC NUISANCE. ▷late Middle English (in the sense 'injury, hurt'): from Old French, 'hurt,' from the verb *nuire*, from Latin *nocere* 'to harm.'

nui·sance val·ue ▸*n.* the significance of a person or thing arising from their capacity to cause inconvenience or annoyance.

nuit blanche /ˌnwē ˈblänsʜ/ ▸*n.* (*pl.* **nuits blanches** *pronunc.* same) a sleepless night. ▷French, literally 'white night.'

Nu·jol /ˈn(y)o͞oˌjôl; -ˌjäl/ ▸*n. trademark* a paraffin oil used as an emulsifying agent in pharmacy and for making mulls in infrared spectroscopy. ▷early 20th cent.: perhaps from *New J(ersey)*, site of the original manufacturing company, + Latin *oleum* 'oil.'

nuke /n(y)o͞ok/ *informal* ▸*n.* a nuclear weapon. ■ a nuclear power station. ■ a nuclear-powered vessel.

▸*v.* [*trans.*] attack or destroy with nuclear weapons. ■ destroy; get rid of: *I fertilized the lawn and nuked the weeds.* ■ cook or heat up (food) in a microwave oven: *I nuked a quick burger.* ▷1950s: abbreviation of NUCLEAR.

Nu·ku·'a·lo·fa /ˌno͞okəo͞oˈlôfə/ the capital of Tonga, situated on the island of Tongatapu; pop. 30,000.

…o legal or binding … *a new interim govern-* … **2** having or associat… *…hematics* (of a set or ma… …or only zeros as elements. …alities; having no positive … *…is curiously null life.* … ■ a dummy letter in a cipher. …ition of no signal. ■ a direction in …magnetic radiation is detected or …

… *…ronics* combine (a signal) with another … create a null; cancel out. ▷late Middle …rom French *nul, nulle*, from Latin *nullus* …rom *ne* 'not' + *ullus* 'any.'

… /ˈnələ/ ▸*n. Indian* a dry riverbed or ravine. …e 18th cent.: from Hindi *nālā*.

…**l char·ac·ter** ▸*n. Computing* a character denoting …nothing, usually represented by a binary zero.

null hy·poth·e·sis ▸*n.* (in a statistical test) the hypothesis that there is no significant difference between specified populations, any observed difference being due to sampling or experimental error.

nul·li·fid·i·an /ˌnələˈfidēən/ *rare* ▸*n.* a person having no faith or religious belief.
▸*adj.* having no faith or religious belief. ▷mid 16th cent.: from medieval Latin *nullifidius* (from *nullus* 'no, none' + *fides* 'faith') + -AN.

nul·li·fy /ˈnələˌfī/ ▸*v.* (**-fies, -fied**) [*trans.*] make legally null and void; invalidate: *judges were unwilling to nullify government decisions.* See note at VOID. ■ make of no use or value; cancel out: *insulin can block the release of the hormone and thereby nullify the effects of training.* —**nul·li·fi·ca·tion** /ˌnələfəˈkāshən/ *n.* —**nul·li·fi·er** *n.*

nul·lip·a·ra /ˌnəˈlipərə/ ▸*n.* (*pl.* **-rae** /-ˌrē/) *Medicine & Zoology* a woman or female animal that has never given birth. Compare with PRIMIPARA. ▷late 19th cent.: modern Latin, from Latin *nullus* 'none' + *-para* (feminine of *-parus*), from *parere* 'bear children.' —**nul·lip·a·rous** /-ˈlip(ə)rəs/ *adj.*

nul·li·ty /ˈnəlitē/ ▸*n.* (*pl.* **-ties**) **1** *Law* an act or thing that is legally void. ■ the state of being legally void; invalidity, esp. of a marriage. **2** a thing of no importance or worth. ■ nothingness. ▷mid 16th cent.: from French *nullité*, from medieval Latin *nullitas*, from Latin *nullus* 'none.'

null link ▸*n. Computing* a reference incorporated into the last item in a list to indicate that there are no further items in the list.

Num. ▸*abbr. Bible* Numbers.

Nu·ma Pom·pil·i·us /ˈn(y)o͞omə pämˈpilēəs/ the legendary second king of Rome, successor to Romulus, revered by the ancient Romans as the founder of nearly all their religious institutions.

numb /nəm/ ▸*adj.* deprived of the power of sensation: *my feet were numb with cold* | *figurative the tragic events left us shocked and numb.*
▸*v.* [*trans.*] deprive of feeling or responsiveness: *the cold had numbed her senses.* ■ cause (a sensation) to be felt less intensely; deaden: *vodka might numb the pain in my hand.* ▷late Middle English *nome(n)*, past participle of obsolete *nim* 'take.' —**numb·ly** *adv.* —**numb·ness** *n.*

num·bat /ˈnəmˌbat/ ▸*n.* a small termite-eating Australian marsupial with a black and white striped back and a bushy tail. • *Myrmecobius fasciatus*, family Myrmecobiidae. ▷early 20th cent.: from Nyungar.

num·ber /ˈnəmbər/ ▸*n.* **1** an arithmetical value, expressed by a word, symbol, or figure, representing a particular quantity and used in counting and making calculations and for showing order in a series or for identification: *she dialed the number carefully* | *an even number.* ■ (**numbers**) *dated* arithmetic: *the boy was adept at numbers.* **2** a quantity or amount: *the company is seeking to increase the number of women on its staff* | *the exhibition attracted vast numbers of visitors.* ■ (**a number of**) several: *we have discussed the matter on a number of occasions.* ■ a group or company of people: *there were some distinguished names **among our number**.* ■ (**numbers**) a large quantity or amount, often in contrast to a smaller one; numerical preponderance: *the **weight of numbers** turned the battle against them.* **3** a single issue of a magazine: *the October number of "Travel."* ■ a song, dance, piece of music, etc., esp. one of several in a performance: *they go from one melodious number to another.* ■ [usu. with *adj.*] *informal* a thing, typically an item of clothing, of a particular type, regarded with approval or admiration: *Yvonne was wearing a little black number.* **4** *Grammar* a distinction of word form denoting reference to one person or thing or to more than one. See also SINGULAR (sense 2), PLURAL, COUNT NOUN, and MASS NOUN. ■ a particular form so classified.
▸*v.* [*trans.*] **1** amount to (a specified figure or quantity); comprise: *the demonstrators numbered more than 5,000.* ■ include or classify as a member of a group: *the orchestra **numbers** Brahms **among** its past conductors.* **2** (often **be numbered**) mark with a number or assign a number to, typically to indicate position in a series: *each document was numbered consecutively.* ■ count: *strategies like ours can be numbered on the fingers of one hand.* ■ assess or estimate the size or quantity of (something) to be a specified figure: *he **numbers** the fleet **at** a thousand.* ▷Middle English: from Old French *nombre* (noun), *nombrer* (verb), from Latin *numerus.*
▸*PHRASES* □ **any number of** any particular whole quantity of: *the game can involve any number of players.* ■ a large and unlimited quantity or amount of: *the results can be read any number of ways.* □ **by numbers** following simple instructions identified by numbers or as if identified: *painting by numbers.* □ **by the numbers** following standard operating procedure. ■ all together with a shouted-out count. □ **someone's/something's days are numbered** someone or something will not survive or remain in a position of power or advantage for much longer: *my days as director were numbered.* □ **do a number on** *informal* treat someone badly, typically by deceiving, humiliating, or criticizing them in a calculated and thorough way. □ **have someone's number** *informal* understand a person's real motives or character and thereby gain some advantage. □ **have someone's number on it** *informal* (of a bomb, bullet, or other missile) destined to find a specified person as its target. □ **someone's number is up** *informal* the time has come when someone is doomed to die or suffer some other disaster or setback. [with reference to a lottery number or a number by which one may be identified.] □ **without number** too many to count: *they forgot the message times without number.*

USAGE The construction **the number of** + plural noun is used with a singular verb (as in ***the number of people** affected **remains** small*). Thus it is the noun **number** rather than the noun **people** that is taken to agree with the verb (and is therefore functioning as the **head noun**). By contrast, the apparently similar construction **a number of** + plural noun is used with a plural verb (as in ***a number of people remain** to be contacted*). In this case, it is the noun **people** that acts as the head noun and with which the verb agrees. In the latter case, **a number of** works as if it were a single word, such as **some** or **several**.
See also **usage** at COLLECTIVE NOUN and LOT.

num·ber crunch·er (also **num·ber-crunch·er**) ▸*n. informal* **1** a computer or software capable of performing rapid calculations with large amounts of data. **2** *often derogatory* a statistician, accountant, or other person whose job involves dealing with large amounts of numerical data. —**num·ber crunch·ing** *n.*

num·bered ac·count ▸*n.* a bank account, esp. in a Swiss bank, identified only by a number and not bearing the owner's name.

num·ber·less /ˈnəmbərləs/ ▸*adj.* too many to be counted; innumerable.

num·ber line ▸*n. Mathematics* a line on which numbers are marked at intervals, used to illustrate simple numerical operations.

num·ber one *informal* ▸*n.* **1** oneself: *you must look after number one.* **2** a person or thing that is the best or the most important in an activity or area: *businesses that were number one in their markets.* ■ a best-selling record or book: *an album featuring seventeen top movie themes and six number ones.* **3** used euphemistically to refer to urine, esp. in reference to children. **4** a lieutenant junior grade in the navy or the coast guard. **5** (or **number two, etc.**) the shortest (or next shortest, etc.) men's haircut produced with electric hair clippers.
▸*adj.* most important or prevalent: *a number-one priority.* ■ best selling: *a number-one album.*

num·ber op·er·a ▸*n.* an opera in which arias and other sections are clearly separable.

num·ber plate ▸*n.* British term for LICENSE PLATE.

Num·bers /ˈnəmbərz/ the fourth book of the Bible, relating the experiences of the Israelites in the wilderness after Moses led them out of Egypt. ▷named in English from the book's accounts of a census; the title in Hebrew means 'in the wilderness.'

num·bers game ▸*n. often derogatory* the use or manipulation of statistics or figures, esp. in support of an argument: *legislators were today playing the numbers game as the vote drew closer.* ■ (also **the numbers** or **numbers racket**) an illegal lottery based on the occurrence of unpredictable numbers in the results of races, etc.

num·ber the·o·ry ▸*n.* the branch of mathematics that deals with the properties and relationships of numbers, esp. the positive integers.

num·ber two ▸*n. informal* **1** a second in command: *my conscientious number two in the task force.* ■ a person or thing ranked second in ability or size in an activity or area: *copycat strategy is a common resort of number two in a market.* **2** used euphemistically to refer to feces, esp. in reference to children.

numb·fish /ˈnəmˌfish/ ▸*n.* (*pl.* same or **-fishes**) an electric ray, esp. a heavy-bodied Australian ray that lies partly buried on sand flats and estuaries and can give a severe electric shock. • Family Torpedinidae: many species, in particular *Hypnos monopterygium.*

num·bles /ˈnəmbəlz/ ▸*plural n. Brit., archaic* the entrails of an animal, esp. a deer, used for food. ▷Middle English (denoting the back and loins of a deer): from Old French, from Latin *lumbulus*, diminutive of *lumbus* 'loin.' Compare with UMBLES.

numb·skull /ˈnəmˌskəl/ (also **num·skull**) ▸*n. informal* a stupid or foolish person.

num·dah /ˈnəmdə/ ▸*n.* (in the Indian subcontinent and the Middle East) an embroidered rug or carpet made of felt or coarse woolen cloth. ■ cloth of this type. ▷from Urdu *namdā*, from Persian *namad* 'carpet.'

nu·men /ˈn(y)o͞omən/ ▸*n.* (*pl.* **-mi·na** /-mənə/) the spirit or divine power presiding over a thing or place. ▷early 17th cent.: from Latin.

nu·mer·a·ble /ˈn(y)o͞om(ə)rəbəl/ ▸*adj.* able to be counted. ▷mid 16th cent.: from Latin *numerabilis*, from *numerare* 'to number.'

nu·mer·a·cy /ˈn(y)o͞om(ə)rəsē/ ▸*n.* the ability to understand and work with numbers.

nu·me·raire /ˈn(y)o͞oməˌrer; ˌn(y)o͞oməˈre(ə)r/ ▸*n. Economics* an item or commodity acting as a measure of value or as a standard for currency exchange. ▷1960s: from French *numéraire*, from late Latin *numerarius*, from Latin *numerus* 'a number.'

nu·mer·al /ˈn(y)o͞om(ə)rəl/ ▸*n.* a figure, symbol, or group of these denoting a number. ■ a word expressing a number.
▸*adj.* of or denoting a number. ▷late Middle English (as an adjective): from late Latin *numeralis*, adjective from Latin *numerus* 'a number' (see NUMBER).

nu·mer·ate /ˈn(y)o͞om(ə)rət/ ▸*adj.* having a good basic knowledge of arithmetic; able to understand and work with numbers. ▷1950s: from Latin *numerus* 'a number,' on the pattern of *literate*.

nu·mer·a·tion /ˌn(y)o͞oməˈrāshən/ ▸*n.* the action or process of calculating or assigning a number to something. ■ a method or process of numbering, counting, or computing. ▷late Middle English: from Latin *numeratio(n-)* 'payment' (in late Latin 'numbering'), from the verb *numerare* 'to number.'

nu·mer·a·tor /ˈn(y)o͞oməˌrātər/ ▸*n.* the number above the line in a common fraction showing how many of the parts indicated by the denominator are taken, for example, 2 in 2/3.

nu·mer·i·cal /n(y)o͞oˈmerikəl/ ▸*adj.* of, relating to, or expressed as a number or numbers: *the lists are in numerical order.* ▷early 17th cent.: from medieval Latin *numericus* (from Latin *numerus* 'a number') + -AL. —**nu·mer·i·cal·ly** *adv.*

nu·mer·i·cal a·nal·y·sis ▸*n.* the branch of mathematics that deals with the development and use of numerical methods for solving problems.

nu·mer·i·cal con·trol ▸*n. Engineering* computer control of machine tools, where operations are directed by numerical data.

nu·mer·ol·o·gy /ˌn(y)o͞oməˈräləjē/ ▸*n.* the branch of knowledge that deals with the occult significance of numbers. ▷early 20th cent.: from Latin *numerus* 'a number' + -LOGY. —**nu·mer·o·log·i·cal** /-rəˈläjikəl/ *adj.* —**nu·mer·ol·o·gist** /-jist/ *n.*

nu·me·ro u·no /ˈn(y)o͞oməˌrō ˈo͞onō/ ▸*n.* (*pl.* **u·nos**) *informal* the best or most important person or thing. ▷Italian, literally 'number one.'

nu·mer·ous /ˈn(y)o͞om(ə)rəs/ ▸*adj.* great in number; many: *he has attended numerous meetings and social events.* ■ consisting of many members: *the orchestra and chorus were numerous.* ▷late Middle English: from Latin *numerosus*, from *numerus* 'a number.' —**nu·mer·ous·ly** *adv.* —**nu·mer·ous·ness** *n.*

nu·me·rus clau·sus /ˈnyo͞omərəs ˈklousəs/ ▸*n.* a fixed

maximum number of entrants admissible to an academic institution. ▷Latin, literally 'closed number.'

Nu·mid·i·a /n(y)o͞o'midēə/ an ancient kingdom, later a Roman province, which was located in North Africa, north of the Sahara, corresponding roughly to present-day Algeria. **—Nu·mid·i·an** *adj.* & *n.*

nu·mi·na /'n(y)o͞omənə/ ▸ plural form of **NUMEN**.

nu·mi·nous /'n(y)o͞omənəs/ ▸*adj.* having a strong religious or spiritual quality; indicating or suggesting the presence of a divinity: *the strange, numinous beauty of this ancient landmark.* ▷mid 17th cent.: from Latin *numen, numin-* 'divine power' + **-OUS**.

numis. ▸*abbr.* numismatic; numismatics.

nu·mis·mat·ic /ˌn(y)o͞oməz'matik; -məs-/ ▸*adj.* of, relating to, or consisting of coins, paper currency, and medals. ▷late 18th cent.: from French *numismatique*, via Latin from Greek *nomisma, nomismat-* 'current coin,' from *nomizein* 'use currently.' **—nu·mis·mat·i·cal·ly** /-ik(ə)lē/ *adv.*

nu·mis·mat·ics /ˌn(y)o͞oməz'matiks; -məs-/ ▸*plural n.* [usu. treated as *sing.*] the study or collection of coins, paper currency, and medals. **—nu·mis·ma·tist** /n(y)o͞o'mizmətist; -'mis-/ *n.*

num·mu·lar /'nəmyələr/ ▸*adj.* resembling a coin or coins. ▷mid 18th cent.: from Latin *nummulus* (diminutive of *nummus* 'coin') + **-AR**[1].

num·mu·lite /'nəmyəˌlīt/ ▸*n. Paleontology* the flat disk-shaped calcareous shell of a foraminifer, found commonly as a fossil up to 8 cm across in marine Tertiary deposits. • Family Nummulitidae, order Foraminiferida: several genera, including *Nummulites*. ▷early 19th cent.: from Latin *nummulus* (diminutive of *nummus* 'coin') + **-ITE**[1].

num·my /'nəmē/ ▸*adj. informal* (of food) delicious. ▷early 20th cent.: variant of **YUMMY**.

num·nah /'nəmnə/ ▸*n. chiefly Brit.* a pad, typically made of sheepskin or foam, that is placed under a saddle. ▷mid 19th cent.: from Urdu *namdā*.

nump·ty /'nəm(p)tē/ ▸*n.* (*pl.* **-ties**) *Brit. informal* **1** nu **2** a stupid or ineffectual person. ▷1990s: from obsolete *numps*, 'a stupid person,' of unknown origin.

num·skull ▸*n.* variant spelling of **NUMBSKULL**.

nun /nən/ ▸*n.* a member of a religious community of women, esp. a cloistered one, living under vows of poverty, chastity, and obedience. ■ any of a number of birds whose plumage resembles a nun's habit, esp. an Asian mannikin. ■ a pigeon of a breed with a crest on its neck. ▷Old English *nonne*, from ecclesiastical Latin *nonna*, feminine of *nonnus* 'monk,' reinforced by Old French *nonne*. **—nun·like** /-ˌlīk/ *adj.* **—nun·nish** *adj.*

nun·a·tak /'nənəˌtak/ ▸*n.* an isolated peak of rock projecting above a surface of inland ice or snow. ▷late 19th cent.: from Eskimo *nunataq*.

Nu·na·vut /no͞o'näˌvo͞ot; 'no͞onə-; ˌvo͞ot/ a territory in northern Canada that includes the eastern part of the original Northwest Territories and most of the islands of the Arctic Archipelago; capital Iqaluit. It is the homeland of the Inuit people.

nun bu·oy ▸*n.* a buoy that is circular in the middle and tapering to each end. ▷early 18th cent.: from obsolete *nun* 'child's top' and **BUOY**.

Nunc Di·mit·tis /'nəngk də'mitis; 'no͝ongk/ ▸*n.* the Song of Simeon (Luke 2:29–32) used as a canticle in Christian liturgy, esp. at compline and evensong. ▷Latin, the opening words of the canticle, '(Lord), now let (your servant) depart.'

nun·cha·ku /ˌnən'chäko͞o/ (also **nun·chuk** /'nənˌchək/) ▸*n.* (*pl.* same or **-kus**) a Japanese martial arts weapon consisting of two hardwood sticks joined together by a chain, rope, or thong. ▷Japanese, from Okinawa dialect.

nun·ci·a·ture /'nənsēəˌchər; 'no͝on-; -ˌcho͝or/ ▸*n.* the office or tenure of a nuncio in the Roman Catholic Church. ▷early 17th cent.: from Italian *nunziatura*, from *nunzio* 'message-bearer' (see **NUNCIO**).

nun·ci·o /'nənsēˌō; 'no͝on-/ ▸*n.* (*pl.* **-os**) (in the Roman Catholic Church) a papal ambassador to a foreign court or government. ▷early 16th cent.: from Italian, from Latin *nuntius* 'messenger.'

nun·cle /'nəngkəl/ ▸*n. archaic* or *dialect* a person's uncle. ▷late 16th cent.: by misdivision of *mine uncle*.

nun·cu·pa·tive /'nəngkyəˌpātiv/ ▸*adj. Law* (of a will or testament) declared orally as opposed to in writing, esp. by a mortally wounded soldier or sailor. ▷mid 16th cent.: from late Latin *nuncupativus*, from Latin *nuncupat-* 'named, declared,' from the verb *nuncupare*.

nun·ner·y /'nən(ə)rē/ ▸*n.* (*pl.* **-ner·ies**) a building or group of buildings in which nuns live as a religious community; a convent.

nu·oc cham /nə'wäk 'chäm/ ▸*n.* a dipping sauce made from nuoc mam, chilies, garlic, sugar, lime juice, and rice vinegar. ▷Vietnamese.

nuoc mam /nə'wäk 'mäm/ ▸*n.* a spicy Vietnamese fish sauce. ▷Vietnamese.

nup·tial /'nəpshəl; -chəl/ ▸*adj.* of or relating to marriage or weddings: *moments of nuptial bliss.* ■ *Zoology* denoting the characteristic breeding behavior, coloration, or structures of some animals: *nuptial plumage.*

▸*n.* (usu. **nuptials**) a wedding: *the forthcoming nuptials between Richard and Jocelyn.* ▷late 15th cent.: from Old French, or from Latin *nuptialis*, from *nuptiae* 'wedding,' from *nubere* 'to wed'; related to **NUBILE**.

nup·tial mass ▸*n.* (in the Roman Catholic Church) a mass celebrated as part of a wedding ceremony.

nup·tial pad ▸*n. Zoology* a pigmented swelling on the inner side of the hand in some male frogs and toads, assisting grip during copulation.

Nu·rem·berg /'n(y)o͝orəmˌbərg/ a city in southern Germany, in Bavaria; pop. 497,000. During the 1930s, Nazi Party congresses and annual rallies were held here, and in 1945–46 it was the site of the Nuremberg war trials, in which Nazi war criminals were tried by an international military tribunal. German name **NÜRNBERG**.

Nu·re·yev /'no͝orəˌyef; -ˌyev; no͞o'räəf/, Rudolf (1939–93), Austrian ballet dancer and choreographer, born in Russia. He defected to the West in 1961 and joined the Royal Ballet in London, where he began his noted partnership with Margot Fonteyn.

Nürn·berg /'no͝ornˌberk; 'nyrn-/ German name for **NUREMBERG**.

nurse /nərs/ ▸*n.* a person trained to care for the sick or infirm, esp. in a hospital. ■ *dated* a person employed or trained to take charge of young children: *her mother's old nurse.* ■ *archaic* a wet nurse. ■ [often as *adj.*] *Forestry* a tree or crop planted as a shelter to others. ■ *Entomology* a worker bee, ant, or other social insect, caring for a young brood.

▸*v.* [*trans.*] **1** give medical and other attention to (a sick person): *she nursed the girl through a dangerous illness.* ■ [*intrans.*] care for the sick and infirm, esp. as a profession: *she nursed at the hospital for thirty years.* ■ try to cure or alleviate (an injury, injured part, or illness) by treating it carefully and protectively: *he has been nursing a cold* | *figurative he nursed his hurt pride.* ■ hold closely and carefully or caressingly: *he nursed his small case on his lap.* ■ hold (a cup or glass) in one's hands, drinking from it occasionally: *I nursed a double brandy.* ■ harbor (a belief or feeling), esp. for a long time: *I still nurse anger and resentment.* ■ take special care of, esp. to promote development or well-being: *our political unity needs to be protected and nursed.* ■ *Billiards* try to play strokes that keep (the balls) close together. **2** feed (a baby) at the breast: *lionesses who were nursing their own cubs* | [as *adj.*] (**nursing**) *nursing mothers.* ■ [*intrans.*] be fed at the breast: *the baby snuffled as he nursed.* ■ (**be nursed in**) *dated* be brought up in (a specified condition): *he was nursed in the lap of plenty.* ▷late Middle English: contraction of earlier *nourice*, from Old French, from late Latin *nutricia*, feminine of Latin *nutricius* '(person) that nourishes,' from *nutrix, nutric-* 'nurse,' from *nutrire* 'nourish.' The verb was originally a contraction of **NOURISH**, altered under the influence of the noun.

nurse·ling ▸*n.* archaic spelling of **NURSLING**.

nurse·maid /'nərsˌmād/ ▸*n.* a woman or girl employed to look after a young child or children.

▸*v.* [*trans.*] look after or be overprotective toward: *I haven't got time to nursemaid you through these blips.*

nurse prac·ti·tion·er (also **nurse-prac·ti·tion·er**) ▸*n.* a registered nurse who has been specially trained to treat routine or minor ailments, and to perform many tasks ordinarily performed by a doctor.

nurs·er·y /'nərs(ə)rē/ ▸*n.* (*pl.* **-er·ies**) a room in a house for the special use of young children. ■ a place where young children are cared for during the working day; a nursery school. ■ a place where young plants and trees are grown for sale or for planting elsewhere. ■ a place or natural habitat that breeds or supports animals: *this estuary provides a vast nursery for fish.* ■ an institution or environment in which certain types of people or qualities are fostered or bred: *that nursery of traitors.* ▷late Middle English: from Old French *nourice* 'nurse' (see **NURSE**) + **-ERY**.

nurs·er·y·man /'nərs(ə)rēmən/ ▸*n.* (*pl.* **-men**) a worker in or owner of a plant or tree nursery.

nurs·er·y rhyme ▸*n.* a simple traditional song or poem for children.

nurs·er·y school ▸*n.* a school for young children, mainly between the ages of three and five.

nurse's aide ▸*n.* (pl. **nurses' aides**) a person who assists professional nurses in a hospital or other medical facility by performing routine tasks, such a making beds and serving meals, that require little or no formal training.

nurse shark ▸*n.* a shark with barbels on the snout. • Three species in the family Orectolobidae (or Ginglymostomatidae), in particular *Ginglymostoma cirratum*, a slow-swimming brownish shark of warm Atlantic waters. ▷mid 19th cent.: *nurse* 'dogfish shark,' alteration of Middle English *nusse*, perhaps derived (by wrong division) from *an huss* (see **Huss**).

nurs·ing /'nərsiNG/ ▸*n.* the profession or practice of providing care for the sick and infirm.

nurs·ing home ▸*n.* a private institution providing residential accommodations with health care, esp. for the elderly.

nurs·ling /'nərsliNG/ ▸*n.* a baby that is being breast-fed. ■ any young animal or plant that is carefully tended or nurtured.

nur·tur·ance /'nərchərəns/ ▸*n.* emotional and physical nourishment and care given to someone. ■ the ability to provide such care. **—nur·tur·ant** /-rənt/ *adj.*

nur·ture /'nərchər/ ▸*v.* [*trans.*] care for and encourage the growth or development of: *figurative my father nurtured my love of art.* ■ cherish (a hope, belief, or ambition): *for a long time she had nurtured the dream of buying a shop.*

▸*n.* the process of caring for and encouraging the growth or development of someone or something: *the nurture of ethics and integrity.* ■ upbringing, education, and environment, contrasted with inborn characteristics as an influence on or determinant of personality. Often contrasted with **NATURE**. ▷Middle English: from Old French *noureture* 'nourishment,' based on Latin *nutrire* 'feed, cherish.' **—nur·tur·er** *n.*

Nus·selt num·ber /'no͞osəlt/ ▸*n. Physics* a dimensionless parameter used in calculations of heat transfer between a moving fluid and a solid body. • It is equal to hD/k, where h is the rate of heat loss per unit area per degree difference in temperature between the body and its surroundings, D is a characteristic length of the body, and k is the thermal conductivity of the fluid. ▷mid 20th cent.: named after Ernst K. W. *Nusselt* (1882–1957), German engineer.

Nut /no͞ot/ *Egyptian Mythology* the sky goddess, thought to swallow the sun at night and give birth to it in the morning.

nut /nət/ ▸*n.* **1** a fruit consisting of a hard or tough shell around an edible kernel. ■ the hard kernel of such a fruit. ■ *informal* a person's head. ■ (usu. **nuts**) *vulgar slang* testicles. **2** a small flat piece of metal or other material, typically square or hexagonal, with a threaded hole through it for screwing onto a bolt as a fastener. ■ *Music* the part at the lower end of the bow of a violin or similar instrument, with a screw for adjusting the tension of the hair. **3** *informal* a crazy or eccentric person. ■ [with *adj.*] a person who is excessively interested in or enthusiastic about a specified thing: *a football nut.* **4** the fixed ridge on the neck of a stringed instrument over which the strings pass.

▸*v.* (**nut·ted, nut·ting**) **1** [*intrans.*] [usu. as *n.*] (**nutting**) *archaic* gather nuts. **2** [*trans.*] *Brit., informal* butt (someone) with one's head. ▷Old English *hnutu*, of

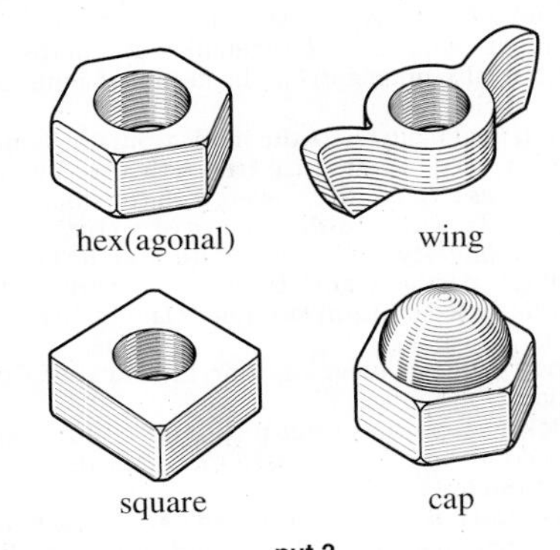

nut 2

Pronunciation Key ə *ago*; ər *over*; 'ə or ˌə *up*; 'ər or ˌər *fur*; a *hat*; ā *rate*; ä *car*; CH *chew*; e *let*; ē *see*; e(ə)r *air*; i *fit*; ī *by*; i(ə)r *ear*; NG *sing*; ō *go*; ô *for*; oi *boy*; o͝o *good*; o͞o *goo*; ou *out*; SH *she*; TH *thin*; TH *then*; (h)w *why*; ZH *vision*

Germanic origin; related to Dutch *noot* and German *Nuss*. —**nut·like** /-ˌlīk/ *adj.*

▸*PHRASES* □ **do one's nut** *Brit., informal* be extremely angry or agitated. □ **nuts and bolts** *informal* the basic practical details: *the nuts and bolts of public policy.* □ **off one's nut** *informal* out of one's mind; crazy. □ **a tough** (or **hard**) **nut** *informal* someone who is difficult to deal with; a formidable person. □ **a tough** (or **hard**) **nut to crack** *informal* a difficult problem or an opponent hard to beat.

nu·ta·tion /n(y)o͞oˈtāsʜən/ ▸*n.* a periodic variation in the inclination of the axis of a rotating object. ■ *Astronomy* a periodic oscillation of the earth's axis that causes the precession of the poles to follow a wavy rather than a circular path. ■ *Botany* the circular swaying movement of the tip of a growing shoot. ▷early 17th cent. (denoting nodding of the head): from Latin *nutatio(n-)*, from *nutare* 'to nod.'

nut-brown ▸*adj.* of a rich dark brown color: *a nut-brown face.*

nut case (also **nut·case**) ▸*n. informal* a crazy or foolish person.

nut·crack·er /ˈnətˌkrakər/ ▸*n.* **1** a device for cracking nuts. **2** a crow that feeds on the seeds of conifers, found widely in Eurasia and in western North America. • Genus *Nucifraga*, family Corvidae: the Eurasian **spotted nutcracker** (*N. caryocatactes*), with white-spotted brown plumage, and the North American **Clark's nutcracker** (*N. columbiana*), with pale gray and black plumage.

Nut·crack·er Man /ˈnətˌkrakər/ ▸*n.* the nickname of a fossil hominid with massive jaws and molar teeth, esp. the original specimen found near Olduvai Gorge in 1959. • *Australopithecus* (or **Zinjanthropus**) *boisei*, family Hominidae. See **AUSTRALOPITHECUS**, **PARANTHROPUS**.

nut·gall /ˈnətˌgôl/ ▸*n.* **1** another term for **ALEPPO GALL**. **2** a gall that forms in response to the presence of mites, esp. one that forms inside the buds of hazel bushes, causing the buds to enlarge greatly. • The mite is *Phytoptus avellanae*, family Eriophyidae.

nut·grass /ˈnətˌgras/ ▸*n.* another term for **NUTSEDGE**.

nut·hatch /ˈnətˌhacʜ/ ▸*n.* a small songbird with a long strong bill, a stiffened square-cut tail, and the habit of climbing down tree trunks head first. • Family Sittidae and genus *Sitta*: numerous species, including the North American **white-breasted nuthatch** (*S. carolinensis*), with a gray back, black cap (male), black eyes, and white face and underparts. ▷Middle English: from **NUT** + obsolete *hatch* (related to **HACK**[1]), from the bird's habit of hacking with the beak at nuts wedged in a crevice.

white-breasted nuthatch

nuth·in /ˈnəᴛʜin/ (also **nuth·in'**) ▸*pron., adj., & adv. informal* nonstandard spelling of **NOTHING**, used to represent informal speech.

nut·house /ˈnətˌhous/ ▸*n. informal, offensive* a home or hospital for people with mental illnesses.

nut·let /ˈnətlət/ ▸*n. Botany* a small nut, esp. an achene.

nut loaf ▸*n.* a baked vegetarian dish made from ground or chopped nuts, vegetables, and herbs.

nut meat (also **nut·meat**) ▸*n.* the kernel of a nut, typically edible.

nut·meg /ˈnətˌmeg/ ▸*n.* **1** the hard, aromatic, almost spherical seed of a tropical tree. ■ this seed grated and used as a spice. **2** the evergreen tree that bears these seeds, native to the Moluccas. • *Myristica fragrans*, family Myristicaceae. ▷late Middle English *notemuge*, partial translation of Old French *nois muguede*, based on Latin *nux* 'nut' + late Latin *muscus* 'musk.'

Nut·meg State a nickname for the state of **CONNECTICUT**.

nut·pick /ˈnətˌpik/ (also **nut pick**) ▸*n.* a thin, sharp-pointed table implement used to dig out the edible meat from nuts.

nu·tra·ceu·ti·cal /ˌn(y)o͞otrəˈso͞otikəl/ ▸*n.* a food containing health-giving additives and having medicinal benefit. ▷1990s: from Latin *nutrire* 'nourish' + **PHARMACEUTICAL**.

nu·tri·a /ˈn(y)o͞otrēə/ ▸*n.* a large semiaquatic beaver-like rodent, native to South America. It is kept in captivity for its fur and has become naturalized in many other areas. • *Myocastor coypus*, the only member of the family Myocastoridae. ■ the pelt of this animal. ▷early 19th cent.: from Spanish, literally 'otter.'

nu·tri·ent /ˈn(y)o͞otrēənt/ ▸*n.* a substance that provides nourishment essential for growth and the maintenance of life: *fish is a source of many important nutrients, including protein, vitamins, and minerals.* ▷mid 17th cent.: from Latin *nutrient-* 'nourishing,' from the verb *nutrire*.

nu·tri·ge·no·mics /ˌn(y)o͞otrijēˈnōmiks; -ˈnäm-/ ▸*plural n.* [treated as *singular*] the scientific study of the interaction of nutrition and genes, especially the role of diet in causing disease: *nutrigenomics holds great promise in fighting obesity and cancer.* ▷blend of *nutrition* and *genomics* 'analysis of an organism's complete set of genes.'

nu·tri·ment /ˈn(y)o͞otrəmənt/ ▸*n. rare* nourishment; sustenance. ▷late Middle English: from Latin *nutrimentum*, from *nutrire* 'feed, nourish.' —**nu·tri·men·tal** /ˌn(y)o͞otrəˈmentl/ *adj.*

nu·tri·tion /n(y)o͞oˈtrisʜən/ ▸*n.* the process of providing or obtaining the food necessary for health and growth: *a guide to good nutrition.* ■ food; nourishment: *a feeding tube gives her nutrition and water.* ■ the branch of science that deals with nutrients and nutrition, particularly in humans: *she took a short course in nutrition* | [as *adj.*] *nutrition experts.* ▷late Middle English: from late Latin *nutritio(n-)*, from *nutrire* 'feed, nourish.' —**nu·tri·tion·al** /-sʜənl/ *adj.* —**nu·tri·tion·al·ly** /-sʜənl-ē/ *adv.*

nu·tri·tion·ist /n(y)o͞oˈtrisʜ(ə)nist/ ▸*n.* a person who studies or is an expert in nutrition.

nu·tri·tious /n(y)o͞oˈtrisʜəs/ ▸*adj.* nourishing; efficient as food: *like all spinach, it is very nutritious and best when young.* ▷mid 17th cent.: from Latin *nutritius* 'that nourishes' (from *nutrex* 'a nurse') + **-OUS**. —**nu·tri·tious·ly** *adv.* —**nu·tri·tious·ness** *n.*

nu·tri·tive /ˈn(y)o͞otrətiv/ ▸*adj.* of or relating to nutrition: *the food was low in nutritive value.* ■ providing nourishment; nutritious: *nutritive food.* ▷late Middle English: from medieval Latin *nutritivus*, from *nutrire* 'feed, nourish.'

nuts /nəts/ ▸*adj.* [*predic.*] *informal* insane: *the way he turns on the television as soon as he walks in drives me nuts.* ▸*exclam. informal* an expression of contempt or derision: *keep up the good work, and* **nuts to** *everyone who doesn't like it.*

▸*PHRASE* □ **be nuts about** (or *Brit.* **on**) *informal* like very much: *I was nuts about him.*

nut·sedge /ˈnətˌsej/ ▸*n.* an invasive sedge with small edible nutlike tubers. Also called **NUTGRASS**. • Genus *Cyperus*, family Cyperaceae: two species, **purple nutsedge** (*C. rotundus*) and **yellow nutsedge** (*C. esculentus*). See also **CHUFA**.

nut·shell /ˈnətˌsʜel/ ▸*n.* the hard woody covering around the kernel of a nut.

▸*PHRASE* □ **in a nutshell** in the fewest possible words: *she put the matter in a nutshell.*

nut·so /ˈnətsō/ *informal* ▸*adj.* insane: *his nutso neighbors.* ▸*n.* (*pl.* **-sos**) an insane or eccentric person.

nut·sy /ˈnətsē/ ▸*adj.* (**-si·er**, **-si·est**) *informal* insane.

nut·ter /ˈnətər/ ▸*n. Brit., informal* a crazy or eccentric person.

nut tree ▸*n.* a tree that bears nuts, esp. the hazel.

nut·ty /ˈnətē/ ▸*adj.* (**nut·ti·er**, **nut·ti·est**) **1** tasting like nuts: *wild rice has a very nutty flavor.* ■ containing a lot of nuts: *a nutty vegetable bake.* **2** *informal* peculiar; insane: *he came up with a few nutty proposals.* —**nut·ti·ness** *n.*

▸*PHRASES* □ **be nutty about** *informal* like very much: *he is nutty about boats.* □ (**as**) **nutty as a fruitcake** *informal* completely insane.

Nuuk /no͝ok/ the capital of Greenland, a port on the Davis Strait; pop. 12,000. It was known by the Danish name Godthåb until 1979.

nux vom·i·ca /ˈnəks ˈvämikə/ ▸*n.* a spiny southern Asian tree with berrylike fruit and toxic seeds that are a commercial source of strychnine. • *Strychnos nux-vomica*, family Loganiaceae. ■ a homeopathic preparation of this plant used esp. for the treatment of symptoms of overeating and overdrinking. ▷late Middle English: from medieval Latin, from Latin *nux* 'nut' + *vomica* 'causing vomiting' (from *vomere* 'to vomit').

nuz·zle /ˈnəzəl/ ▸*v.* [*trans.*] rub or push against gently with the nose and mouth: *he nuzzled her hair* | [*intrans.*] *the foal nuzzled at its mother.* ■ [*intrans.*] (**nuzzle up to/against**) lean or snuggle against: *the dog nuzzled up against me.* ▷late Middle English (in the sense 'grovel'): frequentative from **NOSE**, reinforced by Dutch *neuzelen* 'poke with the nose.'

NV ▸*abbr.* Nevada (in official postal use).

nvCJD ▸*abbr.* see **vCJD**.

NVI ▸*abbr.* no value indicated, a postage stamp that does not bear a monetary value on it but instead shows which postal service it is valid for.

NW ▸*abbr.* ■ northwest. ■ northwestern.

NWbN ▸*abbr.* northwest by north.

NWbW ▸*abbr.* northwest by west.

N-word ▸*n. informal* used instead of or in reference to the word "nigger" because of its taboo nature *I can't believe he used the N-word in front of her.*

NWT ▸*abbr.* Northwest Territories.

n.wt. ▸*abbr.* net weight.

NY ▸*abbr.* New York (in official postal use).

nyah /nyä/ ▸*exclam.* used to express the speaker's feeling of superiority or contempt for another: *I won the gold and she didn't. Nyah, nyah, nyah.* ▷early 20th cent.: imitative of a child's reduplicated phrase used in taunting.

nya·la /ˈnyälə/ ▸*n.* (*pl.* same) a southern African antelope, with a conspicuous crest on the neck and back and lyre-shaped horns. • *Tragelaphus angasi*, family Bovidae. ▷late 19th cent.: from Zulu.

Nyan·ja /ˈnyänjə; ˈnyan-/ ▸*n.* (*pl.* same or **-jas**) **1** a member of a people of Malawi and eastern and central Zambia. **2** the Bantu language of this people. ▸*adj.* of or relating to this people or their language. ▷a local name, literally 'lake.'

Ny·as·a, Lake /ˈnyäsə; ˈnyasə/ a lake in east central Africa, Africa's third largest. About 350 miles (580 km) long, it forms most of the eastern border of Malawi with Mozambique and Tanzania. Also called **MALAWI, LAKE**. ▷*Nyasa*, literally 'lake.'

Ny·as·a·land /nīˈasəˌland; nē-/ former name (until 1966) for **MALAWI**.

NYC ▸*abbr.* New York City.

nyc·ta·lo·pi·a /ˌniktəˈlōpēə/ ▸*n. Medicine* the inability to see in dim light or at night. Also called **NIGHT BLINDNESS**. ▷late 17th cent.: via late Latin from Greek *nuktalōps*, from *nux*, *nukt-* 'night' + *alaos* 'blind' + *ōps* 'eye.'

nyc·ti·nas·tic /ˌniktəˈnastik/ ▸*adj. Botany* (of the periodic movement of flowers or leaves) caused by nightly changes in light intensity or temperature. ▷early 20th cent.: from Greek *nux*, *nukt-* 'night' + *nastos* 'pressed' + **-IC**. —**nyc·ti·nas·ty** /ˈniktəˌnastē/ *n.*

nyc·to·pho·bi·a /ˌniktəˈfōbēə/ ▸*n.* extreme or irrational fear of the night or of darkness. ▷early 20th cent.: from Greek *nux*, *nukt-* 'night' + **PHOBIA**.

Nye·re·re /nyəˈrerē; -ˈrerā/, Julius Kambarage (1922–99), Tanzanian statesman; president of Tanganyika 1962–64 and of Tanzania 1964–85.

ny·lon /ˈnīˌlän/ ▸*n.* a tough, lightweight, elastic synthetic polymer with a proteinlike chemical structure, able to be produced as filaments, sheets, or molded objects. ■ fabric or yarn made from nylon fibers. ■ (**nylons**) stockings or hose made of nylon. ▷1930s: an invented word, on the pattern of *cotton* and *rayon*.

nymph /nimf/ ▸*n.* **1** a mythological spirit of nature imagined as a beautiful maiden inhabiting rivers, woods, or other locations. ■ *chiefly poetic/literary* a beautiful young woman. **2** an immature form of an insect that does not change greatly as it grows, e.g., a dragonfly, mayfly, or locust. Compare with **LARVA**. ■ an artificial fly made to resemble the aquatic nymph of an insect, used in fishing. **3** a mainly brown butterfly that frequents woods and forest glades. • Several genera in the subfamily Satyrinae, family Nymphalidae. See also **WOOD NYMPH**. ▷late Middle English: from Old French *nimphe*, from Latin *nympha*, from Greek *numphē* 'nymph, bride'; related to Latin *nubere* 'be the wife of.' —**nymph·al** /ˈnimfəl/ *adj.* —**nym·phe·an** /ˈnimfēən/ *adj.* —**nymph·like** /-ˌlīk/ *adj.*

nym·phae·um /nimˈfēəm/ ▸*n.* (*pl.* **-phae·a** /-ˈfēə/) a grotto or shrine dedicated to a nymph or nymphs. ▷via Latin from Greek.

nym·pha·lid /nimˈfaləd; ˈnimfəlid/ ▸*n. Entomology* an insect of a large family of strikingly marked butterflies that have small forelegs not used for walking, including many familiar butterflies of temperate regions, such as the monarch and viceroy. • Family Nymphalidae (sometimes restricted to those that are now usually placed in the subfamily Nymphalinae). ▷late 19th cent.: from modern Latin *Nymphalidae*, from Latin *nympha* 'nymph.'

nymph·et /nimˈfet; ˈnimfit/ ▸*n.* an attractive and sexually mature young girl. ▷1950s: from **NYMPH** + **-ET**[1].

nym·pho /ˈnimˈfō/ ▸*n. informal* a nymphomaniac.

nym·pho·lep·sy /ˈnimfəˌlepsē/ ▸*n. poetic/literary* passion aroused in men by beautiful young girls. ■ wild frenzy caused by desire for an unattainable ideal. ▷late 18th cent.: from NYMPHOLEPT, on the pattern of *epilepsy.*

nym·pho·lept /ˈnimfəˌlept/ ▸*n.* a person affected by nympholepsy. ▷early 19th cent.: from Greek *numpholēptos* 'caught by nymphs,' from *numphē* 'nymph' + *lambanein* 'take.' **—nym·pho·lep·tic** /ˌnimfəˈleptik/ *adj.*

nym·pho·ma·ni·a /ˌnimfəˈmānēə/ ▸*n.* uncontrollable or excessive sexual desire in a woman. Compare with SATYRIASIS. ▷late 18th cent.: modern Latin, from Latin *nympha* (see NYMPH) + -MANIA. **—nym·pho·ma·ni·ac** /-ˈmānēˌak/ *n. & adj.* **—nym·pho·ma·ni·a·cal** /-məˈnīəkəl/ *adj.*

Ny·norsk /ˈnoo͞ˌnôrsk; ˌnoo͞ˈnôrsk/ ▸*n.* a literary form of Norwegian, based on country dialects and constructed in the 19th century to serve as a national language more clearly distinct from Danish than Bokmål. See NORWEGIAN (sense 2). ▷Norwegian, from *ny* 'new' + *Norsk* 'Norwegian.'

Nyo·man /ˈnyōˌmän/ ▸ Belorussian name for NEMAN.

NYP ▸*abbr.* not yet published.

Ny·quist cri·te·ri·on /ˈnīkwist/ ▸*n. Electronics* a criterion for determining the stability or instability of a feedback system. ▷1930s: named after Harry *Nyquist* (1889–1976), Swedish-born American engineer.

Ny·quist di·a·gram (also **Nyquist plot**) ▸*n. Electronics* a representation of the vector response of a feedback system (esp. an amplifier) as a complex graphical plot showing the relationship between feedback and gain. ▷1930s: see NYQUIST CRITERION.

Ny·quist fre·quen·cy (also **Nyquist rate**) ▸*n. Electronics* the minimum rate at which a signal can be sampled without introducing errors, which is twice the highest frequency present in the signal. ▷1930s: see NYQUIST CRITERION.

Ny·sa /ˈnisə/ Polish name for NEISSE.

NYSE ▸*abbr.* New York Stock Exchange.

nys·tag·mus /nəˈstagməs/ ▸*n.* rapid involuntary movements of the eyes. ▷early 19th cent.: from Greek *nustagmos* 'nodding, drowsiness,' from *nustazein* 'nod, be sleepy.' **—nys·tag·mic** /-mik/ *adj.*

nys·ta·tin /ˈnistətin; ˈnī-/ ▸*n.* an antibiotic used chiefly to treat fungal infections. • This antibiotic is obtained from the bacterium *Streptomyces noursei.* ▷1950s: from *N(ew) Y(ork) Stat(e)* (where it was developed) + -IN[1].

Nyx /niks/ *Greek Mythology* the female personification of the night, daughter of Chaos.

NZ ▸*abbr.* New Zealand.

O o

O1 /ō/ (also **o**) ▶*n.* (*pl.* **Os** or **O's** /ōz/) **1** the fifteenth letter of the alphabet. ■ denoting the next after N in a set of items, categories, etc. ■ a human blood type (in the ABO system) lacking both the A and B antigens. In blood transfusion, a person with blood of this group is a potential universal donor. **2** (also **oh**) zero (in a sequence of numerals, esp. when spoken). **3** a shape like that of a capital O; a circle.

O2 ▶*abbr.* ■ Ocean. ■ (in prescriptions) a pint. [from Latin *octarius*.] ■ octavo. ■ October. ■ Ohio. ■ old. ■ Ontario. ■ Oregon.
▶*symbol* the chemical element oxygen.

O3 ▶*exclam.* **1** archaic spelling of OH1. **2** *archaic* used before a name in direct address, as in prayers and poetry: *give peace in our time, O Lord.* ▷natural exclamation: first recorded in Middle English.

O' ▶*prefix* in Irish patronymic names such as *O'Neill.* ▷mid 18th cent.: from Irish *ó, ua* 'descendant.'

o ▶*abbr.* ■ pint. [from Latin *octarius*.] ■ octavo. ■ off. ■ old. ■ only. ■ order. ■ *Baseball* out; outs.

o' /ə; ō/ ▶*prep.* short for OF, used to represent an informal pronunciation: *a cup o' coffee.*

o- ▶*abbr.* [used in *combination*] *Chemistry* ortho-: *o-xylene.*

-o ▶*suffix* forming chiefly informal or slang variants or derivatives such as *righto, wino.* ▷perhaps from OH1, reinforced by abbreviated forms such as *hippo, photo.*

-o- ▶*suffix* used as the terminal vowel of combining forms: *chemico-* | *Gallo-.* ▷from Greek.

USAGE The combining-form suffix **-o-** is often elided (that is, omitted) before a vowel, as in *neuralgia* (formed from *neuro-* + *-algia*).

o/a ▶*abbr.* on or about.

oaf /ōf/ ▶*n.* a stupid, uncultured, or clumsy person. ▷early 17th cent.: variant of obsolete *auf,* from Old Norse *álfr* 'elf.' The original meaning was 'elf's child, changeling,' later 'idiot child' and 'halfwit,' generalized in the current sense. **—oaf·ish** *adj.* **—oaf·ish·ly** *adv.* **—oaf·ish·ness** *n.*

Oahe, Lake /ō'ähē/ a reservoir northwest of Pierre in South Dakota, in the Missouri River, created since 1963 by the huge Oahe Dam.

O·a·hu /ō'wähōō/ the third largest of the Hawaiian islands; pop. 838,500. Its principal town, Honolulu, is the capital of Hawaii. It is the site of Pearl Harbor, a U.S. naval base.

oak /ōk/ ▶*n.* (also **oak tree**) a tree that bears acorns as fruit, and typically has lobed deciduous leaves. Oaks are common in many north temperate forests and are an important source of hard and durable wood used chiefly in construction, furniture, and (formerly) shipbuilding. • Genus *Quercus,* family Fagaceae: many species, including the deciduous **Eastern white oak** (*Q. alba*) and **Eastern black oak** (*Q. velutina*) and the evergreen **live oak** (*Q. virginiana*). ■ a smoky flavor or aroma characteristic of wine aged in barrels made from this wood. ▷Old English *āc,* of Germanic origin; related to Dutch *eik* and German *Eiche.* **—oak·en** /'ōkən/ *adj.* **—oak·y** *adj.*
▶*PHRASE* □ **mighty** (or **great**) **oaks from little acorns grow** *proverb* something of small or modest dimensions may grow into something very large or impressive.

oak ap·ple ▶*n.* a spongy spherical gall that forms on oak trees in response to the developing larvae of a gall wasp. • The wasp is *Biorhiza pallida* (in Europe) or *Amphibolips confluenta* (in America), family Cynipidae.

oak fern ▶*n.* a delicate fern of woods and damp places in the uplands of northern Eurasia and North America. • Genus *Gymnocarpium* (formerly *Thelypteris*), family Woodsiaceae: two species, in particular *G. dryopteris.*

oak ker·mes ▶*n.* see KERMES (sense 2).

Oak·land /'ōklənd/ an industrial port in California, on the eastern side of San Francisco Bay; pop. 399,484.

oak leaf clus·ter ▶*n.* an attachment to a military decoration depicting a twig with oak leaves and acorns, indicating distinguished action or a subsequent award of the same decoration.

oak·leaf let·tuce /'ōk,lēf/ (also **oak leaf let·tuce**) ▶*n.* a red or green variety of lettuce that has leaves with serrated edges and a slightly bitter taste.

Oak·ley /'ōklē/, Annie (1860–1926), U.S. markswoman; full name *Phoebe Anne Oakley Mozee.* In 1885, she joined Buffalo Bill's Wild West Show and was the star attraction for the next seventeen years.

Annie Oakley

Oak Park a village in northeastern Illinois, west of Chicago; pop. 53,648.

Oak Ridge a city in eastern Tennessee, on the Clinch River, established in 1942 as part of U.S. nuclear development; pop. 27,310.

oak·tag /'ōk,tag/ (also **oak tag**) ▶*n.* another term for TAGBOARD.

oa·kum /'ōkəm/ ▶*n. chiefly historical* loose fiber obtained by untwisting old rope, used esp. in caulking wooden ships. ▷Old English *ācumbe,* literally 'off-combings.' The current sense dates from Middle English.

oak wilt ▶*n.* a fungal disease of oaks and other trees that makes the foliage wilt and eventually kills the tree. • The fungus is *Ceratocystis fagacearum,* subdivision Ascomycotina.

O. & M. ▶*abbr.* ■ operations and maintenance. ■ organization and methods.

OAPEC /ō,pek/ ▶*abbr.* Organization of Arab Petroleum Exporting Countries.

oar /ôr/ ▶*n.* a pole with a flat blade, pivoting in an oar lock, used to row or steer a boat through the water. ■ a rower.
▶*v.* [*trans.*] row; propel with or as with oars: *oaring the sea like madmen* | [*intrans.*] *oaring through the weeds.* ■ move (something, esp. the hands) like oars: *her slender arms oaring the air.* ▷Old English *ār,* of Germanic origin; related to Danish and Norwegian *åre.* **—oar·less** *adj.*
▶*PHRASES* □ **put in one's oar** *informal* give an opinion without being asked. □ **rest on one's oars** relax one's efforts.

oar·fish /'ôr,fisн/ ▶*n.* (*pl.* same or **-fish·es**) a very long, narrow, silvery marine fish of deep water, with a deep red dorsal fin running the length of the body. Also called RIBBONFISH. • *Regalecus glesne,* family Regalecidae.

oar·lock /'ôr,läk/ ▶*n.* a fitting on the gunwale of a boat that serves as a fulcrum for an oar and keeps it in place.

oarlock

oars·man /'ôrzmən/ ▶*n.* (*pl.* **-men**) a rower, esp. as a member of a racing team. **—oars·man·ship** /'ôrzmən,sнip/ *n.*

oars·wom·an /'ôrz,wŏŏmən/ ▶*n.* (*pl.* **-wom·en**) a female rower, esp. as a member of a racing team.

oar·weed /'ôr,wēd/ ▶*n.* a large brown kelp with a long hard stalk and a large oar-shaped frond divided into ribbonlike strips, growing on rocky shores. Also called TANGLE2. • Genus *Laminaria,* class Phaeophyceae, in particular *L. digitata.*

OAS ▶*abbr.* ORGANIZATION OF AMERICAN STATES.

o·a·sis /ō'āsis/ ▶*n.* (*pl.* **-ses** /ō'āsēz/) **1** a fertile spot in a desert where water is found. ■ *figurative* a pleasant or peaceful area or period in the midst of a difficult, troubled, or hectic place or situation: *an oasis of calm in the center of the city.* **2** (**Oasis**) *trademark* a type of rigid foam into which the stems of flowers can be secured in flower arranging. ▷early 17th cent.: via late Latin from Greek, apparently of Egyptian origin.

oast /ōst/ ▶*n.* a kiln used for drying hops. ▷Old English *āst* (originally denoting any kiln), of Germanic origin; related to Dutch *eest,* from an Indo-European root meaning 'burn.'

oat /ōt/ ▶*n.* a cereal plant cultivated chiefly in cool climates and widely used for animal feed as well as human consumption. • *Avena sativa,* family Gramineae. ■ (**oats**) the grain yielded by this, used as food. ■ used in names of wild grasses related to the cultivated oat, e.g., **wild oat.** ▷Old English *āte,* plural *ātan,* of unknown origin. Unlike other names of cereals (such as *wheat, barley,* etc.), *oat* is not a mass noun and may originally have denoted the individual grain, which may imply that oats were eaten in grains and not as meal. **—oat·en** /'ōtn/ *adj.* (*archaic*). **—oat·y** *adj.*
▶*PHRASES* □ **feel one's oats** *informal* feel lively and energetic. □ **sow one's wild oats** go through a period of wild or promiscuous behavior while young.

oat·cake /'ōt,kāk/ ▶*n.* a thin, unleavened cake made of oatmeal.

oat·er /'ōtər/ ▶*n. informal* a western movie or television show. ▷1950s: derivative of OAT, with allusion to horse feed; compare with the synonym HORSE OPERA.

Oates1 /ōts/, Joyce Carol (1938–) U.S. writer. Her works include *Bellefleur* (1980), *You Must Remember This* (1988), *Zombie* (1995), *Man Crazy* (1997), *Blonde* (2000), and *The Best American Essays of the Century* (2000).

Oates2, Titus (1649–1705), English clergyman and conspirator. He is known as the fabricator of the Popish Plot in 1678.

oat grass ▶*n.* a wild grass that resembles the oat. • *Avenula* and other genera, family Gramineae.

oath /ōтн/ ▶*n.* (*pl.* **oaths** /ōтнs; ōтнz/) **1** a solemn promise, often invoking a divine witness, regarding one's future action or behavior: *they took an oath of allegiance to the king.* ■ a sworn declaration that one will tell the truth, esp. in a court of law. **2** a profane or offensive expression used to express anger or

other strong emotions. ▷Old English *āth*, of Germanic origin; related to Dutch *eed* and German *Eid*.
▶*PHRASE* □ **under oath** having sworn to tell the truth, esp. in a court of law.

oat·meal /ˈōtˌmēl/ ▶*n.* **1** meal made from ground oats, used in breakfast cereals or other food. **2** a grayish-beige color flecked with brown: [as *adj.*] *an oatmeal jacket.*

OAU ▶*abbr.* Organization of African Unity.

Oa·xa·ca /wäˈhäkə; -ˈkhäkä/ a state in southern Mexico. ■ its capital city; pop. 213,000. Full name **OAXACA DE JUÁREZ** .

Ob /äb; ôb/ the principal river of the western Siberian lowlands and one of the largest rivers in Russia. Rising in the Altai Mountains, it flows north and west for 3,481 miles (5,410 km) before entering the Gulf of Ob (or Ob Bay), an inlet of the Kara Sea, a part of the Arctic Ocean.

ob. ▶*abbr.* he or she died: *ob. 1867.* ▷from Latin *obiit.*

ob- ▶*prefix* **1** denoting exposure or openness: *obverse.* ■ expressing meeting or facing: *observe.* **2** denoting opposition, hostility, or resistance: *obstacle.* ■ denoting hindrance, blocking, or concealment: *obliterate* | *obviate.* **3** denoting extensiveness, finality, or completeness: *obdurate* | *obsolete.* **4** (in modern technical words) inversely; in a direction or manner contrary to the usual: *obconical.* ▷from Latin *ob* 'toward, against, in the way of.'

USAGE **Ob-** occurs mainly in words of Latin origin. It is also found assimilated in the following forms: **oc-** before *c*; **of-** before *f*; **op-** before *p*.

Obad. ▶*abbr. Bible* Obadiah.

O·ba·di·ah /ˌōbəˈdīə/ (in the Bible) a Hebrew minor prophet. ■ the shortest book of the Bible, bearing his name.

ob·bli·ga·to /ˌäbləˈgätō/ (also **ob·li·ga·to**) ▶*n.* (*pl.* **-ga·tos** or **-ga·ti** /-ˈgätē/) [usu. with or as *adj.*] an instrumental part, typically distinctive in effect, that is integral to a piece of music and should not be omitted in performance. ▷Italian, literally 'obligatory,' from Latin *obligatus*, past participle of *obligare* (see **OBLIGE**).

ob·con·i·cal /äbˈkänikəl/ (also **ob·con·ic** /-ˈkänik/) ▶*adj. Botany* in the form of an inverted cone.

ob·cor·date /äbˈkôrˌdāt/ ▶*adj. Botany* (of a leaf) in the shape of a heart with the pointed end at the base.

ob·du·rate /ˈäbd(y)ərit/ ▶*adj.* stubbornly refusing to change one's opinion or course of action. See note at **STUBBORN**. ▷late Middle English (originally in the sense 'hardened in sin, impenitent'): from Latin *obduratus*, past participle of *obdurare*, from *ob-* 'in opposition' + *durare* 'harden' (from *durus* 'hard'). **—ob·du·ra·cy** /-rəsē/ *n.* **—ob·du·rate·ly** *adv.* **—ob·du·rate·ness** *n.*

o·be·ah /ˈōbēə/ (also **o·bi** /ˈōbē/) ▶*n.* a kind of sorcery practiced esp. in the Caribbean. ▷Twi, from *bayi* 'sorcery.'

o·be·che /ōˈbēchē/ ▶*n.* a tropical tree native to West and central Africa, grown for its pale timber that is used for plywood and veneers. • *Triplochiton scleroxylon*, family Sterculiaceae. ▷early 20th cent.: a term used in Nigeria.

o·be·di·ence /ōˈbēdēəns/ ▶*n.* compliance with someone's wishes or orders or acknowledgment of their authority: *unquestioning obedience to the commander in chief.* ■ submission to a law or rule: *obedience to moral standards.* ■ observance of a monastic rule: *vows of poverty, chastity, and obedience.* ▷Middle English: via Old French from Latin *oboedientia*, from the verb *oboedire* (see **OBEY**).
▶*PHRASE* □ **in obedience to** in accordance with: *the Communist Party supported sanctions, in obedience to Soviet policy.*

o·be·di·ent /ōˈbēdēənt/ ▶*adj.* complying or willing to comply with orders or requests; submissive to another's will: *she was totally obedient to him.* ▷Middle English: via Old French from Latin *oboedient-* 'obeying,' from the verb *oboedire* (see **OBEY**). **—o·be·di·ent·ly** *adv.*
▶*PHRASE* □ **your obedient servant** *dated* a formula used to end a letter.

THE RIGHT WORD **biddable, compliant, docile, dutiful, obedient**

Children and animals may be expected to obey, but nowadays **obedient** is seldom used to describe adult human beings without a suggestion that they are allowing someone else to assume too great a degree of authority (*are we to believe that Cinderella became the prince's demure, obedient wife?*).

The critical note is stronger in **biddable**. A *biddable* person is excessively meek and ready to obey any instruction, without questioning either its wisdom or the authority of the person giving it (*he could barely think for himself, having been so biddable to his domineering parents*).

Docile (from Latin *docilis* 'teachable') has similar implications, but in addition to unquestioning obedience it suggests a general reluctance to complain or rebel, even where such behavior would be justified (*employers depended on the regime for a cheap and docile workforce*).

Dutiful may evoke a sneer, suggesting the virtuous, yet dull (*his dutiful niece spent most of her life caring for him*), or the perfunctory fulfillment of an obligation (*a dutiful postcard to his mother*).

One of the oldest (and still living) meanings of **compliant** is 'reshaping under pressure' (*conversion of the gel to a much less compliant glass*). This helps to explain the principal modern sense of the adjective, '(excessively) disposed to agree with others or obey rules' (*compliant legislators loyally followed party policy*). In the computer age a further sense, 'technically compatible,' has developed (*the system is Windows compliant*).

o·bei·sance /ōˈbāsəns; ōˈbē-/ ▶*n.* deferential respect: *they* ***paid obeisance to*** *the prince.* See note at **HONOR**. ■ a gesture expressing deferential respect, such as a bow or curtsy: *she made a deep obeisance.* ▷late Middle English (in the sense 'obedience'): from Old French *obeissance*, from *obeissant* 'obeying,' present participle of *obeir.* **—o·bei·sant** /ōˈbāsənt/ *adj.*

ob·e·li /ˈäbəˌlī/ ▶ plural form of **OBELUS**.

o·be·lia /ōˈbēlyə; -ˈbēlēə/ ▶*n. Zoology* a genus of marine animals that bear polyps and produce medusae, and that form colonies that attach to rocks or the ocean bottom. • Genus *Obelia*, class Hydrozoa. ▷modern Latin, from Greek *obelos* 'tapering column.'

ob·e·lisk /ˈäbəˌlisk/ ▶*n.* **1** a stone pillar, typically having a square or rectangular cross section and a pyramidal top, set up as a monument or landmark. ■ a mountain, tree, or other natural object of similar shape. **2** another term for **OBELUS**. ▷mid 16th cent.: via Latin from Greek *obeliskos*, diminutive of *obelos* 'pointed pillar.'

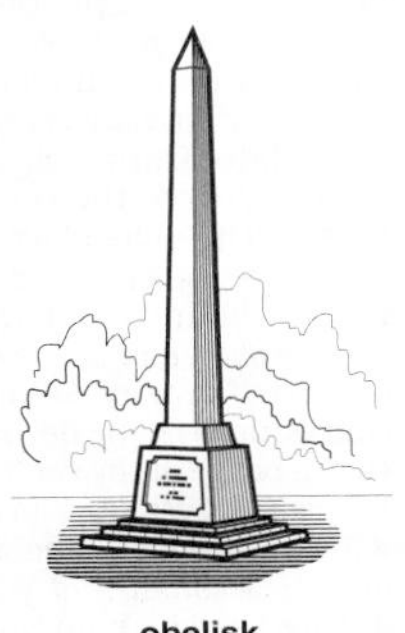

obelisk

ob·e·lize /ˈäbəˌlīz/ ▶*v.* [*trans.*] mark (a word or passage) with an obelus to show that it is spurious, corrupt, or doubtful. ▷mid 17th cent.: from Greek *obelizein*, in the same sense.

ob·e·lus /ˈäbələs/ ▶*n.* (*pl.* **-li** /-ˌlī/) **1** a symbol (†) used as a reference mark in printed matter, or to indicate that a person is deceased. Also called **DAGGER**. **2** a mark (– or ÷) used in ancient texts to mark a word or passage as spurious, corrupt, or doubtful. ▷late Middle English: via Latin from Greek *obelos* 'pointed pillar,' also 'critical mark.'

O·ber·am·mer·gau /ˌōbərˈämərgou/ a village in the Bavarian Alps of southwestern Germany; pop. 5,000. It is the site of one of the few surviving passion plays, which has been performed by the villagers every tenth year (with few exceptions) from 1634 as a result of a vow made during an epidemic of plague.

O·ber·hau·sen /ˈōbərˌhouzən/ an industrial city in western Germany, in the Ruhr valley of North Rhine-Westphalia; pop. 225,000.

O·ber·on /ˈōbəˌrän/ *Astronomy* a satellite of Uranus, the furthest from the planet, discovered by W. Herschel in 1787. It has a heavily cratered surface and a diameter of 963 miles (1,550 km). ▷from the name of the king of the fairies in Shakespeare's *A Midsummer Night's Dream.*

o·bese /ōˈbēs/ ▶*adj.* grossly fat or overweight. ▷mid 17th cent.: from Latin *obesus* 'having eaten until fat,' from *ob-* 'away, completely' + *esus* (past participle of *edere* 'eat'). **—o·be·si·ty** /-sitē/ *n.*

o·bey /ōˈbā/ ▶*v.* [*trans.*] comply with the command, direction, or request of (a person or a law); submit to the authority of: *I always obey my father.* ■ carry out (a command or instruction): *the officer was convicted for refusing to obey orders* | [*intrans.*] *when the order was repeated, he refused to obey.* ■ behave in accordance with (a general principle, natural law, etc.): *the universe was complex but it obeyed certain rules.* ▷Middle English: from Old French *obeir*, from Latin *oboedire*, from *ob-* 'in the direction of' + *audire* 'hear.' **—o·bey·er** *n.*

ob·fus·cate /ˈäbfəˌskāt/ ▶*v.* [*trans.*] render obscure, unclear, or unintelligible: *the spelling changes will deform some familiar words and obfuscate their etymological origins.* ■ bewilder (someone): *it is more likely to obfuscate people than enlighten them.* ▷late Middle English: from late Latin *obfuscat-* 'darkened,' from the verb *obfuscare*, based on Latin *fuscus* 'dark.' **—ob·fus·ca·tion** /ˌäbfəˈskāshən/ *n.* **—ob·fus·ca·to·ry** /äbˈfəskəˌtôrē/ *adj.*

ob-gyn /ˈōˈbē ˈjēˌwīˈen/ ▶*abbr.* obstetrics and gynecology.

o·bi[1] /ˈōbē/ ▶*n.* (*pl.* **o·bis**) a broad sash worn around the waist of a Japanese kimono. ▷Japanese, literally 'belt.'

o·bi[2] ▶*n.* variant form of **OBEAH**.

o·bit /ˈōbit; ōˈbit/ ▶*n. informal* an obituary. ▷late Middle English: now regarded as an abbreviation of **OBITUARY**, but originally also used in the senses 'death' and 'funeral service,' from Latin *obitus* 'going down, death.'

ob·i·ter dic·tum /ˈōbitər ˈdiktəm/ ▶*n.* (*pl.* **dic·ta** /ˈdiktə/) *Law* a judge's incidental expression of opinion, not essential to the decision and not establishing precedent. ■ an incidental remark. ▷Latin *obiter* 'in passing' + *dictum* 'something that is said.'

o·bit·u·ar·y /ōˈbichooˌerē/ ▶*n.* (*pl.* **-ar·ies**) a notice of a death, esp. in a newspaper, typically including a brief biography of the deceased person: *the obituary of a friend* | [as *adj.*] *an obituary notice.* ▷early 18th cent.: from medieval Latin *obituarius*, from Latin *obitus* 'death,' from *obit-* 'perished,' from the verb *obire*. **—o·bit·u·ar·ist** /-ərist/ *n.*

obj. ▶*abbr.* ■ object. ■ objection. ■ objective.

ob·ject ▶*n.* /ˈäbjəkt/ **1** a material thing that can be seen and touched: *he was dragging a large object* | *small objects such as shells.* ■ *Philosophy* a thing external to the thinking mind or subject. **2** a person or thing to which a specified action or feeling is directed: *disease became* ***the object of*** *investigation.* ■ a goal or purpose: *the institute was opened* ***with the object of*** *promoting scientific study.* ■ *Grammar* a noun or noun phrase governed by an active transitive verb or by a preposition. ■ *Computing* a data construct that provides a description of something that may be used by a computer (such as a processor, a peripheral, a document, or a data set) and defines its status, its method of operation, and how it interacts with other objects.
▶*v.* /əbˈjekt/ [*reporting verb*] say something to express one's disapproval of or disagreement with something: [*intrans.*] *residents* ***object to*** *the volume of traffic* | [*with clause*] *the boy's father objected that the police had arrested him unlawfully.* ■ [*trans.*] *archaic* adduce as a reason against something: *Bryant objects this very circumstance to the authenticity of the Iliad.* ▷late Middle English: from medieval Latin *objectum* 'thing presented to the mind,' neuter past participle (used as a noun) of Latin *obicere*, from *ob-* 'in the way of' + *jacere* 'to throw'; the verb may also partly represent the Latin frequentative *objectare*. **—ob·ject·less** /ˈäbjəktləs/ *adj.* **—ob·jec·tor** /əbˈjektər/ *n.*
▶*PHRASE* □ **no object** not influencing or restricting choices or decisions: *a tycoon for whom* ***money is no object.***

ob·ject ball ▶*n. Billiards* any ball other than the cue ball.

ob·ject choice ▶*n. Psychoanalysis* a person or thing external to the ego chosen as a focus of desire or sexual activity.

ob·ject code ▶*n. Computing* code produced by a compiler or assembler.

ob·ject glass (also **ob·ject-glass**) ▶*n.* another term for **OBJECTIVE** (sense 3).

ob·jec·ti·fy /əbˈjektəˌfī/ ▶*v.* (**-fies, -fied**) [*trans.*] express (something abstract) in a concrete form: *good poetry objectifies feeling.* ■ degrade to the status of a mere object: *a deeply sexist attitude that objectifies women.* **—ob·jec·ti·fi·ca·tion** /əbˌjektəfiˈkāshən/ *n.*

ob·jec·tion /əbˈjekshən/ ▶*n.* an expression or feeling of disapproval or opposition; a reason for disagreeing: *they have raised no objections to the latest plans.* ■ the action of challenging or disagreeing with something: *his view is open to objection.* ▷late Middle English: from Old French, or from late Latin *objectio(n-)*, from the verb *obicere* (see **OBJECT**).

Pronunciation Key ə ago; ər over; ˈə or ˌə up; ˈər or ˌər fur; a hat; ā rate; ä car; ch chew; e let; ē see; e(ə)r air; i fit; ī by; i(ə)r ear; ng sing; ō go; ô for; oi boy; o͝o good; o͞o goo; ou out; sh she; th thin; th then; (h)w why; zh vision

ob·jec·tion·a·ble /əbˈjeksHənəbəl/ ▸*adj.* arousing distaste or opposition; unpleasant or offensive: *I find his theory objectionable in its racist undertones.* —**ob·jec·tion·a·ble·ness** *n.* —**ob·jec·tion·a·bly** /-blē/ *adv.*

ob·jec·tive /əbˈjektiv/ ▸*adj.* **1** (of a person or their judgment) not influenced by personal feelings or opinions in considering and representing facts: *historians try to be objective and impartial.* Contrasted with SUBJECTIVE. ■ not dependent on the mind for existence; actual: *a matter of objective fact.* **2** [*attrib.*] *Grammar* of, relating to, or denoting a case of nouns and pronouns used as the object of a transitive verb or a preposition.
▸*n.* **1** a thing aimed at or sought; a goal: *the system has achieved its objective.* **2** (**the objective**) *Grammar* the objective case. **3** (also **objective lens**) the lens in a telescope or microscope nearest to the object observed. ▷early 17th cent.: from medieval Latin *objectivus*, from *objectum* (see OBJECT). —**ob·jec·tive·ly** *adv.* —**ob·jec·tive·ness** *n.* —**ob·jec·tiv·i·ty** /ˌäbjekˈtivitē/ *n.* —**ob·jec·ti·vi·za·tion** /əbˌjektəviˈzāsHən/ *n.* —**ob·jec·tiv·ize** /-ˌvīz/ *v.*

ob·jec·tive cor·rel·a·tive ▸*n.* the artistic and literary technique of representing or evoking a particular emotion by means of symbols that objectify that emotion and are associated with it.

ob·jec·tive func·tion ▸*n.* *Mathematics* (in linear programming) the function that it is desired to maximize or minimize.

ob·jec·tiv·ism /əbˈjektəˌvizəm/ ▸*n.* **1** the tendency to lay stress on what is external to or independent of the mind. **2** *Philosophy* the belief that certain things, esp. moral truths, exist independently of human knowledge or perception of them. —**ob·jec·tiv·ist** *n.* & *adj.* —**ob·jec·ti·vis·tic** /əbˌjektəˈvistik/ *adj.*

ob·ject lan·guage ▸*n.* **1** a language described by means of another language. Compare with META-LANGUAGE, TARGET LANGUAGE. **2** *Computing* a language into which a program is translated by means of a compiler or assembler.

ob·ject les·son ▸*n.* a striking practical example of some principle or ideal: *they responded to emergencies in a way that was an object lesson to us all.*

ob·ject-o·ri·ent·ed ▸*adj.* *Computing* (of a programming language) using a methodology that enables a system to be modeled as a set of objects that can be controlled and manipulated in a modular manner. —**ob·ject o·ri·en·ta·tion** *n.*

ob·ject pro·gram ▸*n.* *Computing* a program into which some other program is translated by an assembler or compiler. —**ob·ject pro·gram·ming** *n.*

ob·ject re·la·tions ▸*n.* *Psychoanalysis* a theory describing the relationship felt or the emotional energy directed by the self or ego toward a chosen object.

ob·ject-world ▸*n.* the world external to the self, apprehended through the objects in it.

ob·jet d'art /ˌôbZHä ˈdär/ ▸*n.* (*pl.* **ob·jets d'art** *pronunc.* same) a small decorative or artistic object, typically when regarded as a collectible item. ▷French, literally 'object of art.'

ob·jet trou·vé /ôb,ZHä trōōˈvā/ ▸*n.* (*pl.* **ob·jets trou·vés** *pronunc.* same) an object found or picked up at random and considered aesthetically pleasing. ▷French, literally 'found object.'

ob·jur·gate /ˈäbjərˌgāt/ ▸*v.* [*trans.*] rebuke severely; scold. ▷early 17th cent.: from Latin *objurgat-* 'chided, rebuked,' from the verb *objurgare*, based on *jurgium* 'strife.' —**ob·jur·ga·tion** /ˌäbjərˈgāsHən/ *n.* —**ob·jur·ga·tor** /-gātər/ *n.* —**ob·jur·ga·to·ry** /əbˈjərgəˌtôrē/ *adj.*

obl. ▸*abbr.* ■ oblique. ■ oblong.

ob·lan·ce·o·late /äbˈlansēəˌlāt/ ▸*adj.* *technical* (esp. of leaves) lanceolate, with the more pointed end at the base.

o·blast /ˈôbləst; ˈäblast/ ▸*n.* an administrative division or region in Russia and the former Soviet Union, and in some constituent republics of the former Soviet Union. ▷Russian.

ob·late[1] /ˈäbˌlāt; ˌōˈblāt/ ▸*adj.* *Geometry* (of a spheroid) flattened at the poles. Often contrasted with PROLATE. ▷early 18th cent.: from modern Latin *oblatus* (from *ob-* 'inversely' + *-latus* 'carried'), on the pattern of Latin *prolatus* 'prolonged.'

ob·late[2] ▸*n.* a person dedicated to a religious life, but typically having not taken full monastic vows. ▷late 17th cent.: from French, from medieval Latin *oblatus*, past participle (used as a noun) of Latin *offerre* 'to offer.'

ob·la·tion /əˈblāsHən/ ▸*n.* a thing presented or offered to God or a god. ■ *Christian Church* the presentation of bread and wine to God in the Eucharist. ▷late Middle English: from Old French, or from late Latin *oblatio(n-)*, from Latin *offerre* 'to offer.' —**ob·la·tion·al** /-sHənl; -sHnəl/ *adj.* —**ob·la·to·ry** /ˈäbləˌtôrē/ *adj.*

ob·li·gate ▸*v.* /ˈäbliˌgāt/ **1** bind or compel (someone), esp. legally or morally: *the medical establishment is obligated to take action in the best interest of the public.* **2** [*trans.*] commit (assets) as security: *the money must be obligated within thirty days.*
▸*adj.* /ˈäbligit/ [*attrib.*] *Biology* restricted to a particular function or mode of life: *an obligate intracellular parasite.* Often contrasted with FACULTATIVE. ▷late Middle English (as an adjective in the sense 'bound by law'): from Latin *obligatus*, past participle of *obligare* (see OBLIGE). The current adjectival use dates from the late 19th cent. —**ob·li·ga·tor** /-ˌgātər/ *n.*

ob·li·ga·tion /ˌäbliˈgāsHən/ ▸*n.* an act or course of action to which a person is morally or legally bound; a duty or commitment: *he has enough cash to meet his present obligations* | [with *infinitive*] *I have an obligation to look after her.* ■ the condition of being morally or legally bound to do something: *they are* ***under no obligation*** *to stick to the scheme.* ■ a debt of gratitude for a service or favor: *she didn't want to be under an obligation to him.* ■ *Law* a binding agreement committing a person to a payment or other action. ■ *Law* a document containing a binding agreement; a written contract or bond. ▷Middle English (in the sense 'formal promise'): via Old French from Latin *obligatio(n-)*, from the verb *obligare* (see OBLIGE). —**ob·li·ga·tion·al** /-sHənl; -sHnəl/ *adj.*

ob·li·ga·to /ˌäbliˈgätō/ ▸*n.* variant spelling of OBBLIGATO.

o·blig·a·to·ry /əˈbligəˌtôrē/ ▸*adj.* required by a legal, moral, or other rule; compulsory: *use of seat belts in cars is now obligatory.* ■ so customary or routine as to be expected of everyone or on every occasion: *after the obligatory preamble on the weather he got down to business.* ■ (of a ruling) having binding force: *a sovereign whose laws are obligatory.* ▷late Middle English: from late Latin *obligatorius*, from Latin *obligat-* 'obliged,' from the verb *obligare* (see OBLIGE). —**ob·lig·a·to·ri·ly** /-ˌtôrəlē/ *adv.*

o·blige /əˈblīj/ ▸*v.* [*trans.*] make (someone) legally or morally bound to an action or course of action: *doctors are obliged by law to keep patients alive while there is a chance of recovery.* See note at COMPEL. ■ [*trans.*] do as (someone) asks or desires in order to help or please them: ***oblige*** *me* ***by*** *not being sorry for yourself* | [*intrans.*] *tell me what you want to know and I'll see if I can oblige.* ■ (**be obliged**) be indebted or grateful: *if you can give me a few minutes of your time I'll be much obliged.* ■ [*trans.*] *archaic* bind (someone) by an oath, promise, or contract. ▷Middle English (in the sense 'bind by oath'): from Old French *obliger*, from Latin *obligare*, from *ob-* 'toward' + *ligare* 'to bind.' —**o·blig·er** *n.*

ob·li·gee /ˌäbliˈjē/ ▸*n.* *Law* a person to whom another is bound by contract or other legal procedure. Compare with OBLIGOR.

o·blig·ing /əˈblījiNG/ ▸*adj.* willing to do a service or kindness; helpful. —**o·blig·ing·ly** *adv.* —**o·blig·ing·ness** *n.*

ob·li·gor /ˌäbliˈgôr/ ▸*n.* *Law* a person who is bound to another by contract or other legal procedure. Compare with OBLIGEE.

o·blique /əˈblēk; ōˈblēk/ ▸*adj.* **1** neither parallel nor at a right angle to a specified or implied line; slanting: *we sat on the settee oblique to the fireplace.* ■ not explicit or direct in addressing a point: *he issued an oblique attack on the president.* ■ *Geometry* (of a line, plane figure, or surface) inclined at other than a right angle. ■ *Geometry* (of an angle) acute or obtuse. ■ *Geometry* (of a cone, cylinder, etc.) with an axis not perpendicular to the plane of its base. ■ *Anatomy* (esp. of a muscle) neither parallel nor perpendicular to the long axis of a body or limb. **2** *Grammar* denoting any case other than the nominative or vocative.
▸*n.* **1** a muscle neither parallel nor perpendicular to the long axis of a body or limb. **2** *Brit.* another term for SLASH[1] (sense 2). ▷late Middle English: from Latin *obliquus*. —**o·blique·ly** *adv.* —**o·blique·ness** *n.* —**o·bliq·ui·ty** /əˈblikwətē/ *n.*

ob·lit·er·ate /əˈblitəˌrāt/ ▸*v.* [*trans.*] destroy utterly; wipe out: *figurative the memory was so painful that he obliterated it from his mind.* ■ cause to become invisible or indistinct; blot out: *clouds were darkening, obliterating the sun.* ▷mid 16th cent.: from Latin *obliterat-* 'struck out, erased,' from the verb *obliterare*, based on *littera* 'letter, something written.' —**ob·lit·er·a·tion** /əˌblitəˈrāsHən/ *n.* —**ob·lit·er·a·tive** /-ˌrātiv/ *adj.* —**o·blit·er·a·tor** /-ˌrātər/ *n.*

ob·liv·i·on /əˈblivēən/ ▸*n.* **1** the state of being unaware or unconscious of what is happening: *they drank themselves into oblivion.* ■ the state of being forgotten, esp. by the public: *his name will fade into oblivion.* ■ *figurative* extinction: *only our armed forces stood between us and oblivion.* **2** *historical Law* amnesty or pardon. ▷late Middle English: via Old French from Latin *oblivio(n-)*, from *oblivisci* 'forget.'

ob·liv·i·ous /əˈblivēəs/ ▸*adj.* not aware of or not concerned about what is happening around one: *she became absorbed,* ***oblivious to*** *the passage of time* | *the women were oblivious of his presence.* ▷late Middle English: from Latin *obliviosus*, from *oblivio(n-)* (see OBLIVION). —**ob·liv·i·ous·ly** *adv.* —**ob·liv·i·ous·ness** *n.*

ob·long /ˈäbˌlôNG; -ˌläNG/ ▸*adj.* having an elongated shape, as a rectangle or an oval.
▸*n.* an object or flat figure in this shape. ▷late Middle English: from Latin *oblongus* 'longish.'

ob·lo·quy /ˈäbləkwē/ ▸*n.* strong public criticism or verbal abuse: *he endured years of contempt and obloquy.* ■ disgrace, esp. that brought about by public abuse: *conduct to which no more obloquy could reasonably attach.* ▷late Middle English: from late Latin *obloquium* 'contradiction,' from Latin *obloqui*, from *ob-* 'against' + *loqui* 'speak.' —**ob·lo·qui·al** /äbˈlōkwēəl/ *adj.* —**ob·lo·qui·ous** /äbˈlōkwēəs/ *adj.*

ob·nox·ious /əbˈnäksHəs/ ▸*adj.* extremely unpleasant. ▷late 16th cent. (in the sense 'vulnerable [to harm]'): from Latin *obnoxiosus*, from *obnoxius* 'exposed to harm,' from *ob-* 'toward' + *noxa* 'harm.' The current sense, influenced by NOXIOUS, dates from the late 17th cent. —**ob·nox·ious·ly** *adv.* —**ob·nox·ious·ness** *n.*

ob·nu·bi·late /äbˈn(y)ōōbəˌlāt/ ▸*v.* [*trans.*] *poetic/literary* darken, dim, or cover with or as if with a cloud; obscure. ▷late 16th cent.: from Latin *obnubilat-* 'covered with clouds or fog,' from the verb *obnubilare*. —**ob·nu·bi·la·tion** /äbˌn(y)ōōbəˈlāsHən/ *n.*

obo (also **o.b.o.**) ▸*abbr.* or best offer (used in advertisements): *$2,700 obo.*

o·boe /ˈōbō/ ▸*n.* a woodwind instrument with a slender, tubular body, played with a double-reed mouthpiece. ■ an organ stop resembling an oboe in tone. ▷early 18th cent.: from Italian, or from French *hautbois*, from *haut* 'high' + *bois* 'wood.' —**o·bo·ist** /-wist/ *n.*

oboe

o·boe d'a·mo·re /ˈōbō däˈmôrā/ ▸*n.* a type of oboe with a bulbous bell, sounding a minor third lower than the ordinary oboe. It has a soft tone and is used in baroque music. ▷late 19th cent.: from Italian, literally 'oboe of love.'

ob·ol /ˈäbəl/ ▸*n.* an ancient Greek coin worth one sixth of a drachma. ▷via Latin from Greek *obolos*, variant of *obelos* (see OBELUS).

O-Bon /ō ˈbôn/ ▸*n.* another name for **BON**.

O·bo·te /ōˈbōtā/, (Apollo) Milton (1924–), Ugandan statesman; prime minister 1962–66; president 1966–71 and 1980–85. Overthrown by Idi Amin in 1971, he was reelected president in 1980 but was removed in a second military coup in 1985.

ob·o·vate /äˈbōˌvāt/ ▸*adj.* *Botany* (of a leaf) ovate with the narrower end at the base.

O'Bri·en[1] /ōˈbrīən/, Edna (1932–), Irish novelist and short-story writer. Her works include the novels *The Country Girls* (1960), *Down by the River* (1997), and *In the Forest* (2002), and the collections *The Love Object and Other Stories* (1968) and *A Fanatic Heart: Selected Stories* (1984).

O'Bri·en[2], Flann (1911–66), Irish novelist and journalist; pseudonym of *Brian O'Nolan*. Writing under the name of Myles na Gopaleen, he contributed a satirical column to the *Irish Times* for nearly twenty years. Notable novels: *At Swim-Two-Birds* (1939); *The Third Policeman* (1967).

O'Bri·en[3], Howard Allen, see **RICE** [1].

O'Bri·en[4], Mary, see **SPRINGFIELD**[2].

obs. (also **Obs.**) ▸*abbr.* ■ observation. ■ observatory. ■ obsolete.

ob·scene /əbˈsēn/ ▸*adj.* (of the portrayal or description of sexual matters) offensive or disgusting by accepted standards of morality and decency: *obscene jokes* | *obscene literature.* ■ offensive to moral principles; repugnant: *using animals' skins for fur coats is obscene.* ▷late 16th cent.: from French *obscène* or Latin *obscaenus* 'ill-omened or abominable.' **—ob·scene·ly** *adv.*

ob·scen·i·ty /əb'senitē/ ▸*n.* (*pl.* **-ties**) the state or quality of being obscene; obscene behavior, language, or images: *the book was banned for obscenity.* ■ an extremely offensive word or expression: *the men scowled and muttered obscenities.* ▷late 16th cent.: from French *obscénité* or Latin *obscaenitas,* from *obscaenus* (see **OBSCENE**).

ob·scu·rant·ism /əb'skyo͝orən,tizəm; äb-; ,äbskyə'ran-/ ▸*n.* the practice of deliberately preventing the facts or full details of something from becoming known. ▷mid 19th cent.: from earlier *obscurant,* denoting a person who obscures something, via German from Latin *obscurant-* 'making dark,' from the verb *obscurare.* **—ob·scu·rant** /'äbskyərənt/ *n.* & *adj.* **—ob·scu·rant·ist** *n.* & *adj.*

ob·scure /əb'skyo͝or/ ▸*adj.* (**-scur·er, -scur·est**) not discovered or known about; uncertain: *his origins and parentage are obscure.* ■ not clearly expressed or easily understood: *obscure references to Proust.* ■ not important or well known: *an obscure religious sect.* ■ hard to make out or define; vague: *figurative I feel an obscure resentment.* ■ (of a color) not sharply defined; dim or dingy.

▸*v.* [*trans.*] keep from being seen; conceal: *gray clouds obscure the sun.* ■ make unclear and difficult to understand: *the debate has become obscured by conflicting ideological perspectives.* ■ overshadow: *none of this should obscure the skill, experience, and perseverance of the workers.* ▷late Middle English: from Old French *obscur,* from Latin *obscurus* 'dark,' from an Indo-European root meaning 'cover.' **—ob·scu·ra·tion** /,äbskyə'rāsʜən/ *n.* **—ob·scure·ly** *adv.*

THE RIGHT WORD **abstruse, obscure, recondite**

Obscure is the general term for something that is unclear or not easy to understand; **abstruse** and **recondite** are more formal terms.

Obscure often expresses dissatisfaction at one's inability to identify something (*the causation of his mental disorder is obscure*), or, more critically, refers to something that's not sufficiently clearly expressed (*the law is too obscure to interpret correctly; we find it difficult to address your obscure complaints*). A reference to, say, "an obscure congressman" is a dismissive comment, suggesting that this is someone not only little known but perhaps deservedly so.

Abstruse is more precise in its meaning—'difficult to understand'—and usually implies that the subject would be puzzling to most anyone (*reading her essays, one wonders if even she can understand her abstruse philosophy*).

Recondite denotes topics that are known and understood by only a few experts: *recondite though their theme may be, they demonstrate that it is not without relevance.* There is often a critical suggestion that difficulty or obscurity has been deliberately sought out or magnified.

ob·scure vow·el ▸*n.* another term for **INDETERMINATE VOWEL.**

ob·scu·ri·ty /əb'skyo͝oritē/ ▸*n.* (*pl.* **-ties**) the state of being unknown, inconspicuous, or unimportant: *he is too good a player to slide into obscurity.* ■ the quality of being difficult to understand: *poems of impenetrable obscurity.* ■ a thing that is unclear or difficult to understand: *the obscurities in his poems and plays.* ▷late Middle English: from Old French *obscurite,* from Latin *obscuritas,* from *obscurus* 'dark.'

obsd. ▸*abbr.* (esp. in medical and scientific abstracts) observed.

ob·se·cra·tion /,äbsə'krāsʜən/ ▸*n. rare* earnest pleading or supplication. ▷late Middle English: from Latin *obsecratio(n-),* from *obsecrare* 'entreat,' based on *sacer, sacr-* 'sacred.'

ob·se·quies /'äbsəkwēz/ ▸*plural n.* funeral rites. ▷late Middle English: plural of obsolete *obsequy,* from Anglo-Norman French *obsequie,* from the medieval Latin plural *obsequiae* (from Latin *exsequiae* 'funeral rites,' influenced by *obsequium* 'dutiful service').

ob·se·qui·ous /əb'sēkwēəs/ ▸*adj.* obedient or attentive to an excessive or servile degree: *they were served by obsequious waiters.* ▷late 15th cent. (not depreciatory in sense in early use): from Latin *obsequiosus,* from *obsequium* 'compliance,' from *obsequi* 'follow, comply with.' **—ob·se·qui·ous·ly** *adv.* **—ob·se·qui·ous·ness** *n.*

THE RIGHT WORD **obsequious, servile, slavish, subservient**

If you want to get ahead with your boss, you might trying being **obsequious**, which suggests an attitude of inferiority that may or may not be genuine, but that is assumed in order to placate a superior in hopes of getting what one wants (*a "goody two shoes" whose obsequious behavior made everyone in the class cringe*).

While **subservient** may connote similar behavior, it is more often applied to those who are genuinely subordinate or dependent and act accordingly (*a timid, subservient child who was terrified of making a mistake*).

Servile is a stronger and more negative term, suggesting a cringing submissiveness (*the dog's servile obedience to her master*).

Slavish, suggesting the status or attitude of a slave, is often used to describe strict adherence to a set of rules or a code of conduct (*a slavish adherence to the rules of etiquette*).

ob·serv·ance /əb'zərvəns/ ▸*n.* **1** the action or practice of fulfilling or respecting the requirements of law, morality, or ritual: *strict* ***observance of*** *the rules | the decline in religious observance.* ■ (usu. **observances**) an act performed for religious or ceremonial reasons: *official anniversary observances.* ■ a rule to be followed by a religious order: *he drew up a body of monastic observances.* ■ *archaic* respect; deference. **2** the action of watching or noticing something: *the baby's motionless observance of me.* ▷Middle English: via Old French from Latin *observantia,* from *observant-* 'watching, paying attention to,' from the verb *observare* (see **OBSERVE**).

ob·serv·ant /əb'zərvənt/ ▸*adj.* **1** quick to notice things: *her observant eye took in every detail.* **2** adhering strictly to the rules of a particular religion, esp. Judaism.

▸*n.* (**Observant**) *historical* a member of a branch of the Franciscan order that followed a strict rule. ▷late Middle English (as a noun): from French, literally 'watching,' present participle of *observer* (see **OBSERVE**).

ob·ser·va·tion /,äbzər'vāsʜən/ ▸*n.* **1** the action or process of observing something or someone carefully or in order to gain information: *she was brought into the hospital for observation | detailed observations were carried out on the students' behavior.* ■ the ability to notice things, esp. significant details: *his powers of observation.* ■ the taking of the altitude of the sun or another celestial body for navigational purposes. **2** a remark, statement, or comment based on something one has seen, heard, or noticed: *he made a telling observation about Hugh.* ▷late Middle English (in the sense 'respectful adherence to the requirements of [rules, a ritual, etc.]'): from Latin *observatio(n-),* from the verb *observare* (see **OBSERVE**). **—ob·ser·va·tion·al** /-sʜənl/ *adj.* **—ob·ser·va·tion·al·ly** /-sʜənl-ē/ *adv.*

▸***PHRASE*** □ **under observation** (esp. of a patient or a suspected criminal) being closely and constantly watched or monitored: *he spent two nights in the hospital under observation.*

ob·ser·va·tion car ▸*n.* a railroad car with large windows designed to provide a good view of passing scenery.

ob·ser·va·tion post ▸*n. Military* a post for watching the movement of enemy forces or the effect of artillery fire.

ob·serv·a·to·ry /əb'zərvə,tôrē/ ▸*n.* (*pl.* **-ries**) a room or building housing an astronomical telescope or other scientific equipment for the study of natural phenomena. ■ a position or building affording an extensive view. ▷late 17th cent.; from modern Latin *observatorium,* from Latin *observat-* 'watched,' from the verb *observare* (see **OBSERVE**).

ob·serve /əb'zərv/ ▸*v.* [*trans.*] **1** notice or perceive (something) and register it as being significant: [with *clause*] *young people observe that decisions are made by others.* ■ watch (someone or something) carefully and attentively: *Rob stood in the hallway, where he could observe the happenings on the street.* ■ take note of or detect (something) in the course of a scientific study: *the behavior observed in groups of chimpanzees.* ■ [*reporting verb*] make a remark or comment: [with *direct speech*] *"It's chilly," she observed |* [with *clause*] *a stockbroker once observed that dealers live and work in hell.* **2** fulfill or comply with (a social, legal, ethical, or religious obligation): *a tribunal must observe the principles of natural justice.* ■ (usu. **be observed**) maintain (silence) in compliance with a rule or custom, or temporarily as a mark of respect: *a minute's silence will be observed.* ■ perform or take part in (a rite or ceremony): *relations gather to observe the funeral rites.* ■ celebrate or acknowledge (an anniversary): *many observed the one-year anniversary of the flood.* ▷late Middle English (sense 2): from Old French *observer,* from Latin *observare* 'to watch,' from *ob-* 'toward' + *servare* 'attend to, look at.' **—ob·serv·a·ble** *adj.* **—ob·serv·a·bly** /-blē/ *adv.*

ob·serv·er /əb'zərvər/ ▸*n.* a person who watches or notices something: *to a casual observer, he was at peace.* ■ a person who follows events, esp. political ones, closely and comments publicly on them: *some observers expect interest rates to rise.* ■ a person posted to an area in an official capacity to monitor political or military events: *elections scrutinized by international observers.* ■ a person who attends a conference, inquiry, etc., to note the proceedings without participating in them. ■ (in science or art) a real or hypothetical person whose observation is regarded as having a particular viewpoint or effect.

ob·sess /əb'ses/ ▸*v.* [*trans.*] (usu. **be obsessed**) preoccupy or fill the mind of (someone) continually, intrusively, and to a troubling extent: *he was obsessed with thoughts of suicide |* [as *adj.*] (**obsessed**) *he became completely obsessed about germs.* ■ [*intrans.*] (of a person) be preoccupied in this way: *her husband, who is* ***obsessing about*** *the wrong she has done him.* ▷late Middle English (in the sense 'haunt, possess,' referring to an evil spirit): from Latin *obsess-* 'besieged,' from the verb *obsidere,* from *ob-* 'opposite' + *sedere* 'sit.' The current sense dates from the late 19th cent. **—ob·ses·sive** /-'sesiv/ *adj.* & *n.* **—ob·ses·sive·ly** /-'sesivlē/ *adv.* **—ob·ses·sive·ness** /-'sesivnis/ *n.*

ob·ses·sion /əb'sesʜən/ ▸*n.* the state of being obsessed with someone or something: *she cared for him with a devotion bordering on obsession.* ■ an idea or thought that continually preoccupies or intrudes on a person's mind: *he was in the grip of an obsession he was powerless to resist.* ▷early 16th cent. (in the sense 'siege'): from Latin *obsessio(n-),* from the verb *obsidere* (see **OBSESS**). **—ob·ses·sion·al** /-sʜənl/ *adj.* **—ob·ses·sion·al·ly** /-sʜənl-ē/ *adv.*

ob·ses·sive–com·pul·sive ▸*adj. Psychiatry* denoting or relating to a disorder in which a person feels compelled to perform certain meaningless actions repeatedly in order to alleviate obsessive fears or intrusive thoughts, typically resulting in severe disruption of daily life.

▸*n.* a person characterized by such obsessive behavior.

ob·sid·i·an /əb'sidēən; äb-/ ▸*n.* a hard, dark, glasslike volcanic rock formed by the rapid solidification of lava without crystallization. ▷mid 17th cent.: from Latin *obsidianus,* error for *obsianus,* from *Obsius,* the name (in Pliny) of the discoverer of a similar stone.

ob·so·les·cent /,äbsə'lesənt/ ▸*adj.* becoming obsolete: *the custom is now obsolescent.* ▷mid 18th cent.: from Latin *obsolescent-* 'falling into disuse,' from the verb *obsolescere.* **—ob·so·lesce** *v. existing systems begin to obsolesce.* **—ob·so·les·cence** *n.*

ob·so·lete /,äbsə'lēt/ ▸*adj.* **1** no longer produced or used; out of date: *the disposal of old and obsolete machinery | the phrase was obsolete after 1625.* See note at **OLD. 2** *Biology* (of a part or characteristic of an organism) less developed than formerly or in a related species; rudimentary; vestigial.

▸*v.* [*trans.*] cause (a product or idea) to be or become obsolete by replacing it with something new: *we're trying to stimulate the business by obsoleting last year's designs.* ▷late 16th cent.: from Latin *obsoletus* 'grown old, worn out,' past participle of *obsolescere* 'fall into disuse.' **—ob·so·lete·ly** *adv.* **—ob·so·lete·ness** *n.* **—ob·so·let·ism** /-'lē,tizəm/ *n.*

ob·sta·cle /'äbstəkəl/ ▸*n.* a thing that blocks one's way or prevents or hinders progress: *the major* ***obstacle to*** *achieving that goal is money.* ▷Middle English: via Old French from Latin *obstaculum,* from *obstare* 'impede,' from *ob-* 'against' + *stare* 'stand.'

ob·sta·cle course ▸*n.* a course over which participants negotiate obstacles to be climbed, crawled under, crossed on suspended ropes, etc., as used for training soldiers. ■ *figurative* any situation that presents a series of challenges or obstacles.

ob·stet·ri·cal /əb'stetrikəl; äb-/ ▸*adj.* of or relating to childbirth and the processes associated with it. ▷mid 18th cent.: from modern Latin *obstetricus* for Latin *obstetricius* (based on *obstetrix* 'midwife'), from *obstare* 'be present.' **—ob·stet·ric** *adj.* **—ob·stet·ri·cal·ly** /-ik(ə)lē/ *adv.*

ob·ste·tri·cian /ˌäbstəˈtrisʜən/ ▸*n.* a physician or surgeon qualified to practice in obstetrics.

ob·stet·rics /əbˈstetriks; äb-/ ▸*plural n.* [usu. treated as *sing.*] the branch of medicine and surgery concerned with childbirth and the care of women giving birth.

ob·sti·nate /ˈäbstənit/ ▸*adj.* stubbornly refusing to change one's opinion or chosen course of action, despite attempts to persuade one to do so. See note at STUBBORN. ■ (of an unwelcome phenomenon or situation) very difficult to change or overcome: *the obstinate problem of unemployment.* ▷Middle English: from Latin *obstinatus*, past participle of *obstinare* 'persist.' **—ob·sti·na·cy** /-nəsē/ *n.* **—ob·sti·nate·ly** *adv.*

ob·sti·pa·tion /ˌäbstəˈpāsʜən/ ▸*n. Medicine* severe or complete constipation. ▷late 16th cent.: alteration of CONSTIPATION, by substitution of the prefix OB- for *con-*.

ob·strep·er·ous /əbˈstrepərəs; äb-/ ▸*adj.* noisy and difficult to control: *the boy is cocky and obstreperous.* See note at VOCIFEROUS. ▷late 16th cent. (in the sense 'clamorous, vociferous'): from Latin *obstreperus* (from *obstrepere*, from *ob-* 'against' + *strepere* 'make a noise') + -OUS. **—ob·strep·er·ous·ly** *adv.* **—ob·strep·er·ous·ness** *n.*

ob·struct /əbˈstrəkt; äb-/ ▸*v.* [*trans.*] block (an opening, path, road, etc.); be or get in the way of: *she was obstructing the entrance.* ■ prevent or hinder (movement or someone or something in motion): *they had to alter the course of the stream and obstruct the natural flow of the water.* See note at HINDER. ■ block (someone's view): *the view of the driver had been obstructed by the bend in the road.* ■ *figurative* put difficulties in the way of: *fears that the regime would obstruct the distribution of food.* ■ *Law* commit the offense of intentionally hindering (a legal process). ■ (in various sports) impede (a player on the opposing team) in a manner that constitutes an offense. ▷late 16th cent.: from Latin *obstruct-* 'blocked up,' from the verb *obstruere*, from *ob-* 'against' + *struere* 'build, pile up.' **—ob·struc·tor** /-tər/ *n.*

ob·struc·tion /əbˈstrəksʜən; äb-/ ▸*n.* the action of obstructing or the state of being obstructed: *they faced obstruction in carrying out their research | walkers could proceed with the minimum of obstruction.* ■ a thing that impedes or prevents passage or progress; an obstacle or blockage: *the tractor hit an obstruction.* ■ (in various sports) the action of unlawfully obstructing a player on the opposing team. ■ *Medicine* blockage of a bodily passageway, as the intestines. ■ *Law* the action of deliberately hindering a legal process. ▷mid 16th cent.: from Latin *obstructio(n-)*, from the verb *obstruere* (see OBSTRUCT).

ob·struc·tion·ism /əbˈstrəksʜəˌnizəm; äb-/ ▸*n.* the practice of deliberately impeding or delaying the course of legal, legislative, or other procedures. **—ob·struc·tion·ist** *n.* & *adj.*

ob·struc·tive /əbˈstrəktiv; äb-/ ▸*adj.* **1** causing a blockage or obstruction: *all tubing should be cleared of obstructive algae and detritus.* ■ of or relating to obstruction of a passage in the body, esp. the intestines or the bronchi: *the child developed severe obstructive symptoms.* **2** causing or tending to cause deliberate difficulties and delays: *instead of being helpful, she had been a shade obstructive.* **—ob·struc·tive·ly** *adv.* **—ob·struc·tive·ness** *n.*

ob·stru·ent /ˈäbstrōōənt/ ▸*n.* **1** *Phonetics* a fricative or plosive speech sound. **2** *Medicine* a medicine or substance that closes the natural passages or pores of the body. ▷mid 17th cent.: from Latin *obstruent-* 'blocking up,' from the verb *obstruere*.

ob·tain /əbˈtān; äb-/ ▸*v.* **1** [*trans.*] get, acquire, or secure (something): *an opportunity to obtain advanced degrees.* See note at GET. **2** [*intrans.*] *formal* be prevalent, customary, or established: *the price of silver fell to that obtaining elsewhere in the ancient world.* ▷late Middle English: from Old French *obtenir*, from Latin *obtinere* 'obtain, gain.' **—ob·tain·a·bil·i·ty** /-nəˈbilətē/ *n.* **—ob·tain·a·ble** *adj.* **—ob·tain·er** *n.* **—ob·tain·ment** *n.* **—ob·ten·tion** /-ˈtencʜən/ *n.*

ob·tect /əbˈtekt/ (also **ob·tect·ed** /-ˈtektid/) ▸*adj. Entomology* (of an insect pupa or chrysalis) covered in a hard case with the legs and wings attached immovably against the body. ▷late 19th cent.: from Latin *obtectus*, past participle of *obtegere* 'cover over.'

ob·ten·tion /əbˈtensʜən; äb-/ ▸*n.* the action of obtaining something: *their protests serve no purpose and will only make their obtention of a diploma almost impossible.* ▷early 17th cent.: French, or from late Latin, *obtentio(n-)*, from *obtinere*, 'obtain, gain.'

ob·trude /əbˈtrōōd/ ▸*v.* [*intrans.*] become noticeable in an unwelcome or intrusive way: *a sound from the reception hall obtruded into his thoughts.* ■ [*trans.*] impose or force (something) on someone in such a way: *I felt unable to obtrude my private sorrow upon anyone.* ▷mid 16th cent.: from Latin *obtrudere*, from *ob-* 'toward' + *trudere* 'to push.' **—ob·trud·er** *n.* **—ob·tru·sion** /-ˈtrōōzʜən/ *n.*

ob·tru·sive /əbˈtrōōsiv; äb-/ ▸*adj.* noticeable or prominent in an unwelcome or intrusive way: *high-powered satellites can reach smaller and less obtrusive antennas.* See note at IMPERTINENT. ▷mid 17th cent.: from Latin *obtrus-* 'thrust forward,' from the verb *obtrudere* (see OBTRUDE). **—ob·tru·sive·ly** *adv.* **—ob·tru·sive·ness** *n.*

ob·tund /äbˈtənd/ ▸*v.* [*trans.*] *dated, chiefly Medicine* dull the sensitivity of; blunt; deaden. ▷late Middle English: from Latin *obtundere*, from *ob-* 'against' + *tundere* 'to beat.'

ob·tu·rate /ˈäbt(y)əˌrāt/ ▸*v.* [*trans.*] *formal* or *technical* block up; obstruct. ▷mid 17th cent.: from Latin *obturat-* 'stopped up,' from the verb *obturare*. **—ob·tu·ra·tion** /-ˈrāsʜən/ *n.*

ob·tu·ra·tor /ˈäbt(y)əˌrātər/ ▸*n. Anatomy* either of two muscles covering the outer front part of the pelvis on each side and involved in movements of the thigh and hip. ■ [as *adj.*] relating to this muscle or to the obturator foramen. ▷early 18th cent.: from medieval Latin, literally 'obstructor,' from *obturare* 'stop up.'

ob·tu·ra·tor fo·ra·men ▸*n. Anatomy* a large opening in the hipbone between the pubis and the ischium.

ob·tuse /əbˈt(y)ōōs; äb-/ ▸*adj.* **1** annoyingly insensitive or slow to understand: *he wondered if the doctor was being deliberately obtuse.* See note at STUPID. ■ difficult to understand: *some of the lyrics are a bit obtuse.* **2** (of an angle) more than 90° and less than 180°. ■ not sharp-pointed or sharp-edged; blunt. ▷late Middle English (in the sense 'blunt'): from Latin *obtusus*, past participle of *obtundere* 'beat against' (see OBTUND). **—ob·tuse·ly** *adv.* **—ob·tuse·ness** *n.* **—ob·tu·si·ty** /-sitē/ *n.*

Ob-U·gric /ˈäb ˈ(y)ōōgrik; ˈôb/ (also **Ob-U·gri·an** /ˈ(y)ōōgrēən/) ▸*adj.* of or denoting a branch of the Finno-Ugric language family containing two languages of western Siberia related to Hungarian.
▸*n.* this group of languages. ▷1930s: from *Ob*, the name of a Siberian river, + UGRIC.

ob·verse ▸*n.* /ˈäbˌvərs/ [usu. in *sing.*] **1** the side of a coin or medal bearing the head or principal design. ■ the design or inscription on this side. **2** the opposite or counterpart of a fact or truth: *true solitude is the obverse of true society.*
▸*adj.* /əbˈvərs; äb-/ [*attrib.*] **1** of or denoting the obverse of a coin or medal. **2** corresponding to something else as its opposite or counterpart. **3** *Biology* narrower at the base or point of attachment than at the apex or top: *an obverse leaf.* ▷mid 17th cent. (in the sense 'turned toward the observer'): from Latin *obversus*, past participle of *obvertere* 'turn toward' (see OBVERT). **—ob·verse·ly** /əbˈvərslē; äb-/ *adv.*

ob·vert /əbˈvərt; äb-/ ▸*v.* [*trans.*] *Logic* alter (a proposition) so as to infer another proposition with a contradictory predicate, e.g., *"no men are immortal"* to *"all men are mortal."* ▷early 17th cent. (in the sense 'turn something until it is facing'): from Latin *obvertere*, from *ob-* 'toward' + *vertere* 'to turn.' **—ob·ver·sion** /əbˈvərzʜən; äb-/ *n.*

ob·vi·ate /ˈäbvēˌāt/ ▸*v.* [*trans.*] remove (a need or difficulty): *the Venetian blinds obviated the need for curtains.* ■ avoid; prevent: *a parachute can be used to obviate disaster.* ▷late 16th cent.: from late Latin *obviat-* 'prevented,' from the verb *obviare*, based on Latin *via* 'way.' **—ob·vi·a·tion** /äbvēˈāsʜən/ *n.* **—ob·vi·a·tor** /-ˌātər/ *n.*

ob·vi·ous /ˈäbvēəs/ ▸*adj.* easily perceived or understood; clear, self-evident, or apparent: *unemployment has been the most obvious cost of the recession |* [with *clause*] *it was obvious a storm was coming in* ■ *derogatory* predictable and lacking in subtlety: *it was an obvious remark to make.* ▷late 16th cent. (in the sense 'frequently encountered'): from Latin *obvius* (from the phrase *ob viam* 'in the way') + -OUS. **—ob·vi·ous·ly** *adv.* **—ob·vi·ous·ness** *n.*

ob·vo·lute /ˈäbvəˌlōōt/ ▸*adj. Botany* (of a leaf) having a margin that alternately overlaps and is overlapped by that of an opposing leaf. ▷mid 18th cent.: from Latin *obvolutus*, past participle of *obvolvere* 'wrap around.' **—ob·vo·lu·tion** /ˌäbvəˈlōōsʜən/ *n.*

oc. (also **Oc.**) ▸*abbr.* ocean.

o.c. ▸*abbr.* ■ *Architecture* on center. ■ in the work cited. [from Latin *opere citato*.]

o/c ▸*abbr.* overcharge.

oc- ▸*prefix* variant spelling of OB- assimilated before *c* (as in *occasion, occlude*).

o·ca /ˈōkə/ ▸*n.* a South American plant related to wood sorrel, long cultivated in Peru for its edible tubers. • *Oxalis tuberosa*, family Oxalidaceae. ▷early 17th cent.: from American Spanish, from Quechua *ócca*.

O·cal·a /ōˈkälə/ an industrial and resort city in north central Florida; pop. 42,045.

oc·a·ri·na /ˌäkəˈrēnə/ ▸*n.* a small egg-shaped wind instrument with a mouthpiece and holes for the fingers. Also called SWEET POTATO. ▷late 19th cent.: from Italian, from *oca* 'goose' (from its shape).

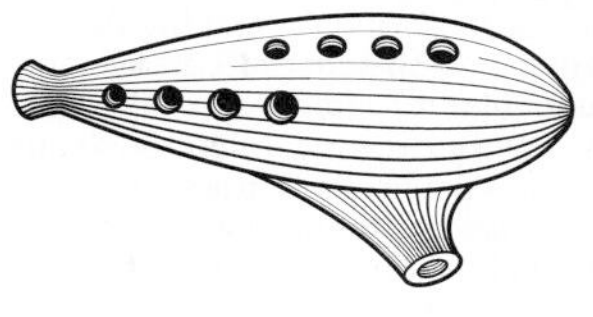

ocarina

OCAS ▸*abbr.* Organization of Central American States.

O'Ca·sey /ōˈkāsē/, Sean (1880–1964), Irish playwright. His plays, such as *The Shadow of a Gunman* (1923) and *Juno and the Paycock* (1924), deal with the Irish poor before and during the civil war that followed the establishment of the Irish Free State in 1922.

occ. ▸*abbr.* ■ occasional; occasionally. ■ Occident; occidental. ■ occupation.

Oc·cam, William of see WILLIAM OF OCCAM.

Oc·cam's ra·zor /ˈäkəmz/ (also **Ock·ham's ra·zor**) the principle (attributed to William of Occam) that in explaining a thing no more assumptions should be made than are necessary. The principle is often invoked to defend reductionism or nominalism. Compare with PRINCIPLE OF PARSIMONY at PARSIMONY.

occas. ▸*abbr.* ■ occasional; occasionally.

oc·ca·sion /əˈkāzʜən/ ▸*n.* **1** a particular time or instance of an event: *on one occasion I stayed up until two in the morning.* ■ a special or noteworthy event, ceremony, or celebration: *she was presented with a gold watch to mark the occasion.* | ■ a suitable or opportune time for doing something: *elections are an occasion for registering protest votes.* **2** *formal* reason; cause: [with *infinitive*] *it's the first time that I've had occasion to complain.*
▸*v.* [*trans.*] *formal* cause (something): *something vital must have occasioned this visit |* [with *two objs.*] *his death occasioned her much grief.* ▷late Middle English: from Latin *occasio(n-)* 'juncture, reason,' from *occidere* 'go down, set,' from *ob-* 'toward' + *cadere* 'to fall.'
▸*PHRASES* □ **on occasion** (or *chiefly Brit.* **occasions**) occasionally; from time to time: *on occasion, the state was asked to intervene.* □ **rise to the occasion** perform very well in response to a special situation or event. □ **take occasion** *archaic* make use of an opportunity to do something.

oc·ca·sion·al /əˈkāzʜənl/ ▸*adj.* occurring, appearing, or done infrequently and irregularly: *the occasional car went by but no taxis.* ■ (of furniture) made or adapted for use on a particular occasion or for irregular use: *an occasional table.* ■ (of a literary composition, speech, religious service, etc.) produced on or intended for a special occasion: *he wrote occasional verse for patrons.* ■ *dated* employed for a particular occasion or on an irregular basis: *occasional freelancer seeks full-time position.* **—oc·ca·sion·al·ly** /-zʜənl-ē/ *adv.*

oc·ca·sion·al·ism /əˈkāzʜənlˌizəm/ ▸*n. Philosophy* the doctrine ascribing the connection between mental and bodily events to the continuing intervention of God.

oc·ca·sion·al ta·ble ▸*n.* a small table for infrequent and varied use.

Oc·ci·dent /ˈäksidənt; -ˌdent/ ▸*n.* (**the Occident**) *formal* or *poetic/literary* the countries of the West, esp. Europe and the Americas (contrasted with ORIENT). ▷late Middle English: via Old French from Latin *occident-* 'going down, setting' (in reference to the sun), from the verb *occidere*.

oc·ci·den·tal /ˌäksəˈdentl/ ▸*adj.* of or relating to the countries of the Occident: *an Asian challenge to occidental dominance.*
▸*n.* (**Occidental**) a native or inhabitant of the Occident. ▷late Middle English: from Old French, or from Latin *occidentalis*, from *occident-* 'going down' (see OCCIDENT). **—oc·ci·den·tal·ism** /-ˌizəm/ *n.* **—oc·ci·den·tal·ize** /-ˌīz/ *v.*

oc·cip·i·tal bone /äk'sipitl/ ▸*n. Anatomy* the bone that forms the back and base of the skull, and through which the spinal cord passes.

oc·cip·i·tal con·dyle ▸*n. Anatomy* each of two rounded knobs on the occipital bone that form a joint with the first cervical vertebra.

oc·cip·i·tal lobe ▸*n. Anatomy* the rearmost lobe in each cerebral hemisphere of the brain.

occipito- ▸*comb. form* relating to the occipital lobe or the occipital bone: *occipitotemporal.* ▷from medieval Latin *occipitalis*, from Latin *caput, capit-* 'head.'

oc·ci·put /'äksəpət/ ▸*n.* (*pl.* **oc·ci·puts** or **oc·cip·i·ta** /äk'sipitə/) *Anatomy* the back of the head or skull. ▷late Middle English: from Latin *occiput*, from *ob-* 'against' + *caput* 'head.' **—oc·cip·i·tal** /äk'sipitl/ *adj.*

Oc·ci·tan /'äksi,tan/ ▸*n.* the medieval or modern language of Languedoc, including literary Provençal of the 12th–14th centuries.
▸*adj.* of or relating to this language. ▷French (see also LANGUE D'OC). **—Oc·ci·ta·ni·an** /,äksə'tānēən/ *n. & adj.*

oc·clude /ə'klōōd/ ▸*v. formal* or *technical* **1** [*trans.*] stop, close up, or obstruct (an opening, orifice, or passage): *thick makeup can occlude the pores.* ■ shut (something) in: *they were occluding the waterfront with a wall of buildings.* ■ *technical* cover (an eye) to prevent its use: *it is placed at eye level with one eye occluded.* ■ *Chemistry* (of a solid) absorb and retain (a gas or impurity). **2** [*intrans.*] (of a tooth) close on or come into contact with another tooth in the opposite jaw. ▷late 16th cent.: from Latin *occludere* 'shut up.'

oc·clud·ed front ▸*n. Meteorology* a composite front produced by occlusion.

oc·clu·sal /ə'klōōsəl/ ▸*adj. Dentistry* of, relating to, or involved in the occlusion of teeth. ■ denoting a portion of a tooth that comes into contact with a tooth in the other jaw.

oc·clu·sion /ə'klōōzhən/ ▸*n.* **1** *Medicine* the blockage or closing of a blood vessel or hollow organ. ■ *Phonetics* the momentary closure of the passage of breath during the articulation of a consonant. **2** *Meteorology* a process in which the cold front of a rotating low pressure system overtakes the warm front, forcing the warm air upward above a wedge of cold air. ■ an occluded front. **3** *Dentistry* the position of the teeth when the jaws are closed. ▷mid 17th cent.: from Latin *occlus-* 'shut up' (from the verb *occludere*) + -ION. **—oc·clu·sive** /-siv/ *adj.*

oc·cult /ə'kəlt/ ▸*n.* (**the occult**) supernatural, mystical, or magical beliefs, practices, or phenomena: *a secret society to study alchemy and the occult.*
▸*adj.* **1** of, involving, or relating to supernatural, mystical, or magical powers or phenomena: *a follower of occult practices similar to voodoo.* ■ beyond the range of ordinary knowledge or experience; mysterious: *a weird occult sensation of having experienced the identical situation before.* ■ communicated only to the initiated; esoteric: *the typically occult language of the time.* **2** *Medicine* (of a disease or process) not accompanied by readily discernible signs or symptoms. ■ (of blood) abnormally present, e.g., in feces, but detectable only chemically or microscopically.
▸*v.* [*trans.*] cut off from view by interposing something: *a wooden screen designed to occult the competitors.* ■ *Astronomy* (of a celestial body) conceal (an apparently smaller body) from view by passing or being in front of it. ▷late 15th cent. (as a verb): from Latin *occultare* 'secrete,' frequentative of *occulere* 'conceal,' based on *celare* 'to hide'; the adjective and noun from *occult-* 'covered over,' from the verb *occulere.* **—oc·cul·ta·tion** /,äkəl'tāshən/ *n.* **—oc·cult·ism** /-,tizəm/ *n.* **—oc·cult·ist** /-tist/ *n.* **—oc·cult·ly** *adv.* **—oc·cult·ness** *n.*

oc·cult·ing light ▸*n.* a light in a lighthouse or buoy that is cut off briefly at regular intervals.

oc·cu·pan·cy /'äkyəpənsē/ ▸*n.* the action or fact of occupying a place: *the house is finally ready for occupancy.* ■ the proportion of accommodations occupied or in use, typically in a hotel: *the 70 percent occupancy needed to give a profit.* ■ *Law* the action of taking possession of something having no owner, as constituting a title to it.

oc·cu·pant /'äkyəpənt/ ▸*n.* a person who resides or is present in a house, vehicle, seat, place, etc., at a given time. ■ the holder of a position or office: *the first occupant of the Oval Office.* ■ *Law* a person holding property, esp. land, in actual possession. ▷late 16th cent. (in the legal sense 'person who establishes a title'): from French, or from Latin *occupant-* 'seizing,' from the verb *occupare.*

oc·cu·pa·tion /,äkyə'pāshən/ ▸*n.* **1** a job or profession: *his prime occupation was as editor.* ■ a way of spending time: *a game of cards is a pretty harmless occupation.* **2** the action, state, or period of occupying or being occupied by military force: *the Roman* ***occupation of*** *Britain | crimes committed during the Nazi occupation.* ■ the action of entering and taking control of a building: *the workers remained* ***in occupation*** *until October 16.* **3** the action or fact of living in or using a building or other place: *a property suitable for occupation by older people.* ▷Middle English: via Old French from Latin *occupatio(n-)*, from the verb *occupare* (see OCCUPY). Sense 2 dates from the mid 16th cent.

oc·cu·pa·tion·al /,äkyə'pāshənl/ ▸*adj.* of or relating to a job or profession: *hepatitis B may be an occupational disease for some health-care workers.* **—oc·cu·pa·tion·al·ly** *adv.*

oc·cu·pa·tion·al haz·ard ▸*n.* a risk accepted as a consequence of a particular occupation.

oc·cu·pa·tion·al med·i·cine ▸*n.* the branch of medicine dealing with the prevention and treatment of job-related injuries and illnesses.

oc·cu·pa·tion·al ther·a·py ▸*n.* a form of therapy for those recuperating from physical or mental illness that encourages rehabilitation through the performance of activities required in daily life. **—oc·cu·pa·tion·al ther·a·pist** *n.*

oc·cu·py /'äkyə,pī/ ▸*v.* (**-pies, -pied**) [*trans.*] **1** reside or have one's place of business in (a building): *the apartment she occupies in Manhattan.* ■ fill or take up (a space or time): *two long windows occupied almost the whole wall.* ■ be situated in or at (a place or position in a system or hierarchy): *on the corporate ladder, they occupy the lowest rungs.* ■ hold (a position or job). **2** (often **be occupied with/in**) fill or preoccupy (the mind or thoughts): *her mind was occupied with alarming questions.* ■ keep (someone) busy and active: *Sarah* ***occupied herself*** *taking the coffee cups over to the sink* | [as *adj.*] (**occupied**) *tasks that kept her occupied for the remainder of the afternoon.* **3** take control of (a place, esp. a country) by military conquest or settlement: *Syria was occupied by France under a League of Nations mandate.* ■ enter, take control of, and stay in (a building) illegally and often forcibly, esp. as a form of protest: *the workers occupied the factory.* ▷Middle English: formed irregularly from Old French *occuper*, from Latin *occupare* 'seize.' A now obsolete vulgar sense 'have sexual relations with' seems to have led to the general avoidance of the word in the 17th and most of the 18th cent. **—oc·cu·pi·er** /-,pīər/ *n.*

oc·cur /ə'kər/ ▸*v.* (**-curred, -cur·ring**) [*intrans.*] happen; take place: *the accident occurred at about 3:30 p.m.* See note at HAPPEN. ■ exist or be found to be present in a place or under a particular set of conditions: *radon occurs naturally in rocks such as granite.* ■ (**occur to**) (of a thought or idea) come into the mind of (someone): [with *clause*] *it occurred to him that he hadn't eaten.* ▷late 15th cent.: from Latin *occurrere* 'go to meet, present itself,' from *ob-* 'against' + *currere* 'to run.'

oc·cur·rence /ə'kərəns/ ▸*n.* an incident or event: *vandalism used to be a rare occurrence.* ■ the fact or frequency of something happening: *the occurrence of cancer increases with age.* ■ the fact of something existing or being found in a place or under a particular set of conditions: *the occurrence of natural gas fields.* ▷mid 16th cent.: probably from the plural of archaic *occurrent*, in the same sense, via French from Latin *occurrent-* 'befalling,' from the verb *occurrere* (see OCCUR).

oc·cur·rent /ə'kərənt/ ▸*adj.* actually occurring or observable, not potential or hypothetical. ▷late 15th cent.: from French, or from Latin *occurrent-* 'befalling,' from the verb *occurrere.*

OCD ▸*abbr.* obsessive-compulsive disorder.

o·cean /'ōshən/ ▸*n.* a very large expanse of sea, in particular, each of the main areas into which the sea is divided geographically: *the Atlantic Ocean.* ■ (usu. **the ocean**) the sea: [as *adj.*] *the ocean floor.* ■ (**an ocean of/oceans of**) *figurative* a very large expanse or quantity: *she had oceans of energy.* ▷Middle English: from Old French *occean*, via Latin from Greek *ōkeanos* 'great stream encircling the earth's disk.' "The ocean" originally denoted the whole body of water regarded as encompassing the earth's single land mass. **—o·cean·ward** /-wərd/ (also **-wards**) *adv. & adj.*

o·cea·nar·i·um /,ōshə'ne(ə)rēəm/ ▸*n.* (*pl.* **-nar·i·ums** or **-nar·i·a** /-'ne(ə)rēə/) a large seawater aquarium in which marine animals are kept for study and public exhibit. ▷1940s: from OCEAN, on the pattern of *aquarium.*

o·cean bo·ni·to ▸*n.* another term for SKIPJACK (sense 1).

o·cean·front /'ōshən,frənt/ ▸*n.* the land that borders an ocean. **—o·cean·front** *adj.*

o·cean·go·ing /'ōshən,gō-iNG/ (also **o·cean-go·ing**) ▸*adj.* (of a ship) designed to cross oceans.

O·ce·an·i·a /,ōshē'anēə; -'änēə/ an area that encompasses the islands of the Pacific Ocean and adjacent seas. ▷modern Latin, from French *Océanie.* **—O·ce·an·i·an** *adj. & n.*

o·ce·an·ic /,ōshē'anik/ ▸*adj.* **1** of or relating to the ocean: *oceanic atolls.* ■ of or inhabiting the part of the ocean beyond the edge of a continental shelf: *stocks of oceanic fish.* ■ (of a climate) governed by the proximity of the ocean. ■ *figurative* of enormous size or extent; huge; vast: *an oceanic failure.* **2** (**Oceanic**) of or relating to Oceania: *a gallery specializing in Oceanic art.*

o·ce·an·ic crust ▸*n. Geology* the relatively thin part of the earth's crust that underlies the ocean basins. It is geologically young compared with the continental crust and consists of basaltic rock overlain by sediments.

O·ce·a·nid /ō'sēənid/ ▸*n.* (*pl.* **O·ce·a·nids** or **O·ce·an·i·des** /,ōsē'anidēz/) *Greek Mythology* a sea nymph; one of the daughters of Oceanus. ▷from French *Océanide*, from Greek *ōkeanis, ōkeanid-.*

O·cean Is·land another name for BANABA.

o·cean lin·er ▸*n.* see LINER[1] (sense 1).

o·cea·nog·ra·phy /,ōshə'nägrəfē/ ▸*n.* the branch of science that deals with the physical and biological properties and phenomena of the sea. **—o·cea·nog·ra·pher** /-fər/ *n.* **—o·cea·no·graph·ic** /-nə'grafik/ *adj.* **—o·cea·no·graph·i·cal** /-nə'grafəkəl/ *adj.*

o·cea·nol·o·gy /,ōshə'näləjē/ ▸*n.* another term for OCEANOGRAPHY. ■ the branch of technology and economics dealing with human use of the sea. **—o·cea·no·log·i·cal** /-nə'läjikəl/ *adj.* **—o·cea·nol·o·gist** /-jist/ *n.*

Ocean·side /'ōshən,sīd/ a residential and commercial city in southwestern California, north of San Diego; pop. 128,398.

O·cean State a nickname for the state of RHODE ISLAND.

O·ce·a·nus /ō'sēənəs/ *Greek Mythology* the son of Uranus (Heaven) and Gaia (Earth), the personification of the great river believed to encircle the whole world.

oc·el·lat·ed /'äsə,lātid/ ▸*adj.* (of an animal, or its plumage or body surface) having one or more ocelli, or eyelike markings.

o·cel·lus /ō'seləs/ ▸*n.* (*pl.* **o·cel·li** /ō'selī; ō'selē/) *Zoology* **1** another term for SIMPLE EYE. **2** another term for EYESPOT (senses 1 and 2). ▷early 19th cent.: from Latin, diminutive of *oculus* 'eye.' **—o·cel·lar** /ō'selər/ *adj.*

oc·e·lot /'äsə,lät; 'ōsə-/ ▸*n.* a medium-sized wild cat that has a tawny yellow coat marked with black blotches and spots, and ranges from southern Texas through South America. • *Felis pardalis*, family Felidae. ■ the fur of the ocelot. ▷late 18th cent.: from French, from Nahuatl *tlatlocelotl*, literally 'field tiger.'

o·cher /'ōkər/ (*chiefly Brit.* also **o·chre**) ▸*n.* an earthy pigment containing ferric oxide, typically with clay, varying from light yellow to brown or red. ■ a pale brownish yellow color. ▷Middle English: from Old French *ocre*, via Latin from Greek *ōkhra* 'yellow ocher.' **—o·cher·ish** /'ōk(ə)rish/ *adj.* **—o·cher·oid** /'ōk(ə)roid/ *adj.* **—o·cher·ous** /'ōk(ə)rəs/ *adj.* **—o·cher·y** *adj.*

och·loc·ra·cy /äk'läkrəsē/ ▸*n.* government by a mob; mob rule. ▷late 16th cent.: via French from Greek *okhlokratia*, from *okhlos* 'mob' + *-kratia* 'power.' **—och·lo·crat** /'äklə,krat/ *n.* **—och·lo·crat·ic** /,äklə'kratik/ *adj.*

och·lo·pho·bi·a /,äklə'fōbēə/ ▸*n.* extreme or irrational fear of or aversion to crowds.

o·chre ▸*n. chiefly Brit.* variant spelling of OCHER.

Ochs /äks/, Adolph Simon (1858–1935), U.S. publisher. He acquired *The New York Times* in 1896 and made it one of the nation's preeminent newspapers.

-ock ▸*suffix* forming nouns originally with diminutive sense: *haddock | pollock.* ■ also occasionally forming words from other sources: *bannock | hassock.* ▷Old English *-uc, -oc*

ock·er /'äkər/ *informal* ▸*n. Austral.* a boorish or aggressive person, esp. an Australian man.
▸*adj.* denoting or characteristic of such a person: *an*

ocker sports writer. ▷alteration of *Oscar*, popularized by the name of a character in an Australian television series (1965–68).

Ock·ham, William of see **WILLIAM OF OCCAM.**

Ock·ham's ra·zor ▸*n.* variant spelling of **OCCAM'S RAZOR.**

o'clock /ə'kläk/ ▸*adv.* used to specify the hour in telling time: *the gates will open at eight o'clock.* ■ used following a numeral to indicate direction or bearing with reference to an imaginary clock face, 12 o'clock being thought of as directly in front or overhead, or at the top of a circular target, etc.: *"I think we've got some action at 11 o'clock," he said, gesturing toward the eastern plains.*

O'Con·nell /ō'känl/, Daniel (1775–1847), Irish nationalist leader and social reformer; known as **the Liberator**. His election to Parliament in 1828 forced the British government to grant emancipation to Catholics in order to enable him to take his seat in the House of Commons.

O'Con·nor[1] /ō'känər/, Carroll (1924–2001), U.S. actor, writer, and producer. He starred as Archie Bunker in the television series "All in the Family" from 1971 until 1979 when it became "Archie's Place" and ran until 1983. He also starred in television's "In the Heat of the Night" (1988–95).

O'Con·nor[2], (Mary) Flannery (1925–64), U.S. novelist and short-story writer. Her short stories are notable for their dark humor and grotesque characters and are published in collections such as *A Good Man Is Hard to Find, and Other Stories* (1955). Notable novels: *Wise Blood* (1952) and *The Violent Bear It Away* (1960).

O'Con·nor[3], Sandra Day (1930–), U.S. Supreme Court associate justice 1981– . Appointed by President Reagan, she was the first woman to sit on the Court.

o·co·til·lo /,ōkə'tēyō/ ▸*n.* (*pl.* **-los**) a spiny, scarlet-flowered desert shrub of the southwestern U.S. and Mexico, sometimes planted as a hedge. • *Fouquieria splendens*, family Fouquieriaceae. ▷mid 19th cent.: via American Spanish (diminutive form) from Nahuatl *ocotl* 'torch.'

OCR ▸*abbr.* ■ optical character reader. ■ optical character recognition.

O·cra·coke Is·land /'ōkrə,kōk/ a barrier island in eastern North Carolina, part of the Outer Banks.

oc·re·a /'äkrēə; 'ōkrēə/ (also **och·re·a**) ▸*n.* (*pl.* **oc·re·ae** /'äkrē-ē; 'ōkrē-ē/ or **oc·re·as**) *Botany* a sheath around a stem formed by the cohesion of two or more stipules, characteristic of the dock family. ▷mid 19th cent.: from Latin, literally 'protective legging.'

OCS ▸*abbr.* ■ *Military* officer candidate school. ■ Old Church Slavonic. ■ outer continental shelf.

Oct. ▸*abbr.* October.

oct. ▸*abbr.* octavo.

oct- ▸*comb. form* variant spelling of **OCTA-** and **OCTO-** assimilated before a vowel (as in *octennial*).

octa- (also **oct-** before a vowel) ▸*comb. form* eight; having eight: *octahedron.* ▷from Greek *oktō* 'eight.'

oc·tad /'äktad/ ▸*n. technical* a group or set of eight. ▷mid 19th cent.: via late Latin from Greek *oktas, oktad-*, from *oktō* 'eight.'

oc·ta·gon /'äktə,gän; -gən/ ▸*n.* a plane figure with eight straight sides and eight angles. ■ an object or building with a plan or cross section of this shape. ▷late 16th cent.: via Latin from Greek *octagōnos* 'eight-angled.' **—oc·tag·o·nal** /äk'tagənl/ *adj.* **—oc·tag·o·nal·ly** /äk'tagənəlē/ *adv.*

oc·ta·he·drite /,äktə'hēdrīt/ ▸*n.* **1** another term for **ANATASE. 2** an iron meteorite containing plates of kamacite and taenite in an octahedral orientation. ▷early 19th cent.: from **OCTAHEDRON** + **-ITE**[1].

oc·ta·he·dron /,äktə'hēdrən/ ▸*n.* (*pl.* **-drons** or **-dra** /-drə/) a three-dimensional shape having eight plane faces, esp. a regular solid figure with eight equal triangular faces. ■ a body, esp. a crystal, in the form of a regular octahedron. ▷late 16th cent.: from Greek *oktaedron*, neuter (used as a noun) of *oktaedros* 'eight-faced.' **—oc·ta·he·dral** /-drəl/ *adj.*

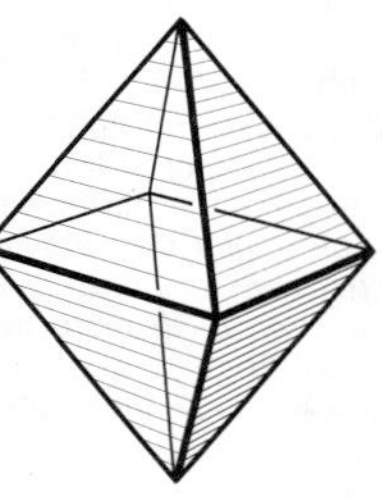

octahedron

oc·tal /'äktl/ ▸*adj.* relating to or using a system of numerical notation that has 8 rather than 10 as a base.
▸*n.* the octal system; octal notation.

oc·tam·er·ous /äk'tamərəs/ ▸*adj. Botany & Zoology* having parts arranged in groups of eight. ■ consisting of eight joints or parts.

oc·tam·e·ter /äk'tamitər/ ▸*n. Prosody* a line of verse consisting of eight metrical feet.

oc·tane /'äktān/ ▸*n. Chemistry* a colorless flammable hydrocarbon of the alkane series, obtained in petroleum refining. • Chem. formula: C_8H_{18}; many isomers, esp. the straight-chain isomer (***n*-octane**). See also **ISOOCTANE.** ▷late 19th cent.: from **OCTO-** 'eight' (denoting eight carbon atoms) + **-ANE**[2].

oc·tane num·ber (also **octane rating**) ▸*n.* a figure indicating the antiknock properties of a fuel, based on a comparison with a mixture of isooctane and heptane.

oc·tan·gu·lar /äk'taNGgyələr/ ▸*adj.* having eight angles.

Oc·tans /'äktanz/ *Astronomy* a faint southern constellation (the Octant), containing the south celestial pole. ■ [as *genitive*] (**Octantis**) used with a preceding letter or numeral to designate a star in this constellation: *the star Delta Octantis.* ▷Latin.

oc·tant /'äktənt/ ▸*n.* an arc of a circle equal to one eighth of its circumference, or the area enclosed by such an arc with two radii of the circle. ■ each of eight parts into which a space or solid body is divided by three planes that intersect (esp. at right angles) at a single point. ■ an obsolete instrument in the form of a graduated eighth of a circle, used in astronomy and navigation. ▷late 17th cent.: from Latin *octans, octant-* 'half-quadrant,' from *octo* 'eight.'

oc·tave /'äktəv; 'äk,tāv/ ▸*n.* **1** *Music* a series of eight notes occupying the interval between (and including) two notes, one having twice or half the frequency of vibration of the other. ■ the interval between these two notes. ■ each of the two notes at the extremes of this interval. ■ these two notes sounding together. **2** a poem or stanza of eight lines; an octet. **3** the eighth day after a church festival, inclusive of the day of the festival. ■ a period of eight days beginning with the day of such a festival. **4** *Fencing* the last of eight standard parrying positions. ▷Middle English (sense 3): via Old French from Latin *octava dies* 'eighth day.'

Oc·ta·vi·an /äk'tāvēən/ see **AUGUSTUS.**

oc·ta·vo /äk'tävō/ (abbr.: **8vo**) ▸*n.* (*pl.* **-vos**) a size of book page that results from the folding of each printed sheet into eight leaves (sixteen pages). ■ a book of this size. ▷late 16th cent.: from Latin *in octavo* 'in an eighth,' from *octavus* 'eighth.'

oc·ten·ni·al /äk'tenēəl/ ▸*adj. rare* recurring every eight years. ■ lasting for or relating to a period of eight years. ▷mid 17th cent.: from late Latin *octennium* 'period of eight years' + **-AL.**

oc·tet /äk'tet/ (also **oc·tette**) ▸*n.* a group of eight people or things, in particular: ■ a group of eight musicians. ■ a musical composition for eight voices or instruments. ■ the first eight lines of a sonnet. ■ *Chemistry* a stable group of eight electrons occupying a single shell in an atom. ▷mid 19th cent.: from Italian *ottetto* or German *Oktett*, on the pattern of *duet* and *quartet*.

octo- (also **oct-** before a vowel) ▸*comb. form* eight; having eight: *octosyllabic.* ▷from Latin *octo* or Greek *oktō* 'eight.'

Oc·to·ber /äk'tōbər/ ▸*n.* the tenth month of the year, in the northern hemisphere usually considered the second month of autumn: *the project started in October* | [as *adj.*] *on an October night.* ▷late Old English, from Latin, from *octo* 'eight' (being originally the eighth month of the Roman year).

Oc·to·ber Rev·o·lu·tion ▸*n.* see **RUSSIAN REVOLUTION.**

Oc·to·ber sur·prise ▸*n.* any political event orchestrated (or apparently orchestrated) in the month before an election, in the hopes of affecting the outcome: *was Osama's videotape supposed to be an October surprise?*

Oc·to·ber War Arab name for **YOM KIPPUR WAR.**

Oc·to·brist /äk'tōbrist/ ▸*n. historical* a member of the moderate party in the Russian Duma that supported Tsar Nicholas II's reforming manifesto of October 30, 1905. ▷suggested by Russian *oktyabrist*.

oc·to·cen·ten·ar·y /,äktōsen'tenərē/ ▸*n.* (*pl.* **-ar·ies**) the eight-hundredth anniversary of a significant event.

oc·to·dec·i·mo /,äktō'desə,mō/ ▸*n.* (*pl.* **-mos**) a size of book page that results from the folding of each printed sheet into eighteen leaves (36 pages). ■ a book of this size. ▷mid 19th cent.: from Latin *in octodecimo* 'in an eighteenth,' from *octodecimus* 'eighteenth.'

oc·to·ge·nar·i·an /,äktəjə'ne(ə)rēən/ ▸*n.* a person who is from 80 to 89 years old: [as *adj.*] *the octogenarian leaders of China.* ▷early 19th cent.: from Latin *octogenarius* (based on *octoginta* 'eighty') + **-AN.**

oc·to·nar·y /'äktə,nerē/ ▸*adj. rare* relating to or based on the number eight.

oc·to·pa·mine /äk'tōpə,mēn/ ▸*n. Biochemistry* a compound that can accumulate in nerves as a result of the use of monoamine oxidase inhibitors and cause a rise in blood pressure. • An amine related to norepinephrine; chem. formula: $HOC_6H_4CHOHCH_2NH_2$. ▷1940s: from **OCTOPUS** (from which it was first extracted) + **AMINE.**

Oc·top·o·da /äk'täpədə/ *Zoology* an order of cephalopod mollusks that comprises the octopuses. ▷modern Latin (plural), from Greek *oktōpous, oktōpod-*, from *oktō* 'eight' + *pous, pod-* 'foot.' **—oc·to·pod** /'äktə,päd/ *n.*

oc·to·pus /'äktəpəs/ ▸*n.* (*pl.* **-pus·es**) **1** a cephalopod mollusk with eight sucker-bearing arms, a soft saclike body, strong beaklike jaws, and no internal shell. • Order Octopoda, class Cephalopoda: *Octopus* and other genera. **2** *figurative* an organization or system perceived to have far-reaching and typically harmful effects: *the octopus of destructive politics.* ▷mid 18th cent.: from Greek *oktōpous* (see also **OCTOPODA**). **—oc·to·poid** /-,poid/ *adj.*

> ***USAGE*** The standard English plural of **octopus** is **octopuses.** However, the word **octopus** comes from Greek, and the Greek plural form is **octopodes** (/äk'täpə,dēz/). Modern usage of **octopodes** is so infrequent that many people mistakenly create the erroneous plural form **octopi**, formed according to rules for Latin plurals.
> See also **usage** at **'-i'.**

oc·to·roon /,äktə'rōōn/ ▸*n. historical* a person whose parents are a quadroon and a white person and who is therefore one-eighth black by descent. ▷mid 19th cent.: from **OCTO-** 'eight,' on the pattern of *quadroon*.

oc·to·syl·la·bic /,äktəsə'labik; ,äktō-/ ▸*adj.* having or written in lines that have eight syllables.
▸*n.* a line of verse that has eight syllables.

oc·to·syl·la·ble /'äktə'siləbəl/ ▸*n.* a word or line of verse with eight syllables.
▸*adj.* having eight syllables.

oc·to·thorp /'äktə,THôrp/ (also **oc·to·thorpe**) ▸*n.* another term for the pound sign (#). ▷1970s: of uncertain origin; probably from **OCTO-** (referring to the eight points on the symbol) + the surname *Thorpe*.

oc·troi /'äktroi; äk'trwä/ ▸*n.* a tax levied in some countries on various goods entering a town or city. ▷late 16th cent. (in the sense 'concession,' esp. one giving an exclusive right of trade): from French *octroyer* 'to grant,' based on medieval Latin *auctorizare* (see **AUTHORIZE**). The current senses dates from the early 18th cent.

oc·tu·ple /äk'təpəl; -'t(y)ōōpəl/ ▸*adj.* [*attrib.*] consisting of eight parts or things. ■ eight times as many or as much.
▸*v.* make or become eight times as numerous or as large. ▷early 17th cent.: from French *octuple* or Latin *octuplus* (both adjectives), from *octo* 'eight' + *-plus* (as in *duplus* 'double').

oc·tup·let /äk'təplit; -'t(y)ōō-/ ▸*n.* (usu. in pl. **octuplets**) each of eight children born at one birth.

oc·tyl /'äktl/ ▸*n.* [as *adj.*] *Chemistry* of or denoting an alkyl radical $-C_8H_{17}$, derived from octane.

oc·u·lar /'äkyələr/ ▸*adj.* [*attrib.*] *Medicine* of or connected with the eyes or vision: *ocular trauma.*
▸*n.* another term for **EYEPIECE.** ▷late 16th cent.: from late Latin *ocularis*, from Latin *oculus* 'eye.' **—oc·u·lar·ly** *adv.*

oc·u·lar dom·i·nance ▸*n.* the priority of one eye over the other as regards preference of use or acuity of vision.

oc·u·lar·ist /'äkyələrist/ ▸*n.* a person who makes artificial eyes. ▷mid 19th cent.: from French *oculariste*, from late Latin *ocularis* (see **OCULAR**).

oc·u·list /'äkyəlist/ ▸*n. dated* a person who specializes in the medical treatment of diseases or defects of the eye; an ophthalmologist. ■ an optometrist. ▷late 16th cent.: from French *oculiste*, from Latin *oculus* 'eye.'

oculo- ▸*comb. form* relating to the eye or the sense of vision: *oculomotor.* ▷from Latin *oculus* 'eye.'

oc·u·lo·mo·tor /,äkyəlō'mōtər/ ▸*adj.* of or relating to the motion of the eye.

oc·u·lo·mo·tor nerve ▸*n. Anatomy* each of the third pair of cranial nerves, supplying most of the muscles around and within the eyeballs.

oc·u·lus /ˈäkyələs/ ▸*n.* (*pl.* **-li** /-ˌlī; -ˌlē/) *Architecture* a round or eyelike opening or design, in particular: ▪ a circular window. ▪ the central boss of a volute. ▪ an opening at the apex of a dome. ▷mid 19th cent.: from Latin, literally 'eye.'

OD[1] ▸*abbr.* ordnance datum.

OD[2] *informal* ▸*v.* (**OD's, OD'd, OD'ing**) [*intrans.*] take an overdose of a drug: *Spike had OD'd on barbiturates.* ▪ *humorous* have too much of something: *I almost OD'd on mushroom salad.*
▸*n.* an overdose of a narcotic drug.

Od /äd/ ▸*n.* an archaic euphemism for God, used in exclamations: *Od damn it all!*

od /äd/ ▸*n.* *historical* a hypothetical power once thought to pervade nature and account for various phenomena, such as magnetism. ▷mid 19th cent.: arbitrary term coined in German by Baron von Reichenbach (1788–1869), German scientist.

o.d. ▸*abbr.* outer diameter.

o·da·lisque /ˈōdlˌisk/ (also **o·da·lisk**) ▸*n.* *historical* a female slave or concubine in a harem, esp. one in the seraglio of the sultan of Turkey. ▷late 17th cent.: from French, from Turkish *odalik*, from *oda* 'chamber' + *lik* 'function.'

odd /äd/ ▸*adj.* **1** different from what is usual or expected; strange: *the neighbors thought him very odd* | [with *clause*] *it's odd that she didn't recognize me.* **2** (of whole numbers such as 3 and 5) having one left over as a remainder when divided by two. ▪ (of things numbered consecutively) represented or indicated by such a number: *he has come to us every odd year since 1981.* ▪ [*postpositive*] [in *combination*] in the region of or somewhat more than a particular number or quantity: *she looked younger than her fifty-odd years.* **3** [*attrib.*] happening or occurring infrequently and irregularly; occasional: *neither did she want a secret affair, snatching odd moments together.* ▪ spare; unoccupied: *when you've got an odd five minutes, could I have a word?* **4** separated from a usual pair or set and therefore out of place or mismatched: *he's wearing odd socks.* ▷Middle English (sense 2): from Old Norse *odda-*, found in combinations such as *odda-mathr* 'third or odd man,' from *oddi* 'angle.' **—odd·ish** *adj.* (in sense 1). **—odd·ly** *adv.* (in sense 1) [*sentence adverb*] *oddly enough, I didn't feel nervous* | [as *submodifier*] *she felt oddly guilty.* **—odd·ness** *n.*

odd·ball /ˈädˌbôl/ *informal* ▸*n.* a strange or eccentric person.
▸*adj.* strange; bizarre: *oddball training methods.*

Odd Fel·low (also **Odd·fel·low**) ▸*n.* a member of the Independent Order of Odd Fellows, a fraternal and benevolent society. **—Odd·fel·low·ship** *n.*

odd·i·ty /ˈäditē/ ▸*n.* (*pl.* **-ties**) a strange or peculiar person, thing, or trait: *she was regarded as a bit of an oddity.* ▪ the quality of being strange or peculiar: *realizing the oddity of the remark, he retracted it.*

odd job ▸*n.* (usu. **odd jobs**) a casual or isolated piece of work, esp. one of a routine domestic or manual nature. **—odd-job·ber** *n.* **—odd-job·bing** *n.*

odd lot ▸*n.* an incomplete set or random mixture of things. ▪ *Stock Exchange* a transaction involving less than the usual round number of shares.

odd man out /ˌäd ˌman ˈout/ ▸*n.* a person differing from all other members of a particular group or set in some way.

odd·ment /ˈädmənt/ ▸*n.* (usu. **oddments**) a remnant or part of something, typically left over from a larger piece or set: *a quilt made from oddments of silk.*

odd-pin·nate ▸*adj.* *Botany* (of a leaf) pinnate with an odd terminal leaflet.

odds /ädz/ ▸*plural n.* the ratio between the amounts staked by the parties to a bet, based on the expected probability either way: *the bookies are offering odds of 8-1* | *it is possible for the race to be won* **at very long odds.** ▪ (usu. **the odds**) the chances or likelihood of something happening or being the case: ***the odds are that*** *he is no longer alive* | ***the odds against*** *this ever happening are high.* ▪ (usu. **the odds**) superiority in strength, power, or resources; advantage: *she clung to the lead* ***against all the odds*** | ***the odds were*** *overwhelmingly* ***in favor of*** *the banks rather than the customer.* ▷early 16th cent.: apparently the plural of the obsolete noun *odd* 'odd number or odd person.'
▸*PHRASES* □ **at odds** in conflict or at variance: *his behavior is* ***at odds with*** *the interests of the company.* □ **by all odds** certainly; by far. □ **lay** (or **give**) **odds** offer a bet with odds favorable to the other bettor. ▪ *figurative* be very sure about something: *I'd lay odds that the person responsible is an insider.* □ **take odds** offer a bet with odds unfavorable to the other bettor.

odds and ends ▸*plural n.* miscellaneous articles or remnants.

odds·mak·er /ˈädzˌmākər/ ▸*n.* a person who calculates or predicts the outcome of a contest, such as a horse race or an election, and sets betting odds.

odds-on ▸*adj.* (esp. of a horse) rated as most likely to win: *the odds-on favorite.*

odd-toed un·gu·late ▸*n.* a hoofed mammal of an order that includes horses, rhinoceroses, and tapirs. Mammals of this group have either one or three toes on each foot. Compare with **EVEN-TOED UNGULATE.** • Order Perissodactyla: three families.

ode /ōd/ ▸*n.* a lyric poem in the form of an address to a particular subject, often elevated in style or manner and written in varied or irregular meter. ▪ *historical* a poem meant to be sung. ▷late 16th cent.: from French, from late Latin *oda*, from Greek *ōidē*, Attic form of *aoidē* 'song,' from *aeidein* 'sing.' **—od·ic** /ˈōdik/ *adj.*

-ode[1] ▸*comb. form* of the nature of a specified thing: *geode.* ▷from Greek adjectival ending *-ōdēs*.

-ode[2] ▸*comb. form* in names of electrodes, or devices having them: *diode.* ▷from Greek *hodos* 'way.'

O·den·se /ˈōdn-sə; ˈōōd-/ a port in eastern Denmark, on the island of Fyn; pop. 178,000.

O·der /ˈōdər/ a river of central Europe that rises in the mountains in western Czech Republic, flows north through western Poland to meet the Neisse River, and then continues north to form the northern part of the border between Poland and Germany before flowing into the Baltic Sea. Czech and Polish name **ODRA.**

O·des·sa /ōˈdesə/ **1** a city and port on the southern coast of Ukraine, on the Black Sea; pop. 1,106,000. Ukrainian name **ODESA** . **2** a city in southwestern Texas, an oil industry center (with its neighbor Midland) in the Permian Basin; pop. 89,699.

O·dets /ōˈdets/, Clifford (1906–63), U.S. playwright. He was a founding member in 1931 of the avant-garde Group Theater, which staged his well-known play, *Waiting for Lefty* (1935).

o·de·um /ˈōdēəm/ ▸*n.* (*pl.* **o·de·ums** or **o·de·a** /ˈōdēə/) (esp. in ancient Greece or Rome) a building used for musical performances. ▷from French *odéum* or Latin *odeum*, from Greek *ōideion* (see **ODE**).

o·dif·er·ous /ōˈdifərəs/ ▸*adj.* variant spelling of **ODORIFEROUS.**

O·din /ˈōdin/ (also **Wo·den** or **Wo·tan**) *Scandinavian Mythology* the supreme god and creator, god of victory and the dead.Wednesday is named after him.

o·di·ous /ˈōdēəs/ ▸*adj.* extremely unpleasant; repulsive. See note at **OFFENSIVE.** ▷late Middle English: from Old French *odieus*, from Latin *odiosus*, from *odium* 'hatred.' **—o·di·ous·ly** *adv.* **—o·di·ous·ness** *n.*

o·di·um /ˈōdēəm/ ▸*n.* general or widespread hatred or disgust directed toward someone as a result of their actions: *his job had made him the target of public hostility and odium.* ▪ disgrace over something hated or shameful; opprobrium. ▷early 17th cent.: from Latin, 'hatred,' from the verb stem *od-* 'hate.'

o·dom·e·ter /ōˈdämitər/ ▸*n.* an instrument for measuring the distance traveled by a vehicle. ▷late 18th cent.: from French *odomètre*, from Greek *hodos* 'way' + **-METER.**

O·do·na·ta /ˌōdnˈätə; ōˈdänə-/ *Entomology* an order of predatory insects that comprises the dragonflies and damselflies. They have long slender bodies, two pairs of membranous wings, large compound eyes, and aquatic larvae. ▪ [as *plural n.*] (**odonata**) insects of this order; dragonflies and damselflies. ▷modern Latin (plural), formed irregularly from Greek *odōn* (variant of *odous*) 'tooth,' with reference to the insect's mandibles. **—o·do·nate** /ˈōdnət; -ˌāt/ *n.* & *adj.*

O'Don·nell /ōˈdänəl/, Rosie (1962–), U.S. actress and talk show host. She hosted "The Rosie O'Donnell Show" on television from 1995. Her acting credits include the revival of the Broadway musical *Grease* (1994) and the movies *A League of Their Own* (1992) and *Harriet the Spy* (1996).

odonto- ▸*comb. form* relating to a tooth or teeth: *odontology* | *odontophore.* ▷from Greek *odous, odont-* 'tooth.'

o·don·to·blast /ōˈdäntəˌblast/ ▸*n.* *Anatomy* a cell in the pulp of a tooth that produces dentin.

O·don·to·ce·ti /ōˌdäntəˈsētē/ *Zoology* the taxonomic division that comprises the toothed whales. • Suborder Odontoceti, order Cetacea. ▷modern Latin (plural), from Greek *odous, odont-* 'tooth' + *ceti* 'of a whale' (genitive of *cetus*, from Greek *kētos* 'whale'). **—o·don·to·cete** /ōˈdän(t)əˌsēt/ *n.* & *adj.*

o·don·toid /ōˈdäntoid/ (also **odontoid process**) ▸*n.* *Anatomy* a toothlike projection from the second cervical vertebra on which the first vertebra pivots. ▷early 19th cent.: from Greek *odontoeidēs*, from *odous, odont-* 'tooth' + *eidos* 'form.'

o·don·tol·o·gy /ˌōdänˈtäləjē/ ▸*n.* the scientific study of the structure and diseases of teeth. **—o·don·to·log·i·cal** /ōˌdäntlˈäjəkəl/ *adj.* **—o·don·tol·o·gist** /-jist/ *n.*

o·don·to·phore /ōˈdäntəˌfôr/ ▸*n.* *Zoology* a projection in the mouth of most mollusks that supports the radula. **—o·don·toph·o·ral** /ˌōdänˈtäfərəl/ *adj.*

o·dor /ˈōdər/ (*Brit.* **o·dour**) ▸*n.* a distinctive smell, esp. an unpleasant or distinctive one: *the odor of cigarette smoke.* See note at **SMELL.** ▪ *figurative* a lingering quality, impression, or feeling attaching to something: *an odor of suspicion.* ▪ [with *adj.*] *figurative* the state of being held in a specified regard: *a decade of bad odor between Britain and the European Community.* ▷Middle English: from Anglo-Norman French, from Latin *odor* 'smell, scent.' **—o·dor·less** *adj.*
▸*PHRASE* □ **be in good** (or **bad**) **odor with someone** be in or out of favor with someone: *the players were in bad odor with the fans.*

o·dor·ant /ˈōdərənt/ ▸*n.* a substance giving off a smell, esp. one used to give a particular scent or odor to a product. ▷late Middle English (as an adjective in the sense 'odorous'): from Old French, present participle of *odorer*, from Latin *odorare* 'give an odor to.' The current sense dates from the 1940s.

o·dor·if·er·ous /ˌōdəˈrifərəs/ ▸*adj.* having or giving off a smell, esp. an unpleasant or distinctive one: *spicily concocted with odoriferous herbs* | *an odoriferous pile of fish remains.* ▷late Middle English: from Latin *odorifer* 'odor-bearing' + **-OUS.** **—o·dor·if·er·ous·ly** *adv.*

o·dor·ize /ˈōdəˌrīz/ ▸*v.* [*trans.*] give an odor or scent to. ▷late 19th cent.: from Latin *odor* 'odor' + **-IZE.** **—o·dor·iz·er** *n.*

o·dor·ous /ˈōdərəs/ ▸*adj.* having or giving off a smell. ▷late Middle English: from Latin *odorus* 'fragrant' (from *odor* 'odor') + **-OUS.**

o·dour ▸*n.* British spelling of **ODOR.**

O·dra /ˈôdrə/ Polish name for **ODER.**

O·dys·se·us /ōˈdisēəs; ōˈdisyōōs/ *Greek Mythology* the king of Ithaca and central figure of the *Odyssey*, renowned for his cunning and resourcefulness. Roman name **ULYSSES.**

Od·ys·sey /ˈädəsē/ a Greek epic poem traditionally ascribed to Homer, describing the travels of Odysseus during his ten years of wandering after the fall of Troy. He eventually returned home to Ithaca and killed the suitors who had plagued his wife Penelope during his absence. **—Od·ys·se·an** /ädəˈsēən/ *adj.*

od·ys·sey ▸*n.* (*pl.* **-seys**) a long and eventful or adventurous journey: *figurative his odyssey from military man to politician.* ▷late 19th cent.: via Latin from Greek *Odusseia* (see **ODYSSEY**). **—od·ys·se·an** *adj.*

OE ▸*abbr.* Old English.

Oe ▸*abbr.* oersted(s).

Oe·a /ˈēə/ ancient name for **TRIPOLI** (sense 1).

OECD ▸*abbr.* Organization for Economic Cooperation and Development.

OED ▸*abbr.* Oxford English Dictionary.

oe·de·ma ▸*n.* variant British spelling of **EDEMA.**

Oed·i·pus /ˈedəpəs; ˈēdə-/ *Greek Mythology* the son of Jocasta and of Laius, king of Thebes.

> Left to die on a mountain by Laius, who had been told by an oracle that he would be killed by his own son, the infant Oedipus was saved by a shepherd. Returning eventually to Thebes, Oedipus solved the riddle of the sphinx, but unwittingly killed his father and married Jocasta. On discovering what he had done, he put out his own eyes in a fit of madness, and Jocasta hanged herself.

Oed·i·pus com·plex ▸*n.* *Psychoanalysis* (in Freudian theory) the complex of emotions aroused in a young child, typically around the age of four, by an unconscious sexual desire for the parent of the opposite sex and a wish to exclude the parent of the same sex. (The term was originally applied to boys, the equivalent in girls being called the **Electra complex.**) ▷early 20th cent.: by association with **OEDIPUS.** **—Oed·i·pal** /-pəl/ *adj.*

oeil-de-boeuf /ˈoi də ˈbœf/ ▸*n.* (*pl.* **oeils-de-boeuf** *pronunc.* same) *Architecture* a small round window. ▷mid 18th cent.: French, literally 'ox-eye.'

OEM ▸*abbr.* original equipment manufacturer (an organization that makes devices from component parts bought from other organizations).

oe·nol·o·gy ▸*n.* variant spelling of ENOLOGY.

Oe·no·ne /ē'nōnē/ *Greek Mythology* a nymph of Mount Ida and lover of Paris, who deserted her for Helen.

oe·no·phile /'ēnə,fīl/ ▸*n.* a connoisseur of wines. **—oe·noph·i·list** /ē'näfəlist/ *n.*

OEO ▸*abbr.* Office of Economic Opportunity.

o'er /ôr/ ▸*adv.* & *prep.* archaic or poetic/literary contraction for OVER.

Oer·sted /'ərsted; 'œrstiTH/, Hans Christian (1777–1851), Danish physicist. He discovered the magnetic effect of an electric current.

oer·sted /'ər,sted/ (abbr.: **Oe**) ▸*n. Physics* a unit of magnetic field strength equivalent to 79.58 amperes per meter. ▹late 19th cent.: named after H. C. OERSTED.

Oer·ter /ôrtər/, Al(fred) (1936–), U.S. track and field athlete. He held an Olympic record for consecutive medals, winning the discus throw in four Olympic games 1956, 1960, 1964, 1968.

oe·soph·a·gus, etc. ▸*n.* British spelling of ESOPHAGUS, etc.

oes·tra·di·ol ▸*n.* British spelling of ESTRADIOL.

oes·tri·ol ▸*n.* British spelling of ESTRIOL.

oes·tro·gen ▸*n.* British spelling of ESTROGEN.

oes·trone ▸*n.* British spelling of ESTRONE.

oes·trus ▸*n. chiefly Brit.* variant spelling of ESTRUS.

oeu·vre /'œvrə/ ▸*n.* the works of a painter, composer, or author regarded collectively: *the complete oeuvre of Mozart.* ■ a work of art, music, or literature: *an early oeuvre.* ▹late 19th cent.: French, literally 'work.'

OF ▸*abbr.* Old French.

of /əv/ ▸*prep.* **1** expressing the relationship between a part and a whole: *the sleeve of his coat | in the back of the car | the days of the week | a series of programs | a piece of cake | a lot of money.* **2** expressing the relationship between a scale or measure and a value: *an increase of 5 percent | a height of 10 feet.* ■ expressing an age: *a boy of fifteen.* **3** indicating an association between two entities, typically one of belonging: *the son of a friend | the government of India | a photograph of the bride |* [with a *possessive*] *a former colleague of John's.* ■ expressing the relationship between an author, artist, or composer and their works collectively: *the plays of Shakespeare | the paintings of Rembrandt.* **4** expressing the relationship between a direction and a point of reference: *north of Chicago | on the left of the picture.* **5** expressing the relationship between a general category and the thing being specified which belongs to such a category: *the city of Prague | the idea of a just society | the set of all genes.* ■ governed by a noun expressing the fact that a category is vague: *this type of book | the general kind of answer that would satisfy me.* **6** indicating the relationship between a verb and an indirect object: ■ with a verb expressing a mental state: *they must be persuaded of the severity of the problem | I don't know of anything that would be suitable.* ■ expressing a cause: *he died of cancer.* **7** indicating the material or substance constituting something: *the house was built of bricks | walls of stone.* **8** expressing time in relation to the following hour: *it would be just a quarter of three in New York.* ▹Old English, of Germanic origin; related to Dutch *af* and German *ab,* from an Indo-European root shared by Latin *ab* and Greek *apo.*

▸*PHRASES* □ **be of** possess intrinsically; give rise to: *this work is of great interest and value.* □ **of all** denoting the least likely or expected example: *Jordan, of all people, committed a flagrant foul.* □ **of all the nerve** (or *Brit.* **cheek**) an expression of indignation. □ **of an evening** (or **morning,** etc.) *informal* **1** on most evenings (or mornings, etc.). **2** at some time in the evenings (or mornings, etc.).

USAGE It is a mistake to use **of** instead of **have** in constructions such as *you should* **have** *asked* (not *you should* **of** *asked*). For more information, see **usage** at HAVE.

of- ▸*prefix* variant spelling of OB- assimilated before *f* (as in *offend*).

O'Fal·lon /ō'falən/ a city in eastern Missouri, northwest of St. Louis; pop. 46,169.

o·fay /'ō,fā/ ▸*n. informal, offensive* an offensive term for a white person, used by black people. ▹1920s: of unknown origin.

off /ôf; äf/ ▸*adv.* **1** away from the place in question; to or at a distance: *the man ran off | she dashed off to her room | we must be off now.* ■ away from the main route: *turning off for Ripon.* **2** so as to be removed or separated: *he whipped off his coat | a section of the runway had been cordoned off.* ■ absent; away from work: *take a day off | he is off on sick leave.* **3** starting a journey or race; leaving: *the gunmen made off on foot | they're off!* **4** so as to bring to an end or be discontinued: *the Christmas party rounded off a hugely successful year | she broke off her reading to look at her husband.* ■ canceled: *tell them the wedding's off.* ■ *Brit., informal* (of a menu item) temporarily unavailable: *strawberries are off.* **5** (of an electrical appliance or power supply) not functioning or so as to cease to function: *switch the TV off | the electricity was off for four days.* **6** *chiefly Brit.* having access to or possession of material goods or wealth to the extent specified: *we'd been rather* **badly off for** *books | how are you off for money?*

▸*prep.* **1** moving away and often down from: *he rolled off the bed | the coat slipped off his arms | trying to get us off the stage.* **2** situated or leading in a direction away from (a main route or intersection): *single wires leading off the main lines | a backstreet off Olympic Boulevard.* ■ out at sea from (a place on the coast): *anchoring off Blue Bay | six miles off Dunkirk.* **3** so as to be removed or separated from: *threatening to tear it off its hinges | they are knocking $2,000 off the price | figurative it's a huge burden off my shoulders.* ■ absent from: *I took a couple of days off work.* ■ *informal* abstaining from: *he managed to stay off alcohol.*

▸*adj.* **1** [*attrib.*] characterized by someone performing or feeling worse than usual; unsatisfactory or inadequate: *even the greatest athletes have* **off days.** **2** [*predic.*] (of food) no longer fresh: *the fish was a bit off.* **3** [*attrib.*] located on the side of a vehicle that is normally furthest from the curb; offside. Compare with NEAR (sense 4). **4** [*predic.*] *Brit., informal* annoying or unfair: *His boss deducted the money from his pay. That was a bit off.* **5** [*predic.*] *Brit., informal* unwell: *I felt decidedly off.*

▸*n.* (also **off side**) *Cricket* the half of the field (as divided lengthways through the pitch) toward which the batsman's feet are pointed when standing to receive the ball. The opposite of LEG.

▸*v. informal* [*trans.*] kill; murder: *she might off a cop, but she wouldn't shoot her boyfriend.* ▹Old English, originally a variant of OF (which combined the senses of 'of' and 'off').

▸*PHRASE* □ **off and on** intermittently; now and then.

USAGE The use of **off of** to mean **off** (*he took the cup off of the table*) is best avoided.

Off. ▸*abbr.* ■ Office. ■ Officer.

Of·fa /'ôfə; 'äfə/ (died 796), king of Mercia 757–796. He organized the construction of Offa's Dyke, a series of earthworks marking the traditional boundary between England and Wales.

of·fa ▸*prep. informal* off of; off from: *get offa your horse!*

off-air ▸*adj.* & *adv.* **1** not being broadcast: [as *adv.*] *he is exactly the same off-air as he is on.* **2** of or relating to the reception of programs not broadcast by cable or satellite: *an area where off-air reception is poor.*

of·fal /'ôfəl; 'äfəl/ ▸*n.* the entrails and internal organs of an animal used as food. ■ refuse or waste material. ■ decomposing animal flesh. ▹late Middle English (in the sense 'refuse from a process'): probably suggested by Middle Dutch *afval,* from *af* 'off' + *vallen* 'to fall.'

Of·fa·ly /'ôfəlē; 'äf-/ a county in the central part of the Republic of Ireland, in the province of Leinster; county town, Tullamore.

off·beat /'ôf,bēt; 'äf-/ ▸*adj.* **1** *Music* not coinciding with the beat. **2** *informal* unconventional; unusual: *she's a little offbeat but she's a wonderful actress.*

▸*n. Music* any of the normally unaccented beats in a bar.

off-brand ▸*adj.* denoting or relating to an item of retail goods of an unknown, unpopular, or inferior brand.

▸*n.* an unknown, unpopular, or inferior brand.

off-Broad·way (also **Off-Broad·way** or **off Broad·way** or **Off Broad·way**) ▸*adj.* & *adv.* (of a theater, play, or performer) located in, appearing in, or associated with an area of New York City other than the Broadway theater district, typically with reference to experimental and less commercial productions.

▸*n.* such theaters and productions collectively.

off-cam·pus ▸*adj.* & *adv.* away from a university or college campus: *asked to live in an off-campus residence.*

off-cen·ter ▸*adj.* & *adv.* not quite in the center of something. ■ [as *adj.*] strange or eccentric: *people say she's off-center.*

off-col·or (also **off col·or**) ▸*adj.* **1** somewhat indecent or in poor taste: *off-color jokes.* **2** of the wrong or an inferior color: *the new paint doesn't match, it's off-color.* ■ (of a diamond) neither white nor any definite color. **3** *chiefly Brit.* slightly unwell: *I'm feeling a bit off-color.*

off-dry ▸*adj.* (of wine) having a nearly dry flavor, with just a trace of sweetness.

Of·fen·bach /'ôfən,bäk; 'äf-/, Jacques (1819–80), German composer, a resident of France from 1833; born *Jacob Offenbach.* He contributed to the rise of the operetta with such works as *Orpheus in the Underworld* (1858) and *The Tales of Hoffmann* (1881).

of·fence ▸*n.* British spelling of OFFENSE.

of·fend /ə'fend/ ▸*v.* **1** [*trans.*] (often **be offended**) cause to feel upset, annoyed, or resentful: *viewers said they had been offended by bad language.* ■ be displeasing to: *he didn't smoke and the smell of ash offended him |* [as *adj.*] (**offending**) *they must redesign the offending section of road.* **2** [*intrans.*] commit an illegal act: *a small hard core of young criminals who offend again and again.* ■ break a commonly accepted rule or principle: *those activities which* **offend against** *public order and decency.* ▹late Middle English: from Old French *offendre,* from Latin *offendere* 'strike against.' **—of·fend·ed·ly** *adv.* **—of·fend·er** *n.*

of·fense /ə'fens/ (*Brit.* **of·fence**) ▸*n.* **1** a breach of a law or rule; an illegal act: *neither offense violates any federal law.* See note at SIN. ■ a thing that constitutes a violation of what is judged to be right or natural: *the outcome is an* **offense to** *basic justice.* **2** annoyance or resentment brought about by a perceived insult to or disregard for oneself or one's standards or principles: *he went out, making it clear he'd* **taken offense** *| I didn't intend to* **give offense.** **3** /'ôfens; 'äf-/ the action of attacking: [as *adj.*] *reductions in strategic offense arsenals.* ■ (in sports) the team or players who are attempting to score or advance the ball. ■ (in sports) the condition of possessing the ball or being on the team attempting to score. ▹late Middle English: from Old French *offens* 'misdeed,' from Latin *offensus* 'annoyance,' reinforced by French *offense,* from Latin *offensa* 'a striking against, a hurt, or displeasure'; based on Latin *offendere* 'strike against.'

▸*PHRASES* □ **no offense** *informal* do not be offended. □ **take offense** be offended; feel resentment.

of·fen·sive ▸*adj.* **1** /ə'fensiv/ causing someone to feel deeply hurt, upset, or angry: *the allegations made are deeply offensive to us | offensive language.* ■ (of a sight or smell) disgusting; repulsive: *an offensive odor.* **2** /'äfensiv/ [*attrib.*] actively aggressive; attacking: *offensive operations against the insurgents.* ■ (of a weapon) meant for use in attack. ■ (in a game) of or relating to the team or player who is seeking to score.

▸*n.* /ə'fensiv/ an attacking military campaign: *an impending military offensive against the guerrillas.* ■ an organized and forceful campaign to achieve something, typically a political or social end: *the need to* **launch an offensive** *against crime.* ▹mid 16th cent.: from French *offensif, -ive* or medieval Latin *offensivus,* from Latin *offens-* 'struck against,' from the verb *offendere* (see OFFEND). **—of·fen·sive·ly** *adv.* **—of·fen·sive·ness** *n.*

▸*PHRASES* □ **be on the offensive** act or be ready to act aggressively. □ **go on** (or **take**) **the offensive** take the initiative by beginning to attack or act aggressively: *security forces took the offensive ten days ago.*

THE RIGHT WORD **abhorrent, abominable, detestable, odious, offensive, repugnant**

Looking for just the right word to express your dislike, distaste, disgust, or aversion to something? **Offensive** is a relatively mild adjective, used to describe anyone or anything that is unpleasant or disagreeable (*she found his remarks offensive; the offensive sight of garbage piled in the alley*).

If you want to express strong dislike for someone or something that deserves to be disliked, use **detestable** (*a detestable man who never had a kind word for anyone*).

If something is so offensive that it provokes a physical as well as a moral or intellectual response, use **odious** (*the odious treatment of women during the war in Bosnia*), and if you instinctively draw back from it, use **repugnant** (*the very thought of piercing one's nose was repugnant to her*).

If your repugnance is extreme, go one step further and use **abhorrent** (*an abhorrent act that could not go unpunished*).

Persons and things that are truly loathsome or terrifying can be called **abominable** (*an abominable act of desecration; the abominable snowman*), although this word is often used as an overstatement to mean "awful" (*abominable taste in clothes*).

of·fer /ˈôfər; ˈäfər/ ▶*v.* [with *two objs.*] present or proffer (something) for (someone) to accept or reject as so desired: *may I offer you a drink?* ■ [*reporting verb*] express readiness or the intention to do something for or on behalf of someone: [with *infinitive*] *he offered to fix the gate* | [with *direct speech*] *"Can I help you, dear?" a kindly voice offered.* ■ [*trans.*] (usu. **be offered**) make available for sale: *the product is offered at a very competitive price.* ■ [*trans.*] provide (something): *the highway offers easy access to the public beaches.* ■ [*trans.*] present (something, esp. an opportunity) for consideration and possible exploitation: *a good understanding of what a particular career can offer.* ■ [*trans.*] present (a prayer or sacrifice) to a deity: *villagers have gone to offer prayers for the souls of the sailors.* ■ [*trans.*] make an attempt at or show one's readiness for (violence or resistance): *he had to offer some resistance to her tirade.* ■ [*trans.*] *archaic* give an opportunity for (battle) to an enemy: *Darius was about to meet him and to offer battle.*
▶*n.* an expression of readiness to do or give something if desired: [with *infinitive*] *he had accepted Mallory's offer to buy him a drink* | *a job offer.* ■ an amount of money that someone is willing to pay for something: *the prospective purchaser who made the highest offer.* ■ a specially reduced price or terms for something on sale: *the offer runs right up until Christmas Eve.* ■ a proposal of marriage. ▷Old English *offrian* 'sacrifice (something) to a deity,' of Germanic origin, from Latin *offerre* 'bestow, present' (in ecclesiastical Latin 'offer to God'), reinforced by French *offrir* (which continued to express the primary sense). The noun (late Middle English) is from French *offre.* **—of·fer·er** (or **of·fer·or**) *n.*
▶*PHRASES* □ **have something to offer** have something available to be used or appreciated. □ **offer one's hand** extend one's hand to be shaken as a sign of friendship. □ **on offer** available: *the number of permanent jobs on offer is relatively small.* □ **open to offers** willing to sell something or do a job for a reasonable price.

of·fer·ing /ˈôf(ə)riNG; äf-/ ▶*n.* a thing offered, esp. as a gift or contribution: *animals as sacrificial offerings.* ■ a thing produced or manufactured for entertainment or sale: *Hollywood's latest offerings for the European market.* ■ a contribution, esp. of money, to a church. ■ a thing offered as a religious sacrifice or token of devotion.

of·fer·ing price ▶*n.* the price at which a dealer or institution is prepared to sell securities or other assets. Compare with BID PRICE.

of·fer·to·ry /ˈôfərˌtôrē; ˈäfər-/ ▶*n.* (*pl.* **-ries**) *Christian Church* **1** the offering of the bread and wine at the Eucharist. ■ prayers or music accompanying this. **2** an offering or collection of money made at a religious service. ■ prayers or music accompanying this. ▷late Middle English: from ecclesiastical Latin *offertorium* 'offering,' from late Latin *offert-* (which replaced Latin *oblat-*) 'offered,' from the verb *offerre* (see OFFER).

off-gas ▶*n.* a gas that is given off, esp. one emitted as the byproduct of a chemical process.
▶*v.* [*intrans.*] give off a chemical, esp. a harmful one, in the form of a gas.

off-glide ▶*n. Phonetics* a glide produced just following the articulation of another speech sound. Compare with ON-GLIDE.

off·hand /ˈôfˈhand; ˈäf-/ ▶*adj.* (also **off·hand·ed**) ungraciously or offensively nonchalant or cool in manner: *his offhand way of talking.*
▶*adv.* without previous thought or consideration: *I can't think of a better answer offhand.* See note at SPONTANEOUS. **—off·hand·ed·ly** *adv.* **—off·hand·ed·ness** *n.*

off-hours ▶*plural n.* the time when one is not at work; one's leisure time.

of·fice /ˈôfis; ˈäf-/ ▶*n.* **1** a room, set of rooms, or building used as a place for commercial, professional, or bureaucratic work: *computers first appeared in offices in the late 1970s* | [as *adj.*] *an office job.* ■ the local center of a large business: *a company that has four U.S. and four European offices.* ■ a room, department, or building used to provide a particular service: *a ticket office* | *a post office.* ■ the consulting room of a professional person. **2** a position of authority, trust, or service, typically one of a public nature: *the office of attorney general.* ■ tenure of an official position, esp. a government position: *a year ago, when the president* **took office** | *he was ejected from office in 1988.* ■ (**Office**) *Brit.* the quarters, staff, or collective authority of a particular government department or agency: *the Foreign Office.* **3** (usu. **offices**) a service or kindness done for another person or group of people. ■ *dated* a duty attaching to one's position; a task or function: *the offices of a nurse* | *his family had escaped to Canada* **through the good offices of** *a Jewish agency in 1923.* **4** (also **Divine Office**) *Christian Church* the series of services of prayers and psalms said (or chanted) daily by Roman Catholic priests, members of religious orders, and other clergy. ■ one of these services: *the noon office.* ▷Middle English: via Old French from Latin *officium* 'performance of a task' (in medieval Latin also 'office, divine service'), based on *opus* 'work' + *facere* 'do.'

of·fice boy (also **of·fice girl**) ▶*n.* a young man (or woman) employed to do less important jobs in a business office.

of·fice·hold·er /ˈôfisˌhōldər/ ▶*n.* a person who holds public office.

of·fice hours ▶*plural n.* the hours during which business is normally conducted. ■ the hours set by a professional person for office consultation.

of·fice park ▶*n.* an area where a number of office buildings are built together on landscaped grounds.

of·fi·cer /ˈôfisər; ˈäf-/ ▶*n.* **1** a person holding a position of command or authority in the armed services, in the merchant marine, or on a passenger ship. ■ a policeman or policewoman. ■ a bailiff. **2** a holder of a public, civil, or ecclesiastical office: *a probation officer* | *the chief medical officer.* ■ a holder of a post in a society, company, or other organization, esp. one who is involved at a senior level in its management: *a chief executive officer.* **3** a member of a certain grade in some honorary orders.
▶*v.* [*trans.*] provide with military officers: *the aristocracy continued to wield considerable political power, officering the army.* ■ act as the commander of (a unit): *foreign mercenaries were hired to officer new regiments.* ▷Middle English: via Anglo-Norman French from medieval Latin *officiarius*, from Latin *officium* (see OFFICE).

of·fi·cer of arms ▶*n. Heraldry* a heraldic official; a herald or pursuivant.

of·fi·cial /əˈfiSHəl/ ▶*adj.* of or relating to an authority or public body and its duties, actions, and responsibilities: *the governor's official engagements.* ■ having the approval or authorization of such a body: *French is the official language of Quebec.* ■ employed by such a body in a position of authority or trust: *an official spokesman.* ■ emanating from or attributable to a person in office; properly authorized: *official statistics.* ■ *often derogatory* perceived as characteristic of officials and bureaucracy; officious: *he sat up straight and became official.*
▶*n.* a person holding public office or having official duties, esp. as a representative of an organization or government department: *a union official.* ▷Middle English (originally as a noun): via Old French from Latin *officialis*, from *officium* (see OFFICE). **—of·fi·cial·dom** *n.* **—of·fi·cial·ism** *n.* **—of·fi·cial·ize** *v.*

of·fi·cial·ese /əˌfiSHəˈlēz/ ▶*n. informal, often derogatory* the formal and typically verbose style of writing considered to be characteristic of official documents, esp. when it is difficult to understand.

of·fi·cial·ly /əˈfiSHəlē/ ▶*adv.* in a formal and public way: *next month the election campaign will officially begin.* ■ with the authority of the government or some other organization: *it was officially acknowledged that the economy was in recession.* ■ in public and for official purposes but not necessarily so in reality: [*sentence adverb*] *there is a possibility he was murdered—officially, he died in a car crash.*

of·fi·ci·ant /əˈfiSHēənt/ ▶*n.* a person, typically a priest or minister, who performs a religious service or ceremony. ▷mid 19th cent.: from medieval Latin *officiant-* 'performing divine service,' from the verb *officiare.*

of·fi·ci·ate /əˈfiSHēˌāt/ ▶*v.* act as an official in charge of something, as a sporting event: *the first woman to officiate a men's basketball game.* ■ perform a religious service or ceremony: *he baptized children and officiated at weddings.* ▷mid 17th cent.: from medieval Latin *officiare* 'perform divine service,' from *officium* (see OFFICE). **—of·fi·ci·a·tion** /əˌfiSHēˈāSHən/ *n.* **—of·fi·ci·a·tor** /-ˌātər/ *n.*

of·fic·i·nal /əˈfisənl/ ▶*adj. chiefly historical* (of an herb or drug) standardly used in medicine. ▷late 17th cent. (as a noun denoting an officinal medicine): from medieval Latin *officinalis* 'storeroom for medicines,' from Latin *officina* 'workshop.' **—of·fic·i·nal·ly** *adv.*

of·fi·cious /əˈfiSHəs/ ▶*adj.* assertive of authority in an annoyingly domineering way, esp. with regard to petty or trivial matters: *a policeman came to move them on, an officious, spiteful man.* ■ intrusively enthusiastic in offering help or advice; interfering: *an officious bystander.* ▷late 15th cent.: from Latin *officiosus* 'obliging,' from *officium* (see OFFICE). The original sense was 'performing its function, efficacious,' whence 'ready to help or please' (mid 16th cent.), later becoming depreciatory (late 16th cent.). **—of·fi·cious·ly** *adv.* **—of·fi·cious·ness** *n.*

off·ing /ˈôfiNG; ˈäf-/ ▶*n.* the more distant part of the sea in view. ▷early 17th cent.: perhaps from OFF + -ING[1].
▶*PHRASE* □ **in the offing** likely to happen or appear soon: *there are several initiatives in the offing.*

off·ish /ˈôfiSH; ˈäf-/ ▶*adj. informal* aloof or distant in manner; not friendly: *he was being offish with her.* **—off·ish·ly** *adv.* **—off·ish·ness** *n.*

off-is·land ▶*adv.* away from an island.
▶*n.* an island off the shore of a larger or central island.
▶*adj.* located on or coming from such an island. **—off-is·land·er** *n.*

off-key ▶*adj.* & *adv.* (of music or singing) not having the correct tone or pitch; out of tune. ■ not in accordance with what is appropriate or correct in the circumstances: [as *adv.*] *some of the cinematic effects are distractingly off-key.*

off-la·bel ▶*adj.* (of a drug) prescribed in a way or for a condition not covered by the original FDA approval: *this drug has been found useful in several off-label treatments* | [as *adverb*] *children with severe anxiety disorders are given antidepressants off label.*

off-li·cence ▶*n. Brit.* a store selling alcoholic beverages for consumption elsewhere. ■ a license for this.

off-lim·its ▶*adj.* not to be entered or used; out of bounds: *the place was* **off-limits to** *Americans.* ■ not to be mentioned or discussed: *no subject is off-limits.*

off·line /ˈôfˈlīn; ˈäf-/ (also **off-line**) *Computing* ▶*adj.* not controlled by or directly connected to a computer or external network.
▶*adv.* (also **off line**) while not directly controlled by or connected to a computer or external network. ■ with a delay between the production of data and its processing.

off·load /ˈôfˌlōd; ˈäf-/ (also **off-load**) ▶*v.* [*trans.*] unload (a cargo): *men were offloading bags of salt.* ■ rid oneself of (something) by selling or passing it on to someone else: *a dealer offloaded 5,000 of these shares on a client.* ■ relieve oneself of (a problem or worry) by talking to someone else: *it would be nice to have been able to offload your worries onto someone.* ■ *Computing* move (data or a task) from one processor to another in order to free the first processor for other tasks: *a system designed to offload the text on to a host computer.*

off-mes·sage ▶*adj.* departing from an expected or regular theme or issue.

off-off-Broad·way (also **off-off Broad·way** or **Off-Off-Broad·way** or **Off-Off Broad·way**) ▶*adj.* & *adv.* denoting or relating to avant-garde, experimental theatrical productions in New York City taking place in small or informal venues.
▶*n.* theatrical productions of this kind.

off-pat·ent /ˈôf ˈpatnt; ˈäf/ ▶*adj.* & *adv.* no longer subject to patent restrictions.

off-peak ▶*adj.* & *adv.* at a time when demand is less: [as *adj.*] *off-peak travel.*

off-piste ▶*adj.* & *adv. Skiing* away from prepared ski runs: [as *adj.*] *challenging expanses of off-piste skiing.*

off-price ▶*n.* a method of retailing in which brand-name goods (esp. clothing) are sold for less than the usual retail price: [as *adj.*] *an off-price store.*
▶*adv.* using this method: *selling goods off-price.*

off·print /ˈôfˌprint; ˈäf-/ ▶*n.* a printed copy of an article that originally appeared as part of a larger publication.

off-put·ting ▶*adj.* unpleasant, disconcerting, or repellent: *his scar is somewhat off-putting.* **—off-put·ting·ly** *adv.*

off-ramp ▶*n.* a one-way road leading off a main highway.

off rhyme ▶*n.* another term for NEAR RHYME.

off-road ▶*adj.* away from a smooth road; on rough terrain. ■ (of a vehicle or bicycle) designed for use over rough terrain.

off-road·ing ▶*n.* the activity or sport of driving a motor vehicle over rough terrain. **—off-road·er** *n.*

off·scour·ings /ˈôfˌskouriNGz; ˈäf-/ (also **off-scour·ings**) ▶*plural n.* refuse, rubbish, or dregs.

Pronunciation Key ə *ago*; ər *over*; ˈə or ˌə *up*; ˈər or ˌər *fur*; a *hat*; ā *rate*; ä *car*; CH *chew*; e *let*; ē *see*; e(ə)r *air*; i *fit*; ī *by*; i(ə)r *ear*; NG *sing*; ō *go*; ô *for*; oi *boy*; o͝o *good*; o͞o *goo*; ou *out*; SH *she*; TH *thin*; TH *then*; (h)w *why*; ZH *vision*

off-screen (also **off screen** or **off•screen**) ▸*adj.* not appearing on a movie or television screen: *he drawls to an off-screen interrogator.* ■ [*attrib.*] happening in real life rather than fictionally on-screen: *they were off-screen lovers.*
▸*adv.* outside what can be seen on a movie or television screen: *the girl is looking off-screen to the right.* ■ in real life rather than fictionally in a movie or on television: *happy endings rarely happen off-screen.*

off-sea•son (also **off•sea•son** or **off sea•son**) ▸*n.* a time of year when a particular activity, typically a sport, is not engaged in: *during baseball's winter off-season.* ■ a time of year when business in a particular sphere is slack: [as *adj.*] *off-season rates.*
▸*adv.* in or during the off-season: *he never trains off-season.*

off•set ▸*n.* /ˈôfˌset; ˈäf-/ **1** a consideration or amount that diminishes or balances the effect of a contrary one: *an offset against taxable profits.* **2** the amount or distance by which something is out of line: *these wheels have an offset of four inches.* ■ *Surveying* a short distance measured perpendicularly from the main line of measurement. ■ *Electronics* a small deviation or bias in a voltage or current. **3** a side shoot from a plant serving for propagation. ■ a spur in a mountain range. **4** *Architecture* a sloping ledge in a wall or other feature where the thickness of the part above is diminished. **5** a bend in a pipe to carry it past an obstacle. **6** [often as *adj.*] a method of printing in which ink is transferred from a plate or stone to a uniform rubber surface and from that to the paper.
▸*v.* /ôfˈset; ˌäf-/ (**-set•ting**; *past* and *past part.* **-set**) **1** [*trans.*] (often **be offset**) counteract (something) by having an opposing force or effect: *the deficit has been more than offset by capital inflows.* **2** [*trans.*] place out of line: *several places where the ridge was offset at right angles to its length.* **3** [*intrans.*] (of ink or a freshly printed page) transfer an impression to the next leaf or sheet.

off•shoot /ˈôfˌSHo͞ot; ˈäf-/ ▸*n.* a side shoot or branch on a plant. ■ a thing that originated or developed from something else: *commercial offshoots of universities.*

off•shore /ˈôfˈSHôr; ˈäf-/ ▸*adj.* & *adv.* **1** situated at sea some distance from the shore: [as *adj.*] *this huge stretch of coastline is dominated by offshore barrier islands* | [as *adv.*] *we dropped anchor offshore.* ■ (of the wind) blowing toward the sea from the land. ■ of or relating to the business of extracting oil or gas from the seabed: *offshore drilling.* **2** made, situated, or conducting business abroad, esp. in order to take advantage of lower costs or less stringent regulation: [as *adj.*] *deposits in offshore accounts.* ■ of, relating to, or derived from a foreign country: [as *adj.*] *offshore politics.*

off•side /ˈôfˈsīd; ˈäf-/ ▸*adj.* & *adv.* (of a player in certain sports) occupying an illegal position on the field, in particular: ■ *Ice Hockey* moving into the attacking zone ahead of the puck. ■ (usu. **offsides**) *Football* over the scrimmage line or otherwise ahead of the ball before the play has begun. ■ *Soccer* in the attacking half ahead of the ball and having fewer than two defenders nearer the goal line at the moment the ball is played. ■ *Field Hockey* in the attacking half of the field when there are fewer than three defenders nearer the goal line at the moment the ball is played.
▸*n.* the fact or an instance of being offside.

off-speed ▸*adj.* slower than expected.

off•spring /ˈôfˌSPRiNG; ˈäf-/ ▸*n.* (*pl.* same) a person's child or children: *the offspring of middle-class parents.* ■ an animal's young. ■ *figurative* the product or result of something: *German nationalism was the offspring of military ambition.* ▷Old English *ofspring* (see **OFF, SPRING**).

off•stage /ˈôfˈstāj; ˈäf-/ (also **off-stage**) ▸*adj.* & *adv.* (in a theater) not on the stage and so not visible to the audience.

off-the-shoul•der ▸*adj.* (esp. of a dress or blouse) not covering the shoulders.

off-track ▸*adj.* (of betting on a race) situated or taking place away from a racetrack.

off-white ▸*n.* a white color with a gray or yellowish tinge: [as *adj.*] *a frilly off-white blouse.*

off-world ▸*n.* in science fiction, any place away from the earth, or from that world that serves as the location of a given narrative or is regarded in a given context as the native world.
▸*adj.* involving, located in, inhabiting, or coming from, a place outside the native world.
▸*adv.* away from the native world. **—off-world•er** *n.*

off year ▸*n.* **1** a year in which there is no major election, esp. one in which there is a congressional election but no presidential election: [as *adj.*] *November was an off-year election month.* **2** a year that is inferior or substandard compared to previous ones: *it's very difficult to make good wines in off years.*

Of•lag /ˈôfˌläg; ˈäf-/ ▸*n.* *historical* a German prison camp for captured enemy officers. Compare with **STALAG**. ▷German, contraction of *Offizier(s)lager* 'officers' camp.'

OFM ▸*abbr.* Order of Friars Minor (Franciscans). ▷Latin *Ordo Fratrum Minorum.*

oft /ôft; äft/ ▸*adv.* archaic, poetic/literary, or jocular form of **OFTEN**: [in *combination*] *an oft-quoted tenet.* ▷Old English, of Germanic origin; related to German *oft.*

of•ten /ˈôf(t)ən; ˈäf-/ ▸*adv.* (**of•ten•er**, **of•ten•est**) frequently; many times: *he often goes for long walks by himself* | *how often do you have your hair cut?* ■ in many instances: *vocabulary often reflects social standing.* ▷Middle English: extended form of **OFT**, probably influenced by *selden* 'seldom.' Early examples appear to be northern English; the word became general in the 16th cent.
▸*PHRASES* □ **as often as not** quite frequently or commonly: *I had two homes really, because as often as not I was down at her house.* □ **more often than not** usually: *food is scarce and more often than not they go hungry.*

> *USAGE* When pronouncing **often**, some speakers sound the *t*, saying 'off-ten'; for others, it is silent, as in *soften, fasten, listen.* Either pronunciation is acceptable, although 'off-en' is more common.

of•ten•times /ˈôf(t)ənˌtīmz; ˈäf-/ ▸*adv.* often. ▷late Middle English: extended form of **OFTTIMES**, influenced by **OFTEN**.

oft•times /ˈôfˌtīmz; ˈäf(t)-/ ▸*adv.* archaic or poetic/literary form of **OFTEN**.

OG ▸*abbr.* officer of the guard.

O•ga•den /ˌôgəˈden; ˌägə-; ōˈgäden/ (**the Ogaden**) a desert region in southeastern Ethiopia, largely inhabited by Somali nomads. It has been claimed by successive governments of neighboring Somalia.

O•gal•la•la Aq•ui•fer /ˌōgəˈläla/ a vast groundwater resource under eight U.S. states, used esp. for crop irrigation, that stretches from southern South Dakota to western Texas and eastern New Mexico.

og•am /ˈägəm/ ▸*n.* variant spelling of **OGHAM**.

Og•bo•mo•sho /ˌägbəˈmōSHō/ a city and agricultural market in southwestern Nigeria, north of Ibadan; pop. 661,000.

Og•den /ˈägdən/ an industrial city in northern Utah, north of Salt Lake City, site of the U.S. Air Force base; pop. 77,226.

og•do•ad /ˈägdəˌwad/ ▸*n.* *rare* a group or set of eight. ▷early 17th cent.: via late Latin from Greek *ogdoas, ogdoad-*, from *ogdoos* 'eighth,' from *oktō* 'eight.'

o•gee /ōˈjē/ *Architecture* ▸*adj.* having a double continuous S-shaped curve.
▸*n.* an S-shaped line or molding. ▷late Middle English: apparently from **OGIVE** (with which it was originally synonymous). The current sense arose in the late 17th cent. **—o•geed** *adj.*

o•gee arch ▸*n.* *Architecture* an arch with two ogee curves meeting at the apex.

og•ham /ˈägəm/ (also **og•am**) ▸*n.* an ancient British and Irish alphabet, consisting of twenty characters formed by parallel strokes on either side of or across a continuous line. ■ an inscription in this alphabet. ■ each of its characters. ▷early 18th cent.: from Irish *ogam*, connected with *Ogma*, the name of its mythical inventor.

o•give /ōˈjīv/ ▸*n.* **1** *Architecture* a pointed or Gothic arch. ■ one of the diagonal groins or ribs of a vault. ■ a thing having the profile of an ogive, esp. the head of a projectile or the nose cone of a rocket. **2** *Statistics* a cumulative frequency graph. ▷late Middle English: from French, of unknown origin. **—o•gi•val** /ōˈjīvəl/ *adj.*

Og•la•la /ögˈlälə/ (also **Og•a•la•la** /ˌōgəˈlälə/) ▸*n.* (*pl.* same or **-las** or **-las**) a member of the chief division of the Lakota people.
▸*adj.* of or relating to this people. ▷the name in Lakota.

o•gle /ˈōgəl/ ▸*v.* [*trans.*] stare at in a lecherous manner: *he was ogling her breasts* | [*intrans.*] *men who had turned up to ogle.*
▸*n.* a lecherous look. ▷late 17th cent.: probably from Low German or Dutch; compare with Low German *oegeln*, frequentative of *oegen* 'look at.' **—o•gler** /ˈōg(ə)lər/ *n.*

O•gle•thorpe /ˈōgəlˌTHôrp/, James Edward (1696–1785), British soldier and politician. A member of Parliament 1722–54, he received the charter for the colony of Georgia in 1732 and founded Savannah 1733. In 1742, he assured the survival of Georgia by defeating the Spanish at Bloody Marsh.

OGPU /ˈägˌpo͞o/ (also **Ogpu**) an organization for investigating and combating counterrevolutionary activities in the former Soviet Union, existing from 1922 (1922–23 as the GPU) to 1934 and replacing the Cheka. It was absorbed into the NKVD in 1934. ▷acronym from Russian *Ob"edinënnoe gosudarstvennoe politicheskoe upravlenie* 'Unified State Political Directorate.'

o•gre /ˈōgər/ ▸*n.* (in folklore) a man-eating giant. ■ a cruel or terrifying person. ▷early 18th cent.: from French, first used by the French writer Perrault in 1697. **—o•gre•ish** /ˈōg(ə)riSH/ (also **o•grish**) *adj.*

o•gress /ˈōgris/ ▸*n.* a female ogre.

OH ▸*abbr.* Ohio (in official postal use).

oh[1] /ō/ ▸*exclam.* used to express a range of emotions including surprise, anger, disappointment, or joy, or when reacting to something that has just been said: *"Oh no," said Daisy, appalled* | *Me? Oh, I'm fine* | *oh, shut up.* ▷mid 16th cent.: variant of **O**[3].
▸*PHRASES* □ **oh boy** used to express surprise or excitement. □ **oh well** used to express resignation: *oh well, please yourself.* □ **oh yeah?** used to express disbelief. ■ used to express a threatening or taunting reaction.

oh[2] ▸*n.* variant spelling of **O**[1] (sense 2).

O'Ha•ra[1] /ōˈhe(ə)rə; ōˈharə/, Frank (1926–66), U.S. poet and art critic; full name *Francis Russell O'Hara.* His poetry reflects his close ties to the art world in New York City and is collected in volumes such as *A City in Winter* (1952), *Meditations in an Emergency* (1956), and *Lunch Poems* (1964).

O'Ha•ra[2], John (Henry) (1905–70), U.S. writer. He wrote *Butterfield 8* (1935), *Pal Joey* (1940), *Ten North Frederick* (1955), and *Waiting for Winter* (1966).

OHC ▸*abbr.* overhead camshaft.

O'Hig•gins /ōˈhiginz; ôˈēgēns/, Bernardo (*c.*1778–1842), Chilean revolutionary leader and statesman; head of state 1817–23. With the help of José de San Martín, he led the army that defeated Spanish forces in 1817 and paved the way for Chilean independence the following year.

O•hi•o /ōˈhi-ō/ a state in the northeastern U.S., bordering on Lake Erie; pop. 11,353,140; capital, Columbus; statehood, Mar. 1, 1803 (17). It was acquired by Britain from France in 1763 and by the U.S. in 1783 after the American Revolution. **—O•hi•o•an** *adj.* & *n.*

O•hi•o Riv•er a river that flows for 980 miles (1,580 km) from Pittsburgh in Pennsylvania, where it is formed by the Allegheny and Monongahela rivers, through the eastern Midwest to join the Mississippi River at Cairo in Illinois.

Ohm /ōm/, Georg Simon (1789–1854), German physicist. The units ohm and mho are named after him, as is Ohm's law on electricity.

ohm /ōm/ ▸*n.* the SI unit of electrical resistance, expressing the resistance in a circuit transmitting a current of one ampere when subjected to a potential difference of one volt. (Symbol: Ω) ▷mid 19th cent.: named after G. S. **OHM**. **—ohm•ic** /ˈōmik/ *adj.* **—ohm•i•cal•ly** /ōmik(ə)lē/ *adv.*

ohm•me•ter /ˈō(m)ˌmētər/ ▸*n.* an instrument for measuring electrical resistance.

OHMS ▸*abbr.* on Her (or His) Majesty's Service.

Ohm's law *Physics* a law stating that electric current is proportional to voltage and inversely proportional to resistance.

o•ho /ōˈhō/ ▸*exclam.* used to express pleased surprise or recognition. ▷Middle English: from **O**[3] + **HO**[2].

oh-oh ▸*exclam.* another spelling for **UH-OH**.

-oholic ▸*suffix* variant spelling of **-AHOLIC**.

o•hone /äˈKHōn/ ▸*exclam.* variant spelling of **OCHONE**.

oh-so ▸*adv.* [as *submodifier*] *informal* extremely: *their oh-so-ordinary lives.*

OHV ▸*abbr.* overhead valve.

oi /oi/ (also **oy**) ▸*exclam.* *Brit., informal* used to attract someone's attention, esp. in a rough or angry way: *oi, don't lean out!*
▸*n.* a type of harsh, aggressive punk music originally popular in the late 1970s and early 1980s. ▷variant of **HOY**[1] : first recorded in the 1930s.

OIC ▸*abbr.* Organization of the Islamic Conference, a permanent delegation to the United Nations representing the interests of Muslims in several dozen countries.

-oid ▸*suffix* forming adjectives and nouns: **1** *Zoology* denoting an animal belonging to a higher taxon with a name ending in *-oidea*: *hominoid* | *percoid.* **2** denoting form or resemblance: *asteroid* | *rhomboid.* ▷from modern Latin *-oides*, from Greek *-oeidēs*; related to *eidos* 'form.'

-oidal ▸*suffix* forming adjectives corresponding to nouns ending in *-oid* (such as *anthropoidal* corresponding to *anthropoidal*). ▷see **-OID, -AL.**

-oidally ▸*suffix* forming adverbs corresponding to nouns adjectives *-oidal* (such as *adenoidally* corresponding to *adenoidal*). ▷see **-OIDAL, -LY.**

o·id·i·um /ō'idēəm/ ▸*n.* (*pl.* **o·id·i·a** /ō'idēə/) **1** *Botany* a type of fungal spore (conidium) formed by the breaking up of fungal hyphae into cells, esp. as produced by powdery mildews. **2** a fungal disease affecting vines, caused by a powdery mildew. • The fungus is *Uncinula necator* (formerly *Oidium tuckeri*), family Erysiphaceae, subdivision Ascomycotina. ▷mid 19th cent.: modern Latin, from Greek *ōion* 'egg' + the diminutive suffix *-idion.*

oik /oik/ (also **oick**) ▸*n. chiefly Brit., informal* an uncouth or obnoxious person. ▷1930s: of unknown origin.

oil /oil/ ▸*n.* **1** a viscous liquid derived from petroleum, esp. for use as a fuel or lubricant. ■ petroleum. ■ [with *adj.*] any of various thick, viscous, typically flammable liquids that are insoluble in water but soluble in organic solvents and are obtained from animals or plants: *potatoes fried in vegetable oil.* ■ a liquid preparation used on the hair or skin as a cosmetic: *suntan oil.* ■ *Chemistry* any of a group of natural esters of glycerol and various fatty acids that are liquid at room temperature. Compare with **FAT. 2** (often **oils**) oil paint: *a portrait in oils.*
▸*v.* [*trans.*] [often as *adj.*] (**oiled**) lubricate or coat (something) with oil: *a lightly oiled baking tray.* ■ impregnate or treat (something) with oil: *her hair was heavily oiled.* ▷Middle English: from Old Northern French *olie*, Old French *oile*, from Latin *oleum* '(olive) oil'; compare with *olea* 'olive.' **—oil·less** *adj.*
▸*PHRASE* □ **oil and water** *figurative* used to refer to two elements, factors, or people that do not agree or blend together.

oil bar·on ▸*n. derogatory* a magnate in the oil industry.

oil bee·tle ▸*n.* a slow-moving flightless beetle that releases a foul-smelling oily secretion when disturbed. The larvae develop as parasites in the nests of solitary bees. • *Meloe* and other genera, family Meloidae.

oil·bird /'oil,bərd/ ▸*n.* chiefly British term for **GUACHARO.** • *Steatornis caripensis*, the only member of the family Steatornithidae.

oil burn·er ▸*n.* a device, esp. a furnace, in which oil is vaporized and burned to produce heat.

oil cake ▸*n.* a mass of compressed linseed or other plant material left after its oil has been extracted, used as fodder or fertilizer.

oil·can /'oil,kan/ ▸*n.* a can containing lubricating oil, esp. one with a long nozzle.

oil·cloth /'oil,klôTH/ ▸*n.* fabric treated on one side with oil to make it waterproof. ■ a canvas coated with linseed or other oil and used to cover a table or floor.

oil col·or ▸*n.* another term for **OIL PAINT.**

oil drum ▸*n.* a metal drum used for transporting oil.

oiled silk ▸*n.* silk treated on one side with oil to make it waterproof.

oil·er /'oilər/ ▸*n.* **1** a thing that holds or supplies oil, in particular: ■ an oil tanker. ■ an oilcan. ■ a person who oils machinery. ■ *informal* an oil well. **2** (**oilers**) *informal* oilskin garments.

oil field (also **oil·field**) ▸*n.* an area of land or seabed underlain by strata yielding petroleum, esp. in amounts that justify commercial exploitation.

oil-fired ▸*adj.* (esp. of a heating system or power station) using oil as fuel.

oil·fish /'oil,fiSH/ ▸*n.* (*pl.* same or **-fish·es**) a large violet or purple-brown escolar, the flesh of which is oily and unpalatable. • *Ruvettus pretiosus*, family Gempylidae.

oil lamp ▸*n.* a lamp using oil as fuel.

oil·man /'oil,man; -mən/ ▸*n.* (*pl.* **-men**) a man who works in the oil industry, specifically: ■ one who owns or operates oil wells. ■ a high executive in an oil company. ■ one who sells or delivers fuel oil.

oil meal ▸*n.* ground oil cake.

oil of cloves ▸*n.* see **CLOVE**[1] (sense 1).

oil of tur·pen·tine ▸*n.* see **TURPENTINE** (sense 1).

oil of vit·ri·ol ▸*n.* archaic term for **SULFURIC ACID.**

oil paint ▸*n.* a paste made with ground pigment and a drying oil such as linseed oil, used chiefly by artists.

oil paint·ing ▸*n.* the art of painting with oil paints. ■ a picture painted with oil paints.

oil palm ▸*n.* a widely cultivated tropical West African palm tree that is the chief source of palm oil. • *Elaeis guineensis*, family Palmae: several cultivars.

oil pan ▸*n.* the bottom section of the crankcase of an internal combustion engine, serving as the reservoir for its lubricating oil.

oil·pa·per /'oil,pāpər/ (also **oil pa·per**) ▸*n.* paper made transparent or waterproof by treatment with oil.

oil plat·form ▸*n.* a structure designed to stand on the seabed to provide a stable base above water for drilling and servicing oil wells.

oil press ▸*n.* an apparatus for pressing oil from seeds, fruits, etc.

oil rig ▸*n.* a structure with equipment for drilling and servicing an oil well.

oil sand ▸*n.* (often **oil sands**) a deposit of loose sand or partially consolidated sandstone containing petroleum or other hydrocarbons.

oil·seed /'oil,sēd/ ▸*n.* any of several seeds from cultivated crops yielding oil, e.g., rape, peanut, soybean, or cotton.

oil·seed rape ▸*n.* see **RAPE**[2].

oil shale ▸*n.* fine-grained sedimentary rock from which oil can be extracted.

oil·skin /'oil,skin/ ▸*n.* heavy cotton cloth waterproofed with oil. ■ (also **oilskins**) a garment or set of garments made of such cloth.

oil slick ▸*n.* a film or layer of oil floating on an expanse of water, esp. one that has leaked or been discharged from a ship.

oil spot ▸*n.* an oily patch or mark. ■ a silvery marking on brown Chinese porcelain (esp. of the Sung period) caused by precipitation of iron in firing: [as *adj.*] *oil-spot glaze.*

oil·stone /'oil,stōn/ ▸*n.* a fine-grained flat stone used with oil for sharpening cutting edges.

oil tank·er ▸*n.* a ship designed to carry oil in bulk.

oil well ▸*n.* a well or shaft drilled through rock, from which petroleum is drawn.

oil·y /'oilē/ ▸*adj.* (**oil·i·er, oil·i·est**) **1** containing oil: *oily fish such as mackerel and sardines.* ■ covered or soaked with oil: *an oily rag.* ■ resembling oil in appearance or behavior: *the oily swell of the river.* **2** *figurative* (of a person or their behavior) unpleasantly smooth and ingratiating: *his oily smile.* **—oil·i·ness** *n.*

oink /oiNGk/ ▸*n.* the characteristic grunting sound of a pig.
▸*v.* [*intrans.*] make such a sound. ▷1940s: imitative.

oint·ment /'ointmənt/ ▸*n.* a smooth oily preparation that is rubbed on the skin for medicinal purposes or as a cosmetic. ▷Middle English: alteration of Old French *oignement*, from a popular Latin form of Latin *unguentum* (see **UNGUENT**); influenced by obsolete *oint* 'anoint' (from Old French, past participle of *oindre* 'anoint').

Oi·sin another name for **OSSIAN.**

OJ ▸*abbr.* orange juice.

O·jib·wa /ō'jib,wā; -wə/ (also **O·jib·way** /-,wā/) ▸*n.* (*pl.* same or **-was** or **-ways**) **1** a member of a North American Indian people native to the region around Lake Superior. Also called **CHIPPEWA. 2** the Algonquian language of this people.
▸*adj.* of or relating to this people or their language. ▷from Ojibwa *očipwē*, probably meaning 'puckered,' with reference to their style of moccasins.

OK[1] (also **o·kay** /'ō'kā/) *informal* ▸*exclam.* used to express assent, agreement, or acceptance: *OK, I'll pass on your message* | *OK, OK, I give in.* ■ used to introduce an utterance: *"OK, let's go."*
▸*adj.* [*predic.*] satisfactory but not exceptionally or especially good: *the flight was OK.* ■ (of a person) in a satisfactory physical or mental state: *are you OK, Ben?* ■ permissible; allowable: *I'm not sure if it's OK to say that to a teacher.*
▸*adv.* in a satisfactory manner or to a satisfactory extent: *the computer continues to work OK.*
▸*n.* [in *sing.*] an authorization or approval: *do you know how long it takes for those pen-pushers to* **give us the OK**?
▸*v.* (**OK's, OK'd, OK'ing**) [*trans.*] sanction or give approval to: *the governor recently OK'd the execution of a man who had committed murder.* ▷mid 19th cent.: probably an abbreviation of *orl korrect*, humorous form of *all correct*, popularized as a slogan during President Van Buren's reelection campaign of 1840; his nickname *Old Kinderhook* (derived from his birthplace) provided the initials.

OK[2] ▸*abbr.* Oklahoma (in official postal use).

o·ka /'ōkə/ (also **o·ke**) ▸*n.* **1** an Egyptian and former Turkish unit of weight, variable but now usually equal to approximately 1.3 kg ($2^3/_4$ lb). **2** an Egyptian and former Turkish unit of capacity equal to approximately 0.2 liter ($^1/_3$ pint). ▷early 17th cent.: via Italian and French *oque* from Turkish *okka*, from Arabic *ūḳiya*, based on Latin *uncia* 'ounce.'

o·ka·pi /ō'käpē/ ▸*n.* (*pl.* same or **-pis**) a large browsing mammal of the giraffe family that lives in the rain forests of the northern Democratic Republic of the Congo (formerly Zaire). It has a dark chestnut coat with stripes on the hindquarters and upper legs. • *Okapia johnstoni*, family Giraffidae. ▷early 20th cent.: a local word.

O·ka·ra /ō'kärə/ a commercial city in northeastern Pakistan, in Punjab province; pop. 154,000.

O·ka·van·go /,ōkə'väNGgō/ a river in southwestern Africa that rises in central Angola and flows 1,000 miles (1,600 km) south and then east to Namibia, where it turns east to form part of the border between Angola and Namibia before entering Botswana, where it drains into the extensive Okavango marshes. Also called **CUBANGO.**

o·kay /'ō'kā/ ▸*exclam., adj., adv., n., & v.* variant spelling of **OK**[1].

O·ka·ya·ma /,ōkä'yämə/ an industrial city and major railroad junction in southwestern Japan, on the southwestern coast of the island of Honshu; pop. 594,000.

O.K. Cor·ral /'ō'kā kə'ral/ see **TOMBSTONE,** Arizona.

oke[1] ▸*n.* variant spelling of **OKA.**

oke[2] /ōk/ ▸*exclam., adj., adv., n., & v.* another term for **OKAY.**

O·kee·cho·bee, Lake /,ōki'CHōbē/ a lake in southern Florida, part of the Okeechobee Waterway that crosses the Florida peninsula from west to east and links the Gulf of Mexico with the Atlantic Ocean.

O'Keeffe /ō'kēf/, Georgia (1887–1986), U.S. painter. A pioneer of modernism in America, she first produced largely abstract work, adopting a more figurative style in the 1920s. Her best-known paintings depict enlarged studies, particularly of flowers, and are often regarded as being sexually symbolic. She married photographer Alfred Stieglitz in 1924.

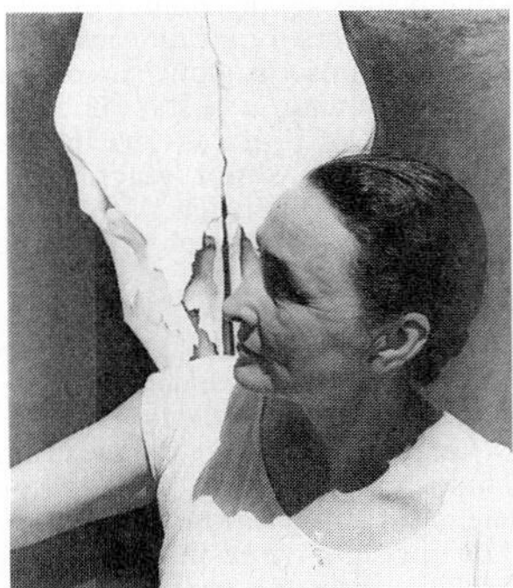

Georgia O'Keeffe

O·ke·fe·no·kee Swamp /,ōkēfə'nōkē/ an area of swampland in southeastern Georgia and northeastern Florida.

o·key-doke /'ōkē 'dōk/ (also **o·key-do·key** /'dōkē/) ▸*exclam., adj., & adv.* variant form of **OK**[1].

O·khotsk, Sea of /ō'kätsk; ə'KHôtsk/ an inlet of the northern Pacific Ocean on the eastern coast of Russia, between the Kamchatka peninsula and the Kurile Islands.

O·kie /'ōkē/ ▸*n.* (*pl.* **O·kies**) *informal* a native or inhabitant of Oklahoma. ■ *historical, derogatory* a migrant agricultural worker from Oklahoma who had been forced to leave during the Depression of the 1930s.

O·ki·na·wa /,ōkə'näwə/ an island in southern Japan, the largest of the Ryukyu Islands; chief town, Naha. An important World War II battle here in 1945 allowed the victorious Allies to establish bases close to the Japanese mainland.

Okla. ▸*abbr.* Oklahoma.

O·kla·ho·ma /,ōklə'hōmə/ a state in the southwestern central U.S., north of Texas; pop. 3,450,654; capital, Oklahoma City; statehood, Nov. 16, 1907 (46). In

1803, most of it was acquired from the French as part of the Louisiana Purchase. **—O·kla·ho·man** *n.* & *adj.*

O·kla·ho·ma Cit·y the capital of Oklahoma, in the central part of the state; pop. 444,719. It expanded rapidly after the discovery of oil in 1928.

o·kou·me /ˌōkəˈmā/ ▸*n.* another term for GABOON.

o·kra /ˈōkrə/ ▸*n.* a plant of the mallow family with long ridged seedpods, native to the Old World tropics. • *Abelmoschus esculentus,* family Malvaceae. ■ the immature seedpods of this plant eaten as a vegetable and also used to thicken soups and stews. Also called GUMBO. ▷early 18th cent.: a West African word, perhaps from the root *nkru;* compare with *nkran,* the name of the town Europeanized as *Accra.*

Ok·to·ber·fest /äkˈtōbərˌfest/ ▸*n.* a traditional autumn festival held in Munich, Germany, every October that features beer-drinking and merrymaking. ■ any similar autumn festival.

-ol ▸*suffix Chemistry* forming names of organic compounds: ■ denoting alcohols and phenols: *glycerol | retinol.* ■ denoting oils and oil-derived compounds: *benzol.* ▷sense 1 from *(alcoh)ol;* sense 2 from Latin *oleum* 'oil.' See also -OLE.

O·laf /ˈōläf/ the name of five kings of Norway: ■ **Olaf I Tryggvason** (969–1000), reigned 995–1000. ■ **Olaf II Haraldsson** (*c.*995–1030), reigned 1016–30; canonized as **St. Olaf** for his attempts to spread Christianity in his kingdom. He is the patron saint of Norway. Feast day, July 29. ■ **Olaf III Haraldsson** (died 1093), reigned 1066–93. ■ **Olaf IV Haakonson** (1370–87), reigned 1380–87. ■ **Olaf V** (1903–91), reigned 1957–91; full name *Olaf Alexander Edmund Christian Frederik.*

O·la·ju·won /əˈlīzhōōˌän/, Hakeem (1963–) U.S. basketball player; born in Nigeria. A center for the Houston Rockets from 1984, he was twice (1994, 1995) named the NBA's most valuable player when his team won the championship title.

Ö·land /ˈəˌländ; ˈœˌländ/ a narrow island in the Baltic Sea, off the southeastern coast of Sweden, separated from the mainland by Kalmar Sound.

O·la·the /ōˈlāTHə/ an industrial city in northeastern Kansas, southwest of Kansas City; pop. 92,962.

Ol·bers' par·a·dox /ˈōlbərz/ *Astronomy* the apparent paradox that if stars are distributed evenly throughout an infinite universe of infinite age, the night sky should display a uniform glow, since every line of sight would terminate at a star. But with an expanding universe of finite age, visible light from very distant stars has not reached the Earth. ▷1950s: named after Heinrich W. M. *Olbers* (1758–1840), the German astronomer who propounded it in 1826.

old /ōld/ ▸*adj.* (**old·er, old·est**) See also ELDER[1], ELDEST. **1** having lived for a long time; no longer young: *the old man lay propped up on cushions.* ■ made or built long ago: *the old quarter of the town.* ■ possessed or used for a long time: *he gave his old clothes away.* ■ having the characteristics or showing the signs of age: *marble now so old that it has turned gray and chipped.* **2** [*attrib.*] belonging only or chiefly to the past; former or previous: *valuation under the old rating system was inexact.* ■ used to refer to the first of two or more similar things: *I was going to try to get my old job back.* ■ dating from far back; long-established or known: *we greet each other like old friends | I get sick of the* **same old** *routine.* ■ (of a form of a language) as used in former or earliest times. **3** [*in combination*] of a specified age: *he was fourteen years old | a seven-month-old baby.* ■ [as *n.*] [*in combination*] a person or animal of the age specified: *a nineteen-year-old.* **4** [*attrib.*] *informal* used to express affection, familiarity, or contempt: *it gets the old adrenaline going | "Good old Mom," she said.* ▷Old English *ald;* related to Dutch *oud* and German *alt,* from an Indo-European root meaning 'grown-up, adult,' shared by Latin *alere* 'nourish.' **—old·ish** *adj.* **—old·ness** *n.*

▸*PHRASES* □ **any old** any item of a specified type (used to show that no particular or special individual is in question): *any old room would have done.* □ **any old way** in no particular order: *they've dropped things just any old way.* □ **as old as the hills** of very long standing or very great age (often used in exaggerated statements). □ **for old times' sake** see SAKE[1]. □ **of old 1** in or belonging to the past: *he was more reticent than of old.* **2** starting long ago; for a long time: *they knew him of old.* □ **the old days** a period in the past, often seen as significantly different from the present, esp. noticeably better or worse: *it was easier in the old days | we are less confident than in* **the good old days** | **the bad old days** *of incoherence and irresponsibility.* □ **old enough to be someone's father** (or **mother**) *informal* of a much greater age than someone (esp. used to suggest that a romantic or sexual relationship between the people concerned is inappropriate).

USAGE Where two, and no more, are involved, they may be **older** and **younger**: *the older of the twins, by ten minutes, is Sam; the younger is Pamela.* Where there are more than two, one may be the **oldest** or **youngest**: *I have four siblings, of whom Jane is the oldest.* See also **usage** at FORMER[1] and LATTER.

THE RIGHT WORD **aged, ancient, antediluvian, antiquated, archaic, obsolete, old**

Almost no one likes to be thought of as **old**, which means having been in existence or use for a relatively long time (*an old washing machine*).

But those who are **aged**, indicating a longer life span than *old* and usually referring to persons of very advanced years, are often proud of the fact that they have outlived most of their peers.

Children may exaggerate and regard their parents as **ancient**, which means dating back to the remote past, often specifically the time before the end of the Roman Empire (*ancient history*), and their attitudes as **antediluvian**, which literally means dating back to the period before the biblical Great Flood and Noah's ark (*an antediluvian transportation system*).

Some people seem older than they really are, simply because their ideas are **antiquated**, which means out of vogue or no longer practiced (*antiquated ideas about dating*).

Things rather than people are usually described as **archaic**, which means having the characteristics of an earlier, sometimes primitive, period (*archaic words like "thou" and "thine"*).

Obsolete also refers to things, implying that they have gone out of use or need to be replaced by something newer (*an obsolete textbook; a machine that will be obsolete within the decade*).

old age ▸*n.* the later part of normal life: *loneliness affects many people* **in old age.** ■ the state of being old: *old age itself is not a disease.*

Old Bai·ley the central criminal court in London, England.

old bean ▸*n.* see BEAN.

Old Be·liev·er ▸*n.* a member of a Russian Orthodox group that refused to accept the liturgical reforms of the patriarch Nikon (1605–81).

old boy ▸*n.* **1** *Brit.* a former male pupil of a school, college, or university. ■ a former male member of a sports team, company, or other organization. **2** *informal* an elderly man. ■ *humorous* an affectionate form of address to a boy or man.

old-boy net·work (also **old boy net·work**) ▸*n.* an informal system of support and friendship through which men use their positions of influence to help others who went to the same school or college as they did or who share a similar social background.

Old Cath·o·lic ▸*n.* a member of any of various religious groups that have separated from the Roman Catholic Church since the Reformation, esp. over the tenets of papal primacy and infallibility. ■ a member of an English family that has remained Roman Catholic since the Reformation.

Old Church Slav·ic (also **Old Church Sla·von·ic**) ▸*n.* the oldest recorded Slavic language, as used by the apostles Cyril and Methodius and surviving in texts from the 9th–12th centuries. It is related particularly to the South Slavic languages. See also CHURCH SLAVIC.

Old Col·o·ny a nickname for the state of MASSACHUSETTS.

old coun·try ▸*n.* (**the old country**) the native country of a person who has gone to live abroad.

Old Del·hi see DELHI.

Old Do·min·ion a nickname for the state of VIRGINIA[1].

olde ▸*adj.* [*attrib.*] pseudoarchaic variant spelling of OLD, intended to be quaint: *Ye Olde Tea Shoppe.*

old·en /ˈōldən/ ▸*adj.* [*attrib.*] *archaic* or *jocular* of or relating to former times: *the olden days.*

Ol·den·burg /ˈōldənˌbərg/, Claes (Thure) (1929–), U.S. pop artist and sculptor; born in Sweden. During the 1960s he conducted "happenings, " participational art events such as *Autobodys* (1964) in which he used actual cars and crowds of people. He later worked with soft materials and foam rubber to create soft sculptures of everyday objects.

Old Eng·lish ▸*n.* the language of the Anglo-Saxons (up to about 1150), a highly inflected language with a largely Germanic vocabulary, very different from modern English. Also called ANGLO-SAXON.

Old Eng·lish sheep·dog ▸*n.* a large sheepdog of a breed with a shaggy blue-gray and white coat.

Old English sheepdog

Old Faith·ful one of the best-known geysers in Yellowstone National Park. Its eruptions occur every 33 to 90 minutes and last about four minutes, sending up a column of hot water and steam that rises 116 to 175 feet (35.4 to 53.4 m).

old-fan·gled /ˈōldˈfaNGgəld/ ▸*adj.* characterized by adherence to what is old; old-fashioned.

old-fash·ioned ▸*adj.* in or according to styles or types no longer current or common; not modern: *an old-fashioned kitchen range.* ■ (of a person or their views) favoring traditional and usually restrictive styles, ideas, or customs: *she's stuffy and old-fashioned.* ▸*n.* a cocktail consisting chiefly of whiskey, bitters, water, and sugar. **—old-fash·ioned·ness** *n.*

Old French ▸*n.* the French language up to *c.*1400.

Old Fri·sian ▸*n.* the Frisian language up to *c.*1400, closely related to both Old English and Old Saxon.

Old Fuss and Feath·ers see SCOTT[6].

old fus·tic ▸*n.* see FUSTIC (sense 2).

Old Glo·ry an informal name for the U.S. national flag.

old gold ▸*n.* a dull brownish-gold color.

old-growth ▸*adj.* (of a tree or forested area) never felled, harvested, or cleared; mature: *old-growth forests.*

old guard (also **Old Guard**) ▸*n.* (usu. **the old guard**) the original or long-standing members of a group or party, esp. ones who are unwilling to accept change or new ideas: *the aging right-wing old guard.* **—old guard·ism** *n.* **—old guards·man** *n.* (*pl.* **-men**)

old hand ▸*n.* a person with a lot of experience in something: *he was an* **old hand at** *red-tape cutting.*

old hat ▸*n. informal* used to refer to something considered uninteresting, predictable, tritely familiar, or old-fashioned.

Old High Ger·man ▸*n.* the language of southern Germany up to *c.*1200, from which modern standard German is derived. See GERMAN.

Old Ice·lan·dic ▸*n.* the Icelandic language up to the 16th century, a form of Old Norse in which medieval sagas were composed.

old·ie /ˈōldē/ ▸*n. informal* an old song, film, or television program that is still well known or popular.

Old I·rish ▸*n.* the Irish Gaelic language up to *c.*1000, from which modern Irish and Scottish Gaelic are derived.

Old I·ron Pants see LE MAY.

Old I·ron·sides nickname for the frigate *Constitution,* the oldest commissioned vessel in the U.S. Navy. Launched in 1797, it defeated four British frigates in the War of 1812 and is permanently berthed at the Boston Navy Yard. ▷early 19th cent.: conferred by her crew when, during her first battle with the British vessel *Guerrière,* the cannon balls glanced off her thick oak hull.

old la·dy ▸*n. informal, often derogatory* one's mother, wife, or girlfriend.

Old Lat·in ▸*n.* Latin before about 100 BC.

old-line ▸*adj.* **1** holding conservative views. **2** well established. **—old-lin·er** *n.*

Old Line State a nickname for the state of MARYLAND.

Old Low Ger·man ▸*n.* the language of northern Germany and the Netherlands up to *c.*1200, from which modern Dutch and modern Low German are derived.

old maid ▸*n.* **1** *derogatory* a single woman regarded as too old for marriage. ■ a prim and fussy person: *he said James was an old maid.* **2** a card game in which players collect pairs and try not to be left with an odd penalty card, typically a black queen. —**old·maid·ish** *adj.*

old man ▶*n.* **1** *informal, often derogatory* one's father, husband, or boyfriend. ■ (**the old man**) a man in authority over others, esp. an employer or commanding officer: *the old man wants a progress report.* ■ used with a surname instead of "Mr.": *old man Roberts.* **2** another term for SOUTHERNWOOD.

old man's beard ▶*n.* **1** a wild clematis that has fluffy gray hairs around the seeds. • Genus *Clematis*, family Ranunculaceae: several species, in particular traveler's joy and virgin's bower. **2** a large lichen that forms shaggy grayish beardlike growths on the branches of trees. • *Usnea barbata* and related species, order Parmeliales.

old mas·ter ▶*n.* a great artist of former times, esp. of the 13th–17th century in Europe. ■ a painting by such a painter: *he formed a large collection of old masters.*

old mon·ey ▶*n.* established, inherited wealth. ■ those whose families have been wealthy for many generations: *the list of Canada's wealthiest people, once dominated by old money, is no longer so exclusive.*

old moon ▶*n.* the moon in its last quarter, before the new moon.

Old Nick /nik/ an informal name for the Devil. ▷mid 17th cent.: probably from a nickname for the given name *Nicholas.*

Old Norse ▶*n.* the North Germanic (Scandinavian) language of medieval Norway, Iceland, Denmark, and Sweden up to the 14th century, from which the modern Scandinavian languages are derived. See also OLD ICELANDIC.

Old North Church an Episcopal church, still active, built in 1723 in the Georgian style in Boston's North End. On April 18, 1775, Robert Newman, the sexton of the church, hung two lanterns from the church steeple, warning Paul Revere that British regulars were moving up the Charles River toward Cambridge to begin their march on Lexington. Revere then rode from Charlestown to Lexington to alert the militia that the British were coming.

Old North Church

Old North State a nickname for the state of NORTH CAROLINA.

Ol·do·wan /ˈōldəwən; ˈōl-/ ▶*adj. Archaeology* of, relating to, or denoting an early Lower Paleolithic culture of Africa, dated to about 2.0–1.5 million years ago. It is characterized by primitive stone tools that are associated chiefly with *Homo habilis.* ■ [as *n.*] (**the Oldowan**) the Oldowan culture or period. ▷1930s: from *Oldoway*, alteration of OLDUVAI GORGE, Tanzania, + -AN.

Old Per·sian ▶*n.* the Persian language up to the 3rd century BC, used in the ancient Persian empire and written in cuneiform.

Old Pre·tend·er see STUART[2].

Old Prus·sian ▶*n.* a Baltic language, related to Lithuanian, spoken in Prussia until the 17th century.

old re·li·gion ▶*n.* a religion that has been supplanted by another, in particular: ■ paganism. ■ witchcraft. ■ Roman Catholicism.

old rose ▶*n.* **1** a double-flowered rose of a variety or hybrid evolved before the development of the hybrid tea rose. **2** a shade of grayish or purplish pink. ▶*adj.* (usu. **old-rose**) of this shade of pink.

Old Sax·on ▶*n.* **1** a member of the Saxon peoples who remained in Germany, as opposed to an Anglo-Saxon. **2** the dialect of Old Low German spoken in Saxony up to *c.*1200. ▶*adj.* of or relating to the Old Saxons or their language.

old school ▶*n.* (often **of/from the old school**) used, usually approvingly, to refer to someone or something that is old-fashioned or traditional: *amenities that my parents, being of the old school, still take for granted.*

old school tie ▶*n. chiefly Brit.* a necktie with a characteristic pattern worn by the former students of an exclusive English public school. ■ used to refer to the group loyalty, mutual assistance, social class, and traditional attitudes associated with people who attended such schools: *appointments based on social class and the old school tie.*

Old Slav·ic (also **Old Sla·von·ic**) ▶*n.* another name for CHURCH SLAVIC.

Old South ▶*n.* (**the Old South**) the Southern States of the U.S. before the Civil War (1861–65).

old·squaw /ˈōldˌskwô/ (also **old squaw** or **old squaw duck**) ▶*n.* a marine diving duck that breeds in Arctic Eurasia and North America, the male having very long tail feathers and mainly white plumage in winter. • *Clangula hyemalis*, family Anatidae.

old stag·er ▶*n.* a person who is experienced at something or who has been in a place or position for a long time: *the changes aroused the suspicions of the old stagers.*

old·ster /ˈōl(d)stər/ ▶*n. informal* an older person. ▷early 19th cent.: from OLD, on the pattern of *youngster.*

Old Stone Age the Paleolithic period.

Old Style (abbr.: **OS**) ▶*n.* [often as *adj.*] the method of calculating dates using the Julian calendar.

old style ▶*n.* a style that is no longer current, common, or fashionable: *the old style of gabled manor.* ■ *Printing* an early style of type characterized by strokes of relatively equal thickness and the use of serifs, often slanted.
▶*adj.* [*attrib.*] denoting or according to such a style: *old-style socialists | urban centers of old-style manufacturing.*

Old Tes·ta·ment ▶*n.* the first part of the Christian Bible, comprising thirty-nine books and corresponding approximately to the Hebrew Bible. Most of the books were originally written in Hebrew, some in Aramaic, between about 1200 and 100 BC. They comprise the chief texts of the law, history, prophecy, and wisdom literature of the ancient people of Israel.

old-time ▶*adj.* [*attrib.*] used to refer to something old-fashioned in an approving or nostalgic way: *old-time dancing.* ■ denoting traditional or folk styles of American popular music, such as gospel or bluegrass.
▶*PHRASE* □ **for old times' sake** see SAKE[1].

old-tim·er ▶*n. informal* a person who has had the same job, membership, or residence, etc., for a long time. ■ *derogatory* an old person.

Ol·du·vai Gorge /ˈôldəˌvī; -ˌwā; -ˌvā/ a gorge in northern Tanzania, 30 miles (48 km) long and up to 300 feet (90 m) deep. The exposed strata contain numerous fossils (esp. hominids) spanning the full range of the Pleistocene period.

Old Vic /ˈvik/ the popular name of the Royal Victoria Theatre in London. Under the management of Lilian Baylis from 1912, it gained an enduring reputation for its Shakespearean productions.

Old Welsh ▶*n.* the Welsh language up to *c.*1150.

old·wife /ˈōldˌwīf/ ▶*n.* **1** any of a number of deep-bodied edible marine fishes, in particular: • a brightly patterned tropical Atlantic triggerfish (*Balistes vetula*, family Balistidae). • a small brightly patterned Australian fish (*Enoplosus armatus*, the only member of the family Enoplosidae). • the black sea bream of European Atlantic waters (*Spondyliosoma cantharus*, family Sparidae). **2** another term for OLDSQUAW.

old wives' tale ▶*n.* a superstition or traditional belief that is regarded as unscientific or incorrect.

old wom·an ▶*n.* **1** *informal, often derogatory* one's mother, wife, or girlfriend. **2** *derogatory* a fussy or timid person, esp. a man: *he's always telling me I'm an old woman about security.* —**old-wom·an·ish** *adj.* (in sense 2).

Old World Europe, Asia, and Africa, regarded collectively as the part of the world known before the discovery of the Americas. Compare with NEW WORLD.

old-world (also **old world**; **Old World**) ▶*adj.* belonging to or associated with former times, esp. when considered quaint and attractive: *medieval towns that still retain old-world charm.* ■ characteristic of the Old World: *transplanting Old World memories into New World soil.*

OLE *Computing* ▶*abbr.* object linking and embedding, denoting a set of techniques for transferring an object from one application to another.

ole /ōl/ ▶*adj. informal* or *humorous* old: *that ole truck of my daddy's.* ▷mid 19th cent.: representing a folk pronunciation.

o·lé /ōˈlā/ ▶*exclam.* a cry of approval, joy, etc. ▷Spanish, a cry used at bullfights.

-ole ▶*comb. form* in names of organic compounds, esp. heterocyclic compounds: *thiazole.* ▷from Latin *oleum* 'oil' (compare with -OL).

o·le·ag·i·nous /ˌōlēˈajənəs/ ▶*adj.* rich in, covered with, or producing oil; oily or greasy. ■ *figurative* exaggeratedly and distastefully complimentary; obsequious: *candidates made the usual oleaginous speeches in the debate.* ▷late Middle English: from French *oléagineux*, from Latin *oleaginus* 'of the olive tree,' from *oleum* 'oil.'

o·le·an·der /ˈōlēˌandər/ ▶*n.* a poisonous evergreen Old World shrub that is widely grown in warm countries for its clusters of white, pink, or red flowers. • *Nerium oleander*, family Apocynaceae. ▷early 16th cent.: from medieval Latin, of unknown ultimate origin.

o·le·as·ter /ˌōlēˈastər/ ▶*n.* a Eurasian shrub or small tree that is often cultivated as an ornamental. • Genus *Elaeagnus*, family Elaeagnaceae: several species, in particular *E. angustifolia*, commonly called **Russian olive**, which bears edible yellow olive-shaped fruit. ▷late Middle English: from Latin, from *olea* 'olive tree.'

o·lec·ra·non /ōˈlekrəˌnän; ˌōləˈkrā-/ ▶*n. Anatomy* the bony prominence of the elbow, on the upper end of the ulna. ▷early 18th cent.: from Greek *ōle(no)kranon*, from *ōlenē* 'elbow' + *kranion* 'head.'

o·le·fin /ˈōləfin/ (also **o·le·fine**) ▶*n. Chemistry* another term for ALKENE. ▷mid 19th cent.: from French *oléfiant* 'oil-forming' (with reference to oily ethylene dichloride). —**o·le·fin·ic** /ˌōləˈfinik/ *adj.*

o·le·ic ac·id /ōˈlē-ik/ ▶*n. Chemistry* an unsaturated fatty acid present in many fats and soaps. • Chem. formula: $CH_3(CH_2)_7CH{=}CH(CH_2)_7COOH$. ▷early 19th cent.: *oleic* from Latin *oleum* 'oil.' —**o·le·ate** /ˈōlēˌāt/ *n.*

o·le·if·er·ous /ˌōlēˈifərəs/ ▶*adj. Botany* (of seeds, glands, etc.) producing oil. ▷early 19th cent.: from Latin *oleum* 'oil' + -FEROUS.

o·le·o /ˈōlēō/ ▶*n.* another term for MARGARINE.

oleo- ▶*comb. form* relating to or containing oil: *oleomargarine | oleoresin.* ▷from Latin *oleum* 'oil.'

o·le·o·chem·i·cal /ˌōlēōˈkemikəl/, ▶*n.* a chemical compound derived industrially from animal or vegetable oils or fats.

o·le·o·graph /ˈōlēəˌgraf/ ▶*n.* a lithographic print textured to resemble an oil painting. —**o·le·o·graph·ic** /ˌōlēəˈgrafik/ *adj.* —**o·le·og·ra·phy** /ˌōlēˈägrəfē/ *n.*

o·le·o·mar·ga·rine /ˌōlēōˈmärj(ə)rən/ ▶*n.* another term for MARGARINE.

o·le·o·res·in /ˌōlē-ōˈrezən/ ▶*n.* a natural or artificial mixture of essential oils and a resin, e.g., balsam. —**o·le·o·res·in·ous** /-nəs/ *adj.*

O·les·tra /ōˈlestrə/ (also **o·les·tra**) ▶*n. trademark* a synthetic cooking oil used as a calorie-free fat substitute in various foods. ▷1980s: from *(p)ol(y)est(e)r* + the suffix *-a.*

o·le·um /ˈōlēəm/ ▶*n.* a dense, corrosive liquid consisting of concentrated sulfuric acid containing excess sulfur trioxide in solution. ▷early 20th cent.: from Latin, literally 'oil.'

O lev·el ▶*n. historical* (in the UK except Scotland) the lower of the two main levels of standardized examinations in secondary schools. Compare with A LEVEL. ▷short for *ordinary level.*

ol·fac·tion /älˈfakshən; ōl-/ ▶*n. technical* the action or capacity of smelling; the sense of smell. ▷mid 19th cent.: from Latin *olfactus* 'a smell' (from *olere* 'to smell' + *fact-* 'made,' from the verb *facere*) + -ION. —**ol·fac·tive** /-tiv/ *adj.*

ol·fac·tom·e·ter /ˌälfakˈtämitər; ˌōl-/ ▶*n.* an instrument for measuring the intensity of an odor or sensitivity to odor. —**ol·fac·tom·e·try** /-ˈtämitrē/ *n.*

ol·fac·to·ry /älˈfakt(ə)rē; ōl-/ ▶*adj.* of or relating to the sense of smell: *the olfactory organs.* ▷mid 17th cent.:

from Latin *olfactare* (frequentative of *olfacere* 'to smell') + **-ORY**[2].

ol·fac·to·ry nerve ▸*n. Anatomy* each of the first pair of cranial nerves, transmitting impulses to the brain from the smell receptors in the mucous membrane of the nose.

o·lib·a·num /ō'libənəm/ ▸*n.* another term for **FRANKINCENSE.** ▷late Middle English: from medieval Latin, from late Latin *libanus,* from Greek *libanos* 'frankincense.'

ol·i·garch /'äli,gärk; 'ōl-/ ▸*n.* a ruler in an oligarchy. ▷late 19th cent.: from Greek *oligarkhēs,* from *oligoi* 'few' + *arkhein* 'to rule.'

ol·i·gar·chy /'äli,gärkē; 'ōli-/ ▸*n.* (*pl.* **-chies**) a small group of people having control of a country, organization, or institution: *the ruling oligarchy of military men around the president.* ■ a state governed by such a group: *the English aristocratic oligarchy of the 19th century.* ■ government by such a group. ▷late 15th cent.: from Greek *oligarkhia* (probably via medieval Latin). **—ol·i·gar·chic** /,äli'gärkik; ,ōli-/ *adj.* **—ol·i·gar·chi·cal** /,äli'gärkikəl; ,ōli-/ *adj.* **—ol·i·gar·chi·cal·ly** /,äli'gärkik(ə)lē; ,ōli-/ *adv.*

USAGE See usage at **ARISTOCRACY.**

ol·i·go /'äligō/ ▸*n.* (*pl.* **-gos**) *Biochemistry* short for **OLIGONUCLEOTIDE.**

oligo- ▸*comb. form* having few; containing a relatively small number of units: *oligopoly* | *oligosaccharide.* ▷from Greek *oligos* 'small,' *oligoi* 'few.'

Ol·i·go·cene /'äligō,sēn/ ▸*adj. Geology* of, relating to, or denoting the third epoch of the Tertiary period, between the Eocene and Miocene epochs. ■ [as *n.*] (**the Oligocene**) the Oligocene epoch or the system of rocks deposited during it.

The Oligocene epoch lasted from 35.4 million to 23.3 million years ago. It was a time of falling temperatures, with evidence of the first primates.

▷mid 19th cent.: from **OLIGO-** 'few' + Greek *kainos* 'new.'

Ol·i·go·chae·ta /,äligō'kētə/ *Zoology* a class of annelid worms that includes the earthworms. They have simple setae projecting from each segment and a small head lacking sensory appendages. ▷modern Latin (plural), from **OLIGO-** 'few' + Greek *khaitē* 'long hair' (taken to mean 'bristle'), because they have fewer setae than polychaetes. **—ol·i·go·chaete** /'äligō,kēt/ *n.*

ol·i·go·clase /'äligō,klās/ ▸*n.* a feldspar mineral common in siliceous igneous rocks, consisting of a sodium-rich plagioclase (with more calcium than albite). ▷mid 19th cent.: from **OLIGO-** 'relatively little' + Greek *klasis* 'breaking' (because thought to have a less perfect cleavage than albite).

ol·i·go·den·dro·cyte /,äligō'dendrə,sīt/ ▸*n. Anatomy* a glial cell similar to an astrocyte but with fewer protuberances, concerned with the production of myelin in the central nervous system. ▷1930s: from **OLIGODENDROGLIA** + **-CYTE.**

ol·i·go·den·drog·li·a /,äligōden'dräglēə/ ▸*plural n. Anatomy* oligodendrocytes collectively. ▷1920s: from **OLIGO-** 'few' + **DENDRO-** 'branching' + a shortened form of **NEUROGLIA. —ol·i·go·den·drog·li·al** *adj.*

o·lig·o·mer /ə'ligəmər/ ▸*n. Chemistry* a polymer whose molecules consist of relatively few repeating units. **—o·lig·o·mer·ic** /ə,ligə'merik/ *adj.*

ol·i·go·nu·cle·o·tide /,äligō'n(y)ōōklēə,tīd/ ▸*n. Biochemistry* a polynucleotide whose molecules contain a relatively small number of nucleotides.

ol·i·go·pep·tide /,äligō'pep,tīd/ ▸*n. Biochemistry* a peptide whose molecules contain a relatively small number of amino-acid residues.

ol·i·gop·o·ly /,äli'gäpəlē/ ▸*n.* (*pl.* **-lies**) a state of limited competition, in which a market is shared by a small number of producers or sellers. ▷late 19th cent.: from **OLIGO-** 'small number,' on the pattern of *monopoly.* **—ol·i·gop·o·list** /-list/ *n.* **—ol·i·gop·o·lis·tic** /,äli,gäpə'listik/ *adj.*

ol·i·gop·so·ny /,äli'gäpsənē/ ▸*n.* (*pl.* **-nies**) a state of the market in which only a small number of buyers exists for a product. ▷1940s: from **OLIGO-** 'small number' + Greek *opsōnein* 'buy provisions,' on the pattern of *monopsony.* **—ol·i·gop·so·nis·tic** /,äli,gäpsə'nistik/ *adj.*

ol·i·go·sac·cha·ride /,äligō'sakə,rīd/ ▸*n. Biochemistry* a carbohydrate whose molecules are composed of a relatively small number of monosaccharide units.

ol·i·go·troph·ic /,äligō'trōfik; -'träfik/ ▸*adj. Ecology* (esp. of a lake) relatively low in plant nutrients and containing abundant oxygen in the deeper parts. Compare with **DYSTROPHIC, EUTROPHIC. —ol·i·got·ro·phy** /,äli'gätrəfē/ *n.*

ol·i·gu·ri·a /,äli'gyōōrēə/ ▸*n. Medicine* the production of abnormally small amounts of urine. **—ol·igu·ric** /-rik/ *adj.*

o·lin·go /ō'liNGō/ ▸*n.* (*pl.* **-gos**) a small nocturnal mammal related to the kinkajou and the raccoon, living in tropical Central and South American rain forests. • Genus *Bassaricyon,* family Procyonidae: between one and five species. ▷1920s: via American Spanish from Mayan.

o·li·o /'ōlēō/ ▸*n.* (*pl.* **-os**) another term for **OLLA PODRIDA.** ■ a miscellaneous collection of things. ■ a variety act or show. ▷mid 17th cent.: from Spanish *olla* 'stew,' from Latin *olla* 'cooking pot.'

ol·i·va·ceous /,älə'vāsHəs/ ▸*adj. technical* of a dusky yellowish green color; olive green.

ol·i·va·ry /'älə,verē/ ▸*adj. Anatomy* relating to or denoting each of the pair of oval bodies of nerve tissue on the medulla oblongata of the brain. ▷late Middle English: from Latin *olivarius* 'relating to olives,' from *oliva* (see **OLIVE**).

ol·ive /'äliv/ ▸*n.* **1** a small oval fruit with a hard pit and bitter flesh, green when unripe and brownish black when ripe, used as food and as a source of oil. **2** (also **olive tree**) the widely cultivated evergreen tree that yields this fruit, native to warm regions of the Old World. • *Olea europaea,* family Oleaceae (the **olive family**). This family also includes the ash, lilac, jasmine, and privet. ■ used in names of other trees that are related to the olive, resemble it, or bear similar fruit, e.g., **Russian olive. 3** (also **olive green**) a grayish-green color like that of an unripe olive. **4** a metal ring or fitting that is tightened under a threaded nut to form a seal, as in a compression joint. **5** (also **olive shell**) a marine mollusk with a smooth, roughly cylindrical shell that is typically brightly colored. • Genus *Oliva,* family Olividae, class Gastropoda.
▸*adj.* grayish-green, like an unripe olive: *a small figure in olive fatigues.* ■ (of the complexion) yellowish brown; sallow. ▷Middle English: via Old French from Latin *oliva,* from Greek *elaia,* from *elaion* 'oil.'

Ol·ive Branch a city in northern Mississippi, just south of the Tennessee border; pop. 21,054.

ol·ive branch ▸*n.* the branch of an olive tree, traditionally regarded as a symbol of peace (in allusion to the story of Noah in Gen. 8:1, in which a dove returns with an olive branch after the Flood). ■ an offer of reconciliation: *the government is* ***holding out an olive branch to*** *the demonstrators.*

ol·ive drab ▸*n.* a dull olive-green color, used in some military uniforms.

ol·ive oil ▸*n.* an oil pressed from ripe olives, used in cooking, medicines, soap, etc.

Ol·i·ver /'äləvər/ the companion of Roland in the *Chanson de Roland* (see **ROLAND**).

O·liv·i·er /ə'livēā; ō'livi-/, Laurence (Kerr), Baron Olivier of Brighton (1907–89), English actor and director. Following his professional debut in 1924, he performed all the major Shakespearean roles; he was also director of the National Theatre (1963–73). His movies include *Wuthering Heights* (1939), *Rebecca* (1940), *Pride and Prejudice* (1940), *Henry V* (1944), and *Hamlet* (1948).

ol·i·vine /'älə,vēn/ ▸*n.* an olive-green, gray-green, or brown mineral occurring widely in basalt, peridotite, and other basic igneous rocks. It is a silicate containing varying proportions of magnesium, iron, and other elements. ▷late 18th cent.: from Latin *oliva* (see **OLIVE**) + **-INE**[1].

ol·la po·dri·da /,älə pə'drēdə; ,ô(l)yə/ ▸*n.* a highly spiced Spanish-style stew containing a mixture of meat and vegetables. ■ any miscellaneous assortment or collection: *an olla podrida of romance, comedy, and tragedy.* ▷Spanish, literally 'rotten pot,' from Latin *olla* 'jar' + *putridus* 'rotten.'

ol·lie /älē/ ▸*n.* (*pl.* **-lies**) (in skateboarding and snowboarding) a jump performed without the aid of a takeoff ramp, executed by pushing the back foot down on the tail of the board, bringing the board off the ground.
▸*v.* (**-lie·ing**) [*intrans.*] perform such a jump. ▷1980s: of unknown origin.

Ol·mec /'äl,mek; 'ōl-/ ▸*n.* (*pl.* same or **-mecs**) **1** a member of a prehistoric people inhabiting the coast of Veracruz and western Tabasco on the Gulf of Mexico (*c.*1200–400 BC), who established what was probably the first Meso-American civilization. **2** a native people living in the same general area during the 15th and 16th centuries. ▷from Nahuatl *Olmecatl,* (plural) *Olmeca,* literally 'inhabitants of the rubber country.'

Olm·sted /'ōm,sted/, Frederick Law (1822–1903) U.S. landscape architect. He designed Central Park in New York City, Fairmount Park in Philadelphia, and the Capitol grounds in Washington, D.C.

ol·o·gy /'äləjē/ ▸*n.* (*pl.* **-gies**) *informal, humorous* a subject of study; a branch of knowledge. **—ol·o·gist** /-jist/ *n.*

-ology ▸*comb. form* common form of **-LOGY.**

O·lo·mouc /'ôlômōts/ an industrial city in the Czech Republic, on the Morava River, in northern Moravia; pop. 106,000.

o·lo·ro·so /,ōlə'rōsō/ ▸*n.* a dry or medium-dry Spanish sherry. ▷Spanish, literally 'fragrant.'

Olsz·tyn /'ôlsHtin/ a city in northern Poland, in the Masuria region; pop. 164,000. Founded in 1348 by the Teutonic Knights, it was part of Prussia from 1772 until 1945. German name **ALLENSTEIN.**

O·lym·pi·a /ə'limpēə; ō'lim-/ **1** a plain in Greece, in the western Peloponnese. In ancient Greece it was the site of the chief sanctuary of the god Zeus, the place where the original Olympic Games were held. **2** the capital of Washington, a port on Puget Sound; pop. 33,840.

O·lym·pi·ad /ō'limpē,ad; ə'lim-/ ▸*n.* a celebration of the ancient or modern Olympic Games. ■ a period of four years between Olympic Games, used by the ancient Greeks in dating events. ■ a major national or international contest in some activity, notably chess or bridge. ▷via French or Latin from Greek *Olumpias, Olumpiad-,* from *Olumpios* (see also **OLYMPIAN** and **OLYMPIC**).

O·lym·pi·an /ə'limpēən; ō'lim-/ ▸*adj.* **1** associated with Mount Olympus in northeastern Greece, or with the Greek gods whose home was traditionally held to be there. ■ resembling or appropriate to a god, esp. in superiority and aloofness: *the court is capable of an Olympian detachment.* **2** [*attrib.*] relating to the ancient or modern Olympic Games.
▸*n.* **1** any of the twelve Greek gods regarded as living on Olympus. ■ a person of great attainments or exalted position. **2** a competitor in the Olympic Games. ▷late 15th cent.: sense 1 from Latin *Olympus* (see **OLYMPUS**) + **-IAN**; sense 2 from *Olympia* (see **OLYMPIA**) + **-AN.**

O·lym·pic /ə'limpik; ō'lim-/ ▸*adj.* [*attrib.*] of or relating to the ancient city of Olympia or the Olympic Games: *an Olympic champion.*
▸*n.* (**the Olympics**) the Olympic Games. ▷late 16th cent.: via Latin from Greek *Olumpikos* 'of Olympus or Olympia,' the latter (see **OLYMPIA**) being the site of games in honor of Zeus of *Olympus.*

O·lym·pic Games (also **the O·lym·pics**) a modern sports festival held traditionally every four years in different venues, instigated by the Frenchman Baron de Coubertin (1863–1937) in 1896. Athletes representing many countries compete for gold, silver, and bronze medals in a great variety of sports. Since 1992 the Summer Games and Winter Games alternate every two years. ■ an ancient Greek festival with athletic, literary, and musical competitions, held at Olympia every four years traditionally from 776 BC until abolished by the Roman emperor Theodosius I in AD 393.

O·lym·pic Pe·nin·su·la a region in northwestern Washington, on the Pacific Ocean and Juan de Fuca Strait. The Olympic Mountains and Olympic National Park are here.

O·lym·pic-sized (also **O·lym·pic-size**) ▸*adj.* (of a swimming pool or other sports venue) of the dimensions prescribed for modern Olympic competitions.

O·lym·pus /ə'limpəs; ō'lim-/ *Greek Mythology* the home of the twelve principal gods, identified in later antiquity with Mount Olympus in northern Greece.

O·lym·pus, Mount 1 a mountain in northern Greece that rises to 9,570 feet (2,917 m), at the eastern end of the range dividing Thessaly from Macedonia. **2** a mountain in Cyprus that rises to 6,400 feet (1,951 m), in the Troodos range. It is the highest peak on the island.

OM ▸*abbr.* (in the UK) Order of Merit.

Om /ōm/ ▸*n. Hinduism & Tibetan Buddhism* a mystic syllable, considered the most sacred mantra. It appears at the beginning and end of most Sanskrit recitations, prayers, and texts. ▷Sanskrit, sometimes regarded as three sounds, *a-u-m,* symbolic of the three major Hindu deities.

-oma ▸*suffix* (forming nouns) denoting tumors and

other abnormal growths: *carcinoma.* ▷modern Latin, from a Greek suffix denoting the result of verbal action.

O·ma·ha[1] /ˈōmə,hô; -,hä/ a city in eastern Nebraska, on the Missouri River; pop. 390,007.

O·ma·ha[2] ▸*n.* (*pl.* same or **-has**) **1** a member of an American Indian people of northeastern Nebraska. **2** the Siouan language of this people.
▸*adj.* of or relating to this people or their language. ▷from Omaha *umą̄hą̄* 'upstream.'

O·ma·ha Beach the name used during the D-Day landing in June 1944 for one part of the Norman coast where U.S. troops landed. It is at the mouth of the Vire River, at the village of Saint-Laurent-sur-Mer, northwest of Bayeux.

O·man /ōˈmän/ a country at the eastern corner of the Arabian peninsula; pop. 2,903,000; capital, Muscat; language, Arabic (official). **—O·ma·ni** /ōˈmänē/ *adj.* & *n.*

An independent sultanate known as Muscat and Oman until 1970, Oman was the most influential power in the region during the 19th century; it controlled Zanzibar and other territory. Since the late 19th century, it has had strong links with Britain. The economy is dependent on oil, discovered in 1964.

O·man, Gulf of an inlet of the Arabian Sea, connected by the Strait of Hormuz to the Persian Gulf.

O·mar I /ˈōmär/ (*c.*581–644), Muslim caliph 634–44. He conquered Syria, Palestine, and Egypt.

O·mar Khay·yám /kīˈäm; -ˈam/ (died 1123), Persian poet, mathematician, and astronomer. His *rubáiyát* (quatrains), found in *The Rubáiyát of Omar Khayyám* (translation published 1859), are meditations on the mysteries of existence and celebrations of worldly pleasures.

o·ma·sum /ōˈmāsəm/ ▸*n.* (*pl.* **-sa** /-sə/) *Zoology* the muscular third stomach of a ruminant animal, between the reticulum and the abomasum. Also called PSALTERIUM. ▷early 18th cent.: from Latin, literally 'bullock's tripe.'

O·may·yad /ōˈmī(y)ad/ variant spelling of **UMAYYAD**.

OMB ▸*abbr.* (in the federal government) Office of Management and Budget.

om·bre /ˈämbər/ ▸*n.* a trick-taking card game for three people using a pack of forty cards, popular in Europe in the 17th–18th centuries. ▷from Spanish *hombre* 'man,' with reference to one player seeking to win the pool.

om·bré /ˈäm,brā/ ▸*adj.* (of a fabric) having a dyed, printed, or woven design in which the color is graduated from light to dark. ▷French, past participle of *ombrer* 'to shade.'

ombro- ▸*comb. form* relating to rain: *ombrotrophic.* ▷from Greek *ombros* 'rain shower.'

om·bro·troph·ic /,ämbrəˈtrōfik; -ˈträfik/ ▸*adj. Ecology* (of a bog or its vegetation) dependent on atmospheric moisture for its nutrients.

om·buds·man /ˈämbədzmən; -,bo͝odz-/ ▸*n.* (*pl.* **-men**) an official appointed to investigate individuals' complaints against maladministration, esp. that of public authorities. ▷1950s: from Swedish, 'legal representative.'

om·buds·per·son /ˈämbədz,pərsən; -bo͝odz-/ ▸*n.* a person acting as an ombudsman.

Om·dur·man /,ämdərˈmän/ a city in central Sudan, on the Nile River opposite Khartoum; pop. 229,000.

-ome ▸*suffix chiefly Biology* forming nouns denoting objects or parts having a specified nature: *rhizome* | *trichome.* ▷variant form of **-OMA**.

o·me·ga /ōˈmāgə; ōˈmē-/ ▸*n.* the twenty-fourth, and last, letter of the Greek alphabet (Ω, ω), transliterated as 'o' or 'ō.' ■ the last of a series; the final development: [as *adj.*] *the omega point.* ■ (**Omega**) [followed by Latin genitive] *Astronomy* the twenty-fourth star in a constellation: *Omega Scorpii.*
▸*symbol* ■ (Ω) ohm(s): *a 100Ω resistor.* ▷from Greek *ō mega* 'big O.'

o·me·ga-3 fat·ty ac·id ▸*n.* an unsaturated fatty acid of a kind occurring chiefly in fish oils, with three double bonds at particular positions in the hydrocarbon chain.

om·e·let /ˈäm(ə)lit/ (also **om·e·lette**) ▸*n.* a dish of beaten eggs cooked in a frying pan until firm, often with a filling added while cooking, and usually served folded over. ▷French *omelette*, earlier *amelette*, alteration of *alumette*, variant of *alumelle*, from *lemele* 'knife blade,' from Latin *lamella* (see **LAMELLA**). The association with 'knife blade' is probably because of the thin flat shape of an omelet.

o·men /ˈōmən/ ▸*n.* an event regarded as a portent of good or evil: *the ghost's appearance was an ill omen* | *a rise in imports might be an* **omen of** *recovery.* See note at **SIGN**. ■ prophetic significance: *the raven seemed a bird of evil omen.* ▷late 16th cent.: from Latin.

o·men·tum /ōˈmentəm/ ▸*n.* (*pl.* **-ta** /-tə/) *Anatomy* a fold of peritoneum connecting the stomach with other abdominal organs. ▷late Middle English: from Latin. **—o·men·tal** /ōˈmentl/ *adj.*

o·mer /ˈōmər; ˈōmer/ ▸*n.* **1** an ancient Hebrew dry measure, the tenth part of an ephah. **2** (**Omer**) *Judaism* a sheaf of corn or omer of grain presented as an offering on the second day of Passover. ■ the period of 49 days between this day and Shavuoth (Pentecost). ▷from Hebrew *'ōmer.*

o·mer·tà /ōˈme(ə)rtə; ,ômerˈtä/ ▸*n.* (as practiced by the Mafia) a code of silence about criminal activity and a refusal to give evidence to authorities.

om·i·cron /ˈämi,krän; ˈōm-/ ▸*n.* the fifteenth letter of the Greek alphabet (Ο, ο), transliterated as 'o.' ■ (**Omicron**) [followed by Latin genitive] *Astronomy* the fifteenth star in a constellation: *Omicron Piscium.* ▷from Greek *o mikron* 'little O.'

om·i·nous /ˈämənəs/ ▸*adj.* giving the impression that something bad or unpleasant is going to happen; threatening; inauspicious: *there were ominous dark clouds gathering overhead.* ▷late 16th cent.: from Latin *ominosus*, from *omen, omin-* 'omen.' **—om·i·nous·ly** *adv.* **—om·i·nous·ness** *n.*

THE RIGHT WORD **fateful, forbidding, foreboding, ominous, portentous, premonitory**

A sky filled with low, dark clouds might look **ominous**, but it probably wouldn't be considered **portentous**, even though the root words *omen* and *portent* are nearly synonymous.

What is *ominous* is usually threatening and may imply impending disaster (*an ominous silence*), while *portentous* is more often used to describe something that provokes awe or amazement (*a portentous show of military strength*) or a very important outcome (*a portentous moment for the American people*).

Like *ominous*, **foreboding** implies that something evil is coming (*foreboding words that sent shivers through us*), while **forbidding** suggests an unfriendly or threatening appearance (*a dark, forbidding castle*).

Fateful and **premonitory** are less frightening words. What is *fateful* appears to have been inevitable or decreed by fate, with an emphasis on decisive importance (*a fateful meeting with her ex-boyfriend; a battle that would prove fateful*).

Anything that serves to warn beforehand is *premonitory*, whether or not the warning concerns something negative (*a premonitory dream about her father's death; a premonitory feeling about the exam*).

o·mis·sion /ōˈmisʜən/ ▸*n.* someone or something that has been left out or excluded: *there are glaring omissions in the report.* ■ the action of excluding or leaving out someone or something: *the omission of recent publications from his bibliography.* ■ a failure to do something, esp. something that one has a moral or legal obligation to do: *to pay compensation for a wrongful act or omission.* ▷late Middle English: from late Latin *omissio(n-)*, from the verb *omittere* (see **OMIT**). **—o·mis·sive** /ōˈmisiv/ *adj.*

o·mit /ōˈmit/ ▸*v.* (**o·mit·ted, o·mit·ting**) [*trans.*] (often **be omitted**) leave out or exclude (someone or something), either intentionally or forgetfully: *a significant detail was* **omitted from** *your story.* ■ fail or neglect to do (something); leave undone: *the final rinse is omitted* | [with *infinitive*] *he modestly omits to mention that he was pole-vault champion.* ▷late Middle English: from Latin *omittere*, from *ob-* 'down' + *mittere* 'let go.' **—o·mis·si·ble** /ōˈmisəbəl/ *adj.*

om·ma·tid·i·um /,äməˈtidēəm/ ▸*n.* (*pl.* **-tid·i·a** /-ˈtidēə/) *Entomology* each of the optical units that make up a compound eye, as of an insect. ▷late 19th cent.: modern Latin, from Greek *ommatidion*, diminutive of *omma, ommat-* 'eye.' **—om·ma·tid·i·al** /-ˈtidēəl/ *adj.*

om·mat·o·phore /əˈmatə,fôr/ ▸*n. Zoology* a part of an invertebrate animal, esp. a stalk or tentacle, that bears an eye. ▷late 19th cent.: from Greek *omma, ommat-* 'eye' + **-PHORE**.

omni- ▸*comb. form* all; of all things: *omniscient* | *omnifarious.* ■ in all ways or places: *omnicompetent* | *omnipresent.* ▷from Latin *omnis* 'all.'

om·ni·bus /ˈämnə,bəs/ ▸*n.* **1** a volume containing several novels or other items previously published separately: *an omnibus of her first trilogy.* **2** *dated* a bus.
▸*adj.* comprising several items: *Congress passed an omnibus anticrime package.* ▷early 19th cent.: via French from Latin, literally 'for all,' dative plural of *omnis.*

om·ni·di·rec·tion·al /,ämni,diˈreksʜənl/ ▸*adj. Telecommunications* receiving signals from or transmitting in all directions.

om·ni·far·i·ous /,ämnəˈfe(ə)rēəs/ ▸*adj. formal* comprising or relating to all sorts or varieties. ▷mid 17th cent.: from late Latin *omnifarius* + **-OUS**; compare with **MULTIFARIOUS**. **—om·ni·far·i·ous·ly** *adv.* **—om·ni·far·i·ous·ness** *n.*

om·nip·o·tent /ämˈnipətənt/ ▸*adj.* (of a deity) having unlimited power; able to do anything. ■ having ultimate power and influence: *an omnipotent sovereign.*
▸*n.* (**the Omnipotent**) God. ▷Middle English (as a divine attribute): via Old French from Latin *omnipotent-* 'all-powerful.' **—om·nip·o·tence** *n.* **—om·nip·o·tent·ly** *adv.*

om·ni·pres·ent /,ämnəˈpreznt/ ▸*adj.* (of God) present everywhere at the same time. ■ widely or constantly encountered; common or widespread: *the omnipresent threat of natural disasters.* ▷early 17th cent.: from medieval Latin *omnipraesent-.* **—om·ni·pres·ence** *n.*

om·ni·range /ˈämni,rānj/ ▸*n.* a navigation system in which short-range omnidirectional VHF transmitters serve as radio beacons.

om·nis·cient /ämˈnisʜənt/ ▸*adj.* knowing everything: *the story is told by an omniscient narrator.* ▷early 17th cent.: from medieval Latin *omniscient-* 'all-knowing,' based on *scire* 'to know.' **—om·nis·cience** *n.* **—om·nis·cient·ly** *adv.*

om·ni·sex·u·al /,ämniˈseksʜo͞oəl/ ▸*adj.* involving, related to, or characterized by a diverse sexual propensity. **—om·ni·sex·u·al·i·ty** /-,seksʜo͞oˈalitē/ *n.*

om·ni·um-gath·er·um /,ämnēəm ˈgat͟ʜərəm/ ▸*n.* a collection of miscellaneous people or things. ▷early 16th cent.: mock Latin, from Latin *omnium* 'of all' and **GATHER** + the Latin suffix *-um.*

om·ni·vore /ˈämnə,vôr/ ▸*n.* an animal or person that eats food of both plant and animal origin. ▷late 19th cent.: from French, from Latin *omnivorus* 'omnivorous.'

om·niv·o·rous /ämˈniv(ə)rəs/ ▸*adj.* (of an animal or person) feeding on food of both plant and animal origin. ■ taking in or using whatever is available: *an omnivorous reader.* ▷mid 17th cent.: from Latin *omnivorus* + **-OUS**. **—om·niv·o·rous·ly** *adv.* **—om·niv·o·rous·ness** *n.*

o·moph·a·gy /ōˈmäfəjē/ (also **o·mo·pha·gia** /,ōməˈfāj(ē)ə/) ▸*n.* the eating of raw food, esp. raw meat. ▷early 18th cent.: from Greek *ōmophagia*, from *ōmos* 'raw' + *-phagia* (from *phagein* 'eat'). **—o·mo·phag·ic** /,ōməˈfajik/ *adj.* **—o·moph·a·gist** /-jist/ *n.* **—o·moph·a·gous** /-gəs/ *adj.*

O·mot·ic /ōˈmätik/ ▸*n.* a subfamily of Afro-Asiatic languages spoken in Ethiopia, with over thirty members.
▸*adj.* denoting or belonging to this subfamily. ▷1970s: from *Omo*, the name of a river in southwestern Ethiopia, + **-OTIC**.

omphalo- ▸*comb. form* relating to the navel. ▷from Greek *omphalos* 'navel.'

om·pha·los /ˈämfələs/ ▸*n.* (*pl.* **-loi** /-loi/) *poetic/literary* the center or hub of something: *this was the omphalos of confusion and strife.* ■ a rounded stone (esp. that at

Pronunciation Key ə *ago*; ər *over*; ˈə or ,ə *up*; ˈər or ,ər *fur*; a *hat*; ā *rate*; ä *car*; ᴄʜ *chew*; e *let*; ē *see*; e(ə)r *air*; i *fit*; ī *by*; i(ə)r *ear*; ɴɢ *sing*; ō *go*; ô *for*; oi *boy*; o͝o *good*; o͞o *goo*; ou *out*; sʜ *she*; ᴛʜ *thin*; t͟ʜ *then*; (h)w *why*; ᴢʜ *vision*

Delphi) representing the navel of the earth in ancient Greek mythology. ▷Greek, literally 'navel.'

Omsk /ômsk/ a city in south central Russia, on the Irtysh River; pop. 1,159,000.

ON[1] ▸*abbr.* Ontario (in official postal use).

ON[2] ▸*abbr.* Old Norse.

on /än; ôn/ ▸*prep.* **1** physically in contact with and supported by (a surface): *on the table was a water jug | she was lying on the floor | a sign on the front gate.* ■ located somewhere in the general surface area of (a place): *an internment camp on the island | the house on the corner.* ■ as a result of accidental physical contact with: *one of the children had cut a foot on some glass | he banged his head on a beam.* ■ supported by (a part of the body): *he was lying on his back.* ■ so as to be supported or held by: *put it on the table.* ■ in the possession of (the person referred to): *she only had a few dollars on her.* **2** forming a distinctive or marked part of (the surface of something): *a scratch on her arm | a smile on her face.* **3** having (the thing mentioned) as a topic: *a book on careers | essays on a wide range of issues.* ■ having (the thing mentioned) as a basis: *modeled on the Mayflower Compact | dependent on availability.* **4** as a member of (a committee, jury, or other body): *they would be allowed to serve on committees.* **5** having (the place or thing mentioned) as a target: *five air raids on the city | thousands marching on Washington.* ■ having (the thing mentioned) as a target for visual focus: *her eyes were fixed on his dark profile.* **6** having (the thing mentioned) as a medium for transmitting or storing information: *put your ideas down on paper | stored on the client's own computer.* ■ being broadcast by (a radio or television channel): *a new TV series on Channel 4.* **7** in the course of (a journey): *he was on his way to see his mother.* ■ while traveling in (a public conveyance): *John got some sleep on the plane.* ■ on to (a public conveyance) with the intention of traveling in it: *we got on the train.* **8** indicating the day or part of a day during which an event takes place: *reported on September 26 | on a very hot evening in July.* ■ at the time of: *she was booed on arriving home.* **9** engaged in: *his attendant was out on errands.* **10** regularly taking (a drug or medicine): *he is on morphine to relieve the pain.* **11** paid for by: *the drinks are on me.* **12** added to: *a few cents on the electric bill is nothing compared with your security.*

▸*adv.* **1** physically in contact with and supported by a surface: *make sure the lid is on.* ■ (of clothing) being worn by a person: *sitting with her coat on | get your shoes on.* **2** indicating continuation of a movement or action: *she burbled on | he drove on | and so on.* ■ further forward; in an advanced state: *later on | time's getting on.* **3** (of an entertainment or other event) taking place or being presented: *what's on at the festival | there's a good film on this afternoon.* ■ due to take place as planned: *the reorganization is still on.* **4** (of an electrical appliance or power supply) functioning: *they always left the lights on.* ■ (of a performer, etc.) broadcasting or acting. ■ (of an employee) working. ▷Old English *on, an,* of Germanic origin; related to Dutch *aan* and German *an,* from an Indo-European root shared by Greek *ana.*

▸*PHRASES* □ **be on about** *Brit., informal* talk about tediously and at length: *she's always on about doing one's duty.* □ **it's not on** *informal, chiefly Brit.* it's impractical or unacceptable. □ **on and off** intermittently: *it rained on and off most of the afternoon.* □ **on and on** continually; at tedious length: *he went on and on about his grandad's trombone.* □ **what are you on?** *informal* said to express incredulity at someone's behavior, with the implication that they must be under the influence of drugs. □ **you're on** *informal* said by way of accepting a challenge or bet.

-on ▸*suffix Physics, Biochemistry, & Chemistry* forming nouns: **1** denoting subatomic particles or quanta: *neutron | photon.* **2** denoting molecular units: *codon.* **3** denoting substances: *interferon.* ▷sense 1 originally in *electron,* from ION, influenced (as in sense 2) by Greek *ōn* 'being'; sense 3 is on the pattern of words such as *cotton* or from German *-on.*

on·a·ger /'änəjər/ ▸*n.* an animal of a race of the Asian wild ass native to northern Iran. • *Equus hemionus onager,* family Equidae. Compare with KIANG . ▷Middle English: via Latin from Greek *onagros,* from *onos* 'ass' + *agrios* 'wild.'

on-air ▸*adj.* broadcasting: *his on-air antics helped breathe new life into the series.*

o·nan·ism /'ōnə,nizəm/ ▸*n. formal* **1** masturbation. **2** coitus interruptus. ▷early 18th cent.: from French *onanisme* or modern Latin *onanismus,* from the biblical story of Onan (Gen. 38:8). **—o·nan·ist** *n.* **—o·nan·is·tic** /,ōnə'nistik/ *adj.*

O·nas·sis[1] /ō'nasis/, Aristotle (Socrates) (1906–75), Greek shipping magnate and international businessman. He owned a substantial shipping empire and founded Olympic Airways, Greece's national airline, in 1957. In 1968, he married Jacqueline Bouvier Kennedy, the widow of John F. Kennedy.

O·nas·sis[2], Jacqueline Lee Bouvier Kennedy (1929–94), U.S. first lady (1961–63); known as **Jackie O.** She worked as a photographer before she married John F. Kennedy in 1953. After he was assassinated, she married Aristotle Onassis in 1968 and, after his death, pursued a career in publishing.

Jacqueline Kennedy Onassis

on·board ▸*adj.* [*attrib.*] **1** available or situated on a ship, aircraft, or other vehicle. **2** *Computing* denoting or controlled from a facility or feature incorporated into the main circuit board of a computer or computerized device.

once /wəns/ ▸*adv.* **1** on one occasion or for one time only: *they deliver once a week.* ■ [usu. with *negative* or *if*] at all; on even one occasion (used for emphasis): *he never once complained | if she once got an idea in her head you'd never move it.* **2** at some time in the past; formerly: *He had once been an Army officer.*

▸*conj.* as soon as; when: *once the grapes were pressed, the juice was put into barrels.* ▷Middle English *ones,* genitive of ONE. The spelling change in the 16th cent. was in order to retain the unvoiced sound of the final consonant.

▸*PHRASES* □ **all at once** **1** without warning; suddenly: *all at once the noise stopped.* **2** all at the same time: *scared and excited all at once.* □ **at once** **1** immediately: *I fell asleep at once.* **2** simultaneously: *computers that can do many things at once.* □ **for once** (or **this once**) on this occasion only, as an exception: *He was glad that for once he had not listened.* □ **once a ——, always a ——** *proverb* a person cannot change their fundamental nature: *once a whiner, always a whiner.* □ **once again** (or **more**) one more time. □ **once and for all** (or **once for all**) now and for the last time; finally. □ **once and future** denoting someone or something that is eternal, enduring, or constant. [1950s: from T. H. White's *Once and Future King* (1958).] □ **once bitten, twice shy** see BITE. □ **once** (or **every once**) **in a while** from time to time; occasionally. □ **once or twice** a few times. □ **once upon a time** at some time in the past (used as a conventional opening of a story). ■ formerly: *once upon a time she would have been jealous, but no longer.*

once-o·ver ▸*n. informal* a rapid inspection or search: *some doctor came and gave us all a once-over.* ■ a piece of work that is done quickly: *a quick once-over with a broom.*

on-chip ▸*adj. Electronics* denoting or relating to circuitry included in a single integrated circuit or in the same integrated circuit as a given device.

on·cho·cer·ci·a·sis /,äNGkōsər'kīəsis/ ▸*n.* technical term for RIVER BLINDNESS. ▷early 20th cent.: from modern Latin *Onchocerca* (from Greek *onkos* 'barb' + *kerkos* 'tail') + -IASIS.

onco- ▸*comb. form* of or relating to tumors: *oncology.* ▷from Greek *onkos* 'mass.'

on·co·gene /'äNGkə,jēn/ ▸*n. Medicine* a gene that in certain circumstances can transform a cell into a tumor cell.

on·co·gen·ic /,äNGkə'jenik/ ▸*adj. Medicine* causing development of a tumor or tumors. **—on·co·gen·e·sis** /-'jenisis/ *n.* **—on·co·ge·nic·i·ty** /-jə'nisitē/ *n.*

on·col·o·gy /än'käləjē; äNG-/ ▸*n. Medicine* the study and treatment of tumors. **—on·co·log·ic** /,änkə'läjik; ,äNG-/ *adj.* **—on·co·log·i·cal** /-kə'läjikəl/ *adj.* **—on·col·o·gist** /-'käləjist/ *n.*

on·com·ing /'än,kəmiNG; 'ôn-/ ▸*adj.* [*attrib.*] approaching; moving toward: *she walked into the path of an oncoming car.* ■ *figurative* due to happen or occur in the near future: *the oncoming Antarctic winter.*

▸*n.* the fact of being about to happen in the near future: *the oncoming of age.*

On·co·Mouse /'äNGkə,mous/ (also **on·co·mouse**) ▸*n. trademark* a transgenic mouse carrying an activated human cancer gene, used in laboratory experiments. ▷from ONCO- + MOUSE.

on·co·pro·tein /,äNGkə'prōtē(ə)n/ ▸*n.* a protein encoded by an oncogene which can cause the transformation of a cell into a tumor cell if introduced into it. ▷from ONCO- + PROTEIN.

OND *historical* ▸*abbr.* (in the UK) Ordinary National Diploma (a qualification in technical subjects).

On·daat·je /än'däjē; än'dätyə/, (Philip) Michael (1943–), Canadian writer, born in Sri Lanka. Notable works: *Running in the Family* (autobiography, 1982), *The English Patient* (novel, Booker Prize, 1992; film 1996), and *Anil's Ghost* (2000).

one /wən/ ▸*cardinal number* the lowest cardinal number; half of two; 1: *there's only room for one person | two could live as cheaply as one | one hundred miles | World War One | a one-bedroom apartment.* (Roman numeral: **i, I**) ■ a single person or thing, viewed as taking the place of a group: *they would straggle home in ones and twos.* ■ single; just one as opposed to any more or to none at all (used for emphasis): *her one concern is to save her daughter.* ■ denoting a particular item of a pair or number of items: *electronics is one of his hobbies | he put one hand over her shoulder and one around her waist | a glass tube closed at one end.* ■ denoting a particular but unspecified occasion or period: *one afternoon in late October.* ■ used before a name to denote a person who is not familiar or has not been previously mentioned; a certain: *he worked as a clerk for one Mr. Ming.* ■ *informal* a noteworthy example of (used for emphasis): *the actor was one smart-mouthed troublemaker | he was **one hell of a** snappy dresser.* ■ identical; the same: *all types of training meet one common standard.* ■ identical and united; forming a unity: *the two things are **one and the same**.* ■ one year old. ■ one o'clock: *it's half past one | I'll be there at one.* ■ *informal* a one-dollar bill. ■ *informal* an alcoholic drink: *a cool one after a day on the water.* ■ *informal* a joke or story: *the one about the chicken farmer and the spaceship.* ■ a size of garment or other merchandise denoted by one. ■ a domino or dice with one spot.

▸*pron.* **1** referring to a person or thing previously mentioned: *her mood changed from one of moroseness to one of joy | her best apron, the white one.* ■ used as the object of a verb or preposition to refer to any example of a noun previously mentioned or easily identified: *they had to buy their own copies rather than waiting to borrow one | do you want one?* **2** a person of a specified kind: *you're the one who ruined her life | Eleanor was never one to be trifled with | my friends and **loved ones**.* ■ a person who is remarkable or extraordinary in some way: *you never saw **such a one** for figures.* **3** [*third person singular*] used to refer to any person as representing people in general: *one must admire him for his willingness.* ■ referring to the speaker as representing people in general: *one gets the impression that he is ahead.* ▷Old English *ān,* of Germanic origin; related to Dutch *een* and German *ein,* from an Indo-European root shared by Latin *unus.* The initial *w* sound developed before the 15th cent. and was occasionally represented in the spelling; it was not accepted into standard English until the late 17th cent.

▸*PHRASES* □ **at one** in agreement or harmony: *they were completely **at one with** their environment.* □ **for one** used to stress that the person named holds the specified view, even if no one else does: *I for one am getting a little sick of writing about it.* □ **one after another** (or **the other**) following one another in quick succession: *one after another the buses drew up.* □ **one and all** everyone: *well done one and all!* □ **one and only** unique; single (used for emphasis or as a designation of a celebrity): *the title of his one and only book | the one and only Muhammad Ali.* □ **one by one** separately and in succession; singly. □ **one day** at a particular but unspecified time in the past or future: *one day a boy started teasing Grady | he would one day be a great president.* □ **one-for-one** denoting or referring to a situation or arrangement in which one thing corresponds to or is exchanged for another: *donations would be matched on a one-for-one basis with public revenues.* □ **one of a kind** see KIND[1]. □ **one-on-one** (or **one-to-one**) denoting or referring to a situation in which two parties come into direct contact, opposition, or correspondence: *maybe we should talk to them one-on-one.* □ **one or another** (or **the other**) denoting or referring to a particular but unspecified one out of a set of items: *not all instances fall neatly into one or another of these categories.* □ **one or two** *informal* a few: *there are one or two signs worth watching for.* □ **one thing and another** *informal* used to cover various unspecified matters, events, or tasks: ***what with one thing and another** she hadn't had much sleep recently.*

USAGE 1 **One** is used as a pronoun to mean 'anyone' or 'me and people in general,' as in ***one** must try **one's** best.* In modern English, it is generally used only in formal and written contexts. In informal and spoken contexts, the normal alternative is **you**, as in ***you** must try **your** best*.
2 Until quite recently, sentences in which **one** is followed by **his** or **him** were considered perfectly correct: ***one** must try **his** best.* These uses are now held to be less than perfectly grammatical (and possibly sexist as well).

-one ▸*suffix Chemistry* forming nouns denoting various compounds, esp. ketones: *acetone | quinone.* ▷from Greek patronymic *-ōnē*.

one-act·er ▸*n.* a one-act play.

O'Neal /ō'nēl/, Shaquille (1972–), U.S. basketball player. He played for the Orlando Magic 1992–96 and the Los Angeles Lakers 1996– . He also made some recordings of rap music and was in several movies, including *Blue Chips* (1994) and *Steel* (1997).

one an·oth·er ▸*pron.* each other: *the children used to tease one another.*

one-armed ban·dit ▸*n. informal* a slot machine operated by pulling a long handle at the side.

one-di·men·sion·al ▸*adj.* having or relating to a single dimension: *one-dimensional curves.* ■ lacking depth; superficial: *the supporting roles are alarmingly one-dimensional creations.* **—one-di·men·sion·al·i·ty** *n.*

one-down ▸*adj. informal* at a psychological disadvantage in a game or a competitive situation.

O·ne·ga, Lake /ō'negə; ə'nyegə/ a lake in northwestern Russia, near the border with Finland, the second largest lake in Europe.

one-horse ▸*adj.* drawn by or using a single horse. ■ *informal* small and insignificant: *a **one-horse town.***
▸*PHRASE* □ **one-horse race** a contest in which one candidate or competitor is clearly superior to all the others and seems certain to win.

O·nei·da /ō'nīdə/ ▸*n.* (*pl.* same or **-das**) **1** a member of an American Indian people formerly inhabiting upper New York state, one of the Five Nations. **2** the Iroquoian language of this people.
▸*adj.* of or relating to this people or their language. ▷from Oneida *onęyóte'* 'erected stone,' referring to the large syenite boulder said to have appeared near the successive principal Oneida settlements.

O·nei·da Com·mu·ni·ty a utopian religious community, founded in New York state in 1848 and originally embracing primitive Christian beliefs and radical social and economic ideas, later relaxed. Successful in various commercial enterprises, it was formed into a joint-stock company in 1881.

O'Neill /ō'nēl/, Eugene (Gladstone) (1888–1953), U.S. playwright. He was awarded the Pulitzer Prize for his first full-length play, *Beyond the Horizon* (1920). Other notable works: *Desire under the Elms* (1924), *Mourning Becomes Electra* (1931), *The Iceman Cometh* (1946), and *Long Day's Journey into Night* (1956, posthumously). Nobel Prize for Literature (1936).

o·nei·ric /ō'nīrik/ ▸*adj. formal* of or relating to dreams or dreaming. ▷mid 19th cent.: from Greek *oneiros* 'dream' + **-IC**.

oneiro- ▸*comb. form* relating to dreams or dreaming: *oneiromancy.* ▷from Greek *oneiros* 'dream.'

o·nei·ro·man·cy /ō'nīrə,mansē/ ▸*n.* the interpretation of dreams in order to foretell the future.

one-lin·er ▸*n. informal* a short joke or witty remark.

one-lung·er /'ləNGər/ ▸*n. informal* a single-cylinder engine. ■ a vehicle or boat driven by such an engine.

one-man ▸*adj.* [*attrib.*] involving, done, or operated by only one person: *a one-man show.*

one-man band ▸*n.* a street entertainer who plays several instruments at the same time. ■ a person who runs a business alone.

one·ness /'wən(n)is/ ▸*n.* **1** the fact or state of being unified or whole, though comprised of two or more parts: *the oneness of man and nature.* ■ identity or harmony with someone or something: *a strong sense of oneness is felt with all things.* **2** the fact or state of being one in number: *belief in the oneness of God.*

one-night stand ▸*n.* **1** *informal* (also **one-night·er**) a sexual relationship lasting only one night. ■ a person with whom one has such a relationship. **2** a single performance of a play or show in a particular place.

one-off *informal, chiefly Brit.* ▸*adj.* done, made, or happening only once and not repeated: *one-off tax deductible donations to charity.*
▸*n.* something done, made, or happening only once, not as part of a regular sequence: *the meeting is a one-off.* ■ a person who is unusual or unique, esp. in an admirable way: *he's a one-off, no one else has his skills.*

101 /'wən,ō'wən/ ▸*adj.* [*postpositive*] (describing education courses, real or imagined) elementary; basic: *stuff that you should learn in hacking 101.*

one-piece ▸*adj.* [*attrib.*] (esp. of an article of clothing) made or consisting of a single piece.
▸*n.* an article of clothing made or consisting of a single piece: *I was wearing a tight black one-piece.*

on·er /'wənər/ ▸*n. informal, archaic chiefly Brit.* a remarkable person or thing.

on·er·ous /'ōnərəs; 'änərəs/ ▸*adj.* (of a task, duty, or responsibility) involving an amount of effort and difficulty that is oppressively burdensome: *he found his duties increasingly onerous.* ■ *Law* involving heavy obligations: *an onerous lease.* ▷late Middle English: from Old French *onereus*, from Latin *onerosus*, from *onus, oner-* 'burden.' **—on·er·ous·ly** *adv.* **—on·er·ous·ness** *n.*

one·self /wən'self/ (also **one's self**) ▸*pron.* [*third person singular*] **1** [*reflexive*] a person's own self: *it is difficult to wrest oneself away | resolves that one makes to oneself.* **2** [*emphatic*] used to emphasize that one does something individually or unaided: *the idea of publishing a book oneself.* **3** in one's normal and individual state of body or mind; not influenced by others: *freedom to be oneself.*
▸*PHRASE* □ **by oneself** see **BY**.

one-sid·ed ▸*adj.* unfairly giving or dealing with only one side of a contentious issue or question; biased or partial: *the press was accused of being one-sided, of not giving a balanced picture.* ■ (of a contest or conflict) having a gross inequality of strength or ability between the opponents. ■ (of a relationship or conversation) having all the effort or activity coming from one participant. ■ having or occurring on one side of something only: *printing one-sided documents.* **—one-sid·ed·ly** *adv.* **—one-sid·ed·ness** *n.*

one·sie /'wənzē/ ▸an infant's one-piece close-fitting lightweight garment, usually having sleeves but leaving the legs uncovered and fastening with snaps at the crotch.

one-star ▸*adj.* (esp. of a hotel or restaurant) given one star in a grading system in which this denotes the lowest class or quality: *a good one-star hotel.* ■ (in the U.S. armed forces) having or denoting the rank of brigadier general, distinguished by one star on the uniform: *a one-star general.*

one-step ▸*n.* a vigorous kind of ballroom dance in duple time.

one-stop ▸*adj.* (of a store or other business) capable of supplying all a customer's needs within a particular range of goods or services: *one-stop shopping.*

one-tailed ▸*adj. Statistics* denoting a test for deviation from the null hypothesis in one direction only.

one-time (also **one·time**) ▸*adj.* **1** former: *a one-time football player.* **2** of or relating to a single occasion: *a one-time charge.*

one-on-one (also *chiefly Brit.* **one-to-one**) ▸*n. informal* a face-to-face encounter.

one-touch ▸*adj.* [*attrib.*] (of an electrical device or facility) able to be operated simply at or as though at the touch of a button.

one-track mind ▸*n.* used in reference to a person whose thoughts are preoccupied with one subject or interest.

one-trick po·ny ▸*n. informal* a person or thing with only one special feature, talent, or area of expertise.

one-two ▸*n.* a pair of punches in quick succession, esp. with alternate hands: [as *adj.*] *a one-two punch.*

one up *informal* ▸*adj.* having a psychological advantage over someone: *you're always trying to be **one up on** whoever you're with.*
▸*v.* [*trans.*] (**one-up**) do better than (someone): *he deftly one-upped the interrogator.*

one-up·man·ship /wən 'əpmən,SHip/ ▸*n. informal* the technique or practice of gaining a feeling of superiority over another person.

one-way ▸*adj.* moving or allowing movement in one direction only: *a one-way valve.* ■ (of a road or system of roads) along which traffic may pass in one direction only. ■ (of a ticket) allowing a person to travel to a place but not back again. ■ (of glass or a mirror) seen as a mirror from one side but transparent from the other. ■ denoting a relationship in which all the action or contribution of a particular kind comes from only one member: *interaction between the organism and the environment is not a one-way process.*

one-wom·an ▸*adj.* involving, done, or operated by only one woman.

one-world ▸*adj.* of, relating to, or holding the view that the world's inhabitants are interdependent and should behave accordingly. **—one-world·er** *n.* **—one-world·ism** *n.*

on-glide ▸*n. Phonetics* a glide produced just before the articulation of another speech sound. Compare with **OFF-GLIDE**.

on·go·ing /'än,gōiNG; 'ôn-/ ▸*adj.* continuing; still in progress: *ongoing negotiations.* **—on·go·ing·ness** *n.*

ONI ▸*abbr.* Office of Naval Intelligence.

on·i·o·man·i·a /,ōnēō'mānēə/ ▸*n.* an obsessive or uncontrollable urge to buy things: *Oniomania can affect either sex but the vast majority of compulsive shoppers are adult females.* ▷from Greek *ōnios* 'for sale,' from *ōnos* 'price, purchase': see **-MANIA**.

on·ion /'ənyən/ ▸*n.* **1** an edible bulb with a pungent taste and smell, composed of several concentric layers, used in cooking. **2** the plant that produces this bulb, with long rolled or straplike leaves and spherical heads of greenish-white flowers. • *Allium cepa*, family Liliaceae (or Alliaceae). ▷Middle English: from Old French *oignon*, based on Latin *unio(n-)*, denoting a kind of onion. **—on·ion·y** *adj.*
▸*PHRASE* □ **know one's onions** *informal* be very knowledgeable about something.

on·ion bag ▸*n. informal Soccer* a goal net (used esp. in the context of scoring a goal).

on·ion dome ▸*n.* a dome that bulges in the middle and rises to a point, used esp. in Russian church architecture. **—on·ion-domed** *adj.*

on·ion set ▸*n.* a small onion bulb planted instead of seed to yield a mature bulb.

on·ion·skin /'ənyən,skin/ (also **onionskin paper**) ▸*n.* very fine smooth translucent paper.

on·li·est /'ōnlē-ist/ ▸*adj. dialect* or *humorous* emphatic form of **ONLY**.

on·line /'änlīn; 'ôn-/ (also **on-line**) *Computing* ▸*adj.* controlled by or connected to another computer or to a network. ■ connected to the Internet or World Wide Web: *the ease and convenience of online shopping.*
▸*adv.* (also **on line**) **1** while so connected or under computer control. ■ with processing of data carried out simultaneously with its production. **2** in or into operation or existence: *the town's new high-tech power plant is expected to go online this month.*

on·look·er /'än,lŏŏkər; 'ôn-/ ▸*n.* a nonparticipating observer; a spectator: *a crowd of fascinated onlookers.* **—on·look·ing** /-,lŏŏkiNG/ *adj.*

on·ly /'ōnlē/ ▸*adv.* **1** and no one or nothing more besides; solely or exclusively: *there are only a limited number of tickets available | only their faith sustained them.* ■ no more than (implying that more was hoped for or expected); merely: *deaths from heart disease have only declined by 10 percent | she was still only in her mid-thirties.* ■ no longer ago than: *genes that were discovered only last year.* ■ not until: *a final report reached him only on January 15.* **2** [with *infinitive*] with the negative or unfortunate result that: *she turned into the parking car, only to find her way blocked.* ■ [with *modal*] inevitably, although unfortunate or undesirable: *if banks canceled the debts, these countries **would only** borrow more | rebellion **will only** bring more unhappiness.*
▸*adj.* [*attrib.*] alone of its or their kind; single or solitary: *the only medal we had ever won | he was an only child.* ■ alone deserving consideration: *it's simply the only place to be seen these days.*
▸*conj. informal* except that; but for the fact that: *he is still a young man, only he seems older because of his careworn expression.* ▷Old English *ānlic* (adjective) (see **ONE**, **-LY**[1]).
▸*PHRASES* □ **only just** by a very small margin; almost not: *the building survived the earthquake, but only just.* ■ very recently: *I'd only just arrived back from Paris.* □ **only too ——** used to emphasize that something is the case to an extreme or regrettable extent: *you should be only too glad to be rid of him | they found that the rumor was only too true.*

USAGE In normal, everyday English, the tendency is to place **only** as early as possible in the sentence, generally just before the verb, and the result is

Pronunciation Key ə *ago*; ər *over*; 'ə or ,ə *up*; 'ər or ,ər *fur*; a *hat*; ā *rate*; ä *car*; CH *chew*; e *let*; ē *see*; e(ə)r *air*; i *fit*; ī *by*; i(ə)r *ear*; NG *sing*; ō *go*; ô *for*; oi *boy*; ŏŏ *good*; ōō *goo*; ou *out*; SH *she*; TH *thin*; TH *then*; (h)w *why*; ZH *vision*

rarely ambiguous. Misunderstandings are possible, however, and grammarians have debated the matter for more than two hundred years. Advice varies, but in general, ambiguity is less likely if **only** is placed as close as is naturally possible to the word(s) to be modified or emphasized. *I saw her **only once*** stresses the single instance; *I **only saw** her once* leaves it unclear whether she was heard (or otherwise perceived) in addition to being seen.

O

O·no /ˈōnō/, Yoko (1933–), U.S. musician and artist, born in Japan. She married John Lennon in 1969 and collaborated with him on various experimental recordings.

on-off ▸*adj.* **1** (of a switch) having two positions, "on" and "off." **2** (of a relationship) not continuous or steady.

on·o·ma·si·ol·o·gy /ˌänəˌmāsēˈäləjē; -ˌmāzē-/ ▸*n.* the branch of knowledge that deals with terminology, in particular contrasting terms for similar concepts. Compare with **SEMASIOLOGY**. ▷early 20th cent.: from Greek *onomasia* 'term' + **-LOGY**. —**on·o·ma·si·o·log·i·cal** /-əˈläjikəl/ *adj.*

on·o·mast /ˈänəˌmast/ ▸*n.* a person who studies proper names, esp. personal names. ▷1980s: back-formation from **ONOMASTIC**.

on·o·mas·tic /ˌänəˈmastik/ ▸*adj.* of or relating to the study of the history and origin of proper names. ▷late 16th cent. (as a noun in the sense 'alphabetical list of proper nouns,' later also 'lexicographer'): from Greek *onomastikos*, from *onoma* 'name.' The adjective dates from the early 18th cent.

on·o·mas·tics /ˌänəˈmastiks/ ▸*plural n.* [usu. treated as *sing.*] the study of the history and origin of proper names, esp. personal names.

on·o·mat·o·poe·ia /ˌänəˌmatəˈpēə; -ˌmätə-/ ▸*n.* the formation of a word from a sound associated with what is named (e.g., *cuckoo, sizzle*). ■ the use of such words for rhetorical effect. ▷late 16th cent.: via late Latin from Greek *onomatopoiia* 'word-making,' from *onoma, onomat-* 'name' + *-poios* 'making' (from *poiein* 'to make'). —**on·o·mat·o·poe·ic** /-ˈpē-ik/ or **on·o·mat·o·po·et·ic** /-pōˈetik/ *adj.* —**on·o·mat·o·poe·i·cal·ly** /-ˈpē-ik(ə)lē/ or **on·o·mat·o·po·et·i·cal·ly** /-pōˈetik(ə)lē/ *adv.*

On·on·da·ga /ˌänənˈdôgə; ˌōnən-; -ˈdägə/ ▸*n.* (*pl.* same or **-gas**) **1** a member of an Iroquois people, one of the Five Nations, formerly inhabiting an area near Syracuse, New York. **2** the Iroquoian language of this people.
▸*adj.* of or relating to this people or their language. ▷from the Onondaga name of their main settlement, literally 'on the hill.'

on-ramp ▸*n.* a lane for traffic entering a turnpike or freeway.

on-road ▸*adj.* denoting or relating to events or conditions on a road, esp. a vehicle's performance.

on·rush /ˈänˌrəsh; ˈôn-/ ▸*n.* a surging rush forward: *the mesmerizing onrush of the sea.*
▸*v.* [*intrans.*] [usu. as *adj.*] (**onrushing**) move forward in a surging rush: *the walls of onrushing whitewater.*

on-screen (also **on screen** or **on·screen**) ▸*adj.* & *adv.* shown or appearing in a movie or television program: [as *adj.*] *on-screen violence.* ■ making use of or performed with the aid of a video screen: [as *adj.*] *on-screen editing facilities.*

on·set /ˈänˌset; ˈôn-/ ▸*n.* the beginning of something, esp. something unpleasant: *the* **onset** *of winter.* ■ *archaic* a military attack.

on·shore /ˈänˈshôr; ˈôn-/ ▸*adj.* & *adv.* situated or occurring on land: [as *adj.*] *an onshore oil field.* ■ (esp. of the direction of the wind) from the sea toward the land.

on·side /ˈänˈsīd; ˈôn-/ ▸*adj.* & *adv.* (of a player, esp. in soccer or hockey) occupying a position on the field where playing the ball or puck is allowed; not offside.

on·side kick (also **on·sides kick**) ▸*n. Football* an intentionally short kickoff that travels forward the required distance of 10 yards, which the kicking team can attempt to recover.

on-site ▸*adj.* & *adv.* taking place or available on a particular site or premises.

on·slaught /ˈänˌslôt; ˈôn-/ ▸*n.* a fierce or destructive attack: *a series of* **onslaughts on** *the citadel.* ■ a large quantity of people or things that is difficult to cope with: *an onslaught of electronic mail.* ▷early 17th cent. (also in the form *anslaight*): from Middle Dutch *aenslag*, from *aen* 'on' + *slag* 'blow.' The change in the ending was due to association with (now obsolete) *slaught* 'slaughter.'

on·stage /ˈänˈstāj; ˈôn-/ (also **on-stage**) ▸*adj.* & *adv.* (in a theater) on the stage and so visible to the audience.

on-stream ▸*adv.* in or into industrial production or useful operation.
▸*adj.* of or relating to normal industrial production.

Ont. ▸*abbr.* Ontario.

-ont ▸*comb. form Biology* denoting an individual or cell of a specified type: *schizont.* ▷from Greek *ont-* 'being,' present participle of *einai* 'be.'

on tar·get ▸*adj.* & *adv.* accurate; hitting a target or achieving an aim: *Saturday's forecast was on target.*

On·tar·i·o[1] /änˈte(ə)rēō/ a province in eastern Canada, between Hudson Bay and the Great Lakes; pop. 9,914,200; capital, Toronto. It was settled by the French and the English in the 1600s, ceded to Britain in 1763, and became one of the original four provinces in the Dominion of Canada in 1867. —**On·tar·i·an** /-ēən/ *adj.* & *n.*

On·tar·i·o[2] a commercial city in southwestern California, east of Los Angeles; pop. 133,179.

On·tar·i·o, Lake the smallest and most easterly of the Great Lakes. It lies on the U.S.–Canadian border between Ontario and New York and is linked to Lake Erie by the Niagara River and to the Atlantic Ocean by the St. Lawrence Seaway.

on·tic /ˈäntik/ ▸*adj. Philosophy* of or relating to entities and the facts about them; relating to real as opposed to phenomenal existence. ▷1940s: from Greek *ōn, ont-* 'being' + **-IC**.

on·to /ˈänˌto͞o; ˈôn-/ ▸*prep.* **1** moving to a location on (the surface of something): *they went up onto the ridge.* **2** moving aboard (a public conveyance) with the intention of traveling in it: *we got onto the train.*
▸*PHRASES* □ **be onto someone** *informal* be close to discovering the truth about an illegal or undesirable activity that someone is engaging in. □ **be onto something** *informal* have an idea or information that is likely to lead to an important discovery.

USAGE The preposition **onto** written as one word (instead of **on to**) is recorded from the early 18th century and has been widely used ever since. In U.S. English, it is the regular form, although it is not wholly accepted in British English.
Nevertheless, it is important to maintain a distinction between the preposition **onto** or **on to** and the use of the adverb **on** followed by the preposition **to**: *she climbed* **onto** (sometimes **on to**) *the roof,* but *let's go* **on to** (never **onto**) *the next chapter.*

on·to·gen·e·sis /ˌäntəˈjenəsis/ ▸*n. Biology* the development of an individual organism or anatomical or behavioral feature from the earliest stage to maturity. Compare with **PHYLOGENESIS**. ▷late 19th cent.: from Greek *ōn, ont-* 'being' + *genesis* 'birth.' —**on·to·ge·net·ic** /-jəˈnetik/ *adj.* —**on·to·ge·net·i·cal·ly** /-jəˈnetik(ə)lē/ *adv.*

on·tog·e·ny /änˈtäjənē/ ▸*n.* the branch of biology that deals with ontogenesis. Compare with **PHYLOGENY**. ■ another term for **ONTOGENESIS**. ▷late 19th cent.: from Greek *ōn, ont-* 'being' + **-GENY**. —**on·to·gen·ic** /ˌäntəˈjenik/ *adj.* —**on·to·gen·i·cal·ly** /ˌäntəˈjenik(ə)lē/ *adv.*

on·to·log·i·cal ar·gu·ment /ˌäntəˈläjikəl/ ▸*n. Philosophy* the argument that God, being defined as most great or perfect, must exist, since a God who exists is greater than a God who does not. Compare with **ARGUMENT FROM DESIGN, COSMOLOGICAL ARGUMENT**, and **TELEOLOGICAL ARGUMENT**.

on·tol·o·gy /änˈtäləjē/ ▸*n.* the branch of metaphysics dealing with the nature of being. ▷early 18th cent.: from modern Latin *ontologia*, from Greek *ōn, ont-* 'being' + **-LOGY**. —**on·to·log·i·cal** /ˌäntəˈläjikəl/ *adj.* —**on·to·log·i·cal·ly** /ˌäntəˈläjik(ə)lē/ *adv.* —**on·tol·o·gist** /-jist/ *n.*

o·nus /ˈōnəs/ ▸*n.* (usu. as **the onus**) used to refer to something that is one's duty or responsibility: **the onus is on** *you to show that you have suffered loss.* ▷mid 17th cent.: from Latin, literally 'load or burden.'

o·nus pro·ban·di /ˈōnəs prōˈbändē; -ˈban-/ ▸*n. Law* the obligation to prove an assertion or allegation one makes; the burden of proof. ▷Latin, 'the burden of proving.'

on·ward /ˈänwərd; ˈôn-/ ▸*adv.* (also **on·wards**) in a continuing forward direction; ahead: *she stumbled onward.* ■ forward in time: *the period* **from 1969 onward.** ■ *figurative* so as to make progress or become more successful: *the business moved* **onward and upward.**
▸*adj.* going further rather than coming to an end or halt; moving forward: *oil was pumped to a port for onward shipment* | *figurative the onward march of history.*

On·y·choph·o·ra /ˌäniˈkäfərə/ *Zoology* a small phylum of terrestrial invertebrates commonly known as velvet worms. They share characteristics with the arthropods and annelids, having a long soft segmented body with stubby legs (lobopods). ▷modern Latin (plural), from Greek *onux, onukh-* 'nail, claw' + *-phoros* 'bearing.' —**on·y·choph·o·ran** *adj.* & *n.*

on·yx /ˈäniks/ ▸*n.* a semiprecious variety of agate with different colors in layers. ▷Middle English: from Old French *oniche, onix*, via Latin from Greek *onux* 'fingernail or onyx.'

on·yx mar·ble ▸*n.* banded calcite or other stone used as a decorative material.

oo- ▸*comb. form Biology* relating to or denoting an egg or ovum. ▷from Greek *ōion* 'egg.'

o-o /ˈō ō/ (also **oo**) ▸*n.* an endangered Hawaiian honeyeater that has a thin curved bill and climbs about on tree trunks. • Genus *Moho*, family Meliphagidae: only two of four species survive. ▷late 19th cent.: from Hawaiian.

o·o·cyst /ˈōəˌsist/ ▸*n. Zoology* a cyst containing a zygote formed by a parasitic protozoan such as the malaria parasite.

o·o·cyte /ˈōəˌsīt/ ▸*n. Biology* a cell in an ovary that may undergo meiotic division to form an ovum.

OOD ▸*abbr.* ■ officer of the deck. ■ officer of the day.

oo·dles /ˈo͞odlz/ ▸*plural n. informal* a very great number or amount of something: *if only I had* **oodles of** *cash.* ▷mid 19th cent. (originally U.S.): of unknown origin.

oof /o͝of/ ▸*exclam.* expressing discomfort, as from sudden exertion or a blow to one's body. ▷natural exclamation: first recorded in English in the mid 19th cent.

o·og·a·mous /ōˈ(w)ägəməs/ ▸*adj. Biology* relating to or denoting reproduction by the union of mobile male and immobile female gametes. —**o·og·a·mous·ly** *adv.* —**o·og·a·my** /-gəmē/ *n.*

o·o·gen·e·sis /ˌōəˈjenəsis/ ▸*n. Biology* the production or development of an ovum.

o·o·go·ni·um /ˌōəˈgōnēəm/ ▸*n.* (*pl.* **-ni·a** /-nēə/) **1** *Botany* the female sex organ of certain algae and fungi, typically a rounded cell or sac containing one or more oospheres. **2** *Biology* an immature female reproductive cell that gives rise to primary oocytes by mitosis. ▷mid 19th cent.: from **oo-** 'of an egg' + Greek *gonos* 'generation' + **-IUM**. —**o·o·go·ni·al** /-nēəl/ *adj.*

ooh /o͞o/ ▸*exclam.* used to express a range of emotions including surprise, delight, or pain: *ooh, this is fun* | *ooh, my feet!*
▸*n.* an utterance of such an exclamation: *the* **oohs and aahs** *of the enthusiastic audience.*
▸*v.* (**oohed, ooh·ing**) [*intrans.*] utter such an exclamation: *visitors* **oohed and aahed** *at the Christmas tree.* ▷natural exclamation: first recorded in English in the early 20th cent.

o·o·lite /ˈōəˌlīt/ ▸*n. Geology* limestone consisting of a mass of rounded grains (ooliths) made up of concentric layers. ▷early 19th cent.: from French *oölithe*, modern Latin *oolites* (see **OO-, -LITE**). —**o·o·lit·ic** /ˌōəˈlitik/ *adj.*

o·o·lith /ˈōəˌlith/ ▸*n. Geology* any of the rounded grains making up oolite.

o·ol·o·gy /ōˈ(w)äləjē/ ▸*n.* the study or collecting of birds' eggs. —**o·o·log·i·cal** /ˌōəˈläjikəl/ *adj.* —**o·ol·o·gist** /-jist/ *n.*

oo·long /ˈo͞oˌlông; -ˌläng/ ▸*n.* a dark-colored China tea made by fermenting the withered leaves to about half the degree usual for black teas. ▷mid 19th cent.: from Chinese *wūlóng*, literally 'black dragon.'

oo·mi·ak ▸*n.* variant spelling of **UMIAK**.

oom·pah /ˈo͞omˌpä; ˈo͝om-/ (also **oom·pah-pah**) *informal* ▸*n.* used to refer to the rhythmical sound of deep-toned brass instruments in a band.
▸*v.* (**-pahed, -pah·ing**) [*intrans.*] make such a sound. ▷late 19th cent.: imitative.

oomph /o͝omf; o͞omf/ (also **umph**) ▸*n. informal* the quality of being exciting, energetic, or sexually attractive: *he showed entrepreneurial oomph.* ▷1930s: perhaps imitative.

-oon ▸*suffix* forming nouns, originally from French words having the final stressed syllable *-on*: *balloon* | *buffoon.* ▷from Latin *-onis*, sometimes via Italian *-one*.

o·o·pho·rec·to·my /ˌōəfəˈrektəmē/ ▸*n.* (*pl.* **-mies**) surgical removal of one or both ovaries; ovariectomy. ▷late 19th cent.: from modern Latin *oophoron* 'ovary' (from Greek *ōophoros* 'egg-bearing') + **-ECTOMY**.

o·o·pho·ri·tis /ˌōəfəˈrītis/ ▸*n. Medicine* inflammation of an ovary; ovaritis.

oops /(w)o͝ops; o͞ops/ ▸*exclam. informal* used to show recognition of a mistake or minor accident, often as part of an apology: *"Oops! I'm sorry. I just made you miss your bus."* ▷natural exclamation: first recorded in English in the 1930s.

oop·sy-dai·sy ▶*exclam.* variant spelling of UPSY-DAISY.

Oort /ôrt/, Jan Hendrik (1900–92), Dutch astronomer. He proved that the galaxy rotates and determined the position and orbital period of the sun within it.

Oort cloud *Astronomy* a spherical cloud of small rocky and icy bodies postulated to orbit the sun beyond the orbit of Pluto and up to 1.5 light years from the sun, and to be the source of comets. Its existence was proposed by J. H. Oort.

o·o·sphere /ˈōəˌsfir/ ▶*n. Botany* the female reproductive cell of certain algae or fungi, which is formed in the oogonium and when fertilized becomes the oospore.

o·o·spore /ˈōəˌspôr/ ▶*n. Botany* the thick-walled zygote of certain algae and fungi, formed by fertilization of an oosphere. Compare with ZYGOSPORE.

Oost·en·de /ōˈstendə/ Flemish name for **OSTEND**.

o·o·the·ca /ˌōəˈTHēkə/ ▶*n.* (*pl.* **-cae** /-ˌsē; -ˌkē/) *Entomology* the egg case of cockroaches, mantises, and related insects. ▷mid 19th cent.: from **oo-** 'of an egg' + Greek *thēkē* 'receptacle.'

o·o·tid /ˈōəˌtid/ ▶*n. Biology* a haploid cell formed by the meiotic division of a secondary oocyte, esp. the ovum, as distinct from the polar bodies. ▷early 20th cent.: from **oo-** 'egg,' on the pattern of *spermatid*.

ooze[1] /o͞oz/ ▶*v.* [*intrans.*] (of a fluid) slowly trickle or seep out of something; flow in a very gradual way: *blood was oozing from a wound in his scalp | honey oozed out of the comb.* ■ [*intrans.*] slowly exude or discharge a viscous fluid: *her mosquito bites were oozing and itching like mad.* ■ [*trans.*] *figurative* give a powerful impression of (a quality): *he oozed charm and poise | the town oozes history.*
▶*n.* **1** the sluggish flow of a fluid. **2** an infusion of oak bark or other vegetable matter, used in tanning. ▷Old English *wōs* 'juice or sap'; the verb dates from late Middle English. **—ooz·y** /ˈo͞ozē/ *adj.*

ooze[2] ▶*n.* wet mud or slime, esp. that found at the bottom of a river, lake, or sea. ■ *Geology* a deposit of white or gray calcareous matter largely composed of foraminiferan remains, covering extensive areas of the ocean floor. ▷Old English *wāse*; related to Old Norse *veisa* 'stagnant pool.' In Middle English and the 16th cent. the spelling was *wose* (rhyming with *repose*), but beginning in 1550 spellings imply a change in pronunciation and influence by OOZE[1]. **—ooz·y** *adj.*

OP ▶*abbr.* ■ observation post. ■ (in the theater) opposite prompt. ■ organophosphate(s). ■ (in the Roman Catholic Church) *Ordo Praedicatorum* Order of Preachers (Dominican).

op /äp/ ▶*n. informal* a surgical or other operation.

op. (also **op.**) ▶*abbr. Music* opus (before a number given to each work of a particular composer, usually indicating the order of publication).

o.p. ▶*abbr.* ■ (of a book) out of print. ■ (of alcohol) overproof.

op- ▶*suffix* **1** variant spelling of OB- **2** assimilated before *p* (as in *oppress, oppugn*).

o·pac·i·fy /ōˈpasəˌfī/ ▶*v.* (**-fies**, **-fied**) *technical* make or become opaque. **—o·pac·i·fi·ca·tion** /ōˌpasəfiˈkāSHən/ *n.* **—o·pac·i·fi·er** *n.*

o·pac·i·ty /ōˈpasitē/ ▶*n.* the condition of lacking transparency or translucence; opaqueness: *thinner paints need black added to increase opacity.* ■ *figurative* obscurity of meaning: *the difficulty and opacity in Barthes' texts.* ▷mid 16th cent.: from French *opacité*, from Latin *opacitas*, from *opacus* 'darkened.'

o·pah /ˈōpə/ ▶*n.* a large deep-bodied fish with a deep blue back, silvery belly, and crimson fins, living in deep oceanic waters. Also called MOONFISH. • *Lampris guttatus*, family Lampridae. ▷mid 18th cent.: a West African word.

o·pal /ˈōpəl/ ▶*n.* a gemstone consisting of hydrated silica, typically semitransparent and showing varying colors against a pale or dark ground. ▷late 16th cent.: from French *opale* or Latin *opalus*, probably based on Sanskrit *upala* 'precious stone' (having been first brought from India).

o·pal·es·cent /ˌōpəˈlesənt/ ▶*adj.* showing varying colors as an opal does. **—o·pal·es·cence** *n.*

o·pal glass ▶*n.* a type of semitranslucent white glass.

o·pal·ine /ˈōpəˌlēn; -ˌlīn/ ▶*adj.* another term for OPALESCENT.
▶*n.* another term for MILK GLASS. ■ translucent glass of a color other than white.

op-amp /ˈäp ˌamp/ ▶*abbr.* operational amplifier.

o·paque /ōˈpāk/ ▶*adj.* (**o·paqu·er**, **o·paqu·est**) not able to be seen through; not transparent: *the windows were opaque with steam.* ■ *figurative* (esp. of language) hard or impossible to understand; unfathomable: *technical jargon that was* **opaque to** *her.*
▶*n.* an opaque thing or substance. ■ *Photography* a substance for producing opaque areas on negatives. ▷late Middle English *opake*, from Latin *opacus* 'darkened.' The current spelling (rare before the 19th cent.) has been influenced by the French form. **—o·paque·ly** *adv.* **—o·paque·ness** *n.*

op art (also **op·ti·cal art**) ▶*n.* a form of abstract art that gives the illusion of movement by the precise use of pattern and color, or in which conflicting patterns emerge and overlap. Bridget Riley and Victor Vasarely are its most famous exponents. ▷1960s: on the pattern of *pop art*.

op. cit. /ˈäp ˌsit/ ▶*adv.* in the work already cited. ▷from Latin *opere citato*.

ope /ōp/ ▶*adj.* & *v.* poetic/literary or archaic form of OPEN.

OPEC /ˈōpek/ ▶*abbr.* Organization of the Petroleum Exporting Countries.

op-ed (also **Op-Ed**) ▶*adj.* denoting or printed on the page opposite the editorial page in a newspaper, devoted to commentary, feature articles, etc. ▷1940s: shortening of *op(posite the) ed(itorial page)*.

O·pel /ˈōpəl/, Wilhelm von (1871–1948), German automobile manufacturer. His company was the first in Germany to introduce assembly-line production. Opel was sold to General Motors in 1929.

Op·e·lou·sas /ˌäpəˈlo͞osəs/ a city in south central Louisiana, north of Lafayette; pop. 22,860.

o·pen /ˈōpən/ ▶*adj.* **1** allowing access, passage, or a view through an empty space; not closed or blocked up: *it was a warm evening and the window was open | the door was* **wide open**. ■ (of a container) not fastened or sealed; in a position or with the lid or other covering in a position allowing access to the inside part or the contents: *the case burst open and its contents flew all over the place.* ■ (of a garment or its fasteners) not buttoned or fastened: *his tie was knotted below the open collar of his shirt.* ■ (of the mouth or eyes) with lips or lids parted: *his eyes were open but he could see nothing.* ■ free from obstructions: *the pass is kept open all year by snowplows.* ■ *informal* (of a car or house) unlocked. ■ *Phonetics* (of a vowel) produced with a relatively wide opening of the mouth and the tongue kept low. ■ *Phonetics* (of a syllable) ending in a vowel. ■ (of the bowels) not constipated. ■ (of a game or style of play) characterized by action that is spread out over the field. **2** [*attrib.*] exposed to the air or to view; not covered: *an open fire burned in the grate.* ■ (of an area of land) not covered with buildings or trees: *increasing numbers of new houses in open countryside.* ■ having spaces or gaps between elements: *air circulates more readily through an open tree.* ■ (of a fabric) loosely knitted or woven. ■ (of a team member in a game) unguarded and therefore able to receive a pass: *the trick is spreading the defense so that at least one receiver gets open.* ■ (of a goalmouth or other object of attack in a game) unprotected; vulnerable. ■ (of a boat) without a deck: *days without food and water in an open boat.* ■ [*predic.*] (**open to**) likely to suffer from or be affected by; vulnerable or subject to: *the system is open to abuse.* ■ (of a town or city) officially declared to be undefended, and so immune under international law from bombardment. ■ with the outer edges or sides drawn away from each other; unfolded: *the trees had buds and a few open flowers.* ■ (of a book or file) with the covers parted or the contents in view, allowing it to be read: *she was copying verses from an open Bible | figurative her mind was an open book to him.* ■ (of a hand) not clenched into a fist. ■ [as *complement*] damaged or injured by a deep cut in the surface: *he had his arm slashed open.* **3** [*predic.*] (of a store, place of entertainment, etc.) officially admitting customers or visitors; available for business: *the store stays open until 9 p.m.* ■ (of a bank account) available for transactions: *the minimum required to keep the account open.* ■ (of a telephone line) ready to take calls: *our free advice line is open from 8:30 to 5:30.* ■ (of a choice, offer, or opportunity) still available; such that people can take advantage of it: *the offer is open while supplies last | we need to consider what options are left open.* **4** (of a person) frank and communicative; not given to deception or concealment: *she was open and naive | I was quite open about my views.* ■ not concealed; manifest: *his eyes showed open admiration.* ■ [*attrib.*] (of conflict) fully developed and unconcealed: *the dispute erupted into open war.* ■ involving no concealment, restraint, or deception; welcoming discussion, criticism, and inquiry: *the conclusions were reached in open discussion.* **5** (of a question, case, or decision) not finally settled; still admitting of debate: *students' choice of major can be kept open until the second year.* ■ (of the mind) accessible to new ideas; unprejudiced: *I'm keeping an open mind about my future.* ■ [*predic.*] (**open to**) receptive to: *the union was open to suggestions for improvements.* ■ [*predic.*] (**open to**) admitting of; making possible: *the message is open to different interpretations.* ■ freely available or accessible; offered without restriction: *the service is* **open to** *all students at the university.* ■ with no restrictions on those allowed to attend or participate: *an open audition was announced.* ■ (also **Open**) (of an award or the competition for it) unrestricted as to who may qualify to compete: *each horse had won two open races.* ■ (of a ticket) not restricted as to day of travel. **6** *Music* (of a string) allowed to vibrate along its whole length. ■ (of a pipe) unstopped at each end. ■ (of a note) sounded from an open string or pipe. **7** (of an electrical circuit) having a break in the conducting path. **8** *Mathematics* (of a set) not containing any of its limit points.
▶*v.* [*trans.*] **1** move or adjust (a door or window) so as to leave a space allowing access and view: *she opened the door and went in | [intrans.] "Open up!" he said.* ■ [*intrans.*] (of a door or window) be moved or adjusted to leave a space allowing access and view: *the door opened and a man came out.* ■ undo or remove the lid, cover, or fastener of (a container) to get access to the contents: *he opened a bottle inexpertly, spilling some of the wine.* ■ remove the covers or wrapping from: *can we open the presents now?* ■ part the lips or lids of (a mouth or eye): *she opened her mouth to argue.* ■ [*intrans.*] (of the mouth or eyes) have the lips or lids parted in this way: *her eyes slowly opened.* ■ (of a wound) lose or lack its protective covering: *old wounds opened and I bled a little bit.* ■ improve or make possible access to or passage through: *the president announced that his government would open the border.* ■ cause evacuation of (the bowels). ■ [*intrans.*] (**open onto/into**) (of a room, door, or window) give access to: *beautiful French doors that opened onto a balcony.* ■ [*intrans.*] (of a panorama) come into view; spread out before someone: *stop to marvel at the views that* **open out** *below.* ■ *Nautical* achieve a clear view of (a place) by sailing past a headland or other obstruction: *we shall open Simon's Bay at any minute now.* **2** spread out; unfold: *the eagle opened its wings and circled up into the air | the tail looks like a fan when it is* **opened out** *fully.* ■ [*intrans.*] be unfolded; spread out to the full extent: *the flowers never opened beyond narrow points.* ■ increase the spaces or gaps between elements of (something): *spacing the scaffolds opens up the tree so light can penetrate.* ■ part the covers or display the contents of (a book or file) to read it: *she opened her book at the prologue.* ■ [*intrans.*] (**open out**) become wider or more spacious: *the path opened out into a glade.* **3** allow public access to: *one woman raised $731 by opening her home and selling coffee and tea.* ■ make available: *the new plan proposed to* **open up** *opportunities to immigrants.* ■ make more widely known; reveal: *the move may force the company to* **open up** *its plans for the future.* ■ [*intrans.*] (**open up**) become more communicative or confiding: *neither one of them had opened up to me about their troubles.* ■ make (one's mind or heart) more receptive or sympathetic: **open** *your mind* **to** *what is going on around you.* ■ (**open someone** (**up**) **to**) make someone vulnerable to: *the process is going to open them to a legal threat.* **4** establish (a new business, movement, or enterprise): *they have opened a new restaurant across the street.* ■ [*intrans.*] (of an enterprise, esp. a commercial one) be established: *two new restaurants open this week.* ■ [*intrans.*] (of a store, place of entertainment, etc.) be officially ready to receive customers or visitors; become ready for business: *the mall didn't open until 10.* ■ take the action required to make ready for use: *they have the $10 necessary to open a savings account | click twice to open a file.* ■ [*intrans.*] (of a meeting or a sporting or artistic event) formally begin: *the incident occurred just before the Olympic Games were due to open.* ■ [*intrans.*] (of a piece of writing or music) begin: *the chapter opens with a discussion of Anglo-American relations.* ■ (**open up**) [*intrans.*] (of a process) start to develop: *a new and dramatic phase was opening up.* ■ officially or ceremonially declare (a building, road, etc.) to be completed and ready for use: *we will have to wait until a new bypass*

Pronunciation Key ə *ago*; ər *over*; ˈə *or* ˌə *up*; ˈər *or* ˌər *fur*; a *hat*; ā *rate*; ä *car*; CH *chew*; e *let*; ē *see*; e(ə)r *air*; i *fit*; ī *by*; i(ə)r *ear*; NG *sing*; ō *go*; ô *for*; oi *boy*; o͝o *good*; o͞o *goo*; ou *out*; SH *she*; TH *thin*; T͟H *then*; (h)w *why*; ZH *vision*

is opened before we can tackle the problem of congestion. ■ (of a counsel in a court of law) make a preliminary statement in (a case) before calling witnesses. ■ [*trans.*] *Bridge* make (the first bid) in the auction. **5** break the conducting path of (an electrical circuit): *the switch opens the motor circuit.* ■ [*intrans.*] (of an electrical circuit or device) suffer a break in its conducting path.

▶*phrasal v.* □ **open up** begin shooting: *the enemy artillery had opened up.* □ **open something up 1** accelerate a motor vehicle. **2** (of an athlete or team) create an advantage for one's side: *he opened up a lead of 14–8.*

▶*n.* **1** (**Open**) a championship or competition with no restrictions on who may qualify to compete: *the venue for the British Open.* **2** an accidental break in the conducting path for an electrical current. ▷Old English *open* (adjective), *openian* (verb), of Germanic origin; related to Dutch *open* and German *offen*, from the root of the adverb **UP**. —**o·pen·a·ble** *adj.* —**o·pen·ness** *n.*

▶*PHRASES* □ **be open with** speak frankly to; conceal nothing from: *I had always been completely open with my mother.* □ **in** (or **into**) **the open** out of doors; not under cover. ■ not subject to concealment or obfuscation; made public: *we have never let our dislike for him come into the open.* □ **in open court** in a court of law, before the judge and the public. □ **open-and-shut** (of a case or argument) admitting no doubt or dispute; straightforward. □ **open the door to** see **DOOR**. □ **open someone's eyes** see **EYE**. □ **open fire** begin to shoot a weapon. □ **an open mind** see **MIND**. □ **with one's eyes open** (or **with open eyes**) fully aware of the risks and other implications of an action or situation: *I went into the job with my eyes open.* □ **with open arms** see **ARM**[1].

o·pen air ▶*n.* a free or unenclosed space outdoors: *getting out* ***in the open air.***

▶*adj.* positioned or taking place out of doors: *an open-air swimming pool.*

o·pen bar ▶*n.* a bar at a special function at which the drinks have been paid for by the host or are prepaid through an admission fee.

o·pen book ▶*n.* a person or thing that is easily understood or interpreted: *my life's an open book.*

O·pen Breth·ren one of the two principal divisions of the Plymouth Brethren (the other is the Exclusive Brethren), formed in 1849 in Plymouth, England, as a result of doctrinal and other differences. The Open Brethren are less rigorous and less exclusive in matters such as conditions for membership and contact with outsiders than the Exclusive Brethren.

o·pen·cast /ˈōpən,kast/ ▶*adj.* British term for **OPEN-PIT**.

o·pen chain ▶*n.* *Chemistry* a molecular structure consisting of a chain of atoms with no closed rings.

o·pen cir·cuit ▶*n.* an electrical circuit that is not complete. —**o·pen-cir·cuit·ed** *adj.*

o·pen class·room ▶*n.* an approach to elementary education that emphasizes spacious classrooms where learning is informally structured, flexible, and individualized. ■ a spacious instructional area shared by several groups of elementary students that facilitates such an approach and the movement of students from one activity to another.

o·pen clus·ter ▶*n.* *Astronomy* a relatively loose grouping of stars.

o·pen com·mun·ion ▶*n.* *Christian Church* communion made available to any Christian believer.

o·pen date ▶*n.* a future date for which no event has yet been arranged.

o·pen door ▶*n.* [*in sing.*] free or unrestricted means of admission or access: [as *adj.*] *many companies encourage open-door management.* ■ the policy or practice by which a country does not restrict the admission of immigrants or foreign imports: [as *adj.*] *an open-door immigration policy.*

o·pen-end·ed (also **o·pen-end**) ▶*adj.* having no determined limit or boundary: *the return invitation was open-ended.* ■ (of a question or set of questions) allowing the formulation of any answer, rather than a selection from a set of possible answers: *the interview includes both open-ended and multiple-choice questions.* —**o·pen-end·ed·ness** *n.*

o·pen en·roll·ment ▶*n.* **1** the unrestricted enrollment of students at schools, colleges, or universities of their choice. **2** a period during which a health insurance company or HMO is statutorily required to accept applicants without regard to health history. ■ such a period when employees can change insurance plans offered by their employer, without proof of insurability.

o·pen·er /ˈōp(ə)nər/ ▶*n.* **1** [usu. with *adj.*] a device for opening something, esp. a container: *a bottle opener | a letter opener.* **2** the first of a series of games, cultural events, etc.: *the league opener is three weeks away.* ■ the first point or points scored in a sports event. ■ a remark used as an excuse to initiate a conversation: *we blurted out the obvious opener.* ■ *Poker* (**openers**) a hand of sufficient value to allow the opening of betting.

▶*PHRASE* □ **for openers** *informal* to start with; first of all: *for openers, the car is roomier than the old model.*

o·pen-eyed ▶*adj.* with the eyes open or wide open. ■ *figurative* clear-sighted; perceptive; fully aware: *an open-eyed approach to political manipulation.* ■ with a sense of wonder, awe, etc.

o·pen-faced ▶*adj.* **1** having a frank or ingenuous expression. **2** (of a watch) having no cover other than the glass. ■ (also **o·pen-face**) (of a sandwich or pie) without an upper layer of bread or pastry.

o·pen·hand·ed /ˈōpənˈhandid/ ▶*adj.* **1** (of a blow) delivered with the palm of the hand: *an openhanded slap to the side of the face.* **2** giving freely; generous: *openhanded philanthropy.* —**o·pen·hand·ed·ly** *adv.* —**o·pen·hand·ed·ness** *n.*

o·pen-heart·ed (also **o·pen·heart·ed**) ▶*adj.* expressing or displaying one's warm and kindly feelings without concealment: *Betty's open-hearted goodwill.* —**o·pen-heart·ed·ness** *n.*

o·pen-hearth ▶*adj.* denoting a steelmaking process in which the charge is laid on a hearth in a shallow furnace and heated by burning gas.

o·pen-heart sur·ger·y ▶*n.* surgery in which the heart is exposed and the blood made to bypass it.

o·pen house ▶*n.* a place or situation in which all visitors are welcome: *they* ***kept open house,*** *entertaining a wide variety of artists and writers.* ■ a day when members of the public are invited to visit a place or institution, esp. one to which they do not normally have access: *the president spent all morning greeting thousands of visitors to a White House open house.* ■ an informal reception or party during which one's home is open to visitors: *on New Year's Day they had an open house.* ■ a time when real estate offered for sale is open to prospective buyers.

o·pen·ing /ˈōp(ə)niNG/ ▶*n.* **1** an aperture or gap, esp. one allowing access: *she peered through one of the smaller openings.* ■ *figurative* an opportunity to achieve something: *they seem to have exploited fully the openings offered.* ■ an available job or position: *an opening for a professional engineer in the public works department.* **2** a beginning; an initial part: *Maya started tapping out the opening of her story.* ■ a formal or official beginning: *the official opening of the tourist season.* ■ the occasion of the first performance of a play, movie, etc., or the start of an exhibition, marked by a celebratory gathering. ■ the occasion of a public building being officially ready for use, marked by a ceremony. ■ *Chess* a recognized sequence of moves at the beginning of a game. ■ an attorney's preliminary statement of a case in a court of law. ■ an open piece of ground in a wooded area; a clearing: *I reached an opening in the forest.*

▶*adj.* [*attrib.*] coming at the beginning of something; initial: *she stole the show with her opening remark.*

o·pen·ing night ▶*n.* the first night of a theatrical play or other entertainment.

o·pen in·ter·est ▶*n.* *Finance* the number of contracts or commitments outstanding in futures and options that are trading on an official exchange at any one time.

o·pen let·ter ▶*n.* a letter, often critical, addressed to a particular person or group of people but intended for publication.

o·pen line ▶*n.* a means of easy access or communication: *to keep an open line to the White House.*

▶*adj.* denoting a radio or television program in which the public can participate by telephone: *the open-line portion of his daily radio show.*

o·pen·ly /ˈōpənlē/ ▶*adv.* without concealment, deception, or prevarication, esp. where these might be expected; frankly or honestly: *he could no longer speak openly of his problems.* ▷Old English *openlīce* (see **OPEN**, **-LY**[2]).

o·pen mar·ket ▶*n.* (often **the open market**) an unrestricted market with free access by and competition of buyers and sellers.

o·pen mar·riage ▶*n.* a marriage in which both partners agree that each may have sexual relations with others.

o·pen mike ▶*n.* a microphone that is in use. ■ [often as *adj.*] a session in a club during which anyone is welcome to sing or perform stand-up comedy.

o·pen-mind·ed ▶*adj.* willing to consider new ideas; unprejudiced. —**o·pen-mind·ed·ly** *adv.* —**o·pen-mind·ed·ness** *n.*

o·pen-mouthed ▶*adj.* with the mouth open, as in surprise or excitement: *open-mouthed astonishment.*

o·pen-necked ▶*adj.* (of a dress shirt) worn with the collar unbuttoned and without a tie.

o·pen out·cry ▶*n.* a system of financial trading in which dealers shout their bids and contracts aloud.

o·pen-pit ▶*adj.* denoting a method of mining in which coal or ore is extracted at or from a level near the earth's surface, rather than from underground workings.

o·pen-plan ▶*adj.* (of a building or floor plan) having large open areas with few or no internal dividing walls: *an open-plan office.*

o·pen pri·ma·ry ▶*n.* a primary election in which voters are not required to declare party affiliation.

o·pen ques·tion ▶*n.* a matter on which differences of opinion are possible; a matter not yet decided.

o·pen range ▶*n.* a large area of grazing land without fences or other barriers.

o·pen-reel ▶*adj.* (of an audiotape recorder) having reels of tape requiring individual threading, as distinct from a cassette.

o·pen road ▶*n.* a road or highway allowing easy travel, esp. one outside an urban area. ■ a path or course of action without care or hindrance.

o·pen sea ▶*n.* (usu. **the open sea**) an expanse of sea away from land.

o·pen sea·son ▶*n.* [*in sing.*] a period when restrictions on the hunting of certain types of wildlife are lifted. ■ a period when all restrictions on a particular activity or product are abandoned or ignored: *an hour before departure, it's open season on all remaining seats.*

o·pen se·cret ▶*n.* a supposed secret that is in fact known to many people.

o·pen ses·a·me ▶*n.* a free or unrestricted means of admission or access: *academic success is not an automatic open sesame to the job market.* [from the magic formula in the tale of Ali Baba and the Forty Thieves (see **ALI BABA**).]

o·pen shop ▶*n.* a system whereby employees in a place of work are not required to join a labor union. Compare with **CLOSED SHOP**, **UNION SHOP**. ■ a place of work following such a system.

o·pen so·ci·e·ty ▶*n.* a society characterized by a flexible structure, freedom of belief, and wide dissemination of information.

o·pen stock ▶*n.* merchandise, esp. china, silverware, and glassware, that is sold in sets and kept in stock so that customers can purchase or replace individual pieces.

o·pen sys·tem ▶*n.* **1** *Computing* a system in which the components and protocols conform to standards independent of a particular supplier. **2** *Physics* a material system in which mass or energy can be lost to or gained from the environment.

o·pen-toed ▶*adj.* (of a shoe) having an upper that does not cover the toes.

o·pen ver·dict ▶*n.* *Law* a verdict of a coroner's jury affirming the occurrence of a suspicious death but not specifying the cause.

o·pen·work /ˈōpən,wərk/ ▶*n.* [usu. as *adj.*] ornamental work in cloth, metal, leather, or other material with regular patterns of openings and holes.

o·per·a[1] /ˈäp(ə)rə/ ▶*n.* a dramatic work in one or more acts, set to music for singers and instrumentalists. ■ such works as a genre of classical music. ■ a building for the performance of opera. ▷mid 17th cent.: from Italian, from Latin, literally 'labor, work.'

o·pe·ra[2] ▶ plural form of **OPUS**.

op·er·a·ble /ˈäp(ə)rəbəl/ ▶*adj.* **1** able to be used: *the storm left only one operable voice channel.* **2** able to be treated by means of a surgical operation: *operable breast cancer.* ▷mid 17th cent.: from late Latin *operabilis*, from Latin *operari* 'expend labor on' (see **OPERATE**). —**op·er·a·bil·i·ty** /,äp(ə)rəˈbilitē/ *n.*

o·pé·ra bouffe /ˈäp(ə)rə ˈbo͞of; ,ôpärä/ ▶*n.* (*pl.* **o·pé·ras bouffes** *pronunc.* same) a French comic opera, with dialogue in recitative and characters drawn from everyday life. ■ such works as a genre. ▷French, from Italian (see **OPERA BUFFA**).

o·pe·ra buf·fa /ˈäp(ə)rə ˈbo͞ofə; ,ōperä ˈbo͞ofä/ ▶*n.* a comic opera, typically in Italian, esp. one with characters drawn from everyday life. ■ such works as a genre. ▷Italian.

o·pe·ra cloak ▸*n.* a cloak of rich material worn over evening clothes, esp. by women.

o·pé·ra co·mique /ˈäp(ə)rə käˈmēk; ˌôpärä kôˈmēk/ ▸*n.* an opera on a lighthearted theme, typically in French and with spoken dialogue. ■ such works as a genre.

op·er·a glass·es (or **op·er·a glass**) ▸*plural n.* small binoculars for use at the opera or theater.

op·er·a·go·er /ˈäp(ə)rəˌgōər/ ▸*n.* one who attends opera performances.

op·er·a hat ▸*n.* a collapsible top hat.

op·er·a house ▸*n.* a theater designed for the performance of opera.

op·er·and /ˈäpəˌrand/ ▸*n. Mathematics* the quantity on which an operation is to be done. ▷late 19th cent.: from Latin *operandum*, neuter gerundive of *operari* 'expend labor on' (see **OPERATE**).

op·er·ant /ˈäpərənt/ *Psychology* ▸*adj.* involving the modification of behavior by the reinforcing or inhibiting effect of its own consequences (instrumental conditioning).
▸*n.* an item of behavior that is initially spontaneous, rather than a response to a prior stimulus, but whose consequences may reinforce or inhibit recurrence of that behavior. ▷late Middle English: from Latin *operant-* 'being at work,' from the verb *operari*.

op·er·a queen ▸*n. informal* a male homosexual who is fanatical about opera, esp. one characterized as being affectedly haughty and overrefined.

o·pe·ra se·ri·a /ˈäp(ə)rə ˈsi(ə)rēə; ˈōpeˌrä ˈserēˌä/ ▸*n.* an opera, typically one of the 18th century in Italian, on a serious, usually classical or mythological theme. ■ such works as a genre. ▷Italian, literally 'serious opera.'

op·er·ate /ˈäpəˌrāt/ ▸*v.* **1** [*trans.*] (of a person) control the functioning of (a machine, process, or system): *a shortage of workers to operate new machines.* ■ [*intrans.*] (of a machine, process, or system) function in a specified manner: *market forces were allowed to operate freely.* ■ [*intrans.*] be in effect: *there is a powerful law that operates in politics.* ■ (of a person or organization) manage and run (a business): *many foreign companies operate factories in the U.S.* ■ [*intrans.*] (of an organization) be managed and run in a specified way: *neither company had operated within the terms of its charter.* ■ [*intrans.*] (of an armed force) conduct military activities in a specified area or from a specified base: *the mountain bases from which the guerrillas were operating.* **2** [*intrans.*] perform a surgical operation: *the surgeons refused to operate | my brother had to be* **operated on** *last week.* **3** [*intrans.*] function; work: *we have as yet no conclusive evidence on how these cells operate.* ▷early 17th cent.: from Latin *operat-* 'done by labor,' from the verb *operari*, from *opus, oper-* 'work.'

op·er·at·ic /ˌäpəˈratik/ ▸*adj.* of, relating to, or characteristic of opera: *operatic arias.* ■ extravagantly theatrical; overly dramatic: *she wrung her hands in operatic despair.* ▷mid 18th cent.: formed irregularly from **OPERA**[1], on the pattern of words such as *dramatic*. **—op·er·at·i·cal·ly** /-ik(ə)lē/ *adv.*

op·er·at·ics /ˌäpəˈratiks/ ▸*plural n.* [often treated as *sing.*] the production or performance of operas. ■ theatrically exaggerated or overemotional behavior.

op·er·at·ing prof·it ▸*n.* profit from business operations (gross profit less operating expenses) before deduction of fixed costs.

op·er·at·ing room (abbr.: **OR**) (*Brit.* **operating theatre**) ▸*n.* a room in a hospital specially equipped for surgical operations.

op·er·at·ing sys·tem ▸*n.* the software that supports a computer's basic functions, such as scheduling tasks, executing applications, and controlling peripherals.

op·er·a·tion /ˌäpəˈrāsʜən/ ▸*n.* **1** the fact or condition of functioning or being active: *the construction and operation of power stations | some of these ideas could be* **put into operation**. ■ an active process; a discharge of a function: *the operations of the mind.* ■ a business organization; a company: *he reopened his operation under a different name.* ■ an activity in which such an organization is involved: *the company is selling most of its commercial banking operations.* **2** an act of surgery performed on a patient. **3** [often with *adj.*] a piece of organized and concerted activity involving a number of people, esp. members of the armed forces or the police: *a rescue operation | military operations.* ■ (**Operation**) preceding a code name for such an activity: *Operation Desert Storm.* **4** *Mathematics* a process in which a number, quantity, expression, etc., is altered or manipulated according to formal rules, such as those of addition, multiplication, and differentiation. ▷late Middle English: via Old French from Latin *operatio(n-)*, from the verb *operari* 'expend labor on' (see **OPERATE**).

op·er·a·tion·al /ˌäpəˈrāsʜənl/ ▸*adj.* in or ready for use: *the new laboratory is fully operational.* ■ of or relating to the routine functioning and activities of a business or organization: *the coffee bar's initial operational costs.* ■ engaged in or relating to active operations of the armed forces, police, or emergency services: *an operational fighter squadron.* **—op·er·a·tion·al·ly** *adv.*

op·er·a·tion·al am·pli·fi·er (abbr.: **op-amp**) ▸*n. Electronics* an amplifier with high gain and high input impedance (usually with external feedback), used esp. in circuits for performing mathematical operations on an input voltage.

op·er·a·tion·al·ism /äpəˈrāsʜənlˌizəm/ ▸*n.* (also **op·er·a·tion·ism**) *Philosophy* a form of positivism that defines scientific concepts in terms of the operations used to determine or prove them. **—op·er·a·tion·al·ist** *n.* & *adj.*

op·er·a·tion·al·ize /ˌäpəˈrāsʜənlˌīz/ ▸*v.* [*trans.*] **1** put into operation or use. **2** *Philosophy* express or define (something) in terms of the operations used to determine or prove it.

op·er·a·tions re·search ▸*n.* the application of scientific principles to business management, providing a quantitative basis for complex decisions.

op·er·a·tive /ˈäp(ə)rītiv; ˈäpəˌrātiv/ ▸*adj.* **1** functioning; having effect: *the transmitter is operative | the mining ban would remain operative.* ■ [*attrib.*] (of a word) having the most relevance or significance in a phrase or sentence: *a young man, and the operative word is young, should go into the armed services at around seventeen.* **2** [*attrib.*] of or relating to surgery: *they had wounds needing operative treatment.*
▸*n.* a worker, esp. a skilled one in a manufacturing industry. ■ a private detective or secret agent. ▷late Middle English: from late Latin *operativus*, from Latin *operat-* 'done by labor,' from the verb *operari* (see **OPERATE**). **—op·er·a·tive·ly** *adv.* **—op·er·a·tive·ness** *n.*

op·er·a·tor /ˈäpəˌrātər/ ▸*n.* **1** [often with *adj.*] a person who operates equipment or a machine: *a radio operator.* ■ (usu. **the operator**) a person who works for a telephone company assisting users, or who works at a telephone switchboard. **2** [usu. with *adj.*] a person or company that engages in or runs a business or enterprise: *a tour operator.* **3** [with *adj.*] *informal* a person who acts in a specified, esp. a manipulative, way: *her reputation as a cool, clever operator.* **4** *Mathematics* a symbol or function denoting an operation (e.g., ×, +).

op·er·a win·dow ▸*n.* a small fixed window usually behind the rear side window of an automobile.

o·per·cu·lum /ōˈpərkyələm/ ▸*n.* (*pl.* **-la** /-lə/) *Zoology* & *Botany* a structure that closes or covers an aperture, in particular: ■ technical term for **GILL COVER**. ■ a secreted plate that serves to close the aperture of a gastropod mollusk's shell when the animal is retracted. ■ a lidlike structure of the spore-containing capsule of a moss. ▷early 18th cent.: from Latin, literally 'lid, covering,' from *operire* 'to cover.' **—o·per·cu·lar** /-lər/ *adj.* **—o·per·cu·late** /-ˌlāt/ *adj.* **—o·per·cu·li-** *comb. form*.

op·er·et·ta /ˌäpəˈretə/ ▸*n.* a short opera, usually on a light or humorous theme and typically having spoken dialogue. Notable composers of operettas include Offenbach, Johann Strauss, Lehár, and Gilbert and Sullivan. ▷late 18th cent.: from Italian, diminutive of *opera* (see **OPERA**[1]).

op·er·on /ˈäpəˌrän/ ▸*n. Biology* a unit made up of linked genes that is thought to regulate other genes responsible for protein synthesis. ▷1960s: from French *opérer* 'to effect, work' + **-ON**.

op·er·ose /ˈäpəˌrōs/ ▸*adj. rare* involving or displaying much industry or effort. ▷late 17th cent.: from Latin *operosus*, from *opus* 'work.'

oph·i·cleide /ˈäfiˌklīd/ ▸*n.* an obsolete bass brass instrument with keys, used in bands in the 19th century but superseded by the tuba. ▷mid 19th cent.: from French *ophicléide*, from Greek *ophis* 'serpent' + *kleis, kleid-* 'key.'

O·phid·i·a /ōˈfidēə/ *Zoology* a group of reptiles that comprises the snakes. Also called **SERPENTES**. • Suborder Ophidia, order Squamata. ▷modern Latin (plural), from Greek *ophis, ophid-* 'snake.' **—o·phid·i·an** *n.* & *adj.*

oph·i·o·lite /ˈäfēəˌlīt; ˈōfē-/ ▸*n. Geology* an igneous rock consisting largely of serpentine, believed to have been formed from the submarine eruption of oceanic crustal and upper mantle material. ▷mid 19th cent.: from Greek *ophis* 'snake' + **-LITE**. **—oph·i·o·lit·ic** /ˌäfēəˈlitik; ˌōfē-/ *adj.*

oph·i·ol·o·gy /ˌäfēˈäləjē; ˌōfē-/ ▸*n.* the branch of zoology that deals with snakes. ▷early 19th cent.: from Greek *ophis* 'snake' + **-LOGY**. **—oph·i·ol·o·gist** /-jist/ *n.*

O·phir /ˈōfər/ (in the Bible) an unidentified region, perhaps in southeastern Arabia, famous for its fine gold and precious stones.

oph·ite /ˈäfīt; ˈōfīt/ ▸*n. Geology* a green rock with spots or markings like a snake that can be either eruptive or metamorphic; serpentine. ▷mid 17th cent.: via Latin from Greek *ophitēs* 'serpentine stone,' from *ophis* 'snake,' + **-ITE**[1].

o·phit·ic /ōˈfitik/ ▸*adj. Geology* relating to or denoting a poikilitic rock texture in which crystals of feldspar are interposed between plates of augite. ▷late 19th cent.: via Latin from Greek *ophitēs* 'serpentine stone' (from *ophis* 'snake') + **-IC**.

Oph·i·u·chus /ˌäfēˈyo͞okəs; ˌōfē-/ *Astronomy* a large constellation (the Serpent Bearer or Holder), said to represent a man in the coils of a snake. Both the celestial equator and the ecliptic pass through it, but it is not counted among the signs of the zodiac. ■ [as *genitive*] (**Ophiuchi**) used with a preceding letter or numeral to designate a star in this constellation: *the star Eta Ophiuchi.* ▷via Latin from Greek *Ophioukos*.

Oph·i·u·roi·de·a /ˌäfēyo͝oroidēə; ˌōfē-/ *Zoology* a class of echinoderms that comprises the brittle stars. ▷modern Latin (plural), based on the genus name *Ophiura*, from Greek *ophis* 'snake' + *oura* 'tail.' **—oph·i·ur·oid** /-ˈyo͝oroid/ *n.* & *adj.*

oph·thal·mi·a /äfˈᴛʜalmēə; äp-/ ▸*n. Medicine* inflammation of the eye, esp. conjunctivitis. ▷late Middle English: via late Latin from Greek, from *ophthalmos* 'eye.'

oph·thal·mic /äfˈᴛʜalmik; äp-/ ▸*adj.* [*attrib.*] of or relating to the eye and its diseases. ▷early 17th cent.: via Latin from Greek *ophthalmikos*, from *ophthalmos* 'eye.'

oph·thal·mi·tis /ˌäfᴛʜəlˈmīdis; ˌäp-/ ▸*n. Medicine* inflammation of the eye.

ophthalmo- ▸*comb. form Medicine* relating to the eyes: *ophthalmoscope.* ▷from Greek *ophthalmos* 'eye.'

oph·thal·mol·o·gy /ˌäfᴛʜə(l)ˈmäləjē; ˌäp-/ ▸*n.* the branch of medicine concerned with the study and treatment of disorders and diseases of the eye. **—oph·thal·mo·log·i·cal** /-məˈläjikəl/ *adj.* **—oph·thal·mol·o·gist** /-jist/ *n.*

oph·thal·mo·ple·gia /äfˌᴛʜalməˈplēj(ē)ə/ ▸*n. Medicine* paralysis of the muscles within or surrounding the eye. **—oph·thal·mo·ple·gic** /-ˈplējik/ *adj.*

oph·thal·mo·scope /äfˈᴛʜalməˌskōp; äp-/ ▸*n.* an instrument for inspecting the retina and other parts of the eye. **—oph·thal·mo·scop·ic** /ˌäfᴛʜəlməˈskäpik; ˌäp-/ *adj.* **—oph·thal·mos·co·py** /ˌäfᴛʜəlˈmäskəpē; ˌäp-/ *n.*

-opia ▸*comb. form* denoting a visual disorder: *myopia.* ▷from Greek *ōps, ōp-* 'eye, face.'

o·pi·ate ▸*adj.* /ˈōpē-it; -ˌāt/ relating to, resembling, or containing opium: *the use of opiate drugs.* ■ *figurative, dated* causing drowsiness or a dulling of the senses.
▸*n.* /ˈōpē-it; -ˌāt/ a drug with morphinelike effects, derived from opium. ■ *figurative* a thing that soothes or stupefies.
▸*v.* /-ˌāt/ [*trans.*] [often as *adj.*] (**opiated**) impregnate with opium. ▷late Middle English (as a noun): from medieval Latin *opiatus* (adjective), *opiatum* (noun), based on Latin *opium* (see **OPIUM**).
▸*PHRASE* □ **the opiate of the masses** (or **people**) something regarded as inducing a false and unrealistic sense of contentment among people. [translating the German phrase *Opium des Volks*, used by Karl Marx in reference to religion (1844).]

o·pine /ōˈpīn/ ▸*v.* [*reporting verb*] *formal* hold and state as one's opinion: [with *direct speech*] *"The man is a genius," he opined* | [with *clause*] *the critic opined that the most exciting musical moment occurred when the orchestra struck up the national anthem.* ▷late Middle English: from Latin *opinari* 'think, believe.'

o·pin·ion /əˈpinyən/ ▸*n.* a view or judgment formed about something, not necessarily based on fact or knowledge: *I'm writing to voice my opinion on an issue of great importance | that,* **in my opinion**, *is dead right.* ■ the beliefs or views of a large number or majority of people about a particular thing: *the changing climate of opinion.* ■ (**opinion of**) an estimation of the quality or worth of someone or something: *I had a higher opinion of myself than I deserved.* ■ a formal

statement of advice by an expert on a professional matter: *seeking a second opinion from a specialist.* ■ *Law* a formal statement of reasons for a judgment given. ■ *Law* a lawyer's advice on the merits of a case. ▷Middle English: via Old French from Latin *opinio(n-)*, from the stem of *opinari* 'think, believe.'
▸*PHRASES* □ **be of the opinion that** believe or maintain that: *economists are of the opinion that the economy could contract.* □ **a matter of opinion** something not capable of being proven either way.

THE RIGHT WORD **belief, conviction, opinion, persuasion, sentiment, view**
When you give your **opinion** on something, you offer a conclusion or a judgment that, although it may be open to question, seems true or probable to you at the time (*she was known for her strong opinions on women in the workplace*).
A **view** is an opinion that is affected by your personal feelings or biases (*his views on life were essentially optimistic*), while a **sentiment** is a more or less settled opinion that may still be colored by emotion (*her sentiments on aging were shared by many other women approaching fifty*).
A **belief** differs from an *opinion* or a *view* in that it is not necessarily the creation of the person who holds it; the emphasis here is on the mental acceptance of an idea, a proposition, or a doctrine and on the assurance of its truth (*religious beliefs; his belief in the power of the body to heal itself*).
A **conviction** is a firmly held and unshakable belief whose truth is not doubted (*she could not be swayed in her convictions*), while a **persuasion** (in this sense) is a strong belief that is unshakable because you want to believe that it's true rather than because there is evidence proving it so (*she was of the persuasion that he was innocent*).

o·pin·ion·at·ed /ə'pinyə,nātid/ ▸*adj.* conceitedly assertive and dogmatic in one's opinions: *an arrogant and opinionated man.* ▷early 17th cent.: from the (rare) verb *opinionate* 'hold the opinion (that),' from **OPINION**.
o·pin·ion poll ▸*n.* an assessment of public opinion obtained by questioning a representative sample.
o·pi·oid /'ōpē,oid/ *Biochemistry* ▸*n.* an opiumlike compound that binds to one or more of the three opioid receptors of the body.
▸*adj.* relating to or denoting such compounds. ▷1950s: from **OPIUM** + **-OID**.
opistho- ▸*prefix* behind; to the rear: *opisthosoma.* ▷from Greek *opisthen* 'behind.'
O·pis·tho·bran·chi·a /ə,pisTHə'braNGkēə/ *Zoology* a group of mollusks that includes the sea slugs and sea hares. They have a small or absent shell and are typically brightly colored with conspicuous external gills. • Subclass Opisthobranchia, class Gastropoda. ▷modern Latin (plural), from **OPISTHO-** 'to the rear' + *brankhia* 'gills.' **—o·pis·tho·branch** /ə'pisTHə,braNGk/ *n.*
op·is·thog·na·thous /'äpis'THägnəTHəs/ ▸*adj. Zoology* (of an animal) having retreating jaws or teeth.
op·is·thot·o·nos /,äpis'THätnəs/ (also **op·is·thot·o·nus**) ▸*n. Medicine* spasm of the muscles causing backward arching of the head, neck, and spine, as in severe tetanus, some kinds of meningitis, and strychnine poisoning. ▷mid 17th cent.: via late Latin from Greek *opisthotonos* 'drawn backward.'
o·pi·um /'ōpēəm/ ▸*n.* a reddish-brown heavy-scented addictive drug prepared from the juice of the opium poppy, used as a narcotic and in medicine as an analgesic. ▷late Middle English: via Latin from Greek *opion* 'poppy juice,' from *opos* 'juice,' from an Indo-European root meaning 'water.'
▸*PHRASE* □ **the opium of the people** (or **masses**) see **THE OPIATE OF THE MASSES** at **OPIATE**.
o·pi·um den ▸*n.* a place where opium is sold and smoked.
o·pi·um pop·py ▸*n.* a Eurasian poppy with ornamental white, red, pink, or purple flowers. Its immature capsules yield a latex from which opium is obtained. • *Papaver somniferum*, family Papaveraceae.
O·pi·um Wars two wars involving Britain and China regarding the question of trading rights.

That between Britain and China (1839–42) followed China's attempt to prohibit the illegal importation of opium from British India into China. The second, involving Britain and France against China (1856–60), followed Chinese restrictions on foreign trade. Defeat of the Chinese resulted in the ceding of Hong Kong to Britain and the opening of five "treaty ports" to traders.

OPM ▸*abbr. informal* other people's money.
O·por·to /ō'pôrtō/ the principal city and port of northern Portugal, near the mouth of the Douro River, known for port wine; pop. 311,000. Portuguese name **PORTO**.
o·pos·sum /(ə)'päsəm/ ▸*n.* an American marsupial that has a ratlike prehensile tail and hind feet with an opposable thumb. • Family Didelphidae: several genera and numerous species, in particular the catsized **common opossum** (*Didelphis marsupialis*) of North, Central, and South America, which in North America was formerly known as the **Virginia opossum** and was considered a distinct species (*D. virginiana*). ▷early 17th cent.: from Virginia Algonquian *opassom*, from *op* 'white' + *assom* 'dog.'

opossum

o·pos·sum shrimp ▸*n.* a small shrimplike crustacean that has a long abdomen, conspicuous eyes and is typically transparent. • Order Mysidacea: *Praunus* and other genera. See also **MYSID**.
opp. ▸*abbr.* opposite.
Op·pen·heim·er /'äpən,hīmər/, Julius Robert (1904–67), U.S. theoretical physicist. He was director of the laboratory at Los Alamos, New Mexico, during the development of the first atom bomb, but opposed the development of the hydrogen bomb after World War II.
op·po·nens /ə'pōnənz/ ▸*n. Anatomy* another term for **OPPONENT MUSCLE.** ▷late 18th cent.: from Latin, literally 'setting against.'
op·po·nent /ə'pōnənt/ ▸*n.* someone who competes against or fights another in a contest, game, or argument; a rival or adversary: *he beat his opponent by a landslide margin.* ■ a person who disagrees with or resists a proposal or practice: *an* **opponent of** *the economic reforms.* ▷late 16th cent. (denoting a person opening an academic debate by proposing objections to a philosophical or religious thesis): from Latin *opponent-* 'setting against,' from the verb *opponere*, from *ob-* 'against' + *ponere* 'place.'
op·po·nent mus·cle ▸*n. Anatomy* any of several muscles enabling the thumb to be moved toward a finger of the same hand.
op·por·tune /,äpər't(y)ōōn/ ▸*adj.* (of a time) well-chosen or particularly favorable or appropriate: *he couldn't have arrived at a less opportune moment.* See note at **TIMELY.** ■ done or occurring at a favorable or useful time; well-timed: *the opportune use of humor to lower tension.* ▷late Middle English: from Old French *opportun(e)*, from Latin *opportunus*, from *ob-* 'in the direction of' + *portus* 'harbor,' originally describing the wind driving toward the harbor, hence 'seasonable.' **—op·por·tune·ly** *adv.* **—op·por·tune·ness** *n.*
op·por·tun·ist /,äpər't(y)ōōnist/ ▸*n.* a person who exploits circumstances to gain immediate advantage rather than being guided by consistent principles or plans: *most burglaries are committed by casual opportunists.*
▸*adj.* opportunistic: *the calculating and opportunist politician.* ▷late 19th cent.: from **OPPORTUNE** + **-IST.** **—op·por·tun·ism** /-,nizəm/ *n.*
op·por·tun·is·tic /,äpərt(y)ōō'nistik/ ▸*adj.* exploiting chances offered by immediate circumstances without reference to a general plan or moral principle: *the change was cynical and opportunistic.* ■ *Ecology* (of a plant or animal) able to spread quickly in a previously unexploited habitat. ■ *Medicine* (of a microorganism or an infection caused by it) rarely affecting patients except in unusual circumstances, typically when the immune system is depressed. **—op·por·tun·is·ti·cal·ly** /-ik(ə)lē/ *adv.*
op·por·tu·ni·ty /,äpər't(y)ōōnitē/ ▸*n.* (*pl.* **-ties**) a set of circumstances that makes it possible to do something: *we may see increased* **opportunities for** *export* | *the collection gives students the* **opportunity of** *reading works by well-known authors.* ■ a chance for employment or promotion: *career opportunities in our New York headquarters.* ▷late Middle English: from Old French *opportunite*, from Latin *opportunitas*, from *opportunus* (see **OPPORTUNE**).
▸*PHRASE* □ **opportunity knocks** a chance for success or advancement occurs.
op·por·tu·ni·ty cost ▸*n. Economics* the loss of potential gain from other alternatives when one alternative is chosen: *idle cash balances represent an opportunity cost in terms of lost interest.*
op·pos·a·ble /ə'pōzəbəl/ ▸*adj. Zoology* (of the thumb of a primate) capable of moving toward and touching the other digits on the same hand.
op·pose /ə'pōz/ ▸*v.* [*trans.*] disapprove of and attempt to prevent, esp. by argument: *those of you who oppose capital punishment.* ■ actively resist or refuse to comply with (a person or a system): *off-roaders who adamantly opposed new trail restrictions.* ■ compete against (someone) in a contest: *a candidate to oppose the leader in the presidential contest.* ▷late Middle English: from Old French *opposer*, from Latin *opponere* (see **OPPONENT**), but influenced by Latin *oppositus* 'set or placed against' and Old French *poser* 'to place.' **—op·pos·er** *n.*
op·posed /ə'pōzd/ ▸*adj.* **1** [*predic.*] (**opposed to**) eager to prevent or put an end to; disapproving of or disagreeing with: *opposed to the construction of nuclear power plants.* ■ in conflict or disagreement with; hostile to: *both groups were opposed to communism.* **2** (of two or more things) contrasting or conflicting with each other: *the agency is being asked to do two* **diametrically opposed** *things.*
▸*PHRASE* □ **as opposed to** distinguished from or in contrast with: *an approach that is theoretical as opposed to practical.*
op·pos·ing /ə'pōziNG/ ▸*adj.* [*attrib.*] in conflict or competition with a specified or implied subject: *the opposing team.* ■ (of two or more subjects) differing from or in conflict with each other: *the brothers fought on opposing sides in the war.* ■ facing; opposite: *on the opposing page there were two addresses.*
op·po·site /'äpəzit/ ▸*adj.* **1** [*attrib.*] having a position on the other or further side of something; facing something, esp. something of the same type: *a crowd gathered on the opposite side of the street.* ■ [*postpositive*] facing the speaker or a specified person or thing: *he went into the store opposite.* ■ *Botany* (of leaves or shoots) arising in opposed pairs, one on each side of the stem. **2** diametrically different; of a contrary kind: *a word that is* **opposite** *in meaning* **to** *another* | *currents flowing in* **opposite directions.** ■ [*attrib.*] being the other of a contrasted pair: *the opposite ends of the price range.*
▸*n.* a person or thing that is totally different from or the reverse of someone or something else: *we* **were opposites** *in temperament* | *the literal is* **the opposite of** *the figurative.*
▸*adv.* in a position facing a specified or implied subject: *she was sitting almost opposite.*
▸*prep.* in a position on the other side of a specific area from; facing: *they sat opposite one another.* ■ *figurative* (of someone taking a leading part in a play or movie) in a complementary role to (another performer). ▷late Middle English: via Old French from Latin *oppositus*, past participle of *opponere* 'set against.' **—op·po·site·ly** *adv.* **—op·po·site·ness** *n.*

THE RIGHT WORD **contradictory, antithetical, contrary, opposite, reverse**
All of these adjectives are usually applied to abstractions and are used to describe ideas, statements, qualities, forces, etc., that are so far apart as to seem irreconcilable.
Opposite refers to ideas or things that are symmetrically opposed in position, direction, or character—in other words, that are set against each other in such a way that the contrast or conflict between them is highlighted (*they sat opposite one another at the table*).
Contradictory goes a little further, implying that if one of two opposing statements, propositions, or principles is true, the other must be false (*he assured us the fee would be under $500; his partner gave us contradictory information, saying costs could go as high as $800.*). Two contradictory elements are mutually exclusive; for example, *alive* and *dead* are contradictory terms because logically they cannot be applied to the same thing.
Antithetical implies that the two things being contrasted are diametrically opposed—as far apart or as different from each other as is possible (*they debated the antithetical theories of creationism and evolution*).
Contrary adds connotations of conflict or

antagonism (*the group's discussion was hindered by his contrary remarks*).

Reverse applies to that which moves or faces in the opposite direction (*he scribbled something on the reverse side of her business card*).

op·po·site num·ber ▸*n.* (**someone's opposite number**) a person whose position or rank in another group, organization, or country is equivalent to that held by someone already mentioned.

op·po·site prompt ▸*n. Brit.* the offstage area of a theater stage to the right of an actor facing the audience.

op·po·site sex ▸*n.* women in relation to men or vice versa.

op·po·si·tion /ˌäpəˈzisHən/ ▸*n.* resistance or dissent, expressed in action or argument: *there was considerable* **opposition to** *the proposal | the regime cracked down against the threat of opposition.* ■ (often **the opposition**) a group of adversaries or competitors, esp. a rival political party or athletic team. ■ (**the opposition**) the principal political party opposed to the one in office. ■ a contrast or antithesis: *a nature-culture opposition.* ■ *Logic* (of two propositions) the relation of having the same subject and predicate, but differing in quantity, quality, or both. ■ *Astronomy & Astrology* the apparent position of two celestial objects that are directly opposite each other in the sky, esp. when a superior planet is opposite the sun. ▷late Middle English: from Latin *oppositio(n-)*, from *opponere* 'set against.' **—op·po·si·tion·al** /-SHənl/ *adj.*
▸*PHRASE* □ **in opposition** in contrast or conflict: *they found themselves* **in opposition to** *federal policy.*

op·press /əˈpres/ ▸*v.* [*trans.*] (often **be oppressed**) keep (someone) in subservience and hardship, esp. by the unjust exercise of authority: *a system that oppressed working people* | [as *adj.*] (**oppressed**) *oppressed racial minorities.* ■ cause (someone) to feel distressed, anxious, or uncomfortable: *he was oppressed by some secret worry.* ▷late Middle English: from Old French *oppresser*, from medieval Latin *oppressare*, from Latin *oppress-* 'pressed against,' from the verb *opprimere.* **—op·pres·sor** /əˈpresər/ *n.*

op·pres·sion /əˈpresHən/ ▸*n.* prolonged cruel or unjust treatment or control: *a region shattered by oppression and killing.* ■ the state of being subject to such treatment or control. ■ mental pressure or distress: *her mood had initially been alarm and a sense of oppression.* ▷Middle English: from Old French, from Latin *oppressio(n-)*, from the verb *opprimere* (see **OPPRESS**).

op·pres·sive /əˈpresiv/ ▸*adj.* unjustly inflicting hardship and constraint, esp. on a minority or other subordinate group: *an oppressive dictatorship.* ■ weighing heavily on the mind or spirits; causing depression or discomfort: *a profound loneliness, an oppressive emptiness.* ■ (of weather) excessively hot and humid. ▷late 16th cent.: from medieval Latin *oppressivus*, from Latin *oppress-* 'pressed against,' from the verb *opprimere* (see **OPPRESS**). **—op·pres·sive·ly** *adv.* **—op·pres·sive·ness** *n.*

op·pro·bri·ous /əˈprōbrēəs/ ▸*adj.* (of language) expressing opprobrium. ■ disgraceful; shameful: *their opprobrious conduct.* ▷late Middle English: from late Latin *opprobriosus*, from *opprobrium* (see **OPPROBRIUM**). **—op·pro·bri·ous·ly** *adv.*

op·pro·bri·um /əˈprōbrēəm/ ▸*n.* harsh criticism or censure: *his films and the critical opprobrium they have generated.* ■ the public disgrace arising from someone's shameful conduct: *the opprobrium of being closely associated with thugs and gangsters.* ■ *archaic* an occasion or cause of reproach or disgrace. ▷mid 17th cent.: from Latin, literally 'infamy,' from *opprobrum*, from *ob-* 'against' + *probrum* 'disgraceful act.'

op·pugn /əˈpyo͞on/ ▸*v.* [*trans.*] *rare* call into question the truth or validity of. ▷late Middle English (in the sense 'fight against'): from Latin *oppugnare* 'attack, besiege,' from *ob-* 'against' + *pugnare* 'to fight.' **—op·pugn·er** *n.*

op·pug·nant /əˈpəgnənt/ ▸*adj. rare* opposing; antagonistic. ▷early 16th cent.: from Latin *oppugnant-* 'fighting against,' from the verb *oppugnare* (see **OPPUGN**). **—op·pug·nan·cy** /-nənsē/ *n.*

O·prah·i·za·tion /ˌōprəiˈzāsHən/ ▸*n.* the increasing tendency of public and private citizens to discuss their personal problems or feelings in public forums, especially talk shows: *going against the trend of Oprahization, he refused to talk about his divorce to the press.* ▷from *Oprah Winfrey* (1954–), U.S. talk-show host + *-ation.*

OP·SEC ▸*abbr.* operations (or operational) security.

op·si·math /ˈäpsəˌmaTH/ ▸*n.* a person who begins to learn or study only late in life. ▷late 19th cent.: from Greek *opsimathēs*, from *opse* 'late' + the stem *math-* 'learn.'

op·sin /ˈäpsin/ ▸*n. Biochemistry* a protein that forms part of the visual pigment rhodopsin and is released by the action of light. ▷1950s: shortening of **RHODOPSIN**.

op·so·nin /ˈäpsənin/ ▸*n. Biochemistry* an antibody or other substance that binds to foreign microorganisms or cells, making them more susceptible to phagocytosis. ▷early 20th cent.: from Latin *opsonare* 'buy provisions' (from Greek *opsōnein*) + **-IN**[1]. **—op·son·ic** /äpˈsänik/ *adj.*

op·so·nize /ˈäpsəˌnīz/ ▸*v.* [*trans.*] *Medicine* make (a foreign cell) more susceptible to phagocytosis. **—op·so·ni·za·tion** /ˌäpsəniˈzāsHən/ *n.*

opt /äpt/ ▸*v.* [*intrans.*] make a choice from a range of possibilities: *consumers will* **opt for** *low-priced goods* | [with *infinitive*] *students opting to continue with physics.*
▸*phrasal v.* □ **opt out** choose not to participate in or carry on with something: *they had both* **opted out of** *the medical plan.* ▷late 19th cent.: from French *opter*, from Latin *optare* 'choose, wish.'

opt. ▸*abbr.* ■ optative. ■ optical. ■ optician. ■ optics. ■ optional.

op·ta·tive /ˈäptətiv/ *Grammar* ▸*adj.* relating to or denoting a mood of verbs in Greek and other languages, expressing a wish, equivalent to English expressions *if only.*
▸*n.* a verb in the optative mood. ■ (**the optative**) the optative mood. ▷mid 16th cent.: from French *optatif, -ive*, from late Latin *optativus*, from *optat-* 'chosen,' from the verb *optare* (see **OPT**). **—op·ta·tive·ly** *adv.*

op·tic /ˈäptik/ ▸*adj.* of or relating to the eye or vision.
▸*n.* **1** a lens or other optical component in an optical instrument. **2** *archaic* or *humorous* the eye. ▷late Middle English: from French *optique* or medieval Latin *opticus*, from Greek *optikos*, from *optos* 'seen.'

op·ti·cal /ˈäptikəl/ ▸*adj.* **1** of or relating to sight, esp. in relation to the physical action of light: *optical illusions.* ■ constructed to assist sight. ■ devised on the principles of optics. **2** *Physics* operating in or employing the visible part of the electromagnetic spectrum: *optical telescopes.* ■ *Electronics* (of a device) requiring electromagnetic radiation for its operation: *integrated optical circuits.* **—op·ti·cal·ly** /-ik(ə)lē/ *adv.*

op·ti·cal ac·tiv·i·ty ▸*n. Chemistry* the property (displayed by solutions of some compounds, notably many sugars) of rotating the plane of polarization of plane-polarized light.

op·ti·cal art ▸*n.* another term for **OP ART**.

op·ti·cal ax·is ▸*n. Physics* a line passing through the center of curvature of a lens or spherical mirror and parallel to the axis of symmetry. ■ *Crystallography* a direction in a doubly refracting crystal along which a light ray does not undergo double refraction.

op·ti·cal bench ▸*n.* a straight rigid bar, typically marked with a scale, to which lenses, light sources, and other optical components can be attached.

op·ti·cal bright·en·er ▸*n.* a fluorescent substance added to detergents in order to produce a whitening effect on laundry.

op·ti·cal char·ac·ter rec·og·ni·tion (abbr.: **OCR**) ▸*n.* the identification of printed characters using photoelectric devices and computer software.

op·ti·cal den·si·ty ▸*n. Physics* the degree to which a refractive medium retards transmitted rays of light.

op·ti·cal disk ▸*n.* see **DISK** (sense 1).

op·ti·cal dou·ble ▸*n. Astronomy* two stars that are in the same line of sight as seen from the earth, but that may be at far different distances. See also **DOUBLE STAR**.

op·ti·cal fi·ber ▸*n.* a thin glass fiber through which light can be transmitted.

op·ti·cal glass ▸*n.* a very pure kind of glass used for lenses.

op·ti·cal il·lu·sion ▸*n.* an experience of seeming to see something that does not exist or that is other than it appears. ■ something that deceives one's eyes and causes such an experience.

op·ti·cal i·so·mer ▸*n. Chemistry* each of two or more forms of a compound that have the same structure but are mirror images of each other and typically differ in optical activity. **—op·ti·cal i·som·er·ism** *n.*

op·ti·cal mi·cro·scope ▸*n.* a microscope using visible light, typically viewed directly by the eye.

op·ti·cal path ▸*n. Physics* the distance of the path that in a vacuum would contain the same number of wavelengths as the actual path taken by a ray of light traveling through a medium.

op·ti·cal ro·ta·tion ▸*n. Chemistry* the rotation of the plane of polarization of plane-polarized light by an optically active substance.

op·ti·cal scan·ner ▸*n. Electronics* a device that performs optical character recognition and produces coded signals corresponding to the characters identified.

op·ti·cal turn·stile ▸*n.* an access control system without barriers in which those attempting to enter are evaluated by closed-circuit television or other visual means.

op·ti·cal tweez·ers ▸*plural n.* a device that uses light from a low-wattage laser to manipulate individual molecules within cells. Also called **LASER TWEEZERS**.

op·tic ax·is ▸*n.* another term for **OPTICAL AXIS**.

op·tic chi·as·ma ▸*n.* (also **op·tic chi·asm**) *Anatomy* the X-shaped structure formed at the point below the brain where the two optic nerves cross over each other.

op·tic cup ▸*n. Anatomy* a cuplike outgrowth of the brain of an embryo that develops into the retina.

op·tic disk ▸*n.* (also **op·tic disc**) *Anatomy* the raised disk on the retina at the point of entry of the optic nerve, lacking visual receptors and so creating a blind spot.

op·ti·cian /äpˈtisHən/ ▸*n.* a person qualified to make and supply eyeglasses and contact lenses for correction of vision. ■ *rare* a person who makes or sells optical instruments. ▷late 17th cent.: from French *opticien*, from medieval Latin *optica* 'optics.'

op·tic lobe ▸*n. Anatomy* a lobe in the midbrain from which the optic nerve partly arises.

op·tic nerve ▸*n. Anatomy* each of the second pair of cranial nerves, transmitting impulses to the brain from the retina at the back of the eye.

op·tics /ˈäptiks/ ▸*plural n.* [usu. treated as *sing.*] the scientific study of sight and the behavior of light, or the properties of transmission and deflection of other forms of radiation.

op·tic tract ▸*n. Anatomy* the pathway between the optic chiasma and the brain.

op·ti·ma /ˈäptəmə/ ▸ plural form of **OPTIMUM**.

op·ti·mal /ˈäptəməl/ ▸*adj.* best or most favorable; optimum: *seeking the optimal solution.* ▷late 19th cent.: from Latin *optimus* 'best' + **-AL**. **—op·ti·mal·i·ty** /ˌäptəˈmalitē/ *n.* **—op·ti·mal·ly** /-(ə)lē/ *adv.*

op·ti·mism /ˈäptəˌmizəm/ ▸*n.* **1** hopefulness and confidence about the future or the successful outcome of something: *the talks had been amicable, and there were grounds for optimism.* **2** *Philosophy* the doctrine, esp. as set forth by Leibniz, that this world is the best of all possible worlds. ■ the belief that good must ultimately prevail over evil in the universe. ▷mid 18th cent.: from French *optimisme*, from Latin *optimum* 'best thing' (see **OPTIMUM**). **—op·ti·mist** *n.*

op·ti·mis·tic /ˌäptəˈmistik/ ▸*adj.* hopeful and confident about the future: *the optimistic mood of the sixties | he was optimistic about the deal.* ■ involving an overestimate: *previous estimates may be wildly optimistic.* **—op·ti·mis·ti·cal·ly** /-ik(ə)lē/ *adv.*

op·ti·mize /ˈäptəˌmīz/ ▸*v.* [*trans.*] make the best or most effective use of (a situation, opportunity, or resource): *to optimize viewing conditions the microscope should be correctly adjusted.* ■ *Computing* rearrange or rewrite data to improve efficiency of retrieval or processing. ▷early 19th cent.: from Latin *optimus* 'best' + **-IZE**. **—op·ti·mi·za·tion** /ˌäptəˌmīˈzāsHən/ *n.* **—op·ti·miz·er** *n.*

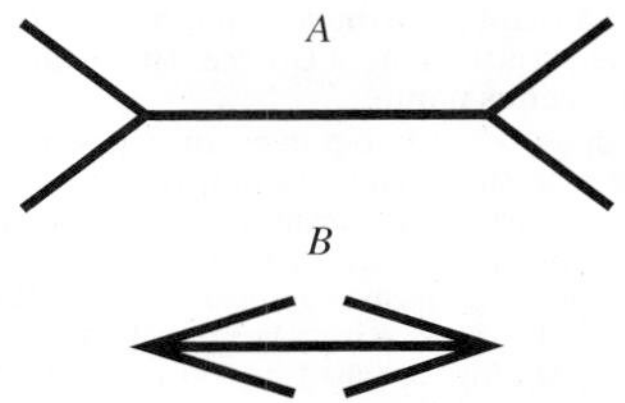

(horizontal line *A* appears to be longer than horizontal line *B*, but in fact, they are of equal length)

optical illusion

op·ti·mum /ˈäptəməm/ ▸*adj.* most conducive to a favorable outcome; best: *the optimum childbearing age.*
▸*n.* (*pl.* **-ma** /-mə/ or **-mums**) the most favorable conditions or level for growth, reproduction, or success. ▷late 19th cent.: from Latin, neuter (used as a noun) of *optimus* 'best.'

op·tion /ˈäpSHən/ ▸*n.* **1** a thing that is or may be chosen: *choose the cheapest options for supplying energy.* ■ [in *sing.*] the freedom, power, or right to choose something: *she was* **given the option** *of resigning or being dismissed* | *he has* **no option but** *to pay up.* ■ a right to buy or sell a particular thing at a specified price within a set time: *Columbia Pictures* **has an option on** *the script* | [with *infinitive*] *an option to buy the land.* **2** *Football* an offensive play in which the ball carrier has the option to run, pass, hand off, or lateral.
▸*v.* [*trans.*] buy or sell an option on (something): *his second script will have been optioned by the time you read this.* ■ *Sports* transfer a player (to a minor league team) with an option to recall him. ▷mid 16th cent.: from French, or from Latin *optio(n-)*, from the stem of *optare* 'choose.' The verb dates from the 1930s.
▸*PHRASES* □ **keep** (or **leave**) **one's options open** not commit oneself. □ **not be an option** not be feasible: *traveling by road is not an option here.*

op·tion·aire /ˌäpSHəˈne(ə)r; ˈäpSHəˌne(ə)r/ ▸*n. informal* a person whose great wealth is based on owning or exercising employee stock options. ▷late 1990s: on the pattern of *millionaire.*

op·tion·al /ˈäpSHənl/ ▸*adj.* available to be chosen but not obligatory: *a wide range of optional excursions is offered.* **—op·tion·al·i·ty** /ˌäpSHəˈnalitē/ *n.* **—op·tion·al·ly** *adv.*

op·tion·ee /ˌäpSHəˈnē/ ▸*n.* a recipient or holder of stock options.

op·to·cou·pler /ˈäptōˌkəplər/ ▸*n. Electronics* a device containing light-emitting and light-sensitive components, used to couple isolated circuits.

op·to·e·lec·tron·ics /ˈäptōəlekˈträniks; -ēˌlek-/ ▸*plural n.* [treated as *sing.*] the branch of technology concerned with the combined use of electronics and light. ■ [treated as *pl.*] circuitry constructed using this technology. **—op·to·e·lec·tron·ic** *adj.*

op·tom·e·ter /äpˈtämitər/ ▸*n.* an instrument for testing the refractive power of the eye. ▷mid 18th cent.: from Greek *optos* 'seen' + **-METER**.

op·tom·e·trist /äpˈtämitrist/ ▸*n.* a person who practices optometry.

op·tom·e·try /äpˈtämitrē/ ▸*n.* the practice or profession of examining the eyes for visual defects and prescribing corrective lenses. **—op·to·met·ric** /ˌäptəˈmetrik/ *adj.*

op·to·phone /ˈäptəˌfōn/ ▸*n.* an instrument that scans printed characters and converts them into sound, thus enabling the blind to read by ear. ▷early 20th cent.: from Greek *optos* 'seen' + **-PHONE**.

opt-out ▸*n.* an instance of choosing not to participate in something: *opt-outs from key parts of the treaty.*

op·tron·ics /äpˈträniks/ ▸*plural n.* [treated as *sing.*] short for **OPTOELECTRONICS**. **—op·tron·ic** *adj.*

op·u·lent /ˈäpyələnt/ ▸*adj.* ostentatiously rich and luxurious or lavish: *the opulent comfort of a limousine.* ■ wealthy: *his more opulent tenants.* See note at **WEALTHY**. ▷mid 16th cent. (in the sense 'wealthy, affluent'): from Latin *opulent-* 'wealthy, splendid,' from *opes* 'wealth.' **—op·u·lence** *n.* **—op·u·lent·ly** *adv.*

o·pun·tia /ōˈpənSH(ē)ə/ ▸*n.* a cactus of a genus that comprises the prickly pears. • Genus *Opuntia*, family Cactaceae. ▷early 17th cent.: from Latin, a name given to a plant growing around *Opus* (stem *Opunt-*), a city in Locris in ancient Greece. The term was later used as a genus name.

o·pus /ˈōpəs/ ▸*n.* (*pl.* **o·pus·es** or **o·pe·ra** /ˈäp(ə)rə/) **1** *Music* a separate composition or set of compositions by a particular composer, usually ordered by date of publication: The Gambler *was Prokofiev's sixth opera, despite its early* **opus number**. See also **OP.** **2** any artistic work, esp. one on a large scale: *he was writing an opus on Mexico.* ▷early 18th cent.: from Latin, literally 'work.'

o·pus·cule /ōˈpəskyo͞ol/ (also **o·pus·cu·lum** /ōˈpəskyələm/) ▸*n.* (*pl.* **-cules** or **-cu·la** /-kyələ/) *rare* a small or minor literary or musical work. ▷mid 17th cent.: from French, from Latin *opusculum*, diminutive of *opus* 'work.'

o·pus De·i /ˌōpəs ˈdā-ē/ ▸*n.* (**Opus Dei**) a Roman Catholic organization of laymen and priests founded in Spain in 1928 with the aim of reestablishing Christian ideals in society. ▷late 19th cent.: from medieval Latin, literally 'work of God.'

OR ▸*abbr.* ■ operational research. ■ Oregon (in official postal use). ■ *Brit. Military* other ranks (as opposed to commissioned officers).

or[1] /ôr/ ▸*conj.* **1** used to link alternatives: *a cup of tea or coffee* | *are you coming* **or not**? | *she couldn't read or write* | *I* **either** *take taxis* **or** *walk everywhere* | *it doesn't matter* **whether** *the theory is right* **or** *wrong.* **2** introducing a synonym or explanation of a preceding word or phrase: *the espionage novel, or, as it is known in the trade, the thriller.* **3** otherwise (used to introduce the consequences of something not being done or not being the case): *hurry up, or you'll miss it all.* **4** introducing an afterthought, usually in the form of a question: *John's indifference—or was it?—left her unsettled.* **5** *poetic/literary* either: *to love is the one way to know* **or** *God* **or** *man.*
▸*n.* (often **OR**) *Electronics* a Boolean operator that gives the value one if at least one operand (or input) has a value of one, and otherwise has a value of zero. ■ (also **OR gate**) a circuit that gives an output signal if there is a signal on any of its inputs. ▷Middle English: a reduced form of the obsolete conjunction *other* (which superseded Old English *oththe* 'or'), of uncertain ultimate origin.
▸*PHRASES* □ **or else** see **ELSE**. □ **or so** (after a quantity) approximately: *a dozen or so people.*

USAGE **1** Where a verb follows a list separated by **or**, the traditional rule is that the verb should be singular, as long as the things in the list are individually singular, as in *a sandwich* **or** *other snack* **is** *included in the price* (rather than *a sandwich* **or** *other snack* **are** *included in the price*). The argument is that each of the elements agrees separately with the verb. The opposite rule applies when the elements are joined by **and**—here the verb should be plural: *a sandwich* **and** *a cup of coffee* **are** *included in the price.* These traditional rules are observed in good English writing style but are often disregarded in speech.
2 On the use of **either . . . or**, see **usage** at **EITHER**.

or[2] ▸*n.* gold or yellow, as a heraldic tincture: [*postpositive*] *a bend or.* ▷early 16th cent.: from French, from Latin *aurum* 'gold.'

-or[1] ▸*suffix* (forming nouns) denoting a person or thing performing the action of a verb, or denoting another agent: *escalator* | *governor* | *resistor.* ▷from Latin, sometimes via Anglo-Norman French *-eour* or Old French *-eor* (see also **-ATOR**, **-ITOR**).

-or[2] ▸*suffix* forming nouns denoting a state or condition: *error* | *pallor* | *terror.* ▷from Latin, sometimes via Old French *-or, -ur.*

-or[3] ▸*suffix* forming adjectives expressing a comparative sense: *minor* | *major.* ▷via Anglo-Norman French from Latin.

o·ra /ˈôrə/ ▸ plural form of **OS**[2].

or·ache /ˈôrəCH; ˈär-/ (also **or·ach**) ▸*n.* a plant of the goosefoot family with leaves that are sometimes covered in a white mealy substance. Several kinds are edible and can be used as a substitute for spinach or sorrel. • Genus *Atriplex*, family Chenopodiaceae: several species, in particular the **common orache** (*A. hortensis*), which is cultivated in some areas. ▷Middle English *orage*, from Anglo-Norman French *arasche*, from Latin *atriplex*, from Greek *atraphaxus.*

or·a·cle /ˈôrəkəl/ ▸*n.* **1** a priest or priestess acting as a medium through whom advice or prophecy was sought from the gods in classical antiquity. ■ a place at which such advice or prophecy was sought. ■ a person or thing regarded as an infallible authority or guide on something: *casting the attorney general as the oracle for and guardian of the public interest is simply impossible.* **2** a response or message given by an oracle, typically one that is ambiguous or obscure. ▷late Middle English: via Old French from Latin *oraculum*, from *orare* 'speak.'

o·rac·u·lar /ôˈrakyələr/ ▸*adj.* of or relating to an oracle: *the oracular shrine.* ■ (of an utterance, advice, etc.) hard to interpret; enigmatic: *an ambiguous, oracular remark.* ■ holding or claiming the authority of an oracle: *he holds forth in oracular fashion.* ▷mid 17th cent.: from Latin *oraculum* (see **ORACLE**) + **-AR**[1]. **—o·rac·u·lar·i·ty** /ôˌrakyəˈlaritē/ *n.* **—o·rac·u·lar·ly** *adv.*

o·ra·cy /ˈôrəsē/ ▸*n.* the ability to express oneself fluently and grammatically in speech. ▷1960s: from Latin *os, or-* 'mouth,' on the pattern of *literacy.*

O·ra·dea /ôˈrädyä/ an industrial city in western Romania, near the border with Hungary; pop. 222,000.

o·ral /ˈôrəl/ ▸*adj.* **1** by word of mouth; spoken rather than written: *they had reached an oral agreement.* ■ relating to the transmission of information or literature by word of mouth rather than in writing: *oral literature.* ■ (of a society) not having reached the stage of literacy. **2** of or relating to the mouth: *oral hygiene.* ■ done or taken by the mouth: *oral contraceptives.* ■ *Phonetics* pronounced by the voice resonating in the mouth, as the vowels in English. Compare with **NASAL** (sense 2). ■ *Psychoanalysis* (in Freudian theory) relating to or denoting a stage of infantile psychosexual development in which the mouth is the main source of pleasure and the center of experience.
▸*n.* (often **orals**) a spoken examination or test: *he was preparing for his orals* | *a French oral.* ▷early 17th cent.: from late Latin *oralis*, from Latin *os, or-* 'mouth.' **—o·ral·ly** *adv.*

USAGE See **usage** at **VERBAL**.

o·ral-for·mu·la·ic ▸*adj.* relating to or denoting poetry belonging to an early spoken tradition characterized by the use of poetic formulas, e.g., the Homeric poems.

o·ral his·to·ry ▸*n.* the collection and study of historical information using sound recordings of interviews with people having personal knowledge of past events. ■ a record of this kind: *their own oral histories.*

o·ral·ism /ˈôrəˌlizəm/ ▸*n.* the system of teaching the deaf to communicate by the use of speech and lip-reading rather than sign language.

o·ral·ist /ˈôrəlist/ ▸*adj.* relating to or advocating oralism.
▸*n.* a deaf person who uses speech and lip-reading to communicate, rather than sign language.

o·ral·i·ty /ôˈralitē/ ▸*n.* **1** the quality of being spoken or verbally communicated. ■ preference for or tendency to use spoken forms of language. **2** *Psychoanalysis* the focusing of sexual energy and feeling on the mouth.

o·ral sex ▸*n.* sexual activity in which the genitals of one partner are stimulated by the mouth of the other; fellatio or cunnilingus.

O·ran /ôˈrän/ a port on the Mediterranean coast of Algeria; pop. 664,000.

o·rang /ōˈraNG/ ▸*n.* short for **ORANGUTAN**.

Or·ange /ôˈränZH; ˈär-/ **1** a town in southern France, on the Rhône River, home of the ancestors of the Dutch royal house. See **ORANGE, HOUSE OF.** **2** a city in southwestern California, southeast of Los Angeles in an agricultural area; pop. 110,658.

Or·ange, House of the Dutch royal house, originally a princely dynasty of the principality centered on the town of Orange in the 16th century.

Or·ange, William of William III of Great Britain and Ireland (see **WILLIAM**).

or·ange /ˈôrənj; ˈär-/ ▸*n.* **1** a round juicy citrus fruit with a tough bright reddish-yellow rind. ■ a drink made from or flavored with orange: *a vodka and orange.* **2** (also **orange tree**) the leathery-leaved evergreen tree that bears this fruit, native to warm regions of south and Southeast Asia. Oranges are a major commercial crop in many warm regions of the world. • Genus *Citrus*, family Rutaceae: several species, in particular the **sweet orange** (*C. sinensis*) and the **Seville orange**. ■ used in names of other plants with similar fruit or flowers, e.g., **mock orange**. **3** a bright reddish-yellow color like that of the skin of a ripe orange.
▸*adj.* **1** reddish yellow, like a ripe orange in color: *an orange glow in the sky.* **2** made from or flavored with oranges, or having an orangelike flavoring. ▷late Middle English: from Old French *orenge* (in the phrase *pomme d'orenge*), based on Arabic *nāranj*, from Persian *nārang.* **—or·ang·ey** (also **or·ang·y**) *adj.* **—or·ang·ish** (also **or·ange·ish**) *adj.*

or·ange·ade /ˌôrənjˈād; ˌär-/ ▸*n.* a drink made with orange juice, sweetener, and water, sometimes carbonated.

or·ange blos·som ▸*n.* **1** flowers from an orange tree, traditionally worn by the bride at a wedding. **2** a cocktail made of gin, sugar, and orange juice.

Or·ange Coun·ty a county in southwestern California, between Los Angeles and San Diego; pop. 2,846,289.

or·ange flow·er wa·ter ▸*n.* a solution of neroli in water, used in perfumery and as a food flavoring.

Or·ange Free State an area and former province in central South Africa, north of the Orange River. First settled by Boers after the Great Trek, the area became a province of the Union of South Africa in 1910 and in 1994 became one of the new provinces of South Africa. Province named **FREE STATE** in 1995.

Members of the family held the position of stadtholder or magistrate from the mid-16th until the late 18th century. In 1689 William of Orange became King William III of Great Britain and Ireland, and the son of the last stadtholder became King William I of the United Netherlands in 1815.

Or·ange·man /'ôrənjmən; 'är-/ ▸*n.* (*pl.* **-men**) a member of the Orange Order, a Protestant political society in Northern Ireland.

or·ange pe·koe ▸*n.* a type of black tea made from young leaves.

Or·ange Riv·er the longest river in South Africa, which rises in the Drakensberg Mountains in northeastern Lesotho and flows westward for 1,155 miles (1,859 km) to the Atlantic Ocean. It forms the border between Namibia and South Africa in its lower course.

or·ange·ry /'ôrənjrē; 'är-/ ▸*n.* (*pl.* **-ries**) a greenhouse where orange trees are grown.

or·ange stick ▸*n.* a thin stick, pointed at one end and typically made of orange wood, used for manicuring the fingernails.

o·rang·u·tan /ə'raNG(g)ə,tan/ (also **o·rang·u·tang, o·rang-ou·tang** /ō'raNG(g)ə,taNG/, **o·rang-u·tan**) ▸*n.* a large mainly solitary arboreal ape with long reddish hair, long arms, and hooked hands and feet, native to Borneo and Sumatra. The mature male develops fleshy cheek pads and a throat pouch. • *Pongo pygmaeus*, family Pongidae. ▷late 17th cent.: from Malay *orang huan* 'forest person.'

orangutan

O·ran·je·stad /ô'rānyə,stät/ the capital of the Dutch island of Aruba in the Caribbean Sea; pop. 25,000.

Or·a·şul Sta·lin /ôr'äSHŏŏl 'stälin/ former name for **BRAŞOV**.

o·rate /ô'rāt; 'ôr,āt/ ▸*v.* [*intrans.*] make a speech, esp. pompously or at length. ▷early 17th cent.: back-formation from **ORATION**.

o·ra·tion /ô'rāSHən/ ▸*n.* a formal speech, esp. one given on a ceremonial occasion. ■ the style or manner in which such a speech is given: *there is nothing quite like his messianic oration.* ▷late Middle English (denoting a prayer): from Latin *oratio(n-)* 'discourse, prayer,' from *orare* 'speak, pray.'

or·a·tor /'ôrətər; 'är-/ ▸*n.* a public speaker, esp. one who is eloquent or skilled. ▷late Middle English: from Anglo-Norman French *oratour*, from Latin *orator* 'speaker, pleader.' **—or·a·to·ri·al** /,ôrə'tôrēəl/ *adj.*

or·a·to·ri·o /,ôrə'tôrē,ō; ,är-/ ▸*n.* (*pl.* **-os**) a large-scale musical work for orchestra and voices, typically a narrative on a religious theme, performed without the use of costumes, scenery, or action.Well-known examples include Bach's *Christmas Oratorio*, Handel's *Messiah*, and Haydn's *The Creation*. ▷Italian, from ecclesiastical Latin *oratorium* 'oratory,' from the musical services held in the Church of the Oratory of St. Philip Neri in Rome.

or·a·to·ry[1] /'ôrə,tôrē; 'är-/ ▸*n.* (*pl.* **-ries**) **1** a small chapel, esp. for private worship. [Middle English: from Anglo-Norman French *oratorie*, from ecclesiastical Latin *oratorium*, based on Latin *orare* 'pray, speak.'] **2** (**Oratory**) (in the Roman Catholic Church) a religious society of secular priests founded in Rome in 1564 to provide plain preaching and popular services and established in various countries. [from *Congregation of the Fathers of the Oratory*.] **—Or·a·to·ri·an** /,ôə'tôrēən; 'är-/ *n.* & *adj.* (sense 2).

or·a·to·ry[2] ▸*n.* the art or practice of formal speaking in public. ■ exaggerated, eloquent, or highly colored language: *learned discussions degenerated into pompous oratory.* ▷early 16th cent.: from Latin *oratoria*, feminine (used as a noun) of *oratorius* 'relating to an orator.' **—or·a·tor·i·cal** /,ôrə'tôrikəl/ *adj.*

orb /ôrb/ ▸*n.* a spherical body; a globe. ■ a golden globe surmounted by a cross, forming part of the regalia of a monarch. ■ *poetic/literary* a celestial body. ■ (usu. **orbs**) *poetic/literary* an eyeball; an eye. ■ *Astrology* a circle of up to 10° radius around the position of a celestial object: *within an orb of 1° of Mars.* ▸*v.* [*trans.*] *poetic/literary* encircle; enclose. ■ form (something) into an orb; make circular or globular. ▷late Middle English (denoting a circle): from Latin *orbis* 'ring.'

or·bic·u·lar /ôr'bikyələr/ ▸*adj. technical* **1** having the shape of a flat ring or disk. **2** having a rounded convex or globular shape. ■ *Geology* (of a rock) containing spheroidal igneous inclusions. ▷late Middle English: from late Latin *orbicularis*, from Latin *orbiculus*, diminutive of *orbis* 'ring.' **—or·bic·u·lar·i·ty** /ôr,bikyə'laritē/ *n.* **—or·bic·u·lar·ly** *adv.*

Or·bi·son /'ôrbisən/, Roy (1936–88), U.S. singer and composer. After writing country music songs for other artists, he established himself as a singer with the ballads "Only the Lonely" (1960) and "Oh, Pretty Woman" (1964).

or·bit /'ôrbit/ ▸*n.* **1** the curved path of a celestial object or spacecraft around a star, planet, or moon, esp. a periodic elliptical revolution. ■ one complete circuit around an orbited body. ■ the state of being on or moving in such a course: *the earth is* **in orbit** *around the sun.* ■ the path of an electron around an atomic nucleus. **2** a sphere of activity, interest, or application: *he moved into the orbit of two great anticommunist socialists of the 1940s and 1950s.* **3** *Anatomy* the cavity in the skull of a vertebrate that contains the eye; the eye socket. ■ the area around the eye of a bird or other animal.
▸*v.* (**-bit·ed, -bit·ing**) [*trans.*] (of a celestial object or spacecraft) move in orbit around (a star, planet, or moon): *Mercury orbits the Sun.* ■ [*intrans.*] fly or move around in a circle: *the mobile's disks spun and orbited slowly.* ■ put (a satellite) into orbit. ▷mid 16th cent. (sense 3): from Latin *orbita* 'course, track' (in medieval Latin 'eye socket'), feminine of *orbitus* 'circular,' from *orbis* 'ring.'
▸*PHRASE* □ **into orbit** *informal* into a state of heightened performance, activity, anger, or excitement: *his goal sent the fans into orbit.*

or·bit·al /'ôrbitl/ ▸*adj.* of or relating to an orbit or orbits. ■ *Brit.* (of a road) passing around the outside of a town.
▸*n. Physics* each of the actual or potential patterns of electron density that may be formed in an atom or molecule by one or more electrons, and that can be represented as a wave function. ▷mid 16th cent. (referring to the eye socket): probably from medieval Latin *orbitalis*, from Latin *orbita* (see **ORBIT**).

or·bit·al sand·er ▸*n.* a sander in which the sanding surface moves in a very tight orbital motion, driven at high speed by an electric motor.

or·bit·er /'ôrbitər/ ▸*n.* a spacecraft designed to go into orbit, esp. one not intended to land. Compare with **LANDER**.

or·bi·to·sphe·noid /,ôrbitō'sfē,noid/ (also **orbitosphenoid bone**) ▸*n. Anatomy & Zoology* a bone in the floor of the mammalian cranium, in the region of the optic nerve. In the human skull it is represented by the lesser wings of the sphenoid bone.

orb web ▸*n.* a generally circular, upright spider's web formed of threads radiating from a central point, crossed by radial links that spiral in from the edge.

orc /ôrk/ ▸*n.* (in fantasy literature and games) a member of an imaginary race of humanlike creatures, characterized as ugly, warlike, and malevolent. ▷late 16th cent. (denoting an ogre): perhaps from Latin *orcus* 'hell' or Italian *orco* 'demon, monster,' influenced by obsolete *orc* 'ferocious sea creature' and by Old English *orcneas* 'monsters.' The current sense is due to the use of the word in Tolkien's fantasy adventures.

or·ca /'ôrkə/ ▸*n.* a large toothed whale with distinctive black-and-white markings and a prominent dorsal fin. It lives in groups that cooperatively hunt fish, seals, and penguins. Also called **KILLER WHALE**. • *Orcinus orca*, family Delphinidae. ▷mid 19th cent.: from French *orque* or Latin *orca*, denoting a kind of whale.

or·ce·in /'ôrsēin/ ▸*n. Chemistry* a red dye obtained from orchil, used as a stain in microscopic study. ▷mid 19th cent.: alteration of *orcin*, another name for **ORCINOL**.

orch. ▸*abbr.* ■ orchestra. ■ orchestrated by.

or·chard /'ôrCHərd/ ▸*n.* a piece of land planted with fruit trees. ▷Old English *ortgeard*; the first element from Latin *hortus* 'garden,' the second representing **YARD**[2]. **—or·char·dist** /-ist/ *n.*

or·chard grass ▸*n.* a pasture grass with broad leaves and green or purplish flowering spikes. • *Dactylis glomerata*, family Gramineae.

or·ches·tra /'ôrkistrə; -,kestrə/ ▸*n.* **1** a group of instrumentalists, esp. one combining string, woodwind, brass, and percussion sections and playing classical music. **2** (also **orchestra pit**) the part of a theater where the orchestra plays, typically in front of the stage and on a lower level than the audience. ■ the seats on the ground floor in a theater. **3** the semicircular space in front of an ancient Greek theater stage where the chorus danced and sang. ▷early 17th cent.: via Latin from Greek *orkhēstra*, from *orkheisthai* 'to dance.'

or·ches·tral /ôr'kestrəl/ ▸*adj.* written for an orchestra to play: *orchestral music.* ■ of or relating to an orchestra: *an orchestral conductor.* **—or·ches·tral·ly** *adv.*

or·ches·trate /'ôrki,strāt/ ▸*v.* [*trans.*] **1** arrange or score (music) for orchestral performance. **2** arrange or direct the elements of (a situation) to produce a desired effect, esp. surreptitiously: *the developers were able to orchestrate a favorable media campaign.* ▷late 19th cent.: from **ORCHESTRA**, perhaps suggested by French *orchestrer*. **—or·ches·tra·tion** /,ôrkə'strāSHən/ *n.* **—or·ches·tra·tor** /-,strātər/ *n.*

or·ches·tri·on /ôr'kestrēən/ (also **or·ches·tri·na** /,ôrki'strēnə/) ▸*n.* a large mechanical musical instrument designed to imitate the sound of an orchestra. ▷mid 19th cent.: from **ORCHESTRA**, on the pattern of *accordion*.

or·chid /'ôrkid/ ▸*n.* a plant with complex flowers that are typically showy or bizarrely shaped, having a large specialized lip (labellum) and frequently a spur. Orchids occur worldwide, esp. as epiphytes in tropical forests, and are valuable hothouse plants. • Family Orchidaceae: numerous genera and species. ■ the flowering stem of a cultivated orchid. ▷mid 19th cent.: from modern Latin *Orchid(ac)eae*, formed irregularly from Latin *orchis* (see **ORCHIS**). **—or·chid·ist** /-ist/ *n.*

or·chi·da·ceous /,ôrki'dāSHəs/ ▸*adj. Botany* of, relating to, or denoting plants of the orchid family (Orchidaceae). ▷mid 19th cent.: from modern Latin *Orchidaceae* (plural) + **-OUS**.

or·chi·ec·to·my /,ôrkē'ektəmē/ (also **or·chi·dec·to·my** /,ôrki'dektəmē/) ▸*n.* surgical removal of one or both testicles. ▷late 19th cent.: from modern Latin *orchido-* (from a Latinized stem of Greek *orkhis* 'testicle') + **-ECTOMY**.

or·chil /'ôrkəl; -CHil/ ▸*n.* **1** a red or violet dye obtained from certain lichens, used as a source of litmus, orcinol, and other pigments. **2** a lichen with flattened fronds from which such a dye can be obtained. • *Roccella* (order Graphidiales) and other genera: several species, including the Mediterranean *R. tinctoria*, used for dyeing, and the Madagascan *R. montagnei*, used for litmus. ▷late 15th cent.: from Old French *orcheil*, related to Spanish *urchilla*; of uncertain origin.

or·chis /'ôrkis/ ▸*n.* an orchid of (or formerly of) a genus native to north temperate regions, characterized by a tuberous root and an erect fleshy stem bearing a spike of typically purple or pinkish flowers. • Genus *Orchis* (or *Dactylorhiza*), family Orchidaceae. ■ [with *adj.*] *dated* any wild orchid occurring in temperate regions. ▷modern Latin, based on Greek *orkhis*, literally 'testicle' (with reference to the shape of its tuber).

or·chi·tis /ôr'kītis/ ▸*n. Medicine* inflammation of one or both of the testicles. ▷late 18th cent.: modern Latin, from Greek *orkhis* 'testicle' + **-ITIS**.

or·ci·nol /'ôrsə,näl; -,nôl/ ▸*n. Chemistry* a crystalline compound extracted from certain lichens and used to make dyes. • Alternative name: **2-hydroxyphenylmethanol**; chem. formula: $C_7H_8O_2$. ▷mid 19th cent.: from modern Latin *orcina*, from Italian *orcello* 'orchil.'

Or·czy /'ôrtsē/, Baroness Emmusca (1865–1947), British novelist, born in Hungary. She wrote *The Scarlet Pimpernel* (1905).

ord. ▸*abbr.* ■ order. ■ ordinary.

or·dain /ôr'dān/ ▸*v.* [*trans.*] **1** make (someone) a priest or minister; confer holy orders on. **2** order or decree (something) officially: *equal punishment was ordained for the two crimes.* ■ (esp. of God or fate) prescribe; determine (something): *the path ordained by God.* ▷Middle English (also in the sense 'put in order'): from Anglo-Norman French *ordeiner*, from

Pronunciation Key ə *ago*; ər *over*; 'ə or ,ə *up*; 'ər or ,ər *fur*; a *hat*; ā *rate*; ä *car*; CH *chew*; e *let*; ē *see*; e(ə)r *air*; i *fit*; ī *by*; i(ə)r *ear*; NG *sing*; ō *go*; ô *for*; oi *boy*; ŏŏ *good*; o͞o *goo*; ou *out*; SH *she*; TH *thin*; T͟H *then*; (h)w *why*; ZH *vision*

Latin *ordinare*, from *ordo, ordin-* (see **ORDER**). **—or·dain·er** *n.* **—or·dain·ment** *n.*

or·deal /ôrˈdēl/ ▸*n.* **1** a painful or horrific experience, esp. a protracted one: *the* ***ordeal of*** *having to give evidence.* **2** *historical* an ancient test of guilt or innocence by subjection of the accused to severe pain, survival of which was taken as divine proof of innocence. ▷Old English *ordāl, ordēl*, of Germanic origin; related to German *urteilen* 'give judgment,' from a base meaning 'share out.' The word is not found in Middle English (except once in Chaucer's *Troylus*); modern use of sense 2 began in the late 16th cent., whence sense 1 (mid 17th cent.).

or·der /ˈôrdər/ ▸*n.* **1** the arrangement or disposition of people or things in relation to each other according to a particular sequence, pattern, or method: *I filed the cards in alphabetical order.* ■ a state in which everything is in its correct or appropriate place: *she tried to put her shattered thoughts into some semblance of order.* ■ a state in which the laws and rules regulating the public behavior of members of a community are observed and authority is obeyed: *the army was deployed to keep order.* ■ [with *adj.*] the overall state or condition of something: *the house had just been vacated and was in good order.* ■ a particular social, political, or economic system: *if only the peasantry would rise up against the established order | the social order of Britain.* ■ the prescribed or established procedure followed by a meeting, legislative assembly, debate, or court of law: *the meeting was* ***called to order.*** ■ a stated form of liturgical service, or of administration of a rite or ceremony, prescribed by ecclesiastical authority. **2** an authoritative command, direction, or instruction: *he was not going to take orders from a mere administrator* | [with *infinitive*] *the skipper gave the order to abandon ship.* ■ an oral or written request for something to be made, supplied, or served: *the company has won an order for six tankers.* ■ a thing made, supplied, or served as a result of such a request: *orders will be delivered the next business day.* ■ a written direction of a court or judge: *a judge's order forbidding the reporting of evidence.* ■ a written direction to pay money or deliver property. **3** (often **orders**) a social class: *the upper social orders.* ■ *Biology* a principal taxonomic category that ranks below class and above family. ■ a grade or rank in the Christian ministry, esp. that of bishop, priest, or deacon. ■ (**orders**) the rank or position of a member of the clergy or an ordained minister of a church: *he took priest's orders.* See also **HOLY ORDERS**. ■ *Theology* any of the nine grades of angelic beings in the celestial hierarchy. **4** (also **Order**) a society of monks, priests, nuns, etc., living according to certain religious and social regulations and discipline and at least some of whose members take solemn vows: *the Franciscan Order.* ■ *historical* a society of knights bound by a common rule of life and having a combined military and monastic character. ■ an institution founded by a monarch for the purpose of conferring an honor or honors for merit on those appointed to it. ■ the insignia worn by members of such an institution. ■ a Masonic or similar fraternal organization. **5** [in *sing.*] used to describe the quality, nature, or importance of something: *with musical talent of this order, von Karajan would have been a phenomenon in any age.* **6** any of the five classical styles of architecture (Doric, Ionic, Corinthian, Tuscan, and Composite) based on the proportions of columns, amount of decoration, etc. ■ any style or mode of architecture subject to uniform established proportions. **7** [with *adj.*] *Military* equipment or uniform for a specified purpose or of a specified type: *drill order.* ■ (**the order**) the position in which a rifle is held after ordering arms. See **ORDER ARMS** below. **8** *Mathematics* the degree of complexity of an equation, expression, etc., as denoted by an ordinal number. ■ the number of differentiations required to reach the highest derivative in a differential equation. ■ the number of elements in a finite group. ■ the number of rows or columns in a square matrix.
▸*v.* **1** [*reporting verb*] give an authoritative direction or instruction to do something: [*trans.*] *she ordered me to leave* | [with *direct speech*] *"Stop frowning," he ordered* | [with *clause*] *the court ordered that the case should be heard at the end of August* | [*trans.*] *her father ordered her back home | the judge ordered a retrial.* ■ [*trans.*] (**order someone around/about**) continually tell someone in an overbearing way what to do. ■ command (something) to be done or (someone) to be treated in a particular way: *he ordered the anchor dropped.* **2** [*trans.*] request (something) to be made, supplied, or served: *my friend ordered the tickets last week* | [with *two objs.*] *I asked the security guard to order me a taxi* | [*intrans.*] *Are you ready to order, sir?* **3** [*trans.*] arrange (something) in a methodical or appropriate way: *all entries are ordered by date* | [as *adj.* in *combination*] (**-ordered**) *her normally well-ordered life.* ▷Middle English: from Old French *ordre*, from Latin *ordo, ordin-* 'row, series, rank.' **—or·der·er** *n.*
▸*PHRASES* □ **by order of** according to directions given by the proper authority: *he was released from prison by order of the court.* □ **in order 1** according to a particular sequence. **2** in the correct condition for operation or use. **3** in accordance with the rules of procedure at a meeting, legislative assembly, etc. ■ appropriate in the circumstances: *a little bit of flattery was now in order.* □ **in order for** so that: *employees must be committed to the change in order for it to succeed.* □ **in order that** with the intention; so that: *she used her mother's kitchen in order that the turkey might be properly cooked.* □ **in order to** as a means to: *he slouched into his seat in order to avoid drawing attention to himself.* □ **of the order of 1** approximately: *sales increases are of the order of 20%.* **2** *Mathematics* having the order of magnitude specified by. □ **on order** (of goods) requested but not yet received from the supplier or manufacturer. □ **on the order of 1** another term for **OF THE ORDER OF** (sense 1) above. **2** along the lines of; similar to: *singers on the order of Janis Joplin.* □ **Order!** a call for silence or the observance of prescribed procedures by someone in charge of a trial, legislative assembly, etc. □ **order arms** *Military* hold a rifle with its butt on the ground close to one's right side. □ **order of battle** the units, formations, and equipment of a military force. □ **orders are orders** commands must be obeyed, however much one may disagree with them. □ **out of order 1** (of an electrical or mechanical device) not working properly or at all. **2** not in the correct sequence. **3** not according to the rules of a meeting, legislative assembly, etc. ■ *informal* (of a person or their behavior) unacceptable or wrong: *he's getting away with things that are out of order.* □ **to order** according to a customer's specific request or requirements: *the sweaters are knitted to order.*

or·dered pair ▸*n.* *Mathematics* a pair of elements *a, b* having the property that *(a, b) = (u, v)* if and only if *a = u, b = v.*

or·der·ly /ˈôrdərlē/ ▸*adj.* neatly and methodically arranged: *an orderly arrangement of objects.* ■ (of a person or group) well behaved; disciplined.
▸*n.* (*pl.* **-lies**) **1** an attendant in a hospital responsible for the nonmedical care of patients and the maintenance of order and cleanliness. **2** a soldier who carries out orders or performs minor tasks for an officer. **—or·der·li·ness** *n.*

or·der·ly room ▸*n.* *Military* the room used for regimental or company business.

or·der of busi·ness (pl. **or·ders of busi·ness**) ▸*n.* a task assigned or a matter to be addressed: *the first order of business is learning who the hitters are.*

or·der of mag·ni·tude ▸*n.* a class in a system of classification determined by size, each class being a number of times (usually ten) greater or smaller than the one before: *values might be compared by order of magnitude, a staple in making ballpark estimates.* ■ relative size, quantity, quality, etc.: *the new problems were of a different order of magnitude.* ■ the arrangement of a number of items determined by their relative size: *the items are arranged in ascending order of magnitude.*

or·der of the day ▸*n.* (**the order of the day**) **1** the prevailing state of things: *confusion would seem to be the order of the day.* **2** something that is required or recommended: *on Sundays, a black suit was the order of the day.* **3** a program or agenda.

Or·der of the Gar·ter the highest order of English knighthood, founded by Edward III *c.*1344. According to tradition the garter was that of the Countess of Salisbury, which the king placed on his own leg after it fell off while she was dancing with him. The king's comment to those present, "Honi soit qui mal y pense" (shame be to him who thinks evil of it), was adopted as the motto of the order.

or·di·nal /ˈôrdn-əl/ ▸*n.* **1** short for **ORDINAL NUMBER**. **2** *Christian Church, chiefly historical* a service book, esp. one with the forms of service used at ordinations.
▸*adj.* of or relating to a thing's position in a series: *ordinal position of birth.* ■ of or relating to an ordinal number. ■ *Biology* of or relating to a taxonomic order. ▷Middle English (sense 2): the noun from medieval Latin *ordinale* (neuter); the adjective from late Latin *ordinalis* 'relating to order in a series,' from Latin *ordo, ordin-* (see **ORDER**).

or·di·nal num·ber ▸*n.* a number defining a thing's position in a series, such as "first," "second," or "third." Ordinal numbers are used as adjectives, nouns, and pronouns. Compare with **CARDINAL NUMBER**.

or·di·nance /ˈôrdn-əns/ ▸*n.* **1** a piece of legislation enacted by a municipal authority: *a city ordinance banned smoking in nearly all types of restaurants.* **2** an authoritative order; a decree. **3** a prescribed religious rite: *Talmudic ordinances.* ▷Middle English (also in the sense 'arrangement in ranks'): from Old French *ordenance*, from medieval Latin *ordinantia*, from Latin *ordinare* 'put in order' (see **ORDAIN**).

or·di·nand /ˈôrdn,and/ ▸*n.* a candidate for ordination. ▷mid 19th cent.: from Latin *ordinandus*, gerundive of *ordinare* 'put in order' (see **ORDAIN**).

or·di·nar·i·ly /,ôrdnˈe(ə)rəlē/ ▸*adv.* **1** usually: *the fixings that would ordinarily appear at a grand turkey dinner* [*sentence adverb*] *ordinarily, Linda was the handy one around the house.* **2** in a normal way: *an effort to behave ordinarily.*

or·di·nar·y /ˈôrdn,erē/ ▸*adj.* **1** with no special or distinctive features; normal: *he sets out to depict ordinary people | it was just an ordinary evening.* See note at **NORMAL**. ■ uninteresting; commonplace: *ordinary items of everyday wear.* **2** (esp. of a judge or bishop) exercising authority by virtue of office and not by delegation.
▸*n.* (*pl.* **-nar·ies**) **1** [in *sing.*] what is commonplace or standard: *their clichés were vested with enough emotion to elevate them above the ordinary.* **2** *Law Brit.* a person, esp. a judge, exercising authority by virtue of office and not by delegation. ■ in some U.S. states, a judge of probate. **3** (usu. **Ordinary**) those parts of a Roman Catholic service, esp. the Mass, that do not vary from day to day. ■ a rule or book giving the order for saying the Mass. **4** *Heraldry* any of the simplest principal charges used in coats of arms (esp. chief, pale, bend, fess, bar, chevron, and saltire). **5** *Brit., archaic* a meal provided at a fixed time and price at an inn. ■ an inn providing this. **6** *historical* an early type of bicycle with one large and one very small wheel; a penny-farthing. ▷late Middle English: the noun partly via Old French; the adjective from Latin *ordinarius* 'orderly' (reinforced by French *ordinaire*), from *ordo, ordin-* 'order.' **—or·di·nar·i·ness** *n.*
▸*PHRASE* □ **out of the ordinary** unusual: *nothing out of the ordinary happened.*

or·di·nar·y ray ▸*n.* *Optics* (in double refraction) the ray that obeys the ordinary laws of refraction.

or·di·nar·y sea·man ▸*n.* the lowest rank of merchant seaman, below able-bodied seaman.

or·di·nar·y share ▸*n.* British term for **COMMON STOCK**.

or·di·nate /ˈôrdnit; -,āt/ ▸*n.* *Mathematics* (in a system of coordinates) the *y*-coordinate, representing the distance from a point to the horizontal or *x*-axis measured parallel to the vertical or *y*-axis. ▷late 17th cent.: from Latin *linea ordinata applicata* 'line applied parallel,' from *ordinare* 'put in order.'

or·di·na·tion /,ôrdnˈāshən/ ▸*n.* **1** the action of ordaining or conferring holy orders on someone. ■ a ceremony in which someone is ordained. **2** *chiefly Ecology* a statistical technique in which data from a large number of sites or populations are represented as points in a two- or three-dimensional coordinate frame. ▷late Middle English (in the general sense 'arrangement in order'): from Latin *ordinatio(n-)*, from *ordinare* 'put in order' (see **ORDAIN**).

ordn. ▸*abbr.* ordnance.

ord·nance /ˈôrdnəns/ ▸*n.* **1** mounted guns; artillery. ■ military weapons, ammunition, and equipment used in connection with them. **2** a branch of the armed forces dealing with the supply and storage of weapons, ammunition, and related equipment. ▷late Middle English: variant of **ORDINANCE**.

Ord·nance Sur·vey (in the UK) an official survey organization that prepares large-scale detailed maps of the whole country.

or·don·nance /ˈôrdn-əns; ,ôdōˈnäns/ ▸*n.* the systematic or orderly arrangement of parts, esp. in art and architecture. ▷mid 17th cent.: from French, alteration of Old French *ordenance* (see **ORDINANCE**).

Or·do·vi·cian /,ôrdəˈvishən/ ▸*adj.* *Geology* of, relating to, or denoting the second period of the Paleozoic era, between the Cambrian and Silurian periods. ■ [as *n.*] (**the Ordovician**) the Ordovician period or the system of rocks deposited during it.

The Ordovician lasted from about 510 million to 439 million years ago. It saw the diversification of many invertebrate groups and the appearance of the first vertebrates (jawless fish).

▷late 19th cent.: from *Ordovices*, the Latin name of an ancient British tribe in North Wales, + **-IAN**.

or·dure /ˈôrjər/ ▸*n.* excrement; dung. ■ something regarded as vile or abhorrent. ▷Middle English: from Old French, from *ord* 'foul,' from Latin *horridus* (see **HORRID**).

Or·dzho·ni·kid·ze /ˌôrjäniˈkidzə; ərjənyiˈkyēdzyə/ former name (1954–93) for **VLADIKAVKAZ**.

ore /ôr/ ▸*n.* a naturally occurring solid material from which a metal or valuable mineral can be profitably extracted. ▷Old English *ōra* 'unwrought metal'; influenced in form by Old English *ār* 'bronze' (related to Latin *aes* 'crude metal, bronze').

ø·re /ˈərə/ ▸*n.* (*pl.* same) a monetary unit of Denmark and Norway, equal to one hundredth of a krone. ▷Danish and Norwegian.

ö·re /ˈərə/ ▸*n.* (*pl.* same) a monetary unit of Sweden, equal to one hundredth of a krona.

Ore. ▸*abbr.* Oregon.

o·re·ad /ˈôrēˌad/ ▸*n. Greek and Roman Mythology* a nymph believed to inhabit mountains. ▷from Latin *Oreas, Oread-*, from Greek *Oreias*, from *oros* 'mountain.'

ore·bod·y /ˈôrˌbädē/ ▸*n.* a connected mass of ore in a mine or suitable for mining.

Ö·re·bro /ˌərəˈbrōō; ˌœrə-/ an industrial city in southern central Sweden; pop. 121,000.

o·rec·chi·et·te /ˌôriˈkyetē/ ▸ *n.* a small ear-shaped pasta. ▷Italian, literally 'little ears.'

o·rec·tic /ôˈrektik/ ▸*adj. technical, rare* of or concerning desire or appetite. ▷late 17th cent. (as a noun in the sense 'stimulant for the appetite'): from Greek *orektikos*, from *oregein* 'stretch out, reach for.' The current sense dates from the late 18th cent.

Oreg. ▸*abbr.* Oregon.

o·reg·a·no /əˈregəˌnō/ ▸*n.* an aromatic plant related to marjoram, with leaves that are used fresh or dried as a culinary herb. • *Origanum vulgare*, family Labiatae. ▷late 18th cent.: from Spanish, variant of **ORIGANUM**.

Or·e·gon /ˈôriˌgən; ˈär-; -ˌgän/ a state in the northwestern U.S., on the Pacific coast; pop. 3,421,399; capital, Salem; statehood, Feb. 14, 1859 (33). Many Americans arrived via the Oregon Trail during the early 1840s; by 1846, Britain formally ceded the territory to the U.S. **—Or·e·go·ni·an** /ˌôriˈgōnēən/ *adj.* & *n.*

Or·e·gon fir ▸*n.* (also **Oregon pine**) another term for **DOUGLAS FIR**.

Or·e·gon grape (also **Oregon grape holly**) ▸*n.* an evergreen shrub of the western coastal U.S. bearing yellow flowers and edible blue berries. • *Mahonia aquifolium*, family Berberidaceae.

Or·e·gon Trail a route across the central and western U.S. used esp. from 1840 until 1860 by settlers moving west. It extends about 2,000 miles (3,200 km) from Missouri to Oregon.

O·rel /ôˈrel; əˈryôl/ an industrial city in southwestern Russia; pop. 342,000.

O·rem /ˈôrəm/ a city in north central Utah, northwest of Provo; pop. 84,324.

Ore Moun·tains another name for the **ERZGEBIRGE**.

O·ren·burg /ˈôrənbərg; əryinˈbōōrk/ a city in southern Russia, on the Ural River; pop. 552,000. It was known as Chkalov from 1938 to 1957.

O·re·o /ˈôrēˌō/ ▸*n.* (*pl.* **-os**) *trademark* a brand of chocolate sandwich cookie with a creamy white filling. ■ *derogatory* an African-American who is seen, esp. by other blacks, as wishing to be part of the white establishment.

O·res·tes /ôˈrestēz/ *Greek Mythology* the son of Agamemnon and Clytemnestra and the brother of Electra and Iphigenia. He killed his mother and her lover Aegisthus to avenge the murder of Agamemnon.

Ø·re·sund /ˈôrəˌsōōnd; ˈœrə-/ a narrow channel between Sweden and the Danish island of Zealand. Also called **THE SOUND**.

o·rex·in ▸*n.* either of two hormones (**orexin-A** or **orexin-B**) produced by the mammalian hypothalamus and functional in the regulation of appetite and sleep. Also called **HYPOCRETIN**.

org /ôrg/ (usu. **.org**) ▸*abbr.* organization (in internet addresses).

org. ▸*abbr.* ■ organic. ■ organization or organized.

or·gan /ˈôrgən/ ▸*n.* **1** (also **pipe organ**) a large musical instrument having rows of tuned pipes sounded by compressed air, and played using one or more keyboards to produce a wide range of musical effects. The pipes are generally arranged in ranks of a particular type, each controlled by a stop, and often into larger sets linked to separate keyboards. ■ a smaller instrument without pipes, producing similar sounds electronically. See also **REED ORGAN**. **2** *Biology* a part of an organism that is typically self-contained and has a specific vital function, such as the heart or liver in humans. ■ a department or organization that performs a specified function: *the central **organs of** administration and business.* ■ a medium of communication, esp. a newspaper or periodical that serves a particular organization, political party, etc.: *the People's Daily, the official organ of the Chinese Communist Party.* ■ (used euphemistically) the penis. ■ *archaic* a region of the brain formerly held to be the seat of a particular faculty. ▷late Old English, via Latin from Greek *organon* 'tool, instrument, sense organ,' reinforced in Middle English by Old French *organe*.

or·gan·dy /ˈôrgəndē/ (also **or·gan·die**) ▸*n.* (*pl.* **-dies**) a fine translucent cotton or silk fabric that is usually stiffened and is used for women's clothing. ▷early 19th cent.: from French *organdi*, of unknown origin.

or·gan·elle /ˌôrgəˈnel/ ▸*n. Biology* any of a number of organized or specialized structures within a living cell. ▷early 20th cent.: from modern Latin *organella*, diminutive of *organum* 'instrument, tool' (see **ORGAN**).

or·gan grind·er ▸*n.* a street musician who plays a barrel organ.

or·gan·ic /ôrˈganik/ ▸*adj.* **1** of, relating to, or derived from living matter: *organic soils.* ■ *Chemistry* of, relating to, or denoting compounds containing carbon (other than simple binary compounds and salts) and chiefly or ultimately of biological origin. Compare with **INORGANIC**. ■ (of food or farming methods) produced or involving production without the use of chemical fertilizers, pesticides, or other artificial agents. **2** *Physiology* of or relating to a bodily organ or organs. ■ *Medicine* (of a disease) affecting the structure of an organ. **3** denoting a relation between elements of something such that they fit together harmoniously as necessary parts of a whole: *the organic unity of the integral work of art.* ■ characterized by continuous or natural development: *companies expand as much by acquisition as by organic growth.* ▷late Middle English: via Latin from Greek *organikos* 'relating to an organ or instrument.' **—or·gan·i·cal·ly** /-ik(ə)lē/ *adv.*

or·gan·ic chem·is·try ▸*n.* the chemistry of carbon compounds (other than simple salts such as carbonates, oxides, and carbides).

or·gan·i·cism /ôrˈganiˌsizəm/ ▸*n.* **1** the doctrine that everything in nature has an organic basis or is part of an organic whole. **2** the use or advocacy of literary or artistic forms in which the parts are connected or coordinated to the whole. ▷mid 19th cent.: from French *organicisme*. **—or·gan·i·cist** *adj.* & *n.* **—or·gan·i·cis·tic** /ôrˌganiˈsistik/ *adj.*

or·gan·ism /ˈôrgəˌnizəm/ ▸*n.* an individual animal, plant, or single-celled life form. ■ the material structure of such an individual: *the heart's contribution to the maintenance of the human organism.* ■ a whole with interdependent parts, likened to a living being: *the upper strata of the American social organism.* ▷early 18th cent. (in the sense 'organization,' from **ORGANIZE**): current senses derive from French *organisme*. **—or·gan·is·mal** /ˌôrgəˈnizməl/ *adj.* **—or·gan·is·mic** /ˌôrgəˈnizmik/ *adj.*

or·gan·ist /ˈôrgənist/ ▸*n.* a person who plays the organ.

or·gan·i·za·tion /ˌôrgəniˈzāSHən/ ▸*n.* **1** the action of organizing something: *the organization of conferences and seminars.* ■ the structure or arrangement of related or connected items: *the spatial organization of the cells.* ■ an efficient and orderly approach to tasks: *apparent disorder and lack of organization.* **2** an organized body of people with a particular purpose, esp. a business, society, association, etc.: *a research organization.* **—or·gan·i·za·tion·al** /-SHənl/ *adj.* **—or·gan·i·za·tion·al·ly** /-SHən-lē/ *adv.*

or·gan·i·za·tion chart ▸*n.* a graphic representation of the structure of an organization, showing the relationships of the positions or jobs within it.

or·gan·i·za·tion man ▸*n. derogatory* a man who lets his individuality and personal life be dominated by the organization he works for.

Or·gan·i·za·tion of Af·ri·can U·ni·ty (abbr.: **OAU**) an association of African states founded in 1963 for mutual cooperation and the elimination of colonialism in Africa. It is based in Addis Ababa, Ethiopia.

Or·gan·i·za·tion of A·mer·i·can States (abbr.: **OAS**) an association including most of the countries of North and South America, chartered in 1948 by members of the former Pan American Union. It has aimed to work for peace and prosperity in the region and to uphold the sovereignty of member nations. Its headquarters are in Washington, D.C.

Or·gan·i·za·tion of the Pe·tro·le·um Ex·port·ing Coun·tries (abbr.: **OPEC**) an association of eleven major oil-producing countries, founded in 1960 to coordinate policies and prices, with headquarters in Vienna. Members are Algeria, Indonesia, Iran, Iraq, Kuwait, Libya, Nigeria, Qatar, Saudi Arabia, the United Arab Emirates, and Venezuela.

or·gan·ize /ˈôrgəˌnīz/ ▸*v.* [*trans.*] **1** arrange into a structured whole; order: *organize lessons in a planned way.* ■ coordinate the activities of (a person or group of people) efficiently: *organize and lead a group of people.* ■ form (a number of people) into a labor union, political group, etc.: *an attempt to organize unskilled workers* | [*intrans.*] *campaigns brought women together to organize.* ■ form (a labor union, political group, etc.). ■ *archaic* arrange or form into a living being or tissue: *the soul doth organize the body.* **2** make arrangements or preparations for (an event or activity); coordinate: *the union organized a 24-hour general strike* | *social and cultural programs are organized by the committee.* ■ take responsibility for providing or arranging: *he is sometimes asked to stay behind, organizing transportation.* ▷late Middle English: from medieval Latin *organizare*, from Latin *organum* 'instrument, tool' (see **ORGAN**). **—or·gan·iz·a·ble** *adj.*

or·gan·ized /ˈôrgəˌnīzd/ ▸*adj.* arranged in a systematic way, esp. on a large scale: *organized crime.* ■ having one's affairs in order so as to deal with them efficiently: *I am systematic and organized enough to save things.* ■ having formed a labor union, political group, etc.: *a repressive regime that crushed organized labor.*

or·gan·iz·er /ˈôrgəˌnīzər/ ▸*n.* **1** a person who organizes: *the organizers of the demonstration* | *he worked as a union organizer all around the state of New Jersey.* **2** a thing used for organizing. See also **ELECTRONIC ORGANIZER, PERSONAL ORGANIZER**.

or·gan loft ▸*n.* a balcony in a church or concert hall for an organ.

organo- ▸*comb. form* **1** *chiefly Biology* relating to bodily organs: *organogenesis.* **2** *Chemistry* (forming names of classes of organic compounds containing a particular element or group) organic: *organochlorine* | *organophosphate.* ▷from Greek *organon* 'organ'; sense 2 from **ORGANIC**.

or·ga·no·chlo·rine /ˌôrgənōˈklôrēn/ ▸*n.* [often as *adj.*] any of a large group of pesticides and other synthetic organic compounds with chlorinated aromatic molecules.

or·gan of Cor·ti /ˈkôrtē/ ▸*n. Anatomy* a structure in the cochlea of the inner ear that produces nerve impulses in response to sound vibrations. ▷late 19th cent.: named after Alfonso *Corti* (1822–76), Italian anatomist.

or·ga·no·gen·e·sis /ˌôrgənōˈjenisis/ ▸*n.* (also **or·ga·nog·e·ny** /ˌôrgəˈnäjənē/) *Biology* the production and development of the organs of an animal or plant.

or·ga·no·lep·tic /ˌôrgənōˈleptik/ ▸*adj.* acting on or involving the use of the sense organs. ▷mid 19th cent.: from French *organoleptique*, from Greek *organon* 'organ' + *lēptikos* 'disposed to take' (from *lambanein* 'take').

or·ga·no·me·tal·lic /ˌôrgənōməˈtalik/ ▸*adj. Chemistry* (of a compound) containing a metal atom bonded to an organic group or groups.

or·ga·non /ˈôrgəˌnän/ ▸*n.* an instrument of thought, esp. a means of reasoning or a system of logic. ▷late 16th cent. (denoting a bodily organ): from Greek, literally 'instrument, organ.' *Organon* was the title of Aristotle's logical treatises.

or·ga·no·phos·pho·rus /ˌôrgənəˈfäsf(ə)rəs; ôrˌganō'-/ ▸*adj.* [*attrib.*] denoting synthetic organic compounds containing phosphorus, esp. pesticides and nerve gases of this kind. **—or·ga·no·phos·phate** /-ˈfäsˌfāt/ *n.*

or·ga·no·ther·a·py /ˌôrgənōˈTHerəpē; ôrˌganō-/ ▸*n.* the treatment of disease with extracts from animal organs, esp. glands. **—or·ga·no·ther·a·peu·tic** /-ˌTHerəˈpyōōtik/ *adj.*

or·gan-pipe cac·tus (also **or·gan pipe cac·tus**) ▸*n.* a large cactus native to the southwestern U.S., having columnar stems or branches and typically flowering

Pronunciation Key ə *ago*; ər *over*; ˈə *or* ˌə *up*; ˈər *or* ˌər *fur*; a *hat*; ā *rate*; ä *car*; CH *chew*; e *let*; ē *see*; e(ə)r *air*; i *fit*; ī *by*; i(ə)r *ear*; NG *sing*; ō *go*; ô *for*; oi *boy*; ŏŏ *good*; ōō *goo*; ou *out*; SH *she*; TH *thin*; TH *then*; (h)w *why*; ZH *vision*

at night. • Several species in the family Cactaceae, including *Lemaireocereus marginatus* and *Cereus thurberi*.

or·gan-pipe cor·al ▸*n.* a tropical coral that forms narrow parallel calcareous tubes linked by transverse plates. • Genus *Tubipora*, order Stolonifera.

or·gan-screen ▸*n.* an ornamental screen above which the organ is placed in some cathedrals and large churches, typically between the choir and the nave.

or·gan stop ▸*n.* a set of pipes of a similar tone in an organ. ■ the handle of the mechanism that brings such a set into action.

or·ga·num /ˈôrgənəm/ ▸*n.* (*pl.* **-na** /-nə/) (in medieval music) a form of early polyphony based on an existing plainsong. ▷Latin, from Greek *organon*, literally 'instrument, organ.'

or·gan·za /ôrˈganzə/ ▸*n.* a thin, stiff, transparent fabric made of silk or a synthetic yarn. ▷early 19th cent.: probably from *Lorganza*, a U.S. trademark.

or·gan·zine /ˈôrgən,zēn/ ▸*n.* a silk thread made of strands twisted together in the contrary direction to that of each individual strand. ▷late 17th cent.: from French *organsin*, from Italian *organzino*, of unknown ultimate origin.

or·gasm /ˈôr,gazəm/ ▸*n.* a climax of sexual excitement, characterized by feelings of pleasure centered in the genitals and (in men) experienced as an accompaniment to ejaculation.
▸*v.* [*intrans.*] experience an orgasm. ▷late 17th cent.: from French *orgasme*, or from modern Latin *orgasmus*, from Greek *orgasmos*, from *organ* 'swell or be excited.'

or·gas·mic /ôrˈgazmik/ ▸*adj.* of or relating to orgasm. ■ (of a person) able to achieve orgasm. ■ *informal, figurative* very enjoyable or exciting: *the album is an orgasmic whirl of techno soundscapes.* —**or·gas·mi·cal·ly** /-mik(ə)lē/ *adv.* —**or·gas·tic** /-ˈgastik/ *adj.* —**or·gas·ti·cal·ly** /-ˈgastik(ə)lē/ *adv.*

OR gate ▸*n.* see OR[1].

or·geat /ˈôr,ZHät; -,ZHä/ ▸*n.* a cooling drink made from orange flower water and either barley or almonds. ▷French, from Provençal *orjat*, from *ordi* 'barley,' from Latin *hordeum* 'barley.'

or·gi·as·tic /,ôrjēˈastik/ ▸*adj.* of or resembling an orgy. ▷late 17th cent.: from Greek *orgiastikos*, from *orgiastēs*, agent noun from *orgiazein* 'hold an orgy.' —**or·gi·as·ti·cal·ly** /-ik(ə)lē/ *adv.*

or·gone /ˈôrgōn/ ▸*n.* (in the theory of Wilhelm Reich) a supposed sexual energy or life force distributed throughout the universe that can be collected and stored (in an orgone box) for therapeutic use. ▷1940s: coined by Wilhelm Reich (1897–1957), Austrian-born psychoanalyst.

or·gu·lous /ˈôrg(y)ələs/ ▸*adj. poetic/literary* haughty. ▷Middle English: from Old French *orguillus*, from *orguill* 'pride.' The word was rare from the 16th cent. until used by Robert Southey and Sir Walter Scott as a historical archaism and affected by 19th-cent. journalists.

or·gy /ˈôrjē/ ▸*n.* (*pl.* **-gies**) a wild party, esp. one involving excessive drinking and unrestrained sexual activity: *he had a reputation for drunken orgies.* ■ excessive indulgence in a specified activity: *an* **orgy of** *buying.* ■ (usu. **orgies**) *historical* secret rites used in the worship of Bacchus, Dionysus, and other Greek and Roman deities, celebrated with dancing, drunkenness, and singing. ▷early 16th cent.: originally plural, from French *orgies*, via Latin from Greek *orgia* 'secret rites or revels.'

-orial ▸*suffix* forming adjectives corresponding to nouns ending in *-ory* (such as *accusatorial* corresponding to *accusatory*). ▷see -ORY, -AL.

or·i·bi /ˈôrəbē; ˈär-/ ▸*n.* (*pl.* same or **-bis**) a small antelope of the African savanna, having a reddish-beige back, white underparts, and short vertical horns. • *Ourebia ourebi*, family Bovidae. ▷late 18th cent.: from Afrikaans, from Khoikhoi.

or·i·chal·cum /,ôriˈkalkəm/ (also **or·i·chalc** /ˈôri,kalk/) ▸*n.* a yellow metal prized in ancient times, probably a form of brass or a similar alloy. ▷late Middle English: via Latin from Greek *oreikhalkon*, literally 'mountain copper.'

oriel

o·ri·el /ˈôrēəl/ ▸*n.* a projection from the wall of a building, typically supported from the ground or by corbels. ■ (also **oriel window**) a window in such a structure. ■ a projecting window, often on an upper story; a bay window. ▷late Middle English: from Old French *oriol* 'gallery,' of unknown origin; compare with medieval Latin *oriolum* 'upper chamber.'

o·ri·ent /ˈôrē,ənt/ ▸*n.* **1** (**the Orient**) *poetic/literary* the countries of Asia, esp. eastern Asia. **2** the special luster of a pearl of the finest quality. ■ a pearl with such a luster.
▸*adj. poetic/literary* situated in or belonging to the east; oriental. ■ (of the sun, daylight, etc.) rising. ■ (esp. of precious stones) lustrous (with reference to fine pearls from the East).
▸*v.* /ˈôrē,ent/ **1** [*trans.*] (often **be oriented**) align or position (something) relative to the points of a compass or other specified positions: *the fires are oriented in direct line with the midsummer sunset.* ■ adjust or tailor (something) to specified circumstances or needs: *magazines oriented to the business community* | [as *adj.*, in *combination*] (**-oriented**) *market-oriented economic reforms.* ■ guide (someone) physically in a specified direction. **2** (**orient oneself**) find one's position in relation to new and strange surroundings: *there are no street names that would enable her to orient herself.* ▷late Middle English: via Old French from Latin *orient-* 'rising or east,' from *oriri* 'to rise.'

o·ri·en·tal /,ôrēˈentl/ (also **O·ri·en·tal**) ▸*adj.* **1** of, from, or characteristic of the Far East: *oriental countries.* ■ *dated* of, from, or characteristic of the countries of Asia. ■ (**Oriental**) *Zoology* of, relating to, or denoting a zoogeographical region comprising Asia south of the Himalayas and Indonesia west of Wallace's line. Distinctive animals include pandas, gibbons, tree shrews, tarsiers, and moonrats. **2** (of a pearl or other jewel) orient.
▸*n.* (**Oriental**) *dated, often offensive* a person of Far Eastern descent. ▷late Middle English: from Old French, or from Latin *orientalis*, from *orient-* (see ORIENT). —**o·ri·en·tal·ize** /-īz/ *v.* —**o·ri·en·tal·ly** *adv.*

> ***USAGE*** The term **Oriental**, denoting a person from the Far East, is regarded as offensive by many Asians, esp. Asian Americans. It has many associations with European imperialism in Asia. Therefore, it has an out-of-date feel and tends to be associated with a rather offensive stereotype of the people and their customs as inscrutable and exotic. **Asian** and more specific terms such as **East Asian**, **Chinese**, and **Japanese** are preferred.

O·ri·en·ta·li·a /,ôrē-enˈtālēə/ ▸*plural n.* books and other items relating to or characteristic of the Orient. ▷early 20th cent.: from Latin, neuter plural of *orientalis* 'oriental.'

O·ri·en·tal·ism /,ôrēˈen(t)l,izəm/ ▸*n.* something considered characteristic of the peoples and cultures of west, east, or central Asia. ■ the knowledge and study of these languages and cultures. —**O·ri·en·tal·ist** *n.*

o·ri·en·tal pop·py ▸*n.* a southwestern Asian poppy with coarse, deeply cut, hairy leaves and large scarlet flowers with a black mark at the base of each petal, widely grown as a garden perennial. • *Papaver orientale*, family Papaveraceae.

o·ri·en·tate /ˈôrēən,tāt/ ▸*v.* another term for ORIENT. ▷mid 19th cent.: probably a back-formation from ORIENTATION.

o·ri·en·ta·tion /,ôrēənˈtāSHən/ ▸*n.* the determination of the relative position of something or someone (esp. oneself): *the child's surroundings provide clues to help in orientation.* ■ the relative physical position or direction of something: *two complex shapes, presented in different orientations.* ■ *Zoology* an animal's change of position in response to an external stimulus, esp. with respect to compass directions. ■ familiarization with something: *their training and orientation comes out of magazine and newspaper distribution.* ■ a program of introduction for students new to a school or college: *she attended freshman orientation.* ■ the direction of someone's interest or attitude, esp. political or sexual: *a common age of consent regardless of gender or sexual orientation.* ▷mid 19th cent.: apparently from ORIENT. —**o·ri·en·ta·tion·al** *adj.*

o·ri·en·teer /,ôrēənˈtir/ ▸*n.* a person who takes part in orienteering.
▸*v.* [*intrans.*] take part in orienteering.

o·ri·en·teer·ing /,ôriənˈti(ə)riNG/ ▸*n.* a competitive sport in which participants find their way to various checkpoints across rough country with the aid of a map and compass, the winner being the one with the lowest elapsed time. ▷1940s: from Swedish *orientering.*

O·ri·ent Ex·press a train that ran between Paris and Istanbul and other Balkan cities, via Vienna, from 1883 to 1961. Since 1961 the name has been used for various trains running in Europe, Asia, and Australia, some of which run over parts of the old route.

or·i·fice /ˈôrəfis/ ▸*n.* an opening, as of a pipe or tube, or one in the body, such as a nostril or the anus. ▷late Middle English: from French, from late Latin *orificium*, from *os, or-* 'mouth' + *facere* 'make.'

or·i·flamme /ˈôrə,flam; ˈär-/ ▸*n. poetic/literary* (in historical use) a scarlet banner or knight's standard. ■ a principle or ideal that serves as a rallying point in a struggle. ▷late Middle English: from Old French, from Latin *aurum* 'gold' + *flamma* 'flame.'

orig. ▸*abbr.* ■ origin. ■ original; originally.

origami

o·ri·ga·mi /,ôrəˈgämē/ ▸*n.* the Japanese art of folding paper into decorative shapes and figures. ▷Japanese, from *oru, -ori* 'fold' + *kami* 'paper.'

o·rig·a·num /əˈrigənəm/ ▸*n.* an aromatic plant of a genus that includes marjoram and oregano. • Genus *Origanum*, family Labiatae. ▷Latin, from Greek *origanon*, perhaps from *oros* 'mountain' + *ganos* 'brightness.'

Or·i·gen /ˈôri,jen; ˈär-/ (*c.*185–*c.*254), Christian scholar and theologian, probably born in Alexandria, Egypt. His most well-known work was the *Hexapla*, an edition of the Old Testament with six or more parallel versions.

or·i·gin /ˈôrəjən/ ▸*n.* **1** the beginning of something's existence: *a novel theory about the origin of oil* | *the name is Norse* **in origin**. ■ a person's social background or ancestry: *they will be asked about their ethnic origin* | *a voice that betrays his Southern origins.* ■ the place or situation from which something comes: *an indication of the country of origin.* **2** *Anatomy* the place or point where a muscle, nerve, or other body part arises, in particular: ■ the more fixed end or attachment of a muscle. ■ a place where a nerve or blood vessel begins or branches from a main nerve or blood vessel. **3** *Mathematics* a fixed point from which coordinates are measured, as where axes intersect. ▷early 16th cent.: from French *origine*, from Latin *origo, origin-*, from *oriri* 'to rise.'

> ***THE RIGHT WORD*** **inception, origin, provenance, root, source**
>
> The **origin** of something is the point from which it starts or sets out, or the person or thing from which it is ultimately derived (*the origin of the custom of carving pumpkins at Halloween; the origin of a word*). It often applies to causes that were in operation before the thing itself was brought into being.
>
> **Source**, on the other hand, applies to that which provides a first and continuous supply (*the source of the river; an ongoing source of inspiration and encouragement*).
>
> **Root**, more often than *source*, applies to what is regarded as the first or final cause of something; it suggests an origin so fundamental as to be the ultimate cause from which something stems (*money is the root of all evil*).
>
> **Inception** refers specifically to the beginning of an undertaking, project, institution, or practice (*she was in charge of the organization from its inception*).
>
> **Provenance** is similarly restricted in meaning, referring to the specific place, or sometimes the race or people, from which something is derived or by whom it was invented or constructed (*in digging, they uncovered an artifact of unknown provenance*).

o·rig·i·nal /əˈrijənl/ ▸*adj.* **1** used or produced at the creation or earliest stage of something: *costumes made from the original designs* | *the plasterwork is probably original.* ■ [*attrib.*] present or existing at the beginning of a series or process; first: *the original owner of the house.* **2** created directly and personally by a particular artist; not a copy or imitation: *original Rembrandts* | *playing original material.* **3** not dependent on other people's ideas; inventive and unusual: *a subtle and original thinker.* See note at CREATIVE.
▸*n.* **1** something serving as a model or basis for imitations or copies: *the portrait may be a copy of the original* | *one set of originals and four photocopies.* ■ (**the original**) the form or language in which something was first produced or created: *the study of Russian texts in the original.* ■ (**the original of**) a person or place on which a character or location in a literary work is based: *the paper where the original of the play's*

Walter Burns worked. ■ a song, picture, etc., produced by a performer or artist personally: *a mix of traditional tunes and originals.* ■ a book or recording that has not been previously made available in a different form: *paperback originals.* ■ a garment made to order from a design specially prepared for a fashion collection. **2** an eccentric or unusual person: *he was one of the true originals.* ▷Middle English (the earliest use being in the phrase *original sin*): from Old French, or from Latin *originalis*, from *origin-* (see ORIGIN).

o·rig·i·nal grav·i·ty ▸*n.* the relative density of the wort before it is fermented to produce beer, being chiefly dependent on the quantity of fermentable sugars in solution. It is regarded as a guide to the alcoholic strength of the finished beer.

o·rig·i·nal in·stru·ment ▸*n.* a musical instrument, or a copy of one, dating from the time the music played on it was composed.

o·rig·i·nal·i·ty /ə,rijə'nalitē/ ▸*n.* the ability to think independently and creatively: *a writer of great originality.* ■ the quality of being novel or unusual: *he congratulated her on the originality of her costume.*

o·rig·i·nal·ly /ə'rijənl-ē/ ▸*adv.* **1** from or in the beginning; at first: *potatoes originally came from South America.* **2** in a novel and inventive way: *suggestions so originally and persuasively outlined.*

o·rig·i·nal sin ▸*n.* *Christian Theology* the tendency to sin innate in all human beings, held to be inherited from Adam in consequence of the Fall. The concept of original sin was developed in the writings of St. Augustine.

o·rig·i·nate /ə'rijə,nāt/ ▸*v.* [*intrans.*] have a specified beginning: *the word originated as a marketing term.* ■ [*trans.*] create or initiate (something): *he is responsible for originating this particular cliché.* ▷mid 17th cent.: from medieval Latin *originat-* 'caused to begin,' from Latin *origo, origin-* 'source, origin.' **—o·rig·i·na·tion** /ə,rijə'nāsHən/ *n.* **—o·rig·i·na·tive** /-,nātiv/ *adj.* **—o·rig·i·na·tor** /-,nātər/ *n.*

o·rig·i·na·tion fee /ə,rijə'nāsHən/ ▸*n.* *Finance* a fee charged by a lender on entering into a loan agreement to cover the cost of processing the loan.

Or·i·mul·sion /äri'məlsHən/ ▸*n.* *trademark* a fuel consisting of an emulsion of bitumen in water. ▷1980s: blend of *Orinoco* (the name of an oil belt in Venezuela, where the bitumen was originally extracted) and EMULSION.

O-ring ▸*n.* a gasket in the form of a ring with a circular cross section, typically made of pliable material, used to seal connections in pipes, tubes, etc.

Or·i·no·co /,ôrə'nōkō/ a river in northern South America that rises in southeastern Venezuela and flows 1,280 miles (2,060 km), entering the Atlantic Ocean through a vast delta. For part of its length it forms the border between Colombia and Venezuela.

o·ri·ole /'ôrē,ōl/ ▸*n.* **1** an Old World bird related to the starlings that feeds on fruit and insects, the male typically having bright yellow and black plumage. • Family Oriolidae and genus *Oriolus*: many species, including the **golden oriole** (*Oriolus oriolus*). **2** a New World bird of the American blackbird family, with black and orange or yellow plumage. • Genus *Icterus*, family Icteridae (sometimes called the **American oriole family**): many species, including the **Baltimore oriole**. ▷late 18th cent.: from medieval Latin *oriolus* (in Old French *oriol*), from Latin *aureolus*, diminutive of *aureus* 'golden,' from *aurum* 'gold.'

O·ri·on /ə'rīən/ **1** *Greek Mythology* a giant and hunter who was changed into a constellation at his death. **2** *Astronomy* a conspicuous constellation (the Hunter), said to represent a hunter holding a club and shield. It lies on the celestial equator and contains many bright stars, including Rigel, Betelgeuse, and a line of three that form **Orion's belt**. ■ [*as genitive*] (**Orionis** /,ôrē'ōnis/) used with a preceding letter or numeral to designate a star in this constellation: *the multiple star Theta Orionis.* ▷via Latin from Greek.

Or·i·sha /'ôrə,sHä/ ▸*n.* (*pl.* same) (in southern Nigeria) any of several minor gods. The term is also used in various religious cults of South America and the Caribbean. ▷Yoruba.

or·i·son /'ôrisən; -zən; 'är-/ ▸*n.* *archaic* a prayer. ▷Middle English: from Old French *oreison*, from Latin *oratio(n-)* 'speech' (see ORATION).

O·ris·sa /ô'risə/ a state in eastern India, on the Bay of Bengal; capital, Bhubaneswar.

-orium ▸*suffix* forming nouns denoting a place for a particular function: *auditorium* | *sanatorium.* ▷from Latin; compare with -ORY[1].

O·ri·ya /ô'rēə/ ▸*n.* (*pl.* same or **-yas**) **1** a native or inhabitant of Orissa. **2** the Indic language of this people, closely related to Bengali. ▷from Hindi *Uṛiyā*.

Ork·ney Is·lands /'ôrknē/ (also **Ork·ney** or **the Ork·neys**) a group of more than 70 islands off the northeastern tip of Scotland, constituting an administrative region of Scotland; pop. 19,000; chief town, Kirkwall.They came into Scottish possession in 1472, having previously been ruled by Norway and Denmark.

Or·lan·do /ôr'landō/ a city in central Florida; pop. 185,951. It is a popular tourist resort.

orle /ôrl/ ▸*n.* *Heraldry* a narrow border inset from the edge of a shield. ▷late 16th cent.: from French *ourle*, from *ourler* 'to hem,' based on Latin *ora* 'edge.'

Or·le·an·ist /'ôrlēənist/ ▸*n.* *historical* a person supporting the claim to the French throne of the descendants of the Duke of Orleans (1640–1701), younger brother of Louis XIV, esp. Louis Philippe (King of France, 1830–48). ▷from French *Orléaniste*, from *Orléans*.

Or·le·ans /'ôrlē(ə)nz; ôr'lē(ə)nz; ôrlā'äN/ a city in central France, on the Loire River; pop. 108,000. In 1429, it was the scene of Joan of Arc's first victory over the English during the Hundred Years War. French name ORLÉANS .

Or·lon /'ôr,län/ ▸*n.* *trademark* a synthetic acrylic fiber used for textiles and knitwear, or a fabric made from it. ▷1950s: invented word, on the pattern of *nylon*.

or·lop /'ôr,läp/ (also **orlop deck**) ▸*n.* the lowest deck of a wooden sailing ship with three or more decks. ▷late Middle English: from Dutch *overloop* 'covering,' from *overlopen* 'run over.'

Or·man·dy /'ôrməndē/, Eugene (1899–1985), U.S. conductor; born in Hungary; born *Jeno Blau*. He was conductor of the Philadelphia Orchestra from 1938 to 1980, the longest directorship of an orchestra in U.S. history.

Or·mazd /'ôrməzd/ (also **Or·muzd**) another name for AHURA MAZDA.

or·mo·lu /'ôrmə,lo͞o/ ▸*n.* a gold-colored alloy of copper, zinc, and sometimes tin, cast into desired shapes and often gilded, used esp. in the 18th century for decorating furniture and making ornaments. ▷mid 18th cent.: from French *or moulu* 'powdered gold' (used in gilding).

Or·mond Beach /'ôrmənd/ a resort city in northeastern Florida, north of Daytona Beach; pop. 29,721.

or·na·ment ▸*n.* /'ôrnəmənt/ a thing used to adorn something but usually having no practical purpose, esp. a small object such as a figurine. ■ a quality or person adding grace, beauty, or honor to something: *the design would be a great* ***ornament to*** *the metropolis.* ■ decoration added to embellish something, esp. a building: *it served more for ornament than for protection.* ■ (**ornaments**) *Music* embellishments and decorations, such as trills or grace notes, added to a melody. ■ (usu. **ornaments**) *Christian Church* the accessories of worship, such as the altar, chalice, and sacred vessels.
▸*v.* /'ôrnə,ment/ [*trans.*] adorn; beautify: *the men and women in the Stone Age ornamented their caves.* ▷Middle English (also in the sense 'accessory'): from Old French *ournement*, from Latin *ornamentum* 'equipment, ornament,' from *ornare* 'adorn.' The verb dates from the early 18th cent.

or·na·men·tal /,ôrnə'mentl/ ▸*adj.* serving or intended as an ornament; decorative: *an ornamental fountain.*
▸*n.* a plant or tree grown for its attractive appearance. **—or·na·men·tal·ism** /-,izəm/ *n.* **—or·na·men·tal·ist** /-ist/ *n.* **—or·na·men·tal·ly** *adv.*

or·na·men·ta·tion /,ôrnəmen'tāsHən/ ▸*n.* things added to something to provide decoration: *a baroque chandelier with plasterwork ornamentation.* ■ the action of decorating something or making it more elaborate: *the rhetorical ornamentation of text.*

or·nate /ôr'nāt/ ▸*adj.* made in an intricate shape or decorated with complex patterns: *an ornate wrought-iron railing.* ■ (of literary style) using unusual words and complex constructions: *peculiarly ornate and metaphorical language.* ■ (of musical composition or performance) using many ornaments such as grace notes and trills. ▷late Middle English: from Latin *ornatus* 'adorned,' past participle of *ornare*. **—or·nate·ly** *adv.* **—or·nate·ness** *n.*

or·ner·y /'ôrn(ə)rē/ ▸*adj.* *informal* bad-tempered and combative: *some hogs are just mean and ornery.* ■ stubborn: *taking the singer's ornery radicalism in a different direction.* ▷early 19th cent.: variant of ORDINARY, representing a dialect pronunciation. **—or·ner·i·ness** *n.*

ornith. ▸*abbr.* ■ ornithological. ■ ornithology.

or·ni·thine /'ôrnə,THēn/ ▸*n.* *Biochemistry* an amino acid produced by the body that is important in protein metabolism. • Chem. formula: $NH_2(CH_2)_3CH(NH_2)COOH$. ▷late 19th cent.: from ORNITHO- (with reference to a constituent found in bird excrement) + -INE[4].

or·nith·is·chi·an /,ôrnə'THiskēən/ *Paleontology* ▸*adj.* of, relating to, or denoting herbivorous dinosaurs of an order distinguished by having a pelvic structure resembling that of birds. Compare with SAURISCHIAN.
▸*n.* an ornithischian dinosaur. • Order Ornithischia, superorder Dinosauria; comprises the stegosaurs, ankylosaurs, ornithopods, pachycephalosaurs, and ceratopsians. ▷early 20th cent.: from modern Latin *Ornithiscia*, from Greek *ornis, ornith-* 'bird' + *iskhion* 'hip joint.'

ornitho- ▸*comb. form* relating to or resembling a bird or birds: *ornithology* | *ornithopod.* ▷from Greek *ornis, ornith-* 'bird.'

or·ni·thol·o·gy /,ôrnə'THäləjē/ ▸*n.* the scientific study of birds. ▷late 17th cent.: from modern Latin *ornithologia*, from Greek *ornithologos* 'treating of birds.' **—or·ni·tho·log·i·cal** /,ôrniTHə'läjikəl/ *adj.* **—or·ni·tho·log·i·cal·ly** /,ôrniTHə'läjik(ə)lē/ *adv.* **—or·ni·thol·o·gist** /-jist/ *n.*

or·nith·o·mi·mo·saur /,ôrnəTHō'mīmə,sôr/ ▸*n.* technical term for OSTRICH DINOSAUR. ▷1980s: from modern Latin *Ornithomimosauria*, from Greek *ornis, ornith-* 'bird' + *mimos* 'mime' + *sauros* 'lizard.'

or·ni·tho·pod /'ôrnəTHə,päd/ ▸*n.* a mainly bipedal herbivorous dinosaur. • Infraorder Ornithopoda, order Ornithischia; includes the hadrosaurs, iguanodon, hypsilophodont, etc. ▷late 19th cent.: from modern Latin *Ornithopoda*, from Greek *ornis, ornith-* 'bird' + *pous, pod-* 'foot.'

or·ni·thop·ter /,ôrnə'THäptər/ ▸*n.* *chiefly historical* a machine designed to achieve flight by means of flapping wings. ▷early 20th cent.: coined in French as *ornithoptère*.

or·ni·tho·rhyn·chus /,ôrnəTHə'riNGkəs/ ▸*n.* another term for PLATYPUS. ▷early 19th cent.: modern Latin, from ORNITHO- + Greek *rhunkhos* 'bill.'

or·ni·tho·sis /,ôrnə'THōsis/ ▸*n.* another term for PSITTACOSIS.

oro- ▸*comb. form* of or relating to mountains: *orogeny.* ▷from Greek *oros* 'mountain.'

or·o·gen /'ôrə,jen; -jən/ ▸*n.* *Geology* a belt of the earth's crust involved in the formation of mountains. ▷1920s: from Greek *oros* 'mountain' + -GEN.

o·rog·e·ny /ô'räjənē/ ▸*n.* *Geology* a process in which a section of the earth's crust is folded and deformed by lateral compression to form a mountain range. **—or·o·gen·e·sis** /,ôrō'jenəsis/ *n.* **—or·o·gen·ic** /,ôrō'jenik/ *adj.*

or·o·graph·ic /,ôrə'grafik/ ▸*adj.* of or relating to mountains, esp. with regard to their position and form. ■ (of clouds or rainfall) resulting from the effects of mountains in forcing moist air to rise. **—or·o·graph·i·cal** *adj.*

o·rog·ra·phy /ô'rägrəfē/ ▸*n.* the branch of physical geography dealing with mountains.

O·ro·mo /ô'rōmō/ ▸*n.* (*pl.* same or **-mos**) **1** a member of the largest ethnic group in Ethiopia. **2** the Cushitic language of this people.
▸*adj.* of or relating to this people or their language. ▷the name in Oromo. An earlier term, *Galla*, remains in use but is not favored by the Oromo themselves.

O·ro·no /'ôrə,nō/ a town in east central Maine, on the Penobscot River, north of Bangor, home to the University of Maine; pop. 10,573.

O·ron·tes /ô'räntēz/ a river in southwestern Asia that rises near Baalbek in northern Lebanon and flows 355 miles (571 km) through western and northern Syria before turning west through southern Turkey to enter the Mediterranean Sea. It is an important source of water for irrigation, esp. in Syria.

o·ro·pen·do·la /,ôrə'pendl-ə/ ▸*n.* a gregarious tropical American bird of the American blackbird family that constructs a pendulous nest and has brown or black plumage with yellow outer tail feathers. • Genus *Psarocolius*, family Icteridae: several species. ▷late 19th cent.: from Spanish, literally 'golden oriole.'

O

o·ro·phar·ynx /ˌôrō'fariNGks/ ▶*n.* (*pl.* **-pha·ryn·ges** /-fə'rinjēz/ or **-phar·ynx·es**) *Anatomy* the part of the pharynx that lies between the soft palate and the hyoid bone. ▷late 19th cent.: formed irregularly from Latin *os*, *-or* 'mouth' + PHARYNX. —**o·ro·pha·ryn·ge·al** /-fə'rinj(ē)əl; -ˌfarən'jēəl/ *adj.*

o·ro·tund /'ôrəˌtənd/ ▶*adj.* (of the voice or phrasing) full, round, and imposing. ■ (of writing, style, or expression) pompous; pretentious. ▷late 18th cent.: from Latin *ore rotundo* 'with rounded mouth.' —**o·ro·tun·di·ty** /ˌôrə'təndite/ *n.*

or·phan /'ôrfən/ ▶*n.* **1** a child whose parents are dead. ■ a person or thing bereft of protection, position, etc.: *radioactive wastes are the main orphan of the nuclear era.* **2** *Printing* the first line of a paragraph set as the last line of a page or column, considered undesirable.

▶*v.* [*trans.*] (usu. **be orphaned**) make (a person or animal) an orphan: *John was orphaned at 12.*

▶*adj.* denoting, of, or for an orphan or orphans. ■ bereft of protection, position, etc.: *orphan garbage barges aimlessly wandering the oceans.* ▷late Middle English: via late Latin from Greek *orphanos* 'bereaved.' —**or·phan·hood** /-ˌho͝od/ *n.*

or·phan·age /'ôrfənij/ ▶*n.* a residential institution for the care and education of orphans. ■ *archaic* the state or condition of being an orphan.

or·phan drug ▶*n.* a pharmaceutical that remains commercially undeveloped owing to limited potential for profitability.

Or·phe·us /'ôrfēəs/ *Greek Mythology* a poet who could entrance wild beasts with the beauty of his singing and lyre playing. He went to the underworld after the death of his wife Eurydice and secured her release from the dead, but lost her because he failed to obey the condition that he must not look back at her until they had reached the world of the living. —**Or·phe·an** /-fēən/ *adj.*

Or·phic /'ôrfik/ ▶*adj.* of or concerning Orpheus or Orphism. ▷late 17th cent.: via Latin from Greek *Orphikos*, from *Orpheus* (see ORPHEUS).

Or·phism /'ôrˌfizəm/ ▶*n.* **1** a mystic religion of ancient Greece, originating in the 7th or 6th century BC and based on poems (now lost) attributed to Orpheus, emphasizing the necessity for individuals to rid themselves of the evil part of their nature by ritual and moral purification throughout a series of reincarnations. **2** a short-lived art movement (*c.*1912) within cubism, pioneered by a group of French painters (including Robert Delaunay, Sonia Delaunay-Terk, and Fernand Léger) and emphasizing the lyrical use of color rather than the austere intellectual cubism of Picasso, Braque, and Gris.

or·phrey /'ôrfrē/ ▶*n.* (*pl.* **-phreys**) an ornamental stripe or border, esp. one on an ecclesiastical vestment such as a chasuble. ▷Middle English: from Old French *orfreis*, from a medieval Latin alteration of *auriphrygium*, from Latin *aurum* 'gold' + *Phrygius* 'Phrygian' (also used in the sense 'embroidered').

or·pi·ment /'ôrpəmənt/ ▶*n.* a bright yellow mineral consisting of arsenic trisulfide, formerly used as a dye and artist's pigment. ▷late Middle English: via Old French from Latin *auripigmentum*, from *aurum* 'gold' + *pigmentum* 'pigment.'

or·pine /'ôrpən/ (also **or·pin**) ▶*n.* a purple-flowered Eurasian plant of the stonecrop family, a naturalized weed of North America. • *Sedum telephium*, family Crassulaceae. ▷Middle English: from Old French *orpine*, probably an alteration of ORPIMENT, originally applied to a yellow-flowered sedum.

Or·ping·ton /'ôrpiNGtən/ ▶*n.* **1** a full-bodied breed of chicken of buff, white, or black color. **2** a duck of a buff or white breed, kept for its meat. ▷late 19th cent.: from *Orpington*, the name of a town in Kent, England.

Orr /ôr/, Bobby (1948–), U.S. hockey player; born in Canada; full name *Robert Gordon Orr*. He signed with the Boston Bruins at the age of eighteen in 1966 and played for them until 1976. He played for the Chicago Blackhawks before retiring in 1978. Hockey Hall of Fame (1979).

or·rer·y /'ôrərē/ ▶*n.* (*pl.* **-rer·ies**) a mechanical model of the solar system, or of just the sun, earth, and moon, used to represent their relative positions and motions. ▷early 18th cent.: named after the fourth Earl of *Orrery*, for whom one was made.

or·ris /'ôris/ (also **or·ris·root**) ▶*n.* a preparation of the fragrant rootstock of an iris, used in perfumery and formerly in medicine. • The root is usually taken from *Iris* × *germanica* var. 'Florentina.' ▷mid 16th cent.: apparently an unexplained alteration of IRIS.

Orsk /ôrsk/ a city in southern Russia, in the Ural Mountains, on the Ural River, near the border with Kazakhstan; pop. 271,000.

ort /ôrt/ (usu. **orts**) ▶*n.* *archaic* or *dialect* a scrap or remainder of food from a meal. ▷late Middle English: from Middle Low German *orte* 'food remains,' originally a compound of which the second element is related to EAT.

ort·a·nique /ˌôrtə'nēk/ ▶*n.* a citrus fruit that is a cross between an orange and a tangerine, developed in Jamaica in the 1920s. • *Citrus sinensis* × *reticulata*, family Rutaceae. ▷blend of ORANGE, TANGERINE, and UNIQUE.

Or·te·ga /ôr'tāgə/, Daniel (1945–), Nicaraguan statesman; president 1985–90; full name *Daniel Ortega Saavedra*. He became the leader of the Sandinista National Liberation Front (FSLN) in 1966 and president after the Sandinista election victory in 1984.

Or·te·ga y Gas·set /ē gä'set/, José (1883–1955), Spanish philosopher. His works include *The Revolt of the Masses* (1930), in which he proposed leadership by an intellectual elite.

orth. ▶*abbr.* ■ orthopedic; orthopedics.

ortho- ▶*comb. form* **1** straight; rectangular; upright: *orthodontics.* ■ right; correct: *orthoepy.* **2** *Chemistry* denoting substitution at two adjacent carbon atoms in a benzene ring, e.g., in 1, 2 positions: *orthodichlorobenzene.* Compare with META- and PARA-[1]. **3** *Chemistry* denoting a compound from which a *meta*-compound is formed by dehydration: *orthophosphoric acid.* ▷from Greek *orthos* 'straight, right.'

or·tho·ce·phal·ic /ˌôrTHōsə'falik/ ▶*adj.* having a head with a medium ratio of breadth to height.

or·tho·chro·mat·ic /ˌôrTHōkrə'matik/ ▶*adj.* (of black-and-white photographic film) sensitive to all visible light except red. Orthochromatic film can therefore be handled in red light in the darkroom but does not produce black-and-white tones that correspond very closely to the colors seen by the eye. Often contrasted with PANCHROMATIC.

or·tho·clase /'ôrTHəˌklās; -ˌklāz/ ▶*n.* a common rock-forming mineral occurring typically as white or pink crystals. It is a potassium-rich alkali feldspar and is used in ceramics and glassmaking. ▷mid 19th cent.: from ORTHO- 'straight' + Greek *klasis* 'breaking' (because of the characteristic two cleavages at right angles).

or·tho·don·tics /ˌôrTHə'däntiks/ (also **or·tho·don·tia** /-'dänsH(ē)ə/) ▶*plural n.* [treated as *sing.*] the treatment of irregularities in the teeth (esp. of alignment and occlusion) and jaws, including the use of braces. ▷early 20th cent.: from ORTHO- 'straight' + Greek *odous, odont-* 'tooth.' —**or·tho·don·tic** *adj.* —**or·tho·don·ti·cal·ly** /-tik(ə)lē/ *adv.* —**or·tho·don·tist** /-tist/ *n.*

or·tho·dox /'ôrTHəˌdäks/ ▶*adj.* **1** (of a person or their views, esp. religious or political ones, or other beliefs or practices) conforming to what is generally or traditionally accepted as right or true; established and approved: *the orthodox economics of today | orthodox medical treatment | orthodox Hindus.* ■ (of a person) not independent-minded; conventional and unoriginal: *a relatively orthodox artist.* **2** (of a thing) of the ordinary or usual type; normal: *they avoided orthodox jazz venues.* **3** (usu. **Orthodox**) (of the Jews or Judaism) strictly keeping to traditional doctrine and ritual. **4** (usu. **Orthodox**) of or relating to the Orthodox Church. ▷late Middle English: from Greek *orthodoxos* (probably via ecclesiastical Latin), from *orthos* 'straight or right' + *doxa* 'opinion.' —**or·tho·dox·ly** *adv.*

Or·tho·dox Church a Christian church or federation of churches originating in the Greek-speaking church of the Byzantine Empire, not accepting the authority of the pope, and using ancient forms of service.

The chief Orthodox churches (often known collectively as the **Eastern Orthodox Church**) include the national churches of Greece, Russia, Bulgaria, Romania, and Serbia. The term is also used by other ancient churches, mainly of African or Asian origin, e.g., the Coptic, Syrian, and Ethiopian churches.

Or·tho·dox Ju·da·ism a major branch within Judaism that teaches strict adherence to rabbinical interpretation of Jewish law and its traditional observances.

or·tho·dox·y /'ôrTHəˌdäksē/ ▶*n.* (*pl.* **-dox·ies**) **1** authorized or generally accepted theory, doctrine, or practice: *monetarist orthodoxy | he challenged many of the established orthodoxies.* ■ the quality of conforming to such theories, doctrines, or practices: *writings of unimpeachable orthodoxy.* **2** the whole community of Orthodox Jews or Orthodox Christians. ▷mid 17th cent.: via late Latin from late Greek *orthodoxia* 'sound doctrine,' from *orthodoxos* (see ORTHODOX).

or·tho·drom·ic /ˌôrTHə'drämik/ ▶*adj.* *Physiology* (of an impulse) traveling in the normal direction in a nerve fiber. The opposite of ANTIDROMIC. ▷1940s: from ORTHO- 'right, correct' + Greek *dromos* 'running' + -IC.

or·tho·e·py /ôr'THōəpē/ ▶*n.* the correct or accepted pronunciation of words. ■ the study of correct or accepted pronunciation. ▷mid 17th cent.: from Greek *orthoepeia* 'correct speech,' from *orthos* 'right or straight' + *epos, epe-* 'word.' —**or·tho·ep·ic** /ˌôrTHō'epik/ *adj.* —**or·tho·e·pist** /-pist/ *n.*

or·tho·gen·e·sis /ˌôrTHō'jenəsis/ ▶*n.* *Biology, chiefly historical* a theory that variations in evolution follow a particular direction and are not merely sporadic and fortuitous. —**or·tho·gen·e·sist** *n.* —**or·tho·ge·net·ic** /-jə'netik/ *adj.* —**or·tho·ge·net·i·cal·ly** /-jə'netik(ə)lē/ *adv.*

or·thog·na·thous /ôr'THägnəTHəs/ ▶*adj.* *Anatomy* (esp. of a person) having a jaw that does not project or recede, so that the facial profile is nearly vertical. ▷mid 19th cent.: from ORTHO- 'straight' + Greek *gnathos* 'jaw' + -OUS.

or·thog·o·nal /ôr'THägənl/ ▶*adj.* **1** of or involving right angles; at right angles. **2** *Statistics* (of variates) statistically independent. ■ (of an experiment) having variates that can be treated as statistically independent. ▷late 16th cent.: from French, based on Greek *orthogōnios* 'right-angled.' —**or·thog·o·nal·i·ty** /ôrˌTHägə'nalitē/ *n.* —**or·thog·o·nal·ly** *adv.*

or·thog·o·nal pro·jec·tion ▶*n.* *Engineering* a system of making engineering drawings showing two or more views of an object at right angles to each other on a single drawing. ■ a drawing made using this method.

or·tho·graph·ic pro·jec·tion /ˌôrTHə'grafik/ ▶*n.* a method of projection in which an object is depicted or a surface mapped using parallel lines to project its shape onto a plane. ■ a drawing or map made using this method.

or·thog·ra·phy /ôr'THägrəfē/ ▶*n.* (*pl.* **-phies**) **1** the conventional spelling system of a language. ■ the study of spelling and how letters combine to represent sounds and form words. **2** another term for ORTHOGRAPHIC PROJECTION. ▷late Middle English: via Old French and Latin from Greek *orthographia*, from *orthos* 'correct' + *-graphia* 'writing.' —**or·thog·ra·pher** /-fər/ *n.* (in sense 1). —**or·tho·graph·ic** /ˌôrTHə'grafik/ *adj.* —**or·tho·graph·i·cal** /ˌôrTHə'grafikəl/ *adj.* —**or·tho·graph·i·cal·ly** /ˌôrTHə'grafik(ə)lē/ *adv.*

or·tho·ker·a·tol·o·gy /ˌôrTHōˌkerə'täləjē/ ▶*n.* the temporary reshaping of the cornea (usually overnight) with specially made rigid contact lenses, in order to correct myopia.

or·tho·mo·lec·u·lar /ˌôrTHōmə'lekyələr/ ▶*adj.* pertaining to a theory that illness can be treated and health maximized by creating the optimal molecular environment for the cells of the body through the introduction of natural substances: *orthomolecular nutrition/psychiatry/oncology.* ▷1968: coined by Linus Pauling.

or·tho·mor·phic /ˌôrTHō'môrfik/ ▶*adj.* see CONFORMAL.

Or·tho·nec·ti·da /ˌôrTHə'nektidə/ *Zoology* a minor phylum of mesozoan worms that are internal parasites of a range of marine invertebrates. ▷modern Latin (plural), from Greek *orthos* 'straight' + *nektos* 'swimming' (see NEKTON). —**or·tho·nec·tid** *n.* & *adj.*

or·tho·nor·mal /ˌôrTHə'nôrməl/ ▶*adj.* *Mathematics* both orthogonal and normalized. —**or·tho·nor·mal·i·ty** /-nôr'malitē/ *n.* —**or·tho·nor·mal·i·za·tion** /-ˌnôrməli'zāsHən/ *n.*

or·tho·pe·dics /ˌôrTHə'pēdiks/ (*Brit.* **or·tho·pae·dics**) ▶*plural n.* [treated as *sing.*] the branch of medicine dealing with the correction of deformities of bones or muscles. [originally relating specifically to children.] ▷mid 19th cent.: from French *orthopédie*, from Greek *orthos* 'right or straight' + *paideia* 'rearing of children.' —**or·tho·pe·dic** *adj.* —**or·tho·pe·di·cal·ly** /-ik(ə)lē/ *adv.* —**or·tho·pe·dist** /-dist/ *n.*

or·tho·phos·phor·ic ac·id /ˌôTHōfäs'fôrik; -'fär-/ ▶*n.* another term for PHOSPHORIC ACID. —**or·tho·phos·phate** /-'fäsfāt/ *n.*

or·tho·pox·vi·rus /'ôrTHōˌpäksˌvīrəs/ ▶*n.* any of a set of viruses pathological in humans and animals that includes the cowpox, smallpox, and monkeypox viruses. • Genus*Orthopoxvirus*, family Poxviridae.

or·tho·psy·chi·a·try /ˌôrTHōˌsī'kīətrē/ ▶*n.* the branch of psychiatry concerned with the study and prevention of mental or behavioral disorders, with emphasis on child development and family life.

—**or·tho·psy·chi·at·ric** /-ˌsīkēˈatrik/ *adj.* —**or·tho·psy·chi·a·trist** /-trist/ *n.*

or·thop·ter /ôrˈTHäptər/ ▸*n.* another term for ORNITHOPTER.

Or·thop·ter·a /ôrˈTHäptərə/ *Entomology* an order of insects that comprises the grasshoppers, crickets, katydids, etc. They have a saddle-shaped thorax, hind legs that are typically long and modified for jumping, and a characteristic song that the male produces by stridulation. ■ [as *plural n.*] (**orthoptera**) insects of this order. ▷modern Latin (plural), from ORTHO- 'straight' + Greek *pteros* 'wing.' —**or·thop·ter·an** *n.* & *adj.* —**or·thop·ter·ous** /-tərəs/ *adj.*

or·thop·ter·oid /ôrˈTHäptəˌroid/ ▸*adj. Entomology* of or relating to a group of insect orders that are related to the grasshoppers and crickets, including also the stoneflies, stick insects, earwigs, cockroaches, mantises, and termites.

or·thop·tics /ôrˈTHäptiks/ ▸*plural n.* [treated as *sing.*] the study or treatment of disorders of vision, esp. of eye movements or eye alignment. ▷late 19th cent.: from ORTHO- 'correct' + Greek *optikos* (see OPTIC). —**or·thop·tic** *adj.* —**or·thop·tist** /-tist/ *n.*

or·tho·py·rox·ene /ˌôrTHōpīˈräksēn/ ▸*n.* a mineral of the pyroxene group crystallizing in the orthorhombic system.

or·tho·rex·i·a /ˌôrTHəˈreksēə/ ▸*n.* an obsession with eating foods that one considers healthy. ■ (also **or·tho·rex·i·a ner·vo·sa** /nərˈvōsə/) a medical condition in which the sufferer systematically avoids specific foods in the belief that they are harmful. ▷1990s: from *ortho-* + Greek *orexia*, 'appetite,' after *anorexia*. —**or·tho·rex·ic** *adj.* & *n.*

or·tho·rhom·bic /ˌôrTHəˈrämbik/ ▸*adj.* of or denoting a crystal system or three-dimensional geometric arrangement having three unequal axes at right angles.

or·tho·sis /ôrˈTHōsis/ ▸*n.* (*pl.* **-ses** /-ˌsēz/) *Medicine* the correction of disorders of the limbs or spine by use of braces and other devices to correct alignment or provide support. ■ a brace or other such device; orthotic. ▷1950s: from Greek *orthōsis* 'making straight,' from *orthoun* 'set straight.'

or·tho·stat·ic /ˌôrTHəˈstatik/ ▸*adj. Medicine* relating to or caused by an upright posture.

or·thos·ti·chy /ôrˈTHästikē/ ▸*n.* (*pl.* **-chies**) *Botany* (in phyllotaxis) a vertical row of leaves arranged one directly above another. Contrasted with PARASTICHY. ▷late 19th cent.: from ORTHO- 'upright, straight' + Greek *stikhos* 'row, rank.'

or·thot·ic /ôrˈTHätik/ ▸*adj.* relating to orthotics.
▸*n.* an artificial support or brace for the limbs or spine.

or·thot·ics /ôrˈTHätiks/ ▸*plural n.* [treated as *sing.*] the branch of medicine that deals with the provision and use of artificial devices such as splints and braces. ■ a treatment prescribing such a device, esp. for the foot. —**or·thot·ist** *n.*

or·tho·trop·ic /ˌôrTHəˈtrōpik; -ˈträp-/ ▸*adj.* **1** *Botany* (of a shoot, stem, or axis) growing vertically. **2** *Engineering* (of a material) having elastic properties in two or three planes perpendicular to each other.

or·thot·ro·pous /ôrˈTHätrəpəs/ ▸*adj. Botany* (of a plant ovule) having the nucleus straight, i.e., not inverted, so that the micropyle is at the end opposite the base.

or·to·lan /ˈôrtl-ən/ (also **ortolan bunting**) ▸*n.* a small Eurasian songbird that was formerly eaten as a delicacy, the male having an olive-green head and yellow throat. • *Emberiza hortulana*, family Emberizidae (subfamily Emberizinae). ▷early 16th cent.: from French, from Provençal, literally 'gardener,' based on a diminutive of Latin *hortus* 'garden.'

O·ru·ro /ōˈrŏŏrō/ a city in western Bolivia; pop. 183,000. It is the center of an important mining region, with rich deposits of tin, zinc, silver, copper, and gold.

ORV ▸*abbr.* off-road vehicle.

Or·vie·to[1] /ôrˈvyetō/ a town in Umbria, in central Italy in the middle of a wine-producing area; pop. 22,000.

Or·vi·e·to[2] /ôrˈvyedō/ ▸*n.* a white wine made near Orvieto.

Or·well /ˈôrwel/, George (1903–50), British novelist and essayist, born in India; pseudonym of *Eric Arthur Blair*. His work is characterized by his concern about social injustice. His most well-known works are *Animal Farm* (1945) and *Nineteen Eighty-Four* (1949). —**Or·well·i·an** /ôrˈwelēən/ *adj.*

-ory[1] ▸*suffix* (forming nouns) denoting a place for a particular function: *dormitory* | *repository*. ▷from Latin *-oria, -orium*, sometimes via Anglo-Norman French *-orie*, Old French *-oire*.

-ory[2] ▸*suffix* forming adjectives (and occasionally nouns) relating to or involving a verbal action: *compulsory* | *directory* | *mandatory*. ▷from Latin *-orius*, sometimes via Anglo-Norman French *-ori(e)*.

o·ryx /ˈôriks/ ▸*n.* any of several species of antelopes native to arid regions of Africa and Asia, having dark markings on the face and long, pointed horns. • Genus *Oryx*, family Bovidae: several species, including the **Arabian oryx** (*O. leucoryx*). See also GEMSBOK, SCIMITAR ORYX. ▷late Middle English: via Latin from Greek *orux* 'stonemason's pickax' (because of its pointed horns).

or·zo /ˈôrzō/ ▸*n.* a variety of pasta shaped like grains of barley or rice. ▷Italian, literally 'barley.'

OS ▸*abbr.* ■ (in calculating dates) Old Style. ■ *Computing* operating system. ■ Ordinary Seaman. ■ (in the UK) Ordnance Survey. ■ (as a size of clothing) outsize. ■ out of stock.

Os ▸*symbol* the chemical element osmium.

os[1] /äs/ ▸*n.* (*pl.* **os·sa** /ˈäsə/) *Anatomy* a bone (used chiefly in Latin names of individual bones, e.g., *os trapezium*). ▷Latin.

os[2] ▸*n.* (*pl.* **o·ra** /ˈôrə/) *Anatomy* an opening or entrance to a passage, esp. one at either end of the cervix of the uterus. ▷mid 18th cent.: from Latin *os* 'mouth.'

o.s. ▸*abbr.* ■ (in prescriptions) the left eye. [Latin, *oculus sinister*.]

OSA ▸*abbr.* Order of St. Augustine (Augustinians).

O·sage /ˈōˌsāj/ ▸*n.* (*pl.* same or **O·sages**) **1** a member of an American Indian people formerly inhabiting the Osage River valley in Missouri. **2** the Siouan language of this people.
▸*adj.* of or relating to this people or their language. ▷via French, from Osage *wažaže*, the name of one of the three groups that compose this people.

O·sage or·ange ▸*n.* a small spiny North American deciduous tree that bears inedible green orangelike fruit. Its durable yellowish-orange wood was formerly used by American Indians for bows and other weapons. Also called BOWWOOD. • *Maclura pomifera*, family Moraceae.

O·sage Riv·er a river that flows for 360 miles (580 km) through Missouri to the Missouri River.

O·sa·ka /ōˈsäkə/ a port and commercial city in central Japan, on the island of Honshu; pop. 2,642,000.

OSB ▸*abbr.* Order of St. Benedict (Benedictines).

Os·borne /ˈäzˌbôrn; -bərn/, John (James) (1929–94), English playwright. His first play, *Look Back in Anger* (1956), ushered in a new era of kitchen-sink drama. Its hero Jimmy Porter personified contemporary disillusioned youth, the so-called "angry young man."

Os·can /ˈäskən/ ▸*n.* an extinct Italic language of southern Italy, related to Umbrian and surviving in inscriptions mainly of the 4th to 1st centuries BC.
▸*adj.* of or relating to this language. ▷late 16th cent.: from Latin *Oscus* 'Oscan' + -AN.

Os·car[1] /ˈäskər/ ▸*n. trademark* the nickname for one of the golden statuettes given as an Academy Award. [one of the several speculative stories of its origin claims that the statuette reminded Margaret Herrick, an executive director of the Academy of Motion Picture Arts and Sciences, of her uncle Oscar.] ■ (**the Oscars**) the annual presentation of the Academy Awards.

Os·car[2] ▸*n.* a code word representing the letter O, used in radio communication.

os·car /ˈäskər/ (also **oscar cichlid**) ▸*n.* a South American cichlid fish with velvety brown young and multicolored adults, popular in aquariums. • *Astronotus ocellatus*, family Cichlidae. Alternative name: **velvet cichlid**.

Os·ce·o·la /ˌäsēˈōlə; ˌōsē-/ (c.1804–38), leader of the Seminole Indians. Resisting all government efforts to remove his people from their homeland in Florida, he led them in the Seminole Wars 1835–42. He was captured while bearing a flag of truce.

os·cil·late /ˈäsəˌlāt/ ▸*v.* [*intrans.*] **1** move or swing back and forth at a regular speed: *a pendulum oscillates about its lowest point.* ■ [with *adverbial*] *figurative* waver between extremes of opinion, action, or quality: *he was* **oscillating between** *fear and bravery.* **2** *Physics* vary in magnitude or position in a regular manner around a central point. ■ (of a circuit or device) cause the electric current or voltage running through it to behave in this way. ▷early 18th cent.: from Latin *oscillat-* 'swung,' from the verb *oscillare*. —**os·cil·la·tion** /ˌäsəˈlāSHən/ *n.* —**os·cil·la·to·ry** /əˈsiləˌtôrē/ *adj.*

os·cil·la·tor /ˈäsəˌlātər/ ▸*n.* a device for generating oscillating electric currents or voltages by nonmechanical means.

oscillo- ▸*comb. form* relating to oscillation, esp. of electric current: *oscilloscope*.

os·cil·lo·gram /əˈsiləˌgram/ ▸*n.* a record produced by an oscillograph.

os·cil·lo·graph /əˈsiləˌgraf/ ▸*n.* a device for recording oscillations, esp. those of an electric current. —**os·cil·lo·graph·ic** /əˌsiləˈgrafik/ *adj.* —**os·cil·log·ra·phy** /ˌäsəˈlägrəfē/ *n.*

os·cil·lo·scope /əˈsiləˌskōp/ ▸*n.* a device for viewing oscillations, as of electrical voltage or current, by a display on the screen of a cathode-ray tube. —**os·cil·lo·scop·ic** /əˌsiləˈskäpik/ *adj.*

os·cine /ˈäsin; ˈäˌsīn/ *Ornithology* ▸*adj.* of, relating to, or denoting passerine birds of a large division that includes the songbirds. Compare with SUBOSCINE. • Suborder Oscines, order Passeriformes.
▸*n.* a bird of this division. ▷late 19th cent.: from Latin *oscen, oscin-* 'songbird' + -INE[1].

Os·co-Um·bri·an /ˈäskō ˈəmbrēən/ ▸*n.* **1** a group of ancient Italic languages including Oscan and Umbrian, spoken in Italy in the 1st millennium BC. **2** a member of any of the peoples who spoke a language of this group.
▸*adj.* of or relating to these peoples or their languages.

os·cu·la /ˈäskyələ/ ▸ plural form of OSCULUM.

os·cu·lar /ˈäskyələr/ ▸*adj.* **1** *humorous* of or relating to kissing. **2** *Zoology* of or relating to an osculum. ▷early 19th cent.: from Latin *osculum* 'mouth, kiss' (diminutive of *os* 'mouth') + -AR[1].

os·cu·late /ˈäskyəˌlāt/ ▸*v.* [*trans.*] **1** *Mathematics* (of a curve or surface) touch (another curve or surface) so as to have a common tangent at the point of contact: [as *adj.*] (**osculating**) *the plots have been drawn using osculating orbital elements.* **2** *formal* or *humorous* kiss. ▷mid 17th cent.: from Latin *osculat-* 'kissed,' from the verb *osculari*, from *osculum* 'little mouth or kiss.' —**os·cu·lant** /-lənt/ *adj.* —**os·cu·la·tion** /ˌäskyəˈlāSHən/ *n.* —**os·cu·la·to·ry** /-ləˌtôrē/ *adj.*

os·cu·lum /ˈäskyələm/ ▸*n.* (*pl.* **-la** /-lə/) *Zoology* a large aperture in a sponge through which water is expelled. ▷early 17th cent.: from Latin, 'little mouth.'

-ose[1] ▸*suffix* (forming adjectives) having a specified quality: *bellicose* | *comatose* | *verbose*. ▷from Latin *-osus*.

-ose[2] ▸*suffix Chemistry* forming names of sugars and other carbohydrates: *cellulose* | *glucose*. ▷on the pattern of *(gluc)ose*.

-osely ▸*suffix* forming adverbs corresponding to adjectives ending in *-ose* (such as *bellicosely* corresponding to *bellicose*). ▷see -OSE, -LY.

-oseness ▸*suffix* forming nouns corresponding to adjectives ending in *-ose* (such as *bellicoseness* corresponding to *bellicose*). Compare with -OSITY. ▷see -OSE, -NESS.

OSF ▸*abbr.* Order of St. Francis (Franciscans).

Osh /ôSH/ a city in western Kyrgyzstan, near the border with Uzbekistan; pop. 236,000. It was, until the 15th century, an important post on an ancient trade route to China and India.

OSHA /ˈōSHə/ ▸*abbr.* (in the U.S.) Occupational Safety and Health Administration.

Osh·a·wa /ˈäSHəwə/ a city in Ontario, Canada, on the northern shores of Lake Ontario, east of Toronto; pop. 174,010.

o·shi /ˈōSHē/ ▸*n.* [*pl.* same] (in sumo wrestling) a move in which an opponent is pushed backward or down. ▷Japanese.

Osh·kosh /ˈäSHkäSH/ an industrial city in east central Wisconsin, on Lake Winnebago; pop. 62,916.

o·sier /ˈōZHər/ ▸*n.* **1** a small Eurasian willow that grows mostly in wet habitats and is a major source of the long flexible shoots (withies) used in basketwork. • *Salix viminalis*, family Salicaceae. ■ a shoot of a willow. ■ *dated* any willow tree. **2** *n.* any of several North American dogwoods. ▷late Middle English: from Old French; compare with medieval Latin *auseria* 'osier bed.'

O·si·jek /ˈōsēˌyek/ a city in eastern Croatia, on the Drava River; pop. 105,000.

O·si·ris /ōˈsīris/ *Egyptian Mythology* a god originally connected with fertility, husband of Isis and father of Horus. He is known chiefly through the story of his death at the hands of his brother Seth and his subsequent restoration to a new life as ruler of the afterlife. —**O·si·ri·an** /-rēən/ *adj.*

-osis ▸*suffix* (*pl.* **-oses**) denoting a process or

condition: *metamorphosis.* ■ denoting a pathological state: *neurosis* | *thrombosis.* ▷via Latin from Greek *-ōsis*, verbal noun ending.

-osity ▶*suffix* forming nouns from adjectives ending in *-ose* (such as *verbosity* from *verbose*) and from adjectives ending in *-ous* (such as *pomposity* from *pompous*). ▷from French *-osité* or Latin *-ositas*.

Os·lo /ˈäz,lō; ˈäs-/ the capital and chief port of Norway, on the southern coast at the head of Oslofjord; pop. 458,000. Founded in the 11th century, it was known as Christiania (or Kristiania) from 1624 until 1924 in honor of Christian IV of Norway and Denmark (1577–1648).

Os·man I /ˈäzmən; ˈäs-; äsˈmän/ (also **Oth·man** /ˈäTH-/) (1259–1326), Turkish conqueror. He founded the Ottoman (Osmanli) dynasty and empire and assumed the title of emir in 1299.

Os·man·li /äzˈmänlē; äs-/ ▶*adj.* & *n.* (*pl.* same or **-lis**) old-fashioned term for **OTTOMAN**. ▷Turkish, from the name *Osman*, from Arabic *ʿuṯmān* (see **OTTOMAN**), + the adjectival suffix *-li*.

os·mic /ˈäzmik/ ▶*adj.* relating to odors or the sense of smell. ▷mid 20th cent.: from Greek *osmē* 'smell, odor' + **-IC**. **—os·mi·cal·ly** /-ik(ə)lē/ *adv.*

os·mic ac·id ▶*n. Chemistry* a solution of osmium tetroxide. ▷mid 19th cent.: *osmic* from **OSMIUM** + **-IC**.

os·mi·um /ˈäzmēəm/ ▶*n.* the chemical element of atomic number 76, a hard, dense, silvery-white metal of the transition series. (Symbol: **Os**) ▷early 19th cent.: modern Latin, from Greek *osmē* 'smell' (from the pungent smell of its tetroxide).

os·mi·um te·trox·ide ▶*n.* a poisonous pale yellow solid with a distinctive pungent smell, used in solution as a biological stain (esp. for lipids) and fixative. • Chem. formula: OsO_4.

osmo- ▶*comb. form* representing **OSMOSIS**.

os·mo·lal·i·ty /,äzməˈlalitē/ ▶*n. Chemistry* the concentration of a solution expressed as the total number of solute particles per kilogram. ▷1950s: blend of *osmotic* (see **OSMOSIS**) and **MOLAL**, + **-ITY**.

os·mo·lar·i·ty /,äzməˈlaritē/ ▶*n. Chemistry* the concentration of a solution expressed as the total number of solute particles per liter. ▷1950s: blend of *osmotic* (see **OSMOSIS**) and **MOLAR**[3], + **-ITY**.

os·mom·e·ter /äzˈmämitər/ ▶*n.* an instrument for demonstrating or measuring osmotic pressure. **—os·mo·met·ric** /-məˈmetrik/ *adj.* **—os·mom·e·try** /-trē/ *n.*

os·mo·reg·u·la·tion /,äzmō,regyəˈlāSHən/ ▶*n. Biology* the maintenance of constant osmotic pressure in the fluids of an organism by the control of water and salt concentrations. **—os·mo·reg·u·la·to·ry** /-ˈregyələ,tôrē/ *adj.*

os·mose /ˈäzmōs; ˈäs-/ ▶*v.* [*intrans.*] *rare* pass by or as if by osmosis. ▷mid 19th cent. (as a noun in the sense 'osmosis'): from the element common to *endosmose* and *exosmose*.

os·mo·sis /äzˈmōsis; äs-/ ▶*n. Biology* & *Chemistry* a process by which molecules of a solvent tend to pass through a semipermeable membrane from a less concentrated solution into a more concentrated one, thus equalizing the concentrations on each side of the membrane. ■ *figurative* the process of gradual or unconscious assimilation of ideas, knowledge, etc.: *what she knows of the blue-blood set she learned not through birthright, not even through wealth, but through osmosis.* ▷mid 19th cent.: Latinized form of earlier *osmose*, from Greek *ōsmos* 'a push.' **—os·mot·ic** /-mätik/ *adj.* **—os·mot·i·cal·ly** /-ˈmädik(ə)lē/ *adv.*

os·mot·ic pres·sure /äzˈmätik/ ▶*n. Chemistry* the pressure that would have to be applied to a pure solvent to prevent it from passing into a given solution by osmosis, often used to express the concentration of the solution.

os·mun·da /äzˈməndə/ ▶*n.* a plant of a genus that includes the royal and cinnamon ferns. • Genus *Osmunda*, family Osmundaceae. ▷Anglo-Latin, from Anglo-Norman French *osmunde*, of unknown origin.

Os·na·brück /ˈäsnə,brŏŏk; ˈôsnä,brʏk/ a city in northwestern Germany, in Lower Saxony; pop. 165,000. In 1648, the Treaty of Westphalia, which ended the Thirty Years War, was signed here and in Münster.

os·na·burg /ˈäznə,bərg/ ▶*n.* a kind of coarse, heavy linen or cotton used for such items as furnishings and sacks. ▷late Middle English: alteration of **OSNABRÜCK**, where the cloth was originally produced.

os pe·nis /äs ˈpēnis/ ▶*n. Zoology* a bone in the penis of carnivores and some other mammals. Also called **BACULUM**.

os·prey /ˈäsprā; -prē/ ▶*n.* (*pl.* **-preys**) a large fish-eating bird of prey with long narrow wings and a white underside and crown, found throughout the world. Also called **FISH HAWK**. • *Pandion haliaetus*, the only member of the family Pandionidae. ▷late Middle English: from Old French *ospres*, apparently based on Latin *ossifraga* (mentioned by Pliny and identified with the lammergeier), from *os* 'bone' + *frangere* 'to break,' probably because of the lammergeier's habit of dropping bones from a height to break them and reach the marrow.

OSS ▶*abbr.* Office of Strategic Services, a U.S. intelligence organization during World War II.

Os·sa, Mount /ˈäsə/ **1** a mountain in Thessaly, in northeastern Greece, south of Mount Olympus, that rises to a height of 6,489 feet (1,978 m). In Greek mythology the giants were said to have piled Mount Olympus and Mount Ossa onto Mount Pelion in an attempt to reach heaven so that they could destroy the gods. **2** the highest mountain on the island of Tasmania. It rises to a height of 5,305 feet (1,617 m).

os·sa /ˈäsə/ ▶ plural form of **OS**[1].

os·se·in /ˈäsē-in/ ▶*n. Biochemistry* the collagen of bones, used for glues and gelatin, derived by dissolving the mineral content in an acid solution. ▷mid 19th cent.: from Latin *osseus* 'bony' + **IN**.

os·se·ous /ˈäsēəs/ ▶*adj. chiefly Zoology Medicine* consisting of or turned into bone; ossified. ▷late Middle English: from Latin *osseus* 'bony' + **-OUS**.

Os·sete /ˈäsēt/ ▶*n.* (also **Os·set**) **1** a native or inhabitant of Ossetia. **2** another term for **OSSETIAN** (the language).
▶*adj.* of or relating to Ossetia or the Ossetes. ▷from Russian *osetin*, from Georgian.

Os·se·tia /ôˈsēSHə; əˈsyetēə/ a region of the central Caucasus. It is divided by the boundary between Russia and Georgia into two parts: North Ossetia and South Ossetia. It was the scene of ethnic conflict 1989–92.

Os·se·tian /äˈsēSHən/ ▶*n.* **1** the Iranian language of the Ossetes. **2** a native or inhabitant of Ossetia.
▶*adj.* of or relating to the Ossetes or their language. **—Os·set·ic** /äˈsetik/ *adj.* & *n.*

Os·si /ˈäsē; ˈôsē/ ▶*n.* (*pl.* **Os·sies** or **Os·sis**) *informal, often derogatory* (in Germany) a citizen of the former German Democratic Republic. Compare with **WESSI**. ▷German, probably an abbreviation of *Ostdeutsche* 'East German.'

Os·sian /ˈäsēən/ a legendary Irish warrior and bard, whose name became well known in 1760–63 when the Scottish poet James Macpherson (1736–96) published his own verse as an alleged translation of 3rd-century Gaelic tales. Irish name **OISIN**. **—Os·si·an·ic** *adj.*

os·si·cle /ˈäsikəl/ ▶*n. Anatomy* & *Zoology* a very small bone, esp. one of those in the middle ear. ■ *Zoology* a small piece of calcified material forming part of the skeleton of an invertebrate animal such as an echinoderm. ▷late 16th cent.: from Latin *ossiculum*, diminutive of *os* 'bone.'

os·sif·er·ous /äˈsifərəs/ ▶*adj. Geology* (of a cave or stratum) containing or yielding deposits of bone, esp. fossil bone. ▷early 19th cent.: from Latin *os, oss-* 'bone' + **-FEROUS**.

os·si·fy /ˈäsə,fī/ ▶*v.* (**-fies**, **-fied**) [*intrans.*] turn into bone or bony tissue: *these tracheal cartilages may ossify.* ■ [often as *adj.*] (**ossified**) *figurative* cease developing; be stagnant or rigid: *ossified political institutions.* ▷early 18th cent.: from French *ossifier*, from Latin *os, oss-* 'bone.' **—os·si·fi·ca·tion** /,äsəfiˈkāSHən/ *n.*

Os·si·ning /ˈäsəniNG/ a town in southeastern New York, on the Hudson River, noted as the home of Sing Sing prison; pop. 34,124.

os·so buc·co /ˈäsō ˈbŏŏkō/ ▶*n.* (also **os·so bu·co**, **os·so·bu·co**) an Italian dish made with veal shank containing marrowbone, stewed in wine with vegetables and seasonings. ▷Italian, literally 'marrowbone.'

os·su·ar·y /ˈäSHōō,erē; ˈäs(y)ōō-/ ▶*n.* (*pl.* **-ar·ies**) a container or room into which the bones of dead people are placed. ▷mid 17th cent.: from late Latin *ossuarium*, formed irregularly from Latin *os, oss-* 'bone.'

OST ▶*abbr.* original soundtrack.

Os·te·ich·thy·es /,ästēˈikTHē-ēz/ *Zoology* a class of fishes that includes those with a bony skeleton. Compare with **CHONDRICHTHYES**. ▷modern Latin (plural), from Greek *osteon* 'bone' + *ikhthus* 'fish.'

os·te·i·tis /,ästēˈītis/ ▶*n. Medicine* inflammation of the substance of a bone. ■ (**osteitis fibrosa cystica**) another term for **VON RECKLINGHAUSEN'S DISEASE** (sense 2). ■ (**osteitis deformans**) another term for **PAGET'S DISEASE** (sense 1). ▷mid 19th cent.: from Greek *osteon* 'bone' + **-ITIS**.

Ost·end /äˈstend; ˈästend/ a port on the North Sea coast of northwestern Belgium, in West Flanders; pop. 68,000. Flemish name **OOSTENDE**; French name **OSTENDE**.

os·ten·si·ble /äˈstensəbəl; əˈsten-/ ▶*adj.* [*attrib.*] stated or appearing to be true, but not necessarily so: *the delay may have a deeper cause than the ostensible reason.* ▷mid 18th cent.: from French, from medieval Latin *ostensibilis* from Latin *ostens-* 'stretched out to view,' from the verb *ostendere*, from *ob-* 'in view of' + *tendere* 'to stretch.' **—os·ten·si·bil·i·ty** /-,stensəˈbilitē/ *n.*

THE RIGHT WORD **apparent, illusory, ostensible, seeming**

The **apparent** reason for something is not necessarily the real reason. In this sense, the word applies to what appears only on the surface, not to what is borne out by scientific investigation or an examination of the relevant facts and circumstances (*the apparent cause was only an illusion*).

The **ostensible** reason for something is the reason that is expressed, declared, or avowed; but it implies that the truth is being concealed (*the ostensible purpose of the meeting was to give the two men a chance to get acquainted*).

Seeming usually refers to the character of the thing observed rather than to a defect in the observation; it implies even more doubt than either *apparent* or *ostensible* (*her seeming innocence fooled no one*).

That which is **illusory** is always deceptive; it has a character or appearance that doesn't really exist (*an illusory beauty that faded quickly in the bright light*).

os·ten·si·bly /äˈstensiblē; əˈsten-/ ▶*adv.* [*sentence adverb*] apparently or purportedly, but perhaps not actually: *portrayed as a blue-collar type, ostensibly a carpenter.*

os·ten·sive /äˈstensiv/ ▶*adj.* directly or clearly demonstrative. ■ ostensible. ■ *Linguistics* denoting a way of defining by direct demonstration, e.g., by pointing. ▷mid 16th cent.: from late Latin *ostensivus*, from *ostens-* 'stretched out to view' (see **OSTENSIBLE**). **—os·ten·sive·ly** *adv.* **—os·ten·sive·ness** *n.*

os·ten·ta·tion /,ästənˈtāSHən/ ▶*n.* pretentious and vulgar display, esp. of wealth and luxury, intended to impress or attract notice: *the office was spacious, but without any trace of ostentation.* ▷late Middle English: via Old French from Latin *ostentatio(n-)*, from the verb *ostentare*, frequentative of *ostendere* 'stretch out to view.'

os·ten·ta·tious /,ästənˈtāSHəs/ ▶*adj.* characterized by vulgar or pretentious display; designed to impress or attract notice: *books that people buy and display ostentatiously but never actually finish.* **—os·ten·ta·tious·ly** *adv.* **—os·ten·ta·tious·ness** *n.*

osteo- ▶*comb. form* of or relating to the bones: *osteoporosis.* ▷from Greek *osteon* 'bone.'

os·te·o·ar·thri·tis /,ästēōärˈTHrītis/ ▶*n. Medicine* degeneration of joint cartilage and the underlying bone, most common from middle age onward. It causes pain and stiffness, esp. in the hip, knee, and thumb joints. Compare with **RHEUMATOID ARTHRITIS**. **—os·te·o·ar·thrit·ic** /-ˈTHritik/ *adj.*

os·te·o·blast /ˈästēə,blast/ ▶*n. Physiology* a cell that secretes the matrix for bone formation. **—os·te·o·blas·tic** /,ästēəˈblastik/ *adj.*

os·te·o·clast /ˈästēə,klast/ ▶*n. Physiology* a large multinucleate bone cell that absorbs bone tissue during growth and healing. ▷late 19th cent.: from **OSTEO-** 'bone' + Greek *klastēs* 'breaker.' **—os·te·o·clas·tic** /,ästēəˈklastik/ *adj.*

os·te·o·cyte /ˈästēə,sīt/ ▶*n. Physiology* a bone cell, formed when an osteoblast becomes embedded in the matrix it has secreted. **—os·te·o·cyt·ic** /,ästēəˈsitik/ *adj.*

os·te·o·gen·e·sis /,ästēōˈjenəsis/ ▶*n.* the formation of bone. **—os·te·o·ge·net·ic** /-jəˈnetik/ *adj.* **—os·te·o·gen·ic** /ˈjenik/ *adj.*

os·te·o·gen·e·sis im·per·fec·ta /,impərˈfektə/ ▶*n. Medicine* an inherited disorder characterized by extreme fragility of the bones. ▷modern Latin, from **OSTEOGENESIS** + Latin *imperfecta* 'imperfect' (feminine of *imperfectus*).

os·te·oid /ˈästē,oid/ ▶*adj. Physiology* & *Medicine* resembling bone in appearance or structure.
▶*n. Physiology* & *Medicine* the unmineralized organic component of bone.

os·te·ol·o·gy /,ästēˈäləjē/ ▶*n.* the study of the structure and function of the skeleton and bony structures. **—os·te·o·log·i·cal** /,ästēəˈläjikəl/ *adj.* **—os·te·o·log·i·cal·ly** /,ästēəˈläjik(ə)lē/ *adv.* **—os·te·ol·o·gist** /-jist/ *n.*

os·te·ol·y·sis /,ästēˈäləsis/ ▶*n. Medicine* the

pathological destruction or disappearance of bone tissue. **—os·te·o·lyt·ic** /-ə'litik/ *adj.*

os·te·o·ma·la·cia /ˌästē-ōmə'lāsH(ē)ə/ ▶*n.* softening of the bones, typically through a deficiency of vitamin D or calcium. ▷early 19th cent.: modern Latin, from OSTEO- 'bone' + Greek *malakos* 'soft.' **—os·te·o·ma·lac·ic** /-'lasik/ *adj.*

os·te·o·my·e·li·tis /ˌästēōˌmīə'lītis/ ▶*n. Medicine* inflammation of bone or bone marrow, usually due to infection.

os·te·o·ne·cro·sis /ˌästēōni'krōsis/ ▶*n. Medicine* the death of bone tissue. **—os·te·o·ne·crot·ic** /-'krätik/ *adj.*

os·te·op·a·thy /ˌästē'äpəTHē/ ▶*n.* a branch of medical practice that emphasizes the treatment of medical disorders through the manipulation and massage of the bones, joints, and muscles. **—os·te·o·path** /'ästēəˌpaTH/ *n.* **—os·te·o·path·ic** /ˌästēə'paTHik/ *adj.* **—os·te·o·path·i·cal·ly** /ˌästēə'paTHik(ə)lē/ *adv.*

os·te·o·pe·ni·a /ˌästēō'pēnēə/ ▶*n.* reduced bone mass of lesser severity than osteoporosis.

os·te·o·phyte /'ästēəˌfīt/ ▶*n. Medicine* a bony outgrowth associated with the degeneration of cartilage at joints. **—os·te·o·phyt·ic** /ˌästēə'fitik/ *adj.*

os·te·o·po·ro·sis /ˌästēōpə'rōsis/ ▶*n.* a medical condition in which the bones become brittle and fragile from loss of tissue, typically as a result of hormonal changes, or deficiency of calcium or vitamin D. ▷mid 19th cent.: from OSTEO- 'bone' + Greek *poros* 'passage, pore' + -OSIS. **—os·te·o·po·rot·ic** /-'rätik/ *adj.*

os·te·o·sar·co·ma /ˌästēōsär'kōmə/ ▶*n.* (*pl.* **-mas** or **-ma·ta** /-mətə/) *Medicine* a malignant tumor of bone in which there is a proliferation of osteoblasts.

os·te·o·sper·mum /ˌästēō'spərməm/ ▶*n.* (*pl.* **-ma** /-mə/) a plant or shrub of the daisy family, native to Africa and the Middle East, some varieties of which are cultivated for their yellow or violet flowers. • Genus *Osteospermum*, family *Compositae*. ▷mid 19th cent.: modern Latin, from Greek, *osteo-*,'bone' + Greek, *sperma*, 'seed.'

os·te·o·tome /'ästēəˌtōm/ ▶*n.* a surgical instrument for cutting bone, typically resembling a chisel.

os·te·ot·o·my /ˌästē'ätəmē/ ▶*n.* (*pl.* **-mies**) the surgical cutting of a bone or removal of a piece of bone.

Os·tia /'ästēə/ an ancient city and harbor that was situated on the western coast of Italy at the mouth of the Tiber River. It was the first colony founded by ancient Rome and was a major port and commercial center.

os·ti·na·to /ˌästi'nätō/ ▶*n.* (*pl.* **-tos** or **-ti** /-tē/) a continually repeated musical phrase or rhythm. ▷Italian, literally 'obstinate.'

os·ti·ole /'ästēˌōl/ ▶*n. Botany* (in some small algae and fungi) a small pore through which spores are discharged. ▷mid 19th cent.: from Latin *ostiolum*, diminutive of *ostium* 'opening.' **—os·ti·o·lar** /-ələr/ *adj.*

os·ti·um /'ästēəm/ ▶*n.* (*pl.* **-ti·a** /-tēə/) *Anatomy & Zoology* an opening into a vessel or cavity of the body. ■ *Zoology* each of a number of pores in the wall of a sponge, through which water is drawn in. ▷early 17th cent.: from Latin, 'door, opening.'

ost·ler /'äslər/ ▶*n.* variant spelling of HOSTLER.

Ost·mark /'ästˌmärk/ ▶*n. historical* the basic monetary unit of the former German Democratic Republic, equal to 100 pfennigs. ▷German, literally 'east mark' (see MARK[2]).

Ost·po·li·tik /'ôstˌpäli'tēk/ ▶*n. historical* the foreign policy of détente of western European countries with reference to the former communist bloc, esp. the opening of relations with the Eastern bloc by the Federal Republic of Germany (West Germany) in the 1960s. ▷German, from *Ost* 'east' + *Politik* 'politics.'

os·tra·cize /'ästrəˌsīz/ ▶*v.* [*trans.*] exclude (someone) from a society or group: *a group of people who have been ridiculed, ostracized, and persecuted for centuries.* ■ (in ancient Greece) banish (an unpopular or too powerful citizen) from a city for five or ten years by popular vote. ▷mid 17th cent.: from Greek *ostrakizein*, from *ostrakon* 'shell or potsherd' (on which names were written, in voting to banish unpopular citizens). **—os·tra·cism** /-ˌsizəm/ *n.*

Os·tra·co·da /ˌästrə'kōdə/ *Zoology* a class of minute aquatic crustaceans that have a hinged shell from which the antennae protrude, and a reduced number of appendages. ▷modern Latin (plural), from Greek *ostrakōdēs* 'testaceous,' from *ostrakon* 'shell.' **—os·tra·cod** /'ästrəˌkäd/ *n.*

os·tra·co·derm /'ästrəkōˌdərm/ ▶*n.* an extinct jawless fish of the Cambrian to Devonian periods, having a heavily armored body. • Class Agnatha: several orders. ▷late 19th cent.: from modern Latin *Ostracodermi* (former taxonomic name), from Greek *ostrakon* 'shell' + *derma* 'skin.'

os·tra·con /'ästrəˌkän/ (also **os·tra·kon**) ▶*n.* (*pl.* **-ca** /-kə/ or **-ka**) a potsherd used as a writing surface. ▷Greek, 'hard shell or potsherd.'

Os·tra·va /'ästrəvə; 'ôsträvä/ an industrial city in northeastern Czech Republic, in the Moravian lowlands; pop. 328,000. It is located in the coal-mining region of Silesia.

os·trich /'ästricH/ ▶*n.* **1** a flightless swift-running African bird with a long neck, long legs, and two toes on each foot. It is the largest living bird, with males reaching an average height of 8 feet (2.5 m). • *Struthio camelus*, the only member of the family Struthionidae. **2** a person who refuses to face reality or accept facts. [from the popular belief that ostriches bury their heads in the sand if pursued.] ▷Middle English: from Old French *ostriche*, from Latin *avis* 'bird' + late Latin *struthio* (from Greek *strouthiōn* 'ostrich,' from *strouthos* 'sparrow or ostrich').

ostrich

os·trich di·no·saur ▶*n.* a lightly built toothless bipedal dinosaur of the late Cretaceous period, adapted for running and somewhat resembling an ostrich. Also called ORNITHOMIMOSAUR. • Infraorder Ornithomimisauria, suborder Theropoda, order Saurischia: several genera, including *Gallimimus*, *Ornithomimus*, and *Struthiomimus*.

Os·tro·goth /'ästrəˌgäTH/ ▶*n.* a member of the eastern branch of the Goths, who conquered Italy in the 5th–6th centuries AD. ▷from late Latin *Ostrogothi* (plural), from the Germanic base of EAST + late Latin *Gothi* 'Goths.' **—Os·tro·goth·ic** /ˌästrə'gäTHik/ *adj.*

Ost·wald /'äs(t)ˌwôld; 'ôstvält/, Friedrich Wilhelm (1853–1932), German physical chemist. He established physical chemistry as a separate discipline.

OSU ▶*abbr.* Order of St. Ursula.

O'Sul·li·van /ō'sələvən/, Maureen (1911–98), U.S. actress; born in Ireland; mother of Mia Farrow. She starred as Jane to Johnny Weissmuller's Tarzan in such movies as *Tarzan the Ape Man* (1932), *Tarzan and His Mate* (1934), and *Tarzan's Secret Treasure* (1941). She also starred in *The Big Clock* (1948) and appeared in *Peggy Sue Got Married* (1986) and *Hannah and Her Sisters* (1986).

Os·wald /'äzˌwôld/, Lee Harvey (1939–63), U.S. alleged assassin of President John F. Kennedy. In November 1963, he was charged with the murder of the president. He denied the charge but was murdered by Jack Ruby, a Dallas nightclub owner, before he could be brought to trial.

Os·wald of York, St. (died 992), English prelate and Benedictine monk. As archbishop of York, he founded several monasteries. Feast day, February 28.

Os·we·go /äs'wēgō/ an industrial port city in north central New York, on Lake Ontario and the Oswego River; pop. 19,195.

Os·we·go tea /äs'wēgō/ ▶*n.* see BERGAMOT (sense 3). ▷mid 18th cent.: named after a river and town in the northern part of the state of New York.

OT ▶*abbr.* ■ occupational therapist. ■ occupational therapy. ■ Old Testament. ■ overnight telegram. ■ overtime.

-ot[1] ▶*suffix* forming nouns that were originally diminutives: *ballot* | *parrot.* ▷from French.

-ot[2] ▶*suffix* (forming nouns) denoting a person of a particular type: *harlot* | *idiot.* ■ denoting a native of a place: *Cypriot.* ▷via French and Latin from Greek *-ōtēs*.

o·ta·ku /ō'täkōō/ ▶*plural n.* (in Japan) young people who are highly skilled in or obsessed with computer technology to the detriment of their social skills. ▷Japanese, literally 'your house,' alluding to the reluctance of such young people to leave the house.

o·tal·gi·a /ō'talj(ē)ə/ ▶*n. Medicine* earache. ▷mid 17th cent.: from Greek *ōtalgia*, from *ous*, *ōt-* 'ear' + *algos* 'pain.'

OTB ▶*abbr.* off-track betting.

OTC ▶*abbr.* ■ over the counter. ■ (in the UK) Officers' Training Corps.

oth·er /'əT͟Hər/ ▶*adj. & pron.* **1** used to refer to a person or thing that is different or distinct from one already mentioned or known about: [as *adj.*] *stick the camera on a tripod or* **some other** *means of support other people found her difficult* | [as *pron.*] *a language unrelated to any other.* ■ the alternative of two: [as *adj.*] *the other side of the page* | [as *pron.*] *flinging up first one arm and then the other* | **one or the other** *of them is bound to be a liar.* ■ those remaining in a group; those not already mentioned: [as *adj.*] *they took the other three away in an ambulance* | [as *pron.*] *Fred set off and* **the others** *followed.* **2** further; additional: [as *adj.*] *one other word of advice* | [as *pron.*] *reporting three stories and rewriting three others.* **3** (**the Other**) [*pron.*] *Philosophy & Sociology* that which is distinct from, different from, or opposite to something or oneself. ▷Old English *ōther*, of Germanic origin; related to Dutch and German *ander*, from an Indo-European root meaning 'different.'

▶*PHRASES* □ **no other** *archaic* nothing else: *we can do no other.* □ **other than** [with *negative* or in *questions*] apart from; except: *he claims not to own anything other than his home.* ■ differently or different from; otherwise than: *there is no suggestion that we are to take this other than literally.* □ **on the other hand** see HAND. □ **the other day** (or **night**, **week**, etc.) a few days (or nights, weeks, etc.) ago. □ **someone** (or **something** or **somehow**, etc.) **or other** some unspecified or unknown person, thing, manner, etc. (used to express vagueness or uncertainty): *they were protesting about something or other.*

oth·er-di·rect·ed ▶*adj. Psychology* (of a person or their behavior) governed by external circumstances and trends.

oth·er half ▶*n.* (**one's other half**) *informal* a person's wife, husband, or partner: *treat your other half to a romantic outing for two.*

▶*PHRASE* □ **how the other half lives** used to allude to the way of life of a different group in society, esp. a wealthier one.

oth·er·ness /'əT͟Hərnis/ ▶*n.* the quality or fact of being different: *the developed world has been celebrating African music while altogether denying its otherness.*

oth·er·where /'əT͟Hərˌ(h)we(ə)r/ ▶*adv. & pron. archaic* or *poetic/literary* elsewhere.

oth·er·wise /'əT͟HərˌwĪz/ ▶*adv.* **1** in circumstances different from those present or considered: *the collection brings visitors who might not come to the college otherwise.* ■ [as *conjunctive adv.*] or else: *I'm not motivated by money, otherwise I would have quit.* **2** in other respects; apart from that: *an otherwise totally black cat with a single white whisker.* **3** in a different way: *he means mischief—it's no good pretending otherwise* | *pretending that they are* **otherwise engaged.** ■ as an alternative: *pre-Renaissance mathematician Leonardo Pisano,* **otherwise known as** *Fibonacci.*

▶*adj.* [*predic.*] in a different state or situation: *if it were otherwise, we would be unable to acquire knowledge.* ▷Old English *on ōthre wīsan* (see OTHER, WISE[2]).

▶*PHRASE* □ **or** (or **and**) **otherwise** indicating the opposite of or a contrast to something stated: *we don't want a president, elected or otherwise.*

oth·er wom·an ▶*n.* (**the other woman**) the lover of a married or similarly attached man.

oth·er world ▶*n.* (**the other world**) the spiritual world or afterlife.

oth·er·world·ly /ˌəT͟Hər'wərldlē/ ▶*adj.* of or relating to an imaginary or spiritual world: *music of an almost otherworldly beauty.* ■ unworldly: *celibate clerics with a very otherworldly outlook.* **—oth·er·world·li·ness** *n.*

Oth·man /'äTHmən; äTH'män/ variant form of OSMAN I.

O·tho /'ōTHō/, Marcus Salvius (AD 32–69), Roman emperor from January until April of 69. Proclaimed emperor after the death of Galba, he was defeated by Vitellius and his German legions and committed suicide.

o·tic /'ōtik; 'ätik/ ▶*adj. Anatomy* of or relating to the ear. ▷mid 17th cent.: from Greek *ōtikos*, from *ous*, *ōt-* 'ear.'

-otic ▶*suffix* forming adjectives and nouns corresponding to nouns ending in *-osis* (such as *neurotic* corresponding to *neurosis*). ▷from French *-otique*, via Latin from the Greek adjectival ending *-ōtikos*.

-otically ▶*suffix* forming adverbs corresponding to adjectives ending in *-otic* (such as *neurotically* corresponding to *neurotic*). ▷see -OTIC, -LY.

o·ti·ose /'ōsHēˌōs; 'ōtēˌōs/ ▶*adj.* serving no practical purpose or result: *he did fuss, uttering otiose explanations.* ■ *archaic* indolent; idle. ▷late 18th cent.: from Latin *otiosus*, from *otium* 'leisure.' **—o·ti·ose·ly** *adv.*

Pronunciation Key ə *ago*; ər *over*; 'ə or ˌə *up*; 'ər or ˌər *fur*; a *hat*; ā *rate*; ä *car*; CH *chew*; e *let*; ē *see*; e(ə)r *air*; i *fit*; ī *by*; i(ə)r *ear*; NG *sing*; ō *go*; ô *for*; oi *boy*; ōō *good*; ōō *goo*; ou *out*; SH *she*; TH *thin*; T͟H *then*; (h)w *why*; ZH *vision*

O·tis[1] /ˈōtis/, Elisha Graves (1811–61), U.S. inventor and manufacturer. In 1852, he produced the first efficient elevator with a safety device. Five years later he installed the first public elevator for passengers in a New York department store.

O·tis[2], James (1725–83), American statesman. He led the majority in the Massachusetts legislature 1766–69 and opposed various revenue acts imposed by the British.

o·ti·tis /ōˈtītis/ ▸*n. Medicine* inflammation of the ear, usually distinguished as **otitis externa** (of the passage of the outer ear), **otitis media** (of the middle ear), and **otitis interna** (of the inner ear; labyrinthitis). ▷late 18th cent.: modern Latin, from Greek *ous, ōt-* 'ear' + **-ITIS**.

oto- ▸*comb. form* (used chiefly in medical terms) of or relating to the ears: *otoscope.* ▷from Greek *ous, ōt-* 'ear.'

o·to·cyst /ˈōtəˌsist/ ▸*n.* another term for **STATOCYST**.

o·to·lar·yn·gol·o·gy /ˈōtōˌlarəNGˈgäləjē/ ▸*n.* the study of diseases of the ear and throat. —**o·to·la·ryn·go·log·i·cal** /-rəNGgəˈläjikəl/ *adj.* —**o·to·lar·yn·gol·o·gist** /-jist/ *n.*

o·to·lith /ˈōtlˌiTH/ ▸*n. Zoology* each of three small oval calcareous bodies in the inner ear of vertebrates, involved in sensing gravity and movement. —**o·to·lith·ic** /ˌōtlˈiTHik/ *adj.*

o·tol·o·gy /ōˈtäləjē/ ▸*n.* the study of the anatomy and diseases of the ear. —**o·to·log·i·cal** /ˌōtəˈläjəkəl/ *adj.* —**o·tol·o·gist** /-jist/ *n.*

O·to·man·gue·an /ˌōtōˈmäNGgēən; -ˈmaNG-/ ▸*adj.* of, relating to, or denoting a family of American Indian languages of central and southern Mexico, including Mixtec and Zapotec. ▷1940s: from **OTOMI** + *Mangue* (an extinct language of Costa Rica) + **-AN**.

O·to·mi /ˌōtəˈmē/ ▸*n.* (*pl.* same) **1** a member of an American Indian people inhabiting parts of central Mexico. **2** the Otomanguean language of this people.
▸*adj.* of or relating to this people or their language. ▷via American Spanish from Nahuatl *otomih*, literally 'unknown.'

O'Toole /ōˈtōōl/, Peter (Seamus) (1932–), British actor, born in Ireland. He is especially noted for his portrayals of eccentric characters. Notable movies: *Lawrence of Arabia* (1962), *Becket* (1964), *Lion in Winter* (1968), *Goodbye, Mr. Chips* (1969), and *The Last Emperor* (1987). He received an honorary Academy Award in 2003.

o·to·plas·ty /ˈōtəˌplastē/ ▸*n.* (*pl.* **-ties**) a surgical operation to restore or enhance the appearance of an ear or the ears.

o·to·rhi·no·lar·yn·gol·o·gy /ˌōtōˌrīnōˌlarəNGˈgäləjē/ ▸*n.* the study of diseases of the ear, nose, and throat. —**o·to·rhi·no·lar·yn·gol·o·gist** /-jist/ *n.*

o·to·scle·ro·sis /ˌōtōskləˈrōsis/ ▸*n. Medicine* a hereditary disorder causing progressive deafness due to overgrowth of bone in the inner ear. —**o·to·scle·rot·ic** /-ˈrätik/ *adj.*

o·to·scope /ˈōtəˌskōp/ ▸*n.* an instrument designed for visual examination of the eardrum and the passage of the outer ear, typically having a light and a set of lenses. Also called **AURISCOPE**. —**o·to·scop·ic** /ˌōtəˈskäpik/ *adj.* —**o·to·scop·i·cal·ly** /ˌōtəˈskäpik(ə)lē/ *adv.*

o·to·tox·ic /ˌōtəˈtäksik/ ▸*adj. Medicine* having a toxic effect on the ear or its nerve supply. —**o·to·tox·ic·i·ty** /-täkˈsisitē/ *n.*

O·tran·to, Strait of /ōˈträntō; ˈōträntō/ a channel that links the Adriatic Sea with the Ionian Sea and separates the "heel" of Italy from Albania.

OTS (also **O.T.S.**) ▸*abbr.* Officers' Training School.

ot·ta·va ri·ma /ōˈtävə ˈrēmə/ ▸*n.* a form of poetry consisting of stanzas of eight lines of ten or eleven syllables, rhyming *abababcc.* ▷late 18th cent.: from Italian, literally 'eighth rhyme.'

Ot·ta·wa /ˈätəwə/ the federal capital of Canada, in southeastern Ontario, on the Ottawa River; pop. 313,987. From its founding in 1827 until 1854, it was named Bytown after Colonel John By (1779–1836).

ot·ter /ˈätər/ ▸*n.* a semiaquatic fish-eating mammal of the weasel family, with an elongated body, dense fur, and webbed feet. • *Lutra* and other genera, family Mustelidae: several species, including the **river otter** (*L. canadensis*). See also **SEA OTTER**. ▷Old English *otr, ot(t)or*, of Germanic origin; related to Greek *hudros* 'water snake.'

river otter

ot·ter board ▸*n.* either of a pair of boards or metal plates attached to each side of the mouth of a trawl net at an angle that keeps the net open as it is pulled through the water.

ot·ter·hound /ˈätərˌhound/ ▸*n.* a large dog of a breed with a long rough coat, used in otter hunting.

ot·ter shrew ▸*n.* a semiaquatic mammal of the tenrec family, with a sleek body and long tail, native to central and West Africa. • Genera *Potamogale* and *Micropotamogale*, family Tenrecidae: three species, including the **giant otter shrew** (*P. velox*), which resembles an otter.

ot·ter trawl ▸*n.* a trawl net fitted with an otter board.

Ot·to /ˈätō; ˈôtō/, Nikolaus August (1832–91), German engineer, whose name is given to **Otto cycle**, the four-stroke cycle on which most internal combustion engines work.

ot·to /ˈätō/ ▸*n.* another term for **ATTAR**.

Ot·to I (912–73), king of the Germans 936–973, Holy Roman Emperor 962–973; known as **Otto the Great**. As king of the Germans he carried out a policy of eastward expansion and as Holy Roman Emperor he established a presence in Italy to rival that of the papacy.

ot·to·cen·to /ˌôtōˈCHentō/ ▸*adj.* of or relating to the 19th century in Italy. ▷Italian, literally '800' (shortened from *milottocento* '1800'), used with reference to the years 1800–99.

Ot·to·man /ˈätəmən/ ▸*adj. historical* **1** of or relating to the Turkish dynasty of Osman I (Othman I). ■ of or relating to the branch of the Turks to which he belonged. ■ of or relating to the Ottoman Empire ruled by his successors. **2** Turkish.
▸*n.* (*pl.* **-mans**) a Turk, esp. of the period of the Ottoman Empire. ▷based on Arabic *'uṯmānī* (adjective), from *'Uṯmān* 'Othman.'

ot·to·man /ˈätəmən/ ▸*n.* (*pl.* **-mans**) **1** a low upholstered seat, or footstool, without a back or arms that typically serves also as a box, with the seat hinged to form a lid. **2** a heavy ribbed fabric made from silk and either cotton or wool, typically used for coats. ▷early 19th cent.: from French *ottomane*, feminine of *ottoman* 'Ottoman.'

Ot·to·man Em·pire the Turkish empire, established in northern Anatolia by Osman I at the end of the 13th century and expanded by his successors to include all of Asia Minor and much of southeastern Europe. After setbacks caused by the invasion of the Mongol ruler Tamerlane in 1402, the Ottomans captured Constantinople in 1453, and the empire reached its zenith under Suleiman in the mid 16th century. It had greatly declined by the 19th century and collapsed after World War I.

Ot·to the Great see **OTTO I**.

ou /ˈōˌōō/ ▸*n.* a fruit-eating Hawaiian honeycreeper with a stout bill and green and yellow plumage. Compare with **o-o**. • *Psittirostra psittacea*, family Drepanididae. ▷late 19th cent.: the name in Hawaiian.

oua·bain /wäˈbī-in; -ˈbā-/ ▸*n. Chemistry* a toxic compound obtained from certain trees, used as a very rapid cardiac stimulant. It is a polycyclic glycoside. ▷late 19th cent.: via French from Somali *wabayo*, denoting a tree that yields poison (used on arrow points) containing ouabain.

Ouach·i·ta Moun·tains /ˈwäSHiˌtô/ a low range in western Arkansas and eastern Oklahoma, south of the Ozark Plateau.

Ouach·i·ta Riv·er a river that flows for 600 miles (970 km) across western Arkansas and into northern Louisiana, where it is known in part as the Black River and empties into the Red River.

Oua·ga·dou·gou /ˌwägəˈdōōgōō/ the capital of Burkina Faso; pop. 634,000.

oua·na·niche /ˌwänäˈnēSH/ ▸*n.* (*pl.* same) *Canadian* a salmon of landlocked populations living in lakes in Labrador and Newfoundland. ▷late 19th cent.: via Canadian French from Algonquian.

ou·bli·ette /ˌōōblēˈet/ ▸*n.* a secret dungeon with access only through a trapdoor in its ceiling. ▷late 18th cent.: from French, from *oublier* 'forget.'

ouch /ouCH/ ▸*exclam.* used to express pain. ▷natural exclamation: first recorded in English in the mid 17th cent.

oud /ōōd/ ▸*n.* a form of lute or mandolin played principally in Arab countries. ▷mid 18th cent.: from Arabic *al-'ūd.*

Oudh /oud/ (also **Audh** or **Awadh**) a region of northern India. Joined with Agra in 1877, it formed the United Provinces of Agra and Oudh in 1902 and was renamed Uttar Pradesh in 1950.

ought[1] /ôt/ ▸*modal verb* (*3rd sing. present* and *past* **ought**) [with *infinitive*] **1** used to indicate duty or correctness, typically when criticizing someone's actions: *they ought to respect the law | it ought not to be allowed.* ■ used to indicate a desirable or expected state: *he ought to be able to take the initiative.* ■ used to give or ask advice: *you ought to go.* **2** used to indicate something that is probable: *five minutes ought to be enough time.* ▷Old English *āhte*, past tense of *āgan* 'owe' (see **OWE**).

USAGE The verb **ought** is a modal verb, which means that, grammatically, it does not behave like ordinary verbs. In particular, the negative is formed with the word **not** by itself, without auxiliary verbs such as **do** or **have**. Thus the standard construction for the negative is *he* ***ought not*** *to go.* Note that the preposition *to* is required in both negative and positive statements: *we ought to accept her offer*, or *we ought not to accept her offer* (not *we ought accept* or *we ought not accept*). The alternative forms *he* ***didn't ought*** *to have gone* and *he* ***hadn't ought*** *to have gone*, formed as if **ought** were an ordinary verb rather than a modal verb, are not acceptable in formal English.
Reserve **ought** for expressing obligation, duty, or necessity, and use **should** for expressing suitability or appropriateness.

ought[2] ▸*n.* archaic term for **AUGHT**[2]. ▷mid 19th cent.: perhaps from *an ought*, by wrong division of *a nought*; compare with **ADDER**[1].

ought[3] ▸*pron.* variant spelling of **AUGHT**[1].

ought·n't /ˈôtnt/ ▸*contraction of* ought not.

ou·gui·ya /ōōˈgēə/ (also **ou·gi·ya**) ▸*n.* the basic monetary unit of Mauritania, equal to five khoums. ▷via French from Mauritanian Arabic, from Arabic *'ūḳiyya*, from Greek *ounkia*, from Latin *uncia* 'ounce.'

Oui·ja board /ˈwējə; -jē/ ▸*n. trademark* a board printed with letters, numbers, and other signs, to which a planchette or movable indicator points, supposedly in answer to questions from people at a seance. ▷late 19th cent.: *Ouija* from French *oui* 'yes' + German *ja* 'yes.'

ounce[1] /ouns/ ▸*n.* **1** (abbr.: **oz**) a unit of weight of one sixteenth of a pound avoirdupois (approximately 28 grams). ■ a unit of one twelfth of a pound troy or apothecaries' measure, equal to 480 grains (approximately 31 grams). **2** a very small amount of something: *Robin summoned up* ***every ounce of*** *strength.* **3** short for **FLUID OUNCE**. ▷Middle English: from Old French *unce*, from Latin *uncia* 'twelfth part (of a pound or foot)'; compare with **INCH**[1].

ounce[2] ▸*n.* another term for **SNOW LEOPARD**. ▷Middle English: from Old French *once*, earlier *lonce* (the *l-* being misinterpreted as the definite article), based on Latin *lynx, lync-* (see **LYNX**).

our /ou(ə)r; är/ ▸*possessive adj.* **1** belonging to or associated with the speaker and one or more other people previously mentioned or easily identified: *Jo and I had our hair cut.* ■ belonging to or associated with people in general: *when we hear a sound, our brains identify the source quickly.* **2** used by a writer, editor, or monarch to refer to something belonging to or associated with himself or herself: *we want to know what you, our readers, think.* ▷Old English *ūre*, of Germanic origin; related to **US** and German *unser.*

-our[1] ▸*suffix chiefly Brit.* variant spelling of **-OR**[1] (as in *saviour*).

-our[2] ▸*suffix chiefly Brit.* variant spelling of **-OR**[2] surviving in some nouns such as *ardour, colour.*

Our Fa·ther *Christian Church* used as a title for God. ■ a name for the Lord's Prayer.

Our La·dy *Christian Church* used as a title for the Virgin Mary.

Our Lord *Christian Church* used as a title for God or Christ.

ou·ro·bo·ros ▸*n.* variant spelling of **UROBOROS**.

ours /ˈou(ə)rz; ärz/ ▸*possessive pron.* used to refer to a thing or things belonging to or associated with the speaker and one or more other people previously mentioned or easily identified: *ours was the ugliest house on the block | this chat* ***of ours*** *is strictly between us.*

our·self /ou(ə)rˈself; är-/ ▸*pron.* [*first person plural*] **1** used instead of "ourselves," typically when "we" refers to people in general rather than a definite group of people: [*reflexive*] *we must choose which aspects of ourself to express to the world* | [*emphatic*] *this is our affair—we deal with it ourself.* **2** *archaic* used instead of "myself" by a sovereign or other person in authority.

USAGE The standard reflexive form corresponding to **we** and **us** is **ourselves**, as in *we can blame only ourselves*. The singular form **ourself**, first recorded in the 15th century, is sometimes used in modern English, typically where **we** refers to people in general. This use, though logical, is uncommon and not widely accepted in standard English.
See also **usage** at THEMSELF and THEY.

our·selves /ou(ə)rˈselvz; är-/ ▶*pron.* [*first person plural*] **1** [*reflexive*] used as the object of a verb or preposition when this is the same as the subject of the clause and the subject is the speaker and one or more other people considered together: *for this we can only blame ourselves.* **2** [*emphatic*] we or us personally (used to emphasize the speaker and one or more other people considered together): *we invented it ourselves.*
▶*PHRASES* □ **(not) be ourselves** see BE ONESELF, NOT BE ONESELF at BE. □ **by ourselves** see BY ONESELF at BY.

-ous ▶*suffix* forming adjectives: **1** characterized by; of the nature of: *dangerous* | *mountainous.* **2** *Chemistry* denoting an element in a lower valence: *ferrous* | *sulfurous.* Compare with **-IC**. ▷from Anglo-Norman French, or Old French *-eus*, from Latin *-osus.*

Ouse /o͞oz/ **1** (also **Great Ouse**) a river in eastern England that rises in the county of Northamptonshire and flows east and then north for 160 miles (257 km) through East Anglia to the Wash near King's Lynn. **2** a river in northeastern England that forms at the confluence of the Ure and Swale rivers and flows southeast for 57 miles (92 km) through York to the Humber estuary. **3** a river in southeastern England that flows southeast for 30 miles (48 km) to the English Channel. **4** (also **Little Ouse**) a river in East Anglia that forms a tributary of the Great Ouse.

ou·sel /ˈo͞ozəl/ ▶*n.* variant spelling of OUZEL.

-ously ▶*suffix* forming adverbs corresponding to adjectives ending in *-ous* (such as *dangerously* corresponding to *dangerous*). ▷see **-OUS**, **-LY**.

-ousness ▶*suffix* forming nouns corresponding to adjectives ending in *-ous* (such as *dangerousness* corresponding to *dangerous*). ▷see **-OUS**, **-NESS**.

oust /oust/ ▶*v.* [*trans.*] drive out or expel (someone) from a position or place: *he ousted a long-term incumbent by only 500 votes.* See note at EJECT. ■ *Law* deprive (someone) of or exclude (someone) from possession of something. ▷late Middle English (as a legal term): from Anglo-Norman French *ouster* 'take away,' from Latin *obstare* 'oppose, hinder.'

oust·er /ˈoustər/ ▶*n.* **1** dismissal or expulsion from a position: *a showdown that may lead to his ouster as leader of the party.* **2** *Law* ejection from a freehold or other possession; deprivation of an inheritance.

out /out/ ▶*adv.* **1** moving or appearing to move away from a particular place, esp. one that is enclosed or hidden: *he walked out into the street* | *watch the stars come out.* ■ situated or operating in the open air, not in buildings: *the search-and-rescue team have been out looking for you.* ■ no longer detained in custody or in jail: *they would be out on bail in no time.* **2** away from one's usual base or residence: *the team had put on a marvelous display out in Georgia.* ■ in a public place for purposes of pleasure or entertainment: *an evening out at a restaurant.* **3** to sea, away from the land: *the fleet put out from Cyprus.* ■ (of the tide) falling or at its lowest level: *the tide was going out.* **4** indicating a specified distance away from the goal line or finishing line: *he scored from 70 meters out.* **5** so as to be revealed or known: *find out what you can.* ■ aloud; so as to be heard: *Miss Beard cried out in horror.* **6** at or to an end: *the romance fizzled out.* ■ so as to be finished or complete: *I'll leave them to fight it out* | *I typed out the poem.* ■ (in various other completive uses): *the crowd had thinned out* | *he crossed out a word.* **7** (of a light or fire) so as to be extinguished or no longer burning: *at ten o'clock the lights went out.* ■ (of a stain or mark) no longer visible; removed: *try to get the stain out.* **8** (of a party, politician, etc.) not in office. **9** (of a jury) considering its verdict in secrecy.
▶*prep.* through to the outside: *he ran out the door.*
▶*adj.* [*predic.*] **1** not at home or at one's place of work: *if he called, she'd pretend to be out.* **2** revealed or made public: *the secret was soon out.* ■ (of a flower) in bloom; open. ■ published: *the book should be out before the end of the month.* ■ *informal* in existence or in use: *it works as well as any system that's out.* ■ not concealing one's homosexuality: *I had been out since I was seventeen.* **3** no longer alight; extinguished: *the fire was nearly out.* **4** at an end: *school was out for the summer.* ■ *informal* no longer in fashion: *life in the fast lane is out.* **5** not possible or worth considering: *a trip to the seaside is out.* **6** in a state of unconsciousness. ■ *Boxing* unable to rise before the count of ten. **7** mistaken; in error: *he was slightly out in his calculations.* **8** (of the ball in tennis and similar games) outside the designated playing area. **9** *Baseball & Cricket* no longer batting or on base, having had one's turn ended by the team in the field: *the Yankees are out in the ninth* | *Johnson was out at second.*
▶*n.* **1** *informal* a way of escaping from a problem or dilemma: *he was desperately looking for an out.* **2** *Baseball* an act of putting a player out. ■ (of a batter or base runner) a play ending in being put out. **3** (**the outs**) the political party or politicians not in office.
▶*v.* **1** [*intrans.*] come or go out; emerge: *the truth will out.* **2** [*trans.*] *informal* reveal the homosexuality of (a prominent person). ▷Old English *ūt* (adverb), *ūtian* (verb), of Germanic origin; related to Dutch *uit* and German *aus.*
▶*PHRASES* □ **on the outs** in disagreement or dispute: *on the outs with established political trends.* □ **out and about** (of a person, esp. after inactivity) engaging in normal activity. □ **out for** intent on having: *he was out for a good time.* □ **out of 1** moving or situated away from (a place, typically one that is enclosed or hidden): *he came out of prison.* ■ situated a specified distance from (a place): *they lived eight miles out of town.* ■ taken or appearing to be taken from (a particular type of writing, genre, or artistic performance): *a romance straight out of a fairy tale.* ■ eliminated from (a competition): *knocked out of the tournament.* **2** spoken by: *still not a word out of Pearsall.* **3** using (a particular thing) as raw material: *a bench fashioned out of a fallen tree trunk.* ■ using (a particular thing) as a source of some benefit: *you should not expect too much out of life.* ■ having (the thing mentioned) as a motivation: *she did it out of spite.* ■ indicating the dam of a pedigree animal, esp. a horse. **4** from among (a number): *nine times out of ten.* **5** not having (a particular thing): *they had run out of cash.* □ **out of it** *informal* **1** not included; rejected: *I hate feeling out of it.* **2** unaware of what is happening as a result of being uninformed. ■ unable to think or react properly as a result of being drowsy. □ **out to** keenly striving to: *they were out to impress.* □ **out with** an exhortation to expel or dismiss (an unwanted person or thing). □ **out with it** [as *imperative*] say what you are thinking.

USAGE The use of **out** as a preposition (rather than the standard prepositional phrase **out of**), as in *he threw it* **out** *the window*, is not widely accepted in standard British English. But in the U.S., it is common in edited prose, and it is found also in Australia and New Zealand. The use of **out** instead of **out of** is usually found in contexts of going, looking, etc.: *going out the door; looking out the window.*

out- ▶*prefix* **1** to the point of surpassing or exceeding: *outfight* | *outperform.* **2** external; separate; from outside: *outbuildings* | *outpatient.* **3** away from; outward: *outbound* | *outpost.*

ou·ta /ˈoutə/ ▶*prep.* variant spelling of OUTTA.

out·act /ˌoutˈakt/ ▶*v.* [*trans.*] surpass (someone) in acting or performing something.

out·age /ˈoutij/ ▶*n.* a period when a power supply or other service is not available or when equipment is closed down.

out-and-out ▶*adj.* [*attrib.*] in every respect; absolute; without question: *an out-and-out crook.*

out-and-out·er ▶*n.* *archaic, informal* a person or thing that possesses a particular quality to an extreme degree.

out·a·sight /ˈoutəˈsīt/ ▶*exclam.* *informal* variant spelling of OUT OF SIGHT (see SIGHT).

out·back /ˈoutˌbak/ ▶*n.* (**the outback**) the remote and usually uninhabited inland regions of Australia. ■ any remote or sparsely populated region. —**out·back·er** *n.*

out·bal·ance /ˌoutˈbaləns/ ▶*v.* [*trans.*] be more valuable, important, or influential than; make up for: *their high capacity outbalances this defect.*

out-bas·ket ▶*n.* an out-box.

out·bid /ˌoutˈbid/ ▶*v.* (**-bid·ding**; *past* and *past part.* **-bid**) [*trans.*] offer to pay a higher price for something (than another person): *residential builders could always outbid any farmer for the land.*

out·board /ˈoutˌbô(ə)rd/ ▶*adj.* & *adv.* on, toward, or near the outside, esp. of a ship or other vehicle: [as *adj.*] *the outboard rear seats* | [as *adv.*] *the chart table faces outboard.* ■ [as *adj.*] (of a motor) portable and usually mounted on the outside of the stern of a boat. ■ [as *adj.*] (of an electronic accessory) in a separate container from the device with which it is used.
▶*n.* an outboard motor. ■ a boat with such a motor.
▶*PHRASE* □ **outboard of** to the outside or on the far side of: *the controls are placed just outboard of the wheel.*

out·bound /ˈoutˈbound/ ▶*adj.* & *adv.* traveling away from a particular place, esp. on the first leg of a round trip: [as *adj.*] *an outbound flight* | [as *adv.*] *flying outbound.*

out·box /ˈoutˌbäks/ ▶*v.* [*trans.*] *Boxing* defeat (an opponent) by superior boxing ability.

out-box ▶*n.* a box or tray on someone's desk for outgoing memos, documents, etc., that have been dealt with.

out·brave /ˌoutˈbrāv/ ▶*v.* [*trans.*] ■ face (something) with a show of brave defiance: *he sat outfacing his accusers, and outbraving their accusations.* ■ *archaic* outdo in bravery.

out·break /ˈoutˌbrāk/ ▶*n.* the sudden or violent start of something unwelcome, such as war, disease, etc.: *the outbreak of World War II.*

out·breed /ˌoutˈbrēd/ ▶*v.* (*past* and *past part.* **-bred**) [*trans.*] [usu. as *n.*] (**outbreeding**) breed from parents not closely related: *many specific genetic factors are known that regulate the degree of outbreeding.*

out·build·ing /ˈoutˌbildiNG/ ▶*n.* a building, such as a shed, barn, or garage, on the same property but separate from a more important one, such as a house.

out·burst /ˈoutˌbərst/ ▶*n.* a sudden release of strong emotion: *"she screamed at him about it one day," said one source who witnessed the outburst.* ■ a sudden outbreak of a particular activity: *a wild outburst of applause.* ■ a volcanic eruption. ■ *Physics* a sudden emission of energy or particles: *a very dramatic outburst of neutrons.*

out·call /ˈoutˌkôl/ ▶*n.* a visit by an escort, prostitute, etc., to the address of the caller.

out·cast /ˈoutˌkast/ ▶*n.* a person who has been rejected by society or a social group.
▶*adj.* rejected or cast out: *made to feel outcast and inadequate.*

out·caste ▶*n.* /ˈoutˌkast/ (in Hindu society) a person who has no caste or has been expelled from a caste.
▶*v.* [*trans.*] cause (someone) to lose one's caste: *he has deliberately elected to outcaste himself.*

out·class /ˌoutˈklas/ ▶*v.* [*trans.*] be far superior to: *they totally outclassed us in the first half.*

out·come /ˈoutˌkəm/ ▶*n.* the way a thing turns out; a consequence: *it is the outcome of the vote that counts.*

out·com·pete /ˌoutkəmˈpēt/ ▶*v.* [*trans.*] surpass (someone) in competition: *they were outcompeted by their foreign rivals.* ■ *Biology* displace (another species) in the competition for space, food, or other resources.

out·crop /ˈoutˌkräp/ ▶*n.* a rock formation that is visible on the surface: *dramatic limestone outcrops.* ■ *figurative* a noticeable manifestation or occurrence.
▶*v.* (**-cropped**, **-crop·ping**) [*intrans.*] [often as *n.*] (**outcropping**) appear as an outcrop: *jumbled outcroppings of bedrock.*

out·cross ▶*v.* /ˌoutˈkrôs; -ˈkräs/ [*trans.*] breed (an animal or plant) with one not closely related.
▶*n.* /ˈoutˌkrôs; -ˈkräs/ an animal or plant produced as the result of such crossbreeding.

out·cry /ˈoutˌkrī/ ▶*n.* (*pl.* **-cries**) an exclamation or shout: *an outcry of spontaneous passion.* ■ a strong expression of public disapproval or anger: *the public outcry over the bombing.*

out·dat·ed /ˌoutˈdātid/ ▶*adj.* out of date; obsolete. —**out·dat·ed·ness** *n.*

out·dis·tance /ˌoutˈdistəns/ ▶*v.* [*trans.*] leave (a competitor or pursuer) far behind: *she could maintain a fast enough pace to outdistance any pursuers.*

out·do /ˌoutˈdo͞o/ ▶*v.* (**-does**, **-doing**; *past* **-did**; *past part.* **-done**) [*trans.*] be more successful than: *the men tried to outdo each other in their generosity* | **not to be outdone**, *Vicky and Laura reached the same standard.*

out·door /ˈoutˈdôr/ ▶*adj.* [*attrib.*] done, situated, or used out of doors: *a huge outdoor concert.* ■ (of a person) fond of the open air or open-air activities: *a rugged, outdoor type.*

out·doors /ˌoutˈdôrz/ ▶*adv.* in or into the open air; outside a building or shelter: *it was warm enough to eat outdoors.*
▶*n.* (usu. **the outdoors**) any area outside buildings or shelter, typically far away from human habitation: *a lover of* **the great outdoors**.

O

out·doors·man /out'dôrzmən/ ▸*n.* (*pl.* **-men**; *fem.* **out·doors·wom·an** /-,wo͝omən/ *pl.* **-wom·en**) a person who spends a lot of time outdoors or doing outdoor activities.

out·doors·y /,out'dôrzē/ ▸*adj. informal* of, associated with, or fond of the outdoors: *the outdoorsy fragrance of pines.*

out·draw /,out'drô/ ▸*v.* (*past* **-drew**; *past part.* **-drawn**) [*trans.*] (of a person or event) attract a larger crowd than (another person or event): *the stores in Paris outdraw both the Louvre and the Eiffel Tower.*

out·drink /,out'driNGk/ ▸*v.* (*past* **-drank**; *past part.* **-drunk**) [*trans.*] drink more alcohol than (another person).

out·drive /,out'drīv/ ▸*v.* (*past* **-drove**; *past part.* **-driven**) [*trans.*] **1** drive a golf ball farther than (another player): *he outdrove his playing partners by as much as seventy-five yards.* **2** drive a vehicle better or faster than (someone else): *he knew he couldn't outdrive the police.*
▸*n.* the portion of an inboard-outboard engine that is outside the hull, providing steering and propulsion.

out·er /'outər/ ▸*adj.* [*attrib.*] outside; external: *the outer door.* ■ further from the center or inside: *the outer hall at the museum's main entrance.* ■ (esp. in place names) more remote: *Outer Mongolia.* ■ objective or physical; not subjective. ▷late Middle English: from OUT + -ER[2], replacing earlier UTTER[1].

Out·er Banks a chain of barrier islands extending southward for 175 miles (282 km) along the coast of North Carolina, consisting largely of sand dunes and serving as a buffer against the Atlantic Ocean.

out·er·course /'outər,kôrs/ ▸*n.* sexual stimulation that excludes penile penetration. ▷1980s: blend of OUTER and INTERCOURSE.

Out·er Mon·go·li·a see MONGOLIA.

out·er·most /'outər,mōst/ ▸*adj.* [*attrib.*] farthest from the center: *the outermost layer of the earth.*
▸*pron.* the one that is farthest from the center: *the orbit of the outermost of these eight planets.*

out·er plan·et ▸*n.* a planet whose orbit lies outside the asteroid belt, i.e., Jupiter, Saturn, Uranus, Neptune, or Pluto.

out·er space ▸*n.* the physical universe beyond the earth's atmosphere.

out·er·wear /'outər,we(ə)r/ ▸*n.* clothing worn over other clothes, esp. for the outdoors.

out·face /,out'fās/ ▸*v.* [*trans.*] disconcert or defeat (an opponent) by bold confrontation: *to outface twenty-five or thirty antagnostic men.*

out·fall /'out,fôl/ ▸*n.* the place where a river, drain, or sewer empties into the sea, a river, or a lake.

out·field /'out,fēld/ ▸*n.* **1** the outer part of the field of play in various sports, in particular: ■ *Baseball* the grassy area beyond the infield. ■ *Cricket* the part of the field furthest from the wicket. ■ [treated as *sing.* or *pl.*] the players stationed in the outfield, collectively. **2** the outlying land of a farm. —**out·field·er** *n.*

out·fight /,out'fit/ ▸*v.* (*past* and *past part.* **-fought**) [*trans.*] fight better than and beat (an opponent).

out·fit /'out,fit/ ▸*n.* a set of clothes worn together, typically for a particular occasion or purpose: *a riding outfit.* ■ [usu. with *adj.*] *informal* a group of people undertaking a particular activity together, as a group of musicians, a military unit, or a business concern: *Tom was the brains of the outfit.* ■ [with *adj.*] a complete set of equipment or articles needed for a particular purpose: *a repair outfit.*
▸*v.* (**-fit·ted**, **-fit·ting**) [*trans.*] (usu. **be outfitted**) provide (someone) with a set of clothes: *an auction of dolls outfitted by world-famous designers | he outfitted himself in the best gray suit he could afford.* ■ provide with equipment: *planes outfitted with sophisticated electronic gear.*

out·fit·ter /'out,fitər/ (also **out·fit·ters**) ▸*n.* an establishment that sells clothing, equipment, and services, esp. for outdoor activities: *an outfitter that provides professional guides.* ■ *Brit., dated* an establishment that sells men's clothing.

out·flank /,out'flaNGk/ ▸*v.* [*trans.*] move around the side of (an enemy) so as to outmaneuver them: *the Germans had sought to outflank them from the northeast.* ■ *figurative* outwit: *an attempt to outflank the opposition.*

out·flow /'out,flō/ ▸*n.* a large amount of money, liquid, or people that moves or is transferred out of a place: *an outflow of foreign currency.* ■ the flowing out of a liquid from a container or cavity: *the combination of arterial inflow and venous outflow.* ■ *Meteorology* the outward flow of air from a weather system, associated with wind shift and temperature drop.

out·fly /,out'flī/ ▸*v.* (**-flies**; *past* **-flew**; *past part.* **-flown**) [*trans.*] fly faster, farther, or with more agility than: *a high-powered combat aircraft that can outfly anything.*

out·fox /,out'fäks/ ▸*v.* [*trans.*] *informal* defeat or deceive (someone) by being more clever or cunning than they are; outwit.

out·gas /,out'gas/ ▸*v.* (**-gas·es**, **-gas·sing**, **-gassed**) [*trans.*] release or give off (a substance) as a gas or vapor: *glue may outgas smelly volatile organic compounds* | [*intrans.*] *samples are heated and begin to outgas.*

out·gen·er·al /,out'jen(ə)rəl/ ▸*v.* (**-gen·er·aled**, **-gen·er·al·ing**; *Brit.* **-gen·er·alled**, **-gen·er·al·ling**) [*trans.*] get the better of by superior strategy or tactics.

out·go ▸*n.* /'out,gō/ the outlay of money: *the secret of success lies in the relation of income to outgo.*
▸*v.* /out'gō/ (**out·goes**; *past* **out·went**; *past part.* **out·gone**) [*trans.*] *archaic* go faster than: *he on horseback outgoes him on foot.*

out·go·ing /'out,gōiNG/ ▸*adj.* **1** friendly and socially confident: *she's an extremely affable, jovial, outgoing type of person.* **2** [*attrib.*] leaving an office or position, esp. after an election defeat or completed term of office: *the outgoing governor.* ■ going out or away from a particular place: *incoming and outgoing calls.*
▸*n. Brit.* (**outgoings**) a person's regular expenditure.

out·gross /'out'grōs/ ▸*v.* [*trans.*] surpass in gross income or profit: *the film has outgrossed all other movie comedies.*

out·group ▸*n.* **1** *Sociology* those people who do not belong to a specific in-group. **2** *Biology* a group of organisms not belonging to the group whose evolutionary relationships are being investigated.

out·grow /,out'grō/ ▸*v.* (*past* **-grew**; *past part.* **-grown**) [*trans.*] grow too big for (something): *babies outgrow their first car seat at six to nine months.* ■ leave behind as one matures: *is it a permanent injury, or will the colt outgrow it?* ■ grow faster or taller than: *the more vigorous plants outgrow their weaker neighbors.*

out·growth /'out,grōTH/ ▸*n.* something that grows out of something else: *outgrowths at the base of the leaf.* ■ a natural development or result of something: *the book is an imaginative outgrowth of practical criticism.* ■ the process of growing out: *with further outgrowth the radius and ulna develop.*

out·guess /,out'ges/ ▸*v.* [*trans.*] outwit (someone) by guessing correctly what they intend to do: *a brilliant military commander outguesses the enemy.*

out·gun /,out'gən/ ▸*v.* (**-gunned**, **-gun·ning**) [*trans.*] [often as *adj.*] (**outgunned**) have better or more weaponry than: *offensives that overwhelmed the outgunned and outmanned armies* | *figurative verbally outgunned by coworkers.*

out·haul /'out,hôl/ ▸*n. Sailing* a rope used to haul out the clew of a boom sail or the tack of a jib.

out·hit /,out'hit/ ▸*v.* (*past* and *past part.* **-hit**; **-hit·ting**) [*trans.*] (in baseball and other sports played with a ball) surpass (a player or a team) in hitting the ball into fair territory: *we outscored them for the Series, 55–27, and outhit them, 91–60.*

out·house /'out,hous/ ▸*n.* an outbuilding containing a toilet, typically with no plumbing. ■ any outbuilding.

out·ing /'outiNG/ ▸*n.* **1** a trip taken for pleasure, esp. one lasting a day or less: *they would go on family outings to the movies.* ■ a brief journey from home: *her daily outing to the stores.* ■ *informal* an appearance in something, as an athletic event or show: *her first screen outing in three years.* **2** the act or practice of revealing the homosexuality of a person. ▷late Middle English (in the sense 'the action of going out or of expelling'): from the verb OUT + -ING[1].

out·ing flan·nel ▸*n.* a type of flannelette with a short nap on both sides, used in infant clothing.

out is·land ▸*n.* an island situated away from the mainland.

out·land /'out,land/ ▸*n.* (often **out·lands**) remote or distant territory: *barbarian chiefs from the outlands.*
▸*adj.* remote; distant. ■ foreign: *in the charge of outland kings.*

out·land·er /'out,landər/ ▸*n.* a foreigner; a stranger.

out·land·ish /out'landiSH/ ▸*adj.* **1** looking or sounding bizarre or unfamiliar: *outlandish brightly colored clothes | the most outlandish ideas.* **2** *archaic* foreign; alien. ▷Old English *ūtlendisc* 'not native,' from *ūtland* 'foreign country.' —**out·land·ish·ly** *adv.* —**out·land·ish·ness** *n.*

out·last /,out'last/ ▸*v.* [*trans.*] outlive; last longer than: *the kind of beauty that will outlast youth.* ■ endure longer so as to overcome (an opponent or challenge).

out·law /'out,lô/ ▸*n.* a person who has broken the law, esp. one who remains at large or is a fugitive. ■ an intractable horse or other animal. ■ *historical* a person deprived of the benefit and protection of the law.
▸*v.* [*trans.*] ban; make illegal: *Maryland outlawed cheap small-caliber pistols* | [as *adj.*] (**outlawed**) *the outlawed terrorist group.* ■ *historical* deprive (someone) of the benefit and protection of the law. ▷late Old English *ūtlaga* (noun), *ūtlagian* (verb), from Old Norse *útlagi*, noun from *útlagr* 'outlawed or banished.' —**out·law·ry** /-,lôrē/ *n.*

out·lay /'out,lā/ ▸*n.* an amount of money spent on something.

out·let /'out,let/ ▸*n.* a means by which something escapes, passes, or is released, in particular: ■ a pipe or hole through which water or gas may escape. ■ the mouth of a river. ■ a point in an electrical circuit from which current may be drawn. ■ a place from which goods are sold or distributed: *a fast-food outlet.* ■ a retail store that sells the goods of a specific manufacturer or brand: [as *adj.*] *an outlet store.* ■ a retail store offering discounted merchandise, esp. overstocked or irregular items. ■ a market for goods: *the indoor markets in Moscow were an outlet for surplus collective-farm produce.* ■ *figurative* a means of expressing one's talents, energy, or emotions: *writing became the main outlet for his energies.* ▷Middle English: from OUT- + the verb LET[1].

out·let box ▸*n.* a box for mounting wall outlets and connecting them to electrical wiring.

out·let pass ▸*n. Basketball* a quick pass from a player who has just taken a rebound to a teammate who can initiate a fast break.

out·li·er /'out,līər/ ▸*n.* a person or thing situated away or detached from the main body or system: *less accessible islands and outliers.* ■ a person or thing excluded from a group; an outsider. ■ *Geology* a younger rock formation isolated among older rocks. ■ *Statistics* a data point on a graph or in a set of results that is very much bigger or smaller than the next nearest data point.

out·line /'out,līn/ ▸*n.* **1** a line or set of lines enclosing or indicating the shape of an object in a sketch or diagram: *fill in the outlines with color.* ■ a line or set of lines of this type, perceived as defining the contours or bounds of an object: *the outlines of her face.* **2** a general plan giving the essential features but not the detail: *an outline of the theory of evolution | a course outline.* ■ a draft of a diagram, plan, proposal, etc., summarizing the main points: *draw up an outline for the essay.* ■ the main features or general principles of something: *the main outlines of Elizabeth's career.*
▸*v.* [*trans.*] **1** draw, trace, or define the outer edge or shape of (something): *her large eyes were darkly outlined with eyeliner.* **2** give a summary of (something): *she outlined the case briefly.*

out·lin·er /'out,līnər/ ▸*n.* a computer application that produces a hierarchically arranged outline of the logical structure of a text document.

out·live /,out'liv/ ▸*v.* [*trans.*] (of a person) live longer than (another person): *women generally outlive men.* ■ survive or last beyond (a specified period or expected lifespan): *the organization had largely* ***outlived its usefulness.*** ■ *archaic* live through (an experience): *the world has outlived much.*

out·look /'out,lo͝ok/ ▸*n.* a person's point of view or general attitude to life: *broaden your* ***outlook on*** *life.* ■ a view: *the pleasant outlook from the lodge window.* ■ a place from which a view is possible: *emerging onto a cliffy outlook over a river.* ■ the prospect for the future: *the deteriorating economic outlook.* ■ the weather as forecast for the near future.
▸*v.* [*trans.*] predict on the basis of current information: *streamflow for the upcoming runoff season is presently outlooked to be much below average.* ■ predict that certain conditions will prevail in (a region): *the Storm Prediction Center outlooked the northeast quarter of Iowa for a moderate risk of severe storms.*

out·ly·ing /'out,lī-iNG/ ▸*adj.* [*attrib.*] situated far from a center; remote: *an outlying village.*

out·man /,out'man/ ▸*v.* (**-manned**, **-man·ning**) [*trans.*] [usu. as *adj.*] (**outmanned**) outnumber: *the rebels are outmanned and outmatched in armaments.* ■ overpower with skill or physical strength: *Mexico controlled the game and ran circles around the outmanned Guatemalan team.*

out·ma·neu·ver /,outmə'no͞ovər/ (*Brit.* **out·ma·noeu·vre**) ▸*v.* [*trans.*] evade (an opponent) by moving faster or with greater agility: *the YF-22 can outmaneuver any fighter flying today.* ■ use skill and cunning to secure an advantage over (someone): *he would be able to outmaneuver his critics.*

out·match /ˌout'mach/ ▸*v.* [*trans.*] be superior to (an opponent or rival).

out·meas·ure /ˌout'mezhər/ ▸*v.* [*trans.*] *archaic* exceed in quantity or extent.

out·mi·grant /'out,migrənt/ ▸*n.* a person who has migrated from one place to another, esp. within a country. **—out·mi·gra·tion** /-mī,grāshən/ *n.*

out·mod·ed /ˌout'mōdid/ ▸*adj.* old-fashioned. **—out·mod·ed·ness** *n.*

out·most /'out,mōst/ ▸*adj.* farthest away: *the outmost reaches of the empire.* ▷Middle English: variant of *utmest* 'utmost.'

out·mus·cle /out'məsəl/ ▸*v.* [*trans.*] to dominate or defeat by virtue of superior strength or force.

out·num·ber /ˌout'nəmbər/ ▸*v.* [*trans.*] be more numerous than: *women outnumbered men by three to one.*

out-of-bod·y ex·pe·ri·ence ▸*n.* a sensation of being outside one's own body, typically of floating and being able to observe oneself from a distance.

out-of-court ▸*adj.* [*attrib.*] (of a settlement) made or done without a court decision.

out of date ▸*adj.* old-fashioned: *everything in her wardrobe must be hopelessly out of date* | *an out-of-date kitchen.* ■ no longer valid or relevant: *your passport is out of date.*

out of pock·et ▸*adj.* (also **out-of-pock·et**) of, pertaining to, or requiring a cash expenditure: *out of pocket expenses* [as *adv.*] *paying for office visits out of pocket.* ■ suffering from a financial loss: *even after our payment, he is still out of pocket.*

out-of-the-way ▸*adj.* (also **out of the way**) (of a place) remote; secluded: *an out-of-the-way rural district.* ■ dealt with or finished: *economic recovery will begin once the election is out of the way.* ■ (of a person) no longer an obstacle or hindrance to someone's plans: *why did Josie want her out of the way?* ■ unusual, exceptional, or remarkable: *something very out of the way had happened.*

out-of-town ▸*adj.* situated, originating from, or taking place outside a given or implied city or town: *a reception for influential out-of-town guests.* **—out-of-town·er** *n.*

out·pace /ˌout'pās/ ▸*v.* [*trans.*] go faster than: *he took the pass and outpaced the defense to score in the corner.* ■ be more than; surpass: *salsa sales now outpace those for ketchup.*

out·par·cel /'out,pärsəl/ ▸*n.* a building lot separated or separable from a commercial development, the selling of which provides liquidity for the developer.

out·pa·tient /'out,pāshənt/ ▸*n.* a patient who receives medical treatment without being admitted to a hospital: *attending a clinic as an outpatient* | [as *adj.*] *treatment is done on an outpatient basis.*

out·per·form /ˌoutpər'fôrm/ ▸*v.* [*trans.*] perform better than: *an experienced employee will outperform the novice.* ■ (of an investment) be more profitable than: *silver has outperformed the stock market.* **—out·per·for·mance** /-'fôrməns/ *n.*

out·place·ment /'outplāsmənt/ ▸*n.* the provision of assistance to laid-off employees in finding new employment, either as a benefit provided by the employer directly, or through a specialist service.

out·play /ˌout'plā/ ▸*v.* [*trans.*] play better than: *they outshot and in general just outplayed us.*

out·point /ˌout'point/ ▸*v.* [*trans.*] **1** defeat (an opponent) on points: *he retained his featherweight title by outpointing the Colombian in twelve rounds.* **2** *Nautical* sail closer to the wind than (another ship).

out·poll /ˌout'pōl/ ▸*v.* [*trans.*] to receive more votes than.

out·port /'out,pôrt/ ▸*n.* a subsidiary port built near an existing one.

out·post /'out,pōst/ ▸*n.* a small military camp or position at some distance from the main force, used esp. as a guard against surprise attack. ■ a remote part of a country or empire. ■ *figurative* something regarded as an isolated or remote branch of something: *the community is the last outpost of civilization in the far north.*

out·pour·ing /'out,pôriNG/ ▸*n.* something that streams out rapidly: *a massive outpouring of high-energy gamma rays.* ■ (often **outpourings**) an outburst of strong emotion: *spontaneous outpourings of affection and support* | *the unprecedented outpouring of tearful grief.*

out·psych /ˌout'sīk/ (also **out·psyche**) ▸*v.* [*trans.*] *informal* defeat by psychological influence or intimidation: *each country tries to outpsych the other.*

out·put /'out,po͝ot/ ▸*n.* **1** the amount of something produced by a person, machine, or industry: *the diverse range of Liszt's output* | *efficiency can lead to higher outputs.* ■ the action or process of producing something: *the output of epinephrine.* ■ the power, energy, or other results supplied by a device or system: *the quality of the output from the printer is very good.* **2** *Electronics* a place where power or information leaves a system.

▸*v.* (**-put·ting**; *past* and *past part.* **-put** or **-put·ted**) [*trans.*] produce, deliver, or supply (data) using a computer or other device: *you can output the image directly to a video recording system.*

out·race /ˌout'rās/ ▸*v.* [*trans.*] exceed in speed, amount, or extent: *demand for trained clergy is outracing the supply.*

out·rage /'out,rāj/ ▸*n.* an extremely strong reaction of anger, shock, or indignation: *her voice trembled with outrage.* ■ an action or event causing such a reaction: *the decision was an outrage.*

▸*v.* [*trans.*] (usu. **be outraged**) arouse fierce anger, shock, or indignation in (someone): *he was outraged at this attempt to take his victory away from him.* ■ violate or infringe flagrantly (a principle, law, etc.): *their behavior outraged all civilized standards.* ▷Middle English (in the senses 'lack of moderation' and 'violent behavior'): from Old French *ou(l)trage*, based on Latin *ultra* 'beyond.' Sense development has been affected by the belief that the word is a compound of **OUT** and **RAGE**.

out·ra·geous /out'rājəs/ ▸*adj.* **1** shockingly bad or excessive: *an outrageous act of bribery.* ■ wildly exaggerated or improbable: *the outrageous claims made by the previous administration.* **2** very bold, unusual, and startling: *her outrageous leotards and sexy routines.* ▷late Middle English: from Old French *outrageus*, from *outrage* 'excess' (see **OUTRAGE**). **—out·ra·geous·ly** *adv.* **—out·ra·geous·ness** *n.*

out·ran /ˌout'ran/ ▸ past of **OUTRUN**.

out·range /ˌout'rānj/ ▸*v.* (of a gun or its user) have a longer range than.

out·rank /ˌout'raNGk/ ▸*v.* [*trans.*] have a higher rank than (someone else): *a father figure to many of the junior officers theoretically outranking him.* ■ be better, more important, or more significant than: *fishing provided the chief employment, outranking both clothing and canning.*

ou·tré /o͞o'trā/ ▸*adj.* unusual and startling: *in 1975 the suggestion was considered outré—today it is orthodox.* ▷French, literally 'exceeded,' past participle of *outrer* (see **OUTRAGE**).

out·reach ▸*n.* /'out,rēch/ the extent or length of reaching out. ■ an organization's involvement with or activity in the community, esp. in the context of social welfare: *her goal is to increase educational outreach* | [as *adj.*] *Phoenix's outreach effort to educate renters and homebuyers about their rights.*

▸*v.* /ˌout'rēch/ [*trans.*] reach further than. ■ [*intrans.*] *poetic/literary* stretch out one's arms.

Ou·tre·mer /ˌo͞otrā'mā/ a name applied to the medieval French crusader states, including Armenia, Antioch, Tripoli, and Jerusalem. ▷from French *outremer* (adverb) 'overseas,' from *outre* 'beyond' + *mer* 'sea.'

out·ride /ˌout'rīd/ ▸*v.* (*past* **-rode**; *past part.* **-rid·den**) [*trans.*] ride better, faster, or farther than.

out·rid·er /'out,rīdər/ ▸*n.* a person in a motor vehicle or on horseback who goes in front of or beside a vehicle as an escort or guard: *an escort of police outriders.* ■ a person or thing that accompanies or precedes another, esp. as a precursor: *gray-white cumulus clouds—outriders of the storm.* ■ a mounted official who escorts racehorses to the starting post. ■ a cowhand who prevents cattle from straying beyond a certain limit. **—out·rid·ing** /ˌout'rīdiNG/ *n.*

out·rig·ger /'out,rigər/ ▸*n.* a beam, spar, or framework projecting from or over the side of a ship or boat. ■ a float or secondary hull fixed parallel to a canoe or other boat to stabilize it. ■ a boat fitted with such a structure. ■ a similar projecting support in another structure or vehicle. ▷mid 18th cent.: perhaps influenced by the obsolete nautical term *outligger*, in the same sense. **—out·rigged** /-,rigd/ *adj.*

outrigger

out·right ▸*adv.* /'out,rīt/ **1** altogether; completely: *logging has been banned outright.* ■ without reservation; openly: *she couldn't ask him outright.* **2** immediately: *the impact killed four horses outright.* ■ not by degrees or installments: *they decided to buy the company outright.*

▸*adj.* [*attrib.*] open and direct; not concealed: *an outright refusal.* ■ total; complete: *the outright abolition of the death penalty.* ■ undisputed; clear: *an outright victory.*

ou·tro /'outrō/ ▸*n.* (*pl.* **-tros**) *informal* the concluding section of a piece of music or a radio or television program: *the intros, outros, and bridges of various segments.* ▷1970s: from **OUT**, on the pattern of *intro*.

out·run /ˌout'rən/ ▸*v.* (**-run·ning**; *past* **-ran**; *past part.* **-run**) [*trans.*] run or travel faster or farther than. ■ escape from: *it's harder than anyone imagines to outrun destiny.* ■ go beyond; exceed: *his courage outran his prudence.*

out·rush /ˌout'rəsh/ ▸*n.* a rushing out of something; a sudden outpouring. **—out·rush·ing** *adj.*

out·sell /ˌout'sel/ ▸*v.* (*past* and *past part.* **-sold**) [*trans.*] be sold in greater quantities than: *his first foray into the assassin/thriller area could well outsell his other books.* ■ (of a person) sell more of something than (someone else): *Garth Brooks is outselling Michael Jackson.*

out·sert /'outsərt/ ▸*n.* a piece of promotional material that is placed on the outside of a package, publication, or other product. ▷1960s: from **OUT** + **INSERT**.

out·set /'out,set/ ▸*n.* [in *sing.*] the start or beginning of something: *a field of which he had known nothing at the outset and learned on the job.*

▸*PHRASE* □ **at** (or **from**) **the outset** at or from the beginning.

out·shine /ˌout'shīn/ ▸*v.* (*past* and *past part.* **-shone**) [*trans.*] shine more brightly than. ■ be much better than (someone) in a particular area: *it is a shame when a mother outshines a daughter.*

out·shoot /ˌout'sho͞ot/ ▸*v.* (*past* and *past part.* **-shot**) [*trans.*] shoot better than (someone else). ■ *Sports* make or take more shots than (another player or team).

out·side /'out'sīd/ ▸*n.* the external side or surface of something: *record the date on the outside of the file.* ■ the side of a bend or curve where the edge or surface is longer in extent. ■ the side of a racetrack further from the center, where the lanes are longer. ■ the external appearance of someone or something: *was he as straight as he appeared* ***on the outside****?* ■ (in basketball) the area beyond the perimeter of the defense: *he often set up the Lakers' plays from the outside.*

▸*adj.* [*attrib.*] **1** situated on or near the exterior or external surface of something: *put the outside lights on.* ■ *Baseball* (of a pitch) passing home plate on the side of the plate away from the batter, not in the strike zone. ■ (in soccer and other sports) denoting positions nearer to the sides of the field. ■ (in basketball) taking place beyond the perimeter of the defense: *he needs work on his outside shot.* **2** not belonging to or coming from within a particular group: *I have some outside help.* ■ beyond one's own immediate personal concerns: *I was able to face the outside world again.* **3** (of an estimate) the greatest or highest possible: *new monthly charges that, according to outside estimates, may total $8 per line.*

▸*prep.* & *adv.* **1** situated or moving beyond the boundaries of (a room, building, or other enclosed space): [as *prep.*] *there was a boy outside the door* | [as *adv.*] *the dog was still barking outside* | *outside, the wind was as wild as ever.* ■ situated beyond the boundaries of (a particular location): [as *prep.*] *Vincennes, just outside Paris* | [as *adv.*] *those in the occupied territories and those outside.* ■ not being a member of (a particular group): [as *prep.*] *those of us outside the university.* ■ (in football, soccer, and other sports) closer to the side of the field than (another player): [as *prep.*] *Swift appeared outside him with Andrews on his left.* **2** [*prep.*] beyond the limits or scope of: *the high cost of shipping has put it outside their price range.*

▸*PHRASES* □ **at the outside** (of an estimate) at the most: *every minute, or at the outside, every ninety seconds.* □ **on the outside** away from or not belonging to a particular circle or institution: *when you're on the outside, then you have a much better view of what they're doing.* □ **on the outside looking in** (of a person) excluded from a group or activity. □ **an outside**

chance a remote possibility. □ **outside of** *informal* beyond the boundaries of: *a village 20 miles outside of New York.* ■ apart from: *outside of his family, nobody cares too much about him.*

USAGE Outside of tends to be more commonly used in the U.S. than in Britain, where **outside** usually suffices, but, like its cousin *off of*, it is colloquial and not recommended for formal writing. (See **usage** at **OFF**.) The adverb **outside** is not problematic when referring to physical space, position, etc. (*I'm going outside*), but the compound preposition **outside of** is often used as a colloquial (and often inferior) way of saying *except for, other than, apart from* (*outside of what I just mentioned, I can't think of any reason not to*).
Besides possibly sounding more informal than desired, **outside of** may cause misunderstanding by suggesting physical space or location when that is not the point to be emphasized, or when no such sense is intended—consider the ambiguity in this sentence: *outside of China, he has few interests.* Does this mean that his primary interest is China? Or does it mean that whenever he is not in China, he has few interests?

out·side in·ter·est ▶*n.* an interest or hobby not connected with one's work or studies. ■ curiosity about a place, situation, or thing on the part of people unconnected with it: *this flurry of outside interest has put many locals on guard.*

out·side line ▶*n.* a telephone connection to an external dial tone, for outgoing calls.

out·side mon·ey ▶*n.* *Economics* money held in a form such as gold that is an asset for the holder and does not represent a corresponding liability for someone else. ■ money or investment from an independent source.

out·sid·er /ˌoutˈsīdər/ ▶*n.* **1** a person who does not belong to a particular group. ■ a person who is not accepted by or who is isolated from society. **2** a competitor, applicant, etc., thought to have little chance of success: *he started as a rank outsider for the title.*

out·sid·er art ▶*n.* art produced by self-taught artists who are not part of the artistic establishment. —**out·sid·er art·ist** *n.*

out·size /ˌoutˈsīz/ ▶*adj.* (also **out·sized**) exceptionally large.
▶*n.* an exceptionally large person or thing, esp. a garment made to measurements larger than the standard.

out·skirts /ˈoutˌskərts/ ▶*plural n.* the outer parts of a town or city: *the park was built* **on the outskirts of** *New York in 1857.* ■ the fringes of something: *he likes to be on the outskirts of a discussion.*

out·smart /ˌoutˈsmärt/ ▶*v.* [*trans.*] *informal* defeat or get the better of (someone) by being clever or cunning: *content with the illusion that they can outsmart the market.*

out·sold /ˌoutˈsōld/ ▶ past and past participle of **OUTSELL**.

out·sole /ˈoutˌsōl/ ▶*n.* the outermost layer of the sole of a boot or shoe, esp. an athletic shoe.

out·source /ˈoutˌsôrs/ ▶*v.* [*trans.*] obtain (goods or a service) from an outside or foreign supplier, esp. in place of an internal source: **outsourcing** *components* **from** *other countries* | [as *n.*] (**outsourcing**) *outsourcing can dramatically lower total costs.* ■ contract (work) out or abroad: *you may choose to* **outsource** *this function* **to** *another company or do it yourself.*

out·spo·ken /ˌoutˈspōkən/ ▶*adj.* frank in stating one's opinions, esp. if they are critical or controversial: *he has been outspoken in his criticism.* —**out·spok·en·ly** *adv.* —**out·spok·en·ness** *n.*

out·spread /ˌoutˈspred/ ▶*adj.* fully extended or expanded: *outspread arms.*
▶*v.* (*past* and *past part.* **-spread**) [*trans.*] *poetic/literary* spread out: *that eagle outspreading his wings for flight.*

out·stand·ing /ˌoutˈstanding; ˈout-/ ▶*adj.* **1** exceptionally good: *the team's outstanding performance.* ■ clearly noticeable: *works of outstanding banality.* See note at **NOTICEABLE**. **2** remaining to be done or dealt with: *how much work is still outstanding?* ■ (of a debt) remaining to be paid or dealt with: *there was a small charge outstanding.*

out·stand·ing·ly /ˌoutˈstandinglē/ ▶*adv.* [usu. as *submodifier*] exceptionally: *outstandingly beautiful gardens.*

out·stare /ˌoutˈste(ə)r/ ▶*v.* [*trans.*] stare at (someone) for longer than they can stare back, typically in order to intimidate or disconcert them.

out·sta·tion /ˈoutˌstāshən/ ▶*n.* a branch of an organization situated at some distance from its headquarters.

out·stay /ˌoutˈstā/ ▶*v.* [*trans.*] stay beyond the limit of (one's expected or permitted time): *employees who had outstayed their coffee break.*
▶*PHRASE* □ **outstay one's welcome** see **WELCOME**.

out·step /ˌoutˈstep/ ▶*v.* (**-stepped, -step·ping**) [*trans.*] *rare* exceed.

out·stretch /ˌoutˈstrech/ ▶*v.* [*trans.*] [usu. as *adj.*] (**outstretched**) extend or stretch out (something, esp. a hand or arm): *I walked with my arms outstretched.* ■ go beyond the limit of: *their good intentions far outstretched their capacity to offer help.*

out·strip /ˌoutˈstrip/ ▶*v.* (**-stripped, -strip·ping**) [*trans.*] move faster than and overtake (someone else). ■ exceed: *supply far outstripped demand.*

out·ta /ˈoutə/ (also **out·a**) ▶*prep.* an informal contraction of "out of," used in representing colloquial speech: *we'd better get outta here.*

out·take /ˈouˌtāk/ ▶*n.* a scene or sequence filmed or recorded for a movie or program but not included in the final version.

out·talk ▶*v.* (also **out-talk**) [*trans.*] outdo or overcome in talking or argumentation: *whether you get ten years or go free can depend on whether your counsel can out-talk the other man's.*

out·think /ˌoutˈthingk/ ▶*v.* [*trans.*] outdo in thinking; outwit: *machines that can outthink humans.*

out·thrust /ˈoutˌthrəst/ ▶*adj.* extended outward: *with his outthrust foot he sent the man keeling over.*
▶*n.* a thing that projects or is extended outward: *root hairs are outthrusts from the root surface.*

out·turn /ˈoutˌtərn/ ▶*n.* the amount of something produced, esp. money; output: *the financial outturn.*

out·vote /ˌoutˈvōt/ ▶*v.* [*trans.*] defeat by tallying a greater number of votes.

out·ward /ˈoutwərd/ ▶*adj.* [*attrib.*] **1** of, on, or from the outside: *the vehicle's outward and interior appearance.* ■ relating to the external appearance of something rather than its true nature or substance: *an outward display of friendliness.* ■ *archaic* outer: *the outward physical body.* **2** going out or away from a place: *the outward voyage.*
▶*adv.* away from the center or a particular point; toward the outside: *a window that opens outward* | *the solar wind that rushes* **outward from** *the sun.* ▷Old English *ūtweard* (see **OUT-, -WARD**). —**out·ward·ness** *n.*

out·ward-bound ▶*adj.* (of a ship or passenger) going away from home or point of origin: *an outward-bound crude oil carrier.*

out·ward·ly /ˈoutwərdlē/ ▶*adv.* [often as *submodifier*] on the surface: *an outwardly normal life* | [*sentence adverb*] *outwardly she seemed no different.* ■ on or from the outside: *outwardly featureless modern offices* | [*sentence adverb*] *outwardly it's not a bad-looking car.*

out·wards /ˈoutwərdz/ ▶*adv.* *chiefly Brit.* variant of **OUTWARD**.

out·wash /ˈoutˌwôsh; -ˌwäsh/ ▶*n.* material carried away from a glacier by meltwater and deposited beyond the moraine.

out·watch /ˌoutˈwäch/ ▶*v.* [*trans.*] *archaic* watch (something) until it disappears. ■ keep awake beyond the end of: *they outwatched the night, ever hopeful of a rescue.*

out·wear /ˌoutˈwe(ə)r/ ▶*v.* (*past* **-wore**; *past part.* **-worn**) [*trans.*] last longer than: *a material that will outwear any other waterproof sheeting.* ■ exhaust; wear out; wear away.

out·weigh /ˌoutˈwā/ ▶*v.* [*trans.*] be heavier than: *Bob outweighed him by more than twenty-five pounds.* ■ be greater or more significant than: *the advantages greatly outweigh the disadvantages.*

out·went /ˌoutˈwent/ ▶ past of **OUTGO**.

out·wit /ˌoutˈwit/ ▶*v.* (**-wit·ted, -wit·ting**) [*trans.*] deceive or defeat by greater ingenuity: *Ray had outwitted many an opponent.*

out·work /ˈoutˌwərk/ ▶*n.* **1** a section of a fortification or system of defense that is in front of the main part. **2** *Brit.* work done outside the factory or office that provides it.
▶*v.* /ˌoutˈwərk/ [*trans.*] work harder, faster, or longer than: *Irwin simply outworks his opponent.* —**out·work·er** *n.* (in sense 2).

out·world /ˈoutˌwərld/ ▶*n.* (in science fiction) an outlying or alien planet. —**out·world·er** *n.*

out·worn /ˌoutˈwôrn/ ▶ past participle of **OUTWEAR**.
▶*adj.* out of date: *outworn prejudices.* ■ no longer usable or serviceable: *outworn lead flashings.*

out·yield /ˌoutˈyēld/ ▶*v.* [*trans.*] produce or yield more than: *plantations outyield managed natural forest.*

ou·zel /ˈōōzəl/ (also **ou·sel**) ▶*n.* a bird that resembles the blackbird, esp. the ring ouzel. See also **WATER OUZEL**. ▷Old English *ōsle* 'blackbird,' of Germanic origin; related to German *Amsel* 'blackbird.'

ou·zo /ˈōōzō/ ▶*n.* a Greek anise-flavored liqueur. ▷modern Greek.

o·va /ˈōvə/ ▶ plural form of **OVUM**.

o·val /ˈōvəl/ ▶*adj.* having a rounded and slightly elongated outline or shape, like that of an egg: *her smooth oval face* | *the game with the oval ball.*
▶*n.* a body, object, or design with such a shape or outline: *cut out two small ovals from the felt.* ■ an oval playing field or racing track. ▷mid 16th cent.: from French, or modern Latin *ovalis*, from Latin *ovum* 'egg.' —**o·val·i·ty** /ōˈvalitē/ *n.* —**o·val·ness** *n.*

ov·al·bu·min /ˌävəlˈbyōōmən; ˌōvəl-/ ▶*n.* *Biochemistry* albumin derived from the white of eggs. ▷mid 19th cent.: from Latin *ovi albumen* 'albumen of egg,' altered on the pattern of *albumin.*

O·val Of·fice the office of the president of the U.S., in the White House. ■ *figurative* this office regarded as representing the power of the executive branch of the U.S. government: *on orders from the Oval Office.*

o·val win·dow ▶*n.* informal term for **FENESTRA OVALIS** (see **FENESTRA**).

Ov·am·bo /ōˈvambō/ ▶*n.* (*pl.* same or **-bos**) **1** a member of a people of northern Namibia. **2** the Bantu language of this people.
▶*adj.* of or relating to the Ovambo or their language. ▷a local name, from *ova-* (prefix denoting a plural) + *ambo* 'man of leisure.'

Ov·am·bo·land /ōˈvämbōˌland/ a semiarid region of northern Namibia, the homeland of the Ovambo people.

o·var·i·an /ōˈve(ə)rēən/ ▶*adj.* of or relating to an ovary or the ovaries: *an ovarian cyst.*

o·var·i·an fol·li·cle ▶*n.* another term for **GRAAFIAN FOLLICLE**.

o·var·i·ec·to·my /ōˌve(ə)rēˈektəmē/ ▶*n.* (*pl.* **-mies**) surgical removal of one or both ovaries; oophorectomy.

o·var·i·ot·o·my /ōˌve(ə)rēˈätəmē/ ▶*n.* **1** surgical incision into an ovary. **2** another term for **OVARIECTOMY**.

o·va·ri·tis /ˌōvəˈrītis/ ▶*n.* another term for **OOPHORITIS**.

o·va·ry /ˈōv(ə)rē/ ▶*n.* (*pl.* **-ries**) a female reproductive organ in which ova or eggs are produced, present in humans and other vertebrates as a pair. ■ *Botany* the hollow base of the carpel of a flower, containing one or more ovules. ▷mid 17th cent.: from modern Latin *ovarium*, from Latin *ovum* 'egg.'

o·vate /ˈōˌvāt/ ▶*adj.* *chiefly Biology* having an oval outline or ovoid shape, like an egg. ▷mid 18th cent.: from Latin *ovatus* 'egg-shaped.'

o·va·tion /ōˈvāshən/ ▶*n.* **1** a sustained and enthusiastic show of appreciation from an audience, esp. by means of applause: *the performance received a thundering ovation.* **2** *Roman History* a processional entrance into Rome by a victorious commander, of lesser honor than a triumph. ▷early 16th cent. (sense 2): from Latin *ovatio(n-)*, from *ovare* 'exult.' The word had the sense 'exultation' from the mid 17th to early 19th cent.

ov·en /ˈəvən/ ▶*n.* an enclosed compartment, as in a kitchen range, for cooking and heating food. ■ a small furnace or kiln. ■ a cremation chamber in a Nazi concentration camp. ▷Old English *ofen*, of Germanic origin; related to Dutch *oven*, German *Ofen*, from an Indo-European root shared by Greek *ipnos.*

ov·en·bird /ˈəvənˌbərd/ ▶*n.* **1** a small tropical American bird belonging to a diverse family, many members of which make domed, ovenlike nests of mud. • Family Furnariidae (the **ovenbird family**): many genera and numerous species. The ovenbird family comprises the horneros, miners,and many others. **2** a migratory brown North American warbler that builds a domed, ovenlike nest on the ground. • *Seiurus aurocapillus*, subfamily Parulinae, family Emberizidae.

ov·en·proof /ˈəvənˌprōōf/ ▶*adj.* (of cookware) suitable for use in an oven; heat-resistant.

ov·en-read·y ▶*adj.* (of food) prepared before sale so as to be ready for cooking in an oven.

ov·en·ware /ˈəvənˌwer/ ▶*n.* dishes that can be used for cooking food in an oven.

o·ver /ˈōvər/ ▶*prep.* **1** extending directly upward from: *I saw flames over Berlin.* ■ above so as to cover or protect: *an oxygen tent over the bed* | *ladle this sauce over fresh pasta.* ■ extending above (a general area) from a vantage point: *views over Hyde Park.* ■ at the other side of; beyond: *over the hill is a small village.* **2** expressing passage or trajectory across: *she trudged over the lawn.* ■ beyond and falling or

o·ver·a·bundant *adj.*
o·ver·a·bun·dance *n.*
o·ver·a·bun·dant·ly *adv.*
o·ver·ac·tive *adj.*
o·ver·ac·tiv·i·ty *n.*
o·ver·am·bi·tious *adj.*
o·ver·am·bi·tion *n.*
o·ver·am·bi·tious·ly *adv.*
o·ver·anx·ious *adj.*
o·ver·anx·i·e·ty *n.*
o·ver·anx·ious·ly *adv.*
o·ver·bold *adj.*
o·ver·bold·ly *adv.*
o·ver·bold·ness *n.*
o·ver·bus·y *adj.*
o·ver·care·ful *adj.*
o·ver·care·ful·ly *adv.*
o·ver·cau·tion *adj.*
o·ver·cau·tious *adj.*
o·ver·cau·tious·ly *adv.*
o·ver·cau·tious·ness *n.*
o·ver·cook *v.*
o·ver·cu·ri·ous *adj.*
o·ver·cu·ri·os·i·ty *n.*
o·ver·del·i·cate *adj.*
o·ver·de·pend·ence *n.*
ov·er·de·pend·ent *adj.*
o·ver·drink *v.*
-drank, -drunk
o·ver·drink·ing *n.*
o·ver·ea·ger *adj.*
o·ver·ea·ger·ly *adv.*
o·ver·ea·ger·ness *n.*
o·ver·eat *v.*; **-ate, -eat·en**
o·ver·eat·er *n.*
o·ver·e·lab·o·rate *adj., v.*
o·ver·em·bel·lished *adj.*
o·ver·em·pha·sis *n.*
o·ver·en·thu·si·asm *n.*
o·ver·en·thu·si·as·tic *adj.*
o·ver·en·thu·si·as·ti·cal·ly *adv.*
o·ver·ex·er·cise *v.*
o·ver·ex·ert *v.*
o·ver·ex·er·tion *n.*
o·ver·ex·pan·sion *n.*
o·ver·fa·tigue *n.*
o·ver·feed *v.*; **-fed**
o·ver·fond *adj.*
o·ver·fond·ly *adv.*
o·ver·fond·ness *n.*
o·ver·full *adj.*
o·ver·gen·er·ous *adj.*
o·ver·hast·y *adj.*
o·ver·im·ag·i·na·tive *adj.*
o·ver·large *adj.*
o·ver·op·ti·mis·tic *adj.*
o·ver·op·ti·mism *n.*
o·ver·op·ti·mis·ti·cal·ly *adv.*
o·ver·re·fine *v.*
o·ver·re·fine·ment *n.*
o·ver·re·stric·tive *adj.*
o·ver·scru·pu·lous *adj.*
o·ver·scru·pu·lous·ness *n.*
o·ver·sen·si·tive *adj.*
o·ver·sen·si·tive·ness *n.*
o·ver·sen·si·tiv·i·ty *n.*
o·ver·sen·ti·men·tal *adj.*
o·ver·spe·cial·ize *v.*
o·ver·staff *v.*
o·ver·stress *v. & n.*
o·ver·stretch *v.*
o·ver·stretched *adj.*
o·ver·sub·tle *adj.*
o·ver·sus·cep·ti·ble *adj.*
o·ver·zeal·ous *adj.*
o·ver·zeal·ous·ness *n.*

---

hanging from: *it toppled over the cliff.* ■ expressing duration: *inventories have been refined over many years | she told me over coffee.* ■ by means of; by the medium of: *over the loudspeaker.* **3** at a higher level or layer than: *watching a television hanging over the bar.* ■ higher in grade or rank than: *over him is the financial director.* ■ expressing authority or control: *editorial control over what is included.* ■ expressing preference: *I'd choose the well-known brand over that one.* ■ expressing greater number: *the predominance of Asian over African managers in the sample.* ■ higher in volume or pitch than: *he shouted over the noise of the taxis.* **4** higher than or more than (a specified number or quantity): *over 40 degrees C | they have lived together for over a year.* **5** on the subject of: *a heated debate over unemployment.*

▸*adv.* **1** expressing passage or trajectory across an area: *he leaned over and tapped me on the hand.* ■ beyond and falling or hanging from a point: *listing over at an acute angle.* **2** in or to the place mentioned or indicated: *over here | come over and cheer us up.* **3** used to express action and result: *the car flipped over | hand the money over.* ■ finished: *the match is over | message understood,* ***over and out.*** **4** used to express repetition of a process: *twice over | the sums will have to be done over again.*

▸*n. Cricket* a sequence of six balls bowled by a bowler from one end of the pitch. ■ the period of play for this. ▷Old English *ofer,* of Germanic origin; related to Dutch *over* and German *über,* from an Indo-European word (originally a comparative of the element represented by *-ove* in *above*) which is also the base of Latin *super* and Greek *huper.*

▸*PHRASES* □ **be over** no longer be affected by: *we were over the worst.* □ **get something over with** do or undergo something unpleasant or difficult, so as to be rid of it. □ **over against** adjacent to: *over against the wall.* ■ in contrast with: *over against heaven is hell.* □ **over and above** in addition to: *exceptional service over and above what normally might be expected.* □ **over and done with** completely finished. □ **over and over** again and again.

over- ▸*prefix* **1** excessively; to an unwanted degree: *overambitious | overcareful.* ■ completely; utterly: *overawe | overjoyed.* **2** upper; outer; extra: *overcoat | overtime.* ■ overhead; above: *overcast | overhang.*

o·ver·a·chieve /ˌōvərəˈCHēv/ ▸*v.* [*intrans.*] do better than is expected, esp. in academic work: *David continued to overachieve all through high school.* ■ be excessively dedicated to the achievement of success in one's work. **—o·ver·a·chieve·ment** *n.* **—o·ver·a·chiev·er** *n.*

o·ver·act /ˌōvərˈakt/ ▸*v.* [*intrans.*] (of an actor) act a role in an exaggerated manner: *a weepy actress with a strong tendency to overact | [as n.]* (**overacting**) *there was a certain amount of overacting.*

o·ver·age[1] /ˈōv(ə)rij/ ▸*n.* an excess or surplus, esp. the amount by which a sum of money is greater than a previous estimate.

o·ver·age[2] /ˌōvərˈāj/ ▸*adj.* over a certain age limit: *a team of overage and underage ball players.*

o·ver·all ▸*adj.* /ˈōvəˌrôl/ [*attrib.*] total: *an overall cut of 30 percent.* ■ taking everything into account: *the overall effect is impressive.*

▸*adv.* /ˈōvəˈrôl/ [*sentence adverb*] in all parts; taken as a whole: *overall, 10,000 jobs will go.*

▸*n.* /ˈōvəˌrôl/ (**overalls**) a garment consisting of trousers with a front flap over the chest held up by straps over the shoulders, made of sturdy material and worn esp. as casual or working clothes. Also called **bib overalls.** ■ *Brit.* a loose-fitting garment such as a smock worn typically over ordinary clothes for protection against dirt or heavy wear. **—o·ver·alled** /ˈōvəˌrôld/ *adj.*

o·ver·arch /ˌōvərˈärCH/ ▸*v.* [*trans.*] form an arch over: *an old dirt road, overarched by forest.*

o·ver·arch·ing /ˌōvərˈärCHiNG/ ▸*adj.* [*attrib.*] forming an arch over something: *the overarching mangroves.* ■ comprehensive; all-embracing: *a single overarching principle.*

o·ver·arm /ˈōvərˌärm/ ▸*adj.* & *adv.* done with the arm moving above the level of the shoulder.

o·ver·awe /ˌōvərˈô/ ▸*v.* [*trans.*] (usu. **be overawed**) impress (someone) so much that they become silent or inhibited: *he used firepower to overawe the hostile tribes.*

o·ver·bal·ance /ˌōvərˈbaləns/ ▸*v.* [*trans.*] outweigh: *I fault the university for many things, but all are overbalanced by its unparalleled resources.* ■ fall or cause to fall over from loss of balance: [*intrans.*] *the ladder overbalanced on top of her.*

▸*n. archaic* excess of weight, value, or amount: *overbalance of propriety.*

o·ver·bear /ˌōvərˈber/ ▸*v.* (*past* **-bore**; *past part.* **-borne**) [*trans.*] overcome by emotional pressure or physical force: *his will had not been overborne by another's influence | he overbore the others who still favored a bold policy.*

o·ver·bear·ing /ˌōvərˈbe(ə)riNG/ ▸*adj.* unpleasantly or arrogantly domineering: *his overbearing, sometimes ruthless desire to succeed.* **—o·ver·bear·ing·ly** *adv.* **—o·ver·bear·ing·ness** *n.*

o·ver·bid ▸*v.* /ˌōvərˈbid/ (**-bid·ding;** *past* and *past part.* **-bid**) [*intrans.*] **1** (in an auction) make a higher bid than a previous bid. **2** (in competitive bidding, the auction in bridge, etc.) bid more than is warranted or manageable.

▸*n.* /ˈōvərˌbid/ a bid that is higher than is justified. **—o·ver·bid·der** *n.*

o·ver·bite /ˈōvərˌbīt/ ▸*n. Dentistry* the overlapping of the lower teeth by the upper.

o·ver·blouse /ˈōvərˌblous; -blouz/ ▸*n.* a blouse designed to be worn without being tucked in at the waist.

o·ver·blow·ing /ˌōvərˈblōiNG/ ▸*n.* a technique for playing a wind instrument so as to produce overtones.

o·ver·blown /ˌōvərˈblōn/ ▸*adj.* **1** excessively inflated or pretentious: *overblown dreams of glory and success.* **2** (of a flower) past its prime: *an overblown rose.*

o·ver·board /ˈōvərˌbôrd/ ▸*adv.* from a ship into the water: *the severe storm washed a man overboard.*

▸*PHRASES* □ **go overboard 1** be very enthusiastic: *Gary went overboard for you.* **2** react in an immoderate way: *Chris has a bit of a temper and can sometimes go overboard.* □ **throw something overboard** abandon or discard something.

o·ver·book /ˌōvərˈbo͝ok/ ▸*v.* [*trans.*] accept more reservations for (a flight, hotel, etc.) than there is room for: *airlines deliberately overbook some scheduled flights.*

o·ver·boot /ˈōvərˌbo͞ot/ ▸*n.* a boot worn over another boot or shoe to protect it or to provide extra warmth.

o·ver·bore /ˌōvərˈbôr/ ▸ past of OVERBEAR.

o·ver·borne /ˌōvərˈbôrn/ ▸ past participle of OVERBEAR.

o·ver·bought /ˌōvərˈbôt/ ▸ past and past participle of OVERBUY.

▸*adj. Stock Market* overvalued owing to excessive buying at unjustifiably high prices: *characterize the sell-off as a healthy correction to an overbought market.*

o·ver·breed /ˌōvərˈbrēd/ ▸*v.* (*past* and *past part.* **-bred**) breed or cause to breed to excess: *the husband and wife were forcing the female dogs to overbreed, and litters grew up with several health problems.*

o·ver·brim·ming /ˌōvərˈbrimiNG/ ▸*adj.* abundant, esp. excessively so: *overbrimming confidence.*

o·ver·build /ˌōvərˈbild/ ▸*v.* (*past* and *past part.* **-built**) [*trans.*] **1** put up too many buildings in (an area): *investors overbuilt the Atlantic and Mediterranean coasts.* ■ build too many: *to overbuild hotels would destroy the setting.* ■ build (something) elaborately or to a very high standard, esp. unnecessarily: *overbuilding something will always be safer than taking shortcuts.* **2** [often as *n.*] (**overbuilding**) build on top of: *the preservation of the medieval field pattern by direct overbuilding.*

o·ver·bur·den ▸*v.* /ˌōvərˈbərdn/ [*trans.*] (often **be overburdened**) load (someone) with too many things to carry: *they were overburdened with luggage.* ■ give (someone) more work or pressure than they can deal with: *the courts became overburdened with large numbers of relatively trivial offenses |* [as *adj.*] (**overburdened**) *overburdened teachers.*

▸*n.* /ˈōvərˌbərdn/ rock or soil overlying a mineral deposit, archaeological site, or other underground feature. ■ an excessive burden: *an overburden of costs.* **—o·ver·bur·den·some** /-səm/ *adj.*

o·ver·buy /ˌōvərˈbī/ ▸*v.* (*past* and *past part.* **-bought**) [*trans.*] buy more of (something) than one needs: *the tendency to overbuy software.*

o·ver·call *Bridge* ▸*v.* /ˌōvərˈkôl/ [*intrans.*] make a higher bid than an opponent's bid.

▸*n.* /ˈōvərˌkôl/ an act or instance of making such a bid.

o·ver·came /ˌōvərˈkām/ ▸ past of OVERCOME.

o·ver·ca·pac·i·ty /ˌōvərkəˈpasitē/ ▸*n.* the situation in which an industry or factory cannot sell as much as it can produce.

o·ver·cap·i·tal·ize /ˌōvərˈkapitlˌīz/ ▸*v.* [*trans.*] [usu. as *adj.*] (**overcapitalized**) provide (a company) with more capital than is advisable or necessary: *a bleak time for the overcapitalized firm.* ■ estimate or set the capital value of (a company) at too high an amount. **—o·ver·cap·i·tal·i·za·tion** /ˈōvərˌkapitl-iˈzāSHən/ *n.*

o·ver·cast ▸*adj.* /ˈōvərˌkast; ˌōvərˈkast/ **1** (of the sky or weather) marked by a covering of gray clouds; dull: *a chilly overcast day.* **2** (in sewing) edged with stitching to prevent fraying.

▸*n.* /ˈōvərˌkast/ clouds covering a large part of the sky: *the sky was leaden with overcast.*

▸*v.* /ˌōvərˈkast/ (*past* and *past part.* **-cast**) [*trans.*] **1** cover with clouds or shade: *the pebbled beach, overcast with the shadows of the high cliffs.* **2** stitch over (an unfinished edge) to prevent fraying: *finish off the raw edge of the hem by overcasting it.*

o·ver·charge ▸*v.* /ˌōvərˈCHärj/ [*trans.*] **1** charge (someone) too high a price for goods or a service: *that makes it easy for wheeler-dealers to overcharge customers.* ■ charge someone (a sum) beyond the correct amount: [with *two objs.*] *the company overcharged the government $3 million.* **2** put too much electric charge into (a battery). ■ put exaggerated or excessive detail into (a text or work of art): *the scenes are overcharged.*

▸*n.* /ˈōvərˌCHärj/ an excessive charge for goods or a service.

o·ver·check[1] /ˈōvərˌCHek/ ▸*n.* a check pattern superimposed on a color or design.

o·ver·check[2] ▸*n.* a strap passing over a horse's head between the ears, to pull up on the bit and make breathing easier.

Pronunciation Key ə ago; ər over; ˈə or ˌə up; ˈər or ˌər fur; a hat; ā rate; ä car; CH chew; e let; ē see; e(ə)r air; i fit; ī by; i(ə)r ear; NG sing; ō go; ô for; oi boy; o͝o good; o͞o goo; ou out; SH she; TH thin; TH then; (h)w why; ZH vision

o•ver•class /ˈōvərˌklas/ ▸*n.* a privileged, wealthy, or powerful subgroup in society.

o•ver•cloud /ˌōvərˈkloud/ ▸*v.* [*trans.*] mar, dim, or obscure.

o•ver•coat /ˈōvərˌkōt/ ▸*n.* **1** a long warm coat worn over other clothing. **2** a top, final layer of paint or a similar covering.

o•ver•come /ˌōvərˈkəm/ ▸*v.* (*past* **-came**; *past part.* **-come**) [*trans.*] succeed in dealing with (a problem or difficulty): *she worked hard to overcome her paralyzing shyness.* ■ defeat (an opponent); prevail: *without firing a shot they overcame the guards* | [*intrans.*] *we shall overcome.* ■ (usu. **be overcome**) (of an emotion) overpower or overwhelm: *she was obviously* ***overcome with*** *excitement.* ▷Old English *ofercuman* (see **OVER-**, **COME**).

o•ver•com•mit /ˌōvərkəˈmit/ ▸*v.* (**-mit•ted**, **-mit•ting**) [*trans.*] oblige (oneself or others) to do more than one is capable of, as to repay a loan one cannot afford: *multiple borrowers who may be overcommitting themselves.* ■ allocate more (resources) to a purpose than can be provided: *they could easily overcommit their budgets.* **—o•ver•com•mit•ment** *n.*

o•ver•com•pen•sate /ˌōvərˈkämpənˌsāt/ ▸*v.* [*intrans.*] take excessive measures in attempting to correct or make amends for an error, weakness, or problem: *he was* ***overcompensating for*** *fears about the future.* **—o•ver•com•pen•sat•ing•ly** /ˈōvərˌkämpənˈsātiNGlē/ *adv.* **—o•ver•com•pen•sa•tion** /ˈōvərˌkämpənˈsāSHən/ *n.* **—o•ver•com•pen•sa•to•ry** /ˈōvərkəmˈpensəˌtôrē/ *adj.*

o•ver•con•fi•dent /ˌōvərˈkänfidənt/ ▸*adj.* excessively or unreasonably confident: *mistakes made through being overconfident.* **—o•ver•con•fi•dence** *n.* **—o•ver•con•fi•dent•ly** *adv.*

o•ver•crit•i•cal /ˌōvərˈkritikəl/ ▸*adj.* inclined to find fault too readily.

o•ver•crop /ˌōvərˈkräp/ ▸*v.* (**-cropped**, **-crop•ping**) [*trans.*] [usu. as *n.*] (**overcropping**) deplete (soil) by growing crops continuously on it.

o•ver•crowd /ˌōvərˈkroud/ ▸*v.* [*trans.*] fill (accommodations or a space) beyond what is usual or comfortable: [as *adj.*] (**overcrowded**) *overcrowded dormitories* | [as *n.*] (**overcrowding**) *trying to eliminate overcrowding in the downtown area.* ■ house (people or animals) in accommodations that are too confined.

o•ver•date /ˈōvərˌdāt/ ▸*n.* a coin on which one date has been superimposed over another. **—o•ver•dat•ing** *n.*

o•ver•de•ter•mine /ˌōvərdiˈtərmən/ ▸*v.* [*trans.*] *technical* determine, account for, or cause (something) in more than one way or with more conditions than are necessary: *every gesture is overdetermined by cultural form, personal biography, historical contingency, and so on.* **—o•ver•de•ter•mi•na•tion** /ˈˌōvərdiˌtərməˈnāSHən/ *n.*

o•ver•de•vel•op /ˌōvərdəˈveləp/ ▸*v.* (**-vel•oped**, **-vel•op•ing**) [*trans.*] develop too much or to excess: *cycling may overdevelop the calf muscles* | [as *adj.*] (**overdeveloped**) *Majorca's overdeveloped coastline.* ■ *Photography* treat with developer for too long: *you can overdevelop the film to make up for underexposure.* **—o•ver•de•vel•op•ment** *n.*

o•ver•do /ˌōvərˈdo͞o/ ▸*v.* (**-does**; *past* **-did**; *past part.* **-done**) [*trans.*] carry to excess; exaggerate: *dramatic yet never overdone.* ■ use too much of (something): *I'd overdone the garlic in the curry.* ■ (**overdo it/things**) exhaust oneself by overwork or overexertion: *I'd simply overdone it in the gym.* ■ [often as *adj.*] (**overdone**) overcook (food): *chewing his overdone steak.* ▷Old English *oferdōn* (see **OVER-**, **DO**[1]).

o•ver•dose ▸*n.* /ˈōvərˌdōs/ an excessive and dangerous dose of a drug: *she took an overdose the day her husband left.*
▸*v.* /ˈōvərˌdōs; ˌōvərˈdōs/ [*intrans.*] take an overdose of a drug: *he was admitted to the hospital after* ***overdosing on*** *cocaine.* ■ [*trans.*] give an overdose to. **—o•ver•dos•age** /-ˈdōsij/ *n.*

o•ver•draft /ˈōvərˌdraft/ ▸*n.* a deficit in a bank account caused by drawing more money than the account holds.

o•ver•dram•a•tize /ˌōvərˈdraməˌtīz; -ˈdrämə-/ ▸*v.* [*trans.*] react to or portray (something) in an excessively dramatic manner. **—o•ver•dra•mat•ic** /-drəˈmatik/ *adj.*

o•ver•draw /ˌōvərˈdrô/ ▸*v.* (*past* **-drew**; *past part.* **-drawn**) [*trans.*] **1** (usu. **be overdrawn**) draw money from (one's bank account) in excess of what the account holds: *you only pay interest if your account is overdrawn.* ■ (**be overdrawn**) (of a person) have taken money out of an account in excess of what it holds: *I'm already overdrawn this month.* **2** exaggerate in describing or depicting (someone or something): *some of the characters were overdrawn.* **3** draw (a bow) too far.

o•ver•dress ▸*v.* /ˌōvərˈdres/ [*intrans.*] (also **be overdressed**) dress with too much display or formality: *Eugenie did not wish to overdress* | *she felt wildly overdressed in her velvet suit.*
▸*n.* /ˈōvərˌdres/ *chiefly Brit.* a dress worn over another dress or other clothing.

o•ver•drive /ˈōvərˌdrīv/ ▸*n.* a gear in a motor vehicle providing a gear ratio higher than that of the drive gear or top gear, so that engine speed and fuel consumption are reduced in highway travel. ■ a state of high or excessive activity: *the city's worried public relations arm* ***went into overdrive.*** ■ a mechanism that permits a higher than normal operating level in a piece of equipment, such as the amplifier of an electric guitar.
▸*v.* [*trans.*] [usu. as *adj.*] (**overdriven**) drive or work to exhaustion: *the overdriven mothers of ten or eleven hungry children.*

o•ver•dub ▸*v.* /ˌōvərˈdəb/ (**-dubbed**, **-dubbing**) record (additional sounds) on an existing recording: [*trans.*] *she'd overdub her parts for a whole album in a single session* | [*intrans.*] *a live tape that I overdubbed on.*
▸*n.* /ˈōvərdəb/ an instance of overdubbing: *a guitar overdub.*

o•ver•due /ˌōvərˈd(y)o͞o/ ▸*adj.* not yet having arrived, happened, or been done, though after the expected time: *reform is now overdue.* ■ (of a payment) not having been made, though required: *the rent was nearly three months overdue.* ■ (of a woman) having gone beyond the expected time for a menstrual period. ■ (of a baby) not having been born, though beyond full gestation: *our daughter was six days overdue.* ■ having deserved or needed something for some time: *she was* ***overdue for*** *some leave.* ■ (of a library book) retained longer than the period allowed.

o•ver eas•y ▸*adj.* (of a fried egg) turned over when the white is nearly done and fried lightly on the other side, so that the yolk remains slightly liquid.

o•ver•e•mo•tion•al /ˌōvəriˈmōSHənl/ ▸*adj.* (of a person) having feelings that are too easily excited and displayed: *we're not an overemotional family.* **—o•ver•e•mo•tion•al•ly** *adv.*

o•ver•em•pha•size /ˌōvərˈemfəˌsīz/ ▸*v.* [*trans.*] (usu. **be overemphasized**) place excessive emphasis on: *the importance of adequate preparation cannot be overemphasized.*

o•ver•es•ti•mate ▸*v.* /ˌōvərˈestəˌmāt/ [*trans.*] estimate (something) to be better, larger, or more important than it really is: *his influence cannot be overestimated.*
▸*n.* /-mit/ an excessively high estimate. **—o•ver•es•ti•ma•tion** /ˈōvərˌestəˈmāSHən/ *n.*

o•ver•ex•cite /ˌōvərikˈsīt/ ▸*v.* [*trans.*] [often as *adj.*] (**overexcited**) excite excessively: *playing an active game can overexcite children.* **—o•ver•ex•cit•a•ble** *adj.* **—o•ver•ex•cite•ment** *n.*

o•ver•ex•pose /ˌōvərikˈspōz/ ▸*v.* [*trans.*] expose too much, esp. to the public eye or to risk: *anybody in the public eye has situations that make them feel overexposed.* ■ *Photography* expose (film or a part of an image) for too long a time or for extra time: *the sunlit background is overexposed.* **—o•ver•ex•po•sure** /-ikˈspōZHər/ *n.*

o•ver•ex•tend /ˌōvərikˈstend/ ▸*v.* [*trans.*] (usu. **be overextended**) **1** make too long: *at nine minutes plus the song is somewhat overextended.* **2** impose on (someone) an excessive burden of work or commitments: *he should not overextend himself on the mortgage.* **—o•ver•ex•ten•sion** /-ˈstenSHən/ *n.*

o•ver•fall /ˈōvərˌfôl/ ▸*n.* a turbulent stretch of open water caused by the wind blowing against a current, by a strong current or tide over an underwater ridge, or by a meeting of currents. ■ a place where surplus water overflows from a dam, pond, etc.

o•ver•fa•mil•iar /ˌōvərfəˈmilyər/ ▸*adj.* too well known: *the overfamiliar teacher's voice.* ■ [*predic.*] (**overfamiliar with**) too well acquainted with: *the researcher is overfamiliar with the community.* ■ behaving or speaking in an inappropriately informal way: *her private detective was dismissed for being* ***overfamiliar with*** *her.* **—o•ver•fa•mil•i•ar•i•ty** /-fəˌmilēˈaritē/ *n.*

o•ver•fill /ˌōvərˈfil/ ▸*v.* [*trans.*] put more into (a container) than it either should or can contain.

o•ver•fine /ˌōvərˈfīn/ ▸*adj.* excessively or extremely fine or particular: *the distinction may seem overfine to Westerners.*

o•ver•fish /ˌōvərˈfiSH/ ▸*v.* [*trans.*] deplete the stock of fish in (a body of water) by too much fishing: *this part of the Mediterranean is terribly overfished.* ■ deplete the stock of (a fish): *yellowfin tuna has been overfished.*

o•ver•flow ▸*v.* /ˌōvərˈflō/ [*intrans.*] (esp. of a liquid) flow over the brim of a receptacle: *chemicals overflowed from a storage tank* | [*trans.*] *the river overflowed its banks.* ■ (of a container) be so full that the contents go over or extend above the sides: *a bath had overflowed upstairs* | *boxes* ***overflowing with*** *bright flowers* | [as *adj.*] (**overflowing**) *an overflowing ashtray.* ■ (of a space) be so crowded that people cannot fit inside: *the waiting area was overflowing.* ■ [*trans.*] flood or flow over (a surface or area): *her hair overflowed her shoulders.* ■ (**overflow with**) *figurative* be very full of (an emotion or quality): *her heart overflowed with joy.*
▸*n.* /ˈōvərˌflō/ **1** [in *sing.*] the excess or surplus not able to be accommodated by an available space: *to accommodate the overflow, five more offices have been built.* ■ the flowing over of a liquid: *there was some overflow after heavy rainfall* | *an overflow of sewage.* **2** (also **overflow pipe**) (in a bathtub or sink) an outlet for excess water. **3** *Computing* the generation of a number or some other data item that is too large for an assigned location or memory space. ▷Old English *oferflōwan* (see **OVER-**, **FLOW**).
▸*PHRASE* □ **full to overflowing** completely full.

o•ver•fly /ˌōvərˈflī/ ▸*v.* (**-flies**; *past* **-flew**; *past part.* **-flown**) [*trans.*] fly over (a place or territory): *there was a delay in obtaining clearance to overfly Israel.* ■ fly beyond (a place or thing): *overfly the radio beacon by approximately fifteen seconds.* **—o•ver•flight** /ˈōvərˌflīt/ *n.*

o•ver•fold /ˈōvərˌfōld/ ▸*n.* a part of something that is folded over another part: *the tunic is belted over a long overfold.*

o•ver•ful•fill /ˌōvərfo͝olˈfil/ (*Brit.* **o•ver•ful•fil**) ▸*v.* (**-filled**, **-fil•ling**) [*trans.*] fulfill (a contract or quota) earlier or in greater quantity than required: *he overfulfilled the quota by forty percent.* **—o•ver•ful•fill•ment** *n.*

o•ver•fund /ˌōvərˈfənd/ ▸*v.* [*trans.*] provide more funding for (something) than is necessary or permitted.

o•ver•gar•ment /ˈōvərˌgärmənt/ ▸*n.* a garment that is worn over others.

o•ver•gen•er•al•ize /ˌōvərˈjen(ə)rəˌlīz/ ▸*v.* [*trans.*] draw a conclusion or make a statement about (something) that is more general than is justified by the available evidence. **—o•ver•gen•er•al•i•za•tion** /-ˌjen(ə)rəliˈzāSHən/ *n.*

o•ver•glaze /ˌōvərˈglāz/ ▸*n.* decoration or a second glaze applied to glazed ceramic ware.
▸*adj.* (of painting, printing, or other decoration) done on a glazed surface: *overglaze enamel.*

o•ver•graze /ˌōvərˈgrāz/ ▸*v.* [*trans.*] graze (grassland) so heavily that the vegetation is damaged and the ground becomes liable to erosion: *their own pastures were overgrazed and arid* | [as *n.*] (**overgrazing**) *the failure of the rains led to overgrazing and deforestation.*

o•ver•ground /ˈōvərˌground/ ▸*adv.* & *adj.* on or above the ground: [as *adv.*] *subway lines that go overground* | [as *attrib. adj.*] *a heating system pipes heat along overground tubes.* ■ [as *attrib. adj.*] legitimate; not underground: *overground political processes.*

o•ver•grow /ˌōvərˈgrō/ ▸*v.* (*past* **-grew**; *past part.* **-grown**) [*trans.*] grow or spread over (something), esp. so as to choke or stifle it: *the mussels overgrow and smother whatever is underneath.*

o•ver•grown /ˌōvərˈgrōn/ ▸*adj.* **1** covered with plants that have been allowed to grow wild: *the garden was overgrown and deserted.* **2** grown too large or beyond its normal size: *the town is only an overgrown village.* ■ *chiefly derogatory* used to describe an adult behaving in a childish manner: *a pair of overgrown schoolboys.*

o•ver•growth /ˈōvərˌgrōTH/ ▸*n.* excessive growth: *intestinal bacterial overgrowth.*

o•ver•hand /ˈōvərˌhand/ ▸*adj.* & *adv.* (chiefly of a throw or a stroke with a racket) made with the hand or arm passing above the level of the shoulder: *pitch overhand* | *sidearm and overhand techniques.* ■ with the palm of the hand over what it grasps: [as *adj.*] *an overhand grip.* ■ *Boxing* (of a punch) passing over the other hand: *caught him with an overhand right.*

o•ver•hand knot ▸*n.* a simple knot made by forming a loop and passing a free end around the standing part and through the loop.

o•ver•hang ▸*v.* /ˌōvərˈhaNG/ (*past* and *past part.* **-hung**) [*trans.*] hang or extend outward over: *a concrete path overhung by trees* | [as *adj.*] (**overhanging**) *overhanging branches.* ■ *figurative* loom over: *the film's mood is overhung with impending death.*
▸*n.* /ˈōvərˌhaNG/ a part of something that sticks out or

hangs over another thing: *he crouched beneath an overhang of bushes.*

o·ver·haul ▶*v.* /ˌōvərˈhôl/ [*trans.*] **1** take apart (a piece of machinery or equipment) in order to examine it and repair it if necessary: *a company that overhauls and repairs aircraft engines | figurative moves to overhaul the income tax system.* **2** *Brit.* overtake (someone), esp. in a sporting event.
▶*n.* /ˈōvərˌhôl/ a thorough examination of machinery or a system, with repairs or changes made if necessary: *a major overhaul of environmental policies.* ▷early 17th cent. (originally in nautical use in the sense 'release (rope tackle) by slackening'): from OVER- + HAUL.

o·ver·head ▶*adv.* /ˈōvərˈhed/ above the level of the head; in the sky: *a helicopter buzzed overhead.*
▶*adj.* /ˈōvərˌhed/ **1** situated above the level of the head: *the sun was directly overhead | overhead power cables.* **2** (of a driving mechanism) above the object driven: *an overhead cam four-cylinder engine.* **3** [*attrib.*] (of a cost or expense) incurred in the general upkeep or running of a plant, premises, or business, and not attributable to specific products or items.
▶*n.* /ˈōvərˌhed/ **1** overhead cost or expense: *research conducted in space requires more overhead.* **2** a transparency designed for use with an overhead projector. **3** short for OVERHEAD PROJECTOR. **4** an overhead compartment: *fits in most airline overheads.* **5** *Tennis* a shot directed sharply downward, hit while the ball is over the head; a smash.

o·ver·head pro·jec·tor ▶*n.* a device that projects an enlarged image of a transparency placed on it onto a wall or screen by means of an overhead mirror.

o·ver·hear /ˌōvərˈhir/ ▶*v.* (*past* and *past part.* **-heard**) [*trans.*] hear (someone or something) without meaning to or without the knowledge of the speaker: *I couldn't help overhearing your conversation.*

o·ver·heat /ˌōvərˈhēt/ ▶*v.* make or become too hot: [*intrans.*] *her car started to overheat* | [*trans.*] *it's vital not to overheat the liquid.* ■ make too excited: [as *adj.*] (**overheated**) *his overheated imagination.* ■ *Economics* (of a country's economy) show marked inflation when increased demand results in rising prices rather than increased output: [*intrans.*] *lending rates could soar as the economy overheats* | [*trans.*] *credit expansion helped overheat the economy.*

o·ver·hit /ˌōvərˈhit/ ▶*v.* (*past* and *past part.* **-hit**; **-hit·ting**) (in tennis and other sports played with a ball) hit the ball too strongly or too far: *Glenders has overhit another ball* | [*intrans.*] *Marat Safin was overhitting, mucking up volleys, but he won anyway.*

o·ver·hype ▶*v.* /ˌōvərˈhīp/ [*trans.*] make exaggerated claims about (a product, idea, or event); publicize or promote excessively: *it would appear that the organizers overhyped the crowd size.*
▶*n.* /ˈōvərˌhīp/ excessive publicity or promotion: *were the media more rational about it, the unmistakable taste of overhype would not be so strong.*

O·ver·ijs·sel /ˌōvərˈīsəl/ a province of the east central Netherlands, north of the IJssel River, on the border with Germany; capital, Zwolle.

o·ver·in·dulge /ˌōvərənˈdəlj/ ▶*v.* [*intrans.*] have too much of something enjoyable, esp. food or drink: *it is easy to* **overindulge in** *these kinds of foods.* ■ [*trans.*] gratify the wishes of (someone) to an excessive extent: *his mother had overindulged him.* **—o·ver·in·dul·gence** /-ˈdəljəns/ *n.* **—o·ver·in·dul·gent** /-ˈdəljənt/ *adj.*

o·ver·in·flat·ed /ˌōvərinˈflātid/ ▶*adj.* **1** (of a price or value) excessive: *overinflated land values.* ■ exaggerated: *there have been so many overinflated claims and unfulfilled promises.* **2** filled with too much air: *an overinflated balloon.* **—o·ver·in·fla·tion** /-ˈflāsʜən/ *n.*

o·ver·in·sured /ˌōvərinˈsʜo͝ord/ ▶*adj.* having insurance coverage beyond what is necessary. **—o·ver·in·sur·ance** /-ˈsʜo͝orəns/ *n.*

o·ver·is·sue /ˌōvərˈisʜo͞o/ ▶*v.* (**-is·sues**, **-is·sued**, **-is·suing**) [*trans.*] issue (bonds, shares of stock, etc.) beyond the authorized amount or the issuer's ability to pay them on demand.
▶*n.* the action of overissuing bonds, shares of stock, etc.

o·ver·joyed /ˌōvərˈjoid/ ▶*adj.* extremely happy: *Joanna will be overjoyed to see you.*

o·ver·kill /ˈōvərˌkil/ ▶*n.* the amount by which destruction or the capacity for destruction exceeds what is necessary: *the existing nuclear overkill.* ■ excessive use, treatment, or action; too much of something: *animators now face a dilemma of technology overkill.*

o·ver·lad·en /ˌōvərˈlādn/ ▶*adj.* having too large or too heavy a load: *an overladen trolley | figurative the film is overladen with tear-jerking moments.*

o·ver·laid /ˌōvərˈlād/ ▶ past and past participle of OVERLAY[1].

o·ver·lain /ˌōvərˈlān/ ▶ past participle of OVERLIE.

o·ver·land /ˈōvərˌland/ ▶*adj.* & *adv.* by land: [as *adj.*] *an overland trade route* | [as *adv.*] *she journeyed overland.*

O·ver·land Park /ˈōvərlənd/ a city in northeastern Kansas, southwest of Kansas City; pop. 149,080.

o·ver·lap ▶*v.* /ˌōvərˈlap/ (**-lapped**, **-lap·ping**) [*trans.*] extend over so as to cover partly: *the canopy overlaps the house roof at one end* | [*intrans.*] *the curtains overlap at the center when closed.* ■ [*intrans.*] cover part of the same area of interest, responsibility, etc.: *their duties sometimes overlapped.* ■ [*intrans.*] partly coincide in time: *two new series overlapped.*
▶*n.* /ˈōvərˌlap/ a part or amount that overlaps: *an overlap of about half an inch.* ■ a common area of interest, responsibility, etc.: *there are many overlaps between the approaches | there is some overlap in requirements.* ■ a period of time in which two events or activities happen together.

o·ver·lay[1] ▶*v.* /ˌōvərˈlā/ (*past* and *past part.* **-laid**) [*trans.*] (often **be overlaid with**) cover the surface of (a thing) with a coating: *their fingernails were overlaid with silver or gold.* ■ lie on top of: *a third screen which will overlay the others.* ■ *figurative* (of a quality or feeling) become more prominent than (a previous quality or feeling): *his openness had been overlaid by his new self-confidence.*
▶*n.* /ˈōvərˌlā/ **1** something laid as a covering over something else: *a durable, cost-effective floor overlay.* ■ a transparency placed over artwork or something such as a map, marked with additional information or detail. ■ a graphical computer display that can be superimposed on another. **2** *Computing* the process of transferring a block of program code or other data into internal memory, replacing what is already stored. ■ a block of code or other data transferred in such a way.

o·ver·lay[2] /ˌōvərˈlā/ ▶ past of OVERLIE.

o·ver·leaf /ˈōvərˌlēf/ ▶*adv.* on the other side of the page: *an information sheet is printed overleaf.*

o·ver·leap /ˌōvərˈlēp/ ▶*v.* (*past* and *past part.* **-leaped** or **-leapt**) [*trans.*] *archaic* jump over or across: *a stream that any five-years' child might overleap.* ■ omit; ignore: *whatever objection made by us, he finds too heavy to remove, he overleaps it.* ▷Old English *oferhlēapan* (see OVER, LEAP).

o·ver·lie /ˌōvərˈlī/ ▶*v.* (**-ly·ing**; *past* **-lay**; *past part.* **-lain**) [*trans.*] lie on top of: *soft clays overlie the basalt | figurative the national situation was overlain by sharp regional differences.*

o·ver·load ▶*v.* /ˌōvərˈlōd/ [*trans.*] load with too great a burden or cargo: [as *adj.*] (**overloaded**) *overloaded vehicles are dangerous.* ■ give too much of something, typically something undesirable, to (someone): *the staff is heavily overloaded with casework.* ■ put too great a demand on (an electrical system): *the wiring had been overloaded.*
▶*n.* /ˈōvərˌlōd/ [in *sing.*] an excessive load or amount: *an overload of stress | momentary surges and overloads in the circuit.*

o·ver·lock /ˌōvərˈläk/ ▶*v.* [*trans.*] strengthen and prevent fraying of (an edge of cloth) by oversewing it. **—o·ver·lock·er** /ˈōvərˌläkər/ *n.*

o·ver·long /ˈōvərˈlôɴɢ; -ˈläɴɢ/ ▶*adj.* & *adv.* too long: [as *adj.*] *an overlong sermon* | [as *adv.*] *the pass was delayed overlong.*

o·ver·look ▶*v.* /ˈōvərˈlo͝ok/ [*trans.*] **1** fail to notice (something): *he seems to have overlooked one important fact.* See note at NEGLECT. ■ ignore or disregard (something, esp. a fault or offense): *she was more than ready to overlook his faults.* ■ pass over (someone) in favor of another: *he was overlooked by the Nobel committee.* **2** have a view of from above: *the chateau overlooks fields of corn and olive trees.* **3** *archaic* supervise; oversee. **4** *archaic* bewitch with the evil eye: *they told them they were overlooked by some unlucky Person.*
▶*n.* /ˈōvərlo͝ok/ a commanding position or view: *he veered off the highway onto an overlook.*

o·ver·lord /ˈōvərˌlôrd/ ▶*n.* a ruler, esp. a feudal lord. ■ a person of great power or authority: *the undisputed overlord of the crime family.* **—o·ver·lord·ship** /-ˌsʜip/ *n.*

o·ver·ly /ˈōvərlē/ ▶*adv.* [as *submodifier*] excessively: *she was a jealous and overly possessive woman.*

o·ver·ly·ing /ˈōvərˈlī-iɴɢ/ ▶ present participle of OVERLIE.

o·ver·man ▶*v.* /ˌōvərˈman/ (**-manned**, **-man·ning**) [*trans.*] provide with more people than necessary: *the company was vastly overmanned.*
▶*n.* /ˈōvərmən; -ˌman/ (*pl.* **-men**) **1** an overseer. **2** *Philosophy* another term for SUPERMAN. [translation of Nietzsche's *Übermensch.*]

o·ver·man·tel /ˈōvərˌmantl/ ▶*n.* an ornamental structure over a mantelpiece, typically of plaster or carved wood and sometimes including a mirror.

o·ver·mas·ter /ˌōvərˈmastər/ ▶*v.* *poetic/literary* [*trans.*] overcome; conquer: *he was overmastered by events* | [as *adj.*] (**overmastering**) *his first grand and overmastering love.*

o·ver·match /ˌōvərˈmacʜ/ ▶*v.* [*trans.*] [usu. as *adj.*] (**overmatched**) be stronger, better armed, or more skillful than: *Bosnia's overmatched forces.*

o·ver·meas·ure /ˌōvərˈmezʜər/ ▶*n.* an amount beyond what is proper or sufficient.

o·ver·much /ˈōvərˈməcʜ/ ▶*adv., adj.,* & *pron.* too much: [as *adv.*] *I would not worry myself overmuch* | [as *adj.*] *the police may have overmuch regard for public order considerations* | [as *pron.*] *she was requiring overmuch from him.*

o·ver·nice /ˌōvərˈnīs/ ▶*adj.* *dated* excessively fussy or fastidious: *Mildred was overnice in regard to their father.*

o·ver·night /ˈōvərˈnīt/ ▶*adv.* for the duration of a night: *they refused to stay overnight.* ■ during the course of a night: *you can recharge the battery overnight.* ■ very quickly; suddenly: *attitudes will not change overnight.*
▶*adj.* /ˈōvərˌnīt/ [*attrib.*] for use overnight: *an overnight bag.* ■ done or happening overnight: *an overnight stay.* ■ sudden, rapid, or instant: *Tom became an overnight celebrity.*
▶*v.* /ˌōvərˈnīt/ [*intrans.*] stay for the night in a particular place: *I overnighted at the Beverly Wilshire.* ■ [*trans.*] ship for delivery the next day: *Forster overnighted the sample to headquarters by courier.*
▶*n.* /ˈōvərˌnīt/ a stop or stay lasting one night: *overnights can be arranged in Kathmandu.*

o·ver·night·er /ˌōvərˈnītər/ ▶*n.* a person who stops at a place overnight. ■ an overnight bag. ■ an overnight trip or stay.

o·ver·pack /ˌōvərˈpak/ ▶*v.* **1** [*trans.*] pack too many items into (a container). **2** [*intrans.*] add a protective layer to items or material packed in a container: *we always overpack, with the usual two inches of packaging material all the way around.*

o·ver·paint /ˌōvərˈpānt/ ▶*v.* [*trans.*] cover with a layer of paint.
▶*n.* paint added as a covering layer.

o·ver·pass ▶*n.* /ˈōvərˌpas/ a bridge by which a road or railroad passes over another.
▶*v.* /ˌōvərˈpas/ [*trans.*] pass over; traverse. ■ surpass: *a capacity to overpass old limits.* ■ *archaic* come to the end of (something): *the time of respite now being overpast, the king demanded surrender.*

o·ver·pay /ˌōvərˈpā/ ▶*v.* (*past* and *past part.* **-paid**) [*trans.*] pay (someone) too highly: *many fans think our top players are overpaid.* ■ pay (money) in excess of what is due: *to overpay taxes.* **—o·ver·pay·ment** *n.*

o·ver·play /ˌōvərˈplā/ ▶*v.* [*trans.*] give undue importance to; overemphasize: *he thinks the idea of a special relationship between sitter and artist is much overplayed.* ■ exaggerate the performance of (a dramatic role): *the uncontrollable urge of ham actors to overplay their parts.* ■ *Sports* play very aggressively.
▶*PHRASE* □ **overplay one's hand 1** (in a card game) play or bet on one's hand with a mistaken optimism. **2** spoil one's chance of success through excessive confidence in one's position.

o·ver·plus /ˈōvərˌpləs/ ▶*n.* *dated* a surplus or excess: *an overplus of one ingredient.* ▷late Middle English: partial translation of French *surplus* or medieval Latin *superplus.*

o·ver·pop·u·late /ˌōvərˈpäpyəˌlāt/ ▶*v.* [*trans.*] populate (an area) in too large numbers: *the country was overpopulated.* ■ [*intrans.*] (of an animal) breed too rapidly: *without natural predators, deer would overpopulate.* **—o·ver·pop·u·la·tion** /ˈōvərˌpäpyəˈlāsʜən/ *n.*

o·ver·pow·er /ˌōvərˈpou(-ə)r/ ▶*v.* [*trans.*] defeat or overcome with superior strength. ■ be too intense for; overwhelm: *they were overpowered by the fumes* | [as *adj.*] (**overpowering**) *a feeling of overpowering sadness.* **—o·ver·pow·er·ing·ly** *adv.*

o·ver·pre·scribe /ˌōvərpriˈskrīb/ ▶*v.* [*trans.*] prescribe (a drug or treatment) in greater amounts or on more occasions than necessary: *doctors have been overprescribing antibiotics for decades.* **—o·ver·pre·scrip·tion** /-ˈskripsʜən/ *n.*

o·ver·price /ˌōvərˈprīs/ ▸*v.* [*trans.*] [often as *adj.*] (**overpriced**) charge too high a price for: *overpriced hotels.*

o·ver·print ▸*v.* /ˌōvərˈprint/ [*trans.*] **1** print additional matter on (a stamp or other surface already bearing print): *menus will be* **overprinted with** *company logos.* ■ print (additional matter) on something already printed. **2** print too many copies or too much of: [as *n.*] (**overprinting**) *the overprinting of paper money.* **3** *Photography* make (a print or other positive) darker than intended.
▸*n.* /ˈōvərˌprint/ words or other matter printed onto something already bearing print. ■ an overprinted postage stamp.

o·ver·pro·duce /ˌōvərprəˈd(y)o͞os/ ▸*v.* [*trans.*] **1** produce more of (a product or commodity) than is wanted or needed: *our unplanned manufacturing system continually overproduces consumer products.* **2** [often as *adj.*] (**overproduced**) record or produce (a song or film) in an elaborate or overdone way: *a series of overproduced albums.* —**o·ver·pro·duc·tion** /-ˈdəksHən/ *n.*

o·ver·proof /ˈōvərˈpro͞of/ ▸*adj.* containing more alcohol than proof spirit does: *overproof rum.*

o·ver·pro·tec·tive /ˌōvərprəˈtektiv/ ▸*adj.* having a tendency to protect someone, esp. a child, excessively. —**o·ver·pro·tect** *v.* —**o·ver·pro·tec·tion** /-ˈteksHən/ *n.* —**o·ver·pro·tec·tive·ness** *n.*

o·ver·qual·i·fied /ˌōvərˈkwôləˌfīd/ ▸*adj.* having qualifications that exceed the requirements of a particular job.

o·ver·ran /ˌōvərˈran/ ▸ past of **OVERRUN**.

o·ver·rate /ˌōvərˈrāt/ ▸*v.* [*trans.*] [often as *adj.*] (**overrated**) have a higher opinion of (someone or something) than is deserved: *dismissing the work as pompous and overrated.*

o·ver·reach /ˌōvərˈrēcH/ ▸*v.* **1** [*intrans.*] reach too far: *never lean sideways from a ladder or overreach.* ■ (**overreach oneself**) defeat one's own purpose by trying to do more than is possible: *he was an arrogant egotist who overreached himself.* ■ (of a horse, dog, or other quadruped) bring the hind feet so far forward that they fall alongside or strike the forefeet: *the horse overreached jumping the first hurdle.* **2** [*trans.*] get the better of (someone) by cunning: *Faustus's lunacy in thinking he can overreach the devil.*
▸*n.* an injury to a forefoot of a horse resulting from its having overreached.

o·ver·reach·er /ˌōvərˈrēcHər/ ▸*n.* an excessively ambitious or haughty person.

o·ver·re·act /ˌōvər-rēˈakt/ ▸*v.* [*intrans.*] respond more emotionally or forcibly than is justified: *they are urging people not to* **overreact to** *the problem.* —**o·ver·re·ac·tion** /-rēˈaksHən/ *n.*

o·ver·re·port /ˌōvər-riˈpôrt/ ▸*v.* [*trans.*] report (an event or instance of something) with disproportionately great frequency or emphasis: *newspapers overreported sexual offenses.*

o·ver·rep·re·sent ▸*v.* [*trans.*] include a disproportionately large number of (a particular category or type of person), as in a statistical study. ■ (**be overrepresented**) form a disproportionately large percentage: *they are relatively overrepresented in semiskilled occupations.* —**o·ver·rep·re·sen·ta·tion** *n.*

o·ver·ride ▸*v.* /ˌōvərˈrīd/ (*past* **-rode**; *past part.* **-rid·den**) [*trans.*] **1** use one's authority to reject or cancel (a decision, view, etc.): *the legislature's insistence on overriding his budget vetoes.* ■ interrupt the action of (an automatic device), typically in order to take manual control: *you can override the cutout by releasing the switch.* ■ be more important than: *this commitment should override all other considerations.* **2** *technical* extend over; overlap: *the external rendering should not override the vapor barrier.* **3** travel or move over (a place or thing): *part of the deposit was overridden and covered by the advancing ice.*
▸*n.* /ˈōvərˌrīd/ **1** a device for suspending an automatic function on a machine. ■ the action or process of suspending an automatic function. **2** an excess or increase on a budget, salary, or cost. ■ a commission paid to a manager on sales made by a subordinate or representative. **3** a cancellation of a decision by exertion of authority or winning of votes: *the House vote in favor of the bill was ten votes short of the requisite majority for an override.*

o·ver·rid·ing /ˌōvərˈrīdiNG/ ▸*adj.* **1** more important than any other considerations: *their overriding need will be for advice.* **2** *technical* extending or moving over something, esp. while remaining in close contact: *oceanic lithosphere beneath an overriding continental plate.*

o·ver·ripe /ˌōvərˈrīp/ ▸*adj.* too ripe; past its best: *overripe tomatoes.* ■ *figurative* decadent: *overripe civilizations wavering on the brink of decay.*

o·ver·ruff /ˌōvərˈrəf/ ▸*v.* another term for **OVERTRUMP**.

o·ver·rule /ˌōvərˈro͞ol/ ▸*v.* [*trans.*] reject or disallow by exercising one's superior authority: *the Supreme Court overruled the lower court.* ■ reject the decision or argument of (someone): *he was overruled by his senior managers.*

o·ver·run ▸*v.* /ˌōvərˈrən/ (**-run·ning**; *past* **-ran**; *past part.* **-run**) [*trans.*] **1** spread over or occupy (a place) in large numbers: *the Mediterranean has been overrun by tourists.* ■ conquer or occupy (territory) by force: *the northern frontier was overrun by invaders.* ■ move or extend over or beyond: *let the text overrun the right-hand margin.* ■ run over or beyond (a thing or place): *she overran third base.* ■ rotate faster than (another part of a machine): [as *adj.*] (**overrunning**) *an overrunning clutch.* **2** continue beyond or above (an expected or allowed time or cost): *he mustn't overrun his budget.*
▸*n.* /ˈōvərˌrən/ **1** an instance of something exceeding an expected or allowed time or cost: *an unexpectedly large cost overrun in the program.* ■ the amount by which this happens: *a $2.7 billion overrun on development and production.* ■ a surplus in manufacturing: *production overruns by some OPEC members.* **2** the movement or extension of something beyond an allotted or particular position or space: *the system acts as a brake to prevent cable overrun.* ■ a clear area beyond the end of an airport runway. **3** the movement of a vehicle at a speed greater than is imparted by the engine. ▷Old English *oferyrnan* (see **OVER-**, **RUN**).

o·ver·sam·pling /ˈōvərˈsampliNG/ ▸*n.* *Electronics* the technique of increasing the apparent sampling frequency of a digital signal by repeating each digit a number of times, in order to facilitate the subsequent filtering of unwanted noise.

o·ver·scan /ˈōvərˌskan/ ▸*n.* the facility on some computer screens or televisions to adjust the picture size so that objects appear bigger but the edges of the picture are lost.

o·ver·seas /ˈōvərˈsēz/ (*Brit.* also **o·ver·sea**) ▸*adv.* in or to a foreign country, esp. one across the sea: *he spent quite a lot of time working overseas.*
▸*adj.* [*attrib.*] from, to, or relating to a foreign country, esp. one across the sea: *overseas trips.*
▸*PHRASE* □ **from overseas** from abroad.

o·ver·see /ˌōvərˈsē/ ▸*v.* (**-sees**; *past* **-saw**; *past part.* **-seen**) [*trans.*] supervise (a person or work), esp. in an official capacity: *a trustee appointed to oversee Corrie's finances.* ▷Old English *oferséon* 'look at from above' (see **OVER-**, **SEE**[1]).

o·ver·se·er /ˈōvərˌsi(ə)r; -ˌsēər/ ▸*n.* a person who supervises others, esp. workers. ▷late Middle English (also denoting a person appointed by a testator to assist the executor of a will): from **OVERSEE**.

o·ver·sell /ˌōvərˈsel/ ▸*v.* (*past* and *past part.* **-sold** /-ˈsōld/) [*trans.*] sell more of (something) than exists or can be delivered: *a surge in airlines overselling flights.* ■ exaggerate the merits of: *computer-aided software engineering has been oversold.*

o·ver·set /ˌōvərˈset/ ▸*v.* (**-set·ting**; *past* and *past part.* **-set**) [*trans.*] **1** upset emotionally: *the small kindness nearly overset her again.* **2** *chiefly Brit.* overturn: *he jumped up and overset the canoe.* **3** *Printing* set up (type) in excess of the available space.

o·ver·sew /ˌōvərˈsō/ ▸*v.* (*past part.* **-sewn** or **-sewed**) [*trans.*] sew (the edges of two pieces of fabric) with every stitch passing over the join: *oversew the two long edges together.* ■ join the sections of (a book) in such a way.

o·ver·sexed /ˌōvərˈsekst/ ▸*adj.* having unusually strong sexual desires.

o·ver·shad·ow /ˌōvərˈsHadō/ ▸*v.* [*trans.*] tower above and cast a shadow over: *an enormous oak tree stood overshadowing the cottage.* ■ *figurative* cast a gloom over: *it is easy to let this feeling of tragedy overshadow his story.* ■ appear much more prominent or important than: *his competitive nature often overshadows the other qualities.* ■ (often **be overshadowed**) be more impressive or successful than (another person): *he was always overshadowed by his brilliant elder brother.* ▷Old English *ofersceadwian* (see **OVER-**, **SHADOW**).

o·ver·shoe /ˈōvərˌsHo͞o/ ▸*n.* a shoe worn over a normal shoe, typically either of waterproof material to protect the normal shoe in wet weather or of fabric to protect a floor surface.

o·ver·shoot ▸*v.* /ˌōvərˈsHo͞ot/ (*past* and *past part.* **-shot**) [*trans.*] go past (a point) unintentionally, esp. through traveling too fast or being unable to stop: *they overshot their intended destination* | [*intrans.*] *he had overshot by fifty yards but backed up to the junction.* ■ (of an aircraft) fly beyond or taxi too far along (the runway) when landing or taking off: *he has overshot the landing strip again.* ■ exceed (a target or limit): *the department may overshoot its cash limit.*
▸*n.* /ˈōvərsHo͞ot/ an act of going past or beyond a point, target, or limit. ■ an amount or distance by which a target is passed.

o·ver·shot /ˈōvərˌsHät/ ▸ past and past participle of **OVERSHOOT**.
▸*adj.* **1** (of a waterwheel) turned by water falling onto it from an overhead channel. **2** denoting an upper jaw that projects beyond the lower jaw.

o·ver·sight /ˈōvərˌsīt/ ▸*n.* **1** an unintentional failure to notice or do something: *he said his failure to pay for the tickets was an oversight* | *was the mistake due to oversight?* **2** the action of overseeing something: *effective oversight of the financial reporting process.*

o·ver·sim·pli·fy /ˌōvərˈsimpləˌfī/ ▸*v.* (**-fies**, **-fied**) [*trans.*] [often as *adj.*] (**oversimplified**) simplify (something) so much that a distorted impression of it is given: *a false and oversimplified view of human personality.* —**o·ver·sim·pli·fi·ca·tion** /ˈōvərˌsimpləfiˈkāsHən/ *n.*

o·ver·sized /ˈōvərˈsīzd/ (also **o·ver·size** /-ˈsīz/) ▸*adj.* bigger than the usual size: *an oversized T-shirt.*

o·ver·skirt /ˈōvərˌskərt/ ▸*n.* an outer skirt worn over the skirt of a dress.

o·ver·slaugh /ˌōvərˈslô/ ▸*v.* [*trans.*] *dated* pass over (someone) in favor of another. ▷mid 18th cent.: from Dutch *overslag* (noun), from *overslaan* 'pass over.'

o·ver·sleep /ˌōvərˈslēp/ ▸*v.* (*past* and *past part.* **-slept**) [*intrans.*] sleep longer or later than one intended: *we talked until the early hours and consequently I overslept.*

o·ver·sold /ˌōvərˈsōld/ ▸ past and past participle of **OVERSELL**.
▸*adj.* *Stock Market* sold to a price below its true value: *technology stocks remain oversold and are considered ripe for buying.*

o·ver·so·lic·i·tous /ˌōvərsəˈlisitəs/ ▸*adj.* showing excessive concern for another person's welfare or interests. —**o·ver·so·lic·i·tude** /-ˌt(y)o͞od/ *n.*

o·ver·soul /ˈōvərˌsōl/ ▸*n.* [in *sing.*] a divine spirit supposed to pervade the universe and to encompass all human souls. The term is associated particularly with Transcendentalism.

o·ver·spend /ˌōvərˈspend/ ▸*v.* (*past* and *past part.* **-spent**) [*intrans.*] spend too much: *she overspent on her husband's funeral.* ■ [*trans.*] spend more than (a specified amount): *the department can see that it is going to overspend its budget.*

o·ver·spill /ˈōvərˌspil/ ▸*n.* *chiefly Brit.* people or things that spill over or are in excess.

o·ver·spin /ˈōvərˌspin/ ▸*n.* a rotating motion given to a ball when throwing or hitting it, used to give it extra speed or distance or to make it bounce awkwardly.

o·ver·spray /ˈōvərˌsprā/ ▸*n.* excess paint or other liquid that spreads or blows beyond an area being sprayed.

o·ver·spread /ˌōvərˈspred/ ▸*v.* (*past* and *past part.* **-spread**) [*trans.*] cover the surface of; spread over: *a broad smile overspread his face.* ▷Old English *ofersprǣdan* (see **OVER-**, **SPREAD**).

o·ver·state /ˌōvərˈstāt/ ▸*v.* [*trans.*] express or state too strongly; exaggerate: *I may have overstated my case to make my point.* —**o·ver·state·ment** *n.*

o·ver·stay /ˌōvərˈstā/ ▸*v.* [*trans.*] stay longer than the time, limits, or duration of: *he was arrested for overstaying his visa.* —**o·ver·stay·er** /ˈōvərˌstāər/ *n.*
▸*PHRASE* □ **overstay one's welcome** see **WELCOME**.

o·ver·steer ▸*v.* /ˌōvərˈstir/ [*intrans.*] (of a motor vehicle) have a tendency to turn more sharply than was intended.
▸*n.* /ˈōvərˌstir/ the tendency of a vehicle to turn in such a way.

o·ver·step /ˌōvərˈstep/ ▸*v.* (**-stepped**, **-step·ping**) pass beyond (a limit): *you must not overstep your borrowing limit.* ■ violate (a rule or standard of behavior): *he has overstepped the bounds of acceptable discipline.*
▸*PHRASE* □ **overstep the mark** behave in an unacceptable way.

o·ver·stim·u·late /ˌōvərˈstimyəˌlāt/ ▸*v.* [*trans.*] stimulate physiologically or mentally to an excessive degree: *caffeine produced by coffee trees overstimulates insects that munch their leaves.* —**overstimulation** /ˈōvərˌstimyəˈlāsHən/ *n.*

o·ver·stitch /ˈōvərˌsticH/ ▸*n.* a stitch made over an edge or over another stitch.
▸*v.* /ˌōvərˈsticH/ [*trans.*] sew with such a stitch.

o·ver·stock ▸*v.* /ˌōvərˈstäk/ [*trans.*] supply with more of something than is necessary or required: *do not overstock the kitchen with food.*
▸*n.* /ˈōvərˌstäk/ (esp. in a manufacturing or retailing context) a supply or quantity in excess of demand or requirements: *factory overstock* | *publishers' overstocks and remainders.*

o·ver·stored /ˌōvərˈstôrd/ ▸*adj.* **1** stored for too long a period: *an overstored apple.* **2** supplied with more retail stores than the market demands: *just at a time when this area is already overstored.*

o·ver·strain /ˌōvərˈstrān/ ▸*v.* [*trans.*] subject to an excessive demand on strength, resources, or abilities: *there was a risk he might overstrain his heart.*
▸*n.* the action or result of subjecting someone or something to such a demand.

o·ver·strike /ˈōvərˌstrīk/ ▸*n.* the superimposing of one printed character or one coin design on another. ■ a coin showing one design superimposed on another. —**o·ver·strik·ing** /ˌōvərˈstrīkiNG/ *n.*

o·ver·strung /ˈōvərˈstrəNG/ ▸*adj.* **1** (of a piano) with strings in sets crossing each other obliquely. **2** *dated* (of a person) extremely nervous or tense.

o·ver·stud·y ▸*n.* /ˈōvərˌstədē/ excessive study.
▸*v.* /ˌōvərˈstədē/ study too long or too intensely: *if your child is a high achiever, but overstudies for fear of not receiving an A+, help her to gradually study a little less.*

o·ver·stuff /ˌōvərˈstəf/ ▸*v.* [*trans.*] [usu. as *adj.*] (**overstuffed**) **1** force too much into (a container): *an overstuffed briefcase.* **2** cover (furniture) completely with padded upholstery: *an overstuffed armchair.*

o·ver·sub·scribed /ˌōvərsəbˈskrībd/ ▸*adj.* applied for in greater quantities than are available or expected: *those bonds were said to be twelve to fourteen times oversubscribed.* ■ (of a course, etc.) having more applications than available places.

o·ver·sup·ply ▸*n.* /ˈōvərsəˌplī/ an excessive supply: *an oversupply of teachers* | *oversupply causes prices to fall.*
▸*v.* /ˌōvərsəˈplī/ (**-plies**, **-plied**) [*trans.*] (usu. **be oversupplied**) supply with too much or too many: *the country was oversupplied with lawyers.*

o·vert /ōˈvərt; ˈōvərt/ ▸*adj.* done or shown openly; plainly or readily apparent, not secret or hidden: *an overt act of aggression* | *in untreated cases, overt psychosis may occur.* ▷Middle English: from Old French, past participle of *ovrir* 'to open,' from Latin *aperire*. —**o·vert·ly** *adv.* —**o·vert·ness** *n.*

o·ver·take /ˌōvərˈtāk/ ▸*v.* (*past* **-took**; *past part.* **-tak·en**) [*trans.*] **1** catch up with and pass while traveling in the same direction: *the driver overtook a line of vehicles.* ■ become greater or more successful than: *Germany rapidly overtook Britain in industrial output.* **2** (esp. of misfortune) come suddenly or unexpectedly upon: *the pattern of economic ruin overtook them.* ■ (of a feeling) affect (someone) suddenly and powerfully: *weariness overtook him and he retired to bed.*

o·ver·task /ˌōvərˈtask/ ▸*v.* [*trans.*] impose too much work on: [as *adj.*] (**overtasked**) *an overtasked school system.*

o·ver·tax /ˌōvərˈtaks/ ▸*v.* [*trans.*] **1** require to pay too much tax: *if you're overtaxed, we want you in our party.* **2** make excessive demands on (a person's strength, abilities, etc.): *do athletes overtax their hearts?* —**o·ver·tax·a·tion** /-takˈsāSHən/ *n.* (in sense 1).

o·ver·throw ▸*v.* /ˌōvərˈTHrō/ (*past* **-threw**; *past part.* **-thrown**) [*trans.*] **1** remove forcibly from power: *military coups which had attempted to overthrow the king.* ■ put an end to (something), typically by the use of force or violence: *their subversive activities are calculated to overthrow parliamentary democracy.* ■ *archaic* knock or throw to the ground: *one who is already prostrate cannot be overthrown.* **2** throw (a ball) further or harder than intended: *he grips the ball too tight and overthrows it.* ■ throw a ball beyond (a receiving player): *he overthrew a receiver in the end zone.*
▸*n.* /ˈōvərˌTHrō/ **1** [in *sing.*] a removal from power; a defeat or downfall: *plotting the overthrow of the government.* **2** (in baseball and other games) a throw that sends a ball past its intended recipient or target. **3** a panel of decorated wrought-iron work above an arch or gateway.

o·ver·thrust /ˈōvərˌTHrəst/ *Geology* ▸*n.* the thrust of one series of rock strata over another, esp. along a fault line at a shallow angle to the horizontal.
▸*v.* (*past* and *past part.* **-thrust**) [*trans.*] force (a body of rock) over another: [as *n.*] (**overthrusting**) *the increased overburden resulting from overthrusting.* ■ (of a body of rock) be forced over (another formation): *the shales are overthrust by Carboniferous rocks.*

o·ver·time /ˈōvərˌtīm/ ▸*n.* time in addition to what is normal, as time worked beyond one's scheduled working hours: *fewer opportunities for overtime* | [as *adj.*] *an overtime ban.* ■ payment for such extra work. ■ extra time played at the end of a game that is tied at the end of the regulation time: *they lost in overtime.*
▸*adv.* in addition to normal working hours: *they were working overtime to fulfill a big order* | *figurative his brain was working overtime.*

o·ver·tip /ˌōvərˈtip/ ▸*v.* (**-tipped**, **-tip·ping**) [*trans.*] give (someone) an excessively generous tip.

o·ver·tire /ˌōvərˈtīr/ ▸*v.* [*trans.*] exhaust (someone): *walk at a pace that does not overtire you.*

o·ver·tone /ˈōvərˌtōn/ ▸*n.* **1** a musical tone that is a part of the harmonic series above a fundamental note and may be heard with it. ■ *Physics* a component of any oscillation whose frequency is an integral multiple of the fundamental frequency. **2** (often **overtones**) a subtle or subsidiary quality, implication, or connotation: *the decision may have political overtones.* ▷mid 19th cent.: from **OVER-** + **TONE**, suggested by German *Oberton*.

o·ver·top /ˌōvərˈtäp/ ▸*v.* (**-top·ped**, **-top·ping**) [*trans.*] exceed in height: *no building is allowed to overtop the cathedral.* ■ (esp. of water) rise over the top of (a barrier constructed to hold it back): *the old sea wall is regularly overtopped by high tides.* ■ be superior to: *none can overtop him in goodness.*

o·ver·trade /ˌōvərˈtrād/ ▸*v.* [*intrans.*] engage in more business than can be supported by the market or by the funds or resources available.

o·ver·train /ˌōvərˈtrān/ ▸*v.* [*intrans.*] (esp. of an athlete) train too hard or for too long. ■ [*trans.*] subject to excessive training: *the team overtrained their young players.*

o·ver·trick /ˈōvərˌtrik/ ▸*n.* *Bridge* a trick taken by the declarer in excess of the contract.

o·ver·trump /ˌōvərˈtrəmp/ ▸*v.* [*intrans.*] (in bridge and similar card games) play a trump that is higher than one already played in the same trick.
▸*n.* an act of overtrumping.

o·ver·ture /ˈōvərCHər; -ˌCHŏŏr/ ▸*n.* **1** an introduction to something more substantial: *the talks were no more than an overture to a long debate.* ■ (usu. **overtures**) an approach or proposal made to someone with the aim of opening negotiations or establishing a relationship: *Coleen listened to his overtures of love.* **2** *Music* an orchestral piece at the beginning of an opera, suite, play, oratorio, or other extended composition. ■ an independent orchestral composition in one movement. ▷late Middle English (in the sense 'aperture'): from Old French, from Latin *apertura* 'aperture.'

o·ver·turn ▸*v.* /ˌōvərˈtərn/ [*trans.*] **1** tip (something) over so that it is on its side or upside down: *the crowd proceeded to overturn cars and set them on fire.* ■ [*intrans.*] turn over and come to rest upside down, typically as the result of an accident: *a large housetrailer overturned in the middle of the road.* **2** abolish, invalidate, or turn around (an established fact, system, etc.): *the results overturned previous findings.* ■ reverse (a legal decision): *he fought for eight years to overturn a conviction for armed robbery.*
▸*n.* /ˈōvərˌtərn/ *rare* an act of turning over or upsetting something; a revolution, subversion, or reversal. ■ *Ecology* the occasional (typically twice yearly) mixing of the water of a thermally stratified lake.

o·ver·type /ˈōvərˌtīp/ ▸*v.* [*trans.*] type over (another character): *overtype it with the correct number and press Return.*
▸*n.* a facility or operating mode allowing overtyping.

o·ver·use ▸*v.* /ˌōvərˈyo͞oz/ [*trans.*] use too much: *young children sometimes overuse "and" in their writing.*
▸*n.* /ˈōvərˈyo͞os/ excessive use: *overuse of natural resources.*

o·ver·val·ue /ˌōvərˈvalyo͞o/ ▸*v.* (**-val·ues**, **-val·ued**, **-val·uing**) [*trans.*] overestimate the importance of: *intelligence can be overvalued.* ■ fix the value of (something, esp. a currency) at too high a level: *sterling was overvalued against the dollar.* —**o·ver·val·u·a·tion** /ˈōvərˌvalyo͞oˈāSHən/ *n.*

o·ver·view /ˈōvərˌvyo͞o/ ▸*n.* a general review or summary of a subject: *a critical overview of the scientific issues of our time.*
▸*v.* [*trans.*] give a general review or summary of: *the report overviews the needs of the community.*

o·ver·wa·ter ▸*v.* /ˌōvərˈwôtər; -ˈwätər/ [*trans.*] water (a plant, a lawn, etc.) too much: *your cutting needs some water, but make sure you don't overwater it.*
▸*adj.* /ˈōvərwôtər; -wätər/ situated or taking place above water: *the airline is to initiate long-haul overwater operations.*

o·ver·wear /ˈōvərˌwe(ə)r/ ▸*n.* outer clothing.

o·ver·ween·ing /ˈōvərˈwēniNG/ ▸*adj.* showing excessive confidence or pride: *overweening ambition.* —**o·ver·ween·ing·ly** *adv.*

o·ver·weight ▸*adj.* /ˈōvərˈwāt/ above a weight considered normal or desirable: *he's forty pounds overweight.* ■ above legal weight: *an overweight truck.*
▸*n.* /ˈōvərˌwāt/ excessive or extra weight.
▸*v.* /ˌōvərˈwāt/ [*trans.*] [usu. as *adj.*] (**overweighted**) put too much weight on; overload. ■ *Finance* invest in (a market sector, industry, etc.) to a greater than normal degree: *we have overweighted the banking sector* | [as *adj.*] *we were overweighted in technology last year.*

o·ver·whelm /ˌōvər'(h)welm/ ▸*v.* [*trans.*] bury or drown beneath a huge mass: *the water flowed through to overwhelm the whole dam and the village beneath.* ■ defeat completely: *his teams overwhelmed their opponents.* ■ (often **be overwhelmed**) give too much of a thing to (someone); inundate: *they were overwhelmed by farewell messages.* ■ (usu. **be overwhelmed**) have a strong emotional effect on: *I was overwhelmed with guilt.* ■ be too strong for; overpower: *the wine doesn't overwhelm the flavor of the trout.*

o·ver·whelm·ing /ˌōvər'(h)welmiNG/ ▸*adj.* very great in amount: *he was elected president by an overwhelming majority.* ■ (esp. of an emotion) very strong: *an overwhelming feeling of gratitude.* —**o·ver·whelm·ing·ly** *adv.* —**o·ver·whelm·ing·ness** *n.*

o·ver·wind /ˌōvərˈwīnd/ ▸*v.* (*past* and *past part.* **-wound**) [*trans.*] wind (a mechanism, esp. a watch) beyond the proper stopping point.

o·ver·win·ter /ˈōvərˈwin(t)ər/ ▸*v.* [*intrans.*] **1** [with *adverbial of place*] spend the winter: *many birds overwinter in equatorial regions.* **2** (of an insect, plant, etc.) live through the winter: *the germinated seeds will overwinter.*

o·ver·with·hold /ˌōvərwiTHˈhōld; -wiT͟H-/ ▸*v.* [*trans.*] to deduct (an amount in withholding tax) in excess of what is owed.

o·ver·work /ˈōvərˈwərk/ ▸*v.* [*trans.*] exhaust with too much work: *executives who are overworked and worried* | [as *adj.*] (**overworked**) *tired, overworked, demoralized staff.* ■ [*intrans.*] (of a person) work too hard: *the doctor advised a complete rest because he had been overworking.* ■ [usu. as *adj.*] (**overworked**) make excessive use of: *the city's overworked sewer system.* ■ [usu. as *adj.*] (**overworked**) use (a word or idea) too much and so make it weaker in meaning or effect: *"Breathtaking" is an overworked brochure cliché.*
▸*n.* excessive work: *his health broke down under the strain of overwork.*

o·ver·write /ˌōvərˈrīt/ ▸*v.* (*past* **-wrote**; *past part.* **-writ·ten**) [*trans.*] **1** write on top of (other writing): *many names had been scratched out or overwritten.* ■ *Computing* destroy (data) or the data in (a file) by entering new data in its place: *an entry stating who is allowed to overwrite the file.* ■ another term for **OVERTYPE**. **2** write too elaborately or ornately: *there is a tendency to overwrite their parts and fall into cliché.*

o·ver·wrought /ˈōvəˈrôt/ ▸*adj.* **1** in a state of nervous excitement or anxiety: *she was too overwrought to listen to reason.* **2** (of a piece of writing or a work of art) too elaborate or complicated in design or construction. ▷late Middle English: archaic past participle of **OVERWORK**.

ovi- ▸*comb. form chiefly Zoology* of or relating to eggs or ova: *oviparous.* ▷from Latin *ovum* 'egg.'

Ov·id /ˈävid/ (43 BC–c.AD 17), Roman poet; full name *Publius Ovidius Naso*. He is especially known for his elegiac love poems (such as the *Amores* and the *Ars Amatoria*) and for the *Metamorphoses*, a hexametric series of tales of mythological, legendary, and historical figures.

o·vi·duct /ˈōviˌdəkt/ ▸*n.* *Anatomy & Zoology* the tube through which an ovum or egg passes from an ovary. —**o·vi·du·cal** /ˌōvəˈdo͞okəl/ *adj.* —**o·vi·duc·tal** /ˌōvəˈdəktəl/ *adj.*

O·vie·do /ôˈvyedō/ a city in northwestern Spain, capital of the Asturias region; pop. 203,000.

o·vi·form /ˈōvəˌfôrm/ ▸*adj.* egg-shaped.

O·vim·bun·du /ˌōvimˈbo͝ondo͞o/ ▸ see **MBUNDU**.

o·vine /ˈōˌvīn/ ▸*adj.* of, relating to, or resembling sheep. ▷early 19th cent.: from late Latin *ovinus*, from Latin *ovis* 'sheep.'

o·vip·a·rous /ōˈvipərəs/ ▸*adj.* *Zoology* (of a bird, etc.) producing young by means of eggs that are hatched after they have been laid by the parent. Compare with **VIVIPAROUS** and **OVOVIVIPAROUS.** **—o·vi·par·i·ty** /-'paritē/ *n.*

o·vi·pos·it /ˌōvə'päzit/ ▶*v.* (**-pos·it·ed, -pos·it·ing**) [*intrans.*] *Zoology* (esp. of an insect) lay an egg or eggs. ▷early 19th cent.: from **OVI-** 'egg' + Latin *posit-* 'placed' (from the verb *ponere*). **—o·vi·po·si·tion** /-pə'zisʜən/ *n.*

o·vi·pos·i·tor /ˌōvə'päzitər/ ▶*n. Zoology* a tubular organ through which a female insect or fish deposits eggs.

O

o·void /'ōˌvoid/ ▶*adj.* (of a solid or a three-dimensional surface) egg-shaped. ■ (of a plane figure) oval, esp. with one end more pointed than the other.
▶*n.* an ovoid body or surface. ▷early 19th cent.: from French *ovoïde*, from modern Latin *ovoides*, from Latin *ovum* 'egg.'

o·vo·lo /'ōvəlō/ ▶*n.* (*pl.* **-li** /-ˌlī/) *Architecture* a rounded convex molding, in cross section a quarter of a circle or ellipse. ▷mid 17th cent.: from Italian, diminutive of *ovo* 'egg,' from Latin *ovum*.

o·vo·tes·tis /ˌōvō'testis/ ▶*n.* (*pl.* **-tes·tes** /-'testēz/) *Zoology* an organ producing both ova and spermatozoa, as in some gastropod mollusks. ▷late 19th cent.: from **OVUM** + **TESTIS.**

o·vo·vi·vip·a·rous /ōˌvōvī'vip(ə)rəs; -və'vip-/ ▶*adj. Zoology* (of an animal) producing young by means of eggs that are hatched within the body of the parent, as in some snakes. Compare with **OVIPAROUS** and **VIVIPAROUS.** **—o·vo·vi·vi·par·i·ty** /-ˌvivə'paritē/ *n.*

ov·u·late /'ōvyəˌlāt; 'äv-/ ▶*v.* [*intrans.*] discharge ova or ovules from the ovary. ▷late 19th cent.: back-formation from *ovulation*, or from medieval Latin *ovulum* 'little egg' (see **OVULE**) + **-ATE**[3]. **—ov·u·la·tion** /ˌōvyə'lāsʜən; -'lāsʜən/ *n.* **—ov·u·la·to·ry** /-ləˌtôrē/ *adj.*

ov·ule /'ōvyo͞ol; 'äv-/ ▶*n.* a small or immature ovum. ■ *Botany* the part of the ovary of seed plants that contains the female germ cell and after fertilization becomes the seed. ▷early 19th cent.: from French, from medieval Latin *ovulum*, diminutive of **OVUM.** **—ov·u·lar** /-lər/ *adj.*

o·vum /'ōvəm/ ▶*n.* (*pl.* **o·va** /'ōvə/) *Biology* a mature female reproductive cell, esp. of a human or other animal, that can divide to give rise to an embryo usually only after fertilization by a male cell. ▷early 18th cent.: from Latin, literally 'egg.'

OW ▶*abbr.* Old Welsh.

ow /ou/ ▶*exclam.* used to express sudden pain: *Ow! You're hurting me!* ▷natural exclamation: first recorded in English in the mid 19th cent.

owe /ō/ ▶*v.* [*trans.*] have an obligation to pay or repay (something, esp. money) in return for something received: *they have denied they owe money to the company* | [with *two objs.*] *I owe you 25 cents.* ■ owe something, esp. money, to (someone): *I owe you for the taxi.* ■ be under a moral obligation to give someone (gratitude, respect, etc.): *I* **owe it to** *him to explain what's happened* | [with *two objs.*] *I owe you an apology.* ■ (**owe something to**) have something because of (someone or something): *he owed his success not to chance but to insight.* ■ be indebted to someone or something for (something): *I owe my life to you.* ▷Old English *āgan* 'own, have it as an obligation,' of Germanic origin; from an Indo-European root shared by Sanskrit *īś* 'possess, own.' Compare with **OUGHT**[1].
▶*PHRASES* □ **owe it to oneself** need to do something to protect one's own interests: *you owe it to yourself to take care of your body.* □ **owe someone one** *informal* feel indebted to someone for a favor done: *thanks, I owe you one for this.* □ **owes someone a living** used to express disapproval of someone who expects to receive financial support or other benefits without doing any work: *they think the world owes them a living.*

Ow·ens /'ō(w)ənz/, Jesse (1913–80), U.S. athlete; born *James Cleveland Owens.* In 1935, he equaled or broke six world records in forty-five minutes, and in 1936, he won four gold medals at the Olympic Games in Berlin. The success of Owens, a black man, in Berlin outraged Hitler.

Ow·ens·bor·o /'ōwənzˌbərō; -ˌbə-rō/ an industrial port city in northwestern Kentucky, on the Ohio River; pop. 54,067.

Ow·ens Val·ley /'ōwənz/ the valley of the Owens River, in east central California, between the Sierra Nevada and the Inyo Mountains, the source since 1913 of much of the water supply for Los Angeles.

ow·ing /'ō-iɴɢ/ ▶*adj.* [*predic.*] (of money) yet to be paid: *no rent was owing.*
▶*PHRASE* □ **owing to** because of or on account of: *his reading was hesitant owing to a stammer.*

owl /oul/ ▶*n.* a nocturnal bird of prey with large forward-facing eyes surrounded by facial disks, a hooked beak, and typically a loud call. • Order Strigiformes: families Strigidae (**typical owls** such as tawny owls and eagle owls) and Tytonidae (**barn owls** and their relatives). ▷Old English *ūle*, of Germanic origin; related to Dutch *uil* and German *Eule*, from a base imitative of the bird's call. **—owl·like** /-ˌlīk/ *adj.*

owl but·ter·fly ▶*n.* a very large South American butterfly that flies at dusk, with a large eyelike marking on the underside of each hind wing. • Genus *Caligo*, subfamily Brassolinae, family Nymphalidae.

owl·et /'oulit/ ▶*n.* **1** a small owl found chiefly in Asia and Africa. • Genus *Glaucidium* and *Athene*, family Strigidae: several species. ■ a young owl of any kind. **2** another term for **NOCTUID.**

owl·et-night·jar ▶*n.* a nocturnal Australasian bird resembling a small nightjar, with an owllike face and a large gape. • Family Aegothelidae and genus *Aegotheles*: several species.

owl-faced mon·key ▶*n.* a guenon that has a black face with white and yellow markings and bright blue skin on the rump, living in the forests of central Africa. • *Cercopithecus hamlyni*, family Cercopithecidae.

owl·ish /'oulisʜ/ ▶*adj.* like an owl, esp. in acting or appearing wise or solemn: *he had an owlish and solemn air.* ■ (of eyeglasses) resembling the large round eyes of an owl. **—owl·ish·ly** *adv.* **—owl·ish·ness** *n.*

owl mon·key ▶*n.* another term for **DOUROUCOULI.**

owl par·rot ▶*n.* another term for **KAKAPO.**

own /ōn/ ▶*adj.* & *pron.* used with a possessive to emphasize that someone or something belongs or relates to the person mentioned: [as *adj.*] *they can't handle their own children I was an outcast among my own kind* | [as *pron.*] *the Church would look after its own.* ■ done or produced by and for the person specified: [as *adj.*] *I used to design all my own clothes* | [as *pron.*] *they claimed the work as their own.* ■ particular to the person or thing mentioned; individual: [as *adj.*] *the style had its own charm* | [as *pron.*] *the film had a quality all its own.*
▶*v.* **1** [*trans.*] have (something) as one's own; possess: *his father owns a restaurant* | [as *adj.*, in *combination*] (**-owned**) *state-owned property.* **2** [*intrans.*] *formal* admit or acknowledge that something is the case or that one feels a certain way: *she* **owned to** *a feeling of profound jealousy* | [with *clause*] *he was reluctant to own that he was indebted.* ■ [*trans.*] *archaic* acknowledge paternity, authorship, or possession of: *he has published little, trivial things which he will not own.*
▶*phrasal v.* □ **own up** admit or confess to having done something wrong or embarrassing: *he* **owns up to** *few mistakes.* ▷Old English *āgen* (adjective and pronoun) 'owned, possessed,' past participle of *āgan* 'owe'; the verb (Old English *āgnian* 'possess,' also 'make own's own') was originally from the adjective, later probably reintroduced from **OWNER.**
▶*PHRASES* □ **as if** (or **like**) **one owns the place** *informal* in an overbearing or self-important manner: *he would have walked in and taken charge as if he owned the place.* □ **be one's own man** (or **woman**) act independently and with confidence. ■ *archaic* be in full possession of one's faculties. □ **come into its** (or **one's**) **own** become fully effective, used, or recognized: *Mexico will come into its own as a vacation spot.* □ **get one's own back** *informal* take action in retaliation for a wrongdoing or insult. □ **hold one's own** retain a position of strength in a challenging situation: *I can hold my own in a fight.* □ **of one's own** belonging to oneself alone: *at last I've got a place of my own.* □ **on one's own** unaccompanied by others; alone or unaided. *I have to do things on my own.*

own·er /'ōnər/ ▶*n.* a person who owns something: *the proud owner of a huge Dalmatian.* **—own·er·less** *adj.* **—own·er·ship** *n.*

own·er-oc·cu·pied ▶*adj.* (of a house or apartment) used as a dwelling by the owner.

own goal ▶*n.* (in soccer) a goal scored inadvertently when the ball is struck into the goal by a player on the defensive team.

ox /äks/ ▶*n.* (*pl.* **ox·en** /'äksən/) a domesticated bovine animal kept for milk or meat; a cow or bull. See **CATTLE** (sense 1). ■ a castrated male of this, formerly much used as a draft animal: [as *adj.*] *an ox cart.* ■ an animal of a group related to the domestic ox. See **CATTLE** (sense 2). ▷Old English *oxa*, of Germanic origin; related to Dutch *os* and German *Ochse*, from an Indo-European root shared by Sanskrit *ukṣán* 'bull.'

ox- ▶*comb. form* variant spelling of **OXY-**[2] reduced before a vowel (as in *oxazole*).

ox·a·cil·lin /ˌäksə'silin/ ▶*n. Medicine* an antibiotic drug made by chemical modification of penicillin and used to treat bacterial infections. ▷1960s: blend of **OXAZOLE** and **PENICILLIN.**

ox·al·ic ac·id /äk'salik/ ▶*n. Chemistry* a poisonous crystalline acid with a sour taste, present in rhubarb leaves, wood sorrel, and other plants. Its uses include bleaching and cleansing. • Alternative name: **ethanedioic acid**; chem. formula: $(COOH)_2$. ▷late 18th cent.: *oxalic* from French *oxalique*, via Latin from Greek *oxalis* 'wood sorrel.' **—ox·a·late** /'äksəˌlāt/ *n.*

ox·a·lis /'äksəlis; äk'salis/ ▶*n.* a plant of a genus that includes the wood sorrel, typically having three-lobed leaves and white, yellow, or pink flowers. • Genus *Oxalis*, family Oxalidaceae. ▷early 17th cent.: via Latin from Greek, from *oxus* 'sour' (because of its sharp-tasting leaves).

ox·a·zole /'äksəˌzōl/ ▶*n. Chemistry* a volatile liquid with weakly basic properties, whose molecule contains a five-membered ring that serves as the basis of a number of medicinal drugs. • A heterocyclic compound; chem. formula: C_3H_3NO. ▷late 19th cent.: from **OX-** 'oxygen' + **AZO-** + **-OLE.**

ox·a·zo·lid·i·none /ˌäksəzō'lidnˌōn/ ▶*n.* any of a class of synthetic antibiotics that inhibit protein synthesis, used against gram-positive bacteria.

ox·bow /'äksˌbō/ ▶*n.* **1** a U-shaped bend in the course of a river. ■ short for **OXBOW LAKE.** **2** a U-shaped collar of an ox yoke.

ox·bow lake ▶*n.* a curved lake formed at a former oxbow where the main stream of the river has cut across the narrow end and no longer flows around the loop of the bend.

Ox·bridge /'äksˌbrij/ ▶*n.* Oxford and Cambridge universities regarded together: [as *adj.*] *Oxbridge colleges.* ▷mid 19th cent.: blend of **OXFORD** and **CAMBRIDGE.**

ox·en /'äksən/ ▶ plural form of **OX.**

ox·eye /'äksˌī/ ▶*n.* a yellow-flowered North American plant of the daisy family. • *Heliopsis helianthoides*, family Compositae.

ox·eye dai·sy ▶*n.* an often-cultivated Eurasian daisy that has large white flowers with yellow centers. Also called **MARGUERITE.** • *Leucanthemum vulgare*, family Compositae.

Oxf. ▶*abbr.* Oxford.

Ox·ford /'äksfərd/ **1** a city in central England, on the Thames River; pop. 109,000. Oxford University is located here. **2** a town in north central Mississippi, home to the University of Mississippi and associated with novelist William Faulkner; pop. 9,984. See also **YOKNAPATAWPHA COUNTY.**

Oxford

ox·ford /'äksfərd/ ▶*n.* **1** (also **oxford shoe**) a type of lace-up shoe with a low heel. **2** (also **oxford cloth**) a heavy cotton cloth chiefly used to make shirts.

Ox·ford Group a Christian movement popularized in Oxford in the late 1920s, advocating discussion of personal problems by groups. Later known as **MORAL REARMAMENT.**

Ox·ford Move·ment a Christian movement started in Oxford, England, in 1833, seeking to restore traditional Catholic teachings and ceremony within the Church of England. Its leaders were John Keble, Edward Pusey, and (until he became a Roman Catholic) John Henry Newman. It formed the basis of the present Anglo-Catholic (or High Church) tradition. Also called **TRACTARIANISM**.

ox·herd /'äks,hərd/ ▶*n. archaic* a cowherd. ▷Old English, from **OX** + obsolete *herd* 'herdsman.'

ox·hide /'äks,hīd/ ▶*n.* leather made from the hide of an ox.

ox·ic /'äksik/ ▶*adj.* designating a process or environment in which oxygen is involved or present. ▷1960s: from *ox(ide)* or *ox(ygen)* + **-IC**.

ox·i·dant /'äksidənt/ ▶*n.* an oxidizing agent. ▷late 19th cent.: from French (modern French *oxydant*), present participle of *oxider* 'oxidize.'

ox·i·dase /'äksi,dās; -,dāz/ ▶*n. Biochemistry* an enzyme that promotes the transfer of a hydrogen atom from a particular substrate to an oxygen molecule, forming water or hydrogen peroxide. ▷late 19th cent.: from French *oxydase*, from *oxyde* 'oxide.'

ox·i·da·tion /,äksi'dāsʜən/ ▶*n. Chemistry* the process or result of oxidizing or being oxidized. ▷late 18th cent.: from French (modern French *oxydation*), from *oxider* 'oxidize.' **—ox·i·da·tion·al** /-sʜənl/ *adj.* **—ox·i·da·tive** /'äksi,dātiv/ *adj.*

ox·i·da·tion num·ber (also **oxidation state**) ▶*n. Chemistry* a number assigned to an element in chemical combination that represents the number of electrons lost (or gained, if the number is negative) by an atom of that element in the compound.

ox·ide /'äk,sīd/ ▶*n. Chemistry* a binary compound of oxygen with another element or group. ▷late 18th cent.: from French, from *oxygène* 'oxygen' + *-ide* (as in *acide* 'acid').

ox·i·dize /'äksi,dīz/ ▶*v.* combine or become combined chemically with oxygen: [*trans.*] *when coal is burned any sulfur is oxidized to sulfur dioxide* | [*intrans.*] *the fats in the food will oxidize, turning it rancid.* ■ *Chemistry* undergo or cause to undergo a reaction in which electrons are lost to another species. The opposite of **REDUCE**. **—ox·i·diz·a·ble** *adj.* **—ox·i·di·za·tion** /,äksidi'zāsʜən/ *n.* **—ox·i·diz·er** *n.*

ox·i·diz·ing a·gent /'äksi,dīzɪɴɢ/ ▶*n. Chemistry* a substance that tends to bring about oxidation by being reduced and gaining electrons.

ox·im·e·ter /äk'simitər/ ▶*n.* an instrument for measuring the proportion of oxygenated hemoglobin in the blood. **—ox·im·e·try** /-trē/ *n.*

ox·i·sol /'äksi,sôl; -säl/ ▶*n. Soil Science* a soil of an order comprising stable, highly weathered, tropical mineral soils with highly oxidized subsurface horizons. ▷1960s: from **OXIC** + **-SOL**.

ox·lip /'äks,lip/ ▶*n.* a woodland Eurasian primula with yellow flowers that hang down one side of the stem. • *Primula elatior*, family Primulaceae. ■ (also **false oxlip**) a natural hybrid between a primrose and a cowslip. ▷Old English *oxanslyppe*, from *oxa* 'ox' + *slyppe* 'slime'; compare with **COWSLIP**.

Ox·nard /'äks,närd/ a city in southwestern California, northwest of Los Angeles, on the Pacific coast; pop. 142,216.

Ox·on /'äks,än/ ▶*abbr.* (esp. in degree titles) of Oxford University: *BA, Oxon.* ▷from medieval Latin *Oxoniensis*, from *Oxonia* (see **OXONIAN**).

Ox·o·ni·an /äk'sōnēən; -'sōnyən/ ▶*adj.* of or relating to Oxford, England, or Oxford University.
▶*n.* a native or inhabitant of Oxford, England. ■ someone who attends or has a degree from Oxford University. ▷mid 16th cent.: from *Oxonia* (Latinized name of Oxford, from its old form *Oxenford*) + **-AN**.

ox·peck·er /'äks,pekər/ ▶*n.* a brown African bird related to the starlings, feeding on parasites that infest the skins of large grazing mammals. • Genus *Buphagus*, family Sturnidae (or Buphagidae): two species.

ox·tail /'äks,tāl/ ▶*n.* the tail of a cow. ■ meat from this, used esp. for making soup.

ox·ter /'äkstər/ ▶*n. Scottish & N. English* a person's armpit. ▷Old English *ōhsta, ōxta*.

ox-tongue ▶*n.* an Old World plant of the daisy family with yellow dandelionlike flowers and prickly hairs on the stem and leaves. • Genus *Picris*, family Compositae: several species, including the **bristly ox-tongue** (*P. echioides*), introduced to and now common in California.

Ox·us /'äksəs/ ancient name for **AMU DARYA**.

oxy-[1] ▶*comb. form* denoting sharpness: *oxytone.* ▷from Greek *oxus* 'sharp.'

oxy-[2] (also **ox-**) ▶*comb. form Chemistry* representing **OXYGEN**.

ox·y·a·cet·y·lene /,äksēə'setl-in; -,ēn/ ▶*adj.* [*attrib.*] of or denoting welding or cutting techniques using a very hot flame produced by mixing acetylene and oxygen.

ox·y·ac·id /,äksē'asid/ ▶*n. Chemistry* an inorganic acid whose molecules contain oxygen, such as sulfuric or nitric acid.

ox·y·an·i·on /,äksē'an,īən/ ▶*n. Chemistry* an anion containing one or more oxygen atoms bonded to another element (as in the sulfate and carbonate ions).

Ox·y·Con·tin /,äksē'käntin/ ▶*n. trademark* a synthetic analgesic drug that is similar to morphine in its effects and subject to abuse and addiction.

ox·y·gen /'äksəjən/ ▶*n.* a colorless, odorless reactive gas, the chemical element of atomic number 8 and the life-supporting component of the air. Oxygen forms about 20 percent of the earth's atmosphere, and is the most abundant element in the earth's crust, mainly in the form of oxides, silicates, and carbonates. (Symbol: **O**) ▷late 18th cent.: from French *(principe) oxygène* 'acidifying constituent' (because at first it was held to be the essential component in the formation of acids). **—ox·yg·e·nous** /äk'sijənəs/ *adj.*

ox·y·gen·ate /'äksəjə,nāt/ ▶*v.* [*trans.*] supply, treat, charge, or enrich with oxygen: [as *adj.*] (**oxygenated**) *a good supply of oxygenated blood.* ▷late 18th cent.: from French *oxygéner* 'supply with oxygen' + **-ATE**[3]. **—ox·y·gen·a·tion** /,äksəjə'nāsʜən/ *n.*

ox·y·gen·a·tor /'äksəjə,nātər/ ▶*n. Medicine* an apparatus for oxygenating the blood. ■ an aquatic plant that enriches the surrounding water with oxygen, esp. in a pond or aquarium.

ox·y·gen bar ▶*n.* an establishment where people pay to inhale pure oxygen for its reputedly therapeutic effects.

ox·y·gen·ize /'äksəjə,nīz/ ▶*v.* alternate term for **OXYGENATE**.

ox·y·gen mask ▶*n.* a mask placed over the nose and mouth and connected to a supply of oxygen, used when the body is not able to gain enough oxygen by breathing air, for example at high altitudes or because of a medical condition.

oxygen mask

ox·y·gen tent ▶*n.* a tentlike enclosure within which the air supply can be enriched with oxygen to aid a patient's breathing.

ox·y·he·mo·glo·bin /,äksē'hēmə,glōbən/ ▶*n. Biochemistry* a bright red substance formed by the combination of hemoglobin with oxygen, present in oxygenated blood.

ox·y·mo·ron /,äksə'môr,än/ ▶*n.* a figure of speech in which apparently contradictory terms appear in conjunction (e.g., *faith unfaithful kept him falsely true*). ▷mid 17th cent.: from Greek *oxumōron*, neuter (used as a noun) of *oxumōros* 'pointedly foolish,' from *oxus* 'sharp' + *mōros* 'foolish.' **—ox·y·mo·ron·ic** /-mə'ränik/ *adj.*

ox·yn·tic /äk'sintik/ ▶*adj.* of or denoting the secretory cells that produce hydrochloric acid in the main part of the stomach, or the glands that they compose. ▷late 19th cent.: from Greek *oxunteos* (verbal noun from *oxunein* 'sharpen') + **-IC**.

ox·y·te·tra·cy·cline /,äksə,tetrə'sīklēn/ ▶*n. Medicine* an antibiotic related to tetracycline, used to treat a variety of bacterial infections.

ox·y·to·cin /,äksə'tōsən/ ▶*n. Biochemistry* a hormone released by the pituitary gland that causes increased contraction of the uterus during labor and stimulates the ejection of milk into the ducts of the breasts. ▷1920s: from Greek *oxutokia* 'sudden delivery' (from *oxus* 'sharp' + *tokos* 'childbirth') + **-IN**[1].

ox·y·tone /'äksə,tōn/ ▶*adj.* (esp. in ancient Greek) having an acute accent on the last syllable.
▶*n.* a word of this kind. ▷mid 18th cent.: from Greek *oxutonos*, from *oxus* 'sharp' + *tonos* 'tone.'

oy /oi/ ▶*exclam.* **1** see **OY VEY**. **2** variant spelling of **OI**.

o·yer and ter·mi·ner /'oi-ər and 'tərmənər/ ▶*n. historical* a court authorized to hear certain criminal cases. ▷late Middle English: from Anglo-Norman French *oyer et terminer* 'hear and determine.'

o·yez /'ō'yā; 'ō'yez/ (also **o·yes**) ▶*exclam.* a call given by a court officer, or formerly by public criers, typically repeated two or three times to command silence and attention, as before court is in session. ▷late Middle English: from Old French *oiez!, oyez!* 'hear!,' imperative plural of *oir*, from Latin *audire* 'hear.'

oys·ter /'oistər/ ▶*n.* **1** any of a number of bivalve mollusks with rough irregular shells. Several kinds are eaten (esp. raw) as a delicacy and may be farmed for food or pearls: • a true oyster (family Ostreidae), in particular the edible **American oyster** (*Crassostrea virginica*). • [with *adj.*] a similar bivalve of another family, in particular the **thorny oysters** (Spondylidae), **wing oysters** (Pteriidae), and **saddle oysters** (Anomiidae). ■ the color oyster white. **2** an oyster-shaped morsel of meat on each side of the backbone in poultry.
▶*v.* [*intrans.*] raise, dredge, or gather oysters: [as *n.*] (**oystering**) *oystering is still the lifeblood of this town.*
▶*adj.* [*attrib.*] of the color oyster white. ▷Middle English: from Old French *oistre*, via Latin from Greek *ostreon*; related to *osteon* 'bone' and *ostrakon* 'shell or tile.'
▶*PHRASE* □ **the world is your oyster** you are in a position to take the opportunities that life has to offer. [from Shakespeare's *Merry Wives of Windsor* (II. ii. 5).]

oys·ter bar ▶*n.* **1** a hotel bar, small restaurant, or other place where oysters are served. **2** (esp. in the southeastern U.S.) an oyster bed.

Oys·ter Bay a town in central Long Island in New York that includes the villages of Hicksville, Farmingdale, and Oyster Bay; pop. 292,657.

oys·ter bed ▶*n.* a part of the sea bottom where oysters breed or are bred.

oys·ter·catch·er /'oistər,kacʜər/ ▶*n.* a coastal wading bird with black-and-white or all-black plumage and a strong orange-red bill, feeding chiefly on shellfish. • Family Haematopodidae and genus *Haematopus*: several species, e.g., the black and white *H. ostralegus* of Eurasia.

oys·ter crab ▶*n.* a minute, soft-bodied crab that lives inside the shell of a bivalve mollusk, where it filters food particles from the water drawn into the shell by its host. Also called **PEA CRAB**. • Family Pinnotheridae: *Pinnotheres* and other genera.

oys·ter crack·er ▶*n.* a small, round soda cracker served with soup, oysters, etc.

oys·ter farm ▶*n.* an area of the seabed used for breeding oysters.

oys·ter·man /'oistərmən/ ▶*n.* a person who gathers, cultivates, or sells oysters. ■ a boat equipped for harvesting oysters.

oys·ter mush·room ▶*n.* a widely distributed edible fungus that has a grayish-brown, oyster-shaped cap and a very short or absent stem, growing on the wood of broad-leaved trees and causing rot. • *Pleurotus ostreatus*, family Pleurotaceae, class Hymenomycetes.

oys·ter plant ▶*n.* another term for **SALSIFY**.

oys·ter sauce ▶*n.* a sauce made with oysters and soy sauce, used esp. in oriental cooking.

oys·ters Rock·e·fel·ler ▶*plural n.* oysters covered with a mixture of spinach, butter, seasonings, and bread crumbs and cooked on the half shell.

oys·ter white ▶*n.* a shade of grayish-white.

oy vey /oi 'vā/ (also **oy**) ▶*exclam.* indicating dismay or grief. ▷late 19th cent.: Yiddish, literally 'oh woe.'

Oz /äz/ *Austral., informal* ▶*adj.* Australian.
▶*n.* Australia. ■ a person from Australia. ▷1940s: representing a pronunciation of an abbreviation of **AUSTRALIA**.

oz. ▶*abbr.* ounce(s). ▷from Italian *onza* 'ounce.'

Oz·a·lid /'äzə,lid/ ▶*n. trademark* a photocopy made by a process in which a diazonium salt and coupler are present in the paper coating, so that the image develops in the presence of ammonia. ▷1920s: by reversal of **DIAZO** and insertion of *-l.*

oz. ap. ▶*abbr.* apothecaries' ounce.

O·zark Moun·tains /'ō,zärk/ (also **the O·zarks**) a heavily forested highland plateau dissected by rivers, valleys, and streams, lying between the Missouri and Arkansas rivers and within the states of Missouri, Arkansas, Oklahoma, Kansas, and Illinois.

oz. av. ▶*abbr.* avoirdupois ounce.

O·za·wa /ō'zäwə/, Seiji (1935–), Japanese conductor. He was conductor of the Toronto Symphony Orchestra 1965–70, music director and conductor of the Boston Symphony Orchestra 1973–2002. In 2002 he became musical director of the Vienna State Opera. He also conducts frequently with major symphony and opera companies.

O·zick /'ō,zik/, Cynthia (1928–), U.S. writer and

critic. Many of her works, such as *Bloodshed and Three Novellas* (1976) and *The Puttermesser Papers* (1997), examine being Jewish in contemporary life. Some of her essays are collected in *Fame and Folly* (1996).

o·zo·ce·rite /ō'zōkə,rīt; -sə,rit; ,ōzō'sirīt/ (also **o·zo·ke·rite**) ▸*n.* a brown or black paraffin wax occurring naturally in some shales and sandstones and formerly used in candles, polishes, and electrical insulation. ▷mid 19th cent.: from German *Ozokerit*, from Greek *ozein* 'to smell' + *kēros* 'wax.'

o·zone /'ō,zōn/ ▸*n.* a colorless unstable toxic gas with a pungent odor and powerful oxidizing properties, formed from oxygen by electrical discharges or ultraviolet light. It differs from normal oxygen (O_2) in having three atoms in its molecule (O_3). ■ short for OZONE LAYER. ■ *informal* fresh invigorating air, esp. that blowing onto the shore from the sea. ▷mid 19th cent.: from German *Ozon*, from Greek *ozein* 'to smell.' **—o·zon·ic** /ō'zänik/ *adj.*

o·zone-friend·ly ▸*adj.* (of manufactured products) not containing chemicals that are destructive to the ozone layer.

o·zone hole ▸*n.* a region of marked thinning of the ozone layer in high latitudes, chiefly in winter, attributed to the chemical action of chlorofluorcarbons and other atmospheric pollutants. The resulting increase in ultraviolet light at ground level gives rise to an increased risk of skin cancer.

o·zone lay·er ▸*n.* a layer in the earth's stratosphere at an altitude of about 10 km (6.2 miles) containing a high concentration of ozone, which absorbs most of the ultraviolet radiation reaching the earth from the sun.

o·zo·nide /'ōzə,nīd/ ▸*n. Chemistry* any of a class of unstable cyclic compounds formed by the addition of ozone to a carbon–carbon double bond. ■ a salt of the anion O_3^-, derived from ozone.

o·zon·ize /'ōzə,nīz/ ▸*v.* [*trans.*] [often as *adj.*] (**ozonized**) convert (oxygen) into ozone. ■ enrich or treat with ozone: *ozonized air.* **—o·zon·i·za·tion** /,ōzəni'zāsʜən/ *n.* **—o·zon·iz·er** *n.*

o·zo·no·sphere /ō'zōnə,sfir/ ▸*n.* technical term for OZONE LAYER.

oz. t. ▸*abbr.* troy ounce.

Pp

P[1] /pē/ (also **p**) ▸*n.* (*pl.* **Ps** or **P's** /pēz/) the sixteenth letter of the alphabet. ■ denoting the next after O (or N if O is omitted) in a set of items, categories, etc.
▸*PHRASE* □ **mind one's Ps and Qs** see **MIND**.

P[2] ▸*abbr.* ■ pastor. ■ father. [Latin *pater*.] ■ (in tables of sports results) games played. ■ (on an automatic gearshift) park. ■ (on road signs and street plans) parking. ■ peseta. ■ peso. ■ [in *combination*] (in units of measurement) peta- (10^{15}): *27 PBq of radioactive material.* ■ *Physics* poise (unit of viscosity). ■ post. ■ president. ■ pressure. ■ priest. ■ prince. ■ proprietary. ■ progressive.
▸*symbol* ■ the chemical element phosphorus.

p ▸*abbr.* ■ page. ■ (**p-**) [in *combination*] *Chemistry* para-: p-*xylene.* ■ *Brit.* penny or pence. ■ *Music* piano (softly). ■ [in *combination*] (in units of measurement) pico- (10^{-12}): *a 220 pf capacitor.* ■ *Chemistry* denoting electrons and orbitals possessing one unit of angular momentum. [from *principal*, originally applied to lines in atomic spectra.]
▸*symbol* ■ *Physics* pressure. ■ *Statistics* probability.

P2P /'pē tə 'pē/ ▸*abbr. Computing* peer-to-peer.

PA ▸*abbr.* ■ Pennsylvania (in official postal use). ■ Press Association. ■ public address.

Pa ▸*abbr.* ■ pascal; pascals. ■ Pennsylvania.
▸*symbol* the chemical element protactinium.

pa /pä/ ▸*n. informal* father: *my pa was no farmer* | [as *name*] *Pa is busy on the telephone.* ▷early 19th cent.: abbreviation of **PAPA**.

p.a. ▸*abbr.* per annum.

pa'an·ga /'pänggə; pä'änggə/ ▸*n.* (*pl.* same) the basic monetary unit of Tonga, equal to 100 seniti. ▷Tongan.

Paarl /pärl/ a town in southwestern South Africa, in the province of Western Cape, northeast of Cape Town; pop. 71,000.

PABA /'päbə; 'pabə/ ▸*abbr.* para-aminobenzoic acid.

pab·lum /'pabləm/ ▸*n.* (also **pab·u·lum** /'pabyələm/) bland or insipid intellectual fare, entertainment, etc.; pap. ■ (**Pablum**) *trademark* a soft breakfast cereal for infants. ▷mid 17th cent. (in the sense 'food'): from Latin, from the stem of *pascere* 'to feed.'

PABX ▸*abbr.* private automatic branch exchange, a private telephone switchboard.

PAC /pak/ ▸*abbr.* ■ Pan-Africanist Congress. ■ political action committee.

pa·ca /'päkə; 'pakə/ ▸*n.* a nocturnal South American rodent that has a reddish-brown coat patterned with rows of white spots. It is hunted for its edible flesh. Also called **SPOTTED CAVY**. • Genus *Agouti* (or *Cuniculus*), family Dasyproctidae: two species, in particular *A. paca.* ▷mid 17th cent.: via Spanish and Portuguese from Tupi.

paca

pace[1] /pās/ ▸*n.* **1** a single step taken when walking or running. ■ a unit of length representing the distance between two successive steps in walking. ■ a gait of a horse or other animal, esp. one of the recognized trained gaits of a horse. ■ *poetic/literary* a person's manner of walking or running: *I steal with quiet pace.* **2** consistent and continuous speed in walking, running, or moving: *most traffic moved at the pace of the riverboat* | [in *sing.*] *walking at a comfortably fast pace.* ■ the speed or rate at which something happens, changes, or develops: *the children work separately in the classroom at their own pace* | *the poor neighborhoods fester at an increasingly rapid pace.* ■ (in sports) the speed or force of a hit or pitched ball.
▸*v.* [*intrans.*] walk at a steady and consistent speed, esp. back and forth and as an expression of one's anxiety or annoyance: *we paced up and down in exasperation* | [*trans.*] *she had been pacing the room.* ■ [*trans.*] measure (a distance) by walking it and counting the number of steps taken: *I* **paced out** *the dimensions of my new home.* ■ [*trans.*] lead (another runner in a race) in order to establish a competitive speed: *Morales paced us for four miles.* ■ (**pace oneself**) do something at a slow and steady rate or speed in order to avoid overexerting oneself: *Frank was pacing himself for the long night and day ahead.* ■ [*trans.*] move or develop (something) at a particular rate or speed: *the action is paced to the beat of a perky march* | [as *adj.* in *combination*] (**-paced**) *our fast-paced daily lives.* ■ [*intrans.*] (of a horse) move in a distinctive lateral gait in which both legs on the same side are lifted together, seen mostly in specially bred or trained horses. ▷Middle English: from Old French *pas*, from Latin *passus* 'stretch (of the leg),' from *pandere* 'to stretch.'
▸*PHRASES* □ **change of pace** a change from what one is used to: *the magenta is a change of pace from traditional red.* □ **keep pace with** move, develop, or progress at the same speed as: *fees have had to be raised a little to keep pace with inflation.* □ **off the pace** behind the leader or leading group in a race or contest. □ **put someone** (or **something**) **through their** (or **its**) **paces** make someone (or something) demonstrate their (or its) qualities or abilities: *the cars are examined by our safety experts and put through their paces by our drivers.* □ **set the pace** be the fastest runner in the early part of a race. ■ lead the way in doing or achieving something: *space movies have set the pace for the development of special effects.*

pace[2] /'pā,sē; 'pä,chā/ ▸*prep.* with due respect to (someone or their opinion), used to express polite disagreement or contradiction: *narrative history, pace some theorists, is by no means dead.* ▷Latin, literally 'in peace,' ablative of *pax*, as in *pace tua* 'by your leave.'

pace car ▸*n. Auto Racing* a car that sets the pace and positions racers for a rolling start in a warm-up lap or laps before a race, or that returns to control the pace in temporarily hazardous conditions.

pace·mak·er /'pās,mākər/ ▸*n.* **1** an artificial device for stimulating the heart muscle and regulating its contractions. ■ the part of the heart muscle (the sinoatrial node) that normally performs this role. ■ the part of an organ or of the body that controls any other rhythmic physiological activity. **2** another term for **PACESETTER**. **—pace·mak·ing** /-,māking/ *adj.* & *n.*

pace notes ▸*plural n.* (in rally driving) notes made before a rally by a competitor about the characteristics of a particular course, esp. with regard to advisable speeds for each section.

pac·er /'pāsər/ ▸*n.* **1** a pacesetter. **2** a horse bred or trained to have a distinctive lateral gait in which both legs on the same side are lifted together, used in some types of racing.

pace·set·ter /'pās,setər/ ▸*n.* a runner or competitor who sets the pace at the beginning of a race or competition, sometimes in order to help another runner break a record. ■ a person or organization viewed as taking the lead or setting standards of achievement for others: *Alaska is the pacesetter when it comes to salaries for teachers.* **—pace·set·ting** *adj.* & *n.*

pa·cha ▸*n.* variant spelling of **PASHA** (sense 1).

pa·chin·ko /pə'chingkō/ ▸*n.* a Japanese form of pinball. ▷Japanese.

pa·chi·si /pə'chēzē/ ▸*n.* a four-person Indian board game in which cowrie shells are thrown to determine the movements of pieces around the board. ■ (also *trademark* **Par·chee·si** /pär'chēzē/) a modern version of this game, using four marbles per player and dice. ▷from Hindi *paccīsī*, literally '(throw) of 25' (the highest of the game).

Pa·chu·ca de So·to /pä'choōkə de 'sōtō/ (also **Pa·chu·ca**) a city in Mexico, capital of the state of Hidalgo; pop. 179,000.

pa·chu·co /pə'choōkō/ ▸*n.* (*pl.* **-cos**) *dated* a juvenile gang member of Mexican-American ethnic origin. ▷Mexican Spanish, literally 'flashily dressed.'

pach·y·ceph·a·lo·saur /,paki'sefələ,sôr/ ▸*n.* a bipedal herbivorous dinosaur of the late Cretaceous period with a thick domed skull. • Infraorder Pachycephalosauria, order Ornithischia: several genera, including *Pachycephalosaurus.* ▷from Greek *pakhus* 'thick' + *kephalē* 'head' + *sauros* 'lizard.'

pach·y·derm /'pakə,dərm/ ▸*n.* a very large mammal with thick skin, esp. an elephant, rhinoceros, or hippopotamus. ▷mid 19th cent.: from French *pachyderme*, from Greek *pakhudermos*, from *pakhus* 'thick' + *derma* 'skin.' **—pach·y·der·mal** /,pakə'dərməl/ *adj.* **—pach·y·der·ma·tous** /,pakə'dərmətəs/ *adj.* **—pach·y·der·mic** /,pakə'dərmik/ *adj.*

pach·y·san·dra /,paki'sandrə/ ▸*n.* an evergreen creeping shrubby plant of the box family. • Genus *Pachysandra*, family Buxaceae: several species, in particular the Japanese *P. terminalis.* ▷formed irregularly from Greek *pakhus* 'thick' + *anēr, andr-* 'male' (with reference to the thick stamens).

pach·y·tene /'pakə,tēn/ ▸*n. Biology* the third stage of the prophase of meiosis, following zygotene, during which the paired chromosomes shorten and thicken, the two chromatids of each separate, and exchange of segments between chromatids may occur. ▷early 20th cent.: from Greek *pakhus* 'thick' + *tainia* 'band.'

pa·cif·ic /pə'sifik/ ▸*adj.* **1** peaceful in character or intent: *a pacific gesture.* **2** (**Pacific**) of or relating to the Pacific Ocean: *the Pacific War.*
▸*n.* (**Pacific**) **1** short for **PACIFIC OCEAN**. **2** a steam locomotive of 4-6-2 wheel arrangement. ▷mid 16th cent.: from French *pacifique* or Latin *pacificus* 'peacemaking,' from *pax, pac-* 'peace.' **—pa·cif·i·cal·ly** /-(ə)lē/ *adv.*

Pa·cif·i·ca /pə'sifikə/ a city in north central California, south of San Francisco, on the Pacific Ocean; pop. 37,670.

Pa·cif·ic Crest Trail a recreational trail that extends from the Mexican to the Canadian border, from California to Washington, and that follows mountain ridges for 2,600 miles (4,200 km).

Pa·cif·ic Is·land·er ▸*n.* a native or inhabitant of any of the islands in the South Pacific, esp. an aboriginal native of Polynesia.

Pa·cif·ic Is·lands, Trust Ter·ri·to·ry of the a UN trusteeship established in 1947 under U.S. administration and dissolved in 1994. It included the Caroline, Marshall, and Mariana islands, today all components of the Marshall Islands, the Northern Mariana Islands, the Federated States of Micronesia, or Palau.

Pa·cif·ic O·cean /pə'sifik/ the largest of the world's oceans. It lies between America on the east and Asia and Australasia on the west.

Pa·cif·ic Rim the countries and regions bordering

the Pacific Ocean, esp. the small nations of eastern Asia.

Pa·cif·ic time the standard time in a zone including the Pacific coastal region of the U.S. and Canada, specifically: • (**Pacific Standard Time**, abbrev.: **PST**) standard time based on the mean solar time at longitude 120° W, eight hours behind GMT. • (**Pacific Daylight Time**, abbrev.: **PDT**) Pacific time during daylight saving time, seven hours behind GMT.

pac·i·fi·er /ˈpasəˌfīər/ ▸*n.* a person or thing that pacifies. ■ a rubber or plastic nipple for a baby to suck on.

pac·i·fism /ˈpasəˌfizəm/ ▸*n.* the belief that any violence, including war, is unjustifiable under any circumstances, and that all disputes should be settled by peaceful means. ■ the refusal to participate in war or military service because of such a belief. ▷early 20th cent.: from French *pacifisme*, from *pacifier* 'pacify.' **—pac·i·fist** *n.* & *adj.* **—pac·i·fis·tic** /ˌpasəˈfistik/ *adj.*

pac·i·fy /ˈpasəˌfī/ ▸*v.* (**-fies**, **-fied**) [*trans.*] quell the anger, agitation, or excitement of: *he had to pacify angry spectators.* ■ bring peace to (a country or warring factions), esp. by the use or threatened use of military force: *the general pacified northern Italy.* ▷late 15th cent.: from Old French *pacefier*, from Latin *pacificare*, based on *pax*, *pac-* 'peace.' **—pa·cif·i·ca·tion** /ˌpasifiˈkāsHən/ *n.* **—pa·cif·i·ca·to·ry** /pəˈsifikəˌtôrē/ *adj.*

THE RIGHT WORD **appease, conciliate, mollify, pacify, placate, propitiate**

You might try to **pacify** a crying baby, to **appease** a demanding boss, to **mollify** a friend whose feelings have been hurt, and to **placate** an angry crowd. While all of these verbs have something to do with quieting people who are upset, excited, or disturbed, each involves taking a slightly different approach.

Pacify suggests soothing or calming (*the mother made soft cooing noises in an attempt to pacify her child*).

Appease implies that you've given in to someone's demands or made concessions in order to please (*she said she would visit his mother just to appease him*), while *mollify* stresses minimizing anger or hurt feelings by taking positive action (*her flattery failed to mollify him*).

Placate suggests changing a hostile or angry attitude to a friendly or favorable one, usually with a more complete or long-lasting effect than *appease* (*they were able to placate their enemies by offering to support them*).

You can **propitiate** a superior or someone who has the power to injure you by allaying or forestalling their anger (*they were able to propitiate the trustees by holding a dinner party in their honor*).

Conciliate implies the use of arbitration or compromise to settle a dispute or to win someone over (*the company made every effort to conciliate its angry competitor*).

Pa·cin·i·an cor·pus·cle /pəˈsinēən / ▸*n. Anatomy* an encapsulated ending of a sensory nerve that acts as a receptor for pressure and vibration. ▷late 19th cent.: named after Filippo *Pacini* (1812–83), Italian anatomist.

Pa·ci·no /pəˈcHēnō/, Al (1940–), U.S. movie actor; full name *Alfred Pacino*. Nominated for an Academy Award eight times, he won one for *Scent of a Woman* (1992). He first achieved recognition with *The Godfather* (1972) and *The Godfather Part II* (1974). Other notable movies: *Serpico* (1973), *Scarface* (1983), *Dick Tracy* (1990), and *Carlito's Way* (1993).

pack[1] /pak/ ▸*n.* **1** a small cardboard or paper container and the items contained within it: ***a pack of*** *cigarettes.* ■ a set of playing cards. ■ a knapsack or backpack. ■ a collection of related documents, esp. one kept in a folder: *an information pack.* ■ (often **the pack**) a quantity of fish, fruit, or other foods packed or canned in a particular season or year. **2** a group of wild animals, esp. wolves, living and hunting together. ■ a group of hounds kept and used for hunting, esp. fox hunting. ■ an organized group of Cub Scouts. ■ (**the pack**) the main body of competitors following the leader or leaders in a race or competition: *figurative the company was demonstrating the kind of innovations needed to keep it ahead of the pack.* ■ *chiefly derogatory* a group or set of similar things or people: *the reports were a* ***pack of*** *lies.* ■ short for PACK ICE. ■ *Rugby* a team's forwards considered as a group. **3** a hot or cold pad of absorbent material, esp. as used for treating an injury. ■ a cosmetic mask.

▸*v.* [*trans.*] fill (a suitcase or bag), esp. with clothes and other items needed when away from home: *I packed a bag with a few of my favorite clothes* | [*intrans.*] *she had packed and checked out of the hotel.* ■ place (something) in a container, esp. for transportation or storage: *I* ***packed up*** *my stuff and drove to Detroit.* ■ [*intrans.*] be capable of being folded up for transportation or storage: *these silver foil blankets pack into a small area.* ■ (**pack something in**) store something perishable in (a specified substance) in order to preserve it: *the organs were packed in ice.* ■ *informal* carry (a gun): *a sixteen-year-old can make a fortune selling drugs and pack a gun in the process.* ■ (often **be packed**) cram a large number of things into (a container or space): *it was a large room, packed with beds jammed side by side.* ■ [often as *adj.*] (**packed**) (of a large number of people) crowd into and fill (a room, building, or place): *the waiting room was packed.* ■ cover, surround, or fill (something): *he packed the wounds with healing malaguetta.* ■ [*intrans.*] *Rugby* (of players) form or take their places in a scrum: *we often* ***packed down*** *with only seven men.*

▸*phrasal v.* □ **pack something in** *informal* give up an activity or job. □ **pack someone off** *informal* send someone somewhere without much warning or notice: *they packed me off to the academy in Baltimore.* □ **pack something out** carry something away rather than leaving it behind (used esp. with respect to refuse at remote campsites): *pack out any garbage you have left.* ▷Middle English: from Middle Dutch, Middle Low German *pak* (noun), *pakken* (verb). The verb appears early in Anglo-Latin and Anglo-Norman French in connection with the wool trade; trade in English wool was chiefly with the Low Countries. **—pack·a·ble** *adj.*

▸*PHRASES* □ **pack heat** *informal* carry a gun. □ **pack it in** *informal* stop what one is doing. □ **pack a punch** be capable of hitting with skill or force: *Rosie could pack a hefty punch.* ■ have a powerful effect: *the Spanish wine packed quite a punch.* □ **packed out** *Brit., informal* (of a place) very crowded. □ **send someone packing** *informal* make someone leave in an abrupt or peremptory way.

pack[2] ▸*v.* [*trans.*] fill (a jury, committee, etc.) with people likely to support a particular verdict or decision: *his efforts to* ***pack*** *the Supreme Court* ***with*** *men who shared his ideology.* ▷early 16th cent. (in the sense 'enter into a private agreement'): probably from the obsolete verb *pact* 'enter into an agreement with,' the final *-t* being interpreted as an inflection of the past tense.

pack·age /ˈpakij/ ▸*n.* an object or group of objects wrapped in paper or plastic, or packed in a box. ■ the box or bag in which things are packed. ■ a packet: *a package of peanuts.* ■ (also **package deal**) a set of proposals or terms offered or agreed to as a whole: *a package of economic reforms.* ■ *informal* a package tour. ■ *Computing* a collection of programs or subroutines with related functionality.

▸*v.* [*trans.*] (usu. **be packaged**) put into a box or wrapping, esp. for sale: *choose products that are packaged in recyclable materials* | [as *adj.*] (**packaged**) *packaged foods.* ■ present (someone or something) in a particular way, esp. to make them more attractive: [as *adj.*, with *submodifier*] (**packaged**) *everything became a carefully packaged photo opportunity.* ■ combine (various products) for sale as one unit: *films would be packaged with the pictures of a production company.* ■ commission and produce (a book, typically a highly illustrated one) to sell as a complete product to publishers: *it's a question of trying to package the book properly.* ▷mid 16th cent. (as a noun denoting the action or mode of packing goods): from the verb PACK[1] + -AGE; compare with Anglo-Latin *paccagium*. The verb dates from the 1920s. **—pack·ag·er** *n.*

pack·age store ▸*n.* a store that sells alcoholic beverages in sealed containers for consumption elsewhere; a liquor store.

pack·age tour ▸*n.* a vacation organized by a travel agent, with arrangements for transportation, accommodations, etc., made at an inclusive price.

pack·ag·ing /ˈpakijiNG/ ▸*n.* materials used to wrap or protect goods. ■ the business or process of packing goods. ■ the presentation of a person, product, or action in a particular way: *diplomatic packaging of the key provisions will make a confrontation unlikely.*

pack an·i·mal ▸*n.* **1** an animal used to carry heavy loads. **2** an animal that lives and hunts in a pack.

pack·cloth /ˈpakˌklôTH/ ▸*n.* a thick, coarse cloth used for packing.

pack drill ▸*n.* a military punishment of marching back and forth carrying full equipment.

▸*PHRASE* □ **no names, no pack drill** punishment will be prevented if names and details are not mentioned.

packed lunch ▸*n. Brit.* a bag lunch.

pack·er /ˈpakər/ ▸*n.* a person or machine that packs something, esp. someone who prepares and packs food for transportation and sale.

pack·et /ˈpakit/ ▸*n.* **1** a paper or cardboard container, typically one in which goods are packed to be sold: ***a packet of*** *cigarettes.* ■ the contents of such a container. ■ a block of data transmitted across a network. **2** (also **packet boat**) *dated* a ship traveling at regular intervals between two ports, originally for the conveyance of mail.

▸*v.* (**-et·ed**, **-et·ing**) [*trans.*] make up into or wrap up in a packet: *packet a basket of take-out and head for Gooseberry Beach.* ▷mid 16th cent.: diminutive of PACK[1], perhaps from Anglo-Norman French; compare with Anglo-Latin *paccettum*.

pack·e·tize /ˈpakəˌtīz/ ▸*v.* [*trans.*] *Computing* partition or separate (data) into units for transmission in a packet-switching network: *this layer packetizes and reassembles messages.*

pack·et net·work ▸*n. Computing* a data transmission network using packet switching.

pack·et ra·di·o ▸*n.* a method of broadcasting that makes use of radio signals carrying packets of data.

pack·et switch·ing ▸*n. Computing & Telecommunications* a mode of data transmission in which a message is broken into a number of parts that are sent independently, over whatever route is optimum for each packet, and reassembled at the destination. Compare with MESSAGE SWITCHING.

pack·frame /ˈpakˌfrām/ ▸*n.* a frame to which a backpack is attached to make it easier to carry.

pack·horse /ˈpakˌhôrs/ ▸*n.* a horse used to carry loads.

pack ice ▸*n.* an expanse of large pieces of floating ice driven together into a nearly continuous mass, as occurs in polar seas.

pack·ing /ˈpakiNG/ ▸*n.* the action or process of packing something: *the handling, packing, and shipping of products.* ■ material used to protect fragile goods, esp. in transit: *polystyrene packing.* ■ material used to seal a joint or assist in lubricating an axle.

pack·ing case (also **packing box** or **packing crate**) ▸*n.* a large strong box, typically a wooden one, in which goods are packed for transportation or storage.

pack·ing den·si·ty ▸*n. Computing* the density of stored information in terms of bits per unit occupied of its storage medium.

pack·man /ˈpakmən/ ▸*n.* (*pl.* **-men**) *archaic* a peddler.

pack rat ▸*n.* a ratlike rodent that accumulates a mound of sticks and debris in the nest hole, native to North and Central America. Also called WOOD RAT. • *Neotoma* and other genera, family Muridae: many species. ■ a person who saves unnecessary objects or hoards things.

pack·sack /ˈpakˌsak/ ▸*n.* a knapsack or backpack.

pack·sad·dle /ˈpakˌsadl/ ▸*n.* a horse's saddle designed for supporting packs.

pack·thread /ˈpakˌTHred/ ▸*n.* thick thread for sewing or tying up packages.

pact /pakt/ ▸*n.* a formal agreement between individuals or parties. ▷late Middle English: from Old French, from Latin *pactum* 'something agreed upon,' neuter past participle (used as a noun) of *paciscere* 'agree.'

pa·cu /ˈpako͞o; paˈko͞o/ ▸*n.* (*pl.* same) a deep-bodied, herbivorous freshwater fish native to northern South America. • *Colossoma nigripinnis*, family Characidae. ▷early 19th cent.: from Tupi *pacú*.

pad[1] /pad/ ▸*n.* **1** a thick piece of soft material used to reduce friction or jarring, enlarge or change the shape of something, or hold or absorb liquid: *sterile gauze pads.* ■ short for INK PAD. ■ the fleshy underpart of an animal's foot or of a human finger. ■ a protective guard worn by a sports player to protect a part of the body from blows. **2** a number of sheets of blank paper fastened together at one edge, used for writing or drawing on. **3** a flat-topped structure or area used for helicopter takeoff and landing or for rocket launching. ■ *Electronics* a flat area on a track of a printed circuit or on the edge of an integrated circuit to which wires or component leads can be attached to make an electrical connection. **4** *informal* a person's home: *the police raided my pad.* **5** short for LILY PAD.

▸*v.* (**pad·ded**, **pad·ding**) [*trans.*] [often as *adj.*] (**padded**) fill or cover (something) with a soft material in order to give it a particular shape, protect it or its contents, or make it more comfortable: *a padded envelope.* ■ add false items to (an expense report or bill) in order to receive unjustified payment: *faked repairs and padded expenses for government work reaped billions of dollars for the Mafia.* ▷mid 16th cent. (in the sense 'bundle of straw to lie on'): the senses may not be of common origin; the meaning 'underpart of an animal's foot' is perhaps related to Low German *pad* 'sole of the foot'; the history remains obscure.

pad[2] ▶*v.* (**pad·ded, pad·ding**) [*intrans.*] walk with steady steps making a soft dull sound: *she padded along the corridor.* ■ [*trans.*] travel along (a road or route) on foot: *he was padding the streets.*
▶*n.* [in *sing.*] the soft dull sound of steady steps: *he heard the pad of feet.* ▷mid 16th cent.: from Low German *padden* 'to tread, go along a path,' partly imitative.

Pa·dang /pä'däNG; 'pädäNG/ a seaport in Indonesia, the largest city on the west coast of Sumatra; pop. 481,000.

pa·dauk /pə'douk/ (also **pa·douk**) ▶*n.* **1** timber from a tropical tree of the pea family, resembling rosewood. **2** the large hardwood tree of the Old World tropics that is widely grown for this timber. Some kinds yield a red dye that is used for religious and ritual purposes. • Genus *Pterocarpus*, family Leguminosae: three species, in particular **African padauk** (*P. soyauxii*). ▷mid 19th cent.: from Burmese.

pad·ded cell ▶*n.* a room in a psychiatric hospital with padding on the walls to prevent violent patients from injuring themselves.

pad·ding /'padiNG/ ▶*n.* soft material such as foam or cloth used to pad or stuff something. ■ superfluous material in a book, speech, etc., introduced in order to make it reach a desired length.

pad·dle[1] /'padl/ ▶*n.* a short pole with a broad blade at one or both ends, used without an oarlock to move a small boat or canoe through the water. ■ an act of using a paddle in a boat: *a gentle paddle on sluggish water.* ■ a short-handled bat used in various ball games, esp. table tennis. ■ a paddle-shaped instrument used for mixing food or for stirring or mixing in industrial processes. ■ another term for PEEL[2]. ■ *informal* a paddle-shaped instrument used for administering corporal punishment. ■ each of the boards fitted around the circumference of a paddle wheel or mill wheel. ■ a flat array of solar cells projecting from a spacecraft. ■ the fin or flipper of an aquatic mammal or bird. ■ *Medicine* a plastic-covered electrode used in cardiac stimulation. ■ short for BIDDING PADDLE.
▶*v.* **1** [*intrans.*] move through the water in a boat using a paddle or paddles: *he paddled along the coast.* ■ [*trans.*] propel (a small boat or canoe) with a paddle or paddles: *he was teaching trainees to paddle canoes.* ■ [*trans.*] travel along (a stretch of water) using such a method: *I had paddled the river through other hot July spells.* ■ (of a bird or other animal) swim with short fast strokes: *the swan paddled away.* **2** [*trans.*] *informal* beat (someone) with a paddle as a punishment: *he was firm in his conviction that his children would never be paddled.* ▷late Middle English (denoting a small spadelike implement): of unknown origin. Current senses date from the 17th cent. **—pad·dler** *n.*
▶PHRASE □ **paddle one's own canoe** *informal* be independent and self-sufficient.

pad·dle[2] ▶*v.* [*intrans.*] walk with bare feet in shallow water: *the children paddled at the water's edge.* ■ dabble the feet or hands in water: *Peter paddled idly in the water with his fingers.*
▶*n.* [in *sing.*] an act of walking with bare feet in shallow water. ▷mid 16th cent.: of obscure origin; compare with Low German *paddeln* 'tramp around'; the association with water remains unexplained. **—pad·dler** *n.*

pad·dle·ball /'padl,bôl/ ▶*n.* a game played with a light ball and wooden bat in a four-walled handball court.

pad·dle·boat /'padl,bōt/ ▶*n.* a small pleasure boat driven by pedals that in turn drive a paddle wheel.

pad·dle·fish /'padl,fiSH/ ▶*n.* (*pl.* same or **-fish·es**) a large, mainly freshwater fish related to the sturgeon, with an elongated snout. • The plankton-feeding *Polyodon spathula* of the Mississippi basin, and the fish-eating *Psephurus gladius* of the Yangtze River, the only surviving members of the family Polyodontidae.

pad·dle steam·er ▶*n.* a boat powered by steam and propelled by paddle wheels.

pad·dle ten·nis ▶*n.* a type of tennis played in a small court with a rubber ball and a wooden or plastic paddle.

pad·dle wheel ▶*n.* a large steam-driven wheel with boards around its circumference, situated at the stern or side of a ship so as to propel the ship through the water by its rotation.

paddle wheel

pad·dling pool /'padliNG / ▶*n.* British term for WADING POOL.

pad·dock /'padək/ ▶*n.* a small field or enclosure where horses are kept or exercised. ■ an enclosure adjoining a racetrack where horses are gathered and displayed before a race.
▶*v.* [*trans.*] (usu. **be paddocked**) keep or enclose (a horse) in a paddock: *horses paddocked on a hillside.* ▷early 17th cent.: apparently a variant of dialect *parrock*, of unknown ultimate origin.

Pad·dy /'padē/ ▶*n.* (*pl.* **-dies**) *informal, often offensive* an Irishman (often as a form of address). ▷late 18th cent.: nickname for the Irish given name *Padraig*.

pad·dy /'padē/ ▶*n.* (*pl.* **-dies**) (also **rice paddy**) a field where rice is grown. ■ rice before threshing or in the husk. ▷early 17th cent.: from Malay *pādī*.

pad·dy·mel·on ▶*n.* variant spelling of PADEMELON.

pad·dy wag·on ▶*n.* *informal* a police van. ▷1930s: *paddy* from PADDY, perhaps because formerly many American police officers were of Irish descent.

pad·e·mel·on /'padē,melən/ (also **pad·dy·mel·on**) ▶*n.* a small wallaby inhabiting the coastal scrub of Australia and New Guinea. • Genus *Thylogale*, family Macropodidae: three species. ▷early 19th cent. (earlier as *paddymelon*): probably an alteration of Dharuk *badimalion.*

Pa·de·rew·ski /,padə'refskē; ,päd-/, Ignacy Jan (1860–1941), Polish pianist, composer, and statesman; prime minister 1919. He was the first prime minister of independent Poland, but resigned after only 10 months in office to resume his musical career.

pad eye ▶*n.* a flat metal plate with a projecting loop or ring, made all in one piece.

pa·di·shah /,pädə'SHä/ ▶*n.* *historical* a title formerly used for various rulers, including the shah of Iran and the sultan of Turkey.

pad·lock /'pad,läk/ ▶*n.* a detachable lock hanging by a pivoted hook on the object fastened.
▶*v.* [*trans.*] [usu. as *adj.*] (**padlocked**) secure with such a lock: *a padlocked door.* ▷late 15th cent.: from *pad-* (of unknown origin) + the noun LOCK[1].

Pad·ma /'padmə/ a river in southern Bangladesh, formed by the confluence of the Ganges and the Brahmaputra rivers near Rajbari.

pa·douk ▶*n.* variant spelling of PADAUK.

Pa·do·va /'pädôvä/ Italian name for PADUA.

pa·dre /'pädrā/ ▶*n.* father; the title of a priest or chaplain in some regions. ■ *informal* a chaplain (typically a Roman Catholic chaplain) in any of the armed services. ▷late 16th cent.: from Italian, Spanish, and Portuguese, literally 'father, priest,' from Latin *pater, patr-* 'father.'

Pad·re Is·land /'pädrā/ a barrier island in southern Texas, on the Gulf of Mexico, 113 miles (183 km) long, noted for its resorts and its wildlife.

pa·dri·no /pə'drēnō/ ▶*n.* (*pl.* **-nos**) a godfather or patron. ■ a best man at a wedding. ▷Spanish.

pa·dro·na /pə'drōnə/ ▶*n.* (*pl.* **-nas**) a female boss or proprietress. ▷Italian.

pa·dro·ne /pə'drōnā; pə'drōnē/ ▶*n.* (*pl.* **-dro·nes** /-'drōnāz; -'drōnz/) a patron or master, in particular: ■ a Mafia boss. ■ *informal* an employer, esp. one who exploits immigrant workers. ■ (in Italy) the proprietor of a hotel. ▷Italian.

pad·saw /'pad,sô/ ▶*n.* a small saw with a narrow blade, for cutting curves.

pad site ▶*n.* a building lot adjacent to a shopping center or mall.

pad thai /,päd 'tī/ ▶*n.* a Thai dish based on rice noodles. ▷Thai.

Pad·u·a /'pajōōə/ a city in northeastern Italy; pop. 218,000. Italian name PADOVA. **—Pad·u·an** *adj.*

pad·u·a·soy /'pajōōə,soi/ ▶*n.* a heavy, rich corded or embossed silk fabric, popular in the 18th century. ▷late 16th cent. (as *poudesoy*), from French *pou-de-soie*, of unknown origin; altered by association with *Padua say*, denoting a cloth resembling serge.

Pa·du·cah /pə'd(y)ōōkə/ a historic commercial city in western Kentucky, on the Ohio River, near the mouth of the Tennessee River; pop. 26,307.

pae·an /'pēən/ ▶*n.* a song of praise or triumph. ■ a thing that expresses enthusiastic praise: *his books are paeans to combat.* ▷late 16th cent.: via Latin from Greek *paian* 'hymn of thanksgiving to Apollo' (invoked by the name *Paian*, originally the Homeric name for the physician of the gods).

pae·di·at·rics ▶*plural n.* British spelling of PEDIATRICS.

paedo- ▶*comb. form* British spelling of PEDO-[1].

pa·el·la /pä'äyä; pə'elə/ ▶*n.* a Spanish dish of rice, saffron, chicken, seafood, etc., cooked and served in a large shallow pan. ▷Catalan, from Old French *paele*, from Latin *patella* 'pan.'

pae·on /'pēən/ ▶*n.* *Prosody* a metrical foot of one long syllable and three short syllables in any order. ▷early 17th cent.: via Latin from Greek *paiōn*, the Attic form of *paian* 'hymn of thanksgiving to Apollo' (see PAEAN). **—pae·on·ic** /pē'änik/ *adj.*

Pa·gan /pə'gän/ ruins in Myanmar (Burma), located on the Irrawaddy River southeast of Mandalay. It is the site of an ancient city that was the capital of a powerful Buddhist dynasty from the 11th to the 13th centuries.

pa·gan /'pāgən/ ▶*n.* a person holding religious beliefs other than those of the main world religions. ■ *dated, derogatory* a non-Christian. ■ an adherent of neopaganism.
▶*adj.* of or relating to such people or beliefs: *a pagan god.* ▷late Middle English: from Latin *paganus* 'villager, rustic,' from *pagus* 'country district.' Latin *paganus* also meant 'civilian,' becoming, in Christian Latin, 'heathen' (i.e., one not enrolled in the army of Christ). **—pa·gan·ish** *adj.* **—pa·gan·ism** /-,nizəm/ *n.* **—pa·gan·ize** /-,nīz/ *v.*

Pa·ga·ni·ni /,pagə'nēnē; ,pä-/, Niccolò (1782–1840), Italian violinist and composer. His virtuoso violin recitals, including widespread use of pizzicato and harmonics, established him as a major figure of the romantic movement.

Page /pāj/, Geraldine (Sue) (1924–87), U.S. actress. Her Broadway credits include *Sweet Bird of Youth* (1959), *Strange Interlude* (1963), and *Agnes of God* (1982). Her movies include *Hondo* (1953), *Summer and Smoke* (1961), and *The Trip to Bountiful* (Academy Award, 1985).

page[1] /pāj/ ▶*n.* one side of a sheet of paper in a collection of sheets bound together, esp. as a book, magazine, or newspaper. ■ the material written or printed on such a sheet of paper: *she silently read several pages.* ■ a sheet of paper of such a kind considered as a whole, comprising both sides. ■ [with *adj.*] a page of a newspaper or magazine set aside for a particular topic: *the editorial page.* ■ *Printing* the type set for the printing of a page. ■ *Computing* a section of stored data, esp. that which can be displayed on a screen at one time. ■ a significant episode or period considered as a part of a longer history: *the inconsistency of this transaction has no parallel on any page of our political history.*
▶*v.* [*intrans.*] (**page through**) leaf through (a book, magazine, or newspaper): *she was paging through an immense pile of Sunday newspapers.* ■ *Computing* move through and display (text) one page at a time. ■ [usu. as *n.*] (**paging**) *Computing* divide (a piece of software or data) into sections, keeping the most frequently accessed in main memory and storing the rest in virtual memory. ■ [*trans.*] assign numbers to the pages in (a book or periodical); paginate. ■ [as *adj.*, in *combination*] (**-paged**) having pages of a particular kind or number: *a many-paged volume.* ▷late 16th cent.: from French, from Latin *pagina*, from *pangere* 'fasten.'
▶PHRASE □ **on the same page** (of two or more people) in agreement.

page[2] ▶*n.* a young person, usually in uniform, employed in a hotel or other establishment to run errands, open doors, etc. ■ a young boy attending a bride at a wedding. ■ *historical* a boy in training for

Pronunciation Key ə ago; ər over; 'ə or ,ə up; 'ər or ,ər fur; a hat; ā rate; ä car; CH chew; e let; ē see; e(ə)r air; i fit; ī by; i(ə)r ear; NG sing; ō go; ô for; oi boy; ōō good; ōō goo; ou out; SH she; TH thin; TH then; (h)w why; ZH vision

knighthood, ranking next below a squire in the personal service of a knight. ■ *historical* a man or boy employed as the personal attendant of a person of rank.
▸*v.* [*trans.*] summon (an individual) by name, typically over a public address system, so as to pass on a message: *no need to interrupt the background music just to page the concierge.* ■ [often as *n.*] (**paging**) contact (someone) by means of a pager: *many systems have paging as a standard feature.* ▷Middle English (in the sense 'youth, male of uncouth manners'): from Old French, perhaps from Italian *paggio*, from Greek *paidion*, diminutive of *pais*, *paid-* 'boy.' Early use of the verb (mid 16th cent.) was in the sense 'follow as or like a page'; its current sense dates from the early 20th cent.

pag·eant /ˈpajənt/ ▸*n.* a public entertainment consisting of a procession of people in elaborate, colorful costumes, or an outdoor performance of a historical scene. ■ (also **beauty pageant**) a beauty contest. ■ a thing that looks impressive or grand, but is actually shallow and empty. ■ *historical* a scene erected on a fixed stage or moving vehicle as a public show. ▷late Middle English *pagyn*, of unknown origin.

pag·eant·ry /ˈpajəntrē/ ▸*n.* elaborate display or ceremony.

page·boy /ˈpājˌboi/ ▸*n.* **1** a woman's hairstyle consisting of a shoulder-length bob with the ends rolled under. **2** a male page, esp. in a hotel or attending a bride at a wedding.

pageboy 1

page-one ▸*adj.* worthy of being featured on the front page of a newspaper or magazine: *page-one news.*

page proof ▸*n.* a printer's proof of a page to be published.

pag·er /ˈpājər/ ▸*n.* an electronic device, usually worn on one's person, that receives messages and signals the user by beeping or vibrating.

Pag·et's dis·ease /ˈpajits/ ▸*n.* **1** a chronic disease of the elderly characterized by deterioration of bone tissue, esp. in the spine, skull, or pelvis, sometimes causing severe pain; osteitis deformans. **2** an inflammation of the nipple associated with breast cancer. ▷late 19th cent.: named after Sir James *Paget* (1814–99), English surgeon.

page-turn·er ▸*n. informal* an exciting book.

pag·i·nal /ˈpajənəl/ ▸*adj.* of or relating to the pages of a book or periodical. ▷mid 17th cent.: from late Latin *paginalis*, from *pagina* (see **PAGE**[1]).

pag·i·na·tion /ˌpajəˈnāshən/ ▸*n.* the sequence of numbers assigned to pages in a book or periodical. ▷mid 19th cent.: noun of action from *paginate*, from French *paginer*, based on Latin *pagina* 'a page' (see **PAGE**[1]). —**pag·i·nate** /ˈpajəˌnāt/ *v.*

Pa·gnol /pänˈyôl/, Marcel (1895–1974), French playwright, movie director, and writer. His novels include *La Gloire de mon père* (1957) and *Le Chateau de ma mère* (1958); the movies *Jean de Florette* and *Manon des Sources* (both 1986) were based on his *L'Eau des collines* (1963).

pa·go·da /pəˈgōdə/ ▸*n.* a Hindu or Buddhist temple or sacred building, typically a many-tiered tower, in India and the Far East. ■ an ornamental imitation of this. ▷late 16th cent.: from Portuguese *pagode*, perhaps based on Persian *butkada* 'temple of idols,' influenced by Prakrit *bhagodī* 'divine.'

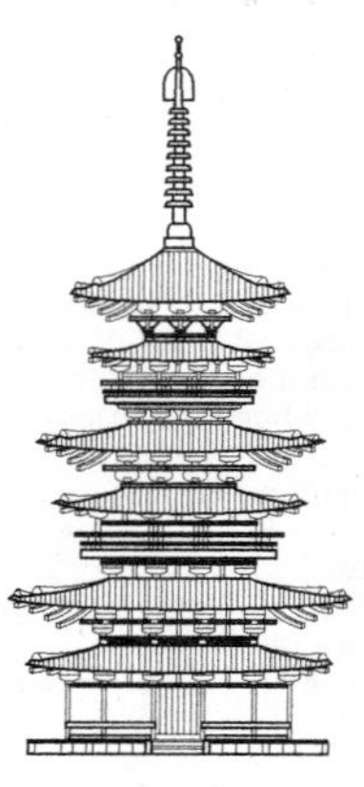
pagoda

pa·go·da sleeve ▸*n.* a funnel-shaped outer sleeve turned back to expose an inner sleeve and lining.

pa·go·da tree ▸*n.* a Southeast Asian tree of the pea family that has hanging clusters of cream flowers and is cultivated as an ornamental. • *Sophora japonica*, family Leguminosae.

Pa·go Pa·go /ˈpäNG(g)ō ˈpäNG(g)ō; ˈpägō ˈpägō/ the chief port of American Samoa, on Tutuila Island; pop. 4,000. Fagatogo, the territorial capital, is just to the east.

PAH ▸*abbr.* polycyclic aromatic hydrocarbon, any of a group of chemicals formed during the incomplete burning of organic substances.

pah /pä/ ▸*exclam.* used to express disgust or contempt: *"Pah! They know nothing."* ▷natural utterance: first recorded in English in the late 16th cent.

Pah·la·vi[1] /ˈpäləˌvē/ the name of two shahs of Iran: ■ **Reza** (1878–1944), ruled 1925–41; born *Reza Khan*. An army officer, he took control of the Persian government after a coup in 1921. He was elected shah in 1925 but abdicated following the occupation of Iran by British and Soviet forces. ■ **Muhammad Reza** (1919–80), ruled 1941–79; son of Reza Pahlavi; also known as **Reza Shah**. Opposition to his regime culminated in the Islamic revolution of 1979 under Ayatollah Khomeini; Reza Shah was forced into exile and died in Egypt.

Pah·la·vi[2] (also **Peh·le·vi**) ▸*n.* an Aramaic-based writing system used in Persia from the 2nd century BC to the advent of Islam in the 7th century AD. It was also used for the recording of ancient Avestan sacred texts. ■ the form of the Middle Persian language written in this script, used in the Sassanian empire. ▷from Persian *pahlawī*, from *pahlav*, from *parthava* 'Parthia.'

pa·ho·e·ho·e /pəˈhōēˌhōē/ ▸*n. Geology* basaltic lava forming smooth undulating or ropy masses. Often contrasted with **AA**. ▷mid 19th cent.: from Hawaiian.

paid /pād/ ▸ past and past participle of **PAY**[1].
▸*adj.* (of work or leave) for or during which one receives pay: *a one-month paid vacation.* ■ [*attrib.*] (of a person in a specified occupation) in receipt of pay: *a paid, anonymous informer.*

pai·deia /pīˈdāə/ ▸*n.* (in ancient Greece) education or upbringing. ■ the culture of a society. ▷Greek.

paid-up ▸*adj.* [*attrib.*] (of a member of an organization, esp. a labor union) having paid the necessary dues in full. ■ denoting the part of the subscribed capital of an undertaking that has actually been paid: *paid-up capital.* ■ denoting an endowment policy in which the policyholder has stopped paying premiums, resulting in the surrender value being used to purchase single-premium whole life insurance.

Paige /pāj/, Satchel (1906–82), U.S. baseball player; born *Leroy Robert Paige*. A pitcher for the Negro leagues 1924–47 and the major leagues, he threw 55 career no-hitters. He pitched for the Cleveland Browns 1948–49, the St. Louis Browns 1951–53, and the Kansas City Athletics 1965. Baseball Hall of Fame (1971).

pail /pāl/ ▸*n.* a bucket. ▷Middle English: origin uncertain; compare with Old English *pægel* 'gill, small measure' and Old French *paelle* 'pan, liquid measure, brazier.' —**pail·ful** /-ˌfo͝ol/ *n.* (*pl.* **-fuls**)

Pai·lin /ˈpäˈlin/ a ruby-mining town in western Cambodia, close to the border with Thailand.

pail·lasse /ˌpalˈyas; ˈpalˌyas/ ▸*n.* variant spelling of **PALLIASSE**.

pail·lette /pīˈyet; pä-; pəˈlet/ ▸*n.* a piece of glittering material used to ornament clothing; a spangle. ■ a piece of bright metal used in enamel painting. ▷mid 19th cent.: from French, diminutive of *paille*, from Latin *palea* 'straw, chaff.'

pain /pān/ ▸*n.* **1** physical suffering or discomfort caused by illness or injury: *she's* ***in great pain*** | *those who suffer from back pain.* ■ a feeling of marked discomfort in a particular part of the body: *he had severe pains in his stomach* | *chest pains.* ■ mental suffering or distress: *the pain of loss.* ■ (also **pain in the neck** or *vulgar slang* **pain in the ass**) [in *sing.*] *informal* an annoying or tedious person or thing: *she's a pain.* **2** (**pains**) careful effort; great care or trouble: *she* ***took pains*** *to see that everyone ate well* | *he* ***is at pains to*** *point out that he isn't like that.*
▸*v.* [*trans.*] cause mental or physical pain to: *it pains me to say this* | *her legs had been paining her.* ■ [*intrans.*] (of a part of the body) hurt: *sometimes my right hand would pain.* ▷Middle English (in the sense 'suffering inflicted as punishment for an offense'): from Old French *peine*, from Latin *poena* 'penalty,' later 'pain.'
▸*PHRASES* □ **for one's pains** *informal* as an unfairly bad return for efforts or trouble: *he was sued for his pains.* □ **no pain, no gain** suffering is necessary in order to achieve something. [originally used as a slogan in fitness classes.] □ **on** (or **under**) **pain of** the penalty for disobedience or shortcoming being: *all persons are commanded to keep silent on pain of imprisonment.*

Paine /pān/, Thomas (1737–1809), English political writer. His pamphlet *Common Sense* (1776) called for American independence, and *The Rights of Man* (1791) defended the French Revolution. His radical views prompted the British government to indict him for treason, and he fled to France. He also wrote *The Age of Reason* (1794).

pained /pānd/ ▸*adj.* affected with pain, esp. mental pain; hurt or troubled: *a pained expression came over his face* | *Susan looked pained.*

pain·ful /ˈpānfəl/ ▸*adj.* (of part of the body) affected with pain: *her ankle was very painful.* ■ causing physical pain: *a painful knock.* ■ causing distress or trouble: *a painful experience* | *change is inevitably slow and painful.* —**pain·ful·ness** *n.*

pain·ful·ly /ˈpānfəlē/ ▸*adv.* in a painful manner or to a painful degree: *she coughed painfully.* ■ [as *submodifier*] (with reference to something bad) exceedingly; acutely: *progress was painfully slow.*

pain·kil·ler /ˈpānˌkilər/ ▸*n.* a drug or medicine for relieving pain. —**pain·kill·ing** /-ˌkiliNG/ *adj.*

pain·less /ˈpānləs/ ▸*adj.* not causing or suffering physical pain: *a painless death.* ■ involving little effort or stress: *a painless way to travel.* —**pain·less·ly** *adv.* —**pain·less·ness** *n.*

pain per·du /ˈpān perˈdo͞o; paN perˈdY/ ▸*n.* French term for **FRENCH TOAST**. ▷French, literally 'lost bread.'

pains·tak·ing /ˈpānzˌtākiNG; ˈpānˌstākiNG/ ▸*adj.* done with or employing great care and thoroughness: *painstaking attention to detail* | *he is a gentle, painstaking man.* —**pains·tak·ing·ly** *adv.* —**pains·tak·ing·ness** *n.*

paint /pānt/ ▸*n.* **1** a colored substance that is spread over a surface and dries to leave a thin decorative or protective coating: *a can of paint* | *the paint has been applied to the surface with a palette knife.* ■ an act of covering something with paint: *it looked in need of a good paint.* ■ *informal* cosmetic makeup: *one has false curls, another too much paint.* ■ *Basketball* the rectangular area marked near the basket at each end of the court; the foul lane: *the two players jostled* ***in the paint.*** ■ *Computing* the function or capability of producing graphics, esp. those that mimic the effect of real paint: [as *adj.*] *a paint program.* **2** a piebald horse: [as *adj.*] *a paint mare.*
▸*v.* [*trans.*] **1** (often **be painted**) cover the surface of (something) with paint, as decoration or protection: *the walls hadn't been painted for years* | [*trans.*] *the ceiling was painted dark gray* | [as *adj.* with *submodifier*] (**painted**) *a brightly painted trailer.* ■ apply cosmetics to (the face or skin): *she couldn't have been more than fourteen but her face was thickly painted.* ■ apply (a liquid) to a surface with a brush. ■ (**paint something out**) efface something with paint: *the markings on the plane were hurriedly painted out.* ■ *Computing* create (a graphic or screen display) using a paint program. ■ display a mark representing (an aircraft or vehicle) on a radar screen. **2** depict (an object, person, or scene) with paint: *I painted a woman sitting next to a table lamp.* ■ produce (a picture) in such a way: *Marr is a self-taught artist who paints portraits* | [*intrans.*] *she paints and she makes sculptures.* ■ give a description of (someone or something): *I'm painted as some nut case living in the woods.* ▷Middle English: from *peint* 'painted,' past participle of Old French *peindre*, from Latin *pingere* 'to paint.' —**paint·a·ble** *adj.* —**paint·y** *adj.* (**paint·i·er**, **paint·i·est**).
▸*PHRASES* □ **like watching paint dry** (of an activity or experience) extremely boring. □ **paint oneself into a corner** leave oneself no means of escape or room to maneuver. □ **paint the town (red)** *informal* go out and enjoy oneself flamboyantly.

paint·ball /ˈpāntˌbôl/ ▸*n.* a game in which participants simulate military combat using air guns to shoot capsules of paint at each other. ■ a capsule of paint used in this game. —**paint·ball·er** *n.*

paint·box /ˈpāntˌbäks/ ▸*n.* a box holding dry paints for painting pictures. ■ (**Paintbox**) *trademark* an electronic system used to create video graphics by storing filmed material on disk and manipulating it using a graphics tablet.

paint·brush /ˈpāntˌbrəsh/ ▸*n.* **1** a brush for applying paint. **2** [with *adj.*] a North American plant that bears brightly colored flowering spikes with a brushlike appearance. See also **DEVIL'S PAINTBRUSH**. • Genus *Castilleja*, family Scrophulariaceae: several species, including the **Indian paintbrush** (*C. coccinea*), also called **painted cup**.

paint-by-num·ber ▸*adj.* denoting a picture marked out in advance into sections that are numbered according to the color to be used. ■ *figurative* denoting something mechanical or formulaic rather than imaginative, original, or natural: *a paint-by-number way to feel or act.*

paint chip ▶*n.* a card showing a color or a range of related colors available in a type of paint.

paint·ed bunt·ing ▶*n.* see BUNTING[1].

paint·ed cup ▶*n.* see PAINTBRUSH (sense 2).

Paint·ed Des·ert a region in northeastern Arizona that is noted for its colorful eroded landscapes.

paint·ed la·dy ▶*n.* **1** a migratory butterfly with predominantly orange-brown wings and darker markings. • Genus *Cynthia*, subfamily Nymphalinae, family Nymphalidae: the widely distributed *C. cardui*, with black and white markings, and the **American painted lady** (*C. virginiensis*), with eyemarks on the undersides of the wings. **2** (also **Painted Lady**) a Victorian house, the exterior of which is painted in three or more colors, effectively highlighting the architecture.

painted lady 1

paint·ed snipe ▶*n.* a small long-billed wading bird that has brown plumage with colorful markings. • Family Rostratulidae: two species, in particular *Rostratula benghalensis* of the Old World.

paint·ed tur·tle ▶*n.* a small American freshwater turtle with a smooth shell and colorful patterns of red, yellow, and black that appear along the border of the carapace and (in certain subspecies) on the plastron. • *Chrysemys picta*, family Emydidae.

painted turtle

paint·er[1] /ˈpāntər/ ▶*n.* **1** an artist who paints pictures: *a German landscape painter.* **2** a person who paints buildings, walls, ceilings, and woodwork, esp. as a job. ▷Middle English: from Anglo-Norman French *peintour*, based on Latin *pictor*, from the verb *pingere* 'to paint.'

paint·er[2] ▶*n.* a rope attached to the bow of a boat for making it fast. ▷Middle English: of uncertain origin; compare with Old French *pentoir* 'something from which to hang things.'

paint·er[3] ▶*n.* another term for COUGAR.

paint·er·ly /ˈpāntərlē/ ▶*adj.* of or appropriate to a painter; artistic: *she has a painterly eye.* ■ (of a painting or its style) characterized by qualities of color, stroke, and texture rather than of line. **—paint·er·li·ness** *n.*

paint gun ▶*n.* an air gun firing capsules of paint, used in the game of paintball.

pain thresh·old ▶*n.* the point beyond which a stimulus causes pain. ■ the upper limit of tolerance to pain.

paint·ing /ˈpāntiNG/ ▶*n.* the process or art of using paint, in a picture, as a protective coating, or as decoration. ■ a painted picture: *an oil painting.*

paint job ▶*n.* the decorative or finishing application of paint to an object. ■ *derogatory* a cosmetic treatment that does not address underlying problems: *this administration will settle for a paint job to try to hide the fact that it lives in a La-La Land of its own construction.*

paint roll·er ▶*n.* a roller covered in wool, sponge, synthetic fiber, or other absorbent material for applying paint to a surface, esp. in interior decorating.

paint shop ▶*n.* the part of a factory where goods are painted, typically by spraying.

paint stick /pānt stik/ ▶*n.* a stick of water-soluble paint used like a crayon.

paint·work /ˈpāntˌwərk/ ▶*n.* painted surfaces in a building or vehicle.

pair /pe(ə)r/ ▶*n.* a set of two things used together or regarded as a unit: *a pair of gloves.* ■ an article or object consisting of two joined or corresponding parts not used separately: *a pair of jeans.* ■ two playing cards of the same denomination: *I have a pair of jacks.* ■ two people related in some way or considered together: *a company run by a pair of brothers | every naughty thing* ***the pair of them*** *did made their faces look worse | students work alone or* ***in pairs.*** ■ the second member of a pair in relation to the first: *each course member tries to persuade his pair of the merits of his model.* ■ a mated couple of animals: *nine breeding pairs of birds.* ■ two horses harnessed side by side. ■ either or both of two members of a legislative assembly on opposite sides who absent themselves from voting by mutual arrangement, leaving the relative position of the parties unaffected.
▶*v.* [*trans.*] (often **be paired**) join or connect to form a pair: *a cardigan* ***paired with*** *a matching skirt.* ■ [*intrans.*] (of animals) mate: *they bought a rooster to* ***pair with*** *the hen.* ■ [*intrans.*] (**pair off/up**) form a couple: *Rachel has* ***paired up with*** *Tommy.* ■ give (a member of a legislative assembly) another member as a pair, to allow both to absent themselves from a vote without affecting the result: *an absent member on one side is to be* ***paired with*** *an absentee on the other.* ▷Middle English: from Old French *paire*, from Latin *paria* 'equal things,' neuter plural of *par* 'equal.' Formerly phrases such as *a pair of gloves* were expressed without *of*, as in *a pair gloves* (compare with German *ein Paar Handschuhe*). **—pair·wise** /-ˌwīz/ *adj.* & *adv.*
▶*PHRASE* □ **pair of hands** a person seen in terms of their participation in a task: *we can always do with an extra pair of hands.*

pair-bond ▶*v.* [*intrans.*] (of an animal or person) form a close relationship through courtship and sexual activity with one other animal or person.
▶*n.* (**pair bond**) a relationship so formed.

paired /pe(ə)rd/ ▶*adj.* occurring in pairs or as a pair: *a characteristic arrangement of paired fins.*

pair·ing /ˈpe(ə)riNG/ ▶*n.* an arrangement or match resulting from organizing or forming people or things into pairs: *the dancers made a fine pairing.* ■ the action of pairing things or people: *the pairing of food and wine | the step occurs very late in meiosis, well after the time of chromosome pairing.*

pair pro·duc·tion ▶*n.* *Physics* the conversion of a radiation quantum into an electron and a positron.

pai·sa /ˈpīsä/ ▶*n.* (*pl.* **-se** /-sā/) a monetary unit of Bangladesh, India, Pakistan, and Nepal, equal to one hundredth of a rupee. ▷from Hindi *paisā*.

pai·san /pīˈzän/ ▶*n.* *informal* (among people of Italian or Spanish descent) a fellow countryman or friend (often as a term of address). ▷from Italian *paisano* 'peasant, rustic.'

pai·sa·no /pīˈzänō/ ▶*n.* (*pl.* **-nos**) a peasant of Spanish or Italian ethnic origin. ▷Spanish.

pais·ley /ˈpāzlē/ ▶*n.* [usu. as *adj.*] a distinctive intricate pattern of curved, feather-shaped figures based on a pine-cone design from India: *a paisley silk tie.* ▷early 19th cent.: named after the town *Paisley*, Scotland, the original place of manufacture.

paisley

Pai·ute /ˈpī(y)o͞ot; pīˈ(y)o͞ot/ ▶*n.* (*pl.* same or **-utes**) **1** a member of either of two culturally similar but geographically separate and linguistically distinct American Indian peoples, the **Southern Paiute** of the southwestern U.S. and the **Northern Paiute** of Oregon and Nevada. **2** either of the Uto-Aztecan languages of these peoples.
▶*adj.* of or relating to the Paiute or their languages. ▷from Spanish *Payuchi, Payuta*, influenced by UTE.

pa·ja·mas /pəˈjäməz; -ˈjaməz/ (*Brit.* **py·ja·mas**) ▶*plural n.* a suit of loose pants and jacket or shirt for sleeping in: *a pair of pajamas* | [as *adj.*] (**pajama**) *pajama bottoms.* ■ [in *sing.*] (**pajama**) a pair of loose pants tied by a drawstring around the waist, worn by both sexes in some Asian countries. ▷early 19th cent.: from Urdu and Persian, from *pāy* 'leg' + *jāma* 'clothing.'

pak choi /ˌbäk ˈCHoi/ ▶*n.* another term for BOK CHOY. ▷from Chinese (Cantonese dialect) *paâk ts'oì* 'white vegetable.'

pa·ke·ha /ˈpäkiˌhä; -kēˌä/ ▶*n.* *Austral./NZ* a white New Zealander, as opposed to a Maori.
▶*adj.* of or relating to white New Zealanders and their languages and culture. ▷Maori.

Pakh·tun /pəkˈto͞on/ ▶a form of PATHAN, used especially in Asia.

Pak·i /ˈpakē/ ▶*n.* (*pl.* **Pak·is**) *Brit., informal, offensive* a person from Pakistan or the Indian subcontinent by birth or descent, esp. one living in Britain. ▷1960s: abbreviation.

Pak·i·stan /ˈpakiˌstan; ˌpäkiˈstän/ a country in the Indian subcontinent; pop. 159,196,000; capital, Islamabad; languages, Urdu (official), English (official), Punjabi, Sindhi, and Pashto. ▷from Punjab, Afghan Frontier, Kashmir, Baluch*istan*, lands where Muslims predominated. **—Pak·i·sta·ni** /ˌpakəˈstanē; ˌpäkiˈstänē/ *adj.* & *n.*

Pakistan was created as a separate country in 1947, following Britain's withdrawal from India. It originally included two territories—one to the east and one to the west of India—in which the population was predominantly Muslim. Civil war in East Pakistan led to the establishment of the independent state of Bangladesh in 1972. Pakistan withdrew from the Commonwealth of Nations in 1972, but rejoined in 1989.

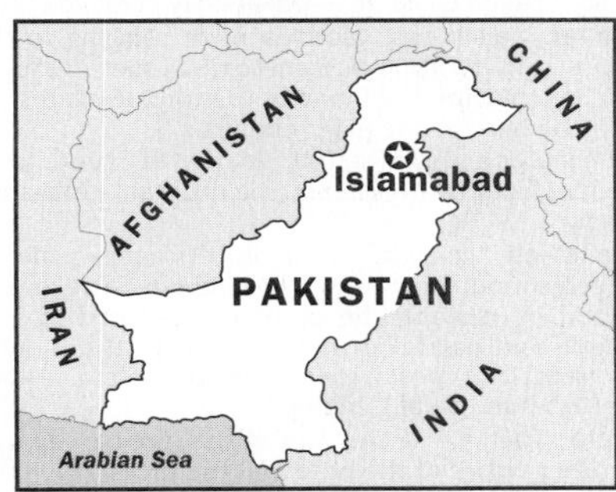

Pa·ki·stan Peo·ple's Par·ty (abbr.: **PPP**) one of the main political parties in Pakistan. It was founded in 1967 by Zulfikar Ali Bhutto, and has been led since 1984 by his daughter Benazir Bhutto.

pa·ko·ra /pəˈkôrə/ ▶*n.* (in Indian cooking) a piece of vegetable or meat, coated in seasoned batter and deep-fried. ▷from Hindi *pakoṛā*, denoting a dish of vegetables in gram flour.

pa kua /pä ˈkwä/ ▶*n.* variant spelling of BA GUA.

PAL /pal/ ▶*n.* the television broadcasting system used in most of Europe. ▷acronym from *Phase Alternate Line* (so named because the color information in alternate lines is inverted in phase).

pal /pal/ *informal* ▶*n.* a friend: *we're best pals.* ■ used as a form of address, esp. to indicate anger or aggression: *back off, pal.*
▶*v.* (**palled, pal·ling**) [*intrans.*] (**pal around**) spend time with a friend: *we got acquainted but we never really palled around.* ▷late 17th cent.: from Romany, 'brother, mate,' based on Sanskrit *bhrātṛ* 'brother.'

pal·ace /ˈpalis/ ▶*n.* the official residence of a sovereign, archbishop, bishop, or other exalted person: *the royal palace.* ■ *informal* a large, splendid house. ▷Middle English: from Old French *paleis*, from Latin *Palatium*, the name of the Palatine hill in Rome, where the house of the emperor was situated.

pal·ace car ▶*n.* *chiefly historical* a luxurious railroad car.

pal·ace coup (also **palace revolution**) ▶*n.* the nonviolent overthrow of a sovereign or government by senior officials within the ruling group.

pa·lac·sin·ta /ˌpälətˈsintə/ ▶*n.* (*pl.* same or **-tas**) (in Hungarian cuisine) a thin pancake eaten as a dessert, typically with a filling. ▷Hungarian.

pal·a·din /ˈpalədin/ ▶*n.* *historical* any of the twelve peers of Charlemagne's court, of whom the count palatine was the chief. ■ a knight renowned for heroism and chivalry. ▷late 16th cent.: from French *paladin*, from Italian *paladino*, from Latin *palatinus* '(officer) of the palace' (see PALATINE[1]).

Pronunciation Key ə ago; ər over; ˈə or ˌə up; ˈər or ˌər fur; a hat; ā rate; ä car; CH chew; e let; ē see; e(ə)r air; i fit; ī by; i(ə)r ear; NG sing; ō go; ô for; oi boy; o͝o good; o͞o goo; ou out; SH she; TH thin; T͟H then; (h)w why; ZH vision

Pa·lae·arc·tic ▸*adj.* British spelling of **PALEARCTIC**.

palaeo- ▸*comb. form* British spelling of **PALEO-**.

pa·laes·tra /pəˈlestrə/ (also **pa·les·tra**) ▸*n.* (in ancient Greece and Rome) a wrestling school or gymnasium. ▷via Latin from Greek *palaistra*, from *palaiein* 'wrestle.'

Pa·lais de Jus·tice /pəˈl ā də jəˈstēs/ ▸*n.* (*pl.* same) (in France and French-speaking countries) a court of law. ▷French, literally 'palace of justice.'

pal·am·pore /ˈpaləm,pôr/ ▸*n.* *Indian* a type of chintz, used especially for bedspreads. ■ a palampore bedspread. ▷late 17th cent.: origin uncertain; perhaps from Portuguese, *palangapuz(es)* plural, from Urdu, Persian, *palangpoš*, 'bedcover,' or perhaps from *Pālanpur*, a town in Gujarat, India.

pal·an·quin /,palənˈkēn/ (also **pal·an·keen**) ▸*n.* (in India and the East) a covered litter for one passenger, consisting of a large box carried on two horizontal poles by four or six bearers. ▷late 16th cent.: from Portuguese *palanquim*, from Oriya *pālaṅki*, based on Sanskrit *palyanka* 'bed, couch.'

pa·la·pa /pəˈläpə/ ▸*n.* a traditional Mexican shelter roofed with palm leaves or branches. ■ a structure, esp. on a beach, of a similar kind. ▷Mexican Spanish, denoting the palm *Orbignya cohune*.

pal·at·a·ble /ˈpalətəbəl/ ▸*adj.* (of food or drink) pleasant to taste: *a very palatable local red wine.* ■ (of an action or proposal) acceptable or satisfactory: *a device that made increased taxation more palatable.* —**pal·at·a·bil·i·ty** /,palətəˈbilətē/ *n.* —**pal·at·a·bly** /-blē/ *adv.*

pal·a·tal /ˈpalətl/ ▸*adj.* *technical* of or relating to the palate: *a palatal lesion.* ■ *Phonetics* (of a speech sound) made by placing the blade of the tongue against or near the hard palate (e.g., *y* in *yes*).
▸*n.* *Phonetics* a palatal sound. ▷early 18th cent.: from French, from Latin *palatum* (see **PALATE**). —**pal·a·tal·ly** *adv.*

pal·a·tal·ize /ˈpalətl,īz/ ▸*v.* [*trans.*] *Phonetics* make (a speech sound) palatal, esp. by changing a velar to a palatal by moving the point of contact between tongue and palate further forward in the mouth. ■ [*intrans.*] (of a speech sound) become palatal. —**pal·a·tal·i·za·tion** /,palətl-iˈzāsHən/ *n.*

pal·ate /ˈpalit/ ▸*n.* **1** the roof of the mouth, separating the cavities of the nose and the mouth in vertebrates. **2** a person's appreciation of taste and flavor, esp. when sophisticated and discriminating: *a fine range of drink for sophisticated palates.* ■ a person's taste or liking: *the suggestions may not suit everyone's palate.* ■ taste or flavor of wine or beer: *a wine with a zingy, peachy palate.* ▷late Middle English: from Latin *palatum*.

pa·la·tial /pəˈlāsHəl/ ▸*adj.* resembling a palace in being spacious and splendid: *her palatial apartment in Chicago.* ▷mid 18th cent.: from Latin *palatium* 'palace' (see **PALACE**) + **-AL**. —**pa·la·tial·ly** *adv.*

pa·lat·i·nate /pəˈlatn,āt; -,it/ ▸*n.* *historical* a territory under the jurisdiction of a count palatine. ■ (**the Palatinate**) the territory of the German Empire ruled by the count palatine of the Rhine.

Pal·a·tine /ˈpalə,tīn/ a village in northeastern Illinois, northwest of Chicago; pop. 39,253.

pal·a·tine[1] /ˈpalə,tīn/ ▸*adj.* [usu. *postpositive*] *chiefly historical* (of an official or feudal lord) having local authority that elsewhere belongs only to a sovereign. ■ (of a territory) subject to this authority. ▷late Middle English: from French *palatin(e)*, from Latin *palatinus* 'of the palace.'

pal·a·tine[2] *chiefly Anatomy* ▸*adj.* of or relating to the palate or esp. the palatine bone.
▸*n.* (also **palatine bone**) each of two bones within the skull forming parts of the eye socket, the nasal cavity, and the hard palate. ▷mid 17th cent.: from French *palatin(e)*, from Latin *palatum* 'palate.'

Pa·lau /pəˈlou/ (also **Be·lau** /bəˈlou/) a republic in the western Pacific Ocean, a group of about 100 of the Caroline Islands; pop. 20,000; capital, Koror; languages, English, Palauan, Sonsorolese, Tobi, and Angaur.

It became a part of the U.S. Trust Territory of the Pacific Islands in 1947, began self-governing internally in 1980, and achieved independence in 1994.

pa·lav·er /pəˈlavər; -ˈläv-/ ▸*n.* prolonged and idle discussion: *an hour of aimless palaver.* ■ *dated* a parley or improvised conference between two sides.
▸*v.* [*intrans.*] talk unnecessarily at length: *it's too hot for palavering.* ▷mid 18th cent. (in the sense 'a talk between tribespeople and traders'): from Portuguese *palavra* 'word,' from Latin *parabola* 'comparison' (see **PARABLE**).

Pa·la·wan /pəˈläwən; pä-/ a long, narrow island in the western Philippines that separates the Sulu Sea from the South China Sea.

pa·laz·zo /pəˈlätsō/ ▸*n.* (*pl.* **-laz·zos** or **-laz·zi** /-ˈlätsē/) a palatial building, esp. in Italy. ▷Italian, 'palace.'

pa·laz·zo pants ▸*plural n.* a woman's loose, wide-legged pants.

pale[1] /pāl/ ▸*adj.* light in color or having little color: *choose pale floral patterns for walls.* ■ (of a person's face or complexion) having less color than usual, typically as a result of shock, fear, or ill health: *she looked pale and drawn.* ■ *figurative* feeble and unimpressive: *unconvincing rock that came across as* ***a pale imitation of*** *Bruce Springsteen.*
▸*v.* [*intrans.*] **1** become pale in one's face from shock or fear: *I paled at the thought of what she might say.* **2** seem less impressive or important: *all else pales by comparison | his own problems* ***paled into insignificance*** *compared to the plight of this child.* ▷Middle English: from Old French *pale*, from Latin *pallidus*; the verb is from Old French *palir*. —**pale·ly** *adv.* —**pale·ness** *n.* —**pal·ish** *adj.*

THE RIGHT WORD **ashen, livid, pale, pallid, wan**
Someone of fair complexion who usually stays indoors and spends little time in the sun is apt to be **pale**, referring to an unusually white or colorless complexion; one can also become *pale* out of fear or illness.
Someone who has lost color from being ill or under stress may be described as **pallid**, which suggests a paleness that is the result of some abnormal condition (*she appeared pallid when she left the police station*).
Wan also connotes an unhealthy condition or sickly paleness (*her wan face smiled at him from the hospital bed*).
Someone who is **ashen** has skin the pale grayish color of ashes (*ashen with fear*), while **livid** can mean either bluish to describe loss of normal coloring (*the livid face of a drowned corpse*) or reddish or flushed (*livid with rage*).

pale[2] ▸*n.* **1** a wooden stake or post used as an upright along with others to form a fence. ■ *figurative* a boundary: *bring these things back within the pale of decency.* ■ *archaic* or *historical* an area within determined bounds, or subject to a particular jurisdiction. **2** (**the Pale**) *historical* another term for **ENGLISH PALE**. ■ the areas of Russia to which Jewish residence was restricted. **3** *Heraldry* a broad vertical stripe down the middle of a shield. ▷Middle English: from Old French *pal*, from Latin *palus* 'stake.'
▸***PHRASES*** □ **beyond the pale** outside the bounds of acceptable behavior: *the language my father used was beyond the pale.* □ **in pale** *Heraldry* arranged vertically. □ **per pale** *Heraldry* divided by a vertical line.

pa·le·a /ˈpālēə/ ▸*n.* (*pl.* **-le·ae** /-lē,ē; -lē,ī/) *Botany* the upper bract of the floret of a grass. Compare with **LEMMA**[2]. ▷mid 18th cent.: from Latin, literally 'chaff.'

Pa·le·arc·tic /,pālēˈärktik; -ˈärtik/ (*Brit.* **Pa·lae·arc·tic**) ▸*adj.* *Zoology* of, relating to, or denoting a zoogeographical region comprising Eurasia north of the Himalayas, together with North Africa and the temperate part of the Arabian peninsula. The fauna is closely related to that of the Nearctic region. Compare with **HOLARCTIC**. ■ [as *n.*] (**the Palearctic**) the Palearctic region.

pale·face /ˈpāl,fās/ ▸*n.* a name supposedly used by North American Indians for a white person.

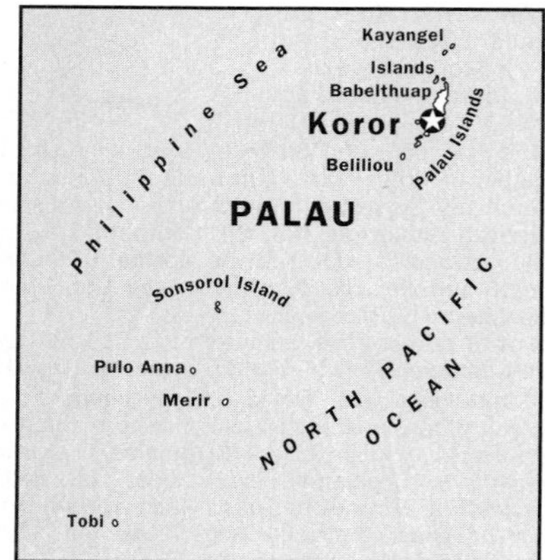

Pa·lekh /ˈpä,lek; -,leKH/ ▸*n.* [as *adj.*] denoting a type of Russian iconography or a style of miniature painting on boxes, trays, and other small items. ▷from the name of a town northeast of Moscow renowned for this type of work.

Pa·lem·bang /pä'lem,bäNG/ a city in Indonesia, in the southeastern part of Sumatra, a river port on the Musi River; pop. 1,141,000.

paleo- (*Brit.* **palaeo-**) ▸*comb. form* older or ancient, esp. relating to the geological past: *Paleolithic | paleomagnetism.* ▷from Greek *palaios* 'ancient.'

pa·le·o·an·thro·pol·o·gy /,pālēō,anTHrəˈpäləjē/ ▸*n.* the branch of anthropology concerned with fossil hominids. —**pa·le·o·an·thro·po·log·i·cal** /-pəˈläjikəl/ *adj.* —**pa·le·o·an·thro·pol·o·gist** /-jist/ *n.*

pa·le·o·bi·ol·o·gy /,pālēōbīˈäləjē/ ▸*n.* the biology of fossil animals and plants. —**pa·le·o·bi·o·log·i·cal** /-,bīəˈläjikəl/ *adj.* —**pa·le·o·bi·ol·o·gist** /-jist/ *n.*

pa·le·o·bot·a·ny /,pālēōˈbätn-ē/ ▸*n.* the study of fossil plants. —**pa·le·o·bo·tan·i·cal** /-bəˈtanikəl/ *adj.* —**pa·le·o·bot·a·nist** /-ˈbätn-ist/ *n.*

Pa·le·o·cene /ˈpālēə,sēn/ ▸*adj.* *Geology* of, relating to, or denoting the earliest epoch of the Tertiary period, between the Cretaceous period and the Eocene epoch. ■ [as *n.*] (**the Paleocene**) the Paleocene epoch or the system of rocks deposited during it.

The Paleocene epoch lasted from 65 million to 56.5 million years ago. It was a time of sudden diversification among the mammals, probably as a result of the mass extinctions (notably of the dinosaurs) that occurred at the end of the Cretaceous period (see **CRETACEOUS–TERTIARY BOUNDARY**).

▷late 19th cent.: from **PALEO-** (relating to prehistoric times) + Greek *kainos* 'new.'

pa·le·o·cli·mate /,pālēōˈklīmit/ ▸*n.* a climate prevalent at a particular time in the geological past. —**pa·le·o·cli·mat·ic** /-klīˈmatik/ *adj.* —**pa·le·o·cli·ma·tol·o·gist** /-,klīməˈtäləjist/ *n.* —**pa·le·o·cli·ma·tol·o·gy** /-,klīməˈtäləjē/ *n.*

pa·le·o·con /ˈpālēō,kän/ ▸*n.* *informal* short for **PALEOCONSERVATIVE**.

pa·le·o·con·serv·a·tive /,pālēōkənˈsərvətiv/ ▸*n.* a person who advocates old or traditional forms of conservatism; an extremely right-wing conservative.

pa·le·o·cur·rent /,pālēōˈkərənt; -ˈkə-rənt/ ▸*n.* a current that existed at some time in the geological past, as inferred from the features of sedimentary rocks.

pa·le·o·e·col·o·gy /,pālēō,əˈkäləjē/ ▸*n.* the ecology of fossil animals and plants. —**pa·le·o·e·co·log·i·cal** /-,ekəˈläjikəl; -,ēkə-/ *adj.* —**pa·le·o·e·col·o·gist** /-,əˈkäləjist; -,ēˈkäl-/ *n.*

pa·le·o·en·vi·ron·ment /,pālēōənˈvīrənmənt; -ˈvī(ə)rn-mənt/ ▸*n.* an environment prevailing at a particular time in the geological past. —**pa·le·o·en·vi·ron·men·tal** /-,vīrənˈmentl; -,vī(ə)rn-/ *adj.*

Pa·le·o-Es·ki·mo ▸*n.* a member of a prehistoric people inhabiting the Arctic from Greenland through North America to Siberia.
▸*adj.* of or relating to this people.

pa·le·o·fe·ces /,pālēōˈfē,sēz/ ▸*plural n.* dessicated prehistoric fecal matter, especially from humans: *sunflower-seed shells found in the paleofeces provide evidence that early American Indians in that region farmed the plants.* Compare with **COPROLITE**. —**pa·le·o·fe·cal** /,pālēōˈfēkəl/ *adj.*

Pa·le·o·gene /ˈpālēəjēn/ ▸*adj.* *Geology* of, relating to, or denoting the earlier division of the Tertiary period, comprising the Paleocene, Eocene, and Oligocene epochs. Compare with **NEOGENE**. ■ [as *n.*] (**the Paleogene**) the Paleogene subperiod or the system of rocks deposited during it.

The Paleogene lasted from about 65 million to 23 million years ago. The mammals diversified following the demise of the dinosaurs, and many bizarre and gigantic forms appeared.

▷late 19th cent.: from **PALEO-** (relating to prehistoric times) + Greek *genēs* 'of a specified kind' (see **-GEN**).

pa·le·o·ge·og·ra·phy /,pālēōjēˈägrəfē/ ▸*n.* the study of geographical features at particular times in the geological past. —**pa·le·o·ge·og·ra·pher** /-fər/ *n.* —**pa·le·o·ge·o·graph·i·cal** /-,jēəˈgrafikəl/ *adj.*

pa·le·og·ra·phy /,pālēˈägrəfē/ (*Brit.* **pa·lae·og·ra·phy**) ▸*n.* the study of ancient writing systems and the deciphering and dating of historical manuscripts. —**pa·le·og·ra·pher** /-fər/ *n.* —**pa·le·o·graph·ic** /,pālēəˈgrafik/ *adj.* —**pa·le·o·graph·i·cal** /,pālēəˈgrafikəl/ *adj.* —**pa·le·o·graph·i·cal·ly** /,pālēəˈgrafik(ə)lē/ *adv.*

Pa·le·o-In·di·an ▸*adj.* of, relating to, or denoting the earliest human inhabitants of the Americas, from as early as 40,000 years ago to *c.*5000 BC.
▸*n.* **1** (**the Paleo-Indian**) the Paleo-Indian culture or period. **2** a member of the Paleo-Indian peoples.

pa·le·o·lat·i·tude /ˌpālēōˈlatiˌt(y)o͞od/ ▸*n.* the latitude of a place at some time in the past, measured relative to the earth's magnetic poles in the same period. Differences between this and the present latitude are caused by continental drift and movement of the earth's magnetic poles.

Pa·le·o·lith·ic /ˌpālēəˈlitHik/ ▸*adj. Archaeology* of, relating to, or denoting the early phase of the Stone Age, lasting about 2.5 million years, when primitive stone implements were used. ■ [as *n.*] (**the Paleolithic**) the Paleolithic period. Also called **OLD STONE AGE**.

The Paleolithic period extends from the first appearance of artifacts to the end of the last ice age (about 8,500 years ago). The period has been divided into the **Lower Paleolithic**, with the earliest forms of humankind and the emergence of hand-ax industries (ending about 120,000 years ago), the **Middle Paleolithic**, the era of Neanderthal humans (ending about 35,000 years ago), and the **Upper Paleolithic**, during which only modern *Homo sapiens* is known to have existed.

▷mid 19th cent.: from **PALEO-** 'of prehistoric times' + Greek *lithos* 'stone' + **-IC**.

pa·le·o·mag·net·ism /ˌpālēōˈmagnəˌtizəm/ ▸*n.* the branch of geophysics concerned with the magnetism in rocks that was induced by the earth's magnetic field at the time of their formation. —**pa·le·o·mag·net·ic** /-magˈnetik/ *adj.*

pa·le·on·tol·o·gy /ˌpālēˌənˈtäləjē/ ▸*n.* the branch of science concerned with fossil animals and plants. ▷mid 19th cent.: from **PALEO-** 'of prehistoric times' + Greek *onta* 'beings' (neuter plural of *ōn*, present participle of *einai* 'be') + **-LOGY**. —**pa·le·on·to·log·i·cal** /ˌpālēˌäntəˈläjikəl/ *adj.* —**pa·le·on·tol·o·gist** /-jist/ *n.*

pa·le·o·pal·li·um /ˌpālēōˈpalēəm/ (*Brit.* **pa·lae·o·pal·li·um**) ▸*n.* (*pl.* **-pal·li·a** /-ˈpalēə/) *Anatomy* a phylogenetically older portion of the pallium of the brain, which comprises mainly the pyriform lobe. —**pa·le·o·pal·li·al** /-ˈpalēəl/ *adj.*

pa·le·o·pa·thol·o·gy /ˌpālēōpəˈTHäləjē/ ▸*n.* the branch of science concerned with the pathological conditions found in ancient human and animal remains. —**pa·le·o·path·o·log·i·cal** /-ˌpaTHəˈläjikəl/ *adj.* —**pa·le·o·path·ol·o·gist** /-jist/ *n.*

pa·le·o·pole /ˈpālēəˌpōl/ ▸*n.* a magnetic pole of the earth as it was situated at a particular time in the geological past.

pa·le·o·sol /ˈpālēəˌsôl; -ˌsäl/ ▸*n. Geology* a stratum or soil horizon that was formed as a soil in a past geological period.

pa·le·o·tem·per·a·ture /ˌpālēōˈtemp(ə)rəCHər; -ˌCHo͝or/ ▸*n. Geology* the temperature or mean temperature of a locality at a time in the geological past.

Pa·le·o·trop·i·cal /ˌpālēəˈträpikəl/ ▸*adj. Botany* of, relating to, or denoting a phytogeographical kingdom comprising Africa, tropical Asia, New Guinea, and many Pacific islands (excluding Australia and New Zealand). ■ *Zoology* of, relating to, or denoting a zoogeographical region comprising the tropical parts of the Old World.

Pa·le·o·zo·ic /ˌpālēəˈzōik/ ▸*adj. Geology* of, relating to, or denoting the era between the Precambrian eon and the Mesozoic era. Formerly called **PRIMARY**. ■ [as *n.*] (**the Paleozoic**) the Paleozoic era or the system of rocks deposited during it.

The Paleozoic lasted from about 570 million to 245 million years ago, its end being marked by mass extinctions. The **Lower Paleozoic** sub-era comprises the Cambrian, Ordovician, and Silurian periods, and the **Upper Paleozoic** sub-era comprises the Devonian, Carboniferous, and Permian periods. The era began with the first invertebrates with hard external skeletons, notably trilobites, and ended with the rise to dominance of the reptiles.

▷mid 19th cent.: from **PALEO-** 'of prehistoric times' + Greek *zōē* 'life' + **-IC**.

Pa·ler·mo /pəˈlerˌmō; -ˈle(ə)r-/ a port on the north coast of Sicily; pop. 734,000.

Pal·es·tine /ˈpaliˌstīn/ a territory in the Middle East on the eastern coast of the Mediterranean Sea. The name Palestine was used as the official political title for the land west of the Jordan mandated to Britain in 1920; in 1948, the state of Israel was established in what was traditionally Palestine, but the name continued to be used in the context of the struggle for territory and political rights of displaced Palestinian Arabs. In 1993, an agreement was signed between Israel and the Palestine Liberation Organization that gave some autonomy to the Gaza Strip and the West Bank and setting up the Palestine National Authority and a police force. ▷from Greek *Palaistinē* (used in early Christian writing), from Latin *(Syria) Palaestina* (the name of a Roman province), from *Philistia* 'land of the Philistines.'

Pal·es·tine Lib·er·a·tion Or·gan·i·za·tion (abbr.: **PLO**) a political and military organization formed in 1964 to unite various Palestinian Arab groups and ultimately to bring about an independent state of Palestine. Since 1968 it has been led by Yasser Arafat.

Pal·es·tin·i·an /ˌpaləˈstinēən/ ▸*adj.* of or relating to Palestine or its peoples.
▸*n.* a member of the native Arab population of the region of Palestine (including the modern state of Israel).

pa·les·tra ▸*n.* variant spelling of **PALAESTRA**.

Pa·les·tri·na /ˌpaləˈstrēnə; ˌpäle-/, Giovanni Pierluigi da (*c.*1525–94), Italian composer. He is chiefly known for his sacred music.

pal·ette /ˈpalit/ ▸*n.* a thin board or slab on which an artist lays and mixes colors. ■ the range of colors used by a particular artist or in a particular picture: *I choose a palette of natural, earthy colors.* ■ *figurative* the range or variety of tonal or instrumental color in a musical piece: *he commands the sort of tonal palette that this music needs.* ■ (in computer graphics) the range of colors or shapes available to the user. ▷late 18th cent.: from French, diminutive of *pale* 'shovel,' from Latin *pala* 'spade.'

pal·ette knife ▸*n.* a thin steel blade with a handle for mixing colors or applying or removing paint.

pal·frey /ˈpôlfrē/ ▸*n.* (*pl.* **-freys**) *archaic* a docile horse used for ordinary riding, esp. by women. ▷Middle English: from Old French *palefrei*, from medieval Latin *palefredus*, alteration of late Latin *paraveredus*, from Greek *para* 'beside, extra' + Latin *veredus* 'riding horse.'

Pa·li /ˈpälē/ ▸*n.* an Indic language, closely related to Sanskrit, in which the sacred texts of Theravada Buddhism are written. Pali developed in northern India in the 5th–2nd centuries BC.
▸*adj.* of or relating to this language. ▷from Pali *pāli(-bhāsā)* 'canonical texts.'

pa·li /ˈpälē/ ▸*n.* (*pl.* same or **pa·lis**) (in Hawaii) a cliff. ▷Hawaiian.

pali·la·lia /ˌpaləˈlālēə/ ▸*n. Medicine* a speech disorder characterized by involuntary repetition of words, phrases, or sentences. ▷early 20th cent.: from French *palilalie*, from Greek *palin* 'again' + *lalia* 'speech, chatter.'

pal·i·mo·ny /ˈpaləˌmōnē/ ▸*n. informal* compensation made by one member of an unmarried couple to the other after separation. ▷1970s: from **PAL** + a shortened form of **ALIMONY**.

pal·imp·sest /ˈpalimpˌsest/ ▸*n.* a manuscript or piece of writing material on which the original writing has been effaced to make room for later writing but of which traces remain. ■ *figurative* something reused or altered but still bearing visible traces of its earlier form: *Sutton Place is a palimpsest of the taste of successive owners.* ▷mid 17th cent.: via Latin from Greek *palimpsēstos*, from *palin* 'again' + *psēstos* 'rubbed smooth.' —**pal·imp·ses·tic** /ˌpalimpˈsestik/ *adj.*

pal·in·drome /ˈpalinˌdrōm/ ▸*n.* a word, phrase, or sequence that reads the same backward as forward, e.g., *madam* or *nurses run*. ▷early 17th cent.: from Greek *palindromos* 'running back again,' from *palin* 'again' + *drom-* (from *dramein* 'to run'). —**pal·in·drom·ic** /ˌpalinˈdrämik/ *adj.* —**pa·lin·dro·mist** /pəˈlindrəmist/ *n.*

pal·ing /ˈpāliNG/ ▸*n.* a fence made from pointed wooden or metal stakes. ■ a stake used in such a fence.

pal·in·gen·e·sis /ˌpalinˈjenəsis/ ▸*n.* **1** *Biology* the exact reproduction of ancestral characteristics in ontogenesis. **2** rebirth or regeneration. ▷early 19th cent.: from Greek *palin* 'again' + *genesis* 'birth.' —**pal·in·ge·net·ic** /ˌpalinjəˈnetik/ *adj.*

pal·i·node /ˈpaləˌnōd/ ▸*n.* a poem in which the poet retracts a view or sentiment expressed in a former poem. ▷late 16th cent.: via Latin from Greek *palinōidia*, from *palin* 'again' + *ōidē* 'song.'

Pal·i·o /ˈpälēō/ (*pl.* **Pal·i·i** /ˈpäləˌē/) a traditional horse race held in Siena, Italy, twice a year, in July and August. ▷Italian, from Latin *pallium* 'covering' (with reference to the cloth given as a prize).

pal·i·sade /ˌpaləˈsād/ ▸*n.* a fence of wooden stakes or iron railings fixed in the ground, forming an enclosure or defense. ■ *historical* a strong pointed wooden stake fixed deeply in the ground with others in a close row, used as a defense. ■ (**palisades**) a line of high cliffs. ■ (**the Palisades**) a ridge of high basalt cliffs that line the western side of the Hudson River, in New Jersey and in New York, beginning across from New York City in New Jersey and extending north to Newburgh in New York.
▸*v.* [*trans.*] [usu. as *adj.*] (**palisaded**) enclose or provide (a building or place) with a palisade. ▷early 17th cent.: from French *palissade*, from Provençal *palissada*, from *palissa* 'paling,' based on Latin *palus* 'stake.'

pal·i·sade lay·er ▸*n. Botany* a layer of parallel elongated cells below the epidermis of a leaf.

Pal·i·sades, the /ˌpaləˈsādz/ (also **Palisades of the Hudson**) cliffs that line the western side of the Hudson River, in New Jersey and in New York, beginning across from New York City in New Jersey and extending north to Newburgh in New York.

Palk Strait /pôk; pôlk/ an inlet of the Bay of Bengal that separates northern Sri Lanka from the coast of Tamil Nadu in India. It lies to the north of Adam's Bridge, which separates it from the Gulf of Mannar.

pall[1] /pôl/ ▸*n.* **1** a cloth spread over a coffin, hearse, or tomb. ■ *figurative* a dark cloud or covering of smoke, dust, or similar matter: *a pall of black smoke hung over the quarry.* ■ *figurative* something regarded as enveloping a situation with an air of gloom, heaviness, or fear: *torture and murder have cast a pall of terror over the villages.* **2** an ecclesiastical pallium. ■ *Heraldry* a Y-shaped charge representing the front of an ecclesiastical pallium. ▷Old English *pæll* 'rich (purple) cloth,' 'cloth cover for a chalice,' from Latin *pallium* 'covering, cloak.'

pall[2] ▸*v.* [*intrans.*] become less appealing or interesting through familiarity: *the novelty of the quiet life palled.* ▷late Middle English: shortening of **APPALL**.

pal·la·di·a /pəˈlādēə/ ▸ plural form of **PALLADIUM**[2].

Pal·la·di·an /pəˈlādēən/ ▸*adj. Architecture* of, relating to, or denoting the neoclassical style of Andrea Palladio, in particular with reference to the phase of English architecture from *c.*1715, when there was a revival of interest in Palladio and his English follower, Inigo Jones, and a reaction against the baroque. —**Pal·la·di·an·ism** /-ˌnizəm/ *n.*

Pal·la·di·an win·dow ▸*n.* a large window consisting of a central arched section flanked by two narrow rectangular sections.

Palladio, Andrea (1508–80), Italian architect. He led a revival of classical architecture, in particular promoting the Roman ideals of harmonic proportions and symmetrical planning. A notable example of his many villas, palaces, and churches is the church of San Giorgio Maggiore in Venice.

pal·la·di·um[1] /pəˈlādēəm/ ▸*n.* the chemical element of atomic number 46, a rare silvery-white metal resembling platinum. (Symbol: **Pd**) ▷early 19th cent.: modern Latin, from *Pallas*, the name given to an asteroid discovered (1803) just before the element.

pal·la·di·um[2] ▸*n.* (*pl.* **-di·a** /-dēə/) *archaic* a safeguard or source of protection. ▷late Middle English (in the Greek sense): via Latin from Greek *palladion*, denoting an image of the goddess Pallas (Athena), on which the safety of Troy was believed to depend.

Pal·las /ˈpaləs/ **1** *Greek Mythology* (also **Pallas Athene**) one of the names (of unknown meaning) of **ATHENA**. **2** *Astronomy* asteroid 2, discovered in 1802. It is the second largest (diameter 523 km).

pal·las·ite /ˈpaləsīt/ ▸*n.* a meteorite consisting of roughly equal proportions of iron and olivine. ▷mid 19th cent.: from the name of Peter S. *Pallas* (1741–1811), German naturalist, + **-ITE**[1].

pall·bear·er /ˈpôlˌbe(ə)rər/ ▸*n.* a person helping to carry or officially escorting a coffin at a funeral.

pal·let[1] /ˈpalit/ ▸*n.* a straw mattress. ■ a crude or makeshift bed. ▷Middle English: from Anglo-Norman French *paillete*, from *paille* 'straw,' from Latin *palea*.

pal·let[2] ▸*n.* **1** a portable platform on which goods can be moved, stacked, and stored, esp. with the aid of a forklift. **2** a flat wooden blade with a handle, used to shape clay or plaster. **3** an artist's palette. **4** a projection on a machine part, serving to change

Pronunciation Key ə *ago*; ər *over*; ˈə *or* ˌə *up*; ˈər *or* ˌər *fur*; a *hat*; ā *rate*; ä *car*; CH *chew*; e *let*; ē *see*; e(ə)r *air*; i *fit*; ī *by*; i(ə)r *ear*; NG *sing*; ō *go*; ô *for*; oi *boy*; o͝o *good*; o͞o *goo*; ou *out*; SH *she*; TH *thin*; T͟H *then*; (h)w *why*; ZH *vision*

the mode of motion of a wheel. ■ (in a clock or watch) a projection transmitting motion from an escapement to a pendulum or balance wheel. ▷late Middle English (sense 2): from French *palette* 'little blade,' from Latin *pala* 'spade'; compare with PALE[2].

pal·let[3] ▸*n. Heraldry* the diminutive of the pale, a narrow vertical strip, usually borne in groups of two or three. ▷late 15th cent.: diminutive of the noun PALE[2].

pal·let·ize /ˈpaləˌtīz/ ▸*v.* [*trans.*] [usu. as *adj.*] (**palletized**) place, stack, or transport (goods) on a pallet or pallets: *a roller system for quick movement of palletized cargo.*

pal·li·a /ˈpalēə/ ▸ plural form of PALLIUM.

pal·liasse /ˌpalˈyas; ˈpalˌyas/ (also **pail·lasse**) ▸*n.* a straw mattress. ▷early 16th cent. (originally Scots): from French *paillasse,* based on Latin *palea* 'straw.'

pal·li·ate /ˈpalēˌāt/ ▸*v.* [*trans.*] make (a disease or its symptoms) less severe or unpleasant without removing the cause: *treatment works by palliating symptoms.* ■ allay or moderate (fears or suspicions): *this eliminated, or at least palliated, suspicions aroused by German unity.* ■ disguise the seriousness or gravity of (an offense): *there is no way to excuse or palliate his dirty deed.* ▷late Middle English: from late Latin *palliat-* 'cloaked,' from the verb *palliare,* from *pallium* 'cloak.' **—pal·li·a·tion** /ˌpalēˈāsHən/ *n.* **—pal·li·a·tor** /-ˌātər/ *n.*

pal·li·a·tive /ˈpalēˌātiv; ˈpalēətiv/ ▸*adj.* (of a treatment or medicine) relieving pain or alleviating a problem without dealing with the underlying cause: *short-term, palliative measures had been taken.*
▸*n.* a remedy, medicine, etc., of such a kind. ▷late Middle English (as an adjective): from French *palliatif, -ive* or medieval Latin *palliativus,* from the verb *palliare* 'to cloak' (see PALLIATE). **—pal·li·a·tive·ly** *adv.*

pal·lid /ˈpalid/ ▸*adj.* (of a person's face) pale, typically because of poor health. See note at PALE. ■ feeble or insipid: *an utterly pallid and charmless character.* ▷late 16th cent.: from Latin *pallidus* 'pale' (related to *pallere* 'be pale'). **—pal·lid·ly** *adv.* **—pal·lid·ness** *n.*

pal·li·um /ˈpalēəm/ ▸*n.* (*pl.* **pal·li·a** /ˈpalēə/ or **pal·li·ums**) **1** a woolen vestment conferred by the pope on an archbishop, consisting of a narrow, circular band placed around the shoulders with short lappets hanging from front and back. **2** *historical* a man's large rectangular cloak, esp. as worn by Greek philosophical and religious teachers. **3** *Zoology* the mantle of a mollusk or brachiopod. **4** *Anatomy* the outer wall of the mammalian cerebrum, corresponding to the cerebral cortex. ▷Middle English: from Latin, literally 'covering.' **—pal·li·al** /ˈpalēəl/ *adj.* (in senses 3 and 4).

pall-mall /ˈpel ˈmel; ˈpôl ˈmôl; ˈpal ˈmal/ ▸*n. historical* a 16th- and 17th-century game in which a boxwood ball was driven through an iron ring suspended at the end of a long alley. ▷from obsolete French *pallemaille,* from Italian *pallamaglio,* from *palla* 'ball' + *maglio* 'mallet.'

pal·lor /ˈpalər/ ▸*n.* [in *sing.*] an unhealthy pale appearance. ▷late Middle English: from Latin, from *pallere* 'be pale.'

pal·ly /ˈpalē/ ▸*adj.* (**pal·li·er, pal·li·est**) [*predic.*] *informal* having a close, friendly relationship: *I see you're getting quite* **pally with** *Carlos.*

palm[1] /pä(l)m/ ▸*n.* (also **palm tree**) an unbranched evergreen tree with a crown of long feathered or fan-shaped leaves, and typically having old leaf scars forming a regular pattern on the trunk. Palms grow in warm regions, esp. the tropics. • Family Palmae (or Arecaceae): numerous genera and species, some of which are of great commercial importance, e.g., the **oil palm, date palm,** and coconut. ■ a leaf of such a tree awarded as a prize or viewed as a symbol of victory or triumph: *the consensus was that the palm should go to Doerner.* ▷Old English *palm(a),* of Germanic origin; related to Dutch *palm* and German *Palme,* from Latin *palma* 'palm (of a hand),' its leaf being likened to a spread hand.

palm[2] ▸*n.* the inner surface of the hand between the wrist and fingers. ■ a part of a glove that covers this part of the hand. ■ a hard shield worn on the hand by sailmakers to protect the palm in sewing. ■ the palmate part of an antler.
▸*v.* **1** [*trans.*] conceal (a card or other small object) in the hand, esp. as part of a trick or theft: *he would spin wild tales while palming your wristwatch.* **2** [*trans.*] hit (something) with the palm of the hand. ■ *Basketball* illegally grip (the ball) with the hand while dribbling.
▸*phrasal v.* □ **palm someone off** *informal* persuade someone to accept something by deception: *most sellers are* **palmed off with** *a fraction of what something is worth.* □ **palm something off** sell or dispose of something by misrepresentation or fraud: *they* **palmed off** *their shoddiest products* **on** *the Russians.* ▷Middle English: from Old French *paume,* from Latin *palma.* Current senses of the verb date from the late 17th cent. **—pal·mar** /ˈpalmər; ˈpä(l)mər/ *adj.* **—palmed** *adj.* [in *combination*] *sweaty-palmed.* **—palm·ful** /-fəl/ *n.*
▸*PHRASES* □ **have** (or **hold**) **someone in the palm of one's hand** have someone under one's control or influence: *she had the audience in the palm of her hand.* □ **read someone's palm** tell someone's fortune by looking at the lines on their palm.

Pal·ma /ˈpälmə/ an industrial port and resort on the island of Majorca in the Balearic Islands; pop. 309,000. Full name PALMA DE MALLORCA.

pal·ma·ro·sa ▸*n.* a fragrant tropical Indian grass related to citronella and lemongrass. It is cultivated for the essential oil it yields, which is used in perfumery and aromatherapy. • *Cymbopogon martinii,* family Gramineae. ■ (also **palmarosa oil**) the essential oil obtained from this grass.

pal·mate /ˈpalˌmāt; ˈpä(l)-/ ▸*adj.* **1** *Botany* (of a leaf) having several lobes (typically 5–7) whose midribs all radiate from one point. **2** *Zoology* (of an antler) in which the angles between the tines are partly filled in to form a broad flat surface, as in fallow deer and moose. ■ web-footed. ▷mid 18th cent.: from Latin *palmatus,* from *palma* 'palm' (see PALM[2]). **—pal·mat·ed** *adj.*

pal·mate newt ▸*n.* a small, olive-brown, smooth-skinned newt native to western Europe, with partially webbed feet. • *Triturus helveticus,* family Salamandridae.

palm ball (also **palm·ball**) ▸*n. Baseball* an off-speed pitch in which the ball is released from the palm and thumb rather than the fingers.

Palm Bay a residential city in east central Florida, southwest of Melbourne; pop. 62,632.

Palm Beach a resort town in southeastern Florida, located on an island just off the coast; pop. 9,814.

palm civ·et ▸*n.* a mainly arboreal civet that typically has powerful curved claws and pale spots or stripes on a dark coat, native to Africa and Asia. It is often a pest of banana plantations. • *Paradoxurus* and other genera, family Viverridae: several species, including the **common palm civet** (*P. hermaphroditus*) of Asia.

palm·cord·er /ˈpä(l)mˌkôrdər/ ▸*n.* a small, hand-held camcorder. ▷1980s: blend of PALM[2] and RECORDER.

Palm·dale /ˈpämˌdāl/ a city in southwestern California, north of Los Angeles, near Edwards Air Force Base; pop. 68,842.

Pal·me /ˈpälmə/, (Sven) Olof (Joachim) (1927–86), Swedish statesman; prime minister 1969–76 and 1982–86. He was killed by an unknown assassin.

Pal·mer /ˈpä(l)mər/, Arnold (Daniel) (1929–), U.S. golfer. His many championship victories included the Masters in 1958, 1960, 1962, and 1964; the U.S. Open in 1960; and the British Open in 1961 and 1962. The huge galleries attracted by Palmer whenever he played were dubbed "Arnie's Army."

palm·er /ˈpä(l)mər/ ▸*n.* **1** *historical* a pilgrim, esp. one who had returned from the Holy Land with a palm frond or leaf as a sign of having undertaken the pilgrimage. ■ *historical* an itinerant monk traveling from shrine to shrine under a vow of poverty. **2** a hairy artificial fly used in angling. ▷Middle English: from Anglo-Norman French, from medieval Latin *palmarius* 'pilgrim,' from Latin *palma* 'palm.'

Pal·mer·ston /ˈpä(l)mərstən/, Henry John Temple, 3rd Viscount (1784–1865), British statesman; prime minister 1855–58 and 1859–65. He declared the second Opium War against China in 1856 and oversaw the successful conclusion of the Crimean War in 1856 and the suppression of the Indian Mutiny in 1858.

pal·mette /palˈmet/ ▸*n. Archaeology* an ornament of radiating petals that resemble the leaflets of a palm. ▷mid 19th cent.: from French, literally 'small palm,' diminutive of *palme.*

pal·met·to /pä(l)ˈmetō; pal-/ ▸*n.* (*pl.* **-tos**) a fan palm, esp. one of a number occurring from the southern U.S. to northern South America. • *Sabal* and other genera, family Palmae: several species, in particular the **cabbage palmetto** (*S. palmetto*), which is the state tree of Florida (where it is better known as the **sabal palm**) and South Carolina. ▷mid 16th cent.: from Spanish *palmito,* literally 'small palm,' diminutive of *palma,* assimilated to Italian words ending in *-etto.*

cabbage palmetto

Pal·met·to State a nickname for the state of SOUTH CAROLINA.

palm·i·er /ˈpä(l)mēā/ ▸*n.* (*pl.* or *pronunc.* same) a sweet, crisp pastry shaped like a palm leaf. ▷French, literally 'palm tree.'

palm·is·try /ˈpä(l)məstrē/ ▸*n.* the art or practice of supposedly interpreting a person's character or predicting their future by examining the lines and other features of the hand, esp. the palm and fingers. ▷late Middle English: from PALM[2] + *-estry* (of unknown origin), later altered to *-istry,* perhaps on the pattern of *sophistry.* **—palm·ist** /ˈpä(l)mist/ *n.*

pal·mit·ic ac·id /pä(l)ˈmitik/ ▸*n. Chemistry* a solid saturated fatty acid obtained from palm oil and other vegetable and animal fats. • Chem. formula: $CH_3(CH_2)_{14}COOH$. ▷mid 19th cent.: *palmitic* from French *palmitique,* from *palme* (see PALM[1]). **—pal·mi·tate** /ˈpä(l)miˌtāt/ *n.*

palm oil ▸*n.* oil from the fruit of certain palms, esp. the West African oil palm.

Palm Pi·lot ▸*n. trademark* a brand of hand-held computer.

Palm Springs a resort city in the desert area of southern California, east of Los Angeles, noted for its hot mineral springs; pop. 40,181.

palm squir·rel ▸*n.* an Old World squirrel that frequents palm trees, esp. a tree squirrel with a striped back and a shrill, birdlike call that is native to the Indian subcontinent. • Genus *Funambulus* and other genera, family Sciuridae: several species, in particular the **five-striped northern palm squirrel** (*F. pennanti*), which is common in and around human habitation in northern India.

Palm Sun·day ▸*n.* the Sunday before Easter, when the triumphal entry of Jesus into Jerusalem is celebrated in many Christian churches by processions in which palm fronds are carried.

palm·top /ˈpä(l)mˌtäp/ ▸*n.* a computer small and lightweight enough to be held in one hand.

palm wine ▸*n.* an alcoholic drink made from fermented palm sap.

palm·y /ˈpä(l)mē/ ▸*adj.* (**palm·i·er, palm·i·est**) **1** (esp. of a previous period of time) flourishing or successful: *the palmy days of the 1970s.* **2** covered with palms.

Pal·my·ra /palˈmīrə/ an ancient city in Syria, an oasis in the Syrian desert northeast of Damascus on the site of present-day Tadmur. ▷Greek form of the city's modern and ancient pre-Semitic name Tadmur or Tadmor, meaning 'city of palms.'

pal·my·ra /palˈmīrə/ ▸*n.* an Asian fan palm that yields a wide range of useful products, including timber, fiber, and fruit. • *Borassus flabellifer,* family Palmae. ▷late 17th cent.: from Portuguese *palmeira* 'palm tree.' The change in the ending was due to association with the name of the ancient city of PALMYRA.

Pal·o Al·to /ˈpalō ˈaltō/ a city in western California, south of San Francisco; pop. 55,900. It is noted for electronics and computer technology and is the site of Stanford University.

pa·lo·lo worm /pəˈlōlō/ ▸*n.* a marine bristle worm that swarms in response to changes in light intensity, particularly that of the moon. The worm's posterior segments detach themselves and swim to the surface where the reproductive cells are released into the sea. • Several species in Eunicidae and other families, in particular the **Samoan palolo worm** (*Palola* (or **Eunice**) *viridis*), which occurs on South Pacific reefs. ▷late 19th cent.: *palolo* from Samoan or Tongan.

Pal·o·mar, Mount /ˈpaləˌmär/ a mountain in southern California, northeast of San Diego, rising to a height of 6,126 feet (1,867 m). It is the site of an astronomical observatory. ▷Spanish *Palomar,* literally 'place of the pigeon.'

pal·o·mi·no /ˌpaləˈmēnō/ ▸*n.* **1** (*pl.* **-nos**) a pale golden or tan-colored horse with a white mane and tail, originally bred in the southwestern U.S. **2** a variety of white grape, originally grown around Jerez in southern Spain, used esp. to make sherry and fortified wines. ▷early 20th cent.: from Latin American Spanish, from Spanish *palomino* 'young pigeon,' from Latin *palumbinus* 'resembling a dove.'

pa·loo·ka /pəˈlo͞okə/ ▸*n. informal, dated* an inferior or average prizefighter. ■ a stupid, uncouth person; a lout. ▷1920s: of unknown origin.

Pa·loo·ka·ville /pəˈlo͞okəˌvil/ ▸*n. informal* **1** a state of obscurity: *a couple of bucks and a one-way ticket to Palookaville.* **2** an economically depressed, working-class community.

Pa·louse /pəˈlo͞os/ ▶*n.* (*pl.* same or **-lous·es**) a member of an American Indian people inhabiting the Palouse River valley in southeastern Washington. ▶*adj.* of or relating to this people. ▷from Sahaptin *palúus* 'which stands in the water,' referring to a large rock in the Snake River.

pal·o·ver·de /ˌpalōˈvərd(ē)/ ▶*n.* a thorny, yellow-flowered tree or shrub that grows along watercourses in the warm desert areas of America. • Genus *Cercidium*, family Leguminosae. ▷early 19th cent.: from Latin American Spanish, literally 'green tree.'

palp /palp/ ▶*n.* another term for **PALPUS**. ▷mid 19th cent.: from Latin *palpus*, literally 'feeler.'

pal·pa·ble /ˈpalpəbəl/ ▶*adj.* able to be touched or felt: *the palpable bump at the bridge of the nose.* See note at **TANGIBLE**. ■ (esp. of a feeling or atmosphere) so intense as to be almost touched or felt: *a palpable sense of loss.* ■ clear to the mind or plain to see: *to talk of dawn raids in the circumstances is palpable nonsense.* ▷late Middle English: from late Latin *palpabilis*, from Latin *palpare* 'feel, touch gently.' —**pal·pa·bil·i·ty** /ˌpalpəˈbilitē/ *n.* —**pal·pa·bly** /-blē/ *adv.*

pal·pate /ˈpalˌpāt/ ▶*v.* [*trans.*] examine (a part of the body) by touch, esp. for medical purposes. ▷mid 19th cent.: from Latin *palpat-* 'touched gently,' from the verb *palpare.* —**pal·pa·tion** /palˈpāsʜən/ *n.*

pal·pe·bral /ˈpalpəbrəl; palˈpē-/ ▶*adj.* [*attrib.*] *Anatomy* of or relating to the eyelids. ▷mid 19th cent.: from late Latin *palpebralis*, from Latin *palpebra* 'eyelid.'

pal·pi·tant /ˈpalpitnt/ ▶*adj. rare* palpitating. ▷mid 19th cent.: from French, present participle of *palpiter*, from Latin *palpitare* 'continue to pat.'

pal·pi·tate /ˈpalpiˌtāt/ ▶*v.* [*intrans.*] [often as *adj.*] (**palpitating**) (of the heart) beat rapidly, strongly, or irregularly: *it wakened him in the night with a palpitating heart.* ■ shake; tremble: *she was palpitating with terror.* ▷early 17th cent.: from Latin *palpitat-* 'patted,' from the verb *palpitare*, frequentative of *palpare* 'touch gently.'

pal·pi·ta·tion /ˌpalpiˈtāsʜən/ ▶*n.* (usu. **palpitations**) a noticeably rapid, strong, or irregular heartbeat due to agitation, exertion, or illness. ▷late Middle English: from Latin *palpitatio(n-)*, from the verb *palpitare* (see **PALPITATE**).

pal·pus /ˈpalpəs/ (also **palp**) ▶*n.* (*pl.* **pal·pi** /ˈpalpī/ or **palps**) *Zoology* each of a pair of elongated segmented appendages near the mouth of an arthropod, usually concerned with the senses of touch and taste. ▷early 19th cent.: Latin, from *palpare* 'to feel.' —**pal·pal** /-pəl/ *adj.*

pals·grave /ˈpôlzˌgrāv; ˈpalz-/ ▶*n. historical* a count palatine. ▷mid 16th cent.: from early modern Dutch *paltsgrave*, from *palts* 'palatinate' + *grave* 'count.'

pal·sy /ˈpôlzē/ ▶*n.* (*pl.* **-sies**) *dated* paralysis, esp. that which is accompanied by involuntary tremors: *a kind of palsy had seized him.* ■ *archaic* a condition of incapacity or helplessness.
▶*v.* (**-sies, -sied**) [*trans.*] (often **be palsied**) affect with paralysis and involuntary tremors: *she feels as if the muscles on her face are palsied* | [as *adj.*] (**palsied**) *figurative the old-boy network laid its palsied hand upon the business of wealth creation.* ▷Middle English: from Old French *paralisie*, from an alteration of Latin *paralysis* (see **PARALYSIS**).

pal·sy-wal·sy /ˈpalzē ˈwalzē/ ▶*adj. informal* very friendly or intimate. ▷1930s (as a noun in the sense 'friend'): from the noun **PAL** + **-SY**, by reduplication.

pal·ter /ˈpôltər/ ▶*v.* [*intrans.*] *archaic* **1** equivocate or prevaricate in action or speech. **2** (**palter with**) trifle with: *this great work should not be paltered with.* ▷mid 16th cent. (in the sense 'mumble or babble'): of unknown origin; no corresponding verb is known in any other language. —**pal·ter·er** *n.*

Pal·trow /ˈpaltrō/, Gwyneth (1972–), U.S. actress. She received an Academy Award for her role in *Shakespeare in Love* (1998). Other films include *Emma* (1996), *Possession* (2001), and *Sylvia* (2003).

pal·try /ˈpôltrē/ ▶*adj.* (**pal·tri·er**, **pal·tri·est**) (of an amount) small or meager: *she would earn a paltry $33 more each month.* ■ petty; trivial: *naval glory struck him as paltry.* ▷mid 16th cent.: apparently based on dialect *pelt* 'trash, esp. rags'; compare with Low German *paltrig* 'ragged.' —**pal·tri·ness** *n.*

pa·lu·dal /pəˈlo͞odl; ˈpalyədl/ ▶*adj. Ecology* (of a plant, animal, or soil) living or occurring in a marshy habitat. ▷early 19th cent.: from Latin *palus, palud-* 'marsh' + **-AL**.

pal·y /ˈpālē/ ▶*adj. Heraldry* divided into equal vertical stripes: *paly of six, argent and gules.* ▷late Middle English: from Old French *pale* 'divided by stakes,' from *pal* 'pale, stake.'

pal·y·nol·o·gy /ˌpaləˈnäləjē/ ▶*n.* the study of pollen grains and other spores, esp. as found in archaeological or geological deposits. ▷1940s: from Greek *palunein* 'sprinkle' + **-LOGY**. —**pal·y·no·log·i·cal** /-nəˈläjikəl/ *adj.* —**pal·y·nol·o·gist** /-jist/ *n.*

pam. ▶*abbr.* pamphlet.

Pa·mir Moun·tains /pəˈmi(ə)r/ (also **the Pa·mirs**) a mountain system of central Asia that is centered in Tajikistan and extends into Kyrgyzstan, Afghanistan, Pakistan, and western China. The highest mountain is Communism Peak in Tajikistan.

Pam·li·co Sound /ˈpamliˌkō/ an inlet of the Atlantic Ocean in eastern North Carolina, inside the islands of the Outer Banks, south of Albemarle Sound.

pam·pas /ˈpampəz; -pəs/ ▶*n.* [treated as *sing.* or *pl.*] extensive, treeless plains in South America. ▷early 18th cent.: via Spanish from Quechua *pampa* 'plain.'

pam·pas grass /ˈpampəs/ ▶*n.* a tall South American grass with silky flowering plumes, widely cultivated as an ornamental plant. • *Cortaderia selloana*, family Gramineae.

pam·per /ˈpampər/ ▶*v.* [*trans.*] indulge with every attention, comfort, and kindness; spoil: *famous people just love being pampered.* ▷late Middle English (in the sense 'cram with food'): probably of Low German or Dutch origin; compare with German dialect *pampfen* 'cram, gorge'; perhaps related to **PAP**[1].

pam·pe·ro /pämˈperō/ ▶*n.* (*pl.* **-ros**) a strong, cold southwesterly wind in South America, blowing from the Andes across the pampas toward the Atlantic. ▷late 18th cent.: from Spanish *pampas* 'plain;' see **PAMPAS**.

pam·phlet /ˈpamflit/ ▶*n.* a small booklet or leaflet containing information or arguments about a single subject.
▶*v.* (**-phlet·ed, -phlet·ing**) [*trans.*] distribute pamphlets to. ▷late Middle English: from *Pamphilet*, the familiar name of the 12th-cent. Latin love poem *Pamphilus, seu de Amore.*

pam·phlet·eer /ˌpamfliˈti(ə)r/ ▶*n.* a writer of pamphlets, esp. ones of a political and controversial nature.
▶*v.* [*intrans.*] [usu. as *n.*] (**pamphleteering**) write and issue such pamphlets.

Pam·phyl·i·a /pamˈfilēə/ an ancient coastal region of southern Asia Minor, between Lycia and Cilicia, to the east of the modern port of Antalya. —**Pam·phyl·i·an** /pamˈfilēən/ *adj. & n.*

Pam·plo·na /pamˈplōnə; päm-/ a city in northern Spain, capital of the former kingdom and modern region of Navarre; pop. 191,000. It is noted for the fiesta of San Fermin, held there in July, which is celebrated with the running of bulls through the streets of the city.

Pan /pan/ *Greek Mythology* a god of flocks and herds, typically represented with the horns, ears, and legs of a goat on a man's body. His sudden appearance was supposed to cause terror similar to that of a frightened and stampeding herd, and the word *panic* is derived from his name. ▷probably originally in the sense 'the feeder' (i.e., herdsman), although the name was regularly associated with Greek *pas* or *pan* (= 'all'), giving rise to his identification as a god of nature or the universe.

pan[1] /pan/ ▶*n.* **1** a container made of metal and used for cooking food in. ■ an amount of something contained in such a container: *a **pan of** hot water.* ■ a large container used in a technical or manufacturing process for subjecting a material to heat or a mechanical or chemical process. ■ a bowl fitted at either end of a balance, in which items to be weighed are set. ■ another term for **STEEL DRUM**. ■ a shallow bowl in which gold is separated from gravel and mud by agitation and washing. ■ a hollow in the ground in which water may collect or in which a deposit of salt remains after water has evaporated. ■ a small ice floe. ■ a part of the lock that held the priming in old types of guns. **2** *informal* a face. **3** a hard stratum of compacted soil.
▶*v.* (**panned, pan·ning**) [*trans.*] **1** (often **be panned**) *informal* criticize (someone or something) severely: *the movie was panned by the critics.* **2** wash gravel in a pan to separate out (gold): *the old-timers panned gold* | [*intrans.*] *prospectors **panned for gold** in the Yukon.*
▶*phrasal v.* □ **pan out** (of gravel) yield gold. ■ turn out well: *Harold's idea had been a good one even if it hadn't panned out.* ■ end up; conclude: *he's happy with the way the deal panned out.* ▷Old English *panne*; related to Dutch *pan*, German *Pfanne*, perhaps based on Latin *patina* 'dish.' —**pan·ful** /-ˌfo͝ol/ *n.* (*pl.* **-fuls**).

pan[2] ▶*v.* (**panned, pan·ning**) [*trans.*] swing (a video or movie camera) in a horizontal or vertical plane, typically to give a panoramic effect or follow a subject. ■ [*intrans.*] (of a camera) be swung in such a way: *the camera panned to the dead dictator.*
▶*n.* a panning movement: *that slow pan over Los Angeles.* ▷early 20th cent.: abbreviation of **PANORAMA**.
▶*PHRASE* □ **pan and scan** a technique for narrowing the aspect ratio of a wide-screen movie to fit the squarer shape of a television screen by continuously selecting the portion of the original picture with the most significance, rather than just the middle portion.

pan- ▶*comb. form* all-inclusive, esp. in relation to the whole of a continent, racial group, religion, etc.: *pan-African* | *pansexual.* ▷from Greek *pan*, neuter of *pas* 'all.'

pan·a·ce·a /ˌpanəˈsēə/ ▶*n.* a solution or remedy for all difficulties or diseases: *the panacea for all corporate ills* | *the time-honored panacea, cod liver oil.* ▷mid 16th cent.: via Latin from Greek *panakeia*, from *panakēs* 'all-healing,' from *pan* 'all' + *akos* 'remedy.' —**pan·a·ce·an** /-ˈsēən/ *adj.*

pa·nache /pəˈnasʜ; -ˈnäsʜ/ ▶*n.* **1** flamboyant confidence of style or manner: *he entertained Palm Springs society **with great panache.*** **2** *historical* a tuft or plume of feathers, esp. as a headdress or on a helmet. ▷mid 16th cent.: from French, from Italian *pennacchio*, from late Latin *pinnaculum*, diminutive of *pinna* 'feather.'

pa·na·da /pəˈnädə; -ˈnādə/ ▶*n.* a dish consisting of bread boiled to a pulp and flavored. ▷late 16th cent.: from Spanish and Portuguese, based on Latin *panis* 'bread.'

pan-Af·ri·can ▶*adj.* of or relating to all people of African birth or descent.

pan-Af·ri·can·ism ▶*n.* the principle or advocacy of the political union of all the indigenous inhabitants of Africa. —**pan-Af·ri·can·ist** *n.*

Pan-Af·ri·can·ist Con·gress (in full **Pan-Africanist Congress of Azania**) (abbr.: **PAC**) a South African political movement formed in 1959 as a militant offshoot of the African National Congress. It was outlawed in 1960 after the Sharpeville massacre, but continued its armed opposition to the South African government until it was legalized in 1990.

Pan·a·ma /ˈpanəˌmä; -ˌmô/ a country in Central America; pop. 3,000,000; capital, Panama City; language, Spanish (official). —**Pan·a·ma·ni·an** /ˌpanəˈmānēən/ *adj. & n.*

Panama occupies the isthmus that connects North and South America. Colonized by Spain in the early 16th century, it was freed from imperial control in 1821 and became a Colombian province. It gained full independence in 1903, although the construction of the Panama Canal and the leasing of the zone around it to the U.S. split the country in two. In 1989, U.S. troops invaded Panama and arrested the country's president, Gen. Manuel Noriega, on charges of drug trafficking. According to an agreement signed in 1977, the Panama Canal and the surrounding zone were turned over to Panama at the end of 1999.

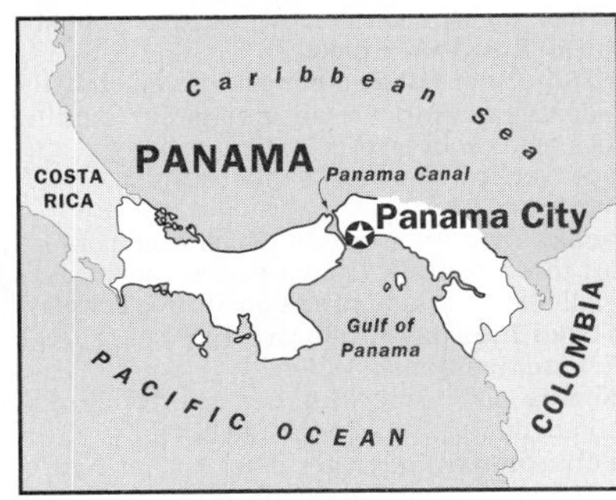

Pan·a·ma, Isth·mus of (formerly the **Isthmus of Darien**) in the narrowest sense, the site of the Panama Canal. More broadly, all the territory of Panama, or the entire region that connects North and South America.

pan·a·ma /ˈpanəˌmä/ (also **panama hat**) ▸*n.* a wide-brimmed hat of strawlike material, originally made from the leaves of a particular tropical palm tree, worn chiefly by men. ▷mid 19th cent.: named after the country of **PANAMA**.

Pan·a·ma Ca·nal a canal about 50 miles (80 km) long, across the Isthmus of Panama, that connects the Atlantic and Pacific oceans. Its construction, begun by Ferdinand de Lesseps in 1881, was abandoned in 1889 and was completed by the U.S., 1904–14. Control of the canal remained with the U.S. until 1999, when it was ceded to Panama.

Pan·a·ma Cit·y 1 the capital of Panama, situated on the Pacific coast close to the Panama Canal; pop. 585,000. **2** a port city in northwestern Florida; pop. 34,378.

Pan·a·ma dis·ease ▸*n.* a fungal disease of bananas producing yellowing and wilting of the leaves. • The fungus is a form of *Fusarium oxysporum*, subdivision Deuteromycotina.

Pan·a·ma Red ▸*n.* a potent variety of marijuana from Panama that is reddish in color.

Pan·a·max /ˈpanəˌmaks/ ▸*adj.* denoting a ship having the maximum permissible dimensions (length, breadth, and draft) for transiting the Panama Canal, with a dead-weight capacity of about 75,000 tons. ▷1980s: blend of **PANAMA** and the adjective **MAXIMUM**.

pan-A·mer·i·can /ˌpan əˈmerikən/ ▸*adj.* of, relating to, representing, or involving all the countries of North and South America.

Pan-A·mer·i·can High·way a road system initiated in the 1920s to link nations of the western hemisphere from Alaska to Chile. Gaps remain in Panama and Colombia. The **Inter-American Highway** is the section from the Texas-Mexico border south to Panama City.

pan-A·mer·i·can·ism ▸*n.* the principle or advocacy of political or commercial and cultural cooperation among all the countries of North and South America.

Pan·a·mint Range /ˈpanəmint/ a mountain range in east central California, west of Death Valley, noted for its high walls and deep canyons.

pan-and-tilt ▸*adj.* denoting a stand, tripod, or other item of mounting equipment that allows a camera to move in both horizontal and vertical planes.

pan-Ar·ab·ism ▸*n.* the principle or advocacy of political alliance or union of all the Arab states. —**pan-Ar·ab** *adj.*

pan·a·tel·a /ˌpanəˈtelə/ ▸*n.* a long thin cigar. ▷mid 19th cent.: from Latin American Spanish *panatela*, denoting a long thin cookie, from Italian *panatello* 'small loaf,' diminutive of *panata*.

Pa·nay /pəˈnī/ an island in the central Philippines; chief town, Iloilo.

pan·cake /ˈpanˌkāk/ ▸*n.* a thin, flat cake of batter, usually fried and turned in a pan. Pancakes are usually eaten with syrup or rolled up with a filling. ■ (also **pancake makeup**) makeup consisting of a flat solid layer of compressed powder, widely used in the theater.
▸*v.* **1** [*intrans.*] (of an aircraft) make a pancake landing. ■ [*trans.*] (of a pilot) cause (an aircraft) to make such a landing: *he pancaked it in about twenty meters.* **2** *informal* flatten or become flattened: [*intrans.*] *the hotel had pancaked into a heap of concrete.* ▷late Middle English: from **PAN**[1] + **CAKE**.
▸*PHRASE* □ **(as) flat as a pancake** completely flat.

pan·cake land·ing ▸*n.* an emergency landing in which an aircraft levels out close to the ground and drops vertically with its undercarriage still retracted.

pan·cake race ▸*n.* a race in which each competitor must toss a pancake from a pan as they run, traditionally held in some places on Shrove Tuesday.

Pan·cake Tues·day ▸*n.* Shrove Tuesday, when pancakes are traditionally eaten.

pan·cet·ta /panˈCHetə/ ▸*n.* Italian cured belly of pork. ▷Italian, diminutive of *pancio* 'belly.'

pan·cha·kar·ma /ˌpənCHəˈkärmə/ ▸*n.* (in Ayurvedic medicine) a fivefold detoxification treatment involving massage, herbal therapy, and other procedures. ▷1980s: from Sanskrit, *panca*, 'five' + *karman*, 'action.'

pan·cha·yat /panˈCHīət/ ▸*n.* *Indian* a village council. ▷from Hindi (originally denoting a council consisting of five members), from Sanskrit *panca* 'five' + *āyatta* 'depending upon.'

Pan·chen La·ma /ˈpänCHən ˈlämə/ ▸*n.* a Tibetan lama ranking next after the Dalai Lama. ▷Tibetan *panchen*, abbreviation of *pandi-tachen-po* 'great learned one'; compare with **PUNDIT**.

Pan·chiao /ˈpanˈCHyou/ (also **Pan-ch'iao**; formerly **Pankiao**) a city in northern Taiwan, southwest of Taipei; pop. 544,000.

pan·chro·mat·ic /ˌpankrōˈmatik/ ▸*adj.* *Photography* (of photographic film) sensitive to all visible colors of the spectrum. Often contrasted with **ORTHOCHROMATIC**.

pan·cre·as /ˈpaNGkrēəs; ˈpankrēəs/ ▸*n.* (*pl.* **-cre·as·es**) a large gland behind the stomach that secretes digestive enzymes into the duodenum. Embedded in the pancreas are the islets of Langerhans, which secrete into the blood the hormones insulin and glucagon. ▷late 16th cent.: modern Latin, from Greek *pankreas*, from *pan* 'all' + *kreas* 'flesh.' —**pan·cre·at·ic** /-krēˈatik/ *adj.*

pan·cre·a·tec·to·my /ˌpaNGkrēəˈtektəmē; ˌpan-/ ▸*n.* (*pl.* **-mies**) surgical removal of the pancreas.

pan·cre·at·ic juice /ˌpaNGkrēˈatik; ˌpan-/ ▸*n.* the clear alkaline digestive fluid secreted by the pancreas.

pan·cre·a·tin /ˈpaNGkrēətn; ˈpan-; ˌpanˈkrēətn/ ▸*n.* a mixture of enzymes obtained from animal pancreases, given as a medicine to aid digestion.

pan·cre·a·ti·tis /ˌpaNGkrēəˈtītis; ˌpan-/ ▸*n.* *Medicine* inflammation of the pancreas.

pan·cre·o·zy·min /ˌpaNGkrēəˈzīmin; ˌpan-/ ▸*n.* *Biochemistry* a hormone that stimulates the production of enzymes by the pancreas.

pan·cy·to·pe·ni·a /ˌpansītəˈpēnēə/ ▸*n.* *Medicine* deficiency of all three cellular components of the blood (red cells, white cells, and platelets). ▷mid 20th cent.: from **PAN-** 'all' + **CYTO-** 'cell' + Greek *penia* 'poverty, lack.'

pan·da /ˈpandə/ (also **giant panda**) ▸*n.* a large bearlike mammal with characteristic black and white markings, native to certain mountain forests of central and western China. It feeds almost entirely on bamboo and has become increasingly rare. See also **RED PANDA**. • *Ailuropoda melanoleuca*; it is now usually placed with the bears (family Ursidae), but was formerly thought to belong with the raccoons (family Procyonidae). ▷mid 19th cent.: from Nepali.

panda

pan·da·nus /panˈdānəs; -ˈdanəs/ (also **pan·dan** /ˈpandən/) ▸*n.* a tropical tree or shrub that has a twisted and branched stem, stilt roots, spiral tufts of long, narrow, typically spiny leaves, and fibrous edible fruit. Also called **SCREW PINE**. • Genus *Pandanus*, family Pandanaceae. ■ fiber from the leaves of this plant, or material woven from this fiber. ▷modern Latin, from Malay *pandan*.

Pan·da·rus /ˈpandərəs/ *Greek Mythology* a Lycian who fought on the side of the Trojans, described in the *Iliad* as breaking the truce with the Greeks by wounding Menelaus with an arrow. The role as the lovers' go-between that he plays in Chaucer's (and later Shakespeare's) story of Troilus and Cressida originated with Boccaccio and is the origin of the word *pander*.

pan·dect /ˈpanˌdekt/ ▸*n.* *chiefly historical* a complete body of the laws of a country. ■ (usu. **the Pandects**) a compendium in 50 books of the Roman civil law made by order of Justinian in the 6th century. ▷mid 16th cent.: from French *pandecte*, from Latin *pandecta*, from Greek *pandektēs* 'all-receiver,' from *pan* 'all' + *dektēs* (from *dekhesthai* 'receive'). —**pan·dect·ist** /panˈdektist/ *n.*

pan·dem·ic /panˈdemik/ ▸*adj.* (of a disease) prevalent over a whole country or the world.
▸*n.* an outbreak of such a disease. See note at **EPIDEMIC**. ▷mid 17th cent.: from Greek *pandēmos* (from *pan* 'all' + *dēmos* 'people') + **-IC**.

USAGE On the difference between **pandemic**, **endemic**, and **epidemic**, see usage at **EPIDEMIC**.

pan·de·mo·ni·um /ˌpandəˈmōnēəm/ ▸*n.* wild and noisy disorder or confusion; uproar: *pandemonium broke out.* ▷mid 17th cent.: modern Latin (denoting the place of all demons, in Milton's *Paradise Lost*), from **PAN-** 'all' + Greek *daimōn* 'demon.'

pan·der /ˈpandər/ ▸*v.* [*intrans.*] (**pander to**) gratify or indulge (an immoral or distasteful desire, need, or habit or a person with such a desire, etc.): *newspapers are pandering to people's baser instincts.*
▸*n.* *dated* a pimp. ■ *archaic* a person who assists the baser urges or evil designs of others: *the lowest panders of a venal press.* ▷late Middle English (as a noun): from *Pandare*, the name of a character in Chaucer's *Troilus and Criseyde* (see **PANDARUS**). The verb dates from the early 17th cent.

Pan·dit /ˈpandit; ˈpən-/, Vijaya (Lakshmi) (1900–90), Indian politician and diplomat, sister of Jawaharlal Nehru. Having been imprisoned three times by the British for nationalist activities, after independence she became the first woman to serve as president of the United Nations General Assembly (1953–54).

pan·dit /ˈpəndit; ˈpan-/ (also **pun·dit**) ▸*n.* a Hindu scholar learned in Sanskrit and Hindu philosophy and religion, typically also a practicing priest: [as *title*] Pandit Misir. ■ *Indian* a wise man or teacher. ■ *Indian* a talented musician (used as a respectful title or form of address). ▷Of the same origin as **PUNDIT**.

P & L ▸*abbr.* profit and loss account.

Pan·do·ra /panˈdôrə/ *Greek Mythology* the first mortal woman. In one story she was created by Zeus and sent to earth with a jar or box of evils in revenge for Prometheus' having brought the gift of fire back to the world. Pandora let out all the evils from the jar to infect the earth; hope alone remained to assuage the lot of humankind. ▷from the Greek name *Pandōra* 'all-gifted' (from *pan* 'all' + *dōron* 'gift').

pan·do·ra /panˈdôrə/ (also **pandora shell** or **Pandora's box shell**) ▸*n.* a burrowing bivalve mollusk with a fragile shell, the unequal valves of which form a "box" with a lid. • Genus *Pandora*, family Pandoridae. ▷modern Latin, from Greek *pandoura* 'three-stringed lute' (because of the shell's resemblance to the sound box of a stringed instrument).

Pan·do·ra's box ▸*n.* a process that generates many complicated problems as the result of unwise interference in something.

pan·dow·dy /panˈdoudē/ ▸*n.* (*pl.* **-dies**) a kind of spiced apple pie baked in a deep dish. ▷of unknown origin.

p. & p. *Brit.* ▸*abbr.* postage and packing.

pane /pān/ ▸*n.* a single sheet of glass in a window or door. ■ *Computing* a separate defined area within a window for the display of, or interaction with, a part of that window's application or output. ■ a sheet or page of postage stamps. ▷late Middle English (originally denoting a section or piece of something, such as a fence or strip of cloth): from Old French *pan*, from Latin *pannus* 'piece of cloth.'

pan·e·gyr·ic /ˌpanəˈjirik/ ▸*n.* a public speech or published text in praise of someone or something: *Vera's panegyric on friendship.* ▷early 17th cent.: from French *panégyrique*, via Latin from Greek *panēgurikos* 'of public assembly,' from *pan* 'all' + *aguris* 'agora, assembly.' —**pan·e·gyr·i·cal** /-ˈjirikəl/ *adj.* —**pan·e·gyr·i·cal·ly** *adv.*

pan·e·gy·rize /ˈpanəjəˌrīz/ ▸*v.* [*trans.*] *archaic* speak or write in praise of; eulogize. —**pan·e·gyr·ist** /ˌpanəˈjirist/ *n.*

pan·el /ˈpanl/ ▸*n.* **1** a thin, typically rectangular piece of wood or glass forming or set into the surface of a door, wall, or ceiling. ■ a thin piece of metal forming part of the outer shell of a vehicle: *body panels for the car business.* ■ a flat board on which instruments or controls are fixed: *a control panel.* ■ a decorated area within a larger design containing a separate subject: *the central panel depicts the Crucifixion.* ■ one of several drawings making up a comic strip. ■ a piece of material forming part of a garment. **2** a small group of people brought together to discuss, investigate, or decide on a particular matter, esp. in the context of business or government: *we assembled a panel of experts.* ■ a list of available jurors or a jury. **3** the soft underside of a saddle, typically of foam or wool.
▸*v.* (**-eled, -el·ing**; *Brit.* **-elled, -el·ling**) [*trans.*] [usu. as *adj.*] (**paneled**) cover (a wall or other surface) with panels: *an elegant paneled dining room.* ▷Middle English: from Old French, literally 'piece of cloth,' based on Latin *pannus* '(piece of) cloth.' The early sense 'piece of parchment' was extended to mean 'list,' whence the notion 'advisory group.' Sense 1 derives from the late Middle English sense 'distinct (usually framed) section of a surface.'

pan·el·ing /ˈpanəliNG/ (*Brit.* **pan·el·ling**) ▸*n.* panels collectively, when used to decorate a wall.

pan·el·ist /ˈpanəlist/ (*Brit.* **pan·el·list**) ▸*n.* a member of a panel, esp. in a formal public discussion.

pan·el stud·y ▸*n.* an investigation of attitude changes using a constant set of people and comparing each individual's opinions at different times.

pan·el truck ▸*n.* a small enclosed delivery truck.

pan·en·the·ism /paˈnenTHēˌizəm/ ▸*n.* the belief or doctrine that God is greater than the universe and includes and interpenetrates it. **—pan·en·the·is·tic** /ˌpanenTHēˈistik/ *adj.*

pan·et·to·ne /ˌpanəˈtōnē/ ▸*n.* (*pl.* **-ni** *pronunc.* same) a rich Italian bread made with eggs, fruit, and butter and typically eaten at Christmas. ▷Italian, from *panetto* 'cake,' diminutive of *pane* 'bread' (from Latin *panis* 'bread').

pan·fish /ˈpanˌfisH/ ▸*n.* (*pl.* same or **-fish·es**) a fish suitable for frying whole in a pan, esp. one caught by an angler rather than bought.
▸*v.* [*intrans.*] [often as *n.*] (**panfishing**) catch, or try to catch, such fish: *panfishing picks up considerably during the fall and spring.*

pan·for·te /panˈfôrˌtā/ ▸*n.* a hard, spicy Sienese cake containing nuts, candied citrus peel, and honey. ▷Italian, from *pane* 'bread' + *forte* 'strong.'

pan-fry ▸*v.* [*trans.*] [often as *adj.*] (**pan-fried**) fry in a pan in a small amount of fat: *pan-fried trout.*

pang /paNG/ ▸*n.* a sudden sharp pain or painful emotion: *Lindsey experienced a sharp* **pang of** *guilt* | *the snack bar will keep those hunger pangs at bay.* ▷late 15th cent.: perhaps an alteration of **PRONG**.

pan·ga /ˈpäNGgə/ ▸*n.* a bladed African tool like a machete. ▷Kiswahili.

Pan·gae·a /panˈjēə/ (also **Pan·ge·a**) a supercontinent comprising all the continental crust of the earth, postulated to have existed in late Paleozoic and Mesozoic times before it broke into Gondwana and Laurasia. ▷early 20th cent.: from **PAN-** 'all' + Greek *gaia* 'earth.'

pan-Ger·man ▸*adj.* of, relating to, or advocating pan-Germanism. ■ of, relating to, or including both East and West Germany. **—pan-Ger·man·ic** *adj.*

pan-Ger·man·ism ▸*n.* the idea or principle of a political unification of all Europeans speaking German or a Germanic language.

Pan·gloss /ˈpanglôs; -gläs/ ▸*n.* a person who is optimistic regardless of the circumstances. ▷mid 19th cent.: from the name of the tutor and philosopher in Voltaire's *Candide* (1759). **—Pan·gloss·i·an** /panˈglôsēən; -ˈgläs-/ *adj.*

pan·go·lin /ˈpaNGgəlin; paNGˈgōlin/ ▸*n.* an African and Asian mammal that has a body covered with horny overlapping scales, a small head with elongated snout, a long sticky tongue for catching ants and termites, and a thick, tapering tail. Also called **SCALY ANTEATER**. • Family Manidae and order Pholidota: genera *Manis* (three species in Asia) and *Phataginus* (four species in Africa). ▷late 18th cent.: from Malay *peng-guling*, literally 'roller' (from its habit of rolling into a ball).

pan·gram /ˈpanˌgram/ ▸*n.* a sentence or verse that contains all the letters of the alphabet.

pan·han·dle /ˈpanˌhandl/ ▸*n.* [often in *place names*] a narrow strip of territory projecting from the main territory of one state into another state: *the Oklahoma Panhandle.*
▸*v.* [*intrans.*] *informal* beg in the street: *she went back to the streets to panhandle for money.* **—pan·han·dler** *n.*

Pan·han·dle State a nickname for the state of **WEST VIRGINIA**.

Pan·hel·len·ic /ˌpanhəˈlenik/ ▸*adj.* of, concerning, or representing all people of Greek origin or ancestry. ■ relating to, advocating, or denoting the idea of a political union of all Greeks. ■ of, concerning, or representing all college fraternities and sororities.

pa·ni /ˈpänē/ ▸*n.* a term used in India for **WATER**. ▷from Hindi *pānī*.

pan·ic[1] /ˈpanik/ ▸*n.* sudden uncontrollable fear or anxiety, often causing wildly unthinking behavior: *she hit him in panic* | [in *sing.*] *he ran to the library in a blind panic.* ■ widespread financial or commercial apprehension provoking hasty action: *he caused an economic panic by his sudden resignation* | [as *adj.*] *panic selling.* ■ *informal* a frenzied hurry to do something: *a workload of constant panics and rush jobs.*
▸*v.* (**-icked**, **-ick·ing**) [*intrans.*] be affected by panic: *the crowd panicked and stampeded for the exit.* ■ [*trans.*] cause to feel panic: *talk of love panicked her.* ▷early 17th cent.: from French *panique*, from modern Latin *panicus*, from Greek *panikos*, from the name of the god **PAN**, noted for causing terror, to whom woodland noises were attributed. **—pan·ick·y** *adj.*

pan·ic[2] (also **panic grass**) ▸*n.* any of a number of cereal and fodder grasses related to millet. • *Panicum* and related genera, family Gramineae. ▷late Middle English: from Latin *panicum*, from *panus* 'ear of millet' (literally 'thread wound on a bobbin'), based on Greek *pēnos* 'web,' *pēnion* 'bobbin.'

pan·ic at·tack ▸*n.* a sudden feeling of acute and disabling anxiety.

pan·ic but·ton ▸*n.* a button for summoning help in an emergency: *personal attack circuits are operated by panic buttons.*
▸PHRASE □ **press** (or **push** or **hit**) **the panic button** *informal* respond to a situation by panicking or taking emergency measures.

pan·ic dis·or·der ▸*n.* a psychiatric disorder in which debilitating anxiety and fear arise frequently and without reasonable cause.

pan·i·cle /ˈpanikəl/ ▸*n. Botany* a loose, branching cluster of flowers, as in oats. ▷late 16th cent.: from Latin *panicula*, diminutive of *panus* 'ear of millet' (see **PANIC**[2]). **—pan·i·cled** *adj.*

pan·ic room ▸another term for a **SAFE ROOM**.

pan·ic-strick·en (also **pan·ic-struck**) ▸*adj.* affected with panic; very frightened: *the panic-stricken victims rushed out of their blazing homes.*

pan-In·di·an ▸*adj.* **1** of or relating to the whole of India, or to all its ethnic, religious, or linguistic groups. **2** denoting or relating to a cultural movement or religious practice participated in by many or all American Indian peoples.

Pa·ni·ni /ˈpäninē/, Indian grammarian. Sources vary as to when he lived, with dates ranging from the 4th to the 7th century BC. He is noted as the author of the *Eight Lectures*, a grammar of Sanskrit.

pa·ni·no /pəˈnēnō/ ▸*n.* (*pl.* **-ni** /-nē/) a sandwich, usu. toasted, made with a baguette or with Italian bread. ▷1950s: from Italian, literally 'bread roll.'

pa·ni pu·ri /ˈpänē ˌpo͝orē/ ▸*n.* (in Indian cooking) a puff-pastry ball filled with spiced mashed potato and tamarind juice and then fried. ▷from Hindi *pānī* 'water' and *pūrī* from Sanskrit *pūrikā* 'small, fried wheaten cake.'

pa·nir /paˈni(ə)r/ (also **pa·neer**) ▸*n.* a type of curd cheese used in Indian, Iranian, and Afghan cooking. ▷Hindi and Persian, 'cheese.'

Pan·ja·bi /pənˈjäbē/ ▸*n.* (*pl.* **-bis**) & *adj.* variant spelling of **PUNJABI**.

pan·jan·drum /panˈjandrəm/ ▸*n.* a person who has or claims to have a great deal of authority or influence. ▷late 19th cent.: from *Grand Panjandrum*, an invented phrase in a nonsense verse (1755) by S. Foote.

Pank·hurst /ˈpaNGkˌhərst/, Mrs. Emmeline (1858–1928), Christabel (1880–1958), and (Estelle) Sylvia (1882–1960), English suffragists. In 1903, Emmeline and her daughters founded the Women's Social and Political Union. When Christabel was imprisoned in 1905, Emmeline initiated the militant suffrage campaign that continued until the outbreak of World War I.

pan·mix·i·a /panˈmiksēə/ ▸*n. Zoology* random mating within a breeding population. ▷late 19th cent.: modern Latin, from German *Panmixie*, from Greek *pan* 'all' + *mixis* 'mixing.' **—pan·mic·tic** /-ˈmiktik/ *adj.*

Pan·mun·jom /ˈˌpanˈmo͝onˈjôm/ a village in the demilitarized zone between North and South Korea. It was here that the armistice ending the Korean War was signed on July 27, 1953.

pan·nage /ˈpanij/ ▸*n. chiefly historical* the right or privilege of feeding pigs or other animals in a wood. ■ pasturage for pigs in woodland. ▷late Middle English: from Old French *pasnage*, from medieval Latin *pastionaticum*, from *pastio(n-)* 'pasturing,' from the verb *pascere* 'to feed.'

panne /pan/ (also **panne velvet**) ▸*n.* a lustrous fabric resembling velvet, made of silk or rayon and having a flattened pile. ▷late 18th cent.: from French, of unknown origin.

pan·nier /ˈpanyər; ˈpanēər/ ▸*n.* **1** a basket, esp. one of a pair carried by a beast of burden. ■ each of a pair of bags or boxes fitted on either side of the rear wheel of a bicycle or motorcycle. **2** *historical* part of a skirt looped up around the hips. ■ a frame supporting this. ▷Middle English: from Old French *panier*, from Latin *panarium* 'breadbasket,' from *panis* 'bread.'

pan·ni·kin /ˈpanikin/ ▸*n.* a small metal drinking cup. ▷early 19th cent.: from **PAN**[1], on the pattern of *cannikin*.

pan·nist /ˈpanist/ ▸*n. W. Indian* a person who plays a pan in a steel band. See **PAN**[1] (sense 1).

Pan·no·ni·a /pəˈnōnēə/ an ancient country of southern Europe that was south and west of the Danube River, in present-day Austria, Hungary, Slovenia, and Croatia.

pan·nus /ˈpanəs/ ▸*n. Medicine* a condition in which a layer of vascular fibrous tissue extends over the surface of an organ or other specialized anatomical structure, esp. the cornea. ▷late Middle English: perhaps from Latin, literally 'cloth.'

pan·o·ply /ˈpanəplē/ ▸*n.* a complete or impressive collection of things: *a deliciously inventive panoply of insults.* ■ a splendid display: *all the panoply of Western religious liturgy.* ■ *historical* or *poetic/literary* a complete set of arms or suit of armor. ▷late 16th cent. (in the sense 'complete protection for spiritual warfare,' often with biblical allusion to Eph. 6:11, 13): from French *panoplie* or modern Latin *panoplia* 'full armor,' from Greek, from *pan* 'all' + *hopla* 'arms.' **—pan·o·plied** /-plēd/ *adj.*

pan·op·tic /paˈnäptik/ ▸*adj.* showing or seeing the whole at one view: *a panoptic aerial view.* ▷early 19th cent.: from Greek *panoptos* 'seen by all,' from *panoptēs* 'all-seeing' + **-IC**.

pan·op·ti·con /paˈnäptiˌkän/ ▸*n. historical* a circular prison with cells arranged around a central well, from which prisoners could at all times be observed. ▷mid 18th cent.: from **PAN-** 'all' + Greek *optikon*, neuter of *optikos* 'optic.'

pan·o·ram·a /ˌpanəˈramə; -ˈrämə/ ▸*n.* an unbroken view of the whole region surrounding an observer: *the tower offers a wonderful panorama of Prague.* ■ a picture or photograph containing a wide view. ■ a complete survey or presentation of a subject or sequence of events: *the galleries will offer a full panorama of 20th-century art.* ▷late 18th cent.: from **PAN-** 'all' + Greek *horama* 'view' (from *horan* 'see'). **—pan·o·ram·ic** /-ˈramik/ *adj.* **—pan·o·ram·i·cal·ly** /-ˈramik(ə)lē/ *adv.*

pan-pan /pan pan/ ▸*n.* an international radio distress signal, of less urgency than a mayday signal. ▷1920s: *pan* from French *panne* 'breakdown.'

pan·pipes /ˈpanˌpīps/ ▸*plural n.* a musical instrument made from a row of short pipes of varying length fixed together and played by blowing across the top. ▷originally associated with the Greek rural god **PAN**.

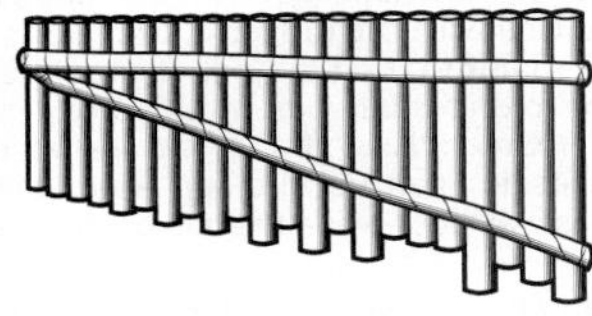

panpipes

pan·psy·chism /panˈsīˌkizəm/ ▸*n.* the doctrine or belief that everything material, however small, has an element of individual consciousness. **—pan·psy·chist** *adj.* & *n.*

pan·sex·u·al /panˈseksHo͞oəl/ ▸*adj.* not limited or inhibited in sexual choice with regard to gender or activity.
▸*n.* a person who is sexually inclusive in this way. **—pan·sex·u·al·i·ty** /-ˌseksHo͞oˈalitē/ *n.*

pan-Slav·ism ▸*n.* the principle or advocacy of the union of all Slavs or all Slavic peoples in one political organization. **—pan-Slav·ist** *adj.* & *n.*

pan·sper·mi·a /panˈspərmēə/ ▸*n.* the theory that life on the earth originated from microorganisms or chemical precursors of life present in outer space and able to initiate life on reaching a suitable environment. ▷mid 19th cent.: from Greek, from *panspermos* 'containing all kinds of seed.'

pan·sy /ˈpanzē/ ▸*n.* **1** a popular cultivated viola with flowers in rich colors, with both summer- and winter-flowering varieties. • Genus *Viola*, family Violaceae: several species and hybrids, in particular the commonly cultivated *V. cornuta*. **2** *informal, offensive* an effeminate or homosexual man. ▷late Middle English: from French *pensée* 'thought; pansy,'

pansy 1

Pronunciation Key ə *ago*; ər *over*; ˈə or ˌə *up*; ˈər or ˌər *fur*; a *hat*; ā *rate*; ä *car*; CH *chew*; e *let*; ē *see*; e(ə)r *air*; i *fit*; ī *by*; i(ə)r *ear*; NG *sing*; ō *go*; ô *for*; oi *boy*; o͝o *good*; o͞o *goo*; ou *out*; SH *she*; TH *thin*; T͟H *then*; (h)w *why*; ZH *vision*

from *penser* 'think,' from Latin *pensare,* frequentative of *pendere* 'weigh, consider.'

pant /pant/ ▶*v.* [*intrans.*] breathe with short, quick breaths, typically from exertion or excitement: *he was panting when he reached the top.* ■ [with *adverbial of direction*] run or go in a specified direction while panting: *they panted up the stairs.* ■ [with *direct speech*] say something breathlessly: *"We'll never have time," she panted.* ■ long for, or long to do, something: *it makes you* **pant for** *more.* ■ *poetic/literary* (of the heart or chest) throb violently from strong emotions.
▶*n.* a short, quick breath. ■ *poetic/literary* a throb or heave of a person's heart or chest. ▷Middle English: related to Old French *pantaisier* 'be agitated, gasp,' based on Greek *phantasioun* 'cause to imagine,' from *phantasia* (see FANTASY). **—pant·ing·ly** *adv.*

Pan·ta·gru·el·i·an /ˌpantəgrōōˈwelēən/ ▶*adj. rare* enormous: *a Pantagruelian banquet.* ▷late 17th cent.: from *Pantagruel* (the name of an enormous giant in Rabelais's *Gargantua and Pantagruel*) + -IAN.

pan·ta·lets /ˌpantlˈets/ (also **pan·ta·lettes**) ▶*plural n.* long underpants with a frill at the bottom of each leg, worn by women and girls in the 19th century.

pan·ta·loon /ˌpantlˈōōn/ ▶*n.* **1** (**pantaloons**) women's baggy trousers gathered at the ankles. ■ *historical* men's close-fitting breeches fastened below the calf or at the foot. ■ *informal* pants. **2** (**Pantaloon**) a Venetian character in Italian commedia dell'arte represented as a foolish old man wearing pantaloons. ▷late 16th cent. (sense 2): from French *pantalon,* from the Italian name *Pantalone* 'Pantaloon' (see sense 2).

pan·tech·ni·con /panˈteknikən; -ˌkän/ ▶*n. Brit., dated* a large van for transporting furniture. ▷mid 19th cent.: from PAN- 'all' + *tekhnikon* 'piece of art,' originally the name of a bazaar in London for all kinds of artistic work, later converted into a furniture warehouse.

Pan·thal·as·sa /ˌpanTHəˈlasə/ a universal sea or single ocean, such as would have surrounded Pangaea. ▷late 19th cent.: from PAN- 'all' + Greek *thalassa* 'sea.'

pan·the·ism /ˈpanTHēˌizəm/ ▶*n.* **1** a doctrine that identifies God with the universe, or regards the universe as a manifestation of God. **2** *rare* worship that admits or tolerates all gods. ▷mid 18th cent.: from PAN- 'all' + Greek *theos* 'god' + -ISM. **—pan·the·ist** *n.* **—pan·the·is·tic** /ˌpanTHēˈistik/ *adj.* **—pan·the·is·ti·cal** /ˌpanTHēˈistikəl/ *adj.* **—pan·the·is·ti·cal·ly** /ˌpanTHēˈistik(ə)lē/ *adv.*

pan·the·on /ˈpanTHēˌän; -THēən/ ▶*n.* all the gods of a people or religion collectively: *the deities of the Hindu and Shinto pantheons.* ■ (also **Pantheon**) (esp. in ancient Greece and Rome) a temple dedicated to all the gods. ■ a building in which the illustrious dead of a nation are buried or honored. ■ a group of particularly respected, famous, or important people: *the pantheon of the all-time greats.* ▷late Middle English (referring esp. to the circular temple built by Hadrian, Severus, and Caracalla in Rome): via Latin from Greek *pantheion,* from *pan* 'all' + *theion* 'holy' (from *theos* 'god').

Pantheon in Rome, Italy

pan·ther /ˈpanTHər/ ▶*n.* a leopard, esp. a black one. ■ a cougar. ▷Middle English: from Old French *pantere,* from Latin *panthera,* from Greek *panthēr.* In Latin, *pardus* 'leopard' also existed; the two terms led to confusion: until the mid 19th cent. many taxonomists regarded the panther and the leopard as separate species.

pan·ther cap ▶*n.* a poisonous toadstool that has a brownish-gray cap with fluffy white spots and white gills, found in woodlands in both Eurasia and North America. • *Amanita pantherina,* family Amanitaceae, class Hymenomycetes.

pant·ies /ˈpantēz/ ▶*plural n. informal* legless underpants worn by women and girls.

pan·tile /ˈpanˌtīl/ ▶*n.* a roof tile curved to form an S-shaped section, fitted to overlap its neighbor. ▷mid 17th cent.: from PAN[1] + TILE, probably suggested by Dutch *dakpan,* literally 'roof pan.' **—pan·tiled** *adj.*

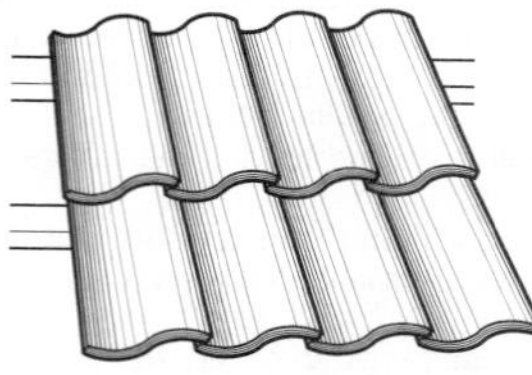

pantile

Pant·i·soc·ra·cy /ˌpantiˈsäkrəsē/ ▶*n.* a form of utopian social organization in which all are equal in social position and responsibility. ▷late 18th cent.: from PANTO- 'all' + Greek *isokratia* 'equality of power.' **—Pant·i·so·cra·tic** /-səˈkratik/ *adj.*

pan·to /ˈpanˌtō/ ▶*n.* (*pl.* **-tos**) *Brit., informal* short for PANTOMIME (sense 1).

panto- ▶*comb. form* all; universal: *pantograph* | *pantomime.* ▷from Greek *pas, pant-* 'all.'

Pan·toc·ra·tor /panˈtäkrətər/ ▶*n.* a title of Christ represented as the ruler of the universe, esp. in Byzantine church decoration. ▷late 19th cent.: via Latin from Greek, 'ruler over all.'

pan·to·graph /ˈpantəˌgraf/ ▶*n.* **1** an instrument for copying a drawing or plan on a different scale by a system of hinged and jointed rods. **2** a jointed framework conveying a current to a train, streetcar, or other electric vehicle from overhead wires. ▷early 18th cent.: from PANTO- 'all, universal' + Greek *-graphos* 'writing.' **—pan·to·graph·ic** /ˌpantəˈgrafik/ *adj.*

pan·to·mime /ˈpantəˌmīm/ ▶*n.* **1** a dramatic entertainment, originating in Roman mime, in which performers express meaning through gestures accompanied by music. ■ an absurdly exaggerated piece of behavior: *he made a pantomime of checking his watch.* ■ *informal* a ridiculous or confused situation or event: *the drive to town was a pantomime.* **2** *Brit.* a theatrical entertainment, mainly for children, that involves music, topical jokes, and slapstick comedy and is based on a fairy tale or nursery story, usually produced around Christmas.
▶*v.* [*trans.*] express or represent (something) by extravagant and exaggerated mime: *the clown candidates pantomimed different emotions.* ▷late 16th cent. (first used in the Latin form and denoting an actor using mime): from French *pantomime* or Latin *pantomimus,* from Greek *pantomimos* 'imitator of all' (see PANTO-, MIME). **—pan·to·mim·ic** /ˌpantəˈmimik/ *adj.* **—pan·to·mim·ist** *n.*

Pan·tone /ˈpanˌtōn/ ▶*n.* [usu. as *adj.*] *trademark* a system for matching colors, used in specifying printing inks: *Pantone colors.*

pan·to·then·ic ac·id /ˌpantəˈTHenik/ ▶*n. Biochemistry* a vitamin of the B complex, found in rice, bran, and many other foods, and essential for the oxidation of fats and carbohydrates. ▷1930s: *pantothenic* from Greek *pantothen* 'from every side' (with allusion to its widespread occurrence.) **—pan·to·then·ate** /panˈtäTHənāt/ *n.*

pan·toum /panˈtōōm/ (also **pan·tun**) ▶*n.* a Malay verse form, imitated in French and English, consisting of quotations with an *abab* rhyme scheme linked by repeated lines. ▷late 18th cent.: Malay *pantun.*

pan·try /ˈpantrē/ ▶*n.* (*pl.* **-tries**) a small room or closet in which food, dishes, and utensils are kept. ▷Middle English: from Anglo-Norman French *panterie,* from *paneter* 'baker,' based on late Latin *panarius* 'bread seller,' from Latin *panis* 'bread.'

pan·try·man /ˈpantrēmən/ ▶*n.* (*pl.* **-men**) a butler or a butler's assistant.

pants /pants/ ▶*plural n.* **1** trousers: *baggy corduroy pants* | [as *adj.*] (**pant**) *his pant leg.* **2** *Brit.* underpants. **3** *Brit. informal* rubbish; nonsense: *he thought we were going to be absolute pants.* ▷mid 19th cent.: abbr. of *pantaloons* (see PANTALOON).
▶*PHRASES* □ **catch someone with their pants down** *informal* catch someone in an embarrassingly unprepared state. □ **fly** (or **drive**) **by the seat of one's pants** *informal* rely on instinct rather than logic or knowledge. □ **scare** (or **bore**, etc.) **the pants off someone** *informal* make someone extremely scared, bored, etc. □ **wear the pants** *informal* be the dominant partner in a relationship: *there's no doubt who'll wear the pants in that house.*

pant·suit /ˈpantˌsōōt/ (also **pants suit**) ▶*n.* a pair of pants and a matching jacket worn by women.

pan·tun ▶*n.* variant spelling of PANTOUM.

pant·y gir·dle ▶*n.* a woman's elasticized undergarment combining girdle and panties.

pant·y·hose /ˈpantēˌhōz/ ▶*plural n.* women's thin nylon tights.

pant·y raid ▶*n. dated* a visit by a group of male students to a women's dormitory with the object of stealing panties.

pant·y·waist /ˈpantēˌwāst/ *informal* ▶*n.* a feeble or effeminate person.
▶*adj.* [*attrib.*] effeminate or feeble. ▷1930s: extended use of the term's literal sense, 'child's garment consisting of panties attached to a bodice.'

pan·za·nel·la /ˌpanzəˈnelə; ˌpansə-/ ▶*n.* a type of Tuscan salad made with anchovies, chopped salad vegetables, and bread soaked in dressing. ▷Italian, from *pane* 'bread' + *zanella* 'small basket.'

pan·zer /ˈpanzər/ ▶*n.* a German armored vehicle, esp. a tank used in World War II: [as *adj.*] *panzer divisions.* ▷from German *Panzer,* literally 'coat of mail.'

pap[1] /pap/ ▶*n. often derogatory* bland soft or semiliquid food such as that suitable for babies or invalids: *trying to eat a trayful of tasteless pap.* ■ *derogatory* reading matter or entertainment that is worthless or lacking in substance: *limitless channels serving up an undemanding diet of pap.* ▷late Middle English: probably from Middle Low German, Middle Dutch *pappe,* probably based on Latin *pappare* 'eat.'

pap[2] ▶*n. archaic* or *dialect* a woman's breast or nipple. ▷Middle English: probably of Scandinavian origin, from a base imitative of the sound of sucking.

pa·pa /ˈpäpə/ ▶*n.* **1** one's father: [as *name*] *Papa had taught her to ride a bicycle.* **2** a code word representing the letter P, used in radio communication. ▷late 17th cent.: from French, via late Latin from Greek *papas.*

pa·pa·bi·le /pəˈpäbəˌlā/ ▶*adj. rare* worthy of being or eligible to be pope. ▷Italian, from Latin *papa* 'pope.'

pa·pa·cy /ˈpāpəsē/ ▶*n.* (*pl.* **-cies**) (usu. **the papacy**) the office or authority of the pope. ■ the tenure of office of a pope: *during the papacy of Pope John.* ▷late Middle English: from medieval Latin *papatia,* from *papa* 'pope.'

Papa Doc ▶ see DUVALIER.

Pap·a·go /ˈpapəˌgō; ˈpäp-/ ▶*n.* (*pl.* same or **-gos**) **1** a member of an American Indian people of southern Arizona and northern Sonora. **2** a dialect of the Uto-Aztecan Pima-Papago language.
▶*adj.* of or relating to this people or their language. ▷via Spanish from an abbreviation of the Papago self-designation *bābāwĭ-ʼoʼodham.*

pa·pa·in /pəˈpā-in; -pī-/ ▶*n.* a protein-digesting enzyme obtained from unripe papaya fruit, used to tenderize meat and as a food supplement to aid digestion. ▷late 19th cent.: from PAPAYA + -IN[1].

pa·pal /ˈpāpəl/ ▶*adj.* of or relating to a pope or to the papacy. ▷late Middle English: from Old French, from medieval Latin *papalis,* from ecclesiastical Latin *papa* 'bishop (of Rome).' **—pa·pal·ly** *adv.*

pa·pal in·fal·li·bil·i·ty ▶*n.* see INFALLIBILITY.

pa·pal·ist /ˈpāpəlist/ *chiefly historical* ▶*n.* a supporter of the papacy, esp. an advocate of papal supremacy.
▶*adj.* supporting the papacy.

Pa·pal States *historical* the temporal dominions belonging to the pope, esp. in central Italy.

pa·pa·raz·zo /ˌpäpəˈrätsō/ ▶*n.* (*pl.* **-raz·zi** /-ˈrätsē/) (usu. **paparazzi**) a freelance photographer who pursues celebrities to get photographs of them. ▷mid 20th cent.: from Italian, from the name of a character in Fellini's film *La Dolce Vita* (1960).

pa·pav·er·a·ceous /pəˌpavəˈrāSHəs/ ▶*adj. Botany* of, relating to, or denoting plants of the poppy family (Papaveraceae). ▷mid 19th cent.: from modern Latin *Papaveraceae* (plural), based on Latin *papaver* 'poppy,' + -OUS.

pa·pav·er·ine /pəˈpavəˌrēn; -rin/ ▶*n. Chemistry* a compound present in opium used medicinally to alleviate muscle spasms and asthma. • An alkaloid; chem. formula: $C_{20}H_{21}NO_4$. ▷mid 19th cent.: from Latin *papaver* 'poppy' + -INE[4].

pa·paw /pəˈpô; ˈpôpô/ ▶*n.* variant spelling of PAWPAW.

pa·pa·ya /pəˈpīyə/ ▶*n.* **1** a tropical fruit shaped like an elongated melon, with edible orange flesh and small black seeds. Also called PAPAW or PAWPAW. **2** (also **papaya tree**) the fast-growing tree that bears this fruit, native to warm regions of America. It is widely cultivated for its fruit, both for eating and for papain production. • *Carica papaya,* family

Caricaceae. ▷late 16th cent.: from Spanish and Portuguese (see PAWPAW).

Pa·pe·e·te /pə'pētē; ˌpäpē'ätā/ the capital of French Polynesia, located on the northwestern coast of Tahiti; pop. 24,000.

pa·per /'pāpər/ ▸*n.* **1** material manufactured in thin sheets from the pulp of wood or other fibrous substances, used for writing, drawing, or printing on, or as wrapping material: *a sheet of paper* | [as *adj.*] *a paper bag.* ■ a newspaper. ■ wallpaper. ■ (usu. **papers**) a piece or sheet of paper with something written or drawn on it: *he riffled through the papers on his desk.* ■ (**papers**) significant or important documents belonging to a person: *the personal papers of major political figures.* ■ [as *adj.*] denoting something that is officially documented but has no real existence or little merit or use: *a paper profit.* ■ a government report or policy document: *a recently leaked cabinet paper.* ■ (**papers**) documents attesting identity; credentials: *two men stopped us and asked us for our papers.* ■ a piece of paper used for wrapping or enclosing something or made into a packet: *toffee papers.* ■ short for COMMERCIAL PAPER. ■ short for CIGARETTE PAPER. **2** an essay or thesis, esp. one read at an academic lecture or seminar or published in an academic journal. **3** *theatrical slang* free passes of admission to a theater or other entertainment.
▸*v.* [*trans.*] **1** (often **be papered**) apply wallpaper to (a wall or room): *the walls were papered in a Regency stripe.* ■ [*intrans.*] (**paper over**) cover (a hole or blemish) with wallpaper. ■ (**paper over**) disguise (an awkward problem) instead of resolving it: *the ill feeling between her and Jenny must have been papered over.* **2** *theatrical slang* fill (a theater) by giving out free tickets. ▷Middle English: from Anglo-Norman French *papir*, from Latin *papyrus* 'paper-reed' (see PAPYRUS). The verb dates from the late 16th cent. **—pa·per·er** *n.* **—pa·per·less** *adj.*
▸*PHRASES* □ **be not worth the paper it is written on** be of no value or validity whatsoever despite having been written down. □ **make the papers** be written about in newspapers and thus become famous or notorious. □ **on paper** in writing. ■ in theory rather than in reality: *the combatants were, on paper at least, evenly matched.*

pa·per·back /'pāpərˌbak/ ▸*adj.* (of a book) bound in stiff paper or flexible cardboard.
▸*n.* a book bound in stiff paper or flexible cardboard.
▸*PHRASE* □ **in paperback** in an edition bound in stiff paper or flexible cardboard: *now available in paperback.*

pa·per bag ▸*n.* a small bag made of paper.
▸*PHRASE* □ **be unable to punch** (or **sing**, **act**, etc.) **one's way out of a paper bag** *informal* be completely ineffectual or inept at the specified activity: *he couldn't act his way out of a paper bag.*

pa·per·bark /'pāpərˌbärk/ ▸*n.* a cajuput tree. ■ used in names of other trees that have a peeling papery bark, e.g., **paperbark maple, paperbark birch.**

pa·per birch (also **pa·per·bark birch**) ▸*n.* a North American birch with peeling white bark. • *Betula papyrifera*, family Betulaceae.

pa·per·board /'pāpərˌbôrd/ ▸*n.* cardboard or pasteboard.

pa·per·boy /'pāpərˌboi/ ▸*n.* a boy who delivers newspapers to people's homes.

pa·per chain ▸*n.* a chain made of colored paper links and used for decorating a room, esp. at Christmas.

pa·per chase ▸*n.* **1** *informal* the action of processing forms and other paperwork, esp. when considered excessive. **2** *informal* the attempt to gain academic qualifications, esp. a law degree.

pa·per clip ▸*n.* a piece of bent wire or plastic used for holding several sheets of paper together.

pa·per cup ▸*n.* a disposable cup made of thin cardboard.

pa·per doll ▸*n.* a piece of paper cut or folded into the shape of a human figure.

pa·per feed ▸*n.* a device for inserting sheets of paper into a printer, typewriter, or similar machine.

pa·per·girl /'pāpərˌgərl/ ▸*n.* a girl who delivers newspapers to people's homes.

pa·per·hang·er /'pāpərˌhaNGər/ ▸*n.* a person who decorates with wallpaper, esp. professionally.

pa·per knife ▸*n.* (*pl.* **pa·per knives**) a blunt knife used for cutting paper, such as when opening envelopes or slitting the uncut pages of books.

pa·per mill ▸*n.* a mill in which paper is made.

pa·per mon·ey ▸*n.* money in the form of banknotes.

pa·per mul·ber·ry ▸*n.* a small tree of the mulberry family, the inner bark of which is used for making paper and tapa cloth, occurring from eastern Asia to Polynesia. • *Broussonetia papyrifera*, family Moraceae.

pa·per nau·ti·lus ▸*n.* another term for ARGONAUT.

pa·per plate ▸*n.* a disposable plate made of cardboard.

pa·per-push·er ▸*n.* *informal* a bureaucrat or menial clerical worker. **—pa·per-push·ing** *n.* & *adj.*

pa·per route (*Brit.* **paper round**) ▸*n.* a job of regularly delivering newspapers. ■ a route taken doing this.

pa·per tape ▸*n.* paper in the form of a long narrow strip. ■ such tape having holes punched in it, used in older computer systems for conveying data or instructions.

pa·per-thin ▸*adj.* extremely thin or insubstantial: *paper-thin pancakes* | *her sophistication was paper-thin.*

pa·per ti·ger ▸*n.* a person or thing that appears threatening but is ineffectual.

pa·per trail ▸*n.* the written evidence of someone's activities: *the paper trail led the FBI to him in just six days.*

pa·per-train ▸*v.* [*trans.*] train a dog to defecate and urinate on paper placed on the floor, rather than directly on the floor.

pa·per wasp ▸*n.* a social wasp that forms a small, umbrella-shaped nest made from wood pulp. • Genus *Polistes*, family Vespidae.

paper wasp

pa·per·weight /'pāpərˌwāt/ ▸*n.* a small, heavy object for keeping loose papers in place.

pa·per·work /'pāpərˌwərk/ ▸*n.* routine work involving written documents such as forms, records, or letters: *I need to catch up on some paperwork.* ■ such written documents.

pa·per·y /'pāpərē/ ▸*adj.* thin and dry like paper.

Pa·pia·men·tu /ˌpäpyə'mentoo/ (also **Pa·pia·men·to** /-tō/) ▸*n.* a Spanish Creole language with admixtures of Portuguese and Dutch, spoken on the Caribbean islands of Aruba, Bonaire, and Curaçao. ▷from Spanish *Papiamento.*

pa·pier col·lé /päp'yā kō'lā/ ▸*n.* (*pl.* **pa·piers col·lés** *pronunc.* same) the technique of using paper for collage. ■ a collage made from paper. ▷French, literally 'glued paper.'

pa·pier mâ·ché /ˌpāpər mə'SHā; pä'p(y)ā/ ▸*n.* a malleable mixture of paper and glue, or paper, flour, and water, that becomes hard when dry: *George was constructing a crocodile out of papier-mâché.* ▷French, literally 'chewed paper.'

pa·pil·i·o·na·ceous /pəˌpilēə'nāSHəs/ ▸*adj.* *Botany* of, relating to, or denoting leguminous plants of a group (subfamily Papilionoideae or family Papilionaceae) with flowers that resemble a butterfly. ▷mid 17th cent.: from modern Latin *Papilionaceae* (plural), based on Latin *papilio* 'butterfly,' + -OUS.

pa·pil·la /pə'pilə/ ▸*n.* (*pl.* **-pil·lae** /-'pilˌē; -'pilˌī/) a small rounded protuberance on a part or organ of the body. ■ a small fleshy projection on a plant. ▷late 17th cent.: from Latin, literally 'nipple,' diminutive of *papula* 'small protuberance.' **—pap·il·lar·y** /'papəˌlerē/ *adj.* **—pap·il·late** /'papəˌlāt; pə'pilit/ *adj.* **—pap·il·lose** /'päpəˌlōs; -ˌlōz/ *adj.*

pap·il·lo·ma /ˌpapə'lōmə/ ▸*n.* (*pl.* **-mas** or **-ma·ta** /-mətə/) *Medicine* a small wartlike growth on the skin or on a mucous membrane, derived from the epidermis and usually benign. ▷mid 19th cent.: from PAPILLA + -OMA.

pap·il·lon /ˌpäpē'yôn/ ▸*n.* a dog of a toy breed with ears suggesting the form of a butterfly. ▷early 20th cent.: from French, literally 'butterfly,' from Latin *papilio(n-).*

pa·pist /'pāpist/ *chiefly derogatory* ▸*n.* a Roman Catholic. ■ another term for PAPALIST.
▸*adj.* of, relating to, or associated with the Roman Catholic Church. ▷mid 16th cent.: from French *papiste* or modern Latin *papista*, from ecclesiastical Latin *papa* 'bishop (of Rome).' **—pa·pism** /-ˌpizəm/ *n.* **—pa·pis·ti·cal** /pə'pistəkəl/ *adj.* (*archaic*). **—pa·pist·ry** /-trē/ *n.*

pa·poose /pa'poos; pə-/ ▸*n.* **1** *dated, offensive* a young North American Indian child. **2** a type of bag used to carry a child on one's back. ▷mid 17th cent.: from Narragansett *papoos.*

Papp /pap/, Joe (1921–91), U.S. producer and director; born *Joseph Papirofsky*. He managed Hollywood's Actors Laboratory 1948–1950 and then founded the Shakespearean Theatre Workshop in 1954 that became the New York Shakespeare Festival. in 1960. He also founded the off-Broadway Public Theater in 1967 and directed the theaters at Lincoln Center from 1973 until 1978.

pap·pa·dam /'päpäˌdəm/ ▸*n.* a thin East Indian bread made with lentil flour. ▷from Tamil.

pap·par·del·le /ˌpapär'delā/ ▸*n.* pasta in the form of broad flat ribbons, usually served with a meat sauce. ▷Italian, from *pappare* 'eat hungrily.'

Pap·pus /'papəs/ (*fl.* c.AD 300–350), Greek mathematician; known as **Pappus of Alexandria**. His *Collection* of six books (another two are missing) is the principal source of knowledge of the mathematics of his predecessors.

pap·pus /'papəs/ ▸*n.* (*pl.* **pap·pi** /'paˌpī; -ˌpē/) *Botany* the tuft of hairs on each seed of thistles, dandelions, and similar plants that assists dispersal by the wind. ▷early 18th cent.: via Latin from Greek *pappos.* **—pap·pose** /'paˌpōs; 'paˌpōz/ *adj.*

pap·py[1] /'papē/ ▸*n.* (*pl.* **-pies**) [usu. as *name*] a child's word for father: *Pappy was always busy.* ▷mid 18th cent.: from PAPA + -Y[2].

pap·py[2] ▸*adj.* of the nature of pap; soft and bland.

pap·ri·ka /pə'prēkə; pa-/ ▸*n.* a powdered spice with a deep orange-red color and a mildly pungent flavor, made from the dried and ground fruits of certain varieties of sweet pepper. ■ a deep orange-red color like that of paprika. ▷late 19th cent.: from Hungarian.

Pap test /pap/ ▸*n.* a test to detect cancer of the cervix or uterus, using a specimen of cellular material from the neck of the uterus spread on a microscope slide (**Pap smear**). ▷1960s: named after George N. *Papanicolaou* (1883–1962), Greek-born American scientist.

Pap·u·a /'päpooə; 'papyooə/ the southeastern part of the island of New Guinea, now part of the independent state of Papua New Guinea. ▷named by a Portuguese navigator who visited it 1526–27, from a Malay word meaning 'woolly-haired.'

Pap·u·an /'päpooən; 'papyooən/ ▸*n.* **1** a native or inhabitant of Papua, or of Papua New Guinea. **2** a heterogeneous group of around 750 languages spoken in Papua New Guinea and neighboring islands.
▸*adj.* of or relating to Papua or its people or their languages.

Pap·u·a New Guin·ea a country in the western Pacific Ocean that includes the eastern half of the island of New Guinea as well as some neighboring islands; pop. 5,420,000; capital, Port Moresby; languages, English (official), Tok Pisin, and several hundred native Austronesian and Papuan languages. **—Pap·u·a New Guin·e·an** *adj.* & *n.*

Papua New Guinea was formed in 1949 from the administrative union of Papua, an Australian Territory since 1906, and the Trust Territory of New Guinea (Northeast New Guinea), which was formerly under German control and an Australian trusteeship since 1921. In 1975, it became an independent state within the Commonwealth of Nations.

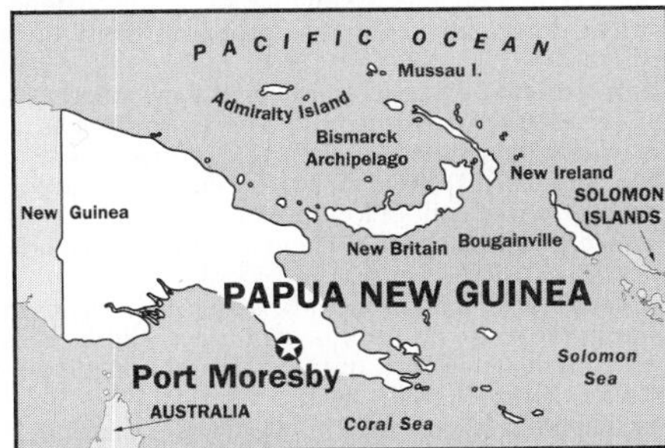

pap·ule /'papˌyool/ (also **pap·u·la** /-yələ/) ▸*n.* (*pl.* **-ules** or **-u·lae** /-yəˌlē/) *Medicine* a small, raised, solid pimple or swelling, often forming part of a rash on the skin and typically inflamed but not producing pus. ▷early 18th cent.: from Latin *papula.* **—pap·u·lar** /-yələr/ *adj.* **—pap·u·lose** /-yəlōs; -lōz/ *adj.* **—pap·u·lous** /-yələs/ *adj.*

pap·y·rol·o·gy /ˌpapə'räləjē/ ▸*n.* the branch of study that deals with ancient papyri. **—pa·py·ro·log·i·cal** /pəˌpīrə'läjikəl; -pi(ə)rə-/ *adj.* **—pap·y·rol·o·gist** /ˌpapə'räləjəst/ *n.*

Pronunciation Key ə *ago*; ər *over*; 'ə or ˌə *up*; 'ər or ˌər *fur*; a *hat*; ā *rate*; ä *car*; CH *chew*; e *let*; ē *see*; e(ə)r *air*; i *fit*; ī *by*; i(ə)r *ear*; NG *sing*; ō *go*; ô *for*; oi *boy*; oo *good*; oo *goo*; ou *out*; SH *she*; TH *thin*; TH *then*; (h)w *why*; ZH *vision*

pa·py·rus /pə'pīrəs/ ▸n. (pl. **-py·ri** /-'pīrī/ or **-py·rus·es**) **1** a material prepared in ancient Egypt from the pithy stem of a water plant, used in sheets throughout the ancient Mediterranean world for writing or painting on and also for making rope, sandals, and boats. ■ a document written on papyrus. **2** the tall aquatic sedge from which this material is obtained, native to central Africa and the Nile valley. • *Cyperus papyrus*, family Cyperaceae. ▷late Middle English (sense 2): via Latin from Greek *papuros*. Sense 1 dates from the early 18th cent.

P

par[1] /pär/ ▸n. **1** *Golf* the number of strokes a first-class player should normally require for a particular hole or course: *the sixteenth is a par five | he had advanced from his overnight position of three* **under par**. ■ a score of this number of strokes at a hole: *a card that showed 16 pars, one eagle, and one birdie.* **2** *Stock Market* the face value of a stock or other security, as distinct from its market value. ■ (also **par of exchange**) the recognized value of one country's currency in terms of another's.

▸v. (**parred, par·ring**) [*trans.*] *Golf* play (a hole) in par. ▷late 16th cent. (in the sense 'equality of value or standing'): from Latin, 'equal,' also 'equality.' The golf term dates from the late 19th cent.

▸*PHRASES* □ **above** (or **below** or **under**) **par** better (or worse) than is usual or expected: *poor nutrition can leave you feeling below par.* □ **on a par with** equal in importance or quality to; on an equal level with: *this home cooking is on a par with the best in the world.* □ **par for the course** what is normal or expected in any given circumstances: *given the high standards of the food, the prices seem par for the course.* □ **up to par** at an expected or usual level or quality.

par[2] /pär/ ▸n. *informal* a paragraph. ▷mid 19th cent.: abbreviation.

par. (also **para.**) ▸*abbr.* paragraph.

par- ▸*comb. form* variant spelling of **PARA-**[1] shortened before a vowel or *h* (as in *paraldehyde, parody, parhelion*).

par·a[1] /'parə/ *informal* ▸n. **1** a paratrooper. **2** a paragraph.

par·a[2] /'pärə/ ▸n. (pl. same or **par·as**) a monetary unit of Bosnia–Herzegovina, Montenegro, and Serbia, equal to one hundredth of a dinar. ▷Turkish, from Persian *pāra* 'piece, portion.'

para-[1] (also **par-**) ▸*prefix* **1** beside; adjacent to: *parameter | parataxis | parathyroid.* ■ *Medicine* denoting a disordered function or faculty: *paresthesia.* ■ distinct from, but analogous to: *paramilitary | paraphrase | paratyphoid.* ■ beyond: *paradox | paranormal | parapsychology.* ■ subsidiary; assisting: *paramedic | paraprofessional.* **2** *Chemistry* denoting substitution at diametrically opposite carbon atoms in a benzene ring, e.g., in 1, 4 positions: *paradichlorobenzene.* Compare with **META-** and **ORTHO-**. ▷from Greek *para* 'beside'; in combinations often meaning 'amiss, irregular' and denoting alteration or modification.

para-[2] ▸*comb. form* denoting something that protects or wards off: *parachute | parasol.* ▷from French, from the Italian imperative singular of *parare* 'defend, shield' (originally meaning 'prepare,' from Latin *parare*).

par·a·a·mi·no·ben·zo·ic ac·id /'parə ə,mēnōben'zōik/ (abbr.: **PABA**) ▸n. *Biochemistry* a crystalline acid that is widely distributed in plant and animal tissue. It has been used to treat rickettsial infections and is widely used in suntan lotions and sunscreens to absorb ultraviolet light. • Chem. formula: $NH_2C_6H_4COOH$.

Par·a·bel·lum /,parə'beləm/ ▸n. *trademark* a make of automatic pistol or machine gun. ▷early 20th cent.: from Latin *para bellum*, from *para!* 'prepare!' (imperative of *parare*) + *bellum* 'war.'

par·a·bi·o·sis /,parəbī'ōsis/ ▸n. *Biology* the anatomical joining of two individuals, esp. artificially in physiological research. ▷early 20th cent.: modern Latin, from **PARA-**[1] 'beside, distinct from' + Greek *biōsis* 'mode of life' (from *bios* 'life'). —**par·a·bi·ot·ic** /-'ätik/ *adj.*

par·a·ble /'parəbəl/ ▸n. a simple story used to illustrate a moral or spiritual lesson, as told by Jesus in the Gospels. ▷Middle English: from Old French *parabole*, from an ecclesiastical Latin sense 'discourse, allegory' of Latin *parabola* 'comparison,' from Greek *parabolē* (see **PARABOLA**).

pa·rab·o·la /pə'rabələ/ ▸n. (pl. **-las** or **-lae** /-lē/) a symmetrical open plane curve formed by the intersection of a cone with a plane parallel to its side. The path of a projectile under the influence of gravity ideally follows a curve of this shape. ▷late 16th cent.: modern Latin, from Greek *parabolē* 'placing side by side, application,' from *para-* 'beside' + *bolē* 'a throw' (from the verb *ballein*).

par·a·bol·ic /,parə'bälik/ ▸*adj.* **1** of or like a parabola or part of one. **2** of or expressed in parables: *parabolic teaching.* ▷late Middle English: via late Latin from Greek *parabolikos*, from *parabolē* 'application' (see **PARABOLA**). —**par·a·bol·i·cal** *adj.* —**par·a·bol·i·cal·ly** /-(ə)lē/ *adv.*

pa·rab·o·loid /pə'rabə,loid/ ▸n. **1** (also **paraboloid of revolution**) a solid generated by the rotation of a parabola around its axis of symmetry. **2** a solid having two or more nonparallel parabolic cross sections. —**pa·rab·o·loi·dal** /pə,rabə'loidl/ *adj.*

Pa·ra·cel Is·lands /,parə'sel/ (also **the Pa·ra·cels**) a group of about 130 small, barren coral islands and reefs in the South China Sea, southeast of Hainan. The islands are claimed by both China and Vietnam.

par·a·cel·lu·lar /,parə'selyələr/ ▸*adj. Biology* passing or situated beside or between cells.

Par·a·cel·sus /,parə'selsəs/ (*c.*1493–1541), Swiss physician: born *Theophrastus Phillipus Aureolus Bombastus von Hohenheim.* He developed a new approach to medicine and philosophy based on observation and experience.

par·a·cen·te·sis /,parəsen'tēsis/ ▸n. (pl. **-ses** /-,sēz/) *Medicine* the perforation of a cavity of the body or of a cyst or similar outgrowth, esp. with a hollow needle to remove fluid or gas. ▷late 16th cent.: via Latin from Greek *parakentēsis*, from *parakentein* 'pierce at the side.'

par·a·cen·tric in·ver·sion /,parə'sentrik/ ▸n. *Genetics* a reversal of the normal order of genes in a chromosome segment involving only the part of a chromosome at one side of the centromere.

par·a·ce·ta·mol /,parə'sētə,mäl; -,môl/ ▸n. (pl. same or **-mols**) British term for **ACETAMINOPHEN**.

pa·rach·ro·nism /pə'rakrə,nizəm/ ▸n. an error in chronology, esp. by assigning too late a date. ▷mid 17th cent.: from **PARA-**[1] 'beyond' + Greek *khronos* 'time' + **-ISM**, perhaps suggested by **ANACHRONISM**.

par·a·chute /'parə,SHo͞ot/ ▸n. a cloth canopy that fills with air and allows a person or heavy object attached to it to descend slowly when dropped from an aircraft, or that is released from the rear of an aircraft on landing to act as a brake.

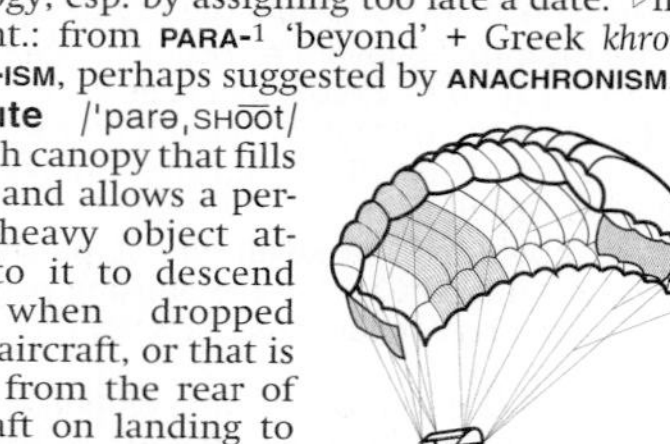

parachute

▸v. **1** drop or cause to drop from an aircraft by parachute: [*intrans.*] *airborne units* **parachuted in** *to secure the airport* | [*trans.*] *an air operation to* **parachute** *relief supplies* **into** *Bosnia.* **2** appoint or be appointed in an emergency or from outside the existing hierarchy: *an old crony of the CEO was controversially* **parachuted into** *the job.* ▷late 18th cent.: from French *para-* 'protection against' + *chute* 'fall.'

par·a·chute flare ▸n. a pyrotechnic signal flare that is carried up into the air by a rocket and floats suspended from a small parachute.

par·a·chut·ist /'parə,SHo͞otist/ ▸n. a person who uses a parachute.

Par·a·clete /'parə,klēt/ ▸n. (in Christian theology) the Holy Spirit as advocate or counselor (John 14:16, 26). ▷via late Latin from Greek *paraklētos* 'called in aid,' from *para-* 'alongside' + *klētos* (from *kalein* 'to call').

par·a·crine /'parəkrin/ ▸*adj. Physiology* of, relating to, or denoting a hormone that has effect only in the vicinity of the gland secreting it. ▷1970s: from **PARA-**[1] 'beside' + a shortened form of **ENDOCRINE** or **EXOCRINE**.

par·a·crys·tal /'parə,kristəl/ ▸n. *Chemistry* a piece of a substance that is not a true crystal but has some degree of order in its structure. —**par·a·crys·tal·line** /,parə'kristəlin/ *adj.*

pa·rade /pə'rād/ ▸n. **1** a public procession, esp. one celebrating a special day or event and including marching bands and floats. ■ a formal march or gathering of troops for inspection or display. ■ a series of people or things appearing or being displayed one after the other: *the parade of Hollywood celebrities who troop onto his show.* ■ a distasteful manifestation of a particular quality or kind of behavior: *the parade of lunacy and corruption will continue.* **2** a parade ground. ■ *Brit.* a public square or promenade. ■ *Brit.* a row of stores: *a shopping parade.*

▸v. [*intrans.*] walk or march in public in a formal procession or in an ostentatious or attention-seeking way: *officers will parade through the town center.* ■ [*trans.*] walk or march in such a way along (the streets of a town): *carefree young men were parading the streets.* ■ [*trans.*] display (someone or something) while marching or moving around a place: *revolutionary guards paraded him through the streets.* ■ [*trans.*] display (something) publicly in order to impress or attract attention: *he paraded his knowledge.* ■ (**parade as**) appear falsely as; masquerade as: *these untruths parading as history.* ■ (of troops) assemble for a formal inspection or ceremonial occasion: *the recruits were due to parade that day.* ▷mid 17th cent.: from French, literally 'a showing,' from Spanish *parada* and Italian *parata*, based on Latin *parare* 'prepare, furnish.' —**pa·rad·er** *n.*

▸*PHRASE* □ **on parade** taking part in a parade. ■ on public display: *politicians are always on parade.*

pa·rade ground ▸n. a place where troops gather for parade.

par·a·did·dle /'parə,didl/ ▸n. *Music* one of the basic patterns (rudiments) of drumming, consisting of four even strokes played in the order left-right-left-left or right-left-right-right. ▷1920s: imitative.

par·a·digm /'parə,dīm/ ▸n. **1** *technical* a typical example or pattern of something; a model: *there is a new paradigm for public art in this country.* See note at **MODEL**. ■ a worldview underlying the theories and methodology of a particular scientific subject: *the discovery of universal gravitation became the paradigm of successful science.* **2** a set of linguistic items that form mutually exclusive choices in particular syntactic roles: *English determiners form a paradigm: we can say "a book" or "his book" but not "a his book."* Often contrasted with **SYNTAGM**. ■ (in the traditional grammar of Latin, Greek, and other inflected languages) a table of all the inflected forms of a particular verb, noun, or adjective, serving as a model for other words of the same conjugation or declension. ▷late 15th cent.: via late Latin from Greek *paradeigma*, from *paradeiknunai* 'show side by side,' from *para-* 'beside' + *deiknunai* 'to show.'

par·a·dig·mat·ic /,parədig'matik/ ▸*adj.* **1** of the nature of a paradigm or model: *they offer this database as a paradigmatic example.* **2** of or denoting the relationship between a set of linguistic items that form mutually exclusive choices in particular syntactic roles. Contrasted with **SYNTAGMATIC**. —**par·a·dig·mat·i·cal·ly** *adv.*

par·a·digm shift ▸n. a fundamental change in approach or underlying assumptions. ▷1970s: term used in the writings of Thomas S. Kuhn (1922–96), philosopher of science.

Par·a·dise /'parə,dīs; 'pe(ə)r-/ a community in southeastern Nevada, south of Las Vegas; pop. 124,682.

par·a·dise /'parə,dīs/ ▸n. (in some religions) heaven as the ultimate abode of the just. ■ (**Paradise**) the abode of Adam and Eve before the Fall in the biblical account of the Creation; the Garden of Eden. ■ an ideal or idyllic place or state: *the surrounding countryside is a walker's paradise my idea of paradise is to relax on the seafront.* ▷Middle English: from Old French *paradis*, via ecclesiastical Latin from Greek *paradeisos* 'royal (enclosed) park,' from Avestan *pairidaēza* 'enclosure, park.' —**par·a·dis·al** /,parə'dīsəl/ *adj.* —**par·a·di·si·a·cal** /,parədi'sīəkəl/ (also **par·a·di·sa·i·cal** /,parədi'sā-ikəl/ or **par·a·di·si·cal** /,parə'disikəl/) *adj.*

par·a·dise fish ▸n. a small colorful labyrinth fish that is native to Southeast Asia and popular in aquariums. • Genus *Macropodus*, family Belontiidae: several species, including *M. opercularis.*

Par·a·dise of the Pa·cif·ic a nickname for the state of **HAWAII**.

pa·ra·dor /'parə,dôr/ ▸n. (pl. **pa·ra·dors** or **pa·ra·do·res** /,parə'dôres/) a hotel in Spain owned and administered by the Spanish government. ▷Spanish, literally 'stopping place.'

par·a·dos /'parə,däs/ ▸n. an elevation of earth behind a fortified place as a protection against attack from the rear, esp. a mound along the back of a trench. ▷mid 19th cent.: from French, from *para-* 'protection against' + *dos* 'back' (from Latin *dorsum*).

par·a·dox /'parə,däks/ ▸n. a statement or proposition that, despite sound (or apparently sound) reasoning from acceptable premises, leads to a conclusion that seems senseless, logically unacceptable, or self-contradictory: *a potentially serious conflict between quantum mechanics and the general theory of relativity known as the information paradox.* See note at **RIDDLE**. ■ a seemingly absurd or self-contradictory statement or proposition that when investigated or explained may prove to be well founded or true: *in a* *paradox, he has discovered that stepping back from his job has increased the rewards he gleans from it.* ■ a situation, person, or thing that combines contradictory features or qualities: *an Arizona canyon where the mingling of deciduous trees with desertic elements of flora forms a fascinating ecological paradox.* ▷mid 16th cent. (originally denoting a statement contrary to accepted opinion): via late Latin from Greek *paradoxon* 'contrary (opinion),' neuter adjective used as a noun, from *para-* 'distinct from' + *doxa* 'opinion.'

par·a·dox·i·cal /ˌparəˈdäksikəl/ ▸*adj.* seemingly absurd or self-contradictory: *by glorifying the acts of violence they achieve the paradoxical effect of making them trivial.* **—par·a·dox·i·cal·ly** *adv.* [*sentence adverb*] *paradoxically, the more fuel a star starts off with, the sooner it runs out.*

par·a·drop /ˈparəˌdräp/ ▸*n.* a descent or delivery by parachute.
▸*v.* (**-dropped, -drop·ping**) [*trans.*] drop (someone or something) by parachute. **—par·a·drop·per** *n.*

par·aes·the·sia ▸*n.* British spelling of PARESTHESIA.

par·af·fin /ˈparəfin/ ▸*n.* (also **paraffin wax**) a flammable, whitish, translucent, waxy solid consisting of a mixture of saturated hydrocarbons, obtained by distillation from petroleum or shale and used in candles, cosmetics, polishes, and sealing and waterproofing compounds. ■ (also **paraffin oil** or **liquid paraffin**) *Brit.* a colorless, flammable, oily liquid similarly obtained and used as fuel, esp. kerosene. ■ *Chemistry* old-fashioned term for ALKANE. ▷mid 19th cent.: from German, from Latin *parum* 'little' + *affinis* 'related' (from its low reactivity).

par·a·gen·e·sis /ˌparəˈjenəsis/ ▸*n.* (*pl.* **-ses**) /-ˌsēz/ *Geology* a set of minerals that were formed together, esp. in a rock, or with a specified mineral. **—par·a·ge·net·ic** /-jəˈnetik/ *adj.*

par·a·glid·ing /ˈparəˌglīdiNG/ ▸*n.* a sport in which a wide canopy resembling a parachute is attached to a person's body by a harness in order to allow them to glide through the air after jumping from or being lifted to a height. **—par·a·glide** /-ˌglīd/ *v.* **—par·a·glid·er** /-ˌglīdər/ *n.*

par·a·gon /ˈparəˌgän; -gən/ ▸*n.* a person or thing regarded as a perfect example of a particular quality: *it would have taken* ***a paragon of*** *virtue not to feel viciously jealous.* ■ a person or thing viewed as a model of excellence: *your cook is a paragon.* ■ a perfect diamond of 100 carats or more. ▷mid 16th cent.: from obsolete French, from Italian *paragone* 'touchstone used to discriminate good (gold) from bad,' from medieval Greek *parakonē* 'whetstone.'

Par·a·gould /ˈparəˌgo͞old/ a city in the northeastern corner of Arkansas, northeast of Jonesboro; pop. 22,017.

par·a·graph /ˈparəˌgraf/ ▸*n.* a distinct section of a piece of writing, usually dealing with a single theme and indicated by a new line, indentation, or numbering.
▸*v.* [*trans.*] arrange (a piece of writing) in paragraphs. ▷late 15th cent.: from French *paragraphe*, via medieval Latin from Greek *paragraphos* 'short stroke marking a break in sense,' from *para-* 'beside' + *graphein* 'write.' **—par·a·graph·ic** /ˌparəˈgrafik/ *adj.*

par·a·graph mark (also **paragraph symbol**) ▸*n.* a symbol (usually ¶) used in printed text to mark a new paragraph or as a reference mark.

Par·a·guay /ˈparəˌgwī; -ˌgwā/ a landlocked country in central South America; pop. 6,191,000; capital, Asunción; languages, Spanish (official) and Guarani. **—Par·a·guay·an** /ˌparəˈgwīən; -ˈgwā-/ *adj.* & *n.*

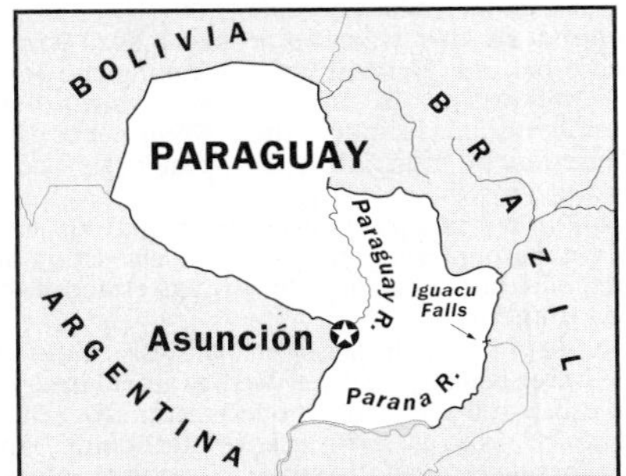

The territory was occupied by seminomadic Guarani peoples before Spanish rule was established in the 16th century. Paraguay achieved independence in 1811. It lost more than half of its population in war, against Brazil, Argentina, and Uruguay 1865–70, but gained land in the Chaco War with Bolivia 1932–35. The country was ruled by military dictator Alfredo Stroessner (1912–) from 1954 until 1989.

Par·a·guay Riv·er a river that flows for 1,584 miles (2,549 km) from the Mato Grosso in western Brazil into Paraguay and into the Paraná River. It is navigable by larger vessels as far as Concepción.

par·a·in·flu·en·za /ˌparəˌinflo͞oˈenzə/ ▸*n.* *Medicine* a disease caused by any of a group of viruses that resemble the influenza viruses.

par·a·keet /ˈparəˌkēt/ ▸*n.* a small parrot with predominantly green plumage and a long tail. • Family Psittacidae: five genera, e.g., *Psittacula* of Asia and Africa and *Cyanoramphus* of Australasia, and many species. ▷mid 16th cent.: from Old French *paroquet*, Italian *parrocchetto*, and Spanish *periquito*; origin uncertain, perhaps (via Italian) based on a diminutive meaning 'little wig,' referring to head plumage, or (via Spanish) based on a diminutive of the given name *Pedro*.

par·a·lan·guage /ˈparəˌlaNGgwij/ ▸*n.* the nonlexical component of communication by speech, for example intonation, pitch and speed of speaking, hesitation noises, gesture, and facial expression.

par·al·de·hyde /pəˈraldəˌhīd/ ▸*n.* *Chemistry* a liquid made by treating acetaldehyde with acid, used medicinally as a sedative, hypnotic, and anticonvulsant. • A cyclic trimer of acetaldehyde; chem. formula: $(CH_3CHO)_3$.

par·a·le·gal /ˌparəˈlēgəl/ ▸*n.* a person trained in subsidiary legal matters but not fully qualified as a lawyer.
▸*adj.* of or relating to auxiliary aspects of the law.

par·a·lin·guis·tic /ˌparəliNGˈgwistik/ ▸*adj.* of, relating to, or denoting paralanguage or the nonlexical elements of communication by speech.

par·a·li·pom·e·na /ˌparəlīˈpämənə; -li-/ (also **par·a·lei·pom·e·na**) ▸*plural n.* (*sing.* **-pom·e·non** /-ˈpäməˌnän/) *formal* things omitted from a work and added as a supplement. ■ (usu. **Paralipomenon**) *archaic* (in the Vulgate Bible and some other versions) the name of the books of Chronicles, regarded as supplementary to the books of Kings. ▷late Middle English: via ecclesiastical Latin from Greek *paraleipomena*, from *paraleipein* 'omit,' from *para-* 'to one side' + *leipein* 'to leave.'

par·a·lip·sis /ˌparəˈlipsis/ ▸*n.* *Rhetoric* the device of giving emphasis by professing to say little or nothing about a subject, as in *not to mention their unpaid debts of several million.* ▷late 16th cent.: via late Latin from Greek *paraleipsis* 'passing over,' from *paraleipein* 'omit,' from *para-* 'aside' + *leipein* 'to leave.'

par·al·lax /ˈparəˌlaks/ ▸*n.* the effect whereby the position or direction of an object appears to differ when viewed from different positions, e.g., through the viewfinder and the lens of a camera. ■ the angular amount of this in a particular case, esp. that of a star viewed from different points in the earth's orbit. ▷late 16th cent. (also in the general sense 'fact of seeing wrongly'): from French *parallaxe*, from Greek *parallaxis* 'a change,' from *parallassein* 'to alternate,' based on *allassein* 'to exchange' (from *allos* 'other'). **—par·al·lac·tic** /ˌparəˈlaktik/ *adj.*

par·al·lel /ˈparəˌlel; -ləl/ ▸*adj.* (of lines, planes, surfaces, or objects) side by side and having the same distance continuously between them: *parallel lines never meet | the road* ***runs parallel to*** *the Ottawa River.* ■ occurring or existing at the same time or in a similar way; corresponding: *a parallel universe | they shared an apartment in Dallas while establishing parallel careers.* ■ *Computing* involving the simultaneous performance of operations. ■ of or denoting electrical components or circuits connected to common points at each end, rather than one to another in sequence. The opposite of SERIES. ■ *Music* containing or denoting successive intervals of the same size in otherwise independent voices: *an answering phrase in parallel thirds.* ■ *Grammar* characterized by parallelism: *a parallel structure of transitive clauses.*
▸*n.* **1** a person or thing that is similar or analogous to another: *a challenge that has* ***no parallel*** *in peacetime this century.* ■ a similarity: *he points to a* ***parallel between*** *biological evolution and cognitive development.* ■ a comparison: *he draws a* ***parallel between*** *personal destiny and social forces.* **2** (also **parallel of latitude**) each of the imaginary parallel circles of constant latitude on the earth's surface. ■ a corresponding line on a map. **3** *Printing* two parallel lines (‖) as a reference mark.
▸*v.* (**-leled, -lel·ing**) [*trans.*] (of something extending in a line) be side by side with (something extending in a line), always keeping the same distance: *a big concrete gutter that paralleled the road.* ■ be similar or corresponding to (something): *U.S. naval and air superiority was paralleled by Soviet superiority in land-based missile systems.* ▷mid 16th cent.: from French *parallèle*, via Latin from Greek *parallēlos*, from *para-* 'alongside' + *allēlos* 'one another.'
▸PHRASE □ **in parallel** occurring at the same time and having some connection. ■ (of electrical components or circuits) connected to common points at each end; not in series.

par·al·lel bars ▸*plural n.* a pair of parallel rails mounted on posts, used in gymnastics.

par·al·lel cous·in ▸*n.* the offspring of a parent's sibling; a first cousin.

par·al·lel dis·trib·ut·ed pro·cess·ing (abbr.: **PDP**) ▸*n.* another term for CONNECTIONISM.

par·al·lel·e·pi·ped /ˌparəˌleləˈpīpid; -ˈpipid/ ▸*n.* *Geometry* a solid body of which each face is a parallelogram. ▷late 16th cent.: from Greek *parallēlepipedon*, from *parallēlos* 'beside another' + *epipedon* 'plane surface.'

par·al·lel·ism /ˈparəlelˌizəm/ ▸*n.* the state of being parallel or of corresponding in some way. ■ the use of successive verbal constructions in poetry or prose that correspond in grammatical structure, sound, meter, meaning, etc. ■ the use of parallel processing in computer systems. **—par·al·lel·is·tic** /ˌparəlelˈistik/ *adj.*

par·al·lel·ize /ˈparələˌlīz; -lelˌīz/ ▸*v.* [*trans.*] *Computing* adapt (a program) for running on a parallel processing system. **—par·al·lel·i·za·tion** /ˌparəˌleləˈzāSHən/ *n.*

par·al·lel·o·gram /ˌparəˈleləˌgram/ ▸*n.* a four-sided plane rectilinear figure with opposite sides parallel. ▷late 16th cent.: from French *parallélogramme*, via late Latin from Greek *parallēlogrammon*, from *parallēlos* 'alongside another' + *grammē* 'line.'
▸PHRASE □ **parallelogram of forces** a parallelogram illustrating the theorem that if two forces acting at a point are represented in magnitude and direction by two sides of a parallelogram meeting at that point, their resultant is represented by the diagonal drawn from that point.

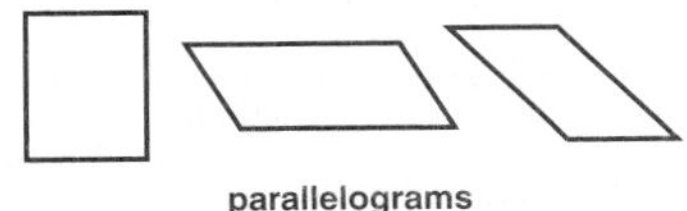

parallelograms

par·al·lel park·ing ▸*n.* the parking of a vehicle or vehicles parallel to the roadside. **—par·al·lel park** *v.*

par·al·lel port ▸*n.* *Computing* a connector for a device that sends or receives several bits of data simultaneously by using more than one wire. Compare with SERIAL PORT.

par·al·lel pro·cess·ing ▸*n.* a mode of computer operation in which a process is split into parts that execute simultaneously on different processors attached to the same computer.

par·al·lel rul·er ▸*n.* an instrument for drawing parallel lines, consisting of two or more rulers connected by jointed crosspieces so as to be always parallel, at whatever distance they are set.

par·al·lel turn ▸*n.* *Skiing* a turn with the skis kept parallel to each other.

par·a·log·i·cal /ˌparəˈläjikəl/ ▸*adj.* of or relating to a form of reasoning that does not conform to the rules of logic. **—par·a·log·i·cal·ly** *adv.*

pa·ral·o·gism /pəˈraləˌjizəm/ ▸*n.* *Logic* a piece of illogical or fallacious reasoning, esp. one that appears superficially logical or that the reasoner believes to be logical. ▷mid 16th cent.: from French *paralogisme*, via late Latin from Greek *paralogismos*, from *paralogizesthai* 'reason falsely.' **—pa·ral·o·gist** *n.*

pa·ral·o·gous /pəˈraləgəs/ ▸*adj.* *Genetics* of or relating to genes that are descended from the same ancestral gene by gene duplication in the course of evolution, esp. when present in different species that have diverged after the duplication.

pa·ral·o·gy /pəˈraləjē/ ▸*n.* **1** *Genetics* the state of being paralogous. **2** paralogical reasoning.

Par·a·lym·pics /ˌparəˈlimpiks/ ▸*plural n.* an international athletic competition for disabled athletes. ▷1950s: blend of *paraplegic* (see PARAPLEGIA) and

Pronunciation Key ə *ago*; ər *over*; ˈə or ˌə *up*; ˈər or ˌər *fur*; a *hat*; ā *rate*; ä *car*; CH *chew*; e *let*; ē *see*; e(ə)r *air*; i *fit*; ī *by*; i(ə)r *ear*; NG *sing*; ō *go*; ô *for*; oi *boy*; o͝o *good*; o͞o *goo*; ou *out*; SH *she*; TH *thin*; T͟H *then*; (h)w *why*; ZH *vision*

Olympics (plural of **Olympic**). **—Par·a·lym·pic** /-pik/ *adj.*

pa·ral·y·sis /pəˈraləsis/ ▶*n.* (*pl.* **-ses** /-sēz/) the loss of the ability to move (and sometimes to feel anything) in part or most of the body, typically as a result of illness, poison, or injury. ■ inability to act or function in a person, organization, or place: *the paralysis gripping the country.* ▷late Old English, via Latin from Greek *paralusis*, from *paraluesthai* 'be disabled at the side,' from *para* 'beside' + *luein* 'loosen.'

pa·ral·y·sis ag·i·tans /ˈajəˌtanz/ ▶*n.* less common term for **Parkinson's disease**. ▷Latin, literally 'shaking paralysis.'

par·a·lyt·ic /ˌparəˈlitik/ ▶*adj.* of or relating to paralysis: *the incidence of paralytic disease.*
▶*n.* a person affected by paralysis. ▷late Middle English: from Old French *paralytique*, via Latin from Greek *paralutikos* 'relating to paralysis' (see **paralysis**). **—par·a·lyt·i·cal·ly** *adv.*

par·a·lyze /ˈparəˌlīz/ (*Brit.* **par·a·lyse**) ▶*v.* [*trans.*] (often **be paralyzed**) cause (a person or part of the body) to become partly or wholly incapable of movement: *Mrs. Burrows had been paralyzed by a stroke* | [as *adj.*] (**paralyzed**) *he became partially paralyzed.* ■ render (someone) unable to think or act normally, esp. through panic or fear: *some people are paralyzed by the thought of failure* | [as *adj.*] (**paralyzing**) *her paralyzing shyness.* ■ bring (a system, place, or organization) to a standstill by causing disruption or chaos: *the regional capital was paralyzed by a general strike.* ▷early 19th cent.: from French *paralyser*, from *paralysie* 'paralysis.' **—par·a·lyz·ing·ly** /-ˌlīziNGlē/ *adv.*

par·a·mag·net·ic /ˌparəmagˈnetik/ ▶*adj.* (of a substance or body) very weakly attracted by the poles of a magnet, but not retaining any permanent magnetism. **—par·a·mag·net·ism** /-ˈmagnəˌtizəm/ *n.*

Par·a·mar·i·bo /ˌparəˈmarəˌbō; ˌperəˈmer-/ the capital of Suriname, a port on the Atlantic coast; pop. 201,000.

par·a·mat·ta /ˌparəˈmatə/ (also **par·ra·mat·ta**) ▶*n.* a fine-quality twill fabric with a weft of worsted and a warp of cotton or silk. ▷early 19th cent.: named after *Parramatta*, a city in New South Wales, Australia, which was the site of a prison whose inmates manufactured the cloth for clothing supplied to the convict servants of settlers.

par·a·me·ci·um /ˌparəˈmēsH(ē)əm; -sēəm/ ▶*n. Zoology* a single-celled freshwater animal that has a characteristic slipperlike shape and is covered with cilia. • Genus *Paramecium*, phylum Ciliophora, kingdom Protista. ▷mid 18th cent.: modern Latin, from Greek *paramēkēs* 'oval,' from *para-* 'against' + *mēkos* 'length.'

par·a·med·ic /ˌparəˈmedik/ ▶*n.* a person who is trained to do medical work, esp. emergency first aid, but is not usually a fully qualified physician.

par·a·med·i·cal /ˌparəˈmedikəl/ ▶*adj.* of or relating to services and professions that supplement and support medical work but do not require a fully qualified physician (such as nursing, radiography, emergency first aid, physical therapy, and dietetics).

pa·ram·e·ter /pəˈramitər/ ▶*n. technical* a numerical or other measurable factor forming one of a set that defines a system or sets the conditions of its operation: *the transmission will not let you downshift unless your speed is within the lower gear's parameters.* ■ *Mathematics* a quantity whose value is selected for the particular circumstances and in relation to which other variable quantities may be expressed. ■ *Statistics* a numerical characteristic of a population, as distinct from a statistic of a sample. ■ (in general use) a limit or boundary that defines the scope of a particular process or activity: *they set the parameters of the debate.* ▷mid 17th cent.: modern Latin, from Greek *para-* 'beside' + *metron* 'measure.'

USAGE Until recently, use of the word **parameter** was confined to mathematics and related technical fields. Since around the mid 20th century, however, it has been used in nontechnical fields as a technical-sounding word for 'a limit or boundary,' as in *they set the* ***parameters*** *of the debate.* This use, probably influenced by the word **perimeter**, has been criticized for being a weakening of the technical sense. Careful writers will leave **parameter** to specialists in mathematics, computer science, and other technical disciplines. As a loose synonym for *limit, boundary, guideline, framework*, it is a vogue word that blurs more than it clarifies. **Perimeter** is a different word, meaning 'border, outer boundary, or the length of such a boundary.'

pa·ram·e·ter·ize /pəˈramitəˌrīz/ ▶*v.* [*trans.*] *technical* describe or represent in terms of a parameter or parameters. **—pa·ram·e·ter·i·za·tion** /pəˌramitəriˈzāsHən/ *n.*

par·a·met·ric /ˌparəˈmetrik/ ▶*adj.* of, relating to, or expressed in terms of a parameter or parameters. ■ *Statistics* assuming the value of a parameter for the purpose of analysis. ■ *Electronics* relating to or denoting a process in which amplification or frequency conversion is obtained using a device modulated by a pumping frequency, which enables power to be transferred from the pumping frequency to the signal.

par·a·met·ric e·qual·iz·er ▶*n.* an electronic device or computer program that allows any specific part of the frequency range of a signal to be selected and altered in strength.

par·a·mil·i·tar·y /ˌparəˈmiliˌterē/ ▶*adj.* (of an unofficial force) organized similarly to a military force: *soldiers and police have been killed in conflicts with the drug cartels and their paramilitary allies.*
▶*n.* (*pl.* **-tar·ies**) a member of an unofficial paramilitary organization.

par·am·ne·sia /ˌparamˈnēzHə/ ▶*n. Psychiatry* a condition or phenomenon involving distorted memory or confusions of fact and fantasy, such as confabulation or déjà vu.

pa·ra·mo /ˈpäraˌmō/ ▶*n.* (*pl.* **-mos**) a high, treeless plateau in tropical South America. ▷Spanish and Portuguese, from Latin *paramus.*

Par·a·mo·tor /ˈparəˌmōtər/ ▶*n. trademark* a motorized steerable paraglider, powered by a motor and propeller harnessed to the pilot's back. **—par·a·mo·tor·ing** *n.*

Par·a·mount[1] /ˈparəˌmount/ a city in southwestern California, southeast of Los Angeles; pop. 47,669.

Par·a·mount[2] a movie production and distribution company established in 1914. A major studio of the silent era, Paramount acted as an outlet for many of the films of Cecil B. De Mille and helped to create stars such as Mary Pickford and Rudolf Valentino; notable later successes included the *Road* movies of Bob Hope and Billy Wilder's *Sunset Boulevard* (1950).

par·a·mount /ˈparəˌmount/ ▶*adj.* more important than anything else; supreme: *the interests of the child are of paramount importance.* ■ [*attrib.*] having supreme power: *a paramount chief.* ▷mid 16th cent. (in the sense 'highest in jurisdiction' in the phrases *lord paramount* and *paramount chief*): from Anglo-Norman French *paramont*, from Old French *par* 'by' + *amont* 'above.' **—par·a·mount·cy** /-sē/ *n.* **—par·a·mount·ly** *adv.*

par·a·mour /ˈparəˌmo͝or/ ▶*n.* a lover, esp. the illicit partner of a married person. ▷Middle English: from Old French *par amour* 'by love'; in English the phrase was written from an early date as one word and came to be treated as a noun.

Pa·ram·us /pəˈraməs/ a borough in northeastern New Jersey, northeast of Paterson; pop. 25,101.

par·a·myx·o·vi·rus /ˌparəˈmiksəˌvīrəs/ ▶*n. Medicine* any of a group of RNA viruses similar to the myxoviruses but larger and hemolytic, including those causing mumps, measles, distemper, rinderpest, and various respiratory infections (parainfluenza).

Pa·ra·ná /ˌpärəˈnä/ **1** a river in South America that rises in southeastern Brazil and flows about 2,060 miles (3,300 km) south to the Plate River estuary in Argentina. For part of its length it forms the southeastern border of Paraguay. **2** a river port in eastern Argentina, on the Paraná River; pop. 276,000.

pa·rang[1] /ˈpäräNG/ ▶*n.* a Malayan machete. ▷Malay.

pa·rang[2] /pəˈräNG/ ▶*n.* a variety of Trinidadian folk music, traditionally played at Christmas by groups that travel from house to house. ▷Spanish Creole, based on Spanish *parranda* 'spree, binge.'

par·a·noi·a /ˌparəˈnoiə/ ▶*n.* a mental condition characterized by delusions of persecution, unwarranted jealousy, or exaggerated self-importance, typically elaborated into an organized system. It may be an aspect of chronic personality disorder, of drug abuse, or of a serious condition such as schizophrenia in which the person loses touch with reality. ■ suspicion and mistrust of people or their actions without evidence or justification: *the global paranoia about hackers and viruses.* ▷early 19th cent.: modern Latin, from Greek, from *paranoos* 'distracted,' from *para* 'irregular' + *noos* 'mind.' **—par·a·noi·ac** /-ˈnoi-ak; -ˈnoi-ik/ *adj.* & *n.* **—par·a·noi·a·cal·ly** *adv.* **—par·a·no·ic** /-ˈnoi-ik/ *adj.* **—par·a·no·i·cal·ly** *adv.*

par·a·noid /ˈparəˌnoid/ ▶*adj.* of, characterized by, or suffering from the mental condition of paranoia: *paranoid schizophrenia.* ■ unreasonably or obsessively anxious, suspicious, or mistrustful: *you think I'm paranoid but I tell you there is something going on.*
▶*n.* a person who is paranoid.

par·a·nor·mal /ˌparəˈnôrməl/ ▶*adj.* denoting events or phenomena such as telekinesis or clairvoyance that are beyond the scope of normal scientific understanding: *a mystic who can prove he has paranormal powers* | [as *n.*] (**the paranormal**) *an investigator of the paranormal.* **—par·a·nor·mal·ly** *adv.*

Par·an·thro·pus /pəˈranTHrəpəs/ ▶*n.* a genus name often applied to robust fossil hominids first found in South Africa in 1938. • *Australopithecus robustus* and *A.* (or **Zinjanthropus**) *boisei*, family Hominidae. See **Australopithecus**. ▷modern Latin, from Greek *para-* (expressing relationship) + *anthrōpos* 'man.'

par·a·pa·re·sis /ˌparəpəˈrēsis/ ▶*n.* partial paralysis of the lower limbs. **—paraparetic** /-ˈretik/ *adj.*

par·a·pente /ˈparəˌpänt/ ▶*n.* the activity of gliding by means of an airfoil parachute launched from high ground. ■ the parachute used for this purpose.
▶*v.* [*intrans.*] glide using an airfoil parachute. ▷1980s: from French, from *para(chute)* + *pente* 'slope.' **—par·a·pent·er** *n.*

par·a·pet /ˈparəpit/ ▶*n.* a low, protective wall along the edge of a roof, bridge, or balcony. ■ a protective wall or earth defense along the top of a trench or other place of concealment for troops. ▷late 16th cent.: from French, or from Italian *parapetto* 'breast-high wall,' from *para-* 'protecting' + *petto* 'breast' (from Latin *pectus*). **—par·a·pet·ed** *adj.*

par·aph /ˈparəf; pəˈraf/ ▶*n.* a flourish after a signature, originally as a precaution against forgery. ▷late Middle English (denoting a paragraph): from French *paraphe*, from medieval Latin *paraphus* (contraction of *paragraphus* 'short horizontal stroke').

par·a·pha·sia /ˌparəˈfāzHə/ ▶*n. Psychology* speech disturbance resulting from brain damage in which words are jumbled and sentences meaningless. **—par·a·pha·sic** /-ˈfāzik/ *adj.*

par·a·pher·na·lia /ˌparəfə(r)ˈnālyə/ ▶*n.* [treated as *sing.* or *pl.*] miscellaneous articles, esp. the equipment needed for a particular activity: *drills, saws, and other paraphernalia necessary for home improvements* | *drugs and drug paraphernalia that had been discovered on the premises.* ■ trappings associated with a particular institution or activity that are regarded as superfluous: *the rituals and paraphernalia of government.* ▷mid 17th cent. (denoting property owned by a married woman): from medieval Latin, based on Greek *parapherna* 'property apart from a dowry,' from *para* 'distinct from' + *pherna* (from *phernē* 'dowry').

par·a·phil·i·a /ˌparəˈfilēə/ ▶*n. Psychiatry* a condition characterized by abnormal sexual desires, typically involving extreme or dangerous activities. **—par·a·phil·i·ac** /-ˈfilēˌak/ *adj.* & *n.*

par·a·phrase /ˈparəˌfrāz/ ▶*v.* [*trans.*] express the meaning of (the writer or speaker or something written or spoken) using different words, esp. to achieve greater clarity: *you can either quote or paraphrase literary texts.*
▶*n.* a rewording of something written or spoken by someone else. ▷mid 16th cent. (as a noun): via Latin from Greek *paraphrasis*, from *paraphrazein*, from *para-* (expressing modification) + *phrazein* 'tell.' **—par·a·phras·a·ble** *adj.* **—par·a·phras·tic** /ˌparəˈfrastik/ *adj.*

par·a·phy·let·ic /ˌparəˌfīˈletik/ ▶*adj. Biology* (of a group of organisms) descended from a common evolutionary ancestor or ancestral group, but not including all the descendant groups.

pa·raph·y·sis /pəˈrafəsəs/ ▶*n.* (*pl.* **-ses** /-ˌsēz/) *Botany* a sterile hairlike filament present among the reproductive organs in many lower plants, esp. bryophytes, algae, and fungi. ▷mid 19th cent.: modern Latin, from Greek *para-* 'beside, subsidiary' + *phusis* 'growth.'

Par·a·Plane /ˈparəˌplān/ (also **Par·a·plane**) ▶*n. trademark* a motor-driven flying machine consisting of a parachute and a pair of fabric wings attached to a rigid framework.

par·a·ple·gi·a /ˌparəˈplēj(ē)ə/ ▶*n.* paralysis of the legs and lower body, typically caused by spinal injury or disease. ▷mid 17th cent.: modern Latin, from Greek *paraplēgia*, from *paraplēssein* 'strike at the side,' from *para* 'beside' + *plēssein* 'to strike.' **—par·a·ple·gic** /-jik/ *adj.* & *n.*

par·a·po·di·um /ˌparəˈpōdēəm/ ▶*n.* (*pl.* **-di·a** /-dēə/) *Zoology* (in a polychaete worm) each of a number of paired muscular bristle-bearing appendages used in locomotion, sensation, or respiration. ■ (in a sea slug or other mollusk) a lateral extension of the foot used as an undulating fin for swimming. ▷late 19th cent.: modern Latin, from Greek *para-* 'subsidiary' + *pous, pod-* 'foot.' —**par·a·po·di·al** /-dēəl/ *adj.*

par·a·pro·fes·sion·al /ˌparəprə'feSHənl/ ▶*n.* a person to whom a particular aspect of a professional task is delegated but who is not licensed to practice as a fully qualified professional.
▶*adj.* of, relating to, or denoting such a person: *the union advocated paraprofessional help for nonteaching duties.*

par·a·pro·tein /ˌparə'prōtē(ə)n/ ▶*n. Medicine* a protein found in the blood only as a result of cancer or other disease.

par·a·psych·ic /ˌparə'sīkik/ ▶*adj.* of, relating to, or denoting mental phenomena for which no adequate scientific explanation exists.

par·a·psy·chol·o·gy /ˌparəsī'käləjē/ ▶*n.* the study of mental phenomena that are excluded from or inexplicable by orthodox scientific psychology (such as hypnosis, telepathy, etc.). —**par·a·psy·cho·log·i·cal** /-ˌsīkə'läjikəl/ *adj.* —**par·a·psy·chol·o·gist** /-jist/ *n.*

par·a·pto·sis /ˌparə(p)'tōsis/ ▶*n.* a system of programmed cell death in which empty spaces form in the cell cytoplasm and the mitochondria swells, causing the cell to lose its vitality. It differs from apoptosis in that the cell does not fragment. ▷based on *para-* 'beside' + Greek *ptōsis* 'a falling.' —**par·a·ptot·ic** /ˌparə(p)'tätik; -'tōtik/ *adj.*

par·a·quat /'parəˌkwät/ ▶*n.* a toxic, fast-acting herbicide that becomes deactivated in the soil. ▷1960s: from **PARA-**[1] (sense 2) + **QUATERNARY** (it is a quaternary ammonium salt containing pyridine rings linked at the para-position).

par·a·rhyme /'parəˌrīm/ ▶*n.* partial rhyme between words with the same pattern of consonants but different vowels, such as *light* and *late.* See also **IMPERFECT RHYME.**

par·a·sag·it·tal /ˌparə'sajitl/ ▶*adj. Anatomy* relating to or situated in a plane adjacent or parallel to the plane that divides the body into right and left halves. —**par·a·sag·it·tal·ly** *adv.*

par·a·sail /'parəˌsāl/ ▶*v.* [*intrans.*] [often as *n.*] (**parasailing**) glide through the air wearing an open parachute while being towed by a motorboat.
▶*n.* a parachute designed for parasailing.

par·a·se·le·ne /ˌparəsə'lēnē/ ▶*n.* (*pl.* **-le·nae** *pronunc.* same) a bright spot in the sky similar to a parhelion but formed by moonlight. Also called **MOCK MOON, MOON DOG.** Compare with **PARHELION.** ▷mid 17th cent.: modern Latin, from Greek *para-* 'beside' + *selēnē* 'moon.'

par·a·site /'parəˌsīt/ ▶*n.* an organism that lives in or on another organism (its host) and benefits by deriving nutrients at the host's expense. ■ *derogatory* a person who habitually relies on or exploits others and gives nothing in return.

Parasites exist in huge variety, including animals, plants, and microorganisms. They may live as ectoparasites on the surface of the host (e.g., arthropods such as ticks, mites, lice, fleas, and many insects infesting plants) or as endoparasites in the gut or tissues (e.g., many kinds of worm), and cause varying degrees of damage or disease to the host.

▷mid 16th cent.: via Latin from Greek *parasitos* '(person) eating at another's table,' from *para-* 'alongside' + *sitos* 'food.'

par·a·sit·e·mi·a /ˌparəsī'tēmēə/ (*Brit.* **par·a·sit·ae·mi·a**) ▶*n. Medicine* the demonstrable presence of parasites in the blood.

par·a·sit·ic /ˌparə'sitik/ ▶*adj.* (of an organism) living as a parasite: *mistletoe is* **parasitic on** *trees.* ■ resulting from infestation by a parasite: *mortality from parasitic diseases.* ■ *derogatory* habitually relying on or exploiting others: *attacks on the parasitic existence of Party functionaries.* ■ *Phonetics* (of a speech sound) inserted without etymological justification (e.g., the *b* in *thimble*); epenthetic. ▷early 17th cent.: via Latin from Greek *parasitikos,* from *parasitos* '(person) eating at another's table.' —**par·a·sit·i·cal** *adj.* —**par·a·sit·i·cal·ly** *adv.* —**par·a·sit·ism** /'parəsiˌtizəm; -ˌsī-/ *n.*

par·a·sit·i·cide /ˌparə'sitəˌsīd/ ▶*n.* a substance used in medicine and veterinary medicine to kill parasites (esp. those other than bacteria or fungi).

par·a·si·tize /'parəsiˌtīz; -sī-/ ▶*v.* [*trans.*] infest or exploit (an organism or part) as a parasite. —**par·a·sit·i·za·tion** /ˌparəsiˌtī'zāSHən; -sī-/ *n.*

par·a·sit·oid /'parəsiˌtoid; -ˌsī-/ *Entomology* ▶*n.* an insect (e.g., the ichneumon wasp) whose larvae live as parasites that eventually kill their hosts (typically other insects).
▶*adj.* of, relating to, or denoting such an insect.

par·a·si·tol·o·gy /ˌparəsi'täləjē; -sī-/ ▶*n.* the branch of biology or medicine concerned with the study of parasitic organisms. —**par·a·si·to·log·i·cal** /ˌparəˌsītl'äjikəl; -ˌsitl-/ *adj.* —**par·a·si·tol·o·gist** /-jist/ *n.*

par·a·ski ▶*v.* [*intrans.*] jump from an aircraft by parachute and ski from the landing place, as a sport or race: [as *adj.*] *he perennially competes in the intermediate class in the para-ski nationals.* —**par·a·ski·ing** *n.*

par·a·sol /'parəˌsôl; -ˌsäl/ ▶*n.* **1** a light umbrella used to give shade from the sun. **2** (also **parasol mushroom**) a widely distributed large mushroom with a broad, scaly, grayish-brown cap and a tall, slender stalk, growing typically in grassy places. • Genus *Lepiota,* family Lepiotaceae, class Hymenomycetes: numerous species, esp. the edible *L. procera.* ▷early 17th cent.: from French, from Italian *parasole,* from *para-* 'protecting against' + *sole* 'sun' (from Latin *sol*).

par·a·stat·al /ˌparə'stātl/ ▶*adj.* (of an organization or industry) having some political authority and serving the state indirectly, esp. in some African countries.
▶*n.* a parastatal organization.

par·a·state /'parəˌstāt/ ▶*n.* a region that seeks or claims but does not have the status of a recognized independent state.

par·a·ster·nal /ˌparə'stərnəl/ ▶*adj. Anatomy* situated beside the sternum.

pa·ras·ti·chy /pə'rastikē/ ▶*n.* (*pl.* **-chies**) *Botany* (in phyllotaxis) an oblique row of leaves arranged in a secondary spiral. Contrasted with **ORTHOSTICHY.** ▷late 19th cent.: from **PARA-**[1] 'adjacent' + Greek *stikhos* 'row, rank.'

par·a·sym·pa·thet·ic /ˌparəˌsimpə'THetik/ ▶*adj. Physiology* of or relating to the part of the automatic nervous system that counterbalances the action of the sympathetic nerves. It consists of nerves arising from the brain and the lower end of the spinal cord and supplying the internal organs, blood vessels, and glands. ▷early 20th cent.: from **PARA-**[1] 'alongside' + **SYMPATHETIC,** because some of these nerves run alongside sympathetic nerves.

par·a·syn·the·sis /ˌparə'sinTHəsis/ ▶*n. Linguistics* a process by which a term is formed by adding a bound morpheme (e.g., *-ed*) to a combination of existing words (e.g., *black-eyed* from *black eye(s)* + *-ed*). ▷mid 19th cent.: from Greek *parasunthesis,* from *para-* 'subsidiary' + **SYNTHESIS.** —**par·a·syn·thet·ic** /-sin'THetik/ *adj.* —**par·a·syn·thet·i·cal·ly** *adv.*

par·a·tax·is /ˌparə'taksis/ ▶*n. Grammar* the placing of clauses or phrases one after another, without words to indicate coordination or subordination, as in *Tell me, how are you?* Contrasted with **HYPOTAXIS.** ▷mid 19th cent.: from Greek *parataxis,* from *para-* 'beside' + *taxis* 'arrangement' (from *tassein* 'arrange'). —**par·a·tac·tic** /-'taktik/ *adj.* —**par·a·tac·ti·cal·ly** /-'taktik(ə)lē/ *adv.*

pa·ra·tha /pə'rätə/ ▶*n.* (in Indian cooking) a flat, thick piece of unleavened bread fried on a griddle. ▷from Hindi *parāṭhā.*

par·a·thi·on /ˌparə'THīˌän/ ▶*n.* a highly toxic synthetic compound containing phosphorus and sulfur, used as an agricultural insecticide. ▷1940s: from **PARA-**[1] (sense 2) + **THIO-** + **-ON.**

par·a·thor·mone /ˌparə'THôrˌmōn/ ▶*n. Physiology* parathyroid hormone.

par·a·thy·roid /ˌparə'THīˌroid/ ▶*n. Anatomy* a gland next to the thyroid that secretes a hormone (**parathyroid hormone**) that regulates calcium levels in a person's body.

par·a·troop·er /'parəˌtrōōpər/ ▶*n.* a member of a paratroop regiment or airborne unit.

par·a·troops /'parəˌtrōōps/ ▶*plural n.* troops equipped to be dropped by parachute from aircraft: [as *adj.*] (usu. **paratroop**) *a paratroop regiment.* ▷1940s: from an abbreviation of **PARACHUTE** + *troops* (plural of **TROOP**).

par·a·ty·phoid /ˌparə'tīˌfoid/ ▶*n.* a fever resembling typhoid but caused by different (though related) bacteria. • The bacteria are species of the genus *Salmonella,* in particular (in humans) *S. paratyphi.*
▶*adj.* [*attrib.*] of or relating to such a fever or the bacteria causing it: *paratyphoid fever.*

par·a·vane /'parəˌvān/ ▶*n.* a device towed behind a boat at a depth regulated by its vanes or planes, so that the cable to which it is attached can cut the moorings of submerged mines. ▷early 20th cent.: from **PARA-**[2] 'protecting' + **VANE.**

par·a·ven·tric·u·lar /ˌparəven'trikyələr/ ▶*adj. Anatomy* situated next to a ventricle of the brain.

par a·vion /ˌpär ä'vyôn/ ▶*adv.* by airmail (written on a letter or parcel to indicate how it is to reach its destination). ▷French, literally 'by airplane.'

par·a·wing /'parəˌwiNG/ ▶*n.* a type of parachute or kite having a flattened shape like a wing, to give greater maneuverability.

par·ax·i·al /pə'raksēəl/ ▶*adj. Anatomy & Zoology* situated alongside, or on each side of, an axis, esp. the central axis of the body.

par·boil /'pärˌboil/ ▶*v.* [*trans.*] partly cook (food) by boiling. ▷late Middle English: from Old French *parbouillir,* from late Latin *perbullire* 'boil thoroughly,' from Latin *per-* 'through, thoroughly' (later confused with **PART**) + *bullire* 'to boil.'

par·buck·le /'pärˌbəkəl/ ▶*n.* a loop of rope arranged like a sling, used for raising or lowering casks and other cylindrical objects along an inclined plane.
▶*v.* [*trans.*] raise or lower with such a device. ▷early 17th cent.: from earlier *parbunkle,* of unknown origin. The change in the ending was due to association with **BUCKLE.**

Par·cae /'pärsē/ *Roman Mythology* Roman name for **THE FATES** (see **FATE**).

par·cel /'pärsəl/ ▶*n.* **1** a thing or collection of things wrapped in paper in order to be carried or sent by mail. **2** a quantity or amount of something, in particular: ■ a piece of land, esp. one considered as part of an estate. ■ a quantity dealt with in one commercial transaction: *a parcel of shares.* ■ *technical* a portion of a larger body of air or other fluid considered as a discrete element.
▶*v.* (**-celed, -cel·ing;** *Brit.* **-celled, -cel·ling**) [*trans.*] make (something) into a parcel by wrapping it: *he* **parceled up** *his only winter suit to take to the pawnbroker.* ■ (**parcel something out**) divide into portions and then distribute: *they will start parceling out radio frequencies for digital cordless telephones.* ■ *Nautical* wrap (rope) with strips of tarred canvas before binding it with yarn as part of a traditional technique to reduce chafing. ▷late Middle English (chiefly in the sense 'small portion'): from Old French *parcelle,* from Latin *particula* 'small part.'
▶*PHRASES* □ **be part and parcel of** see **PART.** □ **pass the parcel** *chiefly Brit.* a children's game in which a parcel is passed around to the accompaniment of music, the child holding the parcel when the music stops being allowed to unwrap a layer.

par·cel post ▶*n.* mail consisting of parcels.

parch /pärCH/ ▶*v.* make or become dry through intense heat: [*trans.*] *a piece of grassland parched by the sun* | [*intrans.*] *his crops parched during the last two summers.* ■ [*trans.*] roast (corn, peas, etc.) lightly. ▷late Middle English: of unknown origin.

parched /pärCHt/ ▶*adj.* dried out with heat: *the parched earth.* See note at **DRY.** ■ [*predic.*] *informal* extremely thirsty: *I'm parched—I'll die without a drink.* ■ lightly roasted: *parched corn.*

par·chee·si /pär'CHēzē/ ▶*n.* variant spelling of **PACHISI.**

parch·ment /'pärCHmənt/ ▶*n.* a stiff, flat, thin material made from the prepared skin of an animal and used as a durable writing surface in ancient and medieval times. ■ a manuscript written on this material: *a large collection of ancient parchments.* ■ (also **parchment paper**) a type of stiff translucent paper treated to resemble parchment and used for lampshades, as a writing surface, and in baking. ■ *informal* a diploma or other formal document. ▷Middle English: from Old French *parchemin,* from a blend of late Latin *pergamina* 'writing material from Pergamum' and *Parthica pellis* 'Parthian skin' (a kind of scarlet leather).

par·close /'pärˌklōz/ ▶*n.* a screen or railing in a church enclosing a tomb or altar or separating off a side chapel. ▷Middle English: from Old French *parclos(e)* 'enclosed,' past participle of *parclore* (from Latin *per-* 'thoroughly' + *claudere* 'to close').

pard /pärd/ ▶*n. archaic* or *poetic/literary* a leopard. ▷late Middle English: from Old French, via Latin from Greek *pardos.*

par·da·lote /'pärdlˌōt/ ▶*n.* a small, short-billed Australian songbird related to the flowerpeckers, typically having white spots or streaks on the dark wings and crown. • Genus *Pardalotus,* family Dicaeidae (or Pardalotidae): several species. ▷mid 19th cent.: from modern Latin *Pardalotus,* from Greek *pardalōtos* 'spotted like a leopard,' based on *pardos* (see **PARD**).

pard·ner /ˈpärdnər/ ▶*n. dated* or *humorous* variant spelling of **PARTNER**, used to represent U.S. dialect speech: *you and me, pardner, against the world.*

par·don /ˈpärdn/ ▶*n.* the action of forgiving or being forgiven for an error or offense: *he obtained pardon for his sins.* ■ a remission of the legal consequences of an offense or conviction: *he offered a full pardon to five convicted men.* ■ *historical Christian Church* an indulgence, as widely sold in medieval Europe.
▶*v.* [*trans.*] forgive or excuse (a person, error, or offense): *I know Catherine will pardon me.* See note at **ABSOLVE**. ■ release (an offender) from the legal consequences of an offense or conviction, and often implicitly from blame: *he was pardoned for his treason.* ■ (usu. **be pardoned**) used to indicate that the actions or thoughts of someone are justified or understandable given the circumstances: *one can be pardoned the suspicion that some of his errors were deliberate.*
▶*exclam.* a request to a speaker to repeat something because one did not hear or understand it: *"Pardon?" I said, cupping a hand to my ear.* ▷Middle English: from Old French *pardun* (noun), *pardoner* (verb), from medieval Latin *perdonare* 'concede, remit,' from *per-* 'completely' + *donare* 'give.' **—par·don·a·ble** *adj.* **—par·don·a·bly** /-əblē/ *adv.*
▶*PHRASES* □ **beg someone's pardon** express polite apology: *I beg your pardon for intruding.* □ **pardon me** (or **I beg your pardon**) used to indicate that one has not heard or understood something. ■ used to express one's anger or indignation at what someone has just said.

par·don·er /ˈpärdn-ər/ ▶*n. historical* a person licensed to sell papal pardons or indulgences. ▷Middle English: from Anglo-Norman French.

pare /pe(ə)r/ ▶*v.* [*trans.*] trim (something) by cutting away its outer edges: *Carlo pared his thumbnails with his knife.* ■ cut off the outer skin of (something): ***pare off** the rind using a peeler.* ■ reduce (something) in size, extent, quantity, or number, usually in a number of small successive stages: *union leaders publicly **pared down** their demands | we pared costs by doing our own cleaning.* ▷Middle English: from Old French *parer* 'adorn, prepare,' also 'peel, trim,' from Latin *parare* 'prepare.' **—par·er** *n.*

par·e·gor·ic /ˌparəˈgôrik/ ▶*n.* a medicine consisting of opium flavored with camphor, aniseed, and benzoic acid, formerly used to treat diarrhea and coughing in children. ▷late 17th cent.: via late Latin from Greek *parēgorikos* 'soothing,' from the verb *parēgorein*, literally 'speak in the assembly,' hence 'soothe, console.'

pa·ren /pəˈren/ ▶*n.* (usu. **parens**) *Printing* a parenthesis. ▷early 20th cent.: abbreviation of **PARENTHESIS**.

paren. ▶*abbr.* parenthesis.

pa·ren·chy·ma /pəˈreNGkəmə/ ▶*n. Anatomy* the functional tissue of an organ as distinguished from the connective and supporting tissue. ■ *Botany* the cellular tissue, typically soft and succulent, found chiefly in the softer parts of leaves, pulp of fruits, bark and pith of stems, etc. ■ *Zoology* cellular tissue lying between the body wall and the organs of invertebrate animals lacking a coelom, such as flatworms. ▷mid 17th cent.: from Greek *parenkhuma* 'something poured in beside,' from *para-* 'beside' + *enkhuma* 'infusion.' **—pa·ren·chy·mal** /-məl/ *adj.* (*chiefly Anatomy*). **—pa·ren·chym·a·tous** /ˌperəNGˈkimətəs/ *adj.* (*chiefly Botany*).

pa·rens pa·tri·ae /ˈparənz ˈpatri-ē/ ▶*n. Law* the government, or any other authority, regarded as the legal protector of citizens unable to protect themselves. ■ the principle that political authority carries with it the responsibility for such protection. ▷modern Latin, literally 'parent of the country.'

par·ent /ˈpe(ə)rənt; ˈpar-/ ▶*n.* a father or mother: *the parents of the bride | his adoptive parents.* ■ *archaic* a forefather or ancestor. ■ an animal or plant from which younger ones are derived. ■ a source or origin of a smaller or less important part. ■ [often as *adj.*] an organization or company that owns or controls a number of subsidiary organizations or companies: *policy considerations were determined largely by the parent institution.*
▶*v.* [*trans.*] [often as *n.*] (**parenting**) be or act as a mother or father to (someone): *the warmth and attention that are the hallmarks of good parenting.* ▷late Middle English: from Old French, from Latin *parent-* 'bringing forth,' from the verb *parere*. The verb dates from the mid 17th cent. **—pa·ren·tal** /pəˈrentl/ *adj.* **—pa·ren·tal·ly** /pəˈrentl-ē/ *adv.* **—par·ent·hood** /-ˌho͝od/ *n.*

par·ent·age /ˈpe(ə)rəntij; ˈpar-/ ▶*n.* the identity and origins of one's parents: *a boy of Jamaican parentage.* ■ *figurative* the origin of something: *this ice cream boasts American parentage.* ▷late 15th cent.: from Old French.

par·en·ter·al /pəˈrentərəl/ ▶*adj. Medicine* administered or occurring elsewhere in the body than the mouth and alimentary canal: *parenteral nutrition.* Often contrasted with **ENTERAL**. ▷early 20th cent.: from **PARA-**[1] 'beside' + Greek *enteron* 'intestine' + **-AL**. **—par·en·ter·al·ly** *adv.*

pa·ren·the·sis /pəˈrenTHəsis/ ▶*n.* (*pl.* **-ses** /-ˌsēz/) a word, clause, or sentence inserted as an explanation or afterthought into a passage that is grammatically complete without it, in writing usually marked off by curved brackets, dashes, or commas. ■ (usu. **parentheses**) one or both of a pair of marks () used to include such a word, clause, or sentence. ■ an interlude or interval: *the three months of coalition government were a lamentable political parenthesis.* ▷mid 16th cent.: via late Latin from Greek, from *parentithenai* 'put in beside.'
▶*PHRASE* □ **in parenthesis** as a digression or afterthought.

pa·ren·the·size /pəˈrenTHəˌsīz/ ▶*v.* [*trans.*] [usu. as *adj.*] (**parenthesized**) put (a word, phrase, or clause) into parentheses: *parenthesized clauses.* ■ insert as a parenthesis; express or state in parenthesis.

par·en·thet·i·cal /ˌparənˈTHetikəl/ ▶*adj.* of, relating to, or inserted as a parenthesis: *ignore the parenthetical remarks that pockmark every page.* ▷late 18th cent.: from **PARENTHESIS**, on the pattern of pairs such as *synthesis, synthetic.* **—par·en·thet·ic** /-ˈTHetik/ *adj.* **—par·en·thet·i·cal·ly** *adv.*

Par·ent-Teach·er As·so·ci·a·tion (abbr.: **PTA**) ▶*n.* a national organization devoted to furthering the safety and interests of children. ■ a local organization of parents and teachers for promoting closer relations and improving educational facilities at a school.

par·er·gon /pəˈrərˌgän/ ▶*n.* (*pl.* **-ga** /-gə/) a piece of work that is supplementary to or a byproduct of a larger work. ■ *archaic* work that is subsidiary to one's ordinary employment: *he pursued astronomy as a parergon.* ▷early 17th cent.: via Latin from Greek *parergon*, from *para-* 'beside, additional' + *ergon* 'work.'

pa·re·sis /pəˈrēsis/ ▶*n.* (*pl.* **-ses** /-sēz/) *Medicine* a condition of muscular weakness caused by nerve damage or disease; partial paralysis. ■ (also **general paresis**) inflammation of the brain in the later stages of syphilis, causing progressive dementia and paralysis. ▷late 17th cent.: modern Latin, from Greek *parienai* 'let go,' from *para-* 'alongside' + *hienai* 'let go.' **—pa·ret·ic** /-ˈretik/ *adj.*

par·es·the·si·a /ˌparəsˈTHēZH(ē)ə/ (*Brit.* **par·aes·the·si·a**) ▶*n.* (*pl.* **-si·ae** /-ZHē-ē/ or **-si·as**) *Medicine* an abnormal sensation, typically tingling or pricking ("pins and needles"), caused chiefly by pressure on or damage to peripheral nerves. ▷late 19th cent.: from **PARA-**[1] 'alongside, irregular' + Greek *aisthēsis* 'sensation' + **-IA**[1].

Pa·re·to /pəˈrētō/ ▶*adj.* [*attrib.*] denoting or involving the theories and methods of the Italian economist and sociologist Vilfredo Pareto (1848–1923), esp. a formula used to express the income distribution of a society.

Pa·re·to-op·ti·mal ▶*adj.* relating to or denoting a distribution of wealth such that any redistribution or other change beneficial to one individual is detrimental to one or more others. **—Pa·re·to-op·ti·mal·i·ty** *n.*

pa·re·u /ˈpärāˌo͞o/ ▶*n.* a kind of sarong made of a single straight piece of printed cotton cloth, worn by Polynesians. ▷Tahitian.

pa·re·ve /ˈpärəvə/ (also **par·ve** ˈpärvə) ▶*adj. Judaism* prepared without meat, milk, or their derivatives and therefore permissible to be eaten with both meat and dairy dishes according to dietary laws. ▷Yiddish.

par ex·cel·lence /ˌpär ˌeksəˈläns/ ▶*adj.* [*postpositive*] better or more than all others of the same kind: *he has won a reputation for being a designer par excellence.* ▷French, literally 'by excellence.'

par·fait /pärˈfā/ ▶*n.* **1** a dessert consisting of layers of ice cream, fruit, etc., served in a tall glass. **2** a rich cold dessert made with whipped cream, eggs, and often fruit. ▷from the French adjective *parfait*, literally 'perfect.'

par·fleche /ˈpärfleSH; pärˈfleSH/ ▶*n.* (in American Indian culture) a hide, esp. a buffalo's hide, dried by being stretched on a frame after the hair has been removed. ■ an article, esp. a bag, made from this. ▷from Canadian French *parflèche*, from French *parer* 'ward off' + *flèche* 'arrow.'

par·fum·er·ie /pärˈfyo͞omərē/ ▶*n.* (*pl.* **-er·ies**) a place where perfume is sold or made. ▷French.

par·get /ˈpärjit/ (also **parge** /pärj/) ▶*v.* (**-get·ed, -get·ing**) [*trans.*] cover (a part of a building, esp. an external brick wall) with plaster or mortar that typically bears an ornamental pattern.
▶*n.* another term for **PARGETING**. ▷late Middle English: from Old French *parjeter*, from *par-* 'all over' + *jeter* 'to throw.'

par·get·ing /ˈpärjitiNG/ (also **parg·ing** /ˈpärjiNG/) ▶*n.* plaster or mortar applied in a layer over a part of a building, esp. ornamental plasterwork.

par·he·li·on /pärˈhēlēən; -ˈhēlyən/ ▶*n.* (*pl.* **-he·li·a** /-ˈhēlēə/) a bright spot in the sky appearing on either side of the sun, formed by refraction of sunlight through ice crystals high in the earth's atmosphere. Also called **SUN DOG**. ▷mid 17th cent.: from Latin *parelion*, from Greek *para-* 'beside' + *hēlios* 'sun.'

pa·ri·ah /pəˈrīə/ ▶*n.* **1** an outcast: *they were treated as social pariahs.* **2** *historical* a member of a low caste or of no caste in southern India. ▷early 17th cent.: from Tamil *paraiyar*, plural of *paraiyan* '(hereditary) drummer,' from *parai* 'a drum' (pariahs not being allowed to join in with a religious procession).

pa·ri·ah dog ▶*n.* another term for **PYE-DOG**.

Par·i·an /ˈpe(ə)rēən; ˈpar-/ ▶*adj.* of or relating to Paros or the fine white marble for which it is renowned. ■ denoting a form of fine white unglazed hard-paste porcelain likened to Parian marble.
▶*n.* **1** a native or inhabitant of Paros. **2** Parian ware (porcelain).

pa·ri·e·tal /pəˈrīətəl/ ▶*adj.* **1** *Anatomy Biology* of, relating to, attached to, or denoting the wall of the body or of a body cavity or hollow structure. ■ of the parietal lobe: *the parietal cortex.* **2** relating to residence in a college or university dormitory and esp. to visits from members of the opposite sex: *parietal rules.* **3** *Archaeology* denoting prehistoric art found on rock walls.
▶*n.* **1** *Anatomy & Zoology* a parietal structure. ■ short for **PARIETAL BONE**. **2** (**parietals**) *informal* dormitory rules governing visits from members of the opposite sex. ▷late Middle English: from late Latin *parietalis*, from Latin *paries, pariet-* 'wall.'

pa·ri·e·tal bone ▶*n.* a bone forming the central side and upper back part of each side of the skull.

pa·ri·e·tal cell ▶*n.* an oxyntic (acid-secreting) cell of the stomach wall.

pa·ri·e·tal lobe ▶*n.* either of the paired lobes of the brain at the top of the head, including areas concerned with the reception and correlation of sensory information.

par·i·mu·tu·el /ˌparəˈmyo͞oCHo͞oəl/ (also **par·i-mu·tu·el**) ▶*n.* [often as *adj.*] a form of betting in which those backing the first three places divide the losers' stakes (less the operator's commission): *pari-mutuel betting.* ■ a booth for placing bets under such a system. ▷French, literally 'mutual stake.'

par·ing knife ▶*n.* a small knife used mainly for peeling fruits and vegetables.

par·ings /ˈpe(ə)riNGz/ ▶*plural n.* thin strips that have been pared off from something: *fingernail parings.*

pa·ri pas·su /ˌpärē ˈpäˌso͞o/ ▶*adv.* side by side; at the same rate or on an equal footing: *early opera developed **pari passu with** solo song.* ▷Latin, literally 'with equal step.'

Par·is[1] /ˈparis/ **1** the capital of France, on the Seine River; pop. 2,175,000. Paris was held by the Romans, who called it Lutetia, and by the Franks, and was established as the capital in 987 under Hugh Capet. It was organized into three parts—the Île de la Cité (an island in the Seine), the Right Bank, and the Left Bank—during the reign of Philippe-Auguste 1180–1223. The city's neoclassical architecture dates from the modernization of the Napoleonic era, which continued under Napoleon III, when the bridges and boulevards of the modern city were built. **2** a commercial city in northeastern Texas; pop. 24,699. ▷named after the *Parisii*, a Gallic people who settled on the Île de la Cité.

Par·is[2] *Greek Mythology* a Trojan prince, the son of Priam and Hecuba. Appointed by the gods to decide who among the three goddesses Hera, Athena, and Aphrodite should win a prize for beauty, he awarded it to Aphrodite, who promised him the most beautiful woman in the world—Helen, wife of King Menelaus of Sparta. He abducted Helen, bringing about the Trojan War, in which he killed Achilles but was later himself killed.

Par·is[3], Matthew, see **MATTHEW PARIS**.

Par·is, Trea·ty of **1** a treaty signed in 1763 by Great Britain, France, and Spain that ended the Seven Years' War in Europe (1756–63) and the French and Indian War in North America. **2** a treaty signed in 1783 by the U.S. and Great Britain that ended the American Revolution. **3** a treaty signed in 1898 by the U.S. and Spain that ended the Spanish-American War.

Par·is club a group of the major creditor nations of the International Monetary Fund whose representatives meet informally in Paris to discuss the financial relations of the IMF member nations.

Par·is Com·mune ▸*n.* see COMMUNE[1] (sense 3).

Par·is green ▸*n.* a vivid green toxic crystalline salt of copper and arsenic, used as a preservative, pigment, and insecticide.

par·ish /ˈpariSH/ ▸*n.* (in the Christian Church) a small administrative district typically having its own church and a priest or pastor: [as *adj.*] *a parish church.* ■ (in Louisiana) a territorial division corresponding to a county in other states. ▷Middle English: from Anglo-Norman French and Old French *paroche*, from late Latin *parochia*, from Greek *paroikia* 'sojourning,' based on *para-* 'beside, subsidiary' + *oikos* 'dwelling.'

pa·ri·shad /ˈpäriSHäd/ ▸*n. Indian* a council or assembly. ▷from Sanskrit, from *pari* 'around' + *sad-* 'sit.'

par·ish·ion·er /pəˈrisHənər/ ▸*n.* an inhabitant of a parish, esp. one who belongs to or attends a particular church.

par·ish-pump ▸*adj.* [*attrib.*] *Brit.* of local importance or interest only; parochial: *I looked down on parish-pump politics.*

Pa·ri·sian /pəˈrēZHən/ ▸*adj.* of or relating to Paris. ▸*n.* a native or inhabitant of Paris. ▷late Middle English: from French *parisien.*

Pa·ri·si·enne /pəˌrēzēˈen/ ▸*n.* a Parisian girl or woman. ▸*adj.* (esp. of a girl or woman) Parisian. ▷mid 17th cent.: French, feminine of *parisien* 'Parisian.'

par·i·son /ˈparəsən/ ▸*n.* a rounded mass of molten glass formed by rolling the substance immediately after removal from the furnace. ▷early 19th cent.: from French *paraison*, from *parer* 'prepare,' from Latin *parare.*

par·i·ty[1] /ˈparitē/ ▸*n.* **1** the state or condition of being equal, esp. regarding status or pay: *parity of incomes between rural workers and those in industrial occupations.* ■ the value of one currency in terms of another at an established exchange rate. ■ a system of providing farmers with consistent purchasing power by regulating prices of farm products, usually with government price supports. **2** *Mathematics* (of a number) the fact of being even or odd. ■ *Physics* the property of a spatial wave equation that either remains the same (**even parity**) or changes sign (**odd parity**) under a given transformation. ■ *Physics* the value of a quantum number corresponding to this property. ■ *Computing* a function whose being even (or odd) provides a check on a set of binary values. ▷late 16th cent.: from late Latin *paritas*, from *par* 'equal.'

par·i·ty[2] ▸*n. Medicine* the fact or condition of having borne children. ■ the number of children previously borne: *very high parity (six children or more).* ▷late 19th cent.: from *parous* 'having borne offspring' (back-formation from adjectives ending in **-PAROUS**) + **-ITY.**

par·i·ty bit ▸*n. Computing* a bit that acts as a check on a set of binary values, calculated in such a way that the number of 1s in the set plus the parity bit should always be even (or occasionally, should always be odd).

Park /pärk/, Mungo (1771–1806), Scottish explorer. He undertook a series of explorations in western Africa (1795–97), among them the navigation of the Niger.

park /pärk/ ▸*n.* **1** a large public green area in a town, used for recreation: *a walk around the park.* ■ a large area of land kept in its natural state for public recreational use. ■ (also **wildlife park**) a large enclosed area of land used to accommodate wild animals in captivity. ■ a stadium or enclosed area used for sports. ■ a large enclosed piece of ground, typically with woodland and pasture, attached to a large country house: *the house is set in its own park.* ■ (in the western U.S.) a broad, flat, mostly open area in a mountainous region. **2** [with *adj.*] an area devoted to a specified purpose: *an industrial park.* ■ [with *adj.*] *chiefly Brit.* a parking lot or garage: *a coach park.* **3** (in a car with automatic transmission) the position of the gear selector in which the gears are locked, preventing the vehicle's movement.
▸*v.* [*trans.*] bring (a vehicle that one is driving) to a halt and leave it temporarily, typically in a parking lot or by the side of the road: *he parked his car outside her house* | [*intrans.*] *he couldn't find anywhere to park.* ■ [*trans.*] *informal* deposit and leave in a convenient place until required: *come on in, and park your bag by the door.* ■ (**park oneself in/on**) *informal* sit down on or in: *after dinner, we parked ourselves on a pair of couches.* ▷Middle English: from Old French *parc*, from medieval Latin *parricus*, of Germanic origin; related to German *Pferch* 'pen, fold,' also to **PADDOCK.** The word was originally a legal term designating land held by royal grant for keeping game animals: this was enclosed and therefore distinct from a *forest* or *chase*, and (also unlike a *forest*) had no special laws or officers. A military sense 'space occupied by artillery, wagons, stores, etc., in an encampment' (late 17th cent.) is the origin of the verb sense (mid 19th cent.) and of sense 2 (early 20th cent.).

par·ka /ˈpärkə/ ▸*n.* a large windproof jacket with a hood, designed to be worn in cold weather. ■ a hooded jacket made of animal skin, worn by Eskimos. ▷late 18th cent.: via Aleut from Russian.

par·kade /pärˈkād/ ▸*n. Canadian* a multistory parking garage. ▷1950s: from **PARK**, on the pattern of *arcade.*

park-and-ride ▸*n.* [often as *adj.*] a system for reducing urban traffic congestion, in which drivers leave their cars in parking lots on the outskirts of a city and travel to the city center on public transportation: *a new park-and-ride system in the town to cut traffic jams.*

Park Avenue /ˈpärk/ a commercial and residential street in Manhattan in New York City, regarded as emblematic of worldly success.

Park Chung Hee /ˈCHəNG ˈhē/ (1917–79), South Korean statesman; president 1963–79. After staging a coup in 1961, he was elected president and by 1971 had assumed dictatorial powers. Under his presidency, South Korea emerged as a leading industrial nation. He was assassinated by the head of the Korean Central Intelligence Agency.

Par·ker[1] /ˈpärkər/, Bonnie (1911–34), U.S. bank robber and murderer. She and her partner, Clyde Barrow, were known for a criminal spree in which they shot and killed at least thirteen people before being stopped and shot to death at a Louisiana roadblock.

Par·ker[2], Charlie (1920–55), U.S. saxophonist; full name *Charles Christopher Parker*; known as **Bird** or **Yardbird**. From 1944, he played with Thelonious Monk and Dizzy Gillespie and became one of the key figures of the bebop movement.

Par·ker[3], Dorothy (Rothschild) (1893–1967), U.S. humorist, literary critic, and writer. From 1927, she wrote book reviews and short stories for the *New Yorker* magazine, becoming one of its legendary wits.

par·ker·iz·ing /ˈpärkərˌīziNG/ ▸*n.* a process for rustproofing iron or steel by brief immersion in a hot acidic solution of a metal phosphate. ▷1920s: from *Parker* Rust-Proof Company of America (which introduced the process) + **-IZE** + **-ING**[1]. **—par·ker·ized** *adj.*

Par·kers·burg /ˈpärkərzˌbərg/ an industrial city in northwestern West Virginia, on the Ohio River; pop. 33,099.

par·kin /ˈpärkin/ ▸*n. Brit.* a kind of dark gingerbread, typically with a soft, dry texture, made with oatmeal and molasses. ▷early 19th cent.: perhaps from the family name *Parkin*, diminutive of *Per* 'Peter.'

park·ing light ▸*n.* [usu. in *pl.*] a small light on each side of a vehicle in the front and rear.

park·ing lot ▸*n.* an area where cars or other vehicles may be left temporarily.

park·ing me·ter ▸*n.* a machine next to a parking space in a street, into which the driver puts money so as to be authorized to park the vehicle for a particular length of time.

park·ing tick·et ▸*n.* a notice telling a driver of a fine imposed for parking illegally, typically attached to a car windshield.

Par·kin·son·ism /ˈpärkinsənˌizəm/ ▸*n.* another term for **PARKINSON'S DISEASE.**

Par·kin·son's dis·ease /ˈpärkinsənz/ ▸*n.* a progressive disease of the nervous system marked by tremor, muscular rigidity, and slow, imprecise movement, chiefly affecting middle-aged and elderly people. It is associated with degeneration of the basal ganglia of the brain and a deficiency of the neurotransmitter dopamine. ▷late 19th cent.: named after James *Parkinson* (1755–1824), English surgeon.

Par·kin·son's law the notion that work expands to fill the time available for its completion. ▷1950s: named after Cyril Northcote *Parkinson* (1909–93), English writer.

park·land /ˈpärkˌland/ ▸*n.* (also **parklands**) open land consisting of fields and scattered groups of trees. ■ land reserved for a public park.

Park·man /ˈpärkmən/, Francis (1823–93), U.S. historian. He traveled the Oregon Trail in 1846 to improve his health and later wrote an account of his journey in *The California and Oregon Trail* (1849). He also wrote *The Discovery of the Great West* (1869) and *A Half-Century of Conflict* (1892).

Park Range a range of the Rocky Mountains in southern Wyoming and northern Colorado, west of the Front Range.

P

Parks[1] /pärks/, Gordon (Roger Alexander Buchanan) (1912–), U.S. photographer, writer, movie director, and composer. He worked as a photographer for the Farm Security Administration 1941–44 before becoming a photojournalist for *Life* magazine 1949–70. He wrote *The Learning Tree* (1963), *Born Black* (1971), and *Shannon* (1981) and directed the movies *Shaft* (1971) and *The Super Cops* (1973).

Parks[2], Rosa (Louise McCauley) (1913–), U.S. civil rights pioneer. On December 1, 1955, she refused to give up her bus seat to a white man in Montgomery, Alabama, an act that inspired the civil rights movement. After the ensuing boycott and NAACP protest, bus segregation was ruled unconstitutional. Congressional Gold Medal (1999).

Rosa Parks

park·way /ˈpärkˌwā/ ▸*n.* an open landscaped highway.

park·y /ˈpärkē/ ▸*adj.* (**park·i·er, park·i·est**) *Brit., informal* chilly. ▷late 19th cent.: of unknown origin.

Parl. *Brit.* ▸*abbr.* ■ Parliament. ■ Parliamentary.

par·lance /ˈpärləns/ ▸*n.* a particular way of speaking or using words, esp. a way common to those with a particular job or interest: *dated terms that were once in common parlance* | *medical parlance.* ▷late 16th cent. (denoting speech or debate): from Old French, from *parler* 'speak,' from Latin *parabola* 'comparison' (in late Latin 'speech').

par·lan·do /pärˈländō/ *Music* ▸*adv.* & *adj.* (with reference to singing) expressive or declamatory in the manner of speech.
▸*n.* composition or performance in this manner: *the high-lying parlando of Siegfried's narration.* ▷Italian, literally 'speaking.'

par·lay /ˈpärˌlā; -lē/ ▸*v.* [*trans.*] (**parlay something into**) turn an initial stake or winnings from a previous bet into (a greater amount) by gambling: *it involved parlaying a small bankroll into big winnings.* ■ *informal* transform into (something greater or more valuable): *a banker who parlayed a sizable inheritance into a financial empire* | *an excellent performance is quickly parlayed into lucrative contracts.*
▸*n.* a cumulative series of bets in which winnings accruing from each transaction are used as a stake for a further bet. ▷late 19th cent.: from French *paroli*, from Italian, from *paro* 'like,' from Latin *par* 'equal.'

par·ley /ˈpärlē/ ▸*n.* (*pl.* **-leys**) a conference between opposing sides in a dispute, esp. a discussion of terms for an armistice. See note at **CONVERSATION.**
▸*v.* (**-leys, -leyed**) [*intrans.*] hold a conference with the opposing side to discuss terms: *they disagreed over*

*whether to **parley with** the enemy.* ▷late Middle English (denoting speech or debate): perhaps from Old French *parlee* 'spoken,' feminine past participle of the verb *parler.*

par·lia·ment /ˈpärləmənt/ ▶*n.* (**Parliament**) (in the UK) the highest legislature, consisting of the sovereign, the House of Lords, and the House of Commons: *the Secretary of State will lay proposals before Parliament.* ■ the members of this legislature for a particular period, esp. between one dissolution and the next: *the act was passed by the last parliament of the reign.* ■ a similar legislature in other nations and states: *the Russian parliament.* ▷Middle English: from Old French *parlement* 'speaking,' from the verb *parler.*

par·lia·men·tar·i·an /ˌpärləmenˈte(ə)rēən/ ▶*n.* **1** a member of a parliament, esp. one well versed in parliamentary procedure and experienced in debate. **2** *historical* a supporter of Parliament in the English Civil War; a Roundhead.

▶*adj.* **1** of or relating to Parliament or its members: *parliamentarian committees.* **2** *historical* of or relating to the Roundheads. —**par·lia·men·tar·i·an·ism** /-ˌnizəm/ *n.*

par·lia·men·ta·ry /ˌpärləˈmentərē/ ▶*adj.* relating to, enacted by, or suitable for a parliament: *parliamentary legislation.*

par·lia·men·ta·ry law ▶*n.* the rules that govern the conduct of legislatures and other deliberative bodies.

par·lia·men·ta·ry pro·ce·dure ▶*n.* **1** a rule that defines how a particular situation is to be handled, or a particular outcome achieved, in a legislature or deliberative body. **2** parliamentary law.

par·lor /ˈpärlər/ (*Brit.* **par·lour**) ▶*n.* **1** *dated* a sitting room in a private house. ■ a room in a public building for receiving guests: *the mayor's parlor.* ■ a room in a monastery or convent that is set aside for conversation. **2** [usu. with *adj.*] a shop or business providing specified goods or services: *an ice-cream parlor | a funeral parlor.* **3** (also **milking parlor**) a room or building equipped for milking cows.

▶*adj.* [*attrib.*] *dated, derogatory* denoting a person who professes but does not actively give support to a specified (esp. radical) political view: *the so-called radicalism of the new "parlor communists."* ▷Middle English: from Anglo-Norman French *parlur* 'place for speaking,' from Latin *parlare* 'speak.'

par·lor car ▶*n.* a luxuriously fitted railroad car, typically with individually reserved seats.

par·lor game ▶*n.* an indoor game, esp. a word game.

par·lor grand ▶*n.* a grand piano intermediate in size between a concert grand and a baby grand.

par·lor·maid /ˈpärlərˌmād/ ▶*n. historical* a maid employed to serve at table.

par·lous /ˈpärləs/ ▶*adj. archaic* or *humorous* full of danger or uncertainty; precarious: *the parlous state of the economy.*

▶*adv. archaic* greatly or excessively: *she is parlous handsome.* ▷late Middle English: contraction of **PERILOUS**. —**par·lous·ly** *adv.* —**par·lous·ness** *n.*

Par·ma /ˈpärmə/ **1** a city in northern Italy, southeast of Milan; pop. 194,000. Founded by the Romans in 183 BC, it became a bishopric in the 9th century AD and capital of the duchy of Parma and Piacenza in about 1547. **2** a city in northeastern Ohio, south of Cleveland; pop. 85,655.

Par·ma ham ▶*n.* a type of ham that is eaten uncooked.

Par·ma vi·o·let ▶*n.* a sweet violet of a variety with a heavy scent and lavender-colored flowers that are often crystallized and used for food decoration.

par·ma wal·la·by ▶*n.* a small dark brown Australian wallaby, restricted to the rain forests of New South Wales. • *Macropus parma*, family Macropodidae. ▷mid 19th cent.: *parma* (probably from a New South Wales Aboriginal language) was applied by George Robert Waterhouse (1810–88), English naturalist.

Par·men·i·des /pärˈmeniˌdēz/ (*fl.* 5th century BC), Greek philosopher. He founded the Eleatic school of philosophers. In his work *On Nature*, he maintained that the apparent motion and changing forms of the universe are in fact manifestations of an unchanging and indivisible reality.

Par·men·tier /ˌpärmenˈtyā/ ▶*adj.* [*postpositive*] cooked or served with potatoes: *soups such as potage Parmentier.* ▷from the name of Antoine A. *Parmentier* (1737–1813), the French agriculturalist who popularized the potato in France.

Par·me·san /ˈpärməˌzän/ ▶*n.* a hard, dry cheese used in grated form, esp. on Italian dishes. ▷early 16th cent.: from French, from Italian *parmigiano* 'of Parma,' where it was originally made.

par·mi·gia·na /ˌpärməˈzhänə/ ▶*adj.* [*postpositive*] cooked or served with Parmesan cheese: *eggplant and veal parmigiana.*

▶*n.* a dish cooked in this way. ▷Italian, feminine of *Parmigiano* 'of Parma.'

Par·nas·si·an /pärˈnasēən/ ▶*adj.* **1** relating to poetry; poetic. **2** of or relating to a group of French poets of the late 19th century who emphasized strictness of form, named from the anthology *Le Parnasse contemporain* (1866).

▶*n.* a member of this group of French poets.

Par·nas·sus, grass of /pärˈnasəs/ ▶*n.* see **GRASS OF PARNASSUS**.

Par·nas·sus, Mount a mountain in central Greece, just north of Delphi, that rises to a height of 8,064 feet (2,457 m). Held to be sacred by the ancient Greeks, it was associated with Apollo and the Muses and was regarded as a symbol of poetry. Greek name **PARNASSÓS** .

Par·nell /pärˈnel; ˈpärnl/, Charles Stewart (1846–91), Irish nationalist leader. He became leader of the Irish Home Rule faction in 1880 and raised the profile of Irish affairs through obstructive parliamentary tactics. —**Par·nell·ite** /-ˈnelīt/ *adj.* & *n.*

pa·ro·chi·al /pəˈrōkēəl/ ▶*adj.* of or relating to a church parish: *the parochial church council.* ■ having a limited or narrow outlook or scope: *this worldview seems incredibly naive and parochial.* ▷late Middle English: from Old French, from ecclesiastical Latin *parochialis* 'relating to an ecclesiastical district,' from *parochia* (see **PARISH**). —**pa·ro·chi·al·ism** /-ˌizəm/ *n.* —**pa·ro·chi·al·i·ty** /-ˌrōkēˈalitē/ *n.* —**pa·ro·chi·al·ly** *adv.*

pa·ro·chi·al school ▶*n.* a private school supported by a particular church or parish.

par·o·dy /ˈparədē/ ▶*n.* (*pl.* **-dies**) an imitation of the style of a particular writer, artist, or genre with deliberate exaggeration for comic effect: *the movie is a parody of the horror genre | his provocative use of parody.* See note at **CARICATURE**. ■ an imitation or a version of something that falls far short of the real thing; a travesty: *he seems like a parody of an educated Englishman.*

▶*v.* (**-dies, -died**) [*trans.*] produce a humorously exaggerated imitation of (a writer, artist, or genre): *his specialty was parodying schoolgirl fiction.* ■ mimic humorously: *he parodied his friend's voice.* ▷late 16th cent.: via late Latin from Greek *parōidia* 'burlesque poem,' from *para-* 'beside' (expressing alteration) + *ōidē* 'ode.' —**pa·rod·ic** /pəˈrädik/ *adj.* —**par·o·dist** /-dist/ *n.*

par of ex·change ▶*n.* see **PAR**[1] (sense 2).

pa·rol /pəˈrōl; ˈparəl/ ▶*adj. Law* given or expressed orally: *the parol evidence.* ■ (of a document) agreed orally, or in writing but not under seal: *there was a parol agreement.* ▷late 15th cent. (as a noun): from Old French *parole* 'word' (see **PAROLE**).

▶*PHRASE* □ **by parol** by oral declaration.

pa·role /pəˈrōl/ ▶*n.* **1** the release of a prisoner temporarily (for a special purpose) or permanently before the completion of a sentence, on the promise of good behavior: *he committed a burglary while **on parole.*** ■ *historical* a promise or undertaking given by a prisoner of war not to escape or, if released, not to engage in hostilities, or to return to custody under stated conditions. **2** *Linguistics* the actual linguistic behavior or performance of individuals, in contrast to the linguistic system of a community. Contrasted with **LANGUE**.

▶*v.* [*trans.*] (usu. **be paroled**) release (a prisoner) on parole: *he was paroled after serving nine months of a two-year sentence.* ▷late 15th cent.: from Old French, literally 'word,' also 'formal promise,' from ecclesiastical Latin *parabola* 'speech'; compare with **PAROL**. —**pa·rol·ee** /-ˌrōˈlē/ *n.*

par·o·no·ma·sia /ˌparənōˈmāzh(ē)ə/ ▶*n.* a play on words; a pun. ▷late 16th cent.: via Latin from Greek *paronomasia*, from *para-* 'beside' (expressing alteration) + *onomasia* 'naming' (from *onomazein* 'to name,' from *onoma* 'a name').

par·o·nym /ˈparənim/ ▶*n. Linguistics* a word that is a derivative of another and has a related meaning: *"wisdom" is a paronym of "wise."* ■ a word formed by adaptation of a foreign word: *"preface" is a paronym of Latin "prefatio."* Contrasted with **HETERONYM**. ▷mid 19th cent.: from Greek *parōnumon*, neuter (used as a noun) of *parōnumos* 'naming by modification,' from *para-* 'beside' + *onuma* 'a name.' —**par·o·nym·ic** /ˌparəˈnimik/ *adj.* —**pa·ron·y·mous** /pəˈränəməs/ *adj.* —**pa·ron·y·my** /pəˈränəmē/ *n.*

Pa·ros /ˈparäs; ˈpe(ə)r-; ˈpärôs/ a Greek island in the southern Aegean Sea, in the Cyclades. It is noted for the translucent white Parian marble, quarried here since the 6th century BC.

pa·rot·id /pəˈrätid/ *Anatomy* ▶*adj.* relating to, situated near, or affecting a parotid gland.

▶*n.* short for **PAROTID GLAND**. ▷late 17th cent.: via Latin from Greek *parōtis, parōtid-*, from *para-* 'beside' + *ous, ōt-* 'ear.'

pa·rot·id gland ▶*n. Anatomy* either of a pair of large salivary glands situated just in front of each ear.

par·o·ti·tis /ˌparəˈtītis/ ▶*n. Medicine* inflammation of a parotid gland, esp. (**infectious parotitis**) mumps.

-parous ▶*comb. form Biology* bearing offspring of a specified number or reproducing in a specified manner: *multiparous | viviparous.* ▷from Latin *-parus* '-bearing' (from *parere* 'bring forth, produce') + **-OUS**.

Par·ou·si·a /pəˈrōōzēə; ˌpärōōˈsēə/ ▶*n. Christian Theology* another term for **SECOND COMING**. ▷Greek, literally 'being present.'

par·ox·ysm /ˈparəkˌsizəm/ ▶*n.* a sudden attack or violent expression of a particular emotion or activity: ***a paroxysm of** weeping.* ■ *Medicine* a sudden recurrence or attack of a disease; a sudden worsening of symptoms. ▷late Middle English: from French *paroxysme*, via medieval Latin from Greek *paroxusmos*, from *paroxunein* 'exasperate,' from *para-* 'beyond' + *oxunein* 'sharpen' (from *oxus* 'sharp'). —**par·ox·ys·mal** /ˌparəkˈsizməl/ *adj.*

par·ox·y·tone /pəˈräksiˌtōn/ ▶*adj.* (esp. in ancient Greek) having an acute accent on the penultimate syllable.

▶*n.* a word with such an accent. ▷mid 18th cent.: from modern Latin *paroxytonus*, from Greek *paroxutonos*, from *para-* 'alongside' + *oxutonos* 'sharp pitch.'

par·pen /ˈpärpən/ ▶*n.* a stone passing through a wall from side to side, with two smooth vertical faces. ▷Middle English: from Old French *parpain* 'length of a stone,' probably based on Latin *perpes* 'continuous.'

par·quet /pärˈkā/ ▶*n.* **1** (also **parquet flooring**) flooring composed of wooden blocks arranged in a geometric pattern. **2** the ground floor of a theater or auditorium. **3** (**the Parquet**) (in France and French-speaking countries) the branch of the administration of the law that deals with the prosecution of crime. ▷late 17th cent. (as a verb, esp. as *parqueted*): from French, literally 'small park (i.e., delineated area).' The noun dates from the early 19th cent.

par·quet·ry /ˈpärkitrē/ ▶*n.* inlaid work of blocks of various woods arranged in a geometric pattern, esp. for flooring or furniture.

Parr[1] /pär/, Jack (Harold) (1918–2004), U.S. television personality. He was host of *The Tonight Show* 1957–62.

Parr [2] /pär/, Katherine (1512–48), English queen; sixth and last wife of Henry VIII. Having married the king in 1543, she influenced his decision to restore the succession to his daughters Mary and Elizabeth (later Mary I and Elizabeth I respectively).

parr /pär/ ▶*n.* (*pl.* same) a young salmon or trout between the stages of fry and smolt, distinguished by dark rounded patches evenly spaced along its sides. ▷early 18th cent.: of unknown origin.

par·ra·keet ▶*n.* variant spelling of **PARAKEET**.

par·ra·mat·ta ▶*n.* variant spelling of **PARAMATTA**.

par·ri·cide /ˈparəˌsīd/ ▶*n.* the killing of a parent or other near relative. ■ a person who commits parricide. ▷late 16th cent.: from French, from Latin *parricidium* 'murder of a parent,' with first element of unknown origin, but long associated with Latin *pater* 'father' and *parens* 'parent.' —**par·ri·cid·al** /ˌparəˈsīdl/ *adj.*

par·rot /ˈparət/ ▶*n.* a bird, often vividly colored, with a short down-curved hooked bill, grasping feet, and a raucous voice, found esp. in the tropics and feeding on fruits and seeds. Many are popular as cage birds, and some are able to mimic the human voice. • Order Psittaciformes: numerous species, sometimes all placed in the family Psittacidae. The order also contains the cockatoos, lories, lovebirds, macaws, conures, and budgerigars.

▶*v.* (**-rot·ed, -rot·ing**) [*trans.*] repeat mechanically: *encouraging students to parrot back information.* ▷early

parrot

16th cent.: probably from dialect French *perrot*, diminutive of the male given name *Pierre* 'Peter.' Compare with PARAKEET.

par·rot·bill /ˈparətˌbil/ ▶*n.* a titlike Asian songbird with brown and gray plumage and a short arched bill. • Family Panuridae (or Paradoxornithidae): two genera and several species.

par·rot fe·ver ▶*n.* less formal term for PSITTACOSIS.

par·rot·fish /ˈparətˌfisн/ ▶*n.* (*pl.* same or **-fish·es**) **1** any of a number of brightly colored marine fish with a parrotlike beak, which they use to scrape food from coral and other hard surfaces: • a widespread fish of warm seas that may secrete a mucous cocoon to deter predators (family Scaridae: *Scarus* and other genera). • an edible fish of the southern Indian ocean (*Oplegnathus conwayi*, family Oplegnathidae). **2** *Austral.* a brightly colored marine fish, esp. one of the wrasse family. • Several species in the family Labridae.

par·rot·let /ˈparətlit/ ▶*n.* a tiny tropical American parrot with mainly green plumage and a short tail. • Family Psittacidae: three genera, in particular *Forpus* and *Touit*, and several species.

par·rot tu·lip ▶*n.* a cultivated tulip of a variety that has irregularly fringed or wavy petals, typically of two colors.

par·ry /ˈparē/ ▶*v.* (**-ries**, **-ried**) [*trans.*] ward off (a weapon or attack), esp. with a countermove: *he parried the blow by holding his sword vertically.* ■ answer (a question or accusation) evasively: *he parried questions from reporters outside the building.*
▶*n.* (*pl.* **-ries**) an act of warding off a blow. ■ *Fencing* block or turn aside (an opponent's blade). ■ an evasive reply: *her question met with a polite parry.* ▷late 17th cent.: probably representing French *parez!* 'ward off!,' imperative of *parer*, from Italian *parare* 'ward off.'

parse /pärs/ ▶*v.* [*trans.*] analyze (a sentence) into its parts and describe their syntactic roles. ■ *Computing* analyze (a string or text) into logical syntactic components, typically in order to test conformability to a logical grammar. ■ examine or analyze minutely: *he has always been quick to parse his own problems in public.*
▶*n. Computing* an act of or the result obtained by parsing a string or a text. ▷mid 16th cent.: perhaps from Middle English *pars* 'parts of speech,' from Old French *pars* 'parts' (influenced by Latin *pars* 'part').

par·sec /ˈpärˌsek/ (abbr.: **pc**) ▶*n.* a unit of distance used in astronomy, equal to about 3.25 light years (3.08×10^{16} meters). One parsec corresponds to the distance at which the mean radius of the earth's orbit subtends an angle of one second of arc. ▷early 20th cent.: blend of PARALLAX and SECOND[2].

Par·see /pärˈsē; ˈpärsē/ (also **Par·si**) ▶*n.* an adherent of Zoroastrianism, esp. a descendant of those Zoroastrians who fled to India from Muslim persecution in Persia during the 7th–8th centuries. ▷from Persian *pārsī* 'Persian,' from *pārs* 'Persia.'

pars·er /ˈpärsər/ ▶*n. Computing* a program for parsing.

Par·si·fal /ˈpärsəfəl; -ˌfäl/ another name for PERCEVAL[1].

par·si·mo·ni·ous /ˌpärsəˈmōnēəs/ ▶*adj.* unwilling to spend money or use resources; stingy or frugal: *parsimonious New Hampshire voters, who have a phobia about taxes.* See note at ECONOMICAL. —**par·si·mo·ni·ous·ly** *adv.* —**par·si·mo·ni·ous·ness** *n.*

par·si·mo·ny /ˈpärsəˌmōnē/ ▶*n.* extreme unwillingness to spend money or use resources: *a great tradition of public design has been shattered by government parsimony.* ▷late Middle English: from Latin *parsimonia*, *parcimonia*, from *parcere* 'be sparing.'
▶*PHRASE* □ **principle** (or **law**) **of parsimony** the scientific principle that things are usually connected or behave in the simplest or most economical way, esp. with reference to alternative evolutionary pathways. Compare with OCCAM'S RAZOR.

Par·sip·pa·ny–Troy Hills /pärˈsipənē troi/ a commercial and residential township in northern New Jersey; pop. 48,478.

pars·ley /ˈpärslē/ ▶*n.* a biennial plant with white flowers and aromatic leaves that are either crinkly or flat and used as a culinary herb and for garnishing food. • *Petroselinum crispum*, family Umbelliferae (or Apiaceae; the **parsley family**). Members of this family have their flowers arranged in umbels and are known as umbellifers; typical members include hogweed and hemlock as well as many food plants and herbs (carrot, parsnip, celery, fennel, anise). ▷Old English *petersilie*, via late Latin based on Greek *petroselinon*, from *petra* 'rock' + *selinon* 'parsley,' influenced in Middle English by Old French *peresil*, of the same origin.

pars·nip /ˈpärsnip/ ▶*n.* **1** a long tapering cream-colored root with a sweet flavor. **2** the widely cultivated Eurasian plant of the parsley family that yields this root. • *Pastinaca sativa*, family Umbelliferae. ▷late Middle English: from Old French *pasnaie*, from Latin *pastinaca* (related to *pastinare* 'dig and trench the ground'). The change in the ending was due to association with NEEP.

par·son /ˈpärsən/ ▶*n.* a beneficed member of the clergy; a rector or a vicar. ■ *informal* any member of the clergy, esp. a Protestant one. ▷Middle English: from Old French *persone*, from Latin *persona* 'person' (in medieval Latin 'rector'). —**par·son·ic** /pärˈsänik/ *adj.* —**par·son·i·cal** /pärˈsänikəl/ *adj.*

par·son·age /ˈpärsənij/ ▶*n.* a church house provided for a member of the clergy.

pars pro to·to /pärz prō ˈtōtō/ ▶*n. formal* a part or aspect of something taken as representative of the whole. ▷Latin, literally 'part for the whole.'

part /pärt/ ▶*n.* **1** a piece or segment of something such as an object, activity, or period of time, which combined with other pieces makes up the whole: *divide the circle into three equal parts | the early part of 1989.* See note at FRAGMENT. ■ an element or constituent that belongs to something and is essential to its nature: *I was part of the family.* ■ a component of a machine: *the production of aircraft parts.* ■ a measure allowing comparison between the amounts of different ingredients used in a mixture: *repot plants in a mixture of three parts soil, one part sand.* ■ a specified fraction of a whole: *they paid a twentieth part of the cost.* ■ a division of a book treated as a unit in which a particular topic is discussed. ■ the amount of a serial that is published or broadcast at one time. ■ (**parts**) *informal* short for PRIVATE PARTS. **2** some but not all of something: *the painting tells only part of the story.* ■ a point on or area of something: *hold the furthest part of your leg that you can reach.* ■ (**parts**) *informal* a region, esp. one not clearly specified or delimited: *they wanted to know why he was loitering in these parts.* **3** a character as represented in a play or movie; a role played by an actor or actress: *she played a lot of leading parts | he took the part of Prospero.* ■ the words and directions to be learned and performed by an actor in such a role: *she was memorizing a part.* ■ *Music* a melody or other constituent of harmony assigned to a particular voice or instrument in a musical work: *he coped well with the percussion part.* ■ the contribution made by someone or something to an action or situation: *he played a key part in ending the revolt | he may be jailed for his part in the robbery.* ■ the behavior appropriate to or expected of a person in a particular role or situation; a person's duty: *in such a place his part is to make good.* ■ the chance to be involved in something: *they were legislating for a future they had no part in.* **4** (**parts**) *archaic* abilities. **5** a line of scalp revealed in a person's hair by combing the hair away in opposite directions on either side.
▶*v.* [*intrans.*] (of two things) move away from each other: *his lips parted in a smile.* ■ divide to leave a central space: *at that moment the mist parted.* ■ [*trans.*] cause to divide or move apart, leaving a central space: *she parted the ferns and looked between them.* ■ leave someone's company: *there was a good deal of kissing and more congratulations before we parted.* ■ (**be parted**) leave the company of someone: *she can't bear to be parted from her daughter again.* ■ (**part with**) give up possession of; hand over: *even quite small companies parted with large sums.* ■ [*trans.*] separate (the hair of the head on either side of the part) with a comb.
▶*adv.* to some extent; partly (often used to contrast different parts of something): *the city is now part slum, part consumer paradise.* ▷Old English (denoting a part of speech), from Latin *pars*, *part-*. The verb (originally in Middle English in the sense 'divide into parts') is from Old French *partir*, from Latin *partire*, *partiri* 'divide, share.'
▶*PHRASES* □ **be part and parcel of** be an essential feature or element of: *it's best to accept that some inconveniences are part and parcel of travel.* □ **for my** (or **his**, **her**, etc.) **part** used to focus attention on one person or group and distinguish them from others involved in a situation: *for my part I was glad when the end of September came.* □ **in part** to some extent though not entirely: *the cause of the illness is at least in part psychological.* □ **look the part** have an appearance or style of dress appropriate to a particular role or situation. □ **a man of** (**many**) **parts** a man showing great ability in many different areas. □ **on the part of** (or **on my**, **their**, etc., **part**) used to ascribe responsibility for something to someone: *there was a series of errors on my part.* □ **part company** (of two or more people) cease to be together; go in different directions: *they parted company outside the Red Lion.* ■ (of two or more parties) cease to associate with each other, esp. as the result of a disagreement: *the chairman has **parted company with** the club.* □ **take part** join in an activity; be involved: *we have come here to **take part in** a major game | they ran away and took no part in the battle.* □ **take the part of** give support and encouragement to (someone) in a dispute.

par·take /pärˈtāk/ ▶*v.* (*past* **-took** /-ˈto͝ok/; *past part.* **-tak·en** /-ˈtākən/) [*intrans.*] (**partake in**) *formal* join in (an activity): *visitors can partake in golfing or clay pigeon shooting.* ■ (**partake of**) be characterized by (a quality): *the birth of twins became an event that partook of the mythic.* ■ (**partake of**) eat or drink (something): *she had partaken of a cheese sandwich and a cup of coffee.* ▷mid 16th cent.: back-formation from earlier *partaker* 'person who takes a part.' —**par·tak·er** *n.*

part·er /ˈpärtər/ ▶*n.* [in *combination*] a broadcast or published work with a specified number of parts: *the first in a six-parter.*

par·terre /pärˈte(ə)r/ ▶*n.* **1** a level space in a garden or yard occupied by an ornamental arrangement of flower beds. **2** the part of the ground floor of an auditorium in the rear and on the sides, esp. the part beneath the balcony. ▷early 17th cent.: from French, from *par terre* 'on the ground.'

par·the·no·car·py /ˈpärтнənōˌkärpē/ ▶*n. Botany* the development of a fruit without prior fertilization. ▷early 20th cent.: from German *Parthenocarpie*, from Greek *parthenos* 'virgin' + *karpos* 'fruit.' —**par·the·no·car·pic** /ˌpärтнənōˈkärpik/ *adj.*

par·the·no·gen·e·sis /ˌpärтнənōˈjenəsis/ ▶*n. Biology* reproduction from an ovum without fertilization, esp. as a normal process in some invertebrates and lower plants. ▷mid 19th cent.: modern Latin, from Greek *parthenos* 'virgin' + *genesis* 'creation.' —**par·the·no·ge·net·ic** /-jəˈnetik/ *adj.* —**par·the·no·ge·net·i·cal·ly** /-jəˈnetik(ə)lē/ *adv.*

Par·the·non /ˈpärтнəˌnän/ the temple of Athena Parthenos, built on the Acropolis in 447–432 BC by Pericles to honor Athens' patron goddess and to commemorate the recent Greek victory over the Persians. It was designed by Ictinus and Callicrates with sculptures by Phidias. ▷from Greek *parthenos* 'virgin.'

Parthenon

Par·thi·a /ˈpärтнēə/ an ancient kingdom that lay southeast of the Caspian Sea in present-day Iran. From *c.*250 BC to *c.*AD 230 the Parthians ruled an empire stretching from the Euphrates to the Indus. —**Par·thi·an** /-тнēən/ *n.* & *adj.*

Par·thi·an shot ▶*n.* another term for PARTING SHOT. ▷late 19th cent.: so named because of the trick used by Parthians of shooting arrows backward while in real or pretended flight.

par·tial /ˈpärsнəl/ ▶*adj.* **1** existing only in part; incomplete: *a question to which we have only partial answers.* **2** favoring one side in a dispute above the other; biased: *the paper gave a distorted and very partial view of the situation.* ■ [*predic.*] (**partial to**) having a liking for: *you know I'm partial to bacon and eggs.*
▶*n. Music* a component of a musical sound; an overtone or harmonic: *the upper partials of the string.* ▷late Middle English (in the sense 'inclined to favor one party in a cause'): from Old French *parcial* (sense 2), French *partiel* (sense 1), from late Latin *partialis*, from *pars*, *part-* 'part.' —**par·tial·ly** *adv.* [as *submodifier*] *a partially open door.* —**par·tial·ness** *n.*

USAGE In the sense 'to some extent, not entirely,' traditionalists prefer **partly** to **partially**: *the piece was written partly in poetry; what we decide will depend partly on the amount of the contract.* Also, in certain

Pronunciation Key ə *ago*; ər *over*; ˈə or ˌə *up*; ˈər or ˌər *fur*; a *hat*; ā *rate*; ä *car*; CH *chew*; e *let*; ē *see*; e(ə)r *air*; i *fit*; ī *by*; i(ə)r *ear*; NG *sing*; ō *go*; ô *for*; oi *boy*; o͝o *good*; o͞o *goo*; ou *out*; SH *she*; TH *thin*; T͟H *then*; (h)w *why*; ZH *vision*

contexts, the use of **partly** could prevent ambiguity: because *partial* can also mean 'biased, taking sides,' something written *partially in poetry* could be interpreted as biased verse. The form **partial**, however, appears in many phrases as the adjectival form of **part**: *partial blindness, partial denture, partial paralysis, partial payment, partial shade, partial vacuum*, etc. **Partially** is therefore widely used, with the same sense as **partly**: *partially blind in one eye.*

par·tial-birth a·bor·tion ▸*n.* a late-term abortion of a fetus that has already died, or is killed before being completely removed from the mother.

USAGE The term **partial-birth abortion** is used primarily in legislation and pro-life writing about this procedure. Pro-choice, scientific, and medical writing uses the term *D&X*, for *dilation and extraction.*

par·tial de·riv·a·tive ▸*n. Mathematics* a derivative of a function of two or more variables with respect to one variable, the other(s) being treated as constant.

par·tial dif·fer·en·tial e·qua·tion ▸*n. Mathematics* an equation containing one or more partial derivatives.

par·tial e·clipse ▸*n.* an eclipse of a celestial body in which only part of the luminary is obscured or darkened.

par·tial frac·tion ▸*n. Mathematics* each of two or more fractions into which a more complex fraction can be decomposed as a sum.

par·ti·al·i·ty /ˌpärsHēˈalitē/ ▸*n.* unfair bias in favor of one thing or person compared with another; favoritism: *an attack on the partiality of judges.* See note at BIAS. ■ a particular liking or fondness for something: *she spoke openly, not concealing her **partiality for** him.* ▷late Middle English: from Old French *parcialite*, from medieval Latin *partialitas*, based on Latin *pars, part-* 'part.'

par·tial or·der (also **partial ordering**) ▸*n. Mathematics* a transitive antisymmetric relation among the elements of a set, which does not necessarily apply to each pair of elements.

par·tial pres·sure ▸*n. Chemistry* the pressure that would be exerted by one of the gases in a mixture if it occupied the same volume on its own.

par·tial prod·uct ▸*n. Mathematics* the product of one term of a multiplicand and one term of its multiplier. ■ the product of the first *n* terms of a large or infinite series, where *n* is a finite integer (including 1).

par·ti·ble /ˈpärtəbəl/ ▸*adj.* involving or denoting a system of inheritance in which a deceased person's estate is divided equally among the heirs. ▷late Middle English (in the sense 'able to be parted'): from late Latin *partibilis*, from Latin *partiri* 'divide into parts.' **—par·ti·bil·i·ty** /ˌpärtəˈbilətē/ *n.*

par·tic·i·pant /pärˈtisəpənt/ ▸*n.* a person who takes part in something: *eager students would become first-hand **participants in** an archaeological exploration.* ▷late Middle English: from Latin *participant-*, literally 'sharing in,' from the verb *participare* (see PARTICIPATE).

par·tic·i·pate /pärˈtisəˌpāt/ ▸*v.* [*intrans.*] **1** take part: *thousands **participated in** a nationwide strike.* **2** (**participate of**) *archaic* have or possess (a particular quality): *both members participate of harmony.* ▷early 16th cent.: from Latin *participat-* 'shared in,' from the verb *participare*, based on *pars, part-* 'part' + *capere* 'take.' **—par·tic·i·pa·tion** /pärˌtisəˈpāsHən/ *n.* **—par·tic·i·pa·tive** /-ˌpātiv; -pətiv/ *adj.* **—par·tic·i·pa·tor** /-ˌpātər/ *n.* **—par·tic·i·pa·to·ry** /-pəˌtôrē/ *adj.*

par·ti·cip·i·al ad·jec·tive /ˌpärtəˈsipēəl/ ▸*n. Grammar* an adjective that is a participle in origin and form, such as *burned, cutting, engaged.*

par·ti·ci·ple /ˈpärtəˌsipəl/ ▸*n. Grammar* a word formed from a verb (e.g., *going, gone, being, been*) and used as an adjective (e.g., *working woman, burned toast*) or a noun (e.g., *good breeding*). In English, participles are also used to make compound verb forms (e.g., *is going, has been*). Compare with GERUND. ▷late Middle English: from Old French, by-form of *participe*, from Latin *participium* '(verbal form) sharing (the functions of a noun),' from *participare* 'share in.' **—par·ti·cip·i·al** /ˌpärtəˈsipēəl/ *adj.* **—par·ti·cip·i·al·ly** /ˌpärtəˈsipēəlē/ *adv.*

par·ti·cle /ˈpärtikəl/ ▸*n.* **1** a minute portion of matter: *tiny **particles of** dust.* ■ [with *negative*] the least possible amount: *he agrees without hearing the least particle of evidence.* ■ *Physics* another term for ELEMENTARY PARTICLE. ■ *Physics* another term for SUBATOMIC PARTICLE. ■ *Mathematics* a hypothetical object having mass but no physical size. **2** *Grammar* a minor function word that has comparatively little meaning and does not inflect, in particular: ■ (in English) any of the class of words such as *in, up, off, over*, used with verbs to make phrasal verbs. ■ (in ancient Greek) any of the class of words such as *de* and *ge*, used for contrast and emphasis. ▷late Middle English: from Latin *particula* 'little part,' diminutive of *pars, part-*.

par·ti·cle ac·cel·er·a·tor ▸*n.* an apparatus for accelerating subatomic particles to high velocities by means of electric or electromagnetic fields. The accelerated particles are generally made to collide with other particles, either as a research technique or for the generation of high-energy X-rays and gamma rays.

par·ti·cle beam ▸*n.* **1** a concentrated stream of subatomic particles, generated in order to cause collisions between particles that will shed new light on their nature and structure. **2** such a stream used in an antimissile defense weapon.

par·ti·cle·board /ˈpärtikəlˌbôrd/ ▸*n.* material made in rigid sheets or panels from compressed wood chips and resin, often coated or veneered, and used in furniture, buildings, etc., where a stronger material is not required.

par·ti·cle phys·ics ▸*plural n.* [treated as *sing.*] the branch of physics that deals with the properties, relationships, and interactions of subatomic particles.

par·ti-col·ored /ˈpärtē ˌkələrd/ (also **par·ti·col·ored**) ▸*adj.* having or consisting of two or more different colors: *their wonderful parti-colored light effects.* ▷early 16th cent.: from the adjective PARTY[2] + COLORED.

par·tic·u·lar /pə(r)ˈtikyələr/ ▸*adj.* **1** [*attrib.*] used to single out an individual member of a specified group or class: *the action seems to discriminate against a particular group of companies.* ■ *Logic* denoting a proposition in which something is asserted of some but not all of a class. Contrasted with UNIVERSAL. **2** [*attrib.*] esp. great or intense: *when handling or checking cash the cashier should exercise particular care.* **3** insisting that something should be correct or suitable in every detail; fastidious: *she is very **particular about** cleanliness.*
▸*n.* **1** *Philosophy* an individual item, as contrasted with a universal quality. **2** a detail: *he is wrong **in every particular.*** ■ (**particulars**) detailed information about someone or something: *a clerk took the woman's particulars.* ▷late Middle English: from Old French *particuler*, from Latin *particularis* 'concerning a small part,' from *particula* 'small part.'
▸*PHRASE* □ **in particular** especially (used to show that a statement applies to one person or thing more than any other): *he socialized with the other young people, one boy in particular.*

Par·tic·u·lar Bap·tist ▸*n.* a member of a Baptist denomination holding the doctrine of the election and redemption of some but not all people.

par·tic·u·lar in·te·gral ▸*n. Mathematics* another term for PARTICULAR SOLUTION.

par·tic·u·lar·ism /pə(r)ˈtikyələˌrizəm/ ▸*n.* exclusive attachment to one's own group, party, or nation. ■ the principle of leaving each state in an empire or federation free to govern itself and promote its own interests, without reference to those of the whole. ■ *Theology* the doctrine that some but not all people are elected and redeemed. ▷early 19th cent.: from French *particularisme*, modern Latin *particularismus*, and German *Partikularismus*, based on Latin *particularis* 'concerning a small part.' **—par·tic·u·lar·ist** *n.* & *adj.* **—par·tic·u·lar·is·tic** /-ˌtikyələˈristik/ *adj.*

par·tic·u·lar·i·ty /pə(r)ˌtikyəˈlaritē/ ▸*n.* (*pl.* **-ties**) the quality of being individual: *the central figures of his novels are stripped of their particularity.* ■ fullness or minuteness of detail in the treatment of something: *parties must present their case with some degree of accuracy and particularity.* ■ (**particularities**) small details: *the tedious particularities of daily life | he wanted to disregard the particularities and establish general laws.* ■ *Christian Theology* God's incarnation as Jesus as a particular person at a particular time and place. ▷early 16th cent. (as *particularities* 'details'): from Old French *particularite* or late Latin *particularitas*, from Latin *particularis* 'concerning a small part.'

par·tic·u·lar·ize /pə(r)ˈtikyələˌrīz/ ▸*v.* [*trans.*] *formal* mention or describe particularly; treat individually or in detail: *he was the first to particularize the theme of the mother in Palestinian poetry.* **—par·tic·u·lar·i·za·tion** /-ˌtikyələriˈzāsHən; pə(r)ˌtikyələˌriˈzāsHən/ *n.*

par·tic·u·lar·ly /pə(r)ˈtikyələrlē/ ▸*adv.* **1** to a higher degree than is usual or average: *I don't particularly want to be reminded of that time |* [as *submodifier*] *particularly able students.* ■ used to single out a subject to which a statement is especially applicable: *the team's defense is excellent, particularly their two center backs.* **2** so as to give special emphasis to a point; specifically: *he particularly asked that I should help you.*

par·tic·u·lar so·lu·tion ▸*n. Mathematics* the most general form of the solution of a differential equation, containing arbitrary constants.

par·tic·u·late /pärˈtikyəlit; -ˌlāt/ ▸*adj.* of, relating to, or in the form of minute separate particles: *particulate pollution.*
▸*n.* (**particulates**) matter in such a form. ▷late 19th cent.: from Latin *particula* 'particle' + -ATE[2].

part·ing /ˈpärtiNG/ ▸*n.* **1** the action of leaving or being separated from someone: *they exchanged a few words on parting.* ■ a leave-taking or departure: *her parting from Stephen | anguished partings at railroad stations.* **2** the action of dividing something into parts: *the parting of the Red Sea.* ■ *Brit.* a part in the hair.
▸*PHRASE* □ **a** (or **the**) **parting of the ways** a point at which two people must separate or at which a decision must be taken: *the best course is to seek an amicable parting of the ways.*

part·ing shot ▸*n.* a final remark, typically a cutting one, made by someone at the moment of departure; compare withPARTHIAN SHOT.: *as her parting shot she told me never to phone her again.*

par·ti pris /ˌpärtē ˈprē/ ▸*n.* (*pl.* **par·tis pris** *pronunc.* same) a preconceived view; a bias.
▸*adj.* prejudiced; biased. ▷French, literally 'side taken.'

par·ti·san /ˈpärtəzən/ ▸*n.* **1** a strong supporter of a party, cause, or person. **2** a member of an armed group formed to fight secretly against an occupying force, in particular one operating in enemy-occupied Yugoslavia, Italy, and parts of eastern Europe in World War II.
▸*adj.* prejudiced in favor of a particular cause: *newspapers have become increasingly partisan.* ▷mid 16th cent.: from French, via Italian dialect from Italian *partigiano*, from *parte* 'part' (from Latin *pars, part-*). **—par·ti·san·ship** /-ˌsHip/ *n.*

par·ti·ta /pärˈtētə/ ▸*n.* (*pl.* **-ti·tas** or **-ti·te** /-ˈtētā/) *Music* a suite, typically for a solo instrument or chamber ensemble. ▷late 19th cent.: from Italian, literally 'divided off,' feminine past participle of *partire*.

par·tite /ˈpärˌtīt/ ▸*adj.* [usu. in *combination*] divided into parts. ■ *Botany & Zoology* (esp. of a leaf or an insect's wing) divided to or nearly to the base. ▷late 16th cent.: from Latin *partitus* 'divided up,' past participle of *partiri*.

par·ti·tion /pärˈtisHən; pər-/ ▸*n.* (esp. with reference to a country with separate areas of government) the action or state of dividing or being divided into parts: *the country's partition into separate states.* ■ a structure dividing a space into two parts, esp. a light interior wall. ■ *Chemistry* the distribution of a solute between two immiscible or slightly miscible solvents in contact with one another, in accordance with its differing solubility in each. ■ *Computing* each of a number of portions into which some operating systems divide memory or storage.
▸*v.* [*trans.*] divide into parts: *an agreement was reached to partition the country.* ■ divide (a room) into smaller rooms or areas by erecting partitions: *the hall was partitioned to contain the noise of the computers.* ■ (**partition something off**) separate a part of a room from the rest by erecting a partition: *partition off part of a large bedroom to create a small bathroom.* ▷late Middle English: from Latin *partitio(n-)*, from *partiri* 'divide into parts.' **—par·ti·tion·er** *n.* **—par·ti·tion·ist** /-ist/ *n.*

par·ti·tion co·ef·fi·cient ▸*n. Chemistry* the ratio of the concentrations of a solute in two immiscible or slightly miscible liquids, or in two solids, when it is in equilibrium across the interface between them.

par·ti·tion·er /pärˈtisHənər/ ▸*n. Computing* a piece of software for apportioning space on a hard disk. A **hard partitioner** does this prior to formatting (i.e., permanently), while a **soft partitioner** does it after formatting.

par·ti·tive /ˈpärtitiv/ *Grammar* ▸*adj.* (of a grammatical construction or case) referring to only a part of a whole, for example *a slice of bacon, a series of accidents, some of the children.*
▸*n.* such a construction. ■ a noun or pronoun used as the first term in such a construction. **—par·ti·tive·ly** *adv.*

par·ti·tive gen·i·tive ▸*n. Grammar* a genitive used to indicate a whole divided into or regarded in parts, expressed in English by *of* as in *most of us.*

par·ti·zan /ˈpärtəzən/ ▸*n.* & *adj.* old-fashioned spelling of PARTISAN.

part·ly /ˈpärtlē/ ▸*adv.* to some extent; not completely: *the result is partly a matter of skill and partly of chance | you're only partly right.*

USAGE See usage at PARTIAL.

part·ner /ˈpärtnər/ ▶*n.* **1** a person who takes part in an undertaking with another or others, esp. in a business or company with shared risks and profits. ■ either of two people dancing together or playing a game or sport on the same side. ■ either member of a married couple or of an established unmarried couple: *she lived with her partner.* ■ a person with whom one has sex; a lover. ■ *dated* or *dialect* a friendly form of address by one man to another: *how you doing, partner?* **2** (**partners**) *Nautical* a timber framework secured to and strengthening the deck of a wooden ship around a hole for a mast.
▶*v.* [*trans.*] be the partner of: *young farmers who partnered Isabel to the village dance.* ■ [*intrans.*] associate as partners: *I never expected to* **partner with** *a man like you.* ▷Middle English: alteration of *parcener* 'partner, joint heir,' from Anglo-Norman French *parcener,* based on Latin *partitio(n-)* 'partition.' The change in the first syllable was due to association with PART. **—part·ner·less** *adj.*

part·ners' desk (also **part·ner·ship desk**) ▶*n.* a large flat-topped desk with space for two people to sit opposite each other.

part·ner·ship /ˈpärtnərˌship/ ▶*n.* the state of being a partner or partners: *we should go on working together in partnership.* ■ an association of two or more people as partners: *an increase in partnerships with housing associations.* ■ a business or firm owned and run by two or more partners. ■ a position as one of the partners in a business or firm.

part of speech ▶*n.* a category to which a word is assigned in accordance with its syntactic functions. In English the main parts of speech are noun, pronoun, adjective, determiner, verb, adverb, preposition, conjunction, and interjection.

Par·ton /ˈpärtn/, Dolly Rebecca (1946–), U.S. singer and songwriter. She is best known as a country music singer. She has also made a number of movies, including *Nine to Five* (1980) and *Steel Magnolias* (1989), and founded Dollywood, a theme park in Tennessee.

par·took /pärˈto͝ok/ ▶ past of PARTAKE.

par·tridge /ˈpärtrij/ ▶*n.* (*pl.* same or **-tridg·es**) a short-tailed game bird with mainly brown plumage, native to Eurasia. • Family Phasianidae: several genera and many species, in particular the **gray partridge** (*Perdix perdix*), introduced into the northern U.S., and the **red-legged partridge** (*Alectoris rufa*), introduced into Colorado. ■ *informal* any of a number of birds, such as the bobwhite or ruffed grouse, that resemble the partridge. ▷Middle English *partrich,* from Old French *pertriz, perdriz,* from Latin *perdix.*

red-legged partridge

par·tridge·ber·ry /ˈpärtrijˌberē/ ▶*n.* (*pl.* **-ries**) a creeping North American plant of the madder family with red berries that are a favored food of game birds. • *Mitchella repens,* family Rubiaceae. ■ the fruit of this plant.

par·tridge pea ▶*n.* a yellow-flowered leguminous plant with sensitive leaves. • *Cassia fasciculata,* family Leguminosae.

part song ▶*n.* an unaccompanied secular song with three or more voice parts, typically homophonic rather than contrapuntal in style.

part-time ▶*adj.* & *adv.* for only part of the usual working day or week: [as *adj.*] *part-time jobs* | *a part-time teacher* | [as *adv.*] *he only worked part-time.* **—part-tim·er** *n.*

par·tu·ri·ent /pärˈt(y)o͝orēənt/ ▶*adj. technical* (of a woman or female mammal) about to give birth; in labor.
▶*n.* a parturient woman. ▷late 16th cent.: from Latin *parturient-* 'being in labor,' from the verb *parturire,* inceptive of *parere* 'bring forth.'

par·tu·ri·tion /ˌpärcho͝oˈrishən/ ▶*n. formal* or *technical* the action of giving birth to young; childbirth: *the weeks following parturition.* ▷mid 17th cent.: from late Latin *parturitio(n-),* from *parturire* 'be in labor' (see PARTURIENT).

part·way /ˈpärtˌwā; ˈpärtˈwā/ ▶*adv.* part of the way: ***partway along*** *the corridor he stopped.*

par·ty[1] /ˈpärtē/ ▶*n.* (*pl.* **-ties**) **1** a social gathering of invited guests, typically involving eating, drinking, and entertainment: *an engagement party.* **2** a formally constituted political group, typically operating on a national basis, that contests elections and attempts to form or take part in a government: *the party's conservative mainstream.* ■ a group of people taking part in a particular activity or trip, esp. one for which they have been chosen: *the fishing party.* **3** a person or people forming one side in an agreement or dispute: *a contract between two parties.* ■ *informal* a person, esp. one with specified characteristics: *will you help the party on line 2?*
▶*v.* (**-ties, -tied**) [*intrans.*] *informal* enjoy oneself at a party or other lively gathering, typically with drinking and music: *put on your glad rags and party!* ▷Middle English (denoting a body of people united in opposition to others, also in sense 2): from Old French *partie,* based on Latin *partiri* 'divide into parts.' Sense 1 dates from the early 18th cent.
▶PHRASE □ **be (a) party to** be involved in: *I felt a wave of revulsion at the manipulations I'd been party to.*

par·ty[2] ▶*adj. Heraldry* divided into parts of different tinctures: *party per fess, or, and azure.* ▷Middle English (in the sense 'particolored'): from Old French *parti* 'parted,' based on Latin *partitus* 'divided into parts' (from the verb *partiri*).

par·ty boat ▶*n.* a boat available for renting by a group of people who want to go fishing.

par·ty fa·vor ▶*n.* a gift, usually small and inexpensive, given to guests at a party.

par·ty·go·er /ˈpärtēˌgōər/ ▶*n.* a person attending a party.

par·ty line ▶*n.* **1** a policy, or the policies collectively, officially adopted by a political party: *they rarely fail to toe the party line* | [as *adj.*] *a party-line voter.* **2** a telephone line or circuit shared by two or more subscribers.

par·ty list ▶*n.* a voting system used with proportional representation, in which people vote for a party rather than a candidate. Each party is assigned a number of seats that reflects its share of the vote. ■ a list of candidates representing a party in this system.

par·ty po·lit·i·cal broad·cast ▶*n.* a television or radio program on which a representative of a political party presents material intended to foster support for it.

par·ty pol·i·tics ▶*plural n.* [also treated as *sing.*] politics that relate to political parties rather than to the good of the general public.

par·ty poop·er ▶*n. informal* a person who throws gloom over social enjoyment: *I hate to be a party pooper, but I've got to catch the last train.* **—par·ty-poop·ing** *n.*

par·ty wall ▶*n.* a wall common to two adjoining buildings or rooms.

pa·rure /pəˈro͝or/ ▶*n.* a set of jewels intended to be worn together. ▷early 19th cent.: from French, from *parer* 'adorn.'

par val·ue ▶*n.* the nominal value of a bond, share of stock, or a coupon as indicated in writing on the document or specified by charter.

Par·va·ti /ˈpärvətē/ *Hinduism* a benevolent goddess, wife of Shiva, mother of Ganesh and Skanda, often identified in her malevolent aspect with Durga and Kali. ▷from Sanskrit *Pārvatī,* literally 'daughter of the mountain.'

par·ve /ˈpärvə/ ▶*n.* variant spelling of PAREVE.

par·ve·nu /ˈpärvəˌn(y)o͞o/ *often derogatory* ▶*n.* a person of obscure origin who has gained wealth, influence, or celebrity: *the political inexperience of a parvenu.*
▶*adj.* having recently achieved, or associated with someone who has recently achieved wealth, influence, or celebrity despite obscure origins: *he concealed the details of his parvenu lifestyle.* ▷early 19th cent.: from French, literally 'arrived,' past participle of *parvenir,* from Latin *pervenire* 'come to, reach.'

par·vis /ˈpärvis/ ▶*n.* an enclosed area in front of a cathedral or church, typically one that is surrounded with colonnades or porticoes. ▷late Middle English: from Old French, based on late Latin *paradisus* 'paradise,' in the Middle Ages denoting a court in front of St. Peter's, Rome.

par·vo·vi·rus /ˈpärvōˌvīrəs/ ▶*n. Medicine* any of a class of very small viruses chiefly affecting animals, esp. one (**canine parvovirus**) that causes contagious disease in dogs. ▷1960s: from Latin *parvus* 'small' + VIRUS.

PAS ▶*abbr.* power-assisted steering.

pas /pä/ ▶*n.* (*pl.* same) a step in dancing, esp. in classical ballet. ▷French.

Pas·a·de·na /ˌpasəˈdēnə/ **1** a city in California, in the San Gabriel Mountains, northeast of Los Angeles; pop. 131,591. It is the site of the Rose Bowl stadium. **2** an industrial port city in southeastern Texas, on the eastern side of Houston; pop. 141,674.

Pas·ca·gou·la /ˌpaskəˈgo͞olə/ an industrial port city in southeastern Mississippi, on the Gulf of Mexico; pop. 26,200.

Pas·cal[1] /paˈskal; päˈskäl/, Blaise (1623–62), French mathematician, physicist, and religious philosopher. He founded the theory of probabilities, but is best known for deriving the principle that the pressure of a fluid at rest is transmitted equally in all directions.

Pas·cal[2] (also **PASCAL**) ▶*n.* a high-level structured computer programming language used for teaching and general programming.

pas·cal /pasˈkäl/ ▶*n.* the SI unit of pressure, equal to one newton per square meter (approximately 0.000145 pounds per square inch, or 9.9×10^{-6} atmospheres). ▷1950s: named after B. *Pascal* (see PASCAL[1]).

Pas·cal's tri·an·gle ▶*n. Mathematics* a triangular array of numbers in which those at the ends of the rows are 1 and each of the others is the sum of the nearest two numbers in the row above (the apex, 1, being at the top).

Pas·cal's wa·ger ▶*n.* [in *sing.*] *Philosophy* the argument that it is in one's own best interest to behave as if God exists, since the possibility of eternal punishment in hell outweighs any advantage of believing otherwise.

pas·chal /ˈpaskəl/ ▶*adj. formal* **1** of or relating to Easter. **2** of or relating to the Jewish Passover. ▷late Middle English: from Old French, from ecclesiastical Latin *paschalis,* from *pascha* 'feast of Passover,' via Greek and Aramaic from Hebrew *Pesaḥ* 'Passover.'

pas·chal can·dle ▶*n. Christian Church* a large candle blessed and lit on Holy Saturday and placed by the altar until Pentecost.

pas·chal lamb ▶*n.* **1** a lamb sacrificed at Passover. **2** Christ.

Pa·schen se·ries /ˈpäshən/ *Physics* a series of lines in the infrared spectrum of atomic hydrogen, between 1.88 and 0.82 micrometers. ▷1920s: named after L. C. H. Friedrich *Paschen* (1865–1947), German physicist.

pas de basque /ˌpä də ˈbäsk/ ▶*n.* (*pl.* same) a ballet step in three beats, with a circular movement of the front leg on the second beat. ■ (esp. in jigs and reels) a step in three beats with one long and two short movements, transferring weight from one foot to the other. ▷French, literally 'step of a Basque.'

pas de bour·rée /ˌpä də bo͞oˈrā/ ▶*n. Ballet* a sideways step in which one foot crosses behind or in front of the other. ▷French, literally 'bourrée step.'

pas de chat /ˌpä də ˈshä/ ▶*n.* (*pl.* same) *Ballet* a jump in which each foot in turn is raised to the opposite knee. ▷French, literally 'step of a cat.'

pas de deux /ˌpä də ˈdo͞o/ ▶*n.* (*pl.* same) a dance for two people, typically a man and a woman. ▷French, literally 'step of two.'

pas de qua·tre /ˌpä də ˈkatrə/ ▶*n.* (*pl.* same) a dance for four people. ▷French, literally 'step of four.'

pas de trois /ˌpä də ˈtwä/ ▶*n.* (*pl.* same) a dance for three people. ▷French, literally 'step of three.'

pa·se /päˈsā/ ▶*n.* a maneuver with the cape in bullfighting, the purpose of which is to get the bull's attention. ▷Spanish, literally 'let him pass'.

pa·se·o /pəˈsāō/ ▶*n.* (*pl.* **-os**) a leisurely walk or stroll, esp. one taken in the evening; a promenade (used with reference to the tradition of taking such a walk in Spain or Spanish-speaking communities). ■ (also **pa·se·o de cua·drill·as** /dā kwäˈdrēlyäs; -ˈdrēäs/) a parade of bullfighters into the arena at the beginning of a bullfight. ■ a plaza or walkway for strolling. ▷Spanish, literally 'step.'

pash /pash/ ▶*n. informal, dated* a brief infatuation: *Kath's got* ***a pash on*** *him.* ▷early 20th cent.: abbreviation of PASSION.

pa·sha /ˈpäshə; ˈpashə; pəˈshä/ ▶*n.* **1** (also **pa·cha**) *historical* the title of a Turkish officer of high rank. **2** (**two-tailed pasha**) a large orange-brown butterfly with two tails on each hind wing and complex patterns on the underwings, occurring around the Mediterranean and in Africa. • *Charaxes jasius,* subfamily Nymphalinae, family Nymphalidae. ▷mid 17th cent.: from Turkish *paşa,* from Pahlavi *pati* 'lord' + *šāh* 'shah.'

Pronunciation Key ə *ago;* ər *over;* ˈə or ˌə *up;* ˈər or ˌər *fur;* a *hat;* ā *rate;* ä *car;* ch *chew;* e *let;* ē *see;* e(ə)r *air;* i *fit;* ī *by;* i(ə)r *ear;* ng *sing;* ō *go;* ô *for;* oi *boy;* o͝o *good;* o͞o *goo;* ou *out;* sh *she;* th *thin;* t͟h *then;* (h)w *why;* zh *vision*

pash·ka /ˈpäshkə/ ▶*n.* variant spelling of PASKHA.

pashm /ˈpəshəm/ ▶*n.* the soft underfur of some Tibetan and Indian goats, of which cashmere represents a particularly fine and soft type. ▷late 19th cent.: from Persian *pašm* 'wool.'

pash·mi·na /pəshˈmēnə/ ▶*n.* fine-quality material made from goat's wool. ▷Persian, from *pašm* 'wool, down.'

Pash·to /ˈpəshtō/ ▶*n.* the Iranian language of the Pathans, also spoken in northern areas of Pakistan, that is an official language of Afghanistan.
▶*adj.* of or relating to this language. ▷the name in Pashto.

Pash·tun /pəshˈto͞on/ ▶*n.* variant spelling of PATHAN.

Pa·siph·a·ë /pəˈsifə,ē/ *Greek Mythology* the wife of Minos and mother of the Minotaur.

pas·kha /ˈpäskə/ (also **pash·ka** /ˈpäshkə/) ▶*n.* a rich Russian dessert made with soft cheese, dried fruit, nuts, and spices, and traditionally eaten at Easter. ▷Russian, literally 'Easter.'

pa·so do·ble /ˌpäsō ˈdōblā/ ▶*n.* (*pl.* **pa·sos do·bles**) a fast-paced ballroom dance based on a Latin American style of marching. ■ a piece of music for this dance, typically in duple time. ■ a quick, light march played at bullfights. ▷1920s: from Spanish, literally 'double step.'

Pa·so·li·ni /ˌpasəˈlēnē; ˌpä-/, Pier Paolo (1922–75), Italian movie director and novelist. A Marxist, he drew on his experiences in the slums of Rome for his work, but became recognized for his controversial, bawdy literary adaptations, such as *The Gospel According to St. Matthew* (1964) and *The Canterbury Tales* (1973).

pas·pa·lum /ˈpaspələm/ ▶*n.* a grass of warm and tropical regions that is grown for fodder, erosion control, and as a pasture grass. • Genus *Paspalum*, family Gramineae. ▷modern Latin, from Greek *paspalos*, denoting a kind of millet.

North American pasqueflower

pasque·flow·er /ˈpask ˌflou(-ə)r/ ▶*n.* a spring-flowering plant of the buttercup family, with purple or white flowers. • Genera *Anemone* and *Pulsatilla*, family Ranunculaceae: several species, in particular the North American *A. patens* and the Eurasian *P. vulgaris*. ▷late 16th cent. (as *passe-flower*): from French *passe-fleur*. The change in spelling of the first word was due to association with archaic *pasque* 'Easter' (because of the plant's early flowering).

pas·quin·ade /ˌpaskwəˈnād/ ▶*n.* a satire or lampoon, originally one displayed or delivered publicly in a public place. ▷late 16th cent.: from Italian *pasquinata*, from *Pasquino*, the name of a statue in Rome on which abusive Latin verses were posted annually.

pass[1] /pas/ ▶*v.* **1** [*intrans.*] move in a specified direction: *he passed through towns and villages | the shells from the Allied guns were passing very low overhead.* ■ [*trans.*] cause (something) to move or lie in a specified direction or position: *he passed a weary hand across his forehead | pass an electric current through it.* ■ change from one state or condition to another: *homes that have passed from public to private ownership.* ■ [*intrans.*] die (used euphemistically): *his father had passed to the afterlife | she* **passed away** *peacefully in her sleep | a good and decent man has* **passed on.** **2** [*trans.*] go past or across; leave behind or on one side in proceeding: *she passed a rest area with a pay phone | the two vehicles had no room to pass each other |* [*intrans.*] *we will not let you pass.* ■ go beyond the limits of; surpass; exceed: *this item has passed its sell-by date.* ■ *Tennis* hit a winning shot past (an opponent). **3** [*intrans.*] (of time or a point in time) elapse; go by: *the day and night passed slowly | the moment had passed.* ■ happen; be done or said: *not another word* **passed between** *them |* [with *complement*] *this fact has passed almost unnoticed.* ■ [*trans.*] spend or use up (a period of time): *this was how they* **passed the time.** ■ come to an end: *the danger had passed.* **4** [*trans.*] transfer (something) to someone, esp. by handing or bequeathing it to the next person in a series: *your letter has been passed to Mr. Rich for action | please pass the fish |* [with *two objs.*] *he passed her a cup.* ■ [*intrans.*] be transferred from one person or place to another, esp. by inheritance: *infections can pass from mother to child at birth | if Ann remarried the estate would* **pass to** *her new husband.* ■ (in football, soccer, hockey, and other games) throw, kick, or hit (the ball or puck) to another player on one's own team. ■ put (something, esp. money) into circulation: *persons who have passed bad checks.* ■ [*intrans.*] (esp. of money) circulate; be current: *cash was passing briskly.* **5** [*trans.*] (of a candidate) be successful in (an examination, test, or course): *she passed her driving test.* ■ judge the performance or standard of (someone or something) to be satisfactory: [*trans.*] *he was passed fit by army doctors.* ■ [*intrans.*] be accepted as adequate; go uncensured: *she couldn't agree, but* **let it pass** *| her rather revealing dress passed without comment.* ■ [*intrans.*] (**pass as/for**) be accepted as or taken for: *he could pass for a native of Sweden.* **6** [*trans.*] (of a legislative or other official body) approve or put into effect (a proposal or law) by voting on it: *the bill was passed despite fierce opposition.* ■ (of a proposal or law) be examined and approved by (a legislative body or process): *bills that passed committees last year.* ■ [*intrans.*] (of a proposal) be approved: *the bill passed by 164 votes to 107.* **7** [*trans.*] pronounce (a judgment or judicial sentence): **passing** *judgment* **on** *these crucial issues | it is now my duty to* **pass** *sentence* **upon** *you.* ■ utter (something, esp. criticism): *she would pass remarks about the Paxtons in their own house.* ■ [*intrans.*] (**pass on/upon**) *archaic* adjudicate or give a judgment on: *a jury could not be trusted to pass upon the question of Endicott's good faith.* **8** [*trans.*] discharge (something, esp. urine or feces) from the body: *frequency of passing urine.* **9** [*intrans.*] forgo one's turn in a game or an offered opportunity: *we* **pass on** *dessert and have coffee.* ■ [as *exclam.*] said when one does not know the answer to a question, for example in a quizzing game: *to the enigmatic question we answered "Pass."* ■ [*trans.*] (of a company) not declare or pay (a dividend). ■ *Bridge* make no bid when it is one's turn during an auction. ■ [*trans.*] *Bridge* make no bid in response to (one's partner's bid): *East had passed his partner's opening bid of one club.*
▶*phrasal v.* □ **pass someone by** happen without being noticed or fully experienced by someone: *sometimes I feel that life is passing me by.* □ **pass off** (of proceedings) happen or be carried through in a specified, usually satisfactory, way: *the weekend had passed off entirely without incident.* □ **pass something off 1** evade or lightly dismiss an awkward remark: *he made a light joke and passed it off.* **2** *Basketball* throw the ball to a teammate who is unguarded: *he scored eight times and passed off six assists.* □ **pass someone/something off as** falsely represent a person or thing as (something else): *the drink was packaged in champagne bottles and was being passed off as the real stuff.* □ **pass out 1** become unconscious: *he consumed enough alcohol to make him pass out.* **2** *Brit.* complete one's initial training in the armed forces. **3** (of bridge players) not play a hand because all players have passed. □ **pass someone over** ignore the claims of someone to promotion or advancement: *he was passed over for a cabinet job.* □ **pass something over** avoid mentioning or considering something: *I shall pass over the matter of the transitional period.* □ **pass something up** refrain from taking up an opportunity: *he passed up a career in pro baseball.*
▶*n.* **1** an act or instance of moving past or through something: *repeated passes with the swipe card | an unmarked plane had been making passes over his house.* ■ *informal* an amorous or sexual advance made to someone: *she* **made a pass at** *Stephen.* ■ an act of passing the hands over anything, as in conjuring or hypnotism. ■ a thrust in fencing. ■ a juggling trick. ■ *Bridge* an act of refraining from bidding during the auction. ■ *Computing* a single scan through a set of data or a program. **2** a successful completion of an examination or course, usually without honors: [as *adj.*] *a 100 percent pass rate.* ■ the grade indicating this. ■ *Brit.* an achievement of a university degree without honors: [as *adj.*] *a pass degree.* **3** a card, ticket, or permit giving authorization for the holder to enter or have access to a place, form of transportation, or event. **4** (in football, soccer, hockey, and other games) an act of throwing, kicking, or hitting the ball or puck to another player on the same team. **5** a state or situation of a specified, usually bad or difficult, nature: *this is a sad pass for a fixture that used to crackle with excitement.* ▷Middle English: from Old French *passer*, based on Latin *passus* 'pace.' —**pass·er** *n. he's a good passer of the ball.*
▶*PHRASES* □ **come to a pretty pass** reach a bad or regrettable state of affairs. □ **pass the baton** see BATON. □ **pass the buck** see BUCK[3]. □ **pass one's eye over** read (a document) cursorily. □ **pass the hat** see HAT. □ **pass one's lips** see LIP. □ **pass muster** see MUSTER. □ **pass the parcel** see PARCEL. □ **pass the time of day** see TIME. □ **pass water** urinate.

pass[2] ▶*n.* a route over or through mountains: *the pass over the mountain was open again after the snows |* [in *place names*] *the Khyber Pass.* ■ a passage for fish over or past a weir or dam. ■ a navigable channel, esp. at the mouth of a river. ▷Middle English (in the sense 'division of a text, passage through'): variant of PACE[1], influenced by PASS[1] and French *pas*.
▶*PHRASE* □ **head** (or **cut**) **someone/something off at the pass** forestall someone or something: *the doctor's aim to head the infection off at the pass.*

pass. ▶*abbr.* ■ passenger. ■ passim. ■ passive.

pass·a·ble /ˈpasəbəl/ ▶*adj.* **1** just good enough to be acceptable; satisfactory: *he spoke passable English.* **2** (of a route or road) clear of obstacles and able to be traveled along or on: *the road was passable with care.* ▷late Middle English: from Old French, from *passer* 'to pass.' —**pass·a·bly** /-əblē/ *adv.*

pas·sa·ca·glia /ˌpäsəˈkälyə/ ▶*n.* *Music* a composition similar to a chaconne, typically in slow triple time with variations over a ground bass. ▷Italian, from Spanish *pasacalle*, from *pasar* 'to pass' + *calle* 'street' (because originally it was a dance often played in the streets).

pas·sade /pəˈsād/ ▶*n.* a movement performed in advanced dressage and classical riding, in which the horse performs a 180° turn, with its forelegs describing a large circle and its hind legs a smaller one. ▷mid 17th cent.: French, from Italian *passata* or Provençal *passada*, from medieval Latin *passare* 'to pass.'

pas·sage[1] /ˈpasij/ ▶*n.* **1** the act or process of moving through, under, over, or past something on the way from one place to another: *there were moorings for boats wanting passage through the lock.* ■ the act or process of moving forward: *despite the passage of time she still loved him.* ■ the right to pass through somewhere: *we obtained a permit for safe passage from the embassy.* ■ a journey or ticket for a journey by sea or air: *he then* **booked passage** *home aboard a Spanish warship.* ■ *Ornithology* (of a migrating bird) the action of passing through a place en route to its final destination: *the species occurs regularly* **on passage** *|* [as *adj.*] *a passage migrant.* ■ *Medicine & Biology* the process of propagating microorganisms or cells in a series of host organisms or culture media, so as to maintain them or modify their virulence. **2** a narrow way, typically having walls on either side, allowing access between buildings or to different rooms within a building; a passageway. ■ a duct, vessel, or other channel in the body. **3** the process of transition from one state to another: *an allegory on the theme of the passage from ignorance to knowledge.* ■ the passing of a bill into law: *a catalyst for the unrest was the passage of a privatization law.* **4** a short extract from a book or other printed material: *he picked up the newspaper and read the passage again.* ■ a section of a piece of music: *nothing obscures the outlines of an orchestral passage more than a drumroll on an unrelated note.* ■ an episode in a longer activity such as a sporting event: *a neat passage of midfield play.*
▶*v.* [*trans.*] *Medicine & Biology* subject (a strain of microorganisms or cells) to a passage: *each recombinant virus was passaged nine times successively.* ▷Middle English: from Old French, based on Latin *passus* 'pace.'
▶*PHRASES* □ **passage of** (or **at**) **arms** a fight or dispute. □ **work one's passage** work in return for a free place on a voyage: *he worked his passage home as a steward.*

pas·sage[2] ▶*n.* a movement performed in advanced dressage and classical riding, in which the horse executes a slow elevated trot, giving the impression of dancing. ▷early 18th cent.: from French *passage*, from an alteration of Italian *passeggiare* 'to walk, pace,' based on Latin *passus* 'pace.'

pas·sage hawk ▶*n.* a hawk caught for training while on migration, esp. as an immature bird of less than twelve months. Compare with HAGGARD.

pas·sage·way /ˈpasij,wā/ ▶*n.* a long, narrow way, typically having walls on either side, that allows access between buildings or to different rooms within a building.

pas·sage·work /ˈpasij,wərk/ ▶*n.* music notable chiefly for the scope it affords for virtuoso playing: *some of the passagework in early Beethoven is very awkward.*

Pas·sa·ic /pəˈsāik/ an industrial city in northeastern New Jersey, on the Passaic River; pop. 67,861.

Pas·sa·ma·quod·dy /ˌpasəməˈkwädē/ ▸*n.* (*pl.* same or **-dies**) **1** a member of a North American Indian people inhabiting parts of southeastern Maine and, formerly, southwestern New Brunswick. **2** the Algonquian language of this people.
▸*adj.* of or relating to this people or their language. ▷from Passamaquoddy *pestəmokhatíyək*, 'place where pollack are plentiful,' referring to *Passamaquoddy* Bay.

Pas·sa·ma·quod·dy Bay /ˌpasəməˈkwädē/ (also **Quoddy Bay**) an inlet of the Bay of Fundy, at the border of Maine and New Brunswick, noted for its powerful tides.

pas·sant /ˈpasənt/ ▸*adj.* [usu. *postpositive*] *Heraldry* (of an animal) represented as walking, with the right front foot raised. The animal is depicted in profile facing the dexter (left) side with the tail raised, unless otherwise specified (e.g., as "passant guardant"). ▷late Middle English: from Old French, literally 'proceeding,' present participle of *passer*.

pas·sa·ta /pəˈsätə/ ▸*n.* a thick paste made from strained tomatoes and used esp. in Italian cooking. ▷Italian.

pass·band /ˈpasˌband/ ▸*n.* a frequency band within which signals are transmitted by a filter without attenuation.

pass·book /ˈpasˌbo͝ok/ ▸*n.* a booklet issued by a bank to an account holder for recording sums deposited and withdrawn.

Pass·chen·daele, Battle of /ˈpasHənˌdāl/ (also **Passen·dale**) a prolonged episode of trench warfare involving appalling loss of life during World War I in 1917, near the village of Passchendaele in western Belgium. It is also known as the third Battle of Ypres.

pass door ▸*n.* a door in a theater connecting the backstage area and the auditorium.

pas·sé /paˈsā/ ▸*adj.* [*predic.*] no longer fashionable; out of date: *miniskirts are passé—the best skirts are knee-length.* ■ *archaic* (esp. of a woman) past one's prime. ▷French, literally 'gone by,' past participle of *passer*.

passed ball ▸*n.* *Baseball* a pitch that the catcher fails to stop or control, enabling a base runner to advance.

passed pawn ▸*n.* *Chess* a pawn that no enemy pawn can stop from queening.

pas·seg·gia·ta /ˌpasəˈjätə/ ▸*n.* (*pl.* **-gia·te** /-ˈjätā/) a leisurely walk or stroll, esp. one taken in the evening; a promenade (used with reference to the tradition of taking such a walk in Italy or Italian-speaking communities). ▷Italian.

pas·sel /ˈpasəl/ ▸*n.* *informal* a large group of people or things of indeterminate number; a pack: ***a passel of*** *journalists.* ▷mid 19th cent.: representing a pronunciation of **PARCEL**.

passe·men·terie /pasˈmentrē/ ▸*n.* decorative textile trimming consisting of gold or silver lace, gimp, or braid. ▷early 17th cent.: from French, from *passement* 'gold lace.'

Pas·sen·dale, Battle of /ˈpasənˌdāl/ variant spelling of **PASSCHENDAELE, BATTLE OF**.

pas·sen·ger /ˈpasinjər/ ▸*n.* a traveler on a public or private conveyance other than the driver, pilot, or crew. ▷Middle English: from the Old French adjective *passager* 'passing, transitory,' used as a noun, from *passage* (see **PASSAGE**[1]).

pas·sen·ger mile ▸*n.* one mile traveled by one passenger, as a unit of traffic.

pas·sen·ger pi·geon ▸*n.* an extinct long-tailed North American pigeon, noted for its long migrations in huge flocks. It was relentlessly hunted, the last individual dying in captivity in 1914. • *Ectopistes migratorius*, family Columbidae.

passe-par·tout /ˌpas pärˈto͞o/ ▸*n.* **1** a picture or photograph simply mounted between a piece of glass and a sheet of cardboard (or two pieces of glass) stuck together at the edges with adhesive tape. ■ adhesive tape or paper used in making such a frame. **2** *archaic* a master key. ▷late 17th cent.: from French, literally 'passes everywhere.'

passe·pied /päsˈpyā/ ▸*n.* a dance like a quick minuet, popular in the 17th and 18th centuries. ▷French, from *passer* 'to pass' + *pied* 'foot.'

pass·er·by /ˈpasərˌbī/ (also **pass·er-by**) ▸*n.* (*pl.* **passers·by**) a person who happens to be going past something, esp. on foot.

pas·ser·ine /ˈpasərin; -ˌrīn/ *Ornithology* ▸*adj.* of, relating to, or denoting birds of a large order distinguished by feet that are adapted for perching, including all songbirds.
▸*n.* a passerine bird; a perching bird.

> The order Passeriformes comprises more than half of all bird species, the remainder being known informally as the **nonpasserines**. All passerines in Europe belong to the suborder Oscines (the **oscine passerines**), so that the term is effectively synonymous with 'songbird' there (see **SONGBIRD**). Those of the suborder Deutero-Oscines (the **suboscine passerines**) are found mainly in America.

▷late 18th cent.: from Latin *passer* 'sparrow' + **-INE**[1].

pas seul /ˌpä ˈsəl/ ▸*n.* a dance for one person. ▷French, literally 'single step.'

Pass·face /ˈpasˌfās/ ▸*n.* **1** *trademark* a security system in which a user must recognize pictures of human faces in order to gain access to a computer or computer network: *their site uses Passface because it's less hackable than regular passwords.* **2** (**pass·face**) a digital photograph of a human face that is used for identification in a Passface system: *the company uses cameras and passfaces to make sure only authorized employees get through the door.* ▷on the pattern of *password*.

pass-fail ▸*adj.* denoting a class, course, or system of grading in which the only two grades given are "pass" and "fail.".

pas·si·ble /ˈpasəbəl/ ▸*adj.* *Christian Theology* capable of feeling or suffering; susceptible to sensation or emotion: *only the humanity of Jesus is regarded as passible.* ▷late Middle English: from Old French, from late Latin *passibilis*, from Latin *pass-* 'suffered,' from the verb *pati*. —**pas·si·bil·i·ty** /ˌpasəˈbilitē/ *n.*

pas·sim /ˈpasim/ ▸*adv.* (of allusions or references in a published work) to be found at various places throughout the text. ▷Latin, from *passus* 'scattered,' from the verb *pandere*.

pass·ing /ˈpasiNG/ ▸*adj.* [*attrib.*] **1** going past: *passing cars.* **2** (of a period of time) going by: *she detested him more with every passing second.* ■ carried out quickly and lightly: *a passing glance.* **3** meeting or surpassing the requirements of a course or examination: *a passing grade.*
▸*n.* [in *sing.*] **1** the passage of something, esp. time: *with **the passing of** the years she had become a little eccentric.* ■ the action of throwing, kicking, or hitting a ball or puck to another team member during a sports match: *his play showed good passing and good control* | [as *adj.*] *a good passing movement.* **2** used euphemistically to refer to a person's death: *her passing will be felt deeply by many people.* ■ the end of something: ***the passing of** the Cold War and the rise of a new Europe.* —**pass·ing·ly** *adv.*
▸*PHRASE* □ **in passing** briefly and casually: *the research was mentioned only in passing.*

pass·ing bell ▸*n.* *chiefly historical* a bell rung immediately after a death as a signal for prayers.

pass·ing note (also **passing tone**) ▸*n.* *Music* a note not belonging to the harmony but interposed to secure a smooth transition from one chord to another.

pass·ing shot ▸*n.* *Tennis* a winning shot beyond and out of reach of one's opponent.

pas·sion /ˈpasHən/ ▸*n.* **1** strong and barely controllable emotion: *a man of impetuous passion.* See note at **EMOTION**. ■ a state or outburst of such emotion: *oratory in which he gradually works himself up into a passion.* ■ intense sexual love: *their all-consuming passion for each other* | *she nurses a passion for Thomas.* ■ an intense desire or enthusiasm for something: *the English have **a passion for** gardens.* ■ a thing arousing enthusiasm: *modern furniture is a particular passion of Bill's.* **2** (**the Passion**) the suffering and death of Jesus: *meditations on the Passion of Christ.* ■ a narrative of this from any of the Gospels. ■ a musical setting of any of these narratives: *an aria from Bach's St. Matthew Passion.* ▷Middle English: from Old French, from late Latin *passio(n-)* (chiefly a term in Christian theology), from Latin *pati* 'suffer.' —**pas·sion·less** *adj.*

pas·sion·al /ˈpasHənl/ ▸*adj.* *rare* of, relating to, or marked by passion: *a current of passional electric energy.*
▸*n.* *Christian Church* a book about the sufferings of saints and martyrs, for reading on their feast days.

pas·sion·ate /ˈpasHənit/ ▸*adj.* showing or caused by strong feelings or a strong belief: *passionate pleas for help* | *he's **passionate about** football.* ■ showing or caused by intense feelings of sexual love: *a passionate kiss.* ■ dominated by or easily affected by intense emotion: *a strong-minded and passionate man.* ▷late Middle English (also in the senses 'easily moved to passion' and 'enraged'): from medieval Latin *passionatus* 'full of passion,' from *passio* (see **PASSION**). —**pas·sion·ate·ly** *adv.* —**pas·sion·ate·ness** *n.*

pas·sion·flow·er /ˈpasHənˌflou(-ə)r/ (also **pas·sion flow·er**) ▸*n.* an evergreen climbing plant of warm regions that bears distinctive flowers with parts that supposedly resemble instruments of the Crucifixion. • Genus *Passiflora*, family Passifloraceae.

pas·sion fruit (also **pas·sion·fruit**) ▸*n.* the edible purple fruit of a kind of passionflower that is grown commercially, esp. in tropical America. Also called **GRANADILLA**. • This fruit is obtained from *Passiflora edulis*, family Passifloraceae.

pas·sion play ▸*n.* a dramatic performance representing Christ's Passion from the Last Supper to the Crucifixion.

Pas·sion Sun·day ▸*n.* the fifth Sunday in Lent.

Pas·sion·tide /ˈpasHənˌtīd/ ▸*n.* the last two weeks of Lent.

Pas·sion Week ▸*n.* **1** the week between Passion Sunday and Palm Sunday. **2** older name for **HOLY WEEK**.

pas·si·vate /ˈpasəˌvāt/ ▸*v.* [*trans.*] [usu. as *adj.*] (**passi·vated**) make (a metal or other substance) unreactive by altering the surface layer or coating the surface with a thin inert layer: *components are made from passivated and anodized aluminum.* ■ *Electronics* coat (a semiconductor) with inert material to protect it from contamination. —**pas·si·va·tion** /ˌpasəˈvāsHən/ *n.*

pas·sive /ˈpasiv/ ▸*adj.* **1** accepting or allowing what happens or what others do, without active response or resistance: *the women were portrayed as passive victims.* ■ *Chemistry* (of a metal) made unreactive by a thin inert surface layer of oxide. ■ (of a circuit or device) containing no source of electromotive force. ■ (of radar or a satellite) receiving or reflecting radiation from a transmitter or target rather than generating its own signal. ■ relating to or denoting heating systems that make use of incident sunlight as an energy source. **2** *Grammar* denoting or relating to a voice of verbs in which the subject undergoes the action of the verb (e.g., *they were killed* as opposed to *he killed them*). The opposite of **ACTIVE**.
▸*n.* *Grammar* a passive form of a verb. ■ (**the passive**) the passive voice. ▷late Middle English (in sense 2, also in the sense '(exposed to) suffering, acted on by an external agency'): from Latin *passivus*, from *pass-* 'suffered,' from the verb *pati*. —**pas·sive·ly** *adv.* —**pas·sive·ness** *n.* —**pas·siv·i·ty** /paˈsivitē/ *n.*

pas·sive-ag·gres·sive ▸*adj.* of or denoting a type of behavior or personality characterized by indirect resistance to the demands of others and an avoidance of direct confrontation, as in procrastinating, pouting, or misplacing important materials.

pas·sive im·mu·ni·ty ▸*n.* *Physiology* the short-term immunity that results from the introduction of antibodies from another person or animal. Compare with **ACTIVE IMMUNITY**.

pas·sive ma·trix ▸*n.* *Electronics* a display system in which individual pixels are selected using two control voltages for the row and column.

pas·sive re·sist·ance ▸*n.* nonviolent opposition to authority, esp. a refusal to cooperate with legal requirements: *they called for protest in the form of passive resistance.*

pas·sive res·traint ▸*n.* a car safety device that is activated by the force of a collision or other sudden stop and that aims to prevent injury to a passenger.

pas·sive smok·ing ▸*n.* the involuntary inhaling of smoke from other people's cigarettes, cigars, or pipes: *children are more susceptible to the effects of passive smoking.*

pas·siv·ize /ˈpasəˌvīz/ ▸*v.* [*trans.*] *Grammar* convert (a verb or clause) into the passive form: *a sentence that has been passivized.* ■ [*intrans.*] (of a verb or clause) be convertible in this way: *transitive verbs in idiomatic expressions frequently will not passivize.* —**pas·siv·iz·a·ble** /-əbəl/ *adj.* —**pas·siv·i·za·tion** /ˌpasəvəˈzāsHən/ *n.*

pass·key /ˈpasˌkē/ ▸*n.* **1** a key to the door of a restricted area, given only to those who are officially allowed access. **2** a master key.

Pas·sos, John Dos, see **DOS PASSOS**.

Pass·o·ver /ˈpasˌōvər/ ▸*n.* the major Jewish spring festival that commemorates the liberation of the Israelites from Egyptian bondage, lasting seven or eight days from the 15th day of Nisan. ■ another term for **PASCHAL LAMB**. ▷from *pass over* 'pass without touching,' with reference to the exemption of

Pronunciation Key ə *ago*; ər *over*; ˈə *or* ˌə *up*; ˈər *or* ˌər *fur*; a *hat*; ā *rate*; ä *car*; CH *chew*; e *let*; ē *see*; e(ə)r *air*; i *fit*; ī *by*; i(ə)r *ear*; NG *sing*; ō *go*; ô *for*; oi *boy*; o͝o *good*; o͞o *goo*; ou *out*; SH *she*; TH *thin*; T͟H *then*; (h)w *why*; ZH *vision*

the Israelites from the death of their firstborn (Exod. 12).

pass·port /ˈpas,pôrt/ ▸*n.* an official document issued by a government, certifying the holder's identity and citizenship and entitling them to travel under its protection to and from foreign countries. ■ [in *sing.*] a thing that ensures admission to or the achievement of something: *the sport utility vehicle seemed like a* ***a passport to*** *new adventures.* ▷late 15th cent. (denoting authorization to enter or depart from a port): from French *passeport,* from *passer* 'to pass' + *port* 'seaport.'

pas·sus /ˈpasəs/ ▸*n.* (*pl.* same) a section, division, or canto of a story or poem, esp. a medieval one. ▷late 16th cent.: from Latin, literally 'step, pace,' in medieval Latin 'passage of a book.'

pass·word /ˈpas,wərd/ ▸*n.* a secret word or phrase that must be used to gain admission to something. ■ a string of characters that allows someone access to a computer system.

past /past/ ▸*adj.* gone by in time and no longer existing: *the danger is now past.* ■ [*attrib.*] belonging to a former time: *they made a study of the reasons why past attempts had failed | he is a past chairman of the society.* ■ [*attrib.*] (of a specified period of time) occurring before and leading up to the time of speaking or writing: *the band has changed over the past twelve months.* ■ *Grammar* (of a tense) expressing an action that has happened or a state that previously existed.
▸*n.* **1** (usu. **the past**) the time or a period of time before the moment of speaking or writing: *she found it hard to make ends meet in the past.* ■ the events of an earlier time: *the war-damaged church is preserved as a reminder of the past.* ■ the history of a person, country, or institution: *the monuments act as guidelines through the country's colorful past.* ■ a part of a person's history that is considered to be shameful: *the heroine was a lady with a past.* **2** *Grammar* a past tense or form of a verb: *a simple past of the first conjugation.*
▸*prep.* to or on the further side of: *he rode on past the crossroads.* ■ in front of or from one side to the other of: *he began to drive slowly past the houses.* ■ beyond in time; later than: *by this time it was past 3:30.* ■ no longer capable of: *he is past giving the best advice.* ■ beyond the scope of: *my hair was past praying for.*
▸*adv.* **1** so as to pass from one side of something to the other: *large angelfish swim slowly past.* ■ used to indicate the lapse of time: *a week went past and nothing changed.* **2** at a time later by a specified amount than a particular known hour: *we're having speeches in the dining room at half past.* ▷Middle English: variant of *passed,* past participle of PASS[1]. —**past·ness** *n.*
▸*PHRASE* □ **not put it past someone** believe someone to be capable of doing something wrong or rash: *I wouldn't put it past him to slip something into the drinks.*

pas·ta /ˈpästə/ ▸*n.* a dish originally from Italy consisting of dough made from durum wheat and water, extruded or stamped into various shapes and typically cooked in boiling water. ▷late 19th cent.: from Italian, literally 'paste.'

paste /pāst/ ▸*n.* a thick, soft, moist substance, usually produced by mixing dry ingredients with a liquid: *blend onions, sugar, and oil to a paste.* ■ a substance such as this that is used as an adhesive, esp. for sticking paper and other light materials: *wallpaper paste.* ■ a mixture consisting mainly of clay and water that is used in making ceramic ware, esp. a mixture of low plasticity based on kaolin for making porcelain. ■ a hard vitreous composition used in making imitation gems: [as *adj.*] *paste brooches.*
▸*v.* [*trans.*] **1** coat with paste: *when coating walls with fabric, paste the wall, not the fabric.* ■ [with *obj.* and *adverbial of place*] fasten or stick (something) onto something with paste: *ads are pasted on the walls.* ■ *Computing* insert (text) into a document. **2** *informal* beat or defeat severely: *he pasted the guy and tied his ankles together.* ▷late Middle English: from Old French, from late Latin *pasta* 'medicinal preparation in the shape of a small square,' probably from Greek *pastē,* (plural) *pasta* 'barley porridge,' from *pastos* 'sprinkled.'

paste·board /ˈpās(t),bôrd/ ▸*n.* a type of thin board made by pasting together sheets of paper.

paste·down /ˈpās(t),doun/ ▸*n.* (in bookbinding) the part of an endpaper that is pasted to the inside of the cover.

pas·tel /paˈstel/ ▸*n.* **1** a crayon made of powdered pigments bound with gum or resin. ■ a work of art created using such crayons: *a pastel entitled "Girl Braiding Her Hair."* **2** a soft and delicate shade of a color: *the subtlest of pastels and creams.*
▸*adj.* of a soft and delicate shade or color: *pastel blue curtains.* ▷mid 17th cent.: via French from Italian *pastello,* diminutive of *pasta* 'paste.' —**pas·tel·ist** /-ist/ (also **pas·tel·list**) *n.*

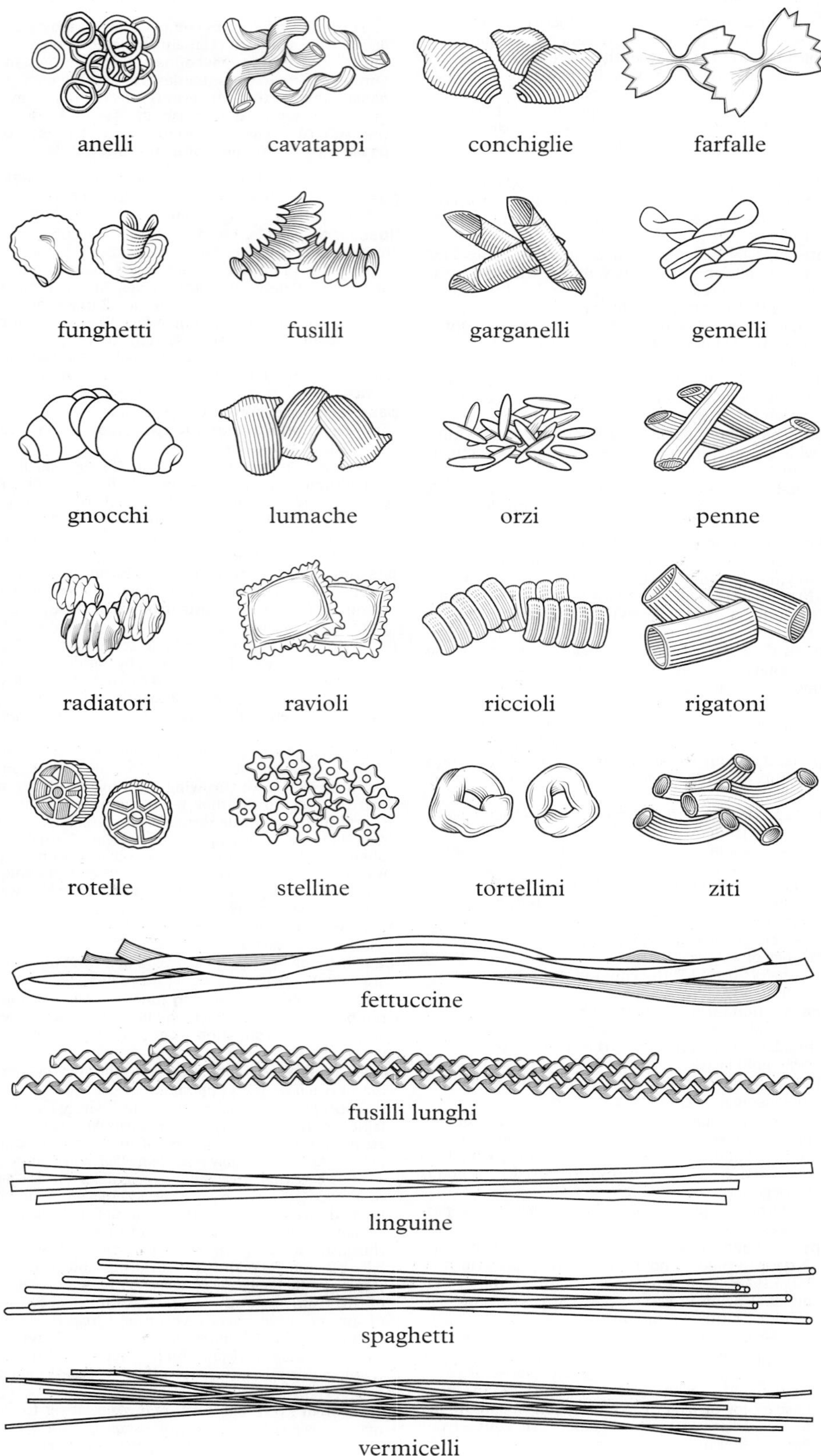

pasta shapes

pas·tern /ˈpastərn/ ▸*n.* the sloping part of a horse's foot between the fetlock and the hoof. ■ a corresponding part in some other domestic animals. ▷Middle English: from Old French *pasturon,* from *pasture* 'strap for hobbling a horse,' transferred in sense to the joint of the foot.

Pas·ter·nak /ˈpastər,nak/, Boris (Leonidovich) (1890–1960), Russian poet, novelist, and translator. His best-known novel, *Doctor Zhivago* (1957), describes the experience of the Russian intelligentsia during the Russian Revolution; it was banned in the Soviet

Union. He was forced by Soviet authorities to turn down the Nobel Prize for Literature in 1958.

paste-up ▸*n.* a document prepared for copying or printing by combining and pasting various sections on a backing.

Pas·teur /pas'tər; pä'stœr/, Louis (1822–95), French chemist and bacteriologist. He introduced pasteurization and made pioneering studies in vaccination techniques.

pas·teu·rel·lo·sis /ˌpastərə'lōsis/ ▸*n.* a bacterial infection commonly affecting animals and sometimes transferred to humans through bites and scratches. • The causative bacteria are Gram-negative rods of the genus *Pasteurella,* in particular *P. multocida.* ▹early 20th cent.: from French *pasteurellose* (from the name **PASTEUR**) + **-OSIS**.

pas·teur·ize /'pascHəˌrīz/ ▸*v.* [*trans.*] [often as *adj.*] (**pasteurized**) subject (milk, wine, or other products) to a process of partial sterilization, esp. one involving heat treatment or irradiation, thus making the product safe for consumption and improving its keeping quality: *pasteurized milk.* ▹late 19th cent.: from the name of L. **PASTEUR** + **-IZE**. **—pas·teur·i·za·tion** /ˌpascHəri'zāsHən/ *n.* **—pas·teur·iz·er** *n.*

Pas·teur pi·pette ▸*n.* a simple glass pipette drawn into a capillary tube at one end, used with a rubber nipple fitted to the other.

pas·tic·cio /pä'stēcHō/ ▸*n.* (*pl.* **-cios**) another term for **PASTICHE**. ▹Italian.

pas·tiche /pa'stēsH; pä-/ ▸*n.* an artistic work in a style that imitates that of another work, artist, or period: *the operetta is **a pastiche of** 18th century styles | the songs amount to much more than blatant pastiche.* ■ an artistic work consisting of a medley of pieces taken from various sources. ■ a confused mixture or jumble: *his speech is a pastiche of false starts and unfinished sentences.*
▸*v.* [*trans.*] imitate the style of (an artist or work): *Gauguin took himself to a Pacific island and pastiched the primitive art he found there.* ▹late 19th cent.: from French, from Italian *pasticcio,* based on late Latin *pasta* 'paste.'

pas·ti·cheur /pas'tēsHər/ ▸*n.* an artist who creates a pastiche: *he was unrivaled as a parodist and pasticheur.*

past·ie ▸*n.* (*pl.* **-ies**) **1** /'pāstē/ (usu. **pasties**) *informal* a decorative covering for the nipple worn by a stripper. **2** /'pastē/ variant spelling of **PASTY**[1].

pas·tille /pa'stēl/ ▸*n.* a small candy or lozenge. ■ a small pellet of aromatic paste burned as a perfume or deodorizer. ▹mid 17th cent.: from French, from Latin *pastillus* 'little loaf, lozenge,' from *panis* 'loaf.'

pas·time /'pasˌtīm/ ▸*n.* an activity that someone does regularly for enjoyment rather than work; a hobby: *his favorite pastimes were shooting and golf.* ▹late 15th cent.: from the verb **PASS**[1] + **TIME**, translating French *passe-temps.*

past·ing /'pāstiNG/ ▸*n. informal* a severe beating or defeat: *an effort to raise party turnout at the polls and avoid a pasting.*

pas·tis /pä'stēs/ ▸*n.* (*pl.* same) an aniseed-flavored aperitif. ▹French.

pas·tit·sio /pä'stētsyō/ ▸*n.* a Greek dish consisting of macaroni, ground lamb, grated cheese, and tomatoes topped with a béchamel sauce. ▹from modern Greek, literally 'hodgepodge.'

past mas·ter ▸*n.* **1** a person who is particularly skilled at a specified activity or art: *he's **a past master at** keeping his whereabouts secret.* **2** a person who has held the position of master in an organization.

pas·tor /'pastər/ ▸*n.* a minister in charge of a Christian church or congregation.
▸*v.* [*trans.*] be pastor of (a church or a congregation): *he pastored Peninsula Bible Church in Palo Alto* | [*intrans.*] *he continued to study law while pastoring in Chicago.* ▹late Middle English: from Anglo-Norman French *pastour,* from Latin *pastor* 'shepherd,' from *past-* 'fed, grazed,' from the verb *pascere.* **—pas·tor·ship** /-ˌsHip/ *n.*

pas·to·ral /'pastərəl; pas'tôrəl/ ▸*adj.* **1** (esp. of land or a farm) used for or related to the keeping or grazing of sheep or cattle: *scattered pastoral farms.* ■ associated with country life: *the view was pastoral, with rolling fields and grazing sheep.* ■ (of a work of art) portraying or evoking country life, typically in a romanticized or idealized form. **2** (in the Christian Church) concerning or appropriate to the giving of spiritual guidance: *pastoral and doctrinal issues | clergy doing pastoral work.*
▸*n.* a work of literature portraying an idealized version of country life: *the story, though a pastoral, has an actual connection with the life of agricultural labor.* ▹late Middle English: from Latin *pastoralis* 'relating to a shepherd,' from *pastor* 'shepherd' (see **PASTOR**). **—pas·to·ral·ism** /'pastərəˌlizəm/ *n.* **—pas·to·ral·ly** *adv.*

pas·to·rale /ˌpastə'räl; -'ral/ ▸*n.* (*pl.* **-rales** or **-ra·li** /-'rälē/) **1** a slow instrumental composition in compound time, usually with drone notes in the bass. **2** a simple musical play with a rural subject. ▹early 18th cent.: from Italian, literally 'pastoral' (adjective used as a noun).

Pas·to·ral E·pis·tles the books of the New Testament comprising the two letters of Paul to Timothy and the one to Titus.

pas·to·ral·ist /'pastərəlist/ ▸*n.* **1** a sheep or cattle farmer. **2** *archaic* a writer of pastorals.

pas·to·ral let·ter ▸*n.* an official letter from a bishop to all the clergy or members of his or her diocese.

pas·to·ral staff ▸*n.* a bishop's crozier.

pas·to·ral the·ol·o·gy ▸*n.* Christian theology that considers religious truth in relation to spiritual needs.

pas·tor·ate /'pastərit/ ▸*n.* the office or period of office of a pastor: *I left the pastorate in 1974.* ■ pastors collectively.

past par·ti·ci·ple ▸*n. Grammar* the form of a verb, typically ending in *-ed* in English, that is used in forming perfect and passive tenses and sometimes as an adjective, e.g., *looked* in *have you looked?* and *lost* in *lost property.*

past per·fect ▸*adj. Grammar* (of a tense) denoting an action completed prior to some past point of time specified or implied, formed in English by *had* and the past participle, as in *he had gone by then.*
▸*n.* the past perfect tense.

pas·tra·mi /pə'strämē/ ▸*n.* highly seasoned smoked beef, typically served in thin slices. ▹Yiddish.

pas·try /'pāstrē/ ▸*n.* (*pl.* **-tries**) a dough of flour, shortening, and water, used as a base and covering in baked dishes such as pies. ■ an item of food consisting of sweet pastry with a cream, jam, or fruit filling. ▹late Middle English (as a collective term): from **PASTE**, influenced by Old French *pastaierie.*

pas·try chef ▸*n.* a professional cook who specializes in making desserts, esp. cakes and pastries.

pas·try cream ▸*n.* a thick, creamy custard used as a filling for cakes or flans.

pas·tur·age /'pascHərij/ ▸*n.* land used for pasture. ■ the occupation or process of pasturing cattle, sheep, or other grazing animals: *the human species has only engaged in pasturage for 12,000 to 15,000 years.* ▹early 16th cent.: from Old French, from *pasture* (see **PASTURE**).

pas·ture /'pascHər/ ▸*n.* land covered with grass and other low plants suitable for grazing animals, esp. cattle or sheep. ■ the grass and herbage growing on such land: *do not let your pasture grow too fast so that the plants become rank.* ■ *figurative* a place or activity regarded as offering new opportunities: *he has departed for the **greener pastures** of a corner office.*
▸*v.* [*trans.*] put (animals) in a pasture to graze: *they pastured their cows in the water meadow.* ■ [*intrans.*] (of animals) graze: *the livestock pastured and the crops grew.* ▹Middle English: from Old French, from late Latin *pastura* 'grazing,' from *past-* 'grazed,' from the verb *pascere.*
▸*PHRASE* □ **put someone out to pasture** force someone to retire.

pas·ture·land /'pascHərˌland/ ▸*n.* land used as pasture.

pas·ture rose ▸*n.* a wild rose of the eastern U.S. with deep pink flowers and straight, thin thorns. Also called **CAROLINA ROSE**. • *Rosa carolina,* family Rosaceae.

pasture rose

past·y[1] /'pastē/ (also **past·ie**) ▸*n.* (*pl.* **past·ies**) *chiefly Brit.* a folded pastry case filled with seasoned meat and vegetables. ▹Middle English: from Old French *paste(e),* based on late Latin *pasta* 'paste.'

past·y[2] /'pāstē/ ▸*adj.* (**past·i·er, past·i·est**) **1** (of a person's face) unhealthily pale: *a pasty complexion.* **2** of or like paste: *a pasty mixture.* **—past·i·ness** /-stēnis/ *n.*

pat[1] /pat/ ▸*v.* (**pat·ted, pat·ting**) [*trans.*] touch quickly and gently with the flat of the hand: *he patted him consolingly on the shoulder* | [*trans.*] *a nurse washed her all over and patted her dry.* ■ draw attention to (something) by tapping it gently: *he patted the bench beside him and I sat down.* ■ [*trans.*] mold into shape or put in position with gentle taps: *she patted down the earth in each pot.*
▸*n.* **1** a light stroke with the hand: *giving him a friendly pat on the arm, she went off to join the others.* **2** a compact mass of soft material: *a **pat of butter**.* ▹late Middle English (as a noun denoting a blow with something flat): probably imitative. The verb dates from the mid 16th cent.
▸*PHRASES* □ **a pat on the back** an expression of approval or congratulation: *they deserve a pat on the back for a job well done.* □ **pat someone on the back** express approval of or admiration for someone: *she needs her own claque to applaud and pat her on the back.*

pat[2] ▸*adj.* simple and somewhat glib or unconvincing: *instead of enlightened minds I found prejudice and pat answers.*
▸*adv.* at exactly the right moment or in the right way; conveniently or opportunely: *the happy ending **came** rather **pat**.* ▹late 16th cent.: related to **PAT**[1]; apparently originally symbolic: a frequently found early use was *hit pat* (i.e., hit as if with a flat blow). **—pat·ly** *adv.* **—pat·ness** *n.*
▸*PHRASES* □ **down pat** see **DOWN**[1]. □ **stand pat** stick stubbornly to one's opinion or decision: *many ranchers stood pat with the old strains of cattle.* ■ (in poker and blackjack) retain one's hand as dealt, without drawing other cards.

Pat. ▸*abbr.* Patent.

pa·ta·gi·um /pə'tājēəm/ ▸*n.* (*pl.* **-gi·a** /-jēə/) *Zoology* a membrane or fold of skin between the forelimbs and hind limbs on each side of a bat or gliding mammal. ■ *Entomology* a lobe that covers the wing joint in many moths. ▹early 19th cent.: from Latin, denoting gold edging on the edge of a Roman lady's tunic, from Greek *patageion.*

Pat·a·go·ni·a /ˌpatə'gōnēə/ a region in South America, in southern Argentina and Chile. Mostly a dry, barren plateau, it extends from the Colorado River in central Argentina to the Strait of Magellan and from the Andes to the Atlantic coast. ▹from obsolete *Patagon,* denoting a member of a native people alleged by travelers of the 17th and 18th cents. to be the tallest known. **—Pat·a·go·ni·an** *adj.* & *n.*

Pat·a·go·ni·an tooth·fish /'tōōTHˌfisH/ ▸*n.* a demersal food fish of Antarctic waters, marketed as Chilean sea bass and recently overfished. • *Dissostichus eleginoides,* family Nototheniidae.

Pa·ta·li·pu·tra /ˌpätälē'pōōtrə/ ancient name for **PATNA**.

pa·ta·phys·ics /ˌpätə'fiziks/ ▸*plural n.* [usu. treated as *sing.*] the branch of philosophy that deals with an imaginary realm additional to metaphysics. ▹1940s: from Greek *ta epi ta metaphusika,* literally 'the (works) imposed on the Metaphysics.' The concept was introduced by Alfred Jarry (1873–1907), French writer of the Absurd.

pa·tas mon·key /pə'tä/ ▸*n.* a central African guenon with reddish-brown fur, a black face, and a white mustache. • *Erythrocebus patas,* family Cercopithecidae. ▹mid 18th cent.: *patas* from Senegalese French, from Wolof *pata.*

Pa·tau's syn·drome /pä'touz/ ▸*n. Medicine* a congenital disorder in which there are three copies of chromosome 13, 14, or 15 instead of the usual two. This results in brain, heart, and kidney defects that are usually fatal soon after birth. ▹1960s: named after Klaus Patau, 20th-cent. German physician.

Pa·ta·vi·um /pə'tāvēəm/ Latin name for **PADUA**.

patch /pacH/ ▸*n.* **1** a piece of cloth or other material used to mend or strengthen a torn or weak point. ■ a pad or shield worn over a sightless or injured eye or an eye socket. ■ a piece of cloth sewn onto clothing as a badge or distinguishing mark. ■ *Computing* a small piece of code inserted into a program to improve its functioning or to correct an error. ■ an adhesive piece of drug-impregnated material worn on the skin so that the drug can be absorbed gradually over a period of time. ■ (on an animal or bird) an area of hair or plumage different in color from that on most of the rest of the body. ■ a part of something marked out from the rest by a particular characteristic: *his hair was combed forward to hide a growing bald patch.* ■ a small area or amount of something: *patches of bluebells in the grass.* ■ *historical* a small disk of black silk attached to the face, esp. as worn by

women in the 17th and 18th centuries for adornment. **2** a small piece of ground, esp. one used for gardening: *they spent Sundays digging their vegetable patch.* ■ *Brit., informal* an area for which someone is responsible or in which they operate: *we didn't want any secret organizations on our patch.* **3** *informal* a period of time seen as a distinct unit with a characteristic quality: *he may have been* ***going through*** *a* ***bad patch.*** **4** a temporary electrical or telephone connection. ■ a preset configuration or sound-data file in an electronic musical instrument, esp. a synthesizer.
▶*v.* [*trans.*] **1** mend or strengthen (fabric or an item of clothing) by putting a piece of material over a hole or weak point in it: *her jeans were neatly patched.* ■ *Medicine* place a patch over (a good eye) in order to encourage a lazy eye to work. ■ *Computing* correct, enhance, or modify (a routine or program) by inserting a patch. ■ (usu. **be patched**) cover small areas of (a surface) with something different, causing it to appear variegated: *the grass was patched with sandy stretches.* ■ (**patch someone/something up**) *informal* treat someone's injuries or repair the damage to something, esp. hastily: *they did their best to patch up the gaping wounds.* ■ (**patch something together**) construct something hastily from unsuitable components: *lean-tos patched together from aluminum siding and planks* | *figurative they were trying to patch together an arrangement for cooperation.* ■ (**patch something up**) *informal* restore peaceful or friendly relations after a quarrel or dispute: *any ill feeling could be patched up with a phone call* | *they sent him home to* ***patch things up with*** *his wife.* **2** [*trans.*] connect by a temporary electrical, radio, or telephonic connection: *Ralph had* ***patched*** *her* ***through*** *to the meeting by walkie-talkie.* ■ [*intrans.*] become connected in this way: *stay on the open line and we'll patch in on you.* ▷late Middle English: perhaps from a variant of Old French *pieche*, dialect variant of *piece* 'piece.' —**patch·er** *n.*
▶*PHRASE* □ **not a patch on** *Brit., informal* greatly inferior to: *he no longer looked so handsome—he wasn't a patch on Peter.*

patch·board /ˈpaCH,bôrd/ ▶*n.* another term for PATCH PANEL.

patch box ▶*n.* *historical* a decorated box for holding black silk patches for the face, used esp. by women in the 17th and 18th centuries.

patch cord ▶*n.* an insulated cord with a plug at each end, for use with a patch panel.

patch·ou·li /pəˈCHo͞olē/ ▶*n.* **1** an aromatic oil obtained from a Southeast Asian shrub and used in perfumery, insecticides, and medicine. **2** the strongly scented shrub of the mint family from which this oil is obtained. • *Pogostemon cablin*, family Labiatae. ▷mid 19th cent.: from Tamil.

patch pan·el (also **patch·board**) ▶*n.* a board in a switchboard, computer, or other device with a number of electric sockets that can be connected in various combinations.

patch pock·et ▶*n.* a pocket made of a separate piece of cloth sewn on to the outside of a garment.

patch reef ▶*n.* a small, isolated platform of coral.

patch test ▶*n.* a test to discover whether a person is allergic to any of several that are applied to the skin in light scratches or under a patch.

patch·work /ˈpaCH,wərk/ ▶*n.* needlework in which small pieces of cloth in different designs, colors, or textures are sewn together: *a quilt of patchwork* | [as *adj.*] *patchwork bell-bottoms.* ■ the craft of sewing in this way: *specialists in quilting and patchwork.* ■ a thing composed of many different elements so as to appear variegated: *a patchwork of stone walls and green fields.*

patch·y /ˈpaCHē/ ▶*adj.* (**patch·i·er, patch·i·est**) existing or happening in small, isolated areas: *patchy fog.* ■ not of the same quality throughout; inconsistent: *your coursework was patchy.* ■ incomplete: *my knowledge of Egyptology is patchy.* —**patch·i·ly** /ˈpaCHəlē/ *adv.* —**patch·i·ness** /ˈpaCHēnis/ *n.*

patd. ▶*abbr.* patented.

pate /pāt/ ▶*n.* *archaic* or *humorous* a person's head: *he scratched his balding pate.* ▷Middle English: of unknown origin.

pâte /pät/ ▶*n.* the paste of which porcelain is made. ▷mid 19th cent.: French, literally 'paste.'

pâ·té /päˈtā/ ▶*n.* a rich, savory paste made from finely minced or mashed ingredients, typically seasoned meat or fish. ▷French, from Old French *paste* 'pie of seasoned meat.'

pâ·té de cam·pag·ne /päˈtā də kämˈpänyə/ ▶*n.* coarse pork and liver pâté. ▷French, literally 'country pâté.'

pâ·té de foie gras /päˈtā ˈdə ,fwä ˈgrä/ ▶*n.* a smooth rich paste made from fattened goose liver. ▷French.

pa·tel·la /pəˈtelə/ ▶*n.* (*pl.* **-lae** /-lē/) *Anatomy* the kneecap. ▷late 16th cent.: from Latin, diminutive of *patina* 'shallow dish.' —**pa·tel·lar** /-ˈtelər/ *adj.* —**pa·tel·late** /-ˈtelit; -,lāt/ *adj.*

pat·en /ˈpatn/ ▶*n.* a plate, typically made of gold or silver, used for holding the bread during the Eucharist and sometimes as a cover for the chalice. ■ a shallow metal plate or dish. ▷Middle English: from Old French *patene*, from Latin *patina* 'shallow dish,' from Greek *patanē* 'a plate.'

pa·ten·cy /ˈpatn-sē; ˈpātn-/ ▶*n.* *Medicine* the condition of being open, expanded, or unobstructed. ■ the condition of showing detectable parasite infection.

pat·ent ▶*n.* /ˈpatnt/ **1** a government authority to an individual or organization conferring a right or title, esp. the sole right to make, use, or sell some invention: *he* ***took out*** *a* ***patent*** *for an improved steam hammer.* [Compare with LETTERS PATENT.] **2** short for PATENT LEATHER.
▶*adj.* **1** /ˈpātnt; ˈpat-/ easily recognizable; obvious: *she was smiling with patent insincerity.* **2** *Medicine* /ˈpātnt; ˈpat-/ (of a vessel, duct, or aperture) open and unobstructed; failing to close. ■ (of a parasitic infection) showing detectable parasites in the tissues or feces. **3** /ˈpatnt/ [*attrib.*] made and marketed under a patent; proprietary: *patent milk powder.*
▶*v.* /ˈpatnt/ [*trans.*] obtain a patent for (an invention): *an invention is not your own until it is patented.* ▷late Middle English: from Old French, from Latin *patent-* 'lying open,' from the verb *patere.* —**pat·ent·a·ble** *adj.* —**pat·ent·ly** /ˈpatntlē; ˈpā-/ *adv.* (in sense 1 of the *adjective*).

pat·ent·ee /,patnˈtē/ ▶*n.* a person or organization that obtains or holds a patent for something.

pat·ent leath·er ▶*n.* leather with a glossy varnished surface, used chiefly for shoes, belts, and purses.

pat·ent log ▶*n.* a mechanical device used to measure the speed and distance traveled through the water of a ship or boat.

pat·ent med·i·cine ▶*n.* a proprietary medicine made and marketed under a patent and available without prescription.

pat·ent of·fice ▶*n.* an office from which patents are issued.

pat·ent right ▶*n.* the exclusive right conferred by a patent: *one of the collaborators has agreed to waive its patent rights to the cowpea gene.*

pa·ter /ˈpātər; ˈpä-; ˈpa-/ ▶*n.* **1** *Brit., informal, dated* father: *the pater gives her fifty pounds a year as a dress allowance.* **2** *Anthropology* a person's legal father. Often contrasted with GENITOR. ▷Latin.

pat·er·a /ˈpatərə/ ▶*n.* (*pl.* **-er·ae** /-ərē/) **1** a broad shallow dish used in ancient Rome for pouring libations. ■ *Architecture* a flat, round ornament resembling a shallow dish. **2** a broad, shallow bowl-shaped feature on a planet's surface. ▷Latin, from *patere* 'be or lie open.'

pa·ter·fa·mil·i·as /,pātərfəˈmilēəs; ,pä-/ ▶*n.* (*pl.* **pa·tres·fa·mil·i·as** /,pātrēzfə-; ,pä-/) the male head of a family or household. Compare with MATERFAMILIAS. ▷Latin, literally 'father of the family.'

pa·ter·nal /pəˈtərnl/ ▶*adj.* of or appropriate to a father: *he reasserted his paternal authority.* ■ showing a kindness and care associated with a father; fatherly: *my elders in the newsroom kept a paternal eye on me.* ■ [*attrib.*] related through the father: *his father and paternal grandfather were porcelain painters.* ▷late Middle English: from late Latin *paternalis*, from Latin *paternus* 'fatherly, belonging to a father,' from *pater* 'father.' —**pa·ter·nal·ly** *adv.*

pa·ter·nal·ism /pəˈtərnl,izəm/ ▶*n.* the policy or practice on the part of people in positions of authority of restricting the freedom and responsibilities of those subordinate to them in the subordinates' supposed best interest: *the arrogance and paternalism that underlies cradle-to-grave employment contracts.* —**pa·ter·nal·ist** *n.* & *adj.* —**pa·ter·nal·is·tic** /-,tərnlˈistik/ *adj.* —**pa·ter·nal·is·ti·cal·ly** /-,tərnlˈistik(ə)lē/ *adv.*

pa·ter·ni·ty /pəˈternitē/ ▶*n.* **1** (esp. in legal contexts) the state of being someone's father: *he refused to admit paternity of the child.* **2** paternal origin: *his enemies made great play of the supposed dubiety of his paternity.* ▷late Middle English: from Old French *paternité*, from late Latin *paternitas*, from *paternus* 'relating to a father.'

pa·ter·ni·ty suit ▶*n.* a court case held to establish formally the identity of a child's father, typically in order to require the man to support the child financially.

pa·ter·ni·ty test ▶*n.* a medical test, typically a blood test, to determine whether a man may be the father of a particular child.

pa·ter·nos·ter /ˈpätər,nästər; ˈpatər-/ ▶*n.* **1** (in the Roman Catholic Church) the Lord's Prayer, esp. in Latin. ■ any of a number of special beads occurring at regular intervals in a rosary, indicating that the Lord's Prayer is to be recited. **2** (also **paternoster lift**) an elevator consisting of a series of linked doorless compartments moving continuously on an endless belt. ▷Old English, from Latin *pater noster* 'our father,' the first words of the Lord's Prayer.

Pat·er·son[1] /ˈpatərsən/ a historic industrial city in northeastern New Jersey, on the Passaic River; pop. 149,222.

Pat·er·son[2], William (1745–1806), U.S. Supreme Court associate justice 1793–1806. A U.S. senator 1789–90 and governor of New Jersey 1790–93, he was appointed to the Court by President Washington.

path /paTH/ ▶*n.* (*pl.* **paths** /pa<u>TH</u>z; paTHs/) a way or track laid down for walking or made by continual treading. ■ [with *adj.*] such a way or track designed for a particular purpose: *a two-mile nature path.* ■ the course or direction in which a person or thing is moving: *the missile traced a fiery path in the sky* | *figurative a chosen career path.* ■ a course of action or conduct: *an ordered, gradual path toward economic liberalization.* ■ *Computing* a definition of the order in which an operating system or program searches for a file or executable program. ■ a schedule available for allocation to an individual railroad train over a given route. ▷Old English *pæth*; related to Dutch *pad*, German *Pfad*, of unknown ultimate origin. —**path·less** *adj.*
▶*PHRASE* □ **the path of least resistance** see RESISTANCE.

path. ▶*abbr.* ■ pathological. ■ pathology.

-path ▶*comb. form* **1** denoting a practitioner of curative treatment: *homeopath.* **2** denoting a person who suffers from a disease: *psychopath.* ▷back-formation from **-PATHY**, or from Greek *-pathēs* '-sufferer.'

Pa·than /pəˈtän/ (also **Pash·tun** /pəshˈto͞on/) ▶*n.* a member of a Pashto-speaking people inhabiting northwestern Pakistan and southeastern Afghanistan. ▷from Hindi *Paṭhān.*

path·break·ing /ˈpaTH,brākiNG/ (also **path-break·ing**) ▶*adj.* pioneering; innovative: *their pathbreaking work opened up a new era in cancer research.* —**path·break·er** *n.*

Pa·thé /päˈtā/, Charles (1863–1957), French movie pioneer. In 1896 he and his brothers founded a company that eventually dominated the production and distribution of movies.

pa·thet·ic /pəˈTHetik/ ▶*adj.* **1** arousing pity, esp. through vulnerability or sadness: *she looked so pathetic that I bent down to comfort her.* See note at MOVING. ■ *informal* miserably inadequate: *his test scores in Chemistry were pathetic.* **2** *archaic* relating to the emotions. ▷late 16th cent. (in the sense 'affecting the emotions'): via late Latin from Greek *pathētikos* 'sensitive,' based on *pathos* 'suffering.' —**pa·thet·i·cal·ly** /-(ə)lē/ *adv.*

pa·thet·ic fal·la·cy ▶*n.* the attribution of human feelings and responses to inanimate things or animals, esp. in art and literature.

Path·find·er /ˈpaTH,fīndər/ (in full **Mars Pathfinder**) an unmanned American spacecraft that landed on Mars in 1997, deploying a small robotic rover (*Sojourner*) to explore the surface and examine the rocks.

path·find·er /ˈpaTH,fīndər/ ▶*n.* a person who goes ahead and discovers or shows others a path or way. ■ an aircraft or its pilot sent ahead to locate and mark the target area for bombing. ■ [usu. as *adj.*] an experimental plan or forecast: *a pathfinder prospectus.*

path length ▶*n.* *Physics* the overall length of the path followed by a light ray or sound wave.

path·name /ˈpaTH,nām/ (also **path name**) ▶*n.* *Computing* a statement of the location of a file or other item in a hierarchy of directories.

patho- ▶*comb. form* relating to disease: *pathogenesis* | *pathology.* ▷from Greek *pathos* 'suffering, disease.'

path·o·gen /ˈpaTHəjən; -,jen/ ▶*n.* *Medicine* a bacterium, virus, or other microorganism that can cause disease. —**path·o·gen·ic** /,paTHəˈjenik/ *adj.* —**path·o·ge·nic·i·ty** /,paTHəjə,nisitē/ *n.* —**pa·thog·e·nous** /pəˈTHäjənəs/ *adj.*

path·o·gen·e·sis /,paTHəˈjenəsis/ ▶*n.* *Medicine* the manner of development of a disease. —**path·o·ge·net·ic** /-jəˈnetik/ *adj.*

pa·thog·no·mon·ic /pə,THägnə'mänik; ,paTHəgnə-/ ▸*adj. Medicine* (of a sign or symptom) specifically characteristic or indicative of a particular disease or condition. ▷early 17th cent.: from Greek *pathognōmonikos* 'skilled in diagnosis,' from *pathos* 'suffering' + *gnōmōn* 'judge.'

pa·thog·ra·phy /pə'THägrəfē/ ▸*n.* (*pl.* **-phies**) a study of the life of an individual or the history of a community with regard to the influence of a particular disease or psychological disorder. ■ writing of such a type as a branch of literature.

path·o·log·i·cal /,paTHə'läjikəl/ (also **path·o·log·ic**) ▸*adj.* of or relating to pathology: *the interpretation of pathological studies.* ■ involving, caused by, or of the nature of a physical or mental disease: *pathological changes associated with senile dementia.* ■ *informal* compulsive; obsessive: *a pathological gambler.* **—path·o·log·i·cal·ly** *adv.*

pa·thol·o·gy /pə'THäləjē/ ▸*n.* the science of the causes and effects of diseases, esp. the branch of medicine that deals with the laboratory examination of samples of body tissue for diagnostic or forensic purposes. ■ *Medicine* pathological features considered collectively; the typical behavior of a disease: *the pathology of Huntington's disease.* ■ *Medicine* a pathological condition: *the dominant pathology is multiple sclerosis.* ■ mental, social, or linguistic abnormality or malfunction: *the city's inability to cope with the pathology of a burgeoning underclass.* ▷early 17th cent.: from modern or medieval Latin *pathologia* (see **PATHO-**, **-LOGY**). **—pa·thol·o·gist** /-jist/ *n.*

path·o·phys·i·ol·o·gy /,paTHə,fizē'äləjē/ ▸*n. Medicine* the disordered physiological processes associated with disease or injury: *intracranial hypertension contributes to the pathophysiology of this condition.* **—path·o·phys·i·o·log·ic** /-,fizēə'läjik/ *adj.* **—path·o·phys·i·o·log·i·cal** /-,fizēə'läjikəl/ *adj.* **—path·o·phys·i·o·log·i·cal·ly** /,fizēə'läjik(ə)lē/ *adv.* **—path·o·phys·i·ol·o·gist** /-jist/ *n.*

pa·thos /'pā,THäs; -,THôs/ ▸*n.* a quality that evokes pity or sadness: *the actor injects his customary humor and pathos into the role.* ▷mid 17th cent.: from Greek *pathos* 'suffering'; related to *paskhein* 'suffer' and *penthos* 'grief.'

path·way /'paTH,wā/ ▸*n.* a way that constitutes or serves as a path. ■ *Physiology* a route, formed by a chain of nerve cells, along which impulses of a particular kind usually travel. ■ (also **metabolic pathway**) *Biochemistry* a sequence of chemical reactions undergone by a compound or class of compounds in a living organism.

-pathy ▸*comb. form* **1** denoting feelings: *telepathy.* **2** denoting disorder in a particular part of the body: *neuropathy.* **3** relating to curative treatment of a specified kind: *hydropathy.* ▷from Greek *patheia* 'suffering, feeling.'

pa·tience /'pāSHəns/ ▸*n.* **1** the capacity to accept or tolerate delay, trouble, or suffering without getting angry or upset: *you can find bargains if you have the patience to sift through the dross.* **2** chiefly British term for **SOLITAIRE** (sense 1). ▷Middle English: from Old French, from Latin *patientia*, from *patient-* 'suffering,' from the verb *pati.*

▸*PHRASE* □ **lose patience** (or **lose one's patience**) become unable to keep one's temper: *even Lawrence finally **lost patience with** him.*

pa·tient /'pāSHənt/ ▸*adj.* able to wait without becoming annoyed or anxious: *be patient, your time will come.* ■ slow to lose one's temper with irritating people or situations: *he was always kindly, patient, and considerate.*

▸*n.* **1** a person receiving or registered to receive medical treatment. **2** *Linguistics* the semantic role of a noun phrase denoting something that is affected or acted upon by the action of a verb. ▷Middle English: from Old French, from Latin *patient-* 'suffering,' from the verb *pati.* **—pa·tient·ly** *adv.*

pa·tient Lu·cy /'lo͞osē/ ▸*n.* chiefly British term for **IMPATIENS.**

pat·i·na /pə'tēnə/ ▸*n.* a green or brown film on the surface of bronze or similar metals, produced by oxidation over a long period. ■ a gloss or sheen on wooden furniture produced by age and polishing. ■ an acquired change in the appearance of a surface: *plankton added a golden patina to the shallow, slowly moving water.* ■ *figurative* an impression or appearance of something: *he carries the patina of old money and good breeding.* ▷mid 18th cent.: from Italian, from Latin *patina* 'shallow dish.' **—pat·i·nat·ed** /'patn,ātid/ *adj.* **—pat·i·na·tion** /,patn'āSHən/ *n.*

pat·i·o /'patē,ō/ ▸*n.* (*pl.* **-os**) a paved outdoor area adjoining a house. ■ a roofless inner courtyard in a Spanish or Spanish-American house. ▷early 19th cent.: from Spanish, denoting an inner courtyard.

pat·i·o rose ▸*n.* a miniature floribunda rose.

pa·tis·se·rie /pə'tisərē/ ▸*n.* a shop where French pastries and cakes are sold. ■ French pastries and cakes collectively. ▷late 16th cent.: from French *pâtisserie*, from medieval Latin *pasticium* 'pastry,' from *pasta* 'paste.'

Pat·mos /'patmäs; -məs; 'patmôs/ a Greek island in the Aegean Sea, one of the Dodecanese group. It is believed that St. John was living here in exile (from AD 95) when he had the visions described in Revelation.

Pat·na /'patnə; 'pət-/ a city in northeastern India, on the Ganges River, capital of the state of Bihar; pop. 917,000. An important city in ancient times, it was deserted by the 7th century but was refounded in 1541 by the Moguls and became a viceregal capital. Former name **PATALIPUTRA.**

pat·ois /'pa,twä; 'pä-/ ▸*n.* (*pl.* same) the dialect of the common people of a region, differing in various respects from the standard language of the rest of the country: *the nurse talked to me in a patois that even Italians would have had difficulty in understanding.* ■ the jargon or informal speech used by a particular social group: *the raunchy patois of inner-city kids.* ▷mid 17th cent.: French, literally 'rough speech,' perhaps from Old French *patoier* 'treat roughly,' from *patte* 'paw.'

Pa·ton /'pātn/, Alan (Stewart) (1903–88), South African writer and politician. He is best known for his novel *Cry, the Beloved Country* (1948), a passionate indictment of the apartheid system.

pa·tonce /pə'täns/ ▸*adj.* [*postpositive*] *Heraldry* (of a cross) with limbs that broaden from the center and end in three pointed lobes: *a cross patonce.* ▷mid 16th cent.: probably related to French *potencé*, a heraldic term denoting T-shaped endings to each limb of a cross, based on medieval Latin *potentia* 'crutch.'

pa·too·tie /pə'to͞otē/ ▸*n.* (*pl.* **-ties**) *informal* **1** *dated* a girlfriend or a pretty girl. **2** *derogatory* a person's or animal's buttocks. ▷1920s: perhaps an alteration of **POTATO.**

Pa·tras /pə'tras; 'patrəs/ an industrial port in the northwestern Peloponnese, on the Gulf of Patras; pop. 155,000. Captured by the Turks in the 18th century, it was the site in 1821 of the outbreak of the Greek war of independence. It was finally freed in 1828. Greek name **PÁTRAI**.

pa·tres·fa·mil·i·as /,patrēzfə'milēəs; ,pä-/ ▸ plural form of **PATERFAMILIAS.**

pa·tri·a /'pātrēə; 'pa-; 'pä-/ ▸*n.* one's native country or homeland: *they remained faithful to their patria, Spain.* ■ *archaic* heaven, regarded as the true home from which the soul is exiled while on earth. ▷Latin.

pa·tri·arch /'pātrē,ärk/ ▸*n.* **1** the male head of a family or tribe. ■ a man who is the oldest or most venerable of a group: *Hollywood's reigning patriarch rose to speak.* ■ a man who behaves in a commanding manner: *Cunningham's authoritative energy marks him out as patriarch within his own company.* ■ a person or thing that is regarded as the founder of something: *the patriarch of all spin doctors.* **2** any of those biblical figures regarded as fathers of the human race, esp. Abraham, Isaac, and Jacob, their forefathers, or the sons of Jacob. **3** the title of a most senior Orthodox or Catholic bishop, in particular: ■ a bishop of one of the most ancient Christian sees (Alexandria, Antioch, Constantinople, Jerusalem, and formerly Rome). ■ the head of an autocephalous or independent Orthodox church. ■ a Roman Catholic bishop ranking above primates and metropolitans and immediately below the pope, often the head of a Uniate community. ▷Middle English: from Old French *patriarche*, via ecclesiastical Latin from Greek *patriarkhēs*, from *patria* 'family' + *arkhēs* 'ruling.'

pa·tri·ar·chal /,pātrē'ärkəl/ ▸*adj.* **1** of, relating to, or characteristic of a patriarch. **2** of, relating to, or characteristic of a system of society or government controlled by men: *patriarchal values.* **—pa·tri·ar·chal·ly** *adv.*

pa·tri·ar·chal cross ▸*n.* a Christian cross with a smaller crossbar above the main one. In heraldry it denotes the rank of bishop or archbishop.

pa·tri·arch·ate /'pātrē,ärkit/ ▸*n.* the office, see, or residence of an ecclesiastical patriarch.

pa·tri·arch·y /'pātrē,ärkē/ ▸*n.* (*pl.* **-arch·ies**) a system of society or government in which the father or eldest male is head of the family and descent is traced through the male line. ■ a system of society or government in which men hold the power and women are largely excluded from it. ■ a society or community organized in this way. ▷mid 17th cent.: via medieval Latin from Greek *patriarkhia*, from *patriarkhēs* 'ruling father' (see **PATRIARCH**).

pa·tri·ate /'pātrē,āt/ ▸*v.* [*trans.*] transfer control over (a constitution) from a mother country to its former dependency: *the Canadian government moved to patriate the constitution from Great Britain.*

pa·tri·cian /pə'triSHən/ ▸*n.* an aristocrat or nobleman. ■ a member of a long-established wealthy family. ■ a member of a noble family or class in ancient Rome.

▸*adj.* belonging to or characteristic of the aristocracy: *a proud, patrician face.* ■ belonging to or characteristic of a long-established and wealthy family. ■ belonging to the nobility of ancient Rome. ▷late Middle English: from Old French *patricien*, from Latin *patricius* 'having a noble father,' from *pater, patr-* 'father.'

pa·tri·ci·ate /pə'triSHē-it; -,āt/ ▸*n.* a noble order or class: *the Venetian merchants became a great hereditary patriciate.* ■ the position or rank of patrician in ancient Rome.

pat·ri·cide /'patrə,sīd/ ▸*n.* the killing of one's father. ■ a person who kills their father. ▷early 17th cent.: from late Latin *patricidium*, alteration of Latin *parricidium* (see **PARRICIDE**). **—pat·ri·cid·al** /,patrə'sīdl/ *adj.*

Pat·rick, St. /'patrik/ (5th century), apostle and patron saint of Ireland. Of Romano-British parentage, he was taken as a slave to Ireland, where he experienced a religious conversion. Feast day, March 17.

pat·ri·lin·e·al /,patrə'linēəl/ ▸*adj.* of, relating to, or based on relationship to the father or descent through the male line: *in Polynesia inheritance of land was predominantly patrilineal.* ▷early 20th cent.: from Latin *pater, patr-* 'father' + **LINEAL.**

pat·ri·lo·cal /,patrə'lōkəl/ ▸*adj.* of or relating to a pattern of marriage in which the couple settles in the husband's home or community: *women moved more often than men because patterns of settlement after marriage tended to be patrilocal.* ▷early 20th cent.: from Latin *pater, patr-* 'father' + **LOCAL.** **—pat·ri·lo·cal·i·ty** /-lō'kalətē/ *n.*

pat·ri·mo·ny /'patrə,mōnē/ ▸*n.* (*pl.* **-nies**) property inherited from one's father or male ancestor. ■ heritage: *an organization that saves the world's cultural patrimony by restoring historic buildings.* ■ *chiefly historical* the estate or property belonging by ancient endowment or right to a church or other institution. ▷Middle English: from Old French *patrimoine*, from Latin *patrimonium*, from *pater, patr-* 'father.' **—pat·ri·mo·ni·al** /,patrə'mōnēəl/ *adj.*

pa·tri·ot /'pātrēət/ ▸*n.* **1** a person who vigorously supports their country and is prepared to defend it against enemies or detractors. **2** (**Patriot**) *trademark* an automated surface-to-air missile system designed for early detection and interception of missiles or aircraft. ■ a missile deployed in this system. ▷late 16th cent. (in the late Latin sense): from French *patriote*, from late Latin *patriota* 'fellow countryman,' from Greek *patriōtēs*, from *patrios* 'of one's fathers,' from *patris* 'fatherland.' **—pa·tri·ot·ism** /-,tizəm/ *n.*

pa·tri·ot·ic /,pātrē'ätik/ ▸*adj.* having or expressing devotion to and vigorous support for one's country: *the wave of relief and patriotic euphoria that followed the president's cease-fire declaration.* ▷mid 17th cent.: via late Latin from Greek *patriōtikos* 'relating to a fellow countryman' (see **PATRIOT**). **—pa·tri·ot·i·cal·ly** /-(ə)lē/ *adv.*

pa·tri·ot·ic front ▸*n.* a militant nationalist political organization.

pa·tris·tic /pə'tristik/ ▸*adj.* of or relating to the early Christian theologians or to patristics. ▷mid 19th cent.: from German *patristisch*, from Latin *pater, patr-* 'father.'

pa·tris·tics /pə'tristiks/ ▸*plural n.* [treated as *sing.*] the branch of Christian theology that deals with the lives, writings, and doctrines of the early Christian theologians.

Pa·tro·clus /pə'trōkləs/ *Greek Mythology* a Greek hero of the Trojan War, the close friend of Achilles.

pa·trol /pə'trōl/ ▸*n.* a person or group of people sent to keep watch over an area, esp. a detachment of guards or police: *a police patrol stopped the man and searched him.* ■ the action of keeping watch over an area by walking or driving around it at regular intervals: *the policemen were **on patrol** when they were*

P

ordered to investigate the incident. ■ an expedition to carry out reconnaissance: *we were ordered to investigate on a night patrol.* ■ a detachment of troops sent out to reconnoiter: *you couldn't go through the country without meeting an enemy patrol.* ■ a routine operational voyage of a ship or aircraft: *a submarine patrol.* ■ a unit of six to eight Girl Scouts or Boy Scouts forming part of a troop.

▸*v.* (**-trolled**, **-trol·ling**) [*trans.*] keep watch over (an area) by regularly walking or traveling around or through it: *the garrison had to patrol the streets to maintain order* | [*intrans.*] *pairs of men were patrolling on each side of the thoroughfare.* ▷mid 17th cent. (as a noun): from German *Patrolle*, from French *patrouille*, from *patrouiller* 'paddle in mud,' from *patte* 'paw' + dialect *(gad)rouille* 'dirty water.' —**pa·trol·ler** *n.*

pa·trol·man /pəˈtrōlmən/ ▸*n.* (*pl.* **-men**) a patrolling police officer.

pa·trol·o·gy /pəˈträləjē/ ▸*n.* another term for PATRISTICS. ▷early 17th cent.: from Greek *patēr, patr-* 'father' + -LOGY. —**pa·trol·o·gist** /-jist/ *n.*

pa·trol wag·on ▸*n.* a police van for transporting prisoners.

pa·tron /ˈpātrən/ ▸*n.* **1** a person who gives financial or other support to a person, organization, cause, or activity: *Charles became a patron of Rubens and van Dyck* | *a celebrated patron of the arts.* **2** a customer, esp. a regular one, of a store, restaurant, or theater: *we surveyed the plushness of the hotel and its sleek, well-dressed patrons.* **3** short for PATRON SAINT. **4** (in ancient Rome) a patrician in relation to a client. See also CLIENT (sense 3). ■ (in ancient Rome) the former owner and (frequently) protector of a freed slave. **5** *Brit., chiefly historical* a person or institution with the right to grant a benefice to a member of the clergy. ▷Middle English: from Old French, from Latin *patronus* 'protector of clients, defender,' from *pater, patr-* 'father.'

pa·tron·age /ˈpatrənij; ˈpā-/ ▸*n.* **1** the support given by a patron: *the arts could no longer depend on private patronage.* **2** the power to control appointments to office or the right to privileges: *recruits are selected on merit, not through political patronage.* **3** a patronizing or condescending manner: *a twang of self-satisfaction—even patronage—about him.* **4** the regular business given to a store, restaurant, or public service by a person or group: *the direct train link was ending because of poor patronage.* **5** (in ancient Rome) the rights and duties or the position of a patron. ▷late Middle English: from Old French, from *patron* 'protector, advocate' (see PATRON).

pa·tron·al /ˈpātrənl/ ▸*adj.* of or relating to a patron saint: *the patronal festival of the parish church of St. Peter.*

pa·tron·ess /ˈpātrənis/ ▸*n.* a female patron.

pa·tron·ize /ˈpātrəˌnīz; ˈpa-/ ▸*v.* **1** [often as *adj.*] (**patronizing**) treat with an apparent kindness that betrays a feeling of superiority: *"She's a good-hearted girl," he said in a patronizing voice* | *she was determined not to be put down or patronized.* **2** frequent (a store, theater, restaurant, or other establishment) as a customer: *restaurants remaining open in the evening were well patronized.* ■ give encouragement and financial support to (a person, esp. an artist, or a cause): *local churches and voluntary organizations were patronized by the family.* —**pa·tron·i·za·tion** /ˌpātrəniˈzāsʜən; ˌpa-/ *n.* —**pa·tron·iz·er** *n.* —**pa·tron·iz·ing·ly** /-ˌnīzinɢlē/ *adv.*

pa·tron saint ▸*n.* the protecting or guiding saint of a person or place.

Pa·trons of Hus·band·ry ▸*n.* see GRANGE (sense 2).

pat·ro·nym·ic /ˌpatrəˈnimik/ ▸*n.* a name derived from the name of a father or ancestor, typically by the addition of a prefix or suffix, e.g., *Johnson, O'Brien, Ivanovich.* ▷early 17th cent.: via late Latin from Greek *patrōnumikos*, from *patrōnumos*, from *patēr, patr-* 'father' + *onuma* 'name.'

pa·troon /pəˈtro͞on/ ▸*n. historical* a person given land and granted certain manorial privileges under the former Dutch governments of New York and New Jersey. ▷mid 17th cent.: from Dutch.

pat·sy /ˈpatsē/ ▸*n.* (*pl.* **-sies**) *informal* a person who is easily taken advantage of, esp. by being cheated or blamed for something. ▷early 20th cent.: of unknown origin.

pat·tée /pəˈtā/ ▸*adj.* [*postpositive*] (of a cross) having almost triangular arms, narrow at the center and broadening to squared ends: *a cross pattée.* ▷late 15th cent.: from French, from *patte* 'paw.'

pat·ten /ˈpatn/ ▸*n. historical* a shoe or clog with a raised sole or set on an iron ring, worn to raise one's feet above wet or muddy ground when walking outdoors. ▷late Middle English: from Old French *patin*, perhaps from *patte* 'paw.'

pat·ter[1] /ˈpatər/ ▸*v.* [*intrans.*] make a repeated light tapping sound: *a flurry of rain pattered against the window.* ■ run with quick light steps: *plovers pattered at the edge of the marsh.*

▸*n.* [in *sing.*] a repeated light tapping: *the rain had stopped its vibrating patter above him.* ▷early 17th cent.: frequentative of PAT[1].

pat·ter[2] ▸*n.* rapid or smooth-flowing continuous talk, such as that used by a comedian or salesman: *slick black hair, flashy clothes, and a New York line of patter.* ■ rapid speech included in a song, esp. for comic effect: [as *adj.*] *a patter song of invective.* ■ the special language or jargon of a profession or other group: *he picked up the patter from watching his dad.*

▸*v.* [*intrans.*] talk at length without saying anything significant: *she pattered on incessantly.* ▷late Middle English (as a verb in the sense 'recite (a prayer, charm, etc.) rapidly'): from PATERNOSTER. The noun dates from the mid 18th cent.

pat·tern /ˈpatərn/ ▸*n.* **1** a repeated decorative design: *a neat blue herringbone pattern.* ■ an arrangement or sequence regularly found in comparable objects or events: *the house had been built on the usual pattern.* ■ a regular and intelligible form or sequence discernible in certain actions or situations: *a complicating factor is the change in working patterns.* **2** a model or design used as a guide in needlework and other crafts. See note at MODEL. ■ a set of instructions to be followed in making a sewn or knitted item. ■ a wooden or metal model from which a mold is made for a casting. ■ an example for others to follow: *he set the pattern for subsequent study.* ■ a sample of cloth or wallpaper.

▸*v.* [*trans.*] **1** [usu. as *adj.*] (**patterned**) decorate with a recurring design: *rosebud patterned wallpapers* | *violet-tinged flowers patterned the grassy banks.* **2** give a regular or intelligible form to: *the brain not only receives information, but interprets and patterns it.* ■ (**pattern something on/after**) give something a form based on that of (something else): *the clothing is patterned on athletes' wear.* ▷Middle English *patron* 'something serving as a model,' from Old French (see PATRON). The change in sense is from the idea of a patron giving an example to be copied. Metathesis in the second syllable occurred in the 16th cent. By 1700 *patron* ceased to be used of things, and the two forms became differentiated in sense.

pat·tern bald·ness ▸*n.* genetically determined baldness in which hair is gradually lost according to a characteristic pattern.

pat·tern bomb·ing ▸*n.* the bombing of a target from a number of aircraft according to a prescribed pattern intended to produce the maximum effect.

pat·tern book ▸*n.* a book containing samples of patterns and designs of cloth or wallpaper.

pat·tern drill ▸*n.* another term for PATTERN PRACTICE.

pat·terned ground ▸*n. Geology* ground showing a pattern of stones, fissures, and vegetation, typically forming polygons, rings, or stripes caused by repeated freezing and thawing.

pat·tern·less /ˈpatərnləs/ ▸*adj.* having no pattern; plain and undecorated: *smooth, patternless paper for covering poor or uneven walls.* ■ forming no discernible pattern: *phenomena that are completely patternless and disorganized.*

pat·tern prac·tice ▸*n.* the intensive repetition of the distinctive constructions and patterns of a foreign language as a means of learning.

pat·ter of ti·ny feet ▸*n. humorous* used in reference to the presence or imminent birth of a child: *I had long ago given up hope of ever* ***hearing the patter of tiny feet.***

Pat·ter·son /ˈpatərsən/, Floyd (1935–), U.S. boxer. An Olympic middleweight champion 1952, he was also the world heavyweight champion 1956–59, 1960–62, becoming the first heavyweight to regain the title.

Pat·ton /ˈpatn/, George Smith, Jr. (1885–1945), U.S. army general. During World War II, he commanded the ground forces in the Allied invasion of northwest Africa 1942–43, the U.S. Seventh Army in the Allied invasion of Sicily 1943, and the U.S. Third Army in the drive through France 1944. His story was told in the movie *Patton* (1971).

pat·ty /ˈpatē/ ▸*n.* (*pl.* **-ties**) a small flat cake of minced or finely chopped food, esp. meat. ■ a small, round, flat chocolate-covered peppermint candy. ■ *chiefly Brit.* a small pie or turnover. ▷mid 17th cent.: alteration of French *pâté*, by association with PASTY[1].

pat·ty-cake (also **pat-a-cake**) ▸*n.* a children's game in which participants gently clap each other's hands and their own in time to the words of a rhyme.

pat·ty·pan /ˈpatēˌpan/ (also **pattypan squash**) ▸*n.* a squash of a saucer-shaped variety with a scalloped rim and creamy white flesh. ▷so named from the resemblance in shape to a pan for baking a patty.

pat·ty shell ▸*n.* a shell of puff pastry with a cooked meat or vegetable filling.

pat·u·lous /ˈpacʜələs/ ▸*adj. rare* (esp. of the branches of a tree) spreading. ▷early 17th cent.: from Latin *patulus* (from *patere* 'be or lie open') + -OUS.

pat·zer /ˈpätsər; ˈpat-/ ▸*n.* a poor chess player. ▷1940s: perhaps related to German *patzen* 'to bungle.'

PAU ▸*abbr.* Pan American Union.

pau·a /ˈpouə/ ▸*n. NZ* a large edible abalone (mollusk). ■ the ornamental shell of this. ▷mid 19th cent.: from Maori.

pau·ci·ty /ˈpôsitē/ ▸*n.* [in *sing.*] the presence of something only in small or insufficient quantities or amounts; scarcity: *a* ***paucity of*** *information.* ▷late Middle English: from Old French *paucite* or Latin *paucitas*, from *paucus* 'few.'

Paul /pôl/, Les (1915–), U.S. jazz guitarist and guitar designer; born *Lester Polfus.* In 1946, he invented the solid-body electric guitar. His style of play influenced many rock guitarists. Notable songs: "Mockin' Bird Hill" (1951) and "Vaya con Dios" (1953).

Paul, St. (died *c.*64), missionary; known as **Paul the Apostle**, **Saul of Tarsus**, or **the Apostle of the Gentiles**. He first opposed the followers of Jesus, but after a vision became one of the first major Christian missionaries and theologians. His epistles form part of the New Testament. Feast day, June 29.

Paul III (1468–1549), Italian pope 1534–49; born *Alessandro Farnese.* He excommunicated Henry VIII of England in 1538, instituted the order of the Jesuits in 1540, and initiated the Council of Trent in 1545.

Paul–Bun·nell test /ˈbənəl/ ▸*n. Medicine* a test in which an antibody reaction to sheep red blood cells confirms a diagnosis of infectious mononucleosis. ▷1930s: named after John R. *Paul* (1893–1936) and Walls W. *Bunnell* (1902–1965), American physicians.

Pau·li /ˈpôlē; ˈpou-/, Wolfgang (1900–58), U.S. physicist, born in Austria. He made a major contribution to quantum theory with his **exclusion principle**, according to which only two electrons in an atom could occupy the same quantum level, provided they had opposite spins. Nobel Prize for Physics (1945).

Pau·li·cian /ˌpôˈlisʜən/ ▸*n. Church History* a member of a sect that arose in Armenia in the 7th century AD, professing a modified form of Manichaeism. ▷from medieval Latin *Pauliciani*, Greek *Paulikianoi*, of unknown origin. —**Pau·li·cian·ism** /-ˌizəm/ *n.*

Pau·li ex·clu·sion prin·ci·ple (also **Pauli's exclusion principle**) *Physics* the assertion that no two fermions can have the same quantum number. ▷1920s: named after W. PAULI.

Pau·line /ˈpôˌlīn; -ˌlēn/ ▸*adj. Christian Theology* of, relating to, or characteristic of St. Paul, his writings, or his doctrines. ■ (in the Roman Catholic Church) of or relating to Pope Paul VI, or the liturgical and doctrinal reforms pursued during his pontificate (1963–78) as a result of the Second Vatican Council.

Paul·ing /ˈpôlinɢ/, Linus Carl (1901–94), U.S. chemist. He is renowned for his study of molecular structure and chemical bonding. His suggestion of a helical structure for proteins formed the foundation for the elucidation of the structure of DNA. Nobel Prize for Chemistry (1954).

Paul Jones ▸*n.* a ballroom dance in which the dancers change partners after circling in concentric rings of men and women. ▷1920s: named after John *Paul Jones* (1747–92), Scottish-born American admiral.

pau·low·ni·a /pôˈlōnēə/ ▸*n.* a small Southeast Asian tree with heart-shaped leaves and fragrant lilac flowers. • Genus *Paulownia*, family Scrophulariaceae. ▷modern Latin, named after Anna *Pavlovna* (1795–1865), a Russian princess.

Paul Pry ▸*n. dated* an inquisitive person. ▷from the name of a character in a U.S. song of 1820.

paunch /pôncʜ; päncʜ/ ▸*n.* **1** a large or protruding abdomen or stomach. **2** *archaic Nautical* a thick strong mat used to give protection from chafing on a mast or other spar. ▷late Middle English: from Anglo-Norman French *pa(u)nche*, based on Latin *pantex, pantic-*, usually in the plural in the sense 'intestines.' —**paunch·i·ness** /ˈpôncʜēnis/ *n.* —**paunch·y** *adj.*

pau·per /ˈpôpər/ ▸*n.* a very poor person. ■ *historical* a recipient of government relief or public charity.

▷late 15th cent.: from Latin, literally 'poor.' The word's use in English originated in the Latin legal phrase *in forma pauperis*, literally 'in the form of a poor person' (allowing nonpayment of costs). **—pau·per·dom** /-dəm/ *n.* **—pau·per·ism** /-ˌrizəm/ *n.* **—pau·per·i·za·tion** /ˌpôpəri'zāshən/ *n.* **—pau·per·ize** /-ˌrīz/ *v.*

pau·piette /pō'pyet/ ▶*n.* a long, thin slice of fish or meat, rolled and stuffed with a filling. ▷French, probably from Italian *polpetta*, from Latin *pulpa* 'pulp.'

pau·ra·que /pou'räkā/ ▶*n.* a long-tailed nightjar found in southern Texas, Mexico, and Central and South America. • Family Caprimulgidae: two genera and species, in particular the **common pauraque** (*Nyctidromus albicollis*). ▷probably a Hispanicized form of a local word.

Pau·rop·o·da /ˌpôrə'pädə/ *Zoology* a small class of myriapod invertebrates that resemble the centipedes. They are small, soft-bodied animals with one pair of legs per segment, living chiefly in forest litter. ▷modern Latin (plural), from Greek *pauros* 'small' + *pous, pod-* 'foot.' **—pau·ro·pod** /'pôrəˌpäd/ *n.* **—pau·rop·o·dan** *n.* & *adj.*

Pau·sa·ni·as /pô'sānēəs/ (2nd century), Greek geographer and historian. His *Description of Greece* (also called the *Itinerary of Greece*) is a guide to the topography and remains of ancient Greece and is still considered an invaluable source of information.

pause /pôz/ ▶*n.* a temporary stop in action or speech: *she dropped me outside during a brief pause in the rain* | *the admiral chattered away* ***without pause.*** ■ *Music* a mark (𝄐) over a note or rest that is to be lengthened by an unspecified amount. ■ (also **pause button**) a control allowing the temporary interruption of an electronic (or mechanical) process, esp. video or audio recording or reproduction.
▶*v.* [*intrans.*] interrupt action or speech briefly: *she paused, at a loss for words.* ■ [*trans.*] temporarily interrupt the operation of (a videotape, audiotape, or computer program): *she had paused a tape on the VCR.* ▷late Middle English: from Old French, from Latin *pausa*, from Greek *pausis*, from *pausein* 'to stop.'
▶*PHRASE* □ **give someone pause** cause someone to think carefully or hesitate before doing something: *public outrage has given him pause.*

pa·vane /pə'vän/ (also **pa·van**) ▶*n.* a stately dance in slow duple time, popular in the 16th and 17th centuries and performed in elaborate clothing. ■ a piece of music for this dance. ▷mid 16th cent.: from French *pavane*, from Italian *pavana*, feminine adjective from *Pavo*, dialect name of Padua.

Pa·va·rot·ti /ˌpävə'rätē; -vä'rôtē/, Luciano (1935–), Italian opera singer. A tenor, he gained international acclaim and popularity for his bel canto singing.

pave /pāv/ ▶*v.* [*trans.*] (often **be paved with**) cover (a piece of ground) with concrete, asphalt, stones, or bricks; lay paving over: *the yard at the front was paved with flagstones* | [as *adj.*] (**paved**) *chrysanthemums provide a cheerful border for the paved area* | *figurative the streets of the big city are not* ***paved with gold.*** ▷Middle English: from Old French *paver* 'pave.' **—pav·er** *n.*
▶*PHRASE* □ **pave the way for** create the circumstances to enable (something) to happen or be done: *the proposals will pave the way for a speedy resolution to the problem.*

pa·vé /pə'vā; pa-/ ▶*n.* **1** a setting of precious stones placed so closely together that no metal shows: *a solid diamond pavé.* **2** *archaic* a paved street, road, or path. ▷French, literally 'paved,' past participle of *paver*.

pave·ment /'pāvmənt/ ▶*n.* any paved area or surface. ■ the hard surface of a road or street. ■ *Brit.* a sidewalk. ■ *Geology* a more or less horizontal expanse of bare rock. ▷Middle English: from Old French, from Latin *pavimentum* 'trodden-down floor,' from *pavire* 'beat, tread down.'
▶*PHRASE* □ **pound the pavement** see POUND[2].

pa·vil·ion /pə'vilyən/ ▶*n.* **1** a building or similar structure used for a specific purpose, in particular: ■ a summerhouse or other decorative building used as a shelter in a park or large garden. ■ in the names of buildings used for theatrical or other entertainments: *the second concert at the White Rock Pavilion.* ■ a detached or semidetached block at a hospital or other building complex. ■ a large tent with a peak and crenellated decorations, used esp. at a show or fair. ■ a temporary building, stand, or other structure in which items are displayed by a dealer or exhibitor at a trade exhibition. **2** a usually highly decorated projecting subdivision of a building. **3** the part of a cut gemstone below the girdle. ▷Middle English (denoting a large decorated tent): from Old French *pavillon*, from Latin *papilio(n-)* 'butterfly; tent.'

pav·ing /'pāviNG/ ▶*n.* pavement. ■ the materials used for a pavement.

pav·ing stone ▶*n.* a large, flat piece of stone or similar material, used in paving.

pav·ior /'pāvyər/ (also *Brit.* **pav·iour**) ▶*n.* a paving stone. ■ a person who lays paving stones. ▷Middle English: from Old French *paveur*, from *paver* 'pave.'

Pa·vlov /'pavˌläv; -lôf; -ləf/, Ivan (Petrovich) (1849–1936), Russian physiologist. He is best known for his studies on the conditioned reflex. He showed by experimenting with dogs how the secretion of saliva can be stimulated not only by food but also by the sound of a bell associated with food. Nobel Prize for Physiology or Medicine (1904).

Pav·lo·va /päv'lōvə; 'pävləvə/ Anna (Pavlovna) (1881–1931), Russian dancer, resident in Britain from 1912. Her highly acclaimed solo dance *The Dying Swan* was created for her by Michel Fokine in 1905. On settling in Britain she formed her own company.

pa·vlo·va /päv'lōvə; 'pavləvə/ ▶*n.* a dessert consisting of a meringue base or shell filled with whipped cream and fruit. ▷named after A. PAVLOVA.

Pav·lov·i·an /pav'lōvēən; -'läv-/ ▶*adj.* of or relating to classical conditioning as described by I. P. Pavlov.

Pa·vo /'pāvō/ *Astronomy* a southern constellation (the Peacock), between Grus and Triangulum Australe. Its brightest star is itself sometimes called "the Peacock." ■ [as *genitive*] (**Pavonis** /pə'vōnis/) used with a preceding letter or numeral to designate a star in this constellation: *the star Beta Pavonis.* ▷Latin.

pav·o·nine /'pavəˌnīn; -nin/ ▶*adj. poetic/literary, rare* of or like a peacock. ▷mid 17th cent.: from Latin *pavoninus*, from *pavo, pavon-* 'peacock.'

paw /pô/ ▶*n.* an animal's foot having claws and pads. ■ *chiefly derogatory* a person's hand: *touch her with your filthy paws and I'll ram my fist into your face.*
▶*v.* [*trans.*] (of an animal) feel or scrape with a paw or hoof: *the horse rose on its strong haunches, its forelegs pawing the air* | [*intrans.*] *young dogs may* ***paw at*** *the floor and whine.* ■ *informal* (of a person) touch or handle awkwardly or roughly: *he had pawed his way through a copious meal.* ■ (of a person) touch (someone) in a lascivious and offensive way: *some overweight, ugly Casanova had tried to paw her.* ▷Middle English: from Old French *poue*, probably of Germanic origin and related to Dutch *poot*.

pawk·y /'pôkē/ ▶*adj.* (**pawk·i·er, pawk·i·est**) *chiefly Brit.* 1having or showing a sly sense of humor: *a gentle man with a pawky wit.* ■ shrewd: *she shakes her head with a look of pawky, knowing skepticism.* ▷mid 17th cent.: from Scots and northern English *pawk* 'trick,' of unknown origin. **—pawk·i·ly** /-kəlē/ *adv.* **—pawk·i·ness** /-kēnis/ *n.*

pawl /pôl/ ▶*n.* a pivoted curved bar or lever whose free end engages with the teeth of a cogwheel or ratchet so that the wheel or ratchet can only turn or move one way. ■ each of a set of short stout bars that engage with the whelps and prevent a capstan, windlass, or winch from recoiling. ▷early 17th cent.: perhaps from Low German and Dutch *pal* (related to *pal* 'fixed').

pawn[1] /pôn/ ▶*n.* a chess piece of the smallest size and value. A pawn moves one square forward along its file if unobstructed (or two on the first move), or one square diagonally forward when making a capture. Each player begins with eight pawns on the second rank, and can promote a pawn to become any other piece (typically a queen) if it reaches the opponent's end of the board. ■ a person used by others for their own purposes: *they had allowed themselves to be used as pawns within the Cold War.* ▷late Middle English: from Anglo-Norman French *poun*, from medieval Latin *pedo, pedon-* 'foot soldier,' from Latin *pes, ped-* 'foot.' Compare with PEON.

pawn[2] ▶*v.* [*trans.*] deposit (an object) with a pawnbroker as security for money lent: *I pawned the necklace to cover the loan.*
▶*phrasal v.* □ **pawn someone/something off** pass off someone or something unwanted: *newly industrialized economies are racing to* ***pawn off*** *old processes* ***on*** *poorer countries.*
▶*n. archaic* an object left as security for money lent. ▷late 15th cent. (as a noun): from Old French *pan* 'pledge, security,' of West Germanic origin; related to Dutch *pand* and German *Pfand*.
▶*PHRASE* □ **in pawn** (of an object) held as security by a pawnbroker: *all our money was gone and everything was in pawn.*

pawn·brok·er /'pônˌbrōkər/ ▶*n.* a person who lends money at interest on the security of an article pawned. **—pawn·brok·ing** /-kiNG/ *n.*

Paw·nee /pô'nē/ ▶*n.* (*pl.* same or **-nees**) **1** a member of an American Indian confederacy formerly in Nebraska, and now mainly in Oklahoma. **2** the Caddoan language of these peoples.
▶*adj.* of or relating to these people or their language. ▷from Canadian French *Pani*, from a Siouan name.

pawn·shop /'pônˌshäp/ ▶*n.* a pawnbroker's shop, esp. one where unredeemed items are sold to the public.

pawn tick·et ▶*n.* a ticket issued by a pawnbroker in exchange for an article pawned, bearing particulars of the loan.

paw·paw /'pôpô/ (also **pa·paw** /pə'pô; 'pôpô/) ▶*n.* **1** another term for PAPAYA. **2** (also **pawpaw tree**) a North American tree of the custard apple family, with purple flowers and edible oblong yellow fruit with sweet pulp. • *Asimina triloba*, family Annonaceae. ■ the fruit of this tree. ▷early 17th cent.: from Spanish and Portuguese *papaya*, of Carib origin. The change in spelling is unexplained.

Paw·tuck·et /pə'təkət; pô-/ an industrial city in northeastern Rhode Island, on the Blackstone River, northeast of Providence, site of pioneering metal and textile plants; pop. 72,958.

Pax /paks; päks/ *Roman Mythology* the goddess of peace. Greek equivalent EIRENE.

pax /paks; päks/ ▶*n. chiefly historical* (in the Christian Church) the kissing of a tablet by all the participants at a mass depicting the Crucifixion or other sacred object; the kiss of peace. ▷Latin, literally 'peace.'

Pax Ro·ma·na /'päks rō'mänə/ ▶*n. historical* the peace that existed between nationalities within the Roman Empire. ▷Latin, literally 'Roman peace.'

Pax·ton /'pakstən/, Sir Joseph (1801–65), English gardener and architect. He designed the Crystal Palace in London in 1851.

pay[1] /pā/ ▶*v.* (*past* **paid**) **1** [*trans.*] give (someone) money that is due for work done, goods received, or a debt incurred: [*trans.*] *he paid the locals to pick his coffee beans* | [*intrans.*] *TV licenses can be* ***paid for*** *by direct debit.* ■ give (a sum of money) in exchange for goods or work done or in discharge of a debt: *he paid $1,000 to have it built in 1977* | [with *two objs.*] *a museum paid him a four-figure sum for it.* ■ hand over or transfer the amount due of (a debt, wages, etc.) to someone: *bonuses were paid to savers whose policies completed their full term.* ■ (of work, an investment, etc.) yield or provide someone with (a specified sum of money): *jobs that pay $5 or $6 an hour.* ■ [*intrans.*] (of a business or undertaking, or an attitude) be profitable or advantageous to someone: *crime doesn't pay* | [with *infinitive*] *it pays to choose varieties carefully.* **2** [*intrans.*] suffer a loss or other misfortune as a consequence of an action: *the destroyer responsible for these atrocities would have to* ***pay with*** *his life.* ■ [*trans.*] give what is due or deserved to (someone); reward or punish. **3** [with *two objs.*] give or bestow (attention, respect, or a compliment) on (someone): *no one paid them any attention.* ■ make (a visit or a call) to (someone): *she has been prevailed upon to pay us a visit.*
▶*phrasal v.* □ **pay someone back** repay a loan to someone: *a regular amount was deducted from my wages to pay her back.* ■ *figurative* take revenge on someone: *a terrorist group had decided to* ***pay him back for*** *shortchanging them.* ■ reward someone for something done earlier: *I took Aunt Shirley a cake to* ***pay her back for*** *solving a problem my grandmother had.* □ **pay something back** repay a loan to someone: *the money should be paid back with interest* | [with *two objs.*] *they did pay me back the money.* □ **pay something in** pay money into a bank account. □ **pay off** *informal* (of a course of action) yield good results; succeed: *all the hard work I had done over the summer paid off.* □ **pay someone off** dismiss someone with a final payment: *when directors are fired, they should not be lavishly paid off.* □ **pay something off** pay a debt in full: *you may have saved up enough to pay off your second mortgage.* □ **pay something out** (or **pay out**) **1** pay a large sum of money from funds under one's control: *insurers can refuse to pay out.* **2** let out (a rope) by slackening it: *I began paying out the nylon line.* □ **pay up** (or **pay something up**) pay a debt in full: *you've got ninety days to pay up the principal.*
▶*n.* the money paid to someone for regular work:

those working on contract may receive higher rates of pay | showing up and collecting your pay. ▷Middle English (in the sense 'pacify'): from Old French *paie* (noun), *payer* (verb), from Latin *pacare* 'appease,' from *pax, pac-* 'peace.' The notion of 'payment' arose from the sense of 'pacifying' a creditor. —**pay·er** *n.*

▸*PHRASES* □ **in the pay of** employed by. □ **pay one's compliments** see COMPLIMENT. □ **pay court to** see COURT. □ **pay dearly** obtain something at a high cost or great effort: *his master must have paid dearly for such a magnificent beast.* ■ suffer for an error or failure: *they paid dearly for wasting goalscoring opportunities.* □ **pay one's dues** see DUE. □ **pay for itself** (of an object or system) earn or save enough money to cover the cost of its purchase: *the best insulation will pay for itself in less than a year.* □ **pay its** (or **one's**) **way** (of an enterprise or person) earn enough to cover its (or one's) costs: *some students are paying their way through college.* □ **pay one's last respects** show respect toward a dead person by attending their funeral. □ **pay one's respects** make a polite visit to someone: *we went to pay our respects to the head lama.* □ **pay through the nose** *informal* pay much more than a fair price.

pay[2] ▸*v.* (*past* and *past part.* **payed**) [*trans.*] *Nautical* seal (the deck or hull seams of a wooden ship) with pitch or tar to prevent leakage. ▷early 17th cent.: from Old Northern French *peier*, from Latin *picare*, from *pix, pic-* 'pitch.'

pay·a·ble /ˈpāəbəl/ ▸*adj.* [*predic.*] **1** (of money) required to be paid; due: *interest is payable on the money owing | send a check, payable to the ASPCA.* **2** able to be paid: *it costs just $195, payable in five monthly installments.*
▸*n.* (**payables**) debts owed by a business; liabilities.

pay-as-you-go ▸*adj.* relating to a system of paying debts or meeting costs as they arise.

pay·back /ˈpāˌbak/ ▸*n.* **1** financial return or reward, esp. profit equal to the initial outlay of an investment: *a long time lag between investment and payback.* **2** an act of revenge or retaliation: *the drive-by shootings are mainly paybacks.*

pay·back pe·ri·od ▸*n.* the length of time required for an investment to recover its initial outlay in terms of profits or savings.

pay ca·ble ▸*n.* a cable television service available on a subscription basis.

pay·check /ˈpāˌCHek/ ▸*n.* a check for salary or wages made out to an employee. ■ *figurative* a salary or income: *socking away money for the time when he wouldn't have a steady paycheck.*

pay·day /ˈpāˌdā/ ▸*n.* a day on which someone is paid or expects to be paid their wages. ■ *informal* money or success won or earned: *his two seasons in Dallas helped him land his first huge payday in the NFL when he signed with the Cardinals.*

pay dirt ▸*n.* *Mining* ground containing ore in sufficient quantity to be profitably extracted. ■ profit; reward: *the gig pays three hundred bucks a week—looks like I just* ***hit pay dirt.***

pay·ee /pāˈē/ ▸*n.* a person to whom money is paid or is to be paid, esp. the person to whom a check is made payable.

pay en·ve·lope ▸*n.* an envelope containing an employee's wages. ■ *figurative* a salary or income: *a company cutting pay envelopes.*

pay·ess /ˈpā-is/ ▸*plural n.* uncut sideburns worn by male Orthodox Jews. ▷mid 20th cent.: Yiddish, from Hebrew *pē'ōṯ* 'corners' (see Lev. 19:27).

pay·ing guest ▸*n.* a person who lives in someone else's house and pays for food and accommodations; a lodger.

pay·load /ˈpāˌlōd/ ▸*n.* the part of a vehicle's load, esp. an aircraft's, from which revenue is derived; passengers and cargo. ■ the total load of bombs carried by a bomber. ■ an explosive warhead carried by a missile. ■ equipment, personnel, or satellites carried by a spacecraft.

pay·mas·ter /ˈpāˌmastər/ ▸*n.* an official who pays troops or workers.

pay·ment /ˈpāmənt/ ▸*n.* **1** the action or process of paying someone or something, or of being paid: *ask for a discount for payment by cash | three interest-free monthly payments.* **2** an amount paid or payable: *an interim compensation payment of $2500.* ■ *figurative* something given as a reward or in recompense for something done: *a suit with a velvet collar that I got as payment for being in the show.* ▷late Middle English: from Old French *paiement*, from *payer* 'to pay.'

Payne's gray /pānz/ ▸*n.* *Printing* a composite pigment composed of blue, red, black, and white permanent pigments, used esp. for watercolors. ▷mid 19th cent.: named after William *Payne* (*fl.* 1800), English artist.

pay·nim /ˈpānim/ ▸*n.* *archaic* a pagan. ■ a non-Christian, esp. a Muslim. ▷Middle English: from Old French *paienime*, from ecclesiastical Latin *paganismus* 'heathenism,' from *paganus* 'heathen' (see PAGAN).

pay·off /ˈpāˌôf/ ▸*n.* *informal* a payment made to someone, esp. as a bribe or reward, or on leaving a job: *widespread rumors of payoffs and kickbacks in the party.* ■ the return on an investment or a bet. ■ a final outcome; a conclusion: *it gave them the idea for the payoff of last night's episode.*

pay·o·la /pāˈōlə/ ▸*n.* the practice of bribing someone to use their influence or position to promote a particular product or interest: *if a record company spends enough money on payola, it can make any record a hit.* ▷1930s: from PAY[1] + *-ola* as in *Victrola*, the name of a make of gramophone.

pay·out /ˈpāˌout/ ▸*n.* a large payment of money, esp. as compensation or a dividend: *an insurance payout.*

pay pack·et ▸*n.* British term for PAY ENVELOPE.

pay-per-view ▸*adj.* see PPV.

pay phone ▸*n.* a public telephone that is operated by coins or by a credit or prepaid card.

pay·roll /ˈpāˌrōl/ ▸*n.* a list of a company's employees and the amount of money they are to be paid: *there are just three employees* ***on the payroll.*** ■ the total amount of wages and salaries paid by a company to its employees: *small employers with a payroll of less than $45,000.*

pay·sage /pāˈzäZH; ˈpāsij/ ▸*n.* a rural scene depicted in art. ■ landscape painting. ▷French, literally 'countryside,' from *pays* 'country.' —**pay·sa·gist** /ˈpāsəjist/ *n.*

pay·san /pāˈzän/ ▸*n.* a peasant or countryman, esp. in France. ▷French.

Pays Basque /ˈpā ˈbäsk/ French name for BASQUE COUNTRY.

pay·slip /ˈpāˌslip/ ▸*n.* a note given to an employee when they have been paid, detailing the amount of pay given and the tax and insurance deducted.

pay sta·tion ▸*n.* *dated* another term for PAY PHONE.

payt. ▸*abbr.* payment.

Pay·ton /ˈpātn/, Walter (1954–99) U.S. football player. A running back, he played for the Chicago Bears 1975–87 and held the NFL's career record for most yards rushed: 16,726. Football Hall of Fame (1993).

pay TV (also **pay television**) ▸*n.* television broadcasting in which viewers pay by subscription to watch a particular channel.

Paz /päz; päs/, Octavio (1914–98), Mexican poet and essayist. His poems reflect his interest in Aztec mythology. Nobel Prize for Literature (1990).

PB ▸*abbr.* ■ British Pharmacopoeia. [Latin *Pharmacopoeia Britannica.*] ■ Prayer Book. ■ petabyte.

Pb ▸*symbol* the chemical element lead. ▷from Latin *plumbum.*

pb ▸*abbr.* paperback: *hb $18.99, pb $6.99.*

PBS ▸*abbr.* Public Broadcasting Service.

PBX ▸*abbr.* private branch exchange, a private telephone switchboard.

PC ▸*abbr.* ■ Past Commander. ■ personal computer. ■ *Brit.* Police Constable. ■ (also **pc**) politically correct; political correctness: *PC language | the cult of PC.* ■ Post Commander. ■ *Brit.* Prince Consort. ■ *Brit.* Privy Council. ■ professional corporation.

pc ▸*abbr.* parsec.

p.c. ▸*abbr.* ■ percent. ■ postcard.

p/c (also **P/C**) ▸*abbr.* ■ petty cash. ■ price current.

PCAS *historical* ▸*abbr.* (in the UK) Polytechnics Central Admissions System (incorporated into UCAS in the 1993–94 academic year).

PCB ▸*abbr.* ■ *Electronics* printed circuit board. ■ *Chemistry* polychlorinated biphenyl.

PC card ▸*n.* *Computing* a printed circuit board for a personal computer, esp. one built to the PCMCIA standard.

P-Celt·ic /ˈkeltik/ ▸*n.* & *adj.* another term for BRYTHONIC. ▷*P*, from the development of the Indo-European *kw* sound into *p* in this group of languages.

PCI ▸*n.* *Computing* a standard for connecting computers and their peripherals. ▷late 20th cent.: abbreviation of *Peripheral Component Interconnect.*

PCM ▸*abbr.* pulse code modulation.

PCMCIA ▸*abbr.* *Computing* Personal Computer Memory Card International Association, denoting a standard specification for memory cards and interfaces in personal computers.

PC mod ▸*n.* *Computing* another term for MOD.

PCN ▸*abbr.* personal communications network, a digital mobile telephone system.

p-code ▸*n.* another term for PSEUDOCODE.

PCP ▸*abbr.* ■ pentachlorophenol. ■ phencyclidine. ■ pneumocystis carinii pneumonia. ■ primary care physician. ■ (in Canada) Progressive-Conservative Party.

PCS ▸*abbr.* personal communications services, a digital mobile telephone system.

pct. ▸*abbr.* percent.

PCV *Brit.* ▸*abbr.* passenger-carrying vehicle.

PD ▸*abbr.* ■ Police Department: *the Chicago PD.* ■ public domain: *PD software.*

Pd ▸*symbol* the chemical element palladium.

pd ▸*abbr.* paid.

p.d. ▸*abbr.* ■ per diem. ■ potential difference.

PDA ▸*n.* a palmtop computer used to store information such as addresses and telephone numbers, and for simple word processing and spreadsheeting. ▷late 20th cent.: abbreviation of *personal digital assistant.*

PDA ▸*abbr.* ■ *informal* public display of affection.

Pd.B. ▸*abbr.* Bachelor of Pedagogy.

PDC ▸*abbr.* program delivery control, a system for broadcasting a coded signal at the beginning and end of a television program which can be recognized by a video recorder and used to begin and end recording.

Pd.D. ▸*abbr.* Doctor of Pedagogy.

PDF ▸*n.* *Computing* a file format that provides an electronic image of text or text and graphics that looks like a printed document and can be viewed, printed, and electronically tramsmitted. ▷abbreviation of *portable document format.*

Pd.M. ▸*abbr.* Master of Pedagogy.

PDP ▸*abbr.* parallel distributed processing.

p.d.q. *informal* ▸*abbr.* pretty damn quick.

PDSA ▸*abbr.* (in the UK) People's Dispensary for Sick Animals.

PDT ▸*abbr.* Pacific Daylight Time (see PACIFIC TIME).

PE ▸*abbr.* ■ physical education. ■ Prince Edward Island (in official postal use).

pea /pē/ ▸*n.* **1** a spherical green seed that is widely eaten as a vegetable. ■ [with *adj.*] any of a number of edible spherical seeds of the pea family, e.g., **chickpea** and **black-eyed pea**. **2** the hardy Eurasian climbing plant that yields pods containing these seeds. • *Pisum sativum*, family Leguminosae (or Fabaceae; the **pea family**). The members of this family (known as legumes) are sometimes divided among three smaller families: Papilionaceae (peas, beans, clovers, vetches, brooms, laburnums, etc.), Mimosaceae (mimosas, acacias), and Caesalpiniaceae (cassia, carob, and many tropical timber trees). ■ used in names of other plants of this family that yield round seeds or have flowers resembling those of the pea, e.g., **sweet pea**. ▷mid 17th cent.: back-formation from PEASE (interpreted as plural).

▸*PHRASE* □ **like peas** (or **two peas**) **in a pod** so similar as to be indistinguishable or nearly so.

pea bean ▸*n.* a variety of kidney bean with small rounded seeds.

pea·ber·ry /ˈpēˌberē/ ▸*n.* (*pl.* **-ries**) a coffee berry containing one rounded seed instead of the usual two, through nonfertilization of one ovule or subsequent abortion. Such beans are esteemed for their fine, strong flavor.

Pea·body /ˈpēˌbädē; -bədē/ an industrial city in northeastern Massachusetts; pop. 47,039.

pea·brain /ˈpēˌbrān/ ▸*n.* *informal* a stupid person.

pea-brained ▸*adj.* *informal* stupid; foolish.

peace /pēs/ ▸*n.* **1** freedom from disturbance; quiet and tranquility: *you can while away an hour or two in peace and seclusion.* ■ mental calm; serenity: *the* ***peace of mind*** *this insurance gives you.* **2** freedom from or the cessation of war or violence: *the Straits were to be open to warships in time of peace.* ■ [in *sing.*] a period of this: *the peace didn't last.* ■ [in *sing.*] a treaty agreeing to the cessation of war between warring states: *support for a negotiated peace.* ■ freedom from civil disorder: *police action to restore peace.* ■ freedom from dispute or dissension between individuals or groups: *the 8.8 percent offer that promises peace with the board.* **3** (**the peace**) a ceremonial handshake or kiss exchanged during a service in some churches (now usually only in the Eucharist), symbolizing Christian love and unity. See also KISS OF PEACE at KISS.
▸*exclam.* **1** used as a greeting. **2** used as an order to remain silent. ▷Middle English: from Old French *pais*, from Latin *pax, pac-* 'peace.'

▸*PHRASES* □ **at peace** **1** free from anxiety or distress.

■ dead (used to suggest that someone has escaped from the difficulties of life). **2** in a state of friendliness: *a man* **at peace with** *the world.* □ **hold one's peace** remain silent about something. □ **keep the peace** refrain or prevent others from disturbing civil order: *the police must play a crucial role in keeping the peace.* □ **make peace** (or **one's peace**) reestablish friendly relations; become reconciled: *not every conservative has* **made peace with** *big government.* □ **no peace for the weary** see NO REST FOR THE WEARY at WEARY.

peace·a·ble /'pēsəbəl/ ▸*adj.* inclined to avoid argument or violent conflict: *they were famed as an industrious, peaceable, practical people.* ■ free from argument or conflict; peaceful: *the mainly peaceable daily demonstrations for democratic reform.* ▷Middle English: from Old French *peisible*, alteration of *plaisible*, from late Latin *placibilis* 'pleasing,' from Latin *placere* 'to please.' **—peace·a·ble·ness** *n.* **—peace·a·bly** /-blē/ *adv.*

Peace Corps /'pēs ˌkôr/ an organization sponsored by the U.S. government that sends young people to work as volunteers in developing countries.

peace div·i·dend ▸*n.* a sum of public money that becomes available for other purposes when spending on defense is reduced.

peace·ful /'pēsfəl/ ▸*adj.* **1** free from disturbance; tranquil: *everything was so quiet and peaceful in the early morning.* See note at CALM. **2** not involving war or violence: *a soldier was shot and seriously wounded at an otherwise peaceful demonstration.* ■ (of a person) inclined to avoid conflict; not aggressive: *Dad was a peaceful, law-abiding citizen.* **—peace·ful·ness** *n.*

peace·ful·ly /'pēsfəlē/ ▸*adv.* **1** without disturbance; tranquilly: *the baby slept peacefully in its cradle.* ■ (of death) without pain: *she suffered a stroke and died peacefully in her sleep.* **2** without war or violence: *the siege ended peacefully.*

Peace Gar·den State a nickname for the state of NORTH DAKOTA.

peace·keep·ing /'pēsˌkēpiNG/ ▸*n.* [usu. as *adj.*] the active maintenance of a truce between nations or communities, esp. by an international military force: *the 2,300-strong UN peacekeeping force.* **—peace·keep·er** /-ˌkēpər/ *n.*

peace·mak·er /'pēsˌmākər/ ▸*n.* a person who brings about peace, esp. by reconciling adversaries. **—peace·mak·ing** /-ˌmākiNG/ *n.* & *adj.*

peace·nik /'pēsˌnik/ ▸*n. informal, often derogatory* a member of a pacifist movement. ▷coined during peace protests in the 1960s.

peace of·fer·ing ▸*n.* **1** a propitiatory or conciliatory gift: *he took the flowers to Jean as a peace offering.* **2** (in biblical use) an offering presented as a thanksgiving to God.

peace of·fi·cer ▸*n.* a civil officer appointed to preserve law and order, such as a sheriff or police officer.

peace or·der ▸*n.* a court order offering protection to certain classes of person who are not eligible to petition for a protective order.

peace pipe ▸*n.* a tobacco pipe offered and smoked as a token of peace among North American Indians.

Peace Riv·er a river that flows for 1,194 miles (1,923 km) from northern British Columbia into Alberta to the Slave River.

peace sign ▸*n.* **1** a sign of peace made by holding up the hand with palm turned outward and the first two fingers extended in a V-shape. **2** a figure representing peace, in the form of a circle with one line bisecting it from top to bottom and two shorter lines radiating downward on either side.

peace sign 2

peace talk ▸*n.* (usu. **peace talks**) a discussion about peace or the ending of hostilities, esp. a conference or series of discussions aimed at achieving peace.

peace·time /'pēsˌtīm/ ▸*n.* a period when a country is not at war.

peach[1] /pēCH/ ▸*n.* **1** a round stone fruit with juicy yellow flesh and downy pinkish-yellow skin. ■ a pinkish-yellow color like that of a peach. ■ *informal* an exceptionally good or attractive person or thing: *what a peach of a shot!* **2** (also **peach tree**) the Chinese tree that bears this fruit. • *Prunus persica*, family Rosaceae: many cultivars, including the nectarine. ▷late Middle English: from Old French *pesche*, from medieval Latin *persica*, from Latin *persicum (malum)*, literally 'Persian apple.'
▸*PHRASE* □ **peaches and cream 1** (of a person's complexion) of a cream color with downy pink cheeks. **2** fine; satisfactory: *all is not quite peaches and cream.*

peach[2] ▸*v.* [*intrans.*] (**peach on**) *informal* inform on: *the other members of the gang would not hesitate to peach on him if it would serve their purpose.* ▷late Middle English: shortening of archaic *appeach*, from Old French *empechier* 'impede' (see IMPEACH).

peach-bloom ▸*n.* a matte glaze of reddish pink, mottled with green and brown, used on fine Chinese porcelain since around 1700. ■ a delicate purplish-pink color. ▷early 19th cent.: applied to the porcelain glaze from the 1880s.

peach-blow ▸*n.* another term for PEACH-BLOOM. ■ a type of late 19th-century American colored glass. ▷early 19th cent.: from PEACH[1] + the noun BLOW[3].

peach fuzz ▸*n. informal* the down on the chin of an adolescent boy whose beard has not yet developed.

pea·chick /'pēˌCHik/ ▸*n.* a young peafowl.

peach Mel·ba ▸*n.* a dish of ice cream and peaches with liqueur or sauce. ▷named after Dame Nellie *Melba* (see MELBA).

Peach State a nickname for the state of GEORGIA.

Peach·tree State /'pēCHˌtrē/ a nickname for the state of GEORGIA.

peach·y /'pēCHē/ ▸*adj.* (**peach·i·er**, **peach·i·est**) *informal* of the nature or appearance of a peach. ■ fine; excellent: *everything is just peachy.* **—peach·i·ness** /-ēnis/ *n.*

peach·y-keen ▸*adj. informal* attractive; outstanding: *I enjoy my life, but it's not that peachy-keen.* ▷mid 20th cent.: from PEACHY in the sense 'excellent' + KEEN[1] in the sense 'wonderful.'

pea·coat /'pēˌkōt/ (also **pea coat**) ▸*n.* another term for PEA JACKET.

pea·cock /'pēˌkäk/ ▸*n.* a male peafowl, which has very long tail feathers that have eyelike markings and that can be erected and expanded in display like a fan. ■ an ostentatious strutting person: *these young men have always considered themselves the peacocks of Europe.*

peacock

▸*v.* [*intrans.*] display oneself ostentatiously; strut like a peacock: *he peacocks in front of the full-length mirror.* ▷Middle English: from Old English *pēa* (from Latin *pavo*) 'peacock' + COCK[1].

pea·cock blue ▸*n.* a greenish-blue color like that of a peacock's neck.

pea·cock but·ter·fly ▸*n.* a brightly colored Eurasian butterfly with conspicuous eyespots on its wings. • *Inachis io*, subfamily Nymphalinae, family Nymphalidae.

pea·cock ore ▸*n.* another term for BORNITE, so named for its iridescence.

pea crab ▸*n.* another term for OYSTER CRAB.

pea flour ▸*n.* flour made from dried split peas.

pea·fowl /'pēˌfoul/ ▸*n.* a large crested pheasant native to Asia. See PEACOCK, PEAHEN. • Two genera and three species in the family Phasianidae, in particular the widely introduced **common peafowl** (*Pavo cristatus*).

pea green ▸*n.* a yellowish green color like that of pea soup.

pea·hen /'pēˌhen/ ▸*n.* a female peafowl, having drabber colors and a shorter tail than the male.

pea jack·et (also **pea·coat**) ▸*n.* a short, double-breasted overcoat of coarse woolen cloth, formerly worn by sailors. ▷early 18th cent.: probably from Dutch *pijjakker*, from *pij* 'coat of coarse cloth' + *jekker* 'jacket.' The change in the ending was due to association with JACKET.

pea jacket

peak[1] /pēk/ ▸*n.* the pointed top of a mountain: *the snowy peaks rose against the blue of a cloudless sky.* ■ a mountain, esp. one with a pointed top: *the rocky outcrops of peaks such as the Cassongrat offer a challenge to rock climbers.* ■ a projecting pointed part or shape: *whisk 2 egg whites to stiff peaks.* ■ a point in a curve or on a graph, or a value of a physical quantity, higher than those around it: *a slight increase in velocity provides a second peak on the general velocity curve.* ■ the point of highest activity, quality, or achievement: *anyone who saw Jones* **at his peak** *looked upon genius.* ■ *chiefly Brit.* a stiff brim at the front of a cap. ■ the narrow part of a ship's hold at the bow or stern. ■ the upper, outer corner of a sail extended by a gaff.
▸*v.* [*intrans.*] reach a highest point, either of a specified value or at a specified time: *its popularity peaked in the 1940s | the rate of increase peaked at 34 percent last autumn.*
▸*adj.* [*attrib.*] greatest; maximum: *he did not expect to be anywhere near peak fitness until Christmas.* ■ characterized by maximum activity or demand: *at peak hours, traffic speeds are reduced considerably.* ▷mid 16th cent.: probably a back-formation from *peaked*, variant of dialect *picked* 'pointed.' **—peak·y** *adj.* **—peak·i·ness** /-kēnis/ *n.*

peak[2] ▸*v.* [*intrans.*] *archaic* decline in health and spirits; waste away. ▷early 17th cent.: of unknown origin. The phrase *peak and pine* derives its currency from Shakespeare.

peaked[1] /pēkt/ ▸*adj.* having a peak: *a peaked cap.*

peak·ed[2] /'pēˌkid/ (also **pe·kid**) ▸*adj.* [*predic.*] (of a person) gaunt and pale from illness or fatigue: *you do look a little peaked.*

peak flow me·ter ▸*n. Medicine* a calibrated instrument used to measure lung capacity in monitoring breathing disorders such as asthma.

peak load ▸*n.* the maximum of electrical power demand.

peal /pēl/ ▸*n.* **1** a loud ringing of a bell or bells. ■ *Bell-ringing* a series of unique changes (strictly, at least five thousand) rung on a set of bells. ■ a set of bells. **2** a loud repeated or reverberating sound of thunder or laughter: *Ross burst into* **peals of laughter**.
▸*v.* [*intrans.*] (of a bell or bells) ring loudly or in a peal: *all the bells of the city began to peal.* ■ (of laughter or thunder) sound in a peal: *Aunt Edie's laughter pealed around the parlor.* ■ [*trans.*] convey or give out by the ringing of bells: *the carillon* **pealed out** *the news to the waiting city.* ▷late Middle English: shortening of APPEAL.

Peale[1] /pēl/, Charles Willson (1741–1827), U.S. artist. He was known for his portraits of well-known Americans, including that of George Washington. His son **Rembrandt** (1778–1860) also painted portraits of well-known people, as well as historical scenes. Another son **Raphaelle** (1774–1825), also an artist, favored silhouettes and still-life paintings.

Peale[2], Norman Vincent (1898–1993), U.S. clergyman. The pastor of the Marble Collegiate Reformed Church in New York City 1932–84, he preached "applied Christianity," that encouraged people to think positively. His books included *The Art of Living* (1937), *The Art of Loving* (1948), and *The Power of Positive Thinking* (1952).

pe·an /'pēən/ ▸*n. Heraldry* fur resembling ermine but with gold spots on a black ground. ▷mid 16th cent.: of unknown origin.

Pe·a·no ax·i·oms /pā'änō 'aksēəmz/ ▸*plural n. Mathematics* a set of axioms from which the properties of the natural numbers can be deduced. ▷early 20th cent.: named after Giuseppe *Peano* (1858–1932), Italian mathematician.

pea·nut /'pēnət/ ▸*n.* **1** the oval seed of a South American plant, widely roasted and salted and eaten as a snack. ■ (**peanuts**) *informal* a paltry thing or amount, esp. a very small amount of money: *he pays peanuts.* ■ a small person (often used as a term of endearment). ■ (**peanuts**) small pieces of Styrofoam used for packing material. **2** the plant of the pea family that bears these seeds, which develop in pods that ripen underground. It is widely cultivated, esp. in the southern U.S., and large quantities are used to make oil or animal feed. • *Arachis hypogaea*, family Leguminosae.

pea·nut but·ter ▸*n.* a paste of ground roasted peanuts, usually eaten spread on bread.

pea·nut gal·ler·y ▸*n. informal* the top gallery in a theater where the cheaper seats are located. ■ a group of people who criticize someone, often by focusing on insignificant details: *he might find that playing the sport he loves isn't worth the aggravation from the peanut gallery's probing of his privacy.*

pea·nut oil ▸*n.* oil produced from peanuts and used

mainly for culinary purposes, but also in some soaps and pharmaceuticals.

pea·nut worm ▸*n.* an unsegmented burrowing marine worm with a stout body and a slender anterior part. The latter bears a terminal mouth surrounded by tentacles, and can be retracted into the trunk. • Phylum Sipuncula.

pear /pe(ə)r/ ▸*n.* **1** a yellowish- or brownish-green edible fruit that is typically narrow at the stalk and wider toward the tip, with sweet, slightly gritty flesh. **2** (also **pear tree**) the Eurasian tree that bears this fruit. • Genus *Pyrus*, family Rosaceae: several species and hybrids, in particular *P. communis.* ▷Old English *pere, peru*; related to Dutch *peer*, from Latin *pirum*.

Pearl a city in central Mississippi, just east of Jackson; pop. 21,961.

pearl /pərl/ ▸*n.* a hard, lustrous spherical mass, typically white or bluish-gray, formed within the shell of a pearl oyster or other bivalve mollusk and highly prized as a gem. ■ an artificial imitation of this. ■ (**pearls**) a necklace of pearls. ■ something resembling a pearl in appearance: *the sweat stood in pearls along his forehead.* ■ short for **MOTHER-OF-PEARL**. ■ *figurative* a precious thing; the finest example of something: *the nation's media were assembled to hear his* ***pearls of wisdom.*** ■ a very pale bluish gray or white like the color of a pearl.
▸*v.* [*intrans.*] **1** *poetic/literary* form pearllike drops: *the juice on the blade pearled into droplets.* ■ [*trans.*] make bluish-gray like a pearl: *the peaked hills, blue and pearled with clouds.* **2** [usu. as *n.*] (**pearling**) dive or fish for pearl oysters. ▷late Middle English: from Old French *perle*, perhaps based on Latin *perna* 'leg,' extended to denote a leg-of-mutton-shaped bivalve. —**pearl·er** *n.*
▸*PHRASE* □ **pearls before swine** valuable things offered or given to people who do not appreciate them. [with biblical allusion to Matt. 7:6.]

pearl ash ▸*n. archaic* commercial potassium carbonate.

pearl bar·ley ▸*n.* barley reduced to small round grains by grinding.

Pearl Cit·y a city in Hawaii, on southern Oahu Island, on Pearl Harbor; pop. 30,976.

pearl div·er ▸*n.* a person who dives for pearl oysters.

pearled /pərld/ ▸*adj.* **1** adorned with pearls: *we saw her pearled like the queen.* **2** *poetic/literary* bluish-gray, like a pearl. **3** formed into pearllike drops or grains.

pearl·es·cent /pər'lesənt/ ▸*adj.* having a luster resembling that of mother-of-pearl: *pearlescent colors.*

pearl ev·er·last·ing ▸*n.* variant of **PEARLY EVERLASTING**.

pearl·eye /'pərl,ī/ ▸*n.* a long-bodied, active fish of open oceans, with tubular eyes that are directed upward and bear a glistening white spot that may be a light organ. • Family Scopelarchidae: several genera and species.

Pearl Har·bor a harbor on the island of Oahu, in Hawaii, the site of a major U.S. naval base, where a surprise attack on December 7, 1941, by Japanese carrier-borne aircraft inflicted heavy damage and brought the U.S. into World War II.

pearl·ite /'pər,līt/ ▸*n. Metallurgy* a finely laminated mixture of ferrite and cementite present in cast iron and steel, formed by the cooling of austenite. ▷late 19th cent.: from **PEARL** + **-ITE**[1].

pearl·ized /'pərlīzd/ ▸*adj.* made to have or give a luster like that of mother-of-pearl.

pearl mil·let ▸*n.* a tall tropical grain with long cylindrical ears, comprising an important food crop in the driest areas of Africa and the Indian subcontinent. • *Pennisetum glaucum* (or **typhoides**) , family Gramineae.

pearl mus·sel ▸*n.* an elongated freshwater bivalve mollusk that occasionally produces small pearls, found in large rivers of the northern hemisphere. • *Margaritifera margaritifera*, family Margaritiferidae.

pearl on·ion ▸*n.* a very small onion used esp. for pickling.

pearl oys·ter ▸*n.* a tropical marine bivalve mollusk that has a ridged scaly shell and produces pearls. • Genus *Pinctada*, family Pteriidae: several species, in particular *P. margaritifera*, a major source of commercial pearls.

Pearl Riv·er **1** a river in southern China that flows from Guangzhou (Canton) south to the South China Sea and forms part of the delta of the Xi River. Its lower reaches widen to form the Pearl River estuary, an inlet between Hong Kong and Macao. **2** a river that flows for 485 miles (780 km) across central Mississippi, to form part of the border with Louisiana, into the Gulf of Mexico.

pearl tea ▸*n.* another term for **BUBBLE TEA**.

pearl·ware /'pərl,we(ə)r/ ▸*n.* fine glazed earthenware pottery, typically white, of a type introduced by Josiah Wedgwood in 1779.

pearl·wort /'pərl,wərt; -,wôrt/ ▸*n.* a small plant of the pink family, with inconspicuous white flowers, native to north temperate regions. • Genus *Sagina*, family Caryophyllaceae.

pearl·y /'pərlē/ ▸*adj.* (**pearl·i·er**, **pearl·i·est**) resembling a pearl in luster or color: *the pearly light of a clear, still dawn.* ■ containing or adorned with pearls or mother-of-pearl. —**pearl·i·ness** /-lēnis/ *n.*
▸*PHRASE* □ **pearly whites** *informal* a person's teeth.

pearl·y ev·er·last·ing ▸*n.* an ornamental North American plant with gray-green foliage and pearly white flowerheads, used in dry flower arrangements. • *Anaphalis margaritacea*, family Compositae.

pearl·y eye ▸*n.* a brown American butterfly with pearly markings and distinctive eyespots on the undersides of the wings. • Genus *Lethe*, subfamily Satyrinae, family Nymphalidae.

Pearl·y Gates ▸*plural n. informal* the gates of heaven: *I am getting less fond of poems about old age as I near the Pearly Gates.*

pearl·y nau·ti·lus ▸*n.* another term for **CHAMBERED NAUTILUS** (see **NAUTILUS**).

Pear·main /'pe(ə)r,mān/ ▸*n.* a pear-shaped apple of a variety with firm white flesh. ▷Middle English (denoting an old variety of baking pear): from Old French *parmain*, probably based on Latin *parmensis* 'of Parma.'

pear-shaped ▸*adj.* shaped like a pear; tapering toward the top. ■ (of a person) having hips that are disproportionately wide in relation to the upper part of the body.

Pear·son[1] /'pi(ə)rsən/, Karl (1857–1936), English mathematician; the principal founder of 20th-century statistics. He defined the concept of standard deviation and devised the chi-square test.

Pear·son[2], Lester Bowles (1897–1972), Canadian diplomat and statesman; prime minister 1963–68. As secretary of state for external affairs 1948–57, he acted as a mediator in the resolution of the Suez crisis in 1956. Nobel Peace Prize (1957).

Pear·son's cor·re·la·tion co·ef·fi·cient (also **Pearson's product-moment correlation coefficient**) ▸*n. Statistics* a statistic measuring the linear interdependence between two variables or two sets of data. ▷early 20th cent.: named after K. *Pearson* (see **PEARSON**[1]).

peart /pərt/ ▸*adj. dialect* lively; cheerful. ▷late 15th cent.: variant of **PERT**.

Pea·ry /'pi(ə)rē/, Robert Edwin (1856–1920), U.S. explorer. On April 6, 1909, he became the first person to reach the North Pole.

Pea·ry Land a mountainous region on the Arctic coast of northern Greenland. It is named after Robert Peary, who explored it in 1892 and 1900.

peas·ant /'pezənt/ ▸*n.* a poor farmer of low social status who owns or rents a small piece of land for cultivation (chiefly in historical use or with reference to subsistence farming in poorer countries). ■ *informal* an ignorant, rude, or unsophisticated person; a person of low social status. ▷late Middle English: from Old French *paisent* 'country dweller,' from *pais* 'country,' based on Latin *pagus* 'country district.' —**peas·ant·ry** /-trē/ *n.* —**peas·ant·y** *adj.*

peas·ant e·con·o·my ▸*n.* an agricultural economy in which the family is the basic unit of production.

Peas·ants' Re·volt an uprising in 1381 among the peasant and artisan classes in England. The rebels marched on London, occupying the city and executing unpopular ministers, but after the death of their leader, Wat Tyler, they were persuaded to disperse by Richard II.

pease /pēz/ ▸*plural n. archaic* peas. ▷Old English *pise* 'pea,' (plural) *pisan*, via Latin from Greek *pison*. Compare with **PEA**.

pea·shoot·er /'pē,sHōōtər/ ▸*n.* a toy weapon consisting of a small tube that is blown through in order to shoot out dried peas.

pea soup ▸*n.* **1** soup made from peas, esp. a thick, yellowish-green soup made from dried split peas. **2** a thick, yellowish fog.

peat /pēt/ ▸*n.* a brown, soil-like material characteristic of boggy, acid ground, consisting of partly decomposed vegetable matter. It is widely cut and dried for use in gardening and as fuel: *cuttings are rooted in a homemade mixture of equal parts peat and sand* | [as *adj.*] *most of Lewis is acid* ***peat bog.*** ▷Middle English: from Anglo-Latin *peta*, perhaps of Celtic origin. —**peat·y** *adj.*

peat·land /'pēt,land/ ▸*n.* (also **peatlands**) land consisting largely of peat or peat bogs.

peat moss ▸*n.* **1** a large absorbent moss that grows in dense masses on boggy ground, where the lower parts decay slowly to form peat deposits. Peat moss is widely used in horticulture, esp. for packing plants and (as peat) for compost. Also called **BOG MOSS**, **SPHAGNUM**. • Genus *Sphagnum*, family Sphagnaceae: many species. **2** a lowland peat bog.

pea tree (also **pea shrub**) ▸*n.* a shrub or small tree with yellow pealike flowers, native to Siberia and grown as an ornamental. • *Caragana arborescens*, family Leguminosae.

peau de soie /'pō də 'swä/ ▸*n.* a smooth, finely ribbed satin fabric of silk or rayon. ▷mid 19th cent.: French, literally 'skin of silk.'

peau d'or·ange /'pō dô'ränzH/ ▸*n.* a pitted or dimpled appearance of the skin, esp. as characteristic of some cases of breast cancer or due to cellulite. ▷French, literally 'orange skin.'

pea·vey /'pēvē/ (also **pea·vy**) ▸*n.* (*pl.* **-veys** or **-vies**) a lumberjack's cant hook with a spike at the end. ▷late 19th cent.: from the surname of the inventor.

pea·vine /'pē,vīn/ ▸*n.* a North American meadow vetch. • *Vicia americana*, family Leguminosae.

peb·ble /'pebəl/ ▸*n.* a small stone made smooth and round by the action of water or sand.
▸*adj.* [*attrib.*] *informal* (of an eyeglass lens) very thick and convex: *pebble glasses.* ▷late Old English, recorded as the first element of *papel-stān* 'pebble-stone,' *pyppelrīpig* 'pebble-stream,' of unknown origin. The word is recorded in place names from the early 12th cent. onward. —**peb·bled** *adj.* —**peb·bly** /-(ə)lē/ *adj.*

Peb·ble Beach a resort on the Monterey Peninsula in west central California, site of a famous golf course.

peb·ble-dash ▸*n. chiefly Brit.* mortar with pebbles in it, used as a coating for exterior walls. —**peb·ble-dashed** *adj.*

peb·ble-grained ▸*adj.* (of leather) having a rough and indented surface as a result of treatment with a patterned roller.

pec /pek/ ▸*n.* (usu. **pecs**) *informal* a pectoral muscle (esp. with reference to the development of these muscles in bodybuilding).

pe·can /pə'kän; 'pē,kan/ ▸*n.* a smooth brown nut with an edible kernel similar to a walnut. • This nut is obtained from a hickory tree (*Carya illinoensis*, family Juglandaceae), native to the southern U.S. ▷late 18th cent.: from French *pacane*, from Illinois (an American Indian language).

pec·ca·ble /'pekəbəl/ ▸*adj. archaic, formal* capable of sinning: *we hold all mankind to be peccable.* ▷early 17th cent.: from French, from medieval Latin *peccabilis*, from Latin *peccare* 'to sin.' —**pec·ca·bil·i·ty** /,pekə'bilitē/ *n.*

pec·ca·dil·lo /,pekə'dilō/ ▸*n.* (*pl.* **-loes** or **-los**) a small, relatively unimportant offense or sin. ▷late 16th cent.: from Spanish *pecadillo*, diminutive of *pecado* 'sin,' from Latin *peccare* 'to sin.'

pec·cant /'pekənt/ ▸*adj. archaic* **1** having committed a fault or sin; offending. **2** diseased or causing disease. ▷late 16th cent. (sense 2): from Latin *peccant-* 'sinning,' from the verb *peccare*. —**pec·can·cy** /'pekənsē/ *n.*

pec·ca·ry /'pekərē/ ▸*n.* (*pl.* **-ries**) a gregarious piglike mammal that is found from the southwestern U.S. to Paraguay. • Family Tayassuidae: two genera and three species, in particular the **collared peccary** (*Tayassu tajacu*). ▷early 17th cent.: from Carib *pakira*.

collared peccary

pec·ca·vi /pə'kävē; -'kāvī/ ▸*exclam. archaic* used to express one's guilt. ▷Latin, literally 'I have sinned.'

Pe·chen·ga /pə'cHenggə; pyi'cHyengə/ a region of northwestern Russia that lies west of Murmansk on the border with Finland. Formerly part of Finland, it was ceded to the Soviet Union in 1940. It was known by its Finnish name, Petsamo, from 1920 until 1944.

Pe·cho·ra /pəˈcʜôrə; pyiˈcʜyôrə/ a river in northern Russia that rises in the Ural Mountains and flows about 1,125 miles (1,800 km) north and then east to the Barents Sea.

Peck /pek/, (Eldred) Gregory (1916– 2002), U.S. actor. His many movies range from the thriller *Spellbound* (1945) to the western *The Big Country* (1958). He won an Academy Award for his role as the lawyer Atticus in *To Kill a Mockingbird* (1962).

peck[1] /pek/ ▶*v.* [*intrans.*] (of a bird) strike or bite something with its beak: *two geese were* ***pecking at*** *some grain* | [*trans.*] *beaks may be cut off to stop the hens pecking each other.* ■ [*trans.*] make (a hole) by striking with the beak: *robins are the worst culprits, pecking holes in every cherry.* ■ [*trans.*] remove or pluck out by biting with the beak: *vultures swooping down to* ***peck out*** *the calf's eyes.* ■ [*trans.*] kiss (someone) lightly or perfunctorily: *she* ***pecked*** *him* ***on the cheek.*** ■ (**peck at**) *informal* (of a person) eat (food) listlessly or daintily: *don't peck at your food, eat a whole mouthful.* ■ (**peck at**) criticize or nag: *defects for a critic to peck at.* ■ [*trans.*] type (something) slowly and laboriously: *his son Paul was* ***pecking out*** *letters with two fingers on his typewriter.* ■ *informal* (of a horse) pitch forward or stumble as a result of striking the ground with the front rather than the flat of the hoof: *her father's horse had pecked slightly on landing.* [variant of obsolete *pick* 'fix (something pointed) in the ground.'] ■ [*trans.*] *archaic* strike with a pick or other tool: *part of a wall was pecked down and carted away.*
▶*n.* **1** a stroke or bite by a bird with its beak: *the bird managed to give its attacker a sharp peck.* ■ a light or perfunctory kiss: *a fatherly* ***peck on the cheek.*** **2** *archaic* food: *he wants a little more peck.* ▷late Middle English: of unknown origin; compare with Middle Low German *pekken* 'peck (with the beak).'

peck[2] ▶*n.* a measure of capacity for dry goods, equal to a quarter of a bushel (8 U.S. quarts = 8.81 liters, or 2 imperial gallons = 9.092 liters). ■ *archaic* a large number or amount of something: *a peck of dirt.* ▷Middle English (used esp. as a measure of oats for horses): from Anglo-Norman French *pek*, of unknown origin.

peck·er /ˈpekər/ ▶*n. vulgar slang* a penis.
▶*PHRASE* □ **keep your pecker up** *Brit., informal* remain cheerful. [*pecker* probably in the sense 'beak, bill.']

peck·er·head /ˈpekərˌhed/ ▶*n. vulgar slang* an aggressive, objectionable person.

peck·er·wood /ˈpekərˌwo͝od/ ▶*n. informal, often derogatory* a white person, esp. a poor one. ▷1920s: from a reversal of the elements of *woodpecker*, originally a dialect word for the bird, used commonly in Mississippi and Tennessee.

Peck·ham /ˈpekəm/, Rufus Wheeler, Jr. (1838–1909), U.S. Supreme Court associate justice 1895–1909. A judge in New York's court of appeals 1886–95, he was appointed to the Court by President Cleveland.

peck·ing or·der (also **peck or·der**) ▶*n.* a hierarchy of status seen among members of a group of people or animals, originally as observed among hens: *the luxurious office accentuated the manager's position in the pecking order.*

peck·ish /ˈpekisʜ/ ▶*adj. informal, chiefly Brit.* hungry: *we were both feeling a bit peckish and there was nothing to eat.*

Peck·sniff·i·an /pekˈsnifēən/ ▶*adj.* affecting benevolence or high moral principles. ▷mid 19th cent.: from *Pecksniff*, the name of a character in Dickens's *Martin Chuzzlewit*, + **-IAN**.

Pe·con·ic Bay /piˈkänik/ an inlet of the Atlantic Ocean at the eastern end of Long Island in New York that separates the North Fork and the South Fork of the island.

pec·o·ri·no /pekəˈrēnō/ ▶*n.* (*pl.* **-nos**) an Italian cheese made from ewes' milk. ▷Italian, from *pecorino* 'of ewes,' from *pecora* 'sheep.'

Pe·cos Riv·er /ˈpāˌkōs/ a river that flows for 925 miles (1,490 km) from northern New Mexico through western Texas to the Rio Grande.

Pécs /pācʜ/ an industrial city in southwestern Hungary; pop. 172,000.

pec·ten /ˈpektən/ ▶*n.* (*pl.* **pec·tens** /ˈpektnz/ or **pec·ti·nes** /ˈpektnēz/) *Zoology* **1** any of a number of comblike structures occurring in animal bodies, in particular: ■ a pigmented vascular projection from the choroid in the eye of a bird. ■ an appendage of an insect consisting of or bearing a row of bristles or chitinous teeth. ■ a sensory appendage on the underside of a scorpion. **2** a scallop. • Genus *Pecten*, family Pectinidae. ▷late Middle English (denoting the metacarpus): from Latin *pecten, pectin-* 'a comb, rake.' —**pec·ti·nate** /ˈpektənit; -ˌnāt/ *adj.* —**pec·ti·nat·ed** /-ˌnātid/ *adj.* —**pec·ti·na·tion** /ˌpektəˈnāsʜən/ *n.* (all in sense 1).

pec·tin /ˈpektin/ ▶*n.* a soluble gelatinous polysaccharide that is present in ripe fruits and is extracted for use as a setting agent in jams and jellies. ▷mid 19th cent.: from Greek *pektos* 'congealed' (from *pēgnuein* 'make solid') + **-IN**[1]. —**pec·tic** /ˈpektik/ *adj.*

pec·to·ral /ˈpektərəl/ ▶*adj.* of or relating to the breast or chest: *pectoral development.* ■ worn on the chest: *a pectoral shield.*
▶*n.* (usu. **pectorals**) a pectoral muscle. ■ a pectoral fin. ■ an ornamental breastplate, esp. one worn by a Jewish high priest. ▷late Middle English (in the sense 'breastplate'): from Latin *pectorale* 'breastplate,' *pectoralis* 'of the breast,' from *pectus, pector-* 'breast, chest.'

pec·to·ral cross ▶*n. Christian Church* a cross or crucifix worn on a long chain around the neck so that it rests on the chest, worn esp. by bishops, abbots, and priests.

pec·to·ral fin ▶*n. Zoology* each of a pair of fins situated on either side just behind a fish's head, helping to control the direction of movement during locomotion. They correspond to the forelimbs of other vertebrates.

pec·to·ral gir·dle ▶*n.* (in vertebrates) the skeletal framework that provides attachment for the forelimbs or pectoral fins, usually consisting of the scapulas and clavicles.

pec·to·ral mus·cle ▶*n.* (usu. **pectoral muscles**) each of the four large paired muscles that cover the front of the rib cage and serve to draw the forelimbs toward the chest.

pec·to·ral sand·pip·er ▶*n.* a migratory sandpiper with dark streaks on the breast and a white belly, breeding chiefly in Arctic Canada. • *Calidris melanotos*, family Scolopacidae.

pec·u·late /ˈpekyəˌlāt/ ▶*v.* [*trans.*] *formal* embezzle or steal (money, esp. public funds): *the people accused them of having peculated the public money.* ▷mid 18th cent.: from Latin *peculat-* 'embezzled,' from the verb *peculari* (related to *peculium* 'property'). —**pec·u·la·tion** /ˌpekyəˈlāsʜən/ *n.* —**pec·u·la·tor** /-ˌlātər/ *n.*

pe·cu·liar /pəˈkyo͞olyər/ ▶*adj.* **1** strange or odd; unusual: *his accent was a peculiar mixture of Cockney and Irish.* ■ [*predic.*] *informal* slightly and indefinably unwell; faint or dizzy: *I* ***felt*** *a little* ***peculiar*** *for a while, but I'm absolutely fine now.* **2** [*predic.*] (**peculiar to**) belonging exclusively to: *the air hung with an antiseptic aroma peculiar to hospitals.* ■ *formal* particular; special: *any attempt to explicate the theme is bound to run into peculiar difficulties.*
▶*n. chiefly Brit.* a parish or church exempt from the jurisdiction of the diocese in which it lies, through being subject to the jurisdiction of the monarch or an archbishop. ▷late Middle English (in the sense 'particular, special'): from Latin *peculiaris* 'of private property,' from *peculium* 'property,' from *pecu* 'cattle' (cattle being private property). The sense 'odd' dates from the early 17th cent.

pe·cu·liar in·sti·tu·tion ▶*n. historical* the system of black slavery in the southern states of the U.S.

pe·cu·li·ar·i·ty /pəˌkyo͞olēˈaritē/ ▶*n.* (*pl.* **-ties**) an odd or unusual feature or habit: *for all his peculiarities, she finds his personality quite endearing.* ■ a characteristic or quality that is distinctive of a particular person or place: *his essays characterized decency as a British peculiarity.* ■ the quality or state of being peculiar: *the peculiarity of their upbringing.*

pe·cu·liar·ly /pəˈkyo͞olyərlē/ ▶*adv.* **1** [as *submodifier*] more than usually; especially: *some patients were peculiarly difficult to cure.* **2** oddly: *the town is peculiarly built.* **3** used to emphasize restriction to an individual or group: *a manner peculiarly his own.*

pe·cu·ni·ar·y /piˈkyo͞onēˌerē/ ▶*adj. formal* of, relating to, or consisting of, money: *he admitted obtaining a pecuniary advantage by deception.* See note at **FINANCIAL**. ▷early 16th cent.: from Latin *pecuniarius*, from *pecunia* 'money,' from *pecu* 'cattle, money.' —**pe·cu·ni·ar·i·ly** /pəˌkyo͞onēˈe(ə)rəlē/ *adv.*

ped·a·gog·ic /ˌpedəˈgäjik/ ▶*adj.* of or relating to teaching: *they show great pedagogic skills.* ■ *rare* of or characteristic of a pedagogue. ▷late 18th cent.: from French *pédagogique*, from Greek *paidagōgikos*. —**ped·a·gog·i·cal** *adj.* —**ped·a·gog·i·cal·ly** /-(ə)lē/ *adv.*

ped·a·gogue /ˈpedəˌgäg/ ▶*n.* a teacher, esp. a strict or pedantic one. ▷late Middle English: via Latin from Greek *paidagōgos*, denoting a slave who accompanied a child to school (from *pais, paid-* 'boy' + *agōgos* 'guide').

ped·a·go·gy /ˈpedəˌgäjē; -ˌgōjē/ ▶*n.* (*pl.* **-gies**) the method and practice of teaching, esp. as an academic subject or theoretical concept: *the relationship between applied linguistics and language pedagogy* | *subject-based pedagogies.* ▷late 16th cent.: from French *pédagogie*, from Greek *paidagōgia* 'office of a pedagogue,' from *paidagōgos* (see **PEDAGOGUE**). —**ped·a·gog·ics** /ˌpedəˈgäjiks/ *n.*

ped·al[1] /ˈpedl/ ▶*n.* a foot-operated lever or control for a vehicle, musical instrument, or other mechanism, in particular: ■ each of a pair of cranks used for powering a bicycle or other vehicle propelled by leg power. ■ a foot-operated throttle, brake, or clutch control in a motor vehicle. ■ each of a set of two or three levers on a piano, particularly (also **sustaining pedal**) one that, when depressed by the foot, prevents the dampers from stopping the sound when the keys are released. The second is the **soft pedal**; a third, if present, produces either selective sustaining or complete muffling of the tone. ■ *Music* (usu. **pedals**) each key of an organ keyboard that is played with the feet. ■ *Music* short for **PEDAL NOTE** (sense 2).
▶*v.* (**ped·aled, ped·al·ing**; *Brit.* **ped·alled, ped·al·ling**) [*intrans.*] move by working the pedals of a bicycle: *they pedaled along the canal towpath.* ■ [*trans.*] move (a bicycle) by working its pedals: *she was pedaling a bicycle around town.* ■ [*intrans.*] work the pedals of a bicycle: *he was coming down the path on his bike, pedaling hard.* ■ [*intrans.*] use the pedals of a piano, esp. in a particular style: [as *n.*] (**pedaling**) *Chopin gave no indications of pedaling in his manuscript.* ▷early 17th cent. (denoting a foot-operated lever of an organ): from French *pédale*, from Italian *pedale*, from Latin *pedalis* 'a foot in length,' from *pes, ped-* 'foot.' —**ped·al·er** (*Brit.* **ped·al·ler**) *n.*
▶*PHRASE* □ **with the pedal to the metal** *informal* with the accelerator of a car pressed to the floor.

ped·al[2] /ˈpēdl/ ▶*adj. chiefly Medicine Zoology* of or relating to the foot or feet. ▷early 17th cent.: from Latin *pedalis*, from *pes, ped-* 'foot.'

ped·al·board /ˈpedlˌbôrd/ ▶*n.* the keyboard of pedals on an organ.

ped·al boat /ˈpedl/ ▶*n.* another term for **PADDLEBOAT**.

ped·al note /ˈpedl/ ▶*n.* (also **pedal tone**) *Music* **1** the lowest or fundamental note of a harmonic series in some brass and wind instruments. **2** (also **pedal point**) a note sustained in one part (usually the bass) through successive harmonies, some of which are independent of it.

ped·al pow·er /ˈpedl/ ▶*n. informal* cycling as a means of transportation.

ped·al push·er /ˈpedl/ ▶*n.* **1** (**pedal pushers**) women's calf-length pants. **2** *informal* a cyclist.

ped·al steel gui·tar /ˈpedl/ (also **pedal steel**) ▶*n.* a musical instrument played like the Hawaiian guitar, but set on a stand with pedals to adjust the tension of the strings.

ped·ant /ˈpednt/ ▶*n.* a person who is excessively concerned with minor details and rules or with displaying academic learning. ▷late 16th cent.: from French *pédant*, from Italian *pedante*, perhaps from the first element of Latin *paedagogus* (see **PEDAGOGUE**). —**ped·ant·ry** /-trē/ *n.*

pe·dan·tic /pəˈdantik/ ▶*adj.* of or like a pedant: *many of the essays are long, dense, and too pedantic to hold great appeal.* —**pe·dan·ti·cal·ly** /-tik(ə)lē/ *adv.*

ped·dle /ˈpedl/ ▶*v.* [*trans.*] try to sell (something, esp. small goods) by going from house to house or place to place: *he peddled art and printing materials around the country.* ■ sell (an illegal drug or stolen item): [as *n.*] (**peddling**) *certain youths who were involved in theft and drug peddling.* ■ *derogatory* promote (an idea or view) persistently or widely: *he criticized his fellow candidate for peddling risky ideas.* ▷early 16th cent.: back-formation from **PEDLAR**.

ped·dler /ˈpedlər; ˈpedl-ər/ (also **ped·lar**) ▶*n.* a person who goes from place to place selling small goods. ■ a person who sells illegal drugs or stolen goods: *a drug peddler.* ■ a person who promotes an idea or view persistently or widely: *peddlers of dangerous Utopianism.* ▷Middle English: perhaps an alteration of synonymous dialect *pedder*, apparently from dialect *ped* 'basket.'

ped·er·ast /ˈpedəˌrast/ ▶*n.* a man who indulges in pederasty. ▷mid 17th cent.: from Greek *paiderastēs*.

ped·er·as·ty /ˈpedəˌrastē/ ▶*n.* sexual activity involving a man and a boy. ▷early 17th cent.: from modern

Pronunciation Key ə *ago*; ər *over*; ˈə or ˌə *up*; ˈər or ˌər *fur*; a *hat*; ā *rate*; ä *car*; cʜ *chew*; e *let*; ē *see*; e(ə)r *air*; i *fit*; ī *by*; i(ə)r *ear*; ɴɢ *sing*; ō *go*; ô *for*; oi *boy*; o͝o *good*; o͞o *goo*; ou *out*; sʜ *she*; ᴛʜ *thin*; <u>TH</u> *then*; (h)w *why*; ᴢʜ *vision*

Latin *paederastia,* from Greek *paiderastia,* from *pais, paid-* 'boy' + *erastēs* 'lover.' —**ped·er·as·tic** /ˌpedəˈrastik/ *adj.*

pe·des /ˈpēdēz; ˈpedēz/ ▸ plural form of PES.

ped·es·tal /ˈpedəstl/ ▸*n.* the base or support on which a statue, obelisk, or column is mounted. ■ *figurative* a position in which one is greatly or uncritically admired: *the heroes they have created and* ***placed on pedestals.*** ■ each of the two supports of a kneehole desk or table, typically containing drawers. ■ the supporting column or base of a washbasin or toilet bowl. ▷mid 16th cent.: from French *piédestal,* from Italian *piedestallo,* from *piè* 'foot' (from Latin *pes, ped-,* which later influenced the spelling) + *di* 'of' + *stallo* 'stall.'

ped·es·tal ta·ble ▸*n.* a table with a single central support.

P

pe·des·tri·an /pəˈdestrēən/ ▸*n.* a person walking along a road or in a developed area.
▸*adj.* lacking inspiration or excitement; dull: *disenchantment with their present, pedestrian lives.* ▷early 18th cent.: from French *pédestre* or Latin *pedester* 'going on foot,' also 'written in prose' + -IAN. Early use in English was in the description of writing as 'prosaic.' —**pe·des·tri·an·ly** *adv.*

pe·des·tri·an cross·ing ▸*n.* British term for CROSSWALK.

pe·des·tri·an·ize /pəˈdestrēəˌnīz/ ▸*v.* [*trans.*] close (a street or area) to traffic, making it accessible only to pedestrians: *the ancient center of the town was pedestrianized.* —**pe·des·tri·an·i·za·tion** /pəˌdestrēəniˈzāshən/ *n.*

pe·di·at·rics /ˌpēdēˈatriks/ (*Brit.* **pae·di·at·rics**) ▸*plural n.* [treated as *sing.*] the branch of medicine dealing with children and their diseases. ▷late 19th cent.: from PEDO-[1] 'of children' + Greek *iatros* 'physician' + -ICS. —**pe·di·at·ric** /-ˈatrik/ *adj.* —**pe·di·a·tri·cian** /ˌpēdēəˈtrishən/ *n.*

ped·i·cab /ˈpedikab/ ▸*n.* a small pedal-operated vehicle, serving as a taxi in some countries.

ped·i·cel /ˈpediˌsel/ ▸*n. Botany* a small stalk bearing an individual flower in an inflorescence. Compare with PEDUNCLE. ■ *Anatomy & Zoology* another term for PEDICLE. ▷late 17th cent.: from modern Latin *pedicellus* 'small foot,' diminutive of *pes, ped-* 'foot.' —**ped·i·cel·late** /ˌpediˈselit; -ˈseˌlāt/ *adj.*

ped·i·cel·lar·i·a /ˌpedisəˈle(ə)rēə/ ▸*n.* (*pl.* **-lar·i·ae** /-ˈle(ə)rēˌē/) *Zoology* a defensive organ like a minute pincer present in large numbers on an echinoderm. ▷late 19th cent.: modern Latin, from Latin *pediculus* 'small foot' (see PEDICEL).

ped·i·cle /ˈpedikəl/ ▸*n. Anatomy & Zoology* a small stalklike structure connecting an organ or other part to the human or animal body. Compare with PEDICEL. ■ *Medicine* part of a graft, esp. a skin graft, left temporarily attached to its original site. ▷early 17th cent.: from Latin *pediculus* 'small foot,' diminutive of *pes, ped-.*

pe·dic·u·li·cide /ˌpediˈkyo͞oləsīd/ ▸*n.* a chemical used to kill lice. ▷early 20th cent.: from Latin *pediculus* 'louse' + -CIDE.

pe·dic·u·lo·sis /pəˌdikyəˈlōsis/ ▸*n. Medicine* infestation with lice. ▷early 19th cent.: from Latin *pediculus* 'louse' + -OSIS.

ped·i·cure /ˈpediˌkyo͝or/ ▸*n.* a cosmetic treatment of the feet and toenails.
▸*v.* [*trans.*] [usu. as *adj.*] (**pedicured**) give such a cosmetic treatment to (the feet). ▷mid 19th cent.: from French *pédicure,* from Latin *pes, ped-* 'foot' + *curare* 'attend to.'

ped·i·gree /ˈpedəˌgrē/ ▸*n.* **1** the record of descent of an animal, showing it to be purebred. ■ *informal* a purebred animal. **2** the recorded ancestry, esp. upper-class ancestry, of a person or family. ■ the background or history of a person or thing, esp. as conferring distinction or quality. ■ a genealogical table. ▷late Middle English: from Anglo-Norman French *pé de grue* 'crane's foot,' a mark used to denote succession in pedigrees. —**ped·i·greed** *adj.*

ped·i·ment /ˈpedəmənt/ ▸*n.* the triangular upper part of the front of a building in classical style, typically surmounting a portico of columns. ■ a similar feature surmounting a door, window, front, or other part of a building in another style. ■ *Geology* a broad, gently sloping expanse of rock debris extending outward from the foot of a mountain slope, esp. in a desert. ▷late 16th cent. (as *periment*): perhaps an alteration of PYRAMID. —**ped·i·men·tal** /ˌpedəˈmentl/ *adj.* —**ped·i·ment·ed** *adj.*

ped·i·palp /ˈpedəˌpalp/ ▸*n. Zoology* each of the second pair of appendages attached to the cephalothorax of most arachnids. They are variously specialized as pincers in scorpions, sensory organs in spiders, and locomotory organs in horseshoe crabs. ▷early 19th cent.: from modern Latin *pedipalpi* (plural), from Latin *pes, ped-* 'foot' + *palpus* 'palp.'

ped·i·plain /ˈpediˌplān/ ▸*n. Geology* an extensive plain formed in a desert by the coalescence of neighboring pediments. ▷1930s: from PEDIMENT + PLAIN[1].

ped·i·pla·na·tion /ˌpediplәˈnāshən/ ▸*n. Geology* the formation of pediplains by coalescence of pediments.

ped·lar ▸*n.* variant spelling of PEDDLER.

pedo-[1] /ˈpedō/ (*Brit.* **paedo-**) ▸*comb. form* of a child; relating to children: *pedophile.* ▷from Greek *pais, paid-* 'child, boy.'

pedo-[2] ▸*comb. form* relating to soil or soil types: *pedogenic.* ▷from Greek *pedon* 'ground.'

pe·do·don·tics /ˌpēdəˈdäntiks/ (*Brit.* **pae·do·don·tics**) ▸*plural n.* [treated as *sing.*] the branch of dentistry that deals with children's teeth. ▷from PEDO-[1] + Greek *odous, odont-* 'tooth.' —**pe·do·don·tic** /-tik/ *adj.* —**pe·do·don·tist** /-ˈdäntist/ *n.*

ped·o·gen·e·sis /ˌpedōˈjenəsəs/ ▸*n. Zoology* see NEOTENY. ▷from PEDO-[1] + GENESIS. —**ped·o·ge·net·ic** *adj.*

pe·do·gen·ic /ˌpedəˈjenik/ ▸*adj.* relating to or denoting processes occurring in soil or leading to the formation of soil. ▷from PEDO-[2] + -GENIC.

pe·dol·o·gy /pəˈdäləjē/ ▸*n.* another term for SOIL SCIENCE. ▷from PEDO-[2] + -OLOGY. —**ped·o·log·i·cal** /ˌpedəˈläjikəl/ *adj.* —**pe·dol·o·gist** /-jist/ *n.*

pe·dom·e·ter /pəˈdämitər/ ▸*n.* an instrument for estimating the distance traveled on foot by recording the number of steps taken. ▷early 18th cent.: from French *pédomètre,* from Latin *pes, ped-* 'foot.'

ped·o·mor·pho·sis /ˌpēdəˈmôrfəsəs/ ▸*n. Zoology* see NEOTENY. ▷from PEDO-[1] + -MORPH + -OSIS. —**pe·do·mor·phic** /-fik/ *adj.*

pe·do·phile /ˈpedəˌfīl/ (*Brit.* **pae·do·phile**) ▸*n.* a person who is sexually attracted to children. ▷from PEDO-[1] + -PHILE.

pe·do·phil·i·a /ˌpedəˈfilēə; ˌpēdə-/ (*Brit.* **pae·do·phil·i·a**) ▸*n.* sexual feelings directed toward children. ▷from PEDO-[1] + -PHILIA. —**pe·do·phil·i·ac** /-ˈfilēˌak/ *n.* & *adj.*

Pe·dro Xi·me·nez /ˌpādrō hiˈmāniz/ (abbr.: **PX** or **px**) ▸*n.* a variety of sweet white Spanish grape used in making sherry and sweet wine. ■ a sweet white wine made from this grape. ▷from the name of the person who introduced the grape.

pe·dun·cle /ˈpēˌdəngkəl; pəˈdəngkəl/ ▸*n. Botany* the stalk bearing a flower or fruit, or the main stalk of an inflorescence. Compare with PEDICEL. ■ *Zoology* a stalklike part by which an organ is attached to an animal's body, or by which a barnacle or other sedentary animal is attached to a substrate. ■ *Anatomy* any of several bundles of nerve fibers connecting two parts of the brain. ▷mid 18th cent.: from modern Latin *pedunculus,* from Latin *pes, ped-* 'foot.' —**pe·dun·cu·lar** /pəˈdəngkyələr/ *adj.*

pe·dun·cu·late /pəˈdəngkyəˌlāt; -lit/ ▸*adj. Botany & Zoology* having a peduncle.

pe·dun·cu·late oak ▸*n.* the common or English oak.

pee /pē/ *informal* ▸*v.* (**pees, peed, pee·ing**) [*intrans.*] urinate: *the puppy was peeing on the carpet.* ■ [*trans.*] (**pee in one's pants**) wet one's underpants by urinating involuntarily (often used to suggest the notion of losing control of oneself through fear or hilarity).
▸*n.* [in *sing.*] an act of urinating: *I really need to* ***take a pee.*** ■ urine. ▷late 18th cent. (as a verb): euphemistic use of the initial letter of PISS.

Pee Dee Riv·er /ˈpēˌdē/ a river that flows for 230 miles (370 km) through North Carolina and South Carolina to an inlet of the Atlantic Ocean south of the Grand Strand.

peek /pēk/ ▸*v.* [*intrans.*] look quickly, typically in a furtive manner: *faces peeked from behind the curtains.*

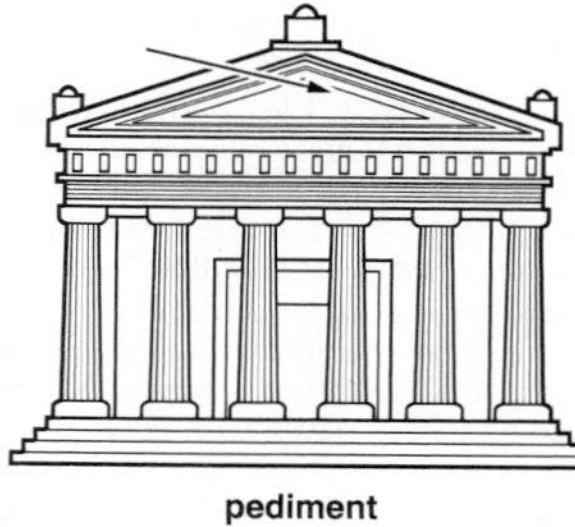
pediment

■ *figurative* protrude slightly so as to be just visible: *his socks were so full of holes his toes peeked through.*
▸*n.* **1** a quick and typically furtive look: *a peek through the window showed that the taxi had arrived.* **2** (usu. **PEEK**) *Computing* a statement or function in BASIC for reading the contents of a specified memory location. Compare with POKE[1] (sense 3). ▷late Middle English *pike, pyke,* of unknown origin.

peek-a-boo /ˈpēkəˌbo͞o/ (also **peek-a-boo**) ▸*n.* a game played with a young child, which involves hiding behind something and suddenly reappearing, saying "peekaboo."
▸*adj.* [*attrib.*] (of a garment) revealing glimpses of the skin or body: *a black lace peekaboo dress.* ■ (of a hairstyle) concealing one eye with a fringe or wave of hair. ▷late 16th cent. (as a noun): from the verb PEEK + BOO.

Peeks·kill /ˈpēkskil/ a commercial city in southeastern New York, on the Hudson River; pop. 19,536.

Peel /pēl/, Sir Robert (1788–1850), British statesman, prime minister 1834–35 and 1841–46. As home secretary 1828–30, he established the Metropolitan Police, whose members are called "bobbies" in his honor. His repeal of the Corn Laws in 1846 split the Conservatives and forced his resignation.

peel[1] /pēl/ ▸*v.* **1** [*trans.*] remove the outer covering or skin from (a fruit, vegetable, or shrimp): *she watched him peel an apple with deliberate care.* ■ remove (the outer covering or skin) from a fruit or vegetable: ***peel off*** *the skins and thickly slice the potatoes.* ■ [*intrans.*] (of a fruit or vegetable) have a skin that can be removed: *oranges that peel easily.* ■ (**peel something away/off**) remove or separate a thin covering or part from the outside or surface of something: *carefully peel away the wax paper.* ■ remove (an article of clothing): *Suzy peeled off her white pullover.* **2** [*intrans.*] (of a surface or object) lose parts of its outer layer or covering in small strips or pieces: *the walls are peeling.* ■ [with *adverbial*] (of an outer layer or covering) come off, esp. in strips or small pieces.
▸*phrasal v.* □ **peel off** (of a member of a formation, esp. a flying formation) leave the formation by veering away to one side: *the pace was much too hot for Beris, and he peeled off after five laps.* □ **peel out** *informal* leave quickly: *he peeled out down the street.*
▸*n.* the outer covering or rind of a fruit or vegetable. ▷Middle English (in the sense 'to plunder'): variant of dialect *pill,* from Latin *pilare* 'to strip hair from,' from *pilus* 'hair.' The differentiation of *peel* and *pill* may have been by association with the French verbs *peler* 'to peel' and *piller* 'to pillage.'

peel[2] ▸*n.* a flat, shovellike implement, esp. one used by baker for carrying loaves, pies, etc., into or out of an oven: *a wooden pizza peel.* ▷late Middle English: from Old French *pele,* from Latin *pala,* from the base of *pangere* 'to fix, plant.'

peel[3] (also **pele** or **peel tower**) ▸*n.* a small square defensive tower of a kind built in the 16th century in the border counties of England and Scotland. ▷probably short for synonymous *peel-house*: *peel* from Anglo-Norman French *pel* 'stake, palisade,' from Latin *palus* 'stake.'

peel[4] ▸*v.* [*trans.*] *Croquet* send (another player's ball) through a wicket: *the better players are capable of peeling a ball through two or three wickets.* ▷late 19th cent.: from the name of Walter H. *Peel,* founder of the All England Croquet Association, a leading exponent of the practice.

peel·er[1] /ˈpēlər/ ▸*n.* [usu. with *adj.*] a device for removing the skin from fruit and vegetables: *a potato peeler.*

peel·er[2] ▸*n. Brit., informal, dated* a police officer. ▷early 19th cent. (originally denoting a member of the Irish constabulary): from the name of Sir Robert *Peel* (see PEEL).

peel·ings /ˈpēlingz/ ▸*plural n.* [usu. with *adj.*] strips of the outer skin of a vegetable or fruit: *potato peelings.*

peen /pēn/ ▸*n.* the end of a hammer head opposite the face, typically wedge-shaped, curved, or spherical.
▸*v.* [*trans.*] strike with a hammer or the peen of a hammer. ■ another term for SHOT-PEEN. ▷early 16th cent. (as a verb): probably of Scandinavian origin; compare with Swedish dialect *pena (ut),* Danish dialect *pene (ud)* 'beat (out).'

Pee·ne·mün·de /ˌpānəˈmo͝ondə; ˌpānəˈmyndə/ a village in northeastern Germany, on a small island just off the Baltic coast. During World War II, it was the chief site of German rocket research and testing.

peep[1] /pēp/ ▸*v.* [*intrans.*] look quickly and furtively at something, esp. through a narrow opening: *the door was ajar and she couldn't resist peeping in.* ■ (**peep out**)

be just visible; appear slowly or partly or through a small opening: *a wad of money that was peeping out of his pocket | the sun began to peep out.*
▸*n.* [usu. in *sing.*] a quick or furtive look: *Jonathan took a peep at his watch.* ■ a momentary or partial view of something: *black curls and a peep of gold earring.* ▷late 15th cent.: symbolic; compare with **PEEK**.

peep2 ▸*n.* a high-pitched feeble sound made by a young bird or mammal. ■ [with *negative*] a slight sound, utterance, or complaint: *not a peep out of them since shortly after eight.* ■ (usu. **peeps**) *informal* a small sandpiper or similar wading bird.
▸*v.* [*intrans.*] make a cheeping or beeping sound. ▷late Middle English: imitative; compare with **CHEEP**.

pee-pee ▸*n. informal* a child's word for an act of urinating. ■ urine. ■ a penis.

peep·er1 /ˈpēpər/ ▸*n.* a person who peeps at someone or something, esp. in a voyeuristic way. ■ (**peepers**) *informal* a person's eyes: *keep your peepers peeled for a familiar face.*

peep·er2 (also **spring peeper**) ▸*n.* a small North American tree frog that has brownish-gray skin with a dark cross on the back, the males of which sing in early spring. • *Hyla crucifer*, family Hylidae.

peep·hole /ˈpēpˌhōl/ ▸*n.* a small hole that may be looked through, esp. one in a door through which visitors may be identified before the door is opened.

peep·ing Tom ▸*n.* a person who gets sexual pleasure from secretly watching people undressing or engaging in sexual activity. ▷from the name of the person said to have watched Lady **GODIVA** ride naked through Coventry.

peep show ▸*n.* a sequence of pictures viewed through a lens or hole set into a box, traditionally offered as a public entertainment. ■ an erotic or pornographic film or show viewed from a coin-operated booth.

peep sight ▸*n.* a rear sight for rifles with a circular hole through which the front sight is brought into line with the object aimed at.

peep-toe ▸*adj. Brit.* (of a shoe) having the tip cut away to leave the large toe partially exposed.
▸*n.* a shoe of such a type.

pee·pul /ˈpēpəl/ (also **pi·pal**) ▸*n.* another term for **BO TREE**. ▷late 18th cent.: via Hindi from Sanskrit *pippala.*

peer1 /pi(ə)r/ ▸*v.* [*intrans.*] look keenly or with difficulty at someone or something: *Blake screwed up his eyes, trying to peer through the fog.* ■ be just visible: *the two towers peer over the roofs.* ■ [*intrans.*] *archaic* come into view; appear. ▷late 16th cent.: perhaps a variant of dialect *pire*; perhaps partly from a shortening of **APPEAR**.

peer2 ▸*n.* **1** a member of the nobility in Britain or Ireland, comprising the ranks of duke, marquess, earl, viscount, and baron.

In the British peerage, earldoms and baronetcies were the earliest to be conferred; dukes were created from 1337, marquesses from the end of the 14th century, and viscounts from 1440. Such peerages are hereditary, although since 1958 there have also been nonhereditary life peerages. Peers are entitled to a seat in the House of Lords and exemption from jury service; they are debarred from election to the House of Commons.

2 a person of the same age, status, or ability as another specified person: *he has incurred much criticism from his academic peers.*
▸*v. archaic* make or become equal with or of the same rank. ▷Middle English: from Old French *peer*, from Latin *par* 'equal.' —**peer·less** *adj.* (in sense 2).
▸*PHRASE* □ **without peer** unequaled; unrivaled: *he is a goalkeeper without peer.*

peer·age /ˈpi(ə)rij/ ▸*n.* the title and rank of peer or peeress: *on his retirement as cabinet secretary, he was given a peerage.* ■ (**the peerage**) peers as a class; those holding a hereditary or honorary title: *he was elevated to the peerage two years ago.* ■ a book containing a list of peers and peeresses, with their genealogy and history.

peer·ess /ˈpi(ə)ris/ ▸*n.* a woman holding the rank of a peer in her own right. ■ the wife or widow of a peer.

peer group ▸*n.* a group of people of approximately the same age, status, and interests.

peer pres·sure ▸*n.* influence from members of one's peer group: *his behavior was affected by drink and peer pressure.*

peer re·view ▸*n.* evaluation of scientific, academic, or professional work by others working in the same field.
▸*v.* [*trans.*] (**peer-review**) subject (someone or something) to such evaluation.

peer-to-peer ▸*adj.* [*attrib.*] denoting computer networks in which each computer can act as a server for the others, allowing shared access to files and peripherals without the need for a central server.

peeve /pēv/ *informal* ▸*v.* [*trans.*] (usu. **be peeved**) annoy; irritate: *he was peeved at being left out of the cabinet* [as *adj.*] (**peeved**) *a somewhat peeved tone.*
▸*n.* a cause of annoyance: *his pet peeve is not having answers for questions from players.* ▷early 20th cent.: back-formation from **PEEVISH**.

peev·ish /ˈpēviSH/ ▸*adj.* easily irritated, esp. by unimportant things: *all this makes Steve fretful and peevish.* ■ querulous: *a peevish, whining voice.* ▷late Middle English (in the sense 'foolish, insane, spiteful'): of unknown origin. —**peev·ish·ly** *adv.* —**peev·ish·ness** *n.*

pee·wee /ˈpēˌwē/ ▸*n.* **1** [usu. as *adj.*] a level of amateur sports, involving children aged eight or nine: *a peewee baseball team.* ■ a player at such a level of amateur sport. **2** variant spelling of **PEWEE**. **3** a small marble.

pee·wit /ˈpēˌwit/ ▸*n.* variant spelling of **PEWIT**.

PEG ▸*abbr.* polyethylene glycol.

peg /peg/ ▸*n.* **1** a short cylindrical piece of wood, metal, or plastic, typically tapered at one end, that is used for holding things together, hanging things on, or marking a position. ■ such an object attached to a wall on which to hang garments. ■ (also **tent peg**) such an object driven into the ground to hold one of the ropes or corners of a tent in position. ■ such an object in the neck of a stringed musical instrument around which the strings are wound, and which are turned to adjust their tension and so tune the instrument. ■ a bung for stoppering a cask. ■ *informal* a person's leg. ■ a point or limit on a scale, esp. of exchange rates. **2** *chiefly Indian* a measure of liquor: *have **a peg of** whiskey.* **3** *informal* a strong throw, esp. in baseball.
▸*v.* (**pegged, peg·ging**) **1** [*trans.*] fix or make fast with a peg or pegs: *drape individual plants with nets, **pegging down** the edges.* ■ [*trans.*] mark (the score) with pegs on a cribbage board. **2** [*trans.*] fix (a price, rate, or amount) at a particular level. ■ *informal* form a fixed opinion of; categorize: *the officer probably **has us pegged as** anarchists.* **3** *informal* throw (a ball) hard and low, esp. in baseball: *the catcher pegs the ball to the first baseman.*
▸*phrasal v.* □ **peg away** *informal* continue working hard at or trying to achieve something, esp. over a long period. □ **peg out 1** *informal, chiefly Brit.* die. **2** score the winning point at cribbage. **3** *Croquet* hit the peg with the ball as the final stroke in a game. □ **peg something out** mark the boundaries of an area of land: *I went out to peg out our assembly area.* ▷late Middle English: probably of Low German origin; compare with Dutch dialect *peg* 'plug, peg.' The verb dates from the mid 16th cent.
▸*PHRASES* □ **a peg to hang a matter on** something used as a pretext or occasion for the discussion or treatment of a wider subject. □ **a square peg in a round hole** a person in a situation unsuited to their abilities or character. □ **take someone down a peg or two** make someone realize that they are less talented or important than they think are.

Peg·a·sus /ˈpegəsəs/ **1** *Greek Mythology* a winged horse that sprang from the blood of Medusa when Perseus cut off her head. **2** *Astronomy* a large northern constellation, said to represent a winged horse. The three brightest stars, together with one star of Andromeda, form the prominent **Square of Pegasus**. ■ [as *genitive*] (**Pegasi** /-sī/) used with a preceding letter or numeral to designate a star in this constellation: *the star Zeta Pegasi.* ▷via Latin from Greek.

peg·board /ˈpegˌbôrd/ ▸*n.* a board having a regular pattern of small holes for pegs, used chiefly for games or the display of information.

peg·box /ˈpegˌbäks/ ▸*n.* a structure at the head of a stringed instrument where the strings are attached to the tuning pegs.

pegged /pegd/ ▸*adj.* another term for **PEGTOP**.

peg·gy /ˈpegē/ ▸*n.* (*pl.* **-gies**) *Nautical slang* a steward in a ship's mess (often used as a form of address). ▷early 20th cent. (earlier denoting a man of feminine habits): alteration of *Meggy*, nickname for the given name *Margaret.*

peg leg ▸*n. informal* an artificial leg, esp. a wooden one. ■ a person with such an artificial leg.

peg·ma·tite /ˈpegməˌtīt/ ▸*n. Geology* a coarsely crystalline granite or other igneous rock with crystals several centimeters to several meters in length. ▷early 19th cent.: from Greek *pēgma, pēgmat-* 'thing joined together' + **-ITE1**.

peg·top /ˈpegˌtäp/ ▸*n.* a pear-shaped spinning top with a metal pin or peg forming the point, spun by the rapid uncoiling of a string wound around it.
▸*adj. dated* (of a garment) wide at the top and narrow at the bottom: *pegtop trousers were very wide in the hips.*

Pe·gu /peˈgo͞o/ a city and river port in southern Myanmar (Burma), on the Pegu River, northeast of Rangoon; pop. 150,000. It is a center of Buddhist culture.

Peh·le·vi /ˈpāləˌvē/ ▸*n.* variant spelling of **PAHLAVI2**.

PEI ▸*abbr.* Prince Edward Island.

Pei /pā/, I. M. (1917–), U.S. architect, born in China; full name *Ieoh Ming Pei.* He designed monumental public buildings, including the east wing of the National Gallery of Art 1978 in Washington, D.C.; the John F. Kennedy Library 1979 in Boston; and the pyramid entrance to the Louvre 1983–89 in Paris.

P

Pei·gan /ˈpēgən/ ▸*n.* (*pl.* same or **-gans**) & *adj.* variant spelling of **PIEGAN**.

peign·oir /ˌpānˈwär/ ▸*n.* a woman's light dressing gown or negligee. ▷French, from *peigner* 'to comb' (because the garment was originally worn while combing the hair).

pein ▸*n.* & *v.* variant spelling of **PEEN**.

Peirce /pi(ə)rs/, Charles Sanders (1839–1914), U.S. philosopher and logician. A founder of pragmatism in the U.S., he argued that the meaning of a belief is to be understood by the actions and uses to which it gives rise.

Pei·sis·tra·tus variant spelling of **PISISTRATUS**.

pe·jo·ra·tive /pəˈjôrətiv; ˈpejəˌrātiv/ ▸*adj.* expressing contempt or disapproval: *permissiveness is used almost universally as a pejorative term.*
▸*n.* a word expressing contempt or disapproval. ▷late 19th cent.: from French *péjoratif, -ive*, from late Latin *pejorare* 'make worse,' from Latin *pejor* 'worse.' —**pe·jo·ra·tive·ly** *adv.*

pek·an /ˈpekən/ ▸*n.* another term for **FISHER** (sense 2). ▷mid 18th cent.: from Canadian French, from New England Algonquian.

peke /pēk/ ▸*n. informal* a Pekingese dog. ▷early 20th cent.: abbreviation.

pe·kid ▸*adj.* variant spelling of **PEAKED2**

Pe·king /ˌpēˈkiNG; ˌpā-/ ▸ Another name for (esp. formerly) **BEIJING**.

Pe·king duck ▸*n.* a Chinese dish consisting of strips of roast duck served with shredded vegetables and a sweet sauce.

Pe·king·ese (also **Pe·kin·ese**) ▸*n.* /ˈpēkəˌnēz; -ˌnēs/ (*pl.* same) a lapdog of a short-legged breed with long hair and a snub nose, originally brought to Europe from the Summer Palace at Beijing (Peking) in 1860.
▸*adj.* /ˌpēkiNGˈēz; -ˈēs/ of or relating to Beijing, its citizens, or their culture or cuisine.

Pekingese

Pe·king man ▸*n.* a fossil hominid of the middle Pleistocene period, identified from remains found near Beijing in 1926. • A late form of *Homo erectus* (formerly *Sinanthropus pekinensis*), family Hominidae.

Pe·king op·er·a ▸*n.* a stylized Chinese form of opera dating from the late 18th century, in which speech, singing, mime, and acrobatics are performed to an instrumental accompaniment.

Pe·kin rob·in /ˈpēkin ˈräbin/ ▸*n.* another term for **LEIOTHRIX**.

pe·koe /ˈpēˌkō/ ▸*n.* a high-quality black tea made from young leaves. ▷early 18th cent.: from Chinese dialect *pekho*, from *pek* 'white' + *ho* 'down' (the leaves being picked young when covered with down).

P

pel·age /ˈpelij/ ▸*n. Zoology* the fur, hair, or wool of a mammal. ▷early 19th cent.: from French, from Old French *pel* 'hair.'

pe·lag·ic /pəˈlajik/ ▸*adj. technical* of or relating to the open sea: *the kittiwakes return from their pelagic winter wanderings.* ■ (chiefly of fish) inhabiting the upper layers of the open sea. Often contrasted with **DEMERSAL**. ▷mid 17th cent.: via Latin from Greek *pelagikos*, from *pelagios* 'of the sea' (from *pelagos* 'level surface of the sea').

Pe·la·gius /pəˈlāj(ē)əs/ (*c.*360–*c.*420), British or Irish monk. He denied the doctrines of original sin and predestination, defending innate human goodness and free will. His beliefs were condemned as heretical by the Synod of Carthage in about 418. —**Pe·la·gi·an** /-jēən/ *adj.* & *n.* —**Pe·la·gi·an·ism** /-ˌnizəm/ *n.*

pel·ar·go·ni·um /ˌpelärˈgōnēəm/ ▸*n.* a tender shrubby plant that is widely cultivated for its red, pink, or white flowers. Some kinds have fragrant leaves that yield an essential oil. See also **GERANIUM**. • Genus *Pelargonium*, family Geraniaceae: many species and several hybrid groups, including the **zonal pelargoniums** (*P.* × *hortorum*), with rounded leaves bearing colored zones, and the trailing **ivy-leaved pelargoniums** (*P. peltatum*). ▷modern Latin, from Greek *pelargos* 'stork,' apparently on the pattern of *geranium* (based on Greek *geranos* 'crane').

Pe·las·gi·an /pəˈlazjēən/ ▸*adj.* relating to or denoting an ancient people inhabiting the coasts and islands of the Aegean Sea and eastern Mediterranean before the arrival of Greek-speaking peoples in the Bronze Age.
▸*n.* a member of this people. ▷late 15th cent.: via Latin from Greek *Pelasgos* + **-IAN**.

pe·lau /pəˈlou/ ▸*n.* a spicy dish consisting of meat (typically chicken), rice, and pigeon peas. ▷from French Creole *pêlao*.

Pe·lé /ˈpāˌlā/ (1940–), Brazilian soccer player; born *Edson Arantes do Nascimento*. Regarded as one of the greatest goal-scorers of all time, he played for the New York Cosmos 1975–77 and is credited with over 1,200 goals in first-class soccer.

pele ▸*n.* variant spelling of **PEEL**3.

pe·lec·y·pod /pəˈlesəˌpäd/ ▸*n.* another term for **BIVALVE**. ▷late 19th cent.: from modern Latin *Pelecypoda* (alternative class name), from Greek *pelekus* 'hatchet' + *-podos* 'footed.'

Pe·lée, Mount /pəˈlā/ a volcano on the island of Martinique, in the Caribbean Sea. Its eruption in 1902 killed about 30,000 people.

pel·er·ine /ˌpeləˈrēn; ˈpelərin/ ▸*n. historical* a woman's cape of lace or silk with pointed ends at the center front, popular in the 19th century. ▷mid 18th cent.: from French *pèlerine*, the sense being a transferred use of the feminine of *pèlerin* 'pilgrim.'

Pe·le's hair /ˈpelāz/ ▸*n.* fine threads of volcanic glass, formed when a spray of lava droplets cools rapidly in the air. ▷mid 19th cent.: translating Hawaiian *lauohu o Pele*, Pele being the goddess of volcanoes in Hawaiian mythology.

Pe·le·us /ˈpēlēəs/ *Greek Mythology* a king of Phthia in Thessaly, who was given as his wife the sea nymph Thetis; their child was Achilles.

pelf /pelf/ ▸*n.* money, esp. when gained in a dishonest or dishonorable way. ▷late Middle English (in the sense 'booty, pilfered property'): from a variant of Old French *pelfre* 'spoils,' of unknown origin. Compare with **PILFER**.

Pel·ham /ˈpeləm/, Henry (1696–1754), British statesman; prime minister 1743–54.

pel·ham /ˈpeləm/ ▸*n.* a horse's bit that combines the action of a curb bit and a snaffle. ▷mid 19th cent.: from the surname *Pelham*.

pel·i·can /ˈpelikən/ ▸*n.* a large gregarious waterbird with a long bill, an extensible throat pouch for scooping up fish, and mainly white or gray plumage. • Genus *Pelecanus*, family Pelecanidae: six species, including the **white pelican** (*P. erythrorhynchos*) of western and central North America, and the **brown pelican** (*P. occidentalis*) of northern and western South America and the southern U.S. ■ a heraldic or artistic representation of a pelican, typically depicted pecking its own breast as a symbol of Christ. [from an ancient legend that the pelican fed its young on its own blood.] ▷late Old English *pellicane*, via late Latin from Greek *pelekan*, probably based on *pelekus* 'ax' (with reference to its bill).

pel·i·can's-foot shell ▸*n.* a burrowing European mollusk that has a heavily sculptured spiral shell with a flared lip that extends into several points. • *Aporrhais pespelecani*, family Aporrhaidae, class Gastropoda.

Pel·i·can State a nickname for the state of **LOUISIANA**.

Pe·li·on /ˈpēlēən/ a wooded mountain in Greece, near the coast of southeastern Thessaly, that rises to 5,079 feet (1,548 m). In Greek mythology it was believed to be the home of the centaurs, and the giants were said to have piled Mounts Olympus and Ossa on its summit in their attempt to reach heaven and destroy the gods.
▸*PHRASE* □ **pile** (or **heap**) **Pelion on Ossa** add a difficulty or task to something that is already difficult or onerous.

pe·lisse /pəˈlēs/ ▸*n. historical* a woman's cloak with armholes or sleeves, reaching to the ankles. ■ a fur-lined cloak, esp. as part of a hussar's uniform. ▷early 18th cent.: from French, from medieval Latin *pellicia (vestis)* '(garment) of fur,' from *pellis* 'skin.'

pe·lite /ˈpēˌlīt/ ▸*n. Geology* a very fine-grained sediment or sedimentary rock composed of clay or mud particles. ▷late 19th cent.: from Greek *pēlos* 'clay, mud' + **-ITE**1.

pel·la·gra /pəˈlagrə; -ˈlāgrə; -ˈlägrə/ ▸*n.* a deficiency disease caused by a lack of nicotinic acid or its precursor tryptophan in the diet. It is characterized by dermatitis, diarrhea, and mental disturbance, and is often linked to overdependence on corn as a staple food. ▷early 19th cent.: from Italian, from *pelle* 'skin,' on the pattern of *podagra*. —**pel·la·grous** /-grəs/ *adj.*

pel·let /ˈpelit/ ▸*n.* a small, rounded, compressed mass of a substance: *fish food pellets.* ■ a piece of small shot or other lightweight bullet. ■ *Ornithology* a small mass of bones and feathers regurgitated by a bird of prey or other bird. ■ a small round piece of animal feces, esp. from a rabbit or rodent.
▸*v.* (**-let·ed, -let·ing**) [*trans.*] **1** form or shape (a substance, esp. animal food) into pellets. **2** hit with or as though with pellets: *the last drops of rain were pelleting the windshield.* ▷late Middle English: from Old French *pelote* 'metal ball,' from a diminutive of Latin *pila* 'ball.'

pel·let·ize /ˈpeliˌtīz/ ▸*v.* [*trans.*] form or shape (a substance) into pellets.

Pei·li /ˈpelē/, Cesar (1926–), U.S. architect; born in Argentina. His designs incorporate the special characteristics of each project, such as the World Financial Center and its Winter Garden 1980–89 in New York City or Founders Hall 1987–92 in Charlotte, North Carolina.

pel·li·cle /ˈpelikəl/ ▸*n. technical* a thin skin, cuticle, membrane, or film. ▷late Middle English: from French *pellicule*, from Latin *pellicula* 'small piece of skin,' diminutive of *pellis*. —**pel·lic·u·lar** /pəˈlikyələr/ *adj.*

pel·li·to·ry /ˈpeliˌtôrē/ ▸*n.* **1** (in full **pellitory of Spain**) a plant of the daisy family, *Anacyclus pyrethrum*, with a pungent-flavored root, used as a local irritant, etc. **2** (also **pellitory of the wall**) a European plant of the nettle family with greenish flowers that grows on or at the foot of walls or in stony places. • *Parietaria judaica*, family Urticaceae. ▷late Middle English: alteration of obsolete *parietary*, from Old French *paritaire*, based on Latin *paries, pariet-* 'wall.'

pell-mell /ˈpel ˈmel/ ▸*adv.* in a confused, rushed, or disorderly manner: *the contents of the sacks were thrown pell-mell to the ground.*
▸*adj.* recklessly hasty or disorganized; headlong: *steering the pell-mell development of Europe onto a new and more gradual course.*
▸*n.* [in *sing.*] a state of affairs or collection of things characterized by haste or confusion: *the pell-mell of ascending gables and roof tiles.* ▷late 16th cent.: from French *pêle-mêle*, from earlier *pesle mesle, mesle pesle*, reduplication from *mesler* 'to mix.'

pel·lu·cid /pəˈlo͞osid/ ▸*adj.* translucently clear: *mountains reflected in the pellucid waters.* ■ lucid in style or meaning; easily understood: *he writes, as always, in pellucid prose.* ■ (of music or other sound) clear and pure in tone: *a smooth legato and pellucid singing tone are his calling cards.* ▷early 17th cent.: from Latin *pellucidus*, from *perlucere* 'shine through.' —**pel·lu·cid·ly** *adv.*

white pelican

Pel·man·ism /ˈpelmənˌizəm/ ▸*n.* a system of memory training originally devised by the Pelman Institute for the Scientific Development of Mind, Memory, and Personality in London in the 1920s. ■ a game based on memorizing cards or other objects placed before the players.

pel·met /ˈpelmit/ ▸*n.* a narrow border of cloth or wood, fitted across the top of a door or window to conceal the curtain fittings. ▷early 20th cent.: probably an alteration of French *palmette*, literally 'small palm' (see **PALMETTE**).

Pel·o·pon·ne·sian War /ˌpeləpəˈnēzHən/ the war of 431–404 BC fought between Athens and Sparta with their respective allies, occasioned largely by Spartan opposition to the Delian League. It ended in the total defeat of Athens and the transfer, for a brief period, of the leadership of Greece to Sparta.

Pel·o·pon·ne·sus /ˌpeləpəˈnēsəs/ (**the Peloponnese** /ˌpeləpəˈnēz; -ˈnēs/) the mountainous southern peninsula of Greece, connected to central Greece by the Isthmus of Corinth. Greek name **PELOPÓNNISOS**, also called **PELOPONNESE** . ▷from Greek, literally 'island of Pelops.'

Pel·ops /ˈpēˌläps/ *Greek Mythology* son of Tantalus, brother of Niobe, and father of Atreus. He was killed by his father and served up as food to the gods, but only one shoulder was eaten, and he was restored to life with an ivory shoulder replacing the one that was missing.

pe·lo·rus /pəˈlôrəs/ ▸*n.* a sighting device on a ship for taking the relative bearings of a distant object. ▷mid 19th cent.: perhaps from *Pelorus*, said to be the name of Hannibal's pilot.

pe·lo·ta /pəˈlōtə/ ▸*n.* a Basque or Spanish game played in a walled court with a ball and basketlike rackets attached to the hand. ■ the ball used in such a game. ▷Spanish, literally 'ball,' augmentative of *pella*, from Latin *pila* 'ball.'

pel·o·ton /ˈpeləˌtän/ ▸*n.* the main field or group of cyclists in a race. ▷1950s: from French, literally 'small ball' (because of the concentrated grouping of the pack).

pelt1 /pelt/ ▸*v.* [*trans.*] attack (someone) by repeatedly hurling things at them: *two little boys* **pelted** *him* **with** *rotten apples.* ■ hurl (something) at someone or something in this way: *he spotted four boys aged about ten pelting stones at ducks.* ■ [*intrans.*] (**pelt down**) (of rain, hail, or snow) fall quickly and very heavily: *the rain was pelting down.* ■ [*intrans.*] *informal* run somewhere very quickly: *I pelted across the road.*
▸*n. archaic* an act of hurling something at someone. ▷late 15th cent.: of unknown origin.

pelt2 ▸*n.* the skin of an animal with the fur, wool, or hair still on it. ■ an animal's coat of fur or hair. ■ the raw skin of a sheep or goat, stripped and ready for tanning. ■ *informal* a person's hair. ▷Middle English: either from obsolete *pellet* 'skin,' from an Old French diminutive of *pel* 'skin,' from Latin *pellis* 'skin,' or a back-formation from **PELTRY**.

pel·tate /ˈpelˌtāt/ ▸*adj. chiefly Botany* shield-shaped. ■ (of a leaf) more or less circular, with the stalk attached at a point on the underside.

Pel·tier ef·fect /ˈpeltēā/ ▸*n. Physics* an effect whereby heat is emitted or absorbed when an electric current passes across a junction between two materials. ▷mid 19th cent.: named after Jean C. A. Peltier (1785–1845), French amateur scientist.

pelt·ry /ˈpeltrē/ ▸*n.* (also **peltries**) animal pelts collectively. ▷late Middle English: from Anglo-Norman French *pelterie*, based on Old French *pel* 'skin,' from Latin *pellis*.

pel·vic /ˈpelvik/ ▸*adj.* of, relating to, or situated within the bony pelvis. ■ of or relating to the renal pelvis.

pel·vic fin ▸*n. Zoology* each of a pair of fins on the underside of a fish's body, attached to the pelvic girdle and helping to control direction. Also called **VENTRAL FIN**.

pel·vic floor ▸*n.* the muscular base of the abdomen, attached to the pelvis.

pel·vic gir·dle ▸*n.* (in vertebrates) the enclosing structure formed by the pelvis, providing attachment for the hind limbs or pelvic fins.

pel·vic in·flam·ma·to·ry dis·ease (abbr.: **PID**) ▸*n.*

inflammation of the female genital tract, accompanied by fever and lower abdominal pain.

pel·vim·e·try /pel'vimətrē/ ▸*n. Medicine* measurement of the dimensions of the pelvis, undertaken chiefly to help determine whether a woman can give birth normally or will require a Caesarean section.

pel·vis /'pelvis/ ▸*n.* (*pl.* **-vis·es** or **-ves** /-vēz/) **1** the large bony structure near the base of the spine to which the hind limbs or legs are attached in humans and many other vertebrates. ■ the part of the abdomen including or enclosed by the pelvis.

In humans the pelvis, connected to the base of the spine, forms a basin-shaped hollow frame at the hips, partly supporting the internal organs and providing attachment for the bones and muscles of the legs.

2 (also **renal pelvis**) the broadened top part of the ureter into which the kidney tubules drain. ▷early 17th cent.: from Latin, literally 'basin.'

pel·y·co·saur /'pelikə,sôr/ ▸*n.* a large extinct reptile of the late Carboniferous and Permian periods, typically having a line of long bony spines along the back supporting a sail-like crest. • Order Pelycosauria, subclass Synapsida: several families and genera, including *Dimetrodon* and *Edaphosaurus*. ▷mid 20th cent.: from Greek *pelux, peluk-* 'bowl' + *sauros* 'lizard.'

Pem·ba /'pembə/ **1** a seaport in northern Mozambique, on the Indian Ocean; pop. 41,000. **2** an island off the coast of Tanzania, in the western Indian Ocean, north of Zanzibar.

Pem·broke Pines /'pem,brōk/ a city in southeastern Florida, northwest of Miami; pop. 137,427.

pem·mi·can /'pemikən/ ▸*n.* a paste of dried and pounded meat mixed with melted fat and other ingredients, originally made by North American Indians and later adapted by Arctic explorers. ▷from Cree *pimikan*, from *pime* 'fat.'

pem·phi·goid /'pemfi,goid/ ▸*n. Medicine* a skin disease resembling pemphigus, chiefly affecting the elderly.

pem·phi·gus /'pemfigəs; pem'figəs/ ▸*n. Medicine* a skin disease in which watery blisters form on the skin. ▷late 18th cent.: modern Latin, from Greek *pemphix, pemphig-* 'bubble.'

PEN ▸*abbr.* International Association of Poets, Playwrights, Editors, Essayists, and Novelists.

pen[1] /pen/ ▸*n.* **1** an instrument for writing or drawing with ink, typically consisting of a metal nib or ball, or a nylon tip, fitted into a metal or plastic holder. ■ (**the pen**) the occupation or practice of writing: *she was forced to support herself not only by the pen, but as a secret agent.* ■ an electronic penlike device used in conjunction with a writing surface to enter commands or data into a computer. **2** *Zoology* the tapering cartilaginous internal shell of a squid.

▸*v.* (**penned, pen·ning**) [*trans.*] write or compose: *he had not penned a line to Lizzie in three years.* ▷Middle English (originally denoting a feather with a sharpened quill): from Old French *penne*, from Latin *penna* 'feather' (in late Latin 'pen').

▸*PHRASES* □ **the pen is mightier than the sword** *proverb* writing is more effective than military power or violence. □ **put** (or **set**) **pen to paper** write or begin to write something.

pen[2] ▸*n.* a small enclosure in which sheep, pigs, cattle, or other domestic animals are kept. ■ a number of animals in or sufficient to fill such an enclosure: *a pen of young horses.* ■ any small enclosure in which someone or something can be confined. ■ a covered dock for a submarine or other warship.

▸*v.* (**penned, pen·ning**) [*trans.*] put or keep (an animal) in a pen: *it was the practice to pen the sheep for clipping.* ■ (**pen someone up/in**) confine someone in a restricted space: *they had been penned up day and night in the house.* ▷Old English *penn*, of unknown origin.

pen[3] ▸*n.* a female swan. ▷mid 16th cent.: of unknown origin.

pen[4] ▸*n. informal* short for PENITENTIARY (sense 1).

Pen. ▸*abbr.* Peninsula.

pe·nal /'pēnəl/ ▸*adj.* of, relating to, or prescribing the punishment of offenders under the legal system: *the campaign for penal reform.* ■ used or designated as a place of punishment: *a former penal colony.* ■ (of an act or offense) punishable by law. ▷late Middle English: from Old French *penal*, from Latin *poenalis*, from *poena* 'pain, penalty.' —**pe·nal·ly** *adv.*

pe·nal·ize /'penəl,īz; 'pē-/ ▸*v.* [*trans.*] (often **be penalized**) subject to some form of punishment: *you'll be penalized if you tap the account before age 59.* ■ (in various sports) punish (a player or team) for a breach of the rules by awarding an advantage to the opposition. ■ put in an unfavorable position or at an unfair disadvantage: *if the bill is not amended, genuine claimants will be penalized.* ■ *Law* make or declare (an act or offense) legally punishable: *section twenty penalizes possession of a firearm when trespassing.* —**pe·nal·i·za·tion** /,penəli'zāsʜən; ,pē-/ *n.*

pe·nal ser·vi·tude ▸*n.* imprisonment with hard labor.

pen·al·ty /'penltē/ ▸*n.* (*pl.* **-ties**) **1** a punishment imposed for breaking a law, rule, or contract: *the charge carries a maximum penalty of ten years' imprisonment.* ■ a disadvantage or unpleasant experience suffered as the result of an action or circumstance: *the cold never leaves my bones these days—one of the penalties of age.* **2** (in sports and games) a disadvantage or handicap imposed on a player or team, typically for infringement of rules. ■ a kick or shot awarded to a team because of a serious infringement of the rules by an opponent. ■ *Bridge* points won by the defenders when a declarer fails to make the contract. ▷early 16th cent.: probably via Anglo-Norman French, from medieval Latin *poenalitas*, based on *poena* 'pain.'

▸*PHRASE* □ **under** (or **on**) **penalty of** under the threat of: *he ordered enterprises to fulfill contracts under penalty of strict fines.*

pen·al·ty ar·e·a ▸*n. Soccer* the rectangular area marked out in front of each goal, within which a foul by a defender involves the award of a penalty kick and outside which the goalkeeper is not allowed to handle the ball.

pen·al·ty box ▸*n. Ice Hockey* an enclosure alongside the rink where players who have been assessed penalties must remain while they serve out their penalties.

pen·al·ty dou·ble ▸*n. Bridge* another term for BUSINESS DOUBLE.

pen·al·ty kick ▸*n.* **1** *Soccer* a free kick at the goal from the penalty spot (which only the goalkeeper is allowed to defend), awarded to the attacking team after a foul within the penalty area by an opponent. **2** *Rugby* a placekick awarded to a team after an offense by an opponent.

pen·al·ty kill·er ▸*n. Hockey* a player specializing in preventing the opposing side from scoring while their own team's strength is reduced through penalties. —**pen·al·ty kill·ing** *n.*

pen·al·ty shoot-out ▸*n.* see SHOOT-OUT.

pen·al·ty spot ▸*n. Soccer* the point within the penalty area from which penalty kicks are taken.

pen·ance /'penəns/ ▸*n.* **1** voluntary self-punishment inflicted as an outward expression of repentance for having done wrong: *he had **done** public **penance for** those hasty words.* **2** a Christian sacrament in which a member of the Church confesses sins to a priest and is given absolution. In the Roman Catholic Church often called SACRAMENT OF RECONCILIATION. ■ a religious observance or other duty required of a person by a priest as part of this sacrament to indicate repentance.

▸*v.* [*trans.*] *archaic* impose a penance on: *a hair shirt to penance him for his folly in offending.* ▷Middle English: from Old French, from Latin *paenitentia* 'repentance,' from the verb *paenitere* 'be sorry.'

Pe·nang /pə'naɴɢ/ (also **Pi·nang**) an island in Malaysia, located off the western coast of the Malay Peninsula. ■ a state of Malaysia, consisting of this island and a coastal strip on the mainland; capital, George Town (on Penang island). ■ another name for GEORGE TOWN (sense 2).

pe·na·tes /pə'nātēz; -'nä-/ ▸*plural n. Roman History* household gods worshiped in conjunction with Vesta and the lares by the ancient Romans. ▷Latin, from *penus* 'provision of food'; related to *penes* 'within.'

pence /pens/ ▸ plural form of PENNY.

pen·chant /'penсʜənt/ ▸*n.* [usu. in *sing.*] a strong or habitual liking for something or tendency to do something: *he has a **penchant for** adopting stray dogs.* ▷late 17th cent.: from French, 'leaning, inclining,' present participle of the verb *pencher.*

pen·cil /'pensəl/ ▸*n.* an instrument for writing or drawing, consisting of a thin stick of graphite or a similar substance enclosed in a long thin piece of wood or fixed in a metal or plastic case. ■ used to refer to the composition, skill, or style of a drawing: *her pencil had captured the dark brooding atmosphere of the place only too well.* ■ graphite or a similar substance used in such a way as a medium for writing or drawing: *the words were scribbled in pencil.* ■ [usu. with *adj.*] a cosmetic in a long thin stick, designed to be applied to a particular part of the face: *an eyebrow pencil.* ■ something with the shape of a pencil: *a pencil of light* | [as *adj.*] *a long pencil beam.* ■ *Physics & Geometry* a set of light rays, lines, etc., converging to or diverging narrowly from a single point.

▸*v.* (**-ciled, -cil·ing**; *Brit.* **-cilled, -cil·ling**) [*trans.*] write, draw, or color (something) with a pencil: *a previous owner has penciled their name inside the cover* | [as *adj.*] (**penciled**) *a penciled note.*

▸*phrasal v.* □ **pencil something in 1** fill in an area or shape with pencil strokes: *a lot of the outlines had been penciled in.* **2** arrange, forecast, or note down something provisionally or tentatively: *May 15 was penciled in as the date for the meeting.* ■ (**pencil someone in**) make a provisional or tentative arrangement with or for someone: *he was penciled in for surgery at the end of the month.* ▷Middle English (denoting a fine paintbrush): from Old French *pincel*, from a diminutive of Latin *peniculus* 'brush,' diminutive of *penis* 'tail.' The verb was originally (early 16th cent.) in the sense 'paint with a fine brush.' —**pen·cil·er** *n.*

pen·cil mus·tache ▸*n.* a very thin mustache.

pen·cil push·er ▸*n. informal* a person with a clerical job involving a lot of tedious and repetitive paperwork.

pen·cil sharp·en·er ▸*n.* a device for sharpening a pencil by rotating a cutter around its point.

pend·ant /'pendənt/ ▸*n.* **1** a piece of jewelry that hangs from a chain worn around the neck. ■ a necklace with such a piece of jewelry. ■ a light designed to hang from the ceiling. ■ the part of a pocket watch by which it is suspended. ■ *Nautical* a short rope hanging from the head of a ship's mast, yardarm, or clew of a sail, used for attaching tackles. **2** an artistic, literary, or musical composition intended to match or complement another: *the triptych's pendant will occupy the corresponding wall in the south transept.*

▸*adj.* hanging downward; pendent: *pendant flowers on frail stems.* ▷Middle English (denoting an architectural decoration projecting downward): from Old French, literally 'hanging,' present participle of the verb *pendre*, from Latin *pendere.*

pend·ent /'pendənt/ ▸*adj.* **1** hanging down or overhanging: *pendent lichens.* **2** undecided; pending: *the use of jurisdiction to decide pendent claims.* **3** *Grammar* (esp. of a sentence) incomplete; not having a finite verb. —**pen·den·cy** *n.*

pen·den·te li·te /pen'dentē 'lītē/ ▸*adv. Law* during litigation. ▷Latin, literally 'with the lawsuit pending.'

pen·den·tive /pen'dentiv/ ▸*n. Architecture* a curved triangle of vaulting formed by the intersection of a dome with its supporting arches. ▷early 18th cent.: from the French adjective *pendentif, -ive*, from Latin *pendent-* 'hanging down,' from the verb *pendere.*

Pen·de·rec·ki /,pendə'retskē/, Krzysztof (1933–), Polish composer. His music frequently features sounds drawn from extramusical sources and note clusters, as in his *Threnody for the Victims of Hiroshima* (1960) for fifty-two strings. Notable religious works: *Stabat Mater* (1962) and *Polish Requiem* (1980–84).

Pen·der·gast /'pendər,gast/, Thomas (Joseph) (1872–1945), U.S. politician. An early supporter of Harry Truman, he was the acknowledged Democratic boss of Kansas City, Missouri. He served time in prison for income tax evasion 1939–40.

pend·ing /'pendiɴɢ/ ▸*adj.* awaiting decision or settlement: *nine cases were still pending.* ■ about to happen; imminent: *with a presidential election pending, it would be wrong to force the changes through now* | *the pending disaster.*

▸*prep.* until (something) happens or takes place: *they were released on bail pending an appeal.* ▷mid 17th cent.: anglicized spelling of French *pendant* 'hanging.'

pen·drag·on /pen'dragən/ ▸*n.* a title given to an ancient British or Welsh prince holding or claiming supreme power. ▷Welsh, literally 'chief war-leader,' from *pen* 'head' + *dragon* 'standard.'

pen·du·lous /'penjələs; 'pendyə-/ ▸*adj.* hanging down loosely: *pendulous branches.* ▷early 17th cent.: from Latin *pendulus* 'hanging down' (from *pendere* 'hang') + -OUS. —**pen·du·lous·ly** *adv.*

pen·du·lum /ˈpenjələm; ˈpendyə-/ ▶*n.* a weight hung from a fixed point so that it can swing freely backward and forward, esp. a rod with a weight at the end that regulates the mechanism of a clock. ■ *figurative* used to refer to the tendency of a situation or state of affairs to oscillate regularly between one extreme and another: *the pendulum of fashion.* ▷mid 17th cent.: from Latin, neuter (used as a noun) of *pendulus* 'hanging down.' **—pen·du·lar** /-lər/ *adj.*

pendulum

pe·nec·to·my /pəˈnektəmē/ ▶*n.* surgical amputation of the penis.

Pe·nel·o·pe /pəˈneləpē/ *Greek Mythology* the wife of Odysseus, who was beset by suitors when her husband did not return after the fall of Troy. See also ODYSSEY.

pe·ne·plain /ˈpēnəˌplān/ (also **pe·ne·plane**) ▶*n. Geology* a more or less level land surface produced by erosion over a long period, undisturbed by crustal movement. ▷late 19th cent.: from Latin *paene* 'almost' + PLAIN[1].

pen·e·tra·li·a /ˌpeniˈtrālēə/ ▶*plural n.* the innermost parts of a building; a secret or hidden place. ▷mid 17th cent.: from Latin, literally 'innermost things,' neuter plural of *penetralis* 'interior.'

pen·e·trance /ˈpenətrəns/ ▶*n. Genetics* the extent to which a particular gene or set of genes is expressed in the phenotypes of individuals carrying it, measured by the proportion of carriers showing the characteristic phenotype. ▷1930s: from German *Penetranz.*

pen·e·trant /ˈpenətrənt/ ▶*adj. Genetics* (of a gene or group of genes) producing characteristic effects in the phenotypes of individuals possessing it.
▶*n.* a substance that can penetrate cracks, pores, and other surface defects.

pen·e·trate /ˈpeniˌtrāt/ ▶*v.* [*trans.*] succeed in forcing a way into or through (a thing): *the shrapnel had penetrated his head and chest* | [*intrans.*] *tunnels that* **penetrate** *deep* **into** *the earth's core.* ■ (of a man) insert the penis into the vagina or anus of (a sexual partner). ■ infiltrate (an enemy group or rival organization) in order to spy on it: *the U.S. media had been penetrated by Soviet stooges.* ■ (of a company) begin to sell its products in (a particular market or area): *Honda has succeeded in penetrating Western motorcycle markets.* ■ succeed in understanding or gaining insight into (something complex or mysterious): *a magician who seemed to have penetrated the mysteries of nature.* ■ [*intrans.*] be fully understood or realized by someone: *as his words penetrated, she saw a mental picture of him with Dawn.* ▷mid 16th cent.: from Latin *penetrat-* 'placed or gone into,' from the verb *penetrare*; related to *penitus* 'inner.' **—pen·e·tra·bil·i·ty** /ˌpenitrəˈbilitē/ *n.* **—pen·e·tra·ble** /-trəbəl/ *adj.*

pen·e·trat·ing /ˈpeniˌtrātiNG/ ▶*adj.* able to make a way through or into something: *the problem of penetrating damp.* See note at KEEN. ■ (of a voice or sound) clearly heard through or above other sounds: *a single penetrating whistle.* ■ (of a smell) strong; pungent: *the penetrating scents of pine and eucalyptus.* ■ (of a person's eyes or expression) reflecting an apparent ability to see into the mind of the person being looked at; piercingly intense: *attempting to avoid her penetrating gaze.* ■ having or showing clear insight: *the students asked some penetrating questions.* **—pen·e·trat·ing·ly** *adv.*

pen·e·tra·tion /ˌpeniˈtrāsHən/ ▶*n.* **1** the action or process of making a way through or into something: *the plant grows in clear, still waters where there is strong sunlight penetration.* ■ the ability to do this: *a weapon that combines the power and penetration of radiation with the precision of the laser.* ■ the insertion by a man of his penis into the vagina or anus of a sexual partner. ■ the infiltration of an enemy group or rival organization in order to spy on it: *the penetration by the KGB of the French intelligence service.* ■ the successful selling of a company's or country's products in a particular market or area: *Japanese import penetration.* ■ the extent to which a product is recognized and bought by customers in a particular market: *the software has attained a high degree of market penetration.* **2** the perceptive understanding of complex matters: *the survey shows subtlety and penetration.* ▷late Middle English: from Latin *penetratio(n-)*, from the verb *penetrare* 'place within or enter.'

pen·e·tra·tive /ˈpeniˌtrātiv/ ▶*adj.* **1** able to make a way into or through something: *the gunpowder weapons have extra penetrative power.* ■ (in various sports) able to break through an opponent's defense: *several times promising movements failed for want of a penetrative final pass.* ■ (of sexual activity) in which a man inserts his penis into the vagina or anus of a sexual partner. **2** having or showing deep understanding and insight: *a remarkably thorough and penetrative survey of the organization's work.*

pen·e·tra·tor /ˈpeniˌtrātər/ ▶*n.* a person or thing that penetrates something. ■ a missile containing a hard alloy rod, designed to penetrate the armor of tanks or fortifications.

pen·e·trom·e·ter /ˌpenəˈträmitər/ ▶*n.* an instrument for determining the consistency or hardness of a substance by measuring the depth or rate of penetration of a rod or needle driven into it by a known force.

pen·gö /ˈpengō/ ▶*n.* (*pl.* same or **-gös**) the basic monetary unit of Hungary from 1927 until 1946, when it was replaced by the forint. ▷Hungarian, literally 'ringing.'

pen·guin /ˈpeNGgwin; ˈpengwin/ ▶*n.* a large flightless seabird of the southern hemisphere, with black upper parts and white underparts and wings developed into flippers for swimming under water. See also ADÉLIE PENGUIN (illustration), EMPEROR PENGUIN, KING PENGUIN, MACARONI PENGUIN. • Family Spheniscidae: six genera and several species. ▷late 16th cent. (originally denoting the great auk): of unknown origin.

pen·i·cil·late /ˌpenəˈsilit; -ˈsilāt/ ▶*adj. Biology* having, forming, or resembling a small tuft or tufts of hair. ▷early 19th cent.: from Latin *penicillus* 'paintbrush' + -ATE[2].

pen·i·cil·lin /ˌpenəˈsilən/ ▶*n.* **1** an antibiotic or group of antibiotics produced naturally by certain blue molds, and now usually prepared synthetically. **2** a blue mold of a type that produces these antibiotics. • Genus *Penicillium*, subdivision Deuteromycotina. ▷from the modern Latin genus name *Penicillium* (from Latin *penicillus* 'paintbrush') + -IN[1].

pen·i·cil·lin·ase /ˌpenəˈsilənās/ ▶*n. Biochemistry* an enzyme that can inactivate penicillin, produced by certain bacteria.

pen·i·cil·li·um /ˌpenəˈsilēəm/ ▶*n.* (*pl.* **-cil·li·a** /-ˈsilēə/) a blue mold that is common on food, being added to some cheeses and used sometimes to produce penicillin. ▷mid 19th cent.: modern Latin, from Latin *penicillus* 'paintbrush' (because of the brushlike fruiting bodies).

pe·nile /ˈpēnəl; -nīl/ ▶*adj.* [*attrib.*] *chiefly technical* of, relating to, or affecting the penis. ▷mid 19th cent.: from modern Latin *penilis*, from *penis* 'tail, penis.'

pen·in·su·la /pəˈninsələ/ ▶*n.* a piece of land almost surrounded by water or projecting out into a body of water. ▷mid 16th cent.: from Latin *paeninsula*, from *paene* 'almost' + *insula* 'island.' **—pen·in·su·lar** /-lər/ *adj.*

pe·nis /ˈpēnis/ ▶*n.* (*pl.* **-nis·es** or **-nes** /-nēz/) the male genital organ of higher vertebrates, carrying the duct for the transfer of sperm during copulation. In humans and most other mammals, it consists largely of erectile tissue and serves also for the elimination of urine. ■ *Zoology* a type of male copulatory organ present in some invertebrates, such as gastropod mollusks. ▷late 17th cent.: from Latin, 'tail, penis.'

pe·nis en·vy ▶*n. Psychoanalysis* supposed envy of the male's possession of a penis, postulated by Freud to account for some aspects of female behavior (notably the castration complex) but controversial among modern theorists.

pen·i·stone /ˈpenistən/ ▶*n.* a kind of coarse woolen cloth formerly used for making clothes. ▷mid 16th cent.: from the name of a town in South Yorkshire, England, where the cloth was made.

pen·i·tent /ˈpenitnt/ ▶*adj.* feeling or showing sorrow and regret for having done wrong; repentant: *a penitent expression.*
▶*n.* a person who repents their sins or wrongdoings and (in the Christian Church) seeks forgiveness from God. ■ (in the Roman Catholic Church) a person who confesses their sins to a priest and submits to the penance that he imposes. ▷Middle English: from Old French, from Latin *paenitent-* 'repenting,' from the verb *paenitere.* **—pen·i·tence** *n.* **—pen·i·tent·ly** *adv.*

pen·i·ten·tial /ˌpenəˈtensHəl/ ▶*adj.* relating to or expressing penitence or penance: *penitential tears.* ▷late 15th cent.: from late Latin *paenitentialis*, from Latin *paenitentia* 'repentance.' **—pen·i·ten·tial·ly** *adv.* (*archaic*).

Pen·i·ten·tial Psalms ▶*plural n.* seven psalms (6, 32, 38, 51, 102, 130, 143) that express penitence.

pen·i·ten·tia·ry /ˌpenəˈtensHərē/ ▶*n.* (*pl.* **-ries**) **1** a prison for people convicted of serious crimes. **2** (in the Roman Catholic Church) a priest charged with certain aspects of the administration of the sacrament of penance. ■ an office in the papal court forming a tribunal for deciding on questions relating to penance, dispensations, and absolution. ▷late Middle English (as a term in ecclesiastical law): from medieval Latin *paenitentiarius*, from Latin *paenitentia* 'repentance.' Sense 1 dates from the early 19th cent.

pen·knife /ˈpenˌnīf/ ▶*n.* (*pl.* **-knives** /-ˌnīvz/) a small pocketknife with a blade that folds into the handle. ▷so named because originally used for making and mending quill pens.

pen·light /ˈpenˌlīt/ ▶*n.* a small flashlight shaped like a fountain pen.

pen·man /ˈpenˌmən/ ▶*n.* (*pl.* **-men**) *chiefly historical* a person who was skilled or professionally engaged in writing by hand, typically, as a clerk, on behalf of others. ■ an author.

pen·man·ship /ˈpenmənˌsHip/ ▶*n.* the art or skill of writing by hand. ■ a person's handwriting.

Penn /pen/, William (1644–1718), English Quaker, founder of Pennsylvania. Having been imprisoned in 1668 for his Quaker writings, he was granted a charter to land in North America by Charles II. He founded the colony of Pennsylvania as a sanctuary for Quakers and other nonconformists in 1682.

Penn. (also **Penna.**) ▶*abbr.* Pennsylvania.

pen name ▶*n.* an assumed name used by a writer instead of their real name.

pen·nant /ˈpenənt/ ▶*n.* **1** a flag denoting a sports championship or other achievement. **2** a tapering flag on a ship, esp. one flown at the masthead of a vessel in commission. Also called PENNON. **3** *Nautical* another term for PENDANT. **4** *Military* another term for PENNON (sense 1). ▷early 17th cent.: blend of PENDANT and PENNON.

pen·nate /ˈpenāt/ ▶*adj. Botany* (of a diatom) bilaterally symmetrical. Compare with CENTRIC. ▷mid 19th cent.: from Latin *pennatus* 'feathered, winged,' from *penna* 'feather.'

pen·ne /ˈpenā/ ▶*n.* pasta in the form of short wide tubes. ▷Italian, plural of *penna* 'quill.'

Pen·ney /ˈpenē/, James Cash (1875–1971), U.S. businessman. He invested in a small store (called the Golden Rule Store) in 1902 and by 1913 had developed 34 stores, the beginning of the J. C. Penney department store chain. He was the company's president 1913–17 and chairman 1917–46.

pen·ni /ˈpenē/ ▶*n.* (*pl.* **pen·niä** /ˈpenēə/) a monetary unit of Finland (until the introduction of the euro), equal to one hundredth of a markka. ▷Finnish.

pen·ni·less /ˈpenēlis/ ▶*adj.* (of a person) having no money; very poor. **—pen·ni·less·ness** *n.*

Pen·nine Hills /ˈpenīn/ (also **Pen·nine Chain** or **the Pen·nines**) a range of hills in northern England that extends from the Scottish border south to the county of Derbyshire.

pen·non /ˈpenən/ ▶*n.* **1** a long triangular or swallow-tailed flag, esp. as the military ensign of lancer regiments. Also called PENNANT. **2** another term for PENNANT (sense 2). ▷late Middle English: from Old French, from a derivative of Latin *penna* 'feather.' **—pen·noned** *adj.*

pen·n'orth /ˈpenərTH/ ▶*n. Brit.* variant spelling of PENNYWORTH.

Penn·syl·va·nia /ˌpensəlˈvānyə/ a state in the northeastern U.S., with a short coastline along Lake Erie in the far northwest; pop. 12,281,054; capital, Harrisburg; statehood, Dec. 12, 1787 (2). Founded in 1682 by William Penn, it became one of the original thirteen states.

Penn·syl·va·nia Av·e·nue a street in Washington, D.C., along which the White House (at number 1600) and Capitol Hill are situated.

Penn·syl·va·nia Dutch (also **Pennsylvania German**) ▶*n.* **1** a dialect of High German spoken in parts of Pennsylvania. **2** [as *plural n.*] (**the Pennsylvania Dutch** or **Germans**) the German-speaking inhabitants of Pennsylvania, descendants of 17th- and 18th-century Protestant immigrants from the Rhineland. ▷*Dutch* from German *Deutsch* 'German.'

Penn·syl·va·nian /ˌpensəlˈvānyən; -ˈvānēən/ ▸*adj.* **1** of or relating to the state of Pennsylvania. **2** *Geology* of, relating to, or denoting the later part of the Carboniferous period in North America, following the Mississippian and preceding the Permian, and corresponding to the Upper Carboniferous of Europe. This period lasted from about 323 to 290 million years ago.
▸*n.* **1** a native or inhabitant of Pennsylvania. **2** (**the Pennsylvanian**) *Geology* the Pennsylvanian period or the system of rocks deposited during it.

pen·ny /ˈpenē/ ▸*n.* **1** a one-cent coin equal to one hundredth of a dollar. ■ (*pl.* for separate coins **pennies**, for a sum of money **pence** /pens/) (abbr.: **p.**) a British bronze coin and monetary unit equal to one hundredth of a pound. ■ (abbr.: **d.**) a former British coin and monetary unit equal to one twelfth of a shilling and one 240th of a pound. ■ (**pennies**) a small sum of money: *in the current economic situation any chance to save a few pennies is welcome.* ■ (in biblical use) a denarius. **2** [with *negative*] (**a penny**) used for emphasis to denote no money at all: *we didn't get paid a penny.* ▷Old English *penig, penning,* of Germanic origin; related to Dutch *penning,* German *Pfennig,* perhaps also to PAWN[2] and (with reference to shape) PAN[1].
▸*PHRASES* □ **be two** (or **ten**) **a penny** *chiefly Brit.* be plentiful or easily obtained and consequently of little value. □ **pinch** (or **count** or **watch**) (**one's**) **pennies** be careful about how much one spends: *he is pinching pennies to save for a movie | she's been watching her pennies.* □ **in for a penny, in for a pound** used to express someone's intention to complete an enterprise once it has been undertaken, however much time, effort, or money this entails. □ **look after the pennies and the pounds will look after themselves** *proverb* if you concentrate on saving small amounts of money, you'll soon amass a large amount. □ **pennies from heaven** unexpected benefits, esp. financial ones. □ **the penny dropped** *informal, chiefly Brit.* used to indicate that someone has finally realized or understood something. □ **a penny for your thoughts** used to ask someone what they are thinking about. □ **a pretty penny** a considerable amount of money: *old Sid charged a pretty penny for his services.* □ **spend a penny** see SPEND.

pen·ny an·te ▸*n.* poker played for very small stakes. ■ [as *adj.*] *informal* petty; contemptible: *a penny-ante scandal of little substance.*

pen·ny ar·cade ▸*n. historical* an indoor area with coin-operated mechanical games, photography booths, picture shows, and other amusements.

pen·ny·cress /ˈpenēˌkres/ ▸*n.* a weed of the cabbage family, similar to shepherd's purse but with deeply notched, flat round pods. Native to Europe, it has become well established in North America. • *Thlaspi arvense,* family Brassicaceae.

pen·ny dread·ful ▸*n.* a cheap, sensational comic or storybook. ▷late 19th cent.: so named because the original cost was one penny.

pen·ny-far·thing ▸*n. historical* an early type of bicycle with a very large front wheel and a small rear wheel. Also called ORDINARY.

pen·ny loaf·er ▸*n.* a casual leather shoe with a decorative slotted leather strip over the upper, in which a coin may be placed.

pen·ny-pinch·ing ▸*adj.* unwilling to spend or share money; miserly; mean.
▸*n.* unwillingness to spend or share money. —**pen·ny-pinch·er** *n.*

pen·ny·roy·al /ˈpenēˌroiəl/ ▸*n.* either of two small-leaved plants of the mint family, used in herbal medicine. • A creeping Eurasian plant (*Mentha pulegium*), and **American pennyroyal** (*Hedeoma pulegioides*), family Labiatae. ▷mid 16th cent.: from Anglo-Norman French *puliol* (based on Latin *pulegium* 'thyme') + *real* 'royal.'

pen·ny stock ▸*n.* a common stock valued at less than one dollar, and therefore highly speculative.

pen·ny·weight /ˈpenēˌwāt/ ▸*n.* a unit of weight, 24 grains or one twentieth of an ounce troy.

pen·ny whis·tle ▸*n.* another term for TIN WHISTLE.

pen·ny wise ▸*adj.* extremely careful about the way one spends even small amounts of money.
▸*PHRASE* □ **penny wise and pound foolish** careful and economical in small matters while being wasteful or extravagant in large ones.

pen·ny·wort /ˈpenēwərt; -ˌwôrt/ ▸*n.* any of a number of plants with rounded leaves, in particular: • a creeping perennial of the genus *Hydrocotyle,* family Umbelliferae: numerous species, including the North American **water pennywort** (*H. americana*).

pen·ny·worth /ˈpenēˌwərTH/ ▸*n. chiefly Brit.* an amount of something that may be bought for a penny: ***a pennyworth of chips.*** ■ (**one's pennyworth**) a person's contribution to a discussion, esp. one that is unwelcome. ■ *archaic* value for one's money; a good bargain.

Pe·nob·scot /pəˈnäbskət; -ˌskät/ ▸*n.* (*pl.* same) **1** a member of an American Indian people of the Penobscot River valley in Maine. **2** the Algonquian language of this people, a dialect of Eastern Abnaki.
▸*adj.* of or relating to this people or their language. ▷from an Abnaki place name *panáwahpskek* 'where the rocks open out.'

Pe·nob·scot Riv·er a river that flows for 350 miles (560 km) through central Maine into Penobscot Bay on the Atlantic Ocean.

pe·nol·o·gy /pēˈnäləjē/ ▸*n.* the study of the punishment of crime and of prison management. ▷mid 19th cent.: from Latin *poena* 'penalty' + -LOGY. —**pe·no·log·i·cal** /ˌpēnəˈläjikəl/ *adj.* —**pe·nol·o·gist** /-jist/ *n.*

pen pal ▸*n.* a person with whom one becomes friendly by exchanging letters, esp. someone in a foreign country whom one has never met.

pen-push·er ▸*n.* another term for PENCIL PUSHER.

Pen·sa·co·la /ˌpensəˈkōlə/ an industrial and port city in northwestern Florida, in the Panhandle, near the Alabama border, site of a naval installation; pop. 58,165.

pen·sée /ˌpänˈsā/ ▸*n.* a thought or reflection put into literary form; an aphorism. ▷French.

pen shell ▸*n.* a large, wedge-shaped, bivalve mollusk of warm seas that burrows into the seabed where it attaches itself by strong byssus threads. • Family Pinnidae: *Pinna* and other genera.

pen·sile /ˈpenˌsīl; -sil/ ▸*adj.* hanging down; pendulous: *pensile nests.* ▷early 17th cent.: from Latin *pensilis,* from the verb *pendere* 'hang.'

pen·sion[1] /ˈpenSHən/ ▸*n.* a regular payment made during a person's retirement from an investment fund to which that person or their employer has contributed during their working life. ■ a regular payment made by the government to people of or above the official retirement age and to some widows and disabled people. ■ *chiefly historical* a regular payment made to a royal favorite or to an artist or scholar to enable them to carry on work that is of public interest or value.
▸*v.* [*trans.*] (**pension someone off**) dismiss someone from employment, typically because of age or ill health, and pay them a pension: *he was pensioned off from the army at the end of the war.* ▷late Middle English (in the sense 'payment, tax, regular sum paid to retain allegiance'): from Old French, from Latin *pensio(n-)* 'payment,' from *pendere* 'to pay.' The current verb sense dates from the mid 19th cent. —**pen·sion·less** *adj.*

pen·sion[2] /pänsēˈōn/ ▸*n.* a boardinghouse in France and other European countries, providing full or partial board at a fixed rate. ▷French.

pen·sion·a·ble /ˈpenSHənəbəl/ ▸*adj.* entitling to or qualifying for a pension: *single and widowed women over pensionable age.* —**pen·sion·a·bil·i·ty** /ˌpenSHənəˈbilitē/ *n.*

pen·sion·ar·y /ˈpenSHəˌnerē/ ▸*adj.* of or concerning a pension.
▸*n.* (*pl.* **-ar·ies**) **1** a pensioner. **2** a creature; a hireling. ▷mid 16th cent.: from medieval Latin *pensionarius* 'receiver or payer of a pension.'

pen·si·o·ne /pänsēˈōnā/ ▸*n.* (*pl.* **-o·ni** /-ˈōnē/) a small hotel or boardinghouse in Italy. ▷Italian.

pen·sion·er /ˈpenSHənər/ ▸*n.* a person who receives a pension.

pen·sion fund ▸*n.* a fund from which pensions are paid, accumulated from contributions from employers, employees, or both.

pen·sive /ˈpensiv/ ▸*adj.* engaged in, involving, or reflecting deep or serious thought: *a pensive mood.* ▷late Middle English: from Old French *pensif, -ive,* from *penser* 'think,' from Latin *pensare* 'ponder,' frequentative of *pendere* 'weigh.' —**pen·sive·ly** *adv.* —**pen·sive·ness** *n.*

pen·ste·mon /penˈstēmən; ˈpenstəmən/ (also **pent·ste·mon**) ▸*n.* another term for BEARDTONGUE. ▷modern Latin, formed irregularly from PENTA- 'five' + Greek *stēmōn* 'warp,' used to mean 'stamen.'

pen·stock /ˈpenˌstäk/ ▸*n.* a sluice or floodgate for regulating the flow of a body of water. ■ a channel for conveying water to a waterwheel or turbine. ▷early 17th cent.: from PEN[2] (in the sense 'milldam') + STOCK.

pent /pent/ ▸*adj. chiefly poetic/literary* another term for PENT-UP: *with pent breath she waited out the meeting.*

penta- ▸*comb. form* five; having five: *pentagram | pentadactyl.* ▷from Greek *pente* 'five.'

pen·ta·chlo·ro·phe·nol /ˌpentəˌklôrəˈfēnäl/ ▸*n. Chemistry* a colorless, crystalline, synthetic compound used in insecticides, fungicides, weed killers, and wood preservatives. • Chem. formula: C_6Cl_5OH.

pen·ta·chord /ˈpentəˌkôrd/ ▸*n.* a musical instrument with five strings. ■ a series of five musical notes.

pen·ta·cle /ˈpentəkəl/ ▸*n.* a talisman or magical object, typically disk-shaped and inscribed with a pentagram or other figure, and used as a symbol of the element of earth. ■ another term for PENTAGRAM. ■ (**pentacles**) one of the suits in some tarot packs, corresponding to coins in others. ▷late 16th cent.: from medieval Latin *pentaculum,* apparently based on Greek *penta-* 'five.'

pen·tad /ˈpenˌtad/ ▸*n. technical* a group or set of five. ▷mid 17th cent.: from Greek *pentas, pentad-,* from *pente* 'five.'

pen·ta·dac·tyl /ˌpentəˈdaktl/ ▸*adj. Zoology* (of a vertebrate limb) having five toes or fingers, or derived from such a form, as characteristic of all tetrapods. ▷early 19th cent.: from PENTA- 'five' + Greek *daktulos* 'finger.' —**pen·ta·dac·tyl·y** *n.*

pen·ta·gas·trin /ˌpentəˈgastrin/ ▸*n. Biochemistry* a synthetic peptide that has the same action as the hormone gastrin. It is used to promote gastric secretions prior to sampling them for tests.

pen·ta·gon /ˈpentəˌgän/ ▸*n.* **1** a plane figure with five straight sides and five angles. **2** (**the Pentagon**) the pentagonal building serving as the headquarters of the U.S. Department of Defense, near Washington, DC. ■ the U.S. Department of Defense: *the Pentagon said 19 of its soldiers had been killed.* ▷late 16th cent.: via Latin from Greek *pentagōnon,* neuter (used as a noun) of *pentagōnos* 'five-angled.' —**pen·tag·o·nal** /penˈtagənəl/ *adj.*

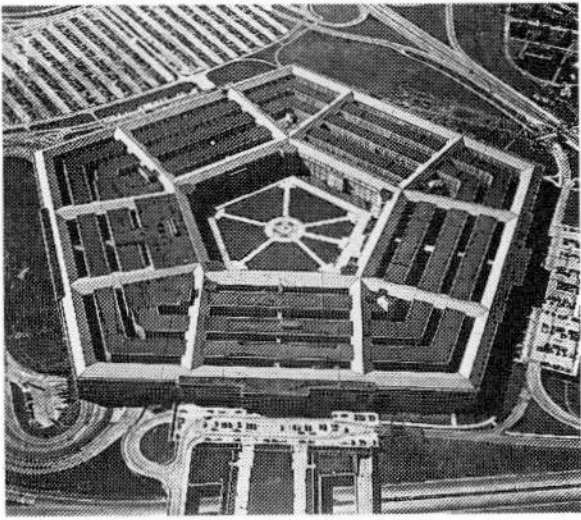

Pentagon

Pen·ta·gon·ese /ˌpentəˌgänˈēz/ ▸*n. informal* the euphemistic or cryptic language supposedly used among high-ranking U.S. military personnel. ▷1950s: from *(the) Pentagon* PENTAGON (see sense 2) + -ESE.

pen·ta·gram /ˈpentəˌgram/ ▸*n.* a five-pointed star that is formed by drawing a continuous line in five straight segments, often used as a mystic and magical symbol. Compare with PENTACLE. ▷mid 19th cent.: from Greek *pentagrammon* (see PENTA-, -GRAM[1]).

pentagram

pen·ta·he·dron /ˌpentəˈhēdrən/ ▸*n.* (*pl.* **-drons** or **-dra** /-drə/) a solid figure with five plane faces. ▷late 18th cent.: from PENTA- 'five' + -HEDRON, on the pattern of words such as *polyhedron.* —**pen·ta·he·dral** /-drəl/ *adj.*

pen·ta·mer /ˈpentəmər/ ▸*n. Chemistry* a polymer comprising five monomer units. —**pen·ta·mer·ic** /ˌpentəˈmerik/ *adj.*

pen·tam·er·al /penˈtamərəl/ ▸*adj. Zoology* (of symmetry) fivefold, as typical of many echinoderms. Compare with PENTAMEROUS. —**pen·tam·er·al·ly** *adv.* —**pen·tam·er·y** /-ˈtamərē/ *n.*

pen·tam·er·ous /penˈtamərəs/ ▸*adj. Botany & Zoology* having parts arranged in groups of five. ■ consisting of five joints or parts. Compare with PENTAMERAL.

pen·tam·e·ter /penˈtamitər/ ▸*n. Prosody* a line of verse consisting of five metrical feet, or (in Greek and

Latin verse) of two halves each of two feet and a long syllable. ▷early 16th cent.: via Latin from Greek *pentametros* (see PENTA-, -METER).

pen·tam·i·dine /pen'tami,dēn/ ▸*n. Medicine* a synthetic antibiotic drug used chiefly in the treatment of pneumocystis carinii pneumonia (PCP) infection. ▷1940s: from PENTANE + AMIDE + -INE[4].

pen·tane /'pen,tān/ ▸*n. Chemistry* a volatile liquid hydrocarbon of the alkane series, present in petroleum-based solvents. • Chem. formula: C_5H_{12}; three isomers, esp. the straight-chain isomer (***n*-pentane**). ▷late 19th cent.: from Greek *pente* 'five' (denoting five carbon atoms) + a shortened form of ALKANE.

pen·tan·gle /'pen,taNGgəl/ ▸*n.* another term for PENTAGRAM. ▷late Middle English: perhaps from medieval Latin *pentaculum* 'pentacle' (*-aculum* assimilated to Latin *angulus* 'an angle').

pen·ta·no·ic ac·id /,pentə'nō-ik/ ▸*n. Chemistry* a colorless liquid fatty acid present in various plant oils, used in making perfumes. • Chem. formula: $CH_3(CH_2)_3COOH$. ▷1920s: *pentanoic* from PENTANE. **—pen·ta·no·ate** /pen'tanə,wāt/ *n.*

pen·ta·ploid /'pentə,ploid/ *Genetics* ▸*adj.* (of a cell or nucleus) containing five homologous sets of chromosomes. ■ (of an organism or species) composed of pentaploid cells.
▸*n.* a pentaploid organism, variety, or species.

pen·ta·prism /'pentə,prizəm/ ▸*n.* a five-sided prism with two silvered surfaces giving a constant deviation of all rays of light through 90°, used chiefly in the viewfinders of single-lens reflex cameras.

pen·ta·quark /'pentə,kwärk; -,kwôrk/ ▸*n.* a baryon consisting of four quarks and an antiquark.

Pen·ta·teuch /'pentə,t(y)o͞ok/ the first five books of the Hebrew Bible (Genesis, Exodus, Leviticus, Numbers, and Deuteronomy). Traditionally ascribed to Moses, it is now held by scholars to be a compilation from texts of the 9th to 5th centuries BC. Jewish name TORAH. ▷via ecclesiastical Latin from ecclesiastical Greek *pentateukhos*, from *penta-* 'five' + *teukhos* 'implement, book.' **—Pen·ta·teuch·al** /-,t(y)o͞okəl/ *adj.*

pen·tath·lon /pen'taTH(ə),län/ ▸*n.* an athletic event comprising five different events for each competitor, in particular (also **modern pentathlon**) a men's event involving fencing, shooting, swimming, riding, and cross-country running. ▷early 17th cent. (denoting the original five events of leaping, running, discus-throwing, spear-throwing, and wrestling): from Greek, from *pente* 'five' + *athlon* 'contest.' **—pen·tath·lete** /-'taTHlēt/ *n.*

pen·ta·thol ▸*n.* variant spelling of PENTOTHAL, regarded as a misspelling in technical use.

pen·ta·ton·ic /,pentə'tänik/ ▸*adj. Music* relating to, based on, or denoting a scale of five notes, esp. one without semitones equivalent to an ordinary major scale with the fourth and seventh omitted. **—pen·ta·ton·i·cism** /-'tänəsizəm/ *n.*

pen·ta·va·lent /,pentə'vālənt/ ▸*adj. Chemistry* having a valence of five.

pen·taz·o·cine /pen'tazə,sēn/ ▸*n. Medicine* a synthetic compound that is a potent, nonaddictive analgesic, often given during childbirth. • A tricyclic compound; chem. formula: $C_{19}H_{27}NO$. ▷1960s: from PENTANE + AZO- + OCTA- + -INE[4].

Pen·te·cost /'pentə,kôst; -,käst/ ▸*n.* **1** the Christian festival celebrating the descent of the Holy Spirit on the disciples of Jesus after his Ascension, held on the seventh Sunday after Easter. ■ the day on which this festival is held. Also called WHITSUNDAY. **2** the Jewish festival of Shavuoth. ▷Old English *pentecosten*, via ecclesiastical Latin from Greek *pentēkostē (hēmera)* 'fiftieth (day)' (because the Jewish festival is held on the fiftieth day after the second day of Passover).

Pen·te·cos·tal /,pentə'kôstl; -'kästl/ ▸*adj.* **1** of or relating to Pentecost. **2** of, relating to, or denoting any of a number of Christian sects and individuals emphasizing baptism in the Holy Spirit, evidenced by speaking in tongues, prophecy, healing, and exorcism. [with reference to the baptism in the Holy Spirit at the first Pentecost (Acts 2: 9-11).]
▸*n.* a member of a Pentecostal sect. **—Pen·te·cos·tal·ism** /-,izəm/ *n.* **—Pen·te·cos·tal·ist** /-ist/ *adj. & n.*

pent·house /'pent,hous/ ▸*n.* **1** an apartment on the top floor of a tall building, typically luxuriously fitted and offering fine views. ■ a structure on the roof of a building housing machinery or equipment. **2** *archaic* an outhouse or shelter built onto the side of a building, having a sloping roof. ▷Middle English *pentis* (sense 2), shortening of Old French *apentis*, based on late Latin *appendicium* 'appendage,' from Latin *appendere* 'hang on.' The change of form in the 16th cent. was by association with French *pente* 'slope' and HOUSE.

pen·ti·men·to /,pentə'mentō/ ▸*n.* (*pl.* **-men·ti** /-'mentē/) a visible trace of earlier painting beneath a layer or layers of paint on a canvas. ▷early 20th cent.: from Italian, literally 'repentance.'

Pent·land Firth /'pentlənd/ a channel that separates the Orkney Islands from the northern tip of mainland Scotland. It links the North Sea with the Atlantic Ocean.

pent·land·ite /'pentlən,dīt/ ▸*n.* a bronze-yellow mineral that consists of a sulfide of iron and nickel and is the principal ore of nickel. ▷mid 19th cent.: from the name of Joseph B. *Pentland* (1797–1873), Irish traveler, + -ITE[1].

pen·to·bar·bi·tal /,pentə'bärbi,täl; -,tôl/ ▸*n. Medicine* a narcotic and sedative barbiturate drug formerly used to relieve insomnia. • Alternative name: **5-ethyl-5-(1-methylbutyl)-barbituric acid**; often used as the sodium salt (**sodium pentobarbitone**, Nembutal). ▷1930s: from PENTANE + BARBITAL (or BARBITONE).

pen·to·bar·bi·tone /,pentə'bärbi,tōn/ ▸*n.* British term for PENTOBARBITAL.

pen·tode /'pentōd/ ▸*n. Electronics* a thermionic tube having five electrodes. ▷early 20th cent.: from Greek *pente* 'five' + *hodos* 'way.'

pen·tose /'pentōs/ ▸*n. Chemistry* any of the class of simple sugars whose molecules contain five carbon atoms, such as ribose and xylose. They generally have the chemical formula $C_5H_{10}O_5$. ▷late 19th cent.: from PENTA- 'five' + -OSE[2].

Pen·to·thal /'pentə,THôl; -,THäl/ ▸*n.* trademark for THIOPENTAL.

pent·ox·ide /pent'äksīd/ ▸*n. Chemistry* an oxide containing five atoms of oxygen in its molecule or empirical formula.

pent roof ▸*n.* a roof consisting of a single sloping surface. ▷mid 19th cent.: from PENTHOUSE + ROOF.

pent·ste·mon /pent'stēmən; 'pentstəmən/ ▸*n.* variant spelling of PENSTEMON.

pent-up ▸*adj.* closely confined or held back: *pent-up frustrations.*

pen·tyl /'pentəl/ ▸*n.* [as *adj.*] *Chemistry* of or denoting an alkyl radical $-C_5H_{11}$. Compare with AMYL. ▷from PENTANE + ALKYL.

pe·nult /'pē,nəlt; pe'nəlt/ ▸*n. Linguistics* the penultimate syllable of a word.
▸*adj.* archaic term for PENULTIMATE.

pe·nul·ti·mate /pe'nəltəmit/ ▸*adj.* [*attrib.*] last but one in a series of things; second to the last: *the penultimate chapter of the book.* ▷late 17th cent.: from Latin *paenultimus*, from *paene* 'almost' + *ultimus* 'last,' on the pattern of *ultimate*.

pe·num·bra /pe'nəmbrə/ ▸*n.* (*pl.* **-brae** /-brē; -brī/ or **-bras**) the partially shaded outer region of the shadow cast by an opaque object. ■ *Astronomy* the shadow cast by the earth or moon over an area experiencing a partial eclipse. ■ *Astronomy* the less dark outer part of a sunspot, surrounding the dark core. ■ any area of partial shade. ▷mid 17th cent.: modern Latin, from Latin *paene* 'almost' + *umbra* 'shadow.' **—pe·num·bral** /-brəl/ *adj.*

pe·nu·ri·ous /pə'n(y)o͝orēəs/ ▸*adj. formal* **1** extremely poor; poverty-stricken: *a penurious old tramp.* ■ characterized by poverty or need: *penurious years.* **2** parsimonious; mean: *he was generous and hospitable in contrast to his stingy and penurious wife.* ▷late 16th cent.: from medieval Latin *penuriosus*, from Latin *penuria* 'need, scarcity' (see PENURY). **—pe·nu·ri·ous·ly** *adv.* **—pe·nu·ri·ous·ness** *n.*

pen·u·ry /'penyərē/ ▸*n.* extreme poverty; destitution: *he died in a state of virtual penury.* ▷late Middle English: from Latin *penuria* 'need, scarcity'; perhaps related to *paene* 'almost.'

Pe·nu·ti·an /pə'no͞oSHən; -'no͞otēən/ ▸*n.* a proposed phylum of American Indian languages including Chinook, Klamath, and Nez Percé, most of which are now extinct or nearly so. Some scholars include certain living languages of Central and South America, principally Mayan and Mapuche, in this group.
▸*adj.* of, relating to, or denoting these languages or any of the peoples speaking them. ▷from *pen* and *uti*, words for 'two' in two groups of Penutian languages + -AN.

Pen·za /'penzə; 'pyen-/ a city in south central Russia; pop. 548,000. Located on the Sura River, a tributary of the Volga River, it is an industrial and transportation center.

pe·on /'pē,än; 'pēən/ ▸*n.* **1** a Spanish-American day laborer or unskilled farm worker. ■ *historical* a debtor held in servitude by a creditor, esp. in the southern U.S. and Mexico. ■ a person who does menial work; a drudge: *racing drivers aren't exactly normal nine-to-five peons.* **2** (in the Indian subcontinent and Southeast Asia) someone of low rank. ■ a foot soldier. ■ an attendant or messenger. ■ a person who does minor jobs in an office. ▷from Portuguese *peão* and Spanish *peón*, from medieval Latin *pedo*, *pedon-* 'walker, foot soldier,' from Latin *pes*, *ped-* 'foot.' Compare with PAWN[1]. **—pe·on·age** /'pēənij/ *n.*

pe·o·ny /'pēənē/ ▸*n.* a herbaceous or shrubby plant of north temperate regions, which has long been cultivated for its showy flowers. • Genus *Paeonia*, family Paeoniaceae. ▷Old English *peonie*, via Latin from Greek *paiōnia*, from *Paiōn*, the name of the physician of the gods.

peo·ple /'pēpəl/ ▸*plural n.* **1** human beings in general or considered collectively: *the earthquake killed 30,000 people.* ■ (**the people**) the citizens of a country, esp. when considered in relation to those who govern them: *his economic reforms no longer have the support of the people.* ■ (**the people**) those without special rank or position in society; the populace: *he is very much a man of the people.* ■ (**one's people**) a person's parents or relatives: *my people live in West Virginia.* ■ (**one's people**) the supporters or employees of a person in a position of power or authority: *I've had my people watching the house for some time now.* ■ (**the People**) the state prosecution in a trial: *pretrial statements made by the People's witnesses.* **2** (*pl.* **peo·ples**) [treated as *sing.* or *pl.*] the men, women, and children of a particular nation, community, or ethnic group: *the native peoples of Canada.*
▸*v.* [*trans.*] (usu. **be peopled**) (of a particular group of people) inhabit (an area or place): *an arid mountain region peopled by warring clans.* ■ fill or be present in (a place, environment, or domain): *the street is peopled with ragamuffined hippies.* ■ fill (an area or place) with a particular group of inhabitants: *it was his intention to people the town with English colonists.* ▷Middle English: from Anglo-Norman French *poeple*, from Latin *populus* 'populace.' **—peo·ple·hood** /-,ho͝od/ *n.* (sense 2 of the *noun*).

USAGE See usage at PERSON.

peo·ple me·ter ▸*n.* an electronic device used to record the television viewing habits of a household so that the information obtained can be used to compile ratings.

peo·ple mov·er ▸*n. informal* a means of transportation, in particular any of a number of automated systems for carrying large numbers of people over short distances.

peo·ple per·son ▸*n. informal* a person who enjoys or is particularly good at interacting with others.

peo·ple's court ▸*n. informal* a small-claims court.

Peo·ple's Lib·er·a·tion Ar·my (abbr.: **PLA**) the armed forces of the People's Republic of China, including all its land, sea, and air forces. The PLA traces its origins to an unsuccessful uprising by communist-led troops against pro-Nationalist forces in Jiangxi (Kiangsi) province on August 1, 1927, a date celebrated annually as its anniversary.

Peo·ple's par·ty ▸*n.* another name for the Populist Party.

Peo·ple's Re·pub·lic ▸*n.* used in the official title of several present or former communist or left-wing states. ■ (**the People's Republic**) short for PEOPLE'S REPUBLIC OF CHINA.

Peo·ple's Re·pub·lic of Chi·na official name (since 1949) of CHINA.

Pe·or·i·a /pē'ôrēə/ **1** a river port and industrial city in central Illinois, on the Illinois River; pop. 112,936. It developed around a fort built by the French in 1680. **2** a city in southwest central Arizona, a northwestern suburb of Phoenix; pop. 108,364. ▷named after the American Indians who occupied the area (in sense 1) when the French arrived.

PEP *Brit.* ▸*abbr.* ■ personal equity plan. ■ Political and Economic Planning.

pep /pep/ *informal* ▸*n.* energy and high spirits; liveliness: *he was an enthusiastic player, full of pep and fight.*
▸*v.* (**pepped, pep·ping**) [*trans.*] (**pep someone/something up**) add liveliness or vigor to someone or something: *measures to pep up the economy.* ▷early 20th cent.: abbreviation of PEPPER.

pep·er·o·mi·a /,pepə'rōmēə/ ▸*n.* a small, fleshy-leaved, tropical plant of the pepper family. Many are grown as houseplants, chiefly for their decorative foliage. • Genus *Peperomia*, family Piperaceae. ▷modern Latin, from Greek *peperi*.

pep·er·o·ni ▸*n.* variant spelling of PEPPERONI.

Pe·pin III /ˈpepin/ (*c.* 714–768) king of the Franks 751–768; called **Pippin the Short;** father of Charlemagne. He founded the Carolingian dynasty in 751.

pe·pi·no /pəˈpēnō/ ▸*n.* (*pl.* **-nos**) a spiny plant of the nightshade family, with edible, purple-streaked yellow fruit, native to the Andes. • *Solanum muricatum*, family Solanaceae. ▷mid 19th cent.: from Spanish, literally 'cucumber' (because of the elongated shape of the fruit).

pep·los /ˈpepləs; ˈpep,läs/ (also **pep·lus**) ▸*n.* a rich outer robe or shawl worn by women in ancient Greece, hanging in loose folds and sometimes drawn over the head. ▷Greek.

pep·lum /ˈpepləm/ ▸*n.* a short flared, gathered, or pleated strip of fabric attached at the waist of a woman's jacket, dress, or blouse to create a hanging frill or flounce. ■ (in ancient Greece) a woman's loose outer tunic or shawl. [via Latin from Greek *peplos*.]

pe·po /ˈpēpō/ ▸*n.* (*pl.* **-pos**) any fleshy, watery fruit of the melon or cucumber type, with numerous seeds and a firm rind. ▷mid 19th cent.: from Latin, literally 'pumpkin,' from Greek *pepōn* (from *pepōn sikuos* 'ripe gourd').

pep·per /ˈpepər/ ▸*n.* **1** a pungent, hot-tasting powder prepared from dried and ground peppercorns, commonly used as a spice or condiment to flavor food. ■ a reddish and typically hot-tasting spice prepared from various forms of capsicum. See also CAYENNE. ■ a capsicum, esp. a sweet pepper. **2** a climbing vine with berries that are dried as black or white peppercorns. • *Piper nigrum*, family Piperaceae. ■ used in names of other plants that are related to this, have hot-tasting leaves, or have fruits used as a pungent spice, e.g., **water pepper**. **3** *Baseball* a practice game in which fielders throw at close range to a batter who hits back to the fielders.
▸*v.* [*trans.*] sprinkle or season (food) with pepper: [as *adj.*] (**peppered**) *peppered beef.* ■ (usu. **be peppered with**) cover or fill with a liberal amount of scattered items: *the script is peppered with four-letter words.* ■ hit repeatedly with small missiles or gunshot: *another burst of enemy bullets peppered his defenseless body* | *figurative he peppered me with questions.* ■ *archaic* inflict severe punishment or suffering upon. ▷Old English *piper, pipor*; related to Dutch *peper* and German *Pfeffer*; via Latin from Greek *peperi*, from Sanskrit *pippalī* 'berry, peppercorn.'

pep·per vine ▸*n.* a bushy vine of the grape family, originally cultivated but now established in much of the southeastern U.S. It bears blackish fruits sought after by wildlife. • *Ampelopsis arborea*, family Vitaceae.

pep·per-and-salt ▸*adj.* another way of saying SALT-AND-PEPPER.

pep·per·box /ˈpepər,bäks/ ▸*n.* **1** a gun or piece of artillery with a revolving set of barrels. **2** *archaic* a pepper shaker.

pep·per·corn /ˈpepər,kôrn/ ▸*n.* the dried berry of a climbing vine, used whole as a spice or crushed or ground to make pepper. See PEPPER (sense 2).

pep·per·grass /ˈpepər,gras/ ▸*n.* a wild cress, particularly one with pungent leaves. • Genus *Lepidium*, family Brassicaceae.

pep·per·idge /ˈpepərij/ ▸*n.* another term for SOURGUM. ▷late 17th cent.: alteration of dialect *pipperidge*, denoting the barberry and its fruit, of unknown origin.

pep·per mill ▸*n.* a device for grinding peppercorns by hand to make pepper.

pep·per·mint /ˈpepər,mint/ ▸*n.* **1** the aromatic leaves of a plant of the mint family, or an essential oil obtained from them, used as a flavoring in food. ■ a candy flavored with such oil. **2** the cultivated Old World plant that yields these leaves or oil. • *Mentha piperita*, family Labiatae. **3** *Austral.* any of a number of trees or shrubs with peppermint-scented foliage, in particular: • a gum tree with leaves that yield an aromatic essential oil (genus *Eucalyptus*, family Myrtaceae). • a myrtle grown as an ornamental tree or shrub (genus *Agonis*, family Myrtaceae). —**pep·per·mint·y** *adj.*

pep·per·o·ni /,pepəˈrōnē/ (also **pep·er·o·ni**) ▸*n.* beef and pork sausage seasoned with pepper. ▷from Italian *peperone* 'cayenne pepper plant.'

pep·per pot ▸*n.* **1** British term for PEPPER SHAKER. **2** a West Indian dish consisting of stewed meat or fish with vegetables, typically flavored with cassareep.

pep·per shak·er ▸*n.* a container with a perforated top for sprinkling pepper.

pep·per·shrike /ˈpepər,SHrīk/ ▸*n.* a tropical American songbird with mainly green and yellow plumage and a heavy bill like that of a shrike. • Genus *Cyclarhis*, family Cyclarhidae (or merged with the vireo family, Vireonidae): two species, including the **rufous-browed peppershrike** (*C. gujanensis*) of Mexico.

pep·per spray ▸*n.* an aerosol spray containing oils derived from cayenne pepper, irritating to the eyes and respiratory passages and used as a disabling weapon.

pep·per tree ▸*n.* any of a number of shrubs or trees that have aromatic leaves or fruit with a pepperlike smell, in particular: • an evergreen Peruvian tree of the cashew family, widely grown as a shade tree in hot countries (*Schinus molle*, family Anacardiaceae).

pep·per·wort /ˈpepər,wərt; -,wôrt/ ▸*n.* another term for PEPPERGRASS.

pep·per·y /ˈpepərē/ ▸*adj.* strongly flavored with pepper or other hot spices: *a hot, peppery dish.* ■ having a flavor or scent like that of pepper. ■ (of a person) irritable and sharp-tongued: *retired generals are expected to be peppery.* —**pep·per·i·ness** /-rēnis/ *n.*

pep pill ▸*n.* *informal* a pill containing a stimulant drug.

pep·py /ˈpepē/ ▸*adj.* (**pep·pi·er**, **pep·pi·est**) *informal* lively and high-spirited: *stickers bearing peppy slogans.* —**pep·pi·ly** /ˈpepəlē/ *adv.* —**pep·pi·ness** /-ēnis/ *n.*

pep ral·ly ▸*n.* *informal* a meeting aimed at inspiring enthusiasm, esp. one held before a sporting event.

pep·sin /ˈpepsin/ ▸*n.* *Biochemistry* the chief digestive enzyme in the stomach, which breaks down proteins into polypeptides. ▷mid 19th cent.: from Greek *pepsis* 'digestion' + -IN[1].

pep·sin·o·gen /pepˈsinəjen/ ▸*n.* *Biochemistry* a substance that is secreted by the stomach wall and converted into the enzyme pepsin by gastric acid.

pep talk ▸*n.* *informal* a talk intended to make someone feel more courageous or enthusiastic.

pep·tic /ˈpeptik/ ▸*adj.* of or relating to digestion, esp. that in which pepsin is concerned. ▷mid 17th cent.: from Greek *peptikos* 'able to digest.'

pep·tic gland ▸*n.* *Anatomy* a gland that secretes the gastric juice containing pepsin.

pep·tic ul·cer ▸*n.* a lesion in the lining (mucosa) of the digestive tract, typically in the stomach or duodenum, caused by the digestive action of pepsin and stomach acid.

pep·ti·dase /ˈpepti,dās/ ▸*n.* *Biochemistry* an enzyme that breaks down peptides into amino acids.

pep·tide /ˈpeptīd/ ▸*n.* *Biochemistry* a compound consisting of two or more amino acids linked in a chain, the carboxyl group of each acid being joined to the amino group of the next by a bond of the type −OC−NH−. ▷early 20th cent.: from German *Peptid*, back-formation from *Polypeptid* 'polypeptide.'

pep·ti·do·gly·can /,peptidōˈglī,kan/ ▸*n.* *Biochemistry* a substance forming the cell walls of many bacteria, consisting of glycosaminoglycan chains interlinked with short peptides.

pep·tone /ˈpeptōn/ ▸*n.* *Biochemistry* a soluble protein formed in the early stage of protein breakdown during digestion. ■ (also **peptone water**) a solution of this in saline, used as a liquid medium for growing bacteria. ▷mid 19th cent.: from German *Pepton*, from Greek *pepton*, neuter of *peptos* 'cooked, digested.'

Pepys /pēps/, Samuel (1633–1703), English diarist and naval administrator. He is particularly remembered for his *Diary* (1660–69), which describes events such as the Great Plague and the Fire of London.

Pé·quiste /,pāˈkēst/ ▸*n.* *Canadian* a member or supporter of the Parti Québecois, a political party originally advocating independent rule for Quebec. ▷from the French pronunciation of the abbreviation *PQ* + the noun suffix *-iste*.

Pe·quot /ˈpē,kwät/ ▸*n.* (*pl.* same or **-quots**) **1** a member of an American Indian people of southern New England. **2** the Algonquian language of this people, closely related to Mohegan.
▸*adj.* of or relating to this people or their language. ▷from Narragansett *pequttôog*, perhaps 'people of the shoals.'

per /pər/ ▸*prep.* **1** for each (used with units to express a rate): *a gas station that charges $1.29 per gallon.* **2** *archaic* by means of: *send it per express.* **3** (**as per**) in accordance with: *made as per instructions.* **4** *Heraldry* divided by a line in the direction of: *per bend* | *per pale* | *per saltire.* ▷Latin, 'through, by means of'; partly via Old French.
▸*PHRASE* □ **as per usual** as usual.

per. ▸*abbr.* ■ percentile. ■ period. ■ person.

per- ▸*prefix* **1** through; all over: *percuss* | *perforation* | *pervade.* ■ completely; very: *perfect* | *perturb.* ■ to destruction; to ill effect: *perdition* | *pervert.* **2** *Chemistry* having the maximum proportion of some element in combination: *peroxide* | *perchloric* | *permanganate.* ▷from Latin (see PER).

per·ad·ven·ture /,pərədˈvenCHər; ,per-/ *archaic humorous* ▸*adv.* *archaic* or *humorous* perhaps: *peradventure I'm not as wealthy as he is.*
▸*n.* *archaic* or *humorous* uncertainty or doubt as to whether something is the case: *that shows* ***beyond peradventure*** *the strength of the economy.* ▷Middle English: from Old French *per* (or *par*) *auenture* 'by chance.'

per·am·bu·late /pəˈrambyə,lāt/ ▸*v.* [*trans.*] *formal* walk or travel through or around (a place or area), esp. for pleasure and in a leisurely way: *she perambulated the square.* ■ [*intrans.*] walk from place to place; walk about: *he grew weary of perambulating over rough countryside in bad weather.* ■ *Brit., historical* walk around (a parish, forest, etc.) in order to officially assert and record its boundaries. ▷late Middle English: from Latin *perambulat-* 'walked around,' from the verb *perambulare*, from *per-* 'all over' + *ambulare* 'to walk.' —**per·am·bu·la·tion** /pə,rambyəˈlāSHən/ *n.* —**per·am·bu·la·to·ry** /-lə,tôrē/ *adj.*

per·am·bu·la·tor /pəˈrambyə,lātər/ ▸*n.* **1** a person who perambulates; a pedestrian. **2** a machine, similar to an odometer, for measuring distances by means of a large wheel pushed along the ground by a long handle, with a mechanism for recording the revolutions. **3** *Brit.* a baby carriage. ▷early 17th cent.: see PERAMBULATE.

per an·num /pər ˈanəm/ ▸*adv.* for each year (used in financial contexts): *an average growth rate of around 2 percent per annum.* ▷early 17th cent.: Latin.

p/e ra·tio ▸*abbr.* price–earnings ratio.

per·bo·rate /pərˈbôr,āt/ ▸*n.* *Chemistry* a salt that is an oxidized borate containing a peroxide linkage, esp. a sodium salt of this kind used as a bleach.

per·cale /pərˈkāl; -ˈkal/ ▸*n.* a closely woven fine cotton or polyester fabric used esp. for sheets. ▷early 17th cent.: from French, of unknown origin.

per cap·i·ta /pər ˈkapitə/ ▸*adv.* & *adj.* for each person; in relation to people taken individually: [as *adv.*] *the state had fewer banks per capita than elsewhere* | [as *adj.*] *per capita spending.* ▷late 17th cent.: Latin, literally 'by heads.'

per·ceive /pərˈsēv/ ▸*v.* [*trans.*] **1** become aware or conscious of (something); come to realize or understand: *his mouth fell open as he perceived the truth* | [with *clause*] *he was quick to perceive that there was little future in such arguments.* ■ become aware of (something) by the use of one of the senses, esp. that of sight: *he perceived the faintest of flushes creeping up her neck.* **2** interpret or look on (someone or something) in a particular way; regard as: *if Guy does not* ***perceive himself as*** *disabled, nobody else should* | [*trans.*] *some geographers perceive hydrology to be a separate field of scientific inquiry.* ▷Middle English: from a variant of Old French *perçoivre*, from Latin *percipere* 'seize, understand,' from *per-* 'entirely' + *capere* 'take.' —**per·ceiv·a·ble** *adj.* —**per·ceiv·er** *n.*

per·cent /pərˈsent/ (also *chiefly Brit.* **per cent**) ▸*adv.* by a specified amount in or for every hundred: *new car sales may be down nineteen percent* | *staff rejected a 1.8 percent increase.*
▸*n.* one part in every hundred: *a reduction of half a percent or so in price.* ■ the rate, number, or amount in each hundred; percentage: *the percent of drug users who are infected.* ▷mid 16th cent.: from PER + CENT, perhaps an abbreviation of pseudo-Latin *per centum*.

USAGE Both spellings, **percent** and **per cent**, are acceptable, but consistency should be maintained. **Percent** is more common in U.S. usage; **per cent** is more common in British usage.

per·cent·age /pərˈsentij/ ▸*n.* a rate, number, or amount in each hundred: *the percentage of Caesareans at the hospital was three percent higher than the national average* | [as *adj.*] *a large percentage increase in the population over 85.* ■ an amount, such as an allowance or commission, that is a proportion of a larger sum of money: *I hope to be on a percentage.* ■ any proportion or share in relation to a whole: *only a small percentage of black Americans have Caribbean roots.* ■ [in *sing.*] *informal* personal benefit or advantage: *you explain to me* **the percentage in** *looking like a hoodlum.*

▸*PHRASE* □ **play the percentages** (or **the percentage game**) *informal* choose a safe and methodical course of action when calculating the odds in favor of success. [referring to the calculated percentage of success from statistics.]

-percenter ▸*comb. form* **1** denoting a member of a group forming a specified and usually small percentage of the population: *he was a one-percenter, riding outside of the law.* **2** denoting a person who takes commission at a specified rate: *ten-percenters.*

per·cen·tile /pər'sen,tīl/ ▸*n. Statistics* each of the 100 equal groups into which a population can be divided according to the distribution of values of a particular variable. ■ each of the 99 intermediate values of a random variable that divide a frequency distribution into 100 such groups: *the tenth percentile for weight.*

per·cept /'pərsept/ ▸*n. Philosophy* an object of perception; something that is perceived. ■ a mental concept that is developed as a consequence of the process of perception. ▷mid 19th cent.: from Latin *perceptum* 'something perceived,' neuter past participle of *percipere* 'seize, understand,' on the pattern of *concept.*

per·cep·ti·ble /pər'septəbəl/ ▸*adj.* (esp. of a slight movement or change of state) able to be seen or noticed: *a perceptible decline in public confidence.* See note at TANGIBLE. ▷late Middle English: from late Latin *perceptibilis,* from Latin *percipere* 'seize, understand' (see PERCEIVE). **—per·cep·ti·bil·i·ty** /pər,septə'bilitē/ *n.* **—per·cep·ti·bly** /-blē/ *adv.*

per·cep·tion /pər'sepSHən/ ▸*n.* the ability to see, hear, or become aware of something through the senses: *the normal limits to human perception.* ■ the state of being or process of becoming aware of something in such a way: *the perception of pain.* ■ a way of regarding, understanding, or interpreting something; a mental impression: *Hollywood's perception of the tastes of the American public | we need to challenge many popular perceptions of old age.* ■ intuitive understanding and insight: *"He wouldn't have accepted," said my mother with unusual perception.* ■ *Psychology & Zoology* the neurophysiological processes, including memory, by which an organism becomes aware of and interprets external stimuli. ▷late Middle English: from Latin *perceptio(n-),* from the verb *percipere* 'seize, understand' (see PERCEIVE). **—per·cep·tion·al** /-SHənl; -SHnəl/ *adj.*

per·cep·tive /pər'septiv/ ▸*adj.* having or showing sensitive insight: *an extraordinarily perceptive account of their relationship.* **—per·cep·tive·ly** *adv.* **—per·cep·tive·ness** *n.* **—per·cep·tiv·i·ty** /,pərsep'tivitē/ *n.*

per·cep·tron /pər'septrän/ ▸*n.* a computer model or computerized machine devised to represent or simulate the ability of the brain to recognize and discriminate.

per·cep·tu·al /pər'sepCHo͞oəl/ ▸*adj.* of or relating to the ability to interpret or become aware of something through the senses: *a patient with perceptual problems who cannot judge distances.* **—per·cep·tu·al·ly** *adv.*

Per·ce·val[1] /'pərsəvəl/ a legendary figure dating back to ancient times, found in French, German, and English poetry from the late 12th century onward. He is the father of Lohengrin and the hero of a number of legends, some of which are associated with the Holy Grail. Also called **PARSIFAL.**

Per·ce·val[2], Spencer (1762–1812), British statesman; prime minister 1809–12. He was shot dead in the lobby of the House of Commons by a bankrupt merchant who blamed the government for his insolvency.

perch[1] /pərCH/ ▸*n.* a thing on which a bird alights or roosts, typically a branch or a horizontal rod or bar in a birdcage. ■ a place where someone or something rests or sits, esp. a place that is high or precarious: *Marian looked down from her perch in a beech tree above the road.*

▸*v.* [*intrans.*] (of a bird) alight or rest on something: *a herring gull perched on the mast.* ■ (of a person) sit somewhere, esp. on something high or narrow: *Eve perched on the side of the armchair.* ■ (**be perched**) (of a building) be situated above or on the edge of something: *the fortress is perched on a crag in the mountains.* ■ [*trans.*] (**perch someone/something on**) set or balance someone or something on (something): *Peter perched a pair of gold-rimmed spectacles on his nose.* ▷late Middle English: the noun from PERCH[3]; the verb from Old French *percher.*

▸*PHRASE* □ **knock someone off their perch** *informal* cause someone to lose a position of superiority or preeminence: *will this knock London off its perch as Europe's leading financial center?*

perch[2] ▸*n.* (*pl.* same or **perch·es**) an edible freshwater fish with a high spiny dorsal fin, dark vertical bars on the body, and orange lower fins. • Genus *Perca,* family Percidae (the **perch family**): three species, in particular *P. fluviatilis* of Europe (also called BASS[2]), and the almost identical **yellow perch** (*P. flavescens*) of North America. The perch family also includes the pikeperches, ruffe, and darters. ■ used in names of other freshwater and marine fishes resembling or related to this, e.g., **climbing perch, sea perch, surfperch.** ▷late Middle English: from Old French *perche,* via Latin from Greek *perkē.*

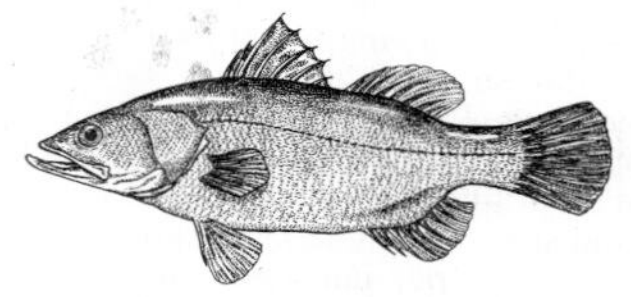

yellow perch

perch[3] ▸*n. chiefly Brit., historical* a linear or square rod; see ROD, sense 3. ▷Middle English (in the general sense 'pole, stick'): from Old French *perche,* from Latin *pertica* 'measuring rod, pole.'

per·chance /pər'CHans/ ▸*adv. archaic* or *poetic/literary* by some chance; perhaps: *we dare not go ashore lest perchance we should fall into some snare.* ▷Middle English: from Old French *par cheance* 'by chance.'

Per·che·ron /'pərSHə,rän; 'pərCHə-/ ▸*n.* a powerful draft horse of a gray or black breed, originally from France. ▷late 19th cent.: from French, originally bred in le *Perche,* the name of a district of northern France.

per·chlo·ric ac·id /pər'klôrik/ ▸*n. Chemistry* a fuming toxic liquid with powerful oxidizing properties. • Chem. formula: $HClO_4$. **—per·chlo·rate** /-,rāt/ *n.*

per·cid /'pərsid/ ▸*n. Zoology* a fish of the perch family (Percidae). ▷late 19th cent.: from modern Latin *Percidae* (plural), from Latin *perca* 'perch.'

per·cip·i·ent /pər'sipēənt/ ▸*adj.* (of a person) having a good understanding of things; perceptive: *he is a percipient interpreter of the public mood.*

▸*n.* (esp. in philosophy or with reference to psychic phenomena) a person who is able to perceive things. ▷mid 17th cent.: from Latin *percipient-* 'seizing, understanding,' from the verb *percipere.* **—per·cip·i·ence** *n.* **—per·cip·i·ent·ly** *adv.*

per·coid /'pərkoid/ *Zoology* ▸*n.* a fish of a large group that includes the perches, basses, jacks, snappers, grunts, sea breams, and drums. • Superfamily Percoidea: many families.

▸*adj.* of or relating to fish of this group. ▷mid 19th cent.: from modern Latin *Percoïdes* (plural), from Latin *perca* 'perch.'

per·co·late /'pərkə,lāt/ ▸*v.* **1** [*intrans.*] (of a liquid or gas) filter gradually through a porous surface or substance: *the water percolating through the soil may leach out minerals.* ■ *figurative* (of information or an idea or feeling) spread gradually through an area or group of people: *this idea soon percolated into the Christian Church.* **2** [*intrans.*] (of coffee) be prepared in a percolator: *he put some coffee on to percolate.* ■ [*trans.*] prepare (coffee) in a percolator: [as *adj.*] (**percolated**) *freshly percolated coffee.* ■ *figurative* be or become full of lively activity or excitement: *the night was percolating with an expectant energy.* ▷early 17th cent.: from Latin *percolat-* 'strained through,' from the verb *percolare,* from *per-* 'through' + *colare* 'to strain' (from *colum* 'strainer'). **—per·co·la·tion** /,pərkə'lāSHən/ *n.*

per·co·la·tor /'pərkə,lātər/ ▸*n.* a machine for making coffee, consisting of a pot in which boiling water is circulated through a small chamber that holds the ground beans.

per con·tra /pər 'käntrə/ ▸*adv. formal* on the other hand; on the contrary: *he had worked very hard on the place; she, per contra, had little to do.*

▸*n.* the opposite side of an account or an assessment. ▷mid 16th cent.: from Italian.

per cu·ri·am /pər 'kyo͝orēəm/ *Law* ▸*adv.* by decision of a judge, or of a court in unanimous agreement.

▸*n.* such a decision: *in only a few cases did the panel publish a per curiam.* ▷Latin, literally 'by a court.'

per·cuss /pər'kəs/ ▸*v.* [*trans.*] *Medicine* gently tap (a part of the body) with a finger or an instrument as part of a diagnosis: *the bladder was percussed.* ▷mid 16th cent. (in the general sense 'give a blow to'): from Latin *percuss-* 'struck forcibly,' from the verb *percutere,* from *per-* 'through' + *quatere* 'to shake, strike.'

per·cus·sion /pər'kəSHən/ ▸*n.* **1** musical instruments played by striking with the hand or with a hand-held or pedal-operated stick or beater, or by shaking, including drums, cymbals, xylophones, gongs, bells, and rattles: [as *adj.*] *percussion instruments | the percussion section.* **2** the striking of one solid object with or against another with some degree of force: *the clattering percussion of objects striking the walls and the shutters.* ■ *Medicine* the action of tapping a part of the body as part of a diagnosis: *the chest sounded dull on percussion.* ▷late Middle English: from Latin *percussio(n-),* from the verb *percutere* 'to strike forcibly' (see PERCUSS). **—per·cus·sion·ist** /-ist/ *n.* (in sense 1) **—per·cus·sive** /-'kəsiv/ *adj.* **—per·cus·sive·ly** /-'kəsivlē/ *adv.* **—per·cus·sive·ness** /-'kəsivnis/ *n.*

per·cus·sion cap ▸*n.* a small amount of explosive powder contained in metal or paper and exploded by striking. Percussion caps are used chiefly in toy guns and formerly in some firearms.

per·cu·ta·ne·ous /,pərkyo͞o'tānēəs/ ▸*adj. Medicine* made, done, or effected through the skin. ▷late 19th cent.: from Latin *per cutem* 'through the skin' + -ANEOUS. **—per·cu·ta·ne·ous·ly** *adv.*

Per·cy[1] /'pərsē/, Sir Henry (1364–1403), English soldier; known as **Hotspur** or **Harry Hotspur**. Son of the 1st Earl of Northumberland, he was killed at the battle of Shrewsbury.

Per·cy[2], Walker (1916–90) U.S. writer. His novels include *The Moviegoer* (1961), *Love in the Ruins* (1971), *The Second Coming* (1980), and *The Thanatos Syndrome* (1987).

per di·em /pər 'dēəm/ ▸*adv.* & *adj.* for each day (used in financial contexts): [as *adv.*] *he agreed to pay at certain specified rates per diem* | [as *adj.*] *they are now demanding a per diem rate.*

▸*n.* an allowance or payment made for each day. ▷early 16th cent.: Latin.

per·di·tion /pər'diSHən/ ▸*n.* (in Christian theology) a state of eternal punishment and damnation into which a sinful and unpenitent person passes after death. ▷late Middle English: from Old French *perdiciun,* from ecclesiastical Latin *perditio(n-),* from Latin *perdere* 'destroy,' from *per-* 'completely, to destruction' + the base of *dare* 'put.'

per·dur·a·ble /pər'd(y)o͝orəbəl/ ▸*adj. formal* enduring continuously; imperishable. ▷late Middle English: via Old French from late Latin *perdurabilis,* from Latin *perdurare* 'endure.' **—per·dur·a·bil·i·ty** /-,d(y)o͝orə'bilitē/ *n.* **—per·dur·a·bly** *adv.*

per·dure /pər'd(y)o͝or/ ▸*v.* [*intrans.*] *formal* remain in existence throughout a substantial period of time; endure: *bell music has perdured in Venice throughout five centuries.* ▷late 15th cent.: from Old French *perdurer,* from Latin *perdurare* 'endure,' from *per-* 'through' + *durare* 'to last.' **—per·dur·ance** /-'d(y)o͝orəns/ *n.*

père /pe(ə)r/ ▸*n.* used after a surname to distinguish a father from a son of the same name: *Alexandre Dumas père.* Compare with FILS[2]. ▷French, literally 'father.'

Père Da·vid's deer /,per 'dāvidz/ ▸*n.* a large deer with a red summer coat that turns dark gray in winter, and long antlers with backward pointing tines. Formerly a native of China, it is now found only in captivity. • *Elaphurus davidianus,* family Cervidae. ▷late 19th cent.: named after Father Armand *David* (1826–1900), French missionary and naturalist.

per·e·gri·nate /'perigrə,nāt/ ▸*v.* [*intrans.*] *archaic* or *humorous* travel or wander around from place to place. ▷late 16th cent.: from Latin *peregrinat-* 'traveled abroad,' from the verb *peregrinari,* from *peregrinus* 'foreign, traveling.' **—per·e·gri·na·tion** /,perigrə'nāSHən/ *n.* **—per·e·gri·na·tor** /-,nātər/ *n.*

per·e·grine /'perəgrin/ ▸*n.* (also **peregrine falcon**) a powerful falcon found on most continents, breeding chiefly on mountains and coastal cliffs and much used for falconry. [translating the modern Latin taxonomic name, literally 'pilgrim falcon,' because the

peregrine

bird was caught full-grown as a passage hawk, not taken from the nest.] • *Falco peregrinus,* family Falconidae.

▸*adj. archaic* coming from another country; foreign or outlandish: *peregrine species of grass.* ▷late Middle English: from Latin *peregrinus* 'foreign,' from *peregre* 'abroad,' from *per-* 'through' + *ager* 'field.'

pe·rei·o·pod /pəˈrīə,päd; -ˈrāə-/ ▸*n. Zoology* each of the eight walking limbs of a crustacean such as a crab or lobster, growing from the thorax. ▷late 19th cent.: from Greek *peraioōn* 'transporting' (present participle of *peraioun*) + *pous, pod-* 'foot.'

Pe·rel·man /ˈpərlmən; ˈperəl-/, S. J. (1904–79), U.S. humorist and writer; full name *Sidney Joseph Perelman.* In the early 1930s he worked in Hollywood as a scriptwriter and from 1934 his name is linked with the *New Yorker* magazine, for which he wrote most of his short stories and sketches.

per·emp·to·ry /pəˈremptərē/ ▸*adj.* (esp. of a person's manner or actions) insisting on immediate attention or obedience, esp. in a brusquely imperious way: *"Just do it!" came the peremptory reply.* ■ *Law* not open to appeal or challenge; final: *there has been no disobedience of a peremptory order of the court.* ▷late Middle English (as a legal term): via Anglo-Norman French from Latin *peremptorius* 'deadly, decisive,' from *perempt-* 'destroyed, cut off,' from the verb *perimere,* from *per-* 'completely' + *emere* 'take, buy.' **—per·emp·to·ri·ly** /-tərəlē/ *adv.* **—per·emp·to·ri·ness** /-rēnis/ *n.*

USAGE **Peremptory** and **preemptive** may sometimes be confused, but they are in no way interchangeable terms. A **peremptory** act or statement is absolute; it cannot be denied: *he issued a peremptory order.* A **preemptive** action is one taken before an adversary can act: *preemptive air strikes stopped the enemy from launching the new warship.*

per·emp·to·ry chal·lenge ▸*n. Law* a defendant's or lawyer's objection to a proposed juror, made without needing to give a reason.

per·en·nate /ˈperə,nāt; pəˈrenāt/ ▸*v.* [*intrans.*] [usu. as *adj.*] (**perennating**) *Botany* (of a plant or part of a plant) live through a number of years, usually with an annual quiescent period. ▷early 17th cent.: from Latin *perennat-* 'continued for many years' (from the verb *perennare*) + **-ATE**[3]. **—per·en·na·tion** /,perəˈnāSHən/ *n.*

per·en·ni·al /pəˈrenēəl/ ▸*adj.* lasting or existing for a long or apparently infinite time; enduring: *his perennial distrust of the media.* ■ (of a plant) living for several years: *tarragon is perennial.* Compare with **ANNUAL, BIENNIAL.** ■ (esp. of a problem or difficult situation) continually occurring: *perennial manifestations of urban crisis.* ■ [*attrib.*] (of a person) apparently permanently engaged in a specified role or way of life: *he's a perennial student.* ■ (of a stream or spring) flowing throughout the year.

▸*n.* a perennial plant. ▷mid 17th cent. (in the sense 'remaining leafy throughout the year, evergreen'): from Latin *perennis* 'lasting the year through' + **-IAL.** **—per·en·ni·al·ly** *adv.*

Pe·res /ˈperez/, Shimon (1923–), Israeli statesman, born in Poland; prime minister 1984–86 and 1995–96; Polish name *Szymon Perski.* As foreign minister under Yitzhak Rabin, he played a major role in negotiating the PLO–Israeli peace accord of 1993. Nobel Peace Prize (1994, shared with Rabin and Yasser Arafat).

pe·re·stroi·ka /,perəˈstroikə/ ▸*n.* (in the former Soviet Union) the policy or practice of restructuring or reforming the economic and political system. First proposed by Leonid Brezhnev in 1979 and actively promoted by Mikhail Gorbachev, perestroika originally referred to increased automation and labor efficiency, but came to entail greater awareness of economic markets and the ending of central planning. See also **GLASNOST.** ▷Russian, literally 'restructuring.'

Pé·rez de Cué·llar /ˈpārās də ˈkwāyär/, Javier (1920–), Peruvian diplomat; secretary-general of the UN 1982–91.

per·fect ▸*adj.* /ˈpərfikt/ **1** having all the required or desirable elements, qualities, or characteristics; as good as it is possible to be: *she strove to be the perfect wife* | *life certainly isn't perfect at the moment.* ■ free from any flaw or defect in condition or quality; faultless: *the equipment was in perfect condition.* ■ precisely accurate; exact: *a perfect circle.* ■ highly suitable for someone or something; exactly right: *Gary was perfect for her—ten years older and with his own career.* ■ *Printing* denoting a way of binding books in which pages are glued to the spine rather than sewn together. ■ *dated* thoroughly trained in or conversant with: *she was perfect in French.* **2** [*attrib.*] absolute; complete (used for emphasis): *a perfect stranger* | *all that Joseph said made perfect sense to me.* **3** *Mathematics* (of a number) equal to the sum of its positive divisors, e.g., the number 6, whose divisors (1, 2, 3) also add up to 6. **4** *Grammar* (of a tense) denoting a completed action or a state or habitual action that began in the past. The perfect tense is formed in English with *have* or *has* and the past participle, as in *they have eaten* and *they have been eating (since dawn)* (**present perfect**), *they had eaten* (**past perfect**), and *they will have eaten* (**future perfect**). **5** *Botany* (of a flower) having both stamens and carpels present and functional. ■ *Botany* denoting the stage or state of a fungus in which the sexually produced spores are formed. ■ *Entomology* (of an insect) fully adult and (typically) winged.

▸*v.* /pərˈfekt/ [*trans.*] make (something) completely free from faults or defects, or as close to such a condition as possible: *he's busy perfecting his bowling technique.* ■ *archaic* bring to completion; finish. ■ complete (a printed sheet of paper) by printing the second side. ■ *Law* satisfy the necessary conditions or requirements for the transfer of (a gift, title, etc.): *equity will not perfect an imperfect gift.*

▸*n.* /ˈpərfikt/ (**the perfect**) *Grammar* the perfect tense. ▷Middle English: from Old French *perfet,* from Latin *perfectus* 'completed,' from the verb *perficere,* from *per-* 'through, completely' + *facere* 'do.' **—per·fect·er** /pərˈfektər/ *n.* **—per·fect·i·bil·i·ty** /pər,fektəˈbilitē/ *n.* **—per·fect·i·ble** /pərˈfektəbəl/ *adj.* **—per·fect·ness** /ˈpərfək(t)nəs/ *n.*

USAGE In the literal sense, **perfect, unique,** etc., are absolute words and should not be modified, as they often are in such phrases as *most perfect, quite unique,* etc.
See also **usage** at **UNIQUE.**

per·fec·ta /pərˈfektə/ ▸*n.* another term for **EXACTA.** ▷1970s: from Latin American Spanish *quiniela perfecta* 'perfect quinella.'

per·fect bind·ing ▸*n.* a form of bookbinding in which the leaves are bound by gluing, after the back folds have been cut off, rather than by sewing.

per·fect ca·dence ▸*n. Music* a cadence in which the chord of the dominant immediately precedes that of the tonic.

per·fect com·pe·ti·tion ▸*n.* the situation prevailing in a market in which buyers and sellers are so numerous and well informed that all elements of monopoly are absent and the market price of a commodity is beyond the control of individual buyers and sellers.

per·fect crime ▸*n.* a crime so ingeniously contrived and carefully executed that it cannot be detected or solved.

per·fect fifth ▸*n. Music* see **FIFTH.**

per·fect fourth ▸*n. Music* see **FOURTH.**

per·fect game ▸*n. Baseball* a game in which all the batters from one team are retired in order, with no one reaching base.

per·fect gas ▸*n.* another term for **IDEAL GAS.**

per·fec·tion /pərˈfekSHən/ ▸*n.* the condition, state, or quality of being free or as free as possible from all flaws or defects: *the satiny perfection of her skin* | *his pursuit of golfing perfection.* ■ a person or thing perceived as the embodiment of such a condition, state, or quality: *I am told that she is perfection itself.* ■ the action or process of improving something until it is faultless or as faultless as possible: *among the key tasks was the perfection of new mechanisms of economic management.* ▷Middle English (in the sense 'completeness'): via Old French from Latin *perfectio(n-),* from *perficere* 'to complete' (see **PERFECT**).

▸*PHRASE* □ **to perfection** in a manner or way that could not be better; perfectly: *a blue suit that showed off her blonde hair to perfection.*

per·fec·tion·ism /pərˈfekSHə,nizəm/ ▸*n.* refusal to accept any standard short of perfection. ■ *Philosophy* a doctrine holding that religious, moral, social, or political perfection is attainable, esp. the theory that human moral or spiritual perfection should be or has been attained. **—per·fec·tion·ist** *n.* & *adj.* **—per·fec·tion·is·tic** /-,fekSHənˈistik/ *adj.*

per·fec·tive /pərˈfektiv/ *Grammar* ▸*adj.* denoting or relating to an aspect of verbs, esp. in Slavic languages that expresses completed action. The opposite of **IMPERFECTIVE.**

▸*n.* a perfective form of a verb. ■ (**the perfective**) the perfective aspect. ▷early 17th cent. (in the general sense 'tending to make complete'): from medieval Latin *perfectivus,* from Latin *perfectus* 'accomplished' (see **PERFECT**).

per·fect·ly /ˈpərfik(t)lē/ ▸*adv.* in a manner or way that could not be better: *the ring fitted perfectly* | [as *submodifier*] *perfectly clean glass bottles.* ■ [as *submodifier*] used for emphasis, esp. in order to assert something that has been challenged or doubted: *you know perfectly well I can't stay.*

per·fec·to /pərˈfektō/ ▸*n.* (*pl.* **-tos**) a type of cigar that is thick in the center and tapered at each end. ▷late 19th cent.: from Spanish, literally 'perfect.'

per·fect pitch ▸*n.* the ability to recognize the pitch of a note or to produce any given note; a sense of absolute pitch.

per·fect rhyme ▸*n.* **1** the rhyme exemplified by homonyms, such as *bear/bare* or *wear/where.* **2** rhyme in which different consonants are followed by identical vowel and consonant sounds, such as in *moon* and *June.*

per·fect square ▸*n.* the product of a rational number multiplied by itself. ■ the product of a polynomial multiplied by itself.

per·fer·vid /pərˈfərvid/ ▸*adj. poetic/literary* intense and impassioned: *perfervid nationalism.* ▷mid 19th cent.: from modern Latin *perfervidus,* from Latin *per-* 'utterly' + *fervidus* 'glowing hot, fiery.' **—per·fer·vid·ly** *adv.*

per·fid·i·ous /pərˈfidēəs/ ▸*adj. poetic/literary* deceitful and untrustworthy: *a perfidious lover.* ▷late 16th cent.: from Latin *perfidiosus,* from *perfidia* 'treachery.' **—per·fid·i·ous·ly** *adv.*

per·fi·dy /ˈpərfidē/ ▸*n. poetic/literary* deceitfulness; untrustworthiness. ▷late 16th cent.: via French from Latin *perfidia,* from *perfidus* 'treacherous,' based on *per-* 'to ill effect' + *fides* 'faith.'

perf·in /ˈpərfin/ ▸*n. Philately* a postage stamp perforated with the initials or insignia of an organization, esp. to prevent misuse. ▷1950s: from *perf(orated) in(itials).*

per·fo·li·ate /pərˈfōlē,āt; -it/ ▸*adj. Botany* (of a stalkless leaf or bract) extended at the base to encircle the node, so that the stem apparently passes through it. ■ (of a plant) having such leaves. ▷late 17th cent.: from modern Latin *perfoliatus,* from Latin *per-* 'through' + *foliatus* 'leaved.'

per·fo·rate ▸*v.* /ˈpərfə,rāt/ [*trans.*] pierce and make a hole or holes in: *the worms had perforated the pages of the book from cover to cover* | [as *adj.*] (**perforated**) *a perforated appendix.* ■ make a row of small holes in (paper) so that a part may be torn off easily.

▸*adj.* /ˈpərfərit; -,rāt/ *Biology & Medicine* perforated: *a perforate shell.* ▷late Middle English (as an adjective): from Latin *perforat-* 'pierced through,' from the verb *perforare,* from *per-* 'through' + *forare* 'pierce.' **—per·fo·ra·tor** /-,rātər/ *n.*

per·fo·ra·tion /,pərfəˈrāSHən/ ▸*n.* a hole made by boring or piercing; an aperture passing through or into something: *the perforations allow water to enter the well.* ■ a small hole or row of small holes punched in a sheet of paper, e.g., of postage stamps, so that a part can be torn off easily. ■ the action or state of perforating or being perforated: *there was evidence of intestinal perforation.* ▷late Middle English: from medieval Latin *perforatio(n-),* from the verb *perforare* (see **PERFORATE**).

per·force /pərˈfôrs/ ▸*adv. formal* used to express necessity or inevitability: *amateurs, perforce, have to settle for less expensive solutions.* ▷Middle English: from Old French *par force* 'by force.'

per·fo·rin /ˈpərfərin/ ▸*n. Biochemistry* a protein, released by killer cells of the immune system, that destroys targeted cells by creating lesions like pores in their membranes. ▷1980s: from the verb **PERFORATE** + **-IN**[1].

per·form /pərˈfôrm/ ▸*v.* [*trans.*] **1** carry out, accomplish, or fulfill (an action, task, or function): *I have my duties to perform.* ■ [*intrans.*] work, function, or do something to a specified standard: *the car performs well at low speeds.* ■ [*intrans.*] (of an investment) yield a profitable return: *our $120 million investment in the company is not performing at present.* ■ [*intrans.*] *informal* have successful or satisfactory sexual intercourse with someone. **2** present (a form of entertainment) to an audience: *Chinese troupes still perform the play.* ■ [*intrans.*] entertain an audience, typically by acting, singing, or dancing on stage: *the band will be performing live in Hyde Park.* ▷Middle English: from

Pronunciation Key ə *ago;* ər *over;* ˈə or ˌə *up;* ˈər or ˌər *fur;* a *hat;* ā *rate;* ä *car;* CH *chew;* e *let;* ē *see;* e(ə)r *air;* i *fit;* ī *by;* i(ə)r *ear;* NG *sing;* ō *go;* ô *for;* oi *boy;* o͝o *good;* o͞o *goo;* ou *out;* SH *she;* TH *thin;* T͟H *then;* (h)w *why;* ZH *vision*

Anglo-Norman French *parfourmer*, alteration (by association with *forme* 'form') of Old French *parfournir*, from *par* 'through, to completion' + *fournir* 'furnish, provide.' **—per·form·a·bil·i·ty** /-ˌfôrməˈbilitē/ *n.* **—per·form·a·ble** *adj.* **—per·form·er** *n.*

per·for·mance /pərˈfôrməns/ ▶*n.* **1** an act of staging or presenting a play, concert, or other form of entertainment: Don Giovanni *had its first performance in 1787.* ■ a person's rendering of a dramatic role, song, or piece of music: *Bailey gives a sound performance as the doctor.* ■ [in *sing.*] *informal* a display of exaggerated behavior or a process involving a great deal of unnecessary time and effort; a fuss: *he stopped to tie his shoe and seemed to be* ***making** quite **a performance** of it.* **2** the action or process of carrying out or accomplishing an action, task, or function: *the continual performance of a single task reduces a man to the level of a machine.* ■ an action, task, or operation, seen in terms of how successfully it was performed: *pay increases are now being linked more closely to performance | a dynamic performance by Davis.* ■ the capabilities of a machine or product, esp. when observed under particular conditions: *the hardware is put through tests which assess the performance of the processor.* ■ a vehicle's capacity to gain speed rapidly and move efficiently and safely at high speed. ■ the extent to which an investment is profitable, esp. in relation to other investments. ■ (also **linguistic performance**) *Linguistics* an individual's use of a language, i.e., what a speaker actually says, including hesitations, false starts, and errors. Often contrasted with **COMPETENCE**.

per·for·mance art ▶*n.* an art form that combines visual art with dramatic performance. **—per·for·mance art·ist** *n.*

per·for·mance bond ▶*n.* a bond issued by a bank or other financial institution, guaranteeing the fulfillment of a particular contract.

per·for·mance cap·ture ▶another term for motion capture.

per·for·mance po·et·ry ▶*n.* a form of poetry intended to be performed as a dramatic monologue or exchange and frequently involving extemporization. **—per·for·mance po·et** *n.*

per·for·mance test·ing ▶*n.* the evaluation of a person's mental or manual ability. ■ the evaluation of the heritable characteristics of a bull or other breeding animal, or of a plant, as determined from the known characteristics of the offspring.

per·for·ma·tive /pərˈfôrmətiv/ ▶*adj. Linguistics & Philosophy* relating to or denoting an utterance by means of which the speaker performs a particular act (e.g., *I bet, I apologize, I promise*). Often contrasted with **CONSTATIVE**.
▶*n. Linguistics & Philosophy* a performative verb, sentence, or utterance.

per·form·ing arts ▶*plural n.* forms of creative activity that are performed in front of an audience, such as drama, music, and dance.

per·fume /ˈpərˌfyo͞om; ˌpərˈfyo͞om/ ▶*n.* a fragrant liquid typically made from essential oils extracted from flowers and spices, used to impart a pleasant smell to one's body or clothes: *I caught a whiff of her fresh lemony perfume | musk-based perfumes.* ■ a pleasant smell: *the heady perfume of lilacs.* See note at **SMELL**.
▶*v.* [*trans.*] impart a pleasant smell to: *just one bloom of jasmine has the power to perfume a whole room.* ■ (usu. **be perfumed**) impregnate (something) with perfume or a sweet-smelling ingredient: *the cream is perfumed with rosemary and iris extracts.* ■ apply perfume to (someone or something): *her hair was oiled and perfumed.* ▷mid 16th cent. (originally denoting pleasant-smelling smoke from a burning substance, esp. one used in fumigation): from French *parfum* (noun), *parfumer* (verb), from obsolete Italian *parfumare*, literally 'to smoke through.' **—per·fum·y** /-mē/ *adj.*

per·fumed /ˌpərˈfyo͞omd/ ▶*adj.* naturally having or producing a sweet, pleasant smell: *the perfumed richness of the wine.* ■ impregnated with a sweet-smelling substance: *perfumed soap.* ■ denoting something to which perfume has been applied: *her perfumed arms.*

per·fum·er /pərˈfyo͞omər/ ▶*n.* a producer or seller of perfumes.

per·fum·er·y /pərˈfyo͞omərē/ ▶*n.* (*pl.* **-er·ies**) the action or business of producing or selling perfumes: *an oil used in perfumery.* ■ a store or store department that sells perfumes.

per·func·to·ry /pərˈfəNGktərē/ ▶*adj.* (of an action or gesture) carried out with a minimum of effort or reflection: *he gave a perfunctory nod.* ▷late 16th cent.: from late Latin *perfunctorius* 'careless,' from Latin *perfunct-* 'done with, discharged,' from the verb *perfungi.* **—per·func·to·ri·ly** /-ˈfəNGktərəlē/ *adv.* **—per·func·to·ri·ness** /-rēnis/ *n.*

per·fus·ate /pərˈfyo͞oˌzāt/ ▶*n. Medicine* a fluid used in perfusion.

per·fuse /pərˈfyo͞oz/ ▶*v.* [*trans.*] permeate or suffuse (something) with a liquid, color, quality, etc.: *Glaser perfused the yellow light with white | figurative such expression is perfused by rhetoric.* ■ *Medicine* supply (an organ, tissue, or body) with a fluid, typically treated blood or a blood substitute, by circulating it through blood vessels or other natural channels. ▷late Middle English (in the sense 'cause to flow through or away'): from Latin *perfus-* 'poured through,' from the verb *perfundere*, from *per-* 'through' + *fundere* 'pour.' **—per·fu·sion** /-ZHən/ *n.* **—per·fu·sion·ist** /-ZHənist/ *n.*

Per·ga·mum /ˈpərgəməm/ a city in ancient Mysia, in western Asia Minor, north of Izmir, capital in the 3rd and 2nd centuries BC of the Attalid dynasty. It was famed for its cultural institutions, esp. its library, which was second only to that at Alexandria. **—Per·ga·mene** /-ˌmēn/ *adj.* & *n.*

per·go·la /ˈpərgələ/ ▶*n.* an archway in a garden or park consisting of a framework covered with trained climbing or trailing plants. ▷mid 17th cent.: from Italian, from Latin *pergula* 'projecting roof,' from *pergere* 'come or go forward.'

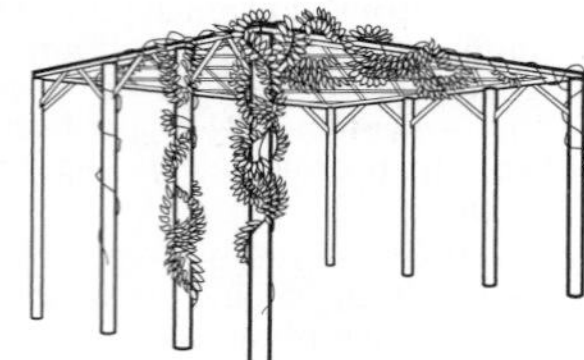

pergola

per·haps /pər(h)aps/ ▶*adv.* used to express uncertainty or possibility: *perhaps I should have been frank with him.* ■ used when one does not wish to be too definite or assertive in the expression of an opinion: *perhaps not surprisingly, he was cautious about committing himself.* ■ used when making a polite request, offer, or suggestion: *would you perhaps consent to act as our guide?* ■ used to express reluctant or qualified agreement or acceptance: *"She understood him better than his wife ever did." "Perhaps so, but . . . "* ▷late 15th cent.: from **PER** + **HAP**.

pe·ri /ˈpi(ə)rē/ ▶*n.* (*pl.* **pe·ris**) (in Persian mythology) a mythical superhuman being, originally represented as evil but subsequently as a good or graceful genie or fairy. ▷from Persian *perī.*

peri- ▶*prefix* **1** around; about: *pericardium | perimeter | peristyle.* **2** *Astronomy* denoting the point nearest to a specified celestial body: *perihelion | perilune.* Compare with **APO-**. ▷from Greek *peri* 'about, around.'

per·i·a·nal /ˌperēˈānəl/ ▶*adj. Medicine* situated in or affecting the area around the anus.

per·i·anth /ˈperēˌanTH/ ▶*n. Botany* the outer part of a flower, consisting of the calyx (sepals) and corolla (petals). ▷early 18th cent.: from French *périanthe*, from modern Latin *perianthium*, from Greek *peri* 'around' + *anthos* 'flower.'

per·i·ap·sis /ˌperēˈapsis/ ▶*n.* (*pl.* **-ses** /-ˌsēz/) *Astronomy* the point in the path of an orbiting body at which it is nearest to the body that it orbits.

per·i·apt /ˈperēˌapt/ ▶*n. archaic* an item worn as a charm or amulet. ▷late 16th cent.: from French *périapte*, from Greek *periapton*, from *peri* 'around' + *haptein* 'fasten.'

per·i·ar·tic·u·lar /ˌperē-ärˈtikyələr/ ▶*adj. Medicine* situated or occurring around a joint of the body.

per·i·as·tron /ˌperēˈastrən/ ▶*n. Astronomy* the point nearest to a star in the path of a body orbiting that star. ▷mid 19th cent.: from **PERI-** 'around' + Greek *astron* 'star,' on the pattern of *perigee* and *perihelion.*

per·i·car·di·tis /ˌperikärˈdītis/ ▶*n. Medicine* inflammation of the pericardium.

per·i·car·di·um /ˌperiˈkärdēəm/ ▶*n.* (*pl.* **-car·di·a** /-ˈkärdēə/) *Anatomy* the membrane enclosing the heart, consisting of an outer fibrous layer and an inner double layer of serous membrane. ▷late Middle English: modern Latin, from Greek *perikardion*, from *peri* 'around' + *kardia* 'heart.' **—per·i·car·di·al** /-ˈkärdēəl/ *adj.*

per·i·carp /ˈperiˌkärp/ ▶*n. Botany* the part of a fruit formed from the wall of the ripened ovary. ▷late 17th cent.: from French *péricarpe*, from Greek *perikarpion* 'pod, shell,' from *peri-* 'around' + *karpos* 'fruit.'

per·i·chon·dri·um /ˌperiˈkändrēəm/ ▶*n. Anatomy* the connective tissue that envelops cartilage where it is not at a joint. ▷mid 18th cent.: modern Latin, from **PERI-** 'around' + Greek *khondros* 'cartilage.'

per·i·clase /ˈperiˌklās; -ˌklāz/ ▶*n.* a colorless mineral consisting of magnesium oxide, occurring chiefly in marble and limestone. ▷mid 19th cent.: from modern Latin *periclasia*, erroneously from Greek *peri* 'utterly' + *klasis* 'breaking' (because it cleaves perfectly).

Per·i·cles /ˈperiˌklēz/ (*c.*495–429 BC), Athenian statesman and general. A champion of Athenian democracy, he pursued an imperialist policy and masterminded Athenian strategy in the Peloponnesian War. He commissioned the building of the Parthenon in 447 and presided over the golden age of Athens.

per·i·cli·nal /ˌperiˈklīnl/ ▶*adj. Botany* (of a cell wall) parallel to the surface of the meristem. ■ (of cell division) taking place by the formation of periclinal walls. ▷late 19th cent.: from Greek *periklinēs* 'sloping on all sides,' from *peri-* 'around' + *klinēs* 'sloping' (from the verb *klinein*). **—per·i·cli·nal·ly** *adv.*

pe·ric·o·pe /pəˈrikəpē/ ▶*n.* an extract from a text, esp. a passage from the Bible. ▷mid 17th cent.: via late Latin from Greek *perikopē* 'section,' from *peri-* 'around' + *kopē* 'cutting' (from *koptein* 'to cut').

per·i·cra·ni·um /ˌperiˈkrānēəm/ ▶*n. Anatomy* the periosteum enveloping the skull. ▷late Middle English: modern Latin, from Greek *peri-* 'around' + *kranion* 'skull.'

per·i·cy·cle /ˈperiˌsīkəl/ ▶*n. Botany* a thin layer of plant tissue between the endodermis and the phloem. ▷late 19th cent.: from Greek *perikuklos* 'spherical,' from *perikukloun* 'encircle.'

per·i·derm /ˈperiˌdərm/ ▶*n. Botany* the corky outer layer of a plant stem formed in secondary thickening or as a response to injury or infection. ▷mid 19th cent.: from **PERI-** 'around' + Greek *derma* 'skin.' **—per·i·der·mal** /ˌperiˈdərməl/ *adj.*

pe·rid·i·um /pəˈridēəm/ ▶*n.* (*pl.* **-rid·i·a** /-ˈridēə/) *Botany* the outer skin of a sporangium or other fruiting body of a fungus. ▷early 19th cent.: from Greek *pēridion*, literally 'small wallet,' diminutive of *pēra.*

per·i·dot /ˈperiˌdät/ ▶*n.* a green semiprecious variety of olivine. ▷early 18th cent.: from French, from Old French *peritot*, of unknown origin.

per·i·do·tite /ˈperidəˌtīt; pəˈridəˌtīt/ ▶*n. Geology* a dense, coarse-grained plutonic rock containing a large amount of olivine, believed to be the main constituent of the earth's mantle. **—per·i·do·tit·ic** /ˌperidəˈtitik; pəˌridə-/ *adj.*

per·i·gee /ˈperəˌjē/ ▶*n. Astronomy* the point in the orbit of the moon or a satellite at which it is nearest to the earth. The opposite of **APOGEE**. ▷late 16th cent.: from French *périgée*, via modern Latin from Greek *perigeion* 'close around the earth,' from *peri-* 'around' + *gē* 'earth.'

per·i·gla·cial /ˌperəˈglāSHəl/ ▶*adj. Geology* relating to or denoting an area adjacent to a glacier or ice sheet or otherwise subject to repeated freezing and thawing.

pe·rig·y·nous /pəˈrijənəs/ ▶*adj. Botany* (of a plant or flower) having the stamens and other floral parts at the same level as the carpels. Compare with **EPIGYNOUS**, **HYPOGYNOUS**. ▷early 19th cent.: from modern Latin *perigynus* (from Greek *peri-* 'around' + *gunē* 'woman') + **-OUS**. **—pe·rig·y·ny** /-ˈrijənē/ *n.*

per·i·he·li·on /ˌperəˈhēlyən; -ˈhēlēən/ ▶*n.* (*pl.* **-he·li·a** /-ˈhēlyə; -ˈhēlēə/ or **-he·li·ons**) *Astronomy* the point in the orbit of a planet, asteroid, or comet at which it is closest to the sun. The opposite of **APHELION**. ▷mid 17th cent.: alteration of modern Latin *perihelium* (by substitution of the Greek ending *-on*), from Greek *peri-* 'around' + *hēlios* 'sun.'

per·i·kar·y·on /periˈkarēˌän/ ▶*n.* (*pl.* **-kar·y·a** /-ˈkarēə/) *Physiology* the cell body of a neuron, containing the nucleus. **—per·i·kar·y·al** /-ˈkarēəl/ *adj.*

per·il /ˈperəl/ ▶*n.* serious and immediate danger: *his family was in peril | a setback to the state could present a peril to the regime.* ■ (**perils**) the dangers or difficulties that arise from a particular situation or activity: *she first witnessed* ***the perils of*** *pop stardom a decade ago.*
▶*v.* (**per·iled, per·il·ing**; *Brit.* **per·illed, per·il·ling**) [*trans.*] *archaic* expose to danger; threaten: *Jonathon periled his life for love of David.* ▷Middle English: from Old French, from Latin *peric(u)lum* 'danger,' from the base of *experiri* 'to try.' The verb dates from the mid 16th cent.
▶*PHRASES* □ **at one's peril** at one's own risk (used esp. in warnings): *neglect our advice at your peril.* □ **in** (or **at**)

peril of very likely to incur or to suffer from: *the movement is in peril of dying.* ■ at risk of losing or injuring: *anyone linked with the Republican cause would be in peril of their life.*

pe·ril·la /pəˈrilə/ ▸*n.* an Asian plant of the mint family with medicinal and culinary uses. It is regarded as an invasive weed in some areas. • *Perilla frutescens*, family Labiatae.

per·il·ous /ˈperələs/ ▸*adj.* full of danger or risk: *a perilous journey south.* ■ exposed to imminent risk of disaster or ruin: *the economy is in a perilous state.* ▷Middle English: from Old French *perillous*, from Latin *periculosus*, from *periculum* 'danger' (see **PERIL**). **—per·il·ous·ly** *adv.* **—per·il·ous·ness** *n.*

per·i·lune /ˈperi,lo͞on/ ▸*n.* the point at which a spacecraft in lunar orbit is closest to the moon. The opposite of **APOLUNE**. ▷1960s: from **PERI-** 'around' + Latin *luna* 'moon,' on the pattern of *perigee*.

per·i·lymph /ˈperi,limf/ ▸*n. Anatomy* the fluid between the membranous labyrinth of the ear and the bone that encloses it. **—per·i·lym·phat·ic** /,perilimˈfatik/ *adj.*

pe·rim·e·ter /pəˈrimitər/ ▸*n.* **1** the continuous line forming the boundary of a closed geometric figure: *the perimeter of a rectangle.* ■ the length of such a line: *the rectangle has a perimeter of 30 cm.* ■ the outermost parts or boundary of an area or object: *the perimeter of the garden* | *figurative my presence on the perimeter of his life.* ■ a defended boundary of a military position or base. ■ *Basketball* an area away from the basket, beyond the reach of the defensive team: *he was very patient in working the ball around the perimeter.* **2** an instrument for measuring the extent and characteristics of a person's field of vision. ▷late Middle English: via Latin from Greek *perimetros*, based on *peri-* 'around' + *metron* 'measure.' **—per·i·met·ric** /,perəˈmetrik/ *adj.*

USAGE See usage at **PARAMETER**.

pe·rim·e·try /pəˈrimətrē/ ▸*n.* measurement of a person's field of vision.

per·i·my·si·um /,perəˈmizēəm; -ˈmizн-/ ▸*n. Anatomy* the sheath of connective tissue surrounding a bundle of muscle fibers. ▷mid 19th cent.: modern Latin, from Greek *peri-* 'around' + *mus* 'muscle.' **—per·i·my·si·al** /-ˈmizēəl; -ˈmizн-/ *adj.*

per·i·na·tal /,perəˈnātl/ ▸*adj. Medicine* of or relating to the time, usually a number of weeks, immediately before and after birth. **—per·i·na·tal·ly** *adv.*

per·i·na·tol·o·gy /,perinā'täləjē/ ▸*n. Medicine* the branch of obstetrics dealing with the period of time around childbirth. **—per·i·na·tol·o·gist** /-jist/ *n.*

per·i·ne·um /,perəˈnēəm/ ▸*n. Anatomy* the area between the anus and the scrotum or vulva. ▷late Middle English: from late Latin, from Greek *perinaion*. **—per·i·ne·al** /-ˈnēəl/ *adj.*

per·i·neu·ri·um /,perəˈn(y)o͝orēəm/ ▸*n. Anatomy* the sheath of connective tissue surrounding a bundle (fascicle) of nerve fibers within a nerve. ▷mid 19th cent.: modern Latin, from Greek *peri-* 'around' + *neuron* 'sinew.' **—per·i·neu·ri·al** /-ˈn(y)o͝orēəl/ *adj.*

pe·ri·od /ˈpi(ə)rēəd/ ▸*n.* **1** a length or portion of time: *he had long periods of depression* | *the ale will be available for a limited period* | *the period 1977–85.* ■ a portion of time in the life of a person, nation, or civilization characterized by the same prevalent features or conditions: *the early medieval period.* ■ one of the set divisions of the day in a school allocated to a lesson or other activity. ■ [with *adj.*] a set period of time during which a particular activity takes place: *the training period is between 16 and 18 months.* ■ each of the intervals into which the playing time of a sporting event is divided. ■ a major division of geological time that is a subdivision of an era and is itself subdivided into epochs, corresponding to a system in chronostratigraphy. **2** a punctuation mark (.) used at the end of a sentence or an abbreviation. ■ *informal* added to the end of a statement to indicate that no further discussion is possible or desirable: *he is the sole owner of the trademark, period.* **3** *Physics* the interval of time between successive occurrences of the same state in an oscillatory or cyclic phenomenon, such as a mechanical vibration, an alternating current, a variable star, or an electromagnetic wave. ■ *Astronomy* the time taken by a celestial object to rotate around its axis, or to make one circuit of its orbit. ■ *Mathematics* the interval between successive equal values of a periodic function. **4** (also **menstrual period**) a flow of blood and other material from the lining of the uterus, lasting for several days and occurring in sexually mature women (who are not pregnant) at intervals of about one lunar month until the onset of menopause. **5** *Chemistry* a set of elements occupying an entire horizontal row in the periodic table. **6** *Rhetoric* a complex sentence, esp. one consisting of several clauses, constructed as part of a formal speech or oration. ■ *Music* a complete idea, typically consisting of two or four phrases.
▸*adj.* [*attrib.*] belonging to or characteristic of a past historical time, esp. in style or design: *a splendid selection of period furniture.* ▷late Middle English (denoting the time during which something, esp. a disease, runs its course): from Old French *periode*, via Latin from Greek *periodos* 'orbit, recurrence, course,' from *peri-* 'around' + *hodos* 'way, course.' The sense 'portion of time' dates from the early 17th cent.

pe·ri·od·ic /,pi(ə)rēˈädik/ ▸*adj.* **1** appearing or occurring at intervals: *the periodic visits she made to her father.* **2** *Chemistry* relating to the periodic table of the elements or the pattern of chemical properties that underlies it. **3** of or relating to a rhetorical period. See **PERIOD** (sense 6). ▷mid 17th cent.: from French *périodique*, or via Latin from Greek *periodikos* 'coming around at intervals,' from *periodos* (see **PERIOD**).

per·i·od·ic ac·id /,pərīˈädik/ ▸*n. Chemistry* a hygroscopic solid acid with strong oxidizing properties. • Chem. formula: H_5IO_6. ▷mid 19th cent.: from sense 2 of **PER-** + **IODIC ACID**. **—per·i·o·date** /pəˈrīə,dāt/ *n.*

pe·ri·od·ic ac·id–Schiff /,pərīˈädik ˈasid ˈsнif/ ▸*adj.* [*attrib.*] *Biochemistry* relating to or denoting a procedure for detecting carbohydrates by oxidizing them with periodic acid and then staining them with Schiff's reagent.

pe·ri·od·i·cal /,pi(ə)rēˈädikəl/ ▸*n.* a magazine or newspaper published at regular intervals.
▸*adj.* [*attrib.*] occurring or appearing at intervals; occasional: *she took periodical gulps of her tea.* ■ (of a magazine or newspaper) published at regular intervals: *a periodical newsletter.* **—pe·ri·od·i·cal·ly** *adv.*

pe·ri·od·i·cal ci·ca·da ▸*n.* an American cicada whose nymphs emerge from the soil in large numbers periodically. The mature nymphs of the northern species (**seventeen-year locust**) emerge every seventeen years; those of the southern species emerge every thirteen years. A cicada brood can be so abundant that the shrill sound emitted by the males can damage the human ear. • Genus *Magicicada*, family Cicadidae, suborder Homoptera: six species.

pe·ri·od·ic func·tion /,pi(ə)rēˈädik/ ▸*n. Mathematics* a function returning to the same value at regular intervals.

pe·ri·o·dic·i·ty /,pi(ə)rēəˈdisitē/ ▸*n. chiefly technical* the quality or character of being periodic; the tendency to recur at intervals: *the periodicity of the sunspot cycle.*

pe·ri·od·ic law /,pi(ə)rēˈädik/ ▸*n. Chemistry* a law stating that the elements, when listed in order of their atomic numbers (originally, atomic weights), fall into recurring groups, so that elements with similar properties occur at regular intervals.

pe·ri·od·ic ta·ble /,pi(ə)rēˈädik/ ▸*n. Chemistry* a table of the chemical elements arranged in order of atomic number, usually in rows, so that elements with similar atomic structure (and hence similar chemical properties) appear in vertical columns.

pe·ri·od·ize /ˈpi(ə)rēə,dīz/ ▸*v.* [*trans.*] *formal* divide (a portion of time) into periods. **—pe·ri·od·i·za·tion** /,pi(ə)rēədəˈzāsнən/ *n.*

per·i·o·don·tics /,perēəˈdäntiks/ (also **per·i·o·don·tia** /ˈdänsн(ē)ə/) ▸*plural n.* [treated as *sing.*] the branch of dentistry concerned with the structures surrounding and supporting the teeth. ▷1940s: from **PERI-** 'around' + Greek *odous*, *odont-* 'tooth' + **-ICS**. **—per·i·o·don·tal** /-ˈdäntl/ *adj.* **—per·i·o·don·tist** /-ˈdäntist/ *n.*

per·i·o·don·ti·tis /,perēədänˈtītis/ ▸*n. Medicine* inflammation of the tissue around the teeth, often causing shrinkage of the gums and loosening of the teeth.

per·i·o·don·tol·o·gy /,perēədänˈtäləjē/ ▸*n.* another term for **PERIODONTICS**.

pe·ri·od piece ▸*n.* an object or work that is set in or strongly reminiscent of an earlier historical period.

per·i·os·te·um /,perēˈästēəm/ ▸*n.* (*pl.* **-os·te·a** /-ˈästēə/) *Anatomy* a dense layer of vascular connective tissue enveloping the bones except at the surfaces of the joints. ▷late 16th cent.: modern Latin, from Greek *periosteon*, from *peri-* 'around' + *osteon* 'bone.' **—per·i·os·te·al** /-ˈästēəl/ *adj.*

per·i·os·ti·tis /,perēäˈstītis/ ▸*n. Medicine* inflammation of the membrane enveloping a bone.

per·i·pa·tet·ic /,peripəˈtetik/ ▸*adj.* **1** traveling from place to place, esp. working or based in various places for relatively short periods: *the peripatetic nature of military life.* **2** (**Peripatetic**) Aristotelian. [with reference to Aristotle's practice of walking to and fro while teaching.]
▸*n.* **1** a person who travels from place to place. **2** (**Peripatetic**) an Aristotelian philosopher. ▷late Middle English (denoting an Aristotelian philosopher): from Old French *peripatetique*, via Latin from Greek *peripatētikos* 'walking up and down,' from the verb *peripatein*. **—per·i·pa·tet·i·cal·ly** /-ik(ə)lē/ *adv.* **—per·i·pa·tet·i·cism** /-ˈtetə,sizəm/ *n.*

per·i·pe·tei·a /,peripəˈtēə; -ˈtīə/ ▸*n. formal* a sudden reversal of fortune or change in circumstances, esp. in reference to fictional narrative. ▷late 16th cent.: from Greek *peripeteia* 'sudden change,' from *peri-* 'around' + the stem of *piptein* 'to fall.'

pe·riph·er·al /pəˈrifərəl/ ▸*adj.* of, relating to, or situated on the edge or periphery of something: *the peripheral areas of Europe.* ■ of secondary or minor importance; marginal: *she will see their problems as* ***peripheral to*** *her own.* ■ [*attrib.*] (of a device) able to be attached to and used with a computer, although not an integral part of it. ■ *Anatomy* near the surface of the body, with special reference to the circulation and nervous system: *lymphocytes from peripheral blood.*
▸*n. Computing* a peripheral device. **—pe·riph·er·al·i·ty** /-,rifəˈralitē/ *n.* **—pe·riph·er·al·i·za·tion** /pə,rifərəliˈzāsнən/ *n.* **—pe·riph·er·al·ize** /-,īz/ *v.* **—pe·riph·er·al·ly** *adv.*

pe·riph·er·al nerv·ous sys·tem ▸*n. Anatomy* the nervous system outside the brain and spinal cord.

pe·riph·er·al vi·sion ▸*n.* side vision; what is seen on the side by the eye when looking straight ahead.

pe·riph·er·y /pəˈrifərē/ ▸*n.* (*pl.* **-er·ies**) the outer limits or edge of an area or object: *new buildings* ***on the periphery of*** *the hospital site.* ■ a marginal or secondary position in, or part or aspect of, a group, subject, or sphere of activity: *a shift in power from the center to the periphery.* ▷late 16th cent. (denoting a line that forms the boundary of something): via late Latin from Greek *periphereia* 'circumference,' from *peripherēs* 'revolving around,' from *peri-* 'around' + *pherein* 'to bear.'

pe·riph·ra·sis /pəˈrifrəsis/ ▸*n.* (*pl.* **-ses** /-,sēz/) the use of indirect and circumlocutory speech or writing. ■ an indirect and circumlocutory phrase. ■ *Grammar* the use of separate words to express a grammatical relationship that is otherwise expressed by inflection, e.g., *did go* as opposed to *went* and *more intelligent* as opposed to *smarter*. ▷mid 16th cent.: via Latin from Greek, from *periphrazein*, from *peri-* 'around' + *phrazein* 'declare.'

per·i·phras·tic /,perəˈfrastik/ ▸*adj.* (of speech or writing) indirect and circumlocutory: *the periphrastic nature of legal syntax.* ■ *Grammar* (of a case or tense) formed by a combination of words rather than by inflection (such as *did go* and *of the people* rather than *went* and *the people's*). ▷early 19th cent.: from Greek *periphrastikos*, from *periphrazein* 'declare in a roundabout way.' **—per·i·phras·ti·cal·ly** /-(ə)lē/ *adv.*

pe·riph·y·ton /pəˈrifi,tän/ ▸*n. Ecology* freshwater organisms attached to or clinging to plants and other objects projecting above the bottom sediments. ▷1960s: from Greek *peri-* 'around' + *phuton* 'plant.' **—per·i·phyt·ic** /,perəˈfitik/ *adj.*

pe·rip·ter·al /pəˈriptərəl/ ▸*adj. Architecture* (of a building) having a single row of pillars on all sides in the style of the temples of ancient Greece. ▷early 19th cent.: from Greek *peripteron* (from *peri-* 'around' + *pteron* 'wing') + **-AL**.

pe·rique /pəˈrēk/ ▸*n.* a strong dark tobacco from Louisiana. ▷late 19th cent.: Louisiana French, apparently from the nickname of Pierre Chenet, who first grew it.

per·i·scope /ˈperə,skōp/ ▸*n.* an apparatus consisting of a tube attached to a set of mirrors or prisms, by which an observer (typically in a submerged submarine or behind a high obstacle) can see things that are otherwise out of sight.

per·i·scop·ic /,perəˈskäpik/ ▸*adj.* of or relating to a periscope. ■ (of a lens or an optical instrument) giving a

periscope

Pronunciation Key ə *ago*; ər *over*; ˈə or ,ə *up*; ˈər or ,ər *fur*; a *hat*; ā *rate*; ä *car*; cн *chew*; e *let*; ē *see*; e(ə)r *air*; i *fit*; ī *by*; i(ə)r *ear*; nG *sing*; ō *go*; ô *for*; oi *boy*; o͝o *good*; o͞o *goo*; ou *out*; sн *she*; тн *thin*; <u>тн</u> *then*; (h)w *why*; zн *vision*

wide field of view: *a periscopic sextant.* **—per·i·scop·i·cal·ly** *adv.*

per·ish /ˈperisн/ ▶*v.* [*intrans.*] suffer death, typically in a violent, sudden, or untimely way: *a great part of his army perished of hunger and disease.* ■ suffer complete ruin or destruction: *the old regime had to perish.* ■ (of rubber, a foodstuff, or other organic substance) lose its normal qualities; rot or decay: *most domestic building was in wood and has perished.* ▷Middle English: from Old French *periss-*, lengthened stem of *perir*, from Latin *perire* 'pass away,' from *per-* 'through, completely' + *ire* 'go.'

▶*PHRASE* □ **perish the thought** *informal* used, often ironically, to show that one finds a suggestion or idea completely ridiculous or unwelcome: *he wasn't out to get drunk—perish the thought!*

per·ish·a·ble /ˈperisнəbəl/ ▶*adj.* (esp. of food) likely to decay or go bad quickly. ■ (of something abstract) having a brief life or significance; transitory: *ballet is the most perishable of arts.*

▶*n.* (**perishables**) things, esp. foodstuffs, likely to decay or go bad quickly. **—per·ish·a·bil·i·ty** /ˌperisнəˈbilitē/ *n.*

Pe·ris·so·dac·ty·la /pəˌrisəˈdaktələ/ *Zoology* an order of mammals that comprises the odd-toed ungulates. Compare with **ARTIODACTYLA**. ▷modern Latin (plural), from Greek *perissos* 'uneven' + *daktulos* 'finger, toe.' **—pe·ris·so·dac·tyl** *n.* & *adj.*

per·i·stal·sis /ˌperəˈstôlsis; -ˈstal-/ ▶*n.* *Physiology* the involuntary constriction and relaxation of the muscles of the intestine or another canal, creating wavelike movements that push the contents of the canal forward. ▷mid 19th cent.: modern Latin, from Greek *peristallein* 'wrap around,' from *peri-* 'around' + *stallein* 'to place.' **—per·i·stal·tic** /-ˈstôltik/ *adj.* **—per·i·stal·ti·cal·ly** *adv.*

per·i·stome /ˈperəˌstōm/ ▶*n.* *Zoology* the parts surrounding the mouth of various invertebrates. ■ *Botany* a fringe of small projections around the mouth of a capsule in mosses and certain fungi. ▷late 18th cent.: from modern Latin *peristoma*, from Greek *peri-* 'around' + *stoma* 'mouth.'

per·i·style /ˈperəˌstīl/ ▶*n.* *Architecture* a row of columns surrounding a space within a building such as a court or internal garden or edging a veranda or porch. ■ an architectural space such as a court or porch that is surrounded or edged by such columns. ▷early 17th cent.: from French *péristyle*, from Latin *peristylum*, from Greek *peristulon*, from *peri-* 'around' + *stulos* 'pillar.'

per·i·the·ci·um /ˌperəˈтнēsн(ē)əm; -sēəm/ ▶*n.* (*pl.* **-the·ci·a** /-ˈтнēsн(ē)ə; -sēə/) *Botany* (in some fungi) a round or flask-shaped fruiting body with a pore through which the spores are discharged. ▷mid 19th cent.: modern Latin, from **PERI-** 'around' + Greek *thēkē* 'case.'

per·i·to·ne·um /ˌperitnˈēəm/ ▶*n.* (*pl.* **-ne·ums** or **-ne·a** /-ˈnēə/) *Anatomy* the serous membrane lining the cavity of the abdomen and covering the abdominal organs. ▷late Middle English: via late Latin from Greek *peritonaion*, from *peritonos* 'stretched around,' from *peri-* 'around' + *-tonos* 'stretched.' **—per·i·to·ne·al** /-ˈēəl/ *adj.*

per·i·to·ni·tis /ˌperitnˈītis/ ▶*n.* *Medicine* inflammation of the peritoneum, typically caused by bacterial infection either via the blood or after rupture of an abdominal organ.

pe·ri·tus /pəˈrētōōs/ ▶*n.* (*pl.* **-ti** /-tē/) a theological adviser or consultant to a council of the Roman Catholic Church. ▷1960s: from Latin; related to *expertus* 'expert.'

per·i·vas·cu·lar /ˌperəˈvaskyələr/ ▶*adj.* *Medicine* situated or occurring around a blood vessel.

per·i·ven·tric·u·lar /ˌperəvenˈtrikyələr/ ▶*n.* *Anatomy* & *Medicine* situated or occurring around a ventricle, esp. a ventricle of the brain.

per·i·wig /ˈperiˌwig/ ▶*n.* a highly styled wig worn formerly as a fashionable headdress by both women and men. ■ archaic term for **WIG**[1]. ▷early 16th cent.: alteration of **PERUKE**, with *-wi-* representing the French *-u-* sound. **—per·i·wigged** *adj.*

periwig

per·i·win·kle[1] /ˈperiˌwiNGkəl/ ▶*n.* an Old World plant with flat, five-petalled flowers and glossy leaves. Some kinds are grown as ornamentals, and some contain alkaloids used in medicine. • Genera *Vinca* and *Catharanthus*, family Apocynaceae. ▷late Old English *peruince*, from late Latin *pervinca*, reinforced in Middle English by Anglo-Norman French *pervenke*. The change of *-v-* to *-w-* and the addition of *-le* seem to have occurred before the appearance of **PERIWINKLE**[2].

per·i·win·kle[2] ▶*n.* another term for **WINKLE**. ▷mid 16th cent.: of unknown origin.

per·jure /ˈpərjər/ ▶*v.* (**perjure oneself**) *Law* willfully tell an untruth when giving evidence to a court; commit perjury. ▷late Middle English (as *perjured* in the sense 'guilty of perjury'): from Old French *parjurer*, from Latin *perjurare* 'swear falsely,' from *per-* 'to ill effect' + *jurare* 'swear.' **—per·jur·er** *n.*

per·jured /ˈpərjərd/ ▶*adj.* *Law* (of evidence) involving willfully told untruths. ■ (of a person) guilty of perjury: *a perjured witness.*

per·ju·ry /ˈpərjərē/ ▶*n.* (*pl.* **-ries**) *Law* the offense of willfully telling an untruth in a court after having taken an oath or affirmation. ▷late Middle English: from Anglo-Norman French *perjurie*, from Latin *perjurium* 'false oath,' from the verb *perjurare* (see **PERJURE**). **—per·ju·ri·ous** /pərˈjŏŏrēəs/ *adj.*

perk[1] /pərk/ ▶*v.* [*intrans.*] (**perk up**) become more cheerful, lively, or interesting: *in the second half, the dance perked up* | *she'd been depressed, but she seemed to perk up last week.* ■ [*trans.*] (**perk someone/something up**) make someone or something more cheerful, lively, or interesting: *the coffee had perked him up long enough to tackle the reviews.*

▶*adj. dialect* perky; pert. ▷late Middle English (in the senses 'perch' and 'be lively'): perhaps from an Old French dialect variant of *percher* 'to perch.'

perk[2] ▶*n.* (usu. **perks**) *informal* money, goods, or other benefit to which one is entitled as an employee or as a shareholder of a company: *many agencies are helping to keep personnel at their jobs by providing perks.* ■ an advantage or benefit following from a job or situation: *they were busy discovering the perks of town life.* ▷early 19th cent.: abbreviation of **PERQUISITE**.

perk[3] *informal* ▶*v.* [*intrans.*] (of coffee) percolate: *while the coffee perks, head out for the morning paper.* ■ [*trans.*] percolate (coffee). ▷1930s: abbreviation of **PERCOLATE**.

Per·kins[1] /ˈpərkinz/, Carl (1932–98), U.S. singer and songwriter. A rockabilly artist, he wrote and recorded "Blue Suede Shoes" (1955), which became his first big hit. His albums include *Matchbox* (1977) and *Go, Cat, Go* (1993).

Per·kins[2], Frances (1882–1965), U.S. public official; born *Fannie Coiralie Perkins*. As U.S. secretary of labor 1933–45, she was the first woman to hold a federal cabinet post. She promoted the Social Security program and the minimum wage.

perk·y /ˈpərkē/ ▶*adj.* (**perk·i·er**, **perk·i·est**) cheerful and lively: *she certainly looked less than her usual perky self.* **—perk·i·ly** /-kəlē/ *adv.* **—perk·i·ness** /-kēnis/ *n.*

per·lite /ˈpərlīt/ ▶*n.* a form of obsidian characterized by spherlulites formed by cracking of the volcanic glass during cooling, used as insulation or in plant growth media. ▷mid 19th cent.: from French, from *perle* 'pearl.'

Perl·man /ˈpərlmən/, Itzhak (1945–) Israeli violinist and social activist. He appeared with most of the world's major orchestras and won many Grammy awards. Crippled by polio, he actively campaigned for the rights of the handicapped.

per·lo·cu·tion /ˌpərləˈkyōōsнən/ ▶*n.* *Philosophy* & *Linguistics* an act of speaking or writing that has an action as its aim but that in itself does not effect or constitute the action, for example persuading or convincing. Compare with **ILLOCUTION**. ▷1950s: from modern Latin *perlocutio(n-)*, from *per-* 'throughout' + *locutio(n-)* 'speaking.' **—per·lo·cu·tion·ar·y** /-ˌnerē/ *adj.*

Perm /pərm; pyerm/ an industrial city in Russia, in the western foothills of the Ural Mountains; pop. 1,094,000. Former name (1940–57) **MOLOTOV**[1]

perm /pərm/ ▶*n.* (also **permanent wave**) a method of setting the hair in waves or curls and then treating it with chemicals so that the style lasts for several months.

▶*v.* [*trans.*] (often **be permed**) treat (the hair) in such a way: *her hair was permed and then set.* ▷1920s: abbreviation of **PERMANENT**.

perm. ▶*abbr.* permanent.

per·ma·cul·ture /ˈpərməˌkəlCHər/ ▶*n.* the development of agricultural ecosystems intended to be sustainable and self-sufficient. ▷1970s: blend of **PERMANENT** and **AGRICULTURE**.

per·ma·frost /ˈpərməˌfrôst; -ˌfräst/ ▶*n.* a thick subsurface layer of soil that remains frozen throughout the year, occurring chiefly in polar regions. ▷1940s: from **PERMANENT** + **FROST**.

per·ma·lanc·er /ˈpərməˌlansər/ ▶*n.* a long-term freelance, part-time, or temporary worker who does not have employee benefits: *the permalancers always have to park in the temporary spaces.* Also called **PERMATEMP**. ▷blend of *permanent* and *freelancer*.

perm·al·loy /ˈpərməˌloi; ˌpərmˈaloi/ ▶*n.* an alloy of nickel and iron that is easily magnetized and demagnetized, used in electrical equipment. ▷1920s: (originally as a trademark) from **PERMEABLE** + **ALLOY**. See **PERMEABILITY** 2.

per·ma·nence /ˈpərmənəns/ ▶*n.* the state or quality of lasting or remaining unchanged indefinitely: *the clarity and permanence of the dyes.* ▷late Middle English: from medieval Latin *permanentia* (perhaps via French), from *permanent-* 'remaining to the end,' from the verb *permanere*. **—per·ma·nen·cy** /-sē/ *n.*

per·ma·nent /ˈpərmənənt/ ▶*adj.* lasting or intended to last or remain unchanged indefinitely: *a permanent ban on the dumping of radioactive waste at sea* | *damage was not thought to be permanent* | *some temporary workers did not want a permanent job.* ■ lasting or continuing without interruption: *he's in a permanent state of rage.*

▶*n.* a perm for the hair. ▷late Middle English: from Latin *permanent-* 'remaining to the end' (perhaps via Old French), from *per-* 'through' + *manere* 'remain.' **—per·ma·nent·ize** /-ˌtīz/ *v.* (*rare*) **—per·ma·nent·ly** *adv.*

per·ma·nent mag·net ▶*n.* a magnet that retains its magnetic properties in the absence of an inducing field or current.

per·ma·nent rev·o·lu·tion ▶*n.* the state or condition, envisaged by Leon Trotsky, of a country's continuing revolutionary progress being dependent on a continuing process of revolution in other countries.

per·ma·nent set ▶*n.* an irreversible deformation that remains in a structure or material after it has been subjected to stress.

per·ma·nent tooth ▶*n.* a tooth in a mammal that replaces a temporary milk tooth and lasts for most of the mammal's life.

per·ma·nent wave ▶*n.* see **PERM**.

per·man·ga·nate /pərˈmaNGgəˌnāt/ ▶*n.* *Chemistry* a salt containing the anion MnO_4^-, typically deep purplish-red and with strong oxidizing properties.

per·ma·temp /ˈpərməˌtemp/ ▶ another term for **PERMALANCER**. ▷a blend of *permanent* and *temporary*.

per·me·a·bil·i·ty /ˌpərmēəˈbilitē/ ▶*n.* **1** the state or quality of a material or membrane that causes it to allow liquids or gases to pass through it. **2** *Physics* a quantity measuring the influence of a substance on the magnetic flux in the region it occupies.

per·me·a·bil·ize /ˈpərmēəbəˌlīz/ ▶*v.* [*trans.*] [often as *adj.*] (**permeabilized**) *technical* make permeable. **—per·me·a·bil·i·za·tion** /ˌpərmēəbəliˈzāsнən/ *n.*

per·me·a·ble /ˈpərmēəbəl/ ▶*adj.* (of a material or membrane) allowing liquids or gases to pass through it: *a frog's skin is* **permeable to** *water.* ▷late Middle English: from Latin *permeabilis*, from *permeare* 'pass through' (see **PERMEATE**).

per·me·ance /ˈpərmēəns/ ▶*n.* *Physics* the property of allowing the passage of lines of magnetic flux.

per·me·ate /ˈpərmēˌāt/ ▶*v.* [*trans.*] spread throughout (something); pervade: *the aroma of soup permeated the air* | [*intrans.*] *his personality has begun to* **permeate through** *the whole organization.* ▷mid 17th cent.: from Latin *permeat-* 'passed through,' from the verb *permeare*, from *per-* 'through' + *meare* 'pass, go.' **—per·me·a·tion** /ˌpərmēˈāsнən/ *n.*

per·meth·rin /pərˈmēтнrin/ ▶*n.* a synthetic insecticide of the pyrethroid class, used chiefly against disease-carrying insects. ▷1970s: from sense 2 of **PER-** + *(res)methrin*, denoting a synthetic pyrethroid.

Per·mi·an /ˈpərmēən/ ▶*adj.* *Geology* of, relating to, or denoting the last period of the Paleozoic era, between the Carboniferous and Triassic periods. See also **PERMO–TRIASSIC**. ■ [as *n.*] (**the Permian**) the Permian period or the system of rocks deposited during it.

The Permian lasted from about 290 million to 245 million years ago. The climate was hot and dry in many parts of the world during this period, which saw the extinction of many marine animals, including trilobites, and the proliferation of reptiles.

▷late 16th cent.: from the name of the Russian province **PERM**, from the extensive development of such strata there.

Per·mi·an Ba·sin /ˈpərmēən/ a region in western Texas and the geologic structure underlying it, a major oil and gas reservoir. The cities of Midland and Odessa are production centers.

per mill (also **per mil**) ▶*n.* one part in every thousand. ▷late 17th cent.: Latin.

per·mis·si·ble /pər'misəbəl/ ▶*adj.* permitted; allowed: *it is permissible to edit and rephrase the statement.* ▷late Middle English: from medieval Latin *permissibilis*, from *permiss-* 'allowed,' from the verb *permittere* (see PERMIT[1]). —**per·mis·si·bil·i·ty** /-,misə'bilitē/ *n.* —**per·mis·si·bly** /-blē/ *adv.*

per·mis·sion /pər'misHən/ ▶*n.* consent; authorization: *they had entered the country without permission* | [with *infinitive*] *he had received permission to go to Brussels.* See note at LIBERTY. ■ an official document giving authorization: *permissions to reproduce copyright material.* ▷late Middle English: from Latin *permissio(n-)*, from the verb *permittere* 'allow' (see PERMIT[1]).

per·mis·sive /pər'misiv/ ▶*adj.* **1** allowing or characterized by great or excessive freedom of behavior: *I was not a permissive parent* | *the permissive society of the 60s and 70s.* See note at LENIENT. **2** *Law* allowed but not obligatory; optional: *the Hague Convention was permissive, not mandatory.* **3** *Biology* allowing a biological or biochemical process to occur: *the mutants grow well at the permissive temperature.* ■ allowing the infection and replication of viruses. ▷late 15th cent. (in the sense 'tolerated, allowed'): from Old French, or from medieval Latin *permissivus*, from *permiss-* 'allowed,' from the verb *permittere* (see PERMIT[1]). —**per·mis·sive·ly** *adv.* —**per·mis·sive·ness** *n.*

per·mit[1] ▶*v.* /pər'mit/ (**-mit·ted, -mit·ting**) [*trans.*] give authorization or consent to (someone) to do something: *the law permits councils to monitor any factory emitting smoke* | [with *two objs.*] *he would not permit anybody access to the library.* ■ [*trans.*] authorize or give permission for (something): *the country is not ready to permit any rice imports.* ■ [*trans.*] (of a thing, circumstance, or condition) provide an opportunity or scope for (something) to take place; make possible: *some properties are too small to permit mechanized farming* | [*intrans.*] *when weather permits, lunches are served outside.* ■ [*intrans.*] (**permit of**) *dated* allow for; admit of: *the camp permits of no really successful defense.*
▶*n.* /'pərmit/ [often with *adj.*] an official document giving someone authorization to do something: *he is only in Britain on a work permit.* ■ official or formal permission to do something: *parking on University grounds is by permit only.* ▷late Middle English (originally in the sense 'commit, hand over'): from Latin *permittere*, from *per-* 'through' + *mittere* 'send, let go.' —**per·mit·tee** /,pərmi'tē/ *n.* —**per·mit·ter** /pər'mitər/ *n.*
▶*PHRASES* □ **permit me** *dated* used for politeness before making a suggestion or used for politeness before making a suggestion or expressing an intention: *permit me to correct you.* □ —— **permitting** if the specified thing does not prevent one from doing something: *weather permitting, guests can dine outside on the veranda.*

per·mit[2] /'pərmit/ ▶*n.* a deep-bodied fish of the jack family, found in warm waters of the western Atlantic and Caribbean and caught for food and sport. • *Trachinotus falcatus*, family Carangidae. ▷alteration of Spanish *palometa* 'little dove.'

per·mit·tiv·i·ty /,pərmi'tivitē/ ▶*n. Physics* the ability of a substance to store electrical energy in an electric field.

pol·li·no·sis /pälə'nōsis/ ▶*n.* a technical term for HAY FEVER.

Per·mo–Car·bon·if·er·ous /,pərmō ,kärbə'nifərəs/ ▶*adj. Geology* of, relating to, or linking the Permian and Carboniferous periods or rock systems together.

Per·mo–Tri·as·sic /,pərmō ,trī'asik/ ▶*adj. Geology* of, relating to, or occurring at the boundary of the Permian and Triassic periods, about 245 million years ago. Mass extinctions occurred at this time, marking the end of the era. ■ of or relating to the Permian and Triassic periods or rock systems considered as a unit. ■ [as *n.*] (**the Permo–Triassic** or **Permo–Trias**) the Permian and Triassic periods together or the system of rocks deposited during them.

per·mu·tate /'pərmyōō,tāt/ ▶*v.* [*trans.*] change the order or arrangement of: *statistics may be sorted and permutated according to requirements.* ▷late 19th cent.: regarded as a back-formation from PERMUTATION.

per·mu·ta·tion /,pərmyōō'tāsHən/ ▶*n.* a way, esp. one of several possible variations, in which a set or number of things can be ordered or arranged: *his thoughts raced ahead to fifty different permutations of what he must do.* ■ *Mathematics* the action of changing the arrangement, esp. the linear order, of a set of items. ▷late Middle English (in the sense 'exchange, barter'): via Old French from Latin *permutatio(n-)*, from the verb *permutare* 'change completely' (see PERMUTE). —**per·mu·ta·tion·al** /-'tāsHənəl/ *adj.*

per·mute /pər'myōōt/ ▶*v.* [*trans.*] *technical* submit to a process of alteration, rearrangement, or permutation: *we wish to permute the order of the bytes.* ▷late Middle English (also in the sense 'interchange'): from Latin *permutare* 'change completely,' from *per-* 'through, completely' + *mutare* 'to change.'

Per·nam·bu·co /,pərnəm'b(y)ōōkō; ,pernäm-/ a state of eastern Brazil, on the Atlantic coast; capital, Recife. ■ former name for RECIFE.

per·nam·bu·co /,pərnəm'b(y)ōōkō/ (also **pernambuco wood**) ▶*n.* the hard reddish timber of a Brazilian tree, used for making violin bows and as a source of red dye. • The tree is *Caesalpinia echinata*, family Leguminosae. ▷late 16th cent.: from the name of the Brazilian state PERNAMBUCO.

per·ni·cious /pər'nisHəs/ ▶*adj.* having a harmful effect, esp. in a gradual or subtle way: *the pernicious influences of the mass media.* ▷late Middle English: from Latin *perniciosus* 'destructive,' from *pernicies* 'ruin,' based on *nex, nec-* 'death.' —**per·ni·cious·ly** *adv.* —**per·ni·cious·ness** *n.*

per·ni·cious a·ne·mi·a ▶*n.* a deficiency in the production of red blood cells through a lack of vitamin B_{12}.

per·nick·et·y /pər'nikitē/ ▶*adj.* British term for PERSNICKETY.

per·noc·tate /pər'näk,tāt/ ▶*v.* [*intrans.*] *formal* pass the night somewhere. ▷early 17th cent.: from Latin *pernoctat-* 'spent the night,' from the verb *pernoctare*, from *per-* 'through' + *nox, noct-* 'night.' —**per·noc·ta·tion** /,pərnäk'tāsHən/ *n.*

Per·nod /per'nō/ ▶*n. trademark* an anise-flavored liqueur. ▷named after the manufacturing firm Pernod Fils.

pe·ro·gi ▶*n.* variant spelling of PIROGI.

Pe·rón[1] /pe'rōn/, Eva (1919–52), Argentine politician; second wife of Juan Perón; full name *María Eva Duarte de Perón*; known as **Evita**. A former actress, after her marriage in 1945 she became de facto minister of health and of labor until her death from cancer. Her social reforms earned her great popularity with the poor.

Pe·rón[2], Juan Domingo (1895–1974), Argentine soldier and statesman; president 1946–55 and 1973–74. The faltering economy and conflict with the Catholic Church led to his removal and exile. He returned to power in 1973, but died in office. —**Pe·ro·nism** /-,nizəm/ *n.* —**Pe·ro·nist** /-nist/ *adj.* & *n.*

per·o·ne·al /,perə'nēəl/ ▶*adj. Anatomy* relating to or situated in the outer side of the calf of the leg. ▷mid 19th cent.: from modern Latin *peronaeus* 'peroneal muscle' (based on Greek *peronē* 'pin, fibula') + -AL.

per·o·rate /'perə,rāt/ ▶*v.* [*intrans.*] *formal* speak at length: *he reportedly would perorate against his colleague.* ■ *archaic* sum up and conclude a speech: *the following innocent conclusion with which she perorates.* ▷early 17th cent.: from Latin *perorat-* 'spoken at length,' from the verb *perorare*, from *per-* 'through' + *orare* 'speak.'

per·o·ra·tion /,perə'rāsHən/ ▶*n.* the concluding part of a speech, typically intended to inspire enthusiasm in the audience. ▷late Middle English: from Latin *peroratio(n-)*, from *perorare* 'speak at length' (see PERORATE).

Pe·rot /pə'rō/, H(enry) Ross (1930–), U.S. businessman and politician. He mounted a third-party candidacy for U.S. president in 1992 and received 19 percent of the popular vote. He established United We Stand America in 1993 to serve as a watchdog for the public and the Reform Party in 1995 to challenge the Democratic and Republican parties. In 1996, as the Reform Party's presidential candidate, he cornered eight percent of the popular vote.

pe·rovsk·ite /pə'rävzkīt; -'räfs-/ ▶*n.* a yellow, brown, or black mineral consisting largely of calcium titanate. ■ any of a group of related minerals and ceramics having the same crystal structure as this. ▷mid 19th cent.: from the name of L. A. *Perovsky* (1792–1856), Russian mineralogist, + -ITE[1].

per·ox·i·dase /pə'räksə,dās/ ▶*n. Biochemistry* an enzyme that catalyzes the oxidation of a particular substrate by hydrogen peroxide.

per·ox·ide /pə'räksīd/ ▶*n. Chemistry* a compound containing two oxygen atoms bonded together in its molecule or as the anion O_2^{2-}. ■ hydrogen peroxide, esp. as used as a bleach for the hair: [as *adj.*] *a peroxide blonde.*
▶*v.* [*trans.*] bleach (hair) with peroxide. ▷early 19th cent.: from sense 2 of PER- + OXIDE.

per·ox·i·some /pə'räksi,sōm/ ▶*n. Biology* a small organelle that is present in the cytoplasm of many cells and that contains the reducing enzyme catalase and usually some oxidases. ▷1960s: from PEROXIDE + -SOME[3]. —**per·ox·i·so·mal** /-,räksi'sōməl/ *adj.*

perp /pərp/ ▶*n. informal* the perpetrator of a crime. ▷1980s: abbreviation.

perp. ▶*abbr.* perpendicular.

per·pend /pər'pend/ ▶*n.* a vertical layer of mortar between two bricks.

per·pen·dic·u·lar /,pərpən'dikyələr/ ▶*adj.* **1** at an angle of 90° to a given line, plane, or surface: *dormers and gables that extend* **perpendicular to** *the main roofline.* ■ at an angle of 90° to the ground; vertical: *the perpendicular cliff.* ■ (of something with a slope) so steep as to be almost vertical: *guest houses seem to cling by faith to the perpendicular hillside.* **2** (**Perpendicular**) denoting the latest stage of English Gothic church architecture, prevalent from the late 14th to mid 16th centuries and characterized by broad arches, elaborate fan vaulting, and large windows with vertical tracery: *the handsome Perpendicular church of St. Andrew.*
▶*n.* a straight line at an angle of 90° to a given line, plane, or surface: *at each division, draw a perpendicular representing the surface line.* ■ (usu. **the perpendicular**) perpendicular position or direction: *the wall declines from the perpendicular a little inward.* ■ an instrument for indicating the vertical line from any point, as a spirit level or plumb line. ▷late Middle English (as an adverb meaning 'at right angles'): via Old French from Latin *perpendicularis*, from *perpendiculum* 'plumb line,' from *per-* 'through' + *pendere* 'to hang.' —**per·pen·dic·u·lar·i·ty** /-,dikyə'laritē/ *n.* —**per·pen·dic·u·lar·ly** *adv.*

per·pe·trate /'pərpə,trāt/ ▶*v.* [*trans.*] carry out or commit (a harmful, illegal, or immoral action): *a crime has been perpetrated against a sovereign state.* ▷mid 16th cent.: from Latin *perpetrat-* 'performed,' from the verb *perpetrare*, from *per-* 'to completion' + *patrare* 'bring about.' In Latin the act perpetrated might be good or bad; in English the verb was first used in the statutes referring to crime, hence the negative association. —**per·pe·tra·tion** /,pərpə'trāsHən/ *n.* —**per·pe·tra·tor** /-,trātər/ *n.*

USAGE To **perpetrate** something is to commit it: *the gang perpetrated outrages against several citizens.* To **perpetuate** something is to cause it to continue or to keep happening: *the stories only serve to perpetuate the legend that the house is haunted.*

per·pet·u·al /pər'pecHōōəl/ ▶*adj.* **1** never ending or changing: *deep caves in perpetual darkness.* ■ [*attrib.*] denoting a position, job, or trophy held for life rather than a limited period, or the person holding it: *a perpetual secretary of the society.* ■ (of an investment) having no fixed maturity date; irredeemable: *a perpetual bond.* **2** occurring repeatedly; so frequent as to seem endless and uninterrupted: *their perpetual money worries.* ■ (of a plant) blooming or fruiting several times in one season: *he grows perpetual carnations.*
▶*n.* a perpetual plant, esp. a hybrid rose. ▷Middle English: from Old French *perpetuel*, from Latin *perpetualis*, from *perpetuus* 'continuing throughout,' from *perpes, perpet-* 'continuous.' —**per·pet·u·al·ly** *adv.*

per·pet·u·al cal·en·dar ▶*n.* a calendar that can be adjusted to show any combination of day, month, and year, and is therefore usable year after year. ■ a set of tables from which the day of the week can be reckoned for any date.

per·pet·u·al check ▶*n. Chess* the situation of play when a draw is obtained by repeated checking of the king.

per·pet·u·al mo·tion ▶*n.* a state in which movement or action is or appears to be continuous and unceasing. ■ the motion of a hypothetical machine that, once activated, would run forever unless subject to an external force or to wear.

per·pet·u·ate /pər'pecHōō,āt/ ▶*v.* [*trans.*] make (something, typically an undesirable situation or an unfounded belief) continue indefinitely: *the law perpetuated the interests of the ruling class.* ■ preserve (something valued) from oblivion or extinction: *how did these first humans survive to perpetuate the species?* ▷early 16th cent.: from Latin *perpetuat-* 'made permanent,' from the verb *perpetuare*, from *perpetuus* 'continuing throughout' (see PERPETUAL). —**per·pet·u·ance** /-o͞oəns/ *n.* —**per·pet·u·a·tion** /pər,peCHo͞o-'āsHən/ *n.* —**per·pet·u·a·tor** *n.*

USAGE See usage at PERPETRATE.

per·pe·tu·i·ty /,pərpi't(y)o͞oitē/ ▸*n.* (*pl.* **-ties**) **1** a thing that lasts forever or for an indefinite period, in particular: ■ a bond or other security with no fixed maturity date. ■ *Law* a restriction making an estate inalienable perpetually or for a period beyond certain limits fixed by law. ■ *Law* an estate so restricted. **2** the state or quality of lasting forever: *he did not believe in the perpetuity of military rule.* ▷late Middle English: from Old French *perpetuite*, from Latin *perpetuitas*, from *perpetuus* 'continuing throughout' (see PERPETUAL).

▸*PHRASE* □ **in** (or **for**) **perpetuity** forever: *all the Bonapartes were banished from France in perpetuity.*

per·pet·u·um mo·bi·le /pər'peCHo͞oəm 'mōbə,lā/ ▸*n.* **1** *Music* a piece of fast-moving instrumental music consisting mainly of notes of equal length. **2** another term for PERPETUAL MOTION. ▷Latin, literally 'continuously moving (thing),' on the pattern of *primum mobile.*

Per·pi·gnan /,perpē'nyäN/ a city in southern France, in the northeastern foothills of the Pyrenees, close to the border with Spain; pop. 108,000.

per·plex /pər'pleks/ ▸*v.* [*trans.*] (often **be perplexed**) (of something complicated or unaccountable) cause (someone) to feel completely baffled: *she was perplexed by her husband's moodiness* | [as *adj.*] (**perplexing**) *a perplexing problem.* ■ *dated* complicate or confuse (a matter): *they were perplexing a subject plain in itself.* ▷late 15th cent. (as the adjective *perplexed*): from the obsolete adjective *perplex* 'bewildered,' from Latin *perplexus* 'entangled,' based on *plexus* 'interwoven,' from the verb *plectere.* —**per·plex·ed·ly** /-'pleksidlē/ *adv.* —**per·plex·ing·ly** *adv.*

per·plex·i·ty /pər'pleksitē/ ▸*n.* (*pl.* **-ties**) **1** inability to deal with or understand something complicated or unaccountable: *she paused in perplexity.* ■ (usu. **perplexities**) a complicated or baffling situation or thing: *the perplexities of international relations.* **2** *archaic* an entangled state: *the dense perplexity of dwarf palm, garlanded creepers, glossy undergrowth.* ▷Middle English: from Old French *perplexite* or late Latin *perplexitas*, from Latin *perplexus* 'entangled, confused' (see PERPLEX).

per pro. /pər 'prō/ ▸*abbr.* per procurationem (used when signing a letter on behalf of someone else; now usually abbreviated to **pp**). ▷Latin.

per·qui·site /'pərkwəzit/ ▸*n.* *formal* another term for PERK[2]. ■ a thing regarded as a special right or privilege enjoyed as a result of one's position: *the wife of a president has all the perquisites of stardom.* ■ *historical* a thing that has served its primary use and is then given to a subordinate or employee as a customary right. ▷late Middle English: from medieval Latin *perquisitum* 'acquisition,' from Latin *perquirere* 'search diligently for,' from *per-* 'thoroughly' + *quaerere* 'seek.'

USAGE **Perquisite** and **prerequisite** are sometimes confused. **Perquisite** usually means 'an extra allowance or privilege': *he had all the perquisites of a movie star, including a stand-in.* **Prerequisite** means 'something required as a condition': *passing the examination was one of the prerequisites for a teaching position.*

Per·rault /pə'rō/, Charles (1628–1703), French writer. He is noted for *Mother Goose Tales* (1697)

Per·ri·er /'perē,yā/ (also **Perrier water**) ▸*n.* *trademark* an effervescent natural mineral water sold as a drink. ▷from the name of a spring at Vergèze, France, from which this water comes.

Per·rin /'perən; pe'raN/, Jean Baptiste (1870–1942), French physical chemist. He provided the definitive proof of the existence of atoms, proved that cathode rays are negatively charged, and investigated Brownian motion. Nobel Prize for Physics (1926).

per·ron /'perən; pə'rōn/ ▸*n.* *Architecture* an exterior set of steps and a platform at the main entrance to a large building such as a church or mansion. ▷late Middle English: from Old French, literally 'large stone,' from Latin *petra* 'stone.'

Per·ry /'perē/, Fred (1909–95), U.S. tennis player, born in Britain; full name *Frederick John Perry.* His record of winning three consecutive singles titles at Wimbledon (1934–36) was unequaled until 1979 when it was broken by Björn Borg.

per·ry /'perē/ ▸*n.* (*pl.* **-ries**) an alcoholic drink made from the fermented juice of pears. ▷Middle English: from Old French *pere*, from an alteration of Latin *pirum* 'pear.'

pers. ▸*abbr.* ■ person. ■ personal.

per se /pər 'sā/ ▸*adv.* by or in itself or themselves; intrinsically: *it is not these facts per se that are important.* ▷Latin.

per·se·cute /'pərsə,kyo͞ot/ ▸*v.* [*trans.*] (often **be persecuted**) subject (someone) to hostility and ill-treatment, esp. because of their race or political or religious beliefs: *Jews who had been persecuted by the Nazi regime.* ■ harass or annoy (someone) persistently: *Hilda was persecuted by some of the other girls.* ▷late Middle English: from Old French *persecuter*, from Latin *persecut-* 'followed with hostility,' from the verb *persequi*, from *per-* 'through, utterly' + *sequi* 'follow, pursue.' —**per·se·cu·tion** /,pərsə'kyo͞osHən/ *n.* —**per·se·cu·tor** /-,kyo͞otər/ *n.* —**per·se·cu·to·ry** /-kyo͞o,tôrē/ *adj.*

per·se·cu·tion com·plex ▸*n.* an irrational and obsessive feeling or fear that one is the object of collective hostility or ill-treatment on the part of others.

Per·se·ids /'pərsēidz/ *Astronomy* an annual meteor shower radiating from a point in the constellation Perseus, reaching a peak about August 12.

Per·seph·o·ne /pər'sefənē/ *Greek Mythology* a goddess, the daughter of Zeus and Demeter. Roman name PROSERPINA.

She was carried off by Hades and made queen of the underworld. Demeter, vainly seeking her, refused to let the earth produce its fruits until her daughter was restored to her, but because Persephone had eaten some pomegranate seeds in the other world, she was obliged to spend part of every year there. Her story symbolizes the return of spring and the life and growth of grain.

Per·sep·o·lis /pər'sepəlis/ a city in ancient Persia, northeast of Shiraz. It was founded in the late 6th century BC by Darius I as the ceremonial capital of Persia under the Achaemenid dynasty.

Per·se·us /'pərsēəs/ **1** *Greek Mythology* the son of Zeus and Danae, a hero celebrated for many achievements. Riding the winged horse Pegasus, he cut off the head of the Gorgon Medusa and gave it to Athena; he also rescued and married Andromeda, and became king of Tiryns in Greece. **2** *Astronomy* a large northern constellation that includes a dense part of the Milky Way. It contains several star clusters and the variable star Algol. ■ [as *genitive*] (**Persei** /-sē-ī/) used with a preceding letter or numeral to designate a star in this constellation: *the star Delta Persei.*

per·se·ver·ance /,pərsə'vi(ə)rəns/ ▸*n.* **1** steadfastness in doing something despite difficulty or delay in achieving success: *his* **perseverance with** *the technique illustrates his single-mindedness* | *medicine is a field which requires dedication and perseverance.* **2** *Theology* continuance in a state of grace leading finally to a state of glory. ▷Middle English: from Old French, from Latin *perseverantia*, from *perseverant-* 'abiding by strictly,' from the verb *perseverare* (see PERSEVERE).

per·sev·er·ate /pər'sevə,rāt/ ▸*v.* [*intrans.*] *Psychology* repeat or prolong an action, thought, or utterance after the stimulus that prompted it has ceased. ▷early 20th cent.: from Latin *perseverat-* 'strictly abided by,' from the verb *perseverare* (see PERSEVERE). —**per·sev·er·a·tion** /pər,sevə'rāsHən/ *n.*

per·se·vere /,pərsə'vi(ə)r/ ▸*v.* [*intrans.*] continue in a course of action even in the face of difficulty or with little or no prospect of success: *his family* **persevered with** *his treatment.* ▷late Middle English: from Old French *perseverer*, from Latin *perseverare* 'abide by strictly,' from *perseverus* 'very strict,' from *per-* 'thoroughly' + *severus* 'severe.' —**per·se·ver·ance** /-'vi(ə)rəns/ *n.* —**per·se·ver·ing·ly** *adv.*

Per·shing[1] /'pərsHiNG; -ZHiNG/, John (Joseph) (1860–1948), U.S. army officer; known as **Black Jack**. His early military years included active duty in Cuba 1889, the Philippines 1899–1903, and Mexico 1916–17 before he became commander in chief of the American Expeditionary Force 1917–19 in World War I. His Meuse-Argonne offensive 1918 led to the final collapse of the German Army. He served as U.S. Army chief of staff 1921–24.

Per·shing[2] (also **Pershing missile**) ▸*n.* a U.S. short-range surface-to-surface ballistic missile, capable of carrying a nuclear or conventional warhead. ▷1950s: named after John J. *Pershing* (1860–1948), American general.

Per·sia /'pərZHə/ a former country in southwestern Asia, now called Iran. The ancient kingdom of Persia became the domain of the Achaemenid dynasty in the 6th century BC. Under Cyrus the Great, Persia became the center of a powerful empire that included western Asia, Egypt, and parts of eastern Europe; it was eventually overthrown by Alexander the Great in 330 BC. The country was conquered by Muslim Arabs between AD 633 and 651. It was renamed Iran in 1935.

Per·sian /'pərZHən/ ▸*n.* **1** a native or national of ancient or modern Persia (or Iran), or a person of Persian descent. ■ (also **Per·sian cat**) a long-haired domestic cat of a breed originating in Persia, having a broad round head, stocky body, and short thick legs. **2** the Iranian language of modern Iran, written in Arabic script. Also called FARSI. ■ an earlier form of this language spoken in ancient or medieval Persia.
▸*adj.* of or relating to ancient Persia or modern Iran or its people or language.

Persian (or Farsi) is spoken by more than 30 million people in Iran, by about 5 million in Afghanistan (as Dari), and by another 2.2 million in Tajikistan (as Tajik). Old Persian, written in cuneiform and attested from the 6th century BC, was the language of the Persian empire, which once extended from the Mediterranean to India. In the 2nd century BC, the Persians created their own alphabet (Pahlavi), which was used until the Islamic conquest in the 7th century.

▷Middle English: from Old French *persien*, from Latin *Persia*, via Greek from Old Persian *pārsa* 'Persia' (modern Persian *pārs*, Arabic *fārs*).

Per·sian car·pet (also **Persian rug**) ▸*n.* a carpet or rug woven in Iran in a traditional design incorporating stylized symbolic imagery, or made elsewhere in such a style.

Per·sian Gulf an arm of the Arabian Sea, to which it is connected by the Strait of Hormuz and the Gulf of Oman. It extends northwest between the Arabian peninsula and the coast of southwestern Iran. Also called ARABIAN GULF; informally THE GULF (see GULF).

Per·sian Gulf War ▸*n.* another name for GULF WAR

Per·sian lamb ▸*n.* a silky, tightly curled fur made from or resembling the fleece of a young karakul, used to make clothing.

Per·sian Wars the wars fought between Greece and Persia in the 5th century BC, in which the Persians sought to extend their rule over the Greek world.

The wars began in 490 BC when Darius I sent an expedition to punish the Greeks for having supported the Ionian cities in their unsuccessful revolt against Persian rule; the Persians were defeated by a small force of Athenians at Marathon. Ten years later, Darius's son Xerxes I attempted an invasion. He devastated Attica, but Persian forces were defeated on land at Plataea and in a sea battle at Salamis (480 BC), and retreated. Intermittent war continued until peace was signed in 449 BC.

per·si·flage /'pərsə,fläZH/ ▸*n.* *formal* light and slightly contemptuous mockery or banter. ▷mid 18th cent.: from French *persifler* 'to banter,' based on *siffler* 'to whistle.'

per·sim·mon /pər'simən/ ▸*n.* **1** an edible fruit that resembles a large tomato and has very sweet flesh. **2** the tree that yields this fruit, related to ebony. • Genus *Diospyros*, family Ebenaceae: the North American *D. virginiana*, an evergreen with dark red fruit, and the **Japanese persimmon** (*D. kaki*), cultivated for its orange fruit. ▷early 17th cent.: alteration of Virginia Algonquian *pessemmins.*

per·sist /pər'sist/ ▸*v.* [*intrans.*] continue firmly or obstinately in an opinion or a course of action in spite of difficulty, opposition, or failure: *the minority of drivers who* **persist in** *drinking* | *we are* **persisting with** *policies that will create jobs for the future.* ■ continue to exist; be prolonged: *if the symptoms persist for more than a few days, contact your doctor.* ▷mid 16th cent.: from Latin *persistere*, from *per-* 'through, steadfastly' + *sistere* 'to stand.'

per·sist·ence /pər'sistəns/ ▸*n.* firm or obstinate continuance in a course of action in spite of difficulty or opposition: *companies must have patience and persistence, but the rewards are there.* ■ the continued or prolonged existence of something: *the persistence of huge environmental problems.* ▷mid 16th cent.: from French *persistance*, from the verb *persister*; influenced in spelling by Latin *persistent-* 'continuing steadfastly.' —**per·sist·en·cy** /-sē/ *n.*

per·sist·ent /pər'sistənt/ ▸*adj.* **1** continuing firmly or obstinately in a course of action in spite of difficulty or opposition: *one of the government's most persistent* critics. ■ [attrib.] characterized by a specified habitual behavior pattern, esp. a dishonest or undesirable one: *they accused officials of persistent discrimination.* **2** continuing to exist or endure over a prolonged period: *persistent rain will affect many areas.* ■ occurring repeatedly over a prolonged period: *persistent reports of human rights abuses by the military.* ■ (of a chemical or radioactivity) remaining within the environment for a long time after its introduction: *PCBs are persistent environmental contaminants.* **3** *Botany & Zoology* (of a part of an animal or plant, such as a horn, leaf, etc.) remaining attached instead of falling off in the normal manner. **—per·sist·ent·ly** *adv.*

per·sist·ent veg·e·ta·tive state ▸*n.* a condition in which a medical patient is completely unresponsive to psychological and physical stimuli and displays no sign of higher brain function, being kept alive only by medical intervention.

per·snick·et·y /pər'snikətē/ ▸*adj. informal* placing too much emphasis on trivial or minor details; fussy: *persnickety gardeners | she's very* ***persnickety about*** *her food.* ■ requiring a particularly precise or careful approach: *it's hard to find a film more persnickety and difficult to use than black-and-white infrared.* ▷early 19th cent. (originally Scots): of unknown origin.

per·son /'pərsən/ ▸*n.* (*pl.* **peo·ple** /'pēpəl/ or **per·sons**) **1** a human being regarded as an individual: *the porter was the last person to see her | she is a person of astonishing energy.* ■ used in legal or formal contexts to refer to an unspecified individual: *the entrance fee is $10.00 per person.* ■ [in *sing.*] [with *adj.*] an individual characterized by a preference or liking for a specified thing: *she's not a cat person.* ■ an individual's body: *I have publicity photographs* ***on my person*** *at all times.* ■ a character in a play or story: *his previous roles in the person of a fallible cop.* **2** *Grammar* a category used in the classification of pronouns, possessive determiners, and verb forms, according to whether they indicate the speaker (**first person**), the addressee (**second person**), or a third party (**third person**). **3** *Christian Theology* each of the three modes of being of God, namely the Father, the Son, or the Holy Spirit, who together constitute the Trinity. ▷Middle English: from Old French *persone*, from Latin *persona* 'actor's mask, character in a play,' later 'human being.'

▸*PHRASES* □ **be one's own person** do or be what one wishes or in accordance with one's own character rather than as influenced by others. □ **in person** with the personal presence or action of the individual specified: *he had to pick up his welfare check in person.* □ **in the person of** in the physical form of: *trouble arrived in the person of a short, mustached Berliner.*

USAGE The words **people** and **persons** can both be used as the plural of **person**, but they are not used in exactly the same way. **People** is by far the more common of the two words and is used in most ordinary contexts: *a group of* ***people****; there were only about ten* ***people****; several thousand* ***people*** *have been rehoused.* **Persons**, on the other hand, tends now to be restricted to official or formal contexts, as in *this vehicle is authorized to carry twenty* ***persons****; no* ***persons*** *admitted without a pass.* In some contexts, **persons**, by pointing to the individual, may sound less friendly than **people**: *the number should not be disclosed to any unauthorized persons.*

-person ▸*comb. form* used as a neutral alternative to *-man* in nouns denoting professional status, a position of authority, etc.: *chairperson | salesperson | sportsperson.*

per·so·na /pər'sōnə/ ▸*n.* (*pl.* **-so·nas** or **-so·nae** /-'sōnē/) the aspect of someone's character that is presented to or perceived by others: *her public persona.* In psychology, often contrasted with **ANIMA**. ■ a role or character adopted by an author or an actor. ▷early 20th cent.: Latin, literally 'mask, character played by an actor.'

per·son·a·ble /'pərsənəbəl/ ▸*adj.* (of a person) having a pleasant appearance and manner. **—per·son·a·ble·ness** *n.* **—per·son·a·bly** /-blē/ *adv.*

per·son·age /'pərsənij/ ▸*n.* a person (often used to express their significance, importance, or elevated status): *it was no less a personage than the bishop.* ■ a character in a play or other work. ▷late Middle English: from Old French, reinforced by medieval Latin *personagium* 'effigy.' In early use the word was qualified by words such as *honorable, eminent*, but since the 19th cent. the notion "significant, notable" has been implied in the word itself.

per·so·na gra·ta /pər'sōnə 'grätə/ ▸*n.* (*pl.* **per·so·nae gra·tae** /pər'sōnē 'grätē/) a person, esp. a diplomat, acceptable to certain others: *I shall no longer be persona grata at the embassy.* Compare with **PERSONA NON GRATA**. ▷Latin, from *persona* (see **PERSONA**) + *grata*, feminine of *gratus* 'pleasing.'

per·son·al /'pərsənəl/ ▸*adj.* **1** [*attrib.*] of, affecting, or belonging to a particular person rather than to anyone else: *her personal fortune was recently estimated at $37 million.* ■ done or made by a particular person; involving the actual presence or action of a particular individual: *the president and his wife made personal appearances for the reelection of the state governor.* ■ done, intended, or made for a particular person: *a personal loan.* **2** of or concerning one's private life, relationships, and emotions rather than matters connected with one's public or professional career: *the book describes his acting career and gives little information about his personal life.* ■ referring to an individual's character, appearance, or private life, esp. in a hostile or critical way: *his personal remarks about Mr. Mellor's work ethic were unprofessional | you look like a drowned rat—nothing personal.* **3** [*attrib.*] of or relating to a person's body: *personal hygiene.* **4** [*attrib.*] *Grammar* of or denoting one of the three persons. See **PERSON** (sense 2). **5** existing as a self-aware entity, not as an abstraction or an impersonal force: *Jews, Christians, and Muslims believe in a personal God.*
▸*n.* an advertisement or message in the personal column of a newspaper; personal ad. ■ (**personals**) another term for **PERSONAL COLUMN**. ▷late Middle English: from Old French, from Latin *personalis* 'of a person,' from *persona* (see **PERSON**).

per·son·al ad ▸*n. informal* a private advertisement or message placed in a newspaper, esp. by someone searching for a romantic partner.

per·son·al as·sis·tant ▸*n.* a secretary or administrative assistant working exclusively for one particular person.

per·son·al col·umn ▸*n.* (usu. **personal columns**) a section of a newspaper devoted to personal ads.

per·son·al com·pu·ter ▸*n.* a microcomputer designed for use by one person at a time.

per·son·al es·tate ▸*n. Law* another term for **PERSONAL PROPERTY**.

per·son·al foul ▸*n. Sports* a rule violation involving illegal contact, as (in basketball) touching a player who is in the act of shooting.

per·son·al i·den·ti·fi·ca·tion num·ber (abbr.: **PIN**) ▸*n.* a number allocated to an individual and used to validate electronic transactions.

per·son·al in·for·ma·tion man·ag·er (abbr.: **PIM**) ▸*n.* a computer program functioning as an address book, organizer, calendar, etc.

per·son·al in·ju·ry ▸*n. Law* physical injury inflicted on a person's body, as opposed to damage to property or reputation.

per·son·al·ism /'pərsənəl,izəm/ ▸*n.* the quality of being personal, esp. a theory or system based on subjective ideas or applications: *his sculpture investigating pure form from which all expressive personalism was eliminated.* ■ *Philosophy* a system of thought that maintains the primacy of the human or divine person on the basis that reality has meaning only through the conscious mind. ■ allegiance to a person, esp. a political leader, rather than to a party or ideology. **—per·son·al·ist** *n.* **—per·son·al·is·tic** /,pərsənəl'istik/ *adj.*

per·son·al·i·ty /,pərsə'nalitē/ ▸*n.* (*pl.* **-ties**) **1** the combination of characteristics or qualities that form an individual's distinctive character: *she had a sunny personality that was very engaging | figurative each brand of gin has its own personality | she has triumphed by sheer force of personality.* ■ qualities that make someone interesting or popular: *she's always had loads of personality.* **2** a famous person, esp. in entertainment or sports: *an official opening by a famous personality.* **3** *archaic* the quality or fact of being a person as distinct from a thing or animal. **4** (**personalities**) *archaic* disparaging remarks about an individual. ▷late Middle English (sense 3): from Old French *personalite*, from medieval Latin *personalitas*, from Latin *personalis* 'of a person' (see **PERSONAL**). Sense 1 dates from the late 18th cent.

per·son·al·i·ty cult ▸*n.* excessive public admiration for or devotion to a famous person, esp. a political leader: *the years of Stalin's personality cult.*

per·son·al·i·ty dis·or·der ▸*n. Psychiatry* a deeply ingrained and maladaptive pattern of behavior of a specified kind, typically manifest by the time one reaches adolescence and causing long-term difficulties in personal relationships or in functioning in society.

per·son·al·i·ty in·ven·to·ry ▸*n.* a type of questionnaire designed to reveal the respondent's personality traits.

per·son·al·i·ty type ▸*n. Psychology* a collection of personality traits that are thought to occur together consistently, esp. as determined by a certain pattern of responses to a personality inventory.

per·son·al·ize /'pərsənəl,īz/ ▸*v.* [*trans.*] **1** (usu. **be personalized**) design or produce (something) to meet someone's individual requirements: *the wedding invitations will be personalized to your exact requirements.* ■ make (something) identifiable as belonging to a particular person, esp. by marking it with their name or initials: [as *adj.*] (**personalized**) *personalized license plates.* **2** cause (something, esp. an issue, argument, or debate) to become concerned with personalities or feelings rather than with general or abstract matters: *the mass media's tendency to personalize politics.* **3** (often **be personalized**) personify (something, esp. a deity or spirit): *evil spirits personalized in Satan.* **—per·son·al·i·za·tion** /,pərsənəli'zāsʜən/ *n.*

P

per·son·al·ly /'pərsənəlē/ ▸*adv.* **1** with the personal presence or action of the individual specified; in person: *she stayed to thank O'Brien personally.* ■ used to indicate that a specified person and no other is involved in something: [as *submodifier*] *he never forgave his father, holding him* ***personally responsible*** *for this betrayal.* ■ used to indicate that one knows or has contact with someone in person rather than indirectly through their work, reputation, or a third party: *they had made conclusions without getting to know me personally.* **2** from someone's personal standpoint or according to their particular nature; in a subjective rather than an objective way: *he had spoken personally and emotionally.* ■ [*sentence adverb*] used to emphasize that one is expressing one's personal opinion: *personally, I think he made a very sensible move.* ■ with regard to one's personal and private rather than public or professional capacity: *nothing had gone well personally or politically.*
▸*PHRASE* □ **take something personally** interpret a remark or action as directed against oneself and be upset or offended by it, even if that was not the speaker's intention: *I took it personally when he yelled at the class.*

per·son·al or·gan·iz·er ▸*n.* a loose-leaf notebook consisting of separate sections including a calendar and pages for recording addresses and telephone numbers. ■ a hand-held microcomputer serving the same purpose.

per·son·al pro·noun ▸*n.* each of the pronouns in English (*I, you, he, she, it, we, they, me, him, her, us,* and *them*) comprising a set that shows contrasts of person, gender, number, and case.

USAGE The correct use of personal pronouns is one of the most debated topics of English usage. **I**, **we**, **they**, **he**, and **she** are **subjective** personal pronouns, which means they are used as the subject of the sentence, often coming before the verb (***she*** *lives in Paris;* ***we*** *are leaving*). **Me**, **us**, **them**, **him**, and **her**, on the other hand, are **objective** personal pronouns, which means that they are used as the object (i.e., they receive the action) of a verb or preposition (*John likes* ***me****; his father left* ***him****; I did it for* ***her***). This explains why it is not correct to say *John and* ***me*** *went to the mall*: the personal pronoun is in subject position, so it must be **I**, not **me**. Using the pronoun alone makes the incorrect use obvious: ***me*** *went to the mall* is clearly not acceptable. This analysis also explains why it is not correct to say *he came with you and I*: the personal pronoun is governed by a preposition (*with*) and is therefore objective, so it must be **me**, not **I**. Again, a simple test for correctness is to use the pronoun alone: *he came with I* is clearly not acceptable.
See also **usage** at **BETWEEN**.

per·son·al prop·er·ty ▸*n. Law* all of someone's property except land and those interests in land that pass to their heirs. Compare with **REAL PROPERTY**.

per·son·al serv·ices ▸*n.* used to refer collectively to commercial services, such as catering and cleaning, that supply the personal needs of customers.

per·son·al shop·per ▸*n.* an individual who is paid to help another to purchase goods, either by accompanying them while shopping or by shopping on their behalf.

per·son·al space ▸*n.* the physical space immediately surrounding someone, into which any encroachment feels threatening to or uncomfortable for them: *he was invading her personal space.* ■ space designated for the use of an individual within a larger communal area such as an office. ■ time in which someone is undisturbed and free to concentrate on their own thoughts and needs.

per·son·al ster·e·o ▸*n.* a small portable electronic device for playing music, used with lightweight headphones.

per·son·al touch ▸*n.* an element or feature contributed by someone to make something less impersonal: *customers prefer to write the messages themselves for more of a personal touch.*

per·son·al·ty /ˈpərsənəltē/ ▸*n.* *Law* a person's personal property. The opposite of REALTY. ▷mid 16th cent. (in the legal phrase *in the personalty* 'for damages'): from Anglo-Norman French *personaltie*, from medieval Latin *personalitas* (see PERSONALITY).

per·son·al wa·ter·craft ▸*n.* (abbr.: **PW** or **PWC**) a small, jet-powered craft, resembling a snowmobile in appearance and ridden astraddle, for individual use on water.

per·so·na non gra·ta /pərˈsōnə nän ˈgrätə/ ▸*n.* (*pl.* **per·so·nae non gra·tae** /pərˈsōnē nän ˈgrätē/) an unacceptable or unwelcome person: *from now on, these yellow journalists can consider themselves personae non grata.* Compare with PERSONA GRATA. ▷Latin, from *persona* (see PERSONA) + *non* 'not' + *grata*, feminine of *gratus* 'pleasing.'

per·son·ate /ˈpərsəˌnāt/ ▸*v.* [*trans.*] *formal* play the part of (a character in a drama). ■ pretend to be (someone else), esp. for fraudulent purposes, such as casting a vote in another person's name. ▷late 16th cent.: from late Latin *personat-* 'represented by acting,' from Latin *persona* 'mask' (see PERSON). —**per·son·a·tion** /ˌpərsəˈnāshən/ *n.* —**per·son·a·tor** /-ˌnātər/ *n.*

per·son·hood /ˈpərsənˌho͝od/ ▸*n.* the quality or condition of being an individual person.

per·son·i·fi·ca·tion /pərˌsänəfiˈkāshən/ ▸*n.* the attribution of a personal nature or human characteristics to something nonhuman, or the representation of an abstract quality in human form. ■ a figure intended to represent an abstract quality: *the design on the franc shows Marianne, the personification of the French republic.* ■ [in *sing.*] a person, animal, or object regarded as representing or embodying a quality, concept, or thing: *he was* **the very personification of** *British pluck and diplomacy.*

per·son·i·fy /pərˈsänəˌfī/ ▸*v.* (**-fies, -fied**) [*trans.*] represent (a quality or concept) by a figure in human form: *public pageants and dramas in which virtues and vices were personified.* ■ (usu. **be personified**) attribute a personal nature or human characteristics to (something nonhuman): *in the poem, the oak trees are personified.* ■ represent or embody (a quality, concept, or thing) in a physical form: *he fairly personifies trustworthiness.* ▷early 18th cent.: from French *personnifier*, from *personne* 'person.' —**per·son·i·fi·er** /-ˌfī(ə)r/ *n.*

per·son·nel /ˌpərsəˈnel/ ▸*plural n.* people employed in an organization or engaged in an organized undertaking such as military service compare with MATERIEL: *many of the personnel involved require training | sales personnel.* ■ short for PERSONNEL DEPARTMENT. ▷early 19th cent.: from French (adjective used as a noun), contrasted with *matériel* 'equipment or materials used in an organization or undertaking.'

per·son·nel car·ri·er ▸*n.* another term for ARMORED PERSONNEL CARRIER.

per·son·nel de·part·ment ▸*n.* the part of an organization concerned with the hiring, training, and welfare of employees.

per·son of col·or ▸*n.* a person who is not white or of European parentage.

USAGE The term **person of color** is first recorded at the end of the 18th century. It was revived in the 1990s as the recommended term to use in some official contexts, esp. in U.S. English, to refer to a person who is not white. The term is not common in general use, however, where terms such as **nonwhite** are still used.
See also **usage** at BLACK, COLORED, and NONWHITE.

per·son-to-per·son ▸*adj.* & *adv.* taking place directly between individuals: [as *adj.*] *person-to-person transmission of the disease* | [as *adv.*] (also **person to person**) *making contact with him person to person.* ■ denoting a phone call made through the operator to a specified person and paid for from the time that person answers the phone.

per·spec·tive /pərˈspektiv/ ▸*n.* **1** the art of drawing solid objects on a two-dimensional surface so as to give the right impression of their height, width, depth, and position in relation to each other when viewed from a particular point: [as *adj.*] *a perspective drawing.* See also LINEAR PERSPECTIVE and AERIAL PERSPECTIVE. ■ a picture drawn in such a way, esp. one appearing to enlarge or extend the actual space, or to give the effect of distance. ■ a view or prospect. ■ *Geometry* the relation of two figures in the same plane, such that pairs of corresponding points lie on concurrent lines, and corresponding lines meet in collinear points. **2** a particular attitude toward or way of regarding something; a point of view: *most guidebook history is written from the editor's perspective.* ■ true understanding of the relative importance of things; a sense of proportion: *we must keep a sense of perspective about what he's done.* **3** an apparent spatial distribution in perceived sound. ▷late Middle English (in the sense 'optics'): from medieval Latin *perspectiva (ars)* 'science of optics,' from *perspect-* 'looked at closely,' from the verb *perspicere*, from *per-* 'through' + *specere* 'to look.' —**per·spec·tiv·al** /-tivəl/ *adj.*

▸*PHRASE* □ **in** (or **out of**) **perspective** showing the right (or wrong) relationship between visible objects. ■ correctly (or incorrectly) regarded in terms of relative importance: *these expenses may seem high, but they need to be* **put into perspective**.

per·spec·tiv·ism /pərˈspektiˌvizəm/ ▸*n.* **1** *Philosophy* the theory that knowledge of a subject is inevitably partial and limited by the individual perspective from which it is viewed. See also RELATIVISM. **2** the practice of regarding and analyzing a situation or work of art from different points of view. —**per·spec·tiv·ist** *n.*

Per·spex /ˈpərspeks/ ▸*n.* *trademark* (often **per·spex**) solid transparent plastic made of polymethyl methacrylate (the same material as plexiglas or lucite). ▷1930s: formed irregularly from Latin *perspicere* 'look through,' from *per-* 'through' + *specere* 'to look.'

per·spi·ca·cious /ˌpərspiˈkāshəs/ ▸*adj.* having a ready insight into and understanding of things: *it offers quite a few facts to the perspicacious reporter.* See note at KEEN. ▷early 17th cent.: from Latin *perspicax*, *perspicac-* 'seeing clearly' + -ACIOUS. —**per·spi·ca·cious·ly** *adv.* —**per·spi·cac·i·ty** /-ˈkasitē/ *n.*

per·spic·u·ous /pərˈspikyo͞owəs/ ▸*adj.* *formal* (of an account or representation) clearly expressed and easily understood; lucid: *it provides simpler and more perspicuous explanations than its rivals.* ■ (of a person) able to give an account or express an idea clearly. ▷late 15th cent. (in the sense 'transparent'): from Latin *perspicuus* 'transparent, clear' (from the verb *perspicere* 'look at closely') + -OUS. —**per·spi·cu·i·ty** /ˌpərspiˈkyo͞oitē/ *n.* —**per·spic·u·ous·ly** *adv.*

per·spi·ra·tion /ˌpərspəˈrāshən/ ▸*n.* the process of sweating: *it causes perspiration and a rapid heartbeat.* ■ sweat: *perspiration ran down his forehead.* ▷early 17th cent.: from French, from *perspirer* (see PERSPIRE). —**per·spir·a·to·ry** /pərˈspīrəˌtôrē/ *adj.*

per·spire /pərˈspīr/ ▸*v.* [*intrans.*] give out sweat through the pores of the skin as the result of heat, physical exertion, or stress: *Will was perspiring heavily.* ▷mid 17th cent.: from French *perspirer*, from Latin *perspirare*, from *per-* 'through' + *spirare* 'breathe.'

per·suade /pərˈswād/ ▸*v.* [*trans.*] cause (someone) to do something through reasoning or argument: *it wasn't easy, but I persuaded him to do the right thing.* ■ [*trans.*] cause (someone) to believe something, esp. after a sustained effort; convince: *they must often be* **persuaded of** *the potential severity of their drinking problems* | [*trans.*] *he did everything he could to persuade the police that he was the robber.* ■ (of a situation or event) provide a sound reason for (someone) to do something: *the cost of the manor's restoration persuaded them to take in guests.* ▷late 15th cent.: from Latin *persuadere*, from *per-* 'through, to completion' + *suadere* 'advise.' —**per·suad·a·bil·i·ty** /-ˌswādəˈbilitē/ *n.* —**per·suad·a·ble** /-əbəl/ *adj.* —**per·sua·si·ble** /-ˈswāzəbəl/ *adj.*

USAGE For a discussion of the difference between **persuade** and **convince**, see **usage** at CONVINCE.

per·suad·er /pərˈswādər/ ▸*n.* a person who persuades someone to do something. ■ *informal* a thing used to compel submission or obedience, typically a gun or other weapon.

per·sua·sion /pərˈswāzhən/ ▸*n.* **1** the action or fact of persuading someone or of being persuaded to do or believe something: *Monica needed plenty of persuasion before she actually left.* ■ a means of persuading someone to do or believe something; an argument or inducement: *he gave way to the persuasions of his half-brother.* **2** a belief or set of beliefs, esp. religious or political ones: *writers of all political persuasions.* See note at OPINION. ■ a group or sect holding a particular religious belief: *the village had two chapels for those of the Methodist persuasion.* ■ *humorous* any group or type of person or thing linked by a specified characteristic, quality, or attribute: *an ancient gas oven* **of the** *enamel* **persuasion**. ▷late Middle English: from Latin *persuasio(n-)*, from the verb *persuadere* (see PERSUADE).

per·sua·sive /pərˈswāsiv; -ziv/ ▸*adj.* good at persuading someone to do or believe something through reasoning or the use of temptation: *an informative and persuasive speech.* ▷late 15th cent.: from French *persuasif, -ive* or medieval Latin *persuasivus*, from *persuas-* 'convinced by reasoning,' from the verb *persuadere* (see PERSUADE). —**per·sua·sive·ly** *adv.* —**per·sua·sive·ness** *n.*

pert /pərt/ ▸*adj.* (of a girl or young woman) sexually attractive because lively or saucy: *a pert Belgian actress.* ■ (of a bodily feature or garment) attractive because neat and jaunty: *she had a pert nose and deep blue eyes.* ■ (of a young person or their speech or behavior) impudent: *no need to be pert, miss.* ■ another term for PEART. ▷Middle English (in the sense 'manifest'): from Old French *apert*, from Latin *apertus* 'opened,' past participle of *aperire*, reinforced by Old French *aspert*, from Latin *expertus* (see EXPERT). —**pert·ly** *adv.* —**pert·ness** *n.*

pert. ▸*abbr.* pertaining.

per·tain /pərˈtān/ ▸*v.* [*intrans.*] be appropriate, related, or applicable: *matters* **pertaining to** *the organization of government.* ■ *chiefly Law* belong to something as a part, appendage, or accessory: *the premises, stock, and all assets* **pertaining to** *the business.* ■ [with *adverbial*] be in effect or existence in a specified place or at a specified time: *their economic circumstances are vastly different from those which pertained in their land of origin.* ▷late Middle English: from Old French *partenir*, from Latin *pertinere* 'extend to, have reference to,' from *per-* 'through' + *tenere* 'to hold.'

Perth /pərth/ the capital of the state of Western Australia, in western Australia, on the Indian Ocean; pop. 1,019,000 (including the port of Fremantle). Founded by the British in 1829, it developed rapidly after the discovery in 1890 of gold in the region and the opening in 1897 of the harbor at Fremantle.

Perth Am·boy /ˈpərth ˈamˌboi/ a historic industrial city in northeastern New Jersey, on the Raritan River, across the Arthur Kill from Staten Island in New York; pop. 41,967.

per·ti·na·cious /ˌpərtnˈāshəs/ ▸*adj.* *formal* holding firmly to an opinion or a course of action: *he worked with a pertinacious resistance to interruptions.* See note at STUBBORN. ▷early 17th cent.: from Latin *pertinax*, *pertinac-* 'holding fast' + -OUS. —**per·ti·na·cious·ly** *adv.* —**per·ti·na·cious·ness** *n.* —**per·ti·nac·i·ty** /-ˈasitē/ *n.*

per·ti·nent /ˈpərtn-ənt/ ▸*adj.* relevant or applicable to a particular matter; apposite: *she asked me a lot of very pertinent questions | the unreleased section of tape was not* **pertinent to** *the investigation.* ▷late Middle English: from Old French, or from Latin *pertinent-* 'having reference to,' from the verb *pertinere* (see PERTAIN). —**per·ti·nence** *n.* —**per·ti·nen·cy** *n.* —**per·ti·nent·ly** *adv.*

per·turb /pərˈtərb/ ▸*v.* [*trans.*] **1** (often **be perturbed**) make (someone) anxious or unsettled: *they were perturbed by her capricious behavior* | [*trans.*] *they were perturbed that the bank had begun switching some of its problem loans.* **2** subject (a system, moving object, or process) to an influence tending to alter its normal or regular state or path: *nuclear weapons could be used to perturb the orbit of an asteroid.* ▷late Middle English: from Old French *pertourber*, from Latin *perturbare*, from *per-* 'completely' + *turbare* 'disturb.' —**per·turb·a·ble** *adj.* —**per·tur·ba·tive** /ˈpərtərˌbātiv; pərˈtərbətiv/ *adj.* (sense 2) —**per·turb·ing·ly** *adv.*

per·tur·ba·tion /ˌpərtərˈbāshən/ ▸*n.* **1** anxiety; mental uneasiness: *she sensed her friend's perturbation.* ■ a cause of such anxiety or uneasiness: *Frank's atheism was more than a perturbation to Michael.* **2** a deviation of a system, moving object, or process from its regular or normal state of path, caused by an outside influence: *some minor perturbation in his house's cash flow.* ■ *Physics* a slight alteration of a physical system, for example of the electrons in an atom, caused by a secondary influence. ■ *Astronomy* a minor deviation in the course of a celestial body, caused by the gravitational attraction of a neighboring body. ▷late Middle English: from Latin *perturbatio(n-)*, from the verb *perturbare* 'disturb greatly' (see PERTURB).

per·tus·sis /pər'təsis/ ▶*n.* medical term for WHOOPING COUGH. ▷late 18th cent.: modern Latin, from PER- 'away, extremely' + Latin *tussis* 'a cough.'

Pe·ru /pə'ro͞o/ a country in South America on the Pacific coast, crossed throughout its length by the Andes; pop. 27,544,000; capital, Lima; languages, Spanish and Quechua. —**Pe·ru·vi·an** /-vēən/ *adj.* & *n.*

The center of the Inca empire, Peru was conquered by the Spanish conquistador Pizarro in 1532. Liberated by Simón Bolívar and José de San Martín in 1820–24, a republic was established. It lost territory in the south in a war with Chile 1879–83 and also had border disputes with Colombia and Ecuador in the 1930s and 1940s. Peru was troubled by revolutionary guerrilla and terrorist activity in the 1980s and 1990s. A new president was elected in 2001.

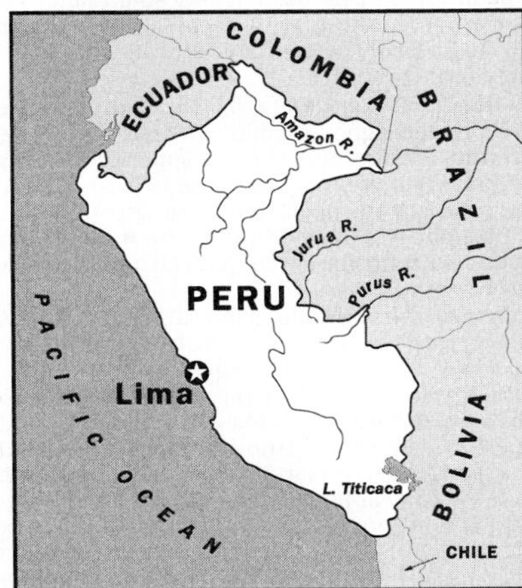

Pe·ru·gia /pə'ro͞oj(ē)ə/ a city in central Italy, the capital of Umbria; pop. 151,000.

pe·ruke /pə'ro͞ok/ ▶*n.* archaic term for PERIWIG. ■ archaic term for WIG[1]. ▷mid 16th cent. (denoting a natural head of hair): from French *perruque*, from Italian *perrucca*, of unknown origin.

pe·rus·al /pə'ro͞ozəl/ ▶*n.* *formal* the action of reading or examining something: *I continued my perusal of the instructions.*

pe·ruse /pə'ro͞oz/ ▶*v.* [*trans.*] *formal* read thoroughly or carefully: *the pursed lips of an auditor perusing an unsatisfactory set of accounts.* ■ examine carefully or at length: *Laura perused a Caravaggio.* ▷late 15th cent. (in the sense 'use up, wear out'): perhaps from PER- 'thoroughly' + USE, but compare with Anglo-Norman French *peruser* 'examine.' —**pe·rus·er** *n.*

USAGE The verb **peruse** means 'read thoroughly and carefully.' It is sometimes mistakenly taken to mean 'read through quickly, glance over,' as in *later documents will be* **perused** *rather than analyzed thoroughly*, a sentence that technically makes no sense.

Pe·ru·vi·an bark /pə'ro͞ovēən/ ▶*n.* cinchona bark.

Pe·ru·vi·an Cur·rent a cold ocean current that moves north from the Antarctic Ocean along the Pacific coast of Chile and Peru before turning west into the South Equatorial Current.

perv /pərv/ *informal* ▶*n.* (also **perv·o** /'pər,vō/) a sexual pervert. ▷1940s: abbreviation of the noun PERVERT.

per·vade /pər'vād/ ▶*v.* [*trans.*] (esp. of a smell) spread through and be perceived in every part of: *a smell of stale cabbage pervaded the air.* ■ (of an influence, feeling, or quality) be present and apparent throughout: *the sense of crisis that pervaded Europe in the 1930s.* ▷mid 17th cent. (also in the sense 'traverse'): from Latin *pervadere*, from *per-* 'throughout' + *vadere* 'go.' —**per·va·sion** /pər'vāzʜən/ *n.*

per·va·sive /pər'vāsiv/ ▶*adj.* (esp. of an unwelcome influence or physical effect) spreading widely throughout an area or a group of people: *ageism is pervasive and entrenched in our society.* ▷mid 18th cent.: from Latin *pervas-* 'passed through' (from the verb *pervadere*) + -IVE. —**per·va·sive·ly** *adv.* —**per·va·sive·ness** *n.*

per·verse /pər'vərs/ ▶*adj.* (of a person or their actions) showing a deliberate and obstinate desire to behave in a way that is unreasonable or unacceptable, often in spite of the consequences: *Kate's perverse decision not to cooperate.* See note at STUBBORN. ■ contrary to the accepted or expected standard or practice: *in two general elections the outcome was quite perverse.* ■ *Law* (of a verdict) against the weight of evidence or the direction of the judge on a point of law. ■ sexually perverted. ▷late Middle English (in the sense 'turned away from what is right or good'): from Old French *pervers(e)*, from Latin *perversus* 'turned around,' from the verb *pervertere* (see PERVERT). —**per·verse·ly** *adv.* [*sentence adverb*] *perversely, she felt nearer to tears now than at any other moment in the conversation.* —**per·verse·ness** *n.* —**per·ver·si·ty** /-'vərsitē/ *n.* (*pl.* **-ties**).

per·ver·sion /pər'vərzʜən/ ▶*n.* the alteration of something from its original course, meaning, or state to a distortion or corruption of what was first intended: *the perversion of Marxist theory to justify Soviet policy-making | a scandalous perversion of the law.* ■ sexual behavior or desire that is considered abnormal or unacceptable. ▷late Middle English: from Latin *perversio(n-)*, from the verb *pervertere* 'turn around' (see PERVERT).

per·vert ▶*v.* /pər'vərt/ [*trans.*] alter (something) from its original course, meaning, or state to a distortion or corruption of what was first intended: *he was charged with conspiring to pervert the course of justice.* ■ lead (someone) away from what is considered right, natural, or acceptable: *Hector is a man who is simply perverted by his time.*

▶*n.* /'pərvərt/ a person whose sexual behavior is regarded as abnormal and unacceptable. ▷late Middle English (as a verb): from Old French *pervertir*, from Latin *pervertere*, from *per-* 'thoroughly, to ill effect' + *vertere* 'to turn.' The current noun sense dates from the late 19th cent. —**per·vert·er** *n.*

per·vert·ed /pər'vərtid/ ▶*adj.* (of a person or their actions) characterized by sexually abnormal and unacceptable practices or tendencies: *he whispered perverted obscenities.* See note at DEPRAVED. ■ (of a thing) having been corrupted or distorted from its original course, meaning, or state: *this sudden surge of perverted patriotism.* —**per·vert·ed·ly** *adv.*

per·vi·ous /'pərvēəs/ ▶*adj.* (of a substance) allowing water to pass through; permeable: *pervious rocks.* ▷early 17th cent.: from Latin *pervius* 'having a passage through' (based on *via* 'way') + -OUS. —**per·vi·ous·ness** *n.*

per·vo /'pər,vō/ ▶*n.* (*pl.* **-vos**) variant of PERV.

pes /pēs; pās/ ▶*n.* (*pl.* **pe·des** /'pēdēz; 'pedēz/) *technical* the human foot, or the corresponding terminal segment of the hind limb of a vertebrate animal. ▷mid 19th cent.: from Latin, 'foot.'

Pe·sach /'pā,säk/ ▶*n.* Jewish term for the Passover festival. ▷from Hebrew *Pesaḥ*.

Pes·ci /'pesʜē/, Joe (1943–), U.S. actor. He appeared in movies such as *Raging Bull* (1980), *Goodfellas* (Academy Award, 1990), *Home Alone* (1990), *My Cousin Vinny* (1992), *Casino* (1995), and *Gone Fishin'* (1997).

pe·se·ta /pə'sātə/ ▶*n.* the basic monetary unit of Spain (until replaced by the euro), equal to 100 centimos. ■ *historical* a silver coin. ▷Spanish, diminutive of *pesa* 'weight,' from Latin *pensa* 'things weighed,' from the verb *pendere* 'weigh.'

pe·se·wa /pā'sāwä/ ▶*n.* a monetary unit of Ghana, equal to one hundredth of a cedi. ▷Akan, literally 'penny.'

Pe·sha·war /pə'sʜäwər/ the capital of North-West Frontier Province, in northwestern Pakistan; pop. 555,000. Situated near the Khyber Pass on the border with Afghanistan, it is of strategic and military importance.

Pe·shit·ta /pə'sʜētə/ (also **Pe·shi·to** /-tō/) ▶*n.* the ancient Syriac version of the Bible, used in Syriac-speaking Christian countries from the early 5th century and still the official Bible of the Syrian Christian Churches. ▷Syriac, literally 'simple, plain.'

pesh·mer·ga /pesʜ'mərgə/ ▶*n.* (*pl.* same or **-gas**) a member of a Kurdish nationalist guerrilla organization. ▷from Kurdish *pêshmerge*, from *pêsh* 'before' + *merg* 'death.'

pes·ky /'peskē/ ▶*adj.* (**-ki·er**, **-ki·est**) *informal* causing trouble; annoying: *pesky mosquitoes.* ▷late 18th cent.: perhaps related to PEST. —**pesk·i·ly** /-kəlē/ *adv.* —**pesk·i·ness** /-kēnis/ *n.*

pe·so /'pāsō/ ▶*n.* (*pl.* **-sos**) the basic monetary unit of Mexico, several other Latin American countries, and the Philippines, equal to 100 centésimos in Uruguay and 100 centavos elsewhere. ▷Spanish, literally 'weight', from Latin *pensum* 'something weighed,' from the verb *pendere* 'weigh.'

pes·sa·ry /'pesərē/ ▶*n.* (*pl.* **-ries**) a small soluble block that is inserted into the vagina to treat infection or as a contraceptive. ■ an elastic or rigid device that is inserted into the vagina to support the uterus. ▷late Middle English: from late Latin *pessarium*, based on Greek *pessos* 'oval stone' (used in board games).

pes·si·mism /'pesə,mizəm/ ▶*n.* a tendency to see the worst aspect of things or believe that the worst will happen; a lack of hope or confidence in the future: *the dispute cast an air of deep pessimism over the future of the peace talks.* ■ *Philosophy* a belief that this world is as bad as it could be or that evil will ultimately prevail over good. ▷late 18th cent.: from Latin *pessimus* 'worst,' on the pattern of *optimism.* —**pes·si·mist** *n.*

pest /pest/ ▶*n.* a destructive insect or other animal that attacks crops, food, livestock, etc. ■ *informal* an annoying person or thing; a nuisance. ■ (**the pest**) *archaic* bubonic plague. ▷late 15th cent. (denoting the bubonic plague): from French *peste* or Latin *pestis* 'plague.'

pes·ter /'pestər/ ▶*v.* [*trans.*] trouble or annoy (someone) with frequent or persistent requests or interruptions: *she constantly pestered him with telephone calls.* ▷mid 16th cent. (in the senses 'overcrowd (a place)' and 'impede (a person)'): from French *empestrer* 'encumber,' influenced by PEST. The current sense is an extension of an earlier use, 'infest,' referring to vermin. —**pes·ter·er** *n.*

pes·ter pow·er ▶*n.* *informal* the ability of children to nag adults, especially to influence their parents to make certain purchases: *advertisers encourage the use of pester power, especially at Christmas.*

pest·house /'pest,hous/ ▶*n.* *historical* a hospital for people suffering from infectious diseases, esp. the plague.

pes·ti·cide /'pestə,sīd/ ▶*n.* a substance used for destroying insects or other organisms harmful to cultivated plants or to animals. —**pes·ti·cid·al** /,pestə'sīdl/ *adj.*

pes·tif·er·ous /pe'stifərəs/ ▶*adj.* *poetic/literary* harboring infection and disease: *the pestiferous area around the prison.* ■ *humorous* constituting a pest or nuisance; annoying: *that pestiferous nephew of yours.* ▷late Middle English (in the sense 'morally corrupting'): from Latin *pestifer* 'bringing pestilence' + -OUS.

pes·ti·lence /'pestələns/ ▶*n.* *archaic* a fatal epidemic disease, esp. bubonic plague. ▷Middle English (also denoting something morally corrupting): from Old French, from Latin *pestilentia*, based on *pestis* 'a plague.'

pes·ti·lent /'pestələnt/ ▶*adj.* destructive to life; deadly: *pestilent diseases.* ■ *informal, dated* causing annoyance; troublesome: *he regarded journalists as a pestilent race.* ■ *archaic, figurative* harmful or dangerous to morals or public order; pernicious: *the pestilent sect of Luther.* ▷late Middle English: from Latin *pestilens*, *pestilent-* 'unhealthy, destructive,' from *pestis* 'plague.' —**pes·ti·lent·ly** *adv.*

pes·ti·len·tial /,pestə'lensʜəl/ ▶*adj.* harmful or destructive to crops or livestock: *these pestilential lichens flourish only in unpolluted air.* ■ *dated* of, relating to, or tending to cause infectious diseases: *you shouldn't be out on a pestilential night like this.* ■ *informal* annoying: *what a pestilential man!* —**pes·ti·len·tial·ly** *adv.*

pes·tle /'pesl; 'pesəl/ ▶*n.* a heavy tool with a rounded end, used for crushing and grinding substances such as spices or drugs, usually in a mortar. ■ a mechanical device for grinding, pounding, or stamping something.

▶*v.* [*trans.*] crush or grind (a substance such as a spice or drug) with a pestle: *she measured seeds into the mortar and pestled them to powder.* ▷Middle English: from Old French *pestel*, from Latin *pistillum*, from *pist-* 'pounded,' from the verb *pinsere*.

pes·to /'pestō/ ▶*n.* a sauce of crushed basil leaves, pine nuts, garlic, Parmesan cheese, and olive oil, typically served with pasta. ▷Italian, from *pestare* 'pound, crush.'

PET /pet/ ▶*abbr.* ■ polyethylene terephthalate. ■ positron emission tomography, used esp. for brain scans.

pet[1] /pet/ ▶*n.* a domestic or tamed animal or bird kept for companionship or pleasure and treated with care and affection: *the pony was a family pet.* ■ a person

Pronunciation Key ə *ago*; ər *over*; 'ə or ,ə *up*; 'ər or ,ər *fur*; a *hat*; ā *rate*; ä *car*; CH *chew*; e *let*; ē *see*; e(ə)r *air*; i *fit*; ī *by*; i(ə)r *ear*; NG *sing*; ō *go*; ô *for*; oi *boy*; o͝o *good*; o͞o *goo*; ou *out*; SH *she*; TH *thin*; T͟H *then*; (h)w *why*; ZH *vision*

treated with special favor, esp. in a way that others regard as unfair: *Liz was teacher's pet.* ■ used as an affectionate form of address: *don't cry, pet, it's all right.* ▸*adj.* [*attrib.*] (of an animal or bird) kept as a pet: *a pet cat.* ■ of or relating to pet animals: *a pet shop | pet food.* ■ denoting a thing that one devotes special attention to or feels particularly strongly about: *another of her pet projects was the arts center | my pet hate is bad telephone manners.* ■ denoting a person or establishment that one regards with particular favor or affection: *his pet performer was Hollander.*

▸*v.* (**pet·ted, pet·ting**) [*trans.*] stroke or pat (an animal) affectionately: *the cats came to be petted.* ■ treat (someone) with affection or favoritism; pamper: *I was cosseted and petted and never shouted at.* ■ [*intrans.*] engage in sexually stimulating caressing and touching: *couples necking and petting in the cars.* ▷early 16th cent. (as a noun; originally Scots and northern English): of unknown origin. —**pet·ter** *n.*

pet[2] ▸*n.* [in *sing.*] a fit of sulking or ill humor: *Mother's **in a pet**.* ▷late 16th cent.: of unknown origin.

Pet. ▸*abbr. Bible* Peter.

PETA /pētə/ ▸*abbr.* People for the Ethical Treatment of Animals.

peta- ▸*comb. form* (used in units of measurement) denoting a factor of 10^{15}: *petabytes.* ▷from *pe(n)ta-* (see **PENTA-**), based on the supposed analogy of *tera-* and *tetra-*.

pe·ta·byte (abbr: **PB**) ▸*n.* 2^{50} bytes; 1024 terabytes, or a million gigabytes: *research projects that generate tens of petabytes of data*

Pé·tain /pe'ten; pā'tan/, (Henri) Philippe (Omer) (1856–1951), French general and statesman; head of state 1940–42. In 1940, he established the French government at Vichy (effectively a puppet regime for the Third Reich) until the German occupation in 1942. After the war, his death sentence for collaboration was commuted to life imprisonment.

pet·al /'petl/ ▸*n.* each of the segments of the corolla of a flower, which are modified leaves and are typically colored. ▷early 18th cent.: from modern Latin *petalum* (in late Latin 'metal plate'), from Greek *petalon* 'leaf,' neuter (used as a noun) of *petalos* 'outspread.' —**pet·al·ine** /'petl,īn; -in/ *adj.* —**pet·aled** *adj.* [*in combination*] *pink-petaled trailing phlox.* —**pet·al·like** /-,līk/ *adj.* —**pet·al·oid** /-,oid/ *adj.*

Pet·a·lu·ma /,petl'ōōmə/ a city in northwestern California, north of San Francisco; pop. 43,184.

pé·tanque /,pā'tängk/ ▸*n.* a lawn game similar to boule, played chiefly in Provence. ▷French, from Provençal *pèd tanco*, literally 'foot fixed (to the ground),' describing the start position.

pe·tard /pi'tärd/ ▸*n. historical* a small bomb made of a metal or wooden box filled with powder, used to blast down a door or to make a hole in a wall. ■ a kind of firework that explodes with a sharp report. ▷mid 16th cent.: from French *pétard*, from *péter* 'break wind.'

▸*PHRASE* □ **hoist with** (or **by**) **one's own petard** have one's plans to cause trouble for others backfire on one. [from Shakespeare's *Hamlet* (III. iv. 207); *hoist* is in the sense 'lifted and removed,' past participle of dialect *hoise* (see **HOIST**).]

pet·a·sus /'petəsəs/ (also **pet·a·sos**) ▸*n.* a hat with a low crown and broad brim, worn in ancient Greece. ■ *Greek Mythology* a winged hat of such a type worn by the god Hermes. ▷via Latin from Greek *petasos*.

pet·a·watt /'petə,wät/ ▸*n.* a quadrillion (10^{15}) watts: *each year warm-core eddies shed southward the equivalent of about 0.3 petawatt of power.*

pet·cock /'pet,käk/ ▸*n.* a small valve, esp. in the pipe of a steam boiler or cylinder of a steam engine for drainage or testing.

pe·te·chi·a /pə'tēkēə/ ▸*n.* (*pl.* **-chi·ae** /-kē,ē/) *Medicine* a small red or purple spot caused by bleeding into the skin. ▷late 18th cent.: modern Latin, from Italian *petecchia*, denoting a freckle or spot on the face, from Latin *petigo* 'scab, eruption.' —**pe·te·chi·al** /-kēəl/ *adj.*

Pe·ter /'pētər/ ▸*n.* either of two books of the New Testament, epistles ascribed to St. Peter.

Pe·ter, St. an apostle; born *Simon*. Peter ("stone") is the name given him by Jesus, signifying the rock on which he would establish his church. He is regarded by Roman Catholics as the first bishop of the Church at Rome, where he is said to have been martyred *c.*AD 67 and is often represented as the keeper of the door of heaven. Feast day, June 29.

pe·ter[1] /'pētər/ ▸*v.* [*intrans.*] decrease or fade gradually before coming to an end: *the storm had **petered out**.* ▷early 19th cent.: of unknown origin.

pe·ter[2] ▸*n. informal* a man's penis. ▷late Middle English: from the given name *Peter*, applied in many transferred uses. The current sense dates from the early 20th cent.

Pe·ter I (1672–1725), tsar of Russia 1682–1725; known as **Peter the Great**. Peter modernized his armed forces and expanded his territory in the Baltic. His extensive administrative reforms were instrumental in transforming Russia into a significant European power. In 1703, he made the new city of St. Petersburg his capital.

Pe·ter·bor·ough /'pētər,bərō/ an industrial city in east central England; pop. 149,000.

pe·ter·man /'pētərmən/ ▸*n.* (*pl.* **-men**) *archaic* a safecracker. ▷early 20th cent.: from slang *peter* 'a safe' + **MAN**.

Pe·ter Pan /,pētər 'pan/ the hero of J. M. Barrie's play of the same name (1904), a boy with magical powers who never grew up. ■ [as *n.*] (**a Peter Pan**) a person, esp. a male who retains youthful features, or who is immature.

Pe·ter Pan col·lar ▸*n.* a flat collar with rounded ends that meet at the front.

Peter Pan collar

Pe·ter Prin·ci·ple the principle that members of a hierarchy are promoted until they reach the level at which they are no longer competent. ▷1960s: named after Laurence J. *Peter* (1919–90), the American educationalist who put forward the theory.

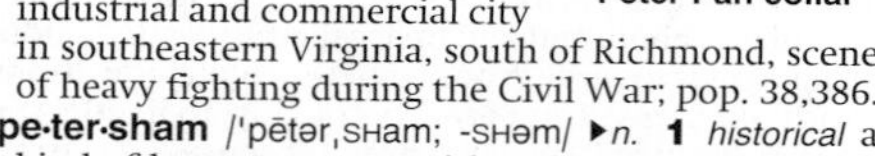

Pe·ters·burg /'pētərz,bərg/ an industrial and commercial city in southeastern Virginia, south of Richmond, scene of heavy fighting during the Civil War; pop. 38,386.

pe·ter·sham /'pētər,sham; -shəm/ ▸*n.* **1** *historical* a kind of heavy overcoat with a short shoulder cape. ■ the thick woolen fabric used to make such coats. **2** a corded tape used for stiffening, esp. in the making of belts and hatbands. ▷early 19th cent.: named after Lord *Petersham* (1790–1851), English army officer.

Pe·ter·son[1] /'pētərsən/, Oscar (Emmanuel) (1925–), Canadian jazz pianist and composer. He often appeared with Ella Fitzgerald.

Pe·ter·son[2], Roger Tory (1908–96), U.S. ornithologist and artist. Peterson produced his first book for identifying birds in the field in 1934, introducing the concept of illustrating similar birds in similar postures with their differences highlighted. The format of his field guides has become standard in field guides.

Pe·ter's pence ▸*plural n.* **1** *historical* an annual tax of one penny from every English householder having land of a certain value, paid to the papal see at Rome from Anglo-Saxon times until it was discontinued in 1534 after Henry VIII's break with Rome. **2** a voluntary payment by Roman Catholics to the papal treasury, made since 1860. ▷named after St. *Peter*, the first pope (see **PETER, ST.**)

Pe·ters pro·jec·tion a world map projection in which areas are shown in correct proportion at the expense of distorted shape, using a rectangular decimal grid to replace latitude and longitude. It was devised in 1973 to be a fairer representation of equatorial (i.e., mainly developing) countries, whose area is underrepresented by the usual projections such as Mercator's. ▷named after Arno *Peters* (born 1916), German historian.

Pe·ter the Her·mit (*c.*1050–1115), French monk. His preaching on the First Crusade rallied thousands of peasants throughout Europe to journey to the Holy Land.

pé·til·lant /,pāti'yän/ ▸*adj.* (of wine) slightly sparkling. ▷French.

pet·i·ole /'petē,ōl/ ▸*n. Botany* the stalk that joins a leaf to a stem; leafstalk. ■ *Zoology* a slender stalk between two structures, esp. that between the abdomen and thorax of a wasp or ant. ▷mid 18th cent.: from French *pétiole*, from Latin *petiolus* 'little foot, stalk.' —**pet·i·o·lar** /,petē'ōlər/ *adj.* —**pet·i·o·late** /'petēə,lāt/ *adj.*

Pe·ti·pa /'petē,pä; petē'pä/, Marius (Ivanovich) (1818–1910), French ballet dancer and choreographer, resident in Russia from 1847. He choreographed more than 50 ballets, working with Tchaikovsky on *Sleeping Beauty* (1890) and *The Nutcracker* (1892).

pet·it /'petē/ ▸*adj. Law* (of a crime) petty: *petit larceny.* ▷late Middle English (in the sense 'small or insignificant'): from Old French, 'small'; the same word as **PETTY**, with retention of the French spelling.

pet·it batte·ment /pə'tē ,batmä/ ▸*n. Ballet* a movement in which one leg is extended and lightly moved forward and backward from the ankle of the supporting leg.

pet·it bour·geois /'petē bŏŏr'zhwä; pə'tē/ ▸*adj.* of or characteristic of the lower middle class, esp. with reference to a perceived conventionalism and conservatism: *the frail facade of petit bourgeois respectability.*

▸*n.* (*pl.* **pet·its bour·geois** *pronunc.* same) a member of the lower middle class, esp. when perceived as conventional and conservative. ▷French, literally 'little citizen.'

pe·tite /pə'tēt/ ▸*adj.* (of a woman) having a small and attractively dainty build: *she was petite and vivacious.* See note at **SMALL**. ■ (of a size of women's clothing) smaller than standard: *it is available in petite sizes.* ▷late 18th cent.: French, feminine of *petit* 'small.'

pe·tite bour·geoi·sie /pə'tēt ,bŏŏrzhwä'zē/ (also **petit bourgeoisie**) ▸*n.* (**the petite bourgeoisie**) [treated as *sing.* or *pl.*] the lower middle class. ▷French, literally 'lesser citizenry.'

pe·tit four /'petē 'fôr/ ▸*n.* (*pl.* **pe·tits fours** /'petē 'fôrz/ or **pe·tit fours** /'petē 'fôrz/) a very small fancy cake, cookie, or confection, typically made with marzipan and traditionally served after a meal. ▷French, literally 'little oven.'

pe·ti·tion /pə'tishən/ ▸*n.* a formal written request, typically one signed by many people, appealing to authority with respect to a particular cause: *she was asked to sign a petition against plans to build on the local playing fields.* ■ an appeal or request, esp. a solemn or humble one to a deity or a superior. ■ *Law* an application to a court for a writ, judicial action in a suit, etc.: *a divorce petition.*

▸*v.* [*trans.*] make or present a formal request to (an authority) with respect to a particular cause: *Americans who moved west **petitioned** Congress **for** admission to the Union as states | [trans.] leaders petitioned the government to hold free elections soon.* ■ make a solemn or humble appeal to (a figure of authority): *Russell **petitioned** her father **for** her hand in marriage.* See note at **BEG**. ■ *Law* make a formal application to (a court) for a writ, judicial action in a suit, etc.: *the custodial parent **petitioned** the court **for** payment of the arrears | [intrans.] the process allows both spouses to jointly **petition for** divorce.* ▷Middle English: from Latin *petitio(n-)*, from *petit-* 'aimed at, sought, laid claim to,' from the verb *petere*. —**pe·ti·tion·ar·y** /-,nerē/ *adj.* —**pe·ti·tion·er** *n.*

pe·ti·ti·o prin·ci·pi·i /pə'tishē,ō prin'sipē,ī/ ▸*n. Logic* a fallacy in which a conclusion is taken for granted in the premises; begging the question. ▷Latin, literally 'laying claim to a principle.'

pe·tit je·té /pə'tē zhə'tā/ ▸*n. Ballet* a jump in which a dancer brushes one leg out to the side in the air then brings it back in again and lands on it with the other leg lifted and bent behind the body.

pe·tit mal /'petē 'mäl/ ▸*n.* a mild form of epilepsy characterized by brief spells of unconsciousness without loss of posture. Compare with **GRAND MAL**. ■ an epileptic fit of this kind. ▷late 19th cent.: from French, literally 'little sickness.'

pe·tit point /'petē ,point/ ▸*n.* a type of embroidery on canvas, consisting of small, diagonal, adjacent stitches. ▷late 19th cent.: from French, literally 'little stitch.'

pe·tits pois /pe'tē 'pwä; pə'tē 'pwä/ ▸*plural n.* young peas that are picked before they are grown to full size; small, fine peas. ▷French, literally 'small peas.'

pet name ▸*n.* a name that is used instead of someone's usual first name to express fondness or familiarity.

petr. ▸*abbr.* petrology.

Pe·tra /'petrə; 'pē-/ an ancient city in southwestern Asia, in present-day Jordan. The city is accessible only through narrow gorges. Its extensive ruins include temples and tombs hewn from the rose-red sandstone cliffs.

Pe·trarch /'pēträrk; 'pet-/ (1304–74), Italian poet; Italian name *Francesco Petrarca*. His reputation is chiefly based on the *Canzoniere* (*c.*1351–53), a sonnet sequence in praise of a woman he calls Laura. He was also an important figure in the rediscovery of Greek and Latin literature.

Pe·trar·chan /pə'trärkən/ ▸*adj.* denoting a sonnet of the kind used by the Italian poet Petrarch, with an octave rhyming *abbaabba*, and a sestet typically rhyming *cdcdcd* or *cdecde*.

pet·rel /'petrəl/ ▸*n.* a seabird related to the shearwaters, typically flying far from land. • Order Procellariiformes, in particular the families

Procellariidae (e.g., the **giant petrel** and **pintado petrel**) or Hydrobatidae (the **storm petrels**). See also DIVING PETREL. ▷early 17th cent.: associated with St. Peter, from the bird's habit of flying low with legs dangling, giving the appearance of walking on the water (see Matt. 14:30).

pe·tri dish /ˈpētrē/ ▸*n.* a shallow, circular, transparent dish with a flat lid, used for the culture of microorganisms. ▷late 19th cent.: named after Julius R. *Petri* (1852–1922), German bacteriologist.

Pe·trie /ˈpetrē; ˈpētrē/, Sir (William Matthew) Flinders (1853–1942), English archaeologist and Egyptologist. He began excavating the Great Pyramid in 1880. He established the system of sequence dating by which sites are excavated layer by layer and historical chronology is determined by the dating of artifacts found *in situ*.

pet·ri·fac·tion /ˌpetrəˈfakSHən/ ▸*n.* another term for PETRIFICATION.

pet·ri·fi·ca·tion /ˌpetrəfiˈkāSHən/ ▸*n.* the process by which organic matter exposed to minerals over a long period is turned into a stony substance. ■ a state of extreme fear, making someone unable to move: *his heavy footfalls served to spur Paul out of his petrification.* ■ an organic object that has been turned to stone.

Pet·ri·fied For·est a highland area in east central Arizona, noted for its agates and plant fossils, now a national park.

pet·ri·fy /ˈpetrəˌfī/ ▸*v.* (**-fies**, **-fied**) [*trans.*] **1** make (someone) so frightened that they are unable to move or think: *his icy controlled quietness petrified her* | [as *adj.*] (**petrified**) *the petrified child clung to her mother.* **2** change (organic matter) into a stony concretion by encrusting or replacing its original substance with a calcareous, siliceous, or other mineral deposit. ■ [*intrans.*] (of organic matter) become converted into stone or a stony substance in such a way. ■ *figurative* deprive or become deprived of vitality or the capacity for change: [*trans.*] *death merely petrifies things for those who go on living* | [*intrans.*] *the inner life of the communist parties petrified.* ▷late Middle English: from French *pétrifier*, from medieval Latin *petrificare*, from Latin *petra* 'rock,' from Greek.

Pe·trine /ˈpēˌtrīn/ ▸*adj.* **1** *Christian Theology* of or relating to St. Peter or his writings or teachings. ■ of or relating to the authority of the pope over the Church, in his role as the successor of St. Peter. **2** of or relating to Peter I of Russia: *the Petrine reforms of the early 18th century.*

petro- ▸*comb. form* **1** of rock; relating to rocks: *petrography.* **2** relating to petroleum: *petrodollar.* ▷sense 1 from Greek *petros* 'stone,' *petra* 'rock'; sense 2 from PETROLEUM.

pet·ro·chem·i·cal /ˌpetrōˈkemikəl/ ▸*adj.* relating to or denoting substances obtained by the refining and processing of petroleum or natural gas: *a huge petrochemical works producing plastics.* ■ of or relating to petrochemistry.
▸*n.* (usu. **petrochemicals**) a chemical obtained from petroleum and natural gas.

pet·ro·chem·is·try /ˌpetrōˈkeməstrē/ ▸*n.* **1** the branch of chemistry concerned with the composition and formation of rocks (as distinct from minerals and ore deposits). **2** the branch of chemistry concerned with petroleum and natural gas, and with their refining and processing.

pet·ro·dol·lar /ˈpetrōˌdälər/ ▸*n.* a notional unit of currency earned by a country from the export of petroleum: *petrodollars were pouring into the kingdom.*

petrog. ▸*abbr.* petrography.

pet·ro·glyph /ˈpetrəˌglif/ ▸*n.* a rock carving, esp. a prehistoric one. ▷late 19th cent.: from PETRO- 'rock' + Greek *gluphē* 'carving.'

Pet·ro·grad /ˈpetrəˌgrad; pyitrəˈgrät/ former name (1914–24) for ST. PETERSBURG.

pe·trog·ra·phy /pəˈträgrəfē/ ▸*n.* the branch of science concerned with the description and classification of rocks, esp. by microscopic study. Compare with PETROLOGY. —**pe·trog·ra·pher** *n.* —**pet·ro·graph·ic** /ˌpetrəˈgrafik/ *adj.* —**pet·ro·graph·i·cal** /ˌpetrəˈgrafikəl/ *adj.*

pet·rol /ˈpetrəl/ ▸*n.* British term for GASOLINE. ▷late 19th cent.: from French *pétrole*, from medieval Latin *petroleum* (see PETROLEUM).

petrol. ▸*abbr.* petrology.

pet·ro·la·tum /ˌpetrəˈlātəm/ ▸*n.* another term for PETROLEUM JELLY. ▷late 19th cent.: modern Latin, from PETROL + the Latin suffix *-atum*.

pe·tro·le·um /pəˈtrōlēəm/ ▸*n.* a liquid mixture of hydrocarbons that is present in certain rock strata and can be extracted and refined to produce fuels including gasoline, kerosene, and diesel oil; oil. ▷late Middle English: from medieval Latin, from Latin *petra* 'rock' (from Greek) + Latin *oleum* 'oil.'

pe·tro·le·um jel·ly ▸*n.* a translucent jelly consisting of a mixture of hydrocarbons, used as a lubricant or ointment.

pet·ro·lif·er·ous /ˌpetrəˈlifərəs/ ▸*adj.* (of rock) yielding or containing petroleum.

pe·trol·o·gy /pəˈträləjē/ ▸*n.* the branch of science concerned with the origin, small-scale structure, and composition of rocks. Compare with LITHOLOGY, PETROGRAPHY. —**pet·ro·log·ic** /ˌpetrəˈläjik/ *adj.* —**pet·ro·log·i·cal** /ˌpetrəˈläjikəl/ *adj.* —**pe·trol·o·gist** /-jist/ *n.*

Pet·ro·nas Tow·ers /pəˈtrōnəs/ twin commercial towers in Kuala Lumpur, Malaysia, completed in 1998, becoming the tallest buildings in the world. The towers are 1,482 feet (452 m) above street level, contain 88 stories topped by steel spires 155 feet (47.2 m) high, and are connected by a double-decked skywalk at the forty-first and forty-second levels.

Petronas Towers

Pe·tro·ni·us /piˈtrōnēəs/, Gaius (died AD 66), Roman writer; known as **Petronius Arbiter**. He is generally accepted as the author of the *Satyricon*, a work in prose and verse satirizing the excesses of Roman society.

Pet·ro·pav·lovsk /ˌpetrəˈpavlôfsk; pyitrəˈpävləfsk/ **1** (also **Petropavlovsk-Kamchatsky**) a Russian fishing port and naval base on the eastern coast of the Kamchatka peninsula in eastern Siberia; pop. 245,000. **2** (also **Pet·ro·pavl** /ˌpetrəˈpävəl/) an industrial and commercial city in northern Kazakhstan, on the Trans-Siberian Railroad; pop. 248,000.

pet·ro·phys·ics /ˌpetrōˈfiziks/ ▸*plural n.* [treated as *sing.*] the branch of geology concerned with the physical properties and behavior of rocks. —**pet·ro·phys·i·cal** /-ˈfizikəl/ *adj.* —**pet·ro·phys·i·cist** /-ˈfizəsist/ *n.*

pe·tro·sal /pəˈtrōsəl/ *Anatomy* ▸*n.* the dense part of the temporal bone at the base of the skull, surrounding the inner ear.
▸*adj.* relating to or denoting this part of the temporal bone, or the nerves that pass through it. ▷mid 18th cent.: from Latin *petrosus* 'stony, rocky' (from *petra* 'rock') + -AL.

pet·rous /ˈpetrəs/ ▸*adj.* *Anatomy* another term for PETROSAL. ▷late Middle English: from Latin *petrosus* 'stony, rocky,' from *petra* 'rock,' from Greek.

Pet·ro·za·vodsk /ˌpetrəzəˈvätsk; pyitrəzəˈvôtsk/ a city in northwestern Russia, on Lake Onega, capital of the republic of Karelia; pop. 252,000.

pe-tsai /ˈbā ˈtsī/ ▸*n.* Chinese cabbage of a pale variety that resembles lettuce. ▷late 18th cent.: from Chinese (Cantonese dialect) *báicài*, literally 'white vegetable.'

Pet·sa·mo /ˈpetsəˌmō/ former name (1920–44) for PECHENGA.

pet sit·ting (also **pet·sit·ting**) ▸*n.* the activity of taking care of pets for absent owners: *an article on how to make money petsitting* [as adj.] *a pet-sitting business.* —**pet·sit** *v.* (**-sit·ting**, **-sat**) —**pet·sit·ter** *n.*

pet·ti·coat /ˈpetēˌkōt/ ▸*n.* a woman's light, loose undergarment hanging from the shoulders or the waist, worn under a skirt or dress. ■ [as *adj.*] *informal, often derogatory* used to denote female control of something regarded as more commonly dominated by men: *he was in danger of succumbing to the petticoat government of Mary and Sarah.* ▷late Middle English: from *petty coat*, literally 'small coat.' —**pet·ti·coat·ed** *adj.*

pet·ti·fog /ˈpetēˌfôg; ˈpetēˌfäg/ ▸*v.* (**-fogged**, **-fog·ging**) [*intrans.*] *rare* quibble about petty points. ■ *archaic* practice legal deception or trickery. ▷early 17th cent.: back-formation from PETTIFOGGER. —**pet·ti·fog·ger·y** /ˌpetēˈfôgərē; -ˈfäg-/ *n.*

pet·ti·fog·ger /ˈpetēˌfôgər; -ˌfäg-/ ▸*n.* *archaic* an inferior legal practitioner, esp. one who deals with petty cases or employs dubious practices. ▷mid 16th cent.: from PETTY + obsolete *fogger* 'underhanded dealer,' probably from *Fugger*, the name of a family of merchants in Augsburg, Germany, in the 15th and 16th centuries.

pet·ti·fog·ging /ˈpetēˌfôgiNG; -ˌfäg-/ ▸*adj.* petty; trivial: *I'm working on the broad business vision here, not pettifogging little details.* ■ (of a person) placing undue emphasis on petty details.

pet·ting zoo ▸*n.* a zoo at which visitors, esp. children, may handle and feed the animals.

pet·tish /ˈpetiSH/ ▸*adj.* (of a person or their behavior) childishly bad-tempered and petulant: *he comes across in his journal entries as spoiled and pettish.* —**pet·tish·ly** *adv.* —**pet·tish·ness** *n.*

Pet·ty /ˈpetē/, Richard (1937–), U.S. race car driver 1960–92. In 1971, he became the first stock car driver to achieve career winnings of $1 million.

pet·ty /ˈpetē/ ▸*adj.* (**pet·ti·er**, **pet·ti·est**) **1** of little importance; trivial: *the petty divisions of party politics.* ■ (of behavior) characterized by an undue concern for trivial matters, esp. in a small-minded or spiteful way: *he was prone to petty revenge on friends and family.* **2** [*attrib.*] of secondary or lesser importance, rank, or scale; minor: *a petty official.* ■ *Law* (of a crime) of lesser importance: *petty theft.* Compare with GRAND. ▷late Middle English (in the sense 'small in size'): from a phonetic spelling of the pronunciation of French *petit* 'small.' Compare with PETIT. —**pet·ti·ly** /ˈpetəlē/ *adv.* —**pet·ti·ness** /ˈpetēnəs/ *n.*

pet·ty bour·geois ▸*n.* another term for PETIT BOURGEOIS.

pet·ty bour·geoi·sie ▸*n.* another term for PETITE BOURGEOISIE.

pet·ty cash ▸*n.* an accessible store of money kept by an organization for expenditure on small items.

pet·ty lar·ce·ny ▸*n.* *Law* theft of personal property having a value less than a legally specified amount.

pet·ty of·fi·cer ▸*n.* a noncommissioned officer in a navy, in particular an NCO in the U.S. Navy or Coast Guard ranking above seaman and below chief petty officer.

pet·ty trea·son ▸*n.* see TREASON.

pet·u·lant /ˈpeCHələnt/ ▸*adj.* (of a person or their manner) childishly sulky or bad-tempered: *he was moody and petulant* | *a petulant shake of the head.* ▷late 16th cent. (in the sense 'immodest'): from French *pétulant*, from Latin *petulant-* 'impudent' (related to *petere* 'aim at, seek'). The current sense (mid 18th cent.) is influenced by PETTISH. —**pet·u·lance** *n.* —**pet·u·lant·ly** *adv.*

pe·tu·nia /pəˈt(y)ōōnyə/ ▸*n.* a plant of the nightshade family with brightly colored funnel-shaped flowers. Native to tropical America, it has been widely developed as an ornamental hybrid, with numerous varieties. • *Petunia* × *hybrida*, family Solanaceae. ▷modern Latin, from French *petun*, from Guarani *petyn* 'tobacco' (to which these plants are related).

pe·tun·tse /pəˈtōōntse/ ▸*n.* a type of weathered volcanic tuff used to make Chinese porcelain. ▷early 18th cent.: from Chinese (Mandarin dialect) *báidūnzi*, from *bái* 'white' + *dūn* 'stone' + the suffix *-zi*.

pew /pyōō/ ▸*n.* a long bench with a back, placed in rows in the main part of some churches to seat the congregation. ■ an enclosure or compartment containing a number of seats, used in some churches to seat a particular worshiper or group of worshipers. ■ (**the pews**) the congregation of a church: *the pews settled down.* ▷late Middle English (originally denoting a raised, enclosed place in a church, provided for particular worshipers): from Old French *puye* 'balcony,' from Latin *podia*, plural of *podium* 'elevated place.'

pe·wee /ˈpēˌwē/ (also **pee·wee**) ▸*n.* a North American tyrant flycatcher with dark olive-gray plumage and a call that sounds like "pee-a-wee." • Genus *Contopus*, family Tyrannidae: several species. ▷late 18th cent.: imitative.

P

pe·wit /ˈpēwit; ˈpyo͞oit/ (also **pee·wit**) ▸*n.* the northern lapwing. ▹early 16th cent.: imitative of the bird's call.

pew·ter /ˈpyo͞otər/ ▸*n.* a gray alloy of tin with copper and antimony (formerly, tin and lead). ■ utensils made of this: *the kitchen pewter.* ■ a shade of bluish or silver gray: *looking back at that pewter sky.* ▹Middle English: from Old French *peutre*, of unknown origin. **—pew·ter·er** *n.*

Pey·er's patch·es /ˈpīərz/ ▸*plural n. Anatomy* the numerous areas of lymphoid tissue in the wall of the small intestine that are involved in the development of immunity to antigens present there. ▹mid 19th cent.: named after Johann K. *Peyer* (1653–1712), Swiss anatomist.

P

pe·yo·te /pāˈyōtē/ ▸*n.* a small, soft, blue-green, spineless cactus, native to Mexico and the southern U.S. Also called **MESCAL.** • *Lophophora williamsii*, family Cactaceae. ■ a hallucinogenic drug prepared from this cactus, containing mescaline. ▹mid 19th cent.: from Latin American Spanish, from Nahuatl *peyotl.*

pe·yo·te but·tons ▸*plural n.* the disk-shaped dried tops of the peyote cactus, eaten or chewed for their hallucinogenic effects. Also called **MESCAL BUTTONS.**

Pf. ▸*abbr.* pfennig.

pf ▸*abbr.* ■ perfect. ■ pfennig. ■ pianoforte; piano. ■ preferred (stock). ■ proof.

PFC (also **Pfc.**) ▸*abbr.* Private First Class.

PFD ▸*abbr.* personal flotation device, a life jacket or similar buoyancy aid.

pfd. ▸*abbr.* preferred (stock).

pfen·nig /ˈfenig/ ▸*n.* a monetary unit of Germany (until the introduction of the euro), equal to one hundredth of a mark. ▹from German *Pfennig*; related to **PENNY.**

pfft /ft/ ▸*exclam.* used to represent a dull abrupt sound as of a slight impact or explosion.
▸*PHRASE* □ **go pfft** *informal* fail to work properly or at all.

pfg. ▸*abbr.* pfennig.

pfu·i /ˈfo͞oē/ ▸*exclam.* variant spelling of **PHOOEY.** ▹mid 19th cent.: from German.

PG ▸*abbr.* ■ parental guidance suggested, a rating in the Voluntary Movie Rating System indicating that some material may not be suitable for children. ■ paying guest.

pg. ▸*abbr.* page.

PG-13 ▸*symbol* parents strongly cautioned, a rating in the Voluntary Movie Rating System indicating that some material may be inappropriate for children under 13.

PGA ▸*abbr.* Professional Golfers' Association (of America).

PH (also **P.H.**) ▸*abbr.* ■ Public Health. ■ Purple Heart.

pH ▸*n. Chemistry* a figure expressing the acidity or alkalinity of a solution on a logarithmic scale on which 7 is neutral, lower values are more acid, and higher values more alkaline. The pH is equal to $-\log_{10} c$, where *c* is the hydrogen ion concentration in moles per liter. ▹early 20th cent.: from *p* representing German *Potenz* 'power' + H, the symbol for hydrogen.

ph. ▸*abbr.* ■ phase. ■ phone.

PHA ▸*abbr.* Public Housing Administration.

pha·ce·li·a /fəˈsēlēə/ ▸*n.* a herbaceous American plant with clustered blue, violet, or white flowers. • Genus *Phacelia*, family Hydrophyllaceae. ▹modern Latin, from Greek *phakelos* 'cluster.'

Phae·a·cian /fēˈāsʜən/ ▸*n.* (in the *Odyssey*) an inhabitant of Scheria (Corfu), whose people were noted for their hedonism. ▹from Latin *Phaeacia*, Greek *Phaiakia*, the name of the island of Scheria, + **-AN.**

Phae·dra /ˈfēdrə; ˈfedrə/ *Greek Mythology* the wife of Theseus. She fell in love with her stepson Hippolytus, who rejected her, whereupon she hanged herself, leaving behind a letter that accused him of raping her. Theseus would not believe his son's protestations of innocence and banished him.

Phae·o·phy·ce·ae /ˌfēəˈfisē/ *Botany* a class of lower plants that comprises the brown algae. • Class Phaeophyceae, division Heterokontophyta (or phylum Heterokonta, kingdom Protista); formerly division Phaeophyta. ▹modern Latin (plural), from Greek *phaios* 'dusky' + *phukos* 'seaweed.'

Pha·e·thon /ˈfāəтʜən; -ˌтʜän/ *Greek Mythology* the son of Helios the sun god. He asked to drive his father's solar chariot for a day, but could not control the immortal horses and the chariot plunged too near to the earth until Zeus killed Phaethon with a thunderbolt in order to save the earth from destruction.

pha·e·ton /ˈfā-itn/ ▸*n. historical* a light, open, four-wheeled horse-drawn carriage. ■ a vintage touring car. ▹mid 18th cent.: from French *phaéton*, via Latin from the Greek name *Phaethōn* (see **PHAETHON**).

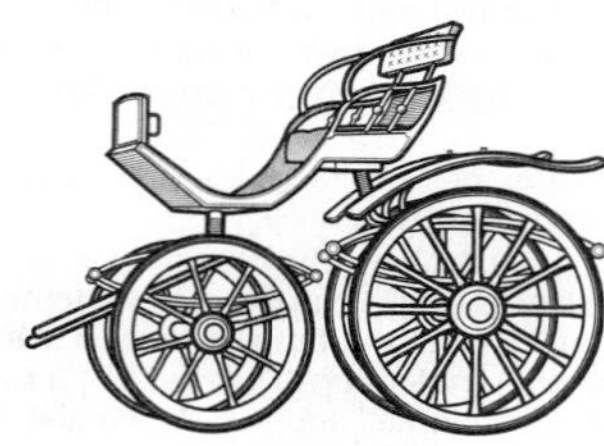

phaeton

phage /fāj/ ▸*n.* short for **BACTERIOPHAGE.**

phage dis·play ▸*n. Biochemistry* a technique for the production and screening of novel proteins and polypeptides by inserting a gene fragment into a gene responsible for the surface protein of a bacteriophage. The new protein appears in the surface coating of the phage, in which it can be manipulated and tested for biological activity.

phag·o·cyte /ˈfagəˌsīt/ ▸*n. Physiology* a type of cell within the body capable of engulfing and absorbing bacteria and other small cells and particles. ▹late 19th cent.: from Greek *phago-* 'eating' (from the verb *phagein*) + **-CYTE.** **—phag·o·cyt·ic** /ˌfagəˈsitik/ *adj.*

phag·o·cy·to·sis /ˌfagəsīˈtōsis/ ▸*n. Biology* the ingestion of bacteria or other material by phagocytes and ameboid protozoans. **—phag·o·cyt·ize** /ˈfagəsiˌtīz/ *v.* **—phag·o·cy·tose** /ˈfagəˌsītōs; ˈfagəˌsītōz/ *v.*

phag·o·some /ˈfagəˌsōm/ ▸*n. Biology* a vacuole in the cytoplasm of a cell, containing a phagocytosed particle enclosed within a part of the cell membrane. **—phag·o·so·mal** /ˌfagəˈsōməl/ *adj.*

-phagous ▸*comb. form* feeding or subsisting on a specified food: *coprophagous.* ▹from Latin *-phagus*, Greek *-phagos* (from *phagein* 'eat') + **-OUS.**

-phagy ▸*comb. form* denoting the practice of eating a specified food: *anthropophagy.* ▹from Greek *-phagia*, from *phagein* 'eat.'

phal·ange /fəˈlanj; ˈfāˌlanj/ ▸*n.* **1** *Anatomy* another term for **PHALANX** (sense 2). [mid 19th cent.: back-formation from *phalanges*, plural of **PHALANX.**] **2** (**Phalange**) a right-wing Maronite party in Lebanon founded in 1936 by Pierre Gemayel. Compare with **FALANGE.** [mid 20th cent.: shortened from French *Phalanges Libanaises* 'Lebanese phalanxes.'] **—Phalangiste** /ˌfälanˈᴢʜēst; fəˈlanjist/ *n.* & *adj.* (in sense 2).

pha·lan·ge·al /fəˈlanjēəl/ ▸*adj. Anatomy* of or relating to a phalanx or the phalanges.

pha·lan·ger /fəˈlanjər/ ▸*n.* a lemurlike tree-dwelling marsupial native to Australia and New Guinea. • Family Phalangeridae: several genera, in particular *Phalanger* and *Spilocuscus*, and including the cuscuses; the **common phalanger** is either the spotted cuscus or the gray cuscus. See also **FLYING PHALANGER.** ▹late 18th cent.: from French, from Greek *phalangion* 'spider's web' (because of the webbed toes of their hind feet).

pha·lan·ges /fəˈlanjēz/ ▸ plural form of **PHALANX** (sense 2).

phal·an·ster·y /ˈfalənˌsterē/ ▸*n.* (*pl.* **-ster·ies**) a group of people living together in community, free of external regulation and holding property in common. ▹mid 19th cent.: from French *phalanstère* (used by Fourier in his socialist scheme for the reorganization of society), blend of Latin *phalanx* 'band (of soldiers), group' and French *monastère* 'monastery.'

pha·lanx /ˈfālaɴɢks; ˈfal-/ ▸*n.* **1** (*pl.* **pha·lanx·es**) a group of people or things of a similar type forming a compact body or brought together for a common purpose: *he headed past the phalanx of waiting reporters to the line of limos.* ■ a body of troops or police officers, standing or moving in close formation: *six hundred marchers set off, led by a phalanx of police.* ■ (in ancient Greece) a body of Macedonian infantry with long spears, drawn up in close order with shields overlapping. **2** (*pl.* **pha·lan·ges** /fəˈlanjēz; fāˈlanjēz/) *Anatomy* a bone of the finger or toe. ▹mid 16th cent. (denoting a body of Macedonian infantry): via Latin from Greek.

phal·a·rope /ˈfaləˌrōp/ ▸*n.* a small wading or swimming bird with a straight bill and lobed feet, unusual in that the female is more brightly colored than the male. • Family Scolopacidae (subfamily Phalaropodinae): three species, **red phalarope** (*Phalaropus fulicarius*), **Wilson's phalarope** (*Steganopus tricolor*), and **northern phalarope** (*Lobipes lobatus*). ▹late 18th cent.: from French, from modern Latin *Phalaropus*, formed irregularly from Greek *phalaris* 'coot' + *pous, pod-* 'foot.'

phal·li /ˈfalī/ ▸ plural form of **PHALLUS.**

phal·lic /ˈfalik/ ▸*adj.* of, relating to, or resembling a phallus or erect penis: *a phallic symbol.* ■ *Psychoanalysis* of or denoting the genital phase of psychosexual development, esp. in males. ▹late 18th cent.: from French *phallique*, from Greek *phallikos*, from *phallos* (see **PHALLUS**). **—phal·li·cal·ly** /-(ə)lē/ *adv.*

phal·lo·cen·tric /ˌfalōˈsentrik/ ▸*adj.* focused on or concerned with the phallus or penis as a symbol of male dominance: *the apartment block was an architectural monument to a phallocentric world.* **—phal·lo·cen·tric·i·ty** /-senˈtrisitē/ *n.* **—phal·lo·cen·trism** /-sentrizəm/ *n.*

phal·loc·ra·cy /faˈläkrəsē/ ▸*n.* (*pl.* **-cies**) a society or system that is dominated by men and in which the male sex is thought superior. ▹1970s: from Greek *phallos* 'phallus' + **-CRACY.** **—phal·lo·crat·ic** /ˌfaləˈkratik/ *adj.*

phal·lo·plas·ty /ˈfaləˌplastē/ ▸*n.* plastic surgery performed to construct, repair, or enlarge the penis. ▹late 19th cent.: from Greek *phallos* 'phallus' + **-PLASTY.**

phal·lus /ˈfaləs/ ▸*n.* (*pl.* **phal·li** /ˈfalī/ or **phal·lus·es**) a penis, esp. when erect (typically used with reference to male potency or dominance). ■ an image or representation of an erect penis, typically symbolizing fertility or potency. ▹early 17th cent.: via late Latin from Greek *phallos.* **—phal·li·cism** /-ˌsizəm/ *n.* **—phal·lism** /ˈfalizəm/ *n.*

phan·er·o·gam /ˈfanərəˌgam/ ▸*n. Botany* old-fashioned term for **SPERMATOPHYTE.** ▹mid 19th cent.: from French *phanérogame*, from Greek *phaneros* 'visible' + *gamos* 'marriage.' **—phan·er·o·gam·ic** /ˌfanərəˈgamik/ *adj.* **—phan·er·og·a·mous** /ˌfanəˈrägəməs/ *adj.*

Phan·er·o·zo·ic /ˌfanərəˈzōik/ ▸*adj. Geology* of, relating to, or denoting the eon covering the whole of time since the beginning of the Cambrian period, and comprising the Paleozoic, Mesozoic, and Cenozoic eras. Compare with **CRYPTOZOIC.** ■ [as *n.*] (**the Phanerozoic**) the Phanerozic eon or the system of rocks deposited during it.

The Phanerozoic began about 570 million years ago and covers the period in which rocks contain evidence of abundant life in the form of macroscopic mineralized fossils.

▹late 19th cent.: from Greek *phaneros* 'visible, evident' + *zōion* 'animal' + **-IC.**

phan·ta·size ▸*v.* variant spelling of **FANTASIZE** (restricted to archaic uses or, in modern use, to the fields of psychology and psychiatry).

phan·tasm /ˈfantazəm/ ▸*n. poetic/literary* a figment of the imagination; an illusion or apparition: *the cart seemed to glide like a terrible phantasm.* ■ *archaic* an illusory likeness of something: *every phantasm of a hope was quickly nullified.* ▹Middle English (in the sense 'deceptive appearance'): from Old French *fantasme*, via Latin from Greek *phantasma*, from *phantazein* 'make visible,' from *phainein* 'to show.' The change from *f-* to *ph-* in the 16th cent. was influenced by the Latin spelling. **—phan·tas·mal** /fanˈtazməl/ *adj.* **—phan·tas·mic** /fanˈtazmik/ *adj.*

phan·tas·ma·go·ri·a /fanˌtazməˈgôrēə/ ▸*n.* a sequence of real or imaginary images like that seen in a dream: *what happened next was a phantasmagoria of horror and mystery.* ▹early 19th cent. (originally the name of a London exhibition (1802) of optical illusions produced chiefly by magic lantern): probably from French *fantasmagorie*, from *fantasme* 'phantasm' + a fanciful suffix. **—phan·tas·ma·gor·ic** /-gôrik/ *adj.* **—phan·tas·ma·gor·i·cal** /gôrikəl/ *adj.*

phan·tast ▸*n.* variant spelling of **FANTAST.**

phan·ta·sy ▸*n.* variant spelling of **FANTASY** (restricted to archaic uses or, in modern use, to the fields of psychology and psychiatry).

phan·tom /ˈfantəm/ ▸*n.* a ghost: *a phantom who haunts lonely roads* | *figurative the centrist and conservative parties were mere phantoms in 1943* | [as *adj.*] *a phantom ship.* ■ a figment of the imagination: *he tried to clear the phantoms from his head and grasp reality* | [as *adj.*] *the women suffered from phantom pain that no physician could ever find.* ■ [as *adj.*] denoting a financial arrangement or transaction that has been invented for fraudulent purposes but that does not really exist: *he diverted an estimated $1,500,000 into "phantom" bank accounts.* ■ [as *adj.*] denoting something, esp. something illegal, that is done by an unknown person: *a series of phantom withdrawals from cash machines.* ▹Middle English (also in the sense 'illusion, delusion'): from Old French *fantosme*, based on Greek *phantasma* (see PHANTASM).

phan·tom limb ▸*n.* a sensation experienced by someone who has had a limb amputated that the limb is still there.

phar. (also **Phar.**) ▸*abbr.* ■ pharmaceutical. ■ pharmacology. ■ pharmacopoeia. ■ pharmacy.

Phar·aoh /ˈfarˌō; ˈfe(ə)rˌō; ˈfāˌrō/ (also **phar·aoh**) ▸*n.* a ruler in ancient Egypt. ▷Middle English: via ecclesiastical Latin from Greek *Pharaō*, from Hebrew *par'ōh*, from Egyptian *pr-'o* 'great house.' **—phar·a·on·ic** /ˌfarāˈnik; ˌfe(ə)r-/ *adj.*

phar·aoh ant (also **pharaoh's ant**) ▸*n.* a small red or yellowish African ant that has established itself worldwide, living as a pest in heated buildings. • *Monomorium pharaonis*, family Formicidae. ▷so named because such ants were believed (erroneously) to be one of the plagues of ancient Egypt.

Phar·aoh hound ▸*n.* a hunting dog of a short-coated tan-colored breed with large, pointed ears. ▷1960s: so named because the breed is said to have been first introduced to Malta and Gozo (a Maltese island) by Phoenician sailors.

Phar.B. ▸*abbr.* Bachelor of Pharmacy.

Phar.D. ▸*abbr.* Doctor of Pharmacy.

Phar·i·see /ˈfarəsē/ ▸*n.* a member of an ancient Jewish sect, distinguished by strict observance of the traditional and written law, and commonly held to have pretensions to superior sanctity. ■ a self-righteous person; a hypocrite.

The Pharisees are mentioned only by Josephus and in the New Testament. Unlike the Sadducees, who tried to apply Mosaic law strictly, the Pharisees allowed some freedom of interpretation. Although in the Gospels they are represented as the chief opponents of Jesus, they seem to have been less hostile than the Sadducees to the nascent Church, with which they shared belief in the Resurrection.

▷Old English *fariseus*, via ecclesiastical Latin from Greek *Pharisaios*, from Aramaic *prīšayyā* 'separated ones' (related to Hebrew *pārūš* 'separated'). **—Phar·i·sa·ic** /ˌfarəˈsāik/ *adj.* **—Phar·i·sa·i·cal** /ˌfarəˈsāikəl/ *adj.* **—Phar·i·sa·ism** /-sāˌizəm/ *n.*

pharm. ▸*abbr.* ■ pharmaceutical. ■ pharmacology. ■ pharmacopoeia. ■ pharmacy.

Phar.M. ▸*abbr.* Master of Pharmacy.

phar·ma·ceu·ti·cal /ˌfärməˈsōōtikəl/ ▸*adj.* of or relating to medicinal drugs, or their preparation, use, or sale.
▸*n.* (usu. **pharmaceuticals**) a compound manufactured for use as a medicinal drug. ■ (**pharmaceuticals**) companies manufacturing medicinal drugs. ▷mid 17th cent.: via late Latin from Greek *pharmakeutikos* (from *pharmakeutēs* 'druggist,' from *pharmakon* 'drug') + -AL. **—phar·ma·ceu·ti·cal·ly** /-(ə)lē/ *adv.* **—phar·ma·ceu·tics** /-sōōtiks/ *n.*

phar·ma·cist /ˈfärməsist/ ▸*n.* a person who is professionally qualified to prepare and dispense medicinal drugs.

pharmaco- ▸*comb. form* relating to drugs: *pharmacogenetics.* ▷from Greek *pharmakon* 'drug, medicine.'

phar·ma·co·dy·nam·ics /ˌfärməkōdīˈnamiks/ ▸*plural n.* [treated as *sing.*] the branch of pharmacology concerned with the effects of drugs and the mechanism of their action. **—phar·ma·co·dy·nam·ic** /-mik/ *adj.*

phar·ma·co·ge·net·ics /ˌfärməkōjəˈnetiks/ ▸*plural n.* [treated as *sing.*] the branch of pharmacology concerned with the effect of genetic factors on reactions to drugs.

phar·ma·cog·no·sy /ˌfärməˈkägnəsē/ ▸*n.* the branch of knowledge concerned with medicinal drugs obtained from plants or other natural sources. ▷mid 19th cent.: from PHARMACO- 'of drugs' + *gnōsis* 'knowledge.' **—phar·ma·cog·no·sist** /-sist/ *n.*

phar·ma·co·ki·net·ics /ˌfärməkōkiˈnetiks/ ▸*plural n.* [treated as *sing.*] the branch of pharmacology concerned with the movement of drugs within the body. **—phar·ma·co·ki·net·ic** /-tik/ *adj.*

phar·ma·col·o·gy /ˌfärməˈkäləjē/ ▸*n.* the branch of medicine concerned with the uses, effects, and modes of action of drugs. ▷early 18th cent.: from modern Latin *pharmacologia*, from Greek *pharmakon* 'drug.' **—phar·ma·co·log·ic** /ˌfärməkəˈläjik/ *adj.* **—phar·ma·co·log·i·cal** /-ˈläjikəl/ *adj.* **—phar·ma·co·log·i·cal·ly** *adv.* **—phar·ma·col·o·gist** /-ˈkäləjist/ *n.*

phar·ma·co·pe·ia /ˌfärməkəˈpēə/ (also **phar·ma·co·poe·ia**) ▸*n.* a book, esp. an official publication, containing a list of medicinal drugs with their effects and directions for their use. ■ a stock of medicinal drugs. ▷early 17th cent.: modern Latin, from Greek *pharmakopoiia* 'art of preparing drugs,' based on *pharmakon* 'drug' + *-poios* 'making.'

phar·ma·co·phore /ˈfärməkəˌfôr/ ▸*n.* a part of a molecular structure that is responsible for a particular biological or pharmacological interaction that it undergoes.

phar·ma·co·ther·a·py /ˌfärməkōˈTHerəpē/ ▸*n.* medical treatment by means of drugs.

phar·ma·cy /ˈfärməsē/ ▸*n.* (*pl.* **-cies**) a store where medicinal drugs are dispensed and sold. ■ the science or practice of the preparation and dispensing of medicinal drugs. ▷late Middle English (denoting the administration of drugs): from Old French *farmacie*, via medieval Latin from Greek *pharmakeia* 'practice of the druggist,' based on *pharmakon* 'drug.'

Pha·ros /ˈfe(ə)rōs/ a lighthouse, often considered one of the Seven Wonders of the World, erected by Ptolemy II (308–246 BC) in *c.*280 BC on the island of Pharos, off the coast of Alexandria. ■ [as *n.*] (**pharos**) a lighthouse or a beacon to guide sailors.

Pharr /fär/ a city in southern Texas, in the Rio Grande valley; pop. 32,921.

pha·ryn·ge·al /fəˈrinj(ē)əl; ˌfarinˈjēəl/ ▸*adj.* of or relating to the pharynx. ■ *Phonetics* (of a speech sound) produced by articulating the root of the tongue with the pharynx, a feature of certain consonants in Arabic, for example.
▸*n.* *Phonetics* a pharyngeal consonant. ▷early 19th cent.: from modern Latin *pharyngeus* (from Greek *pharunx, pharung-* 'throat') + -AL.

pha·ryn·ge·al·ize /fəˈrinjēəˌlīz/ ▸*v.* [*trans.*] *Phonetics* articulate (a speech sound) with constriction of the pharynx. **—pha·ryn·ge·al·i·za·tion** /fəˈrinjēəliˈzāSHən/ *n.*

phar·yn·gi·tis /ˌfarinˈjītis/ ▸*n.* *Medicine* inflammation of the pharynx, causing a sore throat.

pharyngo- ▸*comb. form* of or relating to the pharynx: *pharyngotomy.* ▷from modern Latin *pharynx, pharyng.*

phar·ynx /ˈfariNGks/ ▸*n.* (*pl.* **pha·ryn·ges** /fəˈrinjēz/ or **phar·ynx·es**) *Anatomy & Zoology* the membrane-lined cavity behind the nose and mouth, connecting them to the esophagus. ■ *Zoology* the part of the alimentary canal immediately behind the mouth in invertebrates. ▷late 17th cent.: modern Latin, from Greek *pharunx, pharung-.*

phase /fāz/ ▸*n.* **1** a distinct period or stage in a process of change or forming part of something's development: *the final phases of the war* | [as *adj.*] *phase two of the development is in progress.* ■ a stage in a person's psychological development, esp. a period of temporary unhappiness or difficulty during adolescence or a particular stage during childhood: *you are not obsessed, but you are* ***going through a phase.*** ■ each of the aspects of the moon or a planet, according to the amount of its illumination, esp. the new moon, the first quarter, the full moon, and the last quarter. ■ *Riding* each of the separate events in an eventing competition. **2** *Zoology* a genetic or seasonal variety of an animal's coloration. ■ a stage in the life cycle or annual cycle of an animal. **3** *Chemistry* a distinct and homogeneous form of matter (i.e., a particular solid, liquid, or gas) separated by its surface from other forms. **4** *Physics* the relationship in time between the successive states or cycles of an oscillating or repeating system (such as an alternating electric current or a light or sound wave) and either a fixed reference point or the states or cycles of another system with which it may or may not be in synchrony.
▸*v.* [*trans.*] (usu. **be phased**) **1** carry out (something) in gradual stages: *the work is being phased over a number of years* | [as *adj.*] (**phased**) *a phased withdrawal of troops.* ■ (**phase something in/out**) introduce into (or withdraw from) use in gradual stages: *our armed forces policy was to be phased in over 10 years.* **2** *Physics* adjust the phase of (something), esp. so as to synchronize it with something else. ▷early 19th cent. (denoting each aspect of the moon): from French *phase*, based on Greek *phasis* 'appearance,' from the base of *phainein* 'to show.'
▸*PHRASE* □ **in** (or **out of**) **phase** being or happening in (or out of) synchrony or harmony: *the cabling work should be carried out* ***in phase with*** *the building work.*

phase an·gle ▸*n.* *Physics* an angle representing a difference in phase, 360 degrees (2π radians) corresponding to one complete cycle. ■ *Astronomy* the angle between the lines joining a given planet to the sun and to the earth.

phase con·trast ▸*n.* the technique in microscopy of introducing a phase difference between parts of the light supplied by the condenser so as to enhance the outlines of the sample, or the boundaries between parts differing in optical density.

phase di·a·gram ▸*n.* *Chemistry* a diagram representing the limits of stability of the various phases in a chemical system at equilibrium, with respect to variables such as composition and temperature.

phase-lock ▸*v.* [*trans.*] *Electronics* fix the frequency of (an oscillator or a laser) relative to a stable oscillator of lower frequency by a method that utilizes a correction signal derived from the phase difference generated by any shift in the frequency.

phase mod·u·la·tion /ˌmäjəˈlāSHən/ ▸*n.* *Electronics* variation of the phase of a radio or other wave as a means of carrying information such as an audio signal.

phase·out /ˈfāˌzout/ ▸*n.* an act of discontinuing a process, project, or service in phases.

phas·er / ˈfāzər/ ▸*n.* **1** an instrument that alters a sound signal by phasing it. **2** (in science fiction) a weapon that delivers a beam that can stun or annihilate.

phase rule ▸*n.* *Chemistry* a rule relating the possible numbers of phases, constituents, and degrees of freedom in a chemical system.

phase shift ▸*n.* *Physics* a change in the phase of a waveform.

phase space ▸*n.* *Physics* a multidimensional space in which each axis corresponds to one of the coordinates required to specify the state of a physical system, all the coordinates being thus represented so that a point in the space corresponds to a state of the system.

pha·sic /ˈfāzik/ ▸*adj.* of or relating to a phase or phases. ■ *chiefly Physiology* characterized by occurrence in phases rather than continuously: *phasic and tonic stretch reflexes.*

phas·ing /ˈfāziNG/ ▸*n.* the relationship between the timing of two or more events, or the adjustment of this relationship: *graphical techniques were used to investigate the phasing of traffic lights.* ■ the modification of the sound signal from an electric guitar or other electronic instrument by introducing a phase shift into either of two copies of it and then recombining them. ■ the action of dividing a large task or process into several stages: *the phasing of the overall project.*

Phas·mi·da /ˈfazmidə/ **1** *Entomology* an order of insects that comprises the stick insects and leaf insects. They have very long bodies that resemble twigs or leaves. **2** *Zoology* a class of nematodes that includes the parasitic hookworms and roundworms. Also called SECERNENTEA. ▷modern Latin (plural), from Latin *phasma* 'apparition,' from Greek. **—phas·mid** *n.* & *adj.*

pha·sor /ˈfāzər/ ▸*n.* *Physics* a line used to represent a complex electrical quantity as a vector. ▷1940s: from PHASE, on the pattern of *vector.*

phat /fat/ ▸*adj.* *informal* excellent: *a phat and funky sound.* ▷1970s (originally used to describe a woman, in the sense 'sexy, attractive'): of uncertain origin.

phat·ic /ˈfatik/ ▸*adj.* denoting or relating to language used for general purposes of social interaction, rather than to convey information or ask questions. Utterances such as *hello, how are you?* and *nice morning, isn't it?* are phatic. ▷1920s: from Greek *phatos* 'spoken' or *phatikos* 'affirming.'

Ph.B ▸*abbr.* Bachelor of Philosophy. ▷Latin *Philosophiae Baccalaureus.*

Ph.C. ▸*abbr.* Pharmaceutical Chemist.

PhD ▸*abbr.* Doctor of Philosophy. ▷from Latin *philosophiae doctor.*

pheas·ant /ˈfezənt/ ▸*n.* a large long-tailed game bird native to Asia, the male of which typically has very showy plumage. • Family Phasianidae: several genera and many species, in particular the **ring-necked**

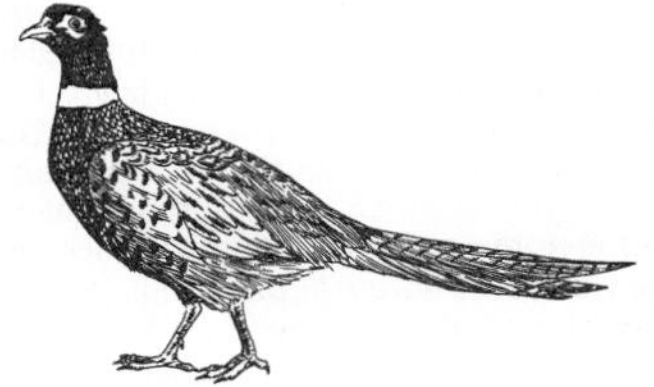

ring-necked pheasant

Pronunciation Key ə *ago;* ər *over;* ˈə or ˌə *up;* ˈər or ˌər *fur;* a *hat;* ā *rate;* ä *car;* CH *chew;* e *let;* ē *see;* e(ə)r *air;* i *fit;* ī *by;* i(ə)r *ear;* NG *sing;* ō *go;* ô *for;* oi *boy;* ŏŏ *good;* ōō *goo;* ou *out;* SH *she;* TH *thin;* T͟H *then;* (h)w *why;* ZH *vision*

pheasant (*Phasianus colchicus*), which has been widely introduced for shooting. ▷Middle English: from Old French *fesan*, via Latin from Greek *phasianos* '(bird) of *Phasis*,' the name of a river in the Caucasus, from which the bird is said to have spread westward.

Phei·dip·pi·des /fī'dipi,dēz/ (5th century BC), Athenian messenger. He was sent to Sparta to ask for help after the Persian landing at Marathon in 490 and is said to have covered the 150 miles (250 km) in two days on foot.

phen- ▶*comb. form* variant spelling of PHENO- shortened before a vowel (as in *phenacetin*).

phe·nac·e·tin /fə'nasitən/ ▶*n. Medicine* a synthetic compound used as a painkilling and antipyretic drug. ▷late 19th cent.: from PHENO- + *acet(yl)* + -IN[1].

phe·nan·threne /fə'nanTHrēn/ ▶*n. Chemistry* a crystalline hydrocarbon present in coal tar, used esp. in making dyes and synthetic drugs. • A tricyclic compound; chem. formula: $C_{14}H_{10}$.

phen·cy·cli·dine /fen'sikli,dēn; -'sik-/ (abbr.: **PCP**) ▶*n.* a synthetic compound derived from piperidine, used as a veterinary anesthetic and in hallucinogenic drugs such as angel dust. ▷1950s: from PHENO- + CYCLO- + a shortened form of PIPERIDINE.

Phe·nix Cit·y /'fēniks/ a city in eastern Alabama, on the west bank of the Chattahoochee River, across from Columbus in Georgia; pop. 28,265.

pheno- (also **phen-** before a vowel) ▶*comb. form* **1** *Chemistry* derived from benzene: *phenobarbital.* **2** showing: *phenotype.* ▷sense 1 from French *phényle* 'phenyl,' from Greek *phaino-* 'shining'; both senses from Greek *phainein* 'to show.'

phe·no·bar·bi·tal /,fēnō'bärbi,tôl/ ▶*n. Medicine* a narcotic and sedative barbiturate drug used chiefly to treat epilepsy.

phe·no·cop·y /'fēnə,käpē/ ▶*n.* (*pl.* **-cop·ies**) *Genetics* an individual showing features characteristic of a genotype other than its own, but produced environmentally rather than genetically.

phe·no·cryst /'fēnə,krist/ ▶*n. Geology* a large or conspicuous crystal in a porphyritic rock, distinct from the groundmass. ▷late 19th cent.: from French *phénocryste*, from Greek *phainein* 'to show' + *krustallos* 'crystal.'

phe·nol /'fē,nôl; -,näl/ ▶*n. Chemistry* a mildly acidic toxic white crystalline solid obtained from coal tar and used in chemical manufacture, and in dilute form (under the name **carbolic**) as a disinfectant. • Chem. formula: C_6H_5OH. ■ any compound with a hydroxyl group linked directly to a benzene ring. ▷mid 19th cent.: from French *phénole*, based on *phène* 'benzene.' **—phe·no·lic** /fi'nälik/ *adj.*

phe·nol·o·gy /fi'näləjē/ ▶*n.* the study of cyclic and seasonal natural phenomena, esp. in relation to climate and plant and animal life. ▷late 19th cent.: from PHENOMENON + -LOGY. **—phe·no·log·i·cal** /,fēnə'läjikəl/ *adj.*

phe·nol·phthal·ein /,fēnəl'THalē(i)n/ ▶*n. Chemistry* a colorless crystalline solid (pink in alkaline solution) used as an acid–base indicator and medicinally as a laxative. • Chem. formula: $C_{20}H_{14}O_4$. ▷late 19th cent.: from PHENOL + *-phthal-* (from NAPHTHALENE) + -IN[1].

phe·nol red ▶*n. Chemistry* a red dye that is used as a pH indicator and (in medicine) injected in testing kidney function.

phe·nom /'fē,näm; fi'näm/ ▶*n. informal* a person who is outstandingly talented or admired; a star. ▷late 19th cent.: abbreviation of PHENOMENON.

phe·nom·e·na /fə'nämənə/ ▶ plural form of PHENOMENON.

phe·nom·e·nal /fə'nämənəl/ ▶*adj.* **1** very remarkable; extraordinary: *the town expanded at a phenomenal rate.* **2** perceptible by the senses or through immediate experience: *the phenomenal world.* **—phe·nom·e·nal·ize** /,iz/ *v.* (in sense 2). **—phe·nom·e·nal·ly** *adv.*

phe·nom·e·nal·ism /fə'nämənəl,izəm/ ▶*n. Philosophy* the doctrine that human knowledge is confined to or founded on the realities or appearances presented to the senses. **—phe·nom·e·nal·ist** *n.* & *adj.* **—phe·nom·e·nal·is·tic** /-,nämənəl'istik/ *adj.*

phe·nom·e·nol·o·gy /fi,nämə'näləjē/ ▶*n. Philosophy* the science of phenomena as distinct from that of the nature of being. ■ an approach that concentrates on the study of consciousness and the objects of direct experience. **—phe·nom·e·no·log·i·cal** /-,nämənə'läjikəl/ *adj.* **—phe·nom·e·no·log·i·cal·ly** /-,nämənə'läjik(ə)lē/ *adv.* **—phe·nom·e·nol·o·gist** /-'näləjist/ *n.*

phe·nom·e·non /fə'nämə,nän; -nən/ ▶*n.* (*pl.* **-na** /-nə/) **1** a fact or situation that is observed to exist or happen, esp. one whose cause or explanation is in question: *glaciers are unique and interesting natural phenomena.* ■ a remarkable person, thing, or event. **2** *Philosophy* the object of a person's perception; what the senses or the mind notice. ▷late 16th cent.: via late Latin from Greek *phainomenon* 'thing appearing to view,' based on *phainein* 'to show.'

USAGE The word **phenomenon** comes from Greek, and its plural form is **phenomena**, as in *these phenomena are not fully understood.* It is a mistake to treat **phenomena** as if it were a singular form, as in *this is a strange* ***phenomena***.

phe·no·thi·a·zine /fēnə'THīə,zēn/ ▶*n. Chemistry* a synthetic compound that is used in veterinary medicine to treat parasitic infestations of animals. • A heterocyclic compound; chem. formula: $C_{12}H_9NS$. ■ *Psychiatry* any of a group of derivatives of this compound with tranquilizing properties, used as tranquilizers in the treatment of mental illness.

phe·no·type /'fēnə,tīp/ ▶*n. Biology* the set of observable characteristics of an individual resulting from the interaction of its genotype with the environment. ▷early 20th cent.: from German *Phaenotypus* (see PHENO-, TYPE). **—phe·no·typ·ic** /,fēnə'tipik/ *adj.* **—phe·no·typ·i·cal** /,fēnə'tipikəl/ *adj.* **—phe·no·typ·i·cal·ly** /,fēnə'tipik(ə)lē/ *adv.*

phen·ter·mine /'fentər,mēn/ ▶*n. Medicine* a prescription appetite-suppressant drug that binds to receptors on the hypothalmus, and is one of the pair of drugs known as fen-phen. It is still prescribed independently for obesity, following the withdrawal of fenfluramine, the other component of fen-phen.

phen·tol·a·mine /fen'tälə,mēn/ ▶*n. Medicine* a synthetic compound used as a vasodilator, esp. in certain cases of hypertension. ▷1950s: from PHEN- + *tol(yl)* (an isomeric cyclic radical derived from toluene) + AMINE.

phen·yl /'fenəl; 'fē-/ ▶*n.* [as *adj.*] *Chemistry* of or denoting the radical $-C_6H_5$, derived from benzene by removal of a hydrogen atom: *a phenyl group.* ▷mid 19th cent.: from French *phényle*, from Greek *phaino-* 'shining' (because first used in names of compounds denoting byproducts of the manufacture of gas used for illumination).

phen·yl·al·a·nine /,fenəl'alə,nēn; ,fēnəl-/ ▶*n. Biochemistry* an amino acid widely distributed in plant proteins. It is an essential nutrient in the diet of vertebrates. • Chem. formula: $C_6H_5CH_2CH(NH_2)COOH$.

phen·yl·bu·ta·zone /,fenəl'byōōtə,zōn; ,fēnəl-/ ▶*n.* a synthetic compound used as an analgesic drug, esp. in the treatment of horses. ▷1950s: from PHENYL + *but(yl)* + AZO- + -ONE.

phen·yl·eph·rine /,fēnəl'efrin; ,fenəl-/ ▶*n. Medicine* a synthetic compound related to epinephrine, used as a vasoconstrictor and nasal decongestant. ▷1940s: from PHENYL + a contraction of EPINEPHRINE.

phen·yl·ke·to·nu·ri·a /,fenl,kētō'n(y)ōōrēə; ,fēnl-/ (abbr.: **PKU**) ▶*n. Medicine* an inherited inability to metabolize phenylalanine that causes brain and nerve damage if untreated.

phen·y·to·in /,feni'tō-in; fə'nitō-in/ ▶*n. Medicine* a synthetic compound related to hydantoin, used as an anticonvulsant in the treatment of epilepsy. ▷1940s: blend of PHENYL and HYDANTOIN.

phe·o·chro·mo·cy·to·ma /,fēō,krōməsī'tōmə/ ▶*n.* (*pl.* **-to·mas** or **-to·ma·ta** /-'tōmətə/) *Medicine* a small vascular tumor of the adrenal medulla, causing irregular secretion of epinephrine and norepinephrine, leading to attacks of raised blood pressure, palpitations, and headache. ▷1920s: from *pheochrome*, another term for chromaffin (from Greek *phaios* 'dusky' + *khrōma* 'color'), + -CYTE.

pher·o·mone /'ferə,mōn/ ▶*n. Zoology* a chemical substance produced and released into the environment by an animal, esp. a mammal or an insect, affecting the behavior or physiology of others of its species. ▷1950s: from Greek *pherein* 'convey' + HORMONE. **—pher·o·mo·nal** /ferə'mōnl/ *adj.*

phew /fyōō/ ▶*exclam. informal* expressing a strong reaction of relief: *phew, what a year!* ▷early 17th cent.: imitative of puffing.

Ph.G. ▶*abbr.* Graduate in Pharmacy.

phi /fī/ ▶*n.* the twenty-first letter of the Greek alphabet (Φ, φ), transliterated as 'ph.' ■ (**Phi**) [followed by Latin genitive] *Astronomy* the twenty-first star in a constellation: *Phi Eridani.*
▶*symbol* ■ (φ) a plane angle. ■ (φ) a polar coordinate. Often coupled with θ.

phi·al /'fīəl/ ▶*n.* another term for VIAL. ▷Middle English: from Old French *fiole*, via Latin from Greek *phialē*, denoting a broad flat container.

Phi Be·ta Kap·pa /'fī 'bātə 'kapə/ ▶*n.* an honorary society of college and university undergraduates and some graduates to which members are elected on the basis of high academic achievement. ■ a member of this society. ▷from the initial letters of a Greek motto *philosophia biou kubernētēs* 'philosophy is the guide to life.'

Phid·i·as /'fidēəs/ (5th century BC), Athenian sculptor. He is noted for the Elgin marbles and his colossal statue of Zeus at Olympia (*c.*430), which was one of the Seven Wonders of the Ancient World.

Phil. ▶*abbr.* ■ *Bible* Philippians. ■ *Bible* Philemon. ■ Philadelphia. ■ Philharmonic. ■ Philippine.

phil- ▶*comb. form* variant spelling of PHILO- shortened before a vowel or *h* (as in *philanthrope*, *philharmonic*).

-phil ▶*comb. form* having a chemical affinity for a substance: *acidophil* | *neutrophil.* ▷see -PHILE.

Phil·a·del·phi·a /,filə'delfēə/ a city in Pennsylvania, on the Delaware River; pop. 1,517,550. Established as a Quaker colony by William Penn and others in 1681, it was the site in 1776 of the signing of the Declaration of Independence and in 1787 of the adoption of the Constitution of the U.S. ▷from Greek *philadelphia* 'brotherly love.' **—Phil·a·del·phi·an** *n.* & *adj.*

Phil·a·del·phi·a cheese steak (also **Phil·ly cheese steak**) ▶*n.* see CHEESE STEAK.

Phil·a·del·phi·a chro·mo·some ▶*n. Genetics* an abnormal small chromosome sometimes found in the leukocytes of leukemia patients.

Phil·a·del·phi·a law·yer ▶*n.* a very shrewd lawyer who is expert in the exploitation of legal technicalities. ▷with reference to Andrew Hamilton of Philadelphia, who successfully defended John Zenger (1735), an American journalist and publisher, from libel charges.

phil·a·del·phus /,filə'delfəs/ ▶*n.* a mock orange. ▷late 18th cent.: modern Latin (adopted by Linnaeus as a genus name), from Greek *philadelphos* 'loving one's brother.'

phi·lan·der /fə'landər/ ▶*v.* [*intrans.*] (of a man) readily or frequently enter into casual sexual relationships with women: *they accepted that their husbands would philander with other women.* ▷mid 18th cent.: from the earlier noun *philander* 'man, husband,' often used in literature as the given name of a lover, from Greek *philandros* 'fond of men,' from *philein* 'to love' + *anēr* 'man.' **—phi·lan·der·er** *n.*

phil·an·thrope /'filən,THrōp/ ▶*n.* archaic term for PHILANTHROPIST. ▷mid 18th cent.: from Greek *philanthrōpos*, from *philein* 'to love' + *anthrōpos* 'human being.'

phil·an·throp·ic /,filən'THräpik/ ▶*adj.* (of a person or organization) seeking to promote the welfare of others, esp. by donating money to good causes; generous and benevolent: *they receive financial support from philanthropic bodies.* ▷late 18th cent.: from French *philanthropique*, from Greek *philanthrōpos* 'man-loving' (see PHILANTHROPE). **—phil·an·throp·i·cal·ly** /-(ə)lē/ *adv.*

phi·lan·thro·pist /fə'lanTHrəpist/ ▶*n.* a person who seeks to promote the welfare of others, esp. by the generous donation of money to good causes.

phi·lan·thro·py /fə'lanTHrəpē/ ▶*n.* the desire to promote the welfare of others, expressed esp. by the generous donation of money to good causes. ■ a philanthropic institution; a charity. ▷early 17th cent.: via late Latin from Greek *philanthrōpia*, from *philanthrōpos* 'man-loving' (see PHILANTHROPE). **—phi·lan·thro·pism** /-pizəm/ *n.* **—phi·lan·thro·pize** /-piz/ *v.*

phi·lat·e·ly /fə'latl-ē/ ▶*n.* the collection and study of postage stamps. ▷mid 19th cent.: from French *philatélie*, from *philo-* 'loving' + Greek *ateleia* 'exemption from payment' (from *a-* 'not' + *telos* 'toll, tax'), used to mean a franking mark or postage stamp exempting the recipient from payment. **—phil·a·tel·ic** /,filə'telik/ *adj.* **—phil·a·tel·i·cal·ly** /,filə'telik(ə)lē/ *adv.* **—phi·lat·e·list** /-ist/ *n.*

-phile ▶*comb. form* denoting fondness for a specified thing: *bibliophile* | *Francophile.* ▷from Greek *philos* 'loving.'

Philem. ▶*abbr. Bible* Philemon.

Phi·le·mon[1] /fə'lēmən; fī-/ *Greek Mythology* a good, old countryman living with his wife Baucis in Phrygia who offered hospitality to Zeus and Hermes when the two gods came to earth, without revealing their identities, to test people's piety. Philemon and Baucis were subsequently saved from a flood that covered the district.

Phi·le·mon[2] a book of the New Testament, an epistle

of St. Paul to a well-to-do Christian living probably at Colossae in Phrygia.

phil·har·mon·ic /ˌfilərˈmänik; ˌfilhär-/ ▸*adj.* devoted to music (chiefly used in the names of orchestras): *the Vienna Philharmonic Orchestra.*

▸*n.* a philharmonic orchestra or the society that sponsors it (chiefly used in names): *the tireless musicians of the Philharmonic.* ▷mid 18th cent.: from French *philharmonique*, from Italian *filarmonico* 'loving harmony' (see **PHIL-, HARMONIC**).

phil·hel·lene /filˈhelēn/ ▸*n.* a lover of Greece and Greek culture: *a romantic philhellene.* ■ *historical* a supporter of Greek independence. ▷early 19th cent.: from Greek *philellēn* 'loving the Greeks' (see **PHIL-, HELLENE**). —**phil·hel·len·ic** /ˌfilheˈlenik/ *adj.* —**phil·hel·len·ism** /filˈheləˌnizəm/ *n.*

-philia ▸*comb. form* denoting fondness, esp. an abnormal love for a specified thing: *pedophilia.* ■ denoting undue inclination: *spasmophilia.* ▷from Greek *philia* 'fondness.'

-philiac ▸*comb. form* in nouns and adjectives corresponding to nouns ending in *-philia* (such as *hemophiliac* coresponding to *hemophilia*).

phil·i·beg ▸*n.* variant spelling of **FILIBEG**.

-philic ▸*comb. form* in adjectives corresponding to nouns ending in *-philia* (such as *paraphilic* corresponding to *paraphilia*).

Phil·ip[1] /ˈfilip/ the name of five kings of ancient Macedonia, notably: ■ **Philip II** (382–336 BC), father of Alexander the Great; reigned 359–336; known as **Philip II of Macedon**. He unified and expanded ancient Macedonia. ■ **Philip V** (238–179 BC), reigned 221–179. His expansionist policies led to a series of confrontations with Rome, culminating in his defeat in 197 and his loss of control over Greece.

Phil·ip[2] the name of six kings of France: ■ **Philip I** (1052–1108), reigned 1059–1108. ■ **Philip II** (1165–1223), son of Louis VII; reigned 1180–1223; known as **Philip Augustus**. After mounting a series of campaigns against the English kings Henry II, Richard I, and John, Philip succeeded in regaining Normandy in 1204, Anjou in 1204, and most of Poitou in 1204–05. ■ **Philip III** (1245–1285), reigned 1270–85; known as **Philip the Bold**. ■ **Philip IV** (1268–1314), son of Philip III; reigned 1285–1314; known as **Philip the Fair**. He continued to extend French dominions, waging wars with England from 1294 until 1303 and with Flanders from 1302 until 05). ■ **Philip V** (1293–1322), reigned 1316–1322; known as **Philip the Tall**. ■ **Philip VI** (1293–1350), reigned 1328–50; known as **Philip of Valois**. The founder of the Valois dynasty, Philip came to the throne on the death of Charles IV, whose only child was a girl and barred from ruling. His claim was challenged by Edward III of England; the dispute developed into the Hundred Years War.

Phil·ip[3] the name of five kings of Spain: ■ **Philip I** (1478–1506), reigned 1504–6; known as **Philip the Handsome**. Son of the Holy Roman Emperor Maximilian I, in 1496 Philip married the infanta Joanna, daughter of Ferdinand of Aragon and Isabella of Castile. After Isabella's death he ruled Castile jointly with Joanna, establishing the Habsburgs as the ruling dynasty in Spain. ■ **Philip II** (1527–98), son of Charles I (Holy Roman Emperor Charles V); reigned 1556–98. Philip came to the throne following his father's abdication. His reign was dominated by an anti-Protestant crusade that exhausted the Spanish economy. His Armada against England (1588) ended in defeat. ■ **Philip III** (1578–1621), reigned 1598–1621. ■ **Philip IV** (1605–1665), reigned 1621–65. ■ **Philip V** (1683–1746), grandson of Louis XIV; reigned 1700–24 and 1724–46. The selection of Philip as successor to Charles II, and Louis XIV's insistence that Philip remain an heir to the French throne, gave rise to the War of the Spanish Succession (1701–14). In 1724, Philip abdicated in favor of his son Louis I, but returned to the throne following Louis's death.

Phil·ip[4], King (c.1639–1676) chief of the Wampanoag Indians; Indian name Metacomet; the son of Massasoit. He waged King Philip's War 1675–76 on the New England colonists because they had taken some of his land and had killed three of his warriors. His defeat and death in battle ended Indian resistance in New England.

Phil·ip, Prince, Duke of Edinburgh (1921–), husband of Elizabeth II. The son of Prince Andrew of Greece and Denmark, he married Princess Elizabeth in 1947; on the eve of his marriage he was created Duke of Edinburgh.

Phil·ip, St.[1], an apostle. He is commemorated with St. James the Less on May 1.

Phil·ip, St.[2], deacon of the early Christian Church; known as **St. Philip the Evangelist**. He was one of seven deacons appointed to superintend the secular business of the Church at Jerusalem (Acts 6:5–6). Feast day, June 6.

Phil·ip II of Mac·e·don, Philip II of Macedonia (see **PHILIP**[1]).

Phil·ip Au·gus·tus, Philip II of France (see **PHILIP**[2]).

Phil·ip of Va·lois, Philip VI of France (see **PHILIP**[2]).

Phi·lip·pi /fəˈliˌpī; ˈfilə-/ a city in ancient Macedonia, close to the Aegean coast in northeastern Greece, near the port of Kaválla (ancient Neapolis). It was the scene in 42 BC of two battles in which Mark Antony and Octavian defeated Brutus and Cassius. Greek name **FÍLIPPOI**.

Phi·lip·pi·ans /fəˈlipēənz/ a book of the New Testament, an epistle of St. Paul to the Church at Philippi in Macedonia.

phi·lip·pic /fəˈlipik/ ▸*n. poetic/literary* a bitter attack or denunciation, esp. a verbal one. ▷late 16th cent.: via Latin from Greek *philippikos*, the name given to Demosthenes' speeches against Philip II of Macedon, also to those of Cicero against Mark Antony.

Phil·ip·pine /ˈfiləˌpēn/ ▸*adj.* of or relating to the Philippines. See also **FILIPINO**.

Phil·ip·pine ma·hog·a·ny ▸*n.* **1** reddish-brown timber from a tropical tree, used for paneling, cabinetry, and furniture. It resembles mahogany but is softer and less expensive. **2** the tree that produces this timber, harvested chiefly in Indonesia and the Philippines. Also called **LAUAN**. • Genus *Shorea*, family Dipterocarpaceae: several species.

Phil·ip·pines /ˈfiləˌpēnz/ a country in Southeast Asia that consists of an archipelago of over 7,000 islands—the main ones being Luzon, Mindanao, Mindoro, Leyte, Samar, Negros, and Panay—that are separated from the Asian mainland by the South China Sea; pop. 86,241,000; capital, Manila; languages, Filipino (based on Tagalog) and English.

Conquered by Spain in 1565, the islands were ceded to the U.S. in 1898, following the Spanish-American War. The Philippines achieved full independence as a republic in 1946. From 1965, the country was under the increasingly dictatorial rule of Ferdinand Marcos (1917–89); he was driven from power in 1986 and replaced by Corazón Aquino (1933–), who was president from 1986 until 1992. Armed radical Muslim insurgents in the south are a major concern.

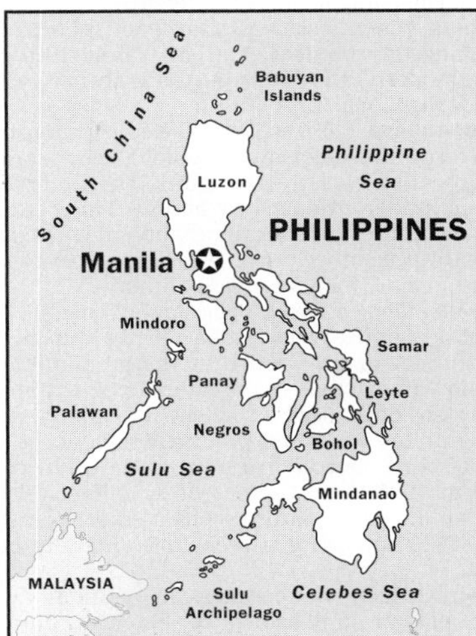

Phil·ip·pine Sea a section of the western Pacific on the east side of the Philippine Islands that extends north to Japan. During World War II, several major battles, including that at **LEYTE GULF**, were fought here.

Phil·ip·pop·o·lis /ˌfiləˈpäpəlis/ ancient Greek name for **PLOVDIV**.

Phil·ip the Bold, Philip III of France (see **PHILIP**[2]).

Phil·ip the Fair, Philip IV of France (see **PHILIP**[2]).

Phil·ip the Hand·some, Philip I of Spain (see **PHILIP**[3]).

Phil·ip the Tall, Philip V of France (see **PHILIP**[2]).

Phil·is·tine /ˈfiləˌstēn; -ˌstīn/ ▸*n.* **1** a member of a non-Semitic (perhaps originally Anatolian) people of southern Palestine in ancient times, who came into conflict with the Israelites during the 12th and 11th centuries BC.

According to the Bible, the Philistines, from whom the country of Palestine took its name, came from Crete and settled the southern coastal plain of Canaan in the 12th century BC.

2 (usu. **philistine**) a person who is hostile or indifferent to culture and the arts, or who has no understanding of them: [as *adj.*] *a philistine government.* ▷from French *Philistin*, via late Latin from Greek *Philistinos*, from Hebrew *pᵊlištī*. Sense 2 arose as a result of a confrontation between the townspeople and the students in Jena, Germany, in the late 17th cent.; a sermon on the conflict quoted: "the Philistines are upon you" (Judges 16), which led to an association between the townspeople and those hostile to culture.See **PALESTINE**. —**phil·is·tin·ism** /ˈfiləstēˌnizəm; fəˈlistə-/ *n.*

Phil·lips /ˈfiləps/ ▸*adj. trademark* denoting a screw with a cross-shaped slot for turning, the head of such a screw, or a corresponding screwdriver: *the screws have deeply cut Phillips heads | a Phillips screwdriver | a Phillips-head screwdriver.* ▷1930s: from the name of Henry F. *Phillips* (died 1958), the original American manufacturer.

Phil·lips curve ▸*n. Economics* a supposed inverse relationship between the level of unemployment and the rate of inflation. ▷1960s: named after Alban W. H. *Phillips* (1914–75), New Zealand economist.

phil·lu·men·ist /fəˈlo͞omənist/ ▸*n.* a collector of matchboxes or matchbooks. ▷1940s: from **PHIL-** 'loving' + Latin *lumen* 'light' + **-IST**. —**phil·lu·men·y** /-mənē/ *n.*

Phil·ly /ˈfilē/ ▸*n. informal* Philadelphia.

Phil·ly cheese·steak ▸*n.* see **CHEESESTEAK**.

philo- (also **phil-** before a vowel or *h*) ▸*comb. form* denoting a liking for a specified thing: *philogynist | philopatric.* ▷from Greek *philein* 'to love' or *philos* 'loving.'

phil·o·den·dron /ˌfiləˈdendrən/ ▸*n.* (*pl.* **-drons** or **-dra** /-drə/) a tropical American climbing plant that is widely grown as a greenhouse or indoor plant. • Genus *Philodendron*, family Araceae. ▷late 19th cent.: from **PHILO-** 'loving' + Greek *dendron* 'tree.'

phi·log·y·nist /fəˈläjənist/ ▸*n. formal* a person who likes or admires women. ▷mid 19th cent.: from **PHILO-** 'loving' + Greek *gunē* 'woman' + **-IST**. —**phi·log·y·ny** /-ˈläjənē/ *n.*

phi·lol·o·gy /fəˈläləjē/ ▸*n.* the branch of knowledge that deals with the structure, historical development, and relationships of a language or languages. ■ literary or classical scholarship. ▷late Middle English (in the Greek sense): current usage (late 17th cent.) from French *philologie*, via Latin from Greek *philologia* 'love of learning' (see **PHILO-, -LOGY**). —**phil·o·lo·gi·an** /ˌfiləˈlōjēən/ *n.* —**phil·o·log·i·cal** /ˌfiləˈläjikəl/ *adj.* —**phil·o·log·i·cal·ly** /ˌfiləˈläjik(ə)lē/ *adv.* —**phi·lol·o·gist** /-jist/ *n.*

Phil·o·me·la /ˌfiləˈmēlə/ (also **Phil·o·mel** /ˈfiləˌmel/) *Greek Mythology* the daughter of Pandion, king of Athens. She was turned into a swallow and her sister Procne into a nightingale (or, in Latin versions, into a nightingale with Procne the swallow) when they were being pursued by the cruel Tereus, who had married Procne and raped Philomela. ▷earlier as *philomene*, from medieval Latin *philomena*, from Latin *philomela* 'nightingale,' from Greek *philomēla*.

phil·o·pat·ric /ˌfiləˈpatrik/ ▸*adj. Zoology* (of an animal or species) tending to return to or remain near a particular site or area. ▷1940s: from **PHILO-** 'liking' + Greek *patra* 'fatherland' + **-IC**. —**phil·op·a·try** /fəˈläpətrē/ *n.*

phil·o·pro·gen·i·tive /ˌfilōprōˈjenitiv/ ▸*adj. formal* having many offspring: *the philoprogenitive senator.* ■ showing love toward one's offspring. —**phil·o·pro·gen·i·tive·ness** *n.*

philos. ▸*abbr.* ■ philosopher. ■ philosophical. ■ philosophy.

phi·los·o·pher /fəˈläsəfər/ ▸*n.* a person engaged or learned in philosophy, esp. as an academic discipline. ▷Middle English: from a variant of Old French *philosophe*, via Latin from Greek *philosophos* 'lover of wisdom,' from *philein* 'to love' + *sophos* 'wise.'

phi·los·o·pher kings ▸*plural n.* (in the political theory of Plato) the elite whose knowledge enables them to rule justly.

phi·los·o·pher's stone ▸*n.* (**the philosopher's stone**) a mythical substance supposed to change any metal into gold or silver and, according to some, to cure all diseases and prolong life indefinitely. Its discovery was the supreme object of alchemy.

phil·o·so·phi·a pe·ren·nis /fə,läsə'fēə pə'renis/ ▸*n.* *Philosophy* a core of philosophical truths that is hypothesized to exist independently of and unaffected by time or place. ▷mid 19th cent.: Latin, literally 'perennial philosophy.'

phil·o·soph·i·cal /,filə'säfikəl/ ▸*adj.* **1** of or relating to the study of the fundamental nature of knowledge, reality, and existence: *philosophical discussions about free will.* ■ devoted to the study of such issues: *the American Philosophical Society.* **2** having or showing a calm attitude toward disappointments or difficulties: *he was* ***philosophical about*** *losing the contract.* **—phil·o·soph·ic** /-'säfik/ *adj.* **—phil·o·soph·i·cal·ly** /-ik(ə)lē/ *adv.*

phi·los·o·phize /fə'läsə,fīz/ ▸*v.* [*intrans.*] speculate or theorize about fundamental or serious issues, esp. in a tedious or pompous way: *he paused for a while to philosophize on racial equality.* ■ [*trans.*] explain or argue (a point or idea) in terms of one's philosophical theories. **—phi·los·o·phiz·er** *n.*

phi·los·o·phy /fə'läsəfē/ ▸*n.* (*pl.* **-phies**) the study of the fundamental nature of knowledge, reality, and existence, esp. when considered as an academic discipline. See also NATURAL PHILOSOPHY. ■ a set of views and theories of a particular philosopher concerning such study or an aspect of it: *a clash of rival socialist philosophies.* ■ the study of the theoretical basis of a particular branch of knowledge or experience: ***the philosophy of*** *science.* ■ a theory or attitude held by a person or organization that acts as a guiding principle for behavior: *don't expect anything and you won't be disappointed, that's my philosophy.* ▷Middle English: from Old French *philosophie*, via Latin from Greek *philosophia* 'love of wisdom.'

-philous ▸*comb. form* in adjectives corresponding to nouns ending in *-philia* (such as *coprophilous* corresponding to *coprophilia*).

phil·ter /'filtər/ (*Brit.* **phil·tre**) ▸*n.* a drink supposed to excite sexual love in the drinker. ▷late 16th cent.: from French *philtre*, via Latin from Greek *philtron*, from *philein* 'to love.'

-phily ▸*comb. form* equivalent to -PHILIA.

phi·mo·sis /fī'mōsis/ ▸*n.* *Medicine* a congenital narrowing of the opening of the foreskin so that it cannot be retracted. ▷late 17th cent.: modern Latin, from Greek, literally 'muzzling.' **—phi·mot·ic** /fī-'mätik/ *adj.*

phish·ing /'fiSHiNG/ ▸*n.* the activity of defrauding an online account holder of financial information by posing as a legitimate company: [as *adj.*] *phishing exercises in which criminals create replicas of commercial Web sites.* ▷1990s: inspired by *fishing*, perhaps borrowing the *ph* from *phony*. **—phish** *v.*

phiz /fiz/ ▸*n.* *Brit., informal* a person's face or expression. ▷late 17th cent.: abbreviation of PHYSIOGNOMY.

phle·bi·tis /flə'bītis/ ▸*n.* *Medicine* inflammation of the walls of a vein. ▷early 19th cent.: modern Latin, from Greek, from *phleps, phleb-* 'vein.' **—phle·bit·ic** /-'bitik/ *adj.*

phle·bog·ra·phy /flə'bägrəfē/ ▸*n.* *Medicine* radiography of the veins carried out after injection of a radiopaque substance. **—phleb·o·graph·ic** /,flebə-'grafik/ *adj.*

phle·bot·o·my /flə'bätəmē/ ▸*n.* (*pl.* **-mies**) the surgical opening or puncture of a vein in order to withdraw blood or introduce a fluid, or (historically) as part of the procedure of letting blood. ▷late Middle English: via Old French from late Latin *phlebotomia*, from Greek, from *phleps, phleb-* 'vein' + *-tomia* 'cutting.' **—phle·bot·o·mist** *n.* **—phle·bot·o·mize** /-'bätə,mīz/ *v.* (*archaic*).

phlegm /flem/ ▸*n.* the thick viscous substance secreted by the mucous membranes of the respiratory passages, esp. when produced in excessive or abnormal quantities, e.g., when someone is suffering from a cold. ■ (in medieval science and medicine) one of the four bodily humors, believed to be associated with a calm, stolid, or apathetic temperament. ■ calmness of temperament: *phlegm and determination carried them through many difficult situations.* ▷Middle English *fleem, fleume*, from Old French *fleume*, from late Latin *phlegma* 'clammy moisture (of the body),' from Greek *phlegma* 'inflammation,' from *phlegein* 'to burn.' The spelling change in the 16th cent. was due to association with the Latin and Greek. **—phlegm·y** *adj.*

phleg·mat·ic /fleg'matik/ ▸*adj.* (of a person) having an unemotional and stolidly calm disposition. ▷Middle English (in the sense 'relating to the humor phlegm'): from Old French *fleumatique*, via Latin from Greek *phlegmatikos*, from *phlegma* 'inflammation' (see PHLEGM). **—phleg·mat·i·cal·ly** /-ik(ə)lē/ *adv.*

phlo·em /'flō,em/ ▸*n.* *Botany* the vascular tissue in plants that conducts sugars and other metabolic products downward from the leaves. ▷late 19th cent.: from Greek *phloos* 'bark' + the passive suffix *-ēma*.

phlo·gis·ton /flō'jistän; -tən/ ▸*n.* a substance supposed by 18th-century chemists to exist in all combustible bodies, and to be released in combustion. ▷mid 18th cent.: modern Latin, from Greek *phlogizein* 'set on fire,' from *phlox, phlog-* 'flame,' from the base of *phlegein* 'to burn.'

phlog·o·pite /'flägə,pīt/ ▸*n.* a brown micaceous mineral that occurs chiefly in metamorphosed limestone and magnesium-rich igneous rocks. ▷mid 19th cent.: from Greek *phlogōpos* 'fiery' (from the base of *phlegein* 'to burn') + *ōps, ōp-* 'face' + -ITE[1].

phlox /fläks/ ▸*n.* a North American plant that typically has dense clusters of colorful scented flowers, widely grown as a rock-garden or border plant. • Genus *Phlox*, family Polemoniaceae. ▷modern Latin, from Latin, denoting a flame-colored flower, from Greek, literally 'flame.'

Ph.M. ▸*abbr.* Master of Philosophy.

Phnom Penh /(pə),näm 'pen/ the capital of Cambodia, a port at the junction of the Mekong and Tonlé Sap rivers; pop. 920,000. Between 1975 and 1979, the Khmer Rouge forced a great many of its inhabitants (then 2.5 million) to leave the city and resettle in the country.

-phobe ▸*comb. form* denoting a person having a fear or dislike of what is specified: *homophobe* | *xenophobe.* ▷from French, via Latin *-phobus* from Greek *-phobos* 'fearing,' from *phobos* 'fear.'

pho·bi·a /'fōbēə/ ▸*n.* an extreme or irrational fear of or aversion to something: *he had a* ***phobia about*** *being under water* | *a* ***phobia of*** *germs* | *a snake phobia.* ▷late 18th cent.: independent usage of -PHOBIA. **—pho·bic** /'fōbik/ *adj.* & *n.*

-phobia ▸*comb. form* extreme or irrational fear or dislike of a specified thing or group: *arachnophobia* | *Russophobia.* ▷via Latin from Greek.

-phobic ▸*comb. form* in adjectives corresponding to nouns ending in *-phobia* (such as *technophobic* corresponding to *technophobia*).

Pho·bos /'fōbəs; 'fōbäs/ *Astronomy* the inner, and larger, of the two satellites of Mars, discovered in 1877. Heavily cratered and shaped like a potato, it is 17 miles (28 km) long. Compare with DEIMOS ▷named after one of the sons of the Greek war god ARES. The name means literally 'fear.'

pho·cine /'fōsīn; 'fōsin/ ▸*adj.* *Zoology* of, relating to, or affecting the true (earless) seals. ▷mid 19th cent.: from modern Latin *Phocinae* (subfamily name), from Greek *phōkē* 'seal.'

pho·co·me·li·a /,fōkō'mēlyə; -'mēlēə/ ▸*n.* *Medicine* a rare congenital deformity in which the hands or feet are attached close to the trunk, the limbs being grossly underdeveloped or absent. This condition was a side effect of the drug thalidomide taken during early pregnancy. ▷late 19th cent.: modern Latin, from Greek *phōkē* 'seal' + *melos* 'limb.'

Phoe·be /'fēbē/ **1** *Greek Mythology* a Titaness, daughter of Uranus (Heaven) and Gaia (Earth). She became the mother of Leto and thus the grandmother of Apollo and Artemis. In the later Greek writers, her name was often used for Selene (Moon). **2** *Astronomy* a satellite of Saturn, the furthest from the planet and with an eccentric retrograde orbit, discovered in 1898. At a distance of 8 million miles (13 million km) from Saturn, it has a diameter of 137 miles (220 km). ▷from Greek *Phoibē*, literally 'bright one.'

phoe·be /'fēbē/ ▸*n.* an American tyrant flycatcher with mainly gray-brown or blackish plumage. • Genus *Sayornis*, family Tyrannidae: three species, in particular the common **eastern phoebe** (*S. phoebe*). ▷early 18th cent.: imitative; influenced by the name PHOEBE.

Phoe·bus /'fēbəs/ *Greek Mythology* an epithet of Apollo, used in contexts in which the god was identified with the sun. ▷from Greek *Phoibos*, literally 'bright one.'

Phoe·ni·cia /fə'niSHə; -'nēSHə/ an ancient country on the shores of the eastern Mediterranean Sea, corresponding to modern Lebanon and the coastal plains of Syria. It consisted of a number of city-states, including Tyre and Sidon, and was a flourishing center of Mediterranean trade and colonization during the early part of the 1st millennium BC. ▷from Latin, from Greek *Phoinikē*.

Phoe·ni·cian /fə'nēSHən/ ▸*n.* **1** a member of a Semitic people inhabiting ancient Phoenicia and its colonies. The Phoenicians prospered from trade and manufacturing until the capital, Tyre, was sacked by Alexander the Great in 332 BC. **2** the Semitic language of this people, written in an alphabet that was the ancestor of the Greek and Roman alphabets.
▸*adj.* of or relating to Phoenicia or its colonies, or its people, language, or alphabet.

Phoe·nix[1] /'fēniks/ *Astronomy* a southern constellation (the Phoenix), west of Grus. ■ [as *genitive*] (**Phoenicis** /fē'nīsis; -'nē-/) used with a preceding letter or numeral to designate a star in this constellation: *the star Delta Phoenicis.* ▷Latin.

Phoe·nix[2] the capital of Arizona; pop. 1,321,045. Its warm dry climate makes it a popular winter resort.

phoe·nix /'fēniks/ ▸*n.* (in classical mythology) a unique bird that lived for five or six centuries in the Arabian desert, after this time burning itself on a funeral pyre and rising from the ashes with renewed youth to live through another cycle. ■ a person or thing regarded as uniquely remarkable in some respect. ▷from Old French *fenix*, via Latin from Greek *phoinix* 'Phoenician, reddish purple, or phoenix.'
▸*PHRASE* □ **rise like a phoenix from the ashes** emerge renewed after apparent disaster or destruction.

Phoe·nix Is·lands a group of eight islands that lie just south of the equator in the western Pacific Ocean. They form a part of Kiribati.

Phol·i·do·ta /,fäli'dōtə/ *Zoology* a small order of mammals that comprises the pangolins. ▷modern Latin (plural), from Greek *pholidōtos* 'scaly,' from *pholis, pholid-* 'scale.'

phon /fän/ ▸*n.* a unit of the perceived loudness of sounds. ▷1930s: from Greek *phōnē* 'sound.'

phon. ▸*abbr.* phonetics.

pho·na·tion /fō'nāSHən/ ▸*n.* *Phonetics* the production or utterance of speech sounds. ▷mid 19th cent.: from Greek *phōnē* 'sound, voice' + -ATION. **—pho·nate** /'fō,nāt/ *v.* **—pho·na·to·ry** /'fōnə,tôrē/ *adj.*

phone[1] /fōn/ ▸*n.* short for TELEPHONE. ■ (**phones**) *informal* headphones or earphones.
▸*v.* short for TELEPHONE.
▸*PHRASE* □ **phone it in** work or perform in a desultory fashion.

phone[2] ▸*n.* *Phonetics* a speech sound; the smallest discrete segment of sound in a stream of speech. ▷mid 19th cent.: from Greek *phōnē* 'sound, voice.'

-phone ▸*comb. form* **1** denoting an instrument using or connected with sound: *megaphone.* **2** denoting a person who uses a specified language: *francophone.* ▷from Greek *phōnē* 'sound, voice.'

phone bank ▸*n.* a battery of telephones: *campaign volunteers have spent countless hours manning phone banks.*

phone book ▸*n.* a telephone directory.

phone card ▸*n.* another term for CALLING CARD (sense 2).

phone-in ▸*n.* & *adj.* another term for CALL-IN.

pho·neme /'fōnēm/ ▸*n.* *Phonetics* any of the perceptually distinct units of sound in a specified language that distinguish one word from another, for example *p, b, d,* and *t* in the English words *pad, pat, bad,* and *bat.* Compare with ALLOPHONE. ▷late 19th cent.: from French *phonème*, from Greek *phōnēma* 'sound, speech,' from *phōnein* 'speak.' **—pho·ne·mic** /fə'nēmik; fō-/ *adj.* **—pho·ne·mics** /fə'nēmiks; fō-/ *n.*

phone sex ▸*n.* a commercial service providing its customers with sexually explicit telephone conversation for the purposes of sexual gratification.

pho·net·ic /fə'netik/ ▸*adj.* *Phonetics* of or relating to speech sounds: *detailed phonetic information.* ■ (of a system of writing) having a direct correspondence between symbols and sounds: *a phonetic alphabet.* ■ of or relating to phonetics: *phonetic training.* ▷early 19th cent.: from modern Latin *phoneticus*, from Greek *phōnētikos*, from *phōnein* 'speak.' **—pho·net·i·cal·ly** /-ik(ə)lē/ *adv.* **—pho·net·i·cism** /-'neti,sizəm/ *n.* **—pho·net·i·cist** /-'netisist/ *n.*

pho·net·ics /fə'netiks/ ▸*plural n.* [treated as *sing.*] the study and classification of speech sounds. **—pho·ne·ti·cian** /,fōnə'tiSHən/ *n.*

pho·ney ▸*adj.* & *n.* variant spelling of PHONY.

phon·ic /'fänik/ ▸*adj.* of or relating to speech sounds. ■ of or relating to phonics: *the English language presents difficulties if a purely phonic approach is attempted.* ▷early 19th cent.: from Greek *phōnē* 'voice' + -IC. **—phon·i·cal·ly** /ik(ə)lē/ *adv.*

phon·ics /'fäniks/ ▸*plural n.* [treated as *sing.*] a method of teaching people to read by correlating sounds with letters or groups of letters in an alphabetic writing system.

pho·no /ˈfōnō/ ▸*n.* short for PHONOGRAPH.
▸*adj.* [*attrib.*] denoting a type of plug, and the corresponding socket, used with audio and video equipment, in which one conductor is cylindrical and the other is a central prong that extends beyond it. ▷1940s: abbreviation of PHONOGRAPH.

phono- ▸*comb. form* relating to sound: *phonograph.* ▷from Greek *phōnē* 'sound, voice.'

pho·no·car·di·o·gram /ˌfōnōˈkärdēəˌgram/ ▸*n. Medicine* a chart or record of the sounds made by the heart.

pho·no·gram /ˈfōnəˌgram/ ▸*n. Phonetics* a symbol representing a vocal sound.

pho·no·graph /ˈfōnəˌgraf/ ▸*n.* a record player. ■ *chiefly historical* an early sound-reproducing machine that used cylinders to record as well as reproduce sound. —**pho·no·graph·ic** /ˌfōnəˈgrafik/ *adj.*

pho·no·graph rec·ord ▸*n.* fuller form of RECORD (sense 4).

pho·no·lite /ˈfōnəˌlīt/ ▸*n. Geology* a fine-grained volcanic rock composed of alkali feldspars and nepheline. ▷early 19th cent.: from PHONO- 'relating to sound' (because of its resonance when struck) + -LITE.

pho·nol·o·gy /fəˈnäləjē; fō-/ ▸*n.* the branch of linguistics that deals with systems of sounds (including or excluding phonetics), esp. in a particular language. ■ the system of relationships among the speech sounds that constitute the fundamental components of a language. —**pho·no·log·i·cal** /ˌfōnəˈläjikəl/ *adj.* —**pho·no·log·i·cal·ly** /ˌfōnəˈläjik(ə)lē/ *adv.* —**pho·nol·o·gist** /-jist/ *n.*

pho·non /ˈfōnän/ ▸*n. Physics* a quantum of energy or a quasiparticle associated with a compressional wave such as sound or a vibration of a crystal lattice. ▷1930s: from Greek *phōnē* 'sound,' on the pattern of *photon.*

pho·no·tac·tics /ˌfōnōˈtaktiks/ ▸*plural n.* [treated as *sing.*] the study of the rules governing the possible phoneme sequences in a language. —**pho·no·tac·tic** /-tik/ *adj.*

pho·ny /ˈfōnē/ (also **pho·ney**) *informal* ▸*adj.* (**-ni·er**, **-ni·est**) not genuine; fraudulent: *I thought your accent was a bit phony.*
▸*n.* (*pl.* **-nies**) a fraudulent person or thing. ▷late 19th cent.: of unknown origin. —**pho·ni·ly** /ˈfōnilē/ *adv.* —**pho·ni·ness** *n.*

pho·ny war the period of comparative inaction at the beginning of World War II between the German invasion of Poland (September 1939) and that of Norway (April 1940).

phoo·ey /ˈfo͞oē/ *informal* ▸*exclam.* (also **pfu·i**) used to express disdain or disbelief: *I say* **phooey** *to all their money and fine clothes.*
▸*n.* nonsense: *those excuses are a lot of phooey.* ▷1920s: imitative.

-phore ▸*comb. form* denoting an agent or bearer of a specified thing: *ionophore | semaphore.* ▷from modern Latin *-phorus*, from Greek *-phoros, -phoron* 'bearing, bearer,' from *pherein* 'to bear.'

phor·e·sy /ˈfôrəsē/ ▸*n. Zoology* an association between two organisms in which one (e.g., a mite) travels on the body of another, without being a parasite. ▷1920s: from French *phorésie*, from Greek *phorēsis* 'being carried.' —**pho·ret·ic** /fəˈretik/ *adj.*

Pho·ron·i·da /fəˈränədə/ *Zoology* a small phylum of wormlike marine invertebrates. ▷modern Latin (plural), from Latin *Phoronis, Phoronid-*, the name of a character in Greek mythology. —**pho·ro·nid** /fəˈrōnid/ *n.*

-phorous ▸*comb. form* in adjectives corresponding to nouns ending in *-phore* (such as *ionophorous* corresponding to *ionophore*).

phos·gene /ˈfäsjēn/ ▸*n. Chemistry* a colorless poisonous gas made by the reaction of chlorine and carbon monoxide. It was used as a poison gas, notably in World War I. • Alternative name: **carbonyl chloride**; chem. formula: $COCl_2$. ▷early 19th cent.: from Greek *phōs* 'light' + -GEN, with reference to its original production by the action of sunlight on chlorine and carbon monoxide.

phos·pha·tase /ˈfäsfəˌtās/ ▸*n. Biochemistry* an enzyme that catalyzes the hydrolysis of organic phosphates in a specified (acid or alkaline) environment.

phos·phate /ˈfäsfāt/ ▸*n.* **1** *Chemistry* a salt or ester of phosphoric acid, containing PO_4^{3-} or a related anion or a group such as $-OPO(OH)_2$. **2** an effervescent soft drink containing phosphoric acid, soda water, and flavoring. ▷late 18th cent.: from French, from *phosphore* 'phosphorus.'

phos·phat·ic /fäsˈfatik/ ▸*adj.* (chiefly of rocks and fertilizer) containing or consisting of phosphates.

phos·pha·tide /ˈfäsfəˌtīd/ ▸*n. Biochemistry* any of a class of compounds that are fatty acid esters of glycerol phosphate with a nitrogen base linked to the phosphate group.

phos·pha·ti·dyl·cho·line /ˌfäsfəˌtīdlˈkōlēn; fäsˌfatədl-/ ▸*n. Biochemistry* another term for LECITHIN.

phos·phene /ˈfäsfēn/ ▸*n.* a ring or spot of light produced by pressure on the eyeball or direct stimulation of the visual system other than by light. ▷late 19th cent.: formed irregularly from Greek *phōs* 'light' + *phainein* 'to show.'

phos·phide /ˈfäsfīd/ ▸*n. Chemistry* a binary compound of phosphorus with another element or group.

phos·phine /ˈfäsfēn/ ▸*n. Chemistry* a colorless foul-smelling gaseous compound of phosphorus and hydrogen, analogous to ammonia, widely used as an insecticidal fumigant in agricultural products. • Chem. formula: PH_3. It forms salts containing the **phosphonium** ion, PH_4^+. ▷late 19th cent.: from PHOSPHO- 'relating to phosphorus' + -INE[4], on the pattern of *amine.*

phos·phite /ˈfäsfīt/ ▸*n. Chemistry* old-fashioned term for PHOSPHONATE (see PHOSPHONIC ACID).

phospho- ▸*comb. form* representing PHOSPHORUS.

phos·pho·cre·a·tine /ˌfäsfōˈkrēətin/ ▸*n. Biochemistry* a phosphate ester of creatine found in vertebrate muscle, where it serves to store phosphates to provide energy for muscular contraction.

phos·pho·di·es·ter·ase /ˌfäsfōdīˈestərās/ ▸*n. Biochemistry* an enzyme that breaks a phosphodiester bond in an oligonucleotide.

phos·pho·di·es·ter bond /ˌfäsfōdīˈestər/ ▸*n. Biochemistry* a chemical bond of the kind joining successive sugar molecules in a polynucleotide.

phos·pho·li·pase /ˌfäsfōˈlīpās/ ▸*n. Biochemistry* an enzyme that hydrolyzes lecithin or a similar phospholipid.

phos·pho·lip·id /ˌfäsfōˈlipid/ ▸*n. Biochemistry* a lipid containing a phosphate group in its molecule, e.g., lecithin.

phos·phon·ic ac·id /fäsˈfänik/ ▸*n. Chemistry* a crystalline acid obtained by the reaction of phosphorus trioxide with water. • A dibasic acid; chem. formula: $HPO(OH)_2$. ▷late 19th cent.: *phosphonic* from PHOSPHO- 'relating to phosphorus,' on the pattern of *sulfonic.* —**phos·pho·nate** /ˈfäsfəˌnāt/ *n.*

phos·pho·ni·um /fäsˈfōnēəm/ ▸*n.* see PHOSPHINE. ▷late 19th cent.: blend of PHOSPHORUS and AMMONIUM.

phos·pho·pro·tein /ˌfäsfōˈprōtēn/ ▸*n. Biochemistry* a protein that contains phosphorus (other than in an associated nucleic acid or phospholipid).

phos·phor /ˈfäsfər/ ▸*n.* a synthetic fluorescent or phosphorescent substance, esp. any of those used to coat the screens of cathode-ray tubes. ■ old-fashioned term for PHOSPHORUS. ▷early 17th cent.: from Latin *phosphorus* (see PHOSPHORUS).

phos·pho·rat·ed /ˈfäsfəˌrātid/ ▸*adj.* combined or impregnated with phosphorus.

phos·phor bronze ▸*n.* a tough, hard form of bronze containing a small amount of phosphorus, used esp. for bearings.

phos·pho·resce /ˌfäsfəˈres/ ▸*v.* [*intrans.*] emit light or radiation by phosphorescence.

phos·pho·res·cence /ˌfäsfəˈresəns/ ▸*n.* light emitted by a substance without combustion or perceptible heat: *the stones overhead gleamed with phosphorescence.* ■ *Physics* the emission of radiation in a similar manner to fluorescence but on a longer timescale, so that emission continues after excitation ceases. —**phos·pho·res·cent** *adj.*

phos·phor·ic /fäsˈfôrik/ ▸*adj.* relating to or containing phosphorus. ■ *Chemistry* of phosphorus with a valence of five. Compare with PHOSPHOROUS. ▷late 18th cent.: from French *phosphorique*, from *phosphore* 'phosphorus.'

phos·phor·ic ac·id ▸*n. Chemistry* a crystalline acid obtained, e.g., by treating phosphates with sulfuric acid, and used in fertilizer and soap manufacture and in food processing. • A tribasic acid; chem. formula: H_3PO_4.

phos·pho·rite /ˈfäsfəˌrīt/ ▸*n.* a sedimentary rock containing a high proportion of calcium phosphate. ▷late 18th cent.: from PHOSPHORUS + -ITE[1].

phos·pho·rous /ˈfäsfərəs; fäsˈfôrəs/ ▸*adj.* relating to or containing phosphorus. Compare with PHOSPHORIC. ■ *Chemistry* of phosphorus with a valence of three. ■ phosphorescent.

USAGE The correct spelling for the noun denoting the chemical element is **phosphorus**, while the correct spelling for the adjective meaning 'relating to or containing phosphorus' is **phosphorous**. A common mistake is to use the spelling **phosphorous** for the noun as well as the adjective.

phos·pho·rous ac·id ▸*n.* another term for PHOSPHONIC ACID.

phos·pho·rus /ˈfäsfərəs/ ▸*n.* the chemical element of atomic number 15, a poisonous, combustible nonmetal that exists in two common allotropic forms, **white phosphorus**, a yellowish waxy solid that ignites spontaneously in air and glows in the dark, and **red phosphorus**, a less reactive form used in making matches. (Symbol: **P**) ▷late 17th cent.: from Latin, from Greek *phōsphoros*, from *phōs* 'light' + *-phoros* '-bringing.'

USAGE See usage at PHOSPHOROUS.

phos·pho·ryl·ase /ˈfäsfərəˌlās; fäsˈfôrəˌlās/ ▸*n. Biochemistry* an enzyme that introduces a phosphate group into an organic molecule, notably glucose.

phos·pho·ryl·ate /ˈfäsfərəˌlāt; fäsˈfôrə-/ ▸*v.* [*trans.*] (often **be phosphorylated**) *chiefly Biochemistry* introduce a phosphate group into (a molecule or compound). —**phos·pho·ryl·a·tion** /ˈfäsfərəˈlāsʜən/ *n.*

phot /fōt/ ▸*n.* a unit of illumination equal to one lumen per square centimeter. ▷early 20th cent.: from Greek *phōs, phōt-* 'light.'

pho·tic /ˈfōtik/ ▸*adj. technical* of or relating to light, esp. as an agent of chemical change or physiological response. ■ *Ecology* denoting the layers of the ocean reached by sufficient sunlight to allow plant growth: *an average depth for the* **photic zone** *is about 300 feet.*

pho·ti·no /fōˈtēnō/ ▸*n.* (*pl.* **-nos**) *Physics* the hypothetical supersymmetric counterpart of the photon, with spin $-1/2$. ▷1970s: from PHOTON + *-ino* from NEUTRINO.

pho·to /ˈfōtō/ ▸*n.* (*pl.* **-tos**) a photograph. ■ *informal* a photo finish. ▷mid 19th cent.: abbreviation.

photo- ▸*comb. form* **1** relating to light: *photochemical.* **2** relating to photography: *photocomposition.* ▷sense 1 from Greek *phōs, phōt-* 'light'; sense 2, abbreviation of PHOTOGRAPHY.

pho·to·ac·tive /ˌfōtōˈaktiv/ ▸*adj.* (of a substance) capable of a chemical or physical change in response to illumination.

pho·to·bi·ol·o·gy /ˌfōtōbīˈäləjē/ ▸*n.* the study of the effects of light on living organisms.

pho·to·bleach·ing /ˌfōtōˈblēcʜiɴɢ/ ▸*n. Biochemistry* loss of color by a pigment (such as chlorophyll or rhodopsin) when illuminated.

pho·to·ca·tal·y·sis /ˌfōtōkəˈtaləsis/ ▸*n. Chemistry* the acceleration of a chemical reaction by light. —**pho·to·cat·a·lyst** /-ˈkatl-ist/ *n.* —**pho·to·cat·a·lyt·ic** /-ˌkatəˈlitik/ *adj.*

pho·to·cath·ode /ˌfōtōˈkaᴛʜōd/ ▸*n.* a cathode that emits electrons when illuminated, causing an electric current.

pho·to CD ▸*n.* a compact disc from which still photographs can be displayed on a television screen or computer monitor. ■ the storing and reproducing of photographs in this way: *photo CD is used in medicine and data storage*

pho·to·cell /ˈfōtōˌsel/ ▸*n.* short for PHOTOELECTRIC CELL.

pho·to·chem·i·cal /ˌfōtōˈkemikəl/ ▸*adj.* of, relating to, or caused by the chemical action of light: *photochemical smog.* ■ of or relating to photochemistry. —**pho·to·chem·i·cal·ly** /-ik(ə)lē/ *adv.*

pho·to·chem·is·try /ˌfōtōˈkeməstrē/ ▸*n.* the branch of chemistry concerned with the chemical effects of light.

pho·to·chro·mic /ˌfōtəˈkrōmik/ ▸*adj.* (of a substance) undergoing a reversible change in color or shade when exposed to light of a particular frequency or intensity: *photochromic sunglasses.* ▷1950s: from PHOTO- 'relating to light' + Greek *khrōma* 'color' + -IC. —**pho·to·chro·mism** /-ˈkrōmizəm/ *n.*

pho·to·co·ag·u·la·tion /ˌfōtōkōˌagyəˈlāsʜən/ ▸*n. Medicine* the use of a laser beam or other intense light source to coagulate and destroy or fuse small areas of tissue, esp. in the retina.

pho·to·com·po·si·tion /ˌfōtōˌkämpəˈzisʜən/ ▸*n. Printing* the setting of material to be printed by projecting it onto photographic film from which the printing surface is prepared.

Pronunciation Key ə ago; ər over; ˈə or ˌə up; ˈər or ˌər fur; a hat; ā rate; ä car; cʜ chew; e let; ē see; e(ə)r air; i fit; ī by; i(ə)r ear; ɴɢ sing; ō go; ô for; oi boy; o͝o good; o͞o goo; ou out; sʜ she; ᴛʜ thin; ᴛʜ then; (h)w why; ᴢʜ vision

pho·to·con·duc·tiv·i·ty /ˌfōtōˌkändəkˈtivitē/ ▸*n.* increased electrical conductivity caused by the presence of light. —**pho·to·con·duc·tive** /-kənˈdəktiv/ *adj.* —**pho·to·con·duc·tor** /-kənˈdəktər/ *n.*

pho·to·cop·i·er /ˈfōtəˌkäpēər/ ▸*n.* a machine for making photocopies.

pho·to·cop·y /ˈfōtəˌkäpē/ ▸*n.* (*pl.* **-cop·ies**) a photographic copy of printed or written material produced by a process involving the action of light on a specially prepared surface.
▸*v.* (**-cop·ies, -cop·ied**) [*trans.*] make a photocopy of. —**pho·to·cop·i·a·ble** /-ˌkäpēəbəl/ *adj.*

pho·to·cur·rent /ˌfōtōˈkərənt/ ▸*n.* an electric current induced by the action of light.

pho·to·de·grad·a·ble /ˌfōtōdəˈgrādəbəl/ ▸*adj.* capable of being decomposed by the action of light, esp. sunlight: *photodegradable plastic.*

pho·to·de·tec·tor /ˌfōtōdəˈtektər/ ▸*n.* a device that detects or responds to incident light by using the electrical effect of individual photons.

pho·to·di·ode /ˈfōtōˌdīōd/ ▸*n.* a semiconductor diode that, when exposed to light, generates a potential difference or changes its electrical resistance.

pho·to·dis·so·ci·a·tion /ˌfōtōdiˌsōsēˈāsʜən/ ▸*n.* *Chemistry* dissociation of a chemical compound by the action of light.

pho·to·dy·nam·ic /ˌfōtōdīˈnamik/ ▸*adj.* *Medicine* denoting treatment for cancer involving the injection of a cytotoxic compound that is relatively inactive until activated by a laser beam after collecting in the tumor.

pho·to·e·lec·tric /ˌfōtōiˈlektrik/ ▸*adj.* characterized by or involving the emission of electrons from a surface by the action of light. —**pho·to·e·lec·tric·i·ty** /ˌfōtōilekˈtrisitē/ *n.*

pho·to·e·lec·tric cell ▸*n.* a device that generates an electric current or voltage dependent on the degree of illumination.

pho·to·e·lec·tron /ˌfōtōiˈlekˌträn/ ▸*n.* an electron emitted from an atom by interaction with a photon, esp. an electron emitted from a solid surface by the action of light. —**pho·to·e·lec·tron·ic** /-ilekˈtränik/ *adj.*

pho·to·e·mis·sion /ˌfōtōiˈmisʜən/ ▸*n.* the emission of electrons from a surface caused by the action of light striking it. —**pho·to·e·mit·ter** /-iˈmitər/ *n.*

pho·to·es·say /ˌfōtōˈesā/ ▸*n.* an essay or short article consisting of text and numerous photographs.

pho·to fin·ish ▸*n.* a close finish of a race in which the winner is identifiable only from a photograph taken as the competitors cross the finish line.

pho·to·fit /ˈfōtōfit/ ▸*n.* *Brit.* a reconstructed picture of a person, especially one wanted by the police, made from composite photographs of facial features.

pho·tog /fəˈtäg/ ▸*n.* *informal* a photographer.

pho·to·gen·ic /ˌfōtəˈjenik/ ▸*adj.* **1** (esp. of a person) looking attractive in photographs or on film: *a photogenic child.* **2** *Biology* (of an organism or tissue) producing or emitting light. —**pho·to·gen·i·cal·ly** /-(ə)lē/ *adv.*

pho·to·ge·ol·o·gy /ˌfōtōjēˈäləjē/ ▸*n.* the field of study concerned with the geological interpretation of aerial photographs. —**pho·to·ge·o·log·i·cal** /-ˌjēəˈläjikəl/ *adj.* —**pho·to·ge·ol·o·gist** /-jist/ *n.*

pho·to·gram /ˈfōtəˌgram/ ▸*n.* a picture produced with photographic materials, such as light-sensitive paper, but without a camera. ■ *archaic* a photograph.

pho·to·gram·me·try /ˌfōtəˈgramitrē/ ▸*n.* the use of photography in surveying and mapping to measure distances between objects. —**pho·to·gram·met·ric** /-grəˈmetrik/ *adj.* —**pho·to·gram·me·trist** /-trist/ *n.*

pho·to·graph /ˈfōtəˌgraf/ ▸*n.* a picture made using a camera, in which an image is focused onto film or other light-sensitive material and then made visible and permanent by chemical treatment.
▸*v.* [*trans.*] take a photograph of. ■ [*intrans.*] appear in a particular way when in a photograph: *that cityscape photographs well.* —**pho·to·graph·a·ble** *adj.* —**pho·tog·ra·pher** /fəˈtägrəfər/ *n.* —**pho·to·graph·ic** /ˌfōtəˈgrafik/ *adj.* —**pho·to·graph·i·cal·ly** /ˌfōtəˈgrafik(ə)lē/ *adv.*

pho·to·graph·ic mem·o·ry /ˌfōtəˈgrafik/ ▸*n.* the ability to remember information or visual images in great detail.

pho·tog·ra·phy /fəˈtägrəfē/ ▸*n.* the art or practice of taking and processing photographs.

Modern photography is based on the property of silver compounds decomposing to metallic silver when exposed to light. The light-sensitive salts are held in an emulsion (in color film, layers of emulsion) usually mounted on transparent roll film.

pho·to·gra·vure /ˌfōtəgrəˈvyo͝or/ ▸*n.* an image produced from a photographic negative transferred to a metal plate and etched in. ■ the production of images in this way. ▷late 19th cent.: from French, from *photo-* 'relating to light' + *gravure* 'engraving.'

pho·to·i·o·ni·za·tion /ˌfōtōˌīəniˈzāsʜən/ ▸*n.* *Physics* ionization produced in a medium by the action of electromagnetic radiation.

pho·to·jour·nal·ism /ˌfōtōˈjərnəˌlizəm/ ▸*n.* the art or practice of communicating news by photographs, esp. in magazines. —**pho·to·jour·nal·ist** *n.*

pho·to·li·thog·ra·phy /ˌfōtōliˈtʜägrəfē/ ▸*n.* lithography using plates made photographically. —**pho·to·lith·o·graph·ic** /-ˌlitʜəˈgrafik/ *adj.* —**pho·to·lith·o·graph·i·cal·ly** /-ˌlitʜəˈgrafik(ə)lē/ *adv.*

pho·tol·y·sis /fōˈtäləsis/ ▸*n.* *Chemistry* the decomposition or separation of molecules by the action of light. —**pho·to·lyze** /ˈfōtlˌīz/ *v.* —**pho·to·lyt·ic** /ˌfōtlˈitik/ *adj.*

photom. ▸*abbr.* photometry.

pho·to·map /ˈfōtōˌmap/ ▸*n.* a map made from or drawn on photographs of the area concerned.

pho·to·mask /ˈfōtōˌmask/ ▸*n.* *Electronics* a photographic pattern used in making microcircuits, ultraviolet light being shone through the mask onto a photoresist in order to transfer the pattern.

pho·to·me·chan·i·cal /ˌfōtōməˈkanikəl/ ▸*adj.* relating to or denoting processes in which photography is involved in the making of a printing plate. —**pho·to·me·chan·i·cal·ly** /-ik(ə)lē/ *adv.*

pho·tom·e·ter /fōˈtämitər/ ▸*n.* an instrument for measuring the intensity of light. —**pho·to·met·ric** /ˌfōtəˈmetrik/ *adj.* —**pho·to·met·ri·cal·ly** /ˌfōtōˈmetrik(ə)lē/ *adv.* —**pho·tom·e·try** /-ˈtämətrē/ *n.*

pho·to·mi·cro·graph /ˌfōtōˈmīkrōˌgraf/ ▸*n.* a photograph of a microscopic object, taken with the aid of a microscope. —**pho·to·mi·crog·ra·pher** /-mīˈkrägrəfər/ *n.* —**pho·to·mi·crog·ra·phy** *n.*

pho·to·mon·tage /ˌfōtōmänˈtäzʜ/ ▸*n.* a montage constructed from photographic images. ■ the technique of constructing such a montage.

pho·to·mor·pho·gen·e·sis /ˌfōtōˌmôrfəˈjenəsis/ ▸*n.* *Botany* development of form and structure in plants that is affected by light, other than that occurring for photosynthesis.

pho·to·mo·sa·ic /ˌfōtōmōˈzāik/ ▸*n.* a large-scale detailed picture or map built up by combining photographs of small areas.

pho·to·mul·ti·pli·er /ˌfōtōˈməltəplīər/ ▸*n.* an instrument containing a photoelectric cell and a series of electrodes, used to detect and amplify the light from very faint sources.

pho·to·mur·al /ˌfōtōˈmyo͝orəl/ ▸*n.* a mural consisting of a single enlarged photograph or a collection of photographs covering a wall.

pho·ton /ˈfōtän/ ▸*n.* *Physics* a particle representing a quantum of light or other electromagnetic radiation. A photon carries energy proportional to the radiation frequency but has zero rest mass. ▷early 20th cent.: from Greek *phōs, phōt-* 'light,' on the pattern of *electron.*

pho·to·neg·a·tive /ˌfōtōˈnegətiv/ ▸*adj.* **1** *Biology* (of an organism) tending to move away from light. **2** *Physics* (of a substance) exhibiting a decrease in electrical conductivity under illumination.

pho·ton·ic crys·tal /fōˈtänik/ ▸*n.* a synthetic crystal that can manipulate or be sensitized to respond to specific wavelengths of light. Its development suggests the possibility of increased miniaturization and efficiency of computing components and other technologies.

pho·ton·ics /fōˈtäniks/ ▸*plural n.* [treated as *sing.*] the branch of technology concerned with the properties and transmission of photons, for example in fiber optics.

pho·to·off·set ▸*n.* offset printing using plates made photographically.

pho·to op /ˈfōtō äp/ ▸*n.* informal term for **PHOTO OPPORTUNITY.**

pho·to op·por·tu·ni·ty ▸*n.* an occasion on which famous people pose for photographers by arrangement.

pho·to·ox·i·da·tion /ˌfōtōˌäksiˈdāsʜən/ ▸*n.* *Chemistry* oxidation caused by the action of light.

pho·to·pe·ri·od /ˈfōtōˌpi(ə)rēəd/ ▸*n.* *Botany & Zoology* the period of time each day during which an organism receives illumination; day length. —**pho·to·pe·ri·od·ic** /ˌfōtōˌpi(ə)rēˈädik/ *adj.*

pho·to·pe·ri·od·ism /ˌfōtōˈpi(ə)rēəˌdizəm/ (also **pho·to·pe·ri·o·dic·i·ty** /-ˌpi(ə)rēəˈdisitē/) ▸*n.* *Botany & Zoology* the response of an organism to seasonal changes in day length.

pho·to·pho·bi·a /ˌfōtəˈfōbēə/ ▸*n.* extreme sensitivity to light. —**pho·to·pho·bic** /ˌfōtəˈfōbik/ *adj.*

pho·to·phore /ˈfōtəˌfôr/ ▸*n.* *Zoology* a light-producing organ in certain fishes and other animals. ▷late 19th cent.: from Greek *phōtophoros* 'light-bearing.'

pho·top·ic /fōˈtäpik/ ▸*adj.* *Physiology* relating to or denoting vision in daylight or other bright light, believed to involve chiefly the cones of the retina. Often contrasted with **SCOTOPIC.** ▷early 20th cent.: from **PHOTO-** 'light' + **-OPIA** + **-IC.**

pho·to·pig·ment /ˌfōtōˈpigmənt/ ▸*n.* a pigment whose chemical state depends on its degree of illumination, such as those in the retina of the eye.

pho·to·po·lar·im·e·ter /ˌfōtəˌpōləˈrimitər/ ▸*n.* a telescopic apparatus for photographing stars, galaxies, etc., and measuring the polarization of light from them.

pho·to·pol·y·mer /ˌfōtōˈpäləmər/ ▸*n.* a light-sensitive polymeric material, esp. one used in printing plates or microfilms.

pho·to·pos·i·tive /ˌfōtōˈpäzitiv/ ▸*adj.* **1** *Biology* (of an organism) tending to move toward light. **2** *Physics* (of a substance) exhibiting an increase in electrical conductivity under illumination.

pho·to·prod·uct /ˈfōtōˌprädəkt/ ▸*n.* a product of a photochemical reaction.

pho·to·pro·tein /ˌfōtōˈprōtēn/ ▸*n.* *Biochemistry* a protein active in the emission of light by a living creature.

pho·to·re·al·ism /ˈfōtōˈrēəˌlizəm/ ▸*n.* **1** detailed and unidealized representation in art, esp. of banal, mundane, or sordid aspects of life. **2** detailed visual representation, like that obtained in a photograph, in a nonphotographic medium such as animation or computer graphics. —**pho·to·re·al·ist** *n.* & *adj.* —**pho·to·re·al·is·tic** /ˌfōtōˌrēəˈlistik/ *adj.*

pho·to·re·cep·tor /ˌfōtōriˈseptər/ ▸*n.* a structure in a living organism, esp. a sensory cell or sense organ, that responds to light falling on it. —**pho·to·re·cep·tive** /ˈseptiv/ *adj.*

pho·to·re·con·nais·sance /ˌfōtōriˈkänəsəns/ ▸*n.* military reconnaissance carried out by means of aerial photography.

pho·to·re·sist /ˌfōtōriˈzist/ ▸*n.* a photosensitive resist that, when exposed to light, loses its resistance or its susceptibility to attack by an etchant or solvent. Such materials are used in making microcircuits.

pho·to·res·pi·ra·tion /ˌfōtōˌrespəˈrāsʜən/ ▸*n.* *Botany* a respiratory process in many higher plants by which they take up oxygen in the light and give out some carbon dioxide, contrary to the general pattern of photosynthesis.

pho·to·re·sponse /ˌfōtōriˈspäns/ ▸*n.* *Biology* a response of a plant or other organism to light, mediated otherwise than through photosynthesis.

pho·to·sen·si·tive /ˌfōtəˈsensitiv/ ▸*adj.* having a chemical, electrical, or other response to light: *photosensitive cells | photosensitive drugs.* —**pho·to·sen·si·tiv·i·ty** /-ˌsensəˈtivitē/ *n.*

pho·to ses·sion ▸*n.* a prearranged session in which a photographer takes photographs of someone for publication.

pho·to shoot ▸*n.* another term for **PHOTO SESSION.**

pho·to·sphere /ˈfōtəˌsfi(ə)r/ ▸*n.* *Astronomy* the luminous envelope of a star from which its light and heat radiate. —**pho·to·spher·ic** /ˌfōtəˈsfi(ə)rik; ˈsferik/ *adj.*

pho·to·stat /ˈfōtōˌstat/ (also **Pho·to·stat**) ▸*n.* *trademark* a type of machine for making photocopies on special paper. ■ a copy made by this means.
▸*v.* (**-stat·ed, -stat·ing**) [*trans.*] make a copy of (a document) using a photostat machine. —**pho·to·stat·ic** /ˌfōtōˈstatik/ *adj.*

pho·to·syn·thate /ˌfōtōˈsinˌtʜāt/ ▸*n.* *Biochemistry* a sugar or other substance made by photosynthesis.

pho·to·syn·the·sis /ˌfōtōˈsintʜəsis/ ▸*n.* the process by which green plants and some other organisms use sunlight to synthesize foods from carbon dioxide and water. Photosynthesis in plants generally involves the green pigment chlorophyll and generates oxygen as a byproduct. —**pho·to·syn·thet·ic** /-ˌsinˈtʜetik/ *adj.* —**pho·to·syn·thet·i·cal·ly** /-ˌsinˈtʜetik(ə)lē/ *adv.*

pho·to·syn·the·size /ˌfōtōˈsintʜəˌsīz/ ▸*v.* [*intrans.*] (of a plant) synthesize sugars or other substances by means of photosynthesis.

pho·to·sys·tem /ˈfōtōˌsistəm/ ▸*n.* a biochemical mechanism in plants by which chlorophyll absorbs light energy for photosynthesis. There are two such mechanisms (**photosystems I** and **II**) involving different chlorophyll–protein complexes.

pho·to·tax·is /ˌfōtō'taksis/ ▸*n.* (*pl.* **-tax·es** /-'taksēz/) *Biology* the bodily movement of a motile organism in response to light, either toward the source of light (**positive phototaxis**) or away from it (**negative phototaxis**). Compare with PHOTOTROPISM. ■ a movement of this kind. —**pho·to·tac·tic** /-'taktik/ *adj.*

pho·to·ther·a·py /ˌfōtō'THerəpē/ ▸*n.* the use of light in the treatment of physical or mental illness.

pho·to·tran·sis·tor /ˌfōtō,tran'zistər/ ▸*n.* a transistor that responds to light striking it by generating and amplifying an electric current.

pho·to·troph /'fōtə,träf/ ▸*n.* *Biology* a phototrophic organism.

pho·to·troph·ic /ˌfōtə'träfik/ ▸*adj.* *Biology* (of an organism) obtaining energy from sunlight to synthesize organic compounds for nutrition.

pho·tot·ro·pism /ˌfōtə'trōpizəm; fō'tätrə,pizəm/ ▸*n.* *Biology* the orientation of a plant or other organism in response to light, either toward the source of light (**positive phototropism**) or away from it (**negative phototropism**). Compare with HELIOTROPISM, PHOTOTAXIS. —**pho·to·trop·ic** /ˌfōtə'trōpik; -'träpik/ *adj.*

pho·to·tube /'fōtō,t(y)o͞ob/ ▸*n.* *Electronics* a photocell in the form of an electron tube with a photoemissive cathode.

pho·to·type·set·ter /ˌfōtō'tīp,setər/ ▸*n.* a machine for photocomposition. —**pho·to·type·set** /-,set/ *adj.* —**pho·to·type·set·ting** /-,setiNG/ *n.*

pho·to·vol·ta·ic /ˌfōtəvōl'tāik; ˌfōtōväl-/ ▸*adj.* relating to the production of electric current at the junction of two substances exposed to light.

pho·to·vol·ta·ics /ˌfōtəvōl'tāiks; ˌfōtōväl-/ ▸*plural n.* [treated as *sing.*] the branch of technology concerned with the production of electric current at the junction of two substances. ■ [treated as *pl.*] devices having such a junction.

phr. ▸*abbr.* phrase.

phrag·mi·tes /frag'mītēz/ ▸*n.* a common and invasive tall reed. • Genus *Phragmites*, family Gramineae: several species, in particular the **common reed** (*P. communis*). ▷modern Latin, from Greek *phragmitēs* 'growing in hedges,' from *phragma* 'hedge.'

phras·al /'frāzəl/ ▸*adj.* [*attrib.*] *Grammar* consisting of a phrase or phrases: *the text fragments itself into phrasal units.* —**phras·al·ly** *adv.*

phras·al verb ▸*n.* *Grammar* an idiomatic phrase consisting of a verb and another element, typically either an adverb, as in *break down*, or a preposition, for example *see to*, or a combination of both, such as *look down on*.

phrase /frāz/ ▸*n.* a small group of words standing together as a conceptual unit, typically forming a component of a clause. ■ an idiomatic or short pithy expression: *his favorite phrase is "it's a pleasure."* ■ *Music* a group of notes forming a distinct unit within a longer passage. ■ *Ballet* a group of steps within a longer sequence or dance.
▸*v.* [*trans.*] put into a particular form of words: *it's important to phrase the question correctly.* ■ divide (music) into phrases in a particular way, esp. in performance: [as *n.*] (**phrasing**) *original phrasing brought out unexpected aspects of the music.* ▷mid 16th cent. (in the sense 'style or manner of expression'): via late Latin from Greek *phrasis*, from *phrazein* 'declare, tell.'
▸*PHRASE* □ **turn of phrase** a manner of expression: *an awkward turn of phrase.*

phrase book ▸*n.* a book for people visiting a foreign country, listing useful expressions in the language of the country together with their equivalent in the visitor's own language.

phra·se·ol·o·gy /ˌfrāzē'äləjē/ ▸*n.* (*pl.* **-gies**) a mode of expression, esp. one characteristic of a particular speaker or writer: *legal phraseology.* ▷mid 17th cent.: from modern Latin *phraseologia*, from Greek *phraseōn*, genitive plural of *phrasis* 'a phrase' + *-logia* (see -LOGY). —**phra·se·o·log·i·cal** /-zēə'läjikəl/ *adj.*

phra·try /'frātrē/ ▸*n.* (*pl.* **-tries**) *Anthropology* a descent group or kinship group in some tribal societies. ▷mid 19th cent.: from Greek *phratria*, from *phratēr* 'clansman.'

phreak·ing /'frēkiNG/ ▸*n.* *informal* the action of hacking into telecommunications systems, esp. to obtain free calls. ▷1970s: alteration of *freaking* (see FREAK). The change from *f-* to *ph-* was due to association with PHONE[1]. —**phreak** *n.* —**phreak·er** /'frēkər/ *n.*

phre·at·ic /frē'atik/ ▸*adj.* *Geology* relating to or denoting underground water in the zone of saturation (beneath the water table). Compare with VADOSE. ■ (of a volcanic eruption) caused by the heating and expansion of groundwater. ▷late 19th cent.: from Greek *phrear, phreat-* 'a well' + -IC.

phre·at·o·mag·mat·ic /frē,atəmag'matik/ ▸*adj.* *Geology* (of a volcanic eruption) in which both magmatic gases and steam from groundwater are expelled. ▷mid 20th cent.: from Greek *phrear, phreat-* 'a well' + *magmatic* (see MAGMA).

phre·at·o·phyte /frē'atə,fit/ ▸*n.* *Botany* a plant with a deep root system that draws its water supply from near the water table. ▷1920s: from Greek *phrear, phreat-* 'a well' + -PHYTE. —**phre·at·o·phyt·ic** /-,atə'fitik/ *adj.*

phren. ▸*abbr.* ■ phrenological. ■ phrenology.

phren·ic /'frenik/ ▸*adj.* [*attrib.*] **1** *Anatomy* of or relating to the diaphragm: *the phrenic nerves.* **2** of or relating to the mind or mental activity. ▷early 18th cent.: from French *phrénique*, from Greek *phrēn, phren-* 'diaphragm, mind' (because the mind was once thought to lie in the diaphragm).

phre·nol·o·gy /fre'näləjē/ ▸*n.* *chiefly historical* the detailed study of the shape and size of the cranium as a supposed indication of character and mental abilities. ▷early 19th cent.: from Greek *phrēn, phren-* 'mind' + -LOGY. —**phre·no·log·i·cal** /ˌfrenə'läjikəl/ *adj.* —**phre·nol·o·gist** /-jist/ *n.*

Phryg·i·a /'frijēə/ an ancient region in west central Asia Minor, to the south of Bithynia. It reached the peak of its power in the 8th century BC under King Midas. It was eventually absorbed into the kingdom of Lydia in the 6th century BC.

Phryg·i·an /'frijēən/ ▸*adj.* of or relating to Phrygia, its people, or their language.
▸*n.* **1** a native or inhabitant of ancient Phrygia. **2** the extinct Indo-European language of the ancient Phrygians, related to Greek and Armenian, of which only a few inscriptions survive.

Phryg·i·an cap ▸*n.* a soft conical cap with the top bent forward, worn in ancient times and now identified with the liberty cap.

Phryg·i·an mode ▸*n.* *Music* the mode represented by the natural diatonic scale E–E (containing a minor 2nd, 3rd, 6th, and 7th).

PHS ▸*abbr.* Public Health Service.

phthal·ic ac·id /'THalik/ ▸*n.* *Chemistry* a crystalline acid derived from benzene, with two carboxylic acid groups attached to the benzene ring. • Chem. formula: $C_6H_4(COOH)_2$; three isomers. ▷mid 19th cent.: *phthalic*, shortening of *naphthalic* (see NAPHTHALENE). —**phthal·ate** /'THal,āt/ *n.*

phthal·ic an·hy·dride ▸*n.* *Chemistry* a crystalline compound made by oxidizing naphthalene, used as an intermediate in the manufacture of plastics, resins, and dyes. • A bicyclic anhydride; chem. formula: $C_6H_4(CO)_2O$. ▷mid 19th cent.: *phthalic*, shortening of *naphthalic* (see NAPHTHALENE).

phthal·o·cy·a·nine /ˌTHalə'sīə,nēn/ ▸*n.* *Chemistry* a greenish-blue crystalline dye of the porphyrin group. • Chem. formula: $C_{32}H_{18}N_8$. ■ any of a large class of green or blue pigments and dyes that are chelate complexes of this compound or one of its derivatives with a metal (in particular, copper). ▷1930s: from *phthalic* (see PHTHALIC ACID) + Greek *kuan(e)os* 'dark blue' + -INE[4].

Phthi·rap·ter·a /THī'raptərə/ *Entomology* an order of insects comprising both the sucking lice and the biting lice. ▷modern Latin (plural), from Greek *phtheir* 'louse' + *pteron* 'wing.'

phthi·sis /'THīsis; 'tī-/ ▸*n.* *archaic Medicine* pulmonary tuberculosis or a similar progressive systemic disease. ▷mid 16th cent.: via Latin from Greek, from *phthinein* 'to decay.' —**phthis·ic** /'tizik; 'THizik/ *adj.* —**phthis·i·cal** /'tizikəl; 'THiz-/ *adj.*

Phu·ket /ˌpo͞o'ket/ **1** an island in Thailand, located at the head of the Strait of Malacca off the western coast of the Malay Peninsula. **2** a port at the south end of Phuket Island, a major resort center and outlet to the Indian Ocean.

phut /fət/ ▸*exclam.* British term for PFFT. ▷late 19th cent.: perhaps from Hindi *phaṭnā* 'to burst.'

phyco- ▸*comb. form* relating to seaweed: *phycology.* ▷from Greek *phukos* 'seaweed.'

phy·co·bilin /ˌfikō'bīlin; -'bilin/ ▸*n.* *Biochemistry* any of a group of red or blue photosynthetic pigments present in some algae.

phy·co·cy·an·in /ˌfikō'sīənin/ ▸*n.* *Biochemistry* any of a group of blue photosynthetic pigments present in cyanobacteria.

phy·co·e·ryth·rin /ˌfikō'erəTHrin; -i'riTHrin/ ▸*n.* *Biochemistry* any of a group of red photosynthetic pigments present in red algae and some cyanobacteria.

phy·col·o·gy /fī'käləjē/ ▸*n.* the branch of botany concerned with seaweeds and other algae. —**phy·co·log·i·cal** /ˌfikə'läjikəl/ *adj.* —**phy·col·o·gist** /-jist/ *n.*

phy·co·my·cete /ˌfikō'mī,sēt; ˌfikōmī'sēt/ ▸*n.* *Botany* any of the lower fungi, which typically form a nonseptate mycelium. • Subdivisions Mastigomycotina and Zygomycotina; formerly placed in a class Phycomycetes.

phy·co·my·co·sis /ˌfikōmī'kōsis/ ▸*n.* *Medicine & Veterinary Medicine* infection with a parasitic fungus that affects the sinuses and the tissues of the lungs, skin, and nerves. • The fungus is typically a phycomycete, typically of the genus *Rhizopus, Absidia*, or *Mucor*.

Phyfe /fīf/, Duncan (1768–1854) U.S. cabinetmaker; born in Scotland. Between 1792 and 1847, working mostly with mahogany, he made chairs, sofas, and tables noted for their graceful proportions and precisely carved simple ornaments.

phy·la /'fīlə/ ▸ plural form of PHYLUM.

phy·lac·ter·y /fī'laktərē/ ▸*n.* (*pl.* **-ter·ies**) a small leather box containing Hebrew texts on vellum, worn by Jewish men at morning prayer as a reminder to keep the law. ▷late Middle English: via late Latin from Greek *phulaktērion* 'amulet,' from *phulassein* 'to guard.'

phylactery

phy·let·ic /fī'letik/ ▸*adj.* *Biology* relating to or denoting the evolutionary development of a species or other group. ▷late 19th cent.: from Greek *phuletikos*, from *phuletēs* 'tribesman,' from *phulē* 'tribe.' —**phy·let·i·cal·ly** /-ik(ə)lē/ *adv.*

phyl·lite /'filīt/ ▸*n.* *Geology* a fine-grained metamorphic rock with a well-developed laminar structure, intermediate between slate and schist in degree of metamorphism. ▷late 19th cent.: from Greek *phullon* 'leaf' + -ITE[1].

phyl·lo /'fēlō/ (also **fi·lo**) ▸*n.* a kind of dough that can be stretched into thin sheets, used in layers to make pastries, esp. in eastern Mediterranean cooking: [as *adj.*] *phyllo pastry.* ▷1950s: from modern Greek *phullo* 'leaf.'

phyllo- ▸*comb. form* of a leaf; relating to leaves: *phyllotaxis.* ▷from Greek *phullon* 'leaf.'

phyl·lo·clade /'filə,klād/ ▸*n.* *Botany* a flattened branch or stem-joint resembling and functioning as a leaf. ▷mid 19th cent.: from modern Latin *phyllocladium*, from Greek *phullōdēs* 'leaflike,' from *phullon* 'leaf.'

phyl·lode /'filōd/ ▸*n.* *Botany* a winged leaf stalk that functions as a leaf. ▷mid 19th cent.: from modern Latin *phyllodium*, from Greek *phullōdēs* 'leaflike,' from *phullon* 'leaf.'

phyl·lo·pod /'filə,päd/ ▸*n.* *Zoology* a branchiopod crustacean. ▷from modern Latin *Phyllopoda* (former class name), from Greek *phullon* 'leaf' + *pous, pod-* 'foot.'

phyl·lo·qui·none /ˌfilō'kwinōn; -kwi'nōn/ ▸*n.* *Biochemistry* one of the K vitamins, found in cabbage, spinach, and other leafy green vegetables, and essential for the blood-clotting process. Also called VITAMIN K_1.

phyl·lo·tax·is /ˌfilə'taksis/ (also **phyl·lo·tax·y** /'filə,taksē/) ▸*n.* *Botany* the arrangement of leaves on an axis or stem. —**phyl·lo·tac·tic** /-'taktik/ *adj.*

phyl·lox·e·ra /fi'läksərə; ˌfilək'si(ə)rə/ ▸*n.* a plant louse that is a pest of vines. • *Phylloxera vitifoliae*, family Phylloxeridae, suborder Homoptera. ▷mid 19th cent.: modern Latin, from Greek *phullon* 'leaf' + *xēros* 'dry.'

phy·lo·gen·e·sis /ˌfilə'jenəsis/ ▸*n.* *Biology* the evolutionary development and diversification of a species or group of organisms, or of a particular feature of an organism. Compare with ONTOGENESIS. ▷late 19th cent.: from Greek *phulon, phulē* 'race, tribe' + GENESIS. —**phy·lo·ge·net·ic** /-jə'netik/ *adj.* —**phy·lo·ge·net·i·cal·ly** /-jə'netik(ə)lē/ *adv.*

phy·log·e·ny /ˌfī'läjənē/ ▸*n.* the branch of biology that deals with phylogenesis. Compare with ONTOGENY. ■ another term for PHYLOGENESIS. ▷late 19th cent.: from Greek *phulon, phulē* 'race, tribe' + -GENY. —**phy·lo·gen·ic** /ˌfilə'jenik/ *adj.* —**phy·lo·gen·i·cal·ly** /ˌfilə'jenik(ə)lē/ *adv.*

phy·lum /'filəm/ ▸*n.* (*pl.* **-la** /-lə/) *Zoology* a principal taxonomic category that ranks above class and below kingdom. ■ *Linguistics* a group of languages related to each other less closely than those forming a family, esp. one in which the relationships are disputed or unclear. ▷late 19th cent.: modern Latin, from Greek *phulon* 'race.'

phys. ▶*abbr.* ■ physical. ■ physician. ■ physics. ■ physiological. ■ physiology.

phy·sa·lis /ˈfīsəlis; ˈfis-/ ▶*n.* a plant of a genus that includes the cape gooseberry and Chinese lantern, which have an inflated, lanternlike calyx. • Genus *Physalis*, family Solanaceae: many species. ▷modern Latin, from Greek *phusallis* 'bladder' (because of the inflated calyx).

phys ed /ˈfiz ˈed/ ▶*n. informal* short for PHYSICAL EDUCATION.

phys·i·at·rics /ˌfizēˈatriks/ ▶*plural n.* [treated as *sing.*] another term for PHYSICAL THERAPY. —**phys·i·at·rist** /ˌfizēˈatrist; fiˈzīəˌtrist/ *n.*

P

phys·ic /ˈfizik/ *archaic* ▶*n.* medicine, esp. a cathartic. ■ the art of healing.
▶*v.* (**phys·icked** /ˈfizikt/, **phys·ick·ing** /ˈfiziking/) [*trans.*] treat with a medicine. ▷Middle English: from Old French *fisique* 'medicine,' from Latin *physica*, from Greek *phusikē* (*epistēmē*) '(knowledge) of nature.'

phys·i·cal /ˈfizikəl/ ▶*adj.* **1** of or relating to the body as opposed to the mind: *a whole range of physical and mental challenges.* ■ involving bodily contact or activity: *verbal or physical abuse | football and other physical games.* ■ sexual: *a physical relationship.* **2** of or relating to things perceived through the senses as opposed to the mind; tangible or concrete: *pleasant physical environments | physical assets such as houses or cars.* ■ of or relating to physics or the operation of natural forces generally: *physical laws.*
▶*n.* (also **physical examination**) a medical examination to determine a person's bodily fitness. ▷late Middle English (in the sense 'medicinal, relating to medicine'): from medieval Latin *physicalis*, from Latin *physica* 'things relating to nature' (see PHYSIC). Sense 2 dates from the late 16th cent. and sense 1 from the late 18th cent. —**phys·i·cal·i·ty** /ˌfiziˈkalitē/ *n.* —**phys·i·cal·ly** /-ik(ə)lē/ *adv.* —**phys·i·cal·ness** *n.*
▶*PHRASE* □ **get physical** *informal* become aggressive or violent. ■ become sexually intimate with someone.

phys·i·cal an·thro·pol·o·gy ▶*n.* see ANTHROPOLOGY.

phys·i·cal chem·is·try ▶*n.* the branch of chemistry concerned with the application of the techniques and theories of physics to the study of chemical systems.

phys·i·cal ed·u·ca·tion ▶*n.* instruction in physical exercise and games, esp. in schools.

phys·i·cal ge·og·ra·phy ▶*n.* the branch of geography dealing with natural features and processes.

phys·i·cal·ism /ˈfizikəlˌizəm/ ▶*n. Philosophy* the doctrine that the real world consists simply of the physical world. —**phys·i·cal·ist** *n.* & *adj.* —**phys·i·cal·is·tic** /ˌfizikəˈlistik/ *adj.*

phys·i·cal·ize /ˈfizikəlˌīz/ ▶*v.* [*trans.*] express or represent by physical means or in physical terms: *physicalizing your anger can help release tension.* —**phys·i·cal·i·za·tion** /ˌfizikəliˈzāshən/ *n.*

phys·i·cal med·i·cine ▶*n.* **1** the branch of medicine concerned with the treatment of disease by physical means such as manipulation, heat, electricity, or radiation, rather than by medication or surgery. **2** the branch of medicine that treats biomechanical disorders and injuries.

phys·i·cal sci·ences ▶*plural n.* the sciences concerned with the study of inanimate natural objects, including physics, chemistry, astronomy, and related subjects. Often contrasted with LIFE SCIENCES.

phys·i·cal the·a·ter ▶*n.* a form of theater that emphasizes the use of physical movement, as in dance and mime, for expression.

phys·i·cal ther·a·py ▶*n.* the treatment of disease, injury, or deformity by physical methods such as massage, heat treatment, and exercise rather than by drugs or surgery. —**phys·i·cal ther·a·pist** *n.*

phys·i·cal train·ing ▶*n.* the systematic use of exercises to promote bodily fitness and strength.

phy·si·cian /fiˈzishən/ ▶*n.* a person qualified to practice medicine. ■ a healer: *physicians of the soul.* ▷Middle English: from Old French *fisicien*, based on Latin *physica* 'things relating to nature' (see PHYSIC).
▶*PHRASE* □ **physician, heal thyself** *proverb* before attempting to correct others, make sure that you aren't guilty of the same faults. [with biblical allusion to Luke 4:23.]

phys·i·cian's as·sis·tant ▶*n.* someone qualified to assist a physician and carry out routine clinical procedures under the supervision of a physician.

phys·i·cist /ˈfizəsist/ ▶*n.* an expert in or student of physics.

physico- ▶*comb. form* physical; physical and . . . : *physico-mental.* ▷from PHYSICS.

phys·i·co·chem·i·cal /ˌfizikōˈkemikəl/ ▶*adj.* of or relating to physics and chemistry or to physical chemistry.

phys·ics /ˈfiziks/ ▶*plural n.* [treated as *sing.*] the branch of science concerned with the nature and properties of matter and energy. The subject matter of physics, distinguished from that of chemistry and biology, includes mechanics, heat, light and other radiation, sound, electricity, magnetism, and the structure of atoms. ■ the physical properties and phenomena of something: *the physics of plasmas.* ▷late 15th cent. (denoting natural science in general, esp. the Aristotelian system): plural of obsolete *physic* 'physical (thing),' suggested by Latin *physica*, Greek *phusika* 'natural things,' from *phusis* 'nature.'

physio- ▶*comb. form* **1** relating to nature and natural phenomena: *physiography.* **2** representing PHYSIOLOGY. ▷from Greek *phusis* 'nature.'

phys·i·o·chem·i·cal /ˌfizēōˈkemikəl/ ▶*adj.* of or relating to physiological chemistry.

phys·i·o·crat /ˈfizēəˌkrat/ ▶*n.* a member of an 18th-century group of French economists who believed that agriculture was the source of all wealth and that agricultural products should be highly priced. Advocating adherence to a supposed natural order of social institutions, they also stressed the necessity of free trade. ▷late 18th cent.: from French *physiocrate*, from *physiocratie* 'physiocracy' (see PHYSIO-, -CRACY). —**phys·i·oc·ra·cy** /ˌfizēˈäkrəsē/ *n.* —**phys·i·o·crat·ic** /ˌfizēəˈkratik/ *adj.*

phys·i·og·no·mist /ˌfizēˈä(g)nəmist/ ▶*n.* a person supposedly able to judge character (or, formerly, to predict the future) from facial characteristics. ▷late 16th cent.: from Old French *physionomiste.*

phys·i·og·no·my /ˌfizēˈä(g)nəmē/ ▶*n.* (*pl.* **-mies**) a person's facial features or expression, esp. when regarded as indicative of character or ethnic origin. ■ the supposed art of judging character from facial characteristics. ■ the general form or appearance of something: *the physiognomy of the landscape.* ▷late Middle English: from Old French *phisonomie*, via medieval Latin from Greek *phusiognōmonia* 'judging of a man's nature (by his features),' based on *gnōmōn* 'a judge, interpreter.' —**phys·i·og·nom·ic** /ˌfizēəˈnämik/ *adj.* —**phys·i·og·nom·i·cal** /ˌfizēəˈnämikəl/ *adj.* —**phys·i·og·nom·i·cal·ly** /ˌfizēəˈnämik(ə)lē/ *adv.*

phys·i·og·ra·phy /ˌfizēˈägrəfē/ ▶*n.* another term for PHYSICAL GEOGRAPHY. ▷early 19th cent.: from French *physiographie* (see PHYSIO-, -GRAPHY). —**phys·i·og·ra·pher** /-fər/ *n.* —**phys·i·o·graph·ic** /ˌfizēəˈgrafik/ *adj.* —**phys·i·o·graph·i·cal** /ˌfizēəˈgrafikəl/ *adj.* —**phys·i·o·graph·i·cal·ly** /ˌfizēəˈgrafik(ə)lē/ *adv.*

physiol. ▶*abbr.* ■ physiological. ■ physiologist. ■ physiology.

phys·i·o·log·i·cal sa·line /ˌfizēəˈläjikəl/ ▶*n.* a solution of salts that is isotonic with the body fluids.

phys·i·ol·o·gy /ˌfizēˈäləjē/ ▶*n.* the branch of biology that deals with the normal functions of living organisms and their parts. ■ the way in which a living organism or bodily part functions: *the physiology of the brain.* ▷early 17th cent.: from Latin *physiologia* (perhaps via French), from Greek *phusiologia* 'natural philosophy' (see PHYSIO-, -LOGY). —**phys·i·o·log·ic** /ˌfizēəˈläjik/ *adj.* —**phys·i·o·log·i·cal** /ˌfizēəˈläjikəl/ *adj.* —**phys·i·o·log·i·cal·ly** /ˌfizēəˈläjik(ə)lē/ *adv.* —**phys·i·ol·o·gist** /-jist/ *n.*

phys·i·o·ther·a·py /ˌfizēōˈTHerəpē/ ▶*n.* British term for PHYSICAL THERAPY. —**phys·i·o·ther·a·pist** /-pist/ *n.*

phy·sique /fiˈzēk/ ▶*n.* the form, size, and development of a person's body: *a sturdy, muscular physique | they were much alike in physique.* ▷early 19th cent.: from French, literally 'physical' (used as a noun).

phy·so·stig·mine /ˌfīsōˈstigˌmēn/ ▶*n. Chemistry* a compound that is the active ingredient of the Calabar bean and is used medicinally in eye drops because of its anticholinergic activity. • A tricyclic alkaloid; chem. formula: $C_{15}H_{21}N_3O_2$. ▷mid 19th cent.: from the modern Latin genus name *Physostigma* (to which the Calabar bean belongs) + -INE[4].

-phyte ▶*comb. form* denoting a plant or plantlike organism: *epiphyte.* ▷from Greek *phuton* 'a plant,' from *phuein* 'come into being.'

-phytic ▶*comb. form.* in adjectives corresponding to nouns ending in *-phyte* (such as *epiphytic* corresponding to *epiphyte*).

phyto- ▶*comb. form* of a plant; relating to plants: *phytogeography.* ▷from Greek *phuton* 'a plant,' from *phuein* 'come into being.'

phy·to·a·lex·in /ˌfītōəˈleksin/ ▶*n. Botany* a substance that is produced by plant tissues in response to contact with a parasite and that specifically inhibits the growth of that parasite. ▷1940s: from PHYTO- 'of plants' + *alexin*, a name for a class of substances found in blood serum, able to destroy bacteria.

phy·to·chem·is·try /ˌfītōˈkeməstrē/ ▶*n.* the branch of chemistry concerned with plants and plant products. —**phy·to·chem·i·cal** /-ˈkemikəl/ *adj.* —**phy·to·chem·ist** /-ˈkemist/ *n.*

phy·to·chrome /ˈfītəˌkrōm/ ▶*n. Biochemistry* a blue-green pigment found in many plants, in which it regulates various developmental processes. ▷late 19th cent.: from PHYTO- 'relating to plants' + Greek *khrōma* 'color.'

phy·to·es·tro·gen /ˌfītōˈestrəjən/ ▶*n.* an estrogen occurring naturally in legumes, considered beneficial in some diets.

phy·to·ge·net·ic /ˌfītōjəˈnetik/ ▶*adj. Botany* of or relating to the origin and evolution of plants.

phy·to·ge·o·graph·i·cal king·dom /ˌfītōˌjēəˈgrafikəl/ ▶*n. Botany* each of a number of major areas of the earth distinguished on the basis of the characteristic plants present. They usually include the Boreal, Paleotropical, Neotropical, Australian, and Antarctic kingdoms.

phy·to·ge·og·ra·phy /ˌfītōjēˈägrəfē/ ▶*n.* the branch of botany that deals with the geographical distribution of plants. —**phy·to·ge·og·ra·pher** /-fər/ *n.* —**phy·to·ge·o·graph·ic** /ˌfītōˌjēəˈgrafik/ *adj.* —**phy·to·ge·o·graph·i·cal** /ˈfītōˌjēəˈgrafikəl/ *adj.* —**phy·to·ge·o·graph·i·cal·ly** /ˌfītōˌjēəˈgrafik(ə)lē/ *adv.*

phy·to·he·mag·glu·ti·nin /ˌfītōˌhēməˈglo͞otn-in/ (*Brit.* **phy·to·hae·mag·glu·ti·nin**) ▶*n. Biochemistry* a toxic plant protein, esp. that extracted from the red kidney bean. It has important medical applications, esp. in immunology, because it can induce mitosis and also causes red blood cells to clump together.

phy·to·lith /ˈfītəlith/ ▶*n. Botany* a minute mineral particle formed inside a plant. ■ *Paleontology* a fossilized particle of plant tissue.

phy·to·nu·tri·ent /ˌfītōˈn(y)o͞otrēənt/ ▶*n.* a substance of plant origin which has nutritional value. ■ a nutritional supplement based on such a substance; a nutraceutical. ▷from PHYTO- + NUTRIENT.

phy·to·pa·thol·o·gy /ˌfītōpəˈTHäləjē/ ▶*n.* the study of plant diseases. —**phy·to·path·o·log·i·cal** /-ˌpaTHəˈläjikəl/ *adj.* —**phy·to·path·ol·o·gist** /-jist/ *n.*

phy·toph·a·gous /fīˈtäfəgəs/ ▶*adj. Zoology* (esp. of an insect or other invertebrate) feeding on plants. —**phy·toph·a·gy** /-əjē/ *n.*

phy·to·plank·ton /ˌfītōˈplaNGktən/ ▶*n. Biology* plankton consisting of microscopic plants.

phy·to·san·i·tar·y /ˌfītōˈsaniterē/ ▶*adj.* (of agricultural goods crossing borders) sanitary with regard to pests and pathogens: *a point-of-origin phytosanitary certificate.*

phy·to·tox·ic /ˌfītəˈtäksik/ ▶*adj. Botany* poisonous to plants. ■ of or relating to a poisonous substance derived from a plant. —**phy·to·tox·ic·i·ty** /-ˌtäkˈsisitē/ *n.*

phy·to·tox·in /ˌfītəˈtäksin/ ▶*n. Botany* a poisonous substance derived from a plant. ■ a substance that is phytotoxic, esp. one produced by a parasite.

PI ▶*abbr.* private investigator

pi /pī/ ▶*n.* the sixteenth letter of the Greek alphabet (Π, π), transliterated as 'p.' ■ the numerical value of the ratio of the circumference of a circle to its diameter (approximately 3.14159). [from the initial letter of Greek *periphereia* 'circumference.'] ■ (**Pi**) [followed by Latin genitive] *Astronomy* the sixteenth star in a constellation: *Pi Herculis.* ■ *Chemistry & Physics* relating to or denoting an electron or orbital with one unit of angular momentum about an internuclear axis.
▶*symbol* ■ (π) the numerical value of pi. ■ (Π) osmotic pressure. ■ (Π) mathematical product. ▷Greek.

pi·a /ˈpīə; ˈpēə/ ▶*n.* short for PIA MATER. —**pi·al** /ˈpīəl; ˈpēəl/ *adj.*

pi·ac·u·lar /pīˈakyələr/ ▶*adj. rare* making or requiring atonement. ▷early 17th cent.: from Latin *piacularis*, from *piaculum* 'expiation,' from *piare* 'appease.'

Piaf /ˈpēäf; pyäf/, Edith (1915–63), French singer; born *Edith Giovanna Gassion.* She became known as a cabaret and music-hall singer in the late 1930s. Her songs included "La Vie en rose" and "Je ne regrette rien."

piaffe /pyaf/ ▶*n.* a movement performed in advanced dressage and classical riding, in which the horse executes a slow, elevated trot without moving forward.
▶*v.* [*intrans.*] (of a horse) perform such a movement. ▷mid 18th cent.: from French *piaffer* 'to strut.'

Pia·get /ˌpēəˈzhä; pyä-/, Jean (1896–1980), Swiss psychologist. His work on the intellectual and logical abilities of children provided the single biggest impact on the study of the development of human thought processes.

pi·a ma·ter /ˈpīə ˈmātər; ˈpēə ˈmätər/ ▸*n. Anatomy* the delicate innermost membrane enveloping the brain and spinal cord. See also MENINGES. ▷late 19th cent.: from medieval Latin, in full literally 'tender mother,' translating Arabic *al-'umm ar-rakīka*.

pia·ni /pēˈänē/ ▸ plural form of PIANO[2].

pi·a·nism /ˈpēəˌnizəm/ ▸*n.* artistry or technical skill in playing the piano, or in composing piano music. **—pi·a·nis·tic** /ˌpēəˈnistik/ *adj.* **—pi·a·nis·ti·cal·ly** /ˌpēəˈnistik(ə)lē/ *adv.*

pi·a·nis·si·mo /ˌpēəˈnisiˌmō/ *Music* ▸*adv. & adj.* (esp. as a direction) very soft or softly.
▸*n.* (*pl.* **-mos** or **-mi** /-ˌmī/) a passage marked to be performed very softly. ▷Italian, superlative of *piano* (see PIANO[2]).

pi·an·ist /ˈpēənist; pēˈanist/ ▸*n.* a person who plays the piano, esp. professionally. ▷mid 19th cent.: from French *pianiste*, from *piano* (see PIANO[1]).

pi·an·o[1] /pēˈanō/ ▸*n.* (*pl.* **-os**) a large keyboard musical instrument with a wooden case enclosing a soundboard and metal strings, which are struck by hammers when the keys are depressed. The strings' vibration is stopped by dampers when the keys are released, and it can be regulated for length and volume by two or three pedals. ▷early 19th cent.: from Italian, abbreviation of PIANOFORTE.

grand piano

pi·a·no[2] /pēˈänō; pēˈanō/ *Music* ▸*adv. & adj.* (esp. as a direction) soft or softly.
▸*n.* (*pl.* **-nos** or **-ni** /-nē/) a passage marked to be performed softly. ▷Italian, literally 'soft.'

pi·an·o ac·cor·di·on ▸*n.* an accordion with the melody played on a small vertical keyboard like that of a piano.

pi·a·no bar ▸*n.* a bar that features live piano music.

pi·a·no bench ▸*n.* a bench for sitting at a piano, often with an adjustable height mechanism and/or a storage area for music.

pi·an·o·forte /pēˈanōˌfôrtā; pēˈanōˌfôrt/ ▸*n. formal* term for PIANO[1]. ▷mid 18th cent.: from Italian, earlier *piano e forte* 'soft and loud,' expressing the gradation in tone.

pi·a·no hinge ▸*n.* a narrow hinge with a pin of the same length as the movable part.

pi·a·no·la /ˌpēəˈnōlə/ ▸*n. trademark* a piano equipped to be played automatically using a piano roll. ▷late 19th cent.: apparently a diminutive of PIANO[1].

pia·no no·bi·le /ˈpyänō ˈnōbēle/ ▸*n. Architecture* the main story of a large house (usually the first floor), containing the principal rooms. ▷Italian, literally 'noble floor.'

pi·an·o roll /pēˈänō/ ▸*n.* a roll of perforated paper that controls the movement of the keys in a player piano or similar instrument, so producing a particular melody.

pi·an·o stool ▸*n.* a stool for a pianist, typically adjustable in height.

pi·an·o tri·o ▸*n.* a trio for piano and two stringed instruments, usually violin and cello.

pi·an·o wire ▸*n.* strong steel wire used esp. for piano strings.

pi·as·sa·va /ˌpēəˈsävə/ (also **pi·as·sa·ba** /-bə/) ▸*n.* a stout fiber obtained from the leaf stalks of a number of South American and African palm trees. ■ a palm tree producing this fiber. ▷mid 19th cent.: via Portuguese from Tupi *piaçába*.

pi·as·ter /pēˈastər/ (also **pi·as·tre**) ▸*n.* a monetary unit of several Middle Eastern countries, equal to one hundredth of a pound. ▷from French, from Italian *piastra (d'argento)* 'plate (of silver).'

pi·az·za /pēˈätsə; pēˈazə/ ▸*n.* **1** /pēˈätsə/ a public square or marketplace, esp. in an Italian town. **2** /pēˈazə/ the veranda of a house. ▷late 16th cent.: Italian.

pi·broch /ˈpēbräk/ ▸*n.* a form of music for the Scottish bagpipes involving elaborate variations on a theme, typically of a martial or funerary character. ■ a piece of such music. ▷early 18th cent.: from Scottish Gaelic *piobaireachd* 'art of piping,' from *piobair* 'piper,' from *piob*, from English PIPE.

pic /pik/ ▸*n.* (*pl.* **pics** or **pix** /piks/) *informal* a photograph or movie; a picture. ▷late 19th cent.: abbreviation.

pi·ca[1] /ˈpīkə/ ▸*n. Printing* a unit of type size and line length equal to 12 points (about 1/6 inch or 4.2 mm). ■ a size of letter in typewriting, with 10 characters to the inch (about 3.9 to the centimeter). ▷late 16th cent.: from Anglo-Latin *pica* (literally 'magpie'), commonly identified with a 15th-cent. book of rules about ecclesiastical feasts, but no edition of such a *pica* printed in "pica" type is known.

pi·ca[2] ▸*n. Medicine* a tendency or craving to eat substances other than normal food (such as clay, plaster, or ashes), occurring during childhood or pregnancy, or as a symptom of disease. ▷mid 16th cent.: modern Latin, from Latin, literally 'magpie,' probably translating Greek *kissa* 'magpie,' also 'false appetite.'

pi·ca·dor /ˈpikəˌdôr/ ▸*n.* a bullfighter on horseback who pricks the bull with a lance to weaken it and goad it. ▷Spanish, from *picar* 'to prick.'

pi·can·te /piˈkantā/ ▸*adj.* (of food) spicy. ▷Spanish, literally 'pricking, biting.'

Pi·card /piˈkärd/ ▸*n.* **1** a native or inhabitant of Picardy. **2** the dialect of French spoken in Picardy.
▸*adj.* relating to Picardy, its inhabitants, or their dialect.

Pic·ar·dy /ˈpikərdē/ a region and former province of northern France. It was the scene of heavy fighting in World War I. French name PICARDIE

pic·a·resque /ˌpikəˈresk/ ▸*adj.* of or relating to an episodic style of fiction dealing with the adventures of a rough and dishonest but appealing hero. ▷early 19th cent.: from French, from Spanish *picaresco*. See PICARO.

pic·a·ro /ˈpēkərō/ ▸*n.* (*pl.* **-ros**) a rogue. ▷early 17th cent.: from Spanish *pícaro* 'rogue'.

pic·a·roon /ˌpikəˈroon/ ▸*n. archaic* a rogue or scoundrel. ▷early 17th cent.: from Spanish *picarón*, augmentative of *pícaro* 'rogue.'

Pi·cas·so /piˈkäsō; -ˈkasō/, Pablo (1881–1973), Spanish painter, sculptor, and graphic artist; resident in France from 1904. His prolific inventiveness and technical versatility made him the dominant figure in avant-garde art in the first half of the 20th century. Following his Blue period (1901–04) and Rose period (1905–06), he developed cubism (1908–14). In the 1920s and 1930s he adopted a neoclassical figurative style. **—Pi·cas·so·esque** /-ˌkäsōˈesk; -ˌkasō-/ *adj.*

Pablo Picasso

pic·a·yune /ˌpikiˈyoon/ ▸*adj. informal* petty; worthless: *the picayune squabbling of party politicians.*
▸*n.* a small coin of little value, esp. a 5-cent piece. ■ *informal* an insignificant person or thing. ▷early 19th cent.: from French *picaillon*, denoting a Piedmontese copper coin, also used to mean 'cash,' from Provençal *picaioun*, of unknown ultimate origin.

Pic·ca·dil·ly /ˌpikəˈdilē; ˈpikəˌdilē/ a street in central London that extends from Hyde Park to Piccadilly Circus, noted for its fashionable shops, hotels, and restaurants.

pic·ca·lil·li /ˈpikəˌlilē/ ▸*n.* (*pl.* **-lies** or **-lis**) a relish of chopped vegetables, mustard, and hot spices. ▷mid 18th cent.: probably from a blend of PICKLE and CHILI.

pic·ca·nin·ny ▸*n.* chiefly British spelling of PICKANINNY.

pic·ca·ta /piˈkätə/ ▸*adj.* cooked in a sauce of lemon, parsley and butter: *chicken piccata | turkey cutlets served piccata style.*

pic·co·lo /ˈpikəˌlō/ ▸*n.* (*pl.* **-los**) a small flute sounding an octave higher than the ordinary one. ■ a player of this instrument in an orchestra. ▷mid 19th cent.: from Italian, 'small (flute).'

pice /pīs/ ▸*n.* (*pl.* same) a former monetary unit in the Indian subcontinent, equal to one quarter of an anna. ▷from Hindi *paisā*.

pi·chi /ˈpichē/ ▸*n.* (*pl.* **pi·chis**) a small armadillo living in open pampas country in southern South America. • *Zaedyus pichiy*, family Dasypodidae. ▷early 19th cent.: via American Spanish from Araucanian, literally 'small.'

pich·i·ci·a·go /ˌpichəsēˈägō/ (also **pich·i·ci·e·go**) ▸*n.* (*pl.* **-gos**) another term for FAIRY ARMADILLO. ▷early 19th cent.: from Spanish, perhaps from Guarani *pichey* 'armadillo' + Spanish *ciego* 'blind' (from Latin *caecus*).

pick[1] /pik/ ▸*v.* **1** [*trans.*] take hold of and remove (a flower, fruit, or vegetable) from where it is growing: *I went to pick some flowers for Jenny's room* | [as *adj.* with *submodifier*] (**picked**) *freshly picked mushrooms.* ■ [*trans.*] take hold of and lift or move: *he picked a match out of the box | **picking** her **up**, he carried her into the next room.* ■ [*intrans.*] (**pick up**) *Golf* lift up one's ball, esp. when conceding a hole. **2** [*trans.*] choose (someone or something) from a number of alternatives, typically after careful thought: *maybe I picked the wrong career after all | she left Jed to **pick out** some toys* | [*intrans.*] *this time, I get to pick.* ■ (**pick one's way**) [with *adverbial of direction*] walk slowly and carefully, selecting the best or safest places to put one's feet: *he picked his way along the edge of the track, avoiding the potholes.* **3** [*intrans.*] repeatedly pull at something with one's fingers: *the old woman was **picking at** the sheet.* ■ [*trans.*] make (a hole) in fabric by doing this. ■ eat food or a meal in small amounts or without much appetite: *she **picked at** her breakfast.* ■ criticize someone in a niggling way: *now, please don't start **picking at** Ruth.* ■ [*trans.*] remove unwanted matter from (one's nose or teeth) by using one's finger or a pointed instrument. ■ [*trans.*] pluck the strings of (a guitar or banjo). ■ [*trans.*] (**pick something out**) play a tune on such an instrument slowly or with difficulty: *she began to pick out a rough melody on the guitar.*
▸*phrasal v.* □ **pick someone/something off** shoot a member of a group of people or things, aiming carefully from a distance. ■ *Baseball* put out a runner by a pickoff. □ **pick on** repeatedly single (someone) out for blame, criticism, or unkind treatment in a way perceived to be unfair. □ **pick someone/something out** distinguish someone or something among a group of people or things: *Lester picked out two familiar voices.* ■ (of a light) illuminate an object by shining directly on it. ■ (usu. **be picked out**) distinguish shapes or letters from their surroundings by painting or fashioning them in a contrasting color or medium: *the initials are picked out in diamonds.* □ **pick something over** (or **pick through**) examine or sort through a number of items carefully: *they picked through the charred remains of their home.* □ **pick up** become better; improve: *my luck's picked up.* ■ become stronger; increase: *the wind has picked up.* □ **pick oneself up** stand up again after a fall. □ **pick someone up** go somewhere to collect someone, typically in one's car and according to a prior arrangement. ■ stop for someone and take them into one's vehicle or vessel. ■ *informal* arrest someone. ■ *informal* casually strike up a relationship with someone one has never met before, as a sexual overture. □ **pick something up 1** collect something that has been left elsewhere: *Wanda came over to pick up her things.* ■ *informal* pay the bill for something, esp. when others have contributed to the expense: *as usual, we had to **pick up the tab**.* ■ tidy a room or building. **2** obtain, acquire, or learn something, esp. without formal arrangements or instruction: *he had picked up a little Russian from his father.* ■ catch an illness or infection. **3** detect or receive a signal or sound, esp. by means of electronic apparatus. ■ (also **pick up on**) become aware of or sensitive to something: *she is very quick to pick up emotional atmospheres.* ■ find and take a particular road or route. **4** (also **pick up**) resume something: *they picked up their friendship without the slightest difficulty.* ■ (also **pick up on**) refer to or develop a point or topic mentioned earlier: *Dawson picked up her earlier remark.* ■ (of an object or color) attractively accentuate the color of something else by being of a similar shade. □ **pick up after** tidy up things left strewn around by (someone).

Pronunciation Key ə *ago*; ər *over*; ˈə or ˌə *up*; ˈər or ˌər *fur*; a *hat*; ā *rate*; ä *car*; ch *chew*; e *let*; ē *see*; e(ə)r *air*; i *fit*; ī *by*; i(ə)r *ear*; ng *sing*; ō *go*; ô *for*; oi *boy*; ŏŏ *good*; ōō *goo*; ou *out*; sh *she*; th *thin*; th *then*; (h)w *why*; zh *vision*

P

▸*n.* **1** [in *sing.*] an act or the right of selecting something from among a group of alternatives: ***take your pick*** *from our extensive menu | Laura should have first pick.* ■ (**the pick of**) *informal* the person or thing perceived as the best in a particular group: *he was the pick of the bunch.* ■ someone or something that has been selected: *the club made him their first pick.* **2** *Basketball* an act of blocking or screening a defensive player from the ball handler, allowing an open shot. ▹Middle English (earlier as *pike*, which continues in dialect use): of unknown origin. Compare with Dutch *pikken* 'pick, peck,' and German *picken* 'peck, puncture,' also with French *piquer* 'to prick.' —**pick·a·ble** /ˈpikəbəl/ *adj.*

▸*PHRASES* □ **pick and choose** select only the best or most desirable from among a number of alternatives. □ **pick someone's** (or **brain**) *informal* obtain information by questioning someone who is better informed about a subject than oneself. □ **pick something clean** completely remove the flesh from a bone or carcass. □ **pick one's feet up** raise one's feet clear of the ground when walking. □ **pick a fight** (or **quarrel**) talk or behave in such a way as to provoke an argument or fight. □ **pick holes in** find fault with. □ **pick a lock** open a lock with an instrument other than the proper key. □ **pick someone's pockets** steal something surreptitiously from another person's pocket. □ **pick someone/something to pieces** (or **apart**) criticize someone or something severely and in detail. □ **pick up the pieces** restore one's life or a situation to a more normal state, typically after a shock or disaster. □ **pick up speed** (or **steam**) (of a vehicle) go faster; accelerate. □ **pick up the threads** resume something that has been interrupted.

pick[2] ▸*n.* **1** a tool consisting of a long handle set at right angles in the middle of a curved iron or steel bar with a point at one end and a chisel edge or point at the other, used for breaking up hard ground or rock. ■ short for ICE PICK. **2** an instrument for picking: [with *adj.*] *an ebony hair pick.* ■ *informal* a plectrum: *a pink guitar pick.* ■ short for TOOTHPICK. ▹Middle English: variant of PIKE[2].

pick·a·back /ˈpikəˌbak/ ▸*n., adv., adj.,* & *v.* old-fashioned term for PIGGYBACK.

pick·a·nin·ny /ˈpikəˌninē/ (also **pic·a·nin·ny** or *chiefly Brit.* **pic·ca·nin·ny**) ▸*n.* (*pl.* **-nies**) *offensive* a small black child.

▸*adj. archaic* very small. ▹mid 17th cent.: from West Indian Creole, from Spanish *pequeño* or Portuguese *pequeno* 'little,' *pequenino* 'tiny.'

pick·ax /ˈpikˌaks/ (also **pick·axe**) ▸*n.* another term for PICK[2] (sense 1).

▸*v.* [*trans.*] break or strike with a pickax. ▹Middle English *pikoys*, from Old French *picois*; related to PIKE[2].

pick·er /ˈpikər/ ▸*n.* [usu. with *adj.*] a person or machine that gathers or collects something: *a tomato picker.* ■ a person who plays a plucked instrument, esp. a guitar, banjo, or mandolin: *a capable singer, writer, and picker.*

pick·er·el /ˈpik(ə)rəl/ ▸*n.* (*pl.* same or **-els**) a small North American pike. • Genus *Esox*, family Esocidae: several species, including the **grass** (or **redfin**) **pickerel** (*E. americanus*). ■ a young pike. ▹Middle English: diminutive of PIKE[1].

pick·er·el·weed /ˈpik(ə)rəlˌwēd/ ▸*n.* a freshwater plant with broad arrow-shaped leaves and spikes of blue flowers that was formerly believed to give rise to, or provide food for, young pike. • *Pontederia cordata*, family Pontederiaceae.

Pick·er·ing[1] /ˈpik(ə)riNG/, John (1777–1846), U.S. linguist and lexicographer; son of Timothy Pickering. He wrote the first dictionary of Americanisms 1816 and studied the languages of North American Indians.

Pick·er·ing[2], Timothy (1745–1829), U.S. government official. He was the U.S. secretary of war 1795 and secretary of state 1795–1800, as well as a member of the U.S. Senate 1803–11 and U.S. House of Representatives 1813–17.

Pick·er·ing[3], William Hayward (1910–2004), U.S. engineer, born in Australia; director of the Jet Propulsion Laboratory (JPL) at the California Institute of Technology 1954–76. During his directorate the JPL launched the U.S.'s first satellite, Explorer I, in 1958.

pick·et /ˈpikit/ ▸*n.* **1** a person or group of people standing outside a place of work or other venue, protesting about something or trying to persuade others not to enter during a strike. ■ a blockade of a workplace or other venue staged by such a person or group. **2** *chiefly historical* a small body of troops or a single soldier sent out to watch for the enemy. ■ a soldier or party of soldiers performing a particular duty: *a* ***picket of*** *soldiers fired a volley over the coffin.* **3** [usu. as *adj.*] a pointed wooden stake driven into the ground, typically to form a fence or palisade or to tether a horse: *a cedar-picket stockade.* See also PICKET FENCE.

▸*v.* (**-et·ed**, **-et·ing**) [*trans.*] **1** act as a picket outside (a place of work or other venue): *strikers picketed the newspaper's main building* | [*intrans.*] *18,000 people turned up to picket.* **2** tether (an animal). ▹late 17th cent. (denoting a pointed stake, on which a soldier was required to stand on one foot as a military punishment): from French *piquet* 'pointed stake,' from *piquer* 'to prick,' from *pic* 'pike.' —**pick·et·er** *n.*

pick·et fence ▸*n.* a wooden fence made of spaced uprights connected by two or more horizontal rails.

pick·et line ▸*n.* a boundary established by workers on strike, esp. at the entrance to the place of work, that others are asked not to cross.

Pick·ett /ˈpikit/, George Edward (1825–75), U.S. army officer. Last in the West Point class of 1846, he was a distinguished Confederate general during the Civil War. In 1863, his military reputation was marred at Gettysburg when, under orders, he led a disastrous charge across an open field that became known as "Pickett's Charge."

Pick·ford /ˈpikfərd/, Mary (1893–1979), U.S. actress, born in Canada; born *Gladys Mary Smith*. A star of silent movies, she usually played the innocent young heroine, as in *Rebecca of Sunnybrook Farm* (1917) and *Pollyanna* (1920). With Douglas Fairbanks, her husband from 1919 to 1936, she was a cofounder of United Artists in 1919.

pick·ings /ˈpikiNGz/ ▸*plural n.* **1** profits or gains that are made effortlessly or dishonestly, as by picking: *thieves found* ***easy pickings*** *from garages and garden sheds | he found, as strays often do,* ***slim pickings.*** **2** remaining scraps or leftovers.

pick·le /ˈpikəl/ ▸*n.* **1** a small cucumber preserved in vinegar, brine, or a similar solution. ■ any food preserved in this way and used as a relish. ■ the liquid used to preserve food or other perishable items. ■ an acid solution for cleaning metal objects. **2** [in *sing.*] *informal* a difficult or messy situation: *I am* ***in a pickle.***

▸*v.* [*trans.*] preserve (food or other perishable items) in vinegar, brine, or a similar solution: *chunks of green tomatoes* ***pickled in*** *brine.* ■ immerse (a metal object) in an acid or other chemical solution for cleaning. ▹late Middle English (denoting a spicy sauce served with meat): from Middle Dutch, Middle Low German *pekel*, of unknown ultimate origin.

pick·led /ˈpikəld/ ▸*adj.* (of food) preserved in vinegar or brine: *pickled onions.* ■ [*predic.*] *informal* drunk.

pick·ler /ˈpik(ə)lər/ ▸*n.* a vegetable or fruit suitable for pickling.

pick·ling /ˈpik(ə)liNG/ ▸*adj.* [*attrib.*] (of food) suitable for being pickled or used in making pickles.

pick·lock /ˈpikˌläk/ ▸*n.* a person who picks locks. ■ an instrument for picking locks.

pick-me-up ▸*n. informal* a thing that makes one feel more energetic or cheerful: *ginseng has long been used as a pick-me-up | your letter was just the pick-me-up I needed.* ■ an alcoholic drink: *I wasn't going to drink tonight, but I need a little pick-me-up.*

pick·ney /ˈpiknē/ ▸*n. black English* a child: *me and the pickney have to survive some way.* Compare with PICKANINNY. ▹contraction of PICKANINNY.

pick·off /ˈpikˌôf; ˈpikˌäf/ ▸*n. Baseball* the putout of a runner leading off base, involving an unexpected throw to a base by the pitcher or the catcher while the batter is still at bat.

pick·pock·et /ˈpikˌpäkət/ ▸*n.* a person who steals from other people's pockets.

▸*v.* [*trans.*] steal from the pockets of (someone): *she stopped in New Orleans where she skillfully pickpocketed tourists.* ■ [*intrans.*] steal from other people's pockets: *an elderly man caught pickpocketing in Times Square.*

Pick's dis·ease /piks/ ▸*n.* a rare form of progressive dementia, typically occurring in late middle age and often familial, involving localized atrophy of the brain. ▹early 20th cent.: named after Arnold *Pick* (1851–1924), Bohemian neurologist.

pick·up /ˈpikˌəp/ ▸*n.* **1** (also **pickup truck**) a small truck with an enclosed cab and open back. **2** an act of collecting a person or goods, esp. in a vehicle: *curbside pickup* | [as *adj.*] *travel by bus from your local pickup point to your hotel.* **3** the reception of signals, esp. interference or noise, by electrical apparatus. **4** *informal* a casual encounter with someone, with a view to having a sexual relationship. ■ a person met in such an encounter. **5** an improvement in an economic indicator: *signs of* ***a pickup in*** *demand.* **6** a device that produces an electrical signal in response to some other kind of signal or change, in particular: ■ the cartridge of a record player, carrying the stylus. ■ a device on a musical instrument, particularly an electric guitar, that converts sound vibrations into electrical signals for amplification. **7** *Music* a series of introductory notes leading into the opening part of a tune. **8** *Fishing* a semicircular loop of metal for guiding the line back onto the spool as it is reeled in.

▸*adj.* informal and spontaneous: *six players had started a full-court pickup basketball game.*

Pick·wick·i·an /pikˈwikēən/ ▸*adj.* of or like Mr. Pickwick in Dickens's *Pickwick Papers*, esp. in being jovial, plump, or generous. ■ (of words or their senses) misunderstood or misused; not literally meant, esp. to avoid offense.

pick·y /ˈpikē/ ▸*adj.* (**pick·i·er**, **pick·i·est**) *informal* fastidious, esp. excessively so: *she had been a picky eater as a child.* —**pick·i·ness** /-ēnis/ *n.*

pick-your-own ▸*adj.* [*attrib.*] of or relating to a system in which commercially grown fruit or vegetables are picked by the customer for purchase at the place of production.

pic·nic /ˈpikˌnik/ ▸*n.* an outing or occasion that involves taking a packed meal to be eaten outdoors. ■ a meal eaten outdoors on such an occasion.

▸*v.* (**-nicked**, **-nick·ing**) [*intrans.*] have or take part in a picnic. ▹mid 18th cent.: from French *pique-nique*, of unknown origin. —**pic·nick·er** *n.*

▸*PHRASE* □ **no picnic** *informal* used of something difficult or unpleasant: *chemotherapy is no picnic.*

pico- ▸*comb. form* (used in units of measurement) denoting a factor of 10^{-12}: *picosecond.* ▹from Spanish *pico*, literally 'beak, peak, little bit.'

Pi·co de O·ri·za·ba /ˈpēkō de ˌôrēˈsäbä/ Spanish name for CITLALTÉPETL.

Pi·co Ri·ve·ra /ˌpēkō riˈverə/ a city in southwestern California, east of Los Angeles; pop. 59,177.

pi·cor·na·vi·rus /piˈkôrnəˌvīrəs/ ▸*n.* any of a group of very small RNA viruses that includes enteroviruses, rhinoviruses, and the virus of foot-and-mouth disease. ▹1960s: from PICO- + **RNA** + VIRUS.

pi·cot /ˈpēkō/ ▸*n.* [often as *adj.*] a small loop or series of small loops of twisted thread in lace or embroidery, typically decorating the border of a fabric. ▹early 17th cent.: from French, literally 'small peak or point,' diminutive of *pic*.

pic·o·tee /ˌpikəˈtē/ ▸*n.* a type of carnation whose light-colored flowers have dark-edged petals. ▹early 18th cent.: from French *picoté(e)* 'marked with points,' past participle of *picoter* 'to prick.'

pic·quet /piˈkāt/ ▸*n.* variant spelling of PIQUET.

pic·ric ac·id /ˈpikrik/ ▸*n. Chemistry* a bitter yellow compound obtained by nitrating phenol, used as a dye and in the manufacture of explosives. • Alternative name: **2,4,6-trinitrophenol**; chem. formula: $C_6H_2(NO_2)_3OH$. ▹mid 19th cent.: *picric* from Greek *pikros* 'bitter' + -IC. —**pic·rate** /ˈpikrāt/ *n.*

pic·rite /ˈpikˌrīt/ ▸*n. Geology* a dark basaltic rock rich in olivine. ▹early 19th cent.: from Greek *pikros* 'bitter' + -ITE[1]. —**pic·rit·ic** /pikˈritik/ *adj.*

pic·ro·tox·in /ˌpikrəˈtäksin/ ▸*n. Medicine* a bitter compound used to stimulate the respiratory and nervous systems, esp. in treating barbiturate poisoning. • This toxin is obtained from the seeds of the shrub *Anamirta cocculus* (family Menispermaceae). ▹mid 19th cent.: from Greek *pikros* 'bitter' + TOXIN.

Pict /pikt/ ▸*n.* a member of an ancient people inhabiting northern Scotland in Roman times.

Roman writings of around AD 300 apply the term *Picti* to the hostile tribes of the area north of the Firth of Forth and the Firth of Clyde. Their origins are uncertain, but they may have been a loose confederation of Celtic tribes.

▹from late Latin *Picti*, perhaps from *pict-* 'painted, tattooed' (from *pingere* 'to paint'), or perhaps influenced by a local name. —**Pict·ish** /-tiSH/ *adj.* & *n.*

pic·to·graph /ˈpiktəˌgraf/ (also **pic·to·gram** /-ˌgram/) ▸*n.* a pictorial symbol for a word or phrase. Pictographs were used as the earliest known form of writing, examples having been discovered in Egypt and Mesopotamia from before 3000 BC. ■ a pictorial representation of statistics on a chart, graph, or computer screen. ▹mid 19th cent.: from Latin *pict-* 'painted' (from the verb *pingere*) + -GRAPH. —**pic·to·graph·ic** /ˌpiktəˈgrafik/ *adj.* —**pic·tog·ra·phy** /pikˈtägrəfē/ *n.*

Pic·tor /ˈpiktər/ *Astronomy* an inconspicuous southern constellation (the Easel or Painter), close to the star Canopus. ■ [as *genitive*] (**Pictoris**) used with a preceding letter or numeral to designate a star in this constellation: *the star Beta Pictoris.* ▷Latin.

pic·to·ri·al /pikˈtôrēəl/ ▶*adj.* of or expressed in pictures; illustrated: *feelings presented in a pictorial form.* See note at **GRAPHIC**. ■ suggestive of pictures: *Blake was concerned not with verisimilitude, but with pictorial ideas.*
▶*n.* a newspaper or periodical with pictures as a main feature. ▷mid 17th cent.: from late Latin *pictorius* (from Latin *pictor* 'painter,' from the verb *pingere* 'to paint') + **-AL**. —**pic·to·ri·al·ly** *adv.*

pic·ture /ˈpikCHər/ ▶*n.* a painting or drawing: *draw a picture of a tree.* ■ a photograph: *we were warned not to* ***take pictures.*** ■ a portrait: *have her picture painted.* ■ *archaic* a person or thing resembling another closely: *she is the very picture of her mother.* ■ *figurative* an impression of something formed from an account or description: *a full picture of the disaster had not yet emerged.* ■ an image on a television screen. ■ a movie: *it took five honors, including best picture.* ■ (**the pictures**) the movies: *I'm* ***going to the pictures*** *with my buddies.*
▶*v.* [*trans.*] (often **be pictured**) represent (someone or something) in a photograph or picture: *he is pictured with party guests.* ■ describe (someone or something) in a certain way: *the markets in London and New York are usually pictured in contrasting terms.* ■ form a mental image of: *she pictured Benjamin waiting.* ▷late Middle English: from Latin *pictura*, from *pict-* 'painted' (from the verb *pingere*).
▶*PHRASES* □ **be in pictures** act in movies or work in the motion-picture industry. □ **be** (or **look**) **a picture** be beautiful. □ **get the picture** *informal* understand a situation. □ **in the picture** fully informed about something. □ **out of the picture** no longer involved; irrelevant: *hostages were better left out of the picture.* □ **the** (or **a**) **picture of ——** the embodiment of a specified state or emotion: *she looked the picture of forbearance.* □ **(as) pretty as a picture** very pretty.

pic·ture book ▶*n.* a book containing many illustrations, esp. one for children.

pic·ture card ▶*n.* an illustrated card, used esp. in games. ■ another term for **FACE CARD**.

pic·ture el·e·ment ▶*n.* see **PIXEL**.

pic·ture hat ▶*n.* a woman's highly decorated hat with a wide brim, as shown in pictures by 18th-century English painters such as Reynolds and Gainsborough.

pic·ture pal·ace ▶*n.* *dated* a movie theater.

pic·ture plane ▶*n.* in perspective, the imaginary plane corresponding to the surface of a picture, perpendicular to the viewer's line of sight.

pic·ture post·card ▶*n.* a postcard with a picture on one side.
▶*adj.* prettily picturesque, like the scenes typically shown on such postcards: *a picture-postcard thatched cottage.*

pic·ture space ▶*n.* the apparent space behind the picture plane of a painting, created by perspective and other techniques.

pic·tur·esque /ˌpikCHəˈresk/ ▶*adj.* visually attractive, esp. in a quaint or pretty style: *the picturesque covered bridges of New England.* See note at **GRAPHIC**. ■ (of language) unusual and vivid: *his picturesque speech contrasted with his rough appearance.* ▷early 18th cent.: from French *pittoresque*, from Italian *pittoresco*, from *pittore* 'painter' (from Latin *pictor*). The change from *-tt-* to *-ct-* was due to association with **PICTURE**. —**pic·tur·esque·ly** *adv.* —**pic·tur·esque·ness** *n.*

pic·ture tube ▶*n.* *Electronics* the cathode-ray tube of a television set designed for the reproduction of television pictures.

pic·ture win·dow ▶*n.* a large window consisting of one pane of glass, typically in a living room.

pic·ture writ·ing ▶*n.* a mode of recording events by pictorial symbols; pictography.

pic·u·let /ˈpikyəlit/ ▶*n.* a tiny tropical woodpecker with a short unstiffened tail, found chiefly in Central and South America. • *Picumnus* and other genera, family Picidae: numerous species, including the **olivaceous piculet** (*P. olivaceus*). ▷mid 19th cent.: apparently a double diminutive of Latin *picus* 'woodpecker.'

PID ▶*abbr.* pelvic inflammatory disease.

pid·dle /ˈpidl/ *informal* ▶*v.* [*intrans.*] urinate.
▶*phrasal v.* □ **piddle around** (or **about**) spend time in trifling activities: *I piddled around the house all day.* [mid 16th cent. (as *piddle*): of unknown origin; compare with the rare synonym *peddle.*]
▶*n.* [in *sing.*] an act of urinating. ■ urine. ▷late 18th cent.: probably from a blend of **PISS** and **PUDDLE**. —**pid·dler** *n.*

pid·dling /ˈpidliNG/ ▶*adj.* *informal* pathetically trivial; trifling: *piddling little questions.*

pid·dock /ˈpidək/ ▶*n.* a bivalve mollusk that bores into soft rock or other firm surfaces. The valves of the shell have a conspicuous gap between them and rough frontal ridges to aid in boring. • *Pholas* and other genera, family Pholadidae. ▷mid 19th cent.: of unknown origin.

pidg·in /ˈpijən/ ▶*n.* [often as *adj.*] a grammatically simplified form of a language, used for communication between people not sharing a common language. Pidgins have a limited vocabulary, some elements of which are taken from local languages, and are not native languages, but arise out of language contact between speakers of other languages. Compare with **CREOLE**, sense 2. ■ (**Pidgin**) another term for **TOK PISIN**. ▷late 19th cent.: Chinese alteration of English *business.*

pie[1] /pī/ ▶*n.* a baked dish of fruit, or meat and vegetables, typically with a top and base of pastry. ■ a pizza. ▷Middle English: probably the same word as **PIE**[2], the various combinations of ingredients being compared to objects randomly collected by a magpie.
▶*PHRASES* □ **(as) easy as pie** *informal* very easy. □ **(as) nice** (or **sweet**) **as pie** extremely pleasant or polite. □ **a piece** (or **slice**) **of the pie** a share of an amount of money or business available to be claimed or distributed: *orchestras have seen cultural rivals get a bigger piece of the pie.* □ **pie in the sky** *informal* used to describe or refer to something that is pleasant to contemplate but is very unlikely to be realized.

pie[2] ▶*n.* short for **MAGPIE**. ▷Middle English: from Old French, from Latin *pica* 'magpie' (related to *picus* 'green woodpecker').

pie[3] ▶*n.* a former monetary unit in the Indian subcontinent, equal to one twelfth of an anna. ▷from Hindi *pā'ī*, from Sanskrit *pada, padī* 'quarter.'

pie·bald /ˈpīˌbôld/ ▶*adj.* (of a horse) having irregular patches of two colors, typically black and white.
▶*n.* a piebald horse or other animal. ▷late 16th cent.: from **PIE**[2] (because of the magpie's black-and-white plumage) + **BALD** (in the obsolete sense 'streaked with white').

piece /pēs/ ▶*n.* a portion of an object or of material, produced by cutting, tearing, or breaking the whole: ***a piece of*** *cheese | the dish lay* ***in pieces*** *upon the floor | she tore his letters* ***to pieces.*** See note at **FRAGMENT**. ■ one of the items that were put together to make something and into which it naturally divides: *take a car* ***to pieces.*** ■ an item of a particular type, esp. one forming one of a set: ***a piece of*** *luggage.* ■ an instance or example: *a crucial piece of evidence.* ■ a financial share: *each employee owns a piece of the company.* ■ a written, musical, or artistic creation or composition: *a hauntingly beautiful piece of music.* ■ [with *adj.*] a coin of specified value: *a 10-cent piece.* ■ a figure or token used to make moves in a board game. ■ *Chess* a king, queen, bishop, knight, or rook, as opposed to a pawn. ■ *informal* a firearm. ■ *informal, offensive* a woman.
▶*v.* [*trans.*] **1** (**piece something together**) assemble something from individual parts: *the children took turns piecing together each other's jigsaw puzzle.* ■ slowly make sense of something from separate facts and pieces of evidence: *Daniel had pieced the story together from the radio.* **2** (**piece something out**) *archaic* extend. **3** *archaic* patch: *if it be broken it must be pieced.* ▷Middle English: from Old French *piece* (compare with medieval Latin *pecia, petium*), of obscure ultimate origin.
▶*PHRASES* □ **a piece of ass** (or **tail**) *vulgar slang* a person, usually a woman, regarded as a sexual partner. □ **a piece of cake** see **CAKE**. □ **a piece of the action** *informal* a share in the excitement of something. ■ a share in the profits accruing from something. □ **go to pieces** become so nervous or upset that one is unable to behave or perform normally. □ **in one piece** unharmed or undamaged, esp. after a dangerous experience. □ **(all) of a piece (with something)** (entirely) consistent (with something): *his rejection of health-care reform is of a piece with his general disregard for the underprivileged.* □ **piece by piece** in slow and small stages. □ **say one's piece** give one's opinion or make a prepared statement. □ **tear** (or **rip**) **someone/something to pieces** criticize someone or something harshly.

pièce de ré·sis·tance /pēˈes də ˌreziˈstäns; -räziˈstäns/ ▶*n.* [in *sing.*] (esp. with reference to creative work or a meal) the most important or remarkable feature: *the pièce de résistance of the meal was flaming ice cream.* ▷French, literally 'piece (i.e., means) of resistance.'

piece goods ▶*plural n.* fabrics woven in standard lengths for sale.

piece·meal /ˈpēsˌmēl/ ▶*adj.* & *adv.* characterized by unsystematic partial measures taken over a period of time: [as *adj.*] *the village is slowly being killed off by piecemeal development* | [as *adv.*] *some can only be had as part of a package, while others can be installed piecemeal.* ▷Middle English: from the noun **PIECE** + *-meal* from Old English *mǣlum*, in the sense 'measure, quantity taken at one time.'

piece of eight ▶*n.* *historical* a Spanish dollar, equivalent to 8 reals.

piec·er /ˈpēsər/ ▶*n.* a person who patches or creates a garment or other item from pieces of fabric. ■ *historical* a child employed in a spinning mill to join the ends of broken threads.

piece rate ▶*n.* a rate of payment for piecework.

piece·work /ˈpēsˌwərk/ ▶*n.* work paid for according to the amount produced. —**piece·work·er** *n.*

pie chart ▶*n.* a type of graph in which a circle is divided into sectors that each represent a proportion of the whole. ▷1920s: because of the resemblance of the graph to a pie divided into portions.

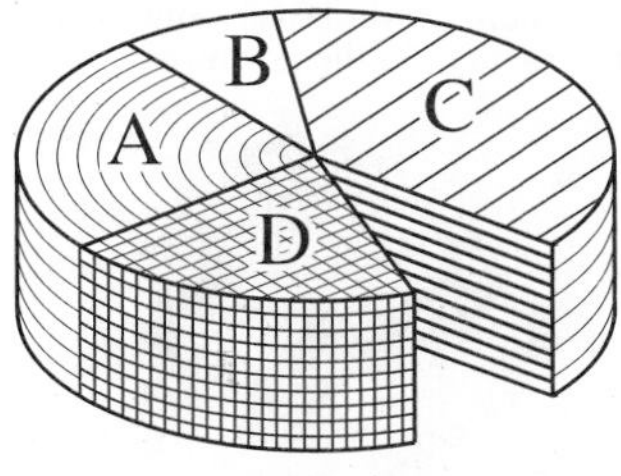

pie chart

pie crust /ˈpīˌkrəst/ (also **pie·crust**) ▶*n.* the baked pastry crust of a pie. ■ the dough used to make pie crusts: *my mother was rolling out pie crust on the table.*

pie·crust ta·ble ▶*n.* a table with an indented edge like a pie crust.

pied /pīd/ ▶*adj.* having two or more different colors: *pied dogs from the Pyrenees.* ▷Middle English (originally in the sense 'black and white like a magpie'): from **PIE**[2] + **-ED**[1].

pied-à-terre /pēˌyād ə ˈter/ ▶*n.* (*pl.* **pieds-à-terre** *pronunc.* same) a small apartment, house, or room kept for occasional use. ▷early 19th cent.: French, literally 'foot to earth.'

Pied·mont /ˈpēdˌmänt/ **1** a region in northwestern Italy, in the foothills of the Alps; capital, Turin. It was the center of the movement for a united Italy in the 19th century. Italian name **PIEMONTE**. **2** in the U.S., a hilly highland region between the Appalachian Mountains and the Atlantic coast. The Piedmont ends at the Fall Line, where rivers drop to the coastal plain. ▷from Italian *piemonte* 'mountain foot.' —**Pied·mon·tese** /ˌpēdmänˈtēz; -ˈtēs/ *n.* & *adj.*

pied·mont /ˈpēdmänt/ ▶*n.* a gentle slope leading from the base of mountains to a region of flat land. ▷mid 19th cent.: from Italian *piemonte*. See **PIEDMONT**.

pied noir /pēˌā ˈnwär/ ▶*n.* (*pl.* **pieds noirs** *pronunc.* same) a person of European origin who lived in Algeria during French rule, esp. one who returned to Europe after Algeria was granted independence. ▷French, literally 'black foot,' so named because of the western-style black leather shoes worn by the first colonists.

Pied Pip·er /ˈpīd ˈpīpər/ the hero of *The Pied Piper of Hamelin*, a poem by Robert Browning (1842), based on an old German legend. The piper, dressed in particolored costume, rid the town of Hamelin (Hameln) in Brunswick of rats by enticing them away with his music, and when refused the promised payment he lured away the children of the citizens. ■ [as *n.*] (**a Pied Piper**) a person who entices people to follow them, esp. to their doom.

Pronunciation Key ə *ago*; ər *over*; ˈə or ˌə *up*; ˈər or ˌər *fur*; a *hat*; ā *rate*; ä *car*; CH *chew*; e *let*; ē *see*; e(ə)r *air*; i *fit*; ī *by*; i(ə)r *ear*; NG *sing*; ō *go*; ô *for*; oi *boy*; o͝o *good*; o͞o *goo*; ou *out*; SH *she*; TH *thin*; T͟H *then*; (h)w *why*; ZH *vision*

pie-eyed ▸*adj. informal* very drunk.

pie-faced ▸*adj. informal* having a roundish face and typically a blank or stupid expression.

Pie·gan /pē'gan/ (also **Pei·gan**) ▸*n.* (*pl.* same or **-gans**) a member of a North American Indian people of the Blackfoot confederacy.

▸*adj.* of or relating to this people. ▷via Cree, from Blackfoot *piikáni* 'Piegan band.'

pie·man /'pīmən/ ▸*n.* (*pl.* **-men**) *archaic* a pie seller.

Pie·mon·te /pye'mônte/ Italian name for **PIEDMONT**.

pie·mon·tite /'pēmən,tīt/ ▸*n.* a brown or black mineral of the epidote group consisting of a silicate of calcium, aluminum, iron, and manganese. ▷late 19th cent.: from Italian *Piemonte* (see **PIEDMONT**) + **-ITE**[1].

pie plate (also **pie pan**) ▸*n.* a shallow metal or glass dish with sloping sides in which pies are baked.

pier /pi(ə)r/ ▸*n.* **1** a structure leading out from the shore into a body of water, in particular: ■ a platform supported on pillars or girders, used as a landing stage for boats. ■ a similar structure leading out to sea and used as an entertainment area, typically incorporating arcades and places to eat. ■ a breakwater or mole. **2** a solid support designed to sustain vertical pressure, in particular: ■ a pillar supporting an arch or a bridge. ■ a section of a wall between windows or other adjacent openings. ▷Middle English: from medieval Latin *pera*, of unknown origin.

Pierce /pi(ə)rs/, Franklin (1804–69), 14th president of the U.S. 1853–57. A New Hampshire Democrat, he served as U.S. congressman 1833–37 and U.S. senator 1837–42. His presidency saw the rise of divisions within the country over slavery and the encouragement of settlement in the northwest.

Franklin Pierce

pierce /pi(ə)rs/ ▸*v.* [*trans.*] (of a sharp pointed object) go into or through (something): *a splinter had pierced the skin.* ■ prick (something) with a sharp instrument: *she pierced the meat with a fork.* ■ make (a hole) with a sharp instrument: *I had to pierce another hole in my belt.* ■ make a hole in (the ears, nose, or other part of the body) so as to wear jewelry in them: [as *adj.*] (**pierced**) *kids with pierced noses.* ■ (usu. **be pierced**) bore a hole or tunnel through: *the dividing wall is pierced by arches and piers.* ■ force or cut a way through: *they were seeking to pierce the antiballistic-missile defenses | a shrill voice pierced the air.* ▷Middle English: from Old French *percer*, based on Latin *pertus-* 'bored through,' from the verb *pertundere*, from *per* 'through' + *tundere* 'thrust.'

pierc·er /'pi(ə)rsər/ ▸*n.* a person or thing that pierces something. ■ [often with *adj.*] a person who pierces the ears, nose, or other parts of the body so jewelry can be worn in them.

pierc·ing /'pi(ə)rsiNG/ ▸*adj.* (of eyes or a look) appearing to see through someone; searching: *he stared at me with those piercing eyes.* ■ (of a voice or sound) extremely high, loud, or shrill: *she let out a piercing scream.* ■ (of wind or extreme temperature) seeming to cut through one: *the piercing cold.* ■ (of a feeling) affecting one keenly or deeply. ■ (of mental attributes) sharp; profound: *her piercing analysis.* —**pierc·ing·ly** *adv.*

pier glass ▸*n.* a large mirror, used originally to fill wall space between windows.

pie·ris /'pīris; 'pi(ə)ris/ ▸*n.* an evergreen shrub of the heath family, typically having pink or red young leaves and loose clusters of waxy white bell-shaped flowers. • Genus *Pieris*, family Ericaceae: many species, in particular *P. floribunda* of North America. ▷modern Latin, from the Latin name of one of the Muses, from *Pieria*, the name of a district in northern Thessaly, Greece, said to be the home of the Muses.

pie·ro·gi ▸*n.* variant spelling of **PIROGI**.

Pierre /'pi(ə)r; pē'e(ə)r/ the capital of South Dakota, in the central part of the state, on the Missouri River; pop. 13,876.

Pi·er·rot /,pēə'rō/ ▸*n.* a stock male character in French pantomime, with a sad white-painted face, a loose white costume, and a pointed hat. ▷French, diminutive of the male given name *Pierre* 'Peter.'

pier ta·ble ▸*n.* a low table or bracket in the space between two windows, typically placed under a pier glass.

pie safe ▸*n.* a cupboard with doors featuring decorative pierced tin panels, originally designed to store pies after baking.

pie·tà /,pēā'tä/ (often **Pie·tà**) ▸*n.* a picture or sculpture of the Virgin Mary holding the dead body of Jesus Christ on her lap or in her arms. ▷Italian, from Latin *pietas* 'dutifulness.'

Pie·ter·mar·itz·burg /,pētər'marits,bərg/ a city in eastern South Africa, the capital of KwaZulu-Natal; pop. 229,000.

pi·e·tism /'pī-i,tizəm/ ▸*n.* pious sentiment, esp. of an exaggerated or affected nature. ■ (usu. **Pietism**) a 17th-century movement for the revival of piety in the Lutheran Church. [from German *Pietismus*, from modern Latin, based on Latin *pietas* (see **PIETY**).] —**pi·e·tist** *n.* —**pi·e·tis·tic** /,pī-i'tistik/ *adj.* —**pi·e·tis·ti·cal** *adj.* —**pi·e·tis·ti·cal·ly** /-tik(ə)lē/ *adv.*

pi·e·ty /'pīətē/ ▸*n.* (*pl.* **-ties**) the quality of being religious or reverent: *acts of piety and charity.* ■ the quality of being dutiful: *filial piety.* ■ a belief or point of view that is accepted with unthinking conventional reverence: *the accepted pieties of our time.* ▷early 16th cent. (in the sense 'devotion to religious observances'): from Old French *piete*, from Latin *pietas* 'dutifulness,' from *pius* (see **PIOUS**).

pi·e·zo /pī'ēzō; pē'äzō/ ▸*adj.* piezoelectric.

pi·e·zo·e·lec·tric·i·ty /pē,äzō,ilek'trisitē; pī,ēz-/ ▸*n.* electric polarization in a substance (esp. certain crystals) resulting from the application of mechanical stress.

Piezoelectric substances are able to convert mechanical signals (such as sound waves) into electrical signals, and vice versa. They are therefore widely used in microphones, phonograph pickups, and earphones, and also to generate a spark for igniting gas.

▷late 19th cent.: from Greek *piezein* 'press, squeeze' + **ELECTRICITY**. —**pi·e·zo·e·lec·tric** /-trik/ *adj.* —**pi·e·zo·e·lec·tri·cal·ly** /-trik(ə)lē/ *adv.*

pi·e·zom·e·ter /pēə'zämitər; pīə'zämitər/ ▸*n.* an instrument for measuring the pressure of a liquid or gas, or something related to pressure (such as the compressibility of liquid). Piezometers are often placed in boreholes to monitor the pressure or depth of groundwater. ▷early 19th cent.: from Greek *piezein* 'press, squeeze' + **-METER**.

pif·fle /'pifəl/ ▸*n.* & *exclam. informal* nonsense. ▷mid 19th cent.: diminutive of imitative *piff-*.

pif·fling /'pifliNG/ ▸*adj. informal* trivial; unimportant.

pig /pig/ ▸*n.* **1** an omnivorous domesticated hoofed mammal with sparse bristly hair and a flat snout for rooting in the soil, kept for its meat. • *Sus domesticus* (with numerous varieties), family Suidae (the **pig family**), descended from the wild boar and domesticated over 8,000 years ago. The pig family also includes the warthog and babirusa, but the similar peccaries are placed in their own family. ■ a wild animal of this family. ■ a young pig; a piglet. ■ the flesh of a pig, esp. a young one, as food. ■ *informal, derogatory* a greedy, dirty, or unpleasant person: *how can she stay married to such a pig?* ■ *informal, derogatory* a police officer. **2** an oblong mass of iron or lead from a smelting furnace. See also **PIG IRON**. ■ a device that fits snugly inside an oil or gas pipeline and is sent through it to clean or test the inside, or to act as a barrier.

▸*v.* (**pigged, pig·ging**) [*intrans.*] **1** *informal* gorge oneself with food: *don't pig out on chips before dinner.* **2** *informal* crowd together with other people in disorderly or dirty conditions: *he and Irving pigged it for years in a shoebox of an apartment | I have no intention of pigging with that bunch for another day.* **3** (of a sow) give birth to piglets; farrow. **4** operate a pig within an oil or gas pipeline. ▷Middle English: probably from an Old English word represented in *picbrēd* 'acorn,' literally 'pig food.' —**pig·like** /'pig,līk/ *adj.* —**pig·ling** /'pigliNG/ *n.*

Chester white pig

▸*PHRASES* □ **bleed like a pig** bleed copiously. □ **in pig** (of a sow) pregnant. □ **in a pig's eye** *informal* expressing scornful disbelief at a statement. □ **make a pig of oneself** *informal* overeat; eat more than one's share. □ **make a pig's ear of** *Brit., informal* handle ineptly. □ **a pig in a poke** something that is bought or accepted without knowing its value or seeing it first. [with reference to the formerly common trick of selling a cat concealed in a bag to someone who was expecting a pig.] □ **squeal like a pig** squeal or yell loudly and shrilly. □ **sweat like a pig** *informal* sweat profusely.

pi·geon[1] /'pijən/ ▸*n.* **1** a stout seed- or fruit-eating bird with a small head, short legs, and a cooing voice, typically having gray and white plumage. See also **DOVE**[1] (sense 1). • Family Columbidae: numerous genera and species. ■ (also **domestic** or **feral pigeon**) a pigeon descended from the wild rock dove, kept for racing, showing, and carrying messages, and common as a feral bird in towns. **2** *informal* a gullible person, esp. someone swindled in gambling or the victim of a confidence trick. **3** *military slang* an aircraft from one's own side. ▷late Middle English: from Old French *pijon*, denoting a young bird, esp. a young dove, from an alteration of late Latin *pipio(n-)* 'young cheeping bird,' of imitative origin.

pi·geon[2] ▸*n.* archaic spelling of **PIDGIN**.

pi·geon breast (also **pigeon chest**) ▸*n.* a deformed human chest with a projecting breastbone. —**pi·geon-breast·ed** (also **pi·geon-chest·ed**) *adj.*

pi·geon hawk ▸*n.* another term for **MERLIN**.

pi·geon-heart·ed ▸*adj.* timid; cowardly.

pi·geon·hole /'pijən,hōl/ ▸*n.* a small recess for a domestic pigeon to nest in. ■ a small compartment, open at the front and forming part of a set, where letters or messages may be left for someone. ■ a similar compartment built into a desk for keeping documents in. ■ *figurative* a category to which someone or something is assigned: *people identified me with a homely farmer's wife and I was never allowed to escape from that pigeonhole.*

▸*v.* [*trans.*] deposit (a document) into a pigeonhole: *he pigeonholed his charts and notes.* ■ assign to a particular category or class, esp. in a manner that is too rigid or exclusive: *a tendency to* **pigeonhole** *him* **as** *a photographer and neglect his work in sculpture and painting.* ■ put aside for future consideration: *she pigeonholed her worry about him.*

pi·geon pea ▸*n.* **1** a dark red tropical pealike seed. **2** the woody Old World plant that yields these seeds, with pods and foliage that are used as fodder. • *Cajanus cajan*, family Leguminosae.

pi·geon's milk ▸*n.* a curdlike secretion from a pigeon's crop, which it regurgitates and feeds to its young.

pi·geon-toed ▸*adj.* having the toes or feet turned inward.

pig·fish /'pig,fisH/ ▸*n.* (*pl.* same or **-fish·es**) **1** a deep-bodied scaleless fish with a protuberant snout, living in the cooler seas of the southern hemisphere. • Family Congiopodidae: several genera and species. **2** [usu. with *adj.*] any of a number of other marine fishes, esp. one that grunts. • a western Atlantic grunt (*Orthopristis chrysoptera*, family Pomadasyidae).

pig·ger·y /'pigərē/ ▸*n.* (*pl.* **-er·ies**) **1** a farm where pigs are bred or kept. ■ a pigpen. **2** behavior regarded as characteristic of pigs in greed or unpleasantness.

pig·gish /'pigisH/ ▸*adj.* resembling a pig, esp. in being greedy or unpleasant. —**pig·gish·ness** *n.*

pig·gy /'pigē/ ▸*n.* (*pl.* **-gies**) (used by or when talking to children) a pig or piglet.

▸*adj.* resembling a pig, esp. in features or appetite: *three pairs of little piggy eyes.*

pig·gy·back /'pigē,bak/ ▸*n.* a ride on someone's back and shoulders.

▸*adv.* on the back and shoulders of another person: *he had to carry him piggyback.* ■ on top of something else: *Dave headed back with the car riding piggyback on his truck.*

▸*v.* [*trans.*] carry by or as if by piggyback. ■ mount on or attach to (an existing object or system): *providers of information have piggybacked their own networks onto*

the system. ■ [*intrans.*] use existing work or an existing product as a basis or support: *we were* ***piggybacking on*** *their training program.*
▸*adj.* on the back and shoulders of another person: *enjoying a piggyback ride.* ■ attached to or riding on a larger object: *a telescope with fittings for piggyback cameras and guidescopes* | *figurative a piggyback income tax, under which taxpayers would pay the state 21 percent of whatever they paid the federal government.* ▷mid 16th cent. (as an adverb): although analyzed by folk etymology in various ways from an early date, the word's origin remains obscure.

pig·gy bank ▸*n.* a container for saving money in, esp. one shaped like a pig, with a slit in the top through which coins are dropped. ■ *figurative* savings: *many people would dip into their piggy banks to pay the higher tax bills.*

pig·head·ed /ˈpig,hedid/ ▸*adj.* stupidly obstinate. **—pig·head·ed·ly** *adv.* **—pig·head·ed·ness** *n.*

pig·ig·no·rant ▸*adj. informal* utterly uneducated: *when I bought my house I was pig-ignorant about the area.*

pig i·ron ▸*n.* crude iron as first obtained from a smelting furnace, in the form of oblong blocks.

pig Lat·in ▸*n.* a made-up language formed from English by transferring the initial consonant or consonant cluster of each word to the end of the word and adding a vocalic syllable (usually /ā/): so *chicken soup* would be translated to *ickenchay oupsay.* Pig Latin is typically spoken playfully, as if to convey secrecy.

pig·let /ˈpiglit/ ▸*n.* a young pig.

pig·ment /ˈpigmənt/ ▸*n.* the natural coloring matter of animal or plant tissue. ■ a substance used for coloring or painting, esp. a dry powder that, when mixed with oil, water, or another medium, constitutes a paint or ink.
▸*v.* [*trans.*] [usu. as *adj.*] (**pigmented**) color (something) with or as if with pigment: *pigmented areas such as freckles.* ▷Middle English, from Latin *pigmentum,* from *pingere* 'to paint.' The verb dates from the early 20th cent. **—pig·men·tar·y** /-,terē/ *adj.*

pig·men·ta·tion /,pigmənˈtāsHən/ ▸*n.* the natural coloring of animal or plant tissue. ■ the coloring of a person's skin, esp. when abnormal or distinctive.

pig·ment ep·i·the·li·um ▸*n. Anatomy* a layer of pigmented cells in the retina of the eye, overlying the choroid.

pig·my ▸*n.* variant spelling of **PYGMY.**

pi·gno·li /pinˈyōlē/ ▸*plural n.* pine nuts. ▷Italian, plural of *pignolo,* from *pigna* 'pine cone,' from Latin *pinea.*

pig·nut /ˈpig,nət/ ▸*n.* **1** a hickory tree that bears nuts with thin husks. • Genus *Carya,* family Juglandaceae: four North American species, **black hickory** (*C. texana*), **pignut hickory** (*C. glabra*), **sand hickory** (*C. pallida*), and **scrub hickory** (*C. floridana*). **2** another term for **EARTHNUT** (sense 1).

pig-out ▸*n. informal* a bout of eating a large amount of food.

pig·pen /ˈpig,pen/ ▸*n.* a pen or enclosure for a pig or pigs. ■ a very dirty or untidy house or room.

Pigs, Bay of a bay on the southwestern coast of Cuba, scene of an unsuccessful attempt in 1961 by U.S.-backed Cuban exiles to invade the country and overthrow the regime of Fidel Castro.

pig·skin /ˈpig,skin/ ▸*n.* **1** the hide of a domestic pig. ■ leather made from this. **2** *informal* a football.

pig·stick·er /ˈpig,stikər/ ▸*n. informal* a long sharp knife or weapon.

pig·stick·ing /ˈpig,stikiNG/ ▸*n.* the sport of hunting wild boar with a spear, typically on horseback.

pig·sty /ˈpig,stī/ ▸*n.* (*pl.* **-sties**) a pigpen.

pig·tail /ˈpig,tāl/ ▸*n.* **1** a braid or gathered hank of hair hanging from the back of the head, or either of a pair at the sides: *she had her hair done* ***in pigtails.*** **2** a short length of flexible braided wire connecting a stationary part to a moving part in an electrical device. **3** a thin twist of tobacco. **—pig·tailed** *adj.*

pig-tailed ma·caque (also **pig·tail ma·caque**) ▸*n.* a forest-dwelling Southeast Asian macaque that has a brown coat with pale underparts, dark markings around the face, and a small piglike tail. • *Macaca nemestrina,* family Cercopithecidae.

pig·weed /ˈpig,wēd/ ▸*n.* **1** an amaranth that grows as a weed or is used for fodder. • Genus *Amaranthus,* family Amaranthaceae: several species, in particular *A. retroflexus* and *A. albus.* **2** another term for **LAMB'S-QUARTERS.**

pi·ka /ˈpīkə; ˈpē-/ ▸*n.* a small mammal related to the rabbits, having rounded ears, short limbs, and a very small tail. • Family Ochotonidae and genus *Ochotona:* many species, including the **collared pika** (*O. collaris*), of western North America. ▷early 19th cent.: from Tungus *piika.*

Pike /pīk/, Zebulon (Montgomery) (1779–1813), U.S. soldier and explorer. He led several expeditions into the Louisiana Purchase region, where he came upon (but never climbed) what is now called Pike's Peak in Colorado. He was killed at York (now Toronto) in Ontario, Canada, while leading a charge against the British during the War of 1812.

pike[1] /pīk/ ▸*n.* (*pl.* same) a long-bodied predatory freshwater fish with a pointed snout and large teeth, of both North America and Eurasia. • Family Esocidae and genus *Esox:* five species, including the widespread **northern pike** (*E. lucius*). ■ any fish with similar characteristics, such as the walleye. ■ used in names of other predatory fish with large teeth, e.g., **garpike.** ▷Middle English: from **PIKE**[2] (because of the fish's pointed jaw).

northern pike

pike[2] ▸*n. historical* an infantry weapon with a pointed steel or iron head on a long wooden shaft. ■ *chiefly Brit.* (in names) a hill with a peaked top: *Scafell pike.* [apparently of Scandinavian origin; compare with West Norwegian dialect *pīk* 'pointed mountain.']
▸*v.* [*trans.*] *historical* kill or thrust (someone) through with a pike. ▷early 16th cent.: from French *pique,* back-formation from *piquer* 'pierce,' from *pic* 'pick, pike'; compare with Old English *pīc* 'point, prick' (of unknown origin).

pike[3] ▸*n.* short for **TURNPIKE.**
▸*PHRASE* □ **come down the pike** appear on the scene; come to notice.

pike[4] (also **pike position**) ▸*n.* [often as *adj.*] a position in diving or gymnastics in which the body is bent at the waist but the legs remain straight. ▷1920s: of unknown origin.

pike·man /ˈpīkmən/ ▸*n.* (*pl.* **-men**) *historical* a soldier armed with a pike.

pike·perch /ˈpīk,pərcH/ ▸*n.* (*pl.* same) a predatory pikelike freshwater fish of the perch family, esp. the walleye. • Genus *Stizostedion,* family Percidae: five species, including the sauger.

pik·er /ˈpīkər/ ▸*n. informal* **1** a gambler who makes only small bets. ■ a stingy or cautious person. **2** *Austral./NZ* a person who withdraws from a commitment. ▷late 19th cent.: from the slang verb *pike,* meaning 'withdraw from an agreement because of overcautiousness.'

Pikes Peak /ˈpīks/ a mountain in the Front Range of the southern Rocky Mountains, near Colorado Springs in Colorado, 14,110 feet (4,300 m) high, named for Zebulon **PIKE.**

pike·staff /ˈpīk,staf/ ▸*n. historical* the wooden shaft of a pike. ▷late 16th cent.: from **PIKE**[2] + **STAFF**[1].
▸*PHRASE* □ **(as) plain as a pikestaff** very obvious. ■ ordinary or unattractive in appearance. [alteration of *as plain as a packstaff,* the staff being that of a peddler, on which he rested his pack of wares.]

pi·ki /ˈpēkē/ ▸*n.* cornmeal bread in the form of very thin sheets, made by the Hopi Indians of the southwestern U.S. ▷Hopi.

Pik Po·be·dy /ˈpēk päbˈyedē/ a mountain in eastern Kyrgyzstan, situated close to the border with China. Rising to a height of 24,406 feet (7,439 m), it is the highest peak in the Tien Shan range. ▷from Russian, literally 'Victory Peak.'

pi·laf /pəˈläf; ˈpēläf/ (also **pi·laff** or **pi·lau** /-ˈlō; -ˈlou; -lō; -lou/ or **pu·lao**) ▸*n.* a Middle Eastern or Indian dish of rice or wheat, with vegetables and spices, typically having added meat or fish. ▷from Turkish *pilav.*

pi·las·ter /pəˈlastər/ ▸*n.* a rectangular column, esp. one projecting from a wall. ▷late 16th cent.: from French *pilastre,* from Italian *pilastro* or medieval Latin *pilastrum,* from Latin *pila* 'pillar.' **—pi·las·tered** *adj.*

Pi·late /ˈpīlət/, Pontius (died c.AD 36), Roman procurator of Judaea *c.*26–*c.*36. He is known for presiding at the trial of Jesus Christ and authorizing his crucifixion.

Pi·la·tes /piˈlätēz/ ▸*n.* a system of exercises using special apparatus, designed to improve physical strength, flexibility, and posture, and enhance mental awareness: *this quest for better training has led many dancers to Pilates* [as *modifier*] *the Pilates method.* ▷1960s: named after German physical fitness specialist Joseph *Pilates* (1880–1967), who devised the system.

pil·chard /ˈpilcHərd/ ▸*n.* a small, edible, commercially valuable marine fish of the herring family. • *Sardinops* and other genera, family Clupeidae: several species, including the European *Sardina pilchardus.* See also **SARDINE**[1]. ▷mid 16th cent.: of unknown origin.

Pil·co·ma·yo Riv·er /,pilkəˈmäyō/ a river that flows for 1,000 miles (1,600 km) from the Andes in western Bolivia along the Argentina-Paraguay border to join the Paraguay River at Asunción in Paraguay.

pile[1] /pīl/ ▸*n.* a heap of things laid or lying one on top of another: *he placed the books in a neat pile.* ■ *informal* a large amount of something: *the growing pile of work.* ■ *informal* a lot of money: *he is admired for having* ***made a pile*** *for himself.* ■ a large imposing building or group of buildings: *a Victorian Gothic pile.* ■ a series of plates of dissimilar metals laid one on another alternately to produce an electric current. ■ dated term for **NUCLEAR REACTOR.** ■ *archaic* a funeral pyre.
▸*v.* **1** [*trans.*] place (things) one on top of another: *she piled all the groceries on the counter.* ■ (**be piled with**) be stacked or loaded with: *his in-box was piled high with papers.* ■ (**pile up**) [*intrans.*] increase in quantity: *the work has piled up.* ■ (**pile something up**) cause to increase in quantity: *the debts he piled up.* ■ (**pile something on**) *informal* intensify or exaggerate something for effect: *you can pile on the guilt, but my heart has turned to stone.* **2** [*intrans.*] (**pile in/out**) (of a group of people) get into or out of a vehicle in a disorganized manner: *we all piled in and headed off to our mysterious destination* | *my students* ***piled out of*** *three cars.* ■ (**pile into**) (of a vehicle) crash into: *60 cars piled into each other on I-95.* ▷late Middle English: from Old French, from Latin *pila* 'pillar, pier.'
▸*PHRASES* □ **make one's pile** *informal* make a lot of money. □ **pile arms** see **STACK ARMS** at **STACK.** □ **pile it on** *informal* exaggerate the seriousness of a situation or of someone's behavior to increase guilt or distress.

pile[2] ▸*n.* **1** a heavy beam or post driven vertically into the bed of a river, soft ground, etc., to support the foundations of a structure. **2** *Heraldry* a triangular charge or ordinary formed by two lines meeting at an acute angle, usually pointing down from the top of the shield.
▸*v.* [*trans.*] strengthen or support (a structure) with piles. ▷Old English *pīl* 'dart, arrow,' also 'pointed stake,' of Germanic origin; related to Dutch *pijl* and German *Pfeil,* from Latin *pilum* '(heavy) javelin.'

pile[3] ▸*n.* the soft projecting surface of a carpet or of a fabric such as velvet or flannel, consisting of many small threads.
▸*v.* [*trans.*] [usu. in *combination*] (**-piled**) furnish with a pile: *a thick-piled carpet.* ▷Middle English (in the sense 'downy feather'): from Latin *pilus* 'hair.' The noun sense dates from the mid 16th cent.

pi·le·a /ˈpīlēə; ˈpil-/ ▸*n.* a plant of the nettle family that lacks stinging hairs, native to warm regions and widely grown as an indoor plant. • Genus *Pilea,* family Urticaceae. ▷modern Latin, from Latin *pileus* 'felt cap.'

pi·le·at·ed wood·peck·er /ˈpīlē,ātid; ˈpil-/ ▸*n.* a large North American woodpecker with mainly black plumage and a red cap and crest. • *Dryocopus pileatus,* family Picidae. ▷late 18th cent.: *pileated* from Latin *pileatus* 'capped,' from *pileus* 'felt cap.'

pile driv·er (also **pile-driv·er**) ▸*n.* a machine for driving piles into the ground. **—pile-driv·ing** *n.* & *adj.*

piles /pīlz/ ▸*plural n.* hemorrhoids. ▷late Middle English: probably from Latin *pila* 'ball' (because of the globular form of external hemorrhoids).

pile·up /ˈpīl,əp/ (also **pile-up**) ▸*n. informal* **1** a crash involving several vehicles. ■ a confused mass of people fallen on top of one another, esp. in a team game. **2** an accumulation of a specified thing: *a massive pileup of data.*

pi·le·us /ˈpīlēəs; ˈpil/ ▸*n.* (*pl.* **-le·i** /-lē,ī/) *Botany* the cap of a mushroom or toadstool. ▷mid 18th cent.: from Latin, literally 'felt cap.'

pile·wort /ˈpīlwərt; -wôrt/ ▸*n.* **1** a plant of the daisy family with clusters of rayless, brush-shaped white flowers and strong-smelling stems. Also called **FIREWEED.** • *Erechtites hieracifolia,* family Compositae. **2** another term for **LESSER CELANDINE** (see

Pronunciation Key ə *ago;* ər *over;* ˈə or ,ə *up;* ˈər or ,ər *fur;* a *hat;* ā *rate;* ä *car;* CH *chew;* e *let;* ē *see;* e(ə)r *air;* i *fit;* ī *by;* i(ə)r *ear;* NG *sing;* ō *go;* ô *for;* oi *boy;* o͝o *good;* o͞o *goo;* ou *out;* SH *she;* TH *thin;* T̲H̲ *then;* (h)w *why;* ZH *vision*

CELANDINE). ▷late Middle English: from PILES (because of its reputed efficacy against piles) + WORT.

pil·fer /ˈpilfər/ ▶v. [trans.] steal (typically things of relatively little value). ▷late Middle English (as a noun in the sense 'action of pilfering, something pilfered'): from Old French *pelfrer* 'to pillage,' of unknown origin. Compare with PELF. —**pil·fer·age** /-rij/ n. —**pil·fer·er** n.

pil·grim /ˈpilgrəm/ ▶n. a person who journeys to a sacred place for religious reasons. ■ (usu. **Pilgrim**) a member of a group of English Puritans fleeing religious persecution who sailed in the *Mayflower* and founded the colony of Plymouth, Massachusetts, in 1620. ■ a person who travels on long journeys. ■ *chiefly poetic/literary* a person whose life is compared to a journey.
▶v. (**-grimed**, **-grim·ing**) [intrans.] *archaic* travel or wander like a pilgrim. ▷Middle English: from Provençal *pelegrin*, from Latin *peregrinus* 'foreign' (see PEREGRINE). —**pil·grim·ize** /-,mīz/ v. (*archaic*).

pil·grim·age /ˈpilgrəmij/ ▶n. a pilgrim's journey. ■ a journey to a place associated with someone or something well known or respected: *making a pilgrimage to the famous racing circuit.* See note at JOURNEY. ■ life viewed as a journey: *life's pilgrimage.*
▶v. [intrans.] go on a pilgrimage. ▷Middle English: from Provençal *pelegrinatge*, from *pelegrin* (see PILGRIM).

pi·li /pēˈlē/ ▶n. the edible seed of a Phillipine tree, which tastes like a sweet almond. ▷from Tagalog.

Pil·i·pi·no /,piləˈpēnō/ ▶n. & adj. variant of FILIPINO.

pill[1] /pil/ ▶n. a small round mass of solid medicine to be swallowed whole. ■ (**the pill** or **the Pill**) a contraceptive pill: *she is **on the pill.*** ■ *informal* a tedious or unpleasant person. ■ *informal* (in some sports) a humorous term for a ball. ▷late Middle English: ultimately from Latin *pilula* 'little ball,' diminutive of *pila*; compare with Middle Dutch, Middle Low German *pille*. —**pil·u·lar** /ˈpilyələr/ adj.
▶PHRASE □ **a bitter pill (to swallow)** an unpleasant or painful necessity (to accept).

pill[2] ▶v. [intrans.] (of knitted fabric) form small balls of fluff on its surface. ▷1960s: from Latin *pilare* 'make bald' and 'pillage.' The verb was recorded in late Old English in the sense 'peel away' (referring esp. to bark or skin).

pil·lage /ˈpilij/ ▶v. [trans.] rob (a place) using violence, esp. in wartime. See note at RAVAGE. ■ steal (something) using violence, esp. in wartime: *artworks pillaged from churches and museums.*
▶n. the action of pillaging a place or property, esp. in wartime. ▷late Middle English (as a noun): from Old French, from *piller* 'to plunder.' —**pil·lag·er** n.

pil·lar /ˈpilər/ ▶n. a tall vertical structure of stone, wood, or metal, used as a support for a building, or as an ornament or monument. ■ something shaped like such a structure: ***a pillar of** smoke.* ■ a person or thing regarded as reliably providing essential support for something: *he was **a pillar of** his local community.* ▷Middle English: from Anglo-Norman French *piler*, based on Latin *pila* ' pillar.' —**pil·lared** adj.
▶PHRASE □ **from pillar to post** from one place to another in an unceremonious or fruitless manner: *the refugees have been pushed from pillar to post in that area.*

pil·lar box ▶n. (in the UK) a large red cylindrical public mailbox.

Pil·lars of Her·cu·les an ancient name for two promontories on either side of the Strait of Gibraltar (the Rock of Gibraltar and Mount Acho in Ceuta), held by legend to have been parted by the arm of Hercules.

pill·box /ˈpil,bäks/ ▶n. a small shallow cylindrical box for holding pills. ■ (usu. **pillbox hat**) a hat of a similar shape. ■ a small, enclosed, partly underground concrete fort used as an outpost.

pill·bug /ˈpil,bəg/ (also **pill bug**) ▶n. a wood louse that has a thick cuticle and is able to roll up into a ball when threatened. • Genus *Armadillidium*, order Isopoda.

pil·lion /ˈpilyən/ ▶n. a seat for a passenger behind a motorcyclist. ■ *historical* a woman's light saddle. ■ *historical* a cushion attached to the back of a saddle for an additional passenger. ▷late 15th cent. (denoting a light saddle): from Scottish Gaelic *pillean*, Irish *pillín* 'small cushion,' diminutive of *pell*, from Latin *pellis* 'skin.'
▶PHRASE □ **ride pillion** travel seated behind a motorcyclist.

pil·lock /ˈpilək/ ▶n. *Brit., informal* a stupid person. ▷mid 16th cent.: variant of archaic *pillicock* 'penis,' the early sense of *pillock* in dialects of northern England.

pil·lo·ry /ˈpilərē/ *historical* ▶n. (pl. **-ries**) a wooden framework with holes for the head and hands, in which an offender was imprisoned and exposed to public abuse.
▶v. (**-ries**, **-ried**) [trans.] put (someone) in the pillory. ■ *figurative* attack or ridicule publicly: *he found himself pilloried by members of his own party.* ▷Middle English: from Old French *pilori*, probably from Provençal *espilori* (associated by some with a Catalan word meaning 'peephole,' of uncertain origin).

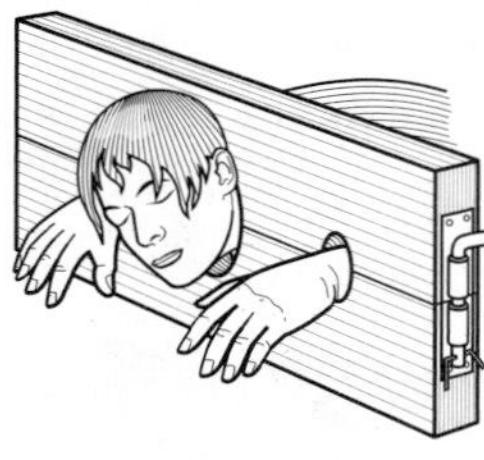
pillory

pil·low /ˈpilō/ ▶n. a rectangular cloth bag stuffed with feathers, foam rubber, or other soft materials, used to support the head when lying down. ■ a piece of wood or metal used as a support; a block or bearing.
▶v. [trans.] rest (one's head) as if on a pillow. ■ *poetic/literary* serve as a pillow for: *her shoulder pillowed his weary head.* ▷Old English *pyle*, *pylu*; related to Dutch *peluw* and German *Pfühl*, based on Latin *pulvinus* 'cushion.' —**pil·low·y** adj.

pil·low block ▶n. the housing for a wheel or journal bearing.

pil·low book ▶n. (in Japanese classical literature) a type of private diary.

pil·low·case /ˈpilō,kās/ ▶n. a removable cloth cover for a pillow.

pil·low fight ▶n. a mock fight in which people hit each other with pillows.

pil·low lace ▶n. lace made by hand using a lace pillow.

pil·low la·va ▶n. lava that has solidified as rounded masses, characteristic of eruption under water.

pil·low sham ▶n. a decorative pillowcase for covering a pillow when it is not in use.

pil·low·slip /ˈpilō,slip/ ▶n. a pillowcase.

pil·low talk ▶n. intimate conversation in bed.

pill pop·per ▶n. *informal* a person who regularly takes large numbers of pills, esp. barbiturates or amphetamines. —**pill-pop·ping** n. & adj.

pill push·er ▶n. *informal* a person, specifically a doctor, who resorts too readily to advocating the use of medication to cure illness rather than considering other treatments. ■ any seller of drugs for profit, such as a pharmaceutical company or a drug dealer. —**pill-push·ing** n. & adj.

pi·lo·car·pine /,piləˈkär,pēn/ ▶n. *Chemistry* a volatile alkaloid obtained from jaborandi leaves, used to contract the pupils and to relieve pressure in the eye in glaucoma patients. ▷late 19th cent.: from modern Latin *Pilocarpus* (genus name of the jaborandi) + -INE[4].

pi·lose /ˈpīlōs/ (also **pi·lous**) ▶adj. *Botany & Zoology* covered with long soft hairs. ▷mid 18th cent.: from Latin *pilosus*, from *pilus* 'hair.' —**pi·los·i·ty** /pīˈläsitē/ n.

pi·lot /ˈpīlət/ ▶n. **1** a person who operates the flying controls of an aircraft. ■ a person with expert local knowledge qualified to take charge of a ship entering or leaving confined waters; a helmsman. ■ *archaic* a guide or leader. ■ [often as adj.] *Telecommunications* an unmodulated reference signal transmitted with another signal for the purposes of control or synchronization. **2** a television program made to test audience reaction with a view to the production of a series. **3** another term for COWCATCHER. **4** short for PILOT LIGHT (sense 1).
▶adj. [attrib.] **1** done as an experiment or test before introducing something more widely: *a two-year pilot study.* **2** leading or guiding: *a pilot boat.*
▶v. (**-lot·ed**, **-lot·ing**) [trans.] **1** act as a pilot of (an aircraft or ship). ■ [trans.] guide; steer: *the task of piloting the economy out of recession.* **2** test (a plan, project, etc.) before introducing it more widely: *other schools were piloting such courses.* ▷early 16th cent. (denoting a person who steers a ship): from French *pilote*, from medieval Latin *pilotus*, an alteration of *pedota*, based on Greek *pēdon* 'oar,' (plural) 'rudder.' —**pi·lot·age** /ˈpīlətij/ n. —**pi·lot·less** adj.

pi·lot bal·loon ▶n. a small meteorological balloon used to track air currents.

pi·lot bis·cuit ▶n. another term for HARDTACK.

pi·lot chute ▶n. a small parachute used to bring the main one into operation.

pi·lot·fish /ˈpīlət fisн/ ▶n. (pl. same or **-fish·es**) a fish of warm seas that is often seen swimming close to large fish such as sharks and sometimes turtles and boats, said to lead sharks to prey. • *Naucrates ductor*, family Carangidae. ■ *figurative* someone who guides someone else: *pilotfish who counsel both predator and quarry in mergers.*

pi·lot hole ▶n. a small hole drilled as a guide for the insertion of a nail or screw, or for the drilling of a larger hole.

pi·lot·house /ˈpīlət,hous/ ▶n. another term for WHEELHOUSE.

pi·lot jack·et ▶n. another term for PEA JACKET.

pi·lot light ▶n. **1** a small gas burner kept continuously burning to light a larger burner when needed, esp. on a gas stove or water heater. **2** an electric indicator light or control light.

pi·lot whale ▶n. a toothed whale that has black skin with a gray anchor-shaped marking on the chin, a low dorsal fin, and a square bulbous head. Also called BLACKFISH. • Genus *Globicephala*, family Delphinidae: the long-finned *G. melas* of subtropical waters, and the short-finned *G. macrorhyncus* of temperate waters.

pi·lous /ˈpīləs/ ▶adj. another term for PILOSE.

Pils /pilz/ (also **pils**) ▶n. short for PILSNER. ▷1960s.

Pil·sen /ˈpilzən/ an industrial city in western Czech Republic; pop. 173,000. Czech name PLZEŇ.

Pil·sner /ˈpilznər/ (also **pil·sner**, **Pil·sen·er**, or **pil·sen·er**) ▶n. a lager beer with a strong hop flavor, originally brewed at Pilsen (Plzeň) in the Czech Republic, and traditionally served in a tall glass tapered at the bottom.

Pilt·down man /ˈpilt,doun/ ▶n. a fraudulent fossil composed of a human cranium and an ape jaw, allegedly discovered in England and presented in 1912 as a genuine hominid of the early Pleistocene, but shown to be a hoax in 1953. ▷*Piltdown*, the name of a village in southern England.

PIM ▶abbr. personal information manager.

Pi·ma /ˈpēmə/ ▶n. (pl. same or **Pi·mas**) **1** a member of either of two American Indian peoples, the (**Upper**) **Pima** living chiefly along the Gila and Salt rivers of southern Arizona, and the **Lower Pima** of central Sonora. **2** the Uto-Aztecan languages of these peoples. See PAPAGO.
▶adj. of or relating to this people or their language. ▷Spanish, shortening of *Pima Ayto*, from Pima *pimaha'icu* 'nothing,' perhaps a shibboleth.

pi·men·to /pəˈmentō/ ▶n. (pl. **-tos**) **1** variant spelling of PIMIENTO. **2** *chiefly W. Indian* another term for ALLSPICE (sense 2). ▷late 17th cent.: from Spanish *pimiento* (see PIMIENTO).

pi me·son /ˈpī ˈmāsän; -,zän/ ▶n. another term for PION.

pi·mien·to /pəˈm(y)entō/ (also **pi·men·to**) ▶n. (pl. **-tos**) a red sweet pepper. ■ a piece of pimiento used as a garnish, esp. stuffed inside a pitted green olive. ▷mid 17th cent.: from Spanish, from medieval Latin *pigmentum* 'spice,' from Latin, 'pigment.'

Pimm's /pimz/ ▶ n. *trademark* a gin-based alcoholic drink, served typically with lemonade or soda water and fresh mint. ▷early 20th cent.: from the name of the proprietor of the restaurant where the drink was created.

pimp /pimp/ ▶n. a man who controls prostitutes and arranges clients for them, taking part of their earnings in return.
▶v. [intrans.] [often as n.] (**pimping**) act as a pimp. ■ [trans.] provide (someone) as a prostitute. ▷late 16th cent.: of unknown origin.

pim·per·nel /ˈpimpər,nel; -pərnəl/ ▶n. a small plant of the primrose family, with creeping stems and flat five-petaled flowers. • Genera *Anagallis* and *Lysimachia*, family Primulaceae: several species, in particular the SCARLET PIMPERNEL. ▷late Middle English (denoting the burnet): from Old French *pimpernelle*, based on Latin *piper* 'pepper' (because of the resemblance of the burnet's fruit to a peppercorn).

pimp·ing /ˈpimpiNG/ ▶adj. *archaic* small or insignificant. ▷late 17th cent.: of unknown origin.

pim·ple /ˈpimpəl/ ▶n. a small hard inflamed spot on the skin. ▷Middle English: related to Old English *pipilian* 'break out in pustules.' —**pim·pled** adj. —**pim·ply** adj.

pimp·mo·bile /ˈpimp-mōˌbēl/ ▸*n. informal* a large ostentatious car, in a style associated with pimps: *like a pimpmobile, with cherry paneling and shag carpet.*

PIN /pin/ (also **PIN number**) ▸*abbr.* personal identification number.

pin /pin/ ▸*n.* **1** a small piece of metal or wood for fastening or attaching things, in particular: ■ a thin piece of metal with a sharp point at one end and a round head at the other, used esp. for fastening pieces of cloth. ■ a small brooch or badge. ■ *Medicine* a steel rod used to join the ends of fractured bones while they heal. ■ a metal peg that holds down the activating lever of a hand grenade, preventing its explosion. ■ short for HAIRPIN. ■ *Music* a peg around which one string of a musical instrument is fastened. **2** a short piece of wood or metal for various purposes, in particular: ■ (in bowling) one of a set of bottle-shaped wooden pieces that are arranged in an upright position at the end of a lane in order to be toppled by a rolling ball. ■ a metal projection from a plug or an integrated circuit that makes an electrical connection with a socket or another part of a circuit. ■ *Golf* a stick with a flag placed in a hole to mark the hole's position. **3** (**pins**) *informal* legs: *she was very nimble on her pins.* **4** *Chess* an attack on a piece or pawn, which is thereby pinned: *the pin of the black queen by the white rook.* **5** *Brit., historical* a half-firkin cask for beer.
▸*v.* (**pinned**, **pin·ning**) [*trans.*] attach with a pin or pins: *pin a note on the door.* ■ fasten (something) with a pin or pins in a specified position: *her hair was pinned back.* ■ (**pin something on**) fix blame or responsibility for something on (someone): *don't pin the blame on me.* ■ hold someone firmly in a specified position so they are unable to move: *she was standing pinned against the door.* ■ [*trans.*] transfix (something) with a pin or other pointed instrument: *carefully pin the preserved insect specimens to the display surface.* ■ [*trans.*] *Chess* hinder or prevent (a piece or pawn) from moving because of the danger to a more valuable piece standing behind it along the line of an attack.
▸*phrasal v.* □ **pin someone down** restrict the actions or movement of an enemy by firing at them. ■ force someone to be specific and make their intentions clear. □ **pin something down** define something precisely. ▷late Old English *pinn*; related to Dutch *pin* 'pin, peg,' from Latin *pinna* 'point, tip, edge.'
▸*PHRASES* □ (**as**) **neat** (or **clean**) **as a pin** extremely neat or clean. □ **hear a pin drop** used to describe absolute silence. □ **on pins and needles** in an agitated state of suspense. □ **pin one's ears back** listen carefully. □ **pin one's hopes** (or **faith**) **on** rely heavily on: *retailers were pinning their hopes on a big-spending Christmas.*

pi·ña /ˈpēnyə/ ▸*n.* a sheer fabric made from the fibers of pineapple leaves.

pi·ña co·la·da /ˈpēnyə kəˈlädə/ ▸*n.* a cocktail made with rum, pineapple juice, and coconut. ▷Spanish, literally 'strained pineapple.'

pin·a·fore /ˈpinəˌfôr/ ▸*n.* a sleeveless apronlike garment worn over a child's dress. ■ a collarless sleeveless dress, tied or buttoned in the back and typically worn as a jumper, over a blouse or sweater. ■ *Brit.* a woman's loose sleeveless garment, typically full length and worn over clothes to keep them clean. ▷late 18th cent.: from PIN + AFORE (because the term originally denoted an apron with a bib pinned on the front of a dress).

child's pinafore

Pi·nang variant spelling of PENANG.

pi·ña·ta /pēnˈyätə/ ▸*n.* (esp. in Spanish-speaking communities) a brightly decorated figure of an animal, usually made of papier mâché, containing toys and candy, and hung in the air so that blindfolded children, taking turns swinging sticks and bats, can smash the figure and share the scattered contents as part of the celebration of a birthday or Christmas or other festival.

Pin·a·tu·bo, Mount /ˌpinəˈto͞obō/ a volcano on the island of Luzon, in the Philippines. It erupted in 1991, killing more than 300 people and destroying the homes of more than 200,000.

pin·ball /ˈpinˌbôl/ ▸*n.* a game in which small metal balls are shot across a sloping board and score points by striking various targets.

pin block ▸*n.* the part of a piano or harpsichord holding the tuning pins.

pince-nez /ˈpansˌnā; ˈpins/ ▸*n.* [treated as *sing.* or *pl.*] a pair of eyeglasses with a nose clip instead of earpieces. ▷late 19th cent.: from French, literally '(that) pinches (the) nose.'

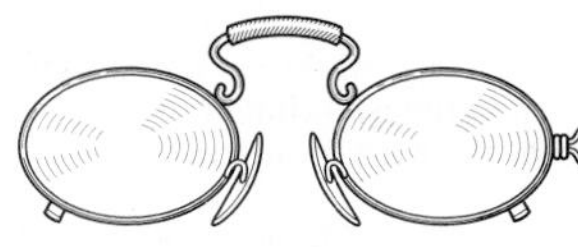
pince-nez

pin·cer /ˈpinsər/ ▸*n.* (usu. **pincers**) (also **a pair of pincers**) a tool made of two pieces of metal bearing blunt concave jaws that are arranged like the blades of scissors, used for gripping and pulling things. ■ a front claw of a lobster, crab, or similar crustacean. ▷Middle English: from Anglo-Norman French, from Old French *pincier* 'to pinch.'

pin·cer move·ment ▸*n.* a movement by two separate bodies of troops converging on the enemy.

pinch /pinCH/ ▸*v.* [*trans.*] **1** grip (the skin of someone's body) tightly and sharply between finger and thumb. ■ grip the skin of a part of the body of (someone) in such a way: *Rosa pinched her hard.* ■ (of a shoe) hurt (a foot) by being too tight. ■ compress (the lips), esp. with worry or tension: *Aunt Rose **pinched** her thin lips **together**.* ■ remove (a bud, leaves, etc.) to encourage bushy growth. **2** [*intrans.*] live in a frugal way: *if I **pinch and scrape**, I might manage.* **3** *informal* arrest (someone): *I was pinched for speeding.* ■ *informal* steal: *he pinched a handful of candies.* **4** *Sailing* sail (a boat) so close to the wind that the sails begin to lose power.
▸*n.* **1** an act of gripping the skin of someone's body between finger and thumb: *he gave her a gentle pinch.* ■ an amount of an ingredient that can be held between fingers and thumb: *add a **pinch of** salt.* **2** *informal* an arrest. ■ an act of theft or plagiarism. ▷Middle English (as a verb): from an Old Northern French variant of Old French *pincier* 'to pinch.' **—pinch·er** *n.*
▸*PHRASES* □ **in a pinch** in a critical situation; if absolutely necessary. □ **feel the pinch** experience hardship, esp. financial. □ **pinch (one's) pennies** see PENNY.

pinch·beck /ˈpinCHˌbek/ ▸*n.* an alloy of copper and zinc resembling gold, used in watchmaking and costume jewelry.
▸*adj.* appearing valuable, but actually cheap or tawdry. ▷mid 18th cent.: named after Christopher *Pinchbeck* (died 1732), English watchmaker.

pinched /pinCHt/ ▸*adj.* **1** (of a person or their face) tense and pale from cold, worry, or hunger. **2** hurt by financial hardship: *consumers feel pinched by rising costs in repairs and housing.*

pinch ef·fect ▸*n. Physics* the constriction of a plasma through which a large electric current is flowing, caused by the attractive force of the current's own magnetic field.

pin cher·ry ▸*n.* see BIRD CHERRY.

pinch-hit ▸*v.* [*intrans.*] *Baseball* bat in place of another player, typically at a critical point in the game: *he **pinch-hit for** O'Brien and hit a grounder.* ■ (of a team manager or coach) assign a player to pinch-hit in place of another: *when National League managers pinch-hit for the pitcher.* ■ *informal* act as a substitute for someone, esp. in an emergency: *last year I briefly pinch-hit for a movie critic on leave.* **—pinch hit·ter** *n.*

Pin·chot /ˈpinSHō/, Gifford (1865–1946), U.S. forester. Chief of the U.S. Department of Agriculture's forestry division 1898–1910, he was the first professional U.S. forester and a leader in the land conservation movement. He was also governor of Pennsylvania 1923–27, 1931–35.

pinch·pen·ny /ˈpinCHˌpenē/ ▸*n.* (*pl.* **-nies**) [usu. as *adj.*] a miserly person.

pinch point ▸*n.* a place between moving equipment parts in which there is a risk of injury: *teach employees how to recognize and avoid pinch point hazards.* ■ *Brit.* a place or point where congestion occurs or is likely to occur, especially on a road: *the planners have suggestions to ease traffic jams at ninety-two pinch points.*

pinch-run ▸*v.* [*intrans.*] *Baseball* substitute for another as a base runner, typically at a critical point in the game. **—pinch run·ner** *n.*

Pinck·ney /ˈpiNGknē/, Charles Cotesworth (1746–1825), U.S. statesman. As minister to France in 1797, he was one of the proposed recipients of the bribery attempts made by the French to U.S. officials in what became known as the XYZ Affair. He ran unsuccessfully for U.S. vice president in 1800 and for president in 1804 and 1808.

pin curl ▸*n.* a curl that is held by a hairpin while setting.

pin·cush·ion /ˈpinˌko͝oSHən/ ▸*n.* a small cushion into which pins are stuck for convenient storage. ■ (also **pincushion distortion**) a form of optical distortion in which straight lines along the edge of a screen or a lens bulge toward the center.

Pin·dar /ˈpindər; -ˌdär/ (*c.*518–*c.*438 BC), Greek lyric poet. He is noted for his odes (the *Epinikia*), which celebrate victories in athletic contests at Olympia and elsewhere and relate them to religious and moral themes. **—Pin·dar·ic** /pinˈdarik/ *adj.*

Pin·dus Moun·tains /ˈpindəs/ a range of mountains in west central Greece that stretch from the border with Albania south to the Gulf of Corinth. The highest peak is Mount Smolikas, which rises to 8,136 feet (2,637 m). Greek name PÍNDHOS.

pine[1] /pīn/ ▸*n.* **1** (also **pine tree**) an evergreen coniferous tree that has clusters of long needle-shaped leaves. Many kinds are grown for their soft timber, which is widely used for furniture and pulp, or for tar and turpentine. • Genus *Pinus*, family Pinaceae: many species, including North America's eastern **white pine** and western **ponderosa pine**. ■ used in names of coniferous trees of other families, e.g., **Norfolk Island pine**. ■ used in names of unrelated plants that resemble the pines in some way, e.g., **ground pine**. ■ [as *adj.*] having the scent of pine needles: *a pine potpourri.* **2** *informal* a pineapple. ▷Old English, from Latin *pinus*, reinforced in Middle English by Old French *pin*. **—pin·er·y** /ˈpīnərē/ *n.*

pine[2] ▸*v.* [*intrans.*] suffer a mental and physical decline, esp. because of a broken heart: *she thinks I am **pining away** from love.* ■ (**pine for**) miss and long for the return of: *I was pining for my boyfriend.* ▷Old English *pīnian* '(cause to) suffer,' of Germanic origin; related to Dutch *pijnen*, German *peinen* 'experience pain,' also to obsolete *pine* 'punishment'; ultimately based on Latin *poena* 'punishment.'

pin·e·al /ˈpinēəl; ˈpī-/ (also **pineal gland**, **pineal body**) ▸*n.* a pea-sized conical mass of tissue behind the third ventricle of the brain, secreting a hormone-like substance in some mammals.
▸*adj.* of, denoting, or relating to the pineal. ▷late 17th cent.: from French *pinéal*, from Latin *pinea* 'pine cone.' The anatomical term refers to the shape of the gland.

pin·e·al eye ▸*n. Zoology* (in some reptiles and lower vertebrates) an eyelike structure on the top of the head, covered by almost transparent skin and derived from or linked to the pineal body.

pine·ap·ple /ˈpīˌnapəl/ ▸*n.* **1** a large juicy tropical fruit consisting of aromatic edible yellow flesh surrounded by a tough segmented skin and topped with a tuft of stiff leaves. **2** the widely cultivated tropical American plant that bears this fruit. It is low-growing, with a spiral of spiny sword-shaped leaves on a thick stem. • *Ananas comosus*, family Bromeliaceae. **3** *informal* a hand grenade. ▷late Middle English (denoting a pine cone): from PINE[1] + APPLE. The word was applied to the fruit in the mid 17th cent., because of its resemblance to a pine cone.

pineapple

pine·ap·ple weed ▸*n.* a small mayweed with flowers that lack ray florets. When crushed, the leaves have a pineapple fragrance. • Genus *Matricaria*, family Compositae: the European *M. matricarioides* and the North American *M. discoidea.*

Pine Barrens a region in southern New Jersey that is lightly populated and is characterized by sandy

Pronunciation Key ə *ago*; ər *over*; ˈə *or* ˌə *up*; ˈər *or* ˌər *fur*; a *hat*; ā *rate*; ä *car*; CH *chew*; e *let*; ē *see*; e(ə)r *air*; i *fit*; ī *by*; i(ə)r *ear*; NG *sing*; ō *go*; ô *for*; oi *boy*; o͝o *good*; o͞o *goo*; ou *out*; SH *she*; TH *thin*; T͟H *then*; (h)w *why*; ZH *vision*

soils, forests of stunted conifers, and numerous small rivers.

Pine Bluff an industrial city in southeastern Arkansas, on the Arkansas River, site of a large arsenal; pop. 55,085.

pine cone

pine cone ▸*n.* the conical or rounded woody fruit of a pine tree, with scales that open to release the seeds.

pine mar·ten ▸*n.* a marten with a dark brown coat, a yellowish throat, and a bushy tail. • Genus *Martes*, family Mustelidae: two species, *M. martes* of northern Eurasia, and *M. americana* of North America, esp. Canada and Alaska.

pi·nene /ˈpīˌnēn/ ▸*n. Chemistry* a colorless flammable liquid present in turpentine, juniper oil, and other natural extracts. • A bicyclic terpene; chem. formula: $C_{10}H_{16}$; four isomers, esp. **α-pinene**, the main constituent of turpentine. ▷late 19th cent.: from Latin *pinus* 'pine' + **-ENE**.

pine nut ▸*n.* the edible seed of various pine trees.

Pine Ridge a village in southwestern South Dakota, headquarters of the Pine Ridge Indian Reservation; pop. 2,596.

pine·sap /ˈpīnˌsap/ ▸*n.* a saprophytic woodland plant related to wintergreen, lacking chlorophyll and bearing one or more waxy bell-shaped flowers. • Two species in the family Monotropaceae (or Pyrolaceae): the yellow or reddish *Monotropa hypopithys* (also called **false beechdrops**), common in eastern North America, and the pinkish or purplish violet-scented *Monotropsis odorata* (also called **sweet pinesap**).

pine snake ▸*n.* a large harmless North American snake with dark markings. When disturbed it hisses loudly and vibrates its tail. • *Pituophis melanoleucus*, family Colubridae.

pine tar ▸*n.* a thick, sticky liquid obtained from the destructive distillation of pinewood, used in soap, roofing, and medicinally for skin infections.

Pine Tree State a nickname for the state of **MAINE**.

pi·ne·tum /pīˈnētəm/ ▸*n.* (*pl.* **-ta** /-tə/) an arboretum of pine trees or other conifers for scientific or ornamental purposes. ▷mid 19th cent.: from Latin, from *pinus* 'pine' + **-ETUM**.

pine vole ▸*n.* a vole with dense molelike fur, found chiefly in forests and orchards in North America and Eurasia. • Genus *Pitymys*, family Muridae: many species, esp. the common *P. pinetorum*, the Florida variety of which is sometimes considered a distinct species (*P. parvulus*).

pine·wood /ˈpīnˌwo͝od/ ▸*n.* **1** [usu. as *adj.*] the timber of the pine: *pinewood furniture.* **2** (usu. **pinewoods**) a forest of pines.

pine·y /ˈpīnē/ (also **pin·y**) ▸*adj.* of, like, or full of pines.

pin·feath·er /ˈpinˌfeTHər/ ▸*n. Ornithology* an immature feather, before the veins have expanded and while the shaft is full of fluid.

pin·fold /ˈpinˌfōld/ *historical* ▸*n.* a pound for stray animals.
▸*v.* [*trans.*] confine (a stray animal) in such a pound. ▷late Old English *pundfald*, from a base shared by **POND** and **POUND**[3] + **FOLD**[2].

ping /piNG/ ▸*n.* **1** a short high-pitched ringing sound, as of a tap on a crystal glass: *the syncopated ping of steel drums.* ■ a percussive knocking sound, esp. in an internal combustion engine: *if any sign of engine ping occurs.* **2** Packet Internet Gopher, a utility which is used to query another computer on a TCP/IP network in order to determine whether there is a connection to it.
▸*v.* [*intrans.*] **1** make such a sound. ■ [*trans.*] cause (something) to make a such a sound. **2** to query another computer on a TCP/IP network to determine whether there is a connection to it. ▷mid 19th cent.: imitative.

ping·er /ˈpiNGər/ ▸*n.* a device that transmits short high-pitched signals at brief intervals for purposes of detection, measurement, or identification.

pin·go /ˈpiNGō/ ▸*n.* (*pl.* **-gos**) *Geology* a dome-shaped mound consisting of a layer of soil over a large core of ice, occurring in permafrost areas. ▷1920s: from Inuit *pinguq* 'nunatak.'

Ping-Pong /ˈpiNG ˌpôNG; -ˌpäNG/ ▸*n. trademark* another term for **TABLE TENNIS**. ▷early 20th cent.: imitative of the sound of a paddle striking a ball.

pin·guid /ˈpiNGgwid/ ▸*adj. formal* of the nature of or resembling fat; oily or greasy. ▷mid 17th cent.: from Latin *pinguis* 'fat' + **-ID**[1]. **—pin·guid·i·ty** /piNGˈgwiditē/ *n.*

pin·head /ˈpinˌhed/ ▸*n.* **1** the flattened head of a pin. ■ [often as *adj.*] a very small rounded object: *pinhead dots.* **2** *informal* a stupid or foolish person.

pin·head·ed /ˈpinˌhedəd/ ▸*adj. informal* stupid; foolish. **—pin·head·ed·ness** *n.*

pin·hole /ˈpinˌhōl/ ▸*n.* a very small hole.

pin·hole bor·er ▸*n.* an ambrosia beetle (family Platypodidae), specifically the larva, which makes minute round holes in timber.

pin·hole cam·er·a ▸*n.* a camera with a pinhole aperture and no lens.

pin·ion[1] /ˈpinyən/ ▸*n.* the outer part of a bird's wing including the flight feathers. ■ *poetic/literary* a bird's wing as used in flight.
▸*v.* [*trans.*] **1** tie or hold the arms or legs of (someone): *he pinioned the limbs of his opponents.* ■ bind (the arms or legs) of someone. **2** cut off the pinion of (a wing or bird) to prevent flight. ▷late Middle English: from Old French *pignon*, based on Latin *pinna, penna* 'feather.'

pin·ion[2] ▸*n.* a small gear or spindle engaging with a large gear. ▷mid 17th cent.: from French *pignon*, alteration of obsolete *pignol*, from Latin *pinea* 'pine cone,' from *pinus* 'pine.'

pink[1] /piNGk/ ▸*adj.* **1** of a color intermediate between red and white, as of coral or salmon: *her healthy pink cheeks | bright pink lipstick.* ■ (of wine) rosé. **2** *informal, often derogatory* having or showing left-wing tendencies: *pale pink politics.* **3** of or associated with homosexuals: *a boom in the pink economy.*
▸*n.* **1** pink color or pigment. ■ pink clothes or material: *she looks good in pink.* ■ (also **hunting pink**) the red clothing or material worn by fox hunters. **2** a pink thing, such as a rosé wine. **3** the best condition or degree: *the economy is not in* **the pink of** *health.* **4** *informal, often derogatory* a person with left-wing tendencies. See also **PINKO**.
▸*v.* [*intrans.*] blush, as from embarrassment: *I tried to hide my embarrassment, but I think I must have pinked a bit.* ▷mid 17th cent.: from **PINK**[2], the early use of the adjective being to describe the color of the flowers of this plant. **—pink·ish** *adj.* **—pink·ly** *adv.* **—pink·ness** *n.* **—pink·y** *adj.*
▸*PHRASES* □ **in the pink** *informal* in very good health and spirits. □ **turn** (or **go**) **pink** blush.

pink[2] ▸*n.* a herbaceous Eurasian plant with sweet-smelling pink or white flowers and slender, typically gray-green, leaves. • Genus *Dianthus*, family Caryophyllaceae (the **pink family**). This family includes the campions, chickweeds, stitchworts, and the cultivated carnations. See also **CLOVE**[1] (sense 3). ▷late 16th cent.: perhaps short for *pink eye*, literally 'small or half-shut eye'; compare with the synonymous French word *oeillet*, literally 'little eye.'

pink[3] ▸*v.* [*trans.*] **1** cut a scalloped or zigzag edge on: [as *adj.*] (**pinked**) *a bonnet with pinked edging.* ■ pierce or nick (someone) slightly with a weapon or missile. **2** *archaic* decorate: *April pinked the earth with flowers.* ▷early 16th cent. (in the sense 'pierce or nick slightly'): compare with Low German *pinken* 'strike, peck.'

pink[4] ▸*n. historical* a small square-rigged sailing ship, typically with a narrow, overhanging stern. ▷late 15th cent.: from Middle Dutch *pin(c)ke*, of unknown ultimate origin; compare with Spanish *pinque* and Italian *pinco*.

pink[5] ▸*n. dated* a yellowish lake pigment made by combining vegetable coloring matter with a white base. ▷mid 17th cent.: of unknown origin.

pink-col·lar ▸*adj.* of or relating to work traditionally associated with women.

pink el·e·phants ▸*plural n. informal* hallucinations supposedly typical of those experienced by a drunk person.

Pin·ker·ton /ˈpiNGkərtən/, Allan (1819–84), U.S. detective, born in Scotland. In 1850, after having solved a series of train robberies, he established the first U.S. private detective agency. He served as chief of the Union's secret service during the Civil War.

pink·eye /ˈpiNGkˌī/ ▸*n.* **1** conjunctivitis in humans and some livestock. **2** a viral disease of horses, symptoms of which include fever, spontaneous abortion, and redness of the eyes. • The virus belongs to the genus *Arterivirus*.

Pink·ham /ˈpiNGkəm/, Lydia (Estes) (1819–83), U.S. inventor and saleswoman. In 1865, she concocted and marketed Mrs. Lydia E. Pinkham's Vegetable Compound, a patented herbal medicine for female complaints.

pink·ie /ˈpiNGkē/ (also **pink·y**) ▸*n. informal* the little finger. ▷early 19th cent.: partly from Dutch *pink* 'the little finger,' reinforced by **PINK**[1].

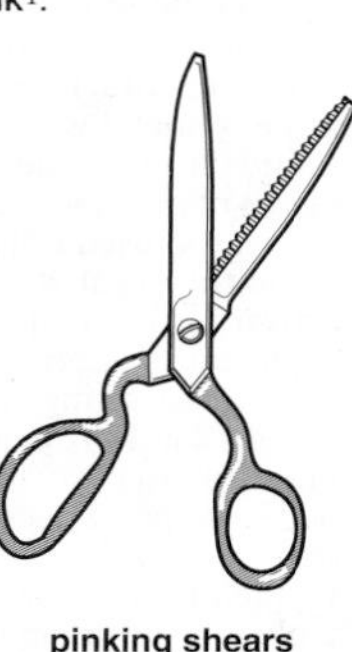
pinking shears

pink·ing shears ▸*plural n.* shears with a serrated blade, used to cut a zigzag edge in fabric to prevent it from fraying.

pink noise ▸*n. Physics* random noise having equal energy per octave, and so having more low-frequency components than white noise.

pink·o /ˈpiNGkō/ ▸*n.* (*pl.* **-os** or **-oes**) *informal, derogatory* a person with left-wing or liberal views.

pink salm·on ▸*n.* a small salmon with dark spots on the back, native to the North Pacific and introduced into the northwestern Atlantic. • *Oncorhynchus gorbuscha*, family Salmonidae. ■ its pale pink flesh used as food.

pink slip *informal* ▸*n.* a notice of dismissal from employment.
▸*v.* (**pink-slip**) [*trans.*] dismiss (someone) from employment.

Pink·ster /ˈpiNGkstər/ ▸*n. dialect* Whitsuntide. ▷mid 18th cent.: from Dutch, 'Pentecost,' from celebrations in areas of former Dutch influence, such as New York.

pin mon·ey ▸*n.* a small sum of money for spending on inessentials. ■ *historical* an allowance to a woman from her husband for clothing and other personal expenses. ▷late 17th cent.: from **PIN** in the sense 'decorative clasp for the hair or a garment' + **MONEY**.

pin·na /ˈpinə/ ▸*n.* (*pl.* **pin·nae** /ˈpinē/) **1** *Anatomy & Zoology* the external part of the ear in humans and other mammals; the auricle. **2** *Botany* a primary division of a pinnate leaf, esp. of a fern. **3** *Zoology* any of a number of animal structures resembling fins or wings. ▷late 18th cent.: modern Latin, from a variant of Latin *penna* 'feather, wing, fin.'

pin·nace /ˈpinis/ ▸*n. chiefly historical* a small boat, with sails or oars, forming part of the equipment of a warship or other large vessel. ▷mid 16th cent.: from French *pinace*, probably based on Latin *pinus* 'pine' (see **PINE**[1]); compare with Italian *pinaccia* and Spanish *pinaza*.

pin·na·cle /ˈpinəkəl/ ▸*n.* a high, pointed piece of rock. ■ a small pointed turret built as an ornament on a roof. ■ the most successful point; the culmination: *he had reached* **the pinnacle of** *his career.*
▸*v.* [*trans.*] *poetic/literary* set on or as if on a pinnacle: *a rustic cross was pinnacled upon the makeshift altar.* ■ form the culminating point or example of. ▷Middle English: from Old French, from late Latin *pinnaculum*, diminutive of *pinna* 'wing, point.' **—pin·na·cled** *adj.*

pin·nae /ˈpinē/ ▸ plural form of **PINNA**.

pin·nate /ˈpināt; -it/ ▸*adj. Botany* (of a compound leaf) having leaflets arranged on either side of the stem, typically in pairs opposite each other. ■ *Zoology* (esp. of an invertebrate animal) having branches, tentacles, etc., on each side of an axis, like the vanes of a feather. ▷early 18th cent.: from Latin *pinnatus* 'feathered,' from *pinna, penna* (see **PINNA**). **—pin·nat·ed** *adj.* **—pin·nate·ly** *adv.* **—pin·na·tion** /piˈnāSHən/ *n.*

pin·nat·i·fid /piˈnatəfid/ ▸*adj. Botany* (of a leaf) pinnately divided, but not all the way down to the central axis. ▷mid 18th cent.: from modern Latin *pinnatifidus*, from Latin *pinnatus* 'feathered' + *fid-* 'cleft' (from the verb *findere*).

pinni- ▸*comb. form* relating to wings or fins: *pinniped.* ▷from Latin *pinna, penna* 'wing, fin.'

Pin·ni·pe·di·a /ˌpinəˈpēdēə/ *Zoology* an order of carnivorous aquatic mammals that comprises the seals, sea lions, and walrus. They are distinguished by their flipperlike limbs. • Order Pinnipedia: three families. ▷modern Latin (plural), from Latin *pinna* 'wing, fin' + *pes, ped-* 'foot.' **—pin·ni·ped** /ˈpinəˌped/ *n.* & *adj.*

pin·nule /ˈpinˌyo͞ol/ ▸*n. Botany* a secondary division of a pinnate leaf, esp. of a fern. ■ *Zoology* a part or organ like a small wing or fin, esp. a side branch on the arm of a crinoid. ▷late 16th cent. (denoting one of the sights of an astrolabe): from Latin *pinnula* 'small wing,' diminutive of *pinna*.

PIN num·ber ▸*n.* see **PIN**.

pin oak ▸*n.* a North American oak with deeply lobed, toothed leaves. Its dead branches remain in position and resemble pegs fixed in the trunk. • *Quercus palustris.*

Pi·no·chet /ˈpēnəˌshä; ˌpēnōˈchet/, Augusto (1915–), Chilean general and statesman; president 1974–90; full name *Augusto Pinochet Ugarte*. He imposed a military dictatorship until forced to call elections, giving way to a democratically elected president in 1990.

pi·noch·le /ˈpēnəkəl/ ▸*n.* a card game for two or more players using a 48-card deck consisting of two of each card from nine to ace, the object being to score points for various combinations and to win tricks. ■ the combination of queen of spades and jack of diamonds in this game. ▷mid 19th cent.: of unknown origin.

pin·o·cy·to·sis /ˌpinəsīˈtōsis; pinə-/ ▸*n. Biology* the ingestion of liquid into a cell by the budding of small vesicles from the cell membrane. ▷late 19th cent.: from Greek *pino* 'drink' + *-cytosis* on the pattern of *phagocytosis*. **—pin·o·cy·tot·ic** /-ˈtätik/ *adj.*

pi·no·le /piˈnōlē/ ▸*n.* a sweetened flour made from ground dried corn mixed with flour made of mesquite beans, sugar, and spices. ▷mid 19th cent.: from Latin American Spanish, from Nahuatl *pinolli*.

pi·ñon /ˈpinyən; ˌpinˈyōn/ (also **pi·nyon** or **pi·ñon pine**) ▸*n.* a small pine tree with edible seeds, native to Mexico and the southwestern U.S. • *Pinus cembroides*, family Pinaceae. ■ (also **piñon nut**) a pine nut obtained from this tree. ▷mid 19th cent.: from Spanish, from Latin *pinea* 'pine cone.'

Pi·not /ˈpēnō; pēˈnō/ ▸*n.* any of several varieties of wine grape, esp. the chief varieties **Pinot Noir**, a black grape, and **Pinot Blanc**, a white grape. ■ a wine made from these grapes. ▷variant of earlier *Pineau*, diminutive of *pin* 'pine' (because of the shape of the grape cluster).

pi·no·tage /ˈpēnōˌtäzh/ ▸*n.* a variety of red wine grape grown in South Africa, produced by crossing Pinot Noir and other varieties. ■ red wine made from this grape. ▷blend of *Pinot (Noir)* and *Hermitage*, names of types of grape.

pin·out /ˈpinˌout/ ▸*n. Electronics* a diagram showing the arrangement of pins on an integrated circuit and their functions.

pin·point /ˈpinˌpoint/ ▸*n.* a tiny dot or point: *a* ***pinpoint of*** *light from a flashlight.*
▸*adj.* [*attrib.*] absolutely precise; to the finest degree: *this weapon fired shells with pinpoint accuracy.* ■ tiny: *a pinpoint laser beam.*
▸*v.* [*trans.*] find or locate exactly: *one flare had pinpointed the target* | *figurative it is difficult to pinpoint the source of his life's inspiration.*

pin·prick /ˈpinˌprik/ ▸*n.* a prick caused by a pin. ■ a cause of minor irritation.

pins and nee·dles ▸*plural n.* a tingling sensation in a limb recovering from numbness.

Pin·sky /ˈpinskē/, Robert (1940–), U.S. poet and writer. He served as U.S. poet laureate 1997–2000. His poetry is collected in volumes such as *History of My Heart* (1984) and *The Figured Wheel: New and Collected Poems, 1966–1996* (1996). His translation of *The Inferno of Dante* was published in 1994.

pin·spot /ˈpinˌspät/ ▸*n.* a small powerful spotlight for sharp illumination of a very small area.
▸*v.* [*trans.*] illuminate with a pinspot.

pin·stripe /ˈpinˌstrīp/ ▸*n.* a very narrow stripe in cloth, esp. of the type used for formal suits. ■ a pinstripe suit.
▸*adj. Sports* of baseball: *a play that instantly became part of pinstripe legend.* [from the fact that many baseball uniforms have pinstripes.] **—pin·striped** *adj.*

pint /pīnt/ (abbr.: **pt**) ▸*n.* a unit of liquid or dry capacity equal to one half of a quart. ■ *Brit., informal* a pint of beer. ▷late Middle English: from Old French *pinte*, of unknown origin.

pin·ta·do pet·rel /pinˈtädō/ ▸*n.* another term for **CAPE PIGEON**. ▷early 17th cent.: from Portuguese and Spanish *pintado* 'guinea fowl', literally'painted,' + **PETREL**.

pin·tail /ˈpinˌtāl/ ▸*n.* a mainly migratory duck with a pointed tail. • Genus *Anas*, family Anatidae: three species, in particular the **common pintail** (*A. acuta*) of North America and Eurasia, the male of which has boldly marked plumage and two long tail streamers. ■ *informal* any of a number of other birds with long pointed tails, esp. a grouse.

Pin·ter /ˈpintər/, Harold (1930–), English playwright, actor, and director. His plays are associated with the Theater of the Absurd and are typically marked by a sense of menace. Notable plays: *The Birthday Party* (1958), *The Caretaker* (1960), and *Party Time* (1991).

pin·tle /ˈpintl/ ▸*n.* one of the pins (on the forward edge of a rudder) that fit into the gudgeons and so suspend the rudder. ▷Old English *pintel* 'penis,' perhaps a diminutive; compare with Dutch *pint* and German *Pint* 'penis,' of unknown ultimate origin.

pin·to /ˈpintō/ ▸*adj.* piebald.
▸*n.* (*pl.* **-tos**) a piebald horse. ▷mid 19th cent.: from Spanish, literally 'mottled,' based on Latin *pictus*, past participle of *pingere* 'to paint.'

pin·to bean ▸*n.* a medium-sized speckled variety of kidney bean. ▷early 20th cent.: *pinto* from **PINTO**, because of the mottled seed of this variety of bean.

pint pot ▸*n. chiefly Brit.* a beer glass or mug that holds a pint, esp. one made of pewter.

pint-sized (also **pint-size**) ▸*adj. informal* very small: *at age seven, he was a pint-sized superstar* | *a pint-sized apartment.*

pin tuck ▸*n.* (in sewing) a very narrow ornamental tuck.

pin·up /ˈpinˌəp/ ▸*n.* a poster showing a famous person or sex symbol, designed to be displayed on a wall. ■ a person shown in such a poster.

pin·wheel /ˈpinˌ(h)wēl/ ▸*n.* a child's toy consisting of a stick with colored vanes that twirl in the wind. ■ a fireworks device that whirls and emits colored fire. ■ something shaped or rotating like a pinwheel.
▸*v.* [*intrans.*] spin or rotate like a pinwheel.

pin·worm /ˈpinˌwərm/ ▸*n.* a small nematode worm that is an internal parasite of vertebrates. • Family Oxyuridae, class Phasmida, including *Enterobius vermicularis* (in humans) and *Oxyuris equi* (in horses).

pinx. ▸*abbr.* pinxit. ▷Latin, 'he painted.'

pin·y /ˈpīnē/ ▸*adj.* variant spelling of **PINEY**.

Pin·yin /ˈpinˈyin/ (also **pin·yin**) ▸*n.* the standard system of romanized spelling for transliterating Chinese. ▷1960s: from Chinese *pīn-yīn*, literally 'spell-sound.'

pin·yon ▸*n.* variant spelling of **PIÑON**.

Pin·za /ˈpinzə/, Ezio (Fortunato) (1892–1957), U.S. opera singer; born in Italy. A bass, he performed with the Metropolitan Opera from 1926 until 1948 and was responsible for the return of Mozart's operas to the Met repertory. In 1949, he branched out and appeared on Broadway in *South Pacific*.

pi·o·let /ˌpēəˈlā/ ▸*n. Climbing* an ice ax. ▷mid 19th cent.: from French dialect, literally 'little pick,' diminutive of *piolo*; related to *pioche* 'pickax.'

pi·on /ˈpīˌän/ ▸*n. Physics* a meson having a mass approximately 270 times that of an electron. Also called **PI MESON**. ▷1950s: from **PI** (the letter used as a symbol for the particle) + **-ON**. **—pi·on·ic** /pīˈänik/ *adj.*

Pi·o·neer /ˌpīəˈnir/ a series of American space probes launched between 1958 and 1973, two of which provided the first clear pictures of Jupiter and Saturn (1973–79).

pi·o·neer /ˌpīəˈnir/ ▸*n.* a person who is among the first to explore or settle a new country or area. ■ a person who is among the first to research and develop a new area of knowledge or activity: *a famous pioneer of birth control.* ■ (in the former USSR and other communist countries) a member of a movement for children below the age of sixteen that aimed to foster communist ideals. ■ a member of an infantry group preparing roads or terrain for the main body of troops. ■ (also **pioneer species**) a plant or animal that establishes itself in an unoccupied area.
▸*v.* [*trans.*] develop or be the first to use or apply (a new method, area of knowledge, or activity): *he has pioneered a number of innovative techniques.* ■ open up (a road or terrain) as a pioneer. ▷early 16th cent. (as a military term denoting a member of the infantry): from French *pionnier* 'foot soldier, pioneer,' Old French *paonier*, from *paon*, from Latin *pedo, pedon-* (see **PAWN**[1]).

pi·o·neer·ing /ˌpīəˈniriNG/ ▸*adj.* involving new ideas or methods: *his pioneering work on consciousness.*

pi·ous /ˈpīəs/ ▸*adj.* devoutly religious. ■ making a hypocritical display of virtue: *there'll be no pious words said over her.* ■ [*attrib.*] (of a hope) sincere but unlikely to be fulfilled. ■ (of a deception) with good or religious intentions, whether professed or real. ■ *archaic* dutiful or loyal, esp. toward one's parents. ▷late Middle English: from Latin *pius* 'dutiful, pious' + **-OUS**. **—pi·ous·ly** *adv.* **—pi·ous·ness** *n.*

pip[1] /pip/ ▸*n.* a small hard seed in a fruit. ▷late 18th cent.: abbreviation of **PIPPIN**. **—pip·less** /ˈpipləs/ *adj.*

pip[2] ▸*n.* a small shape or symbol, in particular: ■ any of the spots on playing cards, dice, or dominoes. ■ a single blossom of a clustered head of flowers. ■ a diamond-shaped segment of the surface of a pineapple. ■ an image of an object on a radar screen; blip. ■ *Brit.* a star (1–3 according to rank) on the shoulder of an army officer's uniform. ▷late 16th cent. (originally *peep*, denoting each of the dots on playing cards, dice, and dominoes): of unknown origin.

pip[3] ▸*n.* a disease of poultry or other birds causing thick mucus in the throat and white scale on the tongue. ▷late Middle English: from Middle Dutch *pippe*, probably from an alteration of Latin *pituita* 'slime.' In the late 15th cent. the word came to be applied humorously to unspecified human diseases, and later to ill humor.
▸*PHRASE* □ **give someone the pip** *informal, dated* make someone angry or depressed.

pip[4] ▸*v.* (**pipped, pip·ping**) [*trans.*] (of a young bird) crack (the shell of the egg) when hatching. ▷late 19th cent.: perhaps of imitative origin.

pip[5] *Brit., informal* ▸*v.* (**pipped, pip·ping**) [*trans.*] (usu. **be pipped**) defeat by a small margin or at the last moment: *you were just pipped for the prize.* ■ *dated* hit or wound (someone) with a gunshot. ▷late 19th cent.: from **PIP**[1] or **PIP**[2].

pi·pa /ˈpēˌpä/ ▸*n.* a shallow-bodied, four-stringed Chinese lute. ▷Chinese.

pi·pal /ˈpēpəl/ ▸*n.* variant spelling of **PEEPUL**.

pipe /pīp/ ▸*n.* **1** a tube of metal, plastic, or other material used to convey water, gas, oil, or other fluid substances. ■ a cylindrical vein of ore or rock, esp. one in which diamonds are found. ■ a cavity in cast metal. ■ *informal* a duct, vessel, or tubular structure in the body, or in an animal or plant. **2** a narrow tube made from wood, clay, etc., with a bowl at one end for containing burning tobacco, the smoke from which is drawn into the mouth. ■ a quantity of tobacco held by this. **3** a wind instrument consisting of a single tube with holes along its length that are covered by the fingers to produce different notes: *a reed pipe.* ■ (usu. **pipes**) bagpipes. ■ (**pipes**) a set of pipes joined together, as in panpipes. ■ a tube by which sound is produced in an organ. ■ [in *sing.*] a high-pitched cry or song, esp. of a bird. ■ a boatswain's whistle. **4** *Computing* a command that causes the output from one routine to be the input for another. **5** *Computing* a connection to the Internet or to a Web site: *although many businesses have high-powered pipes, the vast majority of home users still have to dial up.* **6** a cask for wine, esp. as a measure equal to two hogsheads, usually equivalent to 105 gallons (about 477 liters).
▸*v.* **1** [*trans.*] convey (water, gas, oil, or other fluid substances) through a pipe or pipes: *water from the lakes is piped to several towns.* ■ transmit (music, a radio or television program, signals, etc.) by wire or cable. **2** [*trans.*] play (a tune) on a pipe or pipes. ■ [*intrans.*] (of a bird) sing in a high or shrill voice. ■ [with *direct speech*] say something in a high, shrill voice: *"No, ma'am," piped Lucy.* ■ [*trans.*] use a boatswain's whistle to summon (the crew) to work or a meal: *the hands were piped to breakfast.* **3** [*trans.*] decorate (clothing or soft furnishings) with a thin cord covered in fabric. ■ put (a decorative line or pattern) on a cake or similar dish using icing, whipped cream, etc.
▸*phrasal v.* □ **pipe down** [often in *imperative*] *informal* stop talking; be less noisy. □ **pipe up** say something suddenly. ▷Old English *pīpe* 'musical tube,' *pīpian* 'play a pipe,' of Germanic origin; related to Dutch *pijp* and German *Pfeife*, based on Latin *pipare* 'to peep, chirp,' reinforced in Middle English by Old French *piper* 'to chirp, squeak.' **—pipe·ful** /ˈpīpˌfo͝ol/ *n.* (*pl.* **-fuls**) **—pipe·less** *adj.* **—pip·y** /ˈpīpē/ *adj.* (**pip·i·er, pip·i·est**)
▸*PHRASE* □ **put that in one's pipe and smoke it** *informal* used to indicate that someone should accept what one has said, even if it is unwelcome.

pipe bomb ▸*n.* a homemade bomb, the components of which are contained in a pipe.

pipe-clay (also **pipe·clay** or **pipe clay**) ▸*n.* a fine white clay, used esp. for making tobacco pipes or for whitening leather.
▸*v.* (**pipe-clay** or **pipe·clay**) [*trans.*] whiten (leather) with such clay.

pipe clean·er ▸*n.* a piece of wire covered with tufted fiber, used to clean a tobacco pipe and for a variety of handicrafts.

piped-in mu·sic ▸*n.* prerecorded background music played through loudspeakers in a public place.

pipe dream ▸*n.* an unattainable or fanciful hope or

scheme. ▷late 19th cent.: referring to a dream experienced when smoking an opium pipe.

pipe·fish /ˈpīpˌfisн/ ▸*n.* (*pl.* same or **-fish·es**) a narrow, elongated, chiefly marine fish with segmented bony armor beneath the skin and a long tubular snout. • *Syngnathus* and other genera, family Syngnathidae: numerous species.

pipe·line /ˈpīpˌlīn/ ▸*n.* a long pipe, typically underground, for conveying oil, gas, etc., over long distances. ■ *figurative* a channel supplying goods or information: *the biggest heroin pipeline in history.* ■ (in surfing) the hollow formed by the breaking of a large wave. ■ *Computing* a linear sequence of specialized modules used for pipelining.
▸*v.* [*trans.*] convey (a substance) by a pipeline. ■ [*trans.*] [often as *adj.*] (**pipelined**) *Computing* design or execute (a computer or instruction) using the technique of pipelining.
▸*PHRASE* □ **in the pipeline** awaiting completion or processing; being developed: *new treatments are in the pipeline.*

pipe·lin·ing /ˈpīpˌlīnɪɴɢ/ ▸*n.* **1** the laying of pipelines. ■ transportation by means of pipelines. **2** *Computing* a form of computer organization in which successive steps of an instruction sequence are executed in turn by a sequence of modules able to operate concurrently, so that another instruction can be begun before the previous one is finished.

pipe or·gan ▸*n. Music* see ORGAN (sense 1).

pip·er /ˈpīpər/ ▸*n.* **1** a bagpipe player. **2** a person who plays a pipe, esp. an itinerant musician. ▷Old English *pīpere.*
▸*PHRASE* □ **pay the piper** bear the consequences of an action or activity that one has enjoyed: *we will have to pay the piper, and the price is apt to be a high one.*

pipe rack ▸*n.* **1** a rack for holding tobacco pipes. **2** a rack made of piping on which clothes are hung, as in a store.

pi·per·a·zine /piˈperəˌzēn; pipˈərə-/ ▸*n. Chemistry* a synthetic crystalline compound with basic properties, sometimes used as an anthelmintic and insecticide. • A heterocyclic compound; chem. formula: $C_4H_{10}N_2$. ▷late 19th cent.: from PIPERIDINE + AZINE.

pi·per·i·dine /piˈperiˌdēn; pipˈərə-/ ▸*n. Chemistry* a peppery-smelling liquid formed by the reduction of pyridine. • Chem. formula: $C_5H_{11}N$. ▷mid 19th cent.: from Latin *piper* 'pepper' + -IDE + -INE[4].

pipe snake ▸*n.* any of a number of slender tropical burrowing snakes, in particular: • a South American snake marked with bold red and black stripes (*Anilius scytale,* the only member of the family Aniliidae). • an Asian snake that displays its bright under-tail coloration when alarmed (genus *Cylindrophis,* family Uropeltidae).

pipe stem (also **pipe·stem**) ▸*n.* the shaft of a tobacco pipe. ■ [as *adj.*] used to describe anything resembling this, such as a very narrow pants leg.

pipe·stone /ˈpīpˌstōn/ ▸*n.* hard red clay (catlinite) used by North American Indians for tobacco pipes.

pi·pette /pīˈpet/ (also **pi·pet**) ▸*n.* a slender tube attached to or incorporating a bulb, for transferring or measuring out small quantities of liquid, esp. in a laboratory.
▸*v.* [*trans.*] pour, convey, or draw off using a pipette. ▷mid 19th cent.: from French, literally 'little pipe,' diminutive of *pipe.*

pipe·wort /ˈpīpˌwərt; -ˌwôrt/ ▸*n.* an aquatic or marsh plant with leafless stems bearing heads of inconspicuous flowers, native to North America and parts of the United Kingdom. • *Eriocaulon aquaticum,* family Eriocaulaceae.

pip·ing /ˈpīpɪɴɢ/ ▸*n.* **1** lengths of pipe, or a network of pipes, made of metal, plastic, or other materials. **2** ornamentation on food consisting of lines of icing, whipped cream, etc. ■ thin cord covered in fabric, used to decorate clothing or soft furnishings and reinforce seams. **3** the action or art of playing a pipe or pipes.
▸*adj.* [*attrib.*] **1** (of a voice or sound) high-pitched. **2** (of a time) peaceful; characterized by the playing of pipes.
▸*PHRASE* □ **piping hot** (of food or water) very hot. [*piping,* because of the whistling sound made by very hot liquid or food.]

pip·ing plov·er ▸*n.* a small buff-colored bird of coastal areas in eastern North America. • *Charadrius melodus.*

pip·i·strelle /ˌpipəˈstrel; ˈpipəˌstrel/ (also **pip·i·strel**) ▸*n.* a small insectivorous Old World bat with jerky, erratic flight. • Genus *Pipistrellus,* family Vespertilionidae: numerous species, including *P. pipistrellus,* the most common bat in Eurasia. ▷late 18th cent.: from French, from Italian *pipistrello,* from Latin *vespertilio(n-)* 'bat,' from *vesper* 'evening.'

pip·it /ˈpipit/ ▸*n.* a mainly ground-dwelling songbird of open country, typically having brown streaky plumage. • Family Motacillidae: three genera, in particular *Anthus,* and many species, including the sparrow-sized **water pipit** (*A. spinoletta*) of the northern hemisphere. ▷mid 18th cent.: probably imitative.

pip·kin /ˈpipkin/ ▸*n.* a small earthenware pot or pan. ▷mid 16th cent.: of unknown origin.

pip·pin /ˈpipin/ ▸*n.* a red and yellow dessert apple. ■ an apple grown from seed. ■ *informal* an excellent person or thing. ▷Middle English: from Old French *pepin,* of unknown ultimate origin.

pip pip ▸*exclam. Brit., informal, dated* goodbye. ▷early 20th cent.: imitative, probably of the repeated short blasts on the horn of a car or bicycle.

pip·sis·se·wa /pipˈsisəˌwô; -wə/ ▸*n.* a North American plant of the wintergreen family, with whorled evergreen leaves. • *Chimaphila umbellata,* family Pyrolaceae. ■ a preparation of the leaves of this plant, used as a diuretic and tonic. ▷late 18th cent.: from Abnaki, literally 'flower of the woods.'

pip·squeak /ˈpipˌskwēk/ ▸*n. informal* a person considered to be insignificant, esp. because they are small or young. ▷early 20th cent.: symbolic and imitative.

pi·quant /ˈpēkənt; -känt/ ▸*adj.* having a pleasantly sharp taste or appetizing flavor. ■ pleasantly stimulating or exciting to the mind. ▷early 16th cent. (in the sense 'severe, bitter'): from French, literally 'stinging, pricking,' present participle of *piquer.* **—pi·quan·cy** /-kənsē/ *n.* **—pi·quant·ly** *adv.*

pique /pēk/ ▸*n.* a feeling of irritation or resentment resulting from a slight, esp. to one's pride: *he left **in a fit of pique.***
▸*v.* (**piques** /pēks/, **piqued** /pēkt/, **piqu·ing** /ˈpēkɪɴɢ/) **1** [*trans.*] stimulate (interest or curiosity): *you have piqued my curiosity about the man.* **2** (**be piqued**) feel irritated or resentful: *she was piqued by his curtness.* **3** (**pique oneself**) *archaic* pride oneself. ▷mid 16th cent. (denoting animosity between two or more people): from French *piquer* 'prick, irritate.'

pi·qué /pēˈkā; pi-/ ▸*n.* stiff fabric, typically cotton, woven in a strongly ribbed or raised pattern. ▷mid 19th cent.: from French, literally 'backstitched,' past participle of *piquer.*

pi·quet /piˈkā; ˈket/ (also **pic·quet**) ▸*n.* a trick-taking card game for two players, using a 32-card deck consisting of cards from the seven to the ace. ▷mid 17th cent.: from French, of unknown origin.

PIR ▸*abbr.* passive infrared (denoting a type of sensor).

pir /pi(ə)r/ ▸*n.* a Muslim saint or holy man. ▷from Persian *pir* 'old man.'

pi·ra·cy /ˈpīrəsē/ ▸*n.* the practice of attacking and robbing ships at sea. ■ a similar practice in other contexts, esp. hijacking: *air piracy.* ■ the unauthorized use or reproduction of another's work: *software piracy.* ▷mid 16th cent.: via medieval Latin from Greek *pirateia,* from *peiratēs* (see PIRATE).

Pi·rae·us /pəˈrāəs; pīˈrēəs/ the chief port of Athens, situated on the Saronic Gulf, 5 miles (8 km) southwest of the city; pop. 183,000. Greek name **PIRAIÉVS** or **PIRAIÉUS** .

Pi·ran·del·lo /ˌpirənˈdelō/, Luigi (1867–1936), Italian playwright and novelist. His plays, including *Six Characters in Search of an Author* (1921) and *Henry IV* (1922), challenged the conventions of naturalism. Notable novels: *The Outcast* (1901) and *The Late Mattia Pascal* (1904). Nobel Prize for Literature (1934).

pi·ra·nha /pəˈränə/ ▸*n.* (*pl.* same or **-nhas**) a deep-bodied South American freshwater fish that typically lives in schools and has very sharp teeth that are used to tear flesh from prey. It has a reputation as a fearsome predator. • *Serrasalmus* and other genera, family Characidae: several species, including the **red** (or **red-bellied**) **piranha** (*S. natterei*). ▷mid 18th cent.: via Portuguese from Tupi *pirá* 'fish' + *sainha* 'tooth.'

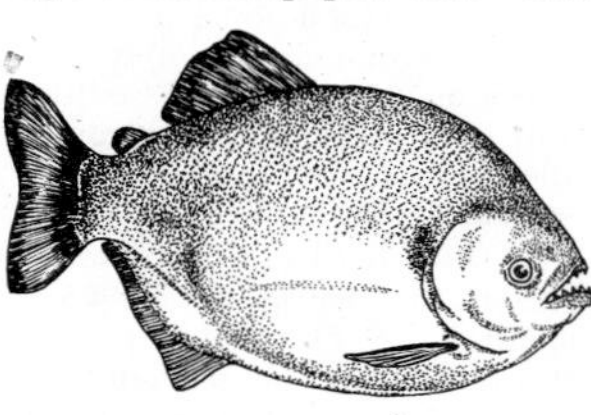
red piranha

pi·rate /ˈpīrət/ ▸*n.* a person who attacks and robs ships at sea. ■ a person who appropriates or reproduces the work of another for profit without permission, usually in contravention of patent or copyright: [with *adj.*] *software pirates.* ■ a person or organization that broadcasts radio or television programs without official authorization: [as *adj.*] *a pirate radio station.*
▸*v.* [*trans.*] **1** *dated* rob or plunder (a ship). **2** [often as *adj.*] (**pirated**) use or reproduce (another's work) for profit without permission, usually in contravention of patent or copyright: *he sold pirated tapes of Hollywood blockbusters | a competing company cannot pirate its intellectual achievements.* ▷Middle English: from Latin *pirata,* from Greek *peiratēs,* from *peirein* 'to attempt, attack' (from *peira* 'an attempt'). **—pi·rat·ic** /pīˈratik; pi-/ *adj.* **—pi·rat·i·cal** /pīˈratikəl; pi-/ *adj.* **—pi·rat·i·cal·ly** /pīˈratiklē; pi-/ *adv.*

pi·rate fish·ing ▸*n.* fishing on the high seas in contravention of national and international laws governing quotas, typically by ships under flags of convenience that are owned by dummy companies.

pir·i·form ▸*adj.* variant spelling of PYRIFORM.

pi·ri-pi·ri /ˈpi(ə)rē ˈpi(ə)rē/ (also **pil-pil** /ˈpēl ˌpēl/) ▸*n.* Portuguese term for hot chilies or the hot sauce made from them.

pi·rog /piˈrōg/ ▸*n.* (*pl.* **-ro·gi** /-ˈrōgē/ or **-ro·gen** /-ˈrōgən/) a large Russian pie. ▷Russian.

pi·ro·gi /piˈrōgē/ (also **pe·ro·gi**) ▸*n.* (*pl.* same or **-gies**) a dough dumpling stuffed with a filling such as potato or cheese, typically served with onions or sour cream. ▷from Polish *pieróg.*

pi·rogue /piˈrōg/ ▸*n.* a long narrow canoe made from a single tree trunk, esp. in Central America and the Caribbean. ▷early 17th cent.: from French, probably from Galibi.

pir·o·plas·mo·sis /ˌpi(ə)rəplazˈmōsis/ ▸*n.* another term for BABESIOSIS.

pi·rosh·ki /piˈrôsнkē; -ˈräsн-/ (also **pi·rozh·ki**) ▸*plural n.* small Russian pastries or patties, filled with meat or fish and rice. ▷from Russian *pirozhki,* plural of *pirozhok,* diminutive of *pirog* (see PIROG).

pir·ou·ette /ˌpiro͝oˈet/ ▸*n. chiefly Ballet* an act of spinning on one foot, typically with the raised foot touching the knee of the supporting leg. ■ a movement performed in advanced dressage and classical riding, in which the horse makes a circle by pivoting on a hind leg while cantering.
▸*v.* [*intrans.*] perform a pirouette. ▷mid 17th cent.: from French, literally 'spinning top,' of unknown ultimate origin.

Pi·sa /ˈpēzə/ a city in northern Italy, in Tuscany, on the Arno River; pop. 101,000. It is noted for the **Leaning Tower of Pisa**, a circular bell tower that leans about 17 feet (5 m) from the perpendicular in its height of 181 feet (55 m).

Leaning Tower of Pisa

pis al·ler /ˌpēz äˈlā/ ▸*n.* a course of action followed as a last resort. ▷French, from *pis* 'worse' + *aller* 'go.'

Pi·sa·no[1] /piˈzänō/, Andrea (*c.*1290–*c.*1348) and Nino, his son (died *c.*1368), Italian sculptors. Andrea created the earliest pair of bronze doors for the baptistery at Florence (completed 1336). Nino was one of the earliest to specialize in freestanding life-size figures.

Pi·sa·no[2] Nicola (*c.*1220–*c.*1278) and Giovanni, his son (*c.*1250–*c.*1314), two Italian sculptors. Nicola's most famous works are the pulpits in the baptistery at Pisa and in Siena cathedral. Giovanni's works include the richly decorated facade of Siena cathedral.

pis·ca·ry /ˈpiskərē/ ▸*n.* (in phrase **common of piscary**) *chiefly historical* the right of fishing in another's water. ▷late 15th cent.: from medieval Latin *piscaria* 'fishing rights,' neuter plural of Latin *piscarius* 'relating to fishing,' from *piscis* 'fish.'

Pis·cat·a·way /pi'skatə,wā/ a township in central New Jersey, across the Raritan River from New Brunswick; pop. 47,089.

pis·ca·to·ri·al /,piskə'tôrēəl/ ▶*adj.* *formal* of or concerning fishermen or fishing. ▷early 19th cent.: from Latin *piscatorius* 'relating to fishing' (from *piscator* 'fisherman,' from *piscis* 'fish') + **-AL**.

pis·ca·to·ry /'piskə,tôrē/ ▶*adj.* another term for **PISCATORIAL**.

Pis·ces /'pīsēz/ **1** *Astronomy* a large constellation (the Fish or Fishes), said to represent a pair of fish tied together by their tails. ■ [as *genitive*] (**Piscium** /'pisHēəm/) used with a preceding letter or numeral to designate a star in this constellation: *the star Alpha Piscium.* **2** *Astrology* the twelfth sign of the zodiac, which the sun enters about February 20. ■ (**a Pisces**) (*pl.* same) a person born when the sun is in this sign. ▷Latin, plural of *piscis* 'fish.' **—Pis·ce·an** /-sēən/ *n.* & *adj.* (in sense 2).

pis·ci·cul·ture /'pisi,kəlCHər/ ▶*n.* the controlled breeding and rearing of fish. ▷mid 19th cent.: from Latin *piscis* 'fish' + **CULTURE**, on the pattern of words such as *agriculture*. **—pis·ci·cul·tur·al** /,pisi',kəlCHərəl/ *adj.* **—pis·ci·cul·tur·ist** /,pisi'kəlCHərist/ *n.*

pis·ci·na /pi'sēnə; -'sīnə/ ▶*n.* (*pl.* **-nas** or **-nae** /-nē/) **1** a stone basin near the altar in Catholic and pre-Reformation churches for draining water used in the Mass. **2** (in ancient Roman architecture) a pool or pond for bathing or swimming. ▷late 16th cent. (sense 2): from Latin, literally 'fishpond,' from *piscis* 'fish'; sense 1 was found in medieval Latin.

pis·cine /'pīsēn; 'pisīn/ ▶*adj.* of or concerning fish. ▷late 18th cent.: from Latin *piscis* 'fish' + **-INE**[1].

Pis·cis Aus·tri·nus /'pīsis ô'strīnəs/ (also **Pis·cis Aus·tra·lis** /ô'strālis/) *Astronomy* a southern constellation (the Southern Fish), south of Aquarius and Capricornus. It contains the bright star Fomalhaut. ■ [as *genitive*] (**Piscis Austrini**) used with a preceding letter or numeral to designate a star in this constellation: *the star Gamma Piscis Austrini.* ▷Latin.

pis·civ·o·rous /pi'sivərəs/ ▶*adj.* *Zoology* (of an animal) feeding on fish. ▷mid 17th cent.: from Latin *piscis* 'fish' + **-VOROUS**. **—pis·ci·vore** /'pisi,vôr/ *n.*

pis·co /'pēskō; 'piskō/ ▶*n.* a white brandy made in Peru from muscat grapes. ▷named after a port in Peru.

pi·sé /pē'zā/ ▶*n.* building material of stiff clay or earth, forced into forms that are removed as it hardens. ▷late 18th cent.: French, literally 'pounded,' past participle of *piser*.

pish /pisH/ ▶*exclam.* *dated* used to express annoyance, impatience, or disgust. ▷natural utterance: first recorded in English in the late 16th cent.

pish·er /'pisHər/ ▶*n.* *informal* an insignificant or contemptible person. ▷1940s: Yiddish, literally 'pisser,' from the verb *pissen*.

Pish·pek /pisH'pek; pi'sHpyek/ former name (until 1926) of **BISHKEK**.

Pi·sid·i·a /pə'sidēə; pī-/ an ancient region in Asia Minor, between Pamphylia and Phrygia. It was incorporated into the Roman province of Galatia in 25 BC. **—Pi·sid·i·an** *adj.* & *n.*

pi·si·form /'pīsə,fôrm/ (also **pisiform bone**) ▶*n.* a small rounded carpal bone situated where the palm of the hand meets the outer edge of the wrist. ▷mid 18th cent.: from modern Latin *pisiformis* 'pea-shaped,' from *pisum* 'pea' + *forma* 'shape.'

Pi·sis·tra·tus /pi'sistrətəs/ (also **Pei·sis·tra·tus**) (*c.*600–*c.*527 BC), tyrant of Athens. He reduced aristocratic power in rural Attica and promoted the financial prosperity and cultural preeminence of Athens.

pis·mire /'pis,mīr/ ▶*n.* *archaic* an ant. ▷Middle English: from **PISS** (alluding to the smell of an anthill) + obsolete *mire* 'ant.'

pis·o·lite /'pīsə,līt/ ▶*n.* *Geology* a sedimentary rock, esp. limestone, made up of small pea-shaped pieces. ▷early 19th cent.: from modern Latin *pisolithus* (see **PISOLITH**) + **-LITE**. **—pis·o·lit·ic** /,pīsə'litik/ *adj.*

pis·o·lith /'pīsəliTH/ ▶*n.* *Geology* any of the component pieces of which pisolite consists. ▷late 18th cent.: from modern Latin *pisolithus*, from Greek *pisos* 'pea' + **-LITE**.

piss /pis/ *vulgar slang* ▶*v.* [*intrans.*] urinate. ■ [*trans.*] wet with urine. ■ [*trans.*] discharge (something, esp. blood) when urinating.
▶*phrasal v.* □ **piss something away** waste something, esp. money or time. □ **piss off** [usu. in *imperative*] go away (usually used to angrily dismiss someone). □ **piss someone off** annoy someone. □ **piss on** show complete contempt for.
▶*n.* urine. ■ [in *sing.*] an act of urinating. ▷Middle English: from Old French *pisser*, probably of imitative origin.
▶*PHRASES* □ **not have a pot to piss in** be very poor. □ **piss in the wind** do something that is ineffective or a waste of time. □ **take a piss** urinate.

pis·sa·la·dière /,pē,säläd'yer/ ▶*n.* a Provençal open tart resembling pizza, typically made with onions, anchovies, and black olives. ▷French, from Provençal *pissaladiero*, from *pissala* 'salt fish.'

piss and vin·e·gar ▶*n.* *vulgar slang* aggressive energy.

piss·ant /'pis,ant/ *vulgar slang* ▶*n.* an insignificant or contemptible person or thing.
▶*adj.* worthless; contemptible. ▷mid 17th cent.: from the noun **PISS** + **-ANT**.

Pis·sar·ro /pi'särō; pēsä'rō/, Camille (1830–1903), French painter and graphic artist. He was a leading figure of the Impressionist movement, typically painting landscapes and cityscapes. He also experimented with pointillism in the 1880s.

pissed /pist/ *vulgar slang* ▶*adj.* **1** (also **pissed off**) very annoyed; angry. **2** (*Brit.* also **pissed up**) drunk.

piss·er /'pisər/ ▶*n.* *vulgar slang* **1** [in *sing.*] an annoying or disappointing event or circumstance. **2** an unpleasant person; a person who causes difficulties.

piss·head /'pis,hed/ ▶*n.* *informal* a drunkard. ■ a stupid or contemptible person.

piss·hole /'pis,hōl/ ▶*n.* *vulgar slang* a hole made in soluble matter by urinating: *making pissholes in the snow.* ■ a squalid place. ■ the opening in the penis through which urine is discharged; the urethral meatus.

pis·soir /pē'swär/ ▶*n.* a public urinal. ▷French.

piss-poor ▶*adj.* *vulgar slang* of a very low standard.

piss·pot /'pis,pät/ ▶*n.* *vulgar slang* a chamber pot.

piss·y /'pisē/ ▶*adj.* (**piss·i·er**, **piss·i·est**) *vulgar slang* **1** of, relating to, or suggestive of urine. ■ inferior; contemptible. **2** arrogantly argumentative.

pis·tach·i·o /pə'stasHē,ō/ ▶*n.* (*pl.* **-os**) **1** (also **pistachio nut**) the edible pale green seed of an Asian tree. ■ (also **pistachio green**) a pale green color. **2** the evergreen tree of the cashew family that produces this nut, with small brownish-green flowers and reddish wrinkled fruit borne in heavy clusters. It is widely cultivated, esp. in the U.S. and around the Mediterranean. • *Pistacia vera*; family Anacardiaceae. ▷late Middle English *pistace*, from Old French, superseded in the 16th cent. by forms from Italian *pistacchio*, via Latin from Greek *pistakion*, from Old Persian.

piste /pēst/ ▶*n.* **1** a ski run of compacted snow. **2** the specially marked-out rectangular playing area in fencing. ▷French, literally 'racetrack.'

pis·til /'pistl/ ▶*n.* *Botany* the female organs of a flower, comprising the stigma, style, and ovary. ▷early 18th cent.: from French *pistile* or Latin *pistillum* 'pestle.'

pis·til·late /'pistəlit; -,lāt/ ▶*adj.* *Botany* (of a plant or flower) having pistils but no stamens. Compare with **STAMINATE**.

pis·tol /'pistl/ ▶*n.* a small firearm designed to be held in one hand.
▶*v.* (**-toled**, **-tol·ing**; *Brit.* **-tolled**, **-tol·ling**) [*trans.*] *dated* shoot (someone) with a pistol. ▷mid 16th cent.: from obsolete French *pistole*, from German *Pistole*, from Czech *pišt'ala*, of which the original meaning was 'whistle,' hence 'a firearm' by the resemblance in shape.

pis·tole /pi'stōl/ ▶*n.* any of various gold coins used in Europe in the 17th and 18th centuries. ▷late 16th cent.: from French, abbreviation of *pistolet*, in the same sense, of uncertain ultimate origin.

pis·to·leer /,pistə'li(ə)r/ ▶*n.* *archaic* a soldier armed with a pistol.

pis·to·le·ro /pistə'le(ə)rō/ ▶*n.* (*pl.* **-ros**) (in Spanish-speaking regions) a gunman or gangster. ▷Spanish.

pis·tol grip ▶*n.* (esp. of a tool) a handle shaped like the butt of a pistol.

Pis·tol Pete see **MARAVICH**.

pis·tol-whip ▶*v.* [*trans.*] hit or beat (someone) with a pistol.

pis·ton /'pistn/ ▶*n.* a disk or short cylinder fitting closely within a tube in which it moves up and down against a liquid or gas, used in an internal combustion engine to derive motion, or in a pump to impart motion. ■ a valve in a brass musical instrument in the form of a piston, depressed to alter the pitch of a note. ▷early 18th cent.: from French, from Italian *pistone*, variant of *pestone* 'large pestle,' augmentative of *pestello* 'pestle.'

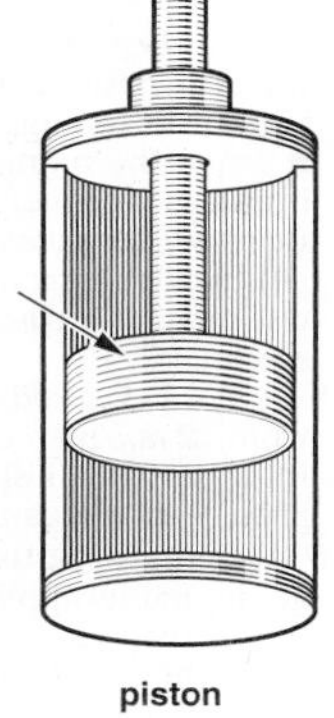
piston

pis·ton en·gine ▶*n.* an engine powered by pistons. **—pis·ton-en·gined** /'pistn ,enjənd/ *adj.*

pis·ton ring ▶*n.* a ring on a piston sealing the gap between the piston and the cylinder wall.

pis·ton rod ▶*n.* a rod or crankshaft attached to a piston to drive a wheel or to impart motion.

pit[1] /pit/ ▶*n.* **1** a large hole in the ground. ■ a large deep hole from which stones or minerals are dug. ■ a coal mine. ■ a sunken enclosure in which certain animals are kept in captivity. ■ short for **ORCHESTRA PIT** (see **ORCHESTRA**). ■ a sunken area in a workshop floor allowing access to a car's underside. ■ *figurative* a low or wretched psychological state: *spiraling downward into the pit of despair.* ■ (**the pit**) *poetic/literary* hell. **2** an area reserved or enclosed for a specific activity, in particular: ■ (usu. **pits**) an area at the side of a track where race cars are serviced and refueled. ■ a part of the floor of an exchange in which a particular stock or commodity is traded, typically by open outcry. ■ *chiefly historical* an enclosure in which animals are made to fight. **3** a hollow or indentation in a surface. ■ a small indentation left on the skin after smallpox, acne, or other diseases; a pockmark.
▶*v.* (**pit·ted**, **pit·ting**) [*trans.*] **1** (**pit someone/something against**) set someone or something in conflict or competition with: *a chance to pit herself against him.* ■ *historical* set an animal to fight against (another animal) for sport. [because formerly set against each other in a 'pit' or enclosure.] **2** make a hollow or indentation in the surface of: *rain poured down, pitting the bare earth.* ■ [*intrans.*] sink in or contract so as to form a pit or hollow. **3** [*intrans.*] drive a race car into the pits for fuel or maintenance. ▷Old English *pytt*; related to Dutch *put* and German *Pfütze*, based on Latin *puteus* 'well, shaft.'
▶*PHRASES* □ **be the pits** *informal* be extremely bad or the worst of its kind. □ **the pit of one's** (or **the**) **stomach** an ill-defined region of the lower abdomen regarded as the seat of strong feelings, esp. anxiety.

pit[2] ▶*n.* the stone of a fruit.
▶*v.* (**pit·ted**, **pit·ting**) [*trans.*] remove the pit from (fruit). ▷mid 19th cent.: apparently from Dutch; related to **PITH**.

pi·ta /'pētə/ (also **pita bread**) ▶*n.* flat hollow unleavened bread that can be split open to hold a filling. ▷modern Greek, literally 'cake or pie'; compare with Turkish *pide*, in a similar sense.

pit·a·ha·ya /,pitə'hīə/ ▶*n.* any tall cactus of Mexico and the southwestern U.S., in particular the saguaro. ■ the edible fruit of such cacti. ▷late 18th cent.: from Spanish, from Haitian Creole.

pit-a-pat /'pit ə ,pat/ (also **pit·a·pat**) ▶*adv.* with a sound like quick light steps or taps: *my heart goes pit-a-pat.*
▶*n.* [in *sing.*] a sound of this kind. ▷early 16th cent.: imitative of alternating sounds.

pit boss ▶*n.* *informal* an employee in a casino in charge of gaming tables. ■ *dated* a foreman in a coal mine.

pit bull (in full **pit bull terrier**) ▶*n.* a dog of an American variety of bull terrier, noted for its muscular build and often associated with ferocity.

Pit·cairn Is·lands /'pit,ke(ə)rn/ a British dependency that consists of a group of volcanic islands in the South Pacific Ocean, east of French Polynesia. Discovered in 1767, the islands remained uninhabited until settled in 1790 by mutineers from HMS *Bounty*. ▷named after the midshipman who first sighted the islands.

pitch[1] /picH/ ▶*n.* **1** the quality of a sound governed by the rate of vibrations producing it; the degree of highness or lowness of a tone: *a car engine seems to change pitch downward as the vehicle passes you.* ■ a standard degree of highness or lowness used in performance: *the guitars were strung and tuned to pitch.* See also **CONCERT PITCH**. **2** the steepness of a slope, esp. of a roof. ■ *Climbing* a section of a climb, esp. a steep one. ■ the height to which a hawk soars before swooping on its prey. **3** [in *sing.*] the level of intensity of something: *he brought the machine to a high pitch of development.* ■ (**a pitch of**) a very high degree of: *rousing herself to a pitch of indignation.* **4** *Baseball* a

Pronunciation Key ə *ago*; ər *over*; 'ə or ,ə *up*; 'ər or ,ər *fur*; a *hat*; ā *rate*; ä *car*; CH *chew*; e *let*; ē *see*; e(ə)r *air*; i *fit*; ī *by*; i(ə)r *ear*; NG *sing*; ō *go*; ô *for*; oi *boy*; o͝o *good*; o͞o *goo*; ou *out*; SH *she*; TH *thin*; T͟H *then*; (h)w *why*; ZH *vision*

legal delivery of the ball by the pitcher. ■ (also **pitch shot**) *Golf* a high approach shot onto the green. ■ *Football* short for PITCHOUT sense 2. **5** *Brit.* a playing field. ■ *Cricket* the strip of ground between the two sets of stumps. **6** a form of words used when trying to persuade someone to buy or accept something: *a good sales pitch.* **7** a swaying or oscillation of a ship, aircraft, or vehicle around a horizontal axis perpendicular to the direction of motion. ■ the degree of slope or angle, as of a roof. **8** *technical* the distance between successive corresponding points or lines, e.g., between the teeth of a cogwheel. ■ a measure of the angle of the blades of a screw propeller, equal to the distance forward a blade would move in one revolution if it exerted no thrust on the medium. ■ the density of typed or printed characters on a line, typically expressed as numbers of characters per inch.

▸*v.* **1** [*trans.*] *Baseball* throw (the ball) for the batter to try to hit. ■ *Baseball* assign (a player) to pitch. ■ [*intrans.*] be a pitcher: *she pitched in a minor-league game* | [*trans.*] *he pitched the entire game.* ■ *Golf* hit (the ball) onto the green with a pitch shot. ■ [*intrans.*] *Golf* (of the ball) strike the ground in a particular spot. **2** [*trans.*] throw or fling roughly or casually: *he crumpled the page up and pitched it into the fireplace.* ■ [*intrans.*] fall heavily, esp. headlong: *she pitched forward into blackness.* **3** [*trans.*] set (one's voice or a piece of music) at a particular pitch: *you've pitched the melody very high.* ■ express at a particular level of difficulty: *he should pitch his talk at a suitable level for the age group.* ■ aim (a product) at a particular section of the market: *the machine is being* ***pitched at*** *banks.* **4** [*intrans.*] make a bid to obtain a contract or other business: *they were* ***pitching for*** *an account.* **5** [*trans.*] set up and fix in a definite position: *we pitched camp for the night.* **6** [*intrans.*] (of a moving ship, aircraft, or vehicle) rock or oscillate around a lateral axis, so that the front and back move up and down: *the little steamer pressed on, pitching gently.* ■ (of a vehicle) move with a vigorous jogging motion: *a jeep came pitching down the hill.* **7** [*trans.*] cause (a roof) to slope downward from the ridge: *the roof was pitched at an angle of 75 degrees* | [as *adj.*] (**pitched**) *a pitched roof.* ■ [*intrans.*] slope downward: *the ravine pitches down to the creek.*

▸*phrasal v.* □ **pitch in** *informal* vigorously join in to help with a task or activity. ■ join in a fight or dispute. □ **pitch into** *informal* vigorously tackle or begin to deal with. ■ forcefully assault. □ **pitch out** throw a pitchout. ▷Middle English (as a verb in the senses 'thrust (something pointed) into the ground' and 'fall headlong'): perhaps related to Old English *picung* 'stigmata,' of unknown ultimate origin. The sense development is obscure.

▸*PHRASE* □ **make a pitch** make a bid to obtain a contract or other business.

pitch[2] ▸*n.* a sticky resinous black or dark brown substance that is semiliquid when hot, hard when cold. It is obtained by distilling tar or petroleum and is used for waterproofing. ■ any of various similar substances, such as asphalt or bitumen. ■ a sticky resinous sap from a conifer.

▸*v.* [*trans.*] cover, coat, or smear with pitch. ▷Old English *pic* (noun), *pician* (verb), of Germanic origin; related to Dutch *pek* and German *Pech*; based on Latin *pix, pic-*.

pitch and putt ▸*n.* a form of golf played on a miniature course in which the green can be reached in one stroke from the tee.

pitch and run ▸*n. Golf* a pitch shot with a low trajectory and no backspin, so that the ball runs forward on landing.

pitch-and-toss ▸*n.* a gambling game in which the player who manages to throw a coin closest to a mark gets to toss all the coins, winning those that land with the head up.

pitch bend ▸*n.* a mechanism in a synthesizer that enables the player to change the pitch of the note played by a small amount.

pitch-black (also **pitch-dark**) ▸*adj.* completely dark; as black as pitch. **—pitch-black·ness** *n.*

pitch·blende /ˈpiCH,blend/ ▸*n.* a form of the mineral uraninite occurring in brown or black pitchlike masses. ▷late 18th cent.: from German *Pechblende*, from *Pech* 'pitch' + *Blende* (see BLENDE).

pitch cir·cle ▸*n. Mechanics* an imaginary circle concentric to a toothed wheel, along which the pitch of the teeth is measured.

pitch con·trol ▸*n.* **1** control of the pitch of a helicopter's rotors or an aircraft's or ship's propellers. **2** control of the pitching motion of an aircraft.

pitched bat·tle /piCHt ˈbatl/ ▸*n.* a planned military encounter on a prearranged battleground. ■ a violent or vigorous confrontation involving large numbers of people.

California pitcher plant

pitch·er[1] /ˈpiCHər/ ▸*n.* a large container, typically earthenware, glass, or plastic, with a handle and a lip, used for holding and pouring liquids. ■ the contents of such a container: ***a pitcher of*** *water.* ■ the modified leaf of a pitcher plant. ▷Middle English: from Old French *pichier* 'pot,' based on late Latin *picarium.* **—pitch·er·ful** /-,fo͝ol/ *n.* (*pl.* **-fuls**).

pitch·er[2] ▸*n. Baseball* the player who delivers the ball to the batter.

pitch·er plant ▸*n.* a plant with a deep pitcher-shaped pouch that contains fluid into which insects are attracted and trapped. The plant then absorbs nutrients from their bodies. • Families Sarraceniaceae (New World), Droseraceae (New World), and Nepenthaceae (Old World): many species, including the purple-flowered *Sarracenia purpurea* of eastern North America and the white-flowered **California pitcher plant** (*Darlingtonia californica*) of the western U.S. See also TRUMPET (sense 2).

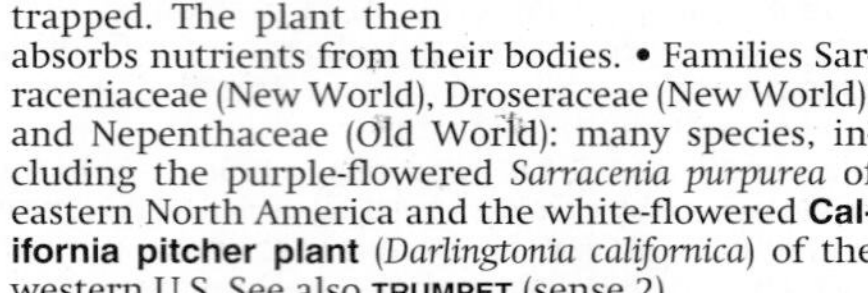

pitch·fork /ˈpiCH,fôrk/ ▸*n.* a farm tool with a long handle and sharp metal prongs, used esp. for lifting hay.

▸*v.* [*trans.*] lift with a pitchfork. ■ *figurative* thrust (someone) suddenly into an unexpected and difficult situation: *a woman of ordinary intellect pitchforked into power by circumstances.* ▷late Middle English: from earlier *pickfork*, influenced by the verb PITCH[1] (because the tool is used for "pitching" or throwing sheaves on to a stack).

pitch·man /ˈpiCHmən/ ▸*n.* (*pl.* **-men**) *informal* a person delivering a sales pitch.

pitch·out /ˈpiCH,out/ ▸*n.* **1** *Baseball* a pitch thrown intentionally away from the reach of the batter to allow the catcher a clear throw to put out a base runner who is stealing or leading off too far. **2** (also **pitch**) *Football* a lateral, esp. from the quarterback to a running back.

pitch pine ▸*n.* a pine tree that is a source of pitch or turpentine, and typically yielding hard, heavy, resinous timber that is used in building, esp. the longleaf *Pinus rigida* of the Appalachians and northeastern U.S.

pitch pipe ▸*n. Music* a small reed pipe or set of pipes blown to set the pitch for singing or tuning an instrument.

pitch·pole /ˈpiCH,pōl/ ▸*v.* [*intrans.*] *dialect* somersault. ■ *Nautical* (of a boat) be overturned so that its stern pitches forward over its bow. ▷mid 17th cent. (as a noun, originally dialect): from the verb PITCH[1] + POLL.

pitch·stone /ˈpiCH,stōn/ ▸*n. Geology* a dull vitreous rock resembling hardened pitch, formed by weathering of obsidian.

pitch·y /ˈpiCHē/ ▸*adj.* (**pitch·i·er, pitch·i·est**) of, like, or as dark as pitch.

pit·e·ous /ˈpitēəs/ ▸*adj.* deserving or arousing pity. ▷Middle English: from Old French *piteus*, from Latin *pietas* 'piety, pity' (see PIETY). **—pit·e·ous·ly** *adv.* **—pit·e·ous·ness** *n.*

pit·fall /ˈpit,fôl/ ▸*n.* a hidden or unsuspected danger or difficulty. ■ a covered pit used as a trap.

pith /piTH/ ▸*n.* **1** soft or spongy tissue in plants or animals, in particular: ■ spongy white tissue lining the rind of an orange, lemon, and other citrus fruits. ■ *Botany* the spongy cellular tissue in the stems and branches of many higher plants. ■ *archaic* spinal marrow. **2** *figurative* the essence of something: *the pith and core of socialism.* **3** *figurative* forceful and concise expression: *he writes with a combination of pith and exactitude.*

▸*v.* [*trans.*] **1** *dated, chiefly figurative* remove the pith from. **2** *rare* pierce or sever the spinal cord of (an animal) so as to kill or immobilize it. ▷Old English *pitha.* **—pith·less** *adj.*

Pith·e·can·thro·pus /,piTHəˈkanTHrəpəs/ ▸*n.* a former genus name applied to some fossilized hominids found in Java in 1891. See JAVA MAN. ▷late 19th cent.: modern Latin, from Greek *pithēkos* 'ape' + *anthrōpos* 'man.'

pith hel·met ▸*n.* a lightweight sun helmet made from the dried pith of the sola or a similar tropical plant.

pith·y /ˈpiTHē/ ▸*adj.* (**pith·i·er, pith·i·est**) **1** (of language or style) concise and forcefully expressive. See note at TERSE. **2** (of a fruit or plant) containing much pith. **—pith·i·ly** /ˈpiTHəlē/ *adv.* **—pith·i·ness** *n.*

pit·i·a·ble /ˈpitēəbəl/ ▸*adj.* deserving or arousing pity. ■ contemptibly poor or small. ▷late Middle English: from Old French *piteable*, from *piteer* 'to pity.' **—pit·i·a·ble·ness** *n.* **—pit·i·a·bly** /-əblē/ *adv.*

pit·i·ful /ˈpitifəl/ ▸*adj.* deserving or arousing pity. ■ very small or poor; inadequate. ■ *archaic* compassionate. **—pit·i·ful·ly** *adv.* **—pit·i·ful·ness** *n.*

pit·i·less /ˈpitēlis/ ▸*adj.* showing no pity; cruel. **—pit·i·less·ly** *adv.* **—pit·i·less·ness** *n.*

Pit·man /ˈpitmən/, Sir Isaac (1813–97), English inventor of a formerly widely used shorthand system.

pit·man /ˈpitmən/ ▸*n.* **1** (*pl.* **-men**) a coal miner. **2** (*pl.* **-mans**) a connecting rod in machinery.

Pit·ney /ˈpitnē/, Mahlon (1858–1924), U.S. Supreme Court associate justice 1912–22. A conservative, he was appointed to the Court by President Taft.

Pi·to·cin /piˈtōsin/ ▸*n. trademark* a synthetic form of oxytocin, used to induce labor.

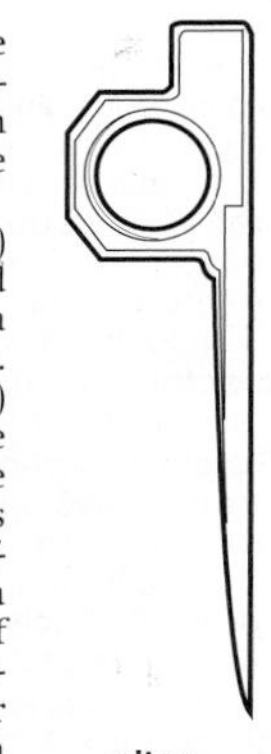

piton

pi·ton /ˈpētän/ ▸*n.* a peg or spike driven into a rock or crack to support a climber or a rope. ▷late 19th cent.: from French, literally 'eye bolt.'

pi·tot tube /ˈpētō; pēˈtō/ (also **pi·tot**) ▸*n.* an open-ended right-angled tube pointing into the flow of a fluid and used to measure pressure. ■ (also **pitot-static tube, pitot head**) a device consisting of a pitot tube inside or adjacent to a parallel tube closed at the end but with holes along its length, the pressure difference between them being a measure of the relative velocity of the fluid or the airspeed of an aircraft. ▷late 19th cent.: named after Henri Pitot (1695–1771), French physicist.

pit saw (also **pit·saw**) ▸*n. historical* a large saw with handles at each end, used in a vertical position by two persons, one standing above the timber to be cut, the other in a pit below it.

pit stop ▸*n. Auto Racing* a stop in the pits for servicing and refueling, esp. during a race. ■ a brief rest, esp. during a journey. ■ *informal* a place where one takes such a rest.

Pitt[1] /pit/ the name of two British statesmen: ■ **William**, 1st Earl of Chatham (1708–78); known as **Pitt the Elder**. As secretary of state (effectively prime minister), he headed coalition governments 1756–61 and 1766–68. He brought the Seven Years War to an end in 1763 and also masterminded the conquest of French possessions overseas. ■ **William** (1759–1806), prime minister 1783–1801 and 1804–6; the son of Pitt the Elder; known as **Pitt the Younger**. The youngest-ever prime minister, he introduced financial reforms to reduce the national debt.

Pitt[2], Brad (1963–), U.S. actor; full name *William Bradley Pitt*. He appeared in movies such as *Legends of the Fall* (1994), *Seven Years in Tibet* (1997), *Meet Joe Black* (1998), and *Ocean's Eleven* (2001).

pit·ta[1] /ˈpitə/ ▸*n.* variant spelling of PITA.

pit·ta[2] ▸*n.* a small ground-dwelling thrushlike bird with brightly colored plumage and a very short tail, found in the Old World tropics. • Family Pittidae and genus *Pitta*: many species. ▷mid 19th cent.: from Telugu *pitta* '(young) bird.'

pit·tance /ˈpitns/ ▸*n.* [usu. in *sing.*] a very small or inadequate amount of money paid to someone as an allowance or wage. ▷Middle English: from Old French *pitance*, from medieval Latin *pitantia*, from Latin *pietas* 'pity.'

pit·ted /ˈpitid/ ▸*adj.* **1** having a hollow or indentation on the surface: *a dusty pitted road.* **2** (of a fruit) having had the stone removed.

pit·ter-pat·ter /ˈpitər ˈpatər/ ▸*n.* a sound as of quick light steps or taps: *the soft* ***pitter-patter of*** *the rain on the leaves.*

▸*adv.* with this sound: *footsteps that go pitter-patter.* ▷late Middle English: reduplication (expressing rhythmic repetition) of the verb PATTER[1].

Pitt Is·land see CHATHAM ISLANDS.

pit·tos·po·rum /pəˈtäspərəm; ,pitəˈspôrəm/ ▸*n.* an evergreen shrub or small tree that typically has small fragrant flowers and is native chiefly to Australasia. • Genus *Pittosporum*, family Pittosporaceae. ▷modern Latin, from Greek *pitta* 'pitch' (because of the resinous pulp around the seeds) + *sporos* 'seed.'

Pitt-Riv·ers /ˈrivərz/, Augustus Henry Lane Fox (1827–1900), English archaeologist and anthropologist. He developed a new scientific approach to archaeology. His collection of weapons and artifacts from different cultures formed the basis of the ethnological museum in Oxford that bears his name.

Pitts·burg /ˈpitsbərg/ an industrial port city in north central California, on Suisun Bay, northeast of Oakland; pop. 47,564.

Pitts·burgh /ˈpits,bərg/ an industrial city in southwestern Pennsylvania, where the Allegheny and Monongahela rivers join to form the Ohio River; pop. 334,563.

Pitts·field /ˈpits,fēld/ an industrial city in western Massachusetts, on the Housatonic River, the commercial center of the Berkshire Hills; pop. 48,622.

pi·tu·i·tar·y /pəˈt(y)o͞oə,terē/ ▶*n.* (*pl.* **-tar·ies**) (in full **pituitary gland** or **pituitary body**) the major endocrine gland. A pea-sized body attached to the base of the brain, the pituitary is important in controlling growth and development and the functioning of the other endocrine glands. Also called HYPOPHYSIS.
▶*adj.* of or relating to this gland. ▷early 17th cent.: from Latin *pituitarius* 'secreting phlegm,' from *pituita* 'phlegm.'

pit vi·per ▶*n.* a venomous snake of a group distinguished by visible sensory pits on the head that can detect heat emitted by their prey. They are found in both America and Asia. • Subfamily Crotalinae, family Viperidae: numerous genera and species, including the rattlesnakes.

pit·y /ˈpitē/ ▶*n.* (*pl.* **pit·ies**) **1** the feeling of sorrow and compassion caused by the suffering and misfortunes of others: *her voice was full of pity.* **2** [in *sing.*] a cause for regret or disappointment: *what a pity we can't be friends.*
▶*v.* (**pit·ies, pit·ied**) [*trans.*] feel sorrow for the misfortunes of: *Clare didn't know whether to envy or pity them* | [as *adj.*] (**pitying**) *he gave her a pitying look.* ▷Middle English (also in the sense 'clemency, mildness'): from Old French *pite* 'compassion,' from Latin *pietas* 'piety'; compare with PIETY. —**pit·y·ing·ly** *adv.*
▶*PHRASES* □ **for pity's sake** *informal* used to express impatience or make an urgent appeal. □ **more's the pity** *informal* used to express regret about a fact that has just been stated. □ **take** (or **have**) **pity** show compassion: *they* **took pity on** *him and gave him food.*

pit·y·ri·a·sis /,pitəˈrīəsis/ ▶*n.* [with *adj.*] *Medicine* a skin disease characterized by the shedding of fine flaky scales. ▷late 17th cent.: modern Latin, from Greek *pituriasis* 'scurf,' from *pituron* 'bran,' + -ASIS.

piu /pyo͞o/ ▶*adj. Music* (esp. as a direction) more.

più mos·so /pyo͞o ˈmōsō/ ▶*adv.* & *adj. Music* (esp. as a direction) more quickly. ▷Italian.

Pi·us XII /ˈpīəs/ (1876–1958), pope 1939–58; born *Eugenio Pacelli.* He upheld the neutrality of the Roman Catholic Church during World War II and was criticized after the war for failing to condemn Nazi atrocities.

piv·ot /ˈpivət/ ▶*n.* the central point, pin, or shaft on which a mechanism turns or oscillates. ■ [usu. in *sing.*] a person or thing that plays a central part in an activity or organization: *the* **pivot of** *community life was the chapel.* ■ the person or people about whom a body of troops wheels. ■ (also **pivotman**) a player in a central position in a team sport. ■ *Basketball* a movement in which the player holding the ball may move in any direction with one foot, while keeping the other (the **pivot foot**) in contact with the floor.
▶*v.* (**piv·ot·ed, piv·ot·ing**) [*intrans.*] turn on or as if on a pivot: *the sail* **pivots around** *the axis of a virtually static mast* | *he swung around,* **pivoting on** *his heel.* ■ (**pivot on**) *figurative* depend on: *your escape pivots on my disappearing with you.* ■ [*trans.*] provide (a mechanism) with a pivot; fix (a mechanism) on a pivot: [as *adj.*] (**pivoted**) *a pivoted bracket.* ▷late Middle English: from French, probably from the root of dialect *pue* 'tooth of a comb' and Spanish *pu(y)a* 'point.' The verb dates from the mid 19th cent. —**piv·ot·a·bil·i·ty** /,pivətəˈbilitē/ *n.* —**piv·ot·a·ble** *adj.*

piv·ot·al /ˈpivətl/ ▶*adj.* of crucial importance in relation to the development or success of something else: *the alliance that played a pivotal role in the revolution.* ■ fixed on or as if on a pivot: *a sliding or pivotal motion.*

pix¹ /piks/ ▶*plural n. informal* pictures, esp. photographs. ▷1930s: pluralized abbreviation.

pix² ▶*n.* variant spelling of PYX.

pix·el /ˈpiksəl/ ▶*n. Electronics* a minute area of illumination on a display screen, one of many from which an image is composed. ▷1960s: abbreviation of *picture element* (compare with PIX¹).

pix·el·ate /ˈpiksəlāt/ (also **pix·el·late** or **pix·il·ate**) ▶*v.* [*trans.*] divide (an image) into pixels, typically for display or storage in a digital format. ■ (**be pixelated**) (of an image on a computer screen or other display) be enlarged so far that the viewer sees the individual pixels that form the image, the enlargement having reached the point at which no further detail can be resolved. ■ display an image of (someone or something) on television as a small number of large pixels, typically in order to disguise someone's identity. —**pix·el·a·tion** /,piksəˈlāsʜən/ *n.*

pix·ie /ˈpiksē/ (also **pix·y**) ▶*n.* (*pl.* **pix·ies**) a supernatural being in folklore and children's stories, typically portrayed as small and humanlike in form, with pointed ears and a pointed hat, and mischievous in character. ▷mid 17th cent.: of unknown origin. —**pix·ie·ish** *adj.*

pix·ie dust ▶*n.* in Sir James Barrie's *Peter Pan*, magic dust taken or shaken from a pixie or fairy, enabling humans to fly. ■ unusually great success, felicity, or luck: *the folks who live there still seem to believe that they've been sprinkled with pixie dust.*

pix·i·late /ˈpiksə,lāt/ ▶*v.* variant spelling of PIXELATE.

pix·il·at·ed /ˈpiksə,lātid/ (*Brit.* also **pix·il·lat·ed**) ▶*adj.* crazy; confused. ▷mid 19th cent.: variant of *pixieled*, literally 'led astray by pixies,' figuratively 'confused,' or from PIXIE, on the pattern of words such as *elated* and *emulated.*

pix·il·a·tion /,piksəˈlāsʜən/ (*Brit.* also **pix·il·la·tion**) ▶*n.* **1** a technique used in film whereby the movements of real people are made to appear like artificial animations. **2** the state of being crazy or confused. **3** variant spelling of PIXELATION (see PIXELATE).

Pi·zar·ro /piˈzärō; pēˈsä-; -ˈᴛʜä-/, Francisco (*c.*1478–1541), Spanish conquistador. He defeated the Inca empire and in 1533 set up a puppet monarchy at Cuzco. He built his own capital at Lima 1535, where he was assassinated.

pizz. ▶*abbr. Music* pizzicato.

piz·za /ˈpētsə/ ▶*n.* a dish of Italian origin consisting of a flat, round base of dough baked with a topping of tomato sauce and cheese, typically with added meat or vegetables. ▷Italian, literally 'pie.'

piz·za box ▶*n.* a computer casing that is not very tall and has a square cross section.

piz·zazz /pəˈzaz/ (also **pi·zazz**) ▶*n. informal* an attractive combination of vitality and glamour: *a new way to add graphic pizzazz to your desktop-publishing project.* ▷said to have been invented by Diana Vreeland, fashion editor of *Harper's Bazaar* in the 1930s.

piz·ze·ri·a /,pētsəˈrēə/ ▶*n.* a place where pizzas are made or sold; a pizza restaurant. ▷Italian.

piz·zi·ca·to /,pitsiˈkätō/ *Music* ▶*adv.* (often as a direction) plucking the strings of a violin or other stringed instrument with one's finger.
▶*adj.* performed in this way.
▶*n.* (*pl.* **-tos** or **-ti** /-tē/) this technique of playing. ■ a note or passage played in this way. ▷Italian, literally 'pinched, twitched,' past participle of *pizzicare*, based on *pizza* 'point, edge.'

piz·zle /ˈpizəl/ ▶*n.* the penis of an animal, esp. a bull. ▷late 15th cent.: from Low German *pēsel* or Flemish *pezel* (diminutives of Middle Low German *pēse* and Middle Dutch *pēze*).

PK ▶*abbr.* ■ psychokinesis.

pK ▶*n. Chemistry* a figure expressing the acidity or alkalinity of a solution of a weak electrolyte in a similar way to pH, equal to $-\log_{10} K$ where K is the dissociation (or ionization) constant of the electrolyte. ▷from *p* as in *pH* and *K* representing a constant.

pk ▶*abbr.* ■ (also **Pk**) park. ■ peak. ■ peck(s).

pkg. ▶*abbr.* (*pl.* **pkgs.**) package.

pkt. ▶*abbr.* ■ packet. ■ pocket.

PKU ▶*abbr.* phenylketonuria.

pkwy ▶*abbr.* parkway.

pky ▶*abbr.* parkway.

PL ▶*abbr.* ■ *Computing* programming language. ■ *Military* patrol leader.

pl. ▶*abbr.* ■ (also **Pl.**) place: *3 Palmerston Pl., Edinburgh.* ■ plate (referring to illustrations in a book). ■ *chiefly Military* platoon. ■ *Grammar* plural.

PL/1 ▶*n. Computing* a high-level programming language used in science, engineering, business, and data processing. ▷from P(rogramming) L(anguage)/1.

PLA ▶*abbr.* ■ People's Liberation Army. ■ (in the UK) Port of London Authority.

plac·a·ble /ˈplakəbəl/ ▶*adj. archaic* easily calmed; gentle and forgiving. ▷late Middle English (in the sense 'pleasing, agreeable'): from Old French, or from Latin *placabilis*, from *placare* 'appease.' —**plac·a·bil·i·ty** /,plakəˈbilitē/ *n.* —**plac·a·bly** /-əblē/ *adv.*

plac·ard /ˈplakärd; -ərd/ ▶*n.* a poster or sign for public display, either fixed to a wall or carried during a demonstration.
▶*v.* [*trans.*] cover with placards: *they were placarding the town with posters.* ▷late 15th cent. (denoting a warrant or license): from Old French *placquart*, from *plaquier* 'to plaster, lay flat,' from Middle Dutch *placken*. The current sense of the verb dates from the early 19th cent.

pla·cate /ˈplākāt/ ▶*v.* [*trans.*] make (someone) less angry or hostile: *they attempted to placate the students with promises.* See note at PACIFY. ▷late 17th cent.: from Latin *placat-* 'appeased,' from the verb *placare*. —**pla·cat·er** *n.* —**pla·cat·ing·ly** /pləˈkātiɴɢ-lē/ *adv.* —**pla·ca·tion** /plāˈkāsʜən/ *n.* —**pla·ca·to·ry** /-kə,tôrē; ˈplakə-/ *adj.*

place /plās/ ▶*n.* **1** a particular position or point in space: *there were still some remote places in the world* | *the monastery was a peaceful place.* ■ used to refer to an area already identified (giving an impression of informality): *we head to a disco—the place is pandemonium.* ■ a particular point on a larger surface or in a larger object or area: *he lashed out and cut the policeman's hand in three places.* ■ a building or area used for a specified purpose or activity: *the town has many excellent eating places.* ■ *informal* a person's home: *what about dinner at my place?* ■ a point in a book or other text reached by a reader at a particular time: *I must have lost my place in the script.* **2** a portion of space occupied by someone: *he was watching from his place across the room.* ■ a portion of space available or designated for someone: *they hurried to their places at the table.* ■ a vacancy or available position: *she won a place to study German at the university.* ■ the regular or proper position of something: *lay each slab* **in place.** ■ [often with *negative*] somewhere where it is appropriate or prudent for someone to be or for something to occur: *that street at that time was* **no place for** *a lady.* ■ a chance to be accepted or to be of use: *the policy left no place for individual initiative.* ■ a person's rank or status: *occupation structures a person's place in society.* ■ [usu. with *negative*] a right or privilege resulting from someone's role or position: *I'm sure she has a story to tell, but it's* **not my place** *to ask.* ■ the role played by or importance attached to someone or something in a particular context: *the place of computers in improving office efficiency varies between companies.* **3** a position in a sequence, in particular: ■ a position in a contest: *his score was good enough to leave him in ninth place.* ■ the second position, esp. in a horse race. ■ *Brit.* any of the first three or sometimes four positions in a race (used esp. of the second, third, or fourth positions). ■ the degree of priority given to something: *accurate reportage* **takes second place to** *lurid detail.* ■ the position of a figure in a series indicated in decimal or similar notation, esp. one after the decimal point: *calculate the ratios* **to** *one decimal* **place.** **4** [in *place names*] a square or a short street: *our new restaurant is in Hilliard Place.* ■ a country house with its grounds.
▶*v.* [*trans.*] **1** [*trans.*] put in a particular position: *a newspaper had been placed beside my plate.* ■ cause to be in a particular situation: *enemy officers were placed under arrest* | *you are not placing yourself under any obligation.* ■ used to express the attitude someone has toward someone or something: *I am not able to place any trust in you.* ■ (**be placed**) used to indicate the degree of advantage or convenience enjoyed by someone or something as a result of their position or circumstances: [with *infinitive*] *the company is well placed to seize the opportunity.* **2** [*trans.*] find a home or employment for: *the children were placed with foster parents* | *the agency had placed 3,000 people in full-time jobs.* ■ dispose of (something, esp. shares) by selling to a customer. ■ arrange for the recognition and implementation of (an order, bet, etc.): *they placed a contract for three boats.* ■ order or obtain a connection for (a telephone call) through an operator. **3** [*trans.*] identify or classify as being of a specified type or as holding a specified position in a sequence or hierarchy: *a survey placed the company 13th for achievement.* ■ [*trans.*] [usu. with *negative*] remember where one has seen or how one comes to recognize (someone

or something): *she eventually said she couldn't place him.* ■ (**be placed**) *Brit.* achieve a specified position in a race: *he was placed eleventh in the long individual race.* ■ [*intrans.*] be among the first three in a race (or the first three or four in the UK). ▷Middle English: from Old French, from an alteration of Latin *platea* 'open space,' from Greek *plateia (hodos)* 'broad (way).' —**place·less** *adj.*

▸*PHRASES* □ **give place to** be succeeded or replaced by. □ **go places** *informal* visit places; travel. ■ be increasingly successful. □ **in place 1** working or ready to work; established. **2** not traveling any distance: *running in place.* □ **in place of** instead of. □ **keep someone in his** (or **her**) **place** keep someone from becoming presumptuous. □ **out of place** not in the proper position; disarranged. ■ in a setting where one is or feels inappropriate or incongruous. □ **place in the sun** a position of favor or advantage. □ **put oneself in someone's place** consider a situation from someone's point of view. □ **put someone in his** (or **her**) **place** deflate or humiliate someone regarded as being presumptuous. □ **take place** occur. □ **take one's place** take up the physical position or status in society that is correct or due for one. □ **take the place of** replace.

pla·ce·bo /plə'sēbō/ ▸*n.* (*pl.* **-bos**) a harmless pill, medicine, or procedure prescribed more for the psychological benefit to the patient than for any physiological effect: *his Aunt Beatrice had been kept alive on sympathy and placebos for thirty years* | [as *adj.*] *placebo drugs.* ■ a substance that has no therapeutic effect, used as a control in testing new drugs. ■ *figurative* a measure designed merely to calm or please someone. ▷late 18th cent.: from Latin, literally 'I shall please,' from *placere* 'to please.'

pla·ce·bo ef·fect ▸*n.* a beneficial effect, produced by a placebo drug or treatment, that cannot be attributed to the properties of the placebo itself, and must therefore be due to the patient's belief in that treatment.

place card ▸*n.* a card bearing a person's name and used to mark their place at a dining or meeting table.

place·hold·er /'plās,hōldər/ ▸*n.* **1** *Mathematics* a significant zero in the decimal representation of a number. ■ a symbol or piece of text used in a mathematical expression or in an instruction in a computer program to denote a missing quantity or operator. **2** *Linguistics* an element of a sentence that is required by syntactic constraints but carries little or no semantic information, for example the word *it* as a subject in *it is a pity that she left*, where the true subject is *that she left*.

place·kick /'plās,kik/ *Football* ▸*n.* a kick made with the ball held on the ground or on a tee.

▸*v.* [*intrans.*] [often as *n.*] (**placekicking**) take such a kick: *our placekicking struggled at times last season.* —**place·kick·er** *n.*

place mat (also **place·mat**) ▸*n.* a small mat beneath a place setting at a dining table.

place·ment /'plāsmənt/ ▸*n.* the action of putting someone or something in a particular place or the fact of being placed: *the proper placement of microphones.* ■ the action of finding a home, job, or school for someone: *a baby put up for adoption may wait up to three years or more for placement* | *a placement in a special school.* ■ *Football* another term for **PLACEKICK.** ■ *Football* the act of holding the ball for a placekick.

place name ▸*n.* the name of a geographical location, such as a town, lake, or range of hills.

pla·cen·ta /plə'sentə/ ▸*n.* (*pl.* **-tae** /-tē/ or **-tas**) **1** a flattened circular organ in the uterus of pregnant eutherian mammals, nourishing and maintaining the fetus through the umbilical cord.

> The placenta consists of vascular tissue in which oxygen and nutrients can pass from the mother's blood into that of the fetus, and waste products can pass in the reverse direction. The placenta is expelled from the uterus at the birth of the fetus, when it is often called the afterbirth. Marsupials and monotremes do not develop placentas.

2 *Botany* (in flowers) part of the ovary wall to which the ovules are attached. ▷late 17th cent.: from Latin, from Greek *plakous, plakount-* 'flat cake,' based on *plax, plak-* 'flat plate.'

pla·cen·tal /plə'sentl/ ▸*adj.* of or relating to a placenta. ■ *Zoology* relating to or denoting mammals that possess a placenta; eutherian.

▸*n. Zoology* a placental mammal. See **EUTHERIA.**

pla·cen·ta pre·vi·a /plə'sentə 'prēvēə/ (*Brit.* **pla·cen·ta prae·vi·a**) ▸*n. Medicine* a condition in which the placenta partially or wholly blocks the neck of the uterus, thus interfering with normal delivery of a baby. ▷early 19th cent.: from **PLACENTA** and Latin *praevia* 'going before.'

plac·en·ta·tion /,plasən'tāSHən/ ▸*n. Anatomy & Zoology* the formation or arrangement of a placenta or placentae in a woman's or female animal's uterus. ■ *Botany* the arrangement of the placenta or placentae in the ovary of a flower.

plac·er[1] /'plāsər/ ▸*n.* [often as *adj.*] a deposit of sand or gravel in the bed of a river or lake, containing particles of valuable minerals: *placer gold deposits.* ▷early 19th cent.: from Latin American Spanish, literally 'deposit, shoal'; related to *placel* 'sandbank,' from *plaza* 'a place.'

plac·er[2] ▸*n.* **1** [with *adj.*] a person or animal gaining a specified position in a competition or race: *last year's fifth placer had a good run.* **2** a person who positions, sets, or arranges something: *he was a shrewd placer of the ball.*

place set·ting ▸*n.* a complete set of dishes and cutlery provided for one person at a meal.

pla·cet /'plāsit/ ▸*n.* an affirmative vote, indicated by an utterance of 'placet.' ▷Latin, literally 'it pleases.'

place val·ue ▸*n.* the numerical value that a digit has by virtue of its position in a number.

plac·id /'plasid/ ▸*adj.* (of a person or animal) not easily upset or excited: *this horse has a placid nature.* ■ (esp. of a place or stretch of water) calm and peaceful, with little movement or activity: *the placid waters of a small lake.* See note at **CALM.** ▷early 17th cent.: from French *placide*, from Latin *placidus*, from *placere* 'to please.' —**pla·cid·i·ty** /plə'siditē/ *n.* —**plac·id·ly** *adv.*

Plac·i·dyl /'plasidil/ ▸*n. trademark* a short-acting sedative and hypnotic drug used to treat insomnia.

plack·et /'plakit/ ▸*n.* an opening or slit in a garment, covering fastenings or giving access to a pocket, or the flap of fabric under such an opening. ▷early 17th cent.: variant of **PLACARD** in an obsolete sense 'garment worn under an open coat or gown.'

plac·o·derm /'plakə,dərm/ ▸*n.* an extinct fish of the Devonian period, having the front part of the body encased in broad flat bony plates. • Class Placodermi: several orders. ▷mid 19th cent.: from Greek *plax, plak-* 'flat plate' + *derma* 'skin.'

plac·o·dont /'plakə,dänt/ ▸*n.* an extinct marine shellfish-eating reptile of the Triassic period, having short flat grinding palatal teeth and sometimes a turtlelike shell. • Suborder Placodontia, superorder Sauropterygia: several families and genera, including *Placodus.* ▷late 19th cent.: from Greek *plax, plak-* 'flat plate' + *odous, odont-* 'tooth.'

plac·oid /'plakoid/ ▸*adj. Zoology* (of fish scales) toothlike, being made of dentin with a pointed backward projection of enamel, as in sharks and rays. Compare with **CTENOID** and **GANOID.** ▷mid 19th cent.: from Greek *plax, plak-* 'flat plate' + **-OID.**

Plac·o·zo·a /,plakə'zōə/ *Zoology* a minor phylum that contains a single minute marine invertebrate (*Trichoplax adhaerens*), which has a flattened body with two cell layers and is the simplest known metazoan. ▷modern Latin (plural), from Greek *plakos* 'flat' + *zōia* 'animals.'

pla·fond /plə'fänd/ ▸*n.* an ornately decorated ceiling. ■ a painting or decoration on a ceiling. ▷French, from *plat* 'flat' + *fond* 'bottom, base.'

pla·gal /'plāgəl/ ▸*adj. Music* (of a church mode) containing notes between the dominant and the note an octave higher, having the final in the middle. Compare with **AUTHENTIC.** ▷late 16th cent.: from medieval Latin *plagalis*, from *plaga* 'plagal mode,' from Latin *plagius*, from medieval Greek *plagios (hēkhos)* 'plagal (mode),' from Greek *plagos* 'side.'

plage /pläZH/ ▸*n.* **1** *dated* a beach by the sea, esp. at a fashionable resort. **2** *Astronomy* an unusually bright region on the sun. ▷late 19th cent.: from French.

pla·gia·rism /'plājə,rizəm/ ▸*n.* the practice of taking someone else's work or ideas and passing them off as one's own. ▷early 17th cent.: from Latin *plagiarius* 'kidnapper' (from *plagium* 'a kidnapping,' from Greek *plagion*) + **-ISM.** —**pla·gia·rist** *n.* —**pla·gia·ris·tic** /,plājə'ristik/ *adj.*

pla·gia·rize /'plājə,rīz/ ▸*v.* [*trans.*] take (the work or an idea of someone else) and pass it off as one's own. ■ copy from (someone) in such a way. —**pla·gia·riz·er** *n.*

plagio- ▸*comb. form* oblique: *plagioclase.* ▷from Greek *plagios* 'slanting,' from *plagos* 'side.'

pla·gi·o·clase /'plājēə,klās/ (also **plagioclase feldspar**) ▸*n.* a form of feldspar consisting of aluminosilicates of sodium and/or calcium, common in igneous rocks and typically white. ▷mid 19th cent.: from **PLAGIO-** + Greek *klasis* 'cleavage' (because originally characterized as having two cleavages at an oblique angle).

plague /plāg/ ▸*n.* a contagious bacterial disease characterized by fever and delirium, typically with the formation of buboes (see **BUBONIC PLAGUE**) and sometimes infection of the lungs (**pneumonic plague**): *an outbreak of plague* | *they died of* ***the plague.*** ■ a contagious disease that spreads rapidly and kills many people. ■ an unusually large number of insects or animals infesting a place and causing damage: *a* ***plague of*** *fleas.* ■ [in *sing.*] a thing causing trouble or irritation: *staff theft is usually* ***the plague of*** *restaurants.* ■ a widespread affliction regarded as divine punishment: *the plagues of Egypt.* ■ [in *sing.*] *archaic* used as a curse or an expression of despair or disgust: *a plague on all their houses!* [in recent use echoing Shakespeare's *Romeo and Juliet* (III. i. 94).]

▸*v.* (**plagues, plagued, pla·guing**) [*trans.*] cause continual trouble or distress to: *the problems that plagued the company* | *he has been plagued by ill health.* ■ pester or harass (someone) continually: *he was* ***plaguing*** *her* ***with*** *questions.* ▷late Middle English: Latin *plaga* 'stroke, wound,' probably from Greek (Doric dialect) *plaga*, from a base meaning 'strike.'

pla·guy /'plāgē/ (also **pla·guey**) ▸*adj.* [*attrib.*] *informal* troublesome; annoying.

plaice /plās/ ▸*n.* (*pl.* same) a North Atlantic flatfish that is a commercially important food fish. • Two species in the family Pleuronectidae: the European *Pleuronectes platessa*, often found in very shallow water, and the American *Hippoglossoides platessoides*, found in deeper waters. ▷Middle English: from Old French *plaiz*, from late Latin *platessa*, from Greek *platus* 'broad.'

plaid /plad/ ▸*n.* checkered or tartan twilled cloth, typically made of wool. ■ any cloth with a tartan pattern. ■ a long piece of plaid worn over the shoulder as part of Scottish Highland dress. ▷early 16th cent.: from Scottish Gaelic *plaide* 'blanket,' of unknown ultimate origin. —**plaid·ed** *adj.*

plain[1] /plān/ ▸*adj.* **1** not decorated or elaborate; simple or ordinary in character: *good plain food* | *everyone dined at a plain wooden table.* ■ without a pattern; in only one color: *a plain fabric.* ■ bearing no indication as to source, contents, or affiliation: *donations can be put in a plain envelope.* ■ (of a person) having no pretensions; not remarkable or special: *a plain, honest man with no nonsense about him.* ■ [*attrib.*] (of a person) without a special title or status: *for years he was just plain Bill.* **2** easy to perceive or understand; clear: *the advantages were* ***plain to see*** | *it was* ***plain that*** *something was very wrong.* ■ [*attrib.*] (of written or spoken usage) clearly expressed, without the use of technical or abstruse terms: *written* ***in plain English.*** ■ not using concealment or deception; frank: *he recalled her plain speaking.* **3** (of a person) not beautiful or attractive: *the dark-haired, rather plain woman.* **4** [*attrib.*] sheer; simple (used for emphasis): *the main problem is* ***just plain*** *exhaustion.* **5** (of a knitting stitch) made using a knit rather than a purl stitch.

▸*adv.* [as *submodifier*] *informal* clearly; unequivocally (used for emphasis): *perhaps the youth was just plain stupid.*

▸*n.* a large area of flat land with few trees. Compare with **PRAIRIE.** ■ (**the Plains**) another term for **GREAT PLAINS.** ▷Middle English: from Old French *plain*, from Latin *planus*, from a base meaning 'flat.' —**plain·ness** *n.*

▸*PHRASES* □ **as plain as the nose on one's face** *informal* very obvious. □ **plain and simple** *informal* used to emphasize the statement preceding or following: *she was a genius, plain and simple.* □ **plain as day** *informal* very clearly.

plain[2] ▸*v.* [*intrans.*] *archaic* mourn; lament. ■ complain. ■ emit a mournful or plaintive sound. ▷Middle English: from Old French *plaindre*, from Latin *plangere* 'to lament.'

plain·chant /'plān,CHant/ ▸*n.* another term for **PLAINSONG.**

plain clothes ▸*plural n.* ordinary clothes rather than uniform, esp. when worn as a disguise by police officers: *a detective* ***in plain clothes.***

▸*adj.* [*attrib.*] (**plainclothes**) (esp. of a police officer) wearing such clothes: *plainclothes troopers.*

plain deal·ing ▸*n.* honest and straightforward behavior toward others.

Plain·field /'plān,fēld/ an industrial city in northeastern New Jersey; pop. 46,567.

plain-laid ▸*adj.* denoting a rope consisting of three strands twisted to the right.

plain·ly /ˈplānlē/ ▸*adv.* **1** [as *submodifier*] able to be perceived easily: *the lake was plainly visible.* ■ [*sentence adverb*] used to state one's belief that something is obviously or undeniably true: *her mother was plainly anxious to leave.* ■ in a frank and direct way; unequivocally: *let me speak plainly.* **2** in a style that is simple and without decoration: *the restaurant was plainly furnished.*

plain-pa·per ▸*adj.* denoting a fax machine or other device that does not require special paper to print on.

Plain Peo·ple ▸*plural n.* the Amish, the Mennonites, and the Dunkers, three strict Christian sects emphasizing a simple way of life.

plain sail·ing ▸*n.* used to describe a process or activity that goes well and is easy and uncomplicated: *he is pleased to report that the tour has been plain sailing.* ▷mid 18th cent.: probably a popular use of *plane sailing*, denoting the practice of determining a ship's position on the theory that it is moving on a plane.

plain-saw ▸*v.* (*past part.* **-sawed** /-sôd/ or **-sawn** /-sôn/) [*trans.*] saw (timber) tangential to the growth rings, so that the rings make angles of less than 45° with the faces of the boards produced: [as *adj.*, in *combination*] (**-sawn**) *plain-sawn logs.* —**plain saw·ing** *n.*

Plains In·di·an ▸*n.* a member of any of various North American Indian peoples who formerly inhabited the Great Plains.

Although a few of the Plains Indian peoples were sedentary farmers, most, including the Blackfoot, Cheyenne, and Comanche, were nomadic buffalo hunters, who gathered in tribes during the summer and dispersed into family groups in the winter. They hunted on foot until they acquired horses from the Spanish in the early 18th century. The introduction of the horse also led other peoples, such as the Sioux and the Cree, to move into the Plains area.

plains·man /ˈplānzmən/ ▸*n.* (*pl.* **-men**) a person who lives on a plain, esp. a frontiersman who lived on the Great Plains of North America.

Plains of A·bra·ham a plateau beside the city of Quebec, overlooking the St. Lawrence River. In 1759 it was the scene of a battle in which the British army under General Wolfe, having scaled the heights above the city under cover of darkness, surprised and defeated the French.

plain·song /ˈplānˌsôNG; -säNG/ ▸*n.* unaccompanied church music sung in unison in medieval modes and in free rhythm corresponding to the accentuation of the words, which are taken from the liturgy. Compare with **GREGORIAN CHANT**. ▷late Middle English: translating Latin *cantus planus.*

plain-spo·ken (also **plain·spo·ken**) ▸*adj.* outspoken; blunt. —**plain-spok·en·ness** *n.*

Plains States the U.S. states dominated by the Great Plains, generally including North and South Dakota, Nebraska, and Kansas and sometimes Iowa and Missouri.

plaint /plānt/ ▸*n. Brit. Law* an accusation; a charge. ■ *chiefly poetic/literary* a complaint; a lamentation. ▷Middle English: from Old French *plainte*, feminine past participle of *plaindre* 'complain,' or from Old French *plaint*, from Latin *planctus* 'beating of the breast.'

plain·text /ˈplānˌtekst/ ▸*n. Computing* an original readable text, as opposed to a coded version.

plain·tiff /ˈplāntif/ ▸*n. Law* a person who brings a case against another in a court of law. Compare with **DEFENDANT**. ▷late Middle English: from Old French *plaintif* 'plaintive' (used as a noun). The *-f* ending has come down through Law French; the word was originally the same as *plaintive*.

plain·tive /ˈplāntiv/ ▸*adj.* sounding sad and mournful: *a plaintive cry.* ▷late Middle English: from Old French *plaintif, -ive*, from *plainte* 'lamentation' (see **PLAINT**). —**plain·tive·ly** *adv.* —**plain·tive·ness** *n.*

plain weave ▸*n.* a common and basic style of weave in which the weft alternates over and under the warp.

plait /plāt; plat/ ▸*n.* a single length of hair or other flexible material made up of three or more interlaced strands; a braid. ■ archaic term for **PLEAT**.
▸*v.* [*trans.*] form (hair or other material) into a plait or plaits. ■ make (something) by forming material into a plait or plaits. ▷late Middle English: from Old French *pleit* 'a fold,' based on Latin *plicare* 'to fold.' The word was formerly often pronounced like "plate," which is the usual American pronunciation; since late Middle English there has arisen an alternative spelling *plat*, to which the current alternative pronunciation corresponds.

plan /plan/ ▸*n.* **1** a detailed proposal for doing or achieving something: *the UN peace plan.* ■ [with *adj.*] a scheme for the regular payment of contributions toward a pension, savings account, or insurance policy: *a personal pension plan.* **2** (usu. **plans**) an intention or decision about what one is going to do: *I have no plans to retire.* **3** a detailed diagram, drawing, or program, in particular: ■ a fairly large-scale map of a town or district: *a street plan.* ■ a drawing or diagram made by projection on a horizontal plane, esp. one showing the layout of a building or one floor of a building. Compare with **ELEVATION** (sense 3). ■ a diagram showing how something will be arranged: *look at the seating plan.*
▸*v.* (**planned**, **plan·ning**) [*trans.*] **1** decide on and arrange in advance: *they were planning a trip to Egypt* | [with *infinitive*] *he plans to fly on Wednesday* | [*intrans.*] *we* **plan on** *getting married in the near future.* See note at **INTEND**. ■ [*intrans.*] make preparations for an anticipated event or time: *we have to* **plan for** *the future.* **2** design or make a plan of (something to be made or built): *they were planning a garden.* ▷late 17th cent.: from French, from earlier *plant* 'ground plan, plane surface,' influenced in sense by Italian *pianta* 'plan of building.' Compare with **PLANT**.
▸*PHRASES* □ **someone's** (or **the**) **best plan** a person's (or the) most sensible course of action. □ **go according to plan** happen as one arranged or intended. □ **plan of action** (or **attack**) an organized program of measures to be taken in order to achieve a goal.

pla·nar /ˈplānər/ ▸*adj. Mathematics* of, relating to, or in the form of a plane: *planar surfaces.*

pla·nar·i·an /pləˈne(ə)rēən/ ▸*n.* a free-living flatworm that has a three-branched intestine and a tubular pharynx, typically located halfway down the body. • Order Tricladida, class Turbellaria: *Planaria* and other genera. ▷mid 19th cent.: from modern Latin *Planaria* (feminine of Latin *planarius* 'lying flat') + **-IAN**.

pla·na·tion /plāˈnāSHən/ ▸*n.* the leveling of a landscape by erosion. ▷late 19th cent.: from **PLANE**1 + **-ATION**.

planch·et /ˈplanCHit/ ▸*n.* a plain metal disk from which a coin is made. ▷early 17th cent.: diminutive of earlier *planch* 'slab of metal,' from Old French *planche* 'plank, slab.'

plan·chette /planˈSHet/ ▸*n.* a small board supported on casters, typically heart-shaped and fitted with a vertical pencil, used for automatic writing and in seances. ▷mid 19th cent.: from French, literally 'small plank,' diminutive of *planche*.

Planck /plaNGk; läNGk/, Max (Karl Ernst Ludwig) (1858–1947), German theoretical physicist. The founder of the quantum theory, he announced the radiation law named after him in 1900. Nobel Prize for Physics (1918).

Planck's con·stant (also **Planck constant**) *Physics* a fundamental constant, equal to the energy of a quantum of electromagnetic radiation divided by its frequency, with a value of 6.626×10^{-34} joule-seconds.

Planck's law *Physics* a law, forming the basis of quantum theory, that states that electromagnetic radiation from heated bodies is not emitted as a continuous flow but is made up of discrete units or quanta of energy, the size of which involve a fundamental physical constant (Planck's constant).

plane1 /plān/ ▸*n.* **1** a flat surface on which a straight line joining any two points on it would wholly lie: *the horizontal plane.* ■ an imaginary flat surface through or joining material objects: *the planets orbit the sun in roughly the same plane.* ■ a flat or level surface of a material object: *the* **plane of** *his forehead.* ■ a flat surface producing lift by the action of air or water over and under it. **2** a level of existence, thought, or development: *everything is connected on the spiritual plane.*
▸*adj.* [*attrib.*] completely level or flat. ■ of or relating to only two-dimensional surfaces or magnitudes: *plane and solid geometry.*
▸*v.* [*intrans.*] (of a bird or an airborne object) soar without moving the wings; glide: *a bird planed down toward the water below.* ■ [*intrans.*] (of a boat, surfboard, etc.) skim over the surface of water as a result of lift produced hydrodynamically. ▷early 17th cent.: from Latin *planum* 'flat surface,' neuter of the adjective *planus* 'plain.' The adjective was suggested by French *plan(e)* 'flat.' The word was introduced to differentiate the geometric senses, previously expressed by **PLAIN**1, from the latter's other meanings.

plane2 ▸*n.* an airplane.
▸*v.* [*intrans.*] *rare* travel in an airplane. ▷early 20th cent.: shortened form.

plane3 ▸*n.* a tool consisting of a block with a projecting steel blade, used to smooth a wooden or other surface by paring shavings from it.
▸*v.* [*trans.*] smooth (wood or other material) with a plane. ■ [*trans.*] reduce or remove (redundant material) with a plane: *high areas can be* **planed down**. ■ *archaic* make smooth or level. ▷Middle English: from a variant of obsolete French *plaine* 'planing tool,' from late Latin *plana* (in the same sense), from Latin *planare* 'make level,' from *planus* 'plain, level.'

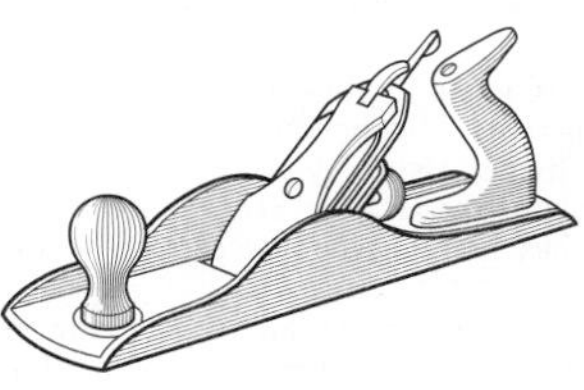

plane3

plane4 (also **plane tree**) ▸*n.* a tall spreading tree of the northern hemisphere, with maplelike leaves and bark that peels in irregular patches. • Genus *Platanus*, family Platanaceae. See also **SYCAMORE**. ▷late Middle English: from Old French, from Latin *platanus*, from Greek *platanos*, from *platus* 'broad.'

plane po·lar·i·za·tion /ˌpōlərəˈzāSHən/ ▸*n.* a process restricting the vibrations of electromagnetic radiation, esp. light, to one direction. —**plane-po·lar·ized** *adj.*

plan·er /ˈplānər/ ▸*n.* another term for **PLANE**3, esp. when power-operated.

planes·man /ˈplānzmən/ ▸*n.* (*pl.* **-men**) a person who operates the hydroplanes on a submarine.

plan·et /ˈplanit/ ▸*n.* a celestial body moving in an elliptical orbit around a star. ■ (**the planet**) the earth: *no generation has the right to pollute the planet.* ■ *chiefly Astrology, historical* a celestial body distinguished from the fixed stars by having an apparent motion of its own (including the moon and sun), esp. with reference to its supposed influence on people and events.

The nine planets of the solar system are either gas giants—Jupiter, Saturn, Uranus, and Neptune—or smaller rocky bodies—Mercury, Venus, Earth, Mars, and Pluto. The minor planets, or asteroids, orbit mainly between the orbits of Mars and Jupiter.

▷Middle English: from Old French *planete*, from late Latin *planeta, planetes*, from Greek *planētēs* 'wanderer, planet,' from *planan* 'wander.' —**plan·e·tol·o·gy** /ˌplaniˈtäləjē/ *n.*

plane ta·ble ▸*n.* a surveying instrument used for direct plotting in the field, with a drawing board and pivoted alidade.

plan·e·tar·i·um /ˌplaniˈte(ə)rēəm/ ▸*n.* (*pl.* **-tar·i·ums** or **-tar·i·a** /-ˈte(ə)rēə/) **1** a building in which images of stars, planets, and constellations are projected on the inner surface of a dome for public entertainment or education. ■ a device used to project such images. **2** another term for **ORRERY**. ▷mid 18th cent.: modern Latin, from Latin *planetarius* 'relating to the planets.'

plan·e·tar·y /ˈplaniˌterē/ ▸*adj.* of, relating to, or belonging to a planet or planets: *the laws of planetary motion.* ■ of or relating to the earth as a planet: *planetary air pollution and climatic change.* ▷late 16th cent.: from late Latin *planetarius* 'relating to the planets' (recorded only as a noun meaning 'astrologer'), from *planeta* 'planet.'

plan·e·tar·y gear (also **planetary wheel**) ▸*n.* see **SUN-AND-PLANET GEAR**.

plan·e·tar·y neb·u·la ▸*n. Astronomy* a ring-shaped nebula formed by an expanding shell of gas around an aging star.

plan·e·tes·i·mal /ˌplaniˈtesəməl/ *Astronomy* ▸*n.* a minute planet; a body that could or did come together with many others under gravitation to form a planet.

▶*adj.* [*attrib.*] denoting or relating to such bodies. ▷early 20th cent.: from PLANET, on the pattern of *infinitesimal.*

plan·et·fall /ˈplanit,fôl/ ▶*n.* (chiefly in science fiction) a landing or arrival on a planet after a journey through space. ▷from PLANET + *-fall,* on the pattern of LANDFALL.

plan·et·oid /ˈplani,toid/ ▶*n.* another term for ASTEROID.

plan·form /ˈplan,fôrm/ ▶*n.* the shape or outline of an aircraft wing as projected onto a horizontal plane.

plan·gent /ˈplanjənt/ ▶*adj. chiefly poetic/literary* (of a sound) loud, reverberating, and often melancholy. ▷early 19th cent.: from Latin *plangent-* 'lamenting,' from the verb *plangere.* **—plan·gen·cy** *n.* **—plan·gent·ly** *adv.*

pla·nig·ra·phy /pləˈnigrəfē/ ▶*n. Medicine* the process of obtaining a visual representation of a plane section through living tissue, by such techniques as tomography, ultrasonography, etc. ▷1930s: from Dutch *planigraphie,* from Latin *planus* 'flat, level' + Greek *-graphia* (see -GRAPHY).

pla·nim·e·ter /pləˈnimitər/ ▶*n.* an instrument for mechanically measuring the area of a plane figure. ▷mid 19th cent.: from French *planimètre,* from Latin *planus* 'level' + *-mètre* '(instrument) measuring.' **—plan·i·met·ric** /,plānəˈmetrik/ *adj.* **—plan·i·met·ri·cal·ly** /-ˈmetrik(ə)lē/ *adv.* **—pla·nim·e·try** /-ˈnimətrē/ *n.*

plan·ish /ˈplanisн/ ▶*v.* [*trans.*] flatten (sheet metal) with a smooth-faced hammer or between rollers. ▷late Middle English (in the sense 'make level'): from obsolete French *planiss-,* lengthened stem of *planir* 'to smooth,' from *plain* 'smooth, level.' **—plan·ish·er** *n.*

plan·i·sphere /ˈplanə,sfi(ə)r/ ▶*n.* a map formed by the projection of a sphere or part of a sphere on a plane, esp. an adjustable circular star map that shows the appearance of the heavens at a specific time and place. ▷late Middle English *planisperie,* from medieval Latin *planisphaerium,* from Latin *planus* 'level' + *sphaera* 'sphere'; later influenced by French *planisphère.* **—plan·i·spher·ic** /,planəˈsfi(ə)rik; -ˈsfer-/ *adj.*

plank /plaNGk/ ▶*n.* **1** a long, thin, flat piece of timber, used esp. in building and flooring. **2** a fundamental point of a political or other program: *the central plank of the bill is the curb on industrial polluters.*

▶*v.* [*trans.*] **1** make, provide, or cover with planks: *the ship was planked with teak* | [as *adj.*] (**planked**) *the planked floor.* **2** *informal* another term for PLUNK (sense 3). **3** cook and serve (meat or fish) on a plank. ▷Middle English: from Old Northern French *planke,* from late Latin *planca* 'board,' feminine (used as a noun) of *plancus* 'flatfooted.'

▶*PHRASE* □ **walk the plank** (formerly) be forced by pirates to walk blindfold along a plank over the side of a ship to one's death in the sea. ■ *informal* lose one's job or position.

plank·ing /ˈplaNGkiNG/ ▶*n.* planks collectively, esp. when used for flooring or as part of a boat. ■ the act or process of laying planks.

plank·ton /ˈplaNGktən/ ▶*n.* the small and microscopic organisms drifting or floating in the sea or fresh water, consisting chiefly of diatoms, protozoans, small crustaceans, and the eggs and larval stages of larger animals. Many animals are adapted to feed on plankton, esp. by filtering the water. Compare with NEKTON. ▷late 19th cent.: from German, from Greek *planktos* 'wandering,' from the base of *plazein* 'wander.' **—plank·tic** /-tik/ *adj.* **—plank·ton·ic** /-ˈtänik/ *adj.*

planned e·con·o·my ▶*n.* another term for COMMAND ECONOMY.

planned ob·so·les·cence /,äbsəˈlesəns/ ▶*n.* a policy of producing consumer goods that rapidly become obsolete and so require replacing, achieved by frequent changes in design, termination of the supply of spare parts, and the use of nondurable materials.

Planned Par·ent·hood ▶*trademark* a nonprofit organization that does research into and gives advice on contraception, family planning, and reproductive problems.

plan·ner /ˈplanər/ ▶*n.* **1** a person who makes plans. ■ a person who controls or plans urban development: *city planners.* **2** [usu. with *adj.*] a list or chart with information that is an aid to planning: *my day planner.*

plan·ning /ˈplaniNG/ ▶*n.* the process of making plans for something. ■ [often as *adj.*] the control of urban development by a local government authority, from which a license must be obtained to build a new property or change an existing one: *the local planning authority.*

Pla·no /ˈplānō/ a city in northeastern Texas, northeast of Dallas; pop. 222,030.

plano- ▶*comb. form* level; flat: *plano-convex* | *planography.* ▷from Latin *planus* 'flat.'

pla·no-con·cave /,plānō,känˈkāv; -ˈkän,kāv/ ▶*adj.* (of a lens) with one surface plane and the opposite one concave.

pla·no-con·vex /,plānō,känˈveks; -ˈkän,veks/ ▶*adj.* (of a lens) with one surface plane and the opposite one convex.

plan·o·gram /ˈplanə,gram/ ▶*n.* a diagram or model that indicates the placement of retail products on shelves in order to maximize sales.

pla·no·graph·ic /,plānəˈgrafik/ ▶*adj. Printing* relating to or denoting a printing process in which the printing surface is flat, as in lithography. **—pla·nog·ra·phy** /pləˈnägrəfē/ *n.*

plant /plant/ ▶*n.* **1** a living organism of the kind exemplified by trees, shrubs, herbs, grasses, ferns, and mosses, typically growing in a permanent site, absorbing water and inorganic substances through its roots, and synthesizing nutrients in its leaves by photosynthesis using the green pigment chlorophyll. ■ a small organism of this kind, as distinct from a shrub or tree: *garden plants.*

> Plants differ from animals in lacking specialized sense organs, having no capacity for voluntary movement, having cell walls, and growing to suit their surroundings rather than having a fixed body plan.

2 a place where an industrial or manufacturing process takes place: *the company has 30 plants in Mexico.* ■ machinery used in an industrial or manufacturing process: *inadequate investment in new plant.* ■ any system that is analyzed and controlled, e.g., the dynamic equations of an aircraft or the equations governing chemical processes. **3** a person placed in a group as a spy or informer: *we thought he was a CIA plant spreading disinformation.* ■ a thing put among someone's belongings to incriminate or compromise them: *he insisted that the cocaine in the glove compartment was a plant.*

▶*v.* [*trans.*] **1** place (a seed, bulb, or plant) in the ground so that it can grow. ■ place a seed, bulb, or plant in (a place) to grow: *the garden is planted with herbs.* ■ *informal* bury (someone). **2** [*trans.*] place or fix in a specified position: *she planted a kiss on his cheek.* ■ (**plant oneself**) position oneself: *she planted herself on the arm of his chair.* ■ establish (an idea) in someone's mind: *the seed of doubt is planted in his mind.* ■ secretly place (a bomb that is set to go off at a later time). ■ put or hide (something) among someone's belongings to compromise or incriminate the owner: *he* **planted** *drugs* **on** *him to extort a bribe.* ■ send (someone) to join a group or organization to act as a spy or informer. ■ found or establish (a colony, city, or community). ■ deposit (young fish, spawn, oysters, etc.) in a river or lake. ▷Old English *plante* 'seedling,' *plantian* (verb), from Latin *planta* 'sprout, cutting' (later influenced by French *plante*) and *plantare* 'plant, fix in a place.' **—plant·a·ble** *adj.* **—plant·let** /-lit/ *n.* **—plant·like** /-,līk/ *adj.*

▶*PHRASE* □ **have** (or **keep**) **one's feet firmly planted on the ground** be (or remain) level-headed and sensible.

Plan·tag·e·net /planˈtajənit/ ▶*adj.* of or relating to the English royal dynasty that held the throne from the accession of Henry II in 1154 until the death of Richard III in 1485.

▶*n.* a member of this dynasty. ▷from Latin *planta genista* 'sprig of broom,' said to be worn as a crest by and given as a nickname to Geoffrey, count of Anjou, the father of Henry II.

plan·tain[1] /ˈplantən/ ▶*n.* a low-growing plant that typically has a rosette of leaves and a slender green flower spike, widely growing as a weed in lawns. • Genus *Plantago,* family Plantaginaceae: many species. ▷late Middle English: from Old French, from Latin *plantago, plantagin-,* from *planta* 'sole of the foot' (because of its broad prostrate leaves).

plan·tain[2] ▶*n.* **1** a banana containing high levels of starch and little sugar, harvested green and widely used as a cooked vegetable in the tropics. **2** the plant that bears this fruit. • *Musa × paradisiaca,* family Musaceae. ▷mid 16th cent.: from Spanish *plá(n)tano,* probably by assimilation of a South American word to the Spanish *plá(n)tano* 'plane tree.'

plan·tain lil·y ▶*n.* another term for HOSTA.

plan·tar /ˈplantər/ ▶*adj. Anatomy* of or relating to the sole of the foot. ▷early 18th cent.: from Latin *plantaris,* from *planta* 'sole.'

Plan·ta·tion /planˈtāsнən/ a city in southeastern Florida, west of Fort Lauderdale; pop. 66,692.

plan·ta·tion /planˈtāsнən/ ▶*n.* [often with *adj.*] an estate on which crops such as coffee, sugar, and tobacco are cultivated by resident labor. ■ an area in which trees have been planted, esp. for commercial purposes. ■ *historical* a colony. ▷late Middle English (denoting the action of planting seeds): from Latin *plantatio(n-),* from the verb *plantare* 'to plant.'

plant·er /ˈplantər/ ▶*n.* **1** [often with *adj.*] a manager or owner of a plantation: *sugar planters.* **2** a decorative container in which plants are grown. **3** a machine or person that plants seeds, bulbs, etc.

plant·er's punch ▶*n.* a cocktail containing rum, lime juice, carbonated water, and sugar.

plant hop·per ▶*n.* a small, widely distributed plant-sucking bug that leaps when disturbed. Some species are pests of rice and sugar cane. • Delphacidae and other families, suborder Homoptera.

plan·ti·grade /ˈplanti,grād/ ▶*adj.* (of a mammal) walking on the soles of the feet, like a human or a bear. Compare with DIGITIGRADE. ▷mid 19th cent.: from French, from modern Latin *plantigradus,* from Latin *planta* 'sole' + *-gradus* '-walking.'

plant louse ▶*n.* a small bug that infests plants and feeds on the sap or tender shoots, esp. an aphid. • Several families in the series Sternorrhyncha, suborder Homoptera.

plan·toc·ra·cy /planˈtäkrəsē/ ▶*n.* (*pl.* **-cies**) a population of planters regarded as the dominant class, esp. in the West Indies.

plants·man /ˈplantsmən/ ▶*n.* (*pl.* **-men**) an expert in garden plants and gardening.

plants·wom·an /ˈplantswŏmən/ ▶*n.* (*pl.* **-wom·en**) a female expert in garden plants and gardening.

plan·u·la /ˈplanyələ/ ▶*n.* (*pl.* **-lae** /-,lē/) *Zoology* a free-swimming coelenterate larva with a flattened, ciliated, solid body. ▷late 19th cent.: modern Latin, diminutive of Latin *planus* 'plane, flat.'

plan view ▶*n.* a view of an object as projected onto a horizontal plane.

plaque /plak/ ▶*n.* **1** an ornamental tablet, typically of metal, porcelain, or wood, that is fixed to a wall or other surface in commemoration of a person or event. **2** a sticky deposit on teeth in which bacteria proliferate. **3** *Medicine* a small, distinct, typically raised patch or region resulting from local damage or deposition of material, such as a fatty deposit on an artery wall in atherosclerosis or a site of localized damage of brain tissue in Alzheimer's disease. ■ *Microbiology* a clear area in a cell culture caused by the inhibition of growth or destruction of cells by an agent such as a virus. ▷mid 19th cent.: from French, from Dutch *plak* 'tablet,' from *plakken* 'to stick.'

plash[1] /plasн/ *poetic/literary* ▶*n.* [in *sing.*] a sound produced by liquid striking something or being struck. ■ a pool or puddle.

▶*v.* [*intrans.*] splash: *gray curtains of rain plashed down.* ■ [*trans.*] strike the surface of (water) with a splashing sound. ▷early 16th cent.: probably imitative. **—plash·y** *adj.*

plash[2] ▶*v.* [*trans.*] *archaic* bend and interweave (branches and twigs) to form a hedge. ■ make or renew (a hedge) in this way. ▷late 15th cent.: from Old French *plaissier,* based on Latin *plectere* 'to plait.' Compare with PLEACH.

plas·ma /ˈplazmə/ (also **plasm** /ˈplazəm/) ▶*n.* **1** the colorless fluid part of blood, lymph, or milk, in which corpuscles or fat globules are suspended. ■ this substance taken from donors or donated blood for administering in transfusions. **2** an ionized gas consisting of positive ions and free electrons in proportions resulting in more or less no overall electric charge, typically at low pressures (as in the upper atmosphere and in fluorescent lamps) or at very high temperatures (as in stars and nuclear fusion reactors). ■ an analogous substance consisting of mobile charged particles (such as a molten salt or the electrons within a metal). **3** a dark green, translucent variety of quartz used in mosaic and for other decorative purposes. **4** another term for CYTOPLASM or PROTOPLASM. ▷early 18th cent. (in the sense 'mold, shape'): from late Latin, literally 'mold,' from Greek *plasma,* from *plassein* 'to shape.' **—plas·mat·ic** /plazˈmatik/ *adj.* **—plas·mic** /-mik/ *adj.*

plas·ma cell ▶*n. Physiology* a fully differentiated B cell that produces a single type of antibody.

plas·ma·lem·ma /,plazməˈlemə/ ▶*n. Biology* a plasma membrane that bounds a cell, esp. one immediately within the wall of a plant cell. ▷1920s: from PLASMA + Greek *lemma* 'rind.' —**plas·ma·lem·mal** /-ˈleməl/ *adj.*

plas·ma mem·brane ▶*n. Biology* a microscopic membrane of lipids and proteins that forms the external boundary of the cytoplasm of a cell or encloses a vacuole, and that regulates the passage of molecules in and out of the cytoplasm.

plas·ma·pause /ˈplazmə,pôz/ ▶*n. Astronomy* the outer limit of a plasmasphere, marked by a sudden change in plasma density.

plas·ma·pher·e·sis /,plazməfəˈrēsis/ ▶*n. Medicine* a method of removing blood plasma from the body by withdrawing blood, separating it into plasma and cells, and transfusing the cells back into the bloodstream. It is performed esp. to remove antibodies in treating autoimmune conditions. ▷1920s: from PLASMA + Greek *aphairesis* 'taking away' (from *apo-* 'from' + *hairein* 'take').

plas·ma sheet ▶*n. Astronomy* a layer of plasma in the magnetotail of the earth (or another planet), lying in the equatorial plane beyond the plasmapause, with two divergent branches that reach the earth at polar latitudes.

plas·ma·sphere /ˈplazmə,sfir/ ▶*n. Astronomy* the roughly toroidal region surrounding and thought to rotate with the earth (or another planet) at latitudes away from the poles, containing a relatively dense plasma of low-energy electrons and protons.

plas·mid /ˈplazmid/ ▶*n. Biology* a genetic structure in a cell that can replicate independently of the chromosomes, typically a small circular DNA strand in the cytoplasm of a bacterium or protozoan. Plasmids are much used in the laboratory manipulation of genes. Compare with EPISOME. ▷1950s: from PLASMA + -ID[2].

plas·min /ˈplazmin/ ▶*n. Biochemistry* an enzyme, formed in the blood in some circumstances, that destroys blood clots by attacking fibrin. ▷mid 19th cent.: from French *plasmine*, from late Latin *plasma* 'mold, image.'

plas·min·o·gen /plazˈminəjen/ ▶*n. Biochemistry* the inactive precursor of the enzyme plasmin, present in blood.

plas·mo·des·ma /,plazməˈdesmə/ ▶*n.* (*pl.* **-des·ma·ta** /-ˈdesmətə/) *Botany* a narrow thread of cytoplasm that passes through the cell walls of adjacent plant cells and allows communication between them. ▷early 20th cent.: from German *Plasmodesma*, from late Latin *plasma* 'mold, formation' + Greek *desma* 'bond, fetter.'

plas·mo·di·um /plazˈmōdēəm/ ▶*n.* (*pl.* **-di·a** /-dēə/) **1** a parasitic protozoan of a genus that includes those causing malaria. • Genus *Plasmodium*, phylum Sporozoa. **2** *Biology* a form within the life cycle of some simple organisms such as slime molds, typically consisting of a mass of naked protoplasm containing many nuclei. ▷late 19th cent.: modern Latin, based on late Latin *plasma* 'mold, formation.' —**plas·mo·di·al** /-mōdēəl/ *adj.*

plas·mol·y·sis /plazˈmäləsis/ ▶*n. Botany* contraction of the protoplast of a plant cell as a result of loss of water from the cell. ▷late 19th cent.: modern Latin, from *plasmo-* 'consisting of protoplasm' (from late Latin *plasma* 'mold, formation') + Greek *lusis* 'loosening' (because of the separation of the plasma membrane from the cell wall).

plas·mo·lyze /ˈplazmə,līz/ (*Brit.* **plas·mo·lyse**) ▶*v.* [*trans.*] *Botany* subject to plasmolysis.

plas·mon /ˈplaz,män/ ▶*n. Physics* a quantum or quasiparticle associated with a local collective oscillation of charge density. ▷1950s: from PLASMA + -ON.

pla·steel /ˈpla,stēl/ ▶*n.* (in science fiction) an ultrastrong nonmetallic material. ▷1970s: blend of PLASTIC and STEEL.

plas·ter /ˈplastər/ ▶*n.* **1** a soft mixture of lime with sand or cement and water for spreading on walls, ceilings, or other structures to form a smooth hard surface when dried. ■ (also **plaster of Paris**) a hard white substance made by the addition of water to powdered and partly dehydrated gypsum, used for holding broken bones in place and making sculptures and casts. [so called because prepared from the gypsum of Paris, France.] ■ the powder from which such a substance is made. **2** *dated* a bandage on which a poultice or liniment is spread for application. See MUSTARD PLASTER. ■ (also **sticking plaster**) *Brit.* an adhesive strip of material for covering cuts and wounds.
▶*v.* [*trans.*] cover (a wall, ceiling, or other structure) with plaster. ■ (**plaster something with/in**) coat or cover something with (a substance), esp. to an extent considered excessive: *a face plastered in heavy makeup.* ■ [*trans.*] make (hair) lie flat by applying a liquid to it: *his hair was plastered down with water.* ■ apply a plaster cast or medical plaster to (a part of the body). ■ (**plaster something with**) cover a surface with (large numbers of pictures or posters): *the store windows are plastered with posters.* ■ (**plaster something over**) present a story or picture conspicuously and sensationally in (a newspaper or magazine): *her story was plastered all over the December issue.* ■ *informal, dated* bomb or shell (a target) heavily. ▷Old English, denoting a bandage spread with a curative substance, from medieval Latin *plastrum* (shortening of Latin *emplastrum*, from Greek *emplastron* 'daub, salve'), later reinforced by the Old French noun *plastre*. Sense 1 dates from late Middle English. —**plas·ter·y** *adj.*

plas·ter·board /ˈplastər,bôrd/ ▶*n.* a type of drywall made of plaster between two sheets of heavy paper.

plas·ter cast ▶*n.* see CAST[1] (sense 1).

plas·tered /ˈplastərd/ ▶*adj.* **1** *informal* very drunk: *I went out and **got totally plastered**.* **2** covered with or made of plaster.

plas·ter·er /ˈplastərər/ ▶*n.* a person whose job it is to apply plaster to walls, ceilings, or other surfaces.

plas·ter saint ▶*n.* a person who makes a show of being without moral faults or human weakness, esp. in a hypocritical way.

plas·ter·work /ˈplastər,wərk/ ▶*n.* plaster as part of the interior of a building, esp. covering the surface of a wall or formed into decorative shapes and patterns.

plas·tic /ˈplastik/ ▶*n.* a synthetic material made from a wide range of organic polymers such as polyethylene, PVC, nylon, etc., that can be molded into shape while soft and then set into a rigid or slightly elastic form. ■ *informal* credit cards or other types of plastic card that can be used as money: *he pays with cash instead of with plastic.*
▶*adj.* **1** made of plastic: *plastic bags.* ■ looking or tasting artificial: *long-distance flights with their plastic food | she smiled a little plastic smile.* **2** (of substances or materials) easily shaped or molded: *rendering the material more plastic.* ■ (in art) of or relating to molding or modeling in three dimensions, or producing three-dimensional effects. ■ (in science and technology) of or relating to the permanent deformation of a solid without fracture by the temporary application of force. ■ offering scope for creativity: *the writer is drawn to words as a plastic medium.* ■ *Biology* exhibiting adaptability to change or variety in the environment. ▷mid 17th cent. (in the sense 'characteristic of molding'): from French *plastique* or Latin *plasticus*, from Greek *plastikos*, from *plassein* 'to mold.' —**plas·ti·cal·ly** /-(ə)lē/ *adv.*

plas·tic arts ▶*plural n.* art forms that involve modeling or molding, such as sculpture and ceramics, or art involving the representation of solid objects with three-dimensional effects.

plas·tic bomb ▶*n.* a bomb containing plastic explosive.

plas·tic ex·plo·sive ▶*n.* a puttylike explosive capable of being molded by hand.

plas·ti·cine /ˈplastə,sēn/ (also **Plas·ti·cine**) ▶*n. trademark* a soft modeling material, used esp. by children. ▷late 19th cent.: from the adjective PLASTIC + -INE[4].

plas·tic·i·ty /plaˈstisitē/ ▶*n.* the quality of being easily shaped or molded. ■ *Biology* the adaptability of an organism to changes in its environment or differences between its various habitats.

plas·ti·cize /ˈplastə,sīz/ ▶*v.* [*trans.*] [often as *adj.*] (**plasticized**) make plastic or moldable, esp. by the addition of a plasticizer. ■ treat or make with plastic: *plasticized cotton.* —**plas·ti·ci·za·tion** /,plastəsiˈzāshən/ *n.*

plas·ti·ciz·er /ˈplastə,sīzər/ ▶*n.* a substance (typically a solvent) added to a synthetic resin to produce or promote plasticity and flexibility and to reduce brittleness.

plas·tick·y /ˈplastikē/ ▶*adj.* resembling plastic. ■ seeming artificial or of inferior quality.

plas·tic sur·ger·y ▶*n.* the process of reconstructing or repairing parts of the body, esp. by the transfer of tissue, either in the treatment of injury or for cosmetic reasons. ▷from PLASTIC in the sense of being possible to (re-)shape. Compare with -PLASTY. —**plas·tic sur·geon** *n.*

plas·tic wood ▶*n.* a moldable material that hardens to resemble wood and is used for filling cracks in wood.

plas·tic wrap ▶*n.* a thin, transparent plastic film that adheres to surfaces and to itself, used chiefly as a wrapping or covering for food.

plas·tid /ˈplastid/ ▶*n. Botany* any of a class of small organelles, such as chloroplasts, in the cytoplasm of plant cells, containing pigment or food. ▷late 19th cent.: from German, based on Greek *plastos* 'shaped.'

plas·tique /plaˈstēk/ ▶*n.* **1** plastic explosive. **2** statuesque poses or slow graceful movements in dancing. ■ the art or technique of performing such movements. ▷mid 20th cent.: French, literally 'plastic' (adjective used as a noun).

plas·ti·sol /ˈplastə,sôl; -,säl/ ▶*n.* a liquid substance that can be converted into a solid plastic simply by heating, consisting of particles of synthetic resin dispersed in a nonvolatile liquid. ▷1940s: from the noun PLASTIC + SOL[2].

plas·tron /ˈplastrən/ ▶*n.* **1** a large pad worn by a fencer to protect the chest. ■ *historical* a lancer's breast covering. **2** an ornamental front of a women's bodice or shirt consisting of colorful material with lace or embroidery, fashionable in the late 19th century. ■ a man's starched shirtfront without pleats. **3** *Zoology* the part of a tortoise's or turtle's shell forming the underside. ■ a similar ventral plate in some invertebrate animals. ■ *Entomology* (in an aquatic insect) a patch of cuticle covered with hairs that retain a thin layer of air, acting like a gill for breathing under water. ▷early 16th cent.: from French, from Italian *piastrone*, augmentative of *piastra* 'breastplate,' from Latin *emplastrum* 'medical dressing' (see PLASTER). —**plas·tral** /ˈplastrəl/ *adj.*

-plasty ▶*comb. form* molding, grafting, or formation of a specified part, esp. a part of the body: *rhinoplasty.* ▷based on Greek *plastos* 'formed, molded.' Compare with PLASTIC SURGERY.

plat[1] /plat/ ▶*n.* a plot of land. ■ a map or plan of an area of land showing actual or proposed features.
▶*v.* [*trans.*] plan out or make a map of (an area of land, esp. a proposed site for construction). ▷late Middle English: variant of the noun PLOT in the sense 'piece of ground.' The current verb sense dates from the early 18th cent.

plat[2] ▶*n.* & *v.* variant spelling of PLAIT.

plat. ▶*abbr.* ■ plateau. ■ platoon.

Pla·tae·a, Battle of /pləˈtēə/ a battle in 479 BC, during the Persian Wars, in which the Persian forces were defeated by the Greeks near the city of Plataea in Boeotia.

plat du jour /,plä də ˈzhŏŏr/ ▶*n.* (*pl.* **plats du jour** *pronunc.* same) a dish specially prepared by a restaurant on a particular day, in addition to the usual menu. ▷French, literally 'dish of the day.'

plate /plāt/ ▶*n.* **1** a flat dish, typically circular and made of china, from which food is eaten or served. ■ an amount of food on such a dish: ***a plate of** spaghetti.* ■ a flat dish, typically made of metal or wood, passed around a church congregation in order to collect donations of money. ■ a course of a meal, served on one plate: *I'll have the salad plate.* ■ an individual meal, with reference to its cost: *a gala $1,000-a-plate dinner.* ■ *Biology* a shallow glass dish on which a culture of cells or microorganisms may be grown. ■ dishes, bowls, cups, and other utensils made of gold, silver, or other metal. [from Old French *vaisselle en plate* 'dishes and plates made of a single piece of metal.'] ■ a silver or gold dish or trophy awarded as a prize in a race or competition: *she lifted the plate in victory.* ■ [in *names*] *Brit.* a race or competition in which such a prize is awarded: *the final of the Ladies' Plate at Henley.* **2** a thin, flat sheet or strip of metal or other material, typically one used to join or strengthen things or forming part of a machine: *he underwent surgery to have a steel plate put into his leg.* ■ a small, flat piece of metal or other material bearing a name or inscription and attached to a door or other object: *a brass plate with her initials.* ■ (usu. **plates**) short for LICENSE PLATE: *the car had Vermont plates.* ■ *Botany & Zoology* a thin, flat organic structure or formation: *the fused bony plates protect the tortoise's soft parts.* ■ *Geology* each of the several rigid pieces of the earth's lithosphere that together make up the earth's surface. (See also PLATE TECTONICS.) ■ *Baseball* short for HOME PLATE. ■ a piece of lumber laid horizontally along the top of a wall to support the ends of joists or rafters. ■ a light horseshoe for a racehorse. **3** a sheet of metal, plastic, or some other material bearing an image of type or illustrations

P

from which multiple copies are printed. ■ a printed photograph, picture, or illustration, esp. one on superior-quality paper in a book. ■ a thin sheet of metal, glass, or other substance coated with a light-sensitive film on which an image is formed, used in larger or older types of cameras. **4** a thin piece of plastic molded to the shape of a person's mouth and gums, to which artificial teeth or another orthodontic appliance are attached. ■ *informal* a complete denture or orthodontic appliance. **5** a thin piece of metal that acts as an electrode in a capacitor, battery, or cell. ■ the anode of a thermionic tube.
▸*v.* [*trans.*] **1** cover (a metal object) with a thin coating or film of a different metal: *she had already taken the coin to a jeweler to be plated* | [as *adj.*, in *combination*] (**-plated**) *the cylinder is nickel-plated.* ■ cover (an object) with plates of metal for decoration, protection, or strength. **2** serve or arrange (food) on a plate or plates before a meal: *overcooked vegetables won't look appetizing, no matter how they are plated.* **3** *Baseball* score (a run or runs); cause (someone) to score. **4** *Biology* inoculate (cells or infective material) onto a culture plate, esp. with the object of isolating a particular strain of microorganisms or estimating viable cell numbers. ▷Middle English (denoting a flat, thin sheet, usually of metal): from Old French, from medieval Latin *plata* 'plate armor,' based on Greek *platus* 'flat.' Sense 1 represents Old French *plat* 'platter, large dish,' also 'dish of meat,' noun use of Old French *plat* 'flat.' **—plate·ful** /-ˌfo͝ol/ *n.* (*pl.* **-fuls**) **—plate·less** *adj.* **—plat·er** /ˈplātər/ *n.*
▸*PHRASE* □ **on one's plate** occupying one's time or energy: *you've* ***got a lot on your plate*** *at the moment.*

plate ap·pear·ance ▸*n.* *Baseball* a player's turn at the plate, the total of which for any player includes all official at bats plus appearances that resulted in a walk, sacrifice, etc. Compare with **AT BAT**.

plate ar·mor ▸*n.* protective armor of metal plates, esp. as worn in medieval times by mounted knights.

pla·teau /plaˈtō/ ▸*n.* (*pl.* **-teaus** or **-teaux** /-ˈtōz/) an area of relatively level high ground. ■ *figurative* a state of little or no change following a period of activity or progress: *the peace process had* ***reached a plateau.*** ■ [as *adj.*] denoting a group of American Indian peoples of the plateau country of western Canada and the U.S., including the Nez Percé.
▸*v.* (**-teaus, -teaued, -teau·ing**) [*intrans.*] reach a state of little or no change after a time of activity or progress: *the industry's problems have* ***plateaued out.*** ▷late 18th cent.: from French, from Old French *platel*, diminutive of *plat* 'level.'

plate glass ▸*n.* [often as *adj.*] (**plate-glass**) thick fine-quality glass, typically used for doors and store windows and originally cast in plates.

plate·let /ˈplāt-lit/ ▸*n.* *Physiology* a small colorless disk-shaped cell fragment without a nucleus, found in large numbers in blood and involved in clotting. Also called **THROMBOCYTE**.

plate·mak·er /ˈplātˌmākər/ ▸*n.* a person or machine that makes printing plates.

plat·en /ˈplatn/ ▸*n.* **1** the plate in a small letterpress printing press that presses the paper against the type. **2** the cylindrical roller in a typewriter against which the paper is held. ▷late 16th cent.: from French *platine* 'flat piece,' from *plat* 'flat.'

plat·er·esque /ˌplatəˈresk/ ▸*adj.* (esp. of Spanish architecture) richly ornamented in a low-relief style suggesting silver work. ▷late 19th cent.: from Spanish *plateresco*, from *platero* 'silversmith,' from *plata* 'silver.'

Plate Riv·er /plāt/ a wide estuary on the Atlantic coast of South America at the border between Argentina and Uruguay that is formed by the confluence of the Paraná and Uruguay rivers. The cities of Buenos Aires and Montevideo lie on its shores. In 1939, it was the scene of a naval battle in which the British defeated the Germans. Spanish name **Río de la Plata**. ▷*Plate* from Spanish *plata* 'silver,' exported from the region in the Spanish colonial period.

plate tec·ton·ics ▸*plural n.* [treated as *sing.*] a theory explaining the structure of the earth's crust and many associated phenomena as resulting from the interaction of rigid lithospheric plates that move slowly over the underlying mantle. **—plate-tec·ton·ic** *adj.*

plat·form /ˈplatfôrm/ ▸*n.* **1** a raised level surface on which people or things can stand: *there are viewing platforms where visitors may gape at the chasm.* ■ a raised floor or stage used by public speakers or performers so that they can be seen by their audience: *earning her living on the concert platform.* ■ a raised structure along the side of a railroad track where passengers get on and off trains at a station. ■ a raised structure standing in the sea from which oil or gas wells can be drilled or regulated. ■ [usu. with *adj.*] a raised structure or orbiting satellite from which rockets or missiles may be launched. ■ *Computing* a standard for the hardware of a computer system, determining what kinds of software it can run. **2** [usu. in *sing.*] the declared policy of a political party or group: *seeking election on a platform of low taxes.* ■ an opportunity to voice one's views or initiate action: *the forum will provide a platform for discussion of communication issues.* **3** (**platforms**) shoes with very thick soles: *chunky platforms* | [as *adj.*] *yellow platform shoes.* ▷mid 16th cent.: from French *plateforme* 'ground plan,' literally 'flat shape.'

plat·form bed ▸*n.* a bed consisting of a mattress supported by a platform, which sometimes contains drawers for storage.

plat·form game ▸*n.* a type of video game featuring two-dimensional graphics in which the player controls a character jumping or climbing between solid platforms at different positions on the screen.

Plath /plaTH/, Sylvia (1932–63), U.S. poet; wife of Ted Hughes. Her life was marked by periods of severe depression, and her work is notable for its treatment of extreme and painful states of mind. In 1963, she committed suicide. Notable works: *Ariel* (1965) and *The Bell Jar* (1963).

Sylvia Plath

plat·ing /ˈplātiNG/ ▸*n.* **1** a thin coating of gold, silver, or other metal. ■ the process of applying such a layer. **2** an outer covering of broad, flattish sections, typically of metal: *the tractors carried steel plating for protection.* **3** the process of knitting two yarns together so that each yarn appears mainly on one side of the finished piece.

plat·i·nize /ˈplatnˌīz/ ▸*v.* [*trans.*] [usu. as *adj.*] (**platinized**) coat (something) with platinum. **—plat·i·ni·za·tion** /ˌplatn-iˈzāSHən/ *n.*

plat·i·noid /ˈplatnˌoid/ ▸*n.* an alloy of copper with zinc, nickel, and sometimes tungsten, used for its high electrical resistance.

plat·i·num /ˈplatn-əm/ ▸*n.* a precious silvery-white metal, the chemical element of atomic number 78. It was first encountered by the Spanish in South America in the 16th century and is used in jewelry, electrical contacts, laboratory equipment, and industrial catalysts. (Symbol: **Pt**) ■ the grayish-white or silvery color of platinum.
▸*adj.* **1** of a platinum color: *a platinum wig.* **2** (of a recording) having sold enough copies to merit a platinum disk. ▷early 19th cent.: alteration of earlier *platina*, from Spanish, diminutive of *plata* 'silver.'
▸*PHRASE* □ **go platinum** (of a recording) achieve sales meriting a platinum disk.

plat·i·num black ▸*n.* platinum in the form of a finely divided black powder, used as a catalyst and absorbent for gases.

plat·i·num blonde ▸*n.* a woman with silvery-blond hair.
▸*adj.* (of a woman's hair) silvery blond.

plat·i·num card ▸*n.* a credit card made available to individuals with high credit ratings, which carries certain privileges that are unavailable to holders of other cards.

plat·i·num disk ▸*n.* a framed disk of platinum awarded to a recording artist or group for sales of a recording exceeding one million copies (for albums) or two million copies (for singles).

plat·i·num met·als ▸*plural n.* *Chemistry* the six metals platinum, palladium, ruthenium, osmium, rhodium, and iridium, which have similar properties and tend to occur together in nature.

plat·i·tude /ˈplatiˌt(y)o͞od/ ▸*n.* a remark or statement, esp. one with a moral content, that has been used too often to be interesting or thoughtful: *she began uttering liberal platitudes.* ■ the quality of being dull, ordinary, or trite: *educators willing to violate the bounds of platitude.* ▷early 19th cent.: from French, from *plat* 'flat.' **—plat·i·tu·di·nize** /ˌplatiˈt(y)o͞odnˌīz/ *v.* **—plat·i·tu·di·nous** /ˌplatiˈt(y)o͞odn-əs/ *adj.*

Pla·to /ˈplātō/ (*c.*429–*c.*347 BC), Greek philosopher. A disciple of Socrates and the teacher of Aristotle, he founded the Academy in Athens. His theory of "ideas" or "forms" contrasts abstract entities or **universals** with their objects or **particulars** in the material world. His philosophical writings are presented in the form of dialogues, and his political theories appear in the *Republic*.

Pla·ton·ic /pləˈtänik/ ▸*adj.* of or associated with the Greek philosopher Plato or his ideas. ■ (**platonic**) (of love or friendship) intimate and affectionate but not sexual: *their relationship is purely platonic.* ■ (**platonic**) confined to words, theories, or ideals, and not leading to practical action. ▷mid 16th cent.: via Latin from Greek *Platōnikos*, from *Platōn* 'Plato.' **—pla·ton·i·cal·ly** /-(ə)lē/ *adv.*

Pla·ton·ic sol·id ▸*n.* one of five regular solids (a tetrahedron, cube, octahedron, dodecahedron, or icosahedron).

Pla·to·nism /ˈplātnˌizəm/ ▸*n.* the philosophy of Plato or his followers. See **PLATO**. ■ any of various revivals of Platonic doctrines or related ideas, esp. Neoplatonism and Cambridge Platonism (a 17th-century attempt to reconcile Christianity with humanism and science). ■ the theory that numbers or other abstract objects are objective, timeless entities, independent of the physical world and of the symbols used to represent them. **—Pla·to·nist** *n.*

pla·toon /pləˈto͞on/ ▸*n.* a subdivision of a company of soldiers, usually forming a tactical unit that is commanded by a lieutenant and divided into several sections. ■ a group of people acting together: *platoons of sharp lawyers.* ■ (in baseball and other sports) a pairing of two or more teammates who play the same position at different times: *in 1982 the Orioles employed a productive left-field platoon of Lowenstein, Ayala, and Roenicke.*
▸*v.* [*trans.*] (in baseball and other sports) have (an athlete) play in rotation with one or more teammates at the same position: *he was underrated because of Stengel's platooning him with Woodling.* ■ [*intrans.*] play a sport in this way: *Polonia mostly platooned in his three years with the A's.* ▷mid 17th cent.: from French *peloton* 'platoon,' literally 'small ball,' diminutive of *pelote*.

pla·toon ser·geant ▸*n.* a noncommissioned officer in the U.S. Army intermediate in rank between a staff sergeant and a first sergeant.

Platt·deutsch /ˈplätˌdoiCH/ ▸*n.* & *adj.* another term for **Low German**. ▷German, from Dutch *Platduits*, from *plat* 'flat, low' + *Duits* 'German.'

plat·ter /ˈplatər/ ▸*n.* **1** a large flat dish or plate, typically oval or circular in shape, used for serving food. ■ a quantity of food served on such a dish: *huge* ***platters of*** *cold cuts.* ■ a meal or selection of food placed on a platter, esp. one served in a restaurant: *I'll have the seafood platter.* **2** something shaped like such a dish or plate, esp. of a circular shape, in particular: ■ *informal, dated* a phonograph record. ■ the rotating metal disk forming the turntable of a record player. ■ *Computing* a rigid rotating disk on which data is stored in a disk drive; a hard disk (considered as a physical object). ▷Middle English: from Anglo-Norman French *plater*, from *plat* 'large dish' (see **PLATE**).
▸*PHRASE* □ **on a (silver) platter** *informal* used to indicate that someone receives or achieves something with little or no effort: *you're being offered this opportunity on a silver platter.*

Platte Riv·er /ˈplat/ a river in southwestern Nebraska that is formed by the North Platte and South Platte rivers and flows for 310 miles (500 km) to join the Missouri River near Omaha.

Platts·burgh /ˈplatsˌbərg/ a city in northeastern New York, on Lake Champlain, the site of battles during the 18th and 19th centuries; pop. 21,255.

platy- ▸*comb. form* broad; flat: *platypus.* ▷from Greek *platus* 'broad, flat.'

plat·y·fish /ˈplatēˌfiSH/ ▸*n.* (*pl.* same or **-fish·es**) a small livebearing freshwater fish of Mexico and Central America, popular in aquariums. • Genus *Xiphophorus*, family Poeciliidae: several species, in particular

X. maculatus, which has been bred in a wide variety of colors. ▷early 20th cent.: colloquial abbreviation of modern Latin *Platypoecilus* (former genus name), from Greek *platus* 'broad' + *poikilos* 'variegated.'

Plat·y·hel·min·thes /ˌplatēhelˈminTHēz/ *Zoology* a phylum of invertebrates that comprises the flatworms. ▷modern Latin (plural), from **PLATY-** 'flat' + Greek *helminth* 'worm.' —**plat·y·hel·minth** /-ˈhelminTH/ *n.*

plat·y·kur·tic /ˌplatiˈkərtik/ ▸*n. Statistics* (of a frequency distribution or its graphical representation) having less kurtosis than the normal distribution. Compare with **LEPTOKURTIC, MESOKURTIC** ▷early 20th cent.: from **PLATY-** 'broad, flat' + Greek *kurtos* 'bulging' + **-IC.** —**plat·y·kur·to·sis** /-ikərˈtōsis/ *n.*

plat·y·pus /ˈplatəpəs; -ˌpo͝os/ ▸*n.* (*pl.* **-pus·es**) a semiaquatic egg-laying mammal that frequents lakes and streams in eastern Australia. It has a sensitive pliable bill shaped like that of a duck, webbed feet with venomous spurs, and dense fur. Also called **DUCKBILL, DUCKBILL PLATYPUS,** or **DUCK-BILLED PLATYPUS.** • *Ornithorhynchus anatinus*, the only member of the family Ornithorhynchidae, order Monotremata. ▷late 18th cent.: modern Latin, from Greek *platupous* 'flatfooted,' from *platus* 'flat' + *pous* 'foot.'

platypus

plat·yr·rhine /ˈplatəˌrīn; -rin/ *Zoology* ▸*adj.* of or relating to primates of a group that comprises the New World monkeys, marmosets, and tamarins. They are distinguished by having nostrils that are far apart and directed forward or sideways, and typically have a prehensile tail. Compare with **CATARRHINE.** ▸*n.* a platyrrhine primate. • Infraorder Platyrrhini, order Primates: families Cebidae and Callitrichidae. ▷mid 19th cent.: from **PLATY-** 'flat' + Greek *rhis, rhin-* 'nose' + **-INE**1.

pla·tys·ma /pləˈtizmə/ ▸*n.* (*pl.* **-mas** or **-ma·ta** /-mətə/) *Anatomy* a broad sheet of muscle fibers extending from the collarbone to the angle of the jaw. ▷late 17th cent.: modern Latin, from Greek *platusma* 'flat piece, plate.'

plau·dits /ˈplôdits/ ▸*plural n.* praise: *the network has received plaudits for its sports coverage.* ■ the applause of an audience: *the plaudits for the winner died down.* ▷early 17th cent.: *plaudit* shortened from Latin *plaudite* 'applaud!' (said by Roman actors at the end of a play), imperative plural of *plaudere.*

plau·si·ble /ˈplôzəbəl/ ▸*adj.* (of an argument or statement) seeming reasonable or probable: *a plausible explanation* | *it seems plausible that one of two things may happen.* See note at **BELIEVABLE.** ■ (of a person) skilled at producing persuasive arguments, esp. ones intended to deceive: *a plausible liar.* ▷mid 16th cent. (also in the sense 'deserving applause or approval'): from Latin *plausibilis*, from *plaus-* 'applauded,' from the verb *plaudere.* —**plau·si·bil·i·ty** /ˌplôzəˈbilitē/ *n.* —**plau·si·bly** /-əblē/ *adv.*

Plau·tus /ˈplôtəs/, Titus Maccius (*c.*250–184 BC), Roman comic playwright. Fantasy and imagination are more important than realism in the development of his plots, and his stock characters are often larger than life.

play /plā/ ▸*v.* **1** [*intrans.*] engage in activity for enjoyment and recreation rather than a serious or practical purpose: *the children were playing outside* | *her friends were **playing with** their dolls.* ■ [*trans.*] engage in (a game or activity) for enjoyment: *I want to play Monopoly.* ■ amuse oneself by engaging in imaginative pretense: *the boys were playing cops and robbers.* ■ (**play at**) engage in without proper seriousness or understanding: *you cannot play at being a Christian.* ■ (**play with**) treat inconsiderately for one's own amusement: *she likes to play with people's emotions.* ■ (**play with**) handle without skill so as to damage or prevent from working: *has somebody been playing with the thermostat?* **2** [*trans.*] take part in (a sport) on a regular basis: *I play softball and tennis.* ■ participate in (an athletic match or contest): *the Red Sox will play two games on Wednesday.* ■ compete against (another player or team) in an athletic match or contest: *the team will play France on Wednesday.* ■ [*intrans.*] [usu. with *negative*] *figurative* be cooperative: *he needs financial backing, but the bank won't play.* ■ [*intrans.*] be part of a team, esp. in a specified position, in a game: *he played shortstop.* ■ strike (a ball) or execute (a stroke) in a game. ■ assign to take part in an athletic contest, esp. in a specified position: *the manager will want to play the right-handed Curtis.* ■ move (a piece) or display (a playing card) in one's turn in a game: *he played his queen.* ■ bet or gamble at or on: *he didn't play the ponies.* **3** [*trans.*] represent (a character) in a theatrical performance or on film: *she played Ophelia.* ■ [*intrans.*] perform in a theatrical production or on film: *he was proud to be playing opposite a famous actor.* ■ put on or take part in (a theatrical performance or concert): *the show was one of the best we ever played.* ■ give a dramatic performance at (a particular theater or place). ■ behave as though one were (a specified type of person): *the skipper played the innocent, but smuggled goods were found on his vessel.* ■ (**play someone for**) treat someone as being of (a specified type): *don't imagine you can play me for a fool.* ■ (**play a trick/joke on**) behave in a deceptive or teasing way toward. **4** [*trans.*] perform on (a musical instrument): *we heard someone playing a harmonica* | [*intrans.*] *a pianist who will play for us.* ■ possess the skill of performing upon (a musical instrument): *he taught himself to play the violin.* ■ produce (notes) from a musical instrument; perform (a piece of music): *they played a violin sonata.* ■ make (an audiotape, CD, radio, etc.) produce sounds. ■ [*intrans.*] (of a musical instrument, audiotape, CD, radio, etc.) produce sounds: *somewhere within, a harp was playing.* ■ [*trans.*] accompany (someone) with music as they are moving in a specified direction: *the bagpipes played them out of the dining room.* **5** [*intrans.*] move lightly and quickly, so as to appear and disappear; flicker: *a smile played about her lips.* ■ (of a fountain or similar source of water) emit a stream of gently moving water. **6** [*trans.*] allow (a fish) to exhaust itself pulling against a line before reeling it in.

▸*phrasal v.* □ **play around** (or **about**) behave in a casual, foolish, or irresponsible way: *you shouldn't **play around with** a child's future.* ■ *informal* (of a married person) have a love affair. □ **play along** pretend to cooperate: *she had to play along and be polite.* □ **play someone along** *informal* deceive or mislead someone over a period of time. □ **play something back** play sounds that one has recently recorded, esp. to monitor recording quality. □ **play something down** represent something as being less important than it in fact is: *he tried to play down the seriousness of his illness.* □ **play someone off** bring people into conflict or competition for one's own advantage: *China can no longer **play** one superpower **off against** the other.* □ **play off** (of two teams or competitors) play an extra game or match to decide a draw or tie. □ **play on** exploit (a weak or vulnerable point in someone): *he played on his opponent's nerves.* □ **play someone out** (usu. **be played out**) drain someone of strength or life. □ **play something out** act the whole of a drama; enact a scene or role. □ **play something up** emphasize the extent or importance of something: *the mystery surrounding his death was played up by the media.* □ **play up to** humor or flatter, esp. to win favor.

▸*n.* **1** activity engaged in for enjoyment and recreation, esp. by children: *a child **at play** may use a stick as an airplane.* ■ behavior or speech that is not intended seriously: *I flinched, but only **in play**.* ■ [as *adj.*] designed to be used in games of pretense; not real: *play families are arranged in play houses.* **2** the conducting of an athletic match or contest: *rain interrupted the second day's play.* ■ the action or manner of engaging in a sport or game: *he maintained the same rhythm of play throughout the game.* ■ the status of the ball in a game as being available to be played according to the rules: *the ball was put in play.* ■ *figurative* the state of being active, operative, or effective: *luck **comes into play**.* ■ a move or maneuver in a sport or game: *the best play is to lead the 3 of clubs.* ■ *archaic* gambling. **3** a dramatic work for the stage or to be broadcast: *the actors put on a new play.* **4** the space in or through which a mechanism can or does move: *the steering rack was loose, and there was a little play.* ■ *figurative* scope or freedom to act or operate: *our policy allows the market to have freer play.* ■ light and constantly changing movement: *the artist exploits the play of light across the surface.* ▷Old English *pleg(i)an* 'to exercise,' *plega* 'brisk movement,' related to Middle Dutch *pleien* 'leap for joy, dance.' —**play·a·bil·i·ty** /ˌplāəˈbilitē/ *n.* —**play·a·ble** *adj.*

▸*PHRASES* □ **make a play for** *informal* attempt to attract or attain. □ **make** (**great**) **play of** (or **with**) draw attention to in an ostentatious manner, typically to gain prestige or advantage: *the company made great play of its recent growth in profits.* □ **not playing with a full deck** see **DECK.** □ **play ball** see **BALL**1. □ **play both ends against the middle** keep one's options open by supporting or favoring opposing sides. □ **play something by ear** perform music without having to read from a score. ■ (**play it by ear**) *informal* proceed instinctively according to results and circumstances rather than according to rules or a plan. □ **play by the rules** follow what is generally held to be the correct line of behavior. □ **play one's cards close to one's chest** see **CHEST.** □ **play one's cards right** (or **well**) see **CARD**1. □ **play ducks and drakes with** see **DUCKS AND DRAKES.** □ **play fair** observe principles of justice; avoid cheating. □ **play someone false** prove treacherous or deceitful toward someone. □ **play fast and loose** behave irresponsibly or immorally. □ **play favorites** show favoritism toward someone or something. □ **play the field** see **FIELD.** □ **play for time** use specious excuses or unnecessary maneuvers to gain time. □ **play the game** see **GAME**1. □ **play God** see **GOD.** □ **play havoc with** see **HAVOC.** □ **play hell** see **HELL.** □ **play hookey** see **HOOKEY.** □ **play a** (or **one's**) **hunch** make an instinctive choice. □ **play into someone's hands** act in such a way as unintentionally to give someone an advantage. □ **play it cool** *informal* make an effort to be or appear to be calm and unemotional. □ **play the market** speculate in stocks. □ **a play on words** a pun. □ **play** (or **play it**) **safe** take precautions; avoid risks. □ **play to the gallery** see **GALLERY.** □ **play truant** see **TRUANT.** □ **play with oneself** *informal* masturbate. □ **play with fire** take foolish risks.

P

pla·ya /ˈplīə/ ▸*n.* an area of flat, dried-up land, esp. a desert basin from which water evaporates quickly. ▷mid 19th cent.: from Spanish, literally 'beach,' from late Latin *plagia.*

play·act /ˈplāˌakt/ ▸*v.* [*intrans.*] act in a play. ■ [*trans.*] act (a scene, role, etc.). ■ [usu. as *n.*] (**playacting**) engage in histrionic pretense: *the defender indulged in some playacting after tumbling to the ground.* —**play·ac·tor** *n.*

play·back /ˈplāˌbak/ ▸*n.* the reproduction of previously recorded sounds or moving images.

play·bill /ˈplāˌbil/ ▸*n.* a poster announcing a theatrical performance. ■ a theater program.

play·boy /ˈplāˌboi/ ▸*n.* a wealthy man who spends his time enjoying himself, esp. one who behaves irresponsibly or is sexually promiscuous.

play-by-play ▸*n.* a detailed running commentary on an athletic contest: *he provided play-by-play as well as interviews* | [as *adj.*] *the play-by-play announcer.*

play date ▸*n.* a date and time set by parents for children to play together.

Play·er /ˈplāər/, Gary (1936–), South African golfer. He won numerous championships including the Masters (1961, 1974, 1978), the PGA (1962, 1972), the U.S. Open (1965), and the British Open (1959, 1968, 1974).

play·er /ˈplāər/ ▸*n.* **1** a person taking part in a sport or game: *a tennis player.* ■ a person or body that is involved and influential in an area or activity: *the country's isolationism made it a secondary player in world political events.* **2** a person who plays a musical instrument: *a guitar player.* ■ a device for playing compact discs, audiocassettes, etc. **3** an actor.

play·er pi·an·o ▸*n.* a piano fitted with an apparatus enabling it to be played automatically.

play·fel·low /ˈplāˌfelō/ ▸*n.* a playmate.

play·ful /ˈplāfəl/ ▸*adj.* fond of games and amusement; lighthearted: *a playful tomboy who loves to dress up.* ■ intended for one's own or others' amusement rather than seriously: *he gave me a playful punch on the arm.* ■ giving or expressing pleasure and amusement: *the ballet accents the playful use of movement.* —**play·ful·ly** *adv.* —**play·ful·ness** *n.*

play·go·er /ˈplāˌgōər/ ▸*n.* a person who goes to the theater, esp. regularly.

play·ground /ˈplāˌground/ ▸*n.* an outdoor area provided for children to play on, esp. at a school or public park. ■ a place where a particular group of people choose to enjoy themselves: *the mountains are **a playground for** hang gliders.*

play group ▸*n.* a regular meeting of a group of preschool children, organized by parents for their children to take part in supervised creative and social play.

play·house /ˈplāˌhous/ ▸*n.* **1** a theater. **2** a toy house for children to play in.

play·ing card ▸*n.* each of a set of rectangular pieces of cardboard or other material with an identical pattern on one side and different numbers and symbols on the other, used to play various games, some involving gambling. A standard deck contains 52 cards divided into four suits.

play·ing field ▸*n.* a field used for outdoor team games.

▸*PHRASE* □ **a level playing field** see LEVEL.

play·let /'plālit/ ▸*n.* a short play or dramatic piece.

play·list /'plā,list/ ▸*n.* a list of recorded songs or pieces of music chosen to be broadcast on a radio show or by a particular radio station.

play·mak·er /'plā,mākər/ ▸*n.* a player in a team game who leads attacks or brings other players on the same side into a position from which they could score. —**play·mak·ing** /-mākiNG/ *n.*

play·mate /'plā,māt/ ▸*n.* **1** a friend with whom a child plays. **2** used euphemistically to refer to a person's lover.

play·off /'plā,ôf/ ▸*n.* an additional game or period of play that decides the outcome of a tied contest: *a sudden-death playoff was required to settle the tournament.* ■ (**playoffs**) a series of contests played to determine the winner of a championship, as between the leading teams in different divisions or leagues: *Chandler was credited with taking his team to the playoffs.*

play·pen /'plā,pen/ ▸*n.* a small portable enclosure in which a baby or small child can play safely.

play·room /'plā,ro͞om; -,ro͝om/ ▸*n.* a room in a house that is set aside for children to play in.

play·scape /'plā,skāp/ ▸*n.* a designed and integrated set of playground equipment, often made of wood.

play·suit /'plā,so͞ot/ ▸*n.* an all-in-one stretchy garment for a baby or very young child, covering the body, arms, and legs.

play ther·a·py ▸*n.* therapy in which emotionally disturbed children are encouraged to act out their fantasies and express their feelings through play, aided by a therapist's interpretations. —**play ther·a·pist** *n.*

play·thing /'plā,THiNG/ ▸*n.* a toy. ■ *figurative* a person treated as amusing but unimportant by someone else: *she was the mistress and plaything of a wealthy businessman.*

play·time /'plā,tīm/ ▸*n.* time for play or recreation.

play·wright /'plā,rīt/ ▸*n.* a person who writes plays.

play·writ·ing /'plā,rītiNG/ ▸*n.* the activity or process of writing plays.

pla·za /'plazə; 'pläzə/ ▸*n.* **1** a public square, marketplace, or similar open space in a built-up area. **2** a shopping center. ■ a service area on a highway, typically with a gas station and restaurants. ▷late 17th cent.: from Spanish, literally 'place.'

plc (also **PLC**) *Brit.* ▸*abbr.* public limited company.

plea /plē/ ▸*n.* **1** a request made in an urgent and emotional manner: *he made a dramatic plea for disarmament.* ■ a claim that a circumstance means that one should not be blamed for or should not be forced to do something: *her plea of a headache was not entirely false.* **2** *Law* a formal statement by or on behalf of a defendant or prisoner, stating guilt or innocence in response to a charge, offering an allegation of fact, or claiming that a point of law should apply: *he changed his plea to not guilty.* ▷Middle English (in the sense 'lawsuit'): from Old French *plait, plaid* 'agreement, discussion,' from Latin *placitum* 'a decree,' neuter past participle of *placere* 'to please.'

plea bar·gain·ing ▸*n.* *Law* an arrangement between a prosecutor and a defendant whereby the defendant pleads guilty to a lesser charge in the expectation of leniency. —**plea-bar·gain** *v.* —**plea bar·gain** *n.*

pleach /plēCH/ ▸*v.* [*trans.*] [usu. as *adj.*] (**pleached**) entwine or interlace (tree branches) to form a hedge or provide cover for an outdoor walkway: *an avenue of pleached limes.* ▷late Middle English: from an Old French variant of *plaissier* (see PLASH[2]).

plead /plēd/ ▸*v.* (*past* **plead·ed** or **pled** /pled/) **1** [*reporting verb*] make an emotional appeal: [*intrans.*] *they* **pleaded with** *Carol to come home again* | [with *direct speech*] *"Don't go," she pleaded* | [with *infinitive*] *Anne pleaded to go with her.* See note at BEG. **2** [*trans.*] present and argue for (a position), esp. in court or in another public context: *using cheap melodrama to plead the case for three prisoners.* ■ [*intrans.*] *Law* address a court as an advocate on behalf of a party. ■ [*intrans.*] *Law* state formally in court whether one is guilty or not guilty of the offense with which one is charged: *he pleaded guilty to the drug charge.* ■ *Law* invoke (a reason or a point of law) as an accusation or defense: *on trial for attempted murder, she pleaded self-defense.* ■ offer or present as an excuse for doing or not doing something: *he pleaded family commitments as a reason for not attending.* ▷Middle English (in the sense 'to wrangle'): from Old French *plaidier* 'resort to legal action,' from *plaid* 'discussion' (see PLEA). —**plead·er** *n.* —**plead·ing·ly** *adv.*

USAGE In a court of law, a person can **plead guilty** or **plead not guilty**. The phrase **plead innocent**, although commonly found in general use, is not a technical legal term. Note that one *pleads guilty to* (not *of*) an offense, and may be *found guilty of* an offense.

See also **usage** at INNOCENT.

plead·a·ble /'plēdəbəl/ ▸*adj.* *Law* able to be offered as a formal plea in court.

plead·ing /'plēdiNG/ ▸*n.* **1** the action of making an emotional or earnest appeal to someone: *he ignored her pleading.* **2** (usu. **pleadings**) *Law* a formal statement of the cause of an action or defense.

pleas·ance /'plezəns/ ▸*n.* a secluded enclosure or part of a garden, esp. one attached to a large house. ▷Middle English (in the sense 'pleasure'): from Old French *plaisance*, from *plaisant* 'pleasing' (see PLEASANT).

pleas·ant /'plezənt/ ▸*adj.* (**pleas·ant·er, pleas·ant·est**) giving a sense of happy satisfaction or enjoyment: *a very pleasant evening* | *what a pleasant surprise!* ■ (of a person or their manner) friendly and considerate; likable: *they found him pleasant and cooperative.* ▷Middle English (in the sense 'pleasing'): from Old French *plaisant* 'pleasing,' from the verb *plaisir* (see PLEASE). —**pleas·ant·ly** *adv.* —**pleas·ant·ness** *n.*

THE RIGHT WORD **agreeable, attractive, congenial, enjoyable, gratifying, pleasant, pleasing**

One might have a **pleasant** smile and a **pleasing** personality, since the former suggests something that is naturally appealing while the latter suggests a conscious attempt to please.

Something that is **enjoyable** is able to give enjoyment or pleasure (*a thoroughly enjoyable evening*), while **agreeable** describes something that is in harmony with one's personal mood or wishes (*an agreeable afternoon spent relaxing in the sun*).

Gratifying is more intense, suggesting that deeper expectations or needs have been met (*the awards ceremony was particularly gratifying for parents*).

Something that is **attractive** gives pleasure because of its appearance or manner (*an attractive house in a wooded setting*), while **congenial** has more to do with compatibility (*a congenial couple*).

Pleas·an·ton /'plesəntən/ a city in north central California, southeast of Oakland; pop. 50,553.

pleas·ant·ry /'plezəntrē/ ▸*n.* (*pl.* **-ries**) (usu. **pleasantries**) an inconsequential remark made as part of a polite conversation: *after an exchange of pleasantries, I proceeded to outline a plan.* ■ a mild joke: *he laughed at his own pleasantry.* ▷late 16th cent.: from French *plaisanterie*, from Old French *plaisant* 'pleasing' (see PLEASANT).

please /plēz/ ▸*v.* [*trans.*] **1** cause to feel happy and satisfied: *he arranged a fishing trip to please his son* | [*trans.*] *it* **pleased** *him to be seen with someone in the news.* ■ [*intrans.*] give satisfaction: *she was quiet and eager to please.* ■ satisfy aesthetically: [as *adj.*] (**pleasing**) *the pleasing austerity of the surroundings.* **2** (**please oneself**) take only one's own wishes into consideration in deciding how to act or proceed: *this is the first time in ages that I can just please myself.* ■ [*intrans.*] wish or desire to do something: *feel free to wander around* **as you please**. ■ (**it pleases, pleased,** etc., **someone to do something**) *dated* it is someone's choice to do something: *instead of attending the meeting, it pleased him to go off hunting.*

▸*adv.* used in polite requests or questions: *please address letters to the Editor* | *what type of fish is this, please?* ■ used to add urgency and emotion to a request: *please, please come home!* ■ used to agree politely to a request: *"May I call you at home?" "Please do."* ■ used in polite or emphatic acceptance of an offer: *"Would you like a drink?" "Yes, please."* ■ used to ask someone to stop doing something of which the speaker disapproves: *Rita, please—people are looking.* ■ used to express incredulity or irritation: *You cleaned out the barn in only two hours? Oh, please!* ▷Middle English: from Old French *plaisir* 'to please,' from Latin *placere*. —**pleas·er** *n.* —**pleas·ing·ly** /'plēziNGlē/ *adv.*

▸*PHRASES* □ **as —— as you please** *informal* used to emphasize the manner in which someone does something, esp. when this is seen as surprising: *she walked forward as calm as you please.* □ **if you please** **1** used in polite requests: *follow me, if you please.* **2** used to express indignation at something perceived as unreasonable: *she wants me to make fifty cakes in time for the festival, if you please!*

pleased /plēzd/ ▸*adj.* feeling or showing pleasure and satisfaction, esp. at an event or a situation: *both girls were* **pleased with** *their new hairstyles* | *he seemed really* **pleased that** *she was there* | *a pleased smile.* ■ [with *infinitive*] willing or glad to do something: *we will be pleased to provide an independent appraisal.* ■ (**pleased with oneself**) proud of one's achievements, esp. excessively so; self-satisfied: *as he led the way, he looked very pleased with himself.*

▸*PHRASES* □ **(as) pleased as Punch** see PUNCH[4]. □ **pleased to meet you** said on being introduced to someone: *"This is my wife." "Pleased to meet you."*

pleas·ur·a·ble /'plezHərəbəl/ ▸*adj.* pleasing; enjoyable. ▷late 16th cent.: from PLEASURE, on the pattern of *comfortable*. —**pleas·ur·a·ble·ness** *n.* —**pleas·ur·a·bly** /-blē/ *adv.*

pleas·ure /'plezHər/ ▸*n.* a feeling of happy satisfaction and enjoyment: *she smiled with pleasure at being praised.* ■ enjoyment and entertainment, contrasted with things done out of necessity: *she had not traveled for pleasure for a long time.* ■ an event or activity from which one derives enjoyment: *the car makes driving in the city a pleasure.* ■ sensual gratification.

▸*adj.* [*attrib.*] used or intended for entertainment rather than business: *pleasure boats.*

▸*v.* [*trans.*] give sexual enjoyment or satisfaction to: *tell me what will pleasure you.* ■ [*intrans.*] (**pleasure in**) derive enjoyment from: *risky verbal exchanges that the pair might pleasure in.* ▷late Middle English: from Old French *plaisir* 'to please' (used as a noun). The second syllable was altered under the influence of abstract nouns ending in *-ure*, such as *measure*.

▸*PHRASES* □ **at someone's pleasure** as and when someone wishes: *the landlord could terminate the agreement at his pleasure.* □ **have the pleasure of something** used in formal requests and descriptions: *he asked if he might have the pleasure of taking her to lunch.* □ **my pleasure** used as a polite reply to thanks: *"Oh, thank you!" "My pleasure."* □ **take pleasure in** derive happiness or enjoyment from: *they take a perverse pleasure in causing trouble.* □ **what's your pleasure?** what would you like? (used esp. when offering someone a choice): *"What's your pleasure?" "A cappuccino, please."* □ **with pleasure** gladly (used to express polite agreement or acceptance).

pleas·ure prin·ci·ple ▸*n.* *Psychoanalysis* the instinctive drive to seek pleasure and avoid pain, expressed by the id as a basic motivating force that reduces psychic tension.

pleat /plēt/ ▸*n.* a double or multiple fold in a garment or other item made of cloth, held by stitching the top or side.

▸*v.* [*trans.*] fold into pleats: *she was absently pleating her skirt between her fingers* | [as *adj.*] (**pleated**) *a short pleated skirt.* ▷late Middle English: a variant of PLAIT. The written form of the word became obsolete between *c.*1700 and the end of the 19th cent. —**pleat·er** *n.*

pleath·er /'pleTHər/ ▸*n.* imitation leather made from polyurethane. ▷1980s: blend of *polyurethane* and *leather*.

pleb /pleb/ ▸*n.* (usu. **plebs**) *derogatory* an ordinary person, esp. one from the lower social classes. ▷mid 17th cent.: originally plural, from Latin *plebs*. Later a shortened form of PLEBEIAN. —**pleb·by** /'plebē/ *adj.*

plebe /plēb/ ▸*n.* *informal* a newly entered cadet or freshman, esp. at a military academy. ▷early 17th cent.: perhaps an abbreviation of PLEBEIAN.

ple·be·ian /pli'bēən/ ▸*n.* (in ancient Rome) a commoner. ■ a member of the lower social classes.

▸*adj.* of or belonging to the commoners of ancient Rome. ■ of or belonging to the lower social classes. ■ lacking in refinement: *he is a man of plebeian tastes.* ▷mid 16th cent.: from Latin *plebeius* (from *plebs, pleb-* 'the common people') + -AN.

pleb·i·scite /'plebə,sīt/ ▸*n.* the direct vote of all the members of an electorate on an important public question such as a change in the constitution. ■ *Roman History* a law enacted by the plebeians' assembly. ▷mid 16th cent. (referring to Roman history): from French *plébiscite*, from Latin *plebiscitum*, from *plebs, pleb-* 'the common people' + *scitum* 'decree' (from *sciscere* 'vote for'). The sense 'direct vote of the whole electorate' dates from the mid 19th cent. —**ple·bis·ci·tar·y** /plə'bisi,terē/ *adj.*

Ple·cop·ter·a /plə'käptərə/ *Entomology* an order of insects that comprises the stoneflies. ■ [as *plural n.*] (**plecoptera**) insects of this order; stoneflies. ▷modern Latin (plural), from Greek *plekos* 'wickerwork' (from *plekein* 'to plait') + *pteron* 'wing.' —**ple·cop·ter·an** /-tərən/ *n.* & *adj.*

plec·trum /'plektrəm/ ▸*n.* (*pl.* **-trums** or **-tra** /-trə/) a thin flat piece of plastic, tortoiseshell, or other slightly flexible material held by or worn on the fingers and used to pluck the strings of a musical instrument such as a guitar. ■ the corresponding mechanical part that plucks the strings of an instrument such as a harpsichord. ▷late Middle English: via Latin from Greek *plēktron* 'something with which to strike,' from *plēssein* 'to strike.'

pled /pled/ ▶ past and past participle of **PLEAD**.

pledge /plej/ ▶*n.* **1** a solemn promise or undertaking: [with *infinitive*] *the conference ended with a joint pledge to limit pollution.* ■ a promise of a donation to charity: *the company's pledge of 10% of profits to environmental concerns.* ■ (**the pledge**) a solemn undertaking to abstain from alcohol: *she persuaded Arthur to* ***take the pledge.*** **2** *Law* a thing that is given as security for the fulfillment of a contract or the payment of a debt and is liable to forfeiture in the event of failure. ■ a thing given as a token of love, favor, or loyalty. **3** a person who has promised to join a fraternity or sorority. **4** *archaic* the drinking to a person's health; a toast.

▶*v.* **1** [*trans.*] commit (a person or organization) by a solemn promise: *the government pledged itself to deal with environmental problems.* ■ [with *clause*] formally declare or promise that something is or will be the case: *the president pledged that 20,000 government buildings would have solar roofs.* ■ [*intrans.*] solemnly undertake to do something: *they pledged to continue the campaign for funding.* ■ [*trans.*] undertake formally to give: *Japan pledged $100 million in humanitarian aid* | *to pledge allegiance.* **2** [*trans.*] *Law* give as security on a loan: *the creditor to whom the land is pledged.* **3** [*trans.*] promise to join (a fraternity or sorority): *Francie and I pledged the same sorority.* **4** [*trans.*] *archaic* drink to the health of. ▷Middle English (denoting a person acting as surety for another): from Old French *plege*, from medieval Latin *plevium*, perhaps related to the Germanic base of **PLIGHT**[1]. —**pledg·er** *n.* —**pledg·or** /'plejər/ *n.* (*Law*).

▶*PHRASE* □ **pledge one's troth** see **TROTH**.

pledg·ee /ple'jē/ ▶*n.* a person to whom a pledge is given.

Pledge of Al·le·giance a solemn oath of loyalty to the U.S., declaimed as part of flag-saluting ceremonies.

pledg·et /'plejit/ ▶*n.* a small wad of absorbent cotton or other soft material used to stop up a wound or other opening in the body. ▷mid 16th cent.: of unknown origin.

ple·iad /'plēəd/ ▶*n. poetic/literary* an outstanding group of seven people or things. ▷early 17th cent.: from **PLEIADES**.

Ple·ia·des /'plēədēz/ **1** *Greek Mythology* the seven daughters of the Titan Atlas and the Oceanid Pleione. They were pursued by the hunter Orion until Zeus changed them into a cluster of stars. **2** *Astronomy* a well-known open cluster of stars in the constellation Taurus. Six (or more) stars are visible to the naked eye but there are actually some five hundred in the cluster, formed very recently in stellar terms. Also called **SEVEN SISTERS**. ▷via Latin from Greek.

plein-air /'plān 'e(ə)r/ ▶*adj.* [*attrib.*] denoting or in the manner of a 19th-century style of painting outdoors, or with a strong sense of the open air, that became a central feature of French Impressionism. ▷from French *en plein air* 'in the open air.'

plei·ot·ro·py /plī'ätrəpē/ ▶*n. Genetics* the production by a single gene of two or more apparently unrelated effects. ▷1930s: from Greek *pleiōn* 'more' + *tropē* 'turning.' —**plei·o·trop·ic** /,plīə'trōpik; -'träpik/ *adj.* —**plei·ot·ro·pism** /,plī'ätrə,pizəm/ *n.*

Pleis·to·cene /'plīstə,sēn/ ▶*adj. Geology* of, relating to, or denoting the first epoch of the Quaternary period, between the Pliocene and Holocene epochs. ■ [as *n.*] (**the Pleistocene**) the Pleistocene epoch or the system of deposits laid down during it.

The Pleistocene epoch lasted from 1,640,000 to about 10,000 years ago. It was marked by great fluctuations in temperature that caused the ice ages, with glacial periods followed by warmer interglacial periods. Several extinct forms of human, forerunners of modern humans, appeared during this epoch.

▷mid 19th cent.: from Greek *pleistos* 'most' + *kainos* 'new.'

ple·na·ry /'plenərē/ ▶*adj.* **1** unqualified; absolute: *crusaders were offered a plenary indulgence by the pope.* **2** (of a meeting) to be attended by all participants at a conference or assembly, who otherwise meet in smaller groups: *a plenary session of the European Parliament.*

▶*n.* a meeting or session of this type. ▷late Middle English: from late Latin *plenarius* 'complete,' from *plenus* 'full.'

plen·i·po·ten·ti·ar·y /,plenəpə'tensHē,erē; -'tensHərē/ ▶*n.* (*pl.* **-ar·ies**) a person, esp. a diplomat, invested with the full power of independent action on behalf of their government, typically in a foreign country.

▶*adj.* having full power to take independent action: [*postpositive*] *he represented the Japanese government in Seoul as minister plenipotentiary.* ■ (of power) absolute. ▷mid 17th cent.: from medieval Latin *plenipotentiarius*, from *plenus* 'full' + *potentia* 'power.'

plen·i·tude /'pleni,t(y)o͞od/ ▶*n.* an abundance: *the farm boasts* ***a plenitude of*** *animals and birds.* ■ the condition of being full or complete: *the plenitude of the pope's powers.* ▷late Middle English: from Old French, from late Latin *plenitudo*, from *plenus* 'full.'

plen·te·ous /'plentēəs/ ▶*adj. poetic/literary* plentiful. ▷Middle English: from Old French *plentivous*, from *plentif*, *-ive*, from *plente* 'plenty.' Compare with **BOUNTEOUS**. —**plen·te·ous·ly** *adv.* —**plen·te·ous·ness** *n.*

plen·ti·ful /'plentəfəl/ ▶*adj.* existing in or yielding great quantities; abundant: *the wine is good, cheap, and plentiful.* See note at **PREVALENT**. —**plen·ti·ful·ly** *adv.* —**plen·ti·ful·ness** *n.*

plent·i·tude /'plenti,t(y)o͞od/ ▶*n.* another term for **PLENITUDE**.

plen·ty /'plentē/ ▶*pron.* a large or sufficient amount or quantity; more than enough: *I would have* ***plenty of*** *time to get home* | *you'll have plenty to keep you busy* | [as *adj.*] *informal* or *dialect there was plenty room.*

▶*n.* a situation in which food and other necessities are available in sufficiently large quantities: *such natural phenomena as famine and plenty.*

▶*adv.* [usu. as *submodifier*] *informal* used to emphasize the degree of something: *she has* ***plenty more*** *ideas.* ▷Middle English (in the sense 'fullness, perfection'): from Old French *plente*, from Latin *plenitas*, from *plenus* 'full.'

ple·num /'plenəm; 'plēnəm/ ▶*n.* **1** an assembly of all the members of a group or committee. [influenced by Russian *plenum* 'plenary session.'] **2** *Physics* a space completely filled with matter, or the whole of space so regarded. ■ an enclosed chamber where a treated substance collects for distribution, as heated or conditioned air through a ventilation system. ▷late 17th cent.: from Latin, literally 'full space,' neuter of *plenus* 'full.'

pleo- ▶*comb. form* having more than the usual or expected number: *pleomorphism.* ▷from Greek *pleōn* 'more.'

ple·o·chro·ic /,plēə'krōik/ ▶*adj.* (of a crystal) absorbing different wavelengths of light differently depending on the direction of incidence of the rays or their plane of polarization, often resulting in the appearance of different colors according to the direction of view. ▷mid 19th cent.: from **PLEO-** 'more' + *khrōs* 'color' + **-IC**. —**ple·och·ro·ism** /-'krō,izəm/ *n.*

ple·o·mor·phism /,plēə'môr,fizəm/ ▶*n.* the occurrence of more than one distinct form of a natural object, such as a crystalline substance, a virus, the cells in a tumor, or an organism at different stages of the life cycle. ▷mid 19th cent.: from Greek *pleiōn* 'more' + *morphē* 'form' + **-ISM**. —**ple·o·mor·phic** /-fik/ *adj.*

ple·o·nasm /'plēə,nazəm/ ▶*n.* the use of more words than are necessary to convey meaning (e.g., *see with one's eyes*), either as a fault of style or for emphasis. ▷mid 16th cent.: via late Latin from Greek *pleonasmos*, from *pleonazein* 'be superfluous.' —**ple·o·nas·tic** /,plēə'nastik/ *adj.* —**ple·o·nas·ti·cal·ly** /,plēə'nastik(ə)lē/ *adv.*

ple·o·pod /'plēə,päd/ ▶*n. Zoology* a forked swimming limb of a crustacean, five pairs of which are typically attached to the abdomen. Also called **SWIMMERET**. ▷mid 19th cent.: from Greek *plein* 'swim, sail' + *pous*, *pod-* 'foot.'

ple·ro·ma /plə'rōmə/ ▶*n.* [in *sing.*] **1** (in Gnosticism) the spiritual universe as the abode of God and of the totality of the divine powers and emanations. **2** (in Christian theology) the totality or fullness of the Godhead that dwells in Christ. ▷mid 18th cent.: from Greek *plērōma* 'that which fills,' from *plēroun* 'make full,' from *plērēs* 'full.' —**ple·ro·mat·ic** /,plerə'matik/ *adj.*

ple·si·o·saur /'plēsēə,sôr/ ▶*n.* a large extinct marine reptile of the Mesozoic era, with a broad flat body, large paddlelike limbs, and typically a long flexible neck and small head. • Infraorder Plesiosauria, superorder Sauropterygia: several families, including Plesiosauridae. ▷mid 19th cent.: from modern Latin *Plesiosaurus*, from Greek *plēsios* 'near' + *sauros* 'lizard.'

ples·sor /'plesər/ ▶*n.* variant spelling of **PLEXOR**.

pleth·o·ra /'plethərə/ ▶*n.* (**a plethora of**) an excess of (something): *a plethora of committees and subcommittees.* ■ *Medicine* an excess of a bodily fluid, particularly blood. ▷mid 16th cent. (in the medical sense): via late Latin from Greek *plēthōrē*, from *plēthein* 'be full.' —**ple·thor·ic** /'plethərik; plə'thôrik/ *adj.* (*archaic* or *Medicine*).

ple·thys·mo·graph /plə'thizmə,graf/ ▶*n. Medicine* an instrument for recording and measuring variation in the volume of a part of the body, esp. as caused by changes in blood pressure. ▷late 19th cent.: from Greek *plēthusmos* 'enlargement' (based on *plēthus* 'fullness') + **-GRAPH**. —**ple·thys·mo·graph·ic** /plə,thizmə'grafik/ *adj.* —**pleth·ys·mog·ra·phy** /,plethiz'mägrəfē/ *n.*

P

pleu·ra[1] /'plo͝orə/ ▶*n.* (*pl.* **pleu·rae** /'plo͝orē/) **1** each of a pair of serous membranes lining the thorax and enveloping the lungs in humans and other mammals. **2** *Zoology* a lateral part in an animal body or structure. Compare with **PLEURON**. ▷late Middle English: via medieval Latin from Greek, literally 'side of the body, rib.' —**pleu·ral** *adj.*

pleu·ra[2] /'plo͝orə/ ▶ plural form of **PLEURON**.

pleu·ri·sy /'plo͝orəsē/ ▶*n. Medicine* inflammation of the pleurae, which impairs their lubricating function and causes pain when breathing. It is caused by pneumonia and other diseases of the chest or abdomen. ▷late Middle English: from Old French *pleurisie*, from late Latin *pleurisis*, alteration of earlier Latin *pleuritis*, from Greek *pleura* 'side of the body, rib.' —**pleu·rit·ic** /plo͞o'ritik/ *adj.*

pleuro- ▶*comb. form* of or relating to the pleura or pleurae: *pleuropneumonia.* ▷from Greek *pleura* 'side,' *pleuron* 'rib.'

pleu·ron /'plo͞o,rän/ ▶*n.* (*pl.* **pleu·ra** /'plo͝orə/) *Zoology* the sidewall of each segment of the body of an arthropod. ▷early 18th cent.: from Greek, literally 'side of the body, rib.'

pleu·ro·pneu·mo·nia /,plo͝orə,n(y)o͞o'mōnyə/ ▶*n.* pneumonia complicated with pleurisy.

Ple·ven /'plevən/ an industrial town in northern Bulgaria, northeast of Sofia; pop. 168,000. An important fortress town and trading center of the Ottoman Empire, it was taken from the Turks by the Russians in the Russo-Turkish War of 1877, after a siege of 143 days.

plew /plo͞o/ ▶*n. historical* a beaver skin, used as a standard unit of value in the fur trade. ▷mid 19th cent.: from Canadian French *pélu* 'hairy,' from French *poil* 'hair, bristle.'

Plex·i·glas /'pleksi,glas/ (also **plex·i·glass**) ▶*n. trademark* a solid transparent plastic made of polymethyl methacrylate (the same material as perspex or Lucite). ▷1930s: from Greek *plēxis* 'percussion' + **GLASS**.

plex·or /'pleksər/ (also **ples·sor**) ▶*n.* a small hammer with a rubber head used to test reflexes and in medical percussion. ▷mid 19th cent.: formed irregularly from Greek *plēxis* 'percussion' (from *plēssein* 'to strike') + **-OR**[1].

plex·us /'pleksəs/ ▶*n.* (*pl.* same or **plex·us·es**) *Anatomy* a network of nerves or vessels in the body. ■ an intricate network or weblike formation. ▷late 17th cent.: from Latin, literally 'plaited formation,' past participle of *plectere* 'to plait.' —**plex·i·form** /'pleksə,fôrm/ *adj.*

plf. (also **plff.**) ▶*abbr.* plaintiff.

pli·a·ble /'plīəbəl/ ▶*adj.* easily bent; flexible: *quality leather is pliable and will not crack.* See note at **FLEXIBLE**. ■ *figurative* easily influenced: *pliable teenage minds.* ▷late Middle English: from French, from *plier* 'to bend' (see **PLY**[1]). —**pli·a·bil·i·ty** /,plīə'bilitē/ *n.* —**pli·a·bly** /-əblē/ *adv.*

pli·ant /'plīənt/ ▶*adj.* pliable: *pliant willow stems* | *figurative an economy pliant to political will.* See note at **FLEXIBLE**. ▷Middle English: from Old French, literally 'bending,' present participle of *plier*. —**pli·an·cy** /'plīənsē/ *n.* —**pli·ant·ly** *adv.*

pli·ca /'plīkə/ ▶*n.* **1** (*pl.* **-cae** /-kē; -sē/ or **-cas**) *Anatomy* a fold or ridge of tissue. ■ *Botany* a small lobe between the petals of a flower. **2** *Medicine* a densely matted condition of the hair. ▷mid 17th cent.: modern Latin, from medieval Latin, 'fold,' from *plicare* 'to fold.'

pli·cate /ˈplīkāt; -kit/ ▸*adj. Biology & Geology* folded, crumpled, or corrugated. ▷mid 18th cent.: from Latin *plicatus* 'folded,' past participle of *plicare*. —**pli·cat·ed** *adj.*

pli·ca·tion /plīˈkāsHən/ ▸*n.* a fold or corrugation. ■ the manner of folding or condition of being folded. ▷late Middle English: via Old French from medieval Latin *plicatio(n-)*, from Latin *plicare* 'to fold.'

pli·é /plēˈā/ *Ballet* ▸*n.* a movement in which a dancer bends the knees and straightens them again, usually with the feet turned out and heels firmly on the ground.
▸*v.* [*intrans.*] perform a plié. ▷French, literally 'bent,' past participle of *plier* (see also **PLY**1).

pli·ers /ˈplīərz/ (also **a pair of pliers**) ▸*plural n.* pincers with parallel, flat, and typically serrated surfaces, used chiefly for gripping small objects or bending wire. ▷mid 16th cent.: from dialect *ply* 'bend,' from French *plier* 'to bend,' from Latin *plicare* 'to fold.'

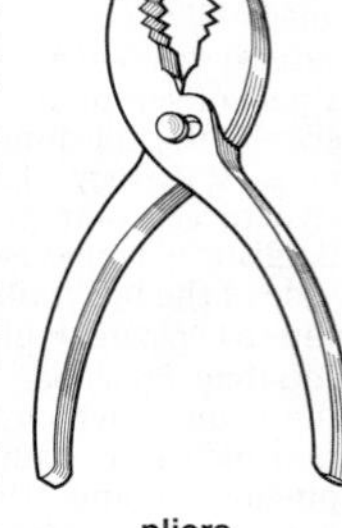
pliers

plight1 /plīt/ ▸*n.* a dangerous, difficult, or otherwise unfortunate situation: *we must direct our efforts toward relieving the plight of children living in poverty.* ▷Middle English: from Anglo-Norman French *plit* 'fold.' The *-gh-* spelling is by association with **PLIGHT**2.

plight2 ▸*v.* [*trans.*] *archaic* pledge or promise solemnly (one's faith or loyalty). ■ (**be plighted to**) be engaged to be married to. ▷Old English *plihtan* 'endanger,' of Germanic origin; related to Dutch *plicht* and German *Pflicht* 'duty.' The current sense is recorded only from Middle English, but is probably original, in view of the related Germanic words.
▸*PHRASE* □ **plight one's troth** see **TROTH**.

plim·soll /ˈplimsəl; -sōl/ (also **plim·sole**) ▸*n. Brit.* a light rubber-soled canvas shoe, worn esp. for sports. ▷late 19th cent.: probably from the resemblance of the side of the sole to a **PLIMSOLL LINE**.

Plim·soll line /ˈplimsəl; -sōl/ (also **Plimsoll mark**) ▸*n.* a marking on a ship's side showing the limit of submersion legal under various conditions. ▷named after Samuel *Plimsoll* (1824–98), the English politician whose agitation in the 1870s resulted in the Merchant Shipping Act of 1876, intended to end the practice of sending to sea overloaded and heavily insured old ships, from which the owners profited if they sank.

Plin·i·an /ˈplinēən/ ▸*adj. Geology* relating to or denoting a type of volcanic eruption in which a narrow stream of gas and ash is violently ejected from a vent to a height of several miles. ▷mid 17th cent.: from Italian *pliniano*, with reference to the eruption of Vesuvius in AD 79, in which Pliny the Elder died.

plink /plingk/ ▸*v.* [*intrans.*] emit a short, sharp, metallic or ringing sound. ■ play a musical instrument in such a way as to produce such sounds. ■ [*trans.*] shoot at (a target) casually.
▸*n.* a short, sharp, metallic or ringing sound. ▷1940s: imitative. —**plink·y** *adj.*

plinth /plinTH/ ▸*n.* a heavy base supporting a statue or vase. ■ *Architecture* the lower square slab at the base of a column. ▷late 16th cent.: from Latin *plinthus*, from Greek *plinthos* 'tile, brick, squared stone.' The Latin form was in early use in English.

Plin·y1 /ˈplinē; ˈplīnē/ (23–79), Roman statesman and scholar; Latin name *Gaius Plinius Secundus*; known as **Pliny the Elder**. His *Natural History* (77) is a vast encyclopedia of the natural and human worlds. He died while observing the eruption of Vesuvius.

Plin·y2 (*c.*61–*c.*112), Roman senator and writer; nephew of Pliny the Elder; Latin name *Gaius Plinius Caecilius Secundus*; known as **Pliny the Younger**. He is noted for his books of letters that deal with both public and private affairs and that include a description of the eruption of Vesuvius in 79.

Pli·o·cene /ˈplīəˌsēn/ ▸*adj. Geology* of, relating to, or denoting the last epoch of the Tertiary period, between the Miocene and Pleistocene epochs. ■ [as *n.*] (**the Pliocene**) the Pliocene epoch or the system of rocks deposited during it.

The Pliocene epoch lasted from 5.2 million to 1.64 million years ago. Temperatures were falling at this time and many mammals became extinct. The first hominids, including *Australopithecus* and *Homo habilis*, appeared.

▷mid 19th cent.: from Greek *pleiōn* 'more' + *kainos* 'new.'

Pli·o–Pleis·to·cene /ˌplīə ˈplīstəˌsēn; ˌplīō-/ ▸*adj. Geology* of, relating to, or linking the Pliocene and Pleistocene epochs or rock systems together. ■ [as *n.*] (**the Plio–Pleistocene**) the Pliocene and Pleistocene epochs together or the system of rocks deposited during them.

pli·o·saur /ˈplīəˌsôr/ ▸*n.* a plesiosaur with a short neck, large head, and massive toothed jaws. • Family Pliosauridae, infraorder Plesiosauria: several genera, including *Pliosaurus*. ▷mid 19th cent.: from modern Latin *Pliosaurus* (genus name), from Greek *pleiōn* 'more' + *sauros* 'lizard' (because of its greater similarity to a lizard than the ichthyosaur).

plis·sé /plēˈsā; pli-/ ▸*adj.* (of fabric) treated to give a permanent puckered or crinkled effect.
▸*n.* material treated in this way. ▷late 19th cent.: French, literally 'pleated,' past participle of *plisser*.

pln. ▸*abbr.* plain.

PLO ▸*abbr.* Palestine Liberation Organization.

plod /pläd/ ▸*v.* (**plod·ded, plod·ding**) [*intrans.*] walk doggedly and slowly with heavy steps: *we plodded back up the hill figurative talks on a new constitution have plodded on.* ■ work slowly and perseveringly at a dull task: *we were plodding through a textbook.*
▸*n.* a slow, heavy walk: *he settled down to a steady plod.* ■ the sound of a heavy, dull tread; a thud. ▷mid 16th cent.: probably symbolic of a heavy gait. —**plod·der** *n.*

plod·ding /ˈplädiNG/ ▸*adj.* slow-moving and unexciting: *a plodding comedy drama.* ■ (of a person) thorough and hardworking but lacking in imagination or intelligence. —**plod·ding·ly** *adv.*

-ploid ▸*comb. form Biology* denoting the number of sets of chromosomes in a cell: *triploid.* ▷based on *(ha)ploid* and *(di)ploid*.

ploi·dy /ˈploidē/ ▸*n. Genetics* the number of sets of chromosomes in a cell, or in the cells of an organism. ▷1940s: from words such as *(di)ploidy* and *(poly)ploidy*.

Plo·ieș·ti /plôˈyesHt(ē)/ an oil-refining city in central Romania, north of Bucharest; pop. 254,000.

plon·geur /ˌplônˈZHər; plänˈjər/ ▸*n.* a person employed to wash dishes and carry out other menial tasks in a restaurant or hotel. ▷French, literally 'person who plunges.'

plonk1 /plängk/ *informal* ▸*v.* **1** [*trans.*] set down heavily or carelessly: *she plonked her glass on the table.* ■ (**plonk oneself**) sit down heavily and without ceremony: *he plonked himself down on the sofa.* **2** [*intrans.*] play on a musical instrument laboriously or unskillfully: *people plonking around on expensive instruments.*
▸*n.* a sound as of something being set down heavily: *he sat down with a plonk.* ▷late 19th cent. (originally dialect): imitative; compare with **PLUNK**.

plonk2 ▸*n. informal* cheap wine of inferior quality. ▷1930s (originally Australian): probably an alteration of *blanc* in French *vin blanc* 'white wine.'

plop /pläp/ ▸*n.* a short sound as of a small, solid object dropping into water without a splash.
▸*v.* (**plopped, plop·ping**) fall or cause to fall with such a sound: [*intrans.*] *the stone plopped into the pond* | [*trans.*] *she plopped a sugar cube into the cup.* ■ (**plop oneself down**) sit or lie down gently but clumsily: *he plopped himself down on the nearest chair.* ▷early 19th cent.: imitative.

plo·sion /ˈplōZHən/ ▸*n. Phonetics* the sudden release of air in the pronunciation of a plosive consonant. ▷early 20th cent.: shortening of **EXPLOSION**.

plo·sive /ˈplōsiv/ *Phonetics* ▸*adj.* denoting a consonant that is produced by stopping the airflow using the lips, teeth, or palate, followed by a sudden release of air.
▸*n.* a plosive speech sound. The basic plosives in English are *t*, *k*, and *p* (voiceless) and *d*, *g*, and *b* (voiced). ▷late 19th cent.: shortening of **EXPLOSIVE**.

plot /plät/ ▸*n.* **1** a plan made in secret by a group of people to do something illegal or harmful: [with *infinitive*] *there's a plot to overthrow the government.* **2** the main events of a play, novel, movie, or similar work, devised and presented by the writer as an interrelated sequence. **3** a small piece of ground marked out for a purpose such as building or gardening: *a vegetable plot.* **4** a graph showing the relation between two variables. ■ a diagram, chart, or map.
▸*v.* (**plot·ted, plot·ting**) [*trans.*] **1** secretly make plans to carry out (an illegal or harmful action): *the two men are serving sentences for plotting a bomb campaign* | [*intrans.*] *Erica has been* ***plotting against*** *me all along.* **2** devise the sequence of events in (a play, novel, movie, or similar work). **3** mark (a route or position) on a chart: *he started to plot lines of ancient sites.* ■ mark out or allocate (points) on a graph. ■ make (a curve) by marking out a number of such points. ■ illustrate by use of a graph: *it is possible to plot fairly closely the rate at which recruitment of girls increased.* ▷late Old English (sense 3 of the *noun*), of unknown origin. The sense 'secret plan,' dating from the late 16th cent., is associated with Old French *complot* 'dense crowd, secret project,' the same term being used occasionally in English from the mid 16th cent. Compare with **PLAT**1. —**plot·less** *adj.* —**plot·ter** /ˈplätər/ *n.*
▸*PHRASES* □ **lose the plot** *informal* lose one's ability to understand or cope with what is happening: *many people believe that he is feeling the strain or has lost the plot.* □ **the plot thickens** see **THICKEN**.

THE RIGHT WORD **cabal, conspiracy, intrigue, machination, plot**

If you come up with a secret plan to do something, especially with evil or mischievous intent, it's called a **plot** (*a plot to seize control of the company*).

If you get other people or groups involved in your plot, it's called a **conspiracy** (*a conspiracy to overthrow the government*).

Cabal usually applies to a small group of political conspirators (*a cabal of right-wing extremists*), while **machination** (usually plural) suggests deceit and cunning in devising a plot intended to harm someone (*the machinations of the would-be assassins*).

An **intrigue** involves more complicated scheming or maneuvering than a plot and often employs underhanded methods in an attempt to gain one's own ends (*she had a passion for intrigue, particularly where romance was involved*).

Plo·ti·nus /plōˈtīnəs/ (*c.*205–270), philosopher, probably of Roman descent. He was the founder and leading exponent of Neoplatonism.

plot line ▸*n.* the course or main features of a narrative such as the plot of a play, novel, or movie: *the plot line might be too complex for audiences to follow.*

Plott hound /plät/ ▸*n.* a hunting dog with a smooth brindle or black coat and large drooping ears. Developed from German stock, it is the only recognized coonhound not descended from the foxhound. ▷late 18th cent.: named after the Plott family of North Carolina, who developed the breed from wild boar hounds brought from Germany in 1750.

plot·ty /ˈplätē/ ▸*adj. informal* (of a novel, play, or movie) having an excessively elaborate or complicated plot.

plotz /pläts/ ▸*v.* [*intrans.*] *informal* collapse or be beside oneself with frustration, annoyance, or other strong emotion: *lots of directors plotz while making their films.* ▷1960s: from Yiddish *platsen*, literally 'to burst,' from Middle High German *platzen*.

plotzed /plätst/ ▸*adj. informal* extremely drunk.

plough /plou/ ▸*n.* & *v.* British spelling of **PLOW**. ■ (**the Plough**) British term for **BIG DIPPER**.

plough·man's lunch /ˈploumənz/ ▸*n. Brit.* a meal of bread and cheese, typically with pickled vegetables and salad.

Plov·div /ˈplôvˌdif/ an industrial and commercial city in southern Bulgaria; pop. 379,000. Known to the ancient Greeks as Philippopolis and to the Romans as Trimontium, it assumed its present name after World War I.

plov·er /ˈpləvər; ˈplō-/ ▸*n.* a short-billed gregarious wading bird, typically found by water but sometimes frequenting grassland, tundra, and mountains. • Family Charadriidae (the **plover family**): several genera and numerous species, esp. the **ringed plovers** (*Charadrius*), **golden plovers** (*Pluvialis*), and lapwings (*Vanellus*). ▷Middle English: from Anglo-Norman French, based on Latin *pluvia* 'rain.'

plow /plou/ (*Brit.* **plough**) ▸*n.* a large farming implement with one or more blades fixed in a frame, drawn by a tractor or by animals and used for cutting furrows in the soil and turning it over, esp. to prepare for the planting of seeds. ■ a snowplow.
▸*v.* [*trans.*] **1** turn up the earth of (an area of land) with a plow, esp. before sowing: *Uncle Vic plowed his garden* | [as *adj.*] (**plowed**) *a plowed field.* ■ cut (a furrow or line) with or as if with a plow: *icebergs have plowed furrows on the seabed.* ■ (of a ship or boat) travel through (an area of water): *cruise liners plow the long-sailed routes.* **2** [*intrans.*] (esp. of a vehicle) move in a fast and uncontrolled manner: *the car* ***plowed into*** *the side of a van.* ■ advance or progress laboriously or forcibly: *they plowed their way through deep snow* |

the students are **plowing through** *a set of grammar exercises.* ■ (**plow on**) continue steadily despite difficulties or warnings to stop: *he plowed on, trying to outline his plans.* **3** clear snow from (a road) using a snowplow: *the roads weren't yet plowed.* **4** *Brit., informal, dated* fail (an examination).

▸*phrasal v.* □ **plow something in/back** plow grass or other material into the soil to enrich it. ■ invest money in a business or reinvest profits in the enterprise producing them: *savings made through greater efficiency will be plowed back into the service.* □ **plow under** bury in the soil by plowing. □ **plow up** till (soil) completely or thoroughly. ■ uncover by plowing. ▷late Old English *plōh*, of Germanic origin; related to Dutch *ploeg* and German *Pflug*. The spelling *plough* became common in England in the 18th cent.; earlier (16th–17th centuries) the noun was normally spelled *plough*, the verb *plow*. —**plow·a·ble** *adj.* —**plow·er** *n.*

▸*PHRASES* □ **plow a lonely** (or **one's own**) **furrow** follow a course of action in which one is isolated or in which one can act independently. □ **put** (or **set**) **one's hand to the plow** embark on a task. [with biblical allusion to Luke 9:62.]

plow·man /ˈploumən/ (*Brit.* **plough·man**) ▸*n.* (*pl.* **-men**) a person who uses a plow.

Plow·right /ˈplou,rīt/, Joan (1929–), British actress. Her films include *The Dressmaker* (1988), *Enchanted April* (1992), and *Tea with Mussolini* (1999). She was married to Laurence Olivier.

plow·share /ˈplou,SHe(ə)r/ (*Brit.* **plough·share**) ▸*n.* the main cutting blade of a plow, behind the coulter. ▷late Middle English: from *plowgh*, an earlier spelling of **PLOW** + Old English *scær, scear* 'plowshare' (related to **SHEAR**).

ploy /ploi/ ▸*n.* a cunning plan or action designed to turn a situation to one's own advantage: *the president has dismissed the referendum as a ploy to buy time.* ▷late 17th cent. (originally Scots and northern English in the senses 'pastime,' 'escapade,' and 'a trick'): of unknown origin. The notion of 'a calculated plan' dates from the 1950s.

PLP ▸*abbr.* (in the UK) Parliamentary Labour Party.

PLR ▸*abbr.* (in the UK) Public Lending Right.

PLSS ▸*abbr.* portable life support system.

plu. ▸*abbr.* plural.

pluck /plək/ ▸*v.* [*trans.*] take hold of (something) and quickly remove it from its place; pick: *she plucked a blade of grass* | *he plucked a tape from the shelf.* ■ catch hold of and pull quickly: *she plucked his sleeve* | [*intrans.*] *brambles* **plucked at** *her jeans.* ■ quickly or suddenly remove someone from a dangerous or unpleasant situation: *the baby was plucked from a grim foster home.* ■ pull the feathers from (a bird's carcass) to prepare it for cooking. ■ pull some of the hairs from (one's eyebrows) to make them look neater. ■ sound (a musical instrument or its strings) with one's finger or a plectrum. ■ select for a move to a new job or position: *many managers were plucked from the company's overseas operations.*

▸*phrasal v.* □ **pluck up courage** see **COURAGE**.

▸*n.* spirited and determined courage; guts. See note at **COURAGE**. ■ the heart, liver, and lungs of an animal as food. ▷late Old English *ploccian, pluccian*, of Germanic origin; related to Flemish *plokken*; probably from the base of Old French *(es)peluchier* 'to pluck.' Sense 1 of the *noun* is originally boxers' slang. —**pluck·er** *n.* [usu. in *combination*] *a goose-plucker.*

pluck·y /ˈpləkē/ ▸*adj.* (**pluck·i·er, pluck·i·est**) having or showing determined courage in the face of difficulties. —**pluck·i·ly** /ˈpləkəlē/ *adv.* —**pluck·i·ness** *n.*

plug /pləg/ ▸*n.* **1** an obstruction blocking a hole, pipe, etc.: *somewhere in the pipes there is a plug of ice blocking the flow.* ■ a circular piece of metal, rubber, or plastic used to stop the drain of a bathtub or basin and keep the water in it. ■ *informal* a baby's pacifier. ■ a mass of solidified lava filling the neck of an old volcano. ■ (in gardening) a young plant or clump of grass with a small mass of soil protecting its roots, for planting in the ground. **2** a device for making an electrical connection, esp. between an appliance and a power supply, consisting of an insulated casing with metal pins that fit into holes in an outlet. ■ short for **SPARK PLUG**. **3** *informal* a piece of publicity promoting a product, event, or establishment: *he threw in a plug, boasting that the restaurant offered many entrées for under $5.* **4** a piece of tobacco cut from a larger cake for chewing. ■ (also **plug tobacco**) tobacco in large cakes designed to be cut for chewing. **5** *Fishing* a lure with one or more hooks attached. **6** short for **FIREPLUG**. **7** *informal* a tired or old horse.

▸*v.* (**plugged, plug·ging**) [*trans.*] **1** block or fill in (a hole or cavity): *trucks arrived loaded with gravel to plug the hole and clear the road* | *figurative the new sanctions are meant to plug the gaps in the trade embargo.* ■ insert (something) into an opening so as to fill it: *the baby plugged his thumb into his mouth.* **2** *informal* mention (a product, event, or establishment) publicly in order to promote it: *during the show he plugged his new record.* **3** *informal* shoot or hit (someone or something). **4** [*intrans.*] *informal* proceed steadily and laboriously with a journey or task: *during the years of poverty, he* **plugged away at** *his writing.*

▸*phrasal v.* □ **plug something in** connect an electrical appliance to a power supply by inserting a plug into an outlet. □ **plug into** (of an electrical appliance) be connected to another appliance by a plug inserted in an outlet. ■ gain or have access to a system of computerized information: *we plug into the research facilities available at the institute.* ■ *figurative* become knowledgeable about and involved with: *the good thing about this job is that I'm plugged into what's going on.* ▷early 17th cent.: from Middle Dutch and Middle Low German *plugge*, of unknown ultimate origin. —**plug·ger** *n.*

▸*PHRASE* □ **pull the plug** see **PULL**.

Plug and Play (also **plug and play**) ▸*n.* a standard for the connection of peripherals to personal computers, whereby a device only needs to be connected to a computer in order to be configured to work perfectly, without any action by the user.

plug·board /ˈpləg,bôrd/ ▸*n.* a board containing several sockets into which plugs can be inserted to interconnect electric circuits, telephone lines, or computer components, by means of short lengths of wire.

plug-com·pat·i·ble ▸*adj.* relating to or denoting computing equipment that is compatible with devices or systems produced by different manufacturers, to the extent that it can be plugged in and operated successfully.

▸*n.* a piece of computing equipment designed in this way.

plug flow ▸*n.* *Geology & Physics* the flow of a body of ice or viscous fluid with no shearing between adjacent layers; idealized flow without any mixing of particles of fluid.

plug fuse ▸*n.* a fuse designed to be pushed into a socket in a panel or board.

plug gauge ▸*n.* a gauge in the form of a plug, used for measuring the diameter of a hole.

plugged-in *informal* ▸*adj.* aware of what is going on or what is up to date; alert: *a small group of plugged-in politicians.*

plug-in ▸*adj.* able to be connected by means of a plug: *a plug-in telephone.* ■ *Computing* (of a module or software) able to be added to a system to give extra features or functions: *a plug-in graphics card.*

▸*n.* **1** *Computing* a module or software of this kind. **2** *Canadian* an electric outlet for plugging in the block heater of a vehicle in order to keep the engine warm.

plug-ug·ly *informal* ▸*n.* (*pl.* **-lies**) a thug or villain.

▸*adj.* very ugly: *that was one plug-ugly dress.* ▷by association with the verb **PLUG** in the informal sense 'hit with the fist.'

plum /pləm/ ▸*n.* **1** an oval fleshy fruit that is purple, reddish, or yellow when ripe and contains a flattish pointed pit. **2** (also **plum tree**) the deciduous tree that bears this fruit. • Several species in the genus *Prunus*, family Rosaceae, in particular *P. domestica*. **3** a reddish-purple color: [as *adj.*] *a plum blazer.* **4** [usu. as *adj.*] *informal* a highly desireable attainment, accomplishment, or acquistion, typically a job: *he landed a plum assistant producer's job.*

▸*adv.* variant spelling of **PLUMB**[1] : *the helicopter crashed plum on the cabins.* ▷Old English *plūme*, from medieval Latin *pruna*, from Latin *prunum* (see **PRUNE**[1]).

plum·age /ˈplo͞omij/ ▸*n.* a bird's feathers collectively. ▷late Middle English: from Old French, from *plume* 'feather.' —**plum·aged** *adj.* [usu. in *combination*] *a gray-plumaged bird.*

plumb[1] /pləm/ ▸*v.* [*trans.*] **1** measure (the depth of a body of water). ■ [*intrans.*] (of water) be of a specified depth: *at its deepest, the lake scarcely plumbed seven feet.* ■ explore or experience fully or to extremes: *she had* **plumbed the depths of** *depravity.* **2** test (an upright surface) to determine the vertical.

▸*n.* a plumb bob.

▸*adv.* **1** *informal* exactly: *a contrabassoonist who sits plumb in the middle of the wind section.* ■ [as *submodifier*] to a very high degree; extremely: *they must both be plumb crazy.* ■ [as *submodifier*] completely: *the transmission was plumb worn out.* **2** *archaic* vertically: *drapery fell from their human forms plumb down.*

▸*adj.* vertical: *ensure that the baseboard is straight and plumb.* ▷Middle English (originally in the sense 'sounding lead'): via Old French from Latin *plumbum* 'lead.'

▸*PHRASE* □ **out of plumb** not exactly vertical: *the towers are inclined, from four to ten feet out of plumb.*

plumb[2] ▸*v.* [*trans.*] install and connect water and drainage pipes in (a building or room): *the house could not be plumbed at all.* ■ (**plumb something in**) *chiefly Brit.* install an appliance and connect it to water and drainage pipes. ▷late 19th cent. (in the sense 'work as a plumber'): back-formation from **PLUMBER**.

plum·ba·go /pləmˈbāgō/ ▸*n.* (*pl.* **-gos**) **1** old-fashioned term for **GRAPHITE**. [early 17th cent. (denoting an ore such as galena containing lead): from Latin, from *plumbum* 'lead.' The sense 'graphite' arose through its use for pencil leads.] **2** an evergreen flowering shrub or climber that is widely distributed in warm regions and grown elsewhere as a greenhouse or indoor plant. Also called **LEADWORT**. [named from the color of the flowers.] • Genus *Plumbago*, family Plumbaginaceae.

plumb bob ▸*n.* a bob of lead or other heavy material forming the weight of a plumb line.

plum·be·ous /ˈpləmbēəs/ ▸*adj.* *chiefly Ornithology* of the dull gray color of lead. ▷late 16th cent.: from Latin *plumbeus* 'leaden' (from *plumbum* 'lead') + **-OUS**.

plumb·er /ˈpləmər/ ▸*n.* a person who installs and repairs the pipes and fittings of water supply, sanitation, or heating systems. ▷late Middle English (originally denoting a person dealing in and working with lead): from Old French *plommier*, from Latin *plumbarius*, from *plumbum* 'lead.'

plumb·er's help·er (**plumb·er's friend**) ▸*n.* *informal* a plunger.

plumb·er's snake ▸*n.* see **SNAKE**.

plum·bic /ˈpləmbik/ ▸*adj.* *Chemistry* of lead with a valence of four; of lead(IV). Compare with **PLUMBOUS**. ■ *Medicine* caused by the presence of lead. ▷late 18th cent.: from Latin *plumbum* 'lead' + **-IC**.

plumb·ing /ˈpləmiNG/ ▸*n.* the system of pipes, tanks, fittings, and other apparatus required for the water supply, heating, and sanitation in a building. ■ the work of installing and maintaining such a system. ■ *informal* used as a humorous euphemism for the excretory tracts and urinary system: *I'd never discuss my plumbing with ladies.*

plum·bism /ˈpləm,bizəm/ ▸*n.* technical term for **LEAD POISONING**.

plumb·less /ˈpləmləs/ ▸*adj.* *poetic/literary* (of a body of water) extremely deep.

plumb line ▸*n.* a line with a plumb attached to it, used for finding the depth of water or determining the vertical on an upright surface.

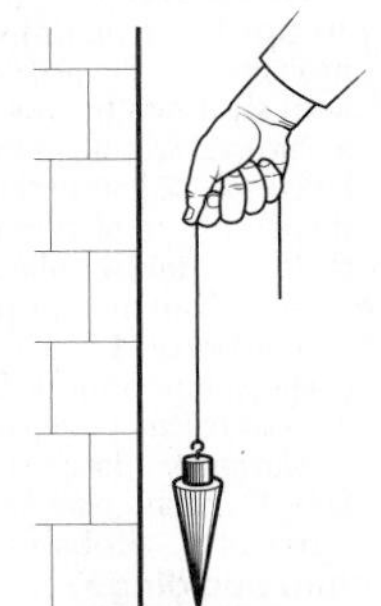

plumb line

plum·bous /ˈpləmbəs/ ▸*adj.* *Chemistry* of lead with a valence of two; of lead(II). Compare with **PLUMBIC**. ▷late 17th cent.: from Latin *plumbosus* 'full of lead.'

plumb rule ▸*n.* a plumb line attached to a board, used by builders and surveyors.

plum duff ▸*n.* a rich, spiced flour pudding made with raisins or currants.

plume /plo͞om/ ▸*n.* a long, soft feather or arrangement of feathers used by a bird for display or worn by a person for ornament: *a hat with a jaunty ostrich plume.* ■ *Zoology* a part of an animal's body that resembles a feather: *the antennae are divided into large feathery plumes.* ■ a long cloud of smoke or vapor resembling a feather as it spreads from its point of origin: *as he spoke, the word was accompanied by a white plume of breath.* ■ a mass of material, typically a pollutant, spreading from a source: *a radioactive plume.* ■ (also **mantle plume**) *Geology* a localized column of hot magma rising by convection in the mantle, believed to cause volcanic activity in hot spots, such as the Hawaiian Islands, away from plate margins.

Pronunciation Key ə *ago*; ər *over*; ˈə or ,ə *up*; ˈər or ,ər *fur*; a *hat*; ā *rate*; ä *car*; CH *chew*; e *let*; ē *see*; e(ə)r *air*; i *fit*; ī *by*; i(ə)r *ear*; NG *sing*; ō *go*; ô *for*; oi *boy*; o͝o *good*; o͞o *goo*; ou *out*; SH *she*; TH *thin*; T͟H *then*; (h)w *why*; ZH *vision*

▸v. **1** [intrans.] spread out in a shape resembling a feather: *smoke plumed from the chimneys.* ■ [trans.] decorate with or as if with feathers: [as adj.] (**plumed**) *a plumed cap.* **2** (**plume oneself**) *chiefly archaic* (of a bird) preen itself. ■ *figurative* feel a great sense of self-satisfaction about something: *she **plumed herself on** being cosmopolitan.* ▷late Middle English: from Old French, from Latin *pluma* 'down.' —**plume·less** *adj.* —**plume·like** /-ˌlīk/ *adj.* —**plum·er·y** /-mərē/ *n.*

Plumed Ser·pent ▸n. a mythical creature depicted as part bird, part snake, in particular Quetzalcóatl, a god of the Toltec and Aztec civilizations having this form.

plume moth ▸n. a small, slender, long-legged moth with narrow wings divided into feathery plumes. At rest, the wings are rolled and held out sideways, giving the moth the shape of a letter T. • Family Pterophoridae: several genera.

plu·me·ri·a /plo͞oˈmi(ə)rēə/ ▸n. a fragrant flowering tropical tree of a genus that includes frangipani. • Genus *Plumeria*, family Apocynaceae. ▷modern Latin, named after Charles *Plumier* (1646–1704), French botanist.

plum·met /ˈpləmit/ ▸v. (**-met·ed, -met·ing**) [intrans.] fall or drop straight down at high speed: *a climber was killed when he plummeted 300 feet down an icy gully.* ■ decrease rapidly in value or amount: *hardware sales plummeted.*

▸n. **1** a steep and rapid fall or drop. **2** a plumb or plumb line. ▷late Middle English (as a noun): from Old French *plommet* 'small sounding lead,' diminutive of *plomb* 'lead.' The current verb sense dates from the 1930s.

plum·my /ˈpləmē/ ▸adj. (**-mi·er, -mi·est**) **1** resembling a plum in taste, scent, or color: *cozy reds and plummy blues.* **2** *Brit., informal* (of a person's voice) having an accent thought typical of the English upper classes. **3** *Brit., informal* choice; highly desirable: *there are some plummy roles for the taking here.*

plu·mose /ˈplo͞oˌmōs/ ▸adj. *chiefly Biology* having many fine filaments or branches that give a feathery appearance. ▷mid 18th cent.: from Latin *plumosus* 'full of down or feathers,' from *pluma* 'down.'

plump[1] /pləmp/ ▸adj. having a full rounded shape: *the berries were plump and sweet.* ■ slightly fat.

▸v. [trans.] shake or pat (a cushion or pillow) to adjust its stuffing and make it rounded and soft: *she **plumped up** her pillows.* ■ [intrans.] (**plump up**) become rounder and fatter: *stew the dried fruits gently until they plump up.* ▷late 15th cent. (in the sense 'blunt, forthright'): related to Middle Dutch *plomp*, Middle Low German *plump, plomp* 'blunt, obtuse, blockish.' The sense has become appreciative, perhaps by association with PLUM. —**plump·ish** *adj.* —**plump·ly** *adv.* —**plump·ness** *n.* —**plump·y** *adj.*

plump[2] ▸v. **1** [trans.] set down heavily or unceremoniously: *she plumped her bag on the table.* ■ (**plump oneself**) sit down in this way: *she plumped herself down in the nearest seat* | [intrans.] *he plumped down on the bench beside me.* **2** [intrans.] (**plump for**) decide definitely in favor of (one of two or more possibilities): *offered a choice of drinks, he plumped for brandy.*

▸n. *archaic* an abrupt plunge; a heavy fall.

▸adv. *informal* **1** with a sudden or heavy fall: *she sat down plump on the bed.* **2** *dated* directly and bluntly: *he must tell her plump and plain that he was collecting unemployment.* ▷late Middle English: related to Middle Low German *plumpen*, Middle Dutch *plompen* 'fall into water,' probably of imitative origin.

plum pud·ding ▸n. a rich boiled or steamed pudding containing raisins, currants, and spices. ▷early 18th cent.: so named because the pudding was originally made with plums, the word *plum* being retained later to denote 'raisin,' which became a substituted ingredient.

plum to·ma·to ▸n. a tomato of an Italian variety that is shaped like a plum, typically used in cooking rather than raw.

plu·mule /ˈplo͞omyo͞ol/ ▸n. **1** *Botany* the rudimentary shoot or stem of an embryo plant. **2** *Ornithology* a bird's down feather, numbers of which form an insulating layer under the contour feathers. ▷early 18th cent.: from French *plumule* or Latin *plumula* 'small feather,' diminutive of *pluma* 'down.'

plum·y /ˈplo͞omē/ ▸adj. (**plum·i·er, plum·i·est**) resembling or decorated with feathers.

plun·der /ˈpləndər/ ▸v. [trans.] steal goods from (a place or person), typically using force and in a time of war or civil disorder: *looters moved into the disaster area to plunder stores* | [intrans.] *the invaders were back and ready to plunder.* See note at RAVAGE. ■ steal (goods) in such a way. ■ take material from (artistic or academic work) for one's own purposes: *we shall plunder related sciences to assist our research.*

▸n. the violent and dishonest acquisition of property: *the farmers suffered the inhumanity and indignities of pillage and plunder.* ■ property acquired illegally and violently: *the army sacked the city and carried off huge quantities of plunder.* ▷mid 17th cent.: from German *plündern*, literally 'rob of household goods,' from Middle High German *plunder* 'household effects.' Early use of the verb was with reference to the Thirty Years' War (1618–48), reflecting German usage; on the outbreak of the English Civil War in 1642, the word and activity were associated with the forces under Prince Rupert. —**plun·der·er** *n.*

plunge /plənj/ ▸v. **1** [intrans.] jump or dive quickly and energetically: *our daughters whooped as they **plunged into** the sea.* ■ fall suddenly and uncontrollably: *a car swerved to avoid a bus and plunged into a ravine.* ■ embark impetuously on a speech or course of action: *overconfident researchers who plunge ahead.* ■ suffer a rapid decrease in value: *their fourth-quarter operating profit plunged 25%.* ■ (of a ship) pitch: *the ship plunged through the 20-foot seas.* **2** [trans.] push or thrust quickly: *he plunged his hands into his pockets.* ■ put (something) in liquid so as to immerse it completely: *cover the cucumbers with boiling water and then plunge them into iced water.* ■ (often **be plunged into**) suddenly bring into a specified condition or state: *for a moment the scene was illuminated, then it was plunged back into darkness.* ■ [trans.] sink (a plant or a pot containing a plant) in the ground.

▸n. an act of jumping or diving into water: *we went straight from the sauna to take a cold plunge.* ■ a swift and drastic fall in value or amount: *the bank declared a 76% plunge in its profits.* ▷late Middle English: from Old French *plungier* 'thrust down,' based on Latin *plumbum* 'lead, plummet.'

▸PHRASE □ **take the plunge** *informal* commit oneself to a course of action about which one is nervous.

plunge pool ▸n. **1** a deep basin excavated at the foot of a waterfall by the action of the falling water. **2** *chiefly Brit.* a small, deep swimming pool, typically one filled with cold water and used to refresh or invigorate the body after a sauna.

plung·er /ˈplənjər/ ▸n. **1** a device consisting of a rubber cup on a long handle, used to clear blocked pipes by means of water pressure. ■ a part of a device or mechanism that works with a plunging or thrusting movement. **2** *informal* a person who gambles or spends money recklessly.

plunge saw ▸n. an electric saw with a projecting blade that can make precision cuts by plunging into dense materials.

plung·ing neck·line ▸n. a low-cut neckline on a woman's dress.

plunk /pləNGk/ *informal* ▸v. **1** [intrans.] play a keyboard or plucked stringed instrument, esp. in an unexpressive or unskilled way. **2** [trans.] hit (someone) abruptly. **3** (also **plank**) [trans.] put or set (something) down heavily or abruptly: *she plunked her purse on top of the bar.* ■ pay (money) on the spot or abruptly: *I gladly **plunked down** my ten dollars.* ■ (**plunk oneself down**) sit down in a hurried or undignified way: *she plunks herself down on the stool.*

▸n. **1** the sound made by abruptly plucking a string of a stringed instrument. **2** a heavy blow. **3** an act of setting something down heavily. ▷early 19th cent.: probably imitative. —**plunk·er** *n.*

plu·per·fect /ˌplo͞oˈpərfikt/ ▸adj. & n. another term for PAST PERFECT. ■ [as adj.] more than perfect: *they have one pluperfect daughter and are expecting an ideal little brother for her.* ▷late 15th cent.: from modern Latin *plusperfectum*, from Latin *(tempus praeteritum) plus quam perfectum* '(past tense) more than perfect.'

plu·ral /ˈplo͝orəl/ ▸adj. more than one in number: *the meanings of the text are plural.* ■ *Grammar* (of a word or form) denoting more than one, or (in languages with dual number) more than two: [postpositive] *the first person plural.*

▸n. *Grammar* a plural word or form. ■ [in sing.] the plural number: *the verb is in the plural.* ▷late Middle English: from Old French *plurel* or Latin *pluralis*, from *plus, plur-* 'more.' —**plu·ral·ly** *adv.*

USAGE 1 The apostrophe is often, but not always, used to form the plural of letters (*r's*) and numbers (*7's*), as well as single words referred to themselves (*four the's in one sentence*).

2 The regular plurals of abbreviations and acronyms may be spelled by simply adding an *s*: *CDs, MiGs.* They may also, esp. if periods are involved, employ an apostrophe: *D.D.S.'s.*

3 The plurals of proper names typically end in *s* or *es*, never with an apostrophe: *the Smiths, the Joneses, the Rosses.* See also **usage** at APOSTROPHE[1].

plu·ral·ism /ˈplo͝orəˌlizəm/ ▸n. **1** a condition or system in which two or more states, groups, principles, sources of authority, etc., coexist. ■ a form of society in which the members of minority groups maintain their independent cultural traditions. ■ a political theory or system of power-sharing among a number of political parties. ■ a theory or system of devolution and autonomy for individual bodies in preference to monolithic state control. ■ *Philosophy* a theory or system that recognizes more than one ultimate principle. Compare with MONISM. **2** the practice of holding more than one office or church benefice at a time. —**plu·ral·ist** *n.* & *adj.* —**plu·ral·is·tic** /-ˈlistik/ *adj.* —**plu·ral·is·ti·cal·ly** /-ˈlistək(ə)lē/ *adv.*

plu·ral·i·ty /plo͝oˈralitē/ ▸n. (pl. **-ties**) **1** the fact or state of being plural: *some languages add an extra syllable to mark plurality.* ■ [in sing.] a large number of people or things: *a plurality of critical approaches.* **2** the number of votes cast for a candidate who receives more than any other but does not receive an absolute majority: *his winning plurality came from creating a reform coalition.* ■ the number by which this exceeds the number of votes cast for the candidate who placed second. **3** *chiefly historical* another term for PLURALISM (sense 2). ▷late Middle English: from Old French *pluralite*, from late Latin *pluralitas*, from Latin *pluralis* 'relating to more than one' (see PLURAL).

USAGE On the difference between **plurality** and **majority**, see **usage** at MAJORITY.

plu·ral·ize /ˈplo͝orəˌlīz/ ▸v. [trans.] **1** cause to become more numerous. ■ cause to be made up of several different elements. **2** give a plural form to (a word). —**plu·ral·i·za·tion** /ˌplo͝orəliˈzāSHən/ *n.*

pluri- ▸comb. form several: *pluripotent.* ▷from Latin *plus, plur-* 'more,' *plures* 'several.'

plu·ri·po·tent /ˌplo͝oriˈpōtnt/ ▸adj. *Biology* (of an immature or stem cell) capable of giving rise to several different cell types. ▷1940s: from PLURI- 'several' + Latin *potent-* 'being able' (see POTENT[1]).

plus /pləs/ ▸prep. with the addition of: *two plus four is six* | *he was awarded the full amount plus interest.* ■ *informal* together with: *all apartments have a small kitchen plus private bathroom.*

▸adj. **1** [postpositive] (after a number or amount) at least: *companies put losses at $500,000 plus.* ■ (after a grade) better than: *B plus.* **2** (before a number) above zero; positive: *plus 60 degrees centigrade.* **3** having a positive electric charge.

▸n. **1** short for PLUS SIGN. ■ a mathematical operation of addition. **2** an advantage: *knowing the language is a decided plus* | [as adj.] ***on the plus side**, the employees are enthusiastic and good-natured.*

▸conj. *informal* furthermore; also: *it's packed full of medical advice, plus it keeps you informed about the latest research.* ▷mid 16th cent.: from Latin, literally 'more.'

▸PHRASE □ **plus or minus** used to define the margin of error of an estimate or calculation: *the coral was estimated to be 840 years old, plus or minus 40 years.*

USAGE The use of **plus** as a conjunction meaning 'furthermore' (*plus, we will be pleased to give you personal financial advice*) is considered informal and should be avoided in formal writing.

plus ça change /ˈplo͞o sä ˈSHÄNZH/ ▸exclam. used to express resigned acknowledgment of the fundamental immutability of human nature and institutions. ▷French, from *plus ça change, plus c'est la même chose* 'the more it changes, the more it stays the same.'

plus fours /pləs fôrz/ ▸plural n. *dated* baggy knickers reaching below the knee, worn esp. by men for playing golf. ▷1920s: so named because the overhang at the knee requires an extra four inches of material.

plush /pləSH/ ▸n. a rich fabric of silk, cotton, wool, or a combination of these, with a long, soft nap: [as adj.] *deep-buttoned plush upholstery.*

▸adj. *informal* richly luxurious and expensive: *the plush chrome and leather office.* ▷late 16th cent.: from obsolete French *pluche*, contraction of *peluche*, from Old French *peluchier* 'to pluck,' based on Latin *pilus* 'hair.' The sense 'luxurious' dates from the 1920s. —**plush·ly** *adv.* —**plush·ness** *n.* —**plush·y** (**plush·i·er, plush·i·est**) *adj.*

plush vel·vet ▸n. a kind of plush with a short, soft, dense nap, resembling velvet.

plus-mi·nus ▸n. [often as adj.] *Ice Hockey* a running total used as an indication of a player's effectiveness, calculated by adding one for each goal scored by the player's team in even-strength play while the player is on the ice, and subtracting one for each goal conceded.

plus sign ▸*n.* the symbol +, indicating addition or a positive value.

plus-size ▸*adj.* (of clothing or people) of a size larger than the normal range: *a new line of plus-size bathing suits.*

Plu·tarch /ˈplo͞oˌtärk/ (*c.*46–*c.*120), Greek biographer and philosopher; Latin name *Lucius Mestrius Plutarchus.* He is chiefly known for *Parallel Lives*, a collection of biographies of prominent Greeks and Romans.

plu·te·us /ˈplo͞otēəs/ ▸*n.* (*pl.* **-te·i** /-tēˌī/) *Zoology* the planktonic larva of some echinoderms, being somewhat triangular with lateral projections. ▷late 19th cent.: from Latin, literally 'barrier' (with reference to its shape).

Plu·to /ˈplo͞otō/ **1** *Greek Mythology* the god of the underworld. Also called **HADES**. **2** *Astronomy* the most remote known planet of the solar system, usually ninth in order from the sun, discovered in 1930 by Clyde Tombaugh.

Pluto usually orbits beyond Neptune at an average distance of 5,900 million km from the sun, although its orbit is so eccentric that at perihelion it is closer to the sun than Neptune (as in 1979–99). Pluto is smaller than earth's moon (diameter about 2,250 km), but it was discovered in 1978 to have its own satellite (Charon), which is so large that the pair should properly be regarded as a double planet.

▷via Latin from *Ploutōn*, the Greek name of the god of the underworld.

plu·toc·ra·cy /plo͞oˈtäkrəsē/ ▸*n.* (*pl.* **-cies**) government by the wealthy. ▪ a country or society governed in this way. ▪ an elite or ruling class of people whose power derives from their wealth. ▷mid 17th cent.: from Greek *ploutokratia*, from *ploutos* 'wealth' + *kratos* 'strength, authority.' —**plu·to·crat·ic** /ˌplo͞otəˈkratik/ *adj.* —**plu·to·crat·i·cal·ly** /ˌplo͞otəˈkratiklē/ *adv.*

USAGE See usage at **ARISTOCRACY**.

plu·to·crat /ˈplo͞otəˌkrat/ ▸*n.* *often derogatory* a person whose power derives from their wealth.

plu·ton /ˈplo͞oˌtän/ ▸*n.* *Geology* a body of intrusive igneous rock. ▷1930s: back-formation from **PLUTONIC**.

Plu·to·ni·an /plo͞oˈtōnēən/ ▸*adj.* **1** of or associated with the underworld. **2** of or relating to the planet Pluto.

plu·ton·ic /plo͞oˈtänik/ ▸*adj.* **1** *Geology* relating to or denoting igneous rock formed by solidification at considerable depth beneath the earth's surface. **2** (**Plutonic**) relating to the underworld or the god Pluto.

plu·to·nism /ˈplo͞otnˌizəm/ ▸*n.* *Geology* the formation of intrusive igneous rock by solidification of magma beneath the earth's surface. ▪ (**Plutonism**) *historical* the theory (now accepted) that rocks such as granite were formed by solidification from the molten state, as proposed by Scottish geologist James Hutton and others, rather than by precipitation from the sea. Compare with **NEPTUNISM**. —**Plu·to·nist** *n.* & *adj.* (*historical*).

plu·to·ni·um /plo͞oˈtōnēəm/ ▸*n.* the chemical element of atomic number 94, a dense silvery radioactive metal of the actinide series, used as a fuel in nuclear reactors and as an explosive in nuclear fission weapons. Plutonium only occurs in trace amounts in nature but is manufactured in nuclear reactors from uranium-238. (Symbol: **Pu**) ▷late 18th cent.: from Greek *Ploutōn* 'Pluto,' on the pattern of *neptunium*, being the next planet beyond Neptune.

plu·vi·al /ˈplo͞ovēəl/ *chiefly Geology* ▸*adj.* relating to or characterized by rainfall.
▸*n.* a period marked by increased rainfall. ▷mid 17th cent.: from Latin *pluvialis*, from *pluvia* 'rain.'

Plu·vi·ose /ˈplo͞ovēˌōs/ (also **Plu·vi·ôse** /plyˈvyôs/) ▸*n.* the fifth month of the French Republican calendar (1793–1805), originally running from January 20 to February 18. ▷French *Pluviôse*, from Latin *pluviosus* 'relating to rain.'

ply[1] /plī/ ▸*n.* (*pl.* **plies**) **1** a thickness or layer of a folded or laminated material. ▪ [usu. in *combination*] a strand of yarn or rope: [as *adj.*] *four-ply yarn.* ▪ the number of layers or strands of which something is made: *the yarn can be any ply from two to eight.* ▪ [usu. in *combination*] a reinforcing layer of fabric in a tire: [as *adj.*] *a six-ply whitewall tire.* **2** short for **PLYWOOD**. **3** (in game theory) the number of levels at which branching occurs in a tree of possible outcomes, typically corresponding to the number of moves ahead (in chess strictly half-moves ahead) considered by a computer program. ▪ a half-move (i.e., one player's move) in computer chess. ▷late Middle English (in the sense 'fold'): from French *pli* 'fold,' from the verb *plier*, from Latin *plicare* 'to fold.'

ply[2] ▸*v.* (**plies, plied**) [*trans.*] **1** work with (a tool, esp. one requiring steady, rhythmic movements): *a tailor delicately plying his needle.* ▪ work steadily at (one's business or trade); conduct: *he plied a profitable export trade.* **2** [*intrans.*] (of a vessel or vehicle) travel regularly over a route, typically for commercial purposes: *ferries ply across a strait to the island.* ▪ [*trans.*] travel over (a route) in this way: *the motion of the big tug as it plied the Jersey coastline.* **3** (**ply someone with**) provide someone with (food or drink) in a continuous or insistent way: *a flight attendant who plied them with soft drinks.* ▪ direct (numerous questions) at someone: *the presiding judge plied him with a series of absurd questions.* ▷late Middle English: shortening of **APPLY**.

Ply·mouth /ˈplimәTH/ **1** a port and naval base in southwestern England, on the Devon coast; pop. 239,000. In 1620 it was the scene of the Pilgrim Fathers' departure to North America in the *Mayflower*. **2** a town in southeastern Massachusetts, on the Atlantic coast; pop. 45,608. The site in 1620 of the landing of the Pilgrim Fathers, it was the earliest permanent European settlement in New England. **3** a city in southeastern Minnesota, northwest of Minneapolis; pop. 65,894. **4** the capital of the island of Montserrat in the Caribbean Sea; pop. 3,500. It was abandoned following the eruption of the Soufrière Hills volcano that began in 1995.

Plym·outh Breth·ren a strict Calvinistic religious body formed at Plymouth in England *c.*1830, having no formal creed and no official order of ministers. Its teaching emphasizes an expected millennium and members renounce many secular occupations, allowing only those compatible with New Testament standards.

Ply·mouth Rock[1] a granite boulder at Plymouth, Massachusetts, on to which the Pilgrim Fathers are said to have stepped when they disembarked from the *Mayflower*.

Plym·outh Rock[2] ▸*n.* a chicken of a large domestic breed of American origin, having gray plumage with blackish stripes, and a yellow beak, legs, and feet.

ply·wood /ˈplīˌwo͝od/ ▸*n.* a type of strong thin wooden board consisting of two or more layers glued and pressed together with the direction of the grain alternating, and usually sold in sheets of four by eight feet.

Pl·zeň /ˈpəlˌzenyə/ Czech name for **PILSEN**.

PM ▸*abbr.* ▪ Past Master. ▪ Paymaster. ▪ Police Magistrate. ▪ Postmaster. ▪ postmortem. ▪ Prime Minister. ▪ Provost Marshal.

Pm ▸*symbol* the chemical element promethium.

p.m. ▸*abbr.* after noon, used after times of day between noon and midnight: *at 3:30 p.m.* ▷from Latin *post meridiem*.

PMG ▸*abbr.* ▪ paymaster general. ▪ postmaster general.

pmk. ▸*abbr.* postmark.

PMS ▸*abbr.* premenstrual syndrome.

pmt. ▸*abbr.* payment.

p.n. ▸*abbr.* promissory note.

PNdB ▸*abbr.* perceived noise decibel(s).

pneum. ▸*abbr.* ▪ pneumatic. ▪ pneumatics.

pneu·ma /ˈn(y)o͞omə/ ▸*n.* *Philosophy* (in Stoic thought) the vital spirit, soul, or creative force of a person. ▷Greek, literally 'that which is breathed or blown.'

pneu·mat·ic /n(y)o͞oˈmatik/ ▸*adj.* **1** containing or operated by air or gas under pressure. ▪ *Zoology* (chiefly of cavities in the bones of birds) containing air. ▪ *informal* (of certain body parts, esp. a woman's breasts) large, as if inflated: *she's the one with the pneumatic lips and breasts.* ▪ *informal* (of a woman) having large breasts: *Lee and his pneumatic wife.* **2** of or relating to the spirit.
▸*n.* (usu. **pneumatics**) an item of pneumatic equipment. ▷mid 17th cent.: from French *pneumatique* or Latin *pneumaticus*, from Greek *pneumatikos*, from *pneuma* 'wind,' from *pnein* 'breathe.' —**pneu·mat·i·cal·ly** /n(y)o͞oˈmadək(ə)lē/ *adv.* —**pneu·ma·tic·i·ty** /ˌn(y)o͞oməˈtisədē/ *n.*

pneu·mat·ic drill ▸*n.* a large, heavy mechanical drill driven by compressed air, used for drilling into hard materials such as rock or concrete.

pneu·mat·ics /n(y)o͞oˈmatiks/ ▸*plural n.* [treated as *sing.*] the branch of physics or technology concerned with the mechanical properties of gases.

pneumato- ▸*comb. form* **1** of or containing air: *pneumatophore.* **2** relating to the spirit: *pneumatology.* ▷from Greek *pneuma, pneumat-* 'wind, breath, spirit.'

pneu·ma·tol·o·gy /ˌn(y)o͞oməˈtäləjē/ ▸*n.* the branch of Christian theology concerned with the Holy Spirit. —**pneu·ma·to·log·i·cal** /ˌn(y)o͞omədəˈläjəkəl/ *adj.*

pneu·ma·tol·y·sis /ˌn(y)o͞oməˈtäləsis/ ▸*n.* *Geology* the chemical alteration of rocks and the formation of minerals by the action of hot magmatic gases. —**pneu·mat·o·lyt·ic** *adj.*

pneu·mat·o·phore /ˌn(y)o͞oˈmatəˌfô(ə)r/ ▸*n.* **1** *Zoology* the gas-filled float of some colonial coelenterates, such as the Portuguese man-of-war. **2** *Botany* (in mangroves and other swamp plants) an aerial root specialized for gaseous exchange.

pneumo- ▸*comb. form* **1** of or relating to the lungs: *pneumogastric.* **2** of or relating to the presence of air or gas: *pneumothorax.* ▷sense 1 from Greek *pneumōn* 'lung'; sense 2 from Greek *pneuma* 'air.'

pneu·mo·coc·cus /ˌn(y)o͞omōˈkäkəs/ ▸*n.* (*pl.* **-coc·ci** /-ˈkäksī; -ˈkäksē/) a bacterium associated with pneumonia and some forms of meningitis. • *Streptococcus pneumoniae*, a Gram-positive diplococcus. —**pneu·mo·coc·cal** *adj.*

pneu·mo·co·ni·o·sis /ˌn(y)o͞omōˌkōnēˈōsəs/ ▸*n.* *Medicine* a disease of the lungs due to inhalation of dust, characterized by inflammation, coughing, and fibrosis. ▷late 19th cent.: from **PNEUMO-** 'relating to the lungs' + Greek *konis* 'dust' + **-OSIS**.

pneu·mo·cys·tis /ˈn(y)o͞omōˌsistis/ ▸*n.* *Medicine* a parasitic protozoan that can cause fatal pneumonia in people affected with immunodeficiency disease. • *Pneumocystis carinii*, phylum Sporozoa.

pneu·mo·en·ceph·a·log·ra·phy /ˌn(y)o͞omōenˌsefəˈlägrəfē/ ▸*n.* *Medicine* a radiographic technique (now largely superseded) for examining the brain. It involved displacing the cerebrospinal fluid in the ventricles of the brain by air or oxygen, which served as a contrast medium. —**pneu·mo·en·ceph·a·lo·gram** /-enˈsefələˌgram/ *n.* —**pneu·mo·en·ceph·a·lo·graph·ic** /ˌsefələˈgrafik/ *adj.*

pneu·mo·gas·tric /ˌn(y)o͞omōˈgastrik/ ▸*adj.* of or relating to the lungs and stomach.

pneu·mo·nec·to·my /ˌn(y)o͞omōˈnektəmē/ ▸*n.* (*pl.* **-mies**) surgical removal of a lung or part of a lung.

pneu·mo·nia /n(y)o͞oˈmōnēə; -ˈmōnyə/ ▸*n.* lung inflammation caused by bacterial or viral infection, in which the air sacs fill with pus and may become solid. Inflammation may affect both lungs (**double pneumonia**), one lung (**single pneumonia**), or only certain lobes (**lobar pneumonia**). ▷early 17th cent.: via Latin from Greek, from *pneumōn* 'lung.' —**pneu·mon·ic** /n(y)o͞oˈmänik/ *adj.*

pneu·mo·ni·tis /ˌn(y)o͞oməˈnītis/ ▸*n.* *Medicine* inflammation of the walls of the alveoli in the lungs, usually caused by a virus.

pneu·mo·tach·o·graph /ˌn(y)o͞omōˈtakəˌgraf/ ▸*n.* an apparatus for recording the rate of airflow during breathing.

pneu·mo·tho·rax /ˌn(y)o͞omōˈTHôˌraks/ ▸*n.* *Medicine* the presence of air or gas in the cavity between the lungs and the chest wall, causing collapse of the lung.

PNG ▸*abbr.* Papua New Guinea.

p-n junc·tion ▸*n.* *Electronics* a boundary between p-type and n-type material in a semiconductor device, functioning as a rectifier.

PNP ▸*adj.* *Electronics* denoting a semiconductor device in which an n-type region is sandwiched between two p-type regions.
▸*abbr.* (in computing) Plug and Play.

PO ▸*abbr.* ▪ Petty Officer. ▪ postal order. ▪ Post Office. ▪ purchase order.

Po[1] /pō/ a river in northern Italy. Italy's longest river, it rises in the Alps near the border with France and flows 415 miles (668 km) east to the Adriatic Sea.

Po[2] ▸*symbol* the chemical element polonium.

po' /pō; po͞oə; pô/ ▸*adj.* short for **POOR**, used to represent dialectal speech.

poach[1] /pōCH/ ▸*v.* [*trans.*] cook (an egg), without its shell, in or over boiling water: [as *adj.*] (**poached**) *a breakfast of poached egg and grilled bacon.* ▪ cook by simmering in a small amount of liquid: *poach the* *salmon in the white wine.* ▷late Middle English: from Old French *pochier*, earlier in the sense 'enclose in a bag,' from *poche* 'bag, pocket.'

poach[2] ▸*v.* [*trans.*] **1** illegally hunt or catch (game or fish) on land that is not one's own, or in contravention of official protection. ■ take or acquire in an unfair or clandestine way: *employers risk having their newly trained workers poached by other companies.* ■ [*intrans.*] (in ball games) take a shot that a partner or teammate would have expected to take. **2** (of an animal) trample or cut up (turf) with its hoofs. ■ [*intrans.*] (of land) become sodden by being trampled. ▷early 16th cent. (in the sense 'push roughly together'): apparently related to POKE[1]; sense 1 is perhaps partly from French *pocher* 'enclose in a bag' (see POACH[1]).

▸*PHRASE* □ **poach on someone's territory** encroach on someone else's rights.

poach·er[1] /ˈpōcHər/ ▸*n.* [usu. with *adj.*] a pan for cooking eggs or other food by poaching: *an egg poacher.*

poach·er[2] ▸*n.* a person who hunts or catches game or fish illegally.

▸*PHRASE* □ **poacher turned gamekeeper** someone who now protects the interests they previously attacked.

poach·er[3] ▸*n.* a small spiny fish that has an armor of overlapping plates and lives chiefly in cooler coastal waters. • Family Agonidae: several genera and species.

POB ▸*abbr.* post office box.

po·bla·no /pōˈblänō/ ▸*n.* a large dark green chili pepper of a mild-flavored variety. ▷Spanish.

Po·ca·hon·tas /ˌpōkəˈhäntəs/ (*c.*1595–1617), American Indian; daughter of Powhatan, an Algonquian chief in Virginia. According to John Smith, she rescued him from death at the hands of her father. In 1612, she was seized as a hostage by the English, and she later married colonist John Rolfe.

Po·ca·tel·lo /ˌpōkəˈtelō/ an industrial and commercial city in southeastern Idaho; pop. 51,466.

po·chard /ˈpōcHərd/ ▸*n.* (*pl.* same or **-chards**) a diving duck, the male of which typically has a reddish-brown head and a black breast. • Genera *Aythya* and *Netta*, family Anatidae: five species, in particular the common *A. ferina* of Eurasia. ▷mid 16th cent.: of unknown origin.

pock /päk/ ▸*n.* a pockmark. ▷Old English *poc* 'pustule,' of Germanic origin; related to Dutch *pok* and German *Pocke*. Compare with POX. —**pocked** *adj.* —**pock·y** *adj.* (*archaic*).

pock·et /ˈpäkət/ ▸*n.* **1** a small bag sewn into or on clothing so as to form part of it, used for carrying small articles. ■ a pouchlike compartment providing separate storage space, for example in a suitcase. ■ *informal* (often **pockets**) a person or organization's financial resources: *the food was all priced to suit the hard-up airman's pocket | our pockets are empty.* ■ *Baseball* the hollow in the center of a baseball glove or mitt where the ball can best be caught. ■ an opening at the corner or on the side of a billiard table into which balls are struck. **2** a small patch of something: *some of the gardens still had pockets of dirty snow in them.* ■ a small, isolated group or area: *there were pockets of disaffection in parts of the country.* ■ *Football* the protected area behind the offensive line from which the quarterback throws passes. ■ (in bowling) the space between the head pin and the pin immediately behind it on the left or right. ■ a cavity in a rock or stratum filled with ore or other distinctive component. ■ *Aeronautics* an air pocket.

▸*adj.* [*attrib.*] of a suitable size for carrying in a pocket: *a pocket dictionary.* ■ on a small scale: *a 6,000-acre pocket paradise.*

▸*v.* (**pock·et·ed, pock·et·ing**) [*trans.*] put into one's pocket: *she watched him lock up and pocket the key.* ■ take or receive (money or other valuables) for oneself, esp. dishonestly: *local politicians were found to have been pocketing the proceeds.* ■ *Billiards* drive (a ball) into a pocket. ■ enclose as though in a pocket: *the fillings can be pocketed in a pita bread.* ■ suppress (one's feelings) and proceed despite them: *they were prepared to pocket their pride.* ■ block passage of (a bill) by a pocket veto. ▷Middle English (in the sense 'bag, sack,' also used as a measure of quantity): from Anglo-Norman French *poket(e)*, diminutive of *poke* 'pouch.' The verb dates from the late 16th cent. Compare with POKE[2]. —**pock·et·a·ble** *adj.* —**pock·et·ful** /-ˌfo͝ol/ (*pl.* **-fuls**) *n.* —**pock·et·less** *adj.*

▸*PHRASES* □ **in pocket** having enough money or money to spare; having gained in a transaction. ■ (of money) gained by someone from a transaction. □ **in someone's pocket 1** dependent on someone financially and therefore under their influence. **2** very close to and closely involved with someone: *I'm tired of towns where everyone lives in everyone else's pocket.* □ **line one's pockets** see LINE[2]. □ **out of pocket** having lost money in a transaction: *the organizer of the concert was $15,000 out of pocket after it was canceled.* ■ (**out-of-pocket**) [as *adj.*] [*attrib.*] (of an expense or cost) paid for directly rather than being put on account or charged to some other person or organization. □ **put one's hand in one's pocket** spend or provide one's own money.

pock·et bat·tle·ship ▸*n.* any of a class of cruisers with large-caliber guns, operated by the German navy in World War II.

pock·et·bil·liards ▸*plural n.* a form of billiards played on a table with six pockets into which balls are shot for points. Also called POOL.

pock·et·book /ˈpäkətˌbo͝ok/ ▸*n.* **1** a woman's handbag. ■ one's financial resources: *they provide packages for every taste and every pocketbook.* **2** (**pocket book**) a paperback or other small or cheap edition of a book. **3** *Brit.* a notebook.

pock·et·book plant ▸*n.* another term for CALCEOLARIA.

pock·et bor·ough ▸*n.* (in the UK) a borough in which the election of political representatives was controlled by one person or family. Such boroughs were abolished by the Reform Acts of 1832 and 1867.

pock·et go·pher ▸*n.* see GOPHER (sense 1).

pock·et·knife /ˈpäkətˌnīf/ ▸*n.* (*pl.* **pocketknives**) a knife with a folding blade or blades, suitable for carrying in a pocket.

pock·et mon·ey ▸*n.* a small amount of money suitable for minor expenses. ■ *Brit.* a child's allowance.

pock·et mouse ▸*n.* a small nocturnal rodent with large cheek pouches for carrying food, native to the deserts of North and Central America. • Genus *Perognathus*, family Heteromyidae: several species.

pock·et ve·to ▸*n.* an indirect veto of a legislative bill by the president or a governor by retaining the bill unsigned until it is too late for it to be dealt with during the legislative session.

pock·et watch ▸*n.* a watch on a chain, intended to be carried in the pocket of a jacket or vest.

pock·mark /ˈpäkˌmärk/ ▸*n.* a pitted scar or mark on the skin left by a pustule or pimple. ■ a scar, mark, or pitted area disfiguring a surface.

▸*v.* [*trans.*] (usu. **be pockmarked**) cover or disfigure with such marks: *the area is pockmarked by gravel pits* | [as *adj.*] (**pockmarked**) *a pockmarked face.*

po·co /ˈpōkō; ˈpô-/ ▸*adv. Music* (in directions) a little; somewhat: *poco adagio.* ▷Italian.

po·co a po·co /ˈpōkō ä ˈpōkō/ ▸*adv* . *Music* (esp. as a direction) little by little; gradually.

Po·co·ma·ni·a /ˌpōkəˈmānēə/ ▸*n.* a Jamaican folk religion combining revivalism with ancestor worship and spirit possession. ▷1930s: probably a Hispanicized form of a local word, the second element being interpreted as -MANIA.

Po·co·no Moun·tains /ˈpōkəˌnō/ (also **the Poconos**) a range in northeastern Pennsylvania, noted for its resorts.

pod[1] /päd/ ▸*n.* **1** an elongated seed vessel of a leguminous plant such as the pea, splitting open on both sides when ripe. ■ the egg case of a locust. ■ *Geology* a body of rock or sediment whose length greatly exceeds its other dimensions: *pods of blue quartz in Virginia.* ■ a narrow-necked purse seine for catching eels. **2** [often with *adj.*] a detachable or self-contained unit on an aircraft, spacecraft, vehicle, or vessel, having a particular function: *the torpedo's sensor pod contains a television camera.*

▸*v.* (**pod·ded, pod·ding**) **1** [*intrans.*] (of a plant) bear or form pods: *the peas have failed to pod.* **2** [*trans.*] remove (peas or beans) from their pods prior to cooking. ▷late 17th cent.: back-formation from dialect *podware, podder* 'field crops,' of unknown origin. —**pod·like** /-ˌlīk/ *adj.*

pod[2] ▸*n.* a small herd or school of marine animals, esp. whales. ▷mid 19th cent. (originally U.S.): of unknown origin.

p.o.'d (also **PO'd, po'd**) ▸*abbr. informal* pissed off: *what was he po'd about?*

po·dag·ra /pəˈdagrə/ ▸*n. Medicine* gout of the foot, esp. the big toe. ▷Middle English: from Latin, from Greek *pous, pod-* 'foot' + *agra* 'seizure.' —**po·dag·ral** /-rəl/ *adj.* —**po·dag·ric** /-rik/ *adj.* —**po·dag·rous** /-rəs/ *adj.*

Pod·go·ri·ca /ˈpôdgôˌrētsə/ the capital of Montenegro and the judicial capital of Serbia and Montenegro, in the southwest; pop. 139,500. Under Turkish rule 1474–1878, it was named Titograd 1946–93 in honor of Marshal Tito.

podg·y /ˈpäjē/ ▸*adj.* (**podg·i·er, podg·i·est**) *chiefly Brit., informal* (of a person or part of their body) somewhat fat; chubby. —**podg·i·ness** *n.*

po·di·a·try /pəˈdīətrē/ ▸*n.* the treatment of the feet and their ailments. ▷early 20th cent.: from Greek *pous, pod-* 'foot' + *iatros* 'physician.' —**po·di·a·trist** /-trəst/ *n.*

po·di·um /ˈpōdēəm/ ▸*n.* (*pl.* **-di·ums** or **-di·a** /-dēə/) a small platform on which a person may stand to be seen by an audience, as when making a speech or conducting an orchestra. ■ a lectern. ■ a continuous projecting base or pedestal under a building. ■ a raised platform surrounding the arena in an ancient amphitheater. ▷mid 18th cent.: via Latin from Greek *podion*, diminutive of *pous, pod-* 'foot.'

pod·o·carp /ˈpädəˌkärp/ ▸*n.* a coniferous tree or shrub that is chiefly native to the southern hemisphere, widely grown as an ornamental or timber tree. • Genus *Podocarpus*, family Podocarpaceae. ▷mid 19th cent.: from modern Latin *Podocarpus*, from Greek *pous, pod-* 'foot' + *karpos* 'fruit.'

Po·dolsk /pəˈdôlsk/ an industrial city in Russia, south of Moscow; pop. 209,000.

Po·dunk /ˈpōˌdəNGk/ ▸*n.* [usu. as *adj.*] *informal* a hypothetical small town regarded as typically dull or insignificant: *she lived in a Podunk town notable for nothing except the girls' school where she taught art.* ▷mid 19th cent.: a place name of southern New England, of Algonquian origin.

pod·zol /ˈpädˌzôl; -ˌzäl/ (also **pod·sol**) ▸*n. Soil Science* an infertile acidic soil having an ashlike subsurface layer (from which minerals have been leached) and a lower dark stratum, occurring typically under temperate coniferous woodland. ▷early 20th cent.: from Russian, from *pod* 'under' + *zola* 'ashes.' —**pod·zol·ic** /-ˈzôlik; -ˈzälik/ *adj.* —**pod·zol·i·za·tion** /ˌpädzələˈzāsHən/ *n.* —**pod·zol·ize** /ˈpädzəˌlīz/ *v.*

Poe /pō/, Edgar Allan (1809–49), U.S. short-story writer, poet, and critic. His fiction and poetry are Gothic in style and characterized by their exploration of the macabre and the grotesque. Notable works: "The Fall of the House of Usher" (1840), "The Murders in the Rue Morgue" (1841), and "The Raven" (1845).

po·em /ˈpōəm; ˈpōim; pōm/ ▸*n.* a piece of writing that partakes of the nature of both speech and song that is nearly always rhythmical, usually metaphorical, and often exhibits such formal elements as meter, rhyme, and stanzaic structure. ■ something that arouses strong emotions because of its beauty: *you make a poem of riding downhill on your bike.* ▷late 15th cent.: from French *poème* or Latin *poema*, from Greek *poēma*, early variant of *poiēma* 'fiction, poem,' from *poiein* 'create.'

po·e·sy /ˈpōəzē; -sē/ ▸*n. archaic* or *poetic/literary* poetry. ■ the art or composition of poetry. ▷late Middle English: from Old French *poesie*, via Latin from Greek *poēsis*, variant of *poiēsis* 'making, poetry,' from *poiein* 'create.'

po·et /ˈpōət; ˈpōit/ ▸*n.* a person who writes poems. ■ a person possessing special powers of imagination or expression. ▷Middle English: from Old French *poete*, via Latin from Greek *poētēs*, variant of *poiētēs* 'maker, poet,' from *poiein* 'create.'

poet. ▸*abbr.* ■ poetic; poetical. ■ poetry.

po·et·as·ter /ˈpōətˌastər/ ▸*n.* a person who writes inferior poetry. ▷late 16th cent.: modern Latin, from Latin *poeta* 'poet' + -ASTER.

poète mau·dit /pōˈet mōˈdē/ ▸*n.* (*pl.* **poètes mau·dits** /mōˈdē(z)/) a poet who is insufficiently appreciated by their contemporaries. ▷French, literally 'cursed poet.'

po·et·ess /ˈpōətəs; ˈpōitəs/ ▸*n. dated* a female poet.

USAGE See usage at -ESS.

po·et·ic /pōˈetik/ ▸*adj.* of, relating to, or used in poetry: *the muse is a poetic convention.* ■ written in verse rather than prose: *a poetic drama.* ■ having an imaginative or sensitively emotional style of expression: *the orchestral playing was colorful and poetic.* ▷mid 16th cent.: from French *poétique*, from Latin *poeticus* 'poetic, relating to poets,' from Greek *po(i)ētikos*, from *po(i)ētēs* (see POET). —**po·et·i·cal** /pōˈetikəl/ *adj.* —**po·et·i·cal·ly** /-ik(ə)lē/ *adv.*

po·et·i·cize /pōˈetəˌsīz/ ▸*v.* [*trans.*] make poetic in character. ■ [*intrans.*] write or speak poetically. —**po·et·i·cism** /-ˌsizəm/ *n.*

po·et·ic jus·tice ▸*n.* the fact of experiencing a fitting or deserved retribution for one's actions: *the noise* *was deafening and it was poetic justice when the amplifiers stalled just before the start.*

po·et·ic li·cense ▸*n.* the freedom to depart from the facts of a matter or from the conventional rules of language when speaking or writing in order to create an effect: *he used a little poetic license to embroider a good tale.*

po·et·ics /pō'etiks/ ▸*plural n.* [treated as *sing.*] the art of writing poetry. ■ writing that deals with the art of poetry or presents a theory of poetry or literary discourse.

po·et·ize /'pōət,īz/ ▸*v.* [*intrans.*] *dated* write or speak in verse or in a poetic style. ■ [*trans.*] represent in poetic form.

po·et lau·re·ate /'lôrēət/ ▸*n.* (*pl.* **po·ets lau·re·ate**) an eminent poet traditionally appointed for life as a member of the British royal household. ■ a poet appointed to, or regarded unofficially as holding, an honorary representative position in a particular country, region, or group: *the New York State poet laureate | the poet laureate of young America.*

In 1999, Andrew Motion was appointed poet laureate of Great Britain for a term of ten years, the first time in British history that the honor was not granted as a lifetime position. In the U.S., an unofficial poet laureateship has existed since 1937, although the position was not compensated until 1985, when the honorific title "Poetry Consultant to the Library of Congress" was changed to "Poet Laureate Consultant in Poetry." The first official American poet laureate was Robert Penn Warren, and since then the post has been filled by such well-known poets as Richard Wilbur, Howard Nemerov, Mark Strand, Robert Hass, and Robert Pinsky. The appointment is for one year only, with the possibility of renewal, and although the official duties are limited to one poetry reading and one public lecture, the poet laureate usually takes it upon himself or herself to promote poetry and to encourage its reading and appreciation. In 2000 Stanley Kunitz, at age 95, became the oldest American poet appointed to the post.

po·et·ry /'pōətrē; 'pōitrē/ ▸*n.* literary work in which special intensity is given to the expression of feelings and ideas by the use of distinctive style and rhythm; poems collectively or as a genre of literature: *he is chiefly famous for his love poetry.* ■ a quality of beauty and intensity of emotion regarded as characteristic of poems: *poetry and fire are nicely balanced in the music.* ■ something regarded as comparable to poetry in its beauty: *the music department is housed in a building that is pure poetry.* ▷late Middle English: from medieval Latin *poetria*, from Latin *poeta* 'poet.' In early use the word sometimes referred to creative literature in general.

po·et·ry slam ▸*n.* a competetion using elimination rounds for the reading or performance of poetry.

Po·ets' Cor·ner part of Westminster Abbey where several poets are buried or commemorated.

po-faced /'pō ,fāst/ ▸*adj. Brit.* humorless and disapproving: *don't be so po-faced about everything.* ▷1930s: perhaps from British slang *po* 'chamber pot,' influenced by *poker-faced*.

Pog /päg; pôg/ ▸*n.* (usu. **Pogs**) *trademark* a cardboard or plastic disk printed with a design or picture, used in a children's game involving the flipping over of piles of such disks. ■ (**Pogs**) a game played with these disks: *a group of boys playing Pogs during recess.* ▷1990s: acronym from *passion fruit, orange, guava*, a trademark for a juice drink originally made by a dairy on Maui, Hawaii: the lids of the drink provided the first game disks.

po·gey /'pōgē/ ▸*n. Canadian, informal* unemployment or welfare benefit: *so you want me to end up* ***on pogey****?* ▷late 19th cent., hobo slang for 'workhouse': of unknown origin.

po·go /'pōgō/ ▸*n.* (also **po·go stick**) (*pl.* **-gos**) a toy for jumping around on, consisting of a long, spring-loaded pole with a handle at the top and rests for a person's feet near the bottom.

▸*v.* (**-goes, -goed**) [*intrans.*] *informal* jump up and down as if on such a toy, typically as a form of dancing to certain types of rock music, esp. punk. ▷1920s: of unknown origin.

Po·go·noph·o·ra /,pōgə'näfərə/ *Zoology* a small phylum of long deep-sea worms that live in upright tubes of protein and chitin. They lack mouths and guts, subsisting mainly on the products of symbiotic bacteria. ▷modern Latin (plural), from Greek *pōgōn* 'beard' + *pherein* 'to bear.' **—po·go·noph·o·ran** /-rən/ *n.* & *adj.*

po·grom /'pōgrəm; pə'gräm/ ▸*n.* an organized massacre of a particular ethnic group, in particular that of Jews in Russia or eastern Europe. ▷early 20th cent.: from Russian, literally 'devastation,' from *gromit'* 'destroy by the use of violence.'

Po Hai /'bō 'hī/ variant of **Bo Hai**.

poi /poi/ ▸*n.* a Hawaiian dish made from the fermented root of the taro, which has been baked and pounded to a paste. ▷of Polynesian origin.

poign·ant /'poinyənt/ ▸*adj.* evoking a keen sense of sadness or regret: *a poignant reminder of the passing of time.* See note at **moving**. ■ keenly felt: *the sensation of being back at home was most poignant in the winter.* ■ *archaic* sharp or pungent in taste or smell. ▷late Middle English: from Old French, literally 'pricking,' present participle of *poindre*, from Latin *pungere* 'to prick.' **—poign·ance** *n.* **—poign·an·cy** /-yənsē/ *n.* **—poign·ant·ly** /-yəntlē/ *adv.*

poi·kil·it·ic /,poikə'litik/ ▸*adj. Geology* relating to or denoting the texture of an igneous rock in which small crystals of one mineral occur within crystals of another. ▷mid 19th cent.: from Greek *poikilos* 'variegated' + **-ite**[1] + **-ic**.

poikilo- ▸*comb. form* variegated: *poikiloblastic.* ■ variable: *poikilotherm.* ▷from Greek *poikilos* 'variegated, varied.'

poi·kil·o·blas·tic /,poi,kēlə'blastik; -,kil-/ ▸*adj. Geology* relating to or denoting the texture of a metamorphic rock in which small crystals of an original mineral occur within crystals of its metamorphic product.

poi·kil·o·therm /poi'kēlə,THərm; -kil-/ ▸*n. Zoology* an organism that cannot regulate its body temperature except by behavioral means such as basking or burrowing. Often contrasted with **homeotherm**; compare with **cold-blooded**. **—poi·ki·lo·ther·mal** /,poi,kēlə'THərməl; -,kil-/ *adj.* **—poi·ki·lo·ther·mic** /,poi,kēlə'THərmik; -,kilə-/ *adj.* **—poi·ki·lo·ther·my** *n.*

poi·lu /pwäl'(y)o͞o/ ▸*n. historical, informal* an infantry soldier in the French army, esp. one who fought in World War I. ▷French, literally 'hairy,' by extension 'brave,' whiskers being associated with virility.

Poin·ca·ré map /,pwanka'rā/ ▸*n. Mathematics & Physics* a representation of the phase space of a dynamic system, indicating all possible trajectories. ■ (also **Poincaré section**) the intersection of this representation with a given line, plane, etc.

poin·ci·an·a /,poinsē'anə; ,p(w)än-/ ▸*n.* a tropical tree of the pea family, with showy red or red and yellow flowers. • Genera *Caesalpinia* and *Delonix* (formerly *Poinciana*), family Leguminosae: several species, including the scarlet-flowered **royal poinciana** (*D. regia*), native to Madagascar. ▷mid 18th cent.: modern Latin, named after M. de *Poinci*, a 17th-cent. governor of the Antilles.

poin·set·ti·a /poin'set(ē)ə/ ▸*n.* a small Mexican shrub with large showy scarlet bracts surrounding the small yellow flowers, popular as a houseplant at Christmas. • *Euphorbia* (formerly **Poinsettia**) *pulcherrima*, family Euphorbiaceae. ▷mid 19th cent.: modern Latin, named after Joel R. *Poinsett* (1779–1851), American diplomat and amateur botanist.

point /point/ ▸*n.* **1** the tapered, sharp end of a tool, weapon, or other object: *the point of his dagger | a pencil point.* ■ *Archaeology* a pointed flake or blade, esp. one that has been worked. ■ see **glazier's point**. ■ *Ballet* another term for **pointe**. ■ *Boxing* the tip of a person's chin as a spot for a blow. ■ the prong of a deer's antler. **2** a dot or other punctuation mark, in particular a period. ■ a decimal point: *fifty-five point nine.* ■ a dot or small stroke used in the alphabets of Semitic languages to indicate vowels or distinguish particular consonants. ■ a very small dot or mark on a surface: *the sky was studded with points of light.* **3** a particular spot, place, or position in an area or on a map, object, or surface: *turn left at the point where you see a sign to Apple Grove | the furthermost point of the gallery | the check-in point.* ■ a particular moment in time or stage in a process: *from this point onward, the teacher was completely won over.* ■ (usu. **the point**) the critical or decisive moment: *when it came to the point, he would probably do what was expected of him.* ■ (**the point of**) the verge or brink of (doing or being something): *she was* ***on the point of*** *leaving.* ■ [usu. with *adj.*] a stage or level at which a change of state occurs: *it is packed to the bursting point.* ■ any of the twenty-four triangles on a backgammon board. ■ (in geometry) something having position but not spatial extent, magnitude, dimension, or direction, for example the intersection of two lines. ■ [with *adj.*] *Brit.* a wall outlet or jack: *a telephone point.* **4** a single item or detail in an extended discussion, list, or text: *you ignore a number of important points.* ■ an argument or idea put forward by a person in discussion: *he* ***made the point that*** *economic regulation involves controls on pricing.* ■ an interesting or convincing idea: *you must admit he does have a point.* ■ (usu. **the point**) the significant or essential element of what is intended or being discussed: *it took her a long time to* ***come to the point****.* ■ [in *sing.*] [usu. with *negative* or in *questions*] advantage or purpose that can be gained from doing something: *there was* ***no point in*** *denying the truth |* ***what's the point of*** *having things I don't need?* ■ relevance or effectiveness. ■ a distinctive feature or characteristic, typically a good one, of a person or thing: *he has his good points.* **5** (in sports and games) a mark or unit of scoring: *he scored 13 of his team's final 19 points against Houston.* ■ (in craps) the combination total of the two thrown dice (4, 5, 6, 8, 9, or 10) that permits a shooter to keep throwing until the shooter throws the same number again and wins. ■ a unit used in measuring value, achievement, or extent: *the shares index was down seven points.* ■ an advantage or success in an argument or discussion: *she smiled, assuming she had* ***won her point****.* ■ a unit of credit toward an award or benefit. ■ a percentage of the profits from a movie or recording offered to certain people involved in its production. ■ a punishment awarded by the courts for a driving offense and recorded cumulatively on a person's driver's license: *operating under the influence meant ten points marked up against the driver.* ■ a unit of weight (one hundredth of a carat, or 2 mg) for diamonds. ■ a unit of varying value, used in quoting the price of stocks, bonds, or futures. ■ *Bridge* a value assigned to certain cards (4 points for an ace, 3 for a king, 2 for a queen, and 1 for a jack, sometimes with extra points for long or short suits) by a player in assessing the strength of a hand. ■ (**point of**) (in piquet) the longest suit in a player's hand, containing a specified number of up to eight cards. **6** each of thirty-two directions marked at equal distances around a compass. ■ the corresponding direction toward the horizon. ■ the angular interval between two successive points of a compass, i.e., one eighth of a right angle (11° 15′). ■ (**points ——**) unspecified places considered in terms of their direction from a specified place: *they headed down I-95 to Philadelphia and points south.* **7** a narrow piece of land jutting out into a lake or ocean: *the boat came around the point |* [in *names*] *Sandy Point.* **8** (usu. **points**) *Brit.* another term for **switch** (sense 4). **9** *Printing* a unit of measurement for type sizes and spacing, which in the U.S. and UK is one twelfth of a pica, or 0.013835 inch (0.351 mm), and in Europe is 0.015 inch (0.376 mm). **10** *Basketball* a frontcourt position, usually manned by the guard who sets up the team's defense. ■ *Ice Hockey* either of two areas in each attacking zone, just inside the blue line where it meets the boards. **11** (usu. **points**) each of a set of electrical contacts in the distributor of a motor vehicle. **12** a small leading party of an advanced guard of troops. ■ the position at the head of a column or wedge of troops: *another marine said he would* ***walk point*** *because I had done it on the last patrol.* ■ short for **point man**. **13** (usu. **points**) the extremities of an animal, typically a horse or cat, such as the face, paws, and tail of a Siamese cat. **14** *Hunting* a spot to which a straight run is made. ■ a run of this type: *our fox* ***made his point to*** *Moorhill.* **15** (usu. **points**) *historical* a tagged piece of ribbon or cord used for lacing a garment or attaching breeches to a doublet. **16** a short piece of cord for tying up a reef in a sail. **17** the action or position of a dog in pointing: *a bird dog* ***on point****.* **18** *Music* an important phrase or subject, esp. in a contrapuntal composition. Compare with **counterpoint**.

▸*v.* **1** [*intrans.*] direct someone's attention to the position or direction of something, typically by extending one's finger: *the boys were nudging each other and* ***pointing at*** *me | he gripped her arm and* ***pointed to*** *the seat | it's rude to point.* ■ [with *adverbial of direction*] indicate a particular time, direction, or reading: *a sign pointing left.* ■ [*trans.*] direct or aim (something) at someone or something: *he* ***pointed*** *the flashlight beam* ***at*** *the floor.* ■ [with *adverbial of direction*] face or be turned in a particular direction: *two of its toes point forward and two point back.* ■ [with *adverbial*] cite or put forward a fact or situation as evidence of something: *he points to several factors supporting this conclusion.* ■ (**point to**) (of a situation) be evidence or an indication that (something) is likely to happen or be the case: *everything pointed to an eastern attack.* ■ [*trans.*] (of a dog) indicate the presence of (game) by acting as pointer. ■ [*trans.*] *chiefly Ballet* extend (the toes or feet) by tensing the foot and ankle so as to form a point. **2** [*trans.*] give force or emphasis to (words or actions): *he wouldn't miss the opportunity to point a moral.* ■ (**point something up**) reveal the true nature or importance of something: *he did so much to point up their plight in the 1960s.* **3** [*trans.*] fill in or repair the joints of (brickwork, a brick structure, or tiling) with smoothly finished mortar or cement. **4** [*trans.*] give a sharp, tapered point to: *he twisted and pointed his mustache.* **5** [*trans.*] insert points in (written Hebrew). ■ mark (Psalms) with signs for chanting. **6** [*intrans.*] *Nautical* (of a sailing vessel) sail close to the wind.

▸*phrasal v.* □ **point something out** direct someone's gaze or attention toward something, esp. by extending one's finger. ■ [*reporting verb*] say something to make someone aware of a fact or circumstance: [with *clause*] *she pointed out that his van had been in the parking lot all day* | [with *direct speech*] *"Most of the people around here are very poor," I pointed out.* ▷Middle English: the noun partly from Old French *point*, from Latin *punctum* 'something that is pricked,' giving rise to the senses 'unit, mark, point in space or time'; partly from Old French *pointe*, from Latin *puncta* 'pricking,' giving rise to the senses 'sharp tip, promontory.' The verb is from Old French *pointer*, and in some senses from the English noun.

▸*PHRASES* □ **beside the point** irrelevant. □ **case in point** an instance or example that illustrates what is being discussed: *the "green revolution" in agriculture is a good case in point.* □ **get the point** understand or accept the validity of someone's idea or argument: *I get the point about not sending rejections.* □ **in point of fact** see FACT. □ **make one's point** put across a proposition clearly and convincingly. □ **make a point of** make a special and noticeable effort to do (a specified thing): *she made a point of taking a walk each day.* □ **off the point** irrelevant. □ **point the finger** openly accuse someone or apportion blame. □ **the point of no return** the point in a journey or enterprise at which it becomes essential or more practical to continue to the end instead of returning to the point of departure. □ **point of sailing** a sailboat's heading in relation to the wind. □ **score points** deliberately make oneself appear superior to someone else by making clever remarks: *she was constantly trying to think of ways to score points off him.* □ **take someone's point** *chiefly Brit.* accept the validity of someone's idea or argument. □ **to the point** relevant: *his evidence was brief and to the point.* □ **up to a point** to some extent but not completely. □ **win on points** *Boxing* win by scoring more points than one's opponent (as awarded by the judges and/or the referee) rather than by a knockout.

point af·ter touch·down ▸*n.* another term for EXTRA POINT.

point-and-click ▸*adj. Computing* (of an interface) giving the user the ability to initiate tasks by using a mouse to move the cursor over an area of the screen and clicking on it.
▸*v.* [*intrans.*] use a mouse in such a way.

point-and-shoot ▸*adj. Photography* of, relating to, or denoting an automatic camera which, when it is pointed at a subject and the shutter release is pressed, will take a properly exposed and focused photograph.

point bar ▸*n. Geology* an alluvial deposit that forms by accretion on the inner side of an expanding loop of a river.

point-blank ▸*adj. & adv.* (of a shot, bullet, or other missile) fired from very close to its target. ■ [as *adj.*] (of the range of a shot, bullet, or other missile) so close as to allow no possibility of missing: *the weapon was inaccurate beyond point-blank range.* ■ (of a statement or question) blunt and direct; without explanation or qualification: [as *adj.*] *this point-blank refusal to discuss the issue* | [as *adv.*] *he refuses point-blank to be photographed or give interviews.* ▷late 16th cent.: probably from POINT + BLANK in the contemporaneous sense 'white spot in the center of a target.'

point blan·ket ▸*n. Canadian* a type of Hudson's Bay blanket with distinctive markings or points woven in to indicate size or weight.

point break ▸*n.* (in surfing) a type of wave characteristic of a coast with a headland.

point charge ▸*n. chiefly Physics* an electric charge regarded as concentrated in a mathematical point, without spatial extent.

point con·tact ▸*n. Electronics* the contact of a metal point with the surface of a semiconductor so as to form a rectifying junction.

point d'ap·pui /ˌpwan dä'pwē/ ▸*n.* (*pl.* **points d'ap·pui** *pronunc.* same) a support or prop; a strategic point. ▷French, literally 'point of support.'

pointe /point; pwant/ ▸*n.* (*pl. pronunc.* same) *Ballet* the tips of the toes. ■ (also **pointe work**) dance performed on the tips of the toes. ▷French, literally 'tip.'

▸*PHRASE* □ **on** (or **en**) **pointe** /än; än; ôn/ on the tips of the toes.

Pointe-à-Pi·tre /'pwant ä 'pētrə/ the chief port and commercial capital of the French island of Guadeloupe in the Caribbean Sea; pop. 26,000.

point·ed /'pointid/ ▸*adj.* **1** having a sharpened or tapered tip or end: *his face tapers to a pointed chin.* **2** (of a remark or look) expressing criticism in a direct and unambiguous way: *pointed comments were made about racial discrimination within the army.* —**point·ed·ly** *adv.* (in sense 2). —**point·ed·ness** *n.*

point·ed arch ▸*n.* an arch with a pointed crown, characteristic of Gothic architecture.

poin·telle /poin'tel/ (also *trademark* **Poin·telle**) ▸*n.* a type of knitwear or woolen fabric with small eyelet holes that create a lacy effect. ▷1950s: probably from *point* in the sense 'lace made entirely with a needle' + the French diminutive suffix *-elle*.

Pointe-Noire /pwant 'nwär/ the chief seaport of the Republic of Congo, an oil terminal on the Atlantic coast; pop. 576,000.

point·er /'pointər/ ▸*n.* **1** a long thin piece of metal on a scale or dial that moves to indicate a figure or position. ■ a rod used for pointing to features on a map or chart. ■ a hint as to what might happen in the future: *the figures were a* ***pointer to*** *gradual economic recovery.* ■ a small piece of advice; a tip: *here are some* ***pointers on*** *how to go about the task.* ■ *Computing* another term for CURSOR. ■ *Computing* a variable whose value is the address of another variable; a link. **2** a dog of a breed that on scenting game stands rigid looking toward it.

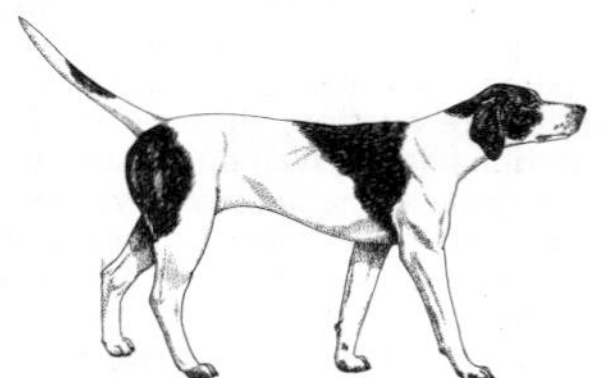

English pointer

Point·ers /'pointərz/ (**the Pointers**) *Astronomy* (in the northern hemisphere) two stars of the Big Dipper in Ursa Major, through which a line points nearly to Polaris. ■ (in the southern hemisphere) two stars in the Southern Cross, through which a line points nearly to the south celestial pole.

point es·ti·mate ▸*n. Statistics* a single value given as an estimate of a parameter of a population. Compare with INTERVAL ESTIMATE.

point guard ▸*n. Basketball* the backcourt player who directs the team's offense.

poin·til·lism /'pwantē,yizəm; 'pointl,izəm/ ▸*n.* a technique of neo-Impressionist painting using tiny dots of various pure colors, which become blended in the viewer's eye. It was developed by Seurat with the aim of producing a greater degree of luminosity and brilliance of color. ▷early 20th cent.: from French *pointillisme*, from *pointiller* 'mark with dots.' —**poin·til·list** /ˌpwantē'yēst; 'pointl-ist/ *n. & adj.* —**poin·til·list·ic** /ˌpwantē'yistik; ˌpointl'istik/ *adj.*

point·ing /'pointiNG/ ▸*n.* cement or mortar used to fill the joints of brickwork, esp. when added externally to a wall to improve its appearance and weatherproofing. ■ the process of adding such cement or mortar.

point·ing de·vice ▸*n. Computing* a generic term for any device (e.g., a graphics tablet, mouse, stylus, pointing stick, or trackball) used to control the movement of a cursor on a computer screen.

point·ing stick ▸*n.* a movable stub embedded in a laptop keyboard that is manipulated to move the screen cursor.

point lace ▸*n.* lace made with a needle on a parchment pattern.

point·less /'pointlis/ ▸*adj.* **1** having little or no sense, use, or purpose: *speculating like this is a pointless exercise* | [with *infinitive*] *it's pointless to plan too far ahead.* **2** (of a contest or competitor) without a point scored. —**point·less·ly** *adv.* —**point·less·ness** *n.*

point man ▸*n.* the soldier at the head of a patrol. ■ (esp. in a political context) a person at the forefront of an activity or endeavor.

point mu·ta·tion ▸*n. Genetics* a mutation affecting only one or very few nucleotides in a gene sequence.

point of de·par·ture ▸*n.* the starting point of a line of thought or course of action; an initial assumption: *historians took Lenin's ideas as their point of departure.* ■ *Nautical* the precise location of a vessel at the outset of a voyage.

point of hon·or ▸*n.* an action or circumstance that affects one's reputation or conscience: *he languished in jail refusing, as a point of honor, to talk.*

point of or·der ▸*n.* a query in a formal debate or meeting as to whether correct procedure is being followed.

point of sale (abbr.: **POS**) ▸*n.* the place at which goods are retailed: *refunds will be provided at the point of sale* | [as *adj.*] *point-of-sale credit card verification.*

point of view ▸*n.* a particular attitude or way of considering a matter: *I'm trying to get Matthew to change his point of view.* ■ (in fictional writing) the narrator's position in relation to the story being told: *this story is told from a child's point of view.* ■ the position from which something or someone is observed: *certain aspects are not visible from a single point of view.*

point set ▸*n.* (in acupuncture) a set of points stimulated simultaneously to treat a particular ailment or bring about a desired effect.

point source ▸*n. Physics* **1** a source of energy, such as light or sound, that can be regarded as having negligible dimensions. **2** a localized and stationary pollution source. Compare with NONPOINT SOURCE.

point spread ▸*n.* **1** a forecast of the number of points by which a stronger team is expected to defeat a weaker one, used for betting purposes. **2** *Physics & Physiology* the spread of energy from a point source, esp. with respect to light coming into an optical instrument or eye.

point sys·tem ▸*n.* a system for distributing or allocating resources or for ranking or evaluating candidates or claimants on the basis of points allocated or accumulated.

point-to-point ▸*n.* (*pl.* **point-to-points**) an amateur steeplechase for horses used in hunting, over a set cross-country course.
▸*adj.* (of a route or journey) from one place to the next without stopping or changing; direct. ■ (of a telecommunications or computer link) directly from the sender to the receiver. —**point-to-point·er** *n.* —**point-to-point·ing** *n.*

point·y /'pointē/ ▸*adj.* (**point·i·er**, **point·i·est**) *informal* having a pointed tip or end: *a pointy goatee.*

point·y-head·ed ▸*adj. informal, chiefly derogatory* intellectual; expert: *some pointy-headed college professor.* ▷by association with EGGHEAD.

poise[1] /poiz/ ▸*n.* **1** graceful and elegant bearing in a person: *poise and good deportment can be cultivated.* ■ composure and dignity of manner: *at least he had a moment to think, to recover his poise.* **2** *archaic* balance; equilibrium.
▸*v.* be or cause to be balanced or suspended: [*intrans.*] *he poised motionless on his toes* | [*trans.*] *figurative the world was poised between peace and war.* ■ (**be poised**) (of a person or organization) be ready to do something: [with *infinitive*] *teachers are poised to resume their attack on government school tests.* ▷late Middle English (in the sense 'weight'): from Old French *pois*, *peis* (noun), *peser* (verb), from an alteration of Latin *pensum* 'weight,' from the verb *pendere* 'weigh.' From the early senses of 'weight' and 'measure of weight' arose the notion of 'equal weight, balance,' leading to the extended senses 'composure' and 'elegant bearing.'

poise[2] ▸*n. Physics* a unit of dynamic viscosity, such that a tangential force of one dyne per square centimeter causes a velocity change of one centimeter per second between two parallel planes separated by one centimeter in a liquid. ▷early 20th cent.: from the name of Jean L. M. *Poiseuille* (1799–1869), French physician.

poised /poizd/ ▸*adj.* having a composed and self-assured manner. ■ having a graceful and elegant bearing.

Poi·seuille flow /pwä'zœ(ē); pwä'zē/ ▸*n. Physics* laminar or streamline flow of an incompressible viscous fluid, esp. through a long narrow cylinder. ▷1940s: named after Jean L. M. *Poiseuille* (1799–1869), French physician.

poi·sha /poisʜə/ ▶*n.* (*pl.* same) a monetary unit of Bangladesh, equal to one hundredth of a taka. ▷Bengali, alteration of PAISA.

poi·son /ˈpoizən/ ▶*n.* a substance that, when introduced into or absorbed by a living organism, causes death or injury, esp. one that kills by rapid action even in a small quantity. ■ *Chemistry* a substance that reduces the activity of a catalyst. ■ *Physics* an additive or impurity in a nuclear reactor that slows a reaction by absorbing neutrons. ■ a person, idea, action, or situation that is considered to have a destructive or corrupting effect or influence: *the late 1930s, when Nazism was spreading its poison.*
▶*v.* [*trans.*] administer poison to (a person or animal), either deliberately or accidentally: *he tried to poison his wife* | [as *n.*] (**poisoning**) *symptoms of poisoning may include nausea, diarrhea, and vomiting.* ■ adulterate or contaminate (food or drink) with poison. ■ [usu. as *adj.*] (**poisoned**) treat (a weapon or missile) with poison in order to augment its lethal effect. ■ (of a dangerous substance) kill or cause to become very ill: *swans are being poisoned by lead from anglers' lines.* ■ contaminate or pollute (an area, the air, or water). ■ *figurative* prove harmful or destructive to: *his disgust had poisoned his attitude toward everyone.* ■ *Chemistry* (of a substance) reduce the activity of (a catalyst). ▷Middle English (denoting a harmful medicinal drink): from Old French *poison* 'magic potion,' from Latin *potio(n-)* 'potion,' related to *potare* 'to drink.' —**poi·son·er** /ˈpoizənər/ *n.*
▶*PHRASE* □ **what's your poison?** *informal* used to ask someone what they would like to drink.

poi·son ar·row frog ▶*n.* a small slender, brightly colored frog of Central and South American rain forests. Its skin secretes a virulent poison, used by American Indians to coat their arrowheads. • Family Dendrobatidae: several genera and numerous species.

poi·soned chal·ice ▶*n. chiefly Brit.* an assignment, award, or honor that is likely to prove a disadvantage or source of problems to the recipient: *many thought the new minister had been handed a poisoned chalice.*

poi·son gas ▶*n.* poisonous gas or vapor, used esp. to disable or kill an enemy in warfare.

poi·son i·vy ▶*n.* a North American climbing plant of the cashew family that secretes an irritant oil from its leaves, which can cause dermatitis. • *Rhus radicans*, family Anacardiaceae.

poison ivy

poi·son oak ▶*n.* a North American climbing shrub of the cashew family, closely related to poison ivy and having similar properties. • *Rhus toxicodendron*, family Anacardiaceae.

poi·son·ous /ˈpoiz(ə)nəs/ ▶*adj.* (of an animal or insect) producing poison as a means of attacking enemies or prey: *a poisonous snake.* ■ (of a plant or substance) causing or capable of causing death or illness if taken into the body: *poisonous chemicals.* ■ *figurative* extremely unpleasant or malicious: *there was a poisonous atmosphere at the office.* —**poi·son·ous·ly** *adv.*

poi·son-pen let·ter ▶*n.* a letter, typically anonymous, that is libelous, abusive, or malicious.

poi·son pill ▶*n. Finance* a tactic used by a company threatened with an unwelcome takeover bid to make itself unattractive to the bidder.

poi·son pill a·mend·ment ▶*n.* an amendment to a legislative bill that considerably weakens the bill's intended effect, or ruins the bill's chances of passing.

poi·son su·mac ▶*n.* see SUMAC.

Pois·son dis·tri·bu·tion /pwäˈsôɴ/ ▶*n. Statistics* a discrete frequency distribution that gives the probability of a number of independent events occurring in a fixed time.

Pois·son's ra·tio /pwäˈsôɴz/ ▶*n. Physics* the ratio of the proportional decrease in a lateral measurement to the proportional increase in length in a sample of material that is elastically stretched.

Poi·tier /ˈpwätē,ā; pwätˈyā/, Sidney (1924–), U.S. actor and movie director, of Bahamian descent; the first black U.S. actor to achieve superstar status. Notable movies: *Lilies of the Field* (1963, Academy Award), *In the Heat of the Night* (1967), and *Guess Who's Coming to Dinner* (1967).

Sidney Poitier

Poi·tiers /pwäˈtyā/ a city in west central France, the chief town of Poitou-Charentes region and capital of the former province of Poitou; pop. 82,000.

Poi·tou /pwäˈto͞o/ a former province of west central France, now united with Charente to form the region of Poitou-Charentes. Formerly part of Aquitaine, it was held by the French and English in succession until it was finally united with France at the end of the Hundred Years War.

poke[1] /pōk/ ▶*v.* **1** [*trans.*] jab or prod (someone or something), esp. with one's finger: *he poked Benny in the ribs and pointed* | [*intrans.*] *they sniffed, felt, and* **poked at** *everything they bought.* ■ [*trans.*] jab (one's finger) at someone or into something: *keep adding water until you can comfortably poke your finger into the soil.* ■ prod and stir (a fire) with a poker to make it burn more fiercely. ■ make (a hole) in something by prodding or jabbing at it. ■ [*trans.*] thrust (something) in a particular direction: *I poked my head around the door to see what was going on* | *she poked her tongue out.* ■ [*intrans.*] protrude and be or become visible: *she had wisps of gray hair poking out from under her bonnet.* ■ *vulgar slang* (of a man) have sexual intercourse with (another person). **2** [*intrans.*] move slowly; dawdle: *I was* **poking along**, *my vision blocked by that curtain of sleet.*
▶*phrasal v.* □ **poke around/about** look around a place, typically in search of something.
▶*n.* **1** an act of poking someone or something: *she gave the fire a poke.* ■ (**a poke around**) *informal* a look or search around a place. ■ *vulgar slang* an act of sexual intercourse. **2** (also **poke bonnet**) a woman's bonnet with a projecting brim or front, popular esp. in the early 19th century. **3** (usu. **POKE**) *Computing* a statement or function in BASIC for altering the contents of a specified memory location. Compare with PEEK (sense 2). **4** *informal, chiefly Brit.* power or acceleration in a car: *I expect you'd prefer something with a bit more poke.* ▷Middle English: origin uncertain; compare with Middle Dutch and Middle Low German *poken*, of unknown ultimate origin. The noun dates from the late 18th cent.
▶*PHRASES* □ **poke fun at** tease or make fun of. □ **poke one's nose into** *informal* take an intrusive interest in. □ **take a poke at someone** *informal* hit or punch someone. ■ criticize someone.

poke[2] ▶*n. dialect* a bag or small sack. ■ *informal* a purse or wallet. ▷Middle English: from Old Northern French *poke*, variant of Old French *poche* 'pocket.' Compare with POUCH.
▶*PHRASE* □ **a pig in a poke** see PIG.

poke[3] ▶*n.* **1** another term for POKEWEED. **2** (**Indian poke**) another term for FALSE HELLEBORE. ▷early 18th cent.: from Virginia Algonquian *poughkone* (see PUCCOON).

poke-check ▶*v.* [*trans.*] *Ice Hockey* poke the puck off the stick of and out of the possession of (an opposing player).

Po·ke·mon /ˈpōki,män/ ▶*n. trademark* a video game, card game, or other toy featuring certain Japanese cartoon characters. ■ a colorful toy model of these Japanese cartoon characters. ▷from the name of the Japanese video game *Pokemon*, itself from the words 'pocket monster.'

pok·er[1] /ˈpōkər/ ▶*n.* a metal rod with a handle, used for prodding and stirring an open fire.

pok·er[2] ▶*n.* a card game played by two or more people who bet on the value of the hands dealt to them. A player wins the pool either by having the highest combination at the showdown or by forcing all opponents to concede without a showing of the hand, sometimes by means of bluff. ▷mid 19th cent.: of U.S. origin; perhaps related to German *pochen* 'to brag,' *Pochspiel* 'bragging game.'

pok·er face ▶*n.* an impassive expression that hides one's true feelings. ■ a person with such an expression. —**pok·er-faced** *adj.*

pok·er·work /ˈpōkər,wərk/ ▶*n.* British term for PYROGRAPHY.

poke·weed /ˈpōk,wēd/ ▶*n.* a North American plant with red stems, spikes of cream flowers, and purple berries. Also called POKE[3], INKBERRY. • *Phytolacca americana*, family Phytolaccaceae. ▷early 18th cent.: from POKE[3].

pok·ey /ˈpōkē/ ▶*n.* (usu. **the pokey**) *informal* prison: *25 years in the pokey.* ▷early 20th cent.: alteration of POGEY (an early sense being 'hostel for the needy'), perhaps influenced by POKY.

pok·y /ˈpōkē/ (also **pok·ey**) ▶*adj.* (**pok·i·er, pok·i·est**) **1** annoyingly slow or dull: *his poky old horse* | *I slept through his poky sermons.* **2** (of a room or building) uncomfortably small and cramped: *five of us shared the poky little room.* ▷mid 19th cent. (in the sense 'concerned with petty matters'): from POKE[1] (in a contemporaneous sense 'confine') + -Y[1]. —**pok·i·ly** /-kəlē/ *adv.* —**pok·i·ness** *n.*

pol /päl/ ▶*n. informal* a politician.

pol. ▶*abbr.* ■ political. ■ politics.

Po·lack /ˈpō,läk; -,lak/ (also **po·lack**) ▶*n. informal, offensive* a person from Poland or of Polish descent.
▶*adj.* of Polish origin or descent. ▷late 16th cent.: from Polish *Polak*.

Po·land /ˈpōlənd/ a country in central Europe with a coastline on the Baltic Sea; pop. 38,183,000; capital, Warsaw; language, Polish (official). Polish name POLSKA.

First united as a nation in the 11th century, Poland became a dominant power in the region in the 16th century but thereafter suffered severely from the rise of Russian, Swedish, Prussian, and Austrian power and was partitioned in the late 18th century. It regained full independence (as a republic) after World War I. Its invasion by German forces in 1939 precipitated World War II, from which it eventually emerged as a communist state under Soviet domination. In the 1980s, the rise of the independent trade union movement Solidarity eventually led to the end of communist rule in 1989. Poland joined NATO in 1999 and the EU in 2004.

Po·land Chi·na ▶*n.* a U.S. breed of hog that is black with white markings.

Po·lan·ski /pəˈlanskē/, Roman (1933–), French movie director. His second wife, actress **Sharon Tate** (1943–69), was one of the victims of a multiple murder by followers of cult leader Charles Manson. Notable movies: *Rosemary's Baby* (1968), *Chinatown* (1974), *Tess* (1979), and *The Pianist* (Academy Award, 2002).

po·lar /ˈpōlər/ ▶*adj.* **1** of or relating to the North or South Pole: *the polar regions.* ■ (of an animal or plant) living in the north or south polar region. ■ *Astronomy* of or relating to the poles of a celestial body.

Pronunciation Key ə *ago*; ər *over*; ˈə or ,ə *up*; ˈər or ,ər *fur*; a *hat*; ā *rate*; ä *car*; ᴄʜ *chew*; e *let*; ē *see*; e(ə)r *air*; i *fit*; ī *by*; i(ə)r *ear*; ɴɢ *sing*; ō *go*; ô *for*; oi *boy*; o͝o *good*; o͞o *goo*; ou *out*; sʜ *she*; ᴛʜ *thin*; T͟H *then*; (h)w *why*; zʜ *vision*

■ *Astronomy* of or relating to a celestial pole. ■ *Geometry* of or relating to the poles of a sphere. See POLE2. ■ *Biology* of or relating to the poles of a cell, organ, or part. **2** *Physics & Chemistry* having electrical or magnetic polarity. ■ (of a liquid, esp. a solvent) consisting of molecules with a dipole moment. ■ (of a solid) ionic. **3** directly opposite in character or tendency: *depression and its polar opposite, mania.*

▸*n.* **1** *Geometry* the straight line joining the two points at which tangents from a fixed point touch a conic section. **2** *Astronomy* a variable binary star that emits strongly polarized light, one component being a strongly magnetic white dwarf. ▷mid 16th cent.: from medieval Latin *polaris* 'heavenly,' from Latin *polus* 'end of an axis' (see POLE2).

po·lar ax·is ▸*n. Astronomy* the axis of an equatorially mounted telescope that is at right angles to the declination axis and parallel to the earth's axis of rotation, about which the telescope is turned to follow the apparent movement of celestial objects resulting from the earth's rotation.

po·lar bear ▸*n.* a large white arctic bear that lives mainly on the pack ice. It is a powerful swimmer and feeds chiefly on seals. • *Thalarctos maritimus*, family Ursidae.

polar bear

po·lar bod·y ▸*n. Biology* each of the small cells that bud off from an oocyte at the two meiotic divisions and do not develop into ova.

po·lar cap ▸*n. Astronomy* a region of ice or other frozen matter surrounding a pole of a planet.

po·lar co·or·di·nates ▸*plural n. Geometry* a pair of coordinates locating the position of a point in a plane, the first being the length of the straight line (*r*) connecting the point to the origin, and the second the angle (*ϑ*) made by this line with a fixed line. ■ the coordinates in a three-dimensional extension of this system.

po·lar dis·tance ▸*n. Geometry* the angular distance of a point on a sphere from the nearest pole.

po·lar·im·e·ter /ˌpōlə'rimitər/ ▸*n.* an instrument for measuring the polarization of light, and esp. (in chemical analysis) for determining the effect of a substance in rotating the plane of polarization of light. ▷mid 19th cent.: from medieval Latin *polaris* 'polar' + -METER. **—po·lar·i·met·ric** /pōˌlarə'metrik/ *adj.* **—po·lar·im·e·try** /-trē/ *n.*

Po·lar·is /pə'larəs/ **1** *Astronomy* a fairly bright star located within one degree of the north celestial pole, in the constellation Ursa Minor. It is a double star, the bright component of which is a cepheid variable. Also called NORTH STAR, POLESTAR. **2** a type of submarine-launched ballistic missile designed to carry nuclear warheads, formerly in service with the U.S. and British navies. ▷mid 19th cent.: from medieval Latin *polaris* 'heavenly,' from Latin *polus* 'end of an axis.'

po·lar·i·scope /pə'larəˌskōp/ ▸*n.* another term for POLARIMETER. ▷early 19th cent.: from medieval Latin *polaris* 'polar' + -SCOPE. **—po·lar·i·scop·ic** /pəˌlarə'skäpik/ *adj.*

po·lar·i·ty /pō'laritē; pə-/ ▸*n.* (*pl.* **-ties**) the property of having poles or being polar: *it exhibits polarity when presented to a magnetic needle.* ■ the relative orientation of poles; the direction of a magnetic or electric field: *the magnetic field peaks in strength immediately after switching polarity.* ■ the state of having two opposite or contradictory tendencies, opinions, or aspects: *the polarity between male and female | the Cold War's neat polarities can hardly be carried on.* ■ *Biology* the tendency of living organisms or parts to develop with distinct anterior and posterior (or uppermost and lowermost) ends, or to grow or orient in a particular direction.

po·lar·i·ty ther·a·py ▸*n.* a system of treatment used in alternative medicine, intended to restore a balanced distribution of the body's energy, and incorporating manipulation, exercise, and dietary restrictions.

po·lar·ize /'pōləˌrīz/ ▸*v.* **1** [*trans.*] *Physics* restrict the vibrations of (a transverse wave, esp. light) wholly or partially to one direction: [as *adj.*] (**polarizing**) *a polarizing microscope.* **2** [*trans.*] *Physics* cause (something) to acquire polarity: *the electrode is polarized in aqueous solution.* **3** divide or cause to divide into two sharply contrasting groups or sets of opinions or beliefs: [*intrans.*] *the cultural sphere has* ***polarized into*** *two competing ideological positions* | [*trans.*] *Vietnam polarized political opinion.* **—po·lar·iz·a·bil·i·ty** /ˌpōləˌrīzə'bilətē/ *n.* **—po·lar·iz·a·ble** *adj.* **—po·lar·i·za·tion** /ˌpōlərə'zāshən/ *n.* **—po·lar·iz·er** *n.*

po·lar·iz·ing fil·ter ▸*n.* a photographic or optical filter that polarizes the light passing through it, used chiefly for reducing reflections and improving contrast. Two polarizing filters are often used together, such that rotation of one of them results in a neutral density filter of variable density.

po·lar·og·ra·phy /ˌpōlə'rägrəfē/ ▸*n. Chemistry* a method of analysis in which a sample is subjected to electrolysis using a special electrode and a range of applied voltages, a plot of current against voltage showing steps corresponding to particular chemical species and proportional to their concentration. ▷1930s: from *polarization* (see POLARIZE) + -GRAPHY. **—po·lar·o·graph·ic** /pōˌlarə'grafik; pə-/ *adj.*

Po·lar·oid /'pōləˌroid/ ▸*n. trademark* **1** material in thin plastic sheets that produces a high degree of plane polarization in light passing through it. ■ (**Polaroids**) sunglasses with lenses made from such material. **2** a photograph taken with a Polaroid camera.

▸*adj. Photography* denoting a type of camera with internal processing that produces a finished print rapidly after each exposure. ■ denoting film for or a photograph taken with such a camera: *a Polaroid snapshot.* ▷1930s: from POLARIZE + -OID.

po·lar or·bit ▸*n.* a satellite orbit that passes over polar regions, esp. one whose plane contains the polar axis.

po·lar star ▸*n. Astronomy* a star at or close to a celestial pole, esp. Polaris.

po·lar wan·der·ing ▸*n.* the slow and erratic, real or apparent, movement of the earth's rotational or magnetic poles relative to the continents throughout geological time, due largely to continental drift.

pol·der /'pōldər/ ▸*n.* a piece of low-lying land reclaimed from the sea or a river and protected by dikes, esp. in the Netherlands. ▷early 17th cent.: from Dutch, from Middle Dutch *polre.*

Pole /pōl/ ▸*n.* a native or national of Poland, or a person of Polish descent. ▷via German from Polish *Polanie*, literally 'field-dwellers,' from *pole* 'field.'

pole1 /pōl/ ▸*n.* **1** a long, slender, rounded piece of wood or metal, typically used with one end placed in the ground as a support for something: *a tent pole.* ■ *Track & Field* a long, slender, flexible rod of wood or fiberglass used by a competitor in pole-vaulting. ■ short for SKI POLE. ■ a wooden shaft fitted to the front of a cart or carriage drawn by animals and attached to their yokes or collars. ■ a simple fishing rod. **2** *n. chiefly Brit., historical* a linear or square rod.

▸*v.* [*trans.*] propel (a boat) by pushing a pole against the bottom of a river, canal, or lake. ▷late Old English *pāl* (in early use without reference to thickness or length), of Germanic origin; related to Dutch *paal* and German *Pfahl*, based on Latin *palus* 'stake.'

▸*PHRASE* □ **under bare poles** *Sailing* with no sail set.

pole2 ▸*n.* either of the two locations (**North Pole** or **South Pole**) on the surface of the earth (or of a celestial object) that are the northern and southern ends of the axis of rotation. See also CELESTIAL POLE, MAGNETIC POLE. ■ *Geometry* either of the two points at which the axis of a sphere intersects its surface. ■ *Geometry* a fixed point to which other points or lines are referred, e.g., the origin of polar coordinates or the point of which a line or curve is a polar. ■ *Biology* an extremity of the main axis of a cell, organ, or part. ■ each of the two opposite points on the surface of a magnet at which magnetic forces are strongest. ■ each of two terminals (positive and negative) of an electric cell, battery, or machine. ■ *figurative* one of two opposed or contradictory principles or ideas: *Miriam and Rebecca represent two poles in the argument about transracial adoption.* ▷late Middle English: from Latin *polus* 'end of an axis,' from Greek *polos* 'pivot, axis, sky.' **—pole·ward** /-wərd/ *adj.* **—pole·wards** /-wərdz/ *adj. & adv.*

▸*PHRASE* □ **be poles apart** have nothing in common.

pole3 ▸*n.* short for POLE POSITION.

pole·ax /'pōˌlaks/ (also **pole·axe**) ▸*n.* another term for BATTLE-AX (sense 1). ■ a short-handled ax with a spike at the back, formerly used in naval warfare for boarding, resisting boarders, and cutting ropes. ■ a butcher's ax with a hammerhead at the back, used to slaughter animals.

▸*v.* [*trans.*] hit, kill, or knock down with or as if with a poleax. ■ (often **be poleaxed**) cause great shock to (someone): *I was poleaxed by this revelation.* ▷Middle English: related to Middle Dutch *pol(l)aex*, Middle Low German *pol(l)exe* (see POLL, AX). The change in the first syllable was due to association with POLE1; the first element *poll-* may have referred to a special head of the ax or to the head of an enemy.

pole barn ▸*n.* a farm building with no foundation and with sides consisting of corrugated steel or aluminum panels supported by poles set in the ground typically at eight-foot intervals.

pole bean ▸*n.* a variety of bean plant that climbs up a wall, tree, or trellis. Compare with BUSH BEAN. ■ the edible bean from such a plant.

pole build·ing ▸*n.* a quickly constructed building in which vertical poles are secured in the ground to serve as both the foundation and framework.

pole·cat /'pōlˌkat/ ▸*n.* a weasellike Eurasian mammal (genus *Mustela*, family Mustelidae) with mainly dark brown fur and a darker mask across the eyes, noted for ejecting a fetid fluid when threatened. ■ another term for SKUNK. ▷Middle English: perhaps from Old French *pole* 'chicken' + CAT1.

po·lem·ic /pə'lemik/ ▸*n.* a strong verbal or written attack on someone or something: *his* ***polemic against*** *the cultural relativism of the sixties | a writer of feminist polemic.* ■ (usu. **polemics**) the art or practice of engaging in controversial debate or dispute: *the history of science has become embroiled in religious polemics.*

▸*adj.* another term for POLEMICAL. ▷mid 17th cent.: via medieval Latin from Greek *polemikos*, from *polemos* 'war.' **—po·lem·i·cist** /pə'leməsist/ *n.* **—po·lem·i·cize** /pə'leməˌsīz/ *v.*

po·lem·i·cal /pə'lemikəl/ ▸*adj.* of, relating to, or involving strongly critical, controversial, or disputatious writing or speech: *a polemical essay.* **—po·lem·i·cal·ly** /-ik(ə)lē/ *adv.*

po·len·ta /pō'lentə/ ▸*n.* cornmeal as used in Italian cooking. ■ a paste or dough made from cornmeal, which is boiled and typically then fried or baked. ▷late 16th cent.: Italian, from Latin, 'pearl barley' (a sense of *polenta* in Old English).

pole piece ▸*n. Physics* a mass of iron forming the end of an electromagnet, through which the lines of magnetic force are concentrated and directed.

pole po·si·tion ▸*n.* the most favorable position at the start of an automobile race, typically on the inside of the front row of competitors. ■ *figurative* a leading or dominant position: *a company boasting the pole position in the communications business.* ▷1950s: from a 19th-cent. use of *pole* in horse racing, denoting the starting position next to the inside boundary fence.

pole·star /'pōlˌstär/ *n. Astronomy* (also **Pole Star**) another term for POLARIS. ■ *figurative* a thing or principle that guides or attracts people: *the store is a polestar for both actual and armchair travelers.*

pole vault ▸*n.* (**the pole vault**) an athletic event in which competitors attempt to vault over a high bar with the end of an extremely long flexible pole held in the hands and used to give extra spring. ■ a vault performed in this way.

▸*v.* (**pole-vault**) [*intrans.*] perform a pole vault. **—pole-vault·er** *n.* **—pole-vault·ing** *n.*

po·lice /pə'lēs/ ▸*n.* [treated as *pl.*] (usu. **the police**) the civil force of a national or local government, responsible for the prevention and detection of crime and the maintenance of public order. ■ members of a police force: *there are fewer women police than men.* ■ [with *adj.*] an organization engaged in the enforcement of official regulations in a specified domain: *transit police figurative, humorous the fashion police.*

▸*v.* [*trans.*] [often as *n.*] (**policing**) (of a police force) have the duty of maintaining law and order in or for (an area or event). ■ enforce regulations or an agreement in (a particular area or domain): *a UN resolution to use military force to police the no-fly zone.* ■ enforce the provisions of (a law, agreement, or treaty): *the regulations will be policed by factory inspectors.* ■ maintain order and neatness in (an area, as a military camp). ▷late 15th cent. (in the sense 'public order'): from French, from medieval Latin *politia* 'citizenship, government' (see POLICY1). Current senses date from the early 19th cent.

po·lice con·sta·ble ▸*n.* see CONSTABLE.

po·lice dog ▸*n.* a dog, esp. a German shepherd, trained for use in police work. ■ *informal* a German shepherd.

po·lice force ▸*n.* an organized body of police officers responsible for a country, district, or town.

po·lice ju·ry ▸*n.* an elected governing body in most Louisiana parishes, corresponding to a county board of commissioners in other states. —**po·lice ju·ror** *n.*

po·lice·man /pə'lēsmən/ ▸*n.* (*pl.* **-men**) a member of a police force.

po·lice of·fi·cer ▸*n.* a policeman or policewoman.

po·lice pro·ce·dur·al ▸*n.* a crime novel in which the emphasis is on the procedures used by the police in solving the crime.

po·lice state ▸*n.* a totalitarian state controlled by a political police force that secretly supervises the citizens' activities.

po·lice sta·tion ▸*n.* the office or headquarters of a local police force.

po·lice·wom·an /pə'lēs,wo͝omən/ ▸*n.* (*pl.* **-wom·en**) a female member of a police force.

po·li·cier /pō,lēs'yā/ ▸*n.* a movie based on a police novel, portraying crime and its detection by police. ▷French, from *roman policier* 'detective novel.'

pol·i·cy[1] /'päləsē/ ▸*n.* (*pl.* **-cies**) a course or principle of action adopted or proposed by a government, party, business, or individual: *the administration's controversial economic policies | it is not company policy to dispense with our older workers.* ■ *archaic* prudent or expedient conduct or action: *a course of policy and wisdom.* ▷late Middle English: from Old French *policie* 'civil administration,' via Latin from Greek *politeia* 'citizenship,' from *politēs* 'citizen,' from *polis* 'city.'

pol·i·cy[2] ▸*n.* (*pl.* **-cies**) **1** a contract of insurance: *they took out a joint policy.* **2** an illegal lottery or numbers game. ▷mid 16th cent.: from French *police* 'bill of lading, contract of insurance,' from Provençal *poliss(i)a*, probably from medieval Latin *apodissa, apodixa*, based on Greek *apodeixis* 'evidence, proof,' from *apodeiknunai* 'demonstrate, show.'

pol·i·cy·hold·er /'päləsē,hōldər/ ▸*n.* a person or group in whose name an insurance policy is held.

po·li·o /'pōlē,ō/ ▸*n.* short for POLIOMYELITIS.

po·li·o·my·e·li·tis /,pōlēō,mīə'lītis/ ▸*n.* *Medicine* an infectious viral disease that affects the central nervous system and can cause temporary or permanent paralysis. ▷late 19th cent.: modern Latin, from Greek *polios* 'gray' + *muelos* 'marrow.'

po·li·o·vi·rus /'pōlēō,vīrəs/ ▸*n.* *Medicine* any of a group of enteroviruses, including those that cause poliomyelitis.

po·lis[1] /'pōləs; 'pä-/ ▸*n.* (*pl.* **po·leis** /'päl,ās/) a city-state in ancient Greece, esp. as considered in its ideal form for philosophical purposes. ▷Greek.

po·lis[2] /'päləs/ ▸*n.* Scottish and Irish form of POLICE.

Po·li·sa·ri·o /,pōlə'särē,ō/ (also **Polisario Front**) ▸*n.* an independence movement in Western (formerly Spanish) Sahara, formed in 1973. ▷Spanish acronym, from *Frente Popular para la Liberación de Saguia el-Hamra y Río de Oro* 'Popular Front for the Liberation of Sagnia el-Hamra and Rio de Oro.'

Pol·ish /'pōlisн/ ▸*adj.* of or relating to Poland, its inhabitants, or their language.
▸*n.* the West Slavic language of Poland.

pol·ish /'pälisн/ ▸*v.* [*trans.*] make the surface of (something) smooth and shiny by rubbing it: *she unloaded the dishwasher and polished the glasses.* ■ improve, refine, or add the finishing touches to: *he's got to* **polish up** *his French for his job.*
▸*phrasal v.* □ **polish something off** finish or consume something quickly: *they polished off most of the sausages.*
▸*n.* a substance used to give something a smooth and shiny surface when rubbed in: *furniture polish.* ■ [in *sing.*] an act of rubbing something to give it a shiny surface: *I could give the cabinet a polish.* ■ smoothness or glossiness produced by rubbing or friction: *the machine refines the shape of the stone and gives it polish.* ■ refinement or elegance in a person or thing: *his poetry has clarity and polish.* ▷Middle English: from Old French *poliss-*, lengthened stem of *polir* 'to polish,' from Latin *polire.* —**pol·ish·a·ble** *adj.* —**pol·ish·er** *n.*

THE RIGHT WORD **gloss, luster, polish, sheen**
All of these words refer to a smooth, shining, or bright surface that reflects light.
If this surface is produced by rubbing or friction, the correct word is **polish** (*the car's mirrorlike polish was the result of regular waxing and buffing*).
Gloss, on the other hand, suggests the hard smoothness associated with lacquered, varnished, or enameled surfaces (*a high-gloss paint*).
Luster is associated with the light reflected from the surfaces of certain materials, such as silk or pearl (*a green stone with a brilliant luster*).
Sheen describes a glistening or radiant brightness that is also associated with specific materials (*her hair had a rich, velvety sheen*).

Po·lish Cor·ri·dor a former region of Poland that extended north to the Baltic coast and separated East Prussia from the rest of Germany, granted to Poland after World War I to ensure Polish access to the coast. Its annexation by Germany in 1939, with the German occupation of the rest of Poland, precipitated World War II. After the war, the area was restored to Poland.

pol·ished /'pälisнt/ ▸*adj.* shiny as a result of being rubbed: *a polished mahogany table.* ■ accomplished and skillful: *his polished performance in the movie.* ■ refined, sophisticated, or elegant: *he was polished and charming.* ■ (of rice) having had the outer husk removed during milling.

Po·lish no·ta·tion ▸*n.* *Logic & Computing* a system of formula notation without brackets or special punctuation, frequently used to represent the order in which arithmetical operations are performed in many computers and calculators. In the usual form (**reverse Polish notation**), operators follow rather than precede their operands.

polit. ▸*abbr.* ■ political. ■ politics.

po·lit·bu·ro /'pälət,byo͝orō; 'pō-/ ▸*n.* (*pl.* **-ros**) the principal policymaking committee of a Communist Party. ■ (**Politburo**) this committee in the former Soviet Union, founded in 1917. Also called (1952–66) the PRESIDIUM. ▷from Russian *politbyuro*, from *polit(icheskoe) byuro* 'political bureau.'

po·lite /pə'līt/ ▸*adj.* (**-lit·er, -lit·est**) having or showing behavior that is respectful and considerate of other people: *they thought she was wrong but were too polite to say so.* ■ [*attrib.*] of or relating to people who regard themselves as more cultured and refined than others: *the picture outraged polite society.* ▷late Middle English (in the Latin sense): from Latin *politus* 'polished, made smooth,' past participle of *polire.* —**po·lite·ly** *adv.* —**po·lite·ness** *n.*

pol·i·tesse /,pälə'tes/ ▸*n.* formal politeness or etiquette. ▷early 18th cent.: French, from Italian *politezza, pulitezza*, from *pulito* 'polite.'

pol·i·tic /'pälə,tik/ ▸*adj.* (of an action) seeming sensible and judicious under the circumstances: [with *infinitive*] *I did not think it politic to express my reservations.* ■ (also **pol·i·tick**) *archaic* (of a person) prudent and sagacious.
▸*v.* (**-ticked, -ticking**) [*intrans.*] [often as *n.*] (**politicking**) *often derogatory* engage in political activity: *news of this unseemly politicking invariably leaks into the press.* ▷late Middle English: from Old French *politique* 'political,' via Latin from Greek *politikos*, from *politēs* 'citizen,' from *polis* 'city.' —**pol·i·tic·ly** *adv.* (*rare*).

po·lit·i·cal /pə'litikəl/ ▸*adj.* of or relating to the government or the public affairs of a country: *a period of political and economic stability.* ■ of or relating to the ideas or strategies of a particular party or group in politics: *a decision taken for purely political reasons.* ■ interested in or active in politics: *I'm not very political.* ■ motivated or caused by a person's beliefs or actions concerning politics: *a political crime.* ■ *chiefly derogatory* relating to, affecting, or acting according to the interests of status or authority within an organization rather than matters of principle. —**po·lit·i·cal·ly** /-ik(ə)lē/ *adv.*

po·lit·i·cal ac·tion com·mit·tee (abbr.: **PAC**) ▸*n.* an organization that raises money privately and employs lobbyists to influence legislation, particularly at the federal level.

po·lit·i·cal a·sy·lum ▸*n.* see ASYLUM.

po·lit·i·cal cor·rect·ness (also **po·lit·i·cal cor·rec·ti·tude**) ▸*n.* the avoidance, often considered as taken to extremes, of forms of expression or action that are perceived to exclude, marginalize, or insult groups of people who are socially disadvantaged or discriminated against.

po·lit·i·cal e·con·o·my ▸*n.* *dated* economics as a branch of knowledge or academic discipline. —**po·lit·i·cal e·con·o·mist** *n.*

po·lit·i·cal ge·og·ra·phy ▸*n.* the branch of geography that deals with the boundaries, divisions, and possessions of countries.

po·lit·i·cal·ly cor·rect /pə'litik(ə)lē/ (or **in·correct**) ▸*adj.* exhibiting (or failing to exhibit) political correctness: *it is not politically correct to laugh at speech impediments.*

po·lit·i·cal pris·on·er ▸*n.* a person imprisoned for their political beliefs or actions.

po·lit·i·cal ref·u·gee ▸*n.* a refugee from an oppressive government.

po·lit·i·cal sci·ence ▸*n.* the branch of knowledge that deals with systems of government; the analysis of political activity and behavior. —**po·lit·i·cal sci·en·tist** *n.*

pol·i·ti·cian /,pälə'tisнən/ ▸*n.* a person who is professionally involved in politics, esp. as a holder of or a candidate for an elected office. ■ a person who acts in a manipulative and devious way, typically to gain advancement within an organization.

po·lit·i·cize /pə'litə,sīz/ ▸*v.* [*trans.*] [often as *adj.*] (**politicized**) cause (an activity or event) to become political in character: *art was becoming politicized | attempts to politicize America's curricula.* ■ make (someone) politically aware, esp. by persuading them of the truth of views considered radical: *we successfully politicized a generation of women.* ■ [*intrans.*] engage in or talk about politics. —**po·lit·i·ci·za·tion** /pə,litəsi'zāsнən/ *n.*

pol·i·tick ▸*adj.* archaic spelling of POLITIC.

po·lit·i·co /pə'litikō/ ▸*n.* (*pl.* **-cos**) informal term for POLITICIAN. ▷Spanish and Italian, 'politic' or 'political person.'

politico- ▸*comb. form* politically: *politico-ethical.* ■ political and . . . : *politico-economic.* ▷from Greek *politikos* 'civic, political.'

pol·i·tics /'pälə,tiks/ ▸*plural n.* [usu. treated as *sing.*] the activities associated with the governance of a country or other area, esp. the debate or conflict among individuals or parties having or hoping to achieve power: *the Communist Party was a major force in French politics | thereafter he dropped out of active politics.* ■ the activities of governments concerning the political relations between countries: *in the conduct of global politics, economic status must be backed by military capacity.* ■ the academic study of government and the state: [as *adj.*] *a politics lecturer.* ■ activities within an organization that are aimed at improving someone's status or position and are typically considered to be devious or divisive: *yet another discussion of office politics and personalities.* ■ a particular set of political beliefs or principles: *people do not buy this newspaper purely for its politics.* ■ (often **the politics of**) the assumptions or principles relating to or inherent in a sphere, theory, or thing, esp. when concerned with power and status in a society: *the politics of gender.*
▸***PHRASE*** □ **play politics** act for political or personal gain rather than from principle.

pol·i·ty /'pälətē/ ▸*n.* (*pl.* **-ties**) a form or process of civil government or constitution. ■ an organized society; a state as a political entity. ▷mid 16th cent.: from obsolete French *politie*, via Latin from Greek *politeia* 'citizenship, government,' from *politēs* 'citizen,' from *polis* 'city.'

Polk /pōk/, James Knox (1795–1849), 11th president of the U.S. 1845–49. A Democrat, his administration oversaw major territorial additions to the U.S. when Texas was admitted to the Union in 1845 and conflict with Mexico resulted in the annexation of California and other parts of the Southwest two years later.

James K. Polk

pol·ka /'pō(l)kə/ ▸*n.* a lively dance of Bohemian origin in duple time. ■ a piece of music for this dance or in its rhythm.
▸*v.* (**pol·kas, pol·kaed** or **pol·ka'd, pol·ka·ing**) [*intrans.*] dance the polka. ▷mid 19th cent.: via French and German from Czech *půlka* 'half step,' from *půl* 'half.'

pol·ka dot ▸*n.* one of a number of large round dots repeated to form a regular pattern on fabric: [as *adj.*] *a red and white polka-dot shirt.* —**pol·ka-dot·ted** *adj.*

poll /pōl/ ▶*n.* **1** (often **the polls**) the process of voting in an election: *the country went to the polls on March 10.* ■ a record of the number of votes cast in an election. ■ (**the polls**) the places where votes are cast in an election: *the polls have only just closed.* ■ short for **OPINION POLL**. **2** *dialect* a person's head. ■ the part of the head on which hair grows; the scalp.
▶*v.* [*trans.*] **1** (often **be polled**) record the opinion or vote of: *focus groups in which customers are polled about merchandise preferences.* ■ [*intrans.*] (of a candidate in an election) receive a specified number of votes: *the Green candidate polled 3.6 percent.* ■ *Telecommunications & Computing* check the status of (a measuring device, part of a computer, or a node in a network), esp. as part of a repeated cycle. **2** cut the horns off (an animal, esp. a young cow). ■ *archaic* cut off the top of (a tree or plant), typically to encourage further growth; pollard. ▷Middle English (in the sense 'head'): perhaps of Low German origin. The original sense was 'head,' and hence 'an individual person among a number,' from which developed the sense 'number of people ascertained by counting of heads' and then 'counting of heads or of votes' (17th cent.). **—poll·ee** /pō'lē/ *n.* (sense 1 of the *verb*).

Pol·lack /'päläk/, Sidney (1934–), U.S. director. He is noted for his direction of movies such as *The Way We Were* (1973), *Out of Africa* (1985), *Havana* (1990), and *The Firm* (1993).

pol·lack /'päläk/ (also **pol·lock**) ▶*n.* (*pl.* same or **-lacks**) an edible greenish-brown fish of the cod family, with a protruding lower jaw. Found in the northeastern Atlantic, it is popular with anglers. • *Pollachius pollachius*, family Gadidae. ▷late Middle English: perhaps of Celtic origin.

pol·lard /'pälərd/ ▶*v.* [*trans.*] [often as *adj.*] (**pollarded**) cut off the top and branches of (a tree) to encourage new growth at the top: *a wide boulevard lined with pollarded linden trees.*
▶*n.* **1** a tree whose top and branches have been cut off for this reason. **2** *archaic* an animal, e.g., a sheep or deer, that has lost its horns or cast its antlers. ▷early 17th cent.: from the verb **POLL** + **-ARD**.

polled /pōld/ ▶*adj.* (of cattle, sheep, or goats) lacking horns, either naturally or because they have been removed.

pol·len /'pälən/ ▶*n.* a fine powdery substance, typically yellow, consisting of microscopic grains discharged from the male part of a flower or from a male cone. Each grain contains a male gamete that can fertilize the female ovule, to which pollen is transported by the wind, insects, or other animals. ▷mid 18th cent.: from Latin, literally 'fine powder.'

pol·len bas·ket ▶*n.* *Entomology* a flattened area fringed with hairs on the hind leg of a social bee, used for carrying pollen. Also called **CORBICULA**.

pol·len count ▶*n.* an index of the amount of pollen in the air, published chiefly for the benefit of those allergic to it.

pol·len grain ▶*n.* each of the microscopic particles, typically single cells, of which pollen is composed. Pollen grains have a tough coat that has a form characteristic of the plant producing it.

pol·len tube ▶*n.* *Botany* a hollow tube that develops from a pollen grain when deposited on the stigma of a flower. It penetrates the style and conveys the male gametes to the ovule.

pol·lex /'päl,eks/ ▶*n.* (*pl.* **pol·li·ces** /'pälə,sēz/) *Anatomy & Zoology* the innermost digit of a forelimb, esp. the thumb in primates. ▷mid 19th cent.: from Latin, literally 'thumb or big toe.'

pol·li·nate /'pälə,nāt/ ▶*v.* [*trans.*] convey pollen to or deposit pollen on (a stigma, ovule, flower, or plant) and so allow fertilization. ▷late 19th cent.: from Latin *pollen, pollin-* 'pollen' + **-ATE**3. **—pol·li·na·tion** /,pälə'nāsHən/ *n.* **—pol·li·na·tor** /-,nātər/ *n.*

poll·ing booth ▶*n.* British and Canadian term for **VOTING BOOTH**.

poll·ing place (also **polling station**) ▶*n.* a building where voting takes place during an election, typically one that normally has another function, such as a school.

pol·lin·i·um /pə'linēəm/ ▶*n.* (*pl.* **pol·lin·ia** /pə'linēə/) *Botany* a coherent mass of pollen grains that is the product of each anther lobe of some flowers, esp. orchids. Single or paired pollinia are often attached to, and carried by, pollinating insects. ▷mid 19th cent.: modern Latin, from Latin *pollen, pollin-* 'pollen.'

pol·li·no·sis /,pälə'nōsis/ ▶*n.* a technical term for hay fever.

pol·li·wog /'pälē,wäg; -,wôg/ (also **pol·ly·wog**) ▶*n.* a tadpole. ▷late Middle English (earlier as *pollywiggle*): from **POLL** in the sense 'head' + the verb **WIGGLE**.

pol·lo /'poi-ō; 'pälō/ ▶*n.* chicken (as used in the names of Italian, Spanish, or Mexican dishes). ▷Spanish and Italian.

Pol·lock /'päläk/, (Paul) Jackson (1912–56), U.S. painter. A leading figure in the abstract expressionist movement, he became the chief exponent of the style known as action painting from 1947. Fixing the canvas to the floor or wall, he poured, splashed, or dripped paint on it, covering the whole canvas and avoiding any point of emphasis.

pol·lock /'päläk/ ▶*n.* **1** a commercially valuable food fish of the cod family, occuring in the North Atlantic. Also called **SAITHE**. • *Pollachius virens*, family Gadidae. **2** variant spelling of **POLLACK**.

poll·ster /'pōlstər/ ▶*n.* a person who conducts or analyzes opinion polls.

poll tax ▶*n.* a tax levied on every adult, without reference to their income or resources.

pol·lute /pə'lōōt/ ▶*v.* [*trans.*] contaminate (water, air, or a place) with harmful or poisonous substances: *the explosion polluted the town with dioxin* | [as *adj.*] (**polluted**) *exposure to polluted air.* ■ *figurative* defile; corrupt: *a society polluted by racism.* ▷late Middle English: from Latin *pollut-* 'soiled, defiled,' from the verb *polluere*, based on the root of *lutum* 'mud.' **—pol·lu·tant** /-'lōōtnt/ *adj.* & *n.* **—pol·lut·er** *n.*

THE RIGHT WORD **adulterate, contaminate, defile, pollute, taint**

When a factory pours harmful chemicals or wastes into the air or water, it is said to **pollute** the environment. But *pollute* may also refer to impairing the purity, integrity, or effectiveness of something (*a campaign polluted by allegations of sexual impropriety*).

To **contaminate** is to spread harmful or undesirable impurities throughout something. Unlike *pollute*, which suggests visible or noticeable impurities, *contaminate* is preferred where the change is unsuspected or not immediately noticeable (*milk contaminated by radioactive fallout from a nuclear plant accident*).

Adulterate often refers to food products to which harmful, low-quality, or low-cost substances have been added in order to defraud the consumer (*cereal adulterated with sawdust*), although this word can apply to any mixture to which the inferior or harmful element is added deliberately and in the hope that no one will notice (*a report adulterated with false statistics*).

To **defile** is to pollute something that should be kept pure or sacred (*a church defiled by vandals*), while **taint** implies that a trace of something toxic or corrupt has been introduced (*he contracted the disease from a tainted blood transfusion; the book is tainted by gratuitous violence*).

pol·lu·tion /pə'lōōsHən/ ▶*n.* the presence in or introduction into the environment of a substance or thing that has harmful or poisonous effects: *the level of pollution in the air is rising.* ▷late Middle English: from Latin *pollutio(n-)*, from the verb *polluere* (see **POLLUTE**).

Pol·lux /'päləks/ **1** *Greek Mythology* the twin brother of Castor. Also called **POLYDEUCES**. See **DIOSCURI**. **2** *Astronomy* the brightest star in the constellation Gemini, close to Castor. ▷Latin, from Greek *Poludeukēs*; compare with **POLYDEUCES**.

Pol·ly·an·na /,pälē'anə/ ▶*n.* an excessively cheerful or optimistic person. ▷early 20th cent.: the name of the optimistic heroine created by Eleanor Hodgman Porter (1868–1920), American author of children's stories. **—Pol·ly·an·na·ish** /-isH/ *adj.* **—Pol·ly·an·na·ism** /-,izəm/ *n.*

pol·ly·wog ▶*n.* variant spelling of **POLLIWOG**.

Po·lo, Marco, see **MARCO POLO**.

po·lo /'pōlō/ ▶*n.* a game of Eastern origin resembling field hockey, played on horseback with a long-handled mallet. ▷late 19th cent.: from Balti, 'ball.'

po·loid·al /pə'loidl/ ▶*adj.* *Physics* relating to or denoting a magnetic field associated with a toroidal electric field, in which each line of force is confined to a radial or meridian plane. ▷1940s: from **POLAR**, on the pattern of *toroidal*.

pol·o·naise /,pälə'nāz; ,pō-/ ▶*n.* **1** a slow dance of Polish origin in triple time, consisting chiefly of an intricate march or procession. ■ a piece of music for this dance or in its rhythm. **2** *historical* a woman's dress with a tight bodice and a skirt open from the waist downward, looped up to show a decorative underskirt.
▶*adj.* (of a dish, esp. a vegetable dish) garnished with chopped hard-boiled egg yolk, breadcrumbs, and parsley. ▷mid 18th cent.: from French, feminine of *polonais* 'Polish,' from medieval Latin *Polonia* 'Poland.'

po·lo neck ▶*n.* British term for **TURTLENECK**. **—po·lo-necked** /'pōlō ,nekt/ *adj.*

po·lo·ni·um /pə'lōnēəm/ ▶*n.* the chemical element of atomic number 84, a radioactive metal occurring in nature only as a product of radioactive decay of uranium. (Symbol: **Po**) ▷late 19th cent.: modern Latin, from medieval Latin *Polonia* 'Poland' (the native country of Marie Curie, the element's codiscoverer).

po·lo po·ny ▶*n.* a horse used in playing polo, typically bred for speed and agility.

po·lo shirt ▶*n.* a casual short-sleeved cotton shirt with a collar and several buttons at the neck. See also **GOLF SHIRT**.

Pol Pot /päl 'pät; pôl/ (*c.*1925–98), Cambodian communist leader of the Khmer Rouge; prime minister 1976–79; born *Saloth Sar*. During his regime the Khmer Rouge embarked on a reconstruction program in which millions were killed. Overthrown in 1979, Pol Pot led the Khmer Rouge in a guerrilla war against the new government.

Pols·ka /'pôlskä/ Polish name for **POLAND**.

Pol·ta·va /pəl'tävə/ a city in east central Ukraine; pop. 317,000.

pol·ter·geist /'pōltər,gīst/ ▶*n.* a ghost or other supernatural being supposedly responsible for physical disturbances such as loud noises and objects thrown around. ▷mid 19th cent.: from German *Poltergeist*, from *poltern* 'create a disturbance' + *Geist* 'ghost.'

Pol·to·ratsk /pəltə'rätsk/ former name (1919–27) of **ASHGABAT**.

pol·troon /päl'trōōn/ ▶*n.* *archaic* or *poetic/literary* an utter coward. ▷early 16th cent.: from French *poltron*, from Italian *poltrone*, perhaps from *poltro* 'sluggard.' **—pol·troon·er·y** /-'trōōnərē/ *n.*

pol·y /'pälē/ ▶*n.* (*pl.* **pol·ys**) *informal* short for: ■ polyester. ■ polytechnic. ■ polyethylene.

poly- ▶*comb. form* many; much: *polyandry* | *polychrome.* ■ *Chemistry* denoting the presence of many atoms or groups of a particular kind in a molecule: *polycarbonate.* ▷from Greek *polus* 'much,' *polloi* 'many.'

pol·y·a·cryl·a·mide /,pälēə'krilə,mīd/ ▶*n.* a synthetic resin made by polymerizing acrylamide, esp. a water-soluble polymer used to form or stabilize gels and as a thickening or clarifying agent.

pol·y·ad·ic /,pälē'adik/ ▶*adj.* involving three or more quantities, elements, or individuals. ▷early 20th cent.: from **POLY-** 'many,' on the pattern of words such as *dyadic, monadic*.

pol·y·am·ide /,pälē'amīd/ ▶*n.* a synthetic polymer of a type made by the linkage of an amino group of one molecule and a carboxylic acid group of another, including many synthetic fibers such as nylon.

pol·y·am·o·ry /,pälē'amərē/ ▶*n.* the philosophy or state of being in love or romantically involved with more than one person at the same time. ▷from *poly-* 'many' + Latin *amor* 'love' + *-y*, on the pattern of *polygamy* and *polyandry*. **—pol·y·am·o·rous** *adj.* **—pol·y·am·o·rist** *n.*

pol·y·an·dry /'pälē,andrē/ ▶*n.* polygamy in which a woman has more than one husband. Compare with **POLYGYNY**. ■ *Zoology* a pattern of mating in which a female animal has more than one male mate. ▷late 17th cent.: from **POLY-** 'many' + Greek *anēr, andr-* 'male.' **—pol·y·an·drous** /,pälē'andrəs/ *adj.*

pol·y·an·thus /,pälē'anTHəs/ ▶*n.* (*pl.* same) a herbaceous flowering plant that is a complex hybrid between the wild primrose and primulas, cultivated in Europe since the 17th century. • *Primula × polyantha*, family Primulaceae. ▷early 18th cent.: modern Latin, from **POLY-** 'many' + Greek *anthos* 'flower.'

pol·y·a·tom·ic /,pälēə'tämik/ ▶*adj.* consisting of many atoms.

pol·y·bu·tyl·ene /,päli'byōōtl,ēn/ ▶*n.* a thermoplastic polymer used in water pipes.

pol·y·car·bon·ate /,päli'kärbə,nāt; -nət/ ▶*n.* a synthetic resin in which the polymer units are linked through carbonate groups, including many molding materials and films.

Pol·y·carp, St. /'pälē,kärp/ (*c.*69–*c.*155), Greek bishop of Smyrna in Asia Minor. The leading Christian figure in Smyrna, he was arrested during a pagan festival, refused to recant his faith, and was burned to death. Feast day, February 23.

Pol·y·chae·ta /,päli'kētə/ *Zoology* a class of marine annelid worms that comprises the bristle worms. ▷modern Latin (plural), from Greek *polu-* 'many' +

khaitē 'mane' (taken to mean 'bristle'). —**pol·y·chaete** /ˈpälēˌkēt/ *n.* & *adj.* —**pol·y·chae·tous** /ˌpäləˈkētəs/ *adj.*

pol·y·chlo·rin·at·ed bi·phen·yl /ˌpälēˈklôrəˌnātid bīˈfenəl/ (abbr.: **PCB**) ▸*n. Chemistry* any of a class of toxic aromatic compounds, often formed as waste in industrial processes, whose molecules contain two benzene rings in which hydrogen atoms have been replaced by chlorine atoms.

pol·y·chro·mat·ic /ˌpälikrōˈmatik/ ▸*adj.* of two or more colors; multicolored. ■ *Physics* (of light or other radiation) of a number of wavelengths or frequencies. —**pol·y·chro·ma·tism** /-ˈkrōməˌtizəm/ *n.*

pol·y·chrome /ˈpäliˌkrōm/ ▸*adj.* painted, printed, or decorated in several colors.
▸*n.* varied coloring. ■ a work of art in several colors, esp. a statue.
▸*v.* [*trans.*] [usu. as *adj.*] (**polychromed**) execute or decorate (a work of art) in several colors. ▷early 19th cent.: from French, from Greek *polukhrōmos*, from *polu-* 'many' + *khrōma* 'color.'

pol·y·chro·my /ˈpäliˌkrōmē/ ▸*n.* the art of painting in several colors, esp. as applied to ancient pottery, sculpture, and architecture.

pol·y·clo·nal /ˌpäliˈklōnl/ ▸*adj. Medicine & Biology* consisting of or derived from many clones.

pol·y·crest ▸*n.* (in homeopathy) a remedy that is frequently used, in general or for a particular condition: *the poison ivy polycrests.* ▷19th cent.: from Greek *polu-* 'many' + *khraosos* 'use.'

pol·y·crys·tal·line /ˌpäliˈkristələn; -ˌlīn; -ˌlēn/ ▸*adj.* (of a metal or other solid) consisting of many crystalline parts that are randomly oriented with respect to each other.

pol·y·cul·ture /ˌpäliˈkəlCHər/ ▸*n.* the simultaneous cultivation or exploitation of several crops or kinds of animals.

pol·y·cy·clic /ˌpäliˈsiklik; -ˈsīklik/ ▸*adj.* of, relating to, or resulting from many cycles. ■ *Chemistry* (of an organic compound) having several rings of atoms in the molecule. ■ *Geology* (of a landform or deposit) having undergone two or more cycles of erosion and deposition.

pol·y·cys·tic /ˌpäliˈsistik/ ▸*adj. Medicine* characterized by multiple cysts.

pol·y·cy·the·mi·a /ˌpäliˌsīˈTHēmēə/ (*Brit.* **pol·y·cy·thae·mi·a**) ▸*n. Medicine* an abnormally increased concentration of hemoglobin in the blood, either through reduction of plasma volume or increase in red cell numbers. It may be a primary disease of unknown cause, or a secondary condition linked to respiratory or circulatory disorder or cancer. ▷mid 19th cent.: from modern Latin *polycythaemia*, from **POLY-** 'many' + **-CYTE** 'cell' + Greek *haima* 'blood' + **-IA**[1].

pol·y·dac·ty·ly /ˌpäliˈdaktəlē/ ▸*n.* a condition in which a person or animal has more than five fingers or toes on one, or on each, hand or foot. ▷late 19th cent.: from Greek *poludaktulos* (from *polu-* 'many' + *daktulos* 'finger') + **-Y**[3]. —**pol·y·dac·tyl** *adj.* & *n.*

Pol·y·deu·ces /ˌpäliˈd(y)o͞oˌsēz/ another name for **POLLUX** (sense 1).

pol·y·dip·si·a /ˌpälēˈdipsēə/ ▸*n. Medicine* abnormally great thirst as a symptom of disease (such as diabetes) or psychological disturbance. ▷mid 17th cent.: from Greek *poludipsios* 'very thirsty,' *poludipsos* 'causing great thirst,' based on *dipsa* 'thirst.'

pol·y·e·lec·tro·lyte /ˌpälēəˈlektrəˌlīt/ ▸*n. Chemistry* a polymer that has several ionizable groups along the molecule, esp. any of those used for coagulating and flocculating particles during water treatment or for making electrophoretic gels.

pol·y·em·bry·o·ny /ˌpäləˈembrēənē; -emˈbrīənē/ ▸*n. Biology* the formation of more than one embryo from a single fertilized ovum or in a single seed. —**pol·y·em·bry·on·ic** /-ˌembrēˈänik/ *adj.*

pol·y·ene /ˈpälēˌēn/ ▸*n. Chemistry* a hydrocarbon with several carbon–carbon double bonds, esp. one having a chain of alternating single and double bonds.

pol·y·es·ter /ˈpälēˌestər/ ▸*n.* a synthetic resin in which the polymer units are linked by ester groups, used chiefly to make synthetic textile fibers. ■ a fabric made from polyester fiber.

pol·y·eth·nic /ˌpālēˈeTHnik/ ▸*adj.* belonging to, comprising, or containing many ethnic groups. —**pol·y·eth·nic·i·ty** /-eTHˈnisətē/ *n.*

pol·y·eth·yl·ene /ˌpälēˈeTHəlēn/ ▸*n.* a tough, light, flexible synthetic resin made by polymerizing ethylene, chiefly used for plastic bags, food containers, and other packaging.

pol·y·eth·yl·ene gly·col ▸*n.* a synthetic resin made by polymerizing ethylene glycol, in particular any of a series of water-soluble oligomers and polymers used chiefly as solvents or waxes.

pol·y·eth·yl·ene ter·eph·thal·ate /ˌterə(f)ˈTHalˌāt/ (abbr.: **PET**) ▸*n.* a synthetic resin made by copolymerizing ethylene glycol and terephthalic acid, widely used to make polyester fibers.

po·lyg·a·mous /pəˈligəməs/ ▸*adj.* practicing, relating to, or involving polygamy: *polygamous societies.* ■ *Zoology* (of an animal) typically having more than one mate. ■ *Botany* (of a plant) bearing some flowers with stamens only, some with pistils only, and some with both, on the same or different plants. ▷early 17th cent.: from Greek *polugamos* (from *polu-* 'much, often' + *-gamos* 'marrying') + **-OUS**. —**po·lyg·a·mous·ly** *adv.*

po·lyg·a·my /pəˈligəmē/ ▸*n.* **1** the practice or custom of having more than one wife or husband at the same time. ■ *Zoology* a pattern of mating in which an animal has more than one mate. **2** *Botany* the condition of bearing some male, some female, and sometimes some perfect flowers on the same plant. ▷late 16th cent.: from French *polygamie*, via late Latin from Greek *polugamia*, from *polugamos* 'often marrying.' —**po·lyg·a·mist** /-mist/ *n.*

pol·y·gene /ˈpäliˌjēn/ ▸*n. Genetics* a gene whose individual effect on a phenotype is too small to be observed, but which can act together with others to produce observable variation. ▷1940s: back-formation from **POLYGENIC**.

pol·y·gen·e·sis /ˌpäliˈjenəsəs/ ▸*n.* origination from several independent sources, in particular: ■ *Biology* the hypothetical origination of a race or species from a number of independent stocks. Compare with **POLYGENY**. ■ the hypothetical origination of language or of a surname from a number of independent sources in different places at different times.

pol·y·ge·net·ic /ˌpälijəˈnetik/ ▸*adj.* of or relating to polygenesis; having more than one origin or source. ■ *Geology* denoting or originating from a volcano that has erupted several times. —**pol·y·ge·net·i·cal·ly** /-ik(ə)lē/ *adv.*

pol·y·gen·ic /ˌpäliˈjenik/ ▸*adj. Genetics* of, relating to, or determined by polygenes. ▷1940s: from Greek *polugenēs* 'of many kinds' + **-IC**. —**pol·y·gen·i·cal·ly** /-ik(ə)lē/ *adv.*

po·lyg·e·nism /pəˈlijəˌnizəm/ ▸*n.* the doctrine of polygeny. —**po·lyg·e·nist** /ˌpəˈlijənist/ *n.* & *adj.*

po·lyg·e·ny /pəˈlijənē/ ▸*n.* the theory (not now generally held) that humans evolved from several independent pairs of ancestors. Compare with **POLYGENESIS**.

pol·y·glot /ˈpäliˌglät/ ▸*adj.* knowing or using several languages: *a polyglot career woman.* ■ (of a book) having the text translated into several languages: *polyglot and bilingual technical dictionaries.*
▸*n.* a person who knows and is able to use several languages. ▷mid 17th cent.: from French *polyglotte*, from Greek *poluglōttos*, from *polu-* 'many' + *glōtta* 'tongue.' —**pol·y·glot·ism** /-ˌglätˌizəm/ *n.*

pol·y·gon /ˈpäliˌgän/ ▸*n. Geometry* a plane figure with at least three straight sides and angles, and typically five or more. ▷late 16th cent.: via late Latin from Greek *polugōnon*, neuter (used as a noun) of *polugōnos* 'many-angled.' —**po·lyg·o·nal** /pəˈligənl/ *adj.* —**po·lyg·o·nal·ly** *adv.*

po·lyg·o·num /pəˈligənəm/ ▸*n.* a plant of a genus that includes knotgrass and knotweed, of which some are weeds and some are garden ornamentals. • Genus *Polygonum*, family Polygonaceae. ▷modern Latin, from Greek *polu-* 'many' + *gonu* 'knee, joint' (because of the swollen joints sheathed by stipules).

pol·y·graph /ˈpäliˌgraf/ ▸*n.* a machine designed to detect and record changes in physiological characteristics, such as a person's pulse and breathing rates, used esp. as a lie detector. ■ a lie-detector test carried out with a machine of this type. —**pol·y·graph·ic** /ˌpäliˈgrafik/ *adj.*

pol·y·gyne /ˈpäliˌjīn/ ▸*adj. Entomology* (of a social insect) having more than one egg-laying queen in each colony.

po·lyg·y·ny /pəˈlijənē/ ▸*n.* polygamy in which a man has more than one wife. Compare with **POLYANDRY**. ■ *Zoology* a pattern of mating in which a male animal has more than one female mate. ▷late 18th cent.: from **POLY-** 'many' + Greek *gunē* 'woman.' —**po·lyg·y·nous** /pəˈlijənəs/ *adj.*

pol·y·he·dron /ˌpäliˈhēdrən/ ▸*n.* (*pl.* **-he·drons** or **-he·dra** /-ˈhēdrə/) *Geometry* a solid figure with many plane faces, typically more than six. ▷late 16th cent.: from Greek *poluedron*, neuter (used as a noun) of *poluedros* 'many-sided.' —**pol·y·he·dral** /-ˈhēdrəl/ *adj.* —**pol·y·he·dric** /-ˈhēdrik/ *adj.*

pol·y·his·tor /ˌpäliˈhistər/ ▸*n.* another term for **POLYMATH**. ▷late 16th cent.: from Greek *poluistōr* 'very learned,' from *polu-* 'much, very' + *histōr* 'wise man.'

Pol·y·hym·ni·a /ˌpäliˈhimnēə/ *Greek & Roman Mythology* the Muse of the art of mime. ▷via Latin from Greek, literally 'she of the many hymns.'

pol·y·math /ˈpäliˌmaTH/ ▸*n.* a person of wide-ranging knowledge or learning. ▷early 17th cent.: from Greek *polumathēs* 'having learned much,' from *polu-* 'much' + the stem of *manthanein* 'learn.' —**pol·y·math·ic** /ˌpäliˈmaTHik/ *adj.* —**po·lym·a·thy** /pəˈliməTHē; ˈpäliˌmaTHē/ *n.*

pol·y·mer /ˈpäləmər/ ▸*n. Chemistry* a substance that has a molecular structure consisting chiefly or entirely of a large number of similar units bonded together, e.g., many synthetic organic materials used as plastics and resins. ▷mid 19th cent.: from German, from Greek *polumeros* 'having many parts,' from *polu-* 'many' + *meros* 'a share.' —**pol·y·mer·ic** /ˌpäləˈmerik/ *adj.*

pol·y·mer·ase /pəˈliməˌrās; -ˌrāz/ ▸*n. Biochemistry* an enzyme that brings about the formation of a particular polymer, esp. DNA or RNA. See also **TRANSCRIPTASE**.

po·lym·er·ize /pəˈliməˌrīz; ˈpäləməˌrīz/ ▸*v. Chemistry* combine or cause to combine to form a polymer. —**po·lym·er·iz·a·ble** /pəˌliməˈrīzəbəl; päləmə-/ *adj.* —**po·lym·er·i·za·tion** /pəˌlimərəˈzāSHən; ˌpäləmərə-/ *n.*

po·lym·er·ous /pəˈlimərəs/ ▸*adj. Biology* having or consisting of many parts.

pol·y·meth·yl meth·ac·ry·late /ˈpäliˌmeTHəl meTHˈakrəˌlāt/ ▸*n.* a glassy synthetic resin obtained by polymerizing methyl methacrylate, used to make perspex, plexiglas, and lucite.

pol·y·morph /ˈpäliˌmôrf/ ▸*n.* an organism or inorganic object or material that takes various forms. ■ *Physiology* a polymorphonuclear leukocyte. ▷early 19th cent.: from Greek *polumorphos*, from *polu-* 'many' + *morphē* 'form.'

pol·y·mor·phism /ˌpäliˈmôrˌfizəm/ ▸*n.* the occurrence of something in several different forms, in particular: ■ *Biology* the occurrence of different forms among the members of a population or colony, or in the life cycle of an individual organism. ■ *Genetics* the presence of genetic variation within a population, upon which natural selection can operate. ■ *Biochemistry* the occurrence of a number of alternative forms within a section of a nucleic acid or protein molecule. ■ *Computing* a feature of a programming language that allows routines to use variables of different types at different times. —**pol·y·mor·phic** /-ˈmôrfik/ *adj.* —**pol·y·mor·phous** /-ˈmôrfəs/ *adj.*

pol·y·mor·pho·nu·cle·ar /ˌpäliˌmôrfōˈn(y)o͞oklēər/ ▸*adj. Physiology* (of a leukocyte) having a nucleus with several lobes and a cytoplasm that contains granules, as in an eosinophil or basophil.

pol·y·mor·phous per·ver·si·ty /ˌpäliˈmôrfəs/ ▸*n. Psychology* a generalized sexual desire that can be excited and gratified in many ways, normal in young children but unusual in adults. —**pol·y·mor·phous·ly per·verse** *adj.*

pol·y·myx·in /ˌpäliˈmiksən/ ▸*n. Medicine* any of a group of polypeptide antibiotics that are active chiefly against Gram-negative bacteria. • Polymyxins are obtained from soil bacteria of the genus *Bacillus*, in particular *B. polymyxa*. ▷1940s: from modern Latin *polymyxa*, from Greek *polu-* 'much' + *muxa* 'slime' + **-IN**[1].

Pol·y·ne·sia /ˌpäləˈnēZHə/ a region of the central Pacific Ocean that lies east of Micronesia and Melanesia and contains the easternmost of the three large groups of Pacific islands, including Hawaii, the Marquesas Islands, Samoa, the Cook Islands, and French Polynesia. ▷from **POLY-** 'many' + Greek *nēsos* 'island.'

Pol·y·ne·sian /ˌpäləˈnēZHən/ ▸*adj.* of or relating to Polynesia, its people, or their languages.
▸*n.* **1** a native or inhabitant of Polynesia, or a person of Polynesian descent. **2** a group of Austronesian languages spoken in Polynesia, including Maori, Hawaiian, and Samoan.

pol·y·neu·ri·tis /ˌpälin(y)o͝oˈrītis/ ▸*n. Medicine* any disorder that affects the peripheral nerves collectively. —**pol·y·neu·rit·ic** /-n(y)o͝oˈritik/ *adj.*

Pronunciation Key ə *ago*; ər *over*; ˈə or ˌə *up*; ˈər or ˌər *fur*; a *hat*; ā *rate*; ä *car*; CH *chew*; e *let*; ē *see*; e(ə)r *air*; i *fit*; ī *by*; i(ə)r *ear*; NG *sing*; ō *go*; ô *for*; oi *boy*; o͝o *good*; o͞o *goo*; ou *out*; SH *she*; TH *thin*; TH *then*; (h)w *why*; ZH *vision*

pol·y·neu·rop·a·thy /ˌpälin(y)o͝orˈäpəTHē/ ▸*n. Medicine* a general degeneration of peripheral nerves that spreads toward the center of the body.

pol·y·no·mi·al /ˌpäləˈnōmēəl/ ▸*adj.* consisting of several terms. ■ *Mathematics* of, relating to, or denoting a polynomial or polynomials.
▸*n. Mathematics* an expression of more than two algebraic terms, esp. the sum of several terms that contain different powers of the same variable(s). ■ *Biology* a Latin name with more than two parts. ▷late 17th cent.: from **POLY-** 'many,' on the pattern of *multinomial*.

pol·y·no·mi·al time ▸*n. Computing* the time required for a computer to solve a problem, where this time is a simple polynomial function of the size of the input.

pol·y·nos·ic /ˌpäliˈnäsik/ ▸*n.* a long-fiber rayon-and-polyester blend with a soft finish, used mainly in clothing.

pol·y·nu·cle·ar /ˌpäliˈn(y)o͞oklēər/ ▸*adj. Chemistry* (of a complex) containing more than one metal atom. ■ (of a compound) polycyclic.

pol·y·nu·cle·o·tide /ˌpäliˈn(y)o͞oklēəˌtīd/ ▸*n. Biochemistry* a linear polymer whose molecule is composed of many nucleotide units, constituting a section of a nucleic acid molecule.

po·lyn·ya /ˌpälənˈyä/ ▸*n.* a stretch of open water surrounded by ice, esp. in Arctic seas. ▷mid 19th cent.: from Russian, from the base of *pole* 'field.'

pol·y·o·ma vi·rus /ˌpälēˈōmə/ ▸*n. Medicine* any of a group of DNA viruses that are usually endemic in their host species without causing disease but that can cause tumors when injected into other species.

pol·yp /ˈpäləp/ ▸*n.* **1** *Zoology* a solitary or colonial sedentary form of a coelenterate such as a sea anemone, typically having a columnar body with the mouth uppermost surrounded by a ring of tentacles. In some species, polyps are a phase in the life cycle that alternates with a medusoid phase. Compare with **MEDUSA**. **2** *Medicine* a small growth, typically benign and with a stalk, protruding from a mucous membrane. ▷late Middle English (sense 2): from Old French *polipe*, from Latin *polypus* (see **POLYPUS**). Sense 1 dates from the mid 18th cent. **—pol·yp·ous** /ˈpäləpəs/ *adj.* (in sense 2).

pol·y·par·y /ˈpäləˌperē/ ▸*n.* (*pl.* **-par·ies**) *Zoology* the common stem or skeletal support of a colony of polyps, to which the individual zooids are attached. ▷mid 18th cent.: from modern Latin *polyparium*, from Latin *polypus* (see **POLYPUS**).

pol·y·pep·tide /ˌpäliˈpepˌtīd/ ▸*n. Biochemistry* a linear organic polymer consisting of a large number of amino-acid residues bonded together in a chain, forming part of (or the whole of) a protein molecule. ▷early 20th cent.: from **POLY-** 'many' + **PEPTONE** + **-IDE**.

po·lyph·a·gous /pəˈlifəgəs/ ▸*adj. Zoology* (of an animal) able to feed on various kinds of food. ▷early 19th cent.: from Greek *poluphagos* 'eating to excess' + **-OUS**.

pol·y·phase /ˈpäliˌfāz/ ▸*adj.* consisting of or occurring in a number of separate stages. ■ (of an electrical device or circuit) designed to supply or use simultaneously several alternating currents of the same voltage and frequency but with different phases. **—pol·y·pha·sic** /ˌpäliˈfāzik/ *adj.*

Pol·y·phe·mus /ˌpäləˈfēməs/ *Greek Mythology* a Cyclops who trapped Odysseus and some of his companions in a cave, from which they escaped by putting out his one eye while he slept. In another story, Polyphemus loved the sea nymph Galatea, and in jealousy killed his rival Acis.

pol·y·phe·nol /ˌpäliˈfēˌnôl; -ˌnōl/ ▸*n. Chemistry* a compound containing more than one phenolic hydroxyl group.

pol·y·phon·ic /ˌpäliˈfänik/ ▸*adj.* producing many sounds simultaneously; many-voiced: *a 64-voice polyphonic sound module.* ■ *Music* (esp. of vocal music) in two or more parts, each having a melody of its own; contrapuntal. Compare with **HOMOPHONIC**. ■ *Music* (of an instrument) capable of producing more than one note at a time. ▷late 18th cent.: from Greek *poluphōnos* (from *polu-* 'many' + *phōnē* 'voice, sound') + **-IC**. **—pol·y·phon·i·cal·ly** /-ik(ə)lē/ *adv.*

po·lyph·o·ny /pəˈlifənē/ ▸*n.* (*pl.* **-nies**) *Music* the style of simultaneously combining a number of parts, each forming an individual melody and harmonizing with each other. ■ a composition written, played, or sung in this style. ■ (on an electronic keyboard or synthesizer) the number of notes or voices that can be played simultaneously without loss. ▷early 19th cent.: from Greek *poluphōnia*, from *polu-* 'many' + *phōnē* 'sound.' **—pol·y·pho·nist** /-fənist/ *n.* **—pol·y·pho·nous** /-fənəs/ *adj.*

pol·y·phy·let·ic /ˌpälifīˈletik/ ▸*adj. Biology* (of a group of organisms) derived from more than one common evolutionary ancestor or ancestral group and therefore not suitable for placing in the same taxon.

pol·y·pi /ˈpäləˌpī; -pē/ ▸ plural form of **POLYPUS**.

pol·y·pill /ˈpäləˌpil/ ▸*n.* a pill containing a number of medicines that all treat the same condition.

pol·y·ploid /ˈpäliˌploid/ *Biology* ▸*adj.* (of a cell or nucleus) containing more than two homologous sets of chromosomes. ■ (of an organism or species) composed of polyploid cells.
▸*n.* a polyploid organism, variety, or species. **—pol·y·ploi·dy** *n.*

pol·y·pod /ˈpäləˌpäd/ ▸*adj. Zoology* having many feet or footlike appendages, esp. denoting a phase of insect larval development characterized by a segmented abdomen with rudimentary or functional appendages. ▷mid 18th cent. (as a noun denoting an animal having many feet): from French *polypode* 'many-footed,' from Greek *polupous, polupod-*, from *polu-* 'many' + *pous, pod-* 'foot.'

pol·y·po·dy /ˈpäləˌpōdē/ ▸*n.* (*pl.* **-dies**) a widely distributed fern that has stout scaly creeping rhizomes and remains green during the winter, growing on trees, walls, and stones, esp. in limestone areas. • Genus *Polypodium*, family Polypodiaceae: several species, in particular the **common polypody** (*P. vulgare*). ▷late Middle English: via Latin from Greek *polupodion*, denoting a kind of fern, from *polu-* 'many' + *pous, pod-* 'foot.'

pol·yp·oid /ˈpäliˌpoid/ ▸*adj.* **1** *Zoology* of, relating to, or resembling a polyp or hydra. ■ of, relating to, or denoting the polyp stage in the life cycle of a coelenterate. Also called **HYDROID**. Compare with **MEDUSOID**. **2** *Medicine* (of a growth) resembling or in the form of a polyp.

pol·y·pore /ˈpäliˌpôr/ ▸*n.* a bracket fungus in which the spores are expelled through fine pores on the underside. • Several families in the order Aphyllophorales, class Hymenomycetes, in particular Polyporaceae, which includes the **DRYAD SADDLE**.

pol·yp·o·sis /ˌpäliˈpōsəs/ ▸*n. Medicine* a condition characterized by the presence of numerous internal polyps, esp. a hereditary disease (**familial adenomatous polyposis**) that affects the colon and in which the polyps may become malignant.

pol·y·pro·pyl·ene /ˌpäliˈprōpəˌlēn/ ▸*n.* a synthetic resin that is a polymer of propylene, used esp. for ropes, fabrics, and molded objects.

pol·yp·tych /ˈpälipˌtik/ ▸*n.* a painting, typically an altarpiece, consisting of more than three leaves or panels joined by hinges or folds. ▷mid 19th cent.: from late Latin *polyptycha* (neuter plural) 'registers,' from Greek *poluptukhos* 'having many folds,' from *polu-* 'many' + *ptukhē* 'fold.'

pol·y·pus /ˈpäləpəs/ ▸*n.* (*pl.* **-pi** /-ˌpī; -ˌpē/) archaic or technical term for **POLYP**. ▷late Middle English: via Latin from a variant of Greek *polupous* 'cuttlefish, polyp,' from *polu-* 'many' + *pous, pod-* 'foot.'

pol·y·rhythm /ˈpäliˌriTHəm/ ▸*n. Music* a rhythm that makes use of two or more different rhythms simultaneously. **—pol·y·rhyth·mic** /ˌpäliˈriTHmik/ *adj.*

pol·y·ri·bo·some /ˌpäliˈrībəˌsōm/ ▸*n.* another term for **POLYSOME**.

pol·y·sac·cha·ride /ˌpäliˈsakəˌrīd/ ▸*n. Biochemistry* a carbohydrate (e.g., starch, cellulose, or glycogen) whose molecules consist of a number of sugar molecules bonded together.

po·ly·se·my /ˈpäliˌsemē/ ▸*n. Linguistics* the coexistence of many possible meanings for a word or phrase. ▷early 20th cent.: from **POLY-** 'many' + Greek *sēma* 'sign.' **—po·ly·se·mic** /ˌpäliˈsēmik/ *adj.* **—po·ly·se·mous** /ˌpäliˈsēməs/ *adj.*

pol·y·some /ˈpäliˌsōm/ ▸*n. Biology* a cluster of ribosomes held together by a strand of messenger RNA that each ribosome is translating.

pol·y·sty·rene /ˌpäliˈstīrēn/ ▸*n.* a synthetic resin that is a polymer of styrene, used chiefly as lightweight rigid foams and films.

pol·y·sul·fide /ˌpäliˈsəlˌfīd/ ▸*n. Chemistry* a compound containing two or more sulfur atoms bonded together as an anion or group. ■ a synthetic rubber or other polymer in which the units are linked through such groups.

pol·y·syl·lab·ic /ˌpäləsəˈlabik/ ▸*adj.* (of a word) having more than one syllable. ■ using or characterized by words of many syllables: *polysyllabic jargon.* **—pol·y·syl·lab·i·cal·ly** /-səˈlabək(ə)lē/ *adv.*

pol·y·syl·la·ble /ˈpäliˌsiləbəl; ˌpäliˈsiləbəl/ ▸*n.* a polysyllabic word.

pol·y·symp·to·mat·ic /ˌpäliˌsimptəˈmatik/ ▸*adj.* (of a disease condition or a person or animal) involving or exhibiting many symptoms.

pol·y·syn·thet·ic /ˌpälisinˈTHetik/ ▸*adj.* denoting or relating to a language characterized by complex words consisting of several morphemes, in which a single word may function as a whole sentence. Many American Indian languages are polysynthetic.

pol·y·tech·nic /ˌpäliˈteknik/ ▸*n.* an institution of higher education offering courses in many subjects, esp. vocational or technical subjects.
▸*adj.* dealing with or devoted to various vocational or technical subjects. ▷early 19th cent.: from French *polytechnique*, from Greek *polutekhnos*, from *polu-* 'many' + *tekhnē* 'art.'

pol·y·tene /ˈpäləˌtēn/ ▸*adj. Genetics* relating to or denoting a giant chromosome that is composed of many parallel copies of the genetic material, as found in *Drosophila* fruit flies where they are much used in genetic research. ▷1930s: from **POLY-** 'many' + *-tene* (from Greek *tainia* 'band, ribbon') denoting stages of the first meiotic division.

pol·y·tet·ra·fluor·o·eth·y·lene /ˌpäliˌtetrəˌflo͝orōˈeTHəˌlēn/ ▸*n.* a tough translucent synthetic resin made by polymerizing tetrafluoroethylene, chiefly used to make seals and bearings and to coat nonstick cooking utensils.

pol·y·the·ism /ˈpäliTHēˌizəm/ ▸*n.* the belief in or worship of more than one god. ▷early 17th cent.: from French *polythéisme*, from Greek *polutheos* 'of many gods,' from *polu-* 'many' + *theos* 'god.' **—pol·y·the·ist** /-ˌTHēist/ *n.* **—pol·y·the·is·tic** /ˌpäliTHēˈistik/ *adj.*

pol·y·thene /ˈpäləTHēn/ ▸*n. chiefly Brit.* another term for **POLYETHYLENE**. ▷1930s: contraction of **POLYETHYLENE**.

pol·y·to·nal·i·ty /ˌpäliˌtōˈnalətē/ ▸*n.* the simultaneous use of two or more keys in a musical composition. **—pol·y·ton·al** /ˌpäliˈtōnl/ *adj.*

pol·y·type /ˈpäliˌtīp/ ▸*n. Crystallography* any of a number of forms of a crystalline substance that differ in only one of the dimensions of the unit cell. **—pol·y·typ·ic** /ˌpäliˈtipik/ *adj.* **—pol·y·typ·ism** /ˌpäliˈtīˌpizəm/ *n.*

pol·y·un·sat·u·rat·ed /ˌpälēənˈsaCHəˌrātid/ ▸*adj. Chemistry* (of an organic compound, esp. a fat or oil molecule) containing several double or triple bonds between carbon atoms. Polyunsaturated fats, which are usually of plant origin, are regarded as healthier in the diet than saturated fats.

pol·y·un·sat·u·rates /ˌpälēənˈsaCHərits/ ▸*plural n.* polyunsaturated fats or fatty acids.

pol·y·u·re·thane /ˌpäliˈyo͞orəˌTHān/ ▸*n.* a synthetic resin in which the polymer units are linked by urethane groups, used chiefly as constituents of paints, varnishes, adhesives, and foams.
▸*v.* [*trans.*] [usu. as *adj.*] (**polyurethaned**) coat or protect with paint or varnish of this kind.

pol·y·u·ri·a /ˌpäliˈyo͞orēə/ ▸*n. Medicine* production of abnormally large volumes of dilute urine. Compare with **DIURESIS**. **—pol·y·u·ric** /-ˈyo͞orik/ *adj.*

pol·y·va·lent /ˌpäliˈvālənt/ ▸*adj. Chemistry* having a valence of three or more. ■ *Medicine* having the property of counteracting several related poisons or affording immunity against different strains of a microorganism. ■ *Medicine* another term for **MULTIVALENT**. ■ *figurative* having many different functions, forms, or facets: *as emotion, love is polyvalent.* **—pol·y·va·lence** *n.*

pol·y·vi·nyl /ˌpäliˈvīnl/ ▸*adj.* [*attrib.*] denoting materials or objects made from polymers of vinyl compounds.

pol·y·vi·nyl ac·e·tate (abbr.: **PVA**) ▸*n.* a synthetic resin made by polymerizing vinyl acetate, used chiefly in paints and adhesives.

pol·y·vi·nyl chlo·ride (abbr.: **PVC**) ▸*n.* a tough, chemically resistant synthetic resin made by polymerizing vinyl chloride and used for a wide variety of products including pipes, flooring, and sheeting.

pol·y·vi·nyl·pyr·rol·i·done /ˌpäliˌvīnl-piˈräləˌdōn/ ▸*n. Chemistry* a water-soluble polymer of vinyl pyrrolidone, used as a synthetic blood plasma substitute and in the cosmetic, drug, and food-processing industries.

pol·y·wa·ter /ˈpäliˌwôtər; -ˌwätər/ ▸*n. historical* a supposed polymeric form of water markedly different from ordinary water, claimed as a new discovery in the early 1970s. The claim was later retracted when its properties were found to be the result of impurities.

Pol·y·zo·a /ˌpäliˈzōə/ *Zoology* British term for **BRYOZOA**. ▷modern Latin (plural), from **POLY-** 'many' + *zōion* 'animal.' **—pol·y·zo·an** *n.* & *adj.*

Pom /päm/ ▸*n.* **1** short for **POMERANIAN**. **2** short for **POMMY**.

pom·ace /ˈpəməs/ ▸*n.* (esp. in cider making) the pulpy residue remaining after fruit has been crushed in order to extract its juice. ■ the pulpy matter remaining after some other substance has been pressed or crushed, for example castor oil seeds after the oil has been extracted. ▷late 16th cent.: apparently from medieval Latin *pomacium* 'cider,' from Latin *pomum* 'apple.'

po·made /pəˈmād; -ˈmäd/ *dated* ▸*n.* a scented ointment applied to the hair or scalp.
▸*v.* [*trans.*] [often as *adj.*] (**pomaded**) apply pomade to. ▷mid 16th cent.: from French *pommade*, based on Latin *pomum* 'apple' (from which it was originally made).

Po·mak /ˈpōˌmak/ ▸*n.* a Muslim Bulgarian. ▷Bulgarian.

po·man·der /pōˈmandər; ˈpōˌmandər/ ▸*n.* a ball or perforated container of sweet-smelling substances such as herbs and spices, placed in a closet, drawer, or room to perfume the air or (formerly) carried as a supposed protection against infection. ■ a piece of fruit, typically an orange or apple, studded with cloves and hung in a closet by a ribbon for a similar purpose. ▷late 15th cent.: from Old French *pome d'embre*, from medieval Latin *pomum de ambra* 'apple of ambergris.'

po·ma·tum /pōˈmātəm; -ˈmätəm/ ▸*n.* & *v.* another term for **POMADE**. ▷mid 16th cent.: modern Latin, from Latin *pomum* 'apple.'

pom·be /ˈpämˌbā/ ▸*n.* (in central and eastern Africa) a fermented drink made from various kinds of grain and fruit. ▷Kiswahili.

pome /pōm/ ▸*n.* *Botany* a fruit consisting of a fleshy enlarged receptacle and a tough central core containing the seeds, e.g., an apple or pear. ▷late Middle English: from Old French, based on Latin *poma*, plural of *pomum* 'apple.'

pome·gran·ate /ˈpäm(ə)ˌgranit; ˈpəm-/ ▸*n.* **1** an orange-sized fruit with a tough reddish outer skin and sweet red gelatinous flesh containing many seeds. **2** the tree that bears this fruit, which is native to North Africa and western Asia and has long been cultivated. • *Punica granatum*, family Punicaceae. ▷Middle English: from Old French *pome grenate*, from *pome* 'apple' + *grenate* 'pomegranate' (from Latin *(malum) granatum* '(apple) having many seeds,' from *granum* 'seed').

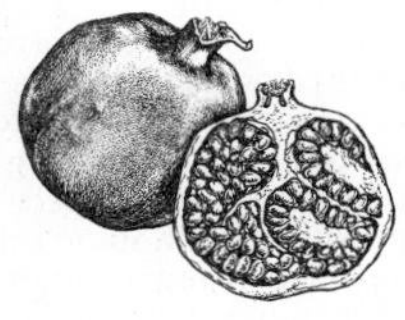
pomegranate 1

pom·e·lo /ˈpäməˌlō; ˈpəm-/ (also **pum·me·lo**) ▸*n.* (*pl.* **-los**) **1** the largest of the citrus fruits, with a thick yellow skin and bitter pulp that resembles grapefruit in flavor. Also called **SHADDOCK**. **2** the tree that bears this fruit. • *Citrus maxima*, family Rutaceae. ▷mid 19th cent.: of unknown origin.

Pom·er·a·ni·a /ˌpäməˈrānēə/ a region of northern Europe that extends along the southern shore of the Baltic Sea in northeastern Germany and Poland. The region was controlled variously by Germany, Poland, the Holy Roman Empire, Prussia, and Sweden until the larger part was restored to Poland in 1945 and the western portion became a part of the German state of Mecklenburg–West Pomerania.

Pom·er·a·ni·an /ˌpäməˈrānēən/ ▸*n.* a small dog of a breed with long silky hair, a pointed muzzle, and pricked ears.

Pomeranian

Pom·e·rol /ˈpäməˌrôl; -ˌrōl/ ▸*n.* a red Bordeaux wine produced in Pomerol, a region in the Gironde, France.

pom·fret /ˈpämfrət; ˈpəm-/ ▸*n.* a deep-bodied fish of open seas that typically has scales on the dorsal and anal fins. • Family Bramidae: several genera and species, including the edible *Brama brama* of the North Atlantic. ▷early 18th cent.: apparently from Portuguese *pampo*.

pom·mel ▸*n.* /ˈpäməl; ˈpəməl/ **1** a rounded knob on the end of the handle of a sword, dagger, or old-fashioned gun. **2** the upward curving or projecting part of a saddle in front of the rider.
▸*v.* /ˈpəməl; ˈpäməl/ (**-meled**, **-mel·ing**; *Brit.* **-melled**, **-mel·ling**) another term for **PUMMEL**. ▷Middle English (denoting a ball or finial at the top point of a tower, corner of an altar, etc.): from Old French *pomel*, from a diminutive of Latin *pomum* 'fruit, apple.'

pom·mel horse ▸*n.* a vaulting horse fitted with a pair of curved handgrips, used for a gymnastic exercise consisting of swings of the legs and body. ■ [in *sing.*] the set of exercises performed on such a piece of equipment.

pommes frites /ˌpəm ˈfrēt/ ▸*plural n.* (esp. in recipes or on menus) French fries. ▷French, from *pommes de terre frites*, literally 'fried potatoes.'

Pom·my /ˈpämē/ (also **Pom·mie**) ▸*n.* (*pl.* **-mies**) *Austral./NZ, informal, offensive* a British person. ▷early 20th cent.: of unknown origin; said by some to be short for *pomegranate*, as a near rhyme to *immigrant*, but evidence is lacking.

Po·mo /ˈpōmō/ ▸*n.* (*pl.* same or **-mos**) **1** a member of an American Indian people of northern California. **2** any of the languages of this people.
▸*adj.* of or relating to this people or their languages. ▷from Pomo *phōmō phóʔma?* 'dweller at the red-earth hole'.

po-mo *informal* ▸*abbr.* postmodern.

po·mol·o·gy /pōˈmäləjē/ ▸*n.* the science of growing fruit. ▷early 19th cent.: from Latin *pomum* 'fruit' + **-LOGY**. **—po·mo·log·i·cal** /ˌpōməˈläjikəl/ *adj.* **—po·mol·o·gist** /-jist/ *n.*

Po·mo·na /pəˈmōnə/ an industrial and commercial city in southwestern California, east of Los Angeles; pop. 131,723.

pomp /pämp/ ▸*n.* ceremony and splendid display, esp. at a public event: *St. Paul's was perfectly adapted to **pomp and circumstance**.* ■ (**pomps**) *archaic* ostentatious boastfulness or vanity: *the pomps and vanities of this world.* ▷Middle English: from Old French *pompe*, via Latin from Greek *pompē* 'procession, pomp,' from *pempein* 'send.'

Pom·pa·dour /ˈpämpəˌdôr; -ˌdo͝or; pônpäˈdo͝or/, Jeanne Antoinette Poisson, Marquise de (1721–64), French noblewoman; known as **Madame de Pompadour**. In 1744, she became the mistress of Louis XV, gaining considerable influence at court.

pom·pa·dour /ˈpämpəˌdôr/ ▸*n.* a man's hairstyle in which the hair is combed up from the forehead without a part. ■ a woman's hairstyle in which the hair is turned back off the forehead in a roll.
▸*v.* [*trans.*] [usu. as *adj.*] (**pompadoured**) arrange (hair) in a pompadour. ▷late 19th cent.: named after Madame de **POMPADOUR**.

pom·pa·no /ˈpämpəˌnō/ ▸*n.* (*pl.* **-nos**) **1** an edible butterfish that lives in shoals along the east coast of North America. • *Peprillus simillimus*, family Stromateidae. **2** another term for **JACK**[1] (sense 11). ▷late 18th cent.: from Spanish *pámpano*, perhaps from *pámpana* 'vine leaf,' because of its shape.

Pom·pa·no Beach /ˈpämpəˌnō/ a resort city in southeastern Florida, north of Fort Lauderdale, on the Atlantic Ocean; pop. 72,411.

Pom·pe·ii /pämˈpā(ē)/ an ancient city in western Italy, southeast of Naples. The city was buried by an eruption of Mount Vesuvius in AD 79; excavations of the site began in 1748 and revealed well-preserved remains of buildings, mosaics, furniture, and the personal possessions of the city's inhabitants.

Pom·pey /ˈpämpē/ (106–48 BC), Roman general and statesman; Latin name *Gnaeus Pompeius Magnus*; known as **Pompey the Great**. He founded the First Triumvirate, but later quarreled with Julius Caesar, who defeated him at the battle of Pharsalus. He then fled to Egypt, where he was murdered.

Pom·pi·dou /ˈpämpiˌdo͞o; pônpēˈdo͞o/, Georges (Jean Raymond) (1911–74), French statesman; prime minister 1962–68 and president 1969–74. He was instrumental in ending the conflict in Algeria between French forces and nationalist guerrillas.

pom·pier /pämˈpyā/ ▸*n.* (*pl.* same) an artist regarded as painting in an academic, imitative, and vulgarly neoclassical style. ▷mid 19th cent.: from French, literally 'fireman,' said to derive from the similarity between firemen's helmets and those worn by the Greek gods and heroes depicted by late Classical artists.

pom-pom[1] /ˈpäm ˌpäm/ (also **pom·pom** or **pom·pon**) ▸*n.* a small woolen ball attached to a garment, esp. a hat, for decoration. ■ a cluster of brightly colored strands of yarn or plastic, waved in pairs by cheerleaders. ■ a dahlia, chrysanthemum, or aster with small tightly clustered petals: [as *adj.*] *miniature, pompom, and border dahlias.* ▷mid 18th cent.: French *pompon*, of unknown origin.

pom-pom[2] (also **pom·pom**) ▸*n.* an automatic quick-firing two-pounder cannon of the World War II period, typically mounted on a ship and used against aircraft. ▷late 19th cent.: imitative of the sound of the discharge.

pomp·ous /ˈpämpəs/ ▸*adj.* affectedly and irritatingly grand, solemn, or self-important: *a pompous ass who pretends he knows everything.* ■ *archaic* characterized by pomp or splendor: *there were many processions and other pompous shows.* See note at **FORMAL**. ▷late Middle English: from Old French *pompeux* 'full of grandeur,' from late Latin *pomposus*, from *pompa* 'pomp.' **—pom·pos·i·ty** /pämˈpäsətē/ *n.* **—pomp·ous·ly** *adv.* **—pomp·ous·ness** *n.*

'pon /pän; pən/ ▸*prep.* short for **UPON**, esp. in poetic use or to represent dialect.

Pon·ca /ˈpängkə; ˈpôngkə/ ▸*n.* (*pl.* same or **-cas**) **1** a member of a Siouan people formerly inhabiting northern Nebraska and southern South Dakota. **2** the Siouan language of this people, related to Omaha.
▸*adj.* of or relating to this people or their language. ▷via French, from the Ponca name *pąka*.

Pon·ca Cit·y /ˈpängkə/ an industrial city in north central Oklahoma; pop. 25,919.

Pon·ce /ˈpônsā/ an industrial port in southern Puerto Rico, on the Caribbean Sea; pop. 159,151.

ponce /päns/ *Brit., informal* ▸*n.* a man who lives off a prostitute's earnings. ■ *derogatory* an effeminate man.
▸*v.* [*intrans.*] live off a prostitute's earnings. ■ [*trans.*] ask for or obtain (something to which one is not strictly entitled): *I **ponced** a cigarette **off** her.*
▸*phrasal v.* □ **ponce around/about** behave in a ridiculous, ineffective, or posturing way: *I ponced around in front of the mirror.* □ **ponce something up** make overly elaborate and unnecessary changes to something in an attempt to improve it. ▷late 19th cent.: perhaps from the verb **POUNCE**[1].

Ponce de Le·ón /ˈpäns də ˈlēən; ˌpônsā de lāˈôn/, Juan (*c.*1460–1521), Spanish explorer. He accompanied Columbus on his second voyage to the New World in 1493, became governor of Puerto Rico 1510–12, and landed on the coast of Florida near what became St. Augustine in 1513, claiming the area for Spain.

pon·cho /ˈpänchō/ ▸*n.* (*pl.* **-chos**) a garment of a type originally worn in South America, made of a thick piece of woolen cloth with a slit in the middle for the head. ■ a garment in this style, esp. a waterproof one worn as a raincoat. ▷early 18th cent.: from South American Spanish, from Araucanian.

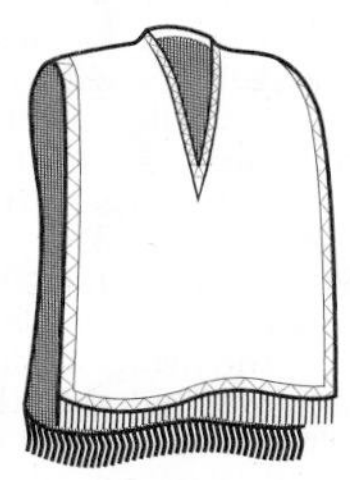
poncho

pon·cy /ˈpänsē/ (also **pon·cey**) ▸*adj.* (**-ci·er**, **-ci·est**) *Brit., informal* pretentious or affected: *a poncy wine bar.*

pond /pänd/ ▸*n.* a small body of still water formed naturally or by hollowing or embanking. ■ (**the pond**) *informal* the Atlantic ocean: *he's relatively unknown on this side of the pond.*
▸*v.* [*trans.*] hold back or dam up (flowing water or another liquid) to form a small lake. ■ [*intrans.*] (of flowing water or other liquids) form such a lake: [as *n.*] (**ponding**) *where a path goes down into a dip, you'll have to ensure that ponding doesn't occur.* ▷Middle English: alteration of **POUND**[3], commonly used in dialect in the same sense.

pon·der /ˈpändər/ ▸*v.* [*trans.*] think about (something) carefully, esp. before making a decision or reaching a conclusion: *I pondered the question of what clothes to* *wear for the occasion* [*intrans.*] *she sat pondering over her problem.* ▷Middle English (in the sense 'appraise, judge the worth of'): from Old French *ponderer* 'consider,' from Latin *ponderare* 'weigh, reflect on,' from *pondus, ponder-* 'weight.' —**pon·der·a·tion** /ˌpändəˈrāsHən/ *n.* (*rare*).

pon·der·a·ble /ˈpändərəbəl/ ▸*adj. poetic/literary* having appreciable weight or significance. ▷mid 17th cent.: from late Latin *ponderabilis*, from *ponderare* 'weigh, reflect on' (see PONDER). —**pon·der·a·bil·i·ty** /ˌpändərəˈbilətē/ *n.*

pon·der·o·sa /ˌpändəˈrōsə/ (also **ponderosa pine**) ▸*n.* a tall slender pine tree, the most widespread conifer of western North America, planted for timber and as an ornamental. • *Pinus ponderosa*, family Pinaceae. ▷late 19th cent.: feminine of Latin *ponderosus* 'massive, ponderous,' used as a specific epithet in *Pinus ponderosa*.

P

pon·der·ous /ˈpändərəs/ ▸*adj.* slow and clumsy because of great weight: *her footsteps were heavy and ponderous.* See note at HEAVY. ■ dull, laborious, or excessively solemn: *Liz could hardly restrain herself from finishing all his ponderous sentences.* ▷late Middle English: via French from Latin *ponderosus*, from *pondus, ponder-* 'weight.' —**pon·der·os·i·ty** /ˌpändəˈräsətē/ *n.* —**pon·der·ous·ly** *adv.* —**pon·der·ous·ness** *n.*

Pon·di·cher·ry /ˌpändiˈcHerē; -ˈsHerē/ a Union Territory of southeastern India, on the Coromandel Coast, formed from several former French territories and incorporated into India in 1954. ■ its capital city; pop. 203,000.

pond scum ▸*n.* a mass of algae forming a green film on the surface of stagnant water. ■ *informal* a person or thing perceived as worthless or contemptible.

pond·weed /ˈpändˌwēd/ ▸*n.* a submerged aquatic plant that grows in still or running water and sometimes has floating leaves. • Genus *Potamogeton*, family Potamogetonaceae.

pone /pōn/ ▸*n.* (also **corn pone** or **pone bread**) unleavened cornbread in the form of flat oval cakes or loaves, originally as prepared with water by North American Indians and cooked in hot ashes. ▷Virginia Algonquian, 'bread.'

pong /pôNG; päNG/ *Brit., informal* ▸*n.* a strong, unpleasant smell.
▸*v.* [*intrans.*] smell strongly and unpleasantly. ▷early 20th cent.: of unknown origin. —**pon·gy** *adj.*

pon·gee /pänˈjē; ˈpänjē/ ▸*n.* a soft and typically unbleached type of Chinese plain-woven fabric, originally made from threads of raw silk and now also other fibers such as cotton, which are usually mercerized. ▷early 18th cent.: from Chinese (Mandarin dialect) *běnjī*, literally 'own loom' or *běnzhì*, literally 'home-woven.'

pon·gid /ˈpänjəd; -gəd/ ▸*n. Zoology* a primate of a family (Pongidae) that comprises the great apes. See also HOMINID. ▷1950s: from modern Latin *Pongidae* (plural), from the genus name *Pongo*, originally from Congolese *mpongo*, used as a term in zoology to refer to the gorilla and other apes.

pon·iard /ˈpänyərd/ ▸*n. historical* a small, slim dagger. ▷mid 16th cent.: from French *poignard*, based on Latin *pugnus* 'fist.'

Pons /pänz/, Lily (1904–76), U.S. opera singer; born in France; born *Alice-Josephine Pons*. A coloratura soprano, she made her debut at the Metropolitan Opera in 1931 and sang there for 25 years. She also appeared in movies.

pons /pänz/ (in full **pons Va·ro·li·i** /vəˈrōlēˌī/) ▸*n.* (*pl.* **pon·tes** /ˈpänˌtēz/) *Anatomy* the part of the brainstem that links the medulla oblongata and the thalamus. ▷late 17th cent.: from Latin, literally 'bridge,' (in full) 'bridge of Varolius,' named after C. Varoli (1543–75), Italian anatomist.

pons as·i·no·rum /ˈpänz ˌasəˈnôrəm/ ▸*n.* the point at which many learners fail, esp. a theory or formula that is difficult to grasp. ▷mid 18th cent.: Latin, literally 'bridge of asses,' term taken from the fifth proposition of the first book of Euclid.

Pon·selle /pänˈsel/, Rosa (1897–1981), U.S. opera singer; born *Rosa Melba Ponzillo*. She sang with the Metropolitan Opera 1918–36, beginning with her debut as Leonora in *Fidelio*.

Pont·char·train, Lake /ˈpäncHərˌtrān/ a shallow lake in southeastern Louisiana, north of New Orleans and Metairie, noted for its long causeway.

pon·tes /ˈpänˌtēz/ ▸ plural form of PONS.

Pon·ti·ac[1] /ˈpäntēˌak/ an industrial city in southeastern Michigan, northwest of Detroit; pop. 71,166.

Pon·ti·ac[2] (c.1720–69), Ottawa Indian chief. He is credited with organizing and leading a rebellion against the British, during which he led a year-long siege of Fort Detroit 1763–64. He agreed to terms of peace in 1766.

Pon·ti·ac fe·ver ▸*n. Medicine* a mild systemic disease with symptoms resembling influenza, probably caused by a legionella infection. ▷1960s: named after *Pontiac*, Michigan, where the first major outbreak was recorded.

Pon·ti·a·nak /ˌpäntēˈänək/ a seaport in Indonesia, on the western coast of Borneo, at the delta of the Kapuas River; pop. 305,000.

Pon·tic /ˈpäntik/ ▸*adj.* of or relating to ancient Pontus.

pon·ti·fex /ˈpäntəˌfeks/ ▸*n.* (*pl.* **pon·tif·i·ces** /pänˈtifəˌsēz/) (in ancient Rome) a member of the principal college of priests. ▷Latin, from *pons, pont-* 'bridge' + *-fex* from *facere* 'make.'

Pon·ti·fex Max·i·mus /ˈmaksəməs/ ▸*n.* (in ancient Rome) the head of the principal college of priests. ■ (in the Roman Catholic Church) a title of the pope. ▷*Maximus*, superlative of Latin *magnus* 'great.'

pon·tiff /ˈpäntəf/ (also **sovereign** or **supreme pontiff**) ▸*n.* the pope. ▷late 17th cent.: from French *pontife*, from Latin *pontifex* (see PONTIFEX).

pon·tif·i·cal /pänˈtifikəl/ ▸*adj.* **1** (in the Roman Catholic Church) of or relating to the pope: *a pontifical commission.* **2** characterized by a pompous and superior air of infallibility: *such explanations were greeted with pontifical disdain.*
▸*n. rare* (in the Roman Catholic Church) an office book of the Western Church containing rites to be performed by the pope or bishops. ■ (**pontificals**) the vestments and insignia of a bishop, cardinal, or abbot: *a bishop in full pontificals.* ▷late Middle English: from Latin *pontificalis*, from *pontifex* (see PONTIFEX). —**pon·tif·i·cal·ly** /-ik(ə)lē/ *adv.*

pon·tif·i·cate ▸*v.* /pänˈtifiˌkāt/ [*intrans.*] **1** (in the Roman Catholic Church) officiate as bishop, esp. at Mass. **2** express one's opinions in a way considered annoyingly pompous and dogmatic: *he was pontificating about art and history.*
▸*n.* /-kət/ (also **Pontificate**) (in the Roman Catholic Church) the office of pope or bishop. ■ the period of such an office: *Pope Gregory VIII enjoyed only a ten-week pontificate.* ▷late Middle English (as a noun): from Latin *pontificatus*, from *pontifex* (see PONTIFEX). The verb dates from the early 19th cent. —**pon·tif·i·ca·tor** /-ˌkātər/ *n.*

pon·tif·i·ces /pänˈtifəˌsēz/ ▸ plural form of PONTIFEX.

pon·til /ˈpäntl/ ▸*n.* another term for PUNTY. ▷mid 19th cent.: from French, apparently from Italian *pontello* 'small point,' diminutive of *punto*.

pon·tine /ˈpänˌtīn/ ▸*adj. Anatomy* of, relating to, or affecting the pons of the brain. ▷late 19th cent.: from Latin *pons, pont-* 'bridge' + -INE[1].

Pon·tine Marsh·es /ˈpänˌtēn; -ˌtīn/ an area of marshland in western Italy, on the Tyrrhenian coast south of Rome. Infested with malaria in ancient Roman times, it was not until 1928 that an extensive program to drain the marshes was begun. Several new towns have since been built in the region, which is now a productive agricultural area. Italian name AGRO PONTINO.

Pont l'É·vêque /ˌpôN ləˈvek/ ▸*n.* a kind of creamy soft cheese made originally at Pont l'Évêque in Normandy, France.

pon·toon[1] /ˌpänˈto͞on/ ▸*n.* a flat-bottomed boat or hollow metal cylinder used with others to support a temporary bridge or floating landing stage. ■ a bridge or landing stage supported by pontoons. ■ a large flat-bottomed barge or lighter equipped with cranes. ■ either of the floats fitted to an aircraft to enable it to land on water. ▷late 17th cent.: from French *ponton*, from Latin *ponto, ponton-*, from *pons, pont-* 'bridge.'

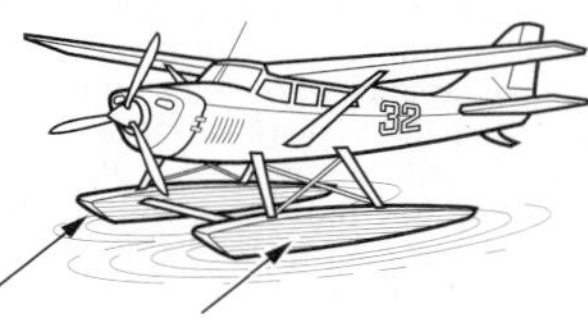

pontoon[1]

pon·toon[2] ▸*n. Brit.* the card game blackjack or vingt-et-un. ■ a hand of two cards totaling 21 in this game. ▷early 20th cent.: probably an alteration of *vingt-et-un* 'twenty-one.'

Pon·tor·mo /pônˈtôrmō/, Jacopo da (1494–1557), Italian painter, whose use of dynamic composition, anatomical exaggeration, and bright colors placed him at the forefront of early mannerism.

Pon·tus /ˈpäntəs/ an ancient region in northern Asia Minor, on the Black Sea coast north of Cappadocia. By the end of the 1st century BC, it had been defeated by Rome and absorbed into the Roman Empire.

po·ny /ˈpōnē/ ▸*n.* (*pl.* **-nies**) **1** a horse of a small breed, esp. one whose height at the withers is below 14 hands 2 inches (58 inches). ■ (**the ponies**) *informal* racehorses: *he had been **playing the ponies** on the side.* **2** *informal* a small drinking glass or the drink contained in it: *a pony of vodka.* **3** a literal translation of a foreign-language text, used illicitly by students; a trot. **4** *Brit., informal* twenty-five pounds sterling.
▸*v.* (**-nies, -nied**) [*intrans.*] (**pony up**) *informal* pay (money), esp. as a contribution or an unavoidable expense: *getting ready to pony up for their children's college education.* ▷mid 17th cent.: probably from French *poulenet* 'small foal,' diminutive of *poulain*, from late Latin *pullanus*, from Latin *pullus* 'young animal.'

Po·ny Ex·press a system of mail delivery operating from 1860 to 1861 over a distance of 1,800 miles (2,900 km) between St. Joseph, Missouri, and Sacramento, California, using continuous relays of horse riders.

po·ny·tail /ˈpōnēˌtāl/ ▸*n.* a hairstyle in which the hair is drawn back and tied at the back of the head, causing it to hang down like a pony's tail. —**po·ny·tailed** *adj.*

Pon·zil·lo /pänˈzilō/, Rosa, see PONSELLE.

Pon·zi scheme /ˈpänzē/ ▸*n.* a form of fraud in which belief in the success of a nonexistent enterprise is fostered by the payment of quick returns to the first investors from money invested by later investors. ▷named after Charles Ponzi (died 1949), who carried out such a fraud (1919–20).

pon·zu /ˈpänˌzo͞o/ ▸*n.* a Japanese dipping sauce made from soy sauce, lime juice, vinegar, and fish flakes. ▷Japanese: 'citrus vinegar.'

poo ▸*exclam., n., & v.* variant spelling of POOH.

pooch[1] /po͞ocH/ ▸*n. informal* a dog. ▷1920s: of unknown origin.

pooch[2] ▸*v. informal* protrude or cause to protrude: [*intrans.*] *a dress that made her stomach pooch out even more than usual.* ▷mid 17th cent.: from the noun POUCH.

poo·dle /ˈpo͞odl/ ▸*n.* a dog of a breed with a curly coat that is usually clipped. The numerous varieties of poodle include standard, miniature, and toy. ■ *Brit.* a person or organization considered to be servile or obsequious: *the council is being made a poodle of central government.* ▷early 19th cent.: from German *Pudel(hund)*, from Low German *pud(d)eln* 'splash in water' (the poodle being a water dog).

poo·dle skirt ▸*n.* a long full skirt in a solid color with a chenille poodle on it, popular in the 1950s with bobbysoxers.

poof[1] /po͞of; po͝of/ (also **pouf**) ▸*exclam.* **1** used to convey the suddenness with which someone or something disappears: *once you've used it, poof—it's gone.* **2** used to express contemptuous dismissal: *"Oh, poof!" said Will. "You say that every year."* ▷early 19th cent.: symbolic.

poof[2] (also **pouf** or **poove**) ▸*n. Brit., informal, offensive* an effeminate or homosexual man. ▷mid 19th cent.: perhaps an alteration of the archaic noun *puff* in the sense 'braggart.' —**poof·y** *adj.*

poof·ter /ˈpo͞oftər; ˈpo͝of-/ ▸*n.* another term for POOF[2]. ▷early 20th cent.: extended form.

pooh /po͞o; po͝o/ (also **poo**) *informal* ▸*exclam.* used to express disgust at an unpleasant smell. ■ used to express impatience or contempt: *Oh pooh! Don't be such a spoilsport.*
▸*n.* excrement. ■ [in *sing.*] an act of defecating.
▸*v.* [*intrans.*] defecate. ▷natural exclamation: first recorded in English in the late 16th cent.

pooh-bah /ˈpo͞o ˌbä/ (also **Pooh-Bah**) ▸*n.* a person having much influence or holding many offices at the same time, esp. one perceived as pompously self-important. ▷from the name of a character in W. S. Gilbert's *The Mikado* (1885).

pooh-pooh /ˈpo͞o ˌpo͞o; po͞o ˈpo͞o/ ▸*v.* [*trans.*] *informal* dismiss (an idea or suggestion) as being foolish or impractical: *until recently, this idea was pooh-poohed by the scientific community.* ▷late 18th cent.: reduplication of POOH.

poo·ja ▸*n.* variant spelling of PUJA.

poo·ka /ˈpo͞okə/ ▸*n.* (in Irish mythology) a hobgoblin. ▷from Irish *púca*.

pool[1] /po͞ol/ ▸*n.* a small area of still water, typically one formed naturally. ■ a small, shallow patch of

liquid lying on a surface: *a pool of blood | figurative the lamps cast pools of light on the wet streets.* ■ a swimming pool. ■ a deep place in a river.
▸*v.* [*intrans.*] (of water or another liquid) form a pool on the ground or another surface: *the oil pooled behind the quay walls, escaping slowly into the river.* ■ (of blood) accumulate in parts of the venous system. ▷Old English *pōl*; related to Dutch *poel* and German *Pfuhl*.

pool[2] ▸*n.* **1** a supply of vehicles or goods available for use when needed: *the oldest vehicle in the motor pool.* ■ a group of people available for work when required: *the typing pool.* ■ a group of people considered as a resource: *a nationwide pool of promising high-school students.* ■ an arrangement, illegal in many countries, between competing parties to fix prices or rates and share business in order to eliminate competition. ■ a common fund into which all contributors pay and from which financial backing is provided: *big public investment pools.* ■ a source of common funding for speculative operations on financial markets: *a huge pool of risk capital.* ■ a group of contestants who compete against each other in a tournament for the right to advance to the next round. ■ the collective amount of players' stakes in gambling or sweepstakes; a kitty. **2** *Billiards* a game played on a table using fifteen colored and numbered balls and a white cue ball. ■ another term for **POCKET BILLIARDS.** ■ short for **STRAIGHT POOL.**
▸*v.* [*trans.*] (of two or more people or organizations) put (money or other assets) into a common fund: *they entered a contract to pool any gains and invest them profitably.* ■ share (things) for the benefit of all those involved: [as *n.*] (**pooling**) *a pooling of ideas.* ▷late 17th cent. (originally denoting a game of cards having a pool): from French *poule* in the sense 'stake, kitty,' associated with **POOL**[1]. **—pool·er** *n.*

Poole[1] /po͞ol/ a port and resort town on the southern coast of England, just west of Bournemouth; pop. 131,000.

Poole[2], Elijah, see **MUHAMMAD**[2].

pool·room /ˈpo͞olˌro͞om; -ˌro͝om/ ▸*n.* (also **pool hall**) a commercial establishment where pool or billiard games are played.

pool·side /ˈpo͞olˌsīd/ ▸*n.* the area adjoining a swimming pool: [as *adj.*] *the poolside bar.*
▸*adv.* toward or beside a swimming pool: *she and her parents lounged poolside.*

poon /po͞on/ ▸*n.* **1** any large Indo-Malayan evergreen tree of the genus *Calophyllum.* **2** short for **POONTANG.**

Poo·na /ˈpo͞onə/ (also **Pu·ne**) an industrial city in Maharashtra, western India, in the hills southeast of Bombay; pop. 1,560,000

poon·tang /ˈpo͞onˌtaNG/ (also **poon**) ▸*n. vulgar slang* sexual activity. ■ a woman or women regarded solely in terms of potential sexual gratification. ▷1920s: perhaps from Limba (a West African language of Sierra Leone) *puntu* 'vagina,' or perhaps alteration of French *putain* 'prostitute.'

poop[1] /po͞op/ ▸*n.* (also **poop deck**) the aftermost and highest deck of a ship, esp. in a sailing ship where it typically forms the roof of a cabin in the stern.
▸*v.* [*trans.*] (usu. **be pooped**) (of a wave) break over the stern of (a ship), sometimes causing it to capsize: *carrying a high sea, we were badly pooped.* ▷late Middle English: from Old French *pupe*, from a variant of Latin *puppis* 'stern.'

poop[2] ▸*v.* [*trans.*] (usu. **be pooped**) *informal* exhaust: *I was pooped and just flopped into bed.*
▸*phrasal v.* □ **poop out** stop functioning: *the analog tape fluttered slightly in pitch but didn't poop out.* ▷1930s: of unknown origin.

poop[3] *informal* ▸*n.* excrement.
▸*v.* [*intrans.*] defecate. ▷early 18th cent.: imitative.

poop[4] ▸*n. informal* up-to-date or inside information: *what's the latest poop from campaign headquarters?* ▷1940s: of unknown origin.

poop[5] ▸*n. informal* a stupid or ineffectual person. ▷early 20th cent.: perhaps a shortening of **NINCOMPOOP.** **—poop·y** *adj.*

poop·er-scoop·er /ˈpo͞opər ˌsko͞opər/ (also **poop·er scoop·er**) ▸*n.* an implement for picking up dog excrement.

poor /po͝or; pôr/ ▸*adj.* **1** lacking sufficient money to live at a standard considered comfortable or normal in a society: *people who were too poor to afford a telephone* | [as *n.*] (**the poor**) *the gap between the rich and the poor has widened.* ■ (of a place) inhabited by people without sufficient money: *a poor area with run-down movie theaters and overcrowded schools.* **2** worse than is usual, expected, or desirable; of a low or inferior standard or quality: *her work was poor | many people are eating a very poor diet.* ■ [*predic.*] (**poor in**) deficient or lacking in: *the water is poor in nutrients.* ■ *dated* used ironically to deprecate something belonging to or offered by oneself: *he is, in my poor opinion, a more handsome young man.* **3** [*attrib.*] (of a person) considered to be deserving of pity or sympathy: *they inquired after poor Dorothy's broken hip.* ▷Middle English: from Old French *poure*, from Latin *pauper*.
▸*PHRASES* □ (**as**) **poor as a church mouse** (or **as church mice**) extremely poor. □ **poor little rich boy** (or **girl**) a wealthy young person whose money brings them no contentment (often used as an expression of mock sympathy). □ **the poor man's ——** an inferior or cheaper substitute for the thing specified: *corduroy has always been the poor man's velvet.* □ **poor relation** a person or thing that is considered inferior or subordinate to others of the same type or group: *for many years radio has been* ***the poor relation of*** *the media.* □ **take a poor view of** regard with disfavor or disapproval.

poor box ▸*n. historical* a collection box, esp. one in a church, for gifts of money or other articles toward the relief of the poor.

poor boy (also **poor-boy**) ▸*n.* another term for **SUBMARINE SANDWICH.**

Poor Clare ▸*n.* a member of an order of Franciscan nuns founded by St. Clare of Assisi in *c.*1212.

poor·house /ˈpo͝orˌhous; ˈpôr-/ ▸*n. historical* an institution where paupers were maintained with public funds.

poo·ri /ˈpo͝orē/ (also **pu·ri**) ▸*n.* (in Indian cooking) a small, round, flat bread, deep-fried and served with meat or vegetables. ▷from Sanskrit.

Poor Law ▸*n. Brit., historical* a law relating to the support of the poor. Originally the responsibility of the parish, the relief and employment of the poor passed over to the workhouses in 1834. In the early 20th century, the Poor Law was replaced by social security.

poor·ly /ˈpo͝orlē; ˈpôr-/ ▸*adv.* in a way or at a level that is considered inadequate: *schools that were performing poorly* | [as *submodifier*] *a few poorly articulated words.* ■ with insufficient money or resources: *he lived as poorly as his peasant parishioners.*
▸*adj.* unwell: *she looked poorly.*

poor-mouth ▸*v. informal* **1** [*trans.*] talk disparagingly about: *I used to poor-mouth corporate jets, but now that I've had the use of one I really appreciate it.* **2** [*intrans.*] claim to be poor: [as *adj.*] (**poor-mouthing**) *the poor-mouthing museum is not exactly eager to publicize this good fortune.*

poor·ness /ˈpo͝ornəs; ˈpôr-/ ▸*n.* the state of lacking or being deficient in some desirable quality or constituent: *the poorness of the food.*

poor-spir·it·ed ▸*adj. archaic* timid; cowardly.

poor white ▸*n. offensive* a member of a group of white people regarded as socially inferior, esp. one living in the southern U.S.

poor-will /ˈpo͝orˌwil/ (also **poor·will**) ▸*n.* a small nightjar found mainly in central and western North America. • Three genera in the family Caprimulgidae: four species, in particular the **common poorwill** (*Phalaenoptilus nuttallii*), which hibernates in cold weather. ▷late 19th cent.: imitative of its call.

Poo·ter·ish /ˈpo͞otəriSH/ ▸*adj.* self-important and mundane or narrow-minded: *Duran has a Pooterish way with an anecdote which makes his book often very funny.* ▷1960s: from the name of Charles Pooter, the fictional diarist in *Diary of a Nobody* (1892) by George and Weedon Grossmith.

poove /po͞ov; po͝ov/ ▸*n.* variant spelling of **POOF**[2].

POP /päp/ (also **PoP**) ▸*abbr.* (in computing) point of presence, denoting equipment that acts as access to the Internet. ■ point of purchase, denoting products or promotions located adjacent to a retail checkout or cashier.

pop[1] /päp/ ▸*v.* (**popped, pop·ping**) **1** [*intrans.*] make a sudden, sharp, explosive sound: *corks popped, glasses tinkled, and delicate canapés were served.* ■ [*trans.*] cause (something) to burst, making such a sound: *they were popping balloons with darts.* ■ (of a person's ears) make a small popping sound within the head as pressure is equalized, typically because of a change of altitude. ■ [*trans.*] heat (popcorn or another foodstuff) until it bursts open, making such a sound. ■ [*intrans.*] (of popcorn or another foodstuff) burst open in such a way. ■ (of a person's eyes) bulge or appear to bulge when opened wide, esp. as an indication of surprise. ■ [*trans.*] shoot (a gun). ■ [*trans.*] shoot (something) with a gun. **2** [*intrans.*] go somewhere, typically for a short time and often without notice: *she* ***popped in*** *to see if she could help.* ■ [*trans.*] put or move (something) somewhere quickly: *he popped his head around the door.* **3** [*intrans.*] *Baseball* (of a batter) hit a pop fly. ■ [*trans.*] (of a pitcher) cause (a batter) to pop up. **4** [*trans.*] *informal* take or inject (a drug): *people who obsessively drink and pop pills.* **5** [*trans.*] *Brit., informal* pawn (something).
▸*phrasal v.* □ **pop off** *informal* **1** die. **2** speak spontaneously and at length, typically angrily: *I've been thinking about it a lot—I don't want you to imagine I'm just popping off.* □ **pop out** make an out in a baseball game by hitting a pop fly that is caught. □ **pop up 1** appear or occur suddenly and unexpectedly: *these memories can pop up from time to time.* **2** hit a baseball high into the air but not deep, providing an easy catch: *in three at bats, he struck out twice and popped up.*
▸*n.* **1** a sudden sharp explosive sound: *at first there were just a few pops, perhaps from pistols.* **2** *informal* short for **SODA POP.** **3** (also **pop fly** or **pop-up**) *Baseball* a ball hit high in the air but not deep, providing an easy catch. **4** an attempt: *he grabs with a paw and hooks about two hundred berries at a pop.*
▸*adv.* with a sudden explosive sound: *the champagne went pop.*
▸*adj.* sudden or unexpected: *a pop quiz on the capitals of South America.* ▷late Middle English (in the senses 'a blow, knock' and 'to strike'): imitative.
▸*PHRASES* □ **—— a pop** *informal* costing a specified amount per item: *those swimsuits she wears are $50 a pop.* □ **have** (or **take**) **a pop at** *informal chiefly Brit.* attack physically or verbally. □ **make someone's eyes pop** (**out**) *informal* cause great astonishment to someone. □ **pop for something** pay for something, esp. a treat for someone else: *I popped for the first three tolls.* □ **pop the question** *informal* propose marriage.

pop[2] ▸*adj.* [*attrib.*] **1** of or relating to commercial popular music: *a pop star | a pop group.* ■ of, denoting, or relating to pop art. **2** *often derogatory* (esp. of a technical, scientific, or academic subject) made accessible to the general public; popularized: *pop psychology.*
▸*n.* (also **pop music**) commercial popular music, in particular accessible, tuneful music of a kind popular since the 1950s and sometimes contrasted with rock, soul, or other forms of popular music. ■ *dated* a pop record or song. ▷late 19th cent.: abbreviation of **POPULAR.**

pop[3] (also **pops**) ▸*n.* informal term for **FATHER.** ▷mid 19th cent.: abbreviation of **POPPA.**

pop. ▸*abbr.* population.

POP3 /ˈpäp ˈTHrē/ ▸*n. Computing* a protocol for receiving e-mail by downloading it to your computer from a mailbox on the server of an Internet service provider. ▷abbreviation of *Post Office Protocol 3*

pop art ▸*n.* art based on modern popular culture and the mass media, esp. as a critical or ironic comment on traditional fine art values.

> The term is applied specifically to the works, largely from the mid 1950s and 1960s, of a group of artists including Andy Warhol, Roy Lichtenstein, and Jasper Johns, who used images from comic books, advertisements, consumer products, television, and the movies.

pop·corn /ˈpäpˌkôrn/ ▸*n.* corn of a variety with hard kernels that swell up and burst open with a pop when heated. ■ these kernels when popped, typically buttered and salted and eaten as a snack.

pop cul·ture ▸*n.* commercial culture based on popular taste.

Pope[1] /pōp/, Alexander (1688–1744), English poet. A major figure of the Augustan age, he is known for his caustic wit and metrical skill, esp. his use of the heroic couplet. Notable works: *The Rape of the Lock* (1712; enlarged 1714) and *An Essay on Man* (1733–34).

Pope[2], John Russell (1874–1937), U.S. architect. He designed the National Archives 1933–35, the Jefferson Memorial 1937–43, and the National Gallery of Art 1941, all in Washington, D.C.

pope[1] /pōp/ ▸*n.* **1** (usu. **the pope** or **the Pope**) the bishop of Rome as head of the Roman Catholic Church. ■ the head of the Coptic Church, the bishop or patriarch of Alexandria. **2** another term for **RUFFE.** ▷Old English, via ecclesiastical Latin from ecclesiastical Greek *papas* 'bishop, patriarch,' variant of Greek *pappas* 'father.' **—pope·dom** /-dəm/ *n.*

pope2 ▸*n.* a parish priest of the Orthodox Church in Russia and the Balkans. ▷mid 17th cent.: from Russian *pop*, from Old Church Slavic *popŭ*.

Pope Joan /jōn/ (according to a legend widely believed in the Middle Ages) a woman in male disguise who (*c.*1100) became a distinguished scholar and then pope, reigned for more than two years, and died after giving birth to a child during a procession.

pope·mo·bile /ˈpōpmə,bēl; -mō,bəl/ ▸*n. informal* a bulletproof vehicle with a raised viewing area, used by the pope on official visits.

pop·er·y /ˈpōpərē/ ▸*n. derogatory, chiefly archaic* the doctrines, practices, and ceremonies associated with the pope or the papal system; Roman Catholicism.

pope's nose ▸*n. informal* the fatty extremity of the rump of a cooked fowl.

pop-eyed ▸*adj. informal* (of a person) having bulging eyes. ■ (of a person) having their eyes wide open, typically in surprise or fear.

pop fly ▸*n. Baseball* see **POP1** (sense 3).

pop·gun /ˈpäp,gən/ ▸*n.* a child's toy gun that shoots a harmless pellet or cork. ■ a small, inefficient, or antiquated gun.

pop·in·jay /ˈpäpən,jā/ ▸*n.* **1** *dated* a vain or conceited person, esp. one who dresses or behaves extravagantly. **2** *archaic* a parrot. ▷Middle English: from Old French *papingay*, via Spanish from Arabic *babbaġā*. The change in the ending was due to association with **JAY**.

pop·ish /ˈpōpisн/ ▸*adj. derogatory* Roman Catholic. **—pop·ish·ly** *adv.*

Pop·ish Plot a fictitious Jesuit plot concocted by Titus Oates in 1678, involving a plan to kill Charles II, massacre Protestants, and put the Catholic Duke of York on the English throne. The "discovery" of the plot led to widespread panic and the execution of about thirty-five Catholics.

pop·lar /ˈpäplər/ ▸*n.* **1** a tall, fast-growing tree of north temperate regions, widely grown in shelter belts and for timber and pulp. • Genus *Populus*, family Salicaceae: many species, including the North American cottonwoods, the quaking aspen, and the balm of Gilead poplars. **2** (**yellow poplar**) another term for **TULIP TREE**. ▷Middle English: from Old French *poplier*, from Latin *populus* 'poplar.'

pop·lin /ˈpäplən/ ▸*n.* a plain-woven fabric, typically a lightweight cotton, with a corded surface. ▷early 18th cent.: from obsolete French *papeline*, perhaps from Italian *papalina* (feminine) 'papal,' referring to the town of Avignon (residence of popes in exile (1309–77), and site of papal property), where it was first made.

pop·lit·e·al /päpˈlitēəl; ,päpləˈtēəl/ ▸*adj. Anatomy* relating to or situated in the hollow at the back of the knee. ▷early 18th cent.: from modern Latin *popliteus* (from Latin *poples, poplit-* 'hollow of the knee') + **-AL**.

pop mu·sic ▸*n.* fuller form of **POP2**.

Po·po·ca·té·petl /,pōpə,katəˈpetl; -ˈkatə,petl; pō,pōkäˈtā,petl/ an active volcano in Mexico that rises to 17,700 feet (5,452 m), southeast of Mexico City.

pop-out ▸*n. Baseball* an act of being put out by a caught fly ball.
▸*adj.* denoting something designed or made so that it is easily removable for use: *a pop-out panel.*

pop·o·ver /ˈpäp,ōvər/ ▸*n.* a light muffin made from a thin batter, which rises to form a hollow shell when baked.

pop·pa /ˈpäpə/ ▸*n.* informal term for **FATHER**. ▷late 19th cent.: alteration of **PAPA**.

Pop·per /ˈpäpər/, Sir Karl Raimund (1902–94), British philosopher; born in Austria. In *The Logic of Scientific Discovery* (1934) he argued that scientific hypotheses can never be finally confirmed as true, but are tested by attempts to falsify them. He also wrote *The Open Society and Its Enemies* (1945), a critique of all totalitarian systems.

pop·per /ˈpäpər/ ▸*n.* a thing that makes a popping sound, in particular: ■ a utensil for popping corn. ■ *informal* a small vial of amyl nitrite used for inhalation that makes a popping sound when opened. ■ (in fishing) an artificial lure that makes a popping sound when reeled in with a jerky motion on the surface of the water.

pop·pet /ˈpäpət/ ▸*n.* **1** (also **poppet valve**) *Engineering* a mushroom-shaped valve with a flat end piece that is lifted in and out of an opening by an axial rod. **2** *chiefly historical* a small figure of a human being used in sorcery and witchcraft. **3** *Brit., informal* an endearingly sweet or pretty child or young girl (often used as an affectionate form of address). ▷late Middle English: based on Latin *pup(p)a* 'girl, doll.' Compare with **PUPPET**.

pop·ple /ˈpäpəl/ *archaic* ▸*v.* [*intrans.*] (of water) flow in a tumbling or rippling way.
▸*n.* [in *sing.*] a rolling or rippling of water. ▷late Middle English: probably from Middle Dutch *popelen* 'to murmur,' of imitative origin. **—pop·ply** /ˈpäplē/ *adj.*

pop·ple2 ▸*n. dialect* any of various poplar trees, especially of northern forests.

pop·py /ˈpäpē/ ▸*n.* a herbaceous plant with showy flowers, milky sap, and rounded seed capsules. Many poppies contain alkaloids and are a source of drugs such as morphine and codeine. • *Papaver, Eschscholzia*, and other genera, family Papaveraceae (the **poppy family**): many species, including the yellow-flowered **arctic poppy** (*P. radicatum*) of the Rocky Mountains. The poppy family also includes the corydalis, greater celandine, and bloodroot. ▷Old English *popig, papæg*, from a medieval Latin alteration of Latin *papaver*. **—pop·pied** *adj.*

pop·py·cock /ˈpäpē,käk/ ▸*n. informal* nonsense. See note at **NONSENSE**. ▷mid 19th cent.: from Dutch dialect *pappekak*, from *pap* 'soft' + *kak* 'dung.'

pop·py·head /ˈpäpē,hed/ ▸*n.* an ornamental top on the end of a church pew.

pop·py·seed /ˈpäpē,sēd/ ▸*n.* the tiny, round seed of the poppy plant, used as a topping or in fillings for baked goods ▷Old English *popig*: from a medieval Latin alteration of Latin *papaver*.

pop quiz ▸*n.* a short test given to students without prior warning. ■ any unexpected question or set of questions: *a dairy farmer who gave the businessman a Vermont pop quiz on farming and geography.*

pop riv·et ▸*n.* a tubular rivet that is inserted into a hole and clinched by the withdrawal of a central rod, used where only one side of the work is accessible.
▸*v.* (**pop-riv·et**) (**-riv·et·ed, -riv·et·ing**) [*trans.*] secure or fasten with pop rivets.

Pop·si·cle /ˈpäp,sikəl/ ▸*n. trademark* a piece of flavored ice or ice cream on a stick. ▷1920s: fanciful formation.

pop·ster /ˈpäpstər/ ▸*n. informal* a pop musician.

pop·sy /ˈpäpsē/ (also **pop·sie**) ▸*n.* (*pl.* **-sies**) *informal, chiefly Brit.* an attractive young woman. ▷mid 19th cent.: alteration of **POPPET**.

pop-top ▸*adj.* (of a can) having a ring or tab that is pulled to open its seal: *a pop-top beer can.*
▸*n.* **1** the ring or tab from a pop-top can. ■ a pop-top can. **2** the top of something that pops up or open: *a wagon with a pop-top that turns it into a makeshift camper.*

pop·u·lace /ˈpäpyələs/ ▸*n.* [treated as *sing.* or *pl.*] the people living in a particular country or area: *the party misjudged the mood of the populace.* ▷late 16th cent.: from French, from Italian *popolaccio* 'common people,' from *popolo* 'people' + the pejorative suffix *-accio*.

pop·u·lar /ˈpäpyələr/ ▸*adj.* **1** liked, admired, or enjoyed by many people or by a particular person or group: *she was one of the most popular girls in the school* | *these cheeses are very popular in Europe.* **2** [*attrib.*] (of cultural activities or products) intended for or suited to the taste, understanding, or means of the general public rather than specialists or intellectuals: *the popular press.* ■ (of a belief or attitude) held by the majority of the general public: *many adult cats, contrary to popular opinion, dislike milk.* **3** [*attrib.*] (of political activity) of or carried on by the people as a whole rather than restricted to politicians or political parties: *a popular revolt against colonial rule.* ▷late Middle English (in the sense 'prevalent among the general public'): from Latin *popularis*, from *populus* 'people.' Sense 1 dates from the early 17th cent. **—pop·u·lar·ism** /-,rizəm/ *n.*

pop·u·lar et·y·mol·o·gy ▸*n.* another term for **FOLK ETYMOLOGY**.

pop·u·lar front ▸*n.* a party or coalition representing left-wing elements, in particular (**the Popular Front**) an alliance of communist, radical, and socialist elements formed and gaining some power in countries such as France and Spain in the 1930s.

pop·u·lar·i·ty /,päpyəˈlaritē/ ▸*n.* the state or condition of being liked, admired, or supported by many people: *he was forced to step down as mayor despite his popularity with the voters.*

pop·u·lar·ize /ˈpäpyələ,rīz/ ▸*v.* [*trans.*] cause (something) to become generally liked: *his books have done much to popularize the sport.* ■ make (something technical, scientific, or academic) accessible or interesting to the general public by presenting it in a readily understandable form: *they are skilled at popularizing the technical aspects of genetics.* **—pop·u·lar·i·za·tion** /,päpyələrəˈzāsнən/ *n.* **—pop·u·lar·iz·er** *n.*

pop·u·lar·ly /ˈpäpyələrlē/ ▸*adv.* by many or most people; generally: *advancing age is popularly associated with a declining capacity to work.* ■ (of a term, name, or title) in informal, common, or nonspecialist use: *polygraph analysis (popularly known as lie-detector testing).* ■ (of a politician or government) chosen by the majority of the voters; democratically: *a governor who is popularly elected.*

pop·u·lar mu·sic ▸*n.* music appealing to the popular taste, including rock and pop and also soul, country, reggae, rap, and dance music.

pop·u·late /ˈpäpyə,lāt/ ▸*v.* [*trans.*] (usu. **be populated**) form the population of (a town, area, or country): *the island is populated by scarcely 40,000 people* | [as *adj.*, with *submodifier*] (**populated**) *a densely populated area.* ■ *figurative* fill or be present in (a place, environment, or domain): *the spirit of the book and the characters who populate its pages.* ■ cause people to settle in (an area or place): *Finland pursues a policy designed to populate its Russian borders.* ■ fill something in, such as a table of values: *use scripts to populate the graph with data.* ▷late 16th cent.: from medieval Latin *populat-* 'supplied with people,' from the verb *populare*, from *populus* 'people.'

pop·u·la·tion /,päpyəˈlāsнən/ ▸*n.* all the inhabitants of a particular town, area, or country: *the island has a population of about 78,000.* ■ [with *adj.*] a particular section, group, or type of people or animals living in an area or country: *the country's immigrant population.* ■ [with *adj.*] the specified extent or degree to which an area is or has been populated: *areas of sparse population.* ■ the action of populating an area. ■ *Biology* a community of animals, plants, or humans among whose members interbreeding occurs. ■ *Statistics* a finite or infinite collection of items under consideration. ■ *Astronomy* each of three groups (designated I, II, and III) into which stars can be approximately divided on the basis of their manner of formation. ▷late 16th cent. (denoting an inhabited place): from late Latin *populatio(n-)*, from the verb *populare*, from *populus* 'people.'

pop·u·la·tion ex·plo·sion ▸*n.* a sudden large increase in the size of a population.

pop·u·la·tion in·ver·sion ▸*n.* see **INVERSION** (sense 1).

pop·u·list /ˈpäpyələst/ ▸*n.* a member or adherent of a political party seeking to represent the interests of ordinary people. ■ a person who holds, or who is concerned with, the views of ordinary people. ■ (**Populist**) a member of the Populist Party, a U.S. political party formed in 1891 that advocated the interests of labor and farmers, free coinage of silver, a graduated income tax, and government control of monopolies.
▸*adj.* of or relating to a populist or populists: *a populist leader.* ▷late 19th cent.: from Latin *populus* 'people' + **-IST**. **—pop·u·lism** /-,lizəm/ *n.* **—pop·u·lis·tic** /,päpyəˈlistik/ *adj.*

pop·u·lous /ˈpäpyələs/ ▸*adj.* having a large population; densely populated. ▷late Middle English: from late Latin *populosus*, from *populus* 'people.' **—pop·u·lous·ly** *adv.* **—pop·u·lous·ness** *n.*

pop-un·der ▸*adj. Computing* of, relating to, or denoting an additional window, usu. an advertisement, that is under a Web browser's main or current window and appears when a user tries to exit: *a plague of flashing pop-under ads.*

pop-up ▸*adj.* [*attrib.*] (of a book or greeting card) containing folded cut-out pictures that rise up to form a three-dimensional scene or figure when the page is turned. ■ (of an electric toaster) operating so as to push up a piece of toast quickly when it is ready. ■ *Computing* (of a menu or other utility) able to be superimposed on the screen being worked on and suppressed rapidly.
▸*n.* **1** a pop-up picture in a book. ■ a book containing such pictures. **2** *Baseball* see **POP1** (sense 3). **3** *Computing* a pop-up menu or other utility.

por. ▸*abbr.* portrait.

por·bea·gle /ˈpôr,bēgəl/ ▸*n.* a large active shark that is found chiefly in the open seas of the North Atlantic and in the Mediterranean. • *Lamna nasus*, family Lamnidae. ▷mid 18th cent.: from Cornish dialect, perhaps from Cornish *porth* 'harbor, cove' + *bugel* 'shepherd.'

por·ce·lain /ˈpôrs(ə)lən/ ▸*n.* a white vitrified translucent ceramic; china. See also **HARD-PASTE, SOFT-PASTE**. ■ (usu. **porcelains**) articles made of this. ■ such articles collectively: *a collection of Chinese* *porcelain.* ▷mid 16th cent.: from French *porcelaine,* from Italian *porcellana* 'cowrie shell,' hence 'chinaware' (from its resemblance to the dense polished shells). **—por·ce·la·ne·ous** /ˌpôrsəˈlānēəs/ *adj.* **—por·cel·la·nous** /-əs/ *adj.*

por·ce·lain·ber·ry /ˈpôrs(ə)lənˌberē/ ▸*n.* a deciduous, woody perennial vine of Asian origin, first cultivated as an ornamental and now regarded as an aggressive invader in most of the eastern U.S. The attractive berries, in multiple colors from white to deep purple, appear in early autumn. • *Ampelopsis brevipedunculata,* family Vitaceae.

por·ce·lain clay ▸*n.* another term for KAOLIN.

porch /pôrCH/ ▸*n.* a covered shelter projecting in front of the entrance of a building. ■ a veranda. ▷Middle English: from Old French *porche,* from Latin *porticus* 'colonnade,' from *porta* 'passage.' **—porched** *adj.* **—porch·less** *adj.*

por·cine /ˈpôrˌsīn/ ▸*adj.* of, affecting, or resembling a pig or pigs: *his flushed, porcine features.* ▷mid 17th cent.: from French *porcin* or Latin *porcinus,* from *porcus* 'pig.'

por·ci·ni /pôrˈCHēnē/ ▸*n.* (*pl.* same) the cep (a wild mushroom), esp. as an item on a menu. ▷Italian, literally 'little pigs.'

por·cu·pine /ˈpôrkyəˌpīn/ ▸*n.* a large rodent with defensive spines or quills on the body and tail. • Suborder Hystricomorpha: families Hystricidae (three Old World genera) and Erethizontidae (four New World genera). The common North American species is *Erethizon dorsatum.* ▷late Middle English: from Old French *porc espin,* from Provençal *porc espi(n),* from Latin *porcus* 'pig' + *spina* 'thorn.'

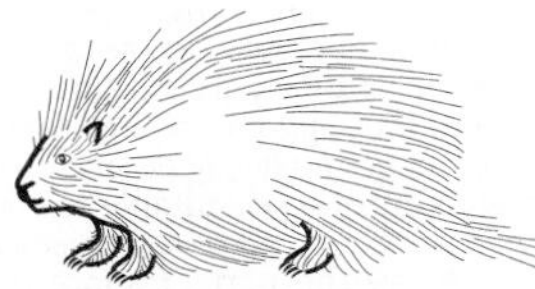

North American porcupine

por·cu·pine fish ▸*n.* a tropical marine fish that has a parrotlike beak and is covered with sharp spines. It inflates itself like a balloon when threatened. • Family Diodontidae: three genera and several species, including the widely distributed *Diodon hystrix.* See also BURRFISH.

Por·cu·pine River /ˈpôrkyəˌpīn/ a river that flows for 450 miles (720 km) from Yukon Territory into northeastern Alaska to join the Yukon River.

pore[1] /pôr/ ▸*n. chiefly Biology* a minute opening in a surface, esp. the skin or integument of an organism, through which gases, liquids, or microscopic particles can pass. ▷late Middle English: from Old French, via Latin from Greek *poros* 'passage, pore.'

pore[2] ▸*v.* [*intrans.*] (**pore over/through**) be absorbed in the reading or study of: *Heather spent hours poring over cookbooks.* ■ *archaic* think intently; ponder: *when he has thought and* **pored on** *it.* ▷Middle English: perhaps related to PEER[1].

pore·wa·ter /ˈpôrˌwôtər; -ˌwä-/ ▸*n. Geology* water contained in pores in soil or rock.

por·gy /ˈpôrgē/ ▸*n.* (*pl.* same or **-gies**) a deep-bodied fish related to the sea breams, typically silvery but sometimes changing to a blotched pattern. It usually lives in warm coastal waters. • *Calamus* and other genera, family Sparidae: many species. ▷mid 17th cent.: alteration of Spanish and Portuguese *pargo.*

Po·rif·er·a /pəˈrifərə/ *Zoology* a phylum of aquatic invertebrate animals that comprises the sponges. ▷modern Latin (plural), from Latin *porus* 'pore' + *-fer* 'bearing.' **—po·rif·er·an** *adj.* & *n.*

po·rin /ˈpôrən/ ▸*n. Biochemistry* any of a class of proteins whose molecules can form channels (large enough to allow the passage of small ions and molecules) through cellular membranes. ▷1970s: from Greek *poros* 'pore' + -IN[1].

pork /pôrk/ ▸*n.* **1** the flesh of a pig used as food, esp. when uncured. **2** short for PORK BARREL.
▸*v.* **1** [*trans.*] *vulgar slang* (of a man) have sexual intercourse with. **2** [*intrans.*] *informal* stuff oneself with food; overeat: *I* **porked out** *on the roast pig.* ▷Middle English: from Old French *porc,* from Latin *porcus* 'pig.'

pork bar·rel ▸*n. informal* the use of government funds for projects designed to please voters or legislators and win votes: *political pork barrel for the benefit of their respective sponsors* | [as *adj.*] *wasteful, pork-barrel spending.* ▷figuratively, from the use of such a barrel by farmers, to keep a reserve supply of meat. **—pork-bar·rel·ing** *n.*

pork·er /ˈpôrkər/ ▸*n.* a pig raised for food. ■ *informal, derogatory* a fat person.

pork·pie hat /ˈpôrkˌpī/ ▸*n.* a hat with a flat crown and a brim turned up all around.

pork·y[1] /ˈpôrkē/ ▸*adj.* (**pork·i·er, pork·i·est**) **1** *informal* (of a person or part of their body) fleshy or fat. **2** of or resembling pork.

pork·y[2] ▸*n.* (*pl.* **pork·ies**) *informal* a porcupine.

porn /pôrn/ (also **porn·o** /ˈpôrnō/) *informal* ▸*n.* **1** pornography. **2** television programs, books, etc., regarded as catering to a voyeuristic or obsessive interest in a specified subject: *a thrilling throwback to the golden age of disaster movies—weather porn of the highest order.*
▸*adj.* pornographic: *a porn video.* ▷1950s: abbr.

por·nog·ra·phy /pôrˈnägrəfē/ ▸*n.* printed or visual material containing the explicit description or display of sexual organs or activity, intended to stimulate erotic rather than aesthetic or emotional feelings. ▷mid 19th cent.: from Greek *pornographos* 'writing about prostitutes,' from *pornē* 'prostitute' + *graphein* 'write.' **—por·nog·ra·pher** /-fər/ *n.* **—por·no·graph·ic** /ˌpôrnəˈgrafik/ *adj.* **—por·no·graph·i·cal·ly** /ˌpôrnəˈgrafik(ə)lē/ *adv.*

po·rous /ˈpôrəs/ ▸*adj.* (of a rock or other material) having minute spaces or holes through which liquid or air may pass. ■ *figurative* not retentive or secure: *he ran through a porous defense to score easily.* ▷late Middle English: from Old French *poreux,* based on Latin *porus* 'pore.' **—po·ros·i·ty** /pəˈräsətē; pôrˈäs-/ *n.* **—po·rous·ness** *n.*

por·phyr·i·a /pôrˈfi(ə)rēə/ ▸*n. Medicine* a rare hereditary disease in which the blood pigment hemoglobin is abnormally metabolized. Porphyrins are excreted in the urine, which becomes dark; other symptoms include mental disturbances and extreme sensitivity of the skin to light. ▷1920s: modern Latin, from PORPHYRIN.

por·phy·rin /ˈpôrfərin/ ▸*n. Biochemistry* any of a class of pigments (including heme and chlorophyll) whose molecules contain a flat ring of four linked heterocyclic groups, sometimes with a central metal atom. ▷early 20th cent.: from Greek *porphura* 'purple' + -IN[1].

por·phy·rit·ic /ˌpôrfəˈritik/ ▸*adj. Geology* relating to or denoting a rock texture, typically found in volcanic rocks, containing distinct crystals or crystalline particles embedded in a fine-grained groundmass.

por·phy·ro·blast /pôrˈfirəˌblast; ˈpôrfərō-/ ▸*n. Geology* a larger recrystallized grain occurring in a finer groundmass in a metamorphic rock. **—por·phy·ro·blas·tic** /pôrˌfirəˈblastik; ˌpôrfərō-/ *adj.*

Por·phy·ry /ˈpôrfərē/ (*c.*232–303), Neoplatonist philosopher; born *Malchus.* He was a student of Plotinus, whose works he edited after the latter's death.

por·phy·ry /ˈpôrfərē/ ▸*n.* (*pl.* **-ries**) a hard igneous rock containing crystals, usually of feldspar, in a fine-grained, typically reddish groundmass. ▷late Middle English: via medieval Latin from Greek *porphuritēs,* from *porphura* 'purple.'

por·poise /ˈpôrpəs/ ▸*n.* a small toothed whale with a low triangular dorsal fin and a blunt rounded snout. • Family Phocoenidae: three genera and several species, in particular the **common** (or **harbor**) **porpoise** (*Phocoena phocoena*), of the North Atlantic and North Pacific.
▸*v.* [*intrans.*] move through the water like a porpoise, alternately rising above it and submerging: *the boat began to porpoise badly.* ▷Middle English: from Old French *porpois,* based on Latin *porcus* 'pig' + *piscis* 'fish,' rendering earlier *porcus marinus* 'sea hog.'

por·ridge /ˈpôrij/ ▸*n.* a dish consisting of oatmeal or another meal or cereal boiled in water or milk. ▷mid 16th cent. (denoting soup thickened with barley): alteration of POTTAGE. **—por·ridg·y** *adj.*

por·rin·ger /ˈpôrənjər/ ▸*n. historical* a small bowl, typically with a handle, used for soup, stew, or similar dishes. ▷late Middle English (earlier as *potager* and *pottinger*): from Old French *potager,* from *potage* 'contents of a pot.'

por·ro prism /ˈpôrō/ (also **Por·ro prism**) ▸*n.* a reflecting prism in which the light is reflected by two 45° surfaces and returned parallel to the incoming beam. Compare with ROOF PRISM. ■ (**porro prisms**) (also **porro-prism binoculars**) a pair of binoculars using two such prisms at right angles, resulting in a conventional instrument with objective lenses that are further apart than the eyepieces. ▷named after Ignazio *Porro* (1801–75), Italian engineer.

Porsche /ˈpôrSH(ə)/, Ferdinand (1875–1952), Austrian car designer. In 1934, he designed the Volkswagen ("people's car"), but his name has since become noted for the high-performance sports and racing cars produced by his company, originally to his designs.

Por·sen·na /ˈpôrsənə/ (also **Por·sen·a**), Lars (6th century BC), a legendary Etruscan chieftain. Summoned by Tarquinius Superbus after the latter's overthrow and exile from Rome, Porsenna subsequently laid siege to the city, but did not succeed in capturing it.

port[1] /pôrt/ ▸*n.* a town or city with a harbor where ships load or unload, esp. one where customs officers are stationed. ■ a harbor: *the port has miles of docks* | [as *adj.*] *an abundant water supply and port facilities.* ■ (also **inland port**) an inland town or city whose connection to the coast by a river or other body of water enables it to act as a port. ▷Old English, from Latin *portus* 'haven, harbor,' reinforced in Middle English by Old French.
▸*PHRASES* □ **any port in a storm** *proverb* in adverse circumstances one welcomes any source of relief or escape. □ **port of entry** a harbor or airport by which people and goods may enter a country.

P

port[2] (also **port wine**) ▸*n.* a strong, sweet, typically dark red fortified wine, originally from Portugal, typically drunk as a dessert wine. ▷shortened form of OPORTO, a major port from which the wine is shipped.

port[3] ▸*n.* the side of a ship or aircraft that is on the left when one is facing forward: *the ferry was listing to port* | [as *adj.*] *the port side of the aircraft.* The opposite of STARBOARD.
▸*v.* [*trans.*] turn (a ship or its helm) to port. ▷mid 16th cent.: probably originally the side facing the shore when the ship was tied up in port.

port[4] ▸*n.* an aperture or opening, in particular: ■ a socket in a computer or network into which a device can be plugged. ■ an opening for the passage of steam, liquid, or gas: *loss of fuel from the exhaust port.* ■ a gunport. ■ a porthole. ■ an opening in the side of a ship for boarding or loading. ■ *chiefly Scottish* a gate or gateway, esp. into a walled city. ▷Old English (in the sense 'gateway'), from Latin *porta* 'gate'; reinforced in Middle English by Old French *porte.* The later sense 'opening in the side of a ship' led to the general sense 'aperture.'

port[5] ▸*v.* **1** [*trans.*] *Computing* transfer (software) from one system or machine to another: *the software can be ported to an IBM RS/6000.* **2** [*trans.*] [often in *imperative*] *Military* carry (a rifle or other weapon) diagonally across and close to the body with the barrel or blade near the left shoulder: *Detail! For inspection—port arms!*
▸*n.* **1** *Military* the position required by an order to port a rifle or other weapon: *Parker had his rifle* **at the port.** **2** *poetic/literary* a person's carriage or bearing: *she has the proud port of a princess.* **3** *Computing* a transfer of software from one system or machine to another. ▷Middle English (sense 2 of the *noun*): from Old French *port* 'bearing, gait,' from the verb *porter,* from Latin *portare* 'carry.' The verb (from French *porter*) dates from the mid 16th cent.
▸*PHRASE* □ **at port arms** *Military* in the position adopted when given a command to port one's weapon.

porta- ▸*comb. form* denoting something that is movable or portable, often used as part of a proprietary name: *Portaloo* | *Portalife.* ▷from PORTABLE.

port·a·ble /ˈpôrtəbəl/ ▸*adj.* able to be easily carried or moved, esp. because of being a lighter and smaller version than usual: *a portable television.* ■ *Computing* (of software) able to be transferred from one machine or system to another.
▸*n.* a version of something, such as a small lightweight television or computer, that can be easily carried. ■ a small transportable building used as a classroom. ▷late Middle English: from Old French *portable,* from late Latin *portabilis,* from Latin *portare* 'carry.' **—port·a·bil·i·ty** /ˌpôrtəˈbilətē/ *n.* **—port·a·bly** /-blē/ *adv.*

Por·tage /ˈpôrtij/ **1** a port city in northwestern Indiana, on Lake Erie, east of Gary; pop. 29,060. **2** a city in southwestern Michigan, south of Kalamazoo; pop. 41,042.

por·tage /ˈpôrtij/ ▸*n.* the carrying of a boat or its cargo between two navigable waters: *the return journey was*

Pronunciation Key ə *ago;* ər *over;* ˈə or ˌə *up;* ˈər or ˌər *fur;* a *hat;* ā *rate;* ä *car;* CH *chew;* e *let;* ē *see;* e(ə)r *air;* i *fit;* ī *by;* i(ə)r *ear;* NG *sing;* ō *go;* ô *for;* oi *boy;* o͝o *good;* o͞o *goo;* ou *out;* SH *she;* TH *thin;* TH *then;* (h)w *why;* ZH *vision*

made much simpler by portage. ■ a place at which this is necessary: *a portage over the dam.* ■ *archaic* the action of carrying or transporting something.
▸*v.* [*trans.*] carry (a boat or its cargo) between navigable waters: *they are incapable of portaging a canoe* | [*intrans.*] *they would only run the rapid if they couldn't portage.* ■ [*intrans.*] (of a boat) be carried between navigable waters: *the cataracts meant that boats had to portage on to the Lualaba.* ▷late Middle English: from French, from *porter* 'carry.' The sense relating to carrying between navigable waters dates from the late 17th cent.

por·tal[1] /ˈpôrtl/ ▸*n.* **1** a doorway, gate, or other entrance, esp. a large and elaborate one. **2** *Computing* an Internet site providing access or links to other sites. ▷late Middle English: from Old French, from medieval Latin *portale,* neuter (used as a noun) of *portalis* 'like a gate,' from Latin *porta* 'door, gate.'

por·tal[2] ▸*adj.* [*attrib.*] *Anatomy* of or relating to an opening in an organ through which major blood vessels pass, esp. the transverse fissure of the liver. ▷mid 19th cent.: from modern Latin *portalis,* from Latin *porta* 'gate.'

por·tal frame ▸*n. Engineering* a rigid structural frame consisting essentially of two uprights connected at the top by a third member.

por·tal sys·tem ▸*n. Anatomy* the system of blood vessels consisting of the portal vein with its tributaries and branches. ■ any system of blood vessels that has a capillary network at each end.

por·tal vein (in full **hepatic portal vein**) ▸*n. Anatomy* a vein conveying blood to the liver from the spleen, stomach, pancreas, and intestines.

por·ta·men·to /ˌpôrtəˈmenˌtō/ ▸*n.* (*pl.* **-tos** or **-ti** /-tē/) *Music* **1** a slide from one note to another, esp. in singing or playing a bowed string instrument. ■ this as a technique or style. **2** piano playing in a manner intermediate between legato and staccato: [as *adj.*] *a portamento style.* ▷Italian, literally 'carrying.'

Por·ta Pot·ti /ˈpôrtə ˌpätē/ ▸*n. trademark* (also **por·ta·pot·ty**) a portable building containing a toilet. ■ a chemical toilet, or one connected to a holding tank, in a vehicle or small boat or aircraft.

Port Ar·thur **1** former name (1898–1905) for **Lushun**. **2** a city in southeastern Texas, on the Neches and Sabine rivers, near the Gulf Coast; pop. 58,724.

por·ta·tive or·gan /ˈpôrtədiv/ ▸*n. chiefly historical* a small portable pipe organ. ▷early 16th cent. (as a compound): *portative* from Old French *portatif, -ive,* apparently an alteration of *portatil,* based on Latin *portare* 'carry.'

Port-au-Prince /ˌpôrt ō ˈprins; ˈpräns/ the capital of Haiti, a port on the western coast of Hispaniola; pop. 1,255,080. Founded by the French in 1749, it became capital of the new republic in 1806.

Port Blair /ble(ə)r/ the capital of the Andaman and Nicobar Islands, a port on the southern tip of South Andaman Island in the Bay of Bengal; pop. 75,000.

portcullis

port·cul·lis /pôrtˈkələs/ ▸*n.* a strong, heavy grating sliding up and down in vertical grooves, lowered to block a gateway to a fortress or town. ▷Middle English: from Old French *porte coleice* 'sliding door,' from *porte* 'door' (from Latin *porta*) + *coleice* 'sliding' (feminine of *couleis,* from Latin *colare* 'to filter'). **—port·cul·lised** *adj.*

port de bras /ˌpôr də ˈbrä/ ▸*n.* (*pl.* **ports de bras** *pronunc.* same) *chiefly Ballet* an act or manner of moving and posing the arms: *one coach told her to change her port de bras.* ■ an exercise designed to develop graceful movement and disposition of the arms, typically involving a bend accompanied by arm movement. ▷French, literally 'bearing of (the) arms.'

Port de France /ˌpôrt də ˈfrans/ former name for **Nouméa**.

Porte /pôrt/ (also **the Sublime Porte**) *historical* the Ottoman court at Constantinople. ▷early 17th cent.: from French *la Sublime Porte* 'the exalted gate,' translation of the Turkish title of the central office of the Ottoman government.

porte co·chère /ˌpôrt kōˈsher(ə)r/ ▸*n. Architecture* a covered entrance large enough for vehicles to pass through, typically opening into a courtyard. ■ a porch where vehicles stop to discharge passengers. ▷late 17th cent.: French, literally 'coach gateway.'

Port E·liz·a·beth a port in South Africa, on the coast of the province of Eastern Cape; pop. 853,000. Settled by the British in 1820, it is now an automobile-manufacturing city and beach resort.

por·tend /pôrˈtend/ ▸*v.* [*trans.*] be a sign or warning that (something, esp. something momentous or calamitous) is likely to happen: *the eclipses portend some major events.* ■ be a signal of: *the gridlock at the top of the leader board portends a sudden-death playoff.* ▷late Middle English: from Latin *portendere,* based on *pro-* 'forth' + *tendere* 'stretch.'

por·tent /ˈpôrˌtent/ ▸*n.* **1** a sign or warning that something, esp. something momentous or calamitous, is likely to happen: *they believed that wild birds in the house were portents of death* | *JFK's political debut was a portent of the fame to come.* ■ future significance: *an omen of grave portent for the tribe.* **2** *archaic* an exceptional or wonderful person or thing: *what portent can be greater than a pious notary?* ▷late 16th cent.: from Latin *portentum* 'omen, token,' from the verb *portendere* (see **portend**).

por·ten·tous /pôrˈtentəs/ ▸*adj.* of or like a portent: *the envelope and its portentous contents.* See note at **ominous**. ■ done in a pompously or overly solemn manner so as to impress: *the author's portentous moralizings.* **—por·ten·tous·ly** *adv.* **—por·ten·tous·ness** *n.*

Por·ter[1] /ˈpôrtər/, Cole (1892–1964), U.S. songwriter. He made his name with a series of Broadway musicals that included *Anything Goes* (1934) and *Kiss Me, Kate* (1948). He also wrote songs for movies, such as *High Society* (1956). Notable songs: "Let's Do It," "Night and Day," and "Begin the Beguine."

Por·ter[2], Katherine Anne (1890–1980), U.S. short-story writer and novelist. Notable works: *Ship of Fools* (1962) and *Collected Short Stories* (1965).

por·ter[1] /ˈpôrtər/ ▸*n.* **1** a person employed to carry luggage and other loads, esp. in a railroad station, airport, or hotel. ■ a person employed to carry supplies on a mountaineering expedition. ■ an attendant in a railroad sleeping car or parlor car. **2** dark brown bitter beer brewed from malt partly charred or browned by drying at a high temperature. [originally made as a drink for porters.] ▷Middle English: from Old French *porteour,* from medieval Latin *portator,* from Latin *portare* 'carry.'

por·ter[2] ▸*n.* an employee in charge of the entrance of a hotel, apartment complex, or other large building. ▷Middle English: from Old French *portier,* from late Latin *portarius,* from *porta* 'gate, door.'

por·ter·age /ˈpôrtərij/ ▸*n.* the work of carrying luggage, supplies, or other materials, done by porters or laborers.

por·ter·house /ˈpôrtərˌhous/ ▸*n.* short for **porterhouse steak**. ■ *historical* an establishment at which porter and sometimes steaks were served. ▷mid 18th cent.: from sense 2 of **porter**[1] + **house**.

por·ter·house steak ▸*n.* a choice steak cut from the thick end of a sirloin.

port-fire ▸*n. historical* a hand-held fuse used for firing cannons, igniting explosives, etc. ▷mid 17th cent.: partial anglicization of French *porte-feu,* from *porter* 'carry' + *feu* 'fire.'

port·fo·li·o /pôrtˈfōlēˌō/ ▸*n.* (*pl.* **-os**) **1** a large, thin, flat case for loose sheets of paper such as drawings or maps. ■ a set of pieces of creative work collected by someone to display their skills, esp. to a potential employer. ■ a varied set of photographs of a model or actor intended to be shown to a potential employer. **2** a range of investments held by a person or organization: *better returns on its investment portfolio.* ■ a range of products or services offered by an organization, esp. when considered as a business asset: *an unrivaled portfolio of quality brands.* **3** the position and duties of a minister of state or a member of a cabinet: *he took on the Foreign Affairs portfolio.*
▸*adj.* relating to, denoting, or engaged in an employment pattern that involves a succession of short-term contracts and part-time work, rather than the more traditional model of a long-term single job: *portfolio careers allow women to balance work with family.* ▷early 18th cent.: from Italian *portafogli,* from *portare* 'carry' + *foglio* 'sheet of paper' (from Latin *folium*).

Port Har·court /ˈhärˌkôrt; -kərt/ a port in southeastern Nigeria, on the Gulf of Guinea at the eastern edge of the Niger delta; pop. 371,000.

port·hole /ˈpôrtˌhōl/ ▸*n.* a small exterior window in a ship or aircraft. ■ *historical* an opening for firing a cannon through.

Port Hue·ne·me /wīˈnēmē/ an industrial and military port city in southwestern California, northwest of Los Angeles; pop. 20,319.

Port Hu·ron /ˈhyo͝orən; -än/ an industrial port city in southeastern Michigan, on Lake Huron and the St. Clair River; pop. 33,694.

por·ti·co /ˈpôrtiˌkō/ ▸*n.* (*pl.* **-coes** or **-cos**) a structure consisting of a roof supported by columns at regular intervals, typically attached as a porch to a building. ▷early 17th cent.: from Italian, from Latin *porticus* 'porch.'

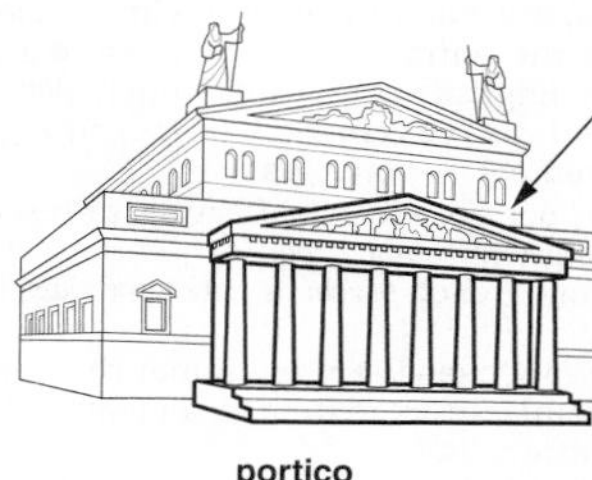
portico

por·tière /ˌpôrtēˈer; -ˈtye(ə)r/ (also **portiere**) ▸*n.* a curtain hung over a door or doorway. ▷mid 19th cent.: French, from *porte* 'door,' from Latin *porta* 'gate, door.'

Por·ţi·le de Fier /pôrtˌsēlə də ˈfyer/ Romanian name for **Iron Gate**.

por·tion /ˈpôrsHən/ ▸*n.* a part of a whole; an amount, section, or piece of something: *a portion of the jetty still stands* See note at **fragment**. *he could repeat large portions of Shakespeare.* ■ a part of something divided between two or more people; a share: *she wanted the right to decide how her portion of the allowance should be spent.* ■ an amount of food suitable for or served to one person: *a portion of ice cream* | *burger joints offering huge portions.* ■ *Law* the part or share of an estate given or descending by law to an heir. ■ *archaic* a person's future as allotted by fate; one's destiny or lot: *what will be my portion?* ■ (also **marriage portion**) *archaic* a dowry given to a bride at her marriage.
▸*v.* [*trans.*] (usu. **be portioned**) divide (something) into shares to be distributed among two or more people: *the fish are **portioned out** to the different families.* ■ [usu. as *adj.*, with *submodifier*] (**portioned**) serve (food) in an amount suitable for one person: *generously portioned lunches.* ■ *archaic* give a dowry to (a bride at her marriage): *my parents will portion me most handsomely.* ▷Middle English: from Old French *porcion,* from Latin *portio(n-),* from the phrase *pro portione* 'in proportion.'

Port·land /ˈpôrtlənd/ **1** the largest city in Maine, on Casco Bay off the Atlantic Ocean, in the southwestern part of the state; pop. 64,249. **2** an industrial port in northwestern Oregon, on the Willamette River near its confluence with the Columbia River; pop. 529,121. The largest city in Oregon, it was founded in 1845 and developed as a supply center for the gold rushes of the 1860s and 1870s and as a port for the lumber trade.

Port·land ce·ment (also **port·land ce·ment**) ▸*n.* cement that is manufactured from limestone and clay and that hardens under water. ▷1810s: named after the Isle of *Portland* in Dorset, England, a limestone peninsula quarried for its fine building stone.

Port Lou·is /ˈlo͞o-is; ˈlo͞o-ē/ the capital of Mauritius, a port on the northwestern coast; pop. 144,000.

port·ly /ˈpôrtlē/ ▸*adj.* (**-li·er, -li·est**) **1** (esp. of a man) having a stout body; somewhat fat. **2** *archaic* of a stately or dignified appearance and manner: *he was a man of portly presence.* ▷late 15th cent.: from **port**[5] in the sense 'bearing' + **-ly**[1]. **—port·li·ness** *n.*

port·man·teau /pôrtˈmantō/ ▸*n.* (*pl.* **-teaus** /-tōz/ or **-teaux** /-tōz/) a large trunk or suitcase, typically made of stiff leather and opening into two equal parts. ■ [as *adj.*] consisting of or combining two or more separable aspects or qualities: *a portmanteau movie composed of excerpts from his most famous films.* ▷mid 16th cent.: from French *portemanteau,* from *porter* 'carry' + *manteau* 'mantle.'

port·man·teau word ▸*n.* a word blending the sounds and combining the meanings of two others, for example *motel* (from 'motor' and hotel') or *brunch* (from 'breakfast' and 'lunch'). ▷*portmanteau* coined, in this sense, by Lewis Carroll in *Through the Looking Glass* (1871).

Port Mores·by /ˈmôrzbē/ the capital of Papua New

Guinea, located on the southern coast of the island of New Guinea, on the Coral Sea; pop. 193,000.

Port Na·tal former name (until 1835) for DURBAN.

Por·to /ˈpôrtŏŏ/ Portuguese name for OPORTO.

Pôr·to A·le·gre /ˈpôrtŏŏ äˈlegrə/ a major port and commercial city in southeastern Brazil, capital of the state of Rio Grande do Sul, on Lagoa dos Patos (a lagoon separated from the Atlantic Ocean by a sandy peninsula); pop. 1,263,000.

por·to·bel·lo /ˌpôrtəˈbelō/ (also **portobello mushroom**) ▸*n.* a large mature edible mushroom with an open flat cap.

port of call ▸*n.* a place where a ship stops on a voyage. ■ any of a number of places that a person visits in succession: *his last port of call that morning was Angela's lawyer | figurative if you're serious about spreadsheeting, then this package must be your first port of call.*

Port-of-Spain the capital of Trinidad and Tobago, a port on the northwestern coast of the island of Trinidad; pop. 46,000.

por·to·lan /ˈpôrtl-ən; -ˌan/ (also **por·to·la·no** /ˌpôrtl-ˈänō/) ▸*n.* (*pl.* **-to·lans** /-tl-ənz/ or **-to·la·nos** /-tlˈänōz/) *historical* a book of sailing directions with charts and descriptions of harbors and coasts. ▷mid 19th cent.: from Italian *portolano*, from *porto* 'harbor.'

Por·to No·vo /ˈpôrtō ˈnōvō/ the capital of Benin, a port on the Gulf of Guinea, close to the border with Nigeria; pop. 179,000. It was a center of the Portuguese slave trade in the 17th century.

Port Or·ford ce·dar /ˈôrfərd/ ▸*n.* a slender conifer with dense foliage and lower branches arising at ground level. Native to a small area of northwestern California and southwestern Oregon, it is widely grown for timber and as an ornamental with many cultivars. Also called LAWSON CYPRESS. • *Chamaecyparis lawsoniana*, family Cupressaceae.

Pôr·to Vel·ho /ˈpôrtŏŏ ˈvelyŏŏ/ a town in western Brazil, capital of the state of Rondônia; pop. 286,000.

Port Pe·trovsk /piˈtrôfsk/ former name (until 1922) for MAKHACHKALA.

por·trait /ˈpôrtrət; -ˌtrāt/ ▸*n.* **1** a painting, drawing, photograph, or engraving of a person, esp. one depicting only the face or head and shoulders. ■ a representation or impression of someone or something in language or on film: *the writer builds up a full and fascinating portrait of a community.* **2** [as *adj.*] (of a page, book, or illustration, or the manner in which it is set or printed) higher than it is wide: *you can print landscape and portrait pages in the same document.* Compare with LANDSCAPE (sense 2). ▷mid 16th cent.: from French, past participle (used as a noun) of Old French *portraire* 'portray.' **—por·trait·ist** /ˈpôrtrətist; -ˌtrātist/ *n.* (in sense 1).

por·trai·ture /ˈpôrtricнər; -ˌcнŏŏr/ ▸*n.* the art of creating portraits. ■ graphic and detailed description, esp. of a person: *it's part murder mystery and part portraiture through poetry.* ■ *formal* a portrait. ▷late Middle English: from Old French, from *portrait* (see PORTRAIT).

por·tray /pôrˈtrā/ ▸*v.* [*trans.*] depict (someone or something) in a work of art or literature: *the author wanted to portray a new type of hero.* ■ (of an actor) represent or play the part of (someone) on film or stage: *he tossed his affable TV persona aside to portray a merciless mobster.* ■ [*trans.*] describe (someone or something) in a particular way: *the book* **portrayed** *him* **as** *a self-serving careerist.* ▷Middle English: from Old French *portraire*, based on *traire* 'to draw,' from an alteration of Latin *trahere*. **—por·tray·a·ble** *adj.* **—por·tray·al** /-ˈtrā(ə)l/ *n.* **—por·tray·er** *n.*

Port Sa·id /sīˈēd/ a port in Egypt, on the Mediterranean coast at the northern end of the Suez Canal; pop. 461,000. It was founded in 1859.

Port Saint Lu·cie /ˈlŏŏsē/ a resort and retirement city in east central Florida; pop. 88,769.

Port Sa·lut /ˌpōr səlŏŏ; səlˈyŏŏ/ ▸*n.* a pale, mild type of cheese. ▷named after the Trappist monastery in France, where it was first produced.

Ports·mouth /ˈpôrtsməтн/ **1** a port and naval base on the southern coast of England; pop. 175,000. The naval dockyard was established here in 1496. **2** a historic port city in southeastern New Hampshire, on the Piscataqua River, off the Atlantic Ocean; pop. 20,784. **3** a commercial and naval city in southeastern Virginia, on Hampton Roads, west of Norfolk; pop. 100,565.

Port Su·dan the chief port of Sudan, on the Red Sea; pop. 206,000.

port tack ▸*n.* a sailboat's heading when the wind is coming from the left, or port, side.

Por·tu·gal /ˈpôrcнəgəl/ a country occupying the western part of the Iberian peninsula in southwestern Europe; pop. 10,393,000; capital, Lisbon; language, Portuguese (official).

Portugal was linked with Spain until it became an independent kingdom in the 12th century. In the 15th and 16th centuries it emerged as one of the leading European colonial powers. It became a republic in 1911 after the expulsion of the monarchy. A long period of dictatorship by Antonio Salazar, who was prime minister 1932–68, and his successor Marcello Caetano (1906–80) was ended in 1974 by a military coup, which led to Portugal's rapid withdrawal from its African colonies and eventually to democratic reform. It became a member of the EC in 1986.

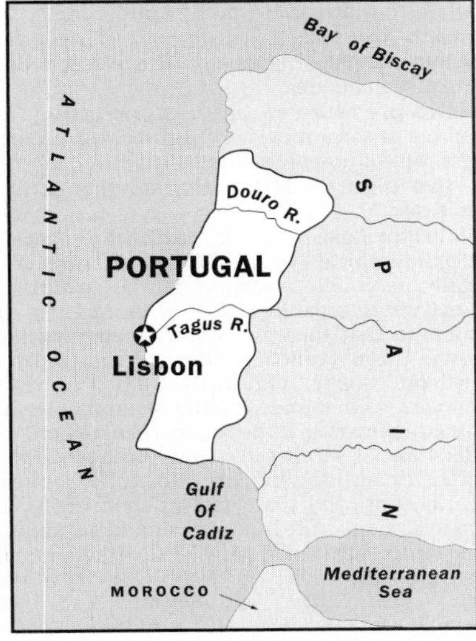

Por·tu·guese /ˈpôrcнəˌgēz/ ▸*adj.* of or relating to Portugal or its people or language.
▸*n.* (*pl.* same) **1** a native or national of Portugal, or a person of Portuguese descent. **2** the Romance language of Portugal and Brazil. ▷from Portuguese *portuguez*, from medieval Latin *portugalensis*.

Por·tu·guese man-of-war ▸*n.* a floating colonial coelenterate with a number of polyps and a conspicuous float. It occurs chiefly in warm seas, and bears long tentacles that can inflict painful stings. • *Physalia physalis*, order Siphonophora, class Hydrozoa.

Port Vi·la another name for VILA.

port watch ▸*n.* see WATCH (sense 2).

port wine ▸*n.* see PORT².

port wine stain ▸*n.* a kind of large, deep red birthmark, a persistent hemangioma or nevus, typically on the face.

POS ▸*abbr.* point of sale.

pos. ▸*abbr.* ■ position. ■ positive. ■ possession. ■ possessive.

po·sa·da /pəˈsädə/ ▸*n.* (in Spanish-speaking regions) a hotel or inn. ■ (also **Las Posadas**) a ritual reenactment of Mary and Joseph's search for a lodging in Bethlehem, performed just before Christmas. ▷Spanish, from *posar* 'to lodge.'

pose¹ /pōz/ ▸*v.* **1** [*trans.*] present or constitute (a problem, danger, or difficulty): *the sheer number of visitors is posing a threat to the area.* ■ raise (a question or matter for consideration): *a statement that posed more questions than it answered.* **2** [*intrans.*] assume a particular attitude or position in order to be photographed, painted, or drawn: *she posed for a swarm of TV cameramen.* ■ [*trans.*] place (someone) in a particular attitude or position in order to be photographed, painted, or drawn: *he posed her on the sofa.* ■ (**pose as**) set oneself up as or pretend to be (someone or something): *a detective posing as a customer | figurative whitewashed chicken coops that posed as villas.* ■ behave affectedly in order to impress others: *some people like to drive these cars, but most just like to pose in them.*
▸*n.* a particular way of standing or sitting, usually adopted for effect or in order to be photographed, painted, or drawn: *photographs of boxers in ferocious poses.* ■ a particular way of behaving adopted in order to give others a false impression or to impress others: *the man dropped his pose of amiability.* ▷Middle English: from Old French *poser* (verb), from late Latin *pausare* 'to pause,' which replaced Latin *ponere* 'to show off.' The noun dates from the early 19th cent.

pose² ▸*v.* [*trans.*] *archaic* puzzle or perplex (someone) with a question or problem: *we have thus posed the mathematician and the historian.* ▷early 16th cent.: shortening of obsolete *appose*, from Old French *aposer*, variant of *oposer* 'oppose.'

Po·sei·don /pəˈsīdn/ *Greek Mythology* the god of the sea, water, earthquakes, and horses, son of Cronus and Rhea and brother of Zeus. He is often depicted with a trident in his hand. Roman equivalent NEPTUNE.

Po·sen /ˈpōzən/ German name for POZNAŃ.

pos·er¹ /ˈpōzər/ ▸*n.* a person who acts in an affected manner in order to impress others.

pos·er² ▸*n.* a difficult or perplexing question or problem.

po·seur /pōˈzər/ ▸*n.* another term for POSER¹. ▷French, from *poser* 'to place.'

po·sey /ˈpōzē/ (also **po·sy**) ▸*adj.* *informal* (of a person or their behavior) affected and attempting to impress others; pretentious.

posh /päsн/ *informal* ▸*adj.* elegant or stylishly luxurious: *a posh Munich hotel.* ■ *chiefly Brit.* typical of or belonging to the upper class of society: *she had a posh accent.*
▸*adv. Brit.* in an upper-class way: *trying to talk posh.*
▸*n. Brit.* the quality or state of being elegant, stylish, or upper-class: *we finally bought a color TV, which seemed the height of posh.* ▷early 20th cent.: perhaps from slang *posh*, denoting a dandy. There is no evidence to support the folk etymology that *posh* is formed from the initials of *port out starboard home* (referring to the practice of using the more comfortable accommodations, out of the heat of the sun, on ships between England and India). **—posh·ly** *adv.* **—posh·ness** *n.*

pos·it /ˈpäzit/ ▸*v.* (**pos·it·ed, pos·it·ing**) **1** [*trans.*] assume as a fact; put forward as a basis of argument: *the Confucian view posits a perfectible human nature |* [with *clause*] *he posited that the world economy is a system with its own particular equilibrium.* ■ (**posit something on**) base something on the truth of (a particular assumption): *these plots are posited on a false premise about women's nature as inferior.* **2** [*trans.*] put in position; place: *the professor posits Cohen in his second category of poets.*
▸*n. Philosophy* a statement that is made on the assumption that it will prove to be true. ▷mid 17th cent.: from Latin *posit-* 'placed,' from the verb *ponere*.

pos·i·tif /ˈpäzəˌtēf/ ▸*n. Music* (in some organs) a separate division of stops with its own manual, similar to a choir organ. ▷French.

po·si·tion /pəˈzisнən/ ▸*n.* **1** a place where someone or something is located or has been put: *the distress call had given the ship's position | Mrs. Snell had taken up her position on the bottom step of the stairs.* ■ the location where someone or something should be; the correct place: *the lid was put* **into position** *and screwed down | make sure that no slates have slipped* **out of position**. ■ (often **positions**) a place where part of a military force is posted for strategic purposes: *the guns were shelling the German positions.* **2** a particular way in which someone or something is placed or arranged: *he moved himself into a reclining position | a cramp forced her to change position.* ■ in a game of chess, the configuration of the pieces and pawns on the board at any point. ■ *Music* a particular location of the hand on the fingerboard of a stringed instrument: *be familiar with the first six positions across the four strings.* ■ *Music* a particular location of the slide of a trombone. ■ *Music* the arrangement of the constituent notes of a chord. **3** a situation or set of circumstances, esp. one that affects one's power to act: *the company's financial position is grim |* [with *infinitive*] *we felt we were not in a position to judge the merits of the case.* ■ a job: *she retired from her position as marketing director.* ■ the state of being placed where one has an advantage over one's rivals in a competitive situation: *his successors were already jockeying for position.* ■ a person's place or rank in relation to others, esp. in a competitive situation: *he made up ground to finish in second position.* ■ high rank or social standing: *a woman of supposed wealth and position.* ■ (in team games) a set of functions considered as the responsibility of a particular player based on the location in which they play: *it gives every player a chance to play* *every fielding position.* **4** a person's particular point of view or attitude toward something: *the official U.S.* ***position on*** *Palestine.* **5** an investor's net holdings in one or more markets at a particular time; the status of an individual or institutional trader's open contracts: *traders were covering short positions.* **6** *Logic* a proposition laid down or asserted; a tenet or assertion.

▸*v.* [*trans.*] put or arrange (someone or something) in a particular place or way: *he pulled out a chair and positioned it between them | she positioned herself on a bench.* ■ promote (a product, service, or business) within a particular sector of a market, or as the fulfillment of that sector's specific requirements: *a comprehensive development plan that will* ***position*** *the city* ***as*** *a major economic force in the region.* ■ [*trans.*] *figurative* portray or regard (someone) as a particular type of person: *I had* ***positioned*** *her* ***as*** *my antagonist.* ▷late Middle English: from Old French, from Latin *positio(n-)*, from *ponere* 'to place.' The current sense of the verb dates from the early 19th cent.

po·si·tion·al /pəˈzisʜənl/ ▸*adj.* of, relating to, or determined by position: *the team will be forced to make several positional changes.* **—po·si·tion·al·ly** *adv.*

po·si·tion pa·per ▸*n.* (in business and politics) a written report outlining someone's attitude or intentions regarding a particular matter.

pos·i·tive /ˈpäzətiv; ˈpäztiv/ ▸*adj.* **1** consisting in or characterized by the presence or possession of features or qualities rather than their absence. ■ (of a statement or decision) expressing or implying affirmation, agreement, or permission: *the company received a positive response from investors.* ■ (of the results of a test or experiment) indicating the presence of something: *three players who had tested positive for cocaine use.* ■ constructive in intention or attitude: *there needs to be a positive approach to youthful offenders.* ■ showing optimism and confidence: *I hope you will be feeling very positive about your chances of success.* ■ showing pleasing progress, gain, or improvement: *the election result will have a positive effect because it will restore people's confidence.* **2** with no possibility of doubt; clear and definite: *he made a positive identification of a glossy ibis.* ■ convinced or confident in one's opinion; certain: *"You are sure it was the same man?" "Positive!"* | [with *clause*] *I am positive that he is not coming back.* ■ [*attrib.*] *informal* downright; complete (used for emphasis): *it's a positive delight to see you.* **3** of, containing, producing, or denoting an electric charge opposite to that carried by electrons. **4** (of a photographic image) showing lights and shades or colors true to the original. **5** *Grammar* (of an adjective or adverb) expressing a quality in its basic, primary degree. Contrasted with **COMPARATIVE** and **SUPERLATIVE**. **6** *chiefly Philosophy* dealing only with matters of fact and experience; not speculative or theoretical. Compare with **POSITIVISM** (sense 1). **7** (of a quantity) greater than zero. **8** *Astrology* of, relating to, or denoting any of the air or fire signs, considered active in nature.

▸*n.* **1** a good, affirmative, or constructive quality or attribute: *take your weaknesses and translate them into positives | to manage your way out of recession, accentuate* ***the positive.*** **2** a photographic image showing lights and shades or colors true to the original, esp. one printed from a negative. **3** a result of a test or experiment indicating the presence of something: *let us look at the distribution of those positives.* **4** the part of an electric circuit that is at a higher electrical potential than another point designated as having zero electrical potential. **5** *Grammar* an adjective or adverb in the positive degree. **6** *Music* another term for **POSITIF**. **7** a number greater than zero. ▷late Middle English: from Old French *positif, -ive* or Latin *positivus*, from *posit-* 'placed,' from the verb *ponere*. The original sense referred to laws as being formally 'laid down,' which gave rise to the sense 'explicitly laid down and admitting no question,' hence 'very sure, convinced.' **—pos·i·tive·ness** *n.* **—pos·i·tiv·i·ty** /ˌpäzəˈtivətē/ *n.*

pos·i·tive dis·crim·i·na·tion ▸*n.* British term for **REVERSE DISCRIMINATION**.

pos·i·tive feed·back ▸*n. chiefly Biology* the enhancement or amplification of an effect by its own influence on the process that gives rise to it. ■ *Electronics* the return of part of an output signal to the input, which is in phase with it, so that the amplifier gain is increased and the output is often distorted.

pos·i·tive ge·ot·ro·pism ▸*n. Botany* the tendency of roots to grow downward.

pos·i·tive law ▸*n.* statutes that have been laid down by a legislature, court, or other human institution and which can take whatever form the authors want. Compare with **NATURAL LAW**.

pos·i·tive·ly /ˈpäzətivlē; ˈpäztivlē; ˌpäzəˈtivlē/ ▸*adv.* in a positive way, in particular: ■ in a constructive or affirmative way: *the negotiations started positively, with agreement on several issues.* ■ with optimism or confidence: *it's time I got down to thinking positively about this show.* ■ with certainty; so as to leave no room for doubt: *experts could not positively identify the voices.* ■ [as *submodifier*] used to emphasize that something is the case, even though it may seem surprising or unlikely: *some of the diets may be positively dangerous.* ■ [*sentence adverb*] used to emphasize that someone means what they are saying: *this is positively the last word on the matter.*

pos·i·tive or·gan ▸*n. chiefly historical* a large but movable pipe organ. Compare with **PORTATIVE ORGAN**. ▷early 18th cent.: *positive* in the sense 'adapted to be placed in position.'

pos·i·tive pole ▸*n. Physics* a north-seeking pole of a magnet. ■ an anode.

pos·i·tive pres·sure ▸*n.* air or gas pressure greater than that of the atmosphere, as used, e.g., in the artificial ventilation of the lungs.

pos·i·tive sign ▸*n. Mathematics* another term for **PLUS SIGN**.

pos·i·tiv·ism /ˈpäzətivˌizəm; ˈpäztiv-/ ▸*n. Philosophy* **1** a philosophical system that holds that every rationally justifiable assertion can be scientifically verified or is capable of logical or mathematical proof, and that therefore rejects metaphysics and theism. [from French *positivisme*, coined by the French philosopher Auguste **COMTE**.] ■ a humanistic religious system founded on this. ■ another term for **LOGICAL POSITIVISM**. **2** the theory that laws are to be understood as social rules, valid because they are enacted by authority or derive logically from existing decisions, and that ideal or moral considerations (e.g., that a rule is unjust) should not limit the scope or operation of the law. **3** the state or quality of being positive: *in this age of illogical positivism, no one wants to sound negative.* **—pos·i·tiv·ist** *n.* & *adj.* **—pos·i·tiv·is·tic** /ˌpäzətəˈvistik/ *adj.* **—pos·i·tiv·is·ti·cal·ly** /ˌpäzətəˈvistik(ə)lē/ *adv.*

pos·i·tron /ˈpäzəˌträn/ ▸*n. Physics* a subatomic particle with the same mass as an electron and a numerically equal but positive charge. ▷1930s: from **POSITIVE** + **-TRON**.

Posix /ˈpäsiks/ (also **POSIX**) ▸*n. Computing* a set of formal descriptions that provide a standard for the design of operating systems, esp. ones that are compatible with Unix. ▷1980s: from the initial letters of *portable operating system* + *-ix* suggested by **UNIX**.

po·sol·o·gy /pəˈzäləjē/ ▸*n. rare* the part of medicine concerned with dosage. ▷early 19th cent.: from French *posologie*, from Greek *posos* 'how much' + *-logia* (see **-LOGY**). **—pos·o·log·i·cal** /ˌpäzəˈläjikəl/ *adj.*

poss /päs/ ▸*abbr.* possible.

poss. ▸*abbr.* ■ possession. ■ possessive. ■ possible; possibly.

pos·se /ˈpäsē/ ▸*n. historical* a body of men, typically armed, summoned by a sheriff to enforce the law. ■ (also **pos·se com·i·ta·tus** /ˌkämiˈtātəs; -ˈtätəs/) *historical* the body of men in a county whom the sheriff could summon to enforce the law. [*comitatus* from medieval Latin, 'of the county.'] ■ *informal* a group of people who have a common characteristic, occupation, or purpose: *he pompously led around* ***a posse of*** *medical students.* ■ *informal* a gang of youths involved in (usually drug-related) crime. ■ *informal* a group of people who socialize together, esp. to go to clubs or raves. ▷mid 17th cent.: from medieval Latin, literally 'power,' from Latin *posse* 'be able.'

Pos·se Com·i·ta·tus Act /ˈpäsē ˌkämiˈtātəs/ ▸*Law* a federal statute prohibiting use of the military in civilian law enforcement. ▷Latin *posse comitatus* 'power of the county.'

pos·sess /pəˈzes/ ▸*v.* [*trans.*] **1** have as belonging to one; own: *I do not possess a television set.* ■ *Law* have possession of as distinct from ownership: *a two-year suspended sentence for possessing cocaine.* ■ have as an ability, quality, or characteristic: *he did not possess a sense of humor* | (**be possessed of**) *a fading blonde possessed of a powerful soprano voice.* ■ (**possess oneself of**) *archaic* take for one's own: *all that the plaintiffs did was to possess themselves of the securities.* **2** (usu. **be possessed**) (of a demon or spirit, esp. an evil one) have complete power over (someone) and be manifested through their speech or actions: *she was possessed by the Devil.* ■ (of an emotion, idea, etc.) dominate the mind of; have an overpowering influence on: *I was possessed by a desire to tell her everything.* **3** *chiefly poetic/literary* have sexual intercourse with (a woman). **4** *archaic* maintain (oneself or one's mind or soul) in a state or condition of patience or quiet: *I tried to* ***possess*** *my soul* ***in*** *patience and to forget how hungry I was.* [often with biblical allusion to Luke 21:19, the proper sense ('gain your souls') being misunderstood.] ▷late Middle English: from Old French *possesser*, from Latin *possess-* 'occupied, held,' from the verb *possidere*, from *potis* 'able, capable' + *sedere* 'sit.'

▸*PHRASE* □ **what possessed you?** used to express surprise at an action regarded as extremely unwise: *what possessed you to come here?*

pos·ses·sion /pəˈzesʜən/ ▸*n.* **1** the state of having, owning, or controlling something: *are you* ***in possession of*** *any items over $500 in value? | he had* ***taken possession of*** *one of the sofas | the book* ***came into my possession.*** ■ *Law* visible power or control over something, as distinct from lawful ownership; holding or occupancy: *both teams attempting to* ***gain possession of*** *the ball | they were imprisoned for possession of explosives.* ■ *informal* the state of possessing an illegal drug: *they're charged with possession.* ■ (in football, basketball, and other ball games) temporary control of the ball by a particular player or team: *the ball hit a defender and Brown's quick reaction put him* ***in possession.*** **2** (usu. **possessions**) an item of property; something belonging to one: *I was alone with no money or possessions | that photograph was Bert's most precious possession.* ■ a territory or country controlled or governed by another: *France's former colonial possessions.* **3** the state of being controlled by a demon or spirit: *they prayed for protection against demonic possession.* ■ the state of being completely under the influence of an idea or emotion: *fear* ***took possession of*** *my soul.* ▷Middle English: from Old French, from Latin *possessio(n-)*, from the verb *possidere* (see **POSSESS**). **—pos·ses·sion·less** *adj.*

pos·ses·sive /pəˈzesiv/ ▸*adj.* **1** demanding someone's total attention and love: *as soon as she'd been out with a guy a few times, he'd get possessive | she was* ***possessive of*** *our eldest son.* ■ showing a desire to own things and an unwillingness to share what one already owns: *young children are proud and* ***possessive of*** *their own property.* **2** *Grammar* relating to or denoting the case of nouns and pronouns expressing possession. [from Latin *possessivus*, translation of Greek *ktētikē (ptōsis)* 'possessive (case).']

▸*n. Grammar* a possessive word or form. ■ (**the possessive**) the possessive case. **—pos·ses·sive·ly** *adv.* **—pos·ses·sive·ness** *n.*

USAGE **1** Form the possessive of all singulars by adding *'s: Ross's, Fox's, Reese's.* A few classical and other foreign names are traditional exceptions to this rule, for example, *Jesus'* and *Euripides'*, which take an apostrophe only.

2 Form the possessive of plurals by adding an apostrophe to the plural form: *the Rosses' house, the Perezes' car.* See also **usage** at **APOSTROPHE**[1], **ITS**, and **PLURAL**.

pos·ses·sive pro·noun ▸*n. Grammar* a pronoun indicating possession, for example *mine, yours, hers, theirs.*

pos·ses·sor /pəˈzesər/ ▸*n.* a person who owns something or has a particular quality: *his father was the possessor of a considerable fortune.* ■ *Law* a person who takes, occupies, or holds something without necessarily having ownership, or as distinguished from the owner. **—pos·ses·so·ry** *adj.*

pos·set /ˈpäsət/ ▸*n. historical* a drink made of hot milk curdled with ale, wine, or other alcoholic liquor and typically flavored with spices, drunk as a delicacy or as a remedy for colds. ▷late Middle English: of unknown origin.

pos·si·bil·i·ty /ˌpäsəˈbilətē/ ▸*n.* (*pl.* **-ties**) a thing that may happen or be the case: *the theoretical* ***possibility of*** *a chain reaction* | [with *clause*] *there was always the possibility that he might be turned down.* ■ the state or fact of being likely or possible; likelihood: *there was* ***no possibility of*** *recompense for him.* ■ a thing that may be chosen or done out of several possible alternatives: *one possibility is to allow all firms to participate | there are three possibilities for obtaining extra money.* ■ (**possibilities**) unspecified qualities of a promising nature; potential: *the house was old but it had possibilities.* ▷late Middle English: from Old French *possibilite*, from late Latin *possibilitas*, from *possibilis* 'able to be done' (see **POSSIBLE**).

pos·si·ble /ˈpäsəbəl/ ▸*adj.* able to be done; within the power or capacity of someone or something: *surely it's not* ***possible for*** *a man to live so long? | what are the possible alternatives? | contact me* ***as soon as possible*** *| I'd* *like the report this afternoon,* ***if possible.*** ■ able to happen although not certain to; denoting a fact, event, or situation that may or may not occur or be so: *a new theory emerged about the possible cause of the plane crash* | [with *clause*] *it is possible that he will have to return to the hospital.* ■ [*attrib.*] able to be or become; potential: *he was a possible future customer.* ■ [with *superlative*] having as much or as little of a specified quality as can be achieved: *children need the best education possible* | *the shortest possible route.* ■ [*attrib.*] (of a number or score) as high as is achievable in a test, competition, or game: *he scored 723 points out of a possible 900.*

▸*n.* a person or thing that has the potential to become or do something, esp. a potential candidate for a job or membership on a team: *I have marked five possibles with an asterisk.* ■ (**the possible**) that which is likely or achievable: *they were living right at the edge of the possible.* ▷late Middle English: from Old French, or from Latin *possibilis,* from *posse* 'be able.'

pos·si·bly /ˈpäsəblē/ ▸*adv.* **1** [*sentence adverb*] perhaps (used to indicate doubt or hesitancy): *he found himself alone, possibly the only surviving officer.* ■ [with *modal*] used in polite requests: *could you possibly pour me another cup of coffee?* **2** [usu. with *modal*] in accordance with what is likely or achievable, in particular: ■ used to emphasize that something is difficult, surprising, or bewildering: *what can you possibly mean?* ■ used to emphasize that someone has or will put all their effort into something: *be as noisy as you possibly can.*

POSSLQ /ˈpäsəl,kyo͞o/ ▸*abbr.* person of the opposite sex sharing living quarters (used to refer to a live-in sexual partner).

pos·sum /ˈpäsəm/ ▸*n.* **1** *informal* an opossum. **2** a tree-dwelling Australasian marsupial that typically has a prehensile tail. • Four families, esp. Petauridae: many species, including the ringtails. ▷early 17th cent.: shortening of OPOSSUM.

▸*PHRASE* □ **play possum 1** pretend to be asleep or unconscious when threatened (in imitation of an opossum's behavior). **2** feign ignorance.

Post[1] /pōst/, Emily (Price) (1873–1960), U.S. writer and columnist. She was an arbiter of social etiquette and was the last word on manners. She wrote *Etiquette* (1922).

Post[2], Wiley (1899–1935), U.S. aviator. He was the first man to fly solo around the world 1933, accomplishing this in 7 days, 18 hours, and 49 minutes. He was flying near Point Barrow, Alaska, with Will Rogers as his passenger when their plane crashed and they were both killed.

post[1] /pōst/ ▸*n.* a long, sturdy piece of timber or metal set upright in the ground and used to support something or as a marker: *follow the blue posts until the track meets a forestry road.* ■ a goalpost: *Robertson, at the near post, headed wide.* ■ (**the post**) a starting post or winning post.

▸*v.* [*trans.*] (often **be posted**) display (a notice) in a public place: *a curt notice had been posted on the door* | *the exam results were posted this morning.* ■ announce or publish (something, esp. a financial result): *the company posted a $460,000 loss.* ■ (of a player or team) achieve or record (a particular score or result): *Smith and Lamb posted a century partnership.* ■ [*trans.*] publish the name of (a member of the armed forces) as missing or dead: *a whole troop had been posted missing.* ■ *Computing* make (information) available on the Internet. ■ put notices on or in: *we have posted all the bars.*

▸*phrasal v.* □ **post up** *Basketball* play in a position near the basket, along the side of the key. ▷Old English, from Latin *postis* 'doorpost,' later 'rod, beam,' probably reinforced in Middle English by Old French *post* 'pillar, beam' and Middle Dutch, Middle Low German *post* 'doorpost.'

post[2] ▸*n.* **1** *chiefly Brit.* the official service or system that delivers letters and parcels: *winners will be notified by post* | *the tickets are in the post.* ■ letters and parcels delivered: *she was opening her post.* ■ [in *sing.*] a single collection or delivery of letters or parcels: *entries must be received no later than first post on Friday, June 14th.* ■ used in names of newspapers: *the Washington Post.* **2** *historical* one of a series of couriers who carried mail on horseback between fixed stages. ■ *archaic* a person or vehicle that carries mail.

▸*v.* **1** [*trans.*] *chiefly Brit.* send (a letter or parcel) via the postal system: *I've just been to post a letter* | ***post off*** *your order form today.* **2** [*trans.*] (in bookkeeping) enter (an item) in a ledger: *post the transaction in the second column.* ■ complete (a ledger) in this way. **3** [*intrans.*] *historical* travel with relays of horses: *we posted in an open carriage.* ■ [with *adverbial of direction*] *archaic* travel with haste; hurry: *he comes posting up the street.*

▸*adv. archaic* with haste: *come now, come post.* ▷early 16th cent. (sense 2 of the *noun*): from French *poste,* from Italian *posta,* from a contraction of Latin *posita,* feminine past participle of *ponere* 'to place.'

▸*PHRASE* □ **keep someone posted** keep someone informed of the latest developments or news.

post[3] ▸*n.* **1** a position of paid employment; a job: *he resigned from the post of foreign minister* | *a teaching post.* **2** a place where someone is on duty or where a particular activity is carried out: *a worker asleep at his post* | *a customs post.* ■ a place where a soldier, guard, or police officer is stationed or which they patrol: *he gave the two armed men orders not to leave their posts* | *a command post.* ■ a force stationed at a permanent position or camp; a garrison. ■ a local group in an organization of military veterans. **3** *Brit., historical* the status or rank of full-grade captain in the Royal Navy: *Captain Miller was* ***made post*** *in 1796.*

▸*v.* [*trans.*] (usu. **be posted**) send (someone) to a particular place to take up an appointment: *he was posted to Washington as military attaché.* ■ station (someone, esp. a soldier, guard, or police officer) in a particular place: *a guard was posted at the entrance.* ▷mid 16th cent.: from French *poste,* from Italian *posto,* from a contraction of popular Latin *positum,* neuter past participle of *ponere* 'to place.'

post- ▸*prefix* after in time or order: *postdate* | *postoperative.* ▷from Latin *post* 'after, behind.'

post·age /ˈpōstij/ ▸*n.* the sending or conveying of letters and parcels by mail: *the free postage that members of Congress enjoy.* ■ the amount required to send a letter or parcel by mail: *the calendar is available for $15.95 including postage and handling.*

post·age due ▸*n.* that part of the postage that was not prepaid. ■ a special postage stamp indicating postage still to be paid on a letter or parcel.

post·age me·ter ▸*n.* a machine that prints an official mark or signature on a letter or parcel to indicate that postage has been paid or does not need to be paid.

post·age stamp ▸*n.* a small adhesive piece of paper of specified value issued by a postal authority to be affixed to a letter or parcel to indicate the amount of postage paid.

post·al /ˈpōstəl/ ▸*adj.* [*attrib.*] of or relating to the post office or the mail: *increased postal rates* | *postal services.* ■ *chiefly Brit.* done through the mail: *a postal ballot* | *a postal survey.*

▸*n.* (in full **postal card**) another term for POSTCARD. ▷mid 19th cent.: from French, from *poste* 'postal service.' —**post·al·ly** *adv.*

▸*PHRASE* □ **go postal** become crazed and violent, esp. as the result of stress. [with reference to cases in which disgruntled employees of the U.S. Postal Service have shot colleagues.]

post·al code ▸*n. Brit.* another term for POSTCODE. ■ *Canadian* a mailing code similar to the U.S. zip code.

post-and-beam ▸*adj.* (of a building or a method of construction) having or using a framework of upright and horizontal beams.

post·bel·lum /pōstˈbeləm/ ▸*adj.* occurring or existing after a war, in particular the American Civil War. ▷late 19th cent.: from Latin *post* 'after' + *bellum* 'war.'

post·box /ˈpōst,bäks/ ▸*n.* British term for MAILBOX.

post·card /ˈpōst,kärd/ ▸*n.* a card for sending a message by mail without an envelope, typically having a photograph or other illustration on one side.

post-chaise /,sHāz/ ▸*n.* (*pl.* **post-chaises** *pronunc.* same or /-,sHāziz/) *historical* a horse-drawn carriage used for transporting passengers or mail, esp. in the 18th and early 19th centuries. ▷late 17th cent.: from POST[2] + CHAISE in the sense 'horse-drawn carriage.'

post·clas·si·cal /,pōstˈklasəkəl/ ▸*adj.* of or relating to a time after the classical period of any language, art, or culture, in particular the classical period of ancient Greek and Latin culture.

post·code /ˈpōst,kōd/ ▸*n. Brit.* a group of numbers or letters and numbers that are added to a postal address to assist the sorting of mail.

post·co·i·tal /,pōstˈkōətl/ ▸*adj.* occurring or done after sexual intercourse: *postcoital contraception.* —**post·co·i·tal·ly** *adv.*

post·date /pōstˈdāt/ ▸*v.* [*trans.*] **1** [usu. as *adj.*] (**postdated**) affix or assign a date later than the actual one to (a document or event): *a postdated check.* **2** occur or come at a later date than: *Stonehenge was presumed to postdate these structures.*

post·doc /ˈpōst,däk/ ▸*n. informal* a person engaged in postdoctoral research. ■ postdoctoral research. ■ a postdoctoral research fellowship.

post·doc·tor·al /pōstˈdäktərəl/ ▸*adj.* of, relating to, or denoting research undertaken after the completion of doctoral research: *a postdoctoral fellowship.*

post·er /ˈpōstər/ ▸*n.* **1** a large printed picture used for decoration. ■ a large printed picture, notice, or advertisement displayed in a public place: [as *adj.*] *a poster campaign.* **2** *Computing* someone who sends a message to a newsgroup.

poste res·tante /,pōst ,resˈtänt/ ▸*n.* written on a letter as an indication that it should be kept at a specified post office until collected by the addressee. ■ *chiefly Brit.* the department in a post office keeping such letters. ▷mid 18th cent.: from French, literally 'mail remaining.'

pos·te·ri·or /päˈsti(ə)rēər; pō-/ ▸*adj.* **1** *chiefly Anatomy, technical* further back in position; of or nearer the rear or hind end, esp. of the body or a part of it: *the posterior part of the gut* **2** a basal body situated just **posterior to** the nucleus. The opposite of ANTERIOR. ■ *Medicine* relating to or denoting presentation of a fetus in which the rear or caudal end is nearest the cervix and emerges first at birth: *a posterior labor.* Compare with BREECH BIRTH. **3** *formal* coming after in time or order; later: *a date posterior to the first Reform Bill.*

▸*n. humorous* a person's buttocks. ▷early 16th cent. (as a plural noun denoting descendants): from Latin, comparative of *posterus* 'following,' from *post* 'after.' —**pos·te·ri·or·i·ty** /pä,sti(ə)rēˈôritē; pō-/ *n.* —**pos·te·ri·or·ly** *adv.*

pos·te·ri·or prob·a·bil·i·ty ▸*n.* the statistical probability that a hypothesis is true calculated in the light of relevant observations. Compare with PRIOR PROBABILITY.

pos·ter·i·ty /päˈsteritē/ ▸*n.* all future generations of people: *the victims' names are recorded for posterity.* ■ [in *sing.*] *archaic* the descendants of a person: *God offered Abraham a posterity like the stars of heaven.* ▷late Middle English: from Old French *posterite,* from Latin *posteritas,* from *posterus* 'following.'

post·er·ize /ˈpōstə,rīz/ ▸*v.* [*trans.*] print or display (a photograph or other image) using only a small number of different tones. —**post·er·i·za·tion** /,pōstərəˈzāsHən/ *n.*

pos·tern /ˈpōstərn; ˈpäs-/ ▸*n.* a back or side entrance: [as *adj.*] *a small postern door.* ▷Middle English: from Old French *posterne,* alteration of *posterle,* from late Latin *posterula,* diminutive of *posterus* 'following.'

pos·ter paint ▸*n.* an opaque paint with a water-soluble binder, used for posters and children's paintings.

post ex·change (abbr.: **PX**) ▸*n.* a store at a U.S. military base selling food, clothing, and other items.

post·face /ˈpōst,fās/ ▸*n.* a brief explanatory comment or note at the end of a book or other piece of writing.

post·fem·i·nist /pōstˈfemənist/ ▸*adj.* coming after the feminism of the 1960s and subsequent decades, in particular moving beyond or rejecting some of the ideas of feminism as out of date.

▸*n.* a person who rejects some feminist ideas for this reason. —**post·fem·i·nism** *n.*

post·fix /pōstˈfiks/ ▸*v.* **1** [*trans.*] (usu. **be postfixed**) *Biology* treat (a biological substance or specimen) with a second fixative. **2** *rare Linguistics* append as a suffix.

▸*n.* a suffix.

post·fron·tal /,pōstˈfrəntl/ ▸*n. Zoology* a bone behind the orbit of the eye in some vertebrates.

post·gla·cial /pōstˈglāsHəl/ ▸*adj. Geology* of or relating to the period since the last continental glaciation (the Wisconsin in North America), beginning with the sudden rise in temperature about 10,000 years ago. Compare with LATE-GLACIAL. ■ [as *n.*] (**the postglacial**) the postglacial period.

post·grad /ˈpōstˈgrad/ ▸*adj.* & *n. informal* short for POSTGRADUATE.

post·grad·u·ate /pōstˈgrajo͞oit/ ▸*adj.* of, relating to, or denoting a course of study undertaken after completing a first degree: *a postgraduate degree.*

▸*n.* a student engaged in such a course of study.

post·haste /ˈpōstˈhāst/ ▸*adv.* with great speed or immediacy: *she would go posthaste to England.* ▷mid 16th cent.: from the direction "haste, post, haste," formerly given on letters.

Pronunciation Key ə *ago;* ər *over;* ˈə *or* ,ə *up;* ˈər *or* ,ər *fur;* a *hat;* ā *rate;* ä *car;* CH *chew;* e *let;* ē *see;* e(ə)r *air;* i *fit;* ī *by;* i(ə)r *ear;* NG *sing;* ō *go;* ô *for;* oi *boy;* o͝o *good;* o͞o *goo;* ou *out;* SH *she;* TH *thin;* T͟H *then;* (h)w *why;* ZH *vision*

post hoc /ˈpōst ˈhäk/ ▸*adj.* & *adv.* occurring or done after the event: *a post hoc justification for the changes.* ▷Latin, literally 'after this.'

▸*PHRASE* □ **post hoc, ergo propter hoc** after this, therefore resulting from it: used to indicate that a causal relationship has erroneously been assumed from a merely sequential one.

post horn ▸*n. historical* a valveless horn used originally to signal the arrival or departure of a mounted courier or mail coach.

post·hu·mous /ˈpäsCHəməs; pästˈ(h)yo͞oməs/ ▸*adj.* occurring, awarded, or appearing after the death of the originator: *he was awarded a posthumous Military Cross* | *a posthumous collection of his articles.* ■ (of a child) born after the death of its father. ▷early 17th cent.: from Latin *postumus* 'last' (superlative from *post* 'after'), in late Latin spelled *posth-* by association with *humus* 'ground.' —**post·hu·mous·ly** *adv.*

post·hyp·not·ic /ˌpōst-(h)ipˈnätik/ ▸*adj.* relating to or denoting the giving of ideas or instructions to a subject under hypnosis that are intended to affect behavior after the hypnotic trance ends: *posthypnotic suggestion.*

pos·til /ˈpästəl/ ▸*n. archaic* a marginal note or comment, esp. on a biblical text. ■ a commentary, homily, or book of homilies. ▷late Middle English: from Old French *postille*, from medieval Latin *postilla*, perhaps from Latin *post illa (verba)* 'after those words,' written as a direction to a scribe.

pos·til·ion /pəˈstilyən; pō-/ (also **pos·til·lion**) ▸*n.* a person who rides the leading left-hand horse of a team or pair drawing a coach or carriage, esp. when there is no coachman. ▷mid 16th cent. (in the sense 'forerunner acting as guide to the post-horse rider'): from French *postillon*, from Italian *postiglione* 'post boy,' from *posta* (see **POST**[2]).

post-Im·pres·sion·ism (also **Post-Im·pres·sion·ism**) ▸*n.* the work or style of a varied group of late 19th-century and early 20th-century artists including Van Gogh, Gauguin, and Cézanne. They reacted against the naturalism of the Impressionists to explore color, line, and form, and the emotional response of the artist, a concern that led to the development of expressionism. —**post-Im·pres·sion·ist** *n.* & *adj.* —**post-Im·pres·sion·is·tic** *adj.*

post·in·dus·tri·al /ˌpōstinˈdəstrēəl/ ▸*adj.* of or relating to an economy that no longer relies on heavy industry: *a postindustrial society.* —**post·in·dus·tri·al·ism** /-ˌlizəm/ *n.*

post·ing /ˈpōstiNG/ ▸*n.* **1** *chiefly Brit.* an appointment to a job, esp. one abroad or in the armed forces: *he requested a posting to Japan.* ■ the location of such an appointment: *Norway was an attractive posting because of its quality of life.* **2** *Computing* a message sent to an Internet bulletin board or newsgroup. ■ the sending of a message to an Internet bulletin board or newsgroup.

Post-it (also **Post-it note**) ▸*n. trademark* a piece of paper with an adhesive strip on one side, designed to be stuck prominently to an object or surface and easily removed when necessary.

post·lap·sar·i·an /ˌpōst,lapˈserēən/ ▸*adj. Theology* or *poetic/literary* occurring or existing after the Fall of Man. ▷mid 18th cent.: from **POST-** 'occurring after,' on the pattern of *sublapsarian.*

post·lude /ˈpōs(t)ˌlo͞od/ ▸*n. Music* a concluding piece of music, esp. an organ piece played at the end of a religious service. ■ a written or spoken epilogue; an afterword. ▷mid 19th cent.: from **POST-** 'later, after,' on the pattern of *prelude.*

post·man /ˈpōstmən/ ▸*n.* (*pl.* **-men**) a mail carrier.

post·mark /ˈpōstˌmärk/ ▸*n.* an official mark stamped on a letter or other postal package, giving the place, date, and time of posting, and serving to cancel the postage stamp: *an envelope with a London postmark.*

▸*v.* [*trans.*] (usu. **be postmarked**) stamp (a letter or other postal package) officially with such a mark: [*trans.*] *the letter was postmarked New York.*

post·mas·ter /ˈpōstˌmastər/ ▸*n.* a person in charge of a post office.

post·mas·ter gen·er·al ▸*n.* (*pl.* **post·mas·ters gen·er·al**) the head of a country's postal service.

post·mil·len·ni·al /ˌpōstməˈlenēəl/ ▸*adj.* (esp. in Christian doctrine) following the millennium.

post·mil·len·ni·al·ism /ˌpōstməˈlenēəˌlizəm/ ▸*n.* (among some Christian Protestants) the doctrine that the Second Coming of Christ will be the culmination of the prophesied millennium of blessedness. Compare with **PREMILLENNIALISM.** —**post·mil·len·ni·al·ist** /-ist/ *n.*

post·mis·tress /ˈpōstˌmistris/ ▸*n.* a woman in charge of a post office.

post·mod·ern·ism /pōstˈmädərˌnizəm/ ▸*n.* a late 20th-century style and concept in the arts, architecture, and criticism that represents a departure from modernism and has at its heart a general distrust of grand theories and ideologies as well as a problematical relationship with any notion of "art."

Typical features include a deliberate mixing of different artistic styles and media, the self-conscious use of earlier styles and conventions, and often the incorporation of images relating to the consumerism and mass communication of late 20th-century postindustrial society. Postmodernist architecture was pioneered by Robert Venturi; the AT&T skyscraper in New York (completed in 1984) is a prime example of the style. Influential literary critics include Jean Baudrillard and Jean-François Lyotard.

—**post·mod·ern** *adj.* —**post·mod·ern·ist** *n.* & *adj.* —**post·mod·er·ni·ty** /ˌpōstməˈdərnətē/ *n.*

post·mod·i·fy /pōstˈmädəˌfī/ ▸*v.* (**-mod·i·fies, -mod·i·fied**) [*trans.*] *Grammar* modify the sense of (a noun or other word) by being placed after it. —**post·mod·i·fi·ca·tion** /ˌpōst,mädifiˈkāSHən/ *n.* —**post·mod·i·fi·er** *n.*

post·mor·tem /pōstˈmôrtəm/ ▸*n.* (also **postmortem examination**) an examination of a dead body to determine the cause of death. ■ an analysis or discussion of an event held soon after it has occurred, esp. in order to determine why it was a failure: *an election postmortem on why the party lost.*

▸*adj.* [*attrib.*] of or relating to a postmortem: *a postmortem report.* ■ happening after death: *postmortem changes in his body* | [as *adv.*] *assessment of morphology in nerves taken postmortem.* ▷mid 18th cent.: from Latin, literally 'after death.'

post·na·tal /pōstˈnātl/ ▸*adj.* of, relating to, characteristic of, or denoting the period after childbirth: *postnatal care.* —**post·na·tal·ly** *adv.*

post·nup·tial /pōstˈnəpSHəl; -CHəl/ ▸*adj.* occurring or relating to the period after marriage. ■ *Zoology* occurring in or relating to the period after the mating season of an animal.

post-o·bit ▸*adj. archaic* taking effect after death. ▷mid 18th cent.: from Latin *post obitum*, from *post* 'after' + *obitus* 'decease' (from *obire* 'to die').

post of·fice ▸*n.* **1** the public department or corporation responsible for postal services and (in some countries) telecommunications. ■ a building where postal business is carried on. **2** a game, played esp. by children, in which imaginary letters are delivered in exchange for kisses.

post of·fice box ▸*n.* a numbered box in a post office assigned to a person or organization, where mail for them is kept until collected.

post-op ▸*abbr.* postoperative.

post·op·er·a·tive /pōstˈäp(ə)rətiv/ ▸*adj.* during, relating to, or denoting the period following a surgical operation: *postoperative care.*

post·or·bit·al /pōstˈôrbətl/ *chiefly Zoology* ▸*adj.* [*attrib.*] situated at the back of the orbit or eye socket, in particular denoting a process of the frontal bone that in some reptiles forms a separate bone.

▸*n.* a postorbital bone.

post·paid /pōstˈpād/ ▸*adj.* & *adv.* (with reference to a letter or parcel) on which postage has already been paid: [as *adj.*] *use the postpaid envelope provided.*

post·par·tum /pōstˈpärtəm/ ▸*adj. Medicine* & *Veterinary Medicine* following childbirth or the birth of young. ▷mid 19th cent.: from Latin *post partum* 'after childbirth.'

post·par·tum de·pres·sion ▸*n.* depression suffered by a mother following childbirth, typically arising from the combination of hormonal changes, psychological adjustment to motherhood, and fatigue.

post·pone /pōstˈpōn/ ▸*v.* [*trans.*] cause or arrange for (something) to take place at a time later than that first scheduled: *the visit had to be postponed for some time* | [with *present participle*] *the judge postponed sentencing a former government spokesman for fraud.* ▷late 15th cent.: from Latin *postponere*, from *post* 'after' + *ponere* 'to place.' —**post·pon·a·ble** *adj.* —**post·pone·ment** *n.* —**post·pon·er** *n.*

THE RIGHT WORD **adjourn, defer, delay, postpone, suspend**

All of these verbs have to do with putting things off.

Defer is the broadest in meaning; it suggests putting something off until a later time (*defer payment; defer a discussion*).

If you **postpone** an event or activity, you put it off intentionally, usually until a definite time in the future (*we postponed the party until the next weekend*).

If you **adjourn** an activity, you postpone its completion until another day or place; *adjourn* is usually associated with meetings or other formal gatherings that are brought to an end and then resumed (*the judge adjourned the hearing until the following morning*).

If you **delay** something, you postpone it because of obstacles (*delayed by severe thunderstorms and highway flooding*) or because you are reluctant to do it (*delay going to the dentist*).

Suspend suggests stopping an activity for a while, usually for a reason (*forced to suspend work on the bridge until the holiday weekend was over*).

post·pose /pōstˈpōz/ ▸*v.* [*trans.*] *Grammar* place (a modifying word or morpheme) after the word that it modifies. ▷late 16th cent. (in the sense 'place later or lower'): from French *postposer*, from *post-* 'after' + *poser* 'to place.' The current sense dates from the 1920s.

post·po·si·tion /ˌpōstpəˈziSHən/ ▸*n. Grammar* a word or morpheme placed after the word it governs, for example *-ward* in *homeward.* ▷mid 19th cent.: from **PREPOSITION**, by substitution of the prefix **POST-** for *pre-*. —**post·po·si·tion·al** /-SHənl/ *adj.*

post·pos·i·tive /ˌpōstˈpäzətiv/ ▸*adj.* (of a word) placed after or as a suffix on the word that it relates to.

▸*n.* a postpositive word. —**post·pos·i·tive·ly** *adv.*

post·pran·di·al /pōstˈprandēəl/ ▸*adj. formal* or *humorous* during or relating to the period after dinner or lunch: *we were jolted from our postprandial torpor.* ■ *Medicine* occurring after a meal. ▷early 19th cent.: from **POST-** 'after' + Latin *prandium* 'a meal' + **-AL**.

post·pro·duc·tion /ˌpōstprəˈdəkSHən/ ▸*n.* [often as *adj.*] work done on a film or recording after filming or recording has taken place: *postproduction editing.*

PostScript ▸*n. trademark Computing* a page description language that is an industry standard for outputting high-resolution text and graphics: [often as modifier] *PostScript files.*

post·script /ˈpō(s)ˌskript/ ▸*n.* an additional remark at the end of a letter, after the signature and introduced by "P.S.": *he added a postscript: "Leaving tomorrow."* ■ an additional statement or action that provides further information on or a sequel to something: *as a* **postscript to** *this, Paul did finally marry.* ▷mid 16th cent.: from Latin *postscriptum*, neuter past participle (used as a noun) of *postscribere* 'write under, add,' from *post* 'after, later' + *scribere* 'write.'

post·sea·son /ˈpō(s)ˌsēzən/ ▸*adj.* (of a sporting event) taking place after the end of the regular season.

▸*n.* the period following the regular season.

post·struc·tur·al·ism /pōstˈstrəkCHərəˌlizəm/ ▸*n.* an extension and critique of structuralism, esp. as used in critical textual analysis.

Emerging in French intellectual life in the late 1960s and early 1970s, poststructuralism departed from the claims to objectivity and comprehensiveness made by structuralism and emphasized instead plurality and deferral of meaning, rejecting the fixed binary oppositions of structuralism and the validity of authorial authority.

—**post·struc·tur·al** *adj.* —**post·struc·tur·al·ist** *n.* & *adj.*

post-synch /SiNGk/ ▸*v.* [*trans.*] add a sound recording to (film or video footage) at a later time.

post-tax ▸*adj. Finance* (of income or profits) remaining after the deduction of taxes.

post-ten·sion ▸*v.* [*trans.*] strengthen (reinforced concrete) by applying tension to the reinforcing rods after the concrete has set: [as *adj.*] (**post-tensioned**) *post-tensioned concrete.* Compare with **PRESTRESSED**, **PRETENSION**[2].

post time ▸*n.* the time at which a race is scheduled to start and entrants must be at their starting positions.

post-trau·mat·ic stress dis·or·der ▸*n. Medicine* a condition of persistent mental and emotional stress occurring as a result of injury or severe psychological shock, typically involving disturbance of sleep and constant vivid recall of the experience, with dulled responses to others and to the outside world.

pos·tu·lant /ˈpäsCHələnt/ ▸*n.* a candidate, esp. one seeking admission into a religious order. ▷mid 18th cent.: from French *postulant* or Latin *postulant-* 'asking,' from the verb *postulare* (see **POSTULATE**).

pos·tu·late ▸*v.* /ˈpäscHəˌlāt/ [*trans.*] **1** suggest or assume the existence, fact, or truth of (something) as a basis for reasoning, discussion, or belief: *his theory postulated a rotatory movement for hurricanes* | [with *clause*] *he postulated that the environmentalists might have a case.* **2** (in ecclesiastical law) nominate or elect (someone) to an ecclesiastical office subject to the sanction of a higher authority.
▸*n.* /ˈpäscHələt/ *formal* a thing suggested or assumed as true as the basis for reasoning, discussion, or belief: *perhaps the postulate of Babylonian influence on Greek astronomy is incorrect.* ■ *Mathematics* an assumption used as a basis for mathematical reasoning. ▷late Middle English (sense 2): from Latin *postulat-* 'asked,' from the verb *postulare.* —**pos·tu·la·tion** /ˌpäscHəˈlāsHən/ *n.*

pos·tu·la·tor /ˈpäscHəˌlātər/ ▸*n.* **1** a person who postulates something. **2** a person who presents a case for the canonization or beatification of someone in the Roman Catholic Church.

pos·ture /ˈpäscHər/ ▸*n.* a position of a person's body when standing or sitting: *he stood in a flamboyant posture with his hands on his hips* | *good posture will protect your spine.* ■ *Zoology* a particular pose adopted by a bird or other animal, interpreted as a signal of a specific pattern of behavior. ■ *figurative* a particular way of dealing with or considering something; an approach or attitude: *labor unions adopted a more militant posture in wage negotiations.* ■ *figurative* a particular way of behaving that is intended to convey a false impression; a pose: *despite pulling back its missiles, the government maintained a defiant posture for home consumption.*
▸*v.* **1** [*intrans.*] [often as *n.*] (**posturing**) behave in a way that is intended to impress or mislead others: *a masking of fear with macho posturing.* ■ [*trans.*] adopt (a certain attitude) so as to impress or mislead: *the companies may posture regret, but they have a vested interest in increasing Third World sales.* **2** [*trans.*] *archaic* place (someone) in a particular attitude or pose: *and still these two were postured motionless.* ▷late 16th cent. (denoting the relative position of one thing to another): from French, from Italian *postura,* from Latin *positura* 'position,' from *posit-* 'placed,' from the verb *ponere.* —**pos·tur·al** *adj.* —**pos·tur·er** *n.*

post·vo·cal·ic /ˌpōs(t)vōˈkalik/ ▸*adj.* (of a speech sound) occurring immediately after a vowel.

post·war /ˈpōstˈwär/ ▸*adj.* occurring or existing after a war (esp. World War II): *postwar Britain* | *postwar reconstruction.*

po·sy[1] /ˈpōzē/ ▸*n.* (*pl.* **-sies**) **1** a small bunch of flowers. **2** *archaic* a short motto or line of verse inscribed inside a ring. ▷late Middle English (sense 2): contraction of POESY.

po·sy[2] ▸*adj.* variant spelling of POSEY.

pot[1] /pät/ ▸*n.* **1** a container, typically rounded or cylindrical and of ceramic ware or metal, used for storage or cooking: *clay pots for keeping water cool in summer* | *a cooking pot.* ■ short for TEAPOT, FLOWERPOT, LOBSTER POT, CHAMBER POT, etc. ■ (**the pot**) a toilet. ■ a container for holding drink, esp. beer. ■ the contents of any of such containers: *a pot of coffee.* **2** (**the pot**) the total sum of the bets made on a round in poker and other card games: *Jim raked in the pot.* ■ all the money contributed by a group of people for a particular purpose: *in insurance, everybody puts money into the pot used to pay claims.* **3** *informal* a potbelly.
▸*v.* (**pot·ted, pot·ting**) [*trans.*] **1** plant in a flowerpot: *pot individual cuttings as soon as you see new young leaves.* **2** *chiefly Brit.* preserve (food, esp. meat or fish) in a sealed pot or jar: *venison can be potted in the same way as tongue.* **3** *Brit., Billiards* another term for POCKET. **4** *informal* hit or kill (someone or something) by shooting: *he was shot in the eye as neighbors potted clay pigeons.* ▷late Old English *pott,* probably reinforced in Middle English by Old French *pot;* of unknown ultimate origin (compare with late Latin *potus* 'drinking cup'). Current senses of the verb date from the early 17th cent. —**pot·ful** /-ˌfo͝ol/ *n.* (*pl.* **-fuls**).
▸*PHRASES* □ **for the pot** for food or cooking: *at the age of fifteen weeks, the snails are ready for the pot.* □ **go to pot** *informal* deteriorate through neglect: *the foundry was allowed to go to pot in the seventies.* □ **the pot calling the kettle black** used to convey that the criticisms a person is aiming at someone else could equally well apply to themselves. □ **pot of gold** see GOLD. □ **shit** (or **piss**) **or get off the pot** *vulgar slang* used to convey that someone should stop wasting time and get on with something.

pot[2] ▸*n. informal* cannabis. ▷1930s: probably from Mexican Spanish *potiguaya* 'cannabis leaves.'

pot. ▸*abbr. Electrical* ■ potential. ■ potentiometer.

po·ta·ble /ˈpōtəbəl/ ▸*adj. formal* safe to drink; drinkable: *there is no supply of potable water available.* ▷late Middle English: from French *potable,* from late Latin *potabilis,* from Latin *potare* 'to drink.' —**po·ta·bil·i·ty** /ˌpōtəˈbilətē/ *n.*

po·tage /pôˈtäzH/ ▸*n.* thick soup. ▷mid 16th cent.: from French. Compare with POTTAGE.

pot·a·mol·o·gy /ˌpätəˈmäləjē/ ▸*n. Geography* the study of rivers. ▷early 19th cent.: from Greek *potamos* 'river' + -LOGY.

pot·ash /ˈpätˌasH/ ▸*n.* an alkaline potassium compound, esp. potassium carbonate or hydroxide. ▷early 17th cent.: from *pot-ashes,* from obsolete Dutch *potasschen,* originally obtained by leaching vegetable ashes and evaporating the solution in iron pots.

pot·ash al·um ▸*n.* see ALUM.

po·tas·si·um /pəˈtasēəm/ ▸*n.* the chemical element of atomic number 19, a soft, silvery-white reactive metal of the alkali metal group. (Symbol: **K**) ▷early 19th cent.: Latinization of POTASH or earlier *potass* (from French *potasse*) by Sir Humphry Lowry, who first separated the element from potash. —**po·tas·sic** /-ˈtasik/ *adj.* (*Mineralogy*).

po·tas·si·um–ar·gon dat·ing ▸*n. Geology* a method of dating rocks from the relative proportions of radioactive potassium-40 and its decay product, argon-40.

po·tas·si·um hy·drox·ide ▸*n.* a strongly alkaline white deliquescent compound used in many industrial processes, e.g., soap manufacture. • Chem. formula: KOH.

po·tas·si·um ni·trate ▸*n.* a white crystalline salt, occurring naturally and produced synthetically, used in fertilizer, as a meat preservative, and as a constituent of gunpowder. Also called SALTPETER and NITER. • Chem. formula: KNO_3.

po·ta·tion /pōˈtāsHən/ ▸*n. archaic* or *humorous* a drink. ■ the action of drinking something, esp. alcohol: *I intend to abstain from potation.* ■ (often **potations**) a drinking bout: *the dreadful potations of his youth.* ▷late Middle English: from Old French, from Latin *potatio(n-),* from *potare* 'to drink.'

po·ta·to /pəˈtātō/ ▸*n.* (*pl.* **-toes**) **1** a starchy plant tuber that is one of the most important food crops, cooked and eaten as a vegetable: *roasted potatoes* | *the meal comes with rice or potato* | [as *adj.*] *leek and potato soup.* ■ see SWEET POTATO. **2** the plant of the nightshade family that produces these tubers on underground runners. • *Solanum tuberosum,* family Solanaceae. It was first cultivated in the Andes about 1,800 years ago and was introduced to Europe in *c.*1570. ▷mid 16th cent.: from Spanish *patata,* variant of Taino *batata* 'sweet potato.' The English word originally denoted the sweet potato and gained its current sense in the late 16th cent.

po·ta·to blight ▸*n.* a destructive fungal disease of potatoes resulting in dry brown rot of the tubers. • **Early blight** is caused by *Alternaria solani* (subdivision Deuteromycotina), and **late blight** is caused by *Phytophthora infestans* (subdivision Mastigomycotina).

po·ta·to chip ▸*n.* a wafer-thin slice of potato fried or baked until crisp and eaten as a snack.

po·ta·to pan·cake ▸*n.* a small flat cake of grated potatoes mixed with flour and egg and fried.

po·ta·to sal·ad ▸*n.* a side dish consisting of cold cooked potato chopped and mixed with a dressing and seasonings.

po·ta·to skin ▸*n.* a strip of deep-fried potato skin, served as an appetizer.

po·ta·to vine ▸*n.* a semievergreen climbing plant with pale blue or white flowers, related to the potato and native to South and Central America. • *Solanum jasminoides,* family Solanaceae.

pot-au-feu /ˌpôt ō ˈfœ/ ▸*n.* a French soup of meat, typically boiled beef, and vegetables cooked in a large pot. ▷French, literally 'pot on the fire.'

Pot·a·wat·o·mi /ˌpätəˈwätəmē/ ▸*n.* (*pl.* same or **-mis**) **1** a member of an American Indian people living originally around Lake Michigan. **2** the Algonquian language of this people.
▸*adj.* of or relating to this people or their language. ▷the name in Ojibwa.

pot·bel·lied pig (in full **Vietnamese potbellied pig**) ▸*n.* a pig of a small, dark breed with short legs and a large stomach, sometimes kept as a pet.

pot·bel·ly /ˈpätˌbelē/ (also **pot bel·ly**) ▸*n.* a large, protruding, rotund stomach. —**pot·bel·lied** *adj.*

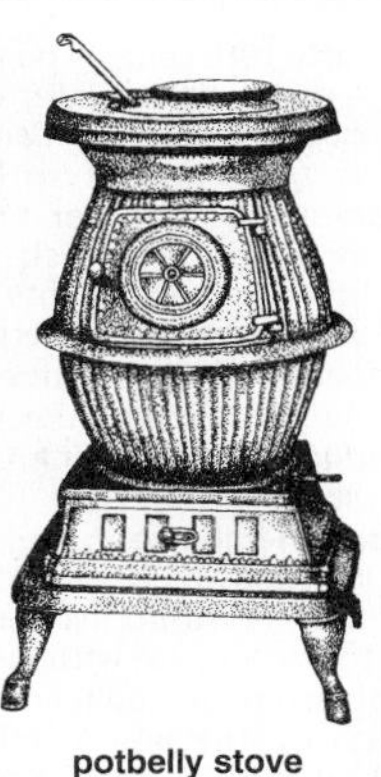
potbelly stove

pot·bel·ly stove (also **pot·bel·lied stove**) ▸*n.* a small, bulbous-sided wood-burning stove.

pot·boil·er ▸*n. informal* a book, painting, or recording produced merely to make the writer or artist a living by catering to popular taste.

pot-bound /pät bound/ ▸*adj.* (of a plant) having roots that fill the flowerpot, leaving no room for them to expand.

pot cheese ▸*n.* a coarse type of cottage cheese.

po·teen /pəˈtēn; -ˈcHēn/ (also **po·theen**) ▸*n. chiefly Irish* alcohol made illicitly, typically from potatoes. ▷early 19th cent.: from Irish *(fuisce) poitín* 'little pot (of whiskey),' diminutive of *pota* 'pot.'

Po·tem·kin[1] /pəˈtem(p)kin/ a battleship whose crew mutinied during the Russian Revolution of 1905 when in the Black Sea, bombarding Odessa before seeking asylum in Romania. The incident persuaded the tsar to agree to a measure of reform.

Po·tem·kin[2] ▸*adj. informal* having a false or deceptive appearance, esp. one presented for the purpose of propaganda: *it proved her to be a Potemkin feminist.* ▷1930s: from Grigori Aleksandrovich *Potyomkin* (often transliterated *Potemkin*), a favorite of Empress Catherine II of Russia, who reputedly gave the order for sham villages to be built for the empress's tour of the Crimea in 1787.

po·ten·cy /ˈpōtnsē/ ▸*n.* (*pl.* **-cies**) **1** power or influence: *a myth of enormous potency.* ■ the strength of an intoxicant, as measured by the amount needed to produce a certain response: *the unexpected potency of the rum punch.* ■ (in homeopathy) the number of times a remedy has been diluted and succussed, taken as a measure of the strength of the effect it will produce: *she was given a low potency twice daily.* ■ *Genetics* the extent of the contribution of an allele toward the production of a phenotypic characteristic. ■ *Biology* a capacity in embryonic tissue for developing into a particular specialized tissue or organ. **2** a male's ability to achieve an erection or to reach orgasm: *medications that diminish sexual potency.*

po·tent[1] /ˈpōtnt/ ▸*adj.* **1** having great power, influence, or effect: *thrones were potent symbols of authority* | *a potent drug* | *a potent argument.* **2** (of a male) able to achieve an erection or to reach an orgasm. ▷late Middle English: from Latin *potent-* 'being powerful, being able,' from the verb *posse.* —**po·tence** *n.* —**po·tent·ly** *adv.*

po·tent[2] *Heraldry* ▸*adj.* [*postpositive*] **1** formed of crutch-shaped pieces; (esp. of a cross) having a straight bar across the end of each extremity: *a cross potent.* **2** of the fur called potent (as a tincture).
▸*n.* fur resembling vair, but with the alternating pieces T-shaped. ▷late Middle English (denoting a crutch): alteration of Old French *potence* 'crutch,' from Latin *potentia* 'power' (in medieval Latin 'crutch'), from *potent-* (see POTENT[1]).

po·ten·tate /ˈpōtnˌtāt/ ▸*n.* a monarch or ruler, esp. an autocratic one. ▷late Middle English: from Latin *potentatus* 'dominion,' from *potent-* 'being able or powerful' (see POTENT[1]).

po·ten·tial /pəˈtencHəl/ ▸*adj.* [*attrib.*] having or showing the capacity to become or develop into something in the future: *a two-pronged campaign to woo potential customers.* See note at LATENT.
▸*n.* **1** latent qualities or abilities that may be developed and lead to future success or usefulness: *a young broadcaster with great potential* | *the potentials of the technology were never wholly controllable.* ■ (often **potential for/to do something**) the possibility of something happening or of someone doing something in the future: *the crane operator's clear view reduces the potential for accidents* | *pesticides with the potential to cause cancer.* **2** *Physics* the quantity determining the energy of mass in a gravitational field or of charge in an electric field. ▷late Middle English: from late Latin *potentialis,* from *potentia* 'power,' from *potent-* 'being able' (see POTENT[1]). The noun dates from the

Pronunciation Key ə *ago;* ər *over;* ˈə or ˌə *up;* ˈər or ˌər *fur;* a *hat;* ā *rate;* ä *car;* CH *chew;* e *let;* ē *see;* e(ə)r *air;* i *fit;* ī *by;* i(ə)r *ear;* NG *sing;* ō *go;* ô *for;* oi *boy;* o͝o *good;* o͞o *goo;* ou *out;* SH *she;* TH *thin;* T͟H *then;* (h)w *why;* ZH *vision*

early 19th cent. **—po·ten·ti·al·i·ty** /pə,tenchē'alətē/ *n.* **—po·ten·tial·ize** /-,līz/ *v.* **—po·ten·tial·ly** *adv.* [as *submodifier*] *potentially dangerous products* | [*sentence adverb*] *potentially an even bigger bombshell is about to burst.*

po·ten·tial bar·ri·er ▸*n. Physics* a region within a force field in which the potential is significantly higher than at points on either side of it, so that a particle requires energy to pass through it.

po·ten·tial dif·fer·ence ▸*n. Physics* the difference of electrical potential between two points.

po·ten·tial di·vid·er ▸*n.* another term for **VOLTAGE DIVIDER.**

po·ten·tial en·er·gy ▸*n. Physics* the energy possessed by a body by virtue of its position relative to others, stresses within itself, electric charge, and other factors. Compare with **KINETIC ENERGY.**

P

po·ten·ti·ate /pə'tenchē,āt/ ▸*v.* [*trans.*] *technical* increase the power, effect, or likelihood of (something, esp. a drug or physiological reaction): *the glucose will potentiate intestinal absorption of sodium.* ▷early 19th cent.: from **POTENT**[1], on the pattern of *substantiate.*

po·ten·ti·a·tion /pə,tenchē'āshən/ ▸*n. Physiology* the increase in strength of nerve impulses along pathways that have been used previously, either short-term or long-term.

po·ten·til·la /,pōtn'tilə/ ▸*n.* a plant of a genus that includes the cinquefoils, esp. (in gardening) a small shrub with bright yellow, red, orange, or pink flowers. • Genus *Potentilla,* family Rosaceae: many species. ▷modern Latin, based on Latin *potent-* 'being powerful' (with reference to its herbal qualities) + the diminutive suffix *-illa.*

po·ten·ti·om·e·ter /pə,tenchē'ämətər/ ▸*n.* **1** an instrument for measuring an electromotive force by balancing it against the potential difference produced by passing a known current through a known variable resistance. **2** a variable resistor with a third adjustable terminal. The potential at the third terminal can be adjusted to give any fraction of the potential across the ends of the resistor.

po·ten·ti·om·e·try /pə,tenchē'ämətrē/ ▸*n. Chemistry* the measurement of electrical potential as a technique in chemical analysis. **—po·ten·ti·o·met·ric** /pə,tenchēə'metrik/ *adj.*

pot·head /'pät,hed/ ▸*n. informal* a person who smokes marijuana, esp. habitually.

po·theen ▸*n. chiefly Irish* variant spelling of **POTEEN.**

poth·er /'pä*th*ər/ ▸*n.* [in *sing.*] *poetic/literary* a commotion or fuss: *don't make such a pother!* ▷late 16th cent.: of unknown origin.

pot·herb /'pät,(h)ərb/ ▸*n.* any herb grown for culinary use.

pot·hold·er /'pät,hōldər/ ▸*n.* a piece of quilted or thick fabric for handling hot dishes and pans.

pot·hole /'pät,hōl/ ▸*n.* a deep natural underground cavity formed by the erosion of rock, esp. by the action of water. ■ a deep circular hole in a riverbed formed by the erosion of the rock by the rotation of stones in an eddy. ■ a depression or hollow in a road surface caused by wear or subsidence. ■ (also **pothole lake**) a pond in a natural hollow in the ground. ▷early 19th cent.: from Middle English *pot* 'pit' (perhaps of Scandinavian origin) + **HOLE.** **—pot·holed** *adj.*

pot·hol·ing /'pät,hōliNG/ ▸*n. Brit.* the exploring of natural potholes as a pasttime.

pot·hook /'pät,ho͝ok/ ▸*n.* **1** *chiefly historical* a hook used for hanging a pot over a hearth or for lifting a hot pot. **2** *dated* a curved stroke in handwriting, esp. as made by children learning to write.

pot·house /'pät,hous/ ▸*n. dated* a small tavern.

pot·hunt·er /'pät,həntər/ ▸*n.* **1** *chiefly archaic* a person who hunts solely to achieve a kill, rather than as a sport. ■ a person who takes part in a contest merely for the sake of the prize. **2** an amateur archaeologist.

po·tion /'pōshən/ ▸*n.* a liquid with healing, magical, or poisonous properties: *a love potion.* ▷Middle English: from Old French, from Latin *potio(n-)* '(poisonous) drink,' related to *potare* 'to drink.'

Pot·i·phar /'pätifər/ (in the Bible) an Egyptian officer whose wife tried to seduce Joseph and then falsely accused him of attempting to rape her (Gen. 39).

pot·latch /'pät,lach/ ▸*n.* (among North American Indian peoples of the northwest coast) an opulent ceremonial feast at which possessions are given away or destroyed to display wealth or enhance prestige.
▸*v.* [*intrans.*] hold such a feast or ceremony. ▷Chinook Jargon *páłač, pátłač,* probably from Nootka.

pot lik·ker ▸*n. informal* nonstandard spelling of **POT LIQUOR,** used in the southern U.S.

pot liq·uor ▸*n.* liquid in which meat, fish, or vegetables have been boiled; stock.

pot·luck /'pät'lək/ ▸*n.* used in reference to a situation in which one must take a chance that whatever is available will prove to be good or acceptable: *he could* **take potluck** *in a town not noted for its hotels.* ■ a meal or party to which each of the guests contributes a dish: [as *adj.*] *a potluck supper.*

Po·tok /'pōtäk/, Chaim (1929–2002), U.S. writer and theologian. A rabbi, his novels include *The Chosen* (1967), *The Book of Lights* (1981), and *I Am the Clay* (1991). He also wrote nonfiction and plays.

Po·to·mac /pə'tōmək/ a river of the eastern U.S. that rises in the Appalachian Mountains in West Virginia and flows about 285 miles (459 km) through Washington, D.C., into Chesapeake Bay.

po·too /pə'to͞o/ ▸*n.* a nocturnal, insectivorous bird resembling a large nightjar. Found in tropical America, it mimics a dead branch when alarmed. • Genus *Nyctibius* and family Nyctibiidae: five species, in particular the **common potoo** (*N. griseus*). ▷mid 19th cent.: from Jamaican Creole, from Twi, of imitative origin.

po·to·roo /,pätə'ro͞o/ ▸*n.* a small, nocturnal rat kangaroo with long hind limbs and typically a hopping gait, native to Australia and Tasmania. • Genus *Potorous,* family Potoroidae: three species. ▷late 18th cent.: probably from Dharuk *badaru.*

Po·to·sí /,pôtô'sē/ a city in southern Bolivia; pop. 112,000. At an altitude of about 13,758 feet (4,205 m), it is one of the highest cities in the world.

pot pie ▸*n.* **1** a meat and vegetable pie baked in a deep dish, often with a top crust only. **2** a stew with dumplings.

pot·pour·ri /,pōpə'rē; pōpo͞o'rē/ ▸*n.* (*pl.* **-ris**) a mixture of dried petals and spices placed in a bowl or small sack to perfume clothing or a room. ■ a mixture of things, esp. a musical or literary medley: *he played* **a potpourri of** *tunes from Gilbert and Sullivan.* ▷early 17th cent. (denoting a stew made of different kinds of meat): from French, literally 'rotten pot.'

po·tre·ro /pə'tre(ə)rō/ ▸*n.* (*pl.* **-ros**) (in the southwestern U.S. and South America) a paddock or pasture for horses or cattle. ▷mid 19th cent.: from Spanish, from *potro* 'colt, pony.'

pot roast ▸*n.* a piece of meat cooked slowly in a covered dish.
▸*v.* (**pot-roast**) [*trans.*] cook (a piece of meat) slowly in a covered dish.

Pots·dam /'päts,dam/ a city in eastern Germany, the capital of Brandenburg state, southwest of Berlin, on the Havel River; pop. 95,000.

Pots·dam Con·fer·ence a meeting held in Potsdam in the summer of 1945 among U.S., Soviet, and British leaders that established principles for the Allied occupation of Germany following the end of World War II.

pot·sherd /'pät,shərd/ ▸*n.* a broken piece of ceramic material, esp. one found on an archaeological site.

pot·shot /'pät,shät/ ▸*n.* a shot aimed unexpectedly or at random at someone or something with no chance of self-defense: *a sniper took a potshot at him.* ■ *figurative* a criticism, esp. a random or unfounded one: *the show takes wickedly funny potshots at movies.* ■ a shot at a game bird or other animal purely to kill it for food, without regard to the rules of the sport. ▷mid 19th cent.: originally a *shot* at an animal intended for the *pot,* i.e., for food, rather than for display (which would require skilled shooting).

pot·still /'pät,stil/ ▸*n.* a still to which heat is applied directly and not by means of a steam jacket.

pot·tage /'pätij/ ▸*n. archaic* soup or stew. ▷Middle English (as *potage*): from Old French *potage* 'that which is put into a pot.' Compare with **POTAGE** and **PORRIDGE.**
▸*PHRASE* □ **sell something for a mess of pottage** sell something for a ridiculously small amount. [with biblical allusion to the story of Esau, who sold his birthright for some bread and pottage of lentils (Gen. 25:31).]

pot·ted /'pätid/ ▸*adj.* **1** (of a plant) planted or grown in a flowerpot and usually kept indoors: *an array of exotic potted palms.* ■ *chiefly Brit.* (of food, esp. meat or fish) preserved in a sealed pot or jar: *potted smoked trout.* ■ *chiefly Brit.* (of a literary work or descriptive account) put into a short and easily assimilable form: *a potted history of the band's career.* **2** [*predic.*] *informal* intoxicated by drink or drugs, esp. marijuana: *a party where everybody was pretty much potted.*

Pot·ter /'pätər/, (Helen) Beatrix (1866–1943), English writer for children. She is known for her series of animal stories, illustrated with her own delicate watercolors, which began with *The Tale of Peter Rabbit* (first published privately in 1900).

pot·ter[1] /'pätər/ ▸*v.* British term for **PUTTER**[3]. ▷late 19th cent.: alteration.

pot·ter[2] ▸*n.* a person who makes pottery. ▷late Old English *pottere* (see **POT**[1], **-ER**[1]).

pot·ter's field ▸*n. historical* a burial place for paupers and strangers. ▷with biblical allusion to Matt. 27:7.

pot·ter's wheel ▸*n.* a horizontal revolving disk on which wet clay is shaped into pots or other round ceramic objects.

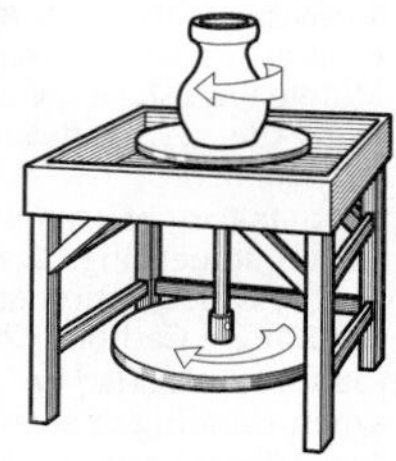

potter's wheel

pot·ter wasp ▸*n.* a solitary wasp that builds a flask-shaped nest of mud into which it seals an egg and a supply of food for the larva. • Genus *Eumenes,* family Eumenidae: many species.

pot·ter·y /'pätərē/ ▸*n.* (*pl.* **-er·ies**) pots, dishes, and other articles made of earthenware or baked clay. Pottery can be broadly divided into earthenware, porcelain, and stoneware. ■ the craft or profession of making such ware: *courses include drawing, painting, and pottery.* ■ a factory or workshop where such ware is made. ▷Middle English: from Old French *poterie,* from *potier* 'a potter.'

pot·ting shed ▸*n.* a shed that is used for potting plants and in which plants and garden tools and supplies are stored.

pot·ting soil ▸*n.* a mixture of loam, peat, sand, and nutrients, used as a growing medium for plants in containers.

pot·tle /'pätl/ ▸*n. archaic* a measure for liquids equal to a half gallon. ■ a pot or container holding this. ▷Middle English: from Old French *potel* 'little pot,' diminutive of *pot.*

pot·to /'pätō/ (also **pot·to gib·bon**) ▸*n.* (*pl.* **-tos**) a small, slow-moving, nocturnal primate with a short tail, living in dense vegetation in the tropical forests of Africa. • *Perodicticus potto,* family Lorisidae, suborder Prosimii. ▷early 18th cent.: perhaps from Guinea dialect.

Potts·town /'päts,toun/ an industrial borough in southeastern Pennsylvania, on the Schuylkill River, northwest of Philadelphia; pop. 21,381.

pot·ty[1] /'pätē/ ▸*n.* (*pl.* **-ties**) *informal* a bowl used by small children as a toilet. ■ *informal* a toilet.

pot·ty[2] ▸*adj.* (**pot·ti·er, pot·ti·est**) *informal, chiefly Brit.* **1** foolish; crazy: *he felt she really had* **gone potty.** ■ [*predic.*] extremely enthusiastic about or fond of someone or something: *I'm* **potty about** *my two sons.* **2** [*attrib.*] insignificant or feeble: *that* **potty little** *mower.* ▷mid 19th cent.: of unknown origin. **—pot·ti·ness** *n.*

pot·ty-train ▸*v.* [*trans.*] train (a small child) to use a potty.

POTUS /'pōtəs/ ▸*abbr.* President of the United States.

pot-val·iant ▸*adj. archaic* (of a person) courageous as a result of being drunk. **—pot-val·or** *n.*

pouch /pouch/ ▸*n.* **1** a small bag or other flexible receptacle, typically carried in a pocket or attached to a belt: *a tobacco pouch* | *webbing with pouches for stun grenades.* ■ a lockable bag for mail or dispatches. **2** a pocketlike abdominal receptacle in which marsupials carry their young during lactation. ■ any of a number of similar animal structures, such as those in the cheeks of rodents.
▸*v.* [*trans.*] **1** put into a pouch: *he stopped, pouched his tickets, and plodded on.* **2** make (part of a garment) hang like a pouch: *the muslin is lightly pouched over the belt.* ▷Middle English (as a noun): from Old Northern French *pouche,* variant of Old French *poche* 'bag.' Compare with **POKE**[2]. **—pouched** *adj.* **—pouch·y** *adj.*

pou·chong /'po͞o'chông; -'chäng/ ▸*n.* a kind of China tea made by fermenting the withered leaves only briefly, typically scented with rose petals. ▷Chinese.

pouf[1] /po͞of/ ▸*n.* variant spelling of **POOF**[2], **POUFFE.**
▸*exclam.* variant spelling of **POOF**[1].

pouf[2] ▸*n.* a dress or part of a dress in which a large mass of material has been gathered so that it stands away from the body: [as *adj.*] *a dress with a pouf skirt.* ■ a bouffant hairstyle: *he grew his hair out in a sort of pouf.* ▷early 19th cent. (denoting an elaborate female headdress fashionable at the time): from French, of imitative origin.

pouffe /po͞of/ (also **pouf**) ▸*n.* a cushioned footstool or low seat with no back. ▷late 19th cent.: from French *pouf*, of imitative origin.

Pough·keep·sie /pə'kipsē/ an industrial city in southeastern New York, on the Hudson River, home of Vassar College; pop. 28,844.

pou·i /'po͞oē/ ▸*n.* (*pl.* same or **pou·is**) a Caribbean and tropical American tree with trumpet-shaped flowers, grown as an ornamental and valued for its timber. • Genus *Tabebuia*, family Bignoniaceae. ▷mid 19th cent.: a local word in Trinidad.

Pouil·ly-Fuis·sé /po͞o,yē fwē'sā/ ▸*n.* a dry white Chardonnay wine from Burgundy.

Pou·lenc /po͞o'leNGk/, Francis (Jean Marcel) (1899–1963), French composer. A member of Les Six, his work is characterized by lyricism as well as by the use of idioms of popular music such as jazz.

poult[1] /pōlt/ ▸*n. Farming* a young domestic chicken, turkey, pheasant, or other fowl being raised for food. ▷late Middle English: contraction of PULLET.

poult[2] /po͞o(lt)/ (also **poult-de-soie** /də 'swä/) ▸*n.* a fine corded silk or taffeta, typically colored and used as a dress fabric. ▷1930s: from French *poult-de-soie*, from *poult* (of unknown origin) + *de soie* 'of silk.'

poul·ter·er /'pōltərər/ ▸*n.* a dealer in poultry and, typically, game. ▷late 16th cent.: from archaic *poulter*, in the same sense, from Old French *pouletier*.

poul·tice /'pōltəs/ ▸*n.* a soft, moist mass of material, typically of plant material or flour, applied to the body to relieve soreness and inflammation and kept in place with a cloth.
▸*v.* [*trans.*] apply a poultice to: *he poulticed the wound.* ▷late Middle English: from Latin *pultes* (plural), from *puls, pult-* 'porridge, pap.'

poul·try /'pōltrē/ ▸*n.* domestic fowl, such as chickens, turkeys, ducks, and geese. ▷Middle English: from Old French *pouletrie*, from *poulet* 'pullet.'

pounce[1] /pouns/ ▸*v.* [*intrans.*] (of an animal or bird of prey) spring or swoop suddenly so as to catch prey: *the wolf* ***pounced on*** *the rat | she looked like a vulture waiting to pounce.* ■ (of a person) spring forward suddenly so as to attack or seize someone or something: *the gang* ***pounced on*** *him and knocked him to the ground.* ■ *figurative* take sudden decisive action so as to grasp an opportunity: *seven insiders pounced, buying 21,900 shares.* ■ *figurative* notice and take swift and eager advantage of a mistake, remark, or sign of weakness: *reporters who are just as eager to* ***pounce on*** *a gaffe as on a significant news story.*
▸*n.* a sudden swoop or spring. ▷late Middle English (as a noun denoting a tool for stamping or punching): origin obscure, perhaps from PUNCHEON[1]. A noun sense 'claw, talon' arose in the late 15th cent., which gave rise to the verb (late 17th cent.). **—pounc·er** *n.*

pounce[2] ▸*n.* a fine resinous powder formerly used to prevent ink from spreading on unglazed paper or to prepare parchment to receive writing. ■ powdered charcoal or other fine powder dusted over a perforated pattern to transfer the design to the object beneath.
▸*v.* [*trans.*] **1** smooth down by rubbing with pounce or pumice. **2** transfer (a design) by the use of pounce. ▷late 16th cent. (as a verb): from French *poncer*, based on Latin *pumex* 'pumice.' **—pounc·er** *n.*

poun·cet box /'pounsət/ ▸*n. archaic* a small box with a perforated lid used for holding perfume. ▷late 16th cent.: perhaps originally erroneously from *pounced* (= perforated) *box*.

Pound /pound/, Ezra (Weston Loomis) (1885–1972), U.S. poet and critic, resident in Europe 1908–45. Initially associated with imagism, he later developed a highly eclectic poetic voice, establishing a reputation as a modernist poet. Notable works: *Hugh Selwyn Mauberley* (1920) and *Cantos* (series, 1917–70).

pound[1] /pound/ ▸*n.* **1** (abbr.: **lb**) a unit of weight in general use equal to 16 oz. avoirdupois (0.4536 kg). ■ a unit of weight equal to 12 oz. troy (0.3732 kg) used for precious metals. **2** (also **pound ster·ling** (*pl.* **pounds ster·ling**)) the basic monetary unit of the UK, equal to 100 pence. ■ another term for PUNT[4]. ■ the basic monetary unit of several Middle Eastern countries, equal to 100 piastres. ■ the basic monetary unit of Cyprus, equal to 100 cents. ■ a monetary unit of the Sudan, equal to one tenth of a dinar. ▷Old English *pund*, of Germanic origin; related to Dutch *pond* and German *Pfund*, from Latin *(libra) pondo*, denoting a Roman '(pound) weight' of 12 ounces.
▸*PHRASE* □ **one's pound of flesh** something that one is strictly or legally entitled to, but that it is ruthless or inhuman to demand. [with allusion to Shakespeare's *Merchant of Venice*.]

pound[2] ▸*v.* [*trans.*] strike or hit heavily and repeatedly: *Patrick pounded the couch with his fists | U.S. gunships pounded the capital |* [*intrans.*] *pounding on the door, she shouted at the top of her voice.* ■ crush or grind (something) into a powder or paste by beating it with an instrument such as a pestle: *pound the cloves with salt and pepper until smooth.* ■ [*intrans.*] beat, throb, or vibrate with a strong regular rhythm: *her heart was pounding.* ■ [*intrans.*] walk or run with heavy steps: *I heard him pounding along the gangway.* ■ *informal* defeat (an opponent) in a resounding way: [*trans.*] *the Yankees pounded the Red Sox 22–1.*
▸*phrasal v.* □ **pound something out** type something with heavy keystrokes: *an old typewriter on which she pounded out her poems.* ■ produce music by striking an instrument heavily and repeatedly: *the women pounded out a ringing tattoo on several oil drums.* ▷Old English *pūnian*; related to Dutch *puin*, Low German *pün* 'rubble.'
▸*PHRASES* □ **pound the beat** (of a police officer) patrol an assigned route or area. □ **pound the pavement** walk the streets in an effort to accomplish something: *I will pound the pavement from city to city in order to explain the dangers.* ■ search diligently for something, typically for a job: *although the country's current jobless rate is small, the number of people pounding the pavement has become a growing worry.*

pound[3] ▸*n.* a place where stray animals, esp. dogs, may be officially taken and kept until claimed by their owners or otherwise disposed of. ■ a place where illegally parked motor vehicles removed by the police are kept until their owners pay a fine in order to reclaim them. ■ *archaic* a place of confinement; a trap or prison.
▸*v.* [*trans.*] *archaic* shut (an animal) in a pound. ▷late Middle English (earlier in compounds): of uncertain origin. Early use referred to an enclosure for the detention of stray or trespassing cattle.

pound·age /'poundij/ ▸*n.* **1** weight, esp. when regarded as excessive: *reduce excess poundage without risking overexertion.* **2** *Brit.* a payment of a particular amount per pound sterling of the sum involved in a transaction. ■ a percentage of the total earnings of a business, paid as wages.

pound·al /'poundəl/ ▸*n. Physics* a unit of force equal to that required to give a mass of one pound an acceleration of one foot per second per second. ▷late 19th cent.: from POUND[1] + the suffix *-al*, perhaps suggested by QUINTAL.

pound cake ▸*n.* a rich cake containing a pound, or equal weights, of each chief ingredient, typically flour, butter, and sugar.

pound coin ▸*n.* a coin worth one British pound sterling.

pound·er /'poundər/ ▸*n.* [usu. in *combination*] **1** a person or thing weighing a specified number of pounds: *Sloan set a blue-shark record with a 184-pounder.* ■ a gun designed to fire a shell weighing a specified number of pounds. **2** a person or thing that pounds something: *he's direct, but not abrasive, not a deskpounder.*

pound·ing /'pounding/ ▸*n.* repeated and heavy striking or hitting of someone or something: *the pounding of the surf on a sandy beach | figurative technology stocks* ***took a pounding*** *in last week's sharp correction.* ■ *informal* a resounding defeat: *the Bulls raised their home record with a 100-86 pounding of the Houston Rockets.*

pound note ▸*n.* a banknote worth one British pound sterling, now replaced by the pound coin in England and Wales.

pound sign ▸*n.* **1** the sign (#), representing a pound as a unit of weight or mass. ■ used to refer to this sign, esp. as represented on a telephone keypad or a computer keyboard. **2** the sign (£), representing a British pound sterling.

pound ster·ling ▸*n.* see POUND[1] (sense 2).

pour /pôr/ ▸*v.* [*intrans.*] (esp. of a liquid) flow rapidly in a steady stream: *water poured off the roof | figurative words poured from his mouth.* ■ [*trans.*] cause (a liquid) to flow from a container in a steady stream by holding the container at an angle: *she poured a little whiskey into a glass.* ■ [*trans.*] serve (a drink) in this way: *she* ***poured out*** *a cup of tea |* [with *two objs.*] *Harry poured her a drink.* ■ [*intrans.*] (of rain) fall heavily: *the storm clouds gathered and the rain* ***poured down*** [*trans.*] *it's pouring rain.* ■ (of people or things) come or go in a steady stream and in large numbers: *letters poured in.* ■ [*trans.*] (**pour something into**) donate something, esp. money, to (a particular enterprise or project) in large amounts: *Belgium has been pouring money into the company.* ■ [*trans.*] (**pour something out**) express one's feelings or thoughts in a full and unrestrained way: *in his letters, Edward poured out his hopes.* ■ (**pour oneself into**) *humorous* dress oneself in (a tight-fitting piece of clothing): *I poured myself into a short Lycra skirt.* ▷Middle English: of unknown origin. **—pour·a·ble** *adj.* **—pour·er** *n.*
▸*PHRASES* □ **when it rains it pours** *proverb* misfortunes or difficult situations tend to follow each other in rapid succession or to arrive all at the same time. □ **pour cold water on** see COLD. □ **pour it on** *informal* progress or work quickly or with all one's energy. □ **pour oil on troubled waters** try to settle a disagreement or dispute with words intended to placate or pacify those involved. □ **pour scorn on** see SCORN.

pour·boire /po͝or'bwär/ ▸*n.* a gratuity; a tip. ▷French, from *pour boire*, literally '(money) for drinking.'

pousse-ca·fé /,po͞os ka'fā/ ▸*n.* (*pl. pronunc.* same) a glass of various liqueurs or cordials poured in successive layers, drunk immediately after coffee. ▷from French, literally 'pushes (the) coffee.'

Pous·sin /po͞o'sen; -'saN/, Nicolas (1594–1665), French painter. Regarded as the chief representative of French classicism and a master of the grand manner, his subject matter included biblical scenes, classical mythology, and historical landscapes.

pous·sin /po͞o'saN/ ▸*n.* a chicken killed young for eating. ▷French.

pout[1] /pout/ ▸*v.* [*intrans.*] push one's lips or one's bottom lip forward as an expression of petulant annoyance or in order to make oneself look sexually attractive: *she lounged on the steps, pouting |* [*trans.*] *he shrugged and pouted his lips.* ■ (of a person's lips) be pushed forward in such a way: *her lips pouted provocatively.*
▸*n.* a pouting expression: *his lower lip protruded in a sulky pout.* ▷Middle English (as a verb): perhaps from the base of Swedish dialect *puta* 'be inflated.' Compare with POUT[2]. **—pout·ing·ly** *adv.* **—pout·y** *adj.*

pout[2] ▸*n.* another term for EELPOUT. ▷Old English *pūta* (only in *ǣlepūta* 'eelpout'); related to Dutch *puit* 'frog, chub,' *puitaal* 'eelpout,' and perhaps to POUT[1].

pout·er /'poutər/ ▸*n.* a kind of pigeon able to inflate its crop considerably.

POV ▸*abbr.* point of view.

pov·er·ty /'pävərtē/ ▸*n.* the state of being extremely poor: *thousands of families are living in abject poverty.* ■ the state of being inferior in quality or insufficient in amount: *the poverty of her imagination.* ■ the renunciation of the right to individual ownership of property as part of a religious vow. ▷Middle English: from Old French *poverte*, from Latin *paupertas*, from *pauper* 'poor.'

pov·er·ty line ▸*n.* the estimated minimum level of income needed to secure the necessities of life.

pov·er·ty-strick·en ▸*adj.* extremely poor: *thousands of poverty-stricken people.*

po·vi·done-i·o·dine /'pōvə,dōn/ ▸*n. Medicine* a brown powder used as an antiseptic for external application, consisting of a complex of polyvinylpyrrolidone and iodine. ▷1950s: *povidone*, contraction of POLYVINYLPYRROLIDONE.

POW ▸*abbr.* prisoner of war.

pow /pou/ ▸*exclam.* expressing the sound of a blow or explosion: *Pow! Bombs went off on six beaches at once.* ▷late 19th cent. (originally U.S.): imitative.

pow·der /'poudər/ ▸*n.* fine dry particles produced by the grinding, crushing, or disintegration of a solid substance: *when the powder is mixed with water, it becomes a creamy white paste | cocoa powder |* [in *sing.*] *crush the poppy seeds to a powder.* ■ (also **face powder**) a cosmetic in this form designed to be applied to a person's face with a brush or soft pad. ■ *dated* a medicine or drug in this form, usually designed to be dissolved in a liquid. ■ (also **powder snow**) light, dry, newly fallen snow: [as *adj.*] *powder skiing.* ■ short for GUNPOWDER (sense 1).
▸*v.* [*trans.*] **1** apply powder to (the face or body): *she powdered her face and put on a dab of perfume.* ■ sprinkle or cover (a surface) with powder or a powdery substance: *broken glass powdered the floor | figurative high cheekbones powdered with freckles.* **2** reduce (a substance) to a powder by drying or crushing it: *then the rose petals are dried and powdered |* [as *adj.*] (**powdered**)

powdered milk. ▷Middle English: from Old French *poudre*, from Latin *pulvis, pulver-* 'dust.'

▸*PHRASES* □ **keep one's powder dry** remain cautious and ready for a possible emergency. □ **take a powder** *informal* depart quickly, esp. in order to avoid a difficult situation.

pow·der blue ▸*n.* a soft, pale blue: [as *adj.*] *a powder-blue jumpsuit.*

pow·der-coat ▸*v.* [*trans.*] cover (an object) with a polyester or epoxy powder, which is then heated to fuse into a protective layer.

pow·dered sug·ar ▸*n.* another term for CONFECTIONERS' SUGAR.

pow·der flask ▸*n. historical* a small container with a nozzle for carrying and dispensing gunpowder.

pow·der horn ▸*n. historical* the horn of an ox, cow, or similar animal used to hold gunpowder, with the wide end filled in and a nozzle at the pointed end.

pow·der hound ▸*n. informal* a person who enjoys skiing on powder snow.

pow·der keg ▸*n.* a barrel of gunpowder. ■ *figurative* a dangerous or volatile situation: *the place had been a powder keg since the uprising.*

Pow·der·ly /ˈpoudərlē/, Terence Vincent (1849–1924), U.S. labor leader. Although he was the mayor of Scranton, Pennsylvania, 1878–84, he also headed the Knights of Labor 1879–93 and was largely responsible for the first Chinese Exclusion Act 1882 and the Contract Labor Act 1885.

pow·der met·al·lur·gy ▸*n.* the production and working of metals as fine powders that can be pressed and sintered to form objects.

pow·der mon·key ▸*n. historical* a boy employed on a sailing warship to carry powder to the guns. ■ *informal* a person who works with explosives.

pow·der-post bee·tle ▸*n.* a small brown beetle whose wood-boring larvae reduce wood to a very fine powder. • Family Lyctidae: several genera.

pow·der puff (also **pow·der·puff**) ▸*n.* a soft pad for applying powder to the skin, esp. the face.
▸*adj.* [*attrib.*] **1** (of sports) played by women or girls only: *a fifth grade powder-puff football game.* **2** *informal* (of a person or thing) ineffectual: *a powder-puff hitter.*

Pow·der Riv·er a river that flows for 485 miles (780 km) from northeastern Wyoming into southern Montana to join the Yellowstone River.

pow·der room ▸*n.* used euphemistically to refer to a women's toilet in a public building.

pow·der snow ▸*n.* see POWDER.

pow·der·y /ˈpoudərē/ ▸*adj.* consisting of or resembling powder: *powdery snow.* ■ covered with powder: *her pale powdery cheeks.*

pow·der·y mil·dew ▸*n.* mildew on a plant that is marked by a white floury covering consisting of conidia. Compare with DOWNY MILDEW. • Family Erysiphaceae, subdivision Ascomycotina.

Pow·ell[1] /ˈpouəl/, Adam Clayton, Jr. (1908–72), U.S. clergyman and politician. A Democrat, he was a member of the U.S. House of Representatives from New York 1945–67, 1969–71 and wrote over 60 pieces of social legislation.

Pow·ell[2], Anthony (Dymoke) (1905–2000), English novelist. He is best known for his sequence of 12 novels *A Dance to the Music of Time* (1951–75), a satire about the English upper middle classes between World War I and World War II.

Pow·ell[3], Colin (Luther) (1937–), U.S. army officer and statesman. Decorated for heroism in Vietnam, he later held a series of command posts and became a White House assistant for national security affairs 1987–89. The first black American to become chairman of the Joint Chiefs of Staff 1989–93, he was commander in chief of the 1990–91 U.S. military operations (Desert Shield and Desert Storm) against Iraq. He served as U.S. secretary of state during President George W. Bush's first term (2001–05).

Pow·ell[4], John Wesley (1834–1902), U.S. geologist and writer. He directed the U.S. Geological Survey 1881–94. He also directed the Smithsonian Institution's Bureau of American Ethnology 1897–1902. He wrote *Report on the Lands of the Arid Region of the United States* (1878).

Pow·ell[5], Lewis Franklin, Jr. (1907–98), U.S. Supreme Court associate justice 1972–87. Considered a moderate, he was appointed to the Court by President Nixon.

Pow·ell, Lake /ˈpouəl/ a reservoir on the Colorado River in southern Utah, formed since the 1960s by the Glen Canyon Dam. The lake inundated Glen Canyon.

pow·er /ˈpou(-ə)r/ ▸*n.* **1** the ability to do something or act in a particular way, esp. as a faculty or quality: *the power of speech* | [with *infinitive*] *the power to raise the dead* | (**powers**) *his powers of concentration.* **2** the capacity or ability to direct or influence the behavior of others or the course of events: *the idea that men should have power over women* | *she had me under her power.* ■ political or social authority or control, esp. that exercised by a government: *the party had been in power for eight years* | [as *adj.*] *a power struggle.* ■ a right or authority that is given or delegated to a person or body: *police do not have the power to stop and search* | *emergency powers.* See note at JURISDICTION. ■ the military strength of a state: *the sea power of Venice.* ■ a state or country, esp. one viewed in terms of its international influence and military strength: *a great colonial power.* ■ a person or organization that is strong or influential within a particular context: *he was a power in the university.* ■ a supernatural being, deity, or force: *the powers of darkness.* ■ (**powers**) (in traditional Christian angelology) the sixth highest order of the ninefold celestial hierarchy. ■ [as *adj.*] *informal* denoting something associated with people who hold authority and influence, esp. in the context of business or politics: *a red power tie.* ■ [with *adj.*] used in the names of movements aiming to enhance the status of a specified group: *gay power.* **3** physical strength and force exerted by something or someone: *the power of the storm.* ■ capacity or performance of an engine or other device: *he applied full power.* ■ the capacity of something to affect the emotions or intellect strongly: *the lyrical power of his prose.* ■ [as *adj.*] denoting a sports player, team, or style of play that makes use of power rather than finesse: *a power pitcher.* ■ the magnifying capacity of a lens. **4** energy that is produced by mechanical, electrical, or other means and used to operate a device: *generating power from waste* | [as *adj.*] *power cables.* ■ electrical energy supplied to an area, building, etc.: *the power went off.* ■ [as *adj.*] driven by such energy: *a power drill.* ■ [as *adj.*] power-assisted: *power brakes.* ■ *Physics* the time-rate of doing work, measured in watts or less frequently horsepower. **5** *Mathematics* the number of times a certain number is to be multiplied by itself: *2* ***to the power of*** *4 equals 16.*
▸*v.* **1** [*trans.*] supply (a device) with mechanical or electrical energy: *the car is powered by a fuel-injected 3.0-liter engine* | [as *adj.* in *combination*] (**-powered**) *a nuclear-powered submarine.* ■ (**power something up/down**) switch a device on or off: *the officer powered up the fighter's radar.* **2** [*intrans.*] move or travel with great speed or force: *they powered past the dock toward the mouth of the creek.* ■ [*trans.*] direct (something, esp. a ball) with great force: *Nicholas powered a header into the net.* ▷Middle English: from Anglo-Norman French *poeir*, from an alteration of Latin *posse* 'be able.'

▸*PHRASES* □ **do someone/something a power of good** *informal* be very beneficial to someone or something. □ **in the power of** under the control of: *a church ministering in the power of the Holy Spirit.* □ **power behind the throne** a person or organization that exerts authority or influence without having formal status. □ **the powers that be** the authorities. [with biblical allusion to Rom. 13:1.]

pow·er-as·sist·ed ▸*adj.* (esp. of steering or brakes in a motor vehicle) using an inanimate source of power to assist manual operation.

pow·er base ▸*n.* a source of authority, influence, or support, esp. in politics or negotiations: *the party's power base was confined to one province.*

pow·er·beads /ˈpou(-ə)rˌbēdz/ ▸*n.* a bracelet or necklace of round beads made of semiprecious stones that are purported to enhance the spiritual well-being of the wearer.

pow·er bloc (also **block**) ▸*n.* an association of groups, esp. nations, having a common interest and acting as a single political force.

pow·er·boat /ˈpou(-ə)rˌbōt/ ▸*n.* a motorboat designed for racing or recreation.

pow·er·bro·ker /ˈpou(-ə)rˌbrōkər/ (also **pow·er brok·er**) ▸*n.* a person who deliberately affects the distribution of political or economic power by exerting influence or by intrigue. —**pow·er·bro·ker·ing** (also **pow·er·brok·ing**) *n.* & *adj.*

pow·er dive ▸*n.* a steep dive of an aircraft with the engines providing thrust.
▸*v.* (**pow·er-dive**) [*intrans.*] perform a power dive.

pow·er fac·tor ▸*n.* the ratio of the actual electrical power dissipated by an AC circuit to the product of the r.m.s. values of current and voltage. The difference between the two is caused by reactance in the circuit and represents power that does no useful work.

pow·er for·ward ▸*n. Basketball* a large forward who plays in the low post and typically has good rebounding skills.

pow·er·ful /ˈpou(-ə)rfəl/ ▸*adj.* having great power or strength: *a fast, powerful car* | *computers are now more compact and powerful.* ■ (of a person, organization, or country) having control and influence over people and events: *the world's most powerful nation.* ■ having a strong effect on people's feelings or thoughts: *his photomontages are powerful antiwar images.*
▸*adv.* [as *submodifier*] *chiefly dialect* very: *walking in this weather is powerful hot work.* —**pow·er·ful·ly** /-f(ə)lē/ *adv.* —**pow·er·ful·ness** *n.*

pow·er·head /ˈpou(-ə)rˌhed/ ▸*n.* **1** *informal* a powerful egomaniac: *record-industry powerheads.* **2** any of various mechanical or electrical devices, including: ■ a submersible pump for an aquarium that creates current within a tank. ■ a vacuum-cleaner attachment that houses an independent motor that drives a carpet-beating rotating brush. See also BEATER BAR. ■ the internal combustion engine of an outboard motor. ■ the power unit of an automatic garage door opener.

pow·er·house /ˈpou(-ə)rˌhous/ ▸*n.* a person or thing of great energy, strength, or power. ■ another term for POWER PLANT.

pow·er law ▸*n. Mathematics* a relationship between two quantities such that one is proportional to a fixed power of the other.

pow·er·less /ˈpou(-ə)rləs/ ▸*adj.* [often with *infinitive*] without ability, influence, or power: *troops were powerless to stop last night's shooting.* —**pow·er·less·ly** *adv.* —**pow·er·less·ness** *n.*

pow·er·lift·ing /ˈpou(-ə)rˌliftiNG/ ▸*n.* a form of competitive weightlifting in which contestants attempt three types of lift in a set sequence. —**pow·er·lift·er** /-tər/ *n.*

pow·er line ▸*n.* a cable carrying electrical power, esp. one supported by pylons or poles.

pow·er of at·tor·ney ▸*n. Law* the authority to act for another person in specified or all legal or financial matters. ■ a legal document giving such authority to someone.

pow·er pack ▸*n.* a self-contained and typically transportable unit that stores and supplies electrical power. ■ a transformer for converting an alternating current to a direct current at a different (usually lower) voltage.

pow·er plant ▸*n.* an installation where electrical power is generated for distribution. ■ an engine or other apparatus that provides power for a machine, building, etc.

pow·er play ▸*n.* **1** tactics exhibiting or intended to increase a person's power or influence: *the sexual power play of their relationship* | *the petty power plays of showbiz.* ■ the use of physical strength to defeat one's opponent in a sport through sheer force. **2** tactics in a team sport involving the concentration of players at a particular point. ■ *Ice Hockey* a situation in which a team has a numerical advantage over its opponents while one or more players is serving a penalty.

pow·er pole ▸*n.* a pole, mast, or tower that carries electric wires.

pow·er pol·i·tics ▸*plural n.* [treated as *sing.* or *pl.*] political action by a person or group that makes use of or is intended to increase their power or influence.

pow·er rat·ing ▸*n.* **1** the amount of electrical power required for a particular device: *a continuous power rating of 150 watts.* **2** a numerical representation of a sports team's strength for betting purposes: *a 99 power rating and a home field edge of four points.*

pow·er se·ries ▸*n. Mathematics* an infinite series of the form $\Sigma a_n x^n$ (where n is a positive integer). ■ a generalization of this for more than one variable.

pow·er-shar·ing ▸*n.* a policy agreed between political parties or within a coalition to share responsibility for decision-making and political action.

pow·er shov·el ▸*n.* a mechanical excavator.

pow·er slide ▸*n.* a deliberate controlled skid in a vehicle, usually done in order to turn corners at high speed.

pow·er spec·trum ▸*n.* (*pl.* **pow·er spec·tra**) *Physics* the distribution of the energy of a waveform among its different frequency components. —**pow·er spec·tral** *adj.*

pow·er sta·tion ▸*n.* another term for POWER PLANT.

pow·er steer·ing ▸*n.* power-assisted steering.

pow·er stroke ▸*n.* the stage of the cycle of an internal combustion engine in which the piston is driven outward by the expansion of gases.

pow·er struc·ture ▸*n.* **1** the hierarchy that encompasses the most powerful people in an organization: *inside the power structure of the American Catholic Church.* **2** the people in such a hierarchy: *there are certain natural leaders of the underclasses, and the power structure interprets what they do as a crime.*

pow·er take-off ▸*n.* a device that transfers mechanical power from an engine to another piece of equipment, esp. on a tractor or similar vehicle.

pow·er train ▸*n.* the mechanism that transmits the drive from the engine of a vehicle to its axle. ■ this mechanism, the engine, and the axle considered collectively.

pow·er trip ▸*n.* a self-aggrandizing quest for ever-increasing control over others.

pow·er-up ▸*n.* the action of switching on an electrical device, esp. a computer. ■ (in a computer game) a bonus that a player can collect and that gives their character an advantage, such as more strength or firepower.

pow·er us·er ▸*n. Computing* a user who needs products having the most features and the fastest performance.

pow·er walk·ing ▸*n.* a form of cardiopulmonary exercise consisting of fast walking with exaggerated swinging of the arms.

Pow·ha·tan[1] /ˌpou-əˈtan; pouˈhatn/ ▸*n.* (*pl.* same or **-tans**) **1** a member of an American Indian people of eastern Virginia. **2** the Algonquian language of this people.
▸*adj.* of or relating to this people or their language. ▷from the chief nicknamed *Powhatan*, referring to his residence at the falls of the James River, from Virginia Algonquian *pawatan* 'river falls.'

Pow·ha·tan [2] (c.1550–1618), Algonquian Indian chief; Indian name **Wa-hun-sen-a-cawh** or **Wahunsonacock**. He was the leader of Powhatan's Confederacy, an alliance of about 30 tribes that were located primarily in eastern Virginia. Often noted for his ruthlessness, he made peace with the colonists after his daughter Pocahontas married Englishman John Rolfe in 1614.

pow·wow /ˈpouˌwou/ ▸*n.* a North American Indian ceremony involving feasting, singing, and dancing. ■ a conference or meeting for discussion, esp. among friends or colleagues.
▸*v.* [*intrans.*] *informal* hold a powwow; confer: *news squads powwowed nervously.* ▷early 17th cent.: from Narragansett *powáw* 'magician' (literally 'he dreams').

Pow·ys /ˈpōis/ a former Welsh kingdom. At its most powerful in the early 12th century, by 1284 it had been conquered by the English.

pox /päks/ ▸*n.* any of several viral diseases producing a rash of pimples that become pus-filled and leave pockmarks on healing. ■ (**the pox**) *informal* syphilis. ■ (**the pox**) *historical* smallpox. ■ a plant disease that causes pocklike spots. ▷late Middle English: alteration of *pocks*, plural of **POCK**.
▸*PHRASE* □ **a pox on** *archaic* used to express anger or intense irritation with someone or something: *a pox on both their houses!*

pox·vi·rus /ˈpäksˌvīrəs/ ▸*n. Medicine* any of a group of large DNA viruses that cause smallpox and similar infectious diseases in vertebrates.

Poz·nań /ˈpōznan; ˈpôzˌnänyə/ a city in northwestern Poland; pop. 590,000. It was overrun by the Germans in 1939 and was severely damaged during World War II. German name **POSEN**.

Po·zsony /ˈpôˌzHônyə/ Hungarian name for **BRATISLAVA**.

poz·zo·la·na /ˌpätsəˈlänə/ ▸*n.* a type of volcanic ash used for mortar or for cement that sets under water. ▷early 18th cent.: from Italian, from *pozz(u)olana* '(earth) of *Pozzuoli*,' a town near Naples.

pp ▸*abbr.* ■ pages: *pp 71–73.* ■ parcel post. ■ past participle. ■ per person. ■ per procurationem (used when signing a letter on someone else's behalf). [Latin.] ■ *Music* pianissimo. ■ postpaid. ■ privately printed.

PPA ▸*abbr.* phenylpropanolamine.

p.p.a. ▸*abbr.* per power of attorney.

ppb (also **p.p.b.**) ▸*abbr.* ■ (in publishing) paper, printing, and binding. ■ parts per billion.

ppd. ▸*abbr.* ■ postpaid. ■ prepaid.

pph. ▸*abbr.* pamphlet.

ppi *Computing* ▸*abbr.* pixels per inch, a measure of the resolution of display screens, scanners, and printers.

PPLO ▸*abbr.* pleuropneumonia-like organism.

ppm ▸*abbr.* ■ part(s) per million: *water containing 1 ppm fluoride.* ■ *Computing* page(s) per minute, a measure of the speed of printers.

PPO ▸*abbr.* preferred-provider organization.

PPP ▸*abbr.* ■ Pakistan People's Party. ■ (in computing) point to point protocol, which allows data conforming to the Internet protocol IP to be handled on a serial line. ■ purchasing power parity (a way of measuring what an amount of money will buy in different countries).

PPS ▸*abbr.* ■ additional postscript: *PS Those photos are awful! PPS Can I have your other address?*

ppt ▸*abbr. Chemistry* precipitate.

pptn. ▸*abbr.* precipitation.

PPV ▸*abbr.* pay-per-view, a system in which television viewers are charged for the length of time that they watch programs.

p.q. ▸*abbr.* previous question.

PQ ▸*abbr.* ■ Parti Québécois. ■ Province of Quebec.

PR ▸*abbr.* ■ parliamentary report. ■ press release. ■ prize ring. ■ proportional representation. ■ public relations. ■ Puerto Rico.

Pr ▸*abbr.* ■ preferred (stock). ■ Priest. ■ Prince. ■ Provençal.
▸*symbol* the chemical element praseodymium.

pr ▸*abbr.* ■ pair: *patterned gloves, $17.95/pr.* ■ *archaic* per: *$6 pr day.*

PRA ▸*abbr.* progressive retinal atrophy (a disease afflicting dogs).

prac·ti·ca·ble /ˈpraktikəbəl/ ▸*adj.* able to be done or put into practice successfully: *the measures will be put into effect as soon as is reasonably practicable.* ■ able to be used; useful: *signal processing can let you transform a signal into a practicable form.* ▷mid 17th cent.: from French *praticable*, from *pratiquer* 'put into practice.' **—prac·ti·ca·bil·i·ty** /ˌpraktikəˈbilətē/ *n.* **—prac·ti·ca·bly** /-blē/ *adv.*

prac·ti·cal /ˈpraktikəl/ ▸*adj.* **1** of or concerned with the actual doing or use of something rather than with theory and ideas: *there are two obvious practical applications of the research.* ■ (of an idea, plan, or method) likely to succeed or be effective in real circumstances; feasible: *neither of these strategies is practical for smaller businesses.* ■ suitable for a particular purpose: *a practical, stylish kitchen.* ■ (of a person) sensible and realistic in their approach to a situation or problem: *I'm not unfeeling, just trying to be practical.* ■ (of a person) skilled at manual tasks: *Steve'll fix it—he's quite practical.* **2** so nearly the case that it can be regarded as so; virtual: *it was a practical certainty that he would try to raise more money.* ▷late 16th cent.: from archaic *practic* 'practical' (from Old French *practique*, via late Latin from Greek *praktikos* 'concerned with action,' from *prattein* 'do, act') + **-AL**.
▸*PHRASE* □ **for all practical purposes** virtually, or essentially: *Zimmerman had become, for all practical purposes, an arms smuggler.*

prac·ti·cal·i·ty /ˌpraktiˈkalətē/ ▸*n.* (*pl.* **-ties**) **1** the quality or state of being practical: *there are still major doubts about the practicality of the proposal.* **2** (**practicalities**) the aspects of a situation that involve the actual doing or experience of something rather than theories or ideas: *the practicalities of living at sea.*

prac·ti·cal joke ▸*n.* a trick played on someone in order to make them look foolish and to amuse others. **—prac·ti·cal jok·er** *n.*

prac·ti·cal·ly /ˈpraktik(ə)lē/ ▸*adv.* **1** virtually; almost: *the risk of default was practically zero* | *the place was practically empty.* **2** in a practical manner. ■ [*sentence adverb*] in practical terms: *the law isn't unreasonable or practically inconvenient.*

prac·ti·cal nurse ▸*n.* a nurse who has completed a training course of a lower standard than a registered nurse, esp. one who is licensed by the state to perform certain duties (a **licensed practical nurse**).

prac·tice /ˈpraktəs/ ▸*n.* **1** the actual application or use of an idea, belief, or method as opposed to theories about such application or use: *the principles and practice of teaching* | *he* **put** *his self-defense training* **into practice** *by helping police arrest the armed robber.* ■ the customary, habitual, or expected procedure of something: *current nursing practice* | *modern child-rearing practices.* ■ the carrying out or exercise of a profession, esp. that of a doctor or lawyer: *he abandoned medical practice for the Church.* ■ the business or premises of a doctor or lawyer: *Dr. Weiss has a practice in Essex.* ■ an established method of legal procedure. **2** repeated exercise in or performance of an activity or skill so as to acquire or maintain proficiency in it: *it must have taken a lot of practice to become so fluent.* ■ a period of time spent doing this: *daily choir practices.*
▸*v.* [*trans.*] (*Brit.* **prac·tise**) **1** perform (an activity) or exercise (a skill) repeatedly or regularly in order to improve or maintain one's proficiency: *I need to practice my French* | [*intrans.*] *they were practicing for the Olympics.* **2** carry out or perform (a particular activity, method, or custom) habitually or regularly: *we still practice some of these rituals today.* ■ actively pursue or be engaged in (a particular profession or occupation): *he began to practice law* | [*intrans.*] *he practiced as an attorney* | [as *adj.*] (**practicing**) *a practicing architect.* ■ observe the teaching and rules of (a particular religion): *non-Muslims were free to practice their religion* | [as *adj.*] (**practicing**) *a practicing Roman Catholic.* ■ [*intrans.*] *archaic* scheme or plot for an evil purpose: *what a tangled web we weave when we first practice to deceive.* ▷late Middle English: the verb from Old French *practiser* or medieval Latin *practizare*, alteration of *practicare* 'perform, carry out,' from *practica* 'practice,' from Greek *praktikē*, feminine (used as a noun) of *praktikos* (see **PRACTICAL**); the noun from the verb in the earlier spelling *practise*, on the pattern of pairs such as *advise, advice.* **—prac·tic·er** *n.*
▸*PHRASES* □ **in practice** in reality (used to refer to what actually happens as opposed to what is meant or believed to happen): *in theory this method is ideal—in practice it is unrealistic.* ■ currently proficient in a particular activity or skill as a result of repeated exercise or performance of it. □ **out of practice** not currently proficient in a particular activity or skill due to not having exercised or performed it for some time: *he was out of practice at interrogation.* □ **practice makes perfect** used to convey that regular exercise of an activity or skill is the way to become proficient in it, esp. when encouraging someone to persist in it. □ **practice what one preaches** do what one advises others to do.

prac·ticed /ˈpraktəst/ (*Brit.* **prac·tised**) ▸*adj.* expert, typically as the result of much experience: *admiring the dress with a practiced eye* | *the waiter was* **practiced at** *disrupting moments of intimacy.*

prac·ti·cian /prakˈtisHən/ ▸*n. archaic* a person who practices a profession or occupation, esp. a practical one; a practitioner. ▷late 15th cent.: from Old French *practicien*, from *practique* 'practical' (see **PRACTICAL**).

prac·ti·cum /ˈpraktikəm/ ▸*n.* (*pl.* **-cums**) a practical section of a course of study. ▷early 20th cent.: from late Latin, neuter of *practicus* 'practical.'

prac·tise ▸*v.* British spelling of **PRACTICE**.

prac·ti·tion·er /prakˈtisHənər/ ▸*n.* a person actively engaged in an art, discipline, or profession, esp. medicine: *patients are treated by skilled practitioners.* ▷mid 16th cent.: extension of obsolete *practitian*, variant of **PRACTICIAN**.

prae- ▸*prefix* (used esp. in words regarded as Latin or relating to Roman antiquity, e.g., *praenomen*) equivalent to **PRE-**. ▷from Latin.

prae·ci·pe /ˈpresəˌpē; ˈprē-/ ▸*n. Law* an order requesting a writ or other legal document. ■ *historical* a writ demanding action or an explanation of nonaction. ▷Latin (the first word of the writ), imperative of *praecipere* 'enjoin, command.' See also **PRECEPT**.

prae·mu·ni·re /ˌprēmyo͝oˈnīrē/ ▸*n. historical* the offense of asserting or maintaining papal jurisdiction in England. ■ a writ charging a sheriff to summon a person accused of this offense. ▷late Middle English: from medieval Latin, 'forewarn,' for Latin *praemonere*, from *prae* 'beforehand' + *monere* 'warn.' The term comes from *praemunire facias* 'that you warn (a person to appear),' part of the wording in the writ.

prae·no·men /prēˈnōmən/ ▸*n.* an ancient Roman's first or personal name, for example *Marcus* Tullius Cicero. ▷Latin, from *prae* 'before' + *nomen* 'name.'

Prae·se·pe /prīˈsēpē/ *Astronomy* a large open cluster of stars in the constellation Cancer; the Beehive. ▷Latin, literally 'manger, hive.'

prae·sid·i·um /priˈsidēəm; prī-/ ▸*n. Brit.* variant spelling of **PRESIDIUM**.

prae·tor /ˈprētər/ (also **pre·tor**) ▸*n. Roman History* each of two ancient Roman magistrates ranking below consul. ▷from Latin *praetor*, perhaps from *prae* 'before' + *it-* 'gone' (from the verb *ire*). **—prae·to·ri·al** /prēˈtôrēəl/ *adj.* **—prae·tor·ship** /ˈprētərˌsHip/ *n.*

prae·to·ri·an /prēˈtôrēən/ (also **pre·to·ri·an**) ▸*adj. Roman History* of or having the powers of a praetor.
▸*n.* a man of praetorian rank.

prae·to·ri·an guard ▸*n. Roman History* the bodyguard of the Roman emperor.

prag·mat·ic /prag'matik/ ▸*adj.* dealing with things sensibly and realistically in a way that is based on practical rather than theoretical considerations: *a pragmatic approach to politics.* ■ relating to philosophical or political pragmatism. ■ *Linguistics* of or relating to pragmatics. ▷late 16th cent. (in the senses 'busy, interfering, conceited'): via Latin from Greek *pragmatikos* 'relating to fact,' from *pragma* 'deed' (from the stem of *prattein* 'do'). The current sense dates from the mid 19th cent. —**prag·mat·i·cal·ly** /-ik(ə)lē/ *adv.*

prag·mat·ics /prag'matiks/ ▸*plural n.* [usu. treated as *sing.*] the branch of linguistics dealing with language in use and the contexts in which it is used, including such matters as deixis, taking turns in conversation, text organization, presupposition, and implicature.

P

prag·mat·ic sanc·tion ▸*n. historical* an imperial or royal ordinance or decree that has the force of law. ▷translating Law Latin *pragmatica sanctio.*

prag·ma·tism /'pragmə,tizəm/ ▸*n.* **1** a pragmatic attitude or policy: *ideology was tempered with pragmatism.* **2** *Philosophy* an approach that assesses the truth of meaning of theories or beliefs in terms of the success of their practical application. ▷mid 19th cent.: from Greek *pragma, pragmat-* 'deed' (see PRAGMATIC) + -ISM. —**prag·ma·tist** *n.* —**prag·ma·tis·tic** /,pragmə'tistik/ *adj.*

Prague /präg/ the capital of the Czech Republic, in the northeastern part of the country, on the Vltava River; pop. 1,212,000. Czech name PRAHA.

Prague School a group of linguists established in Prague in 1926 who developed distinctive-feature theory in phonology and communicative dynamism in language teaching. Leading members were Nikolai Trubetzkoy (1890–1938) and Roman Jakobson.

Prague Spring a brief period of liberalization in Czechoslovakia, ending in August 1968, during which a program of political, economic, and cultural reform was initiated.

Pra·ha /'prähä/ Czech name for PRAGUE.

pra·hu /'prou; 'prä,ōō/ ▸*n.* variant spelling of PROA.

Prai·a /'prīə/ the capital of the Cape Verde Islands, a port on the island of São Tiago; pop. 62,000.

Prai·ri·al /prer'yäl/ ▸*n.* the ninth month of the French Republican calendar (1793–1805), originally running from May 20 to June 18. ▷French, from *prairie* 'meadow.'

prai·rie /'pre(ə)rē/ ▸*n.* **1** a large open area of grassland, esp. in the Mississippi River valley. **2** (**Prairie**) [often as *adj.*] a steam locomotive of 2-6-2 wheel arrangement. ▷late 18th cent.: from French, from Old French *praerie,* from Latin *pratum* 'meadow.'

prai·rie chick·en (also **prairie hen**) ▸*n.* a large North American grouse found on the prairies, the male being noted for the display dance in which it inflates two orange neck pouches and makes a booming sound. • Genus *Tympanuchus,* family Tetraonidae: two species, in particular the **greater prairie chicken** (*T. cupido*).

prai·rie dog ▸*n.* a gregarious ground squirrel that lives in interconnected burrows that may cover many acres. It is native to the grasslands of North America. • Genus *Cynomys,* family Sciuridae: several species.

prai·rie-dog·ging (also **prai·rie dog·ging**) ▸*n. informal* the practice of looking over the wall of an office cubicle to observe coworkers: *stop prairie-dogging and get back to work.*

prai·rie oys·ter ▸*n.* **1** a drink made with a raw egg and seasoning, drunk as a cure for a hangover. **2** (**prairie oysters**) the testicles of a calf cooked and served as food.

prai·rie schoon·er ▸*n.* a covered wagon used by the 19th-century pioneers in crossing the North American prairies. The prairie schooner resembled the Conestoga wagon but was smaller.

Prai·rie State a nickname for the state of ILLINOIS.

prai·rie wolf ▸*n.* another term for COYOTE.

prai·rie wool ▸*n. Canadian* the natural grassy plant cover of prairie land.

praise /prāz/ ▸*v.* [*trans.*] express warm approval or admiration of: *we can't praise Chris enough—he did a brilliant job.* ■ express one's respect and gratitude toward (a deity), esp. in song: *we praise God for past blessings.*

▸*n.* the expression of approval or admiration for someone or something: *the audience was full of praise for the whole production.* ■ the expression of respect and gratitude as an act of worship: *give praise to God.* ▷Middle English (also in the sense 'set a price on, attach value to'): from Old French *preisier* 'to prize, praise,' from late Latin *pretiare,* from Latin *pretium* 'price.' Compare with PRIZE[1]. —**praise·ful** /-fəl/ *adj.*

▸PHRASES □ **praise be** *archaic* used as an expression of relief, joy, or gratitude. □ **sing the praises of** express enthusiastic approval or admiration of (someone or something): *Uncle Felix never stopped singing her praises.*

THE RIGHT WORD **acclaim, commend, eulogize, extol, laud, praise**

If your dog sits when you tell him to sit, you'll want to **praise** him for his obedience. *Praise* is a general term for expressing approval, esteem, or commendation that usually suggests the judgment of a superior (*the teacher's praise for her students*).

If a salesperson goes out of his way to help you, you may want to **commend** him to his superior, which is a more formal, public way of praising someone, either verbally or in writing.

If you're watching a performance and want to express your approval verbally or with applause, **acclaim** is the verb you're looking for.

Laud and **extol** suggest the highest of praise, although *laud* may imply that the praise is excessive (*the accomplishments for which she was lauded were really nothing out of the ordinary*).

Extol, which comes from the Latin meaning to raise up, suggests that you're trying to magnify whatever or whomever you're praising (*to extol her virtues so that everyone would vote for her*).

If you want to praise someone who has died recently, you will **eulogize** him or her, which means to speak or write your praise for a special occasion, such as a funeral.

praise·wor·thy /'prāz,wərTHē/ ▸*adj.* deserving approval and admiration: *they displayed a praiseworthy sense of responsibility.* —**praise·wor·thi·ly** /-,wərTHəlē/ *adv.* —**praise·wor·thi·ness** *n.*

praj·na /'prazHnə/ ▸*n. Buddhism* direct insight into the truth taught by the Buddha, as a faculty required to attain enlightenment. ▷from Sanskrit *prajñā.*

Pra·krit /'präk,rit/ ▸*n.* any of the ancient or medieval vernacular dialects of northern and central India that existed alongside or were derived from Sanskrit. ▷from Sanskrit *prākṛta* 'unrefined, natural.' Compare with SANSKRIT.

pra·kri·ti /'prəkritē/ ▸*n.* (in Vedanta) the prime material energy of which all matter is composed.

pra·line /'prä,lēn/ ▸*n.* a smooth, sweet substance made by boiling nuts in sugar and grinding the mixture, used esp. as a filling for chocolates. ■ a crisp or semicrisp candy made by a similar process and typically consisting of butter, brown sugar, and pecans. ▷early 18th cent.: from French, named after Marshal de Plessis-*Praslin* (1598–1675), the French soldier whose cook invented it.

prall·tril·ler /'präl,trilər/ ▸*n.* a musical ornament consisting of one rapid alternation of the written note with the note immediately above it. ▷mid 19th cent.: from German, from *prallen* 'rebound' + *Triller* 'a trill.'

pram[1] /pram/ ▸*n.* short for PERAMBULATOR. ▷late 19th cent.: contracted abbreviation of PERAMBULATOR.

pram[2] /präm; pram/ ▸*n.* a flat-bottomed sailboat. ■ a small, flat-bottomed rowboat for fishing. ▷late Middle English: from Middle Dutch *prame,* Middle Low German *prāme,* perhaps from Czech *prám* 'raft.'

pra·na /'pränə/ ▸*n. Hinduism* breath, considered as a life-giving force. ▷Sanskrit.

pran·a·ya·ma /,pränə'yämə/ ▸*n.* (in Hindu yoga) the regulation of the breath through certain techniques and exercises. ▷Sanskrit, from *prāṇa* 'breath' + *āyāma* 'restraint.'

prance /prans/ ▸*v.* [*intrans.*] (of a horse) move with high springy steps: *the pony was prancing around the paddock.* ■ (of a person) walk or move around with ostentatious, exaggerated movements: *she pranced around the lounge impersonating her favorite pop stars.*

▸*n.* an act or instance of prancing. ▷late Middle English (as a verb): of unknown origin. —**pranc·er** *n.*

pran·di·al /'prandēəl/ ▸*adj.* [*attrib.*] *formal, often humorous* during or relating to dinner or lunch. ■ *Medicine* during or relating to the eating of food. ▷early 19th cent.: from Latin *prandium* 'meal' + -AL.

Prandtl /'präntl/, Ludwig (1875–1953), German physicist. He established the existence of the boundary layer and made important studies on streamlining.

prang /praNG/ *chiefly Brit., informal* ▸*v.* [*trans.*] crash (a motor vehicle or aircraft). ■ *dated* bomb (a target) successfully from the air.

▸*n.* a crash involving a motor vehicle or aircraft. ■ *dated* a bombing raid. ▷1940s: imitative.

prank /praNGk/ ▸*n.* a practical joke or mischievous act. ▷early 16th cent. (denoting a wicked deed): of unknown origin. —**prank·ish** *adj.* —**prank·ish·ness** *n.*

prank·ster /'praNGkstər/ ▸*n.* a person fond of playing pranks.

prase /'prāz; prās/ ▸*n.* a translucent, greenish variety of chalcedony. ▷late 18th cent.: from French, via Latin from Greek *prasios* 'leek-green,' from *prason* 'leek.'

pra·se·o·dym·i·um /,präzēō'dimēəm/ ▸*n.* the chemical element of atomic number 59, a soft silvery-white metal of the lanthanide series. (Symbol: **Pr**) ▷late 19th cent.: modern Latin, from German *Praseodym,* from Greek *prasios* 'leek-green' (because of its green salts) + German *Didym* 'didymium.'

prat /prat/ ▸*n. informal* **1** a person's buttocks. **2** *Brit.* an incompetent, stupid, or foolish person; an idiot. ▷mid 16th cent. (sense 1): of unknown origin. Sense 2 dates from the 1960s.

prate /prāt/ ▸*v.* [*intrans.*] talk foolishly or tediously about something. ▷late Middle English: from Middle Dutch, Middle Low German *praten,* probably of imitative origin. —**prat·er** *n.* (*rare*).

prat·fall /'prat,fôl/ ▸*n. informal* a fall onto one's buttocks: *he **took a pratfall** into the sand.* ■ a stupid and humiliating action: *the first political pratfalls of the new administration.*

prat·in·cole /'pratn,kōl; 'pratiNG-/ ▸*n.* a long-winged, fork-tailed, insectivorous bird related to the plovers, resembling a swallow in flight and typically living near water. • Genus *Glareola* (and *Stiltia*), family Glareolidae: several species, in particular *G. pratincole* of Africa and the Mediterranean. ▷late 18th cent.: from modern Latin *pratincola,* from Latin *pratum* 'meadow' + *incola* 'inhabitant.'

pra·tique /pra'tēk/ ▸*n. historical* permission granted to a ship to have dealings with a port, given after quarantine or on showing a clean bill of health. ▷early 17th cent.: from French, literally 'practice,' via Italian from medieval Latin *practica,* feminine (used as a noun) of *practicus* 'practical.'

Pra·to /'prätō/ a city in northern Italy, northwest of Florence; pop. 167,000.

prat·tle /'pratl/ ▸*v.* [*intrans.*] talk at length in a foolish or inconsequential way: *she began to **prattle on** about her visit to the dentist.*

▸*n.* foolish or inconsequential talk: *do you intend to keep up this childish prattle?* ▷mid 16th cent.: from Middle Low German *pratelen,* from *praten* (see PRATE). —**prat·tler** /'pratlər; 'pratl-ər/ *n.*

prau /prou/ ▸*n.* variant spelling of PROA.

Prav·da /'prävdə/ a Russian daily newspaper, founded in 1912 and from 1918 to 1991 the official organ of the Soviet Communist Party. ▷Russian, literally 'truth.'

prawn /prôn/ ▸*n.* a marine crustacean that resembles a large shrimp. • *Leander* and other genera, class Malacostraca. ▷late Middle English: of unknown origin.

prax·is /'praksəs/ ▸*n. formal* practice, as distinguished from theory: *the divorce between theory and praxis of Marxism which ensued under Stalinism.* ■ accepted practice or custom: *patterns of Christian praxis in church and society.* ▷late 16th cent.: via medieval Latin from Greek, literally 'doing,' from *prattein* 'do.'

Prax·it·e·les /prak'sitl,ēz/ (mid 4th century BC), Athenian sculptor. Only one of his works, *Hermes Carrying the Infant Dionysus,* survives. He is also noted for a statue of Aphrodite, of which there are only Roman copies.

pray /prā/ ▸*v.* [*intrans.*] address a solemn request or expression of thanks to a deity or other object of worship: *the whole family is praying for Michael* | [*trans.*] *pray God this is true.* ■ wish or hope strongly for a particular outcome or situation: *after several days of rain, we were praying for sun* | [with *clause*] *I prayed that James wouldn't notice.*

▸*adv. formal* or *archaic* used as a preface to polite requests or instructions: *pray continue.* ■ used as a way of adding ironic or sarcastic emphasis to a question: *and what, pray, was the purpose of that?* ▷Middle English (in the sense 'ask earnestly'): from Old French *preier,* from late Latin *precare,* alteration of Latin *precari* 'entreat.'

prayer /pre(ə)r/ ▸*n.* a solemn request for help or expression of thanks addressed to God or an object of worship: *I'll say a prayer for him* | *the peace of God is ours*

through prayer. ■ (**prayers**) a religious service, esp. a regular one, at which people gather in order to pray together: *500 people were detained as they attended Friday prayers.* ■ an earnest hope or wish: *it is our prayer that the current progress on human rights will be sustained.* ▷Middle English: from Old French *preiere,* based on Latin *precarius* 'obtained by entreaty,' from *prex, prec-* 'prayer.'
▸*PHRASE* □ **not have a prayer** *informal* have no chance at all of succeeding at something: *he doesn't have a prayer of toppling Tyson.*

prayer beads ▸*n.* a string of beads used in prayer, esp. a rosary.

prayer book ▸*n.* a book containing the forms of prayer regularly used in Christian worship, esp. the Book of Common Prayer.

prayer flag ▸*n.* (esp. in Tibetan Buddhism) a flag on which prayers are inscribed.

prayer·ful /ˈpre(ə)rfəl/ ▸*adj.* (of an action or event) characterized by or expressive of prayer: *prayerful self-examination.* ■ (of a person) given to praying; devout. **—prayer·ful·ly** *adv.* **—prayer·ful·ness** *n.*

Prayer of Ma·nas·ses /məˈnasəs/ a book of the Apocrypha consisting of a penitential prayer put into the mouth of Manasseh, king of Judah.

prayer plant ▸*n.* a Brazilian plant with variegated leaves that are erect at night but lie flat during the day, grown as a houseplant. • *Maranta leuconeura,* family Marantaceae.

prayer rug ▸*n.* a small carpet used by Muslims for kneeling on when praying.

prayer shawl ▸*n. Judaism* another term for **TALLITH**.

prayer stick ▸*n.* a stick decorated with feathers, used by various American Indian peoples in religious ceremonies.

prayer wheel ▸*n.* a revolving cylinder inscribed with or containing prayers, a revolution of which symbolizes the repetition of a prayer, used by Tibetan Buddhists.

pray·ing man·tis ▸*n.* see **MANTIS**.

pra·zi·quan·tel /ˌpräziˈkwantl; -ˈkwäntl/ ▸*n. Medicine* a synthetic anthelmintic drug used in the treatment of schistosomiasis and other infestations of humans and animals with parasitic trematodes or cestodes. ▷1970s: from *p(y)razi(ne)* + *-quantel* (perhaps from elements of **QUINOLINE** and **ANTHELMINTIC**).

pre- ▸*prefix* before (in time, place, order, degree, or importance): *preadolescent* | *precaution* | *precede.* ▷from Latin *prae-.*

preach /prēcн/ ▸*v.* [*intrans.*] deliver a sermon or religious address to an assembled group of people, typically in church: *he preached to a large congregation* | [*trans.*] *our pastor will preach the sermon.* ■ [*trans.*] publicly proclaim or teach (a religious message or belief): *a church that preaches the good news of Jesus.* ■ [*trans.*] earnestly advocate (a belief or course of action): *my parents have always preached toleration and moderation.* ■ give moral advice to someone in an annoying or pompously self-righteous way: *viewers want to be entertained, not* **preached at.** ▷Middle English: from Old French *prechier,* from Latin *praedicare* 'proclaim,' in ecclesiastical Latin 'preach,' from *prae* 'before' + *dicare* 'declare.'
▸*PHRASE* □ **preach to the choir** (or **the converted**) advocate something to people who already share one's convictions about its merits or importance.

preach·er /ˈprēcнər/ ▸*n.* a person who preaches, esp. a minister of religion. ▷Middle English: from Old French *precheor,* from ecclesiastical Latin *praedicator,* from the verb *praedicare* (see **PREACH**).

preach·i·fy /ˈprēcнiˌfī/ ▸*v.* (**-fies, -fied**) [*intrans.*] *informal* preach or moralize tediously: [as *adj.*] (**preachifying**) *I'm not an admirer of paternalistic, preachifying Christianity.*

preach·ment /ˈprēcнmənt/ ▸*n.* dogmatic instruction and exhortation: *successful leadership is a process of persuasion rather than preachment.* ▷Middle English: from Old French *prechement,* from late Latin *praedicamentum.*

preach·y /ˈprēcнē/ ▸*adj.* (**preach·i·er, preach·i·est**) *informal* having or revealing a tendency to give moral advice in a tedious or self-righteous way: *some were put off by the preachy tone of these stories.* **—preach·i·ness** *n.*

pre·a·dapt /ˌprēəˈdapt/ ▸*v.* [*trans.*] *Biology* adapt (an organism or part of an organism) for life in conditions it has yet to encounter: *the insulation of marine mammals in temperate seas preadapts them for polar seas.* **—pre·ad·ap·ta·tion** /ˈprēˌadˌapˈtāsнən/ *n.*

pre·ad·o·les·cent /ˈprēˌadlˈesənt/ ▸*adj.* (of a child) having nearly reached adolescence. ■ of, relating to, or occurring in the two or three years preceding adolescence: *Mozart's preadolescent sonatas.*
▸*n.* a preadolescent child. **—pre·ad·o·les·cence** *n.*

pre·ag·ri·cul·tur·al /ˈprēˌagriˈkəlcнərəl/ ▸*adj.* denoting a people, tribe, or culture that has not developed agriculture as a means of subsistence.

pre-AIDS /prēˈādz/ ▸*adj.* following infection with HIV but before the full development of AIDS: *pre-AIDS patients.* ■ before the recognition of AIDS as a disease: *we are dealing with an era that was pre-AIDS.*

Preak·ness /ˈprēknis/ ▸*n.* an annual horse race for three-year-olds at Pimlico racetrack in Baltimore, Maryland. Held two weeks after the Kentucky Derby, it is the second race of horse racing's Triple Crown.

pre·am·ble /ˈprēˌambəl/ ▸*n.* a preliminary or preparatory statement; an introduction: *what she said was by way of a preamble* | *I gave him the bad news without preamble.* ■ *Law* the introductory part of a statute or deed, stating its purpose, aims, and justification. ▷late Middle English: from Old French *preambule,* from medieval Latin *praeambulum,* from late Latin *praeambulus* 'going before.' **—pre·am·bu·lar** /prēˈambyələr/ *adj.* (*formal*).

pre·amp /ˈprēˌamp/ ▸*n.* short for **PREAMPLIFIER**.

pre·am·pli·fi·er /prēˈampləˌfīər/ ▸*n.* an electronic device that amplifies a very weak signal, for example from a microphone or pickup, and transmits it to a main amplifier.

pre·ar·range /ˌprēəˈrānj/ ▸*v.* [*trans.*] [usu. as *adj.*] (**prearranged**) arrange or agree upon (something) in advance: *did she have a prearranged meeting?* **—pre·ar·range·ment** *n.*

Preb. ▸*abbr.* Prebendary.

preb·end /ˈprebənd/ ▸*n. historical* the portion of the revenues of a cathedral or collegiate church formerly granted to a canon or member of the chapter as his stipend. ■ the property from which such a stipend was derived. ■ the tenure of this as a benefice. ■ another term for **PREBENDARY**. ▷late Middle English: from Old French *prebende,* from late Latin *praebenda* 'things to be supplied, pension,' neuter plural gerundive of Latin *praebere* 'to grant,' from *prae* 'before' + *habere* 'hold, have.'

pre·ben·dal /priˈbendəl; ˈprebəndəl/ ▸*adj.* of or relating to a prebend or a prebendary: *the prebendal manor.*

preb·en·dar·y /ˈprebənˌderē/ ▸*n.* (*pl.* **-dar·ies**) an honorary canon. ■ *historical* a canon of a cathedral or collegiate church whose income originally came from a prebend. ▷late Middle English: from medieval Latin *praebendarius,* from late Latin *praebenda* 'pension' (see **PREBEND**). **—preb·en·dar·y·ship** /-ˌsнip/ *n.*

pre·bi·ot·ic /ˈprēˌbīˈätik/ ▸*adj.* existing or occurring before the emergence of life.

pre·book /prēˈbo͝ok; ˈprēˌbo͝ok/ ▸*v.* [*trans.*] [usu. as *adj.*] (**prebooked**) book (something) in advance: *a prebooked hotel reservation* | [as *n.*] (**prebooking**) *prebooking is essential.* **—pre·book·a·ble** *adj.*

Pre·bo·re·al /prēˈbôrēəl/ ▸*adj. Geology* of, relating to, or denoting the first climatic stage of the postglacial period in northern Europe, between the Younger Dryas and Boreal stages (about 10,000 to 9,000 years ago). The stage was marked by a rapid spread of birch and pine forests. ■ [as *n.*] (**the Preboreal**) the Preboreal climatic stage.

pre-Böt·zing·er com·plex /prē ˈbœtsiɴgər/ ▸*n.* a structure in the mammalian brain stem that controls respiration.

pre·but·tal /prēˈbətl/ ▸*n.* (in politics) a response formulated in anticipation of a criticism; a preemptive rebuttal. ▷1990s: blend of *pre-* and *(re)buttal.*

prec. ▸*abbr.* ■ preceded. ■ preceding.

pre·cal·cu·lus /prēˈkalkyələs/ ▸*n.* a course in mathematics that prepares a student for calculus.

Pre·cam·bri·an /prēˈkambrēən; -kām-/ ▸*adj. Geology* of, relating to, or denoting the earliest eon, preceding the Cambrian period and the Phanerozoic eon. Compare with **CRYPTOZOIC**. ■ [as *n.*] (**the Precambrian**) the Precambrian eon or the system of rocks deposited during it.

> The Precambrian extended from the origin of the earth (believed to have been about 4,600 million years ago) to about 570 million years ago, representing nearly ninety percent of geological time. The oldest known Precambrian rocks have been dated to about 3,800 million years old, and the earliest living organisms date from the latter part of the eon. The Precambrian is now replaced in formal stratigraphic schemes by the Archean, Proterozoic, and (in some schemes) Priscoan eons.

pre·can·cer·ous /prēˈkansərəs/ ▸*adj. Medicine* (of a cell or medical condition) likely to develop into cancer if untreated: *precancerous skin lesions.*

pre·car·i·ous /priˈke(ə)rēəs/ ▸*adj.* **1** not securely held or in position; dangerously likely to fall or collapse: *a precarious ladder.* **2** dependent on chance; uncertain: *she made a precarious living by writing.* ▷mid 17th cent.: from Latin *precarius* 'obtained by entreaty' (from *prex, prec-* 'prayer') + **-OUS**. **—pre·car·i·ous·ly** *adv.* **—pre·car·i·ous·ness** *n.*

pre·cast /ˈprēˈkast/ ▸*v.* (*past* and *past part.* **pre·cast**) [*trans.*] [usu. as *adj.*] (**precast**) cast (an object or material, typically concrete) in its final shape before positioning: *precast concrete beams.*

prec·a·to·ry /ˈprekəˌtôrē/ ▸*adj. formal* of, relating to, or expressing a wish or request. ■ *Law* (in a will) expressing a wish or intention of the testator: *a trust can be left in precatory words.* ▷mid 17th cent.: from late Latin *precatorius,* from *precat-* 'prayed,' from the verb *precari.*

pre·cau·tion /priˈkôsнən/ ▸*n.* a measure taken in advance to prevent something dangerous, unpleasant, or inconvenient from happening: *he had* **taken the precaution of** *seeking legal advice.* ▷late 16th cent. (in the sense 'prudent foresight'): from French *précaution,* from late Latin *praecautio(n-),* from Latin *praecavere,* from *prae* 'before' + *cavere* 'take heed, beware of.' **—pre·cau·tion·ar·y** /-ˌnerē/ *adj.*

pre·cau·tion·ar·y prin·ci·ple ▸*n.* the principle that the introduction of a new product or process whose ultimate effects are disputed or unknown should be resisted. It has mainly been used to prohibit the importation of genetically modified organisms and food.

pre·cede /priˈsēd/ ▸*v.* [*trans.*] come before (something) in time: *a gun battle had preceded the explosions.* ■ come before in order or position: *take time to read the chapters that precede the recipes* | [as *adj.*] (**preceding**) *the preceding pages.* ■ go in front or ahead of: *he let her precede him through the gate.* ■ (**precede something with**) preface or introduce something with: *he preceded the book with a collection of poems.* ▷late Middle English: from Old French *preceder,* from Latin *praecedere,* from *prae* 'before' + *cedere* 'go.'

prec·e·dence /ˈpresədəns; priˈsēdns/ ▸*n.* the condition of being considered more important than someone or something else; priority in importance, order, or rank: *his desire for power soon* **took precedence over** *any other consideration.* ■ the order to be ceremonially observed by people of different rank, according to an acknowledged or legally determined system: *quarrels over precedence among the Bonaparte family marred the coronation.*

prec·e·dent ▸*n.* /ˈpresid(ə)nt/ an earlier event or action that is regarded as an example or guide to be considered in subsequent similar circumstances: *there are substantial precedents for using interactive media in training* | *breaking with all precedent.* ■ *Law* a previous case or legal decision that may be or (**binding precedent**) must be followed in subsequent similar cases: *the decision* **set a precedent** *for others to be sent to trial in the U.S.*
▸*adj.* /priˈsēd(ə)nt/ preceding in time, order, or importance: *a precedent case.* ▷late Middle English: from Old French, literally 'preceding.'

pre·cen·tor /priˈsentər/ ▸*n.* a person who leads a congregation in its singing or (in a synagogue) prayers. ▷early 17th cent.: from French *précenteur* or Latin *praecentor,* from *praecent-* 'sung before,' from the verb *praecinere,* from *prae* 'before' + *canere* 'sing.' **—pre·cent** *v.* **—pre·cen·tor·ship** /-ˌsнip/ *n.*

pre·cept /ˈprēˌsept/ ▸*n.* **1** a general rule intended to regulate behavior or thought: *moral precepts* | *the legal precept of being innocent until proven guilty* | *children learn far more by example than by precept.* **2** a writ or warrant: *the Commissioner issued precepts requiring the companies to provide information.* ▷late Middle English: from Latin *praeceptum,* neuter past participle of *praecipere* 'warn, instruct,' from *prae* 'before' + *capere* 'take.' **—pre·cep·tive** /priˈseptiv/ *adj.*

pre·cep·tor /ˈprēˌseptər; priˈseptər/ ▸*n.* a teacher or instructor. ▷late Middle English: from Latin *praeceptor,* from *praecept-* 'warned, instructed,' from the verb *praecipere* (see **PRECEPT**). **—pre·cep·to·ri·al** /priˌsepˈtôrēəl; ˈprē-/ *adj.* **—pre·cep·tor·ship** /-ˌsнip/ *n.*

pre·ces·sion /prəˈsesнən/ ▸*n. Physics* the slow movement of the axis of a spinning body around another

P

axis due to a torque (such as gravitational influence) acting to change the direction of the first axis. It is seen in the circle slowly traced out by the pole of a spinning gyroscope. ▷late 16th cent. (as a term in astronomy, referring to the PRECESSION OF THE EQUINOXES): from late Latin *praecessio(n-)*, from *praecedere* 'go before' (see PRECEDE). **—pre·cess** /prē'ses; 'prē,ses/ *v.* **—pre·ces·sion·al** /pri'seSHənl/ *adj.*

pre·ces·sion of the e·qui·nox·es ▸*n. Astronomy* the slow retrograde, or westward, motion of equinoctial points along the ecliptic. ■ the resulting earlier occurrence of equinoxes in each successive sidereal year.

As the earth rotates about its axis, it responds to the gravitational attraction of the sun upon its equatorial bulge, so that its axis of rotation describes a circle in the sky, with a period of about 26,000 years. The precession of the equinoxes was discovered by Hipparchus in *c.*125 BC, when the vernal equinox was in Aries.

pre-Chris·tian /prē'krisCHən/ ▸*adj.* of or relating to a time before Christ or the advent of Christianity: *the pre-Christian world.*

pre·cinct /'prē,siNGkt/ ▸*n.* **1** a district of a city or town as defined for police purposes. ■ the police station situated in such a subdivision: *at the precinct, a desk sergeant ran through her ID.* ■ an electoral district of a city or town served by a single polling place: *with 35 percent of the precincts declaring, he had 51 percent of the vote.* **2** (usu. **precincts**) the area within the walls or perceived boundaries of a particular building or place: *all strata of society live within these precincts* | *figurative beyond the precincts of my own family, I am quite inhibited.* ■ an enclosed or clearly defined area of ground around a cathedral, church, or college. **3** *Brit.* an area in a town designated for specific or restricted use, esp. one that is closed to traffic: *a pedestrian precinct.* ▷late Middle English (denoting an administrative district): from medieval Latin *praecinctum*, neuter past participle (used as a noun) of *praecingere* 'encircle,' from *prae* 'before' + *cingere* 'gird.'

pre·ci·os·i·ty /,presHē'äsətē/ ▸*n.* overrefinement in art, music, or language, esp. in the choice of words. ▷mid 19th cent.: suggested by French *préciosité*, a sense derived from Molière's *Les Précieuses Ridicules* (1659), a comedy in which ladies frequenting the literary salons of Paris were satirized.

pre·cious /'presHəs/ ▸*adj.* **1** (of an object, substance, or resource) of great value; not to be wasted or treated carelessly: *precious works of art* | *my time is precious.* ■ greatly loved or treasured by someone: *look after my daughter—she's very* **precious to** *me.* ■ [*attrib.*] *informal* used to express the speaker's contempt for someone or something greatly valued by another person: *you and your precious schedule—you've got to lighten up!* ■ [*attrib.*] *informal* used for emphasis, often in an ironic context: *a precious lot you know about dogs!* **2** *derogatory* affectedly concerned with elegant or refined behavior, language, or manners: *his exaggerated, precious manner.*
▸*n.* used as a term of address to a beloved person: *don't be frightened, my precious.* ▷Middle English: from Old French *precios*, from Latin *pretiosus* 'of great value,' from *pretium* 'price.' **—pre·cious·ly** *adv.* **—pre·cious·ness** *n.*
▸*PHRASE* □ **precious little/few** extremely little or few (used for emphasis): *police still know precious little about the dead man* | *you will find precious few atheists on operating tables.*

pre·cious cor·al ▸*n.* another term for RED CORAL.

pre·cious met·als ▸*plural n.* gold, silver, and platinum.

pre·cious stone ▸*n.* a highly attractive and valuable piece of mineral or rock, used esp. in jewelry; a gemstone.

prec·i·pice /'presəpəs/ ▸*n.* a very steep rock face or cliff, typically a tall one: *we swerved toward the edge of the precipice* | *figurative the country was teetering on the precipice of political anarchy.* ▷late 16th cent. (denoting a headlong fall): from French *précipice* or Latin *praecipitium* 'abrupt descent,' from *praeceps, praecip(it)-* 'steep, headlong.'

pre·cip·i·tan·cy /pri'sipətənsē/ ▸*n.* rashness or suddenness of action: *matters were taken out of his control by the precipitancy of his commander.*

pre·cip·i·tant /pri'sipətənt/ ▸*n.* a cause of a particular action or event: *the immediate precipitants of the conflict were a succession of undisciplined actions.* ■ *chiefly Psychology* a cause or stimulus that precipitates a particular condition: *depression may be a precipitant in many cases.* ■ *Chemistry* a substance that causes the precipitation of a specified substance: *a protein precipitant.* ▷early 17th cent.: from obsolete French *précipitant* 'precipitating,' present participle of *précipiter.* **—pre·cip·i·tance** *n.*

pre·cip·i·tate ▸*v.* /pri'sipə,tāt/ [*trans.*] **1** cause (an event or situation, typically one that is bad or undesirable) to happen suddenly, unexpectedly, or prematurely: *the incident precipitated a political crisis.* ■ [*trans.*] cause to move suddenly and with force: *suddenly the ladder broke, precipitating them down into a heap.* ■ (**precipitate someone/something into**) send someone or something suddenly into a particular state or condition: *they were precipitated into a conflict for which they were quite unprepared.* **2** (usu. **be precipitated**) *Chemistry* cause (a substance) to be deposited in solid form from a solution. ■ cause (drops of moisture or particles of dust) to be deposited from the atmosphere or from a vapor or suspension.
▸*adj.* /pri'sipətət/ done, made, or acting suddenly or without careful consideration: *I must apologize for my staff—their actions were precipitate.* ■ (of an event or situation) occurring suddenly or abruptly: *a precipitate decline in cultural literacy.*
▸*n.* /pri'sipətət; -ə,tāt/ *Chemistry* a substance precipitated from a solution. [from modern Latin *praecipitatum.*] ▷early 16th cent.: from Latin *praecipitat-* 'thrown headlong,' from the verb *praecipitare*, from *praeceps, praecip(it)-* 'headlong,' from *prae* 'before' + *caput* 'head.' The original sense of the verb was 'hurl down, send violently'; hence 'cause to move rapidly,' which gave rise to sense 1 (early 17th cent.). **—pre·cip·i·ta·ble** /pri'sipətəbəl/ *adj.* **—pre·cip·i·tate·ly** /pri'sipətətlē/ *adv.* **—pre·cip·i·tate·ness** /pri'sipətətnəs/ *n.*

USAGE The adjectives **precipitate** and **precipitous** are sometimes confused. **Precipitate** means 'sudden, hasty': *a precipitate decision; the fugitive's precipitate flight.* **Precipitous** means 'steep': *the precipitous slope of the mountain; a precipitous decline in stock prices.*

pre·cip·i·ta·tion /pri,sipə'tāsHən/ ▸*n.* **1** *Chemistry* the action or process of precipitating a substance from a solution. **2** rain, snow, sleet, or hail that falls to the ground. **3** *archaic* the fact or quality of acting suddenly and rashly: *Cora was already regretting her precipitation.* ▷late Middle English (denoting the action of falling or throwing down): from Latin *praecipitatio(n-)*, from *praecipitare* 'throw down or headlong' (see PRECIPITATE).

pre·cip·i·ta·tor /pri'sipə,tātər/ ▸*n.* an apparatus for causing precipitation, esp. a device for removing dust from a gas.

pre·cip·i·tin /pri'sipətən/ ▸*n. Biochemistry* an antibody that produces a visible precipitate when it reacts with its antigen. ▷early 20th cent.: from the verb PRECIPITATE + -IN[1].

pre·cip·i·tous /pri'sipətəs/ ▸*adj.* **1** dangerously high or steep: *the precipitous cliffs of the North Atlantic coast.* ■ (of a change to a worse situation or condition) sudden and dramatic: *the end of the war led to a precipitous decline in exports.* **2** (of an action) done suddenly and without careful consideration: *precipitous intervention.* ▷mid 17th cent.: from obsolete French *précipiteux*, from Latin *praeceps, praecip(it)-* 'steep, headlong' (see PRECIPITATE). **—pre·cip·i·tous·ly** *adv.* **—pre·cip·i·tous·ness** *n.*

USAGE See usage at PRECIPITATE.

pré·cis /prā'sē; 'prāsē/ ▸*n.* (*pl.* same) a summary or abstract of a text or speech.
▸*v.* (**pré·cises** /prā'sēz; 'prāsēz/, **pré·cised**, **pré·cis·ing**) [*trans.*] make a précis of (a text or speech). ▷mid 18th cent.: from French *précis*, literally 'precise' (adjective used as a noun).

pre·cise /pri'sīs/ ▸*adj.* marked by exactness and accuracy of expression or detail: *precise directions* | *I want as precise a time of death as I can get.* ■ (of a person) exact, accurate, and careful about details: *the director was precise with his camera positions.* ■ [*attrib.*] used to emphasize that one is referring to an exact and particular thing: *at that precise moment the car stopped.* ▷late Middle English: from Old French *prescis*, from Latin *praecis-* 'cut short,' from the verb *praecidere*, from *prae* 'in advance' + *caedere* 'to cut.' **—pre·cise·ness** *n.*
▸*PHRASE* □ **to be precise** used to indicate that one is now giving more exact or detailed information: *there were not many—five, to be precise.*

pre·cise·ly /pri'sīslē/ ▸*adv.* in exact terms; without vagueness: *the guidelines are precisely defined.* ■ exactly (used to emphasize the complete accuracy or truth of a statement): *at 2:00 precisely, the phone rang* | *kids will love it precisely because it will irritate their parents.* ■ used as a reply to assert emphatic agreement with or confirmation of a statement: *"You mean it was a conspiracy?" "Precisely."*

pre·ci·sian /pri'sizHən/ ▸*n. chiefly archaic* a person who is rigidly precise or punctilious, esp. as regards religious rules. **—pre·ci·sian·ism** /-,izəm/ *n.*

pre·ci·sion /pri'sizHən/ ▸*n.* the quality, condition, or fact of being exact and accurate: *the deal was planned and executed with military precision.* ■ [as *adj.*] marked by or adapted for accuracy and exactness: *a precision instrument.* ■ *technical* refinement in a measurement, calculation, or specification, esp. as represented by the number of digits given: *this has brought an unprecedented degree of precision to the business of dating rocks* | *a precision of six decimal figures.* Compare with ACCURACY. ▷mid 18th cent.: from French *précision* or Latin *praecisio(n-)*, from *praecidere* 'cut off' (see PRECISE).

pre·clas·si·cal /prē'klasəkəl/ ▸*adj.* of or relating to a time before a period regarded as classical, esp. in music, literature, or history.

pre·clin·i·cal /prē'klinikəl/ ▸*adj. Medicine* relating to or denoting a stage preceding a clinical stage, in particular: ■ relating to or denoting the first, chiefly theoretical, stage of a medical education: *preclinical students.* ■ relating to or denoting the stage in a disease prior to the appearance of symptoms that make a diagnosis possible. ■ relating to or denoting the stage of drug testing that precedes the clinical stage.

pre·clude /pri'klōōd/ ▸*v.* [*trans.*] prevent from happening; make impossible: *the secret nature of his work precluded official recognition.* See note at PROHIBIT. ■ (**preclude someone from**) (of a situation or condition) prevent someone from doing something: *his difficulties preclude him from leading a normal life.* ▷late 15th cent. (in the sense 'bar (a route or passage)'): from Latin *praecludere*, from *prae* 'before' + *claudere* 'to shut.' **—pre·clu·sion** /-'klōōzHən/ *n.* **—pre·clu·sive** /-'klōōsiv; -ziv/ *adj.*

pre·co·cial /pri'kōsHəl/ *Zoology* ▸*adj.* (of a young bird or other animal) hatched or born in an advanced state and able to feed itself almost immediately. Also called NIDIFUGOUS. Often contrasted with ALTRICIAL. ■ (of a particular species) having such young.
▸*n.* a precocial bird. ▷late 19th cent.: from modern Latin *Praecoces* (the name of a former division of birds, plural of Latin *praecox* 'mature before its time') + -IAL.

pre·co·cious /pri'kōsHəs/ ▸*adj.* (of a child) having developed certain abilities or proclivities at an earlier age than usual: *he was a precocious, solitary boy.* ■ (of behavior or ability) indicative of such development: *a precocious talent for computing.* ■ (of a plant) flowering or fruiting earlier than usual. ▷mid 17th cent.: from Latin *praecox, praecoc-* (from *praecoquere* 'ripen fully,' from *prae* 'before' + *coquere* 'to cook') + -IOUS. **—pre·co·cious·ly** *adv.* **—pre·co·cious·ness** *n.* **—pre·coc·i·ty** /pri'käsətē/ *n.*

pre·cog·ni·tion /,prēkäg'nisHən/ ▸*n.* **1** foreknowledge of an event, esp. foreknowledge of a paranormal kind. **2** *Law, chiefly Scottish* the preliminary examination of witnesses, esp. to decide whether there are grounds for a trial. ▷late Middle English: from late Latin *praecognitio(n-)*, based on Latin *cognoscere* 'know.' **—pre·cog·ni·tive** /prē'kägnətiv/ *adj.* (sense 1).

pre·co·i·tal /prē'kōətl; ,prēkō'ētl/ ▸*adj.* occurring before or as a preliminary to sexual intercourse. **—pre·co·i·tal·ly** *adv.*

pre-Co·lum·bi·an /kə'ləmbēən/ ▸*adj.* of or relating to the history and cultures of the Americas before the arrival of Columbus in 1492.

pre·con·ceived /,prēkən'sēvd/ ▸*adj.* (of an idea or opinion) formed before having the evidence for its truth or usefulness: *the same set of facts can be tailored to fit any preconceived belief.*

pre·con·cep·tion /,prēkən'sepsHən/ ▸*n.* a preconceived idea or prejudice.

pre·con·cert /,prēkən'sərt/ ▸*v.* [*trans.*] *archaic* arrange or organize (something) in advance: [as *adj.*] (**preconcerted**) *a preconcerted signal.*

pre·con·di·tion /,prēkən'disHən/ ▸*n.* a condition that must be fulfilled before other things can happen or be done: *a* **precondition for** *peace.*
▸*v.* [*trans.*] **1** (usu. **be preconditioned**) condition (an action) to happen in a certain way: *inquiries are always preconditioned by cultural assumptions.* ■ condition or influence (a person or animal) by exposing them to stimuli or information prior to the relevant

behavioral situation: [*trans.*] *the anthropologist is not preconditioned to interact with those he studies* | [as *n.*] (**preconditioning**) *the protective effect of preconditioning.* **2** bring (something) into the desired state for use: [as *adj.*] (**preconditioned**) *preconditioned paper.*

pre·Con·quest ▸*adj.* occurring or existing before the Norman conquest of England.

pre·con·scious /prē'känchəs/ ▸*adj. Psychoanalysis* of or associated with a part of the mind below the level of immediate conscious awareness, from which memories and emotions that have not been repressed can be recalled: *beliefs and values that are on a preconscious level.*
▸*n.* (**one's/the preconscious**) *Psychology* the part of the mind in which preconscious thoughts or memories reside. —**pre·con·scious·ness** *n.*

pre·cook /'prē'ko͝ok/ ▸*v.* [*trans.*] cook in advance: [as *adj.*] (**precooked**) *precooked frozen dinners.*

pre·cor·di·um /prē'kôrdēəm/ ▸*n. Anatomy* the region or the thorax immediately in front of the heart. ▷late 19th cent.: singular of Latin *praecordia* 'diaphragm, entrails.' —**pre·cor·dial** /-'kôrdēəl/ *adj.*

pre·cur·sor /'prē,kərsər; pri'kər-/ ▸*n.* a person or thing that comes before another of the same kind; a forerunner: *a three-stringed* **precursor of** *the violin* | [as *adj.*] *precursor cells.* ■ *Biochemistry* a substance from which another is formed, esp. by metabolic reaction: *pepsinogen is the inactive precursor of pepsin.* ▷late Middle English: from Latin *praecursor*, from *praecurs-* 'preceded,' from *praecurrere*, from *prae* 'beforehand' + *currere* 'to run.'

pre·cur·so·ry /pri'kərsərē/ ▸*adj.* preceding something in time, development, or position; preliminary: *precursory seismic activity.* ▷late 16th cent.: from Latin *praecursorius*, from *praecurs-* 'preceded' (see PRECURSOR).

pre·cut /'prē'kət/ ▸*v.* [*trans.*] [usu. as *adj.*] (**precut**) cut into the desired shape or sections in advance: *precut pieces of cloth.*

pred. ▸*abbr.* predicate.

pre·da·cious /pri'dāshəs/ (also **pre·da·ceous**) ▸*adj.* (of an animal) predatory: *predacious insects.* ▷early 18th cent.: from Latin *praeda* 'booty' + -ACIOUS. —**pre·da·cious·ness** *n.* —**pre·dac·i·ty** /pri'dasətē/ *n.*

pre·date /prē'dāt/ ▸*v.* [*trans.*] exist or occur at a date earlier than (something): *this letter predates her illness.*

pre·da·tion /pri'dāshən/ ▸*n. Zoology* the preying of one animal on others: *an effective defense against predation.* ▷late 15th cent. (in the Latin sense): from Latin *praedatio(n-)* 'taking of booty,' from the verb *praedari* 'seize as plunder,' from *praeda* 'booty.' The current sense dates from the 1930s.

pred·a·tor /'predətər/ ▸*n.* an animal that naturally preys on others: *wolves are major predators of rodents* ■ *figurative* a rapacious, exploitative person or group: *her wealth made her vulnerable to predators.* ■ *figurative* a company that tries to take over another. ▷1920s: from Latin *praedator* 'plunderer,' from *praedat-* 'seized as plunder,' from the verb *praedari* (see PREDATION).

pred·a·to·ry /'predə,tôrē/ ▸*adj.* relating to or denoting an animal or animals preying naturally on others: *predatory birds.* ■ *figurative* seeking to exploit or oppress others: *a life destroyed by predatory biographers and yellow journalists.* ▷late 16th cent. (in the sense 'relating to plundering'): from Latin *praedatorius*, from *praedator* 'plunderer' (see PREDATOR). —**pred·a·to·ri·ly** /,predə'tôrəlē/ *adv.* —**pred·a·to·ri·ness** *n.*

pred·a·to·ry pric·ing ▸*n.* the pricing of goods or services at such a low level that other suppliers cannot compete and are forced to leave the market.

pre·dawn /prē'dôn/ ▸*adj.* relating to or taking place before dawn: *Sunday's predawn raid by Israeli warplanes.*

pre·de·cease /,prēdi'sēs/ *formal* ▸*v.* [*trans.*] die before (another person, typically someone related by blood or marriage): *his second wife predeceased him.*

pred·e·ces·sor /'predə,sesər; 'prē-/ ▸*n.* a person who held a job or office before the current holder: *the new president's foreign policy is very similar to that of his predecessor.* ■ a thing that has been followed or replaced by another: *the chapel was built in 1864 on the site of its predecessor.* ▷late Middle English: from late Latin *praedecessor*, from Latin *prae* 'beforehand' + *decessor* 'retiring officer' (from *decedere* 'depart').

pre·de·fined /,prēdi'fīnd/ ▸*adj.* defined, limited, or established in advance: *predefined styles for tables, outlines, paragraphs, and graphics.*

pre·del·la /pri'delə/ ▸*n.* **1** a step or platform on which an altar is placed. **2** a raised shelf above an altar. ■ a painting or sculpture on this, typically forming an appendage to an altarpiece. ▷mid 19th cent.: from Italian, literally 'stool.'

pre·des·ti·nar·i·an /prē,destə'ne(ə)rēən/ ▸*n.* a person who believes in the doctrine of predestination.
▸*adj.* upholding, affirming, or relating to the doctrine of predestination.

pre·des·ti·nate ▸*v.* /prē'destə,nāt/ [*trans.*] predestine.
▸*adj.* /prē'destənit/ predestined. ▷late Middle English: from ecclesiastical Latin *praedestinat-* 'made firm beforehand,' from the verb *praedestinare*, from *prae* 'in advance' + *destinare* 'establish.'

pre·des·ti·na·tion /prē,destə'nāshən/ ▸*n.* (as a doctrine in Christian theology) the divine foreordaining of all that will happen, esp. with regard to the salvation of some and not others. It has been particularly associated with the teachings of St. Augustine of Hippo and of Calvin. ▷Middle English: from ecclesiastical Latin *praedestinatio(n-)*, from *praedestinare* 'make firm beforehand' (see PREDESTINATE).

pre·des·tine /prē'destin/ ▸*v.* [*trans.*] (usu. **be predestined**) (of God) destine (someone) for a particular fate or purpose: *Calvinists believed that every person was predestined by God to go to heaven or to hell.* ■ determine (an outcome or course of events) in advance by divine will or fate: *she was certain that fate was with her and everything was predestined* | [as *adj.*] (**predestined**) *our predestined end.* ▷late Middle English: from Old French *predestiner* or ecclesiastical Latin *praedestinare* (see PREDESTINATE).

pre·de·ter·mine /,prēdi'tərmən/ ▸*v.* [*trans.*] establish or decide in advance: *closed questions almost predetermine the response given* | [as *adj.*] (**predetermined**) *a predetermined level of spending.* ■ (usu. **be predetermined**) predestine (an outcome or course of events): *a strong sense that life had been predetermined.* ▷early 17th cent.: from late Latin *praedeterminare*, from *prae* 'beforehand' + *determinare* 'limit, settle.' —**pre·de·ter·min·a·ble** *adj.* —**pre·de·ter·mi·nate** /-'tərmənit/ *adj.* —**pre·de·ter·mi·na·tion** /-,tərmə'nāshən/ *n.*

pre·de·ter·min·er /,prēdi'tərmənər/ ▸*n. Grammar* a word or phrase that occurs before a determiner, typically quantifying the noun phrase, for example *both* or *a lot of.*

pre·di·al /'prēdēəl/ ▸*adj. archaic* of, relating to, or consisting of land or farming: *political or predial sources of discontent.* ■ *historical* relating to or denoting a slave or tenant attached to farms or the land: *predial service.* ■ *historical* (of a tithe) consisting of agricultural produce.
▸*n. historical* a predial slave. ▷late Middle English: from medieval Latin *praedialis*, from Latin *praedium* 'farm.'

predic. ▸*abbr.* predicate.

pred·i·ca·ble /'predikəbəl/ ▸*adj.* that may be predicated or affirmed.
▸*n.* a thing that is predicable. ■ (usu. **predicables**) (in Aristotelian logic) each of the classes to which predicates belong, usually listed as: genus, species, difference, property, and accident. ▷mid 16th cent.: from medieval Latin *praedicabilis* 'able to be affirmed,' from Latin *praedicare* 'declare' (see PREDICATE). —**pred·i·ca·bil·i·ty** /,predikə'bilətē/ *n.*

pre·dic·a·ment /pri'dikəmənt/ ▸*n.* **1** a difficult, unpleasant, or embarrassing situation: *the club's financial predicament.* **2** *archaic Philosophy* (in Aristotelian logic) each of the ten "categories," often listed as: substance or being, quantity, quality, relation, place, time, posture, having or possession, action, and passion. ▷late Middle English (sense 2): from late Latin *praedicamentum* 'something predicated' (rendering Greek *katēgoria* 'category'), from Latin *praedicare* (see PREDICATE). From the sense 'category' arose the sense 'state of being, condition'; hence 'unpleasant situation.'

pred·i·cate ▸*n.* /'predikət/ *Grammar* the part of a sentence or clause containing a verb and stating something about the subject (e.g., *went home* in *John went home*): [as *adj.*] *predicate adjective.* ■ *Logic* something that is affirmed or denied concerning an argument of a proposition.
▸*v.* /'predə,kāt/ [*trans.*] **1** *Grammar* & *Logic* state, affirm, or assert (something) about the subject of a sentence or an argument of proposition: *a word which predicates something about its subject* | *aggression is* **predicated of** *those who act aggressively.* **2** (**predicate something on/upon**) found or base something on: *the theory of structure on which later chemistry was predicated.* ▷late Middle English (as a noun): from Latin *praedicatum* 'something declared,' neuter of *praedicatus* 'declared, proclaimed,' past participle of the verb *praedicare*, from *prae* 'beforehand' + *dicare* 'make known.' —**pred·i·ca·tion** /,predə'kāshən/ *n.*

pred·i·cate cal·cu·lus /'predəkət/ ▸*n.* the branch of symbolic logic that deals with propositions containing predicates, names, and quantifiers.

pred·i·cate nom·i·na·tive ▸*n. Grammar* a word in the nominative case that completes a copulative verb, such as *son* in the sentence *Charlie is my son.*

pred·i·ca·tive /'predə,kātiv; -ikətiv/ ▸*adj.* **1** *Grammar* (of an adjective or noun) forming or contained in the predicate, as *old* in *the dog is old* (but not in *the old dog*) and *house* in *there is a large house.* Contrasted with ATTRIBUTIVE. ■ denoting a use of the verb *to be* to assert something about the subject. **2** *Logic* acting as a predicate. ▷mid 19th cent.: from Latin *praedicativus*, from *praedicat-* 'declared' (in medieval Latin 'predicated'), from the verb *praedicare* (see PREDICATE). —**pred·i·ca·tive·ly** *adv.*

pred·i·ca·tor /'predə,kātər/ ▸*n.* (in systemic grammar) a verb phrase considered as a constituent of clause structure, along with subject, object, and adjunct.

pre·dict /pri'dikt/ ▸*v.* [*trans.*] say or estimate that (a specified thing) will happen in the future or will be a consequence of something: *it is too early to predict a result* | [with *clause*] *he predicts that the trend will continue* | [as *adj.*] (**predicted**) *the predicted growth is 47 percent.* ▷early 17th cent.: from Latin *praedict-* 'made known beforehand, declared,' from the verb *praedicere*, from *prae-* 'beforehand' + *dicere* 'say.' —**pre·dic·tor** /-tər/ *n.*

THE RIGHT WORD **augur, divine, forecast, foreshadow, foretell, predict, prognosticate, prophesy**

While all of these words refer to telling something before it happens, **predict** is the most commonly used and applies to the widest variety of situations. It can mean anything from hazarding a guess (*they predicted he'd never survive the year*) to making an astute inference based on facts or statistical evidence (*predict that the Republicans would win the election*).

When a meteorologist tells us whether it will rain or snow tomorrow, he or she is said to **forecast** the weather, a word that means *predict* but is used particularly in the context of weather and other phenomena that cannot be predicted easily by the general public (*statistics forecast an influx of women into the labor force*).

Divine and **foreshadow** mean to suggest the future rather than to predict it, especially by giving or evaluating subtle hints or clues. To *divine* something is to perceive it through intuition or insight (*to divine in the current economic situation the disaster that lay ahead*), while *foreshadow* can apply to anyone or anything that gives an indication of what is to come (*her abrupt departure that night foreshadowed the breakdown in their relationship*).

Foretell, like *foreshadow*, can refer to the clue rather than the person who gives it and is often used in reference to the past (*evidence that foretold the young girl's violent end*).

Augur means to foreshadow a favorable or unfavorable outcome for something (*the turnout on opening night augured well for the play's success*).

Prophesy connotes either inspired or mystical knowledge of the future and suggests more authoritative wisdom than *augur* (*a baseball fan for decades, he prophesied the young batter's rise to stardom*).

Although anyone who has inside information or knowledge of signs and symptoms can **prognosticate**, it is usually a doctor who does so by looking at the symptoms of a disease to predict its future outcome.

pre·dict·a·ble /pri'diktəbəl/ ▸*adj.* able to be predicted: *the market is volatile and never predictable.* ■ *chiefly derogatory* behaving or occurring in a way that is expected: *the characters were very stereotyped and extremely predictable.* —**pre·dict·a·bil·i·ty** /-,diktə'bilətē/ *n.* —**pre·dict·a·bly** /-blē/ *adv.* [*sentence adverb*] *predictably, Margaret found an excuse to interrupt him* | [as *submodifier*] *a predictably hostile response.*

pre·dic·tion /pri'dikshən/ ▸*n.* a thing predicted; a forecast: *a prediction that the Greeks would destroy the Persian empire.* ■ the action of predicting something: *the prediction of future behavior.* ▷mid 16th cent.: from Latin *praedictio(n-)*, from *praedicere* 'make known beforehand' (see PREDICT).

pre·dic·tive /pri'diktiv/ ▸*adj.* relating to or having the effect of predicting an event or result: *predictive* *accuracy | rules are not* ***predictive of*** *behavior.* **—pre·dic·tive·ly** *adv.*

pre·di·gest /ˌprēdīˈjest; ˌprēdə-/ ▸*v.* (of an animal) treat (food) by a process similar to digestion in order to make it more digestible when subsequently eaten. ■ *figurative* make (language, ideas, etc.) easier to understand or appreciate, typically by simplification: [as *adj.*] (**predigested**) *predigested news.* **—pre·di·ges·tion** /-ˈjesCHən/ *n.*

pre·di·lec·tion /ˌpredlˈekSHən; ˌprēdl-/ ▸*n.* a preference or special liking for something; a bias in favor of something: *my* ***predilection for*** *Asian food.* ▷mid 18th cent.: from French *prédilection*, from Latin *praedilect-* 'preferred,' from the verb *praediligere*, from *prae* 'in advance' + *diligere* 'to select.'

pre·dis·pose /ˌprēdiˈspōz/ ▸*v.* [*trans.*] (**predispose someone to/to do something**) make someone liable or inclined to a specified attitude, action, or condition: *lack of exercise may predispose an individual to high blood pressure.*

pre·dis·po·si·tion /ˌprēˌdispəˈziSHən/ ▸*n.* a liability or tendency to suffer from a particular condition, hold a particular attitude, or act in a particular way: *a child may inherit a* ***predisposition to*** *schizophrenia | genetic predisposition.*

pred·ni·sone /ˈprednəˌsōn; -ˌzōn/ ▸*n. Medicine* a synthetic drug similar to cortisone, used to relieve rheumatic and allergic conditions and to treat leukemia. ▷1950s: perhaps from *pre(gnane)* (a synthetic hydrocarbon) + *d(ie)n(e)* + *(cort)isone*.

pre·dom·i·nance /priˈdämənəns/ ▸*n.* the state or condition of being greater in number or amount: *the demographic predominance of the Muslims |* [in *sing.*] *there is a predominance of female teachers.* ■ the possession or exertion of control or power: *an area of Soviet predominance.*

pre·dom·i·nant /priˈdämənənt/ ▸*adj.* present as the strongest or main element: *its predominant color was white.* ■ having or exerting control or power: *the predominant political forces.* ▷mid 16th cent.: from Old French, from medieval Latin *predominant-* 'predominating,' from the verb *predominari* (see PREDOMINATE).

pre·dom·i·nant·ly /priˈdämənəntlē/ ▸*adv.* mainly; for the most part: [*sentence adverb*] *it is predominantly a coastal bird |* [as *submodifier*] *predominantly Russian areas.*

pre·dom·i·nate /priˈdäməˌnāt/ ▸*v.* [*intrans.*] be the strongest or main element; be greater in number or amount: *small-scale producers predominate in the south.* ■ have or exert control or power: *private interest was not allowed to* ***predominate over*** *the public good.* ▷late 16th cent.: from medieval Latin *predominat-* 'predominated,' from the verb *predominari* (see PRE-, DOMINATE).

pre·dom·i·nate·ly /priˈdämənətlē/ ▸*adv.* another term for PREDOMINANTLY.

pre·doom /prēˈdo͞om/ ▸*v.* [*trans.*] *poetic/literary* condemn or determine the fate of (someone or something) in advance: *he was predoomed by the decrees of heaven.*

pre·dy·nas·tic /ˌprēˌdīˈnastik; ˌprēdə-/ ▸*adj.* of or relating to a period before the normally recognized dynasties, esp. in ancient Egypt before about 3000 BC.

pre·e·clamp·si·a /ˌprē-iˈklampsēə/ ▸*n.* a condition in pregnancy characterized by high blood pressure, sometimes with fluid retention and proteinuria. **—pre·e·clamp·tic** /-ˈklamptik/ *adj.* & *n.*

pre-e·lec·tion /prē-iˈlekSHən/ (also **pre-e·lec·tor·al**) ▸*adj.* [*attrib.*] occurring or existing in the time leading up to an election: *his pre-election speech.*

pre-em·bry·o /prēˈembrēˌō/ ▸*n. technical* a human embryo or fertilized ovum in the first fourteen days after fertilization, before implantation in the uterus has occurred. **—pre-em·bry·on·ic** /ˌprēˌembrēˈänik/ *adj.*

pree·mie /ˈprēmē/ ▸*n.* (*pl.* **-mies**) *informal* a baby born prematurely. ▷1920s (as *premy*): from PREMATURE + -IE.

pre·em·i·nent /prēˈemənənt/ ▸*adj.* surpassing all others; very distinguished in some way: *the world's preeminent expert on asbestos.* ▷late Middle English: from Latin *praeeminent-* 'towering above, excelling,' from the verb *praeeminere*, from *prae* 'before' + *eminere* 'stand out.' **—pre·em·i·nence** *n.*

pre·em·i·nent·ly /prēˈemənəntlē/ ▸*adv.* [*sentence adverb*] above all; in particular: *this is preeminently the haying month throughout the northern states.*

pre·empt /prēˈempt/ ▸*v.* [*trans.*] **1** take action in order to prevent (an anticipated event) from happening; forestall: *the government preempted a coup attempt.* ■ act in advance of (someone) in order to prevent them from doing something: *it looked as if she'd ask him more, but Parr preempted her.* ■ (of a broadcast) interrupt or replace (a scheduled program): *the violence preempted regular programming.* **2** acquire or appropriate (something) in advance: *many tables were already preempted by family parties.* ■ take (something, esp. public land) for oneself so as to have the right of preemption. **3** [*intrans.*] *Bridge* make a preemptive bid.
▸*n. Bridge* a preemptive bid. ▷mid 19th cent.: back-formation from PREEMPTION. **—pre·emp·tor** /-tər/ *n.*

pre·emp·tion /prēˈempSHən/ ▸*n.* **1** the purchase of goods or shares by one person or party before the opportunity is offered to others: *the commission had the right of preemption.* ■ *historical* the right to purchase public land in this way. **2** the action of preempting or forestalling, esp. of making a preemptive attack: *damaging retaliation for any attempt at preemption.* ■ the interruption or replacement of a scheduled radio or television program. ▷early 17th cent.: from medieval Latin *praeemptio(n-)*, from the verb *praeemere*, from *prae* 'in advance' + *emere* 'buy.'

pre·emp·tive /prēˈemptiv/ ▸*adj.* serving or intended to preempt or forestall something, esp. to prevent attack by disabling the enemy: *preemptive action | a preemptive strike.* ■ relating to the purchase of goods or shares by one person or party before the opportunity is offered to others: *preemptive rights.* ■ *Bridge* denoting a bid, typically an opening bid, intended to be so high that it prevents or interferes with effective bidding by the opponents.

USAGE See usage at PEREMPTORY.

preen /prēn/ ▸*v.* [*intrans.*] (of a bird) straighten and clean its feathers with its beak: *robins preened at the pool's edge |* [*trans.*] *the pigeon preened her feathers.* ■ (of a person) devote effort to making oneself look attractive and then admire one's appearance: *adolescents preening in their bedroom mirrors.* ■ (**preen oneself**) congratulate or pride oneself: *he's busy* ***preening himself on*** *acquiring such a pretty girlfriend.* ▷late Middle English: apparently a variant of obsolete *prune* (based on Latin *ungere* 'anoint'), in the same sense, associated with Scots and northern English dialect *preen* 'pierce, pin' (because of the "pricking" action of the bird's beak). **—preen·er** *n.*

preen gland ▸*n. Ornithology* (on a bird) a gland at the base of the tail that produces the oil used in preening.

pre·es·tab·lish /ˌprē-iˈstabliSH/ ▸*v.* [*trans.*] [usu. as *adj.*] (**preestablished**) establish (something) in advance: *he had no preestablished plan.*

pre·ex·ist /ˌprē-igˈzist/ ▸*v.* [*intrans.*] [usu. as *adj.*] (**preexisting**) exist at or from an earlier time: *a preexisting contractual obligation.* ■ [*trans.*] exist at or from an earlier time than (something): *demons who preexisted the Great Flood.* **—pre·ex·ist·ence** /-ˈzistəns/ *n.* **—pre·ex·ist·ent** /-ˈzistənt/ *adj.*

pre·ex·ist·ing con·di·tion ▸*n.* a medical condition existing at a time when new insurance is applied for. Typically the cost of its treatment is not covered by the insurance.

pre·ex·po·sure /ˌprē-ikˈspōZHər/ ▸*n.* previous or premature exposure to something.
▸*adj.* occurring or existing before exposure, esp. exposure to a disease or infection: *preexposure vaccination.*

pref. ▸*abbr.* ■ preface. ■ preference (with reference to preference shares). ■ preferred (with reference to a preferred stock).

pre·fab /prēˈfab; ˈprēˌfab/ *informal* ▸*n.* a prefabricated building.
▸*adj.* prefabricated: *prefab walls.* ▷1930s: abbreviation.

pre·fab·ri·cate /prēˈfabriˌkāt/ ▸*v.* [*trans.*] [usu. as *adj.*] (**prefabricated**) manufacture sections of (esp. a building or piece of furniture) to enable quick or easy assembly on site: *prefabricated homes.* **—pre·fab·ri·ca·tion** /-ˌfabrəˈkāSHən/ *n.*

pref·ace /ˈprefəs/ ▸*n.* an introduction to a book, typically stating its subject, scope, or aims. ■ the introduction or preliminary part of a speech or event. ■ *Christian Church* the introduction to the central part of the Eucharist, historically forming the first part of the canon or prayer of consecration.
▸*v.* [*trans.*] provide (a book) with a preface: *the book is prefaced by a quotation from William Faulkner.* ■ (**preface something with/by**) introduce or begin (a speech or event) with or by doing something: *it is important to preface the debate with a general comment.* ▷late Middle English: via Old French from medieval Latin *praefatia*, alteration of Latin *praefatio(n-)* 'words spoken beforehand,' from the verb *praefari*, from *prae* 'before' + *fari* 'speak.' **—pref·a·to·ry** /ˈprefəˌtôrē/ *adj.*

pre·fect /ˈprēˌfekt/ ▸*n.* **1** a chief officer, magistrate, or regional governor in certain countries: *the prefect of police.* ■ a senior magistrate or governor in the ancient Roman world: *Avitus was prefect of Gaul from AD 439.* **2** *chiefly Brit.* in some schools, a senior student authorized to enforce discipline. ▷late Middle English (sense 2): from Old French, from Latin *praefectus*, past participle of *praeficere* 'set in authority over,' from *prae* 'before' + *facere* 'make.' Sense 2 dates from the early 19th cent. **—pre·fec·tor·al** /prēˈfektərəl/ *adj.* **—pre·fec·to·ri·al** /ˌprēˌfekˈtôrēəl/ *adj.*

pre·fec·ture /ˈprēˌfekCHər/ ▸*n.* a district under the government of a prefect. ■ a prefect's office or tenure. ■ the official residence or headquarters of a prefect. ▷late Middle English: from Latin *praefectura*, from *praefectus* '(person) set in authority over' (see PREFECT). **—pre·fec·tur·al** /prēˈfekCHərəl/ *adj.*

pre·fer /priˈfər/ ▸*v.* (**pre·ferred**, **pre·fer·ring**) [*trans.*] **1** like (one thing or person) better than another or others; tend to choose: *I* ***prefer*** *Venice* ***to*** *Rome |* [with *infinitive*] *I would prefer to discuss the matter in private |* [with *clause*] *Val would presumably prefer that you didn't get arrested |* [as *adj.*] (**preferred**) *his preferred candidate.* **2** *formal* submit (a charge or a piece of information) for consideration: *the police will prefer charges.* **3** *archaic* promote or advance (someone) to a prestigious position: *he was* ***preferred to*** *the post.* ▷late Middle English: from Old French *preferer*, from Latin *praeferre*, from *prae* 'before' + *ferre* 'to bear, carry.'

pref·er·a·ble /ˈpref(ə)rəbəl/ ▸*adj.* more desirable or suitable: *lower interest rates were* ***preferable to*** *higher ones.* **—pref·er·a·bil·i·ty** /ˌpref(ə)rəˈbilətē/ *n.*

pref·er·a·bly /ˈpref(ə)rəblē/ ▸*adv.* [*sentence adverb*] ideally; if possible: *he would like a place of his own, preferably outside the town.*

pref·er·ence /ˈpref(ə)rəns/ ▸*n.* **1** a greater liking for one alternative over another or others: ***a preference for*** *long walks and tennis over jogging | he chose a clock* ***in preference to*** *a watch.* ■ a thing preferred: *my musical preferences are blues and swing.* ■ favor shown to one person or thing over another or others: *preference is given to those who make a donation.* **2** *Law* a prior right or precedence, esp. in connection with the payment of debts: *debts owed to the community should be accorded a preference.* ▷late Middle English (in the sense 'promotion'): from Old French, from medieval Latin *praeferentia*, from Latin *praeferre* 'carry in front' (see PREFER).

pref·er·ence share ▸*n.* British term for PREFERRED STOCK.

pref·er·en·tial /ˌprefəˈrenCHəl/ ▸*adj.* of or involving preference or partiality; constituting a favor or privilege: *preferential interest rates may be offered to employees.* ■ (of regulations or rates) favoring particular countries: *preferential trade terms.* ■ (of a union shop) giving employment preference to union members: *a preferential shop.* ■ (of voting or an election) in which the voter puts candidates in order of preference. ■ (of a creditor) having a claim on the receipt of payment from a debtor that will be met before those of other creditors. ▷mid 19th cent.: from PREFERENCE, on the pattern of *differential*. **—pref·er·en·tial·ly** *adv.*

pre·fer·ment /priˈfərmənt/ ▸*n.* promotion or appointment to a position or office: *after ordination, preferment was fast | he had passed up endless preferments to remain with her.*

pre·ferred stock ▸*n.* stock that entitles the holder to a fixed dividend, whose payment takes priority over that of common-stock dividends.

pre·fetch *Computing* ▸*v.* /prēˈfeCH/ [*trans.*] transfer (data) from main memory to temporary storage in readiness for later use.
▸*n.* /ˈprēˌfeCH/ a process involving such a transfer.

pre·fig·ure /prēˈfigyər/ ▸*v.* [*trans.*] **1** be an early indication or version of (something): *the Hussite movement prefigured the Reformation.* **2** *archaic* imagine beforehand: *she had prefigured her small pilgrimage as made in solitude.* ▷late Middle English: from ecclesiastical Latin *praefigurare* 'represent beforehand,' from *prae* 'before' + *figurare* 'to form, fashion.' **—pre·fig·u·ra·tion** /prēˌfigyəˈrāSHən/ *n.* **—pre·fig·ur·a·tive** /prēˈfigyərətiv/ *adj.* **—pre·fig·ure·ment** *n.*

pre·fix /ˈprēˌfiks/ ▸*n.* a word, letter, or number placed before another: *add the prefix 83 to the extension number.* ■ an element placed at the beginning of a word to adjust or qualify its meaning, e.g., *ex-*, *non-*, *re-* or (in some languages) as an inflection. ■ a title placed before a name, e.g., *Mr.*

▸*v.* [*trans.*] add (something) at the beginning as a prefix or introduction: *a preface is* ***prefixed to*** *the book.* ■ add a prefix or introduction to (something): *all three-digit numbers will now be* ***prefixed by*** *580.* ▷mid 16th cent. (as a verb): from Old French *prefixer*, from Latin *praefixus* 'fixed in front,' from the verb *praefigere*, from *prae* 'before' + *figere* 'to fix.' The noun is from modern Latin *praefixum*, neuter (used as a noun) of *praefixus*, and dates from the mid 17th cent. **—pre·fix·a·tion** /ˌprēfikˈsāsʜən/ *n.*

pre·flight /ˈprēˈflīt/ ▸*adj.* occurring before a flight in an aircraft: *our detailed preflight briefing.*

pre·fo·cus /ˈprēˈfōkəs/ ▸*adj.* [*attrib.*] relating to or denoting a light bulb that is designed so that its beam is focused automatically when it is fitted inside a lamp, esp. a vehicle headlamp.

pre·form /ˈprēˈfôrm/ ▸*v.* [*trans.*] [usu. as *adj.*] (**preformed**) form (something) beforehand: *a preformed pool.*

pre·for·ma·tion /ˌprēfôrˈmāsʜən/ ▸*n.* the action or process of preforming something. ■ *historical Biology* the theory, now discarded, that an embryo develops from a complete miniature version of the organism. Often contrasted with **EPIGENESIS**. **—pre·for·ma·tion·ist** /-ist/ *n.* & *adj.*

pre·fron·tal /prēˈfrəntl/ ▸*adj.* [*attrib.*] **1** *Anatomy* in or relating to the foremost part of the frontal lobe of the brain: *the prefrontal cortex.* **2** *Zoology* relating to or denoting a bone in front of the eye socket in some lower vertebrates (equivalent to part of the human ethmoid bone).

▸*n. Zoology* a prefrontal bone.

pre·gen·i·tal /prēˈjenətl/ ▸*adj.* **1** *Psychoanalysis* relating to psychosexual development before the genital phase. **2** *Zoology* situated in front of the genital region.

preg·gers /ˈpregərz/ ▸*adj.* [*predic.*] *chiefly Brit. informal* pregnant.

pre·gla·cial /prēˈglāsʜəl/ ▸*adj.* of, relating to, or denoting a time before a glacial period.

preg·na·ble /ˈpregnəbəl/ ▸*adj.* vulnerable to attack; not impregnable: *the fort's pregnable approaches.* ▷late Middle English: from Old French *prenable*, literally 'takable,' from Latin *prehendere* 'seize.' The *g* was sometimes written in French, perhaps indicating palatal *n*, but has come to be pronounced as a separate sound in English.

preg·nan·cy /ˈpregnənsē/ ▸*n.* (*pl.* **-cies**) the condition or period of being pregnant: *the first weeks of pregnancy.* ■ a case or situation of being pregnant: *a straightforward pregnancy.*

preg·nant /ˈpregnənt/ ▸*adj.* **1** (of a woman or female animal) having a child or young developing in the uterus: *a pregnant woman* | *she was heavily* ***pregnant with*** *her second child.* ■ having been in such a condition for a specified time: *she was six months pregnant.* **2** full of meaning; significant or suggestive: *a pregnant pause* | *a development* ***pregnant with*** *implications.* ▷late Middle English: from Latin *praegnant-*, probably from *prae* 'before' + the base of *gnasci* 'be born.' **—preg·nant·ly** *adv.*

pre·heat /prēˈhēt/ ▸*v.* [*trans.*] heat (something, esp. an oven or grill) beforehand: *preheat the oven to 350°.*

pre·hen·sile /prēˈhensəl; -ˌsīl/ ▸*adj.* (chiefly of an animal's limb or tail) capable of grasping. ▷late 18th cent.: from French *préhensile*, from Latin *prehens-* 'grasped,' from the verb *prehendere*, from *prae* 'before' + *hendere* 'to grasp.' **—pre·hen·sil·i·ty** /ˌprēˌhenˈsilətē/ *n.*

pre·hen·sion /prēˈhenCHən/ ▸*n.* **1** *Zoology* & *Psychology* the action of grasping or seizing. **2** *Philosophy* an interaction of a subject with an event or entity that involves perception but not necessarily cognition. ▷early 19th cent.: from Latin *prehensio(n-)*, from *prehendere* 'to grasp.'

pre·his·tor·ic /ˌprē(h)iˈstôrik/ ▸*adj.* of, relating to, or denoting the period before written records: *prehistoric man.* ■ *informal* very old, primitive, or out of date: *my dad's electric typewriter was a prehistoric machine.* ▷mid 19th cent.: from French *préhistorique* (see **PRE-**, **HISTORIC**). **—pre·his·to·ri·an** /-ˈstôrēən/ *n.* **—pre·his·tor·i·cal·ly** /-ik(ə)lē/ *adv.*

pre·his·to·ry /prēˈhist(ə)rē/ ▸*n.* the period of time before written records: *myths that stretch back into prehistory.* ■ the events or conditions leading up to a particular occurrence or phenomenon: *the prehistory of capitalism.*

pre·hos·pi·tal /prēˈhäspitl/ ▸*adj.* relating to procedures administered or care provided prior to a patient's arrival at a hospital: *the bandage was developed primarily for a prehospital setting.*

pre·hy·per·ten·sion /ˌprēˌhipərˈtensʜən/ ▸*n.* the condition of having blood pressure between 120/80 mmHg and 139/89 mmHg, considered an indication of risk for hypertension. ▷early 21st cent. **—pre·hy·per·ten·sive** /-siv/ *adj.*

pre·ig·ni·tion /ˌprē-igˈnisʜən/ ▸*n.* the premature combustion of the fuel–air mixture in an internal combustion engine.

pre·im·plan·ta·tion /ˌprē-imˌplanˈtāsʜən/ (also **pre-implantation**) ▸*adj. Zoology* & *Medicine* occurring or existing between the fertilization of an ovum and its implantation in the wall of the uterus.

pre·in·dus·tri·al /ˌprē-inˈdəstrēəl/ ▸*adj.* of or relating to a time before industrialization: *a preindustrial society.*

pre·in·stall /ˌprē-inˈstôl/ ▸*v.* another term for **PRELOAD**.

pre·judge /prēˈjəj/ ▸*v.* [*trans.*] form a judgment on (an issue or person) prematurely and without having adequate information: *it is wrong to prejudge an issue on the basis of speculation.* **—pre·judg·ment** (also **pre·judge·ment**) *n.*

prej·u·dice /ˈprejədəs/ ▸*n.* **1** preconceived opinion that is not based on reason or actual experience: *English* ***prejudice against*** *foreigners* | *anti-Jewish prejudices.* See note at **BIAS**. ■ dislike, hostility, or unjust behavior formed on such a basis: *accusations of racial prejudice.* **2** *chiefly Law* harm or injury that results or may result from some action or judgment: *prejudice resulting from delay in the institution of the proceedings.*

▸*v.* [*trans.*] **1** give rise to prejudice in (someone); make biased: *the statement might prejudice the jury.* **2** *chiefly Law* cause harm to (a state of affairs): *delay is likely to prejudice the child's welfare.* ▷Middle English (sense 2 of the *noun*): from Old French, from Latin *praejudicium*, from *prae* 'in advance' + *judicium* 'judgment.'

▸*PHRASE* □ **without prejudice** *Law* without detriment to any existing right or claim: *the payment was made* ***without*** *any* ***prejudice to*** *her rights.*

prej·u·diced /ˈprejədəst/ ▸*adj.* having or showing a dislike or distrust that is derived from prejudice; bigoted: *people are* ***prejudiced against*** *us* | *prejudiced views.*

prej·u·di·cial /ˌprejəˈdisʜəl/ ▸*adj.* harmful to someone or something; detrimental: *the behavior is* ***prejudicial to*** *good order and discipline.* ▷late Middle English: from Old French *prejudiciel*, from *prejudice* (see **PREJUDICE**). **—prej·u·di·cial·ly** *adv.*

pre·kin·der·gar·ten /prēˈkindərˌgärtn; -ˌgärdn/ (abbr: **pre-K.**) ▸*n.* day care with some educational content for children younger than five, provided by elementary schools or preschools.

prel·a·cy /ˈpreləsē/ ▸*n.* (*pl.* **-cies**) *chiefly archaic* the government of the Christian Church by clerics of high social rank and power. ■ the office or rank of a prelate. ■ (**the prelacy**) prelates collectively. ▷Middle English: from Anglo-Norman French *prelacie*, from medieval Latin *prelatia*, from *praelatus* (see **PRELATE**).

pre·lap·sar·i·an /ˌprēlapˈse(ə)rēən/ ▸*adj. Theology* or *poetic/literary* characteristic of the time before the Fall of Man; innocent and unspoiled: *a prelapsarian Eden of astonishing plenitude.* ▷late 19th cent.: from **PRE-** 'before,' on the pattern of *sublapsarian*.

prel·ate /ˈprelət/ ▸*n. formal* or *historical* a bishop or other high ecclesiastical dignitary. ▷Middle English: from Old French *prelat*, from medieval Latin *praelatus* 'civil dignitary,' past participle (used as a noun) of Latin *praeferre* 'carry before,' also 'place before in esteem.' **—pre·lat·ic** /priˈlatik/ *adj.* **—pre·lat·i·cal** /priˈlatikəl/ *adj.*

prel·a·ture /ˈpreləCHər; -ˌCHŏŏr/ ▸*n.* the office, rank, or sphere of authority of a prelate. ■ (**the prelature**) prelates collectively. ▷early 17th cent.: from French *prélature*, from medieval Latin *praelatura*, from *praelatus* 'civil dignitary' (see **PRELATE**).

pre·launch /prēˈlônCH; -ˈlänCH/ ▸*adj.* concerning activities or conditions before the launch of a spacecraft, campaign, product, etc.

pre·life /prēˈlīf/ ▸*adj.* **1** prior to the appearance of life forms on earth: *prelife molecules.* **2** (often in religious contexts) prior to a particular life or stage of life.

pre·lim /ˈprēˌlim/ ▸*n. informal* **1** an event that precedes or prepares for another, in particular: ■ a preliminary examination, esp. at a college. ■ a preliminary round in an athletic competition: *the prelims of the 400-meter free relay.* **2** (**prelims**) the pages preceding the main text of a book, including the title, contents, and preface. ▷late 19th cent.: abbreviation of **PRELIMINARY**.

pre·lim·i·nar·y /priˈliməˌnerē/ ▸*adj.* denoting an action or event preceding or done in preparation for something fuller or more important: *preliminary talks* | *the discussions were seen as* ***preliminary to*** *the policy paper.*

▸*n.* (*pl.* **-nar·ies**) an action or event preceding or preparing for something fuller or more important: *the bombardment was resumed as* ***a preliminary to*** *an infantry attack.* ■ (**preliminaries**) business or talk, esp. of a formulaic or polite nature, taking place before an action or event: *she began speaking, without preliminaries.* ■ a preliminary round in a sporting competition. ■ (**preliminaries**) fuller form of **PRELIMS** (see **PRELIM** (sense 2)). ▷mid 17th cent.: from modern Latin *praeliminaris* or French *préliminaire*, from Latin *prae* 'before' + *limen, limin-* 'threshold.' **—pre·lim·i·nar·i·ly** /-ˌliməˈnerəlē/ *adv.*

▸*PHRASE* □ **preliminary to** preparatory to; in advance of.

pre·lin·gual·ly deaf /prēˈliNGg(yə)wəlē/ ▸*adj.* deaf from birth or from a time in infancy before the development of the ability to speak.

pre·lin·guis·tic /ˌprēliNGˈgwistik/ ▸*adj.* of or at a stage before the development of language (by the human species) or the acquisition of speech (by a child).

pre·lit·er·ate /prēˈlitərət/ ▸*adj.* of, relating to, or denoting a society or culture that has not developed the use of writing.

pre·load /prēˈlōd/ ▸*v.* [*trans.*] load beforehand: *the software comes preloaded on the PC.* ■ give (a mechanical component) an internal load independent of any working load, typically in order to reduce distortion or noise in operation.

▸*n.* something loaded or applied as a load beforehand: *prices include DOS and Windows preload.*

pre·loved /prēˈləvd/ (also **pre-loved**) ▸*adj. informal* previously owned; secondhand: *preloved toys are just as appealing.*

prel·ude /ˈprelˌ(y)o͞od; ˈprāˌl(y)o͞od/ ▸*n.* **1** an action or event serving as an introduction to something more important: *education cannot simply be* ***a prelude to*** *a career.* **2** an introductory piece of music, most commonly an orchestral opening to an act of an opera, the first movement of a suite, or a piece preceding a fugue. ■ a short piece of music of a similar style, esp. for the piano. ■ the introductory part of a poem or other literary work.

▸*v.* [*trans.*] serve as a prelude or introduction to: *the bombardment preluded an all-out final attack.* ▷mid 16th cent.: from French *prélude*, from medieval Latin *praeludium*, from Latin *praeludere* 'play beforehand,' from *prae* 'before' + *ludere* 'to play.' **—pre·lu·di·al** /priˈlo͞odēəl; prā-/ *adj.*

prem. ▸*abbr.* premium.

pre·ma·lig·nant /prēməˈlignənt/ ▸*adj.* another term for **PRECANCEROUS**.

pre·mar·i·tal /prēˈmaritl/ ▸*adj.* occurring or existing before marriage: *premarital sex.* **—pre·mar·i·tal·ly** *adv.*

pre·mas·ter /prēˈmastər/ ▸*v.* [*trans.*] *Computing* make a master copy of (data) on a hard disk before writing it to a CD-ROM.

pre·match /prēˈmaCH/ ▸*adj.* in or relating to the period before a sports match: *his prematch press conference.*

pre·ma·ture /ˌprēməˈCHŏŏr; -ˈt(y)ŏŏr/ ▸*adj.* occurring or done before the usual or proper time; too early: *the sun can cause premature aging* | [with *infinitive*] *it would be premature to do so at this stage.* ■ (of a baby) born before the end of the full term of gestation, esp. three or more weeks before. ▷late Middle English (in the sense 'ripe, mature'): from Latin *praematurus* 'very early,' from *prae* 'before' + *maturus* 'ripe.' **—pre·ma·ture·ly** *adv.* [as *submodifier*] *prematurely gray hair.* **—pre·ma·tu·ri·ty** /-ˈCHŏŏritē; -ˈt(y)ŏŏr-/ *n.*

pre·max·il·lar·y /prēˈmaksəˌlerē/ ▸*adj. Anatomy* situated in front of the maxilla.

pre·med /ˈprēˈmed/ ▸*n.* **1** a program of premedical studies. ■ a student in such a program. **2** short for **PREMEDICATION**.

▸*adj.* short for **PREMEDICAL**.

pre·med·i·cal /prēˈmedikəl/ ▸*adj.* of, relating to, or engaged in study in preparation for medical school.

pre·med·i·ca·tion /ˌprēˌmedəˈkāsʜən/ ▸*n.* medication that is given in preparation for an operation or other treatment.

Pronunciation Key ə *ago;* ər *over;* ˈə or ˌə *up;* ˈər or ˌər *fur;* a *hat;* ā *rate;* ä *car;* CH *chew;* e *let;* ē *see;* e(ə)r *air;* i *fit;* ī *by;* i(ə)r *ear;* NG *sing;* ō *go;* ô *for;* oi *boy;* o͝o *good;* o͞o *goo;* ou *out;* SH *she;* TH *thin;* T͟H *then;* (h)w *why;* ZH *vision*

pre·med·i·tate /pri'medə,tāt; prē-/ ▸v. [*trans.*] [usu. as *adj.*] (**premeditated**) think out or plan (an action, esp. a crime) beforehand: *premeditated murder.* ▷mid 16th cent.: from Latin *praemeditat-* 'thought out before,' from the verb *praemeditari,* from *prae* 'before' + *meditari* 'meditate.' —**pre·med·i·ta·tion** /-,medə'tāsʜən/ *n.*

pre·men·o·pau·sal /,prē,menə'pôzəl/ ▸*adj.* of or in the period of a woman's life immediately preceding menopause.

pre·men·stru·al /prē'menstr(o͞o)əl/ ▸*adj.* of, occurring, or experienced before menstruation: *premenstrual tension.* —**pre·men·stru·al·ly** *adv.*

pre·men·stru·al syn·drome (abbr.: **PMS**) ▸*n.* any of a complex of symptoms (including emotional tension and fluid retention) experienced by some women in the days immediately before menstruation.

P

pre·mier /prē'm(y)i(ə)r; 'prēmēər; 'prē,mi(ə)r/ ▸*adj.* [*attrib.*] first in importance, order, or position; leading: *Germany's premier rock band | the premier national publication.* ■ of earliest creation: *the premier issue of the quarterly.*
▸*n.* a Prime Minister or other head of government. ■ (in Australia and Canada) the chief minister of a government of a state or province. ▷late 15th cent.: from Old French, 'first,' from Latin *primarius* 'principal.'

pre·mier cru /prə'myā 'krʏ; 'krē/ ▸*n.* (*pl.* **pre·miers crus** /prə'myā 'krʏ; 'krē(z)/) (chiefly in French official classifications) a wine of a superior grade, or the vineyard that produces it. Compare with GRAND CRU. ▷French, literally 'first growth.'

pre·miere /prē'myer; -'mi(ə)r/ ▸*n.* the first performance of a musical or theatrical work or the first showing of a movie.
▸*v.* [*trans.*] give the first performance of: *his first stage play was premiered at the Birmingham Repertory Theatre.* ■ [*intrans.*] (of a musical or theatrical work or a film) have its first performance: *the show premiered in New York this week.* ▷late 19th cent.: French *première,* feminine of *premier* 'first' (see PREMIER).

pre·mier·ship /prə'm(y)ir,sʜip; 'prēmēər-; 'prē,mi(ə)r-/ ▸*n.* the office or position of a Prime Minister or other head of government.

pre·mil·len·ni·al /,prēmə'leneəl/ ▸*adj.* existing or occurring before a new millennium. ■ *Christian Theology* relating to or believing in premillennialism.

pre·mil·len·ni·al·ism /,prēmə'lenēə,lizəm/ ▸*n.* (among some Christian Protestants) the doctrine that the prophesied millennium of blessedness will begin with the imminent Second Coming of Christ. Compare with POSTMILLENNIALISM. —**pre·mil·len·ni·al·ist** *n.*

Prem·in·ger /'preminjər/, Otto (Ludwig) (1906–86), U.S. movie director, born in Austria. Notable productions: *The Moon Is Blue* (1953), *The Man with the Golden Arm* (1955), and *Bonjour Tristesse* (1959).

prem·ise /'preməs/ ▸*n. Logic* a previous statement or proposition from which another is inferred or follows as a conclusion: *if the premise is true, then the conclusion must be true.* ■ an assertion or proposition which forms the basis for a work or theory: *the fundamental premise of the report.*
▸*v.* [*trans.*] (**premise something on/upon**) base an argument, theory, or undertaking on: *the reforms were premised on our findings.* ■ state or presuppose (something) as a premise: [with *clause*] *one school of thought premised that the cosmos is indestructible.* ■ *archaic* state by way of introduction: [with *clause*] *I will premise generally that I hate lecturing.* ▷late Middle English: from Old French *premisse,* from medieval Latin *praemissa (propositio)* '(proposition) set in front,' from Latin *praemittere,* from *prae* 'before' + *mittere* 'send.'

prem·is·es /'preməsəz/ ▸*plural n.* a house or building, together with its land and outbuildings, occupied by a business or considered in an official context: *business premises | supplying alcoholic liquor for consumption **on the premises.***

pre·mi·um /'prēmēəm/ ▸*n.* (*pl.* **-ums**) **1** an amount to be paid for an insurance policy. **2** a sum added to an ordinary price or charge: *customers are reluctant to pay a premium for organic fruit.* ■ a sum added to interest or wages; a bonus. ■ [as *adj.*] relating to or denoting a commodity or product of superior quality and therefore a higher price: *premium beers.* ■ *Stock Market* the amount by which the price of a share or other security exceeds its issue price, its nominal value, or the value of the assets it represents: *the fund has traded at a premium of 12%.* **3** something given as a reward, prize, or incentive: *the Society of Arts awarded him a premium.* ▷early 17th cent. (in the sense 'reward, prize'): from Latin *praemium* 'booty, reward,' from *prae* 'before' + *emere* 'buy, take.'
▸*PHRASES* □ **at a premium 1** scarce and in demand: *space was at a premium.* **2** above the usual or nominal price: *books with pristine dustjackets are less common and sell at a premium.* □ **put** (or **place**) **a premium on** regard or treat as particularly valuable or important: *he put a premium on peace and stability.*

pre·mix /'prē'miks/ ▸*v.* [*trans.*] mix in advance: *I premix all my colors.*
▸*n.* a mixture that is provided already mixed, in particular: ■ a ready-mixed feed for cattle or horses. ■ a preparation of the dry components of a building material such as concrete or plaster.

pre·mod·ern /prē'mädərn/ ▸*adj.* anticipating the modern phase or period of something while not actually belonging to it: *our nostalgia for premodern times when natural bonds to kith and kin were unshakable continues to surface.*

pre·mo·lar /prē'mōlər/ ▸*n.* a tooth situated between the canine and the molar teeth. An adult human normally has eight, two in each jaw on each side.

pre·mo·ni·tion /,prēmə'nisʜən; ,prem-/ ▸*n.* a strong feeling that something is about to happen, esp. something unpleasant: *he had **a premonition of** imminent disaster.* ▷mid 16th cent. (in the sense ' warning'): from French *prémonition,* from late Latin *praemonitio(n-),* from Latin *praemonere,* from *prae* 'before' + *monere* 'warn.' —**pre·mon·i·to·ry** /prē'mänə,tôrē/ *adj.*

pre·mor·bid /prē'môrbəd/ ▸*adj. Medicine & Psychiatry* preceding the occurrence of symptoms of disease or disorder.

pre·mo·tor /'prē'mōtər/ ▸*adj.* [*attrib.*] *Anatomy* relating to or denoting the anterior part of the motor cortex in the frontal lobe of the brain, which is concerned with coordinating voluntary movement.

pre·mul·ti·ply /prē'məltə,plī/ ▸*v.* (**-plies, -plied**) [*trans.*] *Mathematics* multiply (a vector, matrix, or element of a group) noncommutatively by a preceding factor. —**pre·mul·ti·pli·ca·tion** /-,məltəpli'kāsʜən/ *n.*

pre·na·tal /prē'nātl/ ▸*adj.* before birth; during or relating to pregnancy: *prenatal development.* —**pre·na·tal·ly** /-'nātl-ē/ *adv.*

pre-need ▸*adj.* denoting a scheme in which one pays in advance for a service or facility: *pre-need funeral sales.*

pren·tice /'prentis/ ▸*n.* & *v.* archaic term for APPRENTICE. —**pren·tice·ship** /-,sʜip/ *n.*

pre·nup /prē'nəp/ ▸*n. informal* a prenuptial agreement. ▷1990s: abbreviation.

pre·nup·tial /prē'nəpsʜəl; -cʜəl/ ▸*adj.* existing or occurring before marriage: *prenuptial pregnancy.* ■ *Zoology* existing or occurring before mating.

pre·nup·tial a·gree·ment ▸*n.* an agreement made by a couple before they marry concerning the ownership of their respective assets should the marriage fail.

pre·oc·cu·pa·tion /,prē,äkyə'pāsʜən/ ▸*n.* the state or condition of being preoccupied or engrossed with something: *his **preoccupation with** politics.* ■ a subject or matter that engrosses someone: *their main preoccupation was how to feed their families.* ▷late 16th cent. (first used in rhetoric in the sense 'anticipating and meeting objections beforehand'): from Latin *praeoccupatio(n-),* from *praeoccupare* 'seize beforehand' (see PREOCCUPY).

pre·oc·cu·py /prē'äkyə,pī/ ▸*v.* (**-pies, -pied**) [*trans.*] (of a matter or subject) dominate or engross the mind of (someone) to the exclusion of other thoughts: *his mother was **preoccupied with** paying the bills* | [as *adj.*] (**preoccupied**) *she seemed a bit preoccupied.* ▷mid 16th cent.: from PRE- + OCCUPY, suggested by Latin *praeoccupare* 'seize beforehand.'

pre·oc·u·lar /prē'äkyələr/ ▸*adj.* in front of the eye.

pre-Oed·i·pal /prē'edəpəl; -'ēdə-/ ▸*adj. Psychology* existing or occurring before the onset of the Oedipal phase of development. See OEDIPUS COMPLEX.

pre-op /'prē,äp/ *informal* ▸*adj.* short for PREOPERATIVE.
▸*n.* a tranquilizing injection or other treatment administered in preparation for a surgical operation.

pre·op·er·a·tive /prē'äpərətiv/ ▸*adj.* denoting, administered in, or occurring in the period before a surgical operation. —**pre·op·er·a·tive·ly** *adv.*

pre·or·bit·al /prē'ôrbətl/ ▸*adj. chiefly Zoology* situated in front of the orbit or eye socket.

pre·or·dain /,prēôr'dān/ ▸*v.* [*trans.*] (usu. **be preordained**) decide or determine (an outcome or course of action) beforehand: *you might think the company's success was preordained* | [as *adj.*] (**preordained**) *a divinely preordained plan of creation.*

pre-owned /prē'ōnd/ ▸*adj.* secondhand.

prep[1] /prep/ ▸*n. informal* a student or graduate of a preparatory school: *preps as well as Westerners with Ivy League degrees.* ▷late 19th cent.: abbreviation of PREPARATORY.

prep[2] *informal* ▸*v.* (**prepped, prep·ping**) [*trans.*] prepare (something); make ready: *scores of volunteers help prep the food.* ■ [*intrans.*] prepare oneself for an event: *to prep for his role he trimmed his unruly locks.*
▸*n.* preparation: *I do the prep* | [as *adj.*] *I had virtually no prep time.* ▷1920s: abbreviation of PREPARE or PREPARATION.

prep. ▸*abbr.* preposition.

pre·pack·age /prē'pakij/ ▸*v.* [*trans.*] [usu. as *adj.*] (**prepackaged**) pack or wrap (goods, esp. food) on the site of production or before sale: *prepackaged lasagnas.*

pre·paid /prē'pād/ ▸ past and past participle of PREPAY.

prep·a·ra·tion /,prepə'rāsʜən/ ▸*n.* the action or process of making ready or being made ready for use or consideration: *the preparation of a draft contract | the project is **in preparation.*** ■ (usu. **preparations**) something done to get ready for an event or undertaking: *she continued her **preparations for** the party.* ■ a substance that is specially made up and usually sold, esp. a medicine or food. ■ a specimen that has been prepared for scientific or medical examination: *a microscope preparation.* ■ *Music* (in conventional harmony) the sounding of the discordant note in a chord in the preceding chord where it is not discordant, lessening the effect of the discord. ▷late Middle English: via Old French from Latin *praeparatio(n-),* from *praeparare* 'make ready before' (see PREPARE).

pre·par·a·tive /prē'pe(ə)rətiv; -'par-/ ▸*adj.* preparatory.
▸*n.* a thing that acts as a preparation: *schools where parents send children as a preparative for worldly success.* —**pre·par·a·tive·ly** *adv.*

pre·par·a·to·ry /pri'pe(ə)rə,tôrē; -'parə-; 'prep(ə)rə-/ ▸*adj.* serving as or carrying out preparation for a task or undertaking: *more preparatory work is needed.* ■ *Brit.* relating to education in a preparatory school: *preparatory schooling.* ▷late Middle English: from late Latin *praeparatorius,* from *praeparat-* 'made ready beforehand,' from the verb *praeparare* (see PREPARE).
▸*PHRASE* □ **preparatory to** as a preparation for: *she applied her makeup preparatory to leaving.*

pre·par·a·to·ry school ▸*n.* **1** a private school that prepares students for college. **2** *Brit.* a private school for students between the ages of seven and thirteen.

pre·pare /pri'pe(ə)r/ ▸*v.* [*trans.*] **1** make (something) ready for use or consideration: *prepare a brief summary of the article.* ■ make (food or a meal) ready for cooking or eating: *she was busy preparing lunch.* ■ make (someone) ready or able to do or deal with something: *schools should **prepare** children **for** life | by this time I was **prepared for** anything.* ■ [*intrans.*] make oneself ready to do or deal with something: *she took time off to **prepare for** her exams* | [with *infinitive*] *they're preparing to blast into space.* ■ (**be prepared to do something**) be willing to do something: *I wasn't prepared to go along with that.* ■ make (a chemical product) by a reaction or series of reactions. **2** *Music* (in conventional harmony) lead up to (a discord) by means of preparation. ▷late Middle English: from French *préparer* or Latin *praeparare,* from *prae* 'before' + *parare* 'make ready.' —**pre·par·er** *n.*

pre·par·ed·ness /prə'pe(ə)r(ə)dnis/ ▸*n.* a state of readiness, esp. for war: *the country maintained a high level of military preparedness.*

pre·pared pi·an·o ▸*n.* a piano with objects placed on or between the strings, or some strings retuned, to produce an unusual tonal effect.

pre·pay /prē'pā/ ▸*v.* (*past* and *past part.* **pre·paid**) [*trans.*] [usu. as *adj.*] (**prepaid**) pay for in advance: *prepaid health plans.* —**pre·pay·a·ble** *adj.* —**pre·pay·ment** *n.*

prepd. ▸*abbr.* prepared.

pre·pense /pri'pens/ ▸*adj.* [usu. *postpositive*] *dated chiefly Law* deliberate; intentional: *malice prepense.* ▷early 18th cent.: alteration of *prepensed,* past participle of obsolete *prepense,* from Old French *purpenser,* from *por-* 'beforehand' + *penser* 'think.' The prefix *pre-* was substituted to emphasize the notion of 'beforehand.' —**pre·pense·ly** *adv.*

pre·plan /'prē'plan/ ▸*v.* [*trans.*] [usu. as *adj.*] (**preplanned**) plan in advance: *a preplanned route.*

prepn. ▸*abbr.* preparation.

pre·pol·y·mer /prē'päləmər/ ▸*n. Chemistry* a substance

that represents an intermediate stage in polymerization, and can be usefully manipulated before polymerization is completed.

pre·pon·der·ance /pri'pändərəns/ ▶*n.* the quality or fact of being greater in number, quantity, or importance: *the preponderance of women among older people | forests with a preponderance of Apache pine.*

pre·pon·der·ant /pri'pändərənt/ ▶*adj.* predominant in influence, number, or importance: *the preponderant influence of the U.S. within the alliance.* ▷late Middle English: from Latin *praeponderant-* 'weighing more,' from the verb *praeponderare* (see **PREPONDERATE**). **—pre·pon·der·ant·ly** *adv.*

pre·pon·der·ate /pri'pändə,rāt/ ▶*v.* [*intrans.*] be greater in number, influence, or importance: *the advantages* ***preponderate over*** *this apparent disadvantage.* ▷early 17th cent. (in the sense 'weigh more, have greater intellectual weight'): from Latin *praeponderat-* 'of greater weight,' from the verb *praeponderare*, from *prae* 'before' + *ponderare* 'weigh, consider.'

pre·pose /prē'pōz/ ▶*v.* [*trans.*] *Linguistics* place (an element or word) in front of another. ▷late 15th cent. (in the sense 'place in authority'): from French *préposer*, suggested by Latin *praeponere* 'put before.'

prep·o·si·tion /,prepə'zisʜən/ ▶*n. Grammar* a word governing, and usually preceding, a noun or pronoun and expressing a relation to another word or element in the clause, as in "the man *on* the platform," "she arrived *after* dinner," "what did you do it *for*?" ▷late Middle English: from Latin *praepositio(n-)*, from the verb *praeponere*, from *prae* 'before' + *ponere* 'to place.' **—prep·o·si·tion·al** /-sʜənl/ *adj.* **—prep·o·si·tion·al·ly** /-sʜənl-ē/ *adv.*

USAGE There is a traditional view, as set forth by the 17th-century poet and dramatist John Dryden, that it is incorrect to put a preposition at the end of a sentence, as in *where do you come* ***from****?* or *she's not a writer I've ever come* ***across***. The rule was formulated on the basis that, since in Latin a preposition cannot come after the word it governs or is linked with, the same should be true of English. What this rule fails to take into account is that English is not like Latin in this respect, and in many cases (particularly in questions and with phrasal verbs) the attempt to move the preposition produces awkward, unnatural-sounding results. Winston Churchill famously objected to the rule, saying *"This is the sort of English* ***up with*** *which I will not* ***put****."* In standard English the placing of a preposition at the end of a sentence is widely accepted, provided the use sounds natural and the meaning is clear.

prep·o·si·tion·al ob·ject /,prepə'zisʜənl 'äbjəkt; -jekt/ ▶*n. Grammar* a noun phrase governed by a preposition.

prep·o·si·tion·al phrase ▶*n.* a modifying phrase consisting of a preposition and its object.

pre·pos·i·tive /prē'päzətiv/ ▶*adj. Grammar* (of a word, particle, etc.) placed in front of the word that it governs or modifies. ▷late 16th cent.: from late Latin *praepositivus* (see **PRE-**, **POSITIVE**).

pre·pos·sess·ing /,prēpə'zesiɴɢ/ ▶*adj.* [often with *negative*] attractive or appealing in appearance: *he was not a prepossessing sight.* **—pre·pos·ses·sion** /-'zesʜən/ *n.*

pre·pos·ter·ous /pri'päst(ə)rəs/ ▶*adj.* contrary to reason or common sense; utterly absurd or ridiculous: *a preposterous suggestion.* See note at **ABSURD**. ▷mid 16th cent.: from Latin *praeposterus* 'reversed, absurd' (from *prae* 'before' + *posterus* 'coming after') + **-OUS**. **—pre·pos·ter·ous·ly** *adv.* **—pre·pos·ter·ous·ness** *n.*

pre·po·tent /prē'pōtnt/ ▶*adj.* greater than others in power or influence. ■ (of a breeding animal) showing great effectiveness in transmitting hereditary characteristics to its offspring. ▷late Middle English: from Latin *praepotent-* 'having greater power,' from *prae* 'before, ahead' + *posse* 'be able.' **—pre·po·tence** *n.* **—pre·po·ten·cy** *n.*

prep·py /'prepē/ (also **prep·pie**) *informal* ▶*n.* (*pl.* **-pies**) a student or graduate of an expensive preparatory school or a person resembling such a student in dress or appearance.

▶*adj.* (**-pi·er**, **-pi·est**) of or typical of such a person, esp. with reference to their style of dress: *the preppy look.* ▷early 20th cent.: from **PREP SCHOOL** + **-Y**[2].

pre·pran·di·al /prē'prandēəl/ ▶*adj. formal* or *humorous* done or taken before dinner: *a preprandial glass of sherry.* ■ *Medicine* before a main meal: *urine testing results in the preprandial state.* ▷early 19th cent.: from **PRE-** 'before' + Latin *prandium* 'a meal' + **-AL**.

pre·preg /'prē'preg/ ▶*n.* a fibrous material preimpregnated with a particular synthetic resin, used in making reinforced plastics. ▷1950s: from **PRE-** 'before' + *(im)preg(nated)*.

pre·press /'prē'pres/ ▶*adj.* of or relating to typesetting, page layout, and other work done on a publication before it is actually printed.

pre·print ▶*v.* /prē'print/ [*trans.*] [usu. as *adj.*] (**preprinted**) print (something) in advance: *a preprinted form.*

▶*n.* /'prē,print/ something that is printed in advance, esp. a part of a work printed and issued before general publication of that work.

pre·proc·ess /prē'präs,es; prē'prōs,es; -əs/ ▶*v.* [*trans.*] subject (data) to preliminary processing.

pre·proc·es·sor /prē'präs,esər; -'prōs,esər; -əsər/ ▶*n.* a computer program that modifies data to conform with the input requirements of another program.

pre·pro·duc·tion /,prēprə'dəksʜən/ ▶*n.* work done on a product, esp. a film or broadcast program, before full-scale production begins: [as *adj.*] *the preproduction script.*

pre·pro·gram /prē'prō,gram; -grəm/ ▶*v.* [*trans.*] [usu. as *adj.*] (**preprogrammed**) program (a computer or other electronic device) in advance for ease of use: *a preprogrammed function key.* ■ program (something) into a computer or other electronic device before use: *preprogrammed messages.*

prep school ▶*n.* another term for **PREPARATORY SCHOOL**.

pre·pu·ber·tal /prē'pyoobərtl/ ▶*adj.* another term for **PREPUBESCENT**. **—pre·pu·ber·ty** /-bərtē/ *n.*

pre·pu·bes·cent /,prēpyoo'besənt/ ▶*adj.* relating to or in the period preceding puberty: *a prepubescent girl.*

▶*n.* a prepubescent boy or girl. **—pre·pu·bes·cence** *n.*

pre·pub·li·ca·tion /,prē,pəbli'kāsʜən/ ▶*adj.* issued or occurring before publication: *prepublication censorship.*

▶*n.* publication in advance.

pre·puce /'prē,pyoos/ ▶*n. Anatomy* **1** technical term for **FORESKIN**. **2** the fold of skin surrounding the clitoris. ▷late Middle English: from French *prépuce*, from Latin *praeputium.* **—pre·pu·tial** /prē'pyoosʜəl/ *adj.*

pre·qual·i·fy /prē'kwälə,fī/ ▶*v.* [*intrans.*] qualify in advance to take part in something: [as *adj.*] (**prequalifying**) *players who fail at the prequalifying stage.*

pre·quel /'prēkwəl; -kwil/ ▶*n.* a story or movie containing events that precede those of an existing work: *the film is* ***a prequel to*** *the cult TV series.* ▷1970s: from **PRE-** 'before' + **SEQUEL**.

Pre-Raph·a·el·ite /'rafēə,līt; -rāfē-; -'räfē-/ ▶*n.* a member of a group of English 19th-century artists, including Holman Hunt, Millais, and D. G. Rossetti, who consciously sought to emulate the simplicity and sincerity of the work of Italian artists from before the time of Raphael.

Seven young English artists and writers founded the **Pre-Raphaelite Brotherhood** in 1848 as a reaction against the slick sentimentality and academic convention of much Victorian art. Their work is characterized by strong line and color, naturalistic detail, and often biblical or literary subjects. The group began to disperse in the 1850s, and the term became applied to the rather different later work of Rossetti, and that of Burne-Jones and William Morris, in which a romantic and decorative depiction of classical and medieval themes had come to predominate.

▶*adj.* of or relating to the Pre-Raphaelites. ■ of a style or appearance associated with the later Pre-Raphaelites or esp. with the women they frequently used as models, with long, thick, wavy auburn hair, pale skin, and a fey demeanor. **—Pre-Raph·a·el·it·ism** /-,līt,izəm/ *n.*

pre·re·cord /,prēri'kôrd/ ▶*v.* [*trans.*] [often as *adj.*] (**prerecorded**) record (sound or film) in advance: *a prerecorded talk.* ■ record sound on (a tape or other medium) beforehand.

pre·reg·is·tra·tion /,prē,rejəs'trāsʜən/ ▶*n.* the action of registering or being registered in advance: *members are entitled to free preregistration.*

pre·re·lease /,prērə'lēs; 'prērə,lēs/ ▶*adj.* of, relating to, or denoting a record, movie, or other product that has not yet been generally released: *a prerelease version of the software.* ■ of or relating to the period before the release of a suspect or prisoner.

▶*n.* a movie, record, or other product given restricted availability before being generally released.

pre·req·ui·site /prē'rekwəzət/ ▶*n.* a thing that is required as a prior condition for something else to happen or exist: *sponsorship is not* ***a prerequisite for*** *any of our courses.*

▶*adj.* required as a prior condition: *the student must have the prerequisite skills.*

USAGE See usage at **PERQUISITE**.

pre·rog·a·tive /pri'rägətiv; pə'räg-/ ▶*n.* a right or privilege exclusive to a particular individual or class: *owning an automobile was still the prerogative of the rich.* ■ a faculty or property distinguishing a person or class: *it's not a female prerogative to feel insecure.* ■ (also **royal prerogative**) the right of the sovereign, which in British law is theoretically subject to no restriction.

▶*adj.* [*attrib.*] *Brit. Law* arising from the prerogative of the Crown (usually delegated to the government or the judiciary) and based in common law rather than statutory law: *the monarch retained the formal prerogative power to appoint the Prime Minister.* ▷late Middle English: via Old French from Latin *praerogativa* '(the verdict of) the political division that was chosen to vote first in the assembly,' feminine (used as noun) of *praerogativus* 'asked first,' from *prae* 'before' + *rogare* 'ask.'

pre·rog·a·tive court ▶*n. historical* (in the UK) either of two ecclesiastical courts at Canterbury and York formerly responsible for the probate of wills involving property in more than one diocese.

pre·rog·a·tive of mer·cy ▶*n.* the right and power of a sovereign, president, or other supreme authority to commute a death sentence, to change the mode of execution, or to pardon an offender.

Pres. ▶*abbr.* President.

pres·age /'presij; pri'sāj/ ▶*v.* [*trans.*] (of an event) be a sign or warning that (something, typically something bad) will happen: *the outcome of the game presaged the coming year.* ■ *archaic* (of a person) predict: *lands he could measure, terms and tides presage.*

▶*n.* a sign or warning that something, typically something bad, will happen; an omen or portent: *the fever was a somber presage of his final illness.* ■ *archaic* a feeling of presentiment or foreboding: *he had a strong presage that he had only a very short time to live.* ▷late Middle English (as a noun): via French from Latin *praesagium*, from *praesagire* 'forebode,' from *prae* 'before' + *sagire* 'perceive keenly.' **—pres·ag·er** *n.* (*archaic*)

Presb. ▶*abbr.* Presbyterian.

Presby. ▶*abbr.* Presbyterian.

pres·by·o·pi·a /,prezbē'ōpēə; ,pres-/ ▶*n.* farsightedness caused by loss of elasticity of the lens of the eye, occurring typically in middle and old age. ▷late 18th cent.: modern Latin, from Greek *presbus* 'old man' + *ōps, ōp-* 'eye.' **—pres·by·op·ic** /-'äpik/ *adj.*

pres·by·ter /'prezbitər; 'pres-/ ▶*n. historical* an elder or minister of the Christian Church. ■ *formal* (in Presbyterian churches) an elder. ■ *formal* (in Episcopal churches) a minister of the second order, under the authority of a bishop; a priest. ▷late 16th cent.: via ecclesiastical Latin from Greek *presbuteros* 'elder' (used in the New Testament to denote an elder of the early church), comparative of *presbus* 'old (man).' **—pres·byt·er·al** /prez'bitərəl; pres-/ *adj.* **—pres·byt·er·ate** /prez'bitə,rāt; pres-/ *n.* **—pres·by·te·ri·al** /,prezbi'ti(ə)rēəl; ,pres-/ *adj.* **—pres·by·ter·ship** /-,sʜip/ *n.*

Pres·by·te·ri·an /,prezbə'tirēən; ,pres-/ ▶*adj.* of, relating to, or denoting a Christian Church or denomination governed by elders according to the principles of Presbyterianism.

▶*n.* a member of a Presbyterian Church. ■ an advocate of the Presbyterian system. ▷mid 17th cent.: from ecclesiastical Latin *presbyterium* (see **PRESBYTERY**) + **-AN**.

Pres·by·te·ri·an·ism /,prezbə'tirēə,nizəm; ,pres-/ ▶*n.* a form of Protestant Church government in which the Church is administered locally by the minister with a group of elected elders of equal rank, and regionally and nationally by representative courts of ministers and elders.

Presbyterianism was first introduced in Geneva in 1541 under John Calvin, in the belief that it best represented the pattern of the early church. There are now many Presbyterian Churches (often called Reformed Churches) worldwide, notably in the Netherlands and Scotland and in countries with which they have historic links (including the U.S. and Northern Ireland).

pres·by·ter·y /ˈprezbəˌterē; ˈpres-; -bətrē/ ▸*n.* (*pl.* **-ter·ies**) **1** [treated as *sing.* or *pl.*] a body of church elders and ministers, esp. (in Presbyterian churches) an administrative body (court) representing all the local congregations of a district. ■ a district represented by such a body of elders and ministers. **2** the house of a Roman Catholic parish priest. **3** *chiefly Architecture* the eastern part of a church chancel beyond the choir; the sanctuary. ▷late Middle English (sense 3): from Old French *presbiterie*, via ecclesiastical Latin from Greek *presbuterion*, from *presbuteros* (see PRESBYTER).

pre·school ▸*adj.* /ˈprēˈskōōl/ [*attrib.*] of or relating to the time before a child is old enough to go to elementary school: *a preschool play group.* ■ (of a child) under the age at which compulsory schooling begins.
▸*n.* /ˈprēˌskōōl/ a nursery school: *she goes to preschool.* —**pre·school·er** *n.*

pre·scient /ˈpresH(ē)ənt; ˈprē-/ ▸*adj.* having or showing knowledge of events before they take place: *a prescient warning.* ▷early 17th cent.: from Latin *praescient-* 'knowing beforehand,' from the verb *praescire*, from *prae* 'before' + *scire* 'know.' —**pre·sci·ence** /-əns/ *n.* —**pre·scient·ly** *adv.*

pre·sci·en·tif·ic /ˌprēˌsīənˈtifik/ ▸*adj.* of or relating to the time before the development of modern science or the application of scientific method.

pre·scind /priˈsind/ ▸*v.* [*intrans.*] (**prescind from**) *formal* leave out of consideration: *we have prescinded from many vexing issues.* ■ [*trans.*] cut off or separate from something: *his is an idea entirely prescinded from all of the others.* ▷mid 17th cent. (in the sense 'cut off abruptly or prematurely'): from Latin *praescindere*, from *prae* 'before' + *scindere* 'to cut.'

Pres·cott /ˈpresˌkät/ a historic city in west central Arizona; pop. 33,938.

pre·scribe /priˈskrīb/ ▸*v.* [*trans.*] (of a medical practitioner) advise and authorize the use of (a medicine or treatment) for someone, esp. in writing: *Dr. Greene prescribed magnesium sulfate* | [with *two objs.*] *the doctor prescribed her a drug called amantadine.* ■ recommend (a substance or action) as something beneficial: *marriage is often prescribed as a universal remedy.* ■ state authoritatively or as a rule that (an action or procedure) should be carried out: *rules prescribing five acts for a play are purely arbitrary* | [as *adj.*] (**prescribed**) *doing things in the prescribed manner.* ▷late Middle English (in the sense 'confine within bounds,' also as a legal term meaning 'claim by prescription'): from Latin *praescribere* 'direct in writing,' from *prae* 'before' + *scribere* 'write.' —**pre·scrib·er** *n.*

USAGE The verbs **prescribe** and **proscribe** do not have the same meaning. **Prescribe** is a much more common word than **proscribe** and means either 'issue a medical prescription' or 'recommend with authority': *the doctor* ***prescribed*** *antibiotics.* **Proscribe**, on the other hand, is a formal word meaning 'condemn or forbid': *gambling was strictly* ***proscribed*** *by the authorities.*

pre·script /ˈprēˌskript; priˈskript/ ▸*n. formal* or *dated* an ordinance, law, or command. ▷mid 16th cent.: from Latin *praescriptum* 'something directed in writing,' neuter past participle of *praescribere* (see PRESCRIBE).

pre·scrip·tion /priˈskripsHən/ ▸*n.* **1** an instruction written by a medical practitioner that authorizes a patient to be provided a medicine or treatment: *he scribbled a prescription for tranquilizers* | *antidepressants available only* ***by prescription*** | [as *adj.*] *prescription drugs.* ■ the action of prescribing a medicine or treatment: *the unnecessary prescription of antibiotics.* ■ a medicine or remedy that is prescribed: *I've got to pick up my prescription.* **2** a recommendation that is authoritatively put forward: *effective prescriptions for sustaining rural communities.* ■ the authoritative recommendation of an action or procedure: *rather than prescription there would be guidance.* **3** (also **positive prescription**) *Law* the establishment of a claim founded on the basis of a long or indefinite period of uninterrupted use or of long-standing custom. ▷late Middle English (as a legal term): via Old French from Latin *praescriptio(n-)*, from the verb *praescribere* (see PRESCRIBE). Sense 1 dates from the late 16th cent.

pre·scrip·tive /priˈskriptiv/ ▸*adj.* **1** of or relating to the imposition or enforcement of a rule or method: *these guidelines are not intended to be prescriptive.* ■ *Linguistics* attempting to impose rules of correct usage on the users of a language: *a prescriptive grammar book.* Often contrasted with DESCRIPTIVE. **2** (of a right, title, or institution) having become legally established or accepted by long usage or the passage of time: *a prescriptive right of way.* ■ *archaic* established by long-standing custom or usage: *his regular score at the bar and his prescriptive corner at the winter's fireside.* ▷mid 18th cent.: from late Latin *praescriptivus* 'relating to a legal exception,' from *praescript-* 'directed in writing,' from the verb *praescribere* (see PRESCRIBE). —**pre·scrip·tive·ly** *adv.* —**pre·scrip·tive·ness** *n.* —**pre·scrip·tiv·ism** /-ˈskriptəˌvizəm/ *n.* —**pre·scrip·tiv·ist** /-vist/ *n.* & *adj.*

pre·sea·son /ˈprēˈsēzən/ ▸*adj.* (of a sporting event) taking place before the regular season.
▸*n.* [in *sing.*] the period of time before the regular season.

pre·se·lect /ˌprēsəˈlekt/ ▸*v.* [*trans.*] select or set in advance: *the personal shopper would preselect clothes for a customer.* —**pre·se·lec·tion** /-səˈleksHən/ *n.* —**pre·se·lec·tive** /-səˈlektiv/ *adj.*

pre·se·lec·tor /ˌprēsəˈlektər/ ▸*n.* a device for selecting a mechanical or electrical operation in advance of its execution.

pres·ence /ˈprezəns/ ▸*n.* the state or fact of existing, occurring, or being present in a place or thing: *her presence still comforts me* | *the presence of chlorine in the atmosphere* | *the memorial was unveiled* ***in the presence of*** *24 veterans.* ■ a person or thing that exists or is present in a place but is not seen: *the monks became aware of a strange presence.* ■ [in *sing.*] a group of people, esp. soldiers or police, stationed in a particular place: *the USA would maintain a presence in the Indian Ocean region.* ■ the impressive manner or appearance of a person: *Richard was not a big man, but his presence was overwhelming* | [in *sing.*] *he has a real physical presence.* ▷Middle English: via Old French from Latin *praesentia* 'being at hand,' from the verb *praeesse* (see PRESENT¹).
▸*PHRASES* □ **make one's presence felt** have a strong and obvious effect or influence on others or on a situation. □ **presence of mind** the ability to remain calm and take quick, sensible action: *he had the presence of mind to record the scene on video.*

pres·ence cham·ber ▸*n.* a room, esp. one in a palace, in which a monarch or other distinguished person receives visitors.

pre·se·nile /prēˈsēˌnīl; -ˈsenˌīl/ ▸*adj.* occurring in or characteristic of the period of life preceding old age: *the factors that may predispose women to presenile Alzheimer's disease are not known.*

pres·ent¹ /ˈprezənt/ ▸*adj.* **1** [*predic.*] (of a person) in a particular place: *a doctor must be present at the ringside* | *the speech caused embarrassment to all those present.* ■ (often **present in**) (of a thing) existing or occurring in a place or thing: *organic molecules are present in comets.* **2** [*attrib.*] existing or occurring now: *she did not expect to find herself in her present situation.* ■ now being considered or discussed: *the present article cannot answer every question.* ■ *Grammar* (of a tense or participle) expressing an action now going on or habitually performed or a condition now existing.
▸*n.* [in *sing.*] (usu. **the present**) the period of time now occurring: *they are happy and at peace, refusing to think beyond the present.* ■ *Grammar* a present tense: *the verbs are all in the present.* See also HISTORIC PRESENT. ▷Middle English: via Old French from Latin *praesent-* 'being at hand,' present participle of *praeesse*, from *prae* 'before' + *esse* 'be.'
▸*PHRASES* □ **at present** now: *membership at present stands at about 5,000.* □ **for the present** for now; temporarily. □ (**there is**) **no time like the present** used to suggest that something should be done now rather than later: *"When do you want me to leave?" "No time like the present."* □ **present company excepted** excluding those who are here now. □ **these presents** *formal Law* this document: *the premises outlined in red on the Plan annexed to these presents.*

pre·sent² /priˈzent/ ▸*v.* [*trans.*] **1** (**present something to**) give something to (someone) formally or ceremonially: *a top executive will present an award to employees who built the F-150.* ■ (**present someone with**) give someone (something) in such a way: *my students presented me with some flowers.* ■ show or offer (something) for others to scrutinize or consider: *he stopped and presented his passport.* ■ formally introduce (someone) to someone else: *may I present my wife?* ■ proffer (compliments or good wishes) in a formal manner: *may I present the greetings of my master?* ■ formally deliver (a check or bill) for acceptance or payment: *a check presented by Mr. Jackson was returned by the bank.* ■ *Law* bring (a complaint, petition, or evidence) formally to the notice of a court. ■ (of a company or producer) put (a show or exhibition) before the public. **2** bring about or be the cause of (a problem or difficulty): *this should not present much difficulty.* ■ exhibit (a particular state or appearance) to others: *the EC presented a united front over the crisis.* ■ represent (someone) to others in a particular way, typically one that is false or exaggerated: *he* ***presented himself as*** *a hardworking man.* ■ (**present oneself**) come forward into the presence of another or others, esp. for a formal occasion; appear: *he failed to present himself in court.* ■ (**present itself**) (of an opportunity or idea) occur and be available for use or exploitation: *when a favorable opportunity presented itself, he would submit his proposition.* ■ [*intrans.*] (**present with**) *Medicine* (of a patient) come forward for or undergo initial medical examination for a particular condition or symptom: *the patient presented with mild clinical encephalopathy.* ■ [*intrans.*] *Medicine* (of a part of a fetus) be directed toward the cervix during labor. ■ [*intrans.*] *Medicine* (of an illness) manifest itself. **3** hold out or aim (a firearm) at something so as to be ready to fire: *they were to present their rifles, take aim, and fire.* ▷Middle English: from Old French *presenter*, from Latin *praesentare* 'place before' (in medieval Latin 'present as a gift'), from *praesent-* 'being at hand' (see PRESENT¹). —**pre·sent·er** *n.*
▸*PHRASE* □ **present arms** (usually as a command) hold a rifle vertically in front of the body as a salute.

pres·ent³ /ˈprezənt/ ▸*n.* a thing given to someone as a gift: *a Christmas present.* ▷Middle English: from Old French, originally in the phrase *mettre une chose en present à quelqu'un* 'put a thing into the presence of a person.'
▸*PHRASE* □ **make a present of** give as a gift: *he had made a present of a hacienda to the president.*

THE RIGHT WORD **bonus, donation, gift, gratuity, lagniappe, largesse, present**

What's the difference between a birthday **present** and a Christmas **gift**? Both words refer to something given as an expression of friendship, affection, esteem, etc.

But *gift* is a more formal term, often suggesting something of monetary value that is formally bestowed on an individual, group, or institution (*a gift to the university*).

Present, on the other hand, implies something of less value that is an expression of goodwill (*a housewarming present; a present for the teacher*).

Largesse is a somewhat pompous term for a very generous gift that is conferred in an ostentatious or condescending way, often on many recipients (*the king's largesse; the largesse of our government*).

A **gratuity** is associated with tipping and other forms of voluntary compensation for special attention or service above and beyond what is included in a charge (*known for her generous gratuities, the duchess enjoyed watching the waiters compete with each other to serve her*), while a **lagniappe** is a Southern word, used chiefly in Louisiana and southeast Texas, for either a gratuity or a small gift given to a customer along with a purchase.

If you give money or anything else as a gift to a philanthropic, charitable, or religious organization, it is known as a **donation** (*donations for the poor*).

But if your employer gives you money at the end of the year in addition to your regular salary, it isn't a Christmas *gift*; it's a Christmas **bonus**.

pre·sent·a·ble /priˈzentəbəl/ ▸*adj.* clean, well dressed, or decent enough to be seen in public: *I did my best to make myself look presentable.* —**pre·sent·a·bil·i·ty** /-ˌzentəˈbilətē/ *n.* —**pre·sent·a·bly** /-blē/ *adv.*

pres·en·ta·tion /ˌprēˌzenˈtāsHən; ˌprezən-; ˌprēzən-/ ▸*n.* **1** the proffering or giving of something to someone, esp. as part of a formal ceremony: *the presentation of certificates to new members* | *the trophy presentations.* ■ the manner or style in which something is given, offered, or displayed: *the presentation of foods is designed to stimulate your appetite.* ■ a formal introduction of someone, esp. at court. ■ the official submission of something for consideration in a law court: *the presentation of the bankruptcy petition.* ■ *chiefly historical* the action or right of formally proposing a candidate for a church benefice or other position: *the Earl of Pembroke offered Herbert the presentation of the living of Bremerton.* ■ a demonstration or display of a product or idea: *a sales presentation.* ■ an exhibition or theatrical performance. **2** *Medicine* the position of a fetus in relation to the cervix at the time of delivery: *breech presentation.* ■ the coming forward of a patient for initial examination and diagnosis: *all patients in this group were* *symptomatic at initial presentation.* **3** (**Presentation of Christ**) another term for **CANDLEMAS**. ▷late Middle English: via Old French from late Latin *praesentatio(n-)*, from Latin *praesentare* 'place before' (see **PRESENT**2). —**pres·en·ta·tion·al** /-SHənl/ *adj.* —**pres·en·ta·tion·al·ly** /-SHənl-ē/ *adv.*

pres·en·ta·tion graph·ics ▶ another term for **PRESENTATION SOFTWARE**.

pres·en·ta·tion soft·ware ▶*n.* software used to create a sequence of text and graphics, and often audio and video, to accompany a speech or public presentation. Also called **PRESENTATION GRAPHICS**.

pre·sen·ta·tive /pri'zentətiv/ ▶*adj. historical* (of a benefice) to which a patron has the right of presentation. ▷mid 16th cent.: probably from medieval Latin, based on Latin *praesentare* (see **PRESENT**2).

pres·ent-day ▶*adj.* [*attrib.*] of or relating to the current period of time: *present-day technological developments.*

pres·en·tee /ˌprezən'tē; priˌzen'tē/ ▶*n.* a person nominated or recommended for an office or position, esp. a church benefice. ▷late 15th cent.: from Anglo-Norman French, literally 'presented,' from the verb *presenter* (see **PRESENT**2).

pre·sen·tient /prē'senCHənt/ ▶*adj. rare* having a presentiment. ▷early 19th cent.: from Latin *praesentient-* 'perceiving beforehand,' from the verb *praesentire*, from *prae* 'before' + *sentire* 'to feel.'

pre·sen·ti·ment /pri'zentəmənt/ ▶*n.* an intuitive feeling about the future, esp. one of foreboding: *a presentiment of disaster.* ▷early 18th cent.: from obsolete French *présentiment.*

pres·ent·ism /'prezenˌtizəm/ ▶*n.* uncritical adherence to present-day attitudes, esp. the tendency to interpret past events in terms of modern values and concepts. —**pres·en·tist** *adj.*

pres·ent·ly /'prezəntlē/ ▶*adv.* **1** after a short time; soon: *this will be examined in more detail presently.* **2** at the present time; now: *there are presently 1,128 people on the waiting list*

> ***USAGE*** In *the pain will lessen presently*, the meaning of **presently** is 'soon.' In *limited resources are presently available*, the meaning is 'at this moment.' Both senses are widely used.

pre·sent·ment /pri'zentmənt/ ▶*n. Law, chiefly historical* a formal presentation of information to a court, esp. by a sworn jury regarding an offense or other matter. ▷Middle English: from Old French *presentement*, from *presenter* 'place before' (see **PRESENT**3).

pres·ent par·ti·ci·ple ▶*n. Grammar* the form of a verb, ending in *-ing* in English, which is used in forming continuous tenses, e.g., in *I'm thinking*, alone in nonfinite clauses, e.g., in *sitting here, I haven't a care in the world*, as a noun, e.g., in *good thinking*, and as an adjective, e.g., in *running water*.

pres·ent val·ue (also **net present value**) ▶*n. Finance* the value in the present of a sum of money, in contrast to some future value it will have when it has been invested at compound interest.

pres·er·va·tion /ˌprezər'vāSHən/ ▶*n.* the action of preserving something: *the preservation of the city's green spaces* | *food preservation.* ■ the state of being preserved, esp. to a specified degree: *the homestead is in a fine state of preservation.* ▷late Middle English: via Old French from medieval Latin *praeservatio(n-)*, from late Latin *praeservare* 'to keep' (see **PRESERVE**).

pres·er·va·tion·ist /ˌprezər'vāSHənəst/ ▶*n.* a supporter or advocate of the preservation of something, esp. of historic buildings and artifacts.

pre·serv·a·tive /pri'zərvətiv/ ▶*n.* a substance used to preserve foodstuffs, wood, or other materials against decay.
▶*adj.* acting to preserve something: *the preservative effects of freezing.* ▷late Middle English: via Old French from medieval Latin *praeservativus*, from late Latin *praeservat-* 'kept,' from the verb *praeservare* (see **PRESERVE**).

pre·serve /pri'zərv/ ▶*v.* [*trans.*] maintain (something) in its original or existing state: *all records of the past were zealously preserved* | [as *adj.*] (**preserved**) *a magnificently preserved monastery.* ■ retain (a condition or state of affairs): *a fight to preserve local democracy.* ■ maintain or keep alive (a memory or quality): *the film has preserved all the qualities of the novel.* ■ keep safe from harm or injury: *a place for preserving endangered species.* ■ treat or refrigerate (food) to prevent its decomposition or fermentation. ■ prepare (fruit) for long-term storage by boiling it with sugar: [as *adj.*] (**preserved**) *those sweet preserved fruits associated with Cremona.* ■ keep (game or an area where game is found) undisturbed to allow private hunting or shooting.
▶*n.* **1** (usu. **preserves**) food made with fruit preserved in sugar, such as jam or marmalade: *homemade preserves.* **2** a sphere of activity regarded as being reserved for a particular person or group: *the civil service became* ***the preserve of*** *the educated middle class.* **3** a place where game is protected and kept for private hunting or shooting. ▷late Middle English (in the sense 'keep safe from harm'): from Old French *preserver*, from late Latin *praeservare*, from *prae-* 'before, in advance' + *servare* 'to keep.' —**pre·serv·a·ble** *adj.* —**pre·serv·er** *n.*

pre·served lem·on /pri'zərvd/ ▶*n.* lemons or lemon slices preserved in salt and lemon juice, used as an ingredient in Moroccan cooking.

pre·serv·ice /'prē'sərvəs/ ▶*adj.* of or relating to the period before a person takes a job that requires training, esp. in teaching: *preservice training.*

pre·set /prē'set/ ▶*v.* (**-set·ting**; *past* and *past part.* **-set**) [*trans.*] [usu. as *adj.*] (**preset**) set or adjust (a value that controls the operation of a device) in advance of its use: *the water is heated quickly to a preset temperature.*
▶*n.* a control on electronic equipment or on software that is set or adjusted beforehand to facilitate use.

pre·shrunk /prē'SHrəNGk/ ▶*adj.* (of a fabric or garment) having undergone a shrinking process during manufacture to prevent further shrinking in use. —**pre·shrink** /-'SHriNGk/ *v.*

pre·side /pri'zīd/ ▶*v.* [*intrans.*] **1** be in the position of authority in a meeting or gathering: *Bishop Herbener presided at the meeting* | [as *adj.*] (**presiding**) *the sentence imposed by the presiding judge.* ■ (**preside over**) be in charge of (a place or situation): *he presided over a period of great budgetary recklessness.* **2** (**preside at**) play (a musical instrument, esp. a keyboard instrument) at a public gathering. ▷early 17th cent.: from French *présider*, from Latin *praesidere*, from *prae* 'before' + *sedere* 'sit.'

pres·i·den·cy /'prez(ə)dənsē; 'prezəˌdensē/ ▶*n.* (*pl.* **-cies**) the office of president: *the presidency of the U.S.* ■ the period of this: *the liberal climate that existed during Carter's presidency.* ■ *Christian Church* the role of the priest or minister who conducts a Eucharist. ■ (also **First Presidency**) (in the Mormon church) a council of three officers forming the highest administrative body. ▷late 16th cent.: from medieval Latin *praesidentia*, from *praesidere* 'sit before' (see **PRESIDE**).

pres·i·dent /'prez(ə)dənt; 'prezəˌdent/ ▶*n.* **1** the elected head of a republican state: *the Irish president* | [as *title*] *President Khrushchev.* ■ the head of a society, council, or other organization: *the president of the European Community.* ■ the head of a college or university. ■ the head of a company. **2** *Christian Church* the celebrant at a Eucharist. ▷late Middle English: via Old French from Latin *praesident-* 'sitting before' (see **PRESIDE**). —**pres·i·den·tial** /ˌprezə'denCHəl/ *adj.* —**pres·i·den·tial·ly** /ˌprezə'denCHələ/ *adv.* —**pres·i·dent·ship** /-ˌSHip/ *n.* (*archaic*)

pres·i·dent-e·lect ▶*n.* (*pl.* **pres·i·dents-e·lect**) a person who has been elected president but has not yet taken up office.

Pres·i·den·tial Med·al of Free·dom /ˌprezə'denCHəl/ ▶*n.* (in the U.S.) a medal constituting the highest award that can be given to a civilian in peacetime.

Pres·i·den·tial Range a range in northern New Hampshire's White Mountains that includes Mount Washington, which, at 6,288 feet (1,918 m), is the highest peak in the northeastern U.S.

pres·i·dent pro tem·po·re /'prō 'tempəˌrē/ (also **pres·i·dent pro tem** /'prō 'tem/) ▶*n.* a high-ranking senator of the majority party who presides over the U.S. Senate in the absence of the vice president.

pre·sid·i·o /pri'sidēˌō; -sēdē-/ ▶*n.* (*pl.* **-os**) (in Spain and Spanish America) a fortified military settlement. ▷Spanish, from Latin *praesidium* 'garrison.'

pre·sid·i·um /pri'sidēəm; -'zid-/ (also **prae·sid·i·um**) ▶*n.* a standing executive committee in a communist country. ■ (**Presidium**) the committee of this type in the former USSR, which functioned as the legislative authority when the Supreme Soviet was not sitting. ▷1920s: from Russian *prezidium*, from Latin *praesidium* 'protection, garrison' (see **PRESIDE**).

Pres·ley /'prezlē; 'pres-/, Elvis (Aaron) (1935–77), U.S. singer; known as the **King of Rock and Roll**. He was the dominant personality of early rock and roll with songs such as "Heartbreak Hotel," "Don't Be Cruel," and "Hound Dog" and was noted for the frank sexuality of his performances. He also made numerous movies, including *King Creole* (1958), and became a cult figure after his death.

pre-So·crat·ic ▶*adj.* of, relating to, or denoting the speculative philosophers in the ancient Greek world in the 6th and 5th centuries BC (before the time of Socrates), who attempted to find rational explanations for natural phenomena. They included Parmenides, Anaxagoras, Empedocles, and Heraclitus.
▶*n.* a pre-Socratic philosopher.

pre·sort /prē'sôrt/ ▶*v.* [*trans.*] sort outgoing mail by zip code in order to take advantage of a cheaper rate of postage.

press1 /pres/ ▶*v.* **1** move or cause to move into a position of contact with something by exerting continuous physical force: [*trans.*] *he pressed his face to the glass* | [*intrans.*] *her body pressed against his.* ■ [*trans.*] exert continuous physical force on (something), typically in order to operate a device or machine: *he pressed a button and the doors slid open.* ■ [*trans.*] squeeze (someone's arm or hand) as a sign of affection. ■ [*intrans.*] move in a specified direction by pushing: *the mob was still pressing forward.* ■ *figurative* (of an enemy or opponent) attack persistently and fiercely: [*intrans.*] *their enemies pressed in on all sides* | [*trans.*] *two assailants were pressing Agrippa.* ■ [*intrans.*] (**press on/ahead**) *figurative* continue in one's action: *he stubbornly* ***pressed on with*** *his work.* ■ [*trans.*] *Weightlifting* raise (a specified weight) by first lifting it to shoulder height and then gradually pushing it upward above the head. **2** [*trans.*] apply pressure to (something) to flatten, shape, or smooth it, typically by ironing: *she pressed her nicest blouse* | [as *adj.*] (**pressed**) *immaculately pressed trousers.* ■ apply pressure to (a flower or leaf) between sheets of paper in order to dry and preserve it. ■ extract (juice or oil) by crushing or squeezing fruit, vegetables, etc.: [as *adj.*] (**pressed**) *freshly pressed grape juice.* ■ squeeze or crush (fruit, vegetables, etc.) to extract the juice or oil. ■ manufacture (something, esp. a phonograph record) by molding under pressure. **3** [*trans.*] forcefully put forward (an opinion, claim, or course of action): *Rose did not press the point.* ■ make strong efforts to persuade or force (someone) to do or provide something: *when I* ***pressed*** *him* ***for*** *precise figures, he evaded the subject* | [with *infinitive*] *the marketing directors were pressed to justify their expenditure* | [*intrans.*] *they continued to* ***press for*** *changes in legislation.* ■ [*intrans.*] *Golf* try too hard to achieve distance with a shot, at the risk of inaccuracy. ■ (**press something on/upon**) insist that (someone) accept an offer or gift: *he pressed dinner invitations on her.* ■ [*intrans.*] (of something, esp. time) be in short supply and so demand immediate action. ■ (**be pressed**) have barely enough of something, esp. time: *I'm very* ***pressed for*** *time.* ■ (**be pressed to do something**) have difficulty doing or achieving something: *they may be* ***hard pressed*** *to keep their promise.*
▶*n.* **1** a device for applying pressure to something in order to flatten or shape it or to extract juice or oil: *a flower press* | *a wine press.* ■ a machine that applies pressure to a workpiece by means of a tool, in order to punch shapes. **2** a printing press. ■ [often in *names*] a business that prints or publishes books: *the Clarendon Press.* ■ the process of printing: *the book is ready to* ***go to press.*** **3** (**the press**) [treated as *sing.* or *pl.*] newspapers or journalists viewed collectively: *the press was notified* | [as *adj.*] *press coverage.* ■ coverage in newspapers and magazines: *there's no point in demonstrating if you don't get any press* | [in *sing.*] *the mayor has had a bad press for years.* **4** an act of pressing something: *the system summons medical help at the press of a button.* ■ [in *sing.*] a closely packed crowd or mass of people or things: *among the press of cars he saw a taxi.* ■ *dated* pressure of business. ■ *Weightlifting* an act of raising a weight to shoulder height and then gradually pushing it above the head. ■ *Basketball* any of various forms of close guarding by the defending team. **5** *chiefly Irish Scottish* a large cupboard for clothes, books, and other items, typically in a recess. ▷Middle English: from Old French *presse* (noun), *presser* (verb), from Latin *pressare* 'keep pressing,' frequentative of *premere.*
▶***PHRASES*** □ **press charges** see **CHARGE**. □ **press something home** see **HOME**. □ **press (the) flesh** *informal* (of a celebrity or politician) greet people by shaking hands.

press2 ▶*v.* [*trans.*] (**press someone/something into**) put (someone or something) to a specified use, esp. as a temporary or makeshift measure: *many of these*

stones have been pressed into service as gateposts. ■ *historical* force (a man) to enlist in the army or navy.
▸*n. historical* a forcible enlistment of men, esp. for the navy. ▷late 16th cent.: alteration (by association with **PRESS**[1]) of obsolete *prest* 'pay given on enlistment, enlistment by such payment,' from Old French *prest* 'loan, advance pay,' based on Latin *praestare* 'provide.'

press a·gent ▸*n.* a person employed to organize advertising and publicity in the press on behalf of an organization or well-known person.

press·board /ˈpres,bôrd/ ▸*n.* a hard, dense kind of board with a smooth finish, typically made from wood or textile pulp or laminated wastepaper, and used as an electrical insulator and for making light furniture.

press box ▸*n.* an area reserved for journalists at a sports event.

Press·burg /ˈpresbərg/ German name for **BRATISLAVA**.

press card ▸*n.* an official authorization carried by a reporter, esp. one that gives admission to an event.

press clip·ping ▸*n.* a paragraph or short article cut out of a newspaper or magazine.

press con·fer·ence ▸*n.* an interview given to journalists by a prominent person in order to make an announcement or answer questions.

press·er foot ▸*n.* the footplate of a sewing machine that holds the fabric down onto the part that feeds it under the needle.

press fit ▸*n.* an interference fit between two parts in which one is forced under pressure into a slightly smaller hole in the other. **—press-fit·ted** *adj.*

press gal·ler·y ▸*n.* a place reserved for journalists observing the proceedings in a legislature or court of law.

press gang ▸*n. historical* a body of men employed to enlist men forcibly into service in the army or navy.
▸*v.* [*trans.*] (**press-gang**) *chiefly historical* forcibly enlist (someone) into service in the army or navy. ■ (**press-gang someone into**) force someone to do something: *we press-ganged Simon into playing.*

press·ing /ˈpresiNG/ ▸*adj.* (of a problem, need, or situation) requiring quick or immediate action or attention: *inflation was the most pressing problem.* See note at **CRUCIAL**. ■ (of an engagement or activity) important and requiring one's attendance or presence: *he had pressing business in Albany.* ■ (of an invitation) strongly expressed.
▸*n.* a thing made by the application of force or weight, esp. a phonograph record. ■ a series of such things made at one time: *the first pressing of the live album.* ■ an act or instance of applying force or weight to something: *pure-grade olive oil is the product of the second or third pressings.* **—press·ing·ly** *adv.*

press kit ▸*n.* a package of promotional material provided to members of the press to brief them, esp. about a product, service, or candidate.

press·man /ˈpres,mən; ,man/ ▸*n.* (*pl.* **-men**) **1** *chiefly Brit.* a journalist. **2** a person who operates a printing press.

press·mark /ˈpres,märk/ ▸*n. chiefly Brit.* a call number.

pres·sor /ˈpresər/ ▸*adj.* [*attrib.*] *Physiology* producing an increase in blood pressure by stimulating constriction of the blood vessels: *a pressor response.*

press re·lease ▸*n.* an official statement issued to newspapers giving information on a particular matter.

press run ▸*n.* the operation of a printing press for a single job (the number or entire set of items produced in such an operation): *the paper is increasing its press run from 75,000 to 95,000 copies.*

press time ▸*n.* the moment when a magazine or other publication goes to press.

press-up ▸*n.* British term for **PUSHUP**.

pres·sure /ˈpresHər/ ▸*n.* **1** the continuous physical force exerted on or against an object by something in contact with it: *the slight extra pressure he applied to her hand.* ■ the force exerted per unit area: *gas can be fed to the turbines at a pressure of around 250 psi.* **2** the use of persuasion, influence, or intimidation to make someone do something: *the proposals put pressure on Britain to drop its demand | the many pressures on girls to worry about their looks.* ■ the influence or effect of someone or something: *oil prices came under some downward pressure.* ■ the feeling of stressful urgency caused by the necessity of doing or achieving something, esp. with limited time: *you need to be able to work under pressure and not get flustered | some offenders might find prison a refuge against the pressures of the outside world.*
▸*v.* [*trans.*] attempt to persuade or coerce (someone) into doing something: *it might now be possible to* ***pressure*** *him* ***into*** *resigning | [trans.] she pressured her son to accept a job offer from the bank.* ▷late Middle English: from Old French, from Latin *pressura*, from *press-* 'pressed,' from the verb *premere* (see **PRESS**[1]).

pres·sure cook·er ▸*n.* an airtight pot in which food can be cooked quickly under steam pressure. ■ *figurative* a highly stressful situation or assignment: *being chairman has been a real pressure cooker.* **—pres·sure-cook** *v.*

pres·sure gauge ▸*n.* an instrument indicating pressure: *an oil pressure gauge.*

pres·sure group ▸*n.* a group that tries to influence public policy in the interest of a particular cause: *an environmental pressure group.*

pres·sure hull ▸*n.* the inner hull of a submarine, in which approximately atmospheric pressure is maintained when the vessel is submerged.

pres·sure lamp ▸*n.* a portable oil or kerosene lamp in which the fuel is forced up into the mantle or burner by air pressure in the reservoir, which can be increased by pumping with a plunger.

pres·sure point ▸*n.* a point on the surface of the body sensitive to pressure. ■ a point where an artery can be pressed against a bone to inhibit bleeding. ■ a place in which trouble or difficulty is likely to be found: *the license has been a key pressure point in the struggle.*

pres·sure suit ▸*n.* an inflatable suit that protects the wearer against low pressure, e.g., when flying at a high altitude.

pres·sure ves·sel ▸*n.* a container designed to hold material at high pressures. ■ an enclosed structure containing a nuclear reactor core immersed in pressurized coolant.

pres·sur·ize /ˈpresHə,rīz/ ▸*v.* [*trans.*] **1** produce or maintain raised pressure artificially in (a gas or its container): *the mixture was pressurized to 1,900 atmospheres* | [as *adj.*] (**pressurized**) *a pressurized can.* ■ maintain a tolerable atmospheric pressure in (an aircraft cabin) at a high altitude: [as *adj.*] (**pressurized**) *a pressurized cabin.* **2** [*trans.*] attempt to persuade or coerce (someone) into doing something: *the protests were an attempt to* ***pressurize*** *the government* ***into*** *bringing an end to the violence | [trans.] people had been pressurized to vote.* **—pres·sur·i·za·tion** /,presHərəˈzāsHən/ *n.*

pres·sur·ized-wa·ter re·ac·tor (abbr.: **PWR**) ▸*n.* a nuclear reactor in which the fuel is uranium oxide clad in zircaloy and the coolant and moderator is water maintained at high pressure so that it does not boil at the operating temperature of the reactor.

press·work /ˈpres,wərk/ ▸*n.* **1** the process of using a printing press. ■ printed matter, esp. with regard to its quality. **2** the shaping of metal by pressing or drawing it into a shaped hollow die.

Pres·ter John /ˈprestər ˈjän/ a legendary medieval Christian king of Asia, said to have defeated the Muslims and to be destined to bring help to the Holy Land. ▷Middle English: from Old French *prestre Jehan*, from medieval Latin *presbyter Johannes* 'priest John.'

pres·ti·dig·i·ta·tion /,prestə,dijəˈtāsHən/ ▸*n. formal* magic tricks performed as entertainment. ▷mid 19th cent.: from French, from *preste* 'nimble' + Latin *digitus* 'finger' + **-ATION**. **—pres·ti·dig·i·ta·tor** /-ˈdijə,tātər/ *n.*

pres·tige /presˈtēzH; -ˈtēj/ ▸*n.* widespread respect and admiration felt for someone or something on the basis of a perception of their achievements or quality: *he experienced a tremendous increase in prestige following his victory.* ■ [as *adj.*] denoting something that arouses such respect or admiration: *prestige wines.* ▷mid 17th cent. (in the sense 'illusion, conjuring trick'): from French, literally 'illusion, glamour,' from late Latin *praestigium* 'illusion,' from Latin *praestigiae* (plural) 'conjuring tricks.' The transference of meaning occurred by way of the sense 'dazzling influence, glamour,' at first depreciatory.

pres·tige pric·ing ▸*n.* the practice of pricing goods at a high level in order to give the appearance of quality.

pres·tig·ious /preˈstijəs; -ˈstē-/ ▸*adj.* inspiring respect and admiration; having high status: *a prestigious academic post.* ▷mid 16th cent. (in the sense 'practicing legerdemain'): from late Latin *praestigiosus*, from *praestigiae* 'conjuring tricks.' The current sense dates from the early 20th cent. **—pres·tig·i·ous·ly** *adv.* **—pres·tig·i·ous·ness** *n.*

pres·tis·si·mo /preˈstisə,mō/ *Music* ▸*adv.* & *adj.* (esp. as a direction) in a very quick tempo.
▸*n.* (*pl.* **-mos**) a movement or passage marked to be performed in a very quick tempo. ▷Italian, superlative of *presto* 'quick, quickly' (see **PRESTO**).

pres·to /ˈprestō/ ▸*adv.* & *adj. Music* (esp. as a direction) in a quick tempo.
▸*n.* (*pl.* **-tos**) *Music* a movement or passage marked to be performed in a quick tempo.
▸*exclam.* a phrase announcing the successful completion of a trick, or suggesting that something has been done so easily that it seems to be magic: *just one quick squeeze and presto! A stir fry in seconds.* ▷Italian, 'quick, quickly,' from late Latin *praestus* 'ready,' from Latin *praesto* 'at hand.'

Pres·ton /ˈprestən/ a city in northwestern England, the administrative center of the county of Lancashire, on the Ribble River; pop. 126,000. It was the site in the 18th century of the first English cotton mills.

Pres·ton·pans, Bat·tle of /,prestənˈpanz/ a battle in 1745 near the town of Prestonpans just east of Edinburgh, Scotland, the first major engagement of the Jacobite uprising of 1745–46. The Jacobites routed the Hanoverians, leaving the way clear for Charles Edward Stuart's subsequent invasion of England.

pre·stressed /prēˈstrest/ ▸*adj.* strengthened by the application of stress during manufacture, esp. (of concrete) by means of rods or wires inserted under tension before the material is set. **—pre·stress·ing** /-ˈstresiNG/ *n.*

pre·sum·a·bly /priˈzōōməblē/ ▸*adv.* [*sentence adverb*] used to convey that what is asserted is very likely though not known for certain: *the Yakima Indians presumably came from Asia by way of the Bering Strait.*

pre·sume /priˈzōōm/ ▸*v.* **1** [with *clause*] suppose that something is the case on the basis of probability: *I presumed that the man had been escorted from the building | [trans.] the two men were presumed dead when the wreck of their boat was found.* ■ take for granted that something exists or is the case: *the argument presumes that only one person can do the work | [trans.] the task demands skills which cannot be presumed and therefore require proper training.* **2** [*intrans.*] be audacious enough to do something: *kindly don't presume to issue me orders in my own house.* ■ [*intrans.*] make unjustified demands; take liberties: *forgive me if I have presumed.* ■ [*intrans.*] (**presume on/upon**) unjustifiably regard (something) as entitling one to privileges: *she knew he regarded her as his protegée, but was determined not to presume on that.* ▷late Middle English: from Old French *presumer*, from Latin *praesumere* 'anticipate' (in late Latin 'take for granted'), from *prae* 'before' + *sumere* 'take.' **—pre·sum·a·ble** *adj.*

pre·sum·ing /priˈzōōmiNG/ ▸*adj. archaic* presumptuous. **—pre·sum·ing·ly** *adv.*

pre·sump·tion /priˈzəmpsHən/ ▸*n.* **1** an act or instance of taking something to be true or adopting a particular attitude toward something, esp. at the start of a chain of argument or action: *the* ***presumption of*** *guilt has changed to a presumption of innocence.* ■ an idea that is taken to be true, and often used as the basis for other ideas, although it is not known for certain: *underlying presumptions about human nature.* ■ *chiefly Law* an attitude adopted in law or as a matter of policy toward an action or proposal in the absence of acceptable reasons to the contrary: *the planning policy shows a general* ***presumption in favor of*** *development.* **2** behavior perceived as arrogant, disrespectful, and transgressing the limits of what is permitted or appropriate: *he lifted her off the ground and she was enraged at his presumption.* ▷Middle English: from Old French *presumpcion*, from Latin *praesumptio(n)* 'anticipation,' from the verb *praesumere* (see **PRESUME**).

pre·sump·tive /priˈzəmptiv/ ▸*adj.* of the nature of a presumption; presumed in the absence of further information: *a presumptive diagnosis.* ■ *Law* giving grounds for the inference of a fact or of the appropriate interpretation of the law. ■ another term for **PRESUMPTUOUS**. ▷late Middle English: from French *présomptif, -ive*, from late Latin *praesumptivus*, from *praesumpt-* 'taken before,' from the verb *praesumere* (see **PRESUME**). **—pre·sump·tive·ly** *adv.*

pre·sump·tu·ous /priˈzəmpCH(ōō)əs/ ▸*adj.* (of a person or their behavior) failing to observe the limits of what is permitted or appropriate: *I hope I won't be considered presumptuous if I offer some advice.* See note at **BOLD**. ▷Middle English: from Old French *presumptueux*, from late Latin *praesumptuosus*, variant of *praesumptiosus* 'full of boldness,' from *praesumptio* (see PRESUMPTION). —**pre·sump·tu·ous·ly** *adv.* —**pre·sump·tu·ous·ness** *n.*

pre·sup·pose /ˌprēsəˈpōz/ ▸*v.* [*trans.*] (of an action, process, or argument) require as a precondition of possibility or coherence: *his relationships did not permit the degree of self-revelation that true intimacy presupposes.* ■ [with *clause*] tacitly assume at the beginning of a line of argument or course of action that something is the case: *your argument presupposes that it does not matter who is in power.* ▷late Middle English: from Old French *presupposer*, suggested by medieval Latin *praesupponere*, from *prae* 'before' + *supponere* 'place under' (see SUPPOSE).

pre·sup·po·si·tion /ˌprēˌsəpəˈzisʜən/ ▸*n.* a thing tacitly assumed beforehand at the beginning of a line of argument or course of action: *images that challenge presuppositions about feminine handiwork.* ■ the action or state of presupposing or being presupposed. ▷mid 16th cent.: from medieval Latin *praesuppositio(n-)*, from the verb *praesupponere* (see PRESUPPOSE).

pre·syn·ap·tic /ˌprēsəˈnaptik/ ▸*adj. Physiology* relating to or denoting a nerve cell that releases a transmitter substance into a synapse during transmission of an impulse. —**pre·syn·ap·ti·cal·ly** /-ik(ə)lē/ *adv.*

pret. ▸*abbr.* preterite.

prêt-à-por·ter /ˌpret ä pôrˈtā/ ▸*adj.* (of designer clothes) sold ready-to-wear as opposed to made to measure.

▸*n.* designer clothes sold ready-to-wear. ▷French, literally 'ready to wear.'

pre·tax /ˈprēˈtaks/ ▸*adj.* (of income or profits) considered or calculated before the deduction of taxes: *pretax profits rose 23 percent.*

pre·teen /ˈprēˈtēn/ ▸*adj.* [*attrib.*] of or relating to a child just under the age of thirteen.

▸*n.* a child of such an age.

pre·tence ▸*n.* British spelling of PRETENSE.

pre·tend /priˈtend/ ▸*v.* **1** [with *clause* or *infinitive*] speak and act so as to make it appear that something is the case when in fact it is not: *I closed my eyes and pretended I was asleep | she turned the pages and pretended to read.* ■ engage in a game or fantasy that involves supposing something that is not the case to be so: *children pretending to be grownups.* ■ [*trans.*] give the appearance of feeling or possessing (an emotion or quality); simulate: *she pretended a greater surprise than she felt.* **2** [*intrans.*] (**pretend to**) lay claim to (a quality or title): *he cannot pretend to sophistication.*

▸*adj.* [*attrib.*] *informal* not really what it is represented as being; used in a game or deception: *the children are pouring out pretend tea for the dolls.* ▷late Middle English: from Latin *praetendere* 'stretch forth, claim,' from *prae* 'before' + *tendere* 'stretch.' The adjective dates from the early 20th cent.

pre·tend·er /priˈtendər/ ▸*n.* a person who claims or aspires to a title or position: *the* **pretender to** *the throne.*

pre·tense /ˈprēˌtens; priˈtens/ (*Brit.* **pre·tence**) ▸*n.* **1** an attempt to make something that is not the case appear true: *his anger is masked by a pretense that all is well | they have finally abandoned their secrecy and pretense.* ■ a false display of feelings, attitudes, or intentions: *he asked me questions without any pretense at politeness.* ■ the practice of inventing imaginary situations in play: *before the age of two, children start to engage in pretense.* ■ affected and ostentatious speech and behavior. **2** (**pretense to**) a claim, esp. a false or ambitious one: *he was quick to disclaim any pretense to superiority.* ▷late Middle English: from Anglo-Norman French *pretense*, based on medieval Latin *pretensus* 'pretended,' alteration of Latin *praetentus*, from the verb *praetendere* (see PRETEND).

pre·ten·sion[1] /priˈtenCHən/ ▸*n.* **1** (**pretension to**) a claim or the assertion of a claim to something: *their pretensions to culture | we cannot tolerate pretension to infallibility.* ■ (often **pretensions**) an aspiration or claim to a certain status or quality: *another aging rocker with literary pretensions.* **2** the use of affectation to impress; ostentatiousness: *he spoke simply, without pretension.* ▷late Middle English: from medieval Latin *praetensio(n-)*, from *praetens-* 'alleged,' from the verb *praetendere* (see PRETEND).

pre·ten·sion[2] /prēˈtenCHən/ ▸*v.* [*trans.*] apply tension to (an object) before some other process or event: *the safety system pretensions the seat belts.* ■ strengthen (reinforced concrete) by applying tension to the reinforcing rods before the concrete has set.

pre·ten·sion·er /prēˈtenCHənər/ ▸*n.* a device designed to pull a seat belt tight in an accident.

pre·ten·tious /priˈtenCHəs/ ▸*adj.* attempting to impress by affecting greater importance, talent, culture, etc., than is actually possessed: *a pretentious literary device.* ▷mid 19th cent.: from French *prétentieux*, from *prétention* (see PRETENSION[1]). —**pre·ten·tious·ly** *adv.* —**pre·ten·tious·ness** *n.*

preter- ▸*comb. form* more than: *preternatural.* ▷from Latin *praeter* 'past, beyond.'

pret·er·ite /ˈpretərit/ (also **pret·er·it**) *Grammar* ▸*adj.* expressing a past action or state.

▸*n.* a simple past tense or form. ▷Middle English (in the sense 'bygone, former'): from Latin *praeteritus* 'gone by,' past participle of *praeterire*, from *praeter* 'past, beyond' + *ire* 'go.'

pret·er·i·tion /ˌpretəˈrisʜən/ ▸*n.* **1** the action of passing over or disregarding a matter, esp. the rhetorical technique of making summary mention of something by professing to omit it. **2** (in Calvinist theology) omission from God's elect; nonelection to salvation. ▷late 16th cent.: from late Latin *praeteritio(n-)*, from *praeterire* 'pass, go by.'

pre·term /prēˈtərm/ *Medicine* ▸*adj.* born or occurring after a pregnancy significantly shorter than normal, esp. after no more than 37 weeks of pregnancy: *babies born during preterm labor.*

▸*adv.* after a short pregnancy; prematurely: *babies born preterm are likely to lack surfactant in the lungs.*

pre·ter·mit /ˌprētərˈmit/ ▸*v.* (**-mit·ted, -mit·ting**) [*trans.*] *archaic* **1** omit to do or mention: *some points of conduct we advisedly pretermit.* **2** abandon (a custom or continuous action) for a time: *the pleasant musical evenings were now entirely pretermitted.* ▷late 15th cent.: from Latin *praetermittere*, from *praeter* 'past, beyond' + *mittere* 'let go.' —**pre·ter·mis·sion** /ˌprētərˈmisʜən/ *n.*

pre·ter·nat·u·ral /ˌprētərˈnaCH(ə)rəl/ ▸*adj.* beyond what is normal or natural: *autumn had arrived with preternatural speed.* —**pre·ter·nat·u·ral·ism** /-ˈnaCH(ə)rəˌlizəm/ *n.* —**pre·ter·nat·u·ral·ly** *adv.*

pre·text /ˈprēˌtekst/ ▸*n.* a reason given in justification of a course of action that is not the real reason: *the rebels had the perfect pretext for making their move.* ▷early 16th cent.: from Latin *praetextus* 'outward display,' from the verb *praetexere* 'to disguise,' from *prae* 'before' + *texere* 'weave.'

▸*PHRASE* □ **on** (or **under**) **the pretext** giving the specified reason as one's justification: *the police raided Grand River* **on the pretext of** *looking for moonshiners.*

pre·tor /ˈprētər/ ▸*n.* variant spelling of PRAETOR.

Pre·to·ri·a /prəˈtôrēə/ the administrative capital of South Africa; pop. 1,080,000. It was founded in 1855 by Marthinus Wessel Pretorius (1819–1901), the first president of the South African Republic, and named after his father Andries.

pre·to·ri·an /priˈtôrēən/ ▸*adj.* & *n.* variant spelling of PRAETORIAN.

pre·treat /prēˈtrēt/ ▸*v.* [*trans.*] treat (something) with a chemical before use. —**pre·treat·ment** *n.*

pret·ti·fy /ˈpritəˌfī/ ▸*v.* (**-fies, -fied**) [*trans.*] make (someone or something) appear superficially pretty or attractive: *nothing has been done to prettify the site.* —**pret·ti·fi·ca·tion** /ˌpritəfəˈkāsʜən/ *n.* —**pret·ti·fi·er** *n.*

pret·ty /ˈpritē/ ▸*adj.* (**-ti·er, -ti·est**) attractive in a delicate way without being truly beautiful or handsome: *a pretty little girl with an engaging grin.* ■ [*attrib.*] *informal* used ironically in expressions of annoyance or disgust: *it is a pretty state of affairs when a young fellow prefers the company of Italian fiddlers to taking possession of his own first command.*

▸*adv.* [as *submodifier*] *informal* to a moderately high degree; fairly: *he looked pretty fit for his age.*

▸*n.* (*pl.* **-ties**) *informal* an attractive thing, typically a pleasing but unnecessary accessory: *he buys her lots of pretties—bangles and rings and things.* ■ used to refer in a condescending way to an attractive person, usually a girl or a woman: *six pretties in sequined leotards.*

▸*v.* (**-ties, -tied**) [*trans.*] make pretty or attractive: *she'll be all* **prettied up** *and ready to go in an hour.* ▷Old English *prættig*; related to Middle Dutch *pertich* 'brisk, clever,' obsolete Dutch *prettig* 'humorous, sporty,' from a West Germanic base meaning 'trick.' The sense development 'deceitful, cunning, clever, skillful, admirable, pleasing, nice' has parallels in adjectives such as *canny, fine, nice*, etc. —**pret·ti·ly** /ˈpritl-ē/ *adv.* —**pret·ti·ness** *n.* —**pret·ty·ish** *adj.*

▸*PHRASES* □ **pretty much** (or **nearly** or **well**) *informal* very nearly: *the case is pretty well over.* □ **a pretty penny** *informal* a large sum of money. □ **pretty please** used as an emphatic or wheedling form of request. □ **be sitting pretty** *informal* be in an advantageous position or situation: *if she could get sponsors, she would be sitting pretty.*

pret·ty boy ▸*n. informal, often derogatory* a foppish or effeminate man.

pret·zel /ˈpretsəl/ ▸*n.* a crisp biscuit baked in the form of a knot or stick and flavored with salt.

▸*v.* (**-zeled, -zel·ing**) [*trans.*] twist, bend, or contort: *he found the snake pretzeled into a tangle of knots.* ▷mid 19th cent.: from German *Pretzel.*

prev. ▸*abbr.* ■ previous; previously.

pre·vail /priˈvāl/ ▸*v.* [*intrans.*] prove more powerful than opposing forces; be victorious: *it is hard for logic to* **prevail over** *emotion.* ■ be widespread in a particular area at a particular time; be current: *an atmosphere of crisis prevails |* [as *adj.*] (**prevailing**) *the prevailing political culture.* ■ (**prevail on/upon**) persuade (someone) to do something: *she was prevailed upon to give an account of her work.* ▷late Middle English: from Latin *praevalere* 'have greater power,' from *prae* 'before' + *valere* 'have power.' —**pre·vail·ing·ly** *adv.*

pre·vail·ing wind ▸*n.* a wind from the direction that is predominant at a particular place or season.

prev·a·lent /ˈprevələnt/ ▸*adj.* widespread in a particular area at a particular time: *the social ills prevalent in society today.* ■ *archaic* predominant; powerful. ▷late 16th cent.: from Latin *praevalent-* 'having greater power,' from the verb *praevalere* (see PREVAIL). —**prev·a·lence** *n.* —**prev·a·lent·ly** *adv.*

THE RIGHT WORD **abundant, common, copious, plentiful, prevailing, prevalent, rife**

Wildflowers might be **prevalent** in the mountains during the spring months, but a particular type of wildflower might be the **prevailing** one. *Prevalent*, in other words, implies widespread occurrence or acceptance in a particular place or time (*a prevalent belief during the nineteenth century*), while *prevailing* suggests that something exists in such quantity that it surpasses or leads all others in acceptance, usage, or belief (*the prevailing theory about the evolution of man*).

Wildflowers might also be **abundant** in the valleys—a word that, unlike *prevalent* and *prevailing*, is largely restricted to observations about a place and may suggest oversupply (*an abundant harvest; indications of decay were abundant*).

Plentiful, on the other hand, refers to a large or full supply without the connotations of oversupply (*a country where jobs were plentiful*).

If wildflowers are **rife**, it means that they are not only *prevalent* but spreading rapidly (*speculation was rife among the soldiers*).

If they're **copious**, it means they are being produced in such quantity that they constitute a rich or flowing abundance (*weep copious tears*).

What often happens, with wildflowers as well as with other beautiful things, is that they become so abundant they are regarded as **common**, a word meaning usual or ordinary (*the common cold*).

Like *prevalent*, *common* can apply to a time as well as a place (*an expression common during the Depression*). But neither *abundant* nor *common* connotes dominance as clearly as *prevalent* does.

pre·var·i·cate /priˈvariˌkāt/ ▸*v.* [*intrans.*] speak or act in an evasive way: *he seemed to prevaricate when journalists asked pointed questions.* See note at LIE. ▷mid 16th cent. (in the sense 'go astray, transgress'): from Latin *praevaricat-* 'walked crookedly, deviated,' from the verb *praevaricari*, from *prae* 'before' + *varicari* 'straddle' (from *varus* 'bent, knock-kneed'). —**pre·var·i·ca·tion** /priˌvariˈkāsʜən/ *n.* —**pre·var·i·ca·tor** /-ˌkātər/ *n.*

pre·ven·ient /priˈvēnēənt/ ▸*adj. formal* preceding in time or order; antecedent: *John Wesley referred to God's work in the unconverted as prevenient grace.* ▷early 17th cent.: from Latin *praevenient-* 'coming before,' from the verb *praevenire*, from *prae* 'before' + *venire* 'come.'

pre·vent /priˈvent/ ▸*v.* [*trans.*] **1** keep (something) from happening or arising: *action must be taken to prevent further accidents.* ■ make (someone or something) unable to do something: *window locks won't* **prevent** *a determined burglar* **from** *getting in.* See note at HINDER. **2** *archaic* (of God) go before (someone) with spiritual guidance and help. ▷late Middle English (in the sense 'act in anticipation of'): from Latin *praevent-* 'preceded, hindered,' from the verb *praevenire*, from *prae* 'before' + *venire* 'come.' —**pre·vent·a·bil·i·ty** /priˌventəˈbilətē/ *n.* —**pre·vent·a·ble** (also **pre·vent·i·ble**) *adj.*

pre·ven·ta·tive /prēˈventətiv/ ▸*adj.* & *n.* another term for PREVENTIVE. —**pre·ven·ta·tive·ly** *adv.*

USAGE See **usage** at PREVENTIVE.

Pronunciation Key ə *ago*; ər *over*; ˈə or ˌə *up*; ˈər or ˌər *fur*; a *hat*; ā *rate*; ä *car*; CH *chew*; e *let*; ē *see*; e(ə)r *air*; i *fit*; ī *by*; i(ə)r *ear*; NG *sing*; ō *go*; ô *for*; oi *boy*; o͝o *good*; o͞o *goo*; ou *out*; SH *she*; TH *thin*; T͟H *then*; (h)w *why*; ZH *vision*

pre·vent·er /prē'ventər/ ▶*n.* a person or thing that prevents something: *effective as preventers of further infection.* ■ *Sailing* an extra line or wire rigged to support a piece of rigging under strain, or to hold the boom and prevent it from jybing.

pre·ven·tion /pri'venCHən/ ▶*n.* the action of stopping something from happening or arising: *crime prevention | the treatment and prevention of AIDS.*

▶*PHRASE* □ **an ounce of prevention is worth a pound of cure** *proverb* it's easier to stop something from happening in the first place than to repair the damage after it has happened.

pre·ven·tive /pri'ventiv/ ▶*adj.* designed to keep something undesirable such as illness, harm, or accidents from occurring: *preventive medicine.*

▶*n.* a medicine or other treatment designed to stop disease or ill health from occurring. **—pre·ven·tive·ly** *adv.*

USAGE **Preventive** is the standard form of a word that sometimes appears as the variant form **preventative. Preventive** is used much more often than **preventative**, a form that has been described by some traditionalists as a mere corruption.

pre·ven·tive de·ten·tion ▶*n. Law* the imprisonment of a person with the aim of preventing them from committing further offenses or of maintaining public order.

pre·ver·bal /'prē'vərbəl/ ▶*adj.* **1** existing or occurring before the development of speech: *preverbal communication.* **2** *Grammar* occurring before a verb: *preverbal particles.*

pre·view /'prē,vyo͞o/ ▶*n.* an inspection or viewing of something before it is bought or becomes generally known and available: *you can get a* ***sneak preview*** *of the pictures on sale.* ■ a showing of a movie, play, exhibition, etc., before its official opening. ■ a short extract shown in a movie theater as publicity for a forthcoming film. ■ a commentary on or appraisal of a forthcoming film, play, book, etc., based on an advance viewing. ■ *Computing* a facility for inspecting the appearance of a document prepared in a word-processing or other program before it is printed.

▶*v.* [*trans.*] display (a product, movie, play, etc.) before it officially goes on sale or opens to the public: *the company will preview an enhanced version of its database.* ■ see or inspect (something) before it is used or becomes generally available: *the teacher should preview teaching aids to ensure that they are at the right level.* ■ comment on or appraise (a forthcoming event) in advance: *next week we'll be previewing the new season.*

Prev·in /'prevən/, André (George) (1929–), U.S. conductor, pianist, and composer, born in Germany. He is best known as a conductor, notably with the London Symphony Orchestra (1968–79), the Pittsburgh Symphony Orchestra (1976–86), and the Royal Philharmonic Orchestra (1987–91).

pre·vi·ous /'prēvēəs/ ▶*adj.* **1** [*attrib.*] existing or occurring before in time or order: *she looked tired after her exertions of the previous evening | tickets will be sold on the same basis as in previous years.* **2** *informal* overly hasty in acting or in drawing a conclusion: *I admit I may have been a bit previous.* ▷early 17th cent.: from Latin *praevius* 'going before' (from *prae* 'before' + *via* 'way') + **-OUS. —pre·vi·ous·ly** *adv.*

▶*PHRASE* □ **previous to** before: *the month previous to publication | he seemed to have been in good health previous to the fatal injury.*

pre·vi·ous ques·tion ▶*n.* (in parliamentary procedure) a motion to decide whether to vote on a main question, moved before the main question itself is put.

pre·vise /pri'vīz/ ▶*v.* [*trans.*] *poetic/literary* foresee or predict (an event): *he had intelligence to previse the possible future.* ▷late 16th cent.: from Latin *praevis-* 'foreseen, anticipated,' from the verb *praevidere*, from *prae* 'before' + *videre* 'to see.' **—pre·vi·sion** /-'vizHən/ *n.* **—pre·vi·sion·al** /-'vizHənl/ *adj.*

pre·vo·cal·ic /,prēvō'kalik/ ▶*adj.* occurring immediately before a vowel. **—pre·vo·cal·i·cal·ly** /-ik(ə)lē/ *adv.*

pre·vue /'prē,vyo͞o/ ▶*n.* variant spelling of **PREVIEW**.

pre·war /prē'wôr/ ▶*adj.* existing, occurring, or built before a war: *the prewar years.*

pre·wash /prē'wôsH; -'wäsH/ (also **pre-wash**) ▶*n.* a preliminary wash, esp. one performed as part of a cycle in an automatic washing machine. ■ a substance applied as a treatment before washing.

▶*v.* [*trans.*] give a preliminary wash to (a garment), typically before putting it on sale.

pre·wire /prē'wīr/ ▶*v.* [*trans.*] wire (something requiring electrical circuitry) in advance of usual installation: *we prewired the building.*

prex·y /'preksē/ (also **prex**) ▶*n.* (*pl.* **prex·ies**) *informal* a president, esp. the president of a college or society. ▷early 19th cent. (as *prex*): college slang.

prey /prā/ ▶*n.* an animal that is hunted and killed by another for food: *the kestrel is ready to pounce on unsuspecting prey.* ■ a person or thing easily injured or taken advantage of: *he was* ***easy prey*** *for the two con men.* ■ a person who is vulnerable to distressing emotions or beliefs: *the settlers become* ***prey to*** *nameless fears.* ■ *archaic* plunder or (in biblical use) a prize.

▶*v.* [*intrans.*] (**prey on/upon**) hunt and kill for food: *small birds that prey on insect pests.* ■ take advantage of; exploit or injure: *this is a mean type of theft by ruthless people preying on the elderly.* ■ cause constant trouble and distress to: *the problem had begun to* ***prey on my mind.*** ▷Middle English (also denoting plunder taken in war): the noun from Old French *preie*, from Latin *praeda* 'booty,' the verb from Old French *preier*, based on Latin *praedari* 'seize as plunder,' from *praeda.* **—prey·er** *n.*

▶*PHRASE* □ **fall prey to** be hunted and killed by: *small rodents fell prey to domestic cats.* ■ be vulnerable to or overcome by: *he would often fall prey to melancholy.*

prez /prez/ ▶*n.* informal term for **PRESIDENT**.

PRF ▶*abbr. Telecommunications* pulse repetition frequency.

prf. ▶*abbr.* proof.

Pri·am /'prīəm/ *Greek Mythology* the king of Troy at the time of its destruction by the Greeks under Agamemnon. The father of Paris and Hector and husband of Hecuba, he was slain by Neoptolemus, son of Achilles.

pri·ap·ic /prī'apik; -'āpik/ ▶*adj.* of, relating to, or resembling a phallus: *priapic carvings.* ■ of or relating to male sexuality and sexual activity: *priapic cartoons.* ■ *Medicine* (of a male) having a persistently erect penis. ▷late 18th cent.: from *Priapos* (see **PRIAPISM**) + **-IC**.

pri·a·pism /'prīə,pizəm/ ▶*n. Medicine* persistent and painful erection of the penis. ▷late Middle English: via late Latin from Greek *priapismos*, from *priapizein* 'be lewd,' from *Priapos* (see **PRIAPUS**).

Pri·ap·u·li·da /,prīə'pyo͞olədə/ *Zoology* a small phylum of burrowing wormlike marine invertebrates. A priapulid has a thick body, a large eversible proboscis, and a tail. ▷modern Latin (plural), from *Priapulus* (genus name), diminutive of **PRIAPUS**. **—pri·ap·u·lid** /prī'apyələd/ *n.* & *adj.*

Pri·a·pus /prī'āpəs/ *Greek Mythology* a god of fertility, whose cult spread to Greece (and, later, Italy) from Turkey after Alexander's conquests. He was also a god of gardens and the patron of seafarers and shepherds.

Prib·i·lof Is·lands /'pribə,lôf/ a group of four islands in the Bering Sea, off the coast of southwestern Alaska. First visited in 1786 by Russian explorer Gavriil Loginovich Pribylov (died 1796), they came into U.S. possession after the purchase of Alaska in 1867.

Price[1] /prīs/, (Mary Violet) Leontyne (1927–), U.S. opera singer. Her 1952 Broadway successes in *Four Saints in Three Acts* and *Porgy and Bess* led to an international career as an operatic and concert soprano. She made her Metropolitan Opera debut in 1961 and retired from opera in 1985.

Price[2], Vincent (1911–93), U.S. actor, best known for his performances in a series of movies based on stories by Edgar Allan Poe, including *The Fall of the House of Usher* (1960) and *The Pit and the Pendulum* (1961).

price /prīs/ ▶*n.* the amount of money expected, required, or given in payment for something: *land could be sold for a high price | a wide selection of tools varying in price.* ■ *figurative* an unwelcome experience, event, or action involved as a condition of achieving a desired end: *the price of their success was an entire day spent in discussion.* ■ the odds in betting. ■ *archaic* value; worth: *a pearl of great price.*

▶*v.* [*trans.*] (often **be priced**) decide the amount required as payment for (something offered for sale): *the watches in this range are* ***priced at*** *$14.50.* ▷Middle English: the noun from Old French *pris*, from Latin *pretium* 'value, reward'; the verb, a variant (by assimilation to the noun) of earlier *prise* 'estimate the value of' (see **PRIZE**[1]). Compare with **PRAISE**.

▶*PHRASES* □ **at any price** no matter what expense, sacrifice, or difficulty is involved: *they wanted peace at any price.* □ **at a price** requiring great expense or involving unwelcome consequences: *his generosity comes at a price.* □ **beyond** (or **without**) **price** so valuable that no price can be stated. □ **a price on someone's head** a reward offered for someone's capture or death. □ **price oneself out of the market** become unable to compete commercially. □ **put a price on** determine the value of: *you can't put a price on what she has to offer.* □ **what price ——?** used to ask what has become of something or to suggest that something has or would become worthless: *what price justice if he were allowed to go free?*

price con·trol ▶*n.* a government regulation establishing a maximum price to be charged for specified goods and services, esp. during periods of war or inflation.

price dis·crim·i·na·tion ▶*n.* the action of selling the same product at different prices to different buyers, in order to maximize sales and profits.

price-earn·ings ra·tio (also **price-earnings multiple**) ▶*n. Finance* the current market price of a company share divided by the earnings per share of the company.

price-fix·ing (also **price fix·ing**) ▶*n.* the maintaining of prices at a certain level by agreement between competing sellers.

price·less /'prīsləs/ ▶*adj.* so precious that its value cannot be determined: *priceless works of art.* ■ *informal* used to express great and usually affectionate amusement: *darling, you're priceless!* **—price·less·ly** *adv.* **—price·less·ness** *n.*

price list ▶*n.* a list of current prices of items on sale.

price point ▶*n.* a point on a scale of possible prices at which something might be marketed.

price-sen·si·tive ▶*adj.* denoting a product whose sales are greatly influenced by the price. ■ (of information) likely to affect share prices if it were made public.

price sup·port ▶*n. Economics* government assistance in maintaining the levels of market prices regardless of supply or demand.

price tag ▶*n.* the label on an item for sale, showing its price. ■ *figurative* the cost of a company, enterprise, or undertaking: *a $400 billion price tag was put on the venture.*

price-tak·er ▶*n. Economics* a company that must accept the prevailing prices in the market of its products, its own transactions being unable to affect the market price. **—price-tak·ing** *n.* & *adj.*

price war ▶*n.* a fierce competition in which retailers cut prices in an attempt to increase their share of the market.

pric·ey /'prīsē/ (also **pric·y**) ▶*adj.* (**pric·i·er, pric·i·est**) *informal* expensive: *boutiques selling pricey clothes.* **—pric·i·ness** *n.*

Prich·ard /'pricHərd/ a city in southwestern Alabama, a western suburb of Mobile; pop. 28,633.

prick /prik/ ▶*v.* [*trans.*] **1** make a small hole in (something) with a sharp point; pierce slightly: *prick the potatoes with a fork.* ■ [*intrans.*] feel a sensation as though a sharp point were sticking into one: *she felt her scalp prick and her palms were damp.* ■ (of tears) cause the sensation of imminent weeping in (a person's eyes): *tears of disappointment were pricking her eyelids.* ■ [*intrans.*] (of a person's eyes) experience such a sensation. ■ cause mental or emotional discomfort to: *her conscience pricked her as she told the lie.* ■ arouse or provoke to action: *the police were pricked into action.* **2** (usu. **be pricked**) (esp. of a horse or dog) make (the ears) stand erect when on the alert: *the dog's tail was wagging and her ears were pricked.*

▶*phrasal v.* □ **prick something out** (or **off**) transplant seedlings to a container or bed that provides adequate room for growth: *he was in the garden pricking out marigolds.*

▶*n.* **1** an act of piercing something with a fine, sharp point: *the pin prick had produced a drop of blood.* ■ a small hole or mark made by piercing something with a fine, sharp point. ■ a sharp pain caused by being pierced with a fine point. ■ a sudden feeling of distress, anxiety, or some other unpleasant emotion: *she felt a prick of resentment.* ■ *archaic* a goad for oxen. **2** *vulgar slang* a penis. ■ a man regarded as stupid, unpleasant, or contemptible. ▷Old English *pricca* (noun), *prician* (verb), probably of West Germanic origin and related to Low German and Dutch *prik* (noun), *prikken* (verb). **—prick·er** *n.* **—prick·ing** *n.*

▶*PHRASES* □ **kick against the pricks** hurt oneself by persisting in useless resistance or protest. [with biblical allusion to Acts 9:5.] □ **prick up one's ears** (esp. of a horse or dog) make the ears stand erect when on the alert. ■ (of a person) become suddenly attentive: *he pricked up his ears when he heard them talking about him.*

prick·et /'prikit/ ▶*n.* **1** a male fallow deer in its second year, having straight, unbranched horns. **2** *historical* a spike for holding a candle. ▷late Middle English: from **PRICK** + **-ET**[1].

prick·le /ˈprikəl/ ▶*n.* a short, slender, sharp-pointed outgrowth on the bark or epidermis of a plant; a small thorn: *the prickles of the blackberry bushes.* ■ a small spine or pointed outgrowth on the skin of certain animals. ■ a tingling sensation on someone's skin, typically caused by strong emotion: *Kathleen felt a prickle of excitement.*
▶*v.* [*intrans.*] (of a person's skin or a part of the body) experience a tingling sensation, esp. as a result of strong emotion: *the sound made her skin prickle with horror.* ■ [*trans.*] cause a tingling or mildly painful sensation in: *I hate the way the fibers prickle your skin.* ■ (of a person) react defensively or angrily to something: *she* **prickled at** *the implication that she had led a soft and protected life.* ▷Old English *pricel* 'instrument for pricking, sensation of being pricked'; related to Middle Dutch *prickel*, from the Germanic base of **PRICK**. The verb is partly a diminutive of the verb **PRICK**.

prick·le·back /ˈprikəl,bak/ ▶*n.* a long slender fish with a spiny dorsal fin running the length of the body. It lives in cooler seas of the northern hemisphere, typically in shallow inshore waters. • Family Stichaeidae: many genera and species.

prick·ly /ˈprik(ə)lē/ ▶*adj.* (**-li·er**, **-li·est**) **1** covered in prickles: *masses of prickly brambles.* ■ resembling or feeling like prickles: *his hair was prickly and short.* ■ having or causing a tingling or itching sensation: *a dress that was prickly around the neck | my skin feels prickly.* **2** (of a person) ready to take offense. ■ liable to cause someone to take offense: *this is a prickly subject.* —**prick·li·ness** *n.*

prick·ly-ash ▶*n.* a spiny North American shrub or tree with prickly branches and bark that can be used medicinally. • Genus *Zanthoxylum*, family Rutaceae: the **northern prickly-ash** (*Z. americanum*) (also called **TOOTHACHE TREE**), and the **southern prickly-ash** (see **HERCULES-CLUB**). ■ a medicinal preparation of the bark of these trees.

prick·ly heat ▶*n.* an itchy inflammation of the skin, typically with a rash of small vesicles, common in hot moist weather. Also called **MILIARIA**.

prick·ly pear ▶*n.* a cactus with jointed stems and oval flattened segments, having barbed bristles and large pear-shaped, prickly fruits. • Genus *Opuntia*, family Cactaceae: several species, in particular *O. humifusa* of North America and *O. ficus-indica*, which is cultivated for its fruit and has become naturalized in the Mediterranean. ■ the edible orange or red fruit of this plant.

prickly pear

prick·ly pop·py ▶*n.* a Central American plant with prickly leaves and large scented yellow flowers. It has become a weed in many tropical regions, but is cultivated in cooler regions as an ornamental. • *Argemone mexicana*, family Papaveraceae.

prick-teas·er (also **prick-tease**) ▶*n. vulgar slang* another term for **COCKTEASER**.

pric·y /ˈprīsē/ ▶*adj.* variant spelling of **PRICEY**.

pride /prīd/ ▶*n.* **1** a feeling or deep pleasure or satisfaction derived from one's own achievements, the achievements of those with whom one is closely associated, or from qualities or possessions that are widely admired: *the team was bursting with pride after recording a sensational victory | a woman who* **takes** *great* **pride in** *her appearance.* ■ the consciousness of one's own dignity: *he swallowed his pride and asked for help.* ■ the quality of having an excessively high opinion of oneself or one's importance: *the sin of pride.* ■ a person or thing that is the object or source of a feeling or deep pleasure or satisfaction: *the swimming pool is the pride of the community.* ■ *poetic/literary* the best state or condition of something; the prime: *in* **the pride of** *youth.* **2** a group of lions forming a social unit.
▶*v.* (**pride oneself on/upon**) be especially proud of a particular quality or skill: *she'd always prided herself on her ability to deal with a crisis.* ▷late Old English *prȳde* 'excessive self-esteem,' variant of *prȳtu, prȳte*, from *prūd* (see **PROUD**). —**pride·ful** /-fəl/ *adj.* —**pride·ful·ly** /-fəlē/ *adv.*

▶*PHRASES* □ **one's pride and joy** a person or thing of which one is very proud and which is a source of great pleasure: *the car was his pride and joy.* □ **pride goes** (or **comes**) **before a fall** *proverb* if you're too conceited or self-important, something will happen to make you look foolish. □ **pride of place** the most prominent or important position among a group of things: *the certificate has pride of place on my wall.*

THE RIGHT WORD **arrogance, conceit, egotism, pride, self-esteem, vainglory, vanity**

If you take **pride** in yourself or your accomplishments, it means that you believe in your own worth, merit, or superiority—whether or not that belief is justified (*she took pride in her accomplishments*).

When your opinion of yourself is exaggerated, you're showing **conceit**, a word that combines *pride* with self-obsession.

If you like to be noticed and admired for your appearance or achievements, you're revealing your **vanity**, and if you show off or boast about your accomplishments, you're likely to be accused of **vainglory**, a somewhat literary term for a self-important display of power, skill, or influence.

Arrogance is an overbearing pride combined with disdain for others (*his arrogance led him to assume that everyone else would obey his orders*), while **egotism** implies self-centeredness or an excessive preoccupation with yourself (*blinded by egotism to the suffering of others*).

While no one wants to be accused of *arrogance* or *egotism*, there's a lot to be said for **self-esteem**, which may suggest undue pride but is more often used to describe a healthy belief in oneself and respect for one's worth as a person (*she suffered from low self-esteem*).

prie-dieu /prē ˈdyə(r); -ˈdyœ/ ▶*n.* (*pl.* **prie-dieux** /ˈdyə(r)(z); -ˈdyœ(z)/) a piece of furniture for use during prayer, consisting of a kneeling surface and a narrow upright front with a rest for the elbows or for books. ▷mid 18th cent.: French, literally 'pray God.'

priest /prēst/ ▶*n.* **1** an ordained minister of the Catholic, Orthodox, or Anglican Church having the authority to perform certain rites and administer certain sacraments. ■ a person who performs religious ceremonies and duties in a non-Christian religion. **2** (in full **fish priest**) a mallet used to kill fish caught when angling. [with allusion to the priest's function in performing the last rites.]
▶*v.* [*trans.*] (usu. **be priested**) *formal* ordain to the priesthood. ▷Old English *prēost*, of Germanic origin; related to Dutch *priester*, German *Priester*, based on ecclesiastical Latin *presbyter* 'elder' (see **PRESBYTER**). —**priest·like** /-,līk/ *adj.*

priest·craft /ˈprēst,kraft/ ▶*n. often derogatory* the knowledge and work of a priest.

priest·ess /ˈprēstis/ ▶*n.* a female priest of a non-Christian religion.

priest·hood /ˈprēst,ho͝od; ˈprē,sto͝od/ ▶*n.* (often **the priesthood**) the office or position of a priest. ■ priests in general.

Priest·ley[1] /ˈprēs(t)lē/, J. B. (1894–1984), English novelist, playwright, and critic; full name *John Boynton Priestley*. Notable works: *The Good Companions* (novel, 1929), *Time and the Conways* (play, 1937), and *An Inspector Calls* (play, 1947).

Priest·ley[2], Joseph (1733–1804), English scientist and theologian. His chief work was on the chemistry of gases, in which his most significant discovery was of "dephlogisticated air" (oxygen) in 1774; he demonstrated that it was important to animal life and that plants emit it in sunlight.

priest·ly /ˈprēstlē/ ▶*adj.* of, relating to, or befitting a priest or priests: *performing priestly duties.* ▷Old English *prēostlic* (see **PRIEST**, **-LY**[1]). —**priest·li·ness** *n.*

priest hole (also **priest's hole**) ▶*n. historical* a hiding place for a Roman Catholic priest during times of religious persecution.

prig /prig/ ▶*n.* a self-righteously moralistic person who behaves as if superior to others. ▷mid 16th cent.: of unknown origin. The earliest sense was 'tinker' or 'petty thief,' whence 'disliked person,' esp. 'someone who is affectedly and self-consciously precise' (late 17th cent.). —**prig·ger·y** /ˈprigərē/ *n.* —**prig·gish** *adj.* —**prig·gish·ly** *adv.* —**prig·gish·ness** *n.*

prill /pril/ ▶*n.* a pellet or solid globule of a substance formed by the congealing of a liquid during an industrial process. ▷late 18th cent. (as a term in copper mining, denoting rich copper ore remaining after removal of low-grade material): of unknown origin. —**prilled** *adj.*

prim /prim/ ▶*adj.* (**prim·mer**, **prim·mest**) stiffly formal and respectable; feeling or showing disapproval of anything regarded as improper: *a very prim and proper lady.*
▶*v.* (**primmed**, **prim·ming**) [*trans.*] purse (the mouth or lips) into a prim expression: *Larry* **primmed up** *his mouth.* ▷late 17th cent. (as a verb): probably ultimately from Old French *prin*, Provençal *prim* 'excellent, delicate,' from Latin *primus* 'first.' —**prim·ly** *adv.* —**prim·ness** *n.*

prim. ▶*abbr.* ■ primary. ■ primitive.

pri·ma bal·le·ri·na /ˈprēmə/ ▶*n.* the chief female dancer in a ballet or ballet company. ▷late 19th cent.: Italian, literally 'first ballerina.'

pri·ma·cy /ˈprīməsē/ ▶*n.* **1** the fact of being primary, preeminent, or more important: *the primacy of air power in the modern war.* **2** the office, period of office, or authority of a primate of the Church. **3** [usu. as *adj.*] *Psychology* the fact of an item having been presented earlier to the subject (esp. as increasing its likelihood of being remembered): *the* **primacy effect** *is thought to reflect recall from a long-term memory store.* ▷late Middle English: from Old French *primatie*, from medieval Latin *primatia*, from Latin *primas, primat-* 'of the first rank' (see **PRIMATE**[1]).

pri·ma don·na /,primə ˈdänə; ,prēmə/ ▶*n.* the chief female singer in an opera or opera company. ■ a very temperamental person with an inflated view of their own talent or importance. ▷late 18th cent.: Italian, literally 'first lady.' —**pri·ma don·na·ish** *adj.*

pri·mae·val /prīˈmēvəl/ ▶*adj. Brit.* variant spelling of **PRIMEVAL**.

pri·ma fa·ci·e /,prīmə ˈfāshə; ˈfāshē; ˈfāshē,ē/ ▶*adj.* & *adv. Law* based on the first impression; accepted as correct until proved otherwise: [as *adj.*] *a prima facie case of professional misconduct* | [as *adv.*] *the original lessee prima facie remains liable for the payment of the rent.* ▷Latin, from *primus* 'first' + *facies* 'appearance.'

pri·mal /ˈprīməl/ ▶*adj.* essential; fundamental: *for me, writing is a primal urge.* ■ relating to an early stage in evolutionary development; primeval: *primal hunting societies.* ■ *Psychology* of, relating to, or denoting the needs, fears, or behavior that are postulated (esp. in Freudian theory) to form the origins of emotional life: *he preys on people's primal fears.* See also **PRIMAL SCENE**. ▷early 17th cent.: from medieval Latin *primalis*, from Latin *primus* 'first.' —**pri·mal·ly** *adv.*

pri·mal scene ▶*n. Psychology* (in Freudian theory) the occasion on which a child becomes aware of its parents' sexual intercourse, the timing of which is thought to be crucial in determining predisposition to future neuroses.

pri·mal scream ▶*n.* a release of intense basic frustration, anger, and aggression, esp. that rediscovered by means of primal therapy.

pri·mal ther·a·py ▶*n.* a form of psychotherapy that focuses on a patient's earliest emotional experiences and encourages verbal expression of childhood suffering, typically using an empty chair or other prop to represent a parent toward whom anger is directed.

pri·ma ma·te·ri·a /,prīmə məˈti(ə)rēə; ,prēmə/ (also **materia prima**) ▶*n.* primeval matter; fundamental substance. ▷Latin.

pri·ma·quine /ˈprimə,kwēn; ˈprē-/ ▶*n. Medicine* a synthetic compound derived from quinoline and used in the treatment of malaria. ▷1940s: apparently from Latin *prima* (feminine of *primus* 'first') + *quin(olin)e*.

pri·ma·ri·ly /prīˈme(ə)rəlē/ ▶*adv.* for the most part; mainly: *around 80 percent of personal computers are used primarily for word processing.*

pri·ma·ry /ˈprī,merē; ˈprīm(ə)rē/ ▶*adj.* **1** of chief importance; principal: *the government's primary aim is to see significant reductions in unemployment.* **2** earliest in time or order of development: *the country was in the primary stage of socialism.* ■ not derived from, caused by, or based on anything else: *the research involved the use of primary source materials in national and local archives.* **3** [*attrib.*] of or relating to education for children between the ages of about five and ten: *a primary school.* **4** *Biology* & *Medicine* belonging to or directly derived from the first stage of development or growth: *a primary bone tumor.* **5** (**Primary**) *Geology* former term for **PALEOZOIC**. **6** relating to or

denoting the input side of a device using electromagnetic induction, esp. in a transformer. **7** *Chemistry* (of an organic compound) having its functional group located on a carbon atom that is bonded to no more than one other carbon atom. ■ (chiefly of amines) derived from ammonia by replacement of one hydrogen atom by an organic group.
▸*n.* (*pl.* **-ries**) **1** (also **primary election**) a preliminary election to appoint delegates to a party conference or to select the candidates for a principal, esp. presidential, election. **2** short for: ■ a primary color. ■ *Ornithology* a primary feather. ■ a primary coil or winding in an electrical transformer. **3** *Astronomy* the body orbited by a smaller satellite or companion. **4** (**the Primary**) *dated Geology* the Primary or Paleozoic era. ▷late Middle English (in the sense 'original, not derivative'): from Latin *primarius*, from *primus* 'first.' The noun uses date from the 18th cent.

P

pri·ma·ry ac·cent ▸*n.* another term for PRIMARY STRESS.

pri·ma·ry care (also **primary health care**) ▸*n.* health care at a basic rather than specialized level for people making an initial approach to a doctor or nurse for treatment.

pri·ma·ry cell ▸*n.* an electric cell that produces current by an irreversible chemical reaction.

pri·ma·ry col·or ▸*n.* any of a group of colors from which all other colors can be obtained by mixing.

The primary colors for pigments are red, blue, and yellow. The primary additive colors for light are red, green, and blue; the primary subtractive colors (which give the primary additive colors when subtracted from white light) are magenta, cyan, and yellow.

pri·ma·ry feath·er ▸*n.* any of the largest flight feathers in a bird's wing, growing from the manus.

pri·ma·ry group ▸*n.* *Sociology* a group held together by intimate, face-to-face relationships, formed by family and environmental associations and regarded as basic to social life and culture.

pri·ma·ry in·dus·try ▸*n.* *Economics* industry, such as mining, agriculture, or forestry, that is concerned with obtaining or providing natural raw materials for conversion into commodities and products for the consumer.

pri·ma·ry plan·et ▸*n.* a planet that directly orbits the sun.

pri·ma·ry proc·ess ▸*n.* *Psychoanalysis* an unconscious thought process that arises from the pleasure principle and is irrational and not subject to compulsion, such as condensation, which occurs in dreaming, or displacement, which occurs in the formation of a phobia.

pri·ma·ry qual·i·ties ▸*plural n.* *Philosophy* properties or qualities, such as size, motion, shape, number, etc., belonging to physical matter independently of an observer. ■ the four original qualities of matter (hot, cold, wet, and dry) recognized by Aristotle, from which other qualities were held to derive.

pri·ma·ry stress ▸*n.* *Phonetics* the strongest accent in a word or breath group. Compare with SECONDARY STRESS.

pri·ma·ry struc·ture ▸*n.* **1** *Biochemistry* the characteristic sequence of amino acids forming a protein or polypeptide chain, considered as the most basic element of its structure. **2** *Aeronautics* the parts of an aircraft whose failure would seriously compromise safety.

pri·mate¹ /ˈprīˌmāt; ˈprīmət/ ▸*n.* *Christian Church* the chief bishop or archbishop of a province: *Cardinal Glemp, the primate of Poland.* ▷Middle English: from Old French *primat*, from Latin *primas, primat-* 'of the first rank,' from *primus* 'first.' **—pri·ma·tial** /prīˈmāsʜəl/ *adj.*

pri·mate² /ˈprīˌmāt/ ▸*n.* *Zoology* a mammal of an order that includes the lemurs, bush babies, tarsiers, marmosets, monkeys, apes, and humans. They are distinguished by having hands, handlike feet, and forward-facing eyes, and, with the exception of humans, are typically agile tree-dwellers. • Order Primates: several families. ▷late 19th cent.: from Latin *primas, primat-* 'of the first rank' (see PRIMATE¹).

pri·ma·tol·o·gy /ˌprīməˈtäləjē/ ▸*n.* the branch of zoology that deals with primates. **—pri·ma·to·log·i·cal** /ˌprīmətəˈläjikəl/ *adj.* **—pri·ma·tol·o·gist** /-jist/ *n.*

pri·ma·ve·ra /ˌprēməˈve(ə)rə/ ▸*n.* the hard, light-colored timber of a Central American tree. • The tree is *Cybistax donnellsmithii*, family Bignoniaceae.
▸*adj.* [*postpositive*] (of a pasta dish) made with lightly sautéed spring vegetables: *linguine primavera.* ▷late 19th cent.: from Spanish, denoting the season of spring, from Latin *primus* 'first, earliest' + *ver* 'spring' (alluding to the tree's early flowering).

prime¹ /prīm/ ▸*adj.* **1** of first importance; main: *her prime concern is the well-being of the patient.* ■ from which another thing may derive or proceed: *Diogenes' conclusion that air is the prime matter.* **2** [*attrib.*] of the best possible quality; excellent: *a prime site in the center of Indianapolis | prime cuts of meat.* ■ having all the expected or typical characteristics of something: *the novel is a prime example of the genre.* ■ most suitable or likely: *it's the prime contender for best comedy of the year.* **3** *Mathematics* (of a number) evenly divisible only by itself and one (e.g., 2, 3, 5, 7, 11). ■ [*predic.*] (of two or more numbers in relation to each other) having no common factor but one.
▸*n.* **1** [in *sing.*] a state or time of greatest strength, vigor, or success in a person's life: *you're in the prime of life | he wasn't elderly, but clearly past his prime.* ■ *archaic* the beginning or first period of something: *the prime of the world.* **2** *Christian Church* a service forming part of the Divine Office, traditionally said (or chanted) at the first hour of the day (i.e., 6 a.m.), but now little used. ■ *archaic* this time of day. **3** a prime number. **4** *Printing* a symbol (′) written after a letter or symbol as a distinguishing mark or after a figure as a symbol for minutes or feet. **5** *Fencing* the first of eight standard parrying positions. [French.] **6** short for PRIME RATE. ▷Old English *prīm* (sense 2 of the *noun*), from Latin *prima (hora)* 'first (hour),' reinforced in Middle English by Old French *prime*; the adjective dates from late Middle English, via Old French from Latin *primus* 'first.' **—prime·ness** *n.*

prime² ▸*v.* [*trans.*] **1** make (something) ready for use or action, in particular: ■ prepare (a firearm or explosive device) for firing or detonation. ■ cover (wood, canvas, or metal) with a preparatory coat of paint in order to prevent the absorption of subsequent layers of paint. ■ pour or spray liquid into (a pump) before starting in order to seal the moving parts and facilitate its operation. ■ inject extra fuel into (the cylinder or carburetor of an internal combustion engine) in order to facilitate starting. ■ [*intrans.*] (of a steam engine or its boiler) mix water with the steam being passed into the cylinder. ■ *Biochemistry* serve as a starting material for (a polymerization process). **2** prepare (someone) for a situation or task, typically by supplying them with relevant information: [*trans.*] *the sentries had been primed to admit him without challenge.* ▷early 16th cent. (in the sense 'fill, load'): origin uncertain; probably based on Latin *primus* 'first,' since the sense expressed is a "first" operation before something else.
▸*PHRASE* □ **prime the pump** stimulate or support the growth or success of something by supplying it with money: *capital from overseas that helps prime the U.S. economic pump.*

prime con·tract ▸*n.* a contract whose requirements are partly fulfilled by the awarding of subcontracts. **—prime con·trac·tor** *n.*

prime cost ▸*n.* the direct cost of a commodity in terms of the materials and labor involved in its production, excluding fixed costs.

prime lens ▸*n.* *Photography* a lens of fixed focal length.

prime me·rid·i·an ▸*n.* a planet's meridian adopted as the zero of longitude. ■ (usu. **the prime meridian**) the earth's zero of longitude, which by convention passes through Greenwich, England. See also GREENWICH MERIDIAN.

prime min·is·ter ▸*n.* the head of an elected government; the principal minister of a sovereign or state.

In current use, the terms *premier* and *prime minister* refer to the same office in Britain, but in Canada and Australia the government of a province or state is headed by a premier, that of the federal government by a prime minister. In countries such as France, where the president has an executive function, the prime minister is in a subordinate position.

—prime min·is·ter·ship *n.*

prime mov·er ▸*n.* a person or establishment that is chiefly responsible for the creation or execution of a plan or project. ■ an initial natural or mechanical source of motive power.

prim·er¹ /ˈprīmər/ ▸*n.* a substance used as a preparatory coat on previously unpainted wood, metal, or canvas, esp. to prevent the absorption of subsequent layers of paint or the development of rust. ■ a cap or cylinder containing a compound that responds to friction or an electrical impulse and ignites the charge in a cartridge or explosive. ■ a small pump for pumping fuel to prime an internal combustion engine, esp. in an aircraft. ■ *Biochemistry* a molecule that serves as a starting material for a polymerization process.

prim·er² /ˈprimər/ ▸*n.* an elementary textbook that serves as an introduction to a subject of study or is used for teaching children to read. ▷late Middle English: from medieval Latin *primarius (liber)* 'primary (book)' and *primarium (manuale)* 'primary (manual).'

prime rate ▸*n.* the lowest rate of interest at which money may be borrowed commercially.

prime rib ▸*n.* a roast or steak cut from the seven ribs immediately before the loin.

prime time ▸*n.* the regularly occurring time at which a television or radio audience is expected to be greatest, generally regarded in the television industry as the hours between 8 and 11 p.m.: *the Olympics dominated 59% of prime time.*

prim·eur /prēˈmər/ ▸*n.* **1** (**primeurs**) fruit or vegetables grown to be available very early in the season. **2** (also **Primeur**) newly produced wines that have recently been made available. ▷French, literally 'newness.'

pri·me·val /prīˈmēvəl/ (*Brit.* also **pri·mae·val**) ▸*adj.* of or resembling the earliest ages in the history of the world: *mile after mile of primeval forest.* ■ (of feelings or actions) based on primitive instinct; raw and elementary: *a primeval desire.* ▷mid 17th cent.: from Latin *primaevus* (from *primus* 'first' + *aevum* 'age') + -AL. **—pri·me·val·ly** *adv.*

pri·mi·grav·i·da /ˌprīməˈgravədə/ ▸*n.* (*pl.* **-grav·i·dae** /-ˈgravədē; -gravəˌdī/) *Medicine* a woman who is pregnant for the first time. ▷late 19th cent.: modern Latin (feminine), from Latin *primus* 'first' + *gravidus* 'pregnant' (see GRAVID).

prim·ing /ˈprīmiɴɢ/ ▸*n.* a substance that prepares something for use or action, in particular: ■ another term for PRIMER¹. ■ gunpowder placed in the pan of a firearm to ignite a charge.

pri·mip·a·ra /prīˈmipərə/ ▸*n.* (*pl.* **-ras** or **-rae** /-rē; -ˌrī/) *Medicine* a woman who is giving birth for the first time. ▷mid 19th cent.: modern Latin (feminine), from *primus* 'first' + *-parus* 'bringing forth' (from the verb *parere*). **—pri·mip·a·rous** /-rəs/ *adj.*

prim·i·tive /ˈprimətiv/ ▸*adj.* **1** relating to, denoting, or preserving the character of an early stage in the evolutionary or historical development of something: *primitive mammals | a name corrupted from primitive German.* ■ relating to or denoting a preliterate, nonindustrial society or culture characterized by simple social and economic organization: *primitive people.* ■ having a quality or style that offers an extremely basic level of comfort, convenience, or efficiency: *the accommodations at the camp were a bit primitive.* ■ (of behavior, thought, or emotion) apparently originating in unconscious needs or desires and unaffected by objective reasoning: *the primitive responses we share with many animals.* ■ of or denoting a simple, direct style of art that deliberately rejects sophisticated artistic techniques. **2** not developed or derived from anything else: *the primitive material of the universe.* ■ *Linguistics* denoting a word, base, or root from which another is historically derived. ■ *Linguistics* denoting an irreducible form. ■ *Mathematics* (of an algebraic or geometric expression) from which another is derived, or which is not itself derived from another. **3** *Biology* (of a part or structure) in the first or early stage of formation or growth; rudimentary. See also PRIMITIVE STREAK.
▸*n.* **1** a person belonging to a preliterate, nonindustrial society or culture. **2** a pre-Renaissance painter. ■ a modern painter who imitates the pre-Renaissance style. ■ an artist employing a simple, naive style that deliberately rejects subtlety or conventional techniques. ■ a painting by a primitive artist, or an object in a primitive style. **3** *Linguistics* a word, base, or root from which another is historically derived. ■ *Linguistics* an irreducible form. ■ *Mathematics* an algebraic or geometric expression from which another is derived; a curve of which another is the polar or reciprocal. ■ *Computing* a simple operation or procedure of a limited set from which complex operations or procedures may be constructed, esp. a simple geometric shape that may be generated in computer graphics by such an operation or procedure. ▷late Middle English (in the sense 'original, not derivative'): from Old French *primitif, -ive*, from Latin *primitivus* 'first of its kind,' from *primus* 'first.'

—**prim·i·tive·ly** *adv.* —**prim·i·tive·ness** *n.* —**prim·i·tiv·i·ty** /ˌprimə'tivətē/ *n.*

prim·i·tive cell ▶*n. Crystallography* the smallest possible unit cell of a lattice, having lattice points at each of its eight vertices only.

Prim·i·tive Meth·o·dist ▶*n. historical* a member of a society of Methodists that was formed in 1811 and joined the united Methodist Church in 1932.

prim·i·tive streak ▶*n. Embryology* the faint streak that is the earliest trace of the embryo in the fertilized ovum of a higher vertebrate.

prim·i·tiv·ism /'primətivˌizəm/ ▶*n.* **1** a belief in the value of what is simple and unsophisticated, expressed as a philosophy of life or through art or literature. **2** unsophisticated behavior that is unaffected by objective reasoning. —**prim·i·tiv·ist** *n.* & *adj.*

pri·mo /'prēmō/ ▶*n.* (*pl.* **-mos**) *Music* the leading or upper part in a duet.

▶*adj. informal* of top quality or importance: *the primo team in the land.* ▷mid 18th cent.: Italian, literally 'first.'

Pri·mo de Ri·ve·ra /'prēmō de ri've(ə)rə/, Miguel (1870–1930), Spanish general and statesman; head of state 1923–30. He assumed dictatorial powers after leading a military coup. His son, **José Antonio Primo de Rivera** (1903–36), founded the Falange in 1933 and was executed by Republicans during the Spanish Civil War.

pri·mo·gen·i·tor /ˌprīmō'jenətər/ ▶*n.* an ancestor, esp. the earliest ancestor of a people; a progenitor. ▷mid 17th cent.: variant of **PROGENITOR**, on the pattern of *primogeniture.*

pri·mo·gen·i·ture /ˌprīmō'jeniˌCHər; -ˌCHŏŏr/ ▶*n.* the state of being the firstborn child. ■ (also **right of primogeniture**) the right of succession belonging to the firstborn child, esp. the feudal rule by which the whole real estate of an intestate passed to the eldest son. ▷early 17th cent.: from medieval Latin *primogenitura*, from Latin *primo* 'first' + *genitura* 'geniture.' —**pri·mo·gen·i·tal** /-'jenitl/ *adj.* —**pri·mo·gen·i·tar·y** /-'jeniˌterē/ *adj.*

pri·mor·di·al /prī'môrdēəl/ ▶*adj.* existing at or from the beginning of time; primeval: *the primordial oceans.* ■ (esp. of a state or quality) basic and fundamental: *the primordial needs of the masses.* ■ *Biology* (of a cell, part, or tissue) in the earliest stage of development. ▷late Middle English: from late Latin *primordialis* 'first of all,' from *primordius* 'original' (see **PRIMORDIUM**). —**pri·mor·di·al·i·ty** /ˌprīˌmôrdē'alətē/ *n.* —**pri·mor·di·al·ly** *adv.*

pri·mor·di·al soup ▶*n.* a solution rich in organic compounds in the primitive oceans of the earth, from which life is hypothesized to have originated.

pri·mor·di·um /prī'môrdēəm/ ▶*n.* (*pl.* **-di·a** /-dēə/) *Biology* an organ, structure, or tissue in the earliest stage of development. ▷late 19th cent.: from Latin, neuter of *primordius* 'original,' from *primus* 'first' + *ordiri* 'begin.'

Pri·mor·sky /prē'môrskē/ an administrative territory in the far southeast of Siberian Russia, between the Sea of Japan and the Chinese border; capital, Vladivostok.

pri·mo uo·mo /ˌprēmō 'wōmō/ ▶*n.* (*pl.* **pri·mi uo·mi·ni** /ˌprēmē 'wōmēnē/) the principal male singer in an opera or opera company. ▷Italian, literally 'first man.'

primp /primp/ ▶*v.* [*trans.*] spend time making minor adjustments to (one's hair, makeup, or clothes): *they primped his hair* | [*intrans.*] *the girls who were primping in front of the mirror.* ▷late 16th cent.: related to **PRIM**.

prim·rose /'primˌrōz/ ▶*n.* a commonly cultivated plant of European woodlands that produces pale yellow flowers in the early spring. • *Primula vulgaris*, family Primulaceae (the **primrose family**). This family also includes the cowslips, pimpernels, and cyclamens. ■ (also **primrose yellow**) a pale yellow color. ▷late Middle English: compare with Old French *primerose* and medieval Latin *prima rosa*, literally 'first rose.'

▶*PHRASE* □ **primrose path** the pursuit of pleasure, esp. when it is seen to bring disastrous consequences: *unaware of his doom, he continued down his primrose path.* [with allusion to Shakespeare's *Hamlet* I. iii. 50.]

prim·u·la /'primyələ/ ▶*n.* a plant of a genus that includes primroses, cowslips, and cyclamens. Many kinds are cultivated as ornamentals, bearing flowers in a wide variety of colors in the spring. • Genus *Primula*, family Primulaceae. ▷modern Latin, from medieval Latin, feminine of *primulus*, diminutive of *primus* 'first.'

prim·u·la·ceous /ˌprimyə'lāSHəs/ ▶*adj. Botany* of, relating to, or denoting plants of the primrose family (Primulaceae). ▷mid 19th cent.: from modern Latin *Primulaceae* (plural), based on medieval Latin *primula* (see **PRIMULA**), + **-OUS**.

pri·mum mo·bi·le /ˌprīməm 'mōbəˌlē; ˌprē-/ ▶*n.* **1** the central or most important source of motion or action. **2** (in the medieval version of the Ptolemaic system) an outer sphere supposed to move around the earth in 24 hours, carrying the inner spheres with it. ▷from medieval Latin, literally 'first moving thing.'

pri·mus in·ter pa·res /'prīməs ˌintər 'parˌēz/ ▶*n.* a first among equals; the senior or representative member of a group. ▷Latin.

prin. ▶*abbr.* ■ principal. ■ principally. ■ principle.

Prince /prins/, Hal (1928–) U.S. theatrical producer and director; full name *Harold Smith Prince*. Among the shows that he produced were *Pajama Game* (1954), *West Side Story* (1957), *Fiorello* (1959), and *Fiddler on the Roof* (1964). Some that he also directed included *Cabaret* (1966), *Evita* (1980), and *Phantom of the Opera* (1988).

prince /prins/ ▶*n.* the son of a monarch. ■ a close male relative of a monarch, esp. a son's son. ■ a male royal ruler of a small state, actually, nominally, or originally subject to a king or emperor. ■ (in France, Germany and other European countries) a nobleman, usually ranking next below a duke. ■ (**prince of/among**) a man or thing regarded as outstanding or excellent in a particular sphere or group: *arctic char is a prince among fishes.* ▷Middle English: via Old French from Latin *princeps, princip-* 'first, chief, sovereign,' from *primus* 'first' + *capere* 'take.' —**prince·dom** /dəm/ *n.*

Prince Al·bert, Prince Charles, etc. see **ALBERT, PRINCE; CHARLES, PRINCE,** etc.

Prince Charm·ing (also **prince charm·ing**) an ideal male lover who is both handsome and of admirable character. ▷partial translation of French *Roi Charmant*, literally 'King Charming.'

prince con·sort ▶*n.* (*pl.* **princ·es con·sort**) the husband of a reigning female sovereign who is himself a prince.

Prince Ed·ward Is·land an island in the Gulf of St. Lawrence, in eastern Canada, the country's smallest province; capital, Charlottetown. Explored by Jacques Cartier in 1534 and colonized by the French, it was ceded to the British in 1763 and became a Canadian province in 1873.

Prince George's Coun·ty /'jôrjəz/ a county in south central Maryland, the site of many southeastern suburbs of Washington, D.C.; pop. 801,515.

prince·ling /'prinsliNG/ ▶*n. chiefly derogatory* the ruler of a small principality or domain. ■ a young prince.

prince·ly /'prinslē/ ▶*adj.* of or held by a prince: *the princely states of India* | *princely authority.* ■ sumptuous and splendid: *princely accommodations.* ■ (of a sum of money) large or generous (often used ironically): *she's paying a princely sum.* —**prince·li·ness** *n.*

Prince of Dark·ness ▶*n.* a name for the Devil.

Prince of Peace ▶*n.* a title given to Jesus Christ (in allusion to Isa. 9:6).

Prince of the Church ▶*n. historical* a dignitary in the Church, esp. a wealthy or influential cardinal or bishop.

Prince of Wales ▶*n.* a title traditionally granted to the heir apparent to the British throne (usually the eldest son of the sovereign) since Edward I of England gave the title to his son in 1301 after the conquest of Wales.

Prince of Wales Is·land **1** an island in the Canadian Arctic, in the Northwest Territories, to the east of Victoria Island. **2** former name for **PENANG**. **3** the largest island in the Alexander Archipelago, in southeastern Alaska, home to the Haida people.

prince roy·al ▶*n.* the eldest son of a reigning monarch.

Prince Ru·pert's Land another name for **RUPERT'S LAND**.

Princes in the Tow·er the young sons of Edward IV, namely **Edward, Prince of Wales** (born 1470) and **Richard, Duke of York** (born 1472), supposedly murdered in the Tower of London in or shortly after 1483.

prin·cess /'prinsəs; 'prinˌses; prin'ses/ ▶*n.* the daughter of a monarch. ■ a close female relative of monarch, esp. a son's daughter. ■ the wife or widow of a prince. ■ the female ruler of a small state, actually, nominally, or originally subject to a king or emperor. ■ *informal* a spoiled or arrogant young woman. ▷late Middle English: from Old French *princesse*, from *prince* (see **PRINCE**).

Prin·cess Anne, Prin·cess Mar·gar·et, etc. see **ANNE, PRINCESS; MARGARET, PRINCESS,** etc.

prin·cesse loin·taine /praN'ses lwaN'ten/ ▶*n.* (*pl.* **prin·cesses loin·taines** *pronunc.* same) *poetic/literary* an ideal but unattainable woman. ▷French, literally 'distant princess,' from the title of a play by E. **ROSTAND**, based on a theme in troubadour poetry.

prin·cess roy·al ▶*n.* the eldest daughter of a reigning monarch (esp. as a title conferred by the British monarch).

prin·cess tree ▶*n.* another name for **EMPRESS TREE**.

Prince·ton /'prinstən/ a historic borough in west central New Jersey, home to Princeton University; pop. 12,016.

Prince·ton U·ni·ver·si·ty /'prinstən/ an Ivy League university at Princeton, New Jersey, founded in 1746.

Prince Wil·liam Sound /'wilyəm/ an inlet of the Pacific Ocean in south central Alaska, scene of a huge 1989 oil tanker spill. Cordova and Valdez are the main ports.

prin·ci·pal /'prinsəpəl/ ▶*adj.* [*attrib.*] **1** first in order of importance; main: *the country's principal cities.* **2** (of money) denoting an original sum invested or lent: *the principal amount of your investment.*

▶*n.* **1** the person with the highest authority or most important position in an organization, institution, or group: *a design consultancy whose principal is based in San Francisco.* ■ the head of a school, college, or other educational institution. ■ the leading performer in a concert, play, ballet, or opera. ■ *Music* the leading player in each section of an orchestra. **2** a sum of money lent or invested on which interest is paid: *the winners are paid from the interest without even touching the principal.* **3** a person for whom another acts as an agent or representative: *stockbrokers in Tokyo act as agents rather than as principals.* ■ *Law* the person directly responsible for a crime. ■ *historical* each of the combatants in a duel. **4** a main rafter supporting purlins. **5** an organ stop sounding a main register of open flue pipes typically an octave above the diapason. ▷Middle English: via Old French from Latin *principalis* 'first, original,' from *princeps, princip-* 'first, chief.' —**prin·ci·pal·ship** /-ˌSHip/ *n.*

USAGE Is it **principal** or **principle**? **Principal** means 'most important' or 'person in charge': *my principal reason for coming tonight; the high school principal.* It also means 'a capital sum': *the principal would be repaid in five years.* **Principle** means 'rule, basis for conduct': *her principles kept her from stealing despite her poverty.*

prin·ci·pal ax·is ▶*n. Physics* each of three mutually perpendicular axes in a body about which the moment of inertia is at a maximum. ■ another term for **OPTICAL AXIS**.

prin·ci·pal di·ag·o·nal ▶*n. Mathematics* the set of elements of a matrix that lie on the line joining the top left corner to the bottom right corner.

prin·ci·pal·i·ty /ˌprinsə'palətē/ ▶*n.* (*pl.* **-ties**) **1** a state ruled by a prince. ■ (**the Principality**) *Brit.* Wales. **2** (**principalities**) (in traditional Christian angelology) the fifth highest order of the ninefold celestial hierarchy. ▷Middle English (denoting the rank of a prince): from Old French *principalite*, from late Latin *principalitas*, from Latin *principalis* 'first, original' (see **PRINCIPAL**).

prin·ci·pal·ly /'prinsəp(ə)lē/ ▶*adv.* [*sentence adverb*] for the most part; chiefly: *he was principally a landscape painter.*

prin·ci·pal parts ▶*plural n. Grammar* the forms of a verb from which all other inflected forms can be deduced, for example, *swim, swam, swum.*

prin·ci·pate /'prinsəˌpāt; -pət/ ▶*n.* the rule of the early Roman emperors, during which some features of republican government were retained. ■ supreme office or authority. ▷late Middle English (denoting a principality): from Latin *principatus* 'first place,' from *princeps, princip-* 'first, chief' (see **PRINCE**). The sense 'rule of the emperors' dates from the mid 19th cent.

prin·ci·ple /'prinsəpəl/ ▶*n.* **1** a fundamental truth or proposition that serves as the foundation for a system of belief or behavior or for a chain of reasoning: *the basic principles of Christianity.* ■ (usu. **principles**) a rule or belief governing one's personal behavior: *struggling to be true to their own principles | she resigned over a matter of principle.* ■ morally correct behavior and attitudes: *a man of principle.* ■ a general scientific theorem or law that has numerous special applications across a wide field. ■ a natural law forming the basis for the construction or working of a machine: *these machines all operate on the same general principle.* **2** a fundamental source or basis of something: *the first principle of all things was water.* ■ a fundamental quality or attribute determining the nature of something; an essence: *the combination of male and female principles.* ■ [with *adj.*] *Chemistry* an active or characteristic constituent of a substance, obtained by simple analysis or separation: *the active principle in the medulla is epinephrine.* ▷late Middle English: from Old French, from Latin *principium* 'source,' *principia* (plural) 'foundations,' from *princeps, princip-* 'first, chief.'

▶*PHRASES* □ **in principle** as a general idea or plan, although the details are not yet established or clear: *the government agreed in principle to a peace plan that included a cease-fire.* ■ used to indicate that although something is theoretically possible, it may not actually happen: *in principle, the banks are entitled to withdraw these loans when necessary.* □ **on principle** because of or in order to demonstrate one's adherence to a particular belief: *he refused, on principle, to pay the fine.*

USAGE On the confusion of **principle** and **principal**, see usage at PRINCIPAL.

prin·ci·pled /'prinsəpəld/ ▶*adj.* **1** (of a person or their behavior) acting in accordance with morality and showing recognition of right and wrong: *a principled politician.* **2** (of a system or method) based on a given set of rules: *a coherent and principled approach.*

prin·ci·ple of par·si·mo·ny ▶*n.* see PARSIMONY.

prink /priNGk/ ▶*v.* (**prink oneself**) spend time making minor adjustments to one's appearance; primp: *prinking themselves in front of the mirror.* ▷late 16th cent.: probably related to archaic *prank* 'dress or adorn in a showy manner'; related to Middle Low German *prank* 'pomp,' Dutch *pronk* 'finery.'

print /print/ ▶*v.* [*trans.*] (often **be printed**) **1** produce (books, newspapers, magazines, etc.), esp. in large quantities, by a mechanical process involving the transfer of text, images, or designs to paper: *a thousand copies of the book were printed.* ■ produce (text or a picture) in such a way: *the words had been printed in blue type.* ■ (of a newspaper or magazine) publish (a piece of writing) within its pages: *the article was printed in the first edition.* ■ (of a publisher or printer) arrange for (a book, manuscript, etc.) to be reproduced in large quantities: *Harper printed her memoirs in 1930.* ■ produce a paper copy of (information stored on a computer): *the results of a search can be* **printed out**. ■ send (a computer file) to a printer or to another, temporary file. ■ produce (a photographic print) from a negative: *any make of film can be developed and printed.* ■ write (text) clearly without joining the letters: *print your name and address on the back of the check | [intrans.] it will be easier to read if I print.* **2** mark (a surface, typically a textile or a garment) with a colored design or pattern: *a delicate fabric* **printed with** *roses.* ■ transfer (a colored design or pattern) to a surface: *patterns of birds, flowers, and trees were printed on the cotton.* ■ make (a mark or indentation) on a surface or in a soft substance by pressing something onto it: *he printed a mark on her soft skin.* ■ mark or indent (the surface of a soft substance) in such a way: *we printed the butter with carved wooden butter molds.* ■ *figurative* fix (something) firmly or indelibly in someone's mind: *his face, with its clearly drawn features, was* **printed on** *her memory.*

▶*n.* **1** the text appearing in a book, newspaper, or other printed publication, esp. with reference to its size, form, or style: *squinting at the tiny print | bold print.* ■ the state of being available in published form: *the news will never* **get into print**. ■ a newspaper or magazine: [as *adj.*] *the print media.* ■ [as *adj.*] of or relating to the printing industry or the printed media: *the print unions | a print worker.* **2** an indentation or mark left on a surface or soft substance by pressure, esp. that of a foot or hand: *there were paw prints everywhere.* ■ (**prints**) fingerprints: *the FBI matched the prints to those of the Las Vegas drug suspect.* **3** a picture or design printed from a block or plate or copied from a painting by photography: *the walls were hung with wildlife prints.* ■ a photograph printed on paper from a negative or transparency. ■ a copy of a motion picture on film, esp. a particular version of it. **4** a piece of fabric or clothing with a decorative colored pattern or design printed on it: *light summer prints | [as adj.] a floral print dress.* ■ such a pattern or design. ▷Middle English (denoting the impression made by a stamp or seal): from Old French *preinte* 'pressed,' feminine past participle of *preindre*, from Latin *premere* 'to press.'

▶*PHRASES* □ **appear in print** (of an author) have one's work published. □ **in print 1** (of a book) available from the publisher: *he was surprised to find it was still in print.* **2** in printed or published form: *she did not live to see her work in print.* □ **out of print** (of a book) no longer available from the publisher: *the title I want is out of print.* □ **the printed word** language or ideas as expressed in books, newspapers, or other publications, esp. when contrasted with their expression in speech.

print. ▶*abbr.* printing.

print·a·bil·i·ty /ˌprintə'bilətē/ ▶*n.* the ability of paper to take print: *the paper's printability and porosity.*

print·a·ble /'printəbəl/ ▶*adj.* suitable or fit to be printed or published: *break photographs up into printable form | few people had a good, or even printable, word for him.* ■ *Computing* (of text) able to be printed: *the file is printable.*

print·ed cir·cuit ▶*n.* an electronic circuit consisting of thin strips of a conducting material such as copper, which have been etched from a layer fixed to a flat insulating sheet called a **printed circuit board**, and to which integrated circuits and other components are attached.

print·er /'printər/ ▶*n.* a person whose job or business is commercial printing. ■ a machine for printing text or pictures onto paper, esp. one linked to a computer.

print·er-friend·ly /'printər ˌfrendlē/ ▶*adj.* formatted for output to a printer, with extraneous material deleted or suppressed: *printer-friendly sample ballots to take with you to their polling place.*

print·er's dev·il ▶*n.* *historical* a person, typically a young boy, serving at or below the level of apprentice in a printing establishment.

print·er's mark ▶*n.* a logo serving as a printer's trademark.

print·er·y /'printərē/ ▶*n.* (*pl.* **-ter·ies**) a print shop.

print·head /'print,hed/ (also **print head**) ▶*n.* *Computing* a component in a printer that assembles and holds the characters and from which the images of the characters are transferred to the printing medium.

print·ing /'printiNG/ ▶*n.* the production of books, newspapers, or other printed material: *the invention of printing | [as adj.] the printing industry.* ■ a single impression of a book: *the second printing was ready just after Christmas.* ■ handwriting in which the letters are written separately rather than being joined together.

print·ing press ▶*n.* a machine for printing text or pictures from type or plates.

print·mak·er /'print,mākər/ ▶*n.* a person who makes pictures or designs by printing them from specially prepared plates or blocks. —**print·mak·ing** /-kiNG/ *n.*

print·out /'print,out/ ▶*n.* *Computing* a page or set of pages of printed material produced by a computer's printer.

print queue ▶*n.* *Computing* a series of print jobs waiting to use a printer.

print run ▶*n.* the number of copies of a book, magazine, etc., printed at one time.

print shop (also **print·shop**) ▶*n.* an establishment where the printing of newspapers, books, and other materials takes place.

pri·on[1] /'prī,än/ ▶*n.* a small petrel of southern seas, having a wide bill fringed with comblike plates for feeding on planktonic crustaceans. • Genus *Pachyptila*, family Procellariidae: six species. ▷mid 19th cent.: modern Latin (former genus name), from Greek *priōn* 'a saw' (referring to its sawlike bill).

pri·on[2] /'prē,än/ ▶*n.* *Microbiology* a protein particle that is believed to be the cause of brain diseases such as BSE, scrapie, and Creutzfeldt–Jakob disease. Prions are not visible microscopically, contain no nucleic acid, and are highly resistant to destruction. Compare with VIRINO. ▷1980s: by rearrangement of elements from *pro(teinaceous) in(fectious particle)*.

pri·or[1] /'prīər/ ▶*adj.* [*attrib.*] existing or coming before in time, order, or importance: *he has a prior engagement this evening.*

▶*n.* *informal* a previous criminal conviction: *he had no juvenile record, no priors.* ▷early 18th cent.: from Latin, literally 'former, elder,' related to *prae* 'before.'

▶*PHRASE* □ **prior to** before a particular time or event: *she visited me on the day prior to her death.*

pri·or[2] ▶*n.* a man who is head of a house or group of houses of certain religious orders, in particular: ■ the man next in rank below an abbot. ■ the head of a house of friars. ▷late Old English, from a medieval Latin noun use of Latin *prior* 'elder, former' (see PRIOR[1]). —**pri·or·ate** /'prīərət/ *n.* —**pri·or·ship** /-,SHip/ *n.*

pri·or·ess /'prīərəs/ ▶*n.* a woman who is head of a house of certain orders of nuns. ■ the woman next in rank below an abbess.

pri·or·i·tize /prī'ôrə,tīz; 'prīərə-/ ▶*v.* [*trans.*] designate or treat (something) as more important than other things: *prioritize your credit card debt.* ■ determine the order for dealing with (a series of items or tasks) according to their relative importance: *age affects the way people prioritize their goals | [intrans.] are you able to prioritize?* —**pri·or·i·ti·za·tion** /,prī,ôrətə'zāSHən/ *n.*

pri·or·i·ty /prī'ôrətē/ ▶*n.* (*pl.* **-ties**) a thing that is regarded as more important than another: *housework didn't figure high on her list of priorities.* ■ the fact or condition of being regarded or treated as more important: *the safety of the country* **takes priority over** *any other matter.* ■ the right to take precedence or to proceed before others: *priority is given to those with press passes | [as adj.] clear the left lane for priority traffic.* ▷late Middle English (denoting precedence in time or rank): from Old French *priorite*, from medieval Latin *prioritas*, from Latin *prior* 'former' (see PRIOR[1]).

pri·or prob·a·bil·i·ty ▶*n.* *Statistics* a probability as assessed before making reference to certain relevant observations, esp. subjectively or on the assumption that all possible outcomes be given the same probability. Compare with POSTERIOR PROBABILITY.

pri·or re·straint ▶*n.* *Law* judicial suppression of material that would be published or broadcast, on the grounds that it is libelous or harmful. In U.S. law, the first amendment severely limits the ability of the government to do this.

pri·o·ry /'prīərē/ ▶*n.* (*pl.* **-ries**) a small monastery or nunnery that is governed by a prior or prioress. ▷Middle English: from Anglo-Norman French *priorie*, medieval Latin *prioria*, from Latin *prior* 'elder, superior' (see PRIOR[2]).

Pri·pyat /'prēpyit/ (also **Pri·pet** /'pripit; -et/) a river in northwestern Ukraine and southern Belarus that rises in Ukraine near the border with Poland and flows about 440 miles (710 km) east through the Pripyat Marshes to join the Dnieper River north of Kiev.

Pris·cian /'prisH(ē)ən/ (6th century AD), Byzantine grammarian; full name *Priscianus Caesariensis*. His *Grammatical Institutions* became one of the standard Latin grammatical works in the Middle Ages.

Pris·co·an /pris'kōən/ ▶*adj.* *Geology* of, relating to, or denoting the eon that (in some schemes) constitutes the earliest part of the Precambrian, preceding the Archean eon. It extended from the origin of the earth to about 4 billion years ago and has left no so far identifiable rocks. ■ [as *n.*] (**the Priscoan**) the Priscoan eon. ▷formed irregularly from Latin *priscus* 'ancient' + -AN.

prise ▶*v.* variant spelling of PRIZE[2].

prism /'prizəm/ ▶*n.* *Geometry* a solid geometric figure whose two end faces are similar, equal, and parallel rectilinear figures, and whose sides are parallelograms. ■ *Optics* a glass or other transparent object in this form, esp. one that is triangular with refracting surfaces at an acute angle with each other and that separates white light into a spectrum of colors. ■ used figuratively with reference to the clarification or distortion afforded by a particular viewpoint: *they were forced to imagine the disaster through* **the prism of** *television.* ▷late 16th cent.: via late Latin from Greek *prisma* 'thing sawn,' from *prizein* 'to saw.'

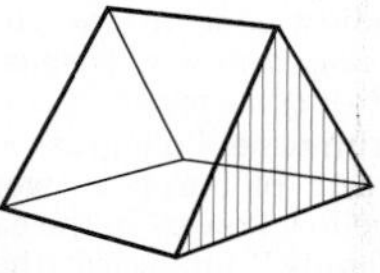

geometric prism

pris·mat·ic /priz'matik/ ▶*adj.* of, relating to, or having the form of a prism or prisms: *a prismatic structure.* ■ (of colors) formed, separated, or distributed by an optical prism or something acting as one: *a flash of prismatic light on the edge of the glass.* ■ (of colors) varied and brilliant: *a hundred prismatic tints.* ■ (of an instrument) incorporating a prism or prisms: *a prismatic compass.* ▷early 18th cent.: from French *prismatique*, from Greek *prisma* 'thing sawn' (see PRISM). —**pris·mat·i·cal·ly** /-ik(ə)lē/ *adv.*

pris·mat·ic lay·er ▸*n. Zoology* the middle layer of the shell of a mollusk, consisting of calcite or aragonite.

pris·moid /ˈpriz,moid/ ▸*n. Geometry* a solid geometric figure like a prism, in which the end faces have the same number of sides but are not equal.

pris·on /ˈprizən/ ▸*n.* a building (or vessel) to which people are legally committed as a punishment for crimes they have committed or while awaiting trial: *he died* ***in prison*** | *both men were* ***sent to prison.*** ■ confinement in such a building: *prison saves one man and hardens another.*
▸*v.* (**-oned, -on·ing**) [*trans.*] *poetic/literary* imprison: *the young man prisoned behind the doors.* ▷late Old English, from Old French *prisun*, from Latin *prensio(n-)*, variant of *prehensio(n-)* 'laying hold of,' from the verb *prehendere.*

pris·on camp ▸*n.* a camp where prisoners of war or political prisoners are kept under guard. ■ a minimum-security prison, typically where prisoners have outdoor work assignments.

pris·on·er /ˈpriz(ə)nər/ ▸*n.* a person legally committed to prison as a punishment for crimes they have committed or while awaiting trial. ■ a person captured and kept confined by an enemy, opponent, or criminal: *American citizens were being* ***held prisoner*** *in Iran* | *200 rebels were* ***taken prisoner.*** ■ *figurative* a person who is or feels confined or trapped by a situation or set of circumstances: *he's become a prisoner of the publicity he's generated.* ▷late Middle English: from Old French *prisonier*, from *prison* (see PRISON).
▸*PHRASE* □ **take no prisoners** be ruthlessly aggressive or uncompromising in the pursuit of one's objectives.

pris·on·er of con·science ▸*n.* a person who has been imprisoned for holding political or religious views that are not tolerated by their own government.

pris·on·er of war (abbr.: **POW**) ▸*n.* a person who has been captured and imprisoned by the enemy in war.

pris·on·er's base ▸*n.* a chasing game played by two groups of children each occupying a distinct base or home.

pris·on·er's di·lem·ma ▸*n.* (in game theory) a situation in which two players each have two options whose outcome depends crucially on the simultaneous choice made by the other, often formulated in terms of two prisoners separately deciding whether to confess to a crime.

pris·sy /ˈprisē/ ▸*adj.* (**-si·er, -si·est**) (of a person or their manner) fussily and excessively respectable: *her prissy mother.* ■ (of clothes) overadorned with details such as ruffles and bows: *prissy little dresses.* ▷late 19th cent.: perhaps a blend of PRIM and SISSY. —**pris·si·ly** /ˈprisəlē/ *adv.* —**pris·si·ness** *n.*

Priš·ti·na /ˈprishti,nä/ a city in southern Serbia, the capital of the autonomous province of Kosovo; pop. 108,000.

pris·tine /ˈpris,tēn; priˈstēn/ ▸*adj.* in its original condition; unspoiled: *pristine copies of an early magazine.* ■ clean and fresh as if new; spotless: *a pristine white shirt.* ▷mid 16th cent. (in the sense 'original, former, primitive and undeveloped'): from Latin *pristinus* 'former.' The senses 'unspoiled' and 'spotless' date from the 1920s. —**pris·tine·ly** *adv.*

Pritch·ett /ˈprichət/, Sir V. S. (1900–97), English writer and critic; full name *Victor Sawdon Pritchett*. His short-story collections include *The Spanish Virgin and Other Stories* (1930). Pritchett is also noted for his novels, such as *Mr. Beluncle* (1951), and for his autobiographies, *A Cab at the Door* (1968) and *Midnight Oil* (1973). His critical works include *The Living Novel* (1946).

prith·ee /ˈpriT͟Hē/ ▸*exclam. archaic* please (used to convey a polite request): *prithee, Jack, answer me honestly.* ▷late 16th cent.: abbreviation of *I pray thee.*

priv. ▸*abbr.* ■ private. ■ privative.

pri·va·cy /ˈprīvəsē/ ▸*n.* the state or condition of being free from being observed or disturbed by other people: *she returned to the privacy of her own home.* ■ the state of being free from public attention: *a law to restrict newspapers' freedom to invade people's privacy.*

pri·vate /ˈprīvit/ ▸*adj.* **1** belonging to or for the use of one particular person or group of people only: *all bedrooms have private facilities* | *his private plane.* ■ (of a situation, activity, or gathering) affecting or involving only a particular person or group of people: *a small private service in the chapel.* ■ (of thoughts and feelings) not to be shared with or revealed to others: *she felt awkward intruding on private grief.* ■ (of a person) not choosing to share thoughts and feelings with others: *he was a very private man.* ■ (of a meeting or discussion) involving only a small number of people and dealing with matters that are not to be disclosed to others: *this is a private conversation.* ■ (of a place) quiet and free from people who can interrupt: *can we go somewhere a little more private?* **2** (of a person) having no official or public role or position: *the paintings were sold to a private collector.* ■ not connected with one's work or official position: *the president was visiting China in a private capacity.* **3** (of a service or industry) provided or owned by an individual or an independent, commercial company rather than by the government: *research projects carried out by private industry* | *more than 1,400 state enterprises that were about to* ***go private.*** ■ of or relating to a system of education or medical treatment conducted outside the system of government and charging fees to the individuals who make use of it. ■ of, relating to, or denoting a transaction between individuals and not involving commercial organizations: *it was a private sale—no agent's commission.*
▸*n.* **1** a soldier of the lowest rank, in particular an enlisted person in the U.S. Army or Marine Corps ranking below private first class. **2** (**privates**) *informal* short for PRIVATE PARTS. ▷late Middle English (originally denoting a person not acting in an official capacity): from Latin *privatus* 'withdrawn from public life,' a use of the past participle of *privare* 'bereave, deprive,' from *privus* 'single, individual.'
▸*PHRASE* □ **in private** with no one else present: *I've got to talk to you in private.*

pri·vate de·tec·tive ▸*n.* another term for PRIVATE INVESTIGATOR.

pri·vate en·ter·prise ▸*n.* business or industry that is managed by independent companies or private individuals rather than by the state.

pri·va·teer /,prīvəˈtir/ ▸*n. chiefly historical* an armed ship owned and officered by private individuals holding a government commission and authorized for use in war, esp. in the capture of enemy merchant shipping. ■ (also **privateersman**) a commander or crew member of such a ship, often regarded as a pirate.
▸*v.* [*intrans.*] engage in the activities of a privateer. ▷mid 17th cent.: from PRIVATE, on the pattern of *volunteer.* —**pri·va·teer·ing** *n.*

pri·vate eye ▸*n. informal* a private investigator.

pri·vate first class ▸*n.* an enlisted person in the armed forces, in particular (in the U.S. Army) an enlisted person ranking above private and below corporal or (in the U.S. Marine Corps) an enlisted person ranking above private and below lance corporal.

pri·vate in·ves·ti·ga·tor (also **private detective**) ▸*n.* a freelance detective who carries out covert investigations on behalf of private clients.

pri·vate key ▸*n.* see PUBLIC KEY.

pri·vate law ▸*n.* a branch of the law that deals with the relations between individuals or institutions, rather than relations between these and the government.

pri·vate·ly /ˈprīvitlē/ ▸*adv.* in a private way, manner, or capacity: *I must insist we speak privately* | *his research is privately financed.* ■ [often *sentence adverb*] used to refer to a situation in which someone's thoughts and feelings are not disclosed to others: *privately, Republican strategists worried about the latest polls.*

pri·vate mem·ber ▸*n.* (in the UK, Canada, Australia, and New Zealand) a member of a parliament who is not a minister or does not hold government office.

pri·vate nui·sance ▸*n. Law* see NUISANCE.

pri·vate parts ▸*plural n.* used euphemistically to refer to a person's genitals.

pri·vate prac·tice ▸*n.* the work of a professional practitioner, such as a doctor or lawyer, who is self-employed.

pri·vate school ▸*n.* **1** a school supported by a private organization or private individuals rather than by the government. **2** *Brit.* a school supported wholly by the payment of fees.

pri·vate sec·re·tar·y ▸*n.* **1** a secretary who deals with the personal and confidential concerns of a business person or public figure. **2** a civil servant acting as an aide to a senior government official.

pri·vate sec·tor ▸*n.* the part of the national economy that is not under direct government control.

pri·vate sol·dier ▸*n.* a soldier of the lowest rank.

pri·vate trea·ty ▸*n.* the agreement for the sale of a property at a price negotiated directly between the vendor and purchaser or their agents.

pri·va·tion /prīˈvāshən/ ▸*n.* a state in which things that are essential for human well-being such as food and warmth are scarce or lacking: *years of rationing and privation* | *the* ***privations of*** *life at the front.* ■ *formal* the loss or absence of a quality or attribute that is normally present: *cold is the privation of heat.* See note at LACK. ▷Middle English: from Latin *privatio(n-)*, from *privat-* 'deprived,' from the verb *privare* (see PRIVATE).

pri·va·tism /ˈprīvə,tizəm/ ▸*n.* a tendency to be concerned with ideas or issues only insofar as they affect one as an individual. —**pri·va·tist** *adj.*

pri·va·tive /ˈprivətiv/ ▸*adj.* (of an action or state) marked by the absence, removal, or loss of some quality or attribute that is normally present. ■ (of a statement or term) denoting the absence or loss of an attribute or quality: *the wording of the privative clause.* ■ *Grammar* (of a particle or affix) expressing absence or negation, for example, the *a-* (from the *alpha privative* in Greek), meaning "not," in *atypical.*
▸*n.* a privative attribute, quality, or proposition. ▷late 16th cent.: from Latin *privativus* 'denoting privation,' from *privat-* 'deprived' (see PRIVATION).

pri·va·tize /ˈprīvə,tīz/ ▸*v.* [*trans.*] transfer (a business, industry, or service) from public to private ownership and control: *a plan for privatizing education.* —**pri·va·ti·za·tion** /,prīvətəˈzāshən/ *n.* —**pri·va·tiz·er** *n.*

priv·et /ˈprivit/ ▸*n.* a shrub of the olive family, with small white, heavily scented flowers and poisonous black berries. • Genus *Ligustrum*, family Oleaceae: several species, in particular the semievergreen **common privet** (*L. vulgare*), often grown as a hedge. ▷mid 16th cent.: of unknown origin.

priv·i·lege /ˈpriv(ə)lij/ ▸*n.* a special right, advantage, or immunity granted or available only to a particular person or group of people: *education is a right, not a privilege* | *he has been accustomed all his life to wealth and privilege.* ■ something regarded as a rare opportunity and bringing particular pleasure: *I have the privilege of awarding you this scholarship.* ■ (also **absolute privilege**) (in a parliamentary context) the right to say or write something without the risk of incurring punishment or legal action for defamation. ■ the right of a lawyer or official to refuse to divulge confidential information. ■ *chiefly historical* a grant to an individual, corporation, or place of special rights or immunities, esp. in the form of a franchise or monopoly.
▸*v.* [*trans.*] *formal* grant a privilege or privileges to: *English inheritance law privileged the eldest son.* ■ (usu. **be privileged from**) exempt (someone) from a liability or obligation to which others are subject. ▷Middle English: via Old French from Latin *privilegium* 'bill or law affecting an individual,' from *privus* 'private' + *lex, leg-* 'law.'

priv·i·leged /ˈpriv(ə)lijd/ ▸*adj.* having special rights, advantages, or immunities: *in the nineteenth century, only a privileged few had the vote.* ■ [with *infinitive*] having the rare opportunity to do something that brings particular pleasure: *I felt I had been privileged to compete in such a race.* ■ (of information) legally protected from being made public: *the intelligence reports are privileged.*

priv·i·ty /ˈprivitē/ ▸*n.* (*pl.* **-ties**) *Law* a relation between two parties that is recognized by law, such as that of blood, lease, or service: *the parties no longer have privity with each other* | *a warehouseman not in privity with the government.* ▷Middle English (in the sense 'secrecy, intimacy'): from Old French *privete*, from medieval Latin *privitas*, from Latin *privus* 'private.'

priv·y /ˈprivē/ ▸*adj.* [*predic.*] (**privy to**) sharing in the knowledge of (something secret or private): *he was no longer privy to her innermost thoughts.* ■ *archaic* hidden; secret: *a privy place.*
▸*n.* (*pl.* **priv·ies**) **1** a toilet located in a small shed outside a house or other building; outhouse. **2** *Law* a person having a part or interest in any action, matter, or thing. ▷Middle English (originally in the sense 'belonging to one's own private circle'): from Old French *prive* 'private' (also used as a noun meaning 'private place' and 'familiar friend'), from Latin *privatus* 'withdrawn from public life' (see PRIVATE). —**priv·i·ly** /ˈprivəlē/ *adv.*

priv·y cham·ber ▸*n.* a private apartment in a royal residence.

priv·y coun·cil ▸*n.* a body of advisers or private counselors appointed by a sovereign or a governor general (now chiefly on an honorary basis and including present and former government ministers). **—priv·y coun·ci·lor** *n.*

priv·y purse ▸*n.* (in the UK) an allowance from the public revenue for the monarch's private expenses.

priv·y seal ▸*n.* (in the UK) a seal affixed to documents that are afterward to pass the Great Seal or that do not require it.

prix fixe /ˈprē ˈfēks; ˈfiks/ ▸*n.* a meal consisting of several courses served at a total fixed price. ▷French, literally 'fixed price.'

prize[1] /prīz/ ▸*n.* a thing given as a reward to the winner of a competition or race or in recognition of another outstanding achievement: *the nation's most prestigious prize for contemporary art.* ■ a thing, esp. an amount of money or a valuable object, that can be won in a lottery or other game of chance: *the grand prize in the drawing* | [as *adj.*] *prize money.* ■ something of great value that is worth struggling to achieve: *the prize will be victory in the general election.* ■ *chiefly historical* an enemy ship captured during the course of naval warfare. [late Middle English: from Old French *prise* 'taking, booty,' from *prendre* 'take.']
▸*adj.* [*attrib.*] (esp. of something entered in a competition) having been or likely to be awarded a prize: *prize onions* | *a prize bull.* ■ denoting something for which a prize is awarded: *a prize crossword.* ■ excellent of its kind; outstanding: *a prize example of how well organic farming can function.* ■ complete; utter: *you must think I'm a prize idiot.*
▸*v.* [*trans.*] (often **be prized**) value extremely highly: *the berries were prized for their healing properties* | [as *adj.*] (**prized**) *the bicycle was her most prized possession.* See note at **ESTEEM**. ▷Middle English: the noun, a variant of **PRICE**; the verb (originally in the sense 'estimate the value of') from Old French *pris-*, stem of *preisier* 'to praise, appraise' (see **PRAISE**).

prize[2] (also **prise**) ▸*v.* another term for **PRY**[2] : *prizing open the door* | *he prized his left leg free.* ▷late 17th cent.: from dialect *prise* 'lever,' from Old French *prise* 'grasp, taking hold.' Compare with **PRY**[2].

prize court ▸*n.* a naval court that adjudicates on the distribution of ships and property captured in the course of naval warfare.

prize·fight /ˈprīzˌfīt/ (also **prize fight**) ▸*n.* a boxing match fought for prize money. **—prize·fight·er** *n.* **—prize·fight·ing** *n.*

prize ring ▸*n.* a ring used for prizefighting. ■ (**the prize ring**) the practice of prizefighting; boxing.

p.r.n. ▸*abbr.* (in prescriptions) as the occasion arises; as needed. ▷Latin *pro re nata.*

PRO ▸*abbr.* ■ public relations officer. ■ *Brit.* Public Record Office.

pro[1] /prō/ ▸*n.* (*pl.* **pros**) *informal* a professional, esp. in sports: *a tennis pro.*
▸*adj.* (of a person or an event) professional: *a pro golfer.* ▷mid 19th cent.: abbreviation.

pro[2] ▸*n.* (*pl.* **pros**) (usu. **pros**) an advantage of something or an argument in favor of a course of action: ***the pros and cons** of joint ownership.*
▸*prep.* & *adv.* in favor of: [as *prep.*] *they were pro the virtues of individualism.* ▷late Middle English (as a noun): from Latin, literally 'for, on behalf of.'

pro-[1] ▸*prefix* **1** favoring; supporting: *pro-choice* | *pro-life.* **2** acting as a substitute or deputy for; on behalf of; for: *proconsul* | *procure.* **3** denoting motion forward, out, or away: *proceed* | *propel* | *prostrate.* ▷from Latin *pro* 'in front of, on behalf of, instead of, on account of.'

pro-[2] ▸*prefix* before in time, place, order, etc.: *proactive* | *prognosis* | *program.* ▷from Greek *pro* 'before.'

pro·a /ˈprōə/ (also **pra·hu** /ˈpräˌo͞o/ or **prau** /prou/) ▸*n.* a type of sailing boat originating in Malaysia and Indonesia that may be sailed with either end at the front, typically having a large triangular sail and an outrigger. ▷late 16th cent.: from Malay *perahu.*

pro·ac·tive /prōˈaktiv/ ▸*adj.* (of a person, policy, or action) creating or controlling a situation by causing something to happen rather than responding to it after it has happened: *be proactive in identifying and preventing potential problems.* ▷1930s: from **PRO-**[2] (denoting earlier occurrence), on the pattern of *reactive.* **—pro·ac·tion** /prōˈakSHən/ *n.* **—pro·ac·tive·ly** *adv.* **—pro·ac·tiv·i·ty** /ˌprōˌakˈtivətē/ *n.*

pro·ac·tive in·hi·bi·tion ▸*n.* *Psychology* the tendency of previously learned material to hinder subsequent learning.

pro-am /ˈprō ˈam/ ▸*adj.* (of a sports event) involving both professionals and amateurs: *a pro-am golf tournament.*
▸*n.* an event of this type.

pro-an·a /ˈprō ˈanə/ ▸*adj.* (of a Web site) encouraging or advocating anorexia: *pro-ana sites share tips on how to trick your parents into believing you're eating.*

prob /präb/ ▸*n.* *informal* problem: *there's no prob.* ▷1930s: abbreviation.

prob. ▸*abbr.* ■ probable or probably. ■ probate. ■ problem.

prob·a·bi·lis·tic /ˌpräbəbəˈlistik/ ▸*adj.* based on or adapted to a theory of probability; subject to or involving chance variation: *the main approaches are either rule-based or probabilistic.* **—prob·a·bi·lism** /ˈpräbəbəˌlizəm/ *n.*

prob·a·bil·i·ty /ˌpräbəˈbilətē/ ▸*n.* (*pl.* **-ties**) the extent to which something is probable; the likelihood of something happening or being the case: *the rain will make the probability of their arrival even greater.* ■ a probable event: *for a time, revolution was a strong probability.* ■ the most probable thing: *the probability is that it will be phased in over a number of years.* ■ *Mathematics* the extent to which an event is likely to occur, measured by the ratio of the favorable cases to the whole number of cases possible: *the area under the curve represents probability* | *a probability of 0.5.* ▷late Middle English: from Latin *probabilitas*, from *probabilis* 'provable, credible' (see **PROBABLE**).
▸**PHRASE** □ **in all probability** used to convey that something is very likely: *he would in all probability make himself known.*

prob·a·bil·i·ty den·si·ty func·tion ▸*n.* *Statistics* a function of a continuous random variable, whose integral across an interval gives the probability that the value of the variable lies within the same interval.

prob·a·bil·i·ty dis·tri·bu·tion ▸*n.* *Statistics* a function of a discrete variable whose integral over any interval is the probability that the random variable specified by it will lie within that interval.

prob·a·bil·i·ty the·o·ry ▸*n.* the branch of mathematics that deals with quantities having random distributions.

prob·a·ble /ˈpräbəbəl/ ▸*adj.* [often with *clause*] likely to be the case or to happen: *it is **probable that** the economic situation will deteriorate further* | *the probable consequences of his action.*
▸*n.* a person who is likely to become or do something, esp. one who is likely to be chosen for a team: *Merson and Wright are probables.* ▷late Middle English (in the sense 'worthy of belief'): via Old French from Latin *probabilis*, from *probare* 'to test, demonstrate.'

prob·a·ble cause ▸*n.* *Law* reasonable grounds (for making a search, pressing a charge, etc.).

prob·a·bly /ˈpräbəblē; ˈpräblē/ ▸*adv.* [*sentence adverb*] almost certainly; as far as one knows or can tell: *she would probably never see him again* | *"Would you recognize them?" "Probably."*

pro·band /ˈprōˌband; prōˈband/ ▸*n.* a person serving as the starting point for the genetic study of a family (used esp. in medicine and psychiatry). ▷1920s: from Latin *probandus* 'to be proved,' gerundive of *probare* 'to test.'

pro·bang /ˈprōˌbaNG/ ▸*n.* *Medicine* a strip of flexible material with a sponge or tuft at the end, used to remove an object from or apply medication to the throat. ▷mid 17th cent. (named *provang* by its inventor): perhaps an alteration suggested by **PROBE**.

pro·bate /ˈprōˌbāt/ ▸*n.* the official proving of a will: *the will was in probate* | [as *adj.*] *a probate court.* ■ a verified copy of a will with a certificate as handed to the executors.
▸*v.* [*trans.*] establish the validity of (a will). ▷late Middle English: from Latin *probatum* 'something proved,' neuter past participle of *probare* 'to test, prove.'

pro·ba·tion /prōˈbāSHən/ ▸*n.* *Law* the release of an offender from detention, subject to a period of good behavior under supervision: *I went to court and was **put on probation.*** ■ the process or period of testing or observing the character or abilities of a person in a certain role, for example, a new employee: *for an initial period of probation, your manager will closely monitor your progress.* ▷late Middle English (denoting testing, investigation, or examination): from Old French *probacion*, from Latin *probatio(n-)*, from *probare* 'to test, prove' (see **PROVE**). The legal use dates from the late 19th cent. **—pro·ba·tion·ar·y** /-ˌnerē/ *adj.*

pro·ba·tion·er /prōˈbāSHənər/ ▸*n.* a person who is serving a probationary or trial period in a job or position to which they are newly appointed. See note at **NOVICE**. ■ an offender on probation.

pro·ba·tion of·fi·cer ▸*n.* a person appointed to supervise offenders who are on probation.

pro·ba·tive /ˈprōbətiv/ ▸*adj.* *chiefly Law* having the quality or function of proving or demonstrating something; affording proof or evidence: *it places the probative burden on the defendant.* ▷late Middle English (describing something that serves as a test): from Latin *probativus*, from *probat-* 'proved,' from the verb *probare* (see **PROVE**).

probe /prōb/ ▸*n.* a blunt-ended surgical instrument used for exploring a wound or part of the body. ■ a small device, esp. an electrode, used for measuring, testing, or obtaining information. ■ a projecting device for engaging in a drogue, either on an aircraft for use in inflight refueling or on a spacecraft for use in docking with another craft. ■ (also **space probe**) an unmanned exploratory spacecraft designed to transmit information about its environment. ■ an investigation into a crime or other matter: *a **probe into** the maritime industry by the FBI.*
▸*v.* [*trans.*] physically explore or examine (something) with the hands or an instrument: *researchers probing the digestive glands of mollusks.* ■ [*intrans.*] seek to uncover information about someone or something: *he began to **probe into** Donald's whereabouts* | [*trans.*] *police are probing another murder.* ▷late Middle English (as a noun): from late Latin *proba* 'proof' (in medieval Latin 'examination'), from Latin *probare* 'to test.' The verb dates from the mid 17th cent. **—prob·er** *n.* **—prob·ing·ly** *adv.*

pro·ben·e·cid /prōˈbenəsid/ ▸*n.* *Medicine* a synthetic compound that promotes increased excretion of uric acid and is used to treat gout. • Chem. formula $C_{13}H_{19}NO_4S$. ▷1950s: from *pro(pyl)* + *ben(zoic)* + *-e-* + *(a)cid.*

pro·bi·ot·ic /ˌprōbīˈätik/ ▸*adj.* denoting a substance that stimulates the growth of microorganisms, especially those with beneficial properties (such as those of the intestinal flora).
▸*n.* a probiotic substance or preparation. ■ a microorganism introduced into the body for its beneficial qualities.

prob·it /ˈpräbit/ ▸*n.* *Statistics* a unit of probability based on deviation from the mean of a standard distribution. ▷1930s: from *prob(ability un)it.*

pro·bi·ty /ˈprōbitē/ ▸*n.* *formal* the quality of having strong moral principles; honesty and decency: *financial probity.* See note at **GOODNESS**. ▷late Middle English: from Latin *probitas*, from *probus* 'good.'

prob·lem /ˈpräbləm/ ▸*n.* **1** a matter or situation regarded as unwelcome or harmful and needing to be dealt with and overcome: *mental health problems* | [as *adj.*] *city planners consider it a problem district.* ■ a thing that is difficult to achieve or accomplish: *motivation of staff can also be a problem.* **2** *Physics & Mathematics* an inquiry starting from given conditions to investigate or demonstrate a fact, result, or law. ■ *Geometry* a proposition in which something has to be constructed. Compare with **THEOREM**. ■ (in various games, esp. chess) an arrangement of pieces in which the solver has to achieve a specified result. ▷late Middle English (originally denoting a riddle or a question for academic discussion): from Old French *probleme*, via Latin from Greek *problēma*, from *proballein* 'put forth,' from *pro* 'before' + *ballein* 'to throw.'
▸**PHRASES** □ **have a problem with** disagree with or have an objection to: *I have no problem with shopping on Sundays.* □ **no problem** used to express one's agreement or acquiescence: *"Can you help?" "No problem."* □ **that's your** (or **his**, or **her**, etc.) **problem** (said with emphatic stress on pronoun) used to express one's lack of interest in or sympathy with the problems or misfortunes of another person: *he'd made a mistake but that was his problem.*

prob·lem·at·ic /ˌpräbləˈmatik/ ▸*adj.* constituting or presenting a problem or difficulty: *the situation was problematic for teachers.* ■ doubtful or questionable. See note at **DOUBTFUL**. ■ *Logic* enunciating or supporting what is possible but not necessarily true.
▸*n.* a thing that constitutes a problem or difficulty: *the **problematics of** artificial intelligence.* ▷early 17th cent.: via French from late Latin *problematicus*, from Greek *problēmatikos*, from *problēma* (see **PROBLEM**). **—prob·lem·at·i·cal** *adj.* **—prob·lem·at·i·cal·ly** /-ik(ə)lē/ *adv.*

prob·lem·a·tize /ˈpräbləməˌtīz/ ▸*v.* [*trans.*] make into or regard as a problem requiring a solution: *he problematized the concept of history.* **—prob·lem·a·ti·za·tion** /ˌpräbləmətəˈzāSHən; -ˌmatə-/ *n.*

pro bo·no pu·bli·co /ˌprō ˈbōnō ˈpo͝obliˌkō; ˈbōnō ˈpəbliˌkō/ ▸*adv.* & *adj.* for the public good: [as *adv.*] *the burden they carried pro bono publico.* ■ (usu. **pro bono**) denoting work undertaken for the public good without charge, esp. legal work for a client with a low income: [as *adv.*] *the attorneys are representing him pro bono* | [as *adj.*] *pro bono legal services.* ▷Latin.

Pro·bos·cid·e·a /ˌprōbəˈsidēə; prəˌbäsˈidēə/ *Zoology* an order of large mammals that comprises the elephants and their extinct relatives. They are distinguished by the possession of a trunk and tusks. ▷modern Latin (plural), from PROBOSCIS. **—pro·bos·cid·e·an** /ˌprōbəˈsidēən; prəˌbäsəˈdēən/ (also **pro·bos·cid·i·an**) *n.* & *adj.*

pro·bos·cis /prəˈbäsəs; -ˈbäskəs/ ▶*n.* (*pl.* **-bos·cis·es**, **-bos·ci·des** /-ˈbäsəˌdēz/, or **-bos·ces** /-ˈbäsēz/) the nose of a mammal, esp. when it is long and mobile, such as the trunk of an elephant or the snout of a tapir. ■ *Entomology* (in many insects) an elongated sucking mouthpart that is typically tubular and flexible. ■ *Zoology* (in some worms) an extensible tubular sucking organ. ▷early 17th cent.: via Latin from Greek *proboskis* 'means of obtaining food,' from *pro* 'before' + *boskein* '(cause to) feed.'

pro·bos·cis mon·key ▶*n.* a leaf-eating monkey native to the forests of Borneo, the male of which is twice the weight of the female and has a large pendulous nose. • *Nasalis larvatus*, family Cercopithecidae.

proc. ▶*abbr.* ■ procedure. ■ proceedings. ■ process. ■ proclamation. ■ proctor.

pro·caine /ˈprōˌkān/ ▶*n.* a synthetic compound derived from benzoic acid, used as a local anesthetic, esp. in dentistry. ▷early 20th cent.: from PRO-[1] (denoting substitution) + *-caine* (from COCAINE).

pro·caine pen·i·cil·lin ▶*n. Medicine* a slow-acting antibiotic made from a salt of procaine and a form of penicillin.

pro·car·y·ote ▶*n.* variant spelling of PROKARYOTE.

pro·ce·dure /prəˈsējər/ ▶*n.* an established or official way of doing something: *the police are now reviewing procedures* | *rules of procedure.* ■ a series of actions conducted in a certain order or manner: *the standard procedure for informing new employees about conditions of work.* ■ a surgical operation: *the procedure is carried out under general anesthesia.* ■ *Computing* another term for SUBROUTINE. ▷late 16th cent.: from French *procédure*, from *procéder* (see PROCEED). **—pro·ce·dur·al** *adj.* **—pro·ce·dur·al·ly** *adv.*

pro·ceed /prəˈsēd; prō-/ ▶*v.* [*intrans.*] begin or continue a course of action: *we can* ***proceed with*** *our investigation.* ■ [*intrans.*] move forward, esp. after reaching a certain point: *the ship could proceed to Milwaukee.* ■ [with *infinitive*] do something as a natural or seemingly inevitable next step: *opposite the front door was a staircase, which I proceeded to climb.* ■ *Law* start a lawsuit against someone: *he may still be able to* ***proceed against*** *the contractor under the common law negligence rules.* ■ (of an action) be started: *negotiations must proceed without delay.* ■ (of an action) be carried on or continued: *as the excavation proceeds, the visible layers can be recorded and studied.* ■ originate from: *his claim that all power* ***proceeded from*** *God.* ▷late Middle English: from Old French *proceder*, from Latin *procedere*, from *pro-* 'forward' + *cedere* 'go.'

pro·ceed·ings /prəˈsēdiNGz; prō-/ ▶*plural n.* an event or a series of activities involving a formal or set procedure: *you complete a form to start proceedings.* ■ *Law* action taken in a court to settle a dispute: *criminal proceedings were brought against him.* ■ a published report of a set of meetings or a conference.

pro·ceeds /ˈprōˌsēdz/ ▶*plural n.* money obtained from an event or activity: *proceeds will help purchase new equipment.* ▷early 17th cent.: plural of the obsolete noun *proceed*, in the same sense, earlier meaning 'procedure.'

proc·ess[1] /ˈpräˌses; ˈpräsəs; ˈprō-/ ▶*n.* **1** a series of actions or steps taken in order to achieve a particular end: *military operations could jeopardize the peace process.* ■ a natural or involuntary series of changes: *the aging process.* ■ a systematic series of mechanized or chemical operations that are performed in order to produce or manufacture something: *the modern block printer needs to accommodate all the traditional factory processes in one shop.* ■ [as *adj.*] *Printing* relating to or denoting printing using ink in three colors (cyan, magenta, and yellow) and black to produce a complete range of color: *process inks.* **2** *Law* a summons or writ requiring a person to appear in court. **3** *Biology* & *Anatomy* a natural appendage or outgrowth on or in an organism, such as a protuberance on a bone.

▶*v.* perform a series of mechanical or chemical operations on (something) in order to change or preserve it: *the various stages in processing the wool.* ■ *Computing* operate on (data) by means of a program. ■ deal with (someone) using an official and established procedure: *the immigration authorities who processed him.* ■ another term for CONK[3]. ▷Middle English: from Old French *proces*, from Latin *processus* 'progression, course,' from the verb *procedere* (see PROCEED). Current senses of the verb date from the late 19th cent. **—proc·ess·a·ble** *adj.*

▶*PHRASES* □ **be in the process of doing something** be continuing with an action already started: *a hurricane that was in the process of devastating South Carolina.* □ **in the process** as an unintended part of a course of action: *she would make him pay for this, even if she killed herself in the process.* □ **in process of time** as time goes on.

pro·cess[2] /prəˈses/ ▶*v.* [*intrans.*] walk or march in procession: *they processed down the aisle.* ▷early 19th cent.: back-formation from PROCESSION.

proc·ess en·gi·neer·ing ▶*n.* the branch of engineering that is concerned with industrial processes, esp. continuous ones such as the production of petrochemicals. **—proc·ess en·gi·neer** *n.*

pro·ces·sion /prəˈseSHən/ ▶*n.* **1** a number of people or vehicles moving forward in an orderly fashion, esp. as part of a ceremony or festival: *a funeral procession.* ■ the action of moving forward in such a way: *the fully robed civic dignitaries walk* ***in procession.*** ■ *figurative* a relentless succession of people or things: *his path was paved by* ***a procession of*** *industry executives.* **2** *Theology* the emanation of the Holy Spirit. ▷late Old English, via Old French from Latin *processio(n-)*, from *procedere* 'move forward' (see PROCEED).

pro·ces·sion·al /prəˈseSHənl/ ▶*adj.* of, for, or used in a religious or ceremonial procession: *a processional cross.*

▶*n.* a book containing litanies and hymns for use in religious processions, esp. at the beginning of a religious service. ■ a hymn or other musical composition sung or played during a procession.

proc·es·sor /ˈpräsˌesər; ˈpräsəsər; ˈprō-/ ▶*n.* a machine that processes something: *the processor overexposed the film.* ■ *Computing* another term for CENTRAL PROCESSING UNIT. ■ short for FOOD PROCESSOR.

proc·ess print·ing /ˈpräˌses; ˈpräsəs; ˈprō-/ ▶*n.* a full-color printing method using four templates, for magenta, cyan, yellow, and black.

proc·ess serv·er ▶*n.* a person, esp. a sheriff or deputy, who serves writs, warrants, subpoenas, etc.

pro·ces·su·al /prəˈseSHo͞oəl/ ▶*adj.* relating to or involving the study of processes rather than discrete events.

pro·cès-ver·bal /prōˌsā vərˈbäl/ ▶*n.* (*pl.* **pro·cès-ver·baux** /vərˈbō/) a written report of proceedings. ■ a written statement of facts in support of a charge. ▷mid 17th cent.: French.

pro·chlor·per·a·zine /ˌprōklôrˈperəˌzēn/ ▶*n. Medicine* a synthetic compound derived from phenothiazine, used as a tranquilizer. ▷1950s: from *pro(pyl)* + *chlor(ine)* + *(pi)perazine.*

pro-choice /prōˈCHois/ (also **pro·choice**) ▶*adj.* advocating legalized abortion: *a pro-choice demonstration.* Compare with PRO-LIFE. **—pro-choic·er** *n.*

pro·claim /prəˈklām; prō-/ ▶*v.* [with *clause*] announce officially or publicly: *the joint manifesto proclaimed that imperialism would be the coalition's chief objective* [*trans.*] *army commanders proclaimed a state of emergency.* See note at ANNOUNCE. ■ declare something one considers important with due emphasis: *she proclaimed that what I had said was untrue* | [*trans.*] *he proclaimed the car to be in sound condition.* ■ [*trans.*] declare officially or publicly to be: *he* ***proclaimed*** *James III* ***as*** *King of England.* ■ [*trans.*] demonstrate or indicate clearly: *the decor proclaimed a family history of taste and tradition* | [*trans.*] *he had a rolling gait that proclaimed him a man of the sea.* ▷late Middle English *proclame*, from Latin *proclamare* 'cry out,' from *pro-* 'forth' + *clamare* 'to shout.' The change in the second syllable was due to association with the verb CLAIM. **—pro·claim·er** *n.* **—pro·clam·a·to·ry** /-ˈklaməˌtôrē/ *adj.*

proc·la·ma·tion /ˌpräkləˈmāSHən/ ▶*n.* a public or official announcement, esp. one dealing with a matter of great importance: *Eisenhower signed a proclamation admitting Alaska to the Union.* ■ the public or official announcement of such a matter: *the government restricted the use of water by proclamation.* ■ a clear declaration of something: *the proclamation of his passion.* ▷late Middle English: via Old French from Latin *proclamatio(n-)*, from *proclamare* 'shout out' (see PROCLAIM).

pro·clit·ic /prōˈklitik/ *Linguistics* ▶*n.* a word pronounced with so little emphasis that it is shortened and forms part of the following word, for example, *you* in *y'all*. Compare with ENCLITIC.

▶*adj.* being or relating to such a word. ▷mid 19th cent.: from modern Latin *procliticus* (from Greek *proklinein* 'lean forward'), on the pattern of late Latin *encliticus* (see ENCLITIC). **—pro·clit·i·cal·ly** /-ik(ə)lē/ *adv.*

pro·cliv·i·ty /prōˈklivətē; prə-/ ▶*n.* (*pl.* **-ties**) a tendency to choose or do something regularly; an inclination or predisposition toward a particular thing: *a* ***proclivity for*** *hard work.* ▷late 16th cent.: from Latin *proclivitas*, from *proclivis* 'inclined,' from *pro-* 'forward, down' + *clivus* 'slope.'

Proc·ne /ˈpräknē/ *Greek Mythology* the sister of PHILOMELA.

pro·co·ag·u·lant /ˌprōkōˈagyələnt/ *Biochemistry* ▶*adj.* relating to or denoting substances that promote the conversion in the blood of the inactive protein prothrombin to the clotting enzyme thrombin.

▶*n.* a substance of this kind.

Pro·con·sul /prōˈkänsəl/ ▶*n.* a fossil hominoid primate found in Lower Miocene deposits in East Africa, one of the last common ancestors of both humans and the great apes. • Genus *Proconsul*, family Pongidae.

pro·con·sul /prōˈkänsəl/ ▶*n.* **1** a governor of a province in ancient Rome, having much of the authority of a consul. **2** a governor or deputy consul of a modern colony. ▷from Latin *pro consule* '(one acting) for the consul.' **—pro·con·su·lar** /-ˈkäns(y)ələr/ *adj.* **—pro·con·su·late** /-ˈkäns(y)ələt/ *n.* **—pro·con·sul·ship** /-SHip/ *n.*

pro·cras·ti·nate /prəˈkrastəˌnāt; prō-/ ▶*v.* [*intrans.*] delay or postpone action; put off doing something: *it won't be this price for long, so don't procrastinate.* ▷late 16th cent.: from Latin *procrastinat-* 'deferred until tomorrow,' from the verb *procrastinare*, from *pro-* 'forward' + *crastinus* 'belonging to tomorrow' (from *cras* 'tomorrow'). **—pro·cras·ti·na·tion** /prəˌkrastəˈnāSHən; prō-/ *n.* **—pro·cras·ti·na·tor** /-ˌnātər/ *n.* **—pro·cras·ti·na·to·ry** /-nəˌtôrē/ *adj.*

pro·cre·ate /ˈprōkrēˌāt/ ▶*v.* [*intrans.*] (of people or animals) produce young; reproduce: *species that procreate by copulation.* ▷late Middle English: from Latin *procreat-* 'generated, brought forth,' from the verb *procreare*, from *pro-* 'forth' + *creare* 'create.' **—pro·cre·ant** /-krēənt/ *adj.* (*archaic*). **—pro·cre·a·tion** /ˌprōkrēˈāSHən/ *n.* **—pro·cre·a·tive** /-krēˌātiv/ *adj.* **—pro·cre·a·tor** /-ˌātər/ *n.*

Pro·crus·te·an /prəˈkrəstēən; prō-/ ▶*adj.* (esp. of a framework or system) enforcing uniformity or conformity without regard to natural variation or individuality: *a fixed Procrustean rule.* ▷mid 19th cent.: from the name PROCRUSTES + -AN.

Pro·crus·tes /prəˈkrəstēz; prō-/ *Greek Mythology* a robber who forced travelers to lie on a bed and made them fit it by stretching their limbs or cutting off the appropriate length of leg. Theseus killed him in like manner. ▷from Greek *prokroustēs*, literally 'stretcher,' from *prokrouein* 'beat out.'

proc·ti·tis /präkˈtītis/ ▶*n. Medicine* inflammation of the rectum and anus. ▷early 19th cent.: from Greek *prōktos* 'anus' + -ITIS.

proc·tol·o·gy /präkˈtäləjē/ ▶*n.* the branch of medicine concerned with the anus and rectum. ▷late 19th cent.: from Greek *prōktos* 'anus' + -LOGY. **—proc·to·log·i·cal** /ˌpräktəˈläjikəl/ *adj.* **—proc·tol·o·gist** /-jist/ *n.*

Proc·tor /ˈpräktər/, William C(ooper) (1862–1934) U.S. businessman. By 1890, he was the general manager of Proctor & Gamble, the company that made and marketed Ivory soap. In 1907, when he became president of the company, he began to institute labor reforms such as profit sharing and pensions.

proc·tor /ˈpräktər/ ▶*n.* **1** a person who monitors students during an examination. **2** *Brit.* an officer (usually one of two) at certain universities, appointed annually and having mainly disciplinary functions.

▶*v.* serve as a proctor. ▷late Middle English: contraction of PROCURATOR. **—proc·to·ri·al** /präkˈtôrēəl/ *adj.* **—proc·tor·ship** /-ˌSHip/ *n.*

proc·to·scope /ˈpräktəˌskōp/ ▶*n.* a medical instrument with an integral lamp for examining the anus and lower part of the rectum or carrying out minor medical procedures. ▷late 19th cent.: from Greek *prōktos* 'anus' + -SCOPE. **—proc·to·scop·ic** /ˌpräktəˈskäpik/ *adj.* **—proc·tos·co·py** /präkˈtäskəpē/ *n.*

pro·cum·bent /prōˈkəmbənt/ ▶*adj. Botany* (of a plant or stem) growing along the ground without setting forth roots. ■ *archaic* (of a person) lying face down; prone; prostrate: ▷mid 17th cent.: from Latin *procumbent-* 'falling forward,' from the verb *procumbere*, from *pro-* 'forward, down' + a verb related to *cubare* 'to lie.'

proc·u·ra·tion /,präkyə'rāsHən/ ▶*n. dated Law* the appointment, authority, or action of an attorney. ■ *archaic* the action of procuring or obtaining something. ▷late Middle English: via Old French from Latin *procuratio(n-)*, from *procurare* 'attend to, take care of' (see **PROCURE**).

proc·u·ra·tor /'präkyə,rātər/ ▶*n. Law* an agent representing others in a court of law in countries retaining Roman civil law. ■ *historical* a treasury officer in a province of the Roman Empire. ▷Middle English (denoting a steward): from Old French *procuratour* or Latin *procurator* 'administrator, agent,' from *procurat-* 'taken care of,' from the verb *procurare* (see **PROCURE**). —**proc·u·ra·to·ri·al** /,präkyərə'tôrēəl/ *adj.* —**proc·u·ra·tor·ship** *n.*

pro·cure /prə'kyŏŏr; prō-/ ▶*v.* [*trans.*] **1** obtain (something), esp. with care or effort: *food procured for the rebels* | [with *two objs.*] *he persuaded a friend to procure him a ticket.* See note at **GET**. ■ obtain (someone) as a prostitute for another person: *he was charged with procuring a minor.* **2** [*trans.*] *Law* persuade or cause (someone) to do something: *he procured his wife to sign the agreement.* ▷Middle English: from Old French *procurer*, from Latin *procurare* 'take care of, manage,' from *pro-* 'on behalf of' + *curare* 'see to.' —**pro·cur·a·ble** *adj.* —**pro·cure·ment** *n.*

pro·cure·ment /prə'kyŏŏrmənt; prō-/ ▶*n.* the action of obtaining or procuring something: *financial assistance for the procurement of legal advice* | *the company's procurements from foreign firms.* ■ the action or occupation of acquiring military equipment and supplies: *defense procurement.*

pro·cur·er /prə'kyŏŏrər; prō-/ ▶*n.* a person who obtains a woman as a prostitute for another person. ▷late Middle English (denoting a steward): from Anglo-Norman French *procurour*, from Latin *procurator* (see **PROCURATOR**). Modern usage dates from the mid 17th cent.

pro·cur·ess /prə'kyŏŏris; prō-/ ▶*n.* a female procurer.

Pro·cy·on /'prōsē,än; -sēən/ *Astronomy* the eighth brightest star in the sky, and the brightest in the constellation Canis Minor. ▷Greek, literally 'before the dog' (because it rises before Sirius, the Dog Star).

prod /präd/ ▶*v.* (**prod·ded**, **prod·ding**) [*trans.*] poke (someone) with a finger, foot, or pointed object: *he prodded her in the ribs to stop her snoring* | [*intrans.*] *a woman* ***prods at*** *a tiger with a stick.* ■ stimulate or persuade (someone who is reluctant or slow) to do something: *he has been trying to* ***prod*** *the White House* ***into*** *launching an antipoverty program.*

▶*n.* **1** a poke with a finger, foot, or pointed object: *he gave the wire netting an experimental prod.* ■ an act of stimulating or reminding someone to do something: *he'll need a little prod to get back to the task at hand.* **2** a pointed implement, typically one discharging an electric current and used as a goad: *a cattle prod.* ▷mid 16th cent. (as a verb): perhaps symbolic of a short poking movement, or a blend of **POKE**[1] and dialect *brod* 'to goad, prod.' The noun dates from the mid 18th cent. —**prod·der** *n.*

prod. ▶*abbr.* ■ produce. ■ produced. ■ producer. ■ product. ■ production.

prod·i·gal /'prädigəl/ ▶*adj.* **1** spending money or resources freely and recklessly; wastefully extravagant: *prodigal habits die hard.* **2** having or giving something on a lavish scale: *the dessert was crunchy with brown sugar and prodigal with whipped cream.* See note at **PROFUSE**.

▶*n.* a person who spends money in a recklessly extravagant way. ■ (also **prodigal son** or **daughter**) a person who leaves home and behaves in such a way, but later makes a repentant return. [with biblical allusion to the parable in Luke 15:11–32.] ▷late Middle English: from late Latin *prodigalis*, from Latin *prodigus* 'lavish.' —**prod·i·gal·i·ty** /,prädə'galətē/ *n.* —**prod·i·gal·ly** /-g(ə)lē/ *adv.*

pro·di·gious /prə'dijəs/ ▶*adj.* **1** remarkably or impressively great in extent, size, or degree: *the stove consumed a prodigious amount of fuel.* **2** *archaic* unnatural or abnormal: *rumors of prodigious happenings, such as monstrous births.* ▷late 15th cent. (in the sense 'portentous'): from Latin *prodigiosus*, from *prodigium* 'portent' (see **PRODIGY**). —**pro·di·gious·ly** *adv.* —**pro·di·gious·ness** *n.*

prod·i·gy /'prädəjē/ ▶*n.* (*pl.* **-gies**) [often with *adj.*] a person, esp. a young one, endowed with exceptional qualities or abilities: *a Russian pianist who was a child prodigy in his day.* ■ an impressive or outstanding example of a particular quality: *Germany seemed* ***a prodigy of*** *industrial discipline.* ■ an amazing or unusual thing, esp. one out of the ordinary course of nature: *omens and prodigies abound in Livy's work.* ▷late 15th cent. (denoting something extraordinary considered to be an omen): from Latin *prodigium* 'portent.'

prod·ro·mal /prō'drōməl/ ▶*adj. Medicine* relating to or denoting the period between the appearance of initial symptoms and the full development of a rash or fever.

pro·drome /'prō,drōm/ ▶*n. Medicine* an early symptom indicating the onset of a disease or illness. ▷early 17th cent.: from French, from modern Latin *prodromus*, from Greek *prodromos* 'precursor,' from *pro* 'before' + *dromos* 'running.' —**pro·drom·ic** /prō'drämik/ *adj.*

pro·drug /'prō,drəg/ ▶*n.* a biologically inactive compound that can be metabolized in the body to produce a drug.

pro·duce ▶*v.* /prə'd(y)o͞os; prō-/ [*trans.*] **1** make or manufacture from components or raw materials: *the company has just produced a luxury version of the aircraft.* ■ (of a region, country, or process) yield, grow, or supply: *the California vineyards produce excellent wines.* ■ create or form (something) as part of a physical, biological, or chemical process: *the plant produces blue flowers in late autumn.* ■ make (something) using creative or mental skills: *the garden where the artist produced many of his flower paintings.* **2** cause (a particular result or situation) to happen or come into existence: *no conventional drugs had produced any significant change.* **3** show or provide (something) for consideration, inspection, or use: *he produced a sheet of paper from his pocket.* **4** administer the financial and managerial aspects of (a movie or broadcast) or the staging of (a play, opera, etc.). ■ supervise the making of a (musical recording), esp. by determining the overall sound. **5** *dated Geometry* extend or continue (a line): *one side of the triangle was produced.*

▶*n.* /'präd(y)o͞os; 'prō-/ things that have been produced or grown, esp. by farming: *dairy produce.* ▷late Middle English (sense 3 of the *verb*): from Latin *producere*, from *pro-* 'forward' + *ducere* 'to lead.' Current noun senses date from the late 17th cent. —**pro·duc·i·bil·i·ty** /prə,d(y)o͞osə'bilətē; prō-/ *n.* —**pro·duc·i·ble** *adj.*

pro·duc·er /prə'd(y)o͞osər; prō-/ ▶*n.* **1** a person, company, or country that makes, grows, or supplies goods or commodities for sale: *an oil producer.* ■ a person or thing that makes or causes something: *the mold is the producer of the toxin aflatoxin.* **2** a person responsible for the financial and managerial aspects of making of a movie or broadcast or for staging a play, opera, etc. ■ a person who supervises the making of a musical recording, esp. by determining the overall sound.

pro·duc·er gas ▶*n.* a low-grade fuel gas consisting largely of nitrogen and carbon monoxide, formed by passing air, or air and steam, through red-hot carbon.

prod·uct /'prädəkt/ ▶*n.* **1** an article or substance that is manufactured or refined for sale: *marketing products and services* | *dairy products.* ■ a substance produced during a natural, chemical, or manufacturing process: *waste products.* ■ a thing or person that is the result of an action or process: *his daughter, the product of his first marriage.* ■ a person whose character and identity have been formed by a particular period or situation: *an aging academic who is a product of the 1960s.* ■ commercially manufactured articles, esp. recordings, viewed collectively: *too much product of too little quality.* **2** *Mathematics* a quantity obtained by multiplying quantities together, or from an analogous algebraic operation. ▷late Middle English (as a mathematical term): from Latin *productum* 'something produced,' neuter past participle (used as a noun) of *producere* 'bring forth' (see **PRODUCE**).

pro·duc·tion /prə'dəksHən; prō-/ ▶*n.* **1** the action of making or manufacturing from components or raw materials, or the process of being so manufactured: *the production of chemical weapons* | *it is no longer* ***in production.*** ■ the harvesting or refinement of something natural: *nonintensive methods of food production.* ■ the total amount of something that is manufactured, harvested, or refined: *steel production had peaked in 1974.* ■ the creation or formation of something as part of a physical, biological, or chemical process: *excess production of collagen by the liver.* ■ [as *adj.*] denoting a car or other vehicle that has been manufactured in large numbers. **2** the process of or financial and administrative management involved in making a movie, play, or record: *the movie was still* ***in production*** | [as *adj.*] *a production company.* ■ a movie, play, or record, esp. when viewed in terms of its making or staging: *this production updates the play and sets it in the sixties.* ■ [in *sing.*] the overall sound of a musical recording; the way a record is produced: *the record's production is gloriously relaxed.* ▷late Middle English: via Old French from Latin *productio(n-)*, from *producere* 'bring forth' (see **PRODUCE**).

▶*PHRASE* □ **make a production of** do (something) in an unnecessarily elaborate or complicated way.

pro·duc·tion line ▶*n.* an arrangement in a factory in which a thing being manufactured is passed through a set linear sequence of mechanical or manual operations. Compare with **ASSEMBLY LINE**.

pro·duc·tion num·ber ▶*n.* a spectacular musical item, typically including song and dance and involving all or most of the cast, in a theatrical show or motion picture.

pro·duc·tion plat·form ▶*n.* a platform housing equipment necessary to keep an oil or gas field in production, with facilities for temporarily storing the output of several wells.

pro·duc·tive /prə'dəktiv; prō-/ ▶*adj.* producing or able to produce large amounts of goods, crops, or other commodities: *the most productive employees.* ■ relating to or engaged in the production of goods, crops, or other commodities: *the country's productive capacity.* ■ achieving or producing a significant amount or result: *a long and productive career* | *the therapy sessions became more productive.* ■ [*predic.*] (**productive of**) producing or giving rise to: *the unconscious is limitlessly productive of dreams, myths, stories.* ■ *Linguistics* (of a morpheme or other linguistic unit) currently used in forming new words or expressions: *many suffixes are common and productive.* ■ *Medicine* (of a cough) that raises mucus from the respiratory tract. ▷early 17th cent.: from French *productif, -ive* or late Latin *productivus*, from *product-* 'brought forth,' from the verb *producere* (see **PRODUCE**). —**pro·duc·tive·ly** *adv.* —**pro·duc·tive·ness** *n.*

pro·duc·tiv·i·ty /,prō,dək'tivətē; ,prädək-; prə,dək-/ ▶*n.* the state or quality of producing something, esp. crops: *the long-term productivity of land* | *agricultural productivity.* ■ the effectiveness of productive effort, esp. in industry, as measured in terms of the rate of output per unit of input: *workers have boosted productivity by 30 percent.* ■ *Ecology* the rate of production of new biomass by an individual, population, or community; the fertility or capacity of a given habitat or area: *nutrient-rich waters with high productivity.*

prod·uct li·a·bil·i·ty ▶*n.* the legal liability a manufacturer or trader incurs for producing or selling a faulty product.

prod·uct place·ment ▶*n.* a practice in which manufacturers of goods or providers of a service gain exposure for their products by paying for them to be featured in movies and television programs.

pro·em /'prō,em; -əm/ ▶*n. formal* a preface or preamble to a book or speech. ▷late Middle English: from Old French *proeme*, via Latin from Greek *prooimion* 'prelude,' from *pro* 'before' + *oimē* 'song.' —**pro·e·mi·al** /prō'ēmēəl; -'əmēəl/ *adj.*

pro·en·zyme /prō'en,zīm/ ▶*n. Biochemistry* a biologically inactive substance that is metabolized into an enzyme.

pro-Eu·ro·pe·an /,prō,yərə'pēən, -,yŏŏrə-/ ▶*adj.* (of a person, attitude, or policy) favoring or supporting closer links with the European Union.

▶*n.* a person who favors or supports closer links with the European Union.

prof /präf/ ▶*n. informal* a professor. ▷mid 19th cent.: abbreviation.

Prof. ▶*abbr.* professor: [as *title*] *Prof. Smith.*

pro-fam·i·ly /prō'fam(ə)lē/ ▶*adj.* promoting family life and traditional moral values.

pro·fane /prə'fān; prō-/ ▶*adj.* **1** relating or devoted to that which is not sacred or biblical; secular rather than religious: *a talk that tackled topics both sacred and profane.* ■ (of a person) not initiated into religious rites or any esoteric knowledge: *he was an agnostic, a profane man.* **2** (of a person or their behavior) not respectful of orthodox religious practice; irreverent: *desecration of the temple by profane adolescents.* ■ (of language) blasphemous or obscene.

▶*v.* [*trans.*] treat (something sacred) with irreverence or disrespect: *it was a serious matter to profane a tomb.* ▷late Middle English (in the sense 'heathen'): from Old French *prophane*, from Latin *profanus* 'outside the temple, not sacred,' from *pro-* (from *pro* 'before') + *fanum* 'temple.' —**prof·a·na·tion** /,präfə'nāsHən;

ˌprō-/ *n.* —**pro·fane·ly** *adv.* —**pro·fane·ness** *n.* —**pro·fan·er** *n.*

pro·fan·i·ty /prəˈfanətē; prō-/ ▸*n.* (*pl.* **-ties**) blasphemous or obscene language: *an outburst of profanity.* ■ a swear word; an oath. ■ irreligious or irreverent behavior. ▷mid 16th cent.: from late Latin *profanitas*, from Latin *profanus* 'not sacred' (see PROFANE).

pro·fess /prəˈfes; prō-/ ▸*v.* [*trans.*] **1** claim openly but often falsely that one has (a quality or feeling): *he had professed his love for her* | [with *infinitive*] *I don't profess to be an expert* | [with *complement*] (**profess oneself**) *he professed himself amazed at the boy's ability.* **2** affirm one's faith in or allegiance to (a religion or set of beliefs): *a people professing Christianity.* ■ (**be professed**) be received into a religious order under vows: *she entered St. Margaret's Convent, and was professed in 1943.* **3** *dated* or *humorous* teach (a subject) as a professor: *a professor—what does he profess?* **4** *archaic* have or claim knowledge or skill in (a subject or accomplishment). ▷Middle English (as *be professed* 'be received into a religious order'): from Latin *profess-* 'declared publicly,' from the verb *profiteri*, from *pro-* 'before' + *fateri* 'confess.'

pro·fessed /prəˈfest; prō-/ ▸*adj.* **1** (of a quality, feeling, or belief) claimed or asserted openly but often falsely: *for all her professed populism, she was seen as remote from ordinary people.* **2** (of a person) self-acknowledged or openly declared to be: *a professed and conforming Anglican.* ■ (of a monk or nun) having taken the vows of a religious order. ■ *archaic* claiming to be qualified as a particular specialist; professional.

pro·fess·ed·ly /prəˈfesədlē; -ˈfestlē/ ▸*adv.* [*sentence adverb*] ostensibly; apparently (used in reference to something claimed or asserted, possibly falsely): *restrictions professedly designed to stop the use of political propaganda.*

pro·fes·sion /prəˈfesHən/ ▸*n.* **1** a paid occupation, esp. one that involves prolonged training and a formal qualification: *his chosen profession of teaching* | *a lawyer* **by profession**. ■ [treated as *sing.* or *pl.*] a body of people engaged in a particular profession: *the profession is divided on the issue.* **2** an open but often false declaration or claim: *a profession of allegiance.* ■ a declaration of belief in a religion. ■ the declaration or vows made on entering a religious order. ■ the ceremony or fact of being professed in a religious order. ▷Middle English (denoting the vow made on entering a religious order): via Old French from Latin *professio(n-)*, from *profiteri* 'declare publicly' (see PROFESS). Sense 1 derives from the notion of an occupation that one "professes" to be skilled in.

▸*PHRASE* □ **the oldest profession** *humorous* the practice of working as a prostitute.

pro·fes·sion·al /prəˈfesHənl/ ▸*adj.* **1** [*attrib.*] of, relating to, or connected with a profession: *young professional people* | *the professional schools of Yale and Harvard.* **2** (of a person) engaged in a specified activity as one's main paid occupation rather than as a pastime: *a professional boxer.* ■ having or showing the skill appropriate to a professional person; competent or skillful: *their music is both memorable and professional.* ■ worthy of or appropriate to a professional person: *his professional expertise.* ■ *informal, derogatory* denoting a person who persistently makes a feature of a particular activity or attribute: *a professional naysayer.*

▸*n.* a person engaged or qualified in a profession: *professionals such as lawyers and surveyors.* ■ a person engaged in a specified activity, esp. a sport or branch of the performing arts, as a main paid occupation rather than as a pastime. ■ a person competent or skilled in a particular activity: *she was a real professional on stage.* —**pro·fes·sion·al·ly** /-sHənl-ē/ *adv.*

pro·fes·sion·al·ism /prəˈfesHənlˌizəm/ ▸*n.* the competence or skill expected of a professional: *the key to quality and efficiency is professionalism.* ■ the practicing of an activity, esp. a sport, by professional rather than amateur players: *the trend toward professionalism.*

pro·fes·sion·al·ize /prəˈfesHənlˌīz/ ▸*v.* [*trans.*] give (an occupation, activity, or group) professional qualities, typically by increasing training or raising required qualifications: *attempts to professionalize the police are resisted by many.* —**pro·fes·sion·al·i·za·tion** /prəˌfesHənl-əˈzāsHən/ *n.*

pro·fes·sor /prəˈfesər/ ▸*n.* **1** (also **full professor**) a teacher of the highest rank in a college or university. ■ an associate professor or an assistant professor. ■ *informal* any instructor, esp. in a specialized field. **2** a person who affirms a faith in or allegiance to something: *the professors of true religion.* ▷late Middle English: from Latin *professor*, from *profess-* 'declared publicly,' from the verb *profiteri* (see PROFESS). —**pro·fes·sor·ate** /-rət/ *n.* —**pro·fes·so·ri·al** /ˌpräfəˈsôrēəl/ *adj.* —**pro·fes·so·ri·al·ly** /ˌpräfəˈsôrēəlē/ *adv.* —**pro·fes·so·ri·ate** /ˌpräfəˈsôrēət/ *n.* —**pro·fes·sor·ship** /-ˌsHip/ *n.*

prof·fer /ˈpräfər/ ▸*v.* [*trans.*] hold out (something) to someone for acceptance; offer: *he proffered his resignation.*

▸*n. poetic/literary* an offer or proposal. ▷Middle English: from Anglo-Norman French *proffrir*, from Latin *pro-* 'before' + *offerre* 'to offer.'

pro·fi·cient /prəˈfisHənt/ ▸*adj.* competent or skilled in doing or using something: *I was* **proficient at** *my job* | *she felt reasonably* **proficient in** *Italian.*

▸*n. rare* a person who is proficient: *he became a proficient in Latin and Greek.* ▷late 16th cent.: from Latin *proficient-* 'advancing,' from the verb *proficere*, from *pro-* 'on behalf of' + *facere* 'do, make.' —**pro·fi·cien·cy** *n.* —**pro·fi·cient·ly** *adv.*

pro·file /ˈprōˌfīl/ ▸*n.* **1** an outline of something, esp. a person's face, as seen from one side: *the man turned and she caught his profile.* ■ a drawing or other representation of such an outline. ■ a vertical cross section of a structure: *skillfully made vessels with an S-shaped profile.* ■ *Geography* an outline of part of the earth's surface, e.g., the course of a river, as seen in a vertical section. ■ *Theater* a flat piece of scenery or stage property that has been cut so as to form an outline or silhouette of an object. ■ a graphical or other representation of information relating to particular characteristics of something, recorded in quantified form: *the blood profiles of cancer patients.* ■ a short article giving a description of a person or organization, esp. a public figure: *a profile of a Texas tycoon.* **2** [in *sing.*] the extent to which a person or organization attracts public notice or comment: *raising the profile of women in industry.*

▸*v.* [*trans.*] **1** describe (a person or organization, esp. a public figure) in a short article: *he was to profile each candidate.* **2** (usu. **be profiled**) represent in outline from one side: *he was standing motionless, profiled on the far side of the swimming pool.* ■ (**be profiled**) have a specified shape or appearance in outline: *a proud bird profiled like a phoenix.* ■ shape (something), esp. by means of a tool guided by a template: [as *adj.*] (**profiled**) *profiled and plain tiles.* ▷mid 17th cent.: from obsolete Italian *profilo*, from the verb *profilare*, from *pro-* 'forth' + *filare* 'to spin,' formerly 'draw a line' (from Latin *filare*, from *filum* 'thread'). —**pro·fil·er** *n.*

▸*PHRASE* □ **in profile** (in reference to someone's face) as seen from one side: *a photograph of Leon in profile.*

pro·fil·ing /ˈprōˌfīliNG/ ▸*n.* the recording and analysis of a person's psychological and behavioral characteristics, so as to assess or predict their capabilities in a certain sphere or to assist in identifying a particular subgroup of people.

prof·it /ˈpräfit/ ▸*n.* a financial gain, esp. the difference between the amount earned and the amount spent in buying, operating, or producing something: *pretax profits* | *his eyes brightened at the prospect of profit.* ■ advantage; benefit: *there's no profit in screaming at referees from the bench.*

▸*v.* (**-it·ed, -it·ing**) [*intrans.*] obtain a financial advantage or benefit, esp. from an investment: *the only people to profit from the entire episode were the lawyers.* ■ obtain an advantage or benefit: *not all children would profit from this kind of schooling.* ■ [*trans.*] be beneficial to: *it would profit us to change our plans.* ▷Middle English (in the sense 'advantage, benefit'): from Old French, from Latin *profectus* 'progress, profit,' from *proficere* 'to advance,' from *pro-* 'on behalf of' + *facere* 'do.' The verb is from Old French *profiter*. —**prof·it·less** *adj.*

▸*PHRASE* □ **at a profit** making more money than is spent buying, operating, or producing something: *fixing up houses and selling them at a profit.*

prof·it·a·ble /ˈpräfitəbəl/ ▸*adj.* **1** (of a business or activity) yielding profit or financial gain. **2** beneficial; useful: *he'd had a profitable day.* ▷Middle English: from Old French, from the verb *profiter* (see PROFIT). —**prof·it·a·bil·i·ty** /ˌpräfitəˈbilətē/ *n.* —**prof·it·a·bly** /-blē/ *adv.*

prof·it and loss ac·count (abbr.: **P & L**) ▸*n. Finance* an account in the books of an organization to which incomes and gains are credited and expenses and losses debited, so as to show the net profit or loss over a given period. ■ a financial statement showing a company's net profit or loss in a given period.

prof·it cen·ter ▸*n.* a part of an organization with assignable revenues and costs and hence ascertainable profitability.

prof·it·eer /ˌpräfəˈti(ə)r/ ▸*v.* [*intrans.*] make or seek to make an excessive or unfair profit, esp. illegally or in a black market: [as *n.*] (**profiteering**) *the profiteering of tabloid journalists.*

▸*n.* a person who profiteers: *a war profiteer.*

pro·fit·er·ole /prəˈfitəˌrōl/ ▸*n.* a small hollow pastry typically filled with cream and covered with chocolate sauce. ▷French, diminutive of *profit* 'profit.'

prof·it mar·gin ▸*n.* the amount by which revenue from sales exceeds costs in a business.

prof·it-shar·ing (also **prof·it shar·ing**) ▸*n.* a system in which the people who work for a company receive a direct share of the profits.

prof·it-tak·ing (also **prof·it tak·ing**) ▸*n. Stock Market* the sale of securities that have risen in price.

prof·li·gate /ˈpräfligət; -ləˌgāt/ ▸*adj.* recklessly extravagant or wasteful in the use of resources: *profligate consumers of energy.* ■ licentious; dissolute: *he succumbed to drink and a profligate lifestyle.*

▸*n.* a licentious, dissolute person. ▷mid 16th cent. (in the sense 'overthrown, routed'): from Latin *profligatus* 'dissolute,' past participle of *profligare* 'overthrow, ruin,' from *pro-* 'forward, down' + *fligere* 'strike down.' —**prof·li·ga·cy** /ˈpräfligəsē/ *n.* —**prof·li·gate·ly** *adv.*

pro-form /ˈprōˌfôrm/ ▸*n. Linguistics* a word or lexical unit that is dependent for its meaning on reference to some other part of the context or sentence in which it occurs, for example, a pronoun replacing a noun or noun phrase, or a verb replacing a clause, such as *do* in *she likes chocolate and so do I.*

pro for·ma /prō ˈfôrmə/ ▸*adv.* as a matter of form or politeness: *he nodded to him pro forma.*

▸*adj.* done or produced as a matter of form: *pro forma reports.* ■ [*attrib.*] denoting a standard document or form, esp. an invoice sent in advance of or with goods supplied. ■ [*attrib.*] (of a financial statement) showing potential or expected income, costs, assets, or liabilities, esp. in relation to some planned or expected act or situation.

▸*n.* a standard document or form or financial statement of such a type. ▷early 16th cent.: from Latin.

pro·found /prəˈfound; prō-/ ▸*adj.* (**-found·er, -found·est**) **1** (of a state, quality, or emotion) very great or intense: *profound social changes* | *profound feelings of disquiet.* ■ (of a disease or disability) very severe; deep-seated: *a case of profound liver failure.* **2** (of a person or statement) having or showing great knowledge or insight: *a profound philosopher.* ■ (of a subject or thought) demanding deep study or thought: *expressing profound truths in simple language.* **3** *archaic* at, from, or extending to a great depth; very deep: *he opened the door with a profound bow.*

▸*n.* (**the profound**) *poetic/literary* the vast depth of the ocean or of the mind. ▷Middle English: from Old French *profund*, from Latin *profundus* 'deep,' from *pro* 'before' + *fundus* 'bottom.' The word was used earliest in the sense 'showing deep insight.' —**pro·found·ly** *adv.* [as *submodifier*] *a profoundly disturbing experience.* —**pro·found·ness** *n.*

Pro·fu·mo /prəˈf(y)o͞omō/, John (Dennis) (1915–), British politician. In 1960, he was appointed secretary of state for war, but three years later he resigned because of his relationship with Christine Keeler (1942–), the mistress of a Soviet diplomat.

pro·fun·di·ty /prəˈfəndətē/ ▸*n.* (*pl.* **-ties**) deep insight; great depth of knowledge or thought: *the simplicity and profundity of the message.* ■ great depth or intensity of a state, quality, or emotion: *the profundity of her misery.* ■ a statement or idea that shows great knowledge or insight.

pro·fuse /prəˈfyo͞os; prō-/ ▸*adj.* (esp. of something offered or discharged) exuberantly plentiful; abundant: *I offered my profuse apologies.* ■ *archaic* (of a person) lavish; extravagant: *they are* **profuse in** *hospitality.* ▷late Middle English (in the sense 'extravagant'): from Latin *profusus* 'lavish, spread out,' past participle of *profundere*, from *pro-* 'forth' + *fundere* 'pour.' —**pro·fuse·ly** *adv.* —**pro·fuse·ness** *n.*

THE RIGHT WORD **extravagant, lavish, lush, luxuriant, prodigal, profuse**

Something that is **profuse** is poured out or given freely, often to the point of exaggeration or excess (*profuse apologies*).

Extravagant also suggests unreasonable excess, but with an emphasis on wasteful spending (*her gift was much too extravagant for the occasion*).

Someone who is **prodigal** is so recklessly extravagant that his or her resources will ultimately be exhausted (*the prodigal heir to the family fortune*).

Another way to end up impoverished is through **lavish** spending, a word that combines extravagance with generosity or a lack of moderation (*lavish praise; lavish furnishings*).

While *lavish, extravagant* and *prodigal* are often used to describe human behavior, **lush** and **luxuriant** normally refer to things. What is *luxuriant* is produced in great quantity, suggesting that it is not only profuse but gorgeous (*luxuriant auburn hair*). Something described as *lush* is not only luxuriant but has reached a peak of perfection (*the lush summer grass*).

P

pro·fu·sion /prəˈfyoōzʜən; prō-/ ▸*n.* [in *sing.*] an abundance or large quantity of something: *a rich* **profusion of** *wildflowers | the foxgloves growing* **in profusion** *among the ferns.* ▷mid 16th cent.: via French from Latin *profusio(n-)*, from *profundere* 'pour out.' Early use expressed the senses 'extravagance,' 'squandering,' and 'waste.'

prog /präg/ *informal* ▸*adj.* [*attrib.*] (of rock music) progressive: *prog rock bands.* ▷1950s: abbreviation.

pro·gen·i·tive /prəˈjenətiv; prō-/ ▸*adj. formal* having the quality of producing offspring; having reproductive power.

pro·gen·i·tor /prəˈjenətər; prō-/ ▸*n.* a person or thing from which a person, animal, or plant is descended or originates; an ancestor or parent: *his sons and daughters were the progenitors of many of Scotland's leading noble families.* ■ a person who originates an artistic, political, or intellectual movement: *the progenitor of modern jazz.* ▷late Middle English: from Old French *progeniteur*, from Latin *progenitor*, from *progenit-* 'begotten,' from the verb *progignere*, from *pro-* 'forward' + *gignere* 'beget.' **—pro·gen·i·to·ri·al** /-ˌjenəˈtôrēəl/ *adj.*

prog·e·ny /ˈpräjənē/ ▸*n.* [treated as *sing.* or *pl.*] a descendant or the descendants of a person, animal, or plant; offspring: *the progeny of mixed marriages.* ▷Middle English: from Old French *progenie*, from Latin *progenies*, from *progignere* 'beget' (see **PROGENITOR**).

pro·ge·ri·a /prōˈji(ə)rēə; prə-/ ▸*n. Medicine* a rare syndrome in children characterized by physical signs and symptoms suggestive of premature old age. ▷early 20th cent.: modern Latin, from Greek *progērōs* 'prematurely old.'

pro·ges·ter·one /prōˈjestəˌrōn; prə-/ ▸*n. Biochemistry* a steroid hormone released by the corpus luteum that stimulates the uterus to prepare for pregnancy. ▷1930s: blend of **PROGESTIN** and the German synonym *Luteosteron* (from **CORPUS LUTEUM** + **STEROL**).

pro·ges·tin /prōˈjestin/ ▸*n. Biochemistry* a natural or synthetic steroid hormone, such as progesterone, that maintains pregnancy and prevents further ovulation during pregnancy.

pro·ges·to·gen /prōˈjestəjən/ ▸*n. Biochemistry* another term for **PROGESTIN.** ▷1940s: from **PROGESTIN** + **-GEN.**

pro·glot·tid /prōˈglätid/ (also **pro·glot·tis** /-ˈglätis/) ▸*n. Zoology* each segment in the strobila of a tapeworm, containing a complete sexually mature reproductive system. ▷late 19th cent.: from Greek *proglōssis, proglōssid-* 'point of the tongue,' based on *glōssa, glōtta* 'tongue' (because of its shape).

prog·na·thous /ˈprägnəᴛʜəs; prägˈnā-/ ▸*adj.* (esp. of a person) having a projecting lower jaw or chin. ■ (of a jaw or chin) projecting. ■ (of an insect) having projecting mouthparts. ▷mid 19th cent.: from **PRO-**[2] 'before' + Greek *gnathos* 'jaw' + **-OUS.** **—prog·nath·ic** /prägˈnaᴛʜik/ *adj.* **—prog·na·thism** /-ˌᴛʜizəm/ *n.*

prog·no·sis /prägˈnōsəs/ ▸*n.* (*pl.* **-ses** /-ˌsēz/) the likely course of a disease or ailment: *the disease has a poor prognosis.* ■ a forecast of the likely course of a disease or ailment: *it is very difficult to make an accurate prognosis.* ■ a forecast of the likely outcome of a situation: *gloomy prognoses about overpopulation.* ▷mid 17th cent.: via late Latin from Greek *prognōsis*, from *pro-* 'before' + *gignōskein* 'know.'

prog·nos·tic /prägˈnästik/ ▸*adj.* serving to predict the likely outcome of a disease or ailment; of or relating to a medical prognosis.

▸*n. archaic* an advance indication or portent of a future event: *a one-banded caterpillar is considered a prognostic of a mild winter.* ▷late Middle English: from Latin *prognosticus*, from Greek *prognōstikos*, from *prognōsis* (see **PROGNOSIS**). **—prog·nos·ti·cal·ly** /-ik(ə)lē/ *adv.*

prog·nos·ti·cate /prägˈnästəˌkāt/ ▸*v.* [*trans.*] foretell or prophesy (an event in the future): *the economists were prognosticating financial Armageddon.* See note at **PREDICT.** ▷late Middle English: from medieval Latin *prognosticat-*, from the verb *prognosticare* 'make a prediction' (see **PROGNOSTIC**). **—prog·nos·ti·ca·tor** /-ˌkātər/ *n.* **—prog·nos·ti·ca·to·ry** /-kəˌtôrē/ *adj.*

prog·nos·ti·ca·tion /prägˌnästəˈkāsʜən/ ▸*n.* the action of foretelling or prophesying future events: *an unprecedented amount of soul-searching and prognostication.* ■ a prophecy: *these gloomy prognostications proved to be unfounded.* ▷late Middle English: from Old French *prognosticacion*, from medieval Latin *prognosticatio(n-)*, from the verb *prognosticare* (see **PROGNOSTICATE**).

pro·grade /ˈprōˌgrād/ ▸*adj.* **1** *Astronomy* (of planetary motion) proceeding from west to east; direct. The opposite of **RETROGRADE.** **2** *Geology* (of a metamorphic change) resulting from an increase in temperature or pressure or both. Compare with **RETROGRADE.**

▸*v.* [*intrans.*] *Geology* (of a beach or coastline) advance toward the sea as a result of the accumulation of waterborne sediment. ▷early 20th cent. (as a verb): from **PRO-**[1] 'forward' + **RETROGRADE.** **—pro·gra·da·tion** /ˌprōˌgrāˈdāsʜən; ˌprōgrə-/ *n.*

pro·gram /ˈprōˌgram; -grəm/ (*Brit.* **pro·gramme**) ▸*n.* **1** a planned series of future events, items, or performances: *a weekly program of films | the program includes Dvorak's New World symphony.* ■ a set of related measures, events, or activities with a particular long-term aim: *the nuclear power program.* **2** a sheet or booklet giving details of items or performers at an event or performance: *a theater program.* **3** a presentation or item on radio or television, esp. one broadcast regularly between stated times: *a nature program.* ■ *dated* a radio or television service or station providing a regular succession of programs on a particular frequency; a channel. **4** (**program**) a series of coded software instructions to control the operation of a computer or other machine.

▸*v.* (**-grammed, -gram·ming;** or **-gramed, -gram·ing**) [*trans.*] **1** (**program**) provide (a computer or other machine) with coded instructions for the automatic performance of a particular task: *it is a simple matter to program the computer to recognize such symbols.* ■ input (instructions for the automatic performance of a task) into a computer or other machine: *simply* **program in** *your desired volume level.* ■ (often **be programmed**) *figurative* cause (a person or animal) to behave in a predetermined way: *all members of a particular species are* **programmed to** *build nests in the same way.* **2** arrange according to a plan or schedule: *we learn how to program our own lives consciously.* ■ schedule (an item) within a framework: *the next stage of the treaty is programmed for 1996.* ■ broadcast (an item): *the station does not program enough contemporary works.* ▷early 17th cent. (in the sense 'written notice'): via late Latin from Greek *programma*, from *prographein* 'write publicly,' from *pro* 'before' + *graphein* 'write.' **—pro·gram·ma·bil·i·ty** /-əˈbilətē/ *n.* **—pro·gram·ma·ble** /ˈprōˌgraməbəl; prōˈgram-/ *adj.*

▸*PHRASE* □ **get with the program** [often in *imperative*] *informal* do what is expected of one; adopt the prevailing viewpoint.

pro·gram·mat·ic /ˌprōgrəˈmatik/ ▸*adj.* of the nature of or according to a program, schedule, or method: *a programmatic approach to change.* ■ of the nature of program music. **—pro·gram·mat·i·cal·ly** /-ik(ə)lē/ *adv.*

pro·grammed cell death ▸*n.* less technical term for **APOPTOSIS.**

pro·gram·mer /ˈprōˌgramər/ ▸*n.* a person who writes computer programs. ■ a device that automatically controls the operation of something in accordance with a prescribed program.

pro·gram·ming /ˈprōˌgramiɴɢ/ ▸*n.* **1** the action or process of writing computer programs. ■ *figurative* predetermined behavior: *men and women are the playthings of programming.* **2** the action or process of scheduling something, esp. radio or television programs: *the programming of shows.* ■ radio or television programs that are scheduled or broadcast: *the station is to expand its late-night programming.*

pro·gram mu·sic ▸*n.* music that is intended to evoke images or convey the impression of events. Compare with **ABSOLUTE MUSIC.**

pro·gram trad·ing ▸*n.* the simultaneous purchase and sale of many different stocks, or of stocks and related futures contracts, with the use of a computer program to exploit price differences in different markets.

pro·gress ▸*n.* /ˈprägrəs; ˈprägˌres; ˈprōˌgres/ forward or onward movement toward a destination: *the darkness did not stop my progress | they failed to* **make** *any* **progress** *up the narrow estuary.* ■ advance or development toward a better, more complete, or more modern condition: *we are* **making progress** *toward equal rights.* ■ *Brit., archaic* a state journey or official tour, esp. by royalty.

▸*v.* /prəˈgres/ [*intrans.*] move forward or onward in space or time: *as the century progressed, the quality of telescopes improved.* ■ advance or develop toward a better, more complete, or more modern state: *work on the pond is progressing.* ■ [*trans.*] [usu. as *adj.*] (**progressed**) *Astrology* calculate the position of (a planet) or of all the planets and coordinates of (a chart) according to the technique of progression. ▷late Middle English (as a noun): from Latin *progressus* 'an advance,' from the verb *progredi*, from *pro-* 'forward' + *gradi* 'to walk.'

▸*PHRASE* □ **in progress** in the course of being done or carried out: *a meeting was in progress.*

pro·gres·sion /prəˈgresʜən/ ▸*n.* a movement or development toward a destination or a more advanced state, esp. gradually or in stages: *the normal progression from junior to senior status | their mode of progression through the forest.* ■ a succession; a series: *counting the twenty-four hours in a single progression from midnight.* ■ *Music* a passage or movement from one note or chord to another: *a blues progression.* ■ *Mathematics* short for **ARITHMETIC PROGRESSION, GEOMETRIC PROGRESSION,** or **HARMONIC PROGRESSION.** ■ *Astrology* a predictive technique in which the daily movement of the planets, starting from the day of birth, represents a year in the subject's life. ▷late Middle English: from Old French, from Latin *progressio(n-)*, from the verb *progredi* (see **PROGRESS**). **—pro·gres·sion·al** /-sʜənl/ *adj.*

pro·gres·sion·ist /prəˈgresʜənist/ *chiefly historical* ▸*n.* **1** *Biology* a supporter of the theory that all life forms gradually progress or evolve to a higher form. **2** an advocate of or believer in political or social progress.

▸*adj. Biology* (of a person or theory) supporting or based on the theory that all life forms progress or evolve to a higher form: *progressionist evolutionists.*

pro·gres·sive /prəˈgresiv/ ▸*adj.* **1** happening or developing gradually or in stages; proceeding step by step: *a progressive decline in popularity.* ■ (of a disease or ailment) increasing in severity or extent: *progressive liver failure.* ■ (of taxation or a tax) increasing as a proportion of the sum taxed as that sum increases: *steeply progressive income taxes.* ■ (of a card game or dance) involving a series of sections for which participants successively change place or relative position. ■ *archaic* engaging in or constituting forward motion. **2** (of a group, person, or idea) favoring or implementing social reform or new, liberal ideas: *a relatively progressive governor.* ■ favoring or promoting change or innovation: *a progressive art school.* ■ relating to or denoting a style of rock music popular esp. in the 1980s and characterized by classical influences, the use of keyboard instruments, and lengthy compositions. **3** *Grammar* denoting an aspect or tense of a verb that expresses an action in progress, e.g., *am writing, was writing.* Also called **CONTINUOUS.**

▸*n.* **1** a person advocating or implementing social reform or new, liberal ideas. **2** *Grammar* a progressive tense or aspect: *the present progressive.* **3** (also **progressive proof**) (usu. **progressives**) *Printing* each of a set of proofs of color work, showing all the colors separately and the cumulative effect of overprinting them. ▷early 17th cent.: from French *progressif, -ive* or medieval Latin *progressivus*, from *progress-* 'gone forward,' from the verb *progredi* (see **PROGRESS**). **—pro·gres·sive·ly** *adv.* **—pro·gres·sive·ness** *n.* **—pro·gres·siv·ism** /-ˈgresəˌvizəm/ *n.* **—pro·gres·siv·ist** /-ˈgresəvist/ *n.* & *adj.*

Pro·gres·sive Con·ser·va·tive Par·ty a Canadian political party advocating free trade and holding moderate views on social policies.

pro·gres·sive din·ner ▸*n.* a social occasion at which the different courses of a meal are eaten at different people's houses.

pro·gres·sive lens ▸ *n.* (usually **progressive lenses**) an eyeglass lens having a smooth transition between parts with different focal lengths, correcting for vision at all distances.

Pro·gres·sive Par·ty ▸*n.* any of three related political parties active in the first half of the twentieth century that favored social reform. The most prominent was that formed under Theodore Roosevelt in 1912.

pro·gres·sives /prəˈgresivz/ ▸*plural n.* a pair of eyeglasses having progressive lenses: *progressives for use when driving, reading, or using a computer.*

pro hac vice /prō ˌhäk ˈwikē; ˈvīsē/ ▸*adv.* for or on this occasion only. ▷Latin.

pro·hib·it /prəˈhibit; prō-/ ▸*v.* (**-hib·it·ed**, **-hib·it·ing**) [*trans.*] formally forbid (something) by law, rule, or other authority: *laws prohibiting cruelty to animals.* ■ (**prohibit someone/something from doing something**) formally forbid a person or group from doing something: *he is prohibited from being a director.* ■ (of a fact or situation) prevent (something); make impossible: *the budget agreement had prohibited any tax cuts.* ▷late Middle English: from Latin *prohibit-* 'kept in check,' from the verb *prohibere,* from *pro-* 'in front' + *habere* 'to hold.' **—pro·hib·it·er** *n.* **—pro·hib·i·tor** /-ər/ *n.* **—pro·hib·i·to·ry** /-ˌtôrē/ *adj.*

THE RIGHT WORD **ban, disallow, enjoin, forbid, hinder, interdict, preclude, prohibit**

There are a number of ways to prevent something from happening. You can **prohibit** it, which assumes that you have legal or other authority and are willing to back up your prohibition with force (*prohibit smoking*); or you can simply **forbid** it and hope that you've got the necessary clout (*forbid teenagers to stay out after midnight*).

Ban carries a little more weight—both legal and moral—and **interdict** suggests that church or civil authorities are behind the idea.

To **enjoin** (in this sense) is to prohibit by legal injunction (*the truckers were enjoined from striking*), which practically guarantees that you'll get what you want.

A government or some other authority may **disallow** an act it might otherwise have permitted (*the IRS disallowed the deduction*), but anyone with a little gumption can **hinder** an activity by putting obstacles in its path (*hinder the thief's getaway by tripping him on his way out the door*).

Of course, the easiest way to prohibit something is to **preclude** it, which means stopping it before it even gets started.

pro·hi·bi·tion /ˌprō(h)əˈbisʜən/ ▸*n.* **1** the action of forbidding something, esp. by law: *they argue that prohibition of drugs will always fail.* ■ a law or regulation forbidding something: *those who favor prohibitions on insider trading.* **2** (**Prohibition**) the prevention by law of the manufacture and sale of alcohol, esp. in the U.S. between 1920 and 1933. ▷late Middle English: from Old French, from Latin *prohibitio(n-),* from *prohibere* 'keep in check' (see **PROHIBIT**). **—pro·hi·bi·tion·ar·y** /-ˌnerē/ *adj.* **—Pro·hi·bi·tion·ist** /-nist/ *n.*

pro·hib·i·tive /prəˈhibitiv; prō-/ ▸*adj.* **1** (of a price or charge) excessively high; difficult or impossible to pay: *the costs involved were prohibitive* | *prohibitive interest rates.* **2** (esp. of a law or rule) forbidding or restricting something: *prohibitive legislation.* ■ (of a condition or situation) preventing someone from doing something: *a wind over force 5 is prohibitive.* ▷late Middle English (sense 2): from French *prohibitif, -ive* or Latin *prohibitivus,* from *prohibit-* 'kept in check,' from the verb *prohibere* (see **PROHIBIT**). **—pro·hib·i·tive·ly** *adv.* **—pro·hib·i·tive·ness** *n.*

pro·in·su·lin /prōˈinsələn/ ▸*n. Biochemistry* a substance produced by the pancreas that is converted to insulin.

pro·ject ▸*n.* /ˈpräjˌekt; -ikt/ **1** an individual or collaborative enterprise that is carefully planned and designed to achieve a particular aim: *a research project* | *a nationwide project to encourage business development.* ■ a school assignment undertaken by a student or group of students, typically as a long-term task that requires independent research: *a history project.* ■ a proposed or planned undertaking: *the novel undermines its own stated project of telling a story.* **2** (also **housing project**) a government-subsidized housing development with relatively low rents: *her family still lives in* ***the projects.***

▸*v.* /prəˈjekt; prōˈjekt/ [*trans.*] **1** (usu. **be projected**) estimate or forecast (something) on the basis of present trends: *spending was* ***projected at*** *$72 million.* ■ [often as *adj.*] (**projected**) plan (a scheme or undertaking): *a projected exhibition of contemporary art.* **2** [*intrans.*] extend outward beyond something else; protrude: *I noticed a slip of paper* ***projecting from*** *the book* | [as *adj.*] (**projecting**) *a projecting bay window.* See note at **BULGE**. **3** [*trans.*] throw or cause to move forward or outward: *seeds are projected from the tree.* ■ cause (light, shadow, or an image) to fall on a surface: *the one light projected shadows on the wall.* ■ cause (a sound, esp. the voice) to be heard at a distance: *being audible depends on your ability to project your voice.* ■ imagine (oneself, a situation, etc.) as having moved to a different place or time: *people may be projecting the present* ***into*** *the past.* **4** present or promote (a particular view or image): *he strives to project an image of youth.* ■ present (someone or something) in a way intended to create a favorable impression: *she liked to project herself more as a friend than a doctor.* ■ display (an emotion or quality) in one's behavior: *everyone would be amazed that a young girl could project such depths of emotion.* ■ (**project something onto**) transfer or attribute one's own emotion or desire to (another person), esp. unconsciously: *men may sometimes project their own fears onto women.* **5** *Geometry* draw straight lines from a center of or parallel lines through every point of (a given figure) to produce a corresponding figure on a surface or a line by intersecting the surface. ■ draw (such lines). ■ produce (such a corresponding figure). **6** make a projection of (the earth, sky, etc.) on a plane surface. ▷late Middle English (in the sense 'preliminary design, tabulated statement'): from Latin *projectum* 'something prominent,' neuter past participle of *proicere* 'throw forth,' from *pro-* 'forth' + *jacere* 'to throw.' Early senses of the verb were 'plan, devise' and 'cause to move forward.' **—pro·ject·a·ble** /prəˈjektəbəl/ *adj.*

pro·jec·tile /prəˈjektl; -ˌtīl/ ▸*n.* a missile designed to be fired from a rocket or gun. ■ an object propelled through the air, esp. one thrown as a weapon: *they tried to shield Johnson from the projectiles that were being thrown.*

▸*adj.* [*attrib.*] of or relating to such a missile or object: *a projectile weapon.* ■ propelled with great force: *projectile vomiting.* ▷mid 17th cent.: modern Latin, from *project-* 'thrown forth,' from the verb *proicere* (see **PROJECT**).

pro·jec·tion /prəˈjeksʜən/ ▸*n.* **1** an estimate or forecast of a future situation or trend based on a study of present ones: *plans based on projections of slow but positive growth* | *population projection is essential for planning.* **2** the presentation of an image on a surface, esp. a movie screen: *quality illustrations for overhead projection.* ■ an image projected in such a way: *the background projections featured humpback whales.* ■ the ability to make a sound, esp. the voice, heard at a distance: *I taught him voice projection.* **3** the presentation or promotion of someone or something in a particular way: *the legal profession's projection of an image of altruism.* ■ a mental image viewed as reality: *monsters can be understood as mental projections of mankind's fears.* ■ the unconscious transfer of one's own desires or emotions to another person: *we protect the self by a number of defense mechanisms, including repression and projection.* **4** a thing that extends outward from something else: *the particle board covered all the sharp projections.* **5** *Geometry* the action of projecting a figure. **6** the representation on a plane surface of any part of the surface of the earth or a celestial sphere. ■ (also **map projection**) a method by which such representation may be done. ▷mid 16th cent. (sense 6): from Latin *projectio(n-),* from *proicere* 'throw forth' (see **PROJECT**). **—pro·jec·tion·ist** /-ist/ *n.* (in sense 2).

pro·jec·tion tel·e·vi·sion (also **pro·jec·tion TV**) ▸*n.* a large television receiver in which the image is projected optically onto a large viewing screen.

pro·jec·tive /prəˈjektiv/ ▸*adj.* **1** *Geometry* relating to or derived by projection: *projective transformations.* ■ (of a property of a figure) unchanged by projection. **2** *Psychology* relating to the unconscious transfer of one's own desires or emotions to another person: *the projective contents of wish fantasies.* ■ relating to or exploiting the unconscious expression or introduction of one's impressions or feelings. **—pro·jec·tive·ly** *adv.* **—pro·jec·tiv·i·ty** /ˌprōˌjekˈtivətē; ˌpräjˌek-/ *n.*

pro·jec·tive ge·om·e·try ▸*n.* the study of the projective properties of geometric figures.

pro·jec·tive test ▸*n.* a psychological test in which words, images, or situations are presented to a person and the responses analyzed for the unconscious expression of elements of personality that they reveal.

pro·jec·tor /prəˈjektər/ ▸*n.* **1** an object that is used to project rays of light, esp. an apparatus with a system of lenses for projecting slides or film onto a screen. **2** *archaic* a person who plans and sets up a project or enterprise. ■ a promoter of a dubious or fraudulent enterprise.

pro·kar·y·ote /prōˈkarēˌōt/ (also **pro·car·y·ote**) ▸*n. Biology* a microscopic single-celled organism, including the bacteria and cyanobacteria, that has neither a distinct nucleus with a membrane nor other specialized organelles. Compare with **EUKARYOTE**. ▷1960s: from **PRO-**[2] 'before' + Greek *karuon* 'nut, kernel' + *-ote* as in **ZYGOTE**. **—pro·kar·y·ot·ic** /prōˌkarēˈätik/ *adj.*

Pro·ko·fi·ev /prōˈkôfēˌef/, Sergei (Sergeevich) (1891–1953), Russian composer. Notable works include the opera *The Love for Three Oranges* (1919), the *Lieutenant Kijé* suite (1934), the ballet music for *Romeo and Juliet* (1935–36), and *Peter and the Wolf* (1936).

Pro·ko·pyevsk /prəˈkôpyifsk/ a coal-mining city in southern Russia, in the Kuznets Basin industrial region, to the south of Kemerovo; pop. 274,000.

pro·lac·tin /prōˈlaktən/ ▸*n. Biochemistry* a hormone released from the anterior pituitary gland that stimulates milk production after childbirth. ▷1930s: from **PRO-**[2] 'before' + **LACTATION**.

pro·lapse ▸*n.* /prōˈlaps; ˈprōˌlaps/ a slipping forward or down of one of the parts or organs of the body: *a rectal prolapse.* ■ a prolapsed part or organ, esp. a uterus or rectum.

▸*v.* /prōˈlaps/ [*intrans.*] [usu. as *adj.*] (**prolapsed**) (of a part or organ of the body) slip forward or down: *a prolapsed uterus.* ▷mid 18th cent.: from Latin *prolaps-* 'slipped forward,' from the verb *prolabi,* from *pro-* 'forward, down' + *labi* 'to slip.'

pro·lap·sus /prōˈlapsəs/ ▸*n.* technical term for **PROLAPSE**. ▷late 18th cent.: modern Latin, from late Latin, literally 'fall.'

pro·late /ˈprōˌlāt/ ▸*adj. Geometry* (of a spheroid) lengthened in the direction of a polar diameter. Often contrasted with **OBLATE**[1]. ▷late 17th cent.: from Latin *prolatus* 'carried forward,' past participle of *proferre* 'prolong,' from *pro-* 'forward' + *ferre* 'carry.'

prole /prōl/ *informal, derogatory* ▸*n.* a member of the working class; a worker.

▸*adj.* working-class: *prole soldiers.* ▷late 19th cent.: abbreviation of **PROLETARIAT**.

pro·leg /ˈprōˌleg/ ▸*n. Entomology* a fleshy abdominal limb of a caterpillar or similar insect larva.

pro·le·gom·e·non /ˌprōləˈgäməˌnän; -nən/ ▸*n.* (*pl.* **-na** /-nə/) a critical or discursive introduction to a book. ▷mid 17th cent.: via Latin from Greek, passive present participle (neuter) of *prolegein* 'say beforehand,' from *pro* 'before' + *legein* 'say.' **—pro·le·gom·e·nous** /-nəs/ *adj.*

pro·lep·sis /prōˈlepsəs/ ▸*n.* (*pl.* **-ses** /-ˌsēz/) **1** *Rhetoric* the anticipation and answering of possible objections in rhetorical speech. ■ *poetic/literary* anticipation: *in the first of the novella's three parts Marlow gives a prolepsis of the climax.* **2** the representation of a thing as existing before it actually does or did so, as in *he was a dead man when he entered.* ▷late Middle English (as a term in rhetoric): via late Latin from Greek *prolēpsis,* from *prolambanein* 'anticipate,' from *pro* 'before' + *lambanein* 'take.' **—pro·lep·tic** /-ˈleptik/ *adj.* **—pro·lep·ti·cal·ly** /-ˈleptik(ə)lē/ *adv.*

pro·le·tar·i·an /ˌprōliˈte(ə)rēən/ ▸*adj.* of or relating to the proletariat: *a proletarian ideology.*

▸*n.* a member of the proletariat. ▷mid 17th cent.: from Latin *proletarius* (from *proles* 'offspring'), denoting a person having no wealth in property, who only served the state by producing offspring, + **-AN**. **—pro·le·tar·i·an·ism** /-ˌnizəm/ *n.* **—pro·le·tar·i·an·i·za·tion** /-ˌterēənəˈzāsʜən/ *n.* **—pro·le·tar·i·an·ize** /-ˌnīz/ *v.*

pro·le·tar·i·at /ˌprōliˈte(ə)rēət/ (also *archaic* **pro·le·tar·i·ate**) ▸*n.* [treated as *sing.* or *pl.*] workers or working-class people, regarded collectively (often used with reference to Marxism): *the growth of the industrial proletariat.* ■ the lowest class of citizens in ancient Rome. ▷mid 19th cent.: from French *prolétariat,* from Latin *proletarius* (see **PROLETARIAN**).

pro-life /prōˈlīf/ ▸*adj.* opposing abortion and euthanasia: *she is a pro-life activist.* Compare with **PRO-CHOICE**. **—pro-lif·er** *n.*

pro·lif·er·ate /prəˈlifəˌrāt/ ▸*v.* [*intrans.*] increase rapidly in numbers; multiply: *the science-fiction magazines which proliferated in the 1920s.* ■ (of a cell, structure, or organism) reproduce rapidly: *the Mediterranean faces an ecological disaster if the seaweed continues to proliferate at its present rate.* ■ [*trans.*] cause (cells, tissue, structures, etc.) to reproduce rapidly: *electromagnetic radiation can only proliferate cancers already present.* ■ [*trans.*] produce (something) in large or increasing quantities: *the promise of new technology proliferating options on every hand* ▷late 19th cent.: back-formation from **PROLIFERATION**. **—pro·lif·er·a·tive** /-ˌrātiv/ *adj.* **—pro·lif·er·a·tor** /-ˌrātər/ *n.*

pro·lif·er·a·tion /prə,lifəˈrāsHən/ ▸*n.* rapid increase in numbers: *a continuing threat of nuclear proliferation.* ■ rapid reproduction of a cell, part, or organism: *we attempted to measure cell proliferation.* ■ [in *sing.*] a large number of something: *stress levels are high, forcing upon them* ***a proliferation of*** *ailments.* ▷mid 19th cent.: from French *prolifération,* from *prolifère* 'proliferous.'

pro·lif·er·ous /prəˈlifərəs/ ▸*adj. Biology* (of a plant) producing buds or side shoots from a flower or other terminal part. ■ (of a plant or invertebrate) propagating or multiplying by means of buds or offsets. ▷mid 17th cent.: from Latin *proles* 'offspring' + **-FEROUS.**

pro·lif·ic /prəˈlifik/ ▸*adj.* **1** (of a plant, animal, or person) producing much fruit or foliage or many offspring: *in captivity, tigers are prolific breeders.* See note at **FERTILE.** ■ (of an artist, author, or composer) producing many works: *he was a prolific composer of operas.* ■ (of a sports player) high-scoring: *a prolific home-run hitter.* **2** present in large numbers or quantities; plentiful: *mahogany was once prolific in the tropical forests.* ■ (of a river, area, or season of the year) characterized by plentiful wildlife or produce: *the prolific rivers and lakes of Franklin County.* ▷mid 17th cent.: from medieval Latin *prolificus,* from Latin *proles* 'offspring' (see **PROLIFEROUS**). **—pro·lif·i·ca·cy** /-ikəsē/ *n.* **—pro·lif·i·cal·ly** /-ik(ə)lē/ *adv.* **—pro·lif·ic·ness** *n.*

pro·line /ˈprō,lēn/ ▸*n. Biochemistry* an amino acid that is a constituent of most proteins, esp. collagen. • A heterocyclic compound; chem. formula: $C_5H_9NO_2$. ▷early 20th cent.: contraction of the chemical name *p(yr)rol(id)ine*-2-carboxylic acid.

pro·lix /prōˈliks/ ▸*adj.* (of speech or writing) using or containing too many words; tediously lengthy: *he found the narrative too prolix and discursive.* ▷late Middle English: from Old French *prolixe* or Latin *prolixus* 'poured forth, extended,' from *pro-* 'outward' + *liquere* 'be liquid.' **—pro·lix·i·ty** /-ˈliksətē/ *n.* **—pro·lix·ly** *adv.*

pro·loc·u·tor /prōˈläkyətər/ ▸*n.* **1** a chairperson of the lower house of convocation in a province of the Church of England. **2** *archaic* or *formal* a spokesperson. ▷late Middle English (sense 2): from Latin, from *prolocut-* 'spoken out,' from the verb *proloqui,* from *pro-* 'before' + *loqui* 'speak.'

Pro·log /ˈprō,lôg; -,läg/ ▸*n. Computing* a high-level computer programming language first devised for artificial intelligence applications. ▷1970s: from the first elements of **PROGRAMMING** and **LOGIC.**

pro·logue /ˈprō,lôg; -,läg/ ▸*n.* a separate introductory section of a literary or musical work: *this idea is outlined in the prologue.* ■ an event or action that leads to another event or situation: *civil unrest in a few isolated villages became the* ***prologue to*** *widespread rebellion.* ■ (in professional cycling) a short preliminary time trial held before a race to establish a leader. ■ the actor who delivers the prologue in a play. ▷Middle English: from Old French, via Latin from Greek *prologos,* from *pro-* 'before' + *logos* 'saying.'

pro·long /prəˈlôNG; -ˈläNG/ (also **pro·lon·gate** /-ˈlôNGgāt; -ˈläNG-/) ▸*v.* [*trans.*] extend the duration of: *an idea that prolonged the life of the engine by many years.* ■ (usu. **be prolonged**) *rare* extend in spatial length: *the line of his lips was prolonged in a short red scar.* ▷late Middle English: from Old French *prolonguer,* from late Latin *prolongare,* from *pro-* 'forward, onward' + *longus* 'long.' **—pro·lon·ga·tion** /prō,lôNGˈgāsHən; prə-/ *n.* **—pro·long·er** *n.*

pro·longed /prəˈlôNGd; -ˈläNGd/ ▸*adj.* continuing for a long time or longer than usual; lengthy: *the region suffered a prolonged drought.* **—pro·long·ed·ly** /-ˈlôNG(ə)dlē; -ˈläNG/ *adv.*

pro·lu·sion /prōˈlo͞ozHən/ ▸*n. archaic* or *formal* a preliminary action or event; a prelude. ■ a preliminary essay or article. ▷early 17th cent.: from Latin *prolusio(n-),* from *prolus-* 'practiced beforehand,' from the verb *proludere,* from *pro* 'before' + *ludere* 'to play.'

PROM /präm/ ▸*n. Computing* a memory chip that can be programmed only once by the manufacturer or user. ▷from p(rogrammable) r(ead-)o(nly) m(emory).

prom /präm/ ▸*n. informal* **1** a formal dance, esp. one held by a class in high school or college at the end of a year. **2** *Brit.* short for **PROMENADE** (sense 1). **3** (also **Prom**) *Brit.* short for **PROMENADE CONCERT**: *the last night of the Proms.*

prom. ▸*abbr.* promontory.

prom·e·nade /,präməˈnād; -ˈnäd/ ▸*n.* **1** a paved public walk, typically one along a waterfront at a resort. ■ a leisurely walk, or sometimes a ride or drive, typically one taken in a public place so as to meet or be seen by others: *she went on a promenade with Jules.* ■ (in country dancing) a movement in which couples follow one another in a given direction, each couple having both hands joined. **2** archaic term for **PROM** (sense 1). ▸*v.* [*intrans.*] take a leisurely walk, ride, or drive in public, esp. to meet or be seen by others: *women who promenaded in the Bois de Boulogne.* ■ [*trans.*] take such a walk through (a place): *people began to promenade the streets.* ■ [*trans.*] *dated* escort (someone) about a place, esp. so as to be seen by others: *the governor of Utah promenades the daughter of the Maryland governor.* ▷mid 16th cent. (denoting a leisurely walk in public): from French, from *se promener* 'to walk,' reflexive of *promener* 'take for a walk.' **—prom·e·nad·er** *n.*

prom·e·nade con·cert ▸*n. Brit.* a concert of classical music at which a part of the audience stands in an area that has no seating, for which tickets are sold at a reduced price. The most famous series of such concerts is the annual BBC Promenade Concerts (known as **the Proms**), instituted by Sir Henry Wood (1869–1944) in 1895 and held since World War II chiefly in the Albert Hall in London.

prom·e·nade deck ▸*n.* an upper deck on a passenger ship for the use of passengers who wish to enjoy the open air.

pro·meth·a·zine /prōˈmeTHə,zēn/ ▸*n. Medicine* a synthetic antihistamine drug derived from phenothiazine, used chiefly to treat the symptoms of allergies and motion sickness. ▷1950s: from *pro(pyl)* + *(di)meth(ylamine)* + *(phenothi)azine.*

Pro·me·the·us /prəˈmēTHēəs; -,TH(y)o͞os/ *Greek Mythology* a demigod, one of the Titans, who was worshiped by craftsmen. When Zeus hid fire from man, Prometheus stole it by trickery and returned it to earth. As punishment, Zeus chained him to a rock where an eagle fed each day on his liver, which grew again each night; he was rescued by Hercules. **—Pro·me·the·an** /-THēən/ *adj.*

pro·me·thi·um /prōˈmēTHēəm/ ▸*n.* the chemical element of atomic number 61, a radioactive metal of the lanthanide series. It was first produced artificially in a nuclear reactor and occurs in nature in traces as a product of uranium fission. (Symbol: **Pm**) ▷1940s: modern Latin, from the name of the Titan **PROMETHEUS.**

prom·i·nence /ˈprämənəns/ ▸*n.* **1** the state of being important or famous: *she* ***came to prominence*** *as an artist in the 1960s* | [in *sing.*] *the commission gave the case a prominence which it might otherwise have escaped.* **2** the fact or condition of standing out from something by physically projecting or being particularly noticeable: *radiographs showed enlargement of the right heart with prominence of the pulmonary outflow tract.* ■ a thing that projects from something, esp. a projecting feature of the landscape or a protuberance on a part of the body: *the rocky prominence resembled a snow-capped mountain.* ■ *Astronomy* a stream of incandescent gas projecting above the sun's chromosphere. ▷late 16th cent. (denoting something that juts out): from obsolete French, from Latin *prominentia* 'jutting out,' from the verb *prominere* (see **PROMINENT**).

prom·i·nent /ˈprämənənt/ ▸*adj.* **1** important; famous: *she was a prominent member of the city council.* **2** projecting from something; protuberant: *a man with big, prominent eyes like a lobster's.* ■ situated so as to catch the attention; noticeable: *the new housing developments are prominent landmarks.* See note at **NOTICEABLE.** ▷late Middle English (in the sense 'projecting'): from Latin *prominent-* 'jutting out,' from the verb *prominere.* Compare with **EMINENT.** **—prom·i·nen·cy** *n.* **—prom·i·nent·ly** *adv.*

pro·mis·cu·ous /prəˈmiskyo͞oəs/ ▸*adj.* **1** *derogatory* (of a person) having many sexual relationships, esp. transient ones: *she's a wild, promiscuous girl.* ■ (of sexual behavior or a society) characterized by such relationships: *they ran wild, indulging in promiscuous sex and experimenting with drugs.* **2** demonstrating or implying an undiscriminating or unselective approach; indiscriminate or casual: *the city fathers were promiscuous with their honors.* ■ consisting of a wide range of different things: *Americans are free to pick and choose from a promiscuous array of values and behavior.* ▷early 17th cent.: from Latin *promiscuus* 'indiscriminate' (based on *miscere* 'to mix') + **-OUS.** The early sense was 'consisting of elements mixed together,' giving rise to 'indiscriminate' and 'undiscriminating,' whence the notion of 'casual.' **—prom·is·cu·i·ty** /,präməˈskyo͞oitē; prə,misˈkyo͞o-/ *n.* **—pro·mis·cu·ous·ly** *adv.* **—pro·mis·cu·ous·ness** *n.*

prom·ise /ˈpräməs/ ▸*n.* a declaration or assurance that one will do a particular thing or that guarantees that a particular thing will happen: *what happened to all those firm promises of support?* | [with *clause*] *he took my fax number with the promise that he would send me a drawing* | [with *infinitive*] *I did not keep my promise to go home early.* ■ the quality of potential excellence: *he showed great promise even as a junior officer.* ■ [in *sing.*] an indication that something specified is expected or likely to occur: *the promise of peace.* ▸*v.* **1** [*reporting verb*] assure someone that one will definitely do, give, or arrange something; undertake or declare that something will happen: [with *infinitive*] *he promised to forward my mail* | [with *clause*] *she made him promise that he wouldn't do it again* | [with *direct speech*] *"I'll bring it right back," she promised* | [with *two objs.*] *he promised her the job.* ■ [*trans.*] (usu. **be promised**) *archaic* pledge (someone, esp. a woman) to marry someone else; betroth: *I've been promised to him for years.* **2** [*trans.*] give good grounds for expecting (a particular occurrence or situation): *forthcoming concerts promise a feast of music from around the world* | [with *infinitive*] *it promised to be a night that all present would long remember.* ■ (of a person, publication, institution, etc.) announce (something) as being expected to happen: *China yesterday promised a record grain harvest* | [with *two objs.*] *we're promised more winter weather tonight.* ■ (**promise oneself**) contemplate the pleasant expectation of: *he tidied up the room, promising himself an early night.* ▷late Middle English: from Latin *promissum* 'something promised,' neuter past participle of *promittere* 'put forth, promise,' from *pro-* 'forward' + *mittere* 'send.' **—prom·is·er** *n.*

▸*PHRASES* □ **I promise** (or **I promise you**) *informal* used for emphasis, esp. so as to reassure, encourage, or threaten someone: *oh, I'm not joking, I promise you.* □ **promise** (**someone**) **the earth** (or **moon**) make extravagant promises to someone that are unlikely to be fulfilled: *interactive technology titillates, promises the earth, but delivers nothing.* □ **promises, promises** *informal* used to indicate that the speaker is skeptical about someone's stated intention to do something.

Prom·ised Land ▸*n.* (in the Bible) the land of Canaan, which was promised to Abraham and his descendants (Gen. 12:7). ■ (**promised land**) a place or situation in which someone expects to find great happiness: *Italy is the promised land for any musician.*

prom·is·ee /,präməˈsē/ ▸*n. Law* a person to whom a promise is made.

prom·is·ing /ˈpräməsiNG/ ▸*adj.* showing signs of future success: *a promising actor* | *a promising start to the season.* **—prom·is·ing·ly** *adv.*

prom·i·sor /ˈpräməsər/ ▸*n. Law* a person who makes a promise.

prom·is·so·ry /ˈprämə,sôrē/ ▸*adj. chiefly Law* conveying or implying a promise: *statements that are promissory in nature* | *promissory words.* ■ *archaic* indicative of something to come; full of promise: *the glow of evening is* ***promissory of*** *the splendid days to come.* ▷late Middle English: from medieval Latin *promissorius,* from *promiss-* 'promised,' from the verb *promittere* (see **PROMISE**).

prom·is·so·ry note ▸*n.* a signed document containing a written promise to pay a stated sum to a specified person or the bearer at a specified date or on demand.

pro·mo /ˈprōmō/ *informal* ▸*n.* (*pl.* **-mos**) a piece of publicity or advertising, esp. in the form of a short film or video: *taping a two-minute promo* | [as *adj.*] *a promo video.* ▷1960s: abbreviation of **PROMOTION.**

prom·on·to·ry /ˈprämən,tôrē/ ▸*n.* (*pl.* **-ries**) a point of high land that juts out into a large body of water; a headland: *a rocky promontory.* ■ *Anatomy* a prominence or protuberance on an organ or other structure in the body. ▷mid 16th cent.: from Latin *promontorium,* variant (influenced by *mons, mont-* 'mountain') of *promunturium.*

Prom·on·to·ry Moun·tains a short range that forms a peninsula in the northern Great Salt Lake, in northern Utah. The first transcontinental railroad passed through Promontory, north of the range. Today, trains pass Promontory Point, at the southern end, via a causeway across the lake.

pro·mote /prəˈmōt/ ▸*v.* [*trans.*] **1** further the progress of (something, esp. a cause, venture, or aim); support or actively encourage: *some regulation is still required to promote competition.* ■ give publicity to (a product, organization, or venture) so as to increase sales or public awareness: *they are using famous personalities to promote the library nationally.* ■ *Chemistry* act as a promoter of (a catalyst). **2** (often **be promoted**) advance or raise (someone) to a higher position or rank: *she was* ***promoted to*** *general manager.* ■ transfer (a sports team) to a higher division of a league: *they were promoted from the Third Division last season.* ■ *Chess* exchange (a pawn) for a more powerful piece of the same color, typically a queen, as part of the move in which it reaches the opponent's end of the board. ■ *Bridge* enable (a relatively low card) to win a trick by playing off the higher ones first. ▷late Middle English: from Latin *promot-* 'moved forward,' from the verb *promovere*, from *pro-* 'forward, onward' + *movere* 'to move.' —**pro·mot·a·bil·i·ty** /prə,mōtə'bilətē/ *n.* —**pro·mot·a·ble** *adj.* —**pro·mo·tive** /-tiv/ *adj.*

pro·mot·er /prə'mōtər/ ▸*n.* a person or thing that promotes something, in particular: ■ a person or company that finances or organizes a sporting event or theatrical production: *a boxing promoter.* ■ a person involved in setting up and funding a new company. ■ a supporter of a cause or aim: *Mitterrand was a fierce promoter of European integration.* ■ (also **pro·mo·tor**) *Chemistry* an additive that increases the activity of a catalyst. ■ *Biology* a region of a DNA molecule that forms the site at which transcription of a gene starts. ▷late Middle English: from Anglo-Norman French *promotour*, from medieval Latin *promotor* (see PROMOTE).

pro·mo·tion /prə'mōsHən/ ▸*n.* **1** activity that supports or provides active encouragement for the furtherance of a cause, venture, or aim: *disease prevention and health promotion.* ■ the publicization of a product, organization, or venture so as to increase sales or public awareness. ■ a publicity campaign for a particular product, organization, or venture: *the paper is reaping the rewards of a series of promotions.* ■ [often as *adj.*] (**promotions**) the activity or business of organizing such publicity or campaigns: *she's the promotions manager for the museum.* ■ a sporting event, esp. a series of boxing matches, staged for profit. ■ *Chemistry* the action of promoting a catalyst. **2** the action of raising someone to a higher position or rank or the fact of being so raised: *majors designated for* **promotion to** *lieutenant colonel | a promotion to divisional sales director.* ■ the transfer of a sports team to a higher division of a league: *they won promotion last season.* ▷late Middle English (sense 2): via Old French from Latin *promotio(n-)*, from *promovere* 'move forward' (see PROMOTE).

pro·mo·tion·al /prə'mōsHənl/ ▸*adj.* of or relating to the publicizing of a product, organization, or venture so as to increase sales or public awareness: *she was on a promotional tour for her books.*

prompt /prämpt/ ▸*v.* [*trans.*] **1** (of an event or fact) cause or bring about (an action or feeling): *his death has prompted an industry-wide investigation of safety violations.* ■ cause (someone) to take a course of action: *a demonstration by 20,000 people prompted the government to step up security.* **2** assist or encourage (a hesitating speaker) to say something: [with *direct speech*] *"And the picture?" he prompted.* ■ supply a forgotten word or line to (an actor) during the performance of a play. ■ *Computing* (of a computer) request input from (a user).
▸*n.* **1** an act of assisting or encouraging a hesitating speaker: *with barely a prompt, Barbara talked on.* ■ the word or phrase spoken as a reminder to an actor of a forgotten word or line. ■ *Computing* a message or symbol on a monitor to show that the system is waiting for input. ■ another term for PROMPTER. **2** the time limit for the payment of an account, as stated on a prompt note.
▸*adj.* done without delay; immediate: *the owner would have died but for the prompt action of two paramedics.* ■ (of a person) acting without delay: *the fans were prompt and courteous in complying with police requests.* ■ (of goods) for immediate delivery and payment. ▷Middle English (as a verb): based on Old French *prompt* or Latin *promptus* 'brought to light,' also 'prepared, ready,' past participle of *promere* 'to produce,' from *pro-* 'out, forth' + *emere* 'take.' —**promp·ti·tude** /'prämptə,t(y)o͞od/ *n.* —**prompt·ly** *adv.* —**prompt·ness** *n.*

prompt·book /'prämpt ,bo͝ok/ ▸*n.* an annotated copy of a play for the use of a prompter during a performance.

prompt·er /'prämptər/ ▸*n.* a person seated out of sight of the audience who supplies a forgotten word or line to an actor during the performance of a play.

prompt·ing /'prämptiNG/ ▸*n.* the action of saying something to persuade, encourage, or remind someone to do or say something: *after some prompting, the defendant gave the police his name.*

prompt side ▸*n.* the side of the stage where the prompter sits, usually to the actor's right in the U.S. and to the the actor's left in the UK.

prom·ul·gate /'präməl,gāt; prō'məl-/ ▸*v.* [*trans.*] promote or make widely known (an idea or cause): *these objectives have to be promulgated within the organization.* See note at ANNOUNCE. ■ put (a law or decree) into effect by official proclamation: *in January 1852, the new constitution was promulgated.* ▷mid 16th cent.: from Latin *promulgat-* 'exposed to public view,' from the verb *promulgare*, from *pro-* 'out, publicly' + *mulgere* 'cause to come forth' (literally 'to milk'). —**prom·ul·ga·tion** /,präməl'gāsHən; ,prōməl-/ *n.* —**prom·ul·ga·tor** /-,gātər/ *n.*

pro·mulge /prō'məlj/ ▸*v.* archaic variant of PROMULGATE. ▷late 15th cent.: from Latin *promulgare*.

pron. ▸*abbr.* ■ pronominal. ■ pronoun. ■ pronounced. ■ pronunciation.

pro·na·os /prō'nā,äs/ ▸*n.* (*pl.* **-na·oi** /-'nā,oi/) a vestibule at the front of a classical temple, enclosed by a portico and projecting sidewalls. ▷via Latin from Greek *pronaos* 'hall of a temple,' from *pro* 'before' + *naos* 'temple.'

pro·nate /'prō,nāt/ ▸*v.* [*trans.*] *technical* **1** put or hold (a hand, foot, or limb) with the palm or sole turned downward: [as *adj.*] (**pronated**) *a pronated foot.* Compare with SUPINATE. **2** walk or run with most of the weight on the outside of the feet. ▷mid 19th cent.: back-formation from *pronation*, based on Latin *pronus* 'leaning forward.' —**pro·na·tion** /prō'nāsHən/ *n.*

pro·na·tor /'prō,nātər/ ▸*n.* *Anatomy* **1** a muscle whose contraction produces or assists in the pronation of a limb or part of a limb. ■ any of several specific muscles in the forearm. **2** one who pronates when walking or running.

prone /prōn/ ▸*adj.* **1** [*predic.*] (**prone to/prone to do something**) likely to or liable to suffer from, do, or experience something, typically something regrettable or unwelcome: *years of logging had left the mountains prone to mudslides | he is prone to jump to conclusions.* **2** lying flat, esp. face downward: *I was lying prone on a foam mattress | a prone position.* ■ *technical* denoting the position of the forearm with the palm of the hand facing downward. **3** *archaic* with a downward slope or direction. ▷late Middle English: from Latin *pronus* 'leaning forward,' from *pro* 'forward.' —**prone·ness** *n.*

prong /prôNG/ ▸*n.* each of two or more projecting pointed parts at the end of a fork. ■ a projecting part on various other devices: *a small rubber brush with large prongs.* ■ *figurative* each of the separate parts of an attack or operation: *the three main prongs of the new government's program.*
▸*v.* [*trans.*] pierce or stab with a fork: *pronging the bread with a fondue fork.* ▷late 15th cent. (denoting a forked implement): perhaps related to Middle Low German *prange* 'pinching instrument.' The verb dates from the mid 19th cent. —**pronged** /prôNGd/ *adj.* [in *combination*] *a three-pronged attack.*

prong·horn /'prôNG,hôrn/ (also **pronghorn antelope**) ▸*n.* a deerlike North American mammal with a stocky body, long slim legs, and black horns that are shed and regrown annually. • *Antilocapra americana*, the only member of the family Antilocapridae.

pronk /prôNGk; präNGk/ ▸*v.* [*intrans.*] (of a springbok or other antelope) leap in the air with an arched back and stiff legs, typically as a form of display or when threatened. ▷late 19th cent.: from Afrikaans, literally 'show off,' from Dutch *pronken* 'to strut.'

pro·nom·i·nal /prō'nämənl/ ▸*adj.* of, relating to, or serving as a pronoun: *a pronominal form.* ▷mid 17th cent.: from late Latin *pronominalis* 'belonging to a pronoun,' from Latin *pronomen* (see PRONOUN). —**pro·nom·i·nal·i·za·tion** /,prō,nämənl-ə'zāsHən/ *n.* —**pro·nom·i·nal·ize** /-īz/ *v.* —**pro·nom·i·nal·ly** *adv.*

pro·noun /'prō,noun/ ▸*n.* a word that can function by itself as a noun phrase and that refers either to the participants in the discourse (e.g., *I, you*) or to someone or something mentioned elsewhere in the discourse (e.g., *she, it, this*). ▷late Middle English: from PRO-[1] 'on behalf of' + NOUN, suggested by French *pronom*, Latin *pronomen* (from *pro-* 'for, in place of' + *nomen* 'name').

pro·nounce /prə'nouns/ ▸*v.* [*trans.*] **1** make the sound of (a word or part of a word), typically in the correct or a particular way: *Gerry pronounced the hero's name "Cahoolin" | a refugee whose name no one could pronounce.* **2** declare or announce, typically formally or solemnly: *allow history to pronounce the verdict* | [with *complement*] *she was pronounced dead at the scene* | [with *clause*] *the doctors pronounced that he would never improve.* ■ [*intrans.*] (**pronounce on**) pass judgment or make a decision on: *the secretary of state will shortly pronounce on alternative measures.* ▷late Middle English: from Old French *pronuncier*, from Latin *pronuntiare*, from *pro-* 'out, forth' + *nuntiare* 'announce' (from *nuntius* 'messenger'). —**pro·nounce·a·bil·i·ty** /prə,nounsə'bilətē/ *n.* —**pro·nounce·a·ble** *adj.* —**pro·nounce·ment** *n.* —**pro·nounc·er** *n.*

pro·nounced /prə'nounst/ ▸*adj.* very noticeable or marked; conspicuous: *he had a pronounced squint.* —**pro·nounc·ed·ly** /-'nounsədlē; -'nounstlē/ *adv.*

pron·to /'präntō/ ▸*adv.* *informal* promptly; quickly: *put it in the refrigerator, pronto.* ▷early 20th cent.: from Spanish, from Latin *promptus* (see PROMPT).

pro·nu·cle·us /prō'n(y)o͞oklēəs/ ▸*n.* (*pl.* **-cle·i** /-klē,ī/) *Biology* either of a pair of gametic nuclei, in the stage following meiosis but before their fusion leads to the formation of the nucleus of the zygote. —**pro·nu·cle·ar** /-klēər/ *adj.*

pro·nun·ci·a·men·to /prō,nənsēə'mentō/ ▸*n.* (*pl.* **-tos**) (esp. in Spain and Spanish-speaking countries) a political manifesto or proclamation. ▷Spanish *pronunciamiento*, from *pronunciar* 'pronounce.'

P

pro·nun·ci·a·tion /prə,nənsē'āsHən/ ▸*n.* the way in which a word is pronounced: *spelling does not determine pronunciation | similar pronunciations are heard in Brooklyn.* ▷late Middle English: from Latin *pronuntiatio(n-)*, from the verb *pronuntiare* (see PRONOUNCE).

pro·nun·ci·o /prō'nənsē,ō/ ▸*n.* (*pl.* **-os**) a papal ambassador to a country that does not accord the pope's ambassador automatic precedence over other ambassadors. ▷1960s: from Italian *pro-nunzio*, from *pro-* 'before' + *nunzio* 'nuncio.'

proof /pro͞of/ ▸*n.* **1** evidence or argument establishing or helping to establish a fact or the truth of a statement: *you will be asked to give proof of your identity | this is not a proof for the existence of God.* ■ *Law* the spoken or written evidence in a trial. ■ the action or process of establishing the truth of a statement: *it shifts the onus of proof in convictions from the police to the public.* ■ *archaic* a test or trial. ■ a series of stages in the resolution of a mathematical or philosophical problem. **2** a trial print of something, in particular: ■ *Printing* a trial impression of a page, taken from type or film and used for making corrections before final printing. ■ a trial photographic print made for initial selection. ■ each of a number of impressions from an engraved plate, esp. (in commercial printing) of a limited number before the ordinary issue is printed and before an inscription or signature is added. ■ any of various preliminary impressions of coins struck as specimens. **3** the strength of distilled alcoholic liquor, relative to proof spirit taken as a standard of 100: [in *combination*] *powerful 132-proof rum.*
▸*adj.* **1** able to withstand something damaging; resistant: *the marine battle armor was* **proof against** *most weapons* | [in *combination*] *the system comes with idiot-proof instructions.* **2** [*attrib.*] denoting a trial impression of a page or printed work: *a proof copy is sent up for checking.*
▸*v.* [*trans.*] **1** make (fabric) waterproof: [as *adj.*] (**proofed**) *the tent is made from proofed nylon.* **2** make a proof of (a printed work, engraving, etc.): [as *n.*] (**proofing**) *proofing could be done on a low-cost printer.* ■ proofread (a text): *a book about dinosaurs was being proofed by the publisher.* **3** activate (yeast) by the addition of liquid. ■ knead (dough) until light and smooth. ■ [*intrans.*] (of dough) prove: *shape into a baguette and let proof for a few minutes.* ▷Middle English *preve*, from Old French *proeve*, from late Latin *proba*, from Latin *probare* 'to test, prove.' The change of vowel in late Middle English was due to the influence of PROVE. Current senses of the verb date from the late 19th cent.
▸*PHRASE* □ **the proof of the pudding is in the eating** *proverb* the real value of something can be judged only from practical experience or results and not from appearance or theory.

proof-of-pur·chase ▸*adj.* designating a feature or symbol on a product that can be removed by the buyer to prove that the product was purchased, in order to claim a rebate or refund.

proof pos·i·tive ▸*n.* evidence taken to be final or absolute proof of the existence of something: *he still needs proof positive of her love.*

proof·read /'pro͞of,rēd/ (also **proof-read**) ▸*v.* (*past* and *past part.* **-read** /-,red/) [*trans.*] read (printer's proofs or other written or printed material) and mark any errors. —**proof·read·er** *n.*

proof sheet ▸*n.* *Printing* a page of proofed text; a proof.

proof spir·it ▸*n.* a mixture of alcohol and water containing (in the U.S.) 50 percent alcohol by volume, or (in the UK) 57.1 percent alcohol by volume, used as a standard of strength of distilled alcoholic liquor.

proof·text /ˈpro͞of,tekst/ ▸*n.* a passage of the Bible to which appeal is made in support of an argument or position in theology.

prop[1] /präp/ ▸*n.* a pole or beam used as a support or to keep something in position, typically one that is not an integral part of the thing supported: *300 tubular steel props.* ■ *figurative* a person or thing that is a major source of support or assistance: *the second institutional prop of conservative Spain was the army.* ■ *Grammar* a word used to fill a syntactic role without any specific meaning of its own, for example *one* in *it's a nice one* and *it* in *it is raining.*
▸*v.* (**propped**, **prop·ping**) [*trans.*] position something underneath (someone or something) for support: *she propped her chin in the palm of her right hand.* ■ position (something or someone) more or less upright by leaning it against something else: *a jug of milk with a note propped against it | she* ***propped*** *the picture* ***up*** *on the mantlepiece.* ■ use an object to keep (something) in position: *he found that the door to the office was* ***propped open.***
▸*phrasal v.* □ **prop someone/something up** provide support or assistance for someone or something that would otherwise fail or decline: *foreign aid tends to prop up incompetent governments.* ▷late Middle English: probably from Middle Dutch *proppe* 'support (for vines).'

prop[2] ▸*n.* (usu. **props**) a portable object other than furniture or costumes used on the set of a play or movie. ▷mid 19th cent.: abbreviation of **PROPERTY**.

prop[3] ▸*n.* *informal* an aircraft propeller. ▷early 20th cent.: abbreviation.

prop. ▸*abbr.* ■ proposition. ■ proprietor.

pro·pae·deu·tic /,prōpiˈd(y)o͞otik/ ▸*adj.* *formal* (of an area of study) serving as a preliminary instruction or as an introduction to further study. ▷late 18th cent.: from **PRO-**[2] 'before' + Greek *paideutikos* 'of or for teaching,' suggested by Greek *propaideuein* 'teach beforehand.' —**pro·pae·deu·ti·cal** *adj.*

prop·a·gan·da /,präpəˈgandə/ ▸*n.* **1** *chiefly derogatory* information, esp. of a biased or misleading nature, used to promote or publicize a particular political cause or point of view: *he was charged with distributing enemy propaganda.* ■ the dissemination of such information as a political strategy: *the party's leaders believed that a long period of education and propaganda would be necessary .* **2** (**Propaganda**) a committee of cardinals of the Roman Catholic Church responsible for foreign missions, founded in 1622 by Pope Gregory XV. ▷Italian, from modern Latin *congregatio de propaganda fide* 'congregation for propagation of the faith' (see sense 2). Sense 1 dates from the early 20th cent.

prop·a·gan·dist /,präpəˈgandist/ *chiefly derogatory* ▸*n.* a person who promotes or publicizes a particular organization or cause: *a highly persuasive political propagandist.*
▸*adj.* consisting of or spreading propaganda: *propagandist films.* —**prop·a·gan·dism** /-,dizəm/ *n.* —**prop·a·gan·dis·tic** /-,ganˈdistik/ *adj.* —**prop·a·gan·dis·ti·cal·ly** /-,ganˈdistik(ə)lē/ *adv.*

prop·a·gan·dize /,präpəˈgan,dīz/ ▸*v.* [*intrans.*] *chiefly derogatory* promote or publicize a particular cause, organization, or view, esp. in a biased or misleading way: *abolitionist leaders had not specifically* ***propagandized for*** *emancipation.* ■ [*trans.*] (often **be propagandized**) attempt to influence (someone) in such a way: *people who have to be emotionalized and propagandized by logical arguments.*

prop·a·gate /ˈpräpə,gāt/ ▸*v.* [*trans.*] **1** breed specimens of (a plant, animal, etc.) by natural processes from the parent stock: *try propagating your own houseplants from cuttings.* ■ [*intrans.*] (of a plant, animal, etc.) reproduce in such a way: *the plant propagates freely from stem cuttings.* ■ cause (something) to increase in number or amount: *operational error includes those errors propagated during the digitizing process.* **2** spread and promote (an idea, theory, knowledge, etc.) widely: *the French propagated the idea that the English were violent and gluttonous drunkards.* **3** [*trans.*] transmit (motion, light, sound, etc.) in a particular direction or through a medium: *electromagnetic effects can be propagated at a finite velocity only through material substances |* [as *adj.*] (**propagated**) *a propagated electrical signal.* ■ [*intrans.*] (of motion, light, sound, etc.) be transmitted or travel in such a way: *a hydraulic fracture is generally expected to propagate in a vertical plane.* ▷late Middle English: from Latin *propagat-* 'multiplied from layers or shoots,' from the verb *propagare*; related to *propago* 'young shoot' (from a base meaning 'fix'). —**prop·a·ga·tion** /,präpəˈgāsHən/ *n.* —**prop·a·ga·tive** /-,gātiv/ *adj.* —**prop·a·ga·tor** /-,gātər/ *n.*

prop·a·gule /ˈpräpə,gyo͞ol/ ▸*n.* *Botany* a vegetative structure that can become detached from a plant and give rise to a new plant, e.g., a bud, sucker, or spore. ▷mid 19th cent.: from modern Latin *propagulum* 'small shoot,' diminutive of *propago* 'shoot, runner.'

pro·pane /ˈprō,pān/ ▸*n.* *Chemistry* a flammable hydrocarbon gas of the alkane series, present in natural gas and used as bottled fuel. • Chem. formula: C_3H_8. ▷mid 19th cent.: from **PROPIONIC ACID** + **-ANE**[2].

pro·pa·nol /ˈprōpə,nôl; -,näl/ ▸*n.* *Chemistry* each of two isomeric liquid alcohols used as solvents; propyl alcohol. • Chem. formula: C_3H_7OH. ▷late 19th cent.: from **PROPANE** + **-OL**.

pro·pel /prəˈpel/ ▸*v.* (**-pelled**, **-pel·ling**) [*trans.*] drive, push, or cause to move in a particular direction, typically forward: *the boat is propelled by using a very long paddle |* [as *adj.* in *combination*] (**-propelled**) *a rocket-propelled grenade launcher.* ■ [*trans.*] *figurative* spur or drive into a particular situation: *fear propelled her out of her stillness.* ▷late Middle English (in the sense 'expel, drive out'): from Latin *propellere*, from *pro-* 'forward' + *pellere* 'to drive.'

pro·pel·lant /prəˈpelənt/ ▸*n.* a thing or substance that causes something to move or be driven forward or outward, in particular: ■ an inert fluid, liquefied under pressure, in which the active contents of an aerosol are dispersed. ■ an explosive that fires bullets from a firearm. ■ a substance used as a reagent in a rocket engine to provide thrust.
▸*adj.* another term for **PROPELLENT**. ▷mid 17th cent.: originally from Latin *propellent-* 'driving ahead (of oneself),' from the verb *propellere*, later from **PROPEL**.

pro·pel·lent /prəˈpelənt/ ▸*adj.* capable of driving, pushing, or moving something in a particular direction: *propellent gases.*

pro·pel·ler /prəˈpelər/ ▸*n.* a mechanical device for propelling a boat or aircraft, consisting of a revolving shaft with two or more broad, angled blades attached to it.

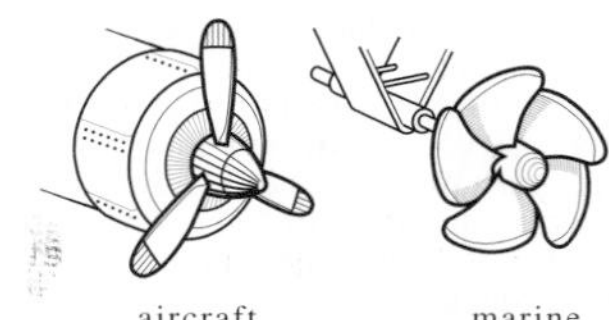

propellers

pro·pel·ler-head (also **pro·pel·ler head** or **pro·pel·ler·head**) ▸*n.* *informal* a person who has an obsessive interest in computers or technology. ▷1980s: probably with reference to a beanie hat with a propeller on top, popularized by science-fiction enthusiasts.

pro·pel·ler shaft ▸*n.* a shaft transmitting power from an engine to a propeller or to the wheels of a motor vehicle; drive shaft.

pro·pene /ˈprō,pēn/ ▸*n.* *Chemistry* another term for **PROPYLENE**. ▷mid 19th cent.: blend of **PROPANE** and **ALKENE**.

pro·pen·si·ty /prəˈpensətē/ ▸*n.* (*pl.* **-ties**) an inclination or natural tendency to behave in a particular way: ***a propensity for*** *violence |* [with *infinitive*] *their innate propensity to attack one another.* ▷late 16th cent.: from archaic *propense* (from Latin *propensus* 'inclined,' past participle of *propendere*, from *pro-* 'forward, down' + *pendere* 'hang') + **-ITY**.

prop·er /ˈpräpər/ ▸*adj.* **1** [*attrib.*] truly what something is said or regarded to be; genuine: *she's never had a proper job | a proper meal.* ■ [*postpositive*] strictly so called; in its true form: *some of the dos and don'ts in espionage proper.* ■ *informal chiefly Brit.* used as an intensifier, often in derogatory contexts: *she looked like a proper harlot.* **2** [*attrib.*] of the required type; suitable or appropriate: *an artist needs the proper tools.* ■ according to what is correct or prescribed for a particular situation or thing: *they had not followed the proper procedures.* See note at **FORMAL**. ■ according to or respecting recognized social standards or conventions; respectable, esp. excessively so: *her parents' view of what was* ***proper for*** *a well-bred girl | a very prim and proper Swiss lady.* **3** [*predic.*] (**proper to**) belonging or relating exclusively or distinctively to; particular to: *the two elephant types proper to Africa and to southern Asia.* ■ (of a psalm, lesson, prayer, etc.) appointed for a particular day, occasion, or season. ■ *archaic* belonging to oneself or itself; own: *to judge with my proper eyes.* **4** [usu. *postpositive*] *Heraldry* in the natural colors. **5** *archaic* (of a person) good-looking: *he is a proper youth!* **6** *Mathematics* denoting a subset or subgroup that does not constitute the entire set or group, esp. one that has more than one element.
▸*adv.* *Brit., informal dialect* satisfactorily or correctly: *my eyes were all blurry and I couldn't see proper.* ■ thoroughly: *I had been fooled* ***good and proper.***
▸*n.* the part of a church service that varies with the season or festival. ▷Middle English: from Old French *propre*, from Latin *proprius* 'one's own, special.' —**prop·er·ness** *n.*

prop·er ad·jec·tive ▸*n.* an adjective, typically capitalized, derived from a proper noun.

prop·er·din /prōˈpərdn/ ▸*n.* *Biochemistry* a protein present in the blood, involved in the body's response to certain kinds of infection. ▷1950s: from **PRO-**[2] 'before' + Latin *perdere* 'destroy' + **-IN**[1].

prop·er frac·tion ▸*n.* a fraction that is less than one, with the numerator less than the denominator.

prop·er·ly /ˈpräpərlē/ ▸*adv.* **1** correctly or satisfactorily: *ensuring the work is carried out properly | a properly drafted agreement.* ■ appropriately for the circumstances; suitably; respectably: *I'm trying to get my mother to behave properly.* ■ [*sentence adverb*] in the strict sense; exactly: *algebra is,* ***properly speaking,*** *the analysis of equations.* **2** [usu. as *submodifier*] *informal, chiefly Brit.* thoroughly; completely: *this is the first day she has felt properly well.*

prop·er mo·tion ▸*n.* *Astronomy* the part of the apparent motion of a fixed star that is due to its actual movement in space relative to the sun.

prop·er noun (also **proper name**) ▸*n.* a name used for an individual person, place, or organization, spelled with initial capital letters, e.g., *Larry, Mexico,* and *Boston Red Sox.* Often contrasted with **COMMON NOUN**.

prop·er·tied /ˈpräpərtēd/ ▸*adj.* (of a person or group) owning property and land, esp. in large amounts: *a propertied country gentleman.*

Pro·per·tius /prōˈpərsH(ē)əs/, Sextus (*c.*50–*c.*16 BC), Roman poet. His four books of elegies are largely concerned with his love affair with a woman whom he called Cynthia.

prop·er·ty /ˈpräpərtē/ ▸*n.* (*pl.* **-ties**) **1** a thing or things belonging to someone; possessions collectively: *she wanted Oliver and his property out of her house | the stolen property was not recovered.* ■ a building or buildings and the land belonging to it or them: *he's expanding now, buying property | the renovation of commercial properties.* ■ *Law* the right to the possession, use, or disposal of something; ownership: *rights of property.* ■ old-fashioned term for **PROP**[2]. **2** an attribute, quality, or characteristic of something: *the property of heat to expand metal at uniform rates.* ▷Middle English: from an Anglo-Norman French variant of Old French *propriete*, from Latin *proprietas*, from *proprius* 'one's own, particular' (see **PROPER**).

prop·er·ty man ▸*n.* *dated* a man in charge of theatrical props.

prop·er·ty mis·tress ▸*n.* *dated* a woman in charge of theatrical props.

prop·er·ty qual·i·fi·ca·tion ▸*n.* *chiefly historical* a qualification for office or for the exercise of a right, esp. the right to vote, based on the ownership of property.

pro·phage /ˈprō,fāj/ ▸*n.* *Microbiology* the genetic material of a bacteriophage, incorporated into the genome of a bacterium and able to produce phages if specifically activated. ▷1950s: from **PRO-**[2] 'before' + **PHAGE**.

pro·phase /ˈprō,fāz/ ▸*n.* *Biology* the first stage of cell division, before metaphase, during which the chromosomes become visible as paired chromatids and the nuclear envelope disappears. The first prophase of meiosis includes the reduction division. ▷late 19th cent.: from **PRO-**[2] 'before' + **PHASE**.

proph·e·cy /ˈpräfəsē/ ▸*n.* (*pl.* **-cies**) a prediction: *a bleak prophecy of war and ruin.* ■ the faculty, function, or practice of prophesying: *the gift of prophecy.* ▷Middle English: from Old French *profecie*, via late Latin from Greek *prophēteia*, from *prophētēs* (see **PROPHET**).

USAGE To avoid a common usage mistake, note the spelling and pronunciation differences between **prophecy** (the noun) and **prophesy** (the verb).

proph·e·sy /ˈpräfəˌsī/ ▸*v.* (**-sies, -sied**) [*trans.*] say that (a specified thing) will happen in the future: *Jacques was prophesying a bumper harvest* | [with *clause*] *the papers prophesied that he would resign after the weekend.* See note at **PREDICT.** ■ [*intrans.*] speak or write by divine inspiration; act as a prophet: *when a man prophesies, it is because the Spirit of the Lord comes upon him.* ▷Middle English: from Old French *profecier,* from *profecie* (see **PROPHECY**). The differentiation of the spellings *prophesy* and *prophecy* as verb and noun was not established until after 1700. **—proph·e·si·er** /-ˌsīər/ *n.*

USAGE See usage at **PROPHECY.**

proph·et /ˈpräfit/ ▸*n.* **1** a person regarded as an inspired teacher or proclaimer of the will of God: *the Old Testament prophet Jeremiah.* ■ (**the Prophet**) (among Muslims) Muhammad. ■ (**the Prophet**) (among Mormons) Joseph Smith or one of his successors. ■ a person who advocates or speaks in a visionary way about a new belief, cause, or theory: *he was a prophet of revolutionary socialism.* ■ a person who makes or claims to be able to make predictions: *the anti-technology* ***prophets of doom.*** **2** (**the Prophets**) the prophetic writings of the Old Testament or Hebrew scriptures, in particular: ■ (in Christian use) the books of Isaiah, Jeremiah, Ezekiel, Daniel, and the twelve minor prophets. ■ (in Jewish use) one of the three canonical divisions of the Hebrew Bible, distinguished from the Law and the Hagiographa, and comprising the books of Joshua, Judges, Samuel, Kings, Jeremiah, Ezekiel, Isaiah, and the twelve minor prophets. ▷Middle English: from Old French *prophete,* via Latin from Greek *prophētēs* 'spokesman,' from *pro* 'before' + *phētēs* 'speaker' (from *phēnai* 'speak'). **—proph·et·hood** /-ˌho͝od/ *n.*

▸*PHRASE* □ **a prophet is not without honor, but** (or **save**) **in his own country** *proverb* a person's gifts and talents are rarely appreciated by those close to him. [with biblical allusion to Matt. 13:57.]

proph·et·ess /ˈpräfətəs/ ▸*n.* a female prophet.

pro·phet·ic /prəˈfetik/ ▸*adj.* **1** accurately describing or predicting what will happen in the future: *his warnings proved prophetic.* **2** of, relating to, or characteristic of a prophet or prophecy: *the prophetic books of the Old Testament.* ▷late 15th cent.: from French *prophétique* or late Latin *propheticus,* from Greek *prophētikos* 'predicting' (see **PROPHET**). **—pro·phet·i·cal** *adj.* **—pro·phet·i·cal·ly** /-ik(ə)lē/ *adv.*

pro·phy·lac·tic /ˌprōfəˈlaktik/ ▸*adj.* intended to prevent disease: *prophylactic measures.*

▸*n.* a medicine or course of action used to prevent disease: *I took malaria prophylactics.* ■ a condom. ▷late 16th cent.: from French *prophylactique,* from Greek *prophulaktikos,* from *pro* 'before' + *phulassein* 'to guard.' **—pro·phy·lac·ti·cal·ly** /-ik(ə)lē/ *adv.*

pro·phy·lax·is /ˌprōfəˈlaksəs/ ▸*n.* action taken to prevent disease, esp. by specified means or against a specified disease: *the treatment and prophylaxis of angina pectoris.* ▷mid 19th cent.: modern Latin, from **PRO-**[2] 'before' + Greek *phulaxis* 'act of guarding.'

pro·pin·qui·ty /prəˈpiNGkwətē/ ▸*n.* **1** the state of being close to someone or something; proximity: *he kept his distance as though afraid propinquity might lead him into temptation.* **2** *technical* close kinship. ▷late Middle English: from Old French *propinquité,* from Latin *propinquitas,* from *propinquus* 'near,' from *prope* 'near to.'

pro·pi·on·i·bac·te·ri·um /ˌprōpēˌänəˌbakˈti(ə)rēəm/ ▸*n.* (*pl.* **-te·ri·a** /-ˈti(ə)rēə/) a bacterium that metabolizes carbohydrate, some kinds being involved in the fermentation of dairy products and the etiology of acne. • Genus *Propionibacterium;* Gram-positive rods. ▷modern Latin, from *propionic* (see **PROPIONIC ACID**) + **BACTERIUM.**

pro·pi·on·ic ac·id /ˌprōpēˈänik/ ▸*n.* *Chemistry* a colorless pungent liquid organic acid produced in some forms of fermentation and used for inhibiting the growth of mold in bread. • Alternative name: **propanoic acid**; chem. formula: C_2H_5COOH. ▷mid 19th cent.: *propionic* from French *propionique,* from Greek *pro* 'before' + *piōn* 'fat,' it being the first or lowest molecular-weight member of the fatty acid series to form fats. **—pro·pi·o·nate** /ˈprōpēəˌnāt/ *n.*

pro·pi·ti·ate /prəˈpishēˌāt/ ▸*v.* [*trans.*] win or regain the favor of (a god, spirit, or person) by doing something that pleases them: *the pagans thought it was important to propitiate the gods with sacrifices.* See note at **PACIFY.** ▷late 16th cent.: from Latin *propitiat-* 'made favorable,' from the verb *propitiare,* from *propitius* 'favorable, gracious' (see **PROPITIOUS**). **—pro·pi·ti·a·tor** /-ˌātər/ *n.* **—pro·pi·ti·a·to·ry** /-ˈpishēəˌtôrē/ *adj.*

pro·pi·ti·a·tion /prəˌpishēˈāshən/ ▸*n.* the action of propitiating or appeasing a god, spirit, or person: *he lifted his hands in propitiation.* ■ atonement, esp. that of Jesus Christ. ▷late Middle English: from late Latin *propitiatio(n-),* from the verb *propitiare* (see **PROPITIATE**).

pro·pi·tious /prəˈpishəs/ ▸*adj.* giving or indicating a good chance of success; favorable: *the timing for such a meeting seemed propitious.* See note at **TIMELY.** ■ *archaic* favorably disposed toward someone: *there were points on which they did not agree, moments in which she did not seem propitious.* ▷late Middle English: from Old French *propicieus* or Latin *propitius* 'favorable, gracious.' **—pro·pi·tious·ly** *adv.* **—pro·pi·tious·ness** *n.*

prop jet ▸*n.* a turboprop aircraft or engine.

prop·o·lis /ˈpräpələs/ ▸*n.* a red or brown resinous substance collected by honeybees from tree buds, used by them to fill crevices and to seal and varnish honeycombs. ▷early 17th cent.: via Latin from Greek *propolis* 'suburb,' also 'bee glue,' from *pro* 'before' + *polis* 'city.'

pro·po·nent /prəˈpōnənt/ ▸*n.* a person who advocates a theory, proposal, or project: *a collection of essays by both critics and proponents of graphology.* ▷late 16th cent.: from Latin *proponent-* 'putting forth,' from the verb *proponere* (see **PROPOUND**).

Pro·pon·tis /prəˈpäntəs/ ancient name for the Sea of Marmara (see **MARMARA, SEA OF**). ▷from Latin, from Greek *pro-* 'before' + *Pontos* 'Black Sea.'

pro·por·tion /prəˈpôrshən/ ▸*n.* a part, share, or number considered in comparative relation to a whole: *the proportion of greenhouse gases in the atmosphere is rising.* ■ the relationship of one thing to another in terms of quantity, size, or number; the ratio: *the* ***proportion of*** *exams* ***to*** *schoolwork* | *the bleach can be diluted with water in the proportion one part bleach to ten parts water.* ■ (**proportions**) the comparative measurements or size of different parts of a whole: *the view of what constitutes perfect bodily proportions changes from one generation to the next.* ■ (**proportions**) dimensions; size: *the room, despite its ample proportions, seemed too small for him.* ■ the correct, attractive, or ideal relationship in size or shape between one thing and another or between the parts of a whole: *perceptions of color, form, harmony, and proportion.*

▸*v.* [*trans.*] *formal* adjust or regulate (something) so that it has a particular or suitable relationship to something else: *a life after death in which happiness can be* ***proportioned to*** *virtue.* ▷late Middle English: from Old French, from Latin *proportio(n-),* from *pro portione* 'with respect to (its or a person's) share.' **—pro·por·tion·less** *adj.*

▸*PHRASES* □ **in proportion** according to a particular relationship in size, amount, or degree: *each region was represented* ***in proportion to*** *its population.* ■ in comparison with; in relation to: *the cuckoo's eggs are unusually small* ***in proportion to*** *its size.* ■ in the correct or appropriate relation to the size, shape, or position of other things: *her figure was completely in proportion.* ■ correctly or realistically regarded in terms of relative importance or seriousness: *the problem has to be* ***kept in proportion.*** □ **out of proportion** in the wrong relation to the size, shape, or position of other things: *the sculpture seemed* ***out of proportion to*** *its surroundings.* ■ greater or more serious than is necessary or appropriate: *the award was* ***out of all proportion to*** *the alleged libel.* ■ wrongly or unrealistically regarded in terms of relative importance or seriousness. □ **sense of proportion** the ability to judge the relative importance or seriousness of things.

pro·por·tion·a·ble /prəˈpôrshənəbəl/ ▸*adj.* archaic term for **PROPORTIONAL.** **—pro·por·tion·a·bly** /-blē/ *adv.*

pro·por·tion·al /prəˈpôrshənl/ ▸*adj.* corresponding in size or amount to something else: *the punishment should be* ***proportional to*** *the crime.* ■ *Mathematics* (of a variable quantity) having a constant ratio to another quantity. ▷late Middle English: from late Latin *proportionalis,* from *proportio(n-)* (see **PROPORTION**). **—pro·por·tion·al·i·ty** /prəˌpôrshəˈnalətē; pərˌpôrshəˈnalədē/ *n.* **—pro·por·tion·al·ly** /-shənl-ē/ *adv.*

USAGE Except in certain long-established phrases, such as *proportional representation,* the adjectives **proportional** and **proportionate** may be used interchangeably.

pro·por·tion·al count·er ▸*n.* *Physics* an ionization chamber in which the operating voltage is large enough to produce amplification but not so large that the output pulse ceases to be proportional to the initial ionization.

pro·por·tion·al rep·re·sen·ta·tion (abbr.: **PR**) ▸*n.* an electoral system in which parties gain seats in proportion to the number of votes cast for them.

pro·por·tion·ate /prəˈpôrshənət/ ▸*adj.* another term for **PROPORTIONAL.** **—pro·por·tion·ate·ly** *adv.*

USAGE See usage at **PROPORTIONAL.**

pro·por·tioned /prəˈpôrshənd/ ▸*adj.* [with *submodifier*] having dimensions or a comparative relationship of parts of a specified type: *she was tall and perfectly proportioned.*

pro·pos·al /prəˈpōzəl/ ▸*n.* **1** a plan or suggestion, esp. a formal or written one, put forward for consideration or discussion by others: *a set of* ***proposals for*** *a major new high-speed rail link.* ■ the action of putting forward such a plan or suggestion: *the proposal of flexible work hours.* **2** an offer of marriage.

P

pro·pose /prəˈpōz/ ▸*v.* **1** [*trans.*] put forward (an idea or plan) for consideration or discussion by others: *he proposed a new nine-point peace plan* | [with *infinitive*] *we propose to be away for six months* | [with *clause*] *I proposed that the government should retain a 51 percent stake in the company.* See note at **INTEND.** ■ nominate (someone) for an elected office or as a member of a society: *Thomson was proposed as chairman.* ■ put forward (a motion) to a legislature or committee: *the government put its slim majority to the test by proposing a vote of confidence.* **2** [*intrans.*] make an offer of marriage to someone: *I have already* ***proposed to*** *Sarah.* ▷Middle English: from Old French *proposer,* from Latin *proponere* (see **PROPONENT**), but influenced by Latin *propositus* 'put or set forth' and Old French *poser* 'to place.' **—pro·pos·er** *n.*

▸*PHRASES* □ **propose marriage** make an offer of marriage to someone. □ **propose a toast** ask a group of people at a social occasion to drink to the health and happiness of a specified person: *I hereby* ***propose a toast to*** *the bride and groom.*

prop·o·si·tion /ˌpräpəˈzishən/ ▸*n.* **1** a statement or assertion that expresses a judgment or opinion: *the proposition that all men are created equal.* ■ *Logic* a statement that expresses a concept that can be true or false. ■ *Mathematics* a formal statement of a theorem or problem, typically including the demonstration. **2** a suggested scheme or plan of action, esp. in a business context: *a detailed investment proposition.* ■ (in the U.S.) a constitutional proposal; a bill. ■ *informal* an offer of sexual intercourse made to a person with whom one is not sexually involved, esp. one that is made in an unsubtle or offensive way. **3** [with *adj.*] a project, task, or idea considered in terms of its likely success or difficulty, esp. in a commercial context: *a paper that has lost half its readers is unlikely to be an attractive proposition.* ■ a person considered in terms of the likely success or difficulty of one's dealings with them: *as a potential manager, Sandy is a better proposition than Dave.*

▸*v.* [*trans.*] *informal* make a suggestion of sexual intercourse to (someone with whom one is not sexually involved), esp. in an unsubtle or offensive way: *she had been propositioned at the party by an accountant.* ■ make an offer or suggestion to (someone): *I was propositioned by the editor about becoming film critic of the paper.* ▷Middle English: from Old French, from Latin *propositio(n-),* from the verb *proponere* (see **PROPOUND**). The verb dates from the 1920s. **—prop·o·si·tion·al** /-shənl/ *adj.* (*chiefly Logic*).

prop·o·si·tion·al cal·cu·lus ▸*n.* the branch of symbolic logic that deals with propositions and the relations between them, without examination of their content.

pro·pound /prəˈpound/ ▸*v.* [*trans.*] put forward (an idea, theory, or point of view) for consideration by others: *he began to propound the idea of a "social monarchy" as an alternative to Franco.* ▷mid 16th cent.: alteration of archaic *propone,* from Latin *proponere* 'set forth,' from *pro-* 'forward' + *ponere* 'put.' The addition of the final *-d* can be compared with that in *expound* and *compound.* **—pro·pound·er** *n.*

pro·pox·y·phene /prōˈpäksəˌfēn/ ▸*n.* *Medicine* a synthetic compound chemically related to methadone, used as a mild narcotic analgesic. ▷1950s: from **PROPYL** + **OXY-**[2] + *-phene* (from **PHENYL**).

propr. ▸*abbr.* proprietor.

pro·pran·o·lol /prōˈpranlˌôl; -ˌäl/ ▸*n.* *Medicine* a synthetic compound that acts as a beta blocker and is used mainly in the treatment of cardiac arrhythmia.

• Chem. formula: $C_{16}H_{21}NO_2$ ▷1960s: from *pro(pyl)* + *pr(op)anol*, with the reduplication of *-ol*.

pro·pri·e·tar·y /p(r)ə'prī-i,terē/ ▸*adj.* of or relating to an owner or ownership: *the company has a proprietary right to the property.* ■ (of a product) marketed under and protected by a registered trade name: *proprietary brands of insecticide.* ■ behaving as if one were the owner of someone or something: *he looked about him with a proprietary air.*
▸*n.* an owner; proprietor. ■ *historical* esp. in North America, a grantee or owner of a colony who has been granted, as an individual or as part of a group, the full rights of self-government. ▷late Middle English (as a noun denoting a member of a religious order who held property): from late Latin *proprietarius* 'proprietor,' from *proprietas* (see PROPERTY).

pro·pri·e·tar·y name ▸*n.* a name of a product or service registered by its owner as a trademark and not usable by others without permission.

pro·pri·e·tor /p(r)ə'prīətər/ ▸*n.* the owner of a business. ■ a holder of property. **—pro·pri·e·to·ri·al** /p(r)ə,prīə'tôrēəl/ *adj.* **—pro·pri·e·to·ri·al·ly** /p(r)ə,prīə'tôrēəlē/ *adv.* **—pro·pri·e·tor·ship** /-,SHip/ *n.*

pro·pri·e·tress /p(r)ə'prīətrəs/ ▸*n.* a female proprietor.

pro·pri·e·ty /p(r)ə'prīətē/ ▸*n.* (*pl.* **-ties**) the state or quality of conforming to conventionally accepted standards of behavior or morals: *he always behaved with the utmost propriety.* ■ (**proprieties**) the details or rules of behavior conventionally considered to be correct: *she's a great one for the proprieties.* ■ the condition of being right, appropriate, or fitting: *they questioned the propriety of certain investments made by the council.* ▷late Middle English (in the sense 'peculiarity, essential quality'): from Old French *propriete*, from Latin *proprietas* (see PROPERTY).

pro·pri·o·cep·tive /,prōprēə'septiv/ ▸*adj. Physiology* relating to stimuli that are produced and perceived within an organism, esp. those connected with the position and movement of the body. Compare with EXTEROCEPTIVE and INTEROCEPTIVE. ▷early 20th cent.: from Latin *proprius* 'own' + RECEPTIVE. **—pro·pri·o·cep·tion** /-'sepSHən/ *n.* **—pro·pri·o·cep·tive·ly** *adv.*

pro·pri·o·cep·tor /,prōprēə'septər/ ▸*n. Physiology* a sensory receptor that receives stimuli from within the body, esp. one that responds to position and movement. ▷early 20th cent.: from Latin *proprius* 'own' + RECEPTOR.

props /präps/ ▸*plural n. informal* respect or credit due to a person: *Erika gets props for the great work she did on the music.*

prop·to·sis /präp'tōsəs/ ▸*n. Medicine* abnormal protrusion or displacement of an eye or other body part. ▷late 17th cent.: via late Latin from Greek *proptōsis*, from *pro* 'before' + *piptein* 'to fall.'

pro·pul·sion /prə'pəlSHən/ ▸*n.* the action of driving or pushing forward: *they dive and use their wings for propulsion under water.* ▷early 17th cent. (in the sense 'expulsion'): from medieval Latin *propulsio(n-)*, from Latin *propellere* 'drive before (oneself).' **—pro·pul·sive** /-siv/ *adj.*

prop wash ▸*n.* a current of water or air created by the action of a propeller or rotor.

pro·pyl /'prōpəl/ ▸*n.* [as *adj.*] *Chemistry* of or denoting the alkyl radical $-C_3H_7$, derived notionally from propane. Compare with ISOPROPYL.

prop·y·la /'präpələ/ ▸ plural form of PROPYLON.

prop·y·lae·um /,präpə'lēəm; ,prō-/ ▸*n.* (*pl.* **-lae·a** /-'lēə/) the structure forming the entrance to a temple. ■ (**the Propylaeum**) the entrance to the Acropolis at Athens. ▷via Latin from Greek *propulaion*, neuter (used as a noun) of *propulaios* 'before the gate,' from *pro* 'before' + *pulē* 'gate.'

pro·pyl·ene /'prōpə,lēn/ ▸*n. Chemistry* a gaseous hydrocarbon of the alkene series, made by cracking alkanes. • Alternative name: **propene**; chem. formula: C_3H_6.

pro·pyl·ene gly·col ▸*n. Chemistry* a liquid alcohol that is used as a solvent, in antifreeze, and in the food, plastics, and perfume industries. • Chem. formula: $C_3H_6(OH)_2$: two isomers.

prop·y·lon /'präpə,län/ ▸*n.* (*pl.* **-lons** or **-la** /-lə/) another term for PROPYLAEUM. ▷mid 19th cent.: via Latin from Greek *propulon*, from *pro* 'before' + *pulē* 'gate.'

pro ra·ta /prō 'rātə; 'rätə; 'ratə/ ▸*adj.* proportional: *as the dollar has fallen, costs have risen on a pro rata basis* | *pro-rata ownership.*
▸*adv.* proportionally: *their fees will rise pro rata with salaries.* ▷late 16th cent.: Latin, literally 'according to the rate.'

pro·rate /prō'rāt; 'prō,rāt/ ▸*v.* [*trans.*] (usu. **be prorated**) allocate, distribute, or assess pro rata: *bonuses are prorated over the life of a player's contract.* **—pro·ra·tion** /prō'rāSHən/ *n.*

pro·rogue /p(r)ə'rōg/ ▸*v.* (**-rogues, -rogued, -rogu·ing**) [*trans.*] discontinue a session of (a parliament or other legislative assembly) without dissolving it: *James prorogued Parliament in 1685 and ruled without it.* ■ [*intrans.*] (of such an assembly) be discontinued in this way: *the House was all set to prorogue.* ▷late Middle English: from Old French *proroger*, from Latin *prorogare* 'prolong, extend,' from *pro-* 'in front of, publicly' + *rogare* 'ask.' **—pro·ro·ga·tion** /,prōrə'gāSHən/ *n.*

pros. ▸*abbr.* ■ proscenium. ■ prosody.

pro·sa·ic /prō'zāik/ ▸*adj.* having the style or diction of prose; lacking poetic beauty: *prosaic language can't convey the experience.* ■ commonplace; unromantic: *the masses were too preoccupied by prosaic day-to-day concerns.* ▷late 16th cent. (as a noun denoting a prose writer): from late Latin *prosaicus*, from Latin *prosa* 'straightforward (discourse)' (see PROSE). Current senses of the adjective date from the mid 18th cent. **—pro·sa·i·cal·ly** /-ik(ə)lē/ *adv.* **—pro·sa·ic·ness** *n.*

Pros. Atty. ▸*abbr.* prosecuting attorney.

pro·sau·ro·pod /prō'sôrə,päd/ ▸*n.* an elongated, partly bipedal herbivorous dinosaur of the late Triassic and early Jurassic periods, related to the ancestors of sauropods. • Infraorder Prosauropoda, suborder Sauropodomorpha, order Saurischia. ▷1950s: from PRO-[2] 'before in time' + SAUROPOD.

pro·sce·ni·um /prə'sēnēəm; prō-/ ▸*n.* (*pl.* **-ni·ums** or **-ni·a** /-nēə/) the part of a theater stage in front of the curtain. ■ short for PROSCENIUM ARCH. ■ the stage of an ancient theater. ▷early 17th cent.: via Latin from Greek *proskēnion*, from *pro* 'before' + *skēnē* 'stage.'

pro·sce·ni·um arch ▸*n.* an arch framing the opening between the stage and the auditorium in some theaters.

pro·sciut·to /prə'SHōōtō/ ▸*n.* Italian ham cured by drying and typically served in very thin slices. ▷Italian.

pro·scribe /prō'skrīb/ ▸*v.* [*trans.*] forbid, esp. by law: *strikes remained proscribed in the armed forces.* ■ denounce or condemn: *certain practices which the Catholic Church proscribed, such as polygyny.* ■ *historical* outlaw (someone). ▷late Middle English (in the sense 'to outlaw'): from Latin *proscribere*, from *pro-* 'in front of' + *scribere* 'write.' **—pro·scrip·tion** /-'skripSHən/ *n.* **—pro·scrip·tive** /-'skriptiv/ *adj.*

USAGE **Proscribe** does not have the same meaning as **prescribe**: see **usage** at PRESCRIBE.

prose /prōz/ ▸*n.* **1** written or spoken language in its ordinary form, without metrical structure: *a short story in prose* | [as *adj.*] *a prose passage.* ■ *figurative* plain or dull writing, discourse, or expression: *medical and scientific prose.* **2** another term for SEQUENCE (sense 4).
▸*v.* **1** [*intrans.*] talk tediously: *prosing on about female beauty.* **2** [*trans.*] *dated* compose or convert into prose. ▷Middle English: via Old French from Latin *prosa (oratio)* 'straightforward (discourse),' feminine of *prosus*, earlier *prorsus* 'direct.' **—pros·er** *n.*

pro·sec·tor /prō'sektər/ ▸*n.* a person who dissects corpses for examination or anatomical demonstration. ▷mid 19th cent.: from late Latin, literally 'anatomist,' based on Latin *secare* 'to cut,' perhaps via French *prosecteur*.

pros·e·cute /'präsi,kyōōt/ ▸*v.* [*trans.*] **1** institute legal proceedings against (a person or organization): *they were prosecuted for obstructing the highway.* ■ institute legal proceedings in respect of (a claim or offense): *the state's attorney's office seemed to decide that this was a case worth prosecuting* | [*intrans.*] *the company didn't prosecute because of his age.* ■ [*intrans.*] (of a lawyer) conduct the case against the party being accused or sued in a lawsuit: *Mr. Ryan will be prosecuting this morning.* **2** continue with (a course of action) with a view to its completion: *a serious threat to the government's ability to prosecute the war.* ■ *archaic* carry on (a trade or pursuit): *waiting for permission to prosecute my craft.* ▷late Middle English (sense 2): from Latin *prosecut-* 'pursued, accompanied,' from the verb *prosequi*, from *pro-* 'onward' + *sequi* 'follow.' **—pros·e·cut·a·ble** *adj.*

pros·e·cu·tion /,präsi'kyōōSHən/ ▸*n.* **1** the institution and conducting of legal proceedings against someone in respect of a criminal charge: *Olesky faces prosecution on charges he spied for Russian intelligence* | *they lacked the funds to embark on private prosecutions.* ■ (**the prosecution**) [treated as *sing.* or *pl.*] the party instituting or conducting legal proceedings against someone in a lawsuit: *the main witness for the prosecution.* **2** the continuation of a course of action with a view to its completion: *the network's prosecution of its commercial ends.* ▷mid 16th cent. (sense 2): from Old French, or from late Latin *prosecutio(n-)*, from *prosequi* 'pursue, accompany' (see PROSECUTE).

pros·e·cu·tor /'präsi,kyōōtər/ ▸*n.* a person, esp. a public official, who institutes legal proceedings against someone. ■ a lawyer who conducts the case against a defendant in a criminal court. Also called **prosecuting attorney**. **—pros·e·cu·to·ri·al** /,präsikyə'tôrēəl/ *adj.*

pros·e·lyte /'präsə,līt/ ▸*n.* a person who has converted from one opinion, religion, or party to another, esp. recently. ■ a Gentile who has converted to Judaism.
▸*v.* another term for PROSELYTIZE. ▷late Middle English: via late Latin from Greek *prosēluthos* 'stranger, convert,' from *prosēluth-*, past stem of *proserkhesthai* 'approach.' **—pros·e·lyt·ism** /-lə,tizəm/ *n.*

pros·e·lyt·ize /'präsələ,tīz/ ▸*v.* [*trans.*] convert or attempt to convert (someone) from one religion, belief, or opinion to another: *the program did have a tremendous evangelical effect, proselytizing many* | [*intrans.*] *proselytizing for converts* | [as *n.*] (**proselytizing**) *no amount of proselytizing was going to change their minds.* ■ advocate or promote (a belief or course of action): *Davis wanted to share his concept and proselytize his ideas.* **—pros·e·lyt·iz·er** *n.*

pro·sem·i·nar /prō'semə,när/ ▸*n.* a seminar that accepts graduate and advanced undergraduate students alike.

pros·en·ceph·a·lon /,präs,en'sefə,län; -lən/ ▸*n.* another term for FOREBRAIN. ▷mid 19th cent.: from Greek *prosō* 'forward' + *enkephalos* 'brain.'

pros·en·chy·ma /präs'eNGkəmə/ ▸*n. Biology* a plant tissue consisting of elongated cells with interpenetrating tapering ends, occurring esp. in vascular tissue. ▷mid 19th cent.: from Greek *pros* 'toward' + *enkhuma* 'infusion,' on the pattern of *parenchyma.* **—pros·en·chym·a·tous** /,präsən'kimətəs/ *adj.*

prose po·em ▸*n.* a piece of writing in prose having obvious poetic qualities, including intensity, compactness, prominent rhythms, and imagery. **—prose po·et·ry** *n.*

Pro·ser·pi·na /prə'sərpənə/ (also **Pro·ser·pi·ne** /-pənē/) *Roman Mythology* Roman name for PERSEPHONE.

pro shop ▸*n.* a retail outlet at a golf club, typically run by the resident professional, where golfing equipment is sold or repaired.

pro·sim·i·an /prō'simēən/ *Zoology* ▸*n.* a primitive primate of a group that includes the lemurs, lorises, bush babies, and tarsiers. • Suborder Prosimii, order Primates: several families.
▸*adj.* of or relating to the prosimians. Compare with SIMIAN. ▷late 19th cent.: from PRO-[2] 'before' + SIMIAN.

pro·sit /'prōzət; -sət/ ▸*exclam.* an expression used as a toast when drinking to a person's health. ▷German, from Latin, literally 'may it benefit.'

Pros·o·bran·chi·a /,präsə'braNGkēə/ *Zoology* a group of mollusks that includes the limpets, abalones, and many terrestrial and aquatic snails. They all have a shell, and many have an operculum. • Subclass Prosobranchia, class Gastropoda. ▷modern Latin (plural), from Greek *prosō* 'forward' + *brankhia* 'gills.' **—pros·o·branch** /'präsə,braNGk/ *n.*

pro·so·cial /prō'sōSHəl/ ▸*adj. Psychology* relating to or denoting behavior that is positive, helpful, and intended to promote social acceptance and friendship.

pro·sod·ic a·nal·y·sis /prə'sädik; -'zädik/ ▸*n. Linguistics* analysis of a language based on its patterns of stress and intonation in various contexts.

pros·o·dy /'präsədē/ ▸*n.* the patterns of rhythm and sound used in poetry: *the translator is not obliged to reproduce the prosody of the original.* ■ the theory or study of these patterns, or the rules governing them. ■ the patterns of stress and intonation in a language: *the salience of prosody in child language acquisition* | *early English prosodies.* ▷late 15th cent.: from Latin *prosodia* 'accent of a syllable,' from Greek *prosōidia* 'song sung to music, tone of a syllable,' from *pros* 'toward' + *ōidē* 'song.' **—pro·sod·ic** /prə'sädik; -zädik/ or **pro·sod·i·cal** /prə'sädikəl; -'zäd-/ *adj.* **—pros·o·dist** /'präsədist; 'präz-/ *n.*

pro·so·ma /prō'sōmə/ ▸*n.* (*pl.* **-mas** or **-ma·ta** /-mətə/) another term for CEPHALOTHORAX. ▷late 19th cent.: from PRO-[2] 'before' + Greek *sōma* 'body.'

pros·o·pag·no·sia /,präsəpag'nōZH(ē)ə/ ▸*n. Psychiatry*

an inability to recognize the faces of familiar people, typically as a result of damage to the brain. ▷1950s: modern Latin, from Greek *prosōpon* 'face' + *agnōsia* 'ignorance.' —**pros·o·pag·nos·ic** /-'nōzik; -'nōsik/ *n.*

pros·o·pog·ra·phy /,präsə'pägrəfē/ ▶*n.* (*pl.* **-phies**) a description of a person's social and family connections, career, etc., or a collection of such descriptions. ■ the study of such descriptions, esp. in Roman history. ▷1920s: from modern Latin *prosopographia*, from Greek *prosōpon* 'face, person' + *-graphia* 'writing.' —**pros·o·pog·ra·pher** /-fər/ *n.* —**pros·o·po·graph·i·cal** /-pə'grafikəl/ *adj.*

pro·so·po·poe·ia /prə,sōpə'pēə; ,präsə-/ ▶*n.* **1** a figure of speech in which an abstract thing is personified. **2** a figure of speech in which an imagined or absent person or thing is represented as speaking. ▷mid 16th cent.: via Latin from Greek *prosōpopoiia*, from *prosōpon* 'person' + *poiein* 'to make.'

pros·pect /'präs,pekt/ ▶*n.* **1** the possibility or likelihood of some future event occurring: *there was no prospect of a reconciliation | training that offered a prospect of continuous employment.* ■ [in *sing.*] a mental picture of a future or anticipated event: *this presents a disturbing prospect of one-party government.* ■ (usu. **prospects**) chances or opportunities for success or wealth: *the poor prospects for the steel industry.* **2** a person regarded as a potential customer or subscriber to something: *clients deemed likely prospects for active party membership.* ■ a person regarded as likely to succeed, esp. in a sporting event: *a great young pitching prospect.* ■ a place likely to yield mineral deposits. ■ a place being explored for mineral deposits. **3** an extensive view of landscape: *a viewpoint commanding a magnificent prospect of the estuary.*
▶*v.* [*intrans.*] search for mineral deposits in a place, esp. by means of experimental drilling and excavation: *the company is also* **prospecting for** *gold.* ■ (**prospect for**) *figurative* look out for; search for: *the responsibilities of salespeople to prospect for customers.* ▷late Middle English (as a noun denoting the action of looking toward a distant object): from Latin *prospectus* 'view,' from *prospicere* 'look forward,' from *pro-* 'forward' + *specere* 'to look.' Early use, referring to a view of landscape, gave rise to the meaning 'mental picture' (mid 16th cent.), whence 'anticipated event.' —**pros·pec·tor** /-tər/ *n.*

pro·spec·tive /prə'spektiv/ ▶*adj.* [*attrib.*] (of a person) expected or expecting to be something particular in the future: *she showed a prospective buyer around the house.* ■ likely to happen at a future date; concerned with or applying to the future: *a meeting to discuss prospective changes in government legislation.* ▷late 16th cent. (in the sense 'looking forward, having foresight'): from obsolete French *prospectif, -ive* or late Latin *prospectivus*, from Latin *prospectus* 'view' (see **PROSPECT**). —**pro·spec·tive·ly** *adv.* —**pro·spec·tive·ness** *n.*

pro·spec·tus /prə'spektəs/ ▶*n.* (*pl.* **-tus·es**) a printed document that advertises or describes a school, commercial enterprise, forthcoming book, etc., in order to attract or inform clients, members, buyers, or investors. ▷mid 18th cent.: from Latin, literally 'view, prospect,' from the verb *prospicere*, from *pro-* 'forward' + *specere* 'to look.'

pros·per /'präspər/ ▶*v.* [*intrans.*] succeed in material terms; be financially successful: *his business prospered | the nation plans to prosper from free trade with the U.S.* ■ flourish physically; grow strong and healthy: *areas where gray squirrels cannot prosper.* ■ [*trans.*] *archaic* make successful: *God has wonderfully prospered this nation.* ▷late Middle English: from Old French *prosperer*, from Latin *prosperare*, from *prosperus* 'doing well.'

pros·per·i·ty /prä'sperité/ ▶*n.* the state of being prosperous: *a long period of prosperity.* ▷Middle English: from Old French *prosperite*, from Latin *prosperitas*, from *prosperus* 'doing well.'

pros·per·ous /'präspərəs/ ▶*adj.* successful in material terms; flourishing financially: *prosperous middle-class professionals.* See note at **WEALTHY**. ■ bringing wealth and success: *we wish you a prosperous New Year.* ▷late Middle English: from Old French *prospereus*, from Latin *prosperus* 'doing well.' —**pros·per·ous·ly** *adv.* —**pros·per·ous·ness** *n.*

Prost /prôst/, Alain (1955–), French race car driver. He won the Formula One world championship in 1985, 1986, 1989, and 1993.

pros·ta·cy·clin /,prästə'sīklin/ ▶*n.* *Biochemistry* a compound of the prostaglandin type that is produced in arterial walls and that functions as an anticoagulant and vasodilator. ▷1970s: from **PROSTAGLANDIN** + **CYCLIC** + **-IN**[1].

pros·ta·glan·din /,prästə'glandin/ ▶*n.* *Biochemistry* any of a group of cyclic fatty acid compounds with varying hormonelike effects, notably the promotion of uterine contractions. ▷1930s: from **PROSTATE** + **GLAND**[1] + **-IN**[1].

pros·tate /'präs,tāt/ (also **prostate gland**) ▶*n.* a gland surrounding the neck of the bladder in male mammals and releasing prostatic fluid. ▷mid 17th cent.: via French from modern Latin *prostata*, from Greek *prostatēs* 'one that stands before,' from *pro* 'before' + *statos* 'standing.' —**pros·tat·ic** /prä'statik/ *adj.*

pros·ta·tec·to·my /,prästə'tektəmē/ ▶*n.* (*pl.* **-mies**) a surgical operation to remove all or part of the prostate gland.

pros·tate-spe·cif·ic an·ti·gen (abbr.: **PSA**) ▶*n.* *Medicine* an antigenic enzyme released by the prostate and found in abnormally high concentrations in the blood of men with prostate cancer.

prostatic fluid ▶*n.* *Medicine* an alkaline fluid secreted by the prostate gland during ejaculation that forms part of the semen.

pros·ta·ti·tis /,prästə'tītəs/ ▶*n.* *Medicine* inflammation of the prostate gland.

pros·the·sis /präs'THēsis/ ▶*n.* (*pl.* **-ses** /-sēz/) **1** an artificial body part, such as a leg, a heart, or a breast implant: *his upper jaw was removed and a prosthesis was fitted.* **2** (also **prothesis**) the addition of a letter or syllable at the beginning of a word, as in Spanish *escribo* derived from Latin *scribo*. ▷mid 16th cent. (sense 2): via late Latin from Greek, from *prostithenai*, from *pros* 'in addition' + *tithenai* 'to place.' —**pros·thet·ic** /-'THetik/ *adj.* —**pros·thet·i·cal·ly** /-'THetik(ə)lē/ *adv.*

pros·thet·ic group ▶*n.* *Biochemistry* a nonprotein group forming part of or combined with a protein.

pros·thet·ics /präs'THetiks/ ▶*plural n.* artificial body parts; prostheses. ■ pieces of flexible material applied to actors' faces to transform their appearance. ■ [treated as *sing.*] the making and fitting of artificial body parts.

pros·the·tist /'präsTHətist/ ▶*n.* a specialist in prosthetics.

pros·tho·don·tics /,präsTHə'däntiks/ ▶*plural n.* [treated as *sing.*] the branch of dentistry concerned with the design, manufacture, and fitting of artificial replacements for teeth and other parts of the mouth. ▷1940s: from **PROSTHESIS**, on the pattern of *orthodontics*. —**pros·tho·don·tist** /-'däntist/ *n.*

pros·ti·tute /'prästə,t(y)o͞ot/ ▶*n.* a person, typically a woman, who engages in sexual activity for payment. ■ *figurative* a person who misuses their talents or who sacrifices their self-respect for the sake of personal or financial gain: *careerist political prostitutes.*
▶*v.* [*trans.*] offer (someone, typically a woman) for sexual activity in exchange for payment: *although she was paid $15 to join a man at his table, she never* **prostituted herself.** ■ *figurative* put (oneself or one's talents) to an unworthy or corrupt use or purpose for the sake of personal or financial gain: *his willingness to prostitute himself to the worst instincts of the electorate.* ▷mid 16th cent. (as a verb): from Latin *prostitut-* 'exposed publicly, offered for sale,' from the verb *prostituere*, from *pro-* 'before' + *statuere* 'set up, place.' —**pros·ti·tu·tor** /-,t(y)o͞otər/ *n.*

pros·ti·tu·tion /,prästə't(y)o͞oSHən/ ▶*n.* the practice or occupation of engaging in sexual activity with someone for payment. ■ *figurative* the unworthy or corrupt use of one's talents for the sake of personal or financial gain.

pros·trate /'präs,trāt/ ▶*adj.* lying stretched out on the ground with one's face downward. ■ [*predic.*] *figurative* completely overcome or helpless, esp. with illness, distress, or exhaustion: *his wife was* **prostrate with** *shock.* ■ *Botany* growing along the ground.
▶*v.* [*trans.*] (**prostrate oneself**) lay oneself flat on the ground face downward, esp. in reverence or submission: *she prostrated herself on the bare floor of the church.* ■ (often **be prostrated**) (of distress, exhaustion, or illness) reduce (someone) to extreme physical weakness: *she was so prostrated by a migraine that she could scarcely get up the stairs.* ▷Middle English: from Latin *prostratus* 'thrown down,' past participle of *prosternere*, from *pro-* 'before' + *sternere* 'lay flat.' —**pros·tra·tion** /prä'sträSHən/ *n.*

pro·style /'prō,stīl/ ▶*n.* *Architecture* a portico with a maximum of four columns. ▷late 17th cent.: from Latin *prostylos* '(building) having pillars in front,' from Greek *pro* 'before' + *stulos* 'column.'

pro·sum·er /prō'so͞omər/ ▶*n.* **1** an amateur who purchases equipment with quality or features suitable for professional use: *the magazine is aimed at the prosumer who uses a $10,000 camera to make home movies of his dog.* **2** a prospective consumer who is involved in the design, manufacture, or development of a product or service: *a panel of prosumers weighed in on the plans for the new shampoo.* ■ a person who designs or produces a product for personal use or for sale: *she's a driven prosumer with one idea: to make a better-smelling toothpaste.* ■ a well-informed and proactive consumer: *prosumers read labels, sometimes obsessively.* ▷blend of *professional* or *producer* or *proactive* and *consumer.*

pros·y /'prōzē/ ▶*adj.* (**pros·i·er, pros·i·est**) (esp. of speech or writing) showing no imagination; commonplace or dull. —**pros·i·ly** /-əlē/ *adv.* —**pros·i·ness** *n.*

prot- ▶*comb. form* variant spelling of **PROTO-** before a vowel (as in *protamine*).

prot·ac·tin·i·um /,prō,tak'tinēəm/ ▶*n.* the chemical element of atomic number 91, a radioactive metal of the actinide series, occurring in small amounts as a product of the natural decay of uranium. (Symbol: **Pa**) ▷early 20th cent.: from **PROTO-** 'original, earlier' + **ACTINIUM**, so named because one of its isotopes decays to form actinium.

pro·tag·o·nist /prō'tagənist; prō-/ ▶*n.* the leading character or one of the major characters in a drama, movie, novel, or other fictional text. ■ the main figure or one of the most prominent figures in a real situation: *in this colonial struggle, the main protagonists were Great Britain and France.* ■ an advocate or champion of a particular cause or idea: *a strenuous protagonist of the new agricultural policy.* ▷late 17th cent.: from Greek *prōtagōnistēs*, from *prōtos* 'first in importance' + *agōnistēs* 'actor.'

USAGE The first sense of **protagonist**, as originally used in connection with ancient Greek drama, is 'the main character in a play.' In the early 20th century, a new sense arose meaning 'a supporter of a cause': *a strenuous* **protagonist** *of the new agricultural policy.* This new sense probably arose by analogy with **antagonist**, the **pro-** in **protagonist** being interpreted as meaning 'in favor of.' In fact, the **prot-** in **protagonist** derives from the Greek root meaning 'first.' **Protagonist** is best used in its original dramatic, theatrical sense, not as a synonym for *supporter* or *proponent.* Further, because of its basic meaning of 'leading character,' such usage as *the play's half-dozen protagonists were well cast* blurs the word's distinctiveness; *characters*, instead of *protagonists*, would be more accurate and more widely understood.

prot·a·mine /'prōtə,mēn/ ▶*n.* *Biochemistry* any of a group of simple proteins found combined with nucleic acids, esp. in fish sperm. ▷late 19th cent.: from **PROTO-** 'original' + **AMINE**.

prot·an·drous /prōt'andrəs/ ▶*adj.* *Botany & Zoology* (of a hermaphrodite flower or animal) having the male reproductive organs come to maturity before the female. The opposite of **PROTOGYNOUS**. —**prot·an·dry** /-'andrē/ *n.*

pro·ta·nope /'prōtə,nōp/ ▶*n.* a person suffering from protanopia.

pro·ta·no·pi·a /,prōtə'nōpēə/ ▶*n.* color-blindness resulting from insensitivity to red light, causing confusion of greens, reds, and yellows. It is hereditary and is the most common form of color-blindness. Also called **DALTONISM**. Compare with **DEUTERANOPIA**, **TRITANOPIA**. ▷early 20th cent.: from **PROTO-** 'original' (red being regarded as the first component of color vision) + **AN-**[1] 'lacking' + **-OPIA**.

pro tan·to /prō 'tan,tō/ ▶*adj.* & *adv.* to such an extent; to that extent. ▷Latin, literally 'for so much.'

prot·a·sis /'prätəsəs/ ▶*n.* (*pl.* **-ses** /-,sēz/) *Grammar* the clause expressing the condition in a conditional sentence (e.g., *if you asked me* in *if you asked me I would agree*). Often contrasted with **APODOSIS**. ▷late 16th cent.: via Latin from Greek *protasis* 'proposition,' from *pro* 'before' + *teinein* 'to stretch.'

pro·te·a /'prōtēə/ ▶*n.* an evergreen shrub or small tree with large nectar-rich conelike flowerheads surrounded by brightly colored bracts, chiefly native to South Africa. • Genus *Protea*, family Proteaceae: many species, including *P. repens*, which was formerly used as a source of sweet syrup. ▷modern Latin, from **PROTEUS**, with reference to the many species of the genus.

P

pro·te·an /ˈprōtēən; prōˈtēən/ ▸*adj.* tending or able to change frequently or easily: *it is difficult to comprehend the whole of this protean subject.* ■ able to do many different things; versatile: *Shostakovich was a remarkably protean composer, one at home in a wide range of styles.* ▷late 16th cent.: from **PROTEUS** + **-AN**. **—pro·te·an·ism** /-ˌnizəm/ *n.*

pro·te·ase /ˈprōtēˌāz; -ˌās/ ▸*n. Biochemistry* an enzyme that breaks down proteins and peptides. ▷early 20th cent.: from **PROTEIN** + **-ASE**.

pro·te·ase in·hib·i·tor ▸*n.* a substance that breaks down protease, thereby inhibiting the replication of certain cells and viruses, including HIV.

pro·te·a·some /ˈprōtēəˌsōm/ ▸*n.* a protein complex in cells containing proteases; it breaks down proteins that have been tagged by ubiquitin.

protec. ▸*abbr.* protectorate.

pro·tect /prəˈtekt/ ▸*v.* [*trans.*] keep safe from harm or injury: *he tried to* ***protect*** *Kelly* ***from*** *the attack* | [*intrans.*] *certain vitamins may* ***protect against*** *heart disease.* ■ [often as *adj.*] (**protected**) aim to preserve (a threatened plant or animal species) by legislating against collecting or hunting. ■ [often as *adj.*] (**protected**) restrict by law access to or development of (land) so as to preserve its natural state: *logging is continuing in protected areas in violation of an international agreement.* ■ (often **be protected**) (of an insurance policy) promise to pay (someone) an agreed amount in the event of loss, injury, fire, theft, or other misfortune: *in the event of your death, your family will be protected against any financial problems that may arise.* ■ *Economics* shield (a domestic industry) from competition by imposing import duties on foreign goods. ■ *Computing* restrict access to or use of (data or a memory location): *security products are designed to* ***protect*** *information* ***from*** *unauthorized access.* ■ provide funds to meet (a bill of exchange or commercial draft). ▷late Middle English: from Latin *protect-* 'covered in front,' from the verb *protegere*, from *pro-* 'in front' + *tegere* 'to cover.' **—pro·tect·a·ble** *adj.*

pro·tect·ant /prəˈtektənt/ ▸*n.* a substance that provides protection, e.g., against disease or ultraviolet radiation.

pro·tec·tion /prəˈtekSHən/ ▸*n.* the action of protecting someone or something, or the state of being protected: *the B vitamins give protection against infection* | *his son was put under police protection.* ■ a person or thing that prevents someone or something from suffering harm or injury: *the castle was built as protection against the Saxons* | [in *sing.*] *a protection against the evil eye.* ■ the cover provided by an insurance policy. ■ (usu. **protections**) a legal or other formal measure intended to preserve civil liberties and rights. ■ a document guaranteeing immunity from harm to the person specified in it. ■ the practice of paying money to criminals so as to prevent them from attacking oneself or one's property: [as *adj.*] *a protection racket.* ■ (also **protection money**) the money so paid to criminals, esp. on a regular basis. ■ *archaic* used euphemistically to refer to the keeping of a mistress by her lover in a separate establishment: *she was living* ***under his lordship's protection*** *at Gloucester Gate.* ▷Middle English: from Old French, from late Latin *protectio(n-)*, from *protegere* 'cover in front' (see **PROTECT**).

pro·tec·tion·ism /prəˈteksHəˌnizəm/ ▸*n. Economics* the theory or practice of shielding a country's domestic industries from foreign competition by taxing imports. **—pro·tec·tion·ist** *n.* & *adj.*

pro·tec·tive /prəˈtektiv/ ▸*adj.* capable of or intended to protect someone or something: *protective gloves are worn to minimize injury.* ■ having or showing a strong wish to keep someone or something safe from harm: *I felt protective toward her* | *Marco wrapped a protective arm around her shoulder.* ■ *Economics* of or relating to the protection of domestic industries from foreign competition: *protective tariffs.* **—pro·tec·tive·ly** *adv.* **—pro·tec·tive·ness** *n.*

pro·tec·tive col·or·a·tion (also **pro·tec·tive col·or·ing**) ▸*n.* coloring that disguises or camouflages a plant or animal.

pro·tec·tive cus·to·dy ▸*n.* the detention of a person for their own protection: *they were being held* ***in protective custody*** *during the trial.*

pro·tec·tive or·der ▸*n.* a court order instructing a person to desist from abusing or harassing the petitioner (usu. a related person) for a fixed period: *a protective order against the man accused of setting his wife on fire.*

pro·tec·tor /prəˈtektər/ ▸*n.* **1** a person who protects or defends someone or something: *a passionate protector of animal rights.* **2** [often with *adj.*] a thing that protects someone or something from injury: *ear protectors.* **3** (chiefly **Protector**) *historical* a regent in charge of a kingdom during the minority, absence, or incapacity of the sovereign. ■ (also **Lord Protector**) the title of the head of state in England during the later period of the Commonwealth between 1653 and 1659, first Oliver Cromwell (1653–58), then his son Richard (1658–59). **—pro·tec·tor·al** /-rəl/ *adj.* **—pro·tec·tor·ship** /-ˌSHip/ *n.*

pro·tec·tor·ate /prəˈtektərət/ ▸*n.* **1** a state that is controlled and protected by another. ■ the relationship between a state of this kind and the one that controls it: *a French protectorate had been established over Tunis.* **2** (usu. **Protectorate**) *historical* the position or period of office of a Protector, esp. that in England of Oliver and Richard Cromwell.

pro·tect·ress /ˈprōtektrəs/ ▸*n.* a female protector.

pro·té·gé /ˈprōtəˌZHā; ˌprōtəˈZHā/ (also **pro·te·ge**) ▸*n.* a person who is guided and supported by an older and more experienced or influential person: *he was an aide and protégé of the former Tennessee senator.* ▷late 18th cent.: French, literally 'protected,' past participle of *protéger*, from Latin *protegere* 'cover in front' (see **PROTECT**).

pro·té·gée /ˈprōtəˌZHā; ˌprōtəˈZHā/ (also **pro·te·gee**) ▸*n.* a female protégé.

pro·tein /ˈprōˌtē(ə)n/ ▸*n.* any of a class of nitrogenous organic compounds that consist of large molecules composed of one or more long chains of amino acids and are an essential part of all living organisms, esp. as structural components of body tissues such as muscle, hair, collagen, etc., and as enzymes and antibodies. ■ such substances collectively, esp. as a dietary component: *a diet high in protein.* ▷mid 19th cent.: from French *protéine*, German *Protein*, from Greek *prōteios* 'primary,' from *prōtos* 'first.' **—pro·tein·a·ceous** /ˌprōˌtē(ə)ˈnāSHəs; ˌprōtnˈā-/ *adj.*

pro·tein·ase /ˈprōtnˌās; ˈprōˌtēn-; -ˌāz/ ▸*n.* another term for **ENDOPEPTIDASE**.

pro·tein·oid /ˈprōtnˌoid; ˈprōˌtēn-/ ▸*n. Biochemistry* a polypeptide or mixture of polypeptides obtained by heating a mixture of amino acids.

pro·tein·u·ri·a /ˌprōtnˈ(y)o͝orēə; ˌprōˌtēn-/ ▸*n. Medicine* the presence of abnormal quantities of protein in the urine, which may indicate damage to the kidneys.

pro tem /prō ˈtem/ ▸*adv.* & *adj.* for the time being: [as *adv.*] *a printer that Marisa could use pro tem* | [as *adj.*] *a pro tem committee* | [as *postpositive adj.*] *the president pro tem of the Senate.* ▷abbreviation of Latin *pro tempore.*

pro·te·o·gly·can /ˌprōtēəˈglīˌkan/ ▸*n. Biochemistry* a compound consisting of a protein bonded to glycosaminoglycan groups, present esp. in connective tissue.

pro·te·ol·y·sis /ˌprōtēˈäləsəs/ ▸*n. Biochemistry* the breakdown of proteins or peptides into amino acids by the action of enzymes. ▷late 19th cent.: modern Latin, from **PROTEIN** + **-LYSIS**. **—pro·te·o·lyt·ic** /-əˈlitik/ *adj.* **—pro·te·o·lyt·i·cal·ly** /-əˈlitik(ə)lē/ *adv.*

pro·te·ome /ˈprōtēˌōm/ ▸*n. Genetics* the entire complement of proteins that is or can be expressed by a cell, tissue, or organism: *now that the human genome has been deciphered, much of the fanfare surrounding it has transferred to the proteome.* ▷1990s: a blend of *protein* and *genome.*

pro·te·om·ics /ˌprōtēˈämiks/ ▸*plural n.* [treated as *singular*] the branch of molecular biology concerned with determining the proteome. **—pro·te·om·ic** *adj.*

Prot·er·o·zo·ic /ˌprōtərəˈzōik/ ▸*adj. Geology* of, relating to, or denoting the eon that constitutes the later part of the Precambrian, between the Archean eon and the Cambrian period, in which the earliest forms of life evolved. ■ [as *n.*] (**the Proterozoic**) the Proterozoic eon or the system of rocks deposited during it.

> The Proterozoic lasted from about 2,500 million to 570 million years ago. For millions of years only bacteria, algae, and other simple organisms existed, and the early invertebrates that followed were soft-bodied and rarely left any trace in the form of fossils.

▷early 20th cent.: from Greek *proteros* 'former' + *zōē* 'life,' *zōos* 'living' + **-IC**.

pro·test ▸*n.* /ˈprōˌtest/ **1** a statement or action expressing disapproval of or objection to something: *the Hungarian team lodged an official protest* | *two senior scientists resigned* ***in protest.*** ■ an organized public demonstration expressing strong objection to a policy or course of action adopted by those in authority: [as *adj.*] *a protest march.* **2** *Law* a written declaration, typically by a notary public, that a bill has been presented and payment or acceptance refused.

▸*v.* /prəˈtest; prōˈtest; ˈprōˌtest/ **1** [*intrans.*] express an objection to what someone has said or done: *she wouldn't let him pay, and he didn't protest.* ■ publicly demonstrate strong objection to a policy or course of action adopted by those in authority: *doctors and patients* ***protested against*** *plans to cut services at the hospital.* ■ [*trans.*] publicly demonstrate such objection to (a policy or course of action): *the workers were protesting economic measures enacted a week earlier.* **2** [*reporting verb*] declare (something) firmly and emphatically in the face of stated or implied doubt or in response to an accusation: [with *direct speech*] *"I'm not being coy!" Lucy protested* | [*trans.*] *she has always protested her innocence.* **3** [*trans.*] *Law* write or obtain a protest in regard to (a bill). ▷late Middle English (as a verb in the sense 'make a solemn declaration'): from Old French *protester*, from Latin *protestari*, from *pro-* 'forth, publicly' + *testari* 'assert' (from *testis* 'witness'). **—pro·test·er** /ˈprōˌtestər; prəˈtes-/ *n.* **—pro·test·ing·ly** *adv.* **—pro·tes·tor** /ˈprōˌtestər; prəˈtes-/ *n.*

▸*PHRASE* □ **under protest** after expressing one's objection or reluctance; unwillingly: *"I'm only here under protest," Jenna said shortly.*

Prot·es·tant /ˈprätəstənt/ ▸*n.* a member or follower of any of the Western Christian churches that are separate from the Roman Catholic Church and follow the principles of the Reformation, including the Baptist, Presbyterian, and Lutheran churches.

> Protestants are so called after the declaration (*protestatio*) of Martin Luther and his supporters dissenting from the decision of the Diet of Spires (1529), which reaffirmed the edict of the Diet of Worms against the Reformation. All Protestants reject the authority of the papacy, both religious and political, and find authority in the text of the Bible.

▸*adj.* of, relating to, or belonging to any of the Protestant churches. ▷mid 16th cent.: via German or French from Latin *protestant-* 'protesting,' from *protestari* (see **PROTEST**). **—Prot·es·tant·i·za·tion** /ˌprätəstəntəˈzāSHən/ *n.* **—Prot·es·tant·ize** /-īz/ *v.*

Prot·es·tant eth·ic (also **Protestant work ethic**) ▸*n.* the view that a person's duty is to achieve success through hard work and thrift, such success being a sign that one is saved. ▷translating German *die protestantische Ethik*, coined (1904) by the economist Max Weber in his thesis on the relationship between the teachings of Calvin and the rise of capitalism.

Prot·es·tant·ism /ˈprätəstəntˌizəm/ ▸*n.* the faith, practice, and church order of the Protestant churches. ■ adherence to the forms of Christian doctrine that are generally regarded as Protestant rather than Catholic or Eastern Orthodox.

prot·es·ta·tion /ˌprätəˈstāSHən; ˌprōˌtesˈtā-/ ▸*n.* an emphatic declaration that something is or is not the case: *her protestations of innocence were in vain* | *no amount of protestation to the contrary made any difference.* ■ an objection or protest: *he was warned by the referee for his loud protestations.* ▷Middle English: from Old French, from late Latin *protestatio(n-)*, from *protestari* 'to protest' (see **PROTEST**).

Pro·te·us /ˈprōtēəs; ˈprōˌt(y)o͞os/ **1** *Greek Mythology* a minor sea god who had the power of prophecy but who would assume different shapes to avoid answering questions. **2** *Astronomy* a satellite of Neptune, the sixth closest to the planet, discovered by the Voyager 2 space probe in 1989, and having a diameter of 261 miles (420 km).

pro·te·us /ˈprōtēəs/ ▸*n.* a bacterium found in the intestines of animals and in the soil. • Genus *Proteus*; motile Gram-negative rods. ▷early 19th cent.: from **PROTEUS**.

pro·tha·la·mi·on /ˌprōTHəˈlāmēən/ (also **pro·tha·la·mi·um** /-mēəm/) ▸*n.* (*pl.* **-mi·a** /-mēə/) *poetic/literary* a song or poem celebrating an upcoming wedding. ▷late 16th cent.: from *Prothalamion*, the title of a poem by Spenser, on the pattern of **EPITHALAMIUM**.

pro·thal·lus /prōˈTHaləs/ ▸*n.* (*pl.* **-thal·li** /-ˈTHalē; ˈTHalˌī/) *Botany* the gametophyte of ferns and other primitive plants. ▷mid 19th cent.: modern Latin, from **PRO-**[2] 'before, earlier' + Greek *thallos* 'green shoot.' **—pro·thal·li·al** /-ˈTHalēəl/ *adj.*

proth·e·sis /ˈpräTHəsəs/ ▸*n.* (*pl.* **-ses** /-ˌsēz/) **1** *Christian Church* (esp. in the Orthodox Church) the action of placing the Eucharistic elements on the credence table. ■ a credence table. ■ the part of a church where the credence table stands. **2** another term for **PROSTHESIS** (sense 2). ▷late 16th cent. (sense 2):

from Greek, 'placing before or in public view,' from *pro* 'before' + *thesis* 'placing.' —**pro·thet·ic** /prə 'THetik/ *adj.*

pro·thon·o·tar·y /prō'THänə,terē; ,prōTHə'nōtərē/ ▸*n.* variant spelling of PROTONOTARY.

pro·thon·o·tar·y war·bler ▸*n.* a North American warbler, the male of which has a golden-yellow head, breast, and underparts. • *Protonotaria citrea*, subfamily Parulinae, family Emberizidae. ▷late 18th cent.: named with reference to the saffron color of the robes worn by clerks to the pope (see **PROTONOTARY APOSTOLIC**).

pro·tho·rax /prō'THôr,aks/ ▸*n.* (*pl.* **-tho·rax·es** or **-tho·ra·ces** /-'THôrə,sēz/) *Entomology* the anterior segment of the thorax of an insect, not bearing any wings. —**pro·tho·rac·ic** /,prōTHə'rasik/ *adj.*

pro·throm·bin /prō'THrämbən/ ▸*n.* *Biochemistry* a protein present in blood plasma that is converted into active thrombin during coagulation.

Pro·tis·ta /prō'tistə/ *Biology* a kingdom or large grouping that comprises mostly single-celled organisms such as the protozoa, simple algae and fungi, slime molds, and (formerly) the bacteria. They are now divided among up to thirty phyla, and some have both plant and animal characteristics. ▷modern Latin (plural), from Greek *prōtista*, neuter plural of *prōtistos* 'very first,' superlative of *prōtos* 'first.' —**pro·tist** /'prōtəst; 'prō,tist/ *n.* —**pro·tis·tan** /prō'tistən/ *adj.* & *n.* —**pro·tis·tol·o·gy** /,prōtə'stäləjē; ,prō,tis'täl-/ *n.*

pro·ti·um /'prōtēəm; 'prōSH(ē)əm/ ▸*n.* *Chemistry* the common, stable isotope of hydrogen, as distinct from deuterium and tritium. ▷1930s: modern Latin, from Greek *prōtos* 'first.'

proto- (usu. **prot-** before a vowel) ▸*comb. form* original; primitive: *prototherian* | *prototype*. ■ first; anterior; relating to a precursor: *protomartyr* | *protozoan*. ▷from Greek *prōtos* 'first.'

pro·to·cer·a·tops /,prōtə'serə,täps/ ▸*n.* a small quadrupedal dinosaur of the late Cretaceous period, having a bony frill above the neck and probably ancestral to triceratops. The fossilized remains of many individuals and their eggs have been found in Mongolia. • Genus *Protoceratops*, infraorder Ceratopsia, order Ornithischia.

pro·to·col /'prōtə,kôl; -,käl/ ▸*n.* **1** the official procedure or system of rules governing affairs of state or diplomatic occasions: *protocol forbids the prince from making any public statement in his defense.* ■ the accepted or established code of procedure or behavior in any group, organization, or situation: *what is the protocol at a conference if one's neighbor dozes off during the speeches?* ■ *Computing* a set of rules governing the exchange or transmission of data electronically between devices. **2** the original draft of a diplomatic document, esp. of the terms of a treaty agreed to in conference and signed by the parties. ■ an amendment or addition to a treaty or convention: *a protocol to the treaty allowed for this Danish referendum.* **3** a formal or official record of scientific experimental observations. ■ a procedure for carrying out a scientific experiment or a course of medical treatment. ▷late Middle English (denoting the original record of an agreement, forming the legal authority for future dealings relating to it): from Old French *prothocole*, via medieval Latin from Greek *prōtokollon* 'first page, flyleaf,' from *prōtos* 'first' + *kolla* 'glue.' Sense 1 derives from French *protocole*, the collection of set forms of etiquette to be observed by the French head of state, and the name of the government department responsible for this (in the 19th cent.).

Pro·toc·tis·ta /,prōtäk'tistə/ *Biology* a kingdom or large grouping that is either synonymous with the Protista or equivalent to the Protista together with their multicellular descendants. ▷modern Latin (plural), based on Greek *prōtos* 'first.' —**pro·toc·tist** /'prōtäk,tist/ *n.*

pro·to·gal·ax·y /,prōtō'galəksē/ ▸*n.* (*pl.* **-ax·ies**) *Astronomy* a vast mass of gas from which a galaxy is thought to develop. —**pro·to·ga·lac·tic** /-gə'laktik/ *adj.*

Pro·to-Ger·man·ic /,prōtō jər'mänik/ ▸*n.* see **GERMANIC**.

pro·to·gy·nous /,prōtə'jīnəs; prō'täjənəs/ ▸*adj.* *Botany* & *Zoology* (of a hermaphrodite flower or animal) having the female reproductive organs come to maturity before the male. The opposite of **PROTANDROUS**. —**pro·tog·y·ny** /'prōtə,jīnē; prō'täjənē/ *n.*

pro·to·hu·man /,prōtō'(h)yōōmən/ *Anthropology* ▸*n.* a hypothetical prehistoric primate, resembling humans and thought to be their ancestor, whose profile has been compiled mainly from fossil evidence. ▸*adj.* relating to or denoting such a primate.

Pro·to-In·do-Eu·ro·pe·an ▸*n.* the unrecorded language from which all Indo-European languages are hypothesized to derive. See **INDO-EUROPEAN**. ▸*adj.* of or relating to this language.

pro·to·lan·guage /'prōtō,laNG(g)wij/ ▸*n.* a hypothetical undocumented parent language from which actual languages are derived.

pro·to·mar·tyr /'prōtō,märtər/ ▸*n.* the first martyr for a cause, esp. the first Christian martyr, St. Stephen.

pro·ton /'prō,tän/ ▸*n.* *Physics* a stable subatomic particle occurring in all atomic nuclei, with a positive electric charge equal in magnitude to that of an electron, but of opposite sign.

> The mass of the proton is 1,836 times greater than that of the electron. The atoms of each chemical element have a characteristic number of protons in the nucleus; this is known as the atomic number. The common isotope of hydrogen has a nucleus consisting of a single proton.

▷1920s: from Greek, neuter of *prōtos* 'first.' —**pro·ton·ic** /prō'tänik/ *adj.*

pro·ton·ate /'prōtn,āt/ ▸*v.* [*trans.*] (often **be protonated**) *Chemistry* transfer a proton to (a molecule, group, or atom), so that a coordinate bond to the proton is formed. —**pro·to·na·tion** /,prōtn'āSHən/ *n.*

pro·ton·o·tar·y /prō'tänə,terē; ,prōtə'nōtərē/ (also **prothon·o·tar·y**) ▸*n.* (*pl.* **-tar·ies**) *chiefly historical* a chief clerk in some courts of law, originally in the Byzantine court. ▷late Middle English: via medieval Latin from late Greek *prōtonotarios*, from *prōtos* 'first' + *notarios* 'notary.'

Pro·ton·o·tar·y Ap·os·tol·ic ▸*n.* (*pl.* **Pro·ton·o·tar·ies Ap·os·tol·ic**) a member of the Roman Catholic college of prelates who register papal acts and direct the canonization of saints.

pro·to·path·ic /,prōtə'paTHik/ ▸*adj.* *Physiology* relating to or denoting those sensory nerve fibers of the skin that are capable of discriminating only among such relatively coarse stimuli as heat, cold, and pain. Often contrasted with **EPICRITIC**. ▷mid 19th cent.: from **PROTO-** 'primitive' + Greek *pathos* 'suffering, feeling' + **-IC**.

pro·to·plasm /'prōtə,plazəm/ ▸*n.* *Biology* the colorless material comprising the living part of a cell, including the cytoplasm, nucleus, and other organelles. ▷mid 19th cent.: from Greek *prōtoplasma* (see **PROTO-**, **PLASMA**). —**pro·to·plas·mic** /,prōtə'plazmik/ *adj.*

pro·to·plast /'prōtə,plast/ ▸*n.* *chiefly Botany* the protoplasm of a living plant or bacterial cell whose cell wall has been removed. ▷late 19th cent.: from Greek *prōtoplastos* 'first formed,' from *prōtos* 'first' + *plassein* 'to mold.' —**pro·to·plas·tic** /,prōtə'plastik/ *adj.*

pro·top·o·dite /prə'täpə,dīt/ (also **pro·to·pod** /'prōtə ,päd/) ▸*n.* *Zoology* the basal segments of the biramous limb or appendage of a crustacean. Compare with **ENDOPODITE**, **EXOPODITE**. ▷late 19th cent.: from **PROTO-** 'early, original' + Greek *pous*, *pod-* 'foot' + **-ITE**[1].

pro·to·star /'prōtə,stär/ ▸*n.* *Astronomy* a contracting mass of gas that represents an early stage in the formation of a star, before nucleosynthesis has begun.

pro·to·stome /'prōtə,stōm/ ▸*n.* *Zoology* a multicellular organism whose mouth develops from a primary embryonic opening, such as an annelid, mollusk, or arthropod. ▷1950s: from **PROTO-** 'primitive' + Greek *stoma* 'mouth.'

Pro·to·the·ri·a /,prōtə'THirēə/ *Zoology* a group of mammals that comprises the monotremes and their extinct relatives. Compare with **THERIA**. • Subclass Prototheria, class Mammalia. ▷modern Latin (plural), from **PROTO-** 'first, original' + Greek *thēr* 'wild beast.' —**pro·to·the·ri·an** *n.* & *adj.*

pro·to·type /'prōtə,tīp/ ▸*n.* a first or preliminary model of something, esp. a machine, from which other forms are developed or copied: *the firm is testing a prototype of the weapon.* See note at **MODEL**. ■ a typical example of something: *the prototype of all careerists is Judas.* ■ the archetypal example of a class of living organisms, astronomical objects, or other items: *these objects are the prototypes of a category of rapidly spinning neutron stars.* ■ a building, vehicle, or other object that acts as a pattern for a full-scale model. ■ *Electronics* a basic filter network with specified cutoff frequencies, from which other networks may be derived to obtain sharper cutoffs, constancy of characteristic impedance with frequency, etc. ▸*v.* [*trans.*] make a prototype of (a product). ▷late 16th cent. (denoting the original of which something else is a copy or derivative): via French or late Latin from Greek *prōtotupos* (see **PROTO-**, **TYPE**). —**pro·to·typ·al** /,prōtə'tīpəl/ *adj.* —**pro·to·typ·ic** /,prōtə'tipik/ *adj.* —**pro·to·typ·i·cal** /,prōtə'tipikəl/ *adj.* —**pro·to·typ·i·cal·ly** /,prōtə'tipik(ə)lē/ *adv.*

Pro·to·zo·a /,prōtə'zōə/ *Zoology* a phylum or group of phyla that comprises the single-celled microscopic animals, which include amebas, flagellates, ciliates, sporozoans, and many other forms. They are now usually treated as a number of phyla belonging to the kingdom Protista. ■ [as *plural n.*] (**protozoa**) organisms of this group. ▷modern Latin (plural), from **PROTO-** 'first' + Greek *zōion* 'animal.' —**pro·to·zo·al** *adj.* —**pro·to·zo·an** *n.* & *adj.* —**pro·to·zo·ic** /-'zōik/ *adj.* —**pro·to·zo·on** /-'zō,än/ *n.*

pro·tract /prə'trakt; prō-/ ▸*v.* [*trans.*] **1** prolong: *he had certainly taken his time, even protracting the process.* **2** extend a part of the body. **3** draw (a plan, etc.) to scale. ▷mid 16th cent.: from Latin *protract-* 'prolonged,' from the verb *protrahere*, from *pro-* 'out' + *trahere* 'to draw.' —**pro·trac·tion** /-'trakSHən/ *n.*

pro·tract·ed /prə'traktəd; prō-/ ▸*adj.* lasting for a long time or longer than expected or usual: *a protracted and bitter dispute.* —**pro·tract·ed·ly** *adv.* —**pro·tract·ed·ness** *n.*

pro·trac·tile /prə'traktəl; prō-; -'trak,tīl/ ▸*adj.* another term for **PROTRUSIBLE**.

pro·trac·tor /'prō,traktər/ ▸*n.* **1** an instrument for measuring angles, typically in the form of a flat semicircle marked with degrees along the curved edge. **2** (also **protractor muscle**) *chiefly Zoology* a muscle serving to extend a part of the body. Compare with **RETRACTOR**.

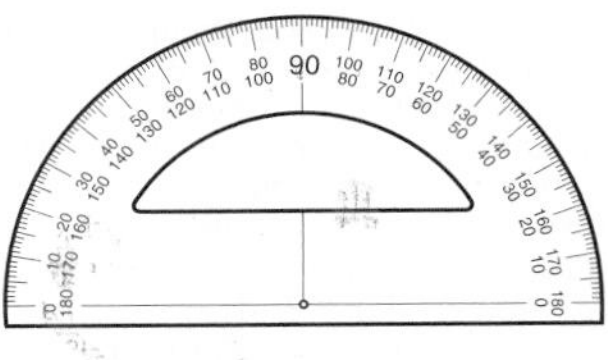

protractor 1

pro·trude /prə'trōōd; prō-/ ▸*v.* [*intrans.*] extend beyond or above a surface: *something like a fin protruded from the water.* See note at **BULGE**. ■ [*trans.*] (of an animal) cause (a body part) to do this. ▷early 17th cent. (in the sense 'thrust (something) forward or onward'): from Latin *protrudere*, from *pro-* 'forward, out' + *trudere* 'to thrust.' —**pro·tru·sion** /-'trōōZHən/ *n.* —**pro·tru·sive** /-'trōōsiv; -ziv/ *adj.*

pro·tru·si·ble /prə'trōōsəbəl; prō-; -zəbəl/ ▸*adj.* *Zoology* (of a body part, such as the jaws of a fish) capable of being protruded or extended. ▷mid 19th cent.: from Latin *protrus-* 'extended or thrust forward' (from the verb *protrudere*) + **-IBLE**.

pro·tru·sile /prə'trōōsəl; prō-; -zəl/ ▸*adj.* (of a limb or other body part) able to be thrust forward. ▷mid 19th cent.: from Latin *protrus-* 'extended or thrust forward' (from the verb *protrudere*), on the pattern of *extrusile*.

pro·tu·ber·ance /prə't(y)ōōb(ə)rəns; prō-/ ▸*n.* a thing that protrudes from something else: *some dinosaurs evolved protuberances on top of their heads.* ■ the fact or state of protruding: *the large size and protuberance of the incisors.*

pro·tu·ber·ant /prə't(y)ōōb(ə)rənt; prō-/ ▸*adj.* protruding; bulging: *his protuberant eyes fluttered open.* ▷mid 17th cent.: from late Latin *protuberant-* 'swelling out,' from the verb *protuberare*, from *pro-* 'forward, out' + *tuber* 'bump.'

Pro·tu·ra /prə't(y)ōōrə/ *Entomology* an order of minute white wingless insects with slender bodies. They lack eyes and antennae, using the first pair of legs as sensory organs. • Order Protura, subclass Apterygota, class Insecta (or Hexapoda). ▷modern Latin (plural), from Greek *prōtos* 'first, primitive.' —**pro·tu·ran** *n.* & *adj.*

proud /proud/ ▸*adj.* **1** feeling deep pleasure or satisfaction as a result of one's own achievements, qualities, or possessions or those of someone with whom one is closely associated: *a proud grandma of three boys* | *she got nine As and he was so* **proud of** *her.* ■ (of an event, achievement, etc.) causing someone to feel this way: *we have a proud history of innovation.* ■ having or showing a consciousness of one's own

Pronunciation Key ə *ago*; ər *over*; 'ə or ,ə *up*; 'ər or ,ər *fur*; a *hat*; ā *rate*; ä *car*; CH *chew*; e *let*; ē *see*; e(ə)r *air*; i *fit*; ī *by*; i(ə)r *ear*; NG *sing*; ō *go*; ô *for*; oi *boy*; ŏŏ *good*; ōō *goo*; ou *out*; SH *she*; TH *thin*; TH *then*; (h)w *why*; ZH *vision*

dignity: *I was too proud to go home.* ■ having or showing a high or excessively high opinion of oneself or one's importance: *a proud, arrogant man.* ■ imposing; splendid: *bulrushes emerge tall and proud from the middle of the pond.* **2** [*predic.*] *Brit.* slightly projecting from a surface: *when the brake is engaged, the lever does not stand* **proud of** *the horizontal.* ▷late Old English *prūt, prūd* 'having a high opinion of one's own worth,' from Old French *prud* 'valiant,' based on Latin *prodesse* 'be of value.' The phrase *proud flesh* dates back to late Middle English, but the sense 'slightly projecting' is first recorded in British dialect of the 19th cent. **—proud·ly** *adv.* **—proud·ness** *n.*

▸*PHRASE* □ **do someone proud** *informal* act in a way that gives someone cause to feel pleased or satisfied: *they did themselves proud in a game that sent the fans home happy.* ■ treat someone very well, typically by lavishly feeding or entertaining them.

proud flesh ▸*n.* another name for GRANULATION TISSUE.

proud·heart·ed /'proud'härtəd/ ▸*adj.* arrogant.

Prou·dhon /prōō'dôN/, Pierre Joseph (1809–65), French social philosopher and journalist. His pamphlet *What is Property?* (1840) argues that property, in the sense of the exploitation of one person's labor by another, is theft.

Proust[1] /prōōst/, Joseph Louis (1754–1826), French analytical chemist. He proposed the law of constant proportions, demonstrating that any pure sample of a chemical compound (such as an oxide of a metal) always contains the same elements in fixed proportions.

Proust[2], Marcel (1871–1922), French novelist, essayist, and critic. He devoted much of his life to writing his novel *À la recherche du temps perdu* (1913–27). Its central theme is the recovery of the lost past and the releasing of its creative energies through the stimulation of unconscious memory.

Prov. ▸*abbr.* ■ *Bible* Proverbs. ■ *chiefly Canadian* Province or Provincial. ■ Provost.

prove /prōōv/ ▸*v.* (*past part.* **proved** or **prov·en** /'prōōvən/) **1** [*trans.*] demonstrate the truth or existence of (something) by evidence or argument: *the concept is difficult to prove* | [as *adj.*] **(proven)** *a proven ability to work hard.* ■ [*trans.*] demonstrate by evidence or argument (someone or something) to be: *innocent until proven guilty.* ■ *Law* establish the genuineness and validity of (a will). ■ (in homeopathy) demonstrate the action of (a remedy) by seeing what effect it produces in a healthy individual. ■ [*intrans.*] be seen or found to be: *the plan has proved a great success.* ■ **(prove oneself)** demonstrate one's abilities or courage: *a new lieutenant, very green and very desperate to prove himself.* ■ [*trans.*] *rare* test the accuracy of (a mathematical calculation). ■ subject (a gun or other item) to a testing process. **2** [*intrans.*] (of bread dough) become aerated by the action of yeast; rise. ▷Middle English: from Old French *prover*, from Latin *probare* 'test, approve, demonstrate,' from *probus* 'good.' **—prov·a·bil·i·ty** /ˌprōōvə'bilətē/ *n.* **—prov·a·ble** *adj.* **—prov·a·bly** /-blē/ *adv.* **—prov·er** *n.*

USAGE For complex historical reasons, **prove** developed two past participles: **proved** and **proven**. Both are correct and can be used more or less interchangeably: *this hasn't been* **proved** *yet; this hasn't been* **proven** *yet.* **Proven** is the more common form when used as an adjective before the noun it modifies: *a proven talent* (not *a proved talent*). Otherwise, the choice between *proved* and *proven* is not a matter of correctness, but usually of sound and rhythm—and often, consequently, a matter of familiarity, as in the legal idiom *innocent until proven guilty.*

prov·e·nance /'prävənəns/ ▸*n.* the place of origin or earliest known history of something: *an orange rug of Iranian provenance.* ■ the beginning of something's existence; something's origin: *they try to understand the whole universe, its provenance and fate.* See note at ORIGIN. ■ a record of ownership of a work of art or an antique, used as a guide to authenticity or quality: *the manuscript has a distinguished provenance.* ▷late 18th cent.: from French, from the verb *provenir* 'come or stem from,' from Latin *provenire*, from *pro-* 'forth' + *venire* 'come.'

Pro·ven·çal /ˌprävən'säl; ˌprōvən-; ˌprōˌvän-/ ▸*adj.* of, relating to, or denoting Provence or its people or language.

▸*n.* **1** a native or inhabitant of Provence. **2** the Romance language of Provence.

Provençal is closely related to French, Italian, and Catalan; it is sometimes called *langue d'oc* (or Occitan), though strictly speaking it is one dialect of this. In the 12th–14th centuries it was the language of the troubadours and cultured speakers of southern France, but the spread of the northern dialects of French led to its decline.

▷French, from Latin *provincialis* 'provincial.'

pro·ven·çale /ˌprävən'säl; ˌprō-; prə'vensəl/ ▸*adj.* [*postpositive*] denoting a dish cooked in a sauce made with tomatoes, garlic, and olive oil: *chicken provençale.* ▷from French *à la provençale* 'in the Provençal style.'

Pro·vence /prō'väns/ a former province of southeastern France, on the Mediterranean coast, east of the Rhône River. It is now part of the region of Provence–Alpes–Côte d'Azur. ▷from Latin *provincia* 'province,' a colloquial name for southern Gaul, the first Roman province to be established outside Italy.

Pro·vence–Al·pes–Côte d'A·zur /prə'väNs ˌälp ˌkōtdä'zHōōr/ a mountainous region in southeastern France, on the border with Italy and including the French Riviera.

prov·en·der /'prävəndər/ ▸*n.* *often humorous* food. ■ *dated* animal fodder. ▷Middle English: from Old French *provendre*, based on an alteration of Latin *praebenda* 'things to be supplied' (see PREBEND).

pro·ve·ni·ence /prə'vinyəns/ ▸*n.* another term for PROVENANCE.

pro·ven·tric·u·lus /ˌprōven'trikyələs/ ▸*n.* (*pl.* **-li** /-ˌlī; -ˌlē/) *Zoology* the narrow glandular first region of a bird's stomach between the crop and the gizzard. ■ the thick-walled muscular expansion of the esophagus above the stomach of crustaceans and insects. ▷mid 19th cent.: from PRO-[2] 'before' + Latin *ventriculus* 'small belly,' diminutive of *venter, ventr-* 'belly.'

prov·erb /'prävˌərb/ ▸*n.* a short pithy saying in general use, stating a general truth or piece of advice. See note at SAYING. ▷Middle English: from Old French *proverbe*, from Latin *proverbium*, from *pro-* '(put) forth' + *verbum* 'word.'

pro·ver·bi·al /prə'vərbēəl/ ▸*adj.* (of a word or phrase) referred to in a proverb or idiom: *I'm going to stick out like the proverbial sore thumb.* ■ well known, esp. so as to be stereotypical: *the Welsh people, whose hospitality is proverbial.* ▷late Middle English: from Latin *proverbialis*, from *proverbium* (see PROVERB). **—pro·ver·bi·al·i·ty** /-ˌvərbē'alətē/ *n.* **—pro·ver·bi·al·ly** *adv.*

Prov·erbs /'prävˌərbz/ (also **Book of Proverbs**) a book of the Bible containing maxims attributed mainly to Solomon.

pro·vide /prə'vīd/ ▸*v.* **1** [*trans.*] make available for use; supply: *these clubs provide a much appreciated service for this area.* ■ **(provide someone with)** equip or supply someone with (something useful or necessary): *we were provided with a map of the area.* ■ present or yield (something useful): *neither will provide answers to these problems.* **2** [*intrans.*] **(provide for)** make adequate preparation for (a possible event): *new qualifications must provide for changes in technology.* ■ supply sufficient money to ensure the maintenance of (someone): *Emma was handsomely provided for in Frank's will.* ■ (of a law) enable or allow (something to be done). **3** [with *clause*] stipulate in a will or other legal document: *the order should be varied to provide that there would be no contact with the father.* **4** **(provide someone to)** *historical Christian Church* appoint an incumbent to (a benefice). ▷late Middle English (also in the sense 'prepare to do, get ready'): from Latin *providere* 'foresee, attend to,' from *pro-* 'before' + *videre* 'to see.'

pro·vid·ed /prə'vīdid/ ▸*conj.* on the condition or understanding that: *cutting corners was acceptable, provided that you could get away with it.*

Prov·i·dence /'prävəˌdens; -dəns/ the capital of Rhode Island, a port near the head of the Providence River, on the Atlantic coast; pop. 173,618. It was founded in 1636 by Roger Williams (1604–83) as a haven for religious dissenters.

prov·i·dence /'prävədəns; -ˌdens/ ▸*n.* the protective care of God or of nature as a spiritual power: *they found their trust in divine providence to be a source of comfort.* ■ **(Providence)** God or nature as providing such care: *I live out my life as Providence decrees.* ■ timely preparation for future eventualities: *it was considered a duty to encourage providence.* ▷late Middle English: from Old French, from Latin *providentia*, from *providere* 'foresee, attend to' (see PROVIDE).

Prov·i·dence Plan·ta·tions the mainland portion of the state of Rhode Island.

prov·i·dent /'prävədənt; -ˌdent/ ▸*adj.* making or indicative of timely preparation for the future: *she had learned to be provident.* See note at ECONOMICAL. ▷late Middle English: from Latin *provident-* 'foreseeing, attending to,' from the verb *providere* (see PROVIDE). **—prov·i·dent·ly** *adv.*

prov·i·den·tial /ˌprävə'denCHəl/ ▸*adj.* **1** occurring at a favorable time; opportune: *thanks to that providential snowstorm, the attack had been repulsed.* **2** involving divine foresight or intervention: *God's providential care for each of us.* ▷mid 17th cent.: from PROVIDENCE, on the pattern of *evidential.* **—prov·i·den·tial·ly** *adv.*

pro·vid·er /prə'vīdər/ ▸*n.* a person or thing that provides something: *a leading provider of personal financial services.* ■ a breadwinner.

pro·vid·ing /prə'vīdiNG/ ▸*conj.* on the condition or understanding that: *we have the team that can win the championship, providing we avoid bad injuries.*

prov·ince /'prävins/ ▸*n.* **1** a principal administrative division of certain countries or empires: *Chengdu, capital of Sichuan province.* ■ **(the provinces)** the whole of a country outside the capital, esp. when regarded as lacking in sophistication or culture: *I made my way home to the dreary provinces by train.* ■ an area of the world with respect to its flora, fauna, or physical characteristics: *the inaccessibility of underwater igneous provinces.* ■ *Christian Church* a district under an archbishop or a metropolitan. ■ *Roman History* a territory outside Italy under a Roman governor. **2** **(one's province)** an area of special knowledge, interest, or responsibility: *she knew little about wine—that had been her father's province.* ▷late Middle English: from Old French, from Latin *provincia* 'charge, province,' of uncertain ultimate origin.

Prov·ince·town /'prävinsˌtoun/ a port town in southeastern Massachusetts, a noted resort and artists' community at the northern tip of Cape Cod; pop. 3,561.

pro·vin·cial /prə'vinsHəl/ ▸*adj.* **1** of or concerning a province of a country or empire: *provincial elections.* ■ of or pertaining to a style of architecture or furniture in fashion in the provinces of various European countries: *French Provincial furnishing.* **2** of or concerning the regions outside the capital city of a country: *scenes of violence were reported in provincial towns.* ■ unsophisticated or narrow-minded, esp. when considered as typical of such regions.

▸*n.* **1** an inhabitant of a province of a country or empire. ■ **(provincials)** (in Canada) athletic contests held between teams representing the country's administrative divisions. **2** an inhabitant of the regions outside the capital city of a country, esp. when regarded as unsophisticated or narrow-minded. **3** *Christian Church* the head or chief of a province or of a religious order in a province. ▷late Middle English: from Old French, from Latin *provincialis* 'belonging to a province' (see PROVINCE). **—pro·vin·ci·al·i·ty** /prəˌvinsHē'alətē/ *n.* **—pro·vin·cial·i·za·tion** /prəˌvinsHələ'zāsHən/ *n.* **—pro·vin·cial·ly** *adv.*

pro·vin·cial·ism /prə'vincHəˌlizəm/ ▸*n.* **1** the way of life or mode of thought characteristic of the regions outside the capital city of a country, esp. when regarded as unsophisticated or narrow-minded. ■ narrow-mindedness, insularity, or lack of sophistication: *the myopic provincialism of women's studies.* See note at BIAS. **2** concern for one's own area or region at the expense of national or supranational unity. **3** a word or phrase peculiar to a local area. **4** the degree to which plant or animal communities are restricted to particular areas. **—pro·vin·cial·ist** *n.* & *adj.*

prov·ing /'prōōviNG/ ▸*n.* (in homeopathy) the testing of a remedy: *Many such provings are required to fully test the powers of a medicinal substance.*

prov·ing ground ▸*n.* an environment that serves to demonstrate whether something, such as a theory or product, really works: *Bay County is the proving ground for a new gutter-cleaning vacuum.* ■ a military facility for the testing of materiel and equipment.

pro·vi·rus /prō'vīrəs/ ▸*n.* *Microbiology* the genetic material of a virus as incorporated into, and able to replicate with, the genome of a host cell. **—pro·vi·ral** /-rəl/ *adj.*

pro·vi·sion /prə'vizHən/ ▸*n.* **1** the action of providing or supplying something for use: *new contracts for the provision of services.* ■ **(provision for/against)** financial or other arrangements for future eventualities or requirements: *farmers have been slow to* **make provision** *for their retirement.* ■ an amount set aside out of profits in the accounts of an organization for a known liability, esp. a bad debt or the diminution in value of an asset. **2** an amount or thing supplied or provided: *low levels of social provision.* ■ **(provisions)** supplies of food, drink, or equipment, esp. for a journey. **3** a condition or requirement in a legal document: *a key provision in civil rights law | an appraisal* ***under the provisions of*** *the National Housing Act.* **4** *historical Christian Church* an appointment to a benefice, esp. directly by the pope rather than by the patron, and originally before it became vacant.

▶*v.* **1** [*trans.*] supply with food, drink, or equipment, esp. for a journey: *civilian contractors were responsible for provisioning these armies.* **2** [*intrans.*] set aside an amount in an organization's accounts for a known liability: *financial institutions have to* ***provision against*** *loan losses.* ▷late Middle English (also in the sense 'foresight'): via Old French from Latin *provisio(n-)*, from *providere* 'foresee, attend to' (see **PROVIDE**). The verb dates from the early 19th cent. —**pro·vi·sion·er** *n.*

pro·vi·sion·al /prəˈvizʜənl/ ▶*adj.* **1** arranged or existing for the present, possibly to be changed later: *a provisional government | a provisional construction permit.* ■ (of a postage stamp) put into circulation temporarily, usually owing to the unavailability of the definitive issue. **2** (**Provisional**) [*attrib.*] of or relating to the unofficial wings of the Irish Republican Army and Sinn Fein established in 1969 and advocating terrorism.

▶*n.* **1** a provisional postage stamp. **2** (**Provisional**) a member of the Provisional wings of the Irish Republican Army or Sinn Fein. —**pro·vi·sion·al·i·ty** /prəˌvizʜəˈnalətē/ *n.* —**pro·vi·sion·al·ly** /-zʜənl-ē/ *adv.*

pro·vi·so /prəˈvīzō/ ▶*n.* (*pl.* **-sos**) a condition attached to an agreement: *he left his unborn grandchild a trust fund* ***with the proviso that*** *he be named after the old man.* ▷late Middle English: from the medieval Latin phrase *proviso (quod)* 'it being provided (that),' from Latin *providere* 'foresee, provide.'

pro·vi·sor /prəˈvīzər/ ▶*n.* **1** (in the Roman Catholic Church) a deputy of a bishop or archbishop. **2** *historical Christian Church* the holder of a provision. ▷late Middle English: from Anglo-Norman French *provisour*, from Latin *provisor*, from *provis-* 'provided' (see **PROVISION**).

pro·vi·so·ry /prəˈvīzərē/ ▶*adj.* **1** *rare* subject to a proviso; conditional. **2** another term for **PROVISIONAL** (sense 1). ▷early 17th cent.: from French *provisoire* or medieval Latin *provisorius*, from *provis-* 'foreseen, attended to,' from the verb *providere* (see **PROVIDE**).

pro·vi·ta·min /prōˈvītəmən/ ▶*n.* *Biochemistry* a substance that is converted into a vitamin within an organism.

Pro·vo[1] /ˈprōvō/ an industrial and commercial city in north central Utah, south of Salt Lake City, home to Brigham Young University; pop. 105,166.

Pro·vo[2] ▶*n.* (*pl.* **-vos**) informal term for **PROVISIONAL** (sense 2).

prov·o·ca·tion /ˌprävəˈkāsʜən/ ▶*n.* **1** action or speech that makes someone annoyed or angry, esp. deliberately: *you should remain calm and not respond to provocation | he burst into tears* ***at the slightest provocation.*** ■ *Law* action or speech held to be likely to prompt physical retaliation: *the assault had taken place* ***under provocation.*** **2** *Medicine* testing to elicit a particular response or reflex: *twenty patients had a high increase of serum gastrin after provocation with secretin.* ▷late Middle English: from Old French, from Latin *provocatio(n-)*, from the verb *provocare* (see **PROVOKE**).

pro·voc·a·tive /prəˈväkətiv/ ▶*adj.* causing annoyance, anger, or another strong reaction, esp. deliberately: *a provocative article | his provocative remarks on race.* ■ arousing sexual desire or interest, esp. deliberately. ▷late Middle English: from Old French *provocatif, -ive*, from late Latin *provocativus*, from *provocat-* 'called forth, challenged,' from the verb *provocare* (see **PROVOKE**). —**pro·voc·a·tive·ly** *adv.* —**pro·voc·a·tive·ness** *n.*

pro·voke /prəˈvōk/ ▶*v.* [*trans.*] stimulate or give rise to (a reaction or emotion, typically a strong or unwelcome one) in someone: *the decision provoked a storm of protest from civil rights organizations |* [as *adj.*, in *combination*] (**-provoking**) *anxiety-provoking situations.* ■ stimulate or incite (someone) to do or feel something, esp. by arousing anger in them: *a teacher can* ***provoke*** *you* ***into*** *working harder.* See note at **INCITE**. ■ deliberately make (someone) annoyed or angry: *Rachel refused to be provoked.* ▷late Middle English (also in the sense 'invoke, summon'): from Old French *provoquer*, from Latin *provocare* 'challenge,' from *pro-* 'forth' + *vocare* 'to call.' —**pro·vok·a·ble** *adj.* —**pro·vok·er** *n.* —**pro·vok·ing·ly** *adv.*

pro·vo·lo·ne /ˌprōvəˈlōnē/ ▶*n.* an Italian soft smoked cheese made from cow's milk and having a mellow flavor. ▷Italian, from *provola* 'buffalo-milk cheese.'

pro·vost /ˈprōˌvōst/ ▶*n.* **1** a senior administrative officer in certain colleges and universities. ■ *Brit.* the head of certain university colleges, esp. at Oxford or Cambridge, and public schools. **2** the head of a chapter in a cathedral. ■ the Protestant minister of the principal church of a town or district in Germany and certain other European countries. ■ *historical* the head of a Christian community. [translating German *Propst*, Dutch *proost*, etc.] **3** short for **PROVOST MARSHAL**. **4** Scottish term for **MAYOR**. **5** *historical* the chief magistrate of a French or other European town. ▷late Old English *profost* 'head of a chapter, prior,' reinforced in Middle English by Anglo-Norman French *provost*, from medieval Latin *propositus*, synonym of Latin *praepositus* 'head, chief.' —**pro·vost·ship** /-ˌsʜip/ *n.*

pro·vost mar·shal ▶*n.* the head of military police in camp or on active service.

prow /prou/ ▶*n.* the portion of a ship's bow above water. ■ the pointed or projecting front part of something such as a car or building. ▷mid 16th cent.: from Old French *proue*, from Provençal *proa*, probably via Latin from Greek *prōira*, from a base meaning 'in front.'

prow·ess /ˈprou-əs; ˈprōəs/ ▶*n.* **1** skill or expertise in a particular activity or field: *his prowess as a fisherman.* **2** bravery in battle. ▷Middle English (sense 2): from Old French *proesce*, from *prou* 'valiant.' Sense 1 dates from the early 20th cent.

prowl /proul/ ▶*v.* [*trans.*] (of a person or animal) move around (a place) in search of or as if in search of prey: *black bears prowl the canyons.* ■ [*intrans.*] (of a person or animal) move stealthily or restlessly as or like a hunter: *committee members prowling around the offices at night with flashlights.*

▶*n.* an act of prowling: *I met her once on one of my off-duty bookstore prowls.* ▷late Middle English: of unknown origin.

▶*PHRASE* □ **on the prowl** (of a person or animal) moving around in search or as if in search of prey.

prowl car ▶*n.* a police squad car.

prowl·er /ˈproulər/ ▶*n.* a person who moves stealthily around or loiters near a place with a view to committing a crime, esp. burglary.

prox. ▶*abbr.* proximo.

prox. acc. ▶*abbr.* proxime accessit.

prox·e·mics /präkˈsēmiks/ ▶*plural n.* [treated as *sing.*] the branch of knowledge that deals with the amount of space that people feel it necessary to set between themselves and others. ▷1960s: from **PROXIMITY**, on the pattern of words such as *phonemics.* —**prox·e·mic** *adj.*

Prox·i·ma Cen·tau·ri /ˈpräksəmə ˌsenˈtôrē; -ˈtôrˌī/ *Astronomy* a faint red dwarf star associated with the bright binary star Alpha Centauri. It is the closest known star to the solar system (distance 4.24 light years). ▷Latin, 'nearest (star) of Centaurus.'

prox·i·mal /ˈpräksəməl/ ▶*adj.* *Anatomy* situated nearer to the center of the body or the point of attachment: *the proximal end of the forearm.* The opposite of **DISTAL**. ■ *Geology* relating to or denoting an area close to a center of a geological process such as sedimentation or volcanism. Often contrasted with **DISTAL**. ▷early 19th cent. (as a term in anatomy and zoology): from Latin *proximus* 'nearest' + **-AL**. In geology, usage dates from the 1940s. —**prox·i·mal·ly** *adv.*

prox·i·mate /ˈpräksəmit/ ▶*adj.* **1** (esp. of a cause of something) closest in relationship; immediate: *that storm was the proximate cause of damage to it.* ■ closest in space or time: *the failure of the proximate military power to lend assistance.* **2** nearly accurate; approximate: *he would try to change her speech into proximate ladylikeness.* ▷late 16th cent.: from Latin *proximatus* 'drawn near,' past participle of *proximare*, from *proximus* 'nearest.' —**prox·i·mate·ly** *adv.* —**prox·i·ma·tion** /ˌpräksəˈmāsʜən/ *n.*

prox·im·i·ty /präkˈsimətē/ ▶*n.* nearness in space, time, or relationship: *do not operate microphones in close proximity to television sets.* ▷late 15th cent.: from French *proximité*, from Latin *proximitas*, from *proximus* 'nearest.'

prox·im·i·ty fuse ▶*n.* an electronic detonator that causes a projectile to explode when it comes within a preset distance of its target.

prox·i·mo /ˈpräksəˌmō/ ▶*adj.* [*postpositive*] *dated* of next month: *he must be in San Francisco on 1st proximo.* Compare with **INSTANT**, **ULTIMO**. ▷from Latin *proximo mense* 'in the next month.'

prox·y /ˈpräksē/ ▶*n.* (*pl.* **prox·ies**) **1** the authority to represent someone else, esp. in voting: *they may register to vote* ***by proxy.*** ■ a person authorized to act on behalf of another. ■ a document authorizing a person to vote on another's behalf. **2** a figure that can be used to represent the value of something in a calculation: *the use of a U.S. wealth measure as a* ***proxy for*** *the true worldwide measure.* ▷late Middle English: contraction of **PROCURACY**.

prox·y war ▶*n.* a war instigated by a major power that does not itself become involved.

Pro·zac /ˈprōˌzak/ ▶*n.* trademark for **FLUOXETINE**. ▷1980s: an invented name.

pro·zone /ˈprōˌzōn/ ▶*n.* *Immunology* (in testing for antigens) the range of relative quantities of precipitin (or agglutinin) and antigen within which any precipitation (or agglutination) is inhibited by the predominance of one component. ▷early 20th cent.: from **PRO-**[2] 'before' + *(agglutination) zone.*

PRS ▶*abbr.* ■ Performing Rights Society. ■ (in the UK) President of the Royal Society.

prude /pro͞od/ ▶*n.* a person who is or claims to be easily shocked by matters relating to sex or nudity. ▷early 18th cent.: from French, back-formation from *prudefemme*, feminine of *prud'homme* 'good man and true,' from *prou* 'worthy.' —**prud·er·y** /ˈpro͞odərē/ *n.* —**prud·ish** *adj.* —**prud·ish·ly** *adv.* —**prud·ish·ness** *n.*

pru·dent /ˈpro͞odnt/ ▶*adj.* acting with or showing care and thought for the future: *no prudent money manager would authorize a loan without first knowing its purpose.* See note at **ECONOMICAL**. ▷late Middle English: from Old French, or from Latin *prudent-*, contraction of *provident-* 'foreseeing, attending to' (see **PROVIDENT**). —**pru·dence** *n.* —**pru·dent·ly** *adv.*

pru·den·tial /pro͞oˈdenсʜəl/ ▶*adj.* involving or showing care and forethought, typically in business. ▷late Middle English: from **PRUDENT**, on the pattern of words such as *evidential.* —**pru·den·tial·ly** *adv.*

Prud·hoe Bay /ˈpro͞od(h)ō/ an inlet of the Arctic Ocean, on the northern coast of Alaska. It is a major center of Alaskan oil production.

pru·i·nose /ˈpro͞oəˌnōs/ ▶*adj.* *chiefly Botany* (of a surface, such as that of a grape) covered with white powdery granules; frosted in appearance. ▷early 19th cent.: from Latin *pruinosus*, from *pruina* 'hoarfrost.'

prune[1] /pro͞on/ ▶*n.* a plum preserved by drying, having a black, wrinkled appearance. ■ *informal* an unpleasant or disagreeable person: *he was a good leader, but a miserable old prune.* ▷Middle English: from Old French, via Latin from Greek *prou(m)non* 'plum.'

prune[2] ▶*v.* [*trans.*] trim (a tree, shrub, or bush) by cutting away dead or overgrown branches or stems, esp. to increase fruitfulness and growth. ■ cut away (a branch or stem) in this way: ***prune back*** *the branches.* ■ reduce the extent of (something) by removing superfluous or unwanted parts: *reduction achieved by working harder or pruning costs.* ■ remove (superfluous or unwanted parts) from something: *Elliot deliberately* ***pruned away*** *details.* ▷late 15th cent. (in the sense 'abbreviate'): from Old French *pro(o)ignier*, possibly based on Latin *rotundus* 'round.' —**prun·er** *n.*

pru·nel·la[1] /pro͞oˈnelə/ ▶*n.* a plant of a genus that includes self-heal. Several kinds are cultivated as ground cover and rock garden plants. • Genus *Prunella*, family Labiatae. ▷modern Latin, literally 'quinsy,' in medieval Latin *brunella*, diminutive of *brunus* 'brown,' denoting a disease causing a brown coating on the tongue. Self-heal was a reputed cure for the disease.

pru·nel·la[2] ▶*n.* a strong silk or worsted twill fabric used formerly for legal robes and the uppers of women's shoes. ▷mid 17th cent.: perhaps from French *prunelle* 'sloe' (because of its dark color).

prun·ing hook ▶*n.* a cutting tool used for pruning, consisting of a hooked blade on a long handle.

prun·ing knife ▶*n.* a knife specifically designed for pruning, typically having a sharp, slightly curved blade and a hooked end.

pru·nus /ˈpro͞onəs/ ▶*n.* a tree or shrub of a large genus that includes many varieties grown for their spring blossom (cherry and almond) or for their fruit (plum, peach, and apricot). • Genus *Prunus*, family Rosaceae. ▷modern Latin, from Latin, literally 'plum tree.'

pru·ri·ent /ˈpro͝orēənt/ ▶*adj.* having or encouraging an excessive interest in sexual matters: *she'd been the subject of much prurient curiosity.* ▷late 16th cent. (in the sense 'having a mental itching'): from Latin *prurient-* 'itching, longing' and 'being wanton,' from the verb *prurire*. —**pru·ri·ence** *n.* —**pru·ri·en·cy** *n.* —**pru·ri·ent·ly** *adv.*

pru·ri·go /prōō'rīgō; -'rēgō/ ▸*n. Medicine* a chronic skin disease causing severe itching. ▷mid 17th cent.: from Latin, from *prurire* 'to itch.' —**pru·rig·i·nous** /prōō'rijənəs/ *adj.*

pru·ri·tus /prōō'rītəs/ ▸*n. Medicine* severe itching of the skin, as a symptom of various ailments. ▷mid 17th cent.: from Latin, 'itching' (see PRURIGO). —**pru·rit·ic** /-'ritik/ *adj.*

prus·ik /'prəsik/ *Climbing* ▸*n.* a method of ascending or descending a rope by means of two loops, each attached to it by a special knot tightening when weight is applied and slackening when it is removed, enabling the loop to be moved along the rope. ■ (also **prusik knot**) a sliding knot that locks under pressure, enabling a person to climb in this way.

▸*v.* (**prus·iked, prus·ik·ing**) [*intrans.*] [usu. as *n.*] (**prusiking**) climb using this method. ▷1930s: from the name of Karl *Prusik*, the Austrian mountaineer who devised this method of climbing.

Prus·sia /'prəshə/ a former kingdom of Germany. Originally a small country on the southeastern shores of the Baltic Sea, it became a major European power, covering much of modern northeastern Germany and Poland, under Frederick the Great. After the Franco-Prussian War of 1870–71, it became the center of Bismarck's new German Empire, but was abolished following Germany's defeat in World War I. —**Prus·sian** *adj.* & *n.*

Prus·sian blue /'prəshən/ ▸*n.* a deep blue pigment used in painting and dyeing, made from or in imitation of ferric ferrocyanide. ■ the deep blue color of this pigment.

prus·sic ac·id /'prəsik/ ▸*n.* old-fashioned term for HYDROCYANIC ACID. ▷late 18th cent.: *prussic* from French *prussique* 'relating to Prussian blue.' —**prus·si·ate** /'prəsē,āt/ *n.*

Prut /prōōt/ (also **Pruth**) a river in southeastern Europe that rises in the Carpathian Mountains in southern Ukraine and flows southeast for 530 miles (850 km) to join the Danube River near Galaţi in Romania. For much of its course it forms the border between Romania and Moldova.

pry[1] /prī/ ▸*v.* (**pries, pried**) [*intrans.*] inquire too closely into a person's private affairs: *I'm sick of you* **prying into** *my personal life* | [as *adj.*] (**prying**) *she felt there was no place where she could escape from the prying eyes.* ▷Middle English (in the sense 'peer inquisitively'): of unknown origin. —**pry·ing·ly** *adv.*

pry[2] ▸*v.* (**pries, pried**) [*trans.*] use force in order to move or open (something) or to separate (something) from something else: *using a screwdriver, he pried open the window.* ■ (**pry something out of/from**) obtain something from (someone) with effort or difficulty: *I got the loan, though I had to pry it out of him.* ▷early 19th cent.: from the verb PRIZE[2], interpreted as *pries*, third person singular of the present tense.

pry bar ▸*n.* a small, flattish iron bar used in the same way as a crowbar.

Prze·wal·ski's horse /,pərzhə'välskēz/ ▸*n.* a stocky wild Mongolian horse with a dun-colored coat and a dark brown erect mane, now extinct in the wild. It is the only true wild horse, and is the ancestor of the domestic horse. • *Equus ferus*, family Equidae. ▷late 19th cent.: named after Nikolai M. *Przheval'sky* (1839–88), Russian explorer.

PS ▸*abbr.* ■ passenger steamer. ■ permanent secretary. ■ police sergeant. ■ postscript. ■ private secretary. ■ Privy Seal. ■ *Theater* prompt side. ■ Public School.

Ps. (*pl.* **Pss.**) ▸*abbr. Bible* Psalm or Psalms.

psalm /sä(l)m/ (also **Psalm**) ▸*n.* a sacred song or hymn, in particular any of those contained in the biblical Book of Psalms and used in Christian and Jewish worship: *a delightful setting of Psalm 150.* ■ (**the Psalms** or **the Book of Psalms**) a book of the Bible comprising a collection of religious verses, sung or recited in both Jewish and Christian worship. Many are traditionally ascribed to King David. ▷Old English *(p)sealm*, via ecclesiastical Latin from Greek *psalmos* 'song sung to harp music,' from *psallein* 'to pluck.' —**psalm·ic** /'sä(l)mik/ *adj.*

psalm·book /'sä(l)m,bōōk/ ▸*n.* a book containing psalms, esp. with metrical settings for worship.

psalm·ist /'sä(l)mist/ ▸*n.* the author or composer of a psalm, esp. of any of the biblical Psalms. ▷late 15th cent.: from late Latin *psalmista*, from *psalmus* 'song sung to harp music' (see PSALM).

psal·mo·dy /'sä(l)mədē/ ▸*n.* the singing of psalms or similar sacred canticles, esp. in public worship. ■ psalms arranged for singing: *these books offer a useful collection of psalmody.* ▷Middle English: via late Latin from Greek *psalmōidia* 'singing to a harp,' from *psalmos* (see PSALM) + *ōidē* 'song.' —**psal·mod·ic** /sä(l)'mädik/ *adj.* —**psal·mo·dist** /-dist/ *n.*

psal·ter /'sôltər/ ▸*n.* (**the psalter** or **the Psalter**) the Book of Psalms. ■ a copy of the biblical Psalms, esp. for liturgical use. ▷Old English *(p)saltere*, via Latin *psalterium* from Greek *psaltērion* 'stringed instrument.'

psal·te·ri·um /,sôl'ti(ə)rēəm/ ▸*n.* another term for OMASUM. ▷mid 19th cent.: from Latin, literally 'psalter' (see PSALTER), because of its many folds of tissue, resembling pages of a book.

psal·ter·y /'sôltərē/ ▸*n.* (*pl.* **-ter·ies**) an ancient and medieval musical instrument like a dulcimer but played by plucking the strings with the fingers or a plectrum. ▷Middle English *sautrie*, from Old French *sauterie*, from Latin *psalterium* (see PSALTER).

PSAT ▸*abbr.* Preliminary Scholastic Aptitude Test.

PSBR *Brit.* ▸*abbr.* public-sector borrowing requirement.

psec. (also **ps**) ▸*abbr.* picosecond; picoseconds.

pse·phol·o·gy /sē'fäləjē/ ▸*n.* the statistical study of elections and trends in voting. ▷1950s: from Greek *psēphos* 'pebble, vote' + -LOGY. —**pse·pho·log·i·cal** /,sēfə'läjikəl/ *adj.* —**pse·pho·log·i·cal·ly** /-ik(ə)lē/ *adv.* —**pse·phol·o·gist** /-jist/ *n.*

pseud /sōōd/ *informal* ▸*adj.* intellectually or socially pretentious.

▸*n.* a pretentious person; a poseur. ▷1960s: abbreviation of PSEUDO.

pseud. ▸*abbr.* pseudonym.

pseud- ▸*comb. form* variant spelling of PSEUDO- reduced before a vowel (as in *pseudepigrapha*).

pseud·e·pig·ra·pha /,sōōdə'pigrəfə/ ▸*plural n.* spurious or pseudonymous writings, esp. Jewish writings ascribed to various biblical patriarchs and prophets but composed within approximately 200 years of the birth of Jesus Christ. ▷late 17th cent.: neuter plural of Greek *pseudepigraphos* 'with false title' (see PSEUDO-, EPIGRAPH). —**pseud·e·pig·ra·phal** *adj.* —**pseud·e·pi·graph·ic** /,sōōd,epi'grafik/ *adj.*

pseu·do /'sōōdō/ ▸*adj.* not genuine; sham: *we are talking about real journalists and not the pseudo kind.* ▷late Middle English: independent use of PSEUDO-.

pseudo- (also **pseud-** before a vowel) ▸*comb. form* **1** supposed or purporting to be but not really so; false; not genuine: *pseudonym* | *pseudoscience.* **2** resembling or imitating: *pseudohallucination* | *pseudo-French.* ▷from Greek *pseudēs* 'false,' *pseudos* 'falsehood.'

pseu·do·bulb /'sōōdō,bəlb/ ▸*n. Botany* a bulblike enlargement of the stem in many orchids, esp. tropical and epiphytic ones.

pseu·do·carp /'sōōdō,kärp/ ▸*n.* technical term for FALSE FRUIT. ▷mid 19th cent.: from PSEUDO- 'false' + Greek *karpos* 'fruit.'

pseu·do·cho·lin·es·ter·ase /,sōōdō,kōlə'nestə,rās; -rāz/ ▸*n. Biochemistry* an enzyme present in the blood and certain organs that hydrolyzes acetylcholine more slowly than acetylcholinesterase.

pseu·do·clas·si·cal /,sōōdō'klasikəl/ ▸*adj.* having a false or spurious classical style: *a pretentious pseudoclassical building.*

pseu·do-cleft *Grammar* ▸*n.* a sentence that resembles a cleft sentence by conveying emphasis or politeness through the use of a relative clause, such as *what we want is* representing *we want.*

▸*adj.* relating to or denoting a sentence of this kind.

pseu·do·code /'sōōdō,kōd/ ▸*n. Computing* a notation resembling a simplified programming language, used in program design.

pseu·do·cop·u·la·tion /,sōōdō,käpyə'lāshən/ ▸*n. Biology* attempted copulation by a male insect with a flower (esp. an orchid) that resembles the female, carrying pollen to it in the process.

pseu·do·cy·e·sis /,sōōdōsī'ēsis/ ▸*n.* technical term for FALSE PREGNANCY. ▷mid 19th cent.: from PSEUDO- 'false' + Greek *kuēsis* 'conception.'

pseu·do·cyst /'sōōdō,sist/ ▸*n. Medicine* a fluid-filled cavity resembling a cyst but lacking a wall or lining.

Pseu·do-Di·o·ny·si·us /'sōōdō ,dīə'nisēəs/ (6th century AD), the unidentified author of important theological works formerly attributed to Dionysius the Areopagite.

pseu·do·e·vent ▸*n. informal* an event arranged or brought about merely for the sake of the publicity or entertainment value it generates: *since real cultural events do not always occur on schedule, we invent pseudo-events for tour operators.*

pseu·do·ex·tinc·tion /,sōōdō-ik'stiNGkSHən/ ▸*n. Paleontology* the apparent extinction of a group of organisms with the survival of modified descendant forms.

pseu·do·gene /'sōōdō,jēn/ ▸*n. Genetics* a section of a chromosome that is an imperfect copy of a functional gene.

pseu·do·her·maph·ro·dit·ism /,sōōdōhər'mafrə,dīt,izəm/ ▸*n. Medicine* the condition in which an individual of one sex has external genitalia superficially resembling those of the other sex. —**pseu·do·her·maph·ro·dite** /-'mafrə,dīt/ *n.*

pseu·do·mem·brane /,sōōdō'mem,brān/ ▸*n. Medicine* a layer of exudate resembling a membrane, formed on the surface of the skin or of a mucous membrane, esp. the conjunctiva. —**pseu·do·mem·bra·nous** /-'membrənəs/ *adj.*

pseu·dom·o·nas /,sōōdō'mōnəs/ ▸*n. Microbiology* a bacterium of a genus that occurs in soil and detritus, including a number that are pathogens of plants or animals. • Genus *Pseudomonas*; aerobic Gram-negative bacteria. ▷modern Latin, from PSEUDO- 'false' + *monas* 'monad.' —**pseu·dom·o·nad** /-'mō,nad/ *n.*

pseu·do·morph /'sōōdə,môrf/ *Crystallography* ▸*n.* a crystal consisting of one mineral but having the form of another which it has replaced.

▸*v.* [*trans.*] replace (another substance) to form a pseudomorph. ▷mid 19th cent.: from PSEUDO- 'false' + Greek *morphē* 'form.' —**pseu·do·mor·phic** /,sōōdō'môrfik/ *adj.* —**pseu·do·mor·phism** /,sōōdō-'môr,fizəm/ *n.* —**pseu·do·mor·phous** /,sōōdō'môrfəs/ *adj.*

pseu·do·nym /'sōōdn-im/ ▸*n.* a fictitious name, esp. one used by an author. ▷mid 19th cent.: from French *pseudonyme*, from Greek *pseudōnymos*, from *pseudēs* 'false' + *onoma* 'name.' —**pseu·do·nym·i·ty** /,sōōdn'imətē/ *n.*

pseu·don·y·mous /sōō'dänəməs/ ▸*adj.* writing or written under a false name: *the pseudonymous author of this mystery.* —**pseu·don·y·mous·ly** *adv.*

pseu·do·pod /'sōōdə,päd/ ▸*n.* another term for PSEUDOPODIUM.

pseu·do·po·di·um /,sōōdə'pōdēəm/ ▸*n.* (*pl.* **-po·di·a** /-'pōdēə/) *Biology* a temporary protrusion of the surface of an ameboid cell for movement and feeding. ▷mid 19th cent.: modern Latin, from PSEUDO- + PODIUM.

pseu·do·preg·nan·cy /,sōōdō'pregnənsē/ ▸*n.* (*pl.* **-cies**) another term for FALSE PREGNANCY. —**pseu·do·preg·nant** /-'pregnənt/ *adj.*

pseu·do·ra·bies /,sōōdō'rābēz/ ▸*n. Veterinary Medicine* an infectious herpesvirus disease of the central nervous system in domestic animals that causes convulsions and intense itching and is usually fatal.

pseu·do·ran·dom /,sōōdō'randəm/ ▸*adj.* (of a number, a sequence of numbers, or any digital data) satisfying one or more statistical tests for randomness but produced by a definite mathematical procedure. —**pseu·do·ran·dom·ly** *adv.*

pseu·do·sci·ence /,sōōdō'sīəns/ ▸*n.* a collection of beliefs or practices mistakenly regarded as being based on scientific method. —**pseu·do·sci·en·tif·ic** /-,sīən'tifik/ *adj.* —**pseu·do·sci·en·tist** /-'sīəntist/ *n.*

pseu·do·scor·pi·on /,sōōdō'skôrpēən/ ▸*n.* a minute arachnid that has pincers but no long abdomen or sting, occurring abundantly in leaf litter. Also called FALSE SCORPION. • Order Pseudoscorpiones.

pseu·do·u·ri·dine /,sōōdō'yōōrə,dēn/ ▸*n. Biochemistry* a nucleoside present in transfer RNA and differing from uridine in having the sugar residue attached at a carbon atom instead of nitrogen.

pshaw /(p)shô/ ▸*exclam. dated* or *humorous* an expression of contempt or impatience: *"Poison? Pshaw! The very idea!"*

▸*v.* [*intrans.*] *dated* or *humorous* utter such an exclamation: *when I suggested that free trade might dilute Canadian culture, he pshawed.* ▷natural exclamation: first recorded in English in the late 17th cent.

psi /(p)sī/ ▸*n.* **1** the twenty-third letter of the Greek alphabet (Ψ, ψ), transliterated as 'ps.' ■ (**Psi**) [followed by Latin genitive] *Astronomy* the twenty-third star in a constellation: *Psi Aquarii.* **2** supposed parapsychological or psychic faculties or phenomena: *he turns to anecdotal evidence to prove that psi exists.*

p.s.i. ▸*abbr.* pounds per square inch.

psil·o·cy·bin /,silə'sībin/ ▸*n. Chemistry* a hallucinogenic alkaloid, found in some toadstools. ▷1950s:

from modern Latin *Psilocybe* (genus name), from Greek *psilos* 'bald' + *kubē* 'head.'

psi·on·ic /sī'änik/ ▸*adj.* relating to or denoting the practical use of psychic powers or paranormal phenomena: *psionic communication.* ▷1950s: from PSI, on the pattern of *electronic.* **—psi·on·i·cal·ly** /-ik(ə)lē/ *adv.*

psit·ta·cine /'sitə,sīn/ ▸*adj. Ornithology* of, relating to, or denoting birds of the parrot family: *psittacine beak and feather disease.* ■ parrotlike (esp. referring to parrots' ability to copy human speech): *issues are thought through in a distinctive way, rather than by psittacine repetition.*
▸*n. Ornithology* a bird of the parrot family. ▷late 19th cent.: from Latin *psittacinus* 'of a parrot,' from *psittacus,* from Greek *psittakos* 'parrot.'

psit·ta·co·sau·rus /,sitəkō'sôrəs/ ▸*n.* a partly bipedal herbivorous dinosaur of the mid Cretaceous period, having a parrotlike beak and probably ancestral to other ceratopsians. • Genus *Psittacosaurus,* infraorder Ceratopsia, order Ornithischia. ▷modern Latin, from Greek *psittakos* 'parrot' + *sauros* 'lizard.'

psit·ta·co·sis /,sitə'kōsəs/ ▸*n.* a contagious disease of birds, caused by chlamydiae and transmissible (esp. from parrots) to human beings as a form of pneumonia. ▷late 19th cent.: from Latin *psittacus* 'parrot' + -OSIS.

pso·as /'sōəs/ (also **psoas major**) ▸*n. Anatomy* each of a pair of large muscles that run from the lumbar spine through the groin on either side and, with the iliacus, flex the hip. A second muscle, the **psoas minor**, has a similar action but is often absent. ▷late 17th cent.: from Greek, accusative plural of *psoa,* interpreted as singular.

pso·cid /'sōsəd/ ▸*n. Entomology* a small or minute insect of an order that includes the booklice. Many psocids are wingless and somewhat resemble lice or aphids, and most live on bark and among foliage. • Order Psocoptera: many families, including the large family Psocidae. ▷late 19th cent.: from modern Latin *Psocidae* (plural), from *Psocus* (genus name), from Greek *psōkhein* 'to grind.'

Pso·cop·ter·a /sō'käptərə/ *Entomology* an order of insects that comprises the booklice and other psocids. ▷modern Latin (plural), from *Psocus* (genus name) + *pteron* 'wing.' **—pso·cop·ter·an** *n.* & *adj.*

pso·ra·len /'sôrələn; -,len/ ▸*n. Chemistry* a compound present in certain plants that is used in perfumery and (in combination with ultraviolet light) to treat psoriasis and other skin disorders. • A tricyclic lactone; chem. formula: $C_{11}H_6O_3$. ▷1930s: from modern Latin *Psorolea* (former genus name), from Greek *psōraleos* 'itchy' (from *psōra* 'itch') + the suffix *-en* (compare with -ENE).

pso·ri·a·sis /sə'rīəsəs/ ▸*n. Medicine* a skin disease marked by red, itchy, scaly patches. ▷late 17th cent.: modern Latin, from Greek *psōriasis,* from *psōrian* 'have an itch,' (from *psōra* 'itch') + -ASIS. **—pso·ri·at·ic** /,sôrē'atik/ *adj.*

psst /pst/ ▸*exclam.* used to attract someone's attention surreptitiously: *Psst! Want to know a secret?* ▷1920s: imitative.

PST ▸*abbr.* Pacific Standard Time (see PACIFIC TIME).

PSV *Brit.* ▸*abbr.* public service vehicle.

psych /sīk/ (also **psyche**) ▸*v.* **1** [*trans.*] *informal* mentally prepare (someone) for a testing task or occasion: *we had to* **psych** *ourselves* **up** *for the race.* **2** (usu. **psyche**) [*intrans.*] *Bridge* make a psychic bid.
▸*phrasal v.* □ **psych someone out** *informal* intimidate an opponent or rival by appearing confident or aggressive: *guys who try to lift heavy weights in a mistaken attempt to psych out the other guys.* □ **psych something out** *informal* analyze something in psychological terms.
▸*n.* **1** *informal* short for PSYCHIATRIST or PSYCHOLOGIST. ■ short for PSYCHIATRY or PSYCHOLOGY. **2** (usu. **psyche**) *Bridge* a psychic bid.
▸*adj.* [*attrib.*] **1** *informal* short for PSYCHIATRIC. **2** short for PSYCHEDELIC: *a rare old psych album.*

psych. ▸*abbr.* ■ psychological. ■ psychologist. ■ psychology.

Psy·che /'sīkē/ *Greek Mythology* a Hellenistic personification of the soul as female, or sometimes as a butterfly. The allegory of Psyche's love for Cupid is told in *The Golden Ass* by Apuleius.

psy·che[1] /'sīkē/ ▸*n.* the human soul, mind, or spirit: *I will never really fathom the female psyche.* ▷mid 17th cent.: via Latin from Greek *psukhē* 'breath, life, soul.'

psy·che[2] /sīk/ ▸*v., n.,* & *adj.* variant spelling of PSYCH.

psych·e·de·lia /,sīkə'dēlyə/ ▸*n.* music, culture, or art based on the experiences produced by psychedelic drugs. ▷1960s: back-formation from PSYCHEDELIC.

psy·che·del·ic /,sīkə'delik/ ▸*adj.* relating to or denoting drugs (esp. LSD) that produce hallucinations and apparent expansion of consciousness. ■ relating to or denoting a style of rock music originating in the mid-1960s, characterized by musical experimentation and drug-related lyrics. ■ denoting or having an intense, vivid color or a swirling abstract pattern: *a psychedelic T-shirt.*
▸*n.* a psychedelic drug. ▷1950s: formed irregularly from PSYCHE[1] + Greek *dēlos* 'clear, manifest' + -IC. **—psy·che·del·i·cal·ly** /-ik(ə)lē/ *adv.*

psy·chi·at·ric /,sīkē'atrik/ ▸*adj.* of or relating to mental illness or its treatment: *a psychiatric disorder.* **—psy·chi·at·ri·cal·ly** /-ik(ə)lē/ *adv.*

psy·chi·a·trist /sə'kīətrist; sī-/ ▸*n.* a medical practitioner specializing in the diagnosis and treatment of mental illness.

psy·chi·a·try /sə'kīətrē; sī-/ ▸*n.* the study and treatment of mental illness, emotional disturbance, and abnormal behavior. ▷mid 19th cent.: from Greek *psukhē* 'soul, mind' + *iatreia* 'healing' (from *iatros* 'healer').

psy·chic /'sīkik/ ▸*adj.* **1** relating to or denoting faculties or phenomena that are apparently inexplicable by natural laws, esp. involving telepathy or clairvoyance: *psychic powers.* ■ (of a person) appearing or considered to have powers of telepathy or clairvoyance: *I could sense it—I must be psychic.* **2** of or relating to the soul or mind: *he dulled his psychic pain with gin.* **3** *Bridge* denoting a bid that deliberately misrepresents the bidder's hand, in order to mislead the opponents.
▸*n.* a person considered or claiming to have psychic powers; a medium. ■ (**psychics**) [treated as *sing.* or *pl.*] the study of psychic phenomena. ▷early 19th cent.: from Greek *psukhikos* (see PSYCHE[1]). **—psy·chi·cal** /'sīkikəl/ *adj.* (usu. in sense 1). **—psy·chi·cal·ly** /'sīkik(ə)lē/ *adv.* **—psy·chism** /'sī,kizəm/ *n.* (in sense 1).

psy·chic in·come ▸*n. Economics* the nonmonetary or nonmaterial satisfactions that accompany an occupation or economic activity.

psy·cho /'sīkō/ *informal* ▸*n.* (*pl.* **-chos**) a psychopath. ▸*adj.* psychopathic. ▷1930s: abbreviation.

psycho- ▸*comb. form* relating to the mind or psychology: *psychobabble* | *psychometrics.* ▷from Greek *psukhē* 'breath, soul, mind.'

psy·cho·a·cous·tics /,sīkōə'kōōstiks/ ▸*plural n.* [treated as *sing.*] the branch of psychology concerned with the perception of sound and its physiological effects. **—psy·cho·a·cous·tic** *adj.*

psy·cho·ac·tive /,sīkō'aktiv/ ▸*adj.* (chiefly of a drug) affecting the mind.

psy·cho·a·nal·y·sis /,sīkōə'naləsəs/ ▸*n.* a system of psychological theory and therapy that aims to treat mental disorders by investigating the interaction of conscious and unconscious elements in the mind and bringing repressed fears and conflicts into the conscious mind by techniques such as dream interpretation and free association. **—psy·cho·an·a·lyze** /,sīkō'anl,īz/ (*Brit.* **psy·cho·an·a·lyse**) *v.* **—psy·cho·an·a·lyt·ic** /,sīkō,anl'itik/ *adj.* **—psy·cho·an·a·lyt·i·cal** /,sīkō,anl'itikəl/ *adj.* **—psy·cho·an·a·lyt·i·cal·ly** /,sīkō,anl'itik(ə)lē/ *adv.*

psy·cho·an·a·lyst /,sīkō'anl-əst/ ▸*n.* a person who practices psychoanalysis.

psy·cho·bab·ble /'sīkō,babəl/ ▸*n. informal, derogatory* jargon used in popular psychology.

psy·cho·bi·ol·o·gy /,sīkō,bī'äləjē/ ▸*n.* the branch of science that deals with the biological basis of behavior and mental phenomena. **—psy·cho·bi·o·log·i·cal** /-,bīə'läjəkəl/ *adj.* **—psy·cho·bi·ol·o·gist** /-jist/ *n.*

psy·cho·dra·ma /,sīkō'drämə; -'dramə/ ▸*n.* **1** a form of psychotherapy in which patients act out events from their past. **2** a play, movie, or novel in which psychological elements are the main interest. ■ the genre to which such works belong. **—psy·cho·dra·mat·ic** /-drə'matik/ *adj.*

psy·cho·dy·nam·ics /,sīkōdī'namiks/ ▸*plural n.* [treated as *sing.*] the interrelation of the unconscious and conscious mental and emotional forces that determine personality and motivation. ■ the branch of psychology that deals with this. **—psy·cho·dy·nam·ic** *adj.* **—psy·cho·dy·nam·i·cal·ly** /-ik(ə)lē/ *adv.*

psy·cho·gen·e·sis /,sīkō'jenəsis/ ▸*n.* [in *sing.*] the psychological cause to which a mental illness or behavioral disturbance may be attributed (as distinct from a physical cause).

psy·cho·gen·ic /,sīkō'jenik/ ▸*adj.* having a psychological origin or cause rather than a physical one: *psychogenic ill health.*

psy·cho·ger·i·at·rics /,sīkō,jerē'atriks/ ▸*plural n.* [treated as *sing.*] the branch of health care concerned with mental illness and disturbance in elderly people, particularly those who have suffered distress as a result of moving into an institution. **—psy·cho·ger·i·at·ric** *adj.* **—psy·cho·ger·i·a·tri·cian** /-,jerēə'trisнən/ *n.*

psy·cho·graph·ics /,sīkō'grafiks/ ▸*plural n.* [treated as *sing.*] the study and classification of people according to their attitudes, aspirations, and other psychological criteria, esp. in market research. **—psy·cho·graph·ic** *adj.*

psy·cho·his·to·ry /'sīkō,hist(ə)rē/ ▸*n.* (*pl.* **-ries**) the interpretation of historical events with the aid of psychological theory. ■ a work that interprets historical events in such a way: *modern writers often substitute psychohistory for biography.* ■ a psychological history of an individual. **—psy·cho·his·to·ri·an** /,sīkō(h)i'stôrēən/ *n.* **—psy·cho·his·to·ri·cal** /,sīkō(h)i'stôrikəl/ *adj.*

psy·cho·ki·ne·sis /,sīkōkə'nēsis/ ▸*n.* the supposed ability to move objects by mental effort alone. **—psy·cho·ki·net·ic** /-'netik/ *adj.*

psychol. ▸*abbr.* ■ psychological. ■ psychologist. ■ psychology.

psy·cho·lin·guis·tics /,sīkōlɪɴɢ'gwistiks/ ▸*plural n.* [treated as *sing.*] the study of the relationships between linguistic behavior and psychological processes, including the process of language acquisition. **—psy·cho·lin·guist** /-'lɪɴɢgwist/ *n.* **—psy·cho·lin·guis·tic** *adj.*

psy·chol·o·gese /,sī,kälə'jēz/ ▸*n. informal* psychological jargon or technical terms used for effect.

psy·cho·log·i·cal /,sīkə'läjəkəl/ ▸*adj.* of, affecting, or arising in the mind; related to the mental and emotional state of a person: *the victim had sustained physical and psychological damage.* ■ of or relating to psychology: *psychological research.* ■ (of an ailment or problem) having a mental rather than a physical cause: *it was concluded that her pain was psychological.* **—psy·cho·log·i·cal·ly** /-ik(ə)lē/ *adv.*

psy·cho·log·i·cal mo·ment ▸*n.* [in *sing.*] the moment at which something will or would have the greatest psychological effect: *there was a psychological moment when they might have accepted the report.*

psy·cho·log·i·cal war·fare ▸*n.* actions intended to reduce an opponent's morale.

psy·chol·o·gism /sī'kälə,jizəm/ ▸*n. Philosophy* a tendency to interpret events or arguments in subjective terms, or to exaggerate the relevance of psychological factors.

psy·chol·o·gist /sī'käləjist/ ▸*n.* an expert or specialist in psychology.

psy·chol·o·gize /sī'kälə,jīz/ ▸*v.* [*trans.*] analyze or regard in psychological terms, esp. in an uninformed way: *he lets few of Kinsey's quirks and opinions pass without psychologizing them away.* ■ [*intrans.*] theorize or speculate concerning the psychology of something or someone.

psy·chol·o·gy /sī'käləjē/ ▸*n.* the scientific study of the human mind and its functions, esp. those affecting behavior in a given context. ■ [in *sing.*] the mental characteristics or attitude of a person or group: *the psychology of Americans in the 1920s.* ■ [in *sing.*] the mental and emotional factors governing a situation or activity: *the psychology of interpersonal relationships.* ▷late 17th cent.: from modern Latin *psychologia* (see PSYCHO-, -LOGY).

psy·cho·met·ric /,sīkə'metrik/ ▸*adj.* of, relating to, or deriving from psychometry or psychometrics. **—psy·cho·met·ri·cal·ly** /-ik(ə)lē/ *adv.*

psy·cho·met·rics /,sīkə'metriks/ ▸*plural n.* [treated as *sing.*] the science of measuring mental capacities and processes. **—psy·chom·e·tri·cian** /-mə'trisнən/ *n.*

psy·chom·e·try /sī'kämətrē/ ▸*n.* **1** the supposed ability to discover facts about an event or person by touching inanimate objects associated with them. **2** another term for PSYCHOMETRICS. **—psy·chom·e·trist** /-trist/ *n.*

psy·cho·mo·tor /,sīkō'mōtər/ ▸*adj.* [*attrib.*] of or relating to the origination of movement in conscious mental activity.

psy·cho·neu·ro·im·mu·nol·o·gy /,sīkō,n(y)ōōrō,imyə'näləjē/ ▸*n. Medicine* the study of the effect of the mind on health and resistance to disease.

psy·cho·neu·ro·sis /,sīkōn(y)ōō'rōsəs/ ▸*n.* (*pl.* **-ro·ses** /-'rō,sēz/) another term for NEUROSIS. **—psy·cho·neu·rot·ic** /-,n(y)ōō'rätik/ *adj.*

psy·cho·path /'sīkə,paтн/ ▸*n.* a person suffering

Pronunciation Key ə *ago;* ər *over;* 'ə or ,ə *up;* 'ər or ,ər *fur;* a *hat;* ā *rate;* ä *car;* CH *chew;* e *let;* ē *see;* e(ə)r *air;* i *fit;* ī *by;* i(ə)r *ear;* NG *sing;* ō *go;* ô *for;* oi *boy;* ŏŏ *good;* ōō *goo;* ou *out;* SH *she;* TH *thin;* TH *then;* (h)w *why;* ZH *vision*

from chronic mental disorder with abnormal or violent social behavior. **—psy·cho·path·ic** /ˌsīkə'paTHik/ *adj.* **—psy·cho·path·i·cal·ly** /ˌsīkə'paTHik(ə)lē/ *adv.*

psy·cho·pa·thol·o·gy /ˌsīkōpə'THäləjē; -paTH'äl-/ ▸*n.* the scientific study of mental disorders. ■ features of people's mental health considered collectively: *ageism, family discord and psychopathology all play their part in abuse.* ■ mental or behavioral disorder: *she showed evidence of genuine psychopathology.* **—psy·cho·path·o·log·i·cal** /-paTHō'läjikəl/ *adj.* **—psy·cho·pa·thol·o·gist** /-THäləjist/ *n.*

psy·chop·a·thy /sī'käpəTHē/ ▸*n.* mental illness or disorder.

psy·cho·phar·ma·col·o·gy /ˌsīkōˌfärmə'käləjē/ ▸*n.* the branch of psychology concerned with the effects of drugs on the mind and behavior. **—psy·cho·phar·ma·co·log·i·cal** /-ˌfärməkə'läjikəl/ *adj.* **—psy·cho·phar·ma·col·o·gist** /-jist/ *n.*

psy·cho·phys·ics /ˌsīkō'fiziks/ ▸*plural n.* [treated as *sing.*] the branch of psychology that deals with the relationships between physical stimuli and mental phenomena. **—psy·cho·phys·i·cal** /-'fizikəl/ *adj.*

psy·cho·phys·i·ol·o·gy /ˌsīkōˌfizē'äləjē/ ▸*n. Psychology* the study of the relationship between physiological and psychological phenomena. ■ the way in which the mind and body interact. **—psy·cho·phys·i·o·log·i·cal** /-ˌfizēə'läjikəl/ *adj.* **—psy·cho·phys·i·ol·o·gist** /-jist/ *n.*

psy·cho·pomp /'sīkōˌpämp/ (also **psy·cho·pom·pos** /ˌsīkō'pämpəs; -'pämpäs/) ▸*n.* (in Greek mythology) a guide of souls to the place of the dead. ■ the spiritual guide of a living person's soul. ▷from Greek *psukhopompos*, from *psukhē* 'soul' + *pompos* 'conductor.'

psy·cho·sex·u·al /ˌsīkō'sekSHōōəl/ ▸*adj.* of or involving the psychological aspects of the sexual impulse. **—psy·cho·sex·u·al·ly** *adv.*

psy·cho·sis /sī'kōsəs/ ▸*n.* (*pl.* **-ses** /-ˌsēz/) a severe mental disorder in which thought and emotions are so impaired that contact is lost with external reality. ▷mid 19th cent.: from Greek *psukhōsis* 'animation,' from *psukhoun* 'give life to,' from *psukhē* 'soul, mind.'

psy·cho·so·cial /ˌsīkō'sōSHəl/ ▸*adj.* of or relating to the interrelation of social factors and individual thought and behavior. **—psy·cho·so·cial·ly** *adv.*

psy·cho·so·mat·ic /ˌsīkōsə'matik/ ▸*adj.* (of a physical illness or other condition) caused or aggravated by a mental factor such as internal conflict or stress: *her doctor was convinced that most of Edith's problems were psychosomatic.* ■ of or relating to the interaction of mind and body. **—psy·cho·so·mat·i·cal·ly** /-ik(ə)lē/ *adv.*

psy·cho·sur·ger·y /ˌsīkō'sərjərē/ ▸*n.* brain surgery, such as lobotomy, used to treat mental disorder. **—psy·cho·sur·gi·cal** /-'sərjikəl/ *adj.*

psy·cho·syn·the·sis /ˌsīkō'sinTHəsəs/ ▸*n. Psychoanalysis* the integration of separated elements of the psyche or personality.

psy·cho·ther·a·py /ˌsīkō'THerəpē/ ▸*n.* the treatment of mental disorder by psychological rather than medical means. **—psy·cho·ther·a·peu·tic** /-ˌTHerə'pyōōtik/ *adj.* **—psy·cho·ther·a·pist** /-'THerəpist/ *n.*

psy·chot·ic /sī'kätik/ ▸*adj.* of, denoting, or suffering from a psychosis: *a psychotic disturbance.*
▸*n.* a person suffering from a psychosis. **—psy·chot·i·cal·ly** /-ik(ə)lē/ *adv.*

psy·chot·o·mi·met·ic /ˌsīˌkätōmə'metik/ ▸*adj.* relating to or denoting drugs that are capable of producing an effect on the mind similar to a psychotic state.
▸*n.* a drug of this kind.

psy·cho·tron·ic /ˌsīkə'tränik/ ▸*adj.* **1** denoting or relating to a genre of movies, typically with a science fiction, horror, or fantasy theme, that were made on a low budget or poorly received by critics. [1980s: coined in this sense by Michael Weldon, who edited a weekly New York guide to the best and worst films on local television.] **2** of or relating to psychotronics.

psy·cho·tron·ics /ˌsīkə'träniks/ ▸*plural n.* [treated as *sing.*] a particular branch of parapsychology that supposes an energy or force to emanate from living organisms and affect matter. ▷1970s: from **PSYCHO-**, on the pattern of *electronics.*

psy·cho·tro·pic /ˌsīkə'trōpik; -'träpik/ ▸*adj.* relating to or denoting drugs that affect a person's mental state.
▸*n.* a drug of this kind.

psy·chrom·e·ter /sī'krämətər/ ▸*n.* a hygrometer consisting of a wet-bulb and a dry-bulb thermometer, the difference in the two thermometer readings being used to determine atmospheric humidity. ▷early 18th cent.: from Greek *psukhros* 'cold' + **-METER.**

psyl·la /'silə/ (also **psyl·lid** /'silid/) ▸*n. Entomology* a minute insect of a family (Psyllidae) that comprises the jumping plant lice. ▷late 19th cent.: from modern Latin *Psyllidae* (plural), from Greek *psulla* 'flea.'

psyl·li·um /'silēəm/ ▸*n.* a leafy-stemmed Eurasian plantain, the seeds of which are used as a laxative and as a bulking agent in the treatment of obesity. • *Plantago afra*, family Plantaginaceae. ▷mid 16th cent.: via Latin from Greek *psullion*, from *psulla* 'flea' (because the seeds resemble fleas).

Psy·Ops ▸*abbr.* psychological operations.

PT ▸*abbr.* ■ Pacific Time. ■ physical therapy. ■ physical training. ■ postal telegraph. ■ post town. ■ *Brit.* pupil teacher.

Pt ▸*symbol* the chemical element platinum.

pt. ▸*abbr.* ■ part: *Pt 1 of the Consumer Protection Act 1987.* ■ payment. ■ pint; pints. ■ point. ■ *Printing* point (as a unit of measurement): *12 pt type.* ■ (denoting a side of a ship or aircraft) port. ■ preterit.

p.t. ▸*abbr.* ■ past tense. ■ post town. ■ pro tempore.

PTA ▸*abbr.* ■ parent–teacher association.

pta. (also **Pta.**) ▸*abbr.* (*pl.* **ptas.**) peseta.

Ptah /tä/ *Egyptian Mythology* an ancient deity of Memphis, creator of the universe, god of artisans, and husband of Sekhmet. He became one of the chief deities of Egypt, and was identified by the Greeks with Hephaestus.

ptar·mi·gan /'tärməgən/ ▸*n.* (*pl.* same or **-gans**) a northern grouse of mountainous and Arctic regions, with feathered legs and feet and plumage that typically changes to white in winter. • Genus *Lagopus*, family Tetraonidae: two species, in particular the (**rock**) **ptarmigan** (*L. mutus*) of Eurasia and North America. ▷late 16th cent.: from Scottish Gaelic *tàrmachan*. The spelling with *p-* was introduced later, suggested by Greek words starting with *pt-*.

PT boat ▸*n.* a motorboat equipped with torpedoes and used by the military, esp. during World War II. ▷1940s: from *P(atrol) T(orpedo) boat.*

PTC ▸*abbr. Biochemistry* phenylthiocarbamide.

pter·an·o·don /tə'ranəˌdän; -dən/ ▸*n.* a large tailless pterosaur of the Cretaceous period, with a long toothless beak, a long bony crest, and a wingspan of up to 7 m. • Genus *Pteranodon*, family Pteranodontidae, order Pterosauria. ▷modern Latin, from Greek *pteron* 'wing' + *an-* 'without' + *odous, odont-* 'tooth.'

pter·i·dol·o·gy /ˌterə'däləjē/ ▸*n.* the study of ferns and related plants. ▷mid 19th cent.: from Greek *pteris, pterid-* 'fern' + **-LOGY.** **—pter·i·do·log·i·cal** /-dl'äjikəl/ *adj.* **—pter·i·dol·o·gist** /-jist/ *n.*

Pter·i·doph·y·ta /ˌterə'däfitə/ *Botany* a division of flowerless green plants that comprises the ferns and their relatives. • Division Pteridophyta: classes Filicopsida (ferns), Sphenopsida (horsetails), and Lycopsida (club mosses). ▷modern Latin (plural), from Greek *pteris, pterid-* 'fern' + *phuton* 'plant.' **—pte·rid·o·phyte** /tə'ridəˌfit; 'teridə-/ *n.*

pte·rid·o·phyte /tə'ridəˌfit; 'teridə-/ ▸*n. Botany* a member of the Pteridphyta, a division of plants including the ferns and their allies (horsetails, club mosses).

pte·rid·o·sperm /tə'ridəˌspərm; 'teridə-/ ▸*n.* an extinct plant that is intermediate between the ferns and seed-bearing plants, dying out in the Triassic period. Also called **SEED FERN.** • Formerly placed in their own taxon (class Pteridospermeae), but now included with the gymnosperms. ▷early 20th cent.: from modern Latin *pteridospermeae*, from Greek *pteris, pterid-* 'fern.'

ptero- ▸*comb. form* relating to wings; having wings: *pterosaur.* ▷from Greek *pteron* 'feather, wing.'

pter·o·branch /'terəˌbraNGk/ ▸*n. Zoology* a minute tube-dwelling colonial acorn worm found chiefly in deep water. • Class Pterobranchia, phylum Hemichordata.

pter·o·dac·tyl /ˌterə'daktəl/ ▸*n.* a pterosaur of the late Jurassic period, with a long slender head and neck and a very short tail. • Family Pterodactylidae, order Pterosauria: several genera, including *Pterodactylus.* ■ (in general use) any pterosaur. ▷early 19th cent.: from modern Latin *Pterodactylus* (genus name), from Greek *pteron* 'wing' + *daktulos* 'finger.'

pter·o·pod /'terəˌpäd/ ▸*n. Zoology* a small mollusk with winglike extensions to its body that it uses for swimming. • Orders Thecosomata (with shells) and Gymnosomata (lacking shells), class Gastropoda. ▷mid 19th cent.: from modern Latin *Pteropoda* (plural), from Greek *pteron* 'wing' + *pous, pod-* 'foot.'

pter·o·saur /'terəˌsôr/ ▸*n.* an extinct warm-blooded flying reptile of the Jurassic and Cretaceous periods, with membranous wings supported by a greatly lengthened fourth finger, and probably covered with fur. • Order Pterosauria, subdivision Archosauria: several families, including pterodactyls, pteranodons, etc. ▷mid 19th cent.: from modern Latin *Pterosauria* (plural), from Greek *pteron* 'wing' + *sauros* 'lizard.'

pter·o·yl·glu·tam·ic ac·id /ˌteröilˌglōō'tamik/ ▸*n.* another term for **FOLIC ACID.** ▷1940s: the initial element of *pteroylglutamic* is from Greek *pteron* 'wing,' with reference to insect pigments. **—pter·o·yl·glu·ta·mate** /-'glōōtəˌmāt/ *n.*

pter·y·goid proc·ess /'teriˌgoid 'präˌses; 'präsəs/ ▸*n. Anatomy* each of a pair of projections from the sphenoid bone in the skull. ▷early 18th cent.: from modern Latin *pterygoides* (plural), from Greek *pterux, pterug-* 'wing.'

Pter·y·go·ta /ˌterə'gōtə/ *Entomology* a large group of insects that comprises those that have wings or winged ancestors, including the majority of modern species. Compare with **APTERYGOTA.** • Subclass Pterygota, class Insecta (or Hexapoda): many orders. ▷modern Latin (plural), from Greek *pterugōtos* 'winged,' from *pterux, pterug-* 'wing.' **—pter·y·gote** /'terəˌgōt/ *n.*

PTFE ▸*abbr.* polytetrafluoroethylene.

ptg. ▸*abbr.* printing.

PTH ▸*abbr.* parathyroid hormone.

ptis·an /tə'zan; 'tizən/ ▸*n.* a nourishing drink, esp. barley water. ▷late Middle English: from Latin *ptisana*, from Greek *ptisanē* 'peeled barley.' Compare with **TISANE.**

PTO ▸*abbr.* ■ please turn over (written at the foot of a page to indicate that the text continues on the reverse). ■ (also **pto**) (in a tractor or other vehicle) power takeoff. ■ Parent-Teacher Organization.

Ptol·e·ma·ic /ˌtälə'mā-ik/ ▸*adj.* **1** of or relating to the Greek astronomer Ptolemy or his theories. **2** of or relating to the Ptolemies of Egypt (see **PTOLEMY**[1].)

Ptol·e·ma·ic sys·tem (also **Ptolemaic theory**) ▸*n. historical & Astronomy* the theory that the earth is the stationary center of the universe, with the planets moving in epicyclic orbits within surrounding concentric spheres. Compare with **COPERNICAN SYSTEM.**

Ptol·e·my[1] /'täləmē/ the name of all the Macedonian rulers of Egypt, a dynasty founded by Ptolemy, a close friend and general of Alexander the Great, who took charge of Egypt after the latter's death and declared himself king (Ptolemy I) in 304 BC. The dynasty ended with the death of Cleopatra in 30 BC.

Ptol·e·my[2] Greek astronomer and geographer of the 2nd century A.D. His teachings had enormous influence on medieval thought, the geocentric view of the cosmos being adopted as Christian doctrine until the late Renaissance. His *Geography* was also a standard work for centuries, despite its inaccuracies.

pto·maine /'tōˌmān; tō'mān/ ▸*n. dated Chemistry* any of a group of amine compounds of unpleasant taste and odor formed in putrefying animal and vegetable matter and formerly thought to cause food poisoning. ▷late 19th cent.: from French *ptomaïne*, from Italian *ptomaina*, formed irregularly from Greek *ptōma* 'corpse.'

P2P /'pētə'pē/ ▸*abbr. Computing* peer-to-peer; denoting a network or data communications in which no dedicated server is involved: [mainly as *adj.*] *popular P2P programs such as Kazaa, Grokster and Gnutella.*

pto·sis /'tōsəs/ ▸*n. Medicine* drooping of the upper eyelid due to paralysis or disease, or as a congenital condition. ▷mid 18th cent.: from Greek *ptōsis*, from *piptein* 'to fall.' **—pto·tic** /'tōˌtik; 'tätik/ *adj.*

PTSD ▸*abbr.* post-traumatic stress disorder.

pty. ▸*abbr.* proprietary.

pty·a·lin /'tīələn/ ▸*n. Biochemistry* a form of amylase found in the saliva of humans and some other animals. ▷mid 19th cent.: from Greek *ptualon* 'spittle' + **-IN**[1].

p-type ▸*adj. Electronics* denoting a region in a semiconductor in which electrical conduction is due chiefly to the movement of positive holes. Often contrasted with **N-TYPE.**

Pu ▸*symbol* the chemical element plutonium.

pub /pəb/ *Brit.* ▸*n.* a tavern or bar. ■ *Austral.* a hotel.
▸*v.* [*intrans.*] [usu. as *n.*] (**pubbing**) *informal* spend time in pubs. ▷mid 19th cent.: abbreviation of **PUBLIC HOUSE.**

pub. ▸*abbr.* ■ publication(s). ■ published. ■ publisher.

pub·cast·er /ˈpəbˌkastər/ ▸*n.* a publically owned broadcasting station or network: *a reality show developed for Norwegian pubcaster NRK.*

pub crawl *informal, chiefly Brit.* ▸*n.* a tour taking in several pubs or bars, with one or more drinks at each.
▸*v.* [*intrans.*] (**pub-crawl**) go on a pub crawl.

pu·ber·ty /ˈpyo͞obərtē/ ▸*n.* the period during which adolescents reach sexual maturity and become capable of reproduction. ▷late Middle English: from Latin *pubertas,* from *puber* 'adult,' related to *pubes* (see **PUBES**). **—pu·ber·tal** /-bərtl/ *adj.*

pu·bes /ˈpyo͞obēz/ ▸*n.* **1** (*pl.* same) the lower part of the abdomen at the front of the pelvis, covered with hair from puberty. **2** plural form of **PUBIS**. ▷late 16th cent.: from Latin, 'pubic hair, groin, genitals.'

pu·bes·cence /pyo͞oˈbesəns/ ▸*n.* **1** the time when puberty begins. **2** *Botany & Zoology* soft down or fine short hairs on the leaves and stems of plants or on various parts of animals, esp. insects. ▷late Middle English: from French, or from medieval Latin *pubescentia,* from Latin *pubescent-* 'reaching puberty' (see **PUBESCENT**).

pu·bes·cent /pyo͞oˈbesənt/ ▸*adj.* **1** relating to or denoting a person at or approaching the age of puberty. **2** *Botany & Zoology* covered with short soft hair; downy.
▸*n.* a person at or approaching the age of puberty. ▷mid 17th cent.: from French, or from Latin *pubescent-* 'reaching puberty,' from the verb *pubescere.*

pu·bic /ˈpyo͞obik/ ▸*adj.* [*attrib.*] of or relating to the pubes or pubis: *pubic hair.*

pu·bic louse ▸*n.* another term for **CRAB**[1] (sense 2).

pu·bis /ˈpyo͞obəs/ ▸*n.* (*pl.* **-bes** /-bēz/) either of a pair of bones forming the two sides of the pelvis. ▷late 16th cent.: from Latin *os pubis* 'bone of the pubes.'

publ. ▸*abbr.* ■ public. ■ publication. ■ publicity. ■ published. ■ publisher.

pub·lic /ˈpəblik/ ▸*adj.* **1** of or concerning the people as a whole: *public concern | public affairs.* ■ open to or shared by all the people of an area or country: *a public library.* ■ of or provided by the government rather than an independent, commercial company: *public spending.* ■ of or involved in the affairs of the community, esp. in government: *his public career was destroyed by tenacious reporters.* ■ known to many people; famous: *a public figure.* **2** done, perceived, or existing in open view: *he wanted a public apology in the* Wall Street Journal | *we should talk somewhere less public.* **3** *Brit.* of, for, or acting for a university: *public examination results.*
▸*n.* (**the public**) [treated as *sing.* or *pl.*] ordinary people in general; the community: *the library is open to the public | the public has made an informed choice.* ■ [with *adj.*] a section of the community having a particular interest or connection: *the reading public.* ■ (**one's public**) the people who watch or are interested in an artist, writer, or performer: *some famous last words to give my public.* ▷late Middle English: from Old French, from Latin *publicus,* blend of *poplicus* 'of the people' (from *populus* 'people') and *pubes* 'adult.'
▸*PHRASES* □ **go public 1** become a public company. **2** reveal details about a previously private concern: *Bates* **went public with** *the news at a press conference.* □ **in public** in view of other people; when others are present: *men don't cry in public.* □ **the public eye** the state of being known or of interest to people in general, esp. through the media: *the pressures of being constantly* **in the public eye**.

pub·lic act ▸*n.* an act of legislation affecting the public as a whole.

pub·lic-ad·dress sys·tem ▸*n.* a system of microphones, amplifiers, and loudspeakers used to amplify speech or music in a large building or at an outdoor gathering.

pub·li·can /ˈpəblikən/ ▸*n.* **1** *Brit.* a person who owns or manages a pub. **2** (in ancient Roman and biblical times) a collector of taxes. ▷Middle English (sense 2): from Old French *publicain,* from Latin *publicanus,* from *publicum* 'public revenue,' neuter (used as a noun) of *publicus* 'of the people.' Sense 1 dates from the early 18th cent.

pub·lic as·sis·tance ▸*n.* government benefits provided to the needy, usually in the form of cash or vouchers.

pub·li·ca·tion /ˌpəbliˈkāsʜən/ ▸*n.* the preparation and issuing of a book, journal, piece of music, or other work for public sale: *the publication of her first novel.* ■ a book, journal, etc. issued for public sale: *scientific publications.* ■ the action of making something generally known: *the publication of April trade figures.* ▷late Middle English (in the sense 'public announcement or declaration'): via Old French from Latin *publicatio(n-),* from *publicare* 'make public' (see **PUBLISH**).

pub·lic com·pa·ny ▸*n.* a company whose shares are traded freely on a stock exchange.

pub·lic de·fend·er ▸*n. Law* a lawyer employed at public expense in a criminal trial to represent a defendant who is unable to afford legal assistance.

pub·lic do·main ▸*n.* the state of belonging or being available to the public as a whole. ■ not subject to copyright: *the photograph had been in the public domain for 15 years* | [as *adj.*] *public-domain software.* ■ public land: *a grazing permit on public domain.*

pub·lic en·e·my ▸*n.* a notorious wanted criminal. ■ *figurative* a person or thing regarded as the greatest threat to a group or community: *he identified inflation as public enemy number one.*

pub·lic good ▸*n.* **1** *Economics* a commodity or service that is provided without profit to all members of a society, either by the government or a private individual or organization: *a conviction that library informational services are a public good, not a commercial commodity.* **2** the benefit or well-being of the public: *the public good clearly demands independent action.*

pub·lic house ▸*n. chiefly Brit.* a tavern.

pub·li·cist /ˈpəbləsist/ ▸*n.* **1** a person responsible for publicizing a product, person, or company. **2** *dated* a journalist, esp. one concerned with current affairs. ■ *archaic* a writer or other person skilled in international law. ▷late 18th cent.: from French *publiciste,* from Latin *(jus) publicum* 'public (law).' **—pub·li·cis·tic** /ˌpəbləˈsistik/ *adj.*

pub·lic·i·ty /pəˈblisətē/ ▸*n.* the notice or attention given to someone or something by the media: *the case attracted wide publicity in the press.* ■ public exposure; notoriety: *the only passage that has been found worthy of nationwide publicity.* ■ the giving out of information about a product, person, or company for advertising or promotional purposes: *head of publicity and marketing* | [as *adj.*] *publicity photographs.* ■ material or information used for such a purpose: *we distributed publicity from a stall in the marketplace.* ▷late 18th cent.: from French *publicité,* from *public* 'public' (see **PUBLIC**).

pub·lic·i·ty a·gent ▸*n.* another term for **PUBLICIST** (sense 1).

pub·li·cize /ˈpəbləˌsīz/ ▸*v.* [*trans.*] make (something) widely known: *use the magazine to publicize human rights abuses.* ■ give out publicity about (a product, person, or company) for advertising or promotional purposes: *Judy had started to publicize books and celebrities.*

pub·lic key ▸*n.* a cryptographic key that can be obtained and used by anyone to encrypt messages intended for a particular recipient, such that the encrypted messages can be deciphered only by using a second key that is known only to the recipient (the **private key**).

pub·lic law ▸*n.* the law of relationships between individuals and the government.

pub·lic lend·ing right (abbr.: **PLR**) ▸*n.* (in the UK) the right of authors to receive payment when their books or other works are loaned out by public libraries.

pub·lic·ly /ˈpəbliklē/ ▸*adv.* so as to be seen by other people; in public: *some weep publicly.* ■ [often *sentence adverb*] used in reference to views expressed to others and not necessarily genuinely felt: *publicly, officials criticized the resolution, but privately they thought it tolerable.* ■ by a government or the public rather than an independent, commercial company: *publicly funded organizations | a publicly owned company.*

pub·lic nui·sance ▸*n.* an act, condition, or thing that is illegal because it interferes with the rights of the public generally. ■ *informal* an obnoxious or dangerous person or group of people.

pub·lic o·pin·ion ▸*n.* views prevalent among the general public.

pub·lic or·a·tor ▸*n.* another term for **ORATOR**.

pub·lic pol·i·cy ▸*n.* **1** the principles, often unwritten, on which social laws are based. **2** *Law* the principle that injury to the public good is a basis for denying the legality of a contract or other transaction.

pub·lic pros·e·cu·tor ▸*n.* a law officer who conducts criminal proceedings on behalf of the government or in the public interest.

pub·lic purse ▸*n.* the funds raised by a government by taxation or other means.

pub·lic re·la·tions ▸*plural n.* [also treated as *sing.*] the professional maintenance of a favorable public image by a company or other organization or a famous person. ■ the state of the relationship between the public and a company or other organization or a famous person: *companies justify the cost in terms of improved public relations.*

pub·lic school ▸*n.* **1** (chiefly in North America) a school supported by public funds. **2** (in the UK) a private for-fee secondary school. ▷late 16th cent.: from Latin *publica schola,* denoting a school maintained at the public expense; in England *public school* (a term recorded from 1580) originally denoted a grammar school under public management, founded for the benefit of the public (contrasting with *private school,* run for the profit of the proprietor); since the 19th cent. the term has been applied to the old endowed English grammar schools, and newer schools modeled on them, which have developed into for-fee boarding schools.

pub·lic sec·tor ▸*n.* the part of an economy that is controlled by the government.

pub·lic serv·ant ▸*n.* a government official.

pub·lic-serv·ice cor·po·ra·tion ▸*n.* a public utility.

pub·lic spir·it ▸*n.* willingness to do things that help the public. **—pub·lic-spir·it·ed** *adj.* **—pub·lic-spir·it·ed·ly** *adv.* **—pub·lic-spir·it·ed·ness** *n.*

pub·lic trans·por·ta·tion ▸*n.* buses, trains, subways, and other forms of transportation that charge set fares, run on fixed routes, and are available to the public.

pub·lic u·til·i·ty ▸*n.* an organization supplying a community with electricity, gas, water, or sewerage.

pub·lic works ▸*plural n.* the work of building such things as roads, schools, and reservoirs, carried out by the government for the community.

pub·lish /ˈpəblisʜ/ ▸*v.* [*trans.*] **1** (of an author or company) prepare and issue (a book, journal, piece of music, or other work) for public sale: *we publish practical reference books* | [*intrans.*] *the pressures on researchers to publish.* ■ print (something) in a book or journal so as to make it generally known: *we pay $10 for every letter we publish.* ■ [usu. as *adj.*] (**published**) prepare and issue the works of (a particular writer): *a published author.* ■ formally announce or read (an edict or marriage banns). See note at **ANNOUNCE**. **2** *Law* communicate (a libel) to a third party. ▷Middle English (in the sense 'make generally known'): from the stem of Old French *puplier,* from Latin *publicare* 'make public,' from *publicus* (see **PUBLIC**). **—pub·lish·a·ble** *adj.*

pub·lish·er /ˈpəblisʜər/ ▸*n.* (also **publishers**) a person or company that prepares and issues books, journals, music, or other works for sale: *the publishers of* Vogue | *a commercial music publisher.* ■ a newspaper proprietor.

pub·lish·ing /ˈpəblisʜiɴɢ/ ▸*n.* the occupation, business, or activity of preparing and issuing books, journals, and other material for sale: *she worked in publishing.*

Puc·ci·ni /po͞oˈcʜēnē/, Giacomo (1858–1924), Italian composer. His sense of the dramatic, gift for melody, and skillful use of the orchestra have contributed to his enduring popularity. Notable operas: *La Bohème* (1896), *Tosca* (1900), and *Madama Butterfly* (1904).

puc·coon /pəˈko͞on/ ▸*n.* a North American plant that yields a pigment from which dye or medicinal products are obtained, esp. formerly. • Genus *Lithospermum,* family Boraginaceae): several species, including **hoary puccoon** (*L. canescens*). ▷early 17th cent.: from Virginia Algonquian *poughkone.*

puce /pyo͞os/ ▸*adj.* of a dark red or purple-brown color: *his face was puce with rage and frustration.*
▸*n.* a dark red or purple-brown color. ▷late 18th cent.: from French, literally 'flea(-color),' from Latin *pulex, pulic-.*

Puck /pək/ ▸*n.* another name for **ROBIN GOODFELLOW**. ■ (**puck**) a mischievous or evil sprite. ▷Old English *pūca.* **—puck·like** /-ˌlīk/ *adj.*

puck /pək/ ▸*n.* **1** a black disk made of hard rubber, the focus of play in ice hockey. **2** *Computing* an input device similar to a mouse that is dragged across a sensitive surface, which notes the puck's position to move the cursor on the screen. ▷late 19th cent.: of unknown origin.

puck·a ▸*adj.* variant spelling of **PUKKA**.

puck·er /ˈpəkər/ ▸v. [intrans.] (esp. of a person's face or a facial feature) tightly gather or contract into wrinkles or small folds: *her brows puckered in a frown.* ■ [trans.] cause to do this: *the baby stirred, **puckering** up its tiny face.*
▸n. a tightly gathered wrinkle or small fold, esp. on a person's face: *a pucker between his eyebrows.* ▷late 16th cent. (as a verb): probably frequentative, from the base of POKE² and POCKET (suggesting the formation of small purselike gatherings). —**puck·er·y** /ˈpəkərē/ adj.
▸PHRASE □ **pucker up** contract one's lips as in preparation for a kiss.

Puck·ett /ˈpəkit/, Kirby (1961–) U.S. baseball player. An outfielder for the Minnesota Twins 1984–96, he was noted for both his hitting and fielding. He helped his team to win two World Series 1987 and 1991. Baseball Hall of Fame (2001).

puck·ish /ˈpəkisн/ ▸adj. playful, esp. in a mischievous way: *a puckish sense of humor.* —**puck·ish·ly** adv. —**puck·ish·ness** n.

pud /po͝od/ ▸n. Brit., informal short for PUDDING.

pud·ding /ˈpo͝odiNG/ ▸n. **1** a dessert with a creamy consistency: *chocolate pudding | a rice pudding.* ■ chiefly Brit. any dessert. ■ chiefly Brit. the dessert course of a meal: *what's for pudding?* **2** a sweet or savory steamed dish made with flour: *Yorkshire pudding.* ■ the intestines of a pig or sheep stuffed with oatmeal, spices, and meat and boiled. See also BLACK PUDDING, BLOOD PUDDING. ■ informal a fat, dumpy, or stupid person: *away with you, you big pudding!* ▷Middle English (denoting a sausage such as *black pudding*): apparently from Old French *boudin* 'black pudding,' from Latin *botellus* 'sausage, small intestine.' —**pud·ding·y** adj.
▸PHRASE □ **in the pudding club** Brit., informal pregnant.

pud·ding face ▸n. informal a large chubby face. —**pud·ding-faced** adj.

pud·ding·stone /ˈpo͝odiNG,stōn/ ▸n. a conglomerate rock in which dark-colored rounded pebbles contrast with a paler fine-grained matrix.

pud·dle /ˈpədl/ ▸n. **1** a small pool of liquid, esp. of rainwater on the ground: *splashing through deep puddles | figurative a little puddle of light.* **2** clay and sand mixed with water and used as a watertight covering for embankments.
▸v. [trans.] **1** wet or cover (a surface) with water, esp. rainwater: *the cobbles under our feet were wet and puddled.* ■ [intrans.] (of liquid) form a small pool: *rivulets of water coursed down the panes, puddling on the sill.* ■ [intrans.] archaic dabble or wallow in mud or shallow water: *children are playing and puddling about in the dirt.* ■ [intrans.] (**puddle around/about**) informal occupy oneself in a disorganized or unproductive way: *the Internet is just the latest excuse for puddling around at work.* **2** line (a hole) with puddle. ■ knead (clay and sand) into puddle. ■ work (mixed water and clay) to separate gold or opal. ■ [usu. as n.] (**puddling**) chiefly historical stir (molten iron) with iron oxide in a furnace, to produce wrought iron by oxidizing carbon. ▷Middle English: diminutive of Old English *pudd* 'ditch, furrow'; compare with German dialect *Pfudel* 'pool.' —**pud·dler** /ˈpədlər; ˈpədl-ər/ n. —**pud·dly** /ˈpədlē; ˈpədl-ē/ adj.

pud·dle jump·er (also **pud·dle-jump·er**) ▸n. informal a small light airplane that is fast and highly maneuverable and used for short trips.

pu·den·cy /ˈpyo͞odn-sē/ ▸n. poetic/literary modesty; shame. ▷early 17th cent.: from late Latin *pudentia.*

pu·den·dum /pyo͞oˈdendəm/ ▸n. (pl. **-den·da** /-ˈdendə/) (often **pudenda**) a person's external genitals, esp. a woman's. ▷mid 17th cent.: from Latin *pudenda (membra)* '(parts) to be ashamed of,' neuter plural of the gerundive of *pudere* 'be ashamed.' —**pu·den·dal** /-ˈdendəl/ adj. —**pu·dic** /ˈpyo͞odik/ adj.

pu·deur /pyo͞oˈdər/ ▸n. a sense of shame or embarrassment, esp. with regard to matters of a sexual or personal nature. ▷mid 20th cent.: French, literally 'modesty.'

pudge /pəj/ ▸n. informal fat on a person's body: *subtle makeup that sharpened the pudge out of her cheekbones.* ▷early 19th cent. (denoting a fat person): of unknown origin.

pudg·y /ˈpəjē/ ▸adj. (**pudg·i·er**, **pudg·i·est**) informal (of a person or part of their body) slightly fat: *his pudgy fingers.* —**pudg·i·ly** /ˈpəjəlē/ adv. —**pudg·i·ness** n.

pu·du /ˈpo͞odo͞o/ ▸n. a very small and rare deer found in the lower Andes of South America. • Genus *Pudu,* family Cervidae: two species. ▷late 19th cent.: from Araucanian.

Pue·bla /ˈpweblä/ a state in south central Mexico. ■ its capital city that lies at the edge of the central Mexican plateau; pop. 1,055,000. Full name **Puebla de Zaragoza.**

Pueb·lo /ˈpweblō/ an industrial city in south central Colorado, on the Arkansas River, at the foot of the Front Range of the Rocky Mountains; pop. 102,121.

pueb·lo /ˈpweblō; po͞oˈeb-/ ▸n. (pl. **-los**) **1** an American Indian settlement of the southwestern U.S., esp. one consisting of multistoried adobe houses built by the Pueblo people. ■ (in Spanish-speaking regions) a town or village. **2** (**Pueblo**) (pl. same or **-los**) a member of any of various American Indian peoples, including the Hopi, occupying pueblo settlements chiefly in New Mexico and Arizona. Their prehistoric period is known as the Anasazi culture.
▸adj. (**Pueblo**) of, relating to, or denoting the Pueblos or their culture. ▷Spanish, literally 'people,' from Latin *populus.*

pu·er·ile /ˈpyo͞o(ə)rəl; ˈpyo͞or,īl/ ▸adj. childishly silly and trivial: *you're making puerile excuses.* See note at YOUTHFUL. ▷late 16th cent. (in the sense 'like a boy'): from French *puéril* or Latin *puerilis,* from *puer* 'boy.' —**pu·er·ile·ly** adv. —**pu·er·il·i·ty** /pyo͞o(ə)ˈrilətē/ n. (pl. **-ties**)

pu·er·per·al fe·ver /pyo͞oˈərpərəl/ ▸n. fever caused by uterine infection following childbirth.

pu·er·pe·ri·um /,pyo͞oərˈpi(ə)rēəm/ ▸n. Medicine the period of about six weeks after childbirth during which the mother's reproductive organs return to their original nonpregnant condition. ▷early 17th cent.: from Latin, from *puerperus* 'parturient' (from *puer* 'child' + *-parus* 'bearing'). —**pu·er·per·al** /pyo͞oˈərpərəl/ adj.

Puer·to Cor·tés /ˈpwertō kôrˈtes/ a port in northwestern Honduras, on the Caribbean coast at the mouth of the Ulua River; pop. 40,000.

Puer·to Pla·ta /ˈpwertō ˈplätä/ a resort town in the Dominican Republic, on the northern coast; pop. 96,000.

Puer·to Ri·co /,pôrtə ˈrēkō; ,pwertə/ an island in the Greater Antilles in the Caribbean Sea; pop. 3,808,610; capital, San Juan. One of the earliest Spanish settlements in the New World, it was ceded to the U.S. in 1898 after the Spanish-American War. In 1952 it became a commonwealth in voluntary association with the U.S. with full powers of local government. —**Puer·to Ri·can** /ˈrēkən/ adj. & n.

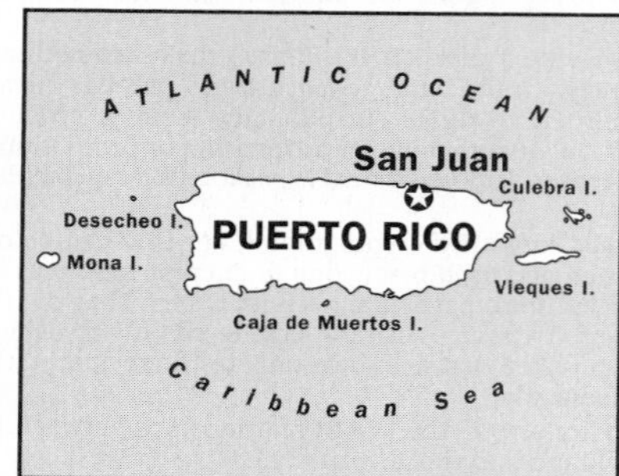

Puer·to Ri·co Trench an ocean trench north of Puerto Rico and the Leeward Islands that extends in an east–west direction. It reaches a depth of 28,397 feet (9,220 m).

puff /pəf/ ▸n. **1** a short, explosive burst of breath or wind: *a puff of wind swung the weathervane around.* ■ the sound of air or vapor escaping suddenly: *the whistle and puff of steam.* ■ a small quantity of vapor or smoke, emitted in one blast: *the fire breathed out **a puff of** blue smoke.* ■ an act of drawing quickly on a pipe, cigarette, or cigar: *he took a puff of his cigar.* **2** [usu. with adj. or in combination] a light pastry case, typically one made of puff pastry, containing a sweet or savory filling: *a cream puff.* ■ a gathered mass of material in a dress or other garment. ■ a rolled protuberant mass of hair. ■ a powder puff. ■ a soft quilt: *the plump pillows and puffs with which the snowy beds were piled.* **3** informal a review of a work of art, book, or theatrical production, esp. an excessively complimentary one: *the publishers sent him a copy of the book hoping for a puff.* ■ Brit. an advertisement, esp. one exaggerating the value of the goods advertised.
▸v. **1** [intrans.] breathe in repeated short gasps: *exercises that make you puff.* ■ [with adverbial] (of a person, engine, etc.) move with short, noisy breaths or bursts of air or steam: *the train came puffing in.* ■ smoke a pipe, cigarette, or cigar: *he **puffed on** his pipe contentedly.* ■ [trans.] blow (dust, smoke, or a light object) in a specified direction with a quick breath or blast of air: *he lighted his pipe and puffed forth smoke.* ■ move through the air in short bursts: *his breath puffed out like white smoke.* **2** (**puff something out/up** or **puff out/up**) cause to swell or become swollen: [trans.] *he suddenly sucked his stomach in and puffed his chest out* | [intrans.] *when he was in a temper, his cheeks puffed up and his eyes shrank.* ■ [trans.] (usu. **be puffed up**) figurative cause to become conceited: *he was never puffed up about his writing.* **3** [trans.] advertise with exaggerated or false praise: *publishers have puffed the book on the grounds that it contains new discoveries.* ▷Middle English: imitative of the sound of a breath, perhaps from Old English *pyf* (noun), *pyffan* (verb).

puff ad·der ▸n. a large, sluggish, mainly nocturnal African viper that inflates the upper part of its body and hisses loudly in threat. • *Bitis arietans,* family Viperidae. ■ another term for HOGNOSE SNAKE.

puff·back /ˈpəf,bak/ (also **puff-back shrike**) ▸n. a small black-and-white African shrike, the male of which displays by puffing up the feathers of the lower back. • Genus *Dryoscopus,* family Laniidae: several species, in particular *D. gambensis.*

puff·ball /ˈpəf,bôl/ ▸n. **1** a fungus that produces a spherical or pear-shaped fruiting body that ruptures when ripe to release a cloud of spores. • Families Lycoperdaceae, class Gasteromycetes, in particular genus *Lycoperdon.* See also GIANT PUFFBALL. **2** anything round and fluffy, such as a powder puff: *puffballs of smoke.*

puff·bird /ˈpəf,bərd/ ▸n. a stocky large-headed bird somewhat resembling a kingfisher, found in tropical American forests. • Family Bucconidae: several genera and many species.

puffed /pəft/ ▸adj. (also **puffed up**) swollen: *symptoms include puffed eyelids.* ■ (of a sleeve or other part of a garment) gathered so as to have a rounded shape.

puff·er /ˈpəfər/ ▸n. **1** informal a person or thing that puffs, in particular, a person who smokes. **2** short for PUFFERFISH.

puff·er·fish /ˈpəfər,fisн/ (also **puff·er fish**) ▸n. (pl. same or **-fish·es**) a stout-bodied marine or freshwater fish (family Tetraodontidae: several genera and many species) that typically has spiny skin and inflates itself like a balloon when threatened. It is sometimes used as food, but some parts are highly toxic.

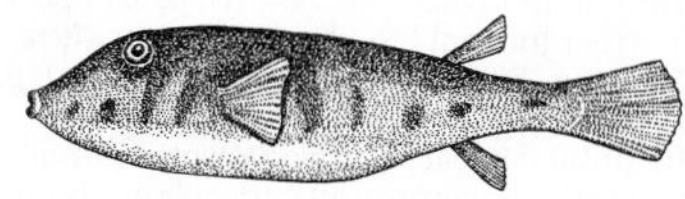
northern pufferfish

puff·er·y /ˈpəfərē/ ▸n. exaggerated or false praise.

puf·fin /ˈpəfən/ ▸n. a hole-nesting auk of northern and Arctic waters, with a large head and a massive, brightly colored triangular bill. • Genera *Fratercula* and *Lunda,* family Alcidae: three species, in particular the **Atlantic puffin** (*F. arctica*). ▷Middle English (denoting the Manx shearwater): apparently from PUFF + -ING³, with reference to the Manx shearwater's fat nestlings. The later use is a confusion, by association of nesting habits and habitat.

Atlantic puffin

puff pas·try ▸n. light flaky pastry, used for pie crusts, canapés, etc.

puff piece ▸n. informal a newspaper article or item on a television show using exaggerated praise to advertise or promote a celebrity, book, or event.

puff sleeve ▸n. a short sleeve gathered at the top and cuff and full in the middle.

puff·y /ˈpəfē/ ▸adj. (**puff·i·er**, **puff·i·est**) **1** (esp. of part of the body) unusually swollen and soft: *her eyes were puffy and full of tears.* ■ soft, rounded, and light: *small puffy clouds.* ■ (of a garment or part of a garment) padded or gathered to give a rounded shape: *a puffy blue ski jacket.* ■ figurative (of a piece of writing) overembellished and pompous: *prose at its most labored and puffy.* **2** (of wind or breath) coming in short bursts: *his breath was puffy and fast.* —**puff·i·ly** /ˈpəfəlē/ adv. —**puff·i·ness** n.

pug[1] /pəg/ ▶*n.* (also **pug dog**) a dog of a dwarf breed like a bulldog with a broad flat nose and deeply wrinkled face. ▷mid 18th cent.: perhaps of Low German origin. **—pug·gish** *adj.* **—pug·gy** /ˈpəgē/ *adj.*

pug dog

pug[2] ▶*n.* loam or clay mixed and worked into a soft, plastic condition without air pockets for making bricks or pottery.
▶*v.* (**pugged, pug·ging**) [*trans.*] **1** [usu. as *adj.*] (**pugged**) prepare (clay) in this way, typically in a machine with rotating blades. **2** [usu. as *n.*] (**pugging**) pack (a space, typically the space under a floor) with pug, sawdust, or other material in order to deaden sound. ▷early 19th cent.: of unknown origin.

pug[3] ▶*n. informal* a boxer. ▷mid 19th cent.: abbreviation of PUGILIST.

pug[4] ▶*n.* the footprint of an animal: [as *adj.*] *I saw the pug marks of the tigress in the soft earth.*
▶*v.* (**pugged, pug·ging**) [*trans.*] track (an animal) by its footprints. ▷mid 19th cent.: from Hindi *pag* 'footprint.'

pug dog ▶*n.* another term for PUG[1].

Pu·get Sound /ˈpyo͞ojit/ an inlet of the Pacific Ocean on the coast of the state of Washington. It is linked to the ocean by the Strait of Juan de Fuca. Seattle is situated on its eastern shore. ▷named after Peter *Puget*, aide to George Vancouver who explored it in 1792.

pug·ga·ree /ˈpəg(ə)rē/ ▶*n.* an Indian turban. ■ a thin muslin scarf tied around a sun helmet so as to hang down over the wearer's neck and shield it from the sun. ▷from Hindi *pagrī* 'turban.'

pu·gi·list /ˈpyo͞ojəlist/ ▶*n. dated* or *humorous* a boxer, esp. a professional one. ▷mid 18th cent.: from Latin *pugil* 'boxer' + -IST. **—pu·gi·lism** /-ˌlizəm/ *n.* **—pu·gi·lis·tic** /ˌpyo͞ojəˈlistik/ *adj.*

pug mill ▶*n.* a machine for mixing and working clay and other materials into pug. (See PUG[2].)

pug·na·cious /pəgˈnāsHəs/ ▶*adj.* eager or quick to argue, quarrel, or fight: *the increasingly pugnacious demeanor of politicians.* ■ having the appearance of a willing fighter: *the set of her pugnacious jaw.* ▷mid 17th cent.: from Latin *pugnax, pugnac-* (from *pugnare* 'to fight,' from *pugnus* 'fist') + -IOUS. **—pug·na·cious·ly** *adv.* **—pug·nac·i·ty** /ˌpəgˈnasətē/ *n.*

pug nose ▶*n.* a short nose with an upturned tip. **—pug-nosed** *adj.*

Pug·wash con·fer·en·ces /ˈpəgˌwôsH; -ˌwäsH/ a series of international conferences first held in Pugwash (a village in Nova Scotia) in 1957 by scientists to promote the peaceful application of scientific discoveries.

puis·ne /ˈpyo͞onē/ ▶*adj.* [*attrib.*] *Law* (in the UK and some other countries) denoting a judge of a superior court inferior in rank to chief justices. ▷late 16th cent. (as a noun, denoting a junior or inferior person): from Old French, from *puis* (from Latin *postea* 'afterwards') + *ne* 'born' (from Latin *natus*). Compare with PUNY.

puis·ne mort·gage ▶*n. Law, chiefly Brit.* a second or subsequent mortgage of unregistered land of which the title deeds are retained by a first mortgagee.

pu·is·sance /ˈpwisəns; ˈpwē-; pyo͞oˈisəns/ ▶*n.* **1** (**Puissance**) [in *sing.*] a competitive test of a horse's ability to jump large obstacles in show jumping. **2** *archaic* or *poetic/literary* great power, influence, or prowess. ▷late Middle English (sense 2): from Old French, 'power,' from *puissant* 'having power' (see PUISSANT). Sense 1 dates from the 1950s.

pu·is·sant /ˈpwisənt; ˈpwēsənt; ˈpyo͞oəsənt/ ▶*adj. archaic* or *poetic/literary* having great power or influence. ▷late Middle English: via Old French from Latin *posse* 'be able.' **—pu·is·sant·ly** *adv.*

pu·ja /ˈpo͞ojə/ (also **poo·ja**) ▶*n. Hinduism & Buddhism* the act of worship. ▷from Sanskrit *pūjā* 'worship.'

puke /pyo͞ok/ *informal* ▶*v.* vomit: [*intrans.*] *I had eaten to the point of puking* | [*trans.*] *he* **puked up** *his pizza.*
▶*n.* vomit. ▷late 16th cent.: probably imitative; first recorded as a verb in: "At first the infant, mewling, and puking in the nurse's arms," in Shakespeare's *As you like it* (II. vii. 144). **—puk·ey** *adj.*

puk·ka /ˈpəkə/ (also **puk·kah**) ▶*adj. chiefly Brit.* genuine: *the more expensive brands are pukka natural mineral waters.* ■ of or appropriate to high or respectable society: *it wouldn't be considered the pukka thing to do.* ■ *informal* excellent: *"That Danny is totally gorgeous." "Yeah, pukka haircut."* ▷late 17th cent.: from Hindi *pakkā* 'cooked, ripe, substantial.'

pul /po͞ol/ ▶*n.* (*pl.* **puls** or **pu·li** /ˈpo͞olē/) a monetary unit of Afghanistan, equal to one hundredth of an afghani. ▷Pashto, from Persian *pūl* 'copper coin.'

pu·la /ˈp(y)o͞olə/ ▶*n.* (*pl.* same) the basic monetary unit of Botswana, equal to 100 thebe. ▷Setswana, literally 'rain.'

pu·lao /pəˈlou; pəˈlō; ˈpərlo͞o/ ▶*n.* variant spelling of PILAF.

Pu·las·ki[1] /pəˈlaskē/, Casimir (1747–79) Polish count and commissioned American cavalry officer; name in Polish *Kazimierz Pulaski*. Having fled from involvement in a Polish rebellion 1768–72, he arrived in America 1777 and joined the cause of American independence. Commissioned a general in 1778, he was invaluable in the defense of Charleston 1779 but was mortally wounded at the siege of Savannah.

Pu·las·ki[2] ▶*n.* (*pl.* **-kis**) a tool with a head that has an ax blade on one side and an adze on the other. ▷1920s: named after Edward C. *Pulaski* (1866–1931), the American forest ranger who designed it.

Pu·lau Se·ri·bu /ˌpo͞olou ˈseribo͞o/ Indonesian name for THOUSAND ISLANDS (sense 2).

pul·chri·tude /ˈpəlkrəˌt(y)o͞od/ ▶*n. poetic/literary* beauty. ▷late Middle English: from Latin *pulchritudo*, from *pulcher, pulchr-* 'beautiful.' **—pul·chri·tu·di·nous** /ˌpəlkrəˈt(y)o͞odn-əs/ *adj.*

pule /pyo͞ol/ ▶*v.* [*intrans.*] [often as *adj.*] (**puling**) *poetic/literary* cry querulously or weakly: *she's no puling infant.* ▷late Middle English (originally referring to a bird's cry): probably imitative; compare with French *piauler*, in the same sense.

pu·li /ˈpo͞olē/ ▶*n.* (*pl.* **pu·lik** /ˈpo͞olik/) a sheepdog of a black, gray, or white breed with a long thick coat. ▷mid 20th cent.: from Hungarian.

Pul·it·zer /ˈpo͝olitsər; ˈpyo͞ol-/, Joseph (1847–1911), U.S. newspaper publisher and editor, born in Hungary. A pioneer of popular journalism, he owned a number of newspapers, including the *New York World*. He made provisions in his will for the establishment of the annual Pulitzer Prizes.

Pu·litz·er Prize ▶*n.* an award for an achievement in American journalism, literature, or music. There are thirteen made each year.

pull /po͝ol/ ▶*v.* [*trans.*] **1** exert force on (someone or something), typically by taking hold of them, in order to move or try to move them toward oneself or the origin of the force: *he pulled the car door handle and began to get out* | [*intrans.*] *the little boy* **pulled at** *her skirt.* ■ (of an animal or vehicle) be attached to the front and be the source of forward movement of (a vehicle): *the carriage was pulled by four horses.* ■ [*trans.*] take hold of and exert force on (something) so as to move it from a specified position or in a specified direction: *she pulled a handkerchief out of her pocket* | *he pulled on his boots* | *I pulled up some onions.* ■ *informal* bring out (a weapon) to attack or threaten someone: *it's not every day a young woman* **pulls** *a gun* **on** *a burglar.* ■ [*intrans.*] (**pull at/on**) inhale deeply while smoking (a pipe or cigar). ■ damage (a muscle, ligament, etc.) by abnormal strain. ■ print (a proof). ■ *Computing* retrieve (an item of data) from the top of a stack. **2** [*intrans.*] (of a vehicle or person) move steadily in a specified direction or to reach a specified point: *the bus was about to pull away* | *the boy pulled ahead and disappeared around the corner.* ■ [with *adverbial of direction*] (**pull oneself**) move in a specified direction with effort, esp. by taking hold of something and exerting force: *he pulled himself into the saddle.* ■ [*intrans.*] move one's body in a specified direction, esp. against resistance: *she tried to pull away from him.* ■ [*intrans.*] (of an engine) exert propulsive force; deliver power: *the engine warmed up quickly and pulled well.* ■ [*intrans.*] work oars to cause a boat to move: *he* **pulled at** *the oars, and the boat moved swiftly through the water.* **3** cause (someone) to patronize, buy, or show interest in something; attract: *tourist attractions that* **pull in** *millions of foreign visitors.* ■ influence in favor of a particular course of action: *they are pulled in incompatible directions by external factors and their own beliefs.* ■ *informal* carry out or achieve (something requiring skill, luck, or planning): *the magazine pulled its trick of producing the right issue at the right time.* **4** *informal* cancel or withdraw (an entertainment or advertisement): *the gig was pulled at the first sign of difficulty.* ■ withdraw (a player) from a game: *four of the leading eight runners were pulled.* ■ check the speed of (a horse), esp. so as to make it lose a race. **5** *chiefly Baseball Golf* strike (a ball) in the direction of one's follow-through so that it travels to the left (or, with a left-handed player, to the right: *he pulled the ball every time he hit a grounder.* **6** [*intrans.*] *Football* (of a lineman) withdraw from position and cross parallel to and behind the line of scrimmage to block opposing players for a runner.
▶*phrasal v.* □ **pull back** (or **pull someone/something back**) retreat or cause troops to retreat from an area: *the pact called on the rival forces to pull back and allow a neutral force to take control.* ■ (**pull back**) withdraw from an undertaking: *the party pulled back from its only positive policy.* □ **pull something down 1** demolish a building. **2** *informal* earn a sum of money: *he was pulling down sixty grand.* □ **pull in 1** (of a vehicle or its driver) move to the side of or off the road: *he pulled in at the curb.* **2** (of a bus or train) arrive to take passengers. □ **pull someone/something in 1** succeed in securing or obtaining something: *the Reform Party pulled in 10% of the vote.* ■ *informal* earn a sum of money: *you could pull in $100,000.* **2** *informal* arrest someone: *I'd pull him in for questioning.* **3** use reins to check a horse. □ **pull something off** *informal* succeed in achieving or winning something difficult: *he pulled off a brilliant first round win.* □ **pull out 1** withdraw from an undertaking: *he was forced to* **pull out of** *the championship because of an injury.* ■ retreat or cause to retreat from an area: *the army pulled out, leaving the city in ruins* | (**pull someone out**) *the CIA had pulled its operatives out of Tripoli.* **2** (of a bus or train) leave with its passengers. **3** (of a vehicle or its driver) move out from the side of the road, or from its normal position in order to pass: *as he turned the corner, a police car pulled out in front of him.* □ **pull over** (of a vehicle or its driver) move to the side of or off the road. □ **pull someone over** cause a driver to move to the side of the road to be charged for a traffic offense: *he was pulled over for speeding.* □ **pull through** (or **pull someone/something through**) get through or enable someone or something to get through an illness or other dangerous or difficult situation: *the illness is difficult to overcome, but we hope she'll pull through.* □ **pull up 1** (of a vehicle or its driver) come to a halt: *he pulled up outside the cabin.* **2** increase the altitude of an aircraft. □ **pull someone up** cause someone to stop or pause; check someone: *the shock of his words* **pulled her up short.** ■ reprimand someone.
▶*n.* **1** an act of taking hold of something and exerting force to draw it toward one: *give the hair a quick pull, and it comes out by the roots.* ■ a handle to hold while performing such an action: *the Cowboy Collection offers hand-forged iron drawer pulls.* ■ a deep draft of a drink: *he unscrewed the cap from the flask and took another pull.* ■ an act of sucking at a cigar or pipe: *he took a pull on his cheroot.* ■ an injury to a muscle or ligament caused by abnormal strain: *he was ruled out of the game with a hamstring pull.* ■ a printer's proof. **2** [in *sing.*] a force drawing someone or something in a particular direction: *the pull of the water tore her away.* ■ a powerful influence or compulsion: *the pull of her hometown was a strong one.* ■ something exerting an influence or attraction: *one of the pulls of urban life is the opportunity of finding work.* ■ the condition of being able to exercise influence: *they were hamstrung without the political pull of the mayor's office.* ▷Old English *pullian* 'pluck, snatch'; origin uncertain; the sense has developed from expressing a short sharp action to one of sustained force. **—pull·er** *n.*
▶*PHRASES* □ **like pulling teeth** *informal* extremely difficult to do: *it had been like pulling teeth to extract these two small items from Moore.* □ **pull a face** (or **faces**) see FACE. □ **pull a fast one** see FAST[1] □ **pull someone's leg** deceive someone playfully; tease someone. □ **pull out all the stops** see STOP. □ **pull the plug 1** *informal* prevent something from happening or continuing: *the company* **pulled the plug on** *the deal because it was not satisfied with the terms.* **2** *informal* remove (a patient) from life support: *we'll be talking to people who* **pulled the plug on** *their mothers.* □ **pull**

(**one's**) **punches** [usu. with *negative*] be less forceful, severe, or violent than one could be: *a smooth-tongued critic who doesn't pull his punches.* □ **pull rank** see RANK[1]. □ **pull one's socks up** see SOCK. □ **pull strings** make use of one's influence and contacts to gain an advantage unofficially or unfairly. □ **pull the strings** be in control of events or of other people's actions. □ **pull together** cooperate in a task or undertaking. □ **pull oneself together** recover control of one's emotions. □ **pull one's weight** do one's fair share of work. □ **pull wires** another way of saying PULL STRINGS above. □ **pull the wool over someone's eyes** see WOOL.

pull-a·part ▸*adj.* [*attrib.*] *Geology* denoting an area that has been ruptured or stretched by tensional stresses or the resulting faulting.

pull·back /ˈpo͝olˌbak/ ▸*n.* **1** an act of withdrawing troops. **2** a reduction in price or demand: *there is no sign of a consumer pullback.*

pull cord ▸*n.* a cord that operates a mechanism when pulled.

pull-down ▸*adj.* [*attrib.*] designed to be worked or made operable by being pulled down: *guests may be put up on folding or pull-down beds.* ■ *Computing* (of a menu) appearing below a menu title only while selected. Compare with DROP-DOWN.
▸*n. Computing* a pull-down menu.

pul·let /ˈpo͝olət/ ▸*n.* a young hen, esp. one less than one year old. ▷late Middle English: from Old French *poulet*, diminutive of *poule*, from the feminine of Latin *pullus* 'chicken, young animal.'

pul·ley /ˈpo͝olē/ ▸*n.* (*pl.* **-leys**) (also **pulley wheel**) a wheel with a grooved rim around which a cord passes. It acts to change the direction of a force applied to the cord and is chiefly used (typically in combination) to raise heavy weights. Compare with BLOCK *n.* 7. ■ (on a bicycle) a wheel with a toothed rim around which the chain passes. ■ a wheel or drum fixed on a shaft and turned by a belt, used esp. to increase speed or power.

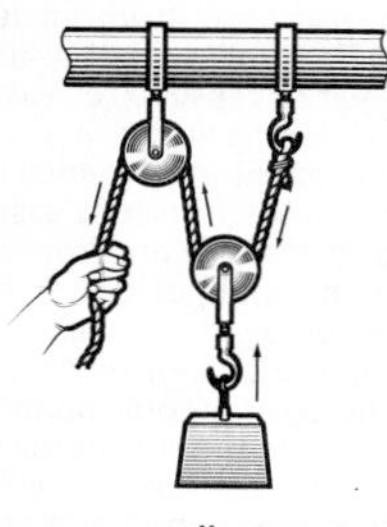
pulley

▸*v.* (**-leys, -leyed**) [*trans.*] hoist with a pulley. ▷Middle English: from Old French *polie*, probably from a medieval Greek diminutive of *polos* 'pivot, axis.'

pul·ley block ▸*n.* a block or casing in which one or more pulleys are mounted.

pull hit·ter ▸*n. Baseball* a hitter who normally drives the ball in the direction of the follow-through of the bat.

pull-in ▸*n. chiefly Brit.* an area at the side of the road where motorists may pull off the road and stop. ■ *Brit., dated* a roadside cafe.

Pull·man[1] /ˈpo͝olmən/ a commercial city in southeastern Washington, on the Palouse River, home to Washington State University; pop. 23,478.

Pull·man[2], George Mortimer (1831–97) U.S. industrialist. The founder of the Pullman Palace Car Company in 1867, he converted railroad coaches into sleeping cars with lower and upper berths. He also designed the first railroad dining car in 1868. The town of Pullman, Illinois, was built to house his workers.

Pull·man[3] ▸*n.* (*pl.* **-mans**) [usu. as *adj.*] a railroad car affording special comfort, esp. one with sleeping berths: *a train of Pullman cars.* ■ a train consisting of such cars. ■ (**pullman**) a large suitcase designed to fit under the seat in a Pullman car. ▷mid 19th cent.: named after George M. *Pullman* (1831–97), its American designer.

Pull·man kitch·en ▸*n.* a kitchenette, especially one recessed and concealable behind doors.

pull-off ▸*n.* an area on the side of a road where a motorist may park, typically in a scenic area.

pull-on ▸*adj.* [*attrib.*] (of a garment) designed to be put on without the need to undo any fastenings: *pull-on trousers with an elastic waist.*
▸*n.* a garment of this type.

pull·out /ˈpo͝olˌout/ (also **pull-out**) ▸*n.* **1** a section of a magazine or newspaper that is designed to be detached and kept for rereading: *don't miss Monday's 8-page NBA pullout.* **2** a withdrawal, esp. from military involvement or participation in a commercial venture.
▸*adj.* [*attrib.*] designed to be pulled out of the usual position: *pullout wire baskets at the bottom of one cupboard.* ■ (of a section of a magazine, newspaper, or other publication) designed to be detached and kept.

pull·o·ver /ˈpo͝olˌōvər/ ▸*n.* a garment, esp. a sweater or jacket, put on over the head and covering the top half of the body.
▸*adj.* (of a sweater, jacket, or shirt) designed to be put on by pulling over the head.

pull-quote ▸*n.* a brief, attention-catching quotation, typically in a distinctive typeface, taken from the main text of an article and used as a subheading or graphic feature.

pull tab ▸*n.* **1** a ring or tab that is pulled to open a can. **2** a gambling card with a tab that can be pulled back to reveal a row or rows of symbols, with prizes for matching symbols.

pul·lu·late /ˈpəlyəˌlāt/ ▸*v.* [*intrans.*] [often as *adj.*] (**pullulating**) breed or spread so as to become extremely common: *the pullulating family.* ■ be very crowded; be full of life and activity: *the supertowers of our pullulating megalopolis.* ▷early 17th cent.: from Latin *pullulat-* 'sprouted,' from the verb *pullulare*, from *pullulus*, diminutive of *pullus* 'young animal.' —**pul·lu·la·tion** /ˌpəlyəˈlāsʜən/ *n.*

pull-up ▸*n.* **1** an exercise involving raising oneself with one's arms by pulling up against a horizontal bar fixed above one's head. **2** an act of pulling up; a sudden stop.

pul·mo·nar·y /ˈpo͝olməˌnerē; ˈpəl-/ ▸*adj.* [*attrib.*] of or relating to the lungs: *pulmonary blood flow.* ▷mid 17th cent.: from Latin *pulmonarius*, from *pulmo*, *pulmon-* 'lung.'

pul·mo·nar·y ar·ter·y ▸*n.* the artery carrying blood from the right ventricle of the heart to the lungs for oxygenation.

pul·mo·nar·y tu·ber·cu·lo·sis ▸*n.* see TUBERCULOSIS.

pul·mo·nar·y vein ▸*n.* a vein carrying oxygenated blood from the lungs to the left atrium of the heart.

Pul·mo·na·ta /ˌpo͝oləˈnätə; pəl-; -ˈnātə/ *Zoology* a group of mollusks that includes the land snails and slugs and many freshwater snails. They have a modified mantle cavity that acts as a lung for breathing air. • Subclass Pulmonata, class Gastropoda. ▷modern Latin (plural), from Latin *pulmo*, *pulmon-* 'lung.' —**pul·mo·nate** /ˈpo͝olməˌnāt; ˈpəl-/ *n. & adj.*

pul·mon·ic /po͝olˈmänik; pəl-/ ▸*adj.* another term for PULMONARY.

pulp /pəlp/ ▸*n.* a soft, wet, shapeless mass of material: *boiling with soda will reduce your peas to pulp.* ■ the soft fleshy part of a fruit. ■ a soft wet mass of fibers derived from rags or wood, used in papermaking. ■ vascular tissue filling the interior cavity and root canals of a tooth. ■ *Mining* pulverized ore mixed with water. ■ [usu. as *adj.*] *figurative* popular or sensational writing that is generally regarded as being of poor quality: *the story is a mix of pulp fiction and Greek tragedy.* [formerly printed on rough paper.]
▸*v.* [*trans.*] crush into a soft, shapeless mass. ■ withdraw (a publication) from the market and recycle the paper. ▷late Middle English (denoting the soft fleshy part of fruit): from Latin *pulpa*. The verb dates from the mid 17th cent. —**pulp·er** *n.* —**pulp·i·ness** *n.* —**pulp·y** *adj.*
▸*PHRASE* □ **beat** (or **smash**) **someone to a pulp** beat someone severely.

pulp cav·i·ty ▸*n.* the space in the interior of a tooth that contains the pulp.

pul·pit /ˈpo͝olˌpit; ˈpəl-; -pət/ ▸*n.* a raised platform or lectern in a church or chapel from which the preacher delivers a sermon. ■ (**the pulpit**) religious teaching as expressed in sermons; preachers collectively: *the movies could rival the pulpit as an agency molding the ideas of the mass public.* ■ a raised platform in the bow of a fishing boat or whaler. ■ a guard rail enclosing a small area at the bow of a yacht. ▷Middle English: from Latin *pulpitum* 'scaffold, platform,' in medieval Latin 'pulpit.'

pulp·wood /ˈpəlpˌwo͝od/ ▸*n.* wood suitable for making into pulp for making paper.

pul·que /ˈpo͝olˌkā; -kē/ ▸*n.* a Mexican alcoholic drink made by fermenting sap from the maguey. ▷via American Spanish from Nahuatl *puliúhki* 'decomposed.'

pul·sar /ˈpəlˌsär/ ▸*n. Astronomy* a celestial object, thought to be a rapidly rotating neutron star, that emits regular pulses of radio waves and other electromagnetic radiation at rates of up to one thousand pulses per second. ▷from *puls(ating st)ar*, on the pattern of *quasar*.

pul·sate /ˈpəlˌsāt/ ▸*v.* [*intrans.*] expand and contract with strong regular movements: *blood vessels throb and pulsate.* ■ [often as *adj.*] (**pulsating**) produce a regular throbbing sensation or sound: *a pulsating headache.* ■ [usu. as *adj.*] (**pulsating**) be very exciting: *victory in a pulsating semifinal.* ▷late 18th cent.: from Latin *pulsat-* 'throbbed, pulsed,' from the verb *pulsare*, frequentative of *pellere* 'to drive, beat.' —**pul·sa·tion** /ˌpəlˈsāsʜən/ *n.* —**pul·sa·tor** /-ˌsātər/ *n.* —**pul·sa·to·ry** /-səˌtôrē/ *adj.*

pul·sa·tile /ˈpəlsətl; -səˌtīl/ ▸*adj. chiefly Physiology* pulsating; relating to pulsation: *pulsatile tinnitus.* ▷late Middle English: from medieval Latin *pulsatilis* (in *vena pulsatilis* 'artery'), from the verb *pulsare* (see PULSATE).

pul·sa·til·la /ˌpəlsəˈtilə/ ▸*n.* a plant of a genus that includes the pasqueflower. • Genus *Pulsatilla*, family Ranunculaceae. ▷modern Latin, diminutive of *pulsatus* 'battered,' expressing the notion 'small flower battered by the wind.'

pulse[1] /pəls/ ▸*n.* a rhythmical throbbing of the arteries as blood is propelled through them, typically as felt in the wrists or neck: *the doctor found a faint pulse.* ■ the rate of this throbbing, used to ascertain the rate of someone's heartbeat and so their state of health or emotions: *the idea was enough to set my* ***pulse racing.*** ■ (usu. **pulses**) each successive throb of the arteries or heart. ■ a single vibration or short burst of sound, electric current, light, or other wave: *radio pulses* | [as *adj.*] *a pulse generator.* ■ a musical beat or other regular rhythm. ■ *figurative* the central point of energy and organization in an area or activity: *those close to the financial and economic pulse maintain that there have been fundamental changes.* ■ *Biochemistry* a measured amount of an isotopic label given to a culture of cells.
▸*v.* [*intrans.*] throb rhythmically; pulsate: *a knot of muscles at the side of his jaw pulsed.* ■ [*trans.*] transmit in rhythmical beats: *the sun pulsed fire into her eyes.* ■ [*trans.*] modulate (a wave or beam) so that it becomes a series of pulses. ■ [*trans.*] apply a pulsed signal to (a device). ■ *Biochemistry* short for PULSE-LABEL. ▷late Middle English: from Latin *pulsus* 'beating,' from *pellere* 'to drive, beat.' —**pulse·less** *adj.* —**puls·er** *n.*
▸*PHRASE* □ **take** (or **feel**) **the pulse of** determine the heart rate of (someone) by feeling and timing the pulsation of an artery: *a nurse came in and took his pulse.* ■ *figurative* ascertain the general mood or opinion of: *he hopped around the country to visit stores and take the pulse of consumers.*

pulse[2] ▸*n.* (usu. **pulses**) the edible seeds of various leguminous plants, for example chickpeas, lentils, and beans. ■ the plant or plants producing such seeds. ▷Middle English: from Old French *pols*, from Latin *puls* 'porridge of meal or pulse'; related to POLLEN.

pulse code mod·u·la·tion (abbr.: **PCM**) ▸*n. Electronics* a pulse modulation technique in which the amplitude of an analog signal is converted to a binary value represented as a series of pulses.

pulse di·al·ing ▸*n.* a method of telephone dialing in which each digit is transmitted as a corresponding number of electronic pulses. Compare with TONE DIALING.

pulse jet ▸*n.* a type of jet engine in which combustion is intermittent, with the ignition and expulsion of each charge of mixture causing the intake of a fresh charge.

pulse-la·bel ▸*v.* [*trans.*] *Biochemistry* subject (cells in a culture) to a pulse of an isotopic label.

pulse mod·u·la·tion ▸*n. Electronics* a type of modulation in which pulses are varied in some respect, such as width or amplitude, to represent the amplitude of a signal.

pul·trude /po͝olˈtro͞od; pəl-/ ▸*v.* [*trans.*] [usu. as *adj.*] (**pultruded**) make (a reinforced plastic article) by drawing resin-coated glass fibers through a heated die. ▷1960s: from *pul(ling)* + EXTRUDE. —**pul·tru·sion** /-ˈtro͞ozʜən/ *n.*

pul·ver·ize /ˈpəlvəˌrīz/ ▸*v.* [*trans.*] reduce to fine particles: *the brick of the villages was pulverized by the bombardment.* ■ *informal* defeat utterly: *he had a winning car and pulverized the opposition.* ▷late Middle English: from late Latin *pulverizare*, from *pulvis*, *pulver-* 'dust.' —**pul·ver·iz·a·ble** *adj.* —**pul·ver·i·za·tion** /ˌpəlvərəˈzāsʜən/ *n.* —**pul·ver·iz·er** *n.*

pul·ver·u·lent /ˌpəlˈver(y)ələnt/ ▸*adj. archaic* consisting of fine particles; powdery or crumbly. ▷mid 17th cent.: from Latin *pulverulentus*, from *pulvis*, *pulver-* 'dust.'

pul·vi·nus /pəlˈvīnəs; -ˈvēnəs/ ▸*n.* (*pl.* **-ni** /-ˌnī; -nē/) *Botany* an enlarged section at the base of a leaf stalk in some plants that is subject to changes of turgor, leading to movements of the leaf or leaflet. ▷mid 19th cent.: from Latin, literally 'cushion.'

pu·ma /ˈp(y)o͞omə/ ▸*n.* another term for COUGAR. ▷late 18th cent.: via Spanish from Quechua.

pum·ice /ˈpəməs/ ▸*n.* a very light and porous volcanic rock formed when a gas-rich froth of glassy lava solidifies rapidly. ■ (also **pumice stone**) a piece of such rock or a similar substance used as an abrasive, esp. for removing hard skin.
▸*v.* [*trans.*] rub with pumice to smooth or clean. ▷late Middle English: from Old French *pomis*, from a Latin dialect variant of *pumex*, *pumic-*. Compare with POUNCE2. —**pu·mi·ceous** /pyo͞oˈmishəs; ˌpəmˈish-/ *adj.*

pum·mel /ˈpəməl/ ▸*v.* (**-meled**, **-mel·ing**; *Brit.* **-mel·led**, **-mel·ling**) [*trans.*] strike repeatedly, typically with the fists: *Bob did not fight back for the fifteen minutes that the half-dozen men pummeled him.* ■ *informal* criticize adversely: *he has been pummeled by the reviewers.* ▷mid 16th cent.: variant of POMMEL.

pum·me·lo ▸*n.* variant spelling of POMELO.

pump1 /pəmp/ ▸*n.* a mechanical device using suction or pressure to raise or move liquids, compress gases, or force air into inflatable objects such as tires: *a gas pump.* ■ [in *sing.*] an instance of moving something or being moved by or as if by such a machine: *the pump of blood to her heart.* ■ [with *adj.*] *Physiology* an active transport mechanism in living cells by which specific ions are moved through the cell membrane against a concentration gradient: *the bacterium's sodium pump.* ■ a pump-action shotgun.
▸*v.* **1** [*trans.*] force (liquid, gas, etc.) to move in a specified direction by or as if by means of a pump: *the blood is pumped around the body* | [*intrans.*] *if we pump long enough, we should bring the level up.* ■ [*intrans.*] move in spurts as though driven by a pump: *blood was pumping from a wound in his shoulder.* ■ fill with something: *my veins had been **pumped full** of glucose.* ■ shoot (bullets) into a target. ■ (**pump something in/into**) *informal* invest a large amount of money in (something): *he pumped all his savings into building the boat.* ■ [*trans.*] *informal* try to elicit information from (someone) by persistent questioning: *she began to **pump** her friend **for** details.* **2** [*trans.*] move (something) vigorously up and down: *we had to pump the handle like mad.* ■ [*intrans.*] move vigorously up and down or back and forth: *that's superb running—look at his legs pumping.* ■ apply and release (a brake pedal or lever) several times in quick succession, typically to prevent skidding. ■ move one's arm as if throwing a ball held in the hand, but without releasing the ball: [in *combination*] *behind the plate Howard double-pumped then threw to second.*
▸*phrasal v.* □ **pump out** produce or emit (something) in large quantities or amounts: *that little printing press pumped out our brochures for more than twenty years.* □ **pump up** inflate (a tire, balloon, etc.) ■ *informal* increase: *she needs to read and pump up her political grip.* ■ *informal* turn up the volume of (music): *let's pump up those tunes, man.* ■ *informal* give inappropriate support and encouragement to: *we let them pump up our egos.* ▷late Middle English (originally in nautical use): related to Dutch *pomp* 'ship's pump' (earlier in the sense 'wooden or metal conduit'), probably partly of imitative origin.
▸*PHRASES* □ **pump someone's hand** shake a person's hand vigorously. □ **pump iron** *informal* exercise with weights.

pump2 ▸*n.* a light shoe, in particular: ■ a woman's plain, lightweight shoe that has a low-cut upper, no fastening, and typically a medium heel. ■ a man's slip-on patent leather shoe for formal wear. ▷mid 16th cent.: of unknown origin.

pump-ac·tion ▸*adj.* [*attrib.*] **1** denoting a repeating firearm, typically a shotgun, in which a new round is brought from the magazine into the breech by a slide action in line with the barrel. **2** denoting a spray dispenser for a liquid such as deodorant or cooking oil that is worked by finger action rather than by internal pressure (as in an aerosol).

pumped /pəmpt/ (also **pumped up**) ▸*adj. informal* (of a person) stimulated or filled with enthusiasm or excitement: *I was so pumped that I overdid everything.*

pump·er /ˈpəmpər/ ▸*n.* a fire engine that carries a hose and pumps water.

pum·per·nick·el /ˈpəmpərˌnikəl/ ▸*n.* dark, dense German bread made from coarsely ground whole-grain rye. ▷mid 18th cent.: transferred use of German *Pumpernickel* 'lout, bumpkin,' of unknown origin.

pump gun ▸*n.* a pump-action rifle with a tubular magazine.

pump jock·ey ▸*n. informal* a service station attendant.

pump·kin /ˈpəm(p)kən; ˈpəNGkən/ ▸*n.* **1** a large rounded orange-yellow fruit with a thick rind, edible flesh, and many seeds. ■ the flesh of this fruit, esp. used as food. ■ *informal* used as an affectionate term of address, esp. to a child. **2** the plant of the gourd family that produces this fruit, having tendrils and large lobed leaves and native to warm regions of America. • Genus *Cucurbita*, family Cucurbitaceae: several species, in particular *C. pepo*. ■ *Brit.* another term for SQUASH2 ▷late 17th cent.: alteration of earlier *pumpion*, from obsolete French *pompon*, via Latin from Greek *pepōn* 'large melon' (see PEPO).

pumpkin 1

pump·kin·seed /ˈpəm(p)kənˌsēd; ˈpəNGkən-/ ▸*n.* (*pl.* same or **-seeds**) a small, edible, brightly colored freshwater fish of the sunfish family, native to North America. It is popular in aquariums and has been introduced into many European waters. • *Lepomis gibbosus*, family Centrarchidae.

pump-prim·ing ▸*n.* **1** the introduction of fluid into a pump to prepare it for working. **2** the stimulation of economic activity by investment: [as *adj.*] *a pump-priming fund.* —**pump-prim·er** *n.*

pump room ▸*n.* a room, building, or compartment in which pumps are housed or from which they are controlled. ■ a room at a spa where medicinal water is dispensed. ■ a common name for a drinking establishment.

pun /pən/ ▸*n.* a joke exploiting the different possible meanings of a word or the fact that there are words that sound alike but have different meanings: *the pigs were a squeal (if you'll forgive the pun).*
▸*v.* (**punned**, **pun·ning**) [*intrans.*] make a joke exploiting the different possible meanings of a word: *his first puzzle punned on composers, with answers like "Handel with care" and "Haydn go seek"* [as *adj.*] (**punning**) *a punning riddle.* ▷mid 17th cent.: perhaps an abbreviation of obsolete *pundigrion*, as a fanciful alteration of PUNCTILIO. —**pun·ning·ly** *adv.* —**pun·ster** /ˈpənstər/ *n.*

pu·na /ˈpo͞onə/ ▸*n.* **1** a high treeless plateau in the Peruvian Andes. **2** another term for ALTITUDE SICKNESS. ▷via American Spanish from Quechua.

punch1 /pənCH/ ▸*v.* [*trans.*] **1** strike with the fist: *he **punched** her **in** the face and ran off.* ■ drive with a blow from the fist: *he punched the ball into his own goal.* **2** press (a button or key on a machine). ■ (**punch something in/into**) enter information by this action. **3** drive (cattle) by prodding them with a stick.
▸*phrasal v.* □ **punch in** (or **out**) register one's arrival at (or departure from) work, esp. by means of a time clock: *she couldn't punch in, because there were no time clocks.*
▸*n.* a blow with the fist. ■ *informal* the strength needed to deliver such a blow: *he has the punch to knock out anyone in his division.* ■ [in *sing.*] *informal* the power to impress or startle: *photos give their arguments an extra visual punch.* ▷late Middle English (as a verb in the sense 'puncture, prod'): variant of POUNCE1. —**punch·er** *n.*
▸*PHRASES* □ **beat someone to the punch** *informal* anticipate or forestall someone's actions. □ **punch the (time) clock** (of an employee) punch in or out. ■ be employed in a conventional job with regular hours. □ **punch someone's lights out** beat someone up; knock someone unconscious. [*Lights* in the sense 'lungs' (see LIGHTS.] □ **punch something up 1** use a computer keyboard to call something to the screen: *people will be able to punch up Andy Warhol and get text, photographs, and video on the entire Pop Art period.* **2** *informal* enliven: *he needed to punch up his meandering presentation.*

punch2 ▸*n.* **1** a device or machine for making holes in materials such as paper, leather, metal, and plaster. **2** a tool or machine for impressing a design or stamping a die on a material.
▸*v.* [*trans.*] pierce a hole in (metal, paper, leather, etc.) with or as though with a punch. ■ pierce (a hole) with or as though with a punch. ▷early 16th cent.: perhaps an abbreviation of PUNCHEON1, or from the verb PUNCH1.

punch3 ▸*n.* a drink made with fruit juices, soda, spices, and sometimes liquor, typically served in small cups from a large bowl. ▷mid 17th cent.: apparently from Sanskrit *pañca* 'five, five kinds of' (because the drink had five ingredients).

punch4 ▸*n.* (**Punch**) a grotesque, hook-nosed, humpbacked buffoon, the chief male character of the Punch and Judy show. Punch is the English variant of a stock character derived ultimately from Italian *commedia dell'arte*. Also called PUNCHINELLO. ▷mid 17th cent. (as a dialect term denoting a short, fat person): abbreviation of PUNCHINELLO.
▸*PHRASE* □ **pleased as Punch** feeling great delight or pride. [with allusion to the delight displayed by the character *Punch* of the PUNCH AND JUDY show.]

Punch and Ju·dy /ˈpənCH and ˈjo͞odē/ a puppet show presented on the miniature stage of a tall collapsible booth traditionally covered with striped canvas. The show was probably introduced to England from the Continent in the 17th century. Punch is on the manipulator's right hand, remaining on stage all the time, while the left hand provides a series of characters—baby, wife (Judy), priest, doctor, policeman, hangman— for him to nag, beat, and finally kill.

punch·bag /ˈpənCHˌbag/ ▸*n.* British term for PUNCHING BAG.

punch·ball /ˈpənCHˌbôl/ ▸*n.* **1** a team ball game in which a rubber ball is punched or headed. **2** *Brit.* another term for PUNCHING BAG.

punch·board /ˈpənCHˌbôrd/ ▸*n.* a board with holes containing slips of paper that are punched out as a form of gambling, with the object of locating a winning slip.

punch bowl ▸*n.* a bowl used for mixing and serving punch. ■ (**punch·bowl**) *chiefly Brit.* a deep round hollow in a hilly area.

punch-drunk ▸*adj.* stupefied by or as if by a series of heavy blows.

punched card (also **punch card**) ▸*n.* a card perforated according to a code, for controlling the operation of a machine, used in voting machines and formerly in programming and entering data into computers.

punched tape ▸*n.* a paper tape perforated according to a code, formerly used for conveying instructions or data to a data processor.

pun·cheon1 /pənCHən/ ▸*n.* **1** a short post, esp. one used for supporting the roof in a coal mine. ■ a rough board or other length of wood, usually with one flattened side, used for flooring or building. **2** another term for PUNCH2. ▷Middle English: from Old French *poinchon*, probably based on Latin *punct-* 'punctured,' from the verb *pungere*. Compare with the noun POUNCE1.

pun·cheon2 ▸*n. historical* a large cask for liquids or other commodities holding from 72 to 120 gallons. ▷late Middle English: from Old French *poinchon*, of uncertain origin although forms in Old French and English correspond to those of PUNCHEON1.

Pun·chi·nel·lo /ˌpənCHəˈnelō/ ▸*n.* (*pl.* **-los**) another name for PUNCH4. ■ *archaic* a short, stout, comical-looking person. ▷mid 17th cent.: alteration of Neapolitan dialect *Polecenella*, perhaps a diminutive of *pollecena* 'young turkey cock with a hooked beak,' from *pulcino* 'chicken,' from Latin *pullus*.

punch·ing bag ▸*n.* a stuffed or inflated bag, typically cylindrical or pear-shaped, suspended so it can be punched for exercise or training, esp. by boxers. ■ a person on whom another person vents their anger.

punch line ▸*n.* the final phrase or sentence of a joke or story, providing the humor or some other crucial element.

punch press ▸*n.* a press that is designed to drive a punch for shaping metal.

punch·y /ˈpənCHē/ ▸*adj.* (**punch·i·er**, **punch·i·est**) **1** having an immediate impact; forceful: *his style is journalistic, with short punchy sentences.* **2** another term for PUNCH-DRUNK. —**punch·i·ly** /ˈpənCHəlē/ *adv.* —**punch·i·ness** *n.*

punc·ta /ˈpəNGktə/ ▸ plural form of PUNCTUM.

punc·tae /ˈpəNGktē; -ˌtī/ ▸*plural n. Biology* minute rounded dots or spots of color, or small elevations or depressions on a surface. ▷modern Latin (plural).

punc·tate /ˈpəNGkˌtāt/ ▸*adj. Biology* studded with or denoting dots or tiny holes. ▷mid 18th cent.: from Latin *punctum* 'point' + -ATE2. —**punc·ta·tion** /ˌpəNGkˈtāSHən/ *n.*

punc·til·i·o /ˌpəNGkˈtilēˌō/ ▸*n.* (*pl.* **-os**) a fine or petty point of conduct or procedure. ▷late 16th cent.:

from Italian *puntiglio(n-)* and Spanish *puntillo*, diminutive of *punto* 'a point.'

punc·til·i·ous /ˌpəNGk'tilēəs/ ▸*adj.* showing great attention to detail or correct behavior: *he was punctilious in providing every amenity for his guests.* See note at **FORMAL**. ▷mid 17th cent.: from French *pointilleux*, from *pointille*, from Italian *puntiglio* (see **PUNCTILIO**). —**punc·til·i·ous·ly** *adv.* —**punc·til·i·ous·ness** *n.*

punc·tu·al /'pəNGkCHo͞oəl/ ▸*adj.* happening or doing something at the agreed or proper time; on time: *he's the sort of man who's always punctual.* ■ *Grammar* denoting or relating to an action that takes place at a particular point in time. Contrasted with **DURATIVE**. ▷late 17th cent.: from medieval Latin *punctualis*, from Latin *punctum* 'a point.' —**punc·tu·al·i·ty** /ˌpəNGkCHo͞o'alitē/ *n.* —**punc·tu·al·ly** *adv.*

punc·tu·ate /'pəNGkCHo͞oˌāt/ ▸*v.* [*trans.*] **1** (often **be punctuated**) occur at intervals throughout (a continuing event or a place): *the country's history has been* ***punctuated by*** *coups.* ■ (**punctuate something with**) interrupt or intersperse (an activity) with: *she punctuates her conversation with snatches of song.* **2** insert punctuation marks in (text). **3** accentuate; emphasize: *the end of the Cold War was punctuated by an extraordinary assertion of American power.* ▷mid 17th cent. (in the sense 'point out'): from medieval Latin *punctuat-* 'brought to a point,' from the verb *punctuare*, from *punctum* 'a point.'

punc·tu·at·ed e·qui·lib·ri·um ▸*n. Biology* the hypothesis that evolutionary development is marked by isolated episodes of rapid speciation between long periods of little or no change.

punc·tu·a·tion /ˌpəNGkCHo͞o'āSHən/ ▸*n.* **1** the marks, such as period, comma, and parentheses, used in writing to separate sentences and their elements and to clarify meaning. **2** *Biology* rapid or sudden speciation, as posited by the theory of punctuated equilibrium. ▷mid 17th cent.: from medieval Latin *punctuatio(n-)*, from the verb *punctuare* (see **PUNCTUATE**). —**punc·tu·a·tion·al** /-SHənl/ *adj.*

punc·tu·a·tion·ist /ˌpəNGkCHo͞o'āSHənist/ ▸*n. Biology* a person who believes in or advocates the hypothesis of punctuated equilibrium. —**punc·tu·a·tion·al·ism** /-'āSHənlˌizəm/ *n.* —**punc·tu·a·tion·al·ist** /-'āSHənl-ist/ *adj.* —**punc·tu·a·tion·ism** /-'āSHəˌnizəm/ *n.*

punc·tum /'pəNGktəm/ ▸*n.* (*pl.* **-ta** /-tə/) *technical* a small, distinct point. ■ *Anatomy* the opening of a tear duct. ▷late 16th cent. (figuratively, denoting a point): from Latin, literally 'a point.'

punc·ture /'pəNGkCHər/ ▸*n.* a small hole in a tire resulting in an escape of air: *she was on her way home when she had a puncture.* ■ a small hole in something such as the skin, caused by a sharp object: *surgeons operate through small punctures in the skin* | [as *adj.*] *a puncture wound.*

▸*v.* [*trans.*] make such a hole in (something): *one of the knife blows had punctured a lung.* ■ [*intrans.*] sustain such a small hole: *the tire had punctured and it would have to be replaced.* ■ *figurative* bring about a dramatic reversal in (mood or behavior) resembling a sudden deflation or collapse: *the earlier mood of optimism was punctured.* ▷late Middle English: from Latin *punctura*, from *punct-* 'pricked,' from the verb *pungere*. The verb dates from the late 17th cent.

pun·dit /'pəndit/ ▸*n.* **1** an expert in a particular subject or field who is frequently called on to give opinions about it to the public: *a globe-trotting financial pundit.* **2** variant spelling of **PANDIT**. ▷from Sanskrit *paṇḍita* 'learned.' —**pun·dit·ry** /-trē/ *n.* (in sense 1).

pun·di·toc·ra·cy /ˌpəndi'täkrəsē/ ▸*n. informal* media commentators, viewed collectively: *The financial markets and the punditocracy continue to believe that Greenspan is the closest thing to God on Earth.*

Pu·ne variant spelling of **POONA**.

pun·gent /'pənjənt/ ▸*adj.* having a sharply strong taste or smell: *the pungent smell of frying onions.* ■ (of comment, criticism, or humor) having a sharp and caustic quality. ▷late 16th cent. (in the sense 'very painful or distressing'): from Latin *pungent-* 'pricking,' from the verb *pungere*. —**pun·gen·cy** /'pənjənsē/ *n.* —**pun·gent·ly** *adv.*

Pu·nic /'pyo͞onik/ ▸*adj.* of or relating to Carthage.

▸*n.* the language of ancient Carthage, related to Phoenician. ▷from Latin *Punicus* (earlier *Poenicus*), from *Poenus*, from Greek *Phoinix* 'Phoenician.'

Pu·nic Wars three wars between Rome and Carthage that led to the undisputed dominance of Rome in the western Mediterranean.

In the first Punic War (264–241 BC), Rome secured Sicily from Carthage and established itself as a naval power; in the second (218–201 BC), the defeat of Hannibal (largely through the generalship of Fabius Cunctator and Scipio Africanus) put an end to Carthage's position as a Mediterranean power; the third (149–146 BC) ended in the total destruction of the city of Carthage.

pun·ish /'pəniSH/ ▸*v.* [*trans.*] inflict a penalty or sanction on (someone) as retribution for an offense, esp. a transgression of a legal or moral code: *I have done wrong and I'm being* ***punished for*** *it.* ■ inflict a penalty or sanction on someone for (such an offense): *fraudulent acts would be punished by up to two years in prison.* ■ treat (someone) in an unfairly harsh way: *a rise in prescription charges would punish the poor.* ■ [usu. as *adj.*] (**punishing**) subject (someone or something) to severe and debilitating treatment: *the recession was having a punishing effect on our business.* ▷Middle English: from Old French *puniss-*, lengthened stem of *punir* 'punish,' from Latin *punire*, from *poena* 'penalty.' —**pun·ish·a·ble** *adj.* —**pun·ish·er** *n.* —**pun·ish·ing·ly** *adv.*

pun·ish·ment /'pəniSHmənt/ ▸*n.* the infliction or imposition of a penalty as retribution for an offense: *crime demands just punishment.* ■ the penalty inflicted: *she assisted her husband to escape* ***punishment for*** *the crime* | *he approved of stiff punishments for criminals.* ■ *informal* rough treatment or handling inflicted on or suffered by a person or thing: *your machine can* ***take a*** *fair amount of* ***punishment*** *before falling to pieces.* ▷late Middle English: from Old French *punissement*, from the verb *punir* (see **PUNISH**).

pu·ni·tive /'pyo͞onətiv/ ▸*adj.* inflicting or intended as punishment: *he called for punitive measures against the Eastern bloc.* ■ (of a tax or other charge) extremely high: *a current punitive interest rate of 31.3%.* ▷early 17th cent.: from French *punitif, -ive* or medieval Latin *punitivus*, from Latin *punit-* 'punished,' from the verb *punire* (see **PUNISH**). —**pu·ni·tive·ly** *adv.* —**pu·ni·tive·ness** *n.*

pu·ni·tive damages ▸*plural n. Law* damages exceeding simple compensation and awarded to punish the defendant.

Pun·jab /'pənˌjäb; pən'jäb/ (also **the Punjab**) a region of northwestern India and Pakistan, a wide, fertile plain traversed by the Indus River and the five tributaries that gave the region its name. ■ a province of Pakistan; capital, Lahore. ■ a state of India; capital, Chandigarh. ▷from Hindi *panj* 'five' + *āb* 'waters.'

Pun·ja·bi /ˌpən'jäbē; po͝on-/ (also **Pan·ja·bi** /ˌpən-/) ▸*n.* (*pl.* **-bis**) **1** a native or inhabitant of Punjab. **2** the Indic language of Punjab.

▸*adj.* of or relating to Punjab or its people or language. ▷from Hindi *pājābī*.

pun·ji stick /'pənjē/ (also **punji stake**) ▸*n.* a sharpened bamboo stake, typically one tipped with poison, set in a camouflaged hole in the ground as a means of defense, esp. in Southeast Asia. ▷late 19th cent.: *punji* probably of Tibeto-Burman origin.

punk /pəNGk/ ▸*n.* **1** *informal* a worthless person (often used as a general term of abuse). ■ a criminal or hoodlum. ■ *derogatory* (in prison slang) a passive male homosexual. ■ an inexperienced young person; a novice. **2** (also **punk rock**) a loud, fast-moving, and aggressive form of rock music, popular in the late 1970s and early 1980s. ■ (also **punk rocker**) an admirer or player of such music, typically characterized by colored spiked hair and clothing decorated with safety pins or zippers. **3** soft, crumbly wood that has been attacked by fungus, sometimes used as tinder.

▸*adj.* **1** *informal* in poor or bad condition: *I felt too punk to eat.* **2** of or relating to punk rock and its associated subculture: *a punk band* | *a punk haircut.* ▷late 17th cent. (sense 3): perhaps, in some senses, related to archaic *punk* 'prostitute,' also to **SPUNK**. —**punk·ish** *adj.* —**punk·y** *adj.*

pun·kah /'pəNGkə/ ▸*n. chiefly historical* (in India) a large cloth fan on a frame suspended from the ceiling, moved backward and forward by pulling on a cord. ■ *Indian* an electric fan. ▷via Hindi from Sanskrit *pakṣaka*, from *pakṣa* 'wing.'

punk·er /'pəNGkər/ ▸*n.* a punk rocker.

punk·ette /ˌpəNG'ket/ ▸*n.* a female punk rocker. ▷1980s: from **PUNK** + the feminine suffix **-ETTE**.

pun·net /'pənət/ ▸*n. Brit.* a small light basket or other container for fruit or vegetables: ***a punnet of*** *strawberries.* ▷early 19th cent.: perhaps a diminutive of dialect *pun* 'a pound.'

punt[1] /pənt/ ▸*n.* a long, narrow, flat-bottomed boat, square at both ends and propelled with a long pole, used on inland waters chiefly for recreation.

▸*v.* [*intrans.*] travel in such a boat. ■ [*trans.*] convey in such a boat. ▷Old English, from Latin *ponto*, denoting a flat-bottomed ferryboat; readopted in the early 16th cent. from Middle Low German *punte* or Middle Dutch *ponte* 'ferryboat,' of the same origin.

punt[2] ▸*v.* **1** [*trans.*] *Football* kick (the ball) after it is dropped from the hands and before it reaches the ground: *he used to be able to punt a football farther than anyone.* ■ [*intrans.*] (of an offensive team) turn possession over to the defensive team by punting the ball after failing to make a first down: *the Raiders could get nowhere with their possession, and had to punt.* ■ (of a player) act as the punter. **2** [*intrans.*] delay in answering or taking action; equivocate: *he would continue to punt on questions of Medicare.*

▸*n.* a kick of this kind. ▷mid 19th cent.: probably from dialect *punt* 'push forcibly.' Compare with **BUNT**[3].

punt[3] ▸*v.* [*intrans.*] (in some gambling card games) place a bet against the bank. ■ *Brit., informal* bet or speculate on something: *investors are* ***punting on*** *a takeover.*

▸*n. informal, chiefly Brit.* a bet: *those* ***taking a punt on*** *the company's success.* ▷early 18th cent.: from French *ponte* 'player against the bank,' from Spanish *punto* 'a point.'

punt[4] ▸*n.* the basic monetary unit of the Republic of Ireland (until replaced by the euro), equal to 100 Irish pence. ▷Irish, literally 'pound.'

Pun·ta A·re·nas /'po͞ontə ə'rānəs/ a port in southern Chile, on the Strait of Magellan; pop. 114,000.

punt·er /'pəntər/ ▸*n.* **1** *Football & Rugby* a player who punts. **2** a person who propels or travels in a punt. **3** *informal, chiefly Brit.* a person who gambles, places a bet, or makes a risky investment. ■ a customer or client, esp. a member of an audience. ■ a prostitute's client. ■ the victim of a swindler or confidence trickster.

pun·ty /'pəntē/ (also **pon·til** /'päntil/) ▸*n.* (*pl.* **-ties**) (in glassmaking) an iron rod used to hold or shape soft glass. ▷mid 17th cent.: from French *pontil* (see **PONTIL**).

Punx·su·taw·ney /ˌpəNGksə'tônē/ a borough in west central Pennsylvania, the home of Punxsutawney Phil, a groundhog whose movements are closely observed by the media each February 2 in order to predict the length of winter.

pu·ny /'pyo͞onē/ ▸*adj.* (**-ni·er**, **-ni·est**) small and weak: *skeletal, white-faced, puny children.* ■ poor in quality, amount, or size: *the army was reduced to a puny 100,000 men.* ▷mid 16th cent. (as a noun denoting a younger or more junior person): phonetic spelling of **PUISNE**. —**pu·ni·ly** /'pyo͞onl-ē/ *adv.* —**pu·ni·ness** *n.*

pup /pəp/ ▸*n.* a young dog. ■ a young wolf, seal, rat, or other mammal. ■ *dated chiefly Brit.* a cheeky or arrogant boy or young man: *you saucy* ***young pup!***

▸*v.* (**pupped**, **pup·ping**) [*intrans.*] (of female dogs and certain other animals) give birth to young. ▷late 16th cent. (in the sense 'arrogant young man'): back-formation from **PUPPY**, interpreted as a diminutive.

▸*PHRASES* □ **in pup** (of a female dog) pregnant. □ **sell someone** (or **buy**) **a pup** *Brit., informal* swindle someone (or be swindled), esp. by selling (or buying) something worthless.

pu·pa /'pyo͞opə/ ▸*n.* (*pl.* **-pae** /-ˌpē; -ˌpī/) an insect in its inactive immature form between larva and adult, e.g., a chrysalis. ▷late 18th cent.: modern Latin, from Latin *pupa* 'girl, doll.' —**pu·pal** *adj.*

pu·par·i·um /pyo͞o'pe(ə)rēəm/ ▸*n.* (*pl.* **-par·i·a** /-'pe(ə)rēə/) *Entomology* the hardened last larval skin that encloses the pupa in some insects, esp. higher diptera. ■ a pupa enclosed in such a skin. ▷early 19th cent.: modern Latin, from **PUPA**, on the pattern of words such as *herbarium*.

pu·pate /'pyo͞oˌpāt/ ▸*v.* [*intrans.*] (of a larva) become a pupa. —**pu·pa·tion** /pyo͞o'pāSHən/ *n.*

pup·fish /'pəpˌfiSH/ ▸*n.* (*pl.* same or **-fish·es**) a small fish found in fresh or brackish water in the deserts of the southwestern U.S. and northern Mexico. • Genus *Cyprinodon*, family Cyprinodontidae: several species, some of which are confined to single pools.

pu·pil[1] /'pyo͞opəl/ ▸*n.* a student in school. ▷late Middle English (in the sense 'orphan, ward'): from Old French *pupille*, from Latin *pupillus* (diminutive of *pupus* 'boy') and *pupilla* (diminutive of *pupa* 'girl').

pu·pil[2] ▸*n.* the dark circular opening in the center of the iris of the eye, varying in size to regulate the amount of light reaching the retina. ▷late Middle English: from Old French *pupille* or Latin *pupilla*, diminutive of *pupa* 'doll' (so named from the tiny reflected images visible in the eye). **—pu·pil·lar·y** /ˈpyo͞opəˌlerē/ (also **pu·pil·ar·y**) *adj.*

pu·pil·age /ˈpyo͞opəlij/ (also **pu·pil·lage**) ▸*n.* the state of being a pupil or student.

pu·pip·a·rous /pyo͞oˈpipərəs/ ▸*adj. Entomology* (of certain flies, e.g., the tsetse) producing young that are already ready to pupate. ▷early 19th cent.: from modern Latin *pupipara* (neuter plural of *pupiparus* 'bringing forth young') + **-OUS**.

pup·pet /ˈpəpət/ ▸*n.* a movable model of a person or animal that is used in entertainment and is typically moved either by strings controlled from above or by a hand inside it. ■ *figurative* a person, party, or state under the control of another person, group, or power: *the new Shah began his reign as an Anglo-Soviet puppet.* ▷mid 16th cent. (denoting a doll): later form of **POPPET**, generally having a more unfavorable connotation. **—pup·pet·ry** /-trē/ *n.*

pup·pet·eer /ˌpəpəˈtir/ ▸*n.* a person who works puppets. **—pup·pet·eer·ing** *n.*

Pup·pis /ˈpəpis/ *Astronomy* a southern constellation (the Poop or Stern), lying partly in the Milky Way south of Canis Major and originally part of Argo. ■ [as *genitive*] (**Puppis**) used with a preceding letter or numeral to designate a star in this constellation: *the star Zeta Puppis.* ▷Latin.

pup·py /ˈpəpē/ ▸*n.* (*pl.* **-pies**) a young dog. ■ *informal, dated* a conceited or arrogant young man: *you ungrateful puppy.* ▷late 15th cent. (denoting a lapdog): perhaps from Old French *poupee* 'doll, plaything'; compare with **PUPPET**, synonymous with dialect *puppy* (as in *puppy-show* 'puppet show'). **—pup·py·hood** /-ˌho͝od/ *n.* **—pup·py·ish** *adj.*

pup·py dog ▸*n.* a child's word for a puppy. ■ *figurative* a gentle or devotedly loyal person.

pup·py fat ▸*n. chiefly Brit.* fat on the body of a baby or child that disappears around adolescence.

pup·py love ▸*n.* an intense but relatively shallow romantic attachment, typically associated with adolescents.

pup tent ▸*n.* a small triangular tent, esp. one with a pole at either end and room for one or two people.

pur- ▸*prefix* equivalent to **PRO-**[1] (as in *purloin, pursue*). ▷from Anglo-Norman French, from Latin *por-, pro-*.

Pu·ra·na /po͞oˈränə/ ▸*n.* (usu. **Puranas**) any of a class of Sanskrit sacred writings containing Hindu legends and folklore of varying date and origin, the most ancient of which dates from the 4th century AD. ▷from Sanskrit *purāṇa* 'ancient (legend),' from *purā* 'formerly.' **—Pu·ra·nic** /-ˈränik/ *adj.*

pur·blind /ˈpərˌblīnd/ ▸*adj.* having impaired or defective vision. ■ *figurative* slow or unable to understand; dim-witted. ▷Middle English (as two words in the sense 'completely blind'): from the adverb **PURE** 'utterly' (later assimilated to **PUR-**) + **BLIND**. **—pur·blind·ness** *n.*

Pur·cell /pərˈsel; ˈpərsəl/, Henry (1659–95), English composer. He composed the first English opera, *Dido and Aeneas* (1689), and the incidental music for many plays.

pur·chase /ˈpərCHəs/ ▸*v.* [*trans.*] **1** acquire (something) by paying for it; buy: *Mr. Gill spotted the manuscript at a local auction and purchased it for $1,500.* ■ *archaic* obtain or achieve with effort or suffering: *the victory was purchased by the death of Rhiwallon.* **2** *Nautical* haul in (a rope or cable) or haul up (an anchor) by means of a pulley, lever, etc.
▸*n.* **1** the action of buying something: *the large number of videos currently available for purchase | we carefully* ***make** our **purchases** after consulting each other.* ■ a thing that has been bought: *she stowed her purchases in the car.* ■ *Law* the acquisition of property by means other than inheritance. ■ *archaic* the annual rent or return from land. **2** a hold or position on something for applying power advantageously, or the advantage gained by such application: *the horse's hooves fought for* ***purchase on*** *the slippery pavement |* [in *sing.*] *an attempt to gain a purchase on the soft earth.* ■ a block and tackle. ▷Middle English: from Old French *pourchacier* 'seek to obtain or bring about,' the earliest sense also in English, which soon gave rise to the senses 'gain' (hence, in nautical use, the notion of "gaining" one portion of rope after another) and 'buy.' **—pur·chas·a·ble** *adj.* **—pur·chas·er** *n.*

pur·dah /ˈpərdə/ ▸*n.* the practice among women in certain Muslim and Hindu societies of living in a separate room or behind a curtain, or of dressing in all-enveloping clothes, in order to stay out of the sight of men or strangers: *he never required them to observe purdah.* ■ the state of living in such a place or dressing in this way: *she was supposed to be* ***in purdah*** *upstairs.* ■ *figurative* isolation or hiding: *in the thirties and seventies, legs went into purdah.* ■ a curtain used for screening off women in this way. ▷early 19th cent.: from Urdu and Persian *parda* 'veil, curtain.'

pure /pyo͝or/ ▸*adj.* not mixed or adulterated with any other substance or material: *cars can run on pure alcohol | the jacket was pure wool.* ■ without any extraneous and unnecessary elements: *the romantic notion of pure art devoid of social responsibility.* ■ free of any contamination: *the pure, clear waters of Montana.* ■ wholesome and untainted by immorality, esp. that of a sexual nature: *our fondness for each other is pure and innocent.* ■ (of a sound) perfectly in tune and with a clear tone. ■ (of an animal or plant) of unmixed origin or descent: *the pure Charolais is white or light wheat in the coat.* ■ (of a subject of study) dealing with abstract concepts and not practical application: *a theoretical discipline such as pure physics.* Compare with **APPLIED**. ■ *Phonetics* (of a vowel) not joined with another to form a diphthong. ■ [*attrib.*] involving or containing nothing else but; sheer (used for emphasis): *a shout of pure anger | an outcome that may be a matter of pure chance.* ▷Middle English: from Old French *pur* 'pure,' from Latin *purus.* **—pure·ness** *n.*
▸*PHRASE* □ **pure and simple** and nothing else (used for emphasis): *it was revenge, pure and simple.*

pure·bred /ˈpyo͝orˌbred/ ▸*adj.* (of an animal) bred from parents of the same breed or variety.
▸*n.* an animal of this kind.

pure cul·ture ▸*n. Microbiology* a culture in which only one strain or clone is present.

pu·rée /pyo͞oˈrā; -ˈrē/ ▸*n.* a smooth, creamy substance made of liquidized or crushed fruit or vegetables: *stir in the tomato purée.*
▸*v.* (**pu·rées, pu·réed, pu·rée·ing**) [*trans.*] make a purée of (fruit or vegetables). ▷early 18th cent.: French, literally 'purified,' feminine past participle of *purer.*

pure line ▸*n. Biology* an inbred line of genetic descent.

pure·ly /ˈpyo͝orlē/ ▸*adv.* in a pure manner: *act nobly, speak purely, and think charitably.* ■ entirely; exclusively: *the purpose of the meeting was purely to give information.*

pure math·e·mat·ics *plural n.* ▸ see **MATHEMATICS**.

pure sci·ence ▸*n.* a science depending on deductions from demonstrated truths, such as mathematics or logic, or studied without regard to practical applications.

pur·fle /ˈpərfəl/ ▸*n.* an ornamental border, typically one inlaid on the back or belly of a violin. ■ *archaic* an ornamental or embroidered edge of a garment.
▸*v.* [*trans.*] [often as *n.*] (**purfling**) decorate (something) with an ornamental border. ▷Middle English (as a verb): from Old French *porfil* (noun), *porfiler* (verb), based on Latin *pro* 'forward' + *filum* 'thread.'

pur·ga·tion /ˌpərˈgāSHən/ ▸*n.* the purification or cleansing of someone or something: *the purgation by ritual violence of morbid social emotions.* ■ (in Roman Catholic doctrine) the spiritual cleansing of a soul in purgatory. ■ *historical* the action of clearing oneself of accusation or suspicion by an oath or ordeal. ■ evacuation of the bowels brought about by laxatives. ▷late Middle English: from Old French *purgacion*, from Latin *purgatio(n-)*, from *purgare* 'purify' (see **PURGE**).

pur·ga·tive /ˈpərgətiv/ ▸*adj.* strongly laxative in effect. ■ *figurative* having the effect of ridding someone of unwanted feelings or memories: *the purgative action of language.*
▸*n.* a laxative. ■ *figurative* a thing that rids someone of unwanted feelings or memories: *confrontation would be a purgative.* ▷late Middle English: from Old French *purgatif, -ive*, from late Latin *purgativus*, from *purgat-* 'purified,' from the verb *purgare* (see **PURGE**).

pur·ga·to·ry /ˈpərgəˌtôrē/ ▸*n.* (*pl.* **-ries**) (in Roman Catholic doctrine) a place or state of suffering inhabited by the souls of sinners who are expiating their sins before going to heaven. ■ mental anguish or suffering: *this was purgatory, worse than anything she'd faced in her life.*
▸*adj. archaic* having the quality of cleansing or purifying: *infernal punishments are purgatory and medicinal.* ▷Middle English: from Anglo-Norman French *purgatorie* or medieval Latin *purgatorium*, neuter (used as a noun) of late Latin *purgatorius* 'purifying,' from the verb *purgare* (see **PURGE**). **—pur·ga·to·ri·al** /ˌpərgəˈtôrēəl/ *adj.*

purge /pərj/ ▸*v.* [*trans.*] rid (someone) of an unwanted feeling, memory, or condition, typically giving a sense of cathartic release: *Bob had helped* ***purge*** *Martha* ***of*** *the terrible guilt that had haunted her.* ■ remove (an unwanted feeling, memory, or condition) in such a way. ■ remove (a group of people considered undesirable) from an organization or place, typically in an abrupt or violent manner: *he purged all but 26 of the central committee members.* ■ remove someone from (an organization or place) in such a way: *an opportunity to* ***purge*** *the party* ***of*** *unsatisfactory members.* ■ *Law* atone for or wipe out (contempt of court). ■ physically remove (something) completely: *a cold air blower* ***purges*** *residual solvents* ***from*** *the body.* ■ [*intrans.*] [often as *n.*] (**purging**) evacuate one's bowels, esp. as a result of taking a laxative.
▸*n.* an abrupt or violent removal of a group of people from an organization or place: *a purge of the ruling class is absolutely necessary | the Stalinist purges.* ■ *dated* a laxative. ▷Middle English (in the legal sense 'clear oneself of a charge'): from Old French *purgier*, from Latin *purgare* 'purify,' from *purus* 'pure.' **—purg·er** *n.*

pu·ri /ˈpo͝orē/ (also **poo·ri**) ▸*n.* (*pl.* **pu·ris**) (in Indian cooking) a small, round, flat piece of bread made of unleavened wheat flour, deep-fried and served with meat or vegetables. ▷via Hindi from Sanskrit *pūrikā*.

pu·ri·fy /ˈpyo͝orəˌfī/ ▸*v.* (**-fies, -fied**) [*trans.*] remove contaminants from: *the filtration plant is able to purify 70 tons of water a day |* [as *adj.*] (**purified**) *purified linseed oil.* ■ make ceremonially clean: *a ritual bath to purify the soul.* ■ rid (something) of an unwanted element: *Mao's campaign to purify the Communist Party hierarchy.* ■ (**purify something from**) extract something from: *genomic DNA was purified from whole blood.* ▷Middle English: from Old French *purifier*, from Latin *purificare*, from *purus* 'pure.' **—pu·ri·fi·ca·tion** /ˌpyo͝orəfiˈkāSHən/ *n.* **—pu·rif·i·ca·to·ry** /pyo͞oˈrifikəˌtôrē/ *adj.* **—pu·ri·fi·er** *n.*

Pu·rim /ˈpo͝orim; po͞oˈrēm/ ▸*n.* a lesser Jewish festival held in spring (on the 14th or 15th day of Adar) to commemorate the defeat of Haman's plot to massacre the Jews as recorded in the book of Esther. ▷Hebrew, plural of *pūr*, explained in the book of Esther (3:7, 9:24) as meaning 'lot,' with allusion to the casting of lots by Haman.

pu·rine /ˈpyo͝orˌēn/ ▸*n. Chemistry* a colorless crystalline compound with basic properties, forming uric acid on oxidation. • A bicyclic compound; chem. formula: $C_5H_4N_4$. ■ (also **purine base**) a substituted derivative of this, esp. the bases adenine and guanine present in DNA and RNA. ▷late 19th cent.: from German *Purin*, from Latin *purus* 'pure' + *uricum* 'uric acid' + **-INE**[4].

pur·ism /ˈpyo͝orˌizəm/ ▸*n.* **1** scrupulous or exaggerated observance of or insistence on traditional rules or structures, esp. in language or style. **2** (**Purism**) an early 20th-century artistic style and movement founded by Le Corbusier and the French painter Amédée Ozenfant (1886–1966) and emphasizing purity of geometric form. It arose out of a rejection of cubism and was characterized by a return to the representation of recognizable objects.

pur·ist /ˈpyo͝orist/ ▸*n.* **1** a person who insists on absolute adherence to traditional rules or structures, esp. in language or style. **2** (**Purist**) an adherent of Purism. ▷early 18th cent.: from French *puriste*, from *pur* 'pure.' **—pu·ris·tic** /pyo͝orˈistik/ *adj.*

Pu·ri·tan /ˈpyo͝oritn/ ▸*n.* a member of a group of English Protestants of the late 16th and 17th centuries who regarded the Reformation of the Church of England under Elizabeth as incomplete and sought to simplify and regulate forms of worship. ■ (**puritan**) a person with censorious moral beliefs, esp. about pleasure and sex.
▸*adj.* of or relating to the Puritans. ■ (**puritan**) having or displaying censorious moral beliefs, esp. about pleasure and sex. ▷late 16th cent.: from late Latin *puritas* 'purity' + **-AN**. **—Pu·ri·tan·ism** (also **pu·ri·tan·ism**) *n.*

pu·ri·tan·i·cal /ˌpyo͝oriˈtanikəl/ ▸*adj. often derogatory* practicing or affecting strict religious or moral behavior. **—pu·ri·tan·i·cal·ly** *adv.*

Pu·ri·tan State a nickname for the state of **MASSACHUSETTS**.

pu·ri·ty /ˈpyo͝oritē/ ▸*n.* freedom from adulteration or contamination: *the purity of our drinking water.* ■ freedom from immorality, esp. of a sexual nature: *white is meant to represent purity and innocence.* ▷Middle English: from Old French *purete*, later assimilated to late Latin *puritas*, from Latin *purus* 'pure.'

Pur·kin·je cell /pərˈkinjē/ ▸*n. Anatomy* a nerve cell of a large, branched type found in the cortex of the cerebellum. ▷mid 19th cent.: named after Jan E. *Purkinje* (1787–1869), Bohemian physiologist.

purl[1] /pərl/ ▶*adj.* [*attrib.*] denoting or relating to a knitting stitch made by putting the needle through the front of the stitch from right to left. Compare with **KNIT**.
▶*n.* a purl stitch.
▶*v.* [*trans.*] knit with a purl stitch: *knit one, purl one.* ▷mid 17th cent. (as a noun): of uncertain origin.

purl[2] ▶*v.* [*intrans.*] (of a stream or river) flow with a swirling motion and babbling sound.
▶*n.* [in *sing.*] a motion or sound of this kind. ▷early 16th cent. (denoting a small swirling stream): probably imitative; compare with Norwegian *purla* 'bubble up.'

pur·lieu /ˈpərl(y)o͞o/ ▶*n.* (*pl.* **-lieus** or **-lieux** /-l(y)o͞o(z)/) the area near or surrounding a place: *the photogenic* **purlieus of** *the Princeton.* ■ *figurative* a person's usual haunts. ■ *Brit., historical* a tract on the border of a forest, esp. one earlier included in it and still partly subject to forest laws. ▷late 15th cent. (denoting a tract on the border of a forest): probably an alteration (suggested by French *lieu* 'place') of Anglo-Norman French *puralee* 'a going around to settle the boundaries.'

pur·lin /ˈpərlən/ ▶*n.* a horizontal beam along the length of a roof, resting on a main rafter and supporting the common rafters or boards. ▷late Middle English: perhaps of French origin.

pur·loin /pərˈloin/ ▶*v.* [*trans.*] steal (something): *he must have managed to purloin a copy of the key.* ▷Middle English (in the sense 'put at a distance'): from Anglo-Norman French *purloigner* 'put away,' from *pur-* 'forth' + *loign* 'far.' **—pur·loin·er** *n.*

pu·ro /ˈpo͝orō/ ▶*n.* (*pl.* **-ros**) (in Spanish-speaking regions) a cigar. ▷Spanish, literally 'pure.'

pu·ro·my·cin /ˌpyo͝orəˈmīsin/ ▶*n. Medicine* an antibiotic used to treat sleeping sickness and amebic dysentery. • This antibiotic is produced by the bacterium *Streptomyces alboniger.* ▷1950s: from **PURINE** + **-MYCIN**.

pur·ple /ˈpərpəl/ ▶*n.* a color intermediate between red and blue: *the painting was mostly in shades of blue and purple.* ■ purple clothing or material. ■ (also **Tyrian purple**) a crimson dye obtained from some mollusks, formerly used for fabric worn by an emperor or senior magistrate in ancient Rome or Byzantium. ■ (**the purple**) (in ancient Rome or Byzantium) clothing of this color. ■ (**the purple**) (in ancient Rome) a position of rank, authority, or privilege: *he was too young to assume the purple.* ■ (**the purple**) the scarlet official dress of a cardinal.
▶*adj.* of a color intermediate between red and blue: *a faded purple T-shirt.*
▶*v.* become or make purple in color: [*intrans.*] *Ed's cheeks purpled.* | [*trans.*] *the neon was purpling the horizon above the highway.* ▷Old English (describing the clothing of an emperor), alteration of *purpre*, from Latin *purpura* 'purple,' from Greek *porphura*, denoting mollusks that yielded a crimson dye, also cloth dyed with this. **—pur·ple·ness** *n.* **—pur·plish** /ˈpərp(ə)lisн/ *adj.* **—pur·ply** /ˈpərp(ə)lē/ *adj.*
▶*PHRASE* □ **born in** (or **to**) **the purple** born into a reigning family or privileged class.

pur·ple gal·li·nule ▶*n.* **1** another term for **GALLINULE**. **2** a marsh bird of the rail family, with a purplish-blue head and breast and a large red bill, found throughout the Old World. • *Porphyrio porphyrio*, family Rallidae.

pur·ple heart ▶*n.* **1** (**Purple Heart**) (in the U.S.) a military decoration for those wounded or killed in action, established in 1782 and reestablished in 1932. **2** a large tree of the rain forests of Central and South America, with dark purplish-brown timber that blackens on contact with water. • Genus *Peltogyne*, family Leguminosae: several species, in particular *P. paniculata.* **3** *Brit., informal* a mauve-colored heart-shaped stimulant tablet, esp. of amphetamine.

pur·ple-leaf plum ▶*n.* a shrub or small tree with white flowers and small red and yellow edible fruit. Native to southwestern Asia, it is used as stock for commercial varieties of plum. Also called **FLOWERING PLUM, MYROBALAN**. • *Prunus cerasifera*, family Rosaceae. ■ the fruit of this tree.

pur·ple mar·tin ▶*n.* a martin with purplish-blue plumage. It is the largest North American swallow, and the male is the only swallow with uniform dark plumage on its belly. • *Progne subis*, family Hirundinidae.

pur·ple pas·sage ▶*n.* an elaborate or excessively ornate passage in a literary composition.

pur·ple patch ▶*n.* **1** *informal, chiefly Brit.* a run of success or good luck. **2** another term for **PURPLE PASSAGE**.

pur·ple prose ▶*n.* prose that is too elaborate or ornate.

pur·port ▶*v.* /pərˈpôrt/ [with *infinitive*] appear or claim to be or do something, esp. falsely; profess: *she is not the person she purports to be.*
▶*n.* /ˈpərˌpôrt/ the meaning or substance of something, typically a document or speech: *I do not understand the purport of your remarks.* ■ the purpose of a person or thing: *the purport of existence.* ▷late Middle English (in the sense 'express, signify'): from Old French *purporter*, from medieval Latin *proportare*, from Latin *pro-* 'forth' + *portare* 'carry, bear.' The sense 'appear to be' dates from the late 18th cent. **—pur·port·ed·ly** *adv.*

pur·pose /ˈpərpəs/ ▶*n.* the reason for which something is done or created or for which something exists: *the purpose of the meeting is to appoint a trustee* | *the building is no longer needed for its original purpose.* ■ a person's sense of resolve or determination: *there was a new* **sense of purpose** *in her step as she set off.* ■ (usu. **purposes**) a particular requirement or consideration, typically one that is temporary or restricted in scope or extent: *pensions are considered as earned income for tax purposes.*
▶*v.* [*trans.*] *formal* have as one's intention or objective: *God has allowed suffering, even purposed it.* See note at **INTEND**. ▷Middle English: from Old French *porpos*, from the verb *porposer*, variant of *proposer* (see **PROPOSE**).
▶*PHRASES* □ **on purpose** intentionally. □ **to no purpose** with no result or effect; pointlessly. □ **to the purpose** relevant or useful: *you may have heard something from them that is to the purpose.*

pur·pose-built ▶*adj. chiefly Brit.* built for a particular purpose: *purpose-built accommodations for the elderly.*

pur·pose·ful /ˈpərpəsfəl/ ▶*adj.* having or showing determination or resolve: *the purposeful stride of a great lawyer.* ■ having a useful purpose: *purposeful activities.* ■ intentional: *if his sudden death was not accidental, it must have been purposeful.* **—pur·pose·ful·ly** *adv.* **—pur·pose·ful·ness** *n.*

pur·pose·less /ˈpərpəslis/ ▶*adj.* done or made with no discernible point or purpose: *purposeless vandalism.* ■ having no aim or plan: *his purposeless life.* **—pur·pose·less·ly** *adv.* **—pur·pose·less·ness** *n.*

pur·pose·ly /ˈpərpəslē/ ▶*adv.* on purpose; intentionally: *she had purposely made it difficult.*

pur·pos·ive /ˈpərpəsiv; pərˈpō-/ ▶*adj.* having, serving, or done with a purpose: *teaching is a purposive activity.* **—pur·pos·ive·ly** *adv.* **—pur·pos·ive·ness** *n.*

pur·pu·ra /ˈpərp(y)ərə/ ▶*n. Medicine* a rash of purple spots on the skin caused by internal bleeding from small blood vessels. ■ [with *adj.*] any of a number of diseases characterized by such a rash: *psychogenic purpura.* ▷mid 18th cent.: from Latin, from Greek *porphura* 'purple.' **—pur·pu·ric** /pərˈpyo͝orik/ *adj.*

pur·pure /ˈpərpyər/ ▶*n.* purple, as a heraldic tincture. ▷Old English (in the sense 'purple garment'), from Latin *purpura* (see **PURPURA**), reinforced by Old French *purpre* and influenced by words ending in *-ure.*

pur·pu·rin /ˈpərpyərin/ ▶*n. Chemistry* a red dye originally extracted from madder and also prepared artificially by the oxidation of alizarin. • An anthraquinone derivative; chem. formula: $C_{14}H_8O_5$. ▷mid 19th cent.: from Latin *purpura* 'purple' + **-IN**[1].

purr /pər/ ▶*v.* [*intrans.*] (of a cat) make a low continuous vibratory sound usually expressing contentment. ■ (of a vehicle or machine) make such a sound when running smoothly at low speed. ■ [*intrans.*] (of a vehicle or engine) move smoothly while making such a sound: *a sleek blue BMW purred past him.* ■ speak in a low soft voice, esp. when expressing contentment or acting seductively: [with *direct speech*] *"Would you like coffee?" she purred* | [*trans.*] *she purred her lines seductively.*
▶*n.* a low continuous vibratory sound, typically that made by a cat or vehicle. ▷early 17th cent.: imitative.

purse /pərs/ ▶*n.* a small bag used esp. by a woman to carry everyday personal items. ■ a small pouch of leather or plastic used for carrying money, typically by a woman. ■ the money possessed or available to a person or country: *institutions are funded from the same general purse.* ■ a sum of money given as a prize in a sporting contest, esp. a boxing match.
▶*v.* (with reference to the lips) pucker or contract, typically to express disapproval or irritation: [*trans.*] *Marianne took a glance at her reflection and pursed her lips disgustedly* | [*intrans.*] *under stress his lips would purse slightly.* ▷late Old English, alteration of late Latin *bursa* 'purse,' from Greek *bursa* 'hide, leather.' The current verb sense (from the notion of drawing purse strings) dates from the early 17th cent.
▶*PHRASES* □ **hold the purse strings** have control of expenditure. □ **tighten** (or **loosen**) **the purse strings** restrict (or increase) the amount of money available to be spent.

purse net ▶*n.* another term for **PURSE SEINE**.

purs·er /ˈpərsər/ ▶*n.* an officer on a ship who keeps the accounts, esp. the head steward on a passenger vessel.

purse seine ▶*n.* [usu. as *adj.*] a seine that can be drawn into the shape of a bag using the line along the bottom of the net like the drawstring of a purse. **—purse sein·er** *n.*

purs·lane /ˈpərslən; -ˌslān/ ▶*n.* any of a number of small, typically fleshy-leaved plants that grow in damp habitats or waste places, in particular: • *Portulaca oleracea*, a prostrate North American plant with tiny yellow flowers. • *Sesuvium maritimum* (**sea-purslane**), an edible plant that grows in damp sand along coastal shores. ▷late Middle English: from Old French *porcelaine*, probably from Latin *porcil(l)aca*, variant of *portulaca*, influenced by French *porcelaine* 'porcelain.'

pur·su·ance /pərˈso͞oəns/ ▶*n. formal* the carrying out of a plan or action: *you have a right to use public areas* **in the pursuance of** *your lawful hobby.* ■ the action of trying to achieve something: *they are considering a walkout in pursuance of a better deal.*

pur·su·ant /pərˈso͞oənt/ ▶*adv.* (**pursuant to**) *formal* in accordance with (a law or a legal document or resolution): *conversations that they wiretap pursuant to court order.*
▶*adj. archaic* following; going in pursuit: *the pursuant lady.* ▷late Middle English *poursuiant* (as a noun in the sense 'prosecutor'): from Old French, 'pursuing,' from the verb *poursuir*; later influenced in spelling by **PURSUE**. **—pur·su·ant·ly** *adv.*

pur·sue /pərˈso͞o/ ▶*v.* (**-sues, -sued, -su·ing**) [*trans.*] **1** follow (someone or something) in order to catch or attack them: *the officer pursued the van* | *figurative a heavily indebted businessman was being pursued by creditors.* ■ seek to form a sexual relationship with (someone) in a persistent way: *Sophie was being pursued by a number of men.* ■ seek to attain or accomplish (a goal), esp. over a long period: *should people pursue their own happiness at the expense of others?* ■ *archaic* or *poetic/literary* (of something unpleasant) persistently afflict (someone): *mercy lasts as long as sin pursues man.* **2** (of a person or way) continue or proceed along (a path or route): *the road pursued a straight course over the scrubland.* ■ engage in (an activity or course of action): *Andrew was determined to pursue a computer career* | *the council decided not to pursue an appeal.* ■ continue to investigate, explore, or discuss (a topic, idea, or argument): *we shall not pursue the matter any further.* ▷Middle English (originally in the sense 'follow with enmity'): from Anglo-Norman French *pursuer*, from an alteration of Latin *prosequi* 'prosecute.' **—pur·su·a·ble** *adj.* **—pur·su·er** *n.*

pur·suit /pərˈso͞ot/ ▶*n.* **1** the action of following or pursuing someone or something: *the cat crouched in the grass* **in pursuit of** *a bird* | *those whose business is the pursuit of knowledge.* ■ a bicycle race in which competitors start from different parts of a track and attempt to overtake one another. ■ *Physiology* the action of the eye in following a moving object. **2** [with *adj.*] (often **pursuits**) an activity of a specified kind, esp. a recreational or athletic one: *a whole range of leisure pursuits.* ▷late Middle English: from Anglo-Norman French *purseute* 'following after,' from *pursuer* (see **PURSUE**). Early senses included 'persecution, annoyance' and in legal contexts 'petition, prosecution.'
▶*PHRASE* □ **give pursuit** (of a person, animal, or vehicle) start to chase another.

pur·sui·vant /ˈpərs(w)ivənt/ ▶*n.* **1** *Brit.* an officer of the College of Arms. **2** *archaic* a follower or attendant. ▷late Middle English (denoting a junior heraldic officer): from Old French *pursivant*, present participle (used as a noun) of *pursivre* 'follow after.'

pur·sy /ˈpərsē/ ▶*adj. archaic* **1** (esp. of a horse) short of breath; asthmatic. **2** (of a person) fat. ▷late Middle English: reduction of Anglo-Norman French *porsif*, alteration of Old French *polsif*, from *polser* 'breathe with difficulty,' from Latin *pulsare* 'set in violent motion.' **—pur·si·ness** *n.*

pu·ru·lent /ˈpyo͝or(y)ələnt/ ▶*adj. Medicine* consisting of, containing, or discharging pus. ▷late Middle

English: from Latin *purulentus* 'festering,' from *pus*, *pur-* (see **PUS**).

Pu·rus Riv·er /pəˈro͞os/ a river that flows northeast for 2,100 miles (3,400 km) from the Andes Mountains in eastern Peru into northwestern Brazil, where it joins the Amazon River.

pur·vey /pərˈvā/ ▸*v.* [*trans.*] provide or supply (food, drink, or other goods) as one's business: *shops purveying cooked food* | *figurative this magazine feels like a concerted effort to purvey gloom and doom.* ▷Middle English: from Anglo-Norman French *purveier*, from Latin *providere* 'foresee, attend to' (see **PROVIDE**). Early senses included 'foresee,' 'attend to in advance,' and 'equip.' **—pur·vey·or** /-ˈvāər/ *n.*

pur·vey·ance /pərˈvāəns/ ▸*n.* the action of purveying something. ■ *Brit., historical* the right of the sovereign to buy provisions and use horses and vehicles for a fixed price lower than the market value. ▷Middle English (in the senses 'foresight' and 'prearrangement'): from Old French *porveance*, from Latin *providentia* 'foresight' (see **PROVIDENCE**).

pur·view /ˈpərˌvyo͞o/ ▸*n.* [in *sing.*] the scope of the influence or concerns of something: *such a case might be within the purview of the legislation.* ■ a range of experience or thought: *social taboos meant that little information was likely to come within the purview of women generally.* ▷late Middle English: from Anglo-Norman French *purveu* 'foreseen,' past participle of *purveier* (see **PURVEY**). Early use was as a legal term specifying the body of a statute following the words "be it enacted."

pus /pəs/ ▸*n.* a thick yellowish or greenish opaque liquid produced in infected tissue, consisting of dead white blood cells and bacteria with tissue debris and serum. ▷late Middle English: from Latin.

Pu·san /ˈpo͞oˈsän/ an industrial city and seaport on the southeastern coast of South Korea; pop. 3,798,000.

Pu·sey /ˈpyo͞ozē/, Edward Bouverie (1800–82), English theologian. In 1833, while professor of Hebrew at Oxford, he founded the Oxford Movement and became its leader after the withdrawal of John Henry Newman in 1841.

push /po͝osн/ ▸*v.* **1** [*trans.*] exert force on (someone or something), typically with one's hand, in order to move them away from oneself or the origin of the force: *she pushed her glass toward him* | *he pushed a card under the door* | [*intrans.*] *he* **pushed at** *the skylight, but it wouldn't budge.* ■ [*trans.*] hold and exert force on (something) so as to cause it to move along in front of one: *a woman was pushing a stroller.* ■ move one's body or a part of it into a specified position, esp. forcefully or with effort: *she pushed her hands into her pockets.* ■ [*trans.*] press (a part of a machine or other device): *he pushed the button for the twentieth floor.* ■ *figurative* affect (something) so that it reaches a specified level or state: *they expect that the huge crop will push down prices.* **2** [*intrans.*] move forward by using force to pass people or cause them to move aside: *she pushed her way through the crowded streets* | *he pushed past an old woman in his haste.* ■ (of an army) advance over territory: *the guerrillas have pushed south to within 100 miles of the capital.* ■ exert oneself to attain something or surpass others: *I was pushing hard until about 10 laps from the finish.* ■ (**push for**) demand persistently: *the council continued to push for the better management of water resources.* ■ [*trans.*] compel or urge (someone) to do something, esp. to work hard: *she believed he was pushing their daughter too hard.* ■ (**be pushed**) *informal* have very little of something, esp. time: *I'm a bit* **pushed for** *time at the moment.* ■ (**be pushing**) *informal* be nearly (a particular age): *she must be pushing forty, but she's still a good looker.* **3** [*trans.*] *informal* promote the use, sale, or acceptance of: *the company is pushing a $500 asking price.* ■ put forward (an argument or demand) with undue force or in too extreme a form: *he thought that the belief in individualism had been pushed too far.* ■ sell (a narcotic drug) illegally. **4** [*trans.*] *Computing* prepare (a stack) to receive a piece of data on the top. ■ transfer (data) to the top of a stack. **5** [*trans.*] *Photography* develop (film) so as to compensate for deliberate underexposure.

▸*phrasal v.* □ **push ahead** proceed with or continue a course of action or policy: *he promised to* **push ahead with** *economic reform.* □ **push along** *Brit., informal* go away; depart. □ **push someone around** *informal* treat someone roughly or inconsiderately. □ **push off** use an oar, boathook, etc., to exert pressure so as to move a boat out from shore or away from another vessel. □ **push on** continue on a journey: *the light was already fading, but she pushed on.* □ **push something through** get a proposed measure completed or accepted quickly.

▸*n.* **1** an act of exerting force on someone or something in order to move them away from oneself: *he closed the door with a push.* ■ an act of pressing a part of a machine or device: *the door locks at the push of a button.* ■ *figurative* something that encourages or assists something else: *the fall in prices was given a push by official policy.* **2** a vigorous effort to do or obtain something: *many clubs are joining in the fund-raising push* | *he determined to make one last push for success.* ■ a military attack in force: *the army was engaged in a push against guerrilla strongholds.* ■ forcefulness and enterprise: *an investor with the necessary money and push.* ▷Middle English (as a verb): from Old French *pousser*, from Latin *pulsare* 'to push, beat, pulse' (see **PULSE**[1]). The early sense was 'exert force on,' giving rise later to 'make a strenuous effort, endeavor.'

▸*PHRASES* □ **get** (or **give someone**) **the push** (or **shove**) *Brit., informal* be dismissed (or dismiss someone) from a job. ■ be rejected in (or end) a relationship. □ **push the boat out** see **BOAT**. □ **push someone's buttons** see **BUTTON**. □ **pushing up daisies** see **DAISY**. □ **push one's luck** *informal* take a risk on the assumption that one will continue to be successful or in favor. □ **when push comes to shove** *informal* when one must commit oneself to an action or decision: *when push came to shove, I always stood up for him.*

push·bike /ˈpo͝osнˌbīk/ ▸*n. Brit., informal* a bicycle.

push broom ▸*n.* a broom consisting of a handle attached at an angle to a wide brush that is worked by pushing.

push but·ton ▸*n.* a button that is pushed to operate an electrical device: *some kind of push button on their TV sets* | [as *adj.*] *a push-button telephone.*

push·cart /ˈpo͝osнˌkärt/ ▸*n.* a small handcart or barrow.

push·chair /ˈpo͝osнˌснe(ə)r/ ▸*n. Brit.* a stroller.

push·er /ˈpo͝osнər/ ▸*n.* **1** *informal* a person who sells illegal drugs. **2** a person or thing that pushes something. ■ *informal* a forceful or pushy person: *she got things moving, she was a tremendous pusher.*

push fit ▸*n.* a fit between two parts in which one is connected to the other by manually pushing or sliding them together.

push·ful /ˈpo͝osнfəl/ ▸*adj.* arrogantly self-assertive; pushy. **—push·ful·ly** *adv.* **—push·ful·ness** *n.*

Push·kin /ˈpo͝osнkin; -kyin/, Aleksandr (Sergeevich) (1799–1837), Russian poet, novelist, and dramatist. His first success was the romantic narrative poem *Ruslan and Ludmilla* (1820). Other notable works: *Eugene Onegin* (1833) and *Boris Godunov* (1831).

push·o·ver /ˈpo͝osнˌōvər/ ▸*n. informal* a person who is easy to overcome or influence: *Colonel Moore was benevolent but no pushover.* ■ a thing that is very easily done: *this is going to be a pushover.*

push·pin /ˈpo͝osнˌpin/ ▸*n.* a thumbtack with a spherical or cylindrical head of colored plastic, used to fasten papers to a bulletin board or to indicate positions on charts and maps.

push poll ▸*n.* an ostensible opinion poll in which the true objective is to sway voters using loaded or manipulative questions. **—push-poll·ing** *n.*

push proc·ess·ing ▸*n. Photography* the development of film so as to compensate for deliberate underexposure, thereby increasing the effective film speed.

push-pull ▸*adj.* [*attrib.*] operated by pushing and pulling. ■ *Electronics* having or involving two matched tubes or transistors that operate 180 degrees out of phase, conducting alternately for increased output.

▸*n.* a push-pull arrangement, state, or action: *a locomotive converted to push-pull.*

push·rod /ˈpo͝osнˌräd/ ▸*n.* a rod operated by cams that opens and closes the valves in an internal combustion engine.

push-start ▸*v.* [*trans.*] start (a motor vehicle) by pushing it and putting it in gear in order to make the engine turn.

▸*n.* an act of starting a motor vehicle in this way.

Push·tu /ˈpəsнto͞o/ ▸*n.* variant of **PASHTO**.

push·up /ˈpo͝osнˌəp/ (also **push-up**) ▸*n.* an exercise in which a person lies facing the floor and, keeping their back straight, raises their body by pressing down on their hands.

▸*adj.* (**push-up**) denoting a padded or underwired bra or similar garment that gives uplift to the breasts.

push·y /ˈpo͝osнē/ ▸*adj.* (**push·i·er**, **push·i·est**) excessively or unpleasantly self-assertive or ambitious. **—push·i·ly** /ˈpo͝osнəlē/ *adv.* **—push·i·ness** *n.*

pu·sil·lan·i·mous /ˌpyo͞osəˈlanəməs/ ▸*adj.* showing a lack of courage or determination; timid. ▷late Middle English: from ecclesiastical Latin *pusillanimis* (translating Greek *olugopsukhos*), from *pusillus* 'very small' + *animus* 'mind,' + **-OUS**. **—pu·sil·la·nim·i·ty** /-ləˈnimətē/ *n.* **—pu·sil·lan·i·mous·ly** *adv.*

puss[1] /po͝os/ ▸*n. informal* a cat (esp. as a form of address): *You naughty little puss!* ■ [usu. with *adj.*] a playful or coquettish girl or young woman: *you old snuggle puss.* ▷early 16th cent.: probably from Middle Low German *pūs* (also *pūskatte*) or Dutch *poes*, of unknown origin.

puss[2] ▸*n. informal* a person's face or mouth. ▷late 19th cent.: from Irish *pus* 'lip, mouth.'

pus·sy /ˈpo͝osē/ ▸*n.* (*pl.* **-sies**) **1** (also **pus·sy·cat**) *informal* a cat. **2** *vulgar slang* a woman's genitals. ■ *offensive* women in general, considered sexually. ■ *offensive* sexual intercourse with a woman. ■ *informal* a weak, cowardly, or effeminate man.

pus·sy·foot /ˈpo͝osēˌfo͝ot/ ▸*v.* [*intrans.*] act in a cautious or noncommittal way: *I realized I could no longer* **pussyfoot around.** ■ move stealthily or warily: *they make a great show of pussyfooting through the greenery.* **—pus·sy·foot·er** /-ˌfo͝otər/ *n.*

pus·sy-whip ▸*v.* [*trans.*] [usu. as *adj.*] (**pussy-whipped**) *vulgar slang* henpeck (a man).

pus·sy wil·low ▸*n.* a willow with soft fluffy silvery or yellow catkins that appear before the leaves. • Genus *Salix*, family Salicaceae: several species, in particular the common North American (*S. discolor*). ▷mid 19th cent.: originally a child's word, because of the resemblance of the soft fluffy catkins to a cat's fur.

pussy willow

pus·tu·late ▸*v.* /ˈpəscнəˌlāt; ˈpəstyə-/ [*intrans.*] form into pustules: [as *adj.*] (**pustulating**) *pustulating epidermal ulcers.*

▸*adj.* /ˈpəscнəlit; ˈpəstyə-/ *chiefly Biology* having or covered with pustules: *the surface is coarsely pustulate.* ▷late Middle English (as an adjective): from late Latin *pustulatus*, past participle of *pustulare* 'to blister,' from *pustula* 'pustule.' **—pus·tu·la·tion** /ˌpəscнəˈlāsнən; ˌpəstyə-/ *n.*

pus·tule /ˈpəscнo͞ol; ˈpəst(y)o͞ol/ ▸*n. Medicine* a small blister or pimple on the skin containing pus. ■ *Biology* a small raised spot or rounded swelling, esp. one on a plant resulting from fungal infection. ▷late Middle English: from Latin *pustula*. **—pus·tu·lar** /ˈpəscнələr; ˈpəstyə-/ *adj.*

put /po͝ot/ ▸*v.* (**put·ting**; *past* **put**) [*trans.*] **1** move to or place in a particular position: *Harry put down his cup* | *I put my hand out toward her* | *watch where you're putting your feet!* ■ cause (someone or something) to go to a particular place and remain there for a time: *India has put three experimental satellites into space.* ■ [*intrans.*] (of a ship or the people on it) proceed in a particular direction: *she stepped into the boat and* **put out to sea.** ■ write or print (something) in a particular place: *they put my name on the cover page.* ■ [*intrans.*] *archaic* (of a river) flow in a particular direction. **2** bring into a particular state or condition: *they tried to put me at ease* | *a large aid program was put into effect* | *he* **is putting himself** *at risk.* ■ (**put oneself in**) imagine oneself in (a particular situation): *it was no use trying to put herself in his place.* ■ express (a thought or comment) in a particular way, form, or language: *to put it bluntly, he was not really divorced.* **3** (**put something on/on to**) cause (someone or something) to carry or be subject to something: *commentators put some of the blame on Congress.* ■ assign a particular value, figure, or limit to: *it is very difficult to put a figure on the size of the budget.* ■ (**put something at**) estimate something to be (a particular amount): *estimates put the war's cost at $1,000,000 a day.* **4** throw (a shot or weight) as an athletic sport: *she set a women's record by putting the shot 56′ 7″.*

▸*phrasal v.* □ **put about** *Nautical* (of a ship) turn on the opposite tack. □ **put something about** (often **be put about**) spread information or rumors. □ **put something across** (or **over**) communicate something effectively. □ **put something aside 1** save money for future use. **2** forget or disregard something, typically a feeling or a past difference. □ **put someone away** (often **be put away**) *informal* confine someone in a prison or psychiatric hospital: *he deserves to be put away forever.* □ **put something away 1** save money for future use. **2** *informal* consume food or drink in large quantities. **3** another way of saying PUT SOMETHING DOWN (sense 3 below). **4** *informal* (in sports) dispatch or deal with a goal or shot. □ **put something back** reschedule a planned event to a later time or date. ■ delay something: *greater public control may put back the modernization of the industry.* □ **put something by** another way of saying PUT SOMETHING ASIDE (sense 1 above). □ **put someone down 1** *informal* lower someone's self-esteem by criticizing them in front of others. **2** lay a baby down to sleep. □ **put something down 1** record something in writing: *he's putting a few thoughts down on paper.* **2** suppress a rebellion, riot, or other disturbance by force. **3** (usu. **be put down**) kill an animal because it is sick, injured, or old. **4** pay a specified sum as a deposit: *he put a thousand down and paid the rest over six months.* **5** preserve or store food or wine for future use. **6** (also **put down**) land an aircraft. □ **put someone down as** consider or judge someone or something to be: *I'd have put you down as a Vivaldi man.* □ **put something down to** attribute something to: *if I forget anything, put it down to old age.* □ **put someone forward** recommend someone as a suitable candidate for a job or position: *he put me forward as head of publicity.* □ **put something forward** submit a plan, proposal, or theory for consideration. □ **put in** [with *direct speech*] interrupt a conversation or discussion: *"But you're a sybarite, Roger," put in Isobel.* □ **put in at/into** (of a ship) enter (a port or harbor). □ **put someone in** appoint someone to fulfill a particular role or job: *he was put in to rescue the company by the stockbrokers.* ■ (in team sports) send a player out to participate into a game. □ **put something in/into 1** present or submit something formally: *the airport had put in a claim for damages.* ■ **(put in for)** apply formally for: *Adam put in for six months' leave.* **2** devote time or effort to something: *employed mothers put in the longest hours of all women.* **3** invest money or resources in. □ **put someone off 1** cancel or postpone an appointment with someone: *he'd put off Martin until nine o'clock.* **2** cause someone to lose interest or enthusiasm: *she wanted to be a nurse, but the thought of night shifts put her off.* ■ cause someone to feel dislike or distrust: *she had a coldness that just put me off.* **3** distract someone: *you're just trying to put me off my game.* □ **put something off** postpone something: *they can't put off a decision much longer.* □ **put someone on** *informal* deceive or hoax someone. □ **put something on 1** place a garment, glasses, or jewelry on part of one's body: *Julie had put on a cotton dress.* ■ attach or apply something: *she put on fresh makeup.* **2** cause a device to operate: *shall I put the light on?* ■ start cooking something: *she was moaning that he hadn't put the dinner on.* ■ play recorded music or a video. **3** organize or present a play, exhibition, or event. ■ provide a public transportation service: *so many people wanted to visit this spot that an extra flight had to be put on.* **4** add a specified amount to (the cost of something): *the news put 12 cents on the share price.* ■ increase in body weight; become heavier by a specified amount: *she's given up her diet and put on 20 lbs.* **5** assume a particular expression, accent, etc.: *he put on a lugubrious look.* ■ behave deceptively: *she doesn't feel she has to* ***put on an act.*** **6** bet a specified amount of money on: *he put $1,000 on the horse to win.* □ **put someone on to** draw someone's attention to (someone or something useful, notable, or interesting): *Pike put me on to the department's legal section.* □ **put out** *vulgar slang* be willing to have sexual intercourse. □ **put someone out 1** cause someone trouble or inconvenience: *would it put you out too much to let her visit you for a couple of hours?* ■ (often **be put out**) upset or annoy someone: *he was not put out by the rebuff.* **2** (in sports) defeat a player or team and so cause them to be out of a competition. **3** make someone unconscious, typically by means of drugs or an anesthetic. □ **put something out 1** extinguish something that is burning: *firefighters from Georgetown put out the blaze.* ■ turn off a light. **2** lay something out ready for use: *she put out glasses and paper napkins.* **3** issue or broadcast something: *a limited-edition single was put out to promote the album.* **4** dislocate a joint: *she fell off her horse and put her shoulder out.* **5** (of a company) allocate work to a contractor or freelancer to be done off the premises. **6** (of an engine or motor) produce a particular amount of power: *the new motor is expected to put out about 250 h.p.* □ **put something over 1** another way of saying PUT SOMETHING ACROSS above. **2** postpone something: *let's put the case over for a few weeks.* □ **put someone through 1** connect someone by telephone to another person or place: ***put*** *me* ***through to*** *the mayor, please.* **2** subject someone to an unpleasant or demanding experience: *I hate Brian for what he put me through.* **3** pay for someone to attend school or college. □ **put something through** initiate something and see it through to a successful conclusion: *he put through a reform program to try to save the regime.* □ **put someone to** cause inconvenience or difficulty to someone: *I don't want to put you to any trouble.* □ **put something to 1** submit something to (someone) for consideration or attention: *we are making a takeover bid and putting an offer to the shareholders.* ■ **2** devote something to (a particular use or purpose): *they put the land to productive use.* □ **put something together** make something by assembling different parts or people: *he can take a clock apart and* ***put it back together*** *again | they decided to put a new band together.* ■ assemble things or people to make something: *a carpenter puts together shaped pieces of wood to make a table.* □ **put someone under** another way of saying PUT SOMEONE OUT (sense 3 above). □ **put up 1** offer or show (a particular degree of resistance, effort, or skill) in a fight or competitive situation: *he put up a brave fight.* **2** stay temporarily in lodgings other than one's own home: *we* ***put up at*** *a hotel in the city center.* □ **put someone up 1** accommodate someone temporarily. **2** propose someone for election or adoption: *they should have* ***put themselves up for*** *election.* □ **put something up 1** construct or erect something: *I put up the tent and cooked a meal.* **2** raise one's hand to signal that one wishes to answer or ask a question. **3** display a notice, sign, or poster. ■ present a proposal, theory, or argument for discussion or consideration. **4** *chiefly Brit.* increase the cost of something: *I'm afraid I've got to put your rent up.* **5** provide money as backing for an enterprise: *the sponsors are putting up $5,000 for the event.* **6** (often **be put up for**) offer something for sale or auction. **7** *archaic* return a sword to its sheath. □ **put upon** [often as *adj.*] **(put-upon)** *informal* take advantage of (someone) by exploiting their good nature: *a put-upon drudge who slaved for her employer.* □ **put someone up to** *informal* encourage someone to do (something wrong or unwise): *Who else would play a trick like that on me? I expect Rose put him up to it.* □ **put up with** tolerate; endure: *I'm too tired to put up with any nonsense.*

▸*n.* **1** a throw of the shot or weight. **2** *Stock Market* short for PUT OPTION. ▷Old English (recorded only in the verbal noun *putung*), of unknown origin; compare with dialect *pote* 'to push, thrust' (an early sense of the verb *put*).

▸*PHRASES* □ **put something behind one** get over a bad experience by distancing oneself from it: *they have tried to put their grief behind them and rebuild their lives.* □ **put the clocks back** (or **forward**) adjust clocks or watches backward (or forward) to take account of official changes in time. □ **put someone's eyes out** blind someone, typically in a violent way. □ **put one's hands together** applaud; clap: *I want you all to put your hands together for Barry.* □ **put one's hands up** raise one's hands in surrender. □ **put it there** [in *imperative*] *informal* used to indicate that the speaker wishes to shake hands with someone in agreement or congratulation: *put it there, Steven, we beat them.* □ **put it to** [with *clause*] make a statement or allegation to (someone) and challenge them to deny it: *I put it to him that he was just a political groupie.* □ **put one over on** *informal* deceive (someone) into accepting something false. □ **put up or shut up** *informal* justify oneself or remain silent: *they called for the alderman to either put up or shut up.*

pu·ta /'po͞o,tä/ ▸*n. informal* (in Spanish-speaking regions) a prostitute or slut. ▷Spanish.

pu·ta·men /pyo͞o'tāmən/ ▸*n.* (*pl.* **-tam·i·na** /-'tamənə/ or **-ta·mens**) *Anatomy* the outer part of the lentiform nucleus of the brain. ▷late 19th cent.: from Latin, literally 'shell remaining after pruning.' **—pu·tam·i·nal** /-'tamənl/ *adj.*

put-and-take ▸*adj.* [*attrib.*] denoting a system whereby waters are stocked with fish for anglers to catch.

pu·ta·tive /'pyo͞otətiv/ ▸*adj.* [*attrib.*] generally considered or reputed to be: *the putative father of a boy of two.* ▷late Middle English: from Old French *putatif, -ive* or late Latin *putativus*, from Latin *putat-* 'thought,' from the verb *putare*. **—pu·ta·tive·ly** *adv.*

put-down ▸*n. informal* a remark intended to humiliate or criticize someone.

Pu·tin /'po͞otin; 'po͞otn/, Vladimir (1952–), Russian statesman; president of the Russian Federation from 2000. A former KGB officer, he was appointed head of the Security Council and then prime minister by Boris Yeltsin; he became acting president on Yeltsin's resignation December 31, 1999, and was elected president in 2000.

put·log /'po͝ot,lôg; -,läg/ (also **put·lock** /-,läk/) ▸*n.* a short horizontal pole projecting from a wall, on which the floorboards of scaffolding rest. ▷mid 17th cent.: of unknown origin.

put-off ▸*n. informal* **1** an evasive reply. **2** an unpleasant or deterrent quality or feature.

put-on ▸*n. informal* a deception; a hoax.

pu·tong·hua /'po͞o'to͝oNG'hwä/ ▸*n.* the standard spoken form of modern Chinese, based on the dialect of Beijing. ▷Chinese, literally 'common spoken language.'

put op·tion ▸*n. Stock Market* an option to sell assets at an agreed price on or before a particular date.

put-out /'po͝ot,out/ ▸*n. Baseball* an act of a fielder in retiring a batter or runner.

pu·tre·fac·tion /,pyo͞otrə'fakSHən/ ▸*n.* the process of decay or rotting in a body or other organic matter. ▷late Middle English: from Old French, or from late Latin *putrefactio(n-)*, from *putrefacere* 'make rotten' (see PUTREFY).

pu·tre·fac·tive /,pyo͞otrə'faktiv/ ▸*adj.* relating to or causing decay: *they were killed by the putrefactive bacteria.*

pu·tre·fy /'pyo͞otrə,fī/ ▸*v.* (**-fies, -fied**) [*intrans.*] (of a body or other organic matter) decay or rot and produce a fetid smell. ▷late Middle English: via French from Latin *putrefacere*, from *puter, putr-* 'rotten.'

pu·tres·cent /pyo͞o'tresənt/ ▸*adj.* undergoing the process of decay; rotting: *the odor of putrescent flesh.* ▷mid 18th cent.: from Latin *putrescent-* 'beginning to go rotten,' inceptive of *putrere* 'to rot' (see PUTRID). **—pu·tres·cence** *n.*

pu·tres·ci·ble /pyo͞o'tresəbəl/ ▸*adj.* liable to decay; subject to putrefaction: *putrescible domestic waste.* ▸*n.* (usu. **putrescibles**) something that is liable to decay.

pu·tres·cine /pyo͞o'tresēn/ ▸*n. Chemistry* an oily amine formed from arginine during putrefaction. • Alternative name: **1,4-diaminobutane**; chem. formula: $C_4H_{12}N_2$.

pu·trid /'pyo͞otrid/ ▸*adj.* (of organic matter) decaying or rotting and emitting a fetid smell. ■ of or characteristic of rotting matter: *the putrid smells from the slaughterhouses.* ■ *informal* very unpleasant; repulsive: *the cocktail is a putrid pink color.* ▷late Middle English: from Latin *putridus*, from *putrere* 'to rot,' from *puter, putr-* 'rotten.' **—pu·trid·i·ty** /pyo͞o'tridətē/ *n.* **—pu·trid·ly** *adv.* **—pu·trid·ness** *n.*

putsch /po͝oCH/ ▸*n.* a violent attempt to overthrow a government. ▷1920s: from Swiss German, literally 'thrust, blow.'

putt /pət/ ▸*v.* (**put·ted, put·ting**) [*intrans.*] try to hit a golf ball into a hole by striking it gently so that it rolls across the green: *Nicklaus putted for eagle on 11 of the 16 par 5s* | [*trans.*] *putt the balls into the hole.* ▸*n.* a stroke of this kind made in an attempt to hole the ball. ▷mid 17th cent. (originally Scots): differentiated from PUT.

put·ta·nes·ca /,po͞otə'neskə; ,po͞otn'eskə/ ▸*adj.* [usually *postpositive*] denoting a pasta sauce typically including tomatoes, garlic, olives, and anchovies: *pasta puttanesca.* ▷Italian, from *puttana* 'prostitute' (the sauce is said to have been devised by prostitutes as one that could be cooked quickly between clients' visits).

put·tee /,pə'tē/ ▸*n.* a long strip of cloth wound spirally around the leg from ankle to knee for protection and support. ■ a leather legging. ▷late 19th cent.: from Hindi *paṭṭī* 'band, bandage.'

put·ter[1] /'pətər/ ▸*n.* **1** a golf club designed for use in putting, typically with a flat-faced malletlike head. **2** [with *adj.*] a golfer considered in terms of putting ability: *you'll need to be a good putter to break par.*

put·ter[2] ▸*n.* & *v.* another term for PUTT-PUTT. ▷1940s: imitative.

put·ter[3] (*Brit.* **pot·ter**) ▸*v.* [*intrans.*] occupy oneself in a desultory but pleasant manner, doing a number of small tasks or not concentrating on anything particular: *early morning is the best time of the day to* ***putter around*** *in the garden.* ■ [with *adverbial of direction*] move or go in a casual, unhurried way: *the duck putters on the surface of the pond.* ▷late 19th cent. (originally U.S.): alteration of POTTER[1]. **—put·ter·er** *n.*

put·ting green /'pətiNG/ ▸*n.* a smooth area of short

grass surrounding a hole, either as part of a golf course or as a separate area for putting.

Putt·nam /ˈpətnəm/, Sir David (Terence) (1941–), English movie director. He directed *Chariots of Fire* (1981), which won four Academy Awards; *The Killing Fields* (1984); and *The Mission* (1986).

put·to /ˈpo͞otō/ ▸*n.* (*pl.* **put·ti** /ˈpo͞otē/) a representation of a naked child, esp. a cherub or a cupid in Renaissance art. ▷Italian, literally 'boy,' from Latin *putus.*

putt-putt (also **put-put**) ▸*n.* the rapid intermittent sound of a small gasoline engine: *she heard the putt-putt of a boat coming toward them.*
▸*v.* [*intrans.*] make such a sound: *the machine gun putt-putted behind me.* ■ [*intrans.*] move under the power of an engine that makes such a sound: *the car at last putt-putted down the hill.* ▷early 20th cent.: imitative.

put·ty /ˈpətē/ ▸*n.* **1** a soft, malleable, grayish-yellow paste, made from whiting and raw linseed oil, that hardens after a few hours and is used chiefly for sealing glass panes in wooden window frames. ■ [usu. with *adj.*] any of a number of similar malleable substances used inside and outside buildings, e.g., **plumber's putty**, or used for modeling or casting. **2** a polishing powder, usually made from tin oxide, used in jewelry work.
▸*v.* (**-ties, -tied**) [*trans.*] seal or cover (something) with putty. ▷mid 17th cent.: from French *potée,* literally 'potful,' from *pot* 'pot.'
▸*PHRASE* □ **be** (**like**) **putty in someone's hands** be easily manipulated or dominated by someone.

Put·u·ma·yo Riv·er /ˌpo͞otəˈmī-ō/ a river that flows for 1,000 miles (1,610 km) from the Andes Mountains in southwestern Colombia along the borders with Ecuador and Peru into northwestern Brazil, where it joins the Amazon River.

put-up ▸*adj.* [*attrib.*] arranged beforehand in order to deceive someone: *the whole thing could be a **put-up job.***

putz /ˈpəts; ˈpo͝ots/ *informal* ▸*n.* **1** a stupid or worthless person. **2** *vulgar slang* a penis.
▸*v.* [*intrans.*] engage in inconsequential or unproductive activity: *too much **putzing around** up there would ruin them.* ▷1960s: Yiddish, literally 'penis.'

Pu·zo /ˈpo͞ozō/, Mario (1920–99), U.S. writer. He wrote the novel *The Godfather* in 1969 and the subsequent screenplay for it in 1972. His other works included *Fools Die* (1978) and *The Sicilian* (1984).

puz·zle /ˈpəzəl/ ▸*v.* [*trans.*] cause (someone) to feel confused because they cannot understand or make sense of something: *one remark he made puzzled me* | [as *adj.*] (**puzzling**) *that was the most puzzling aspect of the whole affair.* ■ [*intrans.*] think hard about something difficult to understand or explain: *she was still **puzzling over** this problem when she reached the office.* ■ (**puzzle something out**) solve or understand something by thinking hard.
▸*n.* a game, toy, or problem designed to test ingenuity or knowledge. See note at **RIDDLE.** ■ short for **JIGSAW PUZZLE** (see **JIGSAW**). ■ [usu. in *sing.*] a person or thing that is difficult to understand or explain; an enigma: *the meaning of the poem has always been a puzzle.* ▷late 16th cent. (as a verb): of unknown origin. —**puz·zle·ment** *n.* —**puz·zling·ly** /ˈpəz(ə)liNGlē/ *adv.*

puz·zler /ˈpəz(ə)lər/ ▸*n.* a difficult question or problem. ■ a person who solves puzzles as a pastime. ■ *informal* a computer game in which the player must solve puzzles.

PV ▸*abbr.* polyvinyl.

PVA ▸*abbr.* polyvinyl acetate.

PVC ▸*abbr.* polyvinyl chloride.

PVO ▸*abbr.* private voluntary organization.

PVR ▸*abbr.* personal video recorder.

PVS *Medicine* ▸*abbr.* ■ persistent vegetative state.

Pvt. (also **PVT**) ▸*abbr.* ■ (in the U.S. Army) private. ■ (in company names) private.

PW ▸*abbr.* policewoman.

p.w. ▸*abbr.* per week.

PWA ▸*abbr.* person with AIDS.

PWC ▸*abbr.* personal watercraft.

PWR ▸*abbr.* pressurized-water reactor.

pwr. ▸*abbr.* power.

PX ▸*abbr.* ■ Pedro Ximenes. ■ post exchange.

pxt. ▸*abbr.* pinxit. ▷Latin, abbreviation of *pinxit,* 'he painted.'

pya /pēˈä/ ▸*n.* a monetary unit of Myanmar (Burma), equal to one hundredth of a kyat. ▷Burmese.

py·ae·mi·a ▸*n.* British spelling of **PYEMIA.**

pyc·no·cline /ˈpiknəˌklīn/ ▸*n.* *Geography* a layer in an ocean or other body of water in which water density increases rapidly with depth. ▷1950s: from Greek *puknos* 'thick' + **CLINE.**

pye-dog /ˈpī ˌdôg/ ▸*n.* a stray mongrel, esp. in Asia. ▷mid 19th cent.: from Anglo-Indian *pye,* Hindi *pāhī* 'outsider' + **DOG.**

py·e·li·tis /ˌpīəˈlītis/ ▸*n.* *Medicine* inflammation of the renal pelvis. ▷mid 19th cent.: from Greek *puelos* 'trough, basin' + **-ITIS.**

py·e·log·ra·phy /ˌpīəˈlägrəfē/ ▸*n.* *Medicine* an X-ray technique for producing an image of the renal pelvis and urinary tract by the introduction of a radiopaque fluid. Also called **UROGRAPHY.** ▷early 20th cent.: from Greek *puelos* 'trough, basin' + **-GRAPHY.** —**py·e·lo·gram** /ˈpīəlōˌgram; pīˈelə-/ *n.*

py·e·lo·ne·phri·tis /ˌpīəˌlōniˈfrītis/ ▸*n.* *Medicine* inflammation of the substance of the kidney as a result of bacterial infection. ▷mid 19th cent.: from Greek *puelos* 'trough, basin' + **NEPHRITIS.** —**py·e·lo·ne·phrit·ic** /-ˈfritik/ *adj.*

py·e·mi·a /pīˈēmēə/ (*Brit.* **py·ae·mi·a**) ▸*n.* blood poisoning (septicemia) caused by the spread in the bloodstream of pus-forming bacteria released from an abscess. ▷mid 19th cent.: modern Latin, from Greek *puon* 'pus' + *haima* 'blood.' —**py·e·mic** /pīˈēmik/ *adj.*

py·gid·i·um /pīˈjidēəm/ ▸*n.* (*pl.* **-gid·i·a** /-ˈjidēə/) *Zoology* the terminal part or hind segment of the body in certain invertebrates. ▷mid 19th cent.: modern Latin, from Greek *pugē* 'rump.'

Pyg·ma·li·on /pigˈmālyən; -lēən/ *Greek Mythology* a king of Cyprus who fashioned an ivory statue of a beautiful woman and loved it so deeply that in answer to his prayer Aphrodite gave it life. The woman (at some point named Galatea) bore him a daughter, Paphos.

Pyg·my /ˈpigmē/ (also **Pig·my**) ▸*n.* (*pl.* **-mies**) a member of certain peoples of very short stature in equatorial Africa and parts of Southeast Asia. ■ (**pygmy**) *chiefly derogatory* a very small person, animal, or thing. ■ (**pygmy**) [usu. with *adj.*] an insignificant person, esp. one who is deficient in a particular respect: *he regarded them as intellectual pigmies.*

> Pygmies (e.g., the Mbuti and Twa peoples) are typically dark-skinned, nomadic hunter-gatherers with an average male height not above 150 cm (4 ft. 11 in.).
> See also **NEGRILLO, NEGRITO.**

▸*adj.* [*attrib.*] of, relating to, or denoting the Pygmies: *centuries-old Pygmy chants from central Africa.* ■ (**pygmy**) (of a person or thing) very small. ■ (**pygmy**) used in names of animals and plants that are much smaller than more typical kinds, e.g., **pygmy hippopotamus, pygmy water lily.** ▷late Middle English (originally in the plural, denoting a mythological race of small people): via Latin from Greek *pugmaios* 'dwarf,' from *pugmē* 'the length measured from elbow to knuckles.' —**pyg·me·an** /ˈpigmēən; pigˈmēən/ *adj.* (*archaic*).

pyg·my chim·pan·zee ▸*n.* another term for **BONOBO.**

pyg·my owl ▸*n.* a very small owl found in America and northern Eurasia. • Genus *Glaucidium,* family Strigidae: several species.

pyg·my pos·sum ▸*n.* a very small Australasian marsupial that feeds on insects and nectar, with hand-like feet and a prehensile tail. • Family Burramyidae: two genera and five species.

pyg·my shrew ▸*n.* a shrew that is one of the smallest known mammals. • Genus *Sorex,* family Soricidae: several species, in particular the Eurasian *S. minutus* and the American *S. hoyi.*

py·go·style /ˈpīgəˌstīl/ ▸*n.* *Ornithology* (in a bird) a triangular plate formed of the fused caudal vertebrae, typically supporting the tail feathers. ▷late 19th cent.: from Greek *pugē* 'rump' + *stulos* 'column.'

py·jam·as /pəˈjäməz; -jaməz/ ▸*plural n.* British spelling of **PAJAMAS.**

pyk·nic /ˈpiknik/ ▸*adj.* *Anthropology* of, relating to, or denoting a stocky physique with a rounded body and head, thickset trunk, and a tendency to be fat. ▷1920s: from Greek *puknos* 'thick' + **-IC.** The word was first used by the German psychiatrist, Ernst Kretschmer (1888–1964), in his tripartite classification of human types (the other two being *asthnic* and *athletic*).

Pyle /pīl/, Ernie (1900–1945), U.S. journalist; full name *Ernest Taylor Pyle.* A syndicated war correspondent, he reported on World War II from Africa, Europe, and the South Pacific. He was killed by Japanese forces during the U.S. invasion of Okinawa. He wrote *Here Is Your War* (1943) and *Brave Men* (1944).

py·lon /ˈpīˌlän; -lən/ ▸*n.* an upright structure that is used for support or for navigational guidance, in particular: ■ (also **electricity pylon**) a tower used for carrying power lines high above the ground. ■ a pillarlike structure on the wing of an aircraft used for carrying an engine, weapon, fuel tank, or other load. ■ a tower or post marking a path for light aircraft, cars, or other vehicles, esp. in racing. ■ a monumental gateway to an ancient Egyptian temple formed by two truncated pyramidal towers. ▷mid 19th cent.: from Greek *pulōn,* from *pulē* 'gate.'

py·lor·ic /pīˈlôrik; pə-/ ▸*adj.* *Anatomy & Medicine* relating to or affecting the region where the stomach opens into the duodenum (small intestine): *pyloric stenosis.*

py·lo·rus /pīˈlôrəs; pə-/ ▸*n.* (*pl.* **-lo·ri** /-ˈlôrˌī; -ˈlôrē/) *Anatomy* the opening from the stomach into the duodenum (small intestine). ▷early 17th cent.: via late Latin from Greek *pulouros* 'gatekeeper,' from *pulē* 'gate' + *ouros* 'warder.'

Pyn·chon /ˈpinCHən/, Thomas (Ruggles) (1937–), U.S. novelist. An elusive author who shuns public attention, his works abandon the normal conventions of the novel. Notable works: *V* (1963), *The Crying of Lot 49* (1966), *Gravity's Rainbow* (1972), *Vineland* (1990), and *Mason and Dixon* (1997).

py·o·der·ma /ˌpīəˈdərmə/ ▸*n.* *Medicine* a skin infection with formation of pus. ▷1930s: from Greek *puo-* (from *puon* 'pus') + *derma* 'skin.'

py·o·gen·ic /ˌpīəˈjenik/ ▸*adj.* *Medicine* involving or relating to the production of pus. ▷mid 19th cent.: from Greek *puo-* (from *puon* 'pus') + **-GENIC.**

Pyong·yang /ˈpyəNGˈyäNG; -ˈyaNG; ˈpyäNG-/ the capital of North Korea; pop. 2,000,000. The oldest city on the Korean peninsula, it was first mentioned in records in 108 BC. It developed as an industrial city during the years of Japanese occupation 1910–45.

py·or·rhe·a /ˌpīəˈrēə/ (also **pyorrhea alveolaris,** *Brit.* **py·or·rhoe·a**) ▸*n.* another term for **PERIODONTITIS.** ▷early 19th cent.: from Greek *puo-* (from *puon* 'pus') + *rhoia* 'flux' (from *rhein* 'to flow').

py·ra·can·tha /ˌpīrəˈkanTHə/ ▸*n.* a thorny evergreen Eurasian shrub with white flowers and bright red or yellow berries that is a popular ornamental. Also called **FIRETHORN.** • Genus *Pyracantha,* family Rosaceae. ▷modern Latin, via Latin from Greek *purakantha,* the name of an unidentified plant, from *pur* 'fire' + *akantha* 'thorn.'

pyr·a·lid /ˈpirəˌlid/ ▸*n.* *Entomology* an insect of a family (Pyralidae) of small delicate moths with narrow forewings. The larvae of many species are pests of stored foodstuffs. ▷late 19th cent.: from modern Latin *Pyralidae* (plural), based on Greek *puralis,* denoting a mythical fly said to live in fire.

pyr·a·mid /ˈpirəˌmid/ ▸*n.* **1** a monumental structure with a square or triangular base and sloping sides that meet in a point at the top, esp. one built of stone as a royal tomb in ancient Egypt.

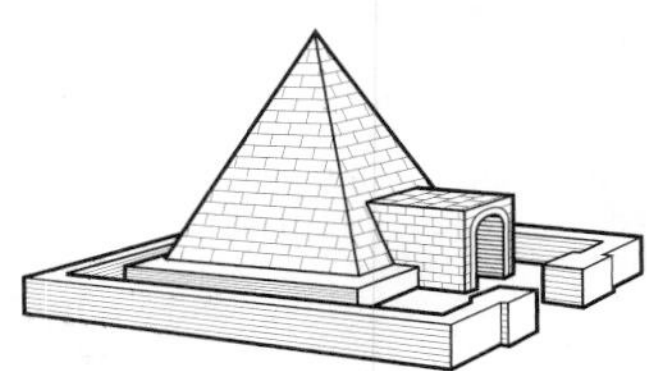

pyramid 1

> Pyramids were built as tombs for Egyptian pharaohs from the 3rd dynasty (*c.*2649 BC) until *c.*1640 BC. Monuments of similar shape are associated with the Aztec and Maya civilizations of *c.*1200 BC–AD 750, and, like those in Egypt, were part of large ritual complexes.

2 a thing, shape, or graph with such a form: *the pyramid of the Matterhorn.* ■ *Geometry* a polyhedron of which one face is a polygon of any number of sides, and the other faces are triangles with a common vertex: *a three-sided pyramid.* ■ a pile of things with such a form: ***a pyramid of** logs.* ■ *Anatomy* a structure of more or less pyramidal form, esp. in the brain or the renal medulla. ■ an organization or system that is structured with fewer people or things at each level as one approaches the top: *the lowest strata of the social pyramid.* ■ a system of financial growth achieved by a small initial investment, with subsequent investments being funded by using unrealized profits as collateral.
▸*v.* [*trans.*] heap or stack in the shape of a pyramid:

Pronunciation Key ə *ago;* ər *over;* ˈə or ˌə *up;* ˈər or ˌər *fur;* a *hat;* ā *rate;* ä *car;* CH *chew;* e *let;* ē *see;* e(ə)r *air;* i *fit;* ī *by;* i(ə)r *ear;* NG *sing;* ō *go;* ô *for;* oi *boy;* o͝o *good;* o͞o *goo;* ou *out;* SH *she;* TH *thin;* T͟H *then;* (h)w *why;* ZH *vision*

debt was pyramided on top of unrealistic debt in an orgy of speculation. ■ achieve a substantial return on (money or property) after making a small initial investment. ▷late Middle English (in the geometric sense): via Latin from Greek *puramis, puramid-*, of unknown ultimate origin. —**py·ram·i·dal** /pi'ramidl/ *adj.* —**py·ram·i·dal·ly** *adv.* —**pyr·a·mid·i·cal** /ˌpirə'midikəl/ *adj.* —**pyr·a·mid·i·cal·ly** *adv.*

pyramid of Giza, in northern Egypt

pyr·a·mid scheme ▶*n.* a system of selling goods in which agency rights are sold to an increasing number of distributors at successively lower levels.

Pyr·a·mus /'pirəməs/ *Roman Mythology* a Babylonian youth, lover of Thisbe.

Forbidden to marry by their parents, who were neighbors, the lovers conversed through a chink in a wall and agreed to meet at a tomb outside the city. There, Thisbe was frightened away by a lioness coming from its kill, and Pyramus, seeing her bloodstained cloak and supposing her dead, stabbed himself. Thisbe, finding his body when she returned, threw herself upon his sword.

py·rar·gy·rite /pī'rärjəˌrīt/ ▶*n.* a dark red mineral consisting of a sulfide of silver and antimony. ▷mid 19th cent.: from Greek *puro-* (from *pur* 'fire') + *arguros* 'silver' + -**ITE**[1].

pyre /pīr/ ▶*n.* a heap of combustible material, esp. one for burning a corpse as part of a funeral ceremony. ▷mid 17th cent.: via Latin from Greek *pura*, from *pur* 'fire.'

py·rene /'pīˌrēn/ ▶*n. Chemistry* a crystalline aromatic hydrocarbon present in coal tar. • A tetracyclic compound; chem. formula: $C_{16}H_{10}$. ▷mid 19th cent.: from Greek *pur* 'fire' + -**ENE**.

Pyr·e·nees /'pirəˌnēz/ a range of mountains that extends along the border between France and Spain from the Atlantic coast to the Mediterranean Sea. Its highest peak is Pico de Aneto in northern Spain, which rises to a height of 11,168 feet (3,404 m). —**Pyr·e·ne·an** /ˌpirə'nēən/ *adj.*

py·re·thrin /pī'rēTHrən; -'reTHrən/ ▶*n. Chemistry* any of a group of insecticidal compounds present in pyrethrum flowers. ▷1920s: from **PYRETHRUM** + -**IN**[1].

py·re·throid /pī'rēTHˌroid; pī'reTH-/ ▶*n. Chemistry* a pyrethrin or related insecticidal compound.

py·re·thrum /pī'rēTHrəm; -'reTHrəm/ ▶*n.* an aromatic plant of the daisy family, typically having feathery foliage and brightly colored flowers. • Genus *Tanacetum* (formerly *Chrysanthemum* or *Pyrethrum*), family Compositae: several species, in particular *T. coccineum*, grown as an ornamental, and *T. cinerariifolium*, grown as a source of the insecticide pyrethrum. ■ an insecticide made from the dried flowers of these plants. ▷Middle English (denoting pellitory): from Latin, from Greek *purethron* 'feverfew.' The current senses (based on the former genus name) date from the late 19th cent.

py·ret·ic /pī'retik/ ▶*adj. rare* fevered, feverish, or inducing fever. ▷early 18th cent. (as a medical term, now only in *antipyretic*): from modern Latin *pyreticus*, from Greek *puretos* 'fever.'

Py·rex /'pīˌreks/ ▶*n.* [usu. as *adj.*] *trademark* a hard, heat-resistant type of glass, typically used for ovenware: *a set of Pyrex dishes.* ▷early 20th cent.: an invented word.

py·rex·i·a /pī'reksēə/ ▶*n. Medicine* raised body temperature; fever. ▷mid 18th cent.: modern Latin, from Greek *purexis*, from *puressein* 'be feverish,' from *pur* 'fire.' —**py·rex·i·al** *adj.* —**py·rex·ic** /-sik/ *adj.*

pyr·i·dine /'pirəˌdēn/ ▶*n. Chemistry* a colorless volatile liquid with an unpleasant odor, present in coal tar and used chiefly as a solvent. • A heteroaromatic compound; chem. formula: C_5H_5N. ▷mid 19th cent.: from Greek *pur* 'fire' + -**IDE** + -**INE**[4].

pyr·i·do·stig·mine /ˌpiridō'stigˌmēn/ ▶*n. Medicine* a synthetic compound related to neostigmine, with similar but weaker and longer-acting effects. ▷1950s: blend of **PYRIDINE** and **NEOSTIGMINE**.

pyr·i·dox·al /ˌpiri'däksəl/ ▶*n. Biochemistry* an oxidized derivative of pyridoxine that acts as a coenzyme in transamination and other processes. ▷1940s: from **PYRIDOXINE** + -**AL**.

pyr·i·dox·ine /ˌpiri'däkˌsēn/ ▶*n. Biochemistry* a colorless weakly basic solid present chiefly in cereals, liver oils, and yeast, and important in the metabolism of unsaturated fatty acids. Also called **VITAMIN B6**. • An alcohol derived from pyridine; chem. formula: $C_8H_{11}NO_3$. ▷1930s: from *pyrid(ine)* + **OX-** 'oxygen' + -**INE**[4].

pyr·i·form /'pirəˌfôrm/ ▶*adj. Anatomy & Biology* pear-shaped: *the pyriform fossa.* ▷mid 18th cent.: from modern Latin *pyriformis*, from *pyrum* (misspelling of *pirum* 'pear') + -**IFORM**.

py·ri·meth·a·mine /ˌpirə'meTHəˌmēn/ ▶*n. Medicine* a synthetic compound derived from pyrimidine, used to treat malaria.

py·rim·i·dine /pə'rimәˌdēn; pī-/ ▶*n. Chemistry* a colorless crystalline compound with basic properties. • A heteroaromatic compound; chem. formula: $C_4H_4N_2$. ■ (also **pyrimidine base**) a substituted derivative of this, esp. the bases thymine and cytosine present in DNA. ▷late 19th cent.: from German *Pyrimidin*, from **PYRIDINE**, with the insertion of *-im-* from **IMIDE**.

py·rite /'pīˌrīt/ (also **py·ri·tes** /pə'rītēz; pī-/) ▶*n.* a shiny yellow mineral consisting of iron disulfide and typically occurring as intersecting cubic crystals; compare with **MARCASITE**. Also called **FOOL'S GOLD**. ▷late Middle English (denoting a mineral used for kindling fire): via Latin from Greek *puritēs* 'of fire,' from *pur* 'fire.' —**py·rit·ic** /pī'ritik; pə-/ *adj.* —**py·rit·i·za·tion** /pəˌritə'zāsHən; pī-/ *n.* —**py·ri·tize** /'pīritˌīz/ *v.* —**py·ri·tous** /pə'rītəs; pī-/ *adj.*

py·ro /'pīrō/ ▶*n.* (*pl.* -**ros**) *informal* a pyromaniac.

pyro. ▶*abbr.* pyrotechnics.

pyro- ▶*comb. form* **1** of or relating to fire: *pyromania.* **2** *Chemistry & Mineralogy* denoting a compound or mineral that is formed or affected by heat or has a fiery color: *pyrophosphate | pyrope.* ▷from Greek *pur* 'fire.'

py·ro·clas·tic /ˌpīrō'klastik/ *Geology* ▶*adj.* relating to, consisting of, or denoting fragments of rock erupted by a volcano. —**py·ro·clast** /'pīrōˌklast/ *n.*

py·ro·clas·tic flow ▶*n. Geology* a dense, destructive mass of very hot ash, lava fragments, and gases ejected explosively from a volcano and typically flowing downslope at great speed.

py·ro·e·lec·tric /ˌpīrō-i'lektrik/ ▶*adj.* having the property of becoming electrically charged when heated. ■ of, relating to, or utilizing this property: *a pyroelectric detector.* —**py·ro·e·lec·tric·i·ty** /-iˌlek'trisitē/ *n.*

py·ro·gal·lol /ˌpīrō'galˌôl; -ˌōl/ ▶*n. Chemistry* a weakly acid crystalline compound chiefly used as a developer in photography. • Alternative name: **1,3,5-trihydroxybenzene**; chem. formula: $C_6H_3(OH)_3$.

py·ro·gen /'pīrəjən/ ▶*n. Medicine* a substance, typically produced by a bacterium, that produces fever when introduced or released into the blood.

py·ro·gen·ic /ˌpīrō'jenik/ ▶*adj. Medicine* inducing fever. ■ caused or produced by combustion or the application of heat: *pyrogenic factors affecting the fluctuation of the forest–savanna boundary.* —**py·ro·ge·nic·i·ty** /ˌpīrōjə'nisitē/ *n.*

py·rog·ra·phy /pī'rägrəfē/ ▶*n.* the art or technique of decorating wood or leather by burning a design on the surface with a heated metallic point.

py·ro·lu·site /ˌpīrō'lōōˌsīt/ ▶*n.* a black or dark gray mineral with a metallic luster, consisting of manganese dioxide. ▷early 19th cent.: from **PYRO-** 'fire, heat' + Greek *lousis* 'washing' (because of the mineral's use in decolorizing glass).

py·rol·y·sis /pī'räləsəs/ ▶*n. Chemistry* decomposition brought about by high temperatures. —**py·ro·lyt·ic** /ˌpīrə'litik/ *adj.*

py·ro·lyze /'pīrəˌlīz/ (*Brit.* **py·ro·lyse**) ▶*v. Chemistry* make or become decomposed through heating to a high temperature. ▷1920s: from **PYROLYSIS**, on the pattern of *analyze*.

py·ro·ma·ni·a /ˌpīrō'mānēə/ ▶*n.* an obsessive desire to set fire to things. —**py·ro·ma·ni·ac** /-'mānēˌak/ *n.* —**py·ro·ma·ni·a·cal** /-mə'nīəkəl/ *adj.* —**py·ro·man·ic** /-'manik/ *adj.*

py·ro·met·al·lur·gy /ˌpīrō'metlˌərjē/ ▶*n.* the branch of science and technology concerned with the use of high temperatures to extract and purify metals. —**py·ro·met·al·lur·gi·cal** /-ˌmetl'ərjikəl/ *adj.*

py·rom·e·ter /pī'rämitər/ ▶*n.* an instrument for measuring high temperatures, esp. in furnaces and kilns. —**py·ro·met·ric** /ˌpīrō'metrik/ *adj.* —**py·ro·met·ri·cal·ly** /ˌpīrō'metrik(ə)lē/ *adv.* —**py·rom·e·try** /-trē/ *n.*

py·ro·met·ric cone /ˌpīrō'metrik/ ▶*n.* see **CONE** (sense 1).

py·ro·mor·phite /ˌpīrə'môrˌfīt/ ▶*n.* a mineral consisting of a chloride and phosphate of lead, typically occurring as green, yellow, or brown crystals in the oxidized zones of lead deposits. ▷early 19th cent.: from **PYRO-** 'fire, heat' + Greek *morphē* 'form' + -**ITE**[1].

py·rope /'pīˌrōp/ (also **pyrope garnet**) ▶*n.* a deep red variety of garnet. ▷early 19th cent.: from German *Pyrop*, via Latin from Greek *purōpos* 'gold-bronze,' literally 'fiery-eyed,' from *pur* 'fire' + *ōps* 'eye.'

py·ro·phor·ic /ˌpīrə'fôrik/ ▶*adj.* liable to ignite spontaneously on exposure to air. ■ (of an alloy) emitting sparks when scratched or struck. ▷mid 19th cent.: from modern Latin *pyrophorus*, from Greek *purophoros* 'fire-bearing,' from *pur* 'fire' + *pherein* 'to bear.'

py·ro·phos·phor·ic ac·id /ˌpīrōˌfäs'fôrik; -'fäsfərik/ ▶*n. Chemistry* a glassy solid obtained by heating phosphoric acid. • A tetrabasic acid; chem. formula: $H_4P_2O_7$. —**py·ro·phos·phate** /-'fäsˌfāt/ *n.*

py·ro·sis /pī'rōsəs/ ▶*n.* another term for **HEARTBURN**. ▷late 18th cent.: modern Latin, from Greek *purōsis*, from *puroun* 'set on fire,' from *pur* 'fire.'

py·ro·tech·nic /ˌpīrə'teknik/ ▶*adj.* of or relating to fireworks: *the sun flickered in the car like a pyrotechnic display.* ■ brilliant or sensational: *his writing contains more pyrotechnic energy, more color and action.* ▷early 19th cent.: from **PYRO-** 'fire' + Greek *tekhnē* 'art' + -**IC**. —**py·ro·tech·ni·cal** *adj.* —**py·ro·tech·nist** /-nist/ *n.*

py·ro·tech·nics /ˌpīrə'tekniks/ ▶*plural n.* a fireworks display. ■ [usu. with *adj.*] a brilliant performance or display, esp. of a specified skill: *he thrilled his audience with vocal pyrotechnics.* ■ [treated as *sing.*] the art of making or displaying fireworks.

py·ro·tech·ny /'pīrəˌteknē/ ▶*n. historical* the use of fire in alchemy. ■ another term for **PYROTECHNICS**. ▷late 16th cent.: from French *pyrotechnie* or modern Latin *pyrotechnia*, from Greek *pur* 'fire' + *tekhnē* 'art.'

py·rox·ene /pī'räkˌsēn; pə-/ ▶*n.* any of a large class of rock-forming silicate minerals, generally containing calcium, magnesium, and iron and typically occurring as prismatic crystals. ▷early 19th cent.: from **PYRO-** 'fire' + Greek *xenos* 'stranger' (because the mineral group was supposed alien to igneous rocks).

py·rox·e·nite /pī'räksəˌnīt; pə-/ ▶*n. Geology* a dark, greenish, granular intrusive igneous rock consisting chiefly of pyroxenes and olivine. ▷mid 19th cent.: from **PYROXENE** + -**ITE**[1].

py·rox·y·lin /pī'räksələn; pə-/ ▶*n. Chemistry* a form of nitrocellulose that is less highly nitrated and is soluble in ether and alcohol. ▷mid 19th cent.: from French *pyroxyline*, from Greek *pur* 'fire' + *xulon* 'wood.'

Pyr·rha /'pirə/ *Greek Mythology* the wife of Deucalion.

Pyr·rhic /'pirik/ (also **pyr·rhic**) ▶*adj.* [*attrib.*] (of a victory) won at too great a cost to have been worthwhile for the victor. ▷late 19th cent.: from the name **PYRRHUS** + -**IC**.

pyr·rhic /'pirik/ ▶*n.* a metrical foot of two short or unaccented syllables.
▶*adj.* written in or based on such a measure. ▷early 17th cent.: via Latin from Greek *purrhikhios (pous)* 'pyrrhic (foot),' the meter of a song accompanying a war dance, named after *Purrhikhos*, inventor of the dance.

Pyr·rho /'pirō/ (*c.*365–*c.*270 BC), Greek philosopher; regarded as the founder of skepticism. He argued that happiness comes from suspending judgment because certainty of knowledge is impossible.

Pyr·rho·nism /'pirəˌnizəm/ ▶*n.* the philosophy of Pyrrho. ■ philosophic doubt; skepticism. —**Pyr·rho·nist** *n.* & *adj.*

pyr·rho·tite /'pirəˌtīt/ ▶*n.* a reddish-bronze mineral consisting of iron sulfide, typically forming massive or granular deposits. ▷mid 19th cent.: from Greek *purrhotēs* 'redness' + -**ITE**[1].

Pyr·rhus /'pirəs/ (*c.*318–272 BC), king of Epirus *c.*307–272. After invading Italy in 280, he defeated the Romans at Asculum in 279, but sustained heavy losses; the term *pyrrhic victory* alludes to this.

pyr·role /'pirˌōl/ ▶*n. Chemistry* a weakly basic sweet-smelling liquid compound present in bone oil and coal tar. • A heteroaromatic compound; chem. formula: C_4H_4NH. ▷mid 19th cent.: from Greek *purrhos* 'reddish' + Latin *oleum* 'oil.'

pyr·rol·i·dine /pə'rōləˌdēn/ ▶*n. Chemistry* a pungent liquid made by reduction of pyrrole. • Chem. formula: C_4H_8NH.

pyr·rol·i·done /pəˈrōlə,dōn/ ▶*n. Chemistry* a colorless weakly basic solid that is a keto derivative of pyrrolidine. • Chem. formula: C_4H_7NO.

py·ru·vic ac·id /pīˈrōōvik/ ▶*n. Biochemistry* a yellowish organic acid that occurs as an intermediate in many metabolic processes, esp. glycolysis. • A keto acid; chem. formula: $CH_3COCOOH$. ▷mid 19th cent.: from modern Latin *acidum pyruvicum*, from *acidum* 'acid' + *pyruvicum* based on **PYRO-** (denoting an acid) + Latin *uva* 'grape.' —**pyr·u·vate** /-,vāt/ *n.*

Py·thag·o·ras /piˈTHagərəs/ *c.*580–500 BC, Greek philosopher; known as **Pythagoras of Samos**. Pythagoras sought to interpret the entire physical world in terms of numbers and founded their systematic and mystical study. He is best known for the theorem of the right-angled triangle. —**Py·thag·o·re·an** /pi,THagəˈrēən; pī-/ *adj.* & *n.*

Py·thag·o·re·an the·o·rem /pə,THagəˈrēən; pī-/ a theorem attributed to Pythagoras that the square of the hypotenuse of a right triangle is equal to the sum of the squares of the other two sides.

Pyth·i·a /ˈpiTHēə/ the priestess of Apollo at Delphi in ancient Greece. See **DELPHI**. ▷from *Puthō*, a former name of Delphi. —**Pyth·i·an** *adj.*

Pyth·i·as /ˈpiTHēəs/ see **DAMON**.

py·thon /ˈpī,THän; ˈpīTHən/ ▶*n.* a large heavy-bodied nonvenomous constrictor snake occurring throughout the Old World tropics. • Family Pythonidae: genera *Python* (of Asia and Africa), and *Morelia* and *Aspidites* (of Australasia). ▷late 16th cent. (in the Greek sense): via Latin from Greek *Puthōn*, the name of a huge serpent killed by Apollo. The current sense dates from the mid 19th cent. —**py·thon·ic** /pīˈTHänik/ *adj.*

Py·thon·esque /,pīTHəˈnesk/ ▶*adj.* after the style of or resembling the absurdist or surrealist humor of *Monty Python's Flying Circus*, a British television comedy series (1969–74).

py·tho·ness /ˈpīTHənəs; ˈpiTH-/ ▶*n. archaic* a female soothsayer or conjuror of spirits. ▷late Middle English: from Old French *phitonise*, from an alteration of late Latin *pythonissa*, based on Greek *puthōn* 'soothsaying demon.' Compare with **PYTHIA**.

py·u·ri·a /pīˈyŏŏrēə/ ▶*n. Medicine* the presence of pus in the urine, typically from bacterial infection. ▷early 19th cent.: from Greek *puon* 'pus' + **-URIA**.

pyx /piks/ ▶*n.* **1** *Christian Church* the container in which the consecrated bread of the Eucharist is kept. **2** (in the UK) a box at the Royal Mint in which specimen gold and silver coins are deposited to be tested annually at the **trial of the pyx**. ▷late Middle English: from Latin *pyxis*, from Greek *puxis* 'box.'

pyx·id·i·um /pikˈsidēəm/ ▶*n.* (*pl.* **-i·a** /-ēə/) *Botany* a seed capsule that splits open so that the top comes off like the lid of a box. ▷mid 19th cent.: modern Latin, from Greek *puxidion*, diminutive of *puxis* 'box.'

Pyx·is /ˈpiksis/ *Astronomy* a small and inconspicuous southern constellation (the Compass Box or Mariner's Compass), lying in the Milky Way between Vela and Puppis. ■ [as *genitive*] (**Pyxidis**) used with a preceding letter or numeral to designate a star in this constellation: *the star Alpha Pyxidis.* ▷Latin.

pzazz /pəˈzaz/ ▶*n.* variant spelling of **PIZZAZZ**.

Qq

Q[1] /kyo͞o/ (also **q**) ▸*n.* (*pl.* **Qs** or **Q's**) the seventeenth letter of the alphabet. ■ denoting the next after P in a set of items, categories, etc.
▸*PHRASE* □ **mind one's Ps and Qs** see **MIND**.

Q[2] ▸*abbr.* ■ quarter (used to refer to a specified quarter of the fiscal year): *we expect to have an exceptional Q4.* ■ queen (used esp. in describing card games and recording moves in chess): *17.Qb4.* ■ question: *Q: What's the problem? A: I don't feel well.* ■ *Theology* denoting the hypothetical source of the passages shared by the gospels of Matthew and Luke, but not found in Mark. [probably from German *Quelle* 'source.']

q ▸*symbol Physics* electric charge. ▹mid 19th cent.: initial letter of *quantity*.

QA ▸*abbr.* quality assurance.

Qab·a·lah /kə'bälə/ ▸*n.* variant spelling of **KABBALAH**.

qa·nat /kə'nät/ ▸*n.* (in the Middle East) a gently sloping underground channel or tunnel constructed to lead water from the interior of a hill to a village below. ▹Persian, from Arabic *ḳanāt* 'reed, pipe, channel.'

q and a /kyo͞o' ən ā'/ ▸*abbr. informal* a question and answer period or exchange.

Qa·ra·ghan·dy /'kärə,gändē/ an industrial city in eastern Kazakhstan, at the center of a major coal-mining region; pop. 613,000. Russian name **KARAGANDA**.

Qa·tar /'kätär; kə'tär/ a sheikhdom that occupies a peninsula on the western coast of the Persian Gulf; pop. 840,000; capital, Doha; language, Arabic (official). **—Qa·tar·i** /'kätärē; kə'tärē/ *adj.* & *n.*

The country was a British protectorate from 1916 until 1971, when it became an independent state. Oil is the chief source of revenue.

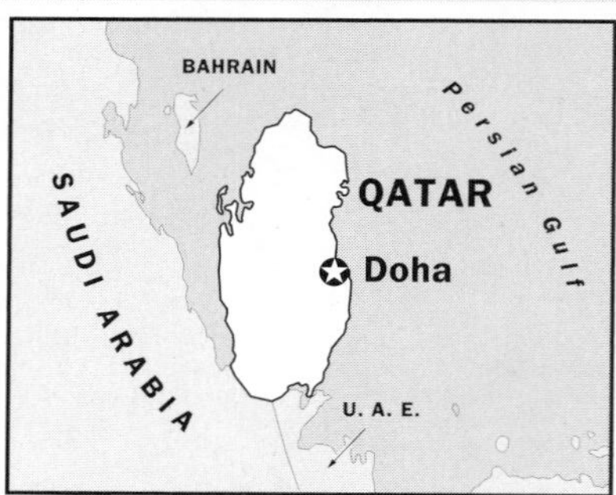

Qat·ta·ra De·pres·sion /kə'tärə/ an extensive, low-lying, and largely impassable area of desert in northeastern Africa, west of Cairo, that is 436 feet (133 m) below sea level.

qaw·wal /kə'väl/ ▸*n.* a performer of qawwali.

qaw·wa·li /kə'välē/ ▸*n.* a style of Muslim devotional music now associated particularly with Sufis in Pakistan. ▹from Arabic *qawwāli*, from *qawwāl* 'loquacious,' also 'singer.'

QB ▸*abbr.* ■ *Football* quarterback. ■ *Law* Queen's Bench.

QC ▸*abbr.* ■ quality control. ■ Quebec (in official postal use). ■ *Law* Queen's Counsel.

QCD ▸*abbr.* quantum chromodynamics.

Q-Celtic /'keltik/ ▸*n.* & *adj.* another term for **GOIDELIC**. ▹*Q*, from the retention of the Indo-European *kw* sound as *q* or *c* in this group of languages.

QED ▸*abbr.* ■ quantum electrodynamics. ■ quod erat demonstrandum.

QEF ▸*abbr.* which was to be done. ▹Latin *quod erat faciendum.*

QF ▸*abbr.* quick-firing.

Q fe·ver ▸*n.* an infectious fever caused by rickettsiae and transmitted to humans from cattle, sheep, and goats by unpasteurized milk. ▹1930s: from *Q* for *query* + **FEVER**.

qi /CHē/ (also **chi** or **ki**) ▸*n.* the circulating life force whose existence and properties are the basis of much Chinese philosophy and medicine. ▹from Chinese (Mandarin dialect) *qì*, literally 'air, breath.'

qib·la /'kiblə/ (also **kib·lah**) ▸*n.* [in *sing.*] the direction of the Kaaba (the sacred building at Mecca), to which Muslims turn at prayer. ▹mid 17th cent.: from Arabic *ḳibla* 'that which is opposite.'

q.i.d. ▸*abbr.* (in prescriptions) four times a day. ▹Latin *quater in die.*

qi·gong /,CHē'gäNG; -'gôNG/ ▸*n.* a Chinese system of physical exercises and breathing control related to tai chi. ▹Chinese.

Qin /CHin/ (also **Ch'in**) a dynasty that ruled China 221–206 BC and was the first to establish rule over a united China. The construction of the Great Wall of China was begun during this period.

Qing /CHiNG/ (also **Ch'ing**) a dynasty established by the Manchus that ruled China 1644–1912. Its overthrow in 1912 by Sun Yat-sen and his supporters ended imperial rule in China.

Qing·dao /'CHiNG'dou/ a port in eastern China, in Shandong province on the Yellow Sea coast; pop. 2,040,000.

Qing·hai /'CHiNG'hī/ (also **Tsing·hai**) a mountainous province in north central China; capital, Xining.

qing·hao·su /,CHiNGgou'so͞o/ ▸*n.* a terpene-based anti-malarial substance used in Chinese medicine. • The drug is obtained from *Artemisia annua*, family Compositae. ▹1970s: from Chinese *qīnghāosù*, from *qīnghāo*, denoting a medicinal plant of the genus *Artemisia*.

qin·tar /kin'tär/ ▸*n.* (*pl.* same, **qin·tars**, or **qin·dar·ka** /kin'darkə/) a monetary unit of Albania, equal to one hundredth of a lek. ▹from Albanian *qindar*, from *qind* 'hundred.'

Qi·qi·har /'CHē'CHē'här/ a port on the Nen River, in Heilongjiang province, in northeastern China; pop. 1,370,000.

QKt ▸*abbr. Chess* queen's knight.

ql. ▸*abbr.* quintal.

Qld ▸*abbr.* Queensland.

qlty. ▸*abbr.* quality.

QM ▸*abbr.* quartermaster.

QMC ▸*abbr.* Quartermaster Corps.

QMG ▸*abbr.* quartermaster general.

qn. ▸*abbr.* question.

Qom /ko͝om/ (also **Qum** or **Kum**) a city in central Iran; pop. 780,000. It is a holy city and center of learning among Shiite Muslims.

QP ▸*abbr. Chess* queen's pawn.

q.p. ▸*abbr.* (in prescriptions) as much as you please. ▹Latin *quantum placet.*

QPM ▸*abbr.* (in the UK) Queen's Police Medal.

qq. ▸*abbr.* questions.

qq.v. ▸*abbr.* which (words, etc.) see. ▹Latin *quae vide.*

qr ▸*abbr.* quarter(s).

q.s. ▸*abbr.* ■ (in prescriptions) enough; as much as is sufficient. ■ quarter section. ▹Latin *quantum sufficit.*

Q-ship ▸*n. historical* a merchant ship with concealed weapons, used by the British in World War I and World War II in an attempt to destroy submarines. ▹World War I: from *Q* as a nonexplicit symbol of the type of vessel + **SHIP**.

QSO ▸*abbr.* quasi-stellar object, a quasar.

QT (also **q.t.**) ▸*n.* (in phrase **on the QT**) *informal* secretly; stealthily: *she'd better get there on the QT.* ▹late 19th cent.: abbreviation of **QUIET**.

qt. ▸*abbr.* quart(s).

qto. ▸*abbr.* quarto.

qty. ▸*abbr.* quantity.

qua /kwä/ ▸*conj.* in the capacity of; as being: *he's hard to pin down if you get him on entertainment qua entertainment.* ▹Latin, ablative feminine singular of *qui* 'who.'

Quaa·lude /'kwā,lo͞od/ ▸*n. trademark* methaqualone. ▹1960s: an invented name.

quack[1] /kwak/ ▸*n.* [in *sing.*] the characteristic harsh sound made by a duck.
▸*v.* [*intrans.*] (of a duck) make this sound. ■ *informal* talk loudly and foolishly. ▹mid-16th cent. (as a verb): imitative.

THE RIGHT WORD **charlatan, dissembler, fake, impostor, mountebank, quack**

There are many different ways to describe a **fake**, a colloquial term for anyone who knowingly practices deception or misrepresentation.

Someone who sells a special tonic that claims to do everything from curing the common cold to making hair grow on a bald man's head is called a **quack**, a term that refers to any fraudulent practitioner of medicine or law.

Mountebank sometimes carries implications of quackery, but more often it refers to a self-promoting person who resorts to cheap tricks or undignified efforts to win attention (*political mountebanks*).

A **charlatan** is usually a writer, speaker, preacher, professor, or some other "expert" who tries to conceal his or her lack of skill or knowledge by resorting to pretentious displays (*supposedly a leading authority in his field, he turned out to be nothing but a charlatan*).

Someone who tries to pass himself or herself off as someone else is an **impostor** (*an impostor who bore a close physical resemblance to the king*), although this term can also refer to anyone who assumes a title or profession that is not his or her own.

Although all of these deceivers are out to fool people, it is the **dissembler** who is primarily interested in concealing his or her true motives or evil purpose (*he is a dissembler who weaves a tangled web of lies*).

quack[2] ▸*n.* a person who dishonestly claims to have special knowledge and skill in some field, typically in medicine: [as *adj.*] *quack cures.* ▹mid 17th cent.: abbreviation of earlier *quacksalver*, from Dutch, probably from obsolete *quacken* 'prattle' + *salf, zalf* (see **SALVE**[1]). **—quack·er·y** /'kwakərē/ *n.* **—quack·ish** *adj.*

quack grass ▸*n.* another term for **COUCH GRASS**. ▹early 19th cent.: *quack*, variant of *quick*, northern English form of **QUITCH**.

quad /kwäd/ ▸*n.* **1** *informal* **SHORT FOR:** ■ a quadrangle. ■ **QUADRUPLET** (sense 1). ■ a quadriceps. ■ a quad bike. ■ quadraphonic sound. ■ a quadriplegic. **2** (in telephony) short for **QUADRAPLEX**. **3** a radio antenna in the form of a square or rectangle broken in the middle of one side. [abbreviation of **QUADRILATERAL**.] **4** a traditional roller skate. [*quad*, with reference to the four wheels.] **5** *Printing* a small metal block in various sizes, lower than type height, used in letterpress printing for filling up short lines. [abbreviation of the late 17th-cent. printing term *quadrat*.]
▸*adj.* [*attrib.*] *informal* **SHORT FOR:** ■ quadruple. ■ quadrophonic.

quad. ▸*abbr.* ■ quadrangle. ■ quadrant.

quad bike ▸*n.* a motorcycle with four large tires, typically used for racing.

quad chair (also **quad chair·lift** or **quad**) ▸*n.* a chairlift with seats for four people at a time.

Quad Cities /kwäd/ an industrial complex of cities on the Mississippi River that includes Davenport and Bettendorf in southeastern Iowa and Moline and Rock Island in northwestern Illinois. A second Quad Cities complex, in northern Alabama on the Tennessee River, consists of the cities of Florence, Sheffield, Tuscumbia, and Muscle Shoals.

quad·plex /ˈkwäd,pleks/ ▸*n.* another term for QUADRIPLEX.

quad·ra·ge·nar·i·an /,kwädrəjəˈne(ə)rēən/ ▸*n.* a person who is from 40 to 49 years old. ▷mid 19th cent.: from late Latin *quadragenarius* (based on Latin *quadraginta* 'forty') + -AN.

Quad·ra·ges·i·ma /,kwädrəˈjesəmə/ (also **Quadragesima Sunday**) *n.* the first Sunday in Lent. ▷from ecclesiastical Latin, feminine of Latin *quadragesimus* 'fortieth,' from *quadraginta* 'forty' (Lent lasting 40 days).

quad·ra·ges·i·mal /,kwädrəˈjesəməl/ ▸*adj.* [*attrib.*] *archaic* (of a fast, esp. one in Lent) lasting forty days. ■ belonging or appropriate to the period of Lent.

quad·ra·min·i·um ▸*n.* variant spelling of QUADROMINIUM.

quad·ran·gle /ˈkwä,draNGgəl/ ▸*n.* *Geometry* a four-sided plane figure, esp. a square or rectangle. ■ a square or rectangular space or courtyard enclosed by buildings. ■ the area shown on a standard topographic map sheet of the U.S. Geological Survey. ▷late Middle English: from Old French, or from late Latin *quadrangulum* 'square,' neuter of *quadrangulus*, from Latin 'four' + *angulus* 'corner, angle.' —**quad·ran·gu·lar** /kwäˈdraNGgyələr/ *adj.*

quad·rant /ˈkwädrənt/ ▸*n.* *technical* each of four quarters of a circle. ■ each of four parts of a plane, sphere, space, or body divided by two lines or planes at right angles: *the right upper quadrant of the kidney.* ■ *historical* an instrument used for taking angular measurements of altitude in astronomy and navigation, typically consisting of a graduated quarter circle and a sighting mechanism. ■ a frame fixed to the head of a ship's rudder, to which the steering mechanism is attached. ■ a panel with slots through which a lever is moved to orient or otherwise control a mechanism. ▷late Middle English (denoting the astronomical instrument): from Latin *quadrans*, *quadrant-* 'quarter,' from *quattuor* four. —**quad·ran·tal** /kwäˈdran(t)l/ *adj.*

Quad·ran·tids /kwäˈdrantidz/ *Astronomy* an annual meteor shower with a radiant in the constellation Boötes, reaching a peak about January 3. ▷from Latin *Quadrans Muralis* 'the Mural Quadrant,' the name of a former constellation.

quad·ra·phon·ic /,kwädrəˈfänik/ (also **quad·ro·phon·ic**) ▸*adj.* (of sound reproduction) transmitted through four channels. ▷1960s: from QUADRI- 'four' + a shortened form of STEREOPHONIC. —**quad·ra·phon·i·cal·ly** /-ik(ə)lē/ *adv.* —**quad·ra·phon·ics** *plural n.* —**qua·draph·o·ny** /kwäˈdräfənē/ *n.*

quad·ra·plex /ˈkwädrə,pleks/ ▸*n.* **1** (in telephony) a group of four insulated conductors twisted together, usually forming two circuits. **2** variant spelling of QUADRIPLEX.

quad·rat /ˈkwädrət/ ▸*n.* *Ecology* each of a number of a small area of habitat, typically of one square meter, selected at random to act as samples for assessing the local distribution of plants or animals. ■ a portable frame, typically with an internal grid, used to mark out such an area. ▷early 20th cent.: variant of QUADRATE.

quad·rate ▸*n.* /ˈkwä,drāt; -rət/ **1** (also **quadrate bone**) *Zoology* (in the skull of a bird or reptile) a squarish bone with which the jaw articulates, thought to be homologous with the incus of the middle ear in mammals. **2** *Anatomy* another term for QUADRATUS.
▸*adj.* /ˈkwädrit/ roughly square or rectangular.
▸*v.* /ˈkwäd,rāt/ *archaic* **1** [*trans.*] make square. **2** conform or cause to conform. ▷late Middle English (as an adjective): from Latin *quadrat-* 'made square,' from the verb *quadrare*, from *quattuor* 'four.'

quad·rat·ic /kwäˈdratik/ ▸*adj.* *Mathematics* involving the second and no higher power of an unknown quantity or variable: *a quadratic equation.*
▸*n.* a quadratic equation. ▷mid 17th cent.: from French *quadratique* or modern Latin *quadraticus*, from *quadratus* 'made square,' past participle of *quadrare* (see QUADRATE).

quad·ra·ture /ˈkwädrə,CHo͝or; -,CHo͝or/ ▸*n.* **1** *Mathematics* the process of constructing a square with an area equal to that of a circle, or of another figure bounded by a curve. **2** *Astronomy* the position of the moon or a planet when it is 90° from the sun as viewed from the earth. **3** *Electronics* a phase difference of 90° between two waves of the same frequency, as in the color difference signals of a television screen. ▷mid 16th cent. (as a mathematical term): from Latin *quadratura* 'a square, squaring,' from *quadrare* (see QUADRATE).

quad·ra·ture am·pli·tude mod·u·la·tion ▸*n.* *Telecommunications* a modulation system used in microwave and satellite communication, involving phase and amplitude modulation of a carrier wave.

qua·dra·tus /kwäˈdrātəs/ ▸*n.* (*pl.* **-dra·ti** /-ˈdrāt,ī/) *Anatomy* any of several roughly square or rectangular muscles, e.g., in the abdomen, thigh, and eye socket. ▷mid 18th cent.: from Latin, literally 'made square.'

quad·ren·ni·al /kwäˈdrenēəl/ ▸*adj.* recurring every four years. ■ lasting for or relating to a period of four years. ▷mid 17th cent.: from QUADRENNIUM + -AL. —**quad·ren·ni·al·ly** *adv.*

quad·ren·ni·um /kwäˈdrenēəm/ ▸*n.* (*pl.* **-dren·ni·a** /-ˈdrenēə/ or **-dren·ni·ums**) a specified period of four years. ▷early 19th cent.: from Latin *quadriennium*, from *quadri-* 'four' + *annus* 'year.'

quadri- ▸*comb. form* four; having four: *quadriceps* | *quadriplegia.* ▷from Latin *quattuor* 'four.'

quad·ric /ˈkwädrik/ *Geometry* ▸*adj.* (of a surface or curve) described by an equation of the second degree.
▸*n.* a quadric surface or curve. ▷mid 19th cent.: from Latin *quadra* 'square' + -IC.

quad·ri·ceps /ˈkwädrə,seps/ ▸*n.* (*pl.* same) *Anatomy* the large muscle at the front of the thigh, which is divided into four distinct portions and acts to extend the leg. ▷mid 16th cent.: from Latin, literally 'four-headed.'

quad·ri·lat·er·al /,kwädrəˈlatərəl/ ▸*n.* a four-sided figure.
▸*adj.* having four straight sides. ▷mid 17th cent.: from late Latin *quadrilaterus* (from Latin *quadri-* 'four' + *latus*, *later-* 'side') + -AL.

quad·rille[1] /kwäˈdril; k(w)ə-/ ▸*n.* a square dance performed typically by four couples and containing five figures, each of which is a complete dance in itself. ■ a piece of music for this dance. ■ each of four groups of riders taking part in a tournament or carousel, distinguished by a special costume or colors. ■ a riding display. ▷mid 18th cent.: from French, from Spanish *cuadrilla* or Italian *quadriglia* 'troop, company,' from *cuadra*, *quadra* 'square,' based on Latin *quadrare* 'make square.'

quad·rille[2] ▸*n.* a trick-taking card game for four players using a deck of forty cards (i.e., one lacking eights, nines, and tens), fashionable in the 18th century. ▷early 18th cent.: from French, perhaps from Spanish *cuartillo* (from *cuarto* 'fourth'). The change in the first syllable was due to association with QUADRILLE[1].

quad·rille[3] ▸*n.* a ruled grid of small squares, esp. on paper. ▷late 19th cent.: from French *quadrillé*, from *quadrille* 'small square,' from Spanish *cuadrillo* 'small block.'

quad·ril·lion /kwäˈdrilyən/ ▸*cardinal number* (*pl.* **-lions** or (with numeral or quantifying word) same) a thousand raised to the power of five (10^{15}). ■ *dated, chiefly Brit.* a septillion, that is, a thousand raised to the power of eight (10^{24}). ▷late 17th cent.: from French, from *million*, by substitution of the prefix *quadri-* 'four' for the initial letters. —**quad·ril·lionth** /-ˈdrilyənTH/ *ordinal number*.

quad·ri·par·tite /,kwädrəˈpärtīt/ ▸*adj.* consisting of four parts. ■ shared by or involving four parties. ▷late Middle English: from Latin *quadripartitus*, from *quadri-* 'four' + *partitus* 'divided.'

quad·ri·ple·gi·a /,kwädrəˈplēj(ē)ə/ ▸*n.* *Medicine* paralysis of all four limbs; tetraplegia. ▷1920s: from QUADRI- 'four' + a shortened form of PARAPLEGIA. —**quad·ri·ple·gic** /-ˈplējik/ *adj.* & *n.*

quad·ri·plex (also **quad·ra·plex**) ▸*n.* a building divided into four self-contained residences. Also called QUADPLEX. ▷1970s: from QUADRI- 'four,' on the pattern of *duplex*.

quad·ri·va·lent /,kwädrəˈvālənt/ ▸*adj.* *Chemistry* another term for TETRAVALENT.

quad·riv·i·um /kwäˈdrivēəm/ ▸*n.* *historical* a medieval university curriculum involving the "mathematical arts" of arithmetic, geometry, astronomy, and music. Compare with TRIVIUM. ▷Latin, literally 'the place where four roads meet' (in late Latin 'the four branches of mathematics'), from *quadri-* 'four' + *via* 'road.'

quad·ro·min·i·um /,kwädrəˈminēəm/ (also **quad·ra·min·i·um**) ▸*n.* a condominium consisting of four apartments. ▷1970s: blend of QUADRI- 'four' and CONDOMINIUM.

quad·roon /kwäˈdro͞on/ ▸*n.* a person whose parents are a mulatto and a white person and who is therefore one-quarter black by descent. ▷early 18th cent. (earlier as *quarteron*): via French from Spanish *cuarterón*, from *cuarto* 'quarter,' from Latin *quartus*; later assimilated to words beginning with QUADRI-.

quad·ro·phon·ic /,kwädrəˈfänik/ ▸*adj.* variant spelling of QUADRAPHONIC.

quad·ru·ma·nous /kwäˈdro͞omənəs/ ▸*adj.* *dated Zoology* (of primates other than humans) having all four feet modified as hands (that is, having opposable digits). ▷late 17th cent.: from modern Latin *Quadrumana* (former order name, neuter plural of *quadrumanus*, from *quadru-* 'four' + Latin *manus* 'hand') + -OUS.

quad·ru·ped /ˈkwädrə,ped/ ▸*n.* an animal that has four feet, esp. an ungulate mammal. ▷mid 17th cent.: from French *quadrupède* or Latin *quadrupes*, *quadruped-*, from *quadru-* 'four' + *pes*, *ped-* 'foot.' —**quad·ru·pe·dal** /,kwädrəˈpedl; kwäˈdro͞opədl/ *adj.*

quad·ru·ple /kwäˈdro͞opəl/ ▸*adj.* [*attrib.*] consisting of four parts or elements: *a quadruple murder.* ■ consisting of four times as much or as many as usual: *a quadruple vodka.* ■ (of time in music) having four beats in a bar.
▸*v.* increase or be increased fourfold: [*intrans.*] *oil prices quadrupled in the 1970s.*
▸*n.* a quadruple thing, number, or amount. ▷late Middle English (as a verb): via French from Latin *quadruplus*, from *quadru-* 'four' + *-plus* as in *duplus* (see DUPLE). —**quad·ru·ply** /-p(ə)lē/ *adv.*

quad·ru·plet /kwäˈdro͞oplit/ ▸*n.* **1** (usu. **quadruplets**) each of four children born at one birth. **2** *Music* a group of four notes to be performed in the time of three. ▷late 18th cent.: from QUADRUPLE, on the pattern of *triplet*.

quad·ru·pli·cate ▸*adj.* /kwäˈdro͞opləkit/ consisting of four parts or elements: ■ of which four copies are made.
▸*v.* /kwäˈdro͞oplə,kāt/ [*trans.*] multiply (something) by four. ■ [usu. as *adj.*] (**quadruplicated**) make or provide in quadruplicate. ▷mid 17th cent.: from Latin *quadruplicat-* 'quadrupled,' from the verb *quadruplicare*, from *quadruplex*, *quadruplic-* 'fourfold,' from *quadru-* 'four' + *plicare* 'to fold.' —**quad·ru·pli·ca·tion** /kwä,dro͞opləˈkāSHən/ *n.*
▸*PHRASE* □ **in quadruplicate** in four identical copies.

quad·ru·plic·i·ty /,kwädrəˈplisətē/ ▸*n.* the state of being fourfold or of forming a set of four. ■ *Astrology* a group of four zodiacal signs of the same quality.

quad·ru·pole /ˈkwädrə,pōl/ ▸*n.* *Physics* a distribution of electric charge or magnetization consisting of four equal monopoles, or two equal dipoles, arranged close together with alternating polarity and operating as a unit. ■ a device using such an arrangement directed at one point to focus beams of subatomic particles.

quad-speed ▸*adj.* (of a CD-ROM drive, esp. formerly) capable of revolving the CD-ROM at a speed of 920 rpm.

quaes·tor /ˈkwestər/ ▸*n.* (in ancient Rome) any of a number of officials who had charge of public revenue and expenditure. ▷Latin, from an old form of *quaesit-* 'sought,' from the verb *quaerere*. —**quaes·to·ri·al** /kweˈstôrēəl/ *adj.* —**quaes·tor·ship** /-SHip/ *n.*

quaff /kwäf/ ▸*v.* [*trans.*] drink (something, esp. an alcoholic drink) heartily.
▸*n.* *informal, dated* an alcoholic drink. ▷early 16th cent.: probably imitative of the sound of drinking. —**quaff·a·ble** *adj.* —**quaff·er** *n.*

quag /kwag/ ▸*n.* *archaic* a marshy or boggy place. ▷late 16th cent.: related to dialect *quag* 'shake, quiver'; probably symbolic, the *qu-* suggesting movement (as in *quake* and *quick*). —**quag·gy** *adj.*

quag·ga /ˈkwagə/ ▸*n.* an extinct South African zebra that had a yellowish-brown coat with darker stripes, exterminated in 1883. • *Equus quagga*, family Equidae; recent studies have shown that it was probably a variety of the common zebra. ▷Afrikaans, probably from Khoikhoi, imitative of its braying.

quag·mire /ˈkwag,mīr/ ▸*n.* a soft boggy area of land that gives way underfoot: *torrential rain turned the building site into a quagmire.* ■ an awkward, complex, or hazardous situation: *a legal quagmire.* ▷late 16th cent.: from QUAG + MIRE.

qua·hog /ˈkwôˌhôg; -ˌhäg; ˈkwō-; ˈkō-/ (also **qua·haug**) ▸*n.* a large, rounded edible clam of the Atlantic coast of North America. Also called HARD CLAM, HARD-SHELL CLAM. • *Venus mercenaria*, family Veneridae. ▷mid 18th cent.: from Narragansett *poquaûhock.*

quaich /kwāk/ ▸*n. Scottish* a shallow drinking cup, typically made of wood and having two handles. ■ a trophy of similar design. ▷mid 16th cent.: from Scottish Gaelic *cuach* 'cup.'

Quai d'Or·say /ˈkē dôrˈsā/ a riverside street on the left bank of the Seine River in Paris. ■ the French ministry of foreign affairs, which has its headquarters on this street.

quail[1] /kwāl/ ▸*n.* (*pl.* same or **quails**) **1** a small, short-tailed Old World game bird resembling a tiny partridge, typically having brown camouflaged plumage. • Family Phasianidae: three genera, in particular *Coturnix*, and several species, e.g., the widespread migratory **common quail** (*C. coturnix*). **2** a small or medium-sized New World game bird, the male of which has distinctive facial markings. • Family Phasianidae (or Odontophoridae): several genera and many species, including the bobwhite. ▷Middle English: from Old French *quaille*, from medieval Latin *coacula* (probably imitative of its call).

quail[2] ▸*v.* [*intrans.*] feel or show fear or apprehension: *she quailed at his heartless words.* ▷late Middle English (in the sense 'waste away, come to nothing'): of unknown origin.

quaint /kwānt/ ▸*adj.* attractively unusual or old-fashioned: *quaint country cottages | a quaint old custom.* ▷Middle English: from Old French *cointe*, from Latin *cognitus* 'ascertained,' past participle of *cognoscere*. The original sense was 'wise, clever,' also 'ingenious, cunningly devised,' hence 'out of the ordinary' and the current sense (late 18th cent.). **—quaint·ly** *adv.* **—quaint·ness** *n.*

quake /kwāk/ ▸*v.* [*intrans.*] (esp. of the earth) shake or tremble: *the rumbling vibrations set the whole valley quaking.* See note at SHAKE. ■ (of a person) shake or shudder with fear: *those words should have them* ***quaking in their boots.***
▸*n. informal* an earthquake. ■ [usu. in *sing.*] an act of shaking or quaking. ▷Old English *cwacian.* **—quak·y** *adj.* (**quak·i·er, quak·i·est**).

Quak·er /ˈkwākər/ ▸*n.* a member of the Religious Society of Friends, a Christian movement founded by George Fox *c.*1650 and devoted to peaceful principles. Central to the Quakers' belief is the doctrine of the "Inner Light," or sense of Christ's direct working in the soul. This has led them to reject both formal ministry and all set forms of worship. ▷from QUAKE + -ER[1], perhaps alluding to George Fox's direction to his followers to "tremble at the name of the Lord," or from fits supposedly experienced by worshipers when moved by the Spirit. Compare with SHAKER (sense 2). **—Quak·er·ish** *adj.* **—Quak·er·ism** /-izəm/ *n.*

Quak·er State a nickname for the state of PENNSYLVANIA.

quak·ie /ˈkwākē/ ▸*n. informal* quaking aspen. (See ASPEN.)

quak·ing bog ▸*n.* a bog formed over water or soft mud that shakes underfoot.

quak·ing grass ▸*n.* a slender-stalked grass with oval or heart-shaped flowerheads that tremble in the wind. • Genus *Briza*, family Gramineae: several species, including *B. media*, which is sometimes cultivated as an ornamental.

qual. ▸*abbr.* qualitative.

qua·le /ˈkwālē/ ▸*n.* (*pl.* **qua·li·a** /ˈkwālēə/) (usu. **qualia**) *Philosophy* a quality or property as perceived or experienced by a person. ▷late 17th cent.: from Latin, neuter of *qualis* 'of what kind.'

qua·li·a ▸*plural n. Philosophy* the internal and subjective component of sense perceptions, arising from stimulation of the senses by phenomena.

qual·i·fi·ca·tion /ˌkwäləfəˈkāshən/ ▸*n.* **1** a quality or accomplishment that makes someone suitable for a particular job or activity: *only one qualification required—fabulous sense of humor.* ■ the action or fact of becoming qualified as a practitioner of a particular profession or activity: *an opportunity for student teachers to share experiences before qualification.* ■ a condition that must be fulfilled before a right can be acquired; an official requirement: *the five-year residency qualification for presidential candidates.* **2** the action or fact of qualifying or being eligible for something: *they need to beat Poland to ensure qualification for the World Cup finals.* **3** a statement or assertion that makes another less absolute: *this important qualification needs to be remembered when interpreting the results | he renounced without qualification all forms of terrorism.* **4** *Grammar* the attribution of a quality to a word, esp. a noun. ▷mid 16th cent.: from medieval Latin *qualificatio(n-)*, from the verb *qualificare* (see QUALIFY). **—qual·i·fi·ca·to·ry** /ˈkwäləfikəˌtôrē/ *adj.*

qual·i·fi·er /ˈkwäləˌfīər/ ▸*n.* **1** a person or team that qualifies for a competition or its final rounds: *he is now 14 and trying to become the youngest qualifier for a PGA Tour event.* ■ a match or contest to decide which individuals or teams qualify for a competition or its final rounds. **2** *Grammar* a word or phrase, esp. an adjective, used to attribute a quality to another word, esp. a noun. ■ (in systemic grammar) a word or phrase added after a noun to qualify its meaning.

qual·i·fy /ˈkwäləˌfī/ ▸*v.* (**-fies, -fied**) **1** [*intrans.*] be entitled to a particular benefit or privilege by fulfilling a necessary condition: *they do not* ***qualify for*** *compensation payments.* ■ become eligible for a competition or its final rounds, by reaching a certain standard or defeating a competitor: *he failed to qualify for the Olympic team |* [as *adj.*] (**qualifying**) *a World Cup qualifying game.* ■ be or make properly entitled to be classed in a particular way: [*intrans.*] *he* ***qualifies as*** *a genuine political refugee.* **2** [*intrans.*] become officially recognized as a practitioner of a particular profession or activity by satisfying the relevant conditions or requirements, typically by undertaking a course of study and passing examinations: *after the war he* ***qualified as*** *a lawyer | I've only just qualified.* ■ [*trans.*] officially recognize or establish (someone) as a practitioner of a particular profession or activity: *the courses qualify you as an instructor of the sport |* [as *adj.*] (**qualified**) *qualified teachers.* ■ [*trans.*] make (someone) competent or knowledgeable enough to do something: *I'm not qualified to write on the subject.* **3** [*trans.*] make (a statement or assertion) less absolute; add reservations to: *she felt obliged to qualify her first short answer |* [as *adj.*] (**qualified**) *qualified welcome.* ■ *archaic* make (something extreme or undesirable) less severe or extreme: *his sincere piety, his large heart alway qualify his errors.* ■ *archaic* alter the strength or flavor of (something, esp. a liquid): *he qualified his mug of water with a plentiful infusion of the liquor.* ■ (**qualify something as**) *archaic* attribute a specified quality to something; describe something as: *the propositions have been qualified as heretical.* ■ [*trans.*] *Grammar* (of a word or phrase) attribute a quality to (another word, esp. a preceding noun). ▷late Middle English (in the sense 'describe in a particular way'): from French *qualifier*, from medieval Latin *qualificare*, from Latin *qualis* 'of what kind, of such a kind' (see QUALITY). **—qual·i·fi·a·ble** *adj.*

qual·i·ta·tive /ˈkwäləˌtātiv/ ▸*adj.* relating to, measuring, or measured by the quality of something rather than its quantity: *a qualitative change in the undergraduate curriculum.* Often contrasted with QUANTITATIVE. ■ *Grammar* (of an adjective) describing the quality of something in size, appearance, value, etc. Such adjectives can be submodified by words such as *very* and have comparative and superlative forms. Contrasted with CLASSIFYING. ▷late Middle English: from late Latin *qualitativus*, from Latin *qualitas* (see QUALITY). **—qual·i·ta·tive·ly** *adv.*

qual·i·ta·tive a·nal·y·sis ▸*n. Chemistry* identification of the constituents, e.g., elements or functional groups, present in a substance.

qual·i·ty /ˈkwälətē/ ▸*n.* (*pl.* **-ties**) **1** the standard of something as measured against other things of a similar kind; the degree of excellence of something: *an improvement in product quality | people today enjoy a better quality of life.* ■ general excellence of standard or level: *a masterpiece for connoisseurs of quality |* [as *adj.*] *a wide choice of quality beers.* ■ *archaic* high social standing: *commanding the admiration of people of quality.* ■ [treated as *pl.*] *archaic* people of high social standing: *he's dazed at being called on to speak before quality.* **2** a distinctive attribute or characteristic possessed by someone or something: *he shows strong leadership qualities | the plant's aphrodisiac qualities.* ■ *Phonetics* the distinguishing characteristic or characteristics of a speech sound. ■ *Music* another term for TIMBRE. ■ *dated Logic* the property of a proposition of being affirmative or negative. ■ *Astrology* any of three properties (cardinal, fixed, or mutable), representing types of movement, that a zodiacal sign can possess. ▷Middle English (in the senses 'character, disposition' and 'particular property or feature'): from Old French *qualite*, from Latin *qualitas* (translating Greek *poiotēs*), from *qualis* 'of what kind, of such a kind.'

qual·i·ty as·sur·ance ▸*n.* the maintenance of a desired level of quality in a service or product, esp. by means of attention to every stage of the process of delivery or production.

qual·i·ty cir·cle ▸*n.* a group of employees that meets regularly to consider ways of resolving problems and improving production in their organization.

qual·i·ty con·trol ▸*n.* a system of maintaining standards in manufactured products by testing a sample of the output against the specification. **—qual·i·ty con·trol·ler** *n.*

qual·i·ty fac·tor ▸*n. Physics* a parameter of an oscillatory system or device, such as a laser, representing the degree to which it is undamped and hence expressing the relationship between stored energy and energy dissipation. ■ a figure expressing the ability of ionizing radiation to cause biological damage, relative to a standard dose of X-rays.

qual·i·ty time ▸*n.* time spent in giving another person one's undivided attention in order to strengthen a relationship, esp. with reference to working parents and their child or children.

qualm /kwä(l)m; kwô(l)m/ ▸*n.* an uneasy feeling of doubt, worry, or fear, esp. about one's own conduct; a misgiving: *military regimes generally* ***have no qualms about*** *controlling the press.* ■ a momentary faint or sick feeling. ▷early 16th cent. (in the sense 'momentary sick feeling'): perhaps related to Old English *cw(e)alm* 'pain,' of Germanic origin. **—qualm·ish** *adj.*

THE RIGHT WORD **compunction, demur, misgiving, qualms, scruple**

To have **qualms** is to have an uneasy feeling that you have acted or are about to act against your better judgment (*she had qualms about leaving a nine-year-old in charge of an infant*).

Misgivings are even stronger, implying a disturbed state of mind because you're no longer confident that what you're doing is right (*his misgivings about letting his 80-year-old mother drive herself home turned out to be justified*).

Compunction implies a momentary pang of conscience because what you are doing or are about to do is unfair, improper, or wrong (*they showed no compunction in carrying out their devious plans*).

Scruples suggest a more highly developed conscience or sense of honor; it implies that you have principles, and that you would be deeply disturbed if you thought you were betraying them (*her scruples would not allow her to participate in what she considered antifeminist activities*).

Demur connotes hesitation to the point of delay, but the delay is usually caused by objections or indecision rather than a sense of conscience (*they accepted his decision without demur*).

quam·ash /ˈkwäˌmash/ ▸*n.* variant spelling of CAMAS.

quan·da·ry /ˈkwänd(ə)rē/ ▸*n.* (*pl.* **-ries**) a state of perplexity or uncertainty over what to do in a difficult situation: *Kate is* ***in a quandary.*** ■ a difficult situation; a practical dilemma: *a legal quandary.* ▷late 16th cent.: perhaps partly from Latin *quando* 'when.'

quan·dong /ˈkwänˌdäng/ ▸*n.* either of two Australian trees: • a small tree of the sandalwood family that has round red fruit with an edible pulp and kernel (*Eucarya acuminata*, family Santalaceae). • (also **blue quandong**) a large tree of the subtropical rain forest that has blue berries (*Elaeocarpus grandis*, family Elaeocarpaceae). ▷mid 19th cent.: from Wiradhuri.

quan·go /ˈkwanggō/ ▸*n.* (*pl.* **-gos**) *Brit., chiefly derogatory* a semipublic administrative body outside the civil service but with financial support from and senior appointments made by the government. ▷1970s (originally U.S.): acronym from *quasi* (or *quasi-autonomous*) *nongovernment(al) organization.*

Quant /kwänt/, Mary (1934–), English fashion designer. She launched the miniskirt in 1966 and promoted bold colors and geometric designs. She was also one of the first to design for the ready-to-wear market.

quant[1] /kwänt/ ▸*n. informal* a quantitative analyst. ▷late 20th cent.: abbreviation.

quant[2] ▸*n. Brit.* a pole for propelling a barge or punt, esp. one with a prong at the bottom to prevent it sinking into the mud. ▷late Middle English: perhaps from Latin *contus*, from Greek *kontos* 'boat pole.'

quant. ▸*abbr.* quantitative.

quan·tal /ˈkwäntl/ ▸*adj. technical* composed of discrete units; varying in steps rather than continuously: *a quantal release of neurotransmitter.* ■ *Physics* of or relating to a quantum or quanta, or to quantum theory. ■ *chiefly Physiology* relating to or denoting an all-or-none response or state. ▷early 20th cent.: from **QUANTUM** + **-AL**. **—quan·tal·ly** /'kwäntl-ē/ *adv.*

quan·tic /'kwäntik/ ▶*n. Mathematics* a homogeneous function of two or more variables having rational and irrational coefficients. ▷mid 19th cent.: from Latin *quantus* 'how great, how much' + **-IC**.

quan·ti·fi·er /'kwäntə,fīər/ ▶*n. Logic* an expression (e.g., *all, some*) that indicates the scope of a term to which it is attached. ■ *Grammar* a determiner or pronoun indicative of quantity (e.g., *all, both*).

quan·ti·fy /'kwäntə,fī/ ▶*v.* (**-fies**, **-fied**) [*trans.*] **1** express or measure the quantity of: *it's very hard to quantify the cost.* **2** *Logic* define the application of (a term or proposition) by the use of *all, some*, etc., e.g., "for all *x* if *x* is A then *x* is B." ▷mid 16th cent.: from medieval Latin *quantificare*, from Latin *quantus* 'how much.' **—quan·ti·fi·a·bil·i·ty** /,kwäntə,fīə'bilətē/ *n.* **—quan·ti·fi·a·ble** /'kwäntə,fīəbəl/ *adj.* **—quan·ti·fi·ca·tion** /,kwäntəfi'kāsʜən/ *n.*

quan·tile /'kwän,tīl/ ▶*n. Statistics* each of any set of values of a variate that divide a frequency distribution into equal groups, each containing the same fraction of the total population. ■ any of the groups so produced, e.g., a quartile or percentile. ▷1940s: from Latin *quantus* 'how great, how much' + **-ILE**.

quan·ti·tate /'kwäntə,tāt/ ▶*v.* [*trans.*] *Medicine & Biology* determine the quantity or extent of (something in numerical terms); quantify. ▷1960s: from **QUANTITY** + **-ATE**[3]. **—quan·ti·ta·tion** /,kwäntə'tāsʜən/ *n.*

quan·ti·ta·tive /'kwäntə,tātiv/ ▶*adj.* relating to, measuring, or measured by the quantity of something rather than its quality: *quantitative analysis.* Often contrasted with **QUALITATIVE**. ■ denoting or relating to verse whose meter is based on the length of syllables, as in Latin, as opposed to the stress, as in English. ▷late 16th cent. (in the sense 'having magnitude or spatial extent'): from medieval Latin *quantitativus*, from Latin *quantitas* (see **QUANTITY**). **—quan·ti·ta·tive·ly** *adv.*

quan·ti·ta·tive a·nal·y·sis ▶*n. Chemistry* measurement of the quantities of particular constituents present in a substance.

quan·ti·ta·tive lin·guis·tics ▶*plural n.* [treated as *sing.*] the comparative study of the frequency and distribution of words and syntactic structures in different texts.

quan·ti·tive /'kwäntətiv/ ▶*adj.* another term for **QUANTITATIVE**. **—quan·ti·tive·ly** *adv.*

quan·ti·ty /'kwäntətē/ ▶*n.* (*pl.* **-ties**) **1** the amount or number of a material or immaterial thing not usually estimated by spatial measurement: *the quantity and quality of the fruit can be controlled | note down the sizes, colors, and quantities that you require.* ■ *Logic* the property of a proposition of being universal or particular. ■ a certain, usually specified, amount or number of something: *a small **quantity of** food | if taken in large quantities, the drug can result in liver failure.* ■ (often **quantities**) a considerable number or amount of something: *she was able to drink quantities of beer without degenerating into giggles | many people like to buy in quantity.* **2** *Phonetics* the perceived length of a vowel sound or syllable. **3** *Mathematics & Physics* a value or component that may be expressed in numbers. ■ the figure or symbol representing this. ▷Middle English: from Old French *quantite*, from Latin *quantitas* (translating Greek *posotēs*), from *quantus* 'how great, how much.'

quan·ti·ty the·o·ry (also **the quantity theory of money**) ▶*n. Economics* the hypothesis that changes in prices correspond to changes in the monetary supply.

quan·tize /'kwän,tīz/ ▶*v.* [*trans.*] **1** *Physics* apply quantum theory to, esp. form into quanta, in particular restrict the number of possible values of (a quantity) or states of (a system) so that certain variables can assume only certain discrete magnitudes. **2** *Electronics* approximate (a continuously varying signal) by one whose amplitude is restricted to a prescribed set of values. **—quan·ti·za·tion** /,kwäntə'zāsʜən/ *n.* **—quan·tiz·er** *n.* (in sense 2).

quan·tum /'kwäntəm/ ▶*n.* (*pl.* **-ta** /-tə/) **1** *Physics* a discrete quantity of energy proportional in magnitude to the frequency of the radiation it represents. ■ an analogous discrete amount of any other physical quantity, such as momentum or electric charge. ■ *Physiology* the unit quantity of acetylcholine released at a neuromuscular junction by a single synaptic vesicle, contributing a discrete small voltage to the measured end-plate potential. **2** a required or allowed amount, esp. an amount of money legally payable in damages. ■ a share or portion: *each man has only a quantum of compassion.* ▷mid 16th cent. (in the general sense 'quantity'): from Latin, neuter of *quantus* (see **QUANTITY**). Sense 1 dates from the early 20th cent.

quan·tum chro·mo·dy·nam·ics (abbr.: **QCD**) ▶*plural n.* [treated as *sing.*] *Physics* a quantum field theory in which the strong interaction is described in terms of an interaction between quarks mediated by gluons, both quarks and gluons being assigned a quantum number called "color."

quan·tum com·put·er ▶*n.* a computer that makes use of the quantum states of subatomic particles to store information. **—quan·tum com·put·ing** *n.*

quan·tum dot ▶*Physics n.* a nanoscale particle of semiconducting material that can be embedded in cells or organisms for various experimental purposes, such as labeling proteins.

quan·tum e·lec·tro·dy·nam·ics ▶*plural n.* [treated as *sing.*] a quantum field theory that deals with the electromagnetic field and its interaction with electrically charged particles.

quan·tum field the·o·ry ▶*n. Physics* a field theory that incorporates quantum mechanics and the principles of the theory of relativity.

quan·tum grav·i·ty ▶*n. Physics* a theory that attempts to explain gravitational physics in terms of quantum mechanics.

quan·tum jump ▶*n. Physics* an abrupt transition of an electron, atom, or molecule from one quantum state to another, with the absorption or emission of a quantum. ■ *figurative* a huge, often sudden, increase or change in something: *the quantum jump in Jamie's grades this semester are extremely encouraging.* Also called **QUANTUM LEAP**.

quan·tum me·chan·ics ▶*plural n.* [treated as *sing.*] *Physics* the branch of mechanics that deals with the mathematical description of the motion and interaction of subatomic particles, incorporating the concepts of quantization of energy, wave-particle duality, the uncertainty principle, and the correspondence principle. **—quan·tum-me·chan·i·cal** *adj.*

quan·tum med·i·cine ▶*n.* a branch of complementary medicine that uses low-dosage electromagnetic radiation in the treatment, diagnosis, and prevention of disease.

quan·tum me·ru·it /,kwäntəm 'merōōit/ ▶*n.* [usu. as *adj.*] *Law* a reasonable sum of money to be paid for services rendered or work done when the amount due is not stipulated in a legally enforceable contract. ▷Latin, literally 'as much as he has deserved.'

quan·tum num·ber ▶*n. Physics* a number that occurs in the theoretical expression for the value of some quantized property of a subatomic particle, atom, or molecule and can only have certain integral or half-integral values.

quan·tum state ▶*n. Physics* a state of a quantized system that is described by a set of quantum numbers.

quan·tum the·o·ry ▶*n. Physics* a theory of matter and energy based on the concept of quanta, esp. quantum mechanics.

Qua·paw /'kwô,pô/ ▶*n.* (*pl.* same or **-paws**) **1** a member of an American Indian people of the Arkansas River region, now living mainly in northeastern Oklahoma. **2** the Siouan language of this people.
▶*adj.* of or relating to this people or their language. ▷from Quapaw *okáxpa*, perhaps meaning 'those downstream,' originally the name of a village.

quar. ▶*abbr.* ■ quarter. ■ quarterly.

quar·an·tine /'kwôrən,tēn/ ▶*n.* a state, period, or place of isolation in which people or animals that have arrived from elsewhere or been exposed to infectious or contagious disease are placed: *many animals die **in quarantine**.*
▶*v.* [*trans.*] impose such isolation on (a person, animal, or place); put in quarantine. ▷mid 17th cent.: from Italian *quarantina* 'forty days,' from *quaranta* 'forty.'

quar·an·tine flag ▶*n.* another term for **YELLOW FLAG**.

quark[1] /kwärk/ ▶*n. Physics* any of a number of subatomic particles carrying a fractional electric charge, postulated as building blocks of the hadrons. Quarks have not been directly observed, but theoretical predictions based on their existence have been confirmed experimentally. ▷1960s: a word invented by Murray **GELL-MANN**. Originally *quork*, the term was changed by association with the line "Three quarks for Muster Mark" in Joyce's *Finnegans Wake* (1939).

quark[2] ▶*n.* a type of low-fat curd cheese. ▷from German *Quark* 'curds.'

quark-glu·on plas·ma ▶*n.* a hypothetical, highly energized form of matter that contains unbound quarks and gluons, believed to have been present ten millionths of a second after the Big Bang.

quar·rel[1] /'kwôrəl; 'kwä-/ ▶*n.* an angry argument or disagreement, typically between people who are usually on good terms: *he made the mistake of **picking a quarrel with** John.* ■ [usu. with *negative*] a reason for disagreement with a person, group, or principle: *we **have no quarrel with** the people of the country, only with the dictator.*
▶*v.* (**-reled**, **-rel·ing**; *Brit.* **-relled**, **-rel·ling**) [*intrans.*] have an angry argument or disagreement: *stop **quarreling with** your sister.* ■ (**quarrel with**) take exception to or disagree with (something): *some people quarrel with this approach.* ▷Middle English (in the sense 'reason for disagreement with a person'): from Old French *querele*, from Latin *querel(l)a* 'complaint,' from *queri* 'complain.' **—quar·rel·er** *n.*

THE RIGHT WORD **altercation, dispute, feud, quarrel, row, spat, squabble, wrangle**

Fighting is an unfriendliness that comes in a variety of shapes and sizes.

A husband and his wife may have a **quarrel**, which suggests a heated verbal argument, with hostility that may persist even after it is over (*it took them almost a week to patch up their quarrel*).

Siblings tend to have **squabbles**, which are childlike disputes over trivial matters, although they are by no means confined to childhood (*frequent squabbles over who would pick up the check*).

A **spat** is also a petty quarrel, but unlike *squabble*, it suggests an angry outburst followed by a quick ending without hard feelings (*another spat in an otherwise loving relationship*).

A **row** is more serious, involving noisy quarreling and the potential for physical violence (*a row that woke the neighbors*).

Neighbors are more likely to have an **altercation**, which is usually confined to verbal blows but may involve actual or threatened physical ones (*an altercation over the location of the fence*).

A **dispute** is also a verbal argument, but one that is carried on over an extended period of time (*an ongoing dispute over who was responsible for taking out the garbage*).

Two families who have been enemies for a long time are probably involved in a **feud**, which suggests a bitter quarrel that lasts for years or even generations (*the feud between the Hatfields and the McCoys*).

There is no dignity at all in being involved in a **wrangle**, which is an angry, noisy, and often futile dispute in which both parties are unwilling to listen to the other's point of view.

quar·rel[2] ▶*n.* **1** *historical* a short, heavy, square-headed arrow or bolt used in a crossbow or arbalest. **2** another term for **QUARRY**[3]. ▷Middle English: from Old French, based on late Latin *quadrus* 'square.' Compare with **QUARRY**[3].

quar·rel·some /'kwôrəlsəm; 'kwä-/ ▶*adj.* given to or characterized by quarreling. **—quar·rel·some·ly** *adv.* **—quar·rel·some·ness** *n.*

quar·ry[1] /'kwôrē; 'kwä-/ ▶*n.* (*pl.* **-ries**) a place, typically a large, deep pit, from which stone or other materials are or have been extracted.
▶*v.* (**-ries**, **-ried**) [*trans.*] extract (stone or other materials) from a quarry. ■ cut into (rock or ground) to obtain stone or other materials. ▷Middle English: from a variant of medieval Latin *quareria*, from Old French *quarriere*, based on Latin *quadrum* 'a square.' The verb dates from the late 18th cent.

quar·ry[2] ▶*n.* (*pl.* **-ries**) an animal pursued by a hunter, hound, predatory mammal, or bird of prey. ■ a thing or person that is chased or sought: *the security police crossed the border in pursuit of their quarry.* ▷Middle English: from Old French *cuiree*, alteration, influenced by *cuir* 'leather' and *curer* 'clean, disembowel,' of *couree*, based on Latin *cor* 'heart.' Originally the term denoted the parts of a deer that were placed on the hide and given as a reward to the hounds.

quar·ry[3] ▶*n.* (*pl.* **-ries**) **1** (also **quar·rel**) a diamond-shaped pane of glass as used in lattice windows. **2** (also **quarry tile**) an unglazed floor tile. ▷mid 16th cent. (sense 2): alteration of **QUARREL**[2], which in late Middle English denoted a lattice windowpane.

quar·ry·man /ˈkwôrēmən; ˈkwär-/ ▶*n.* (*pl.* **-men**) a worker in a quarry.

quart /kwôrt/ ▶*n.* **1** a unit of liquid capacity equal to a quarter of a gallon or two pints, equivalent in the U.S. to approximately 0.94 liter and in Britain to approximately 1.13 liters. ■ a unit of dry capacity equivalent to approximately 1.10 liters. **2** (also **quarte**) *Fencing* the fourth of eight standard parrying positions. [French.] **3** (in piquet) a sequence of four cards of the same suit. ▷Middle English: from Old French *quarte*, from Latin *quarta (pars)* 'fourth (part),' from *quartus* 'fourth,' from *quattuor* 'four.'

quar·tan /ˈkwôrtn/ ▶*adj.* [*attrib.*] *Medicine* denoting a mild form of malaria causing a fever that recurs every third day: *quartan fever.* • Quartan malaria (or quartan ague) is caused by infection with *Plasmodium malariae*. Compare with TERTIAN. ▷late Middle English: from Latin *(febris) quartana*, based on *quartus* 'fourth' (because, by inclusive reckoning, the fever recurs every fourth day).

quar·ter /ˈkwôrtər/ ▶*n.* **1** each of four equal or corresponding parts into which something is or can be divided: *she cut each apple into quarters | a page and a quarter | a quarter of a mile.* ■ a period of three months regarded as one fourth of a year, used esp. in reference to financial transactions such as the payment of bills or a company's earnings: *the payment for each quarter's electricity is made in the next quarter.* ■ a period of fifteen minutes or a point of time marking the transition from one fifteen-minute period to the next: *the baby was born at a quarter past nine.* ■ a coin representing 25 cents, one fourth of a U.S. or Canadian dollar. ■ each of the four parts into which an animal's or bird's carcass may be divided, each including a leg or wing. ■ (**quarters**) the haunches or hindquarters of a horse. ■ one fourth of a lunar month. ■ (in various sports) each of four equal periods into which a game is divided. ■ one of four terms into which a school or college year may be divided. **2** one fourth of a measure of weight, in particular: ■ one fourth of a pound (avoirdupois, equal to 4 ounces). ■ one fourth of a hundredweight (*U.S.* 25 lb or *Brit.* 28 lb). ■ *Brit.* a grain measure equivalent to 8 bushels. **3** [usu. with *adj.* or *n.*] a part of a town or city having a specific character or use: *it is a beautiful port city with a fascinating medieval quarter.* **4** the direction of one of the points of the compass, esp. as a direction from which the wind blows. ■ a particular but unspecified person, group of people, or area: *we have just had help from an unexpected quarter.* ■ either side of a ship aft of the beam: *he trained his glasses over the starboard quarter.* **5** (**quarters**) rooms or lodgings, esp. those allocated to servicemen or to staff in domestic service: *the servants' quarters.* **6** [usu. with *neg.*] pity or mercy shown toward an enemy or opponent who is in one's power: *the riot squad* ***gave no quarter.*** **7** *Heraldry* each of four or more roughly equal divisions of a shield separated by vertical and horizontal lines. ■ a square charge which covers the top left (dexter chief) quarter of the field.
▶*v.* [*trans.*] **1** divide into four equal or corresponding parts: *peel and quarter the bananas.* ■ *historical* cut (the body of an executed person) into four parts: *the plotters were hanged, drawn, and quartered.* ■ cut (a log) into quarters, and these into planks so as to show the grain well. **2** (**be quartered**) be stationed or lodged in a specified place: *many were quartered in tents.* **3** range over or traverse (an area) in every direction: *we watched a pair of kingfishers quartering the river looking for minnows.* ■ [*intrans.*] move at an angle; go in a diagonal or zigzag direction: *his young dog quartered back and forth in quick turns.* **4** *Heraldry* display (different coats of arms) in quarters of a shield, esp. to show arms inherited from heiresses who have married into the bearer's family: *Edward III* ***quartered*** *the French royal arms* ***with*** *his own.* ■ divide (a shield) into four or more parts by vertical and horizontal lines. ▷Middle English: from Old French *quartier*, from Latin *quartarius* 'fourth part of a measure,' from *quartus* 'fourth,' from *quattuor* 'four.'

quar·ter·age /ˈkwôrtərij/ ▶*n. archaic* a sum paid or received quarterly.

quar·ter·back /ˈkwôrtərˌbak/ ▶*n. Football* a player positioned behind the center who directs a team's offensive play. ■ *figurative* a person who directs or coordinates an operation or project.
▶*v.* [*trans.*] *Football* play as a quarterback for (a particular team). ■ *figurative* direct or coordinate (an operation or project).

quar·ter bind·ing ▶*n.* a type of bookbinding in which the spine is covered in one material (usually leather) and the rest of the cover in another. —**quar·ter-bound** *adj.*

quar·ter·deck /ˈkwôrtərˌdek/ ▶*n.* the part of a ship's upper deck near the stern, traditionally reserved for officers. ■ the officers of a ship or the navy.

quar·ter·fi·nal /ˈkwôrtərˌfīnl/ ▶*n.* a match or round of a tournament that precedes the semifinal.

Quar·ter Horse (also **quar·ter horse**) ▶*n.* a horse of a small, stocky breed noted for agility and speed over short distances. It is reputed to be the fastest breed of horse over distances of a quarter of a mile.

quar·ter-hour (also **quarter of an hour**) ▶*n.* a period of 15 minutes. ■ a point of time 15 minutes before or after any hour.

quar·ter·ing /ˈkwôrtəriNG/ ▶*n.* **1** (**quarterings**) *Heraldry* the coats of arms marshalled on a shield to denote the marriages into a family of the heiresses of others. **2** the provision of accommodations or lodgings, esp. for troops. **3** the action of dividing something into four parts.

quar·ter·ly /ˈkwôrtərlē/ ▶*adj.* **1** [*attrib.*] done, produced, or occurring once every quarter of a year: *a quarterly newsletter is distributed to members.* **2** *Heraldry* (of a shield or charge) divided into four (or occasionally more) subdivisions by vertical and horizontal lines.
▶*adv.* **1** once every quarter of a year: *interest is paid quarterly.* **2** *Heraldry* in the four, or in two diagonally opposite, quarters of a shield. [on the pattern of Old French *quartile*.]
▶*n.* (*pl.* **-lies**) a magazine or journal that is published four times a year.

quar·ter·mas·ter /ˈkwôrtərˌmastər/ ▶*n.* **1** a military officer responsible for providing quarters, rations, clothing, and other supplies. **2** a naval petty officer with particular responsibility for steering and signals.

quar·ter·mas·ter gen·er·al ▶*n.* (*pl.* **quar·ter·mas·ters gen·er·al** or **quar·ter·mas·ter gen·er·als**) the head of the army department in charge of the quartering and equipment of troops.

quar·tern /ˈkwôrtərn/ ▶*n. Brit., archaic* a quarter of a pint. ▷Middle English (in the general sense 'a quarter'): from Old French *quart(e)ron*, from *quart(e)* (see QUART).

quar·ter note ▶*n. Music* a musical note having the time value of a quarter of a whole note or half a half note, represented by a large solid dot with a plain stem. Also called CROTCHET.

quar·ter-pipe ▶*n.* a ramp with a slightly convex surface, used by skateboarders, rollerbladers, or snowboarders to perform jumps and other maneuvers.

quar·ter-saw ▶*v.* [*trans.*] [usu. as *adj.*] (**quarter-sawn**) saw (a log) radially into quarters and then into boards: *we quarter-saw the logs at our own mill* [as *adj.*] *quarter-sawn timber from the stand of white ash.* ■ produce (a board or a piece of furniture) using this technique.

quar·ter sec·tion ▶*n.* a quarter of a square mile of land; 160 acres (approximately 64.7 hectares).

quar·ter ses·sions ▶*plural n. historical* (in England, Wales, and Northern Ireland) a court of limited criminal and civil jurisdiction and of appeal, usually held quarterly in counties or boroughs, and replaced in 1972 by crown courts.

quar·ter·staff /ˈkwôrtərˌstaf/ ▶*n. historical* a stout pole 6–8 feet (2–2.5 m) long, tipped with iron, formerly used as a weapon.

quar·ter-tone ▶*n. Music* half a semitone.

quar·tet /kwôrˈtet/ ▶*n.* a group of four people playing music or singing together. ■ a composition for such a group. ■ a set of four people or things. ▷early 17th cent. (in the general sense 'set of four'): from French *quartette*, from Italian *quartetto*, from *quarto* 'fourth,' from Latin *quartus*.

quar·tic /ˈkwôrtik/ *Mathematics* ▶*adj.* involving the fourth and no higher power of an unknown quantity or variable.
▶*n.* a quartic equation, function, curve, or surface. ▷mid 19th cent.: from Latin *quartus* 'fourth' + -IC.

quar·ti·er /ˈkärtē-ā/ ▶*n.* (*pl.* same) a district of a French city. ▷French.

quar·tile /ˈkwôrˌtīl; ˈkwôrtl/ ▶*n. Statistics* each of four equal groups into which a population can be divided according to the distribution of values of a particular variable. ■ each of the three values of the random variable that divide a population into four such groups. ▷late 19th cent.: from medieval Latin *quartilis*, from Latin *quartus* 'fourth.'

quar·to /ˈkwôrtō/ (abbr.: **4to**) ▶*n.* (*pl.* **-tos**) *Printing* a size of book page resulting from folding each printed sheet into four leaves (eight pages). ■ a book of this size. ■ a size of writing paper, 10 in. × 8 in. (254 × 203 mm). ▷late 16th cent.: from Latin *(in) quarto* '(in) the fourth (of a sheet),' ablative of *quartus* 'fourth.'

quartz /kwôrts/ ▶*n.* a hard white or colorless mineral consisting of silicon dioxide, found widely in igneous, metamorphic, and sedimentary rocks. It is often colored by impurities (as in amethyst, citrine, and cairngorm). ▷mid 18th cent.: from German *Quarz*, from Polish dialect *kwardy*, corresponding to standard Polish *twardy* 'hard.'

quartz-hal·o·gen ▶*adj.* (of a high-intensity electric lamp) using a quartz bulb containing the vapor of a halogen, usually iodine.

quartz·ite /ˈkwôrtˌsīt/ ▶*n. Geology* an extremely compact, hard, granular rock consisting essentially of quartz. It often occurs as silicified sandstone, as in sarsen stones.

quartz lamp ▶*n.* an electric lamp in which the envelope is made of quartz, which allows ultraviolet light to pass through it. It may be a bulb containing a halogen or a tube containing mercury vapor.

qua·sar /ˈkwāˌzär/ ▶*n. Astronomy* a massive and extremely remote celestial object, emitting exceptionally large amounts of energy, and typically having a starlike image in a telescope. It has been suggested that quasars contain massive black holes and may represent a stage in the evolution of some galaxies. ▷1960s: contraction of *quasi-stellar*.

quash /kwôSH; kwäSH/ ▶*v.* [*trans.*] reject or void, esp. by legal procedure: *his conviction was quashed on appeal.* ■ put an end to; suppress: *a hospital executive quashed rumors that nursing staff will lose jobs.* ▷Middle English: from Old French *quasser* 'annul,' from late Latin *cassare* (medieval Latin also *quassare*), from *cassus* 'null, void.' Compare with SQUASH[1].

quasi- ▶*comb. form* seemingly; apparently but not really: *quasi-American | quasi-scientific.* ■ being partly or almost: *quasicrystalline.* ▷from Latin *quasi* 'as if, almost.'

qua·si con·tract /ˈkwāˌzī; ˈkwäzē/ ▶*n.* an obligation of one party to another imposed by law independently of an agreement between the parties. —**qua·si-con·trac·tu·al** *adj.*

qua·si·crys·tal /ˌkwāˌzīˈkristəl; ˌkwäzē-/ ▶*n. Physics* a locally regular aggregation of molecules resembling a crystal in certain properties (such as that of diffraction) but not having a consistent spatial periodicity. —**qua·si·crys·tal·line** /-ˈkristəlēn/ *adj.*

Qua·si·mo·do[1] /ˌkwäzēˈmōdō/ the name of the hunchback in Victor Hugo's novel *Notre-Dame de Paris* (1831).

Qua·si·mo·do[2], Salvatore (1901–68), Italian poet. His early work was influenced by French symbolism but his later work was more concerned with political and social issues. Notable works: *Water and Land* (1930) and *And It's Suddenly Evening* (1942). Nobel Prize for Literature (1959).

qua·si·par·ti·cle /ˌkwäzīˈpärtəkəl; ˌkwäzē-/ ▶*n. Physics* a quantum of energy in a crystal lattice or other system of bodies that has momentum and position and can in some respects be regarded as a particle.

quas·sia /ˈkwäSH(ē)ə/ ▶*n.* a South American shrub or small tree related to ailanthus. • Genera *Quassia* and *Picrasma*, family Simaroubaceae: several species, in particular *Q. amara*. ■ the wood, bark, or root of this tree, yielding a bitter medicinal tonic, insecticide, and vermifuge. ▷named after Graman *Quassi*, an 18th-cent. Surinamese slave who discovered its medicinal properties in 1730.

quat·er·cen·ten·ar·y /ˌkwätərsenˈtenərē; -ˈsentnˌerē/ ▶*n.* (*pl.* **-ar·ies**) the four-hundredth anniversary of a significant event.
▶*adj.* of or relating to such an anniversary. ▷late 19th cent.: from Latin *quater* 'four times' + CENTENARY.

qua·ter·nar·y /ˈkwätərˌnerē/ ▶*adj.* **1** fourth in order or rank; belonging to the fourth order. **2** (**Quaternary**) *Geology* of, relating to, or denoting the most recent period in the Cenozoic era, following the Tertiary period and comprising the Pleistocene and Holocene epochs (and thus including the present). **3** *Chemistry* denoting an ammonium compound containing a cation of the form NR_4^+, where R represents organic groups or atoms other than hydrogen. ■ (of a carbon atom) bonded to four other carbon atoms.
▶*n.* (**the Quaternary**) *Geology* the Quaternary period or the system of deposits laid down during it.

The Quaternary began about 1,640,000 years ago. Humans and other mammals evolved into their present forms and were strongly affected by the ice ages of the Pleistocene.

▷late Middle English (as a noun denoting a set of four): from Latin *quaternarius*, from *quaterni* 'four at once,' from *quater* 'four times,' from *quattuor* 'four.'

qua·ter·ni·on /kwəˈtərnēən; kwä-/ ▸*n.* **1** *Mathematics* a complex number of the form $w + xi + yj + zk$, where w, x, y, z are real numbers and i, j, k are imaginary units that satisfy certain conditions. **2** *rare* a set of four people or things. ▷mid 19th cent.: from late Latin *quaternio(n-)*, from Latin *quarterni* (see **QUATERNARY**).

qua·torze /kəˈtôrz/ ▸*n.* (in piquet) a set of four aces, kings, queens, jacks, or tens held in one hand. ▷early 18th cent.: French, literally 'fourteen,' from Latin *quattuordecim*.

quat·rain /ˈkwäˌtrān/ ▸*n.* a stanza of four lines, esp. one having alternate rhymes. ▷late 16th cent.: from French, from *quatre* 'four.'

quat·re·foil /ˈkatərˌfoil; ˈkatrə-/ ▸*n.* an ornamental design of four lobes or leaves as used in architectural tracery, resembling a flower or four-leaf clover. ▷late 15th cent.: from Anglo-Norman French, from Old French *quatre* 'four' + *foil* 'leaf.'

quat·tro·cen·to /ˌkwätrōˈCHentō/ ▸*n.* (**the quattrocento**) the 15th century as a period of Italian art or architecture. ▷Italian, literally '400' (shortened from *milquattrocento* '1400'), used with reference to the years 1400–99.

qua·ver /ˈkwāvər/ ▸*v.* [*intrans.*] (of a person's voice) shake or tremble in speaking, typically through nervousness or emotion.
▸*n.* **1** a shake or tremble in a person's voice. **2** *Music, chiefly Brit.* another term for **EIGHTH NOTE**. ▷late Middle English (as a verb in the general sense 'tremble'): from dialect *quave* 'quake, tremble,' probably from an Old English word related to **QUAKE**. The noun is first recorded (mid 16th cent.) as a musical term. —**qua·ver·ing·ly** *adv.* —**qua·ver·y** *adj.*

quay /kē; k(w)ā/ ▸*n.* a concrete, stone, or metal platform lying alongside or projecting into water for loading and unloading ships. ▷late Middle English *key*, from Old French *kay*, of Celtic origin. The change of spelling in the late 17th cent. was influenced by the modern French spelling *quai*. —**quay·age** /ˈkēij; ˈk(w)āij/ *n.*

Quayle /kwāl/, Dan (1947–), U.S. politician; full name *James Danforth Quayle*. A Republican from Indiana, he served as a member of the U.S. House of Representatives 1977–81 and the U.S. Senate 1981–89 before being elected vice president of the U.S. 1989–93.

quay·side /ˈkēˌsīd; ˈk(w)ā-/ ▸*n.* a quay and the area around it.

Que. ▸*abbr.* Quebec.

quean /kwēn/ ▸*n. archaic* an impudent or ill-behaved girl or woman. ■ a prostitute. ▷Old English *cwene* 'woman,' of Germanic origin; related to Dutch *kween* 'barren cow,' from an Indo-European root shared by Greek *gunē* 'woman.'

quea·sy /ˈkwēzē/ ▸*adj.* (**queas·i·er, queas·i·est**) nauseated; feeling sick: *in the morning he was still pale and queasy.* ■ inducing a feeling of nausea: *the queasy swell of the boat.* ■ *figurative* slightly nervous or worried about something. ▷late Middle English *queisy, coisy* 'causing nausea,' of uncertain origin; perhaps related to Old French *coisier* 'to hurt.' —**quea·si·ly** /-zəlē/ *adv.* —**quea·si·ness** *n.*

Que·bec /k(w)əˈbek; kā-/ **1** a heavily forested province in eastern Canada; pop. 6,845,700. Settled by the French in 1608, it was ceded to the British in 1763 and became one of the original four provinces in the Dominion of Canada in 1867. The majority of its residents are French-speaking, and it is a focal point of the French-Canadian nationalist movement, which advocates independence for Quebec. French name **QUÉBEC**. ■ (also **Quebec City**) its capital city, a port on the St. Lawrence River; pop. 167,517. Founded in 1608, it is Canada's oldest city. It was captured from the French by the British in 1759 after the battle of the Plains of Abraham and became capital of Lower Canada (later Quebec) in 1791. **2** a code word representing the letter Q, used in radio communication. —**Que·beck·er** (also **Que·bec·er**) *n.*

que·bra·cho /kāˈbräˌCHō; kə-/ ▸*n.* (*pl.* **-chos**) a South American tree whose timber and bark are a rich source of tannin. • Genera *Aspidosperma* (family Apocynaceae) and *Schinopsis* (family Anacardiaceae). ▷late 19th cent.: from Spanish, from *quebrar* 'to break' + *hacha* 'ax.'

Quech·ua /ˈkeCHwə/ (also **Quech·a** /ˈkeCHə/, **Quich·ua**) ▸*n.* (*pl.* same or **Quech·uas**) **1** a member of an American Indian people of Peru and parts of Bolivia, Chile, Colombia, and Ecuador. **2** the language or group of languages of this people.
▸*adj.* of or relating to this people or their language. ▷Spanish, abbreviation of Quechua *qheswa simi* 'valley speech,' the designation of a Quechua dialect. —**Quech·uan** /-wən/ (also **Quech·an** /ˈkeCHən/) *adj.* & *n.*

Queen /kwēn/, Ellery, U.S. writer of detective novels; pseudonym of *Frederic Dannay* (1905–82) and *Manfred Lee* (1905–71). The novels feature a detective also called Ellery Queen.

queen /kwēn/ ▸*n.* **1** the female ruler of an independent state, esp. one who inherits the position by right of birth. ■ (also **queen consort**) a king's wife. ■ a woman or thing regarded as excellent or outstanding of its kind: *the queen of romance novelists | Venice: Queen of the Adriatic.* ■ a woman or girl chosen to hold the most important position in a festival or event: *football stars and homecoming queens.* ■ (**the Queen**) *dated* (in the UK) the national anthem when there is a female sovereign. ■ *informal* a man's wife or girlfriend. **2** the most powerful chess piece that each player has, able to move any number of unobstructed squares in any direction along a rank, file, or diagonal on which it stands. **3** a playing card bearing a representation of a queen, normally ranking next below a king and above a jack. **4** *Entomology* a reproductive female in a colony of social ants, bees, wasps, etc. **5** an adult female cat that has not been spayed. **6** *informal, offensive* a male homosexual, typically one regarded as ostentatiously effeminate. ■ [with *modifier*] a man with a particular obsession or fetish: *a size queen | a leather queen.*
▸*v.* [*trans.*] **1** (**queen it over**) (of a woman) behave in an unpleasant and superior way toward. **2** *Chess* convert (a pawn) into a queen when it reaches the opponent's back rank on the board. ▷Old English *cwēn*, of Germanic origin; related to **QUEAN**. —**queen·dom** /-dəm/ *n.* —**queen·like** /-ˌlīk/ *adj.* —**queen·ship** /-ˌSHip/ *n.*

Queen Anne ▸*adj.* denoting a style of English furniture or architecture characteristic of the early 18th century. The furniture is noted for its simple, proportioned style and for its cabriole legs and walnut veneer; the architecture is characterized by the use of red brick in simple, basically rectangular designs.

Queen Anne's lace ▸*n.* the uncultivated form of the carrot, with broad round heads of tiny white flowers that resemble lace. Also called **WILD CARROT**. • *Daucus carota*, family Umbelliferae.

queen bee ▸*n.* the single reproductive female in a hive or colony of honeybees. ■ *informal* a woman who has a dominant or controlling position in a particular group or sphere.

queen cake ▸*n.* a small, soft, typically heart-shaped currant cake.

Queen Char·lotte Is·lands a group of more than 150 islands off the western coast of Canada, in British Columbia.

Queen Cit·y ▸*n.* the preeminent city of a region.

queen con·sort /känˈsôrt/ ▸*n.* see **QUEEN** (sense 1)

queen·fish /ˈkwēnˌfiSH/ ▸*n.* (*pl.* same or **-fish·es**) an edible marine fish, in particular: • a popular sporting fish of the Indo-Pacific (*Chorinemus lysan*, family Carangidae). • a drumfish of the Pacific coast of North America (*Seriphus politus*, family Sciaenidae).

queen·ly /ˈkwēnlē/ ▸*adj.* (**-li·er, -li·est**) fit for or appropriate to a queen. —**queen·li·ness** /-lēnis/ *n.*

Queen Maud Land /môd/ a part of Antarctica that borders the Atlantic Ocean, claimed since 1939 by Norway. ▷named after *Queen Maud* of Norway (1869–1938).

queen of pud·dings ▸*n.* a pudding made with bread, jam, and meringue.

Queens /kwēnz/ a borough of New York City, at the western end of Long Island; pop. 1,951,598.

Queen's Bench (in full **Queen's Bench Di·vi·sion**) ▸*n.* (in the UK) a division of the High Court of Justice.

Queens·ber·ry rules /ˈkwēnzˌberē/ the standard rules of boxing, originally drawn up in 1867 to govern the sport in Britain. ■ standard rules of polite or acceptable behavior. ▷late 19th cent.: named after John Sholto Douglas (1844–1900), 8th Marquess of *Queensberry*, who supervised the preparation of the rules.

queen scal·lop ▸*n.* a small, edible European scallop. • *Chlamys opercularis*, family Pectinidae.

Queen's Coun·sel (abbr.: **QC**) ▸*n. Brit.* a senior barrister appointed on the recommendation of the Lord Chancellor.

Queen's Coun·ty former name for **LAOIS**.

Queen's Eng·lish ▸*n.* (**the Queen's English**) standard English language as written and spoken by educated people in Britain.

queen·side /ˈkwēnˌsīd/ ▸*n. Chess* the half of the board on which both queens stand at the start of a game (the left-hand side for White, right for Black).

Queens·land /ˈkwēnzlənd; -ˌland/ a state that comprises the northeastern part of Australia; pop. 2,922,000; capital, Brisbane. Originally established in 1824 as a penal colony, Queensland was constituted a separate colony in 1859, having previously formed part of New South Wales, and was federated with the other states of Australia in 1901. —**Queens·land·er** *n.*

Queens·land nut ▸*n.* another term for **MACADAMIA**.

queen's pawn ▸*n. Chess* the pawn occupying the square immediately in front of each player's queen at the start of a game.

queens·ware /ˈkwēnzˌwe(ə)r/ ▸*n.* a type of fine, cream-colored Wedgwood pottery. ▷mid 18th cent. (as *Queen's ware*): named in honor of Queen Charlotte (wife of George III), who had been presented with a set in 1765.

queer /kwi(ə)r/ ▸*adj.* **1** strange; odd: *she had a queer feeling that they were being watched.* ■ [*predic.*] *dated* slightly ill. **2** *informal, usu. offensive* (esp. of a man) homosexual.
▸*n. informal, usu. offensive* a homosexual man.
▸*v.* [*trans.*] *informal* spoil or ruin (an agreement, event, or situation): *Reg didn't want someone meddling and queering the deal at the last minute.* ▷early 16th cent.: considered to be from German *quer* 'oblique, perverse,' but the origin is doubtful. —**queer·ish** *adj.* —**queer·ly** *adv.* —**queer·ness** *n.*

USAGE The word **queer** was first used to mean 'homosexual' in the early 20th century: it was originally, and often still is, a deliberately offensive and aggressive term when used by heterosexual people. In recent years, however, many gay people have taken the word **queer** and deliberately used it in place of **gay** or **homosexual**, in an attempt, by using the word positively, to deprive it of its negative power. This use of **queer** is now well established and widely used among gay people (esp. as an adjective or noun modifier, as in *queer rights; queer theory*) and at present exists alongside the other, deliberately offensive, use. The words **fag** and **faggot** are occasionally used in the same way. This use is similar to the way in which a racial epithet may be used *within* a racial group, but not by outsiders.
See also **usage** at **NIGGER**.

queer·core /ˈkwi(ə)rˌkôr/ ▸*n.* a cultural movement among young homosexuals that deliberately rebels against and dissociates itself from the established gay scene, having as its primary form of expression an aggressive type of punk-style music.

que·le·a /ˈkwēlēə/ ▸*n.* a brownish weaverbird found in Africa, the male of which has either a black face or a red head. • Genus *Quelea*, family Ploceidae: three species, in particular the **red-billed quelea** (*Q. quelea*), which occurs in huge numbers and is an important pest of crops. ▷modern Latin, perhaps from medieval Latin *qualea* 'quail.'

quell /kwel/ ▸*v.* [*trans.*] put an end to (a rebellion or other disorder), typically by the use of force: *extra police were called to quell the disturbance.* ■ subdue or silence someone: *Connor quelled him with a look.* ■ suppress (a feeling, esp. an unpleasant one): *he spoke up again to quell any panic among the assembled youngsters.* ▷Old English *cwellan* 'kill,' of Germanic origin; related to German *quälen* 'torture.' —**quell·er** *n.*

quench /kwenCH/ ▸*v.* [*trans.*] **1** satisfy (one's thirst) by drinking. ■ satisfy (a desire): *he only pursued her to quench an aching need.* **2** extinguish (a fire): *firemen hauled on hoses in a desperate bid to quench the flames.* ■ stifle or suppress (a feeling): *fury rose in him, but he quenched it.* ■ rapidly cool (red-hot metal or other material), esp. in cold water or oil. ■ *Physics & Electronics* suppress or damp (an effect such as luminescence, or an oscillation or discharge).

▸n. an act of quenching something very hot. ▷Old English -*cwencan* (in *acwencan* 'put out, extinguish'), of Germanic origin. —**quench·a·ble** *adj.* —**quench·er** *n.* (*chiefly Physics Metallurgy*) —**quench·less** *adj.* (*poetic/literary*).

que·nelle /kə'nel/ ▸n. (usu. **quenelles**) a small seasoned ball of pounded fish or meat. ▷French, probably from Alsatian German *knödel*.

quer·ce·tin /'kwərsətin/ ▸n. *Chemistry* a yellow crystalline pigment present in plants, used as a food supplement to reduce allergic responses or boost immunity. • A flavone derivative; chem. formula: $C_{15}H_{10}O_7$. ▷mid 19th cent.: probably from Latin *quercetum* 'oak grove' (from *quercus* 'oak') + -IN[1].

Quer·cia, Jacopo della, see DELLA QUERCIA.

Que·ré·ta·ro /ke'rātä,rō/ a state in central Mexico. ■ its capital city; pop. 454,000. In 1847, it was the scene of the signing of the treaty that ended the U.S.–Mexican war.

que·rist /'kwi(ə)rist/ ▸n. *chiefly archaic* a person who asks questions; a questioner. ▷mid 17th cent.: from Latin *quaerere* 'ask' + -IST.

quern /kwərn/ ▸n. a simple hand mill for grinding grain, typically consisting of two circular stones, the upper of which is rotated or rubbed to and fro on the lower one. ▷Old English *cweorn(e)*, of Germanic origin; related to Old Norse *kvern* and Dutch *kweern*.

quer·u·lous /'kwer(y)ələs/ ▸adj. complaining in a petulant or whining manner: *she became querulous and demanding.* ▷late 15th cent.: from late Latin *querulosus*, from Latin *querulus*, from *queri* 'complain.' —**quer·u·lous·ly** *adv.* —**quer·u·lous·ness** *n.*

que·ry /'kwi(ə)rē/ ▸n. (*pl.* **-ries**) a question, esp. one addressed to an official or organization: *a spokeswoman said queries could not be answered until Monday.* ■ used in writing or speaking to question the accuracy of a following statement or to introduce a question. ■ *chiefly Printing* a question mark.
▸v. (**-ries, -ried**) [*reporting verb*] ask a question about something, esp. in order to express one's doubts about it or to check its validity or accuracy: [with *clause*] *many people queried whether any harm had been done* | [*trans.*] *he queried the medical database.* | [with *direct speech*] *"Why not?" he queried.* ■ [*trans.*] put a question or questions to (someone): *when these officers were queried, they felt unhappy.* ▷mid 17th cent.: anglicized form of the Latin imperative *quaere!*, used in the 16th cent. in English as a verb in the sense 'inquire' and as a noun meaning 'query,' from Latin *quaerere* 'ask, seek.'

que·ry lan·guage ▸n. *Computing* a language for the specification of procedures for the retrieval (and sometimes also modification) of information from a database.

ques. ▸abbr. question.

que·sa·dil·la /,kāsə'dēyə/ ▸n. a tortilla filled with cheese and heated. ▷Spanish.

que·so blan·co /'kāsō 'blängkō/ ▸n. a fresh white cow's milk cheese used in Latin American cooking. ▷Spanish, 'white cheese.'

que·so fres·co /'kāsō 'freskō/ ▸n. a semisoft fresh Mexican cheese, white in color, typically served shredded over hot foods. ▷Spanish, 'fresh cheese.'

quest /kwest/ ▸n. a long or arduous search for something: ***the quest for** a reliable vaccine has intensified.* ■ (in medieval romance) an expedition made by a knight to accomplish a prescribed task.
▸v. [*intrans.*] search for something: *he was a real scientist, questing after truth.* ■ [*trans.*] *poetic/literary* search for; seek out. ▷late Middle English: from Old French *queste* (noun), *quester* (verb), based on Latin *quaerere* 'ask, seek.' See also INQUEST. —**quest·er** (also **questor**) *n.* —**quest·ing·ly** *adv.*

ques·tion /'kweschən/ ▸n. a sentence worded or expressed so as to elicit information: *we hope this leaflet has been helpful in answering your questions.* ■ a doubt about the truth or validity of something: *there is no question that America faces the threat of Balkanization.* ■ the raising of a doubt about or objection to something: *Edward was the only one she obeyed **without question** | her loyalty is really **beyond question**.* ■ a matter forming the basis of a problem requiring resolution: *we have kept an eye on the question of political authority.* ■ a matter or concern depending on or involving a specified condition or thing: *it was not simply **a question of** age and hierarchy.*
▸v. [*trans.*] ask questions of (someone), esp. in an official context: *four men were being questioned about the killings* | [as *n.*] (**questioning**) *the young lieutenant escorted us to the barracks for questioning.* ■ feel or express doubt about; raise objections to: *members had questioned the cost of the scheme.* ▷late Middle English: from Old French *question* (noun), *questionner* (verb), from Latin *quaestio(n-)*, from *quaerere* 'ask, seek.' —**ques·tion·er** *n.* —**ques·tion·ing·ly** *adv.*
▸PHRASES □ **be (just** or **only) a question of time** be certain to happen sooner or later. □ **bring something into question** raise an issue for further consideration or discussion: *technology had brought into question the whole future of work.* □ **come into question** become an issue for further consideration or discussion: *our Sunday Trading laws have come into question.* □ **in question 1** being considered or discussed: *on the day in question, there were several serious emergencies.* **2** in doubt: *all of the old certainties are in question.* □ **no question of** no possibility of. □ **out of the question** too impracticable or unlikely to merit discussion. □ **question of fact** *Law* an issue to be decided by a jury. □ **question of law** *Law* an issue to be decided by a judge. □ **put the question** (in a formal debate or meeting) require supporters and opponents of a proposal to record their votes.

ques·tion·a·ble /'kweschənəbəl/ ▸adj. doubtful as regards truth or quality: [with *clause*] *it is **questionable whether** any of these exceptions is genuine.* See note at DOUBTFUL. ■ not clearly honest, honorable, or wise: *a few men of allegedly questionable character.* —**ques·tion·a·bil·i·ty** /,kweschənə'bilətē/ *n.* —**ques·tion·a·ble·ness** *n.* —**ques·tion·a·bly** /-əblē/ *adv.*

ques·tion·ar·y /'kweschə,nerē/ ▸n. (*pl.* **-ar·ies**) a questionnaire. ▷late 19th cent.: from French *questionnaire* (see QUESTIONNAIRE).

ques·tion mark ▸n. a punctuation mark (?) indicating a question. ■ *figurative* used to express doubt or uncertainty about something: *there's **a question mark over** his future.*

ques·tion·naire /,kweschə'ne(ə)r/ ▸n. a set of printed or written questions with a choice of answers, devised for the purposes of a survey or statistical study. ▷late 19th cent.: from French, from *questionner* 'to question.'

Quet·ta /'kwetə/ a city in western Pakistan, the capital of Baluchistan province; pop. 350,000.

quet·zal /ket'säl/ ▸n. **1** a bird of the trogon family, with iridescent green plumage and typically red underparts, found in the forests of tropical America. • Genus *Pharomachrus*, family Trogonidae: five species, esp. the **resplendent quetzal** (*P. mocinno*), the male of which has very long tail coverts and was venerated by the Aztecs. **2** the basic monetary unit of Guatemala, equal to 100 centavos. ▷early 19th cent. (sense 1): from Spanish, from Aztec *quetzalli* 'brightly colored tail feather.'

Quet·zal·co·a·tl /,ketsəlkō'ätl/ the plumed serpent god of the Toltec and Aztec civilizations.

Traditionally the god of the morning and evening star, he later became known as the patron of priests, inventor of books and of the calendar, and as the symbol of death and resurrection. His worship involved human sacrifice. Legend said that he would return in another age, and when Montezuma, last king of the Aztecs, received news of the landing of Cortés and his men in 1519, he thought that Quetzalcóatl had returned.

quet·zal·co·a·tlus /,ketsəlkə'wätləs/ ▸n. a giant pterosaur of the late Cretaceous period. It was the largest ever flying animal, with a wingspan of up to 50 feet (15 m). • Genus *Quetzalcoatlus*, family Azhdarchidae, order Pterosauria. ▷modern Latin, from the name of the Aztec god QUETZALCOATL.

queue /kyoo/ ▸n. **1** *chiefly Brit.* a line or sequence of people or vehicles awaiting their turn to be attended to or to proceed. **2** *Computing* a list of data items, commands, etc., stored so as to be retrievable in a definite order, usually the order of insertion. **3** *archaic* a braid of hair worn at the back.
▸v. (**queues, queued, queu·ing** or **queue·ing**) [*intrans.*] *chiefly Brit.* **1** take one's place in a queue: *in the war they had **queued for** food* | [with *infinitive*] *figurative companies are **queuing up** to move to the bay.* **2** [*trans.*] *Computing* arrange in a queue. ▷late 16th cent. (as a heraldic term denoting the tail of an animal): from French, based on Latin *cauda* 'tail.' Compare with CUE[2]. Sense 1 dates from the mid 19th cent.

Que·zon Cit·y /'kāzän; -sōn/ a city on the island of Luzon in the northern Philippines; pop. 1,667,000. Established in 1940, it was the capital of the Philippines 1948–76. ▷named after Manuel Luis *Quezon* (1878–1944), the first president of the republic.

quib·ble /'kwibəl/ ▸n. **1** a slight objection or criticism: *the only quibble about this book is the price.* **2** *archaic* a play on words; a pun.
▸v. [*intrans.*] argue or raise objections about a trivial matter: *they are always quibbling about the amount they are prepared to pay.* ▷early 17th cent. (in the sense 'play on words, pun'): diminutive of obsolete *quib* 'a petty objection,' probably from Latin *quibus*, dative and ablative plural of *qui, quae, quod* 'who, what, which,' frequently used in legal documents and so associated with subtle distinctions or verbal niceties. —**quib·bler** *n.* —**quib·bling·ly** *adv.*

Qui·ché /kē'chā/ ▸n. (*pl.* same or **-chés**) **1** a member of a people inhabiting the western highlands of Guatemala. **2** the Mayan language of this people.
▸adj. of or relating to this people or their language. ▷the name in Quiché.

quiche /kēsh/ ▸n. a baked flan or tart with a savory filling thickened with eggs. ▷French, from Alsatian dialect *Küchen*; related to German *Kuchen* 'cake.'

Quich·ua /'kichwə/ ▸n. & adj. variant spelling of QUECHUA.

quick /kwik/ ▸adj. **1** moving fast or doing something in a short time: *some children are particularly quick learners | I was much quicker than he was and held him at bay for several laps* | [with *infinitive*] *he was always quick to point out her faults.* ■ lasting or taking a short time: *she took a quick look through the drawers | we went to the pub for a quick drink.* ■ happening with little or no delay: prompt: *children like to see quick results from their efforts.* **2** (of a person) prompt to understand, think, or learn; intelligent: *it was quick of him to spot the mistake.* ■ (of a person's eye or ear) keenly perceptive; alert. ■ (of a person's temper) easily roused.
▸adv. *informal* at a fast rate; quickly: *he'll find some place where he can make money quicker* | [as *exclam.*] *Get out, quick!*
▸n. **1** (**the quick**) the soft, tender flesh below the growing part of a fingernail or toenail. ■ *figurative* the central or most sensitive part of someone or something. **2** [as *plural n.*] (**the quick**) *archaic* those who are living: *the quick and the dead.* ▷Old English *cwic, cwicu* 'alive, animated, alert,' of Germanic origin; related to Dutch *kwiek* 'sprightly' and German *keck* 'saucy,' from an Indo-European root shared by Latin *vivus* 'alive' and Greek *bios, zōē* 'life.' —**quick·ly** *adv.* —**quick·ness** *n.*
▸PHRASES □ **cut someone to the quick** cause someone deep distress by a hurtful remark or action. □ **(as) quick as a flash** see FLASH. □ **quick on the draw** see DRAW. □ **quick with child** *archaic* at a stage of pregnancy when movements of the fetus have been felt.

quick-and-dirt·y ▸adj. *informal* makeshift; done or produced hastily: *a quick-and-dirty synopsis of their work.*

quick·en /'kwikən/ ▸v. **1** make or become faster or quicker: [*trans.*] *she quickened her pace, desperate to escape* | [*intrans.*] *I felt my pulse quicken.* **2** [*intrans.*] spring to life; become animated: *her interest quickened* | [as *adj.*] (**quickening**) *he looked with quickening curiosity through the smoke.* ■ [*trans.*] stimulate: *the coroner's words suddenly quickened his own memories.* ■ [*trans.*] give or restore life to: *on the third day after his death the human body of Jesus was quickened by the Spirit.* ■ *archaic* (of a woman) reach a stage in pregnancy when movements of the fetus can be felt. ■ *archaic* (of a fetus) begin to show signs of life. ■ [*trans.*] *archaic* make (a fire) burn brighter.

THE RIGHT WORD **animate, enliven, invigorate, quicken, stimulate, vitalize**

While all of these verbs mean to make alive or lively, **quicken** suggests the rousing or renewal of life, especially life that has been inert or suspended (*she felt the baby quicken during her second trimester of pregnancy*).

Animate means to impart life, motion, or activity to something that previously lacked such a quality (*a discussion animated by the presence of so many young people*).

Stimulate means to goad into activity from a state of inertia, inactivity, or lethargy (*the professor's constant questions stimulated her students to do more research*), while **enliven** refers to a stimulating influence that brightens or makes lively what was previously dull, depressed, or torpid (*a sudden change in the weather enlivened the group's activities*).

Invigorate and **vitalize** both mean to fill with vigor or energy, but the former refers to physical energy (*invigorated by the climb up the mountain*), while the latter implies that energy has been imparted in a nonphysical sense (*to vitalize an otherwise dull meeting*).

quick-freeze ▸v. [*trans.*] freeze (food) rapidly so as to preserve its nutritional value.

quick·ie /ˈkwikē/ *informal* ▸*n.* a thing done or made quickly or hastily, in particular: ■ a rapidly consumed alcoholic drink. ■ a brief act of sexual intercourse.
▸*adj.* done or made quickly: *his wife cooperated with a quickie divorce.*

quick·lime /ˈkwik,līm/ ▸*n.* see LIME[1].

quick march ▸*n.* a brisk military march.
▸*exclam.* a command to begin marching quickly.

quick-re·lease ▸*adj.* (of a device) designed for rapid release: *a quick-release button.*

quick·sand /ˈkwik,sand/ ▸*n.* (also **quicksands**) loose wet sand that yields easily to pressure and sucks in anything resting on or falling into it: *figurative John found himself sinking fast in financial quicksand.*

quick·set /ˈkwik,set/ ▸*n. Brit.* hedging, esp. of hawthorn, grown from slips or cuttings.

quick·sil·ver /ˈkwik,silvər/ ▸*n.* the liquid metal mercury. ■ used in similes and metaphors to describe something that moves or changes very quickly, or that is difficult to hold or contain: *his mood changed like quicksilver.*

quick·step /ˈkwik,step/ ▸*n.* a dance that combines the movements of the waltz and the Charleston. ■ a piece of music written for such a dance, much like a fast foxtrot. ■ a step used when marching in quick time.
▸*v.* (**-stepped**, **-step·ping**) [*intrans.*] dance the quickstep.

quick·thorn /ˈkwik,THôrn/ ▸*n.* another term for HAWTHORN.

quick time ▸*n. Military* marching that is conducted at about 120 paces per minute.

quick trick ▸*n.* (usu. **quick tricks**) *Bridge* a card such as an ace (or a king in a suit where the ace is also held) that can normally be relied on to win a trick.

quick-wit·ted ▸*adj.* showing or characterized by an ability to think or respond quickly or effectively. —**quick-wit·ted·ness** *n.*

quid[1] /kwid/ ▸*n.* (*pl.* same) *Brit., informal* one pound sterling: *we paid him four hundred quid.* ▷late 17th cent.: of obscure origin.

quid[2] ▸*n.* a lump of tobacco for chewing. ▷early 18th cent.: variant of CUD.

quid·di·ty /ˈkwiditē/ ▸*n.* (*pl.* **-ties**) *chiefly Philosophy* the inherent nature or essence of someone or something. ■ a distinctive feature; a peculiarity: *his quirks and quiddities.* ▷late Middle English: from medieval Latin *quidditas*, from Latin *quid* 'what.'

quid·nunc /ˈkwid,nəNGk/ ▸*n. archaic* an inquisitive and gossipy person. ▷early 18th cent.: from Latin *quid nunc?* 'what now?'

quid pro quo /ˈkwid ,prō ˈkwō/ ▸*n.* (*pl.* **quos**) a favor or advantage granted or expected in return for something: *the pardon was a quid pro quo for their help in releasing hostages.* ▷mid 16th cent. (denoting a medicine substituted for another): Latin, 'something for something.'

qui·es·cent /kwēˈesnt; kwī-/ ▸*adj.* in a state or period of inactivity or dormancy: *strikes were headed by groups of workers who had previously been quiescent | quiescent ulcerative colitis.* See note at LATENT. ▷mid 17th cent.: from Latin *quiescent-* 'being still,' from the verb *quiescere*, from *quies* 'quiet.' —**qui·es·cence** *n.* —**qui·es·cent·ly** *adv.*

qui·et /ˈkwīət/ ▸*adj.* (**qui·et·er**, **qui·et·est**) **1** making little or no noise: *the car has a quiet, economical engine | I was as quiet as I could be, but he knew I was there.* ■ (of a place, period of time, or situation) without much activity, disturbance, or excitement: *the street below was quiet, little traffic braving the snow.* ■ without being disturbed or interrupted: *all he wanted was a quiet drink.* **2** carried out discreetly, secretly, or with moderation: *we wanted a quiet wedding | I'll have a quiet word with him.* ■ (of a person) tranquil and reserved by nature; not brash or forceful: *his quiet, middle-aged parents.* ■ [*attrib.*] expressed in a restrained or understated way: *Molly spoke with quiet confidence.* ■ (of a color or garment) unobtrusive; not bright or showy.
▸*n.* absence of noise or bustle; silence; calm: *the ringing of the telephone shattered the early morning quiet.* ■ freedom from disturbance or interruption by others: *he understood her wish for* ***peace and quiet.*** ■ a peaceful or settled state of affairs in social or political life: *after several months of comparative quiet, the scandal reerupted in August.*
▸*v.* make or become silent, calm, or still: [*trans.*] *there are ways of* ***quieting*** *kids* ***down*** | [*intrans.*] *the journalists* ***quieted down*** *as Judy stepped on to the dais.* ▷Middle English (originally as a noun denoting peace as opposed to war): via Old French, based on Latin *quies, quiet-* 'repose, quiet.' —**qui·et·ly** *adv.* —**qui·et·ness** *n.*
▸*PHRASES* □ **do anything for a quiet life** see LIFE. □ **keep quiet** (or **keep someone quiet**) refrain or prevent someone from speaking or from disclosing something secret. □ **keep something quiet** (or **keep quiet about something**) refrain from disclosing information about something; keep something secret. □ **on the quiet** *informal* without anyone knowing or noticing; secretly or unobtrusively. □ (**as**) **quiet as the grave** see GRAVE[1]. □ (**as**) **quiet as a mouse** (of a person or animal) extremely quiet or docile.

qui·et·en /ˈkwīətn/ ▸*v. chiefly Brit.* make or become quiet and calm: [*trans.*] *her mother was trying to quieten her* | [*intrans.*] *things seemed to have* ***quietened down.***

qui·et·ism /ˈkwīə,tizəm/ ▸*n.* (in the Christian faith) devotional contemplation and abandonment of the will as a form of religious mysticism. ■ calm acceptance of things as they are without attempts to resist or change them: *political quietism.* ▷late 17th cent. (denoting the religious mysticism based on the teachings of the Spanish priest Miguel de Molinos (*c.*1640–97)): from Italian *quietismo*, based on Latin *quies, quiet-* 'quiet.' —**qui·et·ist** *n.* & *adj.* —**qui·et·is·tic** /,kwīəˈtistik/ *adj.*

qui·e·tude /ˈkwīə,t(y)o͞od/ ▸*n.* a state of stillness, calmness, and quiet in a person or place. ▷late 16th cent.: from French *quiétude* or medieval Latin *quietudo*, from Latin *quietus* 'quiet.'

qui·e·tus /ˈkwīətəs/ ▸*n.* (*pl.* **qui·et·us·es**) death or something that causes death, regarded as a release from life. ■ *archaic* something that has a calming or soothing effect. ▷late Middle English: abbreviation of medieval Latin *quietus est* 'he is quit' (see QUIT[1]), originally used as a form of receipt or discharge on payment of a debt.

quiff /kwif/ ▸*n. chiefly Brit.* a piece of hair, esp. on a man, brushed upward and backward from the forehead. ▷late 19th cent. (originally denoting a lock of hair plastered down on the forehead, esp. as worn by soldiers): of unknown origin.

quill /kwil/ ▸*n.* **1** (also **quill feather**) any of the main wing or tail feathers of a bird. ■ the hollow shaft of a feather, esp. the lower part or calamus that lacks barbs. ■ (also **quill pen**) a pen made from a main wing or tail feather of a large bird by pointing and slitting the end of the shaft. **2** an object in the form of a thin tube, in particular: ■ the hollow sharp spines of a porcupine, hedgehog, or other spiny mammal. ■ (**quills**) *informal, dated* panpipes. ■ a weaver's spindle.
▸*v.* [*trans.*] **1** form (fabric) into small cylindrical folds. **2** pierce or cover (fabric or bark) with quills. ▷late Middle English (in the senses 'hollow stem' and 'shaft of a feather'): probably from Middle Low German *quiele.*

quill·ing /ˈkwiliNG/ ▸*n.* a piece of quilled lace or other fabric used as a trim. ■ a type of ornamental craftwork involving the shaping of paper, fabric, or glass into delicate pleats or folds.

quill·work /ˈkwil,wərk/ ▸*n.* a type of decoration for clothing and possessions characteristic of certain North American Indian peoples, using softened and dyed porcupine quills to make elaborate applied designs.

quill·wort /ˈkwil,wərt; -,wôrt/ ▸*n.* a plant related to the club mosses, having a dense rosette of long slender leaves, the bases of which contain the spore-producing organs, and occurring typically as a submerged aquatic. • Genus *Isoetes*, family Isoetaceae, class Lycopsida.

quilt /kwilt/ ▸*n.* a warm bed covering made of padding enclosed between layers of fabric and kept in place by lines of stitching, typically applied in a decorative design. ■ a knitted or fabric bedspread with decorative stitching. ■ a layer of padding used for insulation.
▸*v.* [*trans.*] join together (layers of fabric or padding) with lines of stitching to form a bed covering or a warm garment, or for decorative effect. ▷Middle English: from Old French *cuilte*, from Latin *culcita* 'mattress, cushion.' —**quilt·er** *n.*

quilt·ed /ˈkwiltid/ ▸*adj.* (of a garment, bed covering, or sleeping bag) made of two layers of cloth filled with padding held in place by lines of stitching: *a blue quilted jacket.*

quilt·ing /ˈkwiltiNG/ ▸*n.* the making of quilts, esp. as a craft or leisure activity. ■ the work so produced; quilted material. ■ the pattern of stitching used for such work.

quin /kwin/ ▸*n. informal, chiefly Brit.* short for QUINTUPLET.

qui·nac·ri·done /kwəˈnakrə,dōn/ ▸*n. Chemistry* any of a group of synthetic organic compounds whose molecules contain three benzene and two pyridine rings arranged alternately. They include a number of red to violet pigments. ▷early 20th cent.: from *quin(oline)* + *acrid(ine)* + -ONE.

quin·a·crine /ˈkwinə,krin/ ▸*n. Medicine* a synthetic compound derived from acridine, used as an anthelmintic and antimalarial drug. ■ (in full **quinacrine mustard**) *Biochemistry* a nitrogen mustard derived from this, used as a fluorescent stain for chromosomes. ▷1930s: blend of QUININE and ACRIDINE.

qui·na·ry /ˈkwī,nerē/ ▸*adj.* of or relating to the number five, in particular: ■ of the fifth order or rank. ■ *historical Zoology* relating to or denoting a former system of classification in which the animal kingdom is divided into five subkingdoms, and each subkingdom into five classes. ▷early 17th cent.: from Latin *quinarius*, from *quini* 'five at once, a set of five,' from *quinque* 'five.'

quince /kwins/ ▸*n.* **1** a hard, acid, pear-shaped fruit used in preserves or as flavoring. **2** the shrub or small tree that bears this fruit, native to western Asia. • *Cydonia oblonga*, family Rosaceae. ■ (**Japanese quince**) another term for JAPONICA. ▷Middle English (originally a collective plural): from Old French *cooin*, from Latin *(malum) cotoneum*, variant of *(malum) cydonium* 'apple of *Cydonia* (= Canea, in Crete).'

quin·cen·ten·ar·y /,kwinsenˈtenərē; kwinˈsentə,nerē/ ▸*n.* & *adj.* another term for QUINCENTENNIAL.

quin·cen·ten·ni·al /,kwinsenˈtenēəl/ ▸*n.* the five-hundredth anniversary of a significant event.
▸*adj.* of or relating to such an anniversary. ▷late 19th cent.: from Latin *quinque* 'five' + CENTENNIAL.

Quin·cey, Thomas De, see **DE QUINCEY**.

quin·cunx /ˈkwin,kəNGks/ ▸*n.* (*pl.* **quin·cunx·es**) **1** an arrangement of five objects with four at the corners of a square or rectangle and the fifth at its center, used for the five on dice or playing cards, and in planting trees. **2** *Astrology* an aspect of 150°, equivalent to five zodiacal signs. ▷mid 17th cent.: from Latin, literally 'five twelfths,' from *quinque* 'five' + *uncia* 'twelfth.' —**quin·cun·cial** /,kwinˈkənSHəl/ *adj.* —**quin·cun·cial·ly** /,kwinˈkənSHəlē/ *adv.*

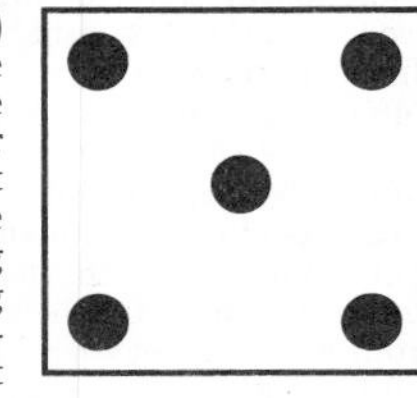
quincunx 1

Quin·cy **1** /ˈkwinsē/ an industrial and commercial city in west central Illinois, on the Mississippi River; pop. 39,681. **2** /-zē/ a historic industrial city in eastern Massachusetts, on Boston Harbor, southeast of Boston, a shipbuilding center; pop. 88,025.

Quine /kwīn/, Willard Van Orman (1908–2000), U.S. philosopher and logician. A radical critic of modern empiricism, he took issue with the philosophy of language proposed by Rudolf Carnap, arguing that "no statement is immune from revision" and that even the principles of logic themselves can be questioned and replaced.

qui·nel·la /kwiˈnelə/ (also **qui·niel·a** /kēnˈyelə/) ▸*n.* a bet in which the first two places in a race must be predicted, but not necessarily in the correct order. Compare with EXACTA. ▷1940s: from Latin American Spanish *quiniela.*

quin·i·dine /ˈkwinə,dēn/ ▸*n. Medicine* a compound obtained from cinchona bark and used to treat irregularities of heart rhythm. It is an isomer of quinine. ▷mid 19th cent.: from Spanish *quina* 'cinchona bark' (from Quechua *kina* 'bark') + -IDE + -INE[4].

qui·nine /ˈkwī,nīn/ ▸*n.* a bitter crystalline compound present in cinchona bark, used as a tonic and formerly as an antimalarial drug. • An alkaloid; chem. formula: $C_{20}H_{24}N_2O_2$. ▷early 19th cent.: from Spanish *quina* 'cinchona bark' (from Quechua *kina* 'bark') + -INE[4].

Quinn /kwin/, Anthony (Rudolph Oaxaca) (1915–2001), U.S. actor; born in Mexico. His many movies include *Viva Zapata* (Academy Award, 1952), *La Strada* (1954), *Lust for Life* (Academy Award, 1956), *Wild Is the Wind* (1957), *Zorba the Greek* (1964), and *A Walk in the Clouds* (1995).

qui·noa /ˈkēnwä/ ▸*n.* a goosefoot found in the Andes, where it was widely cultivated for its edible starchy seeds before the introduction of Old World grains. • *Chenopodium quinoa*, family Chenopodiaceae. ■ the grainlike seeds of this plant, used as food and in the production of alcoholic drinks. ▷early 17th cent.: Spanish spelling of Quechua *kinua, kinoa*.

quin·o·line /ˈkwinəlin/ ▸*n. Chemistry* a pungent oily liquid present in coal tar and bone oil. • A heteroaromatic compound with fused benzene and pyridine rings; chem. formula: C_9H_7N. ▷mid 19th cent.: from Spanish *quina* (see **QUININE**) + **-OL** + **-INE**[4].

quin·o·lone /ˈkwinəˌlōn; ˈkwinl,ōn/ ▸*n.* any of a class of antibiotics used in treating a variety of mainly gram-negative infections, and thought to be responsible for antibiotic resistance in some microbes. Quinolones include the fluoroquinolones, which were developed later and contain fluorine.

qui·none /ˈkwinōn/ ▸*n. Chemistry* another term for 1,4-benzoquinone (see **BENZOQUINONE**). ■ any compound with the same ring structure as 1,4-benzoquinone. ▷mid 19th cent.: from Spanish *quina* (see **QUININE**) + **-ONE**.

Quin·qua·ges·i·ma /ˌkwiNGkwəˈjesəmə/ (also **Quinquagesima Sunday**) *n.* the Sunday before the beginning of Lent. ▷from medieval Latin, feminine of Latin *quinquagesimus* 'fiftieth,' on the pattern of *Quadragesima* (because it is ten days before the forty penitential days of Lent).

quinque- ▸*comb. form* five; having five: *quinquevalent*. ▷from Latin *quinque* 'five.'

quin·quen·ni·al /kwiNGˈkwenēəl/ ▸*adj.* recurring every five years. ■ lasting for or relating to a period of five years. ▷late 15th cent. (in the sense 'lasting five years'): from Latin *quinquennis* (from *quinque* 'five' + *annus* 'year') + **-AL**. **—quin·quen·ni·al·ly** *adv.*

quin·quen·ni·um /kwiNGˈkwenēəm/ ▸*n.* (*pl.* **-quen·ni·a** /-ˈkwenēə/ or **-quen·ni·ums**) a specified period of five years. ▷early 17th cent.: from Latin, from *quinque* 'five' + *annus* 'year.'

quin·que·va·lent /ˌkwiNGkwəˈvālənt/ ▸*adj. Chemistry* another term for **PENTAVALENT**.

quin·sy /ˈkwinzē/ ▸*n.* inflammation of the throat, esp. an abscess in the region of the tonsils. ▷Middle English: from Old French *quinencie*, from medieval Latin *quinancia*, from Greek *kunankhē* 'canine quinsy,' from *kun-* 'dog' + *ankhein* 'throttle.'

quint /kwint/ ▸*n.* **1** (in piquet) a sequence of five cards of the same suit. A run of ace, king, queen, jack, and ten is a **quint major** and one of jack, ten, nine, eight, and seven a **quint minor**. [late 17th cent.: from French, from Latin *quintus* 'fifth,' from *quinque* 'five.'] **2** short for **QUINTUPLET**.

quin·ta /ˈkwintə/ ▸*n.* (in Spain, Portugal, and Latin America) a large house in the country or on the outskirts of a town. ■ a country estate, in particular a wine-growing estate in Portugal. ▷Spanish and Portuguese, from *quinta parte* 'fifth part' (originally referring to the amount of a farm's produce paid in rent).

quin·tain /ˈkwintn/ ▸*n. historical* a post set up as a mark in tilting with a lance, typically with a sandbag attached that would swing around and strike an unsuccessful tilter. ■ (**the quintain**) the medieval military exercise of tilting at such a post. ▷late Middle English: from Old French *quintaine*, perhaps based on Latin *quintana*, a street in a Roman camp separating the fifth and sixth maniples, where military exercises were performed (from *quintus* 'fifth').

quin·tal /ˈkwintl/ ▸*n.* a unit of weight equal to a hundredweight (112 lb) or formerly, 100 lb. ■ a unit of weight equal to 100 kg. ▷late Middle English: via Old French from medieval Latin *quintale*, from Arabic *ḳinṭār*, based on Latin *centenarius* 'containing a hundred.'

Quin·ta·na Roo /kēnˈtänä ˈro͞o/ a state in southeastern Mexico, on the Yucatán Peninsula.

quinte /kant/ ▸*n. Fencing* the fifth of eight standard parrying positions. ▷early 18th cent.: French, from Latin *quintus* 'fifth,' from *quinque* 'five.'

Quin·ter·o /kwinˈte(ə)rō; kēn-/, Jose (1924–99), U.S. theatrical director; born in Panama. He was noted for directing plays by Eugene O'Neill and for founding Circle in the Square, a theater in New York City's Greenwich Village. He directed many Broadway plays, including *Long Day's Journey into Night* (1956), *Strange Interlude* (1963). and *A Moon for the Misbegotten* (1973).

quin·tes·sence /kwinˈtesəns/ ▸*n.* the most perfect or typical example of a quality or class: *he was* ***the quintessence of*** *political professionalism.* ■ the aspect of something regarded as the intrinsic and central constituent of its character: *we were all brought up to believe that advertising is* ***the quintessence of*** *marketing.* ■ a refined essence or extract of a substance. ■ (in classical and medieval philosophy) a fifth substance in addition to the four elements, thought to compose the heavenly bodies and to be latent in all things. ▷late Middle English (as a term in philosophy): via French from medieval Latin *quinta essentia* 'fifth essence.'

quin·tes·sen·tial /ˌkwintəˈsenCHəl/ ▸*adj.* representing the most perfect or typical example of a quality or class: *he was the quintessential tough guy—strong, silent, and self-contained.* **—quin·tes·sen·tial·ly** *adv.*

quin·tet /kwinˈtet/ ▸*n.* a group of five people playing music or singing together. ■ a musical composition for such a group. ■ any group of five people or things: *a novel about a quintet of interrelated lovers.* ▷late 18th cent.: from French *quintette* or Italian *quintetto*, from *quinto* 'fifth,' from Latin *quintus*.

quin·tile /ˈkwin,tīl/ ▸*n.* **1** *Statistics* any of five equal groups into which a population can be divided according to the distribution of values of a particular variable. ■ each of the four values of the random variable that divide a population into five such groups. **2** *Astrology* an aspect of 72° (one fifth of a circle). ▷early 17th cent.: from Latin *quintilis (mensis)* 'fifth month, July,' from *quintus* 'fifth.'

Quin·til·ian /kwinˈtilēən/ (*c.*AD 35–*c.*96), Roman rhetorician; Latin name *Marcus Fabius Quintilianus*. He is noted for his *Education of an Orator*, a comprehensive treatment of the art of rhetoric and the training of an orator.

quin·til·lion /kwinˈtilyən/ ▸*cardinal number* (*pl.* **-lions** or (with numeral) same) a thousand raised to the power of six (10^{18}). ■ *dated, chiefly Brit.* a million raised to the power of five (10^{30}). ▷late 17th cent.: from French, from *million*, by substitution of the prefix *quinti-* 'five' (from Latin *quintus* 'fifth') for the initial letters. **—quin·til·lionth** /-yənTH/ *ordinal number.*

quin·tu·ple /kwinˈt(y)o͞opəl;-ˈtəpəl/ ▸*adj.* [*attrib.*] consisting of five parts or things. ■ five times as much or as many. ■ (of time in music) having five beats in a bar.
▸*v.* increase or cause to increase fivefold.
▸*n.* a fivefold number or amount; a set of five. ▷late 16th cent.: via French from medieval Latin *quintuplus*, from Latin *quintus* 'fifth' + *-plus* as in *duplus* (see **DUPLE**). **—quin·tu·ply** /-(ə)lē/ *adv.*

quin·tu·plet /kwinˈtəplət; -ˈt(y)o͞oplət/ ▸*n.* **1** (usu. **quintuplets**) each of five children born to the same mother at one birth. **2** *Music* a group of five notes to be performed in the time of three or four. ▷late 19th cent.: from **QUINTUPLE**, on the pattern of words such as *triplet*.

quin·tu·pli·cate ▸*adj.* /kwinˈt(y)o͞opləˌkit/ fivefold. ■ of which five copies are made.
▸*v.* /kwinˈt(y)o͞opləˌkāt/ [*trans.*] multiply by five. ▷mid 17th cent.: from **QUINTUPLE**, on the pattern of words such as *quadruplicate*.
▸*PHRASE* □ **in quintuplicate** in five identical copies.■ in groups of five.

quip /kwip/ ▸*n.* a witty remark. ■ *archaic* a verbal equivocation.
▸*v.* (**quipped**, **quip·ping**) [*intrans.*] make a witty remark: [with *direct speech*] *"Flattery will get you nowhere," she quipped.* ▷mid 16th cent.: perhaps from Latin *quippe* 'indeed, forsooth.' **—quip·ster** /-stər/ *n.*

qui·pu /ˈkēpo͞o; ˈkwipo͞o/ ▸*n.* an ancient Inca device for recording information, consisting of variously colored threads knotted in different ways. ▷from Quechua *khipu* 'knot.'

quire /kwīr/ ▸*n.* four sheets of paper or parchment folded to form eight leaves, as in medieval manuscripts. ■ any collection of leaves one within another in a manuscript or book. ■ 25 (formerly 24) sheets of paper; one twentieth of a ream. ▷Middle English: from Old French *quaier*, from Latin *quaterni* 'set of four.'

quirk /kwərk/ ▸*n.* **1** a peculiar behavioral habit: *his distaste for travel is an endearing quirk.* ■ a strange chance occurrence: *a strange quirk of fate had led her to working for Nathan.* ■ a sudden twist, turn, or curve: *wry humor put a slight quirk in his mouth.* **2** *Architecture* an acute hollow between convex or other moldings.
▸*v.* [*intrans.*] (of a person's mouth or eyebrow) move or twist suddenly, esp. to express surprise or amusement. ■ [*trans.*] move or twist (one's mouth or eyebrow) in such a way. ▷early 16th cent. (as a verb): of unknown origin. The early sense of the noun was 'subtle verbal twist, quibble,' later 'unexpected twist.' **—quirk·ish** *adj.*

quirk·y /ˈkwərkē/ ▸*adj.* (**quirk·i·er**, **quirk·i·est**) characterized by peculiar or unexpected traits: *her sense of humor was decidedly quirky.* **—quirk·i·ly** /-kəlē/ *adv.* **—quirk·i·ness** /-kēnis/ *n.*

quirt /kwərt/ ▸*n.* a short-handled riding whip with a braided leather lash.
▸*v.* [*trans.*] hit with a whip of this kind. ▷mid 19th cent. (originally U.S.): from Spanish *cuerda* 'cord' (from Latin *chorda* 'cord') or from Mexican Spanish *cuarta* 'whip.'

quis·ling /ˈkwizliNG/ ▸*n.* a traitor who collaborates with an enemy force occupying their country. ▷World War II: from the name of Major Vidkun *Quisling* (1887–1945), the Norwegian army officer and diplomat who ruled Norway on behalf of the German occupying forces 1940–45.

quit[1] /kwit/ ▸*v.* (**quit·ting**; *past* and *past part.* **quit·ted** or **quit**) **1** [*trans.*] leave (a place), usually permanently: *he was ordered to quit the cabin immediately.* ■ *informal* resign from (a job): *she quit her job in a pizza restaurant* | [*intrans.*] *he* **quit as** *manager of struggling Third Division City.* ■ *informal* stop or discontinue (an action or activity): *quit moaning!* | *I want to quit smoking.* **2** (**quit oneself**) [with *adverbial*] *archaic* behave in a specified way: *quit yourselves like men, and fight.*
▸*adj.* [*predic.*] (**quit of**) rid of: *I want to be quit of him.* ▷Middle English (in the sense 'set free'): from Old French *quiter* (verb), *quite* (adjective), from Latin *quietus*, past participle of *quiescere* 'be still,' from *quies* 'quiet.'
▸*PHRASE* □ **quit hold of** *archaic* let go of.

quit[2] ▸*n.* [in *combination*] used in names of various small songbirds found in the Caribbean area, e.g., **bananaquit**, **grassquit**. ▷mid 19th cent.: probably imitative.

quitch /kwiCH/ (also **quitch grass**) ▸*n.* another term for **COUCH GRASS**. ▷Old English *cwice*, of uncertain origin; perhaps related to **QUICK** (with reference to its vigorous growth).

quit·claim /ˈkwit,klām/ ▸*n. Law* a formal renunciation or relinquishing of a claim.
▸*v.* [*trans.*] renounce or relinquish a claim: *Aikins quitclaimed his interest in the three parcels of real estate.*

quite /kwīt/ ▸*adv.* [usu. as *submodifier*] **1** to the utmost or most absolute extent or degree; absolutely; completely: *it's quite out of the question* | *are you quite certain about this?* | *this is quite a different problem* | *I quite agree* | *quite frankly, I don't blame you.* ■ very; really (used as an intensifier): *"You've no intention of coming back?" "I'm quite sorry, but no, I have not."* **2** to a certain or fairly significant extent or degree; fairly: *it's quite warm outside* | *I was quite embarrassed, actually* | *she did quite well at school* | *he's quite an attractive man.*
▸*exclam.* (also **quite so**) *Brit.* expressing agreement with or understanding of a remark or statement: *"I don't want to talk about that now." "Quite."* ▷Middle English: from the obsolete adjective *quite*, variant of **QUIT**[1].
▸*PHRASES* □ **not quite** not completely or entirely: *my hair's not quite dry* | *she hasn't quite got the hang of it yet.* □ **quite a ——** (also *often ironic* **quite the ——**) used to indicate that the specified person or thing is perceived as particularly notable, remarkable, or impressive: *quite a party, isn't it?* | *it's been quite a year* | *quite the little horsewoman, aren't you?* □ **quite a few** see **FEW**. □ **quite a lot** (or **a bit**) a considerable number or amount of something: *my job involves* ***quite a lot of*** *travel* | *he's quite a bit older than she is.* □ **quite some** **1** a considerable amount of: *she hasn't been seen for quite some time.* **2** informal way of saying **QUITE A**. □ **quite something** see **SOMETHING**. □ **quite the thing** *dated* socially acceptable: *she was quite the thing in heels and stockings and lipstick.*

Qui·to /ˈkētō/ the capital of Ecuador; pop. 1,401,000. It is situated in the Andes just south of the equator, at an altitude of 9,350 feet (2,850 m).

quit-rent ▸*n. historical* a rent, typically a small one, paid by a freeholder or copyholder in lieu of services that might be required of them.

quits /kwits/ ▸*adj.* [*predic.*] (of two people) on even terms, esp. because a debt or score has been settled: *I think we're just about quits now, don't you?* ▷late 15th cent. (in the sense 'freed from a liability or debt'): perhaps a colloquial abbreviation of medieval Latin *quittus*, from Latin *quietus*, used as a receipt (see **QUIETUS**).
▸*PHRASE* □ **call it quits** agree or acknowledge that terms are now equal, esp. on the settlement of a debt: *take this check and we'll call it quits.* ■ decide to abandon an activity or venture: *surely, after covering eleven wars, he could be forgiven for calling it quits?*

quit·tance /ˈkwitns/ ▸*n. archaic, poetic/literary* a release or discharge from a debt or obligation. ■ a document certifying this; a receipt. ▷Middle English: from Old French *quitance*, from *quiter* 'to release' (see **QUIT**[1]).

quit·ter /ˈkwitər/ ▸*n.* [usu. with *negative*] *informal* a person who gives up easily or does not have the courage or determination to finish a task.

quiv·er[1] /ˈkwivər/ ▸*v.* [*intrans.*] tremble or shake with a slight rapid motion: *the tree's branches stopped quivering.* See note at **SHAKE**. ■ (of a person, a part of their body, or their voice) tremble with sudden strong emotion: *Bertha's voice quivered with indignation.* ■ [*trans.*] cause (something) to make a slight rapid motion: *the bird runs along in a zigzag path, quivering its wings.*

▸*n.* a slight trembling movement or sound, esp. one caused by a sudden strong emotion: *Meredith felt a quiver of fear.* ▷Middle English: from Old English *cwifer* 'nimble, quick.' The initial *qu-* is probably symbolic of quick movement (as in *quaver* and *quick*). **—quiv·er·ing·ly** *adv.* **—quiv·er·y** *adj.*

quiv·er[2] ▸*n.* an archer's portable case for holding arrows. ■ a set of surfboards of different lengths and shapes for use with different types of waves. ▷Middle English: from Anglo-Norman French *quiveir*, of West Germanic origin; related to Dutch *koker* and German *Köcher*.

archer's quiver

▸*PHRASE* □ **an arrow in the quiver** one of a number of resources or strategies that can be drawn on or followed.

quiv·er tree ▸*n.* a tropical aloe that forms a tree, the hollow branches of which were formerly used by the San (Bushmen) as quivers. • *Aloe dichotoma*, family Liliaceae (or Aloaceae).

qui vive /ˌkē ˈvēv/ ▸*n.* (in phrase **on the qui vive**) on the alert or lookout: *duty requires the earnest liberal to spend most of his time on the qui vive for fascism.* ▷late 16th cent.: from French, literally '(long) live who?,' i.e., 'on whose side are you?,' used as a sentry's challenge.

Qui·xo·te /kēˈhōtē/ see **DON QUIXOTE**.

quix·ot·ic /kwikˈsätik/ ▸*adj.* exceedingly idealistic; unrealistic and impractical: *a vast and perhaps quixotic project.* ▷late 18th cent.: from **DON QUIXOTE** + **-IC**. **—quix·ot·i·cal·ly** /-ik(ə)lē/ *adv.* **—quix·o·tism** /ˈkwiksəˌtizəm/ *n.* **—quix·o·try** /ˈkwiksətrē/ *n.*

quiz[1] /kwiz/ ▸*n.* (*pl.* **quiz·zes**) a test of knowledge, esp. a brief, informal test given to students.

▸*v.* (**quiz·zes, quizzed, quiz·zing**) [*trans.*] (often **be quizzed**) ask (someone) questions: *four men have been quizzed about the murder.* ■ give (a student or class) an informal test or examination. ▷mid 19th cent. (as a verb; originally U.S.): possibly from **QUIZ**[2], influenced by **INQUISITIVE**.

quiz[2] *archaic* ▸*v.* (**quiz·zes, quizzed, quiz·zing**) [*trans.*] **1** look curiously or intently at (someone) through or as if through an eyeglass: *deep-set eyes quizzed her in the candlelight.* **2** make fun of: *he says there's a great deal of poetry in brewing beer, but of course he's only quizzing us.*

▸*n.* (*pl.* **quiz·zes**) **1** a practical joke or hoax; a piece of banter or ridicule: *I am impatient to know if the whole be not one grand quiz.* ■ a person who ridicules another; a hoaxer or practical joker: *braving the ridicule with which it pleased the quizzes to asperse the husband chosen for her.* **2** a person who is odd or eccentric in character or appearance: *she means to marry that quiz for the sake of his thousands.* ▷late 18th cent.: sometimes said to have been invented by a Dublin theater proprietor who, having made a bet that a nonsense word could be made known within 48 hours throughout the city, and that the public would give it a meaning, had the word written up on walls all over the city. There is no evidence to support this theory. **—quiz·zer** *n.*

quiz·mas·ter /ˈkwizˌmastər/ ▸*n.* a person who asks the questions and enforces the rules in a television or radio quiz program.

quiz show ▸*n.* a television or radio light entertainment program in which people compete in a quiz, typically for prizes.

quiz·zi·cal /ˈkwizəkəl/ ▸*adj.* (of a person's expression or behavior) indicating mild or amused puzzlement: *she gave me a quizzical look.* ■ *rare* causing mild amusement because of its oddness or strangeness. **—quiz·zi·cal·i·ty** /ˌkwiziˈkalətē/ *n.* **—quiz·zi·cal·ly** *adv.* **—quiz·zi·cal·ness** *n.*

Qum /ko͝om/ variant spelling of **QOM**.

Qum·ran /ko͝omˈrän/ a region on the western shore of the Dead Sea. The Dead Sea scrolls were found 1947–56 in caves at nearby Khirbet Qumran, the site of an ancient Jewish settlement.

quod /kwäd/ ▸*n. Brit., informal, dated* prison: *ten years **in quod**.* ▷late 17th cent.: of unknown origin.

quod e·rat de·mon·stran·dum /kwäd ˈerət ˌdemənˈsträndəm/ (abbr.: **QED**) ▸used to convey that a fact or situation demonstrates the truth of one's theory or claim, esp. to mark the conclusion of a formal proof. ▷Latin, literally 'which was to be demonstrated.'

quod·li·bet /ˈkwädləˌbet/ ▸*n.* **1** *archaic* a topic for or exercise in philosophical or theological discussion. **2** *poetic/literary* a lighthearted medley of well-known tunes. ▷late Middle English: from Latin, from *quod* 'what' + *libet* 'it pleases.' **—quod·li·be·tar·i·an** /ˌkwädləbiˈte(ə)rēən/ *n.*

quoin /k(w)oin/ ▸*n.* **1** an external angle of a wall or building. ■ (also **quoin stone**) any of the stones or bricks forming such an angle; a cornerstone. **2** *Printing* a wedge or expanding mechanical device used for locking a letterpress form into a chase. **3** a wedge for raising the level of a gun barrel or for keeping it from rolling.

▸*v.* [*trans.*] **1** provide (a wall) with quoins or corners. **2** *Printing* lock up (a form) with a quoin. ▷Middle English: variant of **COIN**, used earlier in the sense 'cornerstone' and 'wedge.'

quoin·ing /ˈk(w)oiniNG/ ▸*n.* the stone or brick used to form a quoin of a wall or building.

quoit /k(w)oit/ ▸*n.* **1** a ring of iron, rope, or rubber thrown in a game to encircle or land as near as possible to an upright peg. ■ (**quoits**) [treated as *sing.*] a game consisting of aiming and throwing such rings. **2** the flat covering stone of a dolmen. ■ [often in *place names*] the dolmen itself.

▸*v.* [*trans.*] *archaic* throw or propel like a quoit. ▷late Middle English: probably of French origin.

quok·ka /ˈkwäkə/ ▸*n.* a small, short-tailed wallaby with a short face, round ears on top of the head, and some tree-climbing ability, native to Western Australia. • *Setonix brachyurus*, family Macropodidae. ▷mid 19th cent.: from Nyungar *kwaka*.

quoll /kwäl/ ▸*n.* a catlike, carnivorous marsupial with short legs and a white-spotted coat, native to the forests of Australia and New Guinea. Also called **DASYURE**. • Genus *Dasyurus*, family Dasyuridae: several species. ▷late 18th cent.: from Guugu Yimidhirr (an Aboriginal language) *dhigul*.

quon·dam /ˈkwändəm; -ˌdam/ ▸*adj.* [*attrib.*] *formal* that once was; former: *quondam dissidents joined the establishment | its quondam popularity.* ▷late 16th cent.: from Latin, 'formerly.'

Quon·set /ˈkwänsət/ (usu. **Quonset hut**) ▸*n. trademark* a building made of corrugated metal and having a semicircular cross section. ▷World War II: named after *Quonset* Point, Rhode Island, where such huts were first made.

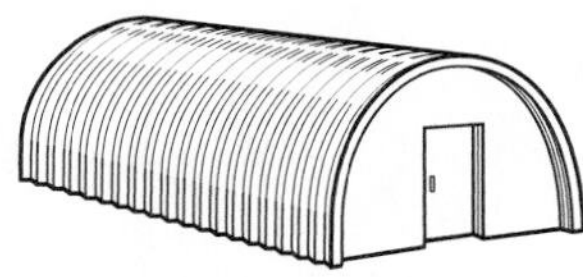
Quonset hut

quo·rum /ˈkwôrəm/ ▸*n.* (*pl.* **quo·rums**) the minimum number of members of an assembly or society that must be present at any of its meetings to make the proceedings of that meeting valid. ▷late Middle English (referring to justices of the peace): used in commissions for committee members designated by the Latin *quorum vos ... unum* (*duos*, etc.) *esse volumus* 'of whom we wish that you ... be one (two, etc.).'

quot. ▸*abbr.* quotation.

quo·ta /ˈkwōtə/ ▸*n.* a limited or fixed number or amount of people or things, in particular: ■ a limited quantity of a particular product that under official controls can be produced, exported, or imported: *the country may be exceeding its OPEC quota of 1,100,000 barrels of oil per day.* ■ a fixed share of something that a person or group is entitled to receive from a total: *the Faeroe Islands' commercial salmon quota.* ■ a person's share of something that must be done: *they were arrested to help fill the quota of arrests the security police had to make during the crackdown.* ■ a fixed minimum or maximum number of a particular group of people allowed to do something, as immigrants to enter a country, workers to undertake a job, or students to enroll for a course: *they demanded a quota for women on the committee.* ■ (in a system of proportional representation) the minimum number of votes required to elect a candidate. ■ *figurative* a person's share of a particular thing, quality, or attribute: *an Irishman with a double ration of blarney and a treble quota of charm.* ▷early 17th cent.: from medieval Latin *quota (pars)* 'how great (a part),' feminine of *quotus*, from *quot* 'how many.'

quot·a·ble /ˈkwōtəbəl/ ▸*adj.* (of a person or remark) suitable for or worth quoting. **—quot·a·bil·i·ty** /ˌkwōtəˈbilətē/ *n.*

quo·ta·tion /ˌkwōˈtāSHən/ ▸*n.* **1** a group of words taken from a text or speech and repeated by someone other than the original author or speaker: *a quotation from Mark Twain | biblical quotations.* ■ a short musical passage or visual image taken from one piece of music or work of art and used in another. ■ the action of quoting from a text, speech, piece of music, or work of art: *a great argument with much quotation of Darwin.* **2** a formal statement setting out the estimated cost for a particular job or service: *you will be sent a written quotation for the cost of repairing your machine.* ■ *Stock Market* a price offered by a broker for the sale or purchase of a stock or other security. ■ *Stock Market* a registration granted to a company enabling their shares to be officially listed and traded. ▷mid 16th cent. (denoting a marginal reference to a passage of text): from medieval Latin *quotatio(n-)*, from the verb *quotare* (see **QUOTE**).

quo·ta·tion mark ▸*n.* each of a set of punctuation marks, single (' ') or double (" "), used either to mark the beginning and end of a title or quoted passage or to indicate that a word or phrase is regarded as slang or jargon or is being discussed rather than used within the sentence.

quote /kwōt/ ▸*v.* [*trans.*] **1** repeat or copy out (a group of words from a text or speech), typically with an indication that one is not the original author or speaker: *he **quoted** a passage **from** the Psalms* | [with *direct speech*] *"The stream mysterious glides beneath," Melinda quoted* | [*intrans.*] *when we told her this she said, and I quote, "Phooey!"* ■ repeat a passage from (a work or author) or statement by (someone): *the prime minister was **quoted as saying** that he would resist all attempts to "sabotage" his government | he quoted Shakespeare, Goethe, and other poets.* ■ mention or refer to (someone or something) to provide evidence or authority for a statement, argument, or opinion: *they won't be here at all in three years time—**you can quote me on that.*** ■ (**quote someone/something as**) put forward or describe someone or something as being: *heavy teaching loads are often quoted as a bad influence on research.* **2** give someone (the estimated price of a job or service): [with *two objs.*] *the agent quoted a fare of $180.* ■ (usu. **be quoted**) *Stock Market* give (a company) a quotation or listing on a stock exchange: *an organization that is **quoted on** the Stock Exchange.*

▸*n.* **1** a quotation from a text or speech: *a quote from Wordsworth.* **2** a quotation giving the estimated cost for a particular job or service: *quotes from different insurance companies.* ■ *Stock Market* a price offered by a broker for the sale or purchase of a stock or other security. ■ *Stock Market* a quotation or listing of a company on a stock exchange. **3** (**quotes**) quotation marks. ▷late Middle English: from medieval Latin *quotare*, from *quot* 'how many,' or from medieval Latin *quota* (see **QUOTA**). The original sense was 'mark a book with numbers, or with marginal references,' later 'give a reference by page or chapter,' hence 'cite a text or person' (late 16th cent.).

▸*PHRASES* □ **quote —— unquote** *informal* used parenthetically when speaking to suggest quotation marks, to indicate the beginning and end of a statement or passage that one is reciting or repeating, in particular: ■ used to indicate the speaker's verbatim recitation of written words: *on page three, the second sentence says, quote, There has never been a better time to invest in the commodities market, unquote.* ■ used to repeat a spoken passage, esp. to emphasize the speaker's detachment from or disagreement with the original: *I swear to you, this is exactly what they told me: quote, You cannot bring a wheelchair into this restaurant during the dinner rush, unquote.* □ **quote, unquote** *informal* **1** used parenthetically when speaking to

Pronunciation Key ə ago; ər over; ˈə or ˌə up; ˈər or ˌər fur; a hat; ā rate; ä car; CH chew; e let; ē see; e(ə)r air; i fit; ī by; i(ə)r ear; NG sing; ō go; ô for; oi boy; o͝o good; o͞o goo; ou out; SH she; TH thin; T͟H then; (h)w why; ZH vision

suggest quotation marks, to precede a statement or passage that one is reciting or repeating, in particular: ■ used to indicate the speaker's verbatim recitation of written words: *the brochure describes the view as, quote, unquote, unforgettably breathtaking.* ■ used to repeat a spoken passage, esp. to emphasize the speaker's detachment from or disagreement with the original: *and then Marty says—quote, unquote—None of those bastards deserve a fair trial.* **2** used parenthetically when speaking to suggest quotation marks, to precede a word or phrase that is meant to be sarcastic, mocking, or disapproving in its context, specifically to challenge a previous assertion that the word or phrase was appropriate in its context: *then she shows up with her quote, unquote sophisticated friends.*

quoth /kwōTH/ ▸*v.* [with *direct speech*] *archaic* or *humorous* said (used only in first and third person singular before the subject): *"Well, the tide is going out" quoth the sailor.* ▷Middle English: past tense of obsolete *quethe* 'say, declare,' of Germanic origin.

quo·tid·i·an /kwō'tidēən/ ▸*adj.* [*attrib.*] of or occurring every day; daily: *the car sped noisily off through the quotidian traffic.* ■ ordinary or everyday, esp. when mundane: *his story is an achingly human one, mired in quotidian details.* ■ *Medicine* denoting the malignant form of malaria. ▷Middle English: via Old French from Latin *quotidianus*, earlier *cotidianus*, from *cotidie* 'daily.'

quo·tient /'kwōSHənt/ ▸*n.* **1** *Mathematics* a result obtained by dividing one quantity by another. **2** [usu. with *adj.*] a degree or amount of a specified quality or characteristic: *the increase in Washington's cynicism quotient.* ▷late Middle English: from Latin *quotiens* 'how many times' (from *quot* 'how many'), by confusion with participial forms ending in *-ens*, *-ent-*.

quo war·ran·to /ˌkwō wə'rän,tō; -'ran-/ ▸*n.* [usu. as *adj.*] *Law* a writ or legal action requiring a person to show by what warrant an office or franchise is held, claimed, or exercised. ▷Law Latin, literally 'by what warrant.'

Qu·r'an /kə'rän; -'ran/ (also **Qu·ran**) ▸*n.* Arabic spelling of **KORAN**.

qursh /kərSH/ ▸*n.* (*pl.* same) a monetary unit of Saudi Arabia, equal to one twentieth of a riyal. ▷from Arabic *ḳirsh*, from Slavic *grossus*.

q.v. ▸*abbr.* used to direct a reader to another part of a book or article for further information. ▷from Latin *quod vide*, literally 'which see.'

qwerty /'kwərtē/ ▸*adj.* denoting the standard layout on English-language typewriters and keyboards, having *q*, *w*, *e*, *r*, *t*, and *y* as the first keys from the left on the top row of letters.

Q

Rr

R[1] /är/ (also **r**) ▸*n.* (*pl.* **Rs** or **R's**) the eighteenth letter of the alphabet. ■ denoting the next after Q in a set of items, categories, etc.
▸*PHRASES* □ **the R months** the months with R in their names (September to April), considered to be the season for eating oysters. □ **the three Rs** reading, writing, and arithmetic, regarded as the fundamentals of learning.

R[2] ▸*abbr.* ■ rand: *a farm worth nearly R1,3-million.* ■ Réaumur: *198.6 °R.* ■ Regina or Rex: *Elizabeth R.* ■ (also ®) registered as a trademark. ■ (in the U.S.) Republican: *congressman Henry Hyde (R-Illinois).* ■ restricted, a rating in the Voluntary Movie Rating System that children under 17 require an accompanying parent or adult guardian for admission. ■ (on a gearshift) reverse. ■ (**R.**) River (chiefly on maps): *R. Cherwell.* ■ roentgen(s). ■ rook (in recording moves in chess): *21.Rh4.*
▸*symbol* ■ *Chemistry* an unspecified alkyl or other organic radical or group. [abbreviation of RADICAL.] ■ electrical resistance. ■ *Chemistry* the gas constant.

r ▸*abbr.* ■ recto. ■ (giving position or direction) right: *l to r: Evan, Nick, and David.* ■ *Law* rule: *under r 7.4 (6) the court may hear an application immediately.*
▸*symbol* ■ radius: *2πr.* ■ *Statistics* correlation coefficient: *sigmoidoscopic and symptom scores also showed a significant correlation with each other (r = 0.91).*

RA ▸*abbr.* ■ regular army. ■ *Astronomy* right ascension.

Ra[1] /rä/ (also **Re**) *Egyptian Mythology* the sun god, the supreme Egyptian deity, worshiped as the creator of all life and typically with a falcon's head bearing the solar disc. From earliest times he was associated with the pharaoh.

Ra[2] ▸*symbol* the chemical element radium.

Ra. ▸*abbr.* range.

RAAF ▸*abbr.* Royal Australian Air Force.

Ra·bat /rəˈbät/ the capital of Morocco, an industrial port on the Atlantic coast; pop. 1,220,000. It was founded as a military fort in the 12th century by the Almohads. ▷from Arabic *Ribat el-Fath* 'fort of victory.'

Ra·baul /räˈboul/ the chief town and port on the island of New Britain in Papua New Guinea; pop. 17,000.

rab·bet /ˈrabit/ ▸*n.* a step-shaped recess cut along the edge or in the face of a piece of wood, typically forming a match to the edge or tongue of another piece: [as *adj.*] *a rabbet joint.*
▸*v.* (**-bet·ed, -bet·ing**) [*trans.*] make a rabbet in (a piece of wood). ■ [*trans.*] join or fix (a piece of wood) to another with a rabbet. ▷late Middle English: from Old French *rabbat* 'abatement, recess.'

rab·bet plane ▸*n.* a plane for making a rabbet in a piece of wood.

rab·bi /ˈrab,ī/ ▸*n.* (*pl.* **-bis**) a Jewish scholar or teacher, esp. one who studies or teaches Jewish law. ■ a person appointed as a Jewish religious leader. ▷late Old English, via ecclesiastical Latin and Greek from Hebrew *rabbī* 'my master,' from *rab* 'master.' **—rab·bin·ate** /ˈrabənət; -,nāt/ *n.*

rab·bin·i·cal /rəˈbinikəl; ra-/ ▸*adj.* [*attrib.*] of or relating to rabbis or to Jewish law or teachings. **—rab·bin·ic** /-ik/ *adj.* **—rab·bin·i·cal·ly** /-ik(ə)lē/ *adv.*

rab·bit /ˈrabit/ ▸*n.* a burrowing, gregarious, plant-eating mammal with long ears, long hind legs, and a short tail. • Family Leporidae: several genera and species, in particular the **European rabbit** (*Oryctolagus cuniculus*), which is often kept as a pet or raised for food. ■ the flesh of the rabbit as food. ■ the fur of the rabbit. ■ another term for HARE. ■ a runner who acts as pacesetter in the first laps of a race.
▸*v.* (**-bit·ed, -bit·ing**) [*intrans.*] **1** [usu. as *n.*] (**rabbiting**) hunt rabbits: *locate the area where you can* **go rabbiting**. **2** *Brit., informal* talk at length, esp. about trivial matters: *stop* **rabbiting on**, *will you, and go to bed!* [from *rabbit and pork*, rhyming slang for 'talk.'] ▷late Middle English: apparently from Old French (compare with French dialect *rabotte* 'young rabbit'), perhaps of Dutch origin (compare with Flemish *robbe*). **—rab·bit·y** *adj.*
▸*PHRASES* □ **breed like rabbits** *informal* reproduce prolifically. □ **pull a rabbit out of the** (or **a**) **hat** used to describe an action that is fortuitous, and may involve sleight of hand or deception: *a rabbit has been pulled out of the political hat.*

rab·bit·brush /ˈrabit,brəsн/ (also **rab·bit·bush** /-,bo͝osн/) ▸*n.* a shrub of the daisy family that bears clusters of pungent small yellow flowers, native to North America, esp. the western U.S. • *Chrysothamnus nauseosus*, family Compositae.

rab·bit fe·ver ▸*n.* informal term for TULAREMIA.

rab·bit·fish /ˈrabit,fisн/ ▸*n.* (*pl.* same or **-fish·es**) a blunt-nosed chimaera with rodentlike front teeth and a long thin tail, found in the northeastern Atlantic and around South Africa. Also called RATFISH, RAT-TAIL. • *Chimaera monstrosa*, family Chimaeridae.

rab·bit food ▸*n. informal, humorous* salad or raw vegetables, characterized as insubstantial or tasteless.

rab·bit punch ▸*n.* a sharp chop with the edge of the hand to the back of the neck.

rab·bit's foot ▸*n.* the foot of a rabbit carried as a good luck charm.

rab·bit's-foot clo·ver ▸*n.* a slender clover with narrow leaflets that are soft and silky and light pink flowerheads that are slightly cylindrical and very fuzzy. • *Trifolium arvense*, family Leguminosae.

rab·bit war·ren ▸*n.* see WARREN.

rab·ble /ˈrabəl/ ▸*n.* a disorderly crowd; a mob: *he was met by a rabble of noisy, angry youths.* ■ (**the rabble**) ordinary people, esp. when regarded as socially inferior or uncouth. ▷late Middle English (in the senses 'string of meaningless words' and 'pack of animals'): perhaps related to dialect *rabble* 'to gabble.'

rab·ble-rous·er ▸*n.* a person who speaks with the intention of inflaming the emotions of a crowd of people, typically for political reasons. **—rab·ble-rous·ing** *adj.* & *n.*

Rab·e·lais /ˈrabə,lā; ,rabəˈlā/, François (*c.*1494–1553), French satirist. His writings are noted for their earthy humor, their parody of medieval learning and literature, and their affirmation of humanist values.

rab·id /ˈrabəd; ˈrā-/ ▸*adj.* **1** having or proceeding from an extreme or fanatical support of or belief in something: *a rabid feminist.* **2** (of an animal) affected with rabies. ■ of or connected with rabies. ▷early 17th cent. (in the sense 'furious, madly violent'): from Latin *rabidus*, from *rabere* 'to rave.' **—ra·bid·i·ty** /rəˈbidətē; ra-; rā-/ *n.* **—rab·id·ly** *adv.* **—rab·id·ness** *n.*

ra·bies /ˈrābēz/ ▸*n.* a contagious and fatal viral disease of dogs and other mammals that causes madness and convulsions, transmissible through the saliva to humans. Also called HYDROPHOBIA. ▷late 16th cent.: from Latin, from *rabere* 'rave.'

Ra·bin /räˈbēn/, Yitzhak (1922–95), Israeli statesman and military leader; prime minister 1974–77 and 1992–95. In 1993, he negotiated a PLO–Israeli peace accord with Yasser Arafat. He was assassinated by a Jewish extremist. Nobel Peace Prize (1994, shared with Arafat and Shimon Peres).

Ra·bin·o·witz /rəˈbinəvits; -wits/, Solomon J., see SHOLOM ALEICHEM.

rac·coon /raˈko͞on; rə-/ (also **ra·coon**) ▸*n.* a grayish-brown American mammal that has a foxlike face with a black mask and a ringed tail. • Genus *Procyon*, family Procyonidae (the **raccoon family**): two species, in particular the **common raccoon** (*P. lotor*), which often occurs in urban areas in North America. The raccoon family also includes the coati, kinkajou, cacomistle, and olingo. ■ the fur of the raccoon. ▷early 17th cent.: from Virginia Algonquian *aroughcun*. The common raccoon's scientific name *lotor* is Latin for 'one who washes,' a name descriptive of the raccoon's habit of using its front feet to forage for food in water.

common raccoon

rac·coon dog ▸*n.* a small wild dog of raccoonlike appearance, with a black facial mask and long brindled fur, native to the forests of southern and eastern Asia. • *Nyctereutes procyonoides*, family Canidae.

race[1] /rās/ ▸*n.* **1** a competition between runners, horses, vehicles, boats, etc., to see which is the fastest in covering a set course: *I won the first 50-lap race.* ■ (**the races**) a series of such competitions for horses or dogs, held at a fixed time on a set course. ■ [in *sing.*] a situation in which individuals or groups compete to be first to achieve a particular objective: *the* **race for** *nuclear power.* ■ *archaic* the course of the sun or moon through the heavens. **2** a strong or rapid current flowing through a narrow channel in the sea or a river: *angling for tuna in turbulent tidal races.* **3** a groove, channel, or passage, in particular: ■ a water channel, esp. one built to lead water to or from a point where its energy is utilized, as in a mill or mine. See also MILLRACE. ■ a smooth, ring-shaped groove or guide in which a ball bearing or roller bearing runs.
▸*v.* **1** [*intrans.*] compete with another or others to see who is fastest at covering a set course or achieving an objective: *the vet took blood samples from the horses before they raced* | [*trans.*] *attorneys have to think twice before they* **race each other** *to the courthouse.* ■ compete regularly in races as a sport or leisure activity: *the next year, he raced again for the team.* ■ [*trans.*] prepare and enter (an animal or vehicle) in races as a sport or leisure activity: *he raced his three horses simply for the fun of it.* **2** [*intrans.*] move or progress swiftly or at full speed: *I raced into the house* | *figurative she spoke automatically, while her mind raced ahead.* ■ (of an engine or other machinery) operate at excessive speed: *the truck came to rest against a tree.* ■ (of a person's heart or pulse) beat faster than usual because of fear or excitement. ■ [*trans.*] cause to move, progress, or operate swiftly or at excessive speed: *she'd driven like a madwoman, racing the engine and swerving around corners.* ▷late Old English, from Old Norse *rás* 'current.'

Pronunciation Key ə *ago*; ər *over*; ˈə *or* ,ə *up*; ˈər *or* ,ər *fur*; a *hat*; ā *rate*; ä *car*; CH *chew*; e *let*; ē *see*; e(ə)r *air*; i *fit*; ī *by*; i(ə)r *ear*; NG *sing*; ō *go*; ô *for*; oi *boy*; o͝o *good*; o͞o *goo*; ou *out*; SH *she*; TH *thin*; T͟H *then*; (h)w *why*; ZH *vision*

R

It was originally a northern English word with the sense 'rapid forward movement,' which gave rise to the senses 'contest of speed' (early 16th cent.) and 'channel, path' (i.e., the space traversed). The verb dates from the late 15th cent.

▶*PHRASE* □ **a race against time** a situation in which something must be done before a particular point in time: *it was a race against time to reach shore before the dinghy sank.*

race2 ▶*n.* each of the major divisions of humankind, having distinct physical characteristics: *people of all races, colors, and creeds.* ■ a group of people sharing the same culture, history, language, etc.; an ethnic group: *we Scots were a bloodthirsty race then.* ■ the fact or condition of belonging to such a division or group; the qualities or characteristics associated with this: *people of mixed race.* ■ a group or set of people or things with a common feature or features: *some male firefighters still regarded women as* ***a race apart.*** ■ *Biology* a population within a species that is distinct in some way, esp. a subspecies: *people have killed so many tigers that two races are probably extinct.* ■ (in nontechnical use) each of the major divisions of living creatures: *a member of the human race | the race of birds.* ■ *poetic/literary* a group of people descended from a common ancestor: *a prince of the race of Solomon.* ■ *archaic* ancestry: *two coursers of ethereal race.*

Although ideas of race are centuries old, it was not until the 19th century that attempts to systematize racial divisions were made. Ideas of supposed racial superiority and social Darwinism reached their culmination in Nazi ideology of the 1930s and gave pseudoscientific justification to policies and attitudes of discrimination, exploitation, slavery, and extermination. Theories of race asserting a link between racial type and intelligence are now discredited. Scientifically it is accepted as obvious that there are subdivisions of the human species, but it is also clear that genetic variation between individuals of the same race can be as great as that between members of different races.

▷early 16th cent. (denoting a group with common features): via French from Italian *razza*, of unknown ultimate origin.

USAGE In recent years, the associations of **race** with the ideologies and theories that grew out of the work of 19th-century anthropologists and physiologists has led to the use of the word **race** itself becoming problematic. Although still used in general contexts (*race relations, racial equality*), it is now often replaced by other words that are less emotionally charged, such as **people(s)** or **community**.

race car ▶*n.* an automobile built or modified for racing.

race·course /ˈrās,kôrs/ ▶*n.* a racetrack.

race driv·er ▶*n.* a person who drives race cars as a profession.

race·horse /ˈrās,hôrs/ ▶*n.* a horse bred, trained, and kept for racing.

race·mate /ˈrās,māt/ ▶*n. Chemistry* a racemic mixture.

ra·ceme /rāˈsēm; rə-/ ▶*n. Botany* a flower cluster with the separate flowers attached by short equal stalks at equal distances along a central stem. The flowers at the base of the central stem develop first. Compare with **CYME** and **SPIKE**2. ▷late 18th cent.: from Latin *racemus* 'bunch of grapes.'

race mem·o·ry ▶*n.* a supposedly inherited subconscious memory of events in human history or prehistory.

ra·ce·mic /rāˈsēmik; rə-/ ▶*adj. Chemistry* composed of dextrorotatory and levorotatory forms of a compound in equal proportion. ▷early 19th cent. (in *racemic acid*): from French *racémique* 'derived from grape juice' (originally referring to tartaric acid in this) + **-IC**. **—rac·e·mize** /rāˈsē,mīz; rəˈsē-; ˈrasə-/ *v.*

rac·e·mose /ˈrasə,mōs; ˈrasə,mōz/ ▶*adj. Botany* (of a flower cluster) taking the form of a raceme. ■ *Anatomy* (esp. of compound glands) having the form of a cluster. ▷late 17th cent.: from Latin *racemosus*, from *racemus* (see **RACEME**).

rac·er /ˈrāsər/ ▶*n.* **1** an animal or means of transportation bred or designed esp. for racing: *tall-masted ocean racers.* ■ a person who competes in races. **2** a fast-moving, harmless, and typically slender-bodied snake. • Several genera in the family Colubridae: genus *Coluber*, including the American *C. constrictor* and the European *C. gemonensis* (see also **WHIP SNAKE**), and the Asian genera *Ptyas* and *Argyrogena* (also called **RAT SNAKE**). **3** a circular horizontal rail along which the carriage or traversing platform of a heavy gun moves.

rac·er·back /ˈrāsər,bak/ ▶*n.* [as *adj.*] denoting an article of clothing with a T-shaped back behind the shoulder blades to allow ease of movement in sports.

race re·la·tions ▶*plural n.* relations between members or communities of different races within one country.

race ri·ot ▶*n.* a public outbreak of violence between two racial groups in a community.

race·run·ner /ˈrās,rənər/ ▶*n.* any of a number of fast-moving active lizards with longitudinal markings and a pointed snout, in particular: • an American lizard (genus *Cnemidophorus*, family Teiidae).

race·track /ˈrās,trak/ ▶*n.* a ground or track for horse or dog racing. ■ a track for auto racing.

race·way /ˈrās,wā/ ▶*n.* **1** a track or channel along which something runs, in particular: ■ a water channel, esp. an artificial one of running water in which fish are reared. ■ a groove or race in which bearings run. ■ a pipe or tubing enclosing electric wires. **2** a track for trotting, pacing, or harness racing. ■ a track for auto racing.

ra·chis /ˈrākis; ˈrak-/ ▶*n.* (*pl.* **rach·i·des** /ˈrakə,dēz; ˈrā-/) **1** *Botany* a stem of a plant, esp. a grass, bearing flower stalks at short intervals. ■ the midrib of a compound leaf or frond. **2** *Anatomy* the vertebral column or the cord from which it develops. **3** *Ornithology* the shaft of a feather, esp. the part bearing the barbs. ▷late 18th cent.: modern Latin, from Greek *rhakhis* 'spine.' The English plural *-ides* is by false analogy.

ra·chi·tis /rəˈkītis/ ▶*n.* old-fashioned medical term for **RICKETS**. ▷early 18th cent.: modern Latin, from Greek *rhakhitis*, from *rhakhis* 'spine.' **—ra·chit·ic** /rəˈkitik/ *adj.*

Rach·ma·ni·nov /räkˈmänənôf; rəKHˈmänyinəf/, Sergei (Vasilevich) (1873–1943), Russian composer and pianist, resident in the U.S. from 1917. Part of the Russian romantic tradition, he is primarily known for his compositions for piano.

ra·cial /ˈrāSHəl/ ▶*adj.* of or relating to race: *a racial minority.* ■ on the grounds of or connected with difference in race: *racial hatred.* **—ra·cial·ly** *adv.*

ra·cial·ism /ˈrāSHə,lizəm/ ▶*n.* another term for **RACISM**. **—ra·cial·ist** /-list/ *n.* & *adj.* **—ra·cial·ize** /-,līz/ *v.*

ra·cial pro·fil·ing ▶*n.* the practice of substituting skin color for evidence as grounds for suspicion by law enforcement officials.

Ra·cine1 /rəˈsēn; rā-/ an industrial city in southeastern Wisconsin, on Lake Michigan; pop. 81,855.

Ra·cine2 /rəˈsēn; rä-/, Jean (1639–99), French playwright. Central to most of his tragedies is a perception of the blind folly of human passion, continually enslaved and unsatisfied. Notable works: *Andromaque* (1667) and *Phèdre* (1677).

rac·ing /ˈrāsiNG/ ▶*n.* short for **HORSE RACING**. ■ any sport that involves competing in races: *bicycle racing | yacht racing.*
▶*adj.* **1** moving swiftly: *he controlled his racing thoughts.* **2** (of a person) following horse racing: *Kevin was not a racing man.*

rac·ism /ˈrā,sizəm/ ▶*n.* the belief that all members of each race possess characteristics or abilities specific to that race, esp. so as to distinguish it as inferior or superior to another race or races. ■ prejudice, discrimination, or antagonism directed against someone of a different race based on such a belief: *a program to combat racism.* **—rac·ist** *n.* & *adj.*

rack1 /rak/ ▶*n.* **1** a framework, typically with rails, bars, hooks, or pegs, for holding or storing things: *a spice rack | a magazine rack.* ■ an overhead shelf on a bus, train, or plane for stowing luggage. ■ a vertically barred frame or wagon for holding animal fodder: *a hay rack.* ■ a lift used for elevating and repairing motor vehicles. ■ a set of antlers. ■ *vulgar slang* a woman's breasts: *Arnie's woman is kinda bossy, but she's got a nice rack.* ■ *informal* a bed. **2** a cogged or toothed bar or rail engaging with a wheel or pinion, or using pegs to adjust the position of something: *a steering rack.* **3** (**the rack**) *historical* an instrument of torture consisting of a frame on which the victim was stretched by turning rollers to which the wrists and ankles were tied. **4** a triangular structure for positioning the balls in pool. Compare with **FRAME** (sense 5). ■ the triangular arrangement of balls set up for the beginning of a game of pool. ■ *Brit.* a single game of snooker. **5** a digital effects unit for a guitar or other instrument, typically giving many different sounds.
▶*v.* [*trans.*] **1** (also **wrack**) (often **be racked**) cause extreme physical or mental pain to; subject to extreme stress: *he was racked with guilt.* ■ *historical* torture (someone) on the rack. **2** [*trans.*] place in or on a rack: *the shoes were racked neatly beneath the dresses.* ■ [*trans.*] put (pool balls) in a rack. **3** *chiefly archaic* raise (rent) above a fair or normal amount.
▶*phrasal v.* □ **rack something up** accumulate or achieve something, typically a score or amount: *Japan is racking up record trade surpluses with the U.S.* ▷Middle English: from Middle Dutch *rec*, Middle Low German *rek* 'horizontal bar or shelf,' probably from *recken* 'to stretch, reach' (possibly the source of sense 1 of the *verb*).
▶*PHRASES* □ **go to rack** (or **wrack**) **and ruin** gradually deteriorate in condition because of neglect: fall into disrepair. [*rack* from Old English *wræc* 'vengeance'; related to **WREAK**.] □ **off the rack** (of clothes) ready-made rather than made to order. □ **on the rack** suffering intense distress or strain. □ **rack** (or **wrack**) **one's brains** (or **brain**) make a great effort to think of or remember something.

USAGE The relationship between the forms **rack** and **wrack** is complicated. The most common noun sense of **rack**, 'a framework for holding and storing things,' is always spelled **rack**, never **wrack**. The figurative senses of the verb, deriving from the type of torture in which someone is stretched on a **rack**, can, however, be spelled either **rack** or **wrack**: thus, ***racked*** *with guilt* or ***wracked*** *with guilt*; ***rack*** *your brains* or ***wrack*** *your brains*. In addition, the phrase ***rack and ruin*** can also be spelled ***wrack and ruin***.

rack2 ▶*n.* a horse's gait in which both hoofs on either side in turn are lifted almost simultaneously, and all four hoofs are off the ground together at certain moments.
▶*v.* [*intrans.*] (of a horse) move with such a gait. ▷mid 16th cent.: of unknown origin.

rack3 ▶*n.* a large cut of meat, typically lamb, that includes the front ribs. ▷late 16th cent.: of unknown origin.

rack4 ▶*v.* [*trans.*] draw off (wine, beer, etc.) from the sediment in the barrel: *the wine is* ***racked off*** *into large oak casks.* ▷late 15th cent.: from Provençal *arracar*, from *raca* 'stems and husks of grapes, dregs.'

rack5 (also **wrack**) ▶*n.* a mass of high, thick, fast-moving clouds: *there was a thin moon, a rack of cloud.*
▶*v.* [*intrans.*] *archaic* (of a cloud) be driven before the wind. ▷Middle English (denoting a rush or collision): probably of Scandinavian origin; compare with Norwegian and Swedish dialect *rak* 'wreckage,' from *reka* 'to drive.'

rack-and-pin·ion ▶*adj.* [*attrib.*] denoting a mechanism, as for a car steering system, using a fixed cogged or toothed bar or rail engaging with a smaller cog.

rack·et1 /ˈrakit/ (also **rac·quet**) ▶*n.* a type of bat with a round or oval frame strung with catgut, nylon, etc., used esp. in tennis, badminton, and squash. ■ a snowshoe resembling such a bat. ▷early 16th cent.: from French *raquette* (see **RACKETS**).

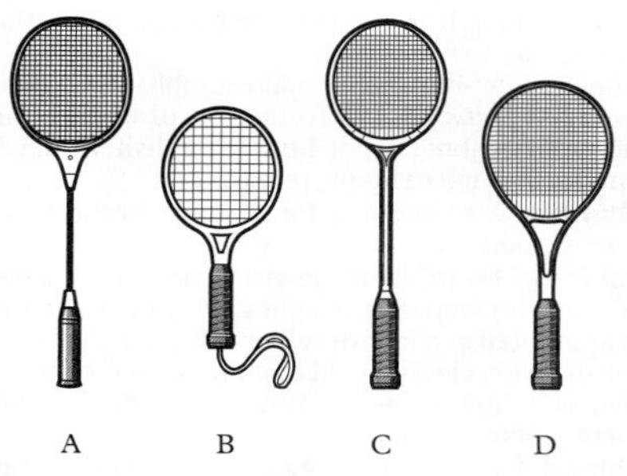

RACKETS

A. badminton racket C. squash racket
B. racquetball racket D. tennis racket

racket1

rack·et2 ▶*n.* **1** [in *sing.*] a loud unpleasant noise; a din: *the kids were* ***making a racket.*** ■ *archaic* the noise and liveliness of fashionable society. **2** *informal* an illegal or dishonest scheme for obtaining money: *a*

protection racket. ■ a person's line of business or way of life: *I'm in the insurance racket.*
▸*v.* (**rack·et·ed**, **rack·et·ing**) [*intrans.*] make a loud unpleasant noise: *trains racketed by.* ■ (**racket around**) enjoy oneself socially; go in pursuit of pleasure or entertainment. ▷mid 16th cent.: perhaps imitative of clattering. —**rack·et·y** *adj.*

rack·et·eer /ˌrakiˈti(ə)r/ ▸*n.* a person who engages in dishonest and fraudulent business dealings. —**rack·et·eer·ing** *n.*

rack·ets /ˈrakits/ ▸*plural n.* [treated as *sing.*] a ball game for two or four people played with rackets in a plain, four-walled court, distinguished from squash in particular by the use of a solid, harder ball. ▷late Middle English (also in the singular): from French *raquette*, via Italian from Arabic *rāḥa*, *rāḥat-* 'palm of the hand.'

rack rail·way ▸*n.* another term for COG RAILWAY.

rack rate ▸*n.* the official or advertised price of a hotel room, on which a discount is usually negotiable.

rack rent ▸*n.* an extortionate or very high rent, esp. an annual rent equivalent to the full value of the property to which it relates.
▸*v.* (**rack-rent**) [*trans.*] exact an excessive or extortionate rent from (a tenant) or for (a property). ▷late 16th cent. (as *rack-rented*): from the verb RACK[1] (in the sense 'cause stress') + the noun RENT[1]. —**rack·rent·er** *n.*

ra·clette /raˈklet; rä-/ ▸*n.* a Swiss dish of melted cheese, typically eaten with potatoes. ▷French, literally 'small scraper,' referring to the practice of holding the cheese over the heat and scraping it on to a plate as it melts.

ra·con /ˈrāˌkän/ ▸*n.* a radar beacon that can be identified and located by its response to a specific radar signal. ▷1940s: blend of RADAR and BEACON.

rac·on·teur /ˌrakˌänˈtər; -ən-/ ▸*n.* a person who tells anecdotes in a skillful and amusing way. ▷early 19th cent.: French, from *raconter* 'relate, recount.'

rac·on·teuse /ˌrakˌänˈtə(r)z/ ▸*n.* a female raconteur. ▷mid 19th cent.: French, feminine of *raconteur* (see RACONTEUR).

ra·coon ▸*n.* variant spelling of RACCOON.

rac·quet /ˈrakit/ ▸*n.* variant spelling of RACKET[1].

rac·quet·ball /ˈrakitˌbôl/ ▸*n.* a game played with a small hard ball and a short-handled racket in a four-walled handball court.

rac·y /ˈrāsē/ ▸*adj.* (**rac·i·er**, **rac·i·est**) (of speech, writing, or behavior) lively, entertaining, and typically mildly titillating sexually: *the novel was considered rather racy at the time.* ■ (of a person or thing) showing vigor or spirit: *a racy fiddle.* ■ (of a wine, flavor, etc.) having a characteristic quality in a high degree. ■ (of a vehicle or animal) designed or bred to be suitable for racing: *the yacht is fast and racy.* —**rac·i·ly** /-səlē/ *adv.* —**rac·i·ness** *n.*

rad[1] ▸*abbr.* radian(s).

rad[2] /rad/ ▸*n. informal* a political radical. ▷early 19th cent.: abbreviation.

rad[3] ▸*n. Physics* a unit of absorbed dose of ionizing radiation, corresponding to the absorption of 0.01 joule per kilogram of absorbing material. ▷early 20th cent.: acronym from *radiation absorbed dose*.

rad[4] ▸*adj. informal* excellent; impressive: *his style is so rad | a really rad game.* ▷1980s: probably an abbreviation of RADICAL.

rad. ▸*abbr. Mathematics* ■ radical. ■ radix.

ra·dar /ˈrāˌdär/ ▸*n.* a system for detecting the presence, direction, distance, and speed of aircraft, ships, and other objects, by sending out pulses of high-frequency electromagnetic waves that are reflected off the object back to the source. ■ an apparatus used for this. ▷1940s: from *ra(dio) d(etection) a(nd) r(anging).*

ra·dar as·tron·o·my ▸*n.* the branch of astronomy that uses radar to map the surfaces of planetary bodies in the solar system.

ra·dar gun ▸*n.* a hand-held radar device used by traffic police to estimate the speed of a passing vehicle. ■ a similar device used to measure the speed of a pitched ball in baseball.

ra·dar trap ▸*n.* a speed trap in which police use radar.

Rad·cliff /ˈradˌklif/ a city in central Kentucky, northwest of Elizabethtown; pop. 21,961.

Rad·cliffe /ˈradklif/, Mrs. Ann (1764–1823), English novelist; a leading exponent of the Gothic novel. Notable works: *The Mysteries of Udolpho* (1794) and *The Italian* (1797).

rad·dle /ˈradl/ ▸*n.* another term for RUDDLE. ▷early 16th cent.: related to RED; compare with RUDDLE.

rad·dled /ˈradld/ ▸*adj.* (of a person or their face) showing signs of age or fatigue: *he's beginning to look quite raddled.* ▷from RADDLE in the sense 'rouge,' by association with its exaggerated use in makeup.

Ra·dha /ˈrädə/ *Hinduism* the favorite consort of the god Krishna, and an incarnation of Lakshmi. ▷from Sanskrit, literally 'prosperity.'

Ra·dha·krish·nan /ˌrädəˈkrishnən/, Sir Sarvepalli (1888–1975), Indian philosopher and statesman; president 1962–67. He introduced classical Indian philosophy to the West through works such as *Indian Philosophy* (1923–27).

ra·di·al /ˈrādēəl/ ▸*adj.* **1** of or arranged like rays or the radii of a circle; diverging in lines from a common center. ■ (or a road or route) running directly from a town or city center to an outlying district. ■ denoting a tire in which the layers of fabric have their cords running at right angles to the circumference of the tire and the tread is strengthened by further layers around the circumference. Compare with BIAS-PLY. ■ denoting an internal combustion engine with its cylinders fixed like the spokes of a wheel around a rotating crankshaft (a type used chiefly in aircraft). **2** *Anatomy & Zoology* of or relating to the radius.
▸*n.* **1** a radial tire. **2** a radial road. **3** *Zoology* a supporting ray in a fish's fin. **4** a radial engine. ▷late 16th cent.: from medieval Latin *radialis*, from Latin *radius* (see RADIUS). —**ra·di·al·ly** *adv.*

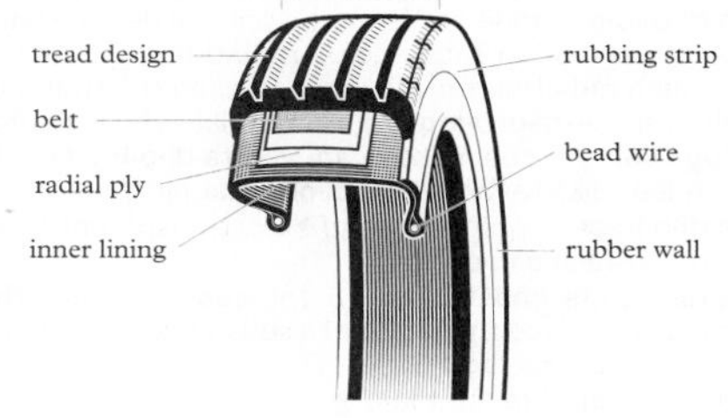

radial tire

ra·di·al ker·a·tot·o·my ▸*n.* see KERATOTOMY.

ra·di·al sym·me·try ▸*n. chiefly Biology* symmetry around a central axis, as in a starfish or a tulip flower.

ra·di·al ve·loc·i·ty ▸*n. chiefly Astronomy* the velocity of a star or other body along the line of sight of an observer.

ra·di·an /ˈrādēən/ ▸*n. Geometry* a unit of angle, equal to an angle at the center of a circle whose arc is equal in length to the radius.

ra·di·ance /ˈrādēəns/ ▸*n.* **1** light or heat as emitted or reflected by something: *the radiance of the sunset dwindled and died.* ■ great happiness, apparent in someone's expression or bearing: *the radiance of the bride's smile.* ■ a glowing quality of the skin, esp. as indicative of good health or youth. **2** *Physics* the flux of radiation emitted per unit solid angle in a given direction by a unit area of a source.

ra·di·ant /ˈrādēənt/ ▸*adj.* **1** sending out light; shining or glowing brightly: *a bird with radiant green and red plumage.* See note at BRIGHT. ■ (of a person or their expression) clearly emanating great joy, love, or health: *she gave him a radiant smile.* ■ (of an emotion or quality) emanating powerfully from someone or something; very intense or conspicuous: *he praised her radiant self-confidence.* **2** [*attrib.*] (of heat) transmitted by radiation, rather than conduction or convection. ■ (of an appliance) designed to emit such energy, esp. for cooking or heating.
▸*n.* a point or object from which light or heat radiates, esp. a heating element in an electric or gas heater. ▷late Middle English: from Latin *radiant-* 'emitting rays,' from the verb *radiare* (see RADIATE). —**ra·di·an·cy** /-ənsē/ *n.* —**ra·di·ant·ly** *adv.*

ra·di·ate ▸*v.* /ˈrādēˌāt/ **1** [*trans.*] emit (energy, esp. light or heat) in the form of rays or waves: *the hot stars radiate energy.* ■ [*intrans.*] (of light, heat, or other energy) be emitted in such a way: *the continual stream of energy that radiates from the sun.* ■ (of a person) clearly emanate (a strong feeling or quality) through their expression or bearing: *she lifted her chin, radiating defiance.* ■ (**radiate from**) (of a feeling or quality) emanate clearly from: *leadership and confidence radiate from her.* **2** [*intrans.*] diverge or spread from or as if from a central point: *he ran down one of the passages that radiated from the room.* ■ *Biology* (of an animal or plant group) evolve into a variety of forms adapted to new situations or ways of life.
▸*adj.* /ˈrādēət; -ˌāt/ *rare* having rays or parts proceeding from a center; arranged in or having a radial pattern: *the radiate crown.* ▷early 17th cent.: from Latin *radiat-* 'emitted in rays,' from the verb *radiare*, from *radius* 'ray, spoke.' —**ra·di·a·tive** /-ˌātiv/ *adj.* (in sense 1).

ra·di·a·tion /ˌrādēˈāshən/ ▸*n.* **1** *Physics* the emission of energy as electromagnetic waves or as moving subatomic particles, esp. high-energy particles that cause ionization. ■ the energy transmitted in this way, as heat, light, electricity, etc. **2** *chiefly Biology* divergence out from a central point, in particular evolution from an ancestral animal or plant group into a variety of new forms. ▷late Middle English (denoting the action of sending out rays of light): from Latin *radiatio(n-)*, from *radiare* 'emit rays' (see RADIATE). —**ra·di·a·tion·al** /-ˈāshənl/ *adj.* —**ra·di·a·tion·al·ly** /-ˈāshənl-ē/ *adv.*

ra·di·a·tion belt ▸*n. Astronomy* a region surrounding a planet where charged particles accumulate under the influence of the planet's magnetic field.

ra·di·a·tion sick·ness ▸*n.* illness caused by exposure of the body to ionizing radiation, characterized by nausea, hair loss, diarrhea, bleeding, and damage to the bone marrow and central nervous system.

ra·di·a·tion ther·a·py (also **ra·di·a·tion treat·ment**) ▸*n.* the treatment of disease, esp. cancer, using X-rays or similar forms of radiation.

ra·di·a·tor /ˈrādēˌātər/ ▸*n.* **1** a thing that radiates or emits light, heat, or sound. ■ a device for heating a room consisting of a metal case connected by pipes through which hot water is pumped by a central heating system. ■ a portable heater resembling such a device. **2** an engine-cooling device in a motor vehicle or aircraft consisting of a bank of thin tubes in which circulating fluid is cooled by the surrounding air.

rad·i·cal /ˈradikəl/ ▸*adj.* **1** (esp. of change or action) relating to or affecting the fundamental nature of something; far-reaching or thorough: *a radical overhaul of the existing regulatory framework.* ■ forming an inherent or fundamental part of the nature of someone or something: *the assumption of radical differences between the mental attributes of literate and nonliterate peoples.* ■ (of surgery or medical treatment) thorough and intended to be completely curative. ■ characterized by departure from tradition; innovative or progressive: *a radical approach to electoral reform.* **2** advocating thorough or complete political or social reform; representing or supporting an extreme section of a political party: *a radical American activist.* ■ (of a measure or policy) following or based on such principles. **3** of or relating to the root of something, in particular: ■ *Mathematics* of the root of a number or quantity. ■ denoting or relating to the roots of a word. ■ denoting the semantic or functional class of a Chinese character. ■ *Music* belonging to the root of a chord. ■ *Botany* of, or springing direct from, the root or stem base of a plant. **4** [usu. as *exclam.*] *informal* very good; excellent: *Okay, then. Seven o'clock. Radical!*
▸*n.* **1** a person who advocates thorough or complete political or social reform; a member of a political party or part of a party pursuing such aims. **2** *Chemistry* a group of atoms behaving as a unit in a number of compounds. See also FREE RADICAL. [early 19th cent.: from French.] **3** the root or base form of a word. ■ any of the basic set of 214 Chinese characters constituting semantically or functionally significant elements in the composition of other characters and used as a means of classifying characters in dictionaries. **4** *Mathematics* a quantity forming or expressed as the root of another. ■ a radical sign. ▷late Middle English (in the senses 'forming the root' and 'inherent'): from late Latin *radicalis*, from Latin *radix*, *radic-* 'root.' —**rad·i·cal·ism** /-ˌlizəm/ *n.* (in sense 1 of the *noun*). —**rad·i·cal·ly** /-ik(ə)lē/ *adv.* [as *submodifier*] *a radically different approach.* —**rad·i·cal·ness** *n.*

rad·i·cal chic ▸*n.* the fashionable affectation of radical left-wing views: [as *adj.*] *completely immersed himself in the subculture of radical chic liberals.* ■ the dress, lifestyle, or people associated with this. ▷1970: coined by U.S. writer Tom Wolfe.

rad·i·cal·ize /ˈradikəˌlīz/ ▸*v.* [*trans.*] cause (someone) to

R

become an advocate of radical political or social reform: *I'm trying to mobilize and radicalize the liberals.* **—rad·i·cal·i·za·tion** /ˌradikəli'zāSHən/ *n.*

rad·i·cal sign ▶*n. Mathematics* the sign √, which indicates the square root of the number following (or a higher root indicated by a preceding superscript numeral).

ra·dic·chi·o /ra'dēkēˌō; rə-/ ▶*n.* (*pl.* **-os**) chicory of a variety that has dark red leaves. ▷Italian.

rad·i·ces /'radəˌsēz; 'rā-/ ▶ plural form of RADIX.

rad·i·cle /'radikəl/ ▶*n. Botany* the part of a plant embryo that develops into the primary root. ■ *Anatomy* a rootlike subdivision of a nerve or vein. ▷late 17th cent.: from Latin *radicula*, diminutive of *radix, radic-* 'root.' **—ra·dic·u·lar** /rə'dikyələr/ *adj.* (*Anatomy*).

ra·di·i /'rādēˌī/ ▶ plural form of RADIUS.

ra·di·o /'rādēˌō/ ▶*n.* (*pl.* **-os**) the transmission and reception of electromagnetic waves of radio frequency, esp. those carrying sound messages: *cellular phones are linked by radio rather than wires.* ■ the activity or industry of broadcasting sound programs to the public: *she has written much material for radio* | [as *adj.*] *a radio station.* ■ radio programs: *we used to listen to a lot of radio.* ■ an apparatus for receiving such programs: *she turned on the radio.* ■ an apparatus capable of both receiving and transmitting radio messages between individuals, ships, planes, etc.: *a ship-to-shore radio.* ■ [in *names*] a broadcasting station or channel: *Monitor Radio.*
▶*v.* (**-oes, -oed**) [*intrans.*] communicate or send a message by radio: *the pilot radioed for help.* ■ [*trans.*] communicate with (a person or place) by radio: *we'll radio Athens right away.* ▷early 20th cent.: abbreviation of RADIOTELEPHONY (see RADIOTELEPHONE).

radio- ▶*comb. form* **1** denoting radio waves or broadcasting: *radio-controlled* | *radiogram.* **2** *Physics* connected with rays, radiation, or radioactivity: *radiogenic* | *radiograph.* ■ denoting artificially prepared radioisotopes of elements: *radio-cobalt.* **3** *Anatomy* belonging to the radius in conjunction with some other part: *radio-carpal.* ▷from RADIO or RADIUS.

ra·di·o·ac·tive /ˌrādēō'aktiv/ ▶*adj.* emitting or relating to the emission of ionizing radiation or particles: *radioactive decay* | *the water was radioactive.* **—ra·di·o·ac·tive·ly** *adv.*

ra·di·o·ac·tiv·i·ty /ˌrādēōak'tivətē/ ▶*n.* the emission of ionizing radiation or particles caused by the spontaneous disintegration of atomic nuclei. ■ radioactive substances, or the radiation emitted by these.

ra·di·o as·tron·o·my ▶*n.* the branch of astronomy concerned with radio emissions from celestial objects.

ra·di·o·bi·ol·o·gy /ˌrādēōbī'äləjē/ ▶*n.* the branch of biology concerned with the effects of ionizing radiation on organisms and the application in biology of radiological techniques. **—ra·di·o·bi·o·log·i·cal** /-ˌbīə'läjikəl/ *adj.* **—ra·di·o·bi·o·log·i·cal·ly** /-ˌbīə'läjik(ə)lē/ *adv.* **—ra·di·o·bi·ol·o·gist** /-jist/ *n.*

ra·di·o but·ton ▶*n. Computing* (in a graphical display) an icon representing one of a set of options, only one of which can be selected at any time.

ra·di·o car ▶*n.* a car, esp. a police car, equipped with a two-way radio.

ra·di·o·car·bon /ˌrādēō'kärbən/ ▶*n. Chemistry* a radioactive isotope of carbon.

ra·di·o·car·bon dat·ing ▶*n.* another term for CARBON DATING.

ra·di·o·chem·is·try /ˌrādēō'keməstrē/ ▶*n.* the branch of chemistry concerned with radioactive substances. **—ra·di·o·chem·i·cal** /-'kemikəl/ *adj.* **—ra·di·o·chem·ist** /-'kemist/ *n.*

ra·di·o·con·trolled ▶*adj.* (esp. of an electronic model toy) controllable from a distance by radio.

ra·di·o·el·e·ment /ˌrādēō'eləmənt/ ▶*n.* a radioactive element or isotope.

ra·di·o fre·quen·cy ▶*n.* a frequency or band of frequencies in the range 10^4 to 10^{11} or 10^{12} Hz, suitable for use in telecommunications.

ra·di·o gal·ax·y ▶*n.* a galaxy emitting radiation in the radio-frequency range of the electromagnetic spectrum.

ra·di·o·gen·ic /ˌrādēō'jenik/ ▶*adj.* produced by radioactivity: *a radiogenic isotope.* **—ra·di·o·gen·i·cal·ly** /-ik(ə)lē/ *adv.*

ra·di·o·go·ni·om·e·ter ▶*n.* an instrument for finding direction using radio waves.

ra·di·o·gram /'rādēōˌgram/ ▶*n.* **1** another term for RADIOGRAPH. **2** a message sent by radiotelegraphy.

ra·di·o·graph /'rādēōˌgraf/ ▶*n.* an image produced on a sensitive plate or film by X-rays, gamma rays, or similar radiation, and typically used in medical examination.
▶*v.* [*trans.*] produce an image of (something) on a sensitive plate or film by X-rays, gamma rays, or similar radiation. **—ra·di·og·ra·pher** /ˌrādē'ägrəfər/ *n.* **—ra·di·o·graph·ic** /ˌrādēō'grafik/ *adj.* **—ra·di·o·graph·i·cal·ly** /-ik(ə)lē/ *adv.* **—ra·di·og·ra·phy** /ˌrādē'ägrəfē/ *n.*

ra·di·o·im·mu·no·as·say /ˌrādēōˌimyənō'aˌsā/ ▶*n. Medicine* a technique for determining antibody levels by introducing an antigen labeled with a radioisotope and measuring the subsequent radioactivity of the antibody component.

ra·di·o·im·mu·nol·o·gy /ˌrādēōˌimyə'näləjē/ ▶*n.* the use of radioactively labeled antigens and antibodies in medical and biological research. **—ra·di·o·im·mu·no·log·i·cal** /-ˌimyənə'läjikəl/ *adj.* **—ra·di·o·im·mu·no·log·i·cal·ly** /-ik(ə)lē/ *adv.*

ra·di·o·i·so·tope /ˌrādēō'īsəˌtōp/ ▶*n. Chemistry* a radioactive isotope. **—ra·di·o·i·so·top·ic** /-ˌīsə'täpik/ *adj.*

ra·di·o·lar·i·a /ˌrādēə'lerēə/ ▶*plural n. Zoology* radiolarians collectively. ▷late 19th cent.: modern Latin (former order name), from late Latin *radiolus* 'faint ray,' diminutive of *radius* 'ray.'

ra·di·o·lar·i·an /ˌrādēə'le(ə)rēən/ *Zoology* ▶*n.* a single-celled aquatic animal that has a spherical, amebalike body with a spiny skeleton of silica. Their skeletons can accumulate as a slimy deposit on the seabed. • Three classes of the phylum Actinopoda, kingdom Protista (formerly subclass or order Radiolaria).
▶*adj.* of, relating to, or formed from radiolarians.

ra·di·ol·o·gy /ˌrādē'äləjē/ ▶*n.* the science dealing with X-rays and other high-energy radiation, esp. the use of such radiation for the diagnosis and treatment of disease. **—ra·di·o·log·ic** /ˌrādēə'läjik/ *adj.* **—ra·di·o·log·i·cal** /ˌrādēə'läjikəl/ *adj.* **—ra·di·o·log·i·cal·ly** /ˌrādēə'läjik(ə)lē/ *adv.* **—ra·di·ol·o·gist** /-jist/ *n.*

ra·di·o·lu·cent /ˌrādēō'lo͞osnt/ ▶*adj.* transparent to X-rays. **—ra·di·o·lu·cen·cy** *n.*

ra·di·ol·y·sis /rādē'äləsis/ ▶*n.* (pl.**-ses**) *Chemistry* the molecular decomposition of a substance by ionizing radiation.

ra·di·o·man /'rādēōˌman/ ▶*n.* a radio operator or technician.

ra·di·om·e·ter /ˌrādē'ämitər/ ▶*n.* an instrument for detecting or measuring the intensity or force of radiation. **—ra·di·o·met·ric** /-dēə'metrik/ *adj.* **—ra·di·o·met·ri·cal·ly** /-dēə'metrik(ə)lē/ *adv.* **—ra·di·om·e·try** /-trē/ *n.*

radiometer

ra·di·o·met·ric dat·ing ▶*n.* a method of dating geological or archeological specimens by determining the relative proportions of particular radioactive isotopes present in a sample.

ra·di·on·ics /ˌrādē'äniks/ ▶*plural n.* [treated as *sing.*] a system of alternative medicine based on the supposition that detectable electromagnetic radiation emitted by living matter can be interpreted diagnostically and transmitted to treat illness at a distance by complex electrical instruments. ▷1940s: from RADIO- 'radiation,' on the pattern of *electronics.*

ra·di·o·nu·clide /ˌrādēō'n(y)o͞oˌklīd/ ▶*n.* a radioactive nuclide.

ra·di·o·paque /ˌrādēō'pāk/ ▶*adj.* (of a substance) opaque to X-rays or similar radiation. **—ra·di·o·pac·i·ty** /ˌrādēō'pasədē/ *n.*

ra·di·o·phar·ma·ceu·ti·cal /ˌrādēōˌfärmə'so͞otikəl/ ▶*n.* a radioactive compound used for diagnostic or therapeutic purposes.

ra·di·o·phon·ic /ˌrādēō'fänik/ ▶*adj.* of, relating to, or denoting sound, esp. music, produced electronically.

ra·di·os·co·py /ˌrādē'äskəpē/ ▶*n. Physics* the examination by X-rays or similar radiation of objects opaque to light. **—ra·di·o·scop·ic** /'ˌrādēə'skäpik/ *adj.*

ra·di·o·sonde /'rādēōˌsänd/ ▶*n. dated* an instrument carried by balloon or other means to various levels of the atmosphere and transmitting measurements by radio. ▷1930s: from RADIO- (relating to broadcasting) + German *Sonde* 'probe.'

ra·di·o·te·leg·ra·phy /ˌrādēōtə'legrəfē/ ▶*n.* telegraphy using radio transmission. **—ra·di·o·tel·e·graph** /-'teləˌgraf/ *n.*

ra·di·o·tel·e·phone /ˌrādēō'teləˌfōn/ ▶*n.* a telephone that uses radio transmission. **—ra·di·o·te·leph·o·ny** /-tə'lefənē/ *n.* **—ra·di·o·tel·e·phon·ic** /-ˌtelə'fänik/ *adj.*

ra·di·o tel·e·scope ▶*n. Astronomy* an instrument used to detect radio emissions from the sky, whether from natural celestial objects or from artificial satellites.

ra·di·o·ther·a·py /ˌrādēō'THerəpē/ ▶*n.* another term for RADIATION THERAPY. **—ra·di·o·ther·a·peu·tic** /-ˌTHerə'pyo͞otik/ *adj.* **—ra·di·o·ther·a·pist** /-pist/ *n.*

ra·di·o wave ▶*n.* an electromagnetic wave of a frequency between about 10^4 and 10^{11} or 10^{12} Hz, as used for long-distance communication.

rad·ish /'radiSH/ ▶*n.* **1** a swollen pungent-tasting edible root, esp. a variety that is small, spherical, and red, and eaten raw with salad. **2** the plant of the cabbage family that yields this root. • *Raphanus sativus*, family Brassicaceae. ▷Old English *rædic*, from Latin *radix, radic-* 'root.'

ra·di·um /'rādēəm/ ▶*n.* the chemical element of atomic number 88, a rare radioactive metal of the alkaline earth series. It was formerly used as a source of radiation for radiotherapy. (Symbol: **Ra**) ▷late 19th cent.: from Latin *radius* 'ray' + -IUM.

ra·di·um em·a·na·tion ▶*n.* archaic term for RADON.

ra·di·us /'rādēəs/ ▶*n.* (*pl.* **ra·di·i** /'rādēˌī/ or **ra·di·us·es**) **1** a straight line from the center to the circumference of a circle or sphere. See also illustration at GEOMETRIC. ■ a radial line from the focus to any point of a curve. ■ the length of the radius of a circle or sphere. ■ a specified distance from a center in all directions: *there are plenty of local pubs within a two-mile radius.* **2** *Anatomy* the thicker and shorter of the two bones in the human forearm. Compare with ULNA. ■ *Zoology* the corresponding bone in a vertebrate's foreleg or a bird's wing. ■ *Zoology* (in an echinoderm or coelenterate) any of the primary axes of radial symmetry. ■ *Entomology* any of the main veins in an insect's wing. ▷late 16th cent. (sense 2): from Latin, literally 'staff, spoke, ray.'

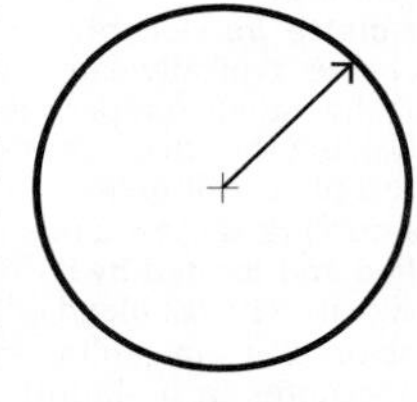

radius 1

ra·di·us of cur·va·ture ▶*n. Mathematics* the radius of a circle that touches a curve at a given point and has the same tangent and curvature at that point.

ra·di·us vec·tor ▶*n. Mathematics* a line of variable length drawn from a fixed origin to a curve. ■ *Astronomy* such a line joining a satellite or other celestial object to its primary.

ra·dix /'rādiks; 'rad-/ ▶*n.* (*pl.* **ra·di·ces** /'radəˌsēz; 'rā-/) **1** *Mathematics* the base of a system of numeration. See also BASE[1] (sense 8). **2** *formal* a source or origin of something: *Judaism is the radix of Christianity.* ▷early 17th cent. (sense 2): from Latin, literally 'root.' Sense 1 dates from the late 18th cent.

RADM (also **RAdm**) ▶*abbr.* rear admiral.

Rad·ner /'radnər/ *n.*, Gilda (1946–82), U.S. comedian and actress. She was an original cast member of television's "Saturday Night Live," where she developed characters such as Roseanne Roseannadana and Emily Litella. She also appeared in movies, including *The Woman in Red* (1984). The first Gilda's Club for support of cancer victims, founded by her husband Gene Wilder, opened in 1995.

Ra·dom /'räˌdôm/ an industrial city in central Poland; pop. 228,000.

ra·dome /'rāˌdōm/ ▶*n.* a dome or other structure protecting radar equipment and made from material transparent to radio waves, esp. one on the outer surface of an aircraft. ▷1940s: blend of RADAR and DOME.

ra·don /'rāˌdän/ ▶*n.* the chemical element of atomic number 86, a rare radioactive gas belonging to the noble gas series. (Symbol: **Rn**) ▷early 20th cent.: from RADIUM, on the pattern of *argon.*

rad·u·la /'rajələ/ ▶*n.* (*pl.* **-lae** /-lē; -ˌlī/) *Zoology* (in a mollusk) a rasplike structure of tiny teeth used for scraping food particles off a surface and drawing them into the mouth. ▷late 19th cent.: from Latin, literally 'scraper,' from *radere* 'to scrape.' **—rad·u·lar** /-lər/ *adj.*

rad·waste /'radˌwāst/ ▶*n. informal* radioactive waste.

Ra·el·i·an /rä'ēlēən/ ▶*n.* a member of an atheistic cult based on the belief that humans originated from alien scientists who came to earth in UFOs.
▶*adj.* relating to the Raelians or their beliefs. ▷1990s:

from *Rael*, assumed name of Claude Vorilhon, French singer and journalist, author of *The Message Given to Me by Extraterrestrials* (1974).

RAF *informal* ▶*abbr.* (in the UK) Royal Air Force.

Raf·fi /ˈrafē/ (1948–), Canadian songwriter and children's entertainer; full name *Raffi Cavoukian*. His many albums include *Singable Songs for the Very Young*, *Baby Beluga* (1980), *Bananaphone* (1994), *Everything Grows* (1996), and *Raffi's Box of Sunshine* (2000).

raf·fi·a /ˈrafēə/ ▶*n.* a palm tree native to tropical Africa and Madagascar, with a short trunk and leaves that may be up to 60 feet (18 m) long. • *Raphia ruffia*, family Palmae. ■ the fiber from these leaves, used for making items such as hats, baskets, and mats. ▷early 18th cent.: from Malagasy.

raf·fi·nate /ˈrafəˌnāt/ ▶*n.* *Chemistry* a liquid from which impurities have been removed by solvent extraction. ▷1920s: from French *raffiner* or German *raffinieren* 'refine' + **-ATE**[1].

raf·fi·nose /ˈrafəˌnōs; -ˌnōz/ ▶*n.* *Chemistry* a sugar present in sugar beet, cotton seed, and many grains. It is a trisaccharide containing glucose, galactose, and fructose units. ▷late 19th cent.: from French *raffiner* 'refine' + **-OSE**[2].

raff·ish /ˈrafisн/ ▶*adj.* unconventional and slightly disreputable, esp. in an attractive manner: *his raffish air.* ▷early 19th cent.: from **RIFFRAFF** + **-ISH**[1]. **—raf·fish·ly** *adv.* **—raf·fish·ness** *n.*

raf·fle[1] /ˈrafəl/ ▶*n.* a means of raising money by selling numbered tickets, one or some of which are subsequently drawn at random, the holder or holders of such tickets winning a prize.

▶*v.* [*trans.*] (usu. **be raffled**) offer (something) as a prize in such a lottery: *a work that will be **raffled off** for a fine arts scholarship.* ▷late Middle English (denoting a kind of dice game): from Old French, of unknown origin. The current sense dates from the mid 18th cent.

raf·fle[2] ▶*n.* rubbish; refuse: *the raffle of the yard below.* ▷late Middle English (in the sense 'rabble, riffraff'): perhaps from Old French *ne rifle ne rafle* 'nothing at all.'

Raf·fles /ˈrafəlz/, Sir (Thomas) Stamford (1781–1826), British colonial administrator. He persuaded the East India Company to purchase the undeveloped island of Singapore in 1819 and undertook much of the preliminary work for transforming it into an international port and center of commerce.

raf·fle·sia /rəˈflēzнə; ra-/ ▶*n.* a parasitic plant that lacks chlorophyll and bears a single, very large flower that smells of carrion, native to Malaysia and Indonesia. • Genus *Rafflesia*, family Rafflesiaceae: several species, including *R. arnoldii*, with flowers over 2 feet (60 cm) across. ▷modern Latin, named after Sir T. Stamford **RAFFLES**.

Raf·san·ja·ni /ˌräfsänˈjänē/, Ali Akbar Hashemi (1934–), Iranian statesman and religious leader; president 1989–97. In 1978, he helped organize the mass demonstrations that led to the shah's overthrow. As leader of Iran he sought to improve the country's relations with the West.

raft[1] /raft/ ▶*n.* a flat buoyant structure of timber or other materials fastened together, used as a boat or floating platform. ■ a small, inflatable rubber or plastic boat, esp. one for use in emergencies. ■ a floating mass of fallen trees, vegetation, ice, or other material. ■ a dense flock of swimming birds or mammals: *great **rafts of** cormorants, often 5,000 strong.* ■ a layer of reinforced concrete forming the foundation of a building.

▶*v.* **1** [*intrans.*] travel on or as if on a raft: *I have rafted along the Rio Grande.* ■ [*trans.*] transport on or as a raft: *the stores were rafted ashore | I rafted 400 logs to my mill.* ■ (of an ice floe) be driven on top of or underneath another floe. ■ [*trans.*] transport (timber) on water in the form of a raft. **2** [*trans.*] bring or fasten together (a number of boats or other objects) side by side. ▷late Middle English (in the sense 'beam, rafter'): from Old Norse *raptr* 'rafter.' The verb dates from the late 17th cent.

raft[2] ▶*n.* a large amount of something: ***a raft of** government initiatives.* ▷mid 19th cent.: alteration of dialect *raff* 'abundance' (perhaps of Scandinavian origin), by association with **RAFT**[1] in the sense 'floating mass.'

raft·er[1] /ˈraftər/ ▶*n.* one of several internal beams extending from the eaves to the peak of a roof and constituting its framework. ▷Old English *ræfter*, of Germanic origin; related to **RAFT**[1].

raft·er[2] ▶*n.* a person who travels on a raft.

raft·ered /ˈraftərd/ ▶*adj.* (of a room or ceiling) having exposed rafters. ■ built using rafters: *raftered roofs.*

raft·ing /ˈraftiNG/ ▶*n.* the sport or pastime of traveling down a river on a raft.

rafts·man /ˈraftsmən/ ▶*n.* (*pl.* **-men**) a man who works on a raft.

rag[1] /rag/ ▶*n.* **1** a piece of old cloth, esp. one torn from a larger piece, used typically for cleaning things: *he wiped his hands on an oily rag | a piece of rag.* ■ (**rags**) old or tattered clothes. ■ (**rags**) *figurative* the remnants of something: *she clung to **the rags of** her self-control.* ■ [with *negative*] *archaic* the smallest scrap of cloth or clothing: *not a rag of clothing has arrived to us this winter.* **2** *informal* a newspaper, typically one regarded as being of low quality: *the local rag.* ▷Middle English: probably a back-formation from **RAGGED** or **RAGGY**.

▶*PHRASES* □ **be on the rag** *informal* be menstruating. [from *rag* in the sense 'sanitary napkin.'] □ **chew the rag** see **CHEW**. □ **in rags** (of clothes) tattered and torn. ■ (of a person) wearing such clothes.

rag[2] ▶*v.* (**ragged** /ragd/, **rag·ging**) [*trans.*] **1** make fun of (someone) in a loud, boisterous manner. **2** rebuke severely.

▶*phrasal v.* □ **rag on** *informal* **1** complain about or criticize continually. **2** make fun of; tease constantly.

▶*n.* [usu. as *adj.*] *Brit.* a program of stunts, parades, and other entertainments organized by students to raise money for charity: *rag week.* ■ *informal, dated* a boisterous prank or practical joke. ▷mid 18th cent.: of unknown origin.

rag[3] ▶*n.* a large, coarse roofing slate. ▷late Middle English (in the sense 'a hard sedimentary rock that can be broken into slabs'): of unknown origin; later associated with **RAG**[1].

rag[4] ▶*n.* a ragtime composition or tune. ▷late 19th cent.: perhaps from **RAGGED**; compare with **RAGTIME**.

rag[5] ▶*n.* variant of **RAGA**.

ra·ga /ˈrägə/ ▶*n.* (in Indian music) a pattern of notes having characteristic intervals, rhythms, and embellishments, used as a basis for improvisation. ■ a piece using a particular raga. ▷late 18th cent.: from Sanskrit, literally 'color, musical tone.'

rag·a·muf·fin /ˈragəˌməfən/ ▶*n.* **1** a person, typically a child, in ragged, dirty clothes. **2** (also **rag·ga·muf·fin**) *chiefly Brit.* an exponent or follower of ragga, typically one dressing in ragged clothes. ■ another term for **RAGGA**. ▷Middle English: probably based on **RAG**[1], with a fanciful suffix.

rag-and-bone man ▶*adj.* an itinerant dealer in old clothes, furniture, and small, cheap secondhand items.

rag·bag /ˈragˌbag/ ▶*n.* a bag in which scraps of fabric and old clothes are kept for use. ■ a miscellaneous collection of something: *Lee threw **a ragbag of** pitches.*

rag doll ▶*n.* a soft doll made from pieces of cloth.

rage /rāj/ ▶*n.* violent, uncontrollable anger: *her face was distorted with rage | she flew into a rage.* ■ *figurative* the violent action of a natural agency: *the rising rage of the sea.* ■ [in *sing.*] a vehement desire or passion: ***a rage for** absolute honesty informs much western art.* ■ [with *modifier*] an instance of aggressive behavior or violent anger caused by a stressful or frustrating situation: *desk rage | sports rage | PC rage.* ■ (**the rage**) a widespread temporary enthusiasm or fashion: *video and computer games are **all the rage**.* ■ *poetic/literary* intense feeling, esp. prophetic, poetic, or martial enthusiasm or ardor.

▶*v.* [*intrans.*] feel or express violent uncontrollable anger: *he **raged at** the futility of it all |* [with *direct speech*] *"That's unfair!" Maggie raged.* ■ [with *adverbial*] (of a natural agency or a conflict) continue violently or with great force: *the argument raged for days.* ■ [with *adverbial of direction*] (of an illness) spread very rapidly or uncontrollably: *the great cholera epidemic that raged across Europe in 1831.* ■ (of an emotion) have or reach a high degree of intensity: *she couldn't hide the fear that raged within her.* ▷Middle English (also in the sense 'madness'): from Old French *rage* (noun), *rager* (verb), from a variant of Latin *rabies* (see **RABIES**).

rag·ga /ˈragə/ ▶*n.* *chiefly Brit.* a style of dance music similiar to dancehall in which a DJ improvises lyrics over a sampled or electronic backing track. ▷1990s: from **RAGAMUFFIN**, because of the style of clothing worn by its followers.

rag·ga·muf·fin /ˈragəˌməfən/ ▶*n.* variant spelling of **RAGAMUFFIN**.

rag·ged /ˈragid/ ▶*adj.* **1** (of cloth or clothes) old and torn. ■ (of a person) wearing such clothes: *a ragged child.* **2** having a rough, irregular, or uneven surface, edge, or outline: *a ragged coastline.* ■ lacking finish, smoothness, or uniformity: *the ragged discipline of the players.* ■ (of a sound) rough or uneven: *his breathing became ragged.* ■ (of an animal) having a rough, shaggy coat: *a pair of ragged ponies.* ■ *Printing* (esp. of a right margin) uneven because the lines are unjustified. **3** suffering from exhaustion or stress: *he looked a little ragged, a little shadowy beneath the eyes.* ▷Middle English: of Scandinavian origin; compare with Old Norse *rǫgvathr* 'tufted' and Norwegian *ragget* 'shaggy.' **—rag·ged·ly** *adv.* **—rag·ged·ness** *n.*

▶*PHRASE* □ **run someone ragged** exhaust someone by making them undertake a lot of physical activity.

rag·ged·y /ˈragədē/ ▶*adj.* *informal* scruffy; shabby.

rag·ged·y-ass (also **rag·ged·y-assed**) ▶*adj.* [*attrib.*] *informal* shabby; miserably inadequate: *she finally sold that raggedy-ass house.* ■ (of a person) new and inexperienced.

rag·gle-tag·gle /ˈragəl ˌtagəl/ ▶*adj.* **UNTIDY AND SCRUFFY.** ▷early 20th cent.: apparently a fanciful variant of **RAGTAG**.

rag·gy /ˈragē/ ▶*adj.* (**-gi·er**, **-gi·est**) *informal* ragged: *his raggy clothes.* ▷late Old English, of Scandinavian origin.

rag·head /ˈragˌhed/ ▶*n.* *informal, offensive* a person who wears a turban.

rag·i /ˈragē/ ▶*n.* *chiefly Indian* another term for **FINGER MILLET** (see **MILLET**). ▷from Sanskrit and Hindi *rāgī*, from Telugu.

rag·ing /ˈrājiNG/ ▶*adj.* showing violent uncontrollable anger: *a raging bull.* ■ (of a natural agency) continuing with overpowering force: *the stream could become a raging torrent in wet weather.* ■ (of a feeling, illness, process, or activity) so powerful as to seem out of control: *her raging thirst.* ■ *informal* tremendous: *he had been a raging success in Spain.*

raglan sleeves

rag·lan /ˈraglən/ ▶*adj.* (of a sleeve) continuing in one piece up to the neck of a garment, without a shoulder seam. ■ (of a garment) having sleeves of this type.

▶*n.* an overcoat with sleeves of this type. ▷mid 19th cent.: named after Lord *Raglan* (1788–1855), a British commander in the Crimean War.

rag·man /ˈragˌman/ ▶*n.* (*pl.* **-men**) a person who collects or deals in rags, old clothes, and other items.

Rag·na·rök /ˈragnəˌräk; -rək/ *Scandinavian Mythology* the final battle between the gods and the powers of evil, the Scandinavian equivalent of the *Götterdämmerung*. ▷from Old Norse *ragnarǫkr* 'twilight of the gods.'

ra·gout /raˈgo͞o/ ▶*n.* a highly seasoned dish of meat cut into small pieces and stewed with vegetables. ▷from French *ragoût*, from *ragoûter* 'revive the taste of.'

rag pa·per ▶*n.* paper made from cotton, originally from cotton rags, but now from cotton linters.

rag·pick·er /ˈragˌpikər/ ▶*n.* *historical* a person who collected and sold rags.

rag-roll ▶*v.* [*trans.*] create a striped or marbled effect on (a surface) by painting it with a rag crumpled up into a roll.

rag rug ▶*n.* a rug made from small strips of fabric hooked into or pushed through a base material such as hessian.

rag·tag /ˈragˌtag/ ▶*adj.* [*attrib.*] untidy, disorganized, or incongruously varied in character: *a ragtag group of idealists.*

▶*n.* (also **rag·tag and bob·tail**) [in *sing.*] a group of people perceived as disreputable or undesirable. ▷early 19th cent.: superseding earlier *tag-rag* and *tag and rag* (see **RAG**[1], **TAG**[1]).

rag·time /ˈragˌtīm/ ▶*n.* music characterized by a syncopated melodic line and regularly accented accompaniment, evolved by black American musicians in the 1890s and played esp. on the piano. ▷probably from **RAG**[4] (from the syncopation) + **TIME**.

rag·top /ˈragˌtäp/ ▶*n.* a car with a convertible roof.

rag trade ▶*n.* (**the rag trade**) *informal* the clothing or fashion industry.

rag·u·ly /ˈragyəlē/ ▶*adj.* [usu. *postpositive*] *Heraldry* having an edge with oblique notches like a row of sawn-off branches. ▷mid 17th cent.: perhaps from RAGGED, on the pattern of *nebuly*.

Ra·gu·sa /rəˈgo͞ozə; räˈgo͞ozä/ Italian name (until 1918) of DUBROVNIK.

rag·weed /ˈrag,wēd/ ▶*n.* a North American plant of the daisy family. Its tiny green flowers produce copious amounts of pollen, making it a major causative agent of hay fever in some areas. • *Ambrosia artemisia*, family Compositae.

rag·wort /ˈrag,wərt; -,wôrt/ ▶*n.* a yellow-flowered plant of the daisy family that is a common weed of grazing land. It is toxic to livestock, esp. when dried. • Genus *Senecio*, family Compositae: several species, including the ragged-leaved **tansy ragwort** (*S. jacobaea*).

rah /rä/ ▶*exclam. informal* a cheer of encouragement or approval. ▷late 19th cent.: shortening of HURRAH.

Rah·man see ABDUL RAHMAN, MUJIBUR RAHMAN.

rah-rah *informal* ▶*adj.* marked by great or uncritical enthusiasm or excitement: *many players were turned off by his rah-rah style.*
▶*n.* great or uncritical enthusiasm and excitement. ▷early 20th cent.: reduplication of RAH.

Rah·way /ˈrô,wā; ˈrä-/ an industrial city in northeastern New Jersey, southwest of Elizabeth; pop. 25,325.

rai /rī/ ▶*n.* a style of music fusing Arabic and Algerian folk elements with Western rock. ▷1980s: perhaps from Arabic *ha er-ray*, literally 'that's the thinking, here is the view,' a phrase frequently found in the songs.

RAID /rād/ ▶*abbr.* redundant array of independent (or inexpensive) disks, a system for providing greater capacity, faster access, and security against data corruption by spreading the data across several disk drives.

raid /rād/ ▶*n.* a sudden attack on an enemy by troops, aircraft, or other armed forces in warfare: *a bombing raid.* ■ a surprise attack to commit a crime, esp. to steal from business premises: *an early morning* ***raid on*** *a bank.* ■ a surprise visit by police to arrest suspected people or seize illicit goods. ■ *Stock Market* a hostile attempt to buy a major or controlling interest in the shares of a company.
▶*v.* [*trans.*] conduct a raid on: *officers raided thirty homes yesterday.* ■ quickly and illicitly take something from (a place): *she crept down the stairs to raid the larder.* ▷late Middle English (as a noun): Scots variant of ROAD in the early senses 'journey on horseback,' 'foray.' The noun became rare from the end of the 16th cent. but was revived by Sir Walter Scott; the verb dates from the mid 19th cent. —**raid·er** *n.*

rail[1] /rāl/ ▶*n.* **1** a bar or series of bars, typically fixed on upright supports, serving as part of a fence or barrier or used to hang things on. ■ (**the rails**) the inside boundary fence of a racecourse. ■ the edge of a surfboard or sailboard. ■ the rim of a billiard or pool table. **2** a steel bar or continuous line of bars laid on the ground as one of a pair forming a railroad track: *trolley rails.* ■ [often as *adj.*] railroads as a means of transportation: *rail fares | traveling by rail.* **3** a horizontal piece in the frame of a paneled door or sash window. Compare with STILE[2]. **4** *Electronics* a conductor that is maintained at a fixed potential and to which other parts of a circuit are connected.
▶*v.* **1** [*trans.*] provide or enclose (a space or place) with a rail or rails: *the altar is* ***railed off from*** *the nave.* **2** [*intrans.*] (in windsurfing) sail the board on its edge, so that it is at a sharp angle to the surface of the water. ▷Middle English: from Old French *reille* 'iron rod,' from Latin *regula* 'straight stick, rule.' —**rail·less** *adj.*
▶*PHRASE* □ **go off the rails** *informal* begin behaving in a strange, abnormal, or wildly uncontrolled way.

rail[2] ▶*v.* [*intrans.*] (**rail against/at/about**) complain or protest strongly and persistently about: *he railed at human fickleness.* ▷late Middle English: from French *railler*, from Provençal *ralhar* 'to jest,' based on an alteration of Latin *rugire* 'to bellow.' —**rail·er** *n.*

rail[3] ▶*n.* a secretive bird with drab gray and brown plumage, typically having a long bill and found in dense waterside vegetation. • Family Rallidae (the **rail family**): several genera, esp. *Rallus*, and numerous species. The rail family also includes the crakes, gallinules, moorhens, and coots. ▷late Middle English: from Old Northern French *raille*, perhaps of imitative origin.

rail·bird /ˈrāl,bərd/ ▶*n.* a spectator, esp. one at a horse race who watches from the railings along the track.

rail car ▶*n.* any railroad car or wagon.

rail fence ▶*n.* a fence, typically a wooden one, made of posts and rails.

rail·head /ˈrāl,hed/ ▶*n.* a point on a railroad from which roads and other transportation routes begin. ■ the furthest point reached in constructing a railroad.

rail·ing /ˈrāliNG/ ▶*n.* (usu. **railings**) a fence or barrier made of rails.

rail·ler·y /ˈrālərē/ ▶*n.* good-humored teasing. ▷mid 17th cent.: from French *raillerie*, from *railler* 'to rail' (see RAIL[2]).

rail·man /ˈrālmən/ ▶*n.* (*pl.* **-men**) chiefly British term for RAILROADER.

rail·road /ˈrāl,rōd/ ▶*n.* **1** a track or set of tracks made of steel rails along which passenger and freight trains run: [as *adj.*] *a railroad line.* ■ a set of tracks for other vehicles. **2** a system of such tracks with the trains, organization, and personnel required for its working: [in *names*] *the Union Pacific Railroad.*
▶*v.* **1** [*trans.*] *informal* press (someone) into doing something by rushing or coercing them: *she hesitated, unwilling to be* ***railroaded into*** *a decision.* ■ cause (a measure) to be passed or approved quickly by applying pressure: *the Bill had been* ***railroaded through*** *the House.* ■ send (someone) to prison without a fair trial or by means of false evidence. **2** [*intrans.*] [usu. as *n.*] (**railroading**) travel or work on the railroads.

rail·road·er ▶*n.* a person who works for a railroad.

rail·way /ˈrāl,wā/ ▶*n.* chiefly British term for RAILROAD.

rail·way·man /ˈrāl,wāmən/ ▶*n.* (*pl.* **-men**) *chiefly Brit.* another term for RAILROADER.

rai·ment /ˈrāmənt/ ▶*n. archaic* or *poetic/literary* clothing: *ladies clothed in raiment bedecked with jewels.* ▷late Middle English: shortening of obsolete *arrayment* 'dress, outfit.'

rain /rān/ ▶*n.* moisture condensed from the atmosphere that falls visibly in separate drops: *the rain had not stopped for days | it's pouring rain.* ■ (**rains**) falls of rain: *the plants were washed away by some unusually heavy rains.* ■ [in *sing.*] a large or overwhelming quantity of things that fall or descend: *he fell under the* ***rain of*** *blows.*
▶*v.* [*intrans.*] (**it rains, it is raining**, etc.) rain falls: *it was beginning to rain.* ■ *poetic/literary* (of the sky, the clouds, etc.) send down rain. ■ [with *adverbial of direction*] (of objects) fall in large or overwhelming quantities: *bombs rained down.* ■ [*trans.*] (**it rains ——, it is raining ——**, etc.) used to convey that a specified thing is falling in large or overwhelming quantities: *it was just raining glass.* ■ [*trans.*] send down in large or overwhelming quantities: *she rained blows onto him.*
▶*phrasal v.* □ **rain something out** (usu. **be rained out**) cause an event to be terminated or canceled because of rain: *the tournament was rained out.* ▷Old English *regn* (noun), *regnian* (verb), of Germanic origin; related to Dutch *regen* and German *Regen*. —**rain·less** *adj.*
▶*PHRASES* □ **be as right as rain** (of a person) be perfectly fit and well. □ **when it rains it pours** see POUR. □ **rain cats and dogs** rain very hard. [origin uncertain; first recorded in 1738, used by Jonathan Swift, but the phrase *rain dogs and polecats* was used a century earlier in Richard Brome's *The City Witt.*] □ **rain on someone's parade** *informal* prevent someone from enjoying an occasion or event; spoil someone's plans. □ (**come**) **rain or shine** whether it rains or not: *he runs six miles every morning, rain or shine.*

rain·bow /ˈrān,bō/ ▶*n.* an arch of colors formed in the sky in certain circumstances, caused by the refraction and dispersion of the sun's light by rain or other water droplets in the atmosphere. ■ any display of the colors of the spectrum produced by dispersion of light. ■ a wide range or variety of related and typically colorful things: ***a rainbow of*** *medals decorated his chest.* ■ [as *adj.*] many-colored: *a big rainbow packet of felt pens.* ■ short for RAINBOW TROUT. ▷Old English *regnboga* (see RAIN, BOW[1]).
▶*PHRASES* □ **at the end of the rainbow** used to refer to something much sought after but impossible to attain. [with allusion to the story of a pot of gold supposedly to be found by anyone reaching the end of a rainbow.] □ **chase rainbows** (or **a rainbow**) pursue an illusory goal.

Rain·bow Bridge a bridge of natural rock, the world's largest natural bridge, situated in southern Utah, just north of the border with Arizona. Its span is 278 feet (86 m).

rain·bow co·a·li·tion ▶*n.* a political alliance of differing groups, typically one comprising minority peoples and other disadvantaged groups.

rain·bow lor·i·keet (also **rain·bow lor·y**) ▶*n.* a small, vividly colored Australasian parrot, found in many different races on southwestern Pacific islands. • *Trichoglossus haematodus*, family Loridae (or Psittacidae).

rain·bow trout ▶*n.* a large trout native to the Pacific seaboard of North America. It has been widely introduced elsewhere, both as a farmed food fish and as a sporting fish. Most rainbow trout remain in streams, but some migrate to lakes and some to the sea (see STEELHEAD). • *Salmo gairdneri*, family Salmonidae.

rain check /ˈrān,CHek/ (also **rain-check**) ▶*n.* a ticket given for later use when a sports event or other outdoor event is interrupted or postponed by rain. ■ a coupon issued to a customer by a store, guaranteeing that a sale item that is out of stock may be purchased by that customer at a later date at the same reduced price.
▶*PHRASE* □ **take a rain check** said when politely refusing an offer, with the implication that one may accept it at a later date: *I can't make it tonight, but I'd like to take a rain check.*

rain·coat /ˈrān,kōt/ ▶*n.* a long coat made from waterproofed or water-resistant fabric.

rain dance ▶*n.* a ritual done to summon rain, as practiced by some Pueblo Indian and other peoples.

rain date ▶*n.* an alternative date for an event in case of inclement weather. ■ *Baseball* the day to which a rained-out game is postponed.

rain·drop /ˈrān,dräp/ ▶*n.* a single drop of rain. ▷Old English *regndropa* (see RAIN, DROP).

Rain·ey /ˈrānē/, Ma (1886–1939), U.S. blues singer; full name *Gertrude Pridgett Rainey*. She made over 100 recordings with Louis Armstrong and with her Georgia Jazz Band.

rain·fall /ˈrān,fôl/ ▶*n.* the fall of rain. ■ the quantity of rain falling within a given area in a given time: *low rainfall.*

rain·fly /ˈrān,flī/ ▶*n.* (*pl.* **-flies**) the flysheet of a tent.

rain for·est (also **rain·for·est**) ▶*n.* a luxuriant, dense forest rich in biodiversity, found typically in tropical areas with consistently heavy rainfall.

rain gauge ▶*n.* a device for collecting and measuring the amount of rain that falls.

Rai·nier, Mount /rəˈni(ə)r; rā-/ a volcanic peak in southwestern Washington state. Rising to a height of 14,410 feet (4,395 m), it is the highest peak in the Cascade Range.

Rain-in-the-Face (c.1835–1905), Native-American Sioux warrior. With Sitting Bull and others, he annihilated the forces under Custer at Little Bighorn in 1876.

rain·mak·er /ˈrān,mākər/ ▶*n.* a person who attempts to cause rain to fall, either by rituals or by a scientific technique such as seeding clouds with crystals. ■ *informal* a person who is highly successful, esp. in business. ■ a person who has influential business or political connections. —**rain·mak·ing** /-,mākiNG/ *n.*

rain·out /ˈrān,out/ ▶*n.* a cancellation or premature ending of an event because of rain.

rain·proof /ˈrān,pro͞of/ ▶*adj.* (esp. of a building or garment) impervious to rain: *a rainproof coat.*

rain scald ▶*n.* a skin disease of horses caused by infection with actinomycete bacteria, typically contracted in persistently rainy conditions.

rain shad·ow ▶*n.* a region having little rainfall because it is sheltered from prevailing rain-bearing winds by a range of hills.

rain·stick ˈrān,stik (also **rain stick**) ▶*n.* a percussion instrument made from a dried cactus branch that is hollowed out, filled with small pebbles, and capped at both ends. When slightly tilted, it makes the sound of falling rain. It originated in Chile, where native people had long used the sticks to serenade the gods in hopes of bringing rain.

rain·storm /ˈrān,stôrm/ ▶*n.* a storm with heavy rain.

rain·swept /ˈrān,swept/ ▶*adj.* exposed to or frequently experiencing rain and wind: *a rainswept day in November.*

rain tree ▶*n.* a large tropical American tree that is widely planted as a street tree. It has grooved bark that typically supports epiphytic plants, and "rain" (as it mimics the sound of rain) that is excreted by cicadas that live in the tree. • *Albizia saman*, family Leguminosae.

rain·wash /ˈrān,wôSH; -,wäSH/ ▶*n.* the washing away of soil or other loose material by rain.

rain·wa·ter /ˈrān,wôtər; -,wätər/ ▶*n.* water that has fallen as or been obtained from rain.

rain·wear /ˈrān,we(ə)r/ ▶*n.* waterproof or water-resistant clothes suitable for wearing in the rain.

rain·worm /ˈrān,wərm/ ▶*n.* **1** the earthworm, which often comes to the surface after rain. **2** a soil-dwelling nematode worm, the juveniles of which parasitize grasshoppers. • *Mermis nigrescens*, class Aphasmida (or Adenophorea).

rain·y /ˈrānē/ ▸*adj.* (**rain·i·er, rain·i·est**) (of weather, a period of time, or an area) having a great deal of rainfall: *a rainy afternoon.* ▷Old English *rēnig* (see RAIN, -Y[1]). —**rain·i·ness** *n.*

▸*PHRASE* □ **a rainy day** used in reference to a possible time in the future when something, esp. money, will be needed: *invest and save for a rainy day.*

Rain·y Riv·er /ˈrānē/ a short river that flows west along the Minnesota-Ontario border, past International Falls, into the Lake of the Woods. One of its sources is Rainy Lake, also on the border.

Rai·pur /ˈrīpo͝or/ a city in central India, in Madhya Pradesh; pop. 438,000.

raise /rāz/ ▸*v.* [*trans.*] **1** lift or move to a higher position or level: *she raised both arms above her head | his flag was raised over the city.* ■ lift or move to a vertical position; set upright: *Melody managed to raise him to his feet.* ■ construct or build (a structure): *a fence was being raised around the property.* ■ cause to rise or form: *the galloping horse raised a cloud of dust.* ■ bring to the surface (something that has sunk). ■ cause (bread) to rise, esp. by the action of yeast: [as *adj.*] (**raised**) *raised doughnuts.* ■ make a (nap) on cloth. **2** increase the amount, level, or strength of: *the bank raised interest rates | the aim was to raise awareness of the plight of the homeless.* ■ promote (someone) to a higher rank: *the king* **raised** *him* **to** *the title of Count Torre Bella.* ■ [usu. as *n.*] (**raising**) *Linguistics* (in transformational grammar) move (an element) from a lower structure to a higher one. ■ (**raise something to**) *Mathematics* multiply a quantity by itself to (a specified power): *3 raised to the 7th power is 2,187.* ■ [with *two objs.*] (in poker or brag) bet (a specified amount) more than (another player): *I'll raise you another hundred dollars.* ■ [*trans.*] *Bridge* make a higher bid in the same suit as that bid by (one's partner). ■ [*trans.*] increase (a bid) in this way. **3** cause to be heard, considered, or discussed: *the alarm was raised when he failed to return home | doubts have been raised about the future of the reprocessing plant.* ■ cause to occur, appear, or be felt: *recent sightings have raised hopes that otters are making a return.* ■ generate (an invoice or other document). **4** collect, levy, or bring together (money or resources): *she was attempting to raise $20,000.* **5** bring up (a child): *he was born and raised in San Francisco.* ■ breed or grow (animals or plants): *they raised pigs and kept a pony.* **6** bring (someone) back from death: *God* **raised** *Jesus* **from the dead.** **7** abandon or force an enemy to abandon (a siege, blockade, or embargo). **8** drive (an animal) from its lair: *the jack rabbit was only 250 yards from where he first raised it.* ■ cause (a ghost or spirit) to appear: *figurative the piece raises the ghosts of a number of twentieth-century art ideas.* ■ *Brit., informal* establish contact with (someone), esp. by telephone or radio: *I raised him on the open line.* ■ (of someone at sea) come in sight of (land or another ship): *they raised the low coast by evening.* **9** *Immunology* stimulate production of (an antiserum, antibody, or other biologically active substance) against the appropriate target cell or substance.

▸*n.* **1** an increase in salary: *he wants a raise and some perks.* **2** (in poker or brag) an increase in a stake. ■ *Bridge* a higher bid in the suit that one's partner has bid. **3** [usu. with *adj.*] *Weightlifting* an act of lifting or raising a part of the body while holding a weight: *bent-over raises.* ▷Middle English: from Old Norse *reisa*; related to the verb REAR[2]. —**rais·a·ble** *adj.* —**rais·er** *n.*

▸*PHRASES* □ **raise Cain** see CAIN. □ **raise the devil** *informal* make a noisy disturbance. □ **raise one's eyebrows** see EYEBROW. □ **raise one's glass** drink a toast: *I* **raised my glass** *to Susan.* □ **raise one's hand** strike or seem to be about to strike someone: *she* **raised her hand to** *me.* □ **raise one's hat** briefly remove one's hat as a gesture of courtesy or respect to someone. □ **raise hell** *informal* make a noisy disturbance. ■ complain vociferously: *he raised hell with real estate developers and polluters.* □ **raise hob** see HOB[2]. □ **raise a laugh** make people laugh. □ **raise the roof** make or cause someone else to make a great deal of noise, esp. through cheering: *when I finally scored, the fans raised the roof.* □ **raise one's voice** speak more loudly. ■ begin to speak or sing.

raised beach ▸*n. Geology* a former beach now lying above water level owing to geological changes since its formation.

rai·sin /ˈrāzən/ ▸*n.* a partially dried grape. ▷Middle English: from Old French, 'grape,' from an alteration of Latin *racemus* 'grape bunch.' —**rai·sin·y** *adj.*

rai·son d'é·tat /rāˈzôɴ dāˈtä/ ▸*n.* (*pl.* **rai·sons d'é·tat** /rāˈzôɴ(z)/) a purely political reason for action on the part of a ruler or government, esp. where a departure from openness, justice, or honesty is involved. ▷French, literally 'reason of state.'

rai·son d'ê·tre /rāˈzôɴ ˈdetr(ə)/ ▸*n.* (*pl.* **rai·sons d'ê·tre** /rāˈzôn(z)/) the most important reason or purpose for someone or something's existence: *an institution whose raison d'être is public service broadcasting.* ▷French, literally 'reason for being.'

rai·ta /ˈrītə/ ▸*n.* an Indian side dish of yogurt containing chopped cucumber or other vegetables, and spices. ▷from Hindi *rāytā.*

raj /räj/ ▸*n.* (**the Raj**) *historical* British sovereignty in India: *the last days of the Raj.* ■ (**raj**) *Indian* rule; government. ▷from Hindi *rāj* 'reign.'

ra·jah /ˈräjə; ˈräzʜə/ (also **ra·ja**) ▸*n. historical* an Indian king or prince. ■ a title extended to petty dignitaries and nobles in India during the British Raj. ■ a title extended by the British to a Malay or Javanese ruler or chief. ▷from Hindi *rājā*, Sanskrit *rājan* 'king.'

ra·jas /ˈrəjəs/ ▸*n.* (in Vedanta) the element or mode of prakriti associated with passion, energy, and movement.

ra·jas·ic /rəˈjasik/ ▸*adj.* (in Ayurveda) denoting a class of foods that are bitter, sour, salty, pungent, hot, or dry, and are thought to promote sensuality, greed, jealousy, anger, delusion, and irreligious feelings. Compare SATTVIC, TAMASIC.

Ra·ja·sthan /ˈräjəˌstän/ a state in western India, on the Pakistani border; capital, Jaipur. The western part of the state consists largely of the Thar Desert and is sparsely populated. —**Ra·ja·stha·ni** /ˌräjəˈstänē/ *n.* & *adj.*

ra·ja yo·ga ▸*n.* a form of Hindu yoga intended to achieve control over the mind and emotions. ▷from Sanskrit, from *rājan* 'king' + YOGA.

Raj·kot /ˈräjkōt/ a city in Gujarat, in western India; pop. 556,000.

Raj·neesh /räjˈnēsʜ/, Bhagwan Shree (1931–90), Indian guru; born *Chandra Mohan Jain*; known as **the Bhagwan** (Sanskrit, "lord"). He founded an ashram in Poona, India, and a commune in Oregon and preached his doctrine of communal therapy and salvation through free love. He was deported from the U.S. in 1985 for immigration violations.

Raj·put /ˈräjˌpo͝ot; ˈräzʜ-/ ▸*n.* a member of a Hindu military caste claiming Kshatriya descent. ▷from Hindi *rājpūt*, from Sanskrit *rājan* 'king' + *putra* 'son.'

Raj·sha·hi /räjˈsʜäˌhē/ a port on the Ganges River in western Bangladesh; pop. 325,000.

Raj·ya Sab·ha /ˈräjə səˈbä/ the upper house of the Indian parliament. Compare with LOK SABHA. ▷from Sanskrit *rājya* 'State' + *sabhā* 'council.'

rake[1] /rāk/ ▸*n.* an implement consisting of a pole with a crossbar toothed like a comb at the end, or with several tines held together by a crosspiece, used esp. for drawing together cut grass or smoothing loose soil or gravel. ■ a wheeled implement used for the same purposes. ■ a similar implement used for other purposes, e.g., by a croupier drawing in money at a gaming table.

▸*v.* [*trans.*] collect, gather, or move with a rake or similar implement: *they started* **raking up** *hay.* ■ make (a stretch of ground) tidy or smooth with a rake: *the infield dirt is meticulously raked.* ■ scratch or scrape (something, esp. a person's flesh) with a long sweeping movement: *her fingers raked Bill's face.* ■ [*trans.*] draw or drag (something) with a long sweeping movement: *she raked a comb through her hair.* ■ sweep (something) from end to end with gunfire, a look, or a beam of light: *Greg let his high beams rake the shrubbery.* ■ [*intrans.*] move across something with a long sweeping movement: *his icy gaze raked mercilessly over Lissa's slender figure.* ■ [*intrans.*] search or rummage through something: *Nina decided to rake through the drawers.*

▸*phrasal v.* □ **rake in something** *informal* make a lot of money, typically very easily: *he was now raking in $250 million a year.* □ **rake something up/over** revive the memory of an incident or period of time that is best forgotten: *I have no desire to rake over the past.* ▷Old English *raca, racu*, of Germanic origin; related to Dutch *raak* and German *Rechen*, from a base meaning 'heap up'; the verb is partly from Old Norse *raka* 'to scrape, shave.' —**rak·er** *n.*

▸*PHRASE* □ (**as**) **thin as a rake** (of a person) very thin.

rake[2] ▸*n.* a fashionable or wealthy man of dissolute or promiscuous habits. ▷mid 17th cent.: abbreviation of archaic *rakehell* in the same sense.

▸*PHRASE* □ **a rake's progress** a progressive deterioration, esp. through self-indulgence. [from the title of a series of engravings (1735) by Hogarth.]

rake[3] ▸*v.* [*trans.*] (often **be raked**) set (something, esp. a stage or the floor of an auditorium) at a sloping angle. ■ [*intrans.*] (of a ship's mast or funnel) incline from the perpendicular toward the stern. ■ [*intrans.*] (of a ship's bow or stern) project at its upper part beyond the keel.

▸*n.* **1** [in *sing.*] the angle at which a thing slopes. **2** the angle of the edge or face of a cutting tool. ▷early 17th cent.: probably related to German *ragen* 'to project,' of unknown ultimate origin; compare with Swedish *raka.*

rake-off ▸*n. informal* a commission or share of the profits from a deal, esp. one that is disreputable.

ra·ki /ˈrəˈkē; ˈrakē; ˈräkē/ ▸*n.* a strong alcoholic spirit made in eastern Europe or the Middle East. ▷from Turkish *rakı.*

rak·ing light ▸*n.* (in art or photography) bright light, usually beamed obliquely, used to reveal such things as texture and detail.

rak·ish[1] /ˈrākisʜ/ ▸*adj.* having or displaying a dashing, jaunty, or slightly disreputable quality or appearance: *he had a rakish, debonair look.* —**rak·ish·ly** *adv.* —**rak·ish·ness** *n.*

rak·ish[2] ▸*adj.* (esp. of a boat or car) trim and fast-looking, with streamlined angles and curves. ▷early 19th cent.: from the noun RAKE[3] + -ISH[1].

Rá·ko·si /ˈräkôsʜē/, Mátyás (1892–1971), Hungarian statesman; first secretary of the Hungarian Socialist Workers' Party 1945–56 and prime minister 1952–53 and 1955–56. After the communists seized power in 1945, he did much to establish a firmly Stalinist regime but was ousted by the more liberal Imre Nagy in 1953.

ra·ku /ˈräˌko͞o/ ▸*n.* [usu. as *adj.*] a kind of lead-glazed Japanese earthenware, typically irregular in shape and used esp. for the tea ceremony. ▷Japanese, literally 'enjoyment.'

rale /räl; ral/ ▸*n.* (usu. **rales**) *Medicine* an abnormal rattling sound heard when examining unhealthy lungs with a stethoscope. ▷early 19th cent.: from French *râle*, from *râler* 'to rattle.'

Ra·leigh[1] /ˈrôlē; ˈrä-/ the capital of North Carolina, in the east central part of the state; pop. 276,093.

Ra·leigh[2] (also **Ra·legh**), Sir Walter (*c.*1552–1618), English explorer, courtier, and writer. A favorite of Elizabeth I, he organized several voyages of exploration and colonization to the Americas and introduced potato and tobacco plants to England.

rall. *Music* ▸*abbr.* rallentando.

ral·len·tan·do /ˌrälənˈtändō; ˌralənˈtandō/ *Music* ▸*adv.*, *adj.*, & *n.* (*pl.* **-dos** or **-di** /-dē/) *Music* another term for RITARDANDO. ▷Italian, literally 'slowing down,' from the verb *rallentare.*

ral·ly[1] /ˈralē/ ▸*v.* (**-lies, -lied**) [*intrans.*] **1** (of troops) come together again in order to continue fighting after a defeat or dispersion: *De Montfort's troops rallied and drove back the king's infantry.* ■ [*trans.*] bring together (forces) again in order to continue fighting: *the king escaped to Perth to rally his own forces.* ■ assemble in a mass meeting: *up to 50,000 people rallied in the city center.* ■ come together in order to support a person or cause or for concerted action: *conservatives in the GOP* **rallied behind** *Goldwater.* ■ [*trans.*] bring together (forces or support) in such a way: *a series of meetings to rally support for the union.* ■ *Sports* come from behind in scoring. ■ (of a person) recover their health, spirits, or poise: *she floundered for a moment, then rallied again.* ■ [*trans.*] revive (a person or their health or spirits): *they rallied her with a drink.* ■ (of share, currency, or commodity prices) increase after a fall: *prices of metals such as aluminum and copper have rallied.* **2** drive in a rally. ■ (in tennis and other racket sports) engage in a rally.

▸*n.* (*pl.* **-lies**) **1** a mass meeting of people making a political protest or showing support for a cause: *a rally attended by around 100,000 people.* ■ an open-air event for people who own a particular kind of vehicle: *a traction engine rally.* **2** (also **rallye**) a competition for motor vehicles in which they are driven a long distance over public roads or rough terrain, typically in stages and through checkpoints: [as *adj.*] *a rally driver.* **3** a quick or marked recovery after a reverse or a period of weakness: *the market staged a late rally.* ■ (in baseball and football) a renewed or sustained offensive, usually by the losing team, that ties or wins the game. **4** (in tennis and other racket sports) an extended exchange of strokes between players. ■ hitting the ball back and forth to warm up before a match begins. ▷early 17th cent. (in the sense 'bring together again'): from French *rallier*, from *re-* 'again' + *allier* 'to ally.' **—ral·li·er** *n.* **—ral·ly·ist** *n.* (in sense 2 of the *noun*).

ral·ly[2] ▸*v.* (**-lies, -lied**) [*trans.*] *archaic* subject (someone) to good-humored ridicule; tease: *he rallied her on the length of her pigtail.* ▷mid 17th cent.: from French *railler* 'to rib, tease' (see RAIL[2]).

ral·ly·ing /ˈralēiNG/ ▸*n.* **1** [often as *adj.*] the action or process of coming together to support a person or cause or take concerted action: *a rallying cry.* **2** the sport or action of participating in a motor rally: *established names in international rallying.*

ral·ox·i·fine /rəˈläksəˌfēn/ ▸*n.* a drug that is prescribed mainly for the prevention and treatment of osteoporosis in post-menopausal women, and that is under study for use against breast cancer.

RAM /ram/ ▸*abbr.* ■ *Computing* random-access memory. ■ (in the UK) Royal Academy of Music.

ram /ram/ ▸*n.* **1** an uncastrated male sheep. ■ (**the Ram**) the zodiacal sign or constellation Aries. **2** short for BATTERING RAM. ■ the falling weight of a pile-driving machine. ■ *historical* a beak or other projecting part of the bow of a warship, for piercing the hulls of other ships. ■ *historical* a warship with such a bow. **3** a hydraulic water-raising or lifting machine. ■ the piston of a hydraulic press. ■ the plunger of a force pump.

▸*v.* (**rammed, ram·ming**) [*trans.*] roughly force (something) into place: *he rammed his stick into the ground.* ■ (of a vehicle or vessel) be driven violently into (something, typically another vehicle or vessel) in an attempt to stop or damage it: *their boat was rammed by a Japanese warship.* ■ [*intrans.*] crash violently against something: *the stolen car rammed into the front of the house.* ■ [*trans.*] [often as *adj.*] (**rammed**) beat (earth or the ground) with a heavy implement to make it hard and firm: *portions of the Great Wall of China are made of rammed earth.* ■ (**ram through**) [*trans.*] force (something) to be accepted: *Sunday's referendum to ram through a new constitution.* ▷Old English *ram(m)*, related to Dutch *ram*. **—ram·mer** *n.*

▸*PHRASES* □ **ram something down someone's throat** see THROAT. □ **ram something home** see HOME.

Ra·ma /ˈrämə/ the hero of the Ramayana, husband of Sita. He is the Hindu model of the ideal man, the seventh incarnation of Vishnu, and is widely venerated, by some sects as the supreme god.

ra·ma·da /rəˈmädə; -ˈmadə/ ▸*n.* an arbor or porch. ▷mid 19th cent.: from Spanish.

Ram·a·dan /ˈräməˌdän; ˈraməˌdan/ ▸*n.* the ninth month of the Muslim year, during which strict fasting is observed from sunrise to sunset. ▷from Arabic *ramaḍān*, from *ramaḍa* 'be hot.' The lunar reckoning of the Muslim calendar brings the fast eleven days earlier each year, eventually causing Ramadan to occur in any season; originally it was supposed to be in one of the hot months.

ram air ▸*n. technical* air that is forced to enter a moving aperture, such as the air intake of an aircraft.

Ra·man /ˈrämən/, Sir Chandrasekhara Venkata (1888–1970), Indian physicist. He discovered the Raman effect, one of the most important proofs of the quantum theory of light. Nobel Prize for Physics (1930).

Ra·man ef·fect ▸*n. Physics* a change of wavelength exhibited by some of the radiation scattered in a medium. The effect is specific to the molecules that cause it, and so can be used in spectroscopic analysis. Compare with RAYLEIGH SCATTERING.

Ra·ma·pith·e·cus /ˌraməˈpiTHikəs; ˌräm-/ ▸*n.* an extinct anthropoid ape of the Miocene epoch, known from remains found in southwestern Asia and East Africa, and probably ancestral to the orangutan. • Genus *Ramapithecus*, family Pongidae. ▷modern Latin, from RAMA + Greek *pithēkos* 'ape.'

Ra·ma·ya·na /ˌrämīˈänə; rəˈmīənə/ one of the two great Sanskrit epics of the Hindus, composed *c.*300 BC. It describes how Rama, aided by his brother and the monkey king Hanuman, rescued his wife Sita from Ravana, the ten-headed demon king of Lanka. ▷Sanskrit, literally 'exploits of Rama.'

ram·ble /ˈrambəl/ ▸*v.* [*intrans.*] **1** walk for pleasure, typically without a definite route. ■ (of a plant) put out long shoots and grow over walls or other plants. **2** talk or write at length in a confused or inconsequential way: *he* **rambled on** *about his acting career.*

▸*n.* a walk taken for pleasure, esp. in the countryside. ▷late Middle English (as a verb in sense 2): probably related to Middle Dutch *rammelen*, used of animals in the sense 'wander around in heat,' also to the noun RAM.

ram·bler /ˈramb(ə)lər/ ▸*n.* **1** a person who walks for pleasure, esp. in the countryside. **2** a straggling or climbing rose. **3** another term for RANCH HOUSE (see RANCH).

ram·bling /ˈramb(ə)liNG/ ▸*adj.* **1** (of writing or speech) lengthy and confused or inconsequential. **2** (of a plant) putting out long shoots and growing over walls or other plants; climbing: *rambling roses.* ■ (of a building or path) spreading or winding irregularly in various directions: *a big old rambling house.* ■ (of a person) traveling from place to place; wandering. **—ram·bling·ly** *adv.*

Ram·bo /ˈrambō/ ▸*n.* an exceptionally tough, aggressive man. ▷the name of the hero of David Morrell's novel *First Blood* (1972), popularized in the movies *First Blood* (1982) and *Rambo: First Blood Part II* (1985).

Ram·bouil·let /ˌrambəˈlā; -bo͞oˈyā/ ▸*n.* (*pl.* same) a sheep of a hardy breed developed from the Spanish merino but bred elsewhere for its meat and its heavy fleece of fine wool.

ram·bunc·tious /ramˈbəNGkSHəs/ ▸*adj. informal* uncontrollably exuberant; boisterous. ▷mid 19th cent.: of unknown origin. **—ram·bunc·tious·ly** *adv.* **—ram·bunc·tious·ness** *n.*

ram·bu·tan /ramˈbo͞otn/ ▸*n.* **1** a red, plum-sized tropical fruit with soft spines and a slightly acidic taste. **2** the Malaysian tree that bears this fruit. • *Nephelium lappaceum*, family Sapindaceae. ▷early 18th cent.: from Malay *rambūtan*, from *rambut* 'hair,' with allusion to the fruit's spines.

ram·e·kin /ˈramikən/ (also **ram·e·kin dish**) ▸*n.* a small dish for baking and serving an individual portion of food. ■ a quantity of food served in such a dish, in particular a small quantity of cheese baked with breadcrumbs, eggs, and seasoning. ▷mid 17th cent.: from French *ramequin*, of Low German or Dutch origin; compare with obsolete Flemish *rameken* 'toasted bread.'

ra·men /ˈrämən/ ▸*plural n.* (in oriental cuisine) quick-cooking noodles, typically served in a broth with meat and vegetables. ▷Japanese, from Chinese *lā* 'to pull' + *miàn* 'noodles.'

ram·ie /ˈramē; ˈrā-/ ▸*n.* **1** a vegetable fiber noted for its length and toughness. ■ cloth woven from this fiber. **2** the plant of the nettle family that yields this fiber, native to tropical Asia and cultivated elsewhere. • *Boehmeria nivea*, family Urticaceae. ▷mid 19th cent.: from Malay *rami*.

ram·i·fi·ca·tion /ˌraməfəˈkāSHən/ ▸*n.* (usu. **ramifications**) a consequence of an action or event, esp. when complex or unwelcome: *any change is bound to have legal ramifications.* ■ a subdivision of a complex structure or process perceived as comparable to a tree's branches: *an extended family with its ramifications of neighboring in-laws.* ■ *formal* or *technical* the action or state of ramifying or being ramified. ▷mid 17th cent.: from French, from *ramifier* 'form branches' (see RAMIFY).

ram·i·fy /ˈraməˌfī/ ▸*v.* (**-fies, -fied**) [*intrans.*] *formal, technical* form branches or offshoots; spread or branch out: *an elaborate system of canals was built, ramifying throughout Britain.* ■ [*trans.*] [often as *adj.*] (**ramified**) cause to branch or spread out: *a ramified genealogical network.* ▷late Middle English: from Old French *ramifier*, from medieval Latin *ramificare*, from Latin *ramus* 'branch.'

ram·jet /ˈramˌjet/ ▸*n.* a type of jet engine in which the air drawn in for combustion is compressed solely by the forward motion of the aircraft.

Ra·món y Ca·jal /rəˈmōn ē kəˈhäl/, Santiago (1852–1934), Spanish physician and histologist. He was a founder of the science of neurology, identifying the neuron as the fundamental unit of the nervous system. Nobel Prize for Physiology or Medicine (1906, shared with Camillo Golgi).

ramp /ramp/ ▸*n.* **1** a slope or inclined plane for joining two different levels, as at the entrance or between floors of a building: *a wheelchair ramp.* ■ a movable set of steps for entering or leaving an aircraft. ■ an inclined road leading onto or off a main road or highway: *an exit ramp.* **2** an upward bend in a stair rail. **3** an electrical waveform in which the voltage increases or decreases linearly with time.

▸*v.* **1** [*trans.*] provide or build (something) with a ramp. **2** [*intrans.*] *archaic* (of an animal) rear up on its hind legs in a threatening posture. ■ [with *adverbial of direction*] rush about violently or uncontrollably: *an awful beast ramping about the woods and fields.* ■ [with *adverbial of direction*] (of a plant) grow or climb luxuriantly: *ivy ramped over the flower beds.* **3** [*intrans.*] (of an electrical waveform) increase or decrease voltage linearly with time.

▸*phrasal v.* □ **ramp something up** (or **ramp up**) (esp. in reference to the production of goods) increase or cause to increase in amount: *they ramped up production to meet booming demand.* ▷Middle English (as a verb in the sense 'rear up,' also used as a heraldic term): from Old French *ramper* 'creep, crawl,' of unknown origin. Sense 1 of the noun dates from the late 18th cent.

ram·page ▸*v.* /ˈramˌpāj/ [*intrans.*] (esp. of a large group of people) rush around in a violent and uncontrollable manner: *several thousand demonstrators rampaged through the city.*

▸*n.* /ˈramˌpāj/ a period of violent and uncontrollable behavior, typically involving a large group of people: *thugs* **went on a rampage** *and wrecked a classroom.* ▷late 17th cent.: perhaps based on the verb RAMP and the noun RAGE. **—ram·pag·er** /ˈramˌpājər/ *n.*

ram·pa·geous /ramˈpājəs/ ▸*adj. archaic* boisterously or violently uncontrollable.

ramp·ant /ˈrampənt/ ▸*adj.* **1** (esp. of something unwelcome or unpleasant) flourishing or spreading unchecked: *political violence was rampant | rampant inflation.* ■ (of a person or activity) violent or unrestrained in action or performance: *rampant sex.* ■ (of a plant) lush in growth; luxuriant: *a rich soil soon becomes home to rampant weeds.* **2** [usu. *postpositive*] *Heraldry* (of an animal) represented standing on one hind foot with its forefeet in the air (typically in profile, facing the dexter (left) side, with right hind foot and tail raised, unless otherwise specified): *two gold lions rampant.* **3** *Architecture* (of an arch) springing from a level of support at one height and resting on the other support at a higher level. ▷Middle English (as a heraldic term): from Old French, literally 'crawling,' present participle of *ramper* (see RAMP). From the original use describing a wild animal, arose the sense 'fierce,' whence the current notion of 'unrestrained.' **—ramp·an·cy** /-pənsē/ *n.* **—ramp·ant·ly** *adv.*

ram·part /ˈramˌpärt/ ▸*n.* (usu. **ramparts**) a defensive wall of a castle or walled city, having a broad top with a walkway and typically a stone parapet. ■ a defensive or protective barrier.

▸*v.* [*trans.*] (usu. **be ramparted**) *rare* fortify or surround with or as if with a rampart. ▷late 16th cent.: from French *rempart*, from *remparer* 'fortify, take possession of again,' based on Latin *ante* 'before' + *parare* 'prepare.'

ram·pi·on /ˈrampēən/ ▸*n.* a Eurasian plant of the bellflower family, some kinds of which have a root that can be eaten in salads. • a Mediterranean plant with a long narrow spike of bluish flowers and a thick taproot (*Campanula rapunculus*, family Campanulaceae). • (**horned rampion**) a grassland plant with dense, rounded flowerheads of inward curving, typically blue, tubular flowers (genus *Phyteuma*, family Campanulaceae). ▷late 16th cent.: from a variant of medieval Latin *rapuncium*; compare with German *Rapunzel* 'corn salad.'

Ram·pling /ˈramˌpliNG/, Anne, see RICE[1].

ram·rod /ˈramˌräd/ ▸*n.* a rod for ramming down the charge of a muzzleloading firearm. ■ used in similes and metaphors to describe someone's erect or rigid posture: *he held himself ramrod straight.* ■ a person, esp. one in a position of leadership, who is strict and uncompromising.

▸*v.* (**-rod·ded, -rod·ding**) [*trans.*] (**ramrod something through**) force a proposed measure to be accepted or completed quickly: *they ramrodded through legislation voiding the court injunctions.*

Ram·say /ˈramzē/, Sir William (1852–1916), Scottish chemist; discoverer of the noble gases. He discovered argon and helium and codiscovered neon, krypton, xenon, and radon. He also determined their atomic weights and places in the periodic table. Nobel Prize for Chemistry (1904).

Ram·ses /ˈramsēz/ (also **Ram·e·ses** /ˈraməˌsēz/) the name of 11 Egyptian pharaohs, notably: ■ **Ramses II** (died *c.*1225 BC), reigned *c.*1292–*c.*1225 BC; known as **Ramses the Great**. The third pharaoh of the 19th dynasty, he built vast monuments and statues, including the two rock temples at Abu Simbel. ■ **Ramses III** (died *c.*1167 BC), reigned *c.*1198–*c.*1167 BC. The second pharaoh of the 20th dynasty, he fought decisive battles against the Libyans and the Sea Peoples. After his death the power of Egypt declined.

ram·shack·le /'ram,SHakəl/ ▸*adj.* (esp. of a house or vehicle) in a state of severe disrepair: *a ramshackle cottage.* ▷early 19th cent. (originally dialect in the sense 'irregular, disorderly'): alteration of earlier *ramshackled*, altered form of obsolete *ransackled* 'ransacked.'

rams·horn snail /'ramz,hôrn/ ▸*n.* a plant-eating European freshwater snail that has a flat spiral shell. • Family Planorbidae: several genera.

ra·mus /'rāməs/ ▸*n.* (*pl.* **-mi** /-,mī/) **1** *Anatomy* an arm or branch of a bone, in particular those of the ischium and pubes or of the jawbone. ■ a major branch of a nerve. **2** *Zoology* a structure in an invertebrate that has the form of a projecting arm, typically one of two or more that are conjoined or adjacent. ■ a barb of a feather. ▷mid 17th cent.: from Latin, literally 'branch.'

ran /ran/ ▸ past of **RUN**.

ranch /ranCH/ ▸*n.* a large farm, esp. in the western U.S. and Canada, where cattle or other animals are bred and raised. ■ (also **ranch house**) a single-story, sometimes split-level, house, typically with a low-pitched roof. ■ short for **RANCH DRESSING**.
▸*v.* [*intrans.*] [often as *n.*] (**ranching**) run a ranch: *cattle ranching.* ■ [*trans.*] [often as *adj.*] (**ranched**) breed (animals) on a ranch. ■ [*trans.*] use (land) as a ranch. ▷early 19th cent.: from Spanish *rancho* 'group of persons eating together.'

ranch dress·ing ▸*n.* a type of thick white salad dressing made with sour cream or buttermilk.

ranch·er /'ranCHər/ ▸*n.* **1** a person who owns or runs a ranch. **2** a ranch house.

ran·cher·a /ran'CHerə; rän-/ ▸*n.* a type of Mexican country music, often played with guitars and horns. ▷early 20th cent.: from Spanish *cancion ranchera*, 'farmers' songs'

ran·che·ria /,ranCHə'rēə/ ▸*n.* (in Spanish America and the western U.S.) a small Indian settlement. ▷Spanish, from *rancho* (see **RANCH**).

ran·che·ro /ran'CHerō/ ▸*n.* (*pl.* **-ros**) a person who farms or works on a ranch, esp. in the southwestern U.S. and Mexico. ▷Spanish, from *rancho* (see **RANCH**).

Ran·chi /'ränCHē/ a city in Bihar, northeastern India; pop. 598,000.

Ran·cho Cor·do·va /'ran,CHō 'kôr,dəvə/ an industrial city in north central California, northeast of Sacramento; pop. 48,731.

Ran·cho Cu·ca·mon·ga /'ranCHō ,ko͞okə'məNGgə; -'mäNG/ (also **Cucamonga**) a city in southwestern California, east of Los Angeles; pop. 101,409.

ran·cid /'ransid/ ▸*adj.* (of foods containing fat or oil) smelling or tasting unpleasant as a result of being old and stale. ▷early 17th cent.: from Latin *rancidus* 'stinking.' —**ran·cid·i·ty** /ran'sidətē/ *n.*

ran·cor /'raNGkər/ (*Brit.* **ran·cour**) ▸*n.* bitterness or resentfulness, esp. when long-standing: *he spoke without rancor.* ▷Middle English: via Old French from late Latin *rancor* 'rankness,' (in the Vulgate 'bitter grudge'), related to Latin *rancidus* 'stinking.' —**ran·cor·ous** /-rəs/ *adj.* —**ran·cor·ous·ly** /-k(ə)rəslē/ *adv.*

Rand[1] /rand/ (**the Rand**) another name for **WITWATERSRAND**.

Rand[2] /rand/, Ayn (1905–82), U.S. writer and philosopher, born in Russia; born *Alissa Rozenbaum*. She developed a philosophy of "objectivism," in *For the New Intellectual* (1961), arguing for "rational self-interest," individualism, and laissez-faire capitalism. Notable novels: *The Fountainhead* (1943) and *Atlas Shrugged* (1957).

rand[1] /rand; ränd; ränt/ ▸*n.* the basic monetary unit of South Africa, equal to 100 cents. ▷from *the Rand*, the name of a goldfield district near Johannesburg.

rand[2] ▸*n.* a strip of leather placed under the back part of a shoe or boot to make it level before the lifts of the heel are attached. ▷Old English (denoting a border): of Germanic origin; related to Dutch *rand* and German *Rand* 'edge.' The current sense dates from the late 16th cent.

Ran·dall /'randl/, Tony 1920–2004, U.S. actor; born *Leonard Rosenberg*. He starred in numerous film and stage productions but is best known for his role as Felix Unger, playing opposite Jack Klugman, in the TV series "The Odd Couple" (1970–75). In 1991 he founded the National Actors Theatre to bring classic works to the New York stage.

R & B ▸*abbr.* rhythm and blues.

R & D ▸*abbr.* research and development.

Rand·olph[1] /'ran,dôlf; -,dälf/ a town in eastern Massachusetts, south of Boston; pop. 30,093.

Ran·dolph[2], A(sa) Philip (1889–1979), U.S. labor and civil rights leader. Believing that unions would benefit African Americans, he founded the Brotherhood of Sleeping Car Porters in 1928 and then served as its president until 1968. He was a major organizer of both the 1941 and 1963 marches on Washington.

ran·dom /'randəm/ ▸*adj.* made, done, happening, or chosen without method or conscious decision: *a random sample of 100 households.* ■ *Statistics* governed by or involving equal chances for each item. ■ (of masonry) with stones of irregular size and shape. ▷Middle English (in the sense 'impetuous headlong rush'): from Old French *randon* 'great speed,' from *randir* 'gallop,' from a Germanic root shared by **RAND**[2]. —**ran·dom·ly** *adv.* —**ran·dom·ness** *n.*
▸*PHRASE* □ **at random** without method or conscious decision: *he opened the book at random.*

ran·dom ac·cess *Computing* ▸*n.* the process of transferring information to or from memory in which every memory location can be accessed directly rather than being accessed in a fixed sequence: [as *adj.*] *random-access programming.*

ran·dom er·ror ▸*n.* *Statistics* an error in measurement caused by factors that vary from one measurement to another.

ran·dom·ize /'randə,mīz/ ▸*v.* [*trans.*] [usu. as *adj.*] (**randomized**) *technical* make unpredictable, unsystematic, or random in order or arrangement; employ random selection or sampling in (an experiment or procedure). —**ran·dom·i·za·tion** /,randəmi'zāSHən/ *n.*

ran·dom var·i·a·ble ▸*n.* *Statistics* a quantity having a numerical value for each member of a group, esp. one whose values occur according to a frequency distribution. Also called **VARIATE**.

ran·dom walk ▸*n.* *Physics* the movements of an object or changes in a variable that follow no discernible pattern or trend.

R & R ▸*abbr.* ■ *informal* rest and recreation. ■ *Medicine* rescue and resuscitation. ■ (also **R'n'R**) rock and roll.

Rand·stad /'rän,städ/ a conurbation in northwestern Netherlands that stretches in a horseshoe shape from Dordrecht and Rotterdam around to Utrecht and Amersfoort via The Hague, Leiden, Haarlem, and Amsterdam. The majority of the people of the Netherlands live in this area.

rand·y /'randē/ ▸*adj.* (**rand·i·er, rand·i·est**) **1** *informal* sexually aroused or excited. **2** *Scottish, archaic* (of a person) having a rude, aggressive manner. ▷mid 17th cent.: perhaps from obsolete *rand* 'rant, rave,' from obsolete Dutch *randen* 'to rant.' —**rand·i·ly** /-dəlē/ *adv.* —**rand·i·ness** *n.*

ra·nee ▸*n.* archaic spelling of **RANI**.

Ra·ney nick·el /'rānī/ ▸*n.* *trademark Chemistry* a form of nickel catalyst with a high surface area, used in organic hydrogenation reactions. ▷1930s: named after Murray *Raney* (1885–1966), U.S. engineer.

rang /raNG/ ▸ past of **RING**[2].

range /rānj/ ▸*n.* **1** the area of variation between upper and lower limits on a particular scale: *the cost is thought to be* ***in the range of*** *$1-5 million a day* | *it's outside my price range.* ■ a set of different things of the same general type: *the area offers a wide range of activities for the tourist.* ■ the scope of a person's knowledge or abilities: *he gave some indication of his range.* ■ the compass of a person's voice or of a musical instrument: *she was gifted with an incredible vocal range.* ■ the extent of time covered by something such as a forecast. See also **LONG-RANGE, SHORT-RANGE**. ■ the area or extent covered by or included in something: *an introductory guide to the range of debate this issue has generated.* ■ *Mathematics* the set of values that a given function can take as its argument varies. **2** the distance within which a person can see or hear: *something lurked just beyond her range of vision.* ■ the maximum distance at which a radio transmission can be effectively received: *planets within radio range of Earth.* ■ the distance that can be covered by a vehicle or aircraft without refueling: *the vans have a range of 125 miles.* ■ the maximum distance to which a gun will shoot or over which a missile will travel: *a duck came within range* | *these rockets have a range of 30 to 40 miles.* ■ the distance between a gun, missile, shot, or blow and its objective: *a dog sidled up to them, stopping just out of range of a kick.* ■ the distance between a camera and the subject to be photographed. ■ *Surveying* the horizontal direction and length of a survey line determined by at least two fixed points. **3** a line or series of mountains or hills: *the coastal ranges of the northwest.* ■ a series of townships extending north and south parallel to the principal meridian of a survey. ■ *Nautical* a line defined by landmarks or beacons, used to locate something offshore, esp. a navigable channel or a hazard. **4** a large area of open land for grazing or hunting. ■ an area of land or sea used as a testing ground for military equipment. ■ an open or enclosed area with targets for shooting practice. ■ the area over which a thing, esp. a plant or animal, is distributed. **5** an electric or gas stove with several burners and one or more ovens. **6** *Building* a course of masonry extending from end to end at one height. ■ a row of buildings. **7** *archaic* the direction or position in which something lies: *the range of the hills and valleys is nearly from north to south.*
▸*v.* **1** [*intrans.*] vary or extend between specified limits: *patients whose ages ranged from 13 to 25 years.* **2** [*trans.*] (usu. **be ranged**) place or arrange in a row or rows or in a specified order or manner: *a table with half a dozen chairs ranged around it.* ■ [*intrans.*] run or extend in a line in a particular direction: *he regularly came to the benches that ranged along the path.* **3** [*intrans.*] (of a person or animal) travel or wander over a wide area: *patrols ranged thousands of miles deep into enemy territory* | [*trans.*] *nomadic tribesmen who ranged the windswept lands of the steppe.* ■ (of a person's eyes) pass from one person or thing to another: *his eyes* ***ranged over*** *them.* ■ (of something written or spoken) cover or embrace a wide number of different topics: *tutorials* ***ranged over*** *a variety of subjects.* **4** [*intrans.*] obtain the range of a target by adjustment after firing past it or short of it, or by the use of radar or laser equipment: *radar-type transmissions which appeared to be* ***ranging on*** *our convoys.* ■ [with *adverbial*] (of a projectile) cover a specified distance. ■ [with *adverbial*] (of a gun) send a projectile over a specified distance. ▷Middle English (in the sense 'line of people or animals'): from Old French *range* 'row, rank,' from *rangier* 'put in order,' from *rang* 'rank.' Early usage also included the notion of 'movement over an area.'
▸*PHRASE* □ **at a range of** with a specified distance between one person or thing and another: *a bat can detect a moth at a range of less than 8 feet.*

THE RIGHT WORD **compass, gamut, latitude, range, reach, scope, sweep**

To say that someone has a wide **range** of interests implies that these interests are not only extensive but varied.

Another way of expressing the same idea would be to say that the person's interests run the **gamut** from TV quiz shows to nuclear physics, a word that suggests a graduated scale or series running from one extreme to another.

Compass implies a range of knowledge or activity that falls within very definite limits reminiscent of a circumference (*within the compass of her abilities*), while **sweep** suggests more of an arc-shaped range of motion or activity (*the sweep of the searchlight*) or a continuous extent or stretch (*a broad sweep of lawn*).

Latitude and **scope** both emphasize the idea of freedom, although *scope* implies great freedom within prescribed limits (*the scope of the investigation*), while *latitude* means freedom from such limits (*she was granted more latitude than usual in interviewing the disaster victims*).

Even someone who has a wide *range* of interests and a broad *scope* of authority will sooner or later come up against something that is beyond his or her **reach**, which suggests the furthest limit of effectiveness or influence.

range·bound /'rānj,bound/ ▸*adj.* (generally of market prices) not straying outside a particular range: *the euro remained rangebound, faltering again in its attempt to regain recent highs.*

range·find·er /'rānj,fīndər/ ▸*n.* an instrument for estimating the distance of an object, esp. for use with a camera or gun.

range·land /'rānj,land/ ▸*n.* (also **rangelands**) open country used for grazing or hunting animals.

Range·ley Lakes /'rānjlē/ a resort region in western Maine, near the New Hampshire border, noted for Rangeley, Mooselookmeguntic, and other lakes, as well as for the Mahoosuc Range, which is to the south.

Rang·er /'rānjər/ a series of nine American moon probes launched between 1961 and 1965, the last three of which took many photographs before crashing into the moon.

R

rang·er /ˈrānjər/ ▸n. **1** a keeper of a park, forest, or area of countryside. **2** a member of a body of armed men, in particular: ■ a mounted soldier. ■ a commando or highly trained infantryman. **3** a person or thing that wanders or ranges over a particular area or domain: *rangers of the mountains.*

Ran·goon /rANGˈgo͞on; ran-/ the capital of Myanmar (Burma), a port in the Irrawaddy delta; pop. 2,495,000. For centuries a Buddhist religious center, it is the site of the Shwe Dagon Pagoda, built over 2,500 years ago. The modern city was established in the mid 19th century and became the capital in 1886. Burmese name **YANGON**.

rang·y /ˈrānjē/ ▸adj. (**rang·i·er, rang·i·est**) **1** (of a person or animal) tall and slim with long, slender limbs. **2** (of land) having a large, open range: *the rangy, hard, scruffy frontier.*

ra·ni /räˈnē/ (also **ra·nee**) ▸n. (*pl.* **ra·nis**) *historical* a Hindu queen, either by marriage to a raja or in her own right. ▷from Hindi *rānī,* Sanskrit *rājñī,* feminine of *rājan* 'king.'

ra·nit·i·dine /rəˈnitəˌdēn/ ▸n. *Medicine* a synthetic compound with antihistamine properties, used to treat ulcers and related conditions. ▷1970s: blend of **FURAN** and **NITRO-**, + **-IDE** + **-INE**[4].

Ran·jit Singh /ˌränjət ˈsiNG/ (1780–1839), Indian maharaja; founder of the Sikh state of Punjab; known as the **Lion of the Punjab**. He proclaimed himself maharaja of Punjab in 1801 and went on to make it the most powerful state in India.

Rank /raNGk/, J. Arthur, 1st Baron (1888–1972), English industrialist and movie executive; full name *Joseph Arthur Rank.* In 1941, he founded the Rank Organization, a movie production and distribution company that acquired control of the leading British studios and movie theater chains in the 1940s and 1950s.

rank[1] /raNGk/ ▸n. **1** a position in the hierarchy of the armed forces: *an army officer of fairly high rank | he was promoted to the rank of Captain.* ■ a position within the hierarchy of an organization or society: *only two cabinet members had held ministerial rank before.* ■ high social position: *persons of rank and breeding.* ■ *Statistics* a number specifying position in a numerically ordered series. **2** a single line of soldiers or police officers drawn up abreast. ■ (**the ranks**) common soldiers as opposed to officers: *he was fined and* **reduced to the ranks.** ■ (**ranks**) the people belonging to or constituting a group or class: *the ranks of the unemployed.* ■ a regular row or line of things or people: *conifer plantations growing in serried ranks.* ■ *Chess* each of the eight rows of eight squares running from side to side across a chessboard. Compare with **FILE**[2]. **3** *Mathematics* the value or the order of the largest nonzero determinant of a given matrix. ■ an analogous quantity in other kinds of groups.

▸v. [*trans.*] **1** give (someone or something) a rank or place within a grading system: *rank them in order of preference | [trans.] she is ranked number four in the world.* ■ [*intrans.*] have a specified rank or place within a grading system: *he ranks with Newman as one of the outstanding English theologians* ■ [*trans.*] take precedence over (someone) in respect to rank; outrank: *the Secretary of State ranks all the other members of the cabinet.* **2** arrange in a rank or ranks: *the tents were ranked in orderly rows.* ▷Middle English: from Old French *ranc,* of Germanic origin; related to **RING**[1].

▸*PHRASES* □ **break rank** (or **ranks**) (of soldiers or police officers) fail to remain in line. ■ *figurative* fail to maintain solidarity: *the government is prepared to* **break ranks with** *the Allied states.* □ **close ranks** (of soldiers or police officers) come closer together in a line. ■ *figurative* unite in order to defend common interests: *the family had always closed ranks in times of crisis.* □ **keep rank** (of soldiers or police officers) remain in line. □ **pull rank** take unfair advantage of one's seniority or privileged position. □ **rise through** (or **from**) **the ranks** (of a private or a noncommissioned officer) receive a commission. ■ advance in an organization by one's own efforts: *he rose through the ranks to become managing director.*

rank[2] ▸adj. **1** (of vegetation) growing too thickly and coarsely. **2** (esp. of air or water) having a foul or offensive smell. **3** [*attrib.*] (esp. of something bad or deficient) complete and utter (used for emphasis): *rank stupidity | rank amateurs | a rank outsider.* ▷Old English *ranc* 'proud, rebellious, sturdy,' also 'fully grown,' of Germanic origin. An early sense 'luxuriant' gave rise to 'too luxuriant,' whence the negative connotation of modern usage. **—rank·ly** *adv.* **—rank·ness** *n.*

rank and file ▸n. [treated as *pl.*] (**the rank and file**) the ordinary members of an organization as opposed to its leaders: *the rank and file of the Labor party are dissatisfied | [as adj.] rank-and-file members.* ▷referring to the "ranks" and "files" into which privates and noncommissioned officers form on parade.

rank cor·re·la·tion ▸n. *Statistics* an assessment of the degree of correlation between two ways of assigning ranks to the members of a set.

rank·er /ˈraNGkər/ ▸n. *chiefly Brit.* a soldier in the ranks; a private. ■ a commissioned officer who has been promoted from the ranks.

rank·ing ▸n. /ˈraNGkiNG/ a position in a scale of achievement or status; a classification: *his number-one world ranking.* ■ the action or process of giving a specified rank or place within a grading system: *the ranking of students.*

▸*adj.* /raNGkiNG/ [in *combination*] having a specified position in a scale of achievement or status: *high-ranking army officers.* ■ [*attrib.*] having a high position in such a scale: *two ranking PLO figures.*

ran·kle /ˈraNGkəl/ ▸v. [*intrans.*] **1** *archaic* (of a wound or sore) continue to be painful; fester. **2** (of a comment, event, or fact) cause annoyance or resentment that persists: *the casual manner of his dismissal still rankles.* ■ [*trans.*] annoy or irritate (someone): *Lisa was rankled by his assertion.* ▷Middle English: from Old French *rancler,* from *rancle, draoncle* 'festering sore,' from an alteration of medieval Latin *dracunculus,* diminutive of *draco* 'serpent.'

Rann of Kutch see **KUTCH, RANN OF.**

ran·sack /ˈranˌsak; ranˈsak/ ▸v. [*trans.*] go hurriedly through (a place) stealing things and causing damage: *burglars ransacked her home.* ■ search through (a place or receptacle) to find something, esp. in such a way as to cause disorder and damage: *Hollywood* **ransacks** *the New York stage* **for** *actors.* ▷Middle English: from Old Norse *rannsaka,* from *rann* 'house' + a second element related to *sœkja* 'seek.' **—ran·sack·er** /ˈranˌsakər/ *n.*

Ran·som /ˈransəm/, John Crowe (1888–1974), U.S. poet and critic. With *The New Criticism* (1941) he started a school of criticism that rejected the Victorian emphasis on literature as a moral force and advocated a close analysis of textual structure in isolation from the social background of the text.

ran·som /ˈransəm/ ▸n. a sum of money or other payment demanded or paid for the release of a prisoner. ■ the holding or freeing of a prisoner in return for payment of such money: *the capture and ransom of the king.*

▸v. [*trans.*] obtain the release of (a prisoner) by making a payment demanded: *the lord was captured in war and had to be ransomed.* ■ hold (a prisoner) and demand payment for their release: *mercenaries burned the village and ransomed the inhabitants.* ■ release (a prisoner) after receiving payment. ▷Middle English: from Old French *ransoun* (noun), *ransouner* (verb), from Latin *redemptio(n-)* 'ransoming, releasing' (see **REDEMPTION**). Early use also occurred in theological contexts expressing 'deliverance' and 'atonement.'

▸*PHRASES* □ **hold someone/something at** (or **for**) **ransom** hold someone prisoner and demand payment for their release. ■ demand concessions from a person or organization by threatening damaging action. □ **a king's ransom** a huge amount of money; a fortune.

rant /rant/ ▸v. [*intrans.*] speak or shout at length in a wild, impassioned way: *she was still* **ranting on** *about the unfairness of it all.*

▸n. a spell of ranting; a tirade: *his rants against organized religion.* ▷late 16th cent. (in the sense 'behave in a boisterous way'): from Dutch *ranten* 'talk nonsense, rave.' **—rant·er** *n.* **—rant·ing·ly** *adv.*

▸*PHRASE* □ **rant and rave** shout and complain angrily and at length.

ra·nun·cu·la·ceous /rəˌnəNGkyəˈlāsHəs/ ▸adj. *Botany* of, relating to, or denoting plants of the buttercup family (Ranunculaceae). ▷mid 19th cent.: from modern Latin *Ranunculaceae* (plural), based on Latin *ranunculus* 'little frog,' + **-OUS**.

ra·nun·cu·lus /rəˈnəNGkyələs/ ▸n. (*pl.* **-lus·es** or **-li** /-ˌlē; -ˌlī/) a temperate plant of a genus that includes the buttercups and water crowfoots, typically having yellow or white bowl-shaped flowers and lobed or toothed leaves. • Genus *Ranunculus,* family Ranunculaceae: many species, including several garden ornamentals. ▷modern Latin, from Latin, literally 'little frog,' diminutive of *rana.*

Ran·vier's node /ränˈvyāz; ˈranvi(ə)rz/ ▸n. see **NODE OF RANVIER.**

rap[1] /rap/ ▸v. (**rapped, rap·ping**) **1** [*trans.*] strike (a hard surface) with a series of rapid audible blows, esp. in order to attract attention: *he stood up and rapped the table | [intrans.] she* **rapped** *angrily* **on** *the window.* ■ strike (something) against a hard surface in such a way: *she rapped her stick on the floor.* ■ strike (someone or something) sharply with stick or similar implement: *she rapped my fingers with a ruler.* ■ *informal* rebuke or criticize sharply: *executives rapped the U.S. for having too little competition in international phone service.* ■ say sharply or suddenly: *the ambassador* **rapped out** *an order.* **2** [*intrans.*] *informal* talk or chat in an easy and familiar manner: *we could be here all night rapping about the finer points of spiritualism.* **3** [*intrans.*] perform rap music.

▸n. **1** a quick, sharp knock or blow: *there was a confident rap at the door.* **2** a type of popular music of U.S. black origin in which words are recited rapidly and rhythmically over a prerecorded, typically electronic instrumental backing. ■ a piece of music performed in this style, or the words themselves. **3** *informal* a talk or discussion, esp. a lengthy or impromptu one: *dropping in after work for a rap over a beer | [as adj.] a rap session.* **4** [usu. with *adj.*] *informal* a criminal charge, esp. of a specified kind: *he's just been acquitted on a murder rap.* ■ a person or thing's reputation, typically a bad one: *there's no reason why drag queens should get a bad rap.* ▷Middle English (originally in the senses 'severe blow with a weapon' and 'deliver a heavy blow'): probably imitative and of Scandinavian origin; compare with Swedish *rappa* 'beat, drub,' also with **CLAP**[1] and **FLAP.**

▸*PHRASES* □ **beat the rap** *informal* escape punishment for or be acquitted of a crime. □ **rap someone on** (or **over**) **the knuckles** rebuke or criticize someone. □ **take the rap** *informal* be punished or blamed, esp. for something that is not one's fault or for which others are equally responsible.

rap[2] ▸n. [in *sing.,* with *negative*] the smallest amount (used to add emphasis to a statement): *he doesn't care a rap whether it's true or not.* ▷early 19th cent.: from Irish *ropaire* 'robber'; used as the name of a counterfeit coin in 18th-cent. Ireland.

ra·pa·cious /rəˈpāsHəs/ ▸adj. aggressively greedy or grasping: *rapacious landlords.* See note at **GREEDY.** ▷mid 17th cent.: from Latin *rapax, rapac-* (from *rapere* 'to snatch') + **-IOUS.** **—ra·pa·cious·ly** *adv.* **—ra·pa·cious·ness** *n.* **—ra·pac·i·ty** /rəˈpasətē/ *n.*

rape[1] /rāp/ ▸n. the crime, committed by a man, of forcing another person to have sexual intercourse with him without their consent and against their will, esp. by the threat or use of violence against them: *he denied two charges of attempted rape | he had committed at least two rapes.* ■ *figurative* the wanton destruction or spoiling of a place or area: *the rape of the Russian countryside.* ■ *poetic/literary* the abduction of a woman, esp. for the purpose of having sexual intercourse with her: *the Rape of the Sabine Women.*

▸v. [*trans.*] (of a man) force (another person) to have sexual intercourse with him without their consent and against their will, esp. by the threat or use of violence against them: *the woman was raped at knifepoint.* ■ *figurative* spoil or destroy (a place): *the timber industry is raping the land.* ▷late Middle English (originally denoting violent seizure of property, later carrying off a woman by force): from Anglo-Norman French *rap* (noun), *raper* (verb), from Latin *rapere* 'seize.' **—rap·er** *n.*

rape[2] ▸n. a plant of the cabbage family with bright yellow, heavily scented flowers, esp. a variety (**oilseed rape**) grown for its oil-rich seed and as stockfeed. Also called **COLE, COLZA.** • Genus *Brassica,* family Brassicaceae, in particular *B. napus* subsp. *oleifera.* ▷late Middle English (originally denoting the turnip plant): from Latin *rapum, rapa* 'turnip.'

rape[3] ▸n. (often **rapes**) the stalks and skins of grapes left after winemaking, used in making vinegar. ▷early 17th cent. (as *rape wine*): from French *râpe,* medieval Latin *raspa* 'bunch of grapes.'

rape[4] ▸n. *historical* (in the UK) any of the six ancient divisions of Sussex. ▷Old English, variant of **ROPE,** with reference to the fencing-off of land.

rape oil (also **rape·seed oil**) ▸n. an oil obtained from rapeseed, used as a lubricant, in alternative fuels, and in foodstuffs.

rape·seed /ˈrāpˌsēd/ ▸n. seeds of the rape plant, used chiefly for oil. See **RAPE**[2].

Raph·a·el[1] /ˈrafēəl; ˈrā-/ (in the Bible) one of the seven archangels in the apocryphal Book of Enoch. He is said to have "healed" the earth when it was defiled by the sins of the fallen angels.

Raph·a·el[2] /ˈrafēəl; ˈrāfēəl; ˌrāfīˈel/ (1483–1520), Italian painter and architect; Italian name *Raffaello Sanzio.* Regarded as one of the greatest artists of the

Renaissance, he is particularly noted for his madonnas, including his altarpiece the *Sistine Madonna* (*c.*1513). As an architect, he was put in charge of the work on St. Peter's Basilica in Rome in 1514.

ra·phe /ˈrāfē/ ▸*n.* (*pl.* **ra·phae** *pronunc.* same) *Anatomy & Biology* a groove, ridge, or seam in an organ or tissue, typically marking the line where two halves fused in the embryo, in particular: ■ the connecting ridge between the two halves of the medulla oblongata or the tegmentum of the midbrain. ■ *Botany* a longitudinal ridge on the side of certain ovules or seeds. ■ *Botany* a longitudinal groove in the valve of many diatoms. ▷mid 18th cent.: modern Latin, from Greek *rhaphē* 'seam.'

ra·phide /ˈrāfīd/ ▸*n. Botany* a needle-shaped crystal of calcium oxalate occurring in clusters within the tissues of certain plants. ▷mid 19th cent.: via French from Greek *rhaphis, rhaphid-* 'needle.'

rap·id /ˈrapid/ ▸*adj.* happening in a short time or at a fast pace: *the country's rapid economic decline | he was disposing of wives in rapid succession.* ■ (of movement or activity) characterized by great speed: *his breathing was rapid and jerky.*
▸*n.* (usu. **rapids**) a fast-flowing and turbulent part of the course of a river. ▷mid 17th cent.: from Latin *rapidus,* from *rapere* 'take by force.' **—ra·pid·i·ty** /rəˈpidətē/ *n.* **—rap·id·ly** *adv.* **—rap·id·ness** *n.*

Rap·id Cit·y a city in southwestern South Dakota, the commercial center for Black Hills and Mount Rushmore tourism; pop. 59,607.

rap·id eye move·ment ▸*n.* a jerky motion of a person's eyes occurring in REM sleep.

rap·id-fire ▸*adj.* [*attrib.*] (esp. of something said in dialogue or done in a sequence) unhesitating and rapid: *a rapid-fire exchange of questions and answers.* ■ (of a gun) able to fire shots in rapid succession.

rap·id tran·sit ▸*n.* [usu. as *adj.*] a form of high-speed urban passenger transportation such as a subway or elevated railroad system.

ra·pi·er /ˈrāpēər/ ▸*n.* a thin, light, sharp-pointed sword used for thrusting. ■ [as *adj.*] (esp. of speech or intelligence) quick and incisive: *rapier wit.* ▷early 16th cent.: from French *rapière,* from *râpe* 'rasp, grater' (because the perforated hilt resembles a rasp or grater).

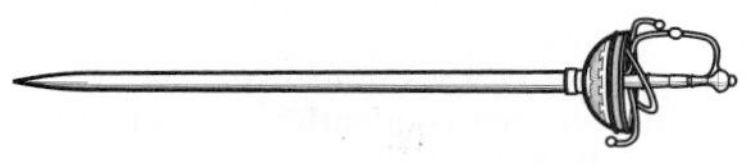

rapier

rap·ine /ˈrapən; -īn/ ▸*n. poetic/literary* the violent seizure of someone's property. ▷late Middle English: from Old French, or from Latin *rapina,* from *rapere* 'seize.'

rap·ist /ˈrāpist/ ▸*n.* a man who commits rape.

Rap·pa·han·nock Riv·er /ˌrapəˈhanək/ a river that flows for 210 miles (340 km) across eastern Virginia into the Tidewater region.

rap·pa·ree /ˌrapəˈrē/ ▸*n.* a bandit or irregular soldier in Ireland in the 17th century. ▷from Irish *rapaire* 'short pike.'

rap·pee /raˈpē; -ˈpā/ ▸*n.* a type of coarse snuff. ▷mid 18th cent.: from French *(tabac) râpé* 'rasped (tobacco).'

rap·pel /rəˈpel/ ▸*v.* (**-pelled, -pel·ling**) [*intrans.*] descend a rock face or other near-vertical surface by using a doubled rope coiled around the body and fixed at a higher point: *they had to rappel down a long steep ice face.*
▸*n.* a descent made by rappeling: *they were careful in setting up the rappel.* ▷1930s: from French, literally 'a recalling,' from *rappeler* in the sense 'bring back to oneself' (with reference to the rope maneuver).

rap·pen /ˈrapən/ ▸*n.* (*pl.* same) a monetary unit in the German-speaking cantons of Switzerland and in Liechtenstein, equal to one hundredth of the Swiss franc. ▷from German *Rappe* 'raven,' with reference to the depiction of the head of a raven, on a medieval coin.

rap·per /ˈrapər/ ▸*n.* a person who performs rap music.

rap·port /raˈpôr; rə-/ ▸*n.* a close and harmonious relationship in which the people or groups concerned understand each other's feelings or ideas and communicate well: *she was able to establish a good rapport with the children | there was little rapport between them.* ▷mid 17th cent.: French, from *rapporter* 'bring back.'

rap·por·teur /ˌraˌpôrˈtər/ ▸*n.* a person appointed by an organization to report on the proceedings of its meetings: *the UN rapporteur.* ▷late 18th cent.: French, from *rapporter* 'bring back.'

rap·proche·ment /ˌrapˌrōshˈmän; -ˌrôsh-/ ▸*n.* (esp. in international relations) an establishment or resumption of harmonious relations: *there were signs of a growing rapprochement between the two countries.* ▷French, from *rapprocher,* from *re-* (expressing intensive force) + *approcher* 'to approach.'

rap·scal·lion /rapˈskalyən/ ▸*n. archaic* or *humorous* a mischievous person. ▷late 17th cent.: alteration of earlier *rascallion,* perhaps from RASCAL.

rap sheet ▸*n. informal* a criminal record.

rapt /rapt/ ▸*adj.* **1** completely fascinated by what one is seeing or hearing: *Andrew looked at her, rapt.* ■ indicating or characterized by such a state of fascination: *they listened with rapt attention.* ■ filled with an intense and pleasurable emotion; enraptured: *she shut her eyes and seemed rapt with desire.* **2** *archaic* or *poetic/literary* having been carried away bodily or transported to heaven: *he was rapt on high.* ▷late Middle English (in the sense 'transported by religious feeling'): from Latin *raptus* 'seized,' past participle of *rapere.* **—rapt·ly** *adv.* **—rapt·ness** *n.*

rap·tor /ˈraptər/ ▸*n.* a bird of prey, e.g., an eagle, hawk, falcon, or owl. ■ *informal* a dromaeosaurid dinosaur, esp. velociraptor or utahraptor. [from VELOCIRAPTOR, a shortened form used originally by paleontologists, popularized by the film *Jurassic Park* (1993).] ▷late Middle English: from Latin, literally 'plunderer,' from *rapt-* 'seized,' from the verb *rapere.*

rap·to·ri·al /rapˈtôrēəl/ ▸*adj. chiefly Zoology* (of a bird or other animal) predatory. ■ (of a limb or other organ) adapted for seizing prey. ▷early 19th cent.: from Latin *raptor* 'plunderer' + -IAL. **—rap·to·ri·al·ly** *adv.*

rap·ture /ˈrapchər/ ▸*n.* **1** a feeling of intense pleasure or joy: *Leonora listened with rapture.* ■ (**raptures**) expressions of intense pleasure or enthusiasm about something: *the tabloids* **went into raptures about** *her.* **2** (**the Rapture**) (according to some millenarian teaching) the transporting of believers to heaven at the second coming of Christ.
▸*v.* [*trans.*] (usu. **be raptured**) (according to some millenarian teaching) transport (a believer) from earth to heaven at the second coming of Christ. ▷late 16th cent. (in the sense 'seizing and carrying off'): from obsolete French, or from medieval Latin *raptura* 'seizing,' partly influenced by RAPT.

THE RIGHT WORD **bliss, ecstasy, euphoria, rapture, transport**

Happiness is one thing; **bliss** is another, suggesting a state of utter joy and contentment (*marital bliss*).

Ecstasy is even more extreme, describing a trancelike state in which one loses consciousness of one's surroundings (*the ecstasy of young love*).

Although **rapture** originally referred to being raised or lifted out of oneself by divine power, nowadays it is used in much the same sense as *ecstasy* to describe an elevated sensation of bliss (*she listened in speechless rapture to her favorite soprano*).

Transport applies to any powerful emotion by which one is carried away (*a transport of delight*).

When happiness is carried to an extreme or crosses over into mania, it is called **euphoria**. *Euphoria* may outwardly resemble *ecstasy* or *rapture,* but upon closer examination, it is usually found to be exaggerated and out of proportion (*the euphoria that came over him whenever he touched alcohol*).

rap·ture of the deep ▸*n.* informal term for NITROGEN NARCOSIS.

rap·tur·ous /ˈrapchərəs/ ▸*adj.* characterized by, feeling, or expressing great pleasure or enthusiasm: *he was greeted with rapturous applause.* **—rap·tur·ous·ly** *adv.* **—rap·tur·ous·ness** *n.*

ra·ra a·vis /ˌre(ə)rə ˈāvis; ˌrärə ˈäwis/ ▸*n.* (*pl.* **ra·rae a·ves** /ˌre(ə)rē ˈāvēs; ˌrärī ˈäwes/) another term for RARE BIRD. ▷Latin.

rare[1] /re(ə)r/ ▸*adj.* (**rar·er, rar·est**) (of an event, situation, or condition) not occurring very often: *a rare genetic disorder |* [with *infinitive*] *it's rare to meet someone who's content with their life.* ■ (of a thing) not found in large numbers and consequently of interest or value: *the jellyfish tree, one of the rarest plants on earth.* ■ unusually good or remarkable: *he plays with rare strength and sensitivity.* ▷late Middle English (in the sense 'widely spaced, infrequent'): from Latin *rarus.* **—rare·ness** *n.*

rare[2] ▸*adj.* (**rar·er, rar·est**) (of meat, esp. beef) lightly cooked, so that the inside is still red. ▷late 18th cent.: variant of obsolete *rear* 'half-cooked' (used to refer to soft-boiled eggs, from the mid 17th to mid 19th centuries).

rare bird ▸*n.* an exceptional person or thing; a rarity: *Irish tenors such as he are rare birds.* ▷translating Latin *rara avis* (Juvenal's *Satires,* vi.165).

rare·bit /ˈre(ə)rbit/ (also **Welsh rare·bit**) ▸*n.* a dish of melted and seasoned cheese on toast, sometimes with other ingredients. ▷late 18th cent.: alteration of *rabbit* in *Welsh rabbit.*

rare earth (also **rare earth el·e·ment** or **rare earth met·al**) ▸*n. Chemistry* any of a group of chemically similar metallic elements comprising the lanthanide series and (usually) scandium and yttrium. They are not esp. rare, but they tend to occur together in nature and are difficult to separate from one another.

rar·ee-show /ˈre(ə)rē ˌshō/ ▸*n. archaic* a form of entertainment, esp. one carried in a box, such as a peep show. ▷late 17th cent.: apparently representing *rare show,* as pronounced by Savoyard showmen in Britain.

rar·e·fac·tion /ˌre(ə)rəˈfakshən/ (also **rar·i·fac·tion**) ▸*n.* diminution in the density of something, esp. air or a gas. ■ *Medicine* the lessening of density of tissue, esp. of nervous tissue or bone. ▷early 17th cent.: from medieval Latin *rarefactio(n-),* from the verb *rarefacere* 'grow thin, become rare.'

rar·e·fied /ˈrerəˌfīd/ (also **rar·i·fied**) ▸*adj.* (of air, esp. that at high altitudes) containing less oxygen than usual. ■ *figurative* esoterically distant from the lives and concerns of ordinary people: *debates about the nature of knowledge can seem very rarefied.*

rare gas ▸*n.* another term for NOBLE GAS.

rare·ly /ˈre(ə)rlē/ ▸*adv.* **1** not often; seldom: *I rarely drive above 60 mph.* **2** *archaic* unusually or remarkably well: *you can write rarely now, after all your schooling.* ■ to an unusual degree; exceptionally: [as *submodifier*] *the rarely fine Sheraton bookcase.*

rar·ing /ˈre(ə)riNG/ ▸*adj.* [with *infinitive*] *informal* very enthusiastic and eager to do something: *she was raring to get back to her work | I'll be ready and* **raring to go.** ▷1920s: present participle of *rare,* dialect variant of ROAR or REAR[2].

Rar·i·tan Riv·er /ˈraritn/ a short river in central New Jersey that flows past New Brunswick and Perth Amboy into Raritan Bay, which is an arm of New York Bay and the Atlantic Ocean.

rar·i·ty /ˈre(ə)ritē/ ▸*n.* (*pl.* **-ties**) the state or quality of being rare: *the rarity of the condition.* ■ a thing that is rare, esp. one having particular value as a result of this: *to take the morning off was a rarity.* ▷late Middle English: from Latin *raritas,* from *rarus* 'far apart, infrequently found' (see RARE[1]).

Ra·ro·tong·a /ˌrarəˈtäNGgə/ a mountainous island in the South Pacific Ocean, the chief island of the Cook Islands. Its chief town, Avarua, is the capital of the islands. **—Ra·ro·tong·an** *n. & adj.*

Ras /räs/ ▸*n.* an Ethiopian king, prince, or feudal lord. ▷from Amharic *rās* 'head.'

ra·sa /ˈrəsə/ ▸*n. Hinduism* essence, flavor, or sentiment, in particular the characteristic quality of music, literature, and drama. ▷Sanskrit, literally 'juice.'

Ras al Khai·mah /ˈräs al ˈkīmə/ one of the seven member states of the United Arab Emirates; pop. 144,000. It joined the United Arab Emirates in 1972, after the British withdrew from the Persian Gulf. ■ its capital, a port on the Persian Gulf; pop. 42,000.

ra·sam /ˈrəsəm/ ▸*n.* a thin, very spicy southern Indian soup served with other dishes, typically as a drink. ▷Tamil.

ras·cal /ˈraskəl/ ▸*n.* a mischievous or cheeky person or child (typically used in an affectionate way). ■ a dishonest person. ▷Middle English (in the senses 'a mob' and 'member of the rabble'): from Old French *rascaille* 'rabble,' of uncertain origin. **—ras·cal·i·ty** /rasˈkalətē/ *n.* (*pl.* **-ties**) **—ras·cal·ly** *adj.*

ras·casse /rasˈkas/ ▸*n.* a small scorpionfish with brick-red skin and spiny fins, found chiefly in the Mediterranean and used as an ingredient of bouillabaisse. • *Scorpaena scrofa,* family Scorpaenidae. ▷1920s: from French.

rase ▸*v. Brit.* variant spelling of RAZE.

rash[1] /rash/ ▸*adj.* displaying or proceeding from a lack of careful consideration of the possible consequences of an action: *it would be extremely rash to make such an assumption | a rash decision.* ▷late Middle English (also in Scots and northern English in the sense 'nimble, eager'); related to German *rasch.* **—rash·ly** *adv.* **—rash·ness** *n.*

R

rash[2] ▸*n.* an area of reddening of a person's skin, sometimes with raised spots, appearing esp. as a result of allergy or illness. ■ a series of things of the same type, esp. when unpleasant or undesirable, occurring or appearing one after the other within a short space of time: *a rash of auto accidents.* ▷early 18th cent.: probably related to Old French *rasche* 'eruptive sores, scurf'; compare with Italian *raschia* 'itch.'

rash·er /ˈrasHər/ ▸*n.* a thin slice of bacon. ■ a serving of several such slices. ▷late 16th cent.: of unknown origin.

rasp /rasp/ ▸*n.* **1** a coarse file or similar metal tool with a roughened surface for scraping, filing, or rubbing down objects of metal, wood, or other hard material. **2** [in *sing.*] a harsh, grating noise: *the rasp of the engine.*

▸*v.* **1** [*trans.*] scrape (something) with a rasp in order to make it smoother. ■ (of a rough surface or object) scrape (something, esp. someone's skin) in a painful or unpleasant way. ■ (**rasp something away/off**) remove something by scraping it off. **2** [*intrans.*] make a harsh, grating noise: *my breath rasped in my throat.* ■ [with *direct speech*] say in a harsh, grating voice: *"Stay where you are!" he rasped.* ▷Middle English (as a verb): from Old French *rasper*, perhaps of Germanic origin. **—rasp·er** *n.* **—rasp·ing·ly** *adv.* **—rasp·y** *adj.*

rasp·ber·ry /ˈrazˌberē; -b(ə)rē/ ▸*n.* **1** an edible soft fruit related to the blackberry, consisting of a cluster of reddish-pink drupelets. **2** the plant that yields this fruit, forming tall, stiff, prickly stems (canes). • *Rubus idaeus*, family Rosaceae; cultivars include the loganberry. **3** a deep reddish-pink color like that of a ripe raspberry: [as *adj.*] *a raspberry tweed jacket.* **4** *informal* a sound made with the tongue and lips in order to express derision or contempt: *Clare* ***blew a raspberry*** *and stood up.* [from *raspberry tart*, rhyming slang for 'fart.'] ▷early 17th cent.: from dialect *rasp*, abbreviation of obsolete *raspis* 'raspberry' (also used as a collective), of unknown origin, + BERRY.

Ra·spu·tin /rasˈpyo͞otn/, Grigori (Efimovich) (1871–1916), Russian monk. He exerted great influence over Tsar Nicholas II and his family during World War I; this influence, combined with his reputation for debauchery, steadily discredited the imperial family, and he was assassinated by a group loyal to the tsar.

ras·sle /ˈrasəl/ ▸*v.* nonstandard spelling of WRESTLE, representing a variant pronunciation. **—ras·sler** /ˈras(ə)lər/ *n.*

Ras·ta /ˈrastə/ ▸*n.* & *adj. informal* short for RASTAFARIAN.

Ras·ta·far·i /ˌrastəˈfe(ə)rē; -ˈfärē/ ▸*n.* [usu. as *adj.*] the Rastafarian movement. ▷from *Ras Tafari*, the name by which Haile Selassie was known (1916–30).

Ras·ta·far·i·an /ˌrastəˈfe(ə)rēən; -ˈfärēən/ ▸*adj.* of or relating to a religious movement of Jamaican origin holding that blacks are the chosen people, that Emperor Haile Selassie of Ethiopia was the Messiah, and that black people will eventually return to their Africa.

▸*n.* a member of the Rastafarian religious movement. Rastafarians have distinctive codes of behavior and dress, including the wearing of dreadlocks, the smoking of cannabis, the rejection of Western medicine, and adherence to a diet that excludes pork, shellfish, and milk. **—Ras·ta·far·i·an·ism** *n.*

Ras·ta·man /ˈrastəˌman/ ▸*n.* (*pl.* **-men**) *informal* a male Rastafarian.

ras·ter /ˈrastər/ ▸*n.* a rectangular pattern of parallel scanning lines followed by the electron beam on a television screen or computer monitor. ▷mid 20th cent.: from German *Raster*, literally 'screen,' from Latin *rastrum* 'rake,' from *ras-* 'scraped,' from the verb *radere*.

ras·ter im·age proc·es·sor (abbr.: **RIP**) ▸*n. Computing* a device that rasterizes an image.

ras·ter·ize /ˈrastəˌrīz/ ▸*v.* [*trans.*] *Computing* convert (an image stored as an outline) into pixels that can be displayed on a screen or printed. **—ras·ter·i·za·tion** /ˌrastərəˈzāsHən/ *n.* **—ras·ter·iz·er** *n.*

Rast·ya·pi·no /rästˈyäpiˌnō/ former name (1919–29) of DZERZHINSK.

rat /rat/ ▸*n.* **1** a rodent that resembles a large mouse, typically having a pointed snout and a long, sparsely haired tail. Some kinds have become cosmopolitan and are sometimes responsible for transmitting diseases. • Family Muridae: many genera, including *Rattus* (the Old World rats), and several hundred species. **2** *informal* a person regarded as despicable, esp. a man who has been deceitful or disloyal. ■ an informer. **3** [with *adj.*] a person who is associated with or frequents a specified place: *you and the rest of the tavern rats will have to find a new hangout* | *LA mall rats.* **4** a pad used to give shape or fullness to a woman's hair.

▸*exclam.* (**rats**) *informal* used to express mild annoyance or irritation.

▸*v.* (**rat·ted, rat·ting**) [*intrans.*] **1** [usu. as *n.*] (**ratting**) (of a person, dog, or cat) hunt or kill rats. **2** *informal* desert one's party, side, or cause. **3** give (hair) shape or fullness with a rat.

▸*phrasal v.* □ **rat on** (also **rat out**) *informal* inform on (someone) to a person in a position of authority: *I never thought Stash would rat on me* | *men will literally choose death over ratting out another prisoner.* ■ break (an agreement or promise): *he accused the government of ratting on an earlier pledge.* ▷Old English *ræt*, probably of Romance origin; reinforced in Middle English by Old French *rat*. The verb dates from the early 19th cent.

rat·a·ble /ˈrātəbəl/ ▸*adj.* able to be rated or estimated. **—rat·a·bil·i·ty** /ˌrātəˈbilətē/ *n.* **—rat·a·bly** /-blē/ *adv.*

rat·a·fi·a /ˌratəˈfēə/ ▸*n.* a liqueur flavored with almonds or the kernels of peaches, apricots, or cherries. ■ (also **rat·a·fi·a bis·cuit**) an almond-flavored cookie like a small macaroon. ▷late 17th cent.: from French; perhaps related to TAFIA.

rat·a·ma·cue /ˈratəməˌkyo͞o/ ▸*n. Music* one of the basic patterns (rudiments) of drumming, consisting of a two-beat figure, the first beat of which is played as a triplet and preceded by two grace notes. ▷1940s: imitative.

Ra·ta·na /räˈtänə/, Tahupotiki Wiremu (1873–1939), Maori political and religious leader. He founded the Ratana Church 1920, a religious revival movement that aimed to unite all Māori people.

rat·a·plan /ˈrätəˌplan/ ▸*n.* [in *sing.*] a drumming or beating sound. ▷mid 19th cent.: from French, of imitative origin.

rat-a-tat /ˈrat ə ˌtat/ (also **rat-a-tat-tat** /ˌrat ə ˌtat ˈtat/ or **rat-tat** or **rat-tat-tat**) ▸*n.* a rapping sound (used esp. in reference to a sequence of two or three knocks on a door or the sound of gunfire). ▷late 17th cent.: imitative.

ra·ta·touille /ˌratəˈto͞o-ē; ˌrä,tä-/ ▸*n.* a vegetable dish consisting of onions, zucchini, tomatoes, eggplant, and peppers, fried and stewed in oil and sometimes served cold. ▷a French dialect word.

rat-bite fe·ver ▸*n. Medicine* a disease contracted from the bite of a rat that causes inflammation of the skin and fever or vomiting. • This disease can be caused by either of two bacteria, *Spirillum minus* or *Streptobacillus moniliformis.*

ratch·et /ˈracHit/ ▸*n.* a device consisting of a bar or wheel with a set of angled teeth in which a pawl, cog, or tooth engages, allowing motion in one direction only. ■ a bar or wheel that has such a set of teeth. ■ *figurative* a situation or process that is perceived to be deteriorating or changing steadily in a series of irreversible steps: *the best way to reverse the ratchet of socialism.*

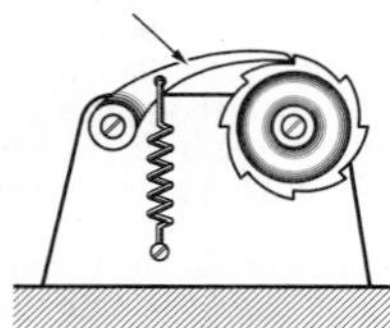
ratchet

▸*v.* (**ratch·et·ed, ratch·et·ing**) [*trans.*] operate by means of a ratchet. ■ (**ratchet something up/down**) *figurative* cause something to rise (or fall) as a step in what is perceived as a steady and irreversible process: *the Bank of Japan ratcheted up interest rates again.* ■ [*intrans.*] make a sound like a ratchet. ▷mid 17th cent.: from French *rochet*, originally denoting a blunt lance head, later in the sense 'bobbin, ratchet'; related to the base of archaic *rock* 'quantity of wool on a distaff for spinning.'

rate[1] /rāt/ ▸*n.* **1** a measure, quantity, or frequency, typically one measured against some other quantity or measure: *the crime rate rose by 26 percent.* ■ the speed with which something moves, happens, or changes: *your heart rate.* **2** a fixed price paid or charged for something, esp. goods or services: *the basic rate of pay* | *advertising rates.* ■ the amount of a charge or payment expressed as a percentage of some other amount, or as a basis of calculation: *you'll find our current interest rate very competitive.* ■ (usu. **rates**) (in the UK) a tax on land and buildings paid to the local authority by a business, and formerly also by occupants of private property.

▸*v.* **1** [*trans.*] assign a standard or value to (something) according to a particular scale: *they were asked to rate their ability at different driving maneuvers* | [*trans.*] *the hotel, rated four star, had no hot water and no sink plugs.* ■ [*trans.*] assign a standard, optimal, or limiting rating to (a piece of equipment): *its fuel economy is* ***rated at*** *25 miles a gallon in the city.* ■ *Brit.* assess the value of (a property) for the purpose of levying a local tax. **2** [*trans.*] consider to be of a certain quality, standard, or rank: *he rates the company's stock a "buy."* | [*trans.*] *the program has been rated a great success.* ■ [*intrans.*] be regarded in a specified way: *Jeff still rates as one of the nicest people I have ever met.* ■ [*trans.*] be worthy of; merit: *the ambassador rated a bulletproof car and a police escort.* ▷late Middle English (expressing a notion of 'estimated value'): from Old French, from medieval Latin *rata* (from Latin *pro rata parte* (or *portione*) 'according to the proportional share'), from *ratus* 'reckoned,' past participle of *reri*.

▸*PHRASES* □ **at any rate** whatever happens or may have happened: *for the moment, at any rate, he was safe.* ■ used to indicate that one is correcting or clarifying a previous statement or emphasizing a following one: *the story, or at any rate, a public version of it, was known and remembered.* □ **at this** (or **that**) **rate** used to introduce the prediction of a particular unwelcome eventuality should things continue as they are or if a certain assumption is true: *at this rate, I won't have a job to go back to.*

rate[2] ▸*v.* [*trans.*] *archaic* scold (someone) angrily: *he rated the young man soundly for his want of respect.* ▷late Middle English: of unknown origin.

rate·a·ble /ˈrātəbəl/ ▸*adj. Brit.* variant spelling of RATABLE.

rate con·stant ▸*n. Chemistry* a coefficient of proportionality relating the rate of a chemical reaction at a given temperature to the concentration of reactant (in a unimolecular reaction) or to the product of the concentrations of reactants.

ra·tel /ˈrätl; ˈrātl/ ▸*n.* a badgerlike mammal with a white or gray back and black underparts, native to Africa and Asia. Also called HONEY BADGER. • *Mellivora capensis*, family Mustelidae. ▷late 18th cent.: from Afrikaans, of unknown ultimate origin.

rate of ex·change ▸*n.* another term for EXCHANGE RATE.

rate·pay·er /ˈrātˌpāər/ ▸*n.* **1** a customer of a public utility. **2** (in the UK) a person required to pay local property taxes.

rat·fish /ˈratˌfisH/ ▸*n.* (*pl.* same or **-fish·es**) **1** a blunt-nosed chimaera with rodentlike front teeth and a long thin tail, found chiefly in cooler waters. See also RABBITFISH. • Genera *Chimaera* and *Hydrolagus*, family Chimaeridae: several species, including *H. colliei* of the eastern North Pacific. **2** another term for RABBITFISH.

Rat·haus /ˈrätˌhous/ ▸*n.* (*pl.* **-häu·ser** /-ˌhoizər/) a town hall in a German-speaking country. ▷German, from *Rat* 'council' + *Haus* 'house.'

rathe /rāT͟H; raTH/ ▸*adj. archaic, poetic/literary* (of a person or their actions) prompt and eager. ■ (of flowers or fruit) blooming or ripening early in the year. ▷Old English *hræth*, *hræd*, of Germanic origin; perhaps related to the base of RASH[1].

Rath·er /ˈraT͟Hər/, Dan (1931–), U.S. journalist. He was managing editor and anchor of "CBS Evening News" from 1981, as well as the anchor for "48 Hours" from 1988. He wrote *The Camera Never Blinks* (1977) and *Deadlines and Datelines* (1999).

rath·er /ˈraT͟Hər; ˈräT͟Hər; ˈrəT͟Hər/ ▸*adv.* **1** (**would rather**) used to indicate one's preference in a particular matter: *would you like some wine, or would you rather stick to sherry?* | *she'd* ***rather*** *die* ***than*** *cause a scene* | [with *clause*] *I'd rather you not tell him "You'd better ask her." "I'd rather not."* **2** [as *submodifier*] to a certain or significant extent or degree: *she's been behaving rather strangely* | *he's rather an unpleasant man.* ■ used before verbs as a way of making the expression of a feeling or opinion less assertive: *I rather think he wants me to marry him* | *we were rather hoping you might do that for us.* **3** on the contrary (used to suggest that the opposite of what has just been implied or stated is the case): [*sentence adverb*] *There is no shortage of basic skills in the workplace. Rather, the problem is poor management.* ■ more precisely (used to modify or clarify something previously stated): *I walked,* ***or rather*** *limped, the two miles home.* ■ instead of; as opposed to: *she seemed indifferent* ***rather than*** *angry.*

▸*exclam. chiefly Brit., dated* used to express emphatic affirmation, agreement, or acceptance: *"You are glad to be home, aren't you?" "Rather!"* ▷Old English *hrathor* 'earlier, sooner,' comparative of *hræthe* 'without delay,' from *hræth* 'prompt' (see RATHE).

▸*PHRASES* □ **had rather** would rather: *I had rather not* *see him.* □ **rather you** (or **him** or **her**, etc.) **than me** used to convey that one would be reluctant oneself to undertake a particular task or project undertaken by someone else: *"I'm picking him up after lunch." "Rather you than me."*

rat·hole /ˈratˌhōl/ ▸*n.* **1** *informal* a cramped or squalid room or building. **2** *informal* used to refer to the waste of money or resources: *pouring our assets* ***down the rathole*** *of military expenditure.*
▸*v.* [*trans.*] *informal* hide (money or goods), typically as part of a fraud or deception.

raths·kel·ler /ˈrätˌskelər; ˈrat-; ˈraTH-/ ▸*n.* a beer hall or restaurant in a basement. ▷early 20th cent.: from obsolete German (now *Ratskeller*), from *Rathaus* 'town hall' + *Keller* 'cellar,' denoting the place where beer and wine were sold.

rat·i·fy /ˈratəˌfī/ ▸*v.* (**-fies**, **-fied**) [*trans.*] sign or give formal consent to (a treaty, contract, or agreement), making it officially valid. See note at **APPROVE**. ▷late Middle English: from Old French *ratifier*, from medieval Latin *ratificare*, from Latin *ratus* 'fixed' (see **RATE**[1]). —**rat·i·fi·a·ble** /ˈratəˌfīəbəl/ *adj.* —**rat·i·fi·ca·tion** /ˌratəfəˈkāSHən/ *n.* —**rat·i·fi·er** *n.*

rat·ing[1] /ˈrātiNG/ ▸*n.* a classification or ranking of someone or something based on a comparative assessment of their quality, standard, or performance: *the hotel regained its five-star rating.* ■ (**ratings**) the estimated audience size of a particular television or radio program: *the soap's ratings have recently picked up.* ■ the value of a property or condition that is claimed to be standard, optimal, or limiting for a substance, material, or item of equipment: *fuel with a low octane rating.* ■ any of the classes into which racing yachts are assigned according to dimensions.

rat·ing[2] ▸*n. dated* an angry reprimand.

ra·tio /ˈrāSHō; ˈrāSHēˌō/ ▸*n.* (*pl.* **-tios**) the quantitative relation between two amounts showing the number of times one value contains or is contained within the other: *the ratio of men's jobs to women's is 8 to 1.* ■ the relative value of silver and gold in a bimetallic system of currency. ▷mid 17th cent.: from Latin, literally 'reckoning,' from *rat-* 'reckoned,' from the verb *reri.*

ra·ti·oc·i·nate /ˌratēˈōsəˌnāt; ˌraSHē-/ ▸*v.* [*intrans.*] *formal* form judgments by a process of logic; reason. ▷mid 17th cent.: from Latin *ratiocinat-* 'deliberated, calculated,' from the verb *ratiocinari*, from *ratio* (see **RATIO**). —**ra·ti·oc·i·na·tion** /-ˌōsəˈnāSHən/ *n.* —**ra·ti·oc·i·na·tive** /-ˈōsəˌnātiv; ˈäs-/ *adj.* —**ra·ti·oc·i·na·tor** /-ˈōsəˌnātər; -ˈäs-/ *n.*

ra·ti·o de·ci·den·di /ˈrātēˌō ˌdesəˈdendē/ ▸*n.* (*pl.* **ra·ti·o·nes de·ci·den·di** /ˌrātēˈōnēz/) *Law* the rule of law on which a judicial decision is based. ▷Latin, literally 'reason for deciding.'

ra·tion /ˈraSHən; ˈrā-/ ▸*n.* a fixed amount of a commodity officially allowed to each person during a time of shortage, as in wartime: *1918 saw the bread ration reduced on two occasions.* ■ (usu. **rations**) an amount of food supplied on a regular basis, esp. to members of the armed forces during a war. ■ (**rations**) food; provisions: *their emergency rations ran out.* ■ *figurative* a fixed amount of a particular thing: *their daily* ***ration of*** *fresh air.*
▸*v.* [*trans.*] (usu. **be rationed**) allow each person to have only a fixed amount of (a particular commodity): *shoes were rationed from 1943.* ■ (**ration someone to**) allow someone to have only (a fixed amount of a certain commodity): *they were requested to ration themselves to one glass of wine each.* ▷early 18th cent.: from French, from Latin *ratio(n-)* 'reckoning, ratio.'

ra·tion·al /ˈraSHənl; ˈraSHnəl/ ▸*adj.* **1** based on or in accordance with reason or logic: *I'm sure there's a perfectly rational explanation.* ■ (of a person) able to think clearly, sensibly, and logically: *Andrea's upset—she's not being very rational.* See note at **SENSIBLE**. ■ endowed with the capacity to reason: *man is a rational being.* **2** *Mathematics* (of a number, quantity, or expression) expressible, or containing quantities that are expressible, as a ratio of whole numbers. When expressed as a decimal, a rational number has a finite or recurring expansion.
▸*n. Mathematics* a rational number. ▷late Middle English (in the sense 'having the ability to reason'): from Latin *rationalis*, from *ratio(n-)* 'reckoning, reason' (see **RATIO**). —**ra·tion·al·i·ty** /ˌraSHəˈnalətē/ *n.* —**ra·tion·al·ly** /ˈraSHənl-ē; ˈraSHnəlē/ *adv.*

ra·tion·ale /ˌraSHəˈnal/ ▸*n.* a set of reasons or a logical basis for a course of action or a particular belief: *he explained the rationale behind the change.* ▷mid 17th cent.: modern Latin, neuter (used as a noun) of Latin *rationalis* 'endowed with reason' (see **RATIONAL**).

ra·tion·al ex·pec·ta·tions hy·poth·e·sis ▸*n. Economics* the hypothesis that an economic agent will make full use of all available information when forming expectations, esp. with regard to inflation, and not just past values of a particular variable. Compare with **ADAPTIVE EXPECTATIONS HYPOTHESIS**.

ra·tion·al·ism /ˈraSHənlˌizəm; ˈraSHnəˌlizəm/ ▸*n.* a belief or theory that opinions and actions should be based on reason and knowledge rather than on religious belief or emotional response: *scientific rationalism.* ■ *Philosophy* the theory that reason rather than experience is the foundation of certainty in knowledge. ■ *Theology* the practice of treating reason as the ultimate authority in religion. —**ra·tion·al·ist** *n.* —**ra·tion·al·is·tic** /ˌraSHənlˈistik; ˌraSHnəˈlistik/ *adj.* —**ra·tion·al·is·ti·cal·ly** /ˌraSHənlˈistik(ə)lē; ˌraSHnəˈlistik(ə)lē/ *adv.*

ra·tion·al·ize /ˈraSHənlˌīz; ˈraSHnəˌlīz/ ▸*v.* [*trans.*] **1** attempt to explain or justify (one's own or another's behavior or attitude) with logical, plausible reasons, even if these are not true or appropriate: *she couldn't rationalize her urge to return to the cottage.* See note at **LIE**. **2** make (a company, process, or industry) more efficient by reorganizing it in such a way as to dispense with unnecessary personnel or equipment: *his success was due primarily to his ability to rationalize production.* **3** *Mathematics* convert (a function or expression) to a rational form. —**ra·tion·al·i·za·tion** /ˌraSHənl-əˈzāSHən; ˌraSHnələ-/ *n.* —**ra·tion·al·iz·er** *n.*

Rat Is·lands an island group in southwestern Alaska, part of the Aleutian Islands, that lie between the Near and Andreanof islands. Amchitka and Kiska islands are also included.

rat·ite /ˈraˌtīt/ *Ornithology* ▸*adj.* (of a bird) having a flat breastbone without a keel, and so unable to fly. Contrasted with **CARINATE**.
▸*n.* any of the mostly large, flightless birds with such a breastbone, i.e., the ostrich, rhea, emu, cassowary, and kiwi, together with the extinct moa and elephant bird. ▷late 19th cent.: from Latin *ratis* 'raft' + **-ITE**[1].

rat kan·ga·roo ▸*n.* a small ratlike Australian marsupial with long hind limbs used for hopping. • Family Potoroidae: several genera and species.

rat·lines /ˈratlənz/ ▸*plural n.* a series of small ropes fastened across a sailing ship's shrouds like the rungs of a ladder, used for climbing the rigging. ▷late Middle English: of unknown origin.

ratlines

ra·toon /rəˈto͞on; ra-/ ▸*n.* a new shoot or sprout springing from the base of a crop plant, esp. sugar cane, after cropping.
▸*v.* [*intrans.*] (of sugar cane) produce ratoons. ■ [*trans.*] cut down (a plant) to cause it to sprout in this way. ▷mid 17th cent. (as a noun): from Spanish *retoño* 'a sprout.'

ra·toon crop ▸*n.* a new crop (esp. of rice, bananas, or sugar cane) that grows from the stubble of the crop already harvested.

Rat Pack ▸*n. informal* a group of five friends and co-performers prominent in the entertainment industries of Hollywood and Las Vegas in the 1950s and 1960s. The group (Frank Sinatra, Dean Martin, Sammy Davis, Jr., Joey Bishop, and Peter Lawford) made several movies together, including *Ocean's Eleven* (1960).

rat race ▸*n. informal* a way of life in which people are caught up in a fiercely competitive struggle for wealth or power. ■ an exhausting, usually competitive routine.

rats·bane /ˈratsˌbān/ ▸*n. poetic/literary* rat poison.

rat snake ▸*n.* a harmless constricting snake that feeds on rats and other small mammals. • Several genera and species in the family Colubridae: genus *Elaphe* of America, in particular *E. obsoleta*, and genera *Ptyas* and *Argyrogena* of Asia (also called **RACER**), in particular *P. mucosus.*

rat-tail ▸*n.* a fish with a long narrow tail, in particular: ■ another term for **GRENADIER** (sense 2). ■ another term for **RABBITFISH**.

rat-tailed mag·got ▸*n.* the aquatic larva of the drone fly, with a taillike telescopic breathing tube that enables it to breathe air while submerged.

rat·tan /raˈtan; rə-/ ▸*n.* **1** the thin pliable stems of a palm, used to make furniture. ■ a length of such a stem used as a walking stick. **2** the tropical Old World climbing palm that yields this product, with long, spiny, jointed stems. • Genus *Calamus*, family Palmae. ▷mid 17th cent.: from Malay *rotan*, probably from *raut* 'pare, trim.'

rat-tat /ˌrat ˈtat/ ▸*n.* variant of **RAT-A-TAT**.

rat·ter /ˈratər/ ▸*n.* a dog or other animal that is used for hunting rats.

rat·tle /ˈratl/ ▸*v.* **1** [*intrans.*] make a rapid succession of short, sharp knocking sounds, typically as a result of being shaken and striking repeatedly against a hard surface or object: *there was a sound of bottles rattling as he stacked the crates.* ■ [*trans.*] cause (something) to make such sounds: *he rattled some change in his pocket.* ■ [with *adverbial of direction*] (of a vehicle or its driver or passengers) move or travel somewhere while making such sounds: *trains rattled past at frequent intervals.* ■ (**rattle around in**) *figurative* be in or occupy (an unnecessarily or undesirably spacious room or building). **2** [*trans.*] (often **be rattled**) *informal* cause (someone) to feel nervous, worried, or irritated: *she turned quickly, rattled by his presence.*
▸*phrasal v.* □ **rattle something off** say, perform, or produce something quickly and effortlessly: *he rattled off some instructions.* □ **rattle on/away** talk rapidly and at length, esp. in an inane or boring way.
▸*n.* **1** a rapid succession of short, sharp, hard sounds: *the rattle of teacups on the tray.* ■ a gurgling sound in the throat of a dying person. **2** a thing used to make a rapid succession of short, sharp sounds, in particular: ■ a baby's toy consisting of a container filled with small pellets that makes a noise when shaken. ■ the set of horny rings at the end of a rattlesnake's tail, shaken with a dry buzzing sound as a warning. ▷Middle English (as a verb): related to Middle Dutch and Low German *ratelen*, of imitative origin. —**rattly** /ˈratl-ē; ˈratlē/ *adj.*
▸*PHRASES* □ **rattle someone's cage** *informal* make someone feel angry or annoyed. □ **rattle sabers** threaten to take aggressive action. See also **SABER-RATTLING**.

rat·tler /ˈratl-ər; ˈratlər/ ▸*n. informal* a rattlesnake.

rat·tle·snake /ˈratlˌsnāk/ ▸*n.* a heavy-bodied American pit viper with a series of horny rings on the tail that, when vibrated, produce a characteristic rattling sound as a warning. • Genera *Crotalus* and *Sistrurus*, family Viperidae: several species.

rat·tle·trap /ˈratlˌtrap/ ▸*n. informal* an old or rickety vehicle.

rat·tling /ˈratl-iNG; ˈratliNG/ ▸*adj.* **1** making a series of short, sharp knocking sounds: *a rattling old bus.* **2** *informal, dated* denoting something very good of its kind (used for emphasis): *a rattling good story.*

rat·trap /ˈratˌtrap/ ▸*n.* **1** a trap for catching rats. **2** *informal* a shabby, squalid, or ramshackle building or establishment. **3** *informal* an unpleasant or restricting situation that offers no prospect of improvement.

rat·ty /ˈratē/ ▸*adj.* (**-ti·er**, **-ti·est**) **1** resembling or characteristic of a rat: *his ratty eyes glittered.* ■ (of a place) infested with rats. ■ *informal* shabby, untidy or in bad condition: *a ratty old armchair.* **2** [*predic.*] *Brit., informal* (of a person) bad-tempered and irritable: *I was ratty with the children.* —**rat·ti·ly** /ˈratl-ē/ *adv.* —**rat·ti·ness** *n.*

rau·cous /ˈrôkəs/ ▸*adj.* making or constituting a disturbingly harsh and loud noise: *raucous youths.* ▷mid 18th cent.: from Latin *raucus* 'hoarse' + **-OUS**. —**rau·cous·ly** *adv.* —**rau·cous·ness** *n.*

raunch /rônCH; ränCH/ ▸*n. informal* energetic earthiness; vulgarity: *the raunch of his first album.* ▷1960s: back-formation from **RAUNCHY**.

raun·chy /ˈrônCHē; ˈrän-/ ▸*adj.* (**-chi·er**, **-chi·est**) *informal* **1** earthy, vulgar, and often sexually explicit: *a raunchy new novel.* **2** (esp. of a person or place) slovenly; grubby: *the restaurant's style is raunchy and the sanitation chancy.* ▷1930s: of unknown origin. —**raunch·i·ly** /-CHəlē/ *adv.* —**raunch·i·ness** *n.*

Rau·schen·berg /ˈrouSHənˌbərg/, Robert (1925–), U.S. artist. His series of "combine" paintings, such as *Charlene* (1954) and *Rebus* (1955), incorporate three-dimensional objects such as nails, rags, and bottles.

rau·wol·fi·a /rouˈwo͝olfēə; rôˈwo͝ol-/ (also **rau·vol·fi·a**) ▸*n.* a tropical shrub or small tree, some kinds of which are cultivated for the medicinal drugs that

Pronunciation Key ə *ago*; ər *over*; ˈə or ˌə *up*; ˈər or ˌər *fur*; a *hat*; ā *rate*; ä *car*; CH *chew*; e *let*; ē *see*; e(ə)r *air*; i *fit*; ī *by*; i(ə)r *ear*; NG *sing*; ō *go*; ô *for*; oi *boy*; o͝o *good*; o͞o *goo*; ou *out*; SH *she*; TH *thin*; T͟H *then*; (h)w *why*; ZH *vision*

R

they yield. • Genus *Rauwolfia* (or *Rauvolfia*), family Apocynaceae: many species, in particular the Indian snakeroot (*R. serpentina*), from which the drug reserpine is obtained. ▷modern Latin, named after Leonhard *Rauwolf* (died 1596), German botanist.

rav /räv/ ▸*n. Judaism* a rabbi, esp. one who holds a position of authority or who acts as a personal mentor. [partly via Yiddish.] ■ (**Rav**) (in orthodox Judaism) a title of respect and form of address preceding a personal name. ▷from Hebrew and Aramaic *rab* 'master.'

rav·age /'ravij/ ▸*v.* [*trans.*] cause severe and extensive damage to: *fears that a war could ravage their country.*
▸*n.* (**ravages**) the severely damaging or destructive effects of something: *his face had withstood **the ravages of time**.* ■ acts of destruction: *the ravages committed by man.* ▷early 17th cent.: from French *ravager*, from earlier *ravage*, alteration of *ravine* 'rush of water.' —**rav·ag·er** *n.*

THE RIGHT WORD **despoil, devastate, pillage, plunder, ravage, sack, waste**

Ravage, pillage, sack, and **plunder** are all verbs associated with the actions of a conquering army during wartime.

Ravage implies violent destruction, usually in a series of raids or invasions over an extended period of time (*the invading forces ravaged the countryside*).

Plunder refers to the roving of soldiers through recently conquered territory in search of money and goods (*they plundered the city and left its inhabitants destitute*), while *pillage* describes the act of stripping a conquered city or people of valuables (*churches pillaged by ruthless invaders*).

Sack is even more extreme than *pillage*, implying not only the seizure of all valuables, but total destruction as well (*the army sacked every village along the coast*).

Despoil also entails the stripping of valuables, but with less violence than *sack*; it is more common in nonmilitary contexts, where it describes a heedless or inadvertent destruction (*forests despoiled by logging companies*).

Devastate emphasizes ruin and desolation, whether it happens to buildings, forests, or crops (*fields of corn devastated by flooding*).

Waste comes close in meaning to *devastate*, but it suggests a less violent or more gradual destruction (*a region of the country wasted by years of drought and periodic fires*).

rave[1] /räv/ ▸*v.* [*intrans.*] **1** talk wildly or incoherently, as if one were delirious or insane: *Nancy's having hysterics and raving about a black ghost.* ■ address someone in an angry, uncontrolled way: [with *direct speech*] *"Never mind how he feels!" Melissa raved.* **2** speak or write about someone or something with great enthusiasm or admiration: *New York's theater critics raved about the acting.* **3** *informal* attend or take part in a rave (party).
▸*n.* **1** *informal* an extremely enthusiastic recommendation or appraisal of someone or something: *the film has won raves from American reviewers* | [as *adj.*] *their recent tour received **rave reviews**.* **2** *informal* a lively party or gathering involving dancing and drinking: *their annual fancy-dress rave.* ■ a party or event attended by large numbers of young people, involving drug use and dancing to fast, electronic music. ■ electronic dance music of the kind played at such events. ▷Middle English (in the sense 'show signs of madness'): probably from Old Northern French *raver*; related obscurely to (Middle) Low German *reven* 'be senseless, rave.'

rave[2] ▸*n.* a rail of a cart. ■ (**raves**) a permanent or removable framework added to the sides of a cart to increase its capacity. ▷mid 16th cent.: variant of the synonymous dialect word *rathe*, of unknown origin.

Rav·el /rə'vel/, Maurice (Joseph) (1875–1937), French composer. His works, which are noted for their colorful orchestration, have a distinctive tone and make use of unresolved dissonances. Notable works: *Daphnis and Chloë* (1912) and *Boléro* (1928).

rav·el /'ravəl/ ▸*v.* (**rav·eled, rav·el·ing**; *Brit.* **rav·el·led, rav·el·ling**) [*trans.*] **1** (**ravel something out**) untangle or unravel something: *Davy had finished raveling out his herring net* | *figurative sleep raveled out the tangles of his mind.* **2** confuse or complicate (a question or situation).
▸*n. rare* a tangle, cluster, or knot: *a lovely yellow ravel of sunflowers.* ▷late Middle English (in the sense 'entangle, confuse'): probably from Dutch *ravelen* 'fray out, tangle.'

rave·lin /'ravlən/ ▸*n. historical* an outwork of fortifications, with two faces forming a salient angle, constructed beyond the main ditch and in front of the curtain. ▷late 16th cent.: from French, from obsolete Italian *ravellino*, of unknown origin.

rav·el·ing /'rav(ə)liNG/ ▸*n.* a thread from a woven or knitted fabric that has frayed or started to unravel.

rav·en[1] /'rāvən/ ▸*n.* **1** a large heavily built crow with mainly black plumage, feeding chiefly on carrion. • Genus *Corvus*, family Corvidae: several species, in particular the widespread all-black **common raven** (*C. corax*) **2** (**the Raven**) the constellation Corvus.
▸*adj.* (esp. of hair) of a glossy black color. ▷Old English *hræfn*, of Germanic origin; related to Dutch *raaf* and German *Rabe*.

rav·en[2] /'ravən/ ▸*v.* [*intrans.*] *archaic* (of a ferocious wild animal) hunt for prey. ■ [*trans.*] devour voraciously. ▷late 15th cent. (in the sense 'take as spoil'): from Old French *raviner*, originally 'to ravage,' based on Latin *rapina* 'pillage.'

rav·en·ing /'ravəniNG/ ▸*adj.* (of a ferocious wild animal) extremely hungry and hunting for prey: *they turned on each other like ravening wolves.*

Ra·ven·na /rə'venə/ a city near the Adriatic coast in northeast central Italy; pop. 137,000. It is noted for its ancient mosaics dating from the early Christian period.

rav·en·ous /'ravənəs/ ▸*adj.* extremely hungry. ■ (of hunger or need) very great; voracious: *a ravenous appetite.* ▷late Middle English: from Old French *ravineus*, from *raviner* 'to ravage' (see RAVEN[2]). —**rav·en·ous·ly** *adv.* —**rav·en·ous·ness** *n.*

rav·er /'rāvər/ ▸*n.* **1** *informal* a person who regularly goes to raves. **2** a person who talks wildly or incoherently, as if delirious or insane.

rave-up ▸*n. informal* another term for RAVE *n.* sense 2.

Ra·vi /'rävē/ a river in the northern Indian subcontinent, one of the headwaters of the Indus River that rises in the Himalayas in Himachel Pradesh, in northwestern India, and flows for 450 miles (725 km) southwest into Pakistan, where it empties into the Chenab River just north of Multan. It is one of the five rivers that gave Punjab its name.

ra·vi·gote /,rävi'gôt/ (also **ra·vi·gotte**) ▸*n.* a mixture of chopped chervil, chives, tarragon, and shallots, used to give piquancy to a sauce or as a base for an herb butter. ▷French, from *ravigoter* 'invigorate.'

rav·in /'ravən/ ▸*n. archaic* or *poetic/literary* violent seizure of prey or property; plunder. ▷Middle English: from Old French *ravine*, from Latin *rapina* 'pillage' (see RAPINE).

ra·vine /rə'vēn/ ▸*n.* a deep, narrow gorge with steep sides. ▷late 18th cent.: from French, 'violent rush (of water)' (see RAVIN). —**ra·vined** *adj.*

rav·ing /'rāviNG/ ▸*n.* (usu. **ravings**) wild, irrational, or incoherent talk: *the ravings of a madwoman.*
▸*adj. informal* used to emphasize the bad or extreme quality of someone or something: *she'd never been a raving beauty* | [as *submodifier*] *have you gone **raving mad**?*

ra·vi·o·li /,ravē'ōlē/ ▸ *n.* small pasta envelopes containing ground meat, cheese, or vegetables. ▷Italian.

rav·ish /'raviSH/ ▸*v.* [*trans.*] **1** *archaic* seize and carry off (someone) by force. ■ *dated* (of a man) force (a woman or girl) to have sexual intercourse against her will; rape. **2** (often **be ravished**) *poetic/literary* fill (someone) with intense delight; enrapture: *ravished by a sunny afternoon, she had agreed without even thinking.* ▷Middle English: from Old French *raviss-*, lengthened stem of *ravir*, from an alteration of Latin *rapere* 'seize.' —**rav·ish·er** *n.* —**rav·ish·ment** *n.*

rav·ish·ing /'raviSHiNG/ ▸*adj.* delightful; entrancing: *she looked ravishing.* —**rav·ish·ing·ly** *adv.*

raw /rô/ ▸*adj.* **1** (of food) uncooked: *raw eggs* | *salsify can be eaten raw in salads or cooked.* ■ (of a material or substance) in its natural state; not yet processed or purified: *raw silk* | *raw sewage.* ■ (of information) not analyzed, evaluated, or processed for use: *there were a number of errors in the raw data.* ■ (of the edge of a piece of cloth) not having a hem or selvage. ■ (of a person) new to an activity or job and therefore lacking experience or skill: *they were replaced by **raw recruits**.* **2** (of a part of the body) red and painful, esp. as the result of skin abrasion: *he scrubbed his hands until they were raw* | *figurative Fran's nerves were raw.* **3** (of the weather) bleak, cold, and damp: *a raw February night.* **4** (of an emotion or quality) strong and undisguised: *he exuded an air of raw, vibrant masculinity.* ■ frank and realistic in the depiction of unpleasant facts or situations: *a raw, uncompromising portrait.* ■ *informal* (of language) coarse or crude, typically in relation to sexual matters. ▷Old English *hrēaw*, of Germanic origin; related to Dutch *rauw* and German *roh*, from an Indo-European root shared by Greek *kreas* 'raw flesh.' —**raw·ly** *adv.* —**raw·ness** *n.*
▸*PHRASE* □ **in the raw 1** in its true state; not made to seem better or more palatable than it actually is: *he didn't much care for nature in the raw.* **2** *informal* (of a person) naked: *I slept in the raw.*

Ra·wal·pin·di /,räwəl'pindē/ a city in Punjab province, in northern Pakistan, in the foothills of the Himalayas; pop. 955,000. A former military station, it was the interim capital of Pakistan 1959–67 during the construction of Islamabad.

raw bar ▸*n.* a bar or counter that sells raw oysters and other seafood.

raw·boned /'rô'bōnd/ ▸*adj.* having a bony or gaunt physique.

raw·hide /'rô,hīd/ ▸*n.* stiff untanned leather. ■ a whip or rope made of such leather.

Rawl·ings /'rôliNGz/, Marjorie Kinnan (1896–53), U.S. writer. She wrote the award-winning *The Yearling* (1938) for young adults; it was made into a movie in 1946. Her other works include *Cross Creek* (1943) and *The Sojourner* (1953).

Rawls /rôlz/, John (1921–2002), U.S. philosopher. His books *A Theory of Justice* (1971) and *Political Liberalism* (1993) consider the basic institutions of a just society as those chosen by rational people under conditions that ensure impartiality.

raw ma·te·ri·al ▸*n.* the basic material from which a product is made.

raw si·en·na ▸*n.* see SIENNA.

raw sug·ar ▸*n.* the residue left after sugarcane has been processed to remove the molasses and refine the sugar crystals. The flavor is similar to that of brown sugar.

raw um·ber ▸*n.* see UMBER (sense 1).

Ray[1] /rā/, John (1627–1705), English naturalist. He was the first to classify flowering plants into monocotyledons and dicotyledons, and he established the species as the basic taxonomic unit.

Ray[2], Man (1890–1976), U.S. photographer, painter, and moviemaker; born *Emmanuel Rudnitsky*. A leading figure in the New York and European Dada movements, he is best known for *Violin d'Ingres* (1924), his photograph in which he made the back of a female nude resemble a violin.

Ray[3] /rī; rā/, Satyajit (1921–92), Indian movie director. He was the first to bring Indian movies to the attention of Western audiences.

ray[1] /rā/ ▸*n.* **1** each of the lines in which light (and heat) may seem to stream from the sun or any luminous body, or pass through a small opening: *a ray of sunlight came through the window.* ■ the straight line in which light or other electromagnetic radiation travels to a given point. ■ [with *adj.*] (**rays**) a specified form of nonluminous radiation: *water reflects and intensifies UV rays.* ■ *Mathematics* any of a set of straight lines passing through one point. ■ (**rays**) *informal,* sunlight considered in the context of sunbathing: ***catch some rays** on a secluded sandy beach.* ■ *figurative* an initial or slight indication of a positive or welcome quality in a time of difficulty or trouble: *if only I could see some **ray of** hope.* **2** a thing that is arranged radially, in particular: ■ *Botany* (in a composite flowerhead of the daisy family) an array of ray florets arranged radially around the central disc, forming the white part of the flowerhead of a daisy. ■ (also **fin ray**) *Zoology* each of the long, slender bony protuberances supporting the fins of most bony fishes. ■ *Zoology* each radial arm of a starfish.
▸*v.* [*intrans.*] spread from or as if from a central point: *delicate lines rayed out at each corner of her eyes.* ■ [*trans.*] *poetic/literary* radiate (light): *the sun rays forth its natural light into the air.* ▷Middle English: from Old French *rai*, based on Latin *radius* 'spoke, ray.' The verb dates from the late 16th cent. —**ray·less** *adj.* (*chiefly Botany*).
▸*PHRASE* □ **ray of sunshine** *informal* a person or thing that brings happiness into the lives of others.

ray[2] ▸*n.* a broad, flat marine or freshwater fish with a cartilaginous skeleton, winglike pectoral fins, and a long slender tail. Many rays have venomous spines or electric organs. • Order Batiformes: several families, including Rajidae (the skates). ▷Middle English: from Old French *raie*, from Latin *raia*.

ray blight ▸*n.* a fungal disease of chrysanthemums that causes collapse and rotting of the leading shoot. • The fungus is *Didymella ligulicola*, also called *Ascochyta chrysanthemi*.

Ray·burn /ˈrāˌbərn/, Sam(uel Taliaferro) (1882–1961), U.S. politician. A Democrat, he was a member of the House of Representatives from Texas 1913–61 and Speaker of the House 1940–46, 1949–53, 1955–61.

rayed /rād/ ▸*adj.* [*in combination*] *chiefly Biology* having rays of a specified number or kind: *white-rayed daisies.*

ray-finned fish ▸*n.* a fish of a large group having thin fins strengthened by slender rays, including all bony fishes apart from the coelacanth and lungfishes. Compare with LOBE-FINNED FISH, TELEOST. • Subclass (or class) Actinopterygii: numerous orders.

ray flo·ret ▸*n.* *Botany* (in a composite flowerhead of the daisy family) any of a number of strap-shaped and typically sterile florets that form the ray. In plants such as dandelions, the flowerhead is composed entirely of ray florets. Compare with DISK FLORET.

ray gun ▸*n.* (in science fiction) a gun causing injury or damage by the emission of rays.

Ray·leigh /ˈrālē/, John William Strutt, 3rd Baron (1842–1919), English physicist. He established the electrical units of resistance, current, and electromotive force. With William Ramsay he discovered argon and other inert gases. Nobel Prize for Physics (1904).

Ray·leigh num·ber ▸*n.* *Physics* a dimensionless parameter that is a measure of the instability of a layer of fluid due to differences of temperature and density at the top and bottom.

Ray·leigh scat·ter·ing ▸*n.* *Physics* the scattering of light by particles in a medium, without change in wavelength. It accounts, for example, for the blue color of the sky, since blue light is scattered slightly more efficiently than red. Compare with RAMAN EFFECT.

Ray·leigh wave ▸*n.* *Physics* an undulating wave that travels over the surface of a solid, esp. of the ground in an earthquake, with a speed independent of wavelength, the motion of the particles being in ellipses.

Ray·naud's dis·ease /rāˈnōz/ (also **Ray·naud's syn·drome**) ▸*n.* a disease characterized by spasm of the arteries in the extremities, esp. the fingers (**Raynaud's phenomenon**). It is typically brought on by constant cold or vibration, and leads to pallor, pain, numbness, and in severe cases, gangrene. ▹late 19th cent.: named after Maurice *Raynaud* (1834–81), French physician.

ray·on /ˈrāˌän/ ▸*n.* a textile fiber made from regenerated cellulose (viscose). ■ fabric or cloth made from this fiber. ▹1920s: an arbitrary formation.

raze /rāz/ ▸*v.* [*trans.*] (usu. **be razed**) completely destroy (a building, town, or other site): *villages were* ***razed to the ground.*** See note at DESTROY. ▹Middle English (in the sense 'scratch, incise'): from Old French *raser* 'shave closely,' from Latin *ras-* 'scraped,' from the verb *radere.*

ra·zor /ˈrāzər/ ▸*n.* an instrument with a sharp blade or combination of blades, used to remove unwanted hair from the face or body.
▸*v.* [*trans.*] cut with a razor. ▹Middle English: from Old French *rasor*, from *raser* 'shave closely' (see RAZE).

ra·zor·back /ˈrāzərˌbak/ ▸*n.* **1** (also **ra·zor·back hog**) a pig of a half-wild breed common in the southern U.S., with the back formed into a high, narrow ridge. **2** (also **ra·zor·back ridge**) a steep-sided, narrow ridge of land.

ra·zor·bill /ˈrāzərˌbil/ ▸*n.* a black-and-white auk with a deep bill that is said to resemble a straight razor, found in the North Atlantic and Baltic Sea. • *Alca torda*, family Alcidae.

ra·zor blade ▸*n.* a blade used in a razor, typically a flat piece of metal with a sharp edge or edges used in a safety razor.

ra·zor clam ▸*n.* a burrowing bivalve mollusk with a long, slender shell that resembles the handle of a straight razor. Also called JACKKNIFE CLAM. • Family Solenidae: *Ensis* and other genera.

ra·zor edge (also **ra·zor's edge**) ▸*n.* a sharp edge of a knife, ax, or similar implement. ■ *figurative* a state of sharp incisiveness: *he had honed his mind to a razor edge.* ■ (**the razor edge**) *figurative* the most advanced stage in the development of something; the cutting edge: *in 1960 jet planes were* ***the razor edge of*** *chic.* **—ra·zor-edged** *adj.*
▸**PHRASE** □ **on the razor's edge** in a precarious or dangerous position: *it is commonplace to believe that Finns live on the razor's edge, at the mercy of their powerful neighbor.*

ra·zor·fish /ˈrāzərˌfisH/ ▸*n.* (*pl.* same or **-fish·es**) **1** a small fish of the Indo-Pacific, with a long, flattened snout and a laterally compressed body encased in thin, bony shields that meet to form a sharp ridge on the belly. • Family Centriscidae: several genera and species, including *Aeoliscus strigatus*, which swims in a head-down vertical posture. **2** a small, brightly colored wrasse with a steeply sloping forehead, living chiefly in sandy coastal waters of the western Atlantic. • Genus *Hemipteronotus*, family Labridae: several species.

Ra·zor scoot·er ▸*n.* *trademark* a type of lightweight aluminum collapsible scooter ridden by adults and children.

ra·zor-sharp ▸*adj.* extremely sharp: *razor-sharp teeth* | *figurative his razor-sharp mind.*

ra·zor shell ▸*n.* British term for RAZOR CLAM.

ra·zor wire ▸*n.* a metal wire or ribbon with sharp edges or studded with small sharp blades, used as a barrier.

razz /raz/ *informal* ▸*v.* [*trans.*] tease (someone) playfully.
▸*n.* another term for RASPBERRY (sense 4). ▹early 20th cent.: from informal *razzberry*, alteration of RASPBERRY.

raz·zi·a /ˈrazēə/ ▸*n.* *historical* a hostile raid for purposes of conquest, plunder, and capture of slaves, esp. one carried out by Moors in North Africa. ▹mid 19th cent.: via French from Algerian Arabic *ġāziya* 'raid.'

raz·zle-daz·zle /ˌrazəl ˈdazəl/ ▸*n.* *informal* noisy, showy, and exciting activity and display designed to attract and impress: *myth, legend, and razzle-dazzle all rolled into one show* | [as *adj.*] *hyped-up, razzle-dazzle gimmicks of quick-sell advertising.* ■ *Football* unusual and often showy offensive maneuvers: *a bit of razzle-dazzle sent Smith into the end zone.* ▹late 19th cent.: reduplication of DAZZLE.

razz·ma·tazz /ˈrazməˌtaz/ ▸*n.* another term for RAZZLE-DAZZLE. ▹late 19th cent.: probably an alteration of RAZZLE-DAZZLE.

Rb ▸*symbol* the chemical element rubidium.

RBC ▸*abbr.* red blood cell.

RBE (also **rbe**) ▸*abbr.* relative biological effectiveness.

RBI *Baseball* ▸*abbr.* run batted in (a run credited to the batter's hitting statistics for enabling a runner to score during his at bat).

RC ▸*abbr.* ■ *Aeronautics* radio compass. ■ *Electronics* radio-controlled. ■ Red Cross. ■ reinforced concrete. ■ *Electronics* resistance/capacitance (or resistor/capacitor). ■ Roman Catholic.

RCA ▸*abbr.* ■ Radio Corporation of America. ■ (in the UK) Royal College of Art.

RCAF ▸*abbr.* Royal Canadian Air Force.

RCCh ▸*abbr.* Roman Catholic Church.

RCMP ▸*abbr.* Royal Canadian Mounted Police.

rcpt. ▸*abbr.* receipt.

rct. (also **Rct.**) ▸*abbr.* ■ receipt. ■ recruit.

Rd ▸*abbr.* Road (used in street names).

rd. ▸*abbr.* rod; rods.

RDA ▸*abbr.* recommended daily (or dietary) allowance, the quantity of a particular nutrient which should be consumed daily in order to maintain good health.

RDBMS *Computing* ▸*abbr.* relational database management system.

RDF ▸*abbr.* ■ radio direction finder (or finding). ■ rapid deployment force.

RDI ▸*abbr.* recommended (or reference) daily intake, another term for **RDA**.

RDS ▸*abbr.* ■ radio data system, in which a digital signal is transmitted with a normal radio signal to provide further data or control the receiver. ■ respiratory distress syndrome.

RDX ▸*n.* a type of high explosive. ▹1940s: from *R(esearch) D(epartment) (E)x(plosive).*

Re[1] /rā/ variant spelling of RA[1].

Re[2] ▸*symbol* the chemical element rhenium.

re[1] /rā; rē/ ▸*prep.* in the matter of (used typically as the first word in the heading of an official document or to introduce a reference in an official letter): *re: invoice 87.* ■ about; concerning: *I saw the deputy re the incident.* ▹Latin, ablative of *res* 'thing.'

USAGE It is often said that, strictly speaking, **re** should be used in headings and references, as in *Re: Harrison versus Ortiz*, but not as a normal word meaning 'regarding,' as in *thanks for your letter* **re** *the job postings.* However, the evidence suggests that **re** is now widely used in the second context in official and semiofficial contexts, and is now generally accepted. Be aware, however, that in certain formal contexts, if **re** is used in mid-sentence, some readers may regard it as business jargon or an inappropriate legalism. Often, *concerning* or *about* would be just as clear (and less likely to annoy).

re[2] /rā/ ▸*n.* *Music* (in solmization) the second note of a major scale. ■ the note D in the fixed-do system. ▹Middle English *re*, representing (as an arbitrary name for the note) the first syllable of *resonare*, taken from a Latin hymn (see SOLMIZATION).

're *informal* ▸*abbr.* are (usually after the pronouns you, we, and they): *we're a bit worried.*

Re. (also **re.**) ▸*abbr.* rupee.

re- ▸*prefix* **1** once more; afresh; anew: *reaccustom* | *reactivate.* ■ with return to a previous state: *restore* | *revert.* **2** (also **red-**) in return; mutually: *react* | *resemble.* ■ in opposition: *repel* | *resistance.* **3** behind or after: *relic* | *remain.* ■ in a withdrawn state: *recluse* | *reticent.* ■ back and away; down: *recede* | *relegation.* **4** with frequentative or intensive force: *redouble* | *resound.* **5** with negative force: *rebuff* | *recant.* ▹from Latin *re-*, *red-* 'again, back.'

USAGE In modern English, the tendency is for words formed with prefixes such as **re-** to be unhyphenated: **reacquaint, reconsider, reshape.** For the sake of clarity, however, hyphenation is sometimes favored when the the root word begins with a vowel: **re-erect**, for instance, may be preferred as a less awkward spelling than **reerect**. A hyphen is often used when the word formed with the prefix would be identical in form with, but different in meaning and pronunciation from, an already existing word: **re-cover** (meaning 'cover again,' as in *we decided to* **re-cover** *the dining-room chairs*), as opposed to **recover** (meaning 'get better in health').

R

reach /rēcH/ ▸*v.* **1** [*intrans.*] stretch out an arm in a specified direction in order to touch or grasp something: *he reached over and turned off his bedside light.* ■ (**reach for**) make a movement with one's hand or arm in an attempt to touch or grasp (something): *Carl reached for the phone.* ■ [*trans.*] (**reach something out**) stretch out one's hand or arm: *he reached out a hand and touched her forehead.* ■ [with *two objs.*] hand (something) to (someone): *reach me those glasses.* ■ [*intrans.*] be able to touch something with an outstretched arm or leg: *I had to stand on tiptoe and even then I could hardly reach.* ■ (**reach out**) extend help, understanding, or influence: *he felt such an urge to reach out to his fellow sufferer.* **2** [*trans.*] arrive at; get as far as: *"Goodbye," she said as they reached the door* | *the show is due to reach our screens early next year.* ■ attain or extend to (a specified point, level, or condition): *unemployment reached a peak in 1933* | [*intrans.*] *in its native habitat it will* ***reach to*** *about 6 m in height.* ■ succeed in achieving: *the intergovernmental conference reached agreement on the draft treaty.* ■ make contact or communicate with (someone) by telephone or other means: *I've been trying to reach you all morning.* ■ (of a broadcast or other communication) be received by: *television reached those parts of the electorate that other news sources could not.* ■ succeed in influencing or having an effect on: *their fresh sound and message reach people who may never set foot in a church.* **3** [*intrans.*] *Sailing* sail with the wind blowing from the side, or from slightly behind the side, of the ship.
▸*n.* **1** an act of reaching out with one's arm: *she made a reach for him.* ■ [in *sing.*] the distance to which someone can stretch out their hand (used esp. of a boxer): *a giant, over six feet seven with a reach of over 81 inches.* ■ the extent or range of application, effect, or influence: *the diameter and the reach of the spark plug varies from engine to engine.* See note at RANGE. **2** (often **reaches**) a continuous extent of land or water, esp. a stretch of river between two bends, or the part of a canal between locks: *the upper reaches of the Nile.* **3** *Sailing* a distance traversed in reaching. ▹Old English *rǣcan*; related to Dutch *reiken* and German *reichen.* **—reach·a·ble** *adj.*
▸**PHRASES** □ **out of** (or **beyond**) **reach** outside the distance to which someone can stretch out their hand. ■ beyond the capacity of someone to attain or achieve something: *she thought college was out of her reach.* □ **within** (or **in**) **reach** inside the distance to which someone can stretch out their hand. ■ inside

re·ab·sorb *v.*
 re·ab·sorp·tion *n.*
re·ac·cept *v.*
 re·ac·cept·ance *n.*
re·ac·cus·tom *v.*
re·ac·quire *v.*
 re·ac·qui·si·tion *n.*
re·ac·ti·vate *v.*
re·a·dapt *v.*
 re·ad·ap·ta·tion *n.*
re·ad·mit *v.*
 re·ad·mis·sion *n.*
re·a·dopt *v.*
 re·a·dop·tion *n.*
re·ad·ver·tise *v.*
 re·ad·ver·tise·ment *n.*
re·al·lot *v.*
 re·al·lot·ment *n.*
re·ap·pear *v.*
 re·ap·pear·ance *n.*
rearrest *v., n.*
re·as·sert *v.*
 re·as·ser·tion *n.*
re·at·tain *v.*
 re·at·tain·ment *n.*
re·at·tempt *v.*
re·bur·y *v.*
 re·bur·i·al *n.*
re·cir·cu·late *v.*
 re·cir·cu·la·tion *n.*
re·com·mence *v.*
 re·com·mence·ment *n.*
re·con·firm *v.*
 re·con·fir·ma·tion *n.*
re·con·quer *v.*
 re·con·quest *n.*
re·con·se·crate *v.*
 re·con·se·cra·tion *n.*
re·con·sol·i·date *v.*
 re·con·sol·i·da·tion *n.*
re·crys·tal·lize *v.*
 re·crys·tal·li·za·tion *n.*
re·ded·i·cate *v.*
 re·ded·i·ca·tion *n.*
re·dis·solve *v.*
 re·dis·so·lu·tion *n.*
re·em·bark *v.*
 re·em·bar·ka·tion *n.*
re·em·pha·size *v.*
 re·em·pha·sis *n.*
re·em·ploy *v.*
 re·em·ploy·ment *n.*
re·en·ter *v.*
 re·en·trance *v.*
re·equip *v.*; **-equipped, -equip·ping**
re·e·rect *v.*
 re·e·rec·tion *n.*
re·es·tab·lish *v.*
 re·es·tab·lish·ment *n.*
re·e·val·u·ate *v.*
 re·e·val·u·a·tion *n.*
re·for·mu·late *v.*
 re·for·mu·la·tion *n.*
re·freeze *v.*; **-froze, -fro·zen**
re·gild *v.*
re·grow *v.*; **-grew, -grown**
 re·growth *n.*
re·meas·ure *v.*
 re·meas·ure·ment *n.*
re·mod·i·fy *v.*; **-fies, -fied**
 re·mod·i·fi·ca·tion *n.*
re·na·tion·al·ize *v.*
 re·na·tion·al·i·za·tion *n.*
re·nom·i·nate *v.*
 re·nom·i·na·tion *n.*
re·num·ber *v.*
re·oc·cu·py *v.*; **-pies, -pied**
 re·oc·cu·pa·tion *n.*
re·oc·cur *v.*; **-curred, -cur·ring**
 re·oc·cur·rence *n.*
re·o·pen *v.*
re·pack *v.*
re·pag·i·nate *v.*
 re·pag·i·na·tion *n.*
re·paint *v., n.*
re·pass *v.*
re·plan *v.*; **-planned, -plan·ning**
re·pol·ish *v., n.*
re·price *v.*
re·pro·gram *v.*; **-grammed, -gram·ming**
 re·pro·gram·ma·ble *adj.*
re·roof *v.*
re·seal *v.*
 re·seal·a·ble *adj.*
re·se·lect *v.*
 re·se·lec·tion *n.*
re·shape *v.*
re·spray *v.*
re·stage *v.*
re·start *v., n.*
re·stud·y *v., n.*; **-ies, -ied**
re·sup·ply *v.*; **-plied, -plies**
re·tag *v.*; **-tagged, -tag·ging**
re·teach *v.*; **-taught**
re·tell *v.*; **-told**
re·tie *v.*; **-ty·ing**
re·time *v.*
re·ti·tle *v.*
re·type *v.*
re·u·ti·lize *v.*
 re·u·ti·li·za·tion *n.*
re·vac·ci·nate *v.*
 re·vac·ci·na·tion *n.*
re·var·nish *v.*
re·wash *v.*
re·weigh *v.*
re·wire *v.*
 re·wir·a·ble *adj.*
re·wrap *v.*; **-wrapped, -wrap·ping**

---

a distance that can be traveled: *Rocky Mountain National Park is **within easy reach** of the city of Denver.* ■ within the capacity of someone to attain or achieve something.

reach·er /ˈrēCHər/ ▸*n.* **1** a thing which reaches, esp. a device that enables a disabled or elderly person to pick up objects that are difficult to reach. **2** a kind of jib on a sailing ship.

re·ac·quaint /ˌrēəˈkwānt/ ▸*v.* [*trans.*] make (someone) acquainted or familiar with someone or something again: *he wants to **reacquaint himself with** the public.* —**re·ac·quaint·ance** /-ˈkwāntns/ *n.*

re·act /rēˈakt/ ▸*v.* [*intrans.*] respond or behave in a particular way in response to something: *Iraq **reacted** angrily **to** Jordan's shift in policy | the market reacted by falling a further 3.1%.* ■ (**react against**) respond with hostility, opposition, or a contrary course of action to: *they reacted against the elite art music of their time.* ■ (of a person) suffer from adverse physiological effects after ingesting, breathing, or touching a substance: *many babies react to soy-based formulas.* ■ *Chemistry & Physics* interact and undergo a chemical or physical change: *the sulfur in the coal **reacts with** the limestone during combustion.* ■ [*trans.*] *Chemistry* cause (a substance) to undergo such a change by interacting with another substance. ■ *Stock Market* (of stock prices) fall or rise in reaction to events, developments, etc. ▷mid 17th cent.: from **RE-** (expressing intensive force or reversal) + **ACT**, originally suggested by medieval Latin *react-* 'done again,' from the verb *reagere*.

re·ac·tance /rēˈaktəns/ ▸*n.* *Physics* the nonresistive component of impedance in an AC circuit, arising from the effect of inductance or capacitance or both and causing the current to be out of phase with the electromotive force causing it.

re·ac·tant /rēˈaktənt/ ▸*n.* *Chemistry* a substance that takes part in and undergoes change during a reaction.

re·ac·tion /rēˈakSHən/ ▸*n.* an action performed or a feeling experienced in response to a situation or event: *Carrie's immediate reaction was one of relief.* ■ (**reactions**) a person's ability to respond physically and mentally to external stimuli: *a skilled driver with quick reactions.* ■ an adverse physiological response to a substance that has been breathed in, ingested, or touched: *such allergic reactions as hay fever and asthma.* ■ a chemical process in which two or more substances act mutually on each other and are changed into different substances, or one substance changes into two or more other substances. ■ *Physics* an analogous transformation of atomic nuclei or other particles. ■ a mode of thinking or behaving that is deliberately different from previous modes of thought and behavior: *the work of these painters was a **reaction against** fauvism.* ■ opposition to political or social progress or reform: *the institution is under threat from the forces of reaction.* ■ *Physics* repulsion or resistance exerted in opposition to the impact or pressure of another body; a force equal and opposite to the force giving rise to it. ▷mid 17th cent.: from **REACT** + **-ION**, originally suggested by medieval Latin *reactio(n-)*, from *react-* 'done again' (see **REACT**). —**re·ac·tion·ist** /-nist/ *n.* & *adj.*

re·ac·tion·ar·y /rēˈakSHəˌnerē/ ▸*adj.* (of a person or a set of views) opposing political or social liberalization or reform.
▸*n.* (*pl.* **-ar·ies**) a person who holds such views.

re·ac·tion for·ma·tion ▸*n.* *Psychoanalysis* the tendency of a repressed wish or feeling to be expressed at a conscious level in a contrasting form.

re·ac·tion shot ▸*n.* (in a film or video recording) a portrayal of a person's response to an event or to a statement made by another.

re·ac·tive /rēˈaktiv/ ▸*adj.* showing a response to a stimulus: *pupils are reactive to light.* ■ acting in response to a situation rather than creating or controlling it: *a proactive rather than a reactive approach.* ■ having a tendency to react chemically: *nitrogen dioxide is a highly reactive gas.* ■ *Physiology* showing an immune response to a specific antigen. ■ (of a disease or illness) caused by a reaction to something: *reactive arthritis | reactive depression.* ■ *Physics* of or relating to reactance: *a reactive load.*

re·ac·tive in·hi·bi·tion ▸*n.* *Psychology* the inhibiting effect of fatigue or boredom on the response to a stimulus and ability to learn.

re·ac·tiv·i·ty /ˌrēˌakˈtivətē/ ▸*n.* the state or power of being reactive or the degree to which a thing is reactive. ■ the extent to which a nuclear reactor deviates from a steady state.

re·ac·tor /rēˈaktər/ ▸*n.* **1** (also **nu·cle·ar re·ac·tor**) an apparatus or structure in which fissile material can be made to undergo a controlled, self-sustaining nuclear reaction with the consequent release of energy. ■ a container or apparatus in which substances are made to react chemically, esp. one in an industrial plant. **2** *Medicine* a person who shows an immune response to a specific antigen or an adverse reaction to a drug or other substance. **3** *Physics* a coil or other component that provides reactance in a circuit.

read /rēd/ ▸*v.* (*past* **read** /red/) [*trans.*] **1** look at and comprehend the meaning of (written or printed matter) by mentally interpreting the characters or symbols of which it is composed: *it's the best novel I've ever read | I never learned to read music | Emily **read over** her notes | [intrans.] I'll go to bed and read for a while.* ■ speak (the written or printed matter that one is reading) aloud, typically to another person: *the charges against him were **read out** | [with two objs.] his mother read him a bedtime story | [intrans.] I'll read to you if you like.* ■ [*intrans.*] have the ability to look at and comprehend the meaning of written or printed matter: *only three of the girls could read and none could write.* ■ habitually read (a particular newspaper or journal). ■ discover (information) by reading it in a written or printed source: *he was arrested yesterday—I read it in the paper | [intrans.] I read about the course in a magazine.* ■ [as *adj.* with *submodifier*] (**read**) (of a person) knowledgeable and informed as a result of extensive reading: *Ada was **well read in** French and German literature.* ■ discern (a fact, emotion, or quality) in someone's eyes or expression: *she looked down, terrified that he would read fear on her face.* ■ understand or interpret the nature or significance of: *he didn't dare look away, in case this was read as a sign of weakness.* ■ [*intrans.*] (of a piece of writing) convey a specified impression to the reader: *the brief note read like a cry for help.* ■ [*intrans.*] (of a passage, text, or sign) contain or consist of specified words; have a certain wording: *the placard read "We want justice."* ■ used to indicate that a particular word in a text or passage is incorrect and that another should be substituted for it: *for madam read madman.* ■ proofread (written or typeset material). ■ [*intrans.*] (**read for**) (of an actor) audition for (a part in a play or film). ■ (of a device) obtain data from (light or other input). **2** inspect and record the figure indicated on (a measuring instrument): *I've come to read the gas meter.* ■ [*intrans.*] (of such an instrument) indicate a specified measurement or figure: *the thermometer read 0° C.* **3** *chiefly Brit.* study (an academic subject) at a university: *I'm reading English at Cambridge | [intrans.] he went to Manchester to **read for** a BA in Economics.* **4** (of a computer) copy or transfer (data). ■ [*trans.*] enter or extract (data) in an electronic storage device: *the commonest way of reading a file into the system.* **5** hear and understand the words of (someone speaking on a radio transmitter): *"Do you read me? Over."* ■ interpret the words formed by (a speaking person's lips) by watching rather than listening.
▸*phrasal v.* □ **read something back** read a message or piece of writing aloud so that its accuracy can be checked. □ **read something into** attribute a meaning or significance to (something) that it may not in fact possess: *was I reading too much into his behavior?* □ **read someone out of** formally expel someone from (an organization or body). [with reference to the reading of the formal sentence of expulsion.] □ **read up on something** acquire information about a particular subject by studying it intensively or systematically: *she spent the time reading up on antenatal care.*
▸*n.* [usu. in *sing.*] a person's interpretation of something: *their **read on** the national situation may be correct.* ■ [with *adj.*] *informal* a book considered in terms of its readability: *the book is a thoroughly entertaining read.* ▷Old English *rǣdan*, of Germanic origin; related to Dutch *raden* and German *raten* 'advise, guess.' Early senses included 'advise' and 'interpret (a riddle or dream)' (see **REDE**).
▸*PHRASES* □ **read between the lines** look for or discover a meaning that is hidden or implied rather than explicitly stated. □ **read someone like a book** understand someone's thoughts and motives clearly or easily. □ **read someone's mind** (or **thoughts**) discern what someone is thinking. □ **read my lips**

informal listen carefully (used to emphasize the importance of the speaker's words or the earnestness of their intent).

read·a·ble /ˈrēdəbəl/ ▸*adj.* (of a text, script, or code) able to be read or deciphered; legible. ■ easy or enjoyable to read: *a marvelously readable book.* —**read·a·bil·i·ty** /ˌrēdəˈbilətē/ *n.* —**read·a·bly** /-blē/ *adv.*

re·ad·dress /ˌrēəˈdres/ ▸*v.* [*trans.*] **1** change the address written or printed on (a letter or parcel). **2** look at or attend to (an issue or problem) once again.

read·er /ˈrēdər/ ▸*n.* **1** a person who reads or who is fond of reading: *the books of Roald Dahl appeal to young readers | she's an avid reader.* ■ a person who reads a particular newspaper, magazine, or text: *Times readers.* ■ short for LAY READER. ■ a person entitled to use a particular library. ■ a person who reads and reports to a publisher or producer on the merits of manuscripts submitted for publication or production, or who provides critical comments on the text prior to publication. ■ a person who reads and grades examinations and papers for a professor. ■ short for PROOFREADER (see PROOFREAD). ■ a person who interprets the significance of tarot cards, horoscopes, lines in the palm of a hand, etc., so as to predict the future: *a tarot reader.* **2** a person who inspects and records the figure indicated on a measuring instrument: *a meter reader.* **3** a book containing extracts of a particular author's work or passages of text designed to give learners of a language practice in reading. **4** (usu. **Reader**) *Brit.* a university lecturer of the highest grade below professor. **5** a machine for producing on a screen a magnified, readable image of any desired part of a microfiche or microfilm. ■ *Computing* a device or piece of software used for reading or obtaining data stored on tape, cards, or other media. ▷Old English *rǣdere* 'interpreter of dreams, reader.'

read·er·ly /ˈrēdərlē/ ▸*adj.* of or relating to a reader: *he tries one's readerly patience to breaking point.*

read·er·ship /ˈrēdərˌship/ ▸*n.* **1** [treated as *sing.* or *pl.*] the readers of a newspaper, magazine, or book regarded collectively: *it has a readership of 100 million.* **2** (usu. **Readership**) *Brit.* the position of Reader at a university.

read·i·ly /ˈredl-ē/ ▸*adv.* without hesitation or reluctance; willingly: *he readily admits that the new car surpasses its predecessors.* ■ without delay or difficulty; easily: [as *submodifier*] *illegal fireworks are readily available.*

read-in ▸*n.* *Computing* the input or entry of data to a computer or storage device.

read·i·ness /ˈredēnis/ ▸*n.* **1** [in *sing.*] [with *infinitive*] willingness to do something: *Spain had indicated a readiness to accept his terms.* **2** the state of being fully prepared for something: *your muscles tense* ***in readiness for*** *action.* **3** immediacy, quickness, or promptness: *quickness of hearing and readiness of speech were essential.*

Read·ing /ˈrediNG/ **1** a town in southern England, on the Kennet River near its junction with the Thames River; pop. 123,000. **2** an industrial and commercial city in southeastern Pennsylvania, on the Schuylkill River; pop. 81,207.

read·ing /ˈrēdiNG/ ▸*n.* **1** the action or skill of reading written or printed matter silently or aloud: *suggestions for further reading* | [as *adj.*] *reading skills | a cursory reading of the minutes.* ■ written or printed matter that can be read: *his main reading was detective stories.* ■ [with *adj.*] used to convey the specified quality of such written or printed matter: *his file certainly* ***makes*** *interesting* ***reading.*** ■ [usu. with *adj.*] knowledge of literature: *a man of wide reading.* ■ the formal reading aloud of a legal document to an audience: *the reading of a will.* ■ an occasion at which poetry or other pieces of literature are read aloud to an audience. ■ a piece of literature or passage of scripture read aloud to a group of people: *readings from the Bible.* **2** an interpretation: *feminist readings of Goethe | his reading of the situation was justified.* ■ a form in which a given passage appears in a particular edition of a text. **3** a figure or amount shown by a meter or other measuring instrument: *radiation readings were taken every hour.* **4** a stage of debate in a parliament through which a bill must pass before it can become law: *the bill returns to the House for its final reading next week.*

re·ad·just /ˌrēəˈjəst/ ▸*v.* [*trans.*] set or adjust (something) again: *I readjusted the rear-view mirror.* ■ [*intrans.*] adjust or adapt to a changed environment or situation: [as *adj.*] (**readjusted**) *she wondered if she could ever become* ***readjusted to*** *this sort of life.* —**re·ad·just·ment** *n.*

read-on·ly mem·o·ry /rēd/ (abbr.: **ROM**) ▸*n.* *Computing* memory read at high speed but not capable of being changed by program instructions.

read·out /ˈrēdˌout/ (also **read-out**) ▸*n.* a visual record or display of the output from a computer or scientific instrument. ■ the process of transferring or displaying such data.

read-through /rēd/ ▸*n.* an initial rehearsal of a play at which actors read their parts from scripts.

read-write /ˈrēd ˈrīt/ ▸*adj.* *Computing* capable of reading existing data and accepting alterations or further input.

read·y /ˈredē/ ▸*adj.* (**read·i·er**, **read·i·est**) **1** [*predic.*] in a suitable state for an activity, action, or situation; fully prepared: *are you ready, Carrie? | I began to* ***get ready for*** *bed* | [with *infinitive*] *she was about ready to leave.* ■ (of a thing) made suitable and available for immediate use: *dinner's ready! | could you have the list ready by this afternoon?* ■ (**ready with**) keen or quick to give: *I'm always ready with a wisecrack.* ■ (**ready for**) in need of or having a desire for: *I expect you're ready for a drink | she always looks ready for a fight.* ■ [with *infinitive*] eager, inclined, or willing to do something: *she is ready to die for her political convictions.* ■ [with *infinitive*] in such a condition as to be likely to do something: *by the time he arrived he was ready to drop.* **2** easily available or obtained; within reach: *there was a ready supply of drink | the murderer knew that the mallet would be* ***ready to hand.*** ■ [*attrib.*] immediate, quick, or prompt: *those who have ready access to the arts | a girl with a ready smile.*

▸*n.* (*pl.* **read·ies**) (**readies** or **the ready**) *Brit., informal* available money; cash.

▸*v.* (**read·ies**, **read·ied**) [*trans.*] prepare (someone or something) for an activity or purpose: *the spare transformer was readied for shipment* | [*trans.*] *she had readied herself to speak first.* ▷Middle English: from Old English *rǣde* (from a Germanic base meaning 'arrange, prepare'; related to Dutch *gereed*) + -Y[1].

▸*PHRASES* □ **at the ready** prepared or available for immediate use: *the men walk with their guns at the ready.* □ **make ready** prepare: *they were told to* ***make ready for*** *the journey home.* □ **ready and waiting** used to emphasize that someone or something is fully prepared or immediately available: *the apartment was all ready and waiting for them.* □ **ready, set, go** used to announce the beginning of a race. □ **ready to roll** *informal* (of a person, vehicle, or thing) fully prepared to start functioning or moving: *the next morning, the plan was ready to roll.*

read·y-made ▸*adj.* (esp. of products such as clothes and curtains) made to a standard size or specification rather than to order. ■ available straight away; not needing to be specially created or devised: *we have no ready-made answers.* ■ (of food) ready to be served without further preparation: *a ready-made Christmas cake.*

▸*n.* (usu. **ready-mades**) a ready-made article: *on the top shelf of ready-mades is Stromboli.* ■ a mass-produced article selected by an artist and displayed as a work of art.

read·y-mix ▸*n.* ready-mixed concrete.

read·y-mixed ▸*adj.* (esp. of a mixture used in building or cooking) having some or all of the constituents already mixed together; commercially prepared.

read·y mon·ey (also **read·y cash**) ▸*n.* money in the form of cash that is immediately available.

read·y-to-wear ▸*adj.* (of clothes) made for the general market and sold through stores rather than made to order for an individual customer; off the rack.

re·af·firm /ˌrēəˈfərm/ ▸*v.* [*reporting verb*] state again as a fact; assert again strongly: *the prime minister reaffirmed his commitment to the agreement* | [with *clause*] *he reaffirmed that it was essential to strengthen the rule of law.* ■ [*trans.*] confirm the validity or correctness of (something previously established): *the election reaffirmed his position as leader.* —**re·af·fir·ma·tion** /ˌrēˌafərˈmāSHən/ *n.*

Rea·gan /ˈrāgən/, Ronald (Wilson) (1911–2004), 40th president of the U.S. 1981–89. He was a movie actor before entering politics and then served as the governor of California 1967–74. A conservative Republican, his administration greatly increased defense spending, cut taxes and social services budgets, and saw a record rise in the national budget deficit. He signed an intermediate nuclear forces nonproliferation treaty in 1987. His reputation was tarnished by his involvement in the Iran-Contra affair. —**Rea·gan·ism** /-ˌnizəm/ *n.*

re·a·gent /rēˈājənt/ ▸*n.* a substance or mixture for use in chemical analysis or other reactions: *this compound is a very sensitive reagent for copper.*

re·a·gin /rēˈājən; -gən/ ▸*n.* *Immunology* the antibody that is involved in allergic reactions, causing the release of histamine when it combines with antigen in tissue, and capable of producing sensitivity to the antigen when introduced into the skin of a normal individual. ■ the substance in the blood that is responsible for a positive response to the Wassermann test. ▷early 20th cent.: coined in German from *reagieren* 'react.' —**re·a·gin·ic** /ˌrēəˈjinik; -ˈginik/ *adj.*

re·al[1] /ˈrē(ə)l/ ▸*adj.* **1** actually existing as a thing or occurring in fact; not imagined or supposed: *Julius Caesar was a real person | a story drawing on real events | her many illnesses, real and imaginary.* ■ used to emphasize the significance or seriousness of a situation or circumstance: *there is a real danger of civil war | the competitive threat from overseas is very real.* ■ *Philosophy* relating to something as it is, not merely as it may be described or distinguished. **2** (of a substance or thing) not imitation or artificial; genuine: *the earring was presumably real gold.* ■ true or actual: *his real name is James | this isn't my real reason for coming.* ■ [*attrib.*] (of a person or thing) rightly so called; proper: *he's my idea of a real man | Jamie is my only real friend.* **3** [*attrib.*] *informal* complete; utter (used for emphasis): *the tour turned out to be a real disaster.* **4** [*attrib.*] adjusted for changes in the value of money; assessed by purchasing power: *real incomes had fallen by 30 percent | an increase* ***in real terms*** *of 11.6 percent.* **5** *Mathematics* (of a number or quantity) having no imaginary part. See IMAGINARY. **6** *Optics* (of an image) of a kind in which the light that forms it actually passes through it; not virtual.

▸*adv.* [as *submodifier*] *informal* really; very: *my head hurts real bad.* ▷late Middle English (as a legal term meaning 'relating to things, esp. real property'): from Anglo-Norman French, from late Latin *realis*, from Latin *res* 'thing.' —**real·ness** *n.*

▸*PHRASES* □ **for real** *informal* used to assert that something is genuine or is actually the case: *I'm not playing games—this is for real!* ■ used in questions to express surprise or to question the truth or seriousness of what one has seen or heard: *are these guys for real?* □ **get real!** *informal* used to convey that an idea or statement is foolish or overly idealistic: *You want teens to have committed sexual relationships? Get real!* □ **real live** *humorous* used to emphasize the existence of something, esp. if it is surprising or unusual: *a real live detective had been at the factory.* □ **real money** *informal* money in a large or significant amount. □ **the real thing** *informal* a thing that is absolutely genuine or authentic: *you've never been in love before, so how can you be sure this is the real thing?*

re·al[2] /rāˈäl/ ▸*n.* (*pl.* **re·als** or **reis** /rāSH; rās/) the basic monetary unit of Brazil since 1994, equal to 100 centavos. ■ (*pl.* **re·a·les** /rāˈäles/ or **re·als**) a former coin and monetary unit of various Spanish-speaking countries. ▷Portuguese and Spanish, literally 'royal' (adjective used as a noun).

real es·tate ▸*n.* another term for REAL PROPERTY.

real es·tate a·gent ▸*n.* a person who sells and rents out buildings and land for clients. —**re·al es·tate a·gen·cy** *n.*

re·al·gar /rēˈalgər; -ˌgär/ ▸*n.* a soft, reddish mineral consisting of arsenic sulfide, formerly used as a pigment and in fireworks. ▷late Middle English: via

Ronald W. Reagan

R

Pronunciation Key ə ago; ər over; ˈə or ˌə up; ˈər or ˌər fur; a hat; ā rate; ä car; CH chew; e let; ē see; e(ə)r air; i fit; ī by; i(ə)r ear; NG sing; ō go; ô for; oi boy; o͝o good; o͞o goo; ou out; SH she; TH thin; T͟H then; (h)w why; ZH vision

medieval Latin from Arabic *rahj al-ġār* 'arsenic,' literally 'dust of the cave.'

re·a·li·a /rē'ālēə; -'ālēə/ ▸*n.* objects and material from everyday life, esp. when used as teaching aids. ▷1950s: from late Latin, neuter plural (used as a noun) of *realis* 'relating to things' (see REAL[1]).

re·a·lign /ˌrēə'līn/ ▸*v.* [*trans.*] change or restore to a different or former position or state: *they worked to relieve his shoulder pain and realign the joint | the president realigned his government to reflect the balance of parties.* ■ (**realign oneself with**) change one's position or attitude with regard to (a person, organization, or cause): *he wished to realign himself with Bagehot's more pessimistic position.* —**re·a·lign·ment** *n.*

re·al·ism /'rēəˌlizəm/ ▸*n.* **1** the attitude or practice of accepting a situation as it is and being prepared to deal with it accordingly: *the summit was marked by a new mood of realism.* ■ the view that the subject matter of politics is political power, not matters of principle: *political realism is the oldest approach to global politics.* **2** the quality or fact of representing a person, thing, or situation accurately or in a way that is true to life: *the earthy realism of Raimu's characters.* ■ (in art and literature) the movement or style of representing familiar things as they actually are. Often contrasted with IDEALISM (sense 1).

While realism in art is often used in the same contexts as naturalism, implying a concern to depict or describe accurately and objectively, it also suggests a deliberate rejection of conventionally beautiful or appropriate subjects in favor of sincerity and a focus on simple and unidealized treatment of contemporary life. Specifically, the term is applied to a late 19th-century movement in French painting and literature represented by Gustave Courbet in the former and Balzac, Stendhal, and Flaubert in the latter.

3 *Philosophy* the doctrine that universals or abstract concepts have an objective or absolute existence. The theory that universals have their own reality is sometimes called **Platonic realism** because it was first outlined by Plato's doctrine of "forms" or ideas. Often contrasted with NOMINALISM. ■ the doctrine that matter as the object of perception has real existence and is neither reducible to universal mind or spirit nor dependent on a perceiving agent. Often contrasted with IDEALISM (sense 2). —**re·al·ist** /'rēələst/ *n.*

re·al·is·tic /ˌrēə'listik/ ▸*adj.* **1** having or showing a sensible and practical idea of what can be achieved or expected: *jobs are scarce at the moment, so you've got to be realistic | a more realistic figure was 20 percent.* **2** representing familiar things in a way that is accurate or true to life: *a realistic human drama.* —**re·al·is·ti·cal·ly** /-ik(ə)lē/ *adv.* [*sentence adverb*] *realistically, there was little prospect of any improvement.*

re·al·i·ty /rē'alətē/ ▸*n.* (*pl.* **-ties**) **1** the world or the state of things as they actually exist, as opposed to an idealistic or notional idea of them: *he refuses to face reality | Laura was losing touch with reality.* ■ a thing that is actually experienced or seen, esp. when this is grim or problematic: *the harsh* ***realities of*** *life in a farming community | the law ignores* ***the reality of*** *the situation.* ■ a thing that exists in fact, having previously only existed in one's mind: *the paperless office may yet become a reality.* ■ the quality of being lifelike or resembling an original: *the reality of Marryat's detail.* **2** the state or quality of having existence or substance: *youth, when death has no reality.* ■ *Philosophy* existence that is absolute, self-sufficient, or objective, and not subject to human decisions or conventions. ▷late 15th cent.: via French from medieval Latin *realitas*, from late Latin *realis* 'relating to things' (see REAL[1]).
▸*PHRASES* □ **in reality** in actual fact (used to contrast a false idea of what is true or possible with one that is more accurate): *she had believed she could control these feelings, but in reality that was not so easy.* □ **the reality is ——** used to assert that the truth of a matter is not what one would think or expect: *the popular view of the Dobermann is of an aggressive guard dog—the reality is very different.*

re·al·i·ty check ▸*n.* [usu. in *sing.*] *informal* an occasion on which one is reminded of the state of things in the real world.

re·al·i·ty prin·ci·ple ▸*n. Psychoanalysis* the ego's control of the pleasure-seeking activity of the id in order to meet the demands of the external world.

re·al·i·ty test·ing ▸*n. Psychology* the objective evaluation of an emotion or thought against real life, as a faculty present in normal individuals but defective in psychotics.

re·al·i·ty TV ▸*n.* staged television programs about real people and situations, designed to be entertaining rather than informative.

re·al·i·za·ble /ˌrēə'līzəbəl/ ▸*adj.* **1** able to be achieved or made to happen: *such a dream, if it is realizable at all, is one for the far future.* **2** in or able to be converted into cash: *10 percent of realizable assets.* —**re·al·iz·a·bil·i·ty** /ˌrēəlīzə'bilətē/ *n.*

re·al·i·za·tion /ˌrē(ə)lə'zāsнən/ ▸*n.* **1** [in *sing.*] an act of becoming fully aware of something as a fact: *there was a growing realization of the need to create common economic structures | realization dawned suddenly.* **2** the fulfillment or achievement of something desired or anticipated: *he did not live to see the realization of his dream.* ■ an actual, complete, or dramatic form given to a concept or work: *a perfect realization of Bartók's Second Violin Concerto on disc.* ■ *Linguistics* the way in which a particular linguistic feature is used in speech or writing on a particular occasion. ■ *Mathematics* an instance or embodiment of an abstract group as the set of symmetry operations of some object or set. ■ *Statistics* a particular series that might be generated by a specified random process. **3** the action of converting an asset into cash. ■ a sale of goods: *auction realizations.*

re·al·ize /'rē(ə)ˌlīz/ ▸*v.* [*trans.*] **1** become fully aware of (something) as a fact; understand clearly: *he realized his mistake at once |* [with *clause*] *they realized that something was wrong | she had not realized how hungry she was.* **2** cause (something desired or anticipated) to happen: *our loans are helping small business realize their dreams | his worst fears have been realized.* ■ fulfill: *it is only now that she is beginning to realize her potential.* **3** (usu. **be realized**) give actual or physical form to: *the stage designs have been beautifully realized.* ■ use (a linguistic feature) in a particular spoken or written form. ■ *Music* add to or complete (a piece of music left sparsely notated by the composer). **4** make (money or a profit) from a transaction: *she realized a profit of $100,000.* ■ (of goods) be sold for (a specified price); fetch: *the drawings are expected to realize $500,000.* ■ convert (an asset) into cash: *he realized all the assets in her trust fund.* ▷early 17th cent.: from REAL[1], on the pattern of French *réaliser.* —**re·al·iz·er** *n.*

real life ▸*n.* life as it is lived in reality, involving unwelcome as well as welcome experiences, as distinct from a fictional world: [as *adj.*] *real-life situations.*

real line ▸*n. Mathematics* a notional line in which every real number is conceived of as represented by a point.

re·al·lo·cate /rē'aləˌkāt/ ▸*v.* [*trans.*] allocate in a different way: *a strong incentive to reallocate their resources overseas.* —**re·al·lo·ca·tion** /ˌrēˌalə'kāsнən/ *n.*

re·al·ly /'rē(ə)lē/ ▸*adv.* **1** in actual fact, as opposed to what is said or imagined to be true or possible: *so what really happened? | they're not really my aunt and uncle |* [*sentence adverb*] *really, there are only three options.* ■ used to add strength, sincerity, or seriousness to a statement or opinion: *I really want to go | I'm sorry, Ruth, I really am | you really ought to tell her.* ■ seriously (used in questions and exclamations with an implied negative answer): *do you really expect me to believe that?* **2** [as *submodifier*] very; thoroughly: *I think she's really great | a really cold day | he writes really well.*
▸*exclam.* used to express interest, surprise, or doubt: *"I've been working hard." "Really?"* ■ used to express mild protest: *really, Marjorie, you do jump to conclusions!* ■ used to express agreement: *"It's a nightmare finding somewhere to live in this town." "Yeah, really."*
▸*PHRASE* □ **really and truly** used to emphasize the sincerity of a statement or opinion: *I sometimes wonder whether you really and truly love me.*

realm /relm/ ▸*n. archaic, poetic/literary,* or *Law* a kingdom: *the peers of the realm | the defense of the realm.* ■ a field or domain of activity or interest: *the realm of applied chemistry.* ■ *Zoology* a primary biogeographical division of the earth's surface. ▷Middle English *rewme*, from Old French *reaume*, from Latin *regimen* 'government' (see REGIMEN). The spelling with *-l-* (standard from *c.*1600) was influenced by Old French *reiel* 'royal.'

re·al·po·li·tik /rā'älˌpōliˌtēk/ ▸*n.* a system of politics or principles based on practical rather than moral or ideological considerations. ▷early 20th cent.: from German *Realpolitik* 'practical politics.'

real pres·ence ▸*n. Christian Theology* the actual presence of Christ's body and blood in the Eucharistic elements.

real prop·er·ty ▸*n. Law* property consisting of land or buildings. Compare with PERSONAL PROPERTY.

real ten·nis ▸*n.* British term for COURT TENNIS.

real time ▸*n.* the actual time during which a process or event occurs: *recent natural experiments in which creolization by children can be observed* ***in real time*** *| information updated in real time.* ■ [as *adj.*] *Computing* of or relating to a system in which input data is processed within milliseconds so that it is available virtually immediately as feedback, e.g., in a missile guidance or airline booking system: *real-time signal processing.* ■ *informal* a two-way conversation, as opposed to the delay of written correspondence: *a place where two people can talk to one another* ***in real time.***

re·al·tor /'rē(ə)ltər; -ˌtôr; 'rē(ə)lətər/ ▸*n. trademark* a person who acts as an agent for the sale and purchase of buildings and land; a real estate agent. ▷early 20th cent.: from REALTY + -OR[1].

re·al·ty /'rē(ə)ltē/ ▸*n. Law* a person's real property. The opposite of PERSONALTY.

ream[1] /rēm/ ▸*n.* 500 (formerly 480) sheets of paper. ■ a large quantity of something, typically paper or writing on paper: ***reams of*** *paper have been used to debate these questions.* ▷late Middle English: from Old French *raime*, based on Arabic *rizma* 'bundle.'

ream[2] ▸*v.* [*trans.*] widen (a bore or hole) with a special tool. ■ widen a bore or hole in (a gun or other metal object) in such a way. ■ clear out or remove (material) from something. ■ *vulgar slang* have anal intercourse with (someone). ■ *informal* rebuke someone fiercely: *the agent was* ***reaming*** *him* ***out*** *for walking away from the deal.* ▷early 19th cent.: of unknown origin.
▸*PHRASE* □ **ream someone's ass** (or **butt**) *vulgar slang* criticize or rebuke someone.

ream·er /'rēmər/ ▸*n.* a tool for widening or finishing drilled holes. ■ an instrument for scraping the burrs off the inside of water pipes. ■ a blade for scraping the carbon layer from the inside of the bowl of a smoking pipe. ■ another term for JUICER (sense 1).

re·an·i·mate /rē'anəˌmāt/ ▸*v.* [*trans.*] restore to life or consciousness; revive. ■ give fresh vigor or impetus to: *his personal dislike of the man was reanimated.* —**re·an·i·ma·tion** /ˌrēˌanə'māsнən/ *n.*

reap /rēp/ ▸*v.* [*trans.*] cut or gather (a crop or harvest): *large numbers of men were employed to reap the harvest | figurative in terms of science, the Apollo program reaped a meager harvest.* ■ harvest the crop from (a piece of land). ■ *figurative* receive (a reward or benefit) as a consequence of one's own or other people's actions: *the company is poised to reap the benefits of this investment.* ▷Old English *ripan, reopan*, of unknown origin.
▸*PHRASES* □ **reap the harvest** (or **fruits**) **of** suffer the results or consequences of: *critics believe we are now reaping the harvest of our permissive ways.* □ **you reap what you sow** *proverb* you eventually have to face up to the consequences of your actions.

reap·er /'rēpər/ ▸*n.* a person or machine that harvests a crop. ■ (**the Reaper**) short for GRIM REAPER.

re·ap·ply /ˌrēə'plī/ ▸*v.* (**-plies, -plied**) **1** [*intrans.*] make another application or request: *he was ordered to take a driving test before reapplying for a license.* **2** [*trans.*] apply (an existing rule or principle) in a different context. **3** [*trans.*] spread (a substance) on a surface again: *reapply the sunscreen hourly.* —**re·ap·pli·ca·tion** /ˌrēˌaplə'kāsнən/ *n.*

re·ap·point /ˌrēə'point/ ▸*v.* [*trans.*] appoint (someone) once again to a position they have previously held. —**re·ap·point·ment** *n.*

re·ap·por·tion /ˌrēə'pôrsнən/ ▸*v.* [*trans.*] assign or distribute (something) again or in a different way. —**re·ap·por·tion·ment** *n.*

re·ap·praise /ˌrēə'prāz/ ▸*v.* [*trans.*] appraise or assess (something) again or in a different way: *it made me reappraise my attitudes.* —**re·ap·prais·al** /-'prāzəl/ *n.*

rear[1] /ri(ə)r/ ▸*n.* [in *sing.*] the back part of something, esp. a building or vehicle: *the kitchen door at the rear of the house.* ■ the space or position at the back of something or someone: *the field at the rear of the church.* ■ the hindmost part of an army, fleet, or line of people: *two blue policemen at the rear fell out of the formation.* ■ (also **rear end**) *informal* a person's buttocks.
▸*adj.* [*attrib.*] at the back: *the car's rear window.* ▷Middle English (first used as a military term): from Old French *rere*, based on Latin *retro* 'back.'
▸*PHRASE* □ **bring up the rear** be at the very end of a line of people. ■ come last in a race or other contest.

rear[2] ▸*v.* **1** [*trans.*] (usu. **be reared**) bring up and care for (a child) until they are fully grown, esp. in a particular manner or place: *he was born and reared in New York City | a generation reared on video.* ■ (of an animal) care for (its young) until they are fully grown.

■ breed and raise (animals): *the calves are reared for beef.* ■ grow or cultivate (plants): [as *adj.*, in *combination*] (**-reared**) *laboratory-reared plantlets.* **2** [*intrans.*] (of a horse or other animal) raise itself upright on its hind legs: *the horse reared in terror.* ■ [with *adverbial of place*] (of a building, mountain, etc.) extend or appear to extend to a great height: *houses reared up on either side.* ■ [*trans.*] *archaic* set (something) upright.
▶*phrasal v.* □ **rear up** (of a person) show anger or irritation; go on the attack: *the press reared up in the wake of the bombings.* ▷Old English *rǣran* 'set upright, construct, elevate,' of Germanic origin; related to RAISE (which has supplanted *rear* in many applications), also to RISE. **—rear·er** *n.*
▶*PHRASE* □ **rear one's head** raise one's head. ■ (**rear its head**) (of an unpleasant matter) emerge; present itself: *elitism is* ***rearing its ugly head*** *again.*

rear ad·mir·al ▶*n.* an officer in the U.S. Navy or Coast Guard ranking above commodore and below vice admiral.

rear com·mo·dore ▶*n.* an officer in a yacht club ranking below vice commodore.

rear ech·e·lon ▶*n.* the section of an army concerned with administrative and supply duties.

rear·guard /ˈri(ə)rˌgärd/ ▶*n.* the soldiers positioned at the rear of a body of troops, esp. those protecting an army when it is in retreat. ■ a defensive or conservative element in an organization or community. ▷late Middle English (denoting the rear part of an army): from Old French *rereguarde.*

rear·guard ac·tion ▶*n.* a defensive action carried out by a retreating army.

re·arm /rēˈärm/ ▶*v.* [*trans.*] provide with a new supply of weapons: *his plan to rearm Germany.* ■ [*intrans.*] acquire or build up a new supply of weapons. **—re·ar·ma·ment** /rēˈärməmənt/ *n.*

rear·most /ˈri(ə)rˌmōst/ ▶*adj.* furthest back: *the rearmost door.*

rear pro·jec·tion (also **rear-pro·jec·tion**) ▶*n.* the projection of a picture onto the back of a translucent screen for viewing or for use as a background in filming. ■ an image projected in this way. **—rear-pro·ject·ed** *adj.*

re·ar·range /ˌrēəˈrānj/ ▶*v.* [*trans.*] move (something) into a more acceptable position or state: *she rearranged her skirt as she sat back in her chair.* ■ change (the position, time, or order of something): *he had rearranged his schedule.* **—re·ar·range·ment** *n.*

rear sight ▶*n.* the sight nearest to the stock on a firearm.

rear·view mir·ror /ˈrirˌvyo͞o/ (also **rear-view mir·ror**) ▶*n.* a small angled mirror fixed inside the windshield of a motor vehicle, enabling the driver to see the vehicle or road behind.

rear·ward /ˈri(ə)rwərd/ ▶*adj.* directed toward the back: *a slight rearward movement.* [early 17th cent.: from REAR[1] + -WARD.]
▶*adv.* (also *chiefly Brit.* **rear·wards**) toward the back: *the engine nozzles point rearward.*
▶*n.* (usu. **in/at/on the rearward**) *archaic* or *poetic/literary* the part or position at the back of something. [Middle English (denoting the rear part of an army): from Anglo-Norman French *rerewarde* 'rearguard.']

rear-wheel drive ▶*n.* a transmission system that provides power to the rear wheels of a motor vehicle: [as *adj.*] *a rear-wheel drive coupé.*

re·as·cend /ˌrēəˈsend/ ▶*v.* [*intrans.*] ascend again or to a former position: *the fallen angel reascends to the upper air.* **—re·as·cen·sion** /ˌrēəˈsenSHən/ *n.*

rea·son /ˈrēzən/ ▶*n.* **1** a cause, explanation, or justification for an action or event: *the minister resigned for personal reasons* | *it is hard to know for the simple reason that few records survive.* ■ good or obvious cause to do something: *we have reason to celebrate.* ■ *Logic* a premise of an argument in support of a belief, esp. a minor premise when given after the conclusion. **2** the power of the mind to think, understand, and form judgments by a process of logic: *there is a close connection between reason and emotion.* ■ what is right, practical, or possible; common sense: *people are willing,* ***within reason,*** *to pay for schooling.* ■ (**one's reason**) one's sanity: *she is in danger of* ***losing her reason.***
▶*v.* [*intrans.*] think, understand, and form judgments by a process of logic: *humans do not reason entirely from facts* | [as *n.*] (**reasoning**) *the present chapter will outline the reasoning behind the review.* ■ [*trans.*] (**reason something out**) find an answer to a problem by considering various possible solutions. ■ (**reason with**) persuade (someone) with rational argument: *I tried to reason with her, but without success.* ▷Middle English: from Old French *reisun* (noun), *raisoner* (verb), from a variant of Latin *ratio(n-)*, from the verb *reri* 'consider.' **—rea·son·er** /ˈrēz(ə)nər/ *n.* **—rea·son·less** *adj.* (*archaic*).
▶*PHRASES* □ **beyond** (**all**) **reason** to a foolishly excessive degree: *he indulged Andrew beyond all reason.* □ **by reason of** *formal* because of: *persons who, by reason of age, are in need of care.* □ **for some reason** used to convey that one doesn't know the reason for a particular state of affairs, often with the implication that one finds it strange or surprising: *for some reason he likes you.* □ **listen to reason** be persuaded to act sensibly: *the child is usually too emotionally overwrought to listen to reason.* □ **theirs** (or **ours**) **not to reason why** used to suggest that it is not someone's (or someone else's) place to question a situation or system. [with allusion to Tennyson's *Charge of the Light Brigade* (1854).] □ **reason of state** another term for RAISON D'ÉTAT. □ (**it**) **stands to reason** it is obvious or logical: *it stands to reason that if you can eradicate the fear, the nervousness will subside.*

USAGE 1 The construction **the reason why . . .** has been objected to on the grounds that the subordinate clause should express a statement, using a *that*-clause, not imply a question with a *why*-clause: ***the reason that*** *I decided not to phone* rather than ***the reason why*** *I decided not to phone. The reason why* has been called a redundancy to be avoided, but it is a mild one, and idiomatic.
2 An objection is also made to the construction **the reason . . . is because,** as in ***the reason*** *I didn't phone* ***is because*** *my mother has been ill.* The objection is made on the grounds that either "because" or "the reason" is redundant; it is better to use the word **that** instead (***the reason*** *I didn't phone* ***is that*** . . .) or rephrase altogether (*I didn't phone* ***because*** . . .).

rea·son·a·ble /ˈrēz(ə)nəbəl/ ▶*adj.* **1** (of a person) having sound judgment; fair and sensible: *no reasonable person could have objected.* ■ based on good sense: *it seems a reasonable enough request* | *the guilt of a person on trial must be proved beyond reasonable doubt.* ■ *archaic* (of a person or animal) able to think, understand, or form judgments by a logical process: *man is by nature reasonable.* **2** as much as is appropriate or fair; moderate: *a police officer may use reasonable force to gain entry.* ■ fairly good; average: *the carpet is in reasonable condition.* ■ (of a price or product) not too expensive: *a restaurant serving excellent food at reasonable prices* | *they are lovely shoes and very reasonable.* ▷Middle English: from Old French *raisonable*, suggested by Latin *rationabilis* 'rational,' from *ratio* (see REASON). **—rea·son·a·ble·ness** *n.*

rea·son·a·ble wom·an stand·ard ▶*n. Law* a guideline for determining what constitutes sexual harassment, based on suppositions about what a reasonable woman would find objectionable.

rea·son·a·bly /ˈrēz(ə)nəblē/ ▶*adv.* **1** in a fair and sensible way: *he began to talk calmly and reasonably about his future.* ■ by fair or sensible standards of judgment; rightly or justifiably: *police must reasonably believe that a threat to the security of the embassy is present.* | [*sentence adverb*] *it was assumed,* ***reasonably enough,*** *that the murder had taken place by the pond.* **2** to a moderate or acceptable degree: fairly; quite: [as *submodifier*] *she played the piano reasonably well.* ■ inexpensively: *ski wear which looks good and is reasonably priced.*

rea·soned /ˈrēzənd/ ▶*adj.* underpinned by logic or good sense: *a reasoned judgment.*

re·as·sem·ble /ˌrēəˈsembəl/ ▶*v.* [*intrans.*] (of a group) gather together again: *after lunch the class reassembled.* ■ [*trans.*] put (something) together again: *the trucks had to be reassembled on arrival.* **—re·as·sem·bly** /-blē/ *n.*

re·as·sess /ˌrēəˈses/ ▶*v.* [*trans.*] consider or assess again, esp. while paying attention to new or different factors: *we have decided to reassess our timetable.* **—re·as·sess·ment** *n.*

re·as·sign /ˌrēəˈsīn/ ▶*v.* [*trans.*] appoint (someone) to a different job or task: *he had been reassigned to another post.* ■ allocate or distribute (work or resources) differently: *a network which continually reassigns costs.* **—re·as·sign·ment** *n.*

re·as·sort·ment ▶*n. Genetics* recombination of genomic material, esp. as it occurs naturally in related viruses: *reassortment also might occur in a person simultaneously infected by both types of flu.*

re·as·sume /ˌrēəˈs(y)o͞om/ ▶*v.* [*trans.*] take on or gain (something) again: *he reassumed the title of Governor General.* **—re·as·sump·tion** /ˌrēəˈsəmpSHən/ *n.*

re·as·sur·ance /ˌrēəˈSHo͝orəns/ ▶*n.* the action of removing someone's doubts or fears: *children need reassurance and praise.* ■ a statement or comment that removes someone's doubts or fears: *we have been given* ***reassurances that*** *the water is safe to drink.*

re·as·sure /ˌrēəˈSHo͝or/ ▶*v.* [*trans.*] say or do something to remove the doubts and fears of someone: *he understood her feelings and tried to reassure her* | [*trans.*] *Joachim reassured him that he was needed* | [as *adj.*] (**reassuring**) *Gina gave her a reassuring smile.* **—re·as·sur·ing·ly** *adv.*

re·at·tach /ˌrēəˈtaCH/ ▶*v.* [*trans.*] attach (something that has fallen or been taken off) in its former position. **—re·at·tach·ment** *n.*

Ré·au·mur scale /ˌrā-ōˈmyo͝or; rāˈōˌmyo͝or/ ▶*n.* an obsolete scale of temperature at which water freezes at 0° and boils at 80° under standard conditions. ▷late 18th cent.: named after René A. F. de *Réaumur* (1683–1757), French naturalist.

reave /rēv/ ▶*v.* (*past* and *past part.* **reft** /reft/) [*intrans.*] *archaic* carry out raids in order to plunder. ■ [*trans.*] rob (a person or place) of something by force: *reft of a crown, he yet may share the feast.* ■ [*trans.*] steal (something). ▷Old English *rēafian*, of Germanic origin; related to Dutch *roven*, German *rauben*, also to ROB. **—reav·er** *n.*

re·a·wak·en /ˌrēəˈwākən/ ▶*v.* [*trans.*] restore (a feeling or state): *his departure reawakened deep divisions within the party.* ■ [*intrans.*] (of a feeling or state) emerge again; return: *the sense of community started to reawaken in the 1970s.*

Reb[1] /reb/ ▶*n.* a traditional Jewish title or form of address, corresponding to Sir, for a man who is not a rabbi (used preceding the forename or surname). ▷Yiddish.

Reb[2] (also **John·ny Reb**) ▶*n. informal* a Confederate soldier in the American Civil War. ▷abbreviation of REBEL.

re·bab /riˈbäb/ ▶*n.* a bowed or plucked stringed instrument of Arab origin, used esp. in North Africa, the Middle East, and the Indian subcontinent. ▷mid 18th cent.: from Arabic *rabāb.*

re·badge /rēˈbaj/ ▶*v.* [*trans.*] relaunch (a product) under a new name or logo.

re·baked /rēˈbākt/ ▶*adj.* another term for TWICE-BAKED.

re·bal·ance /rēˈbaləns/ ▶*v.* [*trans.*] balance again or restore the correct balance to.

re·bar /ˈrēˌbär/ ▶*n.* a steel reinforcing rod in concrete: *a piece of rebar.*

re·bar·ba·tive /rəˈbärbətiv/ ▶*adj. formal* unattractive and objectionable: *rebarbative modern buildings.* ▷late 19th cent.: from French *rébarbatif, -ive*, from Old French *se rebarber* 'face each other "beard to beard" aggressively,' from *barbe* 'beard.'

re·base /rēˈbās/ ▶*v.* [*trans.*] establish a new base level for (a tax level, price index, etc.).

re·bate[1] ▶*n.* /ˈrēˌbāt/ a partial refund to someone who has paid too much money for tax, rent, or a utility. ■ a deduction or discount on a sum of money due.
▶*v.* /ˈrēˌbāt; riˈbāt/ [*trans.*] pay back (such a sum of money). ▷late Middle English (as a verb in the sense 'diminish (a sum or amount)'): from Anglo-Norman French *rebatre* 'beat back,' also 'deduct.' **—re·bat·a·ble** /ˈrēˌbātəbəl; riˈbāt-/ *adj.*

re·bate[2] /ˈrabit; ˈrēˌbāt/ ▶*n.* & *v.* another term for RABBET. ▷late 17th cent.: alteration of RABBET.

reb·be /ˈrebə; -bē/ ▶*n. Judaism* a rabbi, esp. a religious leader of the Hasidic sect. ▷Yiddish, from Hebrew *rabbī* 'rabbi.'

reb·betz·in /rəˈbetsin; ˈrebət-/ (also **reb·bitz·in**) ▶*n. Judaism* the wife of a rabbi. ■ a female religious teacher. ▷Yiddish, feminine of *rebbe* (see REBBE).

re·bec /ˈrēˌbek; ˈrebˌek/ (also **re·beck**) ▶*n.* a medieval stringed instrument played with a bow, typically having three strings. ▷late Middle English: from French, based on Arabic *rabāb.*

reb·el ▶*n.* /ˈrebəl/ a person who rises in opposition or armed resistance against an established government or ruler: *Tory rebels* | [as *adj.*] *rebel forces.* ■ a person who resists authority, control, or convention.
▶*v.* /riˈbel/ (**-elled, -el·ling**) [*intrans.*] rise in opposition or armed resistance to an established government or ruler: *the Earl of Pembroke subsequently rebelled against Henry III.* ■ (of a person) resist authority, control, or convention: *respect did not prevent children from rebelling against their parents.* ■ show or feel repugnance for or resistance to something: *as I came over the hill my legs rebelled—I could walk no further.* ▷Middle English: from Old French *rebelle* (noun),

R

rebeller (verb), from Latin *rebellis* (used originally with reference to a fresh declaration of war by the defeated), based on *bellum* 'war.'

re·bel·lion /ri'belyən/ ▸*n.* an act of violent or open resistance to an established government or ruler: *the authorities put down a rebellion by landless colonials | Simon de Montfort rose in rebellion.* See note at **UPRISING.** ■ the action or process of resisting authority, control, or convention: *an act of teenage rebellion.* ▷Middle English: from Old French, from Latin *rebellio(n-)*, from *rebellis* (see **REBEL**).

re·bel·lious /ri'belyəs/ ▸*adj.* showing a desire to resist authority, control, or convention: *young people with a rebellious streak.* ■ (of a person, city, or state) engaged in opposition or armed resistance to an established government or ruler: *the rebellious republics.* ■ (of a thing) not easily handled or kept in place: *he smoothed back a rebellious lock of hair.* **—re·bel·lious·ly** *adv.* **—re·bel·lious·ness** *n.*

reb·el yell ▸*n.* a shout or battle cry used by the Confederates during the American Civil War.

re·bid ▸*v.* /rē'bid/ (**-bid·ding**; *past* and *past part.* **-bid**) [*intrans.*] bid again: *it will be in an ideal position when it comes to rebidding for its franchise.*
▸*n.* /'rē,bid/ a further bid.

re·bind /rē'bīnd/ ▸*v.* (*past* and *past part.* **-bound**) [*trans.*] give a new binding to (a book).

re·birth /rē'bərTH; 'rē,bərTH/ ▸*n.* the process of being reincarnated or born again: *the endless cycle of birth, death, and rebirth.* ■ the action of reappearing or starting to flourish or increase after a decline; revival: *the rebirth of a defeated nation.*

re·birth·ing /rē'bərTHiNG/ ▸*n.* a form of psychotherapy involving controlled breathing intended to simulate the trauma of being born. **—re·birth·er** /-THər/ *n.*

re·blo·chon /rə,blô'SHôN/ ▸*n.* a kind of soft French cheese, made originally and chiefly in Savoy. ▷French.

re·book /rē'bo͝ok/ ▸*v.* book the same accommodations, seat, ticket, etc.: [*intrans.*] *a third of the tourists had rebooked for next year* | [*trans.*] *passengers were allowed to rebook those flights on Northwest or Pinnacle.*

re·boot /rē'bo͞ot/ ▸*v.* [*trans.*] boot (a computer system) again. ■ [*intrans.*] (of a computer system) be booted again.
▸*n.* an act or instance of booting a computer system again.

re·bore ▸*v.* /rē'bôr/ [*trans.*] bore out (the cylinders of an internal combustion engine) again, typically in order to widen them.
▸*n.* /'rēbôr/ an act of reboring an engine's cylinders. ■ an engine with rebored cylinders.

re·born /rē'bôrn/ ▸*adj.* brought back to life or activity: *the grand concourse stands reborn as a four-star restaurant.* ■ having experienced a complete spiritual change: *a reborn Catholic.*

re·bound[1] ▸*v.* /ri'bound; 'rē,bound/ [*intrans.*] bounce back through the air after hitting a hard surface or object: *his shot hammered into the post and rebounded across the goal.* ■ [*intrans.*] recover in value, amount, or strength after a previous decrease or decline: *NASDAQ rebounded to show a twenty-point gain.* ■ [*intrans.*] (**rebound on/upon**) (of an event or situation) have an unexpected adverse consequence for (someone, esp. the person responsible for it): *Nicholas's tricks are rebounding on him.* ■ [*intrans.*] *Basketball* gain possession of a missed shot after it bounces off the backboard or basket rim.
▸*n.* /'rē,bound/ (in sporting contexts) a ball or shot that bounces back after striking a hard surface: *he blasted the rebound into the net.* ■ *Basketball* a recovery of possession of a missed shot. ■ an instance of increasing in value, amount, or strength after a previous decline: *they revealed a big rebound in profits for last year.* ■ [usu. as *adj.*] the recurrence of a medical condition, esp. after withdrawal of medication: *rebound hypertension.* ▷late Middle English: from Old French *rebondir*, from *re-* 'back' + *bondir* 'bounce up.'
▸**PHRASE** □ **on the rebound** in the process of bouncing back after striking a hard surface. ■ still affected by the emotional distress caused by the ending of a romantic or sexual relationship: *I was on the rebound when I met Jack.*

re·bound[2] ▸ past and past participle of **REBIND.**

re·bound·er /'rē,boundər; ri'boun-/ ▸*n.* *Basketball* a player who rebounds the ball or is especially proficient at doing so.

re·bo·zo /ri'bōzō; -sō/ ▸*n.* (*pl.* **-zos**) a long scarf covering the head and shoulders, traditionally worn by Spanish-American women. ▷Spanish.

re·brand /rē'brand/ ▸*v.* [*trans.*] [usu. as *n.*] (**rebranding**) change the corporate image of (a company or organization).

re·breathe /rē'brēTH/ ▸*v.* [*trans.*] breathe in (exhaled air).

re·breath·er /rē'brēTHər/ ▸*n.* an aqualung in which the diver's exhaled breath is partially purified of carbon dioxide, mixed with more oxygen, and then breathed again by the diver.

re·broad·cast /rē'brôd,kast/ ▸*v.* (*past* **-cast** or **-cast·ed**; *past part.* **-cast**) [*trans.*] broadcast or relay (a program or signal) again.
▸*n.* a repeated or relayed broadcast. **—re·broad·cast·er** *n.*

re·buff /ri'bəf/ ▸*v.* [*trans.*] reject (someone or something) in an abrupt or ungracious manner: *I asked her to be my wife, and was rebuffed in no uncertain terms.*
▸*n.* an abrupt or ungracious refusal or rejection of an offer, request, or friendly gesture: *any attempt to win her friendship was met with rebuffs.* ▷late 16th cent.: from obsolete French *rebuffer* (verb), *rebuffe* (noun), from Italian *ri-* (expressing opposition) + *buffo* 'a gust, puff,' of imitative origin.

re·build /rē'bild/ ▸*v.* (*past* and *past part.* **-built** /-'bilt/) [*trans.*] build (something) again after it has been damaged or destroyed: *he rebuilt the cathedral church | figurative we try to help them rebuild their lives.*
▸*n.* /'rē,bild/ an instance or rebuilding something, esp. a vehicle or other machine. ■ a thing that has been rebuilt, esp. a part of a motor vehicle, e.g., a motor or an alternator. **—re·build·a·ble** *adj.* **—re·build·er** *n.*

re·buke /ri'byo͞ok/ ▸*v.* [*trans.*] express sharp disapproval or criticism of (someone) because of their behavior or actions: *she had* **rebuked** *him* **for** *drinking too much | the judge publicly rebuked the jury.*
▸*n.* an expression of sharp disapproval or criticism: *he hadn't meant it as a rebuke, but Neil flinched.* ▷Middle English (originally in the sense 'force back, repress'): from Anglo-Norman French and Old Northern French *rebuker*, from *re-* 'back, down' + *bukier* 'to beat' (originally 'cut down wood,' from Old French *busche* 'log'). **—re·buk·er** *n.* **—re·buk·ing·ly** *adv.*

THE RIGHT WORD **admonish, censure, rebuke, reprimand, reproach, scold**

All of these verbs mean to criticize or express disapproval, but which one you use depends on how upset you are.

If you want to go easy on someone, you can **admonish** or **reproach**, both of which indicate mild and sometimes kindly disapproval. To *admonish* is to warn or counsel someone, usually because a duty has been forgotten or might be forgotten in the future (*admonish her about leaving the key in the lock*), while *reproach* also suggests mild criticism aimed at correcting a fault or pattern of misbehavior (*he was reproved for his lack of attention in class*).

If you want to express your disapproval formally or in public, use **censure** or **reprimand**. You can *censure* someone either directly or indirectly (*the judge censured the lawyer for violating courtroom procedures; a newspaper article that censured "deadbeat dads"*), while *reprimand* suggests a direct confrontation (*reprimanded by his parole officer for leaving town without reporting his whereabouts*).

If you're irritated enough to want to express your disapproval quite harshly and at some length, you can **scold** (*to scold a child for jaywalking*).

Rebuke is the harshest word of this group, meaning to criticize sharply or sternly, often in the midst of some action (*rebuke a carpenter for walking across an icy roof*).

re·bus /'rēbəs/ ▸*n.* (*pl.* **-bus·es**) a puzzle in which words are represented by combinations of pictures and individual letters; for instance, *apex* might be represented by a picture of an ape followed by a letter *X.* ■ *historical* an ornamental device associated with a person to whose name it punningly alludes. ▷early 17th cent.: from French *rébus*, from Latin *rebus*, ablative plural of *res* 'thing.'

"To be or not to be"

rebus

re·but /ri'bət/ ▸*v.* (**-but·ted, -but·ting**) [*trans.*] **1** claim or prove that (evidence or an accusation) is false: *he had to rebut charges of acting for the convenience of his political friends.* **2** *archaic* drive back or repel (a person or attack). ▷Middle English (in the senses 'rebuke' and 'repulse'): from Anglo-Norman French *rebuter*, from Old French *re-* (expressing opposition) + *boter* 'to butt.' Sense 1 (originally a legal use) dates from the early 19th cent. **—re·but·ta·ble** *adj.*

re·but·tal /ri'bətl/ ▸*n.* a refutation or contradiction. ■ another term for **REBUTTER.**

re·but·ter /ri'bətər/ ▸*n.* *archaic Law* a defendant's reply to the plaintiff's surrejoinder. ▷mid 19th cent.: from Anglo-Norman French *rebuter* (from Old French *rebut* 'a reproach, rebuke') + **-AL.**

rec /rek/ ▸*n.* *informal* recreation: [as *adj.*] *the rec center.* ▷1920s: abbreviation.

rec. ▸*abbr.* ■ receipt. ■ (in prescriptions) fresh. [from Latin *recens.*] ■ recipe. ■ record. ■ recorder. ■ recording.

re·cal·ci·trant /ri'kalsətrənt/ ▸*adj.* having an obstinately uncooperative attitude toward authority or discipline: *a class of recalcitrant fifteen-year-olds.*
▸*n.* a person with such an attitude. ▷mid 19th cent.: from Latin *recalcitrant-* 'kicking out with the heels,' from the verb *recalcitrare*, based on *calx, calc-* 'heel.' **—re·cal·ci·trance** *n.* **—re·cal·ci·trant·ly** *adv.*

re·cal·cu·late /rē'kalkyə,lāt/ ▸*v.* [*trans.*] calculate again, typically using different data. **—re·cal·cu·la·tion** /,rē,kalkyə'lāSHən/ *n.*

re·ca·les·cence /,rēkə'lesəns/ ▸*n.* *Metallurgy* a temporary rise in temperature during cooling of a metal, caused by a change in crystal structure. ▷late 19th cent.: from **RE-** 'again' + Latin *calescere* 'grow hot' + **-ENCE.** **—re·ca·les·cent** *adj.*

re·call ▸*v.* /ri'kôl/ [*trans.*] **1** bring (a fact, event, or situation) back into one's mind, esp. so as to recount it to others; remember: *I can still vaguely recall being taken to the hospital* | [with *direct speech*] *"He was awfully fond of teasing people," she recalled* | [with *clause*] *he recalled how he felt at the time.* ■ cause one to remember or think of: *the film's analysis of contemporary concerns recalls* The Big Chill. ■ (**recall someone/something to**) bring the memory or thought of someone or something to (a person or their mind): *the smell of a black-currant bush has ever since recalled to me that evening.* ■ call up (stored computer data) for processing or display. **2** officially order (someone) to return to a place: *the Panamanian ambassador was recalled from Peru.* ■ select (a sports player) as a member of a team from which they have previously been dropped: *the Fulham defender has been* **recalled to** *the Welsh squad for the World Cup.* ■ (of a manufacturer) request all the purchasers of (a certain product) to return it, as the result of the discovery of a fault. ■ bring (someone) out of a state of inattention or reverie: *her action* **recalled** *him* **to** *the present.* ■ *archaic* revoke or annul (an action or decision).
▸*n.* /'rē,kôl; ri'kôl; rē'kôl/ **1** an act or instance of officially recalling someone or something: *a recall of Parliament.* ■ a request for the return of a faulty product, issued by a manufacturer to all those who have purchased it. ■ the removal of an elected government official from office by a petition followed by voting. **2** the action or faculty of remembering something learned or experienced: *he has amazing recall | people's understanding and subsequent recall of stories or events.* ■ the proportion of the number of relevant documents retrieved from a database in response to an inquiry. ▷late 16th cent. (as a verb): from **RE-** 'again' + **CALL**, suggested by Latin *revocare* or French *rappeler* 'call back.' **—re·call·a·ble** *adj.*
▸**PHRASE** □ **beyond recall** in such a way that restoration is impossible: *shopping developments have already blighted other parts of the city beyond recall.*

re·cant /ri'kant/ ▸*v.* [*intrans.*] say that one no longer holds an opinion or belief, esp. one considered heretical: *heretics were burned if they would not recant* | [*trans.*] *Galileo was forced to recant his assertion that the earth orbited the sun.* ▷mid 16th cent.: from Latin *recantare* 'revoke,' from *re-* (expressing reversal) + *cantare* 'sing, chant.' **—re·can·ta·tion** /,rē,kan'tāSHən/ *n.* **—re·cant·er** *n.*

re·cap *informal* ▸*v.* /rē'kap/ (**-capped, -cap·ping**) [*trans.*] state again as a summary; recapitulate: *a way of recapping the story so far* | [*intrans.*] *to recap, at the end of the Persian Gulf War, he lost control of the northern third of his country.*
▸*n.* /'rē,kap/ a summary of what has been said; a recapitulation: *a quick recap of the idea and its main advantages.* ▷1950s: abbreviation.

re·cap·i·tal·ize /rē'kapətl,īz/ ▸*v.* [*trans.*] provide (a business) with more capital, esp. by replacing debt with stock. **—re·cap·i·tal·i·za·tion** /rē,kapətl-ə'zāSHən/ *n.*

re·ca·pit·u·late /ˌrēkə'picHəˌlāt/ ▶*v.* [*trans.*] summarize and state again the main points of: *he began to recapitulate his argument with care.* ■ *Biology* repeat (an evolutionary or other process) during development and growth. ▷late 16th cent.: from late Latin *recapitulat-* 'gone through heading by heading,' from *re-* 'again' + *capitulum* 'chapter' (diminutive of *caput* 'head'). —**re·ca·pit·u·la·to·ry** /-lə,tôrē/ *adj.*

re·ca·pit·u·la·tion /ˌrēkəˌpicHə'lāsHən/ ▶*n.* an act or instance of summarizing and restating the main points of something: *his recapitulation of the argument.* ■ *Biology* the repetition of an evolutionary or other process during development or growth. ■ *Music* a part of a movement (esp. one in sonata form) in which themes from the exposition are restated.

re·ca·pit·u·la·tion the·o·ry ▶*n.* another term for **BIOGENETIC LAW.**

re·cap·tion /rē'kapsHən/ ▶*n. Law* the action of taking back, without legal process, property of one's own that has been wrongfully taken or withheld. ▷mid 18th cent.: from Anglo-Latin *recaptio(n-)*, from *re-* 'back' + Latin *captio(n-)* 'taking.'

re·cap·ture /rē'kapcHər/ ▶*v.* [*trans.*] capture (a person or animal that has escaped): *armed police have recaptured a prisoner who's been on the run for five days.* ■ recover (something previously captured by an enemy): *Edward I recaptured the castle.* ■ regain (something that has been lost): *Democrats might recapture both the House and the Senate.* ■ recreate or experience again (a past time, event, or feeling): *the programs give viewers a chance to recapture their own childhoods.*
▶*n.* [in *sing.*] an act of recapturing.

re·cast /rē'kast/ ▶*v.* (*past* and *past part.* **-cast**) [*trans.*] **1** give (a metal object) a different form by melting it down and reshaping it. ■ present or organize in a different form or style: *his doctoral thesis has been recast for the general reader.* **2** allocate the parts in (a play or film) to different actors: *there were moves to recast the play.*

recd ▶*abbr.* received.

re·cede /ri'sēd/ ▶*v.* [*intrans.*] go or move back or further away from a previous position: *the flood waters had receded | his footsteps receded down the corridor.* ■ (of a quality, feeling, or possibility) gradually diminish: *the prospects of an early end to the war receded.* ■ (of a man's hair) cease to grow at the temples and above the forehead: *his dark hair was was receding a little* | [as *adj.*] (**receding**) *a receding hairline.* ■ (of a man) begin to go bald in such a way: *Fred was receding a bit.* ■ [usu. as *adj.*] (**receding**) (of a facial feature) slope backward: *a slightly receding chin.* ■ (**recede from**) *archaic* withdraw from (an undertaking, promise, or agreement). ▷late 15th cent. (in the sense 'depart from (a usual state or standard)'): from Latin *recedere*, from *re-* 'back' + *cedere* 'go.'

re·ceipt /ri'sēt/ ▶*n.* **1** the action of receiving something or the fact of its being received: *I would be grateful if you would acknowledge receipt of this letter | this office is already* **in receipt of** *your midterm grades.* ■ a written or printed statement acknowledging that something has been paid for or that goods have been received. ■ (**receipts**) an amount of money received during a particular period by an organization or business: *box-office receipts.* **2** *archaic* a recipe.
▶*v.* [*trans.*] [usu. as *adj.*] (**receipted**) mark (a bill) as paid: *the receipted hotel bill.* ■ write a receipt for (goods or money): *all fish shall be receipted at time of purchase.* ▷late Middle English: from Anglo-Norman French *receite*, from medieval Latin *recepta* 'received,' feminine past participle of Latin *recipere*. The *-p-* was inserted in imitation of the Latin spelling.

re·ceiv·a·ble /ri'sēvəbəl/ ▶*adj.* able to be received.
▶*plural n.* (**receivables**) amounts owed to a business, regarded as assets.

re·ceive /ri'sēv/ ▶*v.* [*trans.*] **1** be given, presented with, or paid (something): *most businesses will receive a tax cut | she received her prize from the manager.* ■ take delivery of (something sent or communicated): *he received fifty inquiries after advertising the job.* ■ buy or accept goods in the knowledge that they have been stolen: *a man convicted of receiving stolen property.* ■ detect or pick up (broadcast signals): *Turkish television began to be received in Tashkent.* ■ form (an idea or impression) as a result of perception or experience: *the impression she received was one of unhurried leisure.* ■ (in tennis and similar games) be the player to whom the server serves (the ball). ■ (in Christian services) eat or drink (the Eucharistic bread or wine): *he received Communion and left.* ■ consent to formally hear (an oath or confession): *he failed to find a magistrate to receive his oath.* ■ serve as a receptacle for: *the basin that receives your blood.* **2** suffer, experience, or be subject to (specified treatment): *the event received wide press coverage | he received an eight-year prison sentence | she received only cuts and bruises.* ■ [*trans.*] (usu. **be received**) respond to (something) in a specified way: *her first poem was not well received.* ■ meet with (a specified response or reaction): *the rulings have received widespread acceptance.* ■ [as *adj.*] (**received**) widely accepted as authoritative or true: *the myths and received wisdom about the country's past.* ■ meet and have to withstand: *the landward slopes receive the full force of the wind.* **3** greet or welcome (a visitor) formally: *representatives of the club will be received by the Mayor.* ■ be visited by: *she was not allowed to receive visitors.* ■ admit as a member: *hundreds of converts were* **received into** *the Church.* ■ provide space or accommodations for: *three lines are reserved for special vehicles, and the remaining lines receive the general rolling stock.* ▷Middle English: from Anglo-Norman French *receivre*, based on Latin *recipere*, from *re-* 'back' + *capere* 'take.'
▶*PHRASE* □ **be at** (or **on**) **the receiving end** be the person to whom a telephone call is made. ■ *informal* be subjected to something unpleasant: *she found herself on the receiving end of a good deal of teasing.*

re·ceived pro·nun·ci·a·tion (also **re·ceived stand·ard**) ▶*n.* the standard form of British English pronunciation, based on educated speech in southern England.

re·ceiv·er /ri'sēvər/ ▶*n.* **1** the part of a telephone apparatus contained in the earpiece, in which electrical signals are converted into sounds. ■ a complete telephone handset: *he picked up the receiver.* ■ a piece of radio or television apparatus that detects broadcast signals and converts them into visible or audible form: *a satellite receiver.* **2** a person who gets or accepts something that has been sent or given to them: *the receiver of a gift.* ■ (in tennis and similar games) the player to whom the ball is served to begin play. ■ *Football* a player who catches a pass or a kick. ■ a person who buys or accepts stolen goods in the knowledge that they have been stolen. **3** a person or company appointed by a court to manage the financial affairs of a business or person that has gone bankrupt: *the company is in the hands of the receivers.* **4** *Chemistry* a container for collecting the products of distillation, chromatography, or other process. **5** the part of a firearm that houses the action and to which the barrel and other parts are attached.

re·ceiv·er·ship /ri'sēvərˌsHip/ ▶*n.* the state of being dealt with by an official receiver: *the company went* **into receivership** *last week.*

re·ceiv·ing line ▶*n.* a collection of people who gather in a row to greet guests as they arrive at a formal social event.

re·cen·sion /ri'sencHən/ ▶*n.* a revised edition of a text; an act of making a revised edition of a text. ▷mid 17th cent. (in the sense 'survey, review'): from Latin *recensio(n-)*, from *recensere* 'revise,' from *re-* 'again' + *censere* 'to review.'

re·cent /'rēsənt/ ▶*adj.* **1** having happened, begun, or been done not long ago or not long before; belonging to a past period of time comparatively close to the present: *his recent visit to Britain | a recent edition of the newspaper.* **2** (**Recent**) *Geology* another term for **HOLOCENE.**
▶*n.* (**the Recent**) *Geology* the Holocene epoch. ▷late Middle English (in the sense 'fresh'): from Latin *recens, recent-* or French *récent.* —**re·cen·cy** *n.* —**re·cent·ly** *adv.* —**re·cent·ness** *n.*

re·cep·ta·cle /ri'septikəl/ ▶*n.* **1** an object or space used to contain something: *trash receptacles.* ■ *chiefly Zoology* an organ or structure that receives a secretion, eggs, sperm, etc. ■ an electrical outlet into which the plug of an electrical device may be inserted. **2** *Botany* an enlarged area at the apex of a stem that bears the organs of a flower or the florets of a flowerhead. ■ a structure supporting the sexual organs in some algae, mosses, and liverworts. ▷late Middle English: from Latin *receptaculum*, from *receptare* 'receive back,' frequentative of *recipere* (see **RECEIVE**).

re·cep·tion /ri'sepsHən/ ▶*n.* **1** the action or process of receiving something sent, given, or inflicted: *the reception of impulses from other neurons | the reception of the sacrament.* ■ the way in which a person or group of people reacts to someone or something: *the proposal continued to get a lukewarm reception on Wall Street.* ■ the receiving of broadcast signals: *a microchip that will allow parents to block reception of violent programs.* ■ the quality of this: *I had to put up with poor radio reception.* ■ the action of admitting someone to a place, group, or institution or the process of being admitted: *their reception into the Church.* ■ the formal or ceremonious welcoming of a guest: *his reception by the Prime Minister.* ■ *Football* an act of catching the ball. **2** a formal social occasion held to welcome someone or to celebrate a particular event: *a wedding reception.* **3** the area in a hotel, office, or other establishment where guests and visitors are greeted and dealt with: [as *adj.*] *the reception desk.* ▷late Middle English: from Old French, or from Latin *receptio(n-)*, from the verb *recipere* (see **RECEIVE**).

re·cep·tion·ist /ri'sepsHənist/ ▶*n.* a person employed in an office or other establishment to answer the telephone, deal with clients, and greet visitors.

re·cep·tion room ▶*n.* a room in a hotel or other building used for functions such as parties and meetings.

re·cep·tive /ri'septiv/ ▶*adj.* able or willing to receive something, esp. signals or stimuli. ■ willing to consider or accept new suggestions and ideas: *a receptive audience | the institution was* **receptive to** *new ideas.* ■ (of a female animal) ready to mate. —**re·cep·tive·ly** *adv.* —**re·cep·tive·ness** *n.* —**re·cep·tiv·i·ty** /ˌrēˌsep'tivətē/ *n.*

re·cep·tor /ri'septər/ ▶*n. Physiology* an organ or cell able to respond to light, heat, or other external stimulus and transmit a signal to a sensory nerve. ■ a region of tissue, or a molecule in a cell membrane, that responds specifically to a particular neurotransmitter, hormone, antigen, or other substance. ▷early 20th cent.: coined in German from Latin *receptor*, from *recept-* 'taken back,' from the verb *recipere* (see **RECEIVE**).

re·cess /'rēˌses; ri'ses/ ▶*n.* **1** a small space created by building part of a wall further back from the rest: *a table set into a recess.* ■ a hollow space inside something: *the concrete block has a recess in its base.* ■ (usu. **recesses**) a remote, secluded, or secret place: *the recesses of the silent pine forest | figurative the dark recesses of his soul.* **2** a period of time when the proceedings of a parliament, committee, court of law, or other official body are temporarily suspended: *talks resumed after a month's recess | the Senate was* **in recess.** ■ a break between school classes: *the mid-morning recess.*
▶*v.* **1** [*trans.*] [often as *adj.*] (**recessed**) attach (a fitment) by setting it back into the wall or surface to which it is fixed: *recessed ceiling lights.* **2** [*intrans.*] (of formal proceedings) be temporarily suspended: *the talks recessed at 2:15.* ■ [*trans.*] suspend (such proceedings) temporarily. ■ (of an official body) suspend its proceedings for a period of time. ▷mid 16th cent. (in the sense 'withdrawal, departure'): from Latin *recessus*, from *recedere* 'go back' (see **RECEDE**). The verb dates from the early 19th cent.

re·ces·sion /ri'sesHən/ ▶*n.* **1** a period of temporary economic decline during which trade and industrial activity are reduced, generally identified by a fall in GDP in two successive quarters. **2** *chiefly Astronomy* the action of receding; motion away from an observer. ▷mid 17th cent.: from Latin *recessio(n-)*, from *recess-* 'gone back,' from the verb *recedere* (see **RECEDE**). —**re·ces·sion·ar·y** /-ˌnerē/ *adj.*

re·ces·sion·al /ri'sesHənl; ri'sesHnəl/ ▶*adj.* of or relating to an economic recession: *recessional times.* ■ *chiefly Astronomy* relating to or denoting motion away from the observer. ■ *Geology* (of a moraine or other deposit) left during a pause in the retreat of a glacier or ice sheet.
▶*n.* a hymn sung while the clergy and choir process out of church at the end of a service. Compare with **PROCESSIONAL.**

re·ces·sive /ri'sesiv/ ▶*adj.* **1** *Genetics* relating to or denoting heritable characteristics controlled by genes that are expressed in offspring only when inherited from both parents, i.e., when not masked by a dominant characteristic inherited from one parent. Often contrasted with **DOMINANT.** **2** undergoing an economic recession: *the recessive housing market.* **3** *Phonetics* (of the stress on a word or phrase) tending to fall on the first syllable.
▶*n. Genetics* a recessive trait or gene. ▷late 17th cent.: from **RECESS**, on the pattern of *excessive.* —**re·ces·sive·ly** *adv.* —**re·ces·sive·ness** *n.* —**re·ces·siv·i·ty** /ˌrēˌses'ivətē/ *n.*

Rech·ab·ite /'rekəˌbīt/ ▶*n.* (in the Bible) a member of an Israelite family, descended from Rechab, who refused to drink wine or live in houses (Jer. 35).

re·charge ▶*v.* /rē'CHärj/ [*trans.*] restore an electric charge to (a battery or a battery-operated device) by connecting it to a device that draws power from another source of electricity: *he plugged his razor in to recharge it.* ■ [*intrans.*] (of a battery or battery-operated device) be refilled with electrical power in such a way: *the drill takes about three hours to recharge.* ■ refill (a container, lake, or aquifer) with water. ■ [*intrans.*] be refilled: *the rate at which the aquifer recharges naturally.* ■ [*intrans.*] *figurative* (of a person) return to a normal state of mind or strength after a period of physical or mental exertion: *she needs a bit of time to recharge after giving so much of herself this morning.*
▶*n.* /'rēCHärj/ the replenishment of an aquifer by the absorption of water. **—re·charge·a·ble** *adj.* **—re·charg·er** *n.*
▶*PHRASE* □ **recharge one's batteries** regain one's strength and energy by resting and relaxing for a time.

ré·chauf·fé /ˌrāˌSHō'fā -'SHōˌfā/ ▶*n.* a dish of warmed-up food left over from a previous meal. ▷French, literally 'reheated,' past participle of *réchauffer.*

re·check ▶*v.* /rē'CHek/ [*trans.*] check or verify again: *recheck all the wiring.*
▶*n.* an act of checking or verifying something again: *a recheck of the data.*

re·cher·ché /rəˌSHer'SHā; rə'SHerˌSHā/ ▶*adj.* rare, exotic, or obscure: *a few linguistic terms are perhaps a bit recherché for the average readership.* ▷French, literally 'carefully sought out,' past participle of *rechercher.*

re·chris·ten /rē'krisən/ ▶*v.* [*trans.*] give a new name to: *he rechristened Zaire the Democratic Republic of the Congo.*

re·cid·i·vist /ri'sidəvist/ ▶*n.* a convicted criminal who reoffends, esp. repeatedly.
▶*adj.* denoting such a person: *recidivist male prisoners | women are rarely recidivist.* ▷late 19th cent.: from French *récidiviste,* from *récidiver* 'fall back,' based on Latin *recidivus* 'falling back,' from the verb *recidere,* from *re-* 'back' + *cadere* 'to fall.' **—re·cid·i·vism** /-ˌvizəm/ *n.* **—re·cid·i·vis·tic** /riˌsidə'vistik/ *adj.*

Re·ci·fe /re'sēfā/ a port on the Atlantic coast of northeastern Brazil, capital of the state of Pernambuco; pop. 1,298,000. Former name **PERNAMBUCO**.

recip. ▶*abbr.* ■ reciprocal. ■ reciprocity.

rec·i·pe /'resəˌpē/ ▶*n.* a set of instructions for preparing a particular dish, including a list of the ingredients required: *a traditional Indonesian recipe.* ■ *figurative* something which is likely to lead to a particular outcome: *sky-high interest rates are* **a recipe for** *disaster.* ■ *archaic* a medical prescription. ▷late Middle English: from Latin, literally 'receive!' (first used as an instruction in medical prescriptions), imperative of *recipere.*

re·cip·i·ent /ri'sipēənt/ ▶*n.* a person or thing that receives or is awarded something: *the recipient of the Nobel Peace Prize.*
▶*adj.* [*attrib.*] receiving or capable or receiving something: *a recipient country.* ▷mid 16th cent.: from Latin *recipient-* 'receiving,' from the verb *recipere.* **—re·cip·i·en·cy** *n.*

re·cip·ro·cal /ri'siprəkəl/ ▶*adj.* **1** given, felt, or done in return: *she was hoping for some reciprocal comment or gesture.* **2** (of an agreement or obligation) bearing on or binding each of two parties equally: *the treaty is a bilateral commitment with reciprocal rights and duties.* ■ *Grammar* (of a pronoun or verb) expressing mutual action or relationship. **3** (of a course or bearing) differing from a given course or bearing by 180 degrees. **4** *Mathematics* (of a quantity or function) related to another so that their product is one.
▶*n.* **1** *technical* a mathematical expression or function so related to another that their product is one; the quantity obtained by dividing the number one by a given quantity. **2** *Grammar* a pronoun or verb expressing mutual action or relationship, e.g., *each other, fight.* ▷late 16th cent.: from Latin *reciprocus* (based on *re-* 'back' + *pro-* 'forward') + **-AL**. **—re·cip·ro·cal·i·ty** /riˌsiprə'kalətē/ *n.* **—re·cip·ro·cal·ly** /-ək(ə)lē/ *adv.*

re·cip·ro·cal cross ▶*n.* *Genetics* a pair of crosses between a male of one strain and a female of another, and vice versa.

re·cip·ro·cate /ri'siprəˌkāt/ ▶*v.* **1** [*trans.*] respond to (a gesture or action) by making a corresponding one: *the favor was reciprocated | [intrans.] perhaps I was expected to reciprocate with some remark of my own.* ■ experience the same (love, liking, or affection) for someone as that person does for oneself: *her passion for him was not reciprocated.* **2** [*intrans.*] [usu. as *adj.*] (**reciprocating**) (of a part of a machine) move backward and forward in a straight line: *a reciprocating blade.* ▷late 16th cent.: from Latin *reciprocat-* 'moved backwards and forwards' from the verb *reciprocare,* from *reciprocus* (see **RECIPROCAL**). **—re·cip·ro·ca·tion** /riˌsiprə'kāSHən/ *n.* **—re·cip·ro·ca·tor** /-ˌkātər/ *n.*

re·cip·ro·cat·ing en·gine ▶*n.* an engine in which one or more pistons move up and down in cylinders; a piston engine.

rec·i·proc·i·ty /ˌresə'präsətē/ ▶*n.* the practice of exchanging things with others for mutual benefit, esp. privileges granted by one country or organization to another. ▷mid 18th cent.: from French *réciprocité,* from *réciproque,* from Latin *reciprocus* 'moving backward and forward' (see **RECIPROCATE**).

rec·i·proc·i·ty fail·ure ▶*n.* *Photography* failure of an emulsion to follow the principle that the degree of darkening is constant for a given product of light intensity and exposure time, typically at very low or very high light intensities.

re·cit·al /ri'sītl/ ▶*n.* **1** the performance of a program of music by a solo instrumentalist or singer or by a small group: *a piano recital.* **2** an enumeration or listing of connected names, facts, or elements; *a recital of their misfortunes.* **3** (usu. **recitals**) *Law* the part of a legal document that explains the purpose of the deed and gives factual information. **—re·cit·al·ist** /-ist/ *n.*

rec·i·ta·tive /ˌres(ə)tə'tēv/ ▶*n.* musical declamation of the kind usual in the narrative and dialogue parts of opera and oratorio, sung in the rhythm of ordinary speech with many words on the same note: *singing in recitative.* ▷mid 17th cent.: from Italian *recitativo,* from Latin *recitare* 'to read out' (see **RECITE**).

rec·i·ta·ti·vo /ˌresətə'tēvō/ ▶*n.* (*pl.* **-vos**) another term for **RECITATIVE**. ▷Italian.

re·cite /ri'sīt/ ▶*v.* [*trans.*] repeat aloud or declaim (a poem or passage) from memory before an audience: *we provided our own entertainment by singing and reciting poetry.* ■ state (names, facts, etc.) in order: *she recited the dates and names of kings and queens.* ▷late Middle English (as a legal term in the sense 'state (a fact) in a document'): from Old French *reciter* or Latin *recitare* 'read out,' from *re-* (expressing intensive force) + *citare* 'cite.' **—rec·i·ta·tion** /ˌresi'tāSHən/ *n.* **—re·cit·er** *n.*

reck /rek/ ▶*v.* [*intrans.*] [with *negative* or in *questions*] *archaic* pay heed to something: *ye* **reck** *not* **of** *lands or goods* | [with *clause*] *little recking where she was wandering* | [*trans.*] *he recks not Syria, recks not Britain.* ■ (**it recks**) it is of importance: *what recks it?* ▷Old English, of Germanic origin; compare with **RECKLESS**. The word became common in rhetorical and poetic language in the 19th cent.

reck·less /'rekləs/ ▶*adj.* (of a person or their actions) without thinking or caring about the consequences of an action: *reckless driving.* ▷Old English *recceléas,* from the Germanic base (meaning 'care') of **RECK**. **—reck·less·ly** *adv.* **—reck·less·ness** *n.*

reck·on /'rekən/ ▶*v.* **1** [*trans.*] establish by counting or calculation; calculate: *his debts were* **reckoned at** *$300,000 | the Byzantine year was reckoned from September 1.* ■ (**reckon someone/something among**) include in (a class or group): *in high school and college he was always reckoned among the brainiest.* **2** [with *clause*] *informal* conclude after calculation; be of the opinion: *he reckons that the army should pull out entirely | I reckon I can manage that.* ■ [*trans.*] (often **be reckoned**) consider or regard in a specified way: *it was generally reckoned a failure.* **3** [*intrans.*] (**reckon on**) rely on or be sure of doing, having, or dealing with: *they had reckoned on a day or two more of privacy.* ■ [with *infinitive*] *informal* expect to do a particular thing: *I reckon to get away by two-thirty.*
▶*phrasal v.* □ **reckon with** (or **without**) **1** take (or fail to take) into account: *it must reckon with two great challenges.* **2** (**reckon with**) *archaic* settle accounts with. ▷Old English *(ge)recenian* 'recount, relate'; related to Dutch *rekenen* and German *rechnen* 'to count (up).' Early senses included 'give an account of items received' and 'mention things in order,' which gave rise to the notion of 'calculation' and hence of 'coming to a conclusion.'
▶*PHRASE* □ **a —— to be reckoned with** (or **to reckon with**) a thing or person of considerable importance or ability that is not to be ignored or underestimated: *the trade unions were a political force to be reckoned with.*

reck·on·er /'rekənər/ ▶*n.* a table or device designed to assist with calculation.

reck·on·ing /'rekəniNG/ ▶*n.* the action or process of calculating or estimating something: *last year was not, by any reckoning, a particularly good one | the system of time reckoning in Babylon.* ■ a person's view, opinion, or judgment: *by ancient reckoning, bacteria are plants.* ■ *archaic* a bill or account, or its settlement. ■ the avenging or punishing of past mistakes or misdeeds: *the fear of being brought to reckoning | there will be a terrible reckoning.*

re·claim /ri'klām/ ▶*v.* [*trans.*] **1** retrieve or recover (something previously lost, given, or paid); obtain the return of: *he returned three years later to reclaim his title as director of advertising | when Dennis emerged I reclaimed my room.* See note at **RECOVER**. ■ redeem (someone) from a state of vice; reform: *societies for reclaiming beggars and prostitutes.* ■ *archaic* tame or civilize (an animal or person). **2** bring (waste land or land formerly under water) under cultivation: *little money is available to reclaim and cultivate the desert* | [as *adj.*] (**reclaimed**) *reclaimed land.* ■ recover (material) for reuse; recycle: *a sufficient weight of plastic could easily be reclaimed.*
▶*n.* the action or process of reclaiming or being reclaimed: *beyond reclaim.* ▷Middle English (used in falconry in the sense 'recall'): from Old French *reclamer,* from Latin *reclamare* 'cry out against,' from *re-* 'back' + *clamare* 'to shout.' **—re·claim·a·ble** *adj.* **—re·claim·er** *n.* **—rec·la·ma·tion** /ˌreklə'māSHən/ *n.*

ré·clame /rā'kläm/ ▶*n.* public acclaim; notoriety. ■ a hunger for publicity or flair for getting attention.

re·clas·si·fy /rē'klasəˌfī/ ▶*v.* (**-fies, -fied**) [*trans.*] (often **be reclassified**) assign to a different class or category: *Hurricane Helene was reclassified as a bad storm.* **—re·clas·si·fi·ca·tion** /rēˌklasəfə'kāSHən/ *n.*

re·cline /ri'klīn/ ▶*v.* [*intrans.*] lean or lie back in a relaxed position with the back supported: *she was reclining in a deck chair* | [as *adj.*] (**reclining**) *a reclining figure.* ■ (of a seat) be able to have the back moved into a sloping position: *all the seats recline.* ■ [*trans.*] move the back of (a seat) into a sloping position. ▷late Middle English (in the sense 'cause to lean back'): from Old French *recliner* or Latin *reclinare* 'bend back, recline,' from *re-* 'back' + *clinare* 'to bend.' **—re·clin·a·ble** *adj.*

re·clin·er /ri'klīnər/ ▶*n.* an upholstered armchair that can be tilted backward, esp. one with a footrest that simultaneously extends from the front.

re·clothe /rē'klōTH/ ▶*v.* [*trans.*] dress again, esp. in different clothes: *she was ceremonially reclothed in a new robe.*

rec·luse /'rekˌlo͞os; ri'klo͞os; 'rekˌlo͞oz/ ▶*n.* a person who lives a solitary life and tends to avoid other people.
▶*adj.* *archaic* favoring a solitary life. ▷Middle English: from Old French *reclus,* past participle of *reclure,* from Latin *recludere* 'enclose,' from *re-* 'again' + *claudere* 'to shut.' **—re·clu·sion** /ri'klo͞oZHən/ *n.*

re·clu·sive /ri'klo͞osiv; -ziv/ ▶*adj.* avoiding the company of other people; solitary: *a reclusive life in rural Ireland.* **—re·clu·sive·ness** *n.*

re·code /rē'kōd/ ▶*v.* [*trans.*] put (something, esp. a computer program) into a different code. ■ assign a different code to.

rec·og·ni·tion /ˌrekig'niSHən/ ▶*n.* the action or process of recognizing or being recognized, in particular: ■ identification of a thing or person from previous encounters or knowledge: *she saw him pass by without a sign of recognition | methods of production have improved* **beyond all recognition.** ■ acknowledgment of something's existence, validity, or legality: *the unions must receive proper recognition.* ■ appreciation or acclaim for an achievement, service, or ability: *his work was slow to gain recognition | she received the award* **in recognition of** *her courageous human rights work.* ■ (also **dip·lo·mat·ic rec·og·ni·tion**) formal acknowledgment by a country that another political entity fulfills the conditions of statehood and is eligible to be dealt with as a member of the international community. ▷late 15th cent. (denoting the acknowledgment of a service): from Latin *recognitio(n-),* from the verb *recognoscere* 'know again, recall to mind' (see **RECOGNIZE**). **—re·cog·ni·to·ry** /ri'kägnəˌtôrē/ *adj.* (*rare*).

rec·og·niz·a·ble /ˌrekig'nīzəbəl/ ▶*adj.* able to be recognized or identified from previous encounters or knowledge. **—rec·og·niz·a·bil·i·ty** /-ˌnīzə'bilətē/ *n.* **—rec·og·niz·a·bly** /-blē/ *adv.*

re·cog·ni·zance /ri'kägnəzəns; -'känəzəns/ ▶*n.* *Law* a bond by which a person undertakes before a court or magistrate to observe some condition, esp. to appear when summoned: *he was released* **on his own recognizance.** ▷Middle English: from Old French *reconnissance,* from *reconnaistre* 'recognize.'

re·cog·ni·zant /ri'kägnəzənt; -'känəzənt/ ▶*adj.* [*predic.*]

(**recognizant of**) *formal* conscious or aware of (something, esp. a favor).

rec·og·nize /ˈrekigˌnīz; ˈrekə(g)ˌnīz/ ▸*v.* [*trans.*] **1** identify (someone or something) from having encountered them before; know again: *I recognized her when her wig fell off* | *Julia hardly recognized Jill when they met.* ■ identify from knowledge of appearance or character: *Pat is very good at recognizing wildflowers.* ■ (of a computer or other machine) automatically identify and respond correctly to (a sound, printed character, etc.). **2** acknowledge the existence, validity, or legality of: *the defense is recognized in Mexican law* | *he was* ***recognized as*** *an international authority* | [with *clause*] *it is important to recognize that a variety of indirect forms of discrimination operate.* ■ officially regard (a qualification) as valid or proper: *these qualifications are recognized by the Department of Education* | [as *adj.*] (**recognized**) *courses that lead to recognized qualifications.* ■ grant diplomatic recognition to (a country or government): *they were refusing to recognize the puppet regime.* ■ show official appreciation of; reward formally: *his work was recognized by an honorary degree from Georgetown University.* ■ (of a person presiding at a meeting or debate) call on (someone) to speak. ▷late Middle English (earliest attested as a term in Scots law): from Old French *reconniss-*, stem of *reconnaistre*, from Latin *recognoscere* 'know again, recall to mind,' from *re-* 'again' + *cognoscere* 'learn.' —**rec·og·niz·er** *n.*

re·coil ▸*v.* /riˈkoil/ [*intrans.*] suddenly spring or flinch back in fear, horror, or disgust: *he recoiled in horror.* See note at WINCE. ■ feel fear, horror, or disgust at the thought or prospect of something; shrink mentally: *Renee felt herself recoil at the very thought.* ■ (of a gun) move abruptly backward as a reaction on firing a bullet, shell, or other missile. ■ rebound or spring back through force of impact or elasticity: *the muscle has the ability to recoil.* ■ (**recoil on/upon**) (of an action) have an adverse reactive effect on (the originator): *the soothsayers agreed that all the dangers would recoil on the heads of those who were in possession of the entrails.*

▸*n.* /ˈrēˌkoil; riˈkoil/ the action of recoiling: *his body jerked with the recoil of the rifle.* ▷Middle English (denoting the act of retreating): from Old French *reculer* 'move back,' based on Latin *culus* 'buttocks.'

rec·ol·lect /ˌrekəˈlekt/ ▸*v.* [*trans.*] remember (something); call to mind: *he could not quite recollect the reason* | [with *clause*] *can you recollect how your brother reacted?* ▷early 16th cent. (in the sense 'gather'): from Latin *recollect-* 'gathered back,' from the verb *recolligere*, from *re-* 'back' + *colligere* 'collect.'

re-col·lect /ˌrēkəˈlekt/ ▸*v.* [*trans.*] collect or gather again: *after re-collecting our apples for the second time, Bruno brought us a couple of nice sturdy sacks.* ▷early 17th cent.: later form of RECOLLECT, from RE- 'once more' + the verb COLLECT[1].

rec·ol·lec·tion /ˌrekəˈlekSHən/ ▸*n.* the action or faculty of remembering something: ***to the best of my recollection*** *no one ever had a bad word to say about him.* ■ a thing recollected; a memory: *a biography based on his wife's recollections.* ■ *Philosophy* (in Platonic thought) anamnesis. ▷late 16th cent. (denoting gathering things together again): from French or medieval Latin *recollectio(n-)*, from the verb *recolligere* 'gather again' (see RECOLLECT). —**rec·ol·lec·tive** /-tiv/ *adj.*

Rec·ol·let /ˌrākôˈlā; ˌrekəˈlet/ (also **Rec·ol·lect** /ˈrekəlekt/) ▸*n. historical* a member of a reformed branch of the Franciscan order, founded in France in the late 16th century. ▷from French *récollet*, from medieval Latin *recollectus* 'gathered together,' expressing a notion of concentration, and absorption in thought.

re·col·o·nize /rēˈkäləˌnīz/ ▸*v.* [*trans.*] (chiefly of a plant or animal species) colonize (a region or habitat) again. —**re·col·o·ni·za·tion** /ˌrēˌkälənəˈzāSHən/ *n.*

re·col·or /rēˈkələr/ (*Brit.* **re·col·our**) ▸*v.* [*trans.*] color again or differently.

re·com·bi·nant /rēˈkämbənənt; ri-/ *Genetics* ▸*adj.* [*attrib.*] of, relating to, or denoting an organism, cell, or genetic material formed by recombination.

▸*n.* a recombinant organism, cell, or piece of genetic material.

re·com·bi·nant DNA ▸*n.* DNA that has been formed artificially by combining constituents from different organisms.

re·com·bi·nase /riˈkämbəˌnās; -ˌnāz/ ▸*n. Biochemistry* an enzyme that promotes genetic recombination.

re·com·bi·na·tion /rēˌkämbəˈnāSHən/ ▸*n.* the process of recombining things. ■ *Genetics* the rearrangement of genetic material, esp. by crossing over in chromosomes or by the artificial joining of segments of DNA from different organisms.

re·com·bine /ˌrēkəmˈbīn/ ▸*v.* combine or cause to combine again or differently: [*intrans.*] *carbohydrates can recombine with oxygen* | [*trans.*] *decompose the calculation into components and recombine them to find the solution.*

rec·om·mend /ˌrekəˈmend/ ▸*v.* [*trans.*] **1** put forward (someone or something) with approval as being suitable for a particular purpose or role: *George had recommended some local architects* | *a book I* ***recommended to*** *a friend of mine.* ■ advise or suggest (something) as a course of action: *some doctors recommend putting a board under the mattress* | [with *clause*] *the report recommended that criminal charges be brought.* ■ [*trans.*] advise (someone) to do something: *you are strongly recommended to seek professional advice.* ■ make (someone or something) appealing or desirable: *the house had much to recommend it.* **2** (**recommend someone/something to**) *archaic* commend or entrust someone or something to (someone): *I devoutly recommended my spirit to its maker.* ▷late Middle English (sense 2): from medieval Latin *recommendare*, from Latin *re-* (expressing intensive force) + *commendare* 'commit to the care of.' —**rec·om·mend·a·ble** *adj.* —**rec·om·men·da·tion** /ˌrekəmənˈdāSHən; -ˌmen-/ *n.* —**rec·om·mend·a·to·ry** /-ˈmendəˌtôrē/ *adj.* —**rec·om·mend·er** *n.*

re·com·mit /ˌrēkəˈmit/ ▸*v.* (**-mit·ted**, **-mit·ting**) [*trans.*] commit again. ■ return (a motion, proposal, or legislative bill) to a committee for further consideration. —**re·com·mit·ment** *n.* —**re·com·mit·tal** /-ˈmitl/ *n.*

rec·om·pense /ˈrekəmˌpens/ ▸*v.* [*trans.*] make amends to (someone) for loss or harm suffered; compensate: *offenders should recompense their victims* | *he was recompensed for the wasted time.* ■ pay or reward (someone) for effort or work: *he was handsomely recompensed.* ■ make amends to or reward someone for (loss, harm, or effort): *he thought his loyalty had been inadequately recompensed.* ■ *archaic* punish or reward (someone) appropriately for an action: *according to their doings will he recompense them.*

▸*n.* compensation or reward given for loss or harm suffered or effort made: *substantial damages were paid* ***in recompense.*** ■ *archaic* restitution made or punishment inflicted for a wrong or injury. ▷late Middle English: from Old French, from the verb *recompenser* 'do a favor to requite a loss,' from late Latin *recompensare*, from Latin *re-* 'again' (also expressing intensive force) + *compensare* 'weigh one thing against another.'

re·com·pile /ˌrēkəmˈpīl/ *Computing* ▸*v.* [*trans.*] compile (a program) again or differently.

▸*n.* a recompilation of a computer program. —**re·com·pi·la·tion** /ˌrēkämpəˈlāSHən/ *n.*

re·com·pose /ˌrēkəmˈpōz/ ▸*v.* [*trans.*] compose again or differently: *a marble panel recomposed from fragments.* —**re·com·po·si·tion** /ˌrēˌkämpəˈziSHən/ *n.*

re·con *informal* ▸*n.* /ˈrēˌkän; riˈkän/ short for RECONNAISSANCE.

▸*v.* /riˈkän/ (**-conned**, **-con·ning**) short for RECONNOITER.

rec·on·cile /ˈrekənˌsīl/ ▸*v.* [*trans.*] (often **be reconciled**) restore friendly relations between: *she wanted to be* ***reconciled with*** *her father* | *the news reconciled us.* ■ cause to coexist in harmony; make or show to be compatible: *a landscape in which inner and outer vision were reconciled* | *you may have to adjust your ideal to* ***reconcile it with*** *reality.* ■ make (one account) consistent with another, esp. by allowing for transactions begun but not yet completed: *it is not necessary to reconcile the cost accounts to the financial accounts.* ■ settle (a disagreement): *advice on how to reconcile the conflict.* ■ (**reconcile someone to**) make someone accept (a disagreeable or unwelcome thing): *he could not reconcile himself to the thought of his mother stocking shelves* | *he was reconciled to leaving.* ▷late Middle English: from Old French *reconcilier* or Latin *reconciliare*, from Latin *re-* 'back' (also expressing intensive force) + *conciliare* 'bring together.' —**rec·on·cil·a·bil·i·ty** /ˌrekənˌsīləˈbilətē/ *n.* —**rec·on·cil·a·ble** /ˌrekənˈsīləbəl/ *adj.* —**rec·on·cile·ment** *n.* —**rec·on·cil·er** *n.* —**rec·on·cil·i·a·tion** /ˌrekənˌsilēˈāSHən/ *n.* —**rec·on·cil·i·a·to·ry** /ˌrekənˈsilēəˌtôrē/ *adj.*

rec·on·dite /ˈrekənˌdīt; riˈkän-/ ▸*adj.* (of a subject or knowledge) little known; abstruse: *the book is full of recondite information.* See note at OBSCURE. ▷mid 17th cent.: from Latin *reconditus* 'hidden, put away,' past participle of *recondere*, from *re-* 'back' + *condere* 'put together, secrete.'

re·con·di·tion /ˌrēkənˈdiSHən/ ▸*v.* [*trans.*] condition again. ■ overhaul or renovate (a vehicle engine or piece of equipment): *a ship was being reconditioned* | [as *adj.*] (**reconditioned**) *a reconditioned engine.*

re·con·fig·ure /ˌrēkənˈfigyər/ ▸*v.* [*trans.*] configure (something) differently: *you don't have to reconfigure the modem each time you make a connection.* —**re·con·fig·ur·a·ble** *adj.* —**re·con·fig·u·ra·tion** /ˌrēkənˌfigyəˈrāSHən/ *n.*

re·con·nais·sance /riˈkänəzəns; -səns/ ▸*n.* military observation of a region to locate an enemy or ascertain strategic features: *an excellent aircraft for low-level reconnaissance* | *after a reconnaissance our forces took the island* | [as *adj.*] *reconnaissance missions.* ■ preliminary surveying or research: *conducting client reconnaissance.* ▷early 19th cent.: from French, from *reconnaître* 'recognize' (see RECONNOITER).

re·con·nect /ˌrēkəˈnekt/ ▸*v.* [*trans.*] connect back together: *surgeons had to reconnect tendons, nerves, and veins.* ■ [*intrans.*] reestablish a bond of communication or emotion: *in order to keep your marriage healthy, it is important to reconnect as mature individuals.* —**re·con·nec·tion** /ˌrēkəˈnekSHən/ *n.*

re·con·noi·ter /ˌrēkəˈnoitər; ˌrek-/ (*Brit.* **re·con·noi·tre**) ▸*v.* [*trans.*] make a military observation of (a region): *they reconnoitered the beach some weeks before the landing* | [*intrans.*] *the raiders were reconnoitering for further attacks.*

▸*n. informal* an act of reconnoitering: *a nocturnal reconnoiter of the camp.* ▷early 18th cent.: from obsolete French *reconnoître*, from Latin *recognoscere* 'know again' (see RECOGNIZE).

re·con·sid·er /ˌrēkənˈsidər/ ▸*v.* [*trans.*] consider (something) again, esp. for a possible change of decision regarding it: *they called on the government to reconsider its policy* | [*intrans.*] *I beg you to reconsider.* —**re·con·sid·er·a·tion** /ˌrēkənˌsidəˈrāSHən/ *n.*

re·con·sign /ˌrēkənˈsīn/ ▸*v.* [*trans.*] consign again or differently. —**re·con·sign·ment** *n.*

re·con·sti·tute /rēˈkänstəˌt(y)o͞ot/ ▸*v.* [*trans.*] build up again from parts; reconstruct. ■ change the form and organization of (an institution): *he reconstituted his cabinet.* ■ restore (something dried, esp. food) to its original state by adding water to it: [as *adj.*] (**reconstituted**) *reconstituted milk.* —**re·con·sti·tu·tion** /ˌrēˌkänstəˈt(y)o͞oSHən/ *n.*

re·con·struct /ˌrēkənˈstrəkt/ ▸*v.* [*trans.*] build or form (something) again after it has been damaged or destroyed: *a small area of painted Roman plaster has been reconstructed.* ■ reorganize (something): *later emperors reconstructed the army.* ■ form an impression, model, or reenactment of (a past event or thing) from the available evidence: *from copies of correspondence it is possible to reconstruct the broad sequence of events.* ■ reenact (a crime or other incident) with the aim of discovering the culprit or cause: *reconstructing the last walk of murdered Tracey.* —**re·con·struct·a·ble** (also **re·con·struct·i·ble**) *adj.* —**re·con·struc·tive** /-tiv/ *adj.* —**re·con·struc·tor** /-tər/ *n.*

re·con·struc·tion /ˌrēkənˈstrəkSHən/ ▸*n.* the action or process of reconstructing or being reconstructed: *the economic reconstruction of Russia* | [as *adj.*] *reconstruction work.* ■ a thing that has been rebuilt after being damaged or destroyed: *comparison between the original and the reconstruction.* ■ an impression, model, or reenactment of a past event formed from the available evidence: *a reconstruction of the accident would be staged to try to discover the cause of the tragedy.* ■ (**Reconstruction**) the period 1865–77 following the Civil War, during which the states of the Confederacy were controlled by federal government and social legislation, including the granting of new rights to African-Americans, was introduced.

re·con·vene /ˌrēkənˈvēn/ ▸*v.* convene or cause to convene again, esp. after a pause in proceedings: [*intrans.*] *as soon as the Senate reconvenes next month* | [*trans.*] *it was agreed to reconvene the permanent commission.*

re·con·vert /ˌrēkənˈvərt/ ▸*v.* [*trans.*] convert back to a former state: *she reconverted the basement back into an apartment.* —**re·con·ver·sion** /-ˈvərZHən/ *n.*

rec·ord ▸*n.* /ˈrekərd/ **1** a thing constituting a piece of evidence about the past, esp. an account of an act or occurrence kept in writing or some other permanent form: *identification was made through dental records* | *a record of meter readings.* ■ (also **court record**) *Law* an official report of the proceedings and judgment in a court. ■ *Computing* a number of related items of information that are handled as a unit.

Pronunciation Key ə **ago**; ər **over**; ˈə or ˌə **up**; ˈər or ˌər **fur**; a **hat**; ā **rate**; ä **car**; CH **chew**; e **let**; ē **see**; e(ə)r **air**; i **fit**; ī **by**; i(ə)r **ear**; NG **sing**; ō **go**; ô **for**; oi **boy**; o͝o **good**; o͞o **goo**; ou **out**; SH **she**; TH **thin**; T͟H **then**; (h)w **why**; ZH **vision**

2 the sum of the past achievements or actions of a person or organization; a person or thing's previous conduct or performance: *the safety record at the airport | the team preserved its unbeaten home record.* ■ short for CRIMINAL RECORD. **3** (esp. in sports) the best performance or most remarkable event of its kind that has been officially measured and noted: *he held the world record for over a decade | he managed to beat the record |* [as *adj.*] *record profits.* **4** a thin plastic disk carrying recorded sound, esp. music, in grooves on each surface, for reproduction by a record player. ■ a piece or collection of music reproduced on such a disk or on another medium, such as compact disc: *my favorite record |* [as *adj.*] *a record company.*

▸*v.* **re·cord** /ri'kôrd/ [*trans.*] **1** set down in writing or some other permanent form for later reference, esp. officially: *they were asked to keep a diary and record everything they ate or drank |* [as *adj.*] (**recorded**) *levels of recorded crime.* ■ state or express publicly or officially; make an official record of: *the coroner recorded a verdict of accidental death.* ■ (of an instrument or observer) show or register (a measurement or result): *the temperature was the lowest recorded since 1926.* ■ achieve (a certain score or result): *they recorded their first win of the season.* **2** convert (sound or a broadcast) into permanent form for later reproduction: *they were recording a guitar recital.* ■ produce (a piece or collection of music or a program) by such means: *they go into the studio next week to record their debut album.* ▷Middle English: from Old French *record* 'remembrance,' from *recorder* 'bring to remembrance,' from Latin *recordari* 'remember,' based on *cor, cord-* 'heart.' The noun was earliest used in law to denote the fact of being written down as evidence. The verb originally meant 'narrate orally or in writing,' also 'repeat so as to commit to memory.' **—re·cord·a·ble** /rə'kôrdəbəl; rē-/ *adj.*

▸*PHRASES* □ **for the record** so that the true facts are recorded or known: *for the record, I have never been to the apartment.* □ **a matter of record** a thing that is established as a fact through being officially recorded. □ **off the record** not made as an official or attributable statement. □ **on record 1** (also **on the record**) used in reference to the making of an official or public statement: *he seems shadowy because he rarely speaks on the record.* **2** officially measured and noted: *it proved to be one of the warmest Decembers on record.* **3** recorded on tape and reproduced on a record or another sound medium: *the material works far better live than on record.* □ **set** (or **put**) **the record straight** give the true version of events that have been reported incorrectly; correct a misapprehension.

rec·ord-break·ing ▸*adj.* surpassing a record or best-ever achievement: *the fair attracted a record-breaking 10,678 visitors.* **—rec·ord-break·er** *n.*

rec·ord club ▸*n.* an organization that sells selected audio recordings to members or subscribers, often from a mail-order catalog or online.

re·cord·ed de·liv·er·y ▸*n.* British term for CERTIFIED MAIL.

re·cord·er /ri'kôrdər/ ▸*n.* **1** an apparatus for recording sound, pictures, or data, esp. a tape recorder. **2** a person who keeps records: *a poet and recorder of rural and industrial life.* **3** a simple woodwind instrument with finger holes and no keys, held vertically and played by blowing air through a shaped mouthpiece against a sharp edge. **4** (**Recorder**) (in England and Wales) a barrister appointed to serve as a part-time judge. ■ *Brit., historical* a judge in certain courts. ▷late Middle English (denoting a kind of judge): from Anglo-Norman French *recordour,* from Old French *recorder* 'bring to remembrance'; partly reinforced by the verb RECORD (also used in the obsolete sense 'practice a tune': see sense 3). **—re·cord·er·ship** /-,SHip/ *n.* (in sense 4).

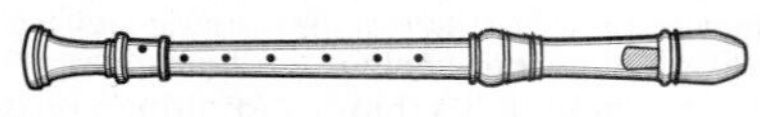

recorder 3

re·cord·ing /ri'kôrdiNG/ ▸*n.* a recorded sound or picture. ■ a tape or disc on which sounds or visual images have been recorded.

re·cord·ist /ri'kôrdist/ ▸*n.* a person who makes recordings, esp. of sound: *a sound recordist.*

rec·ord play·er ▸*n.* an apparatus for reproducing sound from phonograph records, comprising a turntable that spins the record at a constant speed and a stylus that slides along in the groove and picks up the sound, together with an amplifier and a loudspeaker.

rec·ord·set /'rekərd,set/ ▸*n. Computing* a set of records in a database that share an identifiable or isolatable characteristic.

re·count[1] /ri'kount/ ▸*v.* [*reporting verb*] tell someone about something; give an account of an event or experience: [*trans.*] *I recounted the tale to Steve |* [with *clause*] *he recounts how they often talked of politics.*

▸*n.* an act or instance of giving an account of an event or experience: *one woman's recount of a prolonged battle with "huge centipedes."* ▷late Middle English: from Old Northern French *reconter* 'tell again,' based on Old French *counter* (see COUNT[1]).

re·count[2] ▸*v.* /rē'kount; 'rē-/ [*trans.*] count again.

▸*n.* /'rē,kount/ an act of counting something again, esp. votes in an election.

re·coup /ri'ko͞op/ ▸*v.* [*trans.*] regain (something lost): *rains have helped recoup water levels.* See note at RECOVER. ■ regain (money spent or lost), esp. through subsequent profits: *oil companies are keen to recoup their investment.* ■ reimburse or compensate (someone) for money spent or lost. ■ *Law* deduct or keep back (part of a sum due). ■ regain (lost physical or mental resources): *sleep was what she needed to recoup her strength |* [*intrans.*] *he's just resting, recouping from the trial.* ▷early 17th cent. (as a legal term): from French *recouper* 'retrench, cut back,' from *re-* 'back' + *couper* 'to cut.' **—re·coup·a·ble** *adj.* **—re·coup·ment** *n.*

re·course /'rē,kôrs; ri'kôrs/ ▸*n.* [in *sing.*] a source of help in a difficult situation: *surgery may be the only recourse.* ■ (**recourse to**) the use of someone or something as a source of help in a difficult situation: *a means of solving disputes* **without recourse to** *courts of law | all three countries* **had recourse to** *the IMF for standby loans.* ■ the legal right to demand compensation or payment: *the bank* **has recourse against** *the exporter for losses incurred.* ▷late Middle English (also in the sense 'running or flowing back'): from Old French *recours,* from Latin *recursus,* from *re-* 'back, again' + *cursus* 'course, running.'

▸*PHRASE* □ **without recourse** *Finance* a formula used to disclaim responsibility for future nonpayment, esp. of a negotiable financial instrument.

re·cov·er /ri'kəvər/ ▸*v.* **1** [*intrans.*] return to a normal state of health, mind, or strength: *Neil is still* **recovering from** *shock | the economy has begun to recover.* ■ (**be recovered**) (of a person) be well again: *you'll be fully recovered before you know it.* **2** [*trans.*] find or regain possession of (something stolen or lost): *police recovered a stolen video.* ■ regain control of (oneself or of a physical or mental state): *he recovered his balance and sped on | one hour later I had recovered consciousness.* ■ regain or secure (compensation) by means of a legal process or subsequent profits: *many companies recovered their costs within six months.* ■ make up for (a loss in position or time): *the French recovered the lead.* ■ remove or extract (an energy source or industrial chemical) for use, reuse, or waste treatment.

▸*n.* (**the recover**) a defined position of a firearm forming part of a military drill: *bring the firelock* **to the recover.** ▷Middle English (originally with reference to health): from Anglo-Norman French *recoverer,* from Latin *recuperare* 'get again.' **—re·cov·er·er** *n.*

THE RIGHT WORD reclaim, recoup, recover, regain, restore, retrieve

If you lose or let go of something and find it either by chance or with effort, you **recover** it (*recover the stolen artwork*).

Although it is often used interchangeably with *recover,* **regain** puts more emphasis on the search or effort involved in getting back something you have been deprived of (*regain one's position as chairperson; regain one's eyesight*).

Recoup refers to the recovery of something similar or equivalent to what has been lost, usually in the form of compensation (*he tried to recoup his gambling losses*).

Reclaim and **restore** both involve bringing something back to its original condition or to a better or more useful state. *Reclaim* is usually associated with land (*reclaim neglected farmlands*), while *restore* is linked to buildings or objects of art (*restore an eighteenth-century house*).

Retrieve implies that something has slipped beyond reach, and that a concerted effort or search is required to recover it (*her desperate efforts to retrieve the family dog from the flooded house*).

re-cov·er /rē 'kəvər; 'rē-/ ▸*v.* [*trans.*] put a new cover or covering on: *the cost of re-covering the armchair.*

re·cov·er·a·ble /ri'kəvərəbəl/ ▸*adj.* **1** (of something lost) able to be regained or retrieved. ■ (of compensation or money spent or lost) able to be regained or secured by means of a legal process or subsequent profits. **2** (of an energy source or a supply of it) able to be economically extracted from the ground or sea. **—re·cov·er·a·bil·i·ty** /-,kəvərə'bilətē/ *n.*

re·cov·er·y /ri'kəvərē/ ▸*n.* (*pl.* **-er·ies**) **1** a return to a normal state of health, mind, or strength: *signs of recovery in the housing market | he's back at home now and he looks all set to* **make a full recovery.** **2** the action or process of regaining possession or control of something stolen or lost: *a team of salvage experts to ensure the recovery of family possessions | the recovery of his sight.* ■ the action of regaining or securing compensation or money lost or spent by means of a legal process or subsequent profits: *debt recovery.* ■ an object or amount of money recovered: *the recoveries included gold jewelry.* ■ the process of removing or extracting an energy source or industrial chemical for use, reuse, or waste treatment. ■ (also **re·cov·er·y shot**) *Golf* a stroke bringing the ball from the rough or from a hazard back on to the fairway or the green. ■ *Football* an act of taking possession of a fumbled ball. ■ (in rowing, cycling, or swimming) the action of returning the paddle, leg, or arm to its initial position ready to make a new stroke. ▷late Middle English (denoting a means of restoration): from Anglo-Norman French *recoverie,* from *recovrer* 'get back.'

▸*PHRASE* □ **in recovery** in the process of recovering from mental illness, drug addiction, or past abuse: *support groups for parents whose children are in recovery.*

re·cov·er·y stock ▸*n. Finance* a stock that has fallen in price but is thought to have the potential of climbing back to its original level.

re·cov·er·y time ▸*n.* the time required for someone to regain their health after an illness. ■ the time required for a material or piece of equipment to resume its former or usual condition following an action, such as the passage of a current through electrical equipment.

rec·re·ant /'rekrēənt/ *archaic* ▸*adj.* **1** cowardly: *what a recreant figure must he make.* **2** unfaithful to a belief; apostate.

▸*n.* **1** a coward. **2** a person who is unfaithful to a belief; an apostate. ▷Middle English: from Old French, literally 'surrendering,' present participle of *recroire,* from medieval Latin *(se) recredere* 'surrender (oneself),' from *re-* (expressing reversal) + *credere* 'entrust.' **—rec·re·an·cy** /-ənsē/ *n.* **—rec·re·ant·ly** *adv.*

re·cre·ate /,rēkrē'āt/ (also **re-cre·ate**) ▸*v.* [*trans.*] create again: *the door was now open to recreate a single German state.* ■ reproduce; reenact: *he recreated Mallory's 1942 climb for TV.*

rec·re·a·tion[1] /,rekrē'āSHən/ ▸*n.* activity done for enjoyment when one is not working: *areas used for recreation such as hiking or biking |* [as *adj.*] *athletic and recreation facilities.* ▷late Middle English (also in the sense 'mental or spiritual consolation'): via Old French from Latin *recreatio(n-),* from *recreare* 'create again, renew.'

rec·re·a·tion[2] /',rēkrē'āSHən/ (also **re-cre·a·tion**) ▸*n.* the action or process of creating something again: *the periodic destruction and recreation of the universe.* ■ a reenactment or simulation of something. ▷early 16th cent.: from RE- 'again' + CREATION.

rec·re·a·tion·al /,rekrē'āSHənl/ ▸*adj.* relating to or denoting activity done for enjoyment when one is not working: *recreational facilities | recreational cycling in the countryside.* ■ relating to or denoting drugs taken on an occasional basis for enjoyment, esp. when socializing: *recreational drug use.* **—rec·re·a·tion·al·ly** *adv.*

rec·re·a·tion room ▸*n.* a room in an institution or place of work in which people can relax and play games. ■ chiefly dated term for REC ROOM.

rec·re·a·tive /'rekrē,ātiv/ ▸*adj.* another term for RECREATIONAL.

re·crim·i·nate /ri'krimə,nāt/ ▸*v.* [*intrans.*] *archaic* make counteraccusations: *his party would never recriminate, never return evil for evil.* ▷early 17th cent.: from medieval Latin *recriminat-* 'accused in return,' from the verb *recriminari,* from *re-* (expressing opposition) + *criminare* 'accuse' (from *crimen* 'crime').

re·crim·i·na·tion /ri,krimə'nāSHən/ ▸*n.* (usu. **recriminations**) an accusation in response to one from someone else: *there are no tears, no recriminations | there was a period of bitter recrimination.*

re·crim·i·na·tive /ri'krimə,nātiv/ ▸*adj.* archaic term for RECRIMINATORY.

re·crim·i·na·to·ry /ri'krimənə,tôrē/ ▸*adj.* involving or of the nature of mutual accusations or counteraccusations.

rec room (also *chiefly dated* **rec·re·a·tion room**) ▸*n.* a room in a house, esp. in the basement, used for recreation and entertainment.

re·cross /ˌrēˈkrôs/ ▸*v.* [*trans.*] cross or pass over again.

re·cru·desce /ˌrēkro͞oˈdes/ ▸*v.* [*intrans.*] *formal* break out again; recur. ▷late 19th cent.: back-formation from *recrudescence* 'recurrence,' from Latin *recrudescere* 'become raw again,' from *re-* 'again' + *crudus* 'raw.' **—re·cru·des·cence** /-ˈdesns/ *n.* **—re·cru·des·cent** /-ˈdesənt/ *adj.*

re·cruit /riˈkro͞ot/ ▸*v.* [*trans.*] enlist (someone) in the armed forces: *they recruit their toughest soldiers from the desert tribes* | [*intrans.*] *the regiment was still actively recruiting.* ■ form (an army or other force) by enlisting new people: *a basis for recruiting an army.* ■ enroll (someone) as a member or worker in an organization or as a supporter of a cause: *there are plans to recruit more staff later this year.* ■ [*trans.*] *informal* persuade (someone) to do or assist in doing something: *she recruited her children to help run the racket.*

▸*n.* a person newly enlisted in the armed forces and not yet fully trained: *3,000 army recruits at Ft. Benjamin.* ■ a new member of an organization or a new supporter of a cause: *after agreeing on a salary, the new recruit failed to turn up on Monday morning.* ▷mid 17th cent. (in the senses 'fresh body of troops' and 'supplement the numbers in (a group)'): from obsolete French dialect *recrute*, based on Latin *recrescere* 'grow again,' from *re-* 'again' + *crescere* 'grow.' **—re·cruit·a·ble** *adj.* **—re·cruit·er** *n.*

re·cruit·ment /riˈkro͞otmənt/ ▸*n.* the action of enlisting new people in the armed forces. ■ the action of finding new people to join an organization or support a cause: *the recruitment of nurses.* ■ *Ecology* the increase in a natural population as progeny grow and immigrants arrive. ■ *Physiology* the incorporation into a tissue or region of cells from elsewhere in the body.

rec. sec. (also **Rec. Sec.**) ▸*abbr.* recording secretary.

rect. ▸*abbr.* ■ receipt. ■ rectangle. ■ rectangular. ■ (in prescriptions) rectified. [from Latin *rectificatus.*] ■ rector. ■ rectory.

rec·ta /ˈrektə/ ▸ plural form of RECTUM.

rec·tal /ˈrektəl/ ▸*adj.* [*attrib.*] of, relating to, or affecting the rectum: *rectal cancer.* **—rec·tal·ly** *adv.*

rec·tan·gle /ˈrekˌtaNGgəl/ ▸*n.* a plane figure with four straight sides and four right angles, esp. one with unequal adjacent sides, in contrast to a square. ▷late 16th cent.: from medieval Latin *rectangulum*, from late Latin *rectiangulum*, based on Latin *rectus* 'straight' + *angulus* 'an angle.'

rec·tan·gu·lar /rekˈtaNGgyələr/ ▸*adj.* **1** denoting or shaped like a rectangle: *a neat rectangular area.* ■ (of a solid) having a base, section, or side shaped like a rectangle: *a rectangular prism.* **2** placed or having parts placed at right angles. **—rec·tan·gu·lar·i·ty** /rekˌtaNGgyəˈlaritē/ *n.* **—rec·tan·gu·lar·ly** *adv.*

rec·tan·gu·lar co·or·di·nates ▸*plural n.* a pair of coordinates measured along axes at right angles to one another.

rec·tan·gu·lar hy·per·bo·la ▸*n.* a hyperbola with rectangular asymptotes.

rec·ti /ˈrekˌtī; -ˌtē/ ▸ plural form of RECTUS.

rec·ti·fi·er /ˈrektəˌfīər/ ▸*n.* an electrical device that converts an alternating current into a direct one by allowing a current to flow through it in one direction only.

rec·ti·fy /ˈrektəˌfī/ ▸*v.* (**-fies, -fied**) [*trans.*] **1** put (something) right; correct: *mistakes made now cannot be rectified later* | *efforts to rectify the situation.* ■ [usu. as *adj.*] (**rectified**) purify or refine (a substance), esp. by repeated distillation: *add 10 cc of rectified alcohol.* **2** convert (alternating current) to direct current: [as *adj.*] (**rectified**) *rectified AC power systems.* **3** find a straight line equal in length to (a curve). ▷late Middle English: from Old French *rectifier*, from medieval Latin *rectificare*, from Latin *rectus* 'right.' **—rec·ti·fi·a·ble** *adj.* **—rec·ti·fi·ca·tion** /ˌrektəfiˈkāSHən/ *n.*

rec·ti·lin·e·ar /ˌrektəˈlinēər/ (also **rec·ti·lin·e·al** /-ēəl/) ▸*adj.* contained by, consisting of, or moving in a straight line or lines: *a rectilinear waveform.* ■ *Photography* of or relating to a straight line or lines: *rectilinear distortion.* ■ *Photography* (of a wide-angle lens) corrected as much as possible, so that straight lines in the subject appear straight in the image. ▷mid 17th cent.: from late Latin *rectilineus* (from Latin *rectus* 'straight' + *linea* 'line') + -AR[1]. **—rec·ti·lin·e·ar·i·ty** /-ˌlinēˈaritē/ *n.* **—rec·ti·lin·e·ar·ly** *adv.*

rec·ti·tude /ˈrektəˌt(y)o͞od/ ▸*n.* *formal* morally correct behavior or thinking; righteousness: *Maddie is a model of rectitude.* See note at GOODNESS. ▷late Middle English (denoting straightness): from Old French, from late Latin *rectitudo*, from Latin *rectus* 'right, straight.'

rec·to /ˈrektō/ ▸*n.* (*pl.* **-tos**) a right-hand page of an open book, or the front of a loose document. Contrasted with VERSO. ▷early 19th cent.: from Latin *recto (folio)* 'on the right (leaf).'

rec·to·cele /ˈrektəˌsēl/ ▸*n.* *Medicine* a prolapse of the wall between the rectum and the vagina. ▷mid 19th cent.: from RECTUM + -CELE.

rec·tor /ˈrektər/ ▸*n.* **1** (in the Episcopal Church) a member of the clergy who has charge of a parish. ■ (in the Roman Catholic Church) a priest in charge of a church or of a religious institution. ■ (in the Church of England) the incumbent of a parish where all tithes formerly passed to the incumbent. Compare with VICAR. **2** the head of certain universities, colleges, and schools. ▷late Middle English: from Latin *rector* 'ruler,' from *rect-* 'ruled,' from the verb *regere*. **—rec·tor·ate** /-rət/ *n.* **—rec·to·ri·al** /rekˈtôrēəl/ *adj.* **—rec·tor·ship** /-ˌSHip/ *n.*

rec·to·ry /ˈrektərē/ ▸*n.* (*pl.* **-ries**) a rector's house. ■ a Church of England benefice held by a rector. ▷mid 16th cent.: from Old French *rectorie* or medieval Latin *rectoria*, from Latin *rector* (see RECTOR).

rec·trix /ˈrekˌtriks/ ▸ *n.* (*pl.* **-tri·ces** /-ˌtrəsēz/) *Ornithology* any of the larger feathers in a bird's tail, used for steering in flight. Compare with REMEX. ▷mid 18th cent.: from Latin, feminine singular of *rector* 'ruler, governor' (see RECTOR).

rec·tum /ˈrektəm/ ▸*n.* (*pl.* **-tums** or **-ta** /-tə/) the final section of the large intestine, terminating at the anus. ▷mid 16th cent.: from Latin *rectum (intestinum)* 'straight (intestine).'

rec·tus /ˈrektəs/ ▸*n.* (*pl.* **-ti** /-tī/) *Anatomy* any of several straight structures, in particular: ■ (also **rec·tus ab·dom·i·nis** /abˈdämənis/) each of a pair of long flat muscles at the front of the abdomen, joining the sternum to the pubis and acting to bend the whole body forward or sideways. ■ any of a number of muscles controlling the movement of the eyeball. ▷early 18th cent.: from Latin, literally 'straight.'

re·cum·bent /riˈkəmbənt/ ▸*adj.* (esp. of a person or human figure) lying down: *recumbent statues.* ■ (of a bicycle) designed to be ridden lying almost flat on one's back or sitting up with the legs stretched out in front. ■ (of a plant) growing close to the ground: *recumbent shrubs.*

▸*n.* a recumbent bicycle. ▷mid 17th cent.: from Latin *recumbent-* 'reclining,' from the verb *recumbere*, from *re-* 'back' + a verb related to *cubare* 'to lie.' **—re·cum·ben·cy** *n.* **—re·cum·bent·ly** *adv.*

re·cu·per·ate /riˈko͞opəˌrāt/ ▸*v.* **1** [*intrans.*] recover from illness or exertion: *she has been* **recuperating** *from a shoulder wound* | *Christmas is a time to recuperate.* **2** [*trans.*] recover or regain (something lost or taken): *they will seek to recuperate the returns that go with investment.* ▷mid 16th cent.: from Latin *recuperat-* 'regained,' from the verb *recuperare*, from *re-* 'back' + *capere* 'take.' **—re·cu·per·a·ble** /-pərəbəl/ *adj.*

re·cu·per·a·tion /riˌko͞opəˈrāSHən/ ▸*n.* **1** recovery from illness or exertion: *the human body has amazing powers of recuperation.* **2** the recovery or regaining of something: *the recuperation of the avant-garde for art.* ■ the action of a recuperator in imparting heat to incoming air or gaseous fuel from hot waste gases.

re·cu·per·a·tive /riˈko͞opəˌrātiv/ ▸*adj.* **1** having the effect of restoring health or strength. **2** of or relating to the action of a recuperator or a similar heat exchanger.

re·cu·per·a·tor /riˈko͞opəˌrātər/ ▸*n.* a form of heat exchanger in which hot waste gases from a furnace are conducted continuously along a system of flues where they impart heat to incoming air or gaseous fuel.

re·cur /riˈkər/ ▸*v.* (**-curred, -cur·ring**) [*intrans.*] occur again, periodically, or repeatedly: *when the symptoms recurred, the doctor diagnosed something different* | [as *adj.*] (**recurring**) *a recurring theme.* ■ (of a thought, image, or memory) come back to one's mind: *Steve's words kept recurring to him.* ■ (**recur to**) go back to (something) in thought or speech: *the book remained a favorite and she constantly recurred to it.* ▷Middle English (in the sense 'return to'): from Latin *recurrere*, from *re-* 'again, back' + *currere* 'run.' **—re·cur·rence** /riˈkərəns; -ˈkə-rəns/ *n.*

USAGE Recur and recurrence are generally regarded as better style than *reoccur* and *reoccurrence.*

re·cur·rent /riˈkərənt; -ˈkə-rənt/ ▸*adj.* **1** occurring often or repeatedly: *she had a recurrent dream about falling.* ■ (of a disease or symptom) recurring after apparent cure or remission: *recurrent fever.* **2** *Anatomy* (of a nerve or blood vessel) turning back so as to reverse direction. ▷late 16th cent. (sense 2): from Latin *recurrent-* 'running back,' from the verb *recurrere* (see RECUR). **—re·cur·rent·ly** *adv.*

re·cur·ring dec·i·mal ▸*n.* a repeating decimal.

re·cur·sion /riˈkərZHən/ ▸*n.* *Mathematics & Linguistics* the repeated application of a recursive procedure or definition. ■ a recursive definition. ▷1930s: from late Latin *recursio(n-)*, from *recurrere* 'run back' (see RECUR).

re·cur·sion for·mu·la ▸*n.* *Mathematics* an equation relating the value of a function for a given value of its argument (or arguments) to its values for other values of the argument(s).

re·cur·sive /riˈkərsiv/ ▸*adj.* characterized by recurrence or repetition, in particular: ■ *Mathematics & Linguistics* relating to or involving the repeated application of a rule, definition, or procedure to successive results. ■ *Computing* relating to or involving a program or routine of which a part requires the application of the whole, so that its explicit interpretation requires in general many successive executions. ▷late 18th cent. (in the general sense): from late Latin *recurs-* 'returned' (from the verb *recurrere* 'run back') + -IVE. Specific uses have arisen in the 20th cent. **—re·cur·sive·ly** *adv.*

re·curve /rēˈkərv/ ▸*v.* [*intrans.*] *chiefly Biology* bend backward: [as *adj.*] (**recurved**) *large recurved tusks.*

▸*n.* *Archery* a bow that curves forward at the ends, which straighten out under tension when the bow is drawn. ▷late 16th cent.: from Latin *recurvare* 'bend (something) back,' from *re-* 'back' + *curvare* 'to bend.' **—re·cur·va·ture** /-vəCHər/ *n.*

R

rec·u·sant /ˈrekyəzənt; riˈkyo͞ozənt/ ▸*n.* a person who refuses to submit to an authority or to comply with a regulation. ■ *chiefly historical* a Roman Catholic in England who refused to attend services of the Church of England.

▸*adj.* of or denoting a recusant. ▷mid 16th cent.: from Latin *recusant-* 'refusing,' from the verb *recusare* (see RECUSE). **—rec·u·sance** *n.* **—rec·u·san·cy** /-zənsē/ *n.*

re·cuse /riˈkyo͞oz/ ▸*v.* [*trans.*] challenge (a judge, prosecutor, or juror) as unqualified to perform legal duties because of a possible conflict of interest or lack of impartiality: *a motion to recuse the prosecutor.* ■ (**recuse oneself**) (of a judge) excuse oneself from a case because of a possible conflict of interest or lack of impartiality: *the Justice Department demanded that he recuse himself from the case.* ▷late Middle English (in the sense 'reject,' specifically 'object to (a judge) as prejudiced'): from Latin *recusare* 'to refuse,' from *re-* (expressing opposition) + *causa* 'a cause.' The sense 'excuse (oneself from a case)' dates from the early 19th cent. **—re·cus·al** /-zəl/ *n.*

re·cut /rēˈkət/ ▸*v.* [*trans.*] remove further or different material from (a film or screenplay): *director Tony Scott is recutting several key scenes.*

re·cy·cla·ble /rēˈsīk(ə)ləbəl/ ▸*adj.* able to be recycled. ▸*n.* a substance or object that can be recycled. **—re·cy·cla·bil·i·ty** /-ˌsīk(ə)ləˈbilitē/ *n.*

re·cy·cle /rēˈsīkəl/ ▸*v.* [*trans.*] convert (waste) into reusable material: *car hulks were recycled into new steel* | [as *adj.*] (**recycled**) *goods made of recycled materials* | [as *n.*] (**recycling**) *a call for the recycling of all paper.* ■ return (material) to a previous stage in a cyclic process. ■ use again: *he reserves the right to recycle his own text.* **—re·cy·cler** /-k(ə)lər/ *n.*

red /red/ ▸*adj.* (**red·der, red·dest**) **1** of a color at the end of the spectrum next to orange and opposite violet, as of blood, fire, or rubies: *her red lips* | *the sky was turning red outside.* ■ (of a person or their face or complexion) flushed or rosy, esp. with embarrassment, anger, or a healthy glow: *there were some red faces at headquarters.* ■ (of a person's eyes) bloodshot or having pink rims, esp. with tiredness or crying: *her eyes were red and swollen.* ■ (of hair or fur) of a reddish-brown color. ■ *dated, offensive* (of a people) having or regarded as having reddish skin. ■ of or denoting the suits hearts and diamonds in a deck of cards. ■ (of wine) made from dark grapes and colored by their skins. ■ denoting a red light or flag used as a signal to stop. ■ used to denote something forbidden, dangerous, or urgent: *the force went on* **red alert.** ■ (of a ski run) of the second highest level of difficulty, as indicated by colored markers. ■ *Physics* denoting one of three colors of quark.

2 (**Red**) *informal, chiefly derogatory* communist or socialist (used esp. during the Cold War with reference to the Soviet Union): *the Red Menace.* Contrasted with **WHITE** (sense 3). **3** stained or covered with blood: *the red hands and sharp knives of the fishermen.* ■ *archaic* or *poetic/literary* involving bloodshed or violence: *red battle stamps his foot and nations feel the shock.*
▸*n.* **1** red color or pigment: *colors range from yellow to deep red | their work is marked **in red** by the teacher | the reds and browns of wood.* ■ red clothes or material: *she could not wear red.* **2** a red thing or person, in particular: ■ a red wine. ■ a red ball in billiards. ■ a red light. **3** (also **Red**) *informal, chiefly derogatory* a communist or socialist. **4** (**the red**) the situation of owing money or showing a debit: *the company was $4,000,000 **in the red**.* [from the conventional use of *red* to indicate debt items.] ▷Old English *rēad*, of Germanic origin; related to Dutch *rood* and German *rot*, from an Indo-European root shared by Latin *rufus, ruber*, Greek *eruthros*, and Sanskrit *rudhira-* 'red.' —**red·dish** *adj.* —**red·dy** *adj.* —**red·ly** *adv.* —**red·ness** *n.*
▸*PHRASES* □ **better dead than red** (or **better red than dead**) a cold-war slogan claiming that the prospect of nuclear war is preferable to that of a communist society (or vice versa). □ (**as**) **red as a beet** (of a person) red-faced, typically through embarrassment. □ **red in tooth and claw** involving savage or merciless conflict or competition: *nature, red in tooth and claw.* [from Tennyson's *In Memoriam*.] □ **the red planet** a name for Mars. □ **the red, white, and blue** *informal* the U.S. national flag: *learning respect for the red, white, and blue.* □ **see red** *informal* become very angry suddenly: *the mere thought of Peter with Nicole made her see red.*

red. ▸*abbr.* reduction.

red- ▸*prefix* variant spelling of **RE-** before a vowel (as in *redeem, redolent*).

re·dact /ri'dakt/ ▸*v.* [*trans.*] *rare* edit (text) for publication. ▷mid 19th cent.: back-formation from **REDACTION**. —**re·dac·tor** /-tər/ *n.*

re·dac·tion /ri'dakSHən/ ▸*n.* the process of editing text for publication. ■ a version of a text, such as a new edition or an abridged version. ▷late 18th cent.: from French *rédaction*, from late Latin *redactio(n-)*, from *redigere* 'bring back.' —**re·dac·tion·al** /-SHənl/ *adj.*

red ad·mi·ral ▸*n.* a migratory butterfly that has dark wings marked with red-orange bands and white spots. • Genus *Vanessa*, subfamily Nymphalinae, family Nymphalidae: several species, in particular the common and widespread *V. atalanta.*

red admiral

red al·gae ▸*n.* a large group of algae that includes many seaweeds that are mainly red in color. Some kinds yield useful products (agar, alginates) or are used as food (laver, dulse, carrageen). • Division Rhodophyta (or phylum Rhodophyta, kingdom Protista).

re·dan /ri'dan/ ▸*n.* an arrow-shaped embankment forming part of a fortification. ▷late 17th cent.: from French, from *redent* 'notching (of a saw),' from *re-* 'again' (expressing repetition) + *dent* 'tooth.'

Red Ar·my the army of the Soviet Union, formed after the revolution of 1917. The name was officially dropped in 1946. ■ the army of China or some other communist countries.

Red Ar·my Fac·tion a left-wing terrorist group in the former West Germany, active from 1968 onward. It was originally led by Andreas Baader (1943–77) and Ulrike Meinhof (1934–76). Also called **BAADER-MEINHOF GROUP**.

red-backed vole ▸*n.* a vole with a reddish-chestnut back, inhabiting the forest, scrub, and tundra regions of the northern hemisphere. • Genus *Clethrionomys*, family Muridae: several species.

red-bait ▸*v.* [*trans.*] [often as *n.*] (**red-baiting**) *informal* harass or persecute (someone) on account of known or suspected communist sympathies. —**red-bait·er** *n.*

red beds ▸*plural n. Geology* sandstones or other sedimentary strata colored red by hematite coating the grains.

red blood cell ▸*n.* less technical term for **ERYTHROCYTE**.

red-blood·ed ▸*adj.* (of a man) vigorous or virile, esp. in having strong heterosexual appetites: *he was attracted to her, as any red-blooded male would be.* —**red-blood·ed·ness** *n.*

red·bone /'red,bōn/ ▸*n.* a dog with a red or red and tan coat of an American breed formerly used to hunt raccoons.

red·breast /'red,brest/ ▸*n. informal* a robin.

red-brick ▸*adj.* built with red bricks. ■ (of a British university) founded in the late 19th or early 20th century. [with reference to the usual building material (in contrast to the stone used at Oxford and Cambridge).]

Red Bri·gades an extreme left-wing terrorist organization based in Italy that from the early 1970s was responsible for carrying out kidnappings, murders, and acts of sabotage.

red·bud /'red,bəd/ ▸*n.* a North American tree of the pea family, with pink flowers that grow from the trunk, branches, and twigs. • Genus *Cercis*, family Leguminosae: several species, in particular **eastern redbud** (*C. canadensis*).

red·cap /'red,kap/ ▸*n.* **1** a railroad porter. [late 19th cent.: first used because John Williams, a porter in Grand Central Terminal, New York City, wore a cap with a red flannel strip in order to attract attention.] **2** *Brit., informal* a member of the military police.

red card ▸*n.* (in soccer and some other games) a red card shown by the referee to a player who is being ejected from the game. Compare with **YELLOW CARD**.
▸*v.* (**red-card**) [*trans.*] (often **be red-carded**) (of a referee) eject (a player) from the game by showing the red card: *he did his pushing directly in front of the referee and was red-carded.*

red car·pet ▸*n.* a long, narrow red carpet laid on the ground for a distinguished visitor to walk on when arriving. ■ (**the red carpet**) privileged treatment of a distinguished visitor: *they rolled out the red carpet for two special guests.*

red ce·dar ▸*n.* either of two North American coniferous trees with reddish-brown bark. • Two species in the family Cupressaceae: the **western red cedar** (*Thuja plicata*), which yields strong, lightweight timber, and the **eastern red cedar** (*Juniperus virginiana*), found chiefly in the eastern U.S.

red cell ▸*n.* less technical term for **ERYTHROCYTE**.

red cent ▸*n.* a one-cent coin; a penny. ■ [usu. with *negative*] the smallest amount of money: *some of the people don't deserve a single red cent.* ▷early 19th cent.: so named because it was formerly made of copper.

red chan·nel ▸*n.* in many countries, the passage that should be taken (at a customs area in an airport or port) by arriving passengers who have goods to declare: *when we arrived in Bangkok, we were told to proceed to the red channel.*

Red Cloud (1822–1909), leader of the Oglala Sioux Indians; Indian name *Makhpiya-luta*. He opposed, in what became known as Red Cloud's War 1865–68, the U.S. government's attempts to build forts along the Bozeman Trail in Wyoming and Montana. By his forcing of the Fort Laramie Treaty in 1868, peace was guaranteed when the government accepted the territorial claims of the Sioux.

red·coat /'red,kōt/ ▸*n. historical* a British soldier. ▷early 16th cent.: so named because of the color of the uniform.

red cor·al ▸*n.* a branching pinkish-red horny coral that is used in jewelry. Also called **PRECIOUS CORAL**. • Genus *Corallium*, order Gorgonacea, class Anthozoa.

Red Cres·cent a national branch in Muslim countries of the International Movement of the Red Cross and the Red Crescent.

Red Cross the International Movement of the Red Cross and the Red Crescent, an international humanitarian organization that provides relief to victims of war or natural disaster. The Red Cross was set up in 1864 at the instigation of the Swiss philanthropist Henri Dunant (1828–1910) according to the Geneva Convention, and its headquarters are in Geneva.

red cur·rant (*Brit.* also **red·cur·rant**) ▸*n.* **1** a small, sweet, edible red berry. **2** the shrub that produces this fruit. • Genus *Ribes*, family Grossulariaceae: several species, including the European *R. rubrum* and the North American **garden red currant** (*R. sativum*).

redd[1] /red/ ▸*v.* (*past* and *past part.* **redd**) [*trans.*] (**redd something up**) *dialect* put something in order; tidy: *you take this baby while I redd the room up.* ▷late Middle English (in the sense 'clear (space)'): perhaps related to **RID**.

redd[2] ▸*n.* a hollow in a riverbed made by a trout or salmon to spawn in. ▷mid 17th cent. (originally Scots and northern English in the sense 'spawn'): of unknown origin.

red deer ▸*n.* a deer with a rich red-brown summer coat that turns dull brownish-gray in winter, the male having large branched antlers. It is native to North America, Eurasia, and North Africa. • *Cervus elaphus*, family Cervidae. Compare with **ELK**.

Red De·li·cious ▸*n.* a widely grown dessert apple of a soft-fleshed red-skinned variety.

red·den /'redn/ ▸*v.* make or become red: [*trans.*] *bare arms reddened by sun and wind* | [*intrans.*] *the sky is reddening.* ■ [*intrans.*] (of a person) blush: *Lynn reddened at the description of herself.* ■ [*intrans.*] (of the eyes) become pink at the rims as a result of crying.

Red·ding[1] /'rediNG/ a commercial and resort city in northern California, at the northern end of the Sacramento Valley; pop. 66,462.

Red·ding[2], Otis (1941–67), U.S. singer. He was one of the most influential soul singers of the late 1960s. It was not until the Monterey pop festival in 1967 that he gained widespread recognition. "Dock of the Bay," released after his death in an airplane crash, became a number-one U.S. hit in 1968.

red·dle /'redl/ ▸*n.* another term for **RUDDLE**. ▷early 18th cent.: variant of **RUDDLE**.

red dwarf ▸*n. Astronomy* a small, old, relatively cool star.

rede /rēd/ *archaic* ▸*n.* advice or counsel given by one person to another: *what is your rede?*
▸*v.* [*trans.*] **1** advise (someone): [*trans.*] *therefore, my son, I rede thee stay at home.* **2** interpret (a riddle or dream). ▷Old English *rǣd*, of Germanic origin; related to Dutch *raad*, German *Rat*. The verb is a variant of **READ**, of the same origin.

re·dec·o·rate /rē'dekə,rāt/ ▸*v.* [*trans.*] decorate (a room or building) again, typically differently. —**re·dec·o·ra·tion** /,rē,dekə'rāSHən/ *n.*

re·deem /ri'dēm/ ▸*v.* [*trans.*] **1** compensate for the faults or bad aspects of (something): *a disappointing debate redeemed only by an outstanding speech* | [as *adj.*] (**redeeming**) *the splendid views are the one redeeming feature of the center.* ■ (**redeem oneself**) do something that compensates for poor past performance or behavior: *they redeemed themselves in the playoffs by pushing the Detroit Red Wings to a seventh and deciding game.* ■ (of a person) atone or make amends for (error or evil): *the thief on the cross who by a single act redeemed a life of evil.* ■ save (someone) from sin, error, or evil: *he was a sinner, redeemed by the grace of God.* **2** gain or regain possession of (something) in exchange for payment: *his best suit had been redeemed from the pawnbrokers.* ■ *Finance* repay (a stock, bond, or other instrument) at the maturity date. ■ exchange (a coupon, voucher, or trading stamp) for merchandise, a discount, or money. ■ pay the necessary money to clear (a debt): *owners were unable to redeem their mortgages.* ■ exchange (paper money) for gold or silver. ■ fulfill or carry out (a pledge or promise): *the party prepared to redeem the pledges of the past three years.* ■ *archaic* buy the freedom of. ▷late Middle English (in the sense 'buy back'): from Old French *redimer* or Latin *redimere*, from *re(d)-* 'back' + *emere* 'buy.' —**re·deem·a·ble** *adj.*

re·deem·er /ri'dēmər/ ▸*n.* a person who redeems someone or something. ■ (often **the Redeemer**) Christ.

re·de·fine /,rēdi'fīn/ ▸*v.* [*trans.*] define again or differently: *her attempt to redefine postmodernism along more political and sociocultural lines.* —**re·def·i·ni·tion** /,rē,defə'niSHən/ *n.*

re·demp·tion /ri'dempSHən/ ▸*n.* **1** the action of saving or being saved from sin, error, or evil: *God's plans for the redemption of his world.* ■ [in *sing.*] *figurative* a thing that saves someone from error or evil: *his marginalization from the Hollywood jungle proved to be his redemption.* **2** the action of regaining or gaining possession of something in exchange for payment, or clearing a debt. ■ *archaic* the action of buying one's freedom. ▷late Middle English: from Old French, from Latin *redemptio(n-)*, from *redimere* 'buy back' (see **REDEEM**).
▸*PHRASE* □ **beyond** (or **past**) **redemption** (of a person or thing) too bad to be improved or saved.

re·demp·tion yield ▸*n. Finance* the yield of a stock calculated as a percentage of the redemption price with an adjustment made for any capital gain or loss the price represents relative to the current price.

re·demp·tive /ri'demptiv/ ▸*adj.* acting to save someone from error or evil: *the healing power of redemptive love.*

red en·sign ▸*n.* a red flag with the Union Jack in the top corner next to the flagstaff, flown by British-registered ships.

re·de·ploy /ˌrēdə'ploi/ ▸*v.* [*trans.*] assign (troops, employees, or resources) to a new place or task: *units concentrated in Buenos Aires would be redeployed to the provinces.* —**re·de·ploy·ment** *n.*

re·de·sign /ˌrēdi'zīn/ ▸*v.* [*trans.*] design (something) again in a different way: *the front seats have been redesigned.*
▸*n.* the action or process of redesigning something.

re·de·ter·mine /ˌrēdi'tərmən/ ▸*v.* [*trans.*] determine (something) again or differently. —**re·de·ter·mi·na·tion** /-ˌtərmə'nāsHən/ *n.*

re·de·vel·op /ˌrēdi'veləp/ ▸*v.* [*trans.*] develop (something) again or differently. ■ erect new buildings in (an urban area), typically after demolishing the existing buildings: *the riverfront that the city planned to redevelop with family attractions.* —**re·de·vel·op·er** *n.* —**re·de·vel·op·ment** *n.*

red-eye ▸*n.* **1** the undesirable effect in flash photography of people appearing to have red eyes, caused by a reflection from the retina when the flashgun is too near the camera lens. **2** (also **red-eye flight**) [in *sing.*] *informal* an overnight or late-night flight on a commercial airline: *she caught the red-eye back to New York.* **3** a freshwater fish with red eyes, in particular a rock bass. **4** *informal* cheap whiskey.

red-eye gra·vy ▸*n.* gravy made by adding liquid to the fat from cooked ham.

red-faced ▸*adj.* (of a person) having a red face, esp. as a result of exertion, embarrassment, or shame: *Steve was left red-faced when a fan tried to rip his pants off.*

red·fish /'redˌfisH/ ▸*n.* (*pl.* same or **-fish·es**) **1** a bright red edible marine fish, in particular: • a North Atlantic rockfish (genus *Sebastes*, family Scorpaenidae, in particular the commercially important *S. marinus*). • the red drum of the western Atlantic, popular as a game fish (*Sciaenops ocellatus*, family Sciaenidae). **2** *Brit.* a male salmon in the spawning season.

red flag ▸*n.* a red flag as a warning of danger or a problem: *figurative they had overlooked the red flags that should have alerted them to the county's disastrous investment strategy | figurative you have unusually large amounts of deductions or expenses that act as red flags.* ■ a red flag as the symbol of socialist revolution.

red flan·nel hash ▸*n.* a type of hash made with beets.

Red·ford /'redfərd/, (Charles) Robert (1936–), U.S. movie actor and director. He achieved success playing opposite Paul Newman in *Butch Cassidy and the Sundance Kid* (1969) and costarred again with him in *The Sting* (1973). Other notable movies: *Ordinary People* (1980), for which he won an Academy Award as director; *Out of Africa* (1986); *A River Runs through It* (1992); and *The Horse Whisperer* (1998).

red fox ▸*n.* a common fox with a reddish coat, native to both Eurasia and North America and living from the Arctic tundra to the southern temperate regions. • *Vulpes vulpes*, family Canidae.

red fox

red gi·ant ▸*n. Astronomy* a very large star of high luminosity and low surface temperature. Red giants are thought to be in a late stage of evolution when no hydrogen remains in the core to fuel nuclear fusion.

red gold ▸*n.* an alloy of gold and copper.

Red·grave /'redˌgrāv/ the name of a family of English actors, notably: ■ **Sir Michael (Scudamore)** (1908–85), stage actor. He played numerous Shakespearean roles and also starred in movies, such as *The Browning Version* (1951) and *The Importance of Being Ernest* (1952). ■ **Vanessa** (1937–), Sir Michael's eldest daughter. Her acting career includes the movies *Mary Queen of Scots* (1972); *Julia* (1976), for which she won an Academy Award; and *Howard's End* (1992). Sir Michael's other children, **Corin** (1939–) and **Lynn** (1944–), both act. Lynn is best known for such movies as *Georgy Girl* (1966). Vanessa's two daughters **Joely Richardson** (1958–) and **Natasha Richardson** (1963–) are both actresses.

red–green ▸*adj.* [*attrib.*] denoting color-blindness in which reds and greens are confused, either protanopia (daltonism) or deuteranopia.

red grouse ▸*n.* a bird of a race of the willow ptarmigan having entirely reddish-brown plumage, native only to the British Isles. • *Lagopus lagopus scoticus*, family Phasianidae (or Tetraonidae).

Red Guard ▸*n.* any of various radical or socialist groups, in particular a militant youth movement in China (1966–76) that carried out attacks on intellectuals and other disfavored groups as part of Mao Zedong's Cultural Revolution. ■ a member of one of these groups.

red gum ▸*n.* an Australian gum tree with smooth bark and hard dark red timber. • Genera *Eucalyptus* and *Angophora*, family Myrtaceae: many species, in particular the widespread **river red gum** (*E. camaldulensis*). ■ astringent reddish kino gum obtained from some of these trees, used for medicinal purposes and for tanning.

red-hand·ed ▸*adj.* (of a person) having been discovered in or just after the act of doing something wrong or illegal: *I* ***caught him red-handed****, stealing a wallet.*

red hat ▸*n.* a cardinal's hat, esp. as the symbol of a cardinal's office.

red·head /'redˌhed/ ▸*n.* **1** a person with reddish hair. **2** a North American diving duck with a reddish-brown head, related to and resembling the pochard. • *Aythya americana*, family Anatidae.

red-head·ed ▸*adj.* [*attrib.*] (of a person) having reddish-brown hair: *a red-headed man.* ■ used in names of birds, insects, and other animals with red heads, e.g., **red-headed woodpecker**.

red heat ▸*n.* the temperature or state of something so hot that it emits red light.

red her·ring ▸*n.* **1** a dried smoked herring, which is turned red by the smoke. **2** something, esp. a clue, that is or is intended to be misleading or distracting: *the book is fast-paced, exciting, and full of red herrings.* [so named from the practice of using the scent of red herring in training hounds.]

Red Hook an industrial port section of Brooklyn in New York City, on New York Bay, across from Governor's Island.

red-hot ▸*adj.* **1** (of a substance) so hot as to glow red: *red-hot coals.* ■ very hot, esp. too hot to touch: *the red-hot handle burned his hand | figurative the red-hot attack letter they received last week.* **2** extremely exciting or popular: *red-hot jazz.* ■ very passionate: *a red-hot lover.*

red-hot pok·er ▸*n.* a South African plant with tall erect spikes of tubular flowers, the upper ones of which are typically red and the lower ones yellow. • *Kniphofia uvaria*, family Liliaceae: many cultivars.

re·di·al ▸*v.* /rē'dīl/ (**-di·aled, -di·al·ing**; *Brit.* **-di·alled, -di·al·ling**) [*trans.*] dial (a telephone number) again, esp. automatically.
▸*n.* /-'rēˌdīl/ (also **last num·ber re·dial**) the facility on a telephone by which the number just dialed may be automatically redialed by pressing a single button.

re·did /rē'did/ ▸ past of **REDO**.

Red In·di·an ▸*n. chiefly Brit.* old-fashioned term for **AMERICAN INDIAN**.

USAGE See usage at **REDSKIN**.

red·in·gote /'rediNGˌgōt/ ▸*n.* a woman's long coat with a cutaway or contrasting front. ■ a man's double-breasted topcoat with a full skirt. ▷late 18th cent.: French, from English *riding coat.*

red ink ▸*n.* used in reference to financial deficit or debt: *he voted for many of the projects that have left the state awash in red ink.*

red·in·te·grate /ri'dintəˌgrāt/ ▸*v.* [*trans.*] *archaic* restore (something) to a state of wholeness, unity, or perfection. ▷late Middle English: from Latin *redintegrat-* 'made whole,' from the verb *redintegrare*, from *re(d)-* 'again' + *integrare* 'restore.' —**red·in·te·gra·tion** /riˌdintə'grāsHən/ *n.* —**red·in·te·gra·tive** /-ˌgrātiv/ *adj.*

re·di·rect /ˌrēdə'rekt; -dī-/ ▸*v.* [*trans.*] direct (something) to a new or different place or purpose: *get the post office to redirect your mail | resources were redirected to a major project.* —**re·di·rec·tion** /-'reksHən/ *n.*

re·dis·count /rē'disˌkount/ *Finance* ▸*v.* [*trans.*] (of a central bank) discount (a bill of exchange or similar instrument) that has already been discounted by a commercial bank.
▸*n.* the action of rediscounting something.

re·dis·cov·er /ˌrēdis'kəvər/ ▸*v.* [*trans.*] discover (something forgotten or ignored) again: *he was trying to rediscover his Gaelic roots.* —**re·dis·cov·er·y** /-'kəv(ə)rē/ *n.* (*pl.* **-er·ies**).

re·dis·tri·bute /ˌrēdə'stribˌyo͞ot/ ▸*v.* [*trans.*] distribute (something) differently or again, typically to achieve greater social equality: *their primary concern was to redistribute income from rich to poor.* —**re·dis·tri·bu·tion** /ˌrēˌdistrə'byo͞osHən/ *n.* —**re·dis·trib·u·tive** /-'stribyətiv/ *adj.*

re·dis·tri·bu·tion·ist /ˌrēˌdistrə'byo͞osHənist/ ▸*n.* a person who advocates the redistribution of wealth.
▸*adj.* of or relating to the belief that wealth should be redistributed: *redistributionist measures.* —**re·dis·tri·bu·tion·ism** /-ˌnizəm/ *n.*

re·di·vide /ˌrēdi'vīd/ ▸*v.* [*trans.*] divide (something) again or differently: *the Balkans were redivided among Slovene, Croat, and Serb.* —**re·di·vi·sion** /-'vizHən/ *n.*

red·i·vi·vus /ˌredə'vīvəs; -'vēvəs/ ▸*adj.* [*postpositive*] *poetic/literary* come back to life; reborn: *one is tempted to think of Poussin as a sort of Titian redivivus.* ▷late 16th cent.: from Latin, from *re(d)-* 'again' + *vivus* 'living.'

Red Jack·et (c.1758–1830), Native American Seneca leader; Indian name *Sagoyewatha.* A gifted orator, he advised his people at council fires and defended them at treaty sessions and before government agencies. He received a symbolic medal from President Washington in 1792.

red kan·ga·roo ▸*n.* a large kangaroo of Australian grasslands, the male of which has a russet-red coat and the female typically a blue-gray coat. • *Macropus rufus*, family Macropodidae.

Red·lands /'redləndz/ a commercial and resort city in southern California, near the San Bernardino Mountains; pop. 60,394.

red lead ▸*n.* a red form of lead oxide used as a pigment.

Red Leices·ter ▸*n.* see **LEICESTER**[3].

red-let·ter day ▸*n.* a day that is pleasantly noteworthy or memorable. ▷early 18th cent.: from the practice of highlighting a festival in red on a calendar.

red light ▸*n.* a red traffic light or similar signal that instructs moving vehicles to stop. ■ *figurative* a refusal, or an order to stop an action: *some subsidies would get a red light and be prohibited.* ■ a red light used as a signal of warning, danger, or, on a machine, operation: *the winking red light of a video camera.*

red-light dis·trict ▸*n.* an area of a town or city containing many brothels, strip clubs, and other sex businesses. ▷from the use of a red light as the sign of a brothel.

red·line /'redˌlīn/ *informal* ▸*v.* [*trans.*] **1** drive with (a car engine) at or above its rated maximum rpm: *both his engines were redlined now.* **2** refuse (a loan or insurance) to someone because they live in an area deemed to be a poor financial risk. ■ cancel (a project).
▸*n.* the maximum number of revolutions per minute for a car engine. ▷from the use of *red* as a limit marker, in sense 2 a limit marked out by ringing a section of a map.

red man ▸*n. dated, offensive* American Indian.

USAGE See usage at **REDSKIN**.

red meat ▸*n.* meat that is red when raw, for example beef or lamb. Often contrasted with **WHITE MEAT**.

Red·mond /'redmənd/ a city in west central Washington, northeast of Seattle; pop. 45,256.

red mul·let ▸*n.* an elongated fish with long barbels on the chin, living in warmer seas and widely valued as a food fish. • Family Mullidae: several genera and many species, in particular *Muletus surmuletus* of the Mediterranean and eastern Atlantic.

red·neck /'redˌnek/ ▸*n. informal, derogatory* a working-class white person, esp. a politically reactionary one

R

from a rural area: *rednecks in the high, cheap seats stomped their feet and hooted* | [as *adj.*] *a place of redneck biases.* ▷from the back of the neck being sunburned from outdoor work. —**red·necked** *adj.*

re·do ▸*v.* /rē'do͞o/ (**re·does** /rē'dəz/; *past* **re·did** /rē'did/; *past part.* **re·done** /rē'dən/) [*trans.*] do (something) again or differently: *a whole day's work has to be redone.* ■ redecorate (a room or building): *the house is being redone exactly to suit his taste.*

▸*n.* /'rē,do͞o/ a redecoration of a room or building: *a total redo of the second floor shopping concourse.*

red o·cher ▸*n.* a variety of ocher, esp. used for coloring or dyeing.

red·o·lent /'redl-ənt/ ▸*adj.* **1** [*predic.*] (**redolent of/with**) strongly reminiscent or suggestive of (something): *names redolent of history and tradition.* ■ *poetic/literary* strongly smelling of something: *the church was old, dark, and redolent of incense.* **2** *archaic* or *poetic/literary* fragrant or sweet-smelling: *a rich, inky, redolent wine.* ▷late Middle English (in the sense 'fragrant'): from Old French, or from Latin *redolent-* 'giving out a strong smell,' from *re(d)-* 'back, again' + *olere* 'to smell.' —**red·o·lence** *n.* —**red·o·lent·ly** *adv.*

Re·don /rə'dôN/, Odilon (1840–1916), French painter and graphic artist. He was a leading exponent of symbolism and forerunner of surrealism.

Re·don·do Beach /ri'dändō/ a city in southwestern California, on Santa Monica Bay, south of Los Angeles; pop. 60,167.

re·dou·ble /rē'dəbəl/ ▸*v.* [*trans.*] make much greater, more intense, or more numerous: *we will redouble our efforts to reform agricultural policy.* ■ [*intrans.*] become greater or more intense or numerous: *pressure to solve the problem has redoubled.* ■ [*intrans.*] *Bridge* double a bid already doubled by an opponent.

▸*n. Bridge* a call that doubles a bid already doubled by an opponent. ▷late Middle English: from French *redoubler*, from *re-* 'again' + *doubler* 'to double.' The noun dates from the early 20th cent.

re·doubt /ri'dout/ ▸*n. Military* a temporary or supplementary fortification, typically square or polygonal and without flanking defenses. ■ an entrenched stronghold or refuge. ▷early 17th cent.: from French *redoute*, from obsolete Italian *ridotta* and medieval Latin *reductus* 'refuge,' from Latin *reducere* 'withdraw.' The *-b-* was added by association with DOUBT.

re·doubt·a·ble /ri'doutəbəl/ ▸*adj. often humorous* (of a person) formidable, esp. as an opponent: *he was a redoubtable debater.* ▷late Middle English: from Old French *redoutable*, from *redouter* 'to fear,' from *re-* (expressing intensive force) + *douter* 'to doubt.' —**re·doubt·a·bly** /-blē/ *adv.*

re·dound /ri'dound/ ▸*v.* [*intrans.*] **1** (**redound to**) *formal* contribute greatly to (a person's credit or honor): *his latest diplomatic effort will redound to his credit.* **2** (**redound upon**) *archaic* come back upon; rebound on: *may his sin redound upon his head!* [probably by association with REBOUND[1].] ▷late Middle English (in the sense 'surge up, overflow'): from Old French *redonder*, from Latin *redundare* 'surge,' from *re(d)-* 'again' + *unda* 'a wave.'

red·out /'red,out/ ▸*n.* a reddening of the vision resulting from congestion of blood in the eyes when the body is accelerated downward, sometimes followed by loss of consciousness.

re·dox /'rē,däks/ ▸*n.* [usu. as *adj.*] *Chemistry* a process in which one substance or molecule is reduced and another oxidized; oxidation and reduction considered together as complimentary processes: *redox reactions involve electron transfer.* ▷1920s: blend.

red pan·da ▸*n.* a raccoonlike mammal with thick reddish-brown fur and a bushy tail, native to high bamboo forests from the Himalayas to southern China. Also called LESSER PANDA. • *Ailurus fulgens*; it is variously placed with the raccoons or bears, or in its own family (Ailurudae).

red pep·per ▸*n.* the ripe red fruit of a sweet pepper. Compare with GREEN PEPPER. ■ another term for CAYENNE.

red phos·pho·rus ▸*n.* see PHOSPHORUS.

red pine ▸*n.* any of a number of coniferous trees that yield reddish timber, in particular: • a North American pine (*Pinus resinosa*, family Pinaceae).

red·poll /'red,pōl/ ▸*n.* **1** a mainly brown finch with a red forehead, related to the linnet and widespread in Eurasia and North America. • *Acanthis flammea*, family Fringillidae; occurs in a number of races that were formerly regarded as separate species. **2** (**Red Poll**) an animal of a breed of red-haired polled cattle.

Red Queen hy·po·the·sis *Biology* the hypothesis that organisms are constantly struggling to keep up with one another in an evolutionary race between predator and prey species. ▷late 20th cent.: named from a passage in Lewis Carroll's *Alice Through the Looking Glass*, in which the Red Queen tells Alice that "it takes all the running you can do to stay in the same place."

re·draft ▸*v.* /rē'draft/ [*trans.*] draft (a document, text, or map) again in a different way: [as *adj.*] (**redrafted**) *I enclose a redrafted version.*

▸*n.* /'rē,draft/ a document, text, or map that has been redrafted.

re·draw /rē'drô/ ▸*v.* (*past* **re·drew** /rē'dro͞o/; *past part.* **re·drawn** /rē'drôn/) [*trans.*] draw or draw up again or differently: *a judge forced Los Angeles to redraw its districts* | *the diagram was redrawn.*

re·dress /ri'dres; 'rē,dres/ ▸*v.* [*trans.*] remedy or set right (an undesirable or unfair situation): *the power to redress the grievances of our citizens.* ■ *archaic* set upright again: *some ambitious architect being called to redress a leaning wall.*

▸*n.* remedy or compensation for a wrong or grievance: *those seeking redress for an infringement of public law rights.* ▷Middle English: the verb from Old French *redresser*; the noun via Anglo-Norman French *redresse.* —**re·dress·a·ble** *adj.* —**re·dress·al** /-əl/ *n.* —**re·dress·er** *n.*

▸*PHRASE* □ **redress the balance** take action to restore equality in a situation.

re-dress /rē'dres; 'rē-/ ▸*v.* [*trans.*] dress (someone or something) again: *he re-dressed the wound.*

red rib·bon ▸*n.* an award given for coming in second in a competition.

Red Riv·er **1** a river in Southeast Asia that rises in southern China and flows 730 miles (1,175 km) southeast through northern Vietnam to the Gulf of Tonkin. Chinese name YUAN JIANG; Vietnamese name SONG HONG. **2** a river in the southern U.S., a tributary of the Mississippi River, that rises in northern Texas and flows 1,222 miles (1,966 km) southeast, forming part of the border between Texas and Oklahoma. It enters the Mississippi River in Louisiana. Also called RED RIVER OF THE SOUTH. **3** a river in the northern U.S. and Canada that rises in North Dakota and flows 545 miles (877 km) north, forming for most of its length the border between North Dakota and Minnesota, before entering Canada and emptying into Lake Winnipeg. Also called RED RIVER OF THE NORTH.

Red Riv·er cart ▸*n. historical* a strong two-wheeled cart formerly used on the Canadian prairies.

red roan ▸*adj.* denoting an animal's coat consisting of bay or chestnut mixed with white or gray.

▸*n.* a red roan animal.

red salm·on ▸*n.* another term for SOCKEYE. ■ the reddish-pink flesh of the sockeye salmon used as food.

red san·dal·wood ▸*n.* either of two Southeast Asian trees of the pea family that yield red timber. • Two species in the family Leguminosae: *Pterocarpus santalinus*, from which a red dye is obtained, and *Adenanthera pavonina*, whose seeds were formerly used as weights by goldsmiths.

Red Sea a long, narrow, landlocked sea that separates Africa from the Arabian peninsula. It is linked to the Indian Ocean in the south by the Gulf of Aden and to the Mediterranean Sea in the north by the Suez Canal.

red set·ter ▸*n.* less formal term for IRISH SETTER.

red·shank /'red,SHANGK/ ▸*n.* a large Eurasian sandpiper with long red legs and brown, gray, or blackish plumage. • Genus *Tringa*, family Scolopacidae: two species, in particular *T. totanus.*

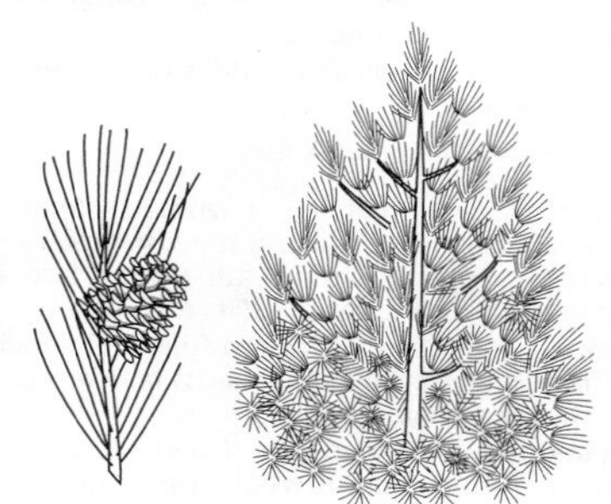
red pine

red·shift /'red'SHift/ (also **red shift**) ▸*n. Astronomy* the displacement of spectral lines toward longer wavelengths (the red end of the spectrum) in radiation from distant galaxies and celestial objects. This is interpreted as a Doppler shift that is proportional to the velocity of recession and thus to distance. Compare with BLUESHIFT. —**red·shift·ed** *adj.*

red·shirt /'red,SHərt/ ▸*n. informal* a college athlete who is withdrawn from college sporting events during one year in order to develop skills and extend the period of playing eligibility by a further year at this level of competition.

▸*v.* [*trans.*] (usu. **be redshirted**) keep (an athlete) out of college competition for a year: *he was less developed at the outset, so he was redshirted.* ▷from the red shirts worn by such athletes in practices with regular team members.

red-shoul·dered hawk ▸*n.* a common North American hawk having reddish-brown shoulders and dark wings with white spots. • *Buteo lineatus.*

red·skin /'red,skin/ ▸*n. dated, offensive* an American Indian.

USAGE **Redskin** is first recorded in the late 17th century and was applied to the Algonquian peoples generally, but specifically to the Delaware (who lived in what is now southern New York State and New York City, New Jersey, and eastern Pennsylvania). **Redskin** referred not to the natural skin color of the Delaware, but to their use of vermilion face paint and body paint. In time, however, through a process that in linguistics is called *pejoration*, by which a neutral term acquires an unfavorable connotation or denotation, **redskin** lost its neutral, accurate descriptive sense and became a term of disparagement.

Red man is first recorded in the early 17th century and was originally neutral in tone. **Red Indian** is first recorded in the early 19th century and was used by the British, far more than by Americans, to distinguish the Indians of the subcontinent from the Indians of the Americas.

All three terms are dated or offensive. **American Indian** and **Native American** are now the standard umbrella terms. Of course, if it is possible or appropriate, one can also use specific tribal names (**Cheyenne, Nez Percé,** etc.).

red snap·per ▸*n.* a reddish marine fish that is of commercial value as a food fish, in particular: • a tropical fish of the snapper family (genus *Lutjanus*, family Lutjanidae). • a North Pacific rockfish (*Sebastes ruberrimus*, family Scorpaenidae).

red spi·der (also **red spi·der mite**) ▸*n.* see SPIDER MITE.

red-spot·ted pur·ple ▸*n.* a North American butterfly that is a form of the white admiral, formerly considered a separate species. Its dark blue wings with red-orange bars and spots mimic the unpalatable pipevine swallowtail.

Red Square a large square in Moscow next to the Kremlin. In existence since the late 15th century, under communism the square was the scene of great parades celebrating May Day and the October Revolution.

red squir·rel ▸*n.* a small tree squirrel with a reddish coat: • a North American squirrel with a pale belly and a black line along the sides during the summer (*Tamiasciurus hudsonicus*, family Sciuridae). • a Eurasian squirrel with distinctive ear tufts during the winter months (*Sciurus vulgaris*, family Sciuridae).

red·start /'red,stärt/ ▸*n.* **1** an American warbler, the male of which is black with either a red belly or orange markings. • Genera *Setophaga* and *Myioborus*, subfamily Parulinae, family Emberizidae: several species, in particular the **American redstart** (*S. ruticilla*). **2** a Eurasian and North African songbird related to the chats, having a reddish tail and underparts. • *Phoenicurus* and other genera, subfamily Turdinae, family Muscicapidae: several species, in particular the widespread *P. phoenicurus.*

red tab·by ▸*n.* a cat with a reddish-orange coat striped or dappled in a deeper red.

red-tailed hawk ▸*n.* the most common and most widespread hawk of North and Central America, with a reddish tail. • *Buteo jamaicensis*, family Accipitridae.

red tape ▸*n.* excessive bureaucracy or adherence to rules and formalities, esp. in public business: *this law will just create more red tape.* ▷early 18th cent.: so named because of the red or pink tape used to bind and secure official documents.

red tide ▸*n.* a discoloration of seawater caused by a bloom of toxic red dinoflagellates.

red top ▸*n. Brit., informal* a tabloid. ▷1990s: from the red background on which the titles of certain British newspapers are printed.

Red To·ry ▸*n.* (in Canada) a member of a political group who, while maintaining some conservative principles, supports many liberal and socialist policies.

re·duce /ri'd(y)o͞os/ ▸*v.* [*trans.*] **1** make smaller or less in amount, degree, or size: *the need for businesses to reduce costs | the workforce has been reduced to some 6,100 |* [as *adj.*] (**reduced**) *a reduced risk of coronary disease.* ■ [*intrans.*] become smaller or less in size, amount, or degree: *the number of priority homeless cases has reduced slightly.* ■ boil (a sauce or other liquid) in cooking so that it becomes thicker and more concentrated. ■ [*intrans.*] (of a person) lose weight, typically by dieting: *by May she had reduced to 125 pounds.* ■ *archaic* conquer (a place), in particular besiege and capture (a town or fortress). ■ *Photography* make (a negative or print) less dense. ■ *Phonetics* articulate (a speech sound) in a way requiring less muscular effort. In vowels, this gives rise to a more central articulatory position. **2** (**reduce someone/something to**) bring someone or something to (a lower or weaker state, condition, or role): *she has been reduced to near poverty | the church was reduced to rubble.* ■ (**be reduced to doing something**) (of a person) be forced by difficult circumstances into doing something desperate: *ordinary soldiers are reduced to begging.* ■ make someone helpless with (an expression of emotion, esp. with hurt, shock, or amusement): *Olga was reduced to stunned silence.* ■ force into (obedience or submission): *he succeeds in reducing his grandees to due obedience.* **3** (**reduce something to**) change a substance to (a different or more basic form): *it is difficult to understand how lava could have been reduced to dust.* ■ present a problem or subject in (a simplified form): *he reduces unimaginable statistics to manageable proportions.* ■ convert a fraction to (the form with the lowest terms). **4** *Chemistry* cause to combine chemically with hydrogen. ■ undergo or cause to undergo a reaction in which electrons are gained by one atom from another. The opposite of OXIDIZE. **5** restore (a dislocated part) to its proper position by manipulation or surgery. ■ remedy (a dislocation) in such a way. ▷late Middle English: from Latin *reducere*, from *re-* 'back, again' + *ducere* 'bring, lead.' The original sense was 'bring back' (hence 'restore,' now surviving in sense 5); this led to 'bring to a different state,' then 'bring to a simpler or lower state' (hence sense 3); and finally 'diminish in size or amount' (sense 1, dating from the late 18th cent.). —**re·duc·er** *n.*
▸*PHRASES* □ **reduced circumstances** used euphemistically to refer to the state of being poor after being relatively wealthy: *a divorcee living in reduced circumstances.* □ **reduce someone to the ranks** demote a noncommissioned officer to an ordinary soldier.

re·duc·i·ble /ri'd(y)o͞osəbəl/ ▸*adj.* **1** [*predic.*] (of a subject or problem) capable of being simplified in presentation or analysis: *Shakespeare's major soliloquies are not* **reducible to** *categories.* **2** *Mathematics* (of a polynomial) able to be factorized into two or more polynomials of lower degree. ■ (of a group) expressible as the direct product of two of its subgroups. —**re·duc·i·bil·i·ty** /ri,d(y)o͞osə'bilətē/ *n.*

re·duc·ing a·gent ▸*n. Chemistry* a substance that tends to bring about reduction by being oxidized and losing electrons.

re·duc·tant /ri'dəktənt/ ▸*n. Chemistry* a reducing agent.

re·duc·tase /ri'dək,tās; -,tāz/ ▸*n.* [usu. with *adj.*] *Biochemistry* an enzyme that promotes the chemical reduction of a specified substance.

re·duc·ti·o ad ab·sur·dum /rə'dəktē,ō ,ad əb'sərdəm; -'dəksHē,ō/ ▸*n. Philosophy* a method of proving the falsity of a premise by showing that its logical consequence is absurd or contradictory. ▷Latin, literally 'reduction to the absurd.'

re·duc·tion /ri'dəksHən/ ▸*n.* **1** the action or fact of making a specified thing smaller or less in amount, degree, or size: *talks on arms reduction | there had been* **a reduction in** *the number of casualties.* ■ the amount by which something is made smaller, less, or lower in price: *special reductions on knitwear.* ■ the simplification of a subject or problem to a particular form in presentation or analysis: *the* **reduction** *of classical genetics* **to** *molecular biology.* ■ *Mathematics* the process of converting an amount from one denomination to a smaller one, or of bringing down a fraction to its lowest terms. ■ *Biology* the halving of the number of chromosomes per cell that occurs at one of the two anaphases of meiosis. **2** a thing that is made smaller or less in size or amount, in particular: ■ an arrangement of an orchestral score for piano or for a smaller group of performers. ■ a thick and concentrated liquid or sauce made by boiling. ■ a copy of a picture or photograph made on a smaller scale than the original. **3** the action of remedying a dislocation or fracture by returning the affected part of the body to its normal position. **4** *Chemistry* the process or result of reducing or being reduced. **5** *Phonetics* substitution of a sound that requires less muscular effort to articulate: *the process of vowel reduction.* ▷late Middle English (denoting the action of bringing back): from Old French, or from Latin *reductio(n-)*, from *reducere* 'bring back, restore' (see REDUCE). The sense development was broadly similar to that of REDUCE; sense 1 dates from the late 17th cent.

re·duc·tion gear ▸*n.* a system of gearwheels in which the driven shaft rotates more slowly than the driving shaft.

re·duc·tion·ism /ri'dəksHə,nizəm/ ▸*n. often derogatory* the practice of analyzing and describing a complex phenomenon, esp. a mental, social, or biological phenomenon, in terms of phenomena that are held to represent a simpler or more fundamental level, esp. when this is said to provide a sufficient explanation. —**re·duc·tion·ist** *n.* & *adj.* —**re·duc·tion·is·tic** /ri,dəksHə'nistik/ *adj.*

re·duc·tive /ri'dəktiv/ ▸*adj.* **1** tending to present a subject or problem in a simplified form, esp. one viewed as crude: *such a conclusion by itself would be reductive.* ■ (with reference to art) minimal: *he combines his reductive abstract shapes with a rippled surface.* **2** of or relating to chemical reduction. —**re·duc·tive·ly** *adv.* —**re·duc·tive·ness** *n.*

re·duc·tiv·ism /ri'dəktə,vizəm/ ▸*n.* **1** another term for MINIMALISM. **2** another term for REDUCTIONISM.

re·dun·dan·cy /ri'dəndənsē/ ▸*n.* (*pl.* **-cies**) the state of being no longer needed or useful: *the redundancy of 19th-century heavy plant machinery.* ■ the use of words or data that could be omitted without loss of meaning or function; repetition or superfluity of information. ■ *Engineering* the inclusion of extra components that are not strictly necessary to functioning, in case of failure in other components: *a high degree of redundancy is built into the machinery installation.* ■ *chiefly Brit.* the state of being no longer employed because there is no more work available: *the factory's workers face redundancy.*

re·dun·dant /ri'dəndənt/ ▸*adj.* no longer needed or useful; superfluous: *an appropriate use for a redundant church | many of the old skills had become redundant.* ■ (of words or data) able to be omitted without loss of meaning or function. ■ *Engineering* (of a component) not strictly necessary to functioning but included in case of failure in another component. ■ *chiefly Brit.* (of a person) no longer employed because there is no more work available: *eight permanent staff* **were made redundant.** ▷late 16th cent. (in the sense 'abundant'): from Latin *redundant-* 'surging up,' from the verb *redundare* (see REDOUND). —**re·dun·dant·ly** *adv.*

re·du·pli·cate /ri'd(y)o͞opli,kāt; 'rē-/ ▸*v.* [*trans.*] repeat or copy so as to form another of the same kind: *the upper parts of the harmony may be reduplicated at the octave above.* ■ repeat (a syllable or other linguistic element) exactly or with a slight change, e.g., *hurly-burly, see-saw.* ▷late 16th cent.: from late Latin *reduplicat-* 'doubled again,' from the verb *reduplicare*, from *re-* 'again' + *duplicare* (see DUPLICATE). —**re·du·pli·ca·tion** /ri,d(y)o͞opli'kāsHən; ,rē-/ *n.* —**re·du·pli·ca·tive** /-,kātiv/ *adj.*

re·dux /rē'dəks; 'rē'dəks/ ▸*adj.* [*postpositive*] brought back; revived: *the 1980s were far more than just the '50s redux.* ▷late 19th cent.: from Latin, from *reducere* 'bring back.'

red va·le·ri·an ▸*n.* see VALERIAN.

red wig·gler ▸*n.* another term for RED WORM (sense 1).

red·wing /'red,wiNG/ ▸*n.* **1** a small migratory thrush that breeds mainly in northern Europe, with red underwings showing in flight. • *Turdus iliacus*, subfamily Turdinae, family Muscicapidae. **2** any of a number of other red-winged birds, esp. the American red-winged blackbird. See BLACKBIRD (sense 2).

red wolf ▸*n.* a fairly small wolf with a cinnamon or tawny-colored coat, native to the southeastern U.S. but possibly extinct in the wild. • *Canis rufus*, family Canidae.

red·wood /'red,wo͝od/ ▸*n.* either of two giant conifers with thick fibrous bark, native to California and Oregon. They are the tallest known trees and are among the largest living organisms. • Two species in the family Taxodiaceae: the **California** (or **coast**) **redwood** (*Sequoia sempervirens*), which can grow to a height of 325 feet (110 m), and the **giant redwood** (*Sequoiadendron giganteum*), which can reach a trunk diameter of 35 feet (11 m). ■ used in names of other, chiefly tropical, trees with reddish timber.

giant redwood tree

Red·wood Cit·y /'red,wo͝od/ a port city in north central California, on the southwestern side of San Francisco Bay, now part of the Silicon Valley complex; pop. 66,072.

red worm ▸*n.* **1** a red earthworm used in composting kitchen waste and as fishing bait. Also called RED WIGGLER. • *Lumbricus rubellus*, family Lumbricidae. **2** a parasitic nematode worm occurring in the intestines of horses. • Genus *Strongylus*, class Phasmida.

red zone ▸*n.* a red sector on a gauge or dial corresponding to conditions that exceed safety limits: *ozone readings edged into the red zone.* ■ a region that is dangerous or forbidden, or in which a particular activity is prohibited: *any officer who parks in the red zone outside the courthouse could receive a ticket.*

ree·bok ▸*n.* variant spelling of RHEBOK.

re·ech·o /rē'ekō/ ▸*v.* (**-ech·oes, -ech·oed**) echo again or repeatedly: [*intrans.*] *Dawn's words reechoed in her mind.*
▸*n.* a reechoed word or sound.

Reed[1] /rēd/, Stanley Forman (1884–1980), U.S. Supreme Court associate justice 1938–57. A supporter of President Franklin D. Roosevelt's New Deal programs, he held various federal positions before being named to the Court.

Reed[2], Walter (1851–1902), U.S. army surgeon. He proved that the yellow fever virus is transmitted by mosquitoes. Walter Reed Hospital in Washington, DC, is named for him.

Reed[3], Willis (1942–), U.S. basketball player. A center for the New York Knickerbockers 1964–74, he was the NBA's most valuable player for the 1969–1970 season. He later coached various professional and college teams. Basketball Hall of Fame (1981).

reed /rēd/ ▸*n.* **1** a tall, slender-leaved plant of the grass family that grows in water or on marshy ground. • Genera *Phragmites* and *Arundo*, family Gramineae: several species, in particular the **common** (or **Norfolk**) **reed** (*P. australis*), which is used for thatching. ■ used in names of similar plants growing in wet habitats, e.g., **bur reed**. ■ a tall, thin, straight stalk of such a plant, used esp. as material for thatching. ■ [often as *adj.*] such plants growing in a mass or used as material, esp. for making thatch or household items: *a reed curtain | clumps of reed and grass.* ■ *poetic/literary* a rustic musical pipe made from such plants or from straw. **2** a thing or person resembling or likened to such plants, in particular: ■ a weak or impressionable person: *the jurors were mere* **reeds in the wind.** ■ *poetic/literary* an arrow. ■ a

Pronunciation Key ə *ago*; ər *over*; 'ə or ,ə *up*; 'ər or ,ər *fur*; a *hat*; ā *rate*; ä *car*; CH *chew*; e *let*; ē *see*; e(ə)r *air*; i *fit*; ī *by*; i(ə)r *ear*; NG *sing*; ō *go*; ô *for*; oi *boy*; o͝o *good*; o͞o *goo*; ou *out*; SH *she*; TH *thin*; T͟H *then*; (h)w *why*; ZH *vision*

weaver's comblike implement for separating the threads of the warp and correctly positioning the weft. ■ (**reeds**) semicylindrical adjacent moldings grouped like reeds laid together. **3** a piece of thin cane or metal, sometimes doubled, that vibrates in a current of air to produce the sound of various musical instruments, as in the mouthpiece of a clarinet or oboe, at the base of some organ pipes, and as part of a set in the accordion and harmonica. ■ a wind instrument played with a reed. ■ an organ stop with reed pipes. **4** an electrical contact used in a magnetically operated switch or relay. ▷Old English *hrēod*; related to Dutch *riet* and German *Ried*. **—reed·like** /-ˌlīk/ *adj.*

reed·buck /ˈrēdˌbək/ ▸*n.* an African antelope with a distinctive whistling call and high bouncing jumps. • Genus *Redunca*, family Bovidae: three species.

reed·ed /ˈrēdid/ ▸*adj.* **1** shaped into or decorated with semicylindrical adjacent moldings. **2** (of a wind instrument) having a reed or reeds: [in *combination*] *a double-reeded oboe.*

reed·ing /ˈrēdiNG/ ▸*n.* a small semicylindrical molding or ornamentation. ■ the making of such moldings.

re·ed·it /rēˈedit/ ▸*v.* (**-ed·it·ed, -ed·it·ing**) [*trans.*] edit (a text or film) again: *the third scene is still too long—we'll have to reedit.* **—re·ed·i·tion** /ˌrēəˈdiSHən/ *n.*

reed mace ▸*n.* another term for CATTAIL.

reed or·gan ▸*n.* a keyboard instrument similar to a harmonium, in which air is drawn upward past metal reeds to produce tones.

reed pipe ▸*n.* a simple wind instrument made from a reed or with the sound produced by a reed. ■ an organ pipe with a reed.

reed stop ▸*n.* an organ stop controlling reed pipes.

re·ed·u·cate /rēˈejəˌkāt/ ▸*v.* [*trans.*] educate or train (someone) in order to change their beliefs or behavior: *criminals are to be reeducated.* **—re·ed·u·ca·tion** /ˌrēˌejəˈkāSHən/ *n.*

reed war·bler ▸*n.* a Eurasian and African songbird with plain plumage, frequenting reed beds. • Genus *Acrocephalus*, family Sylviidae: several species, in particular the common *A. scirpaceus*.

reed·y /ˈrēdē/ ▸*adj.* (**reed·i·er, reed·i·est**) **1** (of a voice, sound, or instrument) high and thin in tone: *Frank's reedy voice | the reedy oboe.* **2** (of water or land) full of or edged with reeds: *they swam in the reedy lake.* **3** (of a person) tall and thin: *a reedy twelve-year-old.* **—reed·i·ness** *n.*

reef1 /rēf/ ▸*n.* a ridge of jagged rock, coral, or sand just above or below the surface of the sea. ■ *Austral.* & *S. African* a metalliferous mineral deposit, esp. one that is bedded and contains gold. ▷late 16th cent. (earlier as *riff*): from Middle Low German and Middle Dutch *rif, ref*, from Old Norse *rif*, literally 'rib,' used in the same sense; compare with REEF2.

reef2 *Sailing* ▸*n.* each of the several strips across a sail that can be taken in or rolled up to reduce the area exposed to the wind.
▸*v.* [*trans.*] take in one or more reefs of (a sail): *reefing the mainsail in strong winds.* ▷Middle English: from Middle Dutch *reef, rif*, from Old Norse *rif*, literally 'rib,' used in the same sense; compare with REEF1.

reef-build·er ▸*n.* a marine organism, esp. a coral, that builds reefs. **—reef-build·ing** *n.*

reef·er1 /ˈrēfər/ ▸*n.* *informal* a marijuana cigarette. ■ marijuana. ▷1930s: perhaps related to Mexican Spanish *grifo* '(smoker of) cannabis.'

reef·er2 ▸*n.* short for REEFER JACKET.

reef·er3 ▸*n.* *informal* a refrigerated truck, railroad car, or ship. ▷early 20th cent.: abbreviation.

reef·er jack·et ▸*n.* a thick, close-fitting, double-breasted jacket.

reef flat ▸*n.* the horizontal upper surface of a coral reef.

reef knot ▸*n.* a square knot, originally used for reefing sails.

reef·point /ˈrēfˌpoint/ ▸*n.* *Sailing* each of several short pieces of rope attached to a sail to secure it when reefed.

reek /rēk/ ▸*v.* [*intrans.*] smell strongly and unpleasantly; stink: *the yard* ***reeked of*** *wet straw and stale horse manure* | [as *adj.*] (**reeking**) *the reeking lavatories.* ■ *figurative* be suggestive of something unpleasant or disapproved of: *the speeches* ***reeked of*** *anti-Semitism.* ■ *archaic* give off smoke, steam, or fumes: *while temples crash, and towers in ashes reek.*
▸*n.* **1** [in *sing.*] a foul smell: *the reek of cattle dung.* **2** *chiefly Scottish* smoke. ▷Old English *rēocan* 'give out smoke or vapor,' *rēc* (noun) 'smoke,' of Germanic origin; related to Dutch *rieken* 'to smell,' *rook* 'smoke,' German *riechen* 'to smell,' *Rauch* 'smoke.' **—reek·y** *adj.*

reel /rēl/ ▸*n.* **1** a cylinder on which film, wire, thread, or other flexible materials can be wound. ■ a length of something wound on to such a device: ***a reel of*** *copper wire.* ■ a part of a movie: *in the final reel he is transformed from unhinged sociopath into local hero.* ■ a device for winding and unwinding a line as required, in particular a fishing reel. **2** a lively Scottish or Irish folk dance. ■ a piece of music for such a dance, typically in simple or duple time. ■ short for VIRGINIA REEL.
▸*v.* **1** [*trans.*] (**reel something in**) wind a line on to a reel by turning the reel. ■ bring something attached to a line, esp. a fish, toward one by turning a reel and winding in the line: *he struck, and reeled in a good perch.* **2** [*intrans.*] lose one's balance and stagger or lurch violently: *he punched Connolly in the ear,* ***sending him reeling*** | *she reeled back against the van.* ■ feel very giddy, disoriented, or bewildered, typically as a result of an unexpected setback: *the unaccustomed intake of alcohol made my head reel* | *figurative the nationalist government is already reeling from 225 percent monthly inflation.* ■ [with *adverbial of direction*] walk in a staggering or lurching manner, esp. while drunk: *the two reeled out of the bar arm in arm.* **3** [*intrans.*] dance a reel.
▸*phrasal v.* □ **reel (something) off** say or recite something rapidly and without apparent effort: *she proceeded to reel off in rapid Italian the various dishes of the day.* ▷Old English *hrēol*, denoting a rotatory device on which spun thread is wound; of unknown origin. **—reel·er** *n.*

re·e·lect /ˌrēəˈlekt/ ▸*v.* [*trans.*] (usu. **be reelected**) elect (someone) to a further term of office: *Wilson was reelected in November 1994.* **—re·e·lec·tion** /-ˈlekSHən/ *n.*

Reel·foot Lake /ˈrēlfo͝ot/ a lake in the northwestern corner of Tennessee, near the Mississippi River, formed during the 1811 earthquake that centered on nearby New Madrid in Missouri.

reel-to-reel ▸*adj.* denoting a tape recorder in which the tape passes between two reels mounted separately rather than within a cassette, now generally superseded by cassette players except for professional use.

re·e·merge /ˌrēəˈmərj/ ▸*v.* [*intrans.*] emerge again; come into sight or prominence once more: *nationalism has reemerged in western Europe.* **—re·e·mer·gence** /-jəns/ *n.* **—re·e·mer·gent** /-jənt/ *adj.*

re·en·act /ˌrēəˈnakt/ ▸*v.* [*trans.*] **1** act out (a past event): *bombers were gathered together to reenact the historic first air attack.* **2** bring (a law) into effect again when the original statute has been repealed. **—re·en·act·ment** *n.*

re·en·gi·neer /ˌrēˌenjəˈnir/ ▸*v.* [*trans.*] redesign (a device or machine). ■ [often as *n.*] (**reengineering**) restructure (a company or part of its operations).

re·en·list /ˌrēənˈlist/ ▸*v.* [*intrans.*] enlist again in the armed forces. **—re·en·list·er** *n.*

re·en·trant /rēˈentrənt/ ▸*adj.* (of an angle) pointing inward. The opposite of SALIENT. ■ having an inward-pointing angle or angles.
▸*n.* **1** a reentrant angle. ■ an indentation or depression in terrain. **2** a person who has reentered something, esp. the labor force.

re·en·try /rē ˈentrē/ ▸*n.* (*pl.* **-tries**) **1** the action or process of reentering something: *programs designed to prepare you for reentry to the profession* | *she feared she would not be granted reentry into Britain.* ■ the return of a spacecraft or missile into the earth's atmosphere. **2** *Law* the action of retaking or repossession. **3** a visible duplication of part of the design for a postage stamp due to an inaccurate first impression. ■ a stamp displaying such a duplication.

Reeve /rēv/, Christopher (1952–2004), U.S. actor. He starred in the *Superman* movie series 1978–87, as well as other movies such as *Somewhere in Time* (1980), *Deathtrap* (1982), and *Rear Window* (1998). A horseback riding accident in 1995 left him paralyzed from the neck down, after which he became a prominent advocate for public awareness of and research support for spinal cord injuries.

reeve1 /rēv/ ▸*n.* *Canadian* the president of a village or town council. ■ *chiefly historical* a local official, in particular the chief magistrate of a town or district in Anglo-Saxon England. ▷Old English *rēfa*.

reeve2 ▸*v.* (*past* and *past part.* **rove** /rōv/ or **reeved**) [*trans.*] *Nautical* thread (a rope or rod) through a ring or other aperture, esp. in a block: *one end of the new rope was* ***reeved through*** *the chain.* ■ fasten (a rope or block) in this way. ▷early 17th cent.: probably from Dutch *reven* 'reef (a sail)' (see REEF2).

reeve3 ▸*n.* a female ruff. See RUFF1 sense 3. ▷early 17th cent.: variant of dialect *ree*, of unknown origin.

re·ex·am·ine /ˌrē-igˈzamən/ ▸*v.* [*trans.*] examine again or further: *I will have the body reexamined.* ■ *Law* examine (a witness) again, after cross-examination by the opposing counsel. **—re·ex·am·i·na·tion** /-ˌzaməˈnāSHən/ *n.*

re·ex·port /rēˈekˌspôrt; rē-ekˈspôrt/ ▸*v.* [*trans.*] export (imported goods), typically after they have undergone further processing or manufacture.
▸*n.* the action of reexporting something. ■ a thing that has or will be reexported. **—re·ex·por·ta·tion** /ˌrēˌekspôrˈtāSHən/ *n.* **—re·ex·port·er** *n.*

ref /ref/ ▸*n.* *informal* (in sports) a referee. ▷late 19th cent.: abbreviation.

ref. ▸*abbr.* ■ reference. ■ refer to.

re·face /rēˈfās/ ▸*v.* [*trans.*] put a new facing on (a building): *part of the tower was refaced with brick.*

re·fash·ion /rēˈfaSHən/ ▸*v.* [*trans.*] fashion (something) again or differently.

re·fec·tion /riˈfekSHən/ ▸*n.* *poetic/literary* refreshment by food or drink. ■ a meal, esp. a light one. ■ *Zoology* the eating of partly digested fecal pellets, as practiced by rabbits. ▷Middle English: from Old French, from Latin *refectio(n-)*, from *reficere* 'renew' (see REFECTORY).

re·fec·to·ry /riˈfekt(ə)rē/ ▸*n.* (*pl.* **-ries**) a room used for communal meals, esp. in an educational or religious institution. ▷late Middle English: from late Latin *refectorium*, from Latin *reficere* 'refresh, renew,' from *re-* 'back' + *facere* 'make.'

re·fec·to·ry ta·ble ▸*n.* a long, narrow table.

re·fer /riˈfər/ ▸*v.* (**-ferred, -fer·ring**) **1** [*intrans.*] (**refer to**) mention or allude to: *the reports of the commission are often referred to in the media* | *New York,* ***referred to as*** *the Big Apple.* ■ [*trans.*] (**refer someone to**) direct the attention of someone to: *I refer my colleague to the reply that I gave some moments ago.* ■ (**refer to**) (of a word or phrase) describe or denote; have as a referent: *the term "rhetoric" almost invariably refers to persuasion.* **2** [*trans.*] (**refer something to**) pass a matter to (another body, typically one with more authority or expertise) for a decision: *disagreement arose and the issue was referred back to the Executive Committee.* ■ send or direct (someone) to a medical specialist: *she was* ***referred to*** *a clinical psychologist for counseling.* ■ [*intrans.*] (**refer to**) read or otherwise use (a source of information) in order to ascertain something; consult: *I always refer to a dictionary when I come across a new word.* **3** [*trans.*] (**refer something to**) *archaic* trace or attribute something to (someone or something) as a cause or source: *the God to whom he habitually referred his highest inspirations.* ■ regard something as belonging to (a certain period, place, or class). ▷late Middle English: from Old French *referer* or Latin *referre* 'carry back,' from *re-* 'back' + *ferre* 'bring.' **—ref·er·a·ble** /ˈref(ə)rəbəl; riˈfər-/ *adj.* **—re·fer·rer** *n.*

ref·er·ee /ˌrefəˈrē/ ▸*n.* **1** an official who watches a game or match closely to ensure that the rules are adhered to and (in some sports) to arbitrate on matters arising from the play. **2** a person whose opinion or judgment is sought in some connection, or who is referred to for a decision in a dispute. ■ a person willing to testify in writing about the character or ability of someone, esp. an applicant for a job. ■ a person appointed to examine and assess for publication a scientific or other academic work.
▸*v.* (**-er·ees, -er·eed, -er·ee·ing**) **1** [*trans.*] officiate as referee at (a game or match): *the man who refereed the World Cup final.* **2** act as referee: [*trans.*] *to referee a split between deficit hawks and doves* | [as *adj.*] (**refereed**) *the only journal that publishes refereed articles.*

ref·er·ence /ˈref(ə)rəns/ ▸*n.* **1** the action of mentioning or alluding to something: *he* ***made reference to*** *the enormous power of the mass media* | *references to Darwinism and evolution.* ■ a mention or citation of a source of information in a book or article. ■ a book or passage cited in such a way. **2** use of a source of information in order to ascertain something: *popular works of reference.* ■ the sending of a matter for decision or consideration to some authority: *demanded the immediate reference of the whole dispute to the United Nations.* **3** a letter from a previous employer testifying to someone's ability or reliability, used when applying for a new job. ■ a person giving this.
▸*v.* [*trans.*] provide (a book or article) with citations of authorities: *each chapter is referenced, citing literature up to 1990.*

▸*adj.* of, denoting, or pertaining to a reference library: *most reference departments house magazine rooms.*
▸*PHRASES* □ **for future reference** for use at a later date: *she lodged this idea in the back of her mind for future reference.* □ **terms of reference** the scope and limitations of an activity or area of knowledge: *the judge will present a plan outlining the inquiry's terms of reference.* □ **with** (or **in**) **reference to** in relation to; as regards: *war can only be explained with reference to complex social factors.*

ref·er·ence book ▸*n.* a book intended to be consulted for information on specific matters rather than read from beginning to end: *a beat-up old grade-school dictionary was the only reference book we ever had in our house.*

ref·er·ence e·lec·trode ▸*n. Electronics* an electrode having an accurately maintained potential, used as a reference for measurement by other electrodes.

ref·er·ence frame ▸*n.* see FRAME OF REFERENCE.

ref·er·ence group ▸*n.* a social group that a person takes as a standard in forming attitudes and behavior.

ref·er·ence li·brar·y ▸*n.* a library, typically one holding many reference books, in which the books are not for loan but may be read on site. ■ a collection of reference books.

ref·er·ence point ▸*n.* a basis or standard for evaluation, assessment, or comparison; a criterion.

ref·er·en·dum /ˌrefəˈrendəm/ ▸*n.* (*pl.* **-dums** or **-da** /-də/) a general vote by the electorate on a single political question that has been referred to them for a direct decision. ■ the process of referring a political question to the electorate for this purpose. ▷mid 19th cent.: from Latin, gerund ('referring'), or neuter gerundive ('something to be brought back or referred') of *referre* (see REFER).

ref·er·ent /ˈref(ə)rənt/ ▸*n. Linguistics* the thing that a word or phrase denotes or stands for: *"the Morning Star" and "the Evening Star" have the same referent (the planet Venus).* ▷mid 19th cent.: from Latin *referent-* 'bringing back,' from the verb *referre* (see REFER).

ref·er·en·tial /ˌrefəˈrenCHəl/ ▸*adj.* **1** containing or of the nature of references or allusions. **2** *Linguistics* of or relating to a referent, in particular having the external world rather than a text or language as a referent. **—ref·er·en·ti·al·i·ty** /ˌrefəˌrenCHēˈalətē/ *n.* **—ref·er·en·tial·ly** *adv.*

re·fer·ral /riˈfərəl/ ▸*n.* an act of referring someone or something for consultation, review, or further action. ■ the directing of a patient to a medical specialist by a primary care physician. ■ a person whose case has been referred to a specialist doctor or a professional body.

re·ferred pain ▸*n. Medicine* pain felt in a part of the body other than its actual source.

re·fi /rēˈfī/ ▸*v.* (**-fies, -fied, -fy·ing**) [*trans.*] refinance (a mortgage):
▸*adj.* relating to refinancing and the refinancing market: *the refi boom is over.* ▷shortening.

re·fill ▸*v.* /rēˈfil/ [*trans.*] fill (a container) again: *she paused and refilled her glass with wine before going on.* ■ replenish the supply of (medicine called for in a prescription): *there's nothing he can do but refill his Valium prescription.* ■ [*intrans.*] (of a container) become full again: *the empty pool will rapidly refill from rain and snow.*
▸*n.* /ˈrēˌfil/ an act of filling a container again: *he proffered his glass for a refill.* ■ a container, esp. a glass, that is so filled: *the waitress appeared with refills.* ■ a replenished supply of medicine called for in a prescription: *an oral contraceptive refill was dispensed.* **—re·fill·a·ble** *adj.*

re·fi·nance /ˌrēfəˈnans; rēˈfīˌnans/ ▸*v.* [*trans.*] finance (something) again, typically with a new loan at a lower rate of interest.

re·fine /riˈfīn/ ▸*v.* [*trans.*] remove impurities or unwanted elements from (a substance), typically as part of an industrial process: *sugar was refined by boiling it in huge iron vats.* ■ improve (something) by making small changes, in particular make (an idea, theory, or method) more subtle and accurate: *ease of access to computers has refined analysis and presentation of data.* ▷late 16th cent.: from RE- 'again' + the verb FINE[1], influenced by French *raffiner.* **—re·fin·er** *n.*

re·fined /riˈfīnd/ ▸*adj.* with impurities or unwanted elements having been removed by processing. ■ elegant and cultured in appearance, manner, or taste: *her voice was very low and refined.* ■ precise; subtle: *a more refined timetable for continental drift.*

re·fine·ment /riˈfīnmənt/ ▸*n.* the process of removing impurities or unwanted elements from a substance: *the refinement of uranium.* ■ the improvement or clarification of something by the making of small changes: *this gross figure needs considerable refinement | recent **refinements to** production techniques.* ■ cultured elegance in behavior or manner: *her carefully cultivated veneer of refinement.* ■ sophisticated and superior good taste: *the refinement of Hellenistic art.*

re·fin·er·y /riˈfīnərē/ ▸*n.* (*pl.* **-er·ies**) an industrial installation where a substance is refined: *an oil refinery.*

re·fin·ish /rēˈfiniSH/ ▸*v.* [*trans.*] apply a new finish to (a surface or object).
▸*n.* an act of refinishing a surface or object.

re·fit ▸*v.* /rēˈfit/ (**-fit·ted, -fit·ting**) [*trans.*] replace or repair machinery, equipment, and fittings in (a ship, building, etc.): *a lucrative contract to refit a submarine fleet.*
▸*n.* /ˈrēˌfit; rēˈfit/ a restoration or repair of machinery, equipment, or fittings.

refl. ▸*abbr.* ■ reflection. ■ reflective. ■ reflex. ■ reflexive.

re·flag /rēˈflag/ ▸*v.* (**-flagged, -flag·ging**) [*trans.*] change the national registry of (a ship).

re·flate /riˈflāt/ ▸*v.* [*trans.*] expand the level of output of (an economy) by government stimulus, using either fiscal or monetary policy. ▷1930s: from RE- 'again,' on the pattern of *inflate, deflate.* **—re·fla·tion** /riˈflāSHən/ *n.* **—re·fla·tion·ar·y** /riˈflāSHəˌnerē/ *n.*

re·flect /riˈflekt/ ▸*v.* **1** [*trans.*] (of a surface or body) throw back (heat, light, or sound) without absorbing it: *when the sun's rays hit the earth a lot of the heat is reflected back into space* | [as *adj.*] (**reflected**) *his eyes gleamed in the reflected light.* ■ (of a mirror or shiny surface) show an image of: *he could see himself reflected in Keith's mirrored glasses.* ■ embody or represent (something) in a faithful or appropriate way: *stocks are priced at a level that reflects a company's prospects | schools should reflect cultural differences.* ■ (of an action or situation) bring (credit or discredit) to the relevant parties: *the main contract is progressing well, which reflects great credit on those involved.* ■ [*intrans.*] (**reflect well/badly on**) bring about a good or bad impression of: *the incident reflects badly on the operating practices of the airlines.* **2** [*intrans.*] (**reflect on/upon**) think deeply or carefully about: *he reflected with sadness on the unhappiness of his marriage* | [with *clause*] *Charles reflected that maybe there was hope for the family after all.* ■ *archaic* make disparaging remarks about. ▷late Middle English: from Old French *reflecter* or Latin *reflectere*, from *re-* 'back' + *flectere* 'to bend.'

re·flect·ance /riˈflektəns/ ▸*n. Physics* the measure of the proportion of light or other radiation striking a surface that is reflected off it.

re·flect·ed glo·ry ▸*n.* fame or approval achieved through association with someone else rather than through one's own efforts.

re·flect·ing tel·e·scope ▸*n.* a telescope in which a mirror is used to collect and focus light.

re·flec·tion /riˈflekSHən/ ▸*n.* **1** the throwing back by a body or surface of light, heat, or sound without absorbing it: *the reflection of light.* ■ an amount of light, heat, or sound that is thrown back in such a way: *the reflections from the streetlights gave us just enough light.* ■ an image seen in a mirror or shiny surface: *Marianne surveyed her reflection in the mirror.* ■ a thing that is a consequence of or arises from something else: *a healthy skin is a reflection of good health in general.* ■ [in *sing.*] a thing bringing discredit to someone or something: *it was a sad **reflection on** society that because of his affliction he was picked on.* ■ *Mathematics* the conceptual operation of inverting a system or event with respect to a plane, each element being transferred perpendicularly through the plane to a point the same distance the other side of it. **2** serious thought or consideration: *he doesn't get much time for reflection.* ■ an idea about something, esp. one that is written down or expressed: *reflections on human destiny and art.* ▷late Middle English: from Old French *reflexion* or late Latin *reflexio(n-)*, from Latin *reflex-* 'bent back,' from the verb *reflectere.*

re·flec·tion co·ef·fi·cient ▸*n.* another term for REFLECTANCE.

re·flec·tive /riˈflektiv/ ▸*adj.* **1** providing a reflection; capable of reflecting light or other radiation: *reflective glass | reflective clothing.* ■ produced by reflection: *a colorful reflective glow.* **2** relating to or characterized by deep thought; thoughtful: *a quiet, reflective, astute man.* **—re·flec·tive·ly** *adv.* **—re·flec·tive·ness** *n.*

re·flec·tiv·i·ty /riˌflekˈtivətē; ˌrēˌflek-/ ▸*n. Physics* the property of reflecting light or radiation, esp. reflectance as measured independently of the thickness of a material.

re·flec·tom·e·ter /riˌflekˈtämətər; ˌrē-/ ▸*n.* an instrument for measuring quantities associated with reflection, in particular (also **time domain reflectometer**) an instrument for locating discontinuities (e.g., faults in electric cables) by detecting and measuring reflected pulses of energy. **—re·flec·tom·e·try** /-ˈtämətrē/ *n.*

re·flec·tor /riˈflektər/ ▸*n.* a piece of glass, metal, or other material for reflecting light in a required direction, e.g., a red one on the back of a motor vehicle or bicycle. ■ an object or device that reflects radio waves, seismic vibrations, sound, or other waves. ■ a reflecting telescope.

re·flet /rəˈflā/ ▸*n.* luster or iridescence, esp. on ceramics. ▷French, literally 'reflection.'

re·flex /ˈrēˌfleks/ ▸*n.* **1** an action that is performed as a response to a stimulus and without conscious thought: *a newborn baby is equipped with basic reflexes.* ■ (**reflexes**) a person's ability to perform such actions, esp. quickly: *he was saved by his superb reflexes.* ■ (in reflexology) a response in a part of the body to stimulation of a corresponding point on the feet, hands, or head: [as *adj.*] *reflex points.* **2** a thing that is determined by and reproduces the essential features or qualities of something else: *politics was no more than a reflex of economics.* ■ a word formed by development from an earlier stage of a language. ■ *archaic* a reflected source of light: *the reflex from the window lit his face.*
▸*adj.* **1** (of an action) performed without conscious thought as an automatic response to a stimulus: *sneezing is a reflex action.* **2** (of an angle) exceeding 180°. ■ *archaic* (of light) reflected. ■ (also **re·flexed**) (esp. of flower petals) bent or turned backward. ■ *archaic* (of a thought) directed or turned back upon the mind itself; introspective. ▷early 16th cent. (as a noun denoting reflection): from Latin *reflexus* 'a bending back,' from *reflectere* 'bend back' (see REFLECT). **—re·flex·ly** /ˈrēˌfleksle; riˈflekslē/ *adv.*

re·flex arc ▸*n. Physiology* the nerve pathway involved in a reflex action including at its simplest a sensory nerve and a motor nerve with a synapse between.

re·flex cam·er·a ▸*n.* a camera with a ground glass focusing screen on which the image is formed by a combination of lens and mirror, enabling the scene to be correctly composed and focused.

re·flex·i·ble /riˈfleksəbəl/ ▸*adj. chiefly technical* capable of being reflected. **—re·flex·i·bil·i·ty** /riˌfleksəˈbilətē/ *n.*

re·flex·ion /riˈflekSHən/ ▸*n. chiefly Brit.* variant spelling of REFLECTION.

re·flex·ive /riˈfleksiv/ ▸*adj.* **1** *Grammar* denoting a pronoun that refers back to the subject of the clause in which it is used, e.g., *myself, themselves.* ■ (of a verb or clause) having a reflexive pronoun as its object, e.g., *wash oneself.* **2** (of an action) performed as a reflex, without conscious thought: *at concerts like this one, standing ovations have become reflexive.* **3** *Logic* (of a relation) always holding between a term and itself. **4** (of a method or theory in the social sciences) taking account of itself or of the effect of the personality or presence of the researcher on what is being investigated.
▸*n.* a reflexive word or form, esp. a pronoun. **—re·flex·ive·ly** *adv.* **—re·flex·ive·ness** *n.* **—re·flex·iv·i·ty** /riˌflekˈsivətē; ˌrēˌflek/ *n.*

re·flex·ol·o·gy /ˌrēˌflekˈsäləjē/ ▸*n.* **1** a system of massage used to relieve tension and treat illness, based on the theory that there are reflex points on the feet, hands, and head linked to every part of the body. **2** *Psychology* the scientific study of reflex action as it affects behavior. **—re·flex·ol·o·gist** /-jist/ *n.* (usu. in sense 1).

re·flow ▸*n.* /ˈrēˌflō/ **1** *Electronics* a soldering technique in which surface-mount components are held in position on a circuit board using a paste containing solder that melts to form soldered joints when the circuit board is heated. **2** (in word processing) the action of rearranging text on a page after having changed such features as type size, line length, and spacing.
▸*v.* /ˈrēˌflō; rēˈflō/ [*trans.*] **1** *Electronics* attach (a surface-mount component) using the reflow technique. **2** (in word processing) rearrange (text) on a page,

Pronunciation Key ə *ago;* ər *over;* ˈə or ˌə *up;* ˈər or ˌər *fur;* a *hat;* ā *rate;* ä *car;* CH *chew;* e *let;* ē *see;* e(ə)r *air;* i *fit;* ī *by;* i(ə)r *ear;* NG *sing;* ō *go;* ô *for;* oi *boy;* o͝o *good;* o͞o *goo;* ou *out;* SH *she;* TH *thin;* T͟H *then;* (h)w *why;* ZH *vision*

having changed such features as type size, line length, and spacing.

ref·lu·ent /ˈref,lo͞oənt; refˈlo͞o-/ ▸*adj. poetic/literary* flowing back; ebbing: *the refluent waters of the Mississippi.* ▹late Middle English: from Latin *refluent-* 'flowing back,' from the verb *refluere,* from *re-* 'back' + *fluere* 'to flow.' **—re·flu·ence** *n.*

re·flux /ˈrē,fləks/ ▸*n. Chemistry* the process of boiling a liquid in such a way that any vapor is liquefied and returned to the stock. ■ *technical* the flowing back of a liquid, esp. that of a fluid in the body.
▸*v.* [*intrans.*] *Chemistry* boil or cause to boil in circumstances such that the vapor returns to the stock of liquid after condensing. ■ [*intrans.*] *technical* (of a liquid, esp. a bodily fluid) flow back.

re·fo·cus /rēˈfōkəs/ ▸*v.* (**-fo·cused, -fo·cus·ing** or **-fo·cussed, -fo·cus·sing**) [*trans.*] adjust the focus of (a lens or one's eyes). ■ focus (attention or resources) on something new or different: *refocus attention on yourself through repeating your main points.*

re·for·est /rēˈfôrəst; -ˈfärəst/ ▸*v.* [*trans.*] replant with trees; cover again with forest: *a project to reforest the country's coastal areas.* **—re·for·est·a·tion** /rē,fôrəˈstāshən; -ˈfärə-/ *n.*

re·forge /rēˈfôrj/ ▸*v.* [*trans.*] forge (something) again or differently: *they wanted to reforge the identity of the nation.*

re·form /riˈfôrm/ ▸*v.* [*trans.*] **1** make changes in (something, typically a social, political, or economic institution or practice) in order to improve it: *an opportunity to reform and restructure an antiquated schooling model.* ■ bring about a change in (someone) so that they no longer behave in an immoral, criminal, or self-destructive manner: *the state has a duty to reform criminals* | [as *adj.*] (**reformed**) *a reformed gambler.* ■ [*intrans.*] (of a person) change oneself in such a way: *it was only when his drunken behavior led to blows that he started to reform.* **2** *Chemistry* subject (hydrocarbons) to a catalytic process in which straight-chain molecules are converted to branched forms for use in gasoline.
▸*n.* the action or process of reforming an institution or practice: *the reform of the divorce laws* | *economic reforms.*
▸*adj.* (**Reform**) of, denoting, or pertaining to Reform Judaism: *a Reform rabbi.* ▹Middle English (as a verb in the senses 'restore (peace)' and 'bring back to the original condition'): from Old French *reformer* or Latin *reformare,* from *re-* 'back' + *formare* 'to form, shape.' The noun dates from the mid 17th cent. **—re·form·a·ble** *adj.* **—re·form·a·tive** /-mətiv/ *adj.* **—re·form·er** *n.*

re-form /ˈrēˈfôrm/ ▸*v.* form or cause to form again: [*intrans.*] *the clouds re-formed over the sun.*

re·for·mat /rēˈfôr,mat/ ▸*v.* (**-mat·ted, -mat·ting**) [*trans.*] *chiefly Computing* give a new format to; revise or represent in another format.

ref·or·ma·tion /,refərˈmāshən/ ▸*n.* **1** the action or process of reforming an institution or practice: *the reformation of the Senate.* **2** (**the Reformation**) a 16th-century movement for the reform of abuses in the Roman Catholic Church ending in the establishment of the Reformed and Protestant Churches.

> The roots of the Reformation go back to the 14th-century attacks on the wealth and hierarchy of the Church made by groups such as the Lollards and the Hussites. But the Reformation is usually thought of as beginning in 1517 when Martin Luther issued ninety-five theses criticizing Church doctrine and practice. In Denmark, Norway, Sweden, Saxony, Hesse, and Brandenburg, supporters broke away and established Protestant churches, while in Switzerland a separate movement was led by Zwingli and later Calvin.

▹late Middle English: from Latin *reformatio(n-),* from *reformare* 'shape again' (see **REFORM**). **—ref·or·ma·tion·al** /-shənl/ *adj.*

re-for·ma·tion /,rē,fôrˈmāshən/ ▸*n.* the action or process of forming again.

re·form·a·to·ry /riˈfôrmə,tôrē/ ▸*n.* (*pl.* **-ries**) an institution to which youthful offenders are sent as an alternative to prison; a reform school.
▸*adj.* tending or intended to produce reform.

Re·formed Church ▸*n.* a church that has accepted the principles of the Reformation, esp. a Calvinist church (as distinct from Lutheran).

re·form·ist /riˈfôrmist/ ▸*adj.* supporting or advancing gradual reform rather than abolition or revolution.
▸*n.* a person who advocates gradual reform rather than abolition or revolution. **—re·form·ism** /-,mizəm/ *n.*

Re·form Ju·da·ism ▸*n.* a form of Judaism, initiated in Germany by the philosopher Moses Mendelssohn (1729–86), that has reformed or abandoned aspects of Orthodox Jewish worship and ritual in an attempt to adapt to modern changes in social, political, and cultural life. **—Re·form Jew** *n.*

re·form school ▸*n.* an institution to which youthful offenders are sent as an alternative to prison.

re·fract /riˈfrakt/ ▸*v.* [*trans.*] (usu. **be refracted**) (of water, air, or glass) make (a ray of light) change direction when it enters at an angle: *the rays of light are refracted by the material of the lens.* ■ measure the focusing characteristics of (an eye) or of the eyes of (someone). ▹early 17th cent.: from Latin *refract-* 'broken up,' from the verb *refringere,* from *re-* 'back' + *frangere* 'to break.'

re·fract·ing tel·e·scope ▸*n.* a telescope that uses a converging lens to collect light.

re·frac·tion /riˈfrakshən/ ▸*n. Physics* the fact or phenomenon of light, radio waves, etc., being deflected in passing obliquely through the interface between one medium and another or through a medium of varying density. ■ change in direction of propagation of any wave as a result of its traveling at different speeds at different points along the wave front. ■ measurement of the focusing characteristics of an eye or eyes. ▹mid 17th cent.: from late Latin *refractio(n-),* from *refringere* 'break up' (see **REFRACT**).

re·frac·tive /riˈfraktiv/ ▸*adj.* of or involving refraction. **—re·frac·tive·ly** *adv.*

re·frac·tive in·dex ▸*n.* the ratio of the velocity of light in a vacuum to its velocity in a specified medium.

re·frac·tom·e·ter /ri,frakˈtämətər; rē-/ ▸*n.* an instrument for measuring a refractive index. **—re·frac·to·met·ric** /ri,fraktəˈmetrik; ,rē-/ *adj.* **—re·frac·tom·e·try** /-trē/ *n.*

re·frac·tor /riˈfraktər/ ▸*n.* a lens or other object that causes refraction. ■ a refracting telescope.

re·frac·to·ry /riˈfraktərē/ ▸*adj. formal* **1** stubborn or unmanageable: *his refractory pony.* **2** resistant to a process or stimulus: *some granules are* ***refractory to*** *secretory stimuli.* ■ *Medicine* (of a person, illness, or diseased tissue) not yielding to treatment: *healing of previously refractory ulcers.* ■ *rare Medicine* (of a person or animal) resistant to infection. ■ *technical* (of a substance) resistant to heat; hard to melt or fuse.
▸*n.* (*pl.* **-ries**) *technical* a substance that is resistant to heat. ▹early 17th cent.: alteration of obsolete *refractary,* from Latin *refractarius* 'stubborn' (see also **REFRACT**). **—re·frac·to·ri·ness** *n.*

re·frac·to·ry pe·ri·od ▸*n. Physiology* a period immediately following stimulation during which a nerve or muscle is unresponsive to further stimulation.

re·frain[1] /riˈfrān/ ▸*v.* [*intrans.*] stop oneself from doing something: *she* ***refrained from*** *comment.* ▹Middle English (in the sense 'restrain (a thought or feeling)'): from Old French *refrener,* from Latin *refrenare,* from *re-* (expressing intensive force) + *frenum* 'bridle.'

re·frain[2] ▸*n.* a repeated line or number of lines in a poem or song, typically at the end of each verse. ■ the musical accompaniment for such a line or number of lines. ■ a comment or complaint that is often repeated: *"Poor Tom" had become the constant refrain of his friends.* ▹late Middle English: from Old French, from *refraindre* 'break,' based on Latin *refringere* 'break up' (because the refrain "broke" the sequence).

re·frame /rēˈfrām/ ▸*v.* [*trans.*] **1** place (a picture or photograph) in a new frame. **2** frame or express (words or a concept or plan) differently.

re·fran·gi·ble /riˈfranjəbəl/ ▸*adj.* able to be refracted. ▹late 17th cent.: from modern Latin *refrangibilis,* from *refrangere* 'break up' (see **REFRACT**). **—re·fran·gi·bil·i·ty** /ri,franjəˈbilətē/ *n.*

re·fresh /riˈfresh/ ▸*v.* [*trans.*] give new strength or energy to; reinvigorate: *the shower had refreshed her* | [as *adj.*] (**refreshed**) *I awoke feeling calm and refreshed.* ■ stimulate or jog (someone's memory) by checking or going over previous information: *he was able to refresh her memory on many points.* ■ revise or update (skills or knowledge): *short-term courses give nurses an opportunity to refresh their skills.* ■ *Computing* update the display on (a screen). ■ pour more (drink) for someone or refill (a container) with drink: *the tea is cold and the pot needs refreshing.* ■ place or keep (food) in cold water so as to cool or maintain freshness.
▸*n. Computing* an act or function of updating the display on a screen. ▹late Middle English: from Old French *refreschier,* from *re-* 'back' + *fres(che)* 'fresh.'

re·fresh·er /riˈfreshər/ ▸*n.* a thing that refreshes, in particular: ■ [usu. as *adj.*] an activity that revises or updates one's skills or knowledge: *candidates take some refresher training before coming back.* ■ *dated* a drink.

re·fresh·er course ▸*n.* a short course reviewing or updating previous studies or training connected with one's profession.

re·fresh·ing /riˈfreshiNG/ ▸*adj.* serving to refresh or reinvigorate someone: *a refreshing drink* | *the morning air was so refreshing.* ■ welcome or stimulating because new or different: *it* ***makes a refreshing change*** *to be able to write about something nice* | *her directness is refreshing.* **—re·fresh·ing·ly** *adv.* [as *submodifier*] *a refreshingly different concept* | [*sentence adverb*] *refreshingly, the current spokesman is very frank.*

re·fresh·ment /riˈfreshmənt/ ▸*n.* **1** (usu. **refreshments**) a light snack or drink, esp. one provided in a public place or at a public event: *light refreshments are available* | *an ample supply of liquid refreshment.* **2** the giving of fresh mental or physical strength or energy: *hobbies and vacations are for refreshment and recreation.* ▹late Middle English (sense 2): from Old French *refreschement,* from the verb *refreschier* (see **REFRESH**).

re·fresh rate ▸*n. Computing* the frequency with which a monitor's display is updated.

re·fried beans /ˈrē,frīd/ ▸*plural n.* pinto beans boiled and fried in advance and reheated when required, used esp. in Mexican cooking.

re·frig·er·ant /riˈfrijərənt/ ▸*n.* a substance used for refrigeration.
▸*adj.* causing cooling or refrigeration. ▹late 16th cent. (denoting a substance that cools or allays fever): from French *réfrigérant* or Latin *refrigerant-* 'making cool,' from the verb *refrigerare* (see **REFRIGERATE**).

re·frig·er·ate /riˈfrijə,rāt/ ▸*v.* [*trans.*] subject (food or drink) to cold in order to chill or preserve it, typically by placing it in a refrigerator: *refrigerate the dough for one hour.* ▹late Middle English: from Latin *refrigerat-* 'made cool,' from the verb *refrigerare,* from *re-* 'back' + *frigus, frigor-* 'cold.' **—re·frig·er·a·tion** /ri,frijəˈrāshən/ *n.* **—re·frig·er·a·to·ry** /riˈfrijərə,tôrē/ *adj.*

re·frig·er·at·ed /riˈfrijə,rātid/ ▸*adj.* (of food or drink) chilled, esp. in a refrigerator: *sandwiches must be kept refrigerated in stores* | *refrigerated meat.* ■ (of a vehicle or container) used to keep or transport food or drink in a chilled condition: *refrigerated display units.*

re·frig·er·a·tor /riˈfrijə,rātər/ ▸*n.* an appliance or compartment that is artificially kept cool and used to store food and drink. Modern refrigerators generally make use of the cooling effect produced when a volatile liquid is forced to evaporate in a sealed system in which it can be condensed back to liquid outside the refrigerator.

re·frin·gent /riˈfrinjənt/ ▸*adj. Physics* refractive. ▹late 18th cent.: from Latin *refringent-,* literally 'breaking again,' from the verb *refringere.* **—re·frin·gence** *n.*

re·froze /rēˈfrōz/ ▸ past of **REFREEZE**.

re·fro·zen /rēˈfrōzən/ ▸ past participle of **REFREEZE**.

reft /reft/ ▸ past and past participle of **REAVE**.

re·fu·el /rēˈfyo͞o(ə)l/ ▸*v.* (**-fu·eled, -fu·el·ing;** *Brit.* **-fu·elled, -fu·el·ling**) [*trans.*] supply (a vehicle) with more fuel: *the authorities agreed to refuel the plane.* ■ [*intrans.*] (of a vehicle) be supplied with more fuel.

ref·uge /ˈref,yo͞oj; -,yo͞ozh/ ▸*n.* a condition of being safe or sheltered from pursuit, danger, or trouble: *he was forced to* ***take refuge in*** *the French embassy* | *I* ***sought refuge in*** *drink.* ■ something providing such shelter: *the family came to be seen as a* ***refuge from*** *a harsh world.* ■ an institution providing safe accommodations for women who have suffered violence from a husband or partner. ▹late Middle English: from Old French, from Latin *refugium,* from *re-* 'back' + *fugere* 'flee.'

ref·u·gee /,refyo͝oˈjē; ˈrefyo͝o,jē/ ▸*n.* a person who has been forced to leave their country in order to escape war, persecution, or natural disaster: *refugees from Nazi persecution* | [as *adj.*] *a refugee camp.* ▹late 17th cent.: from French *réfugié* 'gone in search of refuge,' past participle of *(se) réfugier,* from *refuge* (see **REFUGE**).

re·fu·gi·um /riˈfyo͞ojēəm/ ▸*n.* (*pl.* **-gi·a** /-jēə/) *Biology* an area in which a population of organisms can survive through a period of unfavorable conditions, esp. glaciation. ▹1950s: from Latin, literally 'place of refuge.'

re·ful·gent /riˈfo͝oljənt; -ˈfəl-/ ▸*adj. poetic/literary* shining brightly: *refulgent blue eyes.* ▹late 15th cent.: from

Latin *refulgent-* 'shining out,' from the verb *refulgere*, from *re-* (expressing intensive force) + *fulgere* 'to shine.' —**re·ful·gence** *n.* —**re·ful·gent·ly** *adv.*

re·fund[1] ▶*v.* /ri'fənd; 'rē,fənd/ [*trans.*] pay back (money), typically to a customer who is not satisfied with goods or services bought: *if you're not delighted with your purchase, we guarantee to refund your money in full.* ■ pay back money to (someone): *I'll refund you for the apples and any other damage.*

▶*n.* /'rē,fənd/ a repayment of a sum of money, typically to a dissatisfied customer: *you are entitled to reject it and insist on a refund | you'll get an immediate tax refund.* ▷late Middle English (in the senses 'pour back' and 'restore'): from Old French *refonder* or Latin *refundere*, from *re-* 'back' + *fundere* 'pour,' later associated with the verb **FUND**. The noun dates from the mid 19th cent. —**re·fund·a·ble** *adj.*

re·fund[2] /rē'fənd; 'rē-/ ▶*v.* fund (a debt, etc.) again.

re·fur·bish /ri'fərbisн/ ▶*v.* [*trans.*] (usu. **be refurbished**) renovate and redecorate (something, esp. a building): *the premises have been completely refurbished in our corporate style.* —**re·fur·bish·ment** *n.*

re·fur·nish /rē'fərnisн/ ▶*v.* [*trans.*] (often **be refurnished**) furnish (a room or building) again or differently.

re·fus·al /ri'fyo͞ozəl/ ▶*n.* [usu. with *infinitive*] an act or an instance of refusing; the state of being refused. ■ see **FIRST REFUSAL**.

ref·use[1] /ri'fyo͞oz/ ▶*v.* [*intrans.*] indicate or show that one is not willing to do something: *I refused to answer.* | [*intrans.*] *he was severely beaten when he refused.* ■ [*trans.*] indicate that one is not willing to accept or grant (something offered or requested): *she refused a cigarette* | [with *two objs.*] *the old lady was refused admission to four hospitals.* ■ *informal* (of a thing) fail to perform a required action: *the car refused to start.* ■ [*trans.*] decline to accept an offer of marriage from (someone): *he's so conceited he'd never believe anyone would refuse him.* ■ [*trans.*] (of a horse) stop short or run alongside (a fence or other obstacle) instead of jumping it. ▷Middle English: from Old French *refuser*, probably an alteration of Latin *recusare* 'to refuse,' influenced by *refutare* 'refute.' —**re·fus·er** *n.*

ref·use[2] /'ref,yo͞os; -,yo͞oz/ ▶*n.* matter thrown away or rejected as worthless; trash: *heaps of refuse | refuse collection.* ▷late Middle English : perhaps from Old French *refusé* 'refused,' past participle of *refuser* (see **REFUSE**[1]).

re·fuse·nik /ri'fyo͞oznik/ ▶*n.* **1** a person in the former Soviet Union who was refused permission to emigrate, in particular, a Jew forbidden to emigrate to Israel. **2** a person who refuses to follow orders or obey the law, esp. as a protest. ▷1970s: from **REFUSE**[1] + **-NIK**.

re·fute /ri'fyo͞ot/ ▶*v.* [*trans.*] prove (a statement or theory) to be wrong or false; disprove: *these claims have not been convincingly refuted.* ■ prove that (someone) is wrong. ■ deny or contradict (a statement or accusation): *a spokesman totally refuted the allegation of bias.* ▷mid 16th cent. : from Latin *refutare* 'repel, rebut.' —**re·fut·a·ble** *adj.* —**re·fut·al** /-'fyo͞otl/ *n.* (*rare*) —**ref·u·ta·tion** /,refyo͞o'tāsнən/ *n.* —**re·fut·er** *n.*

USAGE **Refute** and **repudiate** are sometimes confused. **Refute** means 'prove (something or someone) to be false or erroneous': *attempts to* ***refute*** *Einstein's theory.* **Repudiate** means 'reject as baseless, or refuse to acknowledge': *scholars who* ***repudiate*** *the story of Noah's Ark.* One could **repudiate** by silently turning one's back; to **refute** would require disproving by argument. In the second half of the 20th century, a more general sense of **refute** developed from the core one, meaning simply 'deny': *I absolutely* ***refute*** *the charges made against me.* Traditionalists object to the second use on the grounds that it is an unacceptable degradation of the language, but it is now widely accepted in standard English.

re·gain /ri'gān/ ▶*v.* [*trans.*] obtain possession or use of (something) again after losing it: *she died without regaining consciousness | the tyrant was able to regain Sicily.* See note at **RECOVER**. ■ reach (a place, position, or thing) again; get back to: *they were unable to regain their boats.* ▷mid 16th cent.: from French *regagner* (see **RE-**, **GAIN**).

re·gal /'rēgəl/ ▶*adj.* of, resembling, or fit for a monarch, esp. in being magnificent or dignified: *regal authority | her regal bearing.* ▷late Middle English: from Old French, or from Latin *regalis*, from *rex*, *reg-* 'king.' —**re·gal·ly** *adv.*

re·gale /ri'gāl/ ▶*v.* [*trans.*] entertain or amuse (someone) with talk: *he* ***regaled*** *her* ***with*** *a colorful account of that afternoon's meeting.* ■ lavishly supply (someone) with food or drink: *he was regaled with excellent home cooking.* ▷mid 17th cent.: from French *régaler*, from *re-* (expressing intensive force) + Old French *gale* 'pleasure.' —**re·gale·ment** *n.* (*rare*).

re·ga·li·a /ri'gālyə/ ▶*plural n.* [treated as *sing.* or *pl.*] the emblems or insignia of royalty, esp. the crown, scepter, and other ornaments used at a coronation. ■ the distinctive clothing worn and ornaments carried at formal occasions as an indication of status: *the Bishop of Florence* ***in full regalia.*** ■ distinctive, elaborate clothing: *young men, a few in gang regalia.* ▷mid 16th cent. (in the sense 'royal powers'): from medieval Latin, literally 'royal privileges,' from Latin, neuter plural of *regalis* 'regal.'

USAGE The word **regalia** comes from Latin and is, technically speaking, the plural of *regalis*. However, in the way the word is used in English today, it behaves as a collective noun, similar to words like **staff** or **government**. This means that it can be used with either a singular or plural verb (*the* ***regalia*** *of Russian tsardom* ***is*** *now displayed in the Kremlin* or *the* ***regalia*** *of Russian tsardom* ***are*** *now displayed in the Kremlin*). In fact, in English, **regalia** has no other singular form.

re·ga·li·an /ri'gālyən; -lēən/ ▶*adj. formal* belonging or relating to a monarch; regal: *regalian rights.* ▷early 19th cent.: from French *régalien*, from Latin *regalis* 'regal.'

re·gal·i·ty /ri'galətē/ ▶*n.* (*pl.* **-ties**) **1** the state of being a king or queen. ■ the demeanor or dignity appropriate to a king or queen: *Ellen awaited her guests, radiating regality.* **2** *archaic* a royal privilege. ▷late Middle English: from Anglo-Norman French *regalite* or medieval Latin *regalitas*, from *regalis* 'royal' (see **REGAL**).

re·gard /ri'gärd/ ▶*v.* [*trans.*] consider or think of (someone or something) in a specified way: *she regarded Omaha as her base | he was highly regarded by senators of both parties.* ■ gaze at steadily in a specified fashion: *Professor Ryker regarded him with a faint smile.* ■ (of a thing) have relation to or connection with; concern: *if these things regarded only myself, I could stand it with composure.* ■ *archaic* pay attention to; heed: *he talked very wisely, but I regarded him not.*

▶*n.* **1** attention to or concern for something: *the court must have* ***regard to*** *the principle of welfare | she rescued him without* ***regard for*** *herself.* ■ high opinion; liking and respect; esteem: *she had a particular* ***regard for*** *Eliot.* See note at **ESTEEM**. ■ [in *sing.*] a gaze; a steady or significant look: *he shifted uneasily before their clear regard.* **2** (**regards**) best wishes (used to express friendliness in greetings, esp. at the end of letters): *Warm regards, Helen | give her my regards.* ▷Middle English: from Old French *regarder* 'to watch,' from *re-* 'back' (also expressing intensive force) + *garder* 'to guard.'

▶***PHRASES*** □ **as regards** concerning; with respect to: *as regards content, the program will cover important current issues.* □ **in this** (or **that**) **regard** in connection with the point previously mentioned: *there was little incentive for them to be active in this regard.* □ **with** (or **in**) **regard to** as concerns; with respect to: *he made inquiries with regard to Beth.*

re·gard·ant /ri'gärdnt/ ▶*adj.* [usu. *postpositive*] *Heraldry* looking backward. ▷late Middle English: from Anglo-Norman French and Old French, present participle of *regarder* 'look (again).'

re·gard·ful /ri'gärdfəl/ ▶*adj.* [*predic.*] (**regardful of**) *formal* paying attention to; mindful of: *Parker was not overly regardful of public opinion.* —**re·gard·ful·ly** *adv.*

re·gard·ing /ri'gärdiNG/ ▶*prep.* with respect to; concerning: *your recent letter regarding the above proposal.*

re·gard·less /ri'gärdləs/ ▶*adv.* without paying attention to the present situation; despite the prevailing circumstances: *they were determined to carry on regardless.* —**re·gard·less·ly** *adv.* —**re·gard·less·ness** *n.*

▶***PHRASE*** □ **regardless of** without regard or consideration for: *the allowance is paid regardless of age or income.*

USAGE See usage at **IRREGARDLESS**.

re·gath·er /rē'gaTHər/ ▶*v.* **1** [*trans.*] collect or gather (something) again: *after 1910 the workers' movement regathered momentum.* **2** [*intrans.*] meet or come together again: *they regathered at lunchtime to resume their drinking.*

re·gat·ta /ri'gätə; ri'gatə/ ▶*n.* a sporting event consisting of a series of boat or yacht races. ▷early 17th cent.: from Italian (Venetian dialect), literally 'a fight, contest.'

regd ▶*abbr.* registered.

re·ge·late /'rējə,lāt/ ▶*v.* [*intrans.*] *technical* (chiefly of pieces of ice thawed apart) freeze together again. ▷mid 19th cent.: from **RE-** 'again' + Latin *gelat-* 'frozen' (from the verb *gelare*). —**re·ge·la·tion** /,rējə'lāsнən/ *n.*

Ré·gence /rā'zнäns/ ▶*adj.* relating to or denoting a style of costume, furniture, and interior decoration characteristic of the era of the French Regency (1715–23). ▷French, 'Regency.'

re·gen·cy /'rējənsē/ ▶*n.* (*pl.* **-cies**) the office or period of government by a regent. ■ a commission acting as regent. ■ (**the Regency**) the particular period of a regency, esp. (in Britain) from 1811 to 1820 and (in France) from 1715 to 1723.

▶*adj.* (**Regency**) relating to or denoting British architecture, clothing, and furniture of the Regency or, more widely, of the late 18th and early 19th centuries. Regency style was contemporary with the Empire style and shares many of its features: elaborate and ornate, it is generally neoclassical, with a generous borrowing of Greek and Egyptian motifs. ▷late Middle English: from medieval Latin *regentia*, from Latin *regent-* 'ruling' (see **REGENT**).

re·gen·er·ate ▶*v.* /ri'jenə,rāt/ [*trans.*] (of a living organism) regrow (new tissue) to replace lost or injured tissue: *a crab in the process of regenerating a claw.* ■ [*intrans.*] (of an organ or tissue) regrow: *once destroyed, brain cells do not regenerate.* ■ bring into renewed existence; generate again: *the issue was regenerated last month.* ■ bring new and more vigorous life to (an area or institution), esp. in economic terms; revive: *regenerating the inner cities.* ■ (esp. in Christian use) give a new and higher spiritual nature to. ■ [usu. as *adj.*] (**regenerated**) *Chemistry* precipitate (a natural polymer such as cellulose) in a different form following chemical processing, esp. in the form of fibers.

▶*adj.* /ri'jenərət/ reformed or reborn, esp. in a spiritual or moral sense. ▷late Middle English (as an adjective): from Latin *regeneratus* 'created again,' past participle of *regenerare*, from *re-* 'again' + *generare* 'create.' The verb dates from the mid 16th cent. —**re·gen·er·a·tor** /-,rātər/ *n.*

re·gen·er·a·tion /ri,jenə'rāsнən; ,rē-/ ▶*n.* the action or process of regenerating or being regenerated, in particular the formation of new animal or plant tissue. ■ *Electronics* positive feedback. ■ *Chemistry* the action or process of regenerating polymer fibers. ▷Middle English: from Latin *regeneratio(n-)*, from *regenerare* 'create again' (see **REGENERATE**).

re·gen·er·a·tive /ri'jenərətiv; -,rātiv/ ▶*adj.* tending to or characterized by regeneration: *natural regenerative processes.* ■ denoting a method of braking in which energy is extracted from the parts braked, to be stored and reused. —**re·gen·er·a·tive·ly** *adv.*

re·gen·er·a·tive brak·ing ▶*n.* a method of braking in which energy is extracted from the parts braked, to be stored and reused.

re·gent /'rējənt/ ▶*n.* **1** a person appointed to administer a country because the monarch is a minor or is absent or incapacitated. **2** a member of the governing body of a university or other academic institution.

▶*adj.* [*postpositive*] acting as regent for a monarch: *the queen regent of Portugal.* ▷late Middle English: from Old French, or from Latin *regent-* 'ruling,' from the verb *regere*.

re·ger·mi·nate /rē'jərmə,nāt/ ▶*v.* [*intrans.*] germinate again. —**re·ger·mi·na·tion** *n.*

reg·gae /'regā; 'rāgā/ ▶*n.* a style of popular music with a strongly accented subsidiary beat, originating in Jamaica. Reggae evolved in the late 1960s from ska and other local variations on calypso and rhythm and blues, and became widely known in the 1970s through the work of Bob Marley; its lyrics are much influenced by Rastafarian ideas. ▷perhaps related to Jamaican English *rege-rege* 'quarrel, dispute.'

Reg·gio di Ca·la·bri·a /'rej(ē)ō dē kä'läbrēä/ a port at the southern tip of the "toe" of Italy, on the Strait of Messina, capital of Calabria region; pop. 183,000.

reg·i·cide /'rejə,sīd/ ▶*n.* the action of killing a king. ■ a person who kills or takes part in killing a king. ▷mid 16th cent.: from Latin *rex*, *reg-* 'king' + **-CIDE**, probably suggested by French *régicide*. —**reg·i·cid·al** /,rejə'sīdl/ *adj.*

Pronunciation Key ə *ago*; ər *over*; 'ə or ,ə *up*; 'ər or ,ər *fur*; a *hat*; ā *rate*; ä *car*; CH *chew*; e *let*; ē *see*; e(ə)r *air*; i *fit*; ī *by*; i(ə)r *ear*; NG *sing*; ō *go*; ô *for*; oi *boy*; o͝o *good*; o͞o *goo*; ou *out*; SH *she*; TH *thin*; T͟H *then*; (h)w *why*; ZH *vision*

Ré·gie /rā'zhē/ ▸*n.* (in some European countries) a government department that controls an industry or service, historically one with complete control of the importation, manufacture, and taxation of tobacco, salt, and other resources. ▷French, feminine past participle of *régir* 'to rule.'

re·gift /rē'gift/ ▸*v.* [*trans.*] give (a gift one has received) to someone else: *do you think she'll regift that horrendous vase?* [*intrans.*] *the survey showed that 53% of consumers plan to regift this holiday.*
▸*n.* an item that has been regifted: *most of my regifts are more meaningful than the usual bouquet of flowers.* **—re·gift·er** *n.*

re·gime /ri'zhēm; rā-/ (also **ré·gime**) ▸*n.* **1** a government, esp. an authoritarian one. **2** a system or planned way of doing things, esp. one imposed from above: *detention centers with a very tough physical regime.* ■ a coordinated program for the promotion or restoration of health; a regimen: *a low-calorie, low-fat regime.* ■ the conditions under which a scientific or industrial process occurs. ▷late 15th cent. (in the sense 'regimen'): French *régime,* from Latin *regimen* 'rule' (see **REGIMEN**). Sense 1 dates from the late 18th cent. (with original reference to the Ancien Régime).

re·gime change ▸*n.* a change, usually forcible, in leadership or management, as in a government or organization.

reg·i·men /'rejəmən; 'rezh-/ ▸*n.* **1** a prescribed course of medical treatment, way of life, or diet for the promotion or restoration of health: *a regimen of one or two injections per day | a treatment regimen.* **2** *archaic* a system of government. ▷late Middle English (denoting the action of governing): from Latin, from *regere* 'to rule.'

reg·i·ment ▸*n.* /'rejəmənt/ **1** a permanent unit of an army typically commanded by a colonel and divided into several companies, squadrons, or batteries and often into two battalions: *two or three miles inland a highly experienced artillery regiment had established a defensive position.* ■ an operational unit of artillery. ■ a large array or number of people or things: *a neat* **regiment of** *jars and bottles.* **2** *archaic* rule or government over a person, people, or country: *the powers of ecclesiastical regiment which none but the Church should wield.*
▸*v.* /'rejə,ment/ [*trans.*] (usu. **be regimented**) **1** organize according to a strict, sometimes oppressive system or pattern: *every aspect of their life is strictly regimented* | [as *adj.*] (**regimented**) *the regimented environment of the ward.* **2** *rare* form (troops) into a regiment or regiments. ▷late Middle English (in the sense 'rule or government over a person, people, or country'): via Old French from late Latin *regimentum* 'rule,' from *regere* 'to rule.' **—reg·i·men·ta·tion** /,rejəmən'tāshən; -,men-/ *n.*

reg·i·men·tal /,rejə'mentl/ ▸*adj.* of or relating to a regiment: *a regimental band | regimental colors.* **—reg·i·men·tal·ly** /-'mentl-ē/ *adv.*

reg·i·men·tals /,rejə'mentlz/ ▸*plural n. Brit.* military uniform, esp. that of a particular regiment.

Re·gi·na[1] /rə'jīnə/ the capital of Saskatchewan, located in the center of the wheat-growing plains of south central Canada; pop. 179,178.

Re·gi·na[2] /rə'jēnə/ ▸*n.* (in the UK) the reigning queen (used following a name or in the titles of lawsuits, e.g., *Regina v. Jones,* the Crown versus Jones). ▷Latin, literally 'queen.'

Re·gi·o·mon·ta·nus /,rāgē-ō,môn'tänəs; ,rējē-ō,män-'tānəs/, Johannes (1436–76), German astronomer and mathematician; born *Johannes Müller.* Considered the most important astronomer of the 15th century, he translated Ptolemy's *Mathematical Syntaxis* and wrote four monumental works on mathematics and astronomy.

re·gion /'rējən/ ▸*n.* an area or division, esp. part of a country or the world having definable characteristics but not always fixed boundaries: *one of the region's major employers | the equatorial regions | a major wine-producing region.* ■ an administrative district of a city or country. ■ a part of the body, esp. around or near an organ: *an unexpected clenching sensation in the region of her heart.* ■ *figurative* the sphere or realm of something: *his work takes needlework into the region of folk art.* ▷Middle English: from Old French, from Latin *regio(n-)* 'direction, district,' from *regere* 'to rule, direct.'
▸PHRASE □ **in the region of** approximately: *annual sales in the region of $30 million.*

re·gion·al /'rējənl; 'rējnəl/ ▸*adj.* of, relating to, or characteristic of a region: *regional and local needs | regional variations.*
▸*n.* (**regionals**) an athletic contest involving competitors from a particular region: *the opening game of the Little League Senior Division Softball Eastern Regionals.* **—re·gion·al·ly** /'rējənl-ē; 'rējnəlē/ *adv.*

re·gion·al·ism /'rējənl,izəm; 'rējnə-/ ▸*n.* **1** the theory or practice of regional rather than central systems of administration or economic, cultural, or political affiliation: *a strong expression of regionalism.* **2** a linguistic feature peculiar to a particular region and not part of the standard language of a country. **—re·gion·al·ist** *n. & adj.*

re·gion·al·ize /'rējənl,īz; 'rējnə,līz/ ▸*v.* [*trans.*] [usu. as *adj.*] (**regionalized**) organize (a country, area, or enterprise) on a regional basis: *a regionalized system.* **—re·gion·al·i·za·tion** /,rējənl-ə'zāshən; ,rējnələ-/ *n.*

re·gion·al met·a·mor·phism ▸*n. Geology* metamorphism affecting rocks over an extensive area as a result of the large-scale action of heat and pressure. Compare with **CONTACT METAMORPHISM.**

ré·gis·seur /,rāzhē'sər/ ▸*n.* a person who stages a theatrical production, esp. a ballet. ▷from French *régisseur.*

reg·is·ter /'rejəstər/ ▸*n.* **1** an official list or record, for example of births, marriages, and deaths, of shipping, or of historic places. ■ a book or record of attendance, for example of students in a class or school or guests in a hotel. **2** a particular part of the range of a voice or instrument: *his voice moved up a register | she plays a basset horn and relishes the duskiness of its lower register.* ■ a sliding device controlling a set of organ pipes that share a tonal quality. ■ a set of organ pipes so controlled. **3** *Linguistics* a variety of a language or a level of usage, as determined by degree of formality and choice of vocabulary, pronunciation, and syntax, according to the communicative purpose, social context, and social status of the user. **4** *Printing & Photography* the exact correspondence of the position of color components in a printed positive. ■ *Printing* the exact correspondence of the position of printed matter on the two sides of a page. **5** (in electronic devices) a location in a store of data, used for a specific purpose and with quick access time. **6** an adjustable plate for widening or narrowing an opening and regulating a draft, esp. in a fire grate. **7** short for **CASH REGISTER. 8** *Art* one of a number of bands or sections into which a design is divided.
▸*v.* [*trans.*] **1** enter or record in an official list as being in a particular category, having a particular eligibility or entitlement, or in keeping with a requirement: *the vessel is registered as Liberian | her father was late in registering her birth* | [as *adj.*] (**registered**) *a registered trademark.* ■ [*intrans.*] put one's name on an official list under such terms: [with *infinitive*] *34,500 registered to vote.* ■ [*intrans.*] put one's name in a register as a guest in a hotel. ■ [*intrans.*] (of a couple to be married) have a list of wedding gifts compiled and kept at a store for consultation by gift buyers. ■ entrust (a letter or parcel) to a post office for transmission by registered mail: [as *adj.*] (**registered**) *a registered letter.* ■ express (an opinion or emotion): *I wish to register an objection.* **2** (of an instrument) detect and show (a reading) automatically: *the electroscope was too insensitive to register the tiny changes.* ■ [*intrans.*] (of an event) give rise to a specified reading on an instrument: *the blast registered 5.4 on the Richter scale.* ■ [usu. with *negative*] properly notice or become aware of (something): *he had not even registered her presence.* ■ [*intrans.*] [usu. with *negative*] make an impression on a person's mind: *the content of her statement did not register.* ■ [*intrans.*] (of an emotion) show in a person's face or gestures: *nothing registered on their faces.* ■ indicate or convey (a feeling or emotion) by facial expression or gestures: *he did not register much surprise at this.* **3** *Printing & Photography* correspond or cause to correspond exactly in position: [*intrans.*] *they are adjusted until the impressions register.* ▷late Middle English: from Old French *regestre* or medieval Latin *regestrum, registrum,* alteration of *regestum,* singular of late Latin *regesta* 'things recorded,' from *regerere* 'enter, record.' **—reg·is·tra·ble** /-st(ə)rəbəl/ *adj.*

reg·is·tered mail ▸*n.* prepaid first class mail that is recorded by the post office before being sent and at each point along its route to safeguard against loss, theft, or damage.

reg·is·tered nurse (abbr.: **RN**) ▸*n.* a nurse who has graduated from a college's nursing program or from a school of nursing and has passed a national licensure exam. Compare with **PRACTICAL NURSE.**

reg·is·ter ton ▸*n.* see **TON**[1] (sense 1).

reg·is·trant /'rejəstrənt/ ▸*n.* a person who registers.

reg·is·trar /'rejə,strär/ ▸*n.* an official responsible for keeping a register or official records: *the registrar of births and deaths.* ■ an official in a college or university who is responsible for keeping student records. ▷late 17th cent.: from medieval Latin *registrarius,* from *registrum* (see **REGISTER**). **—reg·is·trar·ship** /-,ship/ *n.*

reg·is·tra·tion /,rejə'strāshən/ ▸*n.* the action or process of registering or of being registered: *the registration of births, marriages, and deaths | the number of new private car registrations has increased.* ■ a certificate that attests to the registering of (a person, automobile, etc.). ■ *Music* a combination of stops used when playing the organ. ▷mid 16th cent.: from medieval Latin *registratio(n-),* based on Latin *regerere* 'enter, record' (see **REGISTER**).

reg·is·try /'rejəstrē/ ▸*n.* (*pl.* **-tries**) **1** a place or office where registers or records are kept. **2** an official list or register: *a recognized purebred dog registry.* **3** registration. **4** the nationality of a merchant ship: *converted trawlers of local registry.*

Re·gius pro·fes·sor /'rēj(ē)əs/ ▸*n.* (in the UK) the holder of a university chair founded by a sovereign (esp. one at Oxford or Cambridge instituted by Henry VIII) or filled by Crown appointment. ▷Latin *regius* 'royal,' from *rex, reg-* 'king.'

re·glaze /rē'glāz/ ▸*v.* [*trans.*] glaze (a window) again.

reg·let /'reglit/ ▸*n.* **1** *Printing* a thin strip of wood or metal used to separate type. **2** *Architecture* a narrow strip used to separate moldings or panels from one another. ▷mid 17th cent.: from French *réglet,* diminutive of *règle* 'rule.'

reg·nal /'regnəl/ ▸*adj.* [*attrib.*] of a reign or monarch. ▷early 17th cent.: from Anglo-Latin *regnalis,* from Latin *regnum* 'kingdom.'

reg·nal year ▸*n.* a year reckoned from the date or anniversary of a sovereign's accession.

reg·nant /'regnənt/ ▸*adj.* **1** [often *postpositive*] reigning; ruling: *a queen regnant.* **2** currently having the greatest influence; dominant: *the regnant belief.* ▷early 17th cent.: from Latin *regnant-* 'reigning,' from the verb *regnare.*

reg·o·lith /'regə,lith/ ▸*n. Geology* the layer of unconsolidated rocky material covering bedrock. ▷late 19th cent.: from Greek *rhēgos* 'rug, blanket' + **-LITH.**

re·gorge /rē'gôrj/ ▸*v.* [*trans.*] *archaic* bring up again; disgorge. ■ [*intrans.*] gush or flow back again. ▷early 17th cent.: from French *regorger,* or from **RE-** 'again' + the verb **GORGE.**

re·grade /rē'grād/ ▸*v.* [*trans.*] grade again or differently: [as *n.*] (**regrading**) *a demand for a regrading of pay levels.*

re·gress ▸*v.* /ri'gres/ **1** [*intrans.*] return to a former or less developed state: *art has been regressing toward adolescence for more than a generation now.* ■ return mentally to a former stage of life or a supposed previous life, esp. through hypnosis or mental illness: [*intrans.*] *she claims to be able to regress to the Roman era* | [*trans.*] *I regressed Sylvia to early childhood.* **2** [*trans.*] *Statistics* calculate the coefficient or coefficients of regression of (a variable) against or on another variable. **3** [*intrans.*] *Astronomy* move in a retrograde direction.
▸*n.* /'rē,gres/ **1** the action of returning to a former or less developed state. **2** *Philosophy* a series of statements in which a logical procedure is continually reapplied to its own result without approaching a useful conclusion (e.g., defining something in terms of itself). ▷late Middle English (as a noun): from Latin *regressus,* from *regredi* 'go back, return,' from *re-* 'back' + *gradi* 'walk.'

re·gres·sion /ri'greshən/ ▸*n.* **1** a return to a former or less developed state. ■ a return to an earlier stage of life or a supposed previous life, esp. through hypnosis or mental illness, or as a means of escaping present anxieties: [as *adj.*] *regression therapy.* ■ a lessening of the severity of a disease or its symptoms: *he seemed able to produce a regression in this disease.* **2** *Statistics* a measure of the relation between the mean value of one variable (e.g., output) and corresponding values of other variables (e.g., time and cost).

re·gres·sive /ri'gresiv/ ▸*adj.* **1** becoming less advanced; returning to a former or less developed state: *the regressive, infantile wish for the perfect parent of early childhood.* ■ of, relating to, or marked by psychological regression. **2** (of a tax) taking a proportionally greater amount from those on lower incomes. **3** *Philosophy* proceeding from effect to cause or from particular to universal. **—re·gres·sive·ly** *adv.* **—re·gres·sive·ness** *n.*

R

re·gret /ri'gret/ ▸*v.* (**-gret·ted, -gret·ting**) [*trans.*] feel sad, repentant, or disappointed over (something that has happened or been done, esp. a loss or missed opportunity): *she immediately regretted her words* | [with *clause*] *I regretted that he did not see you.* ■ used in polite formulas to express apology for or sadness over something unfortunate or unpleasant: *any inconvenience to readers is regretted* | [with *clause*] *we regret that no tickets may be exchanged.* ■ *archaic* feel sorrow for the loss or absence of (something pleasant): *my home, when shall I cease to regret you!*
▸*n.* a feeling of sadness, repentance, or disappointment over something that has happened or been done: *she expressed her regret at Virginia's death* | *he had to decline, **to his regret**.* ■ (often **regrets**) an instance or cause of such a feeling: *she had few regrets in leaving the house.* ■ (often **one's regrets**) used in polite formulas to express apology for or sadness at an occurrence or an inability to accept an invitation: *please give your grandmother my regrets.* ▷late Middle English: from Old French *regreter* 'bewail (the dead),' perhaps from the Germanic base of GREET².

re·gret·ful /ri'gretfəl/ ▸*adj.* feeling or showing regret: *he sounded regretful but pointed out that he had committed himself.* **—re·gret·ful·ness** *n.*

USAGE See **usage** at REGRETFULLY.

re·gret·ful·ly /ri'gretfəlē/ ▸*adv.* in a regretful manner. ■ [*sentence adverb*] regrettably: *regretfully, mounting costs and diminishing traffic forced the line to close.*

USAGE The adjectives **regretful** and **regrettable** are distinct in meaning: **regretful** means 'feeling or showing regret' (*she shook her head with a **regretful** smile*), while **regrettable** means 'giving rise to regret, undesirable' (*the loss of jobs is **regrettable***).
The adverbs **regretfully** and **regrettably** have not, however, preserved the same distinction. **Regretfully** is used as a normal manner adverb to mean 'in a regretful manner' (*he sighed **regretfully***), but it is also used as a sentence adverb meaning 'it is regrettable that' (***regretfully**, the trustees must turn down your request*). In this latter use it is synonymous with **regrettably.** Despite objections from traditionalists, this use is now well established and is included in most modern dictionaries without comment.
See also **usage** at HOPEFULLY and SENTENCE ADVERB.

re·gret·ta·ble /ri'gretəbəl/ ▸*adj.* (of conduct or an event) giving rise to regret; undesirable; unwelcome: *the loss of this number of jobs is regrettable* | *irresponsible and regrettable actions.*

USAGE See **usage** at REGRETFULLY.

re·gret·ta·bly /ri'gretəblē/ ▸*adv.* [*sentence adverb*] unfortunately (used to express apology for or sadness at something): *regrettably, last night's audience was a meager one.*

USAGE On the use of **regrettably** and **regretfully**, see **usage** at REGRETFULLY.

re·group /rē'gro͞op/ ▸*v.* [*intrans.*] (of troops) reassemble into organized groups, typically after being attacked or defeated: *their heroic resistance gave American forces time to regroup.* ■ [*trans.*] cause to reassemble in this way: *he regrouped his fighters in the hills.* ■ [*trans.*] rearrange (something) into a new group or groups: *she was regrouping the numeric data.* **—re·group·ment** *n.*

regs /regz/ *informal* ▸*abbr.* regulations.

Regt ▸*abbr.* ■ Regent. ■ Regiment.

reg·u·la·ble /'regyələbəl/ ▸*adj.* able to be regulated.

reg·u·lar /'regyələr; 'reg(ə)lər/ ▸*adj.* **1** arranged in or constituting a constant or definite pattern, esp. with the same space between individual instances: *place the flags at regular intervals* | *a regular arrangement.* ■ happening in such a pattern with the same time between individual instances; recurring at short uniform intervals: *a regular monthly check* | *her breathing became deeper, more regular.* ■ (of a person) doing the same thing or going to the same place with the same time between individual instances: *regular worshipers.* ■ (of a structure or arrangement) arranged in or constituting a symmetrical or harmonious pattern: *beautifully regular, heart-shaped leaves.* ■ (of a person) defecating or menstruating at predictable times. **2** done or happening frequently: *regular border clashes* | *parties were a fairly regular occurrence.* ■ (of a person) doing the same thing or going to the same place frequently: *a regular visitor.* **3** conforming to or governed by an accepted standard of procedure or convention: *policies carried on by his deputies through regular channels.* ■ [*attrib.*] of or belonging to the permanent professional armed forces of a country: *a regular soldier.* ■ (of a person) properly trained or qualified and pursuing a full-time occupation: *a strong distrust of regular doctors.* ■ *Christian Church* subject to or bound by religious rule; belonging to a religious or monastic order: *the regular clergy.* Contrasted with SECULAR (sense 2). ■ *informal* rightly so called; complete; absolute (used for emphasis): *this place is a regular fisherman's paradise.* **4** used, done, or happening on a habitual basis; usual; customary: *I couldn't get an appointment with my regular barber* | *our regular suppliers.* ■ of a normal or ordinary kind; not special: *it's richer than regular pasta.* See note at NORMAL. ■ (chiefly in commercial use) denoting merchandise, esp. food or clothing, of average, medium, or standard size: *a shake and regular fries.* ■ (of a person) not pretentious or arrogant; ordinary and friendly: *advertising agencies who try to portray their candidates as **regular guys**.* ■ (of coffee) of a specified type, such as caffeinated, or prepared in a specified way, such as black or with cream: *one regular coffee and three decafs.* ■ (in surfing and other board sports) with the left leg in front of the right on the board. **5** *Grammar* (of a word) following the normal pattern of inflection: *a regular verb.* **6** *Geometry* (of a figure) having all sides and all angles equal: *a regular polygon.* ■ (of a solid) bounded by a number of equal figures. **7** *Botany* (of a flower) having radial symmetry.
▸*n.* a regular customer or member, for example of a bar, store, or team: *attracting a richer clientele as its regulars.* ■ a regular member of the armed forces. ■ a member of a political party who is faithful to that party: *he plans to sell tickets to the big-money party regulars.* ■ *Christian Church* one of the regular clergy. ▷late Middle English: from Old French *reguler*, from Latin *regularis*, from *regula* 'rule.' **—reg·u·lar·ly** *adv.*
▸*PHRASE* □ **keep regular hours** do the same thing, esp. going to bed and getting up, at the same time each day.

reg·u·lar guy ▸*n. informal* an ordinary, uncomplicated, sociable man.

reg·u·lar·i·ty /ˌregyə'laritē/ ▸*n.* (*pl.* **-ties**) the state or quality of being regular: *he came to see her with increasing regularity.*

reg·u·lar·ize /'regyələˌrīz/ ▸*v.* [*trans.*] make (something) regular. ■ establish (a hitherto temporary or provisional arrangement) on an official or correct basis: *immigrants applying to regularize their status as residents.* **—reg·u·lar·i·za·tion** /ˌregyələrə'zāsʜən/ *n.*

reg·u·late /'regyəˌlāt/ ▸*v.* [*trans.*] control or maintain the rate or speed of (a machine or process) so that it operates properly: *a hormone that regulates metabolism and organ function.* ■ control or supervise (something, esp. a company or business activity) by means of rules and regulations: *the organization that regulates fishing in the region.* ■ set (a clock or other apparatus) according to an external standard. ▷late Middle English (in the sense 'control by rules'): from late Latin *regulat-* 'directed, regulated,' from the verb *regulare*, from Latin *regula* 'rule.' **—reg·u·la·tive** /-ˌlātiv/ *adj.*

reg·u·la·tion /ˌreg(y)ə'lāsʜən/ ▸*n.* **1** a rule or directive made and maintained by an authority: *planning regulations.* ■ [as *adj.*] in accordance with regulations; of the correct type: *regulation army footwear.* ■ [as *adj.*] *informal* of a familiar or predictable type; formulaic; standardized: *a regulation Western parody.* **2** the action or process of regulating or being regulated: *the regulation of financial markets.*

reg·u·la·tor /'regyəˌlātər/ ▸*n.* a person or thing that regulates something, in particular: ■ a person or body that supervises a particular industry or business activity. ■ a device for controlling the rate of working of machinery or for controlling fluid flow, in particular a handle controlling the supply of steam to the cylinders of a steam engine. ■ a device for adjusting the balance of a clock or watch in order to regulate its speed.

reg·u·la·to·ry /'regyələˌtôrē/ ▸*adj.* serving or intended to regulate something: *the existing legal and regulatory framework* | *regulatory enzymes.*

Reg·u·lus /'regyələs/ *Astronomy* the brightest star in the constellation Leo. It is a triple system of which the primary is a hot dwarf star. ▷Latin, literally 'little king.'

reg·u·lus /'regyələs/ ▸*n.* (*pl.* **-lus·es** or **-li** /-ˌlī; -lē/) **1** *archaic Chemistry* a metallic form of a substance obtained by smelting or reduction. **2** a petty king or ruler. ▷late 16th cent.: from Latin, diminutive of *rex, reg-* 'king'; originally in the phrase *regulus of antimony* (denoting metallic antimony), apparently so named because of its readiness to combine with gold. **—reg·u·line** /'regyəˌlīn; -lin/ *adj.* (in sense 1).

re·gur·gi·tate /ri'gərjəˌtāt/ ▸*v.* [*trans.*] bring (swallowed food) up again to the mouth: *gulls regurgitate food for the chicks.* ■ *figurative* repeat (information) without analyzing or comprehending it: *facts that can then be regurgitated at examinations.* ▷late 16th cent.: from medieval Latin *regurgitat-*, from the verb *regurgitare*, from Latin *re-* 'again, back' + *gurges, gurgit-* 'whirlpool.' **—re·gur·gi·ta·tion** /riˌgərjə'tāsʜən/ *n.*

re·hab /'rēˌhab/ *informal* ▸*n.* **1** rehabilitation, in particular: ■ a course of treatment for drug or alcohol addiction, typically at a facility in which the patient is compelled to reside for a period of several weeks or months: *the success of rehab is entirely dependent on the patient's commitment to the process.* ■ a course of treatment, largely physical therapy, designed to reverse the debilitating effects of an injury: *their best hitter has been in rehab since August, after his collision with the left-field wall.* **2** a thing, esp. a building, that has been rehabilitated or restored.
▸*v.* (**-habbed, -hab·bing**) [*trans.*] rehabilitate or restore: *they don't rehab you at all in jail* | [as *adj.*] (**rehabbed**) *newly rehabbed apartments for rent.* ▷1940s: abbreviation. **—re·hab·ber** *n.*

re·ha·bil·i·tate /ˌrē(h)ə'biləˌtāt/ ▸*v.* [*trans.*] restore (someone) to health or normal life by training and therapy after imprisonment, addiction, or illness: *helping to rehabilitate former criminals.* ■ restore (someone) to former privileges or reputation after a period of critical or official disfavor: *with the fall of the government many former dissidents were rehabilitated.* ■ return (something, esp. an environmental feature) to its former condition. ▷late 16th cent. (in the sense 'restore to former privileges'): from medieval Latin *rehabilitat-*, from the verb *rehabilitare* (see RE-, HABILITATE). **—re·ha·bil·i·ta·tion** /-ˌbilə'tāsʜən/ *n.* **—re·ha·bil·i·ta·tive** /-ˌtātiv/ *adj.*

R

re·hang ▸*v.* /rē'haNG/ (*past* and *past part.* **-hung** /-'həNG/) [*trans.*] hang (something) again or differently.
▸*n.* /'rēhaNG/ an act of rehanging works of art in a gallery.

re·hash ▸*v.* /rē'hasʜ/ [*trans.*] put (old ideas or material) into a new form without significant change or improvement: *he contented himself with occasional articles in journals, rehashing his own work.* ■ consider or discuss (something) at length after it has happened: *is it really necessary to rehash that trauma all over again?*
▸*n.* /'rēˌhasʜ/ a reuse of old ideas or material without significant change or improvement: *the spring show was a rehash of the summer show from the previous year.*

re·hear /rē'hi(ə)r/ ▸*v.* (*past* and *past part.* **-heard** /-'hərd/) hear or listen to again. ■ *Law* hear (a case or plaintiff) in a court again: [as *n.*] (**rehearing**) *the parents produced fresh evidence and won a rehearing.*

re·hears·al /ri'hərsəl/ ▸*n.* a practice or trial performance of a play or other work for later public performance: ***rehearsals** for the opera season.* ■ the action or process of rehearsing: *I've had two weeks **in rehearsal*** | [as *adj.*] *a rehearsal room.*

re·hearse /ri'hərs/ ▸*v.* [*trans.*] practice (a play, piece of music, or other work) for later public performance: *we were rehearsing a play* | [*intrans.*] *she was **rehearsing for** her world tour.* ■ supervise (a performer or group) that is practicing in this way: *he listened to Charlie rehearsing the band.* ■ mentally prepare or recite (words one intends to say): *he had rehearsed a thousand fine phrases.* ■ state (a list of points, esp. those that have been made many times before); enumerate: *criticisms of factory farming have been rehearsed often enough.* ▷Middle English (in the sense 'repeat aloud'): from Old French *rehercier*, perhaps from *re-* 'again' + *hercer* 'to harrow,' from *herse* 'harrow' (see HEARSE). **—re·hears·er** *n.*

re·heat ▸*v.* /rē'hēt/ [*trans.*] heat (something, esp. cooked food) again.
▸*n.* /'rēhēt/ the process of using the hot exhaust to burn extra fuel in a jet engine and produce extra power. ■ an afterburner. **—re·heat·er** *n.*

re·heel /rē'hēl/ ▸*v.* [*trans.*] fit (a shoe) with a new heel.

re·hire /rē'hī(ə)r/ ▸*v.* [*trans.*] hire (a former employee) again: *the company dismissed its workers and rehired them on a lower rate.*
▸*n.* a person rehired: *he declined to give any specifics on the number of possible rehires.*

Pronunciation Key ə *ago*; ər *over*; 'ə or ˌə *up*; 'ər or ˌər *fur*; a *hat*; ā *rate*; ä *car*; CH *chew*; e *let*; ē *see*; e(ə)r *air*; i *fit*; ī *by*; i(ə)r *ear*; NG *sing*; ō *go*; ô *for*; oi *boy*; o͝o *good*; o͞o *goo*; ou *out*; SH *she*; TH *thin*; T͟H *then*; (h)w *why*; ZH *vision*

Rehn·quist /ˈrenˌkwist/, William Hubbs (1924–), U.S. chief justice 1986– . As President Nixon's assistant attorney general 1969–71, he held to a conservative stance that opposed civil rights legislation. He was appointed by Nixon as an associate justice to the U.S. Supreme Court in 1972.

William H. Rehnquist

Re·ho·bo·am /ˌrē(h)əˈbōəm/, son of Solomon; king of ancient Israel *c.*930–*c.*915 BC. His reign witnessed the secession of the northern tribes and their establishment of a new kingdom under Jeroboam, leaving Rehoboam as the first king of Judah (1 Kings 11–14).

re·ho·bo·am /ˌrē(h)əˈbōəm/ ▶*n.* a wine bottle of about six times the standard size. ▷late 19th cent.: from the name REHOBOAM.

re·house /rēˈhouz/ ▶*v.* [*trans.*] (usu. **be rehoused**) provide (someone) with new housing: *tenants will be rehoused in hotels until their homes are habitable.*

re·hung /rēˈhəNG/ ▶ past and past participle of RE-HANG.

re·hy·drate /rēˈhīˌdrāt/ ▶*v.* absorb or cause to absorb moisture after dehydration: [*trans.*] *the slides were rehydrated in water.* —**re·hy·drat·a·ble** *adj.* —**re·hy·dra·tion** /ˌrēˌhīˈdrāSHən/ *n.*

Reich[1] /rīk; rīKH/ the former German state, most often used to refer to the Third Reich, the Nazi regime from 1933 to 1945. The **First Reich** was considered to be the Holy Roman Empire, 962–1806, and the **Second Reich** the German Empire, 1871–1918, but neither of these terms are part of normal historical terminology. ▷German, literally 'empire.'

Reich[2] /rīk/, Steve (1936–), U.S. composer; full name *Stephen Michael Reich.* A leading minimalist, he uses the repetition of short phrases within a simple harmonic field. Influences include Balinese and West African music.

Reich·i·an /ˈrīkēən; ˈrīKH-/ ▶*adj.* of or relating to the psychotherapeutic theories of Austrian psychoanalyst Wilhelm Reich (1897–1957), who theorized that sexual repression is the source of all human neuroses and irrational behavior: *he also taught me a kind of Reichian emotional release work, banging pillows and screaming at the top of my lungs.*

Reichs·mark /ˈrīksˌmärk/ ▶*n.* the basic monetary unit of the Third Reich, replaced in 1948 by the Deutschmark. ▷German.

Reichs·tag /ˈrīksˌtäg/ the main legislature of the German state under the Second and Third Reichs. ■ the building in which this met. ▷German, from *Reichs* 'of the empire' + *Tag* 'diet' (see DIET[2]).

Reid /rēd/, Whitelaw (1837–1912), U.S. journalist and diplomat. He was the owner and editor-in-chief of the *New York Tribune* 1872–1905 and the U.S. minister to France 1889–92 and ambassador to England 1905–12.

re·i·fy /ˈrēəˌfī/ ▶*v.* (**-fies**, **-fied**) [*trans.*] *formal* make (something abstract) more concrete or real: *these instincts are, in humans, reified as verbal constructs.* ▷mid 19th cent.: from Latin *res, re-* 'thing' + -FY. —**re·i·fi·ca·tion** /ˌrēəfəˈkāSHən/ *n.* —**re·if·i·ca·to·ry** /rēˈifəkəˌtôrē/ *adj.*

reign /rān/ ▶*v.* [*intrans.*] hold royal office; rule as king or queen: *Queen Elizabeth* **reigns over** *the UK* | *figurative the Nashville sound will* **reign supreme** *once again.* ■ [usu. as *adj.*] (**reigning**) (of an athlete or team) currently hold a particular title: *the reigning world champion.* ■ (of a quality or condition) prevail; predominate: *confusion reigned.*

▶*n.* the period during which a sovereign rules: *the original chapel was built in the reign of Charles I.* ■ the period of prevalence or domination of a specified thing: *these historic seconds inaugurated the reign of negative political advertising.* ■ the period during which an athlete or team holds a specified title. ▷Middle English: from Old French *reignier* 'to reign,' *reigne* 'kingdom,' from Latin *regnum*, related to *rex, reg-* 'king.'

USAGE The correct idiomatic phrase is **free rein**, not **free reign**; see usage at REIN.

re·ig·nite /ˌrēi-gˈnīt/ ▶*v.* ignite or cause to ignite again: [*intrans.*] *oven burners automatically reignite if blown out.*

reign of ter·ror ▶*n.* a period of remorseless repression or bloodshed, in particular (**Reign of Terror**), the period of the Terror during the French Revolution.

rei·ki /ˈrākē/ ▶*n.* a healing technique based on the principle that the therapist can channel energy into the patient by means of touch, to activate the natural healing processes of the patient's body and restore physical and emotional well-being. ▷Japanese, literally 'universal life energy.'

re·im·burse /ˌrē-imˈbərs/ ▶*v.* [*trans.*] (often **be reimbursed**) repay (a person who has spent or lost money): *the investors should be reimbursed for their losses.* ■ repay (a sum of money that has been spent or lost): *they spend thousands of dollars that are not reimbursed by insurance.* ▷early 17th cent.: from RE- 'back, again' + obsolete *imburse* 'put in a purse,' from medieval Latin *imbursare*, from *in-* 'into' + late Latin *bursa* 'purse.' —**re·im·burs·a·ble** *adj.* —**re·im·burse·ment** *n.*

re·im·port /ˌrē-imˈpôrt/ ▶*v.* [*trans.*] import (goods processed or made from exported materials).

▶*n.* the action of reimporting something. ■ a reimported item. —**re·im·por·ta·tion** /ˌrēˌimpôrˈtāSHən/ *n.*

re·im·pose /ˌrē-imˈpōz/ ▶*v.* [*trans.*] impose (something, esp. a law or regulation) again after a lapse. —**re·im·po·si·tion** /ˌrēˌimpəˈziSHən/ *n.*

Reims /rēmz; rans/ (also **Rheims**) a city in northern France, chief town of the Champagne-Ardenne region; pop. 185,000. It was the traditional coronation place for most French kings and is noted for its fine 13th-century Gothic cathedral.

rein /rān/ ▶*n.* (usu. **reins**) a long, narrow strap attached at one end to a horse's bit, typically used in pairs to guide or check a horse while riding or driving. ■ *figurative* the power to direct and control: *management is criticized for its unwillingness to let go of the reins of an organization and delegate routine tasks.*

▶*v.* [*trans.*] cause (a horse) to stop or slow down by pulling on its reins: *he* **reined in** *his horse and waited for her.* ■ cause (a horse) to change direction by pulling on its reins: *he reined the mare's head about and rode off.* ■ keep under control; restrain: *with an effort, she* **reined back** *her impatience* | *critics noted the failure of the administration to* **rein in** *public spending.* ▷Middle English: from Old French *rene*, based on Latin *retinere* 'retain.'

▶*PHRASES* □ **draw rein** stop one's horse. □ (**a**) **free rein** freedom of action or expression: *he was* **given free rein** *to work out his designs.* □ **keep a tight rein on** exercise strict control over; allow little freedom to: *her only chance of survival was to keep a tight rein on her feelings and words.*

USAGE The idiomatic phrase **free rein**, which derives from the literal meaning of using reins to control a horse, is sometimes misinterpreted and written as **free reign**—predictable, perhaps, in a society only vaguely familiar with the **reigns** of royalty or the **reins** of farm animals. Also confused is the related phrase **rein in**, sometimes written incorrectly as **reign in**.

re·in·car·nate ▶*v.* /ˌrē-inˈkärˌnāt/ [*trans.*] (often **be reincarnated**) cause (someone) to undergo rebirth in another body: *a man may be reincarnated in animal form* | [as *adj.*] (**reincarnated**) *a reincarnated soul.* ■ [*intrans.*] (of a person) be reborn in this way: *they were afraid she would reincarnate as a vampire.*

▶*adj.* /-nət/ [usu. *postpositive*] reborn in another body: *he claims that the girl is his dead daughter reincarnate.*

re·in·car·na·tion /ˌrē-inkärˈnāSHən/ ▶*n.* the rebirth of a soul in a new body. ■ a person or animal in whom a particular soul is believed to have been reborn: *he is said to be* **a reincarnation of** *the Hindu god Vishnu.* ■ *figurative* the newest version or closest match of something from the past: *the latest reincarnation of the hippie look.*

re·in·cor·po·rate /ˌrē-inˈkôrpəˌrāt/ ▶*v.* [*trans.*] make (something) a part of something else once more: *a campaign to reincorporate the visual arts into religious devotion.* —**re·in·cor·po·ra·tion** /ˌrē-inˌkôrpəˈrāSHən/ *n.*

rein·deer /ˈrānˌdi(ə)r/ ▶*n.* (*pl.* same or **-deers**) a deer of the tundra and subarctic regions of Eurasia and North America, both sexes of which have large branching antlers. Most Eurasian reindeer are domesticated and used for drawing sleds and as a source of milk, flesh, and hide. • Genus *Rangifer*, family Cervidae: several species, in particular *R. tarandus.* ▷late Middle English: from Old Norse *hreindýri*, from *hreinn* 'reindeer' + *dýr* 'deer.'

rein·deer moss ▶*n.* a large branching bluish-gray lichen that grows in arctic and subarctic regions, sometimes providing the chief winter food of reindeer. • *Cladonia rangiferina*, order Cladoniales.

Rein·er[1] /ˈrīnər/, Carl (1922–), U.S. actor; father of Rob Reiner. He was a writer for television's "Caesar's Hour" (1954–57) and wrote for and acted on "The Dick Van Dyke Show" (1961–66). He also directed movies such as *Oh God!* (1977), *The Jerk* (1979), and *That Old Feeling* (1997).

Rein·er[2], Rob (1947–), U.S. actor and director; son of Carl Reiner. He played Michael Stivic ("Meathead") on television's "All in the Family" 1971–78. He also directed movies such as *The Princess Bride* (1987), *When Harry Met Sally* (1989), *The American President* (1995), and *Ghosts of Mississippi* (1996).

re·in·fect /ˌrē-inˈfekt/ ▶*v.* [*trans.*] (usu. **be reinfected**) cause to become infected again. —**re·in·fec·tion** /-ˈfekSHən/ *n.*

re·in·force /ˌrē-inˈfôrs/ ▶*v.* [*trans.*] strengthen or support, esp. with additional personnel or material: *paratroopers were sent to reinforce the troops already in the area.* ■ strengthen (an existing feeling, idea, or habit): *various actions of the leaders so reinforced fears and suspicions that war became unavoidable.* ▷late Middle English: from French *renforcer*, influenced by *inforce*, an obsolete spelling of ENFORCE; the sense of providing military support is probably from Italian *rinforzare.* —**re·in·forc·er** *n.*

re·in·forced con·crete ▶*n.* concrete in which wire mesh or steel bars are embedded to increase its tensile strength.

re·in·force·ment /ˌrē-inˈfôrsmənt/ ▶*n.* the action or process of reinforcing or strengthening. ■ the process of encouraging or establishing a belief or pattern of behavior, esp. by encouragement or reward. ■ (**reinforcements**) extra personnel sent to increase the strength of an army or similar force: *a small force would hold the position until reinforcements could be sent.* ■ the strengthening structure or material employed in reinforced concrete or plastic.

Rein·hardt /ˈrīnˌhärt/, Max (1873–1943), Austrian director and impresario; born *Max Goldmann.* He produced large-scale versions of such works as Sophocles' *Oedipus Rex* (1910) and helped to establish the Salzburg Festival with Richard Strauss and Hugo von Hofmannsthal.

re·in·sert /ˌrē-inˈsərt/ ▶*v.* [*trans.*] place (something) back into its previous position. —**re·in·ser·tion** /-ˈsərSHən/ *n.*

re·in·stall /ˌrē-inˈstôl/ (*Brit.* also **re·in·stal**) ▶*v.* [*trans.*] install again (used especially of software).

▶*n.* a reinstallation of software: *try performing a "clean" reinstall of your system software.* —**re·in·stal·la·tion** /ˌrēinstəˈlāSHən/ *n.* —**re·in·stall·er** *n.*

re·in·state /ˌrē-inˈstāt/ ▶*v.* [*trans.*] (often **be reinstated**) restore (someone or something) to their former position or condition: *the union is fighting to reinstate the fired journalists.* —**re·in·state·ment** *n.*

re·in·sure /ˌrē-inˈSHŏŏr/ ▶*v.* [*trans.*] (of an insurer) transfer (all or part of a risk) to another insurer to provide protection against the risk of the first insurance. —**re·in·sur·ance** /-ˈSHŏŏrəns/ *n.* —**re·in·sur·er** *n.*

re·in·te·grate /rēˈintəˌgrāt/ ▶*v.* [*trans.*] restore (elements regarded as disparate) to unity. ■ restore to a position as a part fitting easily into a larger whole: *it can be difficult for an offender to be* **reintegrated into** *the community.* —**re·in·te·gra·tion** /ˌrēˌintəˈgrāSHən/ *n.*

re·in·ter /ˌrē-inˈtər/ ▶*v.* [*trans.*] bury (a corpse) again, often in a different place than that of the first burial. —**re·in·ter·ment** *n.*

re·in·ter·me·di·a·tion /reˌintərˈmēdēāSHən/ ▶the transfer or bringing back of borrowing and investments from an outside credit business into the banking system. ■ the insertion of middlemen into transactions between producers and consumers: *instead of connecting people directly with artists, the Web actually causes reintermediation as even more people are put between the artist and the consumer.* ▷from *re-*, 'again, '+ *intermediate,* 'coming between '+ *-ation.*

re·in·ter·pret /ˌrē-inˈtərprət/ ▶*v.* (**-pret·ed**, **-pret·ing**) [*trans.*] (often **be reinterpreted**) interpret (something) in a new or different way. **—re·in·ter·pre·ta·tion** /ˌrē-inˌtərprəˈtāsʜən/ *n.*

re·in·tro·duce /ˌrē-intrəˈd(y)o͞os/ ▸*v.* [*trans.*] bring (something, esp. a law or system) into existence or effect again: *thirty-six states have reintroduced the death penalty.* ■ put (a species of animal or plant) back into a region where it formerly lived: *a plan to reintroduce wolves to Yellowstone National Park.* **—re·in·tro·duc·tion** /-ˈdəksʜən/ *n.*

re·in·vent /ˌrē-inˈvent/ ▸*v.* [*trans.*] change (something) so much that it appears to be entirely new: *he brought opera to the masses and reinvented the waltz.* ■ (**reinvent oneself**) take up a very different job or way of life: *the actor wants to reinvent himself as an independent movie mogul.* **—re·in·ven·tion** /-ˈvenCHən/ *n.*

▸*PHRASE* □ **reinvent the wheel** waste a great deal of time or effort in creating something that already exists.

re·in·vest /ˌrē-inˈvest/ ▸*v.* [*trans.*] put (the profit on a previous investment) back into the same place: *the enterprise had been expanded by reinvesting profits.* **—re·in·vest·ment** /-ˈvestmənt/ *n.*

re·in·vig·or·ate /ˌrē-inˈvigəˌrāt/ ▸*v.* [*trans.*] give new energy or strength to: *we are fully committed to reinvigorating the economy of the area.* **—re·in·vig·or·a·tion** /ˌrē-inˌvigəˈrāsʜən/ *n.*

re·is·sue /rēˈisʜo͞o/ ▸*v.* (**-is·sues, -is·sued, -is·su·ing**) [*trans.*] make a new supply or different form of (a product, esp. a book or record) available for sale: *the book was reissued with a new epilogue.*
▸*n.* a new issue of such a product.

REIT ▸*abbr.* real-estate investment trust.

re·it·er·ate /rēˈitəˌrāt/ ▸*v.* [*reporting verb*] say something again or a number or times, typically for emphasis or clarity: [with *clause*] *she reiterated that the administration would remain steadfast in its support* | [with *direct speech*] *"I just want to forget it all," he reiterated* | [*trans.*] *he reiterated the points made in his earlier speech.* ▷late Middle English (in the sense 'do (an action) repeatedly'): from Latin *reiterat-* 'gone over again,' from the verb *reiterare*, from *re-* 'again' + *iterare* 'do a second time.' **—re·it·er·a·tion** /rēˌitəˈrāsʜən/ *n.* **—re·it·er·a·tive** /-ˌrātiv; -rətiv/ *adj.*

Rei·ter's syn·drome /ˈrītərz/ (also **Rei·ter's dis·ease**) ▸*n.* a medical condition typically affecting young men, characterized by arthritis, conjunctivitis, and urethritis, and caused by an unknown pathogen, possibly a chlamydia. ▷1920s: named after Hans *Reiter* (1881–1969), German bacteriologist.

reive /rēv/ ▸*v.* [*intrans.*] [usu. as *n.*] (**reiving**) *chiefly Scottish* another term for **REAVE**. ▷Middle English: variant of **REAVE**; the usual spelling when referring to the historical practice of cattle raiding on the English-Scottish border. **—reiv·er** *n.*

re·ject ▸*v.* /riˈjekt/ [*trans.*] dismiss as inadequate, inappropriate, or not to one's taste: *union negotiators rejected a 1.5 percent pay increase.* ■ refuse to agree to (a request): *an application to hold a pop concert at the club was rejected.* ■ fail to show due affection or concern for (someone); rebuff: *she didn't want him to feel he had been rejected after his sister was born.* ■ *Medicine* show an immune response to (a transplanted organ or tissue) so that it fails to survive.
▸*n.* /ˈrēˌjekt/ a person or thing dismissed as failing to meet standards or satisfy tastes: *some of the team's rejects have gone on to prove themselves in championships.* ▷late Middle English: from Latin *reject-* 'thrown back,' from the verb *reicere*, from *re-* 'back' + *jacere* 'to throw.' **—re·ject·ee** /riˌjekˈtē; ˌrē-/ *n.* **—re·jec·tion** /riˈjeksʜən/ *n.* **—re·jec·tive** /riˈjektiv/ *adj.* (*rare*). **—re·jec·tor** /-tər/ *n.*

re·jec·tion·ist /riˈjeksʜənist/ ▸*n.* [often as *adj.*] a person who rejects a proposed policy, esp. an Arab who refuses to accept a negotiated peace with Israel.

re·jec·tion slip ▸*n.* a formal notice sent by an editor or publisher to an author with a rejected manuscript or typescript.

re·jig·ger /rēˈjigər/ (*Brit.* **re·jig**) ▸*v.* [*trans.*] organize (something) differently; rearrange: *he rejiggers his stump speech ever so slightly to fit the crowd, then sounds the same messages.*

re·joice /riˈjois/ ▸*v.* [*intrans.*] feel or show great joy or delight: *he rejoiced when he saw his friend alive* | *he* **rejoiced in** *her spontaneity and directness* | [as *n.*] (**rejoicing**) *an occasion for rejoicing.* ■ [*trans.*] *archaic* cause joy to: *I love to rejoice their poor Hearts at this season.* ▷Middle English (in the sense 'cause joy to'): from Old French *rejoiss-*, lengthened stem of *rejoir*, from *re-* (expressing intensive force) + *joir* 'experience joy.' **—re·joic·er** *n.* **—re·joic·ing·ly** *adv.*

re·join[1] /rēˈjoin; ˈrē-/ ▸*v.* [*trans.*] join together again; reunite: *the stone had been cracked and crudely rejoined.* ■ return to (a companion, organization, or route that one has left): *the soldiers were returning from leave to rejoin their unit.*

re·join[2] /riˈjoin/ ▸*v.* [*reporting verb*] say something in answer to a remark, typically rudely or in a discouraging manner: [with *clause*] *Harry said that he longed for a bath and soft towels, to which his father rejoined that he was a gross materialist.* ▷late Middle English (in the sense 'reply to a charge or pleading in a lawsuit'): from Old French *rejoindre*, from *re-* 'again' + *joindre* 'to join.'

re·join·der /riˈjoindər/ ▸*n.* a reply, esp. a sharp or witty one: *she would have made some cutting rejoinder but none came to mind.* ■ *dated Law* a defendant's answer to the plaintiff's reply or replication. ▷late Middle English: from Anglo-Norman French *rejoindre* (infinitive used as a noun) (see **REJOIN**[2]).

re·ju·ve·nate /riˈjo͞ovəˌnāt/ ▸*v.* [*trans.*] make (someone or something) look or feel younger, fresher, or more lively: *a bid to rejuvenate the town center* | [as *adj.*] (**rejuvenating**) *the rejuvenating effects of therapeutic clay.* ■ [often as *adj.*] (**rejuvenated**) restore (a river or stream) to a condition characteristic of a younger landscape. ▷early 19th cent.: from **RE-** 'again' + Latin *juvenis* 'young' + **-ATE**[3], suggested by French *rajeunir*. **—re·ju·ve·na·tion** /riˌjo͞ovəˈnāsʜən/ *n.* **—re·ju·ve·na·tor** /-ˌnātər/ *n.*

re·ju·ve·nes·cence /riˌjo͞ovəˈnesəns/ ▸*n.* the renewal of youth or vitality. ■ *Biology* the reactivation of vegetative cells, resulting in regrowth from old or injured parts. ▷mid 17th cent.: from late Latin *rejuvenescere* (from Latin *re-* 'again' + *juvenis* 'young') + **-ENCE**. **—re·ju·ve·nes·cent** /-ˈnesənt/ *adj.*

re·key /rēˈkē/ ▸*v.* [*trans.*] *chiefly Computing* enter (text or other data) again using a keyboard.

re·kin·dle /rēˈkindəl/ ▸*v.* [*trans.*] relight (a fire). ■ revive (something that has been lost): *he tried to rekindle their friendship* | *the photos rekindled memories.*

rel. ▸*abbr.* ■ relating. ■ relative. ■ relatively. ■ released. ■ religion. ■ religious.

-rel ▸*suffix* forming nouns with diminutive or derogatory force such as *cockerel, pickerel, scoundrel.* ▷from Old French *-erel(le)*.

re·la·bel /rēˈlābəl/ ▸*v.* (**-la·beled, -la·bel·ing**; *Brit.* **-la·belled, -la·bel·ling**) [*trans.*] label (something) again or differently.

re·laid /rēˈlād; ˈrē-/ ▸ past and past participle of **RELAY**[2].

re·lapse ▸*v.* /riˈlaps; ˈrēˌlaps/ [*intrans.*] (of someone suffering from a disease) suffer deterioration after a period of improvement. ■ (**relapse into**) return to (a less active or a worse state): *he relapsed into silence.*
▸*n.* /ˈrēˌlaps/ a deterioration in someone's state of health after a temporary improvement: *he suffered a relapse of schizophrenia after a car crash.* ▷late Middle English: from Latin *relaps-* 'slipped back,' from the verb *relabi*, from *re-* 'back' + *labi* 'to slip.' Early senses referred to a return to heresy or wrongdoing. **—re·laps·er** *n.*

re·laps·ing fe·ver ▸*n.* an infectious bacterial disease marked by recurrent fever. • The disease is caused by spirochetes of the genus *Borrelia*.

re·late /riˈlāt/ ▸*v.* [*trans.*] **1** give an account of (a sequence of events); narrate: *various versions of the chilling story have been related by the locals.* **2** (**be related**) be connected by blood or marriage: *he was* **related to** *my mother* | *people who are related.* ■ be causally connected: *high unemployment is* **related to** *high crime rates.* ■ (**relate something to**) discuss something in such a way as to indicate its connections with (something else): *the study examines social change within the city and relates it to wider developments in the country as a whole.* ■ [*intrans.*] (**relate to**) have reference to; concern: *the new legislation related to corporate activities.* ■ [*intrans.*] (**relate to**) feel sympathy with; identify with: *kids related to him because he was so anti-establishment.* ▷mid 16th cent.: from Latin *relat-* 'brought back,' from the verb *referre* (see **REFER**). **—re·lat·a·ble** *adj.*

re·lat·ed /riˈlātid/ ▸*adj.* belonging to the same family, group, or type; connected: *sleeping sickness and related diseases.* ■ [in *combination*] associated with the specified item or process, esp. causally: *income-related benefits.* **—re·lat·ed·ness** *n.*

re·lat·er /riˈlātər/ (also **re·la·tor**) ▸*n.* a person who tells a story; a narrator.

re·la·tion /riˈlāsʜən/ ▸*n.* **1** the way in which two or more concepts, objects, or people are connected; a thing's effect on or relevance to another: *questions about the* **relation between** *writing and reality* | *the size of the targets* **bore** *no* **relation to** *their importance.* ■ (**relations**) the way in which two or more people, countries, or organizations feel about and behave toward each other: *the improvement in relations between the two countries* | *the meetings helped cement Anglo-American relations.* ■ (**relations**) *chiefly formal* sexual intercourse: *he wanted an excuse to abandon sexual relations with her.* **2** a person who is connected by blood or marriage; a kinsman or kinswoman: *she was no relation at all, but he called her Aunt Nora.* **3** the action of telling a story. ▷Middle English: from Old French, or from Latin *relatio(n-)*, from *referre* 'bring back' (see **RELATE**).
▸*PHRASE* □ **in relation to** in the context of; in connection with: *there is an ambiguity in the provisions in relation to children's hearings.*

re·la·tion·al /riˈlāsʜənl/ ▸*adj.* concerning the way in which two or more people or things are connected: *power is a relational concept that can only be understood in terms of interactions between individuals and groups.* **—re·la·tion·al·ly** *adv.*

rela·tion·al da·ta·base ▸*n.* *Computing* a database structured to recognize relations among stored items of information.

re·la·tion·ship /riˈlāsʜənˌsʜip/ ▸*n.* the way in which two or more concepts, objects, or people are connected, or the state of being connected: *the study will assess the* **relationship between** *unemployment and political attitudes.* ■ the state of being connected by blood or marriage: *they can trace their relationship to a common ancestor.* ■ the way in which two or more people or organizations regard and behave toward each other: *the landlord–tenant relationship* | *she was proud of her good relationship with the household staff.* ■ an emotional and sexual association between two people: *she has a daughter from a previous relationship.*

rel·a·tive /ˈrelətiv/ ▸*adj.* **1** considered in relation or in proportion to something else: *the relative effectiveness of the various mechanisms is not known.* ■ existing or possessing a specified characteristic only in comparison to something else; not absolute: *she went down the steps into the relative darkness of the dining room* | *the companies are relative newcomers to computers.* **2** *Grammar* denoting a pronoun, determiner, or adverb that refers to an expressed or implied antecedent and attaches a subordinate clause to it, e.g., *which, who.* ■ (of a clause) attached to an antecedent by a relative word. **3** *Music* (of major and minor keys) having the same key signature. **4** (of a service rank) corresponding in grade to another in a different service.
▸*n.* **1** a person connected by blood or marriage: *much of my time is spent visiting relatives.* ■ a species related to another by common origin: *the plant is a relative of ivy.* **2** *Grammar* a relative pronoun, determiner, or adverb. **3** *Philosophy* a term, thing, or concept that is dependent on something else. ▷late Middle English: from Old French *relatif, -ive*, from late Latin *relativus* 'having reference or relation' (see **RELATE**). **—rel·a·tiv·al** /ˌreləˈtīvəl/ *adj.* (in sense 2 of the *noun*).
▸*PHRASE* □ **relative to** **1** in comparison with: *the figures suggest that girls are underachieving relative to boys.* ■ in terms of a connection to: *some stars appear to change their position relative to each other.* **2** in connection with; concerning: *if you have any questions relative to payment, please contact us.*

rel·a·tive a·tom·ic mass ▸*n.* *Chemistry* Another term for **ATOMIC MASS**.

rel·a·tive den·si·ty ▸*n.* another term for **SPECIFIC GRAVITY**.

rel·a·tive hu·mid·i·ty ▸*n.* the amount of water vapor present in air expressed as a percentage of the amount needed for saturation at the same temperature.

rel·a·tive·ly /ˈrelətivlē/ ▸*adv.* [*sentence adverb*] in relation, comparison, or proportion to something else: *it is perfectly simple,* **relatively speaking,** *to store a full catalog entry on magnetic tape.* ■ [as *submodifier*] viewed in comparison with something else rather than absolutely: *relatively affluent people* | *the site was cheap and relatively clean.*

rel·a·tiv·ism /ˈreləteˌvizəm/ ▸*n.* the doctrine that knowledge, truth, and morality exist in relation to culture, society, or historical context, and are not absolute. **—rel·a·tiv·ist** *n.*

rel·a·tiv·is·tic /ˌreləteˈvistik/ ▸*adj.* **1** *Physics* accurately described only by the theory of relativity. **2** of or relating to the doctrine of relativism. **—rel·a·tiv·is·ti·cal·ly** /-ik(ə)lē/ *adv.*

R

Pronunciation Key ə *ago*; ər *over*; ˈə or ˌə *up*; ˈər or ˌər *fur*; a *hat*; ā *rate*; ä *car*; CH *chew*; e *let*; ē *see*; e(ə)r *air*; i *fit*; ī *by*; i(ə)r *ear*; NG *sing*; ō *go*; ô *for*; oi *boy*; o͝o *good*; o͞o *goo*; ou *out*; SH *she*; TH *thin*; T͟H *then*; (h)w *why*; ZH *vision*

rel·a·tiv·i·ty /ˌreləˈtivətē/ ▸*n.* **1** the absence of standards of absolute and universal application: *moral relativity.* **2** *Physics* the dependence of various physical phenomena on relative motion of the observer and the observed objects, esp. regarding the nature and behavior of light, space, time, and gravity.

The concept of relativity was set out in Einstein's **special theory of relativity**, published in 1905. This states that all motion is relative and that the velocity of light in a vacuum has a constant value that nothing can exceed. Among its consequences are the following: the mass of a body increases and its length (in the direction of motion) shortens as its speed increases; the time interval between two events occurring in a moving body appears greater to a stationary observer; and mass and energy are equivalent and interconvertible. Einstein's **general theory of relativity**, published in 1915, extended the theory to accelerated motion and gravitation, which was treated as a curvature of the space-time continuum. It predicted that light rays would be deflected and shifted in wavelength when passing through a substantial gravitational field, effects that have been experimentally confirmed.

rel·a·tiv·ize /ˈrelətəˌvīz/ ▸*v.* [*trans.*] *chiefly Linguistics & Philosophy* make or treat as relative to or dependent on something else. ■ *Grammar & Linguistics* make into a relative clause. ■ *Physics* treat (a phenomenon or concept) according to the principles of the theory of relativity. **—rel·a·tiv·i·za·tion** /ˌrelətəvəˈzāsʜən/ *n.*

re·la·tor /riˈlātər/ ▸*n.* **1** *Law* a person who brings a public lawsuit, typically in the name of the attorney general, regarding the abuse of an office or franchise. **2** variant spelling of RELATER.

re·launch ▸*v.* /rēˈlônch; -ˈlänch/ [*trans.*] cause to start again with renewed vigor after a period of inactivity. ■ reintroduce (a product): *he relaunched the paper as a tabloid.*
▸*n.* /ˈrēlônch; -länch/ an instance of reintroducing or restarting something, esp. a product.

re·lax /riˈlaks/ ▸*v.* make or become less tense or anxious: [*intrans.*] *he relaxed and smiled confidently* | [as *adj.*] (**relaxing**) *a relaxing vacation.* ■ [*intrans.*] rest or engage in an enjoyable activity so as to become less tired or anxious: *the team relaxes with a lot of skiing.* ■ [*trans.*] cause (a limb or muscle) to become less rigid: *relax the leg by bringing the knee toward the chest.* ■ make (something) less firm or tight: *Cicely relaxed her hold.* ■ [*trans.*] make (a rule or restriction) less strict while not abolishing it: *they persuaded the local authorities concerned to relax their restrictions.* ▷late Middle English: from Latin *relaxare*, from *re-* (expressing intensive force) + *laxus* 'lax, loose.' **—re·lax·er** *n.*

re·lax·ant /rəˈlaksənt/ ▸*n.* a drug used to promote relaxation or reduce tension: *a muscle relaxant.* ■ a thing having a relaxing effect: *sex can be a great relaxant.*
▸*adj.* causing relaxation.

re·lax·a·tion /riˌlakˈsāsʜən; rē-/ ▸*n.* **1** the state of being free from tension and anxiety. ■ recreation or rest, esp. after a period of work: *his favorite form of relaxation was reading detective novels.* ■ the loss of tension in a part of the body, esp. in a muscle when it ceases to contract. ■ the action of making a rule or restriction less strict: *relaxation of censorship rules.* **2** *Physics* the restoration of equilibrium following disturbance.

re·lax·a·tion os·cil·la·tor ▸*n.* *Electronics* an oscillator in which sharp, sometimes aperiodic oscillations result from the rapid discharge of a capacitor or inductance.

re·laxed /riˈlakst/ ▸*adj.* free from tension and anxiety; at ease: *we were having a great time and feeling very relaxed* | *the relaxed and comfortable atmosphere of the hotel.* ■ (of a muscle or other body part) not tense. **—re·lax·ed·ly** /riˈlaksədlē/ *adv.* **—re·lax·ed·ness** /riˈlaksədnəs/ *n.*

re·lax·in /rəˈlaksin/ ▸*n.* *Biochemistry* a hormone secreted by the placenta that causes the cervix to dilate and prepares the uterus for the action of oxytocin during labor.

re·lay[1] ▸*n.* /ˈrēˌlā/ **1** a group of people or animals engaged in a task or activity for a fixed period of time and then replaced by a similar group: *the wagons were pulled by relays of horses* | *gangs of workers were sent **in relays**.* ■ [usu. as *adj.*] a race between teams usually of sprinters or swimmers, each team member in turn covering part of the total distance: *a 550-meter relay race.* **2** an electrical device, typically incorporating an electromagnet, that is activated by a current or signal in one circuit to open or close another circuit. **3** a device to receive, reinforce, and retransmit a broadcast or program. ■ a message or program transmitted by such a device: *a relay of a performance live from the concert hall.*
▸*v.* /riˈlā; ˈrēˌlā/ [*trans.*] receive and pass on (information or a message): *she intended to relay everything she had learned.* ■ broadcast (something) by passing signals received from elsewhere through a transmitting station: *the speech was relayed live from the White House.* ▷late Middle English (referring to the provision of fresh hounds on the track of a deer): from Old French *relai* (noun), *relayer* (verb), based on Latin *laxare* 'slacken.'

re-lay[2] /rēˈlā/ ▸*v.* (*past* and *past part.* **-laid**) [*trans.*] lay again or differently: *they plan to re-lay about half a mile of the track.*

re·learn /rēˈlərn/ ▸*v.* (*past* and *past part.* **-learned** or *chiefly Brit.* **-learnt** /-ˈlərnt/) [*trans.*] learn (something) again: *I've been relearning my Latin and Greek.*

re·lease /riˈlēs/ ▸*v.* [*trans.*] **1** allow or enable to escape from confinement; set free: *the government announced that the prisoners would be released.* ■ remove restrictions or obligations from (someone or something) so that they become available for other activity: *the strategy would release forces for service in other areas.* ■ allow (information) to be generally available: *no details about the contents of the talks were released.* ■ make (a movie or recording) available for general viewing or purchase: *nine singles and one album had been released.* ■ allow (something concentrated in a small area) to spread and work freely: *growth hormone is released into the blood during the first part of sleep.* ■ remove (part of a machine or appliance) from a fixed position, allowing something else to move or function: *he released the handbrake.* ■ allow (something) to return to its resting position by ceasing to put pressure on it: *press the cap down and release.* **2** *Law* remit or discharge (a debt). ■ surrender (a right). ■ make over (property or money) to another person or entity.
▸*n.* **1** the action or process of releasing or being released: *a campaign by the prisoner's mother resulted in his release.* ■ the action of making a movie, recording, or other product available for general viewing or purchase: *the film was withheld for two years before its release.* ■ a movie or other product issued for viewing or purchase: *his current album release has topped the charts for six months.* ■ a press release. ■ a handle or catch that releases part of a mechanism. **2** *Law* the action of releasing property, money, or a right to another. ■ a document effecting this. ▷Middle English: from Old French *reles* (noun), *relesser* (verb), from Latin *relaxare* 'stretch out again, slacken' (see RELAX). **—re·leas·a·ble** *adj.* **—re·leas·ee** /riˌlēˈsē/ *n.* (*Law*). **—re·leas·er** /riˈlēsər/ *n.* **—re·leas·or** /riˈlēsər/ *n.* (*Law*).

re·leas·ing fac·tor ▸*n.* *Biochemistry* a substance that, when secreted by the hypothalamus, promotes the release of a specified hormone from the anterior lobe of the pituitary gland.

rel·e·gate /ˈreləˌgāt/ ▸*v.* [*trans.*] consign or dismiss to an inferior rank or position: *they aim to prevent women from being **relegated to** a secondary role.* ▷late Middle English (in the sense 'send into exile'): from Latin *relegat-* 'sent away, referred,' from the verb *relegare*, from *re-* 'again' + *legare* 'send.' **—rel·e·ga·tion** /ˌreləˈgāsʜən/ *n.*

re·lent /riˈlent/ ▸*v.* [*intrans.*] abandon or mitigate a harsh intention or cruel treatment: *she was going to refuse his request, but relented.* ■ (esp. of bad weather) become less severe or intense: *by evening the rain relented.* ▷late Middle English (in the sense 'dissolve, melt'): based on Latin *re-* 'back' + *lentare* 'to bend' (from *lentus* 'flexible').

re·lent·less /riˈlentləs/ ▸*adj.* oppressively constant; incessant: *the relentless heat of the desert.* ■ harsh or inflexible: *a patient but relentless taskmaster.* **—re·lent·less·ly** *adv.* **—re·lent·less·ness** *n.*

re·let ▸*v.* /rēˈlet; ˈrē-/ (**-let·ting**; *past* and *past part.* **-let**) [*trans.*] *chiefly Brit.* rent (a property) for a further period or to a new tenant.
▸*n.* /ˈrēlet/ an act of renting a property again.

rel·e·vant /ˈreləvənt/ ▸*adj.* closely connected or appropriate to the matter at hand: *the candidate's experience is **relevant to** the job.* ▷early 16th cent. (as a Scots legal term meaning 'legally pertinent'): from medieval Latin *relevant-* 'raising up,' from Latin *relevare.* **—rel·e·vance** *n.* **—rel·e·van·cy** /-vənsē/ *n.* **—rel·e·vant·ly** *adv.*

re·le·vé /ˌreləˈvā/ ▸*n.* **1** *Ballet* a movement in which the dancer rises on the tips of the toes. **2** *Ecology* each of a number of small plots of vegetation, analyzed as a sample of a wider area. ▷French, literally 'raised up.'

re·li·a·ble /riˈlīəbəl/ ▸*adj.* consistently good in quality or performance; able to be trusted: *a reliable source of information.*
▸*n.* a person or thing with such trustworthy qualities: *the supporting cast includes old reliables like Mitchell.* **—re·li·a·bil·i·ty** /riˌlīəˈbilətē/ *n.* **—re·li·a·ble·ness** *n.* **—re·li·a·bly** /-blē/ *adv.*

re·li·ance /riˈlīəns/ ▸*n.* dependence on or trust in someone or something: *the farmer's **reliance on** pesticides.* ■ *archaic* a person or thing on which someone depends. **—re·li·ant** /-ənt/ *adj.*

rel·ic /ˈrelik/ ▸*n.* an object surviving from an earlier time, esp. one of historical or sentimental interest. ■ a part of a deceased holy person's body or belongings kept as an object of reverence. ■ an object, custom, or belief that has survived from an earlier time but is now outmoded: *individualized computer programming and time-sharing would become expensive relics.* ■ (**relics**) all that is left of something: *relics of a lost civilization.* ▷Middle English: from Old French *relique* (originally plural), from Latin *reliquiae* (see RELIQUIAE).

rel·ict /ˈrelikt/ ▸*n.* **1** a thing that has survived from an earlier period or in a primitive form. ■ an animal or plant that has survived while others of its group have become extinct, e.g., the coelacanth. ■ a species or community that formerly had a wider distribution but now survives in only a few localities such as refugia. [early 20th cent.: from Latin *relictus* 'left behind,' past participle of the verb *relinquere*.] **2** *archaic* a widow. [late Middle English: from Old French *relicte* '(woman) left behind,' from late Latin *relicta*, from the verb *relinquere*.]

re·lief /riˈlēf/ ▸*n.* **1** a feeling of reassurance and relaxation following release from anxiety or distress: *much to her relief, she saw the door open.* ■ a cause of or occasion for such a feeling: *it was a relief to find somewhere to stay.* ■ the alleviation of pain, discomfort, or distress: *tablets for the relief of pain.* ■ a temporary break in a generally tense or tedious situation: *the comic characters aren't part of the plot but just light relief.* **2** assistance, esp. in the form of food, clothing, or money, given to those in special need or difficulty: *raising money for famine relief* | [as *adj.*] *relief workers.* ■ a remission of tax normally due: *people who donate money to charity will receive tax relief.* ■ *chiefly Law* the redress of a hardship or grievance. ■ the action of raising the siege of a beseiged town: *the relief of Mafeking.* **3** a person or group of people replacing others who have been on duty: [as *adj.*] *the relief nurse was late.* ■ *Baseball* the role of a relief pitcher. **4** the state of being clearly visible or obvious due to being accentuated in some way: *the setting sun threw the snow-covered peaks **into relief**.* ■ a method of molding, carving, or stamping in which the design stands out from the surface, to a greater (**high relief**) or lesser (**bas-relief**) extent. ■ a piece of sculpture in relief. ■ a representation of relief given by an arrangement of line or color or shading. ■ *Geography* difference in height from the surrounding terrain; the amount of variation in elevation and slope in a particular area. [via French from Italian *rilievo*, from *rilevare* 'raise,' from Latin *relevare*.] ▷late Middle English: from Old French, from *relever* 'raise up, relieve,' from Latin *relevare* 'raise again, alleviate.'
▸*PHRASES* □ **in relief** **1** *Art* carved, molded, or stamped so as to stand out from the surface. **2** *Baseball* acting as a replacement pitcher. □ **on relief** receiving government assistance because of need.

re·lief map ▸*n.* a map indicating hills and valleys by shading rather than by contour lines alone. ■ a map model with elevations and depressions representing hills and valleys, typically on an exaggerated relative scale.

re·lief pitch·er ▸*n.* *Baseball* a pitcher who enters the game in place of the previous pitcher.

re·lief print·ing ▸*n.* printing from raised images, as in letterpress and flexography.

re·lief road ▸*n.* *Brit.* a road taking traffic around, rather than through, a congested urban area.

re·lieve /riˈlēv/ ▸*v.* [*trans.*] **1** cause (pain, distress, or difficulty) to become less severe or serious: *the drug was used to promote sleep and to relieve pain.* See note at ALLEVIATE. ■ (usu. **be relieved**) cause (someone) to stop feeling distressed or anxious about something: *he was relieved by her change of tone.* ■ make less tedious or monotonous by the introduction of variety or of something striking or pleasing: *the bird's body is* *black, relieved only by white under the tail.* **2** release (someone) from duty by taking their place: *another signalman relieved him at 5:30.* ■ bring military support for (a besieged place): *he dispatched an expedition to relieve the city.* ■ *Baseball* (of a relief pitcher) take the place of (another pitcher) during a game. **3** (**relieve someone of**) take (a burden) from someone: *he relieved her of her baggage.* ■ free someone from (a tiresome responsibility): *she relieved me of the household chores.* ■ used euphemistically to indicate that someone has been deprived of something: *he was relieved of his world title.* **4** (**relieve oneself**) urinate or defecate (used euphemistically). **5** *archaic* make (something) stand out: *the twilight relieving in purple masses the foliage of the island.* ▷Middle English: from Old French *relever*, from Latin *relevare*, from *re-* (expressing intensive force) + *levare* 'raise' (from *levis* 'light'). **—re·liev·a·ble** *adj.* **—re·liev·ed·ly** /ri'lēvədlē/ *adv.* **—re·liev·er** *n.*

re·liev·ing of·fi·cer ▸*n. chiefly Brit., historical* an official appointed to administer relief to the poor.

re·lie·vo /ri'lēvō; rēl'yāvō/ (also **ri·lie·vo**) ▸*n.* (*pl.* **-vos**) *chiefly Art* another term for RELIEF (sense 4). ▷Italian *rilievo*.

re·light /rē'līt; 'rē-/ ▸*v.* (*past* and *past part.* **-light·ed** or **-lit** /-'lit/) [*trans.*] light (something) again: *he reached for the matches to relight his pipe.*

religio- ▸*comb. form* religious and . . . : *religio-political* | *religio-national.* ▷from RELIGION or RELIGIOUS.

re·li·gion /ri'lijən/ ▸*n.* the belief in and worship of a superhuman controlling power, esp. a personal God or gods: *ideas about the relationship between science and religion.* ■ details of belief as taught or discussed: *when the school first opened they taught only religion, Italian, and mathematics.* ■ a particular system of faith and worship: *the world's great religions.* ■ a pursuit or interest to which someone ascribes supreme importance: *consumerism is the new religion.* ▷Middle English (originally in the sense 'life under monastic vows'): from Old French, or from Latin *religio(n-)* 'obligation, bond, reverence,' perhaps based on Latin *religare* 'to bind.' **—re·li·gion·less** *adj.*

▸**PHRASE** □ **get religion** *informal* be converted to religious belief and practices.

re·li·gion·ism /ri'lijə,nizəm/ ▸*n.* excessive religious zeal. **—re·li·gion·ist** *n.*

re·li·gi·ose /ri'lijē,ōs/ ▸*adj.* excessively religious. ▷mid 19th cent.: from Latin *religiosus*, from *religio* 'reverence, obligation.' **—re·li·gi·os·i·ty** /ri,lijē'äsətē/ *n.*

re·li·gious /ri'lijəs/ ▸*adj.* believing in and worshiping a superhuman controlling power or powers, esp. a personal God or gods: *both men were deeply religious, intelligent, and moralistic.* ■ (of a belief or practice) forming part of someone's thought about or worship of a divine being: *he has strong religious convictions.* ■ of or relating to the worship of or a doctrine concerning a divine being or beings: *religious music.* ■ belonging or relating to a monastic order or other group of people who are united by their practice of religion: *religious houses were built on ancient pagan sites.* ■ treated or regarded with a devotion and scrupulousness appropriate to worship: *I have a religious aversion to reading manuals.*

▸*n.* (*pl.* same) a person bound by monastic vows. ▷Middle English: from Old French, from Latin *religiosus*, from *religio* 'reverence, obligation' (see RELIGION). **—re·li·gious·ly** *adv.* **—re·li·gious·ness** *n.*

Re·li·gious So·ci·e·ty of Friends official name for the Quakers (see QUAKER).

re·line /rē'līn; 'rē-/ ▸*v.* [*trans.*] replace the lining of: *the heavily brocaded drapes that she had relined.* ■ attach a new backing canvas to (a painting).

re·lin·quish /ri'liNGkwiSH/ ▸*v.* [*trans.*] voluntarily cease to keep or claim; give up: *he relinquished his managerial role to become chief executive.* ▷late Middle English: from Old French *relinquiss-*, lengthened stem of *relinquir*, from Latin *relinquere*, from *re-* (expressing intensive force) + *linquere* 'to leave.' **—re·lin·quish·ment** *n.*

THE RIGHT WORD **abandon, cede, relinquish, surrender, waive, yield**

Of all these verbs meaning to let go or give up, **relinquish** is the most general. It can imply anything from simply releasing one's grasp (*she relinquished the wheel*) to giving up control or possession reluctantly (*after the defeat, he was forced to relinquish his command*).

Surrender also implies giving up, but usually after a struggle or show of resistance (*the villagers were forced to surrender to the guerrillas*).

Yield is a milder synonym for *surrender*, implying some concession, respect, or even affection on the part of the person who is surrendering (*she yielded to her mother's wishes and stayed home*).

Waive means to give up voluntarily a right or claim to something (*she waived her right to have a lawyer present*), while **cede** is to give up by legal transfer or according to the terms of a treaty (*the French ceded the territory that is now Louisiana*).

If one *relinquishes* something finally and completely, often because of weariness or discouragement, the correct word is **abandon** (*they were told to abandon all hope of being rescued*).

rel·i·quar·y /'relə,kwerē/ ▸*n.* (*pl.* **-quar·ies**) a container for holy relics. ▷mid 16th cent.: from French *reliquaire*, from Old French *relique* (see RELIC).

re·liq·ui·ae /rə'likwē,ī; -wē,ē/ ▸*plural n.* remains. ■ *Geology* fossil remains of animals or plants. ▷mid 17th cent.: Latin, feminine plural (used as a noun) of *reliquus* 'remaining,' based on *linquere* 'to leave.'

rel·ish /'reliSH/ ▸*n.* **1** great enjoyment: *she swigged a mouthful of wine with relish.* ■ liking for or pleasurable anticipation of something: *I was appointed to a position for which I had little relish.* **2** a condiment eaten with plain food to add flavor: *use salsa as a relish with grilled meat or fish.* ■ chopped sweet pickles used as such a condiment: *we could have as many hot dogs as we wanted, smothered in mustard and relish.* **3** *archaic* an appetizing flavor. ■ a distinctive taste or tinge: *the relish of wine.* ■ an attractive quality.

▸*v.* [*trans.*] **1** enjoy greatly: *he was relishing his moment of glory.* ■ be pleased by or about: *I don't relish the thought of waiting on an invalid for the next few months.* **2** *archaic* make pleasant to the taste; add relish to: *I have also a novel to relish my wine.* ▷Middle English: alteration of obsolete *reles*, from Old French, 'remainder,' from *relaisser* 'to release.' The early noun sense was 'odor, taste,' giving rise to 'appetizing flavor, piquant taste' (mid 17th cent.), and hence sense 2 (late 18th cent.). **—rel·ish·a·ble** *adj.*

re·live /rē'liv; 'rē-/ ▸*v.* [*trans.*] live through (an experience or feeling, esp. an unpleasant one) again in one's imagination or memory: *he broke down sobbing as he relived the attack.*

rel·le·no /rə(l)'yānō/ ▸*n.* (*pl.* **-nos**) short for CHILE RELLENO.

re·load /rē'lōd/ ▸*v.* [*trans.*] load (something, esp. a gun that has been fired) again: *he reloaded the chamber of the shotgun with fresh cartridges* | [*intrans.*] *Charlie reloaded and took aim.*

re·lo·cate /rē'lō,kāt; ,rēlō'kāt/ ▸*v.* [*intrans.*] move to a new place and establish one's home or business there: *if you are relocating here from another state* | [*trans.*] *distribution staff will be relocated to Holland.* **—re·lo·ca·tion** /,rēlō'kāSHən/ *n.*

re·luc·tance /ri'ləktəns/ ▸*n.* unwillingness or disinclination to do something: *she sensed his reluctance to continue.* ■ *Physics* the property of a magnetic circuit of opposing the passage of magnetic flux lines, equal to the ratio of the magnetomotive force to the magnetic flux.

re·luc·tant /ri'ləktənt/ ▸*adj.* unwilling and hesitant; disinclined: [with *infinitive*] *she seemed reluctant to discuss the matter.* ▷mid 17th cent. (in the sense 'writhing, offering opposition'): from Latin *reluctant-* 'struggling against,' from the verb *reluctari*, from *re-* (expressing intensive force) + *luctari* 'to struggle.' **—re·luc·tant·ly** *adv.*

re·lume /rē'lo͞om/ ▸*v.* [*trans.*] *poetic/literary* relight or rekindle (a light, flame, etc.): *Oceana stole from her place of concealment, and relumed the taper.* ▷early 17th cent.: from RE- 'again' + ILLUME, partly suggested by French *rallumer*.

re·ly /ri'lī/ ▸*v.* (**-lies, -lied**) [*intrans.*] (**rely on/upon**) depend on with full trust or confidence: *I know I can rely on your discretion.* ■ be dependent on: *the charity has to rely entirely on public donations.* ▷Middle English: from Old French *relier* 'bind together,' from Latin *religare*, from *re-* (expressing intensive force) + *ligare* 'bind.' The original sense was 'gather together,' later 'turn to, associate with,' whence 'depend upon with confidence.'

REM ▸*abbr.* rapid eye movement.

rem /rem/ ▸*n.* (*pl.* same) a unit of effective absorbed dose of ionizing radiation in human tissue, equivalent to one roentgen of X-rays. ▷1940s: acronym from *roentgen equivalent man*.

re·made /rē'mād; 'rē-/ ▸ past and past participle of REMAKE.

re·mail·er /'rē,mālər/ ▸*n. Computing* a service that anonymously forwards e-mail so as to disguise the original sender. ■ a similar service for mail that takes advantage of cheaper or more efficient postal services in other countries.

re·main /ri'mān/ ▸*v.* [*intrans.*] continue to exist, esp. after other similar or related people or things have ceased to exist: *a cloister is all that remains of the monastery.* ■ stay in the place that one has been occupying: *her husband remained at the beach condo.* ■ [with *complement*] continue to possess a particular quality or fulfill a particular role: *he had remained alert the whole time.* ■ be left over after others or other parts have been completed, used, or dealt with: [as *adj.*] (**remaining**) *he would see out the remaining two years of his contract.* ▷late Middle English: from Old French *remain-*, stressed stem of *remanoir*, from Latin *remanere*, from *re-* (expressing intensive force) + *manere* 'to stay.'

▸**PHRASE** □ **remain to be seen** used to express the notion that something is not yet known or certain: *she has broken her leg, but it remains to be seen how badly.*

re·main·der /ri'māndər/ ▸*n.* **1** a part, number, or quantity that is left over: *leave a few mushrooms for garnish and slice the remainder.* ■ a part that is still to come: *the remainder of the year.* ■ the number that is left over in a division in which one quantity does not exactly divide another: *23 divided by 3 is 7, remainder 2.* ■ a copy of a book left unsold when demand has fallen. **2** *Law* an interest in an estate that becomes effective in possession only when a prior interest (devised at the same time) ends.

▸*v.* [*trans.*] (often **be remaindered**) dispose of (a book left unsold) at a reduced price: *titles are being remaindered increasingly quickly to save on overheads.* ▷late Middle English (sense 2): from Anglo-Norman French, from Latin *remanere* (see REMAIN).

re·mains /ri'mānz/ ▸*plural n.* the parts left over after other parts have been removed, used, or destroyed: *the remains of a sandwich lunch were on the table.* ■ historical or archaeological relics: *Roman remains.* ■ a person's body after death. See note at BODY. ▷late Middle English (occasionally treated as singular): from Old French *remain*, from *remaindre*, from an informal form of Latin *remanere* (see REMAIN).

re·make ▸*v.* /rē'māk; 'rē-/ (*past* and *past part.* **-made**) [*trans.*] make (something) again or differently: *the bed would be more comfortable if it were remade.*

▸*n.* /'rē,māk/ a movie or piece of music that has been filmed or recorded again and rereleased.

re·man /rē'man; 'rē-/ ▸*v.* (**-manned, -man·ning**) [*trans.*] **1** equip again or with new personnel. **2** *poetic/literary* make (someone) manly or courageous again.

re·mand /ri'mand/ *Law* ▸*v.* [*trans.*] place (a defendant) on bail or in custody, esp. when a trial is adjourned: *I had a seventeen-year-old son remanded to a drug-addiction program.* ■ return (a case) to a lower court for reconsideration: *the Supreme Court summarily vacated the opinion and remanded the matter back to the California Court of Appeal.*

▸*n.* a committal to custody. ▷late Middle English (as a verb in the sense 'send back again'): from late Latin *remandare*, from *re-* 'back' + *mandare* 'commit.' The noun dates from the late 18th cent.

rem·a·nent /'remənənt/ ▸*adj. technical* remaining; residual. ■ (of magnetism) remaining after the magnetizing field has been removed. ▷late Middle English: from Latin *remanent-* 'remaining,' from the verb *remanere*. **—rem·a·nence** *n.*

re·map /rē'map; 'rē-/ ▸*v.* (**-mapped, -map·ping**) [*trans.*] *Computing* assign (a function) to a different key.

re·mark /ri'märk/ ▸*v.* **1** [*reporting verb*] say something as a comment; mention: [with *direct speech*] *"Tom's looking peaked," she remarked* | [with *clause*] *he remarked that he had some work to finish* | [*intrans.*] *the judges* **remarked on** *the high standard of the entries.* **2** [*trans.*] regard with attention; notice: *he remarked the man's inflamed eyelids.*

▸*n.* a written or spoken comment: *I decided to ignore his rude remarks.* ■ notice or comment: *the landscape was not worthy of remark.* ▷late 16th cent. (sense 2): from French *remarquer* 'note again,' from *re-* (expressing intensive force) + *marquer* 'to mark, note.'

re-mark /rē 'märk; 'rē/ ▸*v.* [*trans.*] mark (an examination paper or piece of academic work) again.

▸*n.* [in *sing.*] an act of marking an examination or piece of academic work again.

re·mark·a·ble /ri'märkəbəl/ ▸*adj.* worthy of attention; striking: *a remarkable coincidence.* See note at NOTICEABLE. ▷early 17th cent.: from French *remarquable*, from *remarquer* 'take note of' (see **REMARK**). **—re·mark·a·ble·ness** *n.* **—re·mark·a·bly** /-blē/ *adv.* [*sentence adverb*] *remarkably, they finished two weeks ahead of schedule* | [as *submodifier*] *the two boys got along remarkably well.*

Re·marque /rəˈmärk/, Erich Maria (1898–1970), U.S. novelist, born in Germany. His first novel, *All Quiet on the Western Front* (1929; movie, 1930), was an international success. The book and its sequel *The Road Back* (1931) were banned by the Nazis in 1933. All of his 10 novels deal with the horror of war and its aftermath.

re·mar·ry /rēˈmarē/ ▸*v.* (**-ries, -ried**) [*intrans.*] marry again: *he remarried shortly after his wife's death.* **—re·mar·riage** /rēˈmarij/ *n.*

re·mas·ter /rēˈmastər/ ▸*v.* [*trans.*] make a new master of (a recording), typically in order to improve the sound quality: *all the tracks have been remastered from the original tapes.*

re·match /ˈrēˌmacн/ ▸*n.* a second match or game between two teams or players.

Rem·brandt /ˈremˌbrant/ (1606–69), Dutch painter; full name *Rembrandt Harmensz van Rijn.* He established his reputation as a portrait painter with the *Anatomy Lesson of Dr. Tulp* (1632). In the *Night Watch* (1642), he used chiaroscuro to give his subjects a more spiritual and introspective quality. Rembrandt is identified with the series of more than sixty self-portraits painted from 1629 to 1669.

REME ▸*abbr.* (in the British army) Royal Electrical and Mechanical Engineers.

re·me·di·al /riˈmēdēəl/ ▸*adj.* giving or intended as a remedy or cure: *remedial surgery.* ■ provided or intended for students who are experiencing learning difficulties: *remedial education.* ▷mid 17th cent.: from late Latin *remedialis*, from Latin *remedium* 'cure, medicine' (see **REMEDY**). **—re·me·di·al·ly** *adv.*

re·me·di·a·tion /riˌmēdēˈāsнən/ ▸*n.* the action of remedying something, in particular of reversing or stopping environmental damage. ■ the giving of remedial teaching or therapy. ▷early 19th cent.: from Latin *remediatio(n-)*, from *remediare* 'heal, cure' (see **REMEDY**). **—re·me·di·ate** /riˈmēdēˌāt/ *v.*

rem·e·dy /ˈremədē/ ▸*n.* (*pl.* **-dies**) **1** a medicine or treatment for a disease or injury: *herbal remedies for aches and pains.* ■ a means of counteracting or eliminating something undesirable: *shopping became a* ***remedy for*** *personal problems.* ■ a means of legal reparation: *the doctrine took away their only* ***remedy against*** *merchants who refused to honor their contracts.* **2** the margin within which coins as minted may differ from the standard fineness and weight.
▸*v.* (**-dies, -died**) [*trans.*] set right (an undesirable situation): *by the time a problem becomes patently obvious, it may be almost too late to remedy it.* ▷Middle English: from Anglo-Norman French *remedie*, from Latin *remedium*, from *re-* 'back' (also expressing intensive force) + *mederi* 'heal.' **—re·me·di·a·ble** /riˈmēdēəbəl/ *adj.* **—rem·e·di·less** *adj.*

re·mem·ber /riˈmembər/ ▸*v.* [*trans.*] have in or be able to bring to one's mind an awareness of (someone or something that one has seen, known, or experienced in the past): *I remember the screech of the horn as the car came toward me* | *no one remembered his name.* ■ [with *infinitive*] do something that one has undertaken to do or that is necessary or advisable: *did you remember to mail the letters?* ■ [with *clause*] used to emphasize the importance of what is asserted: *you must remember that this is a secret.* ■ bear (someone) in mind by making them a gift or making provision for them: *he has remembered the boy in a codicil to his will.* ■ (**remember someone to**) convey greetings from one person to (another): *remember me to Charlie.* ■ pray for the success or well-being of: *the congress should be remembered in our prayers.* ■ (**remember oneself**) recover one's manners after a lapse. ▷Middle English: from Old French *remembrer*, from late Latin *rememorari* 'call to mind,' from *re-* (expressing intensive force) + Latin *memor* 'mindful.' **—re·mem·ber·er** *n.*

re·mem·brance /riˈmembrəns/ ▸*n.* the action of remembering something: *a flash of understanding or remembrance passed between them.* ■ the action of remembering the dead, esp. in a ceremony: *I decided to sell poppies in remembrance of those who died.* ■ a memory or recollection: *the remembrance of her visit came back with startling clarity.* ■ a thing kept or given as a reminder or in commemoration of someone. ▷Middle English: from Old French, from *remembrer* (see **REMEMBER**).

Re·mem·brance Day ▸*n.* **1** (in Canada) November 11, observed in memory of those who died in World Wars I and II; Veterans Day. **2** another term for **REMEMBRANCE SUNDAY**.

re·mem·branc·er /riˈmembrənsər/ ▸*n.* a person with the job or responsibility of reminding others of something; a chronicler.

Re·mem·brance Sun·day *n.* (in the UK) the Sunday nearest to November 11, when those who were killed in World War I and World War II and later conflicts are commemorated.

re·mex /ˈrēˌmeks/ ▸*n.* (*pl.* **remiges** /ˈrēˌmiˌjēz/) *Ornithology* a flight feather. Compare with **RECTRIX**. ▷mid 18th cent.: from Latin, literally 'rower,' based on *remus* 'oar.'

re·mind /riˈmīnd/ ▸*v.* [*trans.*] cause (someone) to remember someone or something: *he would have forgotten the boy's birthday if you hadn't reminded him* | [*trans.*] *"You had an accident," he reminded her.* ■ (**remind someone of**) cause someone to think of (something) because of a resemblance or likeness: *his impassive, fierce stare reminded her of an owl.* ■ bring something, esp. a commitment or necessary course of action, to the attention of (someone): [*trans.*] *the bartender reminded them that singing was not permitted* | [*trans.*] *she reminded me to be respectful.* ▷mid 17th cent.: from **RE-** 'again' + the verb **MIND**, probably suggested by obsolete *rememorate*, in the same sense.

re·mind·er /riˈmīndər/ ▸*n.* a thing that causes someone to remember something: *the watchtower is a reminder of the days when an enemy might appear at any moment.* ■ a message or communication designed to ensure that someone remembers something. ■ a letter sent to remind someone of an obligation, esp. to pay a bill.

re·mind·ful /riˈmīndfəl/ ▸*adj.* acting as a reminder: *his humor is* ***remindful of*** *that of Max.*

re·min·er·al·ize /rēˈminərəˌlīz/ ▸*v.* [*trans.*] restore the depleted mineral content of (a part of the body, esp. the bones or teeth). **—re·min·er·al·i·za·tion** /-ˌminərələˈzāsнən/ *n.*

Rem·ing·ton[1] /ˈremingtən/, Frederic (1861–1909), U.S. painter, sculptor, and writer. He painted scenes of the American West such as "Cavalry Charge on the Southern Plains" (1907). His notable sculptures include "Bronco Buster" (1895) and "Comin' Through the Rye" (1902). He also wrote *The Way of an Indian* (1906).

Rem·ing·ton[2] ▸*n. trademark* **1** a make of firearm. **2** a typewriter, esp. a large manual one formerly used in offices. ▷mid 19th cent.: named after Eliphalet *Remington* (1793–1861) and his son Philo (1816–89), gunsmiths of Ilion, New York, the original manufacturers.

rem·i·nisce /ˌreməˈnis/ ▸*v.* [*intrans.*] indulge in enjoyable recollection of past events: *they reminisced about their summers abroad.* ▷early 19th cent.: back-formation from **REMINISCENCE**. **—rem·i·nis·cer** *n.*

rem·i·nis·cence /ˌreməˈnisəns/ ▸*n.* a story told about a past event remembered by the narrator: *his reminiscences of his early days in Washington.* ■ the enjoyable recollection of past events: *his story made me smile in reminiscence.* ■ (**reminiscences**) a collection in literary form of incidents and experiences that someone remembers. ■ a characteristic of one thing reminding or suggestive of another: *his first works are too full of reminiscences of earlier poetry.* ▷late 16th cent. (denoting the action of remembering): from late Latin *reminiscentia*, from Latin *reminisci* 'remember.' **—rem·i·nis·cen·tial** /ˌremənisˈencнəl/ *adj.* (*archaic*).

rem·i·nis·cent /ˌreməˈnisənt/ ▸*adj.* tending to remind one of something: *the sights were* ***reminiscent of*** *my childhood.* ■ suggesting something by resemblance: *her suit was vaguely* ***reminiscent of*** *military dress.* ■ (of a person or their manner) absorbed in or suggesting absorption in memories: *her expression was wistful and reminiscent.* ▷mid 18th cent.: from Latin *reminiscent-* 'remembering,' from the verb *reminisci*. **—rem·i·nis·cent·ly** *adv.*

re·miss /riˈmis/ ▸*adj.* [*predic.*] lacking care or attention to duty; negligent: *the writer was remiss to have overlooked the group* | *the media have been* ***remiss in*** *portraying bisexuality as a valid identity.* ▷late Middle English: from Latin *remissus* 'slackened,' past participle of *remittere*. The early senses were 'weakened in color or consistency' and (in describing sound) 'faint, soft.' **—re·miss·ly** *adv.* **—re·miss·ness** *n.*

re·mis·si·ble /riˈmisəbəl/ ▸*adj.* (esp. of sins) able to be pardoned. ▷late 16th cent.: from French *rémissible* or late Latin *remissibilis*, from *remiss-* 'slackened,' from the verb *remittere* (see **REMISS**).

re·mis·sion /riˈmisнən/ ▸*n.* the cancellation of a debt, charge, or penalty: *the plan allows for the partial remission of tuition fees.* ■ a diminution of the seriousness or intensity of disease or pain; a temporary recovery: *ten out of twenty patients remained* ***in remission.*** ■ *formal* forgiveness of sins. ■ *Brit.* the reduction of a prison sentence, esp. as a reward for good behavior. ▷Middle English: from Old French, or from Latin *remissio(n-)*, from *remittere* 'send back, restore' (see **REMIT**).

re·mit ▸*v.* /riˈmit/ (**-mit·ted, -mit·ting**) [*trans.*] **1** cancel or refrain from exacting or inflicting (a debt or punishment): *the excess of the sentence over 12 months was remitted.* ■ *Theology* pardon (a sin). **2** send (money) in payment or as a gift: *the income they remitted to their families.* **3** refer (a matter for decision) to some authority: *the request for an investigation was remitted to a special committee.* ■ *Law* send back (a case) to a lower court. ■ *Law* send (someone) from one tribunal to another for a trial or hearing. ■ *archaic* consign again to a previous state: *thus his indiscretion remitted him to the nature of an ordinary person.* **4** *rare* postpone: *the movers refused Mr. Tierney's request to remit the motion.* ■ [*intrans.*] *archaic* diminish: *phobias may remit spontaneously without any treatment.*
▸*n.* /riˈmit; ˈrēˌmit/ **1** the task or area of activity officially assigned to an individual or organization: *the committee was becoming caught up in issues that did not fall within its remit.* **2** an item referred to someone for consideration. ▷late Middle English: from Latin *remittere* 'send back, restore,' from *re-* 'back' + *mittere* 'send.' The noun dates from the early 20th cent. **—re·mit·ta·ble** *adj.* **—re·mit·tal** /-ˈmitl/ *n.* **—re·mit·ter** *n.*

re·mit·tance /riˈmitns/ ▸*n.* a sum of money sent, esp. by mail, in payment for goods or services or as a gift. ■ the action of sending money in such a way.

re·mit·tance man ▸*n. chiefly historical* an emigrant supported or assisted by payments of money from home.

re·mit·tent /riˈmitnt/ ▸*adj.* (of a fever) characterized by fluctuating body temperatures. ▷late 17th cent.: from Latin *remittent-* 'sending back,' from the verb *remittere* (see **REMIT**).

re·mix ▸*v.* /rēˈmiks; ˈrē-/ [*trans.*] mix (something) again. ■ produce a different version of (a musical recording) by altering the balance of the separate tracks.
▸*n.* /ˈrēˌmiks/ a different version of a musical recording produced in such a way. **—re·mix·er** *n.*

rem·nant /ˈremnənt/ ▸*n.* a small remaining quantity of something. ■ a piece of cloth or carpeting left when the greater part has been used or sold. ■ a surviving trace: *a* ***remnant of*** *the past.* See note at **TRACE**. ■ *Christian Theology* a small minority of people who will remain faithful to God and so be saved (in allusion to biblical prophecies concerning Israel).
▸*adj.* [*attrib.*] remaining: *remnant strands of hair.* ▷Middle English: contraction of obsolete *remenant*, from Old French, from *remenoir, remanoir* 'remain.'

re·mod·el /rēˈmädl/ ▸*v.* (**-mod·eled, -mod·el·ing**; *Brit.* **-mod·elled, -mod·el·ling**) [*trans.*] change the structure or form of (something, esp. a building, policy, or procedure): *the station was remodeled and enlarged in 1927.* ■ fashion or shape (a figure or object) again or differently: *she remodeled the head with careful fingers.*

re·mod·el·er /rēˈmädl-ər/ ▸*n.* a person who carries out structural alterations to an existing building, such as adding a new room.

re·mold /rēˈmōld/ (*Brit.* **re·mould**) ▸*v.* [*trans.*] change or refashion the appearance, structure, or character of: *did the welfare state remold capitalism to give it a more human face?*

re·mon·e·tize /rēˈmänəˌtīz/ ▸*v.* [*trans.*] *rare* restore (a metal) to its former position as legal tender. **—re·mon·e·ti·za·tion** /rēˌmänətəˈzāsнən/ *n.*

re·mon·strance /riˈmänstrəns/ ▸*n.* a forcefully reproachful protest: *angry remonstrances in the Senate* | *he shut his ears to any remonstrance.* ■ (**the Remonstrance**) a document drawn up in 1610 by the Arminians of the Dutch Reformed Church, presenting the differences between their doctrines and those of the strict Calvinists. ▷late 16th cent. (in the sense 'evidence'): from Old French, or from medieval Latin *remonstrantia*, from *remonstrare* 'demonstrate, show' (see **REMONSTRATE**).

Re·mon·strant /riˈmänstrənt/ ▸*n.* a member of the Arminian party in the Dutch Reformed Church. ▷early 17th cent.: from medieval Latin *remonstrant-* 'demonstrating' (see also **REMONSTRANCE**).

re·mon·strate /riˈmänˌstrāt; ˈremən-/ ▸*v.* [*intrans.*] make a forcefully reproachful protest: *he turned angrily to* ***remonstrate with*** *Tommy* | [with *direct speech*] *"You don't mean that," she remonstrated.* ▷late 16th cent. (in the sense 'make plain'): from medieval

Latin *remonstrat-* 'demonstrated,' from the verb *remonstrare*, from *re-* (expressing intensive force) + *monstrare* 'to show.' —**re·mon·stra·tion** /ri,män'strāsHən; ,remən-/ *n.* —**re·mon·stra·tive** /-strətiv/ *adj.* —**re·mon·stra·tor** /-,strātər/ *n.*

re·mon·tant /ri'mäntnt/ ▸*adj.* (of a plant) blooming or producing a crop more than once a season.
▸*n.* a remontant plant. ▷late 19th cent.: from French, literally 'coming up again,' from the verb *remonter*.

rem·o·ra /'remərə; ri'môrə/ ▸*n.* a slender marine fish that attaches itself to large fish by means of a sucker on top of its head. It generally feeds on the host's external parasites. Also called SHARKSUCKER, SUCKERFISH. • Family Echeneidae: several genera and species, in particular the widespread *Remora remora*. ▷mid 16th cent.: from Latin, literally 'hindrance,' from *re-* 'back' + *mora* 'delay' (because of the former belief that the fish slowed down ships).

re·morse /ri'môrs/ ▸*n.* deep regret or guilt for a wrong committed: *they were filled with remorse and shame.* ▷late Middle English: from Old French *remors*, from medieval Latin *remorsus*, from Latin *remordere* 'vex,' from *re-* (expressing intensive force) + *mordere* 'to bite.' —**re·morse·ful** /-fəl/ *adj.* —**re·morse·ful·ly** /-fəlē/ *adv.*

re·morse·less /ri'môrsləs/ ▸*adj.* without regret or guilt: *a remorseless killer.* ■ (of something unpleasant) never ending or improving; relentless: *remorseless poverty.* —**re·morse·less·ly** *adv.* —**re·morse·less·ness** *n.*

re·mort·gage /rē'môrgij/ ▸*v.* [*trans.*] take out another or a different kind of mortgage on (a property).
▸*n.* a different or additional mortgage.

re·mote /ri'mōt/ ▸*adj.* (**-mot·er**, **-mot·est**) **1** (of a place) far away; distant: *I'd chosen a spot that looked as* ***remote from*** *any road as possible.* ■ (of a place) situated far from the main centers of population in a country: *a remote Oregon valley.* ■ (of an electronic device) operating or operated by means of radio or infrared signals. ■ distant in time: *a golden age in the remote past.* ■ distantly related: *a remote cousin.* ■ having very little connection with or relationship to: *the theory seems rather intellectual and* ***remote from*** *everyday experience.* ■ (of a person) aloof and unfriendly in manner: *this morning Maria again seemed remote and patronizing.* ■ *Computing* denoting a device that can only be accessed by means of a network. Compare with LOCAL. **2** (of a chance or possibility) unlikely to occur: *chances of a genuine and lasting peace become even more remote.*
▸*n.* a remote control device. ▷late Middle English (in the sense 'far apart'): from Latin *remotus* 'removed,' past participle of *removere* (see REMOVE). —**re·mote·ness** *n.*

re·mote con·trol ▸*n.* control of a machine or apparatus from a distance by means of signals transmitted from a radio or electronic device. ■ (also **re·mote con·trol·ler**) a device that controls an apparatus, esp. a television or VCR, in such a way. —**re·mote-con·trolled** *adj.*

re·mote·ly /ri'mōtlē/ ▸*adv.* **1** from a distance; without physical contact: *new electronic meters that can be read remotely | a new type of remotely controlled torpedo.* **2** [as *submodifier*] [usu. with *negative*] in the slightest degree: *he had never been remotely jealous.*

re·mote sens·ing ▸*n.* the scanning of the earth by satellite or high-flying aircraft in order to obtain information about it.

ré·mou·lade /,rāmə'läd/ (also **re·mou·lade**) ▸*n.* salad or seafood dressing made with hard-boiled egg yolks, oil, and vinegar, and flavored with mustard, capers, and herbs. ▷French from Italian *remolata*.

re·mould /rē'mōld/ ▸*v.* British spelling of REMOLD. ■ *Brit.* put a new tread on (a worn tire).
▸*n.* /'rēmōld/ *Brit.* a tire that has been given a new tread.

re·mount ▸*v.* /rē'mount; 'rē-/ [*trans.*] mount (something) again, in particular: ■ get on (something) in order to ride it again: *she went to remount her horse* | [*intrans.*] *Sandy remounted and rode through the gates.* ■ attach to a new frame or setting: *remount the best photos in glass-fronted mounts.* ■ produce (a play or exhibition) again. ■ organize and embark on (a significant course of action) again: *the raid was remounted in August.*
▸*n.* /'rē,mount/ a fresh horse for a rider. ■ *historical* a supply of fresh horses for a regiment.

re·mov·al /ri'mōōvəl/ ▸*n.* the action of removing someone or something, in particular: ■ the taking away of something unwanted: *the removal of the brain tumor.* ■ the abolition of something: *the removal of all legal barriers to the free movement of goods.* ■ the dismissal of someone from a job or office. ■ [usu. as *adj.*] *chiefly Brit.* the transfer of furniture and other contents when moving from one house to another: *removal men.*

re·move /ri'mōōv/ ▸*v.* [*trans.*] take away (something unwanted or unnecessary) from the position it occupies: *she sat down to remove her makeup.* ■ take (something) from a place in order to take it to another location: *customs officials also* ***removed*** *documents* ***from*** *the premises.* ■ eliminate or get rid of (someone or something): *iron is sometimes found in water as ferric hydroxide, which can be removed by filtration.* ■ take off (clothing): *he sat down on the ground and quickly removed his shoes and socks.* ■ abolish: *the return to real prices as subsidies are removed.* ■ dismiss from a job or office: *a judge was* ***removed from*** *office in 1988 for a number of lapses from proper judicial standards.* ■ [*intrans.*] (**remove to**) *dated* change one's home or place of residence by moving to (another place or area): *he removed to Mexico and began afresh.* ■ (**be removed**) be very different from: *an explanation that is far* ***removed from*** *the truth.* ■ [as *adj.*] (**removed**) separated by a particular number of steps of descent: *his second cousin once removed.*
▸*n.* a degree of remoteness or separation: ***at*** *this* ***remove***, *the whole incident seems insane.* ▷Middle English (as a verb): from the Old French stem *remov-*, from Latin *removere*, from *re-* 'back' + *movere* 'to move.' —**re·mov·a·bil·i·ty** /ri,mōōvə'bilətē/ *n.* —**re·mov·a·ble** *adj.* —**re·mov·er** *n.*

REM sleep /rem/ ▸*n.* a kind of sleep that occurs at intervals during the night and is characterized by rapid eye movements, more dreaming and bodily movement, and faster pulse and breathing.

re·muage /,remōō'äzH/ ▸*n.* the periodic turning or shaking of bottled wine, esp. champagne, to move sediment toward the cork. ▷French, literally 'moving around.'

re·mu·da /ri'm(y)ōōdə/ ▸*n.* a herd of horses that have been saddle-broken, from which ranch hands choose their mounts for the day. ▷late 19th cent.: via American Spanish from Spanish, literally 'exchange, replacement.'

re·mu·ner·ate /ri'myōōnə,rāt/ ▸*v.* [*trans.*] pay (someone) for services rendered or work done: *they should be remunerated fairly for their work.* ▷early 16th cent.: from Latin *remunerat-* 'rewarded, recompensed,' from the verb *remunerari*, from *re-* (expressing intensive force) + *munus, muner-* 'gift.' —**re·mu·ner·a·tive** /-rətiv; -,rātiv/ *adj.*

re·mu·ner·a·tion /ri,myōōnə'rāsHən/ ▸*n.* money paid for work or a service.

Re·mus /'rēməs/ *Roman Mythology* the twin brother of Romulus.

REN ▸*abbr.* ringer equivalent number, a measure of the load a device will place on a telephone line. The maximum REN allowed on a single line is usually limited by telephone companies.

Ren·ais·sance /'renə,säns; -,zäns/ the revival of art and literature under the influence of classical models in the 14th–16th centuries. ■ the culture and style of art and architecture developed during this era. ■ [as *n.*] (**a renaissance**) a revival of or renewed interest in something: *rail travel is enjoying a renaissance.* ▷from French *renaissance*, from *re-* 'back, again' + *naissance* 'birth' (from Latin *nascentia*, from *nasci* 'be born').

> The Renaissance is generally regarded as beginning in Florence, where there was a revival of interest in classical antiquity. Important early figures are the writers Petrarch, Dante, and Boccaccio and the painter Giotto. Music flourished, from madrigals to the polyphonic masses of Palestrina, with a wide variety of instruments such as viols and lutes. The period from the end of the 15th century has become known as the High Renaissance, when Venice and Rome began to share Florence's importance and Raphael, Leonardo da Vinci, and Michelangelo were active. Renaissance thinking spread to the rest of Europe from the early 16th century and was influential for the next hundred years.

Ren·ais·sance man (or **wom·an**) ▸*n.* a person with many talents or interests, esp. in the humanities.

re·nal /'rēnl/ ▸*adj. technical* of or relating to the kidneys: *renal failure.* ▷mid 17th cent.: from French *rénal*, from late Latin *renalis*, from Latin *renes* 'kidneys.'

re·nal cal·cu·lus ▸*n.* another term for KIDNEY STONE.

re·nal pel·vis ▸*n.* see PELVIS (sense 2).

re·nal tu·bule ▸*n.* another term for KIDNEY TUBULE.

re·name /rē'nām; 'rē-/ ▸*v.* [*trans.*] give a new name to (someone or something): *after independence Celebes was renamed Sulawesi.*

re·nas·cence /ri'nasəns; -'nāsəns/ ▸*n. formal* the revival of something that has been dormant: *the renascence of poetry as an oral art.* ■ another term for RENAISSANCE.

re·nas·cent /ri'nasənt; -'nāsənt/ ▸*adj.* becoming active or popular again: *renascent fascism.* ▷early 18th cent.: from Latin *renascent-* 'being born again,' from the verb *renasci*, from *re-* 'back, again' + *nasci* 'be born.'

Re·nault[1] /rə'nō/, Louis (1877–1944), French engineer and automobile manufacturer. He and his brothers established the Renault company in 1898.

Re·nault[2], Mary (1905–83), British novelist; resident in South Africa from 1948; pseudonym of *Mary Challans.* She wrote historical novels set in the ancient world, notably a trilogy dealing with Alexander the Great (1970–81).

ren·con·tre /räN'kôNtr(ə); ren'käntər/ ▸*n. archaic* variant spelling of RENCOUNTER. ▷early 17th cent.: French.

ren·coun·ter /ren'kountər/ *archaic* ▸*n.* a chance meeting with someone. ■ a battle, skirmish, or duel.
▸*v.* [*trans.*] meet by chance: *I wonder who those fellows were we rencountered last night.* ▷early 16th cent.: from French *rencontre* (noun), *rencontrer* 'meet face to face.'

rend /rend/ ▸*v.* (*past* **rent** /rent/) [*trans.*] tear (something) into two or more pieces: *snapping teeth that would rend human flesh to shreds | figurative the speculation and confusion that was rending the civilized world.* ■ [*trans.*] *archaic* wrench (something) violently: *he rent the branch out of the tree.* ■ *poetic/literary* cause great emotional pain to (a person or their heart). ▷Old English *rendan*; related to Middle Low German *rende*.
▸*PHRASES* □ **rend the air** *poetic/literary* sound piercingly: *a shrill scream rent the air.* □ **rend one's garments** tear one's clothes as a sign of extreme grief or distress.

rend·er /'rendər/ ▸*v.* [*trans.*] **1** provide (a service): *money serves as a reward for* ***services rendered.*** ■ give (help): *Mrs. Evans would* ***render*** *assistance* ***to*** *those she thought were in real need.* ■ submit or present for inspection or consideration: *he would render income tax returns at the end of the year.* ■ *poetic/literary* hand over: *he will* ***render up*** *his immortal soul.* ■ deliver (a verdict or judgment): *the jury's finding amounted to the clearest verdict yet rendered upon the scandal.* **2** [*trans.*] cause to be or become; make: *the rains rendered his escape impossible.* **3** represent or depict artistically: *the eyes and the cheeks are exceptionally well rendered.* ■ translate: *the phrase was* ***rendered into*** *English.* ■ *Music* perform (a piece): *a soprano solo reverently rendered by Linda Howie.* ■ *Computing* process (an outline image) using color and shading in order to make it appear solid and three-dimensional. **4** melt down (fat): *the fat was being cut up and rendered for lard.* ■ process (the carcass of an animal) in order to extract proteins, fats, and other usable parts: [as *adj.*] (**rendered**) *the* ***rendered down*** *remains of sheep.* **5** cover (stone or brick) with a coat of plaster: *external walls will be rendered and tiled.*
▸*n.* a first coat of plaster applied to a brick or stone surface. ▷late Middle English: from Old French *rendre*, from an alteration of Latin *reddere* 'give back,' from *re-* 'back' + *dare* 'give.' The earliest senses were 'recite,' 'translate,' and 'give back' (hence 'represent' and 'perform'); 'hand over' (hence 'give (help)' and 'submit for consideration'); 'cause to be'; and 'melt down.' —**ren·der·er** *n.*

rend·er·ing /'rendəriNG/ ▸*n.* **1** a performance of a piece of music or drama: *her fine rendering of "Che farò senza Eurydice" was enough to win her strong commendation.* ■ a translation: *a literal rendering of an idiom.* ■ a work of visual art, esp. a detailed architectural drawing: *a consummately lifelike three-dimensional rendering of a building interior.* ■ *Computing* the processing of an outline image using color and shading to make it appear solid and three-dimensional. **2** the action of applying plaster to a wall. ■ the coating applied in such a way. **3** *formal* the action of giving, yielding, or surrendering something: *the rendering of dues.*

Pronunciation Key ə *ago*; ər *over*; 'ə *or* ,ə *up*; 'ər *or* ,ər *fur*; a *hat*; ā *rate*; ä *car*; CH *chew*; e *let*; ē *see*; e(ə)r *air*; i *fit*; ī *by*; i(ə)r *ear*; NG *sing*; ō *go*; ô *for*; oi *boy*; ŏŏ *good*; ōō *goo*; ou *out*; SH *she*; TH *thin*; TH *then*; (h)w *why*; ZH *vision*

ren·dez·vous /ˈrändi,vo͞o; -dā-/ ▶*n.* (*pl.* same) a meeting at an agreed time and place, typically between two people. ■ a place used for such a meeting. ■ a place, typically a bar or restaurant, that is used as a popular meeting place. ■ a meeting up of troops, ships, or aircraft at an agreed time and place. ■ a prearranged meeting between spacecraft in space.
▶*v.* (**-vouses** /-,vo͞oz/, **-voused** /-,vo͞od/, **-vous·ing** /-,vo͞oiNG/) [*intrans.*] meet at an agreed time and place: *I* **rendezvoused with** *Bea as planned.* ▷late 16th cent.: from French *rendez-vous!* 'present yourselves!,' imperative of *se rendre.*

ren·di·tion /renˈdisHən/ ▶*n.* a performance or interpretation, esp. of a dramatic role or piece of music: *a wonderful rendition of "Nessun Dorma."* ■ a visual representation or reproduction: *a pen-and-ink rendition of Mars with his sword drawn.* ■ a translation or transliteration. ▷early 17th cent.: from obsolete French, from *rendre* 'give back, render.'

Ren·do·va /renˈdōvə/ an island in the west central Solomon Islands, off the coast of New Georgia, the scene of fighting between U.S. and Japanese forces in 1943.

ren·dzi·na /renˈjēnə/ ▶*n.* *Soil Science* a fertile lime-rich soil with dark humus above a pale soft calcareous layer, typical of grassland on chalk or limestone. ▷1920s: via Russian from Polish *rędzina.*

ren·e·gade /ˈreni,gād/ ▶*n.* a person who deserts and betrays an organization, country, or set of principles. ■ a person who behaves in a rebelliously unconventional manner. ■ *archaic* a person who abandons religion; an apostate.
▶*adj.* having treacherously changed allegiance: *a renegade bodyguard.* ■ *archaic* having abandoned one's religious beliefs: *a renegade monk.* ▷late 15th cent.: from Spanish *renegado,* from medieval Latin *renegatus* 'renounced,' past participle (used as a noun) of *renegare,* from *re-* (expressing intensive force) + Latin *negare* 'deny.'

ren·e·ga·do /,renəˈgādō; -ˈgādō/ ▶*n.* (*pl.* **-does**) archaic term for RENEGADE. ▷Spanish.

re·nege /riˈneg; -ˈnig/ (also **re·negue**) ▶*v.* [*intrans.*] go back on a promise, undertaking, or contract: *the administration had* **reneged on** *its election promises.* ■ another term for REVOKE (sense 2). ■ [*trans.*] *archaic* renounce or abandon (someone or something). ▷mid 16th cent. (in the sense 'desert (esp. a faith or a person)'): from medieval Latin *renegare,* from Latin *re-* (expressing intensive force) + *negare* 'deny.' —**re·neg·er** *n.*

re·ne·go·ti·ate /,rēnəˈgōsHē,āt/ ▶*v.* [*trans.*] negotiate (something) again in order to change the original agreed terms: *the parties will renegotiate the price* | [*intrans.*] *she asked to renegotiate after signing the contract.* —**re·ne·go·ti·a·ble** /-ˈgōsH(ē)əbəl/ *adj.* —**re·ne·go·ti·a·tion** /-,gōsHēˈāsHən; -,gōsē-/ *n.*

re·new /riˈn(y)o͞o/ ▶*v.* [*trans.*] resume (an activity) after an interruption: *the parents renewed their campaign to save the school.* ■ reestablish (a relationship): *he had renewed an acquaintance with McCarthy.* ■ repeat (an action or statement): *detectives renewed their appeal for those in the area at the time to contact them.* ■ give fresh life or strength to: [as *adj.*] (**renewed**) *she would face the future with renewed determination.* ■ extend for a further period the validity of (a license, subscription, or contract): *her contract had not been renewed.* ■ replace (something that is broken or worn out): *check the joints—they may need renewing.* —**re·new·er** *n.*

re·new·a·ble /riˈn(y)o͞oəbəl/ ▶*adj.* capable of being renewed: *the 30-day truce is renewable by mutual agreement.* ■ (of energy or its source) not permanently depleted when used: *a shift away from fossil fuels to renewable energy.*
▶*n.* (usu. **renewables**) a source of energy that is not depleted by use, such as water, wind, or solar power. —**re·new·a·bil·i·ty** /ri,n(y)o͞oəˈbilətē/ *n.*

re·new·al /riˈn(y)o͞oəl/ ▶*n.* the action of extending the period of validity of a license, subscription, or contract: *the contracts came up for renewal* | *a renewal of his passport.* ■ an instance of resuming an activity or state after an interruption: *a renewal of hostilities.* ■ the replacing or repair of something that is worn out, run-down, or broken: *the need for urban renewal.* ■ (among charismatic Christians) the state or process of being made spiritually new in the Holy Spirit.

ren·ga /ˈreNGgə/ ▶*n.* (*pl.* same or **-gas**) Japanese linked poetry in the form of a tanka (or series of tanka), with the first three lines composed by one person and the second two by another. A typical renga sequence is comprised of 100 stanzas composed by about three poets in a single sitting. ▷Japanese, from *ren* 'linking' + *ga* (from *ka* 'poetry').

ren·i·form /ˈrēnə,fôrm; ˈren-/ ▶*adj.* *chiefly Mineralogy Botany* kidney-shaped. ▷mid 18th cent.: from Latin *ren* 'kidney' + -IFORM.

re·nin /ˈrēnin; ˈren-/ ▶*n.* *Biochemistry* an enzyme secreted by and stored in the kidneys that promotes the production of the protein angiotensin. ▷late 19th cent.: from Latin *ren* 'kidney' + -IN[1].

ren·min·bi /ˈrenˈminˈbē/ ▶*n.* (*pl.* same) the name of the national currency of the People's Republic of China, introduced in 1948. ■ the yuan. ▷from Chinese *rénmínbì,* from *rénmín* 'people' + *bì* 'currency.'

Rennes /ren(s)/ an industrial city in northwestern France; pop. 204,000.

ren·net /ˈrenit/ ▶*n.* curdled milk from the stomach of an unweaned calf, containing rennin and used in curdling milk for cheese. ■ any preparation containing rennin, esp. a pudding. ▷late 15th cent.: probably related to RUN.

ren·nin /ˈrenin/ ▶*n.* an enzyme secreted into the stomach of unweaned mammals, and in some lower animals and plants, causing the curdling of milk. ▷late 19th cent.: from RENNET + -IN[1].

Re·no[1] /ˈrēnō/ a city in western Nevada, on the Truckee River; pop. 180,480. It is noted as a gambling resort and for its liberal laws that enable quick marriages and divorces.

Re·no[2], Janet (1938–), U.S. lawyer. Before she became the first woman to be appointed to the office of U.S. attorney general 1993–2001, she was the chief prosecutor of Florida's Dade County 1978–93.

Re·noir[1] /ˈren,wär; rənˈwär/, Jean (1894–1979), French movie director; son of Auguste Renoir. His works include *La Grande illusion* (1937) and *La Règle du jeu* (1939).

Re·noir[2], (Pierre) Auguste (1841–1919), French painter. An early Impressionist, he developed a style characterized by light, fresh colors and indistinct, subtle outlines. In his later work he concentrated on the human, esp. female, form. Notable works: *Le Moulin de la galette* (1876) and *The Judgment of Paris* (*c.*1914).

Auguste Renoir

re·nor·mal·i·za·tion /,rē,nôrməliˈzāsHən/ ▶*n.* *Physics* a method used in quantum mechanics in which unwanted infinities are removed from the solutions of equations by redefining parameters such as the mass and charge of subatomic particles. —**re·nor·mal·ize** /rēˈnôrmə,līz/ *v.*

re·nounce /riˈnouns/ ▶*v.* [*trans.*] formally declare one's abandonment of (a claim, right, or possession): *Isabella offered to renounce her son's claim to the French crown.* ■ refuse to recognize or abide by any longer: *these agreements were renounced after the fall of the czarist regime.* ■ declare that one will no longer engage in or support: *they renounced the armed struggle.* ■ reject and stop using or consuming: *he renounced drugs and alcohol completely.* ■ [*intrans.*] *Law* refuse or resign a right or position, esp. one as an heir or trustee: *there will be forms enabling the allottee to renounce.* ▷late Middle English: from Old French *renoncer,* from Latin *renuntiare* 'protest against,' from *re-* (expressing reversal) + *nuntiare* 'announce.' —**re·nounce·a·ble** *adj.* —**re·nounce·ment** *n.* —**re·nounc·er** *n.*
▶*PHRASE* □ **renounce the world** completely withdraw from society or material affairs in order to lead a life considered to be more spiritually fulfilling.

ren·o·vate /ˈrenə,vāt/ ▶*v.* [*trans.*] restore (something old, esp. a building) to a good state of repair: *the old school has been tastefully renovated as a private house.* ■ *archaic* refresh; reinvigorate: *a little warm nourishment renovated him for a short time.* ▷early 16th cent.: from Latin *renovat-* 'made new again,' from the verb *renovare,* from *re-* 'back, again' + *novus* 'new.' —**ren·o·va·tion** /,renəˈvāsHən/ *n.* —**ren·o·va·tor** /-,vātər/ *n.*

re·nown /riˈnoun/ ▶*n.* the condition of being known or talked about by many people; fame: *authors of great renown.* ▷Middle English: from Anglo-Norman French *renoun,* from Old French *renomer* 'make famous,' from *re-* (expressing intensive force) + *nomer* 'to name,' from Latin *nominare.*

re·nowned /riˈnound/ ▶*adj.* known or talked about by many people; famous: *a restaurant* **renowned for** *its Peking duck.*

rent[1] /rent/ ▶*n.* a tenant's regular payment to a landlord for the use of property or land. ■ a sum paid for the hire of equipment.
▶*v.* [*trans.*] pay someone for the use of (something, typically property, land, or a car): *they rented a house together in Spain* | [as *adj.*] (**rented**) *a rented apartment.* ■ (of an owner) let someone use (something) in return for payment: *he purchased a large tract of land and* **rented out** *most of it to local farmers.* ■ [*intrans.*] be let or hired out at a specified rate: *skis or snowboards* **rent for** *$60–80 for six days.* ▷Middle English: from Old French *rente,* from a root shared by RENDER.
▶*PHRASE* □ **for rent** available to be rented.

rent[2] ▶*n.* a large tear in a piece of fabric. ■ an opening or gap resembling such a tear: *they stared at the rents in the clouds.* ▷mid 16th cent.: from obsolete *rent* 'pull to pieces, lacerate,' variant of REND.

rent[3] ▶ past and past participle of REND.

rent-a- ▶*comb. form* denoting availability for hire of a specified thing: *rent-a-car* | *rent-a-tent.* ■ *often humorous* existing in violation of the real thing; not genuine: *rent-a-friend* | *rent-a-mob.*

rent·a·ble /ˈrentəbəl/ ▶*adj.* available or suitable for renting: *rentable office space.* —**rent·a·bil·i·ty** /,rentəˈbilətē/ *n.*

ren·tal /ˈrentl/ ▶*n.* an amount paid or received as rent. ■ the action of renting something: *the office was* **on** *weekly* **rental**. ■ a rented house or car.
▶*adj.* of, relating to, or available for rent: *rental properties.* ▷late Middle English: from Anglo-Norman French, or from Anglo-Latin *rentale,* from Old French *rente* (see RENT[1]).

rent con·trol ▶*n.* government control and regulation of the amounts charged for rented housing.

rent·er /ˈrentər/ ▶*n.* **1** a person who rents an apartment, a car, or other object. **2** a rented car or videocassette.

rent-free ▶*adj. & adv.* with exemption from rent: [as *adj.*] *rent-free periods* | [as *adv.*] *you could live in the cottage rent-free.*

ren·tier /ränˈtyā/ ▶*n.* a person living on income from property or investments. ▷French, from *rente* 'dividend.'

Ren·ton /ˈrentn/ a city in west central Washington, southeast of Seattle, on Lake Washington; pop. 50,052.

rent par·ty ▶*n.* a party held to raise money to pay rent by charging guests for attendance.

re·nun·ci·a·tion /ri,nənsēˈāsHən/ ▶*n.* the formal rejection of something, typically a belief, claim, or course of action: *entry into the priesthood requires renunciation of marriage* | *a renunciation of violence.* ■ *Law* a document expressing renunciation. ▷late Middle English: from late Latin *renuntiatio(n-),* from Latin *renuntiare* 'protest against' (see RENOUNCE). —**re·nun·ci·ant** /riˈnənsēənt/ *n. & adj.*

ren·vers /renˈvərs; ränˈver/ (also **ren·verse**) ▶*n.* a movement performed in dressage, in which the horse moves parallel to the side of the arena, with its hindquarters carried closer to the wall than its shoulders and its body curved away from the center. ▷French.

re·of·fend /,rēəˈfend/ ▶*v.* [*intrans.*] commit a further offense: *people who reoffend while on bail.* —**re·of·fend·er** *n.*

re·or·der /rēˈôrdər/ ▶*v.* [*trans.*] **1** request (something) to be made, supplied, or served again: *the most popular toys will be reordered immediately.* **2** arrange (something) again: *he fixed his bed and reordered his books.*
▶*n.* a renewed or repeated order for goods.

re·org /ˈrē,ôrg; rēˈôrg/ *informal* ▶*n.* a reorganization.
▶*v.* reorganize: [*trans.*] *it reorgs buildings* | [*intrans.*] *the company loves to reorg.*

re·or·gan·ize /rēˈôrgə,nīz/ ▶*v.* [*trans.*] change the way in which (something) is organized: *we have to reorganize the entire workload* | [*intrans.*] *the company reorganized into fewer key areas.* —**re·or·gan·i·za·tion** /,rē,ôrgənəˈzāsHən/ *n.* —**re·or·gan·iz·er** *n.*

re·or·i·ent /rēˈôrē,ent/ ▶*v.* [*trans.*] change the focus or direction of: *the will is dislodged from false values and reoriented toward God.* ■ (**reorient oneself**) find one's position again in relation to one's surroundings: *slowly they advanced, stopping every so often and then reorienting themselves.* —**re·o·ri·en·tate** /-ēən,tāt/ *v.* —**re·o·ri·en·ta·tion** /,rē,ôrēənˈtāsʜən/ *n.*

re·o·vi·rus /ˈrēō,vīrəs/ ▶*n.* any of a group of RNA viruses that are sometimes associated with respiratory and enteric infection. ▷mid 20th cent.: from the initial letters of *respiratory, enteric,* and *orphan* (referring to a virus not identified with a particular disease) + VIRUS.

rep[1] /rep/ *informal* ▶*n.* a representative: *a union rep.* ■ a sales representative.
▶*v.* (**repped, rep·ping**) [*intrans.*] act as a sales representative for a company or product: *at eighteen she was working for her dad, repping on the road.* ▷late 19th cent.: abbreviation.

rep[2] ▶*n. informal* repertory: *once, when I was in rep, I learned the part of Iago in three days.* ■ a repertory theater or company. ▷1920s: abbreviation.

rep[3] (also **repp**) ▶*n.* a fabric with a ribbed surface, used in curtains and upholstery. ▷mid 19th cent.: from French *reps,* of unknown ultimate origin.

rep[4] ▶*n. informal* short for REPUTATION: *I don't know why caffeine's suddenly got such a bad rep.*

rep[5] ▶*n.* (in bodybuilding) a repetition of a set of exercises; compare with SET[2] 1.
▶*v.* [*trans.*] (in knitting patterns) repeat (stitches or part of a design): *rep the last row.* ▷1950s: abbreviation.

Rep. ▶*abbr.* ■ (in the U.S. Congress) Representative. ■ Republic. ■ a Republican.

re·pack·age /rēˈpakij/ ▶*v.* [*trans.*] package again or differently: *excess stock may be given to charities or repackaged.* ■ present in a new way: *the commission has repackaged its ideas.*

re·paid /rēˈpād/ ▶ past and past participle of REPAY.

re·pair[1] /riˈpe(ə)r/ ▶*v.* [*trans.*] fix or mend (a thing suffering from damage or a fault): *faulty electrical appliances should be repaired by an electrician.* ■ make good (such damage) by fixing or repairing it: *an operation to repair damage to his neck.* ■ put right (a damaged relationship or unwelcome situation): *the new government moved quickly to repair relations with the USA.*
▶*n.* the action of fixing or mending something: *the truck was* **beyond repair** | *the abandoned house they bought needs repairs.* ■ a result of such fixing or mending: *a coat of French polish was brushed over the repair.* ■ the relative physical condition of an object: *the existing hospital is in a bad* **state of repair**. ▷late Middle English: from Old French *reparer,* from Latin *reparare,* from *re-* 'back' + *parare* 'make ready.' —**re·pair·a·ble** *adj.* —**re·pair·er** *n.*

re·pair[2] ▶*v.* [*intrans.*] (**repair to**) *formal* or *humorous* go to (a place), esp. in company: *we repaired to the tranquility of a nearby cafe.*
▶*n. archaic* frequent or habitual visiting of a place: *she exhorted repair to the church.* ■ a place that is frequently visited or occupied: *the repairs of wild beasts.* ▷Middle English: from Old French *repairer,* from late Latin *repatriare* 'return to one's country' (see REPATRIATE).

re·pair·man /riˈpe(ə)r,man; -mən/ ▶*n.* (*pl.* **-men**) a person who repairs vehicles, machinery, or appliances.

re·pap·er /rēˈpāpər/ ▶*v.* [*trans.*] apply new wallpaper to (a wall or room).

rep·a·ra·ble /ˈrep(ə)rəbəl/ ▶*adj.* (esp. of an injury or loss) possible to rectify or repair. ▷late 16th cent.: from French *réparable,* from Latin *reparabilis,* from *reparare* 'make ready again' (see REPAIR[1]).

rep·a·ra·tion /,repəˈrāsʜən/ ▶*n.* **1** the making of amends for a wrong one has done, by paying money to or otherwise helping those who have been wronged: *the courts required a convicted offender to* ***make financial reparation to*** *his victim.* ■ (**reparations**) the compensation for war damage paid by a defeated state. **2** *archaic* the action of repairing something: *the old hall was pulled down to avoid the cost of reparation.* ▷late Middle English: from Old French, from late Latin *reparatio(n-),* from *reparare* 'make ready again' (see REPAIR[1]). —**re·par·a·tive** /riˈparətiv/ *adj.*

re·par·a·tive ther·a·py ▶*n.* psychotherapy aimed at changing a person's homosexuality and based on the view that homosexuality is a mental disorder.

rep·ar·tee /,reparˈtē; ,rep,ärˈtē; -ˈtā/ ▶*n.* conversation or speech characterized by quick, witty comments or replies. See note at WIT. ▷mid 17th cent.: from French *repartie* 'replied promptly,' feminine past participle of *repartir,* from *re-* 'again' + *partir* 'divide, depart.'

re·par·ti·tion /,rē,pärˈtisʜən/ ▶*v.* [*trans.*] divide (something) up, or partition or divide (something) again.

re·past /riˈpast; ˈrē,past/ ▶*n. formal* a meal: *a sumptuous repast.* ▷late Middle English: from Old French, based on late Latin *repascere,* from *re-* (expressing intensive force) + *pascere* 'to feed.'

re·pa·tri·ate /rēˈpātrē,āt; rēˈpa-/ ▶*v.* [*trans.*] send (someone) back to their own country: *the government sought to repatriate thousands of Albanian refugees.* ■ send or bring (money) back to one's own country: *foreign firms would be permitted to repatriate all profits.*
▶*n.* a person who has been repatriated. ▷early 17th cent.: from late Latin *repatriat-* 'returned to one's country,' from the verb *repatriare,* from *re-* 'back' + Latin *patria* 'native land.' —**re·pa·tri·a·tion** /,rē,pātrēˈāsʜən; ,rē,pa-/ *n.*

re·pay /rēˈpā/ ▶*v.* (*past* and *past part.* **-paid** /rēˈpād/) [*trans.*] pay back (a loan, debt, or sum of money): *the loans were to be repaid over a 20-year period.* ■ pay back money borrowed from (someone): *most of his fortune had been spent repaying creditors.* ■ do or give something as recompense for (a favor or kindness received): *the manager has given me another chance and I'm desperate to repay that faith.* ▷late Middle English: from Old French *repaier.* —**re·pay·a·ble** *adj.* —**re·pay·ment** *n.*

re·peal /riˈpēl/ ▶*v.* [*trans.*] revoke or annul (a law or congressional act): *the legislation was repealed five months later.*
▶*n.* the action of revoking or annulling a law or congressional act: *the House voted in favor of repeal.* ▷late Middle English: from Anglo-Norman French *repeler,* from Old French *re-* (expressing reversal) + *apeler* 'to call, appeal.' —**re·peal·a·ble** *adj.*

re·peat /riˈpēt/ ▶*v.* **1** [*reporting verb*] say again something one has already said: [with *direct speech*] *"Are you hurt?" he repeated* | [*trans.*] *Billy repeated his question* | [with *clause*] *the landlady repeated that she was being very lenient with him.* ■ say again (something said or written by someone else): *he repeated the words after me* | [with *clause*] *she repeated what I'd said.* ■ (**repeat oneself**) say or do the same thing again. ■ used for emphasis: *force was not—repeat, not—to be used.* **2** [*trans.*] do (something) again, either once or a number of times: *earlier experiments were to be repeated on a far larger scale* | [as *adj.*] (**repeated**) *there were repeated attempts to negotiate.* ■ broadcast (a television or radio program) again. ■ undertake (a course or period of instruction) again: *Mark had to repeat first and second grades.* ■ (**repeat itself**) occur again in the same way or form: *I don't intend to let history repeat itself.* ■ [*intrans.*] illegally vote more than once in an election. ■ [*intrans.*] attain a particular success or achievement again, esp. by winning a championship for the second consecutive time: *the first team in nineteen years to repeat as NBA champions.* ■ [*trans.*] (of a watch or clock) strike (the last hour or quarter) over again when required. **3** [*intrans.*] (of food) be tasted intermittently for some time after being swallowed as a result of belching or indigestion: *it sat rather uncomfortably on my stomach and* **repeated on** *me for hours.*
▶*n.* an action, event, or other thing that occurs or is done again: *the final will be a repeat of last year.* ■ a repeated broadcast of a television or radio program. ■ [as *adj.*] occurring, done, or used more than once: *a repeat prescription.* ■ a consignment of goods similar to one already received. ■ a decorative pattern that is repeated uniformly over a surface. ■ *Music* a passage intended to be repeated. ■ a mark indicating this. ▷late Middle English: from Old French *repeter,* from Latin *repetere,* from *re-* 'back' + *petere* 'seek.' —**re·peat·a·bil·i·ty** /ri,pētəˈbilətē/ *n.* —**re·peat·a·ble** *adj.* —**re·peat·ed·ly** *adv.*

re·peat·er /riˈpētər/ ▶*n.* a person or thing that repeats something, in particular: ■ a firearm that fires several shots without reloading. ■ a watch or clock that can be made to repeat its last strike. ■ a device for the automatic retransmission or amplification of an electrically transmitted message.

re·peat·ing /riˈpētiɴɢ/ ▶*adj.* **1** (of a firearm) capable of firing several shots in succession without reloading. **2** (of a pattern) recurring uniformly over a surface.

re·peat·ing dec·i·mal ▶*n.* a decimal fraction in which a figure or group of figures is repeated indefinitely, as in *0.666 . . .* or as in *1.851851851 . . . .*

re·pê·chage /,repəˈsʜäzʜ/ (also **re·pe·chage**) ▶*n.* (in rowing and other sports) a contest in which the runners-up in the eliminating heats compete for a place in the final. ▷early 20th cent.: French, from *repêcher* 'fish out, rescue.'

re·pel /riˈpel/ ▶*v.* (**-pelled, -pel·ling**) [*trans.*] **1** drive or force (an attack or attacker) back or away: *government units sought to repel the rebels.* ■ [*trans.*] (of a magnetic pole or electric field) force (something similarly magnetized or charged) away from itself: *electrically charged objects attract or repel one another* | [*intrans.*] *like poles repel and unlike poles attract.* ■ (of a substance) resist mixing with or be impervious to (another substance): *boots with good-quality leather uppers to repel moisture.* **2** be repulsive or distasteful to: *she was repelled by the permanent smell of drink on his breath.* **3** *formal* refuse to accept (something, esp. an argument or theory): *the alleged right of lien led by the bankrupt's attorney was repelled.* ▷late Middle English: from Latin *repellere,* from *re-* 'back' + *pellere* 'to drive.' —**re·pel·ler** *n.*

re·pel·lent /riˈpelənt/ (also **re·pel·lant**) ▶*adj.* **1** [often in *combination*] able to repel a particular thing; impervious to a particular substance: *water-repellent nylon.* **2** causing disgust or distaste: *the idea was slightly* ***repellent to*** *her.*
▶*n.* **1** a substance that dissuades particular insects or other pests from approaching or settling: *a flea repellent.* **2** a substance used to treat something, esp. fabric or stone, so as to make it impervious to water: *treat brick with a silicone water repellent.* ▷mid 17th cent.: from Latin *repellent-* 'driving back,' from the verb *repellere* (see REPEL). —**re·pel·lence** *n.* —**re·pel·len·cy** *n.* —**re·pel·lent·ly** *adv.*

USAGE See usage at REPULSIVE.

re·pent /riˈpent/ ▶*v.* [*intrans.*] feel or express sincere regret or remorse about one's wrongdoing or sin: *the priest urged his listeners to repent* | *he* ***repented of*** *his action.* ■ [*trans.*] view or think of (an action or omission) with deep regret or remorse: *Marian came to repent her hasty judgment.* ■ (**repent oneself**) *archaic* feel regret or penitence about: *I repent me of all I did.* ▷Middle English: from Old French *repentir,* from *re-* (expressing intensive force) + *pentir* (based on Latin *paenitere* 'cause to repent'). —**re·pent·ance** /riˈpentns/ *n.* —**re·pent·ant** /riˈpentnt/ *adj.* —**re·pent·er** *n.*

re·peo·ple /rēˈpēpəl; ˈrē-/ ▶*v.* [*trans.*] repopulate (a place).

re·per·cus·sion /,rēpərˈkəsʜən; ,rep-/ ▶*n.* **1** (usu. **repercussions**) an unintended consequence occurring some time after an event or action, esp. an unwelcome one: *the move would have grave repercussions for the entire region.* **2** *archaic* the recoil of something after impact. **3** *archaic* an echo or reverberation. ▷late Middle English (as a medical term meaning 'repressing of infection'): from Old French, or from Latin *repercussio(n-),* from *repercutere* 'cause to rebound, push back,' from *re-* 'back, again' + *percutere* 'to strike.' The early sense 'driving back, rebounding' (mid 16th cent.) gave rise later to 'blow given in return,' hence sense 1 (early 20th cent.). —**re·per·cus·sive** /-ˈkəsiv/ *adj.*

rep·er·toire /ˈrepə(r),twär/ ▶*n.* a stock of plays, dances, or pieces that a company or a performer knows or is prepared to perform. ■ the whole body of items that are regularly performed: *the mainstream concert repertoire.* ■ a stock of skills or types of behavior that a person habitually uses: *his repertoire of threats, stares, and denigratory gestures.* ▷mid 19th cent.: from French *répertoire,* from late Latin *repertorium* (see REPERTORY).

rep·er·to·ry /ˈrepə(r),tôrē/ ▶*n.* (*pl.* **-ries**) **1** the performance of various plays, operas, or ballets by a company at regular short intervals: [as *adj.*] *a repertory actor.* ■ repertory theaters regarded collectively. ■ a repertory company. **2** another term for REPERTOIRE. ■ a repository or collection, esp. of information or retrievable examples. ▷mid 16th cent. (denoting an index or catalog): from late Latin *repertorium,* from Latin *repert-* 'found, discovered,' from the verb *reperire.* Sense 1 (arising from the fact that a company has a "repertory" of pieces for performance) dates from the late 19th cent. —**rep·er·to·ri·al** /,repə(r)ˈtôrēəl/ *adj.*

rep·er·to·ry com·pa·ny ▶*n.* a theatrical company that performs works from its repertoire for regular, short periods of time, moving on from one work to another.

Pronunciation Key ə *ago;* ər *over;* ˈə or ,ə *up;* ˈər or ,ər *fur;* a *hat;* ā *rate;* ä *car;* cʜ *chew;* e *let;* ē *see;* e(ə)r *air;* i *fit;* ī *by;* i(ə)r *ear;* ɴɢ *sing;* ō *go;* ô *for;* oi *boy;* o͝o *good;* o͞o *goo;* ou *out;* sʜ *she;* ᴛʜ *thin;* T̲H̲ *then;* (h)w *why;* zʜ *vision*

R

rep·e·tend /ˈrepəˌtend/ ▶*n.* *Mathematics* the repeating figure or figures of a recurring decimal fraction. ■ *formal* a recurring word or phrase; a refrain. ▷early 18th cent.: from Latin *repetendum* 'something to be repeated,' neuter gerundive of *repetere* (see **REPEAT**).

ré·pé·ti·teur /ˌrāˌpātiˈtər/ ▶*n.* a tutor or coach of ballet dancers or musicians, esp. opera singers. ▷French.

rep·e·ti·tion /ˌrepəˈtisнən/ ▶*n.* the action of repeating something that has already been said or written: *her comments are worthy of repetition | a repetition of his reply to the delegation.* ■ [often with *negative*] the recurrence of an action or event: *there was to be no repetition of the interwar years | I didn't want a repetition of the scene in my office that morning.* ■ a thing repeated: *the geometric repetitions of Islamic art.* ■ a training exercise that is repeated, esp. a series of repeated raisings and lowerings of the weight in weight training. ■ *Music* the repeating of a passage or note. ■ *archaic* a piece set by a teacher to be learned by heart and recited. ▷late Middle English: from Old French *repeticion* or Latin *repetitio(n-)*, from *repetere* (see **REPEAT**). **—rep·e·ti·tion·al** /-sнənl/ *adj.*

rep·e·ti·tious /ˌrepəˈtisнəs/ ▶*adj.* another term for **REPETITIVE**. **—rep·e·ti·tious·ly** *adv.* **—rep·e·ti·tious·ness** *n.*

re·pet·i·tive /riˈpetətiv/ ▶*adj.* containing or characterized by repetition, esp. when unnecessary or tiresome: *a repetitive task.* **—re·pet·i·tive·ly** *adv.* **—re·pet·i·tive·ness** *n.*

re·pet·i·tive-mo·tion dis·or·der ▶*n.* work-related physical symptoms caused by excessive and repeated use of the upper extremities, esp. when typing on a computer keyboard. Also called **re·pet·i·tive in·ju·ry**.

re·pet·i·tive strain in·ju·ry (abbr.: **RSI**) ▶*n.* a condition in which the prolonged performance of repetitive actions, typically with the hands, causes pain or impairment of function in the tendons and muscles involved.

re·phrase /rēˈfrāz/ ▶*v.* [*trans.*] express (an idea or question) in an alternative way, esp. with the purpose of changing the detail or perspective of the original idea or question: *rephrase the statement so that it is clear.*

re·pine /riˈpīn/ ▶*v.* [*intrans.*] *poetic/literary* feel or express discontent; fret: *you mustn't let yourself repine.* ▷early 16th cent.: from **RE-** 'again' + the verb **PINE**[2], on the pattern of *repent.*

re·place /riˈplās/ ▶*v.* [*trans.*] **1** take the place of: *Ian's smile was replaced by a frown.* ■ provide or find a substitute for (something that is broken, old, or inoperative): *the light bulb needs replacing.* ■ fill the role of (someone or something) with a substitute: *the government dismissed 3,000 of its customs inspectors, replacing them with new recruits.* **2** put (something) back in a previous place or position: *he drained his glass and replaced it on the bar.* **—re·plac·er** *n.*

THE RIGHT WORD **displace, replace, supersede, supplant**

When a light bulb burns out, you **replace** it, meaning that you substitute something new or functioning for what is lost, destroyed, or worn out.

If something that is obsolete or ineffective is replaced by something that is superior, more up-to-date, or more authoritative, the correct verb is **supersede** (*the computer superseded the electric typewriter*).

In contrast, **displace** suggests that someone or something has been ousted or dislodged forcibly, without necessarily implying that it was inferior or ineffective (*a growing number of workers were being displaced by machines*).

Supplant is more restricted in meaning; it suggests displacement by force, fraud, or innovation (*the democratic government had been supplanted by a power-hungry tyrant*). It can also mean to uproot or wipe out (*the English immigrants gradually supplanted the island's native inhabitants*).

re·place·a·ble /riˈplāsəbəl/ ▶*adj.* able to be replaced: *a knife with a replaceable blade.* ■ *Chemistry* denoting those hydrogen atoms in an acid that can be displaced by metal atoms when forming salts. **—re·place·a·bil·i·ty** /-ˌplāsəˈbilətē/ *n.*

re·place·ment /riˈplāsmənt/ ▶*n.* the action or process of replacing someone or something: *the replacement of religion by poetry | a hip replacement.* ■ a person or thing that takes the place of another.

re·place·ment ther·a·py ▶*n.* *Medicine* treatment aimed at making up a deficit of a substance normally present in the body.

re·plant /rēˈplant; ˈrē-/ ▶*v.* [*trans.*] plant (a tree or plant that has been dug up) again, esp. when transferring it to a larger pot or new site. ■ provide (an area) with new plants or trees: *38 percent of ancient woodland has been replanted with conifers.* ■ surgically reattach to the body a part that has been removed or severed.

re·plan·ta·tion /ˌrēˌplanˈtāsнən/ ▶*n.* permanent reattachment to the body of a part that has been removed or severed: *successful replantation of the tooth.*

re·play ▶*v.* /rēˈplā; ˈrē-/ [*trans.*] **1** play back (a recording on tape, video, or film): *he could stop the tape and replay it whenever he wished.* ■ *figurative* repeat (something, esp. an event or sequence of events): *she replayed in her mind every detail of the night before.* **2** play (a match or contest) again to decide a winner after the original encounter ended in a draw or contentious result.

▶*n.* /ˈrēˌplā/ **1** the playing again of a section of a recording, esp. so as to be able to watch an incident more closely: *clouds can be studied in speeded-up replay | the umpire studied TV replays.* ■ *figurative* an occurrence that closely follows the pattern of a previous event: *a replay of last summer's civil disturbance.* **2** a replayed match.

re·plen·ish /riˈplenisн/ ▶*v.* [*trans.*] fill (something) up again: *he replenished Justin's glass with mineral water.* ■ restore (a stock or supply of something) to the former level or condition: *all creatures need sleep to replenish their energies.* ▷late Middle English (in the sense 'supply abundantly'): from Old French *repleniss-*, lengthened stem of *replenir*, from *re-* 'again' (also expressing intensive force) + *plenir* 'fill' (from Latin *plenus* 'full'). **—re·plen·ish·er** *n.* **—re·plen·ish·ment** *n.*

re·plete /riˈplēt/ ▶*adj.* [*predic.*] filled or well-supplied with something: *sensational popular fiction,* ***replete with*** *adultery and sudden death.* ■ very full of or sated by food: *I went out into the sun-drenched streets again, replete and relaxed.* ▷late Middle English: from Old French *replet(e)* or Latin *repletus* 'filled up,' past participle of *replere*, from *re-* 'back, again' + *plere* 'fill.' **—re·ple·tion** /riˈplēsнən/ *n.*

re·plev·in /riˈplevən/ ▶*n.* *Law* a procedure whereby seized goods may be provisionally restored to their owner pending the outcome of an action to determine the rights of the parties concerned. ■ an action arising from such a process. ▷late Middle English: from Anglo-Norman French, from Old French *replevir* 'recover' (see **REPLEVY**).

re·plev·y /riˈplevē/ ▶*v.* (**-plev·ies, -plev·ied**) [*trans.*] *Law* recover (seized goods) by replevin. ▷mid 16th cent.: from Old French *replevir* 'recover'; apparently related to **PLEDGE**.

rep·li·ca /ˈreplikə/ ▶*n.* an exact copy or model of something, esp. one on a smaller scale: *a replica of the Empire State Building.* ■ a duplicate of an original artistic work. ▷mid 18th cent. (as a musical term in the sense 'a repeat'): from Italian, from *replicare* 'to reply.'

rep·li·cant /ˈreplikənt/ ▶*n.* **1** (in science fiction) a genetically engineered or artificial being created as an exact replica of a particular human being. **2** a disparaging term for something that imitates or resembles another. ▷from *replica* + *-ant*: first used in the movie *Blade Runner* (1982).

rep·li·case /ˈrepliˌkās; -ˌkāz/ ▶*n.* *Biochemistry* an enzyme that catalyzes the synthesis of a complementary RNA molecule using an RNA template. ▷1960s: from the verb **REPLICATE** + **-ASE**.

rep·li·cate ▶*v.* /ˈrepliˌkāt/ [*trans.*] make an exact copy of; reproduce: *it might be impractical to replicate eastern culture in the west.* ■ (**replicate itself**) (of genetic material or a living organism) reproduce or give rise to a copy of itself: *interleukin-16 prevents the virus from replicating itself | [intrans.] an enzyme that HIV needs in order to replicate.* ■ repeat (a scientific experiment or trial) to obtain a consistent result: *these findings have been replicated by Atwood and Jackson.*

▶*adj.* /-kit/ [*attrib.*] of the nature of a copy: *a replicate Earth.* ■ of the nature of a repetition of a scientific experiment or trial: *the variation of replicate measurements.*

▶*n.* /-kit/ **1** a close or exact copy; a replica. ■ a repetition of an experimental test or procedure. **2** *Music* a tone one or more octaves above or below the given tone. ▷late Middle English (in the sense 'repeat'): from Latin *replicat-*, from the verb *replicare*, from *re-* 'back, again' + *plicare* 'to fold.' The current senses date from the late 19th cent. **—rep·li·ca·bil·i·ty** /ˌreplikəˈbilətē/ *n.* **—rep·li·ca·ble** /ˈreplikəbəl/ *adj.*

rep·li·ca·tion /ˌrepliˈkāsнən/ ▶*n.* **1** the action of copying or reproducing something. ■ a copy: *a twentieth-century building would be cheaper than a replication of what was there before.* ■ the repetition of a scientific experiment or trial to obtain a consistent result. ■ the process by which genetic material or a living organism gives rise to a copy of itself: *HIV replication | a crucial step in cold virus replications.* **2** *dated Law* a plaintiff's reply to the defendant's plea. ▷late Middle English: from Old French *replicacion*, from Latin *replicatio(n-)*, from *replicare* 'fold back, repeat,' later 'make a reply' (see **REPLICATE**).

rep·li·ca·tive /ˈrepliˌkātiv/ ▶*adj.* *Biology* relating to or involving the replication of genetic material or living organisms.

rep·li·ca·tor /ˈrepliˌkātər/ ▶*n.* a thing that replicates or copies something. ■ *Biology* a structural gene at which replication of a specific replicon is believed to be initiated.

rep·li·con /ˈrepliˌkän/ ▶*n.* *Biology* a nucleic acid molecule, or part of one, that replicates as a unit, beginning at a specific site within it. ▷1960s: from **REPLICATION** + **-ON**.

re·ply /riˈplī/ ▶*v.* (**-plies, -plied**) [*reporting verb*] say something in response to something someone has said: [*intrans.*] *he was gone before we could* ***reply to*** *his last remark* | [with *clause*] *she replied that she had been sound asleep* | [with *direct speech*] *"I'm OK—just leave me alone," he replied.* ■ [*intrans.*] write back to someone one has received a letter from: *she replied with a long letter the next day.* ■ [*intrans.*] respond by a similar action or gesture: *they* ***replied to*** *the shelling with a heavy mortar attack on the area.*

▶*n.* (*pl.* **-plies**) a verbal or written answer: *I received a reply from the firm's managing director | "No," was the curt reply.* ■ the action of answering someone or something: *I am writing* ***in reply to*** *your letter of June 1.* ■ a response in the form of a gesture, action, or expression: *we scored the first goal and they hit a late reply.* ■ *Law* a plaintiff's response to the defendant's plea. ▷late Middle English (as a verb): from Old French *replier*, from Latin *replicare* 'repeat,' later 'make a reply' (see **REPLICATE**). **—re·pli·er** *n.*

re·po /ˈrēˌpō/ *informal* ▶*n.* (*pl.* **-pos**) **1** another term for **REPURCHASE AGREEMENT**. [1960s: abbreviation.] **2** a car or other item that has been repossessed.

▶*v.* (**-po's, -po'd**) [*trans.*] repossess (a car or other item) when a buyer defaults on payments. [1970s: abbreviation.]

re·point /rēˈpoint/ ▶*v.* [*trans.*] remortar or repair the joints of (brickwork).

re·po man ▶*n.* *informal* a repossessor.

re·pop·u·late /rēˈpäpyəˌlāt/ ▶*v.* [*trans.*] introduce a population into (a previously occupied area or country): *the area was repopulated largely by Russians.* **—re·population** /ˌrēˌpäpyəˈlāsнən/ *n.*

re·port /riˈpôrt/ ▶*v.* **1** [*reporting verb*] give a spoken or written account of something that one has observed, heard, done, or investigated: [*trans.*] *the representative reported a decline in milk and meat production* | [with *clause*] *police reported that the flood waters were abating* | [*intrans.*] *the teacher should* ***report on*** *the child's progress.* ■ [*intrans.*] cover an event or subject as a journalist or a reporter: *the press* ***reported on*** *Republican sex scandals* | [with *clause*] *the Egyptian news agency reported that a coup attempt had taken place* | [*trans.*] *the paper reported a secret program by the country to build nuclear warheads.* ■ (**be reported**) used to indicate that something has been stated, although one cannot confirm its accuracy: [with *infinitive*] *these hoaxers are reported to be hacking into airline frequencies to impersonate air traffic controllers* | [as *adj.*] (**reported**) *a reported $50,000 in debt.* ■ [*trans.*] make a formal statement or complaint about (someone or something) to the necessary authority: *undisclosed illegalities are* ***reported to*** *the company's directors* | [*trans.*] *eight horses have been reported missing in the last month.* ■ [*trans.*] (of a legislative committee) formally announce that the committee has dealt with (a bill): *the chairman shall report the bill to the House.* See also **REPORT A BILL OUT** below. **2** [*intrans.*] present oneself formally as having arrived at a particular place or as ready to do something: *he was given three days to say goodbye to his family and* ***report for*** *active duty.* **3** [*intrans.*] (**report to**) be responsible to (a superior or supervisor): *the officers now report to the Russian president, not the Politburo.*

▶*phrasal v.* □ **report back** (or **report something back**) **1** deliver a spoken or written account of something one has been asked to do or investigate: *the deadpan voice of a police officer* ***reporting back to*** *his superior | every movement I made was reported back to him.* **2** return to work or duty after a period of absence. □ **report a bill out** (of a committee of Congress) return a bill to the legislative body for action.

▸*n.* **1** an account given of a particular matter, esp. in the form of an official document, after thorough investigation or consideration by an appointed person or body: *the chairman's annual report.* ■ a spoken or written description of an event or situation, esp. one intended for publication or broadcast in the media: *press reports suggested that the government was still using secret police to help maintain public order.* ■ a teacher's written assessment of a student's work, progress, and conduct, issued at the end of a term or academic year. ■ *Law* a detailed formal account of a case heard in a court, giving the main points in the judgment, esp. as prepared for publication. ■ a piece of information that is unsupported by firm evidence and that the speaker feels may or may not be true: *reports were circulating that the chairman was about to resign.* ■ *dated* rumor: ***report has it*** *that the beetles have now virtually disappeared.* ■ *archaic* the way in which someone or something is regarded; reputation: *whatsoever things are lovely and of* ***good report.*** **2** a sudden loud noise of or like an explosion or gunfire. **3** an employee who is supervised by another employee: *all of his reports are twenty-somethings with no concept of proper attire for work.* ▷late Middle English: from Old French *reporter* (verb), *report* (noun), from Latin *reportare* 'bring back,' from *re-* 'back' + *portare* 'carry.' The sense 'give an account' gave rise to 'submit a formal report,' hence 'inform an authority of one's presence' (sense 2, mid 19th cent.) and 'be accountable (to a superior)' (sense 3, late 19th cent.). **—re·port·a·ble** *adj.*

▸*PHRASE* □ **on report** (esp. of a prisoner or member of the armed forces) on a disciplinary charge.

re·port·age /rə'pôrtij; ˌrepôr'täzʜ/ ▸*n.* the reporting of news, for the press and the broadcast media: *extensive reportage of elections.* ■ factual presentation in a book or other text, esp. when this adopts a journalistic style. ▷early 17th cent.: French, from Old French *reporter* 'carry back' (see REPORT).

re·port card ▸*n.* a teacher's written assessment of a student's work, progress, and conduct, sent home to a parent or guardian. ■ an evaluation of performance: *Democrat legislators fared poorly in a recent report card.*

re·port·ed·ly /ri'pôrtədlē/ ▸*adv.* [*sentence adverb*] according to what some say (used to express the speaker's belief that the information given is not necessarily true): *he was in El Salvador, reportedly on his way to Texas.*

re·port·ed speech ▸*n.* a speaker's words reported in subordinate clauses governed by a reporting verb, with the required changes of person and tense (e.g., *he said that he would go,* based on *I will go*). Also called INDIRECT SPEECH. Contrasted with DIRECT SPEECH.

re·port·er /ri'pôrtər/ ▸*n.* a person who reports, esp. one employed to report news or conduct interviews for newspapers or broadcasts.

re·port·ing verb ▸*n.* a verb belonging to a class of verbs conveying the action of speaking and used with both direct and reported speech. Reporting verbs may also be used with a direct object and with an infinitive construction.

rep·or·to·ri·al /ˌrepə(r)'tôrēəl; ˌrē-/ ▸*adj.* of or characteristic of newspaper reporters: *reportorial ambition and curiosity.* ▷mid 19th cent.: from REPORTER, on the pattern of *editorial.* **—rep·or·to·ri·al·ly** *adv.*

re·po·sa·do /ˌrepə'sädō/ ▸*n.* (*pl.* **-dos**) a type of tequila that has been aged in oak for a period of two to twelve months. ▷Spanish, literally 'rested.'

re·pose[1] /ri'pōz/ ▸*n.* temporary rest from activity, excitement, or exertion, esp. sleep or the rest given by sleep: ***in repose*** *her face looked relaxed.* ■ a state of peace: *the repose of the soul of the dead man.* ■ composure: *he had lost none of his grace or his repose.* ■ *Art* harmonious arrangement of colors and forms, providing a restful visual effect.

▸*v.* [*intrans.*] be lying, situated, or kept in a particular place: *the diamond now reposes in the Louvre.* ■ lie down in rest: *how sweetly he would repose in the four-poster bed.* ■ [*trans.*] (**repose something on/in**) *poetic/literary* lay something to rest in or on (something): *I'll go to him, and repose our distresses on his friendly bosom.* ■ [*trans.*] *archaic* give rest to: *he halted to repose his wayworn soldiers.* ▷late Middle English: from Old French *repos* (noun), *reposer* (verb), from late Latin *repausare,* from *re-* (expressing intensive force) + *pausare* 'to pause.' **—re·pose·ful** /-fəl/ *adj.* **—re·pose·ful·ly** /-fəlē/ *adv.*

re·pose[2] ▸*v.* [*trans.*] (**repose something in**) place something, esp. one's confidence or trust, in: *we have never betrayed the trust that you have reposed in us.* ▷late Middle English (in the sense 'put back in the same position'): from RE- 'again' + the verb POSE[1], suggested by Latin *reponere* 'replace,' from *re-* (expressing intensive force) + *ponere* 'to place.'

re·po·si·tion /ˌrēpə'zisʜən/ ▸*v.* [*trans.*] place in a different position; adjust or alter the position of: *try repositioning the thermostat in another room.* ■ change the image of (a company, product, etc.) to target a new or wider market: *our assignment was to reposition coffee from a "rite of passage" drink to a "contemporary experience."*

re·pos·i·to·ry /ri'päzəˌtôrē/ ▸*n.* (*pl.* **-ries**) a place, building, or receptacle where things are or may be stored: *a deep repository for nuclear waste.* ■ a place in which something, esp. a natural resource, has accumulated or where it is found in significant quantities: *accessible repositories of water.* ■ a person or thing regarded as a store of information or in which something abstract is held to exist or be found: *his mind was a rich repository of the past.* ▷late 15th cent.: from Old French *repositoire* or Latin *repositorium,* from *reposit-* 'placed back,' from the verb *reponere* (see RE-POSE[2]).

re·pos·sess /ˌrēpə'zes/ ▸*v.* [*trans.*] retake possession of (something) when a buyer defaults on payments: *565 homes were repossessed for nonpayment of mortgages.* **—re·pos·ses·sion** /-'zesʜən/ *n.*

re·pos·ses·sor /ˌrēpə'zesər/ ▸*n.* a person hired by a credit company to repossess an item when the buyer defaults on payments.

re·pot /rē'pät; 'rē-/ ▸*v.* (**-pot·ted, -pot·ting**) [*trans.*] put (a plant) in another pot, esp. a larger one.

re·pous·sé /rəˌpōō'sā/ ▸*adj.* (of metalwork) hammered into relief from the reverse side.

▸*n.* ornamental metalwork fashioned in this way. ▷mid 19th cent.: French, literally 'pushed back,' past participle of *repousser,* from *re-* (expressing intensive force) + *pousser* 'to push.'

repp /rep/ ▸*n.* variant spelling of REP[3].

repr. ▸*abbr.* reprint or reprinted.

rep·re·hend /ˌrepri'hend/ ▸*v.* [*trans.*] reprimand: *a recklessness that cannot be too severely reprehended.* ▷Middle English: from Latin *reprehendere* 'seize, check, rebuke,' from *re-* (expressing intensive force) + *prehendere* 'seize.' **—rep·re·hen·sion** /-'hencʜən/ *n.*

rep·re·hen·si·ble /ˌrepri'hensəbəl/ ▸*adj.* deserving censure or condemnation: *his complacency and reprehensible laxity.* ▷late Middle English: from late Latin *reprehensibilis,* from *reprehens-* 'rebuked,' from the verb *reprehendere* (see REPREHEND). **—rep·re·hen·si·bil·i·ty** /-ˌhensə'bilətē/ *n.* **—rep·re·hen·si·bly** /-blē/ *adv.*

rep·re·sent /ˌrepri'zent/ ▸*v.* [*trans.*] **1** be entitled or appointed to act or speak for (someone), esp. in an official capacity: *for purposes of litigation, an infant can and must be represented by an adult.* ■ (of a competitor) participate in a sports event or other competition on behalf of (one's club, town, region, or country): *Owens represented the U.S.* ■ be an elected member of a legislature for (a particular constituency, party, or group): *she became the first woman to represent her district.* ■ (usu. **be represented**) act as a substitute for (someone), esp. on an official or ceremonial occasion: *the president was represented by the secretary of state.* **2** constitute; amount to: *this figure represents eleven percent of the company's total sales.* ■ be a specimen or example of; typify: *twenty parents, picked to represent a cross section of rural life.* ■ (**be represented**) (of a group or type of person or thing) be present or found in something, esp. to a particular degree: *abstraction is well represented in this exhibition.* **3** depict (a particular subject) in a picture or other work of art: *santos are small wooden figures representing saints.* ■ [*trans.* or *infinitive*] describe or depict (someone or something) as being of a certain nature; portray in a particular way: *the young were consistently represented as being in need of protection.* ■ (of a sign or symbol) have a particular signification; stand for: *the numbers 1–10 represent the letters A–Z.* ■ be a symbol or embodiment of (a particular quality or thing): *the three heads of Cerberus represent the past, present, and future.* ■ play the part of (someone) in a theatrical production. **4** *formal* state or point out (something) clearly: *it was represented to him that she would be an unsuitable wife.* ■ [with *clause*] allege; claim: *the vendors have represented that such information is accurate.* ▷late Middle English: from Old French *representer* or Latin *repraesentare,* from *re-* (expressing intensive force) + *praesentare* 'to present.' **—rep·re·sent·a·bil·i·ty** /ˌrepriˌzentə'bilətē/ *n.* **—rep·re·sent·a·ble** *adj.*

re-pre·sent /ˌrēpri'zent/ ▸*v.* [*trans.*] present (something) again, esp. for further consideration or in an altered form: *most of today's demonstrations will be represented on Friday.* ■ present (a check or bill) again for payment. **—re-pres·en·ta·tion** /ˌrēˌprezən'tāsʜən; -ˌprēˌzen-/ *n.*

rep·re·sen·ta·tion /ˌrepriˌzen'tāsʜən; -zən-/ ▸*n.* **1** the action of speaking or acting on behalf of someone or the state of being so represented: *asylum-seekers should be guaranteed good legal advice and representation.* **2** the description or portrayal of someone or something in a particular way or as being of a certain nature: *the representation of women in newspapers.* ■ the depiction of someone or something in a picture or other work of art: *Picasso is striving for some absolute representation of reality.* ■ a thing, esp. a picture or model, that depicts a likeness or reproduction of someone or something: *a striking representation of a vase of flowers.* ■ (in some theories of perception) a mental state or concept regarded as corresponding to a thing perceived. **3** (**representations**) formal statements made to a higher authority, esp. so as to communicate an opinion or register a protest: *certain church groups are making strong representations to our government.* ■ a statement or allegation: *any buyer was relying on a representation that the tapes were genuine.* ▷late Middle English (in the sense 'image, likeness'): from Old French *representation* or Latin *repraesentatio(n-),* from *repraesentare* 'bring before, exhibit' (see REPRESENT).

rep·re·sen·ta·tion·al /ˌrepriˌzen'tāsʜənl/ ▸*adj.* of, relating to, or characterized by representation: *representational democracy.* ■ relating to or denoting art that aims to depict the physical appearance of things. Contrasted with ABSTRACT.

rep·re·sen·ta·tion·al·ism /ˌrepriˌzen'tāsʜənlˌizəm/ ▸*n.* **1** the practice or advocacy of representational art. **2** *Philosophy* another term for REPRESENTATIONISM. **—rep·re·sen·ta·tion·al·ist** *adj. & n.*

rep·re·sen·ta·tion·ism /ˌrepriˌzen'tāsʜəˌnizəm; -zən-/ ▸*n.* *Philosophy* the doctrine that thought is the manipulation of mental representations that (somehow) correspond to external states or objects. **—rep·re·sen·ta·tion·ist** *n.*

rep·re·sen·ta·tive /ˌrepri'zentətiv/ ▸*adj.* **1** typical of a class, group, or body of opinion: *these courses are representative of those taken by most Harvard undergraduates.* ■ containing typical examples of many or all types: *a representative sample of young people in the South.* **2** (of a legislative or deliberative assembly) consisting of people chosen to act and speak on behalf of a wider group. ■ (of a government or political system) based on representation of the people by such deputies: *free elections and representative democracy.* **3** serving as a portrayal or symbol of something: *the show should be more* ***representative of*** *how women really are.* ■ (of art) representational: *the bust involves a high degree of representative abstraction.* **4** *Philosophy* of or relating to mental representation.

▸*n.* **1** a person chosen or appointed to act or speak for another or others, in particular: ■ an agent of a firm who travels to potential clients to sell its products. ■ an employee of a travel company who looks after the needs of its vacationing clients. ■ a person chosen or elected to speak and act on behalf of others in a legislative assembly or deliberative body. ■ a delegate who attends a conference, negotiations, legal hearing, etc., so as to represent the interests of another person or group. ■ a person who takes the place of another on a ceremonial or official occasion. **2** an example of a class or group: *fossil representatives of lampreys and hagfishes.* **—rep·re·sent·a·tive·ly** *adv.* **—rep·re·sent·a·tive·ness** *n.*

re·press /ri'pres/ ▸*v.* [*trans.*] subdue (someone or something) by force: *the uprisings were repressed.* ■ restrain or prevent (the expression of a feeling): *Isabel couldn't repress a sharp cry of fear.* ■ suppress (a thought, feeling, or desire) in oneself so that it becomes or remains unconscious: *the thought that he had killed his brother was so terrible that he repressed it.* ■ inhibit the natural development or self-expression of (someone or something): *too much bureaucracy represses creativity.* ■ *Biology* prevent the transcription of (a gene). ▷Middle English (in the sense 'keep back (something objectionable)'): from Latin *repress-* 'pressed back, checked,' from the verb *reprimere,* from *re-* 'back' + *premere* 'to press.' **—re·press·er** *n.* **—re·press·i·ble** /-əbəl/ *adj.* **—re·pres·sion** /ri'presʜən/ *n.*

re·pressed /ri'prest/ ▸*adj.* restrained, inhibited, or oppressed: *repressed indigenous groups | repressed* *energy.* ■ (of a thought, feeling, or desire) kept suppressed and unconscious in one's mind: *repressed memories.* ■ having or characterized by a large number of thoughts, feelings, or desires, esp. sexual ones, that are suppressed in this way: *a very repressed, almost Victorian, household.*

re·pres·sive /ri'presiv/ ▶*adj.* (esp. of a social or political system) inhibiting or restraining the freedom of a person or group of people: *a repressive regime.* ■ inhibiting or preventing the awareness of certain thoughts or feelings: *a repressive moral code.* —**re·pres·sive·ly** *adv.* —**re·pres·sive·ness** *n.*

re·pres·sor /ri'presər/ ▶*n. Biochemistry* a substance that acts on an operon to inhibit messenger RNA synthesis.

re·prieve /ri'prēv/ ▶*v.* [*trans.*] cancel or postpone the punishment of (someone, esp. someone condemned to death): *under the new regime, prisoners under sentence of death were reprieved.* ■ abandon or postpone plans to close or put an end to (something): *the threatened pits could be reprieved.*

▶*n.* a cancellation or postponement of a punishment. ■ a temporary escape from an undesirable fate or unpleasant situation: *a mother who faced eviction has been given a reprieve.* ▷late 15th cent. (as the past participle *repryed*): from Anglo-Norman French *repris,* past participle of *reprendre,* from Latin *re-* 'back' + *prehendere* 'seize.' The insertion of *-v-* (16th cent.) remains unexplained. Sense development has undergone a reversal, from the early meaning 'send back to prison,' via 'postpone (a legal process),' to the current sense 'rescue from impending punishment.'

rep·ri·mand /'reprə,mand/ ▶*n.* a rebuke, esp. an official one.

▶*v.* [*trans.*] rebuke (someone), esp. officially: *officials were dismissed or reprimanded for poor work.* See note at **REBUKE**. ▷mid 17th cent.: from French *réprimande,* via Spanish from Latin *reprimenda* 'things to be held in check,' neuter plural gerundive of *reprimere* (see **REPRESS**).

re·print ▶*v.* /rē'print; 'rē-/ [*trans.*] print again or in a different form: *the story has been reprinted at intervals ever since it first appeared.*

▶*n.* /'rē,print/ an act of printing more copies of a work. ■ a copy of a book or other material that has been reprinted. ■ an offprint. —**re·print·er** *n.*

re·pris·al /ri'prīzəl/ ▶*n.* an act of retaliation: *three youths died in the reprisals that followed | the threat of reprisal.* ■ *historical* the forcible seizure of a foreign subject or their goods as an act of retaliation. ▷late Middle English: from Anglo-Norman French *reprisaille,* from medieval Latin *reprisalia* (neuter plural), based on Latin *repraehens-* 'seized,' from the verb *repraehendere* (see **REPREHEND**). The current sense dates from the early 18th cent.

re·prise /ri'prēz/ ▶*n.* a repeated passage in music. ■ a repetition or further performance of something: *many Syrians fear a reprise of the showdown 12 years ago.*

▶*v.* [*trans.*] repeat (a piece of music or a performance). ▷early 18th cent.: French, literally 'taken up again,' feminine past participle of *reprendre* (see **REPRIEVE**).

re·pro /'rē,prō/ ▶*n.* (*pl.* **-pros**) [usu. as *adj.*] *informal* **1** a reproduction or copy, particularly of a piece of furniture: *a Georgian repro cabinet.* **2** the action or process of copying a document or image: *a repro house.* ▷1940s: abbreviation.

re·proach /ri'prōch/ ▶*v.* [*trans.*] address (someone) in such a way as to express disapproval or disappointment: *critics of the administration* **reproached** *the president* **for** *his failure to tackle the deficiency |* [with *direct speech*] *"You know that isn't true," he reproached her.* See note at **REBUKE**. ■ (**reproach someone with**) accuse someone of: *his wife reproached him with cowardice.* ■ *archaic* censure or rebuke (an offense).

▶*n.* the expression of disapproval or disappointment: *he gave her a look of reproach | a farrago of warnings and pained reproaches.* ■ (**a reproach to**) a thing that makes the failings of someone or something else more apparent: *his elegance is a living reproach to our slovenly habits.* ■ (**Reproaches**) (in the Roman Catholic Church) a set of antiphons and responses for Good Friday representing the reproaches of Jesus Christ to his people. ▷Middle English: from Old French *reprochier* (verb), from a base meaning 'bring back close,' based on Latin *prope* 'near.' —**re·proach·a·ble** *adj.* —**re·proach·er** *n.* —**re·proach·ing·ly** *adv.*

▶*PHRASE* □ **above** (or **beyond**) **reproach** such that no criticism can be made; perfect.

re·proach·ful /ri'prōchfəl/ ▶*adj.* expressing disapproval or disappointment: *she gave him a reproachful look.* —**re·proach·ful·ly** *adv.* —**re·proach·ful·ness** *n.*

rep·ro·bate /'reprə,bāt/ ▶*n.* an unprincipled person (often used humorously or affectionately). ■ *archaic Christian Theology* (esp. in Calvinism) a sinner who is not of the elect and is predestined to damnation.

▶*adj.* unprincipled (often used as a humorous or affectionate reproach): *a long-missed old reprobate drinking comrade.* ■ *Christian Theology, archaic* (in Calvinism) predestined to damnation.

▶*v.* [*trans.*] *archaic* express or feel disapproval of: *his neighbors reprobated his method of proceeding.* ▷late Middle English (as a verb): from Latin *reprobat-* 'disapproved,' from the verb *reprobare,* from *re-* (expressing reversal) + *probare* 'approve.' —**rep·ro·ba·tion** /,reprə'bāshən/ *n.*

re·proc·ess /rē'präs,es; -'präsəs; -'prō-/ ▶*v.* [*trans.*] process (something, esp. spent nuclear fuel) again or differently, typically in order to reuse it: *the costs of reprocessing radioactive waste.*

re·pro·duce /,rēprə'd(y)o͞os/ ▶*v.* [*trans.*] produce again: *a concert performance cannot reproduce all the subtleties of a recording.* ■ produce a copy or representation of: *his works are reproduced on postcards and posters.* ■ create something very similar to (something else), esp. in a different medium or context: *the problems are difficult to reproduce in the laboratory.* ■ (of an organism) produce offspring by a sexual or asexual process: *bacteria normally divide and* **reproduce themselves** *every twenty minutes |* [*intrans.*] *an individual organism needs to avoid being eaten until it has reproduced.* ■ [*intrans.*] be copied with a specified degree of success: *you'll be amazed to see how well halftones reproduce.* —**re·pro·duc·er** *n.* —**re·pro·duc·i·bil·i·ty** /-,d(y)o͞osə'bilətē/ *n.* —**re·pro·duc·i·ble** *adj.* —**re·pro·duc·i·bly** /-əblē/ *adv.*

re·pro·duc·tion /,rēprə'dəkshən/ ▶*n.* the action or process of making a copy of something: *the cost of color reproduction in publication is high.* ■ the production of offspring by a sexual or asexual process. ■ a copy of a work of art, esp. a print or photograph of a painting. ■ [as *adj.*] made to imitate the style of an earlier period or of a particular artist or craftsman: *reproduction French classical beds.* ■ the quality of reproduced sound: *the design was changed to allow louder reproduction.* —**re·pro·duc·tive** /-'dəktiv/ *adj.* —**re·pro·duc·tive·ly** /-'dəktivlē/ *adv.* —**re·pro·duc·tive·ness** /-'dəktivnis/ *n.*

re·pro·graph·ics /,reprə'grafiks; 'rē-/ ▶*plural n.* [treated as *sing.*] reprography.

re·prog·ra·phy /ri'prägrəfē/ ▶*n.* the science and practice of copying and reproducing documents and graphic material. ▷1960s: from **REPRODUCE** + **-GRAPHY**. —**re·prog·ra·pher** /-fər/ *n.* —**re·pro·graph·ic** /,reprə'grafik; ,rē-/ *adj.*

re·prove /ri'pro͞ov/ ▶*v.* [*trans.*] reprimand or censure someone: *he was reproved for obscenity |* [with *direct speech*] *"Don't be childish, Hilary," he reproved mildly |* [as *adj.*] (**reproving**) *a reproving glance.* ▷Middle English (also in the senses 'reject' and 'censure'): from Old French *reprover,* from late Latin *reprobare* 'disapprove' (see **REPROBATE**). —**re·prov·a·ble** *adj.* —**re·prov·er** *n.* —**re·prov·ing·ly** *adv.*

rep·tile /'reptəl; 'rep,tīl/ ▶*n.* **1** a cold-blooded vertebrate of a class that includes snakes, lizards, crocodiles, turtles, and tortoises. They are distinguished by having a dry scaly skin, and typically laying soft-shelled eggs on land. • Class Reptilia: orders Chelonia (turtles and tortoises), Squamata (snakes and lizards), Rhynchocephalia (the tuatara), and Crocodylia (crocodilians). Among several extinct groups are the dinosaurs, pterosaurs, and ichthyosaurs. **2** *informal* a person regarded with loathing and contempt.

▶*adj.* [*attrib.*] belonging to a reptile or to the class of reptiles: *reptile eggs.* ▷late Middle English: from late Latin, neuter of *reptilis,* from Latin *rept-* 'crawled,' from the verb *repere.* —**rep·til·i·an** /rep'tilēən; -'tilyən/ *adj.* & *n.*

Repub. ▶*abbr.* ■ Republic. ■ Republican.

re·pub·lic /ri'pəblik/ ▶*n.* a state in which supreme power is held by the people and their elected representatives, and which has an elected or nominated president rather than a monarch. ■ *archaic, figurative* a community or group with a certain equality between its members. ▷late 16th cent.: from French *république,* from Latin *respublica,* from *res* 'concern' + *publicus* 'of the people, public.'

re·pub·li·can /ri'pəblikən/ ▶*adj.* (of a form of government, constitution, etc.) belonging to, or characteristic of a republic. ■ advocating or supporting republican government: *the republican movement.*

▶*n.* **1** a person advocating or supporting republican government. **2** (**Republican**) a member or supporter of the Republican Party. —**re·pub·li·can·ism** /-,nizəm/ *n.*

Re·pub·li·can Par·ty one of the two main U.S. political parties (the other being the Democratic Party), favoring a conservative stance, limited central government, and a strong national defense.

Re·pub·li·can Riv·er a river that flows for 445 miles (715 km) from northeastern Colorado through southern Nebraska and into Kansas where it joins the Smoky Hill River to form the Kansas River.

Re·pub·lic of Kal·myk·i·a-Khalmg Tangch official name for **KALMYKIA**.

Re·pub·li·crat /ri'pəbli,krat/ (also **re·pub·li·crat** or **Re·pub·lo·crat**) ▶*n.* a Republican or Democrat whose political philosophy is a blend of policies and principles from both parties: *Republicrats are blurring the differences between our two parties* [as *modifier*] *Republicrat senators.* ■ a member of a political faction that includes both Republicans and Democrats. ■ a conservative Democrat with Republican sympathies. ▷blend of *Republican* and *Democrat.* —**Re·pub·li·crat·ic** /ri,pəbli'kratik/ *adj.*

re·pub·lish /rē'pəblish; 'rē-/ ▶*v.* [*trans.*] (often **be republished**) publish (a text) again, esp. in a new edition. —**republication** /,rē,pəblə'kāshən/ *n.*

re·pu·di·ate /ri'pyo͞odē,āt/ ▶*v.* [*trans.*] refuse to accept or be associated with: *she has repudiated policies associated with previous party leaders.* ■ deny the truth or validity of: *the minister repudiated allegations of human rights abuses.* ■ *chiefly Law* refuse to fulfill or discharge (an agreement, obligation, or debt): *breach of a condition gives the other party the right to repudiate a contract.* ■ (esp. in the past or in non-Christian religions) divorce (one's wife). ▷late Middle English (originally an adjective in the sense 'divorced'): from Latin *repudiatus* 'divorced, cast off,' from *repudium* 'divorce.' —**re·pu·di·a·tion** /ri,pyo͞odē'āshən/ *n.* —**re·pu·di·a·tor** /-,ātər/ *n.*

USAGE See usage at **REFUTE**.

re·pug·nance /ri'pəgnəns/ ▶*n.* **1** intense disgust: *our growing repugnance at the bleeding carcasses.* **2** (also **repugnancy**) inconsistency or incompatibility of ideas or statements. ▷late Middle English (in the sense 'opposition'): from Old French *repugnance* or Latin *repugnantia,* from *repugnare* 'oppose,' from *re-* (expressing opposition) + *pugnare* 'to fight.'

re·pug·nant /ri'pəgnənt/ ▶*adj.* **1** extremely distasteful; unacceptable: *the thought of going back into the fog was* **repugnant to** *him.* See note at **OFFENSIVE**. **2** [*predic.*] (**repugnant to**) in conflict with; incompatible with: *a bylaw must not be repugnant to the general law of the country.* ■ *archaic* or *poetic/literary* given to stubborn resistance. ▷late Middle English (in the sense 'offering resistance'): from Old French *repugnant* or Latin *repugnant-* 'opposing,' from the verb *repugnare* (see **REPUGNANCE**). —**re·pug·nant·ly** *adv.*

re·pulse /ri'pəls/ ▶*v.* [*trans.*] **1** drive back (an attack or attacking enemy) by force: *rioters tried to storm ministry buildings but were repulsed by police.* ■ fail to welcome (friendly advances or the person making them); rebuff: *she left, feeling hurt because she had been repulsed.* ■ refuse to accept (an offer): *his bid for the company was repulsed.* **2** (usu. **be repulsed**) cause (someone) to feel intense distaste and aversion: *audiences at early screenings of the film were repulsed by its brutality.*

▶*n.* the action of driving back an attacking force or of being driven back: *the repulse of the invaders.* ■ a discouraging response to friendly advances: *his evasion of her plan had been another repulse.* ▷late Middle English: from Latin *repuls-* 'driven back,' from the verb *repellere* (see **REPEL**).

re·pul·sion /ri'pəlshən/ ▶*n.* **1** a feeling of intense distaste or disgust: *people talk about the case with a mixture of fascination and repulsion.* **2** *Physics* a force under the influence of which objects tend to move away from each other, e.g., through having the same magnetic polarity or electric charge.

re·pul·sive /ri'pəlsiv/ ▶*adj.* **1** arousing intense distaste or disgust: *a repulsive smell.* ■ *archaic* lacking friendliness or sympathy. **2** of or relating to repulsion between physical objects. —**re·pul·sive·ly** *adv.* —**re·pul·sive·ness** *n.*

USAGE **Repulsive** and **repellent** are very close in meaning, but the former, perhaps because of its sound, is felt to express stronger feeling.

re·pur·chase /rē'pərchəs/ ▶*v.* [*trans.*] buy (something) back.

▶*n.* the action of buying something back. —**re·pur·chas·er** *n.*

re·pur·chase a·gree·ment ▸*n.* *Finance* a contract in which the vendor of a security agrees to repurchase it from the buyer at an agreed price.

re·pur·pose /rē'pərpəs/ ▸*v.* [*trans.*] adapt for use in a different purpose: *they've taken a product that was originally designed for a CD-ROM and repurposed it for the Microsoft Network.*

rep·u·ta·ble /'repyətəbəl/ ▸*adj.* having a good reputation: *a reputable company.* ▷early 17th cent.: from obsolete French, or from medieval Latin *reputabilis,* from Latin *reputare* 'reflect upon' (see REPUTE). —**rep·u·ta·bly** /-blē/ *adv.*

rep·u·ta·tion /,repyə'tāsʜən/ ▸*n.* the beliefs or opinions that are generally held about someone or something: *his reputation was tarnished by allegations that he had taken bribes.* ■ a widespread belief that someone or something has a particular habit or characteristic: *his knowledge of his subject earned him a reputation as an expert.* ▷Middle English: from Latin *reputatio(n-),* from *reputare* 'think over' (see REPUTE).

re·pute /ri'pyo͞ot/ ▸*n.* the opinion generally held of someone or something; the state of being generally regarded in a particular way: *pollution could bring the authority's name into bad repute.* ■ the state of being highly thought of; fame: *chefs of international repute.*
▸*v.* (**be reputed**) be generally said or believed to do something or to have particular characteristics: *he was reputed to have a fabulous house.* ■ [usu. as *adj.*] (**reputed**) be generally said or believed to exist or be of a particular type, despite not being so: *this area gave the lie to the reputed flatness of the country.* ■ [usu. as *adj.*] (**reputed**) be widely known and well thought of: *intensive training with reputed coaches.* ▷late Middle English: from Old French *reputer* or Latin *reputare* 'think over,' from *re-* (expressing intensive force) + *putare* 'think.' —**re·put·ed·ly** *adv.*

req. ▸*abbr.* ■ require. ■ required. ■ requisition.

reqd. ▸*abbr.* required.

re·quest /ri'kwest/ ▸*n.* an act of asking politely or formally for something: *a* **request for** *information | the club's excursion was postponed* **at the request of** *some of the members.* ■ a thing that is asked for: *to have our ideas taken seriously is surely a reasonable request.* ■ an instruction to a computer to provide information or perform another function. ■ a tune or song played on a radio program, in some instances accompanied by a personal message, in response to a letter or call asking for it. ■ *archaic* the state of being sought after: *human intelligence, which is in constant request in a family.*
▸*v.* [*trans.*] politely or formally ask for: *he received the information he had requested* | [with *clause*] *the chairman requested that the reports be considered.* ■ [with *infinitive*] politely ask (someone) to do something: *the letter requested him to report to New York immediately.* ▷Middle English: from Old French *requeste* (noun), based on Latin *requirere* (see REQUIRE). —**re·quest·er** *n.*
▸**PHRASE** □ **by** (or **on**) **request** in response to an expressed wish.

USAGE The verb **request** is a more formal word than **ask.** Unlike **ask,** esp. in edited prose, **request** usually sounds better when followed by the conjunction *that,* rather than the infinitive *to.* Thus: *we requested that the staff prepare the suites* (rather than *we requested the staff to prepare the suites*), or *Hilda requested that he not drive across the lawn* (rather than *Hilda requested him not to drive . . .*). This is not a strict rule limiting uses of the verbs **request** and **ask;** it is more a matter of style and preference.

req·ui·em /'rekwēəm; 'rā-/ ▸*n.* (also **req·ui·em mass**) (esp. in the Roman Catholic Church) a Mass for the repose of the souls of the dead. ■ a musical composition setting parts of such a Mass, or of a similar character. ■ an act or token of remembrance: *he designed the epic as a requiem for his wife.* ▷Middle English: from Latin (first word of the Mass), accusative of *requies* 'rest.'

req·ui·em shark ▸*n.* a migratory, livebearing shark of warm seas, sometimes also found in brackish or fresh water. • Family Carcharhinidae: many species, including the tiger shark, blue shark, and tope. ▷mid 17th cent.: from obsolete French *requiem,* variant of *requin* 'shark,' influenced by REQUIEM.

re·qui·es·cat /,rekwē'es,kät; ,rā-/ ▸*n.* a wish or prayer for the repose of a dead person. ▷Latin, from *requiescat in pace* (see RIP[1]).

re·quin·to /rā'kēntō/ ▸*n.* (*pl.* **-tos**) (in Spanish-speaking regions) a small guitar, typically tuned a fifth higher than a standard guitar. ▷Spanish, literally 'second fifth subtracted from a quantity.'

re·quire /ri'kwīr/ ▸*v.* [*trans.*] need for a particular purpose; depend on for success or survival: *three patients required operations.* ■ cause to be necessary: *it would have required much research to produce a comprehensive list.* ■ specify as compulsory: *the minimum car insurance required by law.* ■ [*trans.*] (of someone in authority) instruct or expect (someone) to do something: *you will be required to attend for cross-examination.* ■ (**require something of**) regard an action, ability, or quality as due from (someone) by virtue of their position: *the care and diligence required of him as a trustee.* ■ wish to have: *please indicate how many tickets you require.* ▷late Middle English: from Old French *requere,* from Latin *requirere,* from *re-* (expressing intensive force) + *quaerere* 'seek.' —**re·quire·ment** *n.* —**re·quir·er** *n.*

req·ui·site /'rekwəzət/ ▸*adj.* made necessary by particular circumstances or regulations: *the application will not be processed until the requisite fee is paid.* See note at NECESSARY.
▸*n.* a thing that is necessary for the achievement of a specified end: *she believed privacy to be a* **requisite for** *a peaceful life.* ▷late Middle English: from Latin *requisitus* 'searched for, deemed necessary,' past participle of *requirere* (see REQUIRE). —**req·ui·site·ly** *adv.*

req·ui·si·tion /,rekwə'zisʜən/ ▸*n.* an official order laying claim to the use of property or materials: *I had to make various requisitions for staff and accommodations.* ■ a formal written demand that some duty should be performed or something be put into operation. ■ the appropriation of goods, esp. for military or public use.
▸*v.* [*trans.*] demand the use or supply of, esp. by official order and for military or public use: *the government had assumed powers to requisition cereal products at fixed prices.* ■ demand the performance or occurrence of: *one of the investors has requisitioned a special meeting.* ▷late Middle English (as a noun in the sense 'request, demand'): from Old French, or from Latin *requisitio(n-),* from *requirere* 'search for' (see REQUIRE). The verb dates from the mid 19th cent. —**req·ui·si·tion·er** *n.*

re·quite /ri'kwīt/ ▸*v.* [*trans.*] *formal* make appropriate return for (a favor or service); reward: *they are quick to requite a kindness.* ■ avenge or retaliate for (an injury or wrong). ■ return a favor to (someone): *to win enough to requite my friends.* ■ respond to (love or affection); return: *she did not requite his love.* ▷early 16th cent.: from RE- 'back' + obsolete *quite,* variant of the verb QUIT[1]. —**re·quit·al** /-'kwītl/ *n.*

re·ran /rē'ran/ ▸ past of RERUN.

re·rate /rē'rāt/ ▸*v.* [*trans.*] rate or assess (something, especially shares or a company) again: *the company could be rerated as its share price had not rebounded.*

re-re·cord /,rē ri'kôrd/ ▸*v.* [*trans.*] record (sound, esp. music) again: *the sound will then be rerecorded in binaural stereo. | rerecording a record without a license is illegal* | [as *adj.*] (**rerecorded**) *the track is a rerecorded version of a song from their recent album.*

rere·dos /'rerə,däs; 'ri(ə)rə-/ ▸*n.* (*pl.* same) *Christian Church* an ornamental screen covering the wall at the back of an altar. ▷late Middle English: from Anglo-Norman French, from Old French *areredos,* from *arere* 'behind' + *dos* 'back.'

re·re·lease /,rē-ri'lēs/ (also **re-re·lease**) ▸*v.* [*trans.*] release (a recording or movie) again: *he is rereleasing his 1983 hit single.*
▸*n.* the action of releasing a recording or movie again: *the rerelease of Disney's 1937 classic.* ■ a recording or movie that is released for a second or subsequent time.

reroof /rē'ro͞of; -'ro͝of/ ▸*v.* [*trans.*] provide (a building) with a new or substantially repaired roof.

re·route /rē'ro͞ot; rē'rout/ ▸*v.* [*trans.*] send (someone or something) by or along a different route: *the police had rerouted the march.*

re·run ▸*v.* /rē'rən/ (**-run·ning;** *past* **-ran;** *past part.* **-run**) [*trans.*] show or perform (something, esp. a television program) again.
▸*n.* /'rē,rən/ a program, event, or competition that occurs or is run again: ***a rerun of*** *the Mideast crisis | watching reruns on TV.*

RES ▸*abbr.* reticuloendothelial system.

res. ▸*abbr.* ■ research. ■ reserve. ■ residence or residents. ■ resigned. ■ resolution.

re·sale /'rē,sāl/ ▸*n.* the sale of a thing previously bought: *he is renovating them for resale* | [as *adj.*] *resale value.* —**re·sal·a·ble** /rē'sāləbəl/ (also **re·sale·a·ble**) *adj.*

re·scale /rē'skāl/ ▸*v.* [*trans.*] alter the scale of (something), typically to make it smaller or simpler: *a report to the State Education Department urging that all the science exams be rescaled.*

re·sched·ule /rē'skejo͞o(ə)l/ ▸*v.* [*trans.*] change the time of (a planned event): *the concert has been rescheduled for September.* ■ arrange a new scheme of repayments of (a debt).

re·scind /ri'sind/ ▸*v.* [*trans.*] revoke, cancel, or repeal (a law, order, or agreement): *the government eventually rescinded the directive.* ▷mid 16th cent.: from Latin *rescindere,* from *re-* (expressing intensive force) + *scindere* 'to divide, split.' —**re·scind·a·ble** *adj.*

re·scis·sion /ri'sizʜən/ ▸*n.* *formal* the revocation, cancellation, or repeal of a law, order, or agreement. ▷mid 17th cent.: from late Latin *rescissio(n-),* from *resciss-* 'split again,' from the verb *rescindere* (see RESCIND).

re·script /'rē,skript/ ▸*n.* **1** an official edict or announcement. ■ *historical* a Roman emperor's written reply to an appeal for guidance, esp. on a legal point. ■ the pope's decision on a question of Roman Catholic doctrine or papal law. **2** an official or formal reply to a question. ▷late Middle English (denoting a papal decision): from Latin *rescriptum,* neuter past participle of *rescribere* 'write back,' from *re-* 'back' + *scribere* 'write.'

res·cue /'reskyo͞o/ ▸*v.* (**-cues, -cued, -cu·ing**) [*trans.*] save (someone) from a dangerous or distressing situation: *firemen were called out to rescue a man trapped in the river.* ■ *informal* keep from being lost or abandoned; retrieve: *he got out of his chair to rescue his cup of coffee.*
▸*n.* an act of saving or being saved from danger or distress: *he* ***came to our rescue*** *with a loan of $100.* ■ [as *adj.*] denoting the emergency excavation of archaeological sites threatened by imminent building or road development. ▷Middle English: from Old French *rescoure,* from Latin *re-* (expressing intensive force) + *excutere* 'shake out, discard.' —**res·cu·a·ble** *adj.* —**res·cu·er** *n.*

re·search /'rē,sərcʜ; ri'sərcʜ/ ▸*n.* the systematic investigation into and study of materials and sources in order to establish facts and reach new conclusions: *we are fighting meningitis by raising money for medical research.* ■ (**researches**) acts or periods of such investigation: *his pathological researches were included in official reports.* ■ [as *adj.*] engaged in or intended for use in such investigation and discovery: *a research student | a research paper.*
▸*v.* [*trans.*] investigate systematically: *the biographer spent 25 years researching Stalin's life* | [*intrans.*] *the team has been* **researching into** *flora and fauna.* ■ discover facts by investigation for use in (a book, program, etc.): *I was in New York researching my novel* | [as *adj.,* with *submodifier*] (**researched**) *this is a well-researched and readable account.* ▷late 16th cent.: from obsolete French *recerche* (noun), *recercher* (verb), from Old French *re-* (expressing intensive force) + *cerchier* 'to search.' —**re·search·a·ble** *adj.* —**re·search·er** *n.*

USAGE The traditional pronunciation in British English puts the stress on the second syllable, **-search.** In U.S. English, the stress much more often comes on the **re-**. The U.S. pronunciation is becoming more common in British English and, while some traditionalists view it as incorrect, it is now generally accepted as a standard variant of British English.

re·search and de·vel·op·ment ▸*n.* (in industry) work directed toward the innovation, introduction, and improvement of products and processes.

Re·search Tri·an·gle Park a research complex in central North Carolina, between Durham, Raleigh, and Chapel Hill, that was created in the 1950s by Duke and North Carolina State universities and the University of North Carolina.

re·seat /rē'sēt/ ▸*v.* [*trans.*] **1** cause (someone) to sit down again after they have risen: *he reseated himself in his armchair.* ■ cause to sit in a new position: *we reseated the orchestra for each variation.* ■ realign or repair (a tap, valve, or other object) in order to fit it into its correct position. **2** equip with new seats: *the coaches were reseated last year to increase capacity.*

ré·seau /rā'zō; ri-/ ▸*n.* (*pl.* **-seaux** /-'zōz/) a network or grid. ■ a plain net ground used in lacemaking. ■ a reference marking pattern on a photograph, used in astronomy and surveying. ■ a spy or intelligence network, esp. in the French resistance movement during the German occupation in World War II.

▷late 16th cent. (as a term in lacemaking): French, literally 'net, web.'

re·sect /ri'sekt/ ▸*v.* [*trans.*] [often as *adj.*] (**resected**) *Surgery* cut out (tissue or part of an organ): *a small piece of resected colon.* ▷mid 17th cent. (in the sense 'remove, cut away'): from Latin *resect-* 'cut off,' from the verb *resecare*, from *re-* 'back' + *secare* 'to cut.' **—re·sect·a·ble** *adj.* **—re·sec·tion** /ri'sekSHən/ *n.* **—re·sec·tion·al** /-SHənl/ *adj.* **—re·sec·tion·ist** /-SHənist/ *n.*

re·se·da /rə'sēdə; 'rāzə,dä/ ▸*n.* **1** a plant of the genus *Reseda* (family Resedaceae), esp. (in gardening) a mignonette. **2** the pale green color of mignonette flowers.
▸*adj.* pale green. ▷mid 18th cent.: from Latin, interpreted in the sense 'assuage!,' imperative of *resedare*, with reference to its supposed curative powers.

re·seed /rē'sēd/ ▸*v.* [*trans.*] sow (an area of land) with seed, esp. grass seed, again.

re·sell /rē'sel/ ▸*v.* (*past* and *past part.* **-sold**) [*trans.*] sell (something one has bought) to someone else: *products can be resold on the black market for huge profits.* **—reseller** *n.*

re·sem·blance /ri'zembləns/ ▸*n.* the state of resembling or being alike: *they* ***bear*** *some* ***resemblance to*** *Italian figurines.* See note at **LIKENESS**. ■ a way in which two or more things are alike: *the physical resemblances between humans and apes.* ▷Middle English: from Anglo-Norman French, from the verb *resembler* (see **RESEMBLE**).

re·sem·ble /ri'zembəl/ ▸*v.* [*trans.*] have qualities or features, esp. those of appearance, in common with (someone or something); look or seem like: *some people resemble their dogs | they seemed to* ***resemble each other*** *closely.* ▷Middle English: from Old French *resembler*, based on Latin *similare* (from *similis* 'like'). **—re·sem·bler** /-blər/ *n.* (*rare*).

re·sent /ri'zent/ ▸*v.* [*trans.*] feel bitterness or indignation at (a circumstance, action, or person): *she resented the fact that I had children.* ▷late 16th cent.: from obsolete French *resentir*, from *re-* (expressing intensive force) + *sentir* 'feel' (from Latin *sentire*). The early sense was 'experience (an emotion or sensation),' later 'feel deeply,' giving rise to 'feel aggrieved by.'

re·sent·ful /ri'zentfəl/ ▸*adj.* feeling or expressing bitterness or indignation at having been treated unfairly: *he was angry and* ***resentful of*** *their intrusion.* **—re·sent·ful·ly** *adv.* **—re·sent·ful·ness** *n.*

re·sent·ment /ri'zentmənt/ ▸*n.* bitter indignation at having been treated unfairly: *his* ***resentment at*** *being demoted | some people harbor resentments going back many years.* ▷early 17th cent.: from Italian *risentimento* or French *ressentiment*, from obsolete French *resentir* (see **RESENT**).

re·ser·pine /ri'sər,pēn; -pən/ ▸*n.* *Medicine* a compound of the alkaloid class obtained from Indian snakeroot and other plants and used in the treatment of hypertension. ▷1950s: from the modern Latin species name *R(auwolfia) serp(entina)*, named after Leonhard Rauwolf (see **RAUWOLFIA**), + **-INE**[4].

res·er·va·tion /,rezər'vāSHən/ ▸*n.* **1** the action of reserving something: *the reservation of positions for non-Americans.* ■ an arrangement whereby something, esp. a seat or room, is booked or reserved for a particular person: *do you have a reservation?* ■ an area of land set aside for occupation by North American Indians or Australian Aboriginals. ■ *Law* a right or interest retained in an estate being conveyed. ■ (in the Roman Catholic Church) the practice of retaining a portion of the consecrated elements after mass for communion of the sick or as a focus for devotion. **2** a qualification to an expression of agreement or approval; a doubt: *some generals voiced reservations about making air strikes.* **3** (in the Roman Catholic Church) the action of a superior of reserving to himself the power of absolution. ■ a right reserved to the pope of nomination to a vacant benefice. ▷late Middle English (denoting the pope's right of nomination to a benefice): from Old French, or from late Latin *reservatio(n-)*, from *reservare* 'keep back' (see **RESERVE**).

re·serve /ri'zərv/ ▸*v.* [*trans.*] refrain from using or disposing of (something); retain for future use: *roll out half the dough and reserve the other half.* ■ arrange for (a room, seat, ticket, etc.) to be kept for the use of a particular person and not given to anyone else: *a place was reserved for her in the front row.* ■ retain or hold (an entitlement to something), esp. by formal or legal stipulation: [*trans.*] *the editor reserves the right to edit letters.* ■ refrain from delivering (a judgment or decision) immediately or without due consideration or evidence: *I'll reserve my views on his ability until he's played again.* ■ (**reserve something for**) use or engage in something only in or at (a particular circumstance or time): *Japanese food has been presented as expensive and reserved for special occasions.* ■ (in church use) retain (a portion of the consecrated elements) after mass for communion of the sick or as a focus for devotion.
▸*n.* **1** (often **reserves**) a supply of a commodity not needed for immediate use but available if required: *Australia has major coal, gas, and uranium reserves.* ■ a force or body of troops kept back from action to reinforce or protect others, or additional to the regular forces and available in an emergency. ■ a member of the military reserve. ■ an extra player who is a possible substitute in a team. ■ (**the reserves**) the second-string team. ■ funds kept available by a bank, company, or government: *the foreign exchange reserves.* ■ a part of a company's profits added to capital rather than paid as a dividend. **2** a place set aside for special use, in particular: ■ an area designated as a habitat for a native people. ■ a protected area for wildlife. **3** a lack of warmth or openness in manner or expression: *she smiled and some of her natural reserve melted.* ■ qualification or doubt attached to some statement or claim: *she trusted him* ***without reserve.*** **4** short for **RESERVE PRICE**. **5** (in the decoration of ceramics or textiles) an area that still has the original color of the material or the color of the background. ▷Middle English: from Old French *reserver*, from Latin *reservare* 'keep back,' from *re-* 'back' + *servare* 'to keep.' **—re·serv·a·ble** *adj.* **—re·serv·er** *n.*
▸*PHRASE* □ **in reserve** unused and available if required: *the platoon that had been kept in reserve.*

re·serve /rē 'sərv; 'rē-/ ▸*v.* [*intrans.*] (in various sports) serve again.

re·serve bank ▸*n.* a regional bank operating under and implementing the policies of the U.S. Federal Reserve.

re·served /ri'zərvd/ ▸*adj.* **1** slow to reveal emotion or opinions: *he is a reserved, almost taciturn man.* **2** kept specially for a particular purpose or person: *a reserved seat.* **—re·serv·ed·ly** /ri'zərvədlē/ *adv.* **—re·serv·ed·ness** /ri'zərvədnəs/ *n.*

re·served word ▸*n.* *Computing* a word in a programming language that has a fixed meaning and cannot be redefined by the programmer.

re·serve price ▸*n.* the price stipulated as the lowest acceptable by the seller for an item sold at auction.

re·serv·ist /ri'zərvist/ ▸*n.* a member of the military reserve forces.

res·er·voir /'rezə(r),vwär; -,v(w)ôr/ ▸*n.* a large natural or artificial lake used as a source of water supply. ■ a supply or source of something: *tapping into a universal reservoir of information.* ■ [usu. with *adj.*] a place where fluid collects, esp. in rock strata or in the body. ■ a receptacle or part of a machine designed to hold fluid. ■ *Medicine* a population, tissue, etc., that is chronically infested with the causative agent of a disease and can act as a source of further infection. ▷mid 17th cent.: from French *réservoir*, from *réserver* 'to reserve, keep.'

re·set /rē'set/ ▸*v.* (**-set·ting**; *past* and *past part.* **-set**) [*trans.*] set again or differently: *I must reset the alarm.* ■ *Electronics* cause (a binary device) to enter the state representing the numeral 0. **—re·set·ta·bil·i·ty** /,rē-,setə'bilətē/ *n.* **—re·set·ta·ble** *adj.*

re·set·tle /rē'setl/ ▸*v.* settle or cause to settle in a different place: [*trans.*] *they offered to resettle 300,000 refugees |* [*intrans.*] *144,000 East Germans had resettled in West Germany.* **—re·set·tle·ment** *n.*

res ges·tae /'rās 'ges,tī; 'rēz 'jestē/ ▸*plural n.* *Law* the events, circumstances, remarks, etc., that relate to a particular case, esp. as constituting admissible evidence in a court of law. ▷Latin, literally 'things done.'

re·shoot /rē'SHo͞ot/ ▸*v.* (*past* and *past part.* **-shot**) [*trans.*] shoot (a scene of a film) again or differently: *they had to reshoot the whole thing with another actor |* [*intrans.*] *the insurance was enough to allow them to reshoot or finish with a double.*
▸*n.* an act of reshooting a scene of a film: *the reshoot is scheduled for Thursday.*

re·shuf·fle /rē'SHəfəl/ ▸*v.* [*trans.*] reorganize or change the positions of (government appointees, members of a team, etc.): *the president was forced to reshuffle his cabinet.* ■ put in a new order; rearrange: *genetic constituents are constantly reshuffled into individual organisms.* ■ shuffle playing cards again: *Youngman is requesting that Garcia reshuffle the cards. |* [*intrans.*] *too many pairs are coming up—you better reshuffle.*
▸*n.* an act of reorganizing or rearranging something: *he was brought into the government in the last reshuffle.*

re·side /ri'zīd/ ▸*v.* [*intrans.*] have one's permanent home in a particular place: *people who work in the city actually reside in neighboring towns.* ■ be situated: *the paintings now reside on the walls of a restaurant.* ■ (of power or a right) belong by right to a person or body: *legislative powers reside with the federal assembly.* ■ (of a quality) be present or inherent in something: *the meaning of an utterance does not wholly reside in the semantic meaning.* ▷late Middle English (in the sense 'be in residence as an official'): probably a back-formation from **RESIDENT**, influenced by French *résider* or Latin *residere* 'remain,' from *re-* 'back' + *sedere* 'sit.'

res·i·dence /'rez(ə)dəns; 'rezə,dens/ ▸*n.* a person's home; the place where someone lives. ■ the official house of a government minister or other public and official figure. ■ the fact of living in a particular place: *Rome was his main place of residence.* ▷late Middle English (denoting the fact of living in a place): from Old French, or from medieval Latin *residentia*, from Latin *residere* 'remain' (see **RESIDE**).
▸*PHRASES* □ **in residence** living in or occupying a particular place: *the guests in residence at the hotel.* ■ (**—— in residence**) a person with a particular occupation (esp. an artist or writer) paid to work in a college or other institution. □ **take up residence** start living in a particular place.

res·i·dence time ▸*n.* *technical* the average length of time during which a substance, a portion of material, or an object is in a given location or condition, such as adsorption or suspension.

res·i·den·cy /'rez(ə)dənsē; 'rezə,densē/ ▸*n.* (*pl.* **-cies**) **1** the fact of living in a place: *a government ruling confirmed the returning refugees' right to residency.* ■ a residential post held by a writer, musician, or artist, typically for teaching purposes. **2** *historical* the official residence of the British governor general's representative or other government agent, esp. at the court of an Indian state. ■ a group or organization of intelligence agents in a foreign country. **3** a period of specialized medical training in a hospital; the position of a resident.

res·i·dent /'rez(ə)dənt; 'rezə,dent/ ▸*n.* **1** a person who lives somewhere permanently or on a long-term basis. ■ a bird, butterfly, or other animal of a species that does not migrate. ■ a person who boards at a boarding school. ■ *historical* a British government agent in any semi-independent state, esp. the governor general's agent at the court of an Indian state. **2** a medical graduate engaged in specialized practice under supervision in a hospital.
▸*adj.* living somewhere on a long-term basis: *he has* ***been resident in*** *Brazil for a long time.* ■ living at a school or institution: *resident students.* ■ having quarters on the premises of one's work: *resident farm workers.* ■ attached to and working regularly for a particular institution: *the film studio needed a resident historian.* ■ (of a bird, butterfly, or other animal) nonmigratory; remaining in an area throughout the year. ■ (of a computer program, file, etc.) immediately available in computer memory, rather than having to be loaded from elsewhere. ▷Middle English: from Latin *resident-* 'remaining,' from the verb *residere* (see **RESIDE**). **—res·i·dent·ship** /-,SHip/ *n.* (*historical*).

res·i·dent com·mis·sion·er ▸*n.* a delegate elected to represent a dependency, such as Puerto Rico, in the U.S. House of Representatives. They are able to speak in the House and serve on committees, but may not vote.

res·i·den·tial /,rezə'denCHəl/ ▸*adj.* designed for people to live in: *private residential and nursing homes.* ■ providing accommodations in addition to other services: *a residential college.* ■ occupied by private houses: *quieter traffic in residential areas.* ■ concerning or relating to residence: *land has been diverted from residential use.* **—res·i·den·tial·ly** *adv.*

res·i·den·ti·ar·y /,rezə'denCHē,erē; -'denCHərē/ ▸*adj.* required to live officially in a cathedral or collegiate church. ■ relating to or involving residence in an establishment or place.
▸*n.* (*pl.* **-ar·ies**) a residentiary canon. ▷early 16th cent. (as a noun): from medieval Latin *residentiarius*, from Latin *resident-* 'remaining' (see **RESIDENT**).

re·sid·u·a /ri'zijo͞oə/ ▸ plural form of **RESIDUUM**.

re·sid·u·al /ri'zijo͞oəl/ ▸*adj.* remaining after the greater part or quantity has gone: *the withdrawal of residual occupying forces.* ■ (of a quantity) left after other things have been subtracted: *residual income after tax and mortgage payments.* ■ (of a physical state or property) remaining after the removal of or present in

the absence of a causative agent: *residual stenosis.* ■ (of an experimental or arithmetical error) not accounted for or eliminated. ■ (of a soil or other deposit) formed in situ by weathering.
▸*n.* a quantity remaining after other things have been subtracted or allowed for. ■ a difference between a value measured in a scientific experiment and the theoretical or true value. ■ a royalty paid to a performer, writer, etc., for a repeat of a play, television show, etc. ■ *Geology* a portion of rocky or high ground remaining after erosion. ■ the resale value of a new car or other item at a specified time after purchase, expressed as a percentage of its purchase price. —**re·sid·u·al·ly** *adv.*

re·sid·u·al stress ▸*n. Physics* the stress present in an object in the absence of any external load or force.

re·sid·u·ar·y /ri'zijo͞oˌerē/ ▸*adj. technical* residual. ■ *Law* of or relating to the residue of an estate: *a residuary legatee.* ▷early 18th cent.: from RESIDUUM + -ARY[1].

res·i·due /'rezəˌd(y)o͞o/ ▸*n.* a small amount of something that remains after the main part has gone or been taken or used. ■ *Law* the part of an estate that is left after the payment of charges, debts, and bequests. ■ a substance that remains after a process such as combustion or evaporation. ▷late Middle English: from Old French *residu*, from Latin *residuum* 'something remaining' (see RESIDUUM).

re·sid·u·um /ri'zijo͞oəm/ ▸*n.* (*pl.* **-sid·u·a** /-'zijo͞oə/) *technical* a substance or thing that remains or is left behind, in particular, a chemical residue. ▷late 17th cent.: from Latin, neuter of *residuus* 'remaining,' from the verb *residere.*

re·sign /ri'zīn/ ▸*v.* **1** [*intrans.*] voluntarily leave a job or other position: *he* **resigned from** *the government in protest at the policy.* ■ [*trans.*] give up (an office, power, privilege, etc.): *four deputies resigned their seats.* ■ [*intrans.*] *Chess* end a game by conceding defeat without being checkmated: *he lost his queen and resigned in 45 moves.* **2** (**be resigned**) accept that something undesirable cannot be avoided: *he seems* **resigned to** *a shortened career | she* **resigned herself to** *a lengthy session.* ■ *archaic* surrender oneself to another's guidance: *he vows to resign himself to her direction.* ▷late Middle English: from Old French *resigner*, from Latin *resignare* 'unseal, cancel,' from *re-* 'back' + *signare* 'sign, seal.' —**re·sign·ed·ly** /ri'zīnədlē/ *adv.* —**re·sign·ed·ness** /ri'zīnədnəs/ *n.* —**re·sign·er** *n.*

re-sign /rē'sīn/ ▸*v.* [*trans.*] sign (a document) again. ■ engage (a sports player) to play for a team for a further period. ■ [*intrans.*] (of a sports player) commit oneself to play for a team for a further period.

res·ig·na·tion /ˌrezig'nāsʜən/ ▸*n.* **1** an act of retiring or giving up a position: *he announced his resignation.* ■ a document conveying someone's intention of retiring: *I'm thinking of handing in my resignation.* ■ *Chess* an act of ending a game by conceding defeat without being checkmated. **2** the acceptance of something undesirable but inevitable: *a shrug of resignation.* ▷late Middle English: via Old French from medieval Latin *resignatio(n-)*, from *resignare* 'unseal, cancel' (see RESIGN).

re·sile /ri'zīl/ ▸*v.* [*intrans.*] *formal* abandon a position or a course of action: *can he* **resile from** *the agreement?* ▷early 16th cent.: from obsolete French *resilir* or Latin *resilire* 'to recoil,' from *re-* 'back' + *salire* 'to jump.'

re·sil·ient /ri'zilyənt/ ▸*adj.* (of a substance or object) able to recoil or spring back into shape after bending, stretching, or being compressed. See note at FLEXIBLE. ■ (of a person or animal) able to withstand or recover quickly from difficult conditions: *the fish are* **resilient to** *most infections.* ▷mid 17th cent.: from Latin *resilient-* 'leaping back,' from the verb *resilire* (see RESILE). —**re·sil·ience** *n.* —**re·sil·ien·cy** *n.* —**re·sil·ient·ly** *adv.*

res·i·lin /'rezələn/ ▸*n. Biochemistry* an elastic material formed of cross-linked protein chains, found in insect cuticles, esp. in the hinges and ligaments of wings. ▷1960s: from Latin *resilire* 'leap back, recoil' + -IN[1].

res·in /'rezən/ ▸*n.* a sticky flammable organic substance, insoluble in water, exuded by some trees and other plants (notably fir and pine). Compare with GUM[1] (sense 1). ■ (also **syn·thet·ic res·in**) a solid or liquid synthetic organic polymer used as the basis of plastics, adhesives, varnishes, or other products.
▸*v.* (**res·ined, res·in·ing**) [*trans.*] [usu. as *adj.*] (**resined**) rub or treat with resin: *resined canvas.* ▷late Middle English: from Latin *resina*; related to Greek *rhētinē* 'pine resin.' Compare with ROSIN. —**res·in·ous** /'rezənəs/ *adj.*

res·in·ate ▸*v.* /'rezəˌnāt/ [*trans.*] impregnate or flavor with resin: [as *adj.*] (**resinated**) *resinated white wine.*
▸*n.* /'rezənit/ *Chemistry* a salt of an acid derived from resin.

res ip·sa lo·qui·tur /ˌrēz ˌipsə 'läkwitər; ˌrās; 'lōkwəˌto͝or/ ▸*n. Law* the principle that the occurrence of an accident implies negligence. ▷Latin, literally 'the matter speaks for itself.'

re·sist /ri'zist/ ▸*v.* [*trans.*] withstand the action or effect of: *antibodies help us to resist infection.* ■ try to prevent by action or argument: *we will continue to resist changes to the treaty.* ■ succeed in ignoring the attraction of (something wrong or unwise): *she resisted his advances | I couldn't resist buying the blouse.* ■ [*intrans.*] struggle against someone or something: *without giving her time to resist, he dragged her off her feet.*
▸*n.* a resistant substance applied as a coating to protect a surface during some process, for example to prevent dye or glaze adhering. ▷late Middle English: from Old French *resister* or Latin *resistere*, from *re-* (expressing opposition) + *sistere* 'stop' (reduplication of *stare* 'to stand'). The current sense of the noun dates from the mid 19th cent. —**re·sist·er** *n.* —**re·sist·i·ble** *adj.* —**re·sist·i·bil·i·ty** /riˌzistə'bilətē/ *n.*

re·sist·ance /ri'zistəns/ ▸*n.* **1** the refusal to accept or comply with something; the attempt to prevent something by action or argument: *she* **put up** *no* **resistance to** *being led away.* ■ armed or violent opposition: *government forces were unable to crush guerrilla-style resistance.* ■ (also **re·sist·ance move·ment**) [in *sing.*] a secret organization resisting authority, esp. in an occupied country. ■ (**the Resistance**) the underground movement formed in France during World War II to fight the German occupying forces and the Vichy government. Also called MAQUIS. ■ the impeding, slowing, or stopping effect exerted by one material thing on another: *air resistance would need to be reduced by streamlining.* **2** the ability not to be affected by something, esp. adversely: *some of us have a lower resistance to cold than others.* ■ *Medicine & Biology* lack of sensitivity to a drug, insecticide, etc., esp. as a result of continued exposure or genetic change. **3** the degree to which a substance or device opposes the passage of an electric current, causing energy dissipation. Ohm's law resistance (measured in ohms) is equal to the voltage divided by the current. ■ a resistor or other circuit component that opposes the passage of an electric current. ▷late Middle English: from French *résistance*, from late Latin *resistentia*, from the verb *resistere* 'hold back' (see RESIST).
▸*PHRASE* □ **the line** (or **path**) **of least resistance** an option avoiding difficulty or unpleasantness; the easiest course of action.

re·sist·ant /ri'zistənt/ ▸*adj.* offering resistance to something or someone: *some of the old churches are* **resistant to** *change* | [in *combination*] *a water-resistant adhesive.*

re·sis·tive /ri'zistiv/ ▸*adj. technical* able to withstand the action or effect of something. ■ *Physics* of or concerning electrical resistance.

re·sis·tiv·i·ty /riˌzis'tivətē/ ▸*n. Physics* a measure of the resisting power of a specified material to the flow of an electric current.

re·sist·less /ri'zistlis/ ▸*adj. archaic* powerful and irresistible: *a resistless impulse.* ■ powerless to resist the effect of someone or something; unresisting. —**re·sist·less·ly** *adv.*

re·sis·tor /ri'zistər/ ▸*n. Physics* a device having a designed resistance to the passage of an electric current.

re·size /rē'sīz/ ▸*v.* [*trans.*] alter the size of (something, esp. a computer window or image).

res ju·di·ca·ta /ˌrēz ˌjo͞odi'kätə; ˌrās/ ▸*n.* (*pl.* **res ju·di·ca·tae** /ˌjo͞odi'kätē; -tī/) *Law* a matter that has been adjudicated by a competent court and may not be pursued further by the same parties. ▷Latin, literally 'judged matter.'

re·skin /rē'skin/ ▸*v.* (**-skinned, -skin·ning**) [*trans.*] replace or repair the skin of (an aircraft or motor vehicle).

Res·nais /rə'nā; rə'ne/, Alain (1922–), French movie director. One of the foremost directors of the *nouvelle vague*, he used experimental techniques to explore memory and time. Notable movies: *Hiroshima mon amour* (1959) and *L'Amour à mort* (1984).

re·sold /rē'sōld/ ▸ past and past participle of RESELL.

re·sol·u·ble[1] /ri'zälyəbəl/ ▸*adj. archaic* able to be resolved. ▷early 17th cent.: from French *résoluble* or late Latin *resolubilis*, based on Latin *solvere* 'release, loosen.'

re·sol·u·ble[2] ▸*adj.* able to dissolve or be dissolved again: *the resoluble nature of the paint.*

res·o·lute /'rezəˌlo͞ot; -lət/ ▸*adj.* admirably purposeful, determined, and unwavering: *she was resolute and unswerving.* ▷late Middle English (in the sense 'paid,' describing a rent): from Latin *resolutus* 'loosened, released, paid,' past participle of *resolvere* (see RESOLVE). —**res·o·lute·ly** *adv.* —**res·o·lute·ness** *n.*

THE RIGHT WORD **constant, decisive, determined, faithful, resolute, staunch**

Any of the above adjectives might apply to you if you take a stand on something and stick to it, or show your loyalty to a person, country, or cause.

If you show unswerving loyalty to someone or something you are tied to (as in marriage, friendship, etc.), you would be described as **faithful** (*a faithful wife; a faithful Republican*).

Constant also implies a firm or steady attachment to someone or something, but with less emphasis on vows, pledges, and obligations; it is the opposite of fickleness rather than of unfaithfulness (*my grandfather's constant confidant*).

To be described as **staunch** carries loyalty one step further, implying an unwillingness to be dissuaded or turned aside (*a staunch friend who refused to believe the rumors that were circulating*).

To be called **resolute** means that you are both staunch and steadfast, but the emphasis here is on character and a firm adherence to your own goals and purposes rather than to those of others (*resolute in insisting upon her right to be heard*).

Determined and **decisive** are less forceful words. You can be *decisive* in almost any situation, as long as you have a choice among alternatives and don't hesitate in taking a stand (*decisive as always, she barely glanced at the menu before ordering*).

Determined, unlike *resolute*, suggests a stubborn will rather than a conscious adherence to goals or principles (*he was determined to be home before the holidays*).

res·o·lu·tion /ˌrezə'lo͞osʜən/ ▸*n.* **1** a firm decision to do or not to do something: *she kept her resolution not to see Anne any more | a New Year's resolution.* ■ a formal expression of opinion or intention agreed on by a legislative body, committee, or other formal meeting, typically after taking a vote: *the conference passed two resolutions.* ■ the quality of being determined or resolute: *he handled the last French actions of the war with resolution.* See note at COURAGE. **2** the action of solving a problem, dispute, or contentious matter: *the peaceful resolution of all disputes | a successful resolution to the problem.* ■ *Music* the passing of a discord into a concord during the course of changing harmony. ■ *Medicine* the disappearance of inflammation, or of any other symptom or condition. **3** *chiefly Chemistry* the process of reducing or separating something into its components. ■ *Physics* the replacing of a single force or other vector quantity by two or more jointly equivalent to it. ■ the conversion of something abstract into another form. ■ *Prosody* the substitution of two short syllables for one long one. **4** the smallest interval measurable by a scientific (esp. optical) instrument; the resolving power. ■ the degree of detail visible in a photographic or television image. ▷late Middle English: from Latin *resolutio(n-)*, from *resolvere* 'loosen, release' (see RESOLVE).

re·sol·u·tive /rə'zälyətiv; 'rezəˌlo͞otiv/ ▸*adj. formal* or *archaic* having the power or ability to dissolve or dispel something. ▷late Middle English: from medieval Latin *resolutivus*, from *resolut-* 'released,' from the verb *resolvere* (see RESOLVE).

re·solve /ri'zälv; -'zôlv/ ▸*v.* **1** [*trans.*] settle or find a solution to (a problem, dispute, or contentious matter): *the firm aims to resolve problems within 30 days.* ■ [*trans.*] *Medicine* cause (a symptom or condition) to disperse, subside, or heal: *endoscopic biliary drainage can rapidly resolve jaundice.* ■ [*intrans.*] (of a symptom or condition) disperse, subside, or heal: *symptoms resolved after a median of four weeks.* ■ [*intrans.*] *Music* (of a discord) lead into a concord during the course of harmonic change. ■ [*trans.*] *Music* cause (a discord) to pass into a concord. **2** [*intrans.*] decide firmly on a course of action: [with *infinitive*] *she resolved to call Dana as soon as she got home.* ■ [with *clause*] (of a legislative body, committee, or other formal meeting) make a decision by a formal vote: *the committee*

R

resolved that teachers should make their recommendations without knowledge of test scores | [with *infinitive*] *the conference resolved to support an alliance.* **3** *chiefly Chemistry* separate or cause to be separated into components. ■ [*trans.*] (**resolve something into**) reduce a subject, statement, etc., by mental analysis into (separate elements or a more elementary form): *the ability to resolve facts into their legal categories.* ■ [*intrans.*] (of something seen at a distance) turn into a different form when seen more clearly: *the orange glow* **re-solved itself** *into four lanterns.* ■ [*trans.*] (of optical or photographic equipment) separate or distinguish between (closely adjacent objects): *Hubble was able to resolve six variable stars in M31.* ■ [*trans.*] separately distinguish (peaks in a graph or spectrum). ■ [*trans.*] *Physics* analyze (a force or velocity) into components acting in particular directions.

▶*n.* firm determination to do something: *she received information that strengthened her resolve* | *she intended to stick to her initial resolve.* ■ a formal resolution by a legislative body or public meeting. ▷late Middle English (in the senses 'dissolve, disintegrate' and 'solve (a problem)'): from Latin *resolvere*, from *re-* (expressing intensive force) + *solvere* 'loosen.' **—re·solv·a·bil·i·ty** /ri,zälvə'bilətē; -'zôlvə-/ *n.* **—re·solv·a·ble** *adj.* **—re·solv·er** *n.*

re·solved /ri'zälvd; -'zôlvd/ ▶*adj.* [*predic.*, with *infinitive*] firmly determined to do something: *Constance was resolved not to cry.* **—re·solv·ed·ly** /ri'zälvədlē; -'zôlvədlē/ *adv.*

re·sol·vent /ri'zälvənt; -'zôl-/ *Mathematics* ▶*adj.* denoting an equation, function, or expression that is introduced in order to reach or complete a solution. ▶*n.* an equation, function, or expression of this type.

re·solv·ing pow·er ▶*n.* the ability of an optical instrument or type of film to separate or distinguish small or closely adjacent images. ■ the ability of an electronic device to produce images that can be distinguished.

res·o·nance /'rezənəns/ ▶*n.* the quality in a sound of being deep, full, and reverberating: *the resonance of his voice.* ■ *figurative* the ability to evoke or suggest images, memories, and emotions: *the concepts lose their emotional resonance.* ■ *Physics* the reinforcement or prolongation of sound by reflection from a surface or by the synchronous vibration of a neighboring object. ■ *Mechanics* the condition in which an object or system is subjected to an oscillating force having a frequency close to its own natural frequency. ■ *Physics* the condition in which an electric circuit or device produces the largest possible response to an applied oscillating signal, esp. when its inductive and its capacitative reactances are balanced. ■ *Physics* a short-lived subatomic particle that is an excited state of a more stable particle. ■ *Astronomy* the occurrence of a simple ratio between the periods of revolution of two bodies about a single primary. ■ *Chemistry* the state attributed to certain molecules of having a structure that cannot adequately be represented by a single structural formula but is a composite of two or more structures of higher energy. ▷late Middle English: from Old French, from Latin *resonantia* 'echo,' from *resonare* 'resound' (see **RESONANT**).

res·o·nant /'rezənənt/ ▶*adj.* (of sound) deep, clear, and continuing to sound or ring: *a full-throated and resonant guffaw.* ■ *technical* of, relating to, or bringing about resonance in a circuit, atom, or other object. ■ (of a room, a musical instrument, or a hollow body) tending to reinforce or prolong sounds, esp. by synchronous vibration. ■ (of a color) enhancing or enriching another color or colors by contrast. ■ [*predic.*] (**resonant with**) (of a place) filled or resounding with (the sound of something): *alpine valleys resonant with the sound of church bells.* ■ *figurative* having the ability to evoke or suggest enduring images, memories, or emotions: *the prints are* **resonant with** *traditions of Russian folk art and story.* ▷late 16th cent.: from French *résonnant* or Latin *resonant-* 'resounding,' from the verb *resonare*, from *re-* (expressing intensive force) + *sonare* 'to sound.' **—res·o·nant·ly** *adv.*

res·o·nate /'rezn,āt/ ▶*v.* [*intrans.*] produce or be filled with a deep, full, reverberating sound: *the sound of the siren resonated across the harbor.* ■ *figurative* evoke or suggest images, memories, and emotions: *the words* **resonate with** *so many different meanings.* ■ (of an idea or action) meet with someone's agreement: *the judge's ruling resonated among many of the women.* ■ *technical* produce electrical or mechanical resonance: *the crystal resonates at 16 MHz.* ▷late 19th cent.: from Latin *resonat-* 'resounded,' from the verb *resonare* (see **RESOUND**).

res·o·na·tor /'rezən,ātər/ ▶*n.* an apparatus that increases the resonance of a sound, esp. a hollow part of a musical instrument. ■ a musical or scientific instrument responding to a single sound or note, used for detecting it when it occurs in combination with other sounds. ■ *Physics* a device that displays electrical resonance, esp. one used for the detection of radio waves. ■ *Physics* a hollow enclosure with conducting walls capable of containing electromagnetic fields having particular frequencies of oscillation and exchanging electrical energy with them, used to detect or amplify microwaves.

re·sorb /rē'sôrb; -'zôrb/ ▶*v.* [*trans.*] *technical* absorb (something) again: *the ability to resorb valuable solutes from the urine.* ■ *Physiology* remove (cells, or a tissue or structure) by gradual breakdown into its component materials and dispersal in the circulation: *bone tissue will be resorbed.* ▷mid 17th cent.: from Latin *resorbere*, from *re-* (expressing intensive force) + *sorbere* 'absorb.'

res·or·cin·ol /rə'zôrsə,nôl; -,nōl/ ▶*n.* *Chemistry* a crystalline compound originally obtained from galbanum resin, used in the production of dyes, resins, and cosmetics. • Alternative name: **1,3-dihydroxybenzene**; chem. formula: $C_6H_4(OH)_2$. ▷late 19th cent.: from the earlier term *resorcin* + **-OL**.

re·sorp·tion /rē'sôrpshən; -'zôrp-/ ▶*n.* the process or action by which something is reabsorbed: *the resorption of water.* ■ *Physiology* the absorption into the circulation of cells or tissue: *bone resorption.* ▷early 19th cent.: from **RESORB**, on the pattern of the pair *absorb, absorption.* **—re·sorp·tive** /-tiv/ *adj.*

re·sort /ri'zôrt/ ▶*n.* **1** a place that is a popular destination for vacations or recreation, or which is frequented for a particular purpose: *a seaside resort* | *a health resort.* ■ *archaic* the tendency of a place to be frequented by many people: *places of public resort.* **2** the action of turning to and adopting a strategy or course of action, esp. a disagreeable or undesirable one, so as to resolve a difficult situation: *Germany and Italy tried to resolve their economic and social failures by* **resort to** *fascism.* ■ [in *sing.*] a strategy or course of action that may be adopted in a difficult situation: *her only resort is surgery.*

▶*v.* [*intrans.*] (**resort to**) **1** turn to and adopt (a strategy or course of action, esp. a disagreeable or undesirable one) so as to resolve a difficult situation: *the duke was prepared to resort to force if negotiation failed.* **2** *formal* go often or in large numbers to: *local authorities have a duty to provide adequate sites for gypsies "residing in or resorting to" their areas.* ▷late Middle English (denoting something one can turn to for assistance): from Old French *resortir*, from *re-* 'again' + *sortir* 'come or go out.' The sense 'place frequently visited' dates from the mid 18th cent. **—re·sort·er** *n.*

▶*PHRASES* □ **as a first** (or **last** or **final**) **resort** before anything else is attempted (or when all else has failed). □ **in the last resort** ultimately: *in the last resort what really moves us is our personal convictions.* [suggested by French *en dernier ressort.*]

re-sort /rē 'sôrt/ ▶*v.* [*trans.*] sort (something) again or differently.

re·sound /ri'zound/ ▶*v.* [*intrans.*] (of a sound, voice, etc.) fill a place with sound; be loud enough to echo: *another scream resounded through the school.* ■ (of a place) be filled or echo with a particular sound or sounds: *the office* **resounds with** *the metronomic clicking of keyboards.* ■ *figurative* (of fame, a person's reputation, etc.) be much talked of: *whatever they do in the nineties will not resound in the way that their earlier achievements did.* ■ [*trans.*] *poetic/literary* sing (the praises) of: *Horace resounds the praises of Italy.* ■ [*trans.*] *poetic/literary* (of a place) reecho (a sound): *cliffs, woods, and caves, her viewless steps resound.* ▷late Middle English: from **RE-** 'again' + the verb **SOUND**[1], suggested by Old French *resoner* or Latin *resonare* 'sound again.'

re·sound·ing /ri'zounding/ ▶*adj.* **1** (of a sound) loud enough to reverberate: *a resounding smack across the face.* **2** [*attrib.*] unmistakable; emphatic: *the evening was a resounding success.* **—re·sound·ing·ly** *adv.*

re·source /'rē,sôrs; 'rē,zôrs; ri'sôrs; ri'zôrs/ ▶*n.* **1** (usu. **resources**) a stock or supply of money, materials, staff, and other assets that can be drawn on by a person or organization in order to function effectively: *local authorities complained that they lacked resources.* ■ (**resources**) a country's collective means of supporting itself or becoming wealthier, as represented by its reserves of minerals, land, and other assets. ■ (**resources**) available assets. **2** an action or strategy that may be adopted in adverse circumstances: *sometimes anger is the only resource left in a situation like this.* ■ (**resources**) one's personal attributes and capabilities regarded as able to help or sustain one in adverse circumstances: *we had been left very much to our own resources.* ■ the ability to find quick and clever ways to overcome difficulties: *a man of resource.* ■ a teaching aid. ■ *archaic* the possibility of aid or assistance: *the flower of the French army was lost* **without resource.** **3** *archaic* a leisure occupation.

▶*v.* [*trans.*] provide (a person or organization) with materials, money, staff, and other assets necessary for effective operation: *ensuring that primary health care workers are adequately resourced.* ▷early 17th cent.: from obsolete French *ressourse*, feminine past participle (used as a noun) of Old French dialect *resourdre* 'rise again, recover' (based on Latin *surgere* 'to rise'). **—re·source·less** *adj.* **—re·source·less·ness** *n.*

re·source·ful /ri'sôrsfəl; -'zôrs-/ ▶*adj.* having the ability to find quick and clever ways to overcome difficulties. See note at **CREATIVE**. **—re·source·ful·ly** *adv.* **—re·source·ful·ness** *n.*

resp. ▶*abbr.* ■ respective. ■ respectively. ■ respelled; respelling. ■ respondent.

re·spect /ri'spekt/ ▶*n.* **1** a feeling of deep admiration for someone or something elicited by their abilities, qualities, or achievements: *the director had a lot of* **respect for** *Douglas as an actor.* ■ the state of being admired in such a way: *his first chance in over fifteen years to regain respect in the business.* ■ due regard for the feelings, wishes, rights, or traditions of others: **respect for** *human rights.* ■ (**respects**) a person's polite greetings: *give my respects to your parents.* **2** a particular aspect, point, or detail: *the government's record* **in this respect** *is a mixed one.*

▶*v.* [*trans.*] admire (someone or something) deeply, as a result of their abilities, qualities, or achievements: *she was respected by everyone she worked with* | [as *adj.*] (**respected**) *a respected academic.* See note at **ESTEEM**. ■ have due regard for the feelings, wishes, rights, or traditions of: *I respected his views.* ■ avoid harming or interfering with: *it is incumbent upon all boaters to respect the environment.* ■ agree to recognize and abide by (a legal requirement): *he urged all foreign nationals to respect the laws of their country of residence.* ▷late Middle English: from Latin *respectus*, from the verb *respicere* 'look back at, regard,' from *re-* 'back' + *specere* 'look at.'

▶*PHRASES* □ **with respect to** as regards; with reference to: *the two groups were similar with respect to age, sex, and diagnoses.* □ **in respect that** because. □ **pay one's respects, pay one's last respects** see **PAY**[1]. □ **with** (or **with all due**) **respect** used as a polite formula preceding, and intended to mitigate the effect of, an expression of disagreement or criticism: *with all due respect, Father, I think you've got to be more broadminded these days.*

re·spect·a·bil·i·ty /ri,spektə'bilətē/ ▶*n.* the state or quality of being proper, correct, and socially acceptable: *provincial notions of respectability.* ■ the state or quality of being accepted as valid or important within a particular field: *scientific respectability.*

re·spect·a·ble /ri'spektəbəl/ ▶*adj.* **1** regarded by society to be good, proper, or correct: *they thought the stage no life for a respectable lady.* ■ (of a person's appearance, clothes, or behavior) decent or presentable: *a perfectly respectable pair of pajamas!* **2** of some merit or importance: *a respectable botanical text.* ■ adequate or acceptable in number, size, or amount: *America's GDP grew by a respectable 2.6 percent.* **—re·spect·a·bly** /-blē/ *adv.* [as *submodifier*] *an architecture of respectably high standards.*

re·spect·er /ri'spektər/ ▶*n.* a person who has a high regard for someone or something: *I'm always a respecter of the office of the presidency, but not necessarily of the president.*

▶*PHRASE* □ **be no respecter of** —— not be influenced by status, wealth, etc.: *Jesus was no respecter of people.*

re·spect·ful /ri'spektfəl/ ▶*adj.* feeling or showing deference and respect: *they sit in respectful silence.* **—re·spect·ful·ly** *adv.* **—re·spect·ful·ness** *n.*

re·spect·ing /ri'spekting/ ▶*prep.* *dated* or *formal* with reference or regard to: *he began to have serious worries respecting his car.*

re·spec·tive /ri'spektiv/ ▶*adj.* [*attrib.*] belonging or relating separately to each of two or more people or things: *they chatted about their respective childhoods.* ▷late Middle English (in the sense 'relative, comparative'): from medieval Latin *respectivus*, from *respect-* 'regarded, considered,' from the verb *respicere* (see **RESPECT**), reinforced by French *respectif, -ive.*

re·spec·tive·ly /riˈspektivlē/ ▸*adv.* separately or individually and in the order already mentioned (used when enumerating two or more items or facts that refer back to a previous statement): *they received sentences of one year and eight months, respectively.*

re·spell /rēˈspel/ ▸*v.* (*past* and *past part.* **-spelled** or *chiefly Brit.* **-spelt**) [*trans.*] spell (a word) again or differently, esp. phonetically in order to indicate its pronunciation.

res·pi·ra·ble /ˈrespərəbəl; riˈspīrəbəl/ ▸*adj.* (of the air or a gas) able or fit to be breathed. ■ (of particles in the air) able to be breathed in: *woodworking can create quantities of fine respirable dust.* ▷late 18th cent.: from French *respirable* or late Latin *respirabilis*, from *respirare* 'breathe out' (see **RESPIRE**).

res·pi·rate /ˈrespəˌrāt/ ▸*v.* [*trans.*] *Medicine & Biology* assist (a person or animal) to breathe by means of artificial respiration. ▷mid 17th cent.: back-formation from **RESPIRATION**.

res·pi·ra·tion /ˌrespəˈrāSHən/ ▸*n.* the action of breathing: *opiates affect respiration.* ■ *chiefly Medicine* a single breath. ■ *Biology* a process in living organisms involving the production of energy, typically with the intake of oxygen and the release of carbon dioxide from the oxidation of complex organic substances. ▷late Middle English: from Latin *respiratio(n-)*, from *respirare* 'breathe out' (see **RESPIRE**).

res·pi·ra·tor /ˈrespəˌrātər/ ▸*n.* an apparatus worn over the mouth and nose or the entire face to prevent the inhalation of dust, smoke, or other noxious substances. ■ an apparatus used to induce artificial respiration.

res·pi·ra·to·ry /ˈrespərəˌtôrē; riˈspīrə-/ ▸*adj.* of, relating to, or affecting respiration or the organs of respiration: *respiratory disease.*

res·pi·ra·to·ry dis·tress syn·drome ▸*n.* another term for **HYALINE MEMBRANE DISEASE**.

res·pi·ra·to·ry pig·ment ▸*n.* *Biochemistry* a substance (such as hemoglobin or hemocyanin) with a molecule consisting of protein with a pigmented prosthetic group, involved in the physiological transport of oxygen or electrons.

res·pi·ra·to·ry quo·tient ▸*n.* *Physiology* the ratio of the volume of carbon dioxide evolved to that of oxygen consumed by an organism, tissue, or cell in a given time.

res·pi·ra·to·ry syn·cy·tial vi·rus ▸*n.* *Medicine* a paramyxovirus that causes disease of the respiratory tract. It is a major cause of bronchiolitis and pneumonia in young children and may be a contributing factor in sudden infant death syndrome.

res·pi·ra·to·ry tract ▸*n.* the passage formed by the mouth, nose, throat, and lungs, through which air passes during breathing.

res·pi·ra·to·ry tree ▸*n.* *Zoology* a branched respiratory organ in the body cavity of sea cucumbers.

re·spire /riˈspīr/ ▸*v.* [*intrans.*] breathe: *he lay back, respiring deeply* | [*trans.*] *a country where fresh air seems impossible to respire.* ■ (of a plant) carry out respiration, esp. at night when photosynthesis has ceased. ■ *poetic/literary* recover hope, courage, or strength after a time of difficulty: *the archduke, newly respiring from so long a war.* ▷late Middle English: from Old French *respirer* or Latin *respirare* 'breathe out,' from *re-* 'again' + *spirare* 'breathe.'

res·pi·rom·e·ter /ˌrespəˈrämətər/ ▸*n.* *Biology* a device that measures the rate of consumption of oxygen by a living organism or organic system. ■ *Medicine* an instrument for measuring the air capacity of the lungs.

res·pite /ˈrespət; riˈspīt/ ▸*n.* a short period of rest or relief from something difficult or unpleasant: *the refugee encampments will provide some* ***respite from*** *the suffering* | [in *sing.*] *a brief* ***respite from*** *a dire food shortage.* ■ a short delay permitted before an unpleasant obligation is met or a punishment is carried out.
▸*v.* [*trans.*] *rare* postpone (a sentence, obligation, etc.): *the execution was only respited a few months.* ■ *archaic* grant a delay or extension of time to; reprieve from death or execution: *some poor criminal ... from the gibbet or the wheel, respited for a day.* ▷Middle English: from Old French *respit*, from Latin *respectus* 'refuge, consideration.'

res·pite care ▸*n.* temporary institutional care of a dependent elderly, ill, or handicapped person, providing relief for their usual caregivers.

re·splend·ent /riˈsplendənt/ ▸*adj.* attractive and impressive through being richly colorful or sumptuous: *she was* ***resplendent in*** *a sea-green dress.* See note at **BRIGHT**. ▷late Middle English: from Latin *resplendent-* 'shining out,' from the verb *resplendere*, from *re-* (expressing intensive force) + *splendere* 'to glitter.' —**re·splend·ence** *n.* —**re·splend·en·cy** *n.* —**re·splend·ent·ly** *adv.*

re·spond /riˈspänd/ ▸*v.* [*reporting verb*] say something in reply: [*intrans.*] *she could not get Robert to* ***respond to*** *her words* | [with *clause*] *he responded that it would not be feasible* | [with *direct speech*] *"It's not part of my job," Belinda responded.* ■ (of a congregation) say or sing the response in reply to a priest. ■ [*intrans.*] (of a person) act or behave in reaction to someone or something: *she turned her head,* ***responding to*** *his grin with a smile.* ■ react quickly or positively to a stimulus or treatment: *his back injury has failed to respond to treatment.* ■ [*trans.*] *Bridge* make (a bid) in answer to one's partner's preceding bid.
▸*n.* **1** *Architecture* a half-pillar or half-pier attached to a wall to support an arch, esp. at the end of an arcade. **2** (in church use) a responsory; a response to a versicle. ▷late Middle English (in the noun senses): from Old French, from *respondre* 'to answer,' from Latin *respondere*, from *re-* 'again' + *spondere* 'to pledge.' The verb dates from the mid 16th cent. —**re·spond·ence** /-dəns/ *n.* (*archaic*) —**re·spond·en·cy** /-dənsē/ *n.* (*archaic*) —**re·spond·er** *n.*

re·spond·ent /riˈspändənt/ ▸*n.* **1** a defendant in a lawsuit, esp. one in an appeals or divorce case. **2** a person who replies to something, esp. one supplying information for a survey or questionnaire or responding to an advertisement.
▸*adj.* [*attrib.*] **1** in the position of defendant in a lawsuit: *the respondent defendant.* **2** replying to something, esp. a survey or questionnaire: *the respondent firms in the survey.* **3** *Psychology* involving or denoting a response, esp. a conditioned reflex, to a specific stimulus. ▷early 16th cent. (sense 2 of the *noun*): from Latin *respondent-* 'answering, offering in return,' from the verb *respondere* (see **RESPOND**).

re·spon·sa /riˈspänsə/ ▸ plural form of **RESPONSUM**.

re·sponse /riˈspäns/ ▸*n.* a verbal or written answer: *without waiting for a response, she returned to her newspaper* | *we received 400 applications* ***in response to*** *one job ad.* ■ a written or verbal answer to a question in a test, questionnaire, survey, etc. ■ a reaction to something: *an extended, jazzy piano solo drew the biggest* ***response from*** *the crowd* | *an honors degree course in Japanese has been established* ***in response to*** *an increasing demand.* ■ *Psychology & Physiology* an excitation of a nerve impulse caused by a change or event; a physical reaction to a specific stimulus or situation. ■ the way in which a mechanical or electrical device responds to a stimulus or range of stimuli. ■ (usu. **responses**) a part of a religious liturgy said or sung by a congregation in answer to a minister or cantor. ■ *Bridge* a bid made in answer to one's partner's preceding bid. ▷Middle English: from Old French *respons* or Latin *responsum* 'something offered in return,' neuter past participle of *respondere* (see **RESPOND**).

re·sponse time ▸*n.* the length of time taken for a person or system to react to a given stimulus or event. ■ *Electronics* the time taken for a circuit or measuring device, when subjected to a change in input signal, to change its state by a specified fraction of its total response to that change.

re·sponse var·i·a·ble ▸*n.* another term for **DEPENDENT VARIABLE**.

re·spon·si·bil·i·ty /riˌspänsəˈbilətē/ ▸*n.* (*pl.* **-ties**) the state or fact of having a duty to deal with something or of having control over someone: *women bear children and* ***take responsibility for*** *child care.* ■ the state or fact of being accountable or to blame for something: *the group has claimed responsibility for a string of murders.* ■ the opportunity or ability to act independently and make decisions without authorization: *we would expect individuals lower down the organization to take on more responsibility.* ■ (often **responsibilities**) a thing that one is required to do as part of a job, role, or legal obligation: *he will take over the responsibilities of overseas director.* ■ [in *sing.*] (**responsibility to/toward**) a moral obligation to behave correctly toward or in respect of: *individuals have a responsibility to control personal behavior.*

re·spon·si·ble /riˈspänsəbəl/ ▸*adj.* [*predic.*] having an obligation to do something, or having control over or care for someone, as part of one's job or role: *the department* ***responsible for*** *education.* ■ being the primary cause of something and so able to be blamed or credited for it: *the gene was responsible for a rare type of eye cancer.* ■ [*attrib.*] (of a job or position) involving important duties, independent decision-making, or control over others. ■ [*predic.*] (**responsible to**) having to report to (a superior or someone in authority) and be answerable to them for one's actions: *the team manager is responsible to the league president.* ■ capable of being trusted: *a responsible adult.* ■ morally accountable for one's behavior: *the progressive emergence of the child as a responsible being.* ▷late 16th cent. (in the sense 'answering to, corresponding'): from obsolete French, from Latin *respons-* 'answered, offered in return,' from the verb *respondere* (see **RESPOND**). —**re·spon·si·ble·ness** *n.* —**re·spon·si·bly** /-blē/ *adv.*

THE RIGHT WORD **accountable, answerable, liable, responsible**

Responsible is an adjective that applies to anyone who is in charge of an endeavor or to whom a duty has been delegated, and who is subject to penalty or blame in case of default (*responsible for getting everyone out of the building in the event of a fire*).

Answerable implies a legal or moral obligation for which one must answer (*the parents were held to be answerable for their children's behavior*).

Accountable is more positive than *responsible* or *answerable*, suggesting that something has been entrusted to someone who will be called to account for how that trust has been carried out (*she was directly accountable to the department head for the funds that had been allocated to her group*).

Liable is more restricted in scope than any of the foregoing words; it refers exclusively to the assignment of blame or the payment of monetary damages in the event of a mishap (*because he was responsible for the accident, he was held liable for damages*).

R

re·spon·sive /riˈspänsiv/ ▸*adj.* **1** reacting quickly and positively: *a flexible service that is* ***responsive to*** *changing social and economic patterns.* ■ responding readily and with interest or enthusiasm: *our most enthusiastic and responsive students.* **2** answering: *I'm distracted by a nibble on my line: I jig it several times, but there is no responsive tug.* ■ (of a section of liturgy) using responses. —**re·spon·sive·ly** *adv.* —**re·spon·sive·ness** *n.*

re·spon·so·ri·al /riˌspänˈsôrēəl/ ▸*adj.* (of a psalm or liturgical chant) recited in parts with a congregational response between each part.

re·spon·so·ry /riˈspänsərē/ ▸*n.* (*pl.* **-ries**) (in the Christian Church) an anthem said or sung by a soloist and choir after a lesson. ▷late Middle English: from late Latin *responsorium*, from Latin *respons-* 'answered,' from the verb *respondere* (see **RESPOND**).

re·spon·sum /riˈspänsəm/ ▸*n.* (*pl.* **-sa** /-sə/) a written reply by a rabbi or Talmudic scholar to an inquiry on some matter of Jewish law. ▷Latin, literally 'reply.'

res pu·bli·ca /rās ˈpo͞obliˌkä; ˈpəblikə/ ▸*n.* the state, republic, or commonwealth. ▷Latin, literally 'public matter.'

res·sen·ti·ment /rəˌsäNtēˈmäN/ ▸*n.* a psychological state arising from suppressed feelings of envy and hatred that cannot be acted upon, frequently resulting in some form of self-abasement. ▷via German (used by Nietzsche in this sense) from French *ressentiment* 'feeling.'

rest[1] /rest/ ▸*v.* [*intrans.*] **1** cease work or movement in order to relax, refresh oneself, or recover strength: *he needed to rest after the feverish activity* | *I'm going to* ***rest up*** *before traveling to England.* ■ [*trans.*] allow to be inactive in order to regain strength, health, or energy: *her friend read to her while she rested her eyes.* ■ [*trans.*] leave (a player) out of a team temporarily: *both men were rested for the final game.* ■ (of a dead person or body) lie buried: *the king's body rested in his tomb.* ■ (of a problem or subject) be left without further investigation, discussion, or treatment: *the council has urged the planning committee not to allow the matter to rest.* ■ [*trans.*] allow (land) to lie fallow: *the field should be grazed or rested.* ■ conclude the case for the prosecution or the defense in a law case: *the prosecution rests.* See also **REST ONE'S CASE** below. **2** [*intrans.*] be placed or supported so as to stay in a specified position: *her elbow was resting on the arm of the sofa.* ■ [*trans.*] place (something) so that it is supported in a specified position: *he rested a hand on her shoulder.* ■ (**rest on/upon**) (of a look) alight or be steadily directed on: *his eyes rested briefly on the boy.* ■ (**rest on/upon**) be based on or grounded in; depend on: *the country's security rested on its alliances.* ■ [*trans.*] (**rest something in/on**) place hope, trust, or confidence on or in: *she rested her hopes in* *her attorney.* ■ belong or be located at a specified place or with a specified person: *ultimate control rested with the founders.*

▸*n.* **1** an instance or period of relaxing or ceasing to engage in strenuous or stressful activity: *you look as though you need a rest | a couple of days of complete rest.* ■ refreshment through sleep: *she curled up in a corner to get some rest.* ■ a motionless state: *the car accelerates rapidly from rest.* ■ *Music* an interval of silence of a specified duration. ■ *Music* the sign denoting such an interval. ■ a pause in elocution. ■ a caesura in verse. ■ [in *place names*] a place where people can stay: *we spent the night at Riverview Rest.* **2** [in *combination*] an object that is used to support something: *a chin-rest | a shoulder-rest.* ■ a support or hook for a telephone receiver when not in use. ■ a support for a cue in billiards or pool. ▷Old English *ræst, rest* (noun), *ræstan, restan* (verb), of Germanic origin, from a root meaning 'league' or 'mile' (referring to a distance after which one rests).

▸*PHRASES* □ **at rest** not moving or exerting oneself. ■ not agitated or troubled; tranquil: *he felt at rest, the tension gone.* ■ dead and buried. □ **come to rest** stop moving; settle: *the elevator came to rest at the first floor.* □ **give it a rest** *informal* used to ask someone to stop doing something or talking about something that the speaker finds irritating or tedious. □ **no rest for the weary** see WEARY. □ **put** (or **set**) **someone's mind** (or **doubts** or **fears**) **at rest** relieve someone of anxiety or uncertainty; reassure someone. □ **rest one's case** conclude one's presentation of evidence and arguments in a lawsuit. ■ *humorous* said to show that one believes one has presented sufficient evidence for one's views. □ **rest on one's laurels** see LAUREL. □ **rest** (or **God rest**) **his** (or **her**) **soul** used to express a wish that God should grant someone's soul peace. □ **rest on one's oars** see OAR.

rest[2] ▸*n.* [in *sing.*] the remaining part of something: *what do you want to do for* **the rest of** *your life? | I'll tell you the rest tomorrow night.* ■ [treated as *pl.*] the remaining people or things; the others: **the rest of** *us were experienced skiers.*

▸*v.* [*intrans.*] remain or be left in a specified condition: *you can rest assured she will do everything she can to help her.* ▷late Middle English: from Old French *reste* (noun), *rester* (verb), from Latin *restare* 'remain,' from *re-* 'back' + *stare* 'to stand.'

▸*PHRASES* □ **and** (**all**) **the rest** (**of it**) and everything else that might be mentioned or that one could expect: *social security and pension and the rest of it.* □ **the rest is history** see HISTORY.

rest ar·e·a ▸*n.* a roadside area with restrooms and other facilities for the use of motorists.

re·state /rē'stāt/ ▸*v.* [*trans.*] state (something) again or differently, esp. in order to correct or to make more clear or convincing: *he restated his opposition to abortion | [as adj.] restated earnings.* —**re·state·ment** *n.*

res·tau·rant /'rest(ə)rənt; 'restə,ränt; 'res,tränt/ ▸*n.* a place where people pay to sit and eat meals that are cooked and served on the premises. ▷early 19th cent.: from French, from *restaurer* 'provide food for' (literally 'restore to a former state').

res·tau·ra·teur /,restərə'tər/ ▸*n.* a person who owns and manages a restaurant. ▷late 18th cent.: French, from the verb *restaurer* (see RESTAURANT).

USAGE Despite its close relation to *restaurant*, there is no *n* in **restaurateur**, either in its spelling or in its pronunciation.

rest cure ▸*n.* a period spent in inactivity or leisure with the intention of improving one's physical or mental health.

re·ste·no·sis /,rēstə'nōsəs/ ▸*n. Medicine* the recurrence of abnormal narrowing of an artery or valve after corrective surgery. ▷1950s: from RE- 'again' + STENOSIS.

rest·ful /'restfəl/ ▸*adj.* having a quiet and soothing quality: *the rooms were cool and restful.* —**rest·ful·ly** *adv.* —**rest·ful·ness** *n.*

rest home ▸*n.* a residential institution where old or frail people are cared for.

rest·ing po·ten·tial ▸*n. Physiology* the electrical potential of a neuron or other excitable cell relative to its surroundings when not stimulated or involved in passage of an impulse.

res·ti·tu·tion /,restə't(y)o͞osHən/ ▸*n.* **1** the restoration of something lost or stolen to its proper owner: *seeking the restitution of land taken from blacks under apartheid.* **2** recompense for injury or loss: *he was ordered to pay $6,000 in restitution.* **3** the restoration of something to its original state: *restitution of the damaged mucosa.* ■ *Physics* the resumption of an object's original shape or position through elastic recoil. ▷Middle English: from Old French, or from Latin *restitutio(n-)*, from *restituere* 'restore,' from *re-* 'again' + *statuere* 'establish.' —**res·ti·tu·tive** /'restə,t(y)o͞otiv/ *adj.*

res·tive /'restiv/ ▸*adj.* (of a person) unable to keep still or silent and becoming increasingly difficult to control, esp. because of impatience, dissatisfaction, or boredom. ■ (of a horse) refusing to advance, stubbornly standing still or moving backward or sideways. ▷late 16th cent.: from Old French *restif, -ive*, from Latin *restare* 'remain.' The original sense, 'inclined to remain still, inert,' has undergone a reversal; the association with the refractory movements of a horse gave rise to the current sense 'fidgety, restless.' —**res·tive·ly** *adv.* —**res·tive·ness** *n.*

rest·less /'restləs/ ▸*adj.* (of a person or animal) unable to rest or relax as a result of anxiety or boredom: *the audience grew restless and inattentive.* ■ offering no physical or emotional rest; involving constant activity or motion: *a restless night.* ▷Old English *restlēas* (see REST[1], -LESS). —**rest·less·ly** *adv.* —**rest·less·ness** *n.*

rest mass ▸*n. Physics* the mass of a body when at rest.

re·stock /rē'stäk/ ▸*v.* [*trans.*] replenish (a store) with fresh stock or supplies: *work began at once to restock the fishery.*

Res·ton /'restən/ a planned residential and commercial community in northern Virginia, northwest of Washington, D.C., established in the 1960s; pop. 48,556.

res·to·ra·tion /,restə'rāsHən/ ▸*n.* **1** the action of returning something to a former owner, place, or condition: *the restoration of Andrew's sight.* ■ the process of repairing or renovating a building, work of art, vehicle, etc., so as to restore it to its original condition: *the altar paintings seem in need of restoration.* ■ the reinstatement of a previous practice, right, custom, or situation: *the restoration of capital punishment.* ■ *Dentistry* a structure provided to replace or repair dental tissue so as to restore its form and function, such as a filling, crown, or bridge. ■ a model or drawing representing the supposed original form of an extinct animal, ruined building, etc. **2** the return of a hereditary monarch to a throne, a head of state to government, or a regime to power. ■ (**the Restoration**) the reestablishment of Charles II as King of England in 1660. ■ (**Restoration**) [usu. as *adj.*] the period following this, esp. with regard to its literature or architecture: *Restoration drama.* ▷late 15th cent. (denoting the action of restoring to a former state): partly from Old French, partly an alteration of obsolete *restauration* (from late Latin *restauratio(n-)*, from the verb *restaurare*), suggested by RESTORE.

Res·to·ra·tion com·e·dy ▸*n.* a style of drama that flourished in London after the Restoration in 1660, typically having a complicated plot marked by wit, cynicism, and licentiousness.

res·to·ra·tion·ism /,restə'rāsHə,nizəm/ ▸*n.* a charismatic Christian movement seeking to restore the beliefs and practices of the early Church. —**res·to·ra·tion·ist** *n.* & *adj.*

re·stor·a·tive /ri'stôrətiv/ ▸*adj.* having the ability to restore health, strength, or a feeling of well-being: *the restorative power of long walks.* ■ *Surgery & Dentistry* relating to or concerned with the restoration of form or function to a damaged tooth or other part of the body.

▸*n.* something, esp. a medicine or drink, that restores health, strength, or well-being. ▷late Middle English: from an Old French variant of *restauratif, -ive*, from *restorer* (see RESTORE). —**re·stor·a·tive·ly** *adv.*

re·store /ri'stôr/ ▸*v.* [*trans.*] bring back (a previous right, practice, custom, or situation); reinstate: *the government restored confidence in the housing market.* See note at RECOVER. ■ return (someone or something) to a former condition, place, or position: *the effort to* **restore** *him* **to** *office isn't working.* ■ repair or renovate (a building, work of art, vehicle, etc.) so as to return it to its original condition: *the building has been lovingly restored.* ■ give (something previously stolen, taken away, or lost) back to the original owner or recipient: *the government will* **restore** *land and property* **to** *those who lost it through confiscation.* ▷Middle English: from Old French *restorer*, from Latin *restaurare* 'rebuild, restore.' —**re·stor·a·ble** *adj.* —**re·stor·er** *n.*

re·strain /ri'strān/ ▸*v.* [*trans.*] prevent (someone or something) from doing something; keep under control or within limits: *he had to be* **restrained from** *walking out of the meeting* | [as *adj.*] (**restraining**) *Cara put a restraining hand on his arm.* ■ prevent oneself from displaying or giving way to (a strong urge or emotion: *Amos had to restrain his impatience.* ■ deprive (someone) of freedom of movement or personal liberty: *leg cuffs are used in the U.S. for restraining and transporting extremely violent and dangerous criminals.* ■ (of a seat belt) hold (a person or part of their body) down and back while in a vehicle seat. ▷Middle English: from Old French *restreign-*, stem of *restreindre*, from Latin *restringere*, from *re-* 'back' + *stringere* 'to tie, pull tight.' —**re·strain·a·ble** *adj.* —**re·strain·er** *n.*

re·strained /ri'strānd/ ▸*adj.* characterized by reserve or moderation; unemotional or dispassionate: *he had restrained manners.* ■ (of color, clothes, decoration, etc.) understated and subtle; not excessively showy or ornate. ■ kept under control; prevented from freedom of movement or action: *a patch of land turned into a restrained wilderness.* ■ (of a person) held down and back in a vehicle seat by a seat belt. —**re·strain·ed·ly** /ri'strānidlē/ *adv.*

re·straint /ri'strānt/ ▸*n.* **1** (often **restraints**) a measure or condition that keeps someone or something under control or within limits: *decisions are made within the financial restraints of the budget.* ■ the action of keeping someone or something under control. ■ deprivation or restriction of personal liberty or freedom of movement: *he remained aggressive and required physical restraint.* ■ a device that limits or prevents freedom of movement: *car safety restraints.* **2** unemotional, dispassionate, or moderate behavior; self-control: *he urged the protesters to exercise restraint.* ■ understatement, esp. of artistic expression: *with strings and piano, all restraint vanished.* ▷late Middle English: from Old French *restreinte*, feminine past participle of *restreindre* 'hold back' (see RESTRAIN).

re·straint of trade ▸*n. Law* action that interferes with free competition in a market.

re·strict /ri'strikt/ ▸*v.* [*trans.*] put a limit on; keep under control: *some roads may have to be closed at peak times to restrict the number of visitors.* ■ deprive (someone or something) of freedom of movement or action: *cities can* **restrict** *groups of protesters* **from** *gathering on a residential street.* ■ (**restrict someone to**) limit someone to only doing or having (a particular thing) or staying in (a particular place): *I shall restrict myself to a single example.* ■ (**restrict something to**) limit something, esp. an activity, to (a particular place, time, or category of people): *the zoological gardens were at first restricted to members and their guests.* ■ withhold (information) from general circulation or disclosure: *at first the government tried to restrict news of our involvement in Vietnam.* ▷mid 16th cent.: from Latin *restrict-* 'confined, bound fast,' from the verb *restringere* (see RESTRAIN).

re·strict·ed /ri'striktid/ ▸*adj.* [*attrib.*] limited in extent, number, scope, or action: *Western scientists had only restricted access to the site.* ■ (of a document or information) for limited circulation and not to be revealed to the public for reasons of national security. ■ *Biology* (of a virus) unable to reproduce at its normal rate in certain hosts. ■ *Biochemistry* (of DNA) subject to degradation by a restriction enzyme. —**re·strict·ed·ly** *adv.* —**re·strict·ed·ness** *n.*

re·stric·tion /ri'striksHən/ ▸*n.* (often **restrictions**) a limiting condition or measure, esp. a legal one: *planning restrictions on commercial development.* ■ the limitation or control of someone or something, or the state of being limited or restricted: *the restriction of local government power.* ▷late Middle English: from Old French, or from Latin *restrictio(n-)*, from *restringere* 'bind fast, confine' (see RESTRICT). —**re·stric·tion·ism** /-,nizəm/ *n.* —**re·stric·tion·ist** /-nist/ *adj.* & *n.*

re·stric·tion en·zyme (also **re·stri·ction en·do·nu·cle·ase**) ▸*n. Biochemistry* an enzyme produced chiefly by certain bacteria, having the property of cleaving DNA molecules at or near a specific sequence of bases.

re·stric·tion frag·ment ▸*n. Biochemistry* a fragment of a DNA molecule that has been cleaved by a restriction enzyme.

re·stric·tion frag·ment length pol·y·mor·phism ▸*n. Genetics* a variation in the length of restriction fragments produced by a given restriction enzyme in a sample of DNA. Such variation is used in forensic investigations and to map hereditary disease.

re·stric·tive /ri'striktiv/ ▸*adj.* **1** imposing restrictions or limitations on someone's activities or freedom: *a web of restrictive regulations.* **2** *Grammar* (of a relative clause or descriptive phrase) serving to specify the particular instance or instances being mentioned. —**re·stric·tive·ly** *adv.* —**re·stric·tive·ness** *n.*

USAGE What is the difference between *the books that were on the table once belonged to my aunt* and *the books, which were on the table, once belonged to my aunt?* In the first sentence, the speaker uses the relative clause to pick out specific books (i.e., the ones on the table) in contrast with all others. In the second sentence, the location of the books referred to is unaffected by the relative clause: the speaker merely offers the additional information that the books happened to be on the table.
This distinction is between **restrictive** and **nonrestrictive** relative clauses. In speech, the difference is usually expressed by a difference in intonation. In writing, a **restrictive** relative clause is not set off by commas, and *that* is the preferred subject or object of the clause, although many writers use *which* and *who* or *whom* for such clauses.
A **nonrestrictive** clause is set off within commas, and *which, who,* or *whom,* not *that,* is the relative pronoun to use as the subject or object of the verb of the clause. Without a comma, the clause in *please ask any member of the staff who will be pleased to help* is **restrictive** and therefore implies contrast with another set of staff who will not be pleased to help. It is almost certain that the appropriate intention of such a clause would be **nonrestrictive**—therefore, a comma is needed before **who** (*. . . any member of the staff, who will be pleased . . .*)
For more details, see **usage** at THAT and WHICH.

re·stric·tive cov·e·nant ▸*n. Law* a covenant imposing a restriction on the use of land so that the value and enjoyment of adjoining land will be preserved.

re·string /rēˈstriNG; ˈrē-/ ▸*v.* (*past* and *past part.* **-strung**) [*trans.*] **1** fit new or different strings to (a musical instrument or sports racket). **2** thread (objects such as beads) on a new string.

rest·room /ˈrest,ro͞om; -,ro͝om/ (also **rest room**) ▸*n.* a bathroom in a public building.

re·struc·ture /rēˈstrəkCHər/ ▸*v.* [*trans.*] organize differently: *a plan to strengthen and restructure the department* | [as *n.*] (**restructuring**) *the restructuring of this wing of the Louvre.* ■ *Finance* convert (the debt of a business in difficulty) into another kind of debt, typically one that is repayable at a later time.

re·struc·tur·ing /rēˈstrəkCHəriNG/ ▸*n. Commerce* a reorganization of a company with a view to achieving greater efficiency and profit, or to adapt to a changing market.

re·style ▸*v.* /rēˈstīl/ [*trans.*] **1** rearrange or remake in a new shape or layout: *Nick restyled Rebecca's hair.* **2** give a new designation to: [*trans.*] *the division has restyled the branch the Lovejoy Line.*
▸*n.* /ˈrēstīl/ an instance of reshaping or rearranging something. ■ a new shape or arrangement.

re·sub·mit /,rēsəbˈmit/ ▸*v.* [*trans.*] submit (something, such as a plan, application, or resignation) again. **—re·sub·mis·sion** /-ˈmisHən/ *n.*

re·sult /riˈzəlt/ ▸*n.* a consequence, effect, or outcome of something: *the tower collapsed* ***as a result of*** *safety violations.* ■ an item of information obtained by experiment or some other scientific method; a quantity or formula obtained by calculation. ■ (often **results**) a final score, mark, or placing in a sporting event or examination. ■ (often **results**) a satisfactory or favorable outcome of an undertaking or contest: *determination and persistence guarantee results.* ■ (usu. **results**) the outcome of a business's trading over a given period, expressed as a statement of profit or loss: *oil companies have reported markedly better results.*
▸*v.* [*intrans.*] occur or follow as the consequence of something: *government unpopularity* ***resulting from*** *the state of the economy* | [as *adj.*] (**resulting**) *talk of a general election and the resulting political uncertainty.* ■ (**result in**) have (a specified end or outcome): *talks in July had resulted in stalemate.* ▷late Middle English (as a verb): from medieval Latin *resultare* 'to result,' earlier in the sense 'spring back,' from *re-* (expressing intensive force) + *saltare* (frequentative of *salire* 'to jump'). The noun dates from the early 17th cent.
▸*PHRASE* □ **without result** in vain: *Danny had inquired about getting work, without result.*

re·sult·ant /riˈzəltnt/ ▸*adj.* [*attrib.*] occurring or produced as a result or consequence of something: *restructuring and the resultant cost savings.*
▸*n. technical* a force, velocity, or other vector quantity that is equivalent to the combined effect of two or more component vectors acting at the same point. ▷mid 17th cent. (in the adjectival sense): from Latin *resultant-* 'springing back,' from the verb *resultare* (see RESULT). The noun sense dates from the early 19th cent.

re·sult·a·tive /riˈzəltətiv/ *Grammar* ▸*adj.* expressing, indicating, or relating to the outcome of an action.
▸*n.* a resultative verb, conjunction, or clause.

re·sume /riˈzo͞om/ ▸*v.* [*trans.*] begin to do or pursue (something) again after a pause or interruption: *a day later normal service was resumed.* ■ [*intrans.*] begin to be done, pursued, or used again after a pause or interruption: *hostilities had ceased and normal life had resumed.* ■ [*intrans.*] begin speaking again after a pause or interruption: *he sipped at the glass of water on the lectern and then resumed* | [with *direct speech*] *"As for Joe," the major resumed, "I can't promise anything."* ■ take, pick up, or put on again; return to the use of: *the judge resumed his seat.*
▸*n.* variant spelling of RÉSUMÉ. ▷late Middle English: from Old French *resumer* or Latin *resumere*, from *re-* 'back' + *sumere* 'take.' **—re·sum·a·ble** *adj.* **—re·sump·tion** /riˈzəmpsHən/ *n.*

ré·su·mé /ˈrezə,mā ,rezəˈmā/ (also **re·su·mé** or **re·su·me**) ▸*n.* **1** a curriculum vitae. **2** a summary: *I gave him a quick résumé of events.* ▷early 19th cent.: French, literally 'resumed,' past participle (used as a noun) of *résumer*.

re·su·pi·nate /riˈso͞opə,nāt/ ▸*adj. Botany* (of a leaf, flower, fruiting body, etc.) upside down. ▷late 18th cent.: from Latin *resupinatus* 'bent back,' past participle of *resupinare*, based on *supinus* 'lying on the back.' **—re·su·pi·na·tion** /ri,so͞opəˈnāsHən/ *n.*

re·sur·face /rēˈsərfəs/ ▸*v.* **1** [*trans.*] put a new coating on or reform (a surface such as a road, a floor, or ice). **2** [*intrans.*] come back up to the surface: *he resurfaced beside the boat.* ■ arise or become evident again: *serious concerns about the welfare of animals eventually resurfaced.* ■ (of a person) come out of hiding or obscurity: *he resurfaced under a false identity in Australia.*

re·sur·gent /riˈsərjənt/ ▸*adj.* increasing or reviving after a period of little activity, popularity, or occurrence: *resurgent nationalism.* ▷early 19th cent. (earlier as a noun): from Latin *resurgent-* 'rising again,' from the verb *resurgere*, from *re-* 'again' + *surgere* 'to rise.' **—re·sur·gence** *n.*

res·ur·rect /,rezəˈrekt/ ▸*v.* [*trans.*] restore (a dead person) to life: *he queried whether Jesus was indeed resurrected.* ■ revive the practice, use, or memory of (something); bring new vigor to: *the deal collapsed and has yet to be resurrected.* ▷late 18th cent.: back-formation from RESURRECTION.

res·ur·rec·tion /,rezəˈreksHən/ ▸*n.* the action or fact of resurrecting or being resurrected: *the story of the resurrection of Osiris.* ■ (**the Resurrection**) (in Christian belief) Christ's rising from the dead. ■ (**the Resurrection**) (in Christian belief) the rising of the dead at the Last Judgment. ■ the revitalization or revival of something: *the resurrection of the country under a charismatic leader* | *resurrections of long-forgotten scandals.* ▷Middle English: from Old French, from late Latin *resurrectio(n-)*, from the verb *resurgere* 'rise again' (see RESURGENT).

res·ur·rec·tion plant ▸*n.* any of a number of plants that are able to survive drought, typically folding up when dry and unfolding when moistened, in particular: • a fern of tropical and warm-temperate America (*Polypodium polypodioides*, family Polypodiaceae). • a Californian club moss (*Selaginella lepidophylla*, family Selaginellaceae). • the rose of Jericho.

re·sur·vey /,rēsərˈvā; rēˈsərvā/ ▸*v.* [*trans.*] survey (a district) again. ■ redraw (a map) after surveying a district again. ■ study or investigate again: *the same people surveyed in 1992 will be resurveyed periodically.*
▸*n.* /rēˈsərvā/ an act of surveying a district or studying something again.

re·sus·ci·tate /riˈsəsə,tāt/ ▸*v.* [*trans.*] revive (someone) from unconsciousness or apparent death: *an ambulance crew tried to resuscitate him.* ■ *figurative* make (something such as an idea or enterprise) active or vigorous again: *measures to resuscitate the ailing Japanese economy.* ▷early 16th cent.: from Latin *resuscitat-* 'raised again,' from the verb *resuscitare*, from *re-* 'back' + *suscitare* 'raise.' **—re·sus·ci·ta·tion** /ri,səsəˈtāsHən/ *n.* **—re·sus·ci·ta·tive** /-,tātiv/ *adj.* **—re·sus·ci·ta·tor** /-,tātər/ *n.*

ret /ret/ ▸*v.* (**ret·ted, ret·ting**) [*trans.*] soak (flax or hemp) in water to soften it and separate the fibers. ▷late Middle English: related to Dutch *reten*, also to ROT.

ret. ▸*abbr.* retired.

re·ta·ble /ˈrē,tābəl; ˈretəbəl/ (also **re·ta·blo** /riˈtāblō/) ▸*n.* (*pl.* **-ta·bles** or **-ta·blos**) a frame or shelf enclosing decorated panels or revered objects above and behind an altar. ■ a painting or other image in such a position. ▷early 19th cent.: from French *rétable*, from Spanish *retablo*, from medieval Latin *retrotabulum* 'rear table,' from Latin *retro* 'backward' + *tabula* 'table.'

re·tail /ˈrē,tāl/ ▸*n.* the sale of goods to the public in relatively small quantities for use or consumption rather than for resale: [as *adj.*] *the product's retail price.*
▸*adv.* being sold in such a way: *it is not yet available retail.*
▸*v.* [*trans.*] **1** /ˈrē,tāl/ sell (goods) to the public in such a way: *the difficulties in retailing the new products.* ■ [*intrans.*] (**retail at/for**) (of goods) be sold in this way for (a specified price): *the product retails for around $20.* **2** /ˈrē,tāl; riˈtāl/ recount or relate details of (a story or event) to others: *his inimitable way of retailing a diverting anecdote.* ▷late Middle English: from Anglo-Norman French *retaille* 'a piece cut off,' from *retailler*, from *re-* (expressing intensive force) + *tailler* 'to cut.' **—re·tail·er** *n.*

re·tail park ▸*n.* a shopping development situated outside a town or city, typically containing a number of large chain stores.

re·tail ther·a·py ▸*n. humorous* shopping in order to make oneself feel happier.

re·tain /riˈtān/ ▸*v.* continue to have (something); keep possession of: *built in 1830, the house retains many of its original features.* ■ not abolish, discard, or alter: *the rights of defendants must be retained.* ■ keep in one's memory: *I retained a few French words and phrases.* ■ absorb and continue to hold (a substance): *limestone is known to retain water.* ■ [often as *adj.*] (**retaining**) keep (something) in place; hold fixed: *remove the retaining bar.* ■ keep (someone) engaged in one's service: *he has been retained as a freelance.* ■ secure the services of (a person, esp. an attorney) with a preliminary payment: *retain an attorney to handle the client's business.* ▷late Middle English: via Anglo-Norman French from Old French *retenir*, from Latin *retinere*, from *re-* 'back' + *tenere* 'hold.' **—re·tain·a·bil·i·ty** /ri-,tānəˈbilətē/ *n.* **—re·tain·a·ble** *adj.* **—re·tain·ment** *n.*

re·tain·er /riˈtānər/ ▸*n.* **1** a thing that holds something in place: *a guitar string retainer.* ■ an appliance for keeping a loose tooth, an orthodontic prosthesis, or orthodontically aligned teeth in place. **2** a fee paid in advance to someone, esp. an attorney, in order to secure or keep their services when required. **3** a servant or follower of a noble or wealthy person, esp. one that has worked for a person or family for a long time.

re·tain·ing fee ▸*n.* another term for RETAINER (sense 2).

re·tain·ing wall ▸*n.* a wall that holds back earth or water.

re·take ▸*v.* /rēˈtāk; ˈrē-/ (*past* **-took**; *past part.* **-taken**) [*trans.*] take again, in particular: ■ take (a test or examination) again after a failure or irregularity: *Dan had to retake his driving test.* ■ recapture: *in 799, the Moors retook Barcelona.* ■ regain possession of (something left or lost): *he retook the world driver's championship.* ■ reshoot a movie sequence or a photograph, or re-record a piece of music.
▸*n.* /ˈrē,tāk/ a thing that is retaken, esp. a test or examination. ■ an instance of filming a scene, taking a photograph, or recording a piece of music again.

re·tal·i·ate /riˈtalē,āt/ ▸*v.* [*intrans.*] make an attack or assault in return for a similar attack: *the blow stung and she retaliated immediately.* ■ [*trans.*] *archaic* repay (an injury or insult) in kind: *they used their abilities to retaliate the injury.* ▷early 17th cent.: from Latin *retaliat-* 'returned in kind,' from the verb *retaliare*, from *re-* 'back' + *talis* 'such.' **—re·tal·i·a·tion** /ri,talēˈāsHən/ *n.* **—re·tal·i·a·tive** /riˈtalē,ātiv; -ēətiv/ *adj.* **—re·tal·i·a·tor** /-,ātər/ *n.* **—re·tal·i·a·to·ry** /riˈtalēə,tôrē/ *adj.*

re·tard ▸*v.* /riˈtärd/ [*trans.*] delay or hold back in terms of progress, development, or accomplishment: *his progress was retarded by his limp.*
▸*n.* /ˈrē,tärd/ *offensive* a mentally handicapped person (often used as a general term of abuse). ▷late 15th cent.: from French *retarder*, from Latin *retardare*, from *re-* 'back' + *tardus* 'slow.' **—re·tar·da·tion** /,rē,tärˈdāsHən; ri-/ *n.* **—re·tard·er** *n.* **—re·tard·ment** *n.* (*rare*).

re·tar·dant /riˈtärdnt/ ▸*adj.* [in *combination*] (chiefly of a synthetic or treated fabric or substance) not readily susceptible to fire: *fire-retardant polymers.*
▸*n.* a fabric or substance that prevents or inhibits something, esp. the outbreak of fire. **—re·tard·an·cy** /-ˈtärdnsē/ *n.*

re·tar·da·taire /ri,tärdəˈter/ ▸*adj.* (of a work of art or

Pronunciation Key ə *ago*; ər *over*; ˈə or ,ə *up*; ˈər or ,ər *fur*; a *hat*; ā *rate*; ä *car*; CH *chew*; e *let*; ē *see*; e(ə)r *air*; i *fit*; ī *by*; i(ə)r *ear*; NG *sing*; ō *go*; ô *for*; oi *boy*; o͝o *good*; o͞o *goo*; ou *out*; SH *she*; TH *thin*; TH *then*; (h)w *why*; ZH *vision*

architecture) executed in an earlier or outdated style. ▷French.

re·tar·date /ri'tär,dāt/ ▶*n. dated, offensive* a mentally handicapped person. ▷1950s: from Latin *retardat-* 'slowed down,' from the verb *retardare* (see **RETARD**).

re·tard·ed /ri'tärdid/ ▶*adj.* less advanced in mental, physical, or social development than is usual for one's age.

retch /recH/ ▶*v.* [*intrans.*] make the sound and movement of vomiting. ■ vomit.
▶*n.* a movement or sound of vomiting. ▷mid 19th cent.: variant of dialect *reach*, from a Germanic base meaning 'spittle.'

retd (also **ret.**) ▶*abbr.* retired (used after the name of a retired armed forces officer or in recording that a sports player retired from a game).

re·te /'rētē; 'rātē/ ▶*n.* (*pl.* **-ti·a** /-tēə/) *Anatomy* an elaborate network of blood vessels or nerve cells. ▷mid 16th cent.: from Latin, 'net.'

re·ten·tion /ri'tencHən/ ▶*n.* the continued possession, use, or control of something: *the retention of direct control by central government.* ■ the fact of keeping something in one's memory: *the children's retention of facts.* ■ the action of absorbing and continuing to hold a substance: *the soil's retention of moisture.* ■ failure to eliminate a substance from the body: *eating too much salt can lead to fluid retention.* ▷late Middle English (denoting the power to retain something): from Old French, from Latin *retentio(n-)*, from *retinere* 'hold back' (see **RETAIN**).

re·ten·tive /ri'tentiv/ ▶*adj.* **1** (of a person's memory) having the ability to remember facts and impressions easily. **2** (of a substance) able to absorb and hold moisture. ■ *chiefly Medicine* serving to keep something in place. ▷late Middle English: from Old French *retentif, -ive* or medieval Latin *retentivus*, from *retent-* 'held back,' from the verb *retinere* (see **RETAIN**).
—re·ten·tive·ly *adv.* **—re·ten·tive·ness** *n.*

re·ten·tiv·i·ty /,rē,ten'tivətē; ri-/ ▶*n.* (*pl.* **-ties**) *Physics* the ability of a substance to retain or resist magnetization, frequently measured as the strength of the magnetic field that remains in a sample after removal of an inducing field.

re·test ▶*v.* /rē'test/ [*trans.*] test (someone or something) again.
▶*n.* /'rē,test/ an act of retesting or a repeated test: *he was freed on bond days after the retest and now is seeking a pardon.*

re·tex·ture /rē'teksCHər/ ▶*v.* [*trans.*] treat (skin or hair) so as to restore a healthy or more youthful condition, esp. by moisturizing.

re·think ▶*v.* /rē'THiNGk/ (*past* and *past part.* **-thought**) [*trans.*] think again about (something such as a policy or course of action), esp. in order to make changes to it: *the government was forced to rethink its plans* | [*intrans.*] *I've had to rethink.*
▶*n.* /'rē,THiNGk/ [in *sing.*] a reassessment of something, esp. one that results in changes being made: *a last-minute rethink of their tactics.*

re·tia /'rētēə; 'rā-/ ▶ plural form of **RETE**.

re·ti·ar·i·us /,rēsHē'e(ə)rēəs/ ▶*n.* (*pl.* **-ar·i·i** /-'e(ə)rē,ē; -ē,ī/) an ancient Roman gladiator armed with a net and a spear. ▷Latin, from *rete* 'net.'

ret·i·cent /'retəsənt/ ▶*adj.* not revealing one's thoughts or feelings readily: *she was extremely reticent about her personal affairs.* ▷mid 19th cent.: from Latin *reticent-* 'remaining silent,' from the verb *reticere*, from *re-* (expressing intensive force) + *tacere* 'be silent.' **—ret·i·cence** *n.* **—ret·i·cent·ly** *adv.*

ret·i·cle /'retikəl/ ▶*n.* a series of fine lines or fibers in the eyepiece of an optical device, such as a telescope or microscope, or on the screen of an oscilloscope, used as a measuring scale or an aid in locating objects. ▷mid 18th cent.: from Latin *reticulum* 'net.'

re·tic·u·la /ri'tikyələ/ ▶ plural form of **RETICULUM**.

re·tic·u·lar for·ma·tion /ri'tikyələr/ (also **re·tic·u·lar ac·ti·vat·ing sys·tem**) ▶*n. Anatomy* a diffuse network of nerve pathways in the brainstem connecting the spinal cord, cerebrum, and cerebellum, and mediating the overall level of consciousness.

re·tic·u·late ▶*v.* /ri'tikyə,lāt/ [*trans.*] *rare* divide or mark (something) in such a way as to resemble a net or network: *the numerous canals and branches of the river reticulate the flat alluvial plain.*
▶*adj.* /-lət; -,lāt/ *chiefly Botany Zoology* reticulated. ▷mid 17th cent.: from Latin *reticulatus* 'reticulated,' from *reticulum* (see **RETICULUM**).

re·tic·u·lat·ed /ri'tikyə,lātid/ ▶*adj.* [*attrib.*] constructed, arranged, or marked like a net or network: *a pinafore of a finely reticulated pattern.* ■ (of porcelain) having a pattern of interlacing lines, esp. of pierced work, forming a net or web. ■ *Architecture* relating to or denoting a style of decorated tracery characterized by circular shapes drawn at top and bottom into ogees, resulting in a netlike framework. ■ divided into small squares or sections: *a ranch-style brick home set among reticulated grounds.*

re·tic·u·lat·ed py·thon ▶*n.* a very large Asian python patterned with dark patches outlined in black. It is the longest snake at up to 36 feet (11 m). • *Python reticulatus*, family Pythonidae.

re·tic·u·la·tion /ri,tikyə'lāsHən/ ▶*n.* a pattern or arrangement of interlacing lines resembling a net: *the fish should have a blue back with white reticulation.* ■ *Photography* the formation of a network of wrinkles or cracks in a photographic emulsion.

ret·i·cule /'reti,kyōōl/ ▶*n.* **1** *chiefly historical* a woman's small handbag, originally netted and typically having a drawstring and decorated with embroidery or beading. **2** variant spelling of **RETICLE**. ▷early 18th cent.: from French *réticule*, from Latin *reticulum* (see **RETICULUM**).

re·tic·u·lin /ri'tikyəlin/ ▶*n. Biochemistry* a structural protein resembling collagen, present in connective tissue as a network of fine fibers, esp. around muscle and nerve fibers. ▷late 19th cent.: from *reticular* (see **RETICULUM**) + **-IN**[1].

re·tic·u·lo·cyte /ri'tikyələ,sīt/ ▶*n. Physiology* an immature red blood cell without a nucleus, having a granular or reticulated appearance when suitably stained. ▷1920s: from **RETICULATED** + **-CYTE**.

re·tic·u·lo·en·do·the·li·al /ri,tikyə,lō,endō'THēlēəl/ ▶*adj.* [*attrib.*] *Physiology* relating to or denoting a diverse system of fixed and circulating phagocytic cells (macrophages and monocytes) involved in the immune response. They are spread throughout the body and are especially common in the liver, spleen, and lymphatic system. Also called **LYMPHORETICULAR**. ▷1920s: from **RETICULUM** + *endothelial* (see **ENDOTHELIUM**).

re·tic·u·lo·en·do·the·li·o·sis /ri,tikyə,lō,endō,THēlē'ōsəs/ ▶*n. Medicine* overgrowth of some part of the reticuloendothelial system, causing isolated swelling of the bone marrow and in severe cases the destruction of the bones of the skull.

Re·tic·u·lum /ri'tikyələm/ *Astronomy* a small southern constellation (the Net), between Dorado and Hydrus. ■ [as *genitive*] (**Reticuli**) used with a preceding letter or numeral to designate a star in this constellation: *the star Beta Reticuli.* ▷Latin, diminutive of *rete* 'net.'

re·tic·u·lum /ri'tikyələm/ ▶*n.* (*pl.* **-la** /-lə/) **1** a fine network or netlike structure. See also **ENDOPLASMIC RETICULUM**. **2** *Zoology* the second stomach of a ruminant, having a honeycomblike structure, receiving food from the rumen and passing it to the omasum. ▷mid 17th cent.: from Latin, diminutive of *rete* 'net.' **—re·tic·u·lar** /-lər/ *adj.*

re·ti·form /'retə,fôrm/ ▶*adj. rare* netlike. ▷late 17th cent.: from Latin *rete* 'net' + **-IFORM**.

ret·i·na /'retn-ə/ ▶*n.* (*pl.* **ret·i·nas** or **ret·i·nae** /'retn,ē; 'retn,ī/) a layer at the back of the eyeball containing cells that are sensitive to light and that trigger nerve impulses that pass via the optic nerve to the brain, where a visual image is formed. ▷late Middle English: from medieval Latin, from Latin *rete* 'net.' **—ret·i·nal** /'retn-əl/ *adj.*

Ret·in-A /'retn 'ā/ ▶*n. trademark* a brand of tretinoin, used in the topical treatment of acne and to reduce wrinkles.

ret·i·nal scan·ner ▶*n.* a biometric device that scans a person's or animal's retina in infrared for identification purposes.

ret·i·ni·tis /,retn'ītis/ ▶*n. Medicine* inflammation of the retina of the eye.

ret·i·ni·tis pig·men·to·sa /,pigmən'tōsə; -zə/ ▶*n. Medicine* a chronic hereditary eye disease characterized by black pigmentation and gradual degeneration of the retina. ▷mid 19th cent.: *pigmentosa*, feminine of Latin *pigmentosus*, from *pigmentum* 'pigment.'

ret·ino·blas·to·ma /,retn,ō,bla'stōmə/ ▶*n. Medicine* a rare malignant tumor of the retina, affecting young children.

ret·i·no·ic ac·id /,retn'ōik/ ▶*n.* a carboxylic acid, $C_{19}H_{27}COOH$, obtained from retinol by oxidation and used in ointments to treat acne. ▷1970s: from *retina*.

ret·i·noid /'retn,oid/ ▶*n. Biochemistry* any of a group of compounds having effects in the body like those of vitamin A.

ret·i·nol /'retnôl; -,ōl/ ▶*n. Biochemistry* a yellow compound found in green and yellow vegetables, egg yolk, and fish-liver oil. It is essential for growth and vision in dim light. Also called **VITAMIN A.** • A carotenoid alcohol; chem. formula: $C_{20}H_{29}OH$. ▷1960s: from **RETINA** + **-OL**.

ret·i·nop·a·thy /,retn'äpəTHē/ ▶*n. Medicine* disease of the retina that results in impairment or loss of vision.

ret·i·nue /'retn,(y)ōō/ ▶*n.* a group of advisers, assistants, or others accompanying an important person. ▷late Middle English: from Old French *retenue*, feminine past participle (used as a noun) of *retenir* 'keep back, retain.'

re·tire /ri'tīr/ ▶*v.* **1** [*intrans.*] leave one's job and cease to work, typically upon reaching the normal age for leaving employment: *he* ***retired from*** *the navy in 1966.* ■ [*trans.*] compel (an employee) to leave their job, esp. before they have reached such an age: *the home office retired him.* ■ (of an athlete) cease to play competitively: *he retired from football several years ago.* ■ (of an athlete) withdraw from a race or match, typically as a result of accident or injury: *he was forced to retire to the bench* | [with *complement*] *Stewart retired hurt.* ■ [*trans.*] *Baseball* put out (a batter); cause (a side) to end a turn at bat: *the pitcher retired twelve batters in a row.* ■ [*trans.*] *Economics* withdraw (a bill or note) from circulation or currency. ■ *Finance* pay off or cancel (a debt): *the debt is to be retired from state gaming-tax receipts.* **2** withdraw to or from a particular place: *she retired into the bathroom with her toothbrush.* ■ (of a military force) retreat from an enemy or an attacking position: *lack of numbers compelled the cavalry to retire.* ■ [*trans.*] order (a military force) to retreat: *the general retired all his troops.* ■ (of a jury) leave the courtroom to decide the verdict of a trial. ■ go to bed: *everyone retired early that night.* ▷mid 16th cent. (in the sense 'withdraw (to a place of safety or seclusion)'): from French *retirer*, from *re-* 'back' + *tirer* 'draw.' **—re·tir·er** *n.*

re·ti·ré /rə,tē'rā/ ▶*n.* (*pl.* same) *Ballet* a movement in which one leg is bent and raised at right angles to the body until the toe is in line with the knee of the supporting leg. ▷French, literally 'drawn back.'

re·tired /ri'tīrd/ ▶*adj.* **1** [*attrib.*] having left one's job and ceased to work: *a retired teacher.* **2** *archaic* (of a place) quiet and secluded; not seen or frequented by many people: *this retired corner of the world.* ■ (of a person's way of life) quiet and involving little contact with other people. ■ (of a person) reserved; uncommunicative. **—re·tired·ness** *n.* (*archaic*).

re·tir·ee /ri,tī'rē/ ▶*n.* a person who has retired from full-time work.

re·tire·ment /ri'tīrmənt/ ▶*n.* **1** the action or fact of leaving one's job and ceasing to work: *a man nearing retirement* | *the library has seen a large number of retirements this year.* ■ the period of one's life after leaving one's job and ceasing to work: *he spent much of his retirement traveling in Europe.* ■ the action or fact of ceasing to play a sport competitively. **2** the withdrawal of a jury from the courtroom to decide their verdict. ■ the period of time during which a jury decides their verdict: *a three-hour retirement.* **3** seclusion: *he lived in retirement in Miami.* ■ *archaic* a secluded or private place: *Vermont, where he has a sweet country retirement.*

re·tire·ment home ▶*n.* a house or apartment in which a person lives in old age, esp. one in a complex designed for the needs of old people. ■ an institution for elderly people needing care.

re·tir·ing /ri'tīriNG/ ▶*adj.* shy and fond of being on one's own: *a retiring, acquiescent woman.* **—re·tir·ing·ly** *adv.*

re·told /rē'tōld/ ▶ past and past participle of **RETELL**.

re·took /rē'tŏŏk/ ▶ past of **RETAKE**.

re·tool /rē'tōōl/ ▶*v.* [*trans.*] equip (a factory) with new or adapted tools. ■ adapt or alter (someone or something) to make them more useful or suitable: *he likes to retool the old stories to make them relevant for today's kids.* ■ [*intrans.*] adapt or prepare oneself for something: *perhaps one can even* ***retool for*** *the afterlife.*

re·tort[1] /ri'tôrt/ ▶*v.* **1** [*reporting verb*] say something in answer to a remark or accusation, typically in a sharp, angry, or wittily incisive manner: [with *direct speech*] *"No need to be rude," retorted Isabel* | [with *clause*] *he retorted that this was nonsense* | [*intrans.*] *I resisted the urge to retort.* **2** [*trans.*] *archaic* repay (an insult or injury): *it was now his time to retort the humiliation.* ■ turn (an insult or accusation) back on the person who has issued it: *he was resolute to retort the charge of treason on his foes.* ■ use (an opponent's argument) against them: *the answer they make to us may very easily be retorted.*
▶*n.* a sharp, angry, or wittily incisive reply to a

remark: *she opened her mouth to make a suitably cutting retort.* ▷late 15th cent. (in the sense 'hurl back (an accusation or insult)'): from Latin *retort-* 'twisted back, cast back,' from the verb *retorquere*, from *re-* 'in return' + *torquere* 'to twist.'

re·tort[2] ▶*n.* **1** a container or furnace for carrying out a chemical process on a large or industrial scale. **2** *historical* a glass container with a long neck, used in distilling liquids and other chemical operations.

retort[2] 2

▶*v.* [*trans.*] heat in a retort in order to separate or purify: *the raw shale is retorted at four crude oil works.* ▷early 17th cent.: from French *retorte*, from medieval Latin *retorta*, feminine past participle of *retorquere* 'twist back' (with reference to the long recurved neck of the laboratory container).

re·touch /rē'təCH/ ▶*v.* [*trans.*] improve or repair (a painting, a photograph, makeup, etc.) by making slight additions or alterations. ▷late 17th cent.: probably from French *retoucher*. —**re·touch·er** *n.*

re·trace /rē'trās/ ▶*v.* [*trans.*] go back over (the same route that one has just taken): *he began to* **retrace his steps** *to the parking lot.* ■ discover and follow (a route or course taken by someone else): *I've tried to retrace some of her movements.* ■ trace (something) back to its source or beginning: *I wanted to retrace a particular evolutionary pathway.* ■ trace (lines of drawing or writing) again. ▷late 17th cent.: from French *retracer*.

re·tract /ri'trakt/ ▶*v.* [*trans.*] draw or pull (something) back or back in: *she retracted her hand as if she'd been burned.* ■ withdraw (a statement or accusation) as untrue or unjustified: *he retracted his allegations.* ■ withdraw or go back on (an undertaking or promise): *the parish council was forced to retract a previous resolution.* ■ (of an animal) draw (a part of itself) back into its body: *the cat retracted her claws.* ■ draw (the undercarriage or the wheels) up into the body of an aircraft. ■ [*intrans.*] be drawn back into something: *the tentacle retracted quickly.* ▷late Middle English: from Latin *retract-* 'drawn back,' from the verb *retrahere* (from *re-* 'back' + *trahere* 'drag'); the senses 'withdraw (a statement)' and 'go back on' via Old French from *retractare* 'reconsider' (based on *trahere* 'drag'). —**re·tract·a·ble** *adj.* —**re·trac·tion** /ri'trakSHən/ *n.* —**re·trac·tive** /-tiv/ *adj.*

re·trac·tile /ri'traktəl; -,tīl/ ▶*adj. Zoology* capable of being retracted: *a long retractile proboscis.* ▷late 18th cent.: from RETRACT, on the pattern of *contractile*. —**re·trac·til·i·ty** /,rē,trak'tilətē/ *n.*

re·trac·tor /ri'traktər/ ▶*n.* a device for retracting something: *seat belts with automatic retractors.* ■ (also **re·trac·tor mus·cle**) *chiefly Zoology* a muscle serving to retract a part of the body. Compare with PROTRACTOR.

re·train /rē'trān/ ▶*v.* [*trans.*] teach (someone) new skills, esp. so that they can do a different job. ■ [*intrans.*] learn new skills, esp. so as to be able to do a different job: *a workforce which is willing to retrain.*

re·trans·late /,rētrans'lāt; -tranz-/ ▶*v.* [*trans.*] translate (a translation) back into its original language. —**re·trans·la·tion** /-'lāSHən/ *n.*

re·trans·mit /,rētrans'mit; -tranz-/ ▶*v.* (**-mit·ted**, **-mit·ting**) [*trans.*] transmit (data, a radio signal, or a broadcast program) again or on to another receiver. —**re·trans·mis·sion** /-'misHən/ *n.*

re·tread ▶*v.* /rē'tred/ **1** (*past* **-trod**; *past part.* **-trod·den**) [*trans.*] go back over (a path or one's steps): *they never retread the same ground.* **2** (*past* and *past part.* **-tread·ed**) [*trans.*] put a new tread on (a worn tire).

▶*n.* /'rē,tred/ a tire that has been given a new tread. ■ *informal* a person retrained for new work or recalled for service. ■ *informal* a superficially altered version of an original: *a retread of the 30s romantic comedy.*

re·treat /ri'trēt/ ▶*v.* [*intrans.*] (of an army) withdraw from enemy forces as a result of their superior power or after a defeat: *the French retreated in disarray.* ■ move back or withdraw, esp. so as to remove oneself from a difficult or uncomfortable situation: *it becomes so hot that the lizards retreat into the shade* | [as *adj.*] (**retreating**) *the sound of retreating footsteps.* ■ withdraw to a quiet or secluded place: *after the funeral he retreated to the shore.* ■ (of an expanse of ice or water) become smaller in size or extent: *a series of trenches which filled with water when the ice retreated.* ■ change one's decisions, plans, or attitude, as a result of criticism from others: *his proposals were clearly unreasonable and he was soon forced to retreat.* ■ (of shares of stock) decline in value: [with *complement*] *shares retreated 32 points to 653 points.* ■ [*trans.*] *Chess* move (a piece) back from a forward or threatened position on the board.

▶*n.* **1** an act of moving back or withdrawing: *a speedy retreat* | *the army was* **in retreat**. ■ an act of changing one's decisions, plans, or attitude, esp. as a result of criticism from others: *the unions made a retreat from their earlier position.* ■ a decline in the value of shares of stock. **2** a signal for a military force to withdraw: *the bugle sounded a retreat.* ■ a military musical ceremony carried out at sunset, originating in the playing of drums and bugles to tell soldiers to return to camp for the night. **3** a quiet or secluded place in which one can rest and relax: *their mountain retreat in New Hampshire.* ■ a period of seclusion for the purposes of prayer and meditation: *the bishop is away on his annual retreat* | *before his ordination he* **went on retreat**. ▷late Middle English: from Old French *retret* (noun), *retraiter* (verb), from Latin *retrahere* 'pull back' (see RETRACT).

▶*PHRASE* □ **beat a retreat** see BEAT.

re·trench /ri'trencH/ ▶*v.* [*intrans.*] (of a company, government, or individual) reduce costs or spending in response to economic difficulty: *as a result of the recession the company retrenched* | [*trans.*] *if people are forced to retrench their expenditure trade will suffer.* ■ [*trans.*] *formal* reduce or diminish (something) in extent or quantity: *fortune had retrenched her once abundant gifts.* ▷late 16th cent. (in the now formal usage): from obsolete French *retrencher*, variant of *retrancher*, from *re-* (expressing reversal) + *trancher* 'to cut, slice.' —**re·trench·ment** *n.*

re·tri·al /rē'trīəl; 'rē,trīəl/ ▶*n. Law* a second or further trial.

ret·ri·bu·tion /,retrə'byōōSHən/ ▶*n.* punishment that is considered to be morally right and fully deserved: *settlers drove the Navajo out of Arizona* **in retribution for** *their raids.* ▷late Middle English (also in the sense 'recompense for merit or a service'): from late Latin *retributio(n-)*, from *retribut-* 'assigned again,' from the verb *retribuere*, from *re-* 'back' + *tribuere* 'assign.' —**re·trib·u·tive** /ri'tribyətiv/ *adj.* —**re·trib·u·to·ry** /ri'tribyə,tôrē/ *adj.*

re·triev·al /ri'trēvəl/ ▶*n.* the process of getting something back from somewhere: *the investigation was completed after the retrieval of plane wreckage.* ■ the obtaining or consulting of material stored in a computer system.

re·trieve /ri'trēv/ ▶*v.* [*trans.*] get (something) back; regain possession of: *I was sent to retrieve the balls from his garden.* See note at RECOVER. ■ pick (something) up: *Steven stooped and retrieved his hat.* ■ (of a dog) find and bring back (game or an object). ■ bring (something) back into one's mind: *the police hope to encourage him to retrieve forgotten memories.* ■ find or extract (information stored in a computer). ■ put right or improve (an unwelcome situation): *he made one last desperate attempt to retrieve the situation.* ■ [*intrans.*] reel or bring in a fishing line.

▶*n.* **1** an act of retrieving something, esp. game that has been shot. ■ an act of reeling or drawing in a fishing line. **2** *archaic* the possibility of recovery: *he ruined himself* **beyond retrieve**. ▷late Middle English (in the sense 'find lost game,' said of a hunting dog): from Old French *retroeve-*, stressed stem of *retrover* 'find again.' —**re·triev·a·bil·i·ty** /ri,trēvə'bilətē/ *n.* —**re·triev·a·ble** *adj.*

re·triev·er /ri'trēvər/ ▶*n.* **1** a dog of a breed used for retrieving game. **2** a person or thing that retrieves something.

ret·ro[1] /'retrō/ ▶*adj.* imitative of a style, fashion, or design from the recent past: *retro 60s fashions.*

▶*n.* clothes or music whose style or design is imitative of those of the recent past: *a look that mixes Italian casual wear and American retro.* ▷1960s: from French *rétro*, abbreviation of *rétrograde* 'retrograde.'

ret·ro[2] ▶*n.* (*pl.* **-tros**) short for RETROROCKET.

retro- ▶*comb. form* **1** denoting action that is directed backward or is reciprocal: *retrocede* | *retroject.* **2** denoting location behind: *retrosternal* | *retrochoir.* ▷from Latin *retro* 'backward.'

ret·ro·ac·tive /,retrō'aktiv/ ▶*adj.* (esp. of legislation) taking effect from a date in the past: *a big retroactive tax increase.* —**ret·ro·ac·tion** /-'akSHən/ *n.* —**ret·ro·ac·tive·ly** *adv.* —**ret·ro·ac·tiv·i·ty** /-,ak'tivətē/ *n.*

ret·ro·ac·tive in·hi·bi·tion ▶*n. Psychology* the tendency of later learning to hinder the memory of previously learned material.

ret·ro·bul·bar /,retrō'bəlbər; -,bär/ ▶*adj.* [*attrib.*] *Anatomy & Medicine* situated or occurring behind the eyeball: *a retrobulbar abscess.*

ret·ro·cede /,retrə'sēd/ ▶*v.* [*trans.*] *rare* cede (territory) back again: *the British colony of Hong Kong, retroceded to China.* ▷early 19th cent.: from French *rétrocéder*. —**ret·ro·ces·sion** /-'sesHən/ *n.*

ret·ro·choir /'retrō,kwīr/ ▶*n.* the interior of a cathedral or large church behind the high altar. ▷mid 19th cent.: from medieval Latin *retrochorus* (see RETRO-, CHOIR).

re·trod /rē'träd/ ▶ past of RETREAD (sense 1).

re·trod·den /rē'trädn/ ▶ past participle of RETREAD (sense 1).

ret·ro·dict /,retrō'dikt/ ▶*v.* state a fact about the past based on inference or deduction, rather than evidence: *the model must be able to retrodict a very large quantity of dark matter, and say something about its composition.* | *Can tree ring records be used to retrodict paleofloods?* ▷late 20th cent.: on the pattern of *predict*. —**ret·ro·dic·tion** *n.*

ret·ro·dic·tion /,retrə'dikSHən/ ▶*n.* the explanation or interpretation of past actions or events inferred from the laws that are assumed to have governed them.

ret·ro·fit /,retrō'fit/ ▶*v.* (**-fit·ted**, **-fit·ting**) [*trans.*] add (a component or accessory) to something that did not have it when manufactured: *drivers who retrofit catalysts to older cars.* ■ provide (something) with a component or accessory not fitted to it during manufacture: *buses have been retrofitted with easy-access features.*

▶*n.* an act of adding a component or accessory to something that did not have it when manufactured. ■ a component or accessory added to something after manufacture. ▷1950s: blend of RETROACTIVE and REFIT.

ret·ro·flex /'retrə,fleks/ (also **ret·ro·flexed**) ▶*adj. Anatomy & Medicine* turned backward: *a retroflex fibers.* ■ *Phonetics* pronounced with the tip of the tongue curled up toward the hard palate: *the retroflex /r/.* ▷late 18th cent.: from Latin *retroflex-* 'bent backward,' from the verb *retroflectere*, from *retro* 'backward' + *flectere* 'to bend.' —**ret·ro·flex·ion** /,retrə'flekSHən/ *n.*

ret·ro·gra·da·tion /,retrōgrā'dāSHən/ ▶*n. Astronomy & Astrology* the apparent temporary reverse motion of a planet (from east to west), resulting from the relative orbital progress of the earth and the planet. ■ the orbiting or rotation of a planet or planetary satellite in a reverse direction from that normal in the solar system. ▷mid 16th cent.: from late Latin *retrogradatio(n)-* (see RETRO-, GRADATION).

ret·ro·grade /'retrə,grād/ ▶*adj.* directed or moving backward: *a retrograde flow.* ■ reverting to an earlier and inferior condition: *to go back on the progress that has been made would be a retrograde step.* ■ (of the order of something) reversed; inverse: *the retrograde form of these inscriptions.* ■ (of amnesia) involving the period immediately preceding the causal event. ■ *Geology* (of a metamorphic change) resulting from a decrease in temperature or pressure. ■ *Astronomy & Astrology* (of the apparent motion of a planet) in a reverse direction from normal (from east to west), resulting from the relative orbital progress of the earth and the planet. The opposite of PROGRADE. ■ *Astronomy* (of the orbit or rotation of a planet or planetary satellite) in a reverse direction from that normal in the solar system.

▶*n. rare* a degenerate person.

▶*v.* [*intrans.*] **1** *archaic* go back in position or time: *our history must retrograde for the space of a few pages.* ■ revert to an earlier and usually inferior condition: *people cannot habitually trample on law and justice without retrograding toward barbarism.* **2** *Astronomy* show retrogradation: *all the planets will at some time appear to retrograde.* ▷late Middle English (as a term in astronomy): from Latin *retrogradus*, from *retro* 'backward' + *gradus* 'step' (from *gradi* 'to walk'). —**ret·ro·grade·ly** *adv.* (*rare*).

ret·ro·gress /,retrə'gres/ ▶*v.* [*intrans.*] go back to an earlier state, typically a worse one: *she retrogressed to the starting point of her rehabilitation.* ▷early 19th cent.: from RETRO- 'back,' on the pattern of the verb *progress*.

ret·ro·gres·sion /,retrə'gresHən/ ▶*n.* **1** the process of returning to an earlier state, typically a worse one: *a kind of extreme retrogression to 19th-century attitudes.*

Pronunciation Key ə *ago*; ər *over*; 'ə or ,ə *up*; 'ər or ,ər *fur*; a *hat*; ā *rate*; ä *car*; CH *chew*; e *let*; ē *see*; e(ə)r *air*; i *fit*; ī *by*; i(ə)r *ear*; NG *sing*; ō *go*; ô *for*; oi *boy*; ŏŏ *good*; ōō *goo*; ou *out*; SH *she*; TH *thin*; TH *then*; (h)w *why*; ZH *vision*

2 *Astronomy* another term for **RETROGRADATION.** ▷mid 17th cent.: from **RETRO-** 'backward,' on the pattern of *progression.* **—ret·ro·gres·sive** /-'gresiv/ *adj.*

ret·ro·ject /'retrə,jekt/ ▶*v.* [*trans.*] *rare* project backward: *the rabbinic interpretation is retrojected into the biblical text.* ▷mid 19th cent.: from **RETRO-** 'backward,' on the pattern of the verb *project.*

ret·ro·len·tal fi·bro·pla·sia /,retrə'lentl ,fibrə'plāZHə/ ▶*n. Medicine* abnormal proliferation of fibrous tissue immediately behind the lens of the eye, leading to blindness. It affected many premature babies in the 1950s, owing to the excessive administration of oxygen.

ret·ro·per·i·to·ne·al /,retrō,peratn'ēəl/ ▶*adj. Anatomy & Medicine* situated or occurring behind the peritoneum.

ret·ro·re·flec·tor /,retrōri'flektər/ ▶*n.* a device that reflects light back along the incident path, irrespective of the angle of incidence. **—ret·ro·re·flec·tive** /-'flektiv/ *adj.*

ret·ro·rock·et /'retrō,räkit/ ▶*n.* a small auxiliary rocket on a spacecraft or missile, fired in the direction of travel to slow the craft down, for example, when landing on the surface of a planet.

re·trorse /'rē,trôrs/ ▶*adj. Biology* turned or pointing backward: *retrorse spines.* ▷early 19th cent.: from Latin *retrorsus,* contraction of *retroversus,* from *retro* 'backward' + *versus* 'turned' (past participle of *vertere*).

ret·ro·spect /'retrə,spekt/ ▶*n.* a survey or review of a past course of events or period of time. ▷early 17th cent.: from **RETRO-** 'back,' on the pattern of the noun *prospect.*

▶*PHRASE* □ **in retrospect** when looking back on a past event or situation; with hindsight: *perhaps, in retrospect, I shouldn't have gone.*

ret·ro·spec·tion /,retrə'speksHən/ ▶*n.* the action of looking back on or reviewing past events or situations, esp. those in one's own life: *he was disinclined to indulge in retrospection.* ▷mid 17th cent.: probably from **RETROSPECT** (used as a verb).

ret·ro·spec·tive /,retrə'spektiv/ ▶*adj.* looking back on or dealing with past events or situations: *our survey was retrospective.* ■ (of an exhibition or compilation) showing the development of an artist's work over a period of time. ■ (of a statute or legal decision) taking effect from a date in the past: *retrospective pay awards.*

▶*n.* an exhibition or compilation showing the development of the work of a particular artist over a period of time: *a Georgia O'Keeffe retrospective.* **—ret·ro·spec·tive·ly** *adv.*

ret·ro·ster·nal /,retrō'stərnl/ ▶*adj. Anatomy & Medicine* behind the breastbone.

ret·ro·trans·po·son /,retrōtrans'pō,zän; -tranz-/ ▶*n. Genetics* a transposon whose sequence shows homology with that of a retrovirus.

ret·rous·sé /rə,trōō'sā ,retrōō-/ ▶*adj.* (of a person's nose) turned up at the tip, esp. in an attractive way. ▷early 19th cent.: French, literally 'tucked up,' past participle of *retrousser.*

ret·ro·vert·ed /,retrə'vərtəd/ ▶*adj. Anatomy* (of the uterus) tilted abnormally backward. ▷late 18th cent.: from Latin *retrovertere* 'turn backward' + **-ED**[2]. **—ret·ro·ver·sion** /-'vərZHən/ *n.*

Ret·ro·vir /'retrō,vi(ə)r/ ▶*n.* trademark for **ZIDOVUDINE.** ▷1980s: abbreviation of **RETROVIRUS.**

ret·ro·vi·rus /,retrō'vīrəs; 'retrō,vīrəs/ ▶*n. Biology* any of a group of RNA viruses that insert a DNA copy of their genome into the host cell in order to replicate, e.g., HIV. ▷1970s: modern Latin, from the initial letters of *reverse transcriptase* + **VIRUS.**

re·try /rē'trī/ ▶*v.* (**-tries, -tried**) **1** [*trans.*] *Law* try (a defendant or case) again. **2** [*intrans.*] *Computing* reenter a command, esp. differently because one has made an error the first time. ■ (of a system) transmit data again because the first attempt was unsuccessful.

▶*n.* an instance of reentering a command or retransmitting data.

ret·si·na /ret'sēnə/ ▶*n.* a Greek white or rosé wine flavored with resin. ▷modern Greek.

re·tune /rē't(y)ōōn/ ▶*v.* [*trans.*] tune (something) again or differently, in particular: ■ put (a musical instrument) back in tune or alter its pitch. ■ tune (a radio, television, or other piece of electronic equipment) to a different frequency.

re·turn /ri'tərn/ ▶*v.* **1** [*intrans.*] come or go back to a place or person: *he* ***returned to*** *Canada in the fall.* ■ (**return to**) go back to (a particular state or activity): *Ollie had returned to full health.* ■ (**return to**) turn one's attention back to (something): *he returned to his newspaper.* ■ (esp. of a feeling) come back or recur after a period of absence: *her appetite had returned.* **2** [*trans.*] give, put, or send (something) back to a place or person: *complete the application form and* ***return it to*** *this address.* ■ feel, say, or do (the same feeling, action, etc.) in response: *she returned his kiss.* ■ (in tennis and other sports) hit or send (the ball) back to an opponent. ■ *Football* run upfield with the ball after fielding (a kick), intercepting (a pass), or recovering (a fumble). ■ (of a judge or jury) state or present (a verdict) in response to a formal request. ■ *Bridge* lead (a card of a suit led earlier by one's partner). ■ *Architecture* continue (a wall) in a changed direction, esp. at right angles. **3** [*trans.*] yield or make (a profit): *the company returned a profit of 4.3 million dollars.* **4** [*trans.*] (of an electorate) elect (a person or party) to office: *the Democrat was returned in the third district.*

▶*n.* **1** an act of coming or going back to a place or activity: *he celebrated his safe return from the war* | [as *adj.*] *a return flight.* ■ [in *sing.*] an act of going back to an earlier state or condition: *the designer advocated a return to elegance.* ■ the action of giving, sending, or putting something back: *we demand the return of our books and papers.* ■ *Football* a play in which the ball is caught after a kick or pass interception and is advanced by running; an advance of this kind. ■ (in tennis and other sports) a stroke played in response to a serve or other stroke by one's opponent. ■ a thing that has been given or sent back, esp. an unwanted ticket for a sports event or play. ■ (also **re·turn tick·et**) *chiefly Brit.* a ticket that allows someone to travel to a place and back again; a round trip ticket. ■ an electrical conductor bringing a current back to its source. ■ (also **re·turn game**) a second contest between the same opponents. **2** (often **returns**) a profit from an investment: *product areas are being developed to produce maximum returns.* ■ a good rate of return. **3** an official report or statement submitted in response to a formal demand: *census returns.* ■ *Law* an endorsement or report by a court officer or sheriff on a writ. **4** election to office: *we campaigned for the return of Young and Elkins.* ■ an official report of the results of an election: *falsification of the election return.* **5** (also **car·riage re·turn**) a key pressed to move the carriage of an electric typewriter back to a fixed position. ■ (also **re·turn key**) a key pressed on a computer keyboard to simulate a carriage return in a word-processing program, or to indicate the end of a command or data string. **6** *Architecture* a part receding from the line of the front, for example the side of a house or of a window opening. ▷Middle English: the verb from Old French *retorner,* from Latin *re-* 'back' + *tornare* 'to turn'; the noun via Anglo-Norman French. **—re·turn·a·ble** *adj.* **—re·turn·er** *n.*

▶*PHRASES* □ **in return** as a response, exchange, or reward for something: *he leaves the house to his sister in return for her kindness.* □ **many happy returns (of the day)** used as a greeting to someone on their birthday. □ **return thanks** express thanks, esp. in a grace at a meal or in response to a toast or condolence.

re·turn·ee /ri,tər'nē/ ▶*n.* a person who returns, esp. after a prolonged absence, in particular: ■ a member of the armed forces returning from overseas duty. ■ a traveler returning home. ■ a refugee returning from abroad.

re·turn·ing of·fi·cer ▶*n.* (in the UK, Canada, New Zealand, and Australia) the official in each constituency or electorate who conducts an election and announces the result.

Reu·ben /'rōōbən/ (in the Bible) a Hebrew patriarch, eldest son of Jacob and Leah (Gen. 29:32). ■ the tribe of Israel traditionally descended from him.

re·u·ni·fy /rē'yōōnə,fī/ ▶*v.* (**-fies, -fied**) [*trans.*] restore political unity to (a place or group, esp. a divided territory): *communist insurgents had effectively reunified the country.* **—re·u·ni·fi·ca·tion** /,rē,yōōnəfi'kāsHən/ *n.*

Ré·u·nion /rē'yōōnyən; rā-Y'nyôN/ a volcanically active, subtropical island in the Indian Ocean, east of Madagascar, one of the Mascarene Islands; pop. 597,000; capital, Saint-Denis. A French possession since 1638, the island became an administrative region of France in 1974.

re·un·ion /rē'yōōnyən/ ▶*n.* an instance of two or more people coming together again after a period of separation: *she had a tearful reunion with her parents.* ■ a social gathering attended by members of a certain group of people who have not seen each other for some time: *a school reunion.* ■ the act or process of being brought together again as a unified whole: *the reunion of East and West Germany.* ▷early 17th cent.: from French *réunion* or Anglo-Latin *reunio(n-),* from Latin *reunire* 'unite.'

re·u·nite /,rēyōō'nit/ ▶*v.* come together or cause to come together again after a period of separation or disunity: [*intrans.*] *the three friends reunited in 1959* | [*trans.*] *Stephanie was* ***reunited with*** *her parents.*

re·up·hol·ster /,rēəp'hōlstər; ,rēə'pōl-/ ▶*v.* [*trans.*] upholster with new materials, esp. with a different fabric: *the bed was reupholstered in chintz.* **—re·up·hol·ster·y** /-stərē/ *n.*

re·use ▶*v.* /rē'yōōz/ [*trans.*] use again or more than once: *the tape could be magnetically erased and reused.*

▶*n.* /re'yōōs/ the action of using something again: *the ballast was cleaned and ready for reuse.* **—re·us·a·ble** /rē-'yōōzəbəl/ *adj.*

Reu·ter /'roitər/, Paul Julius, Baron von (1816–99), German pioneer of telegraphy and news reporting; born *Israel Beer Josaphat.* He founded the news agency Reuters.

Reu·ters /'roitərz/ an international news agency founded in London in 1851 by Paul Julius Reuter. The agency pioneered the use of telegraphy, building up a service used today by newspapers and radio and television stations in most countries.

Reu·ther /'rōōTHər/, Walter (Philip) (1907–70), U.S. labor leader. He was president of the United Automobile Workers 1946–70 and of the Congress of Industrial Organizations from 1952 until 1955 when it merged with the American Federation of Labor.

rev /rev/ *informal* ▶*n.* (usu. **revs**) a revolution of an engine per minute: *an engine speed of 1,750 revs.* ■ an act of increasing the speed of revolution of a vehicle's engine by pressing the accelerator, esp. while the clutch is disengaged.

▶*v.* (**revved, rev·ving**) [*trans.*] increase the running speed of (an engine) or the engine speed of (a vehicle) by pressing the accelerator, esp. while the clutch is disengaged: *he got into the car,* ***revved up*** *the engine and drove off* | [*intrans.*] *I* ***revved up*** *enthusiastically.* ■ [*intrans.*] (of an engine or vehicle) operate with increasing speed when the accelerator is pressed, esp. while the clutch is disengaged: *he could hear the sound of an engine revving nearby* | *figurative he's* ***revving up*** *for next week's World Cup game.* ▷early 20th cent.: abbreviation of **REVOLUTION.**

Rev. ▶*abbr.* ■ *Bible* the book of Revelation. ■ (as the title of a priest) Reverend.

re·val·ue /rē'valyōō/ ▶*v.* (**-val·ues, -val·ued, -val·u·ing**) [*trans.*] assess the value of (something) again. ■ *Economics* adjust the value of (a currency) in relation to other currencies. **—re·val·u·a·tion** /rē,valyōō'āsHən/ *n.*

re·vamp /rē'vamp/ ▶*v.* [*trans.*] give new and improved form, structure, or appearance to: *an attempt to revamp the museum's image* | [as *adj.*] (**revamped**) *a revamped magazine.*

▶*n.* [usu. in *sing.*] an act of improving the form, structure, or appearance of something. ■ a new and improved version: *the show was a revamp of an old idea.*

re·vanche /rə'vänsH/ ▶*n.* the policy of a nation to seek the return of lost territory. ▷French, literally 'revenge.'

re·vanch·ism /rə'vän,sHizəm/ ▶*n.* a policy of seeking to retaliate, esp. to recover lost territory. ▷1950s: from French *revanche* (see **REVANCHE**) + **-ISM.** The form *revanchist* dates from the 1920s. **—re·vanch·ist** *adj.* & *n.*

Revd ▶*abbr.* (as the title of a priest) Reverend.

re·veal[1] /ri'vēl/ ▶*v.* [*trans.*] make (previously unknown or secret information) known to others: *Brenda was forced to reveal Robbie's whereabouts* | [with *clause*] *he revealed that he and his children had received death threats.* ■ cause or allow (something) to be seen: *the clouds were breaking up to reveal a clear blue sky.* ■ make (something) known to humans by divine or supernatural means: *the truth revealed at the Incarnation.* ▷late Middle English: from Old French *reveler* or Latin *revelare,* from *re-* 'again' (expressing reversal) + *velum* 'veil.' **—re·veal·a·ble** *adj.* **—re·veal·er** *n.*

re·veal[2] ▶*n.* either side surface of an aperture in a wall for a door or window. ▷late 17th cent.: from obsolete *revale* 'to lower,' from Old French *revaler,* from *re-* 'back' + *avaler* 'go down, sink.'

re·vealed re·li·gion ▶*n.* religion based on divine revelation rather than reason.

re·veal·ing /ri'vēliNG/ ▶*adj.* making interesting or significant information known, esp. about a person's attitude or character: *a revealing radio interview.* ■ (of an item of clothing) allowing more of the wearer's body to be seen than is usual: *a very revealing dress.* **—re·veal·ing·ly** *adv.*

R

re·veg·e·tate /rē'vejə,tāt/ ▸*v.* [*trans.*] produce a new growth of vegetation on (disturbed or barren ground): *each spring we revegetate acre after acre with pine seedlings* | [*intrans.*] *a quarter of the area had revegetated.* —**re·veg·e·ta·tion** /rē,vejə'tāsʜən/ *n.*

rev·eil·le /'revəlē/ ▸*n.* [in *sing.*] a signal sounded esp. on a bugle or drum to wake personnel in the armed forces. ▷mid 17th cent.: from French *réveillez!* 'wake up!,' imperative plural of *réveiller*, based on Latin *vigilare* 'keep watch.'

rev·el /'revəl/ ▸*v.* (**rev·eled, rev·el·ing**; *chiefly Brit.* **rev·elled, rev·el·ling**) [*intrans.*] engage in lively and noisy festivities, esp. those which involve drinking and dancing: [as *n.*] (**reveling**) *a night of drunken reveling.* ■ (**revel in**) get great pleasure from (a situation or experience): *Bill said he was secretly reveling in his newfound fame.*
▸*n.* (**revels**) lively and noisy festivities, esp. those which involve drinking and dancing. ▷late Middle English: from Old French *reveler* 'rise up in rebellion,' from Latin *rebellare* 'to rebel.' —**rev·el·er** or **rev·el·ler** *n.*

rev·e·la·tion /,revə'lāsʜən/ ▸*n.* **1** a surprising and previously unknown fact, esp. one that is made known in a dramatic way: *revelations about his personal life.* ■ the making known of something that was previously secret or unknown: *the revelation of an alleged plot to assassinate the king.* ■ used to emphasize the surprising or remarkable quality of someone or something: *seeing them play at international level was a revelation.* **2** the divine or supernatural disclosure to humans of something relating to human existence or the world: *an attempt to reconcile Darwinian theories with biblical revelation* | *a divine revelation.* ■ (**Revelation** or *informal* **Revelations**) (in full **the Revelation of St. John the Divine**) the last book of the New Testament, recounting a divine revelation of the future to St. John. ▷Middle English (in the theological sense): from Old French, or from late Latin *revelatio(n-)*, from *revelare* 'lay bare' (see **REVEAL**[1]). Sense 1 dates from the mid 19th cent. —**rev·e·la·tion·al** /-sʜənl/ *adj.*

rev·e·la·tion·ist /,revə'lāsʜənist/ ▸*n.* a believer in divine revelation.

re·vel·a·to·ry /'revələ,tôrē; ri'vel-/ ▸*adj.* revealing something hitherto unknown: *an invigorating and revelatory performance.*

rev·el·ry /'revəlrē/ ▸*n.* (*pl.* **-ries**) (also **revelries**) lively and noisy festivities, esp. when these involve drinking a large amount of alcohol: *sounds of revelry issued into the night* | *New Year revelries.*

rev·e·nant /'revə,nän; -nənt/ ▸*n.* a person who has returned, esp. supposedly from the dead. ▷early 19th cent.: French, literally 'coming back,' present participle (used as a noun) of *revenir.*

re·venge /ri'venj/ ▸*n.* the action of inflicting hurt or harm on someone for an injury or wrong suffered at their hands: *other spurned wives have* ***taken*** *public* ***revenge on*** *their husbands.* ■ the desire to inflict such retribution: *it was difficult not to be overwhelmed with feelings of hate and revenge.* ■ (in sports) the defeat of a person or team by whom one was beaten in a previous encounter: *the Yankees wanted to get their revenge for losing to the Dodgers in the 1955 Series.*
▸*v.* (**revenge oneself** or **be revenged**) *chiefly archaic poetic/literary* inflict hurt or harm on someone for an injury or wrong done to oneself: *I'll* ***be revenged on*** *the whole pack of you.* ■ [*trans.*] inflict such retribution on behalf of (someone else): *it's a pity he chose that way to revenge his sister.* ■ inflict retribution for (a wrong or injury done to oneself or another): *her brother was slain, and she revenged his death.* ▷late Middle English: from Old French *revencher*, from late Latin *revindicare*, from *re-* (expressing intensive force) + *vindicare* 'claim, avenge.' —**re·veng·er** *n.* (*poetic/literary*).
▸***PHRASE*** □ **revenge is a dish best served** (or **eaten**) **cold** *proverb* vengeance is often more satisfying if it is not exacted immediately.

re·venge·ful /ri'venjfəl/ ▸*adj.* eager for revenge. —**re·venge·ful·ly** *adv.* —**re·venge·ful·ness** *n.*

re·venge trag·e·dy ▸*n.* a style of drama, popular in England during the late 16th and 17th centuries, in which the basic plot was a quest for vengeance and which typically featured scenes of carnage and mutilation. Examples of the genre include Thomas Kyd's *The Spanish Tragedy* (1592) and John Webster's *The Duchess of Malfi* (1623).

rev·e·nue /'revə,n(y)o͞o/ ▸*n.* income, esp. when of a company or organization and of a substantial nature. ■ a state's annual income from which public expenses are met. ■ (**revenues**) items or amounts constituting such income: *the government's tax revenues.* ■ the government department collecting such income. ▷late Middle English: from Old French *revenu(e)* 'returned,' past participle (used as a noun) of *revenir*, from Latin *revenire* 'return,' from *re-* 'back' + *venire* 'come.'

rev·e·nue shar·ing ▸*n.* the distribution of a portion of federal tax revenues to state and local governments.

rev·e·nue stamp ▸*n.* a stamp showing that a government tax has been paid.

rev·e·nue tar·iff ▸*n.* a tariff imposed principally to raise government revenue rather than to protect domestic industries.

re·verb /'rē,vərb; ri'vərb/ ▸*n.* an effect whereby the sound produced by an amplifier or an amplified musical instrument is made to reverberate slightly. ■ a device for producing such an effect. ▷1960s: abbreviation.

re·ver·ber·ate /ri'vərbə,rāt/ ▸*v.* [*intrans.*] (of a loud noise) be repeated several times as an echo: *her deep booming laugh reverberated around the room.* ■ (of a place) appear to vibrate or be disturbed because of a loud noise: *the hall* ***reverberated with*** *gaiety and laughter.* ■ [*trans.*] *archaic* return or reecho (a sound): *oft did the cliffs reverberate the sound.* ■ have continuing and serious effects: *the statements by the professor reverberated through the capitol.* ▷late 15th cent. (in the sense 'drive or beat back'): from Latin *reverberat-* 'struck again,' from the verb *reverberare*, from *re-* 'back' + *verberare* 'to lash' (from *verbera* (plural) 'scourge'). —**re·ver·ber·ant** /-rənt/ *adj.* —**re·ver·ber·ant·ly** /-rəntlē/ *adv.* —**re·ver·ber·a·tion** /ri,vərbə'rāsʜən/ *n.* —**re·ver·ber·a·tive** /-rətiv/ *adj.* —**re·ver·ber·a·tor** /-,rātər/ *n.* —**re·ver·ber·a·to·ry** /-rə,tôrē/ *adj.*

re·ver·ber·a·to·ry fur·nace ▸*n.* a furnace in which the roof and walls are heated by flames and radiate heat on to material in the center of the furnace.

Re·vere[1] /rə'vi(ə)r/ a city in east central Massachusetts, on Massachusetts Bay, northeast of Boston; pop. 42,786.

Re·vere[2], Paul (1735–1818), American silversmith and patriot. In 1775 he rode from Boston to Lexington to warn fellow American revolutionaries of the approach of British troops. He is the subject of Henry Wadsworth Longfellow's famous poem "Paul Revere's Ride" (1863).

re·vere /ri'vi(ə)r/ ▸*v.* [*trans.*] (often **be revered**) feel deep respect or admiration for (something): *Cézanne's still lifes were revered by his contemporaries* ▷mid 17th cent.: from French *révérer* or Latin *revereri*, from *re-* (expressing intensive force) + *vereri* 'to fear.'

THE RIGHT WORD **admire, adore, idolize, revere, venerate, worship**

We might **admire** someone who walks a tightrope between two skyscrapers, **idolize** a rock star, **adore** our mothers, and **revere** a person like Martin Luther King, Jr. Each of these verbs conveys the idea of regarding someone or something with respect and honor, but they differ considerably in terms of the feelings they connote.

Admire suggests a feeling of delight and enthusiastic appreciation (*admire the courage of the mountain climber*), while *adore* implies the tenderness and warmth of unquestioning love (*he adored babies*).

Idolize is an extreme form of adoration, suggesting a slavish, helpless love, (*he idolized the older quarterback*).

We *revere* individuals and institutions that command our respect for their accomplishments or attributes (*he revered his old English professor*).

Venerate and **worship** are usually found in religious contexts (*venerate saints and worship God*) but both words may be used in other contexts as well.

Venerate is usually associated with dignity and advanced age (*venerate the old man who had founded the company more than 50 years ago*), while *worship* connotes an excessive and uncritical respect (*the young girls who waited outside the stage door worshiped the ground he walked on*).

rev·er·ence /'rev(ə)rəns/ ▸*n.* deep respect for someone or something: *rituals showed honor and reverence for the dead.* See note at **HONOR**. ■ *archaic* a gesture indicative of such respect; a bow or curtsy: *the messenger* ***made his reverence.*** ■ (**His/Your Reverence**) a title given to a member of the clergy, or used in addressing them.
▸*v.* [*trans.*] regard or treat with deep respect: *the many divine beings reverenced by Hindu tradition.* ▷Middle English: from Old French, from Latin *reverentia*, from *revereri* 'stand in awe of' (see **REVERE**).

rev·er·end /'rev(ə)rənd; 'revərnd/ ▸*adj.* (usu. **Reverend**) used as a title or form of address to members of the clergy: *the Reverend Jesse Jackson.* ■ *dated* (of a person) deserving deep respect or reverence on account of advanced age, personal ability, great learning, etc.
▸*n.* *informal* a member of the clergy. ▷late Middle English: from Old French, or from Latin *reverendus* 'person to be revered,' gerundive of *revereri* (see **REVERE**).

USAGE As a title, **Reverend** is used for members of the clergy; the traditionally correct form of address is *the* ***Reverend*** *James Smith* or *the* ***Reverend*** *J. Smith*, rather than ***Reverend*** *Smith* or simply ***Reverend***. In American usage, however, the article *the* is commonly not used, even by the devout and reverent. Careful speakers and writers, however, may choose to include the *the*, in deference to the formerly common and primary use of **reverend** as an adjective ('worthy of being revered, respected').

Rev·er·end Moth·er ▸*n.* the title of the Mother Superior of a convent.

rev·er·ent /'rev(ə)rənt; 'revərnt/ ▸*adj.* feeling or showing deep and solemn respect: *a reverent silence.* ▷late Middle English: from Latin *reverent-* 'revering,' from the verb *revereri* (see **REVERE**). —**rev·er·ent·ly** *adv.*

rev·er·en·tial /,revə'rencʜəl/ ▸*adj.* of the nature of, due to, or characterized by reverence: *their names are always mentioned in reverential tones.* —**rev·er·en·tial·ly** *adv.*

rev·er·ie /'revərē/ ▸*n.* a state of being pleasantly lost in one's thoughts; a daydream: *a knock on the door broke her reverie* | *I slipped into reverie.* ■ *Music* an instrumental piece suggesting a dreamy or musing state. ■ *archaic* a fanciful or impractical idea or theory. ▷early 17th cent.: from obsolete French *resverie*, from Old French *reverie* 'rejoicing, revelry,' from *rever* 'be delirious,' of unknown ultimate origin.

re·vers /ri'vi(ə)r; -'ve(ə)r/ ▸*n.* (*pl.* same) the turned-back edge of a garment revealing the undersurface, esp. at the lapel. ▷mid 19th cent.: from French, literally 'reverse.'

re·ver·sal /ri'vərsəl/ ▸*n.* a change to an opposite direction, position, or course of action: *a dramatic reversal in population decline in the Alps* | *the reversal of tidal currents.* ■ *Law* an annulment of a judgment, sentence, or decree made by a lower court or authority: *the Court has upheld the appellate justices in their reversal of the trial court judgment.* ■ an adverse change of fortune: *the league champions suffered a reversal at the finals last month.* ■ *Photography* direct production of a positive image from an exposed film or plate; direct reproduction of a positive or negative image. ▷late 15th cent. (as a legal term): from the verb **REVERSE** + **-AL**.

re·verse /ri'vərs/ ▸*v.* [*intrans.*] move backward: *the truck reversed into the back of a bus.* ■ [*trans.*] cause (a vehicle) to move backward: *I got in the car, reversed it and drove it up the driveway.* ■ [*trans.*] turn (something) the other way around or up or inside out: [as *adj.*] (**reversed**) *a reversed S-shape.* ■ [*trans.*] make (something) the opposite of what it was: *the damage done to the ozone layer may be reversed.* ■ [*trans.*] exchange (the position or function) of two people or things: *the experimenter and the subject reversed roles and the experiment was repeated.* ■ [*trans.*] *Law* revoke or annul (a judgment, sentence, or decree made by a lower court or authority): *the court reversed his conviction.* ■ (of an engine) work in a contrary direction: *the ship's engines reversed and cut out altogether.* ■ [*trans.*] *Printing* make (type or a design) print as white in a block of solid color or a halftone: *their press ads had a headline* ***reversed out of*** *the illustration.*
▸*adj.* [*attrib.*] going in or turned toward the direction opposite to that previously stated: *the trend appears to be going in the reverse direction.* ■ operating, behaving, or ordered in a way contrary or opposite to that which is usual or expected: *here are the results in reverse order.* ■ *Electronics* (of a voltage applied to a semiconductor junction) in the direction that does not allow significant current to flow. ■ *Geology* denoting a fault or faulting in which a relative downward movement occurred in the strata situated on the underside of the fault plane.
▸*n.* **1** a complete change of direction or action: *the growth actuates a reverse of photosynthesis.* ■ reverse gear on a motor vehicle; the position of a gear lever or selector corresponding to this. See also **IN**

R

REVERSE below. ■ (**the reverse**) the opposite or contrary to that previously stated: *he didn't feel homesick—quite the reverse.* See note at OPPOSITE. ■ an adverse change of fortune; a setback or defeat: *the team suffered its heaviest reverse of the season.* ■ *Football* a play in which the ballcarrier reverses the direction of attack by lateraling or handling the ball to a teammate moving in the opposite direction. **2** the opposite side or face to the observer: *the address is given on the reverse of this leaflet.* ■ a left-hand page of an open book, or the back of a loose document. ■ the side of a coin or medal bearing the value or secondary design. ■ the design or inscription on this side. See also OBVERSE (sense 1). ▷Middle English: from Old French *revers, reverse* (nouns), *reverser* (verb), from Latin *reversus* 'turned back,' past participle of *revertere,* from *re-* 'back' + *vertere* 'to turn.' **—re·verse·ly** *adv.* **—re·vers·er** *n.*

▸*PHRASES* □ **in** (or **into**) **reverse** (of a motor vehicle) in reverse gear so as to travel backward: *he put the Cadillac into reverse.* ■ in the opposite direction or manner from usual: *a similar ride next year will do the route in reverse.* □ **reverse the charges** make the recipient of a telephone call responsible for payment.

re·verse dis·crim·i·na·tion ▸*n.* (in the context of the allocation of resources or employment) the practice or policy of favoring individuals belonging to groups known to have been discriminated against previously.

re·verse en·gi·neer·ing ▸*n.* the reproduction of another manufacturer's product following detailed examination of its construction or composition.

re·verse gear ▸*n.* a gear used to make a vehicle or piece of machinery move or work backward.

re·verse os·mo·sis ▸*n. Chemistry* a process by which a solvent passes through a porous membrane in the direction opposite to that for natural osmosis when subjected to a hydrostatic pressure greater than the osmotic pressure.

re·verse Po·lish no·ta·tion ▸*n.* see POLISH NOTATION.

re·verse split ▸*n.* reduction in the number of a company's traded shares that results in an increase in the par value or earnings per share.

re·verse take·o·ver ▸*n. Finance* a takeover of a public company by a smaller company.

re·verse tran·scrip·tase ▸*n.* an enzyme that catalyzes the formation of DNA from an RNA template in reverse transcription. See also TRANSCRIPTASE.

re·verse tran·scrip·tion ▸*n. Biochemistry* the reverse of normal transcription, occurring in some RNA viruses, in which a sequence of nucleotides is copied from an RNA template during the synthesis of a molecule of DNA.

re·vers·i·ble /ri'vərsəbəl/ ▸*adj.* able to be reversed, in particular: ■ (of a garment, fabric, or bedclothes) faced on both sides so as to be worn or used with either outside. ■ able to be turned the other way around: *a reversible stroller seat.* ■ (of the effects of a process or condition) capable of being reversed so that the previous state or situation is restored: *potentially reversible forms of renal failure.* ■ *Chemistry* (of a reaction) occurring together with its converse, and so yielding an equilibrium mixture of reactants and products. ■ *Physics* (of a change or process) capable of complete and detailed reversal, esp. denoting or undergoing an ideal change in which a system is in thermodynamic equilibrium at all times. ■ *Chemistry* (of a colloid) capable of being changed from a gel into a sol by a reversal of the treatment that turns the sol into a gel. **—re·vers·i·bil·i·ty** /ri,vərsə'bilətē/ *n.* **—re·vers·i·bly** /-blē/ *adv.*

re·ver·sion /ri'vərzHən/ ▸*n.* **1** a return to a previous state, practice, or belief: *there was some reversion to polytheism* | [in *sing.*] *a* **reversion to** *the two-party system.* ■ *Biology* the action of reverting to a former or ancestral type. **2** *Law* the right, esp. of the original owner or their heirs, to possess or succeed to property on the death of the present possessor or at the end of a lease: *the reversion of property.* ■ a property to which someone has such a right. ■ the right of succession to an office or post after the death or retirement of the holder: *he was given a promise of the reversion of Boraston's job.* ▷late Middle English (denoting the action of returning to or from a place): from Old French, or from Latin *reversio(n-),* from *revertere* 'turn back' (see REVERSE). **—re·ver·sion·ar·y** /-,nerē/ *adj.* (in sense 2).

re·ver·sion·er /ri'vərzHənər/ ▸*n. Law* a person who possesses the reversion to a property or privilege.

re·vert /ri'vərt/ ▸*v.* [*intrans.*] (**revert to**) return to (a previous state, condition, practice, etc.): *he reverted to his native language.* ■ return to (a previous topic): *he ignored her words by reverting to the former subject.* ■ *Biology* return to (a former or ancestral type): *it is impossible that a fishlike mammal will actually revert to being a true fish.* ■ *Law* (of property) return or pass to (the original owner) by reversion. ■ [*trans.*] *archaic* turn (one's eyes or steps) back: *on reverting our eyes, every step presented some new and admirable scene.* ▷Middle English: from Old French *revertir* or Latin *revertere* 'turn back.' Early senses included 'recover consciousness,' 'return to a position,' and 'return to a person (after estrangement).' **—re·vert·er** *n.* (*Law*).

re·ver·tant /ri'vərtnt/ *Biology* ▸*adj.* (of a cell, organism, or strain) having reverted to the normal type from a mutant or abnormal form.

▸*n.* a cell, organism, or strain of this type.

re·vet /ri'vet/ ▸*v.* (**-vet·ted, -vet·ting**) [*trans.*] [usu. as *adj.*] (**revetted**) face (a rampart, wall, etc.) with masonry, esp. in fortification: *sandbagged and revetted trenches.* ▷early 19th cent.: from French *revêtir,* from late Latin *revestire,* from *re-* 'again' + *vestire* 'clothe' (from *vestis* 'clothing').

re·vet·ment /ri'vetmənt/ ▸*n.* (esp. in fortification) a retaining wall or facing of masonry or other material, supporting or protecting a rampart, wall, etc. ■ a barricade of earth or sandbags set up to provide protection from blast or to prevent planes from overrunning when landing. ▷late 18th cent.: from French *revêtement,* from the verb *revêtir* (see REVET).

re·view /ri'vyo͞o/ ▸*n.* **1** a formal assessment or examination of something with the possibility or intention of instituting change if necessary: *a comprehensive review of defense policy* | *all areas of the company will come under review.* ■ a critical appraisal of a book, play, movie, exhibition, etc., published in a newspaper or magazine. ■ [often in *names*] a periodical publication with critical articles on current events, the arts, etc. ■ *Law* a reconsideration of a judgment, sentence, etc., by a higher court or authority: *a review of her sentence* | *his case comes up for review in January.* Compare with JUDICIAL REVIEW. ■ a retrospective survey or report on past events: *the CEO's end-of-year review.* ■ a survey or evaluation of a particular subject: *a review of recent developments in multicultural education.* **2** a ceremonial display and formal inspection of military or naval forces, typically by a sovereign, commander in chief, or high-ranking visitor.

▸*v.* [*trans.*] **1** examine or assess (something) formally with the possibility or intention of instituting change if necessary: *the company's safety procedures are being reviewed.* ■ write a critical appraisal of (a book, play, movie, etc.) for publication in a newspaper or magazine: *I reviewed his first novel.* ■ *Law* submit (a sentence, case, etc.) for reconsideration by a higher court or authority: *the attorney general asked the court to review the sentence.* ■ make a retrospective assessment or survey of (past events): *ministers will meet to review progress on conventional arms negotiations in March.* ■ survey or evaluate (a particular subject): *in the next chapter we review a number of recent empirical studies.* **2** (of a sovereign, commander in chief, or high-ranking visitor) make a ceremonial and formal inspection of (military or naval forces). **3** view or inspect visually for a second time or again: *all slides were then reviewed by one pathologist.* ▷late Middle English (as a noun denoting a formal inspection of military or naval forces): from obsolete French *reveue,* from *revoir* 'see again.' **—re·view·a·ble** *adj.* **—re·view·al** /-'vyo͞oəl/ *n.*

re·view·er /ri'vyo͞oər/ ▸*n.* a person who writes critical appraisals of books, plays, movies, etc., for publication. ■ a person who formally assesses or examines something with a view to changing it if necessary: *a rent reviewer.*

re·vile /ri'vīl/ ▸*v.* [*trans.*] (usu. **be reviled**) criticize in an abusive or angrily insulting manner: *he was now reviled by the party that he had helped to lead.* See note at SCOLD. ▷Middle English: from Old French *reviler,* based on *vil* 'vile.' **—re·vile·ment** *n.* **—re·vil·er** *n.*

re·vise /ri'vīz/ ▸*v.* [*trans.*] **1** reconsider and alter (something) in the light of further evidence: *he had cause to revise his opinion a moment after expressing it.* ■ reexamine and make alterations to (written or printed matter): *the book was published in 1960 and revised in 1968* | [as *adj.*] (**revised**) *a revised edition.* ■ alter so as to make more efficient or realistic: [as *adj.*] (**revised**) *the revised finance and administrative groups.* **2** [*intrans.*] *Brit.* reread work done previously to improve one's knowledge of a subject, typically to prepare for an examination: *students frantically revising for exams* | [*trans.*] *revise your lecture notes on the topic.*

▸*n. Printing* a proof including corrections made in an earlier proof. ▷mid 16th cent. (in the sense 'look again or repeatedly (at)'): from French *réviser* 'look at,' or Latin *revisere* 'look at again,' from *re-* 'again' + *visere* (intensive form of *videre* 'to see'). **—re·vis·a·ble** *adj.* **—re·vis·al** /-'vīzəl/ *n.* **—re·vis·er** *n.* **—re·vi·so·ry** /-'vīzərē/ *adj.*

Re·vised Stand·ard Ver·sion (abbr.: **RSV**) ▸*n.* a modern English translation of the Bible, published 1946–57 and based on the American Standard Version of 1901.

Re·vised Ver·sion (abbr.: **RV**) ▸*n.* an English translation of the Bible published in 1881–95 and based on the Authorized Version.

re·vi·sion /ri'vizHən/ ▸*n.* the action of revising: *the plan needs drastic revision.* ■ a revised edition or form of something. **—re·vi·sion·ar·y** /-,nerē/ *adj.*

re·vi·sion·ism /ri'vizHə,nizəm/ ▸*n. often derogatory* a policy of revision or modification, esp. of Marxism on evolutionary socialist (rather than revolutionary) or pluralist principles. ■ the theory or practice of revising one's attitude to a previously accepted situation or point of view. **—re·vi·sion·ist** *n.* & *adj.*

re·vis·it /rē'vizit/ ▸*v.* (**-vis·it·ed, -vis·it·ing**) [*trans.*] come back to or visit again: *he'll revisit old friends* | [as *adj.*] (**revisited**) [*postpositive*] *the battle of Midway revisited* | (*figurative*) *UN to revisit the cloning treaty.*

re·vi·tal·ize /rē'vītl,īz/ ▸*v.* [*trans.*] imbue (something) with new life and vitality: *a package of spending cuts to revitalize the economy.* **—re·vi·tal·i·za·tion** /rē,vītlə'zāsHən/ *n.*

re·viv·al /ri'vīvəl/ ▸*n.* an improvement in the condition or strength of something: *a revival in the fortunes of the party* | *an economic revival.* ■ an instance of something becoming popular, active, or important again: *cross-country skiing is enjoying a revival.* ■ a new production of an old play or similar work. ■ a reawakening of religious fervor, esp. by means of a series of evangelistic meetings: *the revivals of the nineteenth century* | *a wave of religious revival.* ■ such a meeting or series of meetings: *an usher for the revival had the job of helping the sick who went up to seek healing.* ■ a restoration to bodily or mental vigor, to life or consciousness, or to sporting success: *the thunder and lightning affected his revival in the third round.*

re·viv·al·ism /ri'vīvə,lizəm/ ▸*n.* belief in or the promotion of a revival of religious fervor. ■ a tendency or desire to revive a former custom or practice: *French rococo revivalism.* **—re·viv·al·ist** *n.* & *adj.* **—re·viv·al·is·tic** /-,vīvə'listik/ *adj.*

re·vive /ri'vīv/ ▸*v.* [*trans.*] restore to life or consciousness: *both men collapsed, but were revived.* ■ [*intrans.*] regain life, consciousness, or strength: *she was beginning to revive from her faint.* ■ give new strength or energy to: *the cool, refreshing water revived us all.* ■ restore interest in or the popularity of: *many pagan traditions continue or are being revived.* ■ improve the position or condition of: *the paper made panicky attempts to revive falling sales.* ▷late Middle English: from Old French *revivre* or late Latin *revivere,* from Latin *re-* 'back' + *vivere* 'live.' **—re·viv·a·ble** *adj.* **—re·viv·er** *n.*

re·viv·i·fy /rē'vivə,fī/ ▸*v.* (**-fies, -fied**) [*trans.*] give new life or vigor to: *they revivified a wine industry that had all but vanished.* ▷late 17th cent.: from French *revivifier* or late Latin *revivificare* (see RE-, VIVIFY). **—re·viv·i·fi·ca·tion** /,rē,vivəfə'kāsHən/ *n.*

rev·o·ca·ble /'revəkəbəl; ri'vōkəbəl/ ▸*adj.* capable of being revoked or canceled: *a revocable settlement.* **—rev·o·ca·bil·i·ty** /,revəkə'bilətē; ri,vōkə-/ *n.*

re·voke /ri'vōk/ ▸*v.* **1** [*trans.*] put an end to the validity or operation of (a decree, decision, or promise): *the men appealed and the sentence was revoked.* **2** [*intrans.*] (in bridge, whist, and other card games) fail to follow suit despite being able to do so. ▷late Middle English: from Old French *revoquer* or Latin *revocare,* from *re-* 'back' + *vocare* 'to call.' **—rev·o·ca·tion** /,revə'kāsHən; ri,vō-/ *n.* **—rev·o·ca·to·ry** /'revəkə,tôrē; ri'vōkə-/ *adj.* **—re·vok·er** *n.*

re·volt /ri'vōlt/ ▸*v.* **1** [*intrans.*] rise in rebellion: *the insurgents revolted and had to be suppressed.* ■ refuse to acknowledge someone or something as having authority: *voters may revolt when they realize the cost of the measures.* ■ [as *adj.*] (**revolted**) *archaic* having rebelled or revolted: *the revolted Bretons.* **2** [*trans.*] (often **be revolted**) cause to feel disgust: *he was revolted by the stench that greeted him* | [as *adj.*] (**revolting**) *revolting green scum.* ■ [*intrans.*] *archaic* feel strong disgust.

▸*n.* an attempt to put an end to the authority of a person or body by rebelling: *a countrywide* **revolt against** *the central government* | *the peasants rose in revolt.* ■ a refusal to continue to obey or conform: *a revolt over tax increases.* ▷mid 16th cent.: from French *révolte* (noun), *révolter* (verb), from Italian *rivoltare,* based on

Latin *revolvere* 'roll back' (see REVOLVE). **—re·volt·ing·ly** *adv.*

rev·o·lute /ˈrevə,lo͞ot/ ▸*adj. Botany* (esp. of the edge of a leaf) curved or curled back. ▷mid 18th cent.: from Latin *revolutus* 'unrolled,' past participle of *revolvere* (see REVOLVE).

rev·o·lu·tion /,revəˈlo͞oSHən/ ▸*n.* **1** a forcible overthrow of a government or social order in favor of a new system. See note at UPRISING. ■ (**the Revolution**) the American Revolution. ■ (often **the Revolution**) (in Marxism) the class struggle that is expected to lead to political change and the triumph of communism. ■ a dramatic and wide-reaching change in the way something works or is organized or in people's ideas about it: *marketing underwent a revolution.* **2** an instance of revolving: *one revolution a second.* ■ motion in orbit or a circular course or around an axis or center. ■ the single completion of an orbit or rotation. ▷late Middle English: from Old French, or from late Latin *revolutio(n-)*, from *revolvere* 'roll back' (see REVOLVE). **—rev·o·lu·tion·ism** /-,nizəm/ *n.* **—rev·o·lu·tion·ist** /-nist/ *n.*

rev·o·lu·tion·ar·y /,revəˈlo͞oSHə,nerē/ ▸*adj.* engaged in or promoting political revolution: *the revolutionary army.* ■ (**Revolutionary**) of or relating to the American Revolution. ■ involving or causing a complete or dramatic change: *a revolutionary new drug.*
▸*n.* (*pl.* **-ar·ies**) a person who works for or engages in political revolution.

rev·o·lu·tion·ize /,revəˈlo͞oSHə,nīz/ ▸*v.* [*trans.*] change (something) radically or fundamentally: *this fabulous new theory will revolutionize the whole of science.*

re·volve /riˈvälv; riˈvôlv/ ▸*v.* [*intrans.*] move in a circle on a central axis: *overhead, the fan revolved slowly.* ■ (**revolve around/about**) move in a circular orbit around: *the earth revolves around the sun.* ■ (**revolve around**) treat as the most important point or element: *her life revolved around her husband.* ■ [*trans.*] consider (something) repeatedly and from different angles: *her mind revolved the possibilities.* ▷late Middle English (in the senses 'turn (the eyes) back,' 'restore,' 'consider'): from Latin *revolvere*, from *re-* 'back' (also expressing intensive force) + *volvere* 'roll.'

re·volv·er /riˈvälvər; -ˈvôl-/ ▸*n.* a pistol with revolving chambers enabling several shots to be fired without reloading.

revolver

re·volv·ing cred·it ▸*n.* credit that is automatically renewed as debts are paid off.

re·volv·ing door ▸*n.* an entrance to a large building in which four partitions turn about a central axis. ■ used to refer to a situation in which the same events or problems recur in a continuous cycle: *many patients are trapped in a revolving door of admission, discharge, and readmission.* ■ [usu. as *adj.*] a place or organization that people tend to enter and leave very quickly: *the newsroom became a revolving-door workplace.* ■ used to refer to a situation in which someone moves from an influential government position to a position in a private company, or vice versa.

re·volv·ing fund ▸*n.* a fund that is continually replenished as withdrawals are made.

re·vue /riˈvyo͞o/ ▸*n.* a light theatrical entertainment consisting of a series of short sketches, songs, and dances, typically dealing satirically with topical issues. ▷French, literally 'review.'

re·vul·sion /riˈvəlSHən/ ▸*n.* **1** a sense of disgust and loathing: *news of the attack will be met with sorrow and revulsion.* **2** *Medicine, chiefly historical* the drawing of disease or blood congestion from one part of the body to another, e.g., by counterirritation. ▷mid 16th cent. (sense 2): from French, or from Latin *revulsio(n-)*, from *revuls-* 'torn out,' from the verb *revellere* (from *re-* 'back' + *vellere* 'pull'). Sense 1 dates from the early 19th cent.

Rev. Ver. ▸*abbr.* Revised Version (of the Bible).

re·ward /riˈwôrd/ ▸*n.* a thing given in recognition of service, effort, or achievement: *the holiday was a reward for 40 years' service with the company* | *figurative the emotional rewards of being a parent.* ■ a fair return for good or bad behavior: *a slap on the face was his reward for his impudence.* ■ a sum offered for the detection of a criminal, the restoration of lost property, or the giving of information.
▸*v.* [*trans.*] make a gift of something to (someone) in recognition of their services, efforts, or achievements: *the engineer who supervised the work was rewarded with a bonus.* ■ show one's appreciation of (an action or quality) by making a gift: *an effective organization recognizes and rewards creativity and initiative.* ■ (**be rewarded**) receive what one deserves: *their hard work was rewarded by the winning of a five-year contract.* ▷Middle English: from Anglo-Norman French, variant of Old French *reguard* 'regard, heed,' also an early sense of the English word. **—re·ward·less** *adj.*
▸*PHRASE* □ **go to one's (final) reward** used euphemistically to indicate that someone has died.

re·ward·ing /riˈwôrdiNG/ ▸*adj.* providing satisfaction; gratifying: *skiing can be hugely rewarding.* **—re·ward·ing·ly** *adv.*

re·wind ▸*v.* /rēˈwīnd/ (*past* and *past part.* **-wound** /-ˈwound/) [*trans.*] wind (a tape or film) back to the beginning. ■ [*intrans.*] (of a tape or film) wind back to the beginning.
▸*n.* /ˈrē,wīnd/ a mechanism for rewinding a tape or film. **—re·wind·er** /rēˈwīndər/ *n.*

re·word /rēˈwərd/ ▸*v.* put (something) into different words: *there is a sound reason for rewording that clause.*

re·work /rēˈwərk/ ▸*v.* [*trans.*] (often **be reworked**) make changes to something, esp. in order to make it more up to date: *he reworked the orchestral score for two pianos* | [as *n.*] (**reworking**) *a reworking of the Sherwood Forest legend.*

re·wound /rēˈwound/ ▸ past and past participle of REWIND.

re·writ·a·ble /rēˈrītəbəl/ ▸*adj. Computing* (of a storage medium) supporting overwriting of previously recorded data.

re·write ▸*v.* /rēˈrīt/ (*past* **-wrote**; *past part.* **-writ·ten**) [*trans.*] write (something) again so as to alter or improve it: *the songs may have to be rewritten* | [*intrans.*] *he began rewriting, adding more and more layers.*
▸*n.* /ˈrē,rīt/ an instance of writing something again so as to alter or improve it. ■ a piece of text that has been altered or improved in such a way.
▸*PHRASES* □ **rewrite history** select or interpret events from the past in a way that suits one's own particular purposes. □ **rewrite the record books** (of an athlete) break a record or several records.

Rex[1] /reks/ ▸*n.* the reigning king (used following a name or in the titles of lawsuits, e.g., *Rex v. Jones*: the Crown versus Jones). ▷Latin, literally 'king.'

Rex[2] ▸*n.* a cat of a breed with curly fur, which lacks guard hairs. ▷1960s: from Latin, literally 'king.'

Reyes, Point /ˈrāz/ a promontory in northwestern California, north of Drakes Bay, in Marin County, noted for its winds, fog, and wildlife.

Reye's syn·drome /rīz; rāz/ ▸*n.* a life-threatening metabolic disorder in young children, of uncertain cause but sometimes precipitated by aspirin and involving encephalitis and liver failure. ▷1960s: named after Ralph D. K. Reye (1912–78), Australian pediatrician.

Rey·kja·vik /ˈrākyə,vik; -vēk/ the capital of Iceland, a port on the western coast; pop. 98,000. ▷from Icelandic *rejkja* 'smoky,' referring to the steam from its many hot springs.

Reyn·ard /rāˈnärd; ˈrānərd; ˈrenərd/ ▸*n. poetic/literary* a name for a fox. ▷from Old French *renart*; the spelling was influenced by Middle Dutch *Reynaerd*.

Reyn·olds /ˈrenəldz/, Sir Joshua (1723–92), English painter. The first president of the Royal Academy (1768), he sought to raise portraiture to the status of historical painting by adapting poses and settings from classical statues and Renaissance paintings.

Re·za Shah /riˈzä ˈSHä/ see PAHLAVI[1].

Rf ▸*symbol* the chemical element rutherfordium.

rf. ▸*abbr. Baseball* right fielder.

r.f. ▸*abbr.* radio frequency.

RFA ▸*abbr.* (in the UK) Royal Fleet Auxiliary.

RFC ▸*abbr.* ■ (in computing) request for comment, a document circulated on the Internet that forms the basis of a technical standard. ■ *historical* Royal Flying Corps. ■ Rugby Football Club.

RFD (also **R.F.D.**) ▸*abbr.* rural free delivery.

RFID ▸*abbr.* radio frequency identification, denoting technologies that use radio waves to identify people or objects carrying encoded microchips.

RFP ▸*abbr.* request for proposal, a detailed specification of goods or services required by an organization, sent to potential contractors or suppliers.

RGS ▸*abbr.* Royal Geographical Society.

Rh ▸*abbr.* Rhesus (factor).
▸*symbol* the chemical element rhodium.

r.h. ▸*abbr.* right hand.

RHA ▸*abbr.* ■ (in the UK) regional health authority. ■ (in the UK) Royal Horse Artillery.

rhab·dom /ˈrab,däm; -dəm/ (also **rhab·dome** /-,dōm/) ▸*n. Zoology* a translucent cylinder forming part of the light-sensitive receptor in the eye of an arthropod. ▷late 19th cent.: from late Greek *rhabdōma*, from *rhabdos* 'rod.'

rhab·do·man·cy /ˈrabdə,mansē/ ▸*n. formal* dowsing with a rod or stick. ▷mid 17th cent.: from Greek *rhabdomanteia*, from *rhabdos* 'rod.' **—rhab·do·man·cer** /-sər/ *n.*

rhab·do·my·ol·y·sis /,rabdō,mīˈäləsis/ ▸*n. Medicine* the destruction of striated muscle cells; (esp. in horses) azoturia. ▷1950s: from Greek *rhabdos* 'rod' + MYO- + -LYSIS.

rhab·do·my·o·sar·co·ma /,rabdō,mīō,särˈkōmə/ ▸*n.* (*pl.* **-co·mas** or **-co·ma·ta** /-ˈkōmətə/) *Medicine* a rare malignant tumor involving striated muscle tissue. ▷late 19th cent.: from Greek *rhabdos* 'rod' + MYO- + SARCOMA.

Rhad·a·man·thine /,radəˈmanTHən; -,THīn/ ▸*adj. poetic/literary* showing stern and inflexible judgment. ▷mid 17th cent.: from RHADAMANTHUS + -INE[1].

Rhad·a·man·thus /,radəˈmanTHəs/ *Greek Mythology* the son of Zeus and Europa, and brother of Minos, who, as a ruler and judge in the underworld, was renowned for his justice.

Rhae·to-Ro·man·ic /,rētō ,rōˈmanik/ (also **Rhae·to-Ro·mance**) ▸*adj.* of, relating to, or denoting the Romance dialects spoken in parts of southeastern Switzerland, northeastern Italy, and Tyrol, esp. Romansh and Ladin.
▸*n.* any of these dialects. ▷from Latin *Rhaetus* 'of *Rhaetia*' (the name of a Roman province in the Alps) + ROMANIC.

R

rham·nose /ˈram,nōs; -,nōz/ ▸*n. Chemistry* a sugar of the hexose class that occurs widely in plants, esp. in berries of the common buckthorn. ▷late 19th cent.: from modern Latin *rhamnus* (genus name) + -OSE[2].

rhap·sode /ˈrap,sōd/ ▸*n.* a person who recites epic poems, esp. one of a group in ancient Greece whose profession it was to recite the Homeric poems from memory. ▷from Greek *rhapsōidos*, from *rhapsōidia* (see RHAPSODY).

rhap·so·dist /ˈrapsədist/ ▸*n.* **1** a person who rhapsodizes. **2** another term for RHAPSODE.

rhap·so·dize /ˈrapsə,dīz/ ▸*v.* [*intrans.*] speak or write about someone or something with great enthusiasm and delight: *he began to rhapsodize about Gaby's beauty and charm.*

rhap·so·dy /ˈrapsədē/ ▸*n.* (*pl.* **-dies**) **1** an effusively enthusiastic or ecstatic expression of feeling: *rhapsodies of praise.* ■ *Music* a free instrumental composition in one extended movement, typically one that is emotional or exuberant in character. **2** (in ancient Greece) an epic poem, or part of it, of a suitable length for recitation at one time. ▷mid 16th cent. (sense 2): via Latin from Greek *rhapsōidia*, from *rhaptein* 'to stitch' + *ōidē* 'song, ode.' **—rhap·sod·ic** /rapˈsädik/ *adj.*

rhat·a·ny /ˈratn-ē/ ▸*n.* **1** an astringent extract of the root of a South American shrub, used in medicine. **2** the partially parasitic South American shrub that yields this root, which is also used as a source of dye. • Genus *Krameria*, family Krameriaceae. ▷early 19th cent.: from modern Latin *rhatania*, via Portuguese and Spanish from Quechua *ratánya*.

rhbdr. ▸*abbr.* rhombohedron.

Rhe·a /rēə/ **1** *Greek Mythology* one of the Titans, wife of Cronus and mother of Zeus, Demeter, Poseidon, Hera, and Hades. Frightened of betrayal by their children, Cronus ate them; Rhea rescued Zeus from this fate by hiding him and giving Cronus a stone wrapped in blankets instead. **2** *Astronomy* a satellite of Saturn, the fourteenth closest to the planet, discovered by Cassini in 1672, and having a diameter of 951 miles (1,530 km).

rhe·a /ˈrēə/ ▸*n.* a large flightless bird of South American grasslands, resembling a small ostrich, with grayish-brown plumage. • Family Rheidae: two species, *Rhea americana* and *Pterocnemia pennata.* ▷early 19th cent.: modern Latin (genus name), from the name of the Titan RHEA.

rhe·bok /ˈrē,bäk/ ▸*n.* a small South African antelope with a woolly brownish-gray coat, a long slender neck, and short straight horns. • *Pelea capreolus*,

Pronunciation Key ə *ago*; ər *over*; ˈə or ,ə *up*; ˈər or ,ər *fur*; a *hat*; ā *rate*; ä *car*; CH *chew*; e *let*; ē *see*; e(ə)r *air*; i *fit*; ī *by*; i(ə)r *ear*; NG *sing*; ō *go*; ô *for*; oi *boy*; o͝o *good*; o͞o *goo*; ou *out*; SH *she*; TH *thin*; T͟H *then*; (h)w *why*; ZH *vision*

family Bovidae. ▷late 18th cent.: from Dutch *reebok* 'roebuck.'

Rhee /rē/, Syngman (1875–1975), president of the Republic of Korea (South Korea) 1948–60. The principal leader in the movement for Korean independence, he was president of the exiled Korean provisional government 1919–41. After World War II, he became the first elected president of South Korea. Amid social and political unrest, he resigned one month into his fourth term and went into exile in Hawaii.

Rhein /rīn/ German name for **RHINE**.

Rhein·land /ˈrīn,länt/ German name for **RHINELAND**.

Rhein·land-Pfalz /(p)fälts/ German name for **RHINELAND-PALATINATE**.

rheme /rēm/ ▸*n. Linguistics* the part of a clause that gives information about the theme. Compare with **FOCUS** and **THEME**. ▷late 19th cent.: from Greek *rhēma* 'that which is said.'

Rhen·ish /ˈrenish; ˈrē-/ ▸*adj.* of the Rhine and the regions adjoining it.
▸*n.* wine from this area. ▷late Middle English: from Anglo-Norman French *reneis*, from a medieval Latin alteration of Latin *Rhenanus*, from *Rhenus* 'Rhine.'

rhe·ni·um /ˈrēnēəm/ ▸*n.* the chemical element of atomic number 75, a rare silvery-white metal that occurs in trace amounts in ores of molybdenum and other metals. (Symbol: **Re**) ▷1920s: modern Latin, from *Rhenus*, the Latin name of the river **RHINE**.

rheo. ▸*abbr.* rheostat.

rhe·ol·o·gy /rēˈäləjē/ ▸*n.* the branch of physics that deals with the deformation and flow of matter, esp. the non-Newtonian flow of liquids and the plastic flow of solids. ▷1920s: from Greek *rheos* 'stream' + **-LOGY**. **—rhe·o·log·i·cal** /,rēəˈläjikəl/ *adj.* **—rhe·ol·o·gist** /-jist/ *n.*

rhe·o·stat /ˈrēə,stat/ ▸*n.* an electrical instrument used to control a current by varying the resistance. ▷mid 19th cent.: from Greek *rheos* 'stream' + **-STAT**. **—rhe·o·stat·ic** /,rēəˈstatik/ *adj.*

Rhe·sus fac·tor /ˈrēsəs/ (abbr.: **Rh fac·tor**) ▸*n.* [in *sing.*] an antigen occurring on the red blood cells of many humans (around 85 percent) and some other primates. It is particularly important as a cause of hemolytic disease of the newborn and of incompatibility in blood transfusions. ▷1940s: *Rhesus* from **RHESUS MONKEY**, in which the antigen was first observed.

rhe·sus mon·key (also **rhe·sus ma·caque**) ▸*n.* a small brown macaque with red skin on the face and rump, native to southern Asia. It is often kept in captivity and is widely used in medical research. • *Macaca mulatta*, family Cercopithecidae. ▷early 19th cent.: modern Latin *rhesus*, arbitrary use of Latin *Rhesus* (from Greek *Rhēsos*, the name of a mythical king of Thrace).

Rhe·sus neg·a·tive (abbr.: **Rh neg·a·tive**) ▸*adj.* lacking the Rhesus factor.

Rhe·sus pos·i·tive (abbr.: **Rh pos·i·tive**) ▸*adj.* having the Rhesus factor.

rhet. ▸*abbr.* ■ rhetoric. ■ rhetorical.

rhe·tor /ˈretər/ ▸*n.* (in ancient Greece and Rome) a teacher of rhetoric. ■ an orator. ▷via Latin from Greek *rhētōr*.

rhet·o·ric /ˈretərik/ ▸*n.* the art of effective or persuasive speaking or writing, esp. the use of figures of speech and other compositional techniques. ■ language designed to have a persuasive or impressive effect on its audience, but is often regarded as lacking in sincerity or meaningful content: *all we have from the opposition is empty rhetoric.* ▷Middle English: from Old French *rethorique*, via Latin from Greek *rhētorikē (tekhnē)* '(art) of rhetoric,' from *rhētōr* 'rhetor.'

rhe·tor·i·cal /rəˈtôrikəl/ ▸*adj.* of, relating to, or concerned with the art of rhetoric: *repetition is a common rhetorical device.* ■ expressed in terms intended to persuade or impress: *the rhetorical commitment of the government to give priority to primary education.* ■ (of a question) asked in order to produce an effect or to make a statement rather than to elicit information. ▷late Middle English (first used in the sense 'eloquently expressed'): via Latin from Greek *rhētorikos* (from *rhētor* 'rhetor') + **-AL**. **—rhe·tor·i·cal·ly** /-ik(ə)lē/ *adv.*

rhet·o·ri·cian /,retəˈrishən/ ▸*n.* an expert in formal rhetoric. ■ a speaker whose words are primarily intended to impress or persuade. ▷late Middle English: from Old French *rethoricien*, from *rhetorique* (see **RHETORIC**).

rheum /ro͞om/ ▸*n. chiefly poetic/literary* a watery fluid that collects in or drips from the nose or eyes. ▷late Middle English: from Old French *reume*, via Latin from Greek *rheuma* 'stream' (from *rhein* 'to flow').

rheu·mat·ic /ro͞oˈmatik/ ▸*adj.* of, relating to, or caused by rheumatism: *rheumatic pains.* ■ (of a person or part of the body) suffering from or affected by rheumatism.
▸*n.* a person suffering from rheumatism. ▷late Middle English (originally referring to infection characterized by rheum): from Old French *reumatique*, or via Latin from Greek *rheumatikos*, from *rheuma* 'bodily humor, flow' (see **RHEUM**). **—rheu·mat·i·cal·ly** /-ik(ə)lē/ *adv.* **—rheu·ma·tick·y** /ro͞oˈmatikē; ˈro͞omə,tikē/ *adj.* (*informal*).

rheu·mat·ic fe·ver ▸*n.* a noncontagious acute fever marked by inflammation and pain in the joints. It chiefly affects young people and is caused by a streptococcal infection.

rheu·mat·ics /ro͞oˈmatiks/ ▸*plural n.* [usu. treated as *sing.*] *informal* rheumatism; rheumatic pains.

rheu·ma·tism /ˈro͞omə,tizəm/ ▸*n.* any disease marked by inflammation and pain in the joints, muscles, or fibrous tissue, esp. rheumatoid arthritis. ▷late 17th cent.: from French *rhumatisme*, or via Latin from Greek *rheumatismos*, from *rheumatizein* 'to snuffle,' from *rheuma* 'stream': the disease was originally supposed to be caused by the internal flow of "watery" humors.

rheu·ma·toid /ˈro͞omə,toid/ ▸*adj. Medicine* relating to, affected by, or resembling rheumatism.

rheu·ma·toid ar·thri·tis ▸*n.* a chronic progressive disease causing inflammation in the joints and resulting in painful deformity and immobility, esp. in the fingers, wrists, feet, and ankles. Compare with **OSTEOARTHRITIS**.

rheu·ma·toid fac·tor ▸*n. Medicine* any of a group of autoantibodies that are present in the blood of many people with rheumatoid arthritis.

rheu·ma·tol·o·gy /,ro͞oməˈtäləjē/ ▸*n. Medicine* the study of rheumatism, arthritis, and other disorders of the joints, muscles, and ligaments. **—rheu·ma·to·log·i·cal** /,ro͞omətlˈäjikəl/ *adj.* **—rheu·ma·tol·o·gist** /-jist/ *n.*

rheum·y /ˈro͞omē/ ▸*adj.* (esp. of the eyes) full of rheum; watery.

rhi·nal /ˈrīnl/ ▸*adj. Anatomy* of or relating to the nose or the olfactory part of the brain. ▷mid 19th cent.: from Greek *rhis, rhin-* 'nose' + **-AL**.

Rhine /rīn/ a river in western Europe that rises in the Swiss Alps and flows for 820 miles (1,320 km) to the North Sea, forming the German–Swiss border before flowing through Germany and the Netherlands. German name **RHEIN**; French name **RHIN**.

Rhine·land /ˈrīn,land/ the region of western Germany through which the Rhine River flows, esp. the part that is west of the river. German name **RHEINLAND**.

Rhine·land-Pa·lat·i·nate a state in western Germany; capital, Mainz. German name **RHEINLAND-PFALZ**.

rhine·stone /ˈrīn,stōn/ ▸*n.* an imitation diamond used in costume jewelry and to decorate clothes. ▷late 19th cent.: translating French *caillou du Rhin*, literally 'pebble of the Rhine.'

rhi·ni·tis /rīˈnītis/ ▸*n. Medicine* inflammation of the mucous membrane of the nose, caused by a virus infection (e.g., the common cold) or by an allergic reaction (e.g., hay fever).

rhi·no /ˈrīnō/ ▸*n.* (*pl.* same or **-nos**) *informal* a rhinoceros. ▷late 19th cent.: abbreviation.

rhino- ▸*comb. form* of or relating to the nose: *rhinoplasty.* ▷from Greek *rhis, rhin-* 'nose.'

rhi·noc·er·os /rīˈnäs(ə)rəs/ ▸*n.* (*pl.* same or **-os·es**) a large, heavily built plant-eating mammal with one or two horns on the nose and thick folded skin, native to Africa and South Asia. All kinds have become endangered through hunting. • Family Rhinocerotidae: four genera and five species. ▷Middle English: via Latin from Greek *rhinokerōs*, from *rhis, rhin-* 'nose' + *keras* 'horn.'

rhi·noc·er·os bee·tle ▸*n.* a very large mainly tropical beetle, the male of which has a curved horn extending from the head and typically another from the thorax. In some parts of Asia, males are put to fight as a spectator sport. • Several genera and species in the family Scarabaeidae, including the South Asian *Oryctes rhinoceros*, which is a serious pest of coconut palms.

rhi·noc·er·os bird ▸*n.* another term for **OXPECKER**.

rhi·noc·er·os horn ▸*n.* a mass of keratinized fibers that comprises the horn of a rhinoceros, reputed in Eastern medicine to have medicinal or aphrodisiac powers.

rhi·noc·er·os horn·bill ▸*n.* a large Southeast Asian hornbill with black-and-white plumage and an upturned casque. • *Buceros rhinoceros*, family Bucerotidae.

rhi·no·plas·ty /ˈrīnō,plastē/ ▸*n.* (*pl.* **-ties**) plastic surgery performed on the nose. **—rhi·no·plas·tic** /,rīnōˈplastik/ *adj.*

rhi·no·vi·rus /,rīnōˈvīrəs; ˈrīnō,vī-/ ▸*n. Medicine* any of a group of picornaviruses, including those that cause some forms of the common cold.

rhizo- ▸*comb. form Botany* relating to a root or roots: *rhizomorph.* ▷from Greek *rhiza* 'root.'

rhi·zo·bi·um /rīˈzōbēəm/ ▸*n.* a nitrogen-fixing bacterium that is common in the soil, esp. in the root nodules of leguminous plants. • Genus *Rhizobium*; Gram-negative rods. ▷1920s: modern Latin, from **RHIZO-** 'root' + Greek *bios* 'life.'

rhi·zoc·to·ni·a /,rī,zäkˈtōnēə/ ▸*n.* a common soil fungus that sometimes causes plant diseases such as damping off, foot rot, and eyespot. • Genus *Rhizoctonia*, subdivision Deuteromycotina, in particular *R. solani*. ▷late 19th cent.: modern Latin (genus name), from Greek *rhiza* 'root' + *ktonos* 'murder.'

rhi·zoid /ˈrī,zoid/ ▸*n. Botany* a filamentous outgrowth or root hair on the underside of the thallus in some lower plants, esp. mosses and liverworts, serving both to anchor the plant and (in terrestrial forms) to conduct water. **—rhi·zoi·dal** /rīˈzoidl/ *adj.*

rhi·zome /ˈrī,zōm/ ▸*n. Botany* a continuously growing horizontal underground stem that puts out lateral shoots and adventitious roots at intervals. Compare with **BULB** (sense 1), **CORM**. ▷mid 19th cent.: from Greek *rhizōma*, from *rhizousthai* 'take root,' based on *rhiza* 'root.'

rhi·zo·morph /ˈrīzə,môrf/ ▸*n. Botany* a rootlike aggregation of hyphae in certain fungi.

Rhi·zop·o·da /rīˈzäpədə/ *Zoology* a phylum of single-celled animals that includes the amebas and their relatives, which have extensible pseudopodia. ▷modern Latin (plural), from **RHIZO-** 'root' + Greek *pous, pod-* 'foot.' **—rhi·zo·pod** /ˈrīzə,päd/ *n.*

rhi·zo·sphere /ˈrīzə,sfir/ ▸*n. Ecology* the region of soil in the vicinity of plant roots in which the chemistry and microbiology is influenced by their growth, respiration, and nutrient exchange.

rho /rō/ ▸*n.* the seventeenth letter of the Greek alphabet (**Ρ, ρ**), transliterated as 'r' or (when written with a rough breathing) 'rh.' ■ (**Rho**) [followed by Latin genitive] *Astronomy* the seventeenth star in a constellation: *Rho Cassiopeiae.*

rho·da·mine /ˈrōdə,mēn/ ▸*n. Chemistry* any of a number of synthetic dyes derived from xanthene, used to color textiles. ▷late 19th cent.: from **RHODO-** 'rose-colored' + **AMINE**.

Rhode Is·land /rōd/ a state in the northeastern U.S., on the coast of the Atlantic Ocean, one of the six New England states; pop. 1,048,319; capital, Providence; statehood, May 29, 1790 (13). Settled by England in the 17th century, it was one of the original thirteen states. It is the smallest and most densely populated U.S. state. **—Rhode Is·land·er** *n.*

Rhode Is·land Red ▸*n.* a bird of an American breed of reddish-black domestic chicken.

Rhodes[1] /rōdz/ a Greek island in the southeastern Aegean Sea, off the Turkish coast. It is the largest of the Dodecanese Islands and the most easterly of the islands in the Aegean Sea; pop. 98,000. Greek name **RÓDHOS**. ■ its capital, a port on the northern tip; pop. 42,000. It was founded *c.*408 BC and was the site of the Colossus of Rhodes.

Rhodes[2], Cecil (John) (1853–1902), South African statesman, born in Britain; prime minister of Cape Colony 1890–96. He expanded British territory in southern Africa, annexing Bechuanaland (now

Cecil Rhodes

Botswana) in 1884 and developing Rhodesia from 1889. By 1890, he had acquired 90 percent of the world's production of diamonds.

Rho·de·sia /rō'dēzhə/ the former name of a large territory in central and southern Africa that was divided into Southern Rhodesia (now Zambia) in 1923 and into Northern Rhodesia (now Zimbabwe) in 1924. —**Rho·de·sian** *adj.* & *n.*

Rho·de·sian ridge·back /rō'dēzhən/ ▸*n.* a dog of a breed having a short light brown coat and a ridge of hair along the middle of the back, growing in the opposite direction to the rest of the coat.

Rhodes Schol·ar·ship ▸*n.* any of several scholarships awarded annually for study at Oxford University by students from certain Commonwealth countries, South Africa, the U.S., and Germany. ▷named after Cecil *Rhodes* (see **RHODES**[2]), who founded the scholarships in 1902. —**Rhodes schol·ar** *n.*

rho·di·um /'rōdēəm/ ▸*n.* the chemical element of atomic number 45, a hard silvery-white metal of the transition series, typically occurring in association with platinum. (Symbol: **Rh**) ▷mid 17th cent.: modern Latin, from Greek *rhodon* 'rose' (from the color of the solution of its salts).

rhodo- ▸*comb. form chiefly Mineralogy Chemistry* rose-colored: *rhodochrosite.* ▷from Greek *rhodon* 'rose.'

rho·do·chro·site /,rōdə'krō,sīt; rə'däkrə-/ ▸*n.* a mineral consisting of manganese carbonate, typically occurring as pink, brown, or gray rhombohedral crystals. ▷mid 19th cent.: from Greek *rhodokhrōs* 'rose-colored' + **-ITE**[1].

rho·do·den·dron /,rōdə'dendrən/ ▸*n.* a shrub or small tree of the heath family, with large clusters of bell-shaped flowers and typically with large evergreen leaves, widely grown as an ornamental. • Genus *Rhododendron*, family Ericaceae: many cultivars. ▷via Latin from Greek, from *rhodon* 'rose' + *dendron* 'tree.'

rhododendron

rho·do·lite /'rōdl,īt/ ▸*n.* a pale violet or red variety of garnet, used as a gemstone.

rho·do·nite /'rōdn,īt/ ▸*n.* a brownish or rose-pink mineral consisting of a silicate of manganese and other elements. ▷early 19th cent.: from Greek *rhodon* 'rose' + **-ITE**[1].

Rhod·o·pe Moun·tains /'rädəpē/ a mountain system in the Balkans, in southeastern Europe, on the frontier between Bulgaria and Greece, rising to a height of over 6,600 feet (2,000 m) and including the Rila Mountains in the northwest.

Rho·doph·y·ta /rō'däfətə/ *Botany* a division of lower plants that comprises the red algae. ▷modern Latin (plural), from **RHODO-** 'rose-colored' + Greek *phuta* 'plants.' —**rho·do·phyte** /'rōdə,fīt/ *n.*

rho·dop·sin /rō'däpsən/ ▸*n.* a purplish-red light-sensitive pigment present in the retinas of humans and many other animal groups. ▷late 19th cent.: from Greek *rhodon* 'rose' + *opsis* 'sight' + **-IN**[1].

rho·do·ra /rə'dôrə/ ▸*n.* a pink-flowered North American shrub of the heath family. • *Rhododendron canadense*, family Ericaceae. ▷late 18th cent.: modern Latin (former genus name), based on Greek *rhodon* 'rose.'

rhomb /räm(b)/ ▸*n.* a rhombohedral crystal. ■ a rhombus. ▷early 19th cent.: from Latin *rhombus* (see **RHOMBUS**). —**rhom·bic** /'rämbik/ *adj.*

rhomb. ▸*abbr.* rhombic.

rhom·ben·ceph·a·lon /,räm,ben'sefə,län; -lən/ ▸*n.* *Anatomy* another term for **HINDBRAIN**. ▷late 19th cent.: from **RHOMB** + **ENCEPHALON**.

rhom·bi /'räm,bī; -,bē/ ▸ plural form of **RHOMBUS**.

rhom·bo·he·dral /,rämbō'hēdrəl/ ▸*adj.* (chiefly of a crystal) shaped like a rhombohedron.

rhom·bo·he·dron /,rämbō'hēdrən/ ▸*n.* (*pl.* **-drons** or **-dra** /-drə/) a solid figure whose faces are six equal rhombuses. ■ a crystal or other solid object of this form. ▷mid 19th cent.: from **RHOMBUS** + **-HEDRON**, on the pattern of words such as *polyhedron*.

rhom·boid /'räm,boid/ ▸*adj.* having or resembling the shape of a rhombus.
▸*n.* **1** a quadrilateral of which only the opposite sides and angles are equal. **2** (also **rhom·boid mus·cle**) another term for **RHOMBOIDEUS**. ▷late 16th cent. (as a noun): from French *rhomboïde*, or via late Latin from Greek *rhomboeidēs*, from *rhombos* (see **RHOMBUS**). —**rhom·boi·dal** /räm'boidl/ *adj.*

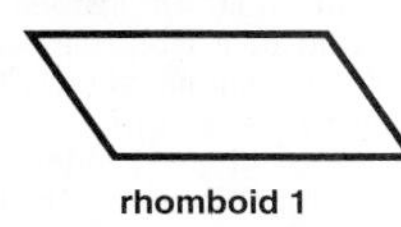
rhomboid 1

rhom·boi·de·us /räm'boidēəs/ ▸*n.* (*pl.* **-de·i** /-dē,ī/) *Anatomy* a muscle connecting the shoulder blade to the vertebrae. ▷mid 19th cent.: modern Latin, from *rhomboideus (musculus)* (see **RHOMBOID**).

Rhom·bo·zoa /,rämbə'zōə/ *Zoology* a minor phylum of mesozoan worms that are parasites in the kidneys of cephalopod mollusks. ▷modern Latin (plural), from Greek *rhombos* 'rhombus' + *zōia* 'animals.' —**rhom·bo·zoan** *n.* & *adj.*

rhom·bus /'rämbəs/ ▸*n.* (*pl.* **-bus·es** or **-bi** /-,bī; -,bē/) a parallelogram with opposite equal acute angles, opposite equal obtuse angles, and four equal sides. ■ any parallelogram with equal sides, including a square. ▷mid 16th cent.: via Latin from Greek *rhombos*.

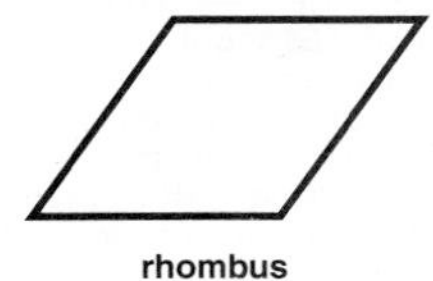
rhombus

Rhône /rōn/ a river in southwestern Europe that rises in the Swiss Alps and flows 505 miles (812 km) through Lake Geneva into France, then to Lyons, Avignon, and the Mediterranean Sea west of Marseilles, where it forms a wide delta.

rho·ta·ci·za·tion /,rōtəsə'zāshən/ ▸*n.* *Linguistics* change of an original *s* or *z* to *r*, as in *was* and *were*. ■ *Phonetics* pronunciation of a vowel to reflect a following *r* in the orthography, e.g., in *farm, bird.* ▷1970s: from *rhotacize* (from Greek *rhōtakizein*) + **-ATION**. —**rho·ta·cized** /'rōtə,sīzd/ *adj.*

rho·tic /'rōtik/ ▸*adj.* *Phonetics* of, relating to, or denoting a dialect or variety of English, e.g., Midwestern American English, in which *r* is pronounced before a consonant (as in *hard*) and at the ends of words (as in *far*). ▷1960s: from Greek *rhot-*, stem of *rho* (see **RHO**) + **-IC**. —**rho·tic·i·ty** /rō'tisətē/ *n.*

rhp (also **r.h.p.**) ▸*abbr.* rated horsepower.

RHS ▸*abbr.* ■ Royal Historical Society. ■ Royal Horticultural Society. ■ Royal Humane Society.

rhu·barb /'ro͞o,bärb/ ▸*n.* **1** the thick leaf stalks of a cultivated plant of the dock family, which are reddish or green and eaten as a fruit after cooking. **2** the large-leaved Eurasian plant that produces these stems. • *Rheum rhaponticum* (or **rhabarbarum**) , family Polygonaceae. ■ used in names of other plants of this genus, several of which are used medicinally, e.g., **Chinese rhubarb**. **3** *chiefly Brit. informal* the noise made by a group of actors to give the impression of indistinct background conversation or to represent the noise of a crowd, esp. by the random repetition of the word "rhubarb" with different intonations. ■ a heated dispute: *rhubarbs often broke out among these less than professional players.* ▷late Middle English (denoting the rootstock of other plants of this genus used medicinally): from Old French *reubarbe*, from a shortening of medieval Latin *rheubarbarum*, alteration (by association with *rheum* 'rhubarb') of *rhabarbarum* 'foreign rhubarb,' from Greek *rha* (also meaning 'rhubarb') + *barbaros* 'foreign.'

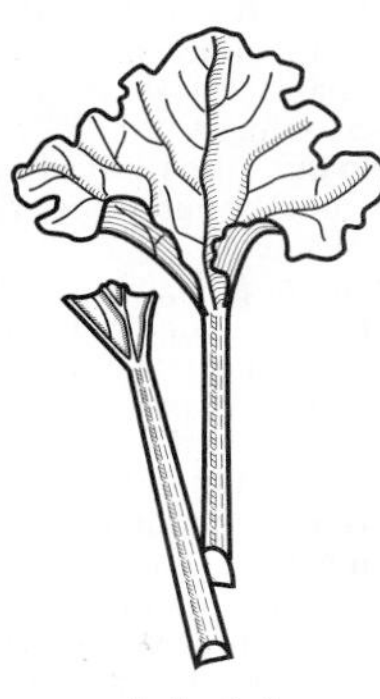
rhubarb 1

rhumb /rəm(b)/ ▸*n.* *Nautical* **1** (also **rhumb line**) an imaginary line on the earth's surface cutting all meridians at the same angle, used as the standard method of plotting a ship's course on a chart. **2** any of the 32 points of the compass. ▷late 16th cent.: from French *rumb* (earlier *ryn (de vent)* 'point of the compass'), probably from Dutch *ruim* 'space, room.' The spelling change was due to association with Latin *rhombus* (see **RHOMBUS**).

rhum·ba ▸*n.* variant spelling of **RUMBA**.

rhyme /rīm/ ▸*n.* correspondence of sound between words or the endings of words, esp. when these are used at the ends of lines of poetry. ■ a short poem in which the sound of the word or syllable at the end of each line corresponds with that at the end of another. ■ poetry or verse marked by such correspondence of sound: *the clues were written* **in rhyme**. ■ a word that has the same sound as another.
▸*v.* [*intrans.*] (of a word, syllable, or line) have or end with a sound that corresponds to another: *balloon* **rhymes with** *moon* | [as *adj.*] (**rhyming**) *rhyming couplets.* ■ (of a poem or song) be composed of lines that end in words or syllables with sounds that correspond with those at the ends of other lines: *the poem would have been better if it had rhymed.* ■ [*trans.*] (**rhyme something with**) put a word together with (another word that has a corresponding sound), as when writing poetry: *I'm not sure about rhyming perestroika with balalaika.* ■ *poetic/literary* compose verse or poetry: *Musa rhymed and sang.* ▷Middle English *rime*, from Old French, from medieval Latin *rithmus*, via Latin from Greek *rhuthmos* (see **RHYTHM**). The current spelling was introduced in the early 17th cent. under the influence of *rhythm.* —**rhym·er** *n.* —**rhym·ist** /-ist/ *n.* (*archaic*).
▸*PHRASE* □ **rhyme or reason** [with *negative*] logical explanation or reason: *without rhyme or reason his mood changed.*

rhyme scheme ▸*n.* the ordered pattern of rhymes at the ends of the lines of a poem or verse.

rhyme·ster /'rīmstər/ ▸*n.* a person who composes rhymes, esp. simple ones.

rhym·ing slang ▸*n.* a type of slang that replaces words with rhyming words or phrases, typically with the rhyming element omitted. For example *butcher's*, short for *butcher's hook*, means "look" in Cockney rhyming slang.

rhy·o·lite /'rīə,līt/ ▸*n.* *Geology* a pale fine-grained volcanic rock of granitic composition, typically porphyritic in texture. ▷mid 19th cent.: from German *Rhyolit*, from Greek *rhuax* 'lava stream' + *lithos* 'stone.' —**rhy·o·lit·ic** /,rīə'litik/ *adj.*

Rhys /rēs/, Jean (1890–1979), British novelist and short-story writer, born in Dominica; pseudonym of *Ella Gwendolen Rees Williams*. Notable novels: *Good Morning, Midnight* (1939) and *Wide Sargasso Sea* (1966).

rhythm /'ri<u>th</u>əm/ ▸*n.* a strong, regular, repeated pattern of movement or sound: *Ruth listened to the rhythm of his breathing.* ■ the systematic arrangement of musical sounds, principally according to duration and periodic stress. ■ a particular type of pattern formed by such arrangement: *guitar melodies with deep African rhythms.* ■ a person's natural feeling for such arrangement: *they've got no rhythm.* ■ the measured flow of words and phrases in verse or prose as determined by the relation of long and short or stressed and unstressed syllables. ■ a regularly recurring sequence of events, actions, or processes: *the twice daily rhythms of the tides.* ■ *Art* a harmonious sequence or correlation of colors or elements. ▷mid 16th cent. (also originally in the sense 'rhyme'): from French *rhythme*, or via Latin from Greek *rhuthmos* (related to *rhein* 'to flow'). —**rhythm·less** *adj.*

rhythm and blues (abbr.: **R & B**) ▸*n.* a form of popular music of African-American origin that arose during the 1940s from blues, with the addition of driving rhythms taken from jazz. It was an immediate precursor of rock and roll.

rhythm gui·tar ▸*n.* a guitar part in a piece of pop music consisting of the chord sequences of a song or melody.

rhyth·mic /'ri<u>th</u>mik/ ▸*adj.* having or relating to rhythm: *a rhythmic dance.* ■ occurring regularly: *there are rhythmic changes in our bodies.* ▷early 17th cent.: from French *rhythmique* or via Latin from Greek *rhuthmikos*, from *rhuthmos* (see **RHYTHM**). —**rhyth·mi·cal** *adj.* —**rhyth·mi·cal·ly** /-ik(ə)lē/ *adv.*

rhyth·mic gym·nas·tics ▸*plural n.* [usu. treated as *sing.*] a form of gymnastics emphasizing dancelike rhythmic routines, typically accentuated by the use of ribbons or hoops. —**rhyth·mic gym·nast** *n.*

rhyth·mic·i·ty /,ri<u>th</u>'misətē/ ▸*n.* rhythmical quality or character: *the nursery rhymes' rhythmicity makes them particularly easy to learn.*

R

rhythm meth·od ▸*n.* a method of avoiding conception by which sexual intercourse is restricted to the times of a woman's menstrual cycle when ovulation is least likely to occur.

rhythm sec·tion ▸*n.* the part of a pop or jazz group supplying the rhythm, generally regarded as consisting of bass and drums and sometimes piano or guitar.

rhy·ton /ˈrīˌtän/ ▸*n.* (*pl.* **rhy·tons** or **rhy·ta** /ˈrītə/) a type of drinking vessel used in ancient Greece, typically having the form of an animal's head or a horn, with the hole for drinking at the bottom. ▹from Greek *rhuton*, neuter of *rhutos* 'flowing'; related to *rhein* 'to flow.'

RI ▸*abbr.* ■ Rex et Imperator (King and Emperor) or Regina et Imperatrix (Queen and Empress). [Latin.] ■ Rhode Island (in official postal use). ■ Royal Institute or Institution.

RIA ▸*abbr.* ■ radioimmunoassay. ■ Royal Irish Academy.

ri·a /ˈrēə/ ▸*n.* *Geography* a long narrow inlet formed by the partial submergence of a river valley. ▹late 19th cent.: from Spanish *ría* 'estuary.'

ri·al /rēˈôl; rēˈäl/ ▸*n.* **1** (also **ri·yal**) the basic monetary unit of Iran and Oman, equal to 100 dinars in Iran and 1000 baiza in Oman. **2** variant spelling of RIYAL. ▹via Persian from Arabic *riyāl* (see RIYAL).

Ri·al·to /rēˈaltō; -ˈäl-/ **1** a city in southwestern California, west of San Bernardino; pop. 72,388. **2** an island in Venice, Italy, that contains the old mercantile quarter of medieval Venice. The Rialto Bridge, completed in 1591, crosses the Grand Canal between the Rialto and the San Marco Islands.

RIB ▸*n.* a small open boat with a fiberglass hull and inflatable rubber sides. ▹acronym from *rigid inflatable boat*.

rib /rib/ ▸*n.* **1** each of a series of slender curved bones articulated in pairs to the spine (twelve pairs in humans), protecting the thoracic cavity and its organs. ■ a rib of an animal with meat adhering to it used as food; a joint or cut from the ribs of an animal. **2** a long raised piece of stronger or thicker material across a surface or through a structure, and typically serving to support or strengthen it, in particular: ■ *Architecture* a curved member supporting a vault or defining its form. ■ any of the curved transverse pieces of metal or timber in a ship, extending up from the keel and forming part of the framework of the hull. ■ each of the curved pieces of wood forming the body of a lute or the sides of a violin. ■ each of the hinged rods supporting the fabric of an umbrella. ■ *Aeronautics* a structural member in an airfoil, extending back from the leading edge and serving to define the contour of the airfoil. ■ a vein of a leaf (esp. the midrib) or an insect's wing. ■ a ridge of rock or land. ■ *Knitting* a combination of alternate knit (plain) and purl stitches producing a ridged, slightly elastic fabric, used esp. for the cuffs and bottom edges of sweaters.
▸*v.* (**ribbed**, **rib·bing**) [*trans.*] **1** (usu. **be ribbed**) mark with or form into raised bands or ridges: *the road ahead was ribbed with furrows of slush.* **2** *informal* tease good-naturedly: *the first time I appeared in the outfit I was ribbed mercilessly.* ▹Old English *rib*, *ribb* (noun), of Germanic origin; related to Dutch *rib(be)* and German *Rippe*. Sense 1 of the *verb* dates from the mid 16th cent.; the sense 'tease' was originally a U.S. slang usage meaning 'to fool, dupe' (1930s). —**rib·less** *adj.*

RIBA ▸*abbr.* Royal Institute of British Architects.

rib·ald /ˈribəld; ˈribˌôld; ˈrīˌbôld/ ▸*adj.* referring to sexual matters in an amusingly rude or irreverent way: *a ribald comment.* ▹Middle English (as a noun denoting a lowly retainer or a licentious or irreverent person): from Old French *ribauld*, from *riber* 'indulge in licentious pleasures,' from a Germanic base meaning 'prostitute.'

rib·ald·ry /ˈribəldrē; ˈrī-/ ▸*n.* ribald talk or behavior.

rib·and /ˈribənd/ ▸*n.* *archaic* a ribbon. ▹Middle English: from Old French *riban*, probably from a Germanic compound of the noun BAND[1].

ribbed /ribd/ ▸*adj.* (esp. of a fabric or garment) having a pattern of raised bands: *a ribbed cashmere sweater.* ■ *Architecture* (of a vault or other structure) strengthened with ribs.

Rib·ben·trop /ˈribənˌtrōp/, Joachim von (1893–1946), German Nazi politician. As foreign minister 1938–45, he signed the nonaggression pact with the Soviet Union in 1939. He was convicted as a war criminal in the Nuremberg trials and hanged.

rib·bie /ˈribē/ ▸*n.* (*pl.* **-bies**) *informal Baseball* a run batted in. See **RBI**. ▹mid 20th cent.: elaboration of **RBI**.

rib·bing /ˈribiNG/ ▸*n.* **1** a riblike structure or pattern, esp. a band of knitting in rib. **2** *informal* good-natured teasing.

rib·bit /ˈribit/ ▸*n.* *informal* the characteristic croaking sound of a frog: *the power of the male's commanding "ribbit" came not from the throat but from vibrations in ear membranes.* ▹imitative.

rib·bon /ˈribən/ ▸*n.* a long, narrow strip of fabric, used esp. for tying something or for decoration: *the tiny pink ribbons in her hair | cut four lengths of ribbon.* ■ a strip of fabric of a special color or design awarded as a prize or worn to indicate the holding of an honor, esp. a small multicolored piece of ribbon worn in place of the medal it represents: *old horse show ribbons and rosettes.* ■ a long, narrow strip of something: *slice the peppers into ribbons lengthwise.* ■ a narrow band of inked material wound on a spool and forming the inking agent in some typewriters and computer printers.
▸*v.* [*intrans.*] extend or move in a long narrow strip like a ribbon: *miles of concrete ribboned behind the bus.* ▹early 16th cent.: variant of RIBAND. The French spelling *ruban* was also frequent in the 16th–18th centuries. —**rib·boned** *adj.* —**rib·bon·like** /-ˌlīk/ *adj.*
▸PHRASES □ **cut a** (or **the**) **ribbon** perform an opening ceremony, typically by formally cutting a ribbon across the entrance to somewhere. □ **cut** (or **tear**) **something to ribbons** cut (or tear) something so badly that only ragged strips remain. ■ *figurative* damage something severely: *the country has seen its economy torn to ribbons by recession.*

rib·bon ca·ble ▸*n.* a cable for transmitting electronic signals consisting of several insulated wires connected together to form a flat ribbon.

rib·bon de·vel·op·ment ▸*n.* *chiefly Brit.* the building of houses along a main road, esp. one leading out of a town or city.

rib·bon·fish /ˈribənˌfiSH/ ▸*n.* (*pl.* same or **-fish·es**) any of a number of long slender fishes that typically have a dorsal fin running the length of the body, in particular: • a fish of the dealfish family (Trachipteridae). • a fish of the cutlassfish family (Trichiuridae). • another term for OARFISH.

rib·bon grass ▸*n.* another term for TAPE GRASS.

rib·bon worm ▸*n.* a chiefly aquatic worm with an elongated, unsegmented, flattened body that is typically brightly colored and tangled in knots, and a long proboscis for catching food. • Phylum Nemertea: two classes.

rib·by /ˈribē/ ▸*adj.* having prominent ribs: *ribby, bony-rumped, horned cattle.*

rib cage ▸*n.* the bony frame formed by the ribs around the chest.

Ri·be·ra /rēˈbärä/, José (or Jusepe) de (*c.*1591–1652), Spanish painter and etcher, resident in Italy from 1616; known as **Lo Spagnoletto** ("the little Spaniard"). He is noted for his religious and genre paintings.

rib eye (also **rib-eye** or **rib-eye steak**) ▸*n.* a cut of beef from the outer side of the ribs: *a menu that runs to gargantuan rib eyes and ten-pound lobsters.*

ri·bi·tol /ˈrībiˌtôl; -ˌtōl/ ▸*n.* *Chemistry* a colorless crystalline compound that is formed by reduction of ribose and occurs in certain plants. • An alcohol; chem. formula: $HOCH_2(CHOH)_3CH_2OH$. ▹1940s: from RIBOSE + -ITE[1] + -OL.

ri·bo·fla·vin /ˌrībəˈflāvin; ˈrībəˌflā-/ ▸*n.* *Biochemistry* a yellow vitamin of the B complex that is essential for metabolic energy production. It is present in many foods, esp. milk, liver, eggs, and green vegetables, and is also synthesized by the intestinal flora. Also called VITAMIN B_2. ▹1930s: from RIBOSE + Latin *flavus* 'yellow' + -IN[1].

ri·bo·nu·cle·ase /ˌrībōˈn(y)o͞oklēˌās; -ˌāz/ ▸*n.* another term for **RN**ASE.

ri·bo·nu·cle·ic ac·id /ˌrībōn(y)o͞oˈklē-ik; -ˈklā-ik/ ▸*n.* see **RNA**. ▹1930s: *ribonucleic* from RIBOSE + NUCLEIC ACID.

ri·bose /ˈrīˌbōs; -ˌbōz/ ▸*n.* *Chemistry* a sugar of the pentose class that occurs widely in nature as a constituent of nucleosides and several vitamins and enzymes. ▹late 19th cent.: arbitrary alteration of ARABINOSE, a related sugar.

ri·bo·some /ˈrībəˌsōm/ ▸*n.* *Biochemistry* a minute particle consisting of RNA and associated proteins, found in large numbers in the cytoplasm of living cells. They bind messenger RNA and transfer RNA to synthesize polypeptides and proteins. ▹1950s: from RIBONUCLEIC ACID + -SOME[3]. —**ri·bo·so·mal** /ˌrībəˈsōməl/ *adj.*

ri·bo·zyme /ˈrībəˌzīm/ ▸*n.* *Biochemistry* an RNA molecule capable of acting as an enzyme. ▹1980s: blend of *ribonucleic* (from RIBONUCLEIC ACID) and ENZYME.

rib-tick·ler ▸*n.* *informal* an amusing joke or story. —**rib-tick·ling** *adj.* —**rib-tick·ling·ly** *adv.*

ri·bu·lose /ˈrībyəˌlōs; -ˌlōz/ ▸*n.* *Chemistry* a sugar of the pentose class that is an important intermediate in carbohydrate metabolism and photosynthesis. ▹1930s: from RIBOSE + *-ulose*.

rib·wort /ˈribˌwərt; -ˌwôrt/ (also **rib·wort plan·tain**) ▸*n.* a Eurasian plantain with erect ribbed leaves and a rounded flower spike, well established as a weed in North America. • *Plantago lanceolata*, family Plantaginaceae.

Ri·car·di·an[1] /riˈkärdēən/ ▸*adj.* of or relating to the time of any of three kings of England, Richard I, II, and III. ■ of or holding the view that Richard III was a just king who was misrepresented by Shakespeare and other writers.
▸*n.* a contemporary or supporter of Richard III. ▹from medieval Latin *Ricardus* 'Richard' + -IAN. —**Ri·car·di·an·ism** /-ˌnizəm/ *n.*

Ri·car·di·an[2] ▸*adj.* relating to or denoting the doctrines of the political economist David Ricardo (1772–1823).

Ric·ci ten·sor /ˈrēCHē; ˈriCHē/ ▸*n.* *Mathematics* a set of components that describes part of the curvature of space-time. It is a symmetric second-order tensor. ▹1920s: named after Curbastro G. *Ricci* (1853–1925), Italian mathematician.

RICE ▸*abbr.* rest, ice, compression, and elevation (treatment method for bruises, strains, and sprains).

Rice[1] /rīs/, Anne (1941–), U.S. writer; born *Howard Allen O'Brien*; pen names **A. N. Roquelaure** and **Anne Rampling**. She is best known for her series called the *Vampire Chronicles*, which includes *Interview with the Vampire* (1976), *The Queen of the Damned* (1988), and *Merrick* (2000).

Rice[2], Condoleeza (1954–), U.S. presidential adviser and stateswoman. Fluent in Russian she became President George H. W. Bush's adviser on Soviet affairs in 1989, and that same year joined the National Security Council. In 2001 she was appointed national security adviser by President George W. Bush, who in November 2004 selected her to replace resigning secretary of state Colin Powell.

Rice[3], Jerry (1962–), U.S. football player. A wide receiver for the San Francisco 49ers 1985–2000 and the Oakland Raiders 2001–, he set NFL records in pass receptions and touchdowns.

Rice[4] /rīs/, Sir Tim (1944–), English lyricist and entertainer; full name *Timothy Miles Bindon Rice*. With Andrew Lloyd Webber, he cowrote a number of hit musicals, including *Joseph and the Amazing Technicolor Dreamcoat* (1968), *Jesus Christ Superstar* (1971), and *Evita* (1978). He also won two Academy Awards for best original movie song in 1992 and 1994.

rice /rīs/ ▸*n.* a swamp grass that is widely cultivated as a source of food, esp. in Asia. • *Oryza sativa*, family Gramineae. **African rice** belongs to the related species *O. glaberrima*, whereas the so-called **wild rice** is not a true rice at all. ■ the grains of this cereal used as food.

Rice provides the staple diet of half the world's population and is second only to wheat in terms of total output. Rice seedlings are usually planted in flooded fields or paddies, so that terraces are necessary on hillsides and a reliable source of water is essential.

▸*v.* [*trans.*] force (cooked potatoes or other vegetables) through a sieve or ricer. ▹Middle English: from Old French *ris*, from Italian *riso*, from Greek *oruza*.

rice bowl ▸*n.* a dish from which rice is eaten. ■ *figurative* one's livelihood (used esp. in reference to Asia): *entrenched vested interests will fight to the death to protect their rice bowl.* ■ an area in which abundant quantities of rice are grown.

rice burn·er ▸*n.* *derogatory* a Japanese motorcycle.

rice pa·per ▸*n.* thin translucent edible paper made from the flattened and dried pith of a shrub, used in painting (esp. oriental) and in baking biscuits and cakes. • This paper is obtained from the Chinese plant *Tetrapanax papyriferus* (family Araliaceae) or from the Indo-Pacific plant *Scaevola sericea* (family Goodeniaceae).

ric·er /ˈrīsər/ ▸*n.* a utensil with small holes through which boiled potatoes or other soft food can be pushed to form particles of a similar size to grains of rice.

rice rat ▸*n.* a nocturnal rat that typically lives in marshy or damp areas, native to America, the Caribbean, and the Galapagos Islands. • *Oryzomys* and other genera, family Muridae: numerous species.

ri·cer·car /ˌrēCHərˈkär/ (also **ri·cer·ca·re** /-ˈkärā/) ▸*n.* (*pl.* **-cars** or **-ca·ri** /-ˈkärē/) *Music* an elaborate instrumental composition in fugal or canonic style, typically of the 16th to 18th centuries. ▷from Italian *ricercare* 'search out.'

Rich /ricH/, Buddy (1917–87), U.S. jazz drummer and bandleader; born *Bernard Rich.* He played for bandleaders such as Artie Shaw and Tommy Dorsey and then formed his own band in 1946.

rich /ricH/ ▸*adj.* **1** having a great deal of money or assets; wealthy: *most of these artists are already quite rich* | [as *plural n.*] (**the rich**) *every day the gap between the rich and the poor widens.* See note at **WEALTHY.** ■ (of a country or region) having valuable natural resources or a successful economy. ■ of expensive materials or workmanship; demonstrating wealth: *rich mahogany furniture.* ■ generating wealth; valuable: *not all football players enjoy rich rewards from the game.* **2** plentiful; abundant: *China's rich and diverse mammalian fauna.* ■ having (a particular thing) in large amounts: *many vegetables and fruits are* **rich in** *antioxidant vitamins* | [in *combination*] *a protein-rich diet.* ■ (of food) containing a large amount of fat, spices, sugar, etc.: *dishes with wonderfully rich sauces.* ■ (of drink) full-bodied: *a rich, hoppy beer.* ■ (of the mixture in an internal combustion engine) containing a high proportion of fuel. ■ (of a color or sound) pleasantly deep and strong: *his rich bass voice.* ■ (of a smell or taste) pleasantly smooth and mellow: *Basmati rice has a rich aroma.* ■ *figurative* interesting because full of diversity or complexity: *what a full, rich life you lead!* **3** producing a large quantity of something: *novels have always been a rich source of material for the film industry.* ■ (of soil or a piece of land) having the properties necessary to produce fertile growth. ■ (of a mine or mineral deposit) yielding a large quantity or proportion of precious metal. **4** *informal* (of a remark) causing ironic amusement or indignation: *these comments are* **a bit rich** *coming from a woman with no money worries.* ▷Old English *rīce* 'powerful, wealthy,' of Germanic origin, related to Dutch *rijk* and German *reich*; ultimately from Celtic; reinforced in Middle English by Old French *riche* 'rich, powerful.' —**rich·ness** *n.*

-rich ▸*comb. form* containing a large amount of something specified: *lime-rich* | *protein-rich.*

Rich·ard[1] /'ricHərd/ the name of three kings of England: ■ **Richard I** (1157–99), son of Henry II and Eleanor of Aquitaine; reigned 1189–99; known as **Richard Coeur de Lion** or **Richard the Lionheart.** He led the Third Crusade, defeating Saladin at Arsuf (1191), but failed to capture Jerusalem. Returning home, he was held hostage by the Holy Roman Emperor Henry VI until being released in 1194 on payment of a huge ransom. ■ **Richard II** (1367–1400), son of the Black Prince; reigned 1377–99. During his minority the government was dominated by his uncle John of Gaunt. Following his minority, he executed or banished most of his former opponents. His confiscation of his uncle John of Gaunt's estate on the latter's death provoked Henry Bolingbroke's return from exile to overthrow him. ■ **Richard III** (1452–85), brother of Edward IV; reigned 1483–85. He served as Protector to his nephew Edward V, who, after two months, was declared illegitimate and subsequently disappeared. Richard's brief rule ended at Bosworth Field, where he was defeated by Henry Tudor and killed.

Rich·ard[2] /rē'sHärd/, Maurice (Joseph Henri) (1921–2000), Canadian hockey player; nickname **The Rocket.** Playing for the Montreal Canadiens 1942–60, he was the first professional hockey player to score 50 goals in one season 1944–45, a record that stood until the early 1980s. Hockey Hall of Fame (1961).

Rich·ards /'ricHərdz/, I. A. (1893–1979), English literary critic and poet; full name *Ivor Armstrong Richards.* He emphasized the importance of close textual study and praised irony, ambiguity, and allusiveness.

Rich·ard·son[1] /'ricHərdsən/ a city in northeastern Texas, northeast of Dallas; pop. 74,840.

Rich·ard·son[2], Sir Ralph (David) (1902–83), English actor. He played many Shakespearean roles as well as leading parts in plays, including Harold Pinter's *No Man's Land* (1975), and movies, including *Oh! What a Lovely War* (1969).

Rich·ard·son[3], Samuel (1689–1761), English novelist. His first novel *Pamela* (1740–41), entirely in the form of letters and journals, popularized the epistolary novel. He experimented further with the genre in *Clarissa Harlowe* (1747–48), in which he explored moral issues in a detailed social context with psychological intensity.

Rich·ard the Li·on·heart /'līən,härt/, Richard I of England (see **RICHARD**[1]).

Rich·e·lieu /'risHəl,(y)o͞o/, Armand Jean du Plessis, duc de (1585–1642), French cardinal and statesman. He was chief minister to Louis XIII 1624–42 and established the Académie française in 1635.

rich·en /'ricHən/ ▸*v.* [*trans.*] make richer: *a town richened by several auto assembly plants.*

rich·es /'ricHiz/ ▸*plural n.* material wealth: *riches beyond their wildest dreams.* ■ valuable natural resources: *the riches of the world's waters* | *figurative the riches of the Serbian oral tradition.* ▷Middle English: variant (later interpreted as a plural form) of archaic *richesse*, from Old French *richeise* (from *riche* 'rich').

Rich·field /'ricH,fēld/ a city in southeastern Minnesota, south of Minneapolis; pop. 35,710.

Rich·ie /'ricHē/, Lionel B. Jr. (1949–), U.S. songwriter, singer, and producer. His hits include "We Are the World" (1985), which he cowrote with Michael Jackson; "Say You, Say Me" (Academy Award, 1986); and "Dancing on the Ceiling" (1987). His works are collected in albums such as *Time* (1998) and *Renaissance* (2001).

Rich·land /'ricHlənd/ a city in southeastern Washington, on the Columbia and Yakima rivers, near Kennewick and Pasco; pop. 32,315.

Ri·chler /'ricHlər/, Mordecai (1931–2001), Canadian writer. One of his best-known novels is *The Apprenticeship of Duddy Kravitz* (1959). Other notable works: *The Incomparable Atuk* (1963), *St. Urbain's Horseman* (1971), and *Simon Gursky Was Here* (1989).

rich·ly /'ricHlē/ ▸*adv.* in an elaborate, generous, or plentiful way: *she was richly dressed in the height of fashion* | *Levkas and its neighboring islands reward explorers richly.* ■ [as *submodifier*] fully (used esp. to indicate that someone or something merits a particular thing): *give your family a richly deserved vacation.*

Rich·mond /'ricHmənd/ **1** an industrial port city in north central California, on the eastern side of San Francisco Bay, north of Berkeley; pop. 87,425. **2** an industrial city in east central Indiana; pop. 39,124. **3** a city in east central Kentucky, southeast of Lexington; pop. 27,152. **4** the capital of Virginia, a port on the James River; pop. 197,790. During the Civil War, it was the Confederate capital from July 1861 until its capture in 1865.

Rich·ter scale /'riktər/ ▸*n.* *Geology* a numerical scale for expressing the magnitude of an earthquake on the basis of seismograph oscillations. The more destructive earthquakes typically have magnitudes between about 5.5 and 8.9; the scale is logarithmic and a difference of one represents an approximate thirtyfold difference in magnitude. ▷1930s: named after Charles F. *Richter* (1900–85), American geologist.

Richt·ho·fen /'rikHt,hōfən; 'rik,tōvən/, Manfred, Freiherr von (1882–1918), German fighter pilot; known as **the Red Baron.** He flew a distinctive bright red aircraft and was eventually shot down, after destroying 80 enemy planes.

ri·cin /'rīsən; 'ris-/ ▸*n.* *Chemistry* a highly toxic protein obtained from the pressed seeds of the castor-oil plant. ▷late 19th cent.: from modern Latin *Ricinus communis* (denoting the castor-oil plant) + **-IN**[1].

rick[1] /rik/ ▸*n.* a stack of hay, corn, straw, or similar material, esp. one built into a regular shape and thatched. ■ a pile of firewood somewhat smaller than a cord. ■ a set of shelving for storing barrels.
▸*v.* [*trans.*] form into rick or ricks; stack: *the nine cords of good spruce wood* **ricked up** *in the back yard.* ▷Old English *hrēac*, of Germanic origin; related to Dutch *rook.*

rick[2] ▸*n.* a slight sprain or strain, esp. in a person's neck or back.
▸*v.* [*trans.*] strain (one's neck or back) slightly. ▷late 18th cent. (as a verb): of dialect origin.

rick·ets /'rikits/ ▸*n.* [treated as *sing.* or *pl.*] *Medicine* a disease of children caused by vitamin D deficiency, characterized by imperfect calcification, softening, and distortion of the bones typically resulting in bow legs. ▷mid 17th cent.: perhaps an alteration of Greek *rhakhitis* (see **RACHITIS**).

rick·ett·si·a /ri'ketsēə/ ▸*n.* (*pl.* **-si·ae** /-sē,ē; -sē,ī/ or **-si·as**) any of a group of very small bacteria that includes the causative agents of typhus and various other febrile diseases in humans. Like viruses, many of them can only grow inside living cells, and they are frequently transmitted by mites, ticks, or lice. • Genus *Rickettsia*, order Rickettsiales; Gram-negative rods. ▷modern Latin, named after Howard Taylor *Ricketts* (1871–1910), American pathologist. —**rick·ett·si·al** *adj.*

rick·et·y /'rikitē/ ▸*adj.* **1** (of a structure or piece of equipment) poorly made and likely to collapse: *we went carefully up the rickety stairs* | *figurative a rickety banking system.* **2** (of a person) suffering from rickets. ▷late 17th cent.: from **RICKETS** + **-Y**[1]. —**rick·et·i·ness** *n.*

rick·ey /'rikē/ ▸*n.* (*pl.* **-eys**) a drink consisting of liquor, typically gin, mixed with lime juice, carbonated water, and ice: *I wanted to drink* **gin rickeys.** ▷late 19th cent.: probably from the surname *Rickey.*

Rick·ov·er /'rik,ōvər/, Hyman (George) (1900–1986), U.S. naval officer; born in Russia (now part of Poland). A rear admiral in 1953 and a vice admiral in 1959, he was the individual most responsible for creating the U.S. nuclear-powered navy. The world's first nuclear-powered submarine, the U.S.S. *Nautilus*, was launched under his direction in 1954. Presidential Medal of Freedom (1980).

rick·rack /'rik,rak/ ▸*n.* braided trimming in a zigzag pattern, used esp. as decoration on clothes. ▷late 19th cent.: of unknown origin.

rick·sha /'rik,sHô/ (also **rick·shaw**) ▸*n.* a light two-wheeled hooded vehicle drawn by one or more people, used chiefly in Asian countries. ■ a similar vehicle like a three-wheeled bicycle, having a seat for passengers behind the driver. ▷late 19th cent.: abbreviation of **JINRIKISHA.**

ricksha

RICO /'rēkō/ ▸*abbr.* (in the U.S.) Racketeer Influenced and Corrupt Organizations Act.

ric·o·chet /'rikə,sHā; -,sHet/ ▸*n.* a shot or hit that rebounds one or more times off a surface. ■ the action or movement of a bullet, shell, or other projectile when rebounding in such a way.
▸*v.* (**-cheted** /-,sHād/, **-chet·ing** /-,sHā-iNG/ or **-chet·ted** /-,sHetid/, **-chet·ting** /-,sHetiNG/) [*intrans.*] (of a bullet, shell, or other projectile) rebound one or more times off a surface: *a bullet ricocheted off a nearby wall.* ■ [*trans.*] cause to rebound in such a way: *they fired off a couple of rounds, ricocheting the bullets against a wall.* ■ *figurative* move or appear to move with a series of such rebounds: *the sound ricocheted around the hall.* ▷mid 18th cent.: from French, of unknown origin.

ri·cot·ta /ri'kätə/ ▸*n.* a soft white unsalted Italian cheese. ▷Italian, literally 'recooked, cooked twice.'

RICS ▸*abbr.* (in the UK) Royal Institution of Chartered Surveyors.

ric·tus /'riktəs/ ▸*n.* a fixed grimace or grin: *Ned's smile had become a rictus of repulsion.* ▷early 19th cent.: from Latin, literally 'open mouth,' from *rict-* 'gaped,' from the verb *ringi.* —**ric·tal** /'riktəl/ *adj.*

rid /rid/ ▸*v.* (**rid·ding;** *past* and *past part.* **rid** or *archaic* **rid·ded**) [*trans.*] (**rid someone/something of**) make someone or something free of (a troublesome or unwanted person or thing): *we now have the greatest chance ever to rid the world of nuclear weapons.* ■ (**be rid of**) be freed or relieved from: *she couldn't wait to be rid of us.* ▷Middle English: from Old Norse *rythja.* The original sense 'to clear' described clearing land of trees and undergrowth; this gave rise to 'free from refuse or encumbrances,' later becoming generalized.
▸*PHRASES* □ **be well rid of** be in a better state for having removed or disposed of (a troublesome or unwanted person or thing). □ **get rid of** take action so as to be free of (a troublesome or unwanted person or thing).

rid·dance /'ridns/ ▸*n.* the action of getting rid of a troublesome or unwanted person or thing.
▸*PHRASE* □ **good riddance** said to express relief at

Pronunciation Key ə *ago*; ər *over*; 'ə *or* ,ə *up*; 'ər *or* ,ər *fur*; a *hat*; ā *rate*; ä *car*; CH *chew*; e *let*; ē *see*; e(ə)r *air*; i *fit*; ī *by*; i(ə)r *ear*; NG *sing*; ō *go*; ô *for*; oi *boy*; o͝o *good*; o͞o *goo*; ou *out*; SH *she*; TH *thin*; T͟H *then*; (h)w *why*; ZH *vision*

being free of a troublesome or unwanted person or thing.

rid·den /ˈridn/ ▶ past participle of RIDE.

rid·dle[1] /ˈridl/ ▶*n.* a question or statement intentionally phrased so as to require ingenuity in ascertaining its answer or meaning, typically presented as a game. ■ a person, event, or fact that is difficult to understand or explain: *the riddle of her death.*

▶*v.* [*intrans.*] *archaic* speak in or pose riddles: *he who knows not how to riddle.* ■ [with *two objs.*] solve or explain (a riddle) to (someone): *riddle me this then.* ▷Old English *rǣdels, rǣdelse* 'opinion, conjecture, riddle'; related to Dutch *raadsel*, German *Rätsel*, also to READ. **—rid·dler** /ˈridlər; ˈridl-ər/ *n.*

▶*PHRASE* □ **talk** (or **speak**) **in riddles** express oneself in an ambiguous or puzzling manner.

THE RIGHT WORD **conundrum, enigma, mystery, paradox, puzzle, riddle**

All of these terms imply something baffling or challenging.

A **mystery** is anything that is incomprehensible to human reason, particularly if it invites speculation (*the mystery surrounding her sudden disappearance*).

An **enigma** is a statement whose meaning is hidden under obscure or ambiguous allusions, so that we can only guess at its significance; it can also refer to a person of puzzling or contradictory character (*he remained an enigma throughout his long career*).

A **riddle** is a mystery involving contradictory statements, with a hidden meaning designed to be guessed at (*the old riddle about how many college graduates it takes to change a light bulb*).

Conundrum applies specifically to a riddle phrased as a question, the answer to which usually involves a pun or a play on words, such as "What is black and white and read all over?"; *conundrum* can also refer to any puzzling or difficult situation.

A **paradox** is a statement that seems self-contradictory or absurd, but in reality expresses a possible truth (*Francis Bacon's well-known paradox, "The most corrected copies are commonly the least correct"*).

A **puzzle** is not necessarily a verbal statement, but it presents a problem with a particularly baffling solution or tests one's ingenuity or skill in coming up with a solution (*a crossword puzzle*).

rid·dle[2] ▶*v.* [*trans.*] **1** (usu. **be riddled**) make many holes in (someone or something), esp. with gunshot: *his car was riddled by sniper fire.* ■ fill or permeate (someone or something), esp. with something unpleasant or undesirable: *the existing law is* **riddled with** *loopholes.* **2** pass (a substance) through a large coarse sieve: *for final potting, the soil mixture is not riddled.* ■ remove ashes or other unwanted material from (something, esp. a fire or stove) in such a way.

▶*n.* a large coarse sieve, esp. one used for separating ashes from cinders or sand from gravel. ▷late Old English *hriddel*, of Germanic origin; from an Indo-European root shared by Latin *cribrum* 'sieve,' *cernere* 'separate,' and Greek *krinein* 'decide.'

rid·dling /ˈridliNG; ˈridl-iNG/ ▶*adj.* speaking or expressed in riddles; enigmatic: *the riddling sphinx.* **—rid·dling·ly** *adv.*

Ride /rīd/, Sally (Kristen) (1951–), U.S. astronaut. She was the first U.S. woman to travel in space, on the shuttle *Challenger* in 1983. She later served on the presidential commission that investigated the 1986 *Challenger* accident.

Sally Ride

ride /rīd/ ▶*v.* (*past* **rode** /rōd/; *past part.* **rid·den** /ˈridn/) [*trans.*] **1** sit on and control the movement of (an animal, esp. a horse), typically as a recreation or sport: *Diana went to watch him ride his horse* | [*intrans.*] *I haven't ridden much since the accident.* ■ [*intrans.*] travel on a horse or other animal: *we* **rode on** *horseback* | *some of the officers were riding back.* ■ sit on and control (a bicycle or motorcycle) for recreation or as a means of transport: *he rode a Harley Davidson across the U.S.* ■ [*intrans.*] (**ride in/on**) travel in or on (a vehicle) as a passenger: *I started riding on the buses.* ■ travel in (a vehicle) or on (a public transport system) as a passenger: *she rides the bus across 42nd Street.* ■ go through or over (an area) on horseback, a bicycle, etc.: *ride the full length of the Ridgeway.* ■ compete in (a race) on horseback or on a bicycle or motorcycle: *I rode a good race.* ■ travel up or down in (an elevator): *the astronauts rode elevators to the launch pad* | [*intrans.*] *we'll ride up in the elevator.* ■ [*intrans.* or *complement*] (of a vehicle, animal, racetrack, etc.) be of a particular character for riding on or in: *the van rode as well as some cars of twice the price.* ■ *informal* transport (someone) in a vehicle: *the taxi driver who rode Kelly into the airport not long ago.* **2** be carried or supported by (something with a great deal of momentum): *a stream of young surfers fighting the elements to ride the waves* | *figurative the fund rode the growth boom in the 1980s.* ■ [*intrans.*] project or overlap: *when two lithospheric plates collide, one tends to* **ride over** *the other.* ■ [*intrans.*] (of a vessel) sail or float: *a large cedar barque* **rode at anchor**. ■ [*intrans.*] float or seem to float: *the moon was riding high in the sky.* ■ yield to (a blow) so as to reduce its impact: *Harrison drew back his jaw as if riding the blow.* ■ *vulgar slang* have sexual intercourse with. ■ (of a supernatural being) take spiritual possession of (someone). ■ annoy, pester, or tease: *if you don't give all the kids a chance to play, the parents ride you.* **3** (**be ridden**) be full of or dominated by: *you must not think him ridden with angst* | [as *adj.* in *combination*] (**-ridden**) *the crime-ridden streets.*

▶*phrasal v.* □ **ride someone down** trample or overtake someone while on horseback. □ **ride on** depend on: *there is a great deal of money riding on the results of these studies.* □ **ride something out** come safely through something, esp. a storm or a period of danger or difficulty: *the fleet had* **ridden out** *the* **storm**. □ **ride up** (of a garment) gradually work or move upward out of its proper position: *her skirt had ridden up.*

▶*n.* **1** a journey made on horseback, on a bicycle or motorcycle, or in a vehicle: *did you enjoy your ride?* | *figurative investors have had a bumpy ride.* ■ a person giving someone a lift in their vehicle: *their ride into town had dropped them off near the bridge.* ■ *informal* a motor vehicle: *that green Chevy over there, that's my ride.* ■ the quality of comfort or smoothness offered by a vehicle while it is being driven, as perceived by the driver or passenger: *the ride is comfortable, though there is a slight roll when cornering.* ■ a path, typically one through woods, for riding horses. ■ *Canadian* a demonstration of horse riding as an entertainment. **2** a roller coaster, merry-go-round, or other amusement ridden at a fair or amusement park. **3** *vulgar slang* an act of sexual intercourse. **4** (also **ride cymbal**) a cymbal used for keeping up a continuous rhythm. ▷Old English *rīdan*, of Germanic origin; related to Dutch *rijden* and German *reiten*. **—ride·a·ble** (also **rid·a·ble**) *adj.*

▶*PHRASES* □ **be riding for a fall** *informal* be acting in a reckless or arrogant way that invites defeat or failure. □ **for the ride** for pleasure or interest, rather than any serious purpose: *I don't need anything at the mall, but I'm happy to go along for the ride.* □ **let something ride** take no immediate action over something. □ **ride herd on** keep watch over: *a man to ride herd on this frenetically paced enterprise.* □ **ride high** be successful: *the economy will be riding high on the top of the next boom.* □ **ride the pine** (or **bench**) *informal* (of an athlete) sit on the sidelines rather than participate in a game or event. □ **ride the rails** (or *chiefly Canadian* **rods**) *informal* **1** ride on a freight train surreptitiously without paying. **2** be a passenger on a train. □ **ride roughshod over** carry out one's own plans or wishes with arrogant disregard for (others or their wishes): *he rode roughshod over everyone else's opinions.* □ **— rides again** used to indicate that someone or something has reappeared unexpectedly and with new vigor. □ **ride shotgun** travel as a guard in the seat next to the driver of a vehicle. ■ ride in the passenger seat of a vehicle. ■ *figurative* act as a protector: The Times *found itself to be riding shotgun for the Red Army.* □ **ride to (the) hounds** *chiefly Brit.* go hunting (esp. fox hunting) on horseback with a pack of dogs. □ **a rough** (or **easy**) **ride** a difficult (or easy) time doing something: *the president has been given a rough ride by this conservative Congress.* □ **take someone for a ride 1** *informal* deceive or cheat someone. **2** *informal* drive someone out somewhere in a car and then kill them.

Ri·deau Ca·nal /riˈdō/ a waterway in eastern Ontario in Canada, created in the 1820s, that links Ottawa and the Ottawa River with Kingston and Lake Ontario.

ride-off ▶*n.* (in a riding competition) a round held to resolve a tie or determine qualifiers for a later stage; a jump-off.

rid·er /ˈrīdər/ ▶*n.* **1** a person who is riding or who can ride something, esp. a horse, bicycle, motorcycle, or snowboard. **2** a condition or proviso added to something already said or decreed: *one* **rider to** *the deal—if the hurricane heads north, we run for shelter.* ■ an addition or amendment to a document, esp. a piece of legislation: *the rules of Congress make it difficult to attach a rider to an appropriations bill* | *a rider to an eligible life insurance policy.* **3** a small weight positioned on the beam of a balance for fine adjustment. ▷late Old English *rīdere* 'mounted warrior, knight' (see RIDE, -ER[1]). **—rid·er·less** *adj.*

rid·er·ship /ˈrīdərˌSHip/ ▶*n.* the number of passengers using a particular form of public transportation.

Ridge /rij/, Tom (1945–), U. S. secretary of homeland security 2001–05; full name *Thomas Joseph Ridge*. The governor of Pennsylvania 1995–2001, he was chosen by President George W. Bush to head the new Office of Homeland Security, a cabinet department created shortly after the terrorist attacks of September 11, 2001.

ridge /rij/ ▶*n.* a long narrow hilltop, mountain range, or watershed: *the northeast ridge of Everest.* ■ the line or edge formed where the two sloping sides of a roof meet at the top. ■ *Meteorology* an elongated region of high atmospheric pressure. ■ a narrow raised band running along or across a surface: *buff your nails in order to smooth ridges.* ■ a raised strip of arable land, esp. (in medieval open fields) one of a set separated by furrows.

▶*v.* [*trans.*] [often as *adj.*] (**ridged**) mark with or form into narrow raised bands: *the ridged sand of the beach.* ■ [*intrans.*] (of a surface) form into or rise up as a narrow raised band: *the crust of the earth ridged.* ■ form (arable land) into raised strips separated by furrows: *a field plowed in narrow stretches that are* **ridged up** *slightly.* ▷Old English *hrycg* 'spine, crest,' of Germanic origin; related to Dutch *rug* and German *Rücken* 'back.' **—ridg·y** *adj.*

ridge·back /ˈrijˌbak/ ▶*n.* short for RHODESIAN RIDGEBACK.

ridge·piece /ˈrijˌpēs/ ▶*n.* another term for RIDGEPOLE.

ridge·pole /ˈrijˌpōl/ ▶*n.* **1** a horizontal beam along the ridge of a roof, into which the rafters are fastened. **2** the horizontal pole of a long tent.

ridge run·ner ▶*n.* *informal* a mountain farmer of the Southern states.

ridge tile ▶*n.* a semicircular or curved tile used in making a roof ridge.

ridge·way /ˈrijˌwā/ ▶*n.* a road or track along a ridge.

rid·i·cule /ˈridiˌkyo͞ol/ ▶*n.* the subjection of someone or something to mockery and derision: *he is held up as* **an object of ridicule**.

▶*v.* [*trans.*] subject (someone or something) to mockery and derision: *his theory was ridiculed and dismissed.* ▷late 17th cent.: from French, or from Latin *ridiculum*, neuter (used as a noun) of *ridiculus* 'laughable,' from *ridere* 'to laugh.'

ri·dic·u·lous /riˈdikyələs/ ▶*adj.* deserving or inviting derision or mockery; absurd: *when you realize how ridiculous these scenarios are, you will have to laugh.* See note at ABSURD. ▷mid 16th cent.: from Latin *ridiculosus*, from *ridiculus* 'laughable' (see RIDICULE). **—ri·dic·u·lous·ness** *n.*

ri·dic·u·lous·ly /riˈdikyələslē/ ▶*adv.* so as to invite mockery or derision; absurdly: [*sentence adverb*] *ridiculously, I felt like crying.* ■ [as *submodifier*] so as to cause surprise or disbelief: *it had been ridiculously easy to track him down.*

ri·ding[1] /ˈrīdiNG/ ▶*n.* the sport or activity of riding horses.

▶*adj.* **1** designed for or associated with the sport of riding: *smartly tailored riding clothes.* **2** (of a machine or device) designed to be operated while riding on it: *a riding mower.*

ri·ding[2] ▶*n.* **1** (usu. **the East/North/West Riding**) one of three former administrative divisions of Yorkshire. **2** an electoral district of Canada. ▷Old English *trithing*, from Old Norse *thrithjungr* 'third part,' from *thrithi* 'third.' The initial *th-* was lost due to assimilation with the preceding *-t* of *East, West*, or with the *-th* of *North*.

rid·ing crop ▶*n.* a short flexible whip with a loop for the hand, used in riding horses.

rid·ing hab·it ▶*n.* a woman's riding dress, consisting of a skirt worn with a double-breasted jacket.

rid·ing light ▸*n.* a light shown by a ship at anchor.

Rid·ley /ˈridlē/, Nicholas (*c.*1500–55), English Protestant bishop and martyr. He was appointed bishop of Rochester in 1547 and then of London in 1550. He opposed the Catholic policies of Mary I, the reason that he was burned at the stake in Oxford.

rid·ley /ˈridlē/ (also **rid·ley tur·tle**) ▸*n.* (*pl.* **-leys**) a small turtle of tropical seas. • Genus *Lepidochelys*, family Cheloniidae: **Kemp's ridley** (*L. kempi*) of the Atlantic, and the larger **olive ridley** (*L. olivacea*) of the Pacific. ▷1940s: of unknown origin.

rie·beck·ite /ˈrēˌbekˌīt/ ▸*n.* a dark blue or black mineral of the amphibole group, occurring chiefly in alkaline igneous rocks or as blue asbestos (crocidolite). ▷late 19th cent.: from the name of Emil *Riebeck* (died 1885), German explorer, + **-ITE**[1].

Rie·fen·stahl /ˈrēfənˌshtäl/, Leni (1902–2003), German filmmaker. She is best known for *Triumph of the Will* (1935), an account of a Nazi rally at Nuremberg.

Ri·el /rēˈel/, Louis (1844–85), Canadian political leader. He led the rebellion of the Metis at Red River Settlement in 1869, later forming a provisional government and negotiating terms for the union of Manitoba with Canada. He was executed for treason after leading a further rebellion.

ri·el /rēˈel/ ▸*n.* the basic monetary unit of Cambodia, equal to 100 sen. ▷Khmer.

Rie·mann /ˈrēmən/, (Georg Friedrich) Bernhard (1826–66), German mathematician. He founded Riemannian geometry, which is of fundamental importance to both mathematics and physics.

Rie·mann·i·an ge·om·e·try /rēˈmänēən; -ˈman-/ ▸*n.* a form of differential non-Euclidean geometry developed by Riemann, used to describe curved space. It provided Einstein with a mathematical basis for his general theory of relativity.

Ries·ling /ˈrēzliNG; ˈrēs-/ ▸*n.* a variety of wine grape grown and developed esp. in Germany and Austria. ■ a dry white wine made from this grape. ▷German.

ri·fam·pin /riˈfampin/ (also **ri·fam·pi·cin** /riˈfampəsin/) ▸*n. Medicine* a reddish-brown antibiotic used chiefly to treat tuberculosis and leprosy. • The antibiotic is obtained from the bacterium *Nocardia mediterranei*. ▷1960s: from *rifam(yci)n* (an antibiotic first isolated from the bacterium *Streptomyces mediterranei*) + the insertion of *pi-* from **PIPERAZINE**.

rife /rīf/ ▸*adj.* [*predic.*] (esp. of something undesirable or harmful) of common occurrence; widespread: *male chauvinism was rife in medicine in those days.* See note at **PREVALENT**. ■ (**rife with**) full of: *the streets were rife with rumor and fear.*
▸*adv.* in an unchecked or widespread manner: *speculation* **ran rife** *that he was an arms dealer.* ▷late Old English *rȳfe*, probably from Old Norse *rífr* 'acceptable.' —**rife·ness** *n.*

riff /rif/ ▸*n.* (in popular music and jazz) a short repeated phrase, frequently played over changing chords or harmonies or used as a background to a solo improvisation: *a brilliant guitar riff.*
▸*v.* [*intrans.*] play such phrases: *the other horns would be riffing behind him.* ▷1930s: abbreviation of the noun **RIFFLE**.

rif·fle /ˈrifəl/ ▸*v.* [*intrans.*] turn over something, esp. the pages of a book, quickly and casually: *he* **riffled through** *the pages* | [*trans.*] *she opened a book with her thumbnail and riffled the pages.* ■ (**riffle through**) search quickly through (something), esp. so as to cause disorder: *she riffled through her leather handbag.* ■ [*trans.*] disturb the surface of; ruffle: *there was a slight breeze that riffled her hair.* ■ [*trans.*] shuffle (playing cards) by flicking up and releasing the corners or sides of two piles of cards so that they intermingle and may be slid together to form a single pile.
▸*n.* **1** [usu. in *sing.*] a quick or casual leaf or search through something. ■ the rustle of paper being leafed through in such a way. ■ a shuffle performed by riffling playing cards. **2** a rocky or shallow part of a stream or river with rough water. ■ a patch of waves or ripples. ▷late 18th cent. (sense 2): perhaps from a variant of the verb **RUFFLE**, influenced by **RIPPLE**.

rif·fler /ˈriflər/ ▸*n.* a narrow elongated tool with a curved file surface at each end, used in filing concave surfaces. ▷late 18th cent.: from French *rifloir*, from Old French *rifler* 'to scrape.'

riff·raff /ˈrifˌraf/ ▸*n.* disreputable or undesirable people: *I don't think they talk to riffraff off the street.* ▷late 15th cent. (as *riff and raff*): from Old French *rif et raf* 'one and all, every bit,' of Germanic origin.

ri·fle[1] /ˈrīfəl/ ▸*n.* a gun, esp. one fired from shoulder level, having a long spirally grooved barrel intended to make a bullet spin and thereby have greater accuracy over a long distance. ■ (**rifles**) troops armed with rifles.
▸*v.* **1** [*trans.*] [usu. as *adj.*] (**rifled**) make spiral grooves in (a gun or its barrel or bore) to make a bullet spin and thereby have greater accuracy over a long distance: *a line of replacement rifled barrels.* **2** [*trans.*] hit, throw, or kick (a ball or puck) hard and straight: *he rifled a hard, rising shot from just inside the blue line.* [1940s: from *rifle* 'gun,' suggestive of explosive speed; compare with the verb *shoot*.] ▷mid 17th cent.: from French *rifler* 'graze, scratch,' of Germanic origin. The earliest noun usage was in *rifle gun*, which had "rifles" or spiral grooves cut into the inside of the barrel.

rifle 1

ri·fle[2] ▸*v.* [*intrans.*] search through something in a hurried way in order to find or steal something: *she* **rifled through** *the cassette tapes* | [*trans.*] *they rifled the house for money.* ■ [*trans.*] steal: *the lieutenant's servant rifled the dead man's possessions.* ▷Middle English: from Old French *rifler* 'graze, plunder,' of Germanic origin.

ri·fle bird ▸*n.* a bird of paradise, the male of which has mainly velvety-black plumage and a display call that sounds like a whistling bullet. • Genus *Ptiloris*, family Paradisaeidae: three species.

ri·fle·man /ˈrīfəlmən/ ▸*n.* (*pl.* **-men**) **1** a soldier armed with a rifle, esp. a private in a rifle regiment. ■ a person skilled at using a rifle. **2** a very small, short-tailed, greenish-yellow songbird that feeds on insects on tree bark, native to New Zealand. [perhaps so named from a comparison between its plumage and an early military uniform.] • *Acanthisitta chloris*, family Xenicidae.

ri·fle mi·cro·phone ▸*n.* a type of gun microphone with several parallel tubes of different lengths in front of the diaphragm to enhance its directional focus.

ri·fle range ▸*n.* a place for practicing shooting with rifles. ■ an attraction at a fairground in which people fire rifles at targets in order to win prizes.

ri·fle·scope /ˈrīfəlˌskōp/ ▸*n. informal* a telescopic sight on a rifle.

ri·fling /ˈrīf(ə)liNG/ ▸*n.* the arrangement of spiral grooves on the inside of a rifle barrel.

Rif Moun·tains /rif/ (also **Er Rif** /er ˈrif/) a mountain range in northern Morocco that runs parallel to the Mediterranean Sea for about 180 miles (290 km) east from Tangier. Rising to over 7,000 feet (2,250 m), it forms a western extension of the Atlas Mountains.

rift /rift/ ▸*n.* a crack, split, or break in something: *the wind had torn open a rift in the clouds.* ■ *Geology* a major fault separating blocks of the earth's surface; a rift valley. ■ *figurative* a serious break in friendly relations: *their demise caused a* **rift between** *the city's town and gown.*
▸*v.* [*intrans.*] *chiefly Geology* form fissures, cracks, or breaks, esp. through large-scale faulting; move apart: *a fragment of continental crust that rifted away from eastern Australia* | [as *n.*] (**rifting**) *active rifting in southwestern Mexico.* ■ [*trans.*] [usu. as *adj.*] (**rifted**) tear or force (something) apart: *the nascent rifted margins of the Red Sea.* ▷Middle English: of Scandinavian origin; compare with Norwegian and Danish *rift* 'cleft, chink.'

rift val·ley ▸*n.* a large elongated depression with steep walls formed by the downward displacement of a block of the earth's surface between nearly parallel faults or fault systems.

rig[1] /rig/ ▸*v.* (**rigged**, **rig·ging**) [*trans.*] make (a sailing ship or boat) ready for sailing by providing it with sails and rigging: *the catamaran will be rigged as a ketch* | [as *adj.*, in *combination*] (**-rigged**) *a gaff-rigged cutter.* ■ assemble and adjust (the equipment of a sailboat, aircraft, etc.) to make it ready for operation: *most sails are kept ready rigged.* ■ set up (equipment or a device or structure), typically hastily or in makeshift fashion: *he had* **rigged up** *a sort of tent* | *the crew began to rig the camera equipment on a platform.* ■ provide (someone) with clothes of a particular style or type: *a cavalry regiment* **rigged out** *in green and gold.*
▸*n.* **1** the particular way in which a sailboat's masts, sails, and rigging are arranged: *the yacht will emerge from the yard with her original rig.* ■ the sail, mast, and boom of a sailboard. **2** an apparatus, device, or piece of equipment designed for a particular purpose: *a lighting rig.* ■ an oil rig or drilling rig. ■ (in CB and shortwave radio) a transmitter and receiver. ■ a particular type of construction for fishing tackle that bears the bait and hook. **3** a person's costume, outfit, or style of dress: *the rig of the Army Air Corps.* **4** a tractor-trailer. ■ another type of vehicle, such as a horse-drawn carriage. ▷late 15th cent. (in nautical use): perhaps of Scandinavian origin: compare with Norwegian *rigga* 'bind or wrap up.' The noun dates from the early 19th cent.
▸*PHRASE* □ (**in**) **full rig** *informal* (wearing) fancy or ceremonial clothes.

rig[2] ▸*v.* (**rigged**, **rig·ging**) [*trans.*] manage or conduct (something) fraudulently so as to produce a result or situation that is advantageous to a particular person: *the results of the elections had been rigged* | [as *n.*, in *combination*] (**-rigging**) *charges of vote-rigging.* ■ cause an artificial rise or fall in prices in (a market, esp. the stock market) with a view to personal profit: *he accused games manufacturers of rigging the market.*
▸*n. archaic* a trick or way of swindling someone. ▷late 18th cent. (in the noun sense): of unknown origin; the verb is related to the noun.

Ri·ga /ˈrēgə/ a port on the Baltic Sea, the capital of Latvia; pop. 915,000.

rig·a·doon /ˌrigəˈdo͞on/ (also **rig·au·don**) ▸*n.* a lively dance for couples, in duple or quadruple time, of Provençal origin. ▷late 17th cent.: from French *rigaudon*, perhaps named after its inventor, said to be a dance teacher called *Rigaud*.

rig·a·to·ni /ˌrigəˈtōnē/ ▸*n.* pasta in the form of short hollow fluted tubes. ▷Italian.

Ri·gel /ˈrījəl; -gəl/ *Astronomy* the seventh brightest star in the sky, and the brightest in the constellation Orion. It is a blue supergiant nearly sixty thousand times as luminous as our sun. ▷from Arabic *rijl* 'foot (of Orion).'

rig·ger[1] /ˈrigər/ ▸*n.* **1** a person who rigs or attends to the rigging of a sailing ship, aircraft, or parachute. ■ a person who erects and maintains scaffolding, lifting tackle, cranes, etc. ■ a person who works on or helps construct an oil rig. **2** (also **rig·ger brush**) an artist's long-haired sable brush. **3** an outrigger carrying a rowlock on a racing rowboat.

rig·ger[2] ▸*n.* a person who fraudulently manipulates something so as to produce a result or situation to their advantage.

rig·ging /ˈrigiNG/ ▸*n.* **1** the system of ropes, cables, or chains employed to support a ship's masts (**standing rigging**) and to control or set the yards and sails (**running rigging**). ■ the action of providing a sailing ship with such gear. **2** the ropes and wires supporting the structure of an airship, biplane, hang glider, or parachute. ■ the system of cables and fittings controlling the flight surfaces and engines of an aircraft. ■ the action of assembling and adjusting such rigging.

right /rīt/ ▸*adj.* **1** morally good, justified, or acceptable: *I hope we're doing the right thing* | [with *infinitive*] *you were quite right to criticize him.* **2** true or correct as a fact: *I'm not sure I know the right answer* | *her theories were proved right.* ■ [*predic.*] correct in one's opinion or judgment: *she was right about Tom having no money.* ■ used as an interrogative at the end of a statement as a way of inviting agreement, approval, or confirmation: *you went to see Angie on Monday, right?* ■ according to what is correct for a particular situation or thing: *is this the right way to the cottage?* | *you're not holding it the right way up.* ■ the best or most suitable of a number of possible choices for a particular purpose or occasion: *he was clearly the right man for the job* | *I was waiting for the right moment to ask him.* ■ socially fashionable or important: *he was seen at all the right places.* ■ [*predic.*] in a satisfactory, sound, or normal state or condition: *that sausage doesn't smell right* | *if only I could have helped* **put** *matters* **right**. **3** denoting or worn on the side of a person's body which is toward the east when they are facing north: *my right elbow* | *her right shoe.* ■ denoting the corresponding side of any other object: *the right edge of the field.* ■ on this side from the point of view of a spectator. **4** [*attrib.*] *informal, chiefly Brit.* complete; absolute (used for emphasis, typically in derogatory contexts): *I felt a right idiot.* **5** of or relating to a person or political party or grouping favoring conservative views: *are you politically right, left, or center?*
▸*adv.* **1** [with *prep. phr.*] to the furthest or most complete extent or degree (used for emphasis): *the car spun right off the track* | *I'm right out of ideas.* ■ exactly; directly (used to emphasize the precise location or

time of something): *Harriet was standing right behind her.* ■ *informal* immediately; without delaying or hesitating: *I'll be right back.* ■ [as *submodifier*] *dialect* or *archaic* very: *it's right spooky in there!* **2** correctly: *he had guessed right.* ■ in the required or necessary way; properly; satisfactorily: *nothing's going right for me this season.* **3** on or to the right side: *turn right at Main Street.*

▸*n.* **1** that which is morally correct, just, or honorable: *she doesn't understand the difference between right and wrong | the rights and wrongs of the matter.* **2** a moral or legal entitlement to have or obtain something or to act in a certain way: [with *infinitive*] *she had every right to be angry | you're quite* ***within your rights*** *to ask for your money back | there is no* ***right of*** *appeal against the decision.* ■ (**rights**) the authority to perform, publish, film, or televise a particular work, event, etc.: *they sold the paperback rights.* **3** (**the right**) the right-hand part, side, or direction: *take the first turning on the right* | (**one's right**) *she seated me on her right.* ■ (in football or a similar sport) the right-hand half of the field when facing the opponent's goal. ■ (**right**) *Baseball* short for RIGHT FIELD: *a looping single to right.* ■ the right wing of an army. ■ a right turn: *he made a right in Dorchester Avenue.* ■ a road or entrance on the right: *take the first right over the stream.* ■ (esp. in the context of boxing) a person's right fist. ■ a blow given with this: *the young cop swung a terrific right.* **4** (often **the Right**) [treated as *sing.* or *pl.*] a grouping or political party favoring conservative views and supporting capitalist economic principles. ■ the section of a group or political party adhering particularly strongly to such views. [see RIGHT WING.]

▸*v.* [*trans.*] restore to a normal or upright position: *we righted the capsized dinghy.* ■ restore to a normal or correct condition or situation: *righting the economy demanded major cuts in defense spending.* ■ redress or rectify (a wrong or mistaken action): *she was determined to right the wrongs done to her father.* ■ (usu. **be righted**) *archaic* make reparation to (someone) for a wrong done to them: *we'll see you righted.*

▸*exclam. informal* used to indicate one's agreement with a suggestion or to acknowledge a statement or order: *"Barry's here." "Oh, right"* | ***right you are,*** *sir.* ■ used as a filler in speech or as a way of confirming that someone is listening to or understanding what one is saying: *and I didn't think any more of it, right, but Mom said I should take him to a doctor.* ■ used to introduce an utterance, exhortation, or suggestion: *right, let's have a drink.* ▷Old English *riht* (adjective and noun), *rihtan* (verb), *rihte* (adverb), of Germanic origin; related to Latin *rectus* 'ruled,' from an Indo-European root denoting movement in a straight line. **—right·a·ble** *adj.* **—right·er** *n.* **—right·ish** *adj.* **—right·ness** *n.*

▸*PHRASES* □ **bang** (or **dead**) **to rights** *informal* (of a criminal) with positive proof of guilt: *we've got you bang to rights handling stolen property.* □ **be in the right** be morally or legally justified in one's views, actions, or decisions. □ **by rights** if things had happened or been done fairly or correctly: *by rights, he should not be playing next week.* □ **do right by** treat (someone) fairly. □ **in one's own right** as a result of one's own claims, qualifications, or efforts, rather than an association with someone else: *he was already established as a poet in his own right.* □ (**not**) **in one's right mind** (not) sane. □ **not right in the head** *informal* (of a person) not completely sane. □ (**as**) **of right** (or **by right**) as a result of having a moral or legal claim or entitlement: *the state will be obliged to provide health care and education as of right.* □ **put** (or **set**) **someone right 1** restore someone to health. **2** make someone understand the true facts of a situation. □ **put** (or **set**) **something to rights** restore something to its correct or normal state or condition. □ (**as**) **right as rain** *informal* (of a person) feeling completely well or healthy, typically after an illness or minor accident. □ **right** (or **straight**) **away** (or *informal* **off**) immediately. □ **right enough** *informal* certainly; undeniably: *your record's bad right enough.* □ **right on** *informal* used an expression of strong support, approval, or encouragement. See also RIGHT-ON. □ **a right one** *Brit., informal* a silly or foolish person. □ **she's** (or **she'll be**) **right** *Austral., informal* that will be all right; don't worry.

right-a·bout (also **right-a·bout face**) ▸*n. Military* a right turn continued through 180° so as to face in the opposite direction: *he did a swift right-about and disappeared.*

right an·gle ▸*n.* an angle of 90°, as in a corner of a square or at the intersection of two perpendicular straight lines.

▸*PHRASE* □ **at right angles** (or **a right angle**) **to** forming an angle of 90° with (something): *hold the brush at right angles to the surface.*

right-an·gled ▸*adj.* containing or being a right angle: *a* ***right-angled triangle.***

right arm ▸*n. dated* one's most reliable helper: *my employer calls me his right arm and depends upon my knowledge and judgment.*

right as·cen·sion (abbr.: **RA**) ▸*n. Astronomy* the distance of a point east of the First Point of Aries, measured along the celestial equator and expressed in hours, minutes, and seconds. Compare with DECLINATION and CELESTIAL LONGITUDE.

Right Bank a district in the city of Paris, located on the right bank of the Seine River, north of the river. The area contains the Champs Élysées and the Louvre.

right bank ▸*n.* the bank of a river, on the right as one faces downstream.

right brain ▸*n.* the right-hand side of the human brain, believed to be associated with creative thought and the emotions. **—right-brain** *adj.* **—right-brained** *adj.*

right-click ▸*v.* [*intrans.*] *Computing* depress the right-hand button on a mouse. ■ [*trans.*] click on a link or other screen object in this way: *right-click a graphic and choose 'Resize.'*

▸*n.* the action of right-clicking: [as *modifier*] *right-click features.*

right·en /ˈrītn/ ▸*v.* [*trans.*] *archaic* make (something) right, correct, or straight: *thy stubborn mind will not be rightened.*

right·eous /ˈrīCHəs/ ▸*adj.* **1** (of a person or conduct) morally right or justifiable; virtuous: *he is a good, righteous man, I am sure | feelings of* ***righteous indignation*** *about pay and conditions.* See note at MORAL. **2** *informal* perfectly wonderful; fine and genuine: *righteous bread pudding.* ▷Old English *rihtwīs,* from *riht* 'right' + *wīs* 'manner, state, condition.' The change in the ending in the 16th cent. was due to association with words such as *bounteous.* **—right·eous·ly** *adv.* **—right·eous·ness** *n.*

right field (also **right**) ▸*n. Baseball* the part of the outfield to the right of center field from the perspective of home plate: *a ball hit* ***to right field.*** ■ the position of the defensive player stationed in right field: *he first gained attention while playing right field.* **—right field·er** *n.*

right-foot·ed ▸*adj.* (of a person) using the right foot more naturally than the left. ■ (of a kick) done with the right foot.

right·ful /ˈrītfəl/ ▸*adj.* [*attrib.*] having a legitimate right to property, position, or status: *the rightful owner of the jewels.* ■ legitimately claimed; fitting: *they are determined to take their* ***rightful place*** *in a new South Africa.* ▷Old English *rihtful* 'upright, righteous' (see RIGHT, -FUL). The notion of 'legitimacy' dates from Middle English. **—right·ful·ly** *adv.* **—right·ful·ness** *n.*

right hand ▸*n.* the hand of a person's right side. ■ the region or direction on the right side of a person or thing: *a great wall loomed above the street on the right hand.* ■ the most important position next to someone: *the place of honor at his host's right hand.* ■ an efficient or indispensable assistant: *she could have helped him, been her father's right hand.*

▸*adj.* [*attrib.*] on or toward the right side of a person or thing: *the top right-hand corner.* ■ done with or using the right hand: *wild right-hand punches.*

right-hand·ed ▸*adj.* **1** (of a person) using the right hand more naturally than the left: *the slant of the stab wounds suggested that the assailant was right-handed.* ■ (of a tool or item of equipment) made to be used with the right hand or by right-handed people: *a right-handed guitar.* ■ made or done with the right hand, or in a manner natural to right-handed people: *right-handed batting.* **2** going toward or turning to the right, in particular: ■ (of a screw) advanced by turning clockwise. ■ *Biology* (of a spiral shell or helix) dextral. ■ (of a racecourse) turning clockwise.

▸*adv.* with the right hand, or in a manner natural to right-handed people: *Jackson bats right-handed.* **—right-hand·ed·ly** *adv.* **—right-hand·ed·ness** *n.*

right-hand·er /ˈhandər/ ▸*n.* a right-handed person, esp. a right-handed baseball pitcher. ■ a blow struck with the right hand.

right-hand man ▸*n.* an indispensable helper or chief assistant.

Right Hon·our·a·ble ▸*n. Brit.* a title given to certain high officials such as government ministers: *the Right Honourable John Major.*

right·ist /ˈrītist/ ▸*n.* a person who supports the political views or policies of the right.

▸*adj.* supportive of the political views or policies of the right: *rightist doctrine.* **—right·ism** /-ˌizəm/ *n.*

right·ly /ˈrītlē/ ▸*adv.* correctly: *if I remember rightly, she never gives interviews.* ■ with good reason: *the delicious cuisine for which her country was rightly famous.* ■ in accordance with justice or what is morally right: *the key rightly belonged to Craig.*

right-mind·ed ▸*adj.* having sound views and principles. **—right-mind·ed·ness** *n.*

right·most /ˈrītˌmōst/ ▸*adj.* [*attrib.*] situated furthest to the right.

right·o /ˈrītˈō/ (also **right·y-ho** /ˈrītē ˈhō/) ▸*exclam. chiefly Brit., informal* expressing agreement or assent: *"Coming to pick up the kids?" "Righto."*

right of a·bode ▸*n. chiefly Brit.* a person's right to take up residence or remain resident in a country.

right of search ▸*n.* the right of a ship of a belligerent state to stop and search a neutral merchant vessel for prohibited goods.

right of way (also **right-of-way**) ▸*n.* **1** the legal right, established by usage or grant, to pass along a specific route through grounds or property belonging to another. ■ a path or thoroughfare subject to such a right. **2** the legal right of a pedestrian, rider, or driver to proceed with precedence over other road users at a particular point: *he waves on other drivers, even when it's not their right of way.* ■ the right of a ship, boat, or aircraft to proceed with precedence over others in a particular situation. **3** the right to build and operate a railroad line, road, or utility on land belonging to another. ■ the land on which a railroad line, road, or utility is built.

right-on ▸*adj. often derogatory* in keeping with fashionable liberal or left-wing opinions and values: *the right-on music press.*

Right Rev·er·end ▸*n.* a title given to a bishop.

right side ▸*n.* the side of something, esp. a garment or fabric, intended to be uppermost or foremost; the better or usable side of something.

▸*PHRASES* □ **on the right side of** on the safe, appropriate, or desirable side of: *her portrayal of his neurotic wife falls just on the right side of caricature.* ■ in a position to be viewed with favor by: *he hasn't always remained on the right side of the law.* ■ somewhat less than (a specified age): *she's on the right side of forty.* □ **right side out** with the side intended to be seen or used uppermost: *turn the skirt right side out.*

rights is·sue ▸*n.* an issue of shares offered at a special price by a company to its existing shareholders in proportion to their holding of old shares.

right·size /ˈrītˌsīz/ ▸*v.* [*trans.*] convert (something) to an appropriate or optimum size: *organizations are beginning to rightsize computer systems to suit themselves.* ■ reduce the size of (a company or organization) by eliminating staff positions, specifically when business conditions necessitate such a reduction.

rights of man ▸*plural n.* rights held to be justifiably belonging to any person; human rights. The phrase is associated with the Declaration of the Rights of Man and of the Citizen, adopted by the French National Assembly in 1789 and used as a preface to the French Constitution of 1791.

right stuff ▸*n.* (in full **the right stuff**) the necessary qualities for a given task or job: *he had the right stuff to enter this business.*

right-think·ing ▸*adj.* right-minded.

right-to-die ▸*adj.* pertaining to, expressing, or advocating the right to refuse extraordinary measures intended to prolong someone's life when they are terminally ill or comatose.

right-to-know ▸*adj.* of or pertaining to laws or policies that make certain government or company records available to any individual who can demonstrate a right or need to know their contents.

right-to-life ▸*adj.* another term for PRO-LIFE. **—right-to-lif·er** /ˈlīfər/ *n.*

right-to-work ▸*adj.* relating to or promoting a worker's right not to be required to join a trade union: *Kansas is a right-to-work state.*

right tri·an·gle ▸*n.* a triangle with a right angle.

right turn ▸*n.* a turn that brings a person's front to face the way their right side did before: *take a right turn onto Sunset Lane.*

right·ward /ˈrītwərd/ ▸*adv.* (also **right·wards** /-wərdz/) (of political views) toward the right: *the party began to shift rightward.*

▸*adj.* going toward or situated on the right: *the rock face is climbed via a rightward curving crack.*

right whale ▸*n.* a baleen whale with a large head and a deeply curved jaw, of Arctic and temperate waters. • Family Balaenidae: two genera and three species, in particular *Balaena glacialis*, which has distinctive patches of callosities on the snout. See also **BOWHEAD**.

right wing ▸*n.* (**the right wing**) **1** the conservative or reactionary section of a political party or system. [with reference to the National Assembly in France (1789–91), where the nobles sat to the president's right and the commons to the left.] **2** the right side of a team on the field in soccer, rugby, and field hockey. ■ the right side of an army.

▸*adj.* conservative or reactionary: *a right-wing Republican senator.* —**right-wing·er** *n.*

right·y /ˈrītē/ ▸*n.* (*pl.* **right·ies**) *informal* **1** a right-handed person. **2** a rightist.

▸*adv.* with the right hand or as customary for a right-handed person: *he bats righty.*

right·y-ho ▸*exclam.* variant spelling of **RIGHTO**.

rig·id /ˈrijid/ ▸*adj.* unable to bend or be forced out of shape; not flexible: *a seat of rigid orange plastic* | *rigid ships are the dirigibles in which the bag is built around a metallic framework.* ■ (of a person or part of the body) stiff and unmoving, esp. as a result of shock or fear: *his face grew* **rigid with** *fear.* ■ *figurative* not able to be changed or adapted: *teachers are being asked to unlearn rigid rules for labeling children.* ■ *figurative* (of a person or their behavior) not adaptable in outlook, belief, or response: *ski instructors have become less rigid about style.* ▹late Middle English: from Latin *rigidus*, from *rigere* 'be stiff.' —**ri·gid·i·fy** /rəˈjidəˌfī/ *v.* —**ri·gid·i·ty** /rəˈjidətē/ *n.* —**rig·id·ly** *adv.* —**rig·id·ness** *n.*

rig·id des·ig·na·tor ▸*n. Philosophy* a term that identifies the same object or individual in every possible world.

Ri·gil Ken·tau·rus /ˈrījəl kenˈtôrəs/ (also **Ri·gil Kent**) *Astronomy* the star Alpha Centauri. ▹Arabic, literally 'the foot of the Centaur.'

rig·ma·role /ˈrig(ə)məˌrōl/ ▸*n.* [usu. in *sing.*] a lengthy and complicated procedure: *he went through the rigmarole of securing the front door.* ■ a long, rambling story or statement. ▹mid 18th cent.: apparently an alteration of *ragman roll*, originally denoting a legal document recording a list of offenses.

rig·or /ˈrigər/ ▸*n.* **1** the quality of being extremely thorough, exhaustive, or accurate: *his analysis is lacking in rigor.* ■ severity or strictness: *the full rigor of the law.* ■ (**rigors**) demanding, difficult, or extreme conditions: *the rigors of a harsh winter.* **2** *Medicine* a sudden feeling of cold with shivering accompanied by a rise in temperature, often with copious sweating, esp. at the onset or height of a fever. ■ short for **RIGOR MORTIS**. ▹late Middle English: from Latin, literally 'stiffness,' from *rigere* 'be stiff.'

rig·or·ism /ˈrigəˌrizəm/ ▸*n.* extreme strictness in interpreting or enforcing a law, precept, or principle. ■ (in the Roman Catholic Church) formerly, the doctrine that in doubtful cases of conscience the strict course is always to be followed. —**rig·or·ist** *n.* & *adj.*

rig·or mor·tis /ˌrigər ˈmôrtəs/ ▸*n. Medicine* stiffening of the joints and muscles of a body a few hours after death, usually lasting from one to four days. ▹mid 19th cent.: from Latin, literally 'stiffness of death.'

rig·or·ous /ˈrigərəs/ ▸*adj.* extremely thorough, exhaustive, or accurate: *the rigorous testing of consumer products.* ■ (of a rule, system, etc.) strictly applied or adhered to: *rigorous controls on mergers.* ■ (of a person) adhering strictly or inflexibly to a belief, opinion, or way of doing something: *a rigorous teetotaler.* ■ (of an activity) physically demanding: *my exercise regime is a little more rigorous than most.* ■ (of the weather or climate) harsh: *the rigorous climate in the regions of perpetual snow high in the Himalayas.* ▹late Middle English: from Old French *rigorous* or late Latin *rigorosus*, from *rigor* 'stiffness' (see **RIGOR**). —**rig·or·ous·ly** *adv.* —**rig·or·ous·ness** *n.*

rig·our ▸*n.* British spelling of **RIGOR** (sense 1).

rig-out ▸*n. informal, chiefly Brit.* an outfit of clothes.

Rig Ve·da /rig ˈvādə; ˈvēdə/ *Hinduism* the oldest and principal of the Vedas, a collection of 1028 hymns composed in the 2nd millennium BC in early Sanskrit. See **VEDA**. ▹from Sanskrit *ṛgveda*, from *ṛk* '(sacred) stanza' + *veda* '(sacred) knowledge.'

Riis /rēs/, Jacob August (1849–1914), U.S. journalist and social reformer; born in Denmark. A police reporter for the *New York Tribune* 1877–88 and the *New York Evening Sun* 1888–99, he was a crusader for parks, playgrounds, and improved schools and housing in urban areas. He wrote *How the Other Half Lives* (1890).

Ri·je·ka /riˈyekə/ a port on the Adriatic coast of Croatia; pop. 168,000. Italian name **FIUME**.

rijst·ta·fel /ˈrīˌstäfəl/ ▸*n.* a meal of Southeast Asian food consisting of a selection of spiced rice dishes. ▹Dutch, from *rijst* 'rice' + *tafel* 'table.'

rik·i·shi /ˈrikəˌshē/ ▸*n.* (*pl.* same) a sumo wrestler. ▹Japanese, from *riki* 'strength' + *shi* 'warrior.'

Riks·mål /ˈrikˌsmôl; ˈrēk-/ ▸*n.* another term for **BOKMÅL**. ▹Norwegian, from *rike* 'state, nation' + *mål* 'language.'

rile /rīl/ ▸*v.* [*trans.*] **1** *informal* make (someone) annoyed or irritated: *it was his air of knowing all the answers that riled her* | *he's getting you all* **riled up**. **2** make (water) turbulent or muddy. ▹early 19th cent.: variant of **ROIL**.

Ri·ley[1] /ˈrīlē/ ▸*n.* (in phrase **the life of Riley**) *informal* a luxurious or carefree existence: *all the older boys are driving big expensive cars and* **living the life of Riley**. ▹early 20th cent.: of unknown origin.

Ri·ley[2], Bridget (Louise) (1931–), English painter. A leading exponent of op art, she worked with flat patterns to create optical illusions of light and movement.

Ri·ley[3], James Whitcomb (1849–1916), U.S. poet; pen name **Benj. F. Johnson, of Boone**. Known as the common people's poet, esp. in Indiana, his most popular poems included "Little Orphant Annie" (1885), "The Raggedy Man" (1890), and "When the Frost Is on the Punkin" (1896).

ri·lie·vo ▸*n.* variant spelling of **RELIEVO**.

Ril·ke /ˈrilkə/, Rainer Maria (1875–1926), Austrian poet, born in Bohemia; pseudonym of *René Karl Wilhelm Josef Maria Rilke*. His conception of art as a quasi-religious vocation culminated in his best-known works, the *Duino Elegies* and *Sonnets to Orpheus* (both 1923).

rill /ril/ ▸*n.* a small stream. ■ a shallow channel cut in the ground by running water. ■ variant spelling of **RILLE**.

▸*v.* [*intrans.*] (of water) flow in or as in a rill: *the springwater rilled over our cold hands.* ■ [as *adj.*] (**rilled**) indented with small grooves: *blocks of butter pounded into artful shapes with rilled paddles.* ▹mid 16th cent.: probably of Low German origin.

rille /ˈrilə/ (also **rill**) ▸*n. Astronomy* a fissure or narrow channel on the moon's surface. ▹mid 19th cent.: from German (see **RILL**).

ril·lettes /rēˈyet/ ▸*plural n.* pâté made of minced pork or other light meat, seasoned and combined with fat. ▹French, diminutive (plural) of Old French *rille* 'strip of pork.'

rim[1] /rim/ ▸*n.* the upper or outer edge of an object, typically something circular or approximately circular: *a china egg cup with a gold rim.* See note at **BORDER**. ■ (also **wheel rim**) the outer edge of a wheel, on which the tire is fitted. ■ the metal hoop from which a basketball net is suspended. ■ (often **rims**) the part of a glasses frame surrounding the lenses. ■ a limit or boundary of something: *the outer rim of the solar system.* ■ an encircling stain or deposit: *a thick rim of suds.*

▸*v.* (**rimmed, rim·ming**) [*trans.*] form or act as an outer edge or rim for: *a huge lake rimmed by glaciers* | [as *adj.*, in *combination*] (**-rimmed**) *steel-rimmed glasses.* ■ (usu. **be rimmed**) mark with an encircling stain or deposit: *his collar was rimmed with dirt.* ▹Old English *rima* 'a border, coast'; compare with Old Norse *rimi* 'ridge, strip of land' (the only known cognate). —**rim·less** *adj.*

rim[2] ▸*v.* (**rimmed, rim·ming**) [*trans.*] *vulgar slang* lick or suck the anus of (someone) as a means of sexual stimulation.

Rim·baud /ramˈbō; raNˈbō/, (Jean Nicholas) Arthur (1854–91), French poet. Known for his symbolist prose poems and for his stormy relationship with Paul Verlaine, he stopped writing at about the age of 20 and spent the rest of his life traveling.

rime[1] /rīm/ ▸*n.* (also **rime ice**) frost formed on cold objects by the rapid freezing of water vapor in cloud or fog. ■ *poetic/literary* hoarfrost.

▸*v.* [*trans.*] *poetic/literary* cover (an object) with hoarfrost: *he does not brush away the frost that rimes his beard.* ▹Old English *hrīm*, of Germanic origin; related to Dutch *rijm*. The word became rare in Middle English but was revived in literary use at the end of the 18th cent.

rime[2] ▸*n.* & *v.* archaic spelling of **RHYME**.

rim·fire /ˈrimˌfīr/ ▸*adj.* [*attrib.*] (of a cartridge) having the primer around the edge of the base. ■ (of a rifle) adapted for such cartridges.

Rim·i·ni /ˈrimənē/ a port and resort on the Adriatic coast of northeastern Italy; pop. 131,000.

rim·land /ˈrimˌland/ ▸*n.* (also **rimlands**) a peripheral area of a country or region.

rim lock ▸*n.* a lock that is fitted to the surface of a door with a matching box fitted into the doorjamb.

Rim·mon /ˈrimən/ (in the Bible) a deity worshiped in ancient Damascus (2 Kings 5: 18).

rim·rock /ˈrimˌräk/ ▸*n.* an outcrop of resistant rock forming a margin to a gravel deposit, esp. one forming a cliff at the edge of a plateau.

rim·shot (also **rim shot**) ▸*n.* **1** a drum stroke in which the stick strikes the rim and the head of the drum simultaneously. **2** in basketball, a toss in which the ball hits the rim of the basket.

Rim·sky-Kor·sa·kov /ˈrimskē ˈkôrsəˌkôf/, Nikolai (Andreevich) (1844–1908), Russian composer. He established his reputation with his orchestral suite *Scheherazade* (1888) and his many operas drawing on Russian and Slavic folk tales.

rim·y /ˈrīmē/ ▸*adj.* (**rim·i·er, rim·i·est**) *poetic/literary* covered with frost.

rind /rīnd/ ▸*n.* the tough outer layer of something, in particular: ■ the tough outer skin of certain fruit, esp. citrus fruit. ■ the hard outer edge of cheese or bacon, usually removed before eating. ■ the bark of a tree or plant. ■ the hard outer layer of a rhizomorph or other part of a fungus. ■ the skin or blubber of a whale.

▸*v.* [*trans.*] strip the bark from (a tree). ▹Old English *rind(e)* 'bark of a tree'; related to Dutch *run* and German *Rinde*, of unknown origin. —**rind·ed** *adj.* [in *combination*] *yellow-rinded lemons.* —**rind·less** *adj.*

R

rin·der·pest /ˈrindərˌpest/ ▸*n. Veterinary Medicine* an infectious disease of ruminants, esp. cattle, caused by a paramyxovirus. It is characterized by fever, dysentery, and inflammation of the mucous membranes. ▹mid 19th cent.: from German, from *Rinder* 'cattle' + *Pest* 'plague.'

ring[1] /riNG/ ▸*n.* **1** a small circular band, typically of precious metal and often set with one or more gemstones, worn on a finger as an ornament or a token of marriage, engagement, or authority. ■ a circular band of any material: *fried onion rings.* ■ *Astronomy* a thin band or disk of rock and ice particles around a planet. ■ a circular marking or pattern: *black rings around her eyes.* ■ short for **TREE RING**. ■ [usu. as *adj.*] *Archaeology* a circular prehistoric earthwork, typically consisting of a bank and ditch: *a ring ditch.* **2** an enclosed space, typically surrounded by seating for spectators, in which a sport, performance, or show takes place: *a circus ring.* ■ a roped enclosure for boxing or wrestling. ■ (**the ring**) the profession, sport, or institution of boxing. **3** a group of people or things arranged in a circle: *he pointed to the ring of trees.* ■ (**in a ring**) arranged or grouped in a circle: *everyone sat in a ring, holding hands.* ■ [usu. with *adj.*] a group of people drawn together due to a shared interest or goal, esp. one involving illegal or unscrupulous activity: *the police had been investigating the drug ring.* ■ *Chemistry* another term for **CLOSED CHAIN**. **4** a circular or spiral course: *they were dancing energetically in a ring.* **5** *Mathematics* a set of elements with two binary operations, addition and multiplication, the second being distributive over the first and associative.

▸*v.* [*trans.*] **1** (often **be ringed**) surround (someone or something), esp. for protection or containment: *the courthouse was ringed with police.* ■ form a line around the edge of (something circular): *dark shadows ringed his eyes.* ■ draw a circle around (something), esp. to focus attention on it: *an area of Tribeca had been ringed in red.* **2** put a circular band through the nose of (a bull, pig, or other farm animal) to lead or otherwise control it. ▹Old English *hring*, of Germanic origin; related to Dutch *ring*, German *Ring*, also to the noun **RANK**[1]. —**ringed** *adj.* [in *combination*] *the five-ringed Olympic emblem.* —**ring·less** *adj.*

▸*PHRASES* □ **run rings around someone** *informal* outclass or outwit someone very easily. □ **throw one's hat in the ring** see **HAT**.

ring[2] ▸*v.* (*past* **rang** /raNG/; *past part.* **rung** /rəNG/) **1** [*intrans.*] make a clear resonant or vibrating sound: *a shot* **rang out** | *a bell rang loudly* | [as *n.*] (**ringing**) *the ringing of fire alarms.* ■ [*trans.*] cause (a bell or alarm) to make such a sound: *he walked up to the door and rang the bell.* ■ (of a telephone) produce a series of resonant or vibrating sounds to signal an incoming call: *the phone rang again as I replaced it.* ■ call for service or attention by sounding a bell: *Ruth, will you* **ring for** *some tea?* ■ (of a person's ears) be filled with a continuous buzzing or humming sound, esp. as the aftereffect of a blow or loud noise: *he yelled so loudly that my eardrums rang.* ■ (**ring with/to**) (of a place) resound or reverberate with (a sound or sounds): *the room rang with laughter.* ■ (**ring with**) *figurative* be filled or permeated with (a particular quality): *those whose names ring with ethnicity.* ■ [*intrans.*] convey a specified impression or quality: *the author's honesty rings true.* ■ [*trans.*] sound (the hour, a peal, etc.) on a bell or bells: *a bell ringing the hour.* **2** [*trans.*] *chiefly Brit.* call by telephone: *I rang her this morning* | *Harriet* **rang** *Dorothy* **up** *next day* | [*intrans.*] *I tried to ring, but the lines to Moscow were engaged.*

▸*phrasal v.* □ **ring in** *Brit.* report or make contact, esp. to or with one's place of work, by telephone: *every morning she coughed she rang in sick.* □ **ring someone/something in** (or **out**) usher someone or something in (or out) by or as if by ringing a bell: *the bells were beginning to ring out the old year.* □ **ring off** *Brit.* end a telephone call by replacing the receiver. □ **ring round** (or **around**) *Brit.* telephone (several people), typically to find something out or arrange something. □ **ring something up** record an amount on a cash register. ■ *figurative* make, spend, or announce a particular amount in sales, profits, or losses.

▸*n.* an act of causing a bell to sound, or the resonant sound caused by this: *there was a ring at the door.* ■ each of a series of resonant or vibrating sounds signaling an incoming telephone call. ■ [in *sing.*] *informal* a telephone call: *I'd better* **give her a ring** *tomorrow.* ■ [in *sing.*] a loud clear sound or tone: *the ring of sledgehammers on metal.* ■ [in *sing.*] a particular quality conveyed by something heard or expressed: *the song had a curious* **ring of** *nostalgia to it.* ■ a set of bells, esp. church bells. ▷Old English *hringan,* of Germanic origin, perhaps imitative.

▸*PHRASES* □ **ring a bell** see BELL[1]. □ **ring the changes** see CHANGE. □ **ring down** (or **up**) **the curtain** cause a theater curtain to be lowered (or raised). ■ *figurative* mark the end (or the beginning) of an enterprise or event: *the sendoff* **rings down the curtain on** *a major chapter in television history.* □ **ring in one's ears** (or **head**) linger in the memory: *he left Washington with the president's praises ringing in his ears.* □ **ring in** (or **out**) **the new** (or **old**) **year** commemorate the new year (or the end of the previous year) with boisterous celebration. □ **ring the knell of** see KNELL. □ **ring off the hook** (of a telephone) be constantly ringing due to a large number of incoming calls.

ring-a·round-a-ro·sy ▸*n.* a singing game played by children, in which the players hold hands and dance in a circle, falling down at the end of the song. ▷said to refer to the inflamed ("rose-colored") ring of buboes, symptomatic of the plague; the final part of the game is symbolic of death.

ring·back /ˈriNG,bak/ ▸*n.* a sound made by a mobile phone that is heard by a person who is calling that phone while waiting for the call to be connected.

ring·bark /ˈriNG,bärk/ ▸*v.* another term for GIRDLE (sense 2).

ring bear·er ▸*n.* the person, typically a young boy, who ceremoniously bears the rings at a wedding.

ring bind·er ▸*n.* a loose-leaf binder with ring-shaped clasps that can be opened to pass through holes in the paper.

ring·bolt /ˈriNG,bōlt/ ▸*n.* a bolt made with a ring for passing a rope through.

ring·bone /ˈriNG,bōn/ ▸*n.* osteoarthritis of the pastern joint of a horse, causing swelling and lameness.

ring-bound ▸*adj.* bound in a ring binder.

ring cir·cuit ▸*n.* an electric circuit serving a number of outlets, with one fuse in the supply to the circuit.

ring·dove /ˈriNG,dəv/ ▸*n.* a dove or pigeon with a ringlike mark on the neck, in particular: • a captive or feral African collared dove (*Streptopelia roseogrisea,* family Columbidae). • *Brit.* the wood pigeon.

ringed plov·er ▸*n.* a small plover found chiefly in Eurasia, with white underparts and a black collar, breeding on sand or shingle beaches. • Genus *Charadrius,* family Charadriidae: three species, in particular *Charadrius hiaticula.*

ringed seal ▸*n.* a seal of arctic and subarctic waters that has pale ring-shaped markings on the back and sides and a short muzzle. • *Phoca hispida,* family Phocidae.

ring·er[1] /ˈriNGər/ ▸*n.* **1** *informal* an athlete or horse fraudulently substituted for another in a competition or event. ■ a person's or thing's double, esp. an impostor: *he's a* **ringer for** *the French actor Fernandel.* ■ a person who is highly proficient at a particular skill or sport and is brought in to supplement a team or group of people: *league eligibility rules had grown flexible to accommodate new teams, and ringers began suiting up.* **2** a person who rings something, esp. a bell-ringer. ■ a device for ringing a bell, esp. on a telephone.

ring·er[2] ▸ **1** in certain games, a tossed object that encircles its intended target, in particular: ■ a tossed horseshoe that encircles the stake: *you never forget the sound of your first ringer.* ■ a tossed quoit that encircles the peg. **2** a game of marbles in which the target marbles are placed in the center of a circular area.

Ring·er's so·lu·tion /ˈriNGərz/ ▸*n. Biology* a physiological saline solution that typically contains, in addition to sodium chloride, salts of potassium and calcium. ▷late 19th cent.: named after Sydney *Ringer* (1834–1910), English physician.

ring·ette /riNGˈet/ ▸*n. Canadian* a game resembling ice hockey, played (esp. by women and girls) with a straight stick and a rubber ring, and in which no intentional body contact is allowed.

ring fin·ger ▸*n.* the finger next to the little finger, esp. of the left hand, on which the wedding band is worn.

ring flash ▸*n. Photography* a circular electronic flash tube that fits around a camera lens to give shadowless lighting of a subject near the lens, esp. for macrophotography.

ring·git /ˈriNGgit/ ▸*n.* (*pl.* same or **-gits**) the basic monetary unit of Malaysia, equivalent to 100 hundred sen. ▷Malay.

ring·hals /ˈriNG,hals/ (also **rink·hals** /ˈriNG,kals/) ▸*n.* a large nocturnal spitting cobra of southern Africa, with one or two white rings across the throat. • *Hemachatus haemachatus,* family Elapidae. ▷late 18th cent.: from Afrikaans *rinkhals,* from *ring* 'ring' + *hals* 'neck.'

ring·ing /ˈriNGiNG/ ▸*adj.* [*attrib.*] having or emitting a clear resonant sound: *a ringing voice.* ■ *figurative* (of a statement) forceful and unequivocal: *the Russian leader received a ringing declaration of support.* **—ring·ing·ly** *adv.*

ring·lead·er /ˈriNG,lēdər/ ▸*n.* a person who initiates or leads an illicit or illegal activity.

ring·let /ˈriNGlit/ ▸*n.* **1** a lock of hair hanging in a corkscrew-shaped curl. **2** a brown butterfly that has wings bearing eyespots that are typically highlighted by a paler color. • *Aphantopus, Erebia,* and other genera in the subfamily Satyrinae, family Nymphalidae: several species. **—ring·let·ed** *adj.* **—ring·let·y** *adj.*

ring main ▸*n. Brit.* **1** an electrical supply serving a series of consumers and returning to the original source, so that each consumer has an alternative path in the event of a failure. ■ another term for RING CIRCUIT. **2** an arrangement of pipes forming a closed loop into which steam, water, or sewage may be fed and whose points of draw-off are supplied by flow from two directions.

ring·mas·ter /ˈriNG,mastər/ ▸*n.* the person directing a circus performance.

ring mod·u·la·tor ▸*n.* an electronic circuit, esp. in a musical instrument, that incorporates a closed loop of four diodes and can be used for the balanced mixing and modulation of signals.

ring-neck (also **ring·neck**) ▸*n.* any of a number of ring-necked birds, in particular: • a ring-necked pheasant. See PHEASANT. • *Austral.* a green parrot with a yellow collar (genus *Barnardius,* family Psittacidae: two species). • a ring-necked duck (*Aythya collaris,* family Anatidae).

ring-necked ▸*adj.* used in names of birds and reptiles with a band or bands of color around the neck, e.g., **ring-necked pheasant**.

Ring of Fire the zone of volcanic activity surrounding the Pacific Ocean.

ring ou·zel (also **ring ou·sel**) ▸*n.* a European thrush that resembles a blackbird with a white crescent across the breast, inhabiting upland moors and mountainous country. • *Turdus torquatus,* subfamily Turdinae, family Muscicapidae.

ring pull ▸*n.* a ring-shaped pull tab on a can or other container.

ring road ▸*n.* a bypass encircling a town.

ring·side /ˈriNG,sīd/ ▸*n.* [often as *adj.*] the area immediately beside a boxing ring or circus ring: *a ringside judge.* ■ *figurative* an advantageous position from which to observe or monitor something: *having* **a ringside seat** *at the healthcare committee hearings.* **—ring·sid·er** *n.*

ring·ster /ˈriNGstər/ ▸*n. archaic* **1** a member of a political or price-fixing ring. **2** a boxer.

ring·tail /ˈriNG,tāl/ ▸*n.* **1** any of a number of mammals or birds having a tail marked with a ring or rings, in particular: ■ a ring-tailed cat or lemur. ■ a female hen harrier or related harrier. ■ a golden eagle up to its third year. **2** (also **ring·tail** or **ring-tailed pos·sum**) a nocturnal tree-dwelling Australian possum that habitually curls its prehensile tail into a ring or spiral. • Genus *Pseudocheirus* and other genera, family Petauridae: several species, in particular the **common ringtail** (*P. peregrinus*), of southern Australia and Tasmania.

ring-tailed ▸*adj.* used in names of mammals and birds that have the tail banded in contrasting colors, e.g., **ring-tailed lemur**, or curled at the end, e.g., **ring-tailed possum**.

ring-tailed cat ▸*n.* a North American cacomistle, a nocturnal raccoonlike mammal with a dark-ringed tail. Also called RINGTAIL. • *Bassariscus astutus,* family Procyonidae.

ring-tailed le·mur ▸*n.* a gregarious lemur with a gray coat, black rings around the eyes, and distinctive black-and-white banding on the tail. • *Lemur catta,* family Lemuridae.

ring-tailed lemur

ring·tone /ˈriNG,tōn/ ▸*n.* a sound made by a mobile phone when an incoming call is received.

ring·toss /ˈriNG,tôs; -,täs/ ▸*n.* a game in which rings are tossed at an upright peg. Points are scored by encircling the peg or coming closer to it than other players.

ring·work /ˈriNG,wərk/ ▸*n. Archaeology* the circular entrenchment of a minor medieval castle.

ring·worm /ˈriNG,wərm/ ▸*n.* a contagious itching skin disease occurring in small circular patches, caused by any of a number of fungi and affecting chiefly the scalp or the feet. The commonest form is athlete's foot. Also called TINEA.

rink /riNGk/ ▸*n.* (also **ice rink** or **hock·ey rink**) an enclosed area of ice for skating, ice hockey, or curling, esp. one artificially prepared. ■ (also **rol·ler rink**) a smooth enclosed floor for roller skating. ■ a building containing either of these. ■ (also **bowl·ing rink**) the strip of a bowling green used for playing a match. ■ a team in curling or lawn bowling. ▷late Middle English (originally Scots in the sense 'jousting ground'): perhaps originally from Old French *renc* 'rank.'

rink·hals /ˈriNG,kals/ ▸*n.* variant spelling of RINGHALS.

rink rat ▸*n. informal* **1** a young person who spends time around an ice-hockey rink in the hope of meeting players, watching practice, and spending time on the ice. **2** a synthetic broom used in the game of curling.

rink·y-dink /ˈriNGkē ,diNGk/ ▸*adj. informal* old-fashioned, amateurish, or shoddy: *the fifty-third issue of the quarterly looked just as rinky-dink as the first.* ▷late 19th cent.: of unknown origin.

Rin·po·che /ˈrinˈpäCHˈā/ ▸*n.* (in Tibetan Buddhism) an incarnate lama or highly respected religious teacher (often used as an honorific title). ▷Tibetan, literally 'precious jewel.'

rinse /rins/ ▸*v.* [*trans.*] wash (something) with clean water to remove soap, detergent, dirt, or impurities: *always rinse your hair thoroughly* | *mussels should be well rinsed before use.* ■ wash (something) quickly, esp. without soap: *Rose* **rinsed out** *a tumbler.* ■ clean (one's mouth) by swilling around and then spitting out a mouthful of water or mouthwash: *Karen* **rinsed** *her* **mouth out.** ■ [*trans.*] remove (soap, detergent, dirt, or impurities) by washing with clean water: *the conditioning mousse doesn't have to be* **rinsed out** | [*intrans.*] *rub salt on to rough areas of skin, then* **rinse off.**

▸*n.* **1** an act of rinsing something: *I gave my hands a quick rinse.* **2** an antiseptic solution for cleansing the mouth. **3** a preparation for conditioning or temporarily tinting the hair. ▷Middle English (as a verb): from Old French *rincer,* of unknown ultimate origin. **—rins·er** *n.*

Ri·o Bran·co /ˈrēō ˈbräNGkō; ˈrē-ōō ˈbräNGkōō/ a city in western Brazil, capital of the state of Acre; pop. 197,000.

Ri·o de Ja·nei·ro /ˈrē-ō ˌdā (d)ZHəˈnerō; ˌdē/ a state in eastern Brazil, on the Atlantic coast. ■ (also **Rio**) its capital; pop. 5,481,000. The chief port of Brazil, it was the country's capital from 1763 until 1960, when it was replaced by Brasilia.

Rí·o de la Pla·ta /ˈrēō dā lä ˈplätä/ Spanish name for the River Plate (see **PLATE, RIVER**).

Rí·o de O·ro /ˈrēō dē ˈôrō/ an arid region on the Atlantic coast of northwestern Africa that forms the southern part of Western Sahara. It was united with Saguia el Hamra in 1958 to form the province of Spanish Sahara (now Western Sahara).

Ri·o Grande /ˌrē-ō ˈgrand(ē)/ a river in North America that rises in the Rocky Mountains of southwestern Colorado and flows 1,880 miles (3,030 km) southeast to the Gulf of Mexico, forming the U.S.–Mexico border from El Paso to the gulf.

Ri·o·ja /rēˈōhä/ ▸*n.* a wine produced in La Rioja, Spain.

Ri·o Mu·ni /ˈrē-ō ˈmōōnē/ the part of Equatorial Guinea that lies on the mainland of West Africa.

Ri·o Ne·gro /ˈrē-ō ˈnegrō/ a river in South America that rises as the Guainia in eastern Colombia and flows for about 1,400 miles (2,255 km) through northwestern Brazil before joining the Amazon River near Manaus.

Rio Ran·cho /ˈrē-ō ˈranCHō/ a city in north central New Mexico, northwest of Albuquerque; pop. 51,765.

ri·ot /ˈrīət/ ▸*n.* **1** a violent disturbance of the peace by a crowd: *riots broke out in the capital.* ■ [as *adj.*] concerned with or used in the suppression of such disturbances: *riot police.* ■ *figurative* an uproar: *the film's sex scenes caused a riot in Cannes.* ■ *figurative* an outburst of uncontrolled feelings: ***a riot of** emotions raged through Frances.* ■ *archaic* uncontrolled revelry; rowdy behavior. **2** [in *sing.*] an impressively large or varied display of something: *the garden was **a riot of** color.* **3** [in *sing.*] *informal* a highly amusing or entertaining person or thing: *everyone thought she was a riot.*

▸*v.* [*intrans.*] take part in a violent public disturbance: *students rioted in Paris* | [as *n.*] (**rioting**) *a night of rioting.* ■ *figurative* behave in an unrestrained way: *another set of emotions rioted through him.* ■ *archaic* act in a dissipated way: *an unrepentant prodigal son, rioting off to far countries.* ▷Middle English (originally in the sense 'dissolute living'): from Old French *riote* 'debate,' from *rioter* 'to quarrel,' of unknown ultimate origin. **—ri·ot·er** *n.*

▸*PHRASE* □ **run riot** behave in a violent and unrestrained way. ■ (of a mental faculty or emotion) function or be expressed without restraint: *her imagination ran riot.* ■ proliferate or spread uncontrollably: *traditional prejudices were allowed to run riot.*

Ri·ot Act a law passed by the British government in 1715 and repealed in 1967, designed to prevent civil disorder.The act made it a felony for an assembly of more than twelve people to refuse to disperse after being ordered to do so and having been read a specified portion of the act by lawful authority.

▸*PHRASE* □ **read the Riot Act** (or **riot act**) give someone a strong warning that they must improve their behavior.

ri·ot gear ▸*n.* protective clothing and equipment worn by police or prison officers in situations of crowd violence.

ri·ot girl (also **riot grrrl**) ▸*n.* a member of a movement of young feminists expressing their resistance to the sexual harassment and exploitation of women, esp. through aggressive punk-style rock music.

ri·ot·ous /ˈrīətəs/ ▸*adj.* marked by or involving public disorder: *a riotous crowd.* ■ characterized by wild and uncontrolled behavior: *a riotous party.* ■ having a vivid, varied appearance: *a riotous display of bright red, green, and yellow vegetables.* ■ hilariously funny: *a riotous account of the making of the movie.* ▷Middle English (in the sense 'troublesome'): from Old French, from *riote* (see **RIOT**). **—ri·ot·ous·ly** *adv.* **—ri·ot·ous·ness** *n.*

RIP[1] ▸*abbr.* rest in peace (used on grave markers). ▷from Latin *requiescat* (or, in the plural, *requiescant*) *in pace.*

RIP[2] /rip; ˈär ˌī ˈpē/ ▸*n.* a raster image processor.

▸*v.* (usu. **rip**) (**ripped, rip·ping**) [*trans.*] rasterize (an image): *once you are happy with the image, you can **rip** it out.* ▷1970s: abbreviation.

rip[1] /rip/ ▸*v.* (**ripped, rip·ping**) **1** [*trans.*] tear or pull (something) quickly or forcibly away from something or someone: *a fan tried to **rip** his pants **off** during a show* | *figurative countries ripped apart by fighting.* ■ [*trans.*] make a long tear or cut in: *you've ripped my jacket* | [as *adj.*] (**ripped**) *ripped jeans.* ■ make (a hole) by force: *the truck was struck by lightning and had a hole ripped out of its roof.* ■ [*intrans.*] come violently apart; tear: *he heard something rip.* ■ cut (wood) in the direction of the grain. **2** [*intrans.*] move forcefully and rapidly: *fire **ripped through** her bungalow.* **3** use a program to copy (a sound sequence on a compact disc) on to a computer's hard drive: *every Beatles song ever made, ripped from my boxed set of CDs.*

▸*phrasal v.* □ **rip into** *informal* make a vehement verbal attack on: *he ripped into me just for going into the trailer.* □ **rip someone off** *informal* cheat someone, esp. financially. □ **rip something off** *informal* steal: *they have ripped off $6.7 billion.* ■ copy; plagiarize: *the film is a shameless collection of ideas ripped off from other movies.* □ **rip something up** tear something violently into small pieces so as to destroy it.

▸*n.* **1** a long tear or cut. ■ [in *sing.*] an act of tearing something forcibly. **2** a fraud or swindle; a rip-off. ▷late Middle English (as a verb): of unknown origin; compare with the verb **REAP**. The noun dates from the early 18th cent.

▸*PHRASES* □ **let rip** *informal* do something or proceed vigorously or without restraint: *the brass sections let rip with sheer gusto.* ■ express oneself vehemently or angrily. □ **let something rip** *informal* allow something, esp. a vehicle, to go at full speed. ■ allow something to happen forcefully or without interference: *once she started a tirade, it was best to let it rip.* ■ utter or express something forcefully and noisily: *when I passed the exam I let rip a "yippee."*

rip[2] ▸*n.* a stretch of fast-flowing and rough water in the sea or in a river, caused by the meeting of currents. ■ short for **RIP CURRENT**. ▷late 18th cent.: perhaps related to **RIP**[1].

rip[3] ▸*n. dated* **1** a dissolute immoral person, esp. a man: *"Where is that old rip?" a deep voice shouted.* ■ a mischievous person, esp. a child. **2** a worthless horse. ▷late 18th cent.: perhaps from *rep*, abbreviation of **REPROBATE**.

ri·par·i·an /riˈpe(ə)rēən; rī-/ ▸*adj. chiefly Law* of, relating to, or situated on the banks of a river: *all the riparian states must sign an agreement.* ■ *Ecology* of or relating to wetlands adjacent to rivers and streams. ▷mid 19th cent.: from Latin *riparius* (from *ripa* 'bank') + **-AN**.

rip·cord /ˈripˌkôrd/ ▸*n.* a cord that is pulled to open a parachute.

rip cur·rent ▸*n.* an intermittent strong surface current flowing seaward from the shore.

ripe /rīp/ ▸*adj.* (of fruit or grain) developed to the point of readiness for harvesting and eating. ■ (of a cheese or wine) fully matured: *a ripe Brie* | *figurative ripe wisdom.* ■ (of a smell or flavor) rich, intense, or pungent: *rich, ripe flavors emanate from this wine.* ■ (of a female fish or insect) ready to lay eggs or spawn. ■ [*predic.*] (**ripe for**) arrived at the fitting stage or time for (a particular action or purpose): *land ripe for development.* ■ [*predic.*] (**ripe with**) full of: *a population ripe with discontent.* ■ [*attrib.*] (of a person's age) advanced: *she lived to a ripe old age.* ■ *informal* (of a person's language) beyond the bounds of propriety; coarse. ▷Old English *rīpe*; related to Dutch *rijp* and German *reif.* **—ripe·ly** *adv.* **—ripe·ness** *n.*

▸*PHRASE* □ **the time is ripe** a suitable time has arrived: *the time was ripe to talk about peace.*

rip·en /ˈrīpən/ ▸*v.* become or make ripe: [*intrans.*] *honeydew melons ripen slowly* | [*trans.*] *for ease of harvesting, the fruit is ripened to order.* See note at **MATURE**.

ri·pie·no /ripˈyānō/ ▸*n.* (*pl.* **-nos** or **-ni** /-nē/) [usu. as *adj.*] *Music* the body of instruments accompanying the concertino in baroque concerto music: *the concertino is accompanied by ripieno strings.* ▷early 18th cent. (in the sense 'supplementary'): from Italian, from *ri-* (expressing intensive force) + *pieno* 'full'.

Rip·ken /ˈripkin/, Cal, Jr. (1960–), U.S. baseball player; nickname **Iron Man**. A shortstop and later a third baseman, he played for the Baltimore Orioles 1982–2001. He holds the major league record of 2,632 consecutive games played.

rip-off ▸*n. informal* a fraud or swindle, esp. something that is grossly overpriced: *designer label clothes are just expensive rip-offs.* ■ an inferior imitation of something: *rip-offs of all the latest styles.*

ri·poste /riˈpōst/ ▸*n.* **1** a quick clever reply to an insult or criticism. **2** *Fencing* a quick return thrust following a parry.

▸*v.* **1** [with *direct speech*] make a quick clever reply to an insult or criticism: *"You've got a strange sense of humor," Grant riposted.* **2** [*intrans.*] make a quick return thrust in fencing. ▷early 18th cent.: from French *risposte* (noun), *risposter* (verb), from Italian *risposta* 'response.'

rip·per /ˈripər/ ▸*n.* **1** a tool that is used to tear or break something. ■ a murderer who mutilates victims' bodies. **2** *informal* a thing that is particularly admirable or excellent.

rip·ping /ˈripiNG/ ▸*adj. Brit., informal, dated* splendid; excellent: *she's going to have a ripping time.* **—rip·ping·ly** *adv.*

rip·ple /ˈripəl/ ▸*n.* **1** a small wave or series of waves on the surface of water, esp. as caused by an object dropping into it or a slight breeze. ■ a thing resembling such a wave or series of waves in appearance or movement: *the sand undulated and was ridged with ripples.* ■ a gentle rising and falling sound, esp. of laughter or conversation, that spreads through a group of people: *a ripple of laughter ran around the room.* ■ a particular feeling or effect that spreads through or to someone or something: *his words set off a ripple of excitement within her.* ■ *Physics* a wave on a fluid surface, the restoring force for which is provided by surface tension rather than gravity, and that consequently has a wavelength shorter than that corresponding to the minimum speed of propagation. ■ *Physics* small periodic, usually undesirable, variations in electrical voltage superposed on a direct voltage or on an alternating voltage of lower frequency. **2** a type of ice cream with wavy lines of colored flavored syrup running through it: *raspberry ripple.*

▸*v.* [*intrans.*] (of water) form or flow with small waves on the surface: *the Mediterranean rippled and sparkled* | [as *adj.*] (**rippling**) *the rippling waters.* ■ [*trans.*] cause (the surface of water) to form small waves: *a cool wind rippled the surface of the estuary.* ■ move or cause to move in a way resembling such waves: [*intrans.*] *fields of grain rippling in the wind.* ■ [*intrans.*] (of a sound or feeling) spread through a person, group, or place: *applause **rippled around** the tables.* ■ [as *adj.*] (**rippled**) having the appearance of small waves: *a broad noodle, rippled on both sides, wider than fettuccine.* ▷late 17th cent. (as a verb): of unknown origin. **—rip·plet** /ˈriplit/ *n.* **—rip·ply** /ˈrip(ə)lē/ *adj.*

rip·ple ef·fect ▸*n.* the continuing and spreading results of an event or action: *while their marriage made an impact on their friends, the ripple effect on family members was even more profound.*

rip·ple marks ▸*plural n.* a system of subparallel wavy ridges and furrows left on sand or mud by the action of water or wind, and sometimes fossilized.

rip·rap /ˈripˌrap/ ▸*n.* loose stone used to form a foundation for a breakwater or other structure.

▸*v.* (**-rapped, -rap·ping**) [*trans.*] strengthen with such a structure. ▷mid 19th cent. (originally U.S.): reduplication of **RAP**[1].

rip-roar·ing ▸*adj.* [*attrib.*] full of energy and vigor: *a rip-roaring rodeo.* **—rip-roar·ing·ly** *adv.*

rip·saw /ˈripˌsô/ ▸*n.* a coarse saw for cutting wood along the grain.

rip·snort·ing /ˈripˈsnôrtiNG/ ▸*adj.* [*attrib.*] *informal* showing great vigor or intensity: *a ripsnorting editorial.* **—rip·snort·er** /-ˈsnôrtər/ *n.* **—rip·snort·ing·ly** *adv.*

rip·stop /ˈripˌstäp/ ▸*n.* nylon fabric that is woven so that a tear will not spread.

rip·tide /ˈripˌtīd/ ▸*n.* another term for **RIP CURRENT**. ■ *figurative* an experience of conflicting psychological forces.

Rip Van Win·kle /ˌrip ˌvan ˈwiNGkəl/ the hero of a story in Washington Irving's *Sketch Book* (1819–20), who fell asleep in the Catskill Mountains and awoke after twenty years to find the world completely changed.

RISC /risk/ ▸*n.* [usu. as *adj.*] *Computing* a computer based on a processor or processors designed to perform a limited set of operations extremely quickly. ■ computing using this kind of computer. ▷1980s: acronym from *reduced instruction set computer* (or *computing*).

rise /rīz/ ▸*v.* (*past* **rose** /rōz/; *past part.* **ris·en** /ˈrizən/) [*intrans.*] **1** move from a lower position to a higher one; come or go up: *the tiny aircraft rose from the ground.* ■ (of the sun, moon, or another celestial body) appear above the horizon: *the sun had just risen.* ■ (of a fish) come to the surface of water: *a fish rose and was hooked and landed.* ■ (of a voice) become

Pronunciation Key ə *ago*; ər *over*; ˈə or ˌə *up*; ˈər or ˌər *fur*; a *hat*; ā *rate*; ä *car*; CH *chew*; e *let*; ē *see*; e(ə)r *air*; i *fit*; ī *by*; i(ə)r *ear*; NG *sing*; ō *go*; ô *for*; oi *boy*; ōō *good*; ōō *goo*; ou *out*; SH *she*; TH *thin*; TH *then*; (h)w *why*; ZH *vision*

R

higher in pitch: *my voice rose an octave or two as I screamed.* ■ reach a higher position in society or one's profession: *the officer was a man of great courage who had* ***risen from the ranks.*** ■ (**rise above**) succeed in not being limited or constrained by (a restrictive environment or situation): *he struggled to rise above his humble background.* ■ (**rise above**) be superior to: *I try to rise above prejudice.* **2** get up from lying, sitting, or kneeling: *she pushed back her chair and rose.* ■ get out of bed, esp. in the morning: *I rose and got dressed.* ■ *chiefly Brit.* (of a meeting or a session of a court) adjourn: *the judge's remark heralded the signal for the court to rise.* ■ be restored to life: *your sister has* ***risen from*** *the dead.* ■ (of a wind) start to blow or to blow more strongly: *the wind continued to rise.* ■ (of a river) have its source: *the Euphrates rises in Turkey.* ■ cease to be submissive, obedient, or peaceful: *the activists urged militant factions to* ***rise up.*** ■ (**rise to**) (of a person) react with annoyance or argument to (provocation): *he didn't rise to my teasing.* ■ (**rise to**) find the strength or ability to respond adequately to (a challenging situation): *many participants in the race had never sailed before, but they rose to the challenge.* **3** (of land or a feature following the contours of the land) incline upward; become higher: *the moorlands rise and fall in gentle folds.* ■ (of a building, mountain, or other high object or structure) be much taller than the surrounding landscape: *the cliff rose more than a hundred feet above us.* ■ (of someone's hair) stand on end: *he felt the hairs rise on the back of his neck.* ■ (of a building) undergo construction from the foundations: *rows of two-story houses are slowly rising.* ■ (of dough) swell by the action of yeast: *leave the dough in a warm place to rise.* ■ (of a bump, blister, or weal) appear as a swelling on the skin: *blisters rose on his burned hand.* ■ (of a person's stomach) become nauseated: *Fabio's stomach* ***rose at*** *the foul bedding.* **4** increase in number, size, amount, or quality: *land prices had risen.* ■ (of the sea, a river, or other body of water) increase in height to a particular level, typically through tidal action or flooding: *the river level rose so high the work had to be abandoned* | *figurative the* ***rising tide of*** *crime.* ■ (of an emotion) develop and become more intense: *he felt a tide of resentment rising in him.* ■ (of a sound) become louder; be audible above other sounds: *her voice rose above the clamor.* ■ (of a person's mood) become more cheerful: *her spirits rose as they left the ugly city behind.* ■ (of the color in a person's face) become deeper, esp. as a result of embarrassment: *he was teasing her, and she could feel her color rising.* ■ (of a barometer or other measuring instrument) give a higher reading. **5** (**rising**) approaching (a specified age): *she was thirty-nine rising forty* | *Polly shall have a young mare rising three years old.*

▸*n.* **1** an upward movement; an instance of becoming higher: *the bird has a display flight of steep flapping rises.* ■ an act of a fish moving to the surface to take a fly or bait. ■ an increase in sound or pitch: *the rise and fall of his voice.* ■ an instance of social, commercial, or political advancement: *few models have had such a meteoric rise.* ■ an upward slope or hill. ■ the vertical height of a step, arch, or incline. ■ another term for RISER (sense 2). **2** an increase in amount, extent, size, or number: *local people are worried by the rise in crime.* ■ *Brit.* an increase in salary or wages. **3** [in *sing.*] a source; an origin: *it was here that the brook had its rise.* ▷Old English *risan* 'make an attack,' 'wake, get out of bed,' of Germanic origin; related to Dutch *rijzen* and German *reisen.*

▸*PHRASES* □ **get** (or **take**) **a rise out of** *informal* provoke an angry or irritated response from (someone), esp. by teasing. □ **on the rise** becoming greater or more numerous; increasing: *prices were on the rise.* ■ becoming more successful: *young stars on the rise.* □ **rise and shine** [usu. in *imperative*] *informal* get out of bed smartly; wake up. □ **rise to the bait** see BAIT. □ **rise with the sun** (or **lark**) get up early in the morning. □ **someone's star is rising** someone is becoming more successful or popular.

ris·er /'rīzər/ ▸*n.* **1** [with *adj.*] a person who habitually gets out of bed at a particular time of the morning: *late risers always exasperate early risers.* **2** a vertical section between the treads of a staircase. **3** a vertical pipe for the upward flow of liquid or gas. **4** a low platform on a stage or in an auditorium, used to give greater prominence to a speaker or performer. **5** a strip of webbing joining the harness and the rigging lines of a parachute or paraglider.

rise time ▸*n. Electronics* the time required for a pulse to rise from 10 percent to 90 percent of its steady value.

rish·i /'rishē/ ▸*n.* (*pl.* **rish·is**) a Hindu sage or saint. ▷from Sanskrit *ṛṣi.*

ris·i·ble /'rizəbəl/ ▸*adj.* such as to provoke laughter: *a risible scene of lovemaking in a tent.* ■ *rare* (of a person) having the faculty or power of laughing; inclined to laugh. ▷mid 16th cent. (in the sense 'inclined to laughter'): from late Latin *risibilis,* from Latin *ris-* 'laughed,' from the verb *ridere.* —**ris·i·bil·i·ty** /ˌrizə'bilətē/ *n.* —**ris·i·bly** /-blē/ *adv.*

ris·ing /'rīziNG/ ▸*adj.* **1** going up; getting higher: *the rising temperature.* ■ increasing: *rising costs.* ■ advancing to maturity or high standing: *the rising generation of American writers.* ■ approaching a higher level, grade, age, etc.: *a rising senior at North Carolina State.* ■ (of ground) sloping upward. ■ *Astrology* (of a sign) ascendant. **2** [*postpositive*] *Heraldry* (of a bird) depicted with the wings open but not fully displayed, as if preparing for flight.

▸*n.* an armed protest against authority; a revolt.

ris·ing main ▸*n. Brit.* a vertical pipe that rises from the ground to supply municipal water to a building. ■ the vertical pipe of a water pump.

risk /risk/ ▸*n.* a situation involving exposure to danger: *flouting the law was too much of a risk* | *all outdoor activities carry an element of risk.* ■ [in *sing.*] the possibility that something unpleasant or unwelcome will happen: ***reduce the risk of*** *heart disease* | [as *adj.*] *a high consumption of caffeine was suggested as a* ***risk factor*** *for loss of bone mass.* ■ [usu. in *sing.*] [with *adj.*] a person or thing regarded as likely to turn out well or badly, as specified, in a particular context or respect: *Western banks regarded Romania as a good risk.* ■ [with *adj.*] a person or thing regarded as a threat to something in need of protection: *she's a security risk.* ■ [with *adj.*] a thing regarded as likely to result in a specified danger: *gloss paint can burn strongly and pose a fire risk.* ■ (usu. **risks**) a possibility of harm or damage against which something is insured. ■ the possibility of financial loss: [as *adj.*] *project finance is essentially an exercise in risk management.*

▸*v.* [*trans.*] expose (someone or something valued) to danger, harm, or loss: *he risked his life to save his dog.* ■ act or fail to act in such a way as to bring about the possibility of (an unpleasant or unwelcome event): *unless you're dealing with pure alcohol you're risking contamination from benzene.* ■ incur the chance of unfortunate consequences by engaging in (an action): *he was far too intelligent to risk attempting to deceive her.* ▷mid 17th cent.: from French *risque* (noun), *risquer* (verb), from Italian *risco* 'danger' and *rischiare* 'run into danger.'

▸*PHRASES* □ **at risk** exposed to harm or danger: *23 million people in Africa are* ***at risk from*** *starvation.* □ **at one's** (**own**) **risk** used to indicate that if harm befalls a person or their possessions through their actions, it is their own responsibility: *they undertook the adventure at their own risk.* □ **at the risk of doing something** although there is the possibility of something unpleasant resulting: *at the risk of boring people to tears, I repeat the most important rule in painting.* □ **at risk to oneself** (or **something**) with the possibility of endangering oneself or something: *he visited prisons at considerable risk to his health.* □ **risk one's neck** put one's life in danger. □ **run the risk** (or **run risks**) expose oneself to the possibility of something unpleasant occurring: *she preferred not to* ***run the risk of*** *encountering his sister.* □ **take a risk** (or **take risks**) proceed in the knowledge that there is a chance of something unpleasant occurring.

risk cap·i·tal ▸*n.* another term for VENTURE CAPITAL.

risk·y /'riskē/ ▸*adj.* (**risk·i·er, risk·i·est**) full of the possibility of danger, failure, or loss: *it was much too risky to try to disarm him.* —**risk·i·ly** /-kəlē/ *adv.* —**risk·i·ness** *n.*

Ri·sor·gi·men·to /rēˌzôrjə'menˌtō; -ˌsôr-/ a movement for the unification and independence of Italy, which was achieved in 1870. ▷Italian, literally 'resurrection.'

> The restoration of repressive regimes after the Napoleonic Wars led to revolts in Naples and Piedmont (1821) and Bologna (1831).With French aid the Austrians were driven out of northern Italy by 1859, and the south was won over by Garibaldi. Voting resulted in the acceptance of Victor Emmanuel II as the first king of a united Italy in 1861.

ri·sot·to /ri'zôtō; -'sôtō/ ▸*n.* (*pl.* **-tos**) an Italian dish of rice cooked in stock with other ingredients such as meat and vegetables. ▷Italian, from *riso* 'rice.'

ris·qué /ri'skā/ ▸*adj.* slightly indecent or liable to shock, esp. by being sexually suggestive: *his risqué humor.* ▷mid 19th cent.: French, past participle of *risquer* 'to risk.'

Riss /ris/ ▸*n.* [usu. as *adj.*] *Geology* the penultimate Pleistocene glaciation in the Alps, possibly corresponding to the Saale of northern Europe. ■ the system of deposits laid down at this time. ▷early 20th cent.: from the name of a tributary of the Danube River in Germany.

ris·sole /ri'sōl; 'risˌōl/ ▸*n.* a compressed mixture of meat and spices, coated in breadcrumbs and fried. ▷early 18th cent.: from French, from Old French dialect *ruissole,* from a feminine form of late Latin *russeolus* 'reddish,' from Latin *russus* 'red.'

Ris·so's dol·phin /'risōz/ ▸*n.* a gray dolphin that has long black flippers and a rounded snout with no beak, living mainly in temperate seas. Also called GRAMPUS. • *Grampus griseus,* family Delphinidae. ▷late 19th cent.: named after Giovanni A. *Risso* (1777–1845), Italian naturalist.

ri·sto·ran·te /ˌristôrän'tā/ ▸*n.* (*pl.* **-ti** /-tē/) an Italian restaurant. ▷Italian.

rit. *Music* ▸*abbr.* ■ ritardando. ■ ritenuto.

Rit·a·lin /'ritl-in/ ▸*n.* trademark for METHYLPHENIDATE.

ri·tar·dan·do /ˌrētär'dändō/ (also **ri·tard** /ri'tärd/) *Music* ▸*adv.* & *adj.* (esp. as a direction) with a gradual decrease of tempo.

▸*n.* (*pl.* **-dan·dos** or **-dan·di** /-'dändē/) a gradual decrease in tempo. ▷Italian.

rite /rīt/ ▸*n.* a religious or other solemn ceremony or act: *the rite of communion* | *fertility rites.* ■ a body of customary observances characteristic of a church or a part of it: *the Byzantine rite.* ■ a social custom, practice, or conventional act: *the family Christmas rite.* ▷Middle English: from Latin *ritus* '(religious) usage.'

▸*PHRASE* □ **rite of passage** a ceremony or event marking an important stage in someone's life, esp. birth, puberty, marriage, and death: *a novel that depicts the state of adolescence and the rites of passage that lead to adulthood.*

ri·te·nu·to /ˌrētə'no͞otō/ *Music* ▸*adv.* & *adj.* (esp. as a direction) with an immediate reduction of tempo.

▸*n.* (*pl.* **-tos** or **-ti** /-tē/) an immediate reduction of tempo. ▷Italian, literally 'retained, restrained.'

ri·tor·nel·lo /ˌritər'nelō/ ▸*n.* (*pl.* **-nel·los** or **-nel·li** /-'nelē/) *Music* a short instrumental refrain or interlude in a vocal work. ■ a recurring tutti section in a concerto. ▷Italian, diminutive of *ritorno* 'return.'

Rit·ter /'ritər/, Tex (1907–74), U.S. country singer, songwriter, and actor; full name *Woodward Maurice Ritter.* He made many singing cowboy movies during the 1930s and 1940s and also wrote and performed songs such as "Jingle, Jangle, Jingle" and "Jealous Heart. " He sang the title song for the movie *High Noon* (1952).

rit·u·al /'riCHo͞oəl/ ▸*n.* a religious or solemn ceremony consisting of a series of actions performed according to a prescribed order: *the ancient rituals of Christian worship* | *the role of ritual in religion.* ■ a prescribed order of performing such a ceremony, esp. one characteristic of a particular religion or church. ■ a series of actions or type of behavior regularly and invariably followed by someone: *her visits to Joy became a ritual.*

▸*adj.* [*attrib.*] of, relating to, or done as a religious or solemn rite: *ritual burial.* ■ (of an action) arising from convention or habit: *the players gathered for the ritual pregame huddle.* ▷late 16th cent. (as an adjective): from Latin *ritualis,* from *ritus* (see RITE). —**rit·u·al·ly** *adv.*

rit·u·al a·buse (also **sa·tan·ic a·buse**) ▸*n.* the alleged sexual abuse or murder of people, esp. children, supposedly committed as part of satanic rituals.

rit·u·al·ism /'riCHo͞oəˌlizəm/ ▸*n.* the regular observance or practice of ritual, esp. when excessive or without regard to its function. —**rit·u·al·ist** *n.* —**rit·u·al·is·tic** /ˌriCHo͞oə'listik/ *adj.* —**rit·u·al·is·ti·cal·ly** *adv.*

rit·u·al·i·za·tion /ˌriCHo͞oələ'zāSHən/ ▸*n.* the action or process of ritualizing something, in particular: ■ the formalization of certain actions expressing a particular emotion or state of mind, whether abnormally (as in obsessive–compulsive disorder) or as part of the symbolism of religion or culture. ■ *Zoology* the evolutionary process by which an action or behavior pattern in an animal loses its original function but is retained for its role in display or other social interaction.

rit·u·al·ize /'riCHo͞oəˌlīz/ ▸*v.* [*trans.*] [usu. as *adj.*] (**ritualized**) make (something) into a ritual by following a pattern of actions or behavior: *hooliganism as a ritualized expression of aggression.* ■ *Zoology* cause (an action or behavior pattern) to undergo ritualization.

ritz /rits/ ▸*n.* *informal* ostentatious luxury and glamour: *removed from all the ritz and glitz.* ▷early 20th cent.: from *Ritz*, a name associated with luxury hotels, from César Ritz (1850–1918), a Swiss hotel owner.

▸*PHRASE* □ **put on the ritz** make a show of luxury or extravagance.

Ritz Broth·ers /rits/, The, U.S. song-and-dance comedy trio 1925–65. The act consisted of the Joachim brothers **Alfred** (1901–65), **Jimmy** (1904–85), and **Harry (Herschel)** (1907–86). They appeared on Broadway in *Sing Baby Sing* (1936) and *On the Avenue* (1937) and in movies such as *Kentucky Moonshine* (1938). After 1965, Jimmy and Harry performed as a duo until 1978.

ritz·y /ˈritsē/ ▸*adj.* (**ritz·i·er, ritz·i·est**) *informal* expensively stylish: *the ritzy Plaza Hotel.* **—ritz·i·ly** /ˈritsilē/ *adv.* **—ritz·i·ness** *n.*

riv. ▸*abbr.* river.

ri·val /ˈrīvəl/ ▸*n.* a person or thing competing with another for the same objective or for superiority in the same field of activity: *he has no serious rival for the job* | [as *adj.*] *gun battles between rival gangs.* ■ [with *negative*] a person or thing that equals another in quality: *she has no rivals as a female rock singer.*

▸*v.* (**-valed, -val·ing**; *Brit.* **-valled, -val·ling**) [*trans.*] compete for superiority with; be or seem to be equal or comparable to: *the efficiency of the Bavarians* ***rivals that of*** *the Viennese.* ▷late 16th cent.: from Latin *rivalis*, originally in the sense 'person using the same stream as another,' from *rivus* 'stream.'

ri·val·rous /ˈrīvəlrəs/ ▸*adj.* prone to or subject to rivalry: *rivalrous presidential aspirants.*

ri·val·ry /ˈrīvəlrē/ ▸*n.* (*pl.* **-ries**) competition for the same objective or for superiority in the same field: *commercial rivalry* | *ethnic rivalries.*

rive /rīv/ ▸*v.* (*past* **rived** /rīvd/; *past part.* **riv·en** /ˈrivən/) (usu. **be riven**) split or tear apart violently: *the party was riven by disagreements over Europe* | *figurative he was* ***riven with*** *guilt.* ■ *archaic* split or crack (wood or stone): *the wood was* ***riven with*** *deep cracks.* ■ [*intrans.*] *archaic* (of wood or stone) split or crack: *I started to chop furiously, the dry wood riving and splintering under the ax.* ▷Middle English: from Old Norse *rífa*, of unknown ultimate origin.

riv·er /ˈrivər/ ▸*n.* a large natural stream of water flowing in a channel to the sea, a lake, or another such stream. ■ a large quantity of a flowing substance: *great* ***rivers of*** *molten lava* | *figurative the trickle of disclosures has grown into a river of revelations.* ■ [as *adj.*] used in names of animals and plants living in or associated with rivers, e.g., **river dolphin, river birch.** ▷Middle English: from Anglo-Norman French, based on Latin *riparius*, from *ripa* 'bank of a river.' **—riv·ered** *adj.* **—riv·er·less** *adj.*

▸*PHRASES* □ **sell someone down the river** *informal* betray someone, esp. so as to benefit oneself. [earlier referring to the sale of a troublesome slave to the owner of a sugarcane plantation on the lower Mississippi, where conditions were harsher.] □ **up the river** *informal* to or in prison. [with allusion to Sing Sing prison, situated up the Hudson River from New York City.]

Ri·ve·ra /riˈve(ə)rə/, Diego (1886–1957), Mexican painter. He inspired a revival of fresco painting in Latin America and the U.S. His largest mural is a history of Mexico for the National Palace in Mexico City (unfinished, 1929–57).

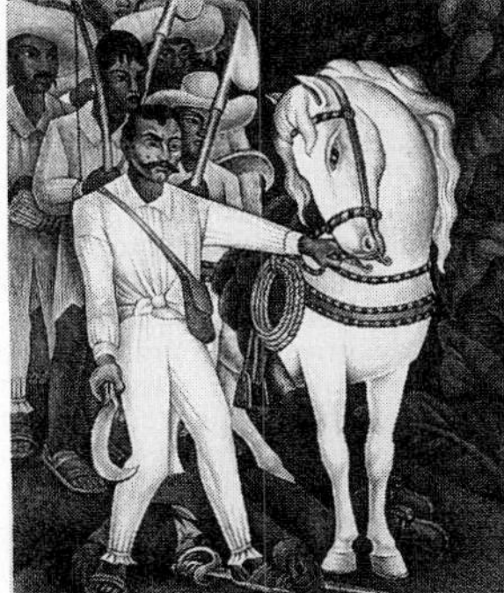

"Agrarian Leader Zapata" (1932) by Diego Rivera

riv·er·bank /ˈrivər,baNGk/ ▸*n.* the bank of a river.

riv·er·bed /ˈrivər,bed/ ▸*n.* the bed or channel in which a river flows. ■ the bottom of a river.

riv·er birch ▸*n.* a North American birch with shaggy reddish-brown or orange bark. • *Betula nigra.*

riv·er blind·ness ▸*n.* a tropical skin disease caused by a parasitic filarial worm, transmitted by the bite of blackflies (*Simulium damnosum*) that breed in fast-flowing rivers. The larvae of the parasite can migrate into the eye and cause blindness. Also called ONCHOCERCIASIS. • The worm is *Onchocerca volvulus*, class Phasmida.

riv·er·boat /ˈrivər,bōt/ ▸*n.* a boat with a shallow draft, designed for use on rivers.

riv·er bot·toms ▸*plural n. N. Amer.* low-lying alluvial land along the banks of a river.

riv·er dol·phin ▸*n.* a solitary dolphin with a long slender beak, a small dorsal fin, and very poor eyesight. It lives in rivers and coastal waters of South America, India, and China, using echolocation to find its prey. • Family Platanistidae: four genera and species.

riv·er·front /ˈrivər,frənt/ ▸*n.* the land or property along a river: *a distinctive feature of Quebec's riverfront.* ▸*adj.* located along a river: *a lovely riverfront park.*

riv·er·ine /ˈrivə,rīn; -,rēn/ ▸*adj.* *technical* or *poetic/literary* of, relating to, or situated on a river or riverbank; riparian: *a riverine village.*

riv·er·scape /ˈrivər,skāp/ ▸*n.* a picturesque view or prospect of a river. ■ a painting of a river or riverside scene.

Riv·er·side /ˈrivər,sīd/ a city in southern California, east of Los Angeles, located in the center of an orange-growing region; pop. 255,166.

riv·er·side /ˈrivər,sīd/ ▸*n.* [often as *adj.*] the ground along a riverbank: *dinner in one of the better riverside hotels.*

riv·et /ˈrivit/ ▸*n.* a short metal pin or bolt for holding together two plates of metal, its headless end being beaten out or pressed down when in place. ■ a similar device for holding seams of clothing together.

▸*v.* (**riv·et·ed, riv·et·ing**) [*trans.*] join or fasten (plates of metal or other material) with a rivet or rivets: *the linings are bonded, not riveted, to the brake shoes for longer wear.* ■ hold (someone or something) fast so as to make them incapable of movement: *the grip on her arm was firm enough to* ***rivet her to the spot.*** ■ attract and completely engross (someone): *he was riveted by the reports shown on television* | [as *adj.*] (**riveting**) *a riveting story.* ■ (usu. **be riveted**) direct (one's eyes or attention) intently: *all eyes were* ***riveted on*** *him.* ▷Middle English: from Old French, from *river* 'fix, clinch,' of unknown ultimate origin. **—riv·et·er** *n.* **—riv·et·ing·ly** *adv.*

rivet

riv·i·er·a /,rivēˈe(ə)rə; riˈvye(ə)rə/ ▸*n.* a coastal region with a subtropical climate and vegetation, esp.: ■ (**the Riviera**) a Mediterranean coastal region from Marseilles in France to La Spezia in Italy, noted for its beauty and climate, site of many resorts. See also CÔTE D'AZUR. ▷mid 18th cent.: from Italian, literally 'seashore.'

Ri·vier·a Beach /riˈvi(ə)rə/ a resort and industrial city in southeastern Florida, north of West Palm Beach; pop. 27,639.

ri·vière /,rivēˈe(ə)r; riˈvye(ə)r/ ▸*n.* a necklace of gems that increase in size toward a large central stone, typically consisting of more than one string. ▷late 19th cent.: French, literally 'river.'

Riv·ne /ˈrivnə/ an industrial city in western Ukraine northeast of Lviv; pop. 233,000. Russian name ROVNO.

riv·u·let /ˈriv(y)ələt/ ▸*n.* a very small stream: *sweat ran in rivulets down his back.* ▷late 16th cent.: alteration of obsolete *riveret* (from French, literally 'small river'), perhaps suggested by Italian *rivoletto*, diminutive of *rivolo*, based on Latin *rivus* 'stream.'

riv·u·lus /ˈrivyələs/ ▸*n.* a small tropical American fish of shallow fresh and brackish water. Often mistaken for a killifish or topminnow, the rivulus is distinguished by its tubular nostrils. • Genus *Rivulus*, family Rivulidae: several species, many of which are spotted, in particular *R. marmoratus.* ▷modern Latin, from Latin, literally 'small stream.'

Ri·yadh /rēˈyäd/ the capital of Saudi Arabia; pop. 2,000,000. It is situated on a high plateau in the center of the country.

ri·yal /rēˈ(y)ôl; rēˈ(y)äl/ ▸*n.* (also **ri·al**) the basic monetary unit of Saudi Arabia, Qatar, and Yemen, equal to 100 halala in Saudi Arabia, 100 dirhams in Qatar, and 100 fils in Yemen. ▷via Persian from Arabic *riyāl*, from Spanish *real* 'royal.'

RJ ▸*abbr.* *Military* road junction.

RKO a movie production and distribution company founded in 1928, which produced classic movies such as *King Kong* (1933) and *Citizen Kane* (1941). It ceased film production in 1953. ▷abbreviation of *Radio–Keith–Orpheum*, which was formed in a merger of Radio Corporation of America (RCA) with the *Keith* and *Orpheum* movie theater chains.

RL ▸*abbr.* ■ rugby league.

rly ▸*abbr.* *Indian & Brit.* railway.

RM ▸*abbr.* ■ (in the UK) Royal Mail. ■ (in the UK) Royal Marines.

rm ▸*abbr.* room.

RMA ▸*abbr.* Royal Military Academy.

RMP ▸*abbr.* Royal Military Police.

r.m.s. *Mathematics* ▸*abbr.* root mean square.

RMT ▸*abbr.* (in the UK) National Union of Rail, Maritime, and Transport Workers. It was formed in 1990 by a merger of the National Union of Railwaymen and National Union of Seamen.

RN ▸*abbr.* ■ (chiefly in North America) Registered Nurse. ■ (in the UK) ROYAL NAVY.

Rn ▸*symbol* the chemical element radon.

RNA ▸*n.* *Biochemistry* ribonucleic acid, a nucleic acid present in all living cells. Its principal role is to act as a messenger carrying instructions from DNA for controlling the synthesis of proteins, although in some viruses RNA rather than DNA carries the genetic information.

RNase /ärˈen,ās; -,āz/ ▸*n.* *Biochemistry* an enzyme that promotes the breakdown of RNA into oligonucleotides and smaller molecules. ▷1950s: from **RNA** + **-ASE.**

RNA vi·rus ▸*n.* a virus in which the genetic information is stored in the form of RNA (as opposed to DNA).

rnd. ▸*abbr.* round.

RNP ▸*abbr.* *Biochemistry* ribonucleoprotein.

RNZAF ▸*abbr.* Royal New Zealand Air Force.

RNZN ▸*abbr.* Royal New Zealand Navy.

ro. ▸*abbr.* ■ recto. ■ roan. ■ rood.

roach[1] /rōCH/ ▸*n.* *informal* **1** a cockroach. [mid 19th cent.: shortened form.] **2** the butt of a marijuana cigarette. [1930s: of unknown origin.]

roach[2] ▸*n.* (*pl.* same) an edible Eurasian freshwater fish of the minnow family, popular with anglers. It can hybridize with related fishes, notably rudd and bream. • *Rutilus rutilus*, family Cyprinidae. ▷Middle English: from Old French *roche*, of unknown ultimate origin.

roach[3] ▸*n.* *Sailing* a curve, in or out, in the edge of a sail, esp. in the leech of a fore-and-aft sail. ▷late 18th cent.: of unknown origin.

roach clip ▸*n.* *informal* a clip for holding the butt of a marijuana cigarette.

roached /rōCHt/ ▸*adj.* **1** (esp. of an animal's back) having an upward curve. **2** (of a person's hair) brushed upward or forward into a roll. ■ (of a horse's mane) clipped or trimmed short so that the hair stands on end.

road /rōd/ ▸*n.* **1** a wide way leading from one place to another, esp. one with a specially prepared surface that vehicles can use. ■ the part of such a way intended for vehicles, esp. in contrast to a shoulder or sidewalk. ■ [with *adj.*] *historical* a regular trade route for a particular commodity: *the Silk Road across Asia to the West.* ■ *Mining* an underground passage or gallery in a mine. ■ a railroad. ■ *Brit.* a railroad track, esp. as clear (or otherwise) for a train to proceed: *they waited for a clear road at Hellifield Junction.* **2** *figurative* a series of events or a course of action that will lead to a particular outcome: *he's well* ***on the road*** *to recovery.* ■ a particular course or direction taken or followed: *the low road of apathy and alienation.* **3** [often in *place names*] (usu. **roads**) another term for ROADSTEAD: *Boston Roads.* ▷Old English *rād* 'journey on horseback,' 'foray'; of Germanic origin; related to the verb RIDE. **—road·less** *adj.*

▸*PHRASES* □ **by road** in or on a road vehicle. □ **down the road** *informal* in the future. □ **the end of the road** see END. □ **hit the road** see HIT. □ **in** (or **out of**) **the** (or **one's**) **road** [often in *imperative*] *informal* in (or out of) someone's way. □ **one for the road** *informal* a final drink, esp. an alcoholic one, before leaving for home. □ **on the road 1** on a long journey or series of journeys, esp. as part of one's job as a sales representative or a performer. ■ (of a person)

Pronunciation Key ə *ago*; ər *over*; ˈə or ,ə *up*; ˈər or ,ər *fur*; a *hat*; ā *rate*; ä *car*; CH *chew*; e *let*; ē *see*; e(ə)r *air*; i *fit*; ī *by*; i(ə)r *ear*; NG *sing*; ō *go*; ô *for*; oi *boy*; o͝o *good*; o͞o *goo*; ou *out*; SH *she*; TH *thin*; T͟H *then*; (h)w *why*; ZH *vision*

without a permanent home and moving from place to place. **2** (of a car) in use; able to be driven. ■ (often **on-the-road**) (of or with reference to the price of a motor vehicle) including the cost of license plates, tax, etc., so the vehicle is fully ready for use on public roads: *we found on-the-road prices from 5,780 to 6,151 dollars.* □ **a road to nowhere** see NOWHERE. □ **take to the road** (or **take the road**) set out on a journey or series of journeys.

road a·gent ▶*n. historical* a highwayman or bandit, esp. along stagecoach routes in the western U.S.

road·bed /ˈrōd,bed/ ▶*n.* the material laid down to form a road. ■ the part of a road on which vehicles travel. ■ the foundation structure on which railroad tracks are laid.

road bike ▶*n.* **1** a motorcycle that meets the legal requirements for use on ordinary roads. **2** a bicycle that is suitable for use on ordinary roads, as opposed to a mountain bike.

road·block /ˈrōd,bläk/ ▶*n.* a barrier or barricade on a road, esp. one set up by the authorities to stop and examine traffic. ■ *figurative* any hindrance: *the tax has become a roadblock against investment incentives.*

road hog ▶*n. informal* a motorist who drives recklessly or inconsiderately, making it difficult for others to proceed safely or at a normal speed.

road·hold·ing /ˈrōd,hōldiNG/ ▶*n.* the ability of a vehicle to remain stable when moving, esp. when cornering at high speeds.

road·house /ˈrōd,hous/ ▶*n.* a tavern, inn, or club on a country road.

R

road·ie /ˈrōdē/ *informal* ▶*n.* a person employed by a touring band of musicians to set up and maintain equipment.
▶*v.* [*intrans.*] work as such a person.

road kill ▶*n.* an animal (or animals, collectively) killed by a vehicle on a road. ■ *informal* someone or something no longer useful or desired: *gee, thanks for making me feel like road kill.*

road man·ag·er ▶*n.* the organizer and supervisor of a musician's tour.

road map ▶*n.* a map, esp. one designed for motorists, showing the roads of a country or area: *you're going to need more than a glove-compartment road map to find your way around* | *figurative we have to have a pretty clear road map of the next season.*

road·map /ˈrōd,map/ ▶*v.* (**-mapped, -map·ping**) [*trans.*] schedule as part of a lengthy or complex program: *originally roadmapped for an early Q4 release, the next generation of the processor will ship in the last few days of the year.*

road met·al ▶*n.* see METAL (sense 2).

road mov·ie ▶*n.* a movie of a genre in which the main character is traveling, either in flight or on a journey of self-discovery.

road noise ▶*n.* noise resulting from the movement of a vehicle's tires over the road surface.

road pric·ing ▶*n. Brit.* the practice of charging motorists for the use of busy roads at certain times, esp. to relieve congestion in urban areas.

road rage ▶*n.* violent anger caused by the stress and frustration involved in driving a motor vehicle in difficult conditions.

road·roll·er /ˈrōd,rōlər/ ▶*n.* a motor vehicle with a heavy roller, used in roadmaking.

road·run·ner /ˈrōd,rənər/ ▶*n.* a slender fast-running bird of the cuckoo family, found chiefly in arid country from the southern U.S. to Central America. • Genus *Geococcyx*, family Cuculidae: two species, in particular the **greater roadrunner** (*G. californianus*). ▷probably a calque from Spanish *correcamino.*

greater roadrunner

road show (also **road·show**) ▶*n.* a touring show of performers, esp. pop musicians. ■ a touring political or promotional campaign. ■ a radio or television program broadcast on location, esp. each of a series done from different venues.

road·side /ˈrōd,sīd/ ▶*n.* the strip of land beside a road: *trash left on the roadside* | [as *adj.*] *roadside cafes.*

road sign ▶*n.* a sign giving information or instructions to road users.

road·stead /ˈrōd,sted/ ▶*n.* a sheltered stretch of water near the shore in which ships can ride at anchor. ▷mid 16th cent.: from ROAD + obsolete *stead* 'a place.'

road·ster /ˈrōdstər/ ▶*n.* an open-top automobile with two seats. ■ *historical* a horse for use on the road.

road test ▶*n.* a test of the performance of a vehicle or engine on the road. ■ *figurative* a test of equipment carried out in working conditions: *he hopes to present a road test of whiskeys and to debate the various aromas and tastes.* ■ a test of a person's competence in driving a motor vehicle that must be passed in order to get a driver's license.
▶*v.* (**road-test**) [*trans.*] test (a vehicle or engine) on the road. ■ *figurative* try out (something) in working conditions for review or prior to purchase or release: *we road-tested a new laptop computer.*

Road Town the capital of the British Virgin Islands, situated on the island of Tortola; pop. 6,000.

road war·ri·or ▶*n. informal* a person who travels, often as part of their job, and does work at the same time.

road·way /ˈrōd,wā/ ▶*n.* a road. ■ the part of a road intended for vehicles, in contrast to a sidewalk or median. ■ the part of a bridge or railroad used by traffic.

road·work /ˈrōd,wərk/ ▶*n.* **1** work done in building or repairing roads. **2** athletic exercise or training involving running on roads. ■ time spent traveling while working or on tour.

road·wor·thy /ˈrōd,wər<u>TH</u>ē/ ▶*adj.* (of a motor vehicle or bicycle) fit to be used on the road. —**road·wor·thi·ness** *n.*

roam /rōm/ ▶*v.* [*intrans.*] move about or travel aimlessly or unsystematically, esp. over a wide area: *tigers once* **roamed over** *most of Asia* | [as *adj.*] (**roaming**) *roaming elephants.* ■ [*trans.*] travel unsystematically over, through, or around (a place): *gangs of youths roamed the streets unopposed.* ■ (of a person's eyes or hands) pass lightly over something without stopping: *her eyes roamed over the chattering women* | [*trans.*] *he let his eyes roam her face.* ■ [*intrans.*] (of a person's mind or thoughts) drift along without dwelling on anything in particular: *he let his mind roam as he walked.* ■ [*trans.*] move from site to site on (the Internet); browse.
▶*n.* [in *sing.*] an aimless walk. ▷Middle English: of unknown origin. —**roam·er** *n.*

roam·ing /ˈrōmiNG/ ▶*n.* [usually as *modifier*] the use of a cellular phone outside of its local area: *the roaming charges were too high.*

roan[1] /rōn/ ▶*adj.* denoting an animal, esp. a horse or cow, having a coat of a main color thickly interspersed with hairs of another color, typically bay, chestnut, or black mixed with white.
▶*n.* an animal with such a coat: *the roan on the right is a stallion.* ▷mid 16th cent.: from Old French, of unknown origin.

roan[2] ▶*n.* soft flexible leather made from sheepskin, used in bookbinding as an inexpensive substitute for morocco. ▷early 19th cent.: perhaps from *Roan*, the old name of the French town of ROUEN.

roan an·te·lope ▶*n.* an African antelope with black-and-white facial markings, a mane of stiff hair, and large backwardly curving horns. • *Hippotragus equinus*, family Bovidae.

Ro·a·noke /ˈrōə,nōk/ an industrial city in west central Virginia, in the Shenandoah Valley; pop. 94,911.

Ro·a·noke Is·land an island in eastern North Carolina, east of Croatan Sound, inside the Outer Banks, site of the first English settlement in America—the "Lost Colony"—that was established in 1585 and had mysteriously disappeared by 1591.

Ro·a·noke Riv·er a river that flows for 410 miles (660 km) from southwestern Virginia across North Carolina to Albemarle Sound.

roar /rôr/ ▶*n.* a full, deep, prolonged cry uttered by a lion or other large wild animal. ■ a loud and deep sound uttered by a person or crowd, generally as an expression of pain, anger, or approval: *he gave a roar of rage.* ■ a loud outburst of laughter. ■ a loud, prolonged sound made by something inanimate, such as a natural force, an engine, or traffic: *the roar of the sea.*
▶*v.* **1** [*intrans.*] (of a lion or other large wild animal) utter a full, deep, prolonged cry. ■ (of something inanimate) make a loud, deep, prolonged sound: *a huge fire roared in the grate.* ■ (of a person or crowd) utter a loud, deep, prolonged sound, typically because of anger, pain, or excitement: *Manny roared with rage.* ■ [*trans.*] utter or express in a loud tone: *the crowd roared its approval* | [with *direct speech*] *"Get out of my way!" he roared.* ■ laugh loudly: *Shirley roared in amusement.* ■ (of a horse) make a loud noise in breathing as a symptom of disease of the larynx. **2** [*intrans.*] (esp. of a vehicle) move at high speed making a loud prolonged sound: *a car roared past.* ■ proceed, act, or happen fast and decisively or conspicuously: *the Clippers came roaring back to outscore the Nets.* ▷Old English *rārian* (verb), imitative of a deep prolonged cry; related to German *röhren*. The noun dates from late Middle English. —**roar·er** *n.*

roar·ing /ˈrôriNG/ ▶*adj.* [*attrib.*] **1** (of a person, crowd, or animal) making a loud and deep sound, esp. as an expression of pain, anger, or approval: *he was greeted everywhere with roaring crowds.* ■ (of something inanimate, esp. a natural phenomenon) making a loud, deep, or harsh prolonged sound: *a swollen, roaring river.* ■ (of a fire) burning fiercely and noisily. ■ (of a period of time) characterized by optimism, buoyancy, or excitement: *the roaring twenties.* ■ (of business) lively; brisk: *cafes that do a roaring trade.* ■ *chiefly archaic* behaving or living in a noisy riotous manner. **2** *informal* obviously or unequivocally the thing mentioned (used for emphasis): *the final week of* Hamlet *was a* **roaring success** | [as *submodifier*] *two roaring drunk firemen.* —**roar·ing·ly** *adv.*

roast /rōst/ ▶*v.* [*trans.*] **1** cook (food, esp. meat) by prolonged exposure to heat in an oven or over a fire: *she was going to roast a leg of lamb for Sunday dinner* | [as *adj.*] (**roasted**) *roasted chestnuts.* ■ [*intrans.*] (of food) be cooked in such a way: *she checked the meat roasting in the oven.* ■ process (a foodstuff, metal ore, etc.) by subjecting it to intense heat: *coffee beans are roasted and ground.* ■ make (someone or something) very warm, esp. by exposure to the heat of the sun or a fire: *the fire was hot enough to roast anyone who stood close to it.* ■ [*intrans.*] become very hot: *Jessica could feel her face begin to roast.* **2** criticize or reprimand severely: *if you waste his time he'll roast you.* ■ offer a mocking tribute to (someone) at a roast.
▶*adj.* [*attrib.*] (of food) having been cooked in an oven or over an open fire: *a plate of cold roast beef.*
▶*n.* **1** a cut of meat that has been roasted or that is intended for roasting: *carving the Sunday roast.* ■ a dish or meal of roasted food. ■ the process of roasting something, esp. coffee, or the result of this. ■ [with *adj.*] a particular type of roasted coffee: *continental roasts.* ■ an outdoor party at which meat, esp. of a particular type, is roasted: *Harold put on a terrific pig roast.* **2** a banquet to honor a person at which the honoree is subjected to good-natured ridicule. ▷Middle English: from Old French *rostir*, of West Germanic origin.

roast·er /ˈrōstər/ ▶*n.* a container, oven, furnace, or apparatus for roasting something. ■ a foodstuff that is particularly suitable for roasting, esp. a chicken. ■ a person or company that processes coffee beans.

roast·ing /ˈrōstiNG/ ▶*adj.* [*attrib.*] (of a container) used for roasting food: *a roasting pan.* ■ (of a foodstuff) particularly suitable for roasting: *a roasting chicken.* ■ (of food) undergoing roasting: *the aroma of a roasting pig.* ■ *informal* very hot and dry: *a roasting day in Miami.*
▶*n.* the action of cooking something in an oven or over an open fire. ■ [in *sing.*] *informal* a severe criticism or reprimand: *I was in for a roasting at the next meeting.*

rob /räb/ ▶*v.* (**robbed, rob·bing**) [*trans.*] take property unlawfully from (a person or place) by force or threat of force: *he tried, with three others, to rob a bank* | *she was* **robbed of** *her handbag* | [*intrans.*] *he was convicted of assault with intent to rob.* ■ (usu. **be robbed**) *informal* overcharge (someone) for something: *Bob thinks my suit cost $100, and even then he thinks I was robbed.* ■ *informal* or *dialect* steal: *he accused her of robbing the cream out of his chocolate eclair.* ■ deprive (someone or something) of something needed, deserved, or significant: *poor health has* **robbed** *her* **of** *a normal social life.* ▷Middle English: from Old French *rober*, of Germanic origin; related to the verb REAVE.

▶*PHRASES* □ **rob Peter to pay Paul** take something away from one person to pay another, leaving the former at a disadvantage; discharge one debt only to incur another. [probably with reference to the apostles *Peter* and *Paul*; the allusion is uncertain, the phrase often showing variations such as 'unclothe Peter and clothe Paul,' 'borrow from Peter . . . ,' etc.] □ **rob someone blind** see BLIND.

USAGE In law, to **rob** is to take something from someone by causing fear of harm, whether or not actual harm occurs. The term is widely, but incorrectly, used to refer to **theft**: *our house was robbed while we were away.* Technically, the more correct statement would be *our house was burglarized while we were away.*

Ro·bards /ˈrō,bärdz/, Jason (Nelson, Jr.) (1922–2000), U.S. actor. Although he began his acting career on the stage, he appeared in many movies, including *Long Day's Journey into Night* (1962), *A Thousand Clowns* (1965), *All The President's Men* (Academy Award, 1976), *Julia* (Academy Award, 1977), *Philadelphia* (1993), and *A Thousand Acres* (1997).

Robbe-Gril·let /,rôb grēˈyā/, Alain (1922–), French novelist. His first novel *The Erasers* (1953) was an early example of the *nouveau roman*. He also wrote essays and screenplays.

rob·ber /ˈräbər/ ▸*n.* a person who commits robbery. ▷Middle English: from Anglo-Norman French and Old French *robere*, from the verb *rober* (see **ROB**).

rob·ber bar·on ▸*n.* an unscrupulous plutocrat, esp. an American capitalist who acquired a fortune in the late nineteenth century by ruthless means. ▷originally denoting a feudal lord who engaged in plundering.

rob·ber crab ▸*n.* another term for **COCONUT CRAB**.

rob·ber fly ▸*n.* a large powerful predatory fly that darts out and grabs insect prey on the wing. • Family Asilidae: many genera.

rob·ber·y /ˈräb(ə)rē/ ▸*n.* (*pl.* **-ber·ies**) the action of robbing a person or place: *he was involved in drugs, violence, extortion, and robbery | an armed robbery.* ■ *Law* the felonious taking of personal property from someone using force or the threat of force. ■ *informal* unashamed swindling or overcharging. ▷Middle English: from Anglo-Norman French and Old French *roberie*, from the verb *rober* (see **ROB**).

Rob·bia /ˈrōbēə; ˈräb-/ see **DELLA ROBBIA**.

Rob·bins[1] /ˈräbənz/, Harold (1916–97), U.S. novelist. Notable works: *The Dream Merchants* (1949), *The Carpetbaggers* (1961), *The Betsy* (1971), and *Tycoon* (1997).

Rob·bins[2], Jerome (1918–98), U.S. ballet dancer and choreographer. He choreographed a number of successful musicals, including *The King and I* (1951), *West Side Story* (1957), and *Fiddler on the Roof* (1964).

robe /rōb/ ▸*n.* **1** a long, loose outer garment. ■ (often **robes**) such a garment worn, esp. on formal or ceremonial occasions, as an indication of the wearer's rank, office, or profession. ■ a dressing gown or bathrobe. **2** *dated* a small blanket; lap robe.
▸*v.* [*trans.*] [usu. as *adj.*] (**robed**) clothe in a long, loose outer garment: *a circle of robed figures* | [in *combination*] *a white-robed Bedouin.* ■ [*intrans.*] put on robes, esp. for a formal or ceremonial occasion: *I went into the vestry and robed for the Mass.* ▷Middle English: from Old French, from the Germanic base (in the sense 'booty') of **ROB** (because clothing was an important component of booty).

Rob·ert /ˈräbərt/ the name of three kings of Scotland: ■ **Robert I** (1274–1329), reigned 1306–29; known as **Robert the Bruce**. He campaigned against Edward I, and defeated Edward II at Bannockburn in 1314. He reestablished Scotland as a separate kingdom, negotiating the Treaty of Northampton in 1328. ■ **Robert II** (1316–90), grandson of Robert the Bruce; reigned 1371–90. He was steward of Scotland from 1326 to 1371 and the first of the Stuart line. ■ **Robert III** (*c.*1337–1406), son of Robert II; reigned 1390–1406; born *John*. An accident rendered him physically disabled, resulting in a power struggle among members of his family.

Rob·erts[1] /ˈräbərts/, Julia (1967–), U.S. actress. She appeared in movies such as *Mystic Pizza* (1988), *Steel Magnolias* (1989), *Pretty Woman* (1990), *Notting Hill* (1999), and *Erin Brockovich* (Academy Award, 2000).

Ro·berts[2], Owen Josephus (1875–1955), U.S. Supreme Court associate justice 1930–45. Appointed to the Court by President Hoover, he usually voted independently although he leaned toward conservatism in many of his decisions. He also served as dean of the University of Pennsylvania Law School 1948–51.

Rob·ert·son /ˈräbərtsən/, Oscar (1938–), U.S. basketball player. A guard, he led the 1960 U.S. Olympic team to a gold medal and then played professionally for the Cincinnati Royals 1960–70 and the Milwaukee Bucks 1970–74. Basketball Hall of Fame (1979).

Rob·ert·so·ni·an /,räbərtˈsōnēən/ ▸*adj. Genetics* denoting a chromosome with a central centromere formed from two chromosomes having noncentral centromeres. ■ (of a karyotypic change or translocation) brought about by this process. ▷1950s: from the name of William R. B. *Robertson* (1881–1941), American biologist, + **-IAN**.

Rob·ert the Bruce /bro͞os/ see **ROBERT**.

Robe·son /ˈrōb(ə)sən/, Paul (Bustill) (1898–1976), U.S. singer and actor. The song "Ol' Man River" in the musical *Showboat* (1927) established his international reputation. As an actor, he was particularly identified with the title role of *Othello*. His black activism and communist sympathies led to ostracism in the 1950s.

Robes·pierre /ˈrōbz,pi(ə)r; -,pye(ə)r/, Maximilien François Marie Isidore de (1758–94), French revolutionary. As leader of the radical Jacobins in the National Assembly, he backed the execution of Louis XVI, implemented a purge of the Girondists, and initiated the Terror. The following year, however, he fell from favor and was guillotined.

rob·in /ˈräbən/ ▸*n.* **1** a large New World thrush that typically has a reddish breast. • genus *Turdus*, subfamily Turdinae, family Muscicapidae, in particular the **American robin** (*T. migratorius*). **2** any of a number of other birds that resemble the American robin, esp. in having a red breast, in particular: ■ a small Old World thrush related to the chats, typically having a brown back with red on the breast or other colorful markings. • *Erithacus* and other genera, subfamily Turdinae, family Muscicapidae: numerous species, in particular the **European robin** (*E. rubecula*). ▷mid 16th cent.: from Old French, nickname for the given name *Robert*.

American robin

Rob·in Good·fel·low /,räbən ˈgo͝od,felō/ a mischievous sprite or goblin believed, esp. in the 16th and 17th centuries, to haunt the English countryside. Also called **PUCK**.

rob·ing room ▸*n.* a room where holders of ceremonial office put on official robes.

Rob·in Hood /ˈräbən ,ho͝od/ a semilegendary English medieval outlaw, reputed to have robbed the rich and helped the poor. Although he is generally associated with Sherwood Forest in Nottinghamshire, it seems likely that the real Robin Hood operated in Yorkshire in the early 13th century. ■ [as *n.*] (**a Robin Hood**) a person considered to be taking from the wealthy and giving to the poor.

rob·in red·breast ▸*n. informal* a robin.

rob·in's-egg (also **rob·in's-egg blue** or **rob·in-egg**) ▸*n.* a greenish-blue color.

Rob·in·son[1] /ˈräbinsən/, Edward Arlington (1869–1935), U.S. poet. His verse was largely unnoticed until 1905 when President Theodore Roosevelt praised his dramatic, often ironic, works, such as "Richard Cory" (1897), "Miniver Cheevy" (1910), and "Tristram" (1927).

Rob·in·son[2] /ˈräbənsən/, Edward G. (1893–1972), U.S. actor, born in Romania; born *Emanuel Goldenberg*. He appeared in a number of gangster movies in the 1930s, beginning with *Little Caesar* (1930). He later played the father in Arthur Miller's *All My Sons* (1948).

Rob·in·son[3], Jackie (1919–72), U.S. baseball player and civil rights activist; full name *Jack Roosevelt Robinson*. Joining the Brooklyn Dodgers in 1947, he became the first black player in the major leagues. In 1949, he led the National League with a .342 batting average and was named the league's Most Valuable Player. He retired in 1957. Baseball Hall of Fame (1962).

Jackie Robinson

Rob·in·son[4], Mary (Terese Winifred) (1944–), Irish stateswoman; president 1990–1997. She was Ireland's first woman president, noted for her platform of religious toleration and her liberal attitude and served as the UN high commissioner for human rights 1997–2002.

Mary Robinson

Rob·in·son[5], Smokey (1940–), U.S. soul singer and songwriter; born *William Robinson*. He is known for a series of successes, such as "Tracks of My Tears" (1965) and "Tears of a Clown" (1970), with his group the Miracles.

Rob·in·son[6], Sugar Ray (1920–89), U.S. boxer; born *Walker Smith*. He was world welterweight champion from 1946 to 1951 and seven times the middleweight champion—in 1951 twice, 1955, and 1957 and from 1958 until 1960.

Rob·in·son Cru·soe /ˈkro͞osō/ the hero of Daniel Defoe's novel *Robinson Crusoe* (1719), who survives a shipwreck and lives on a desert island.

rob·o·rant /ˈräbərənt; ˈrō-/ *Medicine* ▸*adj.* (chiefly of a medicine) having a strengthening effect.
▸*n.* a roborant medicine. ▷mid 17th cent.: from Latin *roborant-* 'strengthening,' from the verb *roborare*, from *robur, robor-* 'strength.'

ro·bot /ˈrō,bät; ˈrōbət/ ▸*n.* a machine capable of carrying out a complex series of actions automatically, esp. one programmable by a computer. ■ (esp. in science fiction) a machine resembling a human being and able to replicate certain human movements and functions automatically. ■ used to refer to a person who behaves in a mechanical or unemotional manner: *terminally bored tour guides chattering like robots.* ▷from Czech, from *robota* 'forced labor.' The term was coined in K. Čapek's play *R.U.R.* 'Rossum's Universal Robots' (1920).

ro·bot·ic /rōˈbätik/ ▸*adj.* of or relating to robots: *a robotic device for performing surgery.* ■ (of a person) mechanical, stiff, or unemotional. **—ro·bot·i·cal·ly** /-ik(ə)lē/ *adv.*

ro·bot·ics /rōˈbätiks/ ▸*plural n.* [treated as *sing.*] the branch of technology that deals with the design, construction, operation, and application of robots. **—ro·bot·i·cist** /-ˈbätəsist/ *n.*

ro·bot·ize /ˈrōbə,tīz/ ▸*v.* [*trans.*] [usu. as *adj.*] (**robotized**) convert (a production system, factory, etc.) to operation by robots. **—ro·bot·i·za·tion** /,rōbətəˈzāsʜən; ,rō,bätə-/ *n.*

Rob Roy[1] /ˈräb ˈroi/ (1671–1734), Scottish outlaw; born *Robert Macgregor*. His reputation as a Robin Hood was exaggerated in Sir Walter Scott's novel of the same name (1817).

Rob Roy[2] ▸*n.* a cocktail made of Scotch whisky and vermouth.

ro·bust /rōˈbəst; ˈrō,bəst/ ▸*adj.* (**-bust·er, -bust·est**) (of a person, animal, or plant) strong and healthy; vigorous: *the Caplans are a robust, healthy lot.* ■ (of an object) sturdy in construction: *a robust metal cabinet.* ■ (of a process or system, esp. an economic one) able to withstand or overcome adverse conditions: *California's robust property market.* ■ (of an intellectual approach or the person taking or expressing it) not perturbed by or attending to subtleties or

Pronunciation Key ə *ago;* ər *over;* ˈə *or* ,ə *up;* ˈər *or* ,ər *fur;* a *hat;* ā *rate;* ä *car;* cʜ *chew;* e *let;* ē *see;* e(ə)r *air;* i *fit;* ī *by;* i(ə)r *ear;* ɴɢ *sing;* ō *go;* ô *for;* oi *boy;* o͝o *good;* o͞o *goo;* ou *out;* sʜ *she;* ᴛʜ *thin;* T̲H̲ *then;* (h)w *why;* zʜ *vision*

difficulties; uncompromising and forceful: *the country's decision to bow to UN pressure was preceded by a robust defense of its policies | he took quite a robust view of my case.* ■ (of action) involving physical force or energy: *a robust game of rugby.* ■ (of wine or food) strong and rich in flavor or smell. ▷mid 16th cent.: from Latin *robustus* 'firm and hard,' from *robus,* earlier form of *robur* 'oak, strength.' **—ro·bust·ly** *adv.* **—ro·bust·ness** *n.*

ro·bus·ta /rō'bəstə/ ▸*n.* **1** coffee or coffee beans from a widely grown kind of coffee plant. Beans of this variety are often used in the manufacture of instant coffee. **2** the tropical West African bush of the bedstraw family that produces these beans. • *Coffea canephora* (formerly **robusta**) , family Rubiaceae. ▷early 20th cent.: modern Latin, feminine of Latin *robustus* 'robust.'

ROC *historical* ▸*abbr.* (in the UK) Royal Observer Corps.

roc /räk/ ▸*n.* a gigantic mythological bird described in the Arabian Nights. ▷late 16th cent.: ultimately from Persian *ruk.*

ro·caille /rō'kī; rä-/ ▸*n.* **1** an 18th-century artistic or architectural style of decoration characterized by elaborate ornamentation with pebbles and shells, typical of grottos and fountains. **2** (**rocailles**) tiny beads. ▷French, from *roc* 'rock.'

roc·am·bole /'räkəm,bōl/ ▸*n.* a Eurasian plant that is closely related to garlic and is sometimes used as a flavoring. • *Allium scorodoprasum,* family Liliaceae (or Alliaceae). ▷late 17th cent.: from French, from German *Rockenbolle.*

ROCE *Finance* ▸*abbr.* return on capital employed.

Roche /rōsʜ/, (Eamonn) Kevin (1922–), U.S. architect; born in Ireland. From 1950 until 1961 he worked with architect Eero Saarinen. After forming his own architectural firm in 1981 with partner John Dinkeloo (1918–81), his projects included the design of the Oakland Museum in California 1961–68, the UN Plaza in New York City 1969–75, and the Jewish Museum in New York City 1985.

Roche lim·it /rōsʜ; rôsʜ/ (also **Roch·e's lim·it**) ▸*n. Astronomy* the closest distance from the center of a planet that a satellite can approach without being pulled apart by the planet's gravitational field. ▷late 19th cent.: named after Edouard Albert *Roche* (1820–83), French mathematician.

Roche lobe ▸*n. Astronomy* either of two lobes that form an hourglass-shaped volume of space around a binary star system. ▷1960s: named after E. A. *Roche* (see **Roche limit**).

roche mou·ton·née /'rōsʜ ,mōōtn'ā; rôsʜ/ ▸*n.* (*pl.* **roches mou·ton·nées** *pronunc.* same or /,mōōtn'āz/) *Geology* a small bare outcrop of rock shaped by glacial erosion, with one side smooth and gently sloping and the other steep, rough, and irregular. ▷mid 19th cent.: French, literally 'fleecy rock.'

Roch·es·ter /'räcʜəstər; 'rä,cʜes-/ **1** an industrial city in southeastern Minnesota, home to the Mayo Clinic that was established in 1889; pop. 85,806. **2** a city in southeastern New Hampshire, northwest of Dover; pop. 28,461. **3** a city in northwestern New York, on Lake Ontario; pop. 219,773.

Roch·es·ter Hills /'rä,cʜestər/ a residential and industrial city in southeastern Michigan, northeast of Pontiac; pop. 61,766.

roch·et /'räcʜit/ ▸*n. Christian Church* a vestment resembling a surplice, used chiefly by bishops and abbots. ▷Middle English: from Old French, a diminutive from a Germanic base shared by German *Rock* 'coat.'

rock[1] /räk/ ▸*n.* **1** the solid mineral material forming part of the surface of the earth and other similar planets, exposed on the surface or underlying the soil or oceans. ■ a mass of such material projecting above the earth's surface or out of the sea: *there are dangerous rocks around the island.* ■ *Geology* any natural material, hard or soft (e.g., clay), having a distinctive mineral composition. ■ (**the Rock**) Gibraltar. ■ (**the Rock**) informal name for **Newfoundland**[1]. **2** a large piece of such material that has become detached from a cliff or mountain; a boulder: *the stream flowed through a jumble of rocks.* ■ a stone of any size, esp. one small enough to be picked up and used as a projectile. ■ *Brit.* a kind of hard confectionery in the form of cylindrical peppermint-flavored sticks. ■ *informal* a precious stone, esp. a diamond. ■ *informal* a small piece of crack cocaine. ■ (**rocks**) *vulgar slang* testicles. **3** used in similes and metaphors to refer to someone or something that is extremely strong, reliable, or hard: *imagining himself as the last rock of civilization being swept over by a wave of barbarism.* ■ (usu. **rocks**) (esp. with allusion to shipwrecks) a source of danger or destruction: *the new system is* ***heading for the rocks.*** **4** (**rocks**) *informal, dated* money. ▷Middle English: from Old French *rocque,* from medieval Latin *rocca,* of unknown ultimate origin. **—rock·less** *adj.* **—rock·like** /-,līk/ *adj.*

▸*PHRASES* □ **between a rock and a hard place** *informal* in a situation where one is faced with two equally difficult alternatives. □ **get one's rocks off** *vulgar slang* have an orgasm. ■ obtain pleasure or satisfaction. □ **on the rocks** *informal* **1** (of a relationship or enterprise) experiencing difficulties and likely to fail. **2** (of a drink) served undiluted and with ice cubes.

rock[2] ▸*v.* **1** [*trans.*] cause (someone or something) to move gently to and fro or from side to side: *she rocked the baby in her arms.* ■ [*intrans.*] move in such a way: *the vase rocked back and forth on its base* | [as *adj.*] (**rocking**) *the rocking movement of the boat.* ■ (with reference to a building or region) shake or cause to shake or vibrate, esp. because of an impact, earthquake, or explosion: [*trans.*] *a terrorist blast rocked a Tube station* | [*intrans.*] *the building began to rock on its foundations.* ■ cause great shock or distress to (someone or something), esp. so as to weaken or destabilize them or it: *diplomatic upheavals that rocked the British Empire.* **2** [*intrans.*] *informal* dance to or play rock music. ■ *figurative* (of a place) have an atmosphere of excitement or much social activity: *the new town really rocks* | [as *adj.*] (**rocking**) *a rocking resort.*

▸*phrasal v.* □ **rock out** *informal* perform rock music loudly and vigorously. ■ enjoy oneself in an enthusiastic and uninhibited way, esp. by dancing to rock music.

▸*n.* **1** rock music: [as *adj.*] *a rock star.* ■ rock and roll. **2** [in *sing.*] a gentle movement to and fro or from side to side: *she placed the baby in the cradle and gave it a rock.* ▷late Old English *roccian,* probably from a Germanic base meaning 'remove, move'; related to Dutch *rukken* 'jerk, tug' and German *rücken* 'move.' The noun dates from the early 19th cent.

▸*PHRASE* □ **rock the boat** see **boat**.

rock·a·bil·ly /'räkə,bilē/ ▸*n.* a type of popular music, originating in the southeastern U.S. in the 1950s, combining elements of rock and roll and country music. ▷1950s: blend of **rock and roll** and **hillbilly**.

rock and roll (also **rock 'n' roll**) ▸*n.* a type of popular dance music originating in the 1950s, characterized by a heavy beat and simple melodies. Rock and roll was an amalgam of black rhythm and blues and white country music, usually based on a twelve-bar structure and an instrumentation of guitar, bass, and drums. **—rock and roll·er** *n.*

rock bass /bas/ ▸*n.* a red-eyed North American freshwater fish of the sunfish family, found chiefly in rocky streams. Also called **red-eye**. • *Ambloplites rupestris,* family Centrarchidae.

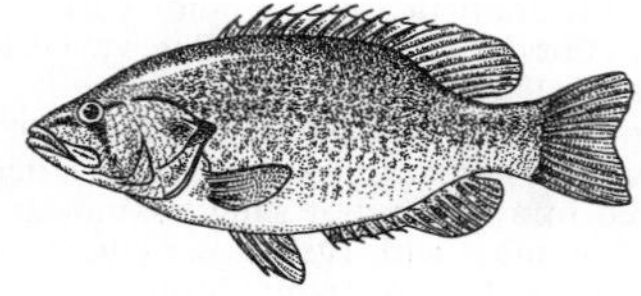

rock bass

rock-bot·tom ▸*adj.* at the lowest possible level: *rock-bottom prices.* ■ fundamental: *a pure, rock-bottom kind of realism.*

▸*n.* (**rock bot·tom**) the lowest possible level: *morale is* ***at rock bottom.***

rock-bound ▸*adj.* (of a coast or shore) rocky and inaccessible.

rock·burst /'räk,bərst/ ▸*n. Mining* a sudden, violent rupture or collapse of highly stressed rock in a mine.

rock cake ▸*n. chiefly Brit.* a small currant cake with a hard rough surface.

rock can·dy ▸*n.* sugar crystallized in large masses onto a string or stick, eaten as candy.

rock climb·ing ▸*n.* the sport or pastime of climbing rock faces, esp. with the aid of ropes and special equipment. **—rock climb** *n.* **—rock climb·er** *n.*

rock cod ▸*n.* any of a number of marine fishes that frequent rocky habitats, esp. in Australian waters. • Several species, chiefly in the families Scorpaenidae and Serranidae.

Rock Cor·nish (also **Rock Cor·nish hen** or **Rock Cor·nish game hen**) ▸*n.* a stocky chicken of a breed that is kept for its meat.

rock cress ▸*n.* another term for **arabis**.

rock crys·tal ▸*n.* transparent quartz, typically in the form of colorless hexagonal crystals.

rock cy·cle ▸*n. Geology* an idealized cycle of processes undergone by rocks in the earth's crust, involving igneous intrusion, uplift, erosion, transportation, deposition as sedimentary rock, metamorphism, remelting, and further igneous intrusion.

rock dove ▸*n.* a mainly gray Old World pigeon that frequents coastal and inland cliffs. It is the ancestor of domestic and feral pigeons. • *Columba livia,* family Columbidae.

Rock·e·fel·ler[1] /'räkə,felər/, John D. (1839–1937), U.S. industrialist and philanthropist; full name *John Davison Rockefeller.* He founded the Standard Oil Company in 1870 and, by 1880, exercised a virtual monopoly over oil refining in the U.S. Both he and his son, **John D. Rockefeller Jr.** (1874–1960), established many philanthropic institutions, including the Rockefeller Foundation in 1913. Rockefeller Center in New York City was built in the 1930s.

Rock·e·fel·ler[2] ▸, John D., IV (1937–), U.S. politician; known as **Jay.** A Democrat, he was governor of West Virginia 1976–84 and a U.S. senator from 1984. He was the great-grandson of John D. Rockefeller and the nephew of Nelson Rockefeller.

Rock·e·fel·ler[3] ▸, Nelson Aldrich (1908–79), U.S. statesman. A moderate Republican, he served as governor of New York 1959–73 and vice president of the U.S. 1974–77. He was the son of John D. Rockefeller Jr.

Rock·e·fel·ler Center /'räkə,felər/ a business building complex in midtown Manhattan in New York City, home to Radio City Music Hall.

rock·er /'räkər/ ▸*n.* **1** a person who performs, dances to, or enjoys rock music, esp. of a particular type: *a punk rocker.* ■ a rock song. **2** a thing that rocks, in particular: ■ a rocking chair. ■ a rocking device forming part of a mechanism, esp. one for controlling the positions of brushes in a generator. **3** a curved bar or similar support on which something such as a chair or cradle can rock. **4** the amount of curvature in the longitudinal contour of a boat or surfboard. **5** any of the curved stripes below the chevron of a noncommissioned officer above the rank of sergeant. ■ the curved strip above the chevron of a chief petty officer.

▸*PHRASE* □ **off one's rocker** *informal* insane.

rock·er arm ▸*n.* a rocking lever in an engine, esp. one in an internal combustion engine that serves to work a valve and is operated by a pushrod from the camshaft.

rock·er pan·el ▸*n.* (in a motor vehicle) a panel forming part of the bodywork below the level of the passenger door.

rock·er switch ▸*n.* an electrical on/off switch incorporating a spring-loaded rocker.

rock·er·y /'räkərē/ ▸*n.* (*pl.* **-er·ies**) a heaped arrangement of rough stones with soil between them, planted with rock plants, esp. alpines.

Rock·et /'räkit/, The, see **Richard**[2].

rock·et[1] /'räkit/ ▸*n.* a cylindrical projectile that can be propelled to a great height or distance by the combustion of its contents, used typically as a firework or signal. ■ (also **rock·et en·gine** or **rock·et mo·tor**) an engine operating on the same principle, providing thrust as in a jet engine but without depending on the intake of air for combustion, an oxidizer being carried on board along with the fuel. ■ an elongated rocket-propelled missile or spacecraft. ■ used, esp. in similes and comparisons, to refer to a person or thing that moves very fast or to an action that is done with great force: *she shot out of her chair like a rocket.*

▸*v.* (**rock·et·ed, rock·et·ing**) **1** [*intrans.*] (of an amount, price, etc.) increase very rapidly and suddenly: *sales of milk in supermarkets are rocketing* | [as *adj.*] (**rocketing**) *rocketing prices.* ■ [with *adverbial of direction*] move or progress very rapidly: *the cab rocketed down a ramp* | *he rocketed to national stardom.* ■ [*trans.*] cause to move or progress very rapidly: *she showed the kind of form that rocketed her to the semifinals last year.* **2** [*trans.*] attack with rocket-propelled missiles: *the city was rocketed and bombed from the air.* ▷early 17th cent.: from French *roquette,* from Italian *rocchetto,* diminutive of *rocca* 'distaff (for spinning),' with reference to its cylindrical shape. **—rock·et·like** /-,līk/ *adj.*

rock·et[2] ▸*n.* (also **gar·den rock·et** or **sal·ad rock·et**) an edible Mediterranean plant of the cabbage family, sometimes eaten in salads. See also **ARUGULA**. • *Eruca vesicaria* subsp. *sativa*, family Brassicaceae. ■ used in names of other fast-growing plants of this family, e.g., **sweet rocket**. ▷late 15th cent.: from French *roquette*, from Italian *ruchetta*, diminutive of *ruca*, from Latin *eruca* 'downy-stemmed plant.'

rock·e·teer /ˌräki'ti(ə)r/ ▸*n.* a person who works with space rockets; a rocket enthusiast.

rock·et·ry /'räkətrē/ ▸*n.* the branch of science that deals with rockets and rocket propulsion. ■ the use of rockets.

rock·et sci·en·tist ▸*n.* a specialist in rocketry. ■ [usu. with *negative*] *informal* an extremely intelligent person: *he's a nice kid—maybe not a rocket scientist, but he should come out okay.*

rock face ▸*n.* a bare vertical surface of natural rock.

rock·fall /'räkˌfôl/ (also **rock fall**) ▸*n.* a descent of loose rocks. ■ a mass of fallen rock.

rock·fish /'räkˌfisH/ ▸*n.* (*pl.* same or **-fish·es**) a marine fish of the scorpionfish family with a laterally compressed body. It is generally a bottom-dweller in rocky areas and is frequently of sporting or commercial value. • Genus *Sebastes*, family Scorpaenidae: numerous species.

rock flour ▸*n.* finely powdered rock formed by glacial or other erosion.

Rock·ford /'räkfərd/ an industrial city in north central Illinois, on the Rock River; pop. 150,115.

rock gar·den ▸*n.* an artificial mound or bank built of earth and stones and planted with rock plants. ■ a garden in which rockeries are the chief feature.

Rock Hill an industrial city in northern South Carolina; pop. 49,765.

rock·hop·per /'räkˌhäpər/ (also **rock·hop·per pen·guin**) ▸*n.* a small penguin with a yellowish crest, breeding on subantarctic coastal cliffs that it ascends by hopping from rock to rock. • *Eudyptes chrysocome*, family Spheniscidae.

rock·hound /'räkˌhound/ ▸*n. informal* a geologist or amateur collector of mineral specimens. —**rock·hound·ing** *n.*

rock hy·rax ▸*n.* an African hyrax that lives on rocky outcrops and cliffs and feeds mainly on grass. Also called **DASSIE**. • Genus *Procavia* (and *Heterohyrax*), family Procaviidae: several species.

Rock·ies another name for the **ROCKY MOUNTAINS**.

rock·ing chair ▸*n.* a chair mounted on rockers or springs, so as to rock back and forth.

rock·ing horse ▸*n.* a model of a horse mounted on rockers or springs for a child to sit on and rock back and forth.

rocking horse

Rock Is·land an industrial city in northwestern Illinois, on the Mississippi River, one of the Quad Cities; pop. 40,552.

rock jock ▸*n. informal* a mountaineer.

Rock·land Coun·ty /'räklənd/ a largely suburban county in southeastern New York, on the western side of the Hudson River and the New Jersey border; pop. 286,753.

rock·ling /'räkliNG/ ▸*n.* a slender marine fish of the cod family, typically occurring in shallow water or tidal pools. • Genera *Ciliata* and *Rhinomenus*, family Gadidae: several species.

rock liz·ard ▸*n.* a small climbing lizard living in mountains and arid rocky habitats, in particular: • (also **banded rock lizard**) a North American lizard (*Streptosaurus mearnsi*, family Iguanidae). • a European and African lizard (genus *Lacerta*, family Lacertidae, including *L. saxicola*).

rock lob·ster ▸*n.* another term for **SPINY LOBSTER**.

rock ma·ple ▸*n.* another term for **SUGAR MAPLE**.

rock mu·sic ▸*n.* a form of popular music that evolved from rock and roll and pop music during the mid- and late 1960s. Harsher and often self-consciously more serious than that which had gone before, it was initially characterized by musical experimentation and drug-related or anti-Establishment lyrics. ■ another term for **ROCK AND ROLL**.

Rock·ne /'räknē/, Knute (Kenneth) (1888–1931), U.S. college football coach; born in Norway. He coached Notre Dame 1918–31 to six national titles and achieved a winning percentage of .881. He was killed in a plane crash in Kansas.

rock 'n' roll ▸*n.* variant spelling of **ROCK AND ROLL**.

Rock of Gi·bral·tar see **GIBRALTAR**.

rock pi·geon ▸*n.* another term for **ROCK DOVE**.

rock plant ▸*n.* a plant that grows on or among rocks.

rock pool ▸*n.* a pool of water among rocks, typically along a shoreline.

rock py·thon ▸*n.* a large dark-skinned constricting snake with paler markings and a distinctive pale mark on the crown. • Genera *Python* and *Morelia*, family Pythonidae: several species, including *P. sebae* of Africa, *P. molurus* of Asia, and *M. amethistina* of Australia.

rock rab·bit ▸*n.* **1** another term for **HYRAX**. **2** another term for **PIKA**.

rock-ribbed ▸*adj.* having ridges or cliffs of rock: *six thousand miles of rock-ribbed coasts.* ■ *figurative* resolute or uncompromising, esp. with respect to political allegiance: *rock-ribbed communists.*

rock·rose /'räkˌrōz/ ▸*n.* **1** a herbaceous or shrubby plant with saucer-shaped, roselike flowers, native to temperate and warm regions. See also **LABDANUM**. • Genera *Cistus* and *Helianthemum*, family Cistaceae. **2** another term for **BITTERROOT**.

rock salm·on ▸*n.* a tropical snapper that occurs both in the sea and in rivers, valuable for food and sport. • *Lutjanus argentimaculatus*, family Lutjanidae.

rock salt ▸*n.* common salt occurring naturally as a mineral; halite.

rock·slide /'räkˌslīd/ ▸*n.* an avalanche of rock. ■ a mass of rock deposited by such an avalanche.

rock snake ▸*n.* the Asian rock python.

rock sol·id ▸*adj.* unlikely to change, fail, or collapse: *her love was rock solid.*

Rock Springs a city in southwestern Wyoming, northeast of Green River; pop. 18,708.

rock stead·y (also **rock·stead·y** /'räk'stedē/) ▸*n.* an early form of reggae music originating in Jamaica in the 1960s, characterized by a slow tempo.

rock·u·men·ta·ry /ˌräkyə'ment(ə)rē/ ▸*n. informal* a documentary about rock music and musicians. ▷1970s: from **ROCK**[2] + **DOCUMENTARY**.

Rock·ville /'räkˌvil/ a city in central Maryland, northwest of Washington, D.C., home to many government offices; pop. 47,381.

rock wal·la·by ▸*n.* an agile Australian wallaby that lives among cliffs and rocks, having feet with thick pads and fringes of stiff hair. • Genus *Petrogale*, family Macropodidae: several species.

Rock·well /'räkˌwel; -wəl/, Norman (Percevel) (1894–1978), U.S. illustrator. Known for his typically sentimental portraits of small-town life in the U.S., he was an illustrator for *Life* and the *Saturday Evening Post*, for whom he created 317 covers between 1916 and 1963.

rock wool ▸*n.* inorganic material made into matted fiber used esp. for insulation or soundproofing.

rock·y[1] /'räkē/ ▸*adj.* (**rock·i·er**, **rock·i·est**) consisting or formed of rock, esp. when exposed to view: *a rocky crag above the village.* ■ full of rocks: *hillsides of dry, rocky soil.* ■ *figurative* difficult; full of obstacles: *a long, rocky road to pop stardom.* —**rock·i·ness** *n.*

rock·y[2] ▸*adj.* (**rock·i·er**, **rock·i·est**) tending to rock or shake; unsteady. ■ *figurative* not stable or firm; full of problems: *the marriage seemingly got off to a rocky start.* —**rock·i·ly** /'räkəlē/ *adv.* —**rock·i·ness** *n.*

Rock·y Mount /'räkē/ an industrial city in east central North Carolina; pop. 55,893.

Rock·y Moun·tain goat ▸*n.* see **MOUNTAIN GOAT** (sense 1).

Rock·y Moun·tains (also **the Rockies**) the chief mountain system in North America. It extends from the U.S.–Mexico border to the Yukon Territory of northern Canada. It separates the Great Plains from the Pacific coast and forms the Continental Divide. Several peaks rise to more than 14,000 feet (4,300 m), the highest being Mount Elbert at 14,431 feet (4,399 m).

Rock·y Moun·tain spot·ted fe·ver ▸*n.* a rickettsial disease transmitted by ticks.

ro·co·co /rə'kōkō; ˌrōkə'kō/ ▸*adj.* (of furniture or architecture) of or characterized by an elaborately ornamental late baroque style of decoration prevalent in 18th-century Continental Europe, with asymmetrical patterns involving motifs and scrollwork. ■ extravagantly or excessively ornate, esp. (of music or literature) highly ornamented and florid.
▸*n.* the rococo style of art, decoration, or architecture. ▷mid 19th cent.: from French, humorous alteration of **ROCAILLE**.

rod /räd/ ▸*n.* **1** a thin straight bar, esp. of wood or metal. ■ a wand or staff as a symbol of office, authority, or power. ■ a slender straight stick or shoot growing on or cut from a tree or bush. ■ a stick used for caning or flogging. ■ (**the rod**) the use of such a stick as punishment: *if you'd been my daughter, you'd have felt the rod.* ■ *vulgar slang* a penis. **2** a fishing rod. **3** *historical* a linear measure, esp. for land, equal to 5½ yards (approximately 5.029 m). ■ (also **square rod**) a square measure, esp. for land, equal to 160th of an acre or 30¼ square yards (approximately 25.29 sq m). **4** *informal* a pistol or revolver. **5** *Anatomy* a light-sensitive cell of one of the two types present in large numbers in the retina of the eye, responsible mainly for monochrome vision in poor light. Compare with **CONE** (sense 3). ▷late Old English *rodd* 'slender shoot growing on or cut from a tree,' also 'straight stick or bundle of twigs used to inflict punishment'; probably related to Old Norse *rudda* 'club.' —**rod·less** *adj.* —**rod·let** /-lət/ *n.* —**rod·like** /-ˌlīk/ *adj.*
▸*PHRASES* □ **ride the rods** steal rides on freight trains: *hundreds of young men took to riding the rods in search of employment.* □ **rule someone or something with a rod of iron** control or govern someone or something very strictly or harshly. □ **spare the rod and spoil the child** *proverb* if children are not physically punished when they do wrong their personal development will suffer.

Rod·den·ber·ry /'rädnˌberē/, Gene (1921–91), U.S. television producer and scriptwriter; full name *Eugene Wesley Roddenberry*. He created and wrote many scripts for the television science-fiction drama series *Star Trek*, first broadcast in 1966. He later worked on movies and launched a follow-up series, *Star Trek: The Next Generation*, in 1987.

rode[1] /rōd/ past of **RIDE**.

rode[2] ▸*v.* [*intrans.*] (of a woodcock) fly on a regular circuit in the evening as a territorial display, making sharp calls and grunts. ▷mid 18th cent. (in the sense 'fly landward in the evening'): of unknown origin.

rode[3] ▸*n. Nautical* a rope, esp. one securing an anchor or trawl. ▷early 17th cent.: of unknown origin.

ro·dent /'rōdnt/ ▸*n.* a gnawing mammal of an order that includes rats, mice, squirrels, hamsters, porcupines, and their relatives, distinguished by strong constantly growing incisors and no canine teeth. They constitute the largest order of mammals. • Order Rodentia: three suborders. See **SCIUROMORPHA**, **MYOMORPHA**, and **HYSTRICOMORPHA**.
▸*adj.* **1** of or relating to mammals of this order. **2** *Medicine* see **RODENT ULCER**. ▷mid 19th cent.: from Latin *rodent-* 'gnawing,' from the verb *rodere*.

ro·den·ti·cide /rō'dentəˌsīd/ ▸*n.* a poison used to kill rodents.

ro·dent ul·cer ▸*n. Medicine* a slow-growing malignant tumor of the face (basal cell carcinoma).

ro·de·o /'rōdēˌō; rə'dāō/ ▸*n.* (*pl.* **-de·os**) **1** an exhibition or contest in which cowboys show their skill at riding broncos, roping calves, wrestling steers, etc. ■ a similar exhibition or contest demonstrating other skills, such as motorcycle riding or canoeing. **2** a roundup of cattle on a ranch for branding, counting, etc. ■ an enclosure for such a roundup.
▸*v.* (**-de·oed**, **-de·o·ing**) [*intrans.*] compete in a rodeo. ▷mid 19th cent.: from Spanish, from *rodear* 'go around,' based on Latin *rotare* 'rotate.'

Rodg·ers /'räjərz/, Richard (Charles) (1902–79), U.S. composer. He worked with librettist **Lorenz Hart** (1895–1942) before collaborating with Oscar Hammerstein II on a succession of popular musicals that included *Oklahoma!* (1943), *South Pacific* (1949), *The King and I* (1951), and *The Sound of Music* (1959).

rodg·er·si·a /rä'jərzēə/ ▸*n.* an Asian plant that is sometimes cultivated for its attractive foliage. • Genus *Rodgersia*, family Saxifragaceae. ▷modern Latin, named after John *Rodgers* (1812–82), American admiral.

Ró·dhos /'rôTHôs/ modern Greek name for **RHODES**[1].

Pronunciation Key ə *ago*; ər *over*; 'ə *or* ˌə *up*; 'ər *or* ˌər *fur*; a *hat*; ā *rate*; ä *car*; CH *chew*; e *let*; ē *see*; e(ə)r *air*; i *fit*; ī *by*; i(ə)r *ear*; NG *sing*; ō *go*; ô *for*; oi *boy*; o͝o *good*; o͞o *goo*; ou *out*; SH *she*; TH *thin*; TH *then*; (h)w *why*; ZH *vision*

R

Ro·din /rō'daN/, Auguste (1840–1917), French sculptor. He was chiefly concerned with the human form, and his first major work, *The Age of Bronze* (1875–76), was considered so lifelike that Rodin was alleged to have taken a cast from a live model. Other notable works: *The Thinker* (1880) and *The Kiss* (1886).

Auguste Rodin

rod·o·mon·tade /ˌrädəmən'tād; ˌrōd-; -'täd/ ▸*n.* boastful or inflated talk or behavior.
▸*v.* [*intrans.*] *archaic* talk boastfully. ▷early 17th cent.: from French, from obsolete Italian *rodomontada*, from Italian *rodomonte*, from the name of a boastful character in the medieval *Orlando* epics.

R

ROE ▸*abbr.* rules of engagement (in combat).

roe[1] /rō/ ▸*n.* (also **hard roe**) the mass of eggs contained in the ovaries of a female fish or shellfish, typically including the ovaries themselves, esp. when ripe and used as food. ■ (**soft roe**) the ripe testes of a male fish, esp. when used as food. ▷late Middle English: related to Middle Low German, Middle Dutch *roge*.

roe[2] (also **roe deer**) ▸*n.* (*pl.* same or **roes**) a small Eurasian deer that lacks a visible tail and has a reddish summer coat that turns grayish in winter. • Genus *Capreolus*, family Cervidae: two species, in particular the **European roe deer** (*C. capreolus*). ▷Old English *rā(ha)*, of Germanic origin; related to Dutch *ree* and German *Reh*.

roe·buck /'rōˌbək/ ▸*n.* a male roe deer.

roent·gen /'rentgən; 'rənt-; -jən/ (abbr.: **R**) ▸*n.* a unit of ionizing radiation, the amount producing one electrostatic unit of positive or negative ionic charge in one cubic centimeter of air under standard conditions. ▷1920s: named after Wilhelm Conrad *Röntgen* (1845–1923), German physicist, discoverer of X-rays.

roent·gen·o·gram /'rentgənəˌgram; 'rənt-; -jə-/ ▸*n.* *chiefly Medicine* an X-ray photograph.

roent·gen·og·ra·phy /ˌrentgə'nägrəfē; ˌrənt-; -jə-/ ▸*n.* *chiefly Medicine* X-ray photography. —**roent·gen·o·graph·ic** /-nə'grafik/ *adj.* —**roent·gen·o·graph·i·cal·ly** /-nə'grafik(ə)lē/ *adv.*

roent·gen·ol·o·gy /ˌrentgə'näləjē; ˌrənt-; -jə-/ ▸*n.* *chiefly Medicine* another term for **RADIOLOGY**. —**roent·gen·o·log·ic** /-nə'läjik/ *adj.*

roent·gen rays ▸*plural n.* *dated* X-rays.

ro·gan josh /'rōgən 'jäsʜ/ ▸*n.* an Indian dish of curried meat, typically lamb, in a rich tomato-based sauce. ▷from Urdu *rogan još*.

ro·ga·tion /rō'gāsʜən/ ▸*n.* [usu. as *adj.*] (in the Christian Church) a solemn supplication consisting of the litany of the saints chanted on the three days before Ascension Day: *Rogation Week.* ▷late Middle English: from Latin *rogatio(n-)*, from *rogare* 'ask.'

Ro·ga·tion Days (in the Western Christian Church) the three days before Ascension Day, traditionally marked by fasting and prayer, particularly for the blessing of the harvest (after the pattern of pre-Christian rituals).

Ro·ga·tion Sun·day ▸*n.* the Sunday preceding the Rogation Days.

rog·er /'räjər/ ▸*exclam.* your message has been received and understood (used in radio communication): *"Roger; we'll be with you in about ten minutes."* ■ *informal* used to express assent or understanding: *"Go light the stove." "Roger, Mister Bossman," Frank replied.*
▸*v.* [*trans.*] *Brit., vulgar slang* have sexual intercourse with (a woman). ■ [*intrans.*] have sexual intercourse. ▷mid 16th cent.: from the given name *Roger*. The verb (dating from the early 18th cent.) is from an obsolete sense 'penis' of the noun.

Rog·ers[1] /'räjərz/ a resort city in northwestern Arkansas, north of Fayetteville; pop. 38,829.

Rog·ers[2], Fred McFeely (1928–2003), U.S. television producer, actor, and writer. He created and starred in the television children's program "Mister Rogers' Neighborhood" 1967–2001.

Rog·ers[3] /'räjərz/, Ginger (1911–95), U.S. actress and dancer; born *Virginia Katherine McMath*. She is known for her dancing partnership with Fred Astaire, during which she appeared in musicals including *Top Hat* (1935) and *Shall We Dance?* (1937). Her acting career included the movie *Kitty Foyle* (1940), for which she won an Academy Award.

Rog·ers[4], Kenny (1938–), U.S. country singer and actor; full name Kenneth Ray Rogers. His hits include "Lucille" (1977), "The Gambler" (1978), and "We've Got Tonight" (1983). He also starred in movies such as *The Gambler* and its sequels (1980–94).

Rog·ers[5], Roy (1912–98), U.S. actor and singer; born *Leonard Franklin Slye*. One of the original Sons of the Pioneers country singers, he starred in many "singing cowboy" westerns, with his horse Trigger and dog Bullet and, from 1944, with Dale Evans (1912–2001), whom he married in 1947. His movies include *Under Western Stars* (1938), *The Yellow Rose of Texas* (1944), and *Apache Rose* (1947).

Rog·ers[6], Will (1879–1935), U.S. humorist and actor; *full name William Penn Adair Rogers*. A vaudeville headliner with his rope twirling and homespun humor from 1905, he wrote a syndicated column for *The New York Times* 1922–35. He died in a plane crash with aviator Wiley Post in Alaska.

Ro·get /rō'zʜā; 'rōˌzʜā/, Peter Mark (1779–1869), English scholar. He worked as a physician but is remembered as the compiler of *Roget's Thesaurus of English Words and Phrases* (1852).

rogue /rōg/ ▸*n.* **1** a dishonest or unprincipled man: *you are a rogue and an embezzler.* ■ a person whose behavior one disapproves of but who is nonetheless likable or attractive (often used as a playful term of reproof): *Cenzo, you old rogue!* **2** [usu. as *adj.*] an elephant or other large wild animal driven away or living apart from the herd and having savage or destructive tendencies: *a rogue elephant.* ■ a person or thing that behaves in an aberrant, faulty, or unpredictable way: *he hacked into data and ran rogue programs.* ■ an inferior or defective specimen among many satisfactory ones, esp. a seedling or plant deviating from the standard variety.
▸*v.* [*trans.*] remove inferior or defective plants or seedlings from (a crop). ▷mid 16th cent. (denoting an idle vagrant): probably from Latin *rogare* 'beg, ask,' and related to obsolete slang *roger* 'vagrant beggar' (many such cant terms were introduced toward the middle of the 16th cent.).

Rogue Riv·er a river that flows west for 200 miles (320 km) across southern Oregon to the Pacific Ocean.

ro·guer·y /'rōgərē/ ▸*n.* (*pl.* **-guer·ies**) conduct characteristic of a rogue, esp. acts of dishonesty or playful mischief: *there has always been roguery associated with horse dealing.*

rogues' gal·ler·y ▸*n.* *informal* a collection of photographs of known criminals, used by police to identify suspects. ■ a collection of people or creatures notable for a certain shared quality or characteristic, typically a disreputable one: *a rogues' gallery of bureaucrats and cold-hearted advocates of "progress."*

rogue trad·er ▸*n.* a securities trader who attempts to hide tremendous losses suffered on speculative trading.

ro·guish /'rōgisʜ/ ▸*adj.* characteristic of a dishonest or unprincipled person: *he led a roguish and uncertain existence.* ■ playfully mischievous, esp. in a way that is sexually attractive: *he gave her a roguish smile.* —**ro·guish·ly** *adv.* —**ro·guish·ness** *n.*

Rohn·ert Park /'rōnərt/ a city in northwestern California, north of San Francisco; pop. 36,326.

Ro·hyp·nol /rō'hipˌnôl; -ˌnōl/ ▸*n.* *trademark* a potent sedative drug of the benzodiazepine class. ▷1980s: invented name.

ROI *Finance* ▸*abbr.* return on investment.

roil /roil/ ▸*v.* **1** [*trans.*] make (a liquid) turbid or muddy by disturbing the sediment: *winds roil these waters.* ■ [*intrans.*] (of a liquid) move in a turbulent, swirling manner: *the sea roiled below her* | *figurative a kind of fear roiled in her.* **2** another term for **RILE** (sense 1). ▷late 16th cent.: perhaps from Old French *ruiler* 'mix mortar,' from late Latin *regulare* 'regulate.'

roil·y /'roilē/ ▸*adj.* (chiefly of water) muddy; turbulent: *those waters were roily, high, and muddy.*

roist·er /'roistər/ ▸*v.* [*intrans.*] enjoy oneself or celebrate in a noisy or boisterous way: *workers from the refinery roistered in the bars.* ▷late 16th cent.: from obsolete *roister* 'roisterer,' from French *rustre* 'ruffian,' variant of *ruste*, from Latin *rusticus* 'rustic.' —**roist·er·er** *n.* —**roist·er·ous** /'roist(ə)rəs/ *adj.*

Ro·land /'rōlənd/ the most famous of Charlemagne's paladins, hero of the *Chanson de Roland* (12th century). He is said to have become a friend of Oliver, another paladin, after engaging him in single combat in which neither won. Roland was killed at the Battle of Roncesvalles.

role /rōl/ ▸*n.* an actor's part in a play, movie, etc.: *Dietrich's role as a wife in war-torn Paris.* ■ the function assumed or part played by a person or thing in a particular situation: *she greeted us all in her various roles of mother, friend, and daughter* | *religion plays a vital role in society.* ▷early 17th cent.: from obsolete French *roule* 'roll,' referring originally to the roll of paper on which the actor's part was written.

role mod·el ▸*n.* a person looked to by others as an example to be imitated.

role-play·ing (also **role-play**) ▸*n.* **1** *chiefly Psychology* the acting out or performance of a particular role, either consciously (as a technique in psychotherapy or training) or unconsciously, in accordance with the perceived expectations of society with regard to a person's behavior in a particular context. **2** participation in a role-playing game. —**role-play** *v.* —**role-play·er** *n.*

role-play·ing game ▸*n.* a game in which players take on the roles of imaginary characters who engage in adventures, typically in a particular computerized fantasy setting overseen by a referee.

role re·ver·sal ▸*n.* a situation in which someone adopts a role the reverse of that which they normally assume in relation to someone else, who typically assumes their role in exchange: *one marriage counselor makes use of role reversal, inviting husband and wife to pretend to be each other.* ■ a complete change from a job, situation, or circumstance to one exactly opposite in character or responsibility: *in a rare role reversal, a justice of the Connecticut Supreme Court found himself in the witness chair.*

Rolfe /rälf/, John (1585–1622), English colonist in Virginia. He perfected the process of curing tobacco. In 1614, he married Pocahontas, the daughter of Indian chief Powhatan.

Rolf·ing /'rôlfiɴɢ/ ▸*n.* *trademark* a massage technique aimed at the vertical realignment of the body, and therefore deep enough to release muscular tension at skeletal level. It can contribute to the relief of long-standing tension and neuroses. ▷1970s: from the name of Ida P. *Rolf* (1897–1979), American physical therapist, + **-ING**[1]. —**Rolf** /rôlf/ *v.*

roll /rōl/ ▸*v.* **1** move or cause to move in a particular direction by turning over and over on an axis: [*intrans.*] *the car rolled down into a ditch* | [*trans.*] *she rolled the ball across the floor.* ■ turn or cause to turn over to face a different direction: [no , with *adverbial*] *she rolled on to her side* | [*trans.*] *they rolled him over on to his back.* ■ [*trans.*] turn (one's eyes) upward, typically to show surprise or disapproval: *Sarah rolled her eyes.* ■ [*trans.*] make (something cylindrical) revolve between two surfaces: *Plummer rolled the glass between his hands.* ■ [*intrans.*] (of a person or animal) lie down and turn over and over while remaining in the same place: *the buffalo rolled in the dust.* ■ [*intrans.*] (of a moving ship, aircraft, or vehicle) rock or oscillate around an axis parallel to the direction of motion: *the ship pitched and rolled.* ■ [*intrans.*] move along or from side to side unsteadily or uncontrollably: *they were rolling about with laughter.* ■ [*trans.*] *informal* overturn (a vehicle): *he rolled his Mercedes in a 100 mph crash.* ■ [*trans.*] throw (a die or dice). ■ [*trans.*] obtain (a particular score) by doing this: *roll a 2, 3, or 12.* **2** [*intrans.*] (of a vehicle) move or run on wheels: *the van was rolling along the highway.* ■ [*trans.*] move or push (a wheeled object): *Pat rolled the cart back and forth.* ■ (**roll something up/down**) make a car window or a window blind move up or down. ■ (of time) elapse steadily: *the years rolled by.* ■ (of a drop of liquid) flow: *huge tears rolled down her cheeks.* ■ (**roll off**) (of a product) issue from (an assembly line or machine): *the first copies of the newspaper rolled off the presses.* ■ (of waves, smoke, cloud, or fog) move or flow forward with an undulating motion: *the fog rolled across the fields.* ■ [*intrans.*] [usu. as *adj.*] (**rolling**) (of land) extend in gentle undulations: *the rolling countryside.* ■ [*intrans.*] (of credits for a movie or television program) be displayed as if moving on a roller up the screen. ■ [*intrans.*] (of a machine, esp. a camera) operate or begin operating: *the cameras started to roll.* ■ [*trans.*] cause (a machine, esp. a camera) to begin operating: *roll the camera.* **3** [*trans.*] turn (something flexible) over and over on itself to form a cylinder, tube, or ball: *she started to roll up her sleeping bag.* ■ [*trans.*] make by forming material into a cylinder or ball: [with *two objs.*] *Harry rolled himself a joint.* ■ [*intrans.*] (of a person or animal) curl up tightly: *the shock made the armadillo roll into a ball.* **4** [*trans.*] flatten (something) by passing a roller over it or by passing it between rollers: *roll out the dough on a floured surface.* **5** [*intrans.*] (of a loud, deep sound such as that of thunder or drums) reverberate: *the first peals of thunder rolled across the sky.* ■ [*trans.*] pronounce (a consonant, typically an r) with a trill: *when he wanted to emphasize a point he rolled his rrrs.* ■ [*trans.*] utter (a word or words) with a reverberating or vibratory effect: *he rolled the word around his mouth.* ■ (of words) flow effortlessly or mellifluously: *the names of his colleagues rolled off his lips.* **6** *informal* rob (someone, typically when they are intoxicated or asleep): *if you don't get drunk, you don't get rolled.*

▸*phrasal v.* □ **roll something back** reverse the progress or reduce the power or importance of something: *the strategy to roll back communism.* □ **roll in** *informal* be received in large amounts: *the money was rolling in.* ■ arrive at a place in a casual way, typically in spite of being late: *Steve rolled in about lunchtime.* □ **roll something on** apply something with a roller: *roll on a decorative paint finish.* □ **roll something out** officially launch or unveil a new product or service: *the firm rolled out its newest generation of supercomputers.* □ **roll something over** *Finance* contrive or extend a particular financial arrangement: *this is not a good time for rolling over corporate debt.* □ **roll up** *informal* arrive in a vehicle: *we rolled up at the same time.* ■ *informal* roll a cigarette, esp. a cannabis cigarette. □ **roll something up** *Military* drive the flank of an enemy line back and round so that the line is shortened or surrounded.

▸*n.* **1** a cylinder formed by winding flexible material around a tube or by turning it over and over on itself without folding: *a roll of carpet.* ■ a cylindrical mass of something or a number of items arranged in a cylindrical shape: *a* **roll of** *mints.* ■ [with *adj.*] an item of food that is made by wrapping a flat sheet of pastry, cake, meat, or fish around a sweet or savory filling: *salmon and rice rolls.* ■ money, typically a quantity of banknotes rolled together. ■ a roller for flattening something, esp. one used to shape metal in a rolling mill. **2** a movement in which someone or something turns or is turned over on itself: *a roll of the dice | the ponies completed two rolls before getting back on their feet.* ■ a gymnastic exercise in which the body is rolled into a tucked position and turned in a forward or backward circle: *a forward roll.* ■ a swaying or oscillation of a ship, aircraft, or vehicle around an axis parallel to the direction of motion: *the car corners capably with a minimum of roll.* ■ undulation of the landscape: *hidden by the roll of the land was a refinery.* **3** a prolonged, deep, reverberating sound, typically made by thunder or a drum: *thunder exploded, roll after roll.* ■ *Music* one of the basic patterns (rudiments) of drumming, consisting of a sustained, rapid alternation of single or double strokes of each stick. **4** a very small loaf of bread, typically eaten with butter or a filling: *a sausage roll.* **5** an official list or register of names. ■ the total numbers on such a list: *a review of secondary schools to assess the effects of falling rolls.* ■ a document, typically an official record, in scroll form. ▷Middle English: from Old French *rolle* (noun), *roller* (verb), from Latin *rotulus* 'a roll,' variant of *rotula* 'little wheel,' diminutive of *rota.* —**roll·a·ble** *adj.*

▸*PHRASES* □ **a roll in the hay** (or **the sack**) *informal* an act of sexual intercourse. □ **be rolling** (**in money**) *informal* be very rich. □ **on a roll** *informal* experiencing a prolonged spell of success or good luck: *the organization is on a roll.* □ **rolled into one** (of characteristics drawn from different people or things) combined in one person or thing: *banks are several businesses rolled into one.* □ **rolling in the aisles** *informal* (of an audience) laughing uncontrollably. □ **roll of honor** a list of people whose deeds or achievements are honored. ■ a list of those who have died in battle. □ **roll of the dice** see DICE. □ **roll one's own** *informal* make one's own cigarettes from loose tobacco. □ **roll up one's sleeves** prepare to fight or work. □ **roll with the punches** (of a boxer) move one's body away from an opponent's blows so as to lessen the impact. ■ *figurative* adapt oneself to adverse circumstances.

Rol·land /rô'läN/, Romain (1866–1944), French novelist, playwright, and essayist. His interest in genius led to a number of biographies, and ultimately to *Jean-Christophe* (1904–12), a cycle of 10 novels about a German composer. Nobel Prize for Literature (1915).

roll·a·way /'rōlə,wā/ ▸*n.* a bed fitted with wheels or casters, allowing it to be moved easily: [as *adj.*] *a rollaway bed.*

roll·back /'rōl,bak/ ▸*n.* **1** a reduction or decrease: *a 5 percent rollback of personal income taxes.* ■ a reversion to a previous state or situation: *they opposed a rollback to Stalinism.* **2** *Computing* the process of restoring a database or program to a previously defined state, typically to recover from an error.

▸*v.* [*trans.*] *Computing* restore (a database) to a previously defined state.

roll bar ▸*n.* a metal bar running up the sides and across the top of a vehicle, esp. one used in motor sports, strengthening its frame and protecting the occupants should the vehicle overturn.

roll bar

roll cage ▸*n.* a framework of reinforcements protecting a car's passenger cabin in the event that it should roll onto its roof.

roll call ▸*n.* the process of calling out a list of names to establish who is present. ■ *figurative* a list or group of people or things that are notable in some specified way: *the roll call of nations that lack full religious rights.*

roll cast ▸*n. Fishing* a cast in which the angler does not throw the line backward.

rolled gold ▸*n.* gold in the form of a thin coating applied to a baser metal by rolling.

rolled oats ▸*plural n.* oats that have been husked and crushed.

roll·er /'rōlər/ ▸*n.* **1** a cylinder that rotates around a central axis and is used in various machines and devices to move, flatten, or spread something. ■ an absorbent revolving cylinder attached to a handle, used to apply paint. ■ a small cylinder on which hair is rolled in order to produce curls. ■ (also **roll·er band·age**) a long surgical bandage rolled up for convenient application. ■ a long swelling wave that appears to roll steadily toward the shore. ■ [as *adj.*] of, relating to, or involving roller skates: *roller hockey.* **2** a brightly colored crow-sized bird with predominantly blue plumage, having a characteristic tumbling display flight. [late 17th cent.: from German *Roller*, from *rollen* 'to roll.'] • Genera *Coracias* and *Eurystomus*, family Coraciidae: several species, esp. the widespread **European roller** (*C. garrulus*). **3** a bird of a breed of tumbler pigeon. **4** a bird of a breed of canary with a trilling song. **5** a broad surcingle, typically padded at the withers.

roll·er·ball /'rōlər,bôl/ ▸*n.* **1** a ballpoint pen using thinner ink than other ballpoints. **2** *Computing* an input device containing a ball that is moved with the fingers to control the cursor.

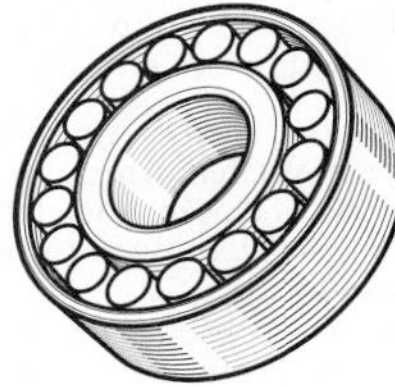

roller bearing

roll·er bear·ing ▸*n.* a bearing similar to a ball bearing but using small cylindrical rollers instead of balls. ■ a roller used in such a bearing.

Roll·er·blade /'rōlər,blād/ ▸*n. trademark* an in-line skate.

▸*v.* [*intrans.*] skate using Rollerblades: *the muscular actor loves to Rollerblade* | [as *n.*] (**rollerblading**) *rollerblading was made to order for runners whose knees are beginning to give out.* —**roll·er·blad·er** *n.*

roll·er coast·er ▸*n.* an amusement park attraction that consists of a light railroad track with many tight turns and steep slopes, on which people ride in small fast open cars. ■ *figurative* a thing that contains or goes through wild and unpredictable changes: *a terrific roller coaster of a book.*

▸*v.* (**roll·er-coast·er**) (also **roll·er-coast**) [*intrans.*] move, change, or occur in the dramatically changeable manner of a roller coaster: *the twentieth century fades behind us and history roller-coasters on.*

Roll·er Der·by (also **roll·er der·by**) ▸*n. trademark* a team skating competition on roller skates, held on a banked oval track.

roll·er rink ▸*n.* see RINK.

roll·er skate ▸*n.* each of a pair of boots, or metal frames attached to shoes, with four or more small wheels, for gliding across a hard surface.

▸*v.* [*intrans.*] (**roller-skate**) glide across a hard surface wearing roller skates. —**roll·er skat·er** *n.* —**roll·er-skat·ing** (also **roll·er skat·ing**) *n.*

roll·er tow·el ▸*n.* a long towel with the ends joined and hung on a roller, or one fed through a device from one roller holding the clean part to another holding the used part.

roll film ▸*n.* photographic film with protective lightproof backing paper wound onto a spool.

rol·lick /'rälik/ ▸*v.* [*intrans.*] *rare* act or behave in a jovial and exuberant fashion. ▷early 19th cent.: probably dialect, perhaps a blend of ROMP and FROLIC.

rol·lick·ing1 /'räliking/ ▸*adj.* [*attrib.*] exuberantly lively and amusing: *good rollicking fun.*

rol·lick·ing2 (also **rol·lock·ing**) ▸*n.* [in *sing.*] *Brit., informal* a severe reprimand.

roll·ing /'rōliNG/ ▸*adj.* steady and continuous: *a rolling program of reforms | a rolling news service.*

roll·ing hitch ▸*n.* a kind of hitch used to attach a rope to a spar or larger rope. It is a clove hitch with an extra turn in the standing part.

roll·ing mill ▸*n.* a factory or machine for rolling steel or other metal into sheets.

roll·ing pin ▸*n.* a cylinder rolled over pastry or dough to flatten or shape it.

roll·ing stock ▸*n.* locomotives, carriages, wagons, or other vehicles used on a railroad. ■ the road vehicles of a trucking company.

roll·ing stone ▸*n.* a person who is unwilling to settle for long in one place.

▸*PHRASE* □ **a rolling stone gathers no moss** *proverb* a person who does not settle in one place will not accumulate wealth, status, responsibilities, or commitments.

roll-in roll-out ▸*n. Computing* a method or the process of switching data or code between main and auxiliary memories in order to process several tasks simultaneously.

roll·mop /'rōl,mäp/ ▸*n.* a rolled uncooked pickled herring fillet. ▷early 20th cent.: from German *Rollmops.*

roll-neck ▸*n.* a high loosely turned-over collar: [as *adj.*] *a black roll-neck sweater.* ■ a garment with such a collar.

rol·lock·ing ▸*n.* variant spelling of ROLLICKING2.

roll-off ▸*n.* the smooth fall of response to zero at either end of the frequency range of a piece of audio equipment.

roll-on ▸*adj.* [*attrib.*] (of deodorant or cosmetic) applied by means of a rotating ball in the neck of the container.

▸*n.* a roll-on deodorant or cosmetic.

roll-on roll-off ▸*adj.* [*attrib.*] denoting a passenger ferry or other method of transportation in which vehicles are driven directly on at the start of the voyage or journey and driven off at the end of it.

roll-out /'rōl,out/ (also **roll-out**) ▸*n.* **1** the unveiling of a new aircraft or spacecraft. ■ the official launch of a new product or service. **2** *Aeronautics* the stage of an aircraft's landing during which it travels along the runway while losing speed. **3** *Football* a play in which the quarterback runs toward the sideline before attempting to pass or advance.

roll·o·ver /'rōl,ōvər/ ▸*n.* **1** *Finance* the extension or transfer of a debt or other financial arrangement. ■ (in a lottery) the accumulative carryover of prize money to the following drawing. **2** *informal* the overturning of a vehicle. **3** a facility on an electronic keyboard enabling one or several keystrokes to be registered correctly while another key is depressed.

Pronunciation Key ə *ago*; ər *over*; 'ə or ,ə *up*; 'ər or ,ər *fur*; a *hat*; ā *rate*; ä *car*; CH *chew*; e *let*; ē *see*; e(ə)r *air*; i *fit*; ī *by*; i(ə)r *ear*; NG *sing*; ō *go*; ô *for*; oi *boy*; o͝o *good*; o͞o *goo*; ou *out*; SH *she*; TH *thin*; T͟H *then*; (h)w *why*; ZH *vision*

Rolls /rōlz/, Charles Stewart (1877–1910), English automobile manufacturer and aviator. He and Henry Royce formed the company Rolls-Royce Ltd. in 1906. Rolls, the first Englishman to fly across the English Channel, was killed in an airplane crash.

roll·top desk /ˈrōl,täp/ ▸*n.* a writing desk with a flexible cover sliding in curved grooves.

roll-up ▸*n. Brit., informal* a hand-rolled cigarette. ■ an article of food rolled up and sometimes stuffed with a filling: *ham roll-ups.*
▸*adj.* [*attrib.*] denoting something that can be rolled up: *roll-up panels.* ■ *Computing* denoting a menu that will display only its title to save screen space.

Ro·lo·dex /ˈrōlə,deks/ ▸*n. trademark* a desktop card index used to record names, addresses, and telephone numbers, in the form of a rotating spindle or a small tray to which removable cards are attached. ■ *informal* a person's list of business contacts and friends.

ro·ly-po·ly /ˈrōlē ˈpōlē/ ▸*adj.* (of a person) having a round, plump appearance: *a roly-poly young boy.*
▸*n.* (also **ro·ly-po·ly pud·ding**) *Brit.* a sweet pastry dough covered with jam or fruit, formed into a roll, and boiled, steamed, or baked. ▷early 17th cent.: fanciful formation from the verb **ROLL**.

ROM /räm/ ▸*abbr. Computing* read-only memory.

Rom /rōm/ ▸*n.* (*pl.* **Ro·ma** /ˈrōmə/) a gypsy, esp. a man. ▷mid 19th cent.: abbreviation of **ROMANY**.

Rom. ▸*abbr. Bible* Romans.

rom. ▸*abbr.* roman (used as an instruction for a typesetter).

Ro·ma /ˈrōmə/ Italian name for **ROME**.

Ro·ma·ic /rōˈmāik/ *dated* ▸*adj. dated* of or relating to the vernacular language of modern Greece.
▸*n.* this language. ▷from modern Greek *romaiikos* 'Roman,' used specifically of the Eastern Roman Empire.

ro·maine /rōˈmān/ ▸*n.* a lettuce of a variety with crisp narrow leaves that form a tall head. ▷early 20th cent.: from French, feminine of *romain* 'Roman.'

ro·ma·ji /ˈrōməjē/ ▸*n.* a system of Romanized spelling used to transliterate Japanese. ▷early 20th cent.: from Japanese, from *rōma* 'Roman' + *ji* 'letter(s).'

Ro·man /ˈrōmən/ ▸*adj.* **1** of or relating to ancient Rome or its empire or people: *an old Roman road.* ■ of or relating to medieval or modern Rome: *the Roman and Pisan lines of popes.* **2** *dated* short for **ROMAN CATHOLIC**: *the Roman Church's instructions to its clergy.* **3** denoting the alphabet (or any of the letters in it) used for writing Latin, English, and most European languages, developed in ancient Rome. ■ (**roman**) (of type) of a plain upright kind used in ordinary print, esp. as distinguished from italic.
▸*n.* **1** a citizen or soldier of the ancient Roman Republic or Empire. ■ a citizen of modern Rome. **2** *dated* a Roman Catholic. **3** (**roman**) roman type. ▷Middle English: from Old French *Romain*, from Latin *Romanus*, from *Roma* 'Rome.'

ro·man à clef /rō,män ä ˈklā/ (also **ro·man-à-clef**) ▸*n.* (*pl.* **ro·mans à clef** *pronunc.* same) a novel in which real people or events appear with invented names. ▷French, literally 'novel with a key.'

Ro·man baths ▸*plural n.* a building containing a complex of rooms designed for bathing, relaxing, and socializing, as used in ancient Rome.

Ro·man can·dle ▸*n.* a firework giving off a series of flaming colored balls and sparks.

Ro·man Cath·o·lic ▸*adj.* of or relating to the Roman Catholic Church: *a Roman Catholic bishop.*
▸*n.* a member of this church. ▷late 16th cent.: translation of Latin *(Ecclesia) Romana Catholica (et Apostolica)* 'Roman Catholic (and Apostolic Church).' It was apparently first used as a conciliatory term in place of the earlier *Roman, Romanist,* or *Romish,* considered derogatory. **—Ro·man Ca·thol·i·cism** *n.*

Ro·man Cath·o·lic Church the part of the Christian Church that acknowledges the pope as its head, esp. as it has developed since the Reformation.

It is the largest Christian church, dominant particularly in South America and southern Europe. Roman Catholicism differs from Protestantism in the importance it grants to tradition, ritual, and the authority of the pope as successor to the Apostle St. Peter, and esp. in its doctrines of papal infallibility (formally defined in 1870) and of the Eucharist (transubstantiation), its celibate male priesthood, its emphasis on confession, and the veneration of the Virgin Mary and other saints. Much modern Roman Catholic thought and practice arises from scholastic theology and from the response to the Reformation made by the Council of Trent (1545–63). It became less rigid after the Second Vatican Council (1962–65), but its continuing opposition to divorce, abortion, and artificial contraception remains controversial.

Ro·mance /rōˈmans; ˈrō,mans/ ▸*n.* the group of Indo-European languages descended from Latin, principally French, Spanish, Portuguese, Italian, Catalan, Occitan, and Romanian.
▸*adj.* of, relating to, or denoting this group of languages: *the Romance languages.* ▷Middle English (originally denoting the vernacular language of France as opposed to Latin): from Old French *romanz*, based on Latin *Romanicus* 'Roman.'

ro·mance /rōˈmans; ˈrō,mans/ ▸*n.* **1** a feeling of excitement and mystery associated with love: *in search of romance.* ■ love, esp. when sentimental or idealized: *he asked her for a date and romance blossomed.* ■ an exciting, enjoyable love affair, esp. one that is not serious or long-lasting: *a summer romance.* ■ a book or movie dealing with love in a sentimental or idealized way: *light historical romances.* ■ a genre of fiction dealing with love in such a way: *wartime passion from the master of romance.* **2** a quality or feeling of mystery, excitement, and remoteness from everyday life: *the beauty and romance of the night.* ■ wild exaggeration; picturesque falsehood: *she slammed the claims as "pure romance, complete fiction."* ■ a work of fiction dealing with events remote from real life. **3** a medieval tale dealing with a hero of chivalry, of the kind common in the Romance languages: *the Arthurian romances.* ■ the literary genre of such works. **4** *Music* a short informal piece.
▸*v.* [*trans.*] **1** court; woo: *the wealthy estate owner romanced her.* ■ *informal* seek the attention or patronage of (someone), esp. by use of flattery: *he is being romanced by the big boys in New York.* ■ [*intrans.*] engage in a love affair: *we start romancing.* **2** another term for **ROMANTICIZE**: *to a certain degree I am romancing the past.* ▷Middle English: from **ROMANCE**, originally denoting a composition in the vernacular as opposed to works in Latin. Early use denoted vernacular verse on the theme of chivalry; the sense 'genre centered on romantic love' dates from the mid 17th cent.

ro·manc·er /rōˈmansər; ˈrō,mansər/ ▸*n.* **1** a person prone to wild exaggeration or falsehood. **2** a writer of medieval romances.

Ro·man Em·pire the empire established by Augustus in 27 BC and divided by Theodosius in AD 395 into the Western or Latin and Eastern or Greek Empire.

Rome was sacked by the Visigoths under Alaric in 410, and the last emperor of the West, Romulus Augustulus, was deposed in 476. The Eastern Empire, whose capital was Constantinople, lasted until 1453 (see **BYZANTINE EMPIRE**).

Ro·man·esque /,rōməˈnesk/ ▸*adj.* of or relating to a style of architecture that prevailed in Europe *c.*900–1200, although sometimes dated back to the end of the Roman Empire (5th century).
▸*n.* Romanesque architecture. ▷French, from *roman* 'romance.'

Romanesque architecture is characterized by round arches and massive vaulting, and by heavy piers, columns, and walls with small windows. Although disseminated throughout western Europe, the style reached its fullest development in central and northern France; the equivalent style in England is usually called Norman.

ro·man-fleuve /rō,män ˈflœv/ ▸*n.* (*pl.* **ro·mans-fleuves** *pronunc.* same) a novel featuring the leisurely description of the lives of closely related people. ■ a sequence of related, self-contained novels. ▷French, literally 'river novel.'

Ro·man hol·i·day ▸*n. poetic/literary* an occasion on which enjoyment or profit is derived from others' suffering or discomfort. ▷early 19th cent.: from Byron's *Childe Harold*, originally with reference to a holiday given for a gladiatorial combat.

Ro·ma·ni·a /rōˈmānēə; rŏŏ-/ (also **Ru·ma·ni·a**) a country in southeastern Europe, on the Black Sea; pop. 22,355,000; capital, Bucharest; language, Romanian (official).

In the Middle Ages, the area consisted of the principalities of Wallachia and Moldavia, which were swallowed up by the Ottoman Empire in the 15th–16th centuries. The two principalities gained independence in 1878. After World War II, during which it had supported Germany, Romania became a communist state under Soviet domination. After 1974, the country pursued an increasingly independent course under the virtual dictatorship of Nicolae Ceaușescu. His regime collapsed in violent popular unrest in 1989, and a new democratic constitution was introduced. Romania joined NATO in 2004.

Ro·ma·ni·an /rōˈmānēən; rŏŏ-/ (also **Ru·ma·ni·an**) ▸*adj.* of or relating to Romania or its people or language.
▸*n.* **1** a native or national of Romania, or a person of Romanian descent. **2** the language of Romania, a Romance language influenced by the neighboring Slavic languages, also spoken by the majority of the population of Moldova.

Ro·man·ic /rōˈmanik/ ▸*n.* & *adj.* less common term for **ROMANCE**. ▷early 18th cent.: from Latin *Romanicus*, from *Romanus* 'Roman.'

Ro·man·ism /ˈrōmə,nizəm/ ▸*n. dated* Roman Catholicism.

Ro·man·ist /ˈrōmənist/ ▸*n.* **1** an expert in or student of Roman antiquities or law, or of the Romance languages. **2** *chiefly derogatory* a member or supporter of the Roman Catholic Church.
▸*adj. usu. derogatory* belonging or adhering to the Roman Catholic Church.

ro·man·ize /ˈrōmə,nīz/ (also **Ro·man·ize**) ▸*v.* [*trans.*] **1** *historical* bring (something, esp. a region or people) under Roman influence or authority: *though not himself a Roman, he was fully Romanized, spoke Latin, and lived in a Roman-style villa.* **2** make Roman Catholic in character: *he has Romanized the services of his church.* **3** put (text) into the Roman alphabet or into roman type: *Atatürk's decision to romanize the written language.* **—ro·man·i·za·tion** /,rōmənəˈzāshən/ *n.*

Ro·man law ▸*n.* the law code of the ancient Romans, which forms the basis of civil law in many countries today.

Ro·man nose ▸*n.* a nose with a high bridge.

Ro·man num·er·al ▸*n.* any of the letters representing numbers in the Roman numerical system: I = 1, V = 5, X = 10, L = 50, C = 100, D = 500, M = 1,000. In this system, a letter placed after another of greater value adds (thus XVI or xvi is 16), whereas a letter placed before another of greater value subtracts (thus XC or xc is 90).

Ro·ma·no /rəˈmänō/ ▸*n.* a strong-tasting hard cheese, originally made in Italy. ▷Italian, literally 'Roman.'

Romano- ▸*comb. form* Roman; Roman and . . . : *Romano-Celtic.*

Ro·ma·nov /rōˈmän,ôf; ˈrōmə,nôf/ a dynasty that ruled in Russia from the accession of Michael Romanov (1596–1645) in 1613 until the overthrow of the last tsar, Nicholas II, in 1917.

Ro·man Re·pub·lic the ancient Roman state from the expulsion of the Etruscan monarchs in 509 BC (see **TARQUINIUS**) until the assumption of power by Augustus (Octavian) in 27 BC.

Ro·mans /ˈrōmənz/ a book of the New Testament, an epistle of St. Paul to the Christian Church at Rome.

Ro·mansh /rōˈmänch; -ˈmanch/ ▸*n.* the Rhaeto-Romanic language that is spoken in the Swiss canton of Grisons and is an official language of Switzerland.
▸*adj.* of or relating to this language. ▷from Romansh *Roman(t)sch*, from medieval Latin *romanice* 'in the Romanic manner.'

ro·man·tic /rōˈmantik; rə-/ ▸*adj.* **1** inclined toward or suggestive of the feeling of excitement and mystery associated with love: *a romantic candlelit dinner.* ■ relating to love, esp. in a sentimental or idealized way: *a romantic comedy.* See note at **SENTIMENTAL**. **2**. of, characterized by, or suggestive of an idealized view of reality: *a romantic attitude toward the past | some romantic dream of country peace.* **3** (usu. **Romantic**) of,

relating to, or denoting the artistic and literary movement of Romanticism: *the Romantic tradition.*
▸*n.* a person with romantic beliefs or attitudes: *I am an incurable romantic.* ■ (usu. **Romantic**) a writer or artist of the Romantic movement. ▷mid 17th cent. (referring to the characteristics of romance in a narrative): from archaic *romaunt* 'tale of chivalry,' from an Old French variant of *romanz* (see **ROMANCE**). **—ro·man·ti·cal·ly** /-ik(ə)lē/ *adv.*

ro·man·ti·cism /rō'mantə,sizəm; rə-/ ▸*n.* **1** (often **Romanticism**) a movement in the arts and literature that originated in the late 18th century, emphasizing inspiration, subjectivity, and the primacy of the individual.

Romanticism was a reaction against the order and restraint of classicism and neoclassicism, and a rejection of the rationalism that characterized the Enlightenment. In music, the period embraces much of the 19th century, with composers including Schubert, Schumann, Liszt, and Wagner. Poets exemplifying the movement include Wordsworth, Coleridge, Byron, Shelley, and Keats; among romantic painters are such stylistically diverse artists as William Blake, J. M. W. Turner, Delacroix, and Goya.

2 the state or quality of being romantic: *a quality of romanticism about women that leads to the creation of a pipe-dream fantasy.*

ro·man·ti·cist /rō'mantəsist; rə-/ ▸*n.* a writer, artist, or musician of the Romantic movement. ■ a person who subscribes to the artistic movement or ideas of Romanticism.

ro·man·ti·cize /rō'mantə,sīz; rə-/ ▸*v.* [*trans.*] deal with or describe in an idealized or unrealistic fashion; make (something) seem better or more appealing than it really is: *the tendency to romanticize nonindustrial societies* | [*intrans.*] *she was romanticizing about the past.* **—ro·man·ti·ci·za·tion** /rō,mantəsə'zāsHən; rə-/ *n.*

Rom·a·ny /'rämənē; 'rō-/ (also **Rom·a·ni**) ▸*n.* (*pl.* **-nies**) **1** the Indic language of the gypsies, spoken in many dialects. **2** a gypsy.
▸*adj.* of or relating to gypsies or their language. ▷early 19th cent.: from Romany *Romani*, feminine and plural of the adjective *Romano*, from *Rom* 'man, husband' (see **ROM**).

Rom·berg /'räm,bərg/, Sigmund (1887–1951), U.S. composer, born in Hungary. He wrote a succession of popular operettas, including *The Student Prince* (1924), *The Desert Song* (1926), and *New Moon* (1928).

rom·com /'räm,käm/ ▸*n. informal* (in movies or television) a romantic comedy. ▷blend.

Rome /rōm/ **1** the capital of Italy, situated in the west central part of the country, on the Tiber River, about 16 miles (25 km) inland; pop. 2,791,000. According to tradition, the ancient city was founded by Romulus (after whom it is named) in 753 BC on the Palatine Hill; as it grew it spread to the other six hills of Rome (Aventine, Caelian, Capitoline, Esquiline, and Quirinal). Rome was made capital of a unified Italy in 1871. Italian name **ROMA**. ■ used allusively to refer to the Roman Catholic Church. **2** an industrial city in northwestern Georgia, on the Coosa River; pop. 34,980. **3** an industrial city in central New York, on the Mohawk River; pop. 44,350.
▸*PHRASES* □ **all roads lead to Rome** *proverb* there are many different ways of reaching the same goal or conclusion. □ **Rome was not built in a day** *proverb* a complex task is bound to take a long time and should not be rushed. □ **when in Rome (do as the Romans do)** *proverb* when abroad or in an unfamiliar environment you should adopt the customs or behavior of those around you.

Ro·me·o /'rōmē,ō/ ▸*n.* **1** (*pl.* **-os**) an attractive, passionate male seducer or lover. **2** a code word representing the letter R, used in radio communication. ▷from the name of the hero of Shakespeare's romantic tragedy *Romeo and Juliet.*

Rom·ish /'rōmisH/ ▸*adj. chiefly derogatory* Roman Catholic: *Romish ideas.*

Rom·mel /'räməl/, Erwin (1891–1944), German field marshal; known as **the Desert Fox**. As commander of the Afrika Korps, he captured Tobruk in 1942, but he was defeated by Montgomery at El Alamein later that year. Implicated in the officers' conspiracy against Hitler in 1944, he committed suicide.

Rom·ney[1] /'rämnē/, George (1734–1802), English portrait painter. From the early 1780s, he produced more than 50 portraits of Lady Hamilton in historical costumes.

Rom·ney[2], George (Wilcken) (1907–95), U.S. businessman and politician; born in Mexico. He was president of American Motors 1954–62, governor of Michigan 1963–69, and U.S. secretary of Housing and Urban Development 1969–72. His son **(Willard) Mitt Romney** (1947–), has been the Republican governor of Massachusetts since 2003.

Rom·ney Marsh ▸*n.* a sheep of a stocky breed with long wool, originally from England and now common in New Zealand.

romp /rämp; rômp/ ▸*v.* [*intrans.*] (esp. of a child or animal) play roughly and energetically: *the noisy pack of children romped around the garden.* ■ [with *adverbial*] *informal* proceed without effort to achieve something: *the Vikings romped to victory.* ■ *informal* engage in sexual activity, esp. illicitly: *a colleague stumbled on the couple romping in an office.*
▸*n.* a spell of rough, energetic play: *a romp in the snow.* ■ a lighthearted movie or other work: *an enjoyably gross sci-fi romp.* ■ *informal* an easy victory: *the 45–28 romp over the Owls yesterday at Alumni Stadium.* ■ *informal* a spell of sexual activity, esp. an illicit one: *three-in-a-bed sex romps.* ▷early 18th cent.: perhaps an alteration of **RAMP**.

romp·er /'rämpər; 'rôm-/ ▸*n.* **1** (also **romp·er suit** or **romp·ers**) a young child's one-piece outer garment. ■ a similar item of clothing for adults, typically worn as overalls or as sports clothing. **2** a person who romps.

Rom·u·lus /'rämyələs/ *Roman Mythology* the traditional founder of Rome, one of the twin sons of Mars by the Vestal Virgin Rhea Silvia. He and his brother Remus were abandoned at birth in a basket on the Tiber River but were found and suckled by a she-wolf and later brought up by a shepherd family.

Ron·ces·valles, Bat·tle of /,rônsəs'vä(l),yäs/ a battle that took place in 778 at a mountain pass in the Pyrenees, near the village of Roncesvalles in northern Spain. The rearguard of Charlemagne's army was attacked by the Basques and massacred; one of the nobles, Roland, was killed, an event celebrated in the *Chanson de Roland* (in which the attackers are wrongly identified as the Moors). French name **RONCEVAUX**.

ron·da·vel /'rändə,vel/ ▸*n. S. African* a traditional circular African dwelling with a conical thatched roof. ■ a building based on the design of such a dwelling, used as a guest room, storeroom, or vacation cottage. ▷from Afrikaans *rondawel.*

rond de jambe /,rôN də 'zHäNb/ ▸*n.* (*pl.* **ronds de jambe** *pronunc.* same) *Ballet* a circular movement of the leg that can be performed on the ground or during a jump. ▷French.

ronde /ränd/ ▸*n.* a dance in which the dancers move in a circle. ▷1930s: French, feminine of *rond* 'round.'

ron·deau /'rändō; rän'dō/ ▸*n.* (*pl.* **-deaux** /-dōz; 'dōz/) a thirteen-line poem, divided into three stanzas of 5, 3, and 5 lines, with only two rhymes throughout and with the opening words of the first line used as a refrain at the end of the second and third stanzas. ▷early 16th cent.: French, later form of *rondel* (see **RONDEL**).

ron·del /'rändəl; rän'del/ ▸*n.* **1** a rondeau, esp. one of three stanzas of thirteen or fourteen lines, with the first two lines of the opening quatrain recurring at the end of the second quatrain and the concluding sestet. **2** a circular object: *at the point where these paths join there is a rondel with a fountain.* ▷Middle English: from Old French, from *rond* 'round'; compare with **ROUNDEL**.

ron·do /'rändō; rän'dō/ ▸*n.* (*pl.* **-dos**) a musical form with a recurring leading theme, often found in the final movement of a sonata or concerto. ▷late 18th cent.: Italian, from French *rondeau* (see **RONDEAU**).

Rong·e·lap /'rängə,lap/ an atoll in the western Pacific, in the northern Marshall Islands at the northwestern end of the Ratak group, east of Bikini. It was evacuated in the 1980s because of contamination from 1950s nuclear tests at Eniwetok.

ro·nin /'rōnən/ ▸*n.* (*pl.* same or **-nins**) *historical* (in feudal Japan) a wandering samurai who had no lord or master. ▷Japanese.

Rönt·gen /'rentgən; 'rencHən/, Wilhelm Conrad (1845–1923), German physicist; the discoverer of X-rays. Nobel Prize for Physics (1901).

rönt·gen, etc. ▸*n.* variant spelling of **ROENTGEN**, etc.

roo /rōō/ ▸*n. Austral., informal* a kangaroo. ▷early 20th cent.: shortened form.

rood /rōōd/ ▸*n.* **1** a crucifix, esp. one positioned above the rood screen of a church or on a beam over the entrance to the chancel. **2** *chiefly Brit., historical* a measure of land area equal to a quarter of an acre. ▷Old English *rōd*; related to Dutch *roede* and German *Rute* 'rod.'

rood screen ▸*n.* a screen, typically of richly carved wood or stone, separating the nave from the chancel of a church. Rood screens are found throughout western Europe and date chiefly from the 14th–16th centuries.

roof /rōōf; rŏŏf/ ▸*n.* (*pl.* **roofs**) the structure forming the upper covering of a building or vehicle. ■ the top inner surface of a covered area or space; the ceiling: *the roof of the cave fell in.* ■ used to signify a house or other building, esp. in the context of hospitality or shelter: *helping those without **a roof over their heads** | they slept **under the same roof**.* ■ (**roof of the mouth**) the palate.
▸*v.* [*trans.*] (usu. **be roofed**) cover with a roof: *the yard had been roughly **roofed over** with corrugated iron.* ■ function as the roof of: *fan vaults roof these magnificent buildings.* ▷Old English *hrōf*, of Germanic origin; related to Old Norse *hróf* 'boat shed,' Dutch *roef* 'deckhouse.' English alone has the general sense 'covering of a house'; other Germanic languages use forms related to *thatch.* **—roof·less** *adj.*
▸*PHRASES* □ **go through the roof** *informal* **1** (of prices or figures) reach extreme or unexpected heights. **2** another way of saying **HIT THE ROOF**. □ **hit the roof** *informal* suddenly become very angry. □ **raise the roof** see **RAISE**. □ **the roof of the world** a nickname given to the Himalayas.

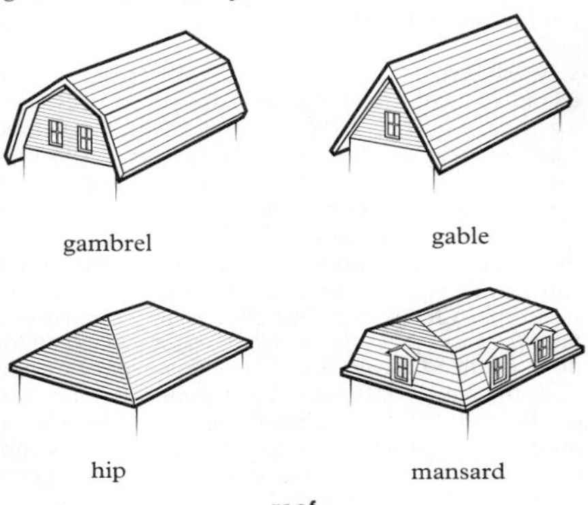

roof

roof·er /'rōōfər; 'rŏŏf-/ ▸*n.* a person who constructs or repairs roofs.

roof gar·den ▸*n.* a garden on the flat roof of a building.

roof·ing /'rōōfiNG; 'rŏŏf-/ ▸*n.* material for constructing a building's roof: *a house with corrugated tin roofing.* ■ the process of constructing a roof or roofs: *jobs such as roofing.*

roof light ▸*n.* a window panel built into a roof to admit light. ■ a small interior light on the ceiling of a motor vehicle. ■ a flashing warning light on the top of a police car or other emergency vehicle.

roof·line /'rōōf,līn; 'rŏŏf-/ ▸*n.* the design or proportions of the roof of a building or vehicle.

roof prism ▸*n.* a reflecting prism in which the reflecting surface is in two parts that are angled like the two sides of a pitched roof. Compare with **PORRO PRISM**. ■ (**roof prisms**) (also **roof-prism bi·noc·u·lars**) a pair of binoculars using two such prisms, resulting in an instrument with parallel sides and objective lenses that are the same distance apart as the eyepieces.

roof rack ▸*n.* a framework for carrying luggage or equipment on the roof of a vehicle.

roof rat ▸*n.* another term for **BLACK RAT**.

roof·top /'rōōf,täp; 'rŏŏf-/ ▸*n.* the outer surface of a building's roof.
▸*PHRASE* □ **shout something from the rooftops** see **SHOUT**.

roof·tree /'rōōf,trē; 'rŏŏf-/ ▸*n.* the ridgepole of a roof.

rook[1] /rŏŏk/ ▸*n.* a gregarious Eurasian crow with black plumage and a bare face, nesting in colonies in treetops. • *Corvus frugilegus*, family Corvidae.
▸*v.* [*trans.*] *informal* take money from (someone) by cheating, defrauding, or overcharging them. ▷Old English *hrōc*, probably imitative and of Germanic origin; related to Dutch *roek.*

rook[2] ▸*n.* a chess piece, typically with its top in the shape of a battlement, that can move in any direction along a rank or file on which it stands. Each player starts the game with two rooks at opposite ends of the first rank. See also CASTLE. ▷Middle English: from Old French *rock*, based on Arabic *rukk* (of which the sense remains uncertain).

rook·er·y /ˈro͝okərē/ ▸*n.* (*pl.* **-er·ies**) a breeding colony of rooks, typically seen as a collection of nests high in a clump of trees. ■ a breeding colony of seabirds (esp. penguins), seals, or turtles. ■ *figurative* a dense collection of housing, esp. in a slum area.

rook·ie /ˈro͝okē/ ▸*n. informal* a new recruit, esp. in the army or police: [as *adj.*] *a rookie cop.* ■ a member of an athletic team in his or her first full season in that sport. ▷late 19th cent.: perhaps an alteration of RECRUIT, influenced by ROOK[1].

room /ro͞om; ro͝om/ ▸*n.* **1** space that can be occupied or where something can be done, esp. viewed in terms of whether there is enough: *there's only room for a single bed in there* | [with *infinitive*] *she was trapped without room to move.* ■ *figurative* opportunity or scope for something to happen or be done, esp. without causing trouble or damage: *there is plenty of room for disagreement in this controversial area* | *there is* **room for improvement**. **2** a part or division of a building enclosed by walls, floor, and ceiling: *he wandered from room to room.* ■ (**rooms**) a set of rooms, typically rented, in which a person, couple, or family live: *my rooms at Mrs. Jenks's house.* ■ [in *sing.*] the people present in a room: *the whole room burst into an uproar of approval.*

▸*v.* [*intrans.*] share a room or house or flat, esp. a rented one at a college or similar institution: *I was rooming with my cousin.* ■ [*trans.*] provide with a shared room or lodging: *they roomed us together.* ▷Old English *rūm*, of Germanic origin; related to Dutch *ruim*, German *Raum*. **—roomed** *adj.* [in *combination*] *a four-roomed house.* **—room·ful** /-ˌfo͝ol/ *n.* (*pl.* **-fuls**).

▸PHRASES □ **make room** move aside or move something aside to allow someone to enter or pass or to clear space for something: *the secretary entered with the coffee tray and made room for it on the desk.* □ **no** (or **not**) **room to swing a cat** *humorous* used in reference to a very confined space. [*cat* in the sense 'cat-o'-nine-tails.'] □ **smoke-filled room** used to refer to political bargaining or decision-making that is conducted privately by a small group of influential people rather than more openly or democratically.

room and board ▸*n.* lodging and food, typically forming part of someone's wages or included in some other agreement: *out-of-state tuition and room and board rates.*

room·er /ˈro͞omər; ˈro͝om-/ ▸*n.* a renter of a room in another person's house.

room·ette /ro͞oˈmet; ro͝omˈet/ ▸*n.* a private single compartment in a railroad sleeping car.

room·ie /ˈro͞omē; ˈro͝omē/ ▸*n. informal* a roommate.

room·ing house ▸*n.* a private house in which rooms are rented for living or staying temporarily.

room·mate /ˈro͞omˌmāt; ˈro͝om-/ ▸*n.* a person occupying the same room as another. ■ a person occupying the same apartment or house as another.

room serv·ice ▸*n.* service provided in a hotel allowing guests to order food and drink to be brought to their rooms.

room tem·per·a·ture ▸*n.* a comfortable ambient temperature, generally taken as about 70°F.

room·y /ˈro͞omē; ˈro͝omē/ ▸*adj.* (**room·i·er**, **room·i·est**) (esp. of accommodations) having plenty of room; spacious. **—room·i·ly** /-məlē/ *adv.* **—room·i·ness** *n.*

Roo·ney /ˈro͞onē/, Mickey (1920–), U.S. actor; born *Joseph Yule, Jr.* He first appeared in *Not to Be Trusted* (1926) before playing Andy Hardy in 16 comedy drama movies over a period of 20 years. He received Academy Award nominations for his roles in *Babes in Arms* (1939) and *The Human Comedy* (1943).

Roo·se·velt[1] /ˈrōzəˌvelt; -vəlt/, (Anna) Eleanor (1884–1962), U.S. humanitarian and diplomat. She was the niece of Theodore Roosevelt and married Franklin D. Roosevelt in 1905. Involved in a wide range of liberal causes, she served as chair of the UN Commission on Human Rights, where she helped to draft the Declaration of Human Rights in 1948.

Roo·se·velt[2], Franklin Delano (1882–1945), 32nd president of the U.S. 1933–45; known as **FDR**. His New Deal programs of the 1930s helped to lift the U.S. out of the Great Depression, and he played an important part in Allied policy during World War II. A Democrat and a victim of polio, he was the only president to be elected to a third (and then a fourth) term in office.

Franklin D. Roosevelt

Roo·se·velt[3], Theodore (1858–1919), 26th president of the U.S. 1901–09; nicknamed **Teddy Roosevelt**. He was responsible for initiating many antitrust laws, and he successfully engineered the U.S. bid to build the Panama Canal (1904–14). He also negotiated the end of the Russo-Japanese War in 1905. The teddy bear is named for him, with reference to his bear-hunting. Nobel Peace Prize (1906).

Theodore Roosevelt

Roo·se·velt Is·land /ˈrōzəˌvelt/ a residential island in the East River in New York City, between Manhattan and Queens.

roost /ro͞ost/ ▸*n.* a place where birds regularly settle or congregate to rest at night, or where bats congregate to rest in the day.

▸*v.* [*intrans.*] (of a bird or bat) settle or congregate for rest or sleep: *migrating martins and swallows were settling to roost.* ▷Old English *hrōst*, related to Dutch *roest*; of unknown ultimate origin.

▸PHRASES □ **come home to roost** (of a scheme, etc.) recoil unfavorably upon the originator: *ensuring that the liability does not come home to roost.* □ **rule the roost** see RULE.

rooster

roost·er /ˈro͞ostər; ˈro͝ostər/ ▸*n.* a male domestic fowl; a cock.

roost·er tail ▸*n. informal* the spray of water thrown up behind a speedboat or surfboard.

Eleanor Roosevelt

root[1] /ro͞ot; ro͝ot/ ▸*n.* **1** the part of a plant that attaches it to the ground or to a support, typically underground, conveying water and nourishment to the rest of the plant via numerous branches and fibers: *cacti have deep and spreading roots* | *a tree root.* ■ the persistent underground part of a plant, esp. when fleshy and enlarged and used as a vegetable, e.g., a turnip or carrot. ■ any plant grown for such a root. ■ the embedded part of a bodily organ or structure such as a hair, tooth, or nail: *her hair was fairer at the roots.* ■ the part of a thing attaching it to a greater or more fundamental whole; the end or base: *a little lever near the root of the barrel.* **2** the basic cause, source, or origin of something: *love of money is the root of all evil* | *jealousy was at the root of it* | [as *adj.*] *the root cause of the problem.* See note at ORIGIN. ■ the essential substance or nature of something: *matters at the heart and root of existence.* ■ (**roots**) family, ethnic, or cultural origins, esp. as the reasons for one's long-standing emotional attachment to a place or community: *it's always nice to return to my roots.* ■ [as *adj.*] (**roots**) denoting or relating to something, esp. music, from a particular ethnic or cultural origin, esp. a non-Western one: *roots music.* ■ (in biblical use) a scion; a descendant: *the root of David.* ■ *Linguistics* a morpheme, not necessarily surviving as a word in itself, from which words have been made by the addition of prefixes or suffixes or by other modification: *many European words stem from this linguistic root* | [as *adj.*] *the root form of the word.* ■ *Music* the fundamental note of a chord. **3** *Mathematics* a number or quantity that when multiplied by itself, typically a specified number of times, gives a specified number or quantity: *find the cube root of the result.* ■ short for SQUARE ROOT. ■ a value of an unknown quantity satisfying a given equation: *the roots of the equation differ by an integer.*

▸*v.* [*trans.*] **1** cause (a plant or cutting) to grow roots: *root your own cuttings from stock plants.* ■ [*intrans.*] (of a plant or cutting) establish roots: *large trees had rooted in the canal bank.* **2** (usu. **be rooted**) establish deeply and firmly: *vegetarianism is* **rooted in** *Indian culture.* ■ (**be rooted in**) have as an origin or cause: *the Latin* dubitare *is rooted in an Indo-European word.* ■ [*trans.*] [often as *adj.*] (**rooted**) cause (someone) to stand immobile through fear or amazement: *she found herself* **rooted to the spot** *in disbelief.*

▸*phrasal v.* □ **root something out** (also **root something up**) dig or pull up a plant by the roots. ■ find and get rid of someone or something regarded as pernicious or dangerous: *a campaign to root out corruption.* ▷late Old English *rōt*, from Old Norse *rót*; related to Latin *radix*, also to WORT. **—root·ed·ness** *n.* **—root·let** /-lət/ *n.* **—root·like** /-ˌlīk/ *adj.* **—root·y** *adj.*

▸PHRASES □ **at root** basically; fundamentally: *it is a moral question at root.* □ **put down roots** (of a plant) begin to draw nourishment from the soil through its roots. ■ (of a person) begin to have a settled life in a particular place. □ **root and branch** used to express the thorough or radical nature of a process or operation: *root and branch reform of personal taxation.* □ **strike at the root** (or **roots**) **of** affect in a vital area with potentially destructive results: *the proposals struck at the roots of community life.* □ **take root** (of a plant) begin to grow and draw nourishment from the soil through its roots. ■ become fixed or established: *the idea had taken root in my mind.*

root[2] ▸*v.* [*intrans.*] (of an animal) turn up the ground with its snout in search of food: *stray dogs rooting around for bones and scraps.* ■ search unsystematically through an untidy mass or area; rummage: *she was rooting through a pile of papers.* ■ [*trans.*] (**root something out**) find or extract something by rummaging: *he managed to root out the cleaning kit.*

▸*phrasal v.* □ **root for** *informal* support or hope for the success of (a person or group entering a contest or undertaking a challenge): *the whole of this club is rooting for him.* □ **root someone on** *informal* cheer or spur someone on: *his mother rooted him on enthusiastically from ringside.*

▸*n.* [in *sing.*] an act of rooting: *I have a root through the open drawers.* ▷Old English *wrōtan*, of Germanic origin; related to Old English *wrōt* 'snout,' German *Rüssel* 'snout,' and perhaps ultimately to Latin *rodere* 'gnaw.'

root·ball /ˈro͞otˌbôl; ˈro͝ot-/ (also **root ball**) ▸*n.* the mass formed by the roots of a plant and the soil surrounding them.

root beer ▸*n.* an effervescent drink made from an extract of the roots and bark of certain plants.

root ca·nal ▸*n.* the pulp-filled cavity in the root of a tooth. ■ a procedure to replace infected pulp in a root canal with an inert material.

root cel·lar ▸*n.* a domestic cellar used for storing root vegetables.

root crop ▸*n.* a crop that is a root vegetable or other root, e.g., sugar beet.

root di·rec·to·ry ▸*n. Computing* the directory at the highest level of a hierarchy.

root·er /ˈrōōtər; ˈrŏŏ-/ ▸*n. informal* a supporter or fan of a sports team or player.

root fly ▸*n.* a dark slender fly whose larvae may cause serious damage to the roots of crops. • Family Anthomyiidae: many genera and species, including the **cabbage root fly**.

root hair ▸*n. Botany* each of a large number of elongated microscopic outgrowths from the outer layer of cells in a root, absorbing moisture and nutrients from the soil.

root·in'-toot·in' /ˈrōōtn ˈtōōtn/ ▸*adj. informal* brashly or boisterously enthusiastic: *their rootin'-tootin' summer adventures.* ▷late 19th cent.: reduplication of *rooting* in the sense 'inquisitive,' an early dialect sense of the compound.

root-knot ▸*n.* a disease of cultivated flowers and vegetables caused by eelworm infestation, resulting in galls on the roots. • The eelworms belong to the genus *Meloidogyne*, class Nematoda.

roo·tle /ˈrōōtl; ˈrŏŏtl/ ▸*v. Brit.* informal term for **ROOT**[2]. ▷early 19th cent.: frequentative of **ROOT**[2].

root·less /ˈrōōtlis; ˈrŏŏt-/ ▸*adj.* **1** having no settled home or social or family ties: *a rootless nomad.* **2** (of a plant) not having roots: *a rootless flowering plant.* **—root·less·ness** *n.*

root mean square ▸*n. Mathematics* the square root of the arithmetic mean of the squares of a set of values, used as a measure of the typical magnitude of a set of numbers, regardless of their sign.

root run ▸*n.* the space over which the roots of a plant extend.

root sign ▸*n. Mathematics* another term for **RADICAL SIGN**.

roots mu·sic ▸*n.* music springing from and identified with a particular culture, typically that of the West Indies.

root·stock /ˈrōōtˌstäk; ˈrŏŏt-/ ▸*n.* a rhizome. ■ a plant onto which another variety is grafted. ■ a primary form or source from which offshoots have arisen: *the rootstock of all post-Triassic ammonites.*

root·sy /ˈrōōtsē; ˈrŏŏt-/ ▸*adj. informal* (of music) uncommercialized and full-blooded, esp. showing traditional or ethnic origins.

root veg·e·ta·ble ▸*n.* the fleshy enlarged root of a plant used as a vegetable, e.g., a carrot, rutabaga, or beet.

rope /rōp/ ▸*n.* **1** a length of strong cord made by twisting together strands of natural fibers such as hemp or artificial fibers such as polypropylene. ■ a lasso. ■ (**the rope**) used in reference to execution by hanging: *executions by the rope continued well into the twentieth century.* ■ (**the ropes**) the ropes enclosing a boxing or wrestling ring. **2** a quantity of roughly spherical objects such as onions or pearls strung together: *a **rope of** pearls.* **3** (**the ropes**) *informal* the established procedures in an organization or area of activity: *I want you to **show her the ropes** | new boys were expected to **learn the ropes** from the old hands.* [mid 19th cent.: with reference to ropes used in sailing.]
▸*v.* [*trans.*] catch, fasten, or secure with rope: *the calves must be roped and led out of the stockade | the climbers were all roped together.* ■ (**rope someone in/into**) persuade someone to take part in (an activity): *anyone who could play an instrument or sing in tune was roped in.* ■ (**rope something off**) enclose or separate an area with a rope or tape: *police roped off the area of the find.* ■ [*intrans.*] *Climbing* (of a party of climbers) connect each other together with a rope: *we stopped at the foot of the Cavales Ridge and **roped up**.* ■ [*intrans.*] (**rope down/up**) *Climbing* climb down or up using a rope: *the party had been roping down a hanging glacier.* ▷Old English *rāp*, of Germanic origin; related to Dutch *reep* and German *Reif*. **—rop·er** *n.*
▸*PHRASES* □ **the end of one's rope** see **END**. □ **give a man enough rope and he will hang himself** *proverb* given enough freedom of action a person will bring about their own downfall. □ **on the rope** *Climbing* roped together: *the technique of moving together on the rope.* □ **on the ropes** *Boxing* forced against the ropes by the opponent's attack. ■ in state of near collapse or defeat: *behind the apparent success the company was on the ropes.*

rope-a-dope /ˈrōp ə ˌdōp/ ▸*n. informal* a boxing tactic of pretending to be trapped against the ropes, goading an opponent to throw tiring ineffective punches. ▷1970s: coined by Muhammad Ali, referring to a tactic in a boxing match with George Foreman.

rope lad·der ▸*n.* two parallel ropes connected by short crosspieces, typically made of wood or metal, used as a ladder.

rope's end *historical* ▸*n.* a short piece of rope used for flogging, esp. on ships.
▸*v.* (**rope's-end**) [*trans.*] flog (someone) with a rope's end.

rope·walk /ˈrōpˌwôk/ ▸*n. historical* a long building or piece of ground where ropes are made.

rope·walk·er /ˈrōpˌwôkər/ ▸*n. dated* a performer on a tightrope. **—rope·walk·ing** /-kiNG/ *n.*

rope·way /ˈrōpˌwā/ ▸*n.* a transportation system for materials or people, used esp. in mines or mountainous areas, in which cars are suspended from moving cables driven by a motor.

rope·y ▸*adj.* variant spelling of **ROPY**.

rope yarn ▸*n.* loosely twisted fibers used for making the strands of rope.

rop·ing /ˈrōpiNG/ ▸*n.* **1** the action of catching or securing something with ropes: *calf roping.* **2** ropes collectively.

rop·y /ˈrōpē/ (also **rop·ey**) ▸*adj.* (**rop·i·er**, **rop·i·est**) **1** resembling a rope in being long, strong, and fibrous: *the ropy roots of the old tree.* ■ (of a liquid) resembling a rope in forming viscous or gelatinous threads: *his spit was thick and ropey as he spat.* **2** *Brit., informal* poor in quality or health; inferior: *a portrait by a pretty ropy artist.* **—rop·i·ly** /ˈrōpəlē/ *adv.* **—rop·i·ness** *n.*

roque /rōk/ ▸*n.* a form of croquet played on a hard court surrounded by a bank. ▷late 19th cent.: alteration of **ROQUET**.

Roque·fort /ˈrōkfərt/ ▸*n. trademark* a soft blue cheese made from ewes' milk. It is ripened in limestone caves and has a strong flavor. ▷from the name of a village in southern France.

Roq·ue·laure /rōkəˈlôr/, A. N., see **RICE**[1].

ro·quet /rōˈkā/ *Croquet* ▸*v.* (**-queted** /-ˈkād/, **-quet·ing** /-ˈkāiNG/) [*trans.*] strike (another ball) with one's own: *once you roquet a ball, you can hit it where you please.*
▸*n.* an act of roqueting. ▷mid 19th cent.: apparently an arbitrary alteration of the verb **CROQUET**, originally used in the same sense.

ro·quette /rōˈket/ ▸*n.* another term for **ROCKET**[2]. ▷French.

ro-ro /ˈrōˌrō/ ▸*abbr.* roll-on roll-off. ▷1960s: abbreviation.

ror·qual /ˈrôrkwəl; -ˌkwôl/ ▸*n.* a baleen whale of streamlined appearance with pleated skin on the underside. • Family Balaenopteridae: two genera and six species, including the **common rorqual** (or fin whale). ▷early 19th cent.: via French from Norwegian *røyrkval*, from Old Norse *reythr*, the specific name, + *hvalr* 'whale.'

Ror·schach test /ˈrôrˌSHäk/ ▸*n. Psychology* a type of projective test used in psychoanalysis, in which a standard set of symmetrical ink blots of different shapes and colors is presented one by one to the subject, who is asked to describe what they suggest or resemble. ▷1920s: named after Hermann *Rorschach* (1884–1922), Swiss psychiatrist.

rort /rôrt/ ▸*n. Austral., informal* **1** [often with *adj.*] a fraudulent or dishonest act or practice: *a tax rort.* **2** a wild party. ▷1930s: back-formation from **RORTY**.

ror·ty /ˈrôrtē/ ▸*adj.* (**-ti·er**, **-ti·est**) *Brit., informal* boisterous and high-spirited. ▷mid 19th cent.: of unknown origin.

ro·sace /rōˈzās; rōˈzäs/ ▸*n.* an ornamentation resembling a rose, in particular a rose window. ▷mid 19th cent.: from French, from Latin *rosaceus* 'roselike' (see **ROSACEOUS**).

ro·sa·ce·a /rōˈzāSH(ə)ə/ (also **ac·ne ro·sa·ce·a**) ▸*n. Medicine* a condition in which certain facial blood vessels enlarge, giving the cheeks and nose a flushed appearance. ▷late 19th cent.: from Latin, feminine of *rosaceus* in the sense 'rose-colored.'

ro·sa·ceous /rōˈzāSHəs/ ▸*adj. Botany* of, relating to, or denoting plants of the rose family (Rosaceae). ▷mid 18th cent.: from modern Latin *Rosaceae* (based on Latin *rosa* 'rose') + **-OUS**.

ros·an·i·line /rōˈzanl-in/ ▸*n. Chemistry* a reddish-brown synthetic compound that is a base used in making a number of red dyes, notably fuchsin. • A triphenylmethane derivative; chem. formula: $C_{20}H_{19}N_3$. ▷mid 19th cent.: from **ROSE**[1] + **ANILINE**.

ro·sar·i·an /rōˈze(ə)rēən/ ▸*n.* a person who cultivates roses, esp. as an occupation. ▷mid 19th cent.: from Latin *rosarium* 'rose garden, rosary' + **-AN**.

Ro·sa·ri·o /rōˈsärēō/ an inland port on the Paraná River in east central Argentina; pop. 1,096,000.

ro·sar·i·um /rōˈze(ə)rēəm/ ▸*n.* (*pl.* **-sar·i·ums** or **-sar·i·a** /-ˈze(ə)rēə/) *formal* a rose garden. ▷mid 19th cent.: from Latin (see **ROSARY**).

ro·sa·ry /ˈrōzərē/ ▸*n.* (*pl.* **-ries**) (in the Roman Catholic Church) a form of devotion in which five (or fifteen) decades of Hail Marys are repeated, each decade preceded by an Our Father and followed by a Glory Be: *the congregation said the rosary.* ■ a string of beads for keeping count in such a devotion or in the devotions of some other religions, in Roman Catholic use 55 or 165 in number. ■ a book containing such a devotion. ▷late Middle English (in the sense 'rose garden'): from Latin *rosarium* 'rose garden,' based on *rosa* 'rose.'

ro·sa·ry pea ▸*n.* a tropical plant of the pea family that produces extremely poisonous, shiny, scarlet beans with a black eye. • Genus *Abrus*, family Leguminosae: several species, in particular *A. precatorius*. ■ the beans of any of these plants.

ros·coe /ˈräskō/ ▸*n. informal, dated* a gun, esp. a pistol or revolver. ▷early 20th cent.: from the surname *Roscoe*.

Ros·com·mon /räsˈkämən/ a county in the north central part of the Republic of Ireland, in the province of Connacht; pop. 52,000. ■ its county town; pop. 18,000.

Rose /rōz/, Pete (1941–), U.S. baseball player and manager; full name *Peter Edward Rose*; nickname **Charlie Hustle**. He played for the Cincinnati Reds 1963–78, the Philadelphia Phillies 1979–83, the Montreal Expos 1984, and the Reds again 1984–86. From 1984 until 1988, he also managed the Reds. He holds the major league record for hits with 4,256. In 1989, amid allegations of betting on baseball games, he was suspended permanently from baseball.

rose[1] /rōz/ ▸*n.* **1** a prickly bush or shrub that typically bears red, pink, yellow, or white fragrant flowers, native to north temperate regions. Numerous hybrids and cultivars have been developed and are widely grown as ornamentals. • Genus *Rosa*, family Rosaceae (the **rose family**). This large family includes most temperate fruits (apple, plum, peach, cherry, blackberry, strawberry) as well as the hawthorns, rowans, potentillas, and avens. ■ the flower of such a plant: *he sent her a dozen red roses* | [as *adj.*] *a rose garden.* ■ used in names of other plants whose flowers resemble roses, e.g., **rose of Sharon**. ■ used in similes and comparisons in reference to the rose flower's beauty or its typical rich red color: *she looked as beautiful as a rose.* ■ [often with *negative*] (**roses**) used to express favorable circumstances or ease of success: *all is not roses in the firm today.* **2** a thing representing or resembling the flower, in particular: ■ a stylized representation of the flower in heraldry or decoration, typically with five petals (esp. as a national emblem of England): *the Tudor rose.* ■ short for **COMPASS ROSE**. ■ short for **ROSE WINDOW**. **3** a perforated cap attached to a shower, the spout of a watering can, or the end of a hose to produce a spray. **4** a warm pink or light crimson color: *the rose and gold of dawn* | [as *adj.*] *the 100% cotton line is available in **rose pink** and ocean blue* | [in *combination*] *leaves with **rose-red** margins.* ■ (usu. **roses**) used in reference to a rosy complexion, esp. that of a young woman: *the fresh air will soon put the roses back in her cheeks.*
▸*v.* [*trans.*] *poetic/literary* make rosy: *a warm flush now rosed her hitherto blue cheeks.* ▷Old English *rōse*, of Germanic origin, from Latin *rosa*; reinforced in Middle English by Old French *rose*. **—rose·like** /-ˌlīk/ *adj.*
▸*PHRASES* □ **a bed of roses** see **BED**. □ **come up roses** (of a situation) develop in a very favorable way: *new boyfriend, successful career—everything was coming up roses.* □ **under the rose** *archaic* in confidence; under pledge of secrecy. See also **SUB ROSA**.

rose[2] ▸ past of **RISE**.

ro·sé /rōˈzā/ ▸*n.* any light pink wine, colored by only brief contact with red grape skins. ▷French, literally 'pink.'

Rose·anne /rōˈzan/ (1952–), U.S. actress; born *Roseanne Barr*. She was the award-winning star of the television program "Roseanne" (1988–97). She also acted in movies such as *She-Devil* (1988).

rose ap·ple ▸*n.* a tropical evergreen tree cultivated for its foliage and fragrant fruit. • Genus *Syzygium*, family Myrtaceae: several species, in particular the Southeast Asian *S. jambos*. ■ the spherical white rose-scented fruit of this tree.

ro·se·ate /ˈrōzēət; -ˌāt/ ▸*adj.* **1** rose-colored: *the early, roseate light.* ■ used in names of birds with partly pink plumage, e.g., **roseate tern, roseate spoonbill. 2** optimistic; promising good fortune: *his letters home give a very good, although somewhat too roseate, idea of how he lived.* ▷late Middle English: from Latin *roseus* 'rosy' (from *rosa* 'rose') + -ATE[2].

Ro·seau /rōˈzō/ the capital of Dominica in the Caribbean; pop. 16,000.

rose·bay /ˈrōzˌbā/ ▸*n.* **1** a rhododendron. • Genus *Rhododendron*, family Ericaceae: several species, including the **great rhododendron** (*R. maximum*) of eastern North America. **2** (also **rose·bay wil·low herb**) *chiefly Brit.* the pink-flowered willow herb *Epilobium angustifolium*, a common fireweed.

rose-breast·ed gros·beak ▸*n.* a North American grosbeak, the male of which is black and white with a pinkish-red breast patch. • *Pheucticus ludovicianus*, family Emberizidae (subfamily Cardinalinae).

rose·bud /ˈrōzˌbəd/ ▸*n.* an unopened flower of a rose.

rose chaf·er ▸*n.* a brilliant green or copper-colored day-flying chafer (beetle) that feeds on roses and other flowers. The larvae typically live in rotting timber. • Genus *Marodactylus*, family Scarabaeidae: three species.

rose-col·ored ▸*adj.* of a warm pink color: *rose-colored silks.* ■ used in reference to a naively optimistic or unrealistic viewpoint: *you are still* **seeing** *the profession* **through rose-colored glasses.**

rose dia·mond ▸*n.* a hemispherical diamond with the curved part cut in triangular facets.

rose·fish /ˈrōzˌfisн/ ▸*n.* (*pl.* same or **-fish·es**) the redfish of the North Atlantic (*Sebastes marinus*).

rose ge·ra·ni·um ▸*n.* a pink-flowered pelargonium with fragrant leaves. • *Pelargonium graveolens*, family Geraniaceae.

rose hip ▸*n.* see HIP[2].

ro·sel·la /rōˈzelə/ ▸*n.* an Australian parakeet with vivid green, red, yellow, or blue plumage. • Genus *Platycercus*, family Psittacidae: several species. ▷mid 19th cent.: alteration of *Rosehill*, New South Wales, where the bird was first found.

rose mad·der ▸*n.* a pale shade of pink.

ro·se·ma·ling /ˈrōzəˌmäliNG; ˈrōsə-/ ▸*n.* the art, originating in Norway, of painting wooden furniture and objects with flower motifs. ■ painted flower motifs of this type. ▷1940s: from Norwegian, literally 'rose painting.' **—ro·se·maled** /-ˌmäld; -ˌmält/ *adj.*

rose mal·low ▸*n.* a plant of the mallow family with typically large pink or white flowers, several species of which are cultivated as ornamentals. • Genus *Hibiscus*, family Malvaceae: many species, including the showy pink-flowered **swamp rose mallow** (*H. palustris*), found esp. in coastal marshes of the eastern U.S.

swamp rose mallow

rose·mar·y /ˈrōzˌme(ə)rē/ ▸*n.* an evergreen aromatic shrub of the mint family, native to southern Europe. The narrow leaves are used as a culinary herb, in perfumery, and as an emblem of remembrance. • *Rosmarinus officinalis*, family Labiatae. ▷Middle English *rosmarine*, based on Latin *ros marinus*, from *ros* 'dew' + *marinus* 'of the sea.' The spelling change was due to association with ROSE[1] and MARY[1].

Rose·mead /ˈrōzˌmēd/ a city in southwestern California, east of Los Angeles; pop. 51,638.

Ros·en·berg /ˈrōzənˌbərg/ U.S. husband and wife spy team. **Julius** (1918–53) and **Ethel Greenglass** (1915–53) were Communist Party members who were tried and convicted of espionage in 1951. They were executed in 1953.

rose of Jer·i·cho ▸*n.* an annual desert plant whose dead branches fold inward around the mature seeds forming a ball that is blown about, native to North Africa and the Middle East. • *Anastatica hierochuntica*, family Brassicaceae.

rose of Shar·on ▸*n.* **1** a shrub of the mallow family, with rose, lavender, or white flowers. • *Hibiscus syriacus*, family Malvaceae. **2** a St. John's wort with dense foliage and large golden-yellow flowers, native to southeastern Europe and Asia Minor and widely cultivated for ground cover. Also called AARON'S BEARD. • *Hypericum calycinum*, family Guttiferae. **3** (in biblical use) a flowering plant of unknown identity.

ro·se·o·la /ˌrōzēˈōlə; rōˈzēələ/ ▸*n.* *Medicine* a rose-colored rash occurring in measles, typhoid fever, syphilis, and some other diseases. ■ (in full **roseola infantum** /inˈfantəm/) a disease of young children in which a fever is followed by a rash, caused by a herpesvirus. ▷early 19th cent.: modern variant of RUBEOLA, from Latin *roseus* 'rose-colored.'

rose quartz ▸*n.* a translucent pink variety of quartz.

rose-tint·ed ▸*adj.* another term for ROSE-COLORED.

Ro·set·ta Stone /rōˈzetə/ an inscribed stone found near Rosetta on the western mouth of the Nile in 1799. Its text is written in three scripts: hieroglyphic, demotic, and Greek. The deciphering of the hieroglyphs by Jean-François Champollion in 1822 led to the interpretation of many other early records of Egyptian civilization. ■ [as *n.*] (**a Rosetta stone**) a key to some previously undecipherable mystery or unattainable understanding: *zero point energy could be the Rosetta stone of physics.*

ro·sette /rōˈzet/ ▸*n.* **1** a rose-shaped decoration, typically made of ribbon and awarded to winners of a competition. **2** a design, arrangement, or growth resembling a rose, in particular: ■ *Architecture* a carved or molded ornament resembling or representing a rose. ■ *Biology* a marking or group of markings resembling a rose. ■ a roselike cluster of parts, esp. a radiating arrangement of horizontally spreading leaves at the base of a low-growing plant. ■ a rose diamond. ▷mid 18th cent.: from French, diminutive of *rose* (see ROSE[1]). **—ro·set·ted** /rōˈzetəd/ *adj.*

Rose·ville /ˈrōzˌvil/ **1** a city in northeastern California, northeast of Sacramento; pop. 44,685. **2** a city in southeastern Michigan, northeast of Detroit; pop. 51,412. **3** a city in southeastern Minnesota, north of St. Paul; pop. 33,485.

rose wa·ter ▸*n.* water scented with rose petals, used as a perfume and for culinary purposes, and formerly in medicinal preparations.

rose win·dow ▸*n.* a circular window with mullions or tracery radiating in a form suggestive of a rose.

rose·wood /ˈrōzˌwo͝od/ ▸*n.* **1** fragrant close-grained tropical timber with a distinctive fragrance, used particularly for making furniture and musical instruments. **2** the tree that produces this timber. • Genus *Dalbergia*, family Leguminosae: several species, including **Indian rosewood** (*D. sissoo*), which is often cultivated in warm areas as an ornamental. ■ used in names of other trees that yield similar timber.

Rosh Ha·sha·nah /ˌrōsн (h)əˈsнōnə; ˌräsн; -ˈsнänə/ (also **Rosh Ha·sha·na**) ▸*n.* the Jewish New Year festival, held on the first (also sometimes the second) day of Tishri (in September). It is marked by the blowing of the shofar, and begins the ten days of penitence culminating in Yom Kippur. ▷Hebrew, literally 'head (i.e., beginning) of the year.'

ro·shi /ˈrōsнē/ ▸*n.* (*pl.* **-shis**) the spiritual leader of a community of Zen Buddhist monks. ▷Japanese.

Ro·si·cru·cian /ˌrōzəˈkro͞osнən; -ˌräzə-/ ▸*n.* a member of a secretive 17th- and 18th-century society devoted to the study of metaphysical, mystical, and alchemical lore. An anonymous pamphlet of 1614 about a mythical 15th-century knight called Christian Rosenkreuz is said to have launched the movement. ■ a member of any of a number of later organizations deriving from this.
▸*adj.* of or relating to the Rosicrucians. ▷from modern Latin *rosa crucis* (or *crux*), Latinization of German *Rosenkreuz*, + -IAN. **—Ro·si·cru·cian·ism** /-ˌnizəm/ *n.*

ros·in /ˈräzən/ ▸*n.* resin, esp. the solid amber residue obtained after the distillation of crude turpentine oleoresin, or of naphtha extract from pine stumps. It is used in adhesives, varnishes, and inks and for treating the bows of stringed instruments.
▸*v.* (**ros·ined, ros·in·ing**) [*trans.*] rub (something, esp. the bow of a stringed instrument) with rosin. ▷Middle English: from medieval Latin *rosina*, from Latin *resina* (see RESIN). **—ros·in·y** *adj.*

ro·so·li·o /rōˈzōlēˌō/ ▸*n.* (*pl.* **-os**) a sweet cordial made in Italy from alcohol, raisins, sugar, rose petals, cloves, and cinnamon. ▷Italian, from modern Latin *ros solis* 'dew of the sun.'

Ross[1] /rôs/, Araminta, see TUBMAN.

Ross[2], Betsy (1752–1836), U.S. patriot and seamstress; full name *Elizabeth Griscom Ross*. She is credited with having made the first flag of the U.S. in June 1776.

Ross[3], Diana (1944–), U.S. pop and soul singer. Originally the lead singer of the Supremes, she went on to become a successful solo artist. She received an Academy Award nomination for her role as Billie Holiday in the movie *Lady Sings the Blues* (1973).

Ross[4], Sir James Clark (1800–62), British explorer. He discovered the north magnetic pole in 1831 and, while heading an expedition to the Antarctic from 1839 to 1843, also discovered Ross Island, Ross Dependency, and the Ross Sea.

Ross[5], Sir John (1777–1856), British explorer. He led an expedition to Baffin Bay in 1818 and another in search of the Northwest Passage between 1829 and 1833.

Ross[6], Sir Ronald (1857–1932), British physician. He confirmed that the *Anopheles* mosquito transmitted malaria and then elucidated the stages in the malarial parasite's life cycle. Nobel Prize for Physiology or Medicine (1902).

Ross De·pend·en·cy the part of Antarctica that lies south of latitude 60° south between longitudes 150° and 160° west that is administered by New Zealand. ▷named after J. C. Ross (see **Ross**[4]).

Ros·sel·li·ni /ˌrôsəˈlēnē; ˌräs-/, Roberto (1906–77), Italian movie director. He is known for his neo-realist movies, particularly his quasi-documentary trilogy about World War II, *Open City* (1945). Other notable works: *Paisà* (1946) and *Germany, Year Zero* (1947).

Ros·set·ti[1] /rəˈzetē/, Christina (Georgina) (1830–94), English poet. She wrote much religious and love poetry and children's verse. She was the sister of Dante Gabriel Rossetti.

Ros·set·ti[2], Dante Gabriel (1828–82), English painter and poet; full name *Gabriel Charles Dante Rossetti*. A founder of the Pre-Raphaelite brotherhood 1848, he is best known for his idealized images of women, including *Beata Beatrix* (*c.*1863) and *The Blessed Damozel* (1871–79). He was the brother of Christina Rossetti.

Ros·si·ni /rəˈsēnē/, Gioacchino Antonio (1792–1868), Italian composer, one of the creators of Italian bel canto. He wrote over 30 operas, including *The Barber of Seville* (1816) and *William Tell* (1829).

Ross Sea a large arm of the Pacific Ocean that forms a deep indentation in the coast of Antarctica. ▷named after J. C. Ross (see **Ross**[2]).

Ross's goose ▸*n.* a small Arctic goose that breeds in northern Canada. • *Anser rossi.*

Ross's gull ▸*n.* a pinkish-white Arctic gull. • *Rhodostethia rosea.*

Ros·tand /ˈräsˌtand; rôˈstäN/, Edmond (1868–1918), French playwright and poet. He romanticized the life of the 17th-century soldier, duelist, and writer Cyrano de Bergerac in his poetic drama of that name (1897).

ros·ter /ˈrästər; ˈrô-/ ▸*n.* a list or plan showing turns of duty or leave for individuals or groups in an organization: *next week's duty roster.* ■ a list of members of a team or organization, in particular of athletes available for team selection.
▸*v.* [*trans.*] (usu. **be rostered**) *chiefly Brit.* assign according to a duty roster: *the locomotive is rostered for service on Sunday.* ▷early 18th cent. (originally denoting a list of duties and leave for military personnel): from Dutch *rooster* 'list,' earlier 'gridiron,' from *roosten* 'to roast,' with reference to its parallel lines.

rösti /ˈrôstē; ˈro͞osнtē/ ▸*n.* (*pl.* same) a Swiss dish of grated potatoes formed into a small flat cake and fried: *place four of the rösti in the pan.* ▷1950s: from Swiss German.

Ros·tock /ˈrästäk; ˈrôstôk/ an industrial port on the Baltic coast of Germany; pop. 244,000.

Ro·stov /rəˈstôf/ a port and industrial city in southwestern Russia, on the Don River near its point of entry into the Sea of Azov; pop. 1,025,000. Full name ROSTOV-ON-DON.

ros·tra /ˈrästrə; ˈrô-/ ▸ plural form of ROSTRUM.

ros·tral /ˈrästrəl; ˈrô-/ ▸*adj.* **1** *Anatomy* situated or occurring near the front end of the body, esp. in the region of the nose and mouth or (in an embryo) near the hypophyseal region: *the rostral portion of the brain.* **2** *Zoology* of or on the rostrum: *in these snakes the rostral shield is enlarged and flattened.* **3** (of a column, etc.) adorned with the rams of ancient warships or with representations of these. ▷early 19th cent.: from ROSTRUM + -AL. —**ros·tral·ly** *adv.*

Ros·tro·po·vich /ˌrästrəˈpōvich/, Mstislav Leopoldovich (1927–), Russian cellist, pianist, and conductor. He came to the U.S. in 1975 and was music director and conductor of the National Symphony Orchestra in Washington, D.C., 1977–94.

ros·trum /ˈrästrəm; ˈrô-/ ▸*n.* (*pl.* **ros·tra** /ˈrästrə; ˈrô-/ or **ros·trums**) **1** a raised platform on which a person stands to make a public speech, receive an award or medal, play music, or conduct an orchestra. ■ a similar platform for supporting a movie or television camera. **2** *chiefly Zoology* a beaklike projection, esp. a stiff snout or anterior prolongation of the head in an insect, crustacean, or cetacean. ▷mid 16th cent.: from Latin, literally 'beak' (from *rodere* 'gnaw'). The word was originally used (at first in the plural *rostra*) to denote part of the Forum in Rome, which was decorated with the beaks of captured galleys, and was used as a platform for public speakers. —**ros·trate** /ˈrásˌtrāt; ˈrôˌstrāt/ *adj.* (in sense 2).

Ros·well /ˈräzwel; -wəl/ **1** a city in northwestern Georgia, north of Atlanta; pop. 79,334. **2** a town in southeastern New Mexico, the scene of a mysterious crash in July 1947. Controversy has surrounded claims by some investigators that the crashed object was a UFO; pop. 45,293.

ros·y /ˈrōzē/ ▸*adj.* (**ros·i·er**, **ros·i·est**) **1** (esp. of a person's skin) colored like a pink or red rose, typically as an indication of health, youth, or embarrassment: *the memory had the power to make her cheeks turn rosy.* **2** promising or suggesting good fortune or happiness; hopeful: *the strategy has produced results beyond the most rosy forecasts.* ■ easy and pleasant: *life could never be rosy for them.* —**ros·i·ly** /ˈrōzəlē/ *adv.* —**ros·i·ness** *n.*

ros·y cross ▸*n.* an equal-armed cross with a rose at its center, the emblem of the Rosicrucians.

ros·y finch ▸*n.* a finch found in Asia and western North America, the male of which has pinkish underparts and rump. • Genus *Leucosticte*, family Fringillictae: three species, in particular *L. arctoa.*

rot /rät/ ▸*v.* (**rot·ted**, **rot·ting**) [*intrans.*] (chiefly of animal or vegetable matter) decompose by the action of bacteria and fungi; decay: *the chalets were neglected and their woodwork was* **rotting away**. ■ [*trans.*] cause to decay: *caries sets in at a weak point and spreads to rot the whole tooth.* ■ *figurative* gradually deteriorate through lack of attention or opportunity: *he cannot understand the way the education system has been allowed to rot.*

▸*n.* **1** the process of decaying: *the leaves were turning black with rot.* ■ rotten or decayed matter: *she was busy cutting the rot from the potatoes.* ■ (**the rot**) a process of deterioration; a decline in standards: *it was when they moved back to the family home that* **the rot set in**. ■ [usu. with *adj.*] any of a number of fungal or bacterial diseases that cause tissue deterioration, esp. in plants. **2** *informal* nonsense; rubbish: *don't talk rot.* ▷Old English *rotian* (verb), of Germanic origin; related to Dutch *rotten*; the noun (Middle English) may have come via Scandinavian.

rot. ▸*abbr.* ■ rotating. ■ rotation.

ro·ta /ˈrōtə/ ▸*n.* **1** *chiefly Brit.* a list showing when each of a number of people has to do a particular job: *a cleaning rota.* Compare with ROSTER. **2** (**the Rota**) the supreme ecclesiastical and secular court of the Roman Catholic Church. ▷early 17th cent.: from Latin, literally 'wheel.'

ro·ta·mer /ˈrōtəmər/ ▸*n.* *Chemistry* any of a number of isomers of a molecule that can be interconverted by rotation of part of the molecule around a particular bond. ▷1960s: from *rotational* (see ROTATION) + -MER.

Ro·ta·ry /ˈrōtərē/ (in full **Ro·ta·ry In·ter·na·tion·al**) a worldwide charitable society of businessmen, businesswomen, and professional people, formed in 1905. ▷so named because members hosted events in rotation. —**Ro·tar·i·an** /rōˈte(ə)rēən/ *n.* & *adj.*

ro·ta·ry /ˈrōtərē/ ▸*adj.* (of motion) revolving around a center or axis; rotational: *a rotary motion.* ■ (of a thing) acting by means of rotation, esp. (of a machine) operating through the rotation of some part: *a rotary mower.*

▸*n.* (*pl.* **-ries**) **1** a rotary machine, engine, or device. **2** a traffic circle. ▷mid 18th cent.: from medieval Latin *rotarius*, from *rota* 'wheel.'

Ro·ta·ry Club ▸*n.* a local branch of Rotary.

ro·ta·ry en·gine ▸*n.* an engine that produces rotary motion or that has a rotating part or parts, in particular: ■ an aircraft engine with a fixed crankshaft around which cylinders and propeller rotate. ■ a Wankel engine.

ro·ta·ry press ▸*n.* a printing press that prints from a rotating cylindrical surface onto paper forced against it by another cylinder.

ro·ta·ry wing ▸*n.* [usu. as *adj.*] an airfoil that rotates in an approximately horizontal plane, providing all or most of the lift in a helicopter or autogiro.

ro·tate /ˈrōˌtāt/ ▸*v.* [*intrans.*] move in a circle around an axis or center: *the wheel continued to rotate* | [as *adj.*] (**rotating**) *a rotating drum.* ■ [*trans.*] cause to move around an axis or in a circle: *the small directional side rockets rotated the craft.* ■ pass to each member of a group in a regularly recurring order: *the job of chairing the meeting rotates.* ■ [*trans.*] grow (different crops) in succession on a particular piece of land to avoid exhausting the soil: *these crops were sometimes rotated with grass.* ■ [*trans.*] change the position of (tires) on a motor vehicle to distribute wear evenly. ▷late 17th cent.: from Latin *rotat-* 'turned in a circle,' from the verb *rotare*, from *rota* 'wheel.' —**ro·tat·a·ble** /ˈrōˌtātəbəl; rōˈtāt-/ *adj.* —**ro·ta·tive** /ˈrōˌtātiv/ *adj.* —**ro·ta·to·ry** /ˈrōtəˌtôrē/ *adj.*

ro·ta·tion /rōˈtāshən/ ▸*n.* the action of rotating around an axis or center: *the moon moves in the same direction as the earth's rotation.* ■ (also **crop ro·ta·tion**) the action or system of rotating crops. ■ *Forestry* the cycle of planting, felling, and replanting. ■ the passing of a privilege or responsibility from one member of a group to another in a regularly recurring succession: *it has become common for senior academics to act as heads of department* **in rotation**. ■ a tour of duty, esp. by a medical practitioner in training: *she was completing a rotation in trauma surgery.* ■ *Mathematics* the conceptual operation of turning a system around an axis. ■ *Mathematics* another term for CURL (sense 2). ▷mid 16th cent.: from Latin *rotatio(n-)*, from the verb *rotare* (see ROTATE). —**ro·ta·tion·al** /-shənl/ *adj.* —**ro·ta·tion·al·ly** /-shənl-ē/ *adv.*

ro·ta·tor /ˈrōˌtātər/ ▸*n.* a thing that rotates or that causes something to rotate. ■ *Anatomy* a muscle whose contraction causes or assists in the rotation of a part of the body.

ro·ta·tor cuff ▸*n.* *Anatomy* a capsule with fused tendons that supports the arm at the shoulder joint and is often subject to athletic injury.

ro·ta·vi·rus /ˈrōtəˌvīrəs/ ▸*n.* *Medicine* any of a group of RNA viruses, some of which cause acute enteritis in humans. ▷1970s: modern Latin, from Latin *rota* 'wheel' + VIRUS.

ROTC /ˈrätsē/ ▸*abbr.* (in the U.S.) Reserve Officers' Training Corps.

rote /rōt/ ▸*n.* mechanical or habitual repetition of something to be learned: *a poem learned* **by rote** *in childhood.* ▷Middle English (also in the sense 'habit, custom'): of unknown origin.

ro·te·none /ˈrōtnˌōn/ ▸*n.* *Chemistry* a toxic crystalline substance obtained from the roots of derris and related plants, widely used as an insecticide. • A polycyclic ketone; chem. formula: $C_{23}H_{22}O_6$. ▷1920s: from Japanese *rotenon* (from *roten* 'derris') + -ONE.

rot·gut /ˈrätˌgət/ ▸*n.* *informal* poor-quality and potentially toxic alcoholic liquor.

Roth /rôth; räth/, Philip (Milton) (1933–), U.S. novelist and short-story writer. He often wrote with irony and humor about the complexity and diversity of contemporary American Jewish life. Notable works: *Portnoy's Complaint* (1969), *Zuckerman Bound* (1985), and *American Pastoral* (1997).

Roth·er·ham /ˈrä*th*ərəm/ an industrial town in northern England; pop. 247,000.

Roth IRA /rôth; räth/ ▸*n.* an individual retirement account allowing a person to set aside after-tax income up to a specified amount each year. Both earnings on the account and withdrawals after age 59½ are tax-free. ▷created in 1997 and named for Senator William Victor Roth II (1921–2003) of Delaware, who proposed this in Congress.

Roth·ko /ˈräthkō/, Mark (1903–70), U.S. painter, born in Latvia; born *Marcus Rothkovich.* A leading figure in color-field painting, he painted hazy and seemingly floating rectangles of color. His series of nine paintings for the Seagram Building in New York City include *Black on Maroon* (1958).

Roth·schild /ˈrôth(s)ˌchīld; ˈrôs-/, Meyer Amschel (1743–1812), German financier. He founded the Rothschild banking house in Frankfurt at the end of the 19th century and was financial adviser to the landgrave of Hesse. His five sons all entered banking.

ro·ti /ˈrōtē/ ▸*n.* (*pl.* **ro·tis**) *Indian* bread, esp. a flat round bread cooked on a griddle. ▷from Hindi *roṭī.*

Ro·tif·er·a /rōˈtifərə/ *Zoology* a small phylum of minute multicellular aquatic animals that have a characteristic wheellike ciliated organ used in swimming and feeding. ▷modern Latin (plural), from Latin *rota* 'wheel' + *ferre* 'to bear.' —**ro·ti·fer** /ˈrōtəfər/ *n.*

ro·ti·ni /rōˈtēnē/ ▸*n.* pasta in short pieces with a helical shape. ▷Italian, literally 'spirals'

ro·tis·ser·ie /rōˈtisərē/ ▸*n.* **1** a cooking appliance with a rotating spit for roasting and barbecuing meat. **2** a restaurant specializing in roasted or barbecued meat. ▷mid 19th cent.: from French *rôtisserie*, from *rôtir* 'to roast.'

ro·tis·se·rie league ▸*n.* an association of individuals who simulate selecting, managing, and playing baseball, using the names and statistics of actual professional players to determine results.

ro·to·gra·vure /ˌrōtəgrəˈvyŏŏr/ ▸*n.* a printing system using a rotary press with intaglio cylinders, typically running at high speed and used for long print runs of magazines and stamps. ■ a sheet or magazine printed with this system, esp. the color magazine of a Sunday newspaper. ▷early 20th cent.: from German *Rotogravur*, part of the name of a printing company.

ro·tor /ˈrōtər/ ▸*n.* a rotary part of a machine or vehicle, in particular: ■ a hub with a number of radiating airfoils that is rotated in an approximately horizontal plane to provide the lift for a rotary-wing aircraft. ■ the rotating assembly in a turbine, esp. a wind turbine. ■ the armature of an electric motor. ■ the rotating part of the distributor of an internal combustion engine that successively makes and breaks electrical contacts so that each spark plug fires in turn. ■ the rotating container in a centrifuge. ■ the rotary winder of a clockwork watch. ■ *Meteorology* a large eddy in which the air circulates around a horizontal axis, esp. in the lee of a mountain. ▷early 20th cent.: formed irregularly from ROTATOR.

ro·tor·craft /ˈrōtərˌkraft/ ▸*n.* (*pl.* same) a rotary-wing aircraft, such as a helicopter or autogiro.

ro·tor wash ▸*n.* air turbulence caused by a helicopter rotor.

ro·to·scope /ˈrōtəˌskōp/ ▸*n.* a device that projects and enlarges individual frames of filmed live action to permit them to be used to create cartoon animation and composite film sequences. ■ a computer application that combines live action and other images in a film.

▸*v.* [*trans.*] transfer (an image from live action film) into another film sequence using a rotoscope. ▷1950s: origin obscure; perhaps the same word as 19th-cent. *rotascope*, denoting a kind of gyroscope.

ro·to·till·er /ˈrōtəˌtilər/ ▸*n.* *trademark* a motor-driven machine with rotating blades for breaking up or tilling the soil. —**ro·to·till** *v.*

rot·ten /ˈrätn/ ▸*adj.* (**-ten·er**, **-ten·est**) suffering from decay: *rotten eggs* | *the supporting beams were rotten.* ■ morally, socially, or politically corrupt: *he believed that the whole art business was rotten.* ■ *informal* very bad: *she was a rotten cook.* ■ *informal* extremely unpleasant: *it's rotten for you having to cope on your own.* ■ [*predic.*] *informal* unwell: *she tried to tell me she felt rotten.*

▸*adv.* *informal* to an extreme degree; very much: *your mother said that I* **spoiled you rotten**. ▷Middle English: from Old Norse *rotinn.* —**rot·ten·ly** *adv.* —**rot·ten·ness** *n.*

rot·ten bor·ough ▸*n.* *Brit., historical* a borough that was able to elect a representative to Parliament though having very few voters, the choice of representative typically being in the hands of one person or family. ▷so named because the borough was found to have "decayed" to the point of no longer having a constituency.

rot·ten·stone /ˈrätnˌstōn/ ▸*n.* weathered siliceous limestone used as a powder or paste for polishing metals.

rot·ter /ˈrätər/ ▸*n.* *informal, dated, chiefly Brit.* a cruel, stingy, or unkind person.

Rot·ter·dam /ˈrätərˌdam/ a city in the Netherlands, at the mouth of the Meuse River, 15 miles (25 km) inland from the North Sea; pop. 582,000. It has extensive shipbuilding and petrochemical industries.

Pronunciation Key ə *ago*; ər *over*; ˈə or ˌə *up*; ˈər or ˌər *fur*; a *hat*; ā *rate*; ä *car*; ch *chew*; e *let*; ē *see*; e(ə)r *air*; i *fit*; ī *by*; i(ə)r *ear*; ng *sing*; ō *go*; ô *for*; oi *boy*; ŏŏ *good*; ōō *goo*; ou *out*; sh *she*; th *thin*; *th* *then*; (h)w *why*; zh *vision*

Rott·wei·ler /ˈrätˌwīlər; ˈrôtˌvīlər/ ▸*n.* a large powerful dog of a tall black-and-tan breed. ▷early 20th cent.: German, from *Rottweil*, the name of a town in southwestern Germany.

Rottweiler

ro·tund /rōˈtənd; ˈrōˌtənd/ ▸*adj.* (of a person) plump. ■ round or spherical: *huge stoves held great rotund cauldrons.* ■ *figurative* (of speech or literary style) indulging in grandiloquent expression. ▷late 15th cent.: from Latin *rotundus*, from *rotare* 'rotate.' **—ro·tun·di·ty** /-ˈtəndətē/ *n.* **—ro·tund·ly** *adv.*

ro·tun·da /rōˈtəndə/ ▸*n.* a round building or room, esp. one with a dome. ▷early 17th cent.: alteration of Italian *rotonda (camera)* 'round (chamber),' feminine of *rotondo* 'round' (see **ROTUND**).

R

Rou·ault /ro͞oˈō/, Georges (Henri) (1871–1958), French painter and engraver. Associated with expressionism, he used vivid colors and simplified forms enclosed in thick black outlines.

rou·ble ▸*n.* variant spelling of **RUBLE**.

rou·é /ro͞oˈā/ ▸*n.* a debauched man, esp. an elderly one. ▷early 19th cent.: French, literally 'broken on a wheel,' referring to the instrument of torture thought to be deserved by such a person.

Rou·en /ro͞oˈän; -äɴ/ a port on the Seine River in northwestern France; pop. 105,000. Joan of Arc was tried and burned at the stake here in 1431.

Rou·en duck ▸*n.* a bird of a breed of large duck resembling the wild mallard in coloring.

Rouge, Riv·er /ˈro͞ozн/ a short river with several branches in and around Detroit in Michigan.

rouge[1] /ro͞ozн/ ▸*n.* a red powder or cream used as a cosmetic for coloring the cheeks or lips. ■ another term for **JEWELER'S ROUGE**.
▸*v.* [*trans.*] [often as *adj.*] (**rouged**) color with rouge: *her brightly rouged cheeks.* ■ [*intrans.*] *archaic* apply rouge to one's cheeks. ▷late Middle English (denoting the color red): from French, 'red,' from Latin *rubeus*. The cosmetic term dates from the mid 18th cent.

rouge[2] ▸*n.* (in Canadian football) a single point awarded when the receiving team fails to run a kick out of its own end zone. ▷late 19th cent.: of unknown origin.

rouge et noir /ˈro͞ozн ā ˈnwär/ ▸*n.* a gambling card game in which cards are turned up on a table marked with red and black diamonds. ▷late 18th cent.: French, literally 'red and black.'

rou·get /ro͞oˈzнā; -ˈzнe/ ▸*n.* French term for **RED MULLET**, used esp. in cooking. ▷French.

rough /rəf/ ▸*adj.* **1** having an uneven or irregular surface; not smooth or level: *take a square of sandpaper, rough side out.* ■ (of ground or terrain) having many bumps or other obstacles; difficult to cross: *they had to carry the victim across the rough, stony ground.* ■ not soft to the touch: *her skin felt dry and rough.* ■ (of a voice) coming out with difficulty so as to sound harsh and rasping: *his voice was rough with barely suppressed fury.* ■ (of wine or another alcoholic drink) sharp or harsh in taste. ■ denoting the face of a tennis or squash racket from which the loops formed in the stringing process project (used as a call when the racket is spun to decide the right to serve first or to choose ends); the opposite of smooth **SMOOTH** (in sense 1). **2** (of a person or their behavior) not gentle; violent or boisterous: *strollers should be capable of withstanding rough treatment.* See note at **RUDE**. ■ (of an area or occasion) characterized by or notorious for the occurrence of violent behavior: *the workmen hate going to the rough areas of town.* ■ (of the sea) having large and dangerous waves: *the lifeboat crew braved rough seas to rescue a couple.* ■ (of weather) wild and stormy. ■ *informal* difficult and unpleasant; hard; severe: *the teachers gave me **a rough time** because my image didn't fit.* | *the first day of a job is **rough on** everyone.* ■ [as *complement*] *informal* unwell: *the altitude had hit her and she was feeling rough.* ■ [as *complement*] *informal* depressed and anxious: *when he's feeling rough, he comes and talks things over to calm him down.* **3** not finished tidily or decoratively; plain and basic: *the customers sat at rough wooden tables.* ■ put together without the proper materials or skill; makeshift: *he had one arm in a rough sling.* ■ (of hair or fur) not smooth; coarse: *the creature's body was covered with rough hair.* ■ lacking sophistication or refinement: *she took care of him in her rough, kindly way.* ■ not worked out or correct in every detail: *he had a rough draft of his new novel.*
▸*adv. informal* in a manner that lacks gentleness; harshly or violently: *treat 'em rough but treat 'em fair.*
▸*n.* **1** *chiefly Brit.* a disreputable and violent person. **2** (on a golf course) longer grass around the fairway and the green: *his second shot was **in the rough** on the left.* **3** a preliminary sketch for a design: *I did a rough to work out the scale of the lettering.* **4** an uncut precious stone.
▸*v.* [*trans.*] **1** work or shape (something) in a rough, preliminary fashion: *flat surfaces of wood are **roughed down**.* ■ (**rough something out**) produce a preliminary and unfinished sketch or version of something: *the engineer roughed out a diagram on his notepad.* ■ make uneven or ruffled: ***rough up** the icing with a palette knife* | *the water was roughed by the wind.* **2** (**rough it**) live in discomfort with only basic necessities: *she had had to rough it alone in a dive.*
▸*phrasal v.* □ **rough someone up** *informal* beat someone up. ▷Old English *rūh*; related to Dutch *ruw* and German *rauh*. **—rough·ish** *adj.* **—rough·ness** *n.*
▸*PHRASES* □ **bit of rough** *Brit. informal* a male sexual partner whose toughness or lack of sophistication is a source of attraction. □ **in the rough 1** in a natural state; without decoration or other treatment: *a diamond in the rough.* **2** in difficulties: *even before the recession hit, the project was in the rough.* □ **rough and ready** crude but effective: *a rough-and-ready estimating method.* ■ (of a person or place) unsophisticated or unrefined. □ **rough around the edges** having a few imperfections: *until we clean up and lay down the new carpet, it's going to look a little rough around the edges.* ■ not refined: *Donnie is a bit rough around the edges, but she loves him.* □ **the rough edge** (or **side**) **of one's tongue** a scolding: *you two stop quarreling or you'll get the rough edge of my tongue.* □ **rough edges** small imperfections in someone or something that is basically satisfactory. □ **rough justice** treatment that is not scrupulously fair or in accordance with the law. □ **rough passage** a journey over rough sea. ■ a difficult process of achieving something or of becoming successful: *the rough passage faced by the legislation.* □ **a rough ride** a difficult time or experience: *rebel shareholders are expected to **give** officials **a rough ride**.* □ **rough stuff** boisterous or violent behavior. □ **sleep rough** *Brit.* sleep in uncomfortable conditions, typically out of doors. □ **take the rough with the smooth** accept the difficult or unpleasant aspects of life as well as the good.

rough·age /ˈrəfij/ ▸*n.* fibrous indigestible material in vegetable foodstuffs that aids the passage of food and waste products through the gut. ■ *Farming* coarse, fibrous fodder.

rough and tum·ble (also **rough-and-tum·ble**) ▸*n.* a situation without rules or organization; a free-for-all: *the rough and tumble of political life* | [as *adj.*] *the rough-and-tumble atmosphere of the dealing room.* ▷early 19th cent.: originally boxing slang.

rough breath·ing ▸*n.* see **BREATHING** (sense 2).

rough·cast /ˈrəfˌkast/ ▸*n.* plaster of lime, cement, and gravel, used on outside walls.
▸*adj.* **1** (of a building or part of a building) coated with roughcast: *a plain stone building, roughcast and whitewashed.* **2** (of a person) lacking refinement: *she thought of the roughcast yeomen she would meet.*
▸*v.* [*trans.*] (usu. **be roughcast**) coat (a wall) with roughcast: *the walls were to have been roughcast at the entrance bay.*

rough-coat·ed ▸*adj.* (of a dog or other animal) having relatively coarse fur that does not lie flat.

rough cut ▸*n.* the first version of a movie after preliminary editing.
▸*v.* (**rough-cut**) [*trans.*] cut (something) rapidly and without particular attention to quality or accuracy: *it would be best to rough-cut the boards to size with a portable saw.*

rough-dry ▸*v.* [*trans.*] dry (something) roughly or imperfectly: *she continued to rough-dry her hair.*

rough·en /ˈrəfən/ ▸*v.* make or become rough: [*trans.*] *the wind was roughening the surface of the river* | [*intrans.*] *his voice roughened.*

rough-hew ▸*v.* [*trans.*] [usu. as *adj.*] (**rough-hewn**) shape (wood or stone) with a tool such as an ax without smoothing it off afterward: *rough-hewn logs* | *figurative his broad, rough-hewn features.* ■ [as *adj.*] (**rough-hewn**) (of a person) uncultivated or uncouth.

rough·house *informal* ▸*v.* /ˈrəfˌhous; -ˌhouz/ [*intrans.*] act in a boisterous, violent manner: *in front of the stage hundreds of teens and young adults roughhouse, flinging themselves into each other.* ■ [*trans.*] handle (someone) roughly or violently: *the police department grabbed Danny as a suspect and roughhoused him.*
▸*n.* /-ˌhous/ a violent disturbance or an instance of boisterous play.

rough·ing /ˈrəfiɴɢ/ ▸*n.* *Ice Hockey* unnecessary or excessive use of force, for which a penalty may be assessed: *both players draw five minutes for roughing.* ■ *Football* illegal bodily contact with the quarterback or kicker, for which a penalty is assessed.

rough·ly /ˈrəflē/ ▸*adv.* **1** in a manner lacking gentleness; harshly or violently: *the man picked me up roughly.* **2** in a manner lacking refinement and precision: *people were crouching over roughly built brick fireplaces.* ■ approximately: *this is a walk of roughly 13 miles* | [*sentence adverb*] *the narrative is, **roughly speaking**, contemporary with the earliest of the gospels.*

rough·neck /ˈrəfˌnek/ ▸*n.* **1** *informal* a rough and uncouth person. **2** an oil rig worker.
▸*v.* [*intrans.*] [usu. as *n.*] (**roughnecking**) work on an oil rig: *his savings from roughnecking are gone.*

rough·rid·er /ˈrəfˈrīdər/ (also **rough rid·er**) ▸*n.* a person who breaks in or can ride unbroken horses. ■ a person who rides horses a lot. ■ (**Rough Rider**) a member of the cavalry unit in which Theodore Roosevelt fought during the Spanish-American War.

rough·shod /ˈrəfˌsнäd/ ▸*adj. archaic* (of a horse) having shoes with nailheads projecting to prevent slipping.
▸*PHRASE* □ **ride roughshod over** see **RIDE**.

rough tim·ber ▸*n.* partly dressed timber, having only the branches removed.

rough trade ▸*n. informal* male homosexual prostitution, esp. when involving brutality or sadism. ■ people involved in prostitution of this type.

rough-winged swal·low ▸*n.* a brown-backed American swallow. • *Stelgidopteryx ruficollis.*

rough·y /ˈrəfē/ ▸*n.* (*pl.* **rough·ies**) *Austral.* **1** a marine fish with a deep laterally compressed body and large rough-edged scales that become spiny on the belly. • Family Trachichthyidae: several genera and species, including the small Australian *Trachichthys australis*, which occurs on rocky reefs. **2** another term for **RUFF**[2] (sense 1).

rou·ille /ˈro͞o-ē; ro͞oˈēy/ ▸*n.* a Provençal sauce made from pounded red chilies, garlic, breadcrumbs, and other ingredients blended with stock, typically added to bouillabaisse. ▷French, literally 'rust,' with reference to the color.

rou·lade /ro͞oˈläd/ ▸*n.* **1** a dish cooked or served in the form of a roll, typically made from a flat piece of meat, fish, or sponge cake, spread with a soft filling and rolled up into a spiral. **2** a florid passage of runs in classical music for a virtuoso singer, esp. one sung to one syllable. ▷French, from *rouler* 'to roll.'

rou·leau /ro͞oˈlō/ ▸*n.* (*pl.* **-leaux** /-ˈlōz/ or **-leaus**) **1** a cylindrical packet of coins. **2** a coil or roll of ribbon, knitted wool, or other material, esp. used as trimming. ▷late 17th cent.: French, from obsolete French *roule* 'a roll.'

rou·lette /ro͞oˈlet/ ▸*n.* **1** a gambling game in which a ball is dropped onto a revolving wheel (**roulette wheel**) with numbered compartments, the players betting on the number at which the ball will come to rest. **2** a tool or machine with a revolving toothed wheel, used in engraving or for making slit-shaped perforations between postage stamps.
▸*v.* [*trans.*] make slit-shaped perforations in (paper, esp. sheets of postage stamps): *the pages are rouletted next to the binding.* ▷mid 18th cent.: from French, diminutive of *rouelle* 'wheel,' from late Latin *rotella*, diminutive of Latin *rota* 'wheel.'

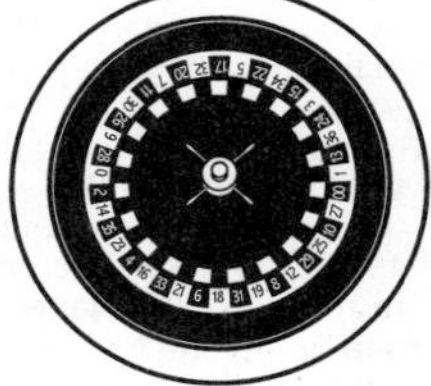

roulette wheel

round /round/ ▸*adj.* **1** shaped like or approximately like a circle or cylinder: *she was seated at a small, round table.* ■ having a curved shape like part of the circumference of a circle: *round arches.* **2** shaped like or approximately like a sphere: *a round glass ball | the grapes are small and round.* ■ (of a person's body) plump. ■ having a curved surface with no sharp or jagged projections: *the boulders look round and smooth.* ■ *figurative* (of a voice) rich and mellow; not harsh. **3** [*attrib.*] (of a number) altered for convenience of expression or calculation, for example to the nearest whole number or multiple of ten or five: *the size of the fleet is given in round numbers.* ■ (of a number) convenient for calculation, typically through being a multiple of ten. ■ used to show that a figure has been completely and exactly reached: *a round dozen.* ■ *archaic* (of a sum of money) considerable: *his business is worth a round sum to me.* **4** *archaic* (of a person or their manner of speaking) not omitting or disguising anything; frank and truthful: *she berated him in good round terms.*

▸*n.* **1** a circular piece of a particular substance: *cut the pastry into rounds.* ■ a thick disk of beef cut from the haunch as a joint. **2** an act of visiting each of a number of people or places: *she* **did the rounds of** *her family to say goodbye | he* **made the rounds of** *the city's churches.* ■ a tour of inspection, typically repeated regularly, in which the safety or well-being of those visited is checked: *the doctor is just* **making his rounds** *in the wards.* **3** one of a sequence of sessions or groups of related actions or events, typically such that development or progress can be seen between one group and another: *the two sides held three rounds of talks.* ■ a division of a contest such as a boxing or wrestling match. ■ one of a succession of stages in a sporting contest or other competition, in each of which more candidates are eliminated: *the playoffs in the second round.* ■ an act of playing all the holes in a golf course once: *Eileen enjoys the occasional* **round of golf.** **4** a regularly recurring sequence of activities or functions: *their lives were a* **daily round** *of housework and laundry.* ■ *Music* a song for three or more unaccompanied voices or parts, each singing the same theme but starting one after another, at the same pitch or in octaves; a simple canon. ■ a set of drinks bought for all the members of a group, typically as part of a sequence in which each member in turn buys such a set: *it's my round.* **5** a measured quantity or number of something, in particular: ■ the amount of ammunition needed to fire one shot. ■ *Archery* a fixed number of arrows shot from a fixed distance.

▸*adv. chiefly Brit.* variant of AROUND.

▸*prep. chiefly Brit.* variant of AROUND.

▸*v.* [*trans.*] **1** pass and go around (something) so as to move on in a changed direction: *the ship rounded the cape and sailed north.* **2** alter (a number) to one less exact but more convenient for calculations: *we'll* **round** *the weight* **up** *to the nearest pound | the committee* **rounded down** *the figure | let's just* **round** *it* **off** *to an even ten dollars.* **3** give a round shape to: *a lathe that rounded chair legs.* ■ [*intrans.*] become circular in shape: *her eyes rounded in dismay.* ■ *Phonetics* pronounce (a vowel) with the lips narrowed and protruded.

▸*phrasal v.* □ **round something off** make the edges or corners of something smooth: *round off the spars with a soft plastic fitting.* ■ complete something in a satisfying or suitable way: *I rounded off my visit to Ganu by purchasing a number of exquisite masks.* □ **round on** make a sudden verbal attack on or unexpected retort to: *she rounded on me angrily.* □ **round something out** make something more complete: *the subtle flavors of a milliard round out the meal.* □ **round someone/something up** drive or collect a number of people or animals together for a particular purpose: *in the afternoon the cows are rounded up for milking.* ■ arrest a number of people. ▷Middle English: from the Old French stem *round-*, from a variant of Latin *rotundus* 'rotund.' **—round·ish** *adj.* **—round·ness** *n.*

▸PHRASES □ **in the round 1** (of sculpture) standing free with all sides shown, rather than carved in relief against a ground. ■ *figurative* treated fully and thoroughly; with all aspects shown or considered: *to understand social phenomena one must see them in the round.* **2** (of a theatrical performance) with the audience placed on at least three sides of the stage. □ **make** (or **go**) **the rounds** (of a story or joke) be passed on from person to person. □ **round about 1** on all sides or in all directions; surrounding someone or something: *everything round about was covered with snow.* **2** at a point or time approximately equal to: *they arrived round about nine.*

USAGE On the difference in use between **round** and **around**, see **usage** at AROUND.

THE RIGHT WORD **annular, circular, globular, round, spherical**

What do a bicycle wheel, a basketball, and a barrel of oil have in common? All are considered to be **round**, an adjective that may be applied to anything shaped like a circle, a sphere, or a cylinder.

But of these three objects, only a basketball is **spherical**, which means having a round body whose surface is equally distant from the center at all points.

Something that is **globular** is shaped like a ball or a globe but is not necessarily a perfect sphere (*globular drops of oil leaking from the seam*).

A wheel is **circular**, as is a Frisbee; in fact, anything with a round, flat surface in the shape of a ring or a disk may be described as *circular*—whether or not it corresponds to a perfect circle.

But only the rings of a tree can be described as **annular**, a word that usually implies having a series of concentric ringlike forms or structures.

round·a·bout /ˈroundəˌbout/ ▸*n.* **1** British term for TRAFFIC CIRCLE. **2** British term for MERRY-GO-ROUND. **3** *historical* a close-fitting, waist-length jacket worn by men and boys.

▸*adj.* not following a short direct route; circuitous: *we need to take a roundabout route to throw off any pursuit.* ■ not saying what is meant clearly and directly; circumlocutory: *in a roundabout way, he was fishing for information.*

round·ball /ˈroundˌbôl/ ▸*n.* informal term for BASKETBALL. **—round·ball·er** *n.*

round brack·ets ▸*plural n. Brit.* parentheses.

round dance ▸*n.* a folk dance in which the dancers form one large circle. ■ a ballroom dance such as a waltz or polka in which couples move in circles around the ballroom.

round·ed /ˈroundid/ ▸*adj.* **1** having a smooth, curved surface: *rounded gray hills.* ■ having a spherical shape: *its rounded, almost bulbous head.* ■ forming circular or elliptical shapes: *his writing was firm and rounded.* ■ *Phonetics* (of a vowel) pronounced with the lips pursed. **2** well developed in all aspects; complete and balanced: *we should educate children to become rounded human beings.*

roun·del /ˈroundl/ ▸*n.* **1** a small disk, esp. a decorative medallion. ■ a picture or pattern contained in a circle. ■ *Heraldry* a plain filled circle as a charge (often with a special name according to color). ■ *Brit.* a circular identifying mark painted on military aircraft, as, for example, the red, white, and blue of the RAF. **2** a short poem consisting of three stanzas of three lines each, rhyming alternately, with the opening words repeated as a refrain after the first and third stanzas. The form, a variant of the rondeau, was developed by Swinburne. ▷Middle English: from Old French *rondel*, from *ro(u)nd-* (see ROUND).

roun·de·lay /ˈroundəˌlā; ˈrän-/ ▸*n. poetic/literary* a short simple song with a refrain. ■ a circle dance. ▷late Middle English: from Old French *rondelet*, from *rondel* (see RONDEL). The change in the ending was due to association with the final syllable of VIRELAY.

round·er /ˈroundər/ ▸*n.* **1** a person who frequents bars and is often drunk. **2** *Brit.* (in rounders) a complete run of a player through all the bases as a unit of scoring.

round·ers /ˈroundərz/ ▸*plural n.* [treated as *sing.*] a ball game similar to baseball, played chiefly in British schools.

round go·by ▸*n.* a Eurasian freshwater goby that threatens native species of fish in the Great Lakes and Mississippi basin. • *Neogobius melanostomus*, family Gobiidae.

round hand ▸*n.* a style of handwriting in which the letters have clear rounded shapes.

Round·head /ˈroundˌhed/ ▸*n. historical* a member or supporter of the Parliamentary party in the English Civil War. ▷so named because of the short-cropped hairstyle of the Puritans, who formed an important element in the party.

round·heel /ˈroundˌhēl/ ▸*n. informal* a promiscuous woman. ▷1950s: with reference to worn-down heels, allowing the wearer to lean backwards. **—round·heeled** *adj.*

round·house /ˈroundˌhous/ ▸*n.* **1** a locomotive maintenance shed built around a turntable. **2** *informal* a blow given with a wide sweep of the arm. ■ a wide turn on a surfboard. **3** *chiefly historical* a cabin or cabins on the after part of the quarterdeck of a sailing ship.

round·house kick ▸*n.* (chiefly in karate) a kick made with a wide sweep of the leg and rotation of the body.

round·ly /ˈroundlē/ ▸*adv.* **1** in a vehement or emphatic manner: *the latest attacks have been roundly condemned by campaigners for peace.* ■ so thoroughly as to leave no doubt: *the army was roundly beaten.* ■ too plainly for politeness; bluntly: *she told him roundly to get to the point.* **2** so as to form a circular or roughly circular shape: *he was a middle-aged, roundly built man.*

round-nose ▸*adj.* **1** (of a tool) having the end rounded, so as to produce a rounded cut or surface or to prevent accidents or damage. **2** (of a bullet) having a rounded front end.

▸*n.* a bullet with a rounded front end. **—round-nosed** *adj.*

round rob·in ▸*n.* **1** [often as *adj.*] a tournament in which each competitor plays in turn against every other: *a round-robin competition.* **2** a petition, esp. one with signatures written in a circle to conceal the order of writing. ■ a letter written by several people in turn, each person adding text before passing the letter on to someone else: [as *adj.*] *a round-robin letter.* **3** a series or sequence: *an inconclusive round robin of talks in Cairo, Washington, and New York.*

Round Rock a city in central Texas, north of Austin; pop. 30,923.

round shot ▸*n. historical* ammunition in the form of cast-iron or steel spherical balls for firing from cannon.

round-shoul·dered ▸*adj.* having the shoulders bent forward so that the back is rounded: *a round-shouldered slouch.*

rounds·man /ˈroundzmən/ ▸*n.* (*pl.* **-men**) **1** a police officer in charge of a patrol. **2** a person on a regular route delivering and taking orders for milk, bread, etc.

Round Ta·ble ▸*n.* **1** the table at which King Arthur and his knights sat so that none should have precedence. It was first mentioned in 1155. **2** an international charitable association that holds discussions and undertakes community service. **3** (**round table**) an assembly for discussion, esp. at a conference: *art historians fly around the world to attend colloquia and round tables* | [as *adj.*] *round-table talks.*

round-the-clock ▸*adj.* lasting all day and all night: *round-the-clock surveillance.*

round trip ▸*n.* a journey to one or more places and back again.

round turn ▸*n.* a complete turn of a rope around another rope or other object.

round·up /ˈroundˌəp/ ▸*n.* a systematic gathering together of people or things: *mass police roundups and detentions | the rites of the cattle drive, the roundup, and the branding.* ■ a summary of facts or events: *a news roundup every fifteen minutes.*

round win·dow ▸*n.* informal term for FENESTRA ROTUNDA (see FENESTRA).

round·wood /ˈroundˌwo͝od/ ▸*n.* timber that is left as small logs, not sawn into planks or chopped for fuel, typically taken from near the tops of trees and used for furniture.

round·worm /ˈroundˌwərm/ ▸*n.* a nematode, esp. a parasitic one found in the intestines of mammals. • Many species in the class Phasmida, including the large *Ascaris lumbricoides* in humans.

roup[1] /ro͞op/ *chiefly Scottish N. English* ▸*n.* an auction.

▸*v.* [*trans.*] (often **be rouped**) sell (something) by auction: *his effects were rouped.* ▷Middle English (in the sense 'roar, croak'): of Scandinavian origin; compare with Old Norse *raupa* 'boast, brag.'

roup[2] ▸*n.* an infectious disease of poultry affecting the respiratory tract. ▷mid 16th cent.: of unknown origin. **—roup·y** *adj.*

rouse /rouz/ ▸*v.* [*trans.*] bring out of sleep; awaken: *she was roused from a deep sleep by a hand on her shoulder.* ■ [*intrans.*] cease to sleep or to be inactive; wake up: *she roused, took off her eyepads, and looked around.* ■ startle out of inactivity; cause to become active: *once the enemy camp was roused, they would move on the castle | she'd just stay a few more minutes, then* **rouse herself** *and go back.* ■ startle (game) from a lair or cover. ■ cause to feel angry or excited: *the crowds were* **roused to** *fever pitch by the drama of the race.* ■ cause or give rise to (an emotion or feeling): *his evasiveness roused my curiosity.* ■ [*trans.*] *archaic Nautical* haul (something) vigorously in the specified direction: *rouse the cable out.* ■ stir (a liquid, esp. beer while brewing): *rouse the beer as the* *hops are introduced.* ▷late Middle English (originally as a hawking and hunting term): probably from Anglo-Norman French, of unknown ultimate origin. —**rous·a·ble** *adj.* —**rous·er** *n.*

rous·ing /ˈrouziNG/ ▸*adj.* **1** exciting; stirring: *a rousing speech.* **2** *archaic* (of a fire) blazing strongly. —**rous·ing·ly** *adv.*

Rous sar·co·ma /rous/ ▸*n.* a form of tumor, caused by an RNA virus, that affects birds, particularly poultry. ▷early 20th cent.: named after Francis P. *Rous* (1879–1970), American physician.

Rous·seau[1] /ro͞oˈsō/, Henri (Julien) (1844–1910), French painter; known as **le Douanier** ("customs officer"). After retiring as a customs official in 1893, he created bold, colorful paintings of fantastic dreams and exotic jungle landscapes.

Rous·seau[2], Jean-Jacques (1712–78), French philosopher and writer, born in Switzerland. He believed that civilization warps the fundamental goodness of human nature, but that the ill effects can be moderated by active participation in democratic consensual politics. Notable works: *Émile* (1762) and *The Social Contract* (1762).

Rous·seau[3], (Pierre Étienne) Théodore (1812–67), French painter. A leading landscapist of the Barbizon School, his works typically depict the scenery and changing light effects of the forest of Fontainebleau.

roust /roust/ ▸*v.* [*trans.*] cause to get up or start moving; rouse: *I rousted him out of his bed with a cup of coffee.* ■ *informal* treat roughly; harass: *the detectives who had rousted him the night of the murder.* ▷mid 17th cent.: perhaps an alteration of **ROUSE**.

roust·a·bout /ˈroustəˌbout/ ▸*n.* an unskilled or casual laborer. ■ a laborer on an oil rig. ■ a dock laborer or deckhand. ■ a circus laborer. ▷mid 19th cent.: from the verb **ROUST**.

rout[1] /rout/ ▸*n.* **1** a disorderly retreat of defeated troops: *the retreat degenerated into a rout* | *the army was in a state of demoralization verging on rout.* ■ a decisive defeat: *the party lost more than half their seats in the rout.* **2** *dated Law* an assembly of people who have made a move toward committing an illegal act that would constitute an offense of riot. ■ *archaic* a disorderly or tumultuous crowd of people: *a rout of strangers ought not to be admitted.* **3** *Brit., archaic* a large evening party or reception.

▸*v.* [*trans.*] defeat and cause to retreat in disorder: *in a matter of minutes the attackers were routed.* ▷Middle English: ultimately based on Latin *ruptus* 'broken,' from the verb *rumpere*; sense 1 and the verb (late 16th cent.) are from obsolete French *route*, probably from Italian *rotta* 'breakup of an army'; the other senses are via Anglo-Norman French *rute*.

▸*PHRASE* □ **put to rout** put to flight; defeat utterly: *I once put a gang to rout.*

rout[2] ▸*v.* **1** [*trans.*] cut a groove, or any pattern not extending to the edges, in (a wooden or metal surface): *you routed each plank all along its length.* **2** another term for **ROOT**[2]. ■ find (someone or something), or force them from a place: *Simon routed him from the stable.* ▷mid 16th cent. (sense 2): alteration of the verb **ROOT**[2]. Sense 1 dates from the early 19th cent.

route /ro͞ot; rout/ ▸*n.* a way or course taken in getting from a starting point to a destination: *our route was via the Jerusalem road.* ■ the line of a road, path, railroad, etc. ■ a circuit traveled in delivering, selling, or collecting goods. ■ a method or process leading to a specified result: *the many routes to a healthier diet will be described.*

▸*v.* (**rout·ing**; *Brit.* also **route·ing**) [*trans.*] send or direct along a specified course: *all lines of communication were routed through Atlanta.* ▷Middle English: from Old French *rute* 'road,' from Latin *rupta (via)* 'broken (way),' feminine past participle of *rumpere*.

route man ▸*n.* another term for **ROUNDSMAN** (sense 2).

route march ▸*n.* a march for troops over a designated route, typically via roads or tracks.

rout·er[1] /ˈroutər/ ▸*n.* a power tool with a shaped cutter, used in carpentry for making grooves for joints, decorative moldings, etc.

rout·er[2] /ˈro͞otər; ˈroutər/ ▸*n.* a device that forwards data packets to the appropriate parts of a computer network.

rou·tine /ro͞oˈtēn/ ▸*n.* a sequence of actions regularly followed; a fixed program: *I settled down into a routine of work and sleep* | *as a matter of routine a report will be sent to the director.* ■ a set sequence in a performance such as a dance or comedy act: *he was trying to persuade her to have a tap routine in the play.* ■ *Computing* a sequence of instructions for performing a task that forms a program or a distinct part of one.

▸*adj.* performed as part of a regular procedure rather than for a special reason: *the principal insisted that this was just a routine annual drill.* ■ monotonous or tedious: *we are set in our dull routine existence.*

▸*v.* [*trans.*] *rare* organize according to a routine: *all had been routined with smoothness.* ▷late 17th cent. (denoting a regular course or procedure): from French, from *route* 'road' (see **ROUTE**). —**rou·tine·ly** *adv.*

rout·ing code ▸*n.* any of various codes used to direct data, documents, or merchandise, including: ■ the magnetically encoded numbers on a check. ■ a numeric code that directs telephone calls or Internet traffic.

rou·tin·ism /ro͞oˈtēˌnizəm; ˈro͞otnˌizəm/ ▸*n.* *archaic* the prevalence or domination of routine. —**rou·tin·ist** *n.* & *adj.*

rou·tin·ize /ro͞oˈtēˌnīz; ˈro͞otnˌīz/ ▸*v.* [*trans.*] (usu. **be routinized**) make (something) into a matter of routine; subject to a routine: *communication was routinized to ensure consistency of information.* —**rou·tin·i·za·tion** /-ˌtēnəˈzāSHən; ˌro͞otn-ə-/ *n.*

roux /ro͞o/ ▸*n.* (*pl.* same) *Cooking* a mixture of fat (esp. butter) and flour used in making sauces. ▷from French *(beurre) roux* 'browned (butter).'

ROV ▸*abbr.* remotely operated vehicle.

rove[1] /rōv/ ▸*v.* [*intrans.*] travel constantly without a fixed destination; wander: *a quarter of a million refugees roved around the country.* ■ [*trans.*] wander over or through (a place) in such a way: *children roving the streets.* ■ [usu. as *adj.*] (**roving**) travel for one's work, having no fixed base: *he trained as a roving reporter.* ■ (of eyes) look in changing directions in order to see something thoroughly: *the policeman's eyes roved around the bar.*

▸*n.* [in *sing.*] a journey, esp. one with no specific destination; an act of wandering: *a new exhibit will electrify campuses on its national rove.* ▷late 15th cent. (originally a term in archery in the sense 'shoot at a casual mark of undetermined range'): perhaps from dialect *rave* 'to stray,' probably of Scandinavian origin.

rove[2] ▸ past of **REEVE**[2].

rove[3] ▸*n.* a sliver of cotton, wool, or other fiber, drawn out and slightly twisted, esp. preparatory to spinning.

▸*v.* [*trans.*] form (slivers of wool, cotton, or other fiber) into roves. ▷late 18th cent.: of unknown origin.

rove[4] ▸*n.* a small metal plate or ring for a rivet to pass through and be clenched over, esp. in boatbuilding. ▷Middle English: from Old Norse *ró*, with the addition of parasitic *-v-*.

rove bee·tle ▸*n.* a long-bodied beetle with very short wing cases, typically found among decaying matter where it may scavenge or prey on other scavengers. • Family Staphylinidae: numerous genera.

rov·er[1] /ˈrōvər/ ▸*n.* **1** a person who spends their time wandering: *they became rovers who departed further and further from civilization.* **2** (in various sports) a player not restricted to a particular position on the field. **3** a vehicle for driving over rough terrain. ■ a vehicle driven by remote control over extraterrestrial terrain. **4** *Croquet* a ball that has passed all the wickets but not pegged out. ■ a player who has such a ball. **5** *Archery* a target for long-distance shooting. ■ a target chosen at random and not at a determined range.

rov·er[2] ▸*n.* *archaic* a sea robber; a pirate. ▷Middle English: from Middle Low German, Middle Dutch *rōver*, from *rōven* 'rob'; related to **REAVE**.

rov·er[3] ▸*n.* a person or machine that makes roves of fiber (see **ROVE**[3]).

rov·ing /ˈrōviNG/ ▸*n.* another term for **ROVE**[3]. ■ roves collectively.

rov·ing eye ▸*n.* [usu. in *sing.*] a tendency to flirt or be constantly looking to start a new sexual relationship: *if his wife wasn't around, he had a roving eye.*

Ro·vno /ˈrôvnə/ Russian name for **RIVNE**.

row[1] /rō/ ▸*n.* a number of people or things in a more or less straight line: *her villa stood in a row of similar ones.* ■ a line of seats in a theater: *they sat in the front row.* ■ a street with a continuous line of houses along one or both of its sides, esp. when specifying houses of a particular type or function: *fraternity row.* ■ a horizontal line of entries in a table. ■ a complete line of stitches in knitting or crochet. ▷Old English *rāw*, of Germanic origin; related to Dutch *rij* and German *Reihe*.

▸*PHRASES* □ **a hard** (or **tough**) **row to hoe** a difficult task. □ **in a row** forming a line: *four chairs were set in a row.* ■ *informal* in succession: *we get six days off in a row.*

row[2] /rō/ ▸*v.* [*trans.*] propel (a boat) with oars: *out in the bay a small figure was rowing a rubber dinghy.* ■ [*intrans.*] travel by propelling a boat in this way: *we rowed down the river all day.* ■ convey (a passenger) in a boat by propelling it with oars: *her father was rowing her across the lake.* ■ [*intrans.*] engage in the sport of rowing, esp. competitively: *he rowed for Yale.*

▸*n.* [in *sing.*] a period of rowing. ▷Old English *rōwan*, of Germanic origin; related to **RUDDER**; from an Indo-European root shared by Latin *remus* 'oar,' Greek *eretmon* 'oar.' —**row·er** *n.*

row[3] /rou/ *informal* ▸*n.* a noisy acrimonious quarrel: *they had a row and she stormed out of the house.* See note at **QUARREL**. ■ a serious dispute: *the director is at the center of a row over policy decisions.* ■ a loud noise or uproar: *if he's at home he must have heard that row.*

▸*v.* [*intrans.*] have a quarrel: *they rowed about who would receive the money from the sale.* ▷mid 18th cent.: of unknown origin.

▸*PHRASE* □ **make** (or **kick up**) **a row** make a noise or commotion. ■ make a vigorous protest.

Row·an /ˈrōən/, Carl (Thomas) (1925–2000), U.S. journalist and specialist in race relations. He wrote a nationally syndicated column from 1965. The U.S. ambassador to Finland 1963–64, he went on to direct the U.S. Information Agency 1964–65.

row·an /ˈrouən; ˈrōən/ (also **row·an tree**) ▸*n.* a mountain ash, in particular the European *Sorbus aucuparia*. ■ (also **row·an ber·ry**) the scarlet berry of this tree. ▷late 15th cent. (originally Scots and northern English): of Scandinavian origin; compare with Norwegian *rogn*.

row·boat /ˈrōˌbōt/ ▸*n.* a small boat propelled by oars.

row·dy /ˈroudē/ ▸*adj.* (**-di·er**, **-di·est**) noisy and disorderly: *it was a rowdy but good-natured crowd.*

▸*n.* (*pl.* **-dies**) a noisy and disorderly person. ▷early 19th cent. (originally U.S. in the sense 'lawless backwoodsman'): of unknown origin. —**row·di·ly** /ˈroudl-ē/ *adv.* —**row·di·ness** *n.* —**row·dy·ism** /-ˌizəm/ *n.*

Rowe /rō/, Nicholas (1674–1718), English playwright. Notable works: *Tamerlane* (1701) and *The Fair Penitent* (1703).

row·el /ˈrou(ə)l/ ▸*n.* a spiked revolving disk at the end of a spur.

▸*v.* (**-eled**, **-el·ing**; *Brit.* **-elled**, **-el·ling**) [*trans.*] use a rowel to urge on (a horse): *he **roweled** his horse **on** as fast as he could.* ▷Middle English: from Old French *roel(e)*, from late Latin *rotella*, diminutive of Latin *rota* 'wheel.'

row·en /ˈrouən/ ▸*n.* a second growth of grass or hay in one season. ▷Middle English: from an Old Northern French variant of Old French *regain* 'an increase.'

row house /rō / ▸*n.* any of a row of houses joined by common sidewalls.

row·ing /ˈrō-iNG/ ▸*n.* the sport or pastime of propelling a boat by means of oars.

> Racing takes place in narrow, light boats (**shells**), between single rowers (**scullers**) with two oars, or between crews of two, four, or eight people with one oar each; crews are often steered by a coxswain.

row·ing boat ▸*n.* British term for **ROWBOAT**.

row·ing ma·chine ▸*n.* an exercise machine with a sliding seat, used to strengthen the muscles used in rowing.

Rowl·ing /ˈrouliNG/, J. K. (1965–), British writer; full name *Joanne Kathleen Rowling*. Her series of children's books featuring the character Harry Potter includes *Harry Potter and the Sorcerer's Stone* (1998), *Harry Potter and the Chamber of Secrets* (1999), *Harry Potter and the Prisoner of Azkaban* (1999), *Harry Potter and the Goblet of Fire* (2000), and *Harry Potter and the Order of the Phoenix* (2003).

row·lock /ˈrōˌläk/ ▸*n.* *chiefly Brit.* an oarlock. ▷mid 18th cent.: alteration of **OARLOCK**, influenced by the verb **ROW**[2].

row vec·tor /rō/ ▸*n.* *Mathematics* a vector represented by a matrix consisting of a single row of elements.

rox·ar·sone /räkˈsärˌsōn/ ▸*n.* an arsenic-containing antibiotic drug that is widely used as a food additive in the poultry industry to promote growth and control intestinal parasites. It is considered a source of arsenic contamination in water near some large poultry producers.

Rox·bury /ˈräksˌberē; -bərē/ a district of Boston in Massachusetts, today the center of the city's black community.

Roy /roi/ a city in northeastern Utah, a southwestern suburb of Ogden; pop. 32,885.

roy·al /ˈroiəl/ ▶*adj.* having the status of a king or queen or a member of their family: *contributors included members of the royal family.* ■ belonging to or carried out or exercised by a king or queen: *the royal palace | the coalition obtained royal approval for the appointment.* ■ [*attrib.*] in the service or under the patronage of a king or queen: *a royal maid.* ■ [*attrib.*] of a quality or size suitable for a king or queen; splendid: *a royal fortune.* ■ *informal* unmitigated; extreme: *he might turn out to be* ***a royal pain.***
▶*n.* **1** *informal* a member of a royal family, esp. in England. **2** short for ROYAL SAIL or ROYAL MAST. **3** (in full **metric royal**) a paper size, now standardized at 636 × 480 mm. ■ (in full **royal octavo**) a book size, now standardized at 234 × 156 mm. ■ (in full **royal quarto**) a book size, now standardized at 312 × 237 mm. ▷late Middle English: from Old French *roial*, from Latin *regalis* 'regal.' —**roy·al·ly** *adv.*
▶*PHRASE* □ **royal road to** a way of attaining or reaching something without trouble: *there is no royal road to teaching.*

Roy·al Air Force (abbr.: **RAF**) the British air force, formed in 1918.

roy·al an·te·lope ▶*n.* a shy West African antelope with an arched back, short neck, and a red and brown coat with white underparts. It is the smallest known antelope. • *Neotragus pygmaeus*, family Bovidae.

roy·al blue ▶*n.* a deep, vivid blue.

Roy·al Ca·na·di·an Mount·ed Po·lice (abbr.: **RCMP**) the national police force of Canada, founded in 1873. A member of the force is informally called a MOUNTIE.

roy·al fern ▶*n.* a large pale green fern that has very long spreading fronds with widely spaced oblong lobes, occurring worldwide in wet habitats. • *Osmunda regalis*, family Osmundaceae.

roy·al flush ▶*n. Poker* a straight flush including ace, king, queen, jack, and ten all in the same suit, which is the hand of the highest possible value when wild cards are not in use.

Roy·al Gorge (also the **Grand Canyon of the Arkansas**) a steep defile on the Arkansas River in south central Colorado, near Cañon City, a noted tourist attraction.

roy·al ic·ing ▶*n. chiefly Brit.* hard white icing made from confectioners' sugar and egg whites, typically used to decorate fruitcakes.

roy·al·ist /ˈroiəlist/ ▶*n.* a person who supports the principle of monarchy or a particular monarchy. ■ a supporter of the king against Parliament in the English Civil War. ■ a supporter of the British during the American Revolution; a Tory.
▶*adj.* giving support to the monarchy: *the paper claims to be royalist.* ■ (in the English Civil War) supporting the king against Parliament: *the royalist army.* —**roy·al·ism** /-ˌizəm/ *n.*

roy·al jel·ly ▶*n.* a substance secreted by honeybee workers and fed by them to larvae that are being raised as potential queen bees.

Roy·al Ma·rines a British armed service (part of the Royal Navy) founded in 1664, trained for service at sea, or on land under specific circumstances.

roy·al mast ▶*n.* a section of a sailing ship's mast above the topgallant.

Roy·al Na·vy (abbr.: **RN**) the British navy. It was the most powerful navy in the world from the 17th century until World War II.

Roy·al Oak a city in southeastern Michigan, northwest of Detroit; pop. 65,410.

roy·al palm ▶*n.* a New World palm that is widely cultivated as a roadside tree. • Genus *Roystonea*, family Palmae: several species, in particular the **Florida royal palm** (*R. elata*) and the **Cuban royal palm** (*R. regia*).

roy·al pur·ple ▶*n.* a rich deep shade of purple.

roy·al sail ▶*n.* a sail above a sailing ship's topgallant sail.

Roy·al So·ci·e·ty (in full **Royal Society of London**) the oldest and most prestigious scientific society in Britain. It was formed by followers of Francis Bacon to promote scientific discussion esp. in the physical sciences, and received its charter from Charles II in 1662.

roy·al stag ▶*n. Brit.* a red deer stag with a head of twelve or more points.

roy·al ten·nis ▶*n.* chiefly Australian term for COURT TENNIS.

roy·al·ty /ˈroiəltē/ ▶*n.* (*pl.* **-ties**) **1** people of royal blood or status: *diplomats, heads of state, and royalty shared tables at the banquet.* ■ a member of a royal family: *she swept by as if she were royalty.* ■ the status or power of a king or queen: *the brilliance of her clothes, her jewels, all revealed her royalty.* **2** a sum of money paid to a patentee for the use of a patent or to an author or composer for each copy of a book sold or for each public performance of a work. **3** a royal right (now esp. over minerals) granted by a sovereign to an individual or corporation. ■ a payment made by a producer of minerals, oil, or natural gas to the owner of the site or of the mineral rights over it. ▷late Middle English: from Old French *roialte*, from *roial* (see ROYAL). The sense 'royal right (esp. over minerals)' (late 15th cent.) developed into the sense 'payment made by a mineral producer to the site owner' (mid 19th cent.), which was then transferred to payments for the use of patents and published materials.

roy·al war·rant ▶*n.* a warrant issued by a sovereign, in particular: ■ (**Royal Warrant**) (in the UK) one authorizing a company to display the royal arms, indicating that goods or services of quality are supplied to the sovereign or to a specified member of the royal family.

roy·al "we" ▶*n.* the use of "we" instead of "I" by an individual person, as traditionally used by a sovereign: *Queen Victoria once remarked, with British understatement, "we are not amused."*

Royce /rois/, Sir (Frederick) Henry (1863–1933), English engine designer. He founded Rolls-Royce Ltd. with Charles Stewart Rolls in 1906.

roz·zer /ˈräzər/ ▶*n. Brit., informal* a police officer. ▷late 19th cent.: of unknown origin.

RP ▶*abbr.* received pronunciation.

RPG ▶*abbr.* ■ report program generator, a high-level commercial computer programming language. ■ rocket-propelled grenade. ■ role-playing game.

rpm ▶*abbr.* ■ resale price maintenance. ■ revolutions per minute.

RPO ▶*abbr.* Royal Philharmonic Orchestra.

rps (also **r.p.s.**) ▶*abbr.* revolutions per second.

rpt ▶*abbr.* repeat.

RPV ▶*abbr.* remotely piloted vehicle.

RQ ▶*abbr.* respiratory quotient.

RR ▶*abbr.* ■ railroad. ■ rural route.

RRB ▶*abbr.* Railroad Retirement Board.

-rrhea (*chiefly Brit.* **-rrhoea**) ▶*comb. form* discharge; flow: *diarrhea.* ▷from Greek *rhoia* 'flow, flux.'

rRNA ▶*abbr. Biochemistry* ribosomal RNA.

RRP *Brit.* ▶*abbr.* recommended retail price.

RRR ▶*abbr.* (of mail) return receipt requested.

RS ▶*abbr.* ■ (in the U.S.) received standard. ■ (in the UK) Royal Scots.

Rs. ▶*abbr.* rupee(s).

RSA ▶*abbr.* ■ Republic of South Africa. ■ Royal Scottish Academy; Royal Scottish Academician.

RSC ▶*abbr.* ■ (in the UK) Royal Society of Chemistry.

RSE ▶*abbr.* Royal Society of Edinburgh.

RSFSR *historical* ▶*abbr.* Russian Soviet Federated Socialist Republic.

RSI ▶*abbr.* repetitive strain injury.

RSJ ▶*abbr.* rolled steel joist.

RSNC ▶*abbr.* (in the UK) Royal Society for Nature Conservation.

RSPCA ▶*abbr.* (in the UK) Royal Society for the Prevention of Cruelty to Animals.

RSV ▶*abbr.* Revised Standard Version (of the Bible).

RSVP ▶*abbr.* répondez s'il vous plaît, or please reply (used at the end of invitations to request a response). ▷French.

RT ▶*abbr.* ■ radiotelegraphy. ■ radiotelephony.

rt. ▶*abbr.* right.

RTA *Brit.* ▶*abbr.* road traffic accident.

rte. ▶*abbr.* route.

RTF ▶*abbr.* rich text format, developed to allow the transfer of graphics and formatted text between different applications and operating systems.

RTFM *informal Computing* ▶*abbr.* read the fucking manual (used esp. in electronic mail in reply to a question whose answer is obvious).

Rt Hon. *Brit.* ▶*abbr.* Right Honourable.

Rt Revd (also **Rt Rev**) ▶*abbr.* Right Reverend.

RTW ▶*abbr.* ready-to-wear.

Ru ▶*symbol* the chemical element ruthenium.

RU-486 (also **RU 486**) ▶*n.* trademark for MIFEPRISTONE.

rub /rəb/ ▶*v.* (**rubbed**, **rub·bing**) [*trans.*] move one's hand or a cloth repeatedly to and fro on the surface of (something) with firm pressure: *she rubbed her arm, where she had a large bruise* | [*intrans.*] *he* ***rubbed at*** *the dirt on his jeans.* ■ [*trans.*] move (one's hand, a cloth, or another object) over a surface in such a way: *he rubbed a finger around the rim of his mug.* ■ [*trans.*] cause (two things) to move to and fro against each other with a certain amount of pressure and friction: *many insects make noises by rubbing parts of their bodies together.* ■ [*intrans.*] move to and fro over something while pressing or grinding against it: *the ice breaks into small floes that rub against each other.* ■ [*intrans.*] (of shoes or other hard items in contact with the skin) cause pain through friction: *badly fitting shoes can rub painfully.* ■ make dry, clean, or smooth with pressure from a hand, cloth, or other object: *she found a towel and began rubbing her hair* | [*trans.*] *she rubbed herself as dry as possible.* ■ [*trans.*] spread (ointment, polish, or a substance of similar consistency) over a surface with repeated movements of one's hand or a cloth: *she took out her sunblock and rubbed some on her nose.* ■ (**rub something in/into/through**) work an ingredient into (a mixture) by breaking and blending it with firm movements of one's fingers: *sift the flour into a bowl and rub in the fat.* ■ reproduce the design of (a gravestone, memorial tablet, etc.) by laying paper on it and rubbing the paper with charcoal, colored chalk, etc. ■ [*intrans.*] *Lawn Bowling* (of a bowl) be slowed or diverted by the unevenness of the ground.
▶*phrasal v.* □ **rub something down** dry, smooth, or clean something by rubbing. ■ rub the sweat from a horse or one's own body after exercise. □ **rub off** be transferred by contact or association: *when parents are having a hard time, their tension can easily* ***rub off on*** *the kids.* □ **rub someone out** *informal* kill someone. □ **rub something out** erase pencil marks with an eraser. □ **rub something up** polish a metal or leather object.
▶*n.* **1** [usu. in *sing.*] an act of rubbing: *she pulled out a towel and gave her head a quick rub.* ■ an ointment designed to be rubbed on the skin to ease pain: *a muscle rub.* **2** (usu. **the rub**) a difficulty, esp. one of central importance in a situation: *that was the rub—she had not cared enough.* [from Shakespeare's *Hamlet* (III. i. 65).] **3** *Lawn Bowling* an inequality of the ground impeding or diverting a bowl; the diversion or hindering of a bowl by this. ▷Middle English (as a verb): perhaps from Low German *rubben*, of unknown ultimate origin. The noun dates from the late 16th cent.
▶*PHRASES* □ **not have two —— to rub together** *informal* have none or hardly any of the specified item, esp. money: *she doesn't have two nickels to rub together.* □ **rub elbows** (or **shoulders**) associate or come into contact (with another person): *he rubbed elbows with TV stars at the party.* □ **rub one's hands** rub one's hands together to show keen satisfaction. □ **rub it in** (or **rub someone's nose in something**) *informal* emphatically draw someone's attention to an embarrassing or painful fact: *they don't just beat you, they rub it in.* □ **rub noses** rub one's nose against someone else's in greeting (esp. as traditional among Maoris and some other peoples). □ **rub of the green** *Golf* any accidental or unpredictable influence on the course or position of the ball. ■ good fortune, esp. as determining events in an athletic contest. □ **rub someone** (or *Brit.* **rub someone up**) **the wrong way** irritate or repel someone as by stroking a cat against the lie of its fur.

Rub' al Kha·li /ˌrōōb al ˈkälē; äl ˈKHälē/ a vast desert in the Arabian peninsula that extends from central Saudi Arabia south to Yemen and east to the United Arab Emirates and Oman. It is also known as the Great Sandy Desert and the Empty Quarter.

ru·ba·to /rōōˈbätō/ *Music* ▶*n.* (*pl.* **-ba·tos** or **-ba·ti** /-ˈbätē/) (also **tem·po ru·ba·to**) the temporary disregarding of strict tempo to allow an expressive quickening or slackening, usually without altering the overall pace.
▶*adj.* performed in this way. ▷Italian, literally 'robbed.'

rub·ber[1] /ˈrəbər/ ▶*n.* a tough elastic polymeric substance made from the latex of a tropical plant or synthetically. ■ (**rubbers**) rubber boots; galoshes. ■ *Baseball* an oblong piece of rubber or similar material embedded in the pitcher's mound, on which the pitcher must keep one foot while delivering the ball. ■ *informal* a condom. ■ *Brit.* an eraser for pencil or ink marks. ▷mid 16th cent.: from the verb RUB + -ER[1]. The original sense was 'an implement (such as a hard brush) used for rubbing and cleaning.' Because an early use of the elastic substance (previously known as CAOUTCHOUC) was to rub out pencil marks, *rubber* gained the sense 'eraser' in the late 18th cent. The sense was subsequently (mid 19th cent.) generalized to refer to the substance in any form or use, at first often differentiated as INDIA RUBBER. —**rub·ber·i·ness** *n.* —**rub·ber·y** *adj.*

rub·ber[2] ▸*n.* a contest consisting of a series of successive matches (typically three or five) between the same sides or people in tennis, cricket, and other games. ■ (usu. **rubber match** or **rubber game**) a game played to determine the winner of a series: *Clemens will pitch in the rubber game of this tied-up series.* ■ *Bridge* a unit of play in which one side scores bonus points for winning the best of three games. ▷late 16th cent.: of unknown origin; early use was as a term in lawn bowling.

rub·ber band ▸*n.* a loop of stretchy rubber for holding things together.

rub·ber bo·a ▸*n.* a short snake with a stout shiny brown body that looks and feels like rubber, found in western North America. • *Charina bottae*, family Boidae.

rub·ber bul·let ▸*n.* a large projectile made of rubber and shot from a firearm, used esp. in riot control.

rub·ber ce·ment ▸*n.* a cement or adhesive containing rubber in a solvent.

rub·ber check ▸*n. informal, humorous* a check that is returned unpaid. ▷1920s (originally U.S.): by association with BOUNCE.

rub·ber chick·en ▸*n. informal* food, typically chicken, consumed at social gatherings, esp. at the events and dinners necessary for a public figure to attend.

rub·ber duck ▸*n. S. African, informal* an inflatable flat-bottomed rubber dinghy, typically motorized. —**rub·ber duck·er** *n.*

rub·ber·ize /ˈrəbəˌrīz/ ▸*v.* [*trans.*] [usu. as *adj.*] (**rubberized**) treat or coat (something) with rubber.

rub·ber·neck /ˈrəbərˌnek/ *informal* ▸*n.* a person who turns their head to stare at something in a foolish manner, esp. while driving a car.
▸*v.* [*intrans.*] stare in such a way: *a passerby rubbernecking at the accident scene.* —**rub·ber·neck·er** *n.*

rub·ber·oid /ˈrəbəˌroid/ ▸*adj.* made of or resembling rubber.

rub·ber plant ▸*n.* **1** an evergreen tree of the fig family that has large dark green shiny leaves and is widely cultivated as a houseplant. Native to Southeast Asia, it was formerly grown as a source of rubber. • *Ficus elastica*, family Moraceae. **2** another term for RUBBER TREE.

rub·ber stamp ▸*n.* a hand-held device for inking and imprinting a message or design on a surface. ■ *figurative* a person or organization that approves the decisions of others, not having the power or ability to reject or alter them: *I hope we never get to the day judges dictate to juries so they become rubber stamps.* ■ an indication of such an approval.
▸*v.* (**rub·ber-stamp**) [*trans.*] approve automatically without proper consideration: *the college would not rubber-stamp its athletes for graduation.*

rub·ber tree ▸*n.* a tree that produces the latex from which rubber is manufactured, native to the Amazonian rain forest and widely cultivated elsewhere. • *Hevea brasiliensis*, family Euphorbiaceae. ■ used in names of other trees from which a similar latex can be obtained.

rub·bing /ˈrəbiNG/ ▸*n.* **1** the action of rubbing something: *dab at the stain—vigorous rubbing could damage the carpet.* **2** an impression of a design on brass or stone, made by rubbing on paper laid over it with colored wax, pencil, chalk, etc.

rub·bing al·co·hol ▸*n.* denatured alcohol, typically perfumed, used as an antiseptic or in massage.

rub·bing strake ▸*n.* a protective strip running along a boat's side below the gunwale to prevent damage when coming alongside something.

rub·bish /ˈrəbiSH/ ▸*n.* waste material; refuse or litter: *an alleyway high with rubbish.* ■ material that is considered unimportant or valueless: *she had to sift through the rubbish in every drawer.* ■ absurd, nonsensical, or worthless talk or ideas: *I suppose you believe that rubbish about vampires.*
▸*v.* [*trans.*] *Brit., informal* criticize severely and reject as worthless: *he has pointedly rubbished professional estimates of the development and running costs.*
▸*adj. Brit., informal* very bad; worthless or useless: *people might say I was a rubbish manager.* ▷late Middle English: from Anglo-Norman French *rubbous*; perhaps related to Old French *robe* 'spoils'; compare with RUBBLE. The change in the ending was due to association with -ISH[1]. The verb (1950s) was originally Australian and New Zealand slang. —**rub·bish·y** *adj.*

rub·ble /ˈrəbəl/ ▸*n.* waste or rough fragments of stone, brick, concrete, etc., esp. as the debris from the demolition of buildings: *two buildings collapsed, trapping scores of people in the rubble.* ■ pieces of rough or undressed stone used in building walls, esp. as filling for cavities. ▷late Middle English: perhaps from an Anglo-Norman French alteration of Old French *robe* 'spoils'; compare with RUBBISH. —**rub·bly** /ˈrəb(ə)lē/ *adj.*

rub·bled /ˈrəbəld/ ▸*adj.* covered in rubble or reduced to rubble.

rub board ▸*n.* **1** a board fitted with teeth, used for making drawnwork from linen. **2** another term for WASHBOARD (sense 2).

rub·by /ˈrəbē/ ▸*n.* (*pl.* **-bies**) *Canadian, informal* an alcoholic who habitually drinks rubbing alcohol.

rub·down /ˈrəbˌdoun/ (also **rub-down**) ▸*n.* a massage. ■ an act of drying, smoothing down, or cleaning something by rubbing: *a shower and a brisk rubdown with a towel* | [as *adj.*] *rubdown decals.*

rube /ro͞ob/ ▸*n. informal, often derogatory* a country bumpkin. ▷late 19th cent.: abbreviation of the given name *Reuben.*

ru·bel·la /ro͞oˈbelə/ ▸*n.* a contagious viral disease, with symptoms like mild measles. It can cause fetal malformation if contracted in early pregnancy. Also called GERMAN MEASLES. ▷late 19th cent.: modern Latin, neuter plural of Latin *rubellus* 'reddish.'

ru·bel·lite /ˈro͞obəˌlīt/ ▸*n.* a red variety of tourmaline. ▷late 18th cent.: from Latin *rubellus* 'reddish' + -ITE[1].

Ru·bens /ˈro͞obənz/, Sir Peter Paul (1577–1640), Flemish painter. He is best known for his portraits and for his paintings of mythological subjects featuring voluptuous female nudes, such as in *Venus and Adonis* (*c.*1635).

ru·be·o·la /ˌro͞obēˈōlə/ ▸*n.* medical term for MEASLES. ▷late 17th cent.: from medieval Latin, diminutive (on the pattern of *variola*) of Latin *rubeus* 'red.'

ru·bes·cent /ro͞oˈbesənt/ ▸*adj. chiefly poetic/literary* reddening; blushing. ▷mid 18th cent.: from Latin *rubescent-* 'reddening,' from the verb *rubescere*, from *ruber* 'red.'

Ru·bi·con /ˈro͞obəˌkän/ a stream in northeastern Italy that marked the ancient boundary between Italy and Cisalpine Gaul. Julius Caesar led his army across it into Italy in 49 BC, breaking the law forbidding a general to lead an army out of his province, and so committing himself to war against the Senate and Pompey. The ensuing civil war resulted in victory for Caesar after three years. ■ [as *n.*] a point of no return: *on the way to political union we are now* ***crossing the Rubicon.***

ru·bi·con ▸*n.* (in piquet) an act of winning a game against an opponent whose total score is less than 100, in which case the loser's score is added to rather than subtracted from the winner's.
▸*v.* (**-coned**, **-con·ing**) [*trans.*] score a rubicon against (one's opponent). ▷late 19th cent.: from RUBICON.

ru·bi·cund /ˈro͞obəˌkənd/ ▸*adj.* (esp. of someone's face) having a ruddy complexion; high-colored. ▷late Middle English (in the general sense 'red'): from Latin *rubicundus*, from *rubere* 'be red.' —**ru·bi·cun·di·ty** /ˌro͞obəˈkəndətē/ *n.*

ru·bid·i·um /ro͞oˈbidēəm/ ▸*n.* the chemical element of atomic number 37, a rare soft silvery reactive metal of the alkali metal group. (Symbol: **Rb**) ▷mid 19th cent.: modern Latin, from Latin *rubidus* 'red' (with reference to its spectral lines).

ru·bid·i·um–stron·ti·um dat·ing ▸*n. Geology* a method of dating rocks from the relative proportions of rubidium-87 and its decay product, strontium-87.

ru·big·i·nous /ro͞oˈbijənəs/ ▸*adj. technical* or *poetic/literary* rust-colored. ▷late 17th cent.: from Latin *rubigo, rubigin-* 'rust' + -OUS.

Ru·bik's Cube /ˈro͞obiks/ ▸*n. trademark* a puzzle in the form of a plastic cube covered with multicolored squares, which the player attempts to twist and turn so that all the squares on each face are of the same color. ▷1980s: named after Erno *Rubik* (born 1944), its Hungarian inventor.

Ru·bin·stein[1] /ˈro͞obənˌstīn/, Artur (1888–1982), U.S. pianist, born in Poland. He toured extensively in Europe and the U.S. Among his many recordings are the complete works of Chopin.

Ru·bin·stein[2], Helena (1882–1965), U.S. beautician and businesswoman. She opened her first beauty salon in Australia in 1902 and then opened salons in London 1908, Paris 1912, and New York City 1915. Her organization became an international cosmetics manufacturer and distributor.

ru·bis·co /ro͞oˈbiskō/ ▸*n. Biochemistry* an enzyme present in plant chloroplasts, involved in fixing atmospheric carbon dioxide during photosynthesis and in oxygenation of the resulting compound during photorespiration. ▷1980s: from *r(ib)u(lose)* + BIS- + *c(arb)o(xyl).*

ru·ble /ˈro͞obəl/ (also **rou·ble**) ▸*n.* the basic monetary unit of Russia and some other former republics of the USSR, equal to 100 kopeks. ▷via French from Russian *rubl'.*

ru·bric /ˈro͞obrik/ ▸*n.* a heading on a document. ■ a direction in a liturgical book as to how a church service should be conducted. ■ a statement of purpose or function: *art of a purpose, not for its own sake, was his rubric.* ■ a category: *party policies on matters falling* ***under the rubric of*** *law and order.* ▷late Middle English *rubrish* (originally referring to a heading, section of text, etc., written in red for distinctiveness), from Old French *rubriche*, from Latin *rubrica (terra)* 'red (earth or ocher as writing material),' from the base of *rubeus* 'red'; the later spelling is influenced by the Latin form. —**ru·bri·cal** *adj.*

ru·bri·cate /ˈro͞obriˌkāt/ ▸*v. chiefly historical* add elaborate, typically red, capital letters or other decorations to (a manuscript). ▷late 16th cent.: from Latin *rubricat-* 'marked in red,' from the verb *rubricare*, from *rubrica* (see RUBRIC). —**ru·bri·ca·tion** /ˌro͞obriˈkāSHən/ *n.* —**ru·bri·ca·tor** /-ˌkātər/ *n.*

Ru·by /ˈro͞obē/, Jack (1911–67), U.S. assassin; born *Jack Rubenstein*. A Dallas, Texas, nightclub owner, on November 24, 1963, he shot and killed Lee Harvey Oswald, the man accused of murdering President Kennedy. The act was captured on national television.

ru·by /ˈro͞obē/ ▸*n.* (*pl.* **-bies**) a precious stone consisting of corundum in color varieties varying from deep crimson or purple to pale rose. ■ an intense purplish-red color. ■ *Printing* an old type size equal to $5\frac{1}{2}$ points (smaller than nonpareil and larger than pearl). ▷Middle English: from Old French *rubi*, from medieval Latin *rubinus*, from the base of Latin *rubeus* 'red.'

ru·by glass ▸*n.* glass colored red by the inclusion of specific impurities such as metal oxides or gold.

Ru·by Moun·tains a range in northeastern Nevada, noted for its alpine scenery.

ru·by port ▸*n.* a deep red port, esp. one matured in wood for only a few years and then fined.

ru·by wed·ding (also **ruby wed·ding an·ni·ver·sa·ry**) ▸*n.* the fortieth anniversary of a wedding.

RUC ▸*abbr.* Royal Ulster Constabulary.

ruche /ro͞oSH/ ▸*n.* a frill or pleat of fabric as decoration on a garment or home furnishing. ▷early 19th cent.: from French, from medieval Latin *rusca* 'tree bark,' of Celtic origin. —**ruched** *adj.* —**ruch·ing** *n.*

ruck[1] /rək/ ▸*n.* a tightly packed crowd of people: *Harry squeezed through the ruck to order another beer.* ■ (**the ruck**) the mass of ordinary people or things: *education was the key to success, a way out of the ruck.* ▷Middle English (in the sense 'stack of fuel, heap'): apparently of Scandinavian origin; compare with Norwegian *ruke* 'heap of hay.'

ruck[2] ▸*v.* [*trans.*] compress or move (cloth or clothing) so that it forms a number of untidy folds or creases: *the baby's nightgown was* ***rucked up*** *to his armpits.* ■ [*intrans.*] (of cloth or clothing) form such folds of creases: *Eleanor's dress rucked up at the front.*
▸*n.* a crease or wrinkle. ▷late 18th cent. (as a noun): from Old Norse *hrukka.*

ruck[3] ▸*n. informal* rucksack: *I barely had time to repack my ruck.*

Ruck·ey·ser /ˈro͞oˌkīzər/, Muriel (1913–80), U.S. poet, writer, and political activist. Her works reflected her liberal political activism in poems such as "The Book of the Dead" (1938) and "The Gates" (1976).

ruck·le /ˈrəkəl/ ▸*v.* & *n. Brit.* another term for RUCK[2].

ruck·sack /ˈrəkˌsak; ˈro͝ok-/ ▸*n.* a bag with shoulder straps that allow it to be carried on someone's back, typically made of a strong, waterproof material and widely used by hikers; a backpack. ▷mid 19th cent.: from German, from *rucken* (dialect variant of *Rücken* 'back') + *Sack* 'bag, sack.'

ruck·us /ˈrəkəs/ ▸*n.* a disturbance or commotion: *a child is raising a ruckus in class* | *the current ruckus over same-sex benefits.* ▷late 19th cent.: perhaps related to RUCTION and RUMPUS.

ru·co·la /ˈro͞okələ/ ▸*n.* another term for ARUGULA.

ruc·tion /ˈrəksʜən/ ▶*n. informal* a disturbance or quarrel. ■ (**ructions**) unpleasant reactions to or complaints about something: *If Mrs. Salt catches her there'll be ructions.* ▷early 19th cent.: of unknown origin.

ru·da·ceous /ˈro͞oˈdāsʜəs/ ▶*adj. Geology* (of rock) composed of relatively large fragments (larger than sand grains). ▷early 20th cent.: from Latin *rudus* 'rubble' + **-ACEOUS**.

rud·beck·i·a /ro͞odˈbekēə; ˌrəd-/ ▶*n.* a North American plant of the daisy family, with yellow or orange flowers and a dark conelike center. • Genus *Rudbeckia*, family Compositae. ▷modern Latin, named after Olaf *Rudbeck* (1660–1740), Swedish botanist.

rudd /rəd/ ▶*n.* (*pl.* same) a freshwater fish of the minnow family with a silvery body and red fins. Native to Eurasia, it has isolated populations in the northeastern U.S. • *Scardinius erythrophthalmus*, family Cyprinidae. ▷early 16th cent.: apparently related to archaic *rud* 'red color.'

rud·der /ˈrədər/ ▶*n.* a flat piece, usu. of wood, metal, or plastic, hinged vertically near the stern of a boat or ship for steering. ■ a vertical airfoil pivoted from the horizontal stabilizer of an aircraft, for controlling movement around the vertical axis. ■ application of a rudder in steering a boat, ship, or aircraft: *bring the aircraft to a stall and apply* ***full rudder*** | *a small amount of extra rudder.* ▷Old English *rōther* 'paddle, oar'; related to Dutch *roer*, German *Ruder*, also to the verb **ROW**[2].

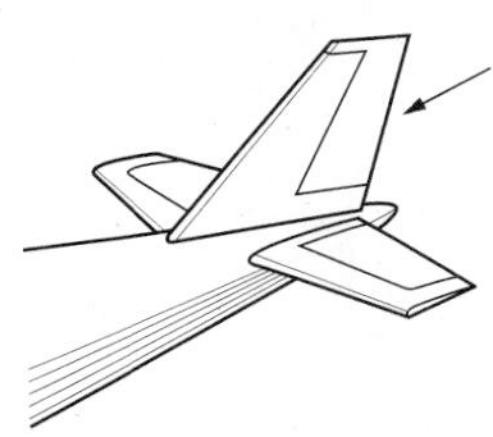

aircraft rudder

rud·der·less /ˈrədərləs/ ▶*adj.* lacking a rudder. ■ lacking a clear sense of one's aims or principles: *today's leadership is rudderless.*

rud·dle /ˈrədl/ ▶*n.* a red pigment consisting of ocher. ■ a small block of ruddle or a similar substance that is attached to the chest of a ram to mark the sheep that it tups. ▷late Middle English: related to obsolete *rud* 'red color' and **RED**.

rud·dy /ˈrədē/ ▶*adj.* (**-di·er, -di·est**) **1** (of a person's face) having a healthy red color: *a cheerful pipe-smoking man of ruddy complexion.* ■ having a reddish color: *the ruddy evening light.* **2** *Brit., informal, dated* used as a euphemism for "bloody."
▶*v.* (**-dies, -died**) [*trans.*] make ruddy in color: *a red flash ruddied the belly of a cloud.* ▷late Old English *rudig*, from the base of archaic *rud* 'red color'; related to **RED**. **—rud·di·ly** /ˈrədl-ē/ *adv.* (*rare*) **—rud·di·ness** *n.*

rud·dy duck ▶*n.* a New World stiff-tailed duck with a broad bill, the male having mainly deep red-brown plumage and white cheeks. • *Oxyura jamaicensis*, family Anatidae.

rud·dy turn·stone ▶*n.* a turnstone of a New World race that breeds on the Arctic coastal tundra.

rude /ro͞od/ ▶*adj.* **1** offensively impolite or ill-mannered: *she had* ***been rude to*** *her boss* | [with *infinitive*] *it's rude to ask a lady her age.* ■ referring to a taboo subject such as sex in a way considered improper and offensive: *he made a rude gesture.* ■ [*attrib.*] having a startling abruptness: *the war came as a very* ***rude awakening.*** **2** roughly made or done; lacking subtlety or sophistication: *a rude coffin.* ■ *archaic* ignorant and uneducated: *the new religion was first promulgated by rude men.* **3** [*attrib.*] *chiefly Brit.* vigorous or hearty: *Isabel had always been in* ***rude health.*** ▷Middle English (in sense 2, also 'uncultured'): from Old French, from Latin *rudis* 'unwrought' (referring to handicraft), figuratively 'uncultivated'; related to *rudus* 'broken stone.' **—rude·ly** *adv.* **—rude·ness** *n.* **—ru·der·y** /-ərē/ *n.*

THE RIGHT WORD **callow, crude, ill-mannered, rough, rude, uncivil, uncouth**

Someone who lacks consideration for the feelings of others and who is deliberately insolent is **rude** (*It was rude of you not to introduce me to your friends*).

Ill-mannered suggests that the person is ignorant of the rules of social behavior rather than deliberately rude (*an ill-mannered child*), while **uncivil** implies disregard for even the most basic rules of social behavior among civilized people (*his uncivil response resulted in his being kicked out of the classroom*).

Rough is used to describe people who lack polish and refinement (*he was a rough but honest man*), while **crude** is a more negative term for people and behavior lacking culture, civility, and tact (*he made a crude gesture*).

Uncouth describes what seems strange, awkward, or unmannerly rather than rude (*his uncouth behavior at the wedding*).

Although people of any age may be rude, crude, ill-mannered, or uncouth, **callow** almost always applies to those who are young or immature; it suggests naiveté and lack of sophistication (*he was surprisingly callow for a man of almost 40*).

rude boy ▶*n.* (in Jamaica) a lawless urban youth who likes ska or reggae music.

ru·der·al /ˈro͞odərəl/ *Botany* ▶*adj.* (of a plant) growing on waste ground or among refuse.
▶*n.* a plant growing on waste ground or among refuse. ▷mid 19th cent.: from modern Latin *ruderalis*, from Latin *rudera*, plural of *rudus* 'rubble.'

ru·di·ment /ˈro͞odəmənt/ ▶*n.* **1** (**the rudiments of**) the first principles of a subject: *she taught the girls the rudiments of reading and writing.* ■ an elementary or primitive form of something: *the rudiments of a hot-water system.* **2** *Biology* an undeveloped or immature part or organ, esp. a structure in an embryo or larva that will develop into an organ, limb, etc.: *the fetal lung rudiment.* **3** *Music* a basic pattern used by drummers, such as the roll, the flam, and the paradiddle. ▷mid 16th cent.: from French, or from Latin *rudimentum*, from *rudis* 'unwrought,' on the pattern of *elementum* 'element.'

ru·di·men·ta·ry /ˌro͞odəˈment(ə)rē/ ▶*adj.* involving or limited to basic principles: *he received a rudimentary education.* ■ of or relating to an immature, undeveloped, or basic form: *a rudimentary stage of evolution.* **—ru·di·men·ta·ri·ly** /-menˈte(ə)rəlē; -ˈment(ə)rəlē/ *adv.* **—ru·di·men·ta·ri·ness** *n.*

ru·dist /ˈro͞odist/ (also **ru·dis·tid** /ˈro͞odistid/) ▶*n.* a cone-shaped extinct bivalve mollusk that formed colonies resembling reefs in the Cretaceous period. • Superfamily Rudistacea, order Hippuritoida. ▷late 19th cent.: from modern Latin *Rudista* (former group name), from Latin *rudis* 'rude'; for the variant spelling see **-ID**[3].

Ru·dolf, Lake /ˈro͞odälf/ former name (until 1979) for Lake Turkana (see **TURKANA, LAKE**).

Ru·dolph /ˈro͞odôlf; -dälf/, Wilma (Glodean) (1940–94), U.S. track athlete. A runner, she was the first woman to win three track and field gold medals in one Olympics, 1960.

Ru·dra /ˈro͞odrə/ *Hinduism* **1** (in the Rig Veda) a Vedic minor god, associated with the storm, father of the Maruts. **2** one of the names of **SHIVA**.

Ru·dras /ˈro͞odrəs/ another term for **MARUTS**.

rue[1] /ro͞o/ ▶*v.* (**rues, rued, ru·ing** or **rue·ing**) [*trans.*] bitterly regret (something one has done or allowed to happen): *Ferguson will* ***rue the day*** *he turned down that offer* | *she might live to rue this impetuous decision.* See note at **MOURN**.
▶*n. archaic* repentance; regret: *with rue my heart is laden.* ■ compassion; pity: *tears of pitying rue.* ▷Old English *hrēow* 'repentance,' *hrēowan* 'affect with contrition,' of Germanic origin; related to Dutch *rouw* 'mourning' and German *Reue* 'remorse.'

rue[2] ▶*n.* a perennial evergreen shrub with bitter strong-scented lobed leaves that are used in herbal medicine. • *Ruta graveolens*, family Rutaceae. ■ used in names of other plants that resemble rue, esp. in leaf shape, e.g., **goat's-rue, meadow rue, wall rue.** ▷Middle English: from Old French, via Latin *ruta* from Greek *rhutē*.

rue·ful /ˈro͞ofəl/ ▶*adj.* expressing sorrow or regret, esp. when in a slightly humorous way: *she gave a rueful grin.* ▷Middle English (also in the sense 'pitiable'): from the noun **RUE**[1] + **-FUL**. **—rue·ful·ly** *adv.* **—rue·ful·ness** *n.*

ru·fes·cent /ro͞oˈfesənt/ ▶*adj.* tinged with red or rufous. ▷early 19th cent.: from Latin *rufescent-* 'becoming reddish,' from the verb *rufescere*, from *rufus* 'reddish.' **—ru·fes·cence** *n.*

ruff[1] /rəf/ ▶*n.* **1** a projecting starched frill worn around the neck, characteristic of Elizabethan and Jacobean costume. **2** a projecting or conspicuously colored ring of feathers or hair around the neck of a bird or mammal. **3** (*pl.* same or **ruffs**) a northern Eurasian wading bird, the male of which has a large variously colored ruff and ear tufts in the breeding season, used in display. • *Philomachus pugnax*, family Scolopacidae; the female is called a **reeve**. ▷early 16th cent. (first used denoting a frill around a sleeve): probably from a variant of **ROUGH**. **—ruffed** *adj.* **—ruff·like** /-ˌlīk/ *adj.*

ruff[1] 1

ruff[2] ▶*n.* **1** an edible marine fish of Australian inshore waters that is related to the Australian salmon. Also called **ROUGHY** in Australia. • *Arripis georgianus*, family Arripidae. **2** variant spelling of **RUFFE**. ▷late 19th cent.: from **RUFFE**.

ruff[3] ▶*v.* [*intrans.*] (in bridge, whist, and similar card games) play a trump in a trick that was led in a different suit. ■ [*trans.*] play a trump on (a card in another suit).
▶*n.* an act of ruffing or opportunity to ruff. ▷late 16th cent. (originally the name of a card game resembling whist): from Old French *rouffle*, a parallel formation to Italian *ronfa* (perhaps an alteration of *trionfo* 'a trump').

ruff[4] ▶*n. Music* one of the basic patterns (rudiments) of drumming, consisting of a single note preceded by either two grace notes played with the other stick (**double-stroke ruff** or **drag**) or three grace notes played with alternating sticks (**four-stroke ruff**). ▷late 17th cent.: probably imitative.

ruffe /rəf/ (also **ruff**) ▶*n.* a freshwater fish of the perch family, with a greenish-brown back and yellow sides and underparts. Native to Eurasia, it has been introduced into Lakes Michigan and Superior. • *Gymnocephalus cernua*, family Percidae. ▷late Middle English: probably from a variant of **ROUGH**.

ruffed grouse ▶*n.* a North American woodland grouse that has a black ruff on the sides of the neck. • *Bonasa umbellus*, family Tetraonidae (or Phasianidae).

ruffed le·mur ▶*n.* a lemur with a prominent muzzle and dense fur that forms a ruff around the neck, living in the Madagascan rain forest. • *Varecia variegata*, family Lemuridae.

ruf·fi·an /ˈrəfēən/ ▶*n.* a violent person, esp. one involved in crime. ▷late 15th cent.: from Old French *ruffian*, from Italian *ruffiano*, perhaps from dialect *rofia* 'scab, scurf,' of Germanic origin. **—ruf·fi·an·ism** /-ˌnizəm/ *n.* **—ruf·fi·an·ly** *adv.*

ruf·fle /ˈrəfəl/ ▶*v.* [*trans.*] **1** disorder or disarrange (someone's hair), typically by running one's hands through it: *he ruffled her hair affectionately.* ■ (of a bird) erect (its feathers) in anger or display: *on his departure to the high wires, the starling ruffled his feathers and flirted his wings.* ■ disturb the smoothness or tranquility of: *the evening breeze ruffled the surface of the pond in the yard.* ■ disconcert or upset the composure of (someone): *Brian had been ruffled by her questions.* **2** [usu. as *adj.*] (**ruffled**) ornament with or gather into a frill: *a blouse with a high ruffled neck.*
▶*n.* **1** an ornamental gathered or goffered frill of lace or other cloth on a garment, esp. around the wrist or neck. **2** a vibrating drumbeat. ▷Middle English (as a verb): of unknown origin. Current noun senses date from the late 17th cent.
▶*PHRASES* □ **ruffle someone's feathers** cause someone to become annoyed or upset: *tampering with the traditional approach would ruffle a few feathers.* □ **smooth someone's ruffled feathers** make someone less angry or irritated by using soothing words.

ru·fi·yaa /ˈro͞ofēˌyä/ ▶*n.* (*pl.* same) the basic monetary unit of the Maldives, equal to 100 laris. ▷Maldivian.

ru·fous /ˈro͞ofəs/ ▶*adj.* reddish brown in color.
▶*n.* a reddish-brown color. ▷late 18th cent.: from Latin *rufus* 'red, reddish' + **-OUS**.

rug /rəg/ ▶*n.* a floor covering of shaggy or woven material, typically not extending over the entire floor. ■ a small carpet woven in a pattern of colors, typically by hand in a traditional style: *Navajo patterned rugs.* ■ *chiefly Brit.* a thick woolen coverlet or wrap, used esp. when traveling. ■ *informal* a toupee or wig. ▷mid 16th cent. (denoting a type of coarse woolen cloth): probably of Scandinavian origin; compare with Norwegian dialect *rugga* 'coverlet,' Swedish *rugg* 'ruffled hair'; related to **RAG**[1]. The sense 'small carpet' dates from the early 19th cent.
▶*PHRASE* □ **pull the rug (out) from under someone** abruptly withdraw support (from someone): *the rug was pulled right out from beneath our feet.*

Pronunciation Key ə *ago*; ər *over*; ˈə *or* ˌə *up*; ˈər *or* ˌər *fur*; a *hat*; ā *rate*; ä *car*; ᴄʜ *chew*; e *let*; ē *see*; e(ə)r *air*; i *fit*; ī *by*; i(ə)r *ear*; ɴɢ *sing*; ō *go*; ô *for*; oi *boy*; o͝o *good*; o͞o *goo*; ou *out*; sʜ *she*; ᴛʜ *thin*; T̲H̲ *then*; (h)w *why*; ᴢʜ *vision*

rug·a·lach /ˈrəgələkн/ (also **rug·e·lach**) ▸*n.* a bite-size cookie made with cream-cheese dough rolled around a filling of nuts, poppy seed paste, chocolate, or jam. ▷Yiddish, literally 'little twists.'

rug·by /ˈrəgbē/ (also **rug·by foot·ball**) ▸*n.* a team game played with an oval ball that may be kicked, carried, and passed from hand to hand. Points are scored by grounding the ball behind the opponents' goal line (thereby scoring a try) or by kicking it between the two posts and over the crossbar of the opponents' goal. See also RUGBY LEAGUE and RUGBY UNION. ▷mid 19th cent.: named after *Rugby* School, where the game was first played.

rug·by league ▸*n.* a form of rugby played in teams of thirteen, originally by a group of northern English clubs that separated from rugby union in 1895. Besides having somewhat different rules, the game differed from rugby union in always allowing professionalism.

rug·by un·ion ▸*n.* a form of rugby played in teams of fifteen. Unlike rugby league, the game was originally strictly amateur, being opened to professionalism only in 1995.

rug·ged /ˈrəgid/ ▸*adj.* (of ground or terrain) having a broken, rocky, and uneven surface: *a rugged coastline.* ■ (of a machine or other manufactured object) strongly made and capable of withstanding rough handling: *the binoculars are compact, lightweight, and rugged.* ■ having or requiring toughness and determination: *a week of rugged, demanding adventure at an outdoor training center.* ■ (of a man's face or looks) having attractively strong, rough-hewn features: *he was known for his rugged good looks.* ▷Middle English (in the sense 'shaggy,' also (of a horse) 'rough-coated'): probably of Scandinavian origin; compare with Swedish *rugga* 'roughen,' also with RUG. **—rug·ged·ly** *adv.* **—rug·ged·ness** *n.*

R

rug·ged·ized /ˈrəgidˌīzd/ ▸*adj.* designed or improved to be hard-wearing or shock-resistant: *ruggedized computers suitable for use on the battlefield.* **—rug·ged·i·za·tion** /ˌrəgədəˈzāsнən/ *n.*

rug·ger /ˈrəgər/ ▸*n.* *Brit., informal* rugby.

ru·go·la /ˈrōōgələ/ ▸*n.* another term for ARUGULA.

ru·go·sa /rōōˈgōsə; -zə/ (also **ru·go·sa rose**) ▸*n.* a widely cultivated Southeast Asian rose with dark green wrinkled leaves and deep pink flowers. • *Rosa rugosa*, family Rosaceae. ▷late 19th cent.: feminine of Latin *rugosus* (see RUGOSE), used as a specific epithet.

ru·gose /ˈrōōˌgōs/ ▸*adj.* *chiefly Biology* wrinkled; corrugated: *rugose corals.* ▷late Middle English: from Latin *rugosus*, from *ruga* 'wrinkle.' **—ru·gos·i·ty** /rōōˈgäsətē/ *n.*

rug rat (also **rug·rat**) ▸*n.* *informal* a child.

Ruhr /rŏŏr/ a region of coal mining and heavy industry in North Rhine-Westphalia, in western Germany. It is named after the Ruhr River, which flows through it and meets the Rhine River near Duisburg. The Ruhr was occupied by French troops 1923–24, after Germany defaulted on war reparation payments.

ru·in /ˈrōōin/ ▸*n.* the physical destruction or disintegration of something or the state of disintegrating or being destroyed: *a large white house* ***falling into*** *gentle* ***ruin.*** ■ the remains of a building, typically an old one, that has suffered much damage or disintegration: ***the ruins of*** *the castle | the church is a ruin now.* ■ the disastrous disintegration of someone's life: *the ruin and heartbreak wrought by alcohol, divorce, and violence.* ■ the cause of such disintegration: *they don't know how to say no, and that's been their ruin.* ■ the complete loss of one's money and other assets: *the financial cost could mean ruin.*

▸*v.* **1** [*trans.*] reduce (a building or place) to a state of decay, collapse, or disintegration: [as *adj.*] (**ruined**) *a ruined castle.* ■ cause great and usually irreparable damage or harm to; have a disastrous effect on: *a noisy freeway has ruined village life.* ■ reduce to a state of poverty: *they were ruined by the highest interest rates this century.* **2** [*intrans.*] *poetic/literary* fall headlong or with a crash: *carriages go ruining over the brink from time to time.* ▷Middle English (in the sense 'collapse of a building'): from Old French *ruine*, from Latin *ruina*, from *ruere* 'to fall.'

▸*PHRASE* □ **in ruins** in a state of complete disorder or disintegration: *the economy was in ruins.*

ru·in·a·tion /ˌrōōəˈnāsнən/ ▸*n.* the action or fact of ruining someone or something or of being ruined: *commercial malpractice causes the ruination of thousands of people.* ■ the state of being ruined: *the headquarters fell into ruination.* ▷mid 17th cent.: from obsolete *ruinate* + -ION.

ru·in·ous /ˈrōōənəs/ ▸*adj.* **1** disastrous or destructive: *a ruinous effect on the environment.* ■ costing far more than can be afforded: *the cost of their ransom might be ruinous.* **2** in ruins; dilapidated: *the castle is ruinous.* ▷late Middle English (also in the sense 'falling down'): from Latin *ruinosus*, from *ruina* (see RUIN). **—ru·in·ous·ly** *adv.* **—ru·in·ous·ness** *n.*

Ruis·dael /ˈroisˌdäl/ (also **Ruys·dael**), Jacob van (*c.*1628–82), Dutch landscape painter. Born in Haarlem, he painted the surrounding landscape until his move to Amsterdam in 1657.

Ru·iz de A·lar·cón y Men·do·za /rōōˈēs dä ˌälärˈkōn ē menˈdōsə/, Juan (1580–1639), Spanish playwright, born in Mexico City.

Ruk·ey·ser /ˈrōōˌkīzər/, Louis (1933–), U.S. economic forecaster and commentator. He hosted the television program "Wall Street Week" 1970–2002. He also publishes two economic newsletters that he began in 1992 and in 1994.

Rukh /rōōкн/ the nationalist movement that established the independence of the Ukraine in 1991. ▷Ukrainian, 'people's movement.'

rukh /rōōk/ ▸*n.* another term for ROC. ▷from Hindi *rūkh.*

rule /rōōl/ ▸*n.* **1** one of a set of explicit or understood regulations or principles governing conduct within a particular activity or sphere: *the rules of the game were understood.* ■ a law or principle that operates within a particular sphere of knowledge, describing or prescribing what is possible or allowable: *the rules of grammar.* ■ a code of practice and discipline for a religious order or community: *the Rule of St. Benedict.* ■ control of or dominion over an area or people: *the revolution brought an end to British rule.* ■ (**the rule**) the normal or customary state of things: *such accidents are the exception rather than the rule.* **2** a strip of wood or other rigid material used for measuring length or marking straight lines; a ruler. ■ a thin printed line or dash, generally used to separate headings, columns, or sections of text. **3** (**Rules**) *Austral.* short for AUSTRALIAN RULES (football). ■ *Law* an order made by a judge or court with reference to a particular case only.

▸*v.* **1** [*trans.*] exercise ultimate power or authority over (an area and its people): *Latin America today is ruled by elected politicians | [intrans.] the period in which Spain* ***ruled over*** *Portugal.* ■ (of a feeling) have a powerful and restricting influence on (a person's life): *her whole life seemed to be ruled by fear.* ■ [*intrans.*] be a dominant or powerful factor or force: [with *complement*] *the black market rules supreme.* ■ [with *clause*] pronounce authoritatively and legally to be the case: *a federal court ruled that he was unfairly dismissed from his job.* ■ *Astrology* (of a planet) have a particular influence over (a sign of the zodiac, house, aspect of life, etc.). **2** [*trans.*] make parallel lines across (paper): [as *adj.*] (**ruled**) *a sheet of ruled paper.* ■ make (a straight line) on paper with a ruler.

▸*phrasal v.* □ **rule something out** (or **in**) exclude (or include) something as a possibility: *the doctor ruled out appendicitis.* ▷Middle English: from Old French *reule* (noun), *reuler* (verb), from late Latin *regulare*, from Latin *regula* 'straight stick.' **—rule·less** *adj.*

▸*PHRASES* □ **as a rule** usually, but not always. □ **make it a rule to do something** have as a habit or general principle to do something: *I make it a rule never to mix business with pleasure.* □ **rule of law** the restriction of the arbitrary exercise of power by subordinating it to well-defined and established laws. □ **rule of thumb** a broadly accurate guide or principle, based on experience or practice rather than theory. □ **rule the roost** be in complete control.

rule of en·gage·ment (abbr.: **ROE**) ▸*n.* (usu. **rules of engagement**) a directive issued by a military authority specifying the circumstances and limitations under which forces will engage in combat with the enemy.

rule of the road ▸*n.* (usu. **rules of the road**) a custom or law regulating the direction in which two vehicles (or riders or ships) should move to pass one another on meeting, or which should yield to the other, so as to avoid collision.

rule of three ▸*n.* *dated Mathematics* a method of finding a number in the same ratio to a given number as exists between two other given numbers.

rul·er /ˈrōōlər/ ▸*n.* **1** a person exercising government or dominion. ■ *Astrology* another term for RULING PLANET. **2** a straight strip or cylinder of plastic, wood, metal, or other rigid material, typically marked at regular intervals, to draw straight lines or measure distances. **—rul·er·ship** /-ˌsнip/ *n.*

Rules Com·mit·tee ▸*n.* a legislative committee responsible for expediting the passage of bills. ■ (**rules committee**) the body of people charged with overseeing the rules of an athletic league: *the NCAA football rules committee considers unsportsmanlike acts to be the game's no. 1 problem.*

rul·ing /ˈrōōliNG/ ▸*n.* an authoritative decision or pronouncement, esp. one made by a judge.

▸*adj.* currently exercising authority or influence: *the ruling coalition.*

rul·ing eld·er ▸*n.* a nominated or elected lay official of any of various Christian churches, esp. of a Presbyterian church.

rul·ing pas·sion ▸*n.* an interest or concern that occupies a large part of someone's time and effort: *football remained their ruling passion.*

rul·ing plan·et ▸*n.* *Astrology* a planet that is held to have a particular influence over a specific sign of the zodiac, house, aspect of life, etc.

rum[1] /rəm/ ▸*n.* an alcoholic liquor distilled from sugar-cane residues or molasses. ■ intoxicating liquor. ▷mid 17th cent.: perhaps an abbreviation of obsolete *rumbullion*, in the same sense.

rum[2] ▸*adj.* (**rum·mer, rum·mest**) *Brit., informal, dated* odd; peculiar: *it's a rum business, certainly | they were a rum bunch.* ▷late 18th cent.: of unknown origin. **—rum·ly** *adv.* **—rum·ness** *n.*

Ru·ma·ni·an /rōōˈmānēən; -nyən/ ▸*adj.* & *n.* variant spelling of ROMANIAN.

rum·ba /ˈrəmbə; ˈrōōm-; ˈrōōm-/ (also **rhum·ba**) ▸*n.* a rhythmic dance with Spanish and African elements, originating in Cuba. ■ a piece of music for this dance or in a similar style. ■ a ballroom dance imitative of this dance.

▸*v.* (**-bas, -baed** /-bəd/, **-ba·ing**) [*intrans.*] dance the rumba. ▷1920s: from Latin American Spanish.

rum ba·ba /ˌrəm ˈbäbə/ ▸*n.* see BABA[1].

rum·ble /ˈrəmbəl/ ▸*v.* **1** [*intrans.*] make a continuous deep, resonant sound: *thunder rumbled, lightning flickered.* ■ [with *adverbial of direction*] (esp. of a large vehicle) move in the specified direction with such a sound: *heavy trucks rumbled through the streets.* ■ [*trans.*] utter in a deep, resonant voice: *the man's low voice rumbled an instruction.* ■ (of a person's stomach) make a deep, resonant sound due to hunger. **2** [*intrans.*] *informal* take part in a street fight between gangs or large groups: *the five of them rumbled with the men in the other car.* **3** [*trans.*] *Brit., informal* discover (an illicit activity or its perpetrator): *it wouldn't need a genius to rumble my little game.*

▸*n.* **1** a continuous deep, resonant sound like distant thunder: *the steady rumble of traffic | figurative rumbles of discontent.* **2** *informal* a street fight between gangs or large groups. ▷late Middle English: probably from Middle Dutch *rommelen, rummelen*, of imitative origin. Sense 3 of the *verb* may be a different word.

rum·bler /ˈrəmb(ə)lər/ ▸*n.* a person or thing that rumbles. ■ a machine for peeling potatoes. ■ *historical* a round bell containing a small hard object placed inside to rattle, formerly used esp. on horses' harnesses.

rum·ble seat ▸*n.* an uncovered folding seat in the rear of an automobile.

rum·ble strip ▸*n.* a series of raised strips across a road or along its edge, changing the noise a vehicle's tires make on the surface and so warning drivers of speed restrictions or of the edge of the road.

rum·bling /ˈrəmb(ə)liNG/ ▸*n.* a continuous deep, resonant sound: *the rumbling of wheels in the distance.* ■ (often **rumblings**) an early indication or rumor of dissatisfaction or incipient change: *there are growing rumblings of discontent.*

▸*adj.* making or constituting a deep resonant sound: *a rumbling ancient air conditioner | a rumbling noise.*

rum·bus·tious /ˌrəmˈbəscнəs/ ▸*adj.* *informal, chiefly Brit.* boisterous or unruly. ▷late 18th cent.: probably an alteration of archaic *robustious* 'boisterous, robust.' **—rum·bus·tious·ly** *adv.* **—rum·bus·tious·ness** *n.*

rum·dum /ˈrəmˌdəm/ ▸*n.* *informal* a drunkard, esp. a derelict alcoholic. ▷late 19th cent.: from RUM[1] + DUMB.

ru·men /ˈrōōmən/ ▸*n.* (*pl.* **-mens** or **-mi·na** /-mənə/) *Zoology* the first stomach of a ruminant, which receives food or cud from the esophagus, partly digests it with the aid of bacteria, and passes it to the reticulum. ▷early 18th cent.: from Latin, literally 'throat.'

ru·mi·nant /ˈrōōmənənt/ ▸*n.* **1** an even-toed ungulate mammal that chews the cud regurgitated from its rumen. The ruminants comprise the cattle, sheep, antelopes, deer, giraffes, and their relatives.

• Suborder Ruminantia, order Artiodactyla: six families. **2** a contemplative person; a person given to meditation.
▸*adj.* of or belonging to ruminants. ▷mid 17th cent.: from Latin *ruminant-* 'chewing over again,' from the verb *ruminari*, from *rumen* 'throat'(see RUMEN).

ru·mi·nate /'ro͞omə,nāt/ ▸*v.* [*intrans.*] **1** think deeply about something: *we sat **ruminating on** the nature of existence.* **2** (of a ruminant) chew the cud. ▷mid 16th cent.: from Latin *ruminat-* 'chewed over,' from the verb *ruminari*. **—ru·mi·na·tion** /,ro͞omə'nāsʜən/ *n.* **—ru·mi·na·tive** /-,nātiv/ *adj.* **—ru·mi·na·tive·ly** /-,nātivlē/ *adv.* **—ru·mi·na·tor** /-,nātər/ *n.*

rum·mage /'rəmij/ ▸*v.* [*intrans.*] search unsystematically and untidily through a mass or receptacle: *he rummaged in his pocket for a handkerchief* | [*trans.*] *he rummaged the drawer for his false teeth.* ■ [*trans.*] find (something) by searching in this way: *Mick **rummaged up** his skateboard.* ■ [*trans.*] (of a customs officer) make a thorough search of (a vessel): *our brief was to rummage as many of the vessels as possible.*
▸*n.* an unsystematic and untidy search through a mass or receptacle. ■ a thorough search of a vessel by a customs officer. ▷late 15th cent.: from Old French *arrumage*, from *arrumer* 'stow (in a hold),' from Middle Dutch *ruim* 'room.' In early use the word referred to the arranging of items such as casks in the hold of a ship, giving rise (early 17th cent.) to the verb sense 'make a search of (a vessel).' **—rum·mag·er** *n.*

rum·mage sale ▸*n.* a sale of miscellaneous secondhand articles, typically held in order to raise money for a charity or a special event.

rum·mer /'rəmər/ ▸*n.* a large drinking glass. ▷mid 17th cent.: of Low Dutch origin; related to Dutch *roemer*; the original meaning is perhaps 'Roman glass.'

rum·my[1] /'rəmē/ ▸*n.* a card game, sometimes played with two decks, in which the players try to form sets and sequences of cards. ▷early 20th cent.: of unknown origin.

rum·my[2] ▸*adj.* (**-mi·er**, **-mi·est**) another term for RUM[2].

ru·mor /'ro͞omər/ (*Brit.* **ru·mour**) ▸*n.* a currently circulating story or report of uncertain or doubtful truth: *they were investigating rumors of a massacre* | ***rumor has it that** he will take a year off.*
▸*v.* (**be rumored**) be circulated as an unverified account: [with *clause*] ***it's rumored that** he lives on a houseboat* | [with *infinitive*] *she is rumored to have gone into hiding.* ▷late Middle English: from Old French *rumur*, from Latin *rumor* 'noise.'

ru·mor·mon·ger /'ro͞omər,mäɴɢgər; -,məɴɢgər/ ▸*n.* *derogatory* a person who spreads rumors. **—ru·mor·mon·ger·ing** *n.*

rump /rəmp/ ▸*n.* **1** the hind part of the body of a mammal or the lower back of a bird. ■ *chiefly humorous* a person's buttocks. **2** a small or unimportant remnant of something originally larger: *once the profitable enterprises have been sold the unprofitable rump will be left.* ▷late Middle English: probably of Scandinavian origin; compare with Danish and Norwegian *rumpe* 'backside.' **—rump·less** *adj.*

rum·ple /'rəmpəl/ ▸*v.* [*trans.*] [usu. as *adj.*] (**rumpled**) give a creased, ruffled, or disheveled appearance to: *a rumpled bed.*
▸*n.* [in *sing.*] an untidy state. ▷early 16th cent. (as a noun in the sense 'wrinkle'): from Middle Dutch *rompel*. **—rum·ply** /'rəmp(ə)lē/ *adj.*

rum·pot /'rəm,pät/ ▸*n.* *informal* an alcoholic.

Rump Par·lia·ment the part of the Long Parliament in Britain that continued to sit after the forced exclusion of Presbyterian members in 1648. It voted for the trial that resulted in the execution of Charles I. ▷origin uncertain: said to derive from *The Bloody Rump*, the name of a paper written before the trial, the word being popularized after a speech by Major General Brown, given at a public assembly; also said to have been coined by Clem Walker in his *History of Independency* (1648), as a term for those strenuously opposing the king.

rump·sprung /'rəmp,spræɴɢ/ ▸*adj.* *informal* (of furniture) baggy and worn in the seat: *a rumpsprung armchair.*

rump steak ▸*n.* a cut of beef from the animal's rump.

rum·pus /'rəmpəs/ ▸*n.* (*pl.* **-pus·es**) [usu. in *sing.*] *informal* a noisy disturbance; a commotion: *he caused a rumpus with his flair for troublemaking.* ▷mid 18th cent.: probably fanciful.

rum·pus room ▸*n.* a room, typically in the basement of a house, used for games and recreation.

Rumsfeld /'rəmzfeld/, Donald Henry (1932–), U.S. secretary of defense. He served in the U.S. House of Representatives 1963–69 as an Illinois Republican before joining the Nixon Administration as an economic adviser 1969–72. Under President Ford, he became the youngest U.S. secretary of defense (1975–77), a cabinet post he was reappointed to in 2001 by President George W. Bush.

run /rən/ ▸*v.* (**run·ning**; *past* **ran** /ran/; *past part.* **run**) **1** [*intrans.*] move at a speed faster than a walk, never having both or all the feet on the ground at the same time: *the dog ran across the road* | *she ran the last few yards, breathing heavily* | *he hasn't paid for his drinks—run and catch him.* ■ run as a sport or for exercise: *I run every morning.* ■ (of an athlete or a racehorse) compete in a race: *she ran in the 200 meters.* | [*trans.*] *Dave has run 42 marathons.* ■ [*trans.*] enter (a racehorse) for a race. ■ *Baseball* (of a batter or base runner) attempt to advance to the next base. ■ (of hounds) chase or hunt their quarry. ■ (of a boat) sail directly before the wind, esp. in bad weather. ■ (of a migratory fish) go upriver from the sea in order to spawn. **2** [*intrans.*] move about in a hurried and hectic way: *I've spent the whole day running around after the kids.* ■ (**run to**) have rapid recourse to (someone) for support or help: *don't come running to me for a handout.* **3** pass or cause to pass quickly or smoothly in a particular direction: [*intrans.*] *the rumor ran through the pack of photographers* | [*trans.*] *Helen ran her fingers through her hair.* ■ move or cause to move somewhere forcefully or with a particular result: [*intrans.*] *the tanker **ran aground** off the Aleutian Islands* | [*trans.*] *a woman ran a stroller into the back of my legs.* ■ [*trans.*] *informal* fail to stop at (a red traffic light). ■ [*trans.*] navigate (rapids or a waterfall) in a boat. ■ extend or cause to extend in a particular direction: [*intrans.*] *cobbled streets run down to a tiny harbor* | [*trans.*] *he ran a wire under the carpet.* ■ [*intrans.*] (**run in**) (of a quality or trait) be common or inherent in members of (a particular family), esp. over several generations: *weight problems run in my family.* ■ [*intrans.*] pass into or reach a specified state or level: *inflation is **running at** 11 percent* | [with *complement*] *the decision ran counter to previous government commitments.* **4** [*intrans.*] (of a liquid) flow in a specified direction: *tears were running down her face.* ■ [*trans.*] cause (a liquid) to flow: [*trans.*] *she ran cold water into the sink.* ■ [*trans.*] cause water to flow over (something): *I ran my hands under the faucet.* ■ [*trans.*] fill (a bath) with water: [with *two objs.*] *I'll run you a nice hot bath.* ■ [*intrans.*] (**run with**) be covered or streaming with (a particular liquid): *his face was running with sweat.* ■ [*intrans.*] emit or exude a liquid: *she was weeping loudly, and her nose was running.* ■ [*intrans.*] (of a solid substance) melt and become fluid: *it was so hot that the butter ran.* ■ [*intrans.*] (of the sea, the tide, or a river) rise higher or flow more quickly: *there was still a heavy sea running.* ■ [*intrans.*] (of dye or color in fabric or paper) dissolve and spread when the fabric or paper becomes wet: *the red dye ran when the socks were washed.* ■ [*intrans.*] (of a stocking or pair of tights) develop a ravel. **5** [*intrans.*] (of a bus, train, ferry, or other form of transportation) make a regular journey on a particular route: *buses run into town every half hour.* ■ [*trans.*] put (a particular form of public transportation) in service: *the group is drawing up plans to run trains on key routes.* ■ [*trans.*] take (someone) somewhere in a car: *I'll run you home.* **6** [*trans.*] be in charge of; manage: *Andrea runs her own catering business* | [as *adj.* in *combination*] (**-run**) *an attractive family-run hotel.* ■ [*intrans.*] (of a system, organization, or plan) operate or proceed in a particular way: *everything's running according to plan.* ■ organize and make available for other people: *we decided to run a series of seminars.* ■ carry out (a test or procedure): *he asked the army to run tests on the anti nerve-gas pills.* ■ own, maintain, and use (a vehicle). **7** be in or cause to be in operation; function or cause to function: [*intrans.*] *the car **runs on** unleaded fuel* | [*trans.*] *a number of peripherals can be **run off** one SCSI port.* ■ move or cause to move between the spools of a recording machine: [*trans.*] *I ran the tape back* | [*intrans.*] *the tape has run out.* **8** [*intrans.*] continue or be valid or operative for a particular period of time: *the course **ran for** two days* | *this particular debate will **run on and on**.* ■ [with *adverbial* or *complement*] happen or arrive at the specified time: *the program was running fifteen minutes late.* ■ (of a play or exhibition) be staged or presented: *the play ran on Broadway last year.* **9** [*intrans.*] be a candidate in a political election: *he announced that he intended to **run for** President.* ■ [*trans.*] (esp. of a political party) sponsor (a candidate) in an election: *they ran their first candidate for the school board.* **10** publish or be published in a newspaper or magazine: [*trans.*] *the tabloids ran the story* | [*intrans.*] *when the story ran, there was a big to-do.* ■ [*intrans.*] (of a story, argument, or piece of writing) have a specified wording or contents: *"Tapestries slashed!" ran the dramatic headline.* **11** [*trans.*] bring (goods) into a country illegally and secretly; smuggle: *they run drugs for the cocaine cartels.* **12** [with *two objs.*] (of an object or act) cost (someone) (a specified amount): *a new photocopier will run us about $1,300.*
▸*phrasal v.* □ **run across** meet or find by chance: *I just thought you might have run across him before.* □ **run after** *informal* seek to acquire or attain; pursue persistently: *businesses that have spent years running after the boomer market.* ■ seek the company of (someone) with the aim of developing a romantic or sexual relationship with them. □ **run against** *archaic* collide with (someone). ■ happen to meet: *I ran against Flanagan the other day.* □ **run along** [in *imperative*] *informal* go away (used typically to address a child): *run along now, there's a good girl.* □ **run around with** see RUN WITH (sense 2). □ **run at** rush toward (someone) to attack or as if to attack them. □ **run away** leave or escape from a place, person, or situation of danger: *children who **run away from** home normally go to big cities.* ■ (also *informal* **run off**) leave one's home or current partner in order to establish a relationship with someone else: *he **ran off with** his wife's best friend* | *Fran, let's **run away together**.* ■ try to avoid acknowledging or facing up to an unpleasant or difficult situation: *the commissioners are **running away from** their responsibilities.* □ **run away with 1** (of one's imagination or emotions) work wildly, so as to overwhelm (one): *Susan's imagination was running away with her.* ■ (of a horse) bolt with (its rider). **2** accept (an idea) without thinking it through properly: *a lot of people ran away with the idea that they were Pacifists.* **3** excel in or win (a competition) easily: *the Yankees ran away with the series.* □ **run something by** (or **past**) tell (someone) about something, esp. in order to ascertain their opinion or reaction. □ **run someone/something down 1** (of a vehicle or its driver) hit a person or animal and knock them to the ground. ■ (of a boat) collide with another vessel. **2** criticize someone or something unfairly or unkindly. **3** find someone or something after a search: *she finally ran the professor down.* **4** *Baseball* (of two or more fielders) try to tag out a base runner who is trapped between two bases, in the process throwing the ball back and forth. □ **run something down** (or **run down**) reduce (or become reduced) in size, numbers, or resources: *hardwood stocks in some countries are rapidly running down.* ■ lose (or cause to lose) power; stop (or cause to stop) functioning: *the battery has run down.* ■ gradually deteriorate (or cause to deteriorate) in quality or condition: *the property had been allowed to run down.* □ **run someone in** *informal* arrest someone. □ **run into 1** collide with: *he ran into a lamp post.* ■ meet by chance: *I ran into Stasia and Katie on the way home.* ■ experience (a problem or difficult situation): *the bank ran into financial difficulties.* **2** reach (a level or amount): *debts running into millions of dollars.* **3** blend into or appear to coalesce with: *her words ran into each other.* □ **run off** see RUN AWAY above. □ **run off with** *informal* steal: *the treasurer had run off with the pension funds.* □ **run something off 1** reproduce copies of a piece of writing on a machine. ■ write or recite something quickly and with little effort. **2** drain liquid from a container: *run off the water that has been standing in the pipes.* □ **run on 1** continue without stopping; go on longer than is expected: *the story ran on for months.* ■ talk incessantly. **2** (also **run upon**) (of a person's mind or a discussion) be preoccupied or concerned with (a particular subject): *my thoughts always ran too much on death.* **3** *Printing* continue on the same line as the preceding matter. □ **run out 1** (of a supply of something) be used up: *our food is about to run out.* ■ use up one's supply of something: *we've **run out of** gasoline.* ■ become no longer valid: *her contract runs out at the end of the year.* **2** (of rope) be paid out: *slowly, he let the cables run out.* **3** [with *adverbial of direction*] extend; project: *a row of buildings ran out to Cityline Avenue.* □ **run out on** *informal* abandon (someone); cease to support or care for. □ **run over 1** (of a container or its contents) overflow: *the bath's running over.* **2** exceed (an expected limit): *the filming ran over schedule and budget.* □ **run someone/something over** (of a vehicle or its driver) knock a person or animal down and pass over their body: *I almost ran over that raccoon.* □ **run through 1** be present in every part of; per-

R

vade: *a sense of personal loss runs through many of his lyrics.* **2** use or spend recklessly or rapidly: *her husband had long since run through her money.* □ **run someone/something through** stab a person or animal so as to kill them. □ **run through** (or **over**) **something** discuss, read, or repeat something quickly or briefly: *I'll just run through the schedule for the weekend.* ■ rehearse a performance or series of actions: *okay, let's run through Scene 3 again.* □ **run to 1** extend to or reach (a specified amount or size): *the document ran to almost 100 pages.* ■ be enough to cover (a particular expense); have the financial resources for: *my income doesn't run to luxuries like taxis.* **2** (of a person) show a tendency to or inclination toward: *she was tall and running to fat.* □ **run something up 1** allow a debt or bill to accumulate quickly: *he ran up debts of $153,000.* ■ achieve a particular score in a game or match: *North Carolina ran up a 62–44 lead.* **2** make something quickly or hurriedly, esp. a piece of clothing: *I'll run up a dress for you.* **3** raise a flag. □ **run up against** experience or meet (a difficulty or problem): *the proposal has been dropped because it could run up against Federal regulations.* □ **run with 1** proceed with; accept: *we do lots of tests before we run with a product.* **2** (also **run around with**) *informal* associate habitually with (someone): *Larry was a good kid until he began running around with the wrong crowd.*

▸*n.* **1** [usu. in *sing.*] an act or spell of running: *I usually go for a run in the morning | a cross-country run.* ■ a running pace: *Bobby set off* ***at a run.*** ■ an opportunity or attempt to achieve something: *their absence means the Russians will have* ***a clear run at*** *the title.* ■ a preliminary test of the efficiency of a procedure or system: *if you are styling your hair yourself, have a practice run.* ■ an attempt to secure election to political office: *his run for the Republican nomination.* ■ an annual mass migration of fish up a river to spawn, or their return migration afterward: *the annual salmon runs.* **2** a journey accomplished or route taken by a vehicle, aircraft, or boat, esp. on a regular basis: *the New York-Washington run.* ■ a short excursion made in a car: *we could take a run out to the country.* ■ the distance covered in a specified period, esp. by a ship: *a record run of 398 miles from noon to noon.* ■ a short flight made by an aircraft on a straight and even course at a constant speed before or while dropping bombs. **3** *Baseball* a point scored when a base runner reaches home plate after touching the other bases. ■ *Cricket* a point scored by hitting the ball so that both batsmen are able to run between the wickets, or awarded in some other circumstances. **4** a continuous spell of a particular situation or condition: *he's had a run of bad luck.* ■ a continuous series of performances: *the play had a long run on Broadway.* ■ a quantity or amount of something produced at one time: *a production run of only 150 cars.* ■ a continuous stretch or length of something: *long runs of copper piping.* ■ a rapid series of musical notes forming a scale. ■ a sequence of cards of the same suit. **5** (**a run on**) a widespread and sudden or continuous demand for (a particular currency or commodity): *there's been a big run on nostalgia toys this year.* ■ a sudden demand for repayment from a bank made by a large number of lenders: *growing nervousness among investors led to a run on some banks.* **6** (**the run of**) free and unrestricted use of or access to: *her cats were given the run of the house.* **7** (**the run**) [usu. with *adj.*] the average or usual type of person or thing: *she stood out from* ***the general run of*** *varsity cheerleaders.* **8** an enclosed area in which domestic animals or birds can run freely in the open: *a chicken run.* ■ [usu. with *adj.*] a track made or regularly used by a particular animal: *a badger run.* ■ a sloping snow-covered course or track used for skiing, bobsledding, or tobogganing: *a ski run.* ■ *Austral./NZ* a large open stretch of land used for pasture or the raising of stock: *one of the richest cattle runs of the district.* **9** a line of unraveled stitches in stockings or tights. **10** a downward trickle of paint or a similar substance when applied too thickly. **11** a small stream or brook. **12** (**the runs**) *informal* diarrhea. **13** *Nautical* the after part of a ship's bottom where it rises and narrows toward the stern. ▷Old English *rinnan, irnan* (verb), of Germanic origin, probably reinforced in Middle English by Old Norse *rinna, renna*. The current form with *-u-* in the present tense is first recorded in the 16th cent. **—run·na·ble** *adj.*

▸*PHRASES* □ **be run off one's feet** see FOOT. □ **come running** be eager to do what someone wants: *he had only to snap his fingers, and she would come running.* □ **give someone/something a** (**good**) **run for their money** provide someone or something with challenging competition or opposition. □ **have a** (**good**) **run for one's money** derive reward or enjoyment in return for one's outlay or efforts. □ **on the run 1** trying to avoid being captured: *a kidnapper on the run from the FBI.* **2** while running: *he took a pass on the run.* ■ continuously active and busy: *I'm on the run every minute of the day.* □ **run a blockade** see BLOCKADE. □ **run afoul** (or **foul**) **of 1** *Nautical* collide or become entangled with (an obstacle or another vessel): *another ship ran afoul of us.* **2** come into conflict with; go against: *the act may run afoul of consumer protection legislation.* □ **run dry** (of a well or river) cease to flow or have any water. ■ *figurative* (esp. of a source of money or information) be completely used up: *municipal relief funds had long since run dry.* □ **run an errand** carry out an errand, typically on someone else's behalf. □ (**make a**) **run for it** attempt to escape someone or something by running away. □ **run the gauntlet** see GAUNTLET[2]. □ **run high** see HIGH. □ **run oneself into the ground** see GROUND[1]. □ **run its course** see COURSE. □ **run low** (or **short**) become depleted: *supplies had run short.* ■ have too little of something: *we're running short of time.* □ **run a mile** see MILE. □ **run off at the mouth** *informal* talk excessively or indiscreetly. □ **run someone out of town** force someone to leave a place. □ **run rings around** see RING[1]. □ **run riot** see RIOT. □ **run the risk** (or **run risks**) see RISK. □ **run the show** *informal* dominate or be in charge of a project, undertaking, or domain. □ **run a temperature** (or **fever**) be suffering from a fever or high temperature. □ **run someone/something to earth** (or **ground**) *Hunting* chase a quarry to its lair. ■ find someone or something, typically after a long search. □ **run to ruin** *archaic* fall into disrepair; gradually deteriorate. □ **run to seed** see SEED. □ **run wild** see WILD.

USAGE On the use of verbs used with **and** instead of a *to* infinitive, as in *run and fetch the paper*, see usage at AND.

run·a·bout /ˈrənəˌbout/ ▸*n.* a small car, motorboat, or light aircraft, esp. one used for short trips.

run·a·round /ˈrənəˌround/ *informal* ▸*n.* difficult or awkward treatment, esp. in which someone is evasive or avoids a question: *the times he* ***got the runaround*** *looking for work.*

run·a·way /ˈrənəˌwā/ ▸*n.* a person who has run away, esp. from their family or an institution. ■ [often as *adj.*] an animal or vehicle that is running out of control: *a runaway train.* ■ [as *adj.*] denoting something happening or done quickly, easily, or uncontrollably: *the runaway success of the book.*

run·back /ˈrənˌbak/ ▸*n. Football* an act of advancing a ball caught after a kickoff, punt, or interception by running while carrying it.

run·ci·ble spoon /ˈrənsəbəl/ ▸*n.* a fork curved like a spoon, with three broad prongs, one of which has a sharpened outer edge for cutting. ▷late 19th cent.: used by Edward Lear, perhaps suggested by late 16th-cent. *rouncival*, denoting a large variety of pea.

run·down ▸*n.* /ˈrənˌdoun/ [usu. in *sing.*] **1** an analysis or summary of something by a knowledgeable person: *he gave his teammates* ***a rundown on*** *the opposition.* **2** a reduction in the productivity or activities of a company or institution: *a rundown in the business would be a devastating blow to the local economy.* **3** *Baseball* an attempt by two or more fielders to tag out a base runner who is trapped between two bases: *he was caught in a rundown and tagged out by the shortstop.*
▸*adj.* /ˈrənˈdoun/ (usu. **run-down**) **1** (esp. of a building or area) in a poor or neglected state after having been prosperous: *a run-down, vandalized inner-city area.* ■ (of a company or industry) in a poor economic state. **2** [*predic.*] tired and somewhat unwell, esp. through overwork: *feeling tired and generally run-down.*

rune /ro͞on/ ▸*n.* a letter of an ancient Germanic alphabet, related to the Roman alphabet. ■ a similar mark of mysterious or magic significance. ■ (**runes**) small stones, pieces of bone, etc., bearing such marks, and used as divinatory symbols: *the casting of the runes.* ■ a spell or incantation. ■ a section of the Kalevala or of an ancient Scandinavian poem. [from Finnish *runo*, from Old Norse.]

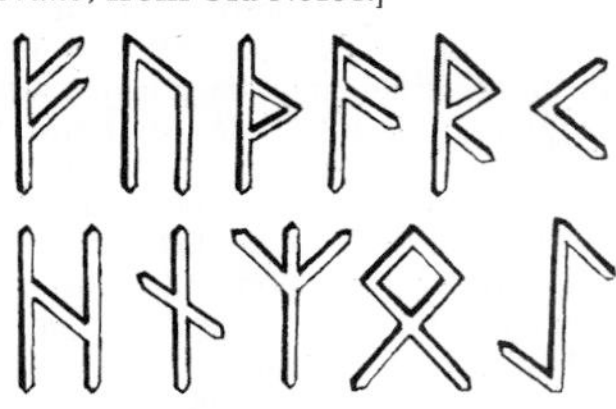

Germanic runes

Runes were used by Scandinavians and Anglo-Saxons from about the 3rd century. They were formed mainly by modifying Roman or Greek characters to suit carving, and were used both in writing and in divination.

▷Old English *rūn* 'a secret, mystery'; not recorded between Middle English and the late 17th cent. when it was reintroduced under the influence of Old Norse *rúnir, rúnar* 'magic signs, hidden lore.' **—ru·nic** /ˈro͞onik/ *adj.*

rune stone ▸*n.* **1** a large stone carved with runes by ancient Scandinavians or Anglo-Saxons. **2** a small stone, piece of bone, etc., marked with a rune and used in divination.

rung[1] /rəNG/ ▸*n.* **1** a horizontal support on a ladder for a person's foot. ■ *figurative* a level in a hierarchical structure, esp. a class or career structure: *we must ensure that the unskilled do not get trapped on the bottom rung.* **2** a strengthening crosspiece in the structure of a chair. ▷Old English *hrung* (sense 2); related to Dutch *rong* and German *Runge*. **—runged** *adj.* **—rung·less** *adj.*

rung[2] ▸ past participle of RING[2].

run-in ▸*n.* **1** *informal* a disagreement or fight, esp. with someone in an official position: *a run-in with armed police in Rio | humorous a run-in with a parking meter.* **2** [usu. in *sing.*] *Brit.* the approach to an action or event: *the final run-in to the World Cup.* ■ the home stretch of a racecourse.

run·let /ˈrənlət/ ▸*n.* a small stream.

run·nel /ˈrənl/ ▸*n.* a narrow channel in the ground for liquid to flow through. ■ a brook or rill. ■ a small stream of a particular liquid: ***a runnel of*** *sweat.* ▷late 16th cent. (denoting a brook or rill): variant of dialect *rindle*, influenced by the verb RUN.

run·ner /ˈrənər/ ▸*n.* **1** a person who runs, esp. in a specified way: *Mary was a fast runner.* ■ a person who runs competitively as a sport or hobby: *a marathon runner.* ■ a horse that runs in a particular race: *there were only four runners.* ■ a messenger, collector, or agent for a bank, bookmaker, or other organization. ■ *Baseball* a base runner. ■ a messenger in the army. **2** [in *combination*] a person who smuggles specified goods into or out of a country or area: *a drug-runner.* **3** a rod, groove, or blade on which something slides. ■ each of the long pieces on the underside of a sled that forms the contact in sliding. ■ (often **runners**) a roller for moving a heavy article. ■ a ring capable of slipping or sliding along a strap or rod or through which something may be passed or drawn. ■ *Nautical* a rope run through a block. **4** a shoot, typically leafless, that grows from the base of a plant along the surface of the ground and can take root at points along its length. ■ a plant that spreads by means of such shoots. ■ a twining plant. **5** a long, narrow rug or strip of carpet, esp. for a hall or stairway. **6** (also **run·ner stone**) a revolving millstone. **7** a fast-swimming fish of the jack family, occurring in tropical seas. • Several species in the family Carangidae, in particular the colorfully striped **rainbow runner** (*Elagatis bipinnulata*) of warm seas worldwide, and the **blue runner** (*Caranx crysos*) of the western Atlantic.
▸*PHRASE* □ **do a runner** *Brit., informal* leave hastily, esp. to avoid paying for something or to escape from somewhere.

run·ner-up ▸*n.* (*pl.* **run·ners-up**) a competitor or team taking second place in a contest: *he was runner-up in the 200 m individual medley.* ■ [with *adj.*] a competitor finishing behind the winner in the specified position: *third runner-up in last year's election.*

run·ning /ˈrəniNG/ ▸*n.* **1** the action or movement of a runner: *he accounted for 31 touchdowns with his running and passing.* ■ the sport of racing on foot: *marathon running.* ■ an act of running a race: *the 122nd running of the Mid-Summer Derby.* **2** the action of managing or operating something: *the day-to-day running of the office.*
▸*adj.* **1** [*attrib.*] denoting something that runs, in particular: ■ (of water) flowing naturally or supplied to a building through pipes and taps: *hot and cold running water.* ■ (of a sore or a part of the body) exuding liquid or pus: *a running sore.* ■ continuous or recurring over a long period: *a running joke.* ■ done while running: *a running jump.* ■ (of a measurement) in a straight line: *today, those same lots are worth $6,000 a running foot.* **2** [*postpositive*] consecutive; in succession: *he failed to produce an essay for the third week running.*
▸*PHRASE* □ **in** (or **out of**) **the running** in (or no longer

in) contention for an award, victory, or a place on a team: *he is in the running for an Oscar.*

run·ning back ▸*n. Football* an offensive player, typically a halfback, who specializes in carrying the ball.

run·ning bat·tle ▸*n.* a military engagement that does not occur at a fixed location. ■ a confrontation that has gone on for a long time.

run·ning be·lay ▸*n. Climbing* a device attached to a rock face through which a climbing rope runs freely, acting as a pulley if the climber falls.

run·ning board ▸*n.* a footboard extending along the side of a vehicle, typically found on trucks, SUVs, and some early models of automobiles.

run·ning com·men·ta·ry ▸*n.* a verbal description of events, given as they occur.

run·ning dog ▸*n.* **1** *informal* a servile follower, esp. of a political system: *the running dogs of capitalism.* [translating Chinese *zǒugǒu.*] **2** a dog bred to run, esp. for racing or pulling a sled.

run·ning fire ▸*n.* successive gunshots from a line of troops. ■ a rapid succession of something: *a running fire of comment in their choicest vernacular.*

run·ning fix ▸*n.* a determination of one's position made by taking bearings at different times and allowing for the distance covered in the meantime.

run·ning gear ▸*n.* the moving parts of a machine, esp. the wheels, steering, and suspension of a vehicle. ■ the moving rope and tackle used in handling a boat.

run·ning head ▸*n.* a heading printed at the top of each page of a book or chapter.

run·ning knot ▸*n.* a knot that slips along the rope and changes the size of the loop it forms.

run·ning lights ▸*plural n.* **1** another term for NAVIGATION LIGHTS. **2** small lights on a motor vehicle that remain illuminated while the vehicle is running.

run·ning mate ▸*n.* **1** an election candidate for the lesser of two closely associated political offices: *a rationale offered by a presidential candidate for choosing his vice presidential running mate.* **2** a horse entered in a race in order to set the pace for another horse from the same stable, which is intended to win.

run·ning re·pairs ▸*plural n.* minor or temporary repairs carried out on machinery while it is in use.

run·ning rig·ging ▸*n.* see RIGGING (sense 1).

run·ning stitch ▸*n.* a simple needlework stitch consisting of a line of small even stitches that run in and out through the cloth without overlapping.

run·ning to·tal ▸*n.* a total that is continually adjusted to take account of items as they are added.

run·ny /'rənē/ ▸*adj.* **(-ni·er, -ni·est) 1** somewhat liquid; not firm: *the soufflé was hard on top and quite runny underneath.* **2** (of a person's nose) producing or discharging mucus; running. ■ dripping: *a runny spout.*

Run·ny·mede /'rəni,mēd/ a meadow on the southern bank of the Thames River, near Windsor. It is noted for its association with the Magna Carta, which was signed by King John in 1215 here or nearby.

run·off /'rən,ôf/ (also **run-off**) ▸*n.* **1** a further competition, election, race, etc., after a tie or inconclusive result. **2** the draining away of water (or substances carried in it) from the surface of an area of land, a building or structure, etc. ■ the water or other material that drains freely off the surface of something.

run-of-the-mill ▸*adj.* lacking unusual or special aspects; ordinary: *a run-of-the-mill job.*

run-on ▸*adj.* **1** [*attrib.*] denoting a line of verse in which a sentence is continued without a pause beyond the end of a line, couplet, or stanza. **2** (of a sentence) containing two or more independent clauses that are not separated by a colon or semicolon: *his sentences were often run-on or confused.*

run·out /'rən,out/ (also **run-out**) ▸*n.* **1** a length of time or stretch of ground over which something gradually ceases or is brought to an end or a halt: *I skied the trail's long runout to the bottom and found the familiar yellow bus waiting.* **2** a slight error in a rotating tool, machine component, etc., such as being off-center or not exactly round.

runt /rənt/ ▸*n.* an animal that is smaller than average, esp. the smallest in a litter. ■ *figurative, derogatory* an undersized or weak person. ▷early 16th cent. (in the sense 'old or decayed tree stump'): of unknown origin. **—runt·y** *adj.*

run-through ▸*n.* **1** a rehearsal: *a run-through of the whole show.* **2** a brief outline or summary: *the textbooks provide a run-through of research findings.*

run-time *Computing* ▸*n.* the length of time a program takes to run. ■ the time at which the program is run. ■ a cut-down version of a program that can be run but not changed: *you can distribute the run-time to your colleagues.*

▸*adj.* (of software) in a reduced version that can be run but not changed.

run-time li·cense ▸*n.* a relatively broad software license enabling the holder to operate software on a network and in some cases to distribute it with other products.

run-up ▸*n.* **1** a marked rise in the value or level of something: *a sharp run-up of land and stock prices.* **2** the period preceding a notable event: *an acrimonious **run-up to** legislative elections.* **3** an act of running briefly to gain momentum before performing a jump in track and field or other sports: *high jumper Steve Smith will use his shortened five-stride run-up.* **4** an act of running an engine or turbine to prepare it for use or to test it. **5** *Golf* a low approach shot that bounces and runs forward.

run·way /'rən,wā/ ▸*n.* **1** a leveled strip of smooth ground along which aircraft take off and land. **2** a raised aisle extending into the audience from a stage, esp. as used for fashion shows. **3** an animal run, esp. one made by small mammals in grass, under snow, etc. **4** an incline or chute down which something slides or runs.

Run·yon /'rənyən/, (Alfred) Damon (1884–1946), U.S. author and journalist. His short stories about New York City's underworld characters are written in a highly individual style with much use of colorful slang. His collection *Guys and Dolls* (1932) formed the basis for the musical of the same name (1950).

ru·o·te /rōō'ōtē/ ▸*n.* pasta that resembles small wheels with five spokes radiating from a hub. ▷Italian, literally 'wheels'.

ru·pee /rōō'pē; 'rōō,pē/ ▸*n.* the basic monetary unit of India, Pakistan, Sri Lanka, Nepal, Mauritius, and the Seychelles, equal to 100 paisa in India, Pakistan, and Nepal, and 100 cents in Sri Lanka, Mauritius, and the Seychelles. ▷via Hindi from Sanskrit *rūpya* 'wrought silver.'

Ru·pert, Prince /'rōōpərt/ (1619–82), English general; son of Frederick V (elector of the Palatinate) and nephew of Charles I. The Royalist leader of cavalry, he initially won a series of victories, but was defeated by Parliamentarian forces at Marston Moor in 1644 and Naseby in 1645.

Ru·pert's Land (also **Prince Ru·pert's Land**) a historical region of northern and western Canada, roughly corresponding to what is now Manitoba, Saskatchewan, Yukon, Alberta, and the southern part of the Northwest Territories.

ru·pes·tri·an /rōō'pestrēən/ ▸*adj.* (of art) done on rock or cave walls. ▷late 18th cent.: from modern Latin *rupestris* 'found on rocks' (from Latin *rupes* 'rock') + -AN.

ru·pi·ah /rōō'pēə/ ▸*n.* the basic monetary unit of Indonesia, equal to 100 sen. ▷Indonesian, from Hindi *rūpyah* (see RUPEE).

rup·ture /'rəpCHər/ ▸*v.* [*intrans.*] (esp. of a pipe, a vessel, or a bodily part such as an organ or membrane) break or burst suddenly: *if the main artery ruptures he could die.* ■ [*trans.*] cause to break or burst suddenly and completely: *the impact ruptured both fuel tanks.* ■ [*trans.*] suffer such a bursting of (a bodily part): *it was her first match since rupturing an Achilles tendon.* ■ **(be ruptured** or **rupture oneself)** suffer an abdominal hernia: *one of the boys was ruptured and needed to be fitted with a truss.* ■ [*trans.*] *figurative* breach or disturb (a harmonious feeling or situation): *once trust has been ruptured it can be difficult to regain.*

▸*n.* an instance of breaking or bursting suddenly and completely: *a small hairline crack could develop into a rupture | the patient died after rupture of an aneurysm.* ■ *figurative* a breach of a harmonious relationship: *the rupture with his father would never be healed.* ■ an abdominal hernia. ▷late Middle English (as a noun): from Old French *rupture* or Latin *ruptura*, from *rumpere* 'to break.' The verb dates from the mid 18th cent.

ru·ral /'rōōrəl/ ▸*adj.* in, relating to, or characteristic of the countryside rather than the town: *remote rural areas.* ▷late Middle English: from Old French, or from late Latin *ruralis*, from *rus, rur-* 'country.' **—ru·ral·ism** *n.* **—ru·ral·ist** *n.* **—ru·ral·i·ty** /rōō'ralitē/ *n.* **—ru·ral·i·za·tion** /,rōōrələ'zāSHən/ *n.* **—ru·ral·ize** *v.* **—ru·ral·ly** *adv.*

ru·ral route (abbr.: **RR**) ▸*n.* a mail delivery route in a rural area.

Ru·rik /'rōōrik/ (also **Ryu·rik**) ▸*n.* a member of a dynasty that ruled Muscovy and much of Russia from the 9th century until the death of Fyodor, son of Ivan the Terrible, in 1598. It was reputedly founded by a Varangian chief who settled in Novgorod in 862.

▸*adj.* of or relating to the Ruriks.

Ru·ri·ta·ni·a /,rōōri'tānēə/ an imaginary kingdom in southeastern Europe used as a fictional background for the adventure novels of courtly intrigue and romance written by Anthony Hope (1863–1933). ▷from RURAL, on the pattern of *Lusitania.* **—Ru·ri·ta·ni·an** /-'tānēən/ *adj.* & *n.*

Ruse /'rōōsā/ (also **Rousse**) an industrial city and the principal port of Bulgaria, on the Danube River; pop. 210,000.

ruse /rōōz; rōōs/ ▸*n.* an action intended to deceive someone; a trick: *Eleanor tried to think of a ruse to get Paul out of the house.* ▷late Middle English (as a hunting term): from Old French, from *ruser* 'use trickery,' earlier 'drive back,' perhaps based on Latin *rursus* 'backward.'

rush[1] /rəSH/ ▸*v.* **1** [*intrans.*] move with urgent haste: *Jason rushed after her | I rushed outside and hailed a taxi.* ■ (of air or a liquid) flow strongly: *the water rushed in through the great oaken gates.* ■ [*intrans.*] act with great haste: *as soon as the campaign started, they **rushed into** action |* [with *infinitive*] *shoppers rushed to buy computers.* ■ [*trans.*] force (someone) to act hastily: *I don't want to **rush** you **into** something.* ■ [*trans.*] take (someone) somewhere with great haste: *an ambulance was waiting to rush him to the hospital.* ■ [with *two objs.*] deliver (something) quickly to (someone): *we'll rush you a copy at once.* ■ **(rush something out)** produce and distribute something, or put something up for sale, very quickly: *a rewritten textbook was rushed out last autumn.* ■ [*trans.*] deal with (something) hurriedly: *panic measures were **rushed through** Congress |* [as *adj.*] **(rushed)** *a rushed job.* ■ [*trans.*] dash toward (someone or something) in an attempt to attack or capture them or it: *he rushed the stronghold.* **2** [*trans.*] *Football* advance rapidly toward (an offensive player, esp. the quarterback). ■ [*intrans.*] gain a specified amount of yardage or score a touchdown or conversion by running from scrimmage with the ball: *he rushed for 100 yards on 22 carries.* **3** [*trans.*] entertain (a new student) in order to assess their suitability for membership in a college fraternity or sorority. ■ (of a student) visit (a college fraternity or sorority) with a view toward joining it: *he rushed three fraternities.*

▸*n.* **1** a sudden quick movement toward something, typically by a number of people: *there was a **rush for** the door.* ■ a flurry of hasty activity: *the pre-Christmas rush |* [as *adj.*] *a rush job.* ■ a sudden strong demand for a commodity: *there's been a **rush on** the Tribune because of the murder.* ■ a sudden flow or flood: *she felt a rush of cold air.* ■ a sudden intense feeling: *Mark felt a rush of anger.* ■ a sudden thrill or feeling of euphoria such as experienced after taking certain drugs: *users experience a rush.* **2** *Football* a rapid advance by a defensive player or players, esp. toward the quarterback. ■ an act of running from scrimmage with the ball to gain yardage. **3** the process whereby college fraternities or sororities entertain new students in order to assess suitability for membership: *ranking pledges during rush |* [as *adj.*] *rush week.* **4 (rushes)** the first prints made of a movie after a period of shooting. ▷late Middle English: from an Anglo-Norman French variant of Old French *ruser* 'drive back,' an early sense of the word in English (see RUSE). **—rush·er** *n.* **—rush·ing·ly** *adv.*

rush[2] ▸*n.* **1** a marsh or waterside plant with slender stemlike pith-filled leaves, widely distributed in temperate areas. Some kinds are used for matting, chair seats, and baskets, and some were formerly used for strewing on floors. • Genus *Juncus*, family Juncaceae. ■ used in names of similar plants of wet habitats, e.g., **flowering rush.** ■ a stem of such a plant. ■ such plants used as a material. **2** *archaic* a thing of no value (used for emphasis): *not one of them is worth a rush.* ▷Old English *risc, rysc*, of Germanic origin. **—rush·like** /-,līk/ *adj.* **—rush·y** *adj.*

Rush·die /'rəSHdē/, (Ahmed) Salman (1947–), British novelist, born in India. His work, chiefly associated with magic realism, includes *Midnight's Children* (1981) and *The Satanic Verses* (1988). The latter, regarded by Muslims as blasphemous, caused Ayatollah Khomeini to issue a fatwa in 1989 that condemned Rushdie to death.

R

rush hour ▸*n.* a time during each day when traffic is at its heaviest.

rush·light /ˈrəsʜ,līt/ ▸*n.* *historical* a candle made by dipping the pith of a rush in tallow.

Rush·more, Mount /ˈrəsʜ,môr/ a mountain in the Black Hills of South Dakota, noted for its giant busts of four U.S. presidents—George Washington, Thomas Jefferson, Theodore Roosevelt, and Abraham Lincoln—carved 1927–41 under the direction of sculptor Gutzon Borglum (1867–1941).

Mount Rushmore

rus in ur·be /,ro͞os in ˈo͝orbe/ ▸*n.* *poetic/literary* an illusion of countryside created by a building or garden, within a city. ▷Latin, literally 'country in the city.'

Rusk /rəsk/, (David) Dean (1909–94), U.S. educator and statesman. He served as secretary of state under Presidents Kennedy and Johnson 1961–69 and was a strong proponent of U.S. involvement in Vietnam.

rusk /rəsk/ ▸*n.* a light, dry biscuit or piece of rebaked bread, esp. one prepared for use as baby food. ■ rebaked bread used as extra filling, for example in sausages, and formerly as rations at sea. ▷late 16th cent.: from Spanish or Portuguese *rosca* 'twist, coil, roll of bread,' of unknown ultimate origin.

Rus·kin /ˈrəskin/, John (1819–1900), English art and social critic. His prolific writings include attacks on Renaissance art in *The Stones of Venice* (1851–53), capitalism in "The Political Economy of Art" (1857), and utilitarianism in *Unto This Last* (1860).

Rus·sell[1] /ˈrəsəl/, Bertrand (Arthur William), 3rd Earl Russell (1872–1970), British philosopher, mathematician, and social reformer. In *Principia Mathematica* (1910–13) he and A. N. Whitehead attempted to express all of mathematics in formal logic terms. He expounded logical atomism in *Our Knowledge of the External World* (1914) and neutral monism in *The Analysis of Mind* (1921). Nobel Prize for Literature (1950).

Rus·sell[2], Bill (1934–), U.S. basketball player and coach; full name *William Felton Russell.* A center, he played for the Boston Celtics 1956–69 and also coached them from 1966, becoming the first African-American head coach in the NBA. He coached the Seattle Supersonics 1973–77. Basketball Hall of Fame (1974).

Rus·sell[3], John, 1st Earl Russell (1792–1878), British statesman; prime minister 1846–52 and 1865–66.

Rus·sell[4], Ken (1927–), English movie director; born *Henry Kenneth Alfred Russell.* Characterized by extravagant and extreme imagery, his movies, such as *Women in Love* (1969), have often attracted controversy for their depiction of sex and violence.

Rus·sell's par·a·dox a logical paradox stated in terms of set theory, concerning the set of all sets that do not contain themselves as members, namely that the condition for it to contain itself is that it should not contain itself. ▷1920s: named after Bertrand *Russell* (see **RUSSELL**[1]).

Rus·sell's vi·per ▸*n.* a large venomous Asian snake that has a yellow-brown body with black markings. • *Daboia* (or **Vipera**) *russelli,* family Viperidae. ▷early 20th cent.: named after Patrick *Russell* (1727–1805), Scottish physician and naturalist.

Rus·sell·ville /ˈrəsəl,vil/ a city in central Arkansas, on the northern shore of the Arkansas River, northwest of Little Rock; pop. 23,682.

rus·set /ˈrəsət/ ▸*adj.* **1** reddish brown in color: *gardens of russet and gold chrysanthemums.* **2** *archaic* rustic; homely.

▸*n.* **1** a reddish-brown color: *the woods in autumn are a riot of russet and gold.* **2** a dessert apple of a variety with a slightly rough greenish-brown skin. **3** *historical* a coarse homespun reddish-brown or gray cloth used for simple clothing.

▸*v.* (**-set·ed, -set·ing**) make or become russet in color. ■ (of smooth-skinned fruit) develop a rough reddish-brown or yellowish-brown skin, or patches of such: [*trans.*] *a week of humid weather has russeted the pears* | [*intrans.*] *this variety of apple tends not to russet.* ▷Middle English: from an Anglo-Norman French variant of Old French *rousset,* diminutive of *rous* 'red,' from Provençal *ros,* from Latin *russus* 'red.' **—rus·set·y** *adj.*

Rus·sia /ˈrəsʜə/ a country in northern Asia and eastern Europe; pop. 143,782,000; capital, Moscow; language, Russian (official). Official name **RUSSIAN FEDERATION.**

> The modern state originated from the expansion of the principality of Muscovy into a great empire. Russia played an increasing role in Europe from the time of Peter the Great in the early 18th century. Following the overthrow of the tsar in the Russian Revolution of 1917, Russia became the largest of the constituent republics of the Soviet Union, with more than three quarters of the area and over half of the population. On the breakup of the Soviet Union and the collapse of communist control in 1991, Russia emerged as an independent state and a founding member of the Commonwealth of Independent States.

Rus·sia leath·er ▸*n.* a durable leather made from calfskin and impregnated with birchbark oil, used for bookbinding.

Rus·sian /ˈrəsʜən/ ▸*adj.* of or relating to Russia, its people, or their language.

▸*n.* **1** a native or national of Russia. ■ a person of Russian descent. ■ *historical* (in general use) a national of the former Soviet Union. **2** the East Slavic language of Russia. ▷mid 16th cent.: from medieval Latin *Russianus.* **—Rus·sian·i·za·tion** /,rəsʜənəˈzāsʜən/ *n.* **—Rus·sian·ize** /-,nīz/ *v.* **—Rus·sian·ness** *n.*

Rus·sian bal·let ▸*n.* a style of ballet developed at the Russian Imperial Ballet Academy, popularized in the West by Sergei Diaghilev's Ballets Russes from 1909.

Rus·sian Blue ▸*n.* a cat of a breed with short grayish-blue fur, green eyes, and large pointed ears.

Rus·sian boot ▸*n.* a boot that loosely encloses the wearer's calf.

Rus·sian doll ▸*n.* another term for **MATRYOSHKA.**

Rus·sian Fed·er·a·tion official name for **RUSSIA.**

Rus·sian ol·ive ▸*n.* see **OLEASTER.**

Rus·sian Or·tho·dox Church the national church of Russia. See **ORTHODOX CHURCH.**

Rus·sian Rev·o·lu·tion the revolution in the Russian empire in 1917, in which the tsarist regime was overthrown and replaced by Bolshevik rule under Lenin.

> There were two phases to the Revolution: the first, in March (Old Style, February, thus **February Revolution**), was sparked by food and fuel shortages during World War I and began with strikes and riots in Petrograd (St. Petersburg). The tsar abdicated, and a provisional government was set up. The second phase, in November 1917 (Old Style, October, thus **October Revolution**), was marked by the seizure of power by the Bolsheviks in a coup led by Lenin. After workers' councils or **soviets** took power in major cities, the new Soviet constitution was declared in 1918.

Rus·sian rou·lette ▸*n.* the practice of loading a bullet into one chamber of a revolver, spinning the cylinder, and then pulling the trigger while pointing the gun at one's own head. ■ *figurative* an activity that is potentially very dangerous.

Rus·sian sal·ad ▸*n.* *Brit.* a salad of mixed diced vegetables with mayonnaise.

Rus·sian tea ▸*n.* tea laced with rum and typically served with lemon.

Rus·sian this·tle ▸*n.* a prickly tumbleweed that is an inland form of saltwort. Native to Eurasia, it was accidentally introduced into North America, where it has become a pest. Also called **Russian tumbleweed.** • *Salsola kali,* family Chenopodiaceae.

Rus·si·fy /ˈrəsə,fī/ ▸*v.* (**-fies, -fied**) [*trans.*] make Russian in character. **—Rus·si·fi·ca·tion** /,rəsəfəˈkāsʜən/ *n.*

Russ·ki /ˈrəskē; ˈro͝oskē/ (also **Russ·ky**) ▸*n.* (*pl.* **-kis** or **-kies**) *informal, often offensive* a Russian. ▷mid 19th cent.: from Russian *russkiĭ* 'Russian,' or from **RUSSIAN**, on the pattern of Russian surnames ending in *-skiĭ.*

Russo- ▸*comb. form* Russian; Russian and . . . : *Russo-Japanese.* ■ relating to Russia.

Rus·so-Jap·an·ese War /ˈrəsō/ a war between the Russian empire and Japan in 1904–05, caused by territorial disputes in Manchuria and Korea. Russia suffered a series of humiliating defeats, and the peace settlement gave Japan the ascendancy in the disputed region.

Rus·so·phile /ˈrəsə,fīl/ ▸*n.* a person who is friendly toward Russia or fond of Russia and Russian things, esp. someone who is sympathetic to the political system and customs of the former Soviet Union. **—Rus·so·phil·i·a** /,rəsəˈfilēə/ *n.*

Rus·so·phobe /ˈrəsə,fōb/ ▸*n.* a person who feels an intense dislike toward Russia and Russian things, esp. the political system or customs of the former Soviet Union. **—Rus·so·pho·bi·a** /,rəsəˈfōbēə/ *n.*

rus·su·la /ˈrəs(y)ələ/ ▸*n.* a widespread woodland toadstool that typically has a brightly colored flattened cap and a white stem and gills. • Genus *Russula,* family Russulaceae, class Hymenomycetes: numerous species. See also **SICKENER** (sense 2). ▷modern Latin, from Latin *russus* 'red' (because many, such as the sickener, have a red cap).

rust /rəst/ ▸*n.* **1** a reddish- or yellowish-brown flaky coating of iron oxide that is formed on iron or steel by oxidation, esp. in the presence of moisture. ■ *figurative* a state of deterioration or disrepair resulting from neglect or lack of use: *they are here to scrape the rust off the derelict machinery of government.* **2** [usu. with *adj.*] a fungal disease of plants that results in reddish or brownish patches. • The fungi belong to *Puccinia* and other genera, order Uredinales, class Teliomycetes. **3** a reddish-brown color: [in *combination*] *his rust-colored hair.*

▸*v.* [*intrans.*] be affected with rust: *the blades had* ***rusted away*** | [as *adj.*] (**rusting**) *rusting machinery.* ■ *figurative* deteriorate through neglect or lack of use. ▷Old English *rūst,* of Germanic origin; related to Dutch *roest,* German *Rost,* also to **RED.** **—rust·less** *adj.*

Rust Belt ▸*n.* (**the Rust Belt**) *informal* parts of the northeastern and midwestern U.S. that are characterized by declining industry, aging factories, and a falling population. Steel-producing cities in Pennsylvania and Ohio are at its center: *the smokestacks of the Rust Belt were no longer allowed to blast wastes into the air* | [as *adj.*] *the state's Rust Belt economy.*

rust buck·et ▸*n.* *informal, often humorous* a car, ship, or other vehicle that is old and badly rusted.

rus·tic /ˈrəstik/ ▸*adj.* **1** having a simplicity and charm that is considered typical of the countryside: *bare plaster walls and a terra-cotta floor give a rustic feel.* ■ *often derogatory* lacking the sophistication of the city; backward and provincial: *you are a rustic halfwit.* **2** constructed or made in a plain and simple fashion, in particular: ■ made of untrimmed branches or rough timber: *a rustic oak bench.* ■ *Architecture* with rough-hewn or roughened surface or with deeply sunk joints: *a rustic bridge.* ■ denoting freely formed lettering, esp. a relatively informal style of handwritten Roman capital letter.

▸*n.* *often derogatory* an unsophisticated country person. ▷late Middle English (in the sense 'rural'): from Latin *rusticus,* from *rus* 'the country.' **—rus·ti·cal·ly** /-ik(ə)lē/ *adv.* **—rus·tic·i·ty** /rəˈstisətē/ *n.*

rus·ti·cate /ˈrəsti,kāt/ ▸*v.* **1** [*intrans.*] go to, live in, or spend time in the country. **2** [*trans.*] fashion (masonry) in large blocks with sunk joints and a roughened surface: [as *adj.*] (**rusticated**) *the stable block was built of rusticated stone.* **3** [*trans.*] *Brit.* suspend (a student) from a university as a punishment (used chiefly at Oxford and Cambridge). ▷late 15th cent. (in the sense 'countrify'): from Latin *rusticat-* '(having) lived in the country,' from the verb *rusticari,* from *rusticus* (see **RUSTIC**). **—rus·ti·ca·tion** /,rəstiˈkāsʜən/ *n.*

Rus·tin /ˈrəstin/, Bayard (1910–87), U.S. civil rights leader. As a special assistant to Martin Luther King, Jr., he helped to organize the 1963 March on Washington. He was the executive director of the A. Philip Randolph Institute 1964–87.

rus·tle /ˈrəsəl/ ▸*v.* **1** [*intrans.*] make a soft, muffled crackling sound like that caused by the movement of dry leaves or paper: *she came closer, her skirt swaying and rustling.* ■ [with *adverbial of direction*] move with such sound: *a nurse rustled in with a syringe.* ■ [*trans.*] move (something), causing it to make such a sound: *Dolly rustled the paper irritably.* **2** [*trans.*] round up and steal (cattle, horses, or sheep). **3** [*intrans.*] *informal* move or act quickly or energetically; hustle: *rustle around the kitchen, see what there is.*

▸*phrasal v.* □ **rustle something up** *informal* produce something quickly when it is needed: *see if you can rustle up a cup of coffee for Paula and me, please.*

▸*n.* [usu. in *sing.*] a soft, muffled crackling sound like that made by the movement of dry leaves or paper:

there was a rustle in the undergrowth behind her. ▷late Middle English (as a verb): imitative; compare with Flemish *rijsselen* and Dutch *ritselen*. The noun dates from the mid 18th cent. **—rus·tler** /ˈrəs(ə)lər/ *n.* (usu. in sense 2).

Rus·ton /ˈrəstən/ a commercial city in northern Louisiana; pop. 20,546.

rust·proof /ˈrəst,pro͞of/ ▶*adj.* (of metal or a metal object) not susceptible to corrosion by rust.
▶*v.* [*trans.*] make resistant to corrosion by rust.

rust·y /ˈrəstē/ ▶*adj.* (**rust·i·er**, **rust·i·est**) **1** (of a metal object) affected by rust: *a rusty hinge.* ■ rust-colored: *green grass turning a rusty brown.* **2** (of knowledge or a skill) impaired by lack of recent practice: *my typing is a little rusty.* ■ stiff with age or disuse: *it was my first race for three months and I felt a bit rusty.* ■ (of a voice) croaking: *her voice sounded rusty.* ▷Old English *rūstig* (see **RUST**, **-Y**[1]). **—rust·i·ly** /ˈrəstəlē/ *adv.* **—rust·i·ness** *n.*

rust·y dust·y ▶*n. black English* a person's buttocks. ▷late 16th cent. (in the sense 'dusty, fusty'): reduplication of **RUSTY**. The current transferred use dates from the 1950s.

rut[1] /rət/ ▶*n.* a long deep track made by the repeated passage of the wheels of vehicles. ■ *figurative* a habit or pattern of behavior that has become dull and unproductive but is hard to change: *the administration was stuck **in a rut** and was losing its direction.* ▷late 16th cent.: probably from Old French *rute* (see **ROUTE**). **—rut·ted** *adj.* **—rut·ty** *adj.*

rut[2] ▶*n.* (**the rut**) an annual period of sexual activity in deer and some other mammals, during which the males fight each other for access to the females.
▶*v.* (**rut·ted**, **rut·ting**) [*intrans.*] [often as *adj.*] (**rutting**) engage in such activity: *a rutting stag.* ▷late Middle English: from Old French, from Latin *rugitus*, from *rugire* 'to roar.' **—rut·tish** *adj.*

ru·ta·ba·ga /ˈro͞otə,bāgə; ˈro͝ot-/ ▶*n.* **1** a large, round, yellow-fleshed root that is eaten as a vegetable. **2** the European plant of the cabbage family that produces this root. • *Brassica napus*, family Brassicaceae: 'napobrassica' group. ▷late 18th cent.: from Swedish dialect *rotabagge*.

Ruth[1] /ro͞oTH/ a book of the Bible telling the story of Ruth, a Moabite woman, who married her deceased husband's kinsman Boaz and bore a son, Obed, who became grandfather to King David.

Ruth[2], Babe (1895–1948), U.S. baseball player; born *George Herman Ruth*; also known as the **Bambino**. He played for the Boston Red Sox 1914–19, the New York Yankees 1919–34, and the Boston Braves 1935. Originally a pitcher, he later became noted for his hitting, setting a record of 714 home runs that remained unbroken until 1974 and a single-season record in 1927 of 60 home runs that was not broken until 1961. Baseball Hall of Fame (1936).

Babe Ruth

ruth /ro͞oTH/ ▶*n. archaic* a feeling of pity, distress, or grief. ▷Middle English: from the verb **RUE**[1], probably influenced by Old Norse *hrygth*.

ru·the·ni·um /ro͞oˈTHēnēəm/ ▶*n.* the chemical element of atomic number 44, a hard silvery-white metal of the transition series. (Symbol: **Ru**) ▷mid 19th cent.: modern Latin, from medieval Latin *Ruthenia*, so named because it was discovered in ores from the Urals.

ruth·er /ˈrə*TH*ər/ ▶*adv.* nonstandard spelling of **RATHER**, used in representing dialectal speech: *I'd ruther walk.* Compare with **DRUTHER**.

Ruth·er·ford[1] /ˈrə*TH*ərfərd/, Sir Ernest, 1st Baron Rutherford of Nelson (1871–1937), New Zealand physicist, regarded as the founder of nuclear physics. Nobel Prize for Chemistry (1908).

Ruth·er·ford[2], Dame Margaret (1892–1972), English actress. Chiefly remembered for her roles as a formidable but jovial eccentric, she won an Academy Award for *The VIPs* (1963).

ruth·er·for·di·um /,rə*TH*ərˈfôrdēəm/ ▶*n.* the chemical element of atomic number 104, a very unstable element made by high-energy atomic collisions. (Symbol: **Rf**) ▷1960s: modern Latin, named after E. *Rutherford* (see **RUTHERFORD**[1]).

ruth·less /ˈro͞oTHləs/ ▶*adj.* having or showing no pity or compassion for others: *a ruthless manipulator.* ▷Middle English: from **RUTH** + **-LESS**. **—ruth·less·ly** *adv.* **—ruth·less·ness** *n.*

ru·ti·lant /ˈro͞otl-ənt/ ▶*adj. poetic/literary* glowing or glittering with red or golden light: *rutilant gems.* ▷late Middle English: from Latin *rutilant-* 'glowing red,' from the verb *rutilare*, from *rutilus* 'reddish.'

ru·tile /ˈro͞o,tēl/ ▶*n.* a black or reddish-brown mineral consisting of titanium dioxide, typically occurring as needlelike crystals. ▷early 19th cent.: from French, or from German *Rutil*, from Latin *rutilus* 'reddish.'

ru·tin /ˈro͞otn/ ▶*n. Chemistry* a flavonoid compound found in common rue, buckwheat, capers, and other plants, and sometimes taken as a dietary supplement. ▷mid 19th cent.: from Latin *ruta* 'rue' + **-IN**[1].

Rut·land /ˈrətlənd/ an industrial and commercial city in south central Vermont; pop. 17,292.

Rut·ledge[1] /ˈrətlij/, John (1739–1800), U.S. Supreme

Sir Ernest Rutherford

Pronunciation Key ə *ago*; ər *over*; ˈə or ,ə *up*; ˈər or ,ər *fur*; a *hat*; ā *rate*; ä *car*; CH *chew*; e *let*; ē *see*; e(ə)r *air*; i *fit*; ī *by*; i(ə)r *ear*; NG *sing*; ō *go*; ô *for*; oi *boy*; o͝o *good*; o͞o *goo*; ou *out*; SH *she*; TH *thin*; *TH* *then*; (h)w *why*; ZH *vision*

Court associate justice 1789–91. He resigned as associate justice to serve as chief justice of South Carolina. In 1795, he was appointed U.S. chief justice by President Washington and served for a short time but he was ultimately rejected by the U.S. Senate.

Rut·ledge2, Wiley Blount, Jr. (1894–1949), U.S. Supreme Court associate justice. Appointed to the Court by President Franklin D. Roosevelt, he tended toward liberalism.

Ru·wen·zo·ri /ˌro͞owənˈzôrē/ a mountain range in central Africa, on the Uganda–Democratic Republic of the Congo (formerly Zaire) border between lakes Edward and Albert. It rises to 16,765 feet (5,110 m) at Margherita Peak on Mount Stanley. The range is generally thought to be the "Mountains of the Moon" mentioned by Ptolemy and, as such, the supposed source of the Nile.

Ruys·dael variant spelling of RUISDAEL.

RV ▸*abbr.* ■ recreational vehicle. ■ a rendezvous point. ■ Revised Version (of the Bible).

Rv. ▸*abbr. Bible* Revelations.

R-val·ue ▸*n.* the capacity of an insulating material to resist heat flow. The higher the R-value, the greater the insulating power.

RVer /ˈärˈvēər/ ▸*n.* a user of a recreational vehicle.

RW ▸*abbr.* ■ Right Worshipful. ■ Right Worthy.

Rwan·da /ro͞oˈändə; rəˈwändə/ a landlocked country in central Africa, north of Burundi and south of Uganda; pop. 7,954,000; capital, Kigali; languages, Rwanda (a Bantu language) and French (both official). Official name RWANDESE REPUBLIC. **—Rwan·dan** *adj.* & *n.* **—Rwan·dese** /-dēz; -dēs/ *adj.* & *n.*

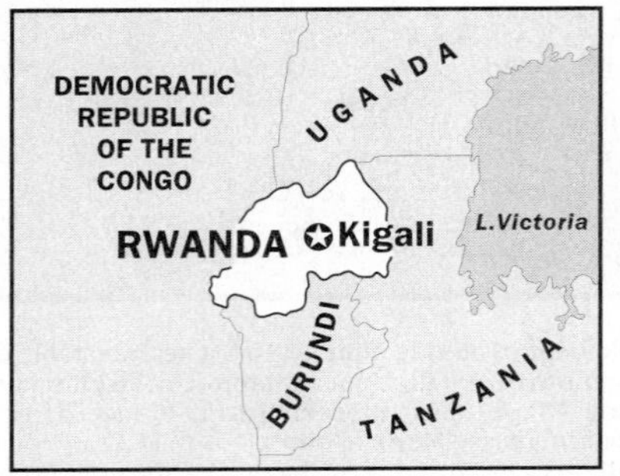

Inhabited largely by Hutu and Tutsi peoples, the area was claimed by Germany from 1890 and after World War I became part of a Belgian trust territory. Rwanda became independent as a republic in 1962, shortly after the violent overthrow of the Tutsi monarchy by the majority Hutu people. In 1994, over 500,000 people, largely Tutsis, were slaughtered by predominantly Hutu supporters of the government, and more than a million fled as refugees into the Democratic Republic of the Congo (formerly Zaire) and neighboring countries. The Tutsi-dominated Rwandan Patriotic Front took power as the new government. Elections were held in 2003, but wars in neighboring countries and a Hutu insurgency cause continuing instability.

rwy. ▸*abbr. Brit.* Railway.

Rx ▸*abbr.* ■ prescription. ■ (in prescriptions) take. ■ tens of rupees.

Ry ▸*abbr.* Railway.

-ry ▸*suffix* a shortened form of -ERY (as in *devilry, rivalry*).

Ry·an /ˈrīən/, (Lynn) Nolan (Jr.) (1948–), U.S. baseball player. He pitched for the New York Mets 1966, 1968–71, the California Angels 1972–79, the Houston Astros 1980–88, and the Texas Rangers 1989–93. He held the pitching records for no-hitters (7) and strikeouts (5,714). Baseball Hall of Fame (1999).

Rya·zan /ˌrēəˈzän; ryi-/ an industrial city in western Russia, southeast of Moscow; pop. 522,000.

Ry·binsk /ˈrib(y)insk/ a city in northwestern Russia, a port on the Volga River; pop. 252,000. It was formerly known as Shcherbakov 1946–57 and as Andropov 1984–89.

Ryd·berg at·om /ˈridˌbərg/ ▸*n. Physics* an atom in a highly excited state in which one electron has almost sufficient energy to escape. Atoms, usually hydrogen atoms, in this **Rydberg state** are used in atomic research. ▷named after J. R. *Rydberg* (see RYDBERG CONSTANT).

Ryd·berg con·stant *Physics* a constant, 1.097 x 10^7 m^{-1}, that appears in the formulae for the wave numbers of lines in atomic spectra and is a function of the rest mass and charge of the electron, the speed of light, and Planck's constant. ▷early 20th cent.: named after Johannes R. *Rydberg* (1854–1919), Swedish physicist.

Ry·der1 /ˈrīdər/, Albert Pinkham (1847–1917), U.S. artist. He is known for seascapes, such as "Toilers of the Sea" (1884), and pastoral landscapes.

Ry·der2, Jonathan, see LUDLUM.

Ry·der Cup /ˈrīdər/ a golf tournament held every two years and played between teams of male professionals from the U.S. and Europe (originally Great Britain), first held in 1927. ▷so named because the trophy was donated by Samuel *Ryder* (1859–1936), English seed merchant.

rye /rī/ ▸*n.* **1** a wheatlike cereal plant that tolerates poor soils and low temperatures. • *Secale cereale*, family Gramineae. ■ grains of this, used mainly for making bread or whiskey and for fodder: [as *adj.*] *rye flour.* **2** (also **rye whis·key**) whiskey in which a significant amount of the grain used in distillation is fermented rye: *half a bottle of rye.* **3** short for RYE BREAD: *pastrami on rye.* ▷Old English *ryge*, of Germanic origin; related to Dutch *rogge* and German *Roggen*.

rye bread ▸*n.* bread made wholly or partly with rye flour, typically with caraway seeds added.

rye·grass /ˈrīˌgras/ ▸*n.* a Eurasian grass that is widely grown as forage. • Genus *Lolium*, family Gramineae: several species, in particular *L. perenne.* ▷early 18th cent.: alteration of obsolete *ray-grass*, of unknown origin.

Ryle1 /rīl/, Gilbert (1900–76), English philosopher. He did much to make Oxford a leading center for philosophical research. In *The Concept of Mind* (1949), he attacked the mind-body dualism of Descartes.

Ryle2, Sir Martin (1918–84), English astronomer. His demonstration that remote objects appeared to be different from closer ones helped to establish the big bang theory of the universe. Nobel Prize for Physics (1974, shared with Anthony Hewish 1924–).

ryo·kan /rēˈōˌkän; -ˌkan/ ▸*n.* a traditional Japanese inn. ▷Japanese.

ry·ot /ˈrīət/ ▸*n.* an Indian peasant or tenant farmer. ▷from Urdu *raiyat*, from Arabic *raʿīyya* 'flock, subjects,' from *raʿā* 'to pasture.'

ry·u /rēˈo͞o/ ▸*n.* (*pl.* same or **ry·us**) a school or style in Japanese arts, esp. in the martial arts. ▷Japanese.

Ryu·kyu Is·lands /rēˈo͞okyo͞o/ a chain of islands in the western Pacific Ocean, stretching about 600 miles (960 km) from the southern tip of the island of Kyushu in Japan to Taiwan. The largest island is Okinawa.

Ry·un /ˈrīən/, Jim (1947–), U.S. athlete and politician; full name *James Ronald Ryun.* In 1964, he became the first high-school male to break the 4-minute mile by running it in 3:59.0 minutes, a record that still stands. He brought home the silver medal for placing second in the 1500-meter run at the 1968 Olympic games. A Republican from Kansas, he served in the U.S. House of Representatives 1997– .

Ryu·rik /rēˈo͞orik; ˈro͞orik/ variant spelling of RURIK.

Ss

S[1] /es/ (also **s**) ▸*n.* (*pl.* **Ss** or **S's** /esiz/) **1** the nineteenth letter of the alphabet. ■ denoting the next after R in a set of items, categories, etc. **2** a shape like that of a capital S: [in *combination*] *an S-bend.*

S[2] ▸*abbr.* ■ (chiefly in Catholic use) Saint: *S Ignatius Loyola.* ■ siemens. ■ small (as a clothes size). ■ South or Southern: *65° S.* ■ *Biochemistry* Svedberg unit(s). ▸*symbol* ■ the chemical element sulfur. ■ *Chemistry* entropy.

s ▸*abbr.* ■ second(s). ■ *Law* section (of an act). ■ shilling(s). ■ *Grammar* singular. ■ *Chemistry* solid. ■ (in genealogies) son(s). ■ succeeded. ■ *Chemistry* denoting electrons and orbitals possessing zero angular momentum and total symmetry: *s-electrons.* [s from *sharp*, originally applied to lines in atomic spectra.]
▸*symbol* (in mathematical formulae) distance.

's *informal* ▸*contraction of* ■ is: *it's raining.* ■ has: *she's gone.* ■ us: *let's go.* ■ does: *what's he do?*

's- ▸*prefix archaic* (used chiefly in oaths) God's: *'sblood.* ▷shortened form.

-s[1] ▸*suffix* denoting the plurals of nouns (as in *apples, wagons*, etc.). Compare with **-ES**[1]. ▷Old English plural ending *-as.*

-s[2] ▸*suffix* forming the third person singular of the present of verbs (as in *sews, vaunts*, etc.). Compare with **-ES**[2]. ▷Old English dialect.

-s[3] ▸*suffix* **1** forming adverbs such as *afterwards, besides.* **2** forming possessive pronouns such as *hers, ours.* ▷Old English *-es*, masculine and neuter genitive singular ending.

-s[4] ▸*suffix* forming nicknames or hypocoristics: *Pops.* ▷suggested by **-S**[1].

-'s[1] ▸*suffix* denoting possession in singular nouns, also in plural nouns not having a final *-s*: *the car's engine | Mrs. Ross's son | the children's teacher.* ▷Old English, masculine and neuter genitive singular ending.

-'s[2] or or depending on the preceding sound. ▸*suffix* denoting the plural of a letter or symbol: *T's | 9's.*

USAGE In the formation of plurals of regular nouns, it is incorrect to use an apostrophe: *six pens* (not *six pen's*). There are a few special occasions, however, in which the apostrophe indicates plurals, as with letters and symbols where s added without punctuation would look odd (or be undecipherable): *ABC's; the five W's; dot your i's and cross your t's; the code is two H's followed by four #'s.*

SA ▸*abbr.* ■ Salvation Army. ■ South Africa. ■ South America. ■ *historical* Sturmabteilung.

s.a. ▸*abbr.* ■ semiannual. ■ sex appeal. ■ without year or date. [from Latin *sine anno.*] ■ subject to approval.

Saa·di variant spelling of **SADI**.

Saa·le[1] /'zälə; 'sä-/ a river in east central Germany. Rising in northern Bavaria near the border with the Czech Republic, it flows 265 miles (425 km) north to join the Elbe River near Magdeburg.

Saa·le[2] ▸*n.* [usu. as *adj.*] *Geology* the penultimate Pleistocene glaciation in northern Europe, corresponding to the Wolstonian of Britain (and possibly the Riss of the Alps). ■ the system of deposits laid down at this time. ▷1930s: from **SAALE**[1]. **—Saa·li·an** /-lēən/ *adj.* & *n.*

Saa·me /'sämē/ ▸*plural n.* variant spelling of **SAMI**.

Saa·mi /'sämē/ ▸*plural n.* variant spelling of **SAMI**.

Saar /sär; zär/ a river in western Europe. Rising in the Vosges Mountains in eastern France, it flows 150 miles (240 km) north to join the Mosel River in Germany, just east of the border with Luxembourg. French name **SARRE**. ■ the Saarland.

Saar·brück·en /sär'brŏŏkən; zär'brykən/ an industrial city in western Germany, the capital of Saarland, on the Saar River, close to the border with France; pop. 362,000.

Saa·ri·nen[1] /'särənən/, Eero (1910–61), U.S. architect; born in Finland; the son of Eliel Saarinen. He designed the Memorial Arch in St. Louis 1948 and the U.S. Embassy in London 1955–60.

Saa·ri·nen[2], (Gottlieb) Eliel (1873–1950), U.S. architect; born in Finland; the father of Eero Saarinen. He designed the Cranbrook Academy of Art in Michigan and served as its president 1932–48.

Saar·land /'sär,land; 'zärlänt/ a state in western Germany, on the border with France; capital, Saarbrücken. Rich in coal and iron ore and historically dominated by France, the area was administered by the League of Nations from the end of World War I until 1935; it became the tenth German state in 1957.

Sab. ▸*abbr.* Sabbath.

Sa·ba /'säbə/ **1** an island in the Netherlands Antilles, in the Caribbean; pop. 1,130. The smallest island in the group, it is located northwest of St. Kitts. **2** an ancient kingdom in southwestern Arabia, known for its trade in gold and spices; the biblical Sheba.

sab·a·dil·la /,sabə'dilə; -'dēyə/ ▸*n.* a Mexican plant of the lily family, whose seeds contain veratrine. • *Schoenocaulon officinale*, family Liliaceae. ■ a preparation of these seeds, used as an agricultural insecticide and in medicines. ▷early 19th cent.: from Spanish *cebadilla*, diminutive of *cebada* 'barley.'

Sa·bae·an /sə'bēən/ ▸*n.* a member of an ancient Semitic people who ruled Saba in southwestern Arabia until overrun by Persians and Arabs in the 6th century AD.
▸*adj.* of or relating to this people. ▷from Latin *Sabaeus* (from Greek *Sabaios*) + **-AN**.

Sa·bah /'säbä/ a state of Malaysia that is comprised of the northern part of Borneo and some offshore islands; capital, Kota Kinabalu.

sa·bal palm /'säbəl/ ▸*n.* see **PALMETTO**.

Sab·a·oth /'sabä,äTH/ ▸*plural n. archaic* the hosts of heaven (in the biblical title "Lord (God) of Sabaoth"). ▷via Latin from Greek *Sabaōth*, from Hebrew *ṣĕḇā'ōṯ*, plural of *ṣāḇā* 'host (of heaven).'

sa·ba·yon /säbī'ōn/ ▸*n.* French term for **ZABAGLIONE**.

sab·ba·tar·i·an /,sabə'te(ə)rēən/ ▸*n.* a Christian who strictly observes Sunday as the sabbath. ■ a Jew who strictly observes the sabbath. ■ a Christian belonging to a denomination or sect that observes Saturday as the sabbath.
▸*adj.* relating to or upholding the observance of the sabbath. ▷early 17th cent.: from late Latin *sabbatarius* (from Latin *sabbatum* 'sabbath') + **-AN**. **—sab·ba·tar·i·an·ism** /-,nizəm/ *n.*

sab·bath /'sabəTH/ ▸*n.* **1** (often **the Sabbath**) a day of religious observance and abstinence from work, kept by Jews from Friday evening to Saturday evening, and by most Christians on Sunday. **2** (also **witch·es' sab·bath**) a supposed annual midnight meeting of witches with the Devil. ▷Old English, from Latin *sabbatum*, via Greek from Hebrew *šabbāṯ*, from *šāḇaṯ* 'to rest.'

sab·bat·i·cal /sə'batikəl/ ▸*n.* a period of paid leave granted to a college teacher for study or travel, traditionally every seventh year: *she's away* ***on sabbatical.***
▸*adj.* **1** of or relating to a sabbatical. **2** *archaic* of or appropriate to the sabbath. ▷late 16th cent.: via late Latin from Greek *sabbatikos* 'of the sabbath' + **-AL**.

sab·bat·i·cal year ▸*n.* **1** a year's sabbatical leave. **2** (in biblical times) a year observed every seventh year under the Mosaic law as a "sabbath" during which the land was allowed to rest.

Sa·bel·li·an /sə'belēən/ ▸*adj.* of or relating to the teachings of Sabellius (*fl.* c.220 in North Africa), who developed a form of the modalist doctrine that the Father, Son, and Holy Spirit are not truly distinct but merely aspects of one divine being.
▸*n.* a follower of the teachings of Sabellius. **—Sa·bel·li·an·ism** /-,izəm/ *n.*

sa·ber /'sābər/ (*Brit.* **sa·bre**) ▸*n.* a heavy cavalry sword with a curved blade and a single cutting edge. ■ a light fencing sword with a tapering blade. ■ the sport of fencing with a saber. ■ *historical* a cavalry soldier and horse.
▸*v.* [*trans.*] *archaic* cut down or wound with a saber. ▷late 17th cent.: from French, alteration of obsolete *sable*, from German *Sabel* (local variant of *Säbel*), from Hungarian *szablya.*

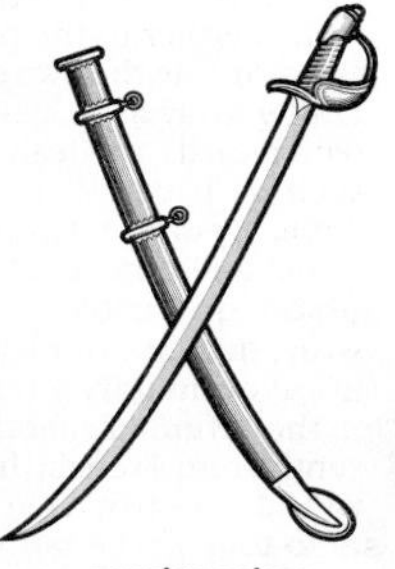
cavalry saber

sa·ber-rat·tling ▸*n.* the display or threat of military force.

sa·ber saw ▸*n.* a portable electric jigsaw.

sa·ber·tooth /'sābər,tōōTH/ ▸*n.* **1** (also **sa·ber-toothed cat** or **sa·ber-toothed ti·ger**) a large extinct carnivorous mammal of the cat family, with large, curved upper canine teeth. • Several genera in the family Felidae, in particular *Smilodon* of the American Pleistocene and *Machairodus* of the Old World Pliocene. **2** a large extinct marsupial mammal with similar teeth, of the South American Pliocene. • Genus *Thylacosmilus*, family Borhyaenidae.

Sa·bi·an /'sābēən/ ▸*adj.* of or relating to a non-Muslim sect classed in the Koran with Jews, Christians, and Zoroastrians as having a faith revealed by the true God. It is not known who the original Sabians were, but the name was adopted by some groups in order to escape religious persecution by Muslims.
▸*n.* a member of this sect. ▷early 17th cent.: from Arabic *ṣābi'* + **-AN**.

sab·i·cu /'sabi,kōō/ ▸*n.* a Caribbean tree of the pea family, with timber that resembles mahogany and is used chiefly in boatbuilding. • *Lysiloma sabicu*, family Leguminosae. ▷mid 19th cent.: from Cuban Spanish *sabicú.*

Sa·bin /'sābin/, Albert Bruce (1906–93), U.S. physician; born in Russia. He developed the orally administered **Sabin vaccine** against poliomyelitis that was adopted by the World Health Organization in the late 1950s.

Sa·bine /'sā,bīn; -,bin/ ▸*adj.* of, relating to, or denoting an ancient Oscan-speaking people of the central Apennines in Italy, northeast of Rome, who feature in early Roman legends and were incorporated into the Roman state in 290 BC.
▸*n.* a member of this people. ▷from Latin *Sabinus.*

Sa·bine Riv·er /sə'bēn/ a river that flows for 360 miles (580 km) from eastern Texas to form the border with Louisiana and reaches the Gulf of Mexico at Sabine Pass.

sab·kha /'sabkə/ ▸*n.* *Geography* an area of coastal flats subject to periodic flooding and evaporation, which result in the accumulation of aeolian clays, evaporites, and salts, typically found in North Africa and Arabia. ▷late 19th cent.: from Arabic *sabḳa* 'salt flat.'

sa·ble[1] /ˈsābəl/ ▸*n.* a marten with a short tail and dark brown fur, native to Japan and Siberia and valued for its fur. • *Martes zibellina*, family Mustelidae. ■ the fur of the sable. ▷late Middle English: from Old French, in the sense 'sable fur,' from medieval Latin *sabelum*, of Slavic origin.

sa·ble[2] ▸*adj. poetic/literary* or *Heraldry* black.
▸*n.* **1** *poetic/literary* or *Heraldry* black. ■ (**sables**) *archaic* mourning garments. **2** (also **sa·ble an·te·lope**) a large African antelope with long curved horns, the male of which has a black coat and the female a russet coat, both having a white belly. • *Hippotragus niger*, family Bovidae. ▷Middle English: from Old French (as a heraldic term), generally taken to be identical with **SABLE**[1], although sable fur is dark brown.

sa·ble·fish /ˈsābəl,fisH/ ▸*n.* (*pl.* same or **-fish·es**) a large commercially important fish with a slate-blue to black back, occurring throughout the North Pacific. • *Anoplopoma fimbria*, family Anoplopomatidae.

sab·ot /saˈbō; ˈsabō/ ▸*n.* **1** a kind of simple shoe, shaped and hollowed out from a single block of wood, traditionally worn by French and Breton peasants. **2** a device that ensures the correct positioning of a bullet or shell in the barrel of a gun, attached either to the projectile or inside the barrel and falling away as it leaves the muzzle. **3** a box from which cards are dealt at casinos in gambling games such as baccarat and chemin de fer. Also called **SHOE**. ▷early 17th cent.: French, blend of *savate* 'shoe' and *botte* 'boot.' —**sa·boted** *adj.* (in sense 1).

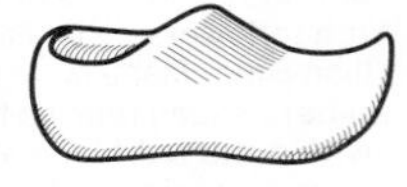
sabot 1

sab·o·tage /ˈsabə,täzH/ ▸*v.* [*trans.*] deliberately destroy, damage, or obstruct (something), esp. for political or military advantage.
▸*n.* the action of sabotaging something. ▷early 20th cent.: from French, from *saboter* 'kick with sabots, willfully destroy' (see **SABOT**).

sab·o·teur /,sabəˈtər/ ▸*n.* a person who engages in sabotage. ▷early 20th cent.: from French, from the verb *saboter* (see **SABOTAGE**).

sa·bra /ˈsäbrə/ ▸*n.* a Jew born in Israel (or before 1948 in Palestine). ▷from modern Hebrew *ṣabbār* 'opuntia fruit' (opuntias being common in coastal regions of Israel).

sa·bre ▸*n.* & *v.* British spelling of **SABER**.

sa·bre·tache /ˈsābər,tasH/ ▸*n. historical* a flat satchel on long straps worn by some cavalry and horse artillery officers from the left of the waist-belt. ▷early 19th cent.: from French, from German *Säbeltasche*, from *Säbel* 'saber' + *Tasche* 'pocket.'

sa·bre·wing /ˈsābər,wiNG/ ▸*n.* a large tropical American hummingbird with a green back and long curved wings. • Genus *Campylopterus*, family Trochilidae: several species.

SAC /sak/ ▸*abbr.* Strategic Air Command.

Sac ▸*n.* variant spelling of **SAUK**.

sac /sak/ ▸*n.* a hollow, flexible structure resembling a bag or pouch: *a fountain pen with an ink sac.* ■ a cavity enclosed by a membrane within a living organism, containing air, liquid, or solid structures. ■ the distended membrane surrounding a hernia, cyst, or tumor. ▷mid 18th cent. (as a term in biology): from French *sac* or Latin *saccus* 'sack, bag.' —**sac·like** /-,līk/ *adj.*

Sac·a·ja·we·a /,sakəjəˈwēə; -ˈwäə/ (c.1786–1812), Shoshone Indian guide and interpreter; also *Sacagawea*. She joined the Lewis and Clark expedition in what is now North Dakota and guided their travels through the wilderness and across the Rockies 1804–06. ▷from Hidatsa *tsakaka-wia*, literally 'bird-woman.'

Sacajawea

sac·cade /səˈkäd; sa-/ ▸*n.* (usu. **saccades**) *technical* a rapid movement of the eye between fixation points. ▷early 18th cent.: from French, literally 'violent pull,' from Old French *saquer* 'to pull.' —**sac·cad·ic** /səˈkadik; sa-/ *adj.*

sac·cate /ˈsa,kāt/ ▸*adj. Botany* dilated to form a sac.

sac·cha·ride /ˈsakə,rīd/ ▸*n. Biochemistry* another term for **SUGAR** (sense 2). ▷mid 19th cent.: from modern Latin *saccharum* 'sugar' + **-IDE**.

sac·cha·rin /ˈsak(ə)rən/ ▸*n.* a sweet-tasting synthetic compound used in food and drink as a substitute for sugar. • Alternative name: ***o*-sulfobenzoic imide**; chem. formula: $C_7H_5NO_3S$. ▷late 19th cent.: from modern Latin *saccharum* 'sugar'+ **-IN**[1].

sac·cha·rine /ˈsak(ə)rin; -rēn; -rīn/ ▸*adj.* [*attrib.*] **1** excessively sweet or sentimental. **2** *dated* relating to or containing sugar; sugary.
▸*n.* another term for **SACCHARIN**. ▷late 17th cent.: from modern Latin *saccharum* + **-INE**[1].

saccharo- ▸*comb. form* of or relating to sugar: *saccharometer.* ▷via Latin from Greek *sakkharon* 'sugar.'

sac·cha·rom·e·ter /,sakəˈrämitər/ ▸*n.* a hydrometer for measuring the sugar content of a solution.

sac·cha·rose /ˈsakə,rōs/ ▸*n. Chemistry* another term for **SUCROSE**. ▷late 19th cent.: from modern Latin *saccharum* 'sugar' + **-OSE**[2].

Sac·co /ˈsakō/, Nicola (1891–1927), U.S. political radical; born in Italy. In 1921, along with Vanzetti, he was accused and convicted of murder in a sensational, controversial trial. In 1927, both men were executed in the electric chair; fifty years later, their names were cleared of any crimes.

sac·cule /ˈsa,kyo͞ol/ ▸*n. Biology* & *Anatomy* a small sac, pouch, or cyst. ■ another term for **SACCULUS**. ▷mid 19th cent.: anglicized form of Latin *sacculus* (see **SACCULUS**). —**sac·cu·lar** /ˈsakyələr/ *adj.* —**sac·cu·lat·ed** /ˈsakyə,lātid/ *adj.* —**sac·cu·la·tion** /,sakyəˈlāsHən/ *n.*

sac·cu·lus /ˈsakyələs/ ▸*n. Anatomy* the smaller of the two fluid-filled sacs forming part of the labyrinth of the inner ear (the other being the utriculus). It contains a region of hair cells and otoliths that send signals to the brain concerning the orientation of the head. ■ another term for **SACCULE**. ▷mid 18th cent.: from Latin, diminutive of *saccus* 'sack.'

sac·er·do·tal /,sasərˈdōtl; ,sakər-/ ▸*adj.* relating to priests or the priesthood; priestly. ■ *Theology* relating to or denoting a doctrine that ascribes sacrificial functions and spiritual or supernatural powers to ordained priests. ▷late Middle English: from Old French, or from Latin *sacerdotalis*, from *sacerdos*, *sacerdot-* 'priest.' —**sac·er·do·tal·ism** /-,izəm/ *n.*

sa·chem /ˈsācHəm/ ▸*n.* (among some American Indian peoples) a chief or leader. ■ *informal* a boss or leader. ▷from Narragansett, 'chief.' Compare with **SAGAMORE**.

Sa·cher·torte /ˈsäkər,tôrt/ ▸*n.* (*pl.* **-tor·ten** /-,tôrtn/) a chocolate gateau with apricot jam filling and chocolate icing. ▷German, from the name of Franz *Sacher*, the pastry chef who created it, + *Torte* 'tart, pastry.'

sa·chet /saˈsHā/ ▸*n.* a small perfumed bag used to scent clothes. ■ *archaic* dried, scented material for use in scenting clothes. ▷mid 19th cent.: from French, 'little bag,' diminutive of *sac*, from Latin *saccus* 'sack, bag.'

Sach·sen /ˈsaksən; ˈzäk-/ German name for **SAXONY**.

Sach·sen-An·halt /ˈänhält/ German name for **SAXONY-ANHALT**.

sack[1] /sak/ ▸*n.* **1** a large bag made of a strong material such as burlap, thick paper, or plastic, used for storing and carrying goods. ■ the contents of such a bag or the amount it can contain: ***a sack of** flour.* **2** a loose, unfitted, or shapeless garment, in particular: ■ *historical* a woman's loose gown. ■ *historical* a decorative piece of dress material fastened to the shoulders of a woman's gown in loose pleats and forming a long train, fashionable in the 18th century. **3** (**the sack**) *informal* bed, esp. as regarded as a place for sex. **4** (**the sack**) *informal* dismissal from employment: *he **got the sack** for swearing | they **were given the sack**.* **5** *informal Baseball* a base. **6** *Football* an act of tackling a quarterback behind the line of scrimmage before he can throw a pass.
▸*v.* [*trans.*] **1** *informal* dismiss from employment: *any official found to be involved would be sacked on the spot.* **2** (**sack out**) *informal* go to sleep or bed. **3** *Football* tackle (a quarterback) behind the line of scrimmage before he can throw a pass. **4** *rare* put into a sack or sacks. ▷Old English *sacc*, from Latin *saccus* 'sack, sackcloth,' from Greek *sakkos*, of Semitic origin. Sense 1 of the *verb* dates from the mid 19th cent. —**sack·a·ble** *adj.* —**sack·like** /-,līk/ *adj.*
▸*PHRASES* □ **hit the sack** *informal* go to bed. □ **a sack of potatoes** *informal* used in similes to refer to clumsiness, inertness, or unceremonious treatment of the person or thing in question: *he drags me in like a sack of potatoes.*

sack[2] ▸*v.* [*trans.*] (chiefly in historical contexts) plunder and destroy (a captured town, building, or other place). See note at **RAVAGE**.
▸*n.* the pillaging of a town or city. ▷mid 16th cent.: from French *sac*, in the phrase *mettre à sac* 'put to sack,' on the model of Italian *fare il sacco*, *mettere a sacco*, which perhaps originally referred to filling a sack with plunder.

sack[3] ▸*n. historical* a dry white wine formerly imported into Britain from Spain and the Canary Islands. ▷early 16th cent.: from the phrase *wyne seck*, from French *vin sec* 'dry wine.'

sack·but /ˈsak,bət/ ▸*n.* an early form of trombone used in Renaissance music. ▷late 15th cent.: from French *saquebute*, from obsolete *saqueboute* 'hook for pulling a man off a horse,' from *saquer* 'to pull' + *bouter* 'to hit.'

sack·cloth /ˈsak,klôTH; -,kläTH/ ▸*n.* a very coarse, rough fabric woven from flax or hemp.
▸*PHRASE* □ **sackcloth and ashes** used with allusion to the wearing of sackcloth and having ashes sprinkled on the head as a sign of penitence or mourning (Matt 11:21).

sack coat ▸*n. historical* a loose-fitting coat hanging straight down from the shoulders, particularly as worn by men (sometimes as part of military uniform) in the 19th and early 20th centuries.

sack dress ▸*n.* a woman's short, loose, unwaisted dress, originally fashionable in the 1950s.

sack·ful /ˈsak,fo͝ol/ ▸*n.* (*pl.* **-fuls**) the quantity of something contained in a sack: ***a sackful of** rice.*

sack·ing /ˈsakiNG/ ▸*n.* **1** an act of sacking someone or something. **2** coarse material for making sacks; sackcloth.

sack lunch ▸*n.* a bag lunch.

sack race ▸*n.* a race in which competitors, typically children, stand in sacks up to the waist or neck and jump forward.

sack suit ▸*n.* a suit with a straight, loose-fitting jacket.

Sack·ville-West /ˈsak,vil ˈwest/, Vita (1892–1962), English novelist and poet; full name *Victoria Mary Sackville-West*. Her works include the novel *All Passion Spent* (1931).

Sa·co /ˈsôkō; ˈsä-/ a city in southern Maine, southwest of Portland; pop. 16,822.

sa·cra /ˈsakrə; ˈsā-/ ▸ plural form of **SACRUM**.

sa·cral /ˈsakrəl; ˈsā-/ ▸*adj.* [*attrib.*] **1** *Anatomy* of or relating to the sacrum. **2** *Anthropology* & *Religion* of, for, or relating to sacred rites or symbols: *sacral horns of a Minoan type.* —**sa·cral·i·ty** /sāˈkralətē; sə-/ *n.* (in sense 2).

sa·cral·ize /ˈsakrə,līz; ˈsā-/ ▸*v.* [*trans.*] imbue with or treat as having a sacred character or quality: *rural images that sacralize country life.* —**sa·cral·i·za·tion** /,sakrəliˈzāsHən; ,sā-/ *n.*

sac·ra·ment /ˈsakrəmənt/ ▸*n.* a religious ceremony or act of the Christian Church that is regarded as an outward and visible sign of inward and spiritual divine grace, in particular: ■ (in the Roman Catholic and many Orthodox Churches) the rites of baptism, confirmation, the Eucharist, penance, anointing of the sick, ordination, and matrimony. ■ (among Protestants) baptism and the Eucharist. ■ (also **the Bless·ed Sac·ra·ment** or **the Ho·ly Sac·ra·ment**) (in Roman Catholic use) the consecrated elements of the Eucharist, esp. the Host: *he heard Mass and received the sacrament.* ■ a thing of mysterious and sacred significance; a religious symbol. ▷Middle English: from Old French *sacrement*, from Latin *sacramentum* 'solemn oath' (from *sacrare* 'to hallow,' from *sacer* 'sacred'), used in Christian Latin as a translation of Greek *mustērion* 'mystery.'

sac·ra·men·tal /,sakrəˈmentl/ ▸*adj.* relating to or constituting a sacrament or the sacraments. ■ attaching great importance to sacraments.
▸*n.* an observance analogous to but not reckoned among the sacraments, such as the use of holy water or the sign of the cross. —**sac·ra·men·tal·ism** /-,izəm/ *n.* —**sac·ra·men·tal·i·ty** /,sakrəmənˈtalitē; -,men-/ *n.* —**sac·ra·men·tal·ize** /-,īz/ *v.* —**sac·ra·men·tal·ly** *adv.*

Sac·ra·men·to /,sakrəˈmentō/ **1** a river in northern California that rises near the border with Oregon and flows about 380 miles (611 km) south to San Francisco Bay. **2** the capital of California, situated on the Sacramento River, northeast of San Francisco; pop. 407,018.

sac·ra·ment of rec·on·cil·i·a·tion (also **sac·ra·ment of pen·ance**) ▸*n.* (chiefly in the Roman Catholic Church) the practice of private confession of sins to a priest and the receiving of absolution.

Sac·ra·men·to Moun·tains a range in southern New Mexico and western Texas comprising the Jicarilla, Sierra Blanca, and Guadalupe mountains.

sa·crar·i·um /səˈkre(ə)rēəm/ ▸*n.* (*pl.* **-crar·i·a** /-ˈkre(ə)rēə/) the sanctuary of a church. ■ (in the Roman Catholic Church) a piscina. ■ (in the ancient Roman world) a shrine, in particular the room in a house containing the penates. ▷Latin, from *sacer, sacr-* 'holy.'

sa·cré bleu /ˈsäkrā ˈblœ/ ▸*exclam.* a French expression of surprise, exasperation, or dismay. ▷alteration of *sacré Dieu* 'holy God.'

sa·cred /ˈsākrid/ ▸*adj.* connected with God (or the gods) or dedicated to a religious purpose and so deserving veneration: *sacred rites | the site at Eleusis is sacred to Demeter.* See note at DIVINE. ■ religious rather than secular: *sacred music.* ■ (of writing or text) embodying the laws or doctrines of a religion: *a sacred Hindu text.* ■ regarded with great respect and reverence by a particular religion, group, or individual: *an animal **sacred to** Mexican culture.* ■ sacrosanct: *to a police officer nothing is sacred.* ▷late Middle English: past participle of archaic *sacre* 'consecrate,' from Old French *sacrer*, from Latin *sacrare*, from *sacer, sacr-* 'holy.' —**sa·cred·ly** *adv.* —**sa·cred·ness** *n.*

sa·cred ba·boon ▸*n.* another term for HAMADRYAS BABOON.

sa·cred bam·boo ▸*n.* another term for NANDINA.

Sa·cred Col·lege another term for COLLEGE OF CARDINALS.

sa·cred cow ▸*n.* an idea, custom, or institution held, esp. unreasonably, to be above criticism (with reference to the Hindus' respect for the cow as a holy animal).

Sa·cred Heart ▸*n.* an image representing the heart of Jesus Christ, used as an object of devotion among Roman Catholics.

sa·cred i·bis ▸*n.* a mainly white ibis with a bare black head and neck and black plumes over the lower back, native to Africa and the Middle East, and venerated by the ancient Egyptians. • *Threskiornis aethiopicus*, family Threskiornithidae.

sa·cred lo·tus ▸*n.* see LOTUS (sense 1).

sa·cred scar·ab ▸*n.* see SCARAB.

sac·ri·fice /ˈsakrəˌfīs/ ▸*n.* an act of slaughtering an animal or person or surrendering a possession as an offering to God or to a divine or supernatural figure: *they offer sacrifices to the spirits | the ancient laws of animal sacrifice.* ■ an animal, person, or object offered in this way. ■ an act of giving up something valued for the sake of something else regarded as more important or worthy: *we must all be prepared to **make sacrifices**.* ■ *Christian Church* Christ's offering of himself in the Crucifixion. ■ *Christian Church* the Eucharist regarded either (in Catholic terms) as a propitiatory offering of the body and blood of Christ or (in Protestant terms) as an act of thanksgiving. ■ *Chess* a move intended to allow the opponent to win a pawn or piece, for strategic or tactical reasons. ■ (also **sac·ri·fice bunt** or **sac·ri·fice hit**) *Baseball* a bunted ball that puts the batter out but allows a base runner or runners to advance. ■ (also **sac·ri·fice bid**) *Bridge* a bid made in the belief that it will be less costly to be defeated in the contract than to allow the opponents to make a contract.
▸*v.* [*trans.*] offer or kill as a religious sacrifice: *the goat was sacrificed at the shrine.* ■ give up (something important or valued) for the sake of other considerations: *working hard doesn't mean sacrificing your social life.* ■ *Chess* deliberately allow one's opponent to win (a pawn or piece). ■ *Baseball* advance (a base runner) by a sacrifice. ■ [*intrans.*] *Bridge* make a sacrifice bid. ▷Middle English: from Old French, from Latin *sacrificium*; related to *sacrificus* 'sacrificial,' from *sacer* 'holy.'

sac·ri·fi·cial /ˌsakrəˈfiSHəl/ ▸*adj.* of, relating to, or constituting a sacrifice: *an altar for sacrificial offerings.* ■ *technical* designed to be used up or destroyed in fulfilling a purpose or function. —**sac·ri·fi·cial·ly** *adv.*

sac·ri·lege /ˈsakrəlij/ ▸*n.* violation or misuse of what is regarded as sacred: *putting ecclesiastical vestments to secular use was considered sacrilege.* ▷Middle English: via Old French from Latin *sacrilegium*, from *sacrilegus* 'stealer of sacred things,' from *sacer, sacr-* 'sacred' + *legere* 'take possession of.' —**sac·ri·le·gious** /ˌsakrəˈlijəs/ *adj.* —**sac·ri·le·gious·ly** /ˌsakrəˈlijəslē/ *adv.*

sa·cring /ˈsākriNG/ ▸*n. archaic* or *historical* the consecration of a bishop, sovereign, or the Eucharistic elements. ▷Middle English: from the obsolete verb *sacre* 'consecrate.'

sa·cring bell ▸*n.* a bell rung in some Christian churches at certain points during the Mass or Eucharist, esp. at the elevation of the consecrated elements.

sac·ris·tan /ˈsakristən/ (also **sa·crist** /ˈsākrist; ˈsak-/) ▸*n.* **1** a person in charge of a sacristy and its contents. **2** *archaic* the sexton of a parish church. ▷Middle English: from medieval Latin *sacristanus*, based on Latin *sacer, sacr-* 'sacred.'

sac·ris·ty /ˈsakristē/ ▸*n.* (*pl.* **-ties**) a room in a church where a priest prepares for a service, and where vestments and other things used in worship are kept. ▷late Middle English: from French *sacristie*, from medieval Latin *sacristia*, based on Latin *sacer, sacr-* 'sacred.'

sacro- ▸*comb. form* of or relating to the sacrum: *sacroiliac.* ▷from Latin *(os) sacrum* 'sacrum.'

sac·ro·il·i·ac /ˌsakrōˈilēˌak/ ▸*adj. Anatomy* relating to the sacrum and the ilium. ■ denoting the rigid joint at the back of the pelvis between the sacrum and the ilium.

sac·ro·sanct /ˈsakrōˌsaNG(k)t/ ▸*adj.* (esp. of a principle, place, or routine) regarded as too important or valuable to be interfered with: *the individual's right to work has been upheld as sacrosanct.* ▷late 15th cent.: from Latin *sacrosanctus*, from *sacro* 'by a sacred rite' (ablative of *sacrum*) + *sanctus* 'holy.' —**sac·ro·sanc·ti·ty** /ˌsakrōˈsaNG(k)titē/ *n.*

sac·rum /ˈsakrəm; ˈsā-/ ▸*n.* (*pl.* **sac·ra** /ˈsakrə; ˈsā-/ or **sac·rums**) *Anatomy* a triangular bone in the lower back formed from fused vertebrae and situated between the two hipbones of the pelvis. ▷mid 18th cent.: from Latin *os sacrum*, translation of Greek *hieron osteon* 'sacred bone' (from the belief that the soul resides in it).

SAD ▸*abbr.* seasonal affective disorder.

sad /sad/ ▸*adj.* (**sad·der, sad·dest**) **1** feeling or showing sorrow; unhappy: *I was sad and subdued | they looked at her with sad, anxious faces.* ■ causing or characterized by sorrow or regret; unfortunate and regrettable: *he told her the sad story of his life | a sad day for us all.* **2** *informal* pathetically inadequate or unfashionable: *somebody's priorities are pretty sad.* **3** (of dough) heavy through having failed to rise. ▷Old English *sæd* 'sated, weary,' also 'weighty, dense,' of Germanic origin; related to Dutch *zat* and German *satt*, from an Indo-European root shared by Latin *satis* 'enough.' The original meaning was replaced in Middle English by the senses 'steadfast, firm' and 'serious, sober,' and later 'sorrowful.' —**sad·dish** *adj.* —**sad·ness** *n.*
▸*PHRASE* □ **sad to say** unfortunately, regrettably.

Sa·dat /səˈdät/, (Muhammad) Anwar al- (1918–81), Egyptian statesman; president 1970–81. He worked to achieve peace in the Middle East, visiting Israel in 1977 and attending talks with Menachim Begin at Camp David in 1978. He was assassinated by members of the Islamic Jihad. Nobel Peace Prize (1978, shared with Begin).

Sad·dam Hus·sein /səˈdäm ho͞oˈsān; ˈsadəm/ see HUSSEIN3.

sad·den /ˈsadn/ ▸*v.* [*trans.*] (often **be saddened**) cause to feel sorrow; make unhappy: *he was greatly saddened by the death of his only son |* [*trans.*] *I was saddened to see their lack of commitment.*

sad·dle /ˈsadl/ ▸*n.* **1** a seat fastened on the back of a horse or other animal for riding, typically made of leather and raised at the front and rear. ■ a seat on a bicycle or motorcycle. **2** something resembling a saddle in appearance, function, or position, in particular: ■ a low part of a ridge between two higher points or peaks. ■ *Mathematics* a low region of a curve between two high points, esp. (in three dimensions) one representing the highest point of a curve in one direction and the lowest point in another direction. ■ the part of a draft horse's harness that supports the straps to which the shafts are attached. ■ a shaped support on which a cable, wire, or pipe rests. ■ a fireclay bar for supporting ceramic ware in a kiln. **3** a large cut of meat consisting of the two loins. ■ the lower part of the back in a mammal or fowl, esp. when distinct in shape or marking.
▸*v.* [*trans.*] put a saddle on (a horse): *he was in the stable saddling up his horse.* ■ (usu. **be saddled with**) burden (someone) with an onerous responsibility or task: *he's saddled with debts of $12 million.* ■ (of a trainer) enter (a horse) for a race. ▷Old English *sadol, sadul*, of Germanic origin; related to Dutch *zadel* and German *Sattel*, perhaps from an Indo-European root shared by Latin *sella* 'seat' and SIT.
▸*PHRASE* □ **in the saddle** on horseback. ■ *figurative* in a position of control or responsibility.

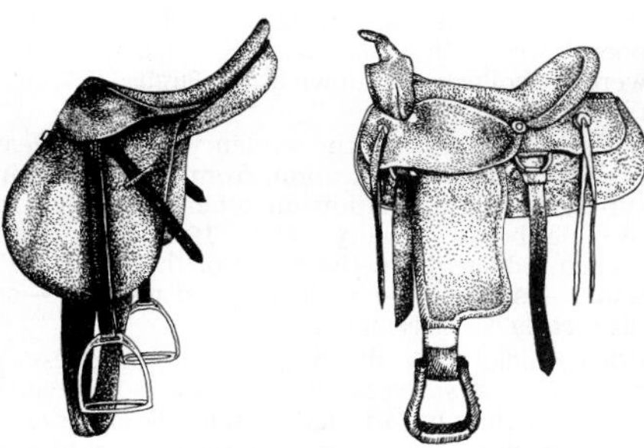

English saddle Western saddle

saddles

sad·dle·back /ˈsadlˌbak/ ▸*n.* **1** *Architecture* a tower roof that has two opposite gables connected by a pitched section. **2** a hill with a ridge along the top that dips in the middle. **3** a pig of a black breed with a white stripe across the back. **4** a New Zealand wattlebird with mainly black plumage, a reddish-brown back, and two small red wattles under the bill. • *Creadion carunculatus*, family Callaeidae. —**sad·dle·backed** *adj.*

sad·dle·bag /ˈsadlˌbag/ ▸*n.* each of a pair of bags attached behind the saddle on a horse, bicycle, or motorcycle. ■ (**saddlebags**) excess fat around the hips and thighs.

sad·dle-bow /bō/ ▸*n. chiefly archaic* the pommel of a saddle, or a similar curved part behind the rider.

sad·dle·bred /ˈsadlˌbred/ ▸*n.* a horse bred to have the gait of an American saddle horse.

sad·dle·cloth /ˈsadlˌklôTH; -ˌkläTH/ ▸*n.* a cloth laid on a horse's back under the saddle.

sad·dle horse ▸*n.* **1** a wooden frame or stand on which saddles are cleaned or stored. **2** a horse kept for riding only.

sad·dler /ˈsadlər/ ▸*n.* someone who makes, repairs, or deals in saddlery.

sad·dler·y /ˈsadlərē; -əlrē; / ▸*n.* (*pl.* **-dler·ies**) saddles, bridles, and other equipment for horses. ■ the making or repairing of such equipment. ■ a saddler's business or premises.

sad·dle shoe ▸*n.* a white oxford shoe with a piece of leather in a contrasting color (typically black or brown) stitched across the instep.

saddle shoe

sad·dle soap ▸*n.* soft soap containing neat's-foot oil, used for cleaning leather.

sad·dle·sore /ˈsadlˌsôr/ ▸*n.* a bruise or sore on a horse's back, caused by pressure or chafing of an ill-fitting saddle.
▸*adj.* (of a person) chafed from riding on a saddle.

sad·dle stitch ▸*n.* a stitch of thread or a wire staple passed through the fold of a magazine or booklet. ■ (in needlework) a decorative stitch made with long stitches on the upper side of the cloth alternated with short stitches on the underside.
▸*v.* (**saddle-stitch**) [*trans.*] sew with such a stitch.

sad·dle tank ▸*n.* a small steam locomotive with a water tank that fits over the top and sides of the boiler like a saddle.

sad·dle tree ▸*n.* a frame around which a saddle is built.

Sad·du·cee /ˈsajəˌsē; ˈsadyə-/ ▸*n.* a member of a Jewish sect or party of the time of Jesus Christ that denied the resurrection of the dead, the existence of spirits, and the obligation of oral tradition, emphasizing acceptance of the written Law alone. Compare with PHARISEE. ▷Old English *sadducēas* (plural), via late Latin from Greek *Saddoukaios*, from Hebrew *ṣĕḏōqī* in the sense 'descendant of Zadok' (2 Sam. 8:17). **—Sad·du·ce·an** /ˌsajəˈsēən; ˌsadyə-/ *adj.*

Sade /säd/, Donatien Alphonse François, Comte de (1740–1814), French writer and soldier; known as **the Marquis de Sade**. His career as a cavalry officer was interrupted by periods of imprisonment for cruelty and debauchery.

sa·dhu /ˈsädo͞o/ ▸*n. Indian* a holy man, sage, or ascetic. ▷Sanskrit.

Sa·di /ˈsädē/ (also **Saa·di**) (*c.*1213–*c.*1291), Persian poet; born *Sheikh Muslih Addin*. His principal works were the collections known as the *Bustan* (1257) and the *Gulistan* (1258).

sa·dism /ˈsāˌdizəm/ ▸*n.* the tendency to derive pleasure, esp. sexual gratification, from inflicting pain, suffering, or humiliation on others. ■ (in general use) deliberate cruelty. ▷late 19th cent.: from French *sadisme*, from the name of the Marquis de SADE. **—sa·dist** *n.* **—sa·dis·tic** /səˈdistik/ *adj.* **—sa·dis·ti·cal·ly** /səˈdistik(ə)lē/ *adv.*

sad·ly /ˈsadlē/ ▸*adv.* showing or feeling sadness: *he smiled sadly.* ■ [*sentence adverb*] it is a sad or regrettable fact that; unfortunately: *sadly, the forests of Sulawesi are now under threat.* ■ [as *submodifier*] to a regrettable extent; regrettably: *his advice is sadly disregarded nowadays.*

sa·do·mas·o·chism /ˌsādōˈmasəˌkizəm; ˌsadō-/ ▸*n.* psychological tendency or sexual practice characterized by both sadism and masochism. **—sa·do·mas·o·chist** *n.* **—sa·do·mas·o·chis·tic** /ˌsādōˌmasəˈkistik; ˌsadō-/ *adj.*

sad sack ▸*n. informal* an inept, blundering person.

sa·fa·ri /səˈfärē/ ▸*n.* (*pl.* **-ris**) an expedition to observe or hunt animals in their natural habitat, esp. in East Africa: *one week* ***on safari***. ▷late 19th cent.: from Kiswahili, from Arabic *safara* 'to travel.'

sa·fa·ri jack·et ▸*n.* a belted lightweight jacket, typically having short sleeves and four patch pockets.

sa·fa·ri park ▸*n.* an area of parkland where wild animals are kept in the open and may be observed by visitors driving through.

sa·fa·ri suit ▸*n.* a lightweight suit consisting of a safari jacket with matching trousers, shorts, or skirt.

Sa·fa·vid /säˈfäˌwēd/ ▸*n.* a member of a dynasty that ruled Persia 1502–1736 and installed Shia rather than Sunni Islam as the state religion.
▸*adj.* of or relating to this dynasty. ▷from Arabic *ṣafawī* 'descended from the ruler Sophy.'

safe /sāf/ ▸*adj.* **1** [*predic.*] protected from or not exposed to danger or risk; not likely to be harmed or lost: *eggs remain in the damp sand,* ***safe from*** *marine predators | she felt safer with them than alone.* ■ *Baseball* having reached a base without being put out: *Davis was safe when the right fielder dropped a fly ball.* ■ *Baseball* allowing the batter to reach base and not involving an error: *a safe hit.* ■ not likely to cause or lead to harm or injury; not involving danger or risk: *we have to cross the river where it's safe for us to do so | a safe investment that produced regular income.* ■ (of a place) affording security or protection: *put it in a safe place.* ■ *often derogatory* cautious and unenterprising: *MacGregor would be a compromise, the safe choice.* ■ based on good reasons or evidence and not likely to be proved wrong: *the verdict is safe and satisfactory | his world,* ***it's safe to say,*** *will not fall apart.* **2** uninjured; with no harm done: *they had returned* ***safe and sound*** *| hopes of her safe return later faded.*
▸*n.* **1** a strong fireproof cabinet with a complex lock, used for the storage of valuables. **2** *informal* a condom. ▷Middle English (as an adjective): from Old French *sauf*, from Latin *salvus* 'uninjured.' The noun is from the verb SAVE[1], later assimilated to the adjectival form. **—safe·ly** *adv.* **—safe·ness** *n.*
▸*PHRASES* □ **in safe hands** see HAND. □ **safe in the knowledge that** used to indicate that one can do something without risk or worry on account of a specified fact: *they used to recruit hundreds a year, safe in the knowledge that many would leave.* □ **to be on the safe side** in order to have a margin of security against risks: *to be on the safe side, she had recorded everything.*

safe ar·e·a ▸*n.* an area not liable to attack, esp. one designated as such by the United Nations.

safe bet ▸*n.* a bet that is certain to succeed. ■ a thing in which confidence can be placed regarding a future outcome: ***it is a safe bet that*** *the current owners will not sell.*

safe con·duct ▸*n.* immunity from arrest or harm when passing through an area. ■ a document securing such a privilege.

safe·crack·er /ˈsāfˌkrakər/ ▸*n.* a person who breaks open and robs safes.

safe de·pos·it (also **safe·ty de·pos·it**) ▸*n.* [usu. as *adj.*] a strongroom or safe in which valuables may be securely stored, typically in a bank or hotel: *a safe-deposit box.*

safe·guard /ˈsāfˌgärd/ ▸*n.* a measure, such as a law or procedure, designed to prevent something undesirable: *there were multiple safeguards to prevent the accidental release of a virus.*
▸*v.* [*trans.*] protect against something undesirable in this way: *low interest rates are offering the opportunity to safeguard their financial futures.* ▷late Middle English (denoting protection or a safe conduct): from Old French *sauve garde*, from *sauve* 'safe' + *garde* 'guard.' Compare with SAGGER.

safe ha·ven ▸*n.* **1** a place of refuge or security. **2** *Law* temporary refuge given to asylum seekers. ■ a country or area within a country where this is provided: *if they merely hunker down in the six existing misnamed safe havens, it will become impossible for them to fulfill those missions.*

safe house ▸*n.* a house in a secret location, used by spies or criminals in hiding.

safe·keep·ing /ˈsāfˈkēpiNG/ ▸*n.* preservation in a safe place: *she'd put her wedding ring in her purse* ***for safekeeping.***

safe·light /ˈsāfˌlīt/ ▸*n.* a light with a colored filter that can be used in a darkroom without affecting photosensitive film or paper.

safe room ▸*n.* a room in a house or other building that is invulnerable to attack or intrusion, and from which security operations can be directed. Also called PANIC ROOM.

safe seat ▸*n.* a legislative seat that is likely to be retained with a large majority in an election.

safe sex ▸*n.* sexual activity in which people take precautions to protect themselves against sexually transmitted diseases such as AIDS.

safe·ty /ˈsāftē/ ▸*n.* (*pl.* **-ties**) **1** the condition of being protected from or unlikely to cause danger, risk, or injury: *they should leave for their own safety | the survivors were airlifted to safety.* ■ [as *adj.*] denoting something designed to prevent injury or damage: *a safety barrier | a safety helmet.* ■ short for SAFETY LOCK. ■ *informal* a condom. **2** *Football* a defensive back who normally is positioned well behind the line of scrimmage. ■ a play in which the offense downs the ball (by accident of the defense, or intentionally) in their own end zone, scoring two points for the defense. ▷Middle English: from Old French *sauvete*, from medieval Latin *salvitas*, from Latin *salvus* 'safe.'
▸*PHRASES* □ **safety first** used to advise caution. □ **there's safety in numbers** *proverb* being in a group of people makes you feel more confident or secure about taking action.

safe·ty belt ▸*n.* another term for SEAT BELT.

safe·ty boat ▸*n.* an accompanying boat providing support in case of emergency, esp. in water sports or competitions.

safe·ty cage ▸*n.* a framework of reinforced struts protecting a car's passenger cabin against crash damage.

safe·ty chain ▸*n.* a chain fitted for security purposes, esp. on a door, watch, or piece of jewelry.

safe·ty-crit·i·cal ▸*adj.* designed or needing to be fail-safe for safety purposes.

safe·ty cur·tain ▸*n.* a fireproof curtain that can be lowered between the stage and the main part of a theater to prevent the spread of fire.

safe·ty de·pos·it ▸*n.* another term for SAFE DEPOSIT.

safe·ty fac·tor ▸*n.* a margin of security against risks. ■ *technical* the ratio of a material's strength to an expected strain.

safe·ty film ▸*n.* fire-resistant motion picture film.

safe·ty fuse ▸*n.* **1** a protective electric fuse. **2** a fuse that burns at a constant slow rate, used for the controlled firing of a detonator.

safe·ty glass ▸*n.* **1** glass that has been toughened or laminated so that it is less likely to splinter when broken. **2** (**safety glasses**) toughened glasses or goggles for protecting the eyes when using power tools or industrial or laboratory equipment.

safe·ty har·ness ▸*n.* a system of belts or restraints to hold a person to prevent falling or injury.

safe·ty lamp ▸*n.* a miner's portable lamp with a flame that is protected, typically by wire gauze, to reduce the risk of explosion from ignited methane (firedamp). The first to be introduced, in the early 19th century, was the Davy lamp.

safe·ty lock (also **safe·ty catch**) ▸*n.* a device that prevents a gun from being fired or a machine from being operated accidentally.

safe·ty match ▸*n.* a match igniting only when struck on a specially prepared surface, esp. the side of a matchbook or matchbox.

safe·ty net ▸*n.* a net placed to catch an acrobat or similar performer in case of a fall. ■ *figurative* a safeguard against possible hardship or adversity: *a safety net for workers who lose their jobs.*

safe·ty pin ▸*n.* a pin with a point that is bent back to the head and is held in a guard when closed.
▸*v.* [*trans.*] (**safety-pin**) fasten with a safety pin.

safe·ty ra·zor ▸*n.* a razor with a guard to reduce the risk of cutting the skin.

safe·ty valve ▸*n.* a valve opening automatically to relieve excessive pressure, esp. in a boiler. ■ *figurative* a means of giving harmless vent to feelings of tension or stress.

saf·flow·er /ˈsafˌlou(-ə)r/ ▸*n.* an orange-flowered, thistlelike Eurasian plant with seeds that yield an edible oil and petals that were formerly used to produce a red or yellow dye. • *Carthamus tinctorius*, family Compositae. ■ (**saf·flow·er oil**) the edible oil obtained from the seeds of this plant. ▷late Middle English: from Dutch *saffloer* or German *Saflor*, via Old French and Italian from Arabic *aṣfar* 'yellow.' The spelling has been influenced by SAFFRON and FLOWER.

saf·fron /ˈsafrən/ ▸*n.* **1** an orange-yellow flavoring, food coloring, and dye made from the dried stigmas of a crocus: [as *adj.*] *saffron buns.* ■ the orange-yellow color of this. **2** (also **saf·fron cro·cus**) an autumn-flowering crocus with reddish-purple flowers, native to warmer regions of Eurasia. Enormous numbers of flowers are required to produce a small quantity of the large red stigmas used for the spice. • *Crocus sativus*, family Iridaceae. See also MEADOW SAFFRON. ▷Middle English: from Old French *safran*, based on Arabic *za'farān*. **—saf·fron·y** *adj.*

Saf·ire /ˈsafˌī(ə)r/, William (1929–), U.S. journalist and writer. With *The New York Times* from 1973, he is a conservative political commentator and also writes the *Times'* "On Language" column.

saf·ra·nine /ˈsafrəˌnēn; -nin/ (also **saf·ra·nin** /-nin/) ▸*n. Chemistry* any of a large group of synthetic azo dyes, mainly red, used as biological stains. ▷mid 19th cent. (denoting the yellow coloring matter in saffron): from French.

sag /sag/ ▸*v.* (**sagged, sag·ging**) [*intrans.*] sink or subside gradually under weight or pressure or through lack of strength: *he closed his eyes and* ***sagged against*** *the wall.* ■ hang down loosely or unevenly: *stockings that sagged at the knees.* ■ have a downward bulge or curve: *the bed sagged in the middle |* [as *adj.*] (**sagging**) *a sagging ceiling about to fall.* ■ (of a ship) bend longitudinally so that the middle is lower than the ends. Compare with HOG. ■ *figurative* decline to a lower level, usually temporarily: *exports are forging ahead while home sales sag.*
▸*n.* a downward curve or bulge in a structure caused by weakness or excessive weight or pressure: *a sag in the middle necessitated a third set of wheels.* ■ *Geometry* the amount of this, measured as the perpendicular distance from the middle of the curve to the straight line between the two supporting points. ■ *figurative* a decline, esp. a temporary one. ▷late Middle English (as a verb): apparently related to Middle Low German *sacken*, Dutch *zakken* 'subside.' **—sag·gy** *adj.*

sa·ga /ˈsägə/ ▸*n.* a long story of heroic achievement, esp. a medieval prose narrative in Old Norse or Old Icelandic: *a figure straight out of a Viking saga.* ■ a long, involved story, account, or series of incidents: *the saga of her engagement.* ▷early 18th cent.: from Old Norse, literally 'narrative'; related to SAW[3].

sa·ga·cious /səˈgāSHəs/ ▸*adj.* having or showing keen mental discernment and good judgment; shrewd: *they were sagacious enough to avoid any outright confrontation.* See note at SENSIBLE. ▷early 17th cent.: from Latin *sagax*, *sagac-* 'wise' + -IOUS. **—sa·ga·cious·ly** *adv.*

sa·gac·i·ty /səˈgasitē/ ▸*n.* the quality of being sagacious: *a man of great political sagacity.*

sag·a·more /ˈsagəˌmôr/ ▸*n.* (among some American Indian peoples) a chief; a sachem. ▷from Eastern Abnaki *sákəmá* 'strong man.' Compare with SACHEM.

Sa·gan[1] /ˈsāgən/, Carl (Edward) (1934–96), U.S. astronomer. He showed that amino acids can be synthesized in an artificial primordial soup irradiated by ultraviolet light, as a model for a possible mechanism of the origin of life on Earth. He wrote several popular science books and coproduced the television series *Cosmos* (1980).

Sa·gan[2] /sä'gän/, Françoise (1935–2004), French novelist, playwright, and short-story writer; pseudonym of *Françoise Quoirez.* She established her reputation with her first novel *Bonjour Tristesse* (1954). Her writing examined the transitory nature of love as experienced in brief liaisons.

sa·ga·na·ki /ˌsägə'näkē; ˌsag-/ ▶*n.* a Greek dish consisting of breaded or floured cheese fried in butter, served as an appetizer. ▷modern Greek, denoting a small two-handled frying pan, in which the dish is traditionally made.

sage[1] /sāj/ ▶*n.* **1** an aromatic plant with grayish-green leaves that are used as a culinary herb, native to southern Europe and the Mediterranean. • *Salvia officinalis,* family Labiatae. ■ used in names of similar aromatic plants of the mint family, e.g., **wood sage**. **2** (also **white sage**) either of two bushy North American plants with silvery-gray leaves: • an aromatic plant that is burned by some American Indian people for its cleansing properties and as an incense (*Artemisia ludoviciana,* family Compositae). • a plant of the goosefoot family (*Krascheninnikovia lanata,* family Chenopodiaceae). **3** short for SAGEBRUSH. ▷Middle English: from Old French *sauge,* from Latin *salvia* 'healing plant,' from *salvus* 'safe.'

sage[2] ▶*n.* a profoundly wise man, esp. one who features in ancient history or legend.
▶*adj.* having, showing, or indicating profound wisdom: *they nodded in agreement with these sage remarks.* ▷Middle English (as an adjective): from Old French, from Latin *sapere* 'be wise.' **—sage·ly** *adv.* **—sage·ness** *n.*

sage·brush /'sājˌbrəsн/ ▶*n.* a shrubby aromatic North American plant of the daisy family. • Genus *Artemisia,* family Compositae: several species, in particular *A. tridentata.* ■ scrub that is dominated by such shrubs, occurring chiefly in semiarid regions of western North America.

Sage·brush State a nickname for the state of NEVADA.

sage green ▶*n.* a grayish-green color like that of sage leaves.

sage grouse ▶*n.* a large grouse of western North America, with long pointed tail feathers, noted for the male's courtship display in which air sacs are inflated to make a popping sound. • *Centrocercus urophasianus,* family Tetraonidae (or Phasianidae).

sag·ger /'sagər/ (also **sag·gar**) ▶*n.* a protective fireclay box enclosing ceramic ware while it is being fired. ▷mid 18th cent.: probably a contraction of the noun SAFEGUARD.

Sag Har·bor /sag/ a resort village in eastern Long Island in New York, noted as a 19th-century whaling port; pop. 2,134.

Sag·i·naw /'sagəˌnô/ an industrial and commercial city in east central Michigan, on the Saginaw River; pop. 69,512.

Sa·git·ta /sə'jitə/ *Astronomy* a small northern constellation (the Arrow), lying in the Milky Way north of Aquila. ■ [as *genitive*] (**Sagittae** /sə'jitē/) used with a preceding letter or numeral to designate a star in this constellation: *the star Beta Sagittae.* ▷Latin.

sag·it·tal /'sajitl/ *Anatomy* ▶*adj.* **1** relating to or denoting the suture on top of the skull that runs between the parietal bones in a front to back direction. **2** of or in a plane parallel to this suture, esp. that dividing the body into left and right halves. ▷late Middle English: from medieval Latin *sagittalis,* from Latin *sagitta* 'arrow.' **—sag·it·tal·ly** *adv.*

sag·it·tal crest ▶*n.* *Zoology* (in many mammals) a bony ridge on the top of the skull to which the jaw muscles are attached.

Sag·it·tar·i·us /ˌsaji'te(ə)rēəs/ **1** *Astronomy* a large constellation (the Archer), said to represent a centaur carrying a bow and arrow. The center of the Galaxy is situated within it. ■ [as *genitive*] (**Sagittarii** /-'terē-ī/) used with a preceding letter or numeral to designate a star in this constellation: *the star Mu Sagittarii.* **2** *Astrology* the ninth sign of the zodiac, which the sun enters about November 22. ■ (**a Sagittarius**) (*pl.* same) a person born when the sun is in this sign. ▷Latin. **—Sag·it·ta·ri·an** /-'te(ə)rēən/ *n.* & *adj.* (in sense 2).

sag·it·tate /'sajəˌtāt/ ▶*adj.* *Botany* & *Zoology* shaped like an arrowhead. ▷mid 18th cent.: from Latin *sagitta* 'arrow' + -ATE[2].

sa·go /'sāgō/ ▶*n.* (*pl.* **-gos**) **1** edible starch that is obtained from a palm and is a staple food in parts of the tropics. The pith inside the trunk is scraped out, washed, and dried to produce a flour or processed to produce the granular sago used in the West. ■ (also **sa·go pud·ding**) a sweet dish made from sago and milk. **2** (**sa·go palm**) the palm from which most sago is obtained, growing in freshwater swamps in Southeast Asia. • *Metroxylon sagu,* family Palmae. ■ any of a number of other palms or cycads that yield a similar starch. ▷mid 16th cent.: from Malay *sagu* (originally via Portuguese).

Sa·gra·da Fa·mi·lia /sä'grädə fə'milyə; -'milēə/ an expiatory temple (not a cathedral) in Barcelona, Spain, begun in 1882 and still unfinished. Antonio Gaudí took over construction of the church in 1883 and in 1891 became its official architect. The spires of the church are more than 328 feet (100 m) tall, and the church has a seating capacity of 13,000. Full name *Templo Expiatorio de la Sagrada Familia* ('Expiatory Temple of the Holy Family').

Sagrada Familia

sa·gua·ro /sə'(g)wärō/ (also **sa·gua·ro cac·tus**) ▶*n.* (*pl.* **-ros**) a giant cactus that can grow to 66 feet (20 m) in height and whose branches are shaped like candelabra, native to Mexico and the southwestern U.S. Its reddish-purple fruit can be used for food and drink. • *Carnegiea gigantea,* family Cactaceae. ▷mid 19th cent.: from Mexican Spanish.

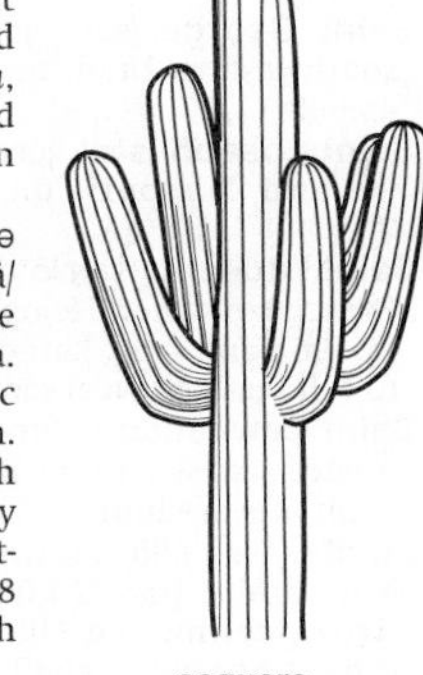

saguaro

Sa·gui·a el Ham·ra /'sägēə el 'hamrə; 'sägyä el 'ämrä/ an intermittent river in the north of Western Sahara. It flows into the Atlantic Ocean west of La'youn. ■ the region through which this river flows. A territory of Spain from 1934, it united with Río de Oro in 1958 to become a part of Spanish Sahara.

Sa·ha /'säˌhä/, Meghnad (1894–1956), Indian theoretical physicist. Saha laid the foundations for modern astrophysics. He devised an equation that expressed the relationship between ionization and temperature.

Sa·hap·ti·an /sä'haptēən/ ▶*adj.* denoting, belonging to, or relating to a family of North American Indian languages, including Nez Percé and Sahaptin, spoken in southern Washington, northern Oregon, and central Idaho.
▶*n.* this family of languages.

Sa·hap·tin /sä'haptin/ ▶*n.* **1** any of several native American peoples of southern Washington and northern Oregon. **2** the Sahaptian language spoken by these peoples.

Sa·har·a Des·ert /sə'harə; -'he(ə)rə; -'härə/ (also **the Sa·har·a**) a vast desert in North Africa that extends from the Atlantic Ocean on the west to the Red Sea on the east and from the Mediterranean Sea and the Atlas Mountains in the north to the Sahel in the south. The largest desert in the world, it covers an area of about 3,500,000 square miles (9,065,000 sq km). ▷*Sahara* from Arabic *ṣaḥrā'* 'desert.' **—Sa·har·an** *adj.*

Sa·hel /sə'hāl; -'hēl; -'hel/ a vast semiarid region of North Africa, south of the Sahara, that forms a transitional zone between the desert and the region known as the Sudan. **—Sa·hel·i·an** /-ēən/ *adj.* & *n.*

sa·hib /'sä(h)ib/ ▶*n.* *Indian* a polite title or form of address for a man: *the Doctor Sahib.* ▷Urdu, via Persian from Arabic *ṣāḥib* 'friend, lord.'

Sa·hi·wal /'sä(h)əˌväl/ ▶*n.* an animal of a breed of cattle that originated in Pakistan but is now used in other tropical regions. Sahiwals have small horns and a hump on the back of the neck. ▷early 20th cent.: from the name of a town in the central Punjab, Pakistan.

sai /sī/ ▶*n.* (*pl.* same) a dagger with two sharp prongs curving outward from the hilt, originating in Okinawa and sometimes used in pairs in martial arts. ▷Japanese.

Sa·id /'säid/, Edward (1935–2003), U.S. literary theorist, critic, journalist, and Palestinian activist, born in Jerusalem. He is best known for his critique of Western culture's false images of the Arab-Islamic world, which he discussed in *Orientalism* (1978).

said /sed/ ▶ past and past participle of SAY.
▶*adj.* used in legal language or humorously to refer to someone or something already mentioned or named: *acting in pursuance of the said agreement.*

Sai·da /'sīdə/ Arabic name for SIDON.

sai·ga /'sīgə/ (also **sai·ga an·te·lope**) ▶*n.* an Asian antelope that has a distinctive convex snout with the nostrils opening downward, living in herds on the cold steppes. • *Saiga tartarica,* family Bovidae. ▷early 19th cent.: from Russian.

Sai·gon /sī'gän; 'sīgän/ official name (until 1975) of HO CHI MINH CITY.

sail /sāl/ ▶*n.* **1** a piece of material extended on a mast to catch the wind and propel a boat, ship, or other vessel: *all the sails were unfurled.* ■ the use of sailing ships as a means of transport: *this led to bigger ships as steam replaced sail.* ■ [in *sing.*] a voyage or excursion in a ship, esp. a sailing ship or boat: *they went for a sail.* ■ *archaic* a sailing ship: *sail ahoy!* **2** something resembling a sail in shape or function, in particular: ■ a wind-catching apparatus, typically one consisting of canvas or a set of boards, attached to the arm of a windmill. ■ the broad fin on the back of a sailfish or of some prehistoric reptiles. ■ a structure by which an animal is propelled across the surface of water by the wind, e.g., the float of a Portuguese man-of-war. ■ the conning tower of a submarine.
▶*v.* [*intrans.*] **1** travel in a boat with sails, esp. as a sport or recreation: *Ian took us out sailing on the lake.* ■ [with *adverbial*] travel in a ship or boat using sails or engine power: *the ferry caught fire sailing between Caen and Portsmouth.* ■ [with *adverbial*] begin a voyage; leave a harbor: *the catamaran sails at 3:30.* ■ [*trans.*] travel by ship on or across (a sea) or on (a route): *plastic ships could be sailing the oceans soon.* ■ [*trans.*] navigate or control (a boat or ship): *I stole a small fishing boat and sailed it to the Delta.* **2** [with *adverbial of direction*] move smoothly and rapidly or in a stately or confident manner: *she sailed into the conference room at 2:30 sharp.* ■ (**sail through**) *informal* succeed easily at (something, esp. a test or examination): *Alex sailed through his exams.* ■ (**sail into**) *informal* attack physically or verbally with force. ▷Old English *segel* (noun), *seglian* (verb), of Germanic origin; related to Dutch *zeil* and German *Segel* (nouns). **—sail·a·ble** *adj.* **—sailed** *adj.* [in *combination*] *a black-sailed ship.*
▶*PHRASES* □ **in** (or **under**) **full sail** with all the sails in position or fully spread: *a galleon in full sail.* □ **sail close to** (or **near**) **the wind** sail as nearly against the wind as possible. ■ *figurative* come close to breaking a rule or the law; behave or operate in a risky way. □ **take in sail** furl the sail or sails of a vessel. □ **under sail** with the sails hoisted: *at a speed of eight knots under sail.*

sail·board /'sālˌbôrd/ ▶*n.* a board with a mast attached to it by a swivel joint, and a sail, used in windsurfing. **—sail·board·er** *n.* **—sail·board·ing** *n.*

sail·boat /'sālˌbōt/ ▶*n.* a boat propelled by sails.

sail·cloth /'sālˌklôтн; -ˌkläтн/ ▶*n.* canvas or other material used for making sails. ■ a canvaslike fabric used for making durable weatherproof clothes.

sail·er /'sālər/ ▶*n.* [usu. with *adj.*] a sailing ship or boat of specified power or manner of sailing: *the great ships were abominable sailers: sluggish and difficult to maneuver | a four-masted motor sailer.*

sail·fin mol·ly /'sālˌfin/ ▶*n.* a small, brightly colored freshwater fish, the male of which has a long, high

Pronunciation Key ə *ago*; ər *over*; 'ə *or* ˌə *up*; 'ər *or* ˌər *fur*; a *hat*; ā *rate*; ä *car*; CH *chew*; e *let*; ē *see*; e(ə)r *air*; i *fit*; ī *by*; i(ə)r *ear*; NG *sing*; ō *go*; ô *for*; oi *boy*; o͝o *good*; o͞o *goo*; ou *out*; SH *she*; TH *thin*; T͟H *then*; (h)w *why*; ZH *vision*

dorsal fin. Native to North and Central America, it is popular in aquariums. • Genus *Poecilia*, family Poeciliidae: *P. latipinna* and *P. velifera*. ▷*sailfin* with reference to the dorsal fin + **MOLLY**.

sail·fish /ˈsālˌfisн/ ▶*n.* (*pl.* same or **-fish·es**) a fish with a high, sail-like dorsal fin, in particular: • an edible migratory billfish that is a prized game fish (genus *Istiophorus*, family Istiophoridae, in particular *I. platypterus*). • (also **Celebes sailfish**) a small tropical freshwater fish of Sulawesi, popular in aquariums (*Telmatherina ladigesi*, family Atherinidae).

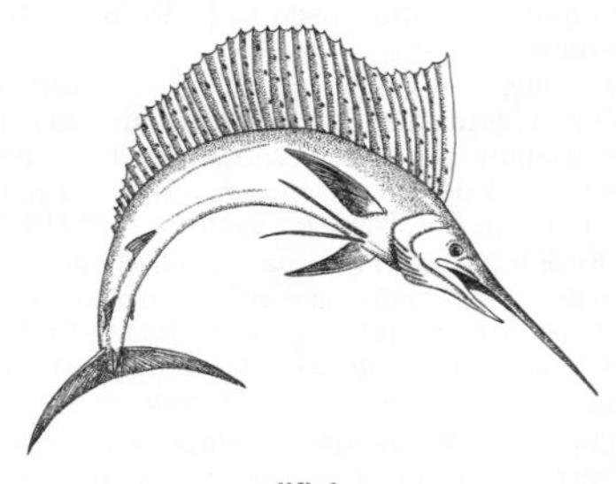

sailfish

sail·ing /ˈsāliNG/ ▶*n.* the action of sailing in a ship or boat: [as *adj.*] *a sailing club.* ■ a voyage made by a ferry or cruise ship, esp. according to a planned schedule: *the company operates five sailings a day.* ■ [in *sing.*] an act of beginning a voyage or of leaving a harbor.

sail·ing boat ▶*n.* British term for **SAILBOAT**.

sail·ing or·ders ▶*plural n.* instructions to the captain of a vessel regarding such matters as time of departure and destination.

sail·ing ship ▶*n.* a ship driven by sails.

sail·mak·er /ˈsālˌmākər/ ▶*n.* a person who makes, repairs, or alters sails as a profession. **—sail·mak·ing** /-ˌmākiNG/ *n.*

sail·or /ˈsālər/ ▶*n.* a person whose job it is to work as a member of the crew of a commercial or naval ship or boat, esp. one who is below the rank of officer. ■ [usu. with *adj.*] a person who goes sailing as a sport or recreation: *she was a keen sailor despite being confined to a wheelchair.* ■ (**a good/bad sailor**) a person who rarely (or often) becomes sick at sea in rough weather. ▷mid 17th cent.: variant of obsolete *sailer*. **—sail·or·ly** *adj.*

sail·or col·lar ▶*n.* a collar cut deep and square at the back, tapering to a V-neck at the front.

sail·or hat ▶*n.* another term for **BOATER** (sense 1). ■ a hat with a turned-up brim in imitation of a sailor's, worn by women and children.

sail·or suit ▶*n.* a suit of blue and white material resembling the dress uniform of an ordinary seaman, esp. as fashionable dress for young boys during the 19th century.

sail plan ▶*n.* a scale diagram of the masts, spars, rigging, and sails of a sailing vessel.

sail·plane /ˈsālˌplān/ ▶*n.* a glider designed for sustained flight.

sain·foin /ˈsānˌfoin/ ▶*n.* a pink-flowered plant of the pea family that is native to Asia and grown widely for fodder. • *Onobrychis viciifolia*, family Leguminosae. ▷mid 17th cent.: from obsolete French *saintfoin*, from modern Latin *sanum foenum* 'wholesome hay' (with reference to its medicinal properties).

saint /sānt/ ▶*n.* **1** a person acknowledged as holy or virtuous and typically regarded as being in heaven after death. ■ (in the Catholic and Orthodox Churches) a person formally recognized or canonized by the Church after death, who may be the object of veneration and prayers for intercession. ■ a person who is admired or venerated because of their virtue: *he was considered a living saint by recipients of his generosity.* ■ (in or alluding to biblical use) a Christian believer. ■ (**Saint**) a member of the Church of Jesus Christ of Latter-Day Saints; a Mormon. **2** (**Saint**) (abbr.: **St.** or **S.**) used in titles of religious saints: *the epistles of Saint Paul | St. John's Church.* ■ used in place names or other dedications: *St. Louis | St. Lawrence River.*

▶*v.* [*trans.*] formally recognize as a saint; canonize. ■ [as *adj.*] (**sainted** /ˈsāntid/) worthy of being a saint; very virtuous: *the story of his sainted sister Eileen.* ▷Middle English, from Old French *seint*, from Latin *sanctus* 'holy,' past participle of *sancire* 'consecrate.' **—saint·hood** /-ˌho͝od/ *n.* **—saint·like** /-ˌlīk/ *adj.*

Saint Au·gus·tine /sānt ˈôgəˌstēn; ôˈgəstin; əˈgəs-/ a historic port city in northeastern Florida, southeast of Jacksonville, near the Atlantic coast. Founded by the Spanish in 1565, it is often noted as the oldest city in America; pop. 11,692.

Saint Cath·e·rines /sānt ˈkaTH(ə)rənz/ an industrial and commercial city in southern Ontario in Canada, on Lake Ontario, northwest of Niagara Falls; pop. 129,300.

Saint Charles /sānt CHärlz/ a historic commercial city in east central Missouri, on the Missouri River; pop. 60,321.

Saint Clair Riv·er /sənt ˈkle(ə)r/ a short river that flows from Lake Huron to Lake Saint Clair, forming part of the boundary between Michigan and Ontario.

Saint Cloud /sānt ˈkloud/ an industrial and commercial city in east central Minnesota, on the Mississippi River, northwest of Minneapolis; pop. 59,107.

Saint Croix Riv·er **1** a river that flows for 75 miles (120 km) from eastern Maine to form the border with New Brunswick in Canada before entering Passamaquoddy Bay. The first French settlement in North America was established in 1604 on Dochet Island, near its mouth. **2** a river that flows for 164 miles (265 km) from northwestern Wisconsin to the Mississippi River and forms part of the border with Minnesota.

Saint-Den·is /saN dəˈnē/ **1** a municipality in France, now a northern suburb of Paris. **2** the capital of the French island of Réunion, a port on the northern coast; pop. 122,000.

Saint Eli·as Moun·tains /ˌsāntlˈīəs; iˈlīəs/ a section of the Coast Ranges in southeastern Alaska and neighboring Yukon Territory in Canada. Mount Logan, the highest point in Canada, is here, along with other high peaks and numerous glaciers.

Saint-Ex·u·pé·ry /ˌsaNt egˌzYpāˈrē/, Antoine (Marie Roger de) (1900–44), French writer and aviator. He is best known for the fable *The Little Prince* (1943).

Saint Fran·cis Riv·er /sānt ˈfransis/ a river that flows for 425 miles (685 km) from southeastern Missouri into eastern Arkansas where it empties into the Mississippi River near Helena.

Saint-Gau·dens /sānt ˈgôdnz/, Augustus (1848–1907), U.S. sculptor; born in Ireland. He is best remembered for his coin designs and for his sculptures, such as "General Sherman on Horseback" (1903).

Saint George /sānt ˈjôrj/ a historic resort city in southwestern Utah, near the Arizona border; pop. 49,663.

Saint Joseph /sānt ˈjōsəf; -zəf/ a port city in northwestern Missouri, on the Missouri River; pop. 73,990.

Saint Lau·rent /ˌsaN lôˈräN/, Yves (Mathieu) (1936–), French couturier. He opened his own fashion house in 1962 and later launched Rive Gauche boutiques to sell ready-to-wear clothing.

Saint Law·rence Is·land /sānt ˈlôrəns/ an island in western Alaska, in the Bering Sea. Most of its few inhabitants are Inuit.

Saint-Lô /saN ˈlō/ a town in northwestern France, in Normandy; pop. 23,000. Almost completely destroyed during the Allied invasion of World War II, it has since been rebuilt.

Saint Lou·is Park /sānt ˈlo͞oəs/ a city in southeastern Minnesota, west of Minneapolis; pop. 43,787.

saint·ly /ˈsāntlē/ ▶*adj.* (**-li·er**, **-li·est**) very holy or virtuous: *a truly saintly woman.* ■ of or relating to a saint: *a crypt for some saintly relic.* **—saint·li·ness** *n.*

Saint-Mihiel /ˌseN mēˈyel/ a commune in northeastern France; pop. 5,000. Fighting independently for the first time in World War I, U.S. troops took the village from the Germans in September 1918.

saint·pau·lia /ˌsāntˈpôlēə/ ▶*n.* a plant of the genus *Saintpaulia* (family Gesneriaceae), esp. (in gardening) an African violet. ▷named after Baron W. von *Saint Paul* (1860–1910), the German explorer who discovered it.

Saint-Saëns /saN ˈsäNs/, (Charles) Camille (1835–1921), French composer, pianist, and organist. He is best known for *Danse macabre* (1874), the opera *Samson and Delila* (1877), and his third symphony and *Carnaval des animaux* (both 1886).

saint's day ▶*n.* a day on which a saint is particularly commemorated in the Christian Church.

Saint-Si·mon[1] /ˌsaN sēmôN/, Claude-Henri de Rouvroy, Comte de (1760–1825), French social reformer and philosopher. He argued that society should be organized by leaders of industry and given spiritual direction by scientists.

Saint-Si·mon[2], Louis de Rouvroy, Duc de (1675–1755), French writer. He is best known for his *Mémoires*, a detailed record of court life between 1694 and 1723 during the reigns of Louis XIV and XV.

Saint-Tro·pez /san trōˈpā/ a fishing port and resort on the Mediterranean coast of southern France, southwest of Cannes; pop. 6,000.

Sai·pan /sīˈpan/ the largest of the islands that make up the Northern Marianas in the western Pacific Ocean.

saith /seTH; ˈsāiTH/ ▶ archaic third person singular present of **SAY**.

saithe /sāT͟H/ ▶*n. chiefly Brit.* another term for **POLLOCK** (sense 1). ▷mid 16th cent.: from Old Norse *seithr*.

Sa·kai /ˈsäkī/ an industrial city in Japan, on Osaka Bay, south of Osaka; pop. 808,000.

sake[1] /sāk/ ▶*n.* **1** (**for the sake of something** or **for something's sake**) for the purpose of; in the interest of; in order to achieve or preserve: *the couple moved to the coast for the sake of her health | for safety's sake, photographers are obliged to stand behind police lines.* ■ used in phrases to comment on the speaker's purpose in choosing a particular way of wording a text or presenting an argument: *let us say, for the sake of argument, that the plotter and the assassin are one and the same person.* ■ (**for its own sake** or **something for something's sake** or **for the sake of it**) used to indicate something that is done as an end in itself rather than to achieve some other purpose: *new ideas amount to change for change's sake.* **2** (**for the sake of someone** or **for someone's sake**) out of consideration for or in order to help someone: *I felt I couldn't give up, for my own sake or the baby's | I have to make an effort for John's sake.* ■ in order to please: *he'd do anything for me—even killed a man for my sake | I've spent a long time doing things for everybody's sake.* **3** (**for God's** or **goodness**, etc., **sake**) used to express impatience, annoyance, urgency, or desperation: *"Oh, for God's sake!" snarled Dyson | where did you get it, for heaven's sake?* ▷Old English *sacu* 'contention, crime,' of Germanic origin; related to Dutch *zaak* and German *Sache*, from a base meaning 'affair, legal action, thing.' The phrase *for the sake of* may be from Old Norse.

▶*PHRASE* □ **for old times' sake** in memory of former times; in acknowledgment of a shared past: *they sat in the back seats for old times' sake.*

sa·ke[2] /ˈsäkē/ (also **sa·ki** or **sa·ké**) ▶*n.* a Japanese alcoholic drink made from fermented rice, traditionally drunk warm in small porcelain cups. ▷Japanese.

sa·ker /ˈsākər/ ▶*n.* **1** a large Eurasian falcon with a brown back and whitish head, used in falconry. • *Falco cherrug*, family Falconidae. **2** an early form of cannon. ▷late Middle English: from Old French *sacre*, from Arabic *ṣaḳr* 'falcon.'

Sa·kha, Republic of /ˈsäkə/ official name for **YAKUTIA**.

Sa·kha·lin /ˈsakəˌlēn; ˌsəKHəlˈyēn/ a large Russian island in the Sea of Okhotsk, situated off the coast of eastern Russia and separated from it by the Tartar Strait; capital, Yuzhno-Sakhalinsk. From 1905 to 1946, it was divided into the northern part, held by Russia, and the southern part, occupied by Japan.

Sa·kha·rov /ˈsäKHəˌrôf; ˈsäk-; -ˌrôv/, Andrei (Dmitrievich) (1921–89), Russian nuclear physicist and civil rights campaigner. Although he helped to develop the Soviet hydrogen bomb, he campaigned against nuclear proliferation. He fought for reform and human rights in the Soviet Union for which he was sentenced to internal exile 1980-86. Nobel Peace Prize (1975).

Sa·ki /ˈsäkē/ (1870–1916), British short-story writer, born in Burma (now Myanmar); pseudonym of *Hector Hugh Munro*. His stories encompass the satiric, comic, macabre, and supernatural, and frequently depict animals as agents seeking revenge on humankind.

sa·ki[1] /ˈsäkē; ˈsakē/ ▶*n.* (*pl.* **-kis**) a tropical American monkey with coarse fur and a long bushy nonprehensile tail. • Genera *Pithecia* and *Chiropotes*, family Cebidae: several species. ▷late 18th cent.: via French from Tupi *saui*.

sa·ki[2] ▶*n.* variant spelling of **SAKE**[2].

sal /sal/ ▶*n.* a northern Indian tree that yields teaklike timber and dammar resin. It is the most commercially important source of timber in India. • *Shorea robusta*, family Dipterocarpaceae. ▷late 18th cent.: from Hindi *sāl*.

sa·laam /səˈläm/ ▶*exclam.* a common greeting in many Arabic-speaking and Muslim countries.

▶*n.* a gesture of greeting or respect, with or without a spoken salutation, typically consisting of a low

bow of the head and body with the hand or fingers touching the forehead. Compare with SHALOM. ■ (**salaams**) respectful compliments.
▸*v.* [*intrans.*] make a salaam. ▷early 17th cent.: from Arabic *(al-)salām ('alaikum)* 'peace (be upon you).'

sal·a·ble /'sāləbəl/ (also **sale·a·ble**) ▸*adj.* fit or able to be sold. —**sal·a·bil·i·ty** /ˌsālə'bilitē/ *n.*

sa·la·cious /sə'lāSHəs/ ▸*adj.* (of writing, pictures, or talk) treating sexual matters in an indecent way and typically conveying undue interest in or enjoyment of the subject: *salacious stories.* ■ lustful; lecherous: *his salacious grin faltered.* ▷mid 17th cent.: from Latin *salax, salac-* (from *salire* 'to leap') + -IOUS. —**sa·la·cious·ly** *adv.* —**sa·la·cious·ness** *n.* —**sa·lac·i·ty** /-'lasitē/ *n.* (*dated*).

sal·ad /'saləd/ ▸*n.* a cold dish of various mixtures of raw or cooked vegetables, usually seasoned with oil, vinegar, or other dressing and sometimes accompanied by meat, fish, or other ingredients: *a green salad* | *bowls of salad.* ■ [with *adj.*] a mixture containing a specified ingredient served with a dressing: *a red pepper filled with tuna salad* | *fruit salad.* ■ a vegetable suitable for eating raw. ▷late Middle English: from Old French *salade*, from Provençal *salada*, based on Latin *sal* 'salt.'

sal·ad days ▸*plural n.* (**one's salad days**) the period when one is young and inexperienced. ■ the peak or heyday of something. ▷from Shakespeare's *Antony and Cleopatra* (I. v. 72).

sal·ad dress·ing ▸*n.* see DRESSING (sense 1).

sa·lade /sə'läd/ ▸*n.* another term for SALLET.

Sal·a·din /'saladn; 'saləˌdin/ (1137–93), sultan of Egypt and Syria 1174–93; Arabic name *Salah-ad-Din Yusuf ibn-Ayyub.* He reconquered Jerusalem from the Christians in 1187, but he was defeated by Richard the Lionheart at Arsuf in 1191.

sa·lal /sə'lal/ ▸*n.* a North American plant of the heath family, with clusters of pink or white flowers and edible purple-black berries. • *Gaultheria shallon*, family Ericaceae. ▷early 19th cent.: from Chinook Jargon *sallal.*

Sa·lam /sä'läm/, Abdus (1926–1996), Pakistani theoretical physicist. He independently developed a unified theory to explain electromagnetic interactions and the weak nuclear force. Nobel Prize for Physics (1979, shared with Sheldon Glashow and Steven Weinberg).

Sal·a·man·ca /ˌsalə'maNGkə; ˌsälə'mäNGkə/ a city in western Spain; pop. 186,000.

sal·a·man·der /'saləˌmandər/ ▸*n.* **1** a newtlike amphibian that typically has bright markings, and that once was thought to be able to endure fire. • Order Urodela: four families, in particular Salamandridae, and numerous species, including the **fire salamander**. **2** a mythical lizardlike creature said to live in fire or to be able to withstand its effects. ■ an elemental spirit living in fire. **3** a metal plate heated and placed over food to brown it. ■ a space-heater, usually fueled by propane. **4** *archaic* a red-hot iron or poker. ▷Middle English (sense 2): from Old French *salamandre*, via Latin from Greek *salamandra.* Sense 1 dates from the early 17th cent. —**sal·a·man·drine** /ˌsalə'mandrin/ *adj.*

sa·la·mi /sə'lämē/ ▸*n.* (*pl.* same or **-mis**) a type of highly seasoned sausage, originally from Italy, usually eaten cold in slices. ■ *informal Baseball* a grand slam home run. [a play on the word 'slam.'] ▷Italian, plural of *salame*, from a late Latin word meaning 'to salt.'

Sal·a·mis /'saləmis/ an island in the Saronic Gulf in Greece, to the west of Athens.

sal am·mo·ni·ac /'sal ə'mōnēˌak/ ▸*n.* old-fashioned term for AMMONIUM CHLORIDE. ▷Middle English: from Latin *sal ammoniacus* 'salt of Ammon' (see AMMONIACAL).

Sa·lang Pass /sä'läNG/ a high-altitude route across the Hindu Kush in Afghanistan. A road and tunnel were built by the Soviet Union during the 1960s to improve the supply route to Kabul.

sa·lar·i·at /sə'le(ə)rēət/ ▸*n.* (**the salariat**) salaried white-collar workers. ▷early 20th cent.: from French, from *salaire* 'salary,' on the pattern of *prolétariat* 'proletariat.'

sal·a·ried /'salərēd/ ▸*adj.* receiving or recompensed by a salary rather than a wage: *salaried employees* | *he was in salaried employment.*

sal·a·ry /'salərē/ ▸*n.* (*pl.* **-ries**) a fixed regular payment, typically paid on a monthly or biweekly basis but often expressed as an annual sum, made by an employer to an employee, esp. a professional or white-collar worker: *he received a salary of $29,000* | [as *adj.*] *a 15 percent salary increase.* Compare with WAGE.
▸*v.* (**-ries, -ried**) [*trans.*] *archaic* pay a salary to. ▷Middle English: from Anglo-Norman French *salarie*, from Latin *salarium*, originally denoting a Roman soldier's allowance to buy salt, from *sal* 'salt.'

sal·a·ry·man /'salərēmən/ ▸*n.* (*pl.* **-men**) (esp. in Japan) a white-collar worker.

sa·lat /sə'lät/ ▸*n.* the ritual prayer of Muslims, performed five times daily in a set form. ▷Arabic, plural of *salāh* 'prayer, worship.'

Sa·la·zar /'saləˌzär/, Antonio de Oliveira (1889–1970), Portuguese statesman; prime minister 1932–68. He maintained Portugal's neutrality throughout the Spanish Civil War and World War II.

sal·bu·ta·mol /sal'byo͞otəˌmôl; -ˌmäl/ ▸*n.* *Medicine* a synthetic compound related to aspirin, used as a bronchodilator in the treatment of asthma and other conditions involving constriction of the airways. ▷1960s: from *sal(icylic acid)* + *but(yl)* + *am(ine)* + -OL.

sal·chow /'salkou/ (also **Sal·chow**) ▸*n.* *Figure Skating* a jump in figure skating with a backward takeoff from the backward inside edge of one skate to the backward outside edge of the other, with one or more full turns in the air. ▷early 20th cent.: named after Ulrich *Salchow* (1877–1949), Swedish skater.

sale /sāl/ ▸*n.* **1** the exchange of a commodity for money; the action of selling something: *we withdrew it from sale* | *the sale has fallen through.* ■ (**sales**) a quantity or amount sold: *price cuts failed to boost sales.* ■ (**sales**) the activity or business of selling products: *director of sales and marketing.* **2** an event for the rapid disposal of goods at reduced prices for a period, esp. at the end of a season: *a clearance sale.* ■ [often with *adj.*] a public or charitable event at which goods are sold. ■ a public auction. ▷late Old English *sala*, from Old Norse *sala*, of Germanic origin; related to SELL.
▸PHRASES □ (**up**) **for sale** offered for purchase; to be bought: *cars for sale at reasonable prices.* □ **on sale** offered for purchase: *the November issue is on sale now.* ■ offered for purchase at a reduced price.

sale·a·ble ▸*adj.* variant spelling of SALABLE.

Sa·lem /'sāləm/ **1** an industrial city in Tamil Nadu in southern India; pop. 364,000. **2** the state capital of Oregon, on the Willamette River, southwest of Portland; pop. 136,924. **3** a city and port in northeastern Massachusetts, on the Atlantic coast, north of Boston; pop. 38,091. First settled in 1626, it was the scene in 1692 of a notorious series of witchcraft trials. **4** a town in southeastern New Hampshire, southeast of Derry; pop. 28,112.

sal·ep /'saləp/ ▸*n.* a starchy preparation of the dried tubers of various orchids, used as a thickener in cooking, and formerly in medicines and tonics. ▷mid 18th cent.: from French, from Turkish *sālep*, from Arabic *(ḵuṣa-'ṯ-) ṯa'lab*, the name of an orchid (literally 'fox's testicles').

sal·e·ra·tus /ˌsalə'rātəs/ ▸*n.* *dated* sodium bicarbonate (or sometimes potassium bicarbonate) as the main ingredient of baking powder. ▷mid 19th cent.: from modern Latin *sal aeratus* 'aerated salt.'

Sa·ler·no /sə'lərnō; -'le(ə)r-/ a port on the western coast of Italy, on the Gulf of Salerno, southeast of Naples; pop. 151,000.

sales·clerk /'sālzˌklərk/ (also **sales clerk**) ▸*n.* an assistant who sells goods in a retail store.

sales·girl /'sālzˌgərl/ ▸*n.* a female salesclerk.

Sa·le·sian /sə'lēZHən/ ▸*adj.* of or relating to a Roman Catholic educational religious order founded near Turin in 1859 and named after St. Francis de Sales.
▸*n.* a member of this order.

sales·la·dy /'sālzˌlādē/ ▸*n.* (*pl.* **-dies**) a saleswoman, esp. one working as a salesclerk.

sales·man /'sālzmən/ ▸*n.* (*pl.* **-men**) a man whose job involves selling or promoting commercial products, either in a store or visiting locations to get orders: *an insurance salesman.* —**sales·man·ship** /-ˌSHip/ *n.*

sales·per·son /'sālzˌpərsən/ ▸*n.* (*pl.* **-per·sons** or **-peo·ple**) a salesman or saleswoman (used as a neutral alternative).

sales·room /'sālzˌro͞om; -ˌro͝om/ ▸*n.* a room in which items are sold at auction. ■ a showroom displaying goods offered for sale.

sales tax ▸*n.* a tax on sales or on the receipts from sales.

sales·wom·an /'sālzˌwo͝omən/ ▸*n.* (*pl.* **-wom·en**) a woman whose job involves selling or promoting commercial products.

Sal·ford /'sôlfərd; 'sal-/ an industrial city in northwestern England, near Manchester; pop. 218,000.

Sa·li·an /'sālēən; -yən/ ▸*adj.* of or relating to the Salii, a 4th-century Frankish people living near the IJssel River, from whom the Merovingians were descended.
▸*n.* a member of this people.

Sal·ic /'salik; 'sal-/ ▸*adj.* another term for SALIAN.

sal·i·cin /'salisin/ ▸*n.* *Chemistry* a bitter compound present in willow bark. It is a glucoside related to aspirin, and accounts for the ancient use of willow bark as a pain-relieving drug. ▷mid 19th cent.: from French *salicine*, from Latin *salix, salic-* 'willow.'

sa·li·cio·nal /sə'lisHənl/ ▸*n.* an organ stop with a soft reedy tone. ▷mid 19th cent.: from German *Salicional*, from Latin *salix, salic-* 'willow' + the obscurely derived suffix *-ional.*

Sal·ic law *historical* ▸*n.* **1** a law excluding females from dynastic succession, esp. as the alleged fundamental law of the French monarchy. **2** a Frankish law book extant in Merovingian and Carolingian times.

sal·i·cyl·ic ac·id /ˌsalə'silik/ ▸*n.* *Chemistry* a bitter compound present in certain plants. It is used as a fungicide and in the manufacture of aspirin and dyestuffs. • Alternative name: ***o*-hydroxybenzoic acid**; chem. formula: $C_6H_4(OH)(COOH)$. ▷mid 19th cent.: *salicylic* from French *salicyle*, the radical of the acid, + -IC. —**sa·lic·y·late** /sə'lisəˌlāt; -lit/ *n.*

sa·li·ent /'sālyənt; -lēənt/ ▸*adj.* **1** most noticeable or important: *it succinctly covered all the salient points of the case.* ■ prominent; conspicuous: *it was always the salient object in my view.* ■ (of an angle) pointing outward. The opposite of REENTRANT. **2** [*postpositive*] *Heraldry* (of an animal) standing on its hind legs with the forepaws raised, as if leaping.
▸*n.* a piece of land or section of fortification that juts out to form an angle. ■ an outward bulge in a line of military attack or defense. ▷mid 16th cent. (as a heraldic term): from Latin *salient-* 'leaping,' from the verb *salire.* The noun dates from the early 19th cent. —**sa·li·ence** *n.* —**sa·li·en·cy** *n.* —**sa·li·ent·ly** *adv.*

Sa·li·en·tia /ˌsālē'enCHə/ *Zoology* another term for ANURA. ▷modern Latin (plural), from Latin *salire* 'to leap.' —**sa·li·en·tian** *n.* & *adj.*

sa·lif·er·ous /sə'lif(ə)rəs/ ▸*adj.* *Geology* (of rock or strata) containing much salt. ▷early 19th cent.: from Latin *sal* 'salt' + -IFEROUS.

Sa·li·na /sə'līnə/ an industrial and commercial city in central Kansas; pop. 45,679.

sa·li·na /sə'līnə; -'lē-/ ▸*n.* (chiefly in the Caribbean or South America) a salt pan, salt lake, or salt marsh. ▷late 16th cent.: from Spanish, from medieval Latin, 'salt pit,' in Latin *salinae* (plural) 'salt pans.'

Sa·li·nas /sə'lēnəs/ a city in west central California, a commercial center in the agriculturally important Salinas Valley; pop. 108,777.

sa·line /'sāˌlēn; -ˌlīn/ ▸*adj.* containing or impregnated with salt: *saline alluvial soils.* ■ *chiefly Medicine* (of a solution) containing sodium chloride and/or a salt or salts of magnesium or another alkali metal.
▸*n.* a solution of salt in water. ■ a saline solution used in medicine. ▷late 15th cent.: from Latin *sal* 'salt' + -INE[1]. —**sa·lin·i·ty** /sə'linitē/ *n.* —**sal·i·ni·za·tion** /ˌsalənə'zāSHən/ *n.* —**sal·i·nize** /'saləˌnīz/ *v.*

Sal·in·ger /'salənjər/, J. D. (1919–), U.S. novelist and short-story writer; full name *Jerome David Salinger.* He is best known for his influential colloquial novel of adolescence *The Catcher in the Rye* (1951). He lives reclusively and did not publish after 1965. Other notable works: *Franny and Zooey* (1961) and *Raise High the Roof Beam, Carpenter* (1963).

sal·i·nom·e·ter /ˌsalə'nämitər/ ▸*n.* an instrument for measuring the salinity of water.

Salis·bur·y[1] /'sôlzˌberē; -b(ə)rē/ **1** a city in southern England; pop. 35,000. It is noted for its 13th-century cathedral. **2** former name (until 1982) of HARARE. **3** a city in southeastern Maryland; pop. 23,743. **4** an industrial city in west central North Carolina; pop. 23,087.

Salis·bur·y[2] /'sôlzˌberē; 'salz-; -b(ə)rē/, Robert Arthur Talbot Gascoigne-Cecil, 3rd Marquess of (1830–1903), British statesman; prime minister 1885–86, 1886–92, and 1895–1902.

Sa·lish /'sāliSH/ ▸*n.* (*pl.* same) **1** a member of a group of American Indian peoples inhabiting areas of the northwestern U.S. and British Columbia. ■ *dated*

another name for the **FLATHEAD** people. **2** the group of related languages spoken by the Salish.
▸*adj.* of or relating to the Salish or their languages. ▷the Flathead name. **—Sa·lish·an** /-ən/ *adj.*

sa·li·va /sə'līvə/ ▸*n.* watery liquid secreted into the mouth by glands, providing lubrication for chewing and swallowing, and aiding digestion. ▷late Middle English: from Latin. **—sal·i·var·y** /'salə,verē/ *adj.*

sal·i·vate /'salə,vāt/ ▸*v.* [*intrans.*] secrete saliva, esp. in anticipation of food. ■ *figurative* display great relish at the sight or prospect of something: *I was fairly* ***salivating at*** *the prospect of a $10 million loan.* ■ [*trans.*] *technical* cause (a person or animal) to produce an unusually copious secretion of saliva. ▷mid 17th cent.: from Latin *salivat-* '(having) produced saliva,' from the verb *salivare*, from *saliva* (see **SALIVA**). **—sal·i·va·tion** /,salə'vāsHən/ *n.*

Salk /sô(l)k/, Jonas Edward (1914–95), U.S. microbiologist. He developed the standard **Salk vaccine** against polio, using virus inactivated by formalin, in the early 1950s. He later became the director of the institute in San Diego that bears his name.

sal·let /'salit/ ▸*n.* *historical* a light helmet with an outward curve extending over the back of the neck, worn as part of medieval armor. ▷late Middle English: from French *salade*, based on Latin *caelare* 'engrave' (from *caelum* 'chisel').

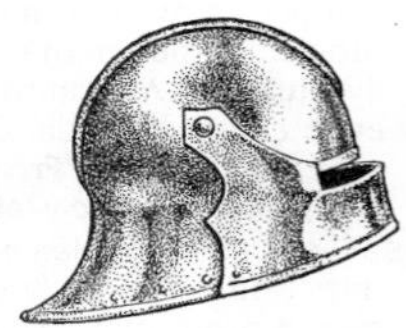
sallet

Sal·lie Mae /'sælē 'mā/ ▸*n.* *Finance informal* the Student Loan Marketing Association, an agency that makes educational loans more widely available to college students.

sal·low[1] /'salō/ ▸*adj.* (**-low·er, -low·est**) (of a person's face or complexion) of an unhealthy yellow or pale brown color.
▸*v.* [*trans.*] *rare* make sallow. ▷Old English *salo* 'dusky,' of Germanic origin; related to Old Norse *sǫlr* 'yellow,' from a base meaning 'dirty.' **—sal·low·ish** *adj.* **—sal·low·ness** *n.*

sal·low[2] ▸*n.* **1** *chiefly Brit.* a willow tree, esp. one of a low-growing or shrubby kind. Also called **PUSSY WILLOW**. • Genus *Salix*, family Salicaceae: several species, in particular the **great sallow** (see **GOAT WILLOW**). **2** a moth with dull yellow, orange, and brown patterned wings. The larvae of some species feed on sallow catkins. • Genus *Xanthia*, family Noctuidae: several species. ▷Old English *salh*, of Germanic origin; related to Old Norse *selja*, and Latin *salix* 'willow.' **—sal·low·y** *adj.*

sal·ly[1] /'salē/ ▸*n.* (*pl.* **-lies**) a sudden charge out of a besieged place against the enemy; a sortie. ■ a brief journey or sudden start into activity. ■ a witty or lively remark, esp. one made as an attack or as a diversion in an argument; a retort.
▸*v.* (**-lies, -lied**) [*intrans.*] make a military sortie: *they sallied out to harass the enemy.* ■ *formal* or *humorous* set out from a place to do something: *I made myself presentable and* ***sallied forth****.* ▷late Middle English: from French *saillie*, feminine past participle (used as a noun) of *saillir* 'come or jut out,' from Old French *salir* 'to leap,' from Latin *salire*.

sal·ly[2] ▸*n.* (*pl.* **-lies**) the part of a bell rope that has colored wool woven into it to provide a grip for the bell-ringer's hands. ▷mid 17th cent. (denoting the first movement of a bell when set for ringing): perhaps from **SALLY**[1] in the sense 'leaping motion.'

Sal·ly Light·foot /'salē 'līt,fŏŏt/ ▸*n.* (*pl.* **Sal·ly Light·foots**) a common active crab of rocky shores in the Caribbean, Central America, and the Galapagos Islands. • *Grapsus grapsus*, family Grapsidae.

Sal·ly Lunn /lən/ ▸*n.* a sweet, light teacake, typically served hot. ▷said to be from the name of a woman selling such cakes in Bath, England, *c.*1800.

sal·ly port ▸*n.* a small exit point in a fortification for the passage of troops when making a sally.

sal·ma·gun·di /,salmə'gəndē/ ▸*n.* (*pl.* **-dis**) a dish of chopped meat, anchovies, eggs, onions, and seasoning. ■ a general mixture; a miscellaneous collection. ▷from French *salmigondis*, of unknown origin.

sal·ma·naz·ar /,salmə'nazər; -'näzər/ ▸*n.* a wine bottle of approximately twelve times the standard size. ▷1930s: named after *Shalmaneser*, a king of Assyria (2 Kings 17–18).

sal·mi /'salmē/ ▸*n.* (*pl.* **-mis**) a ragout or casserole of game stewed in a rich sauce: *a pheasant salmi.* ▷French, abbreviation of *salmigondis* (see **SALMAGUNDI**).

salm·on /'samən/ ▸*n.* (*pl.* same or (esp. of types) **-ons**) **1** a large edible fish that is a popular game fish, much prized for its pink flesh. Salmon mature in the sea but migrate to freshwater streams to spawn. • Family Salmonidae (the **salmon family**): the **Atlantic salmon** (*Salmo salar*), which sometimes returns to spawn two or three times, and five species of Pacific salmon (genus *Oncorhynchus*), which always die after spawning. The salmon family also includes trout, char, whitefish, and their relatives. ■ the flesh of this fish as food. **2** [usu. with *adj.*] any of a number of fishes that resemble the true salmons, in particular: • (**Australian salmon**) a large green and silver fish of Australasian inshore waters, popular as a game fish (*Arripis trutta*, family Arripidae). • a prized food fish of the drum family (Sciaenidae), in particular the **Cape salmon** of the Indian Ocean (*Atractoscion aequidens*) and sea trouts of the western Atlantic (genus *Cynoscion*). **3** a pale pinkish orange color. ▷Middle English *samoun*, from Anglo-Norman French *saumoun*, from Latin *salmo*, *salmon-*. The spelling with *-l-* is influenced by Latin. **—salm·on·y** *adj.*

salm·on·ber·ry /'samən,berē/ ▸*n.* (*pl.* **-ries**) a North American bramble that bears pink raspberrylike fruit. • Genus *Rubus*, family Rosaceae: several species, in particular *R. spectabilis*. ■ the edible fruit of this plant.

sal·mo·nel·la /,salmə'nelə/ ▸*n.* (*pl.* **-nel·lae** /-'nelē/) a bacterium that occurs mainly in the intestine, esp. a serotype causing food poisoning. • Genus *Salmonella*: numerous serotypes; Gram-negative rods. ■ food poisoning caused by infection with a such a bacterium: *an outbreak of salmonella.* ▷modern Latin, named after Daniel E. *Salmon* (1850–1914), American veterinary surgeon. **—sal·mo·nel·lo·sis** /-,ne-'lōsis/ *n.*

sal·mo·nid /'sa(l)mənid/ ▸*n.* *Zoology* a fish of the salmon family (Salmonidae). ▷mid 19th cent.: from modern Latin *Salmonidae* (plural), based on Latin *salmo*, *salmon-* 'salmon.'

salm·on lad·der (also **sal·mon leap**) ▸*n.* a series of natural steps in a cascade or steeply sloping riverbed, or a similar arrangement incorporated into a dam, allowing salmon to pass upstream.

sal·mo·noid /'sa(l)mə,noid/ *Zoology* ▸*n.* a fish of a group that includes the salmon family together with the pikes, smelts, and argentines. • Superfamily Salmonoidea: several families.
▸*adj.* of or relating to fish of this group.

Salm·on Riv·er a river that flows for 425 miles (685 km) through central Idaho. With its branches, it is noted as a salmon breeding resource.

salm·on trout ▸*n.* a large trout or troutlike fish, in particular: ■ a lake trout. ■ *Brit.* a sea trout.

Sa·lo·me /,sälə'mā; sə'lōmē/ (in the New Testament) the daughter of Herodias, who danced before her stepfather Herod Antipas. Given a choice of reward for her dancing, she asked for the head of St. John the Baptist and thus caused him to be beheaded.

sa·lon /sə'län; sa'lôN/ ▸*n.* **1** an establishment where a hairdresser, beautician, or couturier conducts business. **2** a reception room in a large house. ■ *historical* a regular social gathering of eminent people (esp. writers and artists) at the house of a woman prominent in high society. ■ a meeting of intellectuals or other eminent people at the invitation of a celebrity or socialite. **3** (**Salon**) an annual exhibition of the work of living artists held by the Royal Academy of Painting and Sculpture in Paris, originally in the Salon d'Apollon in the Louvre in 1667. ▷late 17th cent.: from French (see **SALOON**).

Sa·lon des Re·fu·sés /sa'lôN dā rəfy'zā/ an exhibition in Paris ordered by Napoleon III in 1863 to display pictures rejected by the Salon. The artists represented included Manet, Cézanne, Pissarro, and Whistler. ▷French, literally 'exhibition of the rejected (works).'

Sa·lon·i·ca /sə'lônikə; ,salə'nēkə/ another name for **THESSALONÍKI**.

sa·lon mu·sic ▸*n.* *often derogatory* light classical music originally considered suitable for playing in a salon.

sa·loon /sə'lo͞on/ ▸*n.* **1** a public room or building used for a specified purpose: *a billiard saloon.* ■ *historical* or *humorous* a place where alcoholic drinks may be bought and drunk. ■ a large public room for use as a lounge on a ship. ■ (also **sa·loon car**) *Brit.* a luxurious railroad car used as a lounge or restaurant or as private accommodations: *a dining saloon.* **2** (also **sa·loon car**) *Brit.* an automobile having a closed body and a closed trunk separated from the part in which the driver and passengers sit; a sedan. ▷early 18th cent. (in the sense 'drawing room'): from French *salon*, from Italian *salone* 'large hall,' augmentative of *sala* 'hall.'

sa·loon deck ▸*n.* a deck on the same level as a ship's saloon, for the use of passengers.

sa·loon·keep·er /sə'lo͞on,kēpər/ (also **sa·loon keep·er**) ▸*n.* a person who runs a bar; a bartender.

sa·lo·pettes /,salə'pets/ ▸*plural n.* a one-piece garment similar to overalls, with a front flap and shoulder straps or a full sleeveless top, worn for skiing, sailing, etc. ▷1970s: from French *salopette* in the same sense + *-s* by analogy with such words as *trousers*.

sa·lot·to /sə'lätō/ ▸*n.* (*pl.* **-lot·ti** /-'lätē/) (esp. in Italy) a reception room. ▷Italian, diminutive of *sala* 'hall.'

salp /salp/ ▸*n.* a free-swimming marine invertebrate related to the sea squirts with a transparent, barrel-shaped body. • Several genera in the class Thaliacea, subphylum Urochordata. ▷mid 19th cent.: from French *salpe*, based on Greek *salpē* 'fish.'

sal·pi·con /,salpi'kän/ ▸*n.* a mixture of finely chopped ingredients bound in a thick sauce and used as a filling or stuffing. ▷via French from Spanish, from *salpicar* 'sprinkle (with salt).'

sal·pi·glos·sis /,salpə'glôsis; -'gläsis/ ▸*n.* a South American plant of the nightshade family, with brightly patterned funnel-shaped flowers. • Genus *Salpiglossis*, family Solanaceae. ▷modern Latin, formed irregularly from Greek *salpinx* 'trumpet' + *glōssa* 'tongue.'

sal·pin·gec·to·my /,salpən'jektəmē/ ▸*n.* (*pl.* **-mies**) surgical removal of the fallopian tubes.

sal·pin·gi·tis /,salpən'jītis/ ▸*n.* *Medicine* inflammation of the fallopian tubes.

salpingo- (also **salping-** before a vowel) ▸*comb. form* relating to the fallopian tubes: *salpingostomy.* ▷from Greek *salpinx*, *salping-* 'trumpet.'

sal·pin·gos·to·my /,salpən'gästəmē/ ▸*n.* surgical unblocking of a blocked fallopian tube.

sal·sa /'sälsə/ ▸*n.* **1** a type of Latin American dance music incorporating elements of jazz and rock. ■ a dance performed to this music. **2** (esp. in Latin American cooking) a spicy tomato sauce. ▷Spanish, literally 'sauce,' extended in American Spanish to denote the dance.

sal·sa ver·de /'sälsə 'verdā/ ▸*n.* **1** an Italian sauce made with olive oil, garlic, capers, anchovies, vinegar or lemon juice, and parsley. **2** a Mexican sauce of finely chopped onion, garlic, coriander, parsley, and hot peppers. ▷Spanish, literally 'green sauce.'

sal·si·fy /'salsəfē; -,fī/ ▸*n.* an edible European plant of the daisy family, with a long root like that of a parsnip. Also called **OYSTER PLANT**. • *Tragopogon porrifolius*, family Compositae. See also **SCORZONERA**. ■ the root of this plant used as a vegetable. ▷late 17th cent.: from French *salsifis*, from obsolete Italian *salsefica*, of unknown ultimate origin.

SALT /sôlt/ ▸*abbr.* Strategic Arms Limitation Talks.

salt /sôlt/ ▸*n.* **1** (also **com·mon salt**) a white crystalline substance that gives seawater its characteristic taste and is used for seasoning or preserving food. • Alternative name: **sodium chloride**; chem. formula: NaCl. See **SEA SALT**. ■ *poetic/literary* something that adds freshness or piquancy: *he described danger as the salt of pleasure.* ■ a saltcellar. ■ table salt mixed with a specified seasoning: *garlic salt.* **2** *Chemistry* any chemical compound formed from the reaction of an acid with a base, with all or part of the hydrogen of the acid replaced by a metal or other cation. **3** (usu. **old salt**) *informal* an experienced sailor.
▸*adj.* [*attrib.*] **1** impregnated with, treated with, or tasting of salt: *salt water* | *salt beef.* **2** (of a plant) growing on the coast or in salt marshes.
▸*v.* [*trans.*] **1** [usu. as *adj.*] (**salted**) season or preserve with salt: *cook the carrots in boiling salted water.* ■ *figurative* make (something) piquant or more interesting: *there was good talk to salt the occasion.* ■ sprinkle (a road or path) with salt in order to melt snow or ice. **2** *informal* fraudulently make (a mine) appear to be a paying one by placing rich ore in it. **3** [as *adj.*] (**salted**) (of a horse) having developed a resistance to disease by surviving it.
▸*phrasal v.* □ **salt something away** *informal* secretly store or put by something, esp. money. □ **salt something out** cause soap to separate from lye by adding salt. ■ *Chemistry* cause an organic compound to separate from an aqueous solution by adding an electrolyte. ▷Old English *sealt* (noun), *sealtan* (verb), of Germanic origin; related to Dutch *zout* and German

Salz (nouns), from an Indo-European root shared by Latin *sal*, Greek *hals* 'salt.' —**salt·ish** *adj.* —**salt·less** *adj.* —**salt·ness** *n.*

▸*PHRASES* □ **rub salt into the** (or **someone's**) **wound** make a painful experience even more painful for someone. □ **the salt of the earth** a person or group of people of great kindness, reliability, or honesty. [with biblical allusion to Matt 5:13.] □ **sit below the salt** be of lower social standing or worth. [from the former custom of placing a large saltcellar in the middle of a dining table with the host at one end.] □ **take something with a grain** (or **pinch**) **of salt** regard something as exaggerated; believe only part of something: *take a stock tip with a grain of salt.* □ **worth one's salt** good or competent at the job or profession specified: *any astrologer worth her salt would have predicted this.*

salt-and-pep·per ▸*adj.* flecked or speckled with intermingled dark and light shades: *his salt-and-pepper hair.*

sal·ta·rel·lo /ˌsaltəˈrelō; ˌsôl-/ ▸*n.* (*pl.* **-rel·los** or **-rel·li** /-ˈrelē/) an energetic Italian or Spanish dance for one couple, characterized by leaps and skips. ▹early 18th cent.: Italian *salterello*, Spanish *saltarelo*, based on Latin *saltare* 'to dance.'

sal·ta·tion /ˌsôlˈtāsʜən/ ▸*n.* **1** *Biology* abrupt evolutionary change; sudden large-scale mutation. **2** *Geology* the movement of hard particles such as sand over an uneven surface in a turbulent flow of air or water. **3** *archaic* the action of leaping or dancing. ▹early 17th cent. (sense 3): from Latin *saltatio(n-)*, from *saltare* 'to dance,' frequentative of *salire* 'to leap.' —**sal·ta·to·ry** /ˈsaltəˌtôrē; ˈsôl-/ *adj.*

sal·ta·to·ri·al /ˌsaltəˈtôrēəl; ˌsôl-/ ▸*adj. chiefly Entomology* (esp. of grasshoppers or their limbs) adapted for leaping.

salt·box /ˈsôltˌbäks/ ▸*n.* a frame house having up to three stories at the front and one fewer at the back with a steeply pitched roof.

salt bridge ▸*n. Chemistry* **1** a tube containing an electrolyte (typically in the form of a gel), providing electrical contact between two solutions. **2** a link between electrically charged acidic and basic groups, esp. on different parts of a large molecule such as a protein.

salt·bush /ˈsôltˌbo͝osʜ/ ▸*n.* a salt-tolerant orache plant sometimes used in the reclamation of saline soils or to provide grazing in areas of salty soil. • Genus *Atriplex*, family Chenopodiaceae: several species, including the **four-wing saltbush** *A. canescens* of the western U.S.

salt ce·dar ▸*n.* a tamarisk with reddish-brown branches and feathery gray foliage. • *Tamarix gallica*, family Tamaricaceae.

salt·cel·lar /ˈsôltˌselər/ ▸*n.* a dish or container for storing salt, now typically a closed container with perforations in the lid for sprinkling. ▹late Middle English: from SALT + obsolete *saler*, from Old French *salier* 'salt-box,' from Latin *salarium* (see SALARY). The change in spelling of the second word was due to association with CELLAR.

salt chuck ▸*n. informal* an inlet of the sea that flows into freshwater lakes or rivers. ■ the sea. ▹from Chinook Jargon.

salt dome ▸*n.* a dome-shaped structure in sedimentary rocks, formed where a large mass of salt has been forced upward. Such structures often form traps for oil or natural gas.

salt·er /ˈsôltər/ ▸*n. historical* a person dealing in or employed in the production of salt. ■ a person whose work involved the preservation of meat or fish in salt. ■ another term for DRY-SALTER. ▹Old English *sealtere* (see SALT, -ER[1]).

sal·tern /ˈsôltərn/ ▸*n.* a set of pools in which seawater is left to evaporate to make salt. ▹Old English *sealtærn* 'salt building' (the original use denoting a saltworks).

salt fin·ger ▸*n. Oceanography* one of several alternating columns of rising and descending water produced when a layer of water is overlain by a denser, saltier layer. —**salt fin·ger·ing** *n.*

salt fish ▸*n.* fish, esp. cod, that has been preserved in salt.

salt flats ▸*plural n.* areas of flat land covered with a layer of salt.

salt glaze ▸*n. Pottery* a hard glaze with a pitted surface, produced on stoneware by adding salt to the kiln during firing. —**salt-glazed** *adj.* —**salt glaz·ing** *n.*

salt grass (also **salt·grass**) ▸*n.* grass growing in salt marshes or in alkaline regions, esp. *Distichlis spicata* (family Gramineae).

salt horse ▸*n. archaic Nautical slang* salted beef.

Sal·ti·llo /sälˈtēyō/ a city in northern Mexico, capital of the state of Coahuila, in the Sierra Madre, southwest of Monterrey; pop. 441,000.

sal·tim·boc·ca /ˌsältimˈbōkə/ ▸*n.* a dish consisting of rolled pieces of veal or poultry cooked with herbs, bacon, and other flavorings. ▹Italian, literally 'leap into the mouth.'

sal·tine /sôlˈtēn/ ▸*n.* a thin, crisp, savory cracker sprinkled with salt. ▹from SALT + -INE[4].

salt·ing /ˈsôltiɴɢ/ ▸*n.* (usu. **saltings**) *Brit.* an area of coastal land that is regularly covered by the tide.

sal·tire /ˈsalˌtīr; ˈsôl-/ ▸*n. Heraldry* another term for **ST. ANDREW'S CROSS.** ■ [as *adj.*] (of a design) incorporating a motif based on such a diagonal cross. ▹late Middle English: from Old French *saultoir* 'stirrup cord, stile, saltire,' based on Latin *saltare* 'to dance.' —**sal·tire·wise** /-ˌwīz/ *adv.*

salt lake ▸*n.* a lake of salt water.

Salt Lake Cit·y the capital of Utah, situated near the southeastern shores of the Great Salt Lake in the northern part of the state; pop. 181,743. Founded in 1847 by Brigham Young, the city is the world headquarters of the Church of Latter-Day Saints (Mormons).

salt lick ▸*n.* a place where animals go to lick salt from the ground. ■ a block of salt provided for animals to lick.

salt marsh ▸*n.* an area of coastal grassland that is regularly flooded by seawater.

salt mead·ow ▸*n.* a meadow that is subject to flooding by seawater; a salt marsh.

Sal·ton Sea /ˈsôltn/ a salt lake in southeastern California, created in the dry **Salton Sink** by a 1905 diversion of the Colorado River.

salt pan ▸*n.* a shallow container or depression in the ground in which salt water evaporates to leave a deposit of salt.

salt·pe·ter /sôltˈpētər/ (*Brit.* **salt·pe·tre**) ▸*n.* another term for POTASSIUM NITRATE. ▹late Middle English: from Old French *salpetre*, from medieval Latin *salpetra*, probably representing *sal petrae* 'salt of rock' (i.e., found as an encrustation). The change in the first element was due to association with SALT.

salt shak·er ▸*n.* a perforated container for sprinkling salt.

salt spoon ▸*n.* a tiny spoon with a roundish deep bowl, used for serving oneself with salt.

sal·tus /ˈsaltəs; ˈsôl-/ ▸*n. poetic/literary* a sudden transition; a breach of continuity. ▹mid 17th cent.: from Latin, literally 'leap.'

salt·wa·ter /ˈsôltˌwôtər; -ˌwätər/ ▸*adj.* [*attrib.*] of or found in salt water; living in the sea: *saltwater fish.*

salt·wa·ter croc·o·dile ▸*n.* a large and dangerous crocodile occurring in estuaries and coastal waters from southwestern India to northern Australia. • *Crocodylus porosus*, family Crocodylidae.

salt·wort /ˈsôltwərt; -ˈwôrt/ ▸*n.* a plant of the goosefoot family that typically grows in salt marshes. It is rich in alkali and its ashes were formerly used in soap-making. • Genus *Salsola*, family Chenopodiaceae.

salt·y /ˈsôltē/ ▸*adj.* (**salt·i·er**, **salt·i·est**) tasting of, containing, or preserved with salt. ■ (of language or humor) down-to-earth; coarse. ■ *informal* tough; aggressive. —**salt·i·ness** *n.*

sa·lu·bri·ous /səˈlo͞obrēəs/ ▸*adj.* health-giving; healthy: *salubrious weather.* See note at SANITARY. ■ (of a place) pleasant; not run-down. ▹mid 16th cent.: from Latin *salubris* (from *salus* 'health') + -OUS. —**sa·lu·bri·ous·ly** *adv.* —**sa·lu·bri·ous·ness** *n.* —**sa·lu·bri·ty** /-britē/ *n.*

Sa·lu·ki /səˈlo͞okē/ (also **sa·lu·ki**) ▸*n.* (*pl.* **-kis**) a tall, swift, slender dog of a silky-coated breed with large drooping ears and fringed feet. ▹early 19th cent.: from Arabic *salūḳī*.

sa·lu·mi /säˈlo͞omē/ ▸*plural n.* cured meats that are sliced and served as an appetizer in an Italian meal. ▹Italian.

sa·lut /saˈlo͞o; säˈly/ ▸*exclam.* used to express friendly feelings toward one's companions before drinking. ▹French.

sal·u·tar·y /ˈsalyəˌterē/ ▸*adj.* (esp. with reference to something unwelcome or unpleasant) producing good effects; beneficial: *a salutary reminder of where we came from.* ■ *archaic* health-giving: *the salutary Atlantic air.* ▹late Middle English (as a noun in the sense 'remedy'): from French *salutaire* or Latin *salutaris*, from *salus, salut-* 'health.'

sal·u·ta·tion /ˌsalyəˈtāsʜən/ ▸*n.* a gesture or utterance made as a greeting or acknowledgment of another's arrival or departure: *we greeted them but no one returned our salutations* | *he raised his glass* ***in salutation.*** ■ a standard formula of words used in a letter to address the person being written to. ▹late Middle English: from Old French, or from Latin *salutatio(n-)*, from *salutare* 'pay one's respects to' (see SALUTE). —**sal·u·ta·tion·al** /-sʜənl/ *adj.*

sa·lu·ta·to·ri·an /səˌlo͞otəˈtôrēən/ ▸*n.* the student who ranks second highest in a graduating class and delivers the salutatory. Compare with VALEDICTORIAN.

sa·lu·ta·to·ry /səˈlo͞otəˌtôrē/ ▸*adj.* (esp. of an address) relating to or of the nature of a salutation.

▸*n.* (*pl.* **-ries**) an address of welcome, esp. one given as an oration by the student ranking second highest in a graduating class at a high school or college. ▹late 17th cent. (as an adjective): from Latin *salutatorius*, from *salutare* 'pay one's respects to' (see SALUTE).

sa·lute /səˈlo͞ot/ ▸*n.* a gesture of respect, homage, or polite recognition or acknowledgment, esp. one made to or by a person when arriving or departing: *he raises his arms in a triumphant salute.* ■ a prescribed or specified movement, typically a raising of a hand to the head, made by a member of a military or similar force as a formal sign of respect or recognition. ■ [often with *adj.*] the discharge of a gun or guns as a formal or ceremonial sign of respect or celebration: *a twenty-one-gun salute.* ■ *Fencing* the formal performance of certain guards or other movements by fencers before engaging.

▸*v.* [*trans.*] make a formal salute to: *don't you usually salute a superior officer?* | [*intrans.*] *he clicked his heels and saluted.* ■ greet: *he saluted her with a smile.* ■ show or express admiration and respect for: *we salute a truly great photographer.* ■ [*trans.*] *archaic* hail (someone) as having a particular high office: *he was saluted king when he entered into Jerusalem.* ▹late Middle English: from Latin *salutare* 'greet, pay one's respects to,' from *salus, salut-* 'health, welfare, greeting'; the noun partly from Old French *salut.* —**sa·lut·er** *n.*

▸*PHRASE* □ **take the salute** (of a senior officer in the armed forces or other person of importance) acknowledge formally a salute given by a body of troops marching past.

Sal·va·dor /ˈsalvəˌdôr; ˌsalvəˈdôr/ a port on the Atlantic coast of eastern Brazil, capital of the state of Bahia; pop. 2,075,000. Former name **BAHIA.**

Sal·va·dor·ean /ˌsalvəˈdôrēən/ ▸*adj.* of or relating to El Salvador.

▸*n.* a native or inhabitant of El Salvador.

sal·vage /ˈsalvij/ ▸*v.* [*trans.*] rescue (a wrecked or disabled ship or its cargo) from loss at sea: *an emerald and gold cross was salvaged from the wreck.* ■ retrieve or preserve (something) from potential loss or adverse circumstances: *it was the only crumb of comfort he could* ***salvage from*** *the ordeal.*

▸*n.* the rescue of a wrecked or disabled ship or its cargo from loss at sea: [as *adj.*] *a salvage operation was under way.* ■ the cargo saved from a wrecked or sunken ship: *salvage taken from a ship that had sunk in the river.* ■ the rescue of property or material from potential loss or destruction. ■ *Law* payment made or due to a person who has saved a ship or its cargo. ▹mid 17th cent. (as a noun denoting payment for saving a ship or its cargo): from French, from medieval Latin *salvagium*, from Latin *salvare* 'to save.' The verb dates from the late 19th cent. —**sal·vage·a·ble** *adj.* —**sal·vag·er** *n.*

sal·vage ther·a·py ▸*n.* a therapeutic regimen, normally based on drugs, that is resorted to when preferred therapies have failed: *forty-eight percent of seriously ill patients survived one month after completing salvage therapy with trimetrexate and leucovorin.*

sal·vage yard ▸*n.* a place where disused vehicles or other machinery is broken up and the parts saved and processed for resale.

Sal·var·san /ˈsalvərˌsan/ ▸*n. historical Medicine* another term for ARSPHENAMINE. ▹early 20th cent.: from German, from Latin *salvare* 'save' + German *Arsenik* 'arsenic' + -AN.

sal·va·tion /salˈvāsʜən/ ▸*n. Theology* deliverance from sin and its consequences, believed by Christians to be brought about by faith in Christ. ■ preservation or deliverance from harm, ruin, or loss: *they try to sell it to us as economic salvation.* ■ (**one's salvation**) a source or means of being saved in this way: *his only salvation was to outfly the enemy.* ▷Middle English: from Old French *salvacion,* from ecclesiastical Latin *salvation-* (from *salvare* 'to save'), translating Greek *sōtēria.*

Sal·va·tion Ar·my (abbr.: **SA**) a worldwide Christian evangelical organization on quasi-military lines. Established by William Booth, it is noted for its work with the poor and for its brass bands.

sal·va·tion·ist /sal'vāsʜənist/ ▶*n.* (**Salvationist**) a member of the Salvation Army.
▶*adj.* of or relating to salvation. ■ (**Salvationist**) of or relating to the Salvation Army. **—sal·va·tion·ism** /-,nizəm/ *n.*

salve[1] /sav; säv/ ▶*n.* an ointment used to promote healing of the skin or as protection. ■ *figurative* something that is soothing or consoling for wounded feelings or an uneasy conscience: *the idea provided him with a* **salve for** *his guilt.*
▶*v.* [*trans.*] *archaic* apply salve to. ■ *figurative* soothe (wounded pride or one's conscience): *charity salves our conscience.* ▷Old English *sealfe* (noun), *sealfian* (verb), of Germanic origin; related to Dutch *zalf* and German *Salbe.*

salve[2] /salv/ ▶*v.* archaic term for **SALVAGE**. ▷early 18th cent.: back-formation from the noun **SALVAGE**. **—salv·a·ble** /'salvəbəl/ *adj.*

sal·ver /'salvər/ ▶*n.* a tray, typically one made of silver and used in formal circumstances. ▷mid 17th cent.: from French *salve* 'tray for presenting food to the king,' from Spanish *salva* 'sampling of food,' from *salvar* 'make safe.'

Sal·ve Re·gi·na /'sälvā rə'jēnə/ ▶*n.* a Roman Catholic hymn or prayer said or sung after compline, and after the Divine Office from Trinity Sunday to Advent. ▷the opening words in Latin, 'hail (holy) queen.'

sal·vi·a /'salvēə/ ▶*n.* a widely distributed plant of the mint family, esp. (in gardening) a bedding plant cultivated for its spikes of bright flowers. • Genus *Salvia,* family Labiatae: many species, in particular the scarlet-flowered *S. splendens.* ▷modern Latin, from Latin *salvia* 'sage.'

sal·vo /'sal,vō/ ▶*n.* (*pl.* **-vos** or **-voes**) a simultaneous discharge of artillery or other guns in a battle. ■ a number of weapons released from one or more aircraft in quick succession. ■ *figurative* a sudden, vigorous, or aggressive act or series of acts: *the pardons provoked* **a salvo of** *accusations.* ▷late 16th cent. (earlier as *salve*): from French *salve,* Italian *salva* 'salutation.'

sal vo·la·ti·le /,sal və'latl-ē/ ▶*n.* a scented solution of ammonium carbonate in alcohol, used as smelling salts. ▷mid 17th cent.: modern Latin, literally 'volatile salt.'

sal·vor /'salvər/ ▶*n.* a person engaged in salvage of a ship or items lost at sea.

sal·war /,səl'wär/ (also **shal·war** /,sʜəl-/) ▶*n.* a pair of light, loose, pleated trousers tapering to a tight fit around the ankles, worn by women from the Indian subcontinent, typically with a kameez. ▷from Persian and Urdu *šalwār.*

Sal·ween /'sal,wēn/ a river in Southeast Asia that rises in Tibet and flows for 1,500 miles (2,400 km) southeast and south through Myanmar (Burma) to the Gulf of Martaban, an inlet of the Andaman Sea.

Sal·yut /'sal,yo͞ot/ a series of seven Soviet manned orbiting space stations, launched between 1971 and 1982. ▷Russian, used as a greeting; compare with French **SALUT**.

Salz·burg /'sôlz,bərg; 'sälz-; 'zälts,bo͝ork/ a city in western Austria, near the border with Germany, the capital of a state of the same name; pop 144,000. It is noted for its annual music festivals.

Salz·git·ter /'zälts,gitər/ an industrial city in Germany, in Lower Saxony, southeast of Hanover; pop. 115,000.

SAM /sam/ ▶*abbr.* surface-to-air missile.

Sam. ▶*abbr. Bible* Samuel.

sa·ma·dhi /sə'mädē/ ▶*n.* (*pl.* **-dhis**) *Hinduism & Buddhism* a state of intense concentration achieved through meditation. In Hindu yoga this is regarded as the final stage, at which union with the divine is reached (before or at death). ■ *Indian* a funerary monument. ▷from Sanskrit *samādhi* 'contemplation.'

sa·man /sə'män/ (also **sa·maan**, **sa·man tree**) ▶*n.* West Indian term for **RAIN TREE**. ▷Latin American Spanish.

Sa·mar /'sä,mär/ an island in the Philippines, southeast of Luzon. It is the third largest island in the group.

Sam·a·ra /sə'märə/ a city and river port in southwestern central Russia, situated on the Volga River at its confluence with the Samara River; pop. 1,258,000. Former name (1935–91) **KUIBYSHEV**.

sam·a·ra /'samərə; sə'me(ə)rə/ ▶*n. Botany* a winged nut or achene containing one seed, as in ash and maple. ▷late 16th cent.: modern Latin, from Latin, denoting an elm seed.

Sa·mar·i·a /sə'me(ə)rēə/ **1** an ancient city in central Palestine, founded in the 9th century BC as the capital of the northern Hebrew kingdom of Israel.The ancient site is situated in the modern West Bank, northwest of Nablus. **2** the region of ancient Palestine around this city, between Galilee in the north and Judaea in the south.

Sam·a·rin·da /,samə'rində/ a city in Indonesia, in eastern Borneo; pop. 265,000.

Sa·mar·i·tan /sə'maritn; -'me(ə)r-/ ▶*n.* **1** (usu. **good Samaritan**) a charitable or helpful person (with reference to Luke 10:33). **2** a member of a people inhabiting Samaria in biblical times, or of the modern community in the region of Nablus claiming descent from them, adhering to a form of Judaism accepting only its own ancient version of the Pentateuch as Scripture. **3** the dialect of Aramaic formerly spoken in Samaria.
▶*adj.* of or relating to Samaria or the Samaritans. ▷from late Latin *Samaritanus,* from Greek *Samareitēs,* from *Samareia* 'Samaria.' The New Testament parable of the Good Samaritan reflects a proverbial hostility between Jews and Samaritans. **—Sa·mar·i·tan·ism** /-,izəm/ *n.*

sa·mar·i·um /sə'me(ə)rēəm/ ▶*n.* the chemical element of atomic number 62, a hard, silvery-white metal of the lanthanide series. (Symbol: **Sm**) ▷late 19th cent.: from *samar(skite),* a mineral in which its spectrum was first observed (named after *Samarsky,* a 19th-cent. Russian official) + **-IUM**.

Sam·ar·kand /'samər,kand; səmər'känt/ (also **Sam·ar·qand**) a city in eastern Uzbekistan; pop. 370,000. One of the oldest cities in Asia, it was founded in the 3rd or 4th millennium BC. It was a prosperous center on the Silk Road and, in the 14th century, became the capital of Tamerlane's Mongol empire.

Sa·ma Ve·da /'sämə 'vādə; 'vēdə/ *Hinduism* one of the four Vedas, a collection of liturgical chants chanted aloud at the sacrifice. Its material is drawn largely from the Rig Veda. See **VEDA**. ▷from Sanskrit *sāmaveda,* from *sāman* 'chant' and *veda* '(sacred) knowledge.'

sam·ba /'sambə; 'säm-/ ▶*n.* a Brazilian dance of African origin. ■ a piece of music for this dance. ■ a lively modern ballroom dance imitating this dance.
▶*v.* (**-bas**, **-baed** /-bəd/ or **-ba'd**, **-ba·ing** /-bə,iɴɢ/) [*intrans.*] dance the samba. ▷late 19th cent.: from Portuguese, of African origin.

sam·bal /'sämbäl/ ▶*n.* (in Indian and Southeast Asian cooking) hot relish made with vegetables or fruit and spices. ▷Malay.

sam·bar /'sämbər; 'sam-/ ▶*n.* a dark brown woodland deer with branched antlers, of South Asia and the Philippines. • *Cervus unicolor,* family Cervidae. ▷late 17th cent.: from Hindi *sābar,* from Sanskrit *śambara.*

sam·bhar /'sämbər; 'sam-/ ▶*n.* a spicy southern Indian dish consisting of lentils and vegetables. ▷from Tamil *cāmpār,* via Marathi from Sanskrit *sambhāra* 'collection, materials.'

Sam·bo /'sambō/ ▶*n.* (*pl.* **-bos** or **-boes**) **1** *offensive* a black person. [early 18th cent.: perhaps from Fula *sambo* 'uncle.'] **2** (**sambo**) *historical* a person of mixed race, esp. of black and Indian or black and European blood. [mid 18th cent.: from American Spanish *zambo,* denoting a kind of yellow monkey.]

Sam Browne belt /sam 'broun/ ▶*n.* a leather belt with a supporting strap that passes over the right shoulder, worn by army and police officers. ▷early 20th cent.: named after Sir Samuel J. *Brown(e)* (1824–1901), the British military commander who invented it.

sam·bu·ca /sam'bo͞okə/ ▶*n.* an Italian aniseed-flavored liqueur. ▷Italian, from Latin *sambucus* 'elder tree.'

Sa·me /'sāmē/ ▶*plural n.* variant spelling of **SAMI**.

same /sām/ ▶*adj.* (**the same**) **1** identical; not different; unchanged: *he's worked at the same place for quite a few years | I'm* **the same age as** *you are* | [with *clause*] *he put on the same costume that he had worn in Ottawa.* ■ (**this/that same**) referring to a person or thing just mentioned: *that same year I went to Boston.* **2** of an identical type: *they all wore the same clothes.*
▶*pron.* **1** (**the same**) the same thing as something previously mentioned: *I'll resign and encourage everyone else to do the same.* ■ people or things that are identical or share the same characteristics: *there are several brands and they're not all the same.* **2** (chiefly in formal or legal use) the person or thing just mentioned: *sighted sub, sank same.*
▶*adv.* similarly; in the same way: *treating women* **the same as** *men | he gave me five dollars,* **same as** *usual.* ▷Middle English: from Old Norse *sami,* from an Indo-European root shared by Sanskrit *sama,* Greek *homos.* **—same·ness** *n.*
▶*PHRASES* □ **all** (or **just**) **the same** in spite of this; nevertheless: *she knew they had meant it kindly, but it had hurt all the same.* ■ in any case; anyway: *I can manage alone, thanks all the same.* □ **at the same time 1** simultaneously. **2** on the other hand; nevertheless; yet: *it's a very creative place, but at the same time it's very relaxing.* □ **be all the same to** be unimportant to (someone) what happens: *it was all the same to me where it was being sold.* □ **by the same token** see **TOKEN**. □ **one and the same** the same person or thing (used for emphasis): *the guy in the glasses and Superman were one and the same.* □ **same difference** *informal* used to express the speaker's belief that two or more things are essentially the same, in spite of apparent differences. □ **same here** *informal* the same applies to me. □ (**the**) **same to you!** may you do or have the same thing (a response to a greeting or insult). □ **the very same** the same (used for emphasis, often to express surprise): *the very same thrillers that flop in theaters become video hits.*

USAGE The phrase *same identical,* more common in speech than in writing, is redundant and should be avoided.

THE RIGHT WORD **equal, equivalent, identical, same, selfsame, tantamount**

All of these adjectives describe something that is not significantly different from something else.

Same may imply, and **selfsame** always implies, that what is referred to is one thing and not two or more distinct things (*they go to the same restaurant every Friday night; this is the selfsame house in which the family once lived*).

In one sense, **identical** is synonymous with *selfsame* (*the identical place where we first met*); but it can also imply exact correspondence in quality, shape, and appearance (*wearing identical raincoats*).

Equivalent describes things that are interchangeable or that amount to the same thing in value, force, or significance (*the equivalent of a free hotel room at a luxury resort*), while **equal** implies exact correspondence in quantity, value, or size (*equal portions of food*).

Tantamount is used to describe one of a pair of things, usually intangible, that are in effect equivalent to each other (*her tears were tantamount to a confession of guilt*).

same-sex ▶*adj.* relating to or involving people of the same sex: *same-sex friendships* ■ relating to or denoting a sexual relationship in which both partners are of the same sex: *same-sex marriage.*

same-store sales /'sām 'stôr ,sālz/ ▶*n. Finance* a figure used to determine what amount of sales growth is attributable to new store openings, based on sales made by stores that have been open more than one year.

Sa·mhain /'souən/ ▶*n.* the first day of November, celebrated by the ancient Celts as a festival marking the beginning of winter and the Celtic new year. ▷Irish, from Old Irish *samain.*

Sam Hill /,sam 'hil/ ▶*n. informal* used in exclamations as a euphemism for "hell": *what in Sam Hill is that smell?* ▷mid 19th cent.: of unknown origin.

Sa·mi /'sāmē/ (also **Saa·mi** /'sä-/, **Sa·me**, or **Saa·me**) ▶*plural n.* the Lapps of northern Scandinavia. ▷Lappish, of unknown origin.

USAGE See **usage** at **LAPP**.

sam·i·sen /'sami,sen/ (also **sham·i·sen** /'sʜam-/) ▶*n.* a traditional Japanese three-stringed lute with a square body, played with a large plectrum. ▷early 17th cent.: Japanese, from Chinese *san-hsien,* from *san* 'three' + *hsien* 'string.'

sam·ite /'samīt; 'sā-/ ▶*n. historical* a rich silk fabric interwoven with gold and silver threads, used for dressmaking and decoration in the Middle Ages. ▷Middle English: from Old French *samit,* via medieval Latin from medieval Greek *hexamiton,* from Greek *hexa-* 'six' + *mitos* 'thread.'

sam·iz·dat /'sämiz,dät; səmyiz'dät/ ▶*n.* the

clandestine copying and distribution of literature banned by the state, esp. formerly in the communist countries of eastern Europe. ▷1960s: Russian, literally 'self-publishing house.'

Sam·nite /ˈsam,nīt/ ▸*n.* a member of an Oscan-speaking people of southern Italy in ancient times, who spent long periods at war with republican Rome in the 4th to 1st centuries BC.
▸*adj.* of or relating to this people. ▷from Latin *Samnites* (plural); related to *Sabinus* (see **SABINE**).

Sa·mo·a /səˈmōə/ a group of islands in Polynesia, divided between American Samoa and the nation of Samoa. ■ a country consisting of the western islands of Samoa; pop. 177,000; capital, Apia; languages, Samoan and English (both official).

Visited by the Dutch in the early 18th century, the islands were divided administratively in 1899 into American Samoa in the east and German Samoa in the west. After World War I, the nine western islands were mandated to New Zealand and became an independent republic known as Western Samoa within the Commonwealth of Nations in 1962. The country became known as Samoa in 1997.

Sa·mo·an /səˈmōən/ ▸*adj.* of or relating to Samoa, its people, or their language.
▸*n.* **1** a native or inhabitant of Samoa. **2** the Polynesian language of Samoa, spoken in Samoa, New Zealand, the U.S., and elsewhere.

Sa·mos /ˈsāmäs; ˈsam-; ˈsämôs/ a Greek island in the Aegean Sea, close to the coast of western Turkey.

sa·mo·sa /səˈmōsə/ ▸*n.* a triangular savory pastry fried in ghee or oil, containing spiced vegetables or meat. ▷Hindi, from Persian and Urdu.

samovar

sam·o·var /ˈsamə,vär/ ▸*n.* a highly decorated tea urn used in Russia. ▷Russian, literally 'self-boiler.'

Sam·o·yed /ˈsamə,yed; səˈmoiyid/ ▸*n.* **1** a member of a group of mainly nomadic peoples of northern Siberia, who traditionally live as reindeer herders. **2** any of several Samoyedic languages of these peoples. ■ another term for **SAMOYEDIC**. **3** a dog of a white Arctic breed. ▷from Russian *samoed* 'self-eater,' a folk etymology from a Lapp (Sami) phrase meaning 'land of the Sami.'

Sam·o·yed·ic /,saməˈyedik/ ▸*n.* a group of Uralic languages of northern Siberia, of which the most widely spoken is Nenets.
▸*adj.* of or relating to the Samoyeds or their languages.

samp /samp/ ▸*n.* coarsely ground corn, or porridge made from this. ▷mid 17th cent.: from Narragansett *nasamp*.

sam·pan /ˈsam,pan/ ▸*n.* a small boat of a kind used in the Far East, typically with an oar or oars at the stern. ▷early 17th cent.: from Chinese *san-ban*, from *san* 'three' + *ban* 'board.'

sam·phire /ˈsam,fīr/ ▸*n.* **1** (also **rock sam·phire**) a European plant of the parsley family that grows on rocks and cliffs by the sea. Its aromatic, fleshy leaves were formerly much used in pickles. • *Crithmum maritimum*, family Umbelliferae. **2** (also **marsh sam·phire**) another term for **GLASSWORT**. ▷mid 16th cent. (earlier as *sampiere*): from French *(herbe de) Saint Pierre* 'St. Peter('s herb).'

sam·ple /ˈsampəl/ ▸*n.* a small part or quantity intended to show what the whole is like: *investigations involved analyzing samples of handwriting.* ■ a specimen taken for scientific testing or analysis: *a urine sample.* ■ *Statistics* a portion drawn from a population, the study of which is intended to lead to statistical estimates of the attributes of the whole population. ■ a small amount of a food or other commodity, esp. one given to a prospective customer. ■ a sound created by sampling.
▸*v.* [*trans.*] take a sample or samples of (something) for analysis: *bone marrow cells were sampled* | [as *adj.*, with *submodifier*] (**sampled**) *a survey of two hundred randomly sampled households.* ■ try the qualities of (food or drink) by tasting it. ■ get a representative experience of: *sample the pleasures of Saint Maarten.* ■ *Electronics* ascertain the momentary value of (an analog signal) many times a second so as to convert the signal to digital form. ■ record or extract a small piece of music or sound digitally for reuse as part of a composition or song. ▷Middle English (as a noun): from an Anglo-Norman French variant of Old French *essample* 'example.' Current senses of the verb date from the mid 18th cent.

sam·ple point ▸*n.* *Statistics* a single possible observed value of a variable.

sam·pler /ˈsamplər/ ▸*n.* **1** a piece of embroidery worked in various stitches as a specimen of skill, typically containing the alphabet and some mottoes. **2** a representative collection or example of something: *a few superb samplers of West Indian dishes.* **3** a person or device that takes and analyzes samples. ■ an electronic device for sampling music and sound. ▷Middle English (denoting an example to be imitated): from Old French *essamplaire* 'exemplar.'

sam·ple space ▸*n.* *Statistics* the range of values of a random variable.

sam·pling /ˈsampliNG/ ▸*n.* **1** the taking of a sample or samples: *routine river sampling is carried out according to a schedule.* ■ *Statistics* a sample. **2** the technique of digitally encoding music or sound and reusing it as part of a composition or recording.

sam·pling er·ror ▸*n.* *Statistics* error in a statistical analysis arising from the unrepresentativeness of the sample taken.

sam·pling frame ▸*n.* *Statistics* a list of the items or people forming a population from which a sample is taken.

Sam·pras /ˈsamprəs/, Peter (1971–), U.S. tennis player. He was men's singles champion at the Australian Open in 1994 and 1997; at the U.S. Open in 1990, 1993, 1995, 1996, and 2002; and holds the record for Wimbledon, winning in 1993, 1994, 1995, 1997, 1998, 1999, and 2000. He was the youngest man ever to win the U.S. Open.

sam·sa·ra /səmˈsärə/ ▸*n.* *Hinduism & Buddhism* the cycle of death and rebirth to which life in the material world is bound. ▷from Sanskrit *saṃsāra*. —**sam·sa·ric** /-ˈsärik/ *adj.*

sam·ska·ra /səmˈskärə/ ▸*n.* *Hinduism* a purificatory ceremony or rite marking a major event in one's life. ▷from Sanskrit *saṃskāra* 'a making perfect, preparation.'

Sam·son /ˈsamsən/ an Israelite leader (probably 11th century BC) famous for his strength (Judges 13–16). He fell in love with Delilah and confided to her that his strength lay in his uncut hair. She betrayed him to the Philistines, who cut off his hair and blinded him, but his hair grew again, and he pulled down the pillars of a house, destroying himself and a large gathering of Philistines.

Sam·son post ▸*n.* a strong pillar fixed to a ship's deck to act as a support for a tackle or other equipment. ▷late 16th cent. (denoting a kind of mousetrap): probably with biblical allusion to **SAMSON**.

sampan

Sam·u·el /ˈsamyə(wə)l/ (in the Bible) a Hebrew prophet who rallied the Israelites after their defeat by the Philistines and became their ruler. ■ either of two books of the Bible covering the history of ancient Israel from Samuel's birth to the end of the reign of David.

Sam·uel·son /ˈsamyo͞o(ə)lsən; -yəl-/, Paul Anthony (1915–), U.S. economist. A professor at Massachusetts Institute of Technology from 1947, he held many international advisory positions, including that of consultant to the Federal Reserve Board 1965– . He wrote the best-selling textbook *Economics: An Introductory Analysis* (1948). Nobel Prize in Economics (1970).

sam·u·rai /ˈsamə,rī/ ▸*n.* (*pl.* same) *historical* a member of a powerful military caste in feudal Japan, esp. a member of the class of military retainers of the daimyos. ▷Japanese.

San /sän/ ▸*n.* (*pl.* same) **1** a member of the aboriginal peoples of southern Africa commonly called Bushmen. See **BUSHMAN**. **2** the group of Khoisan languages spoken by these peoples. ■ any of these languages.
▸*adj.* of or relating to the San or their languages. ▷from Nama *sān* 'aboriginals, settlers.'

Sa·na'a /säˈnä/ (also **Sa·naa**) the capital of Yemen; pop. 500,000.

San An·dre·as fault /,san anˈdrāəs/ a fault line that extends for about 600 miles (965 km) through the length of coastal California. Seismic activity is common along its course, caused by friction between two crustal plates sliding past each other along the line of the fault.

San An·ge·lo /san ˈanjəlō/ a commercial and industrial city in west central Texas; pop. 84,474.

San An·to·ni·o /,san ənˈtōnēō/ an industrial city in south central Texas; pop. 1,144,646. It is the site of the Alamo mission.

san·a·tive /ˈsanətiv/ ▸*adj.* *archaic* conducive to physical or spiritual health and well-being; healing. ▷late Middle English: from Old French *sanatif* or late Latin *sanativus*, from Latin *sanare* 'to cure.'

san·a·to·ri·um /,sanəˈtôrēəm/ ▸*n.* (*pl.* **-ri·ums** or **-ri·a** /-rēə/) another term for **SANITARIUM**. ▷mid 19th cent.: modern Latin, based on Latin *sanare* 'heal.'

San Ber·nar·di·no /,san ,bərnə(r)ˈdēnō/ an industrial and commercial city in southern California, east of Los Angeles, south of the San Bernardino Mountains; pop. 164,164.

San Bru·no /san ˈbro͞onō/ a city in north central California, on San Francisco Bay, south of San Francisco; pop. 38,961.

San·cerre /säNˈser/ ▸*n.* a light wine, typically white, produced in the part of France around Sancerre.

San·chi /ˈsänCHē/ a village in Madhya Pradesh in India that is the location of several well-preserved ancient Buddhist stupas.

San·cho Pan·za /ˈsänCHō ˈpänzə/ the squire of Don Quixote. He is an uneducated peasant but has a store of proverbial wisdom and is thus a foil to his master.

San Cle·men·te /,san kləˈmentē/ a city in southwestern California, on the Pacific Ocean, southeast of Los Angeles; pop; 41,100.

san·coche /sanˈkôSH/ (also **san·co·cho** /-ˈkôCHō/) ▸*n.* (in South America and the Caribbean) a thick soup consisting of meat and root vegetables. ▷from Latin American Spanish *sancocho* 'a stew.'

sanc·ti·fy /ˈsaNG(k)tə,fī/ ▸*v.* (**-fies, -fied**) [*trans.*] set apart as or declare holy; consecrate: *a small Christian shrine was built to sanctify the site.* ■ (often **be sanctified**) make legitimate or binding by religious sanction: *they see their love sanctified by the sacrament of marriage.* ■ free from sin; purify. ■ (often **be sanctified**) *figurative* give the appearance of being right or good; legitimize: *they looked to royalty to sanctify their cause.* ▷late Middle English: from Old French *saintifier* (influenced later by *sanctifier*), from ecclesiastical Latin *sanctificare*, from Latin *sanctus* 'holy.' —**sanc·ti·fi·ca·tion** /-fiˈkāSHən/ *n.* —**sanc·ti·fi·er** *n.*

sanc·ti·mo·ni·ous /,saNG(k)təˈmōnēəs/ ▸*adj.* *derogatory* making a show of being morally superior to other people: *what happened to all the sanctimonious talk about putting his family first?* See note at **MORAL**. ▷early 17th cent. (in the sense 'holy in character'): from Latin *sanctimonia* 'sanctity' (from *sanctus* 'holy') + **-OUS**.

S

—**sanc·ti·mo·ni·ous·ly** *adv.* —**sanc·ti·mo·ni·ous·ness** *n.* —**sanc·ti·mo·ny** /ˈsaNG(k)təˌmōnē/ *n.*

sanc·tion /ˈsaNG(k)SHən/ ▸*n.* **1** a threatened penalty for disobeying a law or rule: *a range of sanctions aimed at deterring insider abuse.* ■ (**sanctions**) measures taken by a nation to coerce another to conform to an international agreement or norms of conduct, typically in the form of restrictions on trade or on participation in official sporting events. ■ *Ethics* a consideration operating to enforce obedience to any rule of conduct. **2** official permission or approval for an action: *he appealed to the bishop for his sanction.* ■ official confirmation or ratification of a law. ■ *historical Law* a law or decree, esp. an ecclesiastical decree.
▸*v.* [*trans.*] **1** (often **be sanctioned**) give official permission or approval for (an action): *only two treatments have been sanctioned by the Food and Drug Administration.* See note at **APPROVE**. **2** impose a sanction or penalty on. ▷late Middle English (as a noun denoting an ecclesiastical decree): from French, from Latin *sanctio(n-)*, from *sancire* 'ratify.' The verb dates from the late 18th cent. —**sanc·tion·a·ble** *adj.*

USAGE **Sanction** is confusing because it has two meanings that are almost opposite. In most domestic contexts, **sanction** means 'approval, permission': *voters gave the measure their sanction.* In foreign affairs, **sanction** means 'penalty, deterrent': *international sanctions against the republic go into effect in January.*

sanc·ti·tude /ˈsaNG(k)təˌt(y)o͞od/ ▸*n. formal* the state or quality of being holy, sacred, or saintly. ▷late Middle English: from Latin *sanctitudo*, from *sanctus* 'holy.'

sanc·ti·ty /ˈsaNG(k)titē/ ▸*n.* (*pl.* **-ties**) the state or quality of being holy, sacred, or saintly: *the site of the tomb was a place of sanctity for the ancient Egyptians.* ■ ultimate importance and inviolability: *the sanctity of human life.* ▷late Middle English (in the sense 'saintliness'): from Old French *saincteté*, reinforced by Latin *sanctitas*, from *sanctus* 'holy.'

sanc·tu·ar·y /ˈsaNG(k)CHo͞oˌerē/ ▸*n.* (*pl.* **-ar·ies**) **1** a place of refuge or safety: *people automatically sought a sanctuary in time of trouble | his sons* ***took sanctuary*** *in the church.* ■ immunity from arrest: *he has been* ***given sanctuary*** *in the U.S. Embassy in Beijing.* **2** [usu. with *adj.*] a nature reserve: *a bird sanctuary.* **3** a holy place; a temple or church. ■ the inmost recess or holiest part of a temple or church. ■ the part of the chancel of a church containing the high altar. ▷Middle English (sense 3): from Old French *sanctuaire*, from Latin *sanctuarium*, from *sanctus* 'holy.' The early sense 'a church or other sacred place where a fugitive was immune, by the law of the medieval church, from arrest' gave rise to senses 1 and 2.

sanc·tu·ar·y lamp ▸*n.* a candle or small light left lit in the sanctuary of a church, esp. (in Catholic churches) a red lamp indicating the presence of the reserved Sacrament.

sanc·tum /ˈsaNG(k)təm/ ▸*n.* (*pl.* **-tums**) a sacred place, esp. a shrine within a temple or church. ■ *figurative* a private place from which most people are excluded. See **INNER SANCTUM**. ▷late 16th cent.: from Latin, neuter of *sanctus* 'holy,' from *sancire* 'consecrate.'

sanc·tum sanc·to·rum /ˈsaNG(k)təm ˌsaNG(k)ˈtôrəm/ ▸*n.* (*pl.* **sanc·ta sanc·to·rum** /ˈsaNG(k)tə/ or **sanc·tum sanc·to·rums**) the holy of holies in the Jewish temple. ■ a very private or secret place. ▷late Middle English: Latin *sanctum* (see **SANCTUM**) + *sanctorum* 'of holy places,' translating Hebrew *qōḏeš haqqŏḏāšîm* 'holy of holies.'

Sanc·tus /ˈsaNG(k)təs/ ▸*n. Christian Church* a hymn beginning *Sanctus, sanctus, sanctus* (Holy, holy, holy) forming a set part of the Mass. ▷late Middle English: from Latin, literally 'holy.'

sanc·tus bell ▸*n.* another term for **SACRING BELL**.

Sand /sand; sän(d)/, George (1804–76), French novelist; pseudonym of *Amandine-Aurore Lucille Dupin, Baronne Dudevant.* Her earlier novels, including *Lélia* (1833), portray women's struggles against conventional morals; she later wrote a number of pastoral novels, such as *La Mare au diable* (1846). Sand had a ten-year affair with Chopin.

sand /sand/ ▸*n.* a loose granular substance, typically pale yellowish brown, resulting from the erosion of siliceous and other rocks and forming a major constituent of beaches, riverbeds, the seabed, and deserts. ■ (**sands**) an expanse of sand, typically along a shore: [in *place names*] *White Sands.* ■ a stratum of sandstone or compacted sand. ■ *technical* sediment whose particles are larger than silt (typically greater than 0.06 mm). ■ *informal* firmness of purpose: *no one has the sand to stand against him.* ■ a light yellow-brown color like that of sand.
▸*v.* [*trans.*] **1** smooth or polish with sandpaper or a mechanical sander: *sand the rusty areas until you expose bare metal* | [as *n.*] (**sanding**) *some recommend a light sanding between the second and third coats.* **2** sprinkle or overlay with sand, to give better purchase on a surface. ▷Old English, of Germanic origin; related to Dutch *zand* and German *Sand.* —**sand·like** /-ˌlīk/ *adj.*
▸***PHRASE*** □ **the sands of time** the allotted time. [with reference to the sand of an hourglass.]

san·dal[1] /ˈsandl/ ▸*n.* a light shoe with either an openwork upper or straps attaching the sole to the foot. ▷late Middle English: via Latin from Greek *sandalion*, diminutive of *sandalon* 'wooden shoe,' probably of Asiatic origin; compare with Persian *sandal.* —**san·daled** /ˈsandld/ (*Brit.* **san·dalled**) *adj.*

san·dal[2] ▸*n.* short for **SANDALWOOD**.

san·dal·wood /ˈsandlˌwo͝od/ ▸*n.* (also **white san·dal·wood**) a widely cultivated Indian tree that yields fragrant timber and oil. • *Santalum album*, family Santalaceae. ■ a perfume or incense derived from this timber. ■ used in names of other trees that yield similar timber, e.g., **red sandalwood**. ▷early 16th cent.: *sandal* from medieval Latin *sandalum* (based on Sanskrit *candana*) + **WOOD**.

San·dal·wood Is·land another name for **SUMBA**.

san·da·rac /ˈsandəˌrak/ (also **gum san·da·rac**) ▸*n.* a gum resin obtained from the alerce (cypress) of Spain and North Africa, used in making varnish. ▷late Middle English (denoting realgar): from Latin *sandaraca*, from Greek *sandarakē*, of Asiatic origin. The current sense dates from the mid 17th cent.

San·da·we /sänˈdäwā/ ▸*n.* **1** (*pl.* same or **-wes**) a member of an indigenous people of Tanzania. **2** the Khoisan language of this people.
▸*adj.* of or relating to this people or their language.

sand·bag /ˈsan(d)ˌbag/ ▸*n.* a bag filled with sand, typically used for defensive purposes or for protection from flooding.
▸*v.* (**-bagged, -bag·ging**) [*trans.*] **1** [usu. as *adj.*] (**sandbagged**) barricade using sandbags: *boarded-up shopfronts and sandbagged doorways.* **2** hit or fell with or as if with a blow from a sandbag. ■ coerce; bully. **3** [*intrans.*] deliberately underperform in a race or competition to gain an unfair advantage. —**sand·bag·ger** *n.*

sand·bank /ˈsan(d)ˌbaNGk/ ▸*n.* a deposit of sand forming a shallow area in the sea or a river.

sand·bar /ˈsan(d)ˌbär/ ▸*n.* a long, narrow sandbank, esp. at the mouth of a river.

sand bath ▸*n.* a container of heated sand, used in a laboratory to supply uniform heating.

sand·blast /ˈsan(d)ˌblast/ ▸*v.* [*trans.*] roughen or clean (a surface) with a jet of sand driven by compressed air or steam.
▸*n.* such a jet of sand. —**sand·blast·er** *n.*

sand·box /ˈsan(d)ˌbäks/ ▸*n.* **1** a shallow box or hollow in the ground partly filled with sand for children to play in. ■ *historical* a perforated container for sprinkling sand onto wet ink in order to dry it. **2** (also **sand·box tree**) a tropical American tree whose seed cases were formerly used to hold sand for blotting ink. • *Hura crepitans*, family Euphorbiaceae.

Sand·burg /ˈsan(d)ˌbərg/, Carl (1878–1967), U.S. poet and biographer. His poetry is collected in *Chicago Poems* (1915), *Smoke and Steel* (1920), *Complete Poems* (1950), and *Honey and Salt* (1963). He is also noted for his biography of Abraham Lincoln, written in six volumes (*Abraham Lincoln: The Prairie Years*, two volumes, and *Abraham Lincoln: The War Years*, four volumes) between 1926 and 1939.

sand cas·tle (also **sand·cas·tle**) ▸*n.* a model of a castle built out of sand, typically by children.

sand cat ▸*n.* a small wild cat with a plain yellow to grayish coat, a dark-ringed tail, and large eyes, of the deserts of North Africa and southwestern Asia. • *Felis margarita*, family Felidae.

sand cher·ry ▸*n.* a dwarf North American wild cherry. • Genus *Prunus*, family Rosaceae: several species, in particular *P. depressa* and *P. pumila.* ■ the fruit of this tree.

sand crab ▸*n.* a crab that lives on or burrows in sand, esp. one related to fiddler and ghost crabs. • Genus *Uca*, family Ocypodidae.

sand crack ▸*n.* a vertical fissure in the wall of a horse's hoof, originating at the top of the hoof.

sand dab ▸*n.* a small flatfish that is found in the Pacific coastal waters of America. • Genus *Citharichthys*, family Bothidae: several species. ■ this fish as food. ■ another term for **WINDOWPANE** (sense 2).

sand dol·lar ▸*n.* a flattened sea urchin that lives partly buried in sand, feeding on detritus. • Order Clypeasteroida, class Echinoidea: several genera and species, including the **common sand dollar** (*Echinarachnius parma*) found mostly along the coasts of North America and Japan.

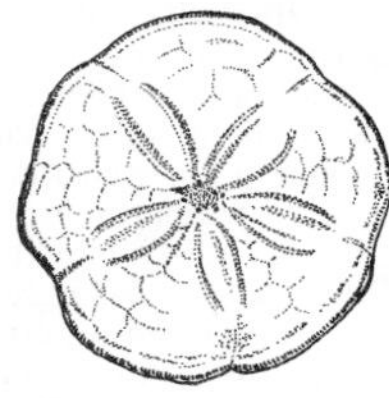
common sand dollar

sand eel ▸*n.* a small elongated marine fish that lives in shallow waters of the northern hemisphere, often found burrowing in the sand. • Family Ammodytidae: several genera and species, including the European *Ammodytes tobianus.*

sand·er /ˈsandər/ ▸*n.* a power tool used for smoothing a surface with sandpaper or other abrasive material.

sand·er·ling /ˈsandərliNG/ ▸*n.* a small migratory sandpiper of northern Eurasia and Canada, typically seen running after receding waves on the beach. • *Calidris alba*, family Scolopacidae. ▷early 17th cent.: of unknown origin.

San·ders[1] /ˈsandərz/, Barry (1968–), U.S. football player. A running back for the Detroit Lions 1989–99, he was named NFL rookie of the year 1989 and player of the year 1997.

San·ders[2], Deion (1967–), U.S. athlete who played both football and baseball professionally. He played football for the Atlanta Falcons 1989–93, the San Francisco 49ers 1994, the Dallas Cowboys 1995–2000, and the Washington Redskins 2000–2001. From 1989 until 1997, he also played baseball with teams such as the New York Yankees, the Atlanta Braves, the Cincinnati Reds, and the San Francisco Giants.

San·ders[3], (Colonel) Harland David (1890–1980), U.S. entrepreneur. He founded Kentucky Fried Chicken (now called KFC), perfecting his secret chicken recipe in 1939 and selling the first franchise in 1952.

San·ders[4], Lawrence (1920–98), U.S. writer. He wrote mostly mysteries and thriller novels such as *The Dream Lover* (1978), *The Seventh Commandment* (1991), and *Guilty Pleasures* (1998). He also wrote some series of novels that featured characters such as Arch McNally (a playboy private eye) and Edward X. Delaney (a retired chief of detectives in New York City).

sand·ers /ˈsandərz/ (also **sand·ers·wood**) ▸*n.* the timber of the red sandalwood, from which a red dye is obtained. • This timber is obtained from *Pterocarpus santalinus*, family Leguminosae. ▷Middle English: from Old French *sandre*, variant of *sandle* 'sandalwood.'

sand fil·ter ▸*n.* a filter used in water purification and consisting of layers of sand arranged with coarseness of texture increasing downward.

sand·fish /ˈsan(d)ˌfiSH/ ▸*n.* (*pl.* same or **-fish·es**) **1** a small marine fish with fringed lips that burrows in the sand, in particular: • an elongated Australian fish (*Crapatulus arenarius*, family Leptoscopidae). • a North Pacific fish (*Trichodon trichodon*, family Trichodontidae). **2** (**belt·ed sand·fish**) a small sea bass that lives only in shallow inshore waters around Florida. • *Serranus subligarius*, family Serranidae.

sand flea ▸*n.* **1** another term for **BEACH FLEA**. **2** another term for **CHIGOE**.

sand·fly /ˈsan(d)ˌflī/ ▸*n.* (*pl.* **-flies**) **1** a small, hairy, biting fly of tropical and subtropical regions that transmits a number of diseases, including leishmaniasis. • Subfamily Phlebotominae, family Psychodidae: several genera, in particular *Phlebotomus.* **2** *Austral.* another term for **BLACK FLY** (sense 2).

sand fox ▸*n.* a small fox with long ears and a thick coat, living in desert and steppe areas from Morocco to Afghanistan. • *Vulpes rueppellii*, family Canidae.

sand·glass /ˈsan(d)ˌglas/ ▸*n.* an hourglass measuring a fixed amount of time (not necessarily one hour).

sand·grouse /ˈsan(d)ˌgrous/ ▸*n.* (*pl.* same) a seed-eating ground-dwelling bird with brownish plumage, allied to the pigeons and found in the deserts and arid regions of the Old World. • Family Pteroclididae, genera *Pterocles* and *Syrrhaptes*: several species.

san·dhi /ˈsandē; ˈsän-/ ▸*n. Phonetics* the process whereby the form of a word changes as a result of its position in an utterance (e.g., the change from *a* to *an* before a vowel). ▷from Sanskrit *saṃdhi* 'putting together.'

sand·hill crane /'sand,hil/ ▸*n.* a chiefly migratory North American crane with grayish plumage and a red crown. • *Grus canadensis*, family Gruidae.

Sand·hills /'sand'hilz/ **1** (also **Sand Hills**) a line of low, sandy hills that lies across North and South Carolina and Georgia, at the boundary of the coastal plain and the Piedmont. **2** a large plains area in west central Nebraska, noted as a ranching district.

sand·hog /'san(d),hôg; -,häg/ ▸*n.* a person who does construction work underground or under water, such as laying foundations or building a tunnel.

sand hop·per /'sand,häpər/ ▸*n.* another term for BEACH FLEA.

San·di·a Moun·tains /san'dēə/ a range in central New Mexico that rises to 10,678 feet (3,255 m) at Sandia Peak, near Albuquerque.

San Di·e·go /,san dē'āgō/ an industrial city and naval port on the Pacific coast of southern California, just north of the U.S.-Mexico border; pop. 1,223,400. It was founded as a mission in 1769.

San·di·nis·ta /,sandə'nēstə/ ▸*n.* a member of a left-wing Nicaraguan political organization, the Sandinista National Liberation Front (FSLN), which came to power in 1979 after overthrowing the dictator Anastasio Somoza. Opposed during most of their period of rule by the U.S.-backed Contras, the Sandinistas were voted out of office in 1990. ▷named after a similar organization founded by the nationalist leader Augusto César *Sandino* (1893–1934).

san·di·ver /'sandəvər/ ▸*n.* a scum that forms on molten glass. ▷late Middle English: apparently from Old French *suin de verre* 'exudation from glass,' from *suer* 'to sweat' + *verre* 'glass.'

S & L ▸*abbr.* savings and loan.

sand lance ▸*n.* another term for SAND EEL.

sand liz·ard ▸*n.* a small, ground-dwelling Old World lizard favoring heathland or sandy areas. • *Lacerta agilis* (of Eurasia), and genus *Pedioplanis* (of Africa), family Lacertidae.

sand·lot /'san(d),lät/ ▸*n.* a piece of unoccupied land used by children for games. ■ [as *adj.*] denoting or relating to sports played by amateurs: *sandlot baseball.*

S & M ▸*abbr.* ■ sadomasochism. ■ (in the insurance industry) stock and machinery.

sand·man /'san(d),man/ ▸*n.* (**the sandman**) a fictional man supposed to make children sleep by sprinkling sand in their eyes.

sand mar·tin ▸*n.* a gregarious swallowlike bird with dark brown and white plumage, excavating nest holes in sandy banks and cliffs near water. • Genus *Riparia*, family Hirundinidae: three species, in particular the widespread *R. riparia* (**bank swallow**).

S & P 500 ▸*abbr. Finance* Standard & Poor's 500.

sand paint·ing ▸*n.* an American Indian ceremonial art form, important among the Navajo and Pueblo peoples, using colored sands, used esp. in connection with healing ceremonies. ■ an example of this art form.

sand·pa·per /'san(d),pāpər/ ▸*n.* paper with sand or another abrasive stuck to it, used for smoothing or polishing woodwork or other surfaces. ■ used to refer to something that feels rough or has a very rough surface.
▸*v.* [*trans.*] smooth with sandpaper. —**sand·pa·per·y** *adj.*

sand·pi·per /'san(d),pīpər/ ▸*n.* a wading bird with a long bill and typically long legs, nesting on the ground near water and frequenting coastal areas on migration. • Family Scolopacidae (the **sandpiper family**): several genera, esp. *Calidris*, *Tringa*, and *Actitis*, and numerous species, including the **western sandpiper** (*C. mauri*), which breeds on the seashores of Alaska and winters from the the southern U.S. to Peru, and the **spotted sandpiper** (*A. macularia*), which prefers lakes and streams and is the most widespread North American sandpiper. The sandpiper family also includes the godwits, curlews, redshanks, turnstones, phalaropes, woodcock, snipe, and ruff.

western sandpiper

sand·pit /'san(d),pit/ ▸*n.* a quarry from which sand is excavated.

sand point well ▸*n.* a well consisting of a pipe with a solid steel point and lateral perforations near the end, which is driven into the earth until groundwater is reached, when a suction pump is applied to the upper end.

sand shark ▸*n.* a voracious, brown-spotted shark of tropical Atlantic waters. • *Odontaspis taurus*, family Odontaspididae. ■ any of a number of mainly harmless rays, dogfish, and sharks found in shallow coastal waters.

sand spur·rey ▸*n.* see SPURREY.

sand star·gaz·er ▸*n.* see STARGAZER (sense 2).

sand·stone /'san(d),stōn/ ▸*n.* sedimentary rock consisting of sand or quartz grains cemented together, typically red, yellow, or brown in color.

sand·storm /'san(d),stôrm/ ▸*n.* a strong wind carrying clouds of sand with it, esp. in a desert.

sand ta·ble ▸*n.* a relief model in sand used to explain military tactics and plan campaigns.

San·dus·ky /sən'dəskē; san-/ an industrial port city in northern Ohio, on Lake Erie at Sandusky Bay; pop. 29,764.

sand wasp ▸*n.* a digger wasp that excavates its burrow in sandy soil and then catches prey with which to furnish it. Sand wasps typically have an abdomen with a very long and slender "waist." • Subfamily Sphecinae, family Sphecidae: *Ammophila* and other genera.

sand wedge ▸*n. Golf* a heavy, lofted iron with a flange on the bottom, used for hitting the ball out of sand.

Sand·wich /'san(d)wicн/ a town in southeastern Massachusetts, on Cape Cod, a resort with a history of glassmaking; pop. 15,489.

sand·wich /'san,(d)wicн/ ▸*n.* an item of food consisting of two pieces of bread with meat, cheese, or other filling between them, eaten as a light meal: *a ham sandwich.* ■ something that is constructed like or has the form of a sandwich.
▸*v.* [*trans.*] (usu. **be sandwiched between**) insert or squeeze (someone or something) between two other people or things, typically in a restricted space or so as to be uncomfortable: *the girl was sandwiched between two burly men in the back of the car.* ▷mid 18th cent.: named after the 4th Earl of *Sandwich* (1718–92), an English nobleman said to have eaten food in this form so as not to leave the gaming table.

sand·wich board ▸*n.* a pair of advertisement boards connected by straps by which they are hung over a person's shoulders.

sand·wich gen·er·a·tion ▸*n.* a generation of people, typically in their thirties or forties, responsible for bringing up their own children and for the care of their aging parents.

Sand·wich Is·lands former name for HAWAII.

sand·wich tern ▸*n.* a large crested tern found in both Europe and North and South America. • *Thalassius sandvicensis*, family Sternidae (or Laridae). ▷late 18th cent.: named after *Sandwich*, a town in Kent, England.

sand·wort /'san(d)wərt; -,wôrt/ ▸*n.* a widely distributed low-growing plant of the pink family, typically having small white flowers and growing in dry sandy ground. • *Arenaria* and other genera, family Caryophyllaceae.

San·dy /'sandē/ a city in north central Utah, south of Salt Lake City; pop. 88,418.

sand·y /'sandē/ ▸*adj.* (**sand·i·er**, **sand·i·est**) **1** covered in or consisting mostly of sand: *pine woods and a fine sandy beach.* **2** (esp. of hair) light yellowish brown. ▷Old English *sandig* (see SAND, -Y[1]). —**sand·i·ness** *n.* —**sand·y·ish** *adj.*

sand yacht ▸*n.* a wind-driven three-wheeled vehicle with a sail, used for racing on beaches.

San·dy Hook a peninsula in northeastern New Jersey that separates Raritan Bay from the Atlantic Ocean, south of New York City.

sane /sān/ ▸*adj.* (of a person) of sound mind; not mad or mentally ill: *hard work kept me sane.* ■ (of an undertaking or manner) reasonable; sensible. See note at SENSIBLE. ▷early 17th cent.: from Latin *sanus* 'healthy.' —**sane·ly** *adv.* —**sane·ness** *n.*

San Fer·nan·do Val·ley /,san fər'nandō/ (popularly **the Valley**) an irrigated district northwest of downtown Los Angeles in California.

San·fi·lip·po's syn·drome /,sanfə'lipōz/ ▸*n. Medicine* a defect in metabolism similar to Hurler's syndrome. ▷1960s: named after Sylvester J. *Sanfilippo*, 20th-cent. American physician.

San·ford[1] /'sanfərd/ **1** a resort and commercial city in north central Florida; pop. 32,387. **2** a town in southern Maine, a southwestern suburb of Portland; pop. 20,806.

San·ford[2], Edward Terry (1865–1930), U.S. Supreme Court associate justice 1923–30. Appointed to the Court by President Harding, he was considered a liberal although he sometimes held more conservative views regarding civil rights.

San·for·ized /'sanfə,rīzd/ ▸*adj. trademark* (of cotton or other fabrics) preshrunk by a controlled compressive process; meeting certain standards of washing shrinkage. ▷1930s: from the name of *Sanford* L. Cluett (1874–1968), the American inventor of the process.

San Fran·cis·co /,san frən'siskō/ a city and seaport in western California, on the coast, on a peninsula between the Pacific Ocean and San Francisco Bay; pop. 776,733. The city suffered severe damage from earthquakes in 1906 and in 1989. —**San Fran·cis·can** /-kən/ *n.* & *adj.*

San Fran·cis·co Peaks a mountain group in northern Arizona, north of Flagstaff. It includes Humphreys Peak, which at 12,633 feet (3,851 m) is the highest point in the state.

sang /sanG/ ▸ past of SING.

San Ga·bri·el /san 'gābrēəl/ a city in southwestern California, east of Los Angeles; pop. 37,120.

San Ga·bri·el Moun·tains a range in southern California, north of (and partly in) the city of Los Angeles. Mount San Antonio, at 10,080 feet (3,105 m), is the high point. The Mount Wilson observatory is here.

san·gam /'sənGgəm/ ▸*n. Indian* a confluence of rivers, esp. that of the Ganges and Jumna at Allahabad. ▷from Sanskrit *saṃgama.*

san·ga·ree /,sanGgə'rē/ ▸*n.* a cold drink of wine mixed with water and spices. ▷from Spanish *sangría* (see SANGRIA).

sang-de-boeuf /'sanG də 'bəf/ ▸*n.* a deep red color, typically found on old Chinese porcelain. ▷French, literally 'ox blood.'

Sang·er[1] /'sanGər/, Frederick (1918–), English biochemist. He determined the complete amino-acid sequence of insulin in 1955 and established the complete nucleotide sequence of a viral DNA in 1977. Nobel Prize for Chemistry (1958 and 1980).

Sang·er[2], Margaret (Higgins) (1883–1966), U.S. birth-control campaigner. Her experiences as a nurse prompted her to distribute the pamphlet *Family Limitation* in 1914 and to found the first U.S. birth-control clinic in 1916. She founded the American Birth Control League in 1921 and became the first president of the International Planned Parenthood Federation in 1953.

Margaret Sanger

sang·froid /säNG'frwä/ (also **sang-froid**) ▸*n.* composure or coolness, sometimes excessive, as shown in danger or under trying circumstances. ▷mid 18th cent.: from French *sang-froid*, literally 'cold blood.'

san·gha /'səNG(g)ə/ ▸*n.* the Buddhist community of monks, nuns, novices, and laity. ▷from Sanskrit *saṃgha* 'community.'

San·gio·vese /,sanjō'vāzē/ ▸*n.* a variety of black wine grape used in making Chianti and other Italian red wines. ■ a red wine made from this grape. ▷Italian.

san·grail /sanG'grāl/ (also **san·greal**) ▸*n.* another term for GRAIL. ▷late Middle English: from Old French *saint graal* 'Holy Grail.'

San·gre de Cris·to Moun·tains /,sanGgrē də 'kristō/ a range in southern Colorado and northern New Mexico, an extension of the Front Range of the Rocky Mountains. The Pecos and Canadian rivers rise here.

Pronunciation Key ə *ago*; ər *over*; 'ə or ,ə *up*; 'ər or ,ər *fur*; a *hat*; ā *rate*; ä *car*; CH *chew*; e *let*; ē *see*; e(ə)r *air*; i *fit*; ī *by*; i(ə)r *ear*; NG *sing*; ō *go*; ô *for*; oi *boy*; o͝o *good*; o͞o *goo*; ou *out*; SH *she*; TH *thin*; T͟H *then*; (h)w *why*; ZH *vision*

san·gri·a /saNG'grēə/ ▸*n.* a Spanish drink of red wine mixed with lemonade, fruit, and spices. ▹Spanish, literally 'bleeding'; compare with SANGAREE.

san·gui·nar·y /'saNGgwə,nerē/ ▸*adj. chiefly archaic* involving or causing much bloodshed. ▹Middle English (in the sense 'relating to blood'): from Latin *sanguinarius*, from *sanguis, sanguin-* 'blood.'

san·guine /'saNGgwin/ ▸*adj.* **1** cheerfully optimistic: *they are not sanguine about the prospect.* ■ (in medieval science and medicine) of or having the constitution associated with the predominance of blood among the bodily humors, supposedly marked by a ruddy complexion and an optimistic disposition. ■ *archaic* (of the complexion) florid; ruddy. ■ *archaic* bloody or bloodthirsty. **2** *poetic/literary & Heraldry* blood-red. ▸*n.* a blood-red color. ■ a deep red-brown crayon or pencil containing iron oxide. ■ *Heraldry* a blood-red stain used in blazoning. ▹Middle English: from Old French *sanguin(e)* 'blood-red,' from Latin *sanguineus* 'of blood,' from *sanguis, sanguin-* 'blood.' —**san·guine·ly** *adv.* —**san·guine·ness** *n.*

San·hed·rin /san'hedrən; -'hēdrin; sän- / the highest court of justice and the supreme council in ancient Jerusalem. ▹from late Hebrew *sanhedrīn*, from Greek *sunedrion* 'council,' from *sun-* 'with'+ *hedra* 'seat.'

San·i·bel Is·land /'sanəbəl/ a resort island in southwestern Florida, southwest of Fort Myers, noted for its seashells.

san·i·cle /'sanikəl/ ▸*n.* a plant of the parsley family that has burrlike fruit. • Genus *Sanicula*, family Umbelliferae: several species, in particular the Eurasian **wood sanicle** (*S. europaea*). ▹late Middle English: via Old French from medieval Latin *sanicula*, perhaps from Latin *sanus* 'healthy.'

san·i·dine /'sani,dēn/ ▸*n.* a glassy mineral of the alkali feldspar group, typically occurring as tabular crystals. ▹early 19th cent.: from Greek *sanis, sanid-* 'board' + -INE[4].

S

sanit. ▸*abbr.* ■ sanitary. ■ sanitation.

san·i·tar·i·an /,sani'te(ə)rēən/ ▸*n. chiefly archaic* an official responsible for public health or a person in favor of public health reform. ▹mid 19th cent.: from SANITARY + -IAN.

san·i·tar·i·um /,sani'te(ə)rēəm/ ▸*n.* (*pl.* **-tar·i·ums** or **-tar·i·a** /-'te(ə)rēə/) an establishment for the medical treatment of people who are convalescing or have a chronic illness. ▹mid 19th cent.: pseudo-Latin, from Latin *sanitas* 'health.'

san·i·tar·y /'sani,terē/ ▸*adj.* of or relating to the conditions that affect hygiene and health, esp. the supply of sewage facilities and clean drinking water: *a sanitary engineer.* ■ hygienic and clean: *the most convenient and sanitary way to get rid of food waste from your kitchen.* ▹mid 19th cent.: from French *sanitaire*, from Latin *sanitas* 'health,' from *sanus* 'healthy.' —**san·i·tar·i·ly** /-,terəlē/ *adv.* —**san·i·tar·i·ness** *n.*

THE RIGHT WORD **antiseptic, healthful, hygienic, salubrious, sanitary, sterile**

Americans thrive on cleanliness and the eradication of germs.

They try to keep their homes **sanitary**, a term that goes beyond cleanliness to imply that measures have been taken to guard against infections or disease.

They demand that their communities provide schools and workplaces that are **hygienic**—in other words, that adhere to the rules or standards promoting public health.

But it would be almost impossible to duplicate the conditions ideally found in a hospital, where everything that comes in contact with patients must be **sterile**, or free of germs entirely.

Most Americans want to make their general environment **healthful**, which means conducive to the health or soundness of the body, but they are not likely to make it **antiseptic**, a word that is similar in meaning to *sterile* but implies preventing infections by destroying germs that are already present (*an antiseptic ointment*).

Many Americans, as they grow older, choose to move to a more **salubrious** climate, a word that means health-giving and applies primarily to an air quality that is invigorating and that avoids harsh extremes.

san·i·tar·y nap·kin ▸*n.* an absorbent pad worn by women to absorb menstrual blood.

san·i·ta·tion /,sani'tāSHən/ ▸*n.* conditions relating to public health, esp. the provision of clean drinking water and adequate sewage disposal. ▹mid 19th cent.: formed irregularly from SANITARY.

san·i·tize /'sani,tīz/ ▸*v.* [*trans.*] make clean and hygienic: *new chemicals for sanitizing a pool.* ■ (usu. **be sanitized**) *derogatory* alter (something regarded as less acceptable) so as to make it more palatable: *lawyers sanitized documents that could have exposed the company to lawsuits.* —**san·i·ti·za·tion** /,sanətə-'zāSHən/ *n.* —**san·i·tiz·er** *n.*

san·i·ty /'sanitē/ ▸*n.* the ability to think and behave in a normal and rational manner; sound mental health: *I began to doubt my own sanity.* ■ reasonable and rational behavior. ▹late Middle English (in the sense 'health'): from Latin *sanitas* 'health,' from *sanus* 'healthy.' Current senses date from the early 17th cent.

San Ja·cin·to Riv·er /,san jə'sin,tō/ a river in southeastern Texas that flows into Galveston Bay east of Houston. The 1836 battle that won Texas independence from Mexico was fought on its bank.

San Joa·quin Riv·er /,san wä'kēn/ a river that flows for 350 miles (560 km) from south central California to join the Sacramento River and enter San Francisco Bay.

San Joa·quin Val·ley fe·ver /,san wä'kēn/ ▸*n.* informal term for COCCIDIOIDOMYCOSIS.

San Jo·se /,san (h)ō'zā/ a city in western California, south of San Francisco Bay; pop. 894,943. It lies in the Santa Clara valley, known as Silicon Valley, a center of the electronics industries.

San Jo·sé /,san (h)ō'zā ,sän hô'sā/ the capital and chief port of Costa Rica; pop. 319,000.

San Juan /san '(h)wän; sän 'hwän/ the capital and chief port of Puerto Rico, on the northern coast of the island; pop. 437,745.

San Juan Cap·is·tra·no /san 'wän ,kapə'stränō/ a city in southwestern California, between Los Angeles and San Diego, the site of a 1776 mission to which migrating swallows return each March 19; pop. 26,183.

San Juan Hill a hill near Santiago de Cuba, in eastern Cuba, the scene of a July 1898 battle during the Spanish-American War.

San Juan Is·lands an island group in northwestern Washington, north of Puget Sound and south of the Strait of Georgia. San Juan and Orcas are the largest islands in the group.

San Juan Moun·tains a range of the Rocky Mountains in southwestern Colorado and northern New Mexico, the source of the Rio Grande.

sank /saNGk/ ▸ past of SINK[1].

San Le·an·dro /,san lē'andrō/ a city in north central California, southeast of Oakland; pop. 68,223.

San Lu·is Obis·po /san ,lo͞oəs ə'bispō/ a city in west central California, northwest of Los Angeles; pop. 41,958.

San Lu·is Po·to·sí /sän lo͞o'ēs ,pôtô'sē/ a state in central Mexico. ■ its capital; pop. 525,000.

San Mar·cos **1** a city in southwestern California, north of San Diego; pop. 38,974. **2** a city in south central Texas, south of Austin; pop. 28,743.

San Ma·ri·no /,san mə'rēnō/ a republic that forms a small enclave in Italy, near Rimini; pop. 28,000; capital, the town of San Marino; language, Italian (official). ▹said to be named after *Marino*, a Dalmatian stonecutter who fled there to escape the persecution of Christians under Diocletian.

It is perhaps Europe's oldest state, claiming to have been independent almost continuously since its founding in the 4th century.

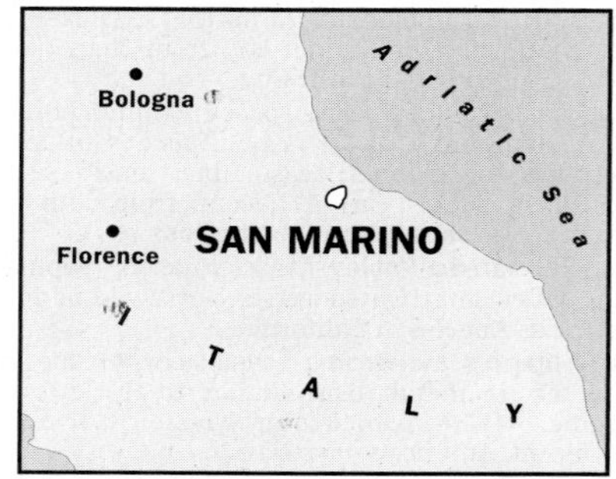

San Mar·tín /,san mär'tēn/, José de (1778–1850), Argentine soldier and statesman. After assisting in the liberation of Argentina from Spanish rule 1812–13, he went on to aid in the liberation of Chile 1817–18 and of Peru 1820–24.

San Ma·te·o /,san mə'tāō/ a commercial and industrial city in north central California, on San Francisco Bay, south of San Francisco; pop. 85,486.

sann·ya·si /sən'yäsē/ (also **san·ya·si** or **sann·ya·sin**) ▸*n.* (*pl.* same) a Hindu religious mendicant. ▹based on Sanskrit *saṃnyāsin* 'laying aside, ascetic,' from *saṃ* 'together' + *ni* 'down' + *as* 'throw.'

San Pab·lo /san 'pablō; 'päb-/ a city in north central California, on San Pablo Bay, north of Oakland; pop. 25,158.

San Pe·dro Su·la /sän 'pedrō 'so͞olä/ a city in northern Honduras, near the Caribbean coast; pop. 325,000.

San Quen·tin /san 'kwentn/ a site in northwestern California, in Marin County, across the Golden Gate from San Francisco, home to a well-known state prison.

San Ra·fael /,san rə'fel/ a city in northwestern California, on San Rafael Bay, north of San Francisco; pop. 48,404.

sans /sanz/ ▸*prep. poetic/literary, humorous* without: *flavorful vegetarian dishes sans meat, eggs, or milk.* ▹Middle English: from Old French *sanz*, from a variant of Latin *sine* 'without,' influenced by Latin *absentia* 'in the absence of.'

san·sa /'sansə/ ▸*n.* another term for THUMB PIANO. ▹based on Arabic *ṣanj* 'cymbal.'

San Sal·va·dor /san 'salvə,dôr; sän ,sälvä'dôr/ **1** an island in the southeastern Bahamas, believed to be the site where Columbus first landed in the New World in 1492; pop. 2,000. **2** the capital of El Salvador; pop. 423,000.

sans-cu·lotte /,sanz k(y)o͞o'lät/ ▸*n.* a lower-class Parisian republican in the French Revolution. ■ an extreme republican or revolutionary. ▹French, literally 'without breeches.' —**sans-cu·lot·tism** /k(y)ə-'lätizəm/ *n.*

San Se·bas·tián /,san sə'basCHən; ,sän sebäst'yän/ a port and resort in northern Spain, on the Bay of Biscay, close to the border with France; pop. 174,000.

san·sei /'sänsā/ ▸*n.* (*pl.* same) a person born in the U.S. or Canada whose grandparents were immigrants from Japan. Compare with NISEI and ISSEI. ▹1940s: Japanese, from *san* 'third' + *sei* 'generation.'

san·se·vi·e·ri·a /,sansəvē'i(ə)rēə; -sə'vi(ə)rēə/ (also **san·se·ve·ri·a**) ▸*n.* a plant of the genus *Sansevieria* in the agave family, esp. (in gardening) mother-in-law's tongue. ▹modern Latin, named after Raimondo di Sangro (1710–71), Prince of *Sanseviero* (now Sansevero), Italy.

San Sim·e·on /san 'simēən/ a community in west central California, on the Pacific coast, site of the Hearst estate that is a popular tourist destination.

San·skrit /'san,skrit/ ▸*n.* an ancient Indic language of India, in which the Hindu scriptures and classical Indian epic poems are written and from which many northern Indian languages are derived. ▸*adj.* of or relating to this language. ▹from Sanskrit *saṃskṛta* 'composed, elaborated,' from *saṃ* 'together' + *kṛ* 'make' + the past participle ending *-ta*. —**San·skrit·ic** /san'skritik/ *adj.* —**San·skrit·ist** /'san,skritist/ *n.*

Sanskrit was spoken in India roughly 1200–400 BC, and continues in use as a language of religion and scholarship. It is written from left to right in the Devanagari script. The suggestion by **Sir William Jones** (1746–94) of its common origin with Latin and Greek was a major advance in the development of historical linguistics.

sans ser·if /,san(z) 'serəf/ *Printing* ▸*n.* a style of type without serifs. ▸*adj.* without serifs. ▹mid 19th cent.: apparently from French *sans* 'without' + SERIF.

sant /sənt/ ▸*n. Hinduism & Sikhism* a saint. ▹from Hindi *santaḥ* 'venerable men.'

San·ta An·a /,säntə 'änə/ **1** a city in El Salvador, close to the border with Guatemala; pop. 202,340. **2** /,säntə 'änə/ a volcano in El Salvador, southwest of the city of Santa Ana. It rises to a height of 7,730 feet (2,381 m). **3** /,santə 'anə/ a city in southern California, southeast of Los Angeles; pop. 337,977. The region gives its name to the hot dry winds that blow from the Santa Ana Mountains on the east across the coastal plain of southern California.

San·ta An·na /,santə 'anə/, Antonio López de (1794–1876), Mexican general and political leader. A militant revolutionary, he controlled Mexico as its president 1833–36, its dictator 1844–45, and again its president 1853–55. In most of the interim years, he was essentially still in control and engaged in several military actions against the U.S., including his victory at the Alamo 1836 and his defeats at San Jacinto 1836 and Buena Vista 1847.

San·ta Bar·ba·ra /ˈsantə ˈbärbrə/ a resort city in California, on the Pacific coast, northwest of Los Angeles; pop. 85,571.

San·ta Bar·ba·ra Is·lands /ˌsantə ˈbärb(ə)rə/ (also **Channel Islands**) an island group in southwestern California, off the Pacific coast. Santa Catalina Island (also called Catalina) is a tourist destination.

San·ta Cla·ra /ˌsantə ˈklarə; ˈkle(ə)rə/ a city in north central California, a longtime fruit-producing center now at the heart of Silicon Valley; pop. 93,613.

San·ta Cla·ri·ta /ˌsantə kləˈrētə/ a city in southwestern California, northwest of Los Angeles; pop. 110,642.

San·ta Claus /ˈsantə ˌklôz/ (also **San·ta**) an imaginary figure said to bring presents for children on Christmas. He is conventionally pictured as a jolly old man from the far north, with a long white beard and red garments trimmed with white fur. Also called **Saint Nicholas** or **Saint Nick**. ▷late 18th cent.: originally a U.S. usage, alteration of Dutch dialect *Sante Klaas* 'St. Nicholas.'

San·ta Cruz 1 /ˌsantə ˈkrōōz; ˌsäntä ˈkrōōs/ a city in central Bolivia; pop. 695,000. **2** /ˌsantə ˈkrōōz; ˌsäntä ˈkrōōth/ a port and the chief city of the island of Tenerife, in the Canary Islands; pop. 192,000. Full name **SANTA CRUZ DE TENERIFE**. **3** a city in west central California, on Monterey Bay; pop. 49,040.

San·ta Cruz Is·lands an island group in the southeastern Solomon Islands, in the southwestern Pacific Ocean, scene of an October 1942 World War II naval battle between U.S. and Japanese forces.

San·ta Fe /ˈsantə ˌfā; ˌsantə ˈfā/ (also **San·ta Fé** /ˌsäntä ˈfā/) **1** a city in northern Argentina, on the Salado River near its confluence with the Paraná River; pop. 395,000. **2** the capital of New Mexico, in the north central part of the state; pop. 62,302. It was founded as a mission by the Spanish in 1610. From 1821 until 1880, it served as the terminus of the Santa Fe Trail. Taken by U.S. forces in 1846 during the Mexican War, it became the capital of New Mexico in 1912.

San·ta Fé de Bo·go·tá ▶ official name for **BOGOTÁ**.

San·ta Fe Trail a historic route, established in the 1820s, from St. Louis in Missouri to Santa Fe in New Mexico. Merchants and settlers used it until the Santa Fe Railroad was built in the 1870s.

San·ta Lu·ci·a Range /ˌsantə lōōˈsēə/ a range in west central California, part of the Coast Ranges

San·ta Ma·ri·a /ˌsantə məˈrēə/ a commercial city in southwestern California; pop. 61,284.

San·ta Mon·i·ca /ˈsantə ˈmänikə/ a resort city on the coast of southwestern California, west of Los Angeles; pop. 86,905.

San·tan·der /ˌsäntänˈder/ a port in northern Spain, on the Bay of Biscay, north of Madrid; pop. 194,220 (1991).

San·ta Ro·sa /ˌsantə ˈrōzə/ a commercial city in northwestern California, north of San Francisco; pop. 113,313.

San·ta·ya·na /ˌsäntəˈyänä/, George (1863–1952), Spanish philosopher and writer; born *Jorge Augustín Nicolás Ruiz de Santayana*. His works include *The Realms of Being* (1924) and *The Last Puritan* (1935).

San·tee Riv·er /sanˈtē/ a river that flows for 140 miles (230 km) through eastern South Carolina, to the Atlantic Ocean.

San·te·ri·a /ˌsantəˈrēə/ (also **San·te·rí·a**) ▶*n.* a pantheistic Afro-Cuban religious cult developed from the beliefs and customs of the Yoruba people and incorporating some elements of the Catholic religion. ▷Spanish, literally 'holiness.'

san·te·ro /sänˈterō/ ▶*n.* (*pl.* **-ros**) **1** (in Mexico and Spanish-speaking areas of the southwestern U.S.) a person who makes religious images. **2** a priest of the Santeria religious cult. ▷Spanish.

San·ti·a·go /ˌsäntēˈägō/ the capital of Chile, west of the Andes, in the central part of the country; pop. 5,181,000.

San·ti·a·go de Com·pos·te·la /də ˌkämpəˈstelə/ a city in northwestern Spain; pop. 106,000. The remains of St. James the Great are said to have been brought there after his death.

San·ti·a·go de Cu·ba /də ˈkyōōbə; de ˈkōōbä/ a port on the coast of southeastern Cuba, the second largest city on the island; pop. 433,000.

san·tim /ˈsäntim/ ▶*n.* (*pl.* **-ti·mi** /-təmē/) a monetary unit of Latvia, equal to one hundredth of a lat. ▷from Latvian *santims*, from French *centime* + the Latvian masculine ending *-s*.

san·to /ˈsantō; ˈsän-/ ▶*n.* (*pl.* **-tos**) (in Mexico and Spanish-speaking areas of the southwestern U.S.) a religious symbol, esp. a wooden representation of a saint. ▷Spanish or Italian.

San·to Do·min·go /ˈsantō dəˈminggō; ˈsäntō dôˈminggô/ the capital of the Dominican Republic, a port on the southern coast; pop. 2,055,000. From 1936 to 1961, it was called Ciudad Trujillo.

san·to·li·na /ˌsantəˈlēnə/ ▶*n.* a plant of the genus *Santolina* in the daisy family, esp. (in gardening) lavender cotton. ▷modern Latin, perhaps an alteration of **SANTONICA**.

san·ton /sänˈtôn/ ▶*n.* (chiefly in Provence) a figurine adorning a representation of the manger in which Jesus was laid. ▷French, from Spanish, from *santo* 'saint.'

san·ton·i·ca /sanˈtänikə/ ▶*n.* the dried flowerheads of a wormwood plant, containing the drug santonin. • The plant is *Artemisia cina* (family Compositae) of Turkestan. ▷mid 17th cent.: from Latin *Santonica (herba)* '(plant) of the Santoni,' referring to a tribe of Aquitania (now **AQUITAINE**[1]).

san·to·nin /ˈsantn-in/ ▶*n. Chemistry* a toxic crystalline compound present in santonica and related plants, used as an anthelmintic. • Chem. formula: $C_{15}H_{18}O_3$. ▷mid 19th cent.: from **SANTONICA** + **-IN**[1].

san·toor /sənˈtŏŏr/ (also **san·tour**) ▶*n.* an Indian musical instrument like a dulcimer, played by striking with a pair of small, spoon-shaped wooden hammers. ▷from Arabic *santīr*, alteration of Greek *psaltērion* 'psaltery.'

San·to·ri·ni /ˌsantəˈrēnē/ another name for **THERA**.

San·tos /ˈsantōs; ˈsän-/ a port on the coast of Brazil, just southeast of São Paulo; pop. 429,000.

san·ya·si ▶*n.* variant spelling of **SANNYASI**.

São Fran·cis·co /ˈsoun frənˈsiskōō/ a river in eastern Brazil that rises in the state of Minas Gerais and flows north and then east for 1,990 miles (3,200 km) to meet the Atlantic Ocean north of Aracajú.

sao·la /ˈsoulə/ ▶*n.* a small two-horned mammal discovered in Vietnam in 1992, with similarities to both antelopes and oxen. • *Pseudoryx nghetinhensis*. ▷1990s: a local name, literally 'spindle horn.'

São Luís /ˈsoun lōōˈēs/ a port in northeastern Brazil, on the Atlantic coast; pop. 695,000.

Saône /sōn/ a river in eastern France that rises in the Vosges Mountains and flows 298 miles (480 km) southwest to join the Rhône River at Lyons.

São Pau·lo /ˌsou ˈpoulō ˌsoun ˈpoulōō/ a state in southern Brazil, on the Atlantic coast. ■ its capital city, the largest city in Brazil and the second largest in South America; pop. 9,700,000.

São To·mé and Prín·ci·pe /ˌsou tōˈmā and ˈprinsəpə; ˌsoun tōōˈmā/ a country that consists of two main islands and several smaller ones in the Gulf of Guinea; pop. 181,000; capital, São Tomé; languages, Portuguese (official) and Portuguese Creole.

The islands were settled by Portugal from 1493 and became an overseas province of that country. São Tomé and Príncipe became independent in 1975.

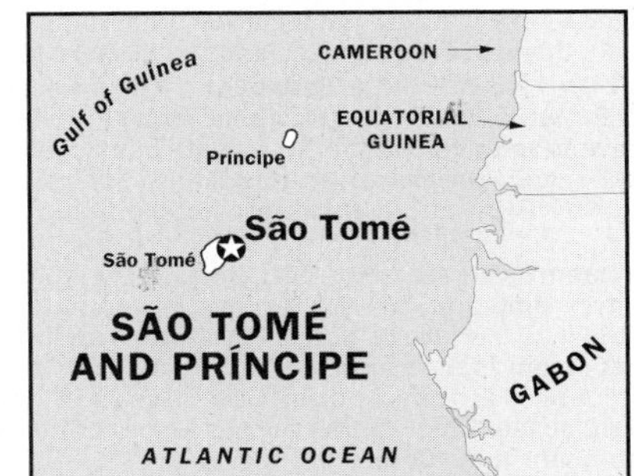

sap[1] /sap/ ▶*n.* the fluid, chiefly water with dissolved sugars and mineral salts, that circulates in the vascular system of a plant. ■ *figurative* vigor or energy, esp. sexual vitality: *the hot, heady days of youth when the sap was rising.*
▶*v.* (**sapped**, **sap·ping**) [*trans.*] gradually weaken or destroy (a person's strength or power): *our energy is being sapped by bureaucrats and politicians.* ■ (**sap someone of**) drain someone of (strength or power): *her illness had sapped her of energy and life.* ▷Old English *sæp*, probably of Germanic origin. The verb (dating from the mid 18th cent.) is often interpreted as a figurative use of the notion "drain the sap from," but is derived originally from the verb **SAP**[2], in the sense 'undermine.' —**sap·less** *adj.*

sap[2] ▶*n. historical* a tunnel or trench to conceal an assailant's approach to a fortified place.
▶*v.* (**sapped**, **sap·ping**) [*intrans.*] *historical* dig a sap or saps. ■ [*trans.*] *archaic* make insecure by removing the foundations of: *a crazy building, sapped and undermined by the rats.* ■ [*trans.*] [often as *n.*] (**sapping**) *Geography* undercut by water or glacial action. ▷late 16th cent. (as a verb in the sense 'dig a sap or covered trench'): from French *saper*, from Italian *zappare*, from *zappa* 'spade, spadework,' probably from Arabic *sarab* 'underground passage,' or *sabora* 'probe a wound, explore.'

sap[3] ▶*n. informal* a foolish and gullible person: *He fell for it! What a sap!* ▷early 19th cent.: abbreviation of dialect *sapskull* 'person with a head like sapwood,' from **SAP**[1] (in the sense 'sapwood') + **SKULL**.

sap[4] *informal* ▶*n.* a bludgeon or club.
▶*v.* (**sapped**, **sap·ping**) [*trans.*] hit with a bludgeon or club. ▷late 19th cent. (as a noun): abbreviation of **SAPLING** (from which such a club was originally made).

s.ap. ▶*abbr.* apothecaries' scruple.

sa·pe·le /səˈpēlē/ ▶*n.* a large, tropical African hardwood tree with reddish-brown timber that resembles mahogany. • Genus *Entandrophragma*, family Meliaceae. ▷early 20th cent.: from the name of a port on the Benin River, Nigeria.

sa·phe·nous /səˈfēnəs/ ▶*adj.* [*attrib.*] *Anatomy* relating to or denoting either of the two large superficial veins in the leg. ▷mid 19th cent.: from medieval Latin *saphena* 'vein' + **-OUS**.

sap·id /ˈsapid/ ▶*adj.* having a strong, pleasant taste. ■ (of talk or writing) pleasant or interesting. ▷early 17th cent.: from Latin *sapidus*, from *sapere* 'to taste.' —**sa·pid·i·ty** /səˈpiditē/ *n.*

sa·pi·ent /ˈsāpēənt/ ▶*adj.* **1** *formal* wise, or attempting to appear wise. ■ (chiefly in science fiction) intelligent: *sapient life forms.* **2** of or relating to the human species (*Homo sapiens*): *our sapient ancestors of 40,000 years ago.*
▶*n.* a human of the species *Homo sapiens*. ▷late Middle English: from Old French, or from Latin *sapient-* 'being wise,' from the verb *sapere*. —**sa·pi·ence** *n.* —**sa·pi·ent·ly** *adv.*

sa·pi·en·tial /ˌsāpēˈenchəl/ ▶*adj. poetic/literary* of or relating to wisdom. ▷late 15th cent.: from Old French, or from ecclesiastical Latin *sapientialis*, from Latin *sapientia* 'wisdom.'

Sa·pir /səˈpi(ə)r/, Edward (1884–1939), U.S. linguistics scholar and anthropologist, born in Germany. One of the founders of American structural linguistics, he carried out important research on American Indian languages and linguistic theory.

Sa·pir-Whorf hy·poth·e·sis /səˈpi(ə)r ˈ(h)wôrf/ *Linguistics* a hypothesis, first advanced by Edward Sapir in 1929 and subsequently developed by Benjamin Whorf, that the structure of a language determines a native speaker's perception and categorization of experience.

sap·ling /ˈsapling/ ▶*n.* a young tree, esp. one with a slender trunk. ■ *poetic/literary* a young and slender or inexperienced person. ▷Middle English: from the noun **SAP**[1] + **-LING**.

sap·o·dil·la /ˌsapəˈdilə/ ▶*n.* a large, evergreen, tropical American tree that has edible fruit and hard, durable wood and yields chicle. • *Manilkara zapota*, family Sapotaceae. ■ (also **sap·o·dil·la plum**) the sweet, brownish, bristly fruit of this tree. ▷late 17th cent.: from Spanish *zapotillo*, diminutive of *zapote*, from Nahuatl *tzápotl*.

sap·o·na·ceous /ˌsapəˈnāshəs/ ▶*adj.* of, like, or containing soap; soapy. ▷early 18th cent.: from modern Latin *saponaceus* (from Latin *sapo*, *sapon-* 'soap') + **-OUS**.

sa·pon·i·fy /səˈpänəˌfī/ ▶*v.* (**-fies**, **-fied**) [*trans.*] *Chemistry* turn (fat or oil) into soap by reaction with an alkali: [as *adj.*] (**saponified**) *saponified vegetable oils.* ■ convert (any ester) into an alcohol and a metal salt by alkaline hydrolysis. ▷early 19th cent.: from French *saponifier*, from Latin *sapo*, *sapon-* 'soap.' —**sa·pon·i·fi·a·ble** *adj.* —**sa·pon·i·fi·ca·tion** /səˌpänəfiˈkāshən/ *n.*

sap·o·nin /ˈsapənən/ ▶*n. Chemistry* a toxic compound that is present in soapwort and makes foam when shaken with water. ■ any of the class of steroid and terpenoid glycosides typified by this, examples of which are used in detergents and foam fire extinguishers. ▷mid 19th cent.: from French *saponine*, from Latin *sapo, sapon-* 'soap'

sap·per /'sapər/ ▸*n.* a military engineer who lays or detects and disarms mines. ▷early 17th cent.: from the verb **SAP**[2] + **-ER**[1].

sap·phic /'safik/ ▸*adj.* **1** *formal* or *humorous* of or relating to lesbians or lesbianism: *sapphic lovers.* **2** (**Sapphic**) of or relating to Sappho or her poetry. ▸*plural n.* (**sapphics**) verse in a meter associated with Sappho. ▷early 16th cent. (sense 2): from French *saphique*, via Latin from Greek *Sapphikos*, from *Sapphō* (see **SAPPHO**).

sap·phire /'saf,ī(ə)r/ ▸*n.* **1** a transparent precious stone, typically blue, which is a variety of corundum (aluminum oxide). ■ a bright blue color. **2** a small hummingbird with shining blue or violet colors in its plumage and a short tail. • *Hylocharis* and other genera, family Trochilidae: several species. ▷Middle English: from Old French *safir*, via Latin from Greek *sappheiros*, probably denoting lapis lazuli. **—sap·phir·ine** /'safərin; -,rēn; -,rīn/ *adj.*

sap·phism /'safizəm/ ▸*n. formal* or *humorous* lesbianism. ▷late 19th cent.: from **SAPPHO** + **-ISM**.

Sap·pho /'safō/ (early 7th century BC), Greek lyric poet who lived on Lesbos. Many of her poems express her affection and love for women and have given rise to her association with female homosexuality.

Sap·po·ro /sə'pôrō/ a city in northern Japan, capital of the island of Hokkaido; pop. 1,672,000.

sap·py /'sapē/ ▸*adj.* (**-pi·er**, **-pi·est**) **1** *informal* oversentimental; mawkish. **2** (of a plant) containing a lot of sap. **—sap·pi·ly** /-əlē/ *adv.* **—sap·pi·ness** *n.*

sapro- ▸*comb. form Biology* relating to putrefaction or decay: *saprogenic.* ▷from Greek *sapros* 'putrid.'

sap·ro·gen·ic /,saprō'jenik/ ▸*adj. Biology* causing or produced by putrefaction or decay.

sap·ro·leg·nia /,saprə'legnēə/ ▸*n.* an aquatic fungus that can attack the bodies of fish and other aquatic animals. • Genus *Saprolegnia*, subdivision Mastigomycotina. ▷modern Latin, from **SAPRO-** 'of decay' + Greek *legnon* 'border.'

sa·proph·a·gous /sə'präfəgəs/ ▸*adj. Biology* (of an organism) feeding on or obtaining nourishment from decaying organic matter. **—sap·ro·phage** /'saprə,fāj/ *n.* **—sa·proph·a·gy** /-'präfəjē/ *n.*

sap·ro·phyte /'saprə,fīt/ ▸*n. Biology* a plant, fungus, or microorganism that lives on dead or decaying organic matter. **—sap·ro·phyt·ic** /,saprə'fitik/ *adj.* **—sap·ro·phyt·i·cal·ly** /-ik(ə)lē/ *adv.*

sap·ro·troph /'saprə,trōf; -,träf/ ▸*n. Biology* an organism that feeds on or derives nourishment from decaying organic matter. ▷back-formation from *saprotrophic.* **—sap·ro·troph·ic** /,saprə'trōfik; -'träfik/ *adj.*

sap·suck·er /'sap,səkər/ ▸*n.* an American woodpecker that pecks rows of small holes in trees and visits them for sap and insects. • *Sphyrapicus*, family Picidae: four species.

sap·wood /'sap,wo͝od/ ▸*n.* the soft outer layers of recently formed wood between the heartwood and the bark, containing the functioning vascular tissue.

Saq·qa·ra /sə'kärə/ (also **Sak·ka·ra**) a vast necropolis at the ancient Egyptian city of Memphis, with monuments dating from the 3rd millennium BC to the Greco-Roman age, notably a step pyramid that is the first known building made entirely of stone (*c.*2650 BC).

SAR ▸*abbr.* search and rescue, an emergency service involving the detection and rescue of those who have met with an accident or mishap in dangerous or isolated locations.

sar·a·band /'sarə,band/ (also **sar·a·bande**) ▸*n.* a slow, stately Spanish dance in triple time. ■ a piece of music written for such a dance. ▷early 17th cent.: from French *sarabande*, from Spanish and Italian *zarabanda.*

Sar·a·cen /'sarəsən/ ▸*n.* an Arab or Muslim, esp. at the time of the Crusades. ■ a nomad of the Syrian and Arabian desert at the time of the Roman Empire. ▷Middle English, from Old French *sarrazin*, via late Latin from late Greek *Sarakēnos*, perhaps from Arabic *šarḳī* 'eastern.' **—Sar·a·cen·ic** /,serə'senik/ *adj.*

Sar·a·cen's head ▸*n.* a conventionalized depiction of the head of a Saracen as a heraldic charge or inn sign.

Sar·a·gos·sa /,sarə'gäsə/ a city in northern Spain, capital of Aragon, situated on the Ebro River; pop. 614,000. Spanish name **ZARAGOZA**. ▷alteration of *Caesaraugusta*, the name given to the ancient settlement on the site, taken by the Romans in the 1st cent. BC.

Sar·ah /'se(ə)rə/ (in the Bible) the wife of Abraham and mother of Isaac (Gen. 17:15 ff.).

Sa·ra·je·vo /,särə'yāvō; -'yěvô/ the capital of Bosnia–Herzegovina; pop. 200,000. It was the scene in June 1914 of the assassination of Archduke Franz Ferdinand (1863–1914), the heir to the Austrian throne, by a Bosnian Serb named Gavrilo Princip—an event that triggered the outbreak of World War I. The city suffered severely from the ethnic conflicts that followed the breakup of Yugoslavia in 1991 and was besieged by Bosnian Serb forces in the surrounding mountains 1992–94.

Sa·ran /sə'ran/ (also **Sa·ran Wrap**) ▸*n.* trademark for **POLYVINYL CHLORIDE**, esp. as plastic wrap. ▷1940s: of unknown origin.

Sar·a·nac Lakes /'sarə,nak/ a group of resort lakes in northeastern New York, in Adirondack Park, site of a pioneering tuberculosis sanatorium.

Sar·an·don /sə'randən/, Susan (1946–), U.S. actress; born *Susan Abigail Tomalin*. She starred in movies such as *Bull Durham* (1988), *Thelma and Louise* (1991) *The Client* (1994), *Dead Man Walking* (Academy Award, 1995), and *Stepmom* (1998).

sa·ran·gi /'särəNGgē/ ▸*n.* (*pl.* **-gis**) an Indian bowed musical instrument about two feet high, with three or four main strings and up to thirty-five sympathetic strings. ▷from Hindi *sāraṅgī*.

Sa·ransk /sə'ränsk/ a city in western Russia, capital of the autonomous republic of Mordvinia, south of Nizhni Novgorod; pop. 316,000.

sa·ra·pe ▸*n.* variant spelling of **SERAPE**.

Sar·a·so·ta /,sarə'sōtə/ a resort city in southwestern Florida, on Sarasota Bay off the Gulf of Mexico, long noted as a winter base for circuses; pop. 50,961.

Sar·a·to·ga /,sarə'tōgə/ an agricultural city in west central California, southwest of San Jose; pop. 28,061.

Sar·a·to·ga, Battle of /,sarə'tōgə/ either of two battles fought in 1777 (September 19 and October 7) during the American Revolution, near the modern city of Saratoga Springs, New York. The defeat of the British in both battles is conventionally regarded as the turning point in the war in favor of the American side.

Sar·a·to·ga Springs a city in eastern New York, north of Albany, a spa noted for horse racing and for two battles fought nearby during the American Revolution; pop. 25,001.

Sa·ra·tov /sə'rätəf/ a city in southwestern central Russia, on the Volga River, north of Volgograd; pop. 909,000.

Sa·ra·wak /sə'räwək/ a state of Malaysia that occupies the northwestern part of Borneo; capital, Kuching.

Sar·a·zen /'sarəzən/, Gene (1902–99), U.S. golfer; born *Eugene Saraceni*. He was the first player to win all four Grand Slam titles: the U.S. Open 1920, the Professional Golfers' Association championship 1920, the British Open 1932, and the Masters 1935.

SarbOx /'särbäks/ (also **Sarb·ox**) ▸*n.* the Sarbanes-Oxley Act, a 2002 Federal law that set new accounting standards for publically traded companies: [*as adj.*] *SarbOx compliance.* ▷after Paul *Sarbanes* and Michael *Oxley*, the legislators who sponsored the law.

sar·casm /'sär,kazəm/ ▸*n.* the use of irony to mock or convey contempt: *his voice, hardened by sarcasm, could not hide his resentment.* See note at **WIT**. ▷mid 16th cent.: from French *sarcasme*, or via late Latin from late Greek *sarkasmos*, from Greek *sarkazein* 'tear flesh,' in late Greek 'gnash the teeth, speak bitterly' (from *sarx, sark-* 'flesh').

sar·cas·tic /sär'kastik/ ▸*adj.* marked by or given to using irony in order to mock or convey contempt: *sarcastic comments on their failures | she's witty and sarcastic.* ▷late 17th cent.: from French *sarcastique*, from *sarcasme* (see **SARCASM**), on the pattern of pairs such as *enthousiasme, enthousiastique.* **—sar·cas·ti·cal·ly** /-ik(ə)lē/ *adv.*

Sar·cee /'särsē/ (also **Sar·si**) ▸*n.* (*pl.* same or **-cees**) **1** a member of an American Indian people of Alberta, Canada. **2** the Athabaskan language of this people.
▸*adj.* of or relating to this people or their language. ▷from Blackfoot *saahsiwa*.

sarce·net /'särsnit/ ▸*n.* variant spelling of **SARSENET**.

sar·coid /'sär,koid/ *Medicine* ▸*adj.* [*attrib.*] relating to, denoting, or suffering from sarcoidosis.
▸*n.* a granuloma of the type present in sarcoidosis. ■ the condition and symptoms of sarcoidosis: *tissues affected by sarcoid.* ▷mid 19th cent. (in the sense 'resembling flesh'): from Greek *sarx, sark-* 'flesh' + **-OID**.

sar·coid·o·sis /,sär,koi'dōsis/ ▸*n.* a chronic disease of unknown cause characterized by the enlargement of lymph nodes in many parts of the body and the widespread appearance of granulomas derived from the reticuloendothelial system.

sar·co·lem·ma /,särkə'lemə/ ▸*n. Physiology* the fine transparent tubular sheath that envelops the fibers of skeletal muscles. ▷mid 19th cent.: from Greek *sarx, sark-* 'flesh' + *lemma* 'husk.' **—sar·co·lem·mal** *adj.*

sar·co·ma /sär'kōmə/ ▸*n.* (*pl.* **-mas** or **-ma·ta** /-mətə/) *Medicine* a malignant tumor of connective or other nonepithelial tissue. ▷early 19th cent.: modern Latin, from Greek *sarkōma*, from *sarkoun* 'become fleshy,' from *sarx, sark-* 'flesh.' **—sar·co·ma·to·sis** /sär,kōmə'tōsis/ *n.* **—sar·co·ma·tous** /-mətəs/ *adj.*

sar·co·mere /'särkə,mi(ə)r/ ▸*n. Anatomy* a structural unit of a myofibril in striated muscle, consisting of a dark band and the nearer half of each adjacent pale band. ▷late 19th cent.: from Greek *sarx, sark-* 'flesh' + *meros* 'part.'

sar·co·pe·ni·a /,särkə'pēnēə/ ▸*n.* loss of muscle tissue as a natural part of the aging process. ▷1990s; from Greek, literally 'lack of flesh'; coined by Irwin H. Rosenberg of the U.S.D.A.

sar·coph·a·gus /sär'käfəgəs/ ▸*n.* (*pl.* **-gi** / -,jī/) a stone coffin, typically adorned with a sculpture or inscription and associated with the ancient civilizations of Egypt, Rome, and Greece. ▷late Middle English: via Latin from Greek *sarkophagos* 'flesh-consuming,' from *sarx, sark-* 'flesh' + *-phagos* '-eating.'

sar·co·plasm /'särkə,plazəm/ ▸*n. Physiology* the cytoplasm of striated muscle cells. ▷late 19th cent.: from Greek *sarx, sark-* 'flesh' + **PLASMA**. **—sar·co·plas·mic** /,särkə'plazmik/ *adj.*

sar·cop·tic mange /sär'käptik/ ▸*n.* a form of mange caused by the itch mite and tending to affect chiefly the abdomen and hindquarters. Compare with **DEMODECTIC MANGE**. ▷late 19th cent.: *sarcoptic* from the modern Latin genus name *Sarcoptes* (from Greek *sarx, sark-* 'flesh') + **-IC**.

sar·co·sine /'särkə,sēn/ ▸*n. Biochemistry* a crystalline amino acid that occurs in the body as a product of the metabolism of creatine. • Alternative name: ***N*-methylglycine**; chem. formula: CH_3NHCH_2COOH. ▷mid 19th cent.: from Greek *sarx, sark-* 'flesh' + **-INE**[4].

sard /särd/ ▸*n.* a yellow or brownish-red variety of chalcedony. ▷late Middle English: from French *sarde* or Latin *sarda*, from Greek *sardios*, probably from *Sardō* 'Sardinia.'

Sar·da·na·pa·lus /,särdn'äpələs/ the name given by ancient Greek historians to the last king of Assyria (died before 600 BC), portrayed as being notorious for his wealth and sensuality. It may not represent a specific historical person.

sar·dar /sər'där/ (also **sir·dar**) ▸*n. chiefly Indian* **1** a leader (often used as a proper name). **2** a Sikh (often used as a title or form of address). ▷from Persian and Urdu *sar-dār*.

Sar·de·gna /sär'denyə/ Italian name for **SARDINIA**.

sar·dine[1] /sär'dēn/ ▸*n.* a young pilchard or other young or small herringlike fish.
▸*v.* [*trans.*] *informal* pack closely together. ▷late Middle English: from French, or from Latin *sardina*, from *sarda*, from Greek, probably from *Sardō* 'Sardinia.'
▸*PHRASE* □ **packed like sardines** crowded very close together, as sardines are in cans.

sar·dine[2] ▸*n.* another term for **SARDIUS**. ▷late Middle English: via late Latin from Greek *sardinos*, variant of *sardios* (see **SARDIUS**).

Sar·din·i·a /sär'dinēə/ a large Italian island in the Mediterranean Sea, west of Italy; pop. 1,664,000; capital, Cagliari. In 1720 it was joined with Savoy and Piedmont to form the kingdom of Sardinia; the kingdom formed the nucleus of the Risorgimento, becoming part of a unified Italy under Victor Emmanuel II of Sardinia in 1861. Italian name **SARDEGNA**.

Sar·din·i·an /sär'dinēən/ ▸*adj.* of or relating to Sardinia, its people, or their language.
▸*n.* **1** a native or inhabitant of Sardinia. **2** the Romance language of Sardinia, which has several distinct dialects.

Sar·dis /ˈsärdis/ an ancient city in Asia Minor whose ruins lie near the western coast of modern Turkey, to the northeast of Izmir, the capital of Lydia.

sar·di·us /ˈsärdēəs/ ▸*n.* a red precious stone mentioned in the Bible (e.g., Exod. 28:17) and in classical writings, probably ruby or carnelian. ▷late Middle English: via late Latin from Greek *sardios.*

sar·don·ic /särˈdänik/ ▸*adj.* grimly mocking or cynical: *Starkey attempted a sardonic smile.* ▷mid 17th cent.: from French *sardonique,* earlier *sardonien,* via Latin from Greek *sardonios* 'of Sardinia,' alteration of *sardanios,* used by Homer to describe bitter or scornful laughter. **—sar·don·i·cal·ly** /-ik(ə)lē/ *adv.* **—sar·don·i·cism** /-ˈdänəˌsizəm/ *n.*

sar·don·yx /särˈdäniks/ ▸*n.* onyx in which white layers alternate with sard. ▷Middle English: via Latin from Greek *sardonux,* probably from *sardios* 'sardius' + *onux* 'onyx.'

sa·ree ▸*n.* variant spelling of **SARI**.

sar·gas·so /särˈgasō/ (also **sar·gas·so weed**) ▸*n.* another term for **SARGASSUM**. ▷late 16th cent.: from Portuguese *sargaço,* of unknown origin.

Sar·gas·so Sea /särˈgasō/ a region of the western Atlantic Ocean between the Azores and the Caribbean Sea, so called because of the prevalence in it of floating sargasso seaweed. It is the breeding place of eels from the rivers of Europe and eastern North America, and is known for its usually calm conditions.

sar·gas·sum /särˈgasəm/ (also **sar·gas·sum weed**) ▸*n.* a brown seaweed with berrylike air bladders, typically forming large floating masses. • Genus *Sargassum,* class Phaeophyceae. ▷modern Latin, from Portuguese *sargaço* (see **SARGASSO**).

sar·gas·sum fish ▸*n.* a small toadfish that occurs worldwide, with a bizarre shape and intricate coloration to camouflage it among the floating sargassum weed that it frequents. • *Histrio histrio,* family Antennariidae.

sarge /särj/ ▸*n. informal* sergeant. ▷mid 19th cent.: abbreviation.

Sar·gent /ˈsärjənt/, John Singer (1856–1925), U.S. painter. He is best known for his portraiture in a style noted for its bold brushwork. He was much in demand in Parisian circles, but following a scandal over the supposed eroticism of *Madame Gautreau* (1884) he moved to London. In World War I, he worked as an official war artist.

Sar·go·dha /sərˈgōdə/ a city in north central Pakistan; pop. 294,000.

Sar·gon /ˈsärˌgän/ (2334–2279 BC), the semilegendary founder of the ancient kingdom of Akkad.

Sar·gon II (died 705 BC), king of Assyria 721–705 BC. Probably a son of Tiglath-pileser III, he is noted for his conquest of cities in Syria and Palestine.

sa·ri /ˈsärē/ (also **sa·ree**) ▸*n.* (*pl.* **-ris** or **-rees**) a garment consisting of a length of cotton or silk elaborately draped around the body, traditionally worn by women from the Indian subcontinent. ▷late 18th cent.: from Hindi *sāṛī.*

sari

sa·rin /säˈrēn/ ▸*n.* an organophosphorus nerve gas, developed in Germany during World War II. ▷from German *Sarin,* of unknown origin.

sark /särk/ ▸*n. Scottish & N. English* a shirt or chemise. ▷Old English *serc,* of Germanic origin.

sar·ky /ˈsärkē/ ▸*adj.* (**-ki·er, -ki·est**) *Brit., informal* sarcastic. ▷early 20th cent.: abbreviation. **—sar·ki·ly** /-kəlē/ *adv.* **—sar·ki·ness** *n.*

Sar·ma·ti·a /särˈmāsн(ē)ə/ an ancient region, located north of the Black Sea, that extended from the Ural Mountains to the Don River. **—Sar·ma·ti·an** /-ˈmāsнən/ *adj.* & *n.*

Sar·noff /ˈsärˌnôf; -ˌnäf/, David (1891–1971), U.S. broadcaster and businessman; born in Russia. A pioneer in the development of radio and television broadcasting in the U.S., he worked for the Radio Corporation of America (RCA) from 1919, founding the National Broadcasting Corporation (NBC) as part of it in 1926. He then served as president and chairman of RCA 1930–70.

sa·rod /səˈrōd/ ▸*n.* a lute used in classical northern Indian music, with four main strings. ▷Urdu, from Persian *surod* 'song, melody.'

sa·rong /səˈrôNG; -ˈräNG/ ▸*n.* a garment consisting of a long piece of cloth worn wrapped around the body and tucked at the waist or under the armpits, traditionally worn in Southeast Asia and now also by women in the West. ▷mid 19th cent.: Malay, literally 'sheath.'

sarong

Sa·ron·ic Gulf /səˈränik/ an inlet of the Aegean Sea on the coast of southeastern Greece. Athens and the port of Piraeus lie on its northern shores.

sa·ros /ˈse(ə)räs/ ▸*n. Astronomy* a period of about 18 years between repetitions of solar and lunar eclipses. ▷early 19th cent.: from Greek, from Babylonian *šār(u)* '3,600 (years),' the sense apparently based on a misinterpretation of the number.

Sa·roy·an /səˈroi-ən/, William (1908–81), U.S. writer. His plays include *The Time of Your Life* (1939) and *Razzle Dazzle* (1942). He also wrote novels such as *The Human Comedy* (1943) and *The Laughing Matter* (1953). Some of his memoirs are recounted in *Places Where I've Done Time* (1972).

sar·ra·ce·nia /ˌsarəˈsēnēə; ˌser-/ ▸*n.* a North American pitcher plant of marshy places, some kinds of which are cultivated as ornamentals. • Genus *Sarracenia,* family Sarraceniaceae: several species, including the purple-flowered *S. purpurea,* which has become naturalized in Ireland. ▷modern Latin, named after Michel *Sarrazin* (died 1734), Canadian botanist.

Sar·raute /säˈrōt/, Nathalie (1902–99), French writer; born in Russia; born *Nathalie Ilyanova Tcherniak.* Her novels included *Portrait of a Man Unknown* (1947) and *Martereau* (1953). Some of her essays are collected in *The Age of Suspicion* (1956).

Sarre /sär/ French name for **SAAR**.

sar·ru·so·phone /səˈro͞ozəˌfōn; -ˈrəsə-/ ▸*n.* a member of a family of wind instruments similar to saxophones but with a double reed like an oboe. ▷late 19th cent.: from the name of W. *Sarrus,* the 19th-cent. French bandmaster who invented it, + **-PHONE**.

SARS /särz/ ▸*n.* a virulently infectious disease originating in China in 2002, caused by a corona virus. ▷2003: acronym from *Severe Acute Respiratory Syndrome .*

sar·sa·pa·ril·la /ˌsärs(ə)pəˈrilə; ˌsaspə-/ ▸*n.* **1** a preparation of the dried rhizomes of various plants, esp. smilax, used to flavor some drinks and medicines and formerly as a tonic. ■ a sweet drink flavored with this. **2** the tropical American climbing plant from which these rhizomes are generally obtained. • Genus *Smilax,* family Liliaceae: several species, in particular *S. regelii,* which is the chief source of commercial sarsaparilla. ▷late 16th cent.: from Spanish *zarzaparilla,* from *zarza* 'bramble' + a diminutive of *parra* 'vine.'

sar·sen /ˈsärsən/ (also **sar·sen stone**) ▸*n. Geology* a silicified sandstone boulder of a kind that occurs on the chalk downs of southern England. Such stones were used in constructing Stonehenge and other prehistoric monuments. ▷late 17th cent.: probably a variant of **SARACEN**.

sarse·net /ˈsärsnit/ (also **sarce·net**) ▸*n.* a fine, soft silk fabric used as a lining material and in dressmaking. ▷late Middle English: from Anglo-Norman French *sarzinett,* perhaps a diminutive of *sarzin* 'Saracen,' suggested by Old French *drap sarrasinois* 'Saracen cloth.'

Sar·to /ˈsärtō/, Andrea del (1486–1531), Italian painter; born *Andrea d'Agnolo.* He worked chiefly in Florence, where his works include fresco cycles in the church of Santa Annunziata and the series of grisailles in the cloister of the Scalzi (1511–26).

Sar·ton /ˈsärtn/, (Eleanor) May (1912–95), U.S. writer and poet; born in Belgium. Her many volumes of poetry include *The Land of Silence* (1953) and *In Time Like Air* (1958). She also wrote novels such as *Faithful Are the Wounds* (1955), *Mrs. Stevens Hears the Mermaids Singing* (1965), and *As We Are Now* (1973) and memoirs such as *I Knew a Phoenix* (1954), *Plant Dreaming Deep* (1968), and *At Eighty-Two* (1995).

sar·to·ri·al /särˈtôrēəl/ ▸*adj.* [*attrib.*] of or relating to tailoring, clothes, or style of dress: *sartorial elegance.* ▷early 19th cent.: from Latin *sartor* 'tailor' (from *sarcire* 'to patch') + **-IAL**. **—sar·to·ri·al·ly** *adv.*

sar·to·ri·us /särˈtôrēəs/ (also **sar·to·ri·us mus·cle**) ▸*n. Anatomy* a long, narrow muscle running obliquely across the front of each thigh from the hipbone to the inside of the leg below the knee. ▷early 18th cent.: modern Latin, from Latin *sartor* 'tailor' (because the muscle is used when adopting a cross-legged position, earlier associated with a tailor's sewing posture).

Sar·tre /ˈsärt(rə)/, Jean-Paul (1905–80), French philosopher, novelist, playwright, and critic. A leading existentialist, he dealt with the nature of human life and the structures of consciousness. He refused the Nobel Prize for Literature in 1964.

Sar·um /ˈse(ə)rəm/ an old name for Salisbury, still used as the name of its diocese.

sa·rus crane /ˈsärəs/ ▸*n.* a large, red-headed crane found from India to the Philippines. • *Grus antigone,* family Gruidae. ▷mid 19th cent.: *sarus* from Sanskrit *sārasa.*

sar·vo·da·ya /särˈvōdiə; -ˈvōdəyə/ ▸*n. Indian* the economic and social development of the community as a whole, esp. as advocated by Mahatma Gandhi. ▷Sanskrit, from *sarva* 'all' + *udaya* 'prosperity.'

SAS ▸*abbr. Brit.* Special Air Service.

sa·san·qua /səˈsäNGkwə/ ▸*n.* a Japanese camellia with fragrant white or pink flowers and seeds that yield tea oil. • *Camellia sasanqua,* family Theaceae. ▷mid 19th cent.: from Japanese *sasank(w)a.*

SASE ▸*abbr.* self-addressed stamped envelope.

sash[1] /sasн/ ▸*n.* a long strip or loop of cloth worn over one shoulder or around the waist, esp. as part of a uniform or official dress. ▷late 16th cent. (earlier as *shash,* denoting fine fabric twisted around the head as a turban): from Arabic *šāš* 'muslin, turban.' **—sashed** /sasнt/ *adj.* **—sash·less** *adj.*

sash[2] ▸*n.* a frame holding the glass in a window, typically one of two sliding frames. ▷late 17th cent.: alteration of **CHASSIS**, interpreted as plural. **—sashed** *adj.*

sa·shay /saˈsнā/ ▸*v.* [*intrans.*] *informal* **1** [with *adverbial of direction*] walk in an ostentatious yet casual manner, typically with exaggerated movements of the hips and shoulders: *Louise was sashaying along in a long black satin dress.* **2** perform the sashay.
▸*n.* (in American square dancing) a figure in which partners circle each other by taking sideways steps. ▷mid 19th cent. (as a verb): alteration of **CHASSÉ**.

sash cord ▸*n.* a strong cord attaching either of the sash weights of a sash window to a sash.

sa·shi·mi /säˈsнēmē/ ▸*n.* a Japanese dish of bite-sized pieces of raw fish eaten with soy sauce and horseradish paste: *tuna sashimi.* ▷Japanese.

sash weight ▸*n.* a weight attached by a cord to each side of a window sash to balance it at any height.

Sask. ▸*abbr.* Saskatchewan.

Sas·katch·e·wan /səˈskacнəwən; -əˌwän/ **1** a province in central Canada; pop. 994,000; capital, Regina. **2** a river in Canada. Rising in two headstreams in the Rocky Mountains, it flows east for 370 miles (596 km) to Lake Winnipeg.

Sas·ka·toon /ˌsaskəˈto͞on/ an industrial city in south central Saskatchewan in Canada, located in the Great Plains on the South Saskatchewan River; pop. 186,060.

Sas·quatch /ˈsaskwäcн; -kwacн/ ▸*n.* another term for **BIGFOOT**. ▷early 20th cent.: Salish *sésq'əc.*

sass /sas/ *informal* ▸*n.* impudence; cheek: *the kind of boy that wouldn't give you any sass.*
▸*v.* [*trans.*] be cheeky or rude to (someone): *we wouldn't have dreamed of sassing our parents.* ▷mid 19th cent.: variant of **SAUCE**.

sas·sa·by /ˈsasəbē/ (also **tses·se·bi** or **tses·se·be** /ˈ(t)sesəbē/) ▸*n.* an antelope of a race found mainly in southern Africa. • *Damaliscus lunatus lunatus,* family Bovidae.

sas·sa·fras /ˈsasəˌfras/ ▸*n.* a deciduous North American tree with aromatic leaves and bark. The leaves are infused to make tea or ground into filé. • *Sassafras albidum,* family Lauraceae. ■ an extract of the leaves or bark of this tree, used medicinally or in perfumery. ▷late 16th cent.: from Spanish *sasafrás,* based on Latin *saxifraga* 'saxifrage.'

Sas·sa·ni·an /səˈsānēən/ (also **Sa·sa·ni·an** or **Sas·sa·nid** /səˈsänid; -ˈsan-; ˈsasənid/) ▸*adj.* of or relating to a dynasty that ruled Persia from the early 3rd century AD until the Arab Muslim conquest of 651.

Pronunciation Key ə *ago;* ər *over;* ˈə *or* ˌə *up;* ˈər *or* ˌər *fur;* a *hat;* ā *rate;* ä *car;* cн *chew;* e *let;* ē *see;* e(ə)r *air;* i *fit;* ī *by;* i(ə)r *ear;* NG *sing;* ō *go;* ô *for;* oi *boy;* o͝o *good;* o͞o *goo;* ou *out;* sн *she;* тн *thin;* тн *then;* (h)w *why;* zн *vision*

▸*n.* a member of this dynasty. ▷from *Sasan* (the name of the grandfather or father of Ardashir, the first Sassanian) + **-IAN**.

Sas·se·nach /'sasə,nak/ *Scottish Irish, derogatory* ▸*n.* an English person.
▸*adj.* English. ▷early 18th cent. (as a noun): from Scottish Gaelic *Sasunnoch*, Irish *Sasanach*, from Latin *Saxones* 'Saxons.'

Sas·soon1 /sə'so͞on; sa-/, Siegfried (Lorraine) (1886–1967), English poet and novelist. His starkly realistic poems, written while serving in World War I, express his contempt for war leaders as well as his compassion for his comrades.

Sas·soon2, Vidal (1928–), English hair stylist. After opening a London salon in 1953, he introduced several popular hairstyles that were named for him.

sas·sy /'sasē/ ▸*adj.* (**-si·er, -si·est**) *informal* lively, bold, and full of spirit; cheeky. ▷mid 19th cent.: variant of **SAUCY**. **—sas·si·ly** /-əlē/ *adv.* **—sas·si·ness** *n.*

sas·tra ▸*n.* variant spelling of **SHASTRA**.

sas·tru·gi /sə'stro͞ogē; sa'-; 'sastrə-/ ▸*plural n.* parallel wavelike ridges caused by winds on the surface of hard snow, esp. in polar regions. ▷mid 19th cent.: from Russian *zastrugi* 'small ridges.'

SAT /'es ,ā 'tē/ ▸*n. trademark* a test of a student's academic skills, used for admission to U.S. colleges. ▷formerly and variously an abbreviation of *Scholastic Assessment Test* and *Scholastic Aptitude Test*.

sat /sat/ ▸ past and past participle of **SIT**.

Sat. ▸*abbr.* Saturday.

Sa·tan /'sātn/ the Devil; Lucifer. ▷Old English, via late Latin and Greek from Hebrew *śāṭān*, literally 'adversary,' from *śāṭan* 'plot against.'

sa·tang /sə'täNG/ ▸*n.* (*pl.* same or **-tangs**) a monetary unit of Thailand, equal to one hundredth of a baht. ▷Thai, from Pali *sata* 'hundred.'

sa·tan·ic /sə'tanik; sā'-/ ▸*adj.* of or characteristic of Satan. ■ connected with Satanism: *a satanic cult*. ■ extremely evil or wicked. **—sa·tan·i·cal·ly** /-ik(ə)lē/ *adv.*

sa·tan·ic rit·u·al a·buse ▸*n.* another term for **RITUAL ABUSE**.

sa·tan·ism /'sātn,izəm/ (also **Sa·tan·ism**) ▸*n.* the worship of Satan, typically involving a travesty of Christian symbols and practices, such as placing a cross upside down. **—sa·tan·ist** *n.* & *adj.*

sa·tan·ize /'sātn,īz/ (also **Sa·tan·ize**) ▸*v.* [*trans.*] *rare* portray as satanic or evil.

sa·tay /'sä,tā/ (also **sa·té**) ▸*n.* an Southeast Asian dish consisting of small pieces of meat grilled on a skewer and usually served with spiced sauce. ▷from Malay *satai*, Indonesian *sate*.

SATB ▸*abbr.* soprano, alto, tenor, and bass (used to describe the constitution of a choir or to specify the singing voices required for a particular piece of music).

satch·el /'sacHəl/ ▸*n.* a bag carried on the shoulder by a long strap and typically closed by a flap. ▷Middle English: from Old French *sachel*, from Latin *saccellus* 'small bag.'

satch·el charge ▸*n.* an explosive on a board fitted with a rope or wire loop for carrying and attaching.

sat·com /'sat,käm/ (also **SATCOM**) ▸*n.* satellite communications. ▷late 20th cent.: blend.

satd. ▸*abbr.* saturated.

sate1 /sāt/ ▸*v.* [*trans.*] satisfy (a desire or an appetite) to the full: *sate your appetite at the resort's restaurant*. ■ supply (someone) with as much as or more of something than is desired or can be managed.
▸*adj.* satisfied completely; fulfilled: *afterward, sated and happy, they both slept*. ▷early 17th cent.: probably an alteration of dialect *sade*, from Old English *sadian* 'become sated or weary' (related to **SAD**). The change in the final consonant was due to association with **SATIATE**. **—sate·less** *adj.* (*poetic/literary*).

sate2 /sat; sāt/ ▸*v.* archaic spelling of **SAT**.

sa·té ▸*n.* variant spelling of **SATAY**.

sa·teen /sa'tēn/ ▸*n.* a cotton fabric woven like satin with a glossy surface. ▷late 19th cent.: alteration of **SATIN**, on the pattern of *velveteen*.

sat·el·lite /'satl,īt/ ▸*n.* **1** (also **ar·ti·fi·cial sat·el·lite**) an artificial body placed in orbit around the earth or moon or another planet in order to collect information or for communication. ■ [as *adj.*] transmitted by satellite; using or relating to satellite technology: *satellite broadcasting*. ■ satellite television: *a news service on satellite*. **2** *Astronomy* a celestial body orbiting the earth or another planet. **3** [usu. as *adj.*] something that is separated from or on the periphery of something else but is nevertheless dependent on or controlled by it: *satellite offices in London and New York*. ■ a small country or state politically or economically dependent on another. **4** *Biology* a portion of the DNA of a genome with repeating base sequences and of different density from the main sequence. ▷mid 16th cent. (in the sense 'follower, obsequious underling'): from French *satellite* or Latin *satelles*, *satellit-* 'attendant.'

sat·el·lite dish ▸*n.* a bowl-shaped antenna with which signals are transmitted to or received from a communications satellite.

sat·el·lite feed ▸*n.* a live broadcast via satellite forming part of another program.

sat·el·lite tel·e·vi·sion ▸*n.* television broadcasting using a satellite to relay signals to appropriately equipped customers in a particular area.

sa·tel·li·ti·um /,satl'itēəm; -'ītēəm/ ▸*n.* *Astrology* a grouping of several planets in a sign.

Sa·ti /,sə'tē; 'sə,tē/ *Hinduism* the wife of Shiva, reborn as Parvati. According to some accounts, she died by throwing herself into the sacred fire.

sa·ti ▸*n.* variant spelling of **SUTTEE**.

sa·ti·ate /'sāsHē,āt/ ▸*v.* another term for **SATE**1: *he folded up his newspaper, his curiosity satiated*.
▸*adj. archaic* satisfied to the full; satiated. ▷late Middle English: from Latin *satiatus*, past participle of *satiare*, from *satis* 'enough.' **—sa·tia·ble** /-sHəbəl/ *adj.* (*archaic*) **—sa·ti·a·tion** /,sāsHē'āsHən/ *n.*

Sa·tie /sä'tē/, Erik (Alfred Leslie) (1866–1925), French avant-garde composer.

sa·ti·e·ty /sə'tīətē/ ▸*n. chiefly technical* the feeling or state of being sated. ▷mid 16th cent.: from Old French *saciete*, from Latin *satietas*, from *satis* 'enough.'

sa·ti·e·ty cen·ter ▸*n. Physiology* an area of the brain situated in the hypothalamus and concerned with the regulation of food intake.

sat·in /'satn/ ▸*n.* a smooth, glossy fabric, typically of silk, produced by a weave in which the threads of the warp are caught and looped by the weft only at certain intervals: [as *adj.*] *a blue satin dress*. ■ [as *adj.*] denoting or having a surface or finish resembling this fabric, produced on metal or other material: *an aluminum alloy with a black satin finish*.
▸*adj.* smooth like satin: *a luxurious satin look*. ▷late Middle English: via Old French from Arabic *zaytūnī* 'of Tsinkiang,' a town in China. **—sat·in·y** *adj.*

sat·i·net /,satn'et/ (also **sat·i·nette**) ▸*n.* a fabric with a similar finish to satin, made partly or wholly of cotton or synthetic fiber.

sat·in pa·per ▸*n.* fine glossy paper, used for writing or printmaking.

sat·in spar ▸*n.* a fibrous variety of gypsum with a pearly luster.

sat·in stitch ▸*n.* a long straight embroidery stitch, closely placed parallel to similar stitches, giving the appearance of satin.

sat·in wal·nut ▸*n.* see **SWEET GUM**.

sat·in weave ▸*n.* a method of weaving fabric in which either the warp or the weft predominates on the surface.

sat·in·wood /'satn,wo͝od/ ▸*n.* **1** glossy yellowish timber from a tropical tree, valued for cabinetwork. **2** the tropical hardwood tree that produces this timber. • Two species in the family Rutaceae: **Ceylon satinwood** (*Chloroxylon swietenia*), native to India and Sri Lanka, and **West Indian** (or **Jamaican**) **satinwood** (*Zanthoxylum flava*), native to the Caribbean, Bermuda, and southern Florida. ■ used in names of other trees that yield high-quality timber, e.g., **Nigerian satinwood**.

sat·ire /'sa,tīr/ ▸*n.* the use of humor, irony, exaggeration, or ridicule to expose and criticize people's stupidity or vices, particularly in the context of contemporary politics and other topical issues. See note at **WIT**. ■ a play, novel, film, or other work that uses satire: *a stinging* **satire on** *American politics*. ■ a genre of literature characterized by the use of satire. ■ (in Latin literature) a literary miscellany, esp. a poem ridiculing prevalent vices or follies. ▷early 16th cent.: from French, or from Latin *satira*, later form of *satura* 'poetic medley.' **—sat·i·rist** /'satərist/ *n.*

sa·tir·i·cal /sə'ti(ə)rikəl/ (also **sa·tir·ic** /-'ti(ə)rik/) ▸*adj.* containing or using satire: *a New York-based satirical magazine*. ■ (of a person or their behavior) sarcastic, critical, and mocking another's weaknesses. ▷early 16th cent.: from late Latin *satiricus* (from *satira* 'poetic medley': see **SATIRE**) + **-AL**. **—sa·tir·i·cal·ly** *adv.*

sat·i·rize /'satə,rīz/ ▸*v.* [*trans.*] deride and criticize by means of satire: *Aristophanes satirized the lack of respect for the laws*. **—sat·i·ri·za·tion** /,satərə'zāsHən/ *n.*

sat·is·fac·tion /,satis'faksHən/ ▸*n.* fulfillment of one's wishes, expectations, or needs, or the pleasure derived from this: *he smiled with satisfaction* | *managing directors seeking greater job satisfaction*. ■ *Law* the payment of a debt or fulfillment of an obligation or claim: *in* **full and final satisfaction** *of the claim*. ■ [with *negative*] what is felt to be owed or due to one, esp. in reparation of an injustice or wrong: *the work will come to a halt if the electricity and telephone people don't* **get satisfaction**. ■ *Christian Theology* Christ's atonement for sin. ■ *historical* the opportunity to defend one's honor in a duel: *I* **demand the satisfaction** *of a gentleman*. ▷Middle English: from Old French, or from Latin *satisfactio(n-)*, from *satisfacere* 'satisfy, content' (see **SATISFY**). The earliest recorded use referred to the last part of religious penance after "contrition" and "confession": this involved fulfillment of the observance required by the confessor, in contrast with the current meaning 'fulfillment of one's own expectations.'
▸*PHRASE* □ **to one's satisfaction** so that one is satisfied: *some amendments were made, not entirely to his satisfaction*.

sat·is·fac·to·ry /,satis'fakt(ə)rē/ ▸*adj.* fulfilling expectations or needs; acceptable, though not outstanding or perfect: *the brakes are satisfactory if not particularly powerful*. ■ (of a patient in a hospital) not deteriorating or likely to die. ■ *Law* (of evidence or a verdict) sufficient for the needs of the case. ▷late Middle English (in the sense 'leading to the atonement of sin'): from Old French *satisfactoire* or medieval Latin *satisfactorius*, from Latin *satisfacere* 'to content' (see **SATISFY**). The current senses date from the mid 17th cent. **—sat·is·fac·to·ri·ly** /-t(ə)rəlē/ *adv.* **—sat·is·fac·to·ri·ness** *n.*

USAGE The adjectives **satisfactory** and **satisfying** are closely related (both deriving from the Latin *satis* 'enough' + *facere* 'to make'), but there is an important distinction. **Satisfactory** denotes the meeting or fulfillment of expectations, standards, or requirements: *the car's* **satisfactory** *performance in its first three road tests*. **Satisfying** denotes the same, but goes further to connote the pleasure or enjoyment derived from the satisfaction: *it was a* **satisfying** *one-dish meal*.

sat·is·fied /'satis,fīd/ ▸*adj.* contented; pleased: *satisfied customers* | *she was very* **satisfied with** *the results*.

sat·is·fy /'satis,fī/ ▸*v.* (**-fies, -fied**) [*trans.*] meet the expectations, needs, or desires of (someone): *I have never been* **satisfied with** *my job* | [*intrans.*] *wealth, the promise of the eighties, has failed to satisfy*. ■ fulfill (a desire or need): *social services is trying to satisfy the needs of so many different groups*. ■ provide (someone) with adequate information or proof so that they are convinced about something: [*trans.*] *people need to be satisfied that the environmental assessments are accurate* | *the chief engineer* **satisfied himself** *that it was not a weapon*. ■ adequately meet or comply with (a condition, obligation, or demand): *the whole team is working to satisfy demand*. ■ *Mathematics* (of a quantity) make (an equation) true. ■ pay off (a debt or creditor): *there was insufficient collateral to satisfy the loan*. ▷late Middle English: from Old French *satisfier*, formed irregularly from Latin *satisfacere* 'to content,' from *satis* 'enough' + *facere* 'make.' **—sat·is·fi·a·bil·i·ty** /,satis,fīə'bilitē/ *n.* **—sat·is·fi·a·ble** *adj.*

sat·is·fy·ing /'satis,fī-iNG/ ▸*adj.* giving fulfillment or the pleasure associated with this: *Fleischer's performance was consummately musical and deeply satisfying*. **—sat·is·fy·ing·ly** *adv.*

USAGE See usage at **SATISFACTORY**.

sat·nav /'sat,nav/ ▸*n.* navigation dependent on information received from satellites. ▷1970s: blend of **SATELLITE** and **NAVIGATION**.

sa·to·ri /sə'tôrē/ ▸*n. Buddhism* sudden enlightenment: *the road that leads to satori*. ▷Japanese, literally 'awakening.'

sa·trap /'sā,trap; 'sa-/ ▸*n.* a provincial governor in the ancient Persian empire. ■ any subordinate or local ruler. ▷late Middle English: from Old French *satrape* or Latin *satrapa*, based on Old Persian *kšathra-pāvan* 'country-protector.'

sa·trap·y /'sātrəpē; 'sa-/ ▸*n.* (*pl.* **-trap·ies**) a province governed by a satrap.

sat·sang /'sat,saNG/ ▸*n. Indian* a spiritual discourse or sacred gathering. ▷from Sanskrit *satsaṅga* 'association with good men.'

Sat·su·ma /sat'so͞omə; 'satsə,mä/ a former province of southwestern Japan that was located on the southwestern peninsula of Kyushu island, also known as the Satsuma Peninsula.

sat·su·ma /sat'sōōmə; 'satsəmə/ ▸n. **1** a tangerine of a hardy loose-skinned variety, originally grown in Japan. **2** (**Sat·su·ma** or **Sat·su·ma ware**) Japanese pottery from Satsuma, ranging from simple 17th-century earthenware to later work made for export to Europe, often elaborately painted, with a crackled cream-colored glaze. ▷late 19th cent.: named after the province SATSUMA.

satt·va /'sətvə/ ▸adj. (in Ayurveda) the element or mode of prakriti associated with purity, wholesomeness, and virtue.

satt·vic /'sətvik/ ▸adj. (in Ayurveda) denoting a class of foods that are fresh, juicy, light, nourishing, and tasty, and thus give necessary energy to the body and help achieve balance. Compare RAJASIC, TAMASIC.

sat·u·rate ▸v. /'sacHə,rāt/ [trans.] (usu. **be saturated**) cause (something) to become thoroughly soaked with liquid so that no more can be absorbed: *the soil is saturated.* ■ cause (a substance) to combine with, dissolve, or hold the greatest possible quantity of another substance: *the groundwater is* **saturated with** *calcium hydroxide.* ■ magnetize or charge (a substance or device) fully. ■ *Electronics* put (a device) into a state in which no further increase in current is achievable. ■ (usu. **be saturated with**) *figurative* fill (something or someone) with something until no more can be held or absorbed: *they've become thoroughly saturated with powerful and seductive messages from the media.* ■ supply (a market) beyond the point at which the demand for a product is satisfied: *Japan's electronics industry began to saturate the world markets.* ■ overwhelm (an enemy target area) by concentrated bombing.
▸n. /-rət/ (usu. **saturates**) a saturated fat.
▸adj. /-rət/ *poetic/literary* saturated with moisture. ▷late Middle English (as an adjective in the sense 'satisfied'): from Latin *saturat-* 'filled, glutted,' from the verb *saturare*, from *satur* 'full.' The early sense of the verb (mid 16th cent.) was 'satisfy'; the noun dates from the 1950s. —**sat·u·ra·ble** /-əbəl/ adj. (*technical*).

sat·u·rat·ed /'sacHə,rātid/ ▸adj. **1** holding as much water or moisture as can be absorbed; thoroughly soaked. ■ *Chemistry* (of a solution) containing the largest possible amount of a particular solute. ■ [often in *combination*] having or holding as much as can be absorbed of something: *the glitzy, media-saturated plasticity of Los Angeles.* **2** *Chemistry* (of an organic molecule) containing the greatest possible number of hydrogen atoms, and so having no carbon–carbon double or triple bonds. ■ denoting fats containing a high proportion of fatty acid molecules without double bonds, considered to be less healthy in the diet than unsaturated fats. **3** (of color) very bright, full, and free from an admixture of white: *intense and saturated color.*

sat·u·ra·tion /,sacHə'rāsHən/ ▸n. the state or process that occurs when no more of something can be absorbed, combined with, or added. ■ *Chemistry* the degree or extent to which something is dissolved or absorbed compared with the maximum possible, usually expressed as a percentage. ■ [as *adj.*] to a very full extent, esp. beyond the point regarded as necessary or desirable: *saturation bombing.* ■ (also **col·or sat·u·ra·tion**) (esp. in photography) the intensity of a color, expressed as the degree to which it differs from white.

sat·u·ra·tion div·ing ▸n. deep-sea diving in which the diver's bloodstream is saturated with helium or other suitable gas at the pressure of the surrounding water, so that the decompression time afterward is independent of the duration of the dive.

sat·u·ra·tion point ▸n. [in *sing.*] *Chemistry* the stage at which no more of a substance can be absorbed into a vapor or dissolved into a solution. ■ *figurative* the stage beyond which no more of something can be absorbed or accepted.

Sat·ur·day /'satər,dā; -dē/ ▸n. the day of the week before Sunday and following Friday, and (together with Sunday) forming part of the weekend: *I am going to see* Twelfth Night **on Saturday** | *the counter is closed on Saturdays and Sundays* | [as *adj.*] *Saturday night.*
▸adv. on Saturday: *he made his first appearance Saturday.* ■ (**Saturdays**) on Saturdays; each Saturday: *they sleep late Saturdays.* ▷Old English *Sætern(es)dæg*, translation of Latin *Saturni dies* 'day of Saturn'; compare with Dutch *zaterdag*.

Sat·ur·day night spe·cial ▸n. *informal* a cheap, low-caliber pistol or revolver, easily obtained and concealed.

Sat·urn /'satərn/ **1** *Roman Mythology* an ancient god, regarded as a god of agriculture. Greek equivalent CRONUS. [from Latin *Saturnus*, perhaps from Etruscan.] **2** *Astronomy* the sixth planet from the sun in the solar system, circled by a system of broad, flat rings.

Saturn orbits between Jupiter and Uranus at an average distance of 887 million miles (1,427 million km) from the sun. It is a gas giant with an equatorial diameter of 74,600 miles (120,000 km), with a conspicuous ring system extending out to a distance twice as great.The planet has a dense, hydrogen-rich atmosphere similar to that of Jupiter but with less distinct banding. There are at least eighteen satellites, the largest of which is Titan, and including small shepherd satellites that orbit close to two of the rings.

3 a series of American space rockets, of which the very large *Saturn V* was used as the launch vehicle for the Apollo missions of 1969–72.

Sat·ur·na·li·a /,satər'nālēə; -nālyə/ ▸n. [treated as *sing.* or *pl.*] the ancient Roman festival of Saturn in December, which was a period of general merrymaking and was the predecessor of Christmas. ■ (**saturnalia**) an occasion of wild revelry. ▷Latin, literally 'matters relating to Saturn,' neuter plural of *Saturnalis*. —**sat·ur·na·li·an** adj.

Sa·tur·ni·an /sə'tərnēən/ ▸adj. **1** of or relating to the planet Saturn. **2** another term for SATURNINE.

sa·tur·ni·id /sə'tərnē-id/ ▸n. *Entomology* a silkworm moth of a family (Saturniidae) that includes the emperor moths and the giant Indian silk moths. They typically have prominent eyespots on the wings. ▷late 19th cent.: from modern Latin *Saturniidae* (plural), from the genus name *Saturnia*.

sat·ur·nine /'satər,nīn/ ▸adj. (of a person or their manner) slow and gloomy: *a saturnine temperament.* See note at GLUM. ■ (of a person or their features) dark in coloring and moody or mysterious: *his saturnine face and dark, watchful eyes.* ■ (of a place or an occasion) gloomy. ▷late Middle English (as a term in astrology): from Old French *saturnin*, from medieval Latin *Saturninus* 'of Saturn' (identified with lead by the alchemists and associated with slowness and gloom by astrologers). —**sat·ur·nine·ly** adv.

sat·ur·nism /'satər,nizəm/ ▸n. archaic term for LEAD POISONING. ▷mid 19th cent.: from SATURN in the obsolete alchemical sense 'lead' + -ISM. —**sa·tur·nic** /sə'tərnik/ adj.

sat·ya·gra·ha /sə'tyägrəhə; 'sətyə,grəhə/ ▸n. a policy of passive political resistance, esp. that advocated by Mahatma Gandhi against British rule in India. ▷Sanskrit, from *satya* 'truth' + *āgraha* 'obstinacy.'

sa·tyr /'satər; 'sātər/ ▸n. **1** *Greek Mythology* one of a class of lustful, drunken woodland gods. In Greek art they were represented as a man with a horse's ears and tail, but in Roman representations as a man with a goat's ears, tail, legs, and horns. ■ a man who has strong sexual desires. **2** a satyrid butterfly with chiefly dark brown wings. • Tribes Satyrini (including the Eurasian genus *Satyrus*) and Euptychiini (the American **wood satyrs**), subfamily Satyrinae, family Nymphalidae. ▷late Middle English: from Old French *satyre*, or via Latin from Greek *saturos*. —**sa·tyr·ic** /sə'tirik/ adj.

sa·ty·ri·a·sis /,satə'rīəsis; ,sā-/ ▸n. uncontrollable or excessive sexual desire in a man. Compare with NYMPHOMANIA. ▷late Middle English: via late Latin from Greek *saturiasis*, from *saturos* (see SATYR).

sa·tyr·id /'satərid; 'sā-/ ▸n. *Entomology* a butterfly of a group that includes the browns, heaths, ringlets, and related species. They typically have brown wings with small eyespots and many live in woodland and breed on grasses. Also called BROWN. • Subfamily Satyrinae, family Nymphalidae (formerly the family Satyridae). ▷early 20th cent.: from modern Latin *Satyridae* (plural), from Latin *Satyrus* (see SATYR), used as a genus name.

sauce /sôs/ ▸n. **1** thick liquid served with food, usually savory dishes, to add moistness and flavor: *tomato sauce* | *the cubes can be added to soups and sauces.* ■ stewed fruit, esp. apples, eaten as dessert or used as a garnish. **2** (**the sauce**) *informal* alcoholic drink: *she's been* **on the sauce** *for years.* **3** *informal, chiefly Brit.* impertinence.
▸v. [trans.] **1** (usu. **be sauced**) provide a sauce for (something); season with a sauce. ■ *figurative* make more interesting and exciting. **2** *informal* be rude or impudent to (someone). ▷Middle English: from Old French, based on Latin *salsus* 'salted,' past participle of *salere* 'to salt,' from *sal* 'salt.' Compare with SALAD. —**sauce·less** adj.
▸PHRASE □ **what's sauce** (or **good**) **for the goose is sauce** (or **good**) **for the gander** *proverb* what is appropriate in one case is also appropriate in the other case in question.

sauce·boat /'sôs,bōt/ ▸n. a boat-shaped vessel used for serving gravy or sauce.

sauced /sôst/ ▸adj. *informal* drunk.

sauce mousse·line ▸n. see MOUSSELINE (sense 3).

sauce·pan /'sôs,pan/ ▸n. a deep cooking pan, typically round, made of metal, and with one long handle and a lid. —**sauce·pan·ful** /-,fōōl/ n. (pl. **-fuls**).

sau·cer /'sôsər/ ▸n. a shallow dish, typically having a circular indentation in the center, on which a cup is placed. ▷Middle English (denoting a condiment dish): from Old French *saussier(e)* 'sauceboat,' probably suggested by late Latin *salsarium*. —**sau·cer·ful** /-,fōōl/ n. (pl. **-fuls**). —**sau·cer·less** adj.
▸PHRASE □ **have eyes like saucers** have one's eyes opened wide in amazement.

sau·cier /sôs'yā; 'sôsēər/ ▸n. a chef who prepares sauces. ▷French.

sau·cis·son /,sōsē'sôN/ ▸n. a large, thick French sausage, typically firm in texture and flavored with herbs. ▷French, literally 'large sausage.'

sau·cy /'sôsē/ ▸adj. (**-ci·er**, **-ci·est**) *informal* **1** impudent; flippant: *a saucy remark.* **2** bold and lively; smart-looking: *a hat with a saucy brim.* **3** sexually suggestive, typically in a way intended to be lighthearted: *saucy songs.* ▷early 16th cent. (in the sense 'savory, flavored with sauce'): from SAUCE + -Y[1]. —**sau·ci·ly** /-səlē/ adv. —**sau·ci·ness** n.

sau·da·de /sou'dädə/ ▸n. a feeling of longing, melancholy, or nostalgia that is supposedly characteristic of the Portuguese or Brazilian temperament. ▷Portuguese.

Sau·di /'soudē; 'sô-/ ▸adj. of or relating to Saudi Arabia or its ruling dynasty.
▸n. (pl. **-dis**) a citizen of Saudi Arabia, or a member of its ruling dynasty. ▷from the name of Abdul-Aziz ibn *Saud* (1880–1953), first king of Saudi Arabia.

Sau·di A·ra·bi·a /'soudē ə'rābēə; 'sôdē/ a country in southwestern Asia that occupies most of the Arabian peninsula; pop. 25,795,000; capital, Riyadh; language, Arabic (official). —**Sau·di A·ra·bi·an** adj. & n.

The birthplace of Islam in the 7th century, Saudi Arabia emerged from the Arab revolt against the Turks during World War I to become an independent kingdom in 1932. Since World War II, the economy has been revolutionized by the exploitation of the area's oil resources, and Saudi Arabia is the largest oil producer in the Middle East. It is ruled by the house of Saud along traditional Islamic lines.

sau·er·bra·ten /'sou(ə)r,brätn/ ▸n. a dish of German origin consisting of beef that is marinated in vinegar with peppercorns, onions, and other seasonings before cooking. ▷from German, from *sauer* 'sour' + *Braten* 'roast meat.'

sau·er·kraut /'sou(ə)r,krout/ ▸n. chopped cabbage that has been pickled in brine. ▷from German, from *sauer* 'sour' + *Kraut* 'vegetable.'

sau·ger /'sôgər/ ▸n. a slender North American pikeperch with silver eyes, which is active at twilight and at night. • *Stizostedion canadense*, family Percidae. ▷late 19th cent.: of unknown origin.

Sau·gus /'sôgəs/ a town in eastern Massachusetts, north of Boston, site of the first U.S. ironworks (established in 1646); pop. 25,549.

Sauk /sôk/ (also **Sac**) ▸n. (pl. same or **Sauks**) **1** a

member of an American Indian people inhabiting parts of the central U.S., formerly in Wisconsin, Illinois, and Iowa, now in Oklahoma and Kansas. **2** the Algonquian language of this people.
▸*adj.* of or relating to this people or their language. ▷from Canadian French *Saki*, from Ojibwa *osākī* '(people of the) river mouth.'

Saul /sôl/ (in the Bible) the first king of Israel (11th century BC).

Saul of Tar·sus see **PAUL, ST.**

Sault Sainte Marie /ˈsoō ˌsānt məˈrē/ each of two North American river ports that face each other across the falls of the St. Mary's River, between lakes Superior and Huron. The northern port (pop. 72,822) lies in Ontario, Canada, while the southern port (pop. 14,700) is in the U.S. state of Michigan. A system of canals serves to bypass the falls on either side of the river.

sau·na /ˈsônə; ˈsou-/ ▸*n.* a small room used as a hot-air or steam bath for cleaning and refreshing the body. ▪ a session in such a room. ▷late 19th cent.: from Finnish.

saun·ders ▸ var. of **SANDERS.**

saun·ter /ˈsôntər/ ▸*v.* [*intrans.*] walk in a slow, relaxed manner, without hurry or effort: *Adam sauntered into the room.*
▸*n.* a leisurely stroll: *a quiet saunter down the road.* ▷late Middle English (in the sense 'to muse, wonder'): of unknown origin. The current sense dates from the mid 17th cent. **—saun·ter·er** *n.*

-saur ▸*comb. form* forming names of reptiles, esp. extinct ones: *ichthyosaur* | *stegosaur.* ▷modern Latin, from Greek *sauros* 'lizard'; compare with **-SAURUS,** a suffix of modern Latin genus names.

Sau·ri·a /ˈsôrēə/ *Zoology* former term for **LACERTILIA.** ▷modern Latin (plural), from Greek *sauros* 'lizard.'

sau·ri·an /ˈsôrēən/ ▸*adj.* of or like a lizard.
▸*n.* any large reptile, esp. a dinosaur or other extinct form. ▷early 19th cent.: from modern Latin *Sauria* (see **SAURIA**) + **-AN.**

saur·is·chi·an /sôˈriskēən/ *Paleontology* ▸*adj.* of, relating to, or denoting dinosaurs of an order distinguished by having a pelvic structure resembling that of lizards. Compare with **ORNITHISCHIAN.**
▸*n.* a saurischian dinosaur. • Order Saurischia, superorder Dinosauria; comprises the carnivorous theropods and the herbivorous sauropods. ▷late 19th cent.: from the modern Latin plural *Saurischia* (from Greek *sauros* 'lizard' + *iskhion* 'hip joint') + **-AN.**

sau·ro·pod /ˈsôrəˌpäd/ ▸*n.* a very large quadrupedal herbivorous dinosaur with a long neck and tail, small head, and massive limbs. • Infraorder Sauropoda, suborder Sauropodomorpha, order Saurischia; e.g., apatosaurus, brachiosaurus, and diplodocus. ▷late 19th cent.: from modern Latin *Sauropoda* (plural), from Greek *sauros* 'lizard' + *pous, pod-* 'foot.'

-saurus ▸*comb. form* forming genus names of reptiles, esp. extinct ones: *stegosaurus.* ▷modern Latin.

sau·ry /ˈsôrē/ ▸*n.* (*pl.* **-ries**) a long slender-bodied edible marine fish with an elongated snout. • Family Scomberesocidae: four genera and species, including *Scomberesox saurus* of the Atlantic (also called **SKIPPER**[2]), and *Cololabis saira* of the Pacific. ▷late 18th cent.: perhaps via late Latin from Greek *sauros* 'horse mackerel.'

sau·sage /ˈsôsij/ ▸*n.* a short cylindrical tube of minced pork, beef, or other meat encased in a skin, typically sold raw to be grilled, boiled, or fried before eating. ▪ a cylindrical tube of minced pork, beef, or other meat seasoned and cooked or preserved, sold mainly to be eaten cold in slices: *smoked German sausage.* ▪ [usu. as *adj.*] used in references to the characteristic cylindrical shape of sausages: *mold into a sausage shape.* ▷late Middle English: from Old Northern French *saussiche*, from medieval Latin *salsicia*, from Latin *salsus* 'salted' (see **SAUCE**).

Sau·sa·li·to /ˌsôsəˈlētō/ a city in northwestern California, across the Golden Gate from San Francisco, a noted artists' colony; pop. 7,152.

Saus·sure /sōˈsoŏr; -ˈsyr/, Ferdinand de (1857–1913), Swiss linguistics scholar. He was one of the founders of modern linguistics, and his work was fundamental to the development of structuralism.

sau·té /sôˈtā; sō-/ ▸*adj.* **1** [*attrib.*] fried quickly in a little hot fat: *sauté potatoes.* **2** *Ballet* (of a step) performed while jumping.
▸*n.* a dish cooked in such a way.
▸*v.* (**-tés, -téed** /-ˈtād/ or **-téd, -téing** /-ˈtāiNG/) [*trans.*] cook in such a way: *sauté the onions in the olive oil.* ▷early 19th cent.: French, literally 'jumped,' past participle of *sauter.*

Sau·ternes /sōˈtərn; sô-/ ▸*n.* a sweet white wine from Sauternes in the Bordeaux region of France.

sauve qui peut /ˌsōv kē ˈpə/ ▸*n. archaic* or *poetic/literary* a general stampede, panic, or disorder. ▷French, literally 'save who can.'

Sau·vi·gnon /ˌsōvinˈyôN; -vēˈnyôN/ (also **Sau·vi·gnon Blanc** /ˈbläN; ˈbläNGk/) ▸*n.* a variety of white wine grape. ▪ a white wine made from this grape. ▷French.

sav·age /ˈsavij/ ▸*adj.* (of an animal or force of nature) fierce, violent, and uncontrolled: *tales of a savage beast* | *a week of savage storms.* ▪ cruel and vicious; aggressively hostile: *they launched a savage attack on the budget.* ▪ (chiefly in historical or literary contexts) primitive; uncivilized. ▪ (of a place) wild-looking and inhospitable; uncultivated. ▪ (of something bad or negative) very great; severe: *this would deal a savage blow to the government's fight.*
▸*n.* (chiefly in historical or literary contexts) a member of a people regarded as primitive and uncivilized. ▪ a brutal or vicious person: *the mother of one of the victims has described his assailants as savages.*
▸*v.* [*trans.*] (esp. of a dog or wild animal) attack ferociously and maul: *ewes savaged by marauding dogs.* ▪ subject to a vicious verbal attack; criticize brutally: *Fowler savaged her in his next review.* ▷Middle English: from Old French *sauvage* 'wild,' from Latin *silvaticus* 'of the woods,' from *silva* 'a wood.' **—sav·age·ly** *adv.* **—sav·age·ness** *n.* **—sav·age·ry** /-rē/ *n.*

Sa·vai'i /səˈvī-ē/ (also **Sa·vai·i**) a mountainous volcanic island in the southwestern Pacific, the largest of the Samoan islands.

sa·van·na /səˈvanə/ (also **sa·van·nah**) ▸*n.* a grassy plain in tropical and subtropical regions, with few trees. ▷mid 16th cent.: from Spanish *sabana*, from Taino *zavana.*

Sa·van·nah /səˈvanə/ a port in Georgia, just south of the border with South Carolina, on the Savannah River close to its outlet on the Atlantic; pop. 131,510.

Sa·vann·ah Riv·er a river that flows for 315 miles (506 km), mostly along the border of Georgia and South Carolina, to reach the Atlantic Ocean near Savannah.

sa·van·nah spar·row /səˈvanə/ ▸*n.* a small sparrow common throughout most of North America. • Family Emberizidae, *Passerculus sandwichensis.*

sa·vant /saˈvänt; sə-/ ▸*n.* a learned person, esp. a distinguished scientist. See also **IDIOT SAVANT.** ▷early 18th cent.: French, literally 'knowing (person),' present participle (used as a noun) of *savoir.*

sav·a·rin /ˈsavərin/ ▸*n.* a light ring-shaped cake made with yeast and soaked in liqueur-flavored syrup. ▷named after Anthelme Brillat-*Savarin* (1755–1826), French gastronome.

sa·vate /səˈvat/ ▸*n.* a French method of fighting in which feet and fists are used. ▷French, originally denoting an ill-fitting shoe.

save[1] /sāv/ ▸*v.* [*trans.*] **1** keep safe or rescue (someone or something) from harm or danger: *she* **saved** *a boy* **from** *drowning.* ▪ prevent (someone) from dying: *the doctors did everything they could to save him.* ▪ (in Christian use) preserve (a person's soul) from damnation. ▪ keep (someone) in health (used in exclamations and formulaic expressions): *God save the Queen.* **2** keep and store up (something, esp. money) for future use: *she had never been able to save much from her salary* | [*intrans.*] *you can* **save up for** *retirement in a number of ways.* ▪ *Computing* keep (data) by moving a copy to a storage location, esp. from memory: *save it to a new file.* ▪ preserve (something) by not expending or using it: *save your strength till later.* ▪ [in *imperative*] (**save it**) *informal* used to tell someone to stop talking: *save it, Joey—I'm in big trouble now.* **3** avoid the need to use up or spend (money, time, or other resources): *save $20* **on** *a new camcorder* | [with *two objs.*] *an efficient dishwasher would save them one year and three months at the sink.* ▪ avoid, lessen, or guard against: *this approach saves wear and tear on the books* | [with *two objs.*] *the statement was made to save the government some embarrassment.* **4** prevent an opponent from scoring (a goal or point) in a game or from winning (the game): *the powerful German saved three match points.* ▪ *Baseball* (of a relief pitcher in certain game situations) finish (a game) while preserving a winning position gained by another pitcher. ▪ *Soccer & Hockey* (of a goalkeeper) stop (a shot) from entering the goal.
▸*n.* **1** *Baseball* an instance of a relief pitcher saving a game. ▪ *chiefly Soccer & Hockey* an act of preventing an opponent's scoring: *the keeper made a great save.* *Bridge* another term for **SACRIFICE. 2** *Computing* an act of saving data to a storage location, usually the hard drive: *the recovery feature enables you to retrieve most of the edits you made since the last save.* ▷Middle English: from Old French *sauver*, from late Latin *salvare*, from Latin *salvus* 'safe.' The noun dates from the late 19th cent. **—sav·a·ble** (also **save·a·ble**) *adj.*
▸***PHRASES*** □ **save one's breath** [often in *imperative*] not bother to say something because it is pointless. □ **save the day** find or provide a solution to a difficulty or disaster. □ **save (someone's) face** see **FACE.** □ **save someone's life** prevent someone's dying by taking specific action. ▪ (**cannot do something to save one's life**) be completely incompetent at doing something: *Adrian couldn't draw to save his life.* □ **save someone's skin** (or **neck** or **hide** or **bacon**) rescue someone from danger or difficulty. □ **save someone the trouble** (or **bother**) avoid involving someone in useless or pointless effort: *write it down and* **save yourself the trouble of** *remembering.*

save[2] ▸*prep.* & *conj. formal* or *poetic/literary* except; other than: *no one needed to know save herself* | *the kitchen was empty* **save for** *Boris.* ▷Middle English: from Old French *sauf, sauve*, from Latin *salvo, salva* (ablative singular of *salvus* 'safe'), used in phrases such as *salvo jure, salva innocentia* 'with no violation of right or innocence.'

sav·er /ˈsāvər/ ▸*n.* **1** a person who regularly saves money through a bank or recognized scheme. **2** [in *combination*] an object, action, or process that prevents a particular kind of resource from being used up or expended: *a great space-saver.*

sav·in /ˈsavin/ ▸*n.* **1** a bushy Eurasian juniper that typically has horizontally spreading branches. • *Juniperus sabina*, family Cupressaceae. ▪ an extract obtained from this plant, formerly used as an abortifacient. **2** another term for **EASTERN RED CEDAR** (see **RED CEDAR**). ▷Old English, from Old French *savine*, from Latin *sabina (herba)* 'Sabine (herb).'

sav·ing /ˈsāviNG/ ▸*n.* **1** an economy of or reduction in money, time, or another resource: *this resulted in a considerable* **saving in** *development costs.* **2** (usu. **one's savings**) the money one has saved, esp. through a bank or official scheme: *the agents were cheating them out of their* **life savings.** **3** *Law* a reservation; an exception.
▸*adj.* [in *combination*] preventing waste of a particular resource: *an energy-saving light bulb.*
▸*prep.* **1** with the exception of; except. **2** *archaic* with due respect to. ▷Middle English: from **SAVE**[1]; the preposition probably from **SAVE**[2], on the pattern of *touching.*

USAGE Use **savings** in the modifying position *(savings bank, savings bond)* and when referring to money saved in a bank: *your* **savings** *are fully insured.* When speaking of an act of saving, as when one obtains a discount on a purchase, the preferred form is **saving:** *with this coupon you will receive a* **saving** *of $3* (not a **savings** *of $3*).

sav·ing grace ▸*n.* [*mass noun*] the redeeming grace of God. ▪ a redeeming quality or characteristic.

sav·ings ac·count ▸*n.* a bank account that earns interest.

sav·ings and loan (also **sav·ings and loan as·so·ci·a·tion**) ▸*n.* an institution that accepts savings at interest and lends money to savers chiefly for home mortgage loans and may offer checking accounts and other services.

sav·ings bank ▸*n.* a financial institution that receives savings accounts and pays interest to depositors.

sav·ings bond ▸*n.* a bond issued by the government and sold to the general public.

sav·ior /ˈsāvyər/ (*Brit.* **sav·iour**) ▸*n.* a person who saves someone or something (esp. a country or cause) from danger, and who is regarded with the veneration of a religious figure. ▪ (**the/our Savior**) (in Christianity) God or Jesus Christ as the redeemer of sin and saver of souls. ▷Middle English: from Old French *sauveour*, from ecclesiastical Latin *salvator* (translating Greek *sōtēr*), from late Latin *salvare* 'to save.'

sav·oir faire /ˌsavwär ˈfe(ə)r/ (also **sav·oir-faire**) ▸*n.* the ability to act or speak appropriately in social situations. ▷early 19th cent.: French, literally 'know how to do.'

Sav·o·na·ro·la /ˌsavənəˈrōlə; səˌvänə-/, Girolamo (1452–98), Italian preacher and religious reformer. A Dominican monk and strict ascetic, he was popular for his passionate preaching against immorality and corruption. Although he became virtual ruler of Florence (1494–95), he was excommunicated in 1497 and later executed as a heretic.

Sa·vonne·rie car·pet /ˈsavənrē/ ▶*n.* a hand-knotted pile carpet, originally made in 17th-century Paris. ▷late 19th cent.: French *savonnerie,* literally 'soap factory,' referring to the original building on the site, converted to carpet manufacture.

sa·vor /ˈsāvər/ (*Brit.* **sa·vour**) ▶*v.* **1** [*trans.*] taste (good food or drink) and enjoy it completely: *gourmets will want to savor our game specialties.* ■ *figurative* enjoy or appreciate (something pleasant) completely, esp. by dwelling on it: *I wanted to savor every moment.* **2** [*intrans.*] (**savor of**) have a suggestion or trace of (something, esp. something bad): *their genuflections savored of superstition and popery.*
▶*n.* a characteristic taste, flavor, or smell, esp. a pleasant one: *the subtle savor of wood smoke.* ■ a suggestion or trace, esp. of something bad. ▷Middle English: from Old French, from Latin *sapor,* from *sapere* 'to taste.' —**sa·vor·less** *adj.*

sa·vor·y[1] /ˈsāv(ə)rē/ ▶*n.* an aromatic plant of the mint family, used as a culinary herb. • Genus *Satureja,* family Labiatae: several species, in particular the annual **summer savory** (*S. hortensis*) and the coarser flavored perennial **winter savory** (*S. montana*). ▷Middle English: perhaps from Old English *sætherie,* or via Old French, from Latin *satureia.*

sa·vor·y[2] (*Brit.* **sa·vour·y**) ▶*adj.* **1** (of food) belonging to the category that is salty or spicy rather than sweet. **2** [usu. with *negative*] morally wholesome or acceptable: *everyone knew it was a front for less savory operations.*
▶*n.* (*pl.* **-vor·ies**) *chiefly Brit.* a savory dish, esp. a snack or an appetizer. ▷Middle English (in the sense 'pleasing to the sense of taste or smell'): from Old French *savoure* 'tasty, fragrant,' based on Latin *sapor* 'taste.' —**sa·vor·i·ly** /-rəlē/ *adv.* —**sa·vor·i·ness** *n.*

Sa·voy /səˈvoi/ an area of southeastern France that borders on northwestern Italy, a former duchy ruled by the counts of Savoy from the 11th century. —**Sa·voy·ard** /səˈvoiərd; ˌsavoiˈärd; -vwäˈyär/ *adj.* & *n.*

sa·voy /səˈvoi/ (also **sa·voy cab·bage**) ▶*n.* a cabbage of a hardy variety with densely wrinkled leaves. ▷late 16th cent.: from **SAVOY**.

Sa·vu Sea /ˈsävoo/ a part of the Indian Ocean that is surrounded by the islands of Sumba, Flores, and Timor.

sav·vy /ˈsavē/ (also **sav·vi·ness**) *informal* ▶*n.* shrewdness and practical knowledge, esp. in politics or business: *the financiers lacked the necessary political savvy.*
▶*v.* (**-vies, -vied**) [with *clause*] know or understand: *Charley would savvy what to do about such a girl* | [*intrans.*] *I've been told, but I want to make sure. Savvy?*
▶*adj.* (**-vi·er, -vi·est**) shrewd and knowledgeable in the realities of life. ▷late 18th cent.: originally black and pidgin English imitating Spanish *sabe usted* 'you know.'

saw[1] /sô/ ▶*n.* a hand tool for cutting wood or other materials, typically with a long, thin serrated steel blade and operated using a backward and forward movement. ■ a mechanical power-driven tool for cutting, typically with a toothed rotating disk or moving band.
▶*v.* (*past part.* **sawed** or **sawn** /sôn/) [*trans.*] cut (something, esp. wood or a tree) using a saw: *the top of each post is **sawed off** at railing height* | [*intrans.*] *thieves escaped after **sawing through** iron bars on a basement window* | [as *adj.*, in *combination*] (**-sawn**) *rough-sawn planks.* ■ make or form (something) using a saw: *the seats are sawed from well-seasoned oak planks.* ■ cut (something) as if with a saw, esp. roughly or so as to leave rough or unfinished edges: *the woman who **sawed off** all my lovely hair.* ■ [*intrans.*] make rapid sawlike motions in cutting something or in playing a stringed instrument: *he was **sawing away** at the loaf of bread.* ▷Old English *saga,* of Germanic origin; related to Dutch *zaag.* —**saw·like** /-ˌlīk/ *adj.*

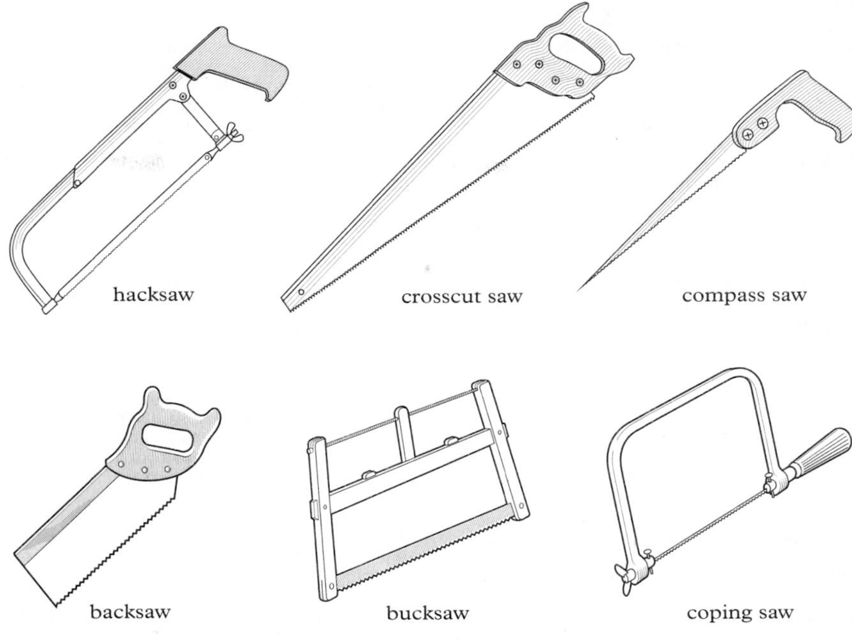

saw[1]

saw[2] ▶ past of **SEE**[1].

saw[3] ▶*n.* a proverb or maxim. ▷Old English *sagu* 'a saying, speech,' of Germanic origin; related to German *Sage,* also to **SAY** and **SAGA**.

Sa·watch Range /səˈwäch/ a range of the Rocky Mountains in central Colorado. Mount Elbert, at 14,433 feet (4,399 m), is the highest peak in the state and in the entire Rocky Mountain system.

saw·bill /ˈsôˌbil/ ▶*n.* another term for **MERGANSER**.

saw·bones /ˈsôˌbōnz/ ▶*n.* (*pl.* same) *informal, humorous* a doctor, esp. a surgeon.

saw·buck /ˈsôˌbək/ ▶*n.* **1** a sawhorse. **2** *informal* a $10 bill. [by association of the X-shaped ends of a sawhorse with the Roman numeral X (= 10).] ▷mid 19th cent.: from Dutch *zaagbok,* from *zaag* 'saw' + *bok* 'vaulting horse.'

saw·dust /ˈsôˌdəst/ ▶*n.* powdery particles of wood produced by sawing.

saw·dust trail (also **Saw·dust Trail**) ▶*n. informal* the itinerary of a traveling gospel preacher: *a retired clergyman who spent his working days as an evangelist on what was left of the old Sawdust Trail.* ■ the process of an erring individual's rehabilitation through repentance: *the president has been on the sawdust trail recently, apologizing hither and yon.*

sawed-off /ˈsôd ˈôf/ (also *chiefly Brit.* **sawn-off**) ▶*adj.* [*attrib.*] (of a gun) having a specially shortened barrel to make handling easier and to give a wider field of fire. ■ *informal* (of an item of clothing) having been cut short. ■ *informal* (of a person) short.
▶*n.* a sawed-off shotgun.

saw·fish /ˈsôˌfish/ ▶*n.* (*pl.* same or **-fish·es**) a large tropical mainly marine fish related to the rays, with an elongated flattened snout that bears large blunt teeth along each side. • Family Pristidae: two genera, in particular *Pristis,* and several species, including the **common sawfish** (*P. pectinata*).

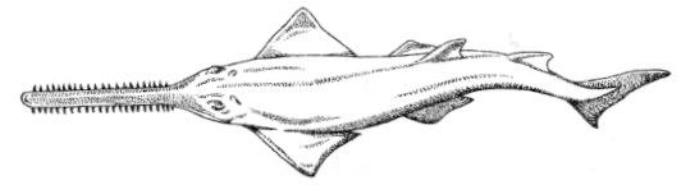
common sawfish

saw·fly /ˈsôˌflī/ ▶*n.* (*pl.* **-flies**) an insect related to the wasps, with a sawlike egg-laying tube used to cut into plant tissue before depositing the eggs. The larvae resemble caterpillars and can be serious pests of crops and foliage. • Suborder Symphyta, order Hymenoptera: many families.

saw·grass /ˈsôˌgras/ (also **saw grass**) ▶*n.* a sedge with spiny-edged leaves. • *Cladium,* family Cyperaceae: two species, in particular the North American *C. jamaicensis,* which is a dominant plant in the Florida everglades.

saw·horse /ˈsôˌhôrs/ ▶*n.* a frame or trestle that supports wood for sawing.

saw·log /ˈsôˌlôg; -ˌläg/ (also **saw log**) ▶*n.* a felled tree trunk suitable for cutting up into timber.

saw·mill /ˈsôˌmil/ ▶*n.* a factory in which logs are sawed into lumber by machine.

sawn /sôn/ ▶ past participle of **SAW**[1].

sawn-off ▶*adj.* & *n. chiefly Brit.* another term for **SAWED-OFF**.

saw pal·met·to ▶*n.* a small palm with fan-shaped leaves that have sharply toothed stalks, native to the southeastern U.S. • Several species in the family Palmae, in particular *Serenoa repens.*

saw pit ▶*n. historical* the pit in which the lower of two men working a pit saw stands.

saw set ▶*n.* a tool for giving the teeth of a saw alternating sideways inclinations.

saw·tooth /ˈsôˌto͞oth/ (also **saw·toothed** or **saw-tooth** or **saw-toothed** /-ˌto͞otht/) ▶*adj.* shaped like the teeth of a saw with alternate steep and gentle slopes. ■ *Physics* (of a waveform) showing a slow linear rise and rapid linear fall or vice versa.

Saw·tooth Range /ˈsôto͞oth/ a range of the northern Rocky Mountains in south central Idaho, noted for its jagged peaks.

saw-whet owl ▶*n.* a small North and Central American owl with a call that resembles the sound of a saw blade being sharpened. • Genus *Aegolius,* family Strigidae: two species, in particular the North American *A. acadicus.*

saw·yer /ˈsôyər/ ▶*n.* **1** a person who saws timber for a living. **2** an uprooted tree floating in a river but held fast at one end. [with allusion to the trapped log's movement up and down.] **3** a large longhorn beetle whose larvae bore tunnels in the wood of injured or recently felled trees, producing an audible chewing sound. • Genus *Monochamus,* family Cerambycidae. ▷Middle English (earlier as *sawer*): from the noun **SAW**[1] + **-YER**.

sax /saks/ ▶*n. informal* a saxophone. ▷early 20th cent.: abbreviation. —**sax·ist** /-ist/ *n.*

Sax. ▶*abbr.* ■ Saxon or Saxony.

sax·a·tile /ˈsaksəˌtīl/ ▶*adj.* living or growing on or among rocks. ▷mid 17th cent.: from French *saxatile* or Latin *saxatilis,* from *saxum* 'rock.'

Saxe-Co·burg-Go·tha /ˈsaks ˈkōbərg ˈgōthə/ the name of the British royal house 1901–17. The name dates from the accession of Edward VII, whose father, Prince Albert, consort of Queen Victoria, was a prince of the German duchy of Saxe-Coburg and Gotha.

sax·horn /ˈsaksˌhôrn/ ▶*n.* a member of a family of brass instruments with valves and a funnel-shaped mouthpiece, used mainly in military and brass bands. ▷from the name of Charles J. *Sax* (1791–1865) and his son Antoine-Joseph "Adolphe" *Sax* (1814–94), Belgian instrument-makers, + **HORN**.

sax·ic·o·line /sakˈsikəˌlīn; -lin/ (also **sax·ic·o·lous** /-ˈsikələs/) ▶*adj.* another term for **SAXATILE**. ▷late 19th cent.: from modern Latin *saxicolus* (from *saxum* 'rock' + *colere* 'inhabit') + **-INE**[1].

sax·i·frage /ˈsaksəˌfrij; -ˌfrāj/ ▶*n.* a low-growing plant of poor soils, bearing small white, yellow, or red flowers and forming rosettes of succulent leaves or hummocks of mossy leaves. Many are grown as alpines in rock gardens. • Genus *Saxifraga,* family Saxifragaceae. ▷late Middle English: from Old

French *saxifrage* or late Latin *saxifraga (herba)*, from Latin *saxum* 'rock' + *frangere* 'break.'

Sax·on /'saksən/ ▸*n.* **1** a member of a Germanic people that inhabited parts of central and northern Germany from Roman times, many of whom conquered and settled in southern England in the 5th–6th centuries. ■ a native of modern Saxony in Germany. **2** the language of the Saxons, in particular: ■ (**Old Saxon**) the West Germanic language of the ancient Saxons. ■ another term for OLD ENGLISH. ■ the Low German dialect of modern Saxony.
▸*adj.* **1** of or relating to the Anglo-Saxons, their language (Old English), or their period of dominance in England (5th–11th centuries). ■ relating to or denoting the style of early Romanesque architecture preceding the Norman in England. **2** of or relating to Saxony or the continental Saxons or their language. ▷Middle English: from Old French, from late Latin *Saxones* (plural), of West Germanic origin; related to Old English *Seaxan, Seaxe* (plural), perhaps from the base of *sax* 'small ax,' from Old English *seax* 'knife,' of Germanic origin, from an Indo-European root meaning 'cut.' —**Sax·on·ize** /-ˌnīz/ *v.*

Sax·o·ny /'saksənē/ a large region and former kingdom in Germany, including the modern states of Saxony, Saxony-Anhalt, and Lower Saxony. German name SACHSEN. ■ a state in eastern Germany, on the upper reaches of the Elbe River; capital, Dresden. ▷from late Latin *Saxonia*, from Latin *Saxo, Saxon-* (see SAXON).

sax·o·ny /'saksənē/ ▸*n.* a fine kind of wool. ■ a fine-quality cloth made from this kind of wool, chiefly used for making coats. ▷mid 19th cent.: from SAXONY.

Sax·o·ny-An·halt /'änhält/ a state in Germany, on the plains of the Elbe and Saale rivers; capital, Magdeburg. It corresponds to the former duchy of Anhalt and the central part of the former kingdom of Saxony. German name SACHSEN-ANHALT.

sax·o·phone /'saksəˌfōn/ ▸*n.* a member of a family of metal wind instruments with a single-reed mouthpiece, used esp. in jazz and dance music. ▷from the name of Adolphe *Sax* (see SAXHORN) + -PHONE. —**sax·o·phon·ic** /ˌsaksə'fänik/ *adj.* —**sax·o·phon·ist** /-ˌfōnist/ *n.*

saxophone

say /sā/ ▸*v.* (**says** /sez/; *past* and *past part.* **said** /sed/) **1** [*reporting verb*] utter words so as to convey information, an opinion, a feeling or intention, or an instruction: [with *direct speech*] *"Thank you," he said* | [with *clause*] *he said the fund stood at $100,000* | [*trans.*] *our parents wouldn't believe a word we said* | [with *infinitive*] *he said to come early.* ■ (of a text or a symbolic representation) convey specified information or instructions: [with *clause*] *the law says such behavior is an offense.* ■ [*trans.*] enable a listener or reader to learn or understand something by conveying or revealing (information or ideas): *I don't want to say too much* | *figurative the movie's title* **says it all**. ■ [*trans.*] (of a clock or watch) indicate (a specified time): *the clock says ten past two.* ■ (**be said**) be asserted or reported (often used to avoid committing the speaker or writer to the truth of the assertion): [with *infinitive*] *they were said to be training freedom fighters* | [with *clause*] *it is said that she lived to be over a hundred.* ■ [*trans.*] (**say something for**) present a consideration in favor of or excusing (someone or something): *all I can say for him is that he's a better writer than some.* ■ [*trans.*] utter the whole of (a speech or other set of words, typically one learned in advance): *we say the Pledge of Allegiance each morning.* **2** [with *clause*] assume something in order to work out what its consequences would be; make a hypothesis: *let's say we pay five thousand dollars in the first year.* ■ used parenthetically to indicate that something is being suggested as possible or likely but not certain: *the form might include, say, a dozen questions.*
▸*exclam. informal* used to express surprise or to draw attention to a remark or question: *say, did you notice any blood?*
▸*n.* [in *sing.*] an opportunity for stating one's opinion or feelings: *the voters are entitled to* **have their say** *on the treaty.* ■ an opportunity to influence developments and policy: *the assessor will* **have a say** *in how the money is spent* | *the households concerned would still* **have** *some* **say** *in what happened.* ▷Old English *secgan*, of Germanic origin; related to Dutch *zeggen* and German *sagen*. —**say·a·ble** *adj.* —**say·er** *n.* [usu. in *combination*] *naysayers*.
▸PHRASES □ **go without saying** be obvious: *it goes without saying that teachers must be selected with care.* [translating French *(cela) va sans dire.*] □ **have something to say for oneself** contribute to a conversation or discussion, esp. as an explanation for one's behavior or actions: *haven't you anything to say for yourself?* □ **how say you?** *Law* how do you find? (addressed to the jury when requesting its verdict). □ **I** (or **he**, **she**, etc.) **cannot** (or **could not**) **say** I (or he, she, etc.) do not know. □ **I'll say** *informal* used to express emphatic agreement: *"That was a good landing." "I'll say!"* □ **I must** (or **have to**) **say** I cannot refrain from saying (used to emphasize an opinion): *you have a nerve, I must say!* □ **I say!** *Brit., dated* used to express surprise or to draw attention to a remark: *I say, that's a bit much!* □ **I wouldn't say no** *informal* used to indicate that one would like something. □ **not to say** used to introduce a stronger alternative or addition to something already said: *it is easy to become sensitive, not to say paranoid.* □ **say no more** *informal* used to indicate that one understands what someone is trying to imply. □ **says you!** *informal* used in speech to express disagreement or disbelief: *"He's guilty." "Says you! I think he's innocent."* □ **say when** *informal* said when helping someone to food or drink to instruct them to indicate when they have enough. □ **say the word** give permission or instructions to do something. □ **that is to say** used to introduce a clarification, interpretation, or correction of something already said. □ **there is no saying** it is impossible to know. □ **they say** it is rumored. □ **to say nothing of** another way of saying NOT TO MENTION (see MENTION). □ **to say the least** see LEAST. □ **what do** (or **would**) **you say** used to make a suggestion or offer: *what do you say to a glass of wine?* □ **when all is said and done** when everything is taken into account (used to indicate that one is making a generalized judgment about a situation. □ **you can say that again!** *informal* used in spoken English to express emphatic agreement. □ **you don't say!** *informal* used to express amazement or disbelief. □ **you said it!** *informal* used to express the feeling that someone's words are true or appropriate.

Say·ers[1] /'sā-ərz; se(ə)rz/, Dorothy L. (1893–1957), English novelist, translator, essayist, and playwright; full name *Dorothy Leigh Sayers.* She is chiefly known for her detective novels that feature amateur detective Lord Peter Wimsey and include *Murder Must Advertise* (1933) and*The Nine Tailors* (1934). She translated the medieval French *La Chanson de Roland* and Dante's *La Divina Commedia.* Her plays include *The Devil to Pay* (1939).

Say·ers[2], Gale (Eugene) (1943–), U.S. football player. Named rookie of the year in 1965, he went on to break touchdown records during his playing career 1965–71, cut short by knee injuries, with the Chicago Bears. Football Hall of Fame (1977).

Say Hey Kid see MAYS.

say·ing /'sāiNG/ ▸*n.* a short, pithy expression that generally contains advice or wisdom. ■ (**sayings**) a collection of such expressions identified with a particular person, esp. a political or religious leader.
▸PHRASE □ **as** (or **so**) **the saying goes** used to introduce or append an expression, drawing attention to its status as a saying or as not part of one's normal language: *I am, as the saying goes, burned out.*

THE RIGHT WORD **adage, aphorism, apothegm, epigram, epigraph, maxim, proverb, saying**

"Once burned, twice shy" is an old **saying** about learning from your mistakes. In fact, *sayings*—a term used to describe any current or habitual expression of wisdom or truth—are a dime a dozen.

Proverbs—sayings that are well known and often repeated, usually expressing metaphorically a truth based on common sense or practical experience—are just as plentiful (*her favorite proverb was "A stitch in time saves nine"*).

An **adage** is a time-honored and widely known proverb, such as "Where's there's smoke, there's fire."

A **maxim** offers a rule of conduct or action in the form of a proverb, such as "Neither a borrower nor a lender be."

Epigram and **epigraph** are often confused, but their meanings are quite separate. An *epigram* is a terse, witty, or satirical statement that often relies on a paradox for its effect (*Oscar Wilde's well-known epigram that "The only way to get rid of temptation is to yield to it"*). An *epigraph*, on the other hand, is a brief quotation used to introduce a piece of writing (*he used a quote from T. S. Eliot as the epigraph to his new novel*).

An **aphorism** requires a little more thought than an *epigram*, since it aims to be profound rather than witty (*as one of Solomon's aphorisms warn, "Better is a living dog than a dead lion"*).

An **apothegm** is a pointed and often startling aphorism, such as Samuel Johnson's remark that "Patriotism is the last refuge of a scoundrel."

sa·yo·na·ra /ˌsīə'närə/ ▸*exclam. informal* goodbye. ▷Japanese.

Sayre·ville /'se(ə)rvil/ an industrial and residential borough in eastern New Jersey; pop. 34,986.

Say's law /säz/ *Economics* a law stating that supply creates its own demand. ▷1930s: named after Jean Baptiste *Say* (1767–1832), French economist.

say-so ▸*n.* [in *sing.*] *informal* the power or act of deciding or allowing something: *no new employees come into the organization* **without his say-so**. ■ (usu. **on someone's say-so**) a person's arbitrary or unauthorized assertion or instruction: *I don't stop on the say-so of anybody's assistant.*

say·yid /'säyid; 'sāyid/ ▸*n.* a Muslim claiming descent from Muhammad through Husayn, the prophet's younger grandson. ■ a respectful Muslim form of address. ▷Arabic, literally 'lord, prince.'

saz /säz; saz/ ▸*n.* a long-necked stringed instrument of the lute family, originating in the Ottoman Empire. ▷late 19th cent.: from Turkish, from Persian *sāz* 'musical instrument.'

SB ▸*abbr.* ■ Bachelor of Science. [Latin *Scientiae Baccalaureus.*] ■ simultaneous broadcast. ■ South Britain (England and Wales).

Sb ▸*symbol* the chemical element antimony. ▷from Latin *stibium*.

sb. ▸*abbr.* substantive.

s.b. ▸*abbr. Baseball* stolen base; stolen bases.

SBA ▸*abbr.* Small Business Administration.

S-Bahn /'es ˌbän/ ▸*n.* (in some German cities) a fast urban railroad line or system. ▷German, abbreviation of *(Stadt) Schnellbahn* '(urban) fast railroad.'

SbE ▸*abbr.* south by east.

SBS ▸*abbr.* Special Boat Service.

SbW ▸*abbr.* south by west.

SC ▸*abbr.* ■ South Carolina (in official postal use). ■ (in the UK) special constable.

Sc ▸*symbol* the chemical element scandium.

sc. ▸*abbr.* that is to say (used to introduce a word to be supplied or an explanation of an ambiguity). ▷from SCILICET.

s.c. ▸*abbr.* small capitals (used as an instruction for a typesetter).

scab /skab/ ▸*n.* **1** a dry, rough protective crust that forms over a cut or wound during healing. ■ mange or a similar skin disease in animals. ■ [usu. with *adj.*] any of a number of fungal diseases of plants in which rough patches develop, esp. on apples and potatoes. **2** *figurative* or *informal* a person or thing regarded with dislike and disgust. ■ *derogatory* a person who refuses to strike or to join a labor union or who takes over the job responsibilities of a striking worker.
▸*v.* (**scabbed**, **scab·bing**) [*intrans.*] **1** [usu. as *adj.*] (**scabbed**) become encrusted or covered with a scab or scabs: *she rested her scabbed fingers on his arm.* **2** act or work as a scab. ▷Middle English (as a noun): from Old Norse *skabb*; related to dialect *shab* (compare with SHABBY). The sense 'contemptible person' (dating from the late 16th cent.) was probably influenced by Middle Dutch *schabbe* 'slut.' —**scab·like** /-ˌlīk/ *adj.*

scab·bard /'skabərd/ ▸*n.* a sheath for the blade of a sword or dagger, typically made of leather or metal. ■ a sheath for a gun or other weapon or tool. ▷Middle English: from Anglo-Norman French *escalberc*, from a Germanic compound of words meaning 'cut' (related to SHEAR) and 'protect' (related to the second element of HAUBERK).

scab·by /'skabē/ ▸*adj.* (**-bi·er**, **-bi·est**) **1** covered in scabs. **2** *informal* loathsome; despicable. —**scab·bi·ness** *n.*

sca·bies /'skābēz/ ▸*n.* a contagious skin disease marked by itching and small raised red spots, caused by the itch mite. ▷late Middle English (denoting various skin diseases): from Latin, from *scabere* 'to scratch.' The current sense dates from the early 19th cent.

sca·bi·ous /'skābēəs/ ▸*n.* a plant of the teasel family, with pink, white, or (most commonly) blue

pincushion-shaped flowers. • *Scabiosa*, *Knautia*, and other genera, family Dipsacaceae: several species.
▸*adj.* affected with mange; scabby. ▷late Middle English: based on Latin *scabiosus* 'rough, scabby'; the noun is from medieval Latin *scabiosa (herba)* 'rough, scabby (plant),' formerly regarded as a cure for skin disease (see **SCABIES**).

scab·lands /'skab,landz/ ▸*plural n. Geology* flat elevated land deeply scarred by channels of glacial or fluvioglacial origin and with poor soil and little vegetation, esp. in the Columbia Plateau of Washington State.

scab·rous /'skabrəs/ ▸*adj.* **1** rough and covered with, or as if with, scabs. **2** indecent; salacious: *scabrous publications.* ▷late 16th cent. (first used to describe an author's style as 'harsh, unmusical, unpolished'): from French *scabreux* or late Latin *scabrosus*, from Latin *scaber* 'rough.' **—scab·rous·ly** *adv.* **—scab·rous·ness** *n.*

scad /skad/ ▸*n.* another term for **JACK**[1] (sense 11) or **HORSE MACKEREL.** ▷early 17th cent.: of unknown origin.

scads /skadz/ ▸*plural n. informal* a large number or quantity: *they raised* **scads of** *children* | [in *sing.*] *he's installed a* **scad of** *microprocessors.* ▷mid 19th cent.: of unknown origin.

scaf·fold /'skafəld; -,fōld/ ▸*n.* **1** a raised wooden platform used formerly for the public execution of criminals. **2** a structure made using scaffolding.
▸*v.* [*trans.*] attach scaffolding to (a building): [as *adj.*] (**scaffolded**) *the soot-black scaffolded structures.* ▷Middle English (denoting a temporary platform from which to repair or erect a building): from Anglo-Norman French, from Old French *(e)schaffaut*, from the base of **CATAFALQUE.** **—scaf·fold·er** *n.*

scaf·fold·ing /'skafəldiNG; -,fōl-/ ▸*n.* a temporary structure on the outside of a building, made usually of wooden planks and metal poles, used by workers while building, repairing, or cleaning the building. ■ the materials used in such a structure.

scag /skag/ ▸*n.* **1** *informal* an unkempt or despicable person; sleazeball. **2** variant spelling of **SKAG.**

scagl·io·la /skal'yōlə/ ▸*n.* imitation marble or other stone, made of plaster mixed with glue and dyes, which is then painted or polished. ▷mid 18th cent.: from Italian *scagliuola*, diminutive of *scaglia* 'a scale.'

scal·a·ble /'skāləbəl/ ▸*adj.* **1** able to be scaled or climbed. **2** able to be changed in size or scale: *scalable fonts.* ■ (of a computing process) able to be used or produced in a range of capabilities: *it is scalable across a range of systems.* **3** *technical* able to be measured or graded according to a scale. **—scal·a·bil·i·ty** /,skālə'bilitē/ *n.*

sca·la me·dia /'skālə 'mēdēə/ ▸*n.* (*pl.* **sca·lae me·di·ae** /'skālē 'mēdē-ē/) *Anatomy* the central duct of the cochlea in the inner ear, containing the sensory cells and separated from the scala tympani and scala vestibuli by membranes. ▷late 19th cent.: from Latin, literally 'middle ladder.'

sca·lar /'skālər/ *Mathematics Physics* ▸*adj. Mathematics & Physics* (of a quantity) having only magnitude, not direction.
▸*n. Mathematics & Physics* a scalar quantity. Compare with **VECTOR** (sense 1). ▷mid 17th cent.: from Latin *scalaris*, from *scala* 'ladder' (see **SCALE**[3]).

sca·lar field ▸*n. Mathematics* a function of a space whose value at each point is a scalar quantity.

sca·lar·i·form /skə'le(ə)rə,fôrm/ ▸*adj. Botany* (esp. of the walls of water-conducting cells) having thickened bands arranged like the rungs of a ladder. ▷mid 19th cent.: from Latin *scalaris* 'of a ladder' + **-IFORM.**

sca·lar prod·uct ▸*n.* another term for **INNER PRODUCT.**

sca·la tym·pa·ni /'skālə 'timpənē/ ▸*n.* (*pl.* **sca·lae tym·pa·ni** /'skālē/) *Anatomy* the lower bony passage of the cochlea. ▷early 18th cent.: from Latin, literally 'ladder of the tympanum.'

sca·la ves·tib·u·li /'skālə ve'stibyəlē/ ▸*n.* (*pl.* **sca·lae ves·tib·u·li** /'skālē/) *Anatomy* the upper bony passage of the cochlea. ▷early 18th cent.: from Latin, literally 'ladder of the vestibule.'

scal·a·wag /'skalə,wag/ (also **scal·ly·wag** /'skalē-/) ▸*n.* *informal* a person who behaves badly but in an amusingly mischievous rather than harmful way; a rascal. ■ *historical* a white Southerner who collaborated with northern Republicans during Reconstruction, often for personal profit. The term was used derisively by white Southern Democrats who opposed Reconstruction legislation. ▷mid 19th cent.: of unknown origin.

scald[1] /skôld/ ▸*v.* [*trans.*] injure with very hot liquid or steam: *the tea scalded his tongue.* See note at **BURN.** ■ heat (milk or other liquid) to near boiling point. ■ immerse (something) briefly in boiling water for various purposes, such as to facilitate the removal of skin from fruit or to preserve meat. ■ cause to feel a searing sensation like that of boiling water on skin: *hot tears scalding her eyes.*
▸*n.* a burn or other injury caused by hot liquid or steam. ■ any of a number of plant diseases that produce a similar effect to that of scalding, esp. a disease of fruit marked by browning and caused by excessive sunlight, bad storage conditions, or atmospheric pollution. See also **SUNSCALD.** ▷Middle English (as a verb): from Anglo-Norman French *escalder*, from late Latin *excaldare*, from Latin *ex-* 'thoroughly' + *calidus* 'hot.' The noun dates from the early 17th cent.

scald[2] ▸*n.* variant spelling of **SKALD.**

scald·ing /'skôldiNG/ ▸*adj.* very hot; burning: *she took a sip of scalding tea* | [as *submodifier*] *the water was scalding hot.* ■ *figurative* intense and painful or distressing: *a scalding tirade of abuse.*

scale[1] /skāl/ ▸*n.* **1** each of the small, thin horny or bony plates protecting the skin of fish and reptiles, typically overlapping one another. **2** something resembling a fish scale in appearance or function, in particular: ■ a thick dry flake of skin. ■ a rudimentary leaf, feather, or bract. ■ each of numerous microscopic tilelike structures covering the wings of butterflies and moths. **3** a flaky deposit, in particular: ■ a white deposit formed in a kettle, boiler, etc., by the evaporation of water containing lime. ■ tartar formed on teeth. ■ a coating of oxide formed on heated metal.
▸*v.* **1** [*trans.*] remove scale or scales from: *he scales the fish and removes the innards.* ■ remove tartar from (teeth) by scraping them. **2** [*intrans.*] [often as *n.*] (**scaling**) (esp. of the skin) form scales: *moisturizers can ease off drying and scaling.* ■ come off in scales or thin pieces; flake off: *the paint was scaling from the brick walls.* ▷Middle English: shortening of Old French *escale*, from the Germanic base of **SCALE**[2]. **—scaled** /skāld/ *adj.* [often in *combination*] *a rough-scaled fish.* **—scale·less** /'skāl(l)is/ *adj.* **—scal·er** *n.*

scale[2] ▸*n.* (usu. **scales**) an instrument for weighing. Scales were originally simple balances (**pairs of scales**) but are now usually devices with an internal weighing mechanism housed under a platform on which the thing to be weighed is placed, with a gauge or electronic display showing the weight. ■ (also **scale·pan**) either of the dishes on a simple balance. ■ (**the Scales**) the zodiacal sign or constellation Libra.
▸*v.* [*trans.*] weigh a specified weight: *some men scaled less than ninety pounds.* ▷Middle English (in the sense 'drinking cup,' surviving in South African English): from Old Norse *skál* 'bowl,' of Germanic origin; related to Dutch *schaal*, German *Schale* 'bowl,' also to English dialect *shale* 'dish.' Compare with **SKOAL.**
▸*PHRASES* □ **tip the scales** see **TIP**[2]. □ **tip the scales at** see **TIP**[2].

scale[3] ▸*n.* **1** a graduated range of values forming a standard system for measuring or grading something: *company employees have hit the top of their pay scales* | *figurative two men at opposite ends of the* **social scale.** ■ a series of marks at regular intervals in a line used in measuring something: *the mean delivery time is plotted against a scale on the right.* ■ a device having such a series of marks: *she read the exact distance off a scale.* ■ a rule determining the distances between such marks: *the vertical axis is given on a logarithmic scale.* **2** [in *sing.*] the relative size or extent of something: *no one foresaw the scale of the disaster* | *everything in the house is* **on a grand scale.** ■ [often as *adj.*] a ratio of size in a map, model, drawing, or plan: *a one-fifth scale model of a seven-story building* | *an Ordnance Survey map* **on a scale of** *1:2500.* ■ (in full **scale of notation**) *Mathematics* a system of numerical notation in which the value of a digit depends upon its position in the number, successive positions representing successive powers of a fixed base: *the conversion of the number to the binary scale.* ■ *Photography* the range of exposures over which a photographic material will give an acceptable variation in density. **3** *Music* an arrangement of the notes in any system of music in ascending or descending order of pitch: *the scale of C major.*
▸*v.* [*trans.*] **1** climb up or over (something high and steep): *thieves scaled an 8-foot fence.* **2** represent in proportional dimensions; reduce or increase in size according to a common scale: [as *adj.*] (**scaled**) *scaled plans of the house.* ■ [*intrans.*] (of a quantity or property) be variable according to a particular scale. **3** estimate the amount of timber that will be produced from (a log or uncut tree).
▸*phrasal v.* □ **scale something back** reduce something in size, number, or extent, esp. by a constant proportion across the board: *in the short term, even scaling back defense costs money.* □ **scale something down** (or **scale down**) reduce something (or be reduced) in size, number or extent, esp. by a constant proportion across the board: *manufacturing capacity has been scaled down* | *his whole income scaled down by 20 percent.* □ **scale something up** (or **scale up**) increase something (or be increased) in size or number: *one cannot suddenly scale up a laboratory procedure by a thousandfold.* ▷late Middle English: from Latin *scala* 'ladder' (the verb via Old French *escaler* or medieval Latin *scalare* 'climb'), from the base of Latin *scandere* 'to climb.' **—scal·er** *n.*
▸*PHRASES* □ **play** (or **sing** or **practice**) **scales** *Music* perform the notes of a scale as an exercise for the fingers or voice. □ **to scale** with a uniform reduction or enlargement: *it is hard to build models to scale from a drawing.* □ **in scale** (of a drawing or model) in proportion to the surroundings.

scale ar·mor ▸*n. historical* armor consisting of small overlapping plates of metal, leather, or horn.

scale in·sect ▸*n.* a small insect with a protective shieldlike scale. It spends most of its life attached by its mouth to a single plant, sometimes occurring in such large numbers that it becomes a serious pest. • Superfamily Coccoidea, suborder Homoptera: several families, in particular Coccidae.

scale leaf ▸*n. Botany* a small modified leaf, esp. a colorless membranous one, such as on a rhizome or forming part of a bulb.

sca·lene /skā'lēn/ ▸*adj.* (of a triangle) having sides unequal in length.
▸*n.* **1** (also **sca·lene mus·cle**) *Anatomy* another term for **SCALENUS.** **2** a scalene triangle. ▷mid 17th cent.: via late Latin from Greek *skalēnos* 'unequal'; related to *skolios* 'bent.'

sca·le·nus /skā'lēnəs/ ▸*n.* (*pl.* **-le·ni** /-'lēnī/) any of several muscles extending from the neck to the first and second ribs. ▷early 18th cent.: modern Latin, from late Latin *scalenus (musculus)* 'unequal (muscle)' (see **SCALENE**).

scale of no·ta·tion ▸*n.* see **SCALE**[3] (sense 2).

scale·pan /'skāl,pan/ ▸*n.* see **SCALE**[2].

scale·worm /'skāl,wərm/ (also **scale worm**) ▸*n.* a marine bristle worm with scales on the upper surface that have a protective function, and in some species are able to luminesce. • Family Aphroditidae: *Aphrodite* and other genera. See also **SEA MOUSE.**

Sca·li·a /skə'lē(y)ə/, Antonin (1936–), U.S. Supreme Court associate justice 1986– . A conservative and an advocate of judicial restraint, he served in several government posts, taught law at various universities, and served on the U.S. Circuit Court of Appeals in Washington, D.C., before being appointed to the Supreme Court by President Reagan.

scal·ing lad·der /'skāliNG/ ▸*n. historical* a ladder used for firefighting or for climbing walls in order to penetrate the defenses of a fortification.

scal·lion /'skalyən/ ▸*n.* a long-necked onion with a small bulb, in particular a shallot or green onion. • A common scallion is *Allium fistulosum*, family Liliaceae (or Alliaceae). ▷late Middle English: from Anglo-Norman French *scaloun*, based on Latin *Ascalonia (caepa)* '(onion) of *Ascalon*,' a port in ancient Palestine.

scal·lop /'skäləp; 'skal-/ ▸*n.* **1** an edible bivalve mollusk with a ribbed fan-shaped shell. Scallops swim by rapidly opening and closing the shell valves. • Family Pectinidae: *Chlamys*, *Pecten*, and other genera. ■ short for **SCALLOP SHELL.** ■ a small pan or dish shaped like a scallop shell and used for baking or serving food. **2** (usu. **scallops**) each of a series of convex rounded projections forming an ornamental edging cut in material or worked in lace or knitting in imitation of the edge of a scallop shell. **3** another term for **ESCALOPE.**
▸*v.* (**-loped, -lop·ing**) **1** [*trans.*] [usu. as *adj.*] (**scalloped**) ornament (an edge or material) with scallops: *a scalloped V-shaped neckline.* ■ cut, shape, or arrange in the form of a scallop shell: *he leaned against the scalloped seat of the limousine.* **2** [*intrans.*] [usu. as *n.*] (**scalloping**)

gather or dredge for scallops. **3** [*trans.*] bake with milk or a sauce: [as *adj.*] (**scalloped**) *scalloped potatoes.* ▷Middle English: shortening of Old French *escalope*, probably of Germanic origin. The verb dates from the mid 18th cent. **—scal·lop·er** *n.*

scal·lop shell ▶*n.* a single valve from the shell of a scallop. ■ *historical* a representation of this shell worn by a pilgrim as a souvenir of the shrine of St. James at Santiago de Compostela in Spain.

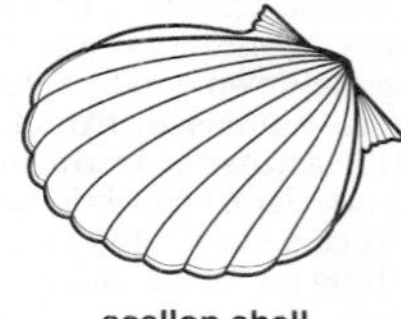

scallop shell

scal·ly·wag /ˈskalē,wag/ ▶*n.* variant spelling of SCALAWAG.

sca·lop·pi·ne /,skäləˈpēnē; ,skal-/ (also **scal·lo·pi·ni**) ▶*plural n.* (in Italian cooking) thin, boneless slices of meat, typically veal, sautéed or fried. ▷Italian, plural of *scaloppina*, diminutive of *scaloppa* 'envelope.'

scalp /skalp/ ▶*n.* the skin covering the head, excluding the face. ■ *historical* the scalp with the hair belonging to it cut or torn away from an enemy's head as a battle trophy, esp. by an American Indian.
▶*v.* [*trans.*] *historical* take the scalp of (an enemy). ■ *informal* punish severely: *if I ever heard anybody doing that, I'd scalp them.* ■ *informal* sell (a ticket) for a popular event at a price higher than the official one: *tickets were scalped for forty times their face value.* ▷Middle English (denoting the skull or cranium): probably of Scandinavian origin.

scal·pel /ˈskalpəl/ ▶*n.* a knife with a small, sharp, sometimes detachable blade, as used by a surgeon. ▷mid 18th cent.: from French, or from Latin *scalpellum*, diminutive of *scalprum* 'chisel,' from *scalpere* 'to scratch.'

scalp·er /ˈskalpər/ ▶*n.* *informal* a person who resells shares or tickets at a large or quick profit.

scalp lock (also **scalp·lock**) ▶*n.* *chiefly historical* a long lock of hair left on a shaved head, esp. as worn by a North American Indian as a challenge to enemies.

scal·y /ˈskālē/ ▶*adj.* (**scal·i·er**, **scal·i·est**) covered in scales. ■ (of skin) dry and flaking. **—scal·i·ness** *n.*

scal·y ant·eat·er ▶*n.* another term for PANGOLIN.

scalpel

scam /skam/ ▶*n.* *informal* a dishonest scheme; a fraud: [with *adj.*] *an insurance scam.*
▶*v.* (**scammed**, **scam·ming**) [*trans.*] swindle: *a guy that scams the elderly out of their savings.* ▷1960s: of unknown origin. **—scam·mer** *n.*

scam·mo·ny /ˈskamənē/ ▶*n.* a plant of the morning glory family, the dried roots of which yield a strong purgative. • Two species in the family Convolvulaceae: *Convolvulus scammonia* of Asia, and *Ipomoea orizabensis* of Mexico. ▷Old English, from Old French *escamonie* or Latin *scammonia*, from Greek *skammōnia.*

sca·mor·za /skəˈmôrtsə/ ▶*n.* a mild white Italian cheese made originally from buffalo's milk, but now chiefly from cow's milk, typically produced in a pear shape. ▷1930s: Italian, from *scamozzare*, 'cut off.'

scamp[1] /skamp/ ▶*n.* *informal* a person, esp. a child, who is mischievous in a likable or amusing way. ■ a wicked or worthless person; a rogue. ▷mid 18th cent. (denoting a highwayman): from obsolete *scamp* 'rob on the highway,' probably from Middle Dutch *schampen* 'slip away,' from Old French *eschamper* 'flee the battlefield,' from *champ* 'field.' **—scamp·ish** *adj.*

scamp[2] ▶*v.* [*trans.*] *dated* do (something) in a perfunctory or inadequate way. ▷mid 19th cent.: perhaps the same word as SCAMP[1], but associated in sense with the verb SKIMP.

scamp·er /ˈskampər/ ▶*v.* [*intrans.*] (esp. of a small animal or child) run with quick light steps, esp. through fear or excitement: *he scampered in like an overgrown puppy.*
▶*n.* [in *sing.*] an act of scampering. ▷late 17th cent. (in the sense 'run away'): probably from SCAMP[2].

scam·pi /ˈskampē/ ▶*n.* [*plural n.*] large shrimp or prawns, esp. when prepared or cooked. ■ a dish of shrimp or prawns, typically sautéed in garlic and butter and often topped with bread crumbs. ▷Italian.

scan /skan/ ▶*v.* (**scanned**, **scan·ning**) [*trans.*] **1** look at all parts of (something) carefully in order to detect some feature: *he raised his binoculars to scan the coast.* ■ look quickly but not very thoroughly through (a document or other text) in order to identify relevant information: *we scan the papers for news from the trouble spots* | [*intrans.*] *I* **scanned through** *the reference materials.* ■ cause (a surface, object, or part of the body) to be traversed by a detector or an electromagnetic beam: *their brains are scanned so that researchers can monitor the progress of the disease.* ■ [*trans.*] cause (a beam) to traverse across a surface or object: *we scanned the beam over a sector of 120°.* ■ resolve (a picture) into its elements of light and shade in a prearranged pattern for the purposes of television transmission. ■ convert (a document or picture) into digital form for storage or processing on a computer: *text and pictures can be* **scanned into** *the computer.* **2** analyze the meter of (a line of verse) by reading with the emphasis on its rhythm or by examining the pattern of feet or syllables. ■ [*intrans.*] (of verse) conform to metrical principles.
▶*n.* an act of scanning someone or something: *a quick scan of the sports page.* ■ a medical examination using a scanner: *a brain scan.* ■ an image obtained by scanning or with a scanner: *we can't predict anything until we have seen the scan.* ▷late Middle English (as a verb in sense 2): from Latin *scandere* 'climb' (in late Latin 'scan (verses)'), by analogy with the raising and lowering of one's foot when marking rhythm. From 'analyze (meter)' arose the senses 'estimate the correctness of' and 'examine minutely,' which led to 'look at searchingly' (late 18th cent.). **—scan·na·ble** *adj.*

scan·dal /ˈskandl/ ▶*n.* an action or event regarded as morally or legally wrong and causing general public outrage: *a bribery scandal involving one of his key supporters.* ■ the outrage or anger caused by such an action or event: *divorce was cause for scandal on the island.* ■ rumor or malicious gossip about such events or actions: *I know that you would want no scandal attached to her name.* ■ [in *sing.*] a state of affairs regarded as wrong or reprehensible and causing general public outrage or anger: *it's a scandal that many older patients are dismissed as untreatable.* ▷Middle English (in the sense 'discredit to religion (by the reprehensible behavior of a religious person)'): from Old French *scandale*, from ecclesiastical Latin *scandalum* 'cause of offense,' from Greek *skandalon* 'snare, stumbling block.'

scan·dal·ize /ˈskandl,īz/ ▶*v.* [*trans.*] **1** shock or horrify (someone) by a real or imagined violation of propriety or morality: *their lack of manners scandalized their hosts.* **2** *Sailing* reduce the area of (a fore-and-aft sail) by lowering the head or raising the boom. [mid 19th cent.: alteration of obsolete *scantelize*, from *scantle* 'make small.'] ▷late 15th cent. (in the sense 'make a public scandal of'): from French *scandaliser* or ecclesiastical Latin *scandalizare*, from Greek *skandalizein.* **—scan·dal·i·za·tion** /,skandl-əˈzāsʜən/ *n.* **—scan·dal·iz·er** *n.*

scan·dal·mon·ger /ˈskandl,mənɢgər; -,mänɢgər/ ▶*n.* a person who stirs up public outrage toward someone or their actions by spreading rumors or malicious gossip.

scan·dal·ous /ˈskandl-əs/ ▶*adj.* causing general public outrage by a perceived offense against morality or law: *a series of scandalous liaisons* | *a scandalous allegation.* ■ (of a state of affairs) disgracefully bad, typically as a result of someone's negligence or irresponsibility: *a scandalous waste of taxpayers' money.* **—scan·dal·ous·ly** *adv.* **—scan·dal·ous·ness** *n.*

scan·dal sheet ▶*n.* *derogatory* a newspaper or magazine giving prominence to scandalous stories or gossip.

scan·dent /ˈskandənt/ ▶*adj.* *chiefly Paleontology* (esp. of a graptolite) having a climbing habit. ▷late 17th cent.: from Latin *scandent-* 'climbing,' from the verb *scandere.*

Scan·den·tia /skanˈdenсʜ(ē)ə/ *Zoology* a small order of mammals that comprises the tree shrews. ▷modern Latin (plural), from Latin *scandent-* 'climbing,' from the verb *scandere.*

Scan·di·na·vi·a /ˈ,skandəˈnāvēə/ a large peninsula in northwestern Europe, occupied by Norway and Sweden. It is bounded by the Arctic Ocean on the north, the Atlantic Ocean on the west, and the Baltic Sea on the south and the east. ■ a cultural region consisting of the countries of Norway, Sweden, and Denmark and sometimes also of Iceland, Finland, and the Faroe Islands. ▷Latin.

Scan·di·na·vi·an /,skandəˈnāvēən/ ▶*adj.* of or relating to Scandinavia, its people, or their languages.
▶*n.* **1** a native or inhabitant of Scandinavia, or a person of Scandinavian descent. **2** the North Germanic languages (Danish, Norwegian, Swedish, Icelandic, Faeroese) descended from Old Norse.

scan·di·um /ˈskandēəm/ ▶*n.* the chemical element of atomic number 21, a soft silvery-white metal resembling the rare earth elements. (Symbol: **Sc**) ▷late 19th cent.: modern Latin, from *Scandia*, contraction of *Scandinavia* (where minerals are found containing this element).

scan·ner /ˈskanər/ ▶*n.* a device for examining, reading, or monitoring something, in particular: ■ *Medicine* a machine that examines the body through the use of radiation, ultrasound, or magnetic resonance imaging, as a diagnostic aid. ■ *Electronics* a device that scans documents and converts them into digital data.

scan·ning e·lec·tron mi·cro·scope (abbr.: **SEM**) ▶*n.* an electron microscope in which the surface of a specimen is scanned by a beam of electrons that are reflected to form an image.

scan·ning tun·nel·ing mi·cro·scope (abbr.: **STM**) ▶*n.* a high-resolution microscope using neither light nor an electron beam, but with an ultrafine tip able to reveal atomic and molecular details of surfaces.

scan·sion /ˈskansʜən/ ▶*n.* the action of scanning a line of verse to determine its rhythm. ■ the rhythm of a line of verse. ▷mid 17th cent.: from Latin *scansio(n-)*, from *scandere* 'to climb'; compare with SCAN.

scant /skant/ ▶*adj.* barely sufficient or adequate: *companies with scant regard for the safety of future generations.* ■ [*attrib.*] barely amounting to a specified number or quantity: *she weighed a scant two pounds.*
▶*v.* [*trans.*] provide grudgingly or in insufficient amounts: *he does not scant his attention to the later writings.* ■ deal with inadequately; neglect: *the press regularly scants a host of issues relating to safety and health.* ▷Middle English: from Old Norse *skamt*, neuter of *skammr* 'short.' **—scant·ly** *adv.* **—scant·ness** *n.*

scant·ling /ˈskantlɪɴɢ/ ▶*n.* **1** a piece of lumber of small cross section. ■ the size to which a piece of wood or stone is measured and cut. **2** (often **scantlings**) a set of standard dimensions for parts of a structure, esp. in shipbuilding. **3** *archaic* a specimen, sample, or small amount of something. ▷early 16th cent. (denoting prescribed size, or a set of standard dimensions): alteration of obsolete *scantillon* (from Old French *escantillon* 'sample'), by association with the suffix -LING.

scant·y /ˈskantē/ ▶*adj.* (**scant·i·er**, **scant·i·est**) small or insufficient in quantity or amount: *scanty wages.* ■ (of clothing) revealing; skimpy: *the women looked cold in their scanty gowns.*
▶*plural n.* (**scanties**) brief underpants. ▷late 16th cent.: from SCANT + -Y[1]. **—scant·i·ly** /ˈskantəlē; ˈskantl-ē/ *adv.* **—scant·i·ness** *n.*

Sca·pa Flow /skapə; ˈskä-/ a strait in the Orkney Islands, Scotland. It was the site of an important British naval base, esp. during World War I. The German High Seas Fleet was interned there after its surrender and was scuttled in 1919 as an act of defiance against the terms of the Versailles peace settlement.

scape /skāp/ ▶*n.* **1** *Botany* a long, leafless flower stalk coming directly from a root. **2** *Entomology* the basal segment of an insect's antenna, esp. when it is enlarged and lengthened (as in a weevil). ▷early 19th cent.: via Latin from Greek *skapos* 'rod'; related to SCEPTER.

-scape ▶*comb. form* denoting a specified type of scene: *moonscape.* ▷on the pattern of *(land)scape.*

scape·goat /ˈskāp,gōt/ ▶*n.* (in the Bible) a goat sent into the wilderness after the Jewish chief priest had symbolically laid the sins of the people upon it (Lev. 16). ■ a person who is blamed for the wrongdoings, mistakes, or faults of others, esp. for reasons of expediency.
▶*v.* [*trans.*] make a scapegoat of. ▷mid 16th cent.: from archaic *scape* 'escape' + GOAT. **—scape·goat·er** *n.* **—scape·goat·ing** *n.* **—scape·goat·ism** /-,izəm/ *n.*

scape·grace /ˈskāp,grās/ ▶*n.* *archaic* a mischievous or wayward person, esp. a young person or child; a rascal. ▷early 19th cent.: from *scape* (see SCAPEGOAT) + GRACE, literally denoting a person who escapes the grace of God.

scaph·oid /ˈskaf,oid/ ▶*n.* *Anatomy* a large carpal bone articulating with the radius below the thumb. ▷mid 18th cent. (in the sense 'boat-shaped'): from modern Latin *scaphoides*, from Greek *skaphoeidēs*, from *skaphos* 'boat.'

Sca·phop·o·da /skəˈfäpədə/ *Zoology* a class of mollusks that comprises the tooth shells. ▷modern Latin (plural), from Greek *skaphē* 'boat' + *pous, pod-* 'foot.' **—scaph·o·pod** /ˈskafə,päd/ *n.*

scap·u·la /ˈskapyələ/ ▸*n.* (*pl.* **-lae** /-ˌlē/ or **-las**) *Anatomy* technical term for SHOULDER BLADE. ▷late 16th cent.: from late Latin, singular of Latin *scapulae* 'shoulder blades.'

scap·u·lar /ˈskapyələr/ ▸*adj. Anatomy & Zoology* of or relating to the shoulder or shoulder blade.
▸*n.* **1** a short monastic cloak covering the shoulders. ■ a symbol of affiliation to an ecclesiastical order, consisting of two strips of cloth hanging down the breast and back and joined across the shoulders. **2** *Medicine* a bandage passing over and around the shoulders. **3** *Ornithology* a scapular feather. ▷late 15th cent. (sense 1 of the *noun*): from late Latin *scapulare*, from *scapula* 'shoulder.' The adjective (late 17th cent.) and the later senses of the noun are from SCAPULA + -AR[1].

scap·u·lar feath·er ▸*n. Ornithology* a feather covering the shoulder, growing above the region where the wing joins the body.

scap·u·lar·y /ˈskapyəˌlerē/ ▸*n.* (*pl.* **-lar·ies**) another term for SCAPULAR (senses 1 and 3). ▷Middle English: from an Anglo-Norman French variant of Old French *eschapeloyre*, based on late Latin *scapulare* (see SCAPULAR).

scar /skär/ ▸*n.* **1** a mark left on the skin or within body tissue where a wound, burn, or sore has not healed quite completely and fibrous connective tissue has developed: *a faint scar ran the length of his left cheek.* ■ *figurative* a lasting effect of grief, fear, or other emotion left on a person's character by a traumatic experience: *the attack has left mental scars on Terry and his family.* ■ a mark left on something following damage of some kind: *Max could see scars of the blast.* ■ a mark left at the point of separation of a leaf, frond, or other part from a plant. **2** a steep high cliff or rock outcrop, esp. of limestone. [Middle English: from Old Norse *sker* 'low reef'; compare with SKERRY.]
▸*v.* (**scarred, scar·ring**) [*trans.*] (often **be scarred**) mark with a scar or scars: *he is likely to be* **scarred for life** *after injuries to his face, arms, and legs* | [as *adj.*, in *combination*] (**-scarred**) *battle-scarred troops.* ■ [*intrans.*] form or be marked with a scar. ▷late Middle English: from Old French *escharre*, via late Latin from Greek *eskhara* 'scab.' —**scar·less** *adj.*

scar·ab /ˈskarəb/ ▸*n.* (also **scar·ab bee·tle** or **sa·cred scar·ab**) a large dung beetle of the eastern Mediterranean area, regarded as sacred in ancient Egypt. • *Scarabaeus sacer*, family Scarabaeidae (the **scarab family**). The scarab family also includes the smaller dung beetles and chafers, together with some very large tropical kinds such as Hercules, goliath, and rhinoceros beetles. ■ an ancient Egyptian gem cut in the form of this beetle, sometimes depicted with the wings spread, and engraved with hieroglyphs on the flat underside. ■ any scarabaeid beetle. ▷late 16th cent. (originally denoting a beetle of any kind): from Latin *scarabaeus*, from Greek *skarabeios*.

scarab beetle

scar·a·bae·id /ˌskarəˈbē-id/ *Entomology* ▸*adj.* of, relating to, or denoting the Scarabaeidae family of beetles.
▸*n.* a beetle of this family, typically having strong spiky forelegs for burrowing. ▷mid 19th cent.: from modern Latin *Scarabaeidae* (plural), from Latin *scarabaeus* (see SCARAB).

scar·a·bae·oid /ˌskarəˈbēˌoid/ ▸*n. Entomology* a beetle of a large group that includes the scarabaeids, dor beetles, and stag beetles. Scarabaeoids include the largest known beetles, and are distinguished by having platelike terminal segments to the antennae. Formerly called LAMELLICORN. • Superfamily Scarabaeoidea (formerly Lamellicornia). ▷late 19th cent.: from modern Latin *Scarabaeoidea* (plural), from Latin *scarabaeus* (see SCARAB).

scar·a·mouch /ˈskarəˌmo͞osн; -ˌmo͞ocн/ ▸*n. archaic* a boastful but cowardly person. ▷mid 17th cent.: from Italian *Scaramuccia*, the name of a stock character in Italian farce, from *scaramuccia* 'skirmish,' ultimately from the same Germanic base as SKIRMISH.

Scar·bor·ough /ˈskärˌbərō/ a town in southern Maine, just south of Portland; pop. 16,970.

scarce /ske(ə)rs/ ▸*adj.* (esp. of food, money, or some other resource) insufficient for the demand: *as raw materials became scarce, synthetics were developed.* ■ occurring in small numbers or quantities; rare: *the freshwater shrimp becomes scarce in soft water.*
▸*adv. archaic* scarcely: *a babe scarce two years old.* ▷Middle English (in the sense 'restricted in quantity or size,' also 'parsimonious'): from a shortening of Anglo-Norman *escars*, from a Romance word meaning 'plucked out, selected.' —**scarce·ness** *n.* —**scar·ci·ty** /ˈskersitē/ *n.*
▸PHRASE □ **make oneself scarce** *informal* leave a place, esp. so as to avoid a difficult situation.

scarce·ly /ˈske(ə)rslē/ ▸*adv.* only just; almost not: *her voice is so low I can scarcely hear what she is saying.* ■ only a very short time before: *she had scarcely dismounted before the door swung open.* ■ used to suggest that something is unlikely to be or certainly not the case: *they could scarcely all be wrong.*

scare /ske(ə)r/ ▸*v.* [*trans.*] cause great fear or nervousness in; frighten: *the rapid questions were designed to* **scare** *her* **into** *blurting out the truth.* ■ [*trans.*] drive or keep (someone) away by frightening them: *the threat of bad weather* **scared away** *the crowds.* ■ [*intrans.*] become scared: *I don't think I scare easily.*
▸*phrasal v.* □ **scare something up** *informal* manage to find or obtain something: *for a price, the box office can usually scare up a pair of tickets.*
▸*n.* a sudden attack of fright: *gosh, that gave me a scare!* ■ [usu. with *adj.*] a general feeling of anxiety or alarm about something: *they were forced to leave the building because of a bomb scare.* ▷Middle English: from Old Norse *skirra* 'frighten,' from *skjarr* 'timid.' —**scar·er** *n.*

scare·crow /ˈske(ə)rˌkrō/ ▸*n.* an object, usually made to resemble a human figure, set up to scare birds away from a field where crops are growing. ■ *informal* a person who is very badly dressed, odd-looking, or thin. ■ *archaic* an object of baseless fear.

scared /ske(ə)rd/ ▸*adj.* fearful; frightened: *she's* **scared stiff** *of her dad* | [with *clause*] *I was scared I was going to kill myself* | [with *infinitive*] *he's scared to come to you and ask for help.*

scared·y-cat /ˈske(ə)rdē ˌkat/ ▸*n. informal* a timid person.

scare·mon·ger /ˈske(ə)rˌməngər; -ˌmänggər/ ▸*n.* a person who spreads frightening or ominous reports or rumors. —**scare·mon·ger·ing** *n.* & *adj.*

scare tac·tics ▸*plural n.* a strategy intended to influence public reaction by the exploitation of fear.

scarf[1] /skärf/ ▸*n.* (*pl.* **scarves** /skärvz/ or **scarfs** /skärfs/) a length or square of fabric worn around the neck or head. ▷mid 16th cent. (in the sense 'sash (around the waist or over the shoulder)'): probably based on Old Northern French *escarpe*, probably identical with Old French *escharpe* 'pilgrim's bag.' —**scarfed** /skärft/ (also **scarved**) *adj.*

scarf[2] ▸*v.* [*trans.*] **1** join the ends of (two pieces of timber or metal) by beveling or notching them so that they fit over or into each other. **2** make an incision in the blubber of (a whale).
▸*n.* **1** (also **scarf joint**) a joint connecting two pieces of timber or metal in which the ends are beveled or notched so that they fit over or into each other. **2** an incision made in the blubber of a whale. ▷Middle English (as a noun): probably via Old French from Old Norse. The verb dates from the early 17th cent.

scarf[3] ▸*v.* [*trans.*] *informal* eat or drink (something) hungrily or enthusiastically: *he* **scarfed down** *the waffles.* ▷1960s: variant of SCOFF[2].

scarf·skin /ˈskärfˌskin/ ▸*n. archaic* the thin outer layer of the skin; the epidermis.

scar·i·fi·er /ˈskarəˌfīər/ ▸*n.* a tool with spikes or prongs used for breaking up matted vegetation in the surface of a lawn. ■ a machine with spikes used for breaking up the surface of a road.

scar·i·fy[1] /ˈskarəˌfī/ ▸*v.* (**-fies, -fied**) [*trans.*] make cuts or scratches in (the surface of something), in particular: ■ break up the surface of (soil or pavement). ■ make shallow incisions in (the skin), esp. as a medical procedure or traditional cosmetic practice: *she scarified the snakebite with a paring knife.* ■ *figurative* criticize severely and hurtfully. ▷late Middle English: from Old French *scarifier*, via late Latin from Greek *skariphasthai* 'scratch an outline,' from *skariphos* 'stylus.' —**scar·i·fi·ca·tion** /-fiˈkāsнən/ *n.*

scar·i·fy[2] /ˈske(ə)rəˌfī/ ▸*v.* (**-fies, -fied**) [*trans.*] [usu. as *adj.*] (**scarifying**) *informal* frighten: *a scarifying mix of extreme violence and absurdist humor.* ▷late 18th cent.: formed irregularly from SCARE, perhaps on the pattern of *terrify*.

scar·la·ti·na /ˌskärləˈtēnə/ (also **scar·le·ti·na**) ▸*n.* another term for SCARLET FEVER. ▷early 19th cent.: modern Latin, from Italian *scarlattina* (feminine), based on *scarlatto* 'scarlet.'

Scar·lat·ti /skärˈlätē/ two Italian composers. **(Pietro) Alessandro (Gaspare)** (1660–1725) was an important and prolific composer of operas that carried Italian opera through the baroque period and into the classical. His son **(Giuseppe) Domenico** (1685–1757) wrote over 550 sonatas for the harpsichord.

scar·let /ˈskärlit/ ▸*adj.* **1** of a brilliant red color: *a mass of scarlet berries.* **2** *chiefly dated* (of an offense or sin) wicked; heinous. ■ immoral, esp. promiscuous or unchaste.
▸*n.* a brilliant red color: *papers lettered* **in scarlet** *and black.* ■ clothes or material of this color. ▷Middle English (originally denoting any brightly colored cloth): shortening of Old French *escarlate*, from medieval Latin *scarlata*, via Arabic and medieval Greek from late Latin *sigillatus* 'decorated with small images,' from *sigillum* 'small image.'

scar·let fe·ver ▸*n.* an infectious bacterial disease affecting esp. children, and causing fever and a scarlet rash. It is caused by streptococci.

scar·le·ti·na ▸*n.* variant spelling of SCARLATINA.

scar·let pim·per·nel ▸*n.* a small plant with scarlet flowers that close in rainy or cloudy weather. Native to Europe, it is also widespread throughout much of North America. • *Anagallis arvensis* subsp. *arvensis*, family Primulaceae.

scar·let run·ner (also **scar·let run·ner bean**) ▸*n.* a twining bean plant with scarlet flowers and very long flat edible pods. Native to Central and South America, it is widely cultivated in North America. • *Phaseolus coccineus*, family Leguminosae. ■ the pod and seed of this plant eaten as food.

scar·let tan·a·ger ▸*n.* a tanager of eastern North America, the breeding male of which is bright red with black wings and tail. • *Piranga olivacea*, family Emberizidae (subfamily Thraupinae).

scarp /skärp/ ▸*n.* a very steep bank or slope; an escarpment. ■ the inner wall of a ditch in a fortification. Compare with COUNTERSCARP.
▸*v.* [*trans.*] cut or erode (a slope or hillside) so that it becomes steep, perpendicular, or precipitous. ■ provide (a ditch in a fortification) with a steep scarp and counterscarp. ▷late 16th cent. (with reference to fortification): from Italian *scarpa*.

scarp·er /ˈskärpər/ ▸*v.* [*intrans.*] *Brit., informal* run away: *they left the stuff where it was and scarpered.* ▷mid 19th cent.: probably from Italian *scappare* 'to escape,' influenced by rhyming slang *Scapa Flow* 'go.'

Scars·dale /ˈskärzˌdāl/ a residential town in southeastern New York, an affluent suburb of New York City; pop. 16,987.

scarves /skärvz/ ▸ plural form of SCARF[1].

scar·y /ˈske(ə)rē/ ▸*adj.* (**scar·i·er, scar·i·est**) *informal* frightening; causing fear: *a scary movie.* ■ uncannily striking or surprising: *it was scary the way they bonded with each other.* —**scar·i·ly** /-əlē/ *adv.* —**scar·i·ness** *n.*

scat[1] /skat/ ▸*v.* (**scat·ted, scat·ting**) [*intrans.*] *informal* go away; leave: *Scat! Leave me alone.* ▷mid 19th cent.: perhaps an abbreviation of SCATTER, or perhaps from the sound of a hiss (used to drive an animal away) + *-cat*.

scat[2] (also **scat sing·ing**) ▸*n.* improvised jazz singing in which the voice is used in imitation of an instrument.
▸*v.* (**scat·ted, scat·ting**) [*intrans.*] sing in such a way. ▷1920s: probably imitative.

scat[3] ▸*n.* droppings, esp. those of carnivorous mammals. ▷1950s: from Greek *skōr, skat-* 'dung'; compare with SCATOLOGY.

scathe /skā*th*/ *archaic* ▸*v.* [*trans.*] (usu. **be scathed**) harm; injure: *he was barely scathed.* ■ *poetic/literary* damage or destroy by fire or lightning.
▸*n.* harm; injury. ▷Middle English: from Old Norse *skathi* (noun), *skatha* (verb); related to Dutch and German *schaden* (verb).

scath·ing /ˈskā*th*ing/ ▸*adj.* witheringly scornful; severely critical: *she launched* **a scathing attack on** *the governor.* —**scath·ing·ly** *adv.*

sca·tol·o·gy /skəˈtäləjē/ ▸*n.* an interest in or preoccupation with excrement and excretion. ■ obscene literature that is concerned with excrement and excretion. ▷late 19th cent.: from Greek *skōr, skat-* 'dung' + -LOGY. Compare with SCAT[3]. —**scat·o·log·i·cal** /ˌskatlˈäjikəl/ *adj.*

scat·ter /ˈskatər/ ▸*v.* [*trans.*] throw in various random directions: ***scatter** the coconut over the icing* | *his family is hoping to scatter his ashes at sea.* ■ (**be scattered**) [usu. with *adverbial*] occur or be found at intervals rather than all together: *there are many mills scattered throughout the marshlands* | [as *adj.*] (**scattered**) *a scattered mountain community.* ■ (of a group of people or animals) separate and move off quickly in different directions: *the roar made the dogs scatter.* ■ [*trans.*] cause (a group or people or animals) to act in such a way: *he charged across the foyer, scattering people.* ■ (usu. **be scattered with**) cover (a surface) with objects thrown or spread randomly over it: *sandy beaches scattered with driftwood.* ■ *Physics* deflect or diffuse (electromagnetic radiation or particles).
▸*n.* a small, dispersed amount of something: ***a scatter of** houses on the north shore.* ■ *Statistics* the degree to which repeated measurements or observations of a quantity differ. ■ *Physics* the scattering of light, other electromagnetic radiation, or particles. ▷Middle English (as a verb): probably a variant of SHATTER. —**scat·ter·a·ble** *adj.* —**scat·ter·a·tion** /ˌskatəˈrāsHən/ *n.* —**scat·ter·er** *n.*

THE RIGHT WORD **broadcast, diffuse, dispel, disperse, disseminate, dissipate, scatter**
If you **scatter** something, you throw it about in different directions, often using force (*the wind scattered leaves around the yard*).
Disperse implies a scattering that completely breaks up a mass or assemblage and spreads the units far and wide (*the crowd dispersed as soon as the storm arrived; the ships were so widely dispersed that they couldn't see each other*).
To **dispel** is to scatter or to drive away something that obscures, confuses, or bothers (*to dispel her fears*), while to **diffuse** is to lessen the intensity of something by spreading it out over a broader area (*the curtains diffused the bright sunlight pouring in the window*).
Dissipate suggests that something has completely dissolved, disintegrated, or vanished (*early-morning mist dissipated by the sun*).
Broadcast originally meant to scatter seed, but it is also used figuratively to mean make public (*the news of the president's defeat was broadcast the next morning*).
Disseminate also means to publish or make public, but it implies a wider audience and usually a longer duration. You can spend a lifetime *disseminating* knowledge, but you would *broadcast* the news of the birth of your first grandchild.

scat·ter·brain /ˈskatərˌbrān/ ▸*n.* a person who tends to be disorganized and lacking in concentration. —**scat·ter·brained** *adj.*
scat·ter di·a·gram ▸*n.* *Statistics* a graph in which the values of two variables are plotted along two axes, the pattern of the resulting points revealing any correlation present.
scat·ter·gram /ˈskatərˌgram/ (also **scat·ter·graph**) ▸*n.* another term for SCATTER DIAGRAM.
scat·ter·gun /ˈskatərˌgən/ ▸*n.* a shotgun.
▸*adj.* another term for SCATTERSHOT.
scat·ter·ing /ˈskatəriNG/ ▸*n.* [in *sing.*] an act of scattering something. ■ a small, dispersed amount of something: *the scattering of freckles across her cheeks and forehead.* ■ *Physics* the process in which electromagnetic radiation or particles are deflected or diffused.
scat·ter·ing an·gle ▸*n.* *Physics* the angle through which a scattered particle or beam is deflected.
scat·ter·plot /ˈskatərˌplät/ (also **scat·ter plot**) ▸*n.* another term for SCATTER DIAGRAM.
scat·ter rug ▸*n.* another term for THROW RUG.
scat·ter·shot /ˈskatərˌSHät/ ▸*adj.* denoting something that is broad but random and haphazard in its range: *a scattershot collection of stories.*
scat·ty /ˈskatē/ ▸*adj.* (**-ti·er**, **-ti·est**) *informal* absent-minded and disorganized. ▷early 20th cent.: abbreviation of SCATTERBRAINED (see SCATTERBRAIN). —**scat·ti·ly** /-əlē/ *adv.* —**scat·ti·ness** *n.*
scaup /skôp/ ▸*n.* a Eurasian, North American, and New Zealand diving duck, the male of which has a black head with a green or purple gloss. • Genus *Aythya*, family Anatidae: three species, in particular the widespread (**greater**) **scaup** (*A. marila*), with a black breast and white sides. ▷late 17th cent.: Scots variant of Scots and northern English *scalp* 'mussel bed,' a feeding ground of the duck.
scau·per /ˈskôpər/ ▸*n.* variant spelling of SCORPER.
scav·enge /ˈskavənj/ ▸*v.* [*trans.*] search for and collect (anything usable) from discarded waste: *people sell junk scavenged from the garbage* | [*intrans.*] *the city dump where the squatters scavenge to survive.* ■ (of an animal) search for (carrion) as food. ■ search for discarded items or food in (a place): *the mink is still commonly seen scavenging the beaches of California.* ■ remove (combustion products) from the cylinder of an internal combustion engine on the return stroke of the piston. ■ *Chemistry* combine with and remove (molecules, radicals, etc.) from a particular medium. ▷mid 17th cent. (in the sense 'clean out (dirt)'): back-formation from SCAVENGER.
scav·eng·er /ˈskavənjər/ ▸*n.* an animal that feeds on carrion, dead plant material, or refuse. ■ a person who searches for and collects discarded items. ■ *Brit., archaic* a person employed to clean the streets. ■ *Chemistry* a substance that reacts with and removes particular molecules, radicals, etc. ▷mid 16th cent.: alteration of earlier *scavager*, from Anglo-Norman French *scawager*, from Old Northern French *escauwer* 'inspect,' from Flemish *scauwen* 'to show.' The term originally denoted an officer who collected *scavage*, a toll on foreign merchants' goods offered for sale in a town, later a person who kept the streets clean.
scav·eng·er cell ▸*n.* another term for PHAGOCYTE.
scav·eng·er hunt ▸*n.* a game, typically played in an extensive outdoor area, in which participants have to collect a number of miscellaneous objects.
Sc.B. ▸*abbr.* Bachelor of Science. ▷from Latin *Scientiae Baccalaureus.*
SCC ▸*abbr.* *Electronics* storage connecting circuit.
ScD ▸*abbr.* Doctor of Science. ▷from Latin *scientiae doctor.*
SCE ▸*abbr.* Scottish Certificate of Education.
sce·na /ˈSHānə/ ▸*n.* a scene in an opera. ■ an elaborate dramatic solo usually including recitative. ▷Italian, from Latin, 'scene.'
sce·nar·i·o /səˈne(ə)rēˌō; -ˈnär-/ ▸*n.* (*pl.* **-os**) a written outline of a movie, novel, or stage work giving details of the plot and individual scenes: *imagine the scenarios for four short stories.* ■ a postulated sequence or development of events: *a possible scenario is that he was attacked after opening the front door.* ■ a setting, in particular for a work of art or literature: *the scenario is World War II.* ▷late 19th cent.: from Italian, from Latin *scena* 'scene.'

USAGE The proper meaning of **scenario** is 'an outline of a plot' or 'a postulated sequence of events': *the worst-case scenario.* It should not be used loosely to mean 'situation,' as in *a nightmare scenario.*

sce·nar·ist /səˈne(ə)rist/ ▸*n.* a screenwriter.
scend /send/ (also **send**) *archaic* ▸*n.* the push or surge created by a wave. ■ a pitching or surging movement of a vessel.
▸*v.* [*intrans.*] (of a vessel) pitch or surge up in a heavy sea. ▷late 15th cent. (as a verb): alteration of SEND[1] or DESCEND. The noun dates from the early 18th cent.
scene /sēn/ ▸*n.* **1** the place where an incident in real life or fiction occurs or occurred: *the emergency team were among the first **on the scene*** | *relatives left flowers **at the scene of** the crash.* ■ a place, with the people, objects, and events in it, regarded as having a particular character or making a particular impression: *a **scene of** carnage.* ■ a landscape: *thick snow had turned the scene outside into a picture postcard.* ■ an incident of a specified nature: *there had already been some scenes of violence.* ■ a place or representation of an incident: *scenes of 1930s America.* ■ [with *adj.*] a specified area of activity or interest: *the country music scene.* ■ [usu. in *sing.*] a public display of emotion or anger: *she was loath to **make a scene** in the office.* **2** a sequence of continuous action in a play, movie, opera, or book: *a scene from Brando's first film.* ■ a subdivision of an act of a play in which the time is continuous and the setting fixed and which does not usually involve a change of characters: *beginning at Act One, Scene One.* ■ [usu. as *adj.*] the pieces of scenery used in a play or opera: *scene changes.* ▷mid 16th cent. (denoting a subdivision of a play, or (a piece of) stage scenery): from Latin *scena*, from Greek *skēnē* 'tent, stage.'
▸***PHRASES*** □ **behind the scenes** out of sight of the public at a theater or organization. ■ *figurative* secretly: *diplomatic maneuvers going on behind the scenes.* □ **change of scene** another way of saying CHANGE OF SCENERY (see SCENERY). □ **come** (or **appear** or **arrive**) **on the scene** arrive; appear. □ **hit** (or **make**) **the scene** informal way of saying COME ON THE SCENE above. □ **not one's scene** *informal* not something one enjoys or is interested in: *sorry, that witchcraft stuff is not my scene.* □ **set the scene** describe a place or situation in which something is about to happen. ■ create the conditions for a future event: *the congressman's speech **set the scene for** a bitter debate.*
scen·er·y /ˈsēn(ə)rē/ ▸*n.* the natural features of a landscape considered in terms of their appearance, esp. when picturesque: *spectacular views of mountain scenery.* ■ the painted background used to represent natural features or other surroundings on a theater stage or movie set.
▸*phrasal v.* □ **chew** (**up**) **the scenery** (of an actor) overact: *he chews up the courtroom scenery as the unscrupulous attorney.* ▷mid 18th cent. (earlier as *scenary*): from Italian *scenario* (see SCENARIO). The change in the ending was due to association with -ERY.
▸***PHRASE*** □ **change of scenery** a move to different surroundings: *we spent the weekend in Seattle just for a change of scenery.*
scene-steal·er ▸*n.* an actor who outshines the rest of the cast, esp. unexpectedly. ■ a person or thing that takes more than their fair share of attention.
scene·ster /ˈsēnstər/ ▸*n.* *informal* a person associated with or immersed in a particular fashionable cultural scene.
sce·nic /ˈsēnik/ ▸*adj.* providing or relating to views of impressive or beautiful natural scenery: *the scenic route to Brussels* | *scenic beauty.* ■ [*attrib.*] of or relating to theatrical scenery: *a scenic artist from the Metropolitan Opera House.* ■ (of a picture) representing an incident: *the trend to scenic figural work.* ▷early 17th cent. (in the sense 'theatrical'): via Latin from Greek *skēnikos* 'of the stage,' from *skēnē* (see SCENE). —**sce·ni·cal·ly** /-ik(ə)lē/ *adv.*
sce·nic rail·way ▸*n.* an attraction at a fair or in a park consisting of a miniature railroad that runs past natural features and artificial scenery.
sce·nog·ra·phy /sēˈnägrəfē/ ▸*n.* the design and painting of theatrical scenery. ■ (in painting and drawing) the representation of objects in perspective. ▷mid 17th cent.: from French *scénographie*, or via Latin from Greek *skēnographia* 'scene-painting,' from *skēnē* (see SCENE). —**sce·no·graph·ic** /ˌsēnəˈgrafik; ˌsenə-/ *adj.*
scent /sent/ ▸*n.* a distinctive smell, esp. one that is pleasant: *the scent of freshly cut hay.* See note at SMELL. ■ pleasant-smelling liquid worn on the skin; perfume: *she sprayed scent over her body.* ■ a trail indicated by the characteristic smell of an animal and perceptible to hounds or other animals: *the hound followed the scent.* ■ *figurative* a trail of evidence or other signs assisting someone in a search or investigation: *once their interest is aroused, they follow the scent with sleuthlike pertinacity.* ■ *archaic* the faculty or sense of smell.
▸*v.* [*trans.*] **1** (usu. **be scented with**) impart a pleasant scent to: *a glass of tea scented with lemon balm* | [as *adj.*] (**scented**) *scented soap.* **2** discern by the sense of smell: *a shark can scent blood from well over half a mile away.* ■ *figurative* sense the presence, existence, or imminence of: *a commander who scented victory.* ■ sniff (the air) for a scent: *the bull advanced, scenting the breeze at every step.* ▷late Middle English (denoting the sense of smell): from Old French *sentir* 'perceive, smell,' from Latin *sentire*. The addition of *-c-* (in the 17th cent.) is unexplained. —**scent·less** *adj.*
▸***PHRASES*** □ **on the scent** in possession of a useful clue in a search or investigation; following a trail that will likely lead to the discovery or acquisition of something. □ **put** (or **throw**) **someone off the scent** mislead someone in the course of a search or investigation.
scent gland ▸*n.* an animal gland that secretes an odorous pheromone or defensive substance, esp. one under the tail of a carnivorous mammal such as a civet or skunk.
scent mark ▸*n.* (also **scent mark·ing**) an odoriferous substance containing a pheromone that is deposited by a mammal from a scent gland or in the urine or feces, typically on prominent objects in an area.
▸*v.* (**scent-mark**) [*intrans.*] (of a mammal) deposit such a substance.
scep·ter /ˈseptər/ (*Brit.* **scep·tre**) ▸*n.* an ornamented staff carried by rulers on ceremonial occasions as a symbol of sovereignty. ▷Middle English: from Old French *ceptre*, via Latin from Greek *skēptron*, from *skēptein* (alteration of *skēptesthai*) 'lean on.' —**scep·tered** *adj.*
scep·tic ▸*n.* British spelling of SKEPTIC.

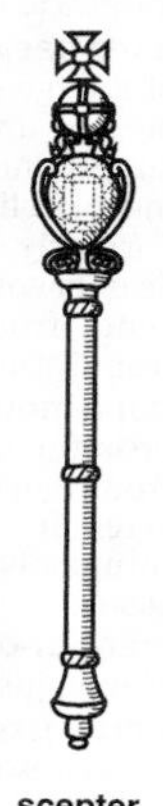
scepter

scep·ti·cal ▸*adj.* British spelling of SKEPTICAL.

scep·tre ▸*n.* British spelling of SCEPTER.

sch. ▸*abbr.* ■ scholar. ■ school. ■ schooner.

scha·den·freu·de /ˈSHädən,froidə/ (also **Scha·den·freu·de**) ▸*n.* pleasure derived by someone from another person's misfortune. ▷German, from *Schaden* 'harm' + *Freude* 'joy.'

Schaum·burg /ˈSHôm,bərg/ a residential and industrial village in northeastern Illinois, northwest of Chicago; pop. 75,386.

Schaw·low /ˈSHô,lō/, Arthur Leonard (1921–99), U.S. inventor. With Charles H. Townes, he invented the laser. Nobel Prize in Physics (1981, shared with Nicolaas Bloembergen 1920– and Kai M. Siegbahn 1918–).

sched·ule /ˈskejo͞ol; -jəl/ ▸*n.* **1** a plan for carrying out a process or procedure, giving lists of intended events and times: *we have drawn up an engineering schedule.* ■ (usu. **one's schedule**) one's day-to-day plans or timetable: *take a moment out of your busy schedule.* ■ a timetable: *information on airline schedules.* **2** *chiefly Law* an appendix to a formal document or statute, esp. as a list, table, or inventory. **3** (with reference to an income tax system) any of the forms (named "A," "B," etc.) issued for completion and relating to the various classes into which taxable income is divided.

▸*v.* [*trans.*] (often **be scheduled**) arrange or plan (an event) to take place at a particular time: *the release of the single is* **scheduled for** *April.* ■ make arrangements for (someone or something) to do something: [*trans.*] *he is scheduled to be released from prison this spring.* ▷late Middle English (in the sense 'scroll, explanatory note, appendix'): from Old French *cedule,* from late Latin *schedula* 'slip of paper,' diminutive of *scheda,* from Greek *skhedē* 'papyrus leaf.' The verb dates from the mid 19th cent. **—sched·u·lar** /-ər/ *adj.*

▸*PHRASES* □ **ahead of** (or **behind**) **schedule** earlier (or later) than planned or expected. □ **on** (or **according to**) **schedule** on time; as planned or expected.

sched·uled /ˈske,jo͞old; -əld/ ▸*adj.* included in or planned according to a schedule: *the bus makes one scheduled thirty-minute stop.* ■ (esp. of an airline or flight) relating to or forming part of a regular service rather than specially chartered.

sched·uled caste (also **Sched·uled Caste**) ▸*n.* the official name given in India to the untouchable castes.

USAGE See usage at UNTOUCHABLE.

sched·ul·er /ˈskejo͞olər; ˈskejələr/ ▸*n.* a person or machine that organizes or maintains schedules. ■ *Computing* a program that arranges jobs or a computer's operations into an appropriate sequence.

scheel·ite /ˈSHā,līt/ ▸*n.* a fluorescent mineral, white when pure, that consists of calcium tungstate and is an important ore of tungsten. ▷mid 19th cent.: from the name of Carl W. *Scheele* (1742–86), Swedish chemist, + -ITE[1].

schef·fler·a /ˈSHeflərə; SHefˈli(ə)rə/ ▸*n.* an evergreen tropical or subtropical shrub or small tree that is widely grown as a houseplant for its decorative foliage. • Genus *Schefflera,* family Araliaceae. ▷modern Latin, named after J. C. *Scheffler,* 18th-cent. German botanist.

Sche·her·a·za·de /SHə,herəˈzäd; -ˈzädə/ the character who narrates the *Arabian Nights.* Her delightful storytelling wins the favor and mercy of her husband, the sultan of India.

Scheldt /SHelt; skelt/ a river in northern Europe. Rising in northern France, it flows 270 miles (432 km) through Belgium and the Netherlands to the North Sea. Also called **SCHELDE**; French name **ESCAUT**.

sche·ma /ˈskēmə/ ▸*n.* (*pl.* **-ma·ta** /-mətə/ or **-mas**) *technical* a representation of a plan or theory in the form of an outline or model: *a schema of scientific reasoning.* ■ *Logic* a syllogistic figure. ■ (in Kantian philosophy) a conception of what is common to all members of a class; a general or essential type or form. ▷late 18th cent. (as a term in philosophy): from Greek *skhēma* 'form, figure.'

sche·mat·ic /skəˈmatik; skē-/ ▸*adj.* (of a diagram or other representation) symbolic and simplified. ■ (of thought, ideas, etc.) simplistic or formulaic in character, usually to an extent inappropriate to the complexities of the subject matter: *a highly schematic reading of the play.*

▸*n.* (in technical contexts) a schematic diagram, in particular of an electric or electronic circuit. **—sche·mat·i·cal·ly** /-ik(ə)lē/ *adv.*

sche·ma·tism /ˈskēmə,tizəm/ ▸*n.* the arrangement or presentation of something according to a scheme or schema. ▷early 17th cent.: from modern Latin *schematismus,* from Greek *skhēmatismos* 'assumption of a certain form,' from *skhēma, skhēmat-* 'form.'

sche·ma·tize /ˈskēmə,tīz/ ▸*v.* [*trans.*] arrange or represent in a schematic form. **—sche·ma·ti·za·tion** /,skēmətiˈzāSHən/ *n.*

scheme /skēm/ ▸*n.* a large-scale systematic plan or arrangement for attaining some particular object or putting a particular idea into effect: *a clever marketing scheme.* ■ a secret or underhanded plan; a plot: *police uncovered a scheme to steal paintings worth more than $250,000.* ■ a particular ordered system or arrangement: *a classical rhyme scheme.*

▸*v.* [*intrans.*] make plans, esp. in a devious way or with intent to do something illegal or wrong: [with *infinitive*] *he schemed to bring about the collapse of the government.* ▷mid 16th cent. (denoting a figure of speech): from Latin *schema,* from Greek (see SCHEMA). An early sense was 'diagram of the position of celestial objects,' giving rise to 'diagram, outline,' whence the current senses. The unfavorable notion "plot"arose in the mid 18th cent.

▸*PHRASE* □ **the scheme of things** a supposed or apparent overall system, within which everything has a place and in relation to which individual details are ultimately to be assessed: *in the overall scheme of things, we didn't do badly.*

schem·er /ˈskēmər/ ▸*n.* a person who is involved in making secret or underhanded plans.

schem·ing /ˈskēmiNG/ ▸*adj.* given to or involved in making secret and underhanded plans: *they had mean, scheming little minds.*

▸*n.* the activity or practice of making such plans. **—schem·ing·ly** *adv.*

sche·moz·zle ▸*n.* variant spelling of SHEMOZZLE.

Sche·nec·ta·dy /skəˈnektədē/ an industrial city in eastern New York, northwest of Albany; pop. 61,821.

Scheng·en a·gree·ment /ˈSHeNGən/ *n.* an intergovernmental agreement on the relaxation of border controls between participating European countries, created in 1985 and ratified under the auspices of the European Union in 1999. Member countries now comprise Austria, Belgium, Denmark, France, Finland, Germany, Greece, Iceland, Italy, Luxembourg, the Netherlands, Norway, Portugal, Spain, and Sweden. ▷1985: named for *Schengen,* a village in Luxembourg on the German border, the site of the original agreement's signing.

scher·zan·do /skərtˈsändō/ *Music* ▸*adv.* & *adj.* (esp. as a direction) in a playful manner. ▷Italian, literally 'joking.'

scher·zo /ˈskertsō/ ▸*n.* (*pl.* **-zos** or **-zi** /-tsē/) *Music* a vigorous, light, or playful composition, typically comprising a movement in a symphony or sonata. ▷Italian, literally 'jest.'

Schia·pa·rel·li /,skyäpəˈrelē; ,SHäpə-/, Elsa (1896–1973), French fashion designer, born in Italy.

Schick test /SHik/ ▸*n. Medicine* a test for previously acquired immunity to diphtheria, using an intradermal injection of diphtheria toxin. ▷early 20th cent.: named after Bela *Schick* (1877–1967), Hungarian-born American pediatrician.

Schil·ler /ˈSHilər/, (Johann Christoph) Friedrich von (1759–1805), German playwright, poet, historian, and critic. Initially influenced by the *Sturm und Drang* movement, he was later an important figure of the Enlightenment. His historical plays include the trilogy *Wallenstein* (1800), *Mary Stuart* (1800), and *William Tell* (1804).

schil·ling /ˈSHiliNG/ ▸*n.* the basic monetary unit of Austria (until replaced by the euro), equal to 100 groschen. ▷from German *Schilling;* compare with SHILLING.

Schin·dler /ˈSHindlər/, Oskar (1908–74), German industrialist. He saved more than 1,200 Jews from concentration camps by employing them first in his enamelware factory in Cracow and then in an armaments factory in Czechoslovakia in 1944. This was celebrated in the film *Schindler's List* (1993), based on *Schindler's Ark* (1982), a novel by Thomas Keneally.

schip·per·ke /ˈskipərkē/ ▸*n.* a small black tailless dog of a breed with a ruff of fur around its neck. ▷late 19th cent.: from Dutch dialect, literally 'little boatman,' with reference to its use as a watchdog on barges.

schism /ˈs(k)izəm/ ▸*n.* a split or division between strongly opposed sections or parties, caused by differences in opinion or belief. ■ the formal separation of a church into two churches or the secession of a group owing to doctrinal and other differences. See also **GREAT SCHISM**. ▷late Middle English: from Old French *scisme,* via ecclesiastical Latin from Greek *skhisma* 'cleft,' from *skhizein* 'to split.'

schis·mat·ic /s(k)izˈmatik/ ▸*adj.* of, characterized by, or favoring schism.

▸*n. chiefly historical* (esp. in the Christian Church) a person who promotes schism; an adherent of a schismatic group. ▷late Middle English: from Old French *scismatique,* via ecclesiastical Latin from ecclesiastical Greek *skhismatikos,* from *skhisma* (see SCHISM). **—schis·mat·i·cal·ly** /-ik(ə)lē/ *adv.*

schist /SHist/ ▸*n. Geology* a coarse-grained metamorphic rock that consists of layers of different minerals and can be split into thin irregular plates. ▷late 18th cent.: from French *schiste,* via Latin from Greek *skhistos* 'split,' from the base of *skhizein* 'cleave.' **—schis·tous** /-təs/ *adj.*

schis·tose /ˈSHistōs/ ▸*adj. Geology* (of metamorphic rock) having a laminar structure like that of schist. **—schis·tos·i·ty** /SHiˈstäsitē/ *n.*

schis·to·some /ˈSHistə,sōm/ ▸*n. Zoology* & *Medicine* a parasitic flatworm that needs two hosts to complete its life cycle. The immature form infests freshwater snails, and the adult lives in the blood vessels of birds and mammals, causing bilharzia in humans. Also called **BLOOD FLUKE**. • Genus *Schistosoma,* subclass Digenea, class Trematoda. ▷early 20th cent.: from modern Latin *Schistosoma,* from Greek *skhistos* 'divided' + *sōma* 'body.'

schis·to·so·mi·a·sis /,SHistōsəˈmīəsis/ ▸*n.* another term for **BILHARZIA** (the disease).

schiz·an·dra /skitˈsandrə/ ▸*n.* a Chinese herb whose berries are credited with various stimulant or medicinal properties. • *Schisandra chinensis,* family Magnoliaceae. Also called magnolia vine. ▷mid 19th cent.: modern Latin, *Schisandra,* formed as *schizo-* + Greek *andr-, anēr* man, on account of the divided stamens.

schi·zan·thus /skiˈzanTHəs/ ▸*n.* a South American plant of the nightshade family, with irregularly lobed showy flowers marked with one or more contrasting colors. • Genus *Schizanthus,* family Solanaceae. ▷modern Latin, from Greek *skhizein* 'to split' + *anthos* 'flower.'

schiz·o /ˈskitsō/ *informal, offensive* ▸*adj.* (of a person or their behavior) schizophrenic.

▸*n.* (*pl.* **-os**) a schizophrenic. ▷1940s: abbreviation.

schizo- ▸*comb. form* divided; split: *schizocarp.* ■ relating to schizophrenia: *schizotype.* ▷from Greek *skhizein* 'to split.'

schiz·o·af·fec·tive (also **schiz·o·af·fec·tive**) ▸*adj.* (of a person or a mental condition) characterized by symptoms of both schizophrenia and manic-depressive psychosis.

schiz·o·carp /ˈskitsō,kärp/ ▸*n. Botany* a dry fruit that splits into single-seeded parts when ripe.

schi·zog·e·nous /skiˈzäjənəs; skitˈsäj-/ ▸*adj. Botany* (of an intercellular space in a plant) formed by the splitting of the common wall of contiguous cells. **—schiz·o·gen·ic** /,skizəjenik; ,skitsə-/ *adj.* **—schi·zog·e·ny** /skiˈzäjənē; skitˈsäj-/ *n.*

schi·zog·o·ny /skiˈzägənē; skitˈsäg-/ ▸*n. Biology* asexual reproduction by multiple fission, found in some protozoa, esp. parasitic sporozoans. ▷late 19th cent.: from SCHIZO- 'divided' + Greek *-gonia* 'production.' **—schi·zog·o·nous** /-nəs/ *adj.*

schiz·oid /ˈskit,soid/ ▸*adj. Psychiatry* denoting or having a personality type characterized by emotional aloofness and solitary habits. ■ *informal* (in general use) resembling schizophrenia in having inconsistent or contradictory elements; mad or crazy: *it's a frenzied, schizoid place.*

▸*n.* a schizoid person.

schiz·ont /ˈskizänt; ˈskitsänt/ ▸*n. Biology* (in certain sporozoan protozoans) a cell that divides by schizogony to form daughter cells. ▷early 20th cent.: from SCHIZO- 'divided' + -ONT.

schiz·o·phre·ni·a /,skitsəˈfrēnēə; -ˈfrenēə/ ▸*n.* a long-term mental disorder of a type involving a breakdown in the relation between thought, emotion, and behavior, leading to faulty perception, inappropriate actions and feelings, withdrawal from reality and personal relationships into fantasy and delusion, and a sense of mental fragmentation. ■ (in general use) a mentality or approach characterized by inconsistent or contradictory elements. ▷early 20th cent.: modern Latin, from Greek *skhizein* 'to split' + *phrēn* 'mind.' **—schiz·o·phren·ic** /-'frenik/ *adj.* & *n.*

schiz·o·type /'skitsə,tīp/ ▶*n.* a personality type in which mild symptoms of schizophrenia are present. **—schiz·o·typ·al** /,skitsə'tīpəl/ *adj.* **—schiz·o·typ·y** /,skit'sätəpē/ *n.*

Schle·gel /'SHlāgəl/, August Wilhelm von (1767–1845), German romantic poet and critic, who was among the founders of art history and comparative philology. His brother, **Friedrich von Schlegel** (1772–1829), was a critic, philosopher, and poet who wrote on comparative literature and philology.

schle·miel /SHlə'mēl/ (also **shle·miel**) ▶*n. informal* a stupid, awkward, or unlucky person. ▷late 19th cent.: from Yiddish *shlemiel.*

schlep /SHlep/ (also **schlepp** or **shlep**) *informal* ▶*v.* (**schlepped**, **schlep·ping**) [*trans.*] haul or carry (something heavy or awkward): *she schlepped her groceries home.* ■ [*intrans.*] (of a person) go or move reluctantly or with effort: *I would have preferred not to schlep all the way over there to run an errand.*
▶*n.* **1** a tedious or difficult journey. **2** another term for **SCHLEPPER.** ▷early 20th cent. (as a verb): from Yiddish *shlepn* 'drag,' from Middle High German *sleppen.*

schlep·per /'SHlepər/ (also **shlep·per**) ▶*n. informal* an inept or stupid person. ▷1930s: Yiddish, from *shlepn* (see **SCHLEP**).

Schles·ing·er[1] /'SHlāziNGər; 'SHlesinjər/, Arthur (Meier) (1888–1965), U.S. historian. He wrote *The Colonial Merchants and the American Revolution, 1763–1776* (1918), *New Viewpoints in American History* (1922), and *The American Reformer* (1950).

Schles·ing·er[2], Arthur (Meier), Jr. (1917–), U.S. historian; the son of Arthur Meier Schlesinger. A professor at Harvard University 1946–61 and advisor to Presidents Kennedy and Lyndon Johnson, he wrote *The Age of Jackson* (1945), *The Age of Roosevelt* in three volumes (1957–60), *A Thousand Days: John F. Kennedy in the White House* (1965), and *The Imperial Presidency* (1973).

Schles·wig /'SHleswig; 'SHläsvikH; -vik/ a former Danish duchy, located on the southern part of the Jutland peninsula.

Schles·wig-Hol·stein /'hōl,stīn; -,SHtīn/ a state in northwestern Germany that occupies the southern part of the Jutland peninsula; capital, Kiel. It consists of the former duchies of Schleswig and Holstein.

Schlick /SHlik/, Moritz (1882–1936), German philosopher and physicist; founder of the Vienna Circle.

Schlie·mann /'SHlē,män/, Heinrich (1822–90), German archaeologist. In 1871, he began excavating the mound of Hissarlik in Turkey, where he discovered the remains of nine superimposed cities, one of which he mistakenly identified as Homer's Troy. By 1876, he had undertaken excavations at Mycenae.

schlie·ren /'SHli(ə)rən/ ▶*plural n. technical* discernible layers in a transparent material that differ from the surrounding material in density or composition. ■ *Geology* irregular streaks or masses in igneous rock that differ from the surrounding rock in texture or composition. ▷late 19th cent.: from German *Schlieren,* plural of *Schliere* 'streak.'

schli·ma·zel /SHlə'mäzəl/ (also **schle·ma·zel**) ▶*n. informal* a consistently unlucky or accident-prone person. ▷Yiddish, from Middle High German, *slim,* 'crooked' + Hebrew, *mazzāl,* 'luck.'

schlock /SHläk/ (also **shlock**) ▶*n. informal* cheap or inferior goods or material; trash: *they peddle their schlock to willing tourists* | [as *adj.*] *schlock journalism* ▷early 20th cent.: apparently from Yiddish *shlak* 'an apoplectic stroke,' *shlog* 'wretch, untidy person, apoplectic stroke.' **—schlock·y** *adj.*

schlock·meis·ter /'SHläk,mīstər/ (also **shlock·meis·ter**) ▶*n. informal* a purveyor of cheap or trashy goods. ▷early 20th cent.: from **SCHLOCK** + German *Meister* 'master.'

schlub /SHləb/ (also **shlub**) ▶*n. informal* a talentless, unattractive, or boorish person. ▷1960s: Yiddish *shlub,* perhaps from Polish *żłób.*

schlump /SHlōōmp/ (also **shlump**) ▶*n. informal* a slow, slovenly, or inept person. ▷1940s: apparently related to Yiddish *shlumperdik* 'dowdy' and German *Schlumpe* 'slattern.'

schmaltz /SHmälts; SHmôlts/ (also **schmalz**) ▶*n. informal* excessive sentimentality, esp. in music or movies. ▷1930s: from Yiddish *shmaltz,* from German *Schmalz* 'drippings, lard.' **—schmaltz·y** *adj.* (**schmaltz·i·er**, **schmaltz·i·est**).

schmat·te /'SHmätə/ (also **shmat·te**) ▶*n. informal* a rag; a ragged or shabby garment. ▷1970s: Yiddish *shmatte,* from Polish *szmata* 'rag.'

schmear /SHmi(ə)r/ (also **schmeer**, **shmeer**, or **shmear**) *informal* ▶*n.* **1** a corrupt or underhanded inducement; a bribe. **2** a smear or spread: *the bagel so perfect with a schmear of low-fat cream cheese.*
▶*v.* [*trans.*] flatter or ingratiate oneself with (someone): *he was constantly buying us drinks and schmearing us up.* ▷1960s: from Yiddish *shmirn* 'flatter, grease.'
▶*PHRASE* □ **the whole schmear** everything possible or available; every aspect of the situation: *I'm going for the whole schmear.*

Schmidt–Cas·se·grain tel·e·scope /'SHmit 'kasi-,grān/ ▶*n.* a type of catadioptric telescope, using the correcting plate of a Schmidt telescope together with the secondary mirror and rear focus of a Cassegrain telescope.

Schmidt tel·e·scope (also **Schmidt cam·er·a**) ▶*n.* a type of catadioptric telescope used solely for wide-angle astronomical photography, with a thin glass plate at the front to correct for spherical aberration. A curved photographic plate is placed at the prime focus inside the telescope. ▷1930s: named after Bernhard V. *Schmidt* (1879–1935), the German inventor.

Schmitt trig·ger /SHmit/ ▶*n. Electronics* a bistable circuit in which the output increases to a steady maximum when the input rises above a certain threshold, and decreases almost to zero when the input voltage falls below another threshold. ▷1940s: named after Otto H. *Schmitt* (born 1913), American electronics engineer.

schmo /SHmō/ (also **shmo**) ▶*n.* (*pl.* **schmoes**) *informal* a fool or a bore. ▷1940s: alteration of **SCHMUCK.**

schmooze /SHmōōz/ (also **shmooze**) ▶*v.* [*intrans.*] talk intimately and cozily; gossip. ■ [*trans.*] talk in such a way to (someone), typically in order to manipulate, flatter, or impress them.
▶*n.* a long and intimate conversation. ▷late 19th cent. (as a verb): from Yiddish *shmuesn* 'converse, chat.' **—schmooz·er** *n.* **—schmooz·y** *adj.*

schmuck /SHmək/ (also **shmuck**) ▶*n. informal* a foolish or contemptible person. ▷late 19th cent.: from Yiddish *shmok* 'penis.'

schnapps /SHnäps; SHnaps/ ▶*n.* a strong alcoholic drink resembling gin and often flavored with fruit: *peach schnapps.* ▷from German *Schnaps,* literally 'dram of liquor,' from Low German and Dutch *snaps* 'mouthful.'

schnau·zer /'SHnouzər/ ▶*n.* a medium- or small-sized dog of a German breed with a close wiry coat and heavy whiskers around the muzzle. ▷early 20th cent.: from German, from *Schnauze* 'muzzle, snout.'

miniature schnauzer

schnit·zel /'SHnitsəl/ ▶*n.* a thin slice of veal or other light meat, coated in breadcrumbs and fried. ▷from German *Schnitzel,* literally 'slice.'

schnook /SHnŏŏk/ (also **shnook**) ▶*n. informal* a person easily duped; a fool. ▷1940s: perhaps from German *Schnucke* 'small sheep' or from Yiddish *shnuk* 'snout.'

schnor·rer /'SHnôrər/ (also **shnor·rer**) ▶*n. informal* a beggar or scrounger; a layabout. ▷late 19th cent.: from Yiddish *shnorrer,* variant of German *Schnurrer.*

schnoz /SHnäz/ (also **schnozz** or **schnoz·zo·la** /SHnä-'zōlə/) ▶*n. informal* a person's nose. ▷1940s: from Yiddish *shnoytz,* from German *Schnauze* 'snout.'

Schoen·berg /'SHə(r)n,bərg; 'SHœn,berk/, Arnold (1874–1951), U.S. composer and music theorist, born in Austria. He introduced atonality into his second string quartet (1907–08), while *Serenade* (1923) is the first example of the technique of serialism.

schol·ar /'skälər/ ▶*n.* a specialist in a particular branch of study, esp. the humanities; a distinguished academic: *a Hebrew scholar.* ■ *chiefly archaic* a person who is highly educated or has an aptitude for study: *Mr. Bell declares himself no scholar.* ■ a student holding a scholarship. ■ *archaic* a student. ▷Old English *scol(i)ere* 'schoolchild, student,' from late Latin *scholaris,* from Latin *schola* (see **SCHOOL**[1]).

schol·ar·ly /'skälərlē/ ▶*adj.* involving or relating to serious academic study: *scholarly journals* | *a scholarly career.* ■ having or showing knowledge, learning, or devotion to academic pursuits: *a scholarly account of the period* | *an earnest, scholarly man.* **—schol·ar·li·ness** *n.*

schol·ar·ship /'skälər,SHip/ ▶*n.* **1** academic study or achievement; learning of a high level. See note at **KNOWLEDGE. 2** a grant or payment made to support a student's education, awarded on the basis of academic or other achievement.

scho·las·tic /skə'lastik/ ▶*adj.* **1** of or concerning schools and education: *scholastic achievement.* ■ of or relating to secondary schools. **2** *Philosophy & Theology* of, relating to, or characteristic of medieval scholasticism. ■ typical of scholasticism in being pedantic or overly subtle.
▶*n.* **1** *historical Philosophy & Theology* an adherent of scholasticism; a schoolman. **2** (in the Roman Catholic Church) a member of a religious order, esp. the Society of Jesus, who is between the novitiate and the priesthood. ▷late 16th cent. (sense 2 of the *adjective*): via Latin from Greek *skholastikos* 'studious,' from *skholazein* 'be at leisure to study,' from *skholē* (see **SCHOOL**[1]). **—scho·las·ti·cal·ly** /-ik(ə)lē/ *adv.*

scho·las·ti·cism /skə'lasti,sizəm/ ▶*n.* the system of theology and philosophy taught in medieval European universities, based on Aristotelian logic and the writings of the early Church Fathers and having a strong emphasis on tradition and dogma. ■ narrow-minded insistence on traditional doctrine.

scho·li·ast /'skōlē,ast/ ▶*n. historical* a commentator on ancient or classical literature. ▷late 16th cent.: from medieval Greek *skholiastēs,* from *skholiazein* 'write scholia' (see **SCHOLIUM**). **—scho·li·as·tic** /,skōlē'astik/ *adj.*

scho·li·um /'skōlēəm/ ▶*n.* (*pl.* **-li·a** /-lēə/) *historical* a marginal note or explanatory comment made by a scholiast. ▷mid 16th cent.: modern Latin, from Greek *skholion,* from *skholē* 'learned discussion.'

school[1] /skōōl/ ▶*n.* **1** an institution for educating children: *Ryder's children did not go to school at all* | [as *adj.*] *school supplies.* ■ the buildings used by such an institution: *the cost of building a new school.* ■ [treated as *pl.*] the students and staff of a school: *the principal was addressing the whole school.* ■ a day's work at school; lessons: *school started at 7 a.m.* ■ [with *adj.*] *figurative* used to describe the type of circumstances in which someone was brought up: *I was brought up in a hard school and I don't forget it.* **2** any institution at which instruction is given in a particular discipline: *a dancing school.* ■ *informal* another term for **UNIVERSITY.** ■ a department or faculty of a college concerned with a particular subject of study: *the School of Dental Medicine.* **3** a group of people, particularly writers, artists, or philosophers, sharing the same or similar ideas, methods, or style: *the Frankfurt school of critical theory.* ■ [with *adj.*] a style, approach, or method of a specified character: *filmmakers are tired of the skin-deep school of cinema.*
▶*v.* [*trans.*] *chiefly formal* send to school; educate: *a scientist born in Taiwan and schooled in California.* ■ train or discipline (someone) in a particular skill or activity: *he* **schooled** *her* **in** *horsemanship* | *it's important to* **school yourself to** *be good at exams.* ▷Old English *scōl, scolu,* via Latin from Greek *skholē* 'leisure, philosophy, place where lectures are given,' reinforced in Middle English by Old French *escole.*
▶*PHRASES* □ **leave school** discontinue one's education: *he left school at 16.* □ **of** (or **from**) **the old school** see **OLD SCHOOL.** □ **the school of hard knocks** see **KNOCK.** □ **school of thought** a particular way of thinking, typically one disputed by the speaker: *a school of thought that calls into question the constitutional foundations of this country.*

school[2] ▶*n.* a large group of fish or sea mammals.
▶*v.* [*intrans.*] (of fish or sea mammals) form a large group. ▷late Middle English: from Middle Low German, Middle Dutch *schōle,* of West Germanic origin; related to Old English *scolu* 'troop.' Compare with **SHOAL**[1].

school age ▶*n.* the age range of children normally attending school. **—school-age** or **school-aged** *adj.*

school board ▶*n.* a local board or authority responsible for the provision and maintenance of schools.

school·book /'skōōl,bŏŏk/ ▶*n.* a textbook used in a school.

school·boy /ˈsko͞olˌboi/ ▸*n.* a boy attending school. ■ [as *adj.*] characteristic of or associated with schoolboys, esp. in being immature: *schoolboy humor.*

school bus ▸*n.* a bus that transports students from home to school, school to home, or to school-sponsored events.

school·child /ˈsko͞olˌchīld/ ▸*n.* (*pl.* **-child·ren**) a child attending school.

school col·ors ▸*plural n.* a badge, cap, or other item in the distinctive colors of a particular school, typically awarded to a student who represents the school as a participant in a competitive sport.

school day ▸*n.* a day on which classes are held in a primary or secondary school.

school·days /ˈsko͞olˌdāz/ ▸*plural n.* the period in someone's life when they attended school: *a close friend from their schooldays.*

school dis·trict ▸*n.* a geographical unit for the local administration of schools.

schooled /sko͞old/ ▸*adj.* [often in *combination*] educated or trained in a specified activity or in a particular way: *a man well* **schooled in** *making money.*

school·er /ˈsko͞olər/ ▸*n.* [in *combination*] a student attending a school of the specified kind or being educated in the specified way: *a high-schooler.*

school·fel·low /ˈsko͞olˌfelō/ ▸*n.* more formal term for **SCHOOLMATE.**

school·girl /ˈsko͞olˌgərl/ ▸*n.* a girl attending school. ■ [as *adj.*] characteristic of or associated with schoolgirls, esp. in being elementary or immature: *schoolgirl French.*

school·house /ˈsko͞olˌhous/ ▸*n.* a building used as a school, esp. in a small community or village.

school·ing /ˈsko͞oliNG/ ▸*n.* education or training received, esp. at school: *his parents paid for his schooling.*

school·man /ˈsko͞olmən; -ˌman/ ▸*n.* (*pl.* **-men**) *historical* **1** a teacher in a university in medieval Europe. ■ a scholar or an educator. **2** a scholastic theologian.

school·marm /ˈsko͞olˌmä(r)m/ ▸*n.* a schoolmistress (typically used with reference to a woman regarded as prim, strict, and brisk in manner). **—school·marm·ish** *adj.*

school·mas·ter /ˈsko͞olˌmastər/ ▸*n. dated* a male teacher in a school. **—school·mas·ter·ly** *adj.*

school·mate /ˈsko͞olˌmāt/ ▸*n. informal* a person who attends or attended the same school as oneself.

school·mis·tress /ˈsko͞olˌmistris/ ▸*n. dated* a female teacher in a school.

school·room /ˈsko͞olˌro͞om; -ˌro͝om/ ▸*n.* a room in which a class of students is taught. ■ (**the schoolroom**) used to refer to school as an institution: *I got most of my education outside of the schoolroom.*

school·teach·er /ˈsko͞olˌtēCHər/ ▸*n.* a person who teaches in a school. **—school·teach·ing** /-ˌtēCHiNG/ *n.*

school vouch·er ▸*n.* a government funded voucher redeemable for tuition fees at a school other than the public school that a student could attend free.

school·work /ˈsko͞olˌwərk/ ▸*n.* work assigned students by their teachers in school: *Brother could do any schoolwork put to him, but he'd answer any spoken question with "I don't know."*

USAGE Although the distinction can be made between **schoolwork** as work assigned to be completed in school and **homework** as work assigned to be completed at home, in practice people often use *schoolwork* to mean the same as *homework*: *they had to do their schoolwork at the kitchen table.*

school·yard /ˈsko͞olˌyärd/ ▸*n.* the grounds of a school, esp. as a place for children to play: *that schoolyard full of kids* [as *adj.*] *the schoolyard bully.*

school year ▸*n.* another term for **ACADEMIC YEAR.**

schoon·er /ˈsko͞onər/ ▸*n.* **1** a sailing ship with two or more masts, typically with the foremast smaller than the mainmast, and having gaff-rigged lower masts. **2** a tall beer glass. ▷early 18th cent.: of unknown origin.

schooner

Scho·pen·hau·er /ˈSHōpənˌhou-ər/, Arthur (1788–1860), German philosopher. According to his philosophy, as expressed in *The World as Will and Idea* (1818), the will is identified with ultimate reality and happiness is only achieved by abnegating the will (as desire).

schorl /SHôrl/ ▸*n.* a black iron-rich variety of tourmaline. ▷late 18th cent.: from German *Schörl*, of unknown origin.

schot·tische /ˈSHätiSH/ ▸*n.* a slow polka. ▷mid 19th cent.: from German *der schottische Tanz* 'the Scottish dance.'

Schott·ky bar·ri·er /ˈSHätkē/ ▸*n. Electronics* an electrostatic depletion layer formed at the junction of a metal and a semiconductor, which causes it to act as an electrical rectifier. ▷1940s: named after Walter *Schottky* (1886–1976), German physicist.

Schreif·fer /ˈSHrēfər/, John R., see **BARDEEN.**

Schrö·der /ˈSHrōdər; ˈSHrā-/, Gerhard (1944–), German statesman; chancellor of Germany from 1998.

Schrö·ding·er /ˈSHrādiNGgər; ˈSHrō-/, Erwin (1887–1961), Austrian theoretical physicist, who founded the study of wave mechanics. His general works influenced scientists in many disciplines. Nobel Prize for Physics (1933).

Schrö·ding·er e·qua·tion *Physics* a differential equation that forms the basis of the quantum-mechanical description of matter in terms of the wavelike properties of particles in a field. Its solution is related to the probability density of a particle in space and time.

schtup ▸*v.* variant spelling of **SHTUP.**

Schu·bert /ˈSHo͞obərt/, Franz (1797–1828), Austrian composer. His music is associated with the romantic movement for its lyricism and emotional intensity, but it belongs in formal terms to the classical age. He composed more than 500 lieder, including the song cycles *Die Schöne Müllerin* (1823) and *Die Winterreise* (1827).

Schulz /SHo͝olts/, Charles (1922–2000), U.S. cartoonist. He is remembered as the creator of the widely syndicated "Peanuts" comic strip that featured a range of characters including Charlie Brown and his dog Snoopy. First published in 1950, the comic strip has since appeared in many publications around the world.

Schu·ma·cher /ˈSHo͞oˌmäKHər/, E. F. (1911–77), German economist and conservationist; full name *Ernst Friedrich Schumacher.* His *Small is Beautiful: Economics as if People Mattered* (1973) argues that mass production needs to be replaced by smaller, more energy-efficient enterprises.

Schu·mann /ˈSHo͞omən; -ˌmän/, Robert (Alexander) (1810–56), German composer. A leading romantic composer, he is particularly noted for his songs and piano music, as well as for four symphonies and much chamber music. His wife **Clara Wieck** (1819–96) was a noted pianist and composer.

schuss /SHo͝os; SHo͞os/ ▸*n.* a straight downhill run on skis.
▸*v.* [*intrans.*] make a straight downhill run on skis. ▷1930s: from German *Schuss*, literally 'shot.'

Schuyl·kill Riv·er /ˈsko͞olˌkil; -kəl/ a river that flows for 130 miles (210 km) through eastern Pennsylvania to join the Delaware River at Philadelphia.

schwa /SHwä/ ▸*n. Phonetics* the unstressed central vowel (as in *a* moment *ago*), represented by the symbol (ə) in the International Phonetic Alphabet. ▷late 19th cent.: from German, from Hebrew *šəwā'*.

Schwa·ben /ˈSHväbən/ German name for **SWABIA.**

Schwann /SHwän; SHfän/, Theodor Ambrose Hubert (1810–82), German physiologist. He showed that animals (as well as plants) are made up of individual cells and that the egg begins life as a single cell. He also discovered the cells that form the myelin sheaths of nerve fibers (Schwann cells).

Schwar·ze·neg·ger /ˈSHwôrtsəˌnegər; ˈswôrt-/, Arnold (1947–), U.S. actor, born in Austria. He is noted for his action roles in movies such as *Conan The Barbarian* (1982) and *The Terminator* (1984). He also starred in movies such as the comedy *Kindergarten Cop* (1990) and the spy thriller *True Lies* (1994). In 2003, he was elected governor of California.

Schwarz·kopf[1] /ˈSHwôrtsˌkô(p)f; ˈswärtsˌkä(p)f/, Dame (Olga Maria) Elisabeth (Friederike) (1915–), German opera singer. She is particularly known for her recitals of German lieder and for her roles in works such as Richard Strauss's *Der Rosenkavalier.*

Schwarz·kopf[2] /ˈSHwôrtsˌkôpf; ˈSHwärts-; -ˌkäpf/, H. Norman, Jr. (1934–), U.S. army officer; nickname **Stormin' Norman.** He was deputy commander of U.S. forces during the invasion of Grenada 1983. Promoted to full general in 1988 and appointed commander in chief of the U.S. Central Command 1988–91, he led the Allied forces against Iraq in the Persian Gulf War 1991. After retirement in 1991, his autobiography, *It Doesn't Take a Hero*, was published in 1992.

Schwarz·schild black hole /ˈSHwôrtsˌCHīld; ˈSHvärtsˌSHilt/ ▸*n. Physics* a black hole of a kind supposed to result from the complete gravitational collapse of an electrically neutral and nonrotating body, having a physical singularity at the center to which infalling matter inevitably proceeds and at which the curvature of space-time is infinite. A **Schwarzschild radius** is the radius of the boundary of a hole of this type. ▷named after Karl *Schwarzschild* (1873–1916), German astronomer.

Schwarz·wald /ˈSHvärtsˌvält/ German name for **BLACK FOREST.**

Schweit·zer /ˈSHwītsər; ˈSHfī-/, Albert (1875–1965), German theologian, musician, and medical missionary. He qualified as a doctor in 1913 and went as a missionary to Gabon, where he established a hospital. Nobel Peace Prize (1952).

Schweiz /SHvīts/ German name for **SWITZERLAND.**

Schwe·rin /SHvāˈrēn/ a city in northeastern Germany, capital of Mecklenburg-West Pomerania, situated on the southwestern shores of Lake Schwerin; pop. 126,000.

Schwyz /SHvēts/ a canton in northeastern Switzerland, one of the three original cantons of the Swiss Confederation, to which it gave its name.

sci·ae·nid /sīˈēnid/ ▸*n. Zoology* a fish of the drum family (Sciaenidae), whose members are mainly marine and important for food or sport. ▷early 20th cent.: from modern Latin *Sciaenidae* (plural), from the genus name *Sciaena*, from Greek *skiaina*, denoting a kind of fish.

sci·ag·ra·phy /sīˈagrəfē/ ▸*n.* British spelling of **SKIAGRAPHY.**

sci·am·a·chy /sīˈaməkē/ ▸*n. archaic* sham fighting for exercise or practice. ■ argument or conflict with an imaginary opponent. ▷early 17th cent.: from Greek *skiamakhia*, from *skia* 'shadow' + *-makhia* '-fighting.'

sci·at·ic /sīˈatik/ ▸*adj.* of or relating to the hip. ■ of or affecting the sciatic nerve. ■ suffering from or liable to sciatica. ▷early 16th cent. (as a noun denoting sciatica): from French *sciatique*, via late Latin from Greek *iskhiadikos* 'relating to the hips, subject to sciatica,' from *iskhion* 'hip joint.' **—sci·at·i·cal·ly** /-ik(ə)lē/ *adv.*

sci·at·i·ca /sīˈatikə/ ▸*n.* pain affecting the back, hip, and outer side of the leg, caused by compression of a spinal nerve root in the lower back, often owing to degeneration of an intervertebral disk. ▷late Middle English: from late Latin *sciatica (passio)* 'sciatic (affliction),' feminine of *sciaticus*, from Greek *iskhiadikos* (see **SCIATIC**).

sci·at·ic nerve ▸*n. Anatomy* a major nerve extending from the lower end of the spinal cord down the back of the thigh, and dividing above the knee joint. It is the nerve with the largest diameter in the human body.

SCID ▸*abbr.* severe combined immune deficiency, a rare genetic disorder in which affected children have no resistance to disease and must be kept isolated from infection from birth.

sci·ence /ˈsīəns/ ▸*n.* the intellectual and practical activity encompassing the systematic study of the structure and behavior of the physical and natural world through observation and experiment: *the world of science and technology.* ■ a particular area of this: *veterinary science* | *the agricultural sciences.* ■ a systematically organized body of knowledge on a particular subject: *the science of criminology.* ■ *archaic* knowledge of any kind. ▷Middle English (denoting knowledge): from Old French, from Latin *scientia*, from *scire* 'know.'

sci·ence fic·tion (abbr.: **SF** or **Sci Fi**) ▸*n.* fiction based on imagined future scientific or technological advances and major social or environmental changes, frequently portraying space or time travel and life on other planets.

sci·ence park ▸*n.* an area devoted to scientific research or the development of science-based or technological industries.

S

sci·en·tial /sī'enchəl/ ▸adj. *archaic* concerning or having knowledge. ▷late Middle English: from late Latin *scientialis*, from *scientia* 'knowledge' (see **SCIENCE**).

sci·en·tif·ic /ˌsīən'tifik/ ▸adj. based on or characterized by the methods and principles of science: *the scientific study of earthquakes.* ■ relating to or used in science: *scientific instruments.* ■ *informal* systematic; methodical: *how many people buy food in an organized, scientific way?* ▷late 16th cent.: from French *scientifique* or late Latin *scientificus* 'producing knowledge,' from *scientia* (see **SCIENCE**). Early use described the liberal arts as opposed to the "mechanic" arts (i.e., arts requiring manual skill). **—sci·en·tif·i·cal·ly** /-ik(ə)lē/ *adv.*

sci·en·tif·ic man·age·ment ▸n. management of a business, industry, or economy, according to principles of efficiency derived from experiments in methods of work and production, esp. from time-and-motion studies.

sci·en·tif·ic meth·od ▸n. a method of procedure that has characterized natural science since the 17th century, consisting in systematic observation, measurement, and experiment, and the formulation, testing, and modification of hypotheses.

sci·en·tif·ic mis·con·duct ▸n. action that willfully compromises the integrity of scientific research, such as plagiarism or the falsification or fabrication of data.

sci·en·tism /'sīənˌtizəm/ ▸n. *rare* thought or expression regarded as characteristic of scientists. ■ excessive belief in the power of scientific knowledge and techniques. **—sci·en·tis·tic** /ˌsīən'tistik/ *adj.*

sci·en·tist /'sīəntist/ ▸n. a person who is studying or has expert knowledge of one or more of the natural or physical sciences.

Sci·en·tol·o·gy /ˌsīən'täləjē/ ▸n. *trademark* a religious system based on the seeking of self-knowledge and spiritual fulfillment through graded courses of study and training. It was founded by American science-fiction writer L. Ron Hubbard (1911–86) in 1955. ▷from Latin *scientia* 'knowledge' + **-LOGY**. **—Sci·en·tol·o·gist** /-jist/ *n.*

S

sci-fi /'sī 'fī/ ▸n. *informal* short for **SCIENCE FICTION**.

scil·i·cet /'siləˌset/ ▸adv. that is to say; namely (introducing a word to be supplied or an explanation of an ambiguity). ▷Latin, from *scire licet* 'one is permitted to know.'

scil·la /'silə/ ▸n. a plant of the lily family that typically bears small blue star- or bell-shaped flowers and glossy straplike leaves, native to Eurasia and temperate Africa. • Genus *Scilla*, family Liliaceae. ▷modern Latin, from Latin *scilla* 'sea onion,' from Greek *skilla*.

Scil·ly Isles /'silē/ (also **Isles of Scil·ly** or **the Scil·lies**) a group of about 140 small islands (of which 5 are inhabited) off the southwestern tip of England; pop. 3,000; capital, Hugh Town (on St. Mary's). **—Scil·lo·ni·an** /sə'lōnēən/ *adj.* & *n.*

scim·i·tar /'simətər; -ˌtär/ ▸n. a short sword with a curved blade that broadens toward the point, used originally in Eastern countries. ▷mid 16th cent.: from French *cimeterre* or Italian *scimitarra*, of unknown origin.

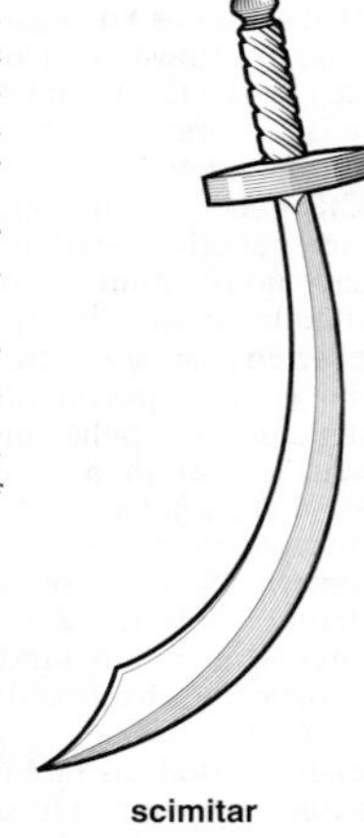
scimitar

scim·i·tar o·ryx (also **scim·i·tar-horned o·ryx**) ▸n. an oryx with scimitar-shaped horns, now living only along the southern edge of the Sahara. • *Oryx dammah*, family Bovidae.

scin·ti·gram /'sintiˌgram/ ▸n. *Medicine* an image of an internal part of the body produced by scintigraphy. ▷1950s: from **SCINTILLATION** + **-GRAM**[1].

scin·tig·ra·phy /sin'tigrəfē/ ▸n. *Medicine* a technique in which a scintillation counter or similar detector is used with a radioactive tracer to obtain an image of a bodily organ or a record of its functioning. ▷1950s: from **SCINTILLATION** + **-GRAPHY**. **—scin·ti·graph·ic** /ˌsinti'grafik/ *adj.*

scin·til·la /sin'tilə/ ▸n. [in *sing.*] a tiny trace or spark of a specified quality or feeling: *a* ***scintilla of*** *doubt.* ▷late 17th cent.: from Latin.

scin·til·late /'sin(t)lˌāt/ ▸v. [*intrans.*] emit flashes of light; sparkle. ■ *Physics* fluoresce momentarily when struck by a photon or charged particle. ▷early 17th cent.: from Latin *scintillat-* 'sparkled,' from the verb *scintillare*, from *scintilla* 'spark.' **—scin·til·lant** /-ənt/ *adj.* & *n.*

scin·til·lat·ing /'sin(t)lˌātiNG/ ▸adj. sparkling or shining brightly: *the scintillating sun.* ■ brilliantly and excitingly clever or skillful: *the audience loved his scintillating wit | the team produced a scintillating second-half performance.* **—scin·til·lat·ing·ly** *adv.*

scin·til·la·tion /ˌsin(t)l'āSHən/ ▸n. a flash or sparkle of light. ■ the process or state of emitting flashes of light. ■ *Physics* a small flash of visible or ultraviolet light emitted by fluorescence in a phosphor when struck by a charged particle or high-energy photon. ■ *Astronomy* the twinkling of the stars, caused by the earth's atmosphere diffracting starlight unevenly.

scin·til·la·tion count·er ▸n. *Physics* a device for detecting and recording scintillations. Also called **scintillometer**.

scin·til·la·tor /'sin(t)lˌātər/ ▸n. *Physics* a material that fluoresces when struck by a charged particle or high-energy photon. ■ a detector for charged particles and gamma rays in which scintillations produced in a phosphor are detected and amplified by a photomultiplier, giving an electrical output signal.

scin·ti·scan /'sin(t)əˌskan/ ▸n. *Medicine* another term for **SCINTIGRAM**. ▷1960s: from **SCINTILLATION** + **SCAN**.

sci·o·list /'sīəlist/ ▸n. *archaic* a person who pretends to be knowledgeable and well informed. ▷early 17th cent.: from late Latin *sciolus* (diminutive of Latin *scius* 'knowing,' from *scire* 'know') + **-IST**. **—sci·o·lism** /-ˌlizəm/ *n.* **—sci·o·lis·tic** /ˌsīə'listik/ *adj.*

sci·on /'sīən/ ▸n. **1** (also **ci·on**) a young shoot or twig of a plant, esp. one cut for grafting or rooting. **2** a descendant of a notable family or one with a long lineage: *he was the scion of a wealthy family.* ▷Middle English: from Old French *ciun* 'shoot, twig,' of unknown origin.

Scip·i·o Ae·mil·i·a·nus /'sipēˌō iˌmilē'ānəs/ (*c.*185–129 BC), Roman general and politician; full name *Publius Cornelius Scipio Aemilianus Africanus Minor*; adoptive grandson of Scipio Africanus. He achieved distinction in the siege of Carthage in 146 during the third Punic War and in his campaign in Spain in 133.

Scip·i·o Af·ri·ca·nus /'sipēˌō ˌafri'kānəs/ (236–*c.*184 BC), Roman general and politician; full name *Publius Cornelius Scipio Africanus Major*. He was successful in concluding the second Punic War, by the defeat of the Carthaginians in Spain in 206 and then by the defeat of Hannibal in Africa at Zama in 202.

sci·re fa·ci·as /ˌsīrē 'fāSHēəs; 'ski(ə)re 'fākēˌäs/ ▸n. *Law* a writ requiring a person to show why a judgment regarding a record or patent should not be enforced or annulled. ▷Latin, literally 'let (the person) know.'

sci·roc·co /SHə'räkō; sə-/ ▸n. variant spelling of **SIROCCO**.

scir·rhus /'s(k)irəs/ ▸n. (*pl.* **scir·rhi** /'s(k)iˌrī; 'skiˌrē/) *Medicine* a carcinoma that is hard to the touch. ▷late Middle English: modern Latin, from Greek *skirros*, from *skiros* 'hard.' **—scir·rhous** /-əs/ *adj.*

scis·sile /'sisəl; -īl/ ▸adj. *chiefly Biochemistry* (of a chemical bond) readily undergoing scission. ▷early 17th cent.: from Latin *scissilis*, from *sciss-* 'cut, divided,' from the verb *scindere*.

scis·sion /'sizHən; 'siSH-/ ▸n. *technical* the action or state of cutting or being cut, in particular: ■ *chiefly Biochemistry* breakage of a chemical bond, esp. one in a long chain molecule so that two smaller chains result. ■ a division or split between people or parties; a schism. ▷late Middle English: from Old French, or from late Latin *scissio(n-)*, from *scindere* 'cut, cleave.'

scis·sor /'sizər/ ▸v. **1** [*trans.*] cut (something) with scissors: *pages scissored out of a magazine.* **2** [*trans.*] move (one's legs) move back and forth in a way resembling the action of scissors: *he was still hanging on, scissoring his legs uselessly.* ■ [*intrans.*] (of a person's legs) move in such a way.
▸n. see **SCISSORS**. ▷early 17th cent.: from **SCISSORS**.

scis·sor hold (also **scis·sors hold**) ▸n. *Wrestling* a hold in which the head or other part of the opponent's body is gripped between the legs, which are then locked by crossing them at the instep or ankles to apply pressure.

scis·sor jack (also **scis·sors jack**) ▸n. a jack for heavy lifting, operated by a horizontal screw that raises or lowers a frame of hinged, rhombus-shaped linkages.

scis·sor kick (also **scis·sors kick**) ▸n. (in various sports, particularly swimming and soccer) a kick in which the legs make a sharp snapping movement like the blades of a pair of scissors. **—scis·sor-kick** *v.*

scis·sors /'sizərz/ (also **a pair of scis·sors**) ▸*plural n.* an instrument used for cutting cloth, paper, and other thin material, consisting of two blades laid one on top of the other and fastened in the middle so as to allow them to be opened and closed by a thumb and finger inserted through rings on the end of their handles. ■ (also **scis·sor**) [often as *adj.*] an action in which two things cross each other or open and close like the blades of a pair of scissors: *as the fish swims, the tail lobes open and close in a slight scissor action.* ▷late Middle English: from Old French *cisoires*, from late Latin *cisoria*, plural of *cisorium* 'cutting instrument,' from *cis-*, variant of *caes-*, stem of *caedere* 'to cut.' The spelling with *sc-* (16th cent.) was by association with the Latin stem *sciss-* 'cut.'

scis·sors and paste ▸n. & *v.* another term for **CUT AND PASTE**.

scis·sor-tailed fly·catch·er ▸n. (also **scis·sor·tail**) a tyrant flycatcher with a very long forked tail, found in the southern U.S. and noted for its spectacular aerial display. • *Tyrannus forficatus*, family Tyrannidae.

Sci·uro·mor·pha /sīˌyŏŏrə'môrfə/ *Zoology* a major division of the rodents that comprises the squirrels, prairie dogs, and marmots. • Suborder Sciuromorpha, order Rodentia. ▷modern Latin (plural), from Greek *skiouros* (from *skia* 'shadow' + *oura* 'tail') + *morphē* 'form.'

scle·ra /'skli(ə)rə/ ▸n. *Anatomy* the white outer layer of the eyeball. At the front of the eye it is continuous with the cornea. ▷late 19th cent.: modern Latin, from Greek *sklēros* 'hard.' **—scle·ral** *adj.*

Scle·rac·tin·i·a /ˌskli(ə)rak'tinēə/ *Zoology* an order of coelenterates that comprises the stony corals. Also called **MADREPORARIA**. ▷modern Latin (plural), from Greek *sklēros* 'hard' + *aktis, aktin-* 'ray.' **—scle·rac·tin·i·an** *n.* & *adj.*

scle·ren·chy·ma /skli'reNGkəmə/ ▸n. *Botany* strengthening tissue in a plant, formed from cells with thickened, typically lignified, walls. ▷mid 19th cent.: modern Latin, from Greek *sklēros* 'hard' + *enkhuma* 'infusion,' on the pattern of *parenchyma*. **—scle·ren·chym·a·tous** /ˌsklireNG'kimətəs/ *adj.*

scle·rite /'skli(ə)rīt/ ▸n. *Zoology* a component section of an exoskeleton, esp. each of the plates forming the skeleton of an arthropod. ▷mid 19th cent.: from Greek *sklēros* 'hard' + **-ITE**[1].

scle·ri·tis /sklə'rītis/ ▸n. *Medicine* inflammation of the sclera.

sclero- ▸*comb. form* hard; hardened; hardening: *scleroderma | sclerotherapy.* ▷from Greek *sklēros* 'hard.'

scle·ro·der·ma /ˌskli(ə)rə'dərmə; ˌskler-/ ▸n. *Medicine* a chronic hardening and contraction of the skin and connective tissue, either locally or throughout the body.

scle·roid /'skli(ə)rˌoid; 'skler-/ ▸adj. *Botany* & *Zoology* having a hard or hardened texture. ▷mid 19th cent.: from Greek *sklēros* 'hard.'

scle·ro·phyll /'skli(ə)rəˌfil; 'skler-/ ▸n. *Botany* a woody plant with evergreen leaves that are tough and thick in order to reduce water loss. ▷early 20th cent.: from Greek *sklēros* 'hard' + *phullon* 'leaf.' **—scle·ro·phyl·lous** /ˌskli(ə)rə'filəs; skli'räfələs/ *adj.*

scle·ro·pro·tein /ˌskli(ə)rō'prōtē(ə)n/ ▸n. *Biochemistry* an insoluble structural protein such as keratin, collagen, or elastin.

scle·rosed /skli'rōst; -'rōzd; 'skli(ə)rōst; 'skler-; -ōzd/ ▸adj. *Medicine* (esp. of blood vessels) affected by sclerosis.

scle·ro·sing cho·lan·gi·tis /ˌsklə'rōsiNG ˌkōlan'jītis/ ▸n. *Medicine* a complication of ulcerative colitis in which the bile ducts become narrow and develop irregularities. ▷1980s: *sclerosing* from the verb *sclerose* (back-formation from **SCLEROSED**); *cholangitis* from Greek *kholē* 'bile' + *angeion* 'vessel' + **-ITIS**.

scle·ro·sis /sklə'rōsis/ ▸n. *Medicine* abnormal hardening of body tissue. ■ see **MULTIPLE SCLEROSIS**. ■ *figurative* excessive resistance to change: *the challenge was to avoid institutional sclerosis.* ▷late Middle English (originally denoting a hard external tumor): via medieval Latin from Greek *sklērōsis*, from *sklēroun* 'harden.'

scle·ro·ther·a·py /ˌskli(ə)rə'THerəpē/ ▸n. *Medicine* the treatment of varicose blood vessels by the injection of an irritant that causes inflammation, coagulation of blood, and narrowing of the blood vessel wall.

scle·rot·ic /sklə'rätik/ ▸adj. **1** *Medicine* of or having sclerosis. ■ *figurative* becoming rigid and unresponsive; losing the ability to adapt: *sclerotic management.* **2** *Anatomy* of or relating to the sclera. ▶*n.* another term for SCLERA.

scle·ro·tin /ˈskli(ə)rətn; ˈskler-/ ▶*n. Biochemistry* a structural protein that forms the cuticles of insects and is hardened and darkened by a natural tanning process in which protein chains are cross-linked by quinone groups. ▷1940s: from SCLERO- 'hardened,' on the pattern of such words as *keratin.*

scle·ro·ti·um /ˌskləˈrōsʜēəm/ ▶*n.* (*pl.* **-ti·a** /-sʜēə/) *Botany* the hard dark resting body of certain fungi, consisting of a mass of hyphal threads, capable of remaining dormant for long periods. ▷mid 19th cent.: modern Latin (former genus name), from Greek *sklēros* 'hard.'

scle·ro·tized /ˈskli(ə)rəˌtīzd; ˈskler-/ (also **scle·ro·tised**) ▶*adj. Entomology* (of an insect's body, or part of one) hardened by conversion into sclerotin. **—scle·ro·ti·za·tion** /ˌskli(ə)rətəˈzāsʜən; ˌskler-/ *n.*

scle·ro·tome /ˈskli(ə)rəˌtōm; ˈskler-/ ▶*n. Embryology* the part of each somite in a vertebrate embryo giving rise to bone or other skeletal tissue. Compare with DERMATOME, MYOTOME.

scle·rous /ˈskli(ə)rəs; ˈskler-/ ▶*adj.* (of tissue) hardened or bony. ▷mid 19th cent.: from Greek *sklēros* 'hard' + -OUS.

scoff[1] /skôf; skäf/ ▶*v.* [*intrans.*] speak to someone or about something in a scornfully derisive or mocking way: *department officials* **scoffed at** *the allegations* | [with *direct speech*] *"You, a scientist?" he scoffed.*
▶*n.* an expression of scornful derision. ■ *archaic* an object of ridicule: *his army was the scoff of all Europe.* ▷Middle English (first used as a noun in the sense 'mockery, scorn'): perhaps of Scandinavian origin. **—scoff·er** *n.* **—scoff·ing·ly** *adv.*

scoff[2] *informal* ▶*v.* [*trans.*] eat (something) quickly and greedily: *she* **scoffed down** *several chops* | *a lizard* **scoffing up** *insects.* Compare with SCARF[3].
▶*n.* food. ▷late 18th cent. (as a verb): originally a variant of Scots and dialect *scaff.* The noun is from Afrikaans *schoff,* representing Dutch *schoft* 'quarter of a day,' (by extension) 'meal.'

scoff·law /ˈskôfˌlô; ˈskäf-/ ▶*n. informal* a person who flouts the law, esp. by failing to comply with a law that is difficult to enforce effectively.

scold /skōld/ ▶*v.* [*trans.*] remonstrate with or rebuke (someone) angrily: *Mom took Anna away, scolding her for her bad behavior.* See note at REBUKE.
▶*n. archaic* a woman who nags or grumbles constantly. ▷Middle English (as a noun): probably from Old Norse *skáld* 'skald.' **—scold·er** *n.* **—scold·ing** *n.* & *adj.*

THE RIGHT WORD **berate, chide, revile, scold, upbraid, vituperate**

A mother might **scold** a child who misbehaves, which means to rebuke in an angry, irritated, and often nagging way, whether or not such treatment is justified.

Chide is a more formal term than *scold,* and it usually implies disapproval for specific failings (*she was chided by her teacher for using "less" instead of "fewer"*).

Berate suggests a prolonged scolding, usually aimed at a pattern of behavior or way of life rather than a single misdeed and often combined with scorn or contempt for the person being criticized (*he berated his parents for being too protective and ruining his social life*).

Upbraid also implies a lengthy expression of displeasure or criticism, but usually with more justification than *scold* and with an eye toward encouraging better behavior in the future (*the tennis coach upbraided her players for missing so many serves*).

Revile and **vituperate** are reserved for very strong or even violent displays of anger. To *revile* is to use highly abusive and contemptuous language (*revile one's opponent in the press*), while **vituperate** connotes even more violence in the attack (*the angry hockey players were held apart by their teammates, but they continued to vituperate each other with the foulest possible language*).

sco·lex /ˈskōˌleks/ ▶*n.* (*pl.* **sco·li·ces** /ˈskäliˌsēz; ˈskō-/) *Zoology* the anterior end of a tapeworm, bearing suckers and hooks for attachment. ▷mid 19th cent.: modern Latin, from Greek *skōlēx* 'worm.'

sco·li·o·sis /ˌskōlēˈōsis/ ▶*n. Medicine* abnormal lateral curvature of the spine. Compare with KYPHOSIS and LORDOSIS. ▷early 18th cent.: modern Latin, from Greek, from *skolios* 'bent.' **—sco·li·ot·ic** /-ˈätik/ *adj.*

scol·lop /ˈskäləp; ˈskal-/ ▶*n.* & *v.* archaic spelling of SCALLOP.

scom·broid /ˈskämˌbroid/ *Zoology* ▶*n.* a fish of the mackerel family, or one of a larger group that also includes the barracudas and billfishes. • Family Scombridae or suborder Scombroidei.
▶*adj.* of or relating to fish of this family or group. ▷mid 19th cent.: from modern Latin *Scombroidea* (superfamily name), from Greek *skombros,* denoting a tuna or mackerel.

sconce[1] /skäns/ ▶*n.* **1** a candle holder, or a holder of another light source, that is attached to a wall with an ornamental bracket. **2** a flaming torch or candle secured in such a holder. ▷late Middle English (originally denoting a portable lantern with a screen to protect the flame): shortening of Old French *esconse* 'lantern,' or from medieval Latin *sconsa,* from Latin *absconsa (laterna)* 'dark (lantern)', literally 'hidden (lantern)' (i.e., a lantern with a device for concealing the light), from *abscondere* 'to hide.'

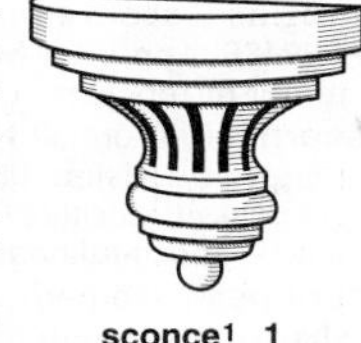

sconce[1] 1

sconce[2] ▶*n. archaic* a small fort or earthwork defending a ford, pass, or castle gate. ■ a shelter or screen serving as protection from fire or the weather. ▷late Middle English: from Dutch *schans* 'brushwood,' from Middle High German *schanze.* The earliest recorded sense 'screen, interior partition' derives perhaps from SCONCE[1]; the later senses date from the late 16th cent.

scone /skōn; skän/ ▶*n.* a small unsweetened or lightly sweetened biscuitlike cake made from flour, fat, and milk and sometimes having added fruit. ▷early 16th cent. (originally Scots): perhaps from Middle Dutch *schoon(broot)* 'fine (bread).'

scoop /sko͞op/ ▶*n.* **1** a utensil resembling a spoon, with a long handle and a deep bowl, used for removing powdered, granulated, or semisolid substances (such as ice cream) from a container. ■ a short-handled deep shovel used for moving grain, coal, etc. ■ a moving bowl-shaped part of a digging machine, dredger, or other mechanism into which material is gathered. ■ a long-handled spoonlike surgical instrument. ■ a quantity taken up by a scoop: *an apple pie with* **scoops of** *ice cream on top.* **2** *informal* a piece of news published by a newspaper or broadcast by a television or radio station in advance of its rivals. ■ (**the scoop**) the latest information about something.
▶*v.* [*trans.*] **1** pick up and move (something) with a scoop: *Philip began to scoop grain into his bag.* ■ create (a hollow or hole) with or as if with a scoop: *a hole was* **scooped out** *in the floor of the dwelling.* ■ pick up (someone or something) in a swift, fluid movement: *he laughed and* **scooped** *her* **up** *in his arms.* **2** *informal* publish a news story before (a rival reporter, newspaper, or radio or television station). ▷Middle English (originally denoting a utensil for pouring liquids): from Middle Dutch, Middle Low German *schōpe* 'waterwheel bucket'; from a West Germanic base meaning 'draw water'; related to the verb SHAPE. **—scoop·er** *n.* **—scoop·ful** *n.*

scoop neck ▶*n.* a deeply curved wide neckline on a garment.

scoot /sko͞ot/ ▶*v.* [*intrans.*] *informal* go or leave somewhere quickly: *I'd better scoot* | *they* **scooted off** *on their bikes.* ▷mid 18th cent.: of unknown origin.

scoot·er /ˈsko͞otər/ ▶*n.* **1** (also **mo·tor scoot·er**) a light two-wheeled open motor vehicle on which the driver sits over an enclosed engine with legs together and feet resting on a floorboard. ■ [often with *adj.*] any small, light, vehicle able to travel quickly across water, ice, or snow. **2** a vehicle typically ridden as a recreation, consisting of a footboard mounted on two wheels and a long steering handle, propelled by resting one foot on the footboard and pushing the other against the ground.
▶*v.* [*intrans.*] travel or ride on a scooter. **—scoot·er·ist** /-ist/ *n.*

scooter 2

sco·pa /ˈskōpə/ ▶*n.* (*pl.* **-pae** /-pē/) *Zoology* a small brushlike tuft of hairs on some insects, esp. that on which pollen collects on the leg of a bee. ▷early 19th cent.: from Latin *scopae* (plural) 'twigs, broom.'

scope[1] /skōp/ ▶*n.* the extent of the area or subject matter that something deals with or to which it is relevant: *we widened the scope of our investigation* | *such questions go well beyond the scope of this book.* See note at RANGE. ■ the opportunity or possibility to do or deal with something: *the* **scope for** *major change is always limited by political realities.* ■ *archaic* a purpose, end, or intention: *Plato maintains religion to be the chief aim and scope of human life.* ■ *Nautical* the length of cable extended when a ship rides at anchor. ■ *Linguistics* & *Logic* the range of the effect of an operator such as a quantifier or conjunction. ▷mid 16th cent. (in the sense 'target for shooting at'): from Italian *scopo* 'aim,' from Greek *skopos* 'target,' from *skeptesthai* 'look out.'

scope[2] *informal* ▶*n.* a telescope, microscope, or other device having a name ending in *-scope.*
▶*v.* [*trans.*] *informal* look at carefully; scan: *they watched him scoping the room, looking for Michael.* ■ assess; weigh up: *they'd* **scoped out** *their market.* ▷early 17th cent. (as a noun): shortened form. The verb dates from the 1970s.

-scope ▶*comb. form* denoting an instrument for observing, viewing, or examining: *microscope* | *telescope.* ▷from modern Latin *-scopium,* from Greek *skopein* 'look at.'

-scopic ▶*comb. form* in adjectives corresponding to nouns ending in *-scope* (such as *telescopic* corresponding to *telescope*).

sco·pol·a·mine /skəˈpäləˌmēn/ ▶*n. Chemistry* a poisonous plant alkaloid used as an antiemetic in motion sickness, as a preoperative medication for examination of the eye, and formerly as a sedative and hypnotic. • Chem. formula: $C_{17}H_{21}NO_4$. It is obtained chiefly from plants of the genus *Scopolia,* family Solanaceae. ▷late 19th cent.: from *Scopolia* (genus name of the plants yielding it) + AMINE.

scops owl /skäps/ ▶*n.* a small owl with distinctive ear tufts, found in Europe, Africa, and Asia. • Genus *Otus,* family Strigidae: many species, in particular the widespread **Eurasian scops owl** (*O. scops*). ▷early 18th cent.: *scops* from modern Latin *Scops* (former genus name), from Greek *skōps.*

scop·u·la /-lə/ ▶*n.* (*pl.* **scop·u·lae** /ˈskäpyəlē; ˈskäpyəlī/) *Zoology* a small brushlike structure, esp. on the legs of spiders. ▷early 19th cent.: from late Latin, diminutive of Latin *scopa* (see SCOPA).

-scopy ▶*comb. form* indicating viewing, observation, or examination, typically with an instrument having a name ending in *-scope*: *endoscopy* | *microscopy.* ▷from Greek *skopia* 'observation,' from *skopein* 'examine, look at.'

scor·bu·tic /skôrˈbyo͞otik/ ▶*adj.* relating to or affected with scurvy. See also ANTISCORBUTIC. ▷mid 17th cent.: from modern Latin *scorbuticus,* from medieval Latin *scorbutus* 'scurvy,' perhaps from Middle Low German *schorbūk* (from *schoren* 'to break' + *būk* 'belly').

scorch /skôrcʜ/ ▶*v.* **1** [*trans.*] burn the surface of (something) with flame or heat: *surrounding houses were scorched by heat from the blast.* See note at BURN. ■ [*intrans.*] become burned when exposed to heat or a flame: *the meat had scorched.* ■ [often as *adj.*] (**scorched**) (of the heat of the sun) cause (vegetation or a place) to become dried out and lifeless: *a desolate, scorched landscape.* **2** [*intrans.*] *informal* (of a person or vehicle) move very fast: *a sports car scorching along the expressway.*
▶*n.* the burning or charring of the surface of something: [as *adj.*] *a scorch mark.* ■ *Botany* a form of plant necrosis, typically of fungal origin, marked by browning of leaf margins. ▷Middle English (as a verb): perhaps related to Old Norse *skorpna* 'be shriveled.'

scorched earth pol·i·cy ▶*n.* a military strategy of burning or destroying buildings, crops, or other resources that might be of use to an invading enemy force. ■ *figurative* a strategy that involves taking extreme action: *a lawyer renowned for his scorched earth policy in divorce cases.*

scorch·er /ˈskôrcʜər/ ▶*n.* [usu. in *sing.*] *informal* **1** a day or period of very hot weather: *next week could be a real scorcher.* **2** a remarkable or extreme example of something, in particular: ■ a very powerfully struck ball: *Winfield hit a scorcher over the left field fence.* ■ sensational book or film. ■ a heated or violent argument.

scorch·ing /ˈskôrcʜiɴɢ/ ▶*adj.* very hot: *the scorching July sun.* ■ (of criticism) harsh; severe. ■ *informal* very fast: *she set a scorching pace.* **—scorch·ing·ly** *adv.*

Pronunciation Key ə *ago*; ər *over*; ˈə or ˌə *up*; ˈər or ˌər *fur*; a *hat*; ā *rate*; ä *car*; cʜ *chew*; e *let*; ē *see*; e(ə)r *air*; i *fit*; ī *by*; i(ə)r *ear*; ɴɢ *sing*; ō *go*; ô *for*; oi *boy*; o͝o *good*; o͞o *goo*; ou *out*; sʜ *she*; ᴛʜ *thin*; T͟H *then*; (h)w *why*; ᴢʜ *vision*

scor·da·tu·ra /ˌskôrdəˈto͝orə/ ▸*n. Music* the technique of altering the normal tuning of a stringed instrument to produce particular effects. ▷late 19th cent.: Italian, from *scordare* 'be out of tune.'

score /skôr/ ▸*n.* **1** the number of points, goals, runs, etc., achieved in a game: *the final score was 25–16 in favor of Washington.* ■ the number of points, goals, runs, etc., achieved by an individual player or a team in a game: *his highest score of the season.* ■ *informal* an act of gaining a point, goal, or run in a game. ■ a rating or grade, such as a mark achieved in a test: *an IQ score of 161.* ■ (**the score**) *informal* the state of affairs; the real facts about the present situation: *"Hey, what's the score here, what's goin' on?"* ■ *informal* an act of buying illegal drugs. ■ *informal* the proceeds of a crime. **2** (*pl.* same) a group or set of twenty or about twenty: *a score of men lost their lives in the battle | Doyle's success brought imitators* **by the score.** ■ (**scores of**) a large amount or number of something: *he sent scores of enthusiastic letters to friends.* **3** a written representation of a musical composition showing all the vocal and instrumental parts arranged one below the other. ■ the music composed for a movie or play. **4** a notch or line cut or scratched into a surface. ■ *historical* a running account kept by marks against a customer's name, typically in a tavern.
▸*v.* [*trans.*] **1** gain (a point, goal, run, etc.) in a competitive game: *Penn State scored two touchdowns in the fourth quarter | [intrans.] Martinez scored on Anderson's sacrifice fly.* ■ decide on the score to be awarded to (a competitor): *the judge must score each dog against this standard.* ■ gain (a number of points) for a competitor; be worth: *each correct answer scores ten points.* ■ decide on the scores to be awarded in (a game or competition). ■ [*intrans.*] record the score during a game; act as scorer. ■ *Baseball* cause (a teammate) to score: *McNab singled, scoring Reynolds and Diaz.* ■ *informal* secure (a success or an advantage): *the band scored a hit single.* ■ [*intrans.*] *informal* be successful: [with *complement*] *his new movie scored big.* ■ *informal* buy or acquire (something, typically illegal drugs): *Sally had scored some acid.* ■ [*intrans.*] *informal* succeed in attracting a sexual partner, typically for a casual encounter. **2** orchestrate or arrange (a piece of music), typically for a specified instrument or instruments: *the Quartet Suite was scored for flute, violin, viola da gamba, and continuo.* ■ compose the music for (a movie or play). **3** cut or scratch a notch or line on (a surface): *score the card until you cut through.* ■ *historical* record (a total owed) by making marks against a customer's name: *a slate on which the old man* **scored up** *vast accounts.* ■ *Medicine & Biology* examine (experimentally treated cells, bacterial colonies, etc.), making a record of the number showing a particular character. ▷late Old English *scoru* 'set of twenty,' from Old Norse *skor* 'notch, tally, twenty,' of Germanic origin; related to **SHEAR**. The verb (late Middle English) is from Old Norse *skora* 'make an incision.' —**score·less** *adj.* —**scor·er** *n.*
▸*PHRASES* □ **keep (the) score** register the score of a game as it proceeds. □ **know the score** *informal* be aware of the essential facts about a situation. □ **on that** (or **this**) **score** so far as that (or this) is concerned: *my priority was to blend new faces into the team, and we have succeeded on that score.* □ **score points** outdo another person, esp. in an argument. □ **settle a** (or **the**) **score 1** take revenge on someone for a past act. **2** *dated* pay off a debt or other obligation.

score·board /ˈskôrˌbôrd/ ▸*n.* a large board on which the score in a game or match is displayed.

score·card /ˈskôrˌkärd/ (also **score·sheet** or **score·book**) ▸*n.* (in sports) a card, sheet, or book in which scores are entered.

score·keep·er /ˈskôrˌkēpər/ ▸*n.* a person who keeps the score of a game.

sco·ri·a /ˈskôrēə/ ▸*n.* (*pl.* **sco·ri·ae** /ˈskôrē-ē/) a cindery, vesicular basaltic lava, typically having a frothy texture. ■ slag separated from molten metal during smelting. ▷late Middle English (denoting slag from molten metal): via Latin from Greek *skōria* 'refuse,' from *skōr* 'dung.' The geological term dates from the late 18th cent. —**sco·ri·a·ceous** /ˌskôrēˈāsнəs/ *adj.*

scor·ing pos·i·tion ▸*n. Baseball* a runner's position on second or third base, from which scoring on a base hit is likely.

scorn /skôrn/ ▸*n.* the feeling or belief that someone or something is worthless or despicable; contempt: *I do not wish to become the object of scorn | [in sing.] a general* **scorn for** *human life.* ■ [in *sing.*] *archaic* a person viewed with such feeling: *a scandal and a scorn to all who look on thee.* ■ *archaic* a statement or gesture indicating such feeling.
▸*v.* [*trans.*] feel or express contempt or derision for: *he accused America of scorning the Arab nation.* See note at **DESPISE**. ■ reject (something) in a contemptuous way: *opponents scorned Noriega's offer to negotiate.* ■ [*intrans.*] refuse to do something because one is too proud: *at her lowest ebb, she would have scorned to stoop to such tactics.* ▷Middle English: shortening of Old French *escarn* (noun), *escharnir* (verb), of Germanic origin. —**scorn·er** *n.* (*rare*).
▸*PHRASE* □ **pour** (or **heap**) **scorn on** speak with contempt or mockery of.

scorn·ful /ˈskôrnfəl/ ▸*adj.* feeling or expressing contempt or derision: *the justices have been* **scornful of** *the government's conduct | scornful laughter.* —**scorn·ful·ly** *adv.* —**scorn·ful·ness** *n.*

scor·per /ˈskôrpər/ (also **scau·per** /ˈskôpər/) ▸*n.* a sharp chisel-like tool with a curved or squared cutting end, used to scoop out broad lines and areas when engraving wood or metal.

Scor·pi·o /ˈskôrpēˌō/ *Astrology* the eighth sign of the zodiac (the Scorpion), which the sun enters about October 23. ■ (**a Scorpio**) (*pl.* **-os**) a person born when the sun is in this sign. ▷Latin. —**Scor·pi·an** /-pēən/ *n.* & *adj.*

scor·pi·oid /ˈskôrpēˌoid/ ▸*adj. Zoology* of, relating to, or resembling a scorpion. ■ *Botany* (of a flower cluster) curled up at the end, and uncurling as the flowers develop. ▷mid 19th cent.: from Greek from *skorpios* 'scorpion' + **-OID**.

scor·pi·on /ˈskôrpēən/ ▸*n.* a terrestrial arachnid with lobsterlike pincers and a poisonous sting at the end of its jointed tail, which it can hold curved over the back. Most kinds live in tropical and subtropical areas. • Order Scorpiones. ■ used in names of other arachnids and insects resembling a scorpion, e.g., **false scorpion, water scorpion.** ■ (**the Scorpion**) the zodiacal sign Scorpio or the constellation Scorpius. ■ (**scorpions**) *poetic/literary* a whip with metal points. [with allusion to 1 Kings 12:11.] ▷Middle English: via Old French from Latin *scorpio(n-)*, based on Greek *skorpios* 'scorpion.'

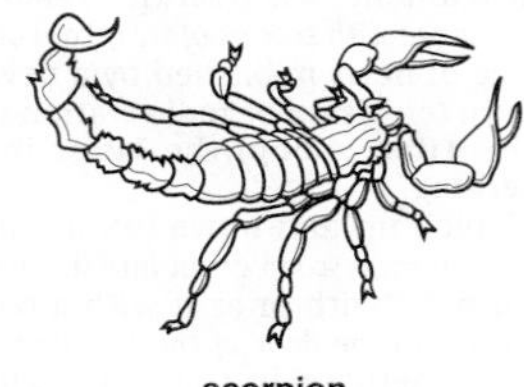

scorpion

scor·pi·on·fish /ˈskôrpēənˌfisн/ ▸*n.* (*pl.* same or **-fish·es**) a chiefly bottom-dwelling marine fish that is typically red in color and has spines on the head that are sometimes venomous. • Family Scorpaenidae: many genera and numerous species, including the redfishes and rockfishes.

scor·pi·on·fly /ˈskôrpēənˌflī/ (also **scor·pi·on fly**) ▸*n.* (*pl.* **-flies**) a slender predatory insect with membranous wings, long legs, and a downward-pointing beak. The terminal swollen section of the male's abdomen is carried curved up like a scorpion's stinger. • Order Mecoptera: several families, in particular Panorpidae.

Scor·pi·us /ˈskôrpēəs/ *Astronomy* a large constellation (the Scorpion). It contains the red giant Antares. ■ [as *genitive*] (**Scorpii** /-pēˌī/) used with a preceding letter or numeral to designate a star in this constellation: *the star Theta Scorpii.* ▷Latin.

Scor·se·se /skôrˈsāzē/, Martin (1942–), U.S. movie director. *Mean Streets* (1973) marked the beginning of his long collaboration with Robert De Niro, which continued in *Taxi Driver* (1976), and *Raging Bull* (1980), *Goodfellas* (1990), *Cape Fear* (1991), and *Casino* (1995). Other movies include the controversial *The Last Temptation of Christ* (1988).

scor·zo·ne·ra /ˌskôrzəˈni(ə)rə/ ▸*n.* a plant of the daisy family with tapering purple-brown edible roots. Also called **BLACK SALSIFY, BLACK OYSTER PLANT.** • *Scorzonera hispanica*, family Compositae. ■ the root of this plant used as a vegetable. ▷early 17th cent.: from Italian, from *scorzone*, from an alteration of medieval Latin *curtio(n-)* 'venomous snake' (against whose venom the plant may have been regarded as an antidote).

Scot /skät/ ▸*n.* a native of Scotland or a person of Scottish descent. ■ a member of a Gaelic people that migrated from Ireland to Scotland around the late 5th century. ▷Old English *Scottas* (plural), from late Latin *Scottus*, of unknown ultimate origin.

USAGE On the different uses of **Scot, Scots, Scottish,** and **Scotch,** see **usage** at **SCOTTISH.**

scot /skät/ ▸*n. archaic* a payment corresponding to a modern tax, rate, or other assessed contribution. ▷late Old English, from Old Norse *skot* 'a shot,' reinforced by Old French *escot*, of Germanic origin; related to **SHOT**[1].

Scot. ▸*abbr.* Scotland. ■ Scottish.

Scotch /skäcн/ ▸*adj.* old-fashioned term for **SCOTTISH.**
▸*n.* **1** short for **SCOTCH WHISKY. 2** [as *plural n.*] (**the Scotch**) *dated* the people of Scotland. **3** *dated* the form of English spoken in Scotland. ▷late 16th cent.: contraction of **SCOTTISH.** —**Scotch·man** (*dated*) *n.* (*pl.* **-men**) —**Scotch·wom·an** (*dated*) *n.* (*pl.* **-wom·en**)

USAGE The use of **Scotch** to mean 'of or relating to Scotland or its people' is disliked by many Scottish people and is now uncommon in modern English. It survives in a number of fixed expressions, such as *Scotch broth* and *Scotch whisky*. For more details, see **usage** at **SCOTTISH.**

scotch[1] /skäcн/ ▸*v.* **1** [*trans.*] decisively put an end to: *a spokesman has scotched the rumors.* ■ *archaic* render (something regarded as dangerous) temporarily harmless: *feudal power in France was scotched, though far from killed.* **2** [*trans.*] wedge (someone or something) somewhere: *he soon scotched himself against a wall.* ■ [*trans.*] *archaic* prevent (a wheel or other rolling object) from moving or slipping by placing a wedge underneath.
▸*n. archaic* a wedge placed under a wheel or other rolling object to prevent its moving or slipping. ▷early 17th cent. (as a noun): of unknown origin; perhaps related to **SKATE**[1]. The sense 'render temporarily harmless' is based on an emendation of Shakespeare's *Macbeth* III. ii. 13 as "We have scotch'd the snake, not kill'd it," originally understood as a use of **SCOTCH**[2]; the sense 'put an end to' (early 19th cent.) results from the influence on this of the notion of wedging or blocking something so as to render it inoperative.

scotch[2] ▸*v.* [*trans.*] *archaic* cut or score the skin or surface of.
▸*n. archaic* a cut or score in skin or another surface. ▷late Middle English: of unknown origin.

Scotch bon·net (also **Scotch bon·net pep·per**) ▸*n.* another term for **HABANERO.**

Scotch broth ▸*n.* a traditional Scottish soup made from beef or mutton stock with pearl barley and vegetables.

Scotch egg ▸*n.* a hard-boiled egg enclosed in sausage meat, rolled in breadcrumbs, and fried.

Scotch·gard /ˈskäcнˌgärd/ ▸*n. trademark* a fluorocarbon preparation for giving a waterproof grease- and stain-resistant finish to textiles, leather, and other materials.
▸*v.* [*trans.*] treat with such a substance.

Scotch pine ▸*n.* a long-lived, medium-sized Eurasian pine tree extensively planted for its timber and other products. It is well established in the northeastern U.S. and the Great Lakes region. • *Pinus sylvestris*, family Pinaceae.

Scotch tape *trademark* ▸*n.* transparent adhesive tape.
▸*v.* (**Scotch-tape**) [*trans.*] stick with transparent adhesive tape.

Scotch whis·ky (also **Scotch whis·key**) ▸*n.* whisky distilled in Scotland, esp. from malted barley.

USAGE The variant spelling **Scotch whiskey** is considered improper. For an explanation of when to use the spelling *whisky* rather than *whiskey*, see **usage** at **WHISKEY.**

sco·ter /ˈskōtər/ ▸*n.* (*pl.* same or **-ters**) a northern diving duck that winters off the coast, the male of which has mainly black plumage. • Genus *Melanitta*, family Anatidae: three species. ▷late 17th cent.: of unknown origin.

scot-free ▸*adv.* without suffering any punishment or injury: *the people who kidnapped you will* **get off scot-free.** ▷from the early sense 'not subject to the payment of scot.'

sco·tia /ˈskōsнə/ ▸*n.* (chiefly in classical architecture) a concave molding, esp. at the base of a column. ▷mid 16th cent.: via Latin from Greek *skotia*, from *skotos* 'darkness,' with reference to the shadow produced.

Scot·land /ˈskätlənd/ a country in northern Great Britain and the United Kingdom; pop. 4,957,300; capital, Edinburgh; languages, English (official) and the Scottish form of Gaelic. Scotland was settled by Celtic peoples during the Bronze and early Iron ages. An independent country in the Middle Ages, it was amalgamated with England as a result of the union of the Crowns in 1603 and of the Parliaments in 1707. The distinctive Celtic society of the Highlands, based on clans, was destroyed in the aftermath of the Jacobite uprisings of 1715 and 1745–46. In 1997, the Scots voted to establish a devolved parliament with tax-raising powers. Scotland's economy has benefited in the 20th century from the discovery of North Sea oil.

Scot·land Yard the headquarters of the London Metropolitan Police, situated from 1829 to 1890 in Great Scotland Yard off Whitehall, from 1890 until 1967 in New Scotland Yard on the Thames Embankment, and from 1967 in New Scotland Yard, Westminster. ■ used to allude to the Criminal Investigation Department of the London Metropolitan Police force.

sco·to·ma /skəˈtōmə/ ▸*n.* (*pl.* **-mas** or **-ma·ta** /-mətə/) *Medicine* a partial loss of vision or a blind spot in an otherwise normal visual field. ▷mid 16th cent. (denoting dizziness and dim vision): via late Latin from Greek *skotōma*, from *skotoun* 'darken,' from *skotos* 'darkness.' —**sco·tom·a·tous** /-mətəs/ *adj.*

sco·top·ic /skəˈtōpik; -ˈtäpik/ ▸*adj. Physiology* relating to or denoting vision in dim light, believed to involve chiefly the rods of the retina. Often contrasted with PHOTOPIC. ▷early 20th cent.: from Greek *skotos* 'darkness' + -OPIA + -IC.

Scots /skäts/ ▸*adj.* another term for SCOTTISH: *a Scots accent.* [northern variant, originally as *Scottis.*]
▸*n.* the form of English used in Scotland.

USAGE On the use of **Scots**, **Scot**, **Scottish**, and **Scotch**, see usage at SCOTTISH.

Scots·man /ˈskätsmən/ ▸*n.* (*pl.* **-men**) a male native or national of Scotland or a man of Scottish descent.

Scots·wom·an /ˈskätsˌwo͝omən/ ▸*n.* (*pl.* **-wom·en**) a female native or national of Scotland or a woman of Scottish descent.

Scott[1] /skät/, Dred (*c.* 1795–1858), U.S. slave. He brought suit for his freedom based on the fact that he had lived in free territories for five years, but the U.S. Supreme Court ruled against him in 1857 in a case that became the focus of much heated political controversy. Scott was emancipated later that year and worked as a hotel porter in St. Louis.

Scott[2], George C(ampbell) (1927–99), U.S. actor and director. His best known movies include *The Hustler* (1961), *Patton* (Academy Award, 1970), *Taps* (1981), and *Malice* (1993).

Scott[3], Ridley (1939–), English movie director. Notable works: *Alien* (1979), *Blade Runner* (1982), *Thelma and Louise* (1991), and *G.I. Jane* (1997). His brother **Tony** (1944–) is also a successful movie director, responsible for such works as *Top Gun* (1986) and *True Romance* (1993).

Scott[4], Sir Robert (Falcon) (1868–1912), English explorer and naval officer. During 1910–12, he and four companions made a journey to the South Pole by sled, arriving there in January 1912 to discover that Roald Amundsen had beaten them by a month. Scott and his companions died on the journey back to base.

Scott[5], Sir Walter (1771–1832), Scottish novelist and poet. He established the form of the historical novel in Britain and was influential in his treatment of rural themes and his use of regional speech. Notable novels: *Waverley* (1814), *Ivanhoe* (1819), and *Kenilworth* (1821).

Scott[6], Winfield (1786–1866), U.S. army officer; known as **Old Fuss and Feathers**. A hero of the War of 1812, he became supreme commander of the U.S. Army 1841–61. During the Mexican War, he waged a victorious campaign from Veracruz to Mexico City in 1847. He ran for the office of U.S. president as the Whig candidate in 1852 but was defeated by Democrat Franklin Pierce.

Scot·ti·cism /ˈskätiˌsizəm/ ▸*n.* a characteristically Scottish phrase, word, or idiom. ▷early 18th cent.: from late Latin *Scot(t)icus* + -ISM.

Scot·tie /ˈskätē/ ▸*n. informal* (also **Scot·tie dog**) a Scottish terrier.

Scot·tish /ˈskätisʜ/ ▸*adj.* of or relating to Scotland or its people: *the Scottish Highlands | Scottish dancing.*
▸*n.* [as *plural n.*] (**the Scottish**) the people of Scotland. See also SCOTS. —**Scot·tish·ness** *n.*

USAGE The terms **Scottish**, **Scot**, **Scots**, and **Scotch** are all variants of the same word. They have had different histories, however, and in modern English they have developed different uses and connotations.
The normal everyday word used to mean 'of or relating to Scotland or its people' is **Scottish**: ***Scottish** people; **Scottish** hills; **Scottish** Gaelic; she's English, not Scottish.*
The normal, neutral word for 'a person from Scotland' is **Scot**, along with **Scotsman**, **Scotswoman**, and the plural form **the Scots** (or, less commonly, **the Scottish**).
Scots is also used, like **Scottish**, as an adjective meaning 'of or relating to Scotland.' However, it tends to be used in a narrower sense to refer specifically to the form of English used in Scotland: ***Scots** accent: the **Scots** word for 'night.'*
The word **Scotch**, meaning either 'of or relating to Scotland' or 'a person/the people from Scotland,' was widely used in the past by Scottish writers such as Robert Burns and Sir Walter Scott. In the 20th century, it became less common. It is disliked by many Scottish people (as being an 'English' invention) and is now regarded as old-fashioned in most contexts. It survives in certain fixed phrases, as, for example, ***Scotch** broth* and ***Scotch** whisky.*

Scot·tish rite ▸*n.* a ceremonial rite in a Masonic order.

Scot·tish ter·ri·er ▸*n.* a small terrier of a rough-haired short-legged breed.

Scotts·dale /ˈskätsˌdāl/ a city in south central Arizona, east of Phoenix; pop. 202,705.

scoun·drel /ˈskoundrəl/ ▸*n.* a dishonest or unscrupulous person; a rogue. ▷late 16th cent.: of unknown origin. —**scoun·drel·ism** /-ˌlizəm/ *n.* —**scoun·drel·ly** *adj.*

scour[1] /skou(ə)r/ ▸*v.* [*trans.*] **1** clean or brighten the surface of (something) by rubbing it hard, typically with an abrasive or detergent: *he scoured the bathtub.* ■ remove (dirt or unwanted matter) by rubbing in such a way: *use an electric toothbrush to **scour off** plaque* | [*intrans.*] *I've spent all day mopping and scouring.* ■ (of water or a watercourse) make (a channel or pool) by flowing forcefully over something and removing soil or rock: *a stream came crashing through a narrow cavern to **scour out** a round pool below.* **2** *archaic* administer a strong purgative to.
▸*n.* **1** the action of scouring or the state of being scoured, esp. by swift-flowing water. ■ [in *sing.*] an act of rubbing something hard to clean or brighten it: *give the floor a good scour.* **2** (also **scours**) diarrhea in livestock, esp. cattle and pigs. ▷Middle English: from Middle Dutch, Middle Low German *schūren*, from Old French *escurer*, from late Latin *excurare* 'clean (off),' from *ex-* 'away' + *curare* 'to clean.' —**scour·er** *n.*

scour[2] ▸*v.* [*trans.*] subject (a place, text, etc.) to a thorough search in order to locate something: *David **scoured** each newspaper **for** an article on the murder.* ■ [*intrans.*] move rapidly in a particular direction, esp. in search or pursuit of someone or something: *he scoured up the ladder.* ▷late Middle English: related to obsolete *scour* 'moving hastily,' of unknown origin.

scourge /skərj/ ▸*n.* **1** *historical* a whip used as an instrument of punishment. **2** a person or thing that causes great trouble or suffering: *the scourge of mass unemployment.*
▸*v.* [*trans.*] **1** *historical* whip (someone) as a punishment. **2** cause great suffering to: *political methods used to scourge and oppress workers.* ▷Middle English: shortening of Old French *escorge* (noun), *escorgier* (verb), from Latin *ex-* 'thoroughly' + *corrigia* 'thong, whip.' —**scourg·er** *n.* (*historical*).

scour·ing rush ▸*n.* a horsetail with a very rough, ridged stem, formerly used for scouring and polishing. • Genus *Equisetum*, family Equisetaceae, in particular *E. hyemale*.

scout[1] /skout/ ▸*n.* **1** a soldier or other person sent out ahead of a main force so as to gather information about the enemy's position, strength, or movements. ■ a ship or aircraft employed for reconnaissance, esp. a small fast aircraft. ■ short for TALENT SCOUT. ■ [usu. in *sing.*] an instance of gathering information, esp. by reconnoitering an area: *I returned from a lengthy scout around the area.* **2** (also **Scout**) a Boy Scout or Girl Scout. **3** *informal, dated* a man or boy: *I've got nothing against Harrison—he's a **good scout**.* **4** a domestic worker at a college at Oxford University.
▸*v.* [*intrans.*] make a search for someone or something in various places: *I was sent to **scout around** for a place to park the camper | we **scouted for** clues.* ■ (esp. of a soldier) go ahead of a main force so as to gather information about an enemy's position, strength, or movements. ■ [*trans.*] explore or examine (a place or area of business) so as to gather information about it: *American companies are keen to **scout out** business opportunities.* ■ look for suitably talented people for recruitment to one's own organization or sports team: *Johnson has been scouting for the Pirates.* ▷late Middle English (as a verb): from Old French *escouter* 'listen,' earlier *ascolter*, from Latin *auscultare*. —**scout·er** *n.*
▸*PHRASE* □ **Scout's honor** the oath taken by a Boy Scout or Girl Scout. ■ *informal* used to indicate that one has the same honorable standards associated with Scouts and so will stand by a promise or tell the truth.

scout[2] ▸*v.* [*trans.*] *rare* reject (a proposal or idea) with scorn. ▷early 17th cent.: of Scandinavian origin; compare with Old Norse *skúta*, *skúti* 'a taunt.'

Scout As·so·ci·a·tion (in the UK) a worldwide youth organization founded for boys in 1908 by Lord Baden-Powell with the aim of developing their character by training them in self-sufficiency and survival techniques in the outdoors.

scout car ▸*n.* a fast armored vehicle used for military reconnaissance and liaison.

scout·ing /ˈskoutiɴɢ/ ▸*n.* **1** the action of gathering information about enemy forces or an area. ■ the activity of a talent scout: [as *adj.*] *What does the scouting report say about Stoddard's change-up pitch?* **2** (also **Scout·ing**) the characteristic activity and occupation of a Boy Scout or Girl Scout; the Scout movement.

scout·mas·ter /ˈskoutˌmastər/ ▸*n.* the adult in charge of a group of Boy Scouts.

scow /skou/ ▸*n.* a wide-beamed sailing dinghy. ■ a flat-bottomed boat with sloping ends used as a lighter and in dredging and other harbor services. ▷mid 17th cent.: from Dutch *schouw* 'ferryboat.'

scowl /skoul/ ▸*n.* an angry or bad-tempered expression.
▸*v.* [*intrans.*] frown in an angry or bad-tempered way: *she **scowled at** him defiantly.* ▷late Middle English (as a verb): probably of Scandinavian origin; compare with Danish *skule* 'scowl.' The noun dates from the early 16th cent. —**scowl·er** *n.*

SCP ▸*abbr.* single-cell protein.

SCPO ▸*abbr.* Senior Chief Petty Officer.

scrab·ble /ˈskrabəl/ ▸*v.* [*intrans.*] scratch or grope around with one's fingers to find, collect, or hold on to something: *she scrabbled at the grassy slope, desperate for a firm grip.* ■ (of an animal) scratch at something with its claws: *a dog was scrabbling at the door.* ■ [with *adverbial of direction*] scramble or crawl quickly: *lizards scrabbling across the walls.* ■ make great efforts to get somewhere or achieve something: *I had to scrabble around to find this apartment.*
▸*n.* **1** [in *sing.*] an act of scratching or scrambling for something: *he heard the scrabble of claws behind him.* ■ a struggle to get somewhere or achieve something: *a scrabble among the salesmen to avoid going to the bottom of the heap.* **2** (**Scrabble**) *trademark* a board game in which players use lettered tiles to create words in a

S

crossword fashion. ▷mid 16th cent. (in the sense 'make marks at random, scrawl'): from Middle Dutch *schrabbelen*, frequentative of *schrabben* 'to scrape.' The noun sense 'struggle to achieve something' is originally a North American usage dating from the late 18th cent. —**scrab·bler** *n.*

scrag /skrag/ ▶*v.* (**scragged**, **scrag·ging**) [*trans.*] *informal, chiefly Brit.* handle roughly; beat up. ■ *dated, informal* kill, esp. by strangling or hanging.
▶*n.* **1** an unattractively thin person or animal. **2** *dated, informal* a person's neck. ▷mid 16th cent. (as a noun): perhaps an alteration of Scots and northern English *crag* 'neck.' The verb (mid 18th cent.) developed the sense 'handle roughly' from the early use 'hang, strangle.'

scrag·gly /ˈskrag(ə)lē/ (also **scrag·gy** /ˈskragē/) ▶*adj.* (**-gli·er**, **-gli·est**) (of a person or animal) thin and bony. ■ ragged, thin, or untidy in form or appearance: *a man with a scraggly beard.* ■ (of a plant, tree, or shrubbery) sparsely foliated or having thin, uneven growth: *it was the scraggliest Christmas tree I had ever seen.* —**scrag·gi·ly** /-əlē/ *adv.* —**scrag·gli·ness** or **scrag·gi·ness** *n.*

scram /skram/ ▶*v.* (**scrammed**, **scram·ming**) **1** [*intrans.*, usu. in *imperative*] *informal* go away from or get out of somewhere quickly: *get out of here, you miserable wretches—scram!* **2** [*trans.*] *informal* shut down (a nuclear reactor) in an emergency.
▶*n. informal* the emergency shutdown of a nuclear reactor: *the power plant was cited for its high rate of scrams over the past year.* ▷early 20th cent.: probably from the verb **SCRAMBLE**.

scram·ble /ˈskrambəl/ ▶*v.* **1** [*intrans.*] make one's way quickly or awkwardly up a steep slope or over rough ground by using one's hands as well as one's feet: *we scrambled over the wet boulders.* ■ move hurriedly or clumsily from or into a particular place or position: *she scrambled out of the car | I tried to scramble to my feet.* ■ (**scramble into**) put (clothes) on hurriedly: *Robbie scrambled into jeans and a T-shirt.* ■ [*trans.*] *informal* perform (an action) or achieve (a result) hurriedly, clumsily, or with difficulty. ■ [with *infinitive*] struggle or compete with others for something in an eager or uncontrolled and undignified way: *firms scrambled to win public-sector contracts.* ■ [*trans.*] (often **be scrambled**) order (a fighter aircraft or its pilot) to take off immediately in an emergency or for action. ■ [*intrans.*] (of a fighter aircraft or its pilot) take off in such a way. ■ [*intrans.*] *Football* (of a quarterback) run around with the ball behind the line of scrimmage while looking for an open receiver. ■ [*intrans.*] *Football* run forward with the ball when unable to pass to an open receiver. **2** [*trans.*] make (something) jumbled or muddled: *maybe the alcohol has scrambled his brains.* ■ prepare (eggs) by beating them with a little liquid and then cooking and stirring them gently. ■ make (a broadcast transmission, a telephone message, or electronic data) unintelligible unless received by an appropriate decoding device: [as *adj.*] (**scrambled**) *scrambled television signals.*
▶*n.* [usu. in *sing.*] **1** a difficult or hurried clamber up or over something: *an undignified scramble over the wall.* ■ a walk up steep terrain involving the use of one's hands. ■ an eager or uncontrolled and undignified struggle with others to obtain or achieve something: *a* **scramble for** *high-priced concert seats.* ■ an emergency takeoff by fighter aircraft. **2** a disordered mixture of things: *the encryptor produced a scramble of the letters of the alphabet.* ▷late 16th cent.: imitative; compare with the dialect words *scamble* 'stumble' and *cramble* 'crawl.' —**scram·bling** /-b(ə)liNG/ *n.*

scram·bled eggs /ˈskrambəld/ ▶*n.* **1** a dish of eggs prepared by beating them with a little liquid and then cooking and stirring gently. **2** *informal* gold braid on a field-grade military officer's cap.

scram·bler /ˈskramb(ə)lər/ ▶*n.* **1** a person or thing that scrambles, esp. a device for scrambling a broadcast transmission, a telephone message, or electronic data. **2** a plant with long slender stems supported by other plants.

scram·jet /ˈskram,jet/ ▶*n. Aeronautics* a ramjet in which combustion takes place in a stream of gas moving at supersonic speed. ▷1960s: from *s(upersonic)* + *c(ombustion)* + **RAMJET**.

Scran·ton /ˈskrantn/ an industrial city in northeastern Pennsylvania; pop. 76,415. ▷named after the *Scranton* family, who established a steelworks on the site in 1840, around which the city developed.

scrap[1] /skrap/ ▶*n.* **1** a small piece or amount of something, esp. one that is left over after the greater part has been used: *I scribbled her address on a* **scrap of** *paper |* **scraps of** *information.* ■ (**scraps**) bits of uneaten food left after a meal, esp. when fed to animals: *he filled Sammy's bowls with fresh water and scraps.* ■ used to emphasize the lack or smallness of something: *there was not* **a scrap of** *aggression in him | every* **scrap of** *green land is up for grabs by development.* ■ *informal* a small person or animal, esp. one regarded with affection or sympathy: *poor little scrap, she's too hot in that coat.* ■ a particularly small thing of its kind: *she was wearing a short black skirt and a tiny scrap of a top.* **2** (also **scrap met·al**) discarded metal for reprocessing: *the steamer was eventually sold for scrap.* ■ [often as *adj.*] any waste articles or discarded material, esp. that which can be put to another purpose: *we're burning scrap lumber.*
▶*v.* (**scrapped**, **scrap·ping**) [*trans.*] (often **be scrapped**) discard or remove from service (a retired, old, or inoperative vehicle, vessel, or machine), esp. so as to convert it to scrap metal: *the decision was made to scrap the entire fleet.* ■ abolish or cancel (something, esp. a plan, policy, or law) that is now regarded as unnecessary, unwanted, or unsuitable: *the station scrapped plans to televise the contest live.* ▷late Middle English (as a plural noun denoting fragments of uneaten food): from Old Norse *skrap* 'scraps'; related to *skrapa* 'to scrape.' The verb dates from the late 19th cent.

scrap[2] *informal* ▶*n.* a fight or quarrel, esp. a minor or spontaneous one.
▶*v.* (**scrapped**, **scrap·ping**) [*intrans.*] engage in such a fight or quarrel. ■ compete fiercely: *the talk-show producers are scrapping for similar audiences.* ▷late 17th cent. (as a noun in the sense 'sinister plot, scheme'): perhaps from the noun **SCRAPE**. —**scrap·per** *n.*

scrap·book /ˈskrap,bo͝ok/ ▶*n.* a book of blank pages for sticking clippings, drawings, or pictures in.
▶*v.* [*intrans.*] [usually as *n.*] (**scrapbooking**) create scrapbooks as a hobby: *I scrapbook with the kids nearly every weekend.*

scrape /skrāp/ ▶*v.* **1** [*trans.*] push or pull a hard or sharp implement across (a surface or object) so as to remove dirt or other matter: *rinse off the carrots and scrape them | we scraped the dishes clean.* ■ use a sharp or hard implement to remove (dirt or unwanted matter) from something: *she scraped the mud off her shoes.* ■ apply (a hard or sharp implement) in this way: *he scraped the razor across the stubble on his cheek.* ■ make (a hollow) by scraping away soil or rock: *he found a ditch, scraped a hole, and put the bag in it.* **2** rub or cause to rub by accident against a rough or hard surface, causing damage or injury: [*intrans.*] *he smashed into the wall and felt his knee* **scrape against** *the plaster |* [*trans.*] *she reversed in a reckless sweep, scraping the left front fender.* ■ [*trans.*] draw or move (something) along or over something else, making a harsh noise: *she* **scraped back** *her chair and stood up.* ■ [*intrans.*] move with or make such a sound: *she lifted the gate to prevent its scraping along the ground.* ■ [*intrans.*] *humorous* play a violin or similar stringed instrument tunelessly: *Katie was scraping away at her cello.* ■ [*trans.*] draw one's hair tightly back off the forehead: *her hair* **was scraped back into** *a ponytail.* **3** [*trans.*] just manage to achieve; accomplish with great effort or difficulty: *for some years he* **scraped a living** *as a tutor.* ■ (**scrape something together/up**) collect or accumulate something with difficulty: *they could hardly scrape up enough money for one ticket, let alone two.* ■ [*intrans.*] try to save as much money as possible; economize: *they had scrimped and scraped and saved for years.* ■ [*intrans.*] (**scrape by/along**) manage to live with difficulty: *she has to* **scrape by on** *Social Security.* ■ [*intrans.*] narrowly pass by or through something: *there was only just room to* **scrape through** *between the tree and the edge of the stream.* ■ [*intrans.*] barely manage to succeed in a particular undertaking: *Clinton* **scraped into** *office in 1992 | he* **scraped through** *the entrance exam.*
▶*n.* **1** an act or sound of scraping: *he heard the scrape of his mother's key in the lock.* ■ an injury or mark caused by scraping: *there was a long, shallow scrape on his shin.* ■ a place where soil has been scraped away, esp. a shallow hollow formed in the ground by a bird during a courtship display or for nesting. ■ *informal, Medicine* a procedure of dilatation of the cervix and curettage of the uterus, or the result of this. ■ *archaic* an obsequious bow in which one foot is drawn backward along the ground. **2** *informal* an embarrassing or difficult predicament caused by one's own unwise behavior: *he'd been in worse scrapes than this before now.* ▷Old English *scrapian* 'scratch with the fingernails,' of Germanic origin, reinforced in Middle English by Old Norse *skrapa* or Middle Dutch *schrapen* 'to scratch.'
▶*PHRASES* □ **scrape acquaintance with** *dated* contrive to get to know: *aboard the ship, a nice girl scraped acquaintance with me.* □ **scrape the bottom of the barrel** *informal* be reduced to using things or people of the poorest quality because there is nothing else available.

scrap·er /ˈskrāpər/ ▶*n.* a tool or device used for scraping, esp. for removing dirt, paint, ice, or other unwanted matter from a surface.

scrap heap ▶*n.* a pile of discarded materials or articles: *cars on a scrap heap |* **figurative** *it should be consigned to the scrap heap of technological history.*

scrap·ie /ˈskrāpē/ ▶*n.* a disease of sheep involving the central nervous system, characterized by a lack of coordination causing affected animals to rub against trees and other objects for support, and thought to be caused by a viruslike agent such as a prion. ▷early 20th cent.: from the verb **SCRAPE** + **-IE**.

scrap·ing /ˈskrāpiNG/ ▶*n.* the action or sound of something scraping or being scraped: *the scraping of the spoon in the bowl |* [in *sing.*] *there was a scraping of chairs.* ■ (usu. **scrapings**) a small amount of something that has been obtained by scraping it from a surface: *I got some scrapings from under the girl's fingernails.*

scrap met·al ▶*n.* another term for **SCRAP**[1] (sense 2).

scrap·ple /ˈskrapəl/ ▶*n.* scraps of pork or other meat stewed with cornmeal and shaped into loaves for slicing and frying, esp. characteristic of eastern Pennsylvania. ▷mid 19th cent.: diminutive of the noun **SCRAP**[1].

scrap·py /ˈskrapē/ ▶*adj.* (**-pi·er**, **-pi·est**) **1** consisting of disorganized, untidy, or incomplete parts: *scrappy lecture notes piled up unread.* [mid 19th cent.: derivative of **SCRAP**[1].] **2** *informal* determined, argumentative, or pugnacious: *he played the part of a scrappy detective.* [late 19th cent.: derivative of **SCRAP**[2].] —**scrap·pi·ly** /-əlē/ *adv.* —**scrap·pi·ness** *n.*

scrap·yard /ˈskrap,yärd/ ▶*n.* British term for **JUNKYARD**.

scratch /skraCH/ ▶*v.* **1** [*trans.*] score or mark the surface of (something) with a sharp or pointed object: *the car's paintwork was battered and scratched |* [*intrans.*] *he scratched at a stain on his jacket.* ■ make a long, narrow superficial wound in the skin of: *her arms were scratched by the thorns | I scratched myself on the tree.* ■ rub (a part of one's body) with one's fingernails to relieve itching: *Jessica lifted her sunglasses and scratched her nose.* ■ make (a mark or hole) by scoring a surface with a sharp or pointed object: *I found two names scratched on one of the windowpanes.* ■ write (something) hurriedly or awkwardly: *pass me my writing things—I'll scratch a few letters before I get up.* ■ [*trans.*] remove (something) from something else by pulling a sharp implement over it: *he scratched away the plaster.* ■ [*intrans.*] make a rasping or grating noise by scraping something over a hard surface: *the dog scratched to be let in |* [as *n.*] (**scratching**) *there was a sound of scratching behind the wall.* ■ [*intrans.*] [often as *n.*] (**scratching**) play a record using the scratch technique (see sense 1 of the *n.* below.) ■ [*intrans.*] (of a bird or mammal, esp. a chicken) rake the ground with the beak or claws in search of food. ■ accomplish (something) with great effort or difficulty: *he* **scratches out a living** *growing strawberries.* **2** [*trans.*] cancel or strike out (writing) with a pen or pencil: *the name of Dr. McNab was* **scratched out** *and that of Dr. Daniels substituted.* ■ withdraw (a competitor) from a competition: *Oswald's Zephyr was the second horse to be* **scratched from** *a race today.* ■ [*intrans.*] (of a competitor) withdraw from a competition: *due to a knee injury she was forced to* **scratch from** *the race.* ■ cancel or abandon (an undertaking or project): *the original filming schedule has been scratched.*
▶*n.* **1** a mark or wound made by scratching: *the scratches on her arm were throbbing |* [as *adj.*] *scratch marks on the door.* ■ [in *sing.*] *informal* a slight or insignificant wound or injury: *it's nothing—just a scratch.* ■ [in *sing.*] an act or spell of scratching oneself to relieve itching: *he gave his scalp a good scratch.* ■ a rasping or grating noise produced by something rubbing against a hard surface: *the scratch of a match lighting a cigarette.* ■ a rough hiss, caused by the friction of the stylus in the groove, heard when a record is played. ■ a technique, used esp. in rap music, of stopping a record by hand and moving it back and forth to give a rhythmic scratching effect. **2** the starting point in a handicap for a competitor receiving no odds. [originally denoting a boundary or starting line for sports competitors.] ■ *Golf* a handicap of zero, indicating that a player is good enough

to achieve par on a course. **3** *informal* money: *he was working to get some scratch together.*

▸*adj.* [*attrib.*] **1** assembled or made from whatever is available, and so unlikely to be of the highest quality: *at least two vessels set sail with scratch crews.* **2** (of a sports competitor or event) with no handicap given. ▷late Middle English: probably a blend of the synonymous dialect words *scrat* and *cratch*, both of uncertain origin; compare with Middle Low German *kratsen* and Old High German *krazzōn.* **—scratch·er** *n.*

▸**PHRASES** □ **from scratch** from the very beginning, esp. without utilizing or relying on any previous work for assistance: *he built his own computer company from scratch.* □ **scratch a —— and find a ——** used to suggest that an investigation of someone or something soon reveals their true nature: *he had been taught to believe "scratch a pious man and find a hypocrite."* □ **scratch one's head** *informal* think hard in order to find a solution to something. ■ feel or express bewilderment. □ **scratch the surface 1** deal with a matter only in the most superficial way: *research has only scratched the surface of the paranormal.* **2** initiate the briefest investigation to discover something concealed: *they have a boring image, but scratch the surface and it's fascinating.* □ **up to scratch** up to the required standard; satisfactory: *her German was not up to scratch.* □ **you scratch my back and I'll scratch yours** *proverb* if you do me a favor, I'll return it.

scratch·board /ˈskraCH,bôrd/ ▸*n.* cardboard with a blackened surface that can be scratched or scraped off for making white line drawings.

scratch coat ▸*n.* a rough coating of plaster scratched before it is quite dry to ensure the adherence of the next coat.

scratch·pad /ˈskraCH,pad/ (also **scratch pad**) ▸*n.* a notepad. ■ *Computing* a small, fast memory for the temporary storage of data.

scratch test ▸*n.* a test for an allergic reaction in which a possible allergen is applied to a scratched area of skin.

scratch·y /ˈskraCHē/ ▸*adj.* (**scratch·i·er**, **scratch·i·est**) (esp. of a fabric or garment) having a rough, uncomfortable texture and tending to cause itching or discomfort. ■ (of a voice or sound) rough; grating: *she dropped her voice to a scratchy whisper.* ■ (of a record) making a crackling or rough sound because of scratches on the surface. ■ (of writing or a drawing) done with quick and jagged strokes: *a scratchy ink sketch of a man on horseback.* **—scratch·i·ly** /-əlē/ *adv.* **—scratch·i·ness** *n.*

scrawl /skrôl/ ▸*v.* [*trans.*] write (something) in a hurried, careless way: *Charlie scrawled his signature* | [*intrans.*] *he was scrawling on the back of a used envelope.*

▸*n.* an example of hurried, careless writing: *the page was covered in scrawls and doodles* | *reams of handwritten scrawl.* ■ a note or message written in this way: *Duncan read the scrawl, then passed it to her.* ▷early 17th cent.: apparently an alteration of the verb **CRAWL**, perhaps influenced by obsolete *scrawl* 'sprawl.' **—scrawl·er** *n.* **—scrawl·y** *adj.*

scrawn·y /ˈskrônē/ ▸*adj.* (**scrawn·i·er**, **scrawn·i·est**) (of a person or animal) unattractively thin and bony. ■ (of vegetation) meager or stunted. ▷mid 19th cent.: variant of dialect *scranny*; compare with archaic *scrannel* 'weak, feeble' (referring to sound). **—scrawn·i·ness** *n.*

scream /skrēm/ ▸*v.* [*intrans.*] give a long, loud, piercing cry or cries expressing excitement, great emotion, or pain: *they could hear him screaming in pain* | [as *adj.*] (**screaming**) *a houseful of barking dogs and screaming children.* ■ [*reporting verb*] cry something in a high-pitched, frenzied way: [*intrans.*] *I ran to the house screaming for help* | [with *direct speech*] *"Get out!" he screamed* | [*trans.*] *he screamed abuse into the phone.* ■ urgently and vociferously call attention to one's views or feelings, esp. ones of anger or distress: [with *clause*] *his supporters scream that he is being done an injustice* | *figurative the creative side of me is screaming out for attention.* ■ make a loud, high-pitched sound: *sirens were screaming from all over the city.* ■ move very rapidly with or as if with such a sound: *a shell screamed overhead.*

▸*n.* a long, loud, piercing cry expressing extreme emotion or pain: *they were awakened by screams for help.* ■ a high-pitched cry made by an animal: *the screams of the seagulls.* ■ a loud, piercing sound: *the scream of a falling bomb.* ■ [in *sing.*] *informal* an irresistibly funny person, thing, or situation: *the movie's a scream.* ▷Middle English: origin uncertain; perhaps from Middle Dutch.

scream·er /ˈskrēmər/ ▸*n.* **1** a person or thing that makes a screaming sound. **2** *informal* a thing remarkable for speed or impact: *he had a screamer of a lap going in his Penske-Chevy.* ■ an extremely fast ball or shot: *Jones hit a screamer against the right-field wall.* ■ a sensational or very large headline: *his death caused a front-page screamer.* ■ *dated* a thing that causes screams of laughter. **3** a large gooselike South American waterbird with a short bill, a sharp bony spur on each wing, and a harsh honking call. • Family Anhimidae: two genera and three species.

scream·ing·ly /ˈskrēmiNGlē/ ▸*adv.* [as *submodifier*] to a very great extent; extremely: *a screamingly dull daily routine.*

scream·ing mee·mies /ˈmēmēz/ ▸*plural n. humorous* an attack of panic or anxiety.

scree /skrē/ ▸*n.* a mass of small loose stones that form or cover a slope on a mountain. ■ a slope covered with such stones. ▷early 18th cent.: probably a back-formation from the plural *screes*, from Old Norse *skritha* 'landslide'; related to *skrítha* 'glide.'

screech /skrēCH/ ▸*v.* [*intrans.*] (of a person or animal) give a loud, harsh, piercing cry: *she hit her brother, causing him to screech with pain.* ■ make a loud, harsh, squealing sound: [as *adj.*] (**screeching**) *she brought the car to a screeching halt.* ■ [*intrans.*] move rapidly with such a sound: *the van screeched around the corner at top speed.*

▸*n.* a loud, harsh, piercing cry. ■ a loud, harsh, squealing sound: *a screech of brakes.* ▷mid 16th cent.: alteration of archaic *scritch*, of imitative origin. **—screech·er** *n.* **—screech·y** *adj.* (**screech·i·er**, **screech·i·est**).

screech owl ▸*n.* a small American owl with a screeching call and distinctive ear tufts. • *Otus asio*, family Strigidae.

screed /skrēd/ ▸*n.* **1** a long speech or piece of writing, typically one regarded as tedious. **2** a leveled layer of material (e.g., cement) applied to a floor or other surface. ■ a strip of plaster or other material placed on a surface as a guide to thickness.

▸*v.* [trans.] level (floors or concrete) with a straight edge using a back and forth motion while moving across the surface. ▷Middle English: probably a variant of the noun **SHRED**. The early sense was 'fragment cut from a main piece,' then 'torn strip, tatter,' whence (via the notion of a long roll or list) sense 1.

screen /skrēn/ ▸*n.* **1** a fixed or movable upright partition used to divide a room, to give shelter from drafts, heat, or light, or to provide concealment or privacy. ■ a thing providing concealment or protection: *his jeep was discreetly parked behind a screen of trees* | *figurative the article is using science as a screen for unexamined prejudice.* ■ *Military* a detachment of troops or ships detailed to cover the movements of the main body. ■ [often with *adj.*] *Architecture* a partition of carved wood or stone separating the nave of a church from the chancel, choir, or sanctuary. See also **ROOD SCREEN**. ■ a frame with fine wire netting used in a window or doorway to keep out mosquitoes and other flying insects: [as *adj.*] *screen door.* ■ a part of an electrical or other instrument that protects it or prevents it from causing electromagnetic interference. ■ *Electronics* (also **screen grid**) a grid placed between the control grid and the anode of a valve to reduce the capacitance between these electrodes. **2** the surface of a cathode-ray tube or similar electronic device, esp. that of a television, VDT, or monitor, on which images and data are displayed. ■ a blank, typically white or silver surface on which a photographic image is projected: *the world's largest movie screen.* ■ (**the screen**) movies or television; the motion-picture industry: *she's a star of the stage as well as the screen.* ■ the data or images displayed on a computer screen: *pressing the F1 key at any time will display a help screen.* ■ *Photography* a flat piece of ground glass on which the image formed by a camera lens is focused. **3** *Printing* a transparent, finely ruled plate or film used in halftone reproduction. **4** a large sieve or riddle, esp. one for sorting substances such as grain or coal into different sizes.

▸*v.* [*trans.*] **1** conceal, protect, or shelter (someone or something) with a screen or something forming a screen: *her hair swung across to screen her face* | *a high hedge screened all of the front from passersby.* ■ (**screen something off**) separate something from something else with or as if with a screen: *an area had been screened off as a waiting room.* ■ protect (someone) from something dangerous or unpleasant: *in my country, a man of my rank would be screened completely from any risk of attack.* ■ prevent from causing or protect from electromagnetic interference: *ensure that your microphone leads are properly screened from hum pickup.* **2** show (a movie or video) or broadcast (a television program): *the show is to be screened by HBO later this year.* **3** test (a person or substance) for the presence or absence of a disease or contaminant: *outpatients were* ***screened for*** *cervical cancer.* ■ check on or investigate (someone), typically to ascertain whether they are suitable for or can be trusted in a particular situation or job: *all prospective presidential candidates would have to screened by the committee.* ■ evaluate or analyze (something) for its suitability for a particular purpose or application: *only one percent of rain forest plants have been* ***screened for*** *medical use.* ■ (**screen someone/something out**) exclude someone or something after such evaluation or investigation: *only those refugees who are screened out are sent back to Vietnam.* **4** pass (a substance such as grain or coal) through a large sieve or screen, esp. so as to sort it into different sizes. **5** *Printing* project (a photograph or other image) through a transparent ruled plate so as to be able to reproduce it as a halftone. ▷Middle English: shortening of Old Northern French *escren*, of Germanic origin. **—screen·a·ble** *adj.* **—screen·er** *n.* **—screen·ful** /-,fo͝ol/ *n.*

screen·ag·er /ˈskrēn,ājər/ ▸*n. informal* a person in their teens or early twenties who has an aptitude for computers and spends much time on the Internet. ▷1990s: blend of *screen* and *teenager.*

screen dump ▸*n.* the process or an instance of causing what is displayed on a VDT screen to be printed out. ■ a resulting printout.

screen·ing /ˈskrēniNG/ ▸*n.* **1** a showing of a movie, video, or television program. **2** the evaluation or investigation of something as part of a methodical survey, to assess suitability for a particular role or purpose. ■ the testing of a person or group of people for the presence of a disease or other condition: *prenatal screening for Down syndrome.* **3** (**screenings**) refuse separated by sieving grain.

screen pass ▸*n. Football* a forward pass to a player protected by a screen of blockers.

screen·play /ˈskrēn,plā/ ▸*n.* the script of a movie, including acting instructions and scene directions.

screen-print ▸*v.* [*trans.*] [often as *adj.*] (**screen-printed**) force ink or metal onto (a surface) through a prepared screen of fine material so as to create a picture or pattern.

▸*n.* (**screen print**) a picture or design produced by screen-printing.

screen sav·er (also **screen·sav·er**) ▸*n. Computing* a program that, after a set time, replaces an unchanging screen display with a moving image, originally to prevent damage to the phosphor and now mostly for decoration or entertainment.

screen shot (also **screen·shot**) ▸*n. Computing* an image of the display on a computer screen to demonstrate the operation of a program.

screen test ▸*n.* a filmed test to ascertain whether an actor is suitable for a movie role.

▸*v.* (**screen-test**) [*trans.*] give such a test to (an actor).

screen·writ·er /ˈskrēn,rītər/ ▸*n.* a person who writes a screenplay. **—screen·writ·ing** /-,rītiNG/ *n.*

screw /skro͞o/ ▸*n.* **1** a short, slender, sharp-pointed metal pin with a raised helical thread running around it and a slotted head, used to join things together by being rotated so that it pierces wood or other material and is held tightly in place. ■ a cylinder with a helical ridge or thread running around the outside (a **male screw**) that can be turned to seal an opening, apply pressure, adjust position, etc., esp. one fitting into a corresponding internally grooved or threaded piece (a **female screw**). ■ (**the screws**) *historical* an instrument of torture acting in this way. ■ (also **screw pro·pel·ler**) a ship's or aircraft's propeller (considered as acting like a screw in moving through water or air). **2** an act of turning a screw or other object having a thread. ■ *Brit. Billiards* another term for **DRAW** ■ *Brit.* a small twisted-up piece of paper, used as a container for a substance such as salt or tobacco. **3** *informal* a prisoner's derogatory term for a prison guard or warden. **4** *vulgar slang* [in *sing.*] an act of sexual intercourse. ■ [with *adj.*] a sexual partner of a specified ability. **5** [in *sing.*] *Brit., informal, dated* an amount of salary or wages: *he's offered me the job with a jolly good screw.*

S

6 *Brit., archaic, informal* a mean or miserly person. **7** *Brit., informal* a worn-out horse.

▸*v.* **1** [*trans.*] fasten or tighten with a screw or screws: *screw the hinge to your new door.* ■ rotate (something) so as to fit it into or on to a surface or object by means of a spiral thread: *Philip screwed the top on the flask.* ■ [*intrans.*] (of an object) be attached or removed by being rotated in this way: *a connector that screws on to the gas cylinder.* ■ (**screw something around**) turn one's head or body around sharply: *he screwed his head around to try and find the enemy.* **2** [*trans.*] (usu. **be screwed**) *informal* cheat or swindle (someone), esp. by charging them too much for something: *if you do what they tell you, you're screwed | we ended up getting more money than what they were trying to* **screw us for.** ■ (**screw something out of**) extort or force something, esp. money, from (someone) by putting them under strong pressure: *your grandmother screwed cash out of him for ten years.* **3** [*trans.*] *vulgar slang* have sexual intercourse with. ■ [*intrans.*] (of a couple) have sexual intercourse. ■ [in *imperative*] *informal* used to express anger or contempt: *Screw him!* **4** [*trans.*] *Billiards, Brit.* another term for DRAW (sense 8).

▸*phrasal v.* □ **screw around 1** *vulgar slang* have many different sexual partners. **2** *informal* fool around. □ **screw someone over** *informal* treat someone unfairly; cheat or swindle someone. □ **screw up** *informal* completely mismanage or mishandle a situation: *I'm sorry, Susan, I screwed up.* □ **screw someone up** *informal* cause someone to be emotionally or mentally disturbed: *this job can really screw you up.* □ **screw something up 1** tense the muscles of one's face or around one's eyes, typically so as to register an emotion or because of bright light. **2** *informal* cause something to fail or go wrong: *why are you trying to screw up your life?* **3** summon up one's courage: *now Stephen had to screw up his courage and confess.* ▷late Middle English (as a noun): from Old French *escroue* 'female screw, nut,' from Latin *scrofa,* literally 'sow,' later 'screw.' The early sense of the verb was 'contort (the features), twist around' (late 16th cent.). —**screw·a·ble** *adj.* —**screw·er** *n.*

▸*PHRASES* □ **have one's head screwed on (the right way)** *informal* have common sense. □ **have a screw loose** *informal* be slightly eccentric or mentally disturbed. □ **put the screws on** *informal* exert strong psychological pressure on (someone) so as to intimidate them into doing something. □ **a turn of the screw** *informal* an additional degree of pressure or hardship added to a situation that is already extremely difficult to bear. □ **turn** (or **tighten**) **the screw** (or **screws**) *informal* exert strong pressure on someone.

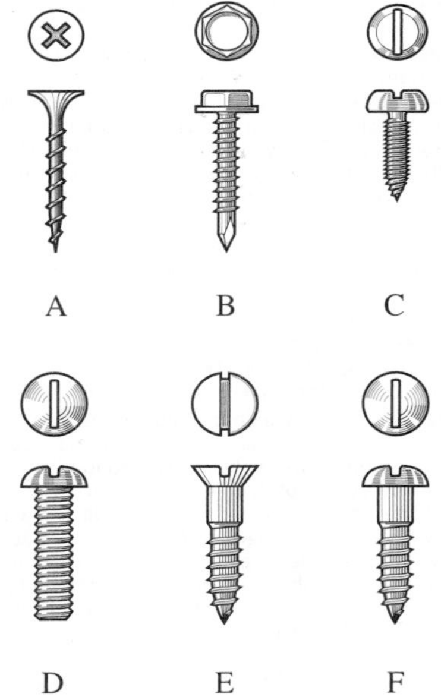

A sheetrock screw, flat head
B self-tapping screw, hex head
C sheet metal screw, pan head
D machine screw, round head
E wood screw, flat head
F wood screw, round head

screw 1

screw·ball /ˈskro͞oˌbôl/ ▸*n.* **1** *Baseball* a pitched ball that moves in a direction opposite to that of a curveball. **2** *informal* a crazy or eccentric person.

▸*adj. informal* crazy; absurd. ■ relating to or denoting a style of fast-moving comedy film involving eccentric characters or ridiculous situations. —**screw·ball·er** *n.* (in sense 1 of the *noun*).

screw cap ▸*n.* a round cap or lid with female thread that can be screwed on to a bottle or jar. —**screw-capped** *adj.*

screw·driv·er /ˈskro͞oˌdrīvər/ ▸*n.* **1** a tool with a flattened, cross-shaped, or star-shaped tip that fits into the head of a screw to turn it. **2** a cocktail made from vodka and orange juice.

screwed /skro͞od/ ▸*adj.* **1** (of a bolt or other device) having a helical ridge or thread running around the outside. **2** *informal* cheated or swindled. ■ ruined; rendered ineffective.

screwed-up ▸*adj. informal* (of a person) emotionally disturbed; neurotic: *the screwed-up children of wealthy parents.* ■ (of an event or a situation) spoiled by being badly managed or carried out: *that was the most screwed-up audition.*

screw eye ▸*n.* a screw with a loop for passing a cord through, instead of a slotted head.

screw jack ▸*n.* another term for JACK SCREW.

screw pine ▸*n.* another term for PANDANUS.

screw pro·pel·ler ▸*n.* see SCREW (sense 1).

screw thread ▸*n.* see THREAD (sense 4).

screw top ▸*n.* a round cap or lid that can be screwed on to a bottle or jar. —**screw-topped** *adj.*

screw·up /ˈskro͞oˌəp/ (also **screw-up**) ▸*n. informal* a situation that has been completely mismanaged or mishandled: *a massive bureaucratic screwup.*

screw·worm /ˈskro͞oˌwərm/ ▸*n.* a large American blowfly larva that enters the wounds of mammals, developing under the skin and often causing death. The adult fly is called the **screwworm fly.** • *Cochliomyia* (or **Callitroga**) *hominivorax,* family Calliphoridae.

screw·y /ˈskro͞oē/ ▸*adj.* (**screw·i·er, screw·i·est**) *informal* rather odd or eccentric. —**screw·i·ness** *n.*

Scria·bin /skrēˈäbən/ (also **Skrya·bin**), Aleksandr (Nikolaevich) (1872–1915), Russian composer and pianist. Much of his later music reflects his interest in mysticism and theosophy, esp. his third symphony. Notable works: *The Divine Poem* (1903) and *Prometheus: The Poem of Fire* (1909–10).

scrib·ble[1] /ˈskribəl/ ▸*v.* [*trans.*] write or draw (something) carelessly or hurriedly: *he took the clipboard and scribbled something illegible |* [as *adj.*] (**scribbled**) *scribbled notes |* [*intrans.*] *hastily he scribbled in the margin.* ■ [*intrans.*] *informal* write for a living or as a hobby: *she spent her last years scribbling and painting.*

▸*n.* a piece of writing or a picture produced in this way: *illegible scribbles | he would never be able to decipher your scribble.* ▷late Middle English: from medieval Latin *scribillare,* diminutive of Latin *scribere* 'write.' —**scrib·bly** /ˈskrib(ə)lē/ *adj.*

scrib·ble[2] ▸*v.* [*trans.*] [often as *n.*] (**scribbling**) card (wool, cotton, etc.) coarsely. ▷late 17th cent.: probably from Low German; compare with German *schrubbeln* (in the same sense), frequentative of Low German *schrubben* 'to scrub.'

scrib·bler /ˈskrib(ə)lər/ ▸*n. informal* a person who writes for a living or as a hobby.

scribe /skrīb/ ▸*n.* **1** *historical* a person who copies out documents, esp. one employed to do this before printing was invented. ■ *informal, often humorous* a writer, esp. a journalist. **2** (also **Scribe**) *Judaism* an ancient Jewish record-keeper or, later, a professional theologian and jurist. **3** another term for SCRIBER.

▸*v.* [*trans.*] **1** *chiefly poetic/literary* write: *he scribed a note that he passed to Dan.* **2** mark with a scriber. ▷Middle English (sense 2 of the *noun*): from Latin *scriba,* from *scribere* 'write.' The verb was first used in the sense 'write down'; in sense 2 it is perhaps partly a shortening of DESCRIBE. —**scrib·al** /-bəl/ *adj.*

scrib·er /ˈskrībər/ ▸*n.* a pointed instrument used for making marks on wood, bricks, etc., to guide a saw or in sign painting.

scrim /skrim/ ▸*n.* strong, coarse fabric, chiefly used for heavy-duty lining or upholstery. ■ *Theater* a piece of gauze cloth that appears opaque until lit from behind, used as a screen or backdrop. ■ a similar heatproof cloth put over film or television lamps to diffuse the light. ■ a thing that conceals or obscures something: *a thin scrim of fog covered the island.* ▷late 18th cent.: of unknown origin.

scrim·mage /ˈskrimij/ ▸*n.* **1** a confused struggle or fight. **2** *Football* the beginning of each down of play, with the ball placed on the ground between the offensive and defensive lines with its longest axis at right angles to the goal line. ■ offensive plays begun in this way: *none of the goals was scored from scrimmage.* ■ *chiefly Football* a session in which teams practice by playing a simulated game.

▸*v.* [*intrans.*] *chiefly Football* engage in a simulated game. ▷late Middle English: alteration of dialect *scrimish,* variant of the noun SKIRMISH. —**scrim·mag·er** *n.*

scrimp /skrimp/ ▸*v.* [*intrans.*] be thrifty or parsimonious; economize: *I have* **scrimped and saved** *to give you a good education.* ▷mid 18th cent. (in the sense 'keep short of (food)'): from Scots *scrimp* 'meager'; perhaps related to SHRIMP.

scrim·shaw /ˈskrimˌshô/ ▸*v.* [*trans.*] adorn (whalebone, ivory, shells, or other materials) with carved or colored designs.

▸*n.* a piece of work done in such a way. ■ the art or technique of producing such work: *craftsmen demonstrate sailmaking and scrimshaw.* ▷early 19th cent.: of unknown origin; perhaps influenced by the surname *Scrimshaw.*

scrip[1] /skrip/ ▸*n.* **1** a provisional certificate of money subscribed to a bank or company, entitling the holder to a formal certificate and dividends. ■ such certificates collectively. ■ (also **scrip issue** or **div·i·dend**) *Finance* an issue of additional shares to shareholders in proportion to the shares already held. **2** (also **land scrip**) a certificate entitling the holder to acquire possession of certain portions of public land. **3** *historical* paper money in amounts of less than a dollar. ▷mid 18th cent.: abbreviation of *subscription receipt.*

scrip[2] ▸*n. historical* a small bag or pouch, typically one carried by a pilgrim, shepherd, or beggar. ▷Middle English: probably a shortening of Old French *escrepe* 'purse.'

scrip[3] ▸*n.* another term for SCRIPT[2].

scri·poph·i·ly /skriˈpäfəlē/ ▸*n.* the collection of old bond and share certificates as a pursuit or hobby. ■ such articles collectively. ▷1970s: from SCRIP[1] + -PHILY. —**scri·poph·i·list** /-list/ *n.*

script[1] /skript/ ▸*n.* **1** handwriting as distinct from print; written characters: *her neat, tidy script.* ■ printed type imitating handwriting. ■ [with *adj.*] writing using a particular alphabet: *Russian script.* **2** the written text of a play, movie, or broadcast. ■ *Computing* an automated series of instructions carried out in a specific order. ■ *Psychology* the social role or behavior appropriate to particular situations that an individual absorbs through cultural influences and association with others.

▸*v.* [*trans.*] write a script for (a play, movie, or broadcast). ▷late Middle English (in the sense 'something written'): shortening of Old French *escript,* from Latin *scriptum,* neuter past participle (used as a noun) of *scribere* 'write.'

script[2] ▸*n. informal* a doctor's prescription.

Script. ▸*abbr.* ■ Scriptural. ■ Scripture.

script kid·die ▸*n. informal, derogatory* a person who uses existing computer scripts or code to hack into computers, lacking the expertise to write their own.

scrip·to·ri·um /ˌskripˈtôrēəm/ ▸*n.* (*pl.* **-to·ri·a** /-ˈtôrēə/ or **-to·ri·ums**) *chiefly historical* a room set apart for writing, esp. one in a monastery where manuscripts were copied. ▷late 18th cent.: from medieval Latin, from Latin *script-* 'written,' from the verb *scribere.*

scrip·tur·al /ˈskripCHərəl/ ▸*adj.* of, from, or relating to the Bible: *scriptural quotations from Genesis.* ▷mid 17th cent.: from late Latin *scripturalis,* from Latin *scriptura* 'writings' (see SCRIPTURE). —**scrip·tur·al·ly** *adv.*

scrip·ture /ˈskripCHər/ ▸*n.* (often **Scrip·ture** or **Scrip·tures**) the sacred writings of Christianity contained in the Bible: *passages of scripture | the fundamental teachings of* **the Scriptures.** ■ the sacred writings of another religion. ▷Middle English: from Latin *scriptura* 'writings,' from *script-* 'written,' from the verb *scribere.*

script·writ·er /ˈskriptˌrītər/ ▸*n.* a person who writes a script for a play, movie, or broadcast. —**script·writ·ing** /-ˌrītiNG/ *n.*

scrive·ner /ˈskriv(ə)nər/ ▸*n. historical* a clerk, scribe, or notary. ▷Middle English: shortening of Old French *escrivein,* from Latin *scriba* (see SCRIBE).

scrod /skräd/ ▸*n.* a young cod, haddock, or similar fish, esp. one prepared for cooking. ▷mid 19th cent.: of unknown origin.

scrof·u·la /ˈskrôfyələ/ ▸*n. chiefly historical* a disease with glandular swellings, probably a form of tuberculosis. Also formerly called KING'S EVIL. ▷late Middle English: from medieval Latin, diminutive of Latin *scrofa* 'breeding sow' (said to be subject to the disease). —**scrof·u·lous** /-ləs/ *adj.*

scroll /skrōl/ ▸*n.* **1** a roll of parchment or paper for writing or painting on. ■ an ancient book or document on such a roll. ■ an ornamental design or carving resembling a partly unrolled scroll of parchment, e.g., on the capital of a column, or at the end of a stringed instrument. ■ *Art & Heraldry* a depiction of a narrow ribbon bearing a motto or inscription. **2** [usu. as *adj.*] the facility that moves a display on a VDT screen in order to view new material.
▸*v.* **1** [*intrans.*] move displayed text or graphics in a particular direction on a computer screen in order to view different parts of them: *she scrolled through her file.* ■ (of displayed text or graphics) move up, down, or across a computer screen. **2** [*trans.*] cause to move like paper rolling or unrolling: *the wind* ***scrolled back*** *the uppermost layer of loose dust.* ▷late Middle English: alteration of obsolete *scrow* 'roll,' shortening of ESCROW. —**scroll·a·ble** *adj.*

scroll bar (also **scroll·bar**) ▸*n.* a long thin section at the edge of a computer display by which material can be scrolled using a mouse.

scrolled /skrōld/ ▸*adj.* having an ornamental design or carving resembling a scroll of parchment.

scroll·er /ˈskrōlər/ ▸*n.* a computer game in which the background scrolls past at a constant rate.

scroll·ing /ˈskrōliNG/ ▸*n.* the action of moving displayed text or graphics up or down on a computer screen in order to view different parts of them.
▸*adj.* [*attrib.*] (of an ornamental design or carving) made to resemble a partly unrolled scroll of parchment.

scroll saw ▸*n.* a narrow-bladed saw for cutting decorative spiral lines or patterns.

scroll·work /ˈskrōl,wərk/ ▸*n.* decoration consisting of spiral lines or patterns, esp. as cut by a scroll saw.

scrooch /skro͞oCH/ ▸*v.* [*intrans.*] *informal* crouch; bend: *he scrooched forward on his chair.* ▷mid 19th cent. (originally U.S.): dialect variant of U.S. *scrouge* 'squeeze, crowd,' perhaps reinforced by the verb CROUCH.

Scrooge /skro͞oj/, Ebenezer, a miserly curmudgeon in Charles Dickens's novel *A Christmas Carol* (1843). ■ [as *n.*] (**a Scrooge**) a person who is miserly.

scro·tum /ˈskrōtəm/ ▸*n.* (*pl.* **scro·ta** or **scro·tums**) a pouch of skin containing the testicles. ▷late 16th cent.: from Latin. —**scro·tal** /ˈskrōtl/ *adj.*

scrounge /skrounj/ *informal* ▸*v.* [*trans.*] seek to obtain (something, typically food or money) at the expense or through the generosity of others or by stealth: *he had managed to scrounge a free meal* | [*intrans.*] *we didn't* ***scrounge off*** *the social security.*
▸*n.* [in *sing.*] an act of seeking to obtain something in such a way. ▷early 20th cent.: variant of dialect *scrunge* 'steal.' —**scroung·er** *n.*

scrub[1] /skrəb/ ▸*v.* (**scrubbed, scrub·bing**) [*trans.*] rub (someone or something) hard so as to clean them, typically with a brush and water: *he had to scrub the floor* | *she was* ***scrubbing*** *herself* ***down*** *at the sink* | [*intrans.*] *she* ***scrubbed*** *furiously* ***at*** *the plates.* ■ (**scrub something away/off**) remove dirt by rubbing hard: *it took ages to scrub off the muck.* ■ [*intrans.*] (**scrub up**) thoroughly clean one's hands and arms, esp. before performing surgery: *the doctor scrubbed up and put on a protective gown.* ■ *informal* cancel or abandon (something): *opposition leaders suggested she should scrub the trip to China.* ■ remove impurities from (gas or vapor). ■ [*intrans.*] (of a rider) rub the arms and legs urgently on a horse's neck and flanks to urge it to move faster.
▸*n.* **1** an act of scrubbing something or someone: ***give*** *the floor* ***a good scrub.*** **2** a semiabrasive cosmetic lotion applied to the face or body in order to cleanse the skin. **3** (**scrubs**) informal term for SCRUB SUIT. ▷late 16th cent.: probably from Middle Low German, Middle Dutch *schrobben, schrubben.* —**scrub·ba·ble** *adj.*

scrub[2] ▸*n.* **1** vegetation consisting mainly of brushwood or stunted forest growth. ■ land covered with such vegetation. **2** [as *adj.*] denoting a shrubby or small form of a plant: *scrub apple trees.* ■ denoting an animal of inferior breed or physique: *a scrub bull.* **3** *informal* an insignificant or contemptible person. ■ (in sports) a player not among the best or most skilled. ▷late Middle English (in the sense 'stunted tree'): variant of SHRUB[1]. —**scrub·by** *adj.*

scrub·ber /ˈskrəbər/ ▸*n.* a brush or other object used to clean something. ■ a person who cleans something. ■ an apparatus using water or a solution for purifying gases or vapors.

scrub jay ▸*n.* a jay with blue and gray plumage and no crest, found in Mexico, the western U.S., and central Florida. • *Aphelocoma coerulescens,* family Corvidae.

scrub·land /ˈskrəb,land/ ▸*n.* (also **scrublands**) land consisting of scrub vegetation.

scrub nurse ▸*n.* a nurse who assists a surgeon by performing certain specialized duties during a surgical operation.

scrub oak ▸*n.* a shrubby dwarf oak that forms thickets. • Genus *Quercus,* family Fagaceae: several species, in particular *Q. ilicifolia* of the northeastern Appalachian region.

scrub suit ▸*n.* a hygienic outfit worn by surgeons and other surgical staff while performing or assisting at an operation.

scrub ty·phus ▸*n.* a rickettsial disease transmitted to humans by mites and found in parts of eastern Asia. Also called TSUTSUGAMUSHI DISEASE.

scrub·wo·man /ˈskrəb,wo͝omən/ ▸*n.* a woman employed to clean floors, walls, windows, etc.

scruff /skrəf/ ▸*n.* the back of a person's or animal's neck: *he grabbed him* ***by the scruff of his neck.*** ▷late 18th cent.: alteration of dialect *scuff,* of obscure origin.

scruff·y /ˈskrəfē/ ▸*adj.* (**scruff·i·er, scruff·i·est**) shabby and untidy or dirty: *dressed in scruffy jeans and a baggy T-shirt.* ▷mid 17th century (in the sense 'covered with scurf'): from *scruff* 'scurf,' variant of SCURF, + -Y[1]. The sense 'shabby' dates from the late 19th cent. —**scruff·i·ly** /-əlē/ *adv.* —**scruff·i·ness** *n.*

scrum /skrəm/ ▸*n. Rugby* an ordered formation of players, used to restart play, in which the forwards of a team form up with arms interlocked and heads down, and push forward against a similar group from the opposing side. The ball is thrown into the scrum and the players try to gain possession of it by kicking it backward toward their own side. ■ *chiefly Brit., informal* a disorderly crowd of people or things: *there was quite a scrum of people at the bar.*
▸*v.* (**scrummed, scrum·ming**) [*intrans.*] *Rugby* form or take part in a scrum. ▷late 19th cent.: abbreviation of SCRUMMAGE.

scrum·mage /ˈskrəmij/ ▸*n.* & *v.* another term for SCRUM. ▷early 19th cent.: variant of SCRIMMAGE. —**scrum·mag·er** *n.*

scrump·tious /ˈskrəm(p)SHəs/ ▸*adj. informal* (of food) extremely appetizing or delicious. ■ (of a person) very attractive. ▷mid 19th cent.: of unknown origin. —**scrump·tious·ly** *adv.* —**scrump·tious·ness** *n.*

scrunch /skrənCH/ ▸*v.* [*intrans.*] make a loud crunching noise: *crisp yellow leaves scrunched underfoot.* ■ [*trans.*] crush or squeeze (something) into a compact mass: *Gloria scrunched the handkerchief into a ball.* ■ [*intrans.*] become crushed or squeezed in such a way: *their faces* ***scrunch up*** *with concentration.* ■ [*trans.*] style (hair) by squeezing or crushing it in the hands to give a tousled look.
▸*n.* [in *sing.*] a loud crunching noise: *Charlotte heard the scrunch of boots on gravel.* ▷late 18th cent. (in the sense 'eat or bite noisily'): probably imitative; compare with CRUNCH.

scrunch·ie /ˈskrənCHē/ ▸*n.* a circular band of fabric-covered elastic used for fastening the hair.

scru·ple /ˈskro͞opəl/ ▸*n.* **1** (usu. **scruples**) a feeling of doubt or hesitation with regard to the morality or propriety of a course of action: *I* ***had no scruples about*** *eavesdropping* | *without scruple, these politicians use fear as a persuasion weapon.* See note at QUALM. **2** *historical* a unit of weight equal to 20 grains, used by apothecaries. ■ *archaic* a very small amount of something, esp. a quality.
▸*v.* [*intrans.*] [usu. with *negative*] hesitate or be reluctant to do something that one thinks may be wrong: *she doesn't scruple to ask her parents for money.* ▷late Middle English: from French *scrupule* or Latin *scrupulus,* from *scrupus,* literally 'rough pebble,' (figuratively) 'anxiety.'

scru·pu·lous /ˈskro͞opyələs/ ▸*adj.* (of a person or process) diligent, thorough, and extremely attentive to details: *the research has been carried out with scrupulous attention to detail.* ■ very concerned to avoid doing wrong: *she's too scrupulous to have an affair with a married man.* ▷late Middle English (in the sense 'troubled with doubts'): from French *scrupuleux* or Latin *scrupulosus,* from *scrupulus* (see SCRUPLE). —**scru·pu·los·i·ty** /,skro͞opyəˈläsitē/ *n.* —**scru·pu·lous·ly** *adv.* [as *submodifier*] *she was scrupulously polite.* —**scru·pu·lous·ness** *n.*

scru·ti·nize /ˈskro͞otn,īz/ ▸*v.* [*trans.*] examine or inspect closely and thoroughly: *customers were warned to scrutinize the small print.* —**scru·ti·ni·za·tion** /,skro͞otn-iˈzāSHən/ *n.* —**scru·ti·niz·er** *n.*

scru·ti·ny /ˈskro͞otn-ē/ ▸*n.* (*pl.* **-nies**) critical observation or examination: *every aspect of local government was placed* ***under scrutiny.*** ▷late Middle English: from Latin *scrutinium,* from *scrutari* 'to search' (originally 'sort trash,' from *scruta* 'trash'). Early use referred to the taking of individual votes in an election procedure.

scry /skrī/ ▸*v.* (**skries, skried**) [*intrans.*] foretell the future using a crystal ball or other reflective object or surface. ▷early 16th cent.: shortening of DESCRY. —**scry·er** *n.*

SCSI /ˈskəzē/ *Computing* ▸*abbr.* small computer system interface, a bus standard for connecting computers and their peripherals.

scu·ba /ˈsko͞obə/ ▸*n.* an aqualung. ■ scuba diving. ▷1950s: acronym from *self-contained underwater breathing apparatus.*

scu·ba div·ing ▸*n.* the sport or pastime of swimming underwater using scuba gear. —**scu·ba dive** (also **scu·ba-dive**) *v.* —**scu·ba div·er** *n.*

scud /skəd/ ▸*v.* (**scud·ded, scud·ding**) [*intrans.*] move fast in a straight line because or as if driven by the wind: *we lie watching the clouds* ***scudding across*** *the sky* | *three small ships were* ***scudding before*** *a brisk breeze.*
▸*n.* **1** *chiefly poetic/literary* a formation of vapory clouds driven fast by the wind. ■ a mass of windblown spray. ■ a driving shower of rain or snow; a gust. ■ the action of moving fast in a straight line when driven by the wind: *the scud of the clouds before the wind.* **2** (**Scud**) (also **Scud mis·sile**) a type of long-range surface-to-surface guided missile able to be fired from a mobile launcher. ▷mid 16th cent. (as a verb): perhaps an alteration of the noun SCUT[1], thus reflecting the sense 'race like a hare.'

scu·do /ˈsko͞odō/ ▸*n.* (*pl.* **-di** /-dē/) *historical* a coin, typically made of silver, formerly used in various Italian states. ▷Italian, from Latin *scutum* 'shield.'

scuff /skəf/ ▸*v.* [*trans.*] scrape or brush the surface of (a shoe or other object) against something: *I scuffed the heel of my shoe on a stone.* ■ mark (a surface) by scraping or brushing it, esp. with one's shoes: *the linoleum on the floor was scuffed.* ■ [*intrans.*] (of an object or surface) become marked by scraping or brushing: *these shoes won't scuff.* ■ drag (one's feet or heels) when walking: *he scuffed his feet boyishly.* ■ [*intrans.*] walk in such a way: *she scuffed along in her slippers.*
▸*n.* a mark made by scraping or grazing a surface or object: *dark colors don't show scuffs.* ▷early 18th cent.: perhaps of imitative origin.

scuf·fle /ˈskəfəl/ ▸*n.* **1** a short, confused fight or struggle at close quarters: *there were minor* ***scuffles with*** *police.* **2** an act or sound of moving in a hurried, confused, or shuffling manner: *he heard the scuffle of feet.*
▸*v.* [*intrans.*] **1** engage in a short, confused fight or struggle at close quarters: *the teacher noticed two students scuffling in the corridor.* **2** [with *adverbial of direction*] move in a hurried, confused, or awkward way, making a rustling or shuffling sound: *a drenched woman scuffled through the doorway.* ■ [*trans.*] (of an animal or person) move (something) in a scrambling or confused manner: *the rabbit struggled free, scuffling his front paws.* ▷late 16th cent. (as a verb): probably of Scandinavian origin; compare with Swedish *skuffa* 'to push'; related to SHOVE and SHUFFLE.

scull[1] /skəl/ ▸*n.* each of a pair of small oars used by a single rower. ■ an oar placed over the stern of a boat to propel it by a side-to-side motion, reversing the blade at each turn. ■ a light, narrow boat propelled with a scull or a pair of sculls. ■ (**sculls**) a race between boats in which each participant uses a pair of oars.
▸*v.* [*intrans.*] propel a boat with sculls. ■ [*trans.*] transport (someone) in a boat propelled with sculls. ■ [*intrans.*] (of an aquatic animal) propel itself with fins or flippers. ▷Middle English: of unknown origin.

scull[2] ▸*n.* *Canadian* a large group of fish that has

S

migrated from the open sea to inshore waters. ■ the season when this happens. ▷variant of SCHOOL².

scul·ler /ˈskələr/ ▸*n.* a person who sculls a boat. ■ a boat propelled with a scull or pair of sculls.

scul·ler·y /ˈskəl(ə)rē/ ▸*n.* (*pl.* **-ler·ies**) a small kitchen or room at the back of a house used for washing dishes and other dirty household work. ▷late Middle English (denoting the department of a household concerned with kitchen utensils): from Old French *escuelerie*, from *escuele* 'dish,' from Latin *scutella* 'salver,' diminutive of *scutra* 'wooden platter.'

scul·lion /ˈskəlyən/ ▸*n. archaic* a servant assigned the most menial kitchen tasks. ▷late 15th cent.: of unknown origin but perhaps influenced by SCULLERY.

sculp. ▸*abbr.* ■ sculptor. ■ sculptural. ■ sculpture.

scul·pin /ˈskəlpən/ ▸*n.* a chiefly marine fish of the northern hemisphere, with a broad flattened head and spiny scales and fins. • Cottidae and related families: many genera and numerous species, including the bullheads. ▷late 17th cent.: perhaps from obsolete *scorpene*, via Latin from Greek *skorpaina*, denoting a kind of fish.

sculpt /skəlpt/ (also **sculp** /skəlp/) ▸*v.* [*trans.*] create or represent (something) by carving, casting, or other shaping techniques: *sculpting human figures from ivory* | [*intrans.*] *she was teaching him how to sculpt.* ▷mid 19th cent.: from French *sculpter*, from *sculpteur* 'sculptor'; later regarded as a back-formation from SCULPTOR or SCULPTURE.

Sculp·tor /ˈskəlptər/ *Astronomy* a faint southern constellation (the Sculptor or Sculptor's Workshop), between Grus and Cetus. ■ [as *genitive*] (**Sculptoris** /skəlpˈtôris/) used with a preceding letter or numeral to designate a star in this constellation: *the star Delta Sculptoris.* ▷Latin.

sculp·tor /ˈskəlptər/ ▸*n.* an artist who makes sculptures. ▷mid 17th cent.: from Latin, from *sculpt-* 'hollowed out,' from the verb *sculpere.*

sculp·tress /ˈskəlptrəs/ ▸*n.* a female artist who makes sculptures.

sculp·tur·al /ˈskəlpCHərəl/ ▸*adj.* of, relating to, or resembling sculpture: *sculptural decoration* | *sculptural works.* **—sculp·tur·al·ly** *adv.*

sculp·ture /ˈskəlpCHər/ ▸*n.* the art of making two- or three-dimensional representative or abstract forms, esp. by carving stone or wood or by casting metal or plaster. ■ a work of such a kind: *a bronze sculpture* | *a collection of sculpture.* ■ *Zoology & Botany* raised or sunken patterns or texture on the surface of a shell, pollen grain, cuticle, or other biological specimen.
▸*v.* [*trans.*] make or represent (a form) by carving, casting, or other shaping techniques: *the choir stalls were each carefully sculptured.* ■ form, shape, or mark as if by sculpture, esp. with strong, smooth curves: [as *adj.*] (**sculptured**) *he had an aquiline nose and sculptured lips.* ▷late Middle English: from Latin *sculptura*, from *sculpere* 'carve.'

sculp·tur·esque /ˌskəlpCHəˈresk/ ▸*adj.* old-fashioned term for SCULPTURAL. **—sculp·tur·esque·ly** *adv.*

sculp·tur·ing /ˈskəlpCHəriNG/ ▸*n.* the action of forming or shaping something by or as if by sculpture: *the gadget is great for blow-drying, sculpturing, and molding.* ■ the shape produced in such a way: *the mountain's graceful sculpturing.* ■ *Zoology & Botany* sculpture: *the external sculpturing consists of a series of corrugations.*

scum /skəm/ ▸*n.* a layer of dirt or froth on the surface of a liquid: *green scum found on stagnant pools.* ■ *informal* a worthless or contemptible person or group of people: *you drug dealers are* **the scum of the earth***.*
▸*v.* (**scummed**, **scum·ming**) [*intrans.*] (of a liquid) become covered with a layer of dirt or froth: *the lagoon* **scummed over***.* ■ [*trans.*] form a layer of dirt or froth on (a liquid): *litter scummed the surface of the harbor.* ▷Middle English: from Middle Low German, Middle Dutch *schūm*, of Germanic origin. **—scum·my** *adj.* (**-mi·er**, **-mi·est**).

scum·bag /ˈskəmˌbag/ ▸*n. informal* a contemptible or objectionable person.

scum·ble /ˈskəmbəl/ *Art* ▸*v.* [*trans.*] modify (a painting or color) by applying a very thin coat of opaque paint to give a softer or duller effect. ■ modify (a drawing) in a similar way with light shading in pencil or charcoal.
▸*n.* a thin, opaque coat of paint or layer of shading applied to give a softer or duller effect. ■ the effect produced by adding such a coat or layer. ▷late 17th cent. (as a verb): perhaps a frequentative of the verb SCUM.

scun·cheon /ˈskənCHən/ ▸*n.* the inside face of a doorjamb or window frame. ▷Middle English: shortening of Old French *escoinson*, based on *coin* 'corner.'

scun·gil·le /sko͞onˈjēlē/ (also **scun·gi·le**) ▸*n.* (*pl.* **-gil·li** /-ˈjēlē/) a mollusk (esp. with reference to its meat eaten as a delicacy). ▷from Italian dialect *scunciglio*, probably an alteration of Italian *conchiglia* 'seashell.'

scun·ner /ˈskənər/ *chiefly Scottish* ▸*n.* a strong dislike: *why have you a scunner against him?* ■ a source of irritation or strong dislike.
▸*v.* [*intrans.*] feel disgust or strong dislike. ▷late Middle English (first used in the sense 'shrink back with fear'): of unknown origin.

scup /skəp/ ▸*n.* (*pl.* same) a common porgy with faint dark vertical bars, occurring off the coasts of the northwestern Atlantic. • *Stenotomus chrysops*, family Sparidae. ▷mid 19th cent.: from Narragansett *mishcup.*

scup·per¹ /ˈskəpər/ ▸*n.* (usu. **scuppers**) a hole in a ship's side to carry water overboard from the deck. ■ an outlet in the side of a building for draining water. ▷late Middle English: perhaps via Anglo-Norman French from Old French *escopir* 'to spit'; compare with German *Speigatt*, literally 'spit hole.'

scup·per² ▸*v.* [*trans.*] *chiefly Brit.* sink (a ship or its crew) deliberately. ■ *informal* prevent from working or succeeding; thwart: *plans for a casino were scuppered by a public inquiry.* ▷late 19th cent. (as military slang in the sense 'kill, esp. in an ambush'): of unknown origin. The sense 'sink' dates from the 1970s.

scup·per·nong /ˈskəpərˌnäNG; -ˌnôNG/ ▸*n.* a variety of the muscadine grape native to the basin of the Scuppernong River in North Carolina. ■ (often **scuppernong wine**) wine made from this grape.

scurf /skərf/ ▸*n.* flakes on the surface of the skin that form as fresh skin develops below, occurring esp. as dandruff. ■ a similar flaky deposit on any surface, esp. one on a plant resulting from a fungal infection. ▷late Old English *sceorf*, from the base of *sceorfan* 'gnaw,' *sceorfian* 'cut to shreds.' **—scurf·y** *adj.*

scur·ril·ous /ˈskərələs/ ▸*adj.* making or spreading scandalous claims about someone with the intention of damaging their reputation: *a scurrilous attack on his integrity.* ■ humorously insulting: *a very funny collection of bawdy and scurrilous writings.* ▷late 16th cent.: from French *scurrile* or Latin *scurrilus* (from *scurra* 'buffoon') + -OUS. **—scur·ril·i·ty** /skəˈrilitē/ *n.* (*pl.* **-ties**) **—scur·ril·ous·ly** *adv.* **—scur·ril·ous·ness** *n.*

scur·ry /ˈskərē/ ▸*v.* (**-ries**, **-ried**) [*intrans.*] (of a person or small animal) move hurriedly with short quick steps: *pedestrians scurried for cover.*
▸*n.* (*pl.* **-ries**) [in *sing.*] a situation of hurried and confused movement: *I was in such a scurry.* ▷early 19th cent.: abbreviation of *hurry-scurry*, reduplication of HURRY.

scur·vy /ˈskərvē/ ▸*n.* a disease caused by a deficiency of vitamin C, characterized by swollen bleeding gums and the opening of previously healed wounds, which particularly affected poorly nourished sailors until the end of the 18th century.
▸*adj.* (**-vi·er**, **-vi·est**) [*attrib.*] *archaic* worthless or contemptible: *that was a scurvy trick.* ▷late Middle English (as an adjective meaning 'scurfy'): from SCURF + -Y¹. The noun use (mid 16th cent.) is by association with French *scorbut* (see SCORBUTIC). **—scur·vi·ly** /-vəlē/ *adv.*

scur·vy grass ▸*n.* a small cresslike European plant with fleshy tar-flavored leaves, growing near the sea. It is rich in vitamin C and was formerly eaten, esp. by sailors, to prevent scurvy. • Genus *Cochlearia*, family Brassicaceae: several species, in particular *C. officinalis.*

scut¹ /skət/ ▸*n.* the short tail of a hare, rabbit, or deer. ▷late Middle English: of unknown origin; compare with obsolete *scut* 'short,' also 'shorten.'

scut² ▸*n. informal, chiefly Irish* a person perceived as foolish, contemptible, or objectionable. ▷late 19th cent.: of unknown origin.

scu·ta /ˈsk(y)o͞otə/ ▸ plural form of SCUTUM.

scu·tage /ˈsk(y)o͞otij/ ▸*n.* (in a feudal society) money paid by a vassal to his lord in lieu of military service. ▷late Middle English: from medieval Latin *scutagium*, from Latin *scutum* 'shield.'

Scu·ta·ri /ˈsko͞otərē; -tärē/ a former name for Üsküdar.

scutch /skəCH/ ▸*v.* [*trans.*] dress (fibrous material, esp. retted flax) by beating it. ▷mid 18th cent.: from obsolete French *escoucher*, from Latin *excutere* 'shake out.' **—scutch·er** *n.*

scutch·eon /ˈskəCHən/ ▸*n.* archaic spelling of ESCUTCHEON.

scute /sk(y)o͞ot/ ▸*n. Zoology* a thickened horny or bony plate on a turtle's shell or on the back of a crocodile, stegosaurus, etc. ▷from Latin *scutum*; see SCUTUM

scu·tel·lum /sk(y)o͞oˈteləm/ ▸*n.* (*pl.* **-tel·la** /-ˈtelə/) *Botany & Zoology* a small shieldlike structure, in particular: ■ a modified cotyledon in the embryo of a grass seed. ■ the third dorsal sclerite in each thoracic segment of an insect. ▷mid 18th cent.: modern Latin, diminutive of Latin *scutum* 'shield.' **—scu·tel·lar** /-ˈtelər/ *adj.*

scut·ter /ˈskətər/ *chiefly Brit.* ▸*v.* [*intrans.*] (esp. of a small animal) move hurriedly with short steps: *a little dog scuttered up from the cabin.*
▸*n.* [in *sing.*] an act or sound of scuttering. ▷late 18th cent.: perhaps an alteration of the verb SCUTTLE².

scut·tle¹ /ˈskətl/ ▸*n.* (in full **coal scut·tle**) a metal container with a sloping hinged lid and a handle, used to fetch and store coal for a domestic fire. ■ the amount of coal held in such a container: *carrying endless* **scuttles of** *coal up from the cellar.* ▷late Old English *scutel* 'dish, platter,' from Old Norse *skutill*, from Latin *scutella* 'dish.'

scut·tle² ▸*v.* [*intrans.*] run hurriedly or furtively with short quick steps: *a mouse scuttled across the floor.*
▸*n.* [in *sing.*] an act or sound of scuttling: *I heard the scuttle of rats across the room.* ▷late 15th cent.: compare with dialect *scuddle*, frequentative of SCUD.

scut·tle³ ▸*v.* [*trans.*] sink (one's own ship) deliberately by holing it or opening its seacocks to let water in. ■ deliberately cause (a scheme) to fail: *some of the stockholders are threatening to scuttle the deal.*
▸*n.* an opening with a lid in a ship's deck or side. ▷late 15th cent. (as a noun): perhaps from Old French *escoutille*, from the Spanish diminutive *escotilla* 'hatchway.' The verb dates from the mid 17th cent.

scut·tle·butt /ˈskətlˌbət/ ▸*n. informal* rumor; gossip: *the* **scuttlebutt has it** *that he was a spy* | *the court cautioned against relying on scuttlebutt.* ▷early 19th cent. (denoting a water butt on the deck of a ship, providing drinking water): from *scuttled butt.*

Scu·tum /ˈsk(y)o͞otəm/ *Astronomy* a small constellation (the Shield) near the celestial equator, lying in the Milky Way between Aquila and Serpens. ■ [as *genitive*] (**Scuti** /-ˌtī/) used with a preceding letter or numeral to designate a star in this constellation: *the star Beta Scuti.* ▷Latin.

scu·tum /ˈsk(y)o͞otəm/ ▸*n.* (*pl.* **-ta** /-tə/) *Zoology* another term for SCUTE. ■ *Entomology* the second dorsal sclerite in each thoracic segment of an insect. ▷late 18th cent.: from Latin, literally 'oblong shield.'

scut work (also **scut·work**) ▸*n. informal* tedious, menial work. ▷1970s: of unknown origin; compare with SCUT².

scuzz /skəz/ ▸*n. informal* something regarded as disgusting, sordid, or disreputable. ■ a disreputable or unpleasant person. ▷1960s: probably an informal abbreviation of DISGUSTING. **—scuzz·y** *adj.*

scuzz·ball /ˈskəzˌbôl/ (also **scuzz·bag** /-ˌbag/) ▸*n. informal* a despicable or disgusting person.

Scyl·la /ˈsilə/ *Greek Mythology* a female sea monster who devoured sailors when they tried to navigate the narrow channel between her cave and the whirlpool Charybdis. In later legend Scylla was a dangerous rock, located on the Italian side of the Strait of Messina.
▸*PHRASE* □ **between Scylla and Charybdis** /kəˈribdis/ used to refer to a situation involving two dangers in which an attempt to avoid one increases the risk from the other.

scy·phis·to·ma /sīˈfistəmə/ ▸*n.* (*pl.* **-mae** /-ˌmē; -ˌmī/ or **-mas**) *Zoology* the fixed polyplike stage in the life cycle of a jellyfish, which reproduces asexually by budding (strobilation). ▷late 19th cent.: from Latin *scyphus* 'cup' + Greek *stoma* 'mouth.'

Scy·pho·zo·a /ˌsīfəˈzōə/ *Zoology* a class of marine coelenterates that comprises the jellyfishes. ▷modern Latin (plural), from Greek *skuphos* 'drinking cup' + *zōion* 'animal.' **—scy·pho·zo·an** *n.* & *adj.*

scythe

scythe /sīTH/ ▸*n.* a tool used for cutting crops such as grass or wheat, with a long curved blade at the end of a long pole attached to which are one or two short handles.
▸*v.* [*trans.*] cut with a scythe. ■ [*intrans.*] move through or penetrate something

rapidly and forcefully: *attacking players can scythe through defenses.* ▷Old English *sīthe*, of Germanic origin; related to Dutch *zeis* and German *Sense*.

Scyth·i·a /ˈsɪTHēə/ an ancient region in southeastern Europe and Asia. The center of the Scythian empire, which existed between the 8th and 2nd centuries BC, was on the northern shores of the Black Sea and extended from southern Russia to the borders of Persia. —**Scyth·i·an** *adj.* & *n.*

SD ▸*abbr.* ■ South Dakota (in official postal use).

sd. ▸*abbr.* sound.

s.d. ▸*abbr.* ■ sine die. ■ *Statistics* standard deviation.

S.Dak. ▸*abbr.* South Dakota.

SDR ▸*abbr.* special drawing right (from the International Monetary Fund).

SDS ▸*abbr.* Students for a Democratic Society; a left-leaning organization of U.S. college students that formed in 1960. It was active in the Civil Rights movement but is best remembered for its resistance to the **VIETNAM WAR**.

SE ▸*abbr.* southeast or southeastern.

Se ▸*symbol* the chemical element selenium.

se- ▸*prefix* (in words adopted from Latin) apart; without: *secede | secure.* ▷from Latin *se-*, from the earlier preposition and adverb *se*.

sea /sē/ ▸*n.* (often **the sea**) the expanse of salt water that covers most of the earth's surface and surrounds its landmasses: *a ban on dumping radioactive wastes in the sea | rocky bays lapped by vivid blue sea |* [as *adj.*] *a sea view.* ■ [often in *place names*] a roughly definable area of this: *the Black Sea.* ■ [in *place names*] a large lake: *the Sea of Galilee.* ■ used to refer to waves as opposed to calm sea: *there was still some sea running.* ■ (**seas**) large waves: *the lifeboat met seas of thirty-five feet head-on.* ■ *figurative* a vast expanse or quantity of something: *she scanned the **sea of** faces for Stephen.* ▷Old English *sǣ*, of Germanic origin; related to Dutch *zee* and German *See*.

▸*PHRASES* □ **at sea** sailing on the sea. ■ (also **all at sea**) confused or unable to decide what to do: *he feels **at sea with** economics.* □ **by sea** by means of a ship or ships: *other army units were sent by sea.* □ **go to sea** set out on a voyage. ■ become a sailor in a navy or a merchant navy. □ **on the sea** situated on the coast. □ **put (out) to sea** leave land on a voyage.

sea an·chor ▸*n.* an object dragged in the water from the bow of a boat in order to keep the bow pointing into the waves or to lessen leeway.

sea a·nem·o·ne ▸*n.* a sedentary marine coelenterate with a columnar body that bears a ring of stinging tentacles around the mouth. • Order Actiniaria, class Anthozoa.

sea·an·gel ▸*n.* an angel shark.

sea·bag /ˈsē,bag/ ▸*n.* a sailor's traveling bag or trunk.

sea bass /bas/ ▸*n.* any of a number of marine fishes that are related to or resemble the common perch, in particular: • a mainly tropical fish of a large family (Serranidae, the **sea bass family**), esp. one of the genus *Centropristis*, including the **giant sea bass** (*C. stiata*). The sea bass family also includes the groupers. • (**white sea bass**) a large game fish of the Pacific coast of North America (*Cynoscion nobilis*, family Sciaenidae).

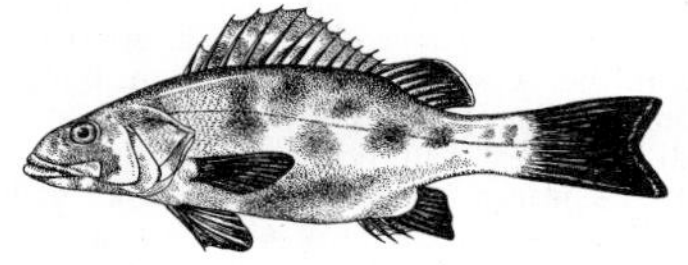

giant sea bass

sea·bed /ˈsē,bed/ ▸*n.* the ground under the sea; the ocean floor.

Sea·bee /ˈsē,bē/ ▸*n.* a member of one of the construction battalions of the Civil Engineer Corps of the U.S. Navy. ▷representing a pronunciation of the letters *CB* (from *construction battalion*).

sea·bird /ˈsē,bərd/ ▸*n.* a bird that frequents the sea or coast.

sea bis·cuit ▸*n.* **1** another term for **HARDTACK**. **2** another term for **SAND DOLLAR**.

sea·board /ˈsē,bôrd/ ▸*n.* a region bordering the sea; the coastline: *the eastern seaboard of the U.S.*

sea boat ▸*n.* [usu. with *adj.*] a boat or ship considered in terms of its ability to cope with conditions at sea: *she was a surprisingly good sea boat.*

Sea·borg /ˈsē,bôrg/, Glenn (Theodore) (1912–99), U.S. nuclear chemist. During 1940–58, he and his colleagues produced nine of the transuranic elements (plutonium to nobelium) in a cyclotron. Nobel Prize for Chemistry (1951, shared with Edwin McMillan (1907–91)).

sea·bor·gi·um /sēˈbôrgēəm/ ▸*n.* the chemical element of atomic number 106, a very unstable element made by high-energy atomic collisions. (Symbol: **Sg**) ▷modern Latin, named after G. *Seaborg* (see **SEABORG**).

sea·borne /ˈsē,bôrn/ ▸*adj.* transported or traveling by sea: *seaborne trade.*

sea bream ▸*n.* a deep-bodied marine fish that resembles the freshwater bream, in particular: • Several genera and species in the family Sparidae (the **sea bream family**), in particular the **red sea bream** (*Pagellus bogaraveo*), which is fished commercially, and the **black sea bream** (*Spondyliosoma cantharus*), a popular angling fish; the sea bream family also includes the porgies. • a fish of Australasian coastal waters, with a purple back and silver underside (*Seriolella brama*, family Centrolophidae).

sea breeze ▸*n.* a breeze blowing toward the land from the sea, esp. during the day owing to the relative warmth of the land.

sea buck·thorn ▸*n.* a bushy Eurasian shrub or small tree that typically grows on sandy coasts. It bears orange berries, and some plants are spiny. • *Hippophae rhamnoides*, Elaeagnaceae.

sea but·ter·fly ▸*n.* another term for **PTEROPOD**.

sea cap·tain ▸*n.* a person who commands a ship, esp. a merchant ship.

Sea·Cat /ˈsē,kat/ ▸*n. trademark* a large, high-speed catamaran used as a passenger and car ferry on short sea crossings.

sea change ▸*n.* a profound or notable transformation. ▷from Shakespeare's *Tempest* (I. ii. 403).

sea chant·ey ▸*n.* see **CHANTEY**.

sea chest ▸*n.* a sailor's storage chest.

sea coal ▸*n. archaic* mineral coal, as distinct from other types of coal such as charcoal.

sea·cock /ˈsē,käk/ ▸*n.* a valve in an opening through a ship's hull below or near the waterline (esp. one connecting a ship's engine-cooling system to the sea).

sea cow ▸*n.* a sirenian, esp. a manatee.

sea cu·cum·ber ▸*n.* an echinoderm that has a thick, wormlike body with tentacles around the mouth. They typically have rows of tube feet along the body and breathe by means of a respiratory tree. • Class Holothuroidea.

sea dog ▸*n.* **1** *informal* an old or experienced sailor. **2** *Heraldry* a mythical beast like a dog with fins, webbed feet, and a scaly tail.

sea duck ▸*n.* any of a number of ducks that frequent the sea, esp. the eiders, scoters, and long-tailed duck. • Tribes Somateriini (and Mergini), family Anatidae: several genera.

sea ea·gle ▸*n.* a large Eurasian fish-eating eagle that frequents coasts and wetlands. • Genus *Haliaeetus*, family Accipitridae: several species, in particular the widespread **white-tailed sea eagle** (*H. albicilla*), recently reintroduced to Scotland.

sea egg ▸*n.* a sea urchin.

sea el·e·phant ▸*n.* another term for **ELEPHANT SEAL**.

sea fan ▸*n.* a horny coral with a vertical treelike or fanlike skeleton, living chiefly in warmer seas. • *Gorgonis* and other genera, order Gorgonacea.

sea·far·ing /ˈsē,fe(ə)rɪNG/ ▸*adj.* (of a person) traveling by sea, esp. regularly.
▸*n.* the practice of traveling by sea, esp. regularly. —**sea·far·er** /-,fe(ə)rər/ *n.*

seafloor spread·ing (also **sea-floor spread·ing**) ▸*n.* *Geology* the formation of new areas of oceanic crust, which occurs through the upwelling of magma at midocean ridges and its subsequent outward movement on either side.

sea·food /ˈsē,fo͞od/ ▸*n.* shellfish and sea fish, served as food.

sea·front /ˈsē,frənt/ ▸*n.* another term for **BEACHFRONT**.

sea-girt ▸*adj. poetic/literary* surrounded by sea.

sea·go·ing /ˈsē,gōɪNG/ ▸*adj.* [*attrib.*] (of a ship) suitable or designed for voyages on the sea. ■ characterized by or relating to traveling by sea, esp. habitually: *a seagoing life.*

sea goose·ber·ry ▸*n.* a common comb jelly with a spherical body bearing two long retractile branching tentacles, typically occurring in swarms. • *Pleurobrachia pileus*, class Tentaculata.

sea grape ▸*n.* a salt-resistant tree of the dock family, bearing grapelike bunches of edible purple fruit and found on the Atlantic coasts of tropical America. • *Coccoloba uvifera*, family Polygonaceae. ■ the fruit of this tree.

sea·grass /ˈsē,gras/ ▸*n.* a grasslike plant that lives in or close to the sea, esp. eelgrass. • Genera *Cymodocea* (family Cymodoceaceae), *Zostera* (family Zosteraceae), and others.

sea-green ▸*adj.* of a pale bluish green color.

sea·gull /ˈsē,gəl/ ▸*n.* a popular name for a gull.

sea hare ▸*n.* a large sea slug that has a minute internal shell and lateral extensions to the foot. Most species can swim, and many secrete distasteful chemicals to deter predators. • *Aplysia* and other genera, order Anaspidea, class Gastropoda.

sea hol·ly ▸*n.* a spiny-leaved plant of the parsley family, with metallic blue teasel-like flowers, growing in sandy places by the sea and native to Europe. • *Eryngium maritimum*, family Umbelliferae. See also **ERYNGIUM**.

sea·horse /ˈsē,hôrs/ (also **sea horse**) ▸*n.* **1** a small marine fish with segmented bony armor, an upright posture, a curled prehensile tail, a tubular snout, and a head and neck suggestive of a horse. • Genus *Hippocampus*, family Syngnathidae: many species, including the European *H. ramulosus* and the American *H. hudsonius*. **2** a mythical creature with a horse's head and fish's tail.

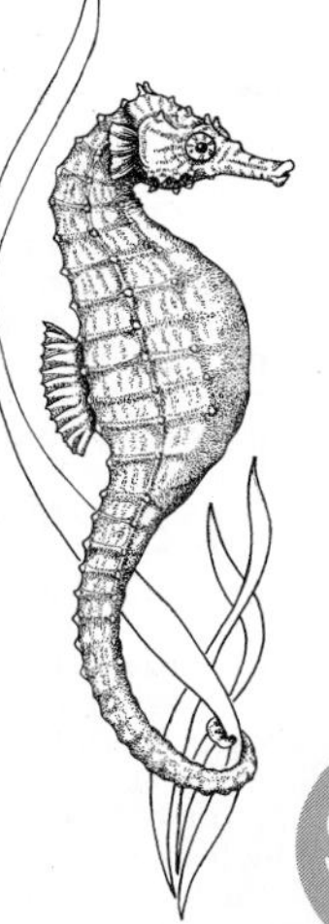

seahorse

Sea Is·land cot·ton ▸*n.* a fine-quality long-staple cotton grown on islands off the southern U.S.

Sea Is·lands a chain of islands off the Atlantic coast of northern Florida, Georgia, and South Carolina. They include many resorts and nature preserves and are noted for their African-derived Gullah culture.

sea·kale /ˈsē,kāl/ ▸*n.* a maritime Eurasian plant of the cabbage family, sometimes cultivated for its edible young shoots. • *Crambe maritima*, family Brassicaceae.

sea·keep·ing /ˈsē,kēpɪNG/ ▸*n.* [usu. as *adj.*] the ability of a vessel to withstand rough conditions at sea.

sea·kind·ly ▸*adj.* (of a ship) easy to handle at sea. —**sea·kind·li·ness** *n.*

sea krait ▸*n.* a venomous sea snake with a compressed tail, occurring in tropical coastal waters of the eastern Indian Ocean and western Pacific, coming ashore to bask and breed. • Genus *Laticauda*, family Elapidae: two species.

SEAL /sēl/ ▸*n.* a member of an elite force within the U.S. Navy specializing in guerrilla warfare and counterinsurgency. ▷abbreviation of *(se)a (a)ir (l)and* (team).

seal[1] /sēl/ ▸*n.* **1** a device or substance that is used to join two things together so as to prevent them from coming apart or to prevent anything from passing between them: *blue smoke from the exhaust suggests worn valve seals.* ■ [in *sing.*] the state or fact of being joined or rendered impervious by such a substance or device: *many fittings have tapered threads for a better seal.* ■ the water standing in the trap of a drain to prevent sewer gas from backing up through the drain, considered in terms of its depth. **2** a piece of wax, lead, or other material with an individual design stamped into it, attached to a document to show that it has come from the person who claims to have issued it. ■ a design embossed in paper for this purpose. ■ an engraved device used for stamping a design that authenticates a document. ■ *figurative* a thing regarded as a confirmation or guarantee of something: *the International Monetary Fund is likely to give a seal of approval to the Mexican plan.* ■ a decorative adhesive stamp. ■ (**the seal**) (also **the seal of confession** or **the seal of the confessional**) the obligation on a priest not to divulge anything said during confession: *I was told **under the seal**.*
▸*v.* [*trans.*] fasten or close securely: *he folded it, sealed the envelope, and walked to the mailbox.* ■ (**seal something in**) prevent something from escaping by closing a

Pronunciation Key ə *ago*; ər *over*; ˈə or ,ə *up*; ˈər or ,ər *fur*; a *hat*; ā *rate*; ä *car*; CH *chew*; e *let*; ē *see*; e(ə)r *air*; i *fit*; ī *by*; i(ə)r *ear*; NG *sing*; ō *go*; ô *for*; oi *boy*; o͝o *good*; o͞o *goo*; ou *out*; SH *she*; TH *thin*; T͟H *then*; (h)w *why*; ZH *vision*

container or opening. ■ (**seal something off**) isolate an area by preventing or monitoring entrance to and exit from it: *anti-terrorist squad officers sealed off the area to search for possible bombs.* ■ apply a nonporous coating to (a surface) to make it impervious: *seal the finish with a satin varnish.* ■ fry (food) briefly in hot fat to prevent it from losing too much of its moisture during subsequent cooking: *heat the oil and seal the lamb on both sides.* ■ fix a piece of wax or lead stamped with a design to (a document) to authenticate it. ■ conclude, establish, or secure (something) definitively, excluding the possibility of reversal or loss: *to seal the deal he offered Thornton a place on the board of the nascent company.* ■ (in the Mormon church) mark (a marriage or adoption) as eternally binding in a formal ceremony. ▷Middle English (sense 2): from Old French *seel* (noun), *seeler* (verb), from Latin *sigillum* 'small picture,' diminutive of *signum* 'a sign.' **—seal·a·ble** *adj.*

▸*PHRASES* □ **my** (or **his**, etc.) **lips are sealed** used to convey that one will not discuss or reveal something. □ **put** (or **set**) **the seal on** give the final authorization to: *the UN envoy hopes to set the seal on a lasting peace.* ■ provide or constitute the final confirmatory or conclusive factor: *the rain set the seal on his depression.* □ **seal someone's fate** see **FATE**. □ **set** (or **put**) **one's seal to** (or **on**) mark with one's distinctive character: *it was the Stewart dynasty which most markedly set its seal on the place.* □ **under seal** under legal protection of secrecy: *the judge ordered that the videotape be kept under seal.*

seal[2] ▸*n.* a fish-eating aquatic mammal with a streamlined body and feet developed as flippers, returning to land to breed or rest. • Families Phocidae (the **true seals**) and Otariidae (the **eared seals**, including the fur seals and sea lions). The latter have external ear flaps and are able to sit upright, and the males are much larger than the females. ■ another term for **SEALSKIN**.

▸*v.* [*intrans.*] [usu. as *n.*] (**sealing**) hunt for seals. ▷Old English *seolh*, of Germanic origin.

sea lane ▸*n.* a route designated for use or regularly used by shipping.

seal·ant /ˈsēlənt/ ▸*n.* material used for sealing something so as to make it airtight or watertight.

sea lav·en·der ▸*n.* a chiefly maritime plant with small pink or lilac funnel-shaped flowers. Several kinds are cultivated and some are used as everlasting flowers. • Genus *Limonium* (formerly *Statice*), family Plumbaginaceae.

sea law·yer ▸*n. informal* an eloquently and obstinately argumentative person.

Seal Beach a city in southwestern California, southeast of Long Beach; pop. 25,098.

seal·coat·ing /ˈsēlˌkōtiNG/ ▸*n.* the application of a sealing coat to a paved surface in order to prolong its integrity. **—seal·coat** *v.* [*trans.*] *How soon can I sealcoat freshly laid asphalt?*

sealed-beam ▸*adj.* denoting a vehicle headlight with a sealed unit consisting of the light source, reflector, and lens.

sealed book ▸*n.* archaic term for **CLOSED BOOK** (see **CLOSED**).

sealed or·ders ▸*plural n. Military* orders that are not to be opened before a specified time.

sea legs ▸*plural n.* (**one's sea legs**) a person's ability to keep their balance and not feel seasick when on board a moving ship.

sea lem·on ▸*n.* a yellowish sea slug. • *Archidoris* and other genera, order Nudibranchia, class Gastropoda.

seal·er[1] /ˈsēlər/ ▸*n.* **1** [usu. with *adj.*] a device or substance used to seal something, esp. with a hermetic or an impervious seal. **2** (also **seal·er jar**) *Canadian* a jar with a hermetic seal designed to preserve food such as fruit, pickles, and jams.

seal·er[2] ▸*n.* a ship or person engaged in hunting seals.

sea let·tuce ▸*n.* an edible seaweed with green fronds that resemble lettuce leaves. • *Ulva lactuca*, division Chlorophyta.

sea lev·el ▸*n.* the level of the sea's surface, used in reckoning the height of geographical features such as hills and as a barometric standard: *it is only 500 feet above sea level.* Compare with **MEAN SEA LEVEL**.

sea·lift /ˈsēˌlift/ ▸*n.* a large-scale transportation of troops, supplies, and equipment by sea.

sea lil·y ▸*n.* a sedentary marine echinoderm that has a small body on a long jointed stalk, with featherlike arms to trap food. • Class Crinoidea.

seal·ing wax ▸*n.* a mixture of shellac and rosin with turpentine and pigment, softened by heating and used to make seals.

sea li·on ▸*n.* **1** an eared seal occurring mainly on Pacific coasts, the large male of which has a mane on the neck and shoulders. • Five genera and species in the family Otariidae. **2** *Heraldry* a mythical beast formed of a lion's head and foreparts and a fish's tail.

sea loch ▸*n.* see **LOCH**.

seal point ▸*n.* a dark brown marking on the fur of the head, tail, and paws of a Siamese cat. ■ a cat with such markings.

seal ring ▸*n. chiefly historical* a finger ring with a seal for impressing sealing wax.

seal·skin /ˈsēlˌskin/ ▸*n.* [often as *adj.*] the skin or prepared fur of a seal, esp. when made into a garment.

seal·stone /ˈsēlˌstōn/ ▸*n.* a gemstone bearing an engraved device for use as a seal.

seal-top ▸*adj.* (of a spoon) having a flat design resembling an embossed seal at the end of its handle. ▸*n.* a spoon with such a handle.

Sea·ly·ham /ˈsēlēəm; -lēˌham/ (in full **Sea·ly·ham ter·ri·er**) ▸*n.* a terrier of a wire-haired, short-legged breed. ▷late 19th cent.: from *Sealyham*, the name of a village in southwestern Wales, where the dog was first bred.

seam /sēm/ ▸*n.* **1** a line along which two pieces of fabric are sewn together in a garment or other article. ■ a line where the edges of two pieces of wood, wallpaper, or another material touch each other. ■ a long thin indentation or scar: *a sun-scorched face fissured with delicate seams.* **2** an underground layer, as of ore or coal.

▸*v.* [*trans.*] **1** join with a seam: *it can be used for seaming garments.* **2** [usu. as *adj.*] (**seamed**) make a long narrow indentation in: *men in middle age have seamed faces.* ▷Old English *sēam*, of Germanic origin; related to Dutch *zoom* and German *Saum*. **—seam·er** *n.*

▸*PHRASES* □ **bursting** (or **bulging**) **at the seams** *informal* (of a place or building) full to overflowing. □ **come** (or **fall**) **apart at the seams** *informal* (of a person or system) be in a very poor condition and near to collapse: *the attitude of the airport guard was symptomatic of a system falling apart at the seams.*

sea·man /ˈsēmən/ ▸*n.* (*pl.* **-men**) a person who works as a sailor, esp. one below the rank of officer. ■ a sailor of the lowest rank in the U.S. Navy or Coast Guard, ranking below petty officer. ■ [with *adj.*] a person regarded in terms of their ability to captain or crew a boat or ship: *he's the best seaman on the coast.* ▷Old English *sǣman* (see **SEA**, **MAN**). **—sea·man·like** /-ˌlīk/ *adj.* **—sea·man·ly** *adj.*

sea·man·ship /ˈsēmənˌSHip/ ▸*n.* the skill, techniques, or practice of handling a ship or boat at sea.

sea·mark /ˈsēˌmärk/ ▸*n.* a conspicuous object distinguishable at sea, serving to guide or warn sailors in navigation.

sea mile ▸*n.* a unit of distance equal to a minute of arc of a great circle and varying (because the earth is not a perfect sphere) between approximately 2,014 yards (1,842 meters) at the equator and 2,035 yards (1,861 meters) at the pole. Compare with **NAUTICAL MILE**.

seam·less /ˈsēmlis/ ▸*adj.* (of a fabric or surface) smooth and without seams or obvious joins: *seamless stockings* | *figurative seamless dialogue between the two pianos.* **—seam·less·ly** *adv.* **—seam·less·ness** *n.*

sea-moth ▸*n.* a small fish with bony plates covering the body and large pectoral fins that spread out horizontally like wings. It lives in the warmer waters of the Indo-Pacific. • Family Pegasidae: several genera and species, including the widely distributed *Eurypegasus draconis*.

sea·mount /ˈsēˌmount/ ▸*n.* a submarine mountain.

sea mouse ▸*n.* a large marine bristle-worm with a stout, oval body that bears matted, furlike, iridescent chaetae. • Genus *Aphrodite*, class Polychaeta.

seam·stress /ˈsēmstris/ ▸*n.* a woman who sews, esp. one who earns her living by sewing. ▷late 16th cent.: from archaic *seamster*, *sempster* 'tailor, seamstress' + **-ESS**[1].

seam·y /ˈsēmē/ ▸*adj.* (**seam·i·er**, **seam·i·est**) sordid and disreputable: *a seamy sex scandal.* ▷late 16th cent.: from **SEAM** + **-Y**[1]. The sense 'disreputable' (early 17th cent.) arose from the notion of 'having the rough edges of seams visible.' **—seam·i·ness** *n.*

Sean·ad /ˈSHônəd; ˈSHänəTH/ (also **Sean·ad Eire·ann** /ˈärən/) the upper House of Parliament in the Republic of Ireland, composed of sixty members, of whom eleven are nominated by the Taoiseach and forty-nine are elected by institutions. ▷Irish, 'senate (of Ireland).'

se·ance /ˈsāˌäns/ ▸*n.* a meeting at which people attempt to make contact with the dead, esp. through the agency of a medium. ▷late 18th cent.: French *séance*, from Old French *seoir*, from Latin *sedere* 'sit.'

sea net·tle ▸*n.* a large, stinging jellyfish. • *Chrysaora* and other genera, class Scyphozoa: numerous species, including the **East Coast sea nettle** (*C. quinquecirrha*), which is particularly common in Chesapeake Bay during midsummer.

East Coast sea nettle

Sea of A·zov, Sea of Gal·i·lee, etc. see **AZOV, SEA OF**; **GALILEE, SEA OF**, etc.

sea ot·ter ▸*n.* an entirely aquatic marine otter of North Pacific coasts, formerly hunted for its dense fur. It is noted for its habit of floating on its back with a stone balanced on the abdomen, in order to crack open bivalve mollusks. • *Enhydra lutris*, family Mustelidae.

sea pen ▸*n.* a marine coelenterate related to the corals, forming a feather-shaped colony with a horny or calcareous skeleton. • Order Pennatulacea, class Anthozoa.

sea perch ▸*n.* any of a number of marine fishes that typically have a long-based dorsal fin and that are popular as sporting fish, in particular: • a fish of the snapper family (Lutjanidae: several genera). • a surfperch.

sea pink ▸*n.* another term for **THRIFT** (sense 2).

sea·plane /ˈsēˌplān/ ▸*n.* an aircraft with floats instead of wheels, designed to land on and take off from water.

sea·port /ˈsēˌpôrt/ ▸*n.* a town or city with a harbor for seagoing ships.

sea po·ta·to ▸*n.* a yellowish-brown European heart urchin. • *Echinocardium cordatum*, class Echinoidea.

sea pow·er ▸*n.* a country's naval strength, esp. as a weapon of war.

SEAQ /ˈsēˌak/ ▸*abbr.* (in the UK) Stock Exchange Automated Quotations (the computer system on which dealers trade shares and seek or provide price quotations on the London Stock Exchange).

sea·quake /ˈsēˌkwāk/ ▸*n.* a sudden disturbance of the sea caused by a submarine eruption or earthquake.

sear /si(ə)r/ ▸*v.* [*trans.*] burn or scorch the surface of (something) with a sudden, intense heat: *the water got so hot that it seared our lips* | *figurative a sharp pang of disappointment seared her.* See note at **BURN**. ■ [*intrans.*] (of pain) be experienced as a sudden, burning sensation: *a crushing pain seared through his chest.* ■ brown (food) quickly at a high temperature so that it will retain its juices in subsequent cooking: [as *adj.*] (**seared**) *seared chicken livers.* ■ *archaic* cause to wither. ■ *archaic* make (someone's conscience, heart, or feelings) insensitive.

▸*adj. poetic/literary* variant spelling of **SERE**. ▷Old English *sēar* (adjective), *sēarian* (verb), of Germanic origin.

search /sərCH/ ▸*v.* [*intrans.*] try to find something by looking or otherwise seeking carefully and thoroughly: *I searched among the rocks, but there was nothing* | *Daniel is then able to* ***search out*** *the most advantageous mortgage* | *Hugh will be* ***searching for*** *the truth.* ■ [*trans.*] examine (a place, vehicle, or person) thoroughly in order to find something or someone: *she searched the house from top to bottom* | *the guards searched him for weapons.* ■ [as *adj.*] (**searching**) scrutinizing thoroughly, esp. in a disconcerting way: *you have to ask yourselves some searching questions.*

▸*n.* an act of searching for someone or something: *the police carried out a thorough search of the premises* | *he plans to go to the Himalayas* ***in search of*** *a yeti.* ■ (usu. **searches**) *Law* an investigation of public records to find if a property is subject to any liabilities or encumbrances. ▷Middle English: from Old French *cerchier* (verb), from late Latin *circare* 'go around,' from Latin *circus* 'circle.' —**search·a·ble** *adj.* —**search·er** *n.* —**search·ing·ly** *adv.*

▶*PHRASE* □ **search me!** *informal* I do not know (used for emphasis).

search coil ▶*n. Physics* a flat coil of insulated wire connected to a galvanometer, used for finding the strength of a magnetic field from the current induced in the coil when it is quickly turned over or withdrawn.

search en·gine ▶*n. Computing* a program for the retrieval of data from a database or network, esp. the Internet.

search·light /'sərcH,līt/ ▶*n.* a powerful outdoor electric light with a concentrated beam that can be turned in the required direction.

search par·ty ▶*n.* a group of people organized to look for someone or something that is lost.

search war·rant ▶*n.* a legal document authorizing a police officer or other official to enter and search premises.

sear·ing /'si(ə)riNG/ ▶*adj.* extremely hot or intense: *the searing heat of the sun | a searing pain.* ■ severely critical: *a searing indictment of the government's performance.*

sea rob·in ▶*n.* a gurnard (fish), esp. one of warm seas that has winglike pectoral fins that are brightly colored. • Family Triglidae: several genera and many species.

sea room ▶*n.* clear space at sea for a ship to maneuver in.

Sears /si(ə)rz/, Richard Warren (1863–1914), U.S. businessman. He founded his first mail-order business, selling watches, in Minneapolis in 1886, moved to Chicago, and sold the business. He then began a partnership with Alvah Curtis Roebuck (1864–1948), a watch repairman, that became Sears, Roebuck & Co. in 1893.

sea-run ▶*adj.* (of a migratory fish, esp. a trout or salmon) having returned to the sea after spawning.

sea salt ▶*n.* salt produced by the evaporation of seawater.

sea·scape /'sē,skāp/ ▶*n.* a view of an expanse of sea. ■ a picture of such a view.

Sea Scout ▶*n.* a participant in a program to train Explorer Scouts in seamanship.

sea ser·pent ▶*n.* a legendary serpentlike sea monster.

sea·shell /'sē,SHel/ ▶*n.* the shell of a marine mollusk.

sea·shore /'sē,SHôr/ ▶*n.* (usu. **the seashore**) an area of sandy, stony, or rocky land bordering and level with the sea. ■ *Law* the land between high- and low-water marks.

sea·sick /'sē,sik/ ▶*adj.* suffering from sickness or nausea caused by the motion of a ship at sea. —**sea·sick·ness** *n.*

sea·side /'sē,sīd/ ▶*n.* (usu. **the seaside**) a place by the sea, esp. a beach area or vacation resort.

sea·side spar·row ▶*n.* a small sparrow found on the Atlantic coast of North America. • *Ammodramus maritimus*, family Emberizidae.

sea slat·er ▶*n.* a common shore-dwelling crustacean that is related to the wood louse. • *Ligia oceanica*, order Isopoda.

sea slug ▶*n.* a shell-less marine mollusk that is typically brightly colored, with external gills and a number of appendages on the upper surface. • Order Nudibranchia, class Gastropoda.

sea snail ▶*n.* **1** a marine mollusk, esp. one with a spiral shell. • Subclass Prosobranchia, class Gastropoda. **2** another term for SNAILFISH.

sea snake ▶*n.* a venomous marine snake with a flattened tail, that lives in the warm coastal waters of the Indian and Pacific oceans and does not come onto land. • Subfamily Hydrophiinae, family Elapidae: several genera and species, including the **yellow-bellied sea snake** (*Pelamis platurus*), the only species found in the open ocean.

sea·son /'sēzən/ ▶*n.* each of the four divisions of the year (spring, summer, autumn, and winter) marked by particular weather patterns and daylight hours, resulting from the earth's changing position with regard to the sun. ■ a period of the year characterized by a particular climatic feature or marked by a particular activity, event, or festivity: *the rainy season | the season for gathering pine needles.* ■ a fixed time in the year when a particular sport is played: *basketball season is over.* ■ the time of year when a particular fruit, vegetable, or other food is plentiful and in good condition: *the pies are made with fruit that is* **in season** | *lobster season.* ■ an indefinite or unspecified period of time; a while: *this most beautiful soul, who walked with me for a season in this world.* ■ *archaic* a proper or suitable time: *to everything there is a season.*
▶*v.* [*trans.*] **1** add salt, herbs, pepper, or other spices to (food): *season the soup to taste with salt and pepper* | [as *adj.*] (**seasoned**) *seasoned flour.* ■ add a quality or feature to (something), esp. so as to make it more lively or exciting: *his conversation is seasoned liberally with exclamation points and punch lines.* **2** make (wood) suitable for use as timber by adjusting its moisture content to that of the environment in which it will be used: [as *adj.*] (**seasoned**) *it was made from seasoned, untreated oak.* ■ [as *adj.*] (**seasoned**) accustomed to particular conditions; experienced: *she is a seasoned traveler.* ▷Middle English: from Old French *seson*, from Latin *satio(n-)* 'sowing,' later 'time of sowing,' from the root of *serere* 'to sow.'

▶*PHRASES* □ **for all seasons** suitable in or appropriate for every kind of weather: *a coat for all seasons.* ■ adaptable to any circumstance: *a singer for all seasons.* □ **season's greetings** used as an expression of goodwill at Christmas or the New Year.

sea·son·a·ble /'sēzənəbəl/ ▶*adj.* **1** usual for or appropriate to a particular season of the year: *seasonable temperatures.* **2** *archaic* coming at the right time or meeting the needs of the occasion; opportune. See note at TIMELY. —**sea·son·a·bil·i·ty** /,sēzənə'bilitē/ *n.* —**sea·son·a·ble·ness** *n.* —**sea·son·a·bly** /-blē/ *adv.*

USAGE Is it **seasonable** or **seasonal**? **Seasonable** means 'usual or suitable for the season' or 'opportune': *although seasonable, the weather was not warm enough for a picnic.* **Seasonal** means 'of, depending on, or varying with the season': *seasonal changes in labor requirements draw migrant workers to the area in spring and fall.*

sea·son·al /'sēzənəl/ ▶*adj.* of, relating to, or characteristic of a particular season of the year: *a selection of seasonal fresh fruit.* ■ fluctuating or restricted according to the season or time of year: *there are companies whose markets are seasonal | seasonal rainfall.* —**sea·son·al·i·ty** /,sēzə'nalitē/ *n.* —**sea·son·al·ly** *adv.*

USAGE See usage at SEASONABLE.

sea·son·al af·fec·tive dis·or·der ▶*n.* depression associated with late autumn and winter and thought to be caused by a lack of light.

sea·son·ing /'sēzəniNG/ ▶*n.* **1** salt, herbs, or spices added to food to enhance the flavor. **2** the process of adjusting the moisture content of wood to make it more suitable for use as timber.

sea·son tick·et ▶*n.* a ticket for a period of travel or a series of events that costs less than purchasing several separate tickets.

sea spi·der ▶*n.* a spiderlike marine arachnid that has a narrow segmented body with a minute abdomen and long legs. • Class Pycnogonida.

sea squill ▶*n.* see SQUILL (sense 1).

sea squirt ▶*n.* a marine tunicate that has a baglike body with orifices through which water flows into and out of a central pharynx. • Class Ascidiacea, subphylum Urochordata.

sea stack ▶*n.* see STACK (sense 2).

sea star ▶*n.* a starfish.

sea state ▶*n.* the degree of turbulence at sea, generally measured on a scale of 0 to 9 according to average wave height.

seat /sēt/ ▶*n.* **1** a thing made or used for sitting on, such as a chair or stool. ■ the roughly horizontal part of a chair, on which one's weight rests directly. ■ a sitting place for a passenger in a vehicle or for a member of an audience: *we have a fairly small theater with about 1,300 seats.* ■ a place in an elected legislative or other body: *he lost his seat in the 1998 election.* ■ a site or location of something specified: *Washington, the seat of the federal government.* ■ short for COUNTRY SEAT. ■ short for COUNTY SEAT. ■ a part of a machine that supports or guides another part. **2** a person's buttocks. ■ the part of a garment that covers the buttocks. ■ a manner of sitting on a horse: *he's got the worst seat on a horse of anyone I've ever seen.*
▶*v.* [*trans.*] arrange for (someone) to sit somewhere: *he seated her next to her husband.* ■ (**seat oneself** or **be seated**) sit down: *she invited them to be seated* | [as *adj.*] (**seated**) *a dummy in a seated position.* ■ (of a place such as a theater or restaurant) have seats for (a specified number of people): *a large tent that seats 100 to 150 people.* ■ [*trans.*] fit in position: *upper boulders were simply seated in the interstices below.* ▷Middle English (as a noun): from Old Norse *sæti*, from the Germanic base of SIT. The verb dates from the late 16th cent. —**seat·less** *adj.*

▶*PHRASES* □ **by the seat of one's pants** *informal* by instinct rather than logic or knowledge. □ **take one's seat** sit down, typically in a seat assigned to one.

seat belt (also **seat·belt**) ▶*n.* a belt or strap securing a person to prevent injury, esp. in a vehicle or aircraft.

-seater ▶*comb. form* denoting a vehicle, sofa, or building with a specified number of seats: *a six-seater.*

seat·ing /'sētiNG/ ▶*n.* **1** the seats with which a building or room is provided: *the restaurant has seating for 80.* **2** the act of directing people to seats: *reservations are only taken for large parties at early seatings.*

SEATO /'sētō/ ▶*abbr.* Southeast Asia Treaty Organization.

sea trout ▶*n.* **1** a troutlike marine fish of the drum family occurring in the western Atlantic. • Genus *Cynoscion*, family Sciaenidae: several species, including the weakfish. **2** *Brit.* a European brown trout of a salmonlike migratory race. Also called SALMON TROUT. • *Salmo trutta trutta*, family Salmonidae.

Se·at·tle[1] /sē'atl/ a port and industrial city in the state of Washington, on the eastern shores of Puget Sound; pop. 563,374. First settled in 1852, it is now the largest city in the northwestern U.S.

Se·at·tle[2] /sē'atl/ (also **Se·atlh**), Chief (1786–1866), Native American leader of the Suquamish and Duwamish tribes. He signed the Treaty of Port Elliott in 1855, guaranteeing a reservation for his people in what became the state of Washington. The city of Seattle is named for him.

sea tur·tle ▶*n.* see TURTLE (sense 2).

sea ur·chin ▶*n.* a marine echinoderm that has a spherical or flattened shell covered in mobile spines, with a mouth on the underside and calcareous jaws. Many species are harvested for food. • Class Echinoidea: several families and genera, and numerous species, including the **Atlantic purple sea urchin** (*Arbacia punctulata*, family Arbaciidae) and the **green sea urchin** (*Strongylocentrotus drobachiensis*, family Strongylocentrotidae).

S

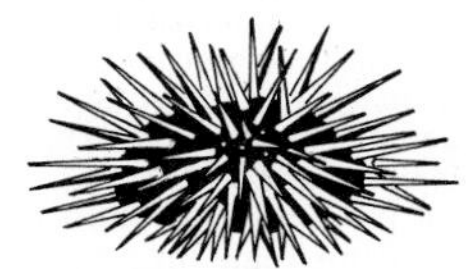

Atlantic purple sea urchin

Seav·er /'sēvər/, Tom (1944–), U.S. baseball player; full name *George Thomas Seaver*. A pitcher for the New York Mets 1966–77 and 1982–83, he won the Cy Young award in 1969, 1973, and 1975. He also pitched for the Cincinnati Reds, the Chicago White Sox, and the Boston Red Sox. Baseball Hall of Fame (1992).

sea wall ▶*n.* a wall or embankment erected to prevent the sea from encroaching on or eroding an area of land.

sea·ward /'sēwərd/ ▶*adv.* toward the sea: *after about a mile they turned seaward.*
▶*adj.* going or pointing toward the sea: *there was a seaward movement of water on the bottom.* ■ nearer or nearest to the sea: *the seaward end of the village.*
▶*n.* [in *sing.*] the side that faces or is nearer to the sea: *breakwaters were extended further* **to seaward**.

sea wasp ▶*n.* a box jellyfish that can inflict a dangerous sting.

sea·wa·ter /'sē,wôtər; -,wätər/ ▶*n.* water in or taken from the sea.

sea·way /'sē,wā/ ▶*n.* **1** an inland waterway capable of accommodating seagoing ships. ■ (**the Seaway**) see ST. LAWRENCE SEAWAY. ■ a natural channel connecting two areas of sea. ■ a route across the sea used by ships. **2** [in *sing.*] a stretch of water in which a sea is running: *with the engine mounted amidship, the boat pitches less* **in a seaway**.

sea·weed /'sē,wēd/ ▶*n.* large algae growing in the sea or on rocks below the high-water mark.

sea wolf ▶*n.* another term for WOLFFISH.

sea·wor·thy /'sē,wər<u>TH</u>ē/ ▶*adj.* (of a vessel) in a good enough condition to sail on the sea. —**sea·wor·thi·ness** *n.*

se·ba·ceous /sə'bāsHəs/ ▶*adj. technical* of or relating

Pronunciation Key ə *ago*; ər *over*; 'ə *or* ,ə *up*; 'ər *or* ,ər *fur*; a *hat*; ā *rate*; ä *car*; CH *chew*; e *let*; ē *see*; e(ə)r *air*; i *fit*; ī *by*; i(ə)r *ear*; NG *sing*; ō *go*; ô *for*; oi *boy*; o͝o *good*; o͞o *goo*; ou *out*; SH *she*; TH *thin*; <u>TH</u> *then*; (h)w *why*; ZH *vision*

to oil or fat. ■ of or relating to a sebaceous gland or its secretion. ▷early 18th cent.: from Latin *sebaceus* (from *sebum* 'tallow') + -OUS.

se·ba·ceous cyst ▸*n.* a swelling in the skin arising in a sebaceous gland, typically filled with yellowish sebum. Also called WEN[1].

se·ba·ceous gland ▸*n.* a small gland in the skin which secretes a lubricating oily matter (sebum) into the hair follicles to lubricate the skin and hair.

Se·bas·tian, St. /si'basCHən/ (late 3rd century), Roman martyr. According to legend he was a soldier who was shot by archers on the orders of Diocletian. When he recovered, he confronted the emperor and was then clubbed to death. Feast day, January 20.

Se·bas·to·pol /sə'bastə,pōl; -,pôl/ a fortress and naval base in Ukraine, near the southern tip of the Crimea; pop. 361,000. It was the focal point of military operations during the Crimean War. Ukrainian and Russian name SEVASTOPOL.

SEbE ▸*abbr.* southeast by east.

seb·or·rhe·a /,sebə'rēə/ (*Brit.* **seb·or·rhoe·a**) ▸*n. Medicine* excessive discharge of sebum from the sebaceous glands. ▷late 19th cent.: from SEBUM + -RRHEA. **—seb·or·rhe·ic** /-'rē-ik/ *adj.*

Se·bring /'sēbriNG/ a city in south central Florida, noted as a car racing center; pop. 8,900.

SEbS ▸*abbr.* southeast by south.

se·bum /'sēbəm/ ▸*n.* an oily secretion of the sebaceous glands. ▷late 19th cent.: modern Latin, from Latin *sebum* 'grease.'

SEC ▸*abbr.* Securities and Exchange Commission, a U.S. governmental agency that monitors trading in securities and company takeovers.

sec[1] /sek/ ▸*abbr.* secant.

sec[2] ▸*n.* (**a sec**) *informal* a second; a very short space of time: *stay put, I'll be back in a sec.* ▷late 19th cent.: abbreviation.

sec[3] ▸*adj.* (of wine) dry. ▷French, from Latin *siccus.*

Sec. ▸*abbr.* secretary.

sec. ▸*abbr.* second(s).

SECAM /'sēkam/ ▸*n.* the television broadcasting system used in France and eastern Europe. ▷from French *séquentiel couleur à mémoire* (so named because the color information is transmitted in sequential blocks to a memory in the receiver).

se·cant /'sē,kant; -kənt/ ▸*n.* **1** (abbr.: **sec**) *Mathematics* the ratio of the hypotenuse to the shorter side adjacent to an acute angle (in a right-angled triangle); the reciprocal of a cosine. **2** *Geometry* a straight line that cuts a curve in two or more parts. ▷late 16th cent.: from French *sécante,* based on Latin *secare* 'to cut.'

sec·a·teurs /'sekə,tərz/ ▸*plural n.* (also **a pair of secateurs**) *chiefly Brit.* a pair of pruning clippers for use with one hand. ▷mid 19th cent.: plural of French *sécateur* 'cutter,' formed irregularly from Latin *secare* 'to cut.'

Sec·chi disc /'sekē/ ▸*n.* an opaque disk, typically white, used to gauge the transparency of water by measuring the depth (**Secchi depth**) at which the disk ceases to be visible from the surface. ▷early 20th cent.: named after Angelo *Secchi* (1818–78), Italian astronomer.

sec·co /'sekō/ (also **fres·co sec·co**) ▸*n.* the technique of painting on dry plaster with pigments mixed in water. ▷mid 19th cent.: from Italian, literally 'dry,' from Latin *siccus.*

se·cede /si'sēd/ ▸*v.* [*intrans.*] withdraw formally from membership in a federal union, an alliance, or a political or religious organization: *the kingdom of Belgium* ***seceded from*** *the Netherlands in 1830.* ▷early 18th cent.: from Latin *secedere,* from *se-* 'apart' + *cedere* 'go.' **—se·ced·er** *n.*

Se·cer·nen·te·a /,sesər'nentēə/ *Zoology* another term for PHASMIDA (sense 2). ▷modern Latin (plural), from Latin *secernent-* 'separating,' from the verb *secernere.*

se·ces·sion /sə'seSHən/ ▸*n.* the action of withdrawing formally from membership of a federation or body, esp. a political state: *the republics want* ***secession from*** *the union.* ■ (**the Secession**) *historical* the withdrawal of eleven Southern states from the Union in 1860, leading to the Civil War. ■ (**the Secession**) variant of SEZESSION. ▷mid 16th cent. (denoting the withdrawal of plebeians from ancient Rome in order to compel the patricians to redress their grievances): from French *sécession* or Latin *secessio(n-),* from *secedere* 'go apart' (see SECEDE). **—se·ces·sion·al** /-SHənl/ *adj.* **—se·ces·sion·ism** /-,nizəm/ *n.* **—se·ces·sion·ist** /-ist/ *n.*

Sech·ua·na /seCH'wänə/ *dated* ▸*n.* & *adj.* variant spelling of SETSWANA.

Seck·el /'sekəl/ ▸*n.* a pear of a small sweet juicy brownish-red variety, grown chiefly in the U.S. ▷early 19th cent.: from the surname of an early grower.

se·clude /si'klōōd/ ▸*v.* [*trans.*] keep (someone) away from other people: *I secluded myself up here for a life of study and meditation.* ▷late Middle English (in the sense 'obstruct access to'): from Latin *secludere,* from *se-* 'apart' + *claudere* 'to shut.'

se·clud·ed /si'klōōdid/ ▸*adj.* (of a place) not seen or visited by many people; sheltered and private: *the gardens are quiet and secluded.*

se·clu·sion /si'klōōZHən/ ▸*n.* the state of being private and away from other people: *they enjoyed ten days of peace and seclusion.* ■ *archaic* a sheltered or private place. ▷early 17th cent.: from medieval Latin *seclusio(n-),* from *secludere* 'shut off' (see SECLUDE). **—se·clu·sive** /-siv/ *adj.*

Sec·o·nal /'sekə,nôl; -,nal/ ▸*n. trademark* a barbiturate drug used as a sedative and hypnotic. ▷1930s: blend of SECONDARY and ALLYL.

sec·ond[1] /'sekənd/ ▸*ordinal number* **1** constituting number two in a sequence; coming after the first in time or order; 2nd: *he married for a second time | Herbie was the second of their six children.* ■ secondly (used to introduce a second point or reason): *second, they are lightly regulated; and third, they do business with nonresident clients.* ■ alternating; other: *auctions are held every second week.* ■ *Music* an interval spanning two consecutive notes in a diatonic scale. ■ the note that is higher by this interval than the tonic of a diatonic scale or root of a chord. ■ the second in a sequence of a vehicle's gears: *he took the corner in second.* ■ *Baseball* second base. ■ the second grade of a school. ■ (**seconds**) *informal* a second course or second helping of food at a meal. ■ denoting someone or something regarded as comparable to or reminiscent of a better-known predecessor: *a fear that the conflict would turn into a second Vietnam.* ■ an act or instance of seconding. **2** subordinate or inferior in position, rank, or importance: *it was* ***second only to*** *Copenhagen among Baltic ports | he is a writer first and a scientist second.* ■ additional to that already existing, used, or possessed: *a second home | French as a second language.* ■ the second finisher or position in a race or competition: *he finished second.* ■ *Brit.* a place in the second-highest grade in an examination, esp. for a degree: *she got a first in moral sciences and a second in history.* ■ *Music* performing a lower or subordinate of two or more parts for the same instrument or voice: *the second violins.* ■ (**seconds**) goods of an inferior quality. ■ coarse flour, or bread made from it. **3** an assistant, in particular: ■ an attendant assisting a combatant in a duel or boxing match.

▸*v.* [*trans.*] formally support or endorse (a nomination or resolution or its proposer) as a necessary preliminary to adoption or further discussion: *Bertonazzi seconded Birmingham's nomination.* ■ express agreement with: *her view is seconded by most Indian leaders today.* ■ *archaic* support; back up: *so well was he seconded by the multitude of laborers at his command.* ▷Middle English: via Old French from Latin *secundus* 'following, second,' from the base of *sequi* 'follow.' The verb dates from the late 16th cent. **—sec·ond·er** *n.*

▸*PHRASES* □ **in the second place** as a second consideration or point. □ **second to none** the best, worst, fastest, etc.

sec·ond[2] /'sekənd/ ▸*n.* **1** (abbr.: **s**) a sixtieth of a minute of time, which as the SI unit of time is defined in terms of the natural periodicity of the radiation of a cesium-133 atom. (Symbol: ″) ■ *informal* a very short time: *his eyes met Charlotte's for a second.* **2** (also **arc second** or **second of arc**) a sixtieth of a minute of angular distance. (Symbol: ″) ▷late Middle English: from medieval Latin *secunda (minuta)* 'second (minute),' feminine (used as a noun) of *secundus,* referring to the "second" operation of dividing an hour by sixty.

sec·ond[3] /si'känd/ ▸*v.* [*trans.*] *Brit.* transfer (a military officer or other official or worker) temporarily to other employment or another position: *I was* ***seconded to*** *a public relations unit.* ▷early 19th cent.: from French *en second* 'in the second rank (of officers).' **—sec·ond·ee** /,sekən'dē/ *n.*

sec·ond Ad·am ▸*n.* (**the second Adam**) (in Christian thought) Jesus Christ. ▷with biblical allusion to 1 Cor. 15: 45–47.

Sec·ond A·dar see ADAR.

Sec·ond Ad·vent ▸*n.* another term for SECOND COMING.

sec·ond·ar·y /'sekən,derē/ ▸*adj.* **1** coming after, less important than, or resulting from someone or something else that is primary: *luck plays a role, but it's ultimately* ***secondary to*** *local knowledge.* ■ [*attrib.*] of or relating to education for children from the age of eleven to sixteen or eighteen: *a secondary school.* ■ having a reversible chemical reaction and therefore able to store energy. ■ relating to or denoting the output side of a device using electromagnetic induction, esp. in a transformer. **2** (**Secondary**) *Geology* former term for MESOZOIC. **3** *Chemistry* (of an organic compound) having its functional group located on a carbon atom that is bonded to two other carbon atoms. ■ (chiefly of amines) derived from ammonia by replacement of two hydrogen atoms by organic groups.

▸*n.* (*pl.* **-ar·ies**) **1** short for: ■ a secondary color. ■ *Ornithology* a secondary feather. ■ a secondary coil or winding in an electrical transformer. **2** *Football* the players in the defensive backfield; the area these players cover. **3** (**the Secondary**) *dated Geology* the Secondary or Mesozoic era. ▷late Middle English: from Latin *secundarius* 'of the second quality or class,' from *secundus* (see SECOND[1]). **—sec·ond·ar·i·ly** /-,derəlē/ *adv.* **—sec·ond·ar·i·ness** *n.*

sec·ond·ar·y ar·tic·u·la·tion ▸*n. Phonetics* an additional feature in the pronunciation of a consonant (besides the actual place of articulation), such as palatalization or lip-rounding.

sec·ond·ar·y boy·cott ▸*n.* industrial action by a union against a company on the grounds that does business with another company engaged in a labor dispute.

sec·ond·ar·y col·or ▸*n.* a color resulting from the mixing of two primary colors.

sec·ond·ar·y ev·i·dence ▸*n. Law* something, in particular documentation, which confirms the existence of unavailable primary evidence.

sec·ond·ar·y feath·er ▸*n.* any of the flight feathers growing from the second joint of a bird's wing.

sec·ond·ar·y in·dus·try ▸*n. Economics* industry that converts the raw materials provided by primary industry into commodities and products for the consumer; manufacturing industry.

sec·ond·ar·y pick·et·ing ▸*n. Brit.* picketing by strikers of the premises of a firm that trades with their employer but is not otherwise involved in the dispute in question.

sec·ond·ar·y plan·et ▸*n.* a satellite of a planet.

sec·ond·ar·y proc·ess ▸*n. Psychoanalysis* a thought process connecting the preconscious and conscious, governed by the reality principle and reflecting the decision-making and problem-solving activity of the ego.

sec·ond·ar·y sec·tor ▸*n. Economics* the sector of the economy concerned with or relating to primary industry.

sec·ond·ar·y sex·u·al char·ac·ter·is·tics ▸*plural n.* physical characteristics developed at puberty that distinguish between the sexes but are not involved in reproduction.

sec·ond·ar·y smoke ▸*n.* British term for SECONDHAND SMOKE.

sec·ond·ar·y smok·ing ▸*n.* another term for PASSIVE SMOKING.

sec·ond·ar·y stress ▸*n. Phonetics* (in a system that postulates three levels of stress) the accent on a syllable of a word or breath group that is weaker than the primary stress but stronger than the lack of stress.

sec·ond·ar·y struc·ture ▸*n. Biochemistry* the local three-dimensional structure of sheets, helices, or other forms adopted by a polynucleotide or polypeptide chain, due to electrostatic attraction between neighboring residues.

sec·ond·ar·y thick·en·ing ▸*n. Botany* (in the stem or root of a woody plant) the increase in girth resulting from the formation of new woody tissue by the cambium.

sec·ond·ar·y treat·ment ▸*n.* the further treatment of sewage effluent by biological methods following sedimentation.

sec·ond bal·lot ▸*n.* a further ballot held to confirm the selection of a candidate where a previous ballot did not yield an absolute majority.

sec·ond best (also **sec·ond-best**) ▸*adj.* next after the best: *his second-best suit.*

▸*n.* a less adequate or less desirable alternative: *he would have to settle for second best.*

▸*PHRASE* □ **come off second best** be defeated in a competition.

sec·ond cause ▸*n. Logic* a cause that is itself caused.

sec·ond cham·ber ▸*n.* the upper house of a parliament with two chambers.

sec·ond child·hood ▸*n.* a period in someone's adult life when they act as a child, either for fun or as a consequence of reduced mental capabilities.

sec·ond class ▸*n.* [in *sing.*] a set of people or things grouped together as the second best. ■ the second-best accommodations in an aircraft, train, or ship. ■ *Brit.* the second-highest division in the results of the examinations for a university degree: *he obtained a second class in modern history.*
▸*adj.* & *adv.* of the second-best quality or in the second division: [as *adj.*] *until 1914 women were thought of as second-class citizens.* ■ of or relating to the second-best accommodations in an aircraft, train, or ship: [as *adj.*] *I want second-class tickets* | [as *adv.*] *they don't fly second-class.* ■ of or relating to a class of mail having lower priority than first-class mail: [as *adj.*] *second-class postage stamps.* ■ (in North America) denoting a class of mail that includes newspapers and periodicals. ■ [as *adj.*] *Brit.* of or relating to the second-highest division in a university examination: *a respectable second-class degree.*

Sec·ond Com·ing ▸*n. Christian Theology* the prophesied return of Christ to earth at the Last Judgment.

sec·ond cous·in ▸*n.* see **COUSIN**.

sec·ond-cut ▸*adj.* another term for **CROSSCUT**.

sec·ond-de·gree ▸*adj.* [*attrib.*] **1** *Medicine* denoting burns that cause blistering but not permanent scars. **2** *Law* denoting a category of a crime, esp. murder, that is less serious than a first-degree crime.

se·conde /sə'känd/ ▸*n. Fencing* the second of eight standard parrying positions. ▷early 18th cent.: from French, feminine of *second* 'second.'

Sec·ond Em·pire the imperial government in France of Napoleon III, 1852–70. ■ this period in France.

sec·ond-gen·er·a·tion ▸*adj.* **1** denoting the offspring of parents who have immigrated to a particular country: *she was a second-generation American.* **2** of a more advanced stage of technology than previous models or systems.

sec·ond growth ▸*n.* **1** woodland growth that replaces harvested or burned virgin forest: [as *adj.*] *a thicket of second-growth Ponderosa pine and Douglas fir.* **2** a wine considered to be the second-best in quality compared to the first growth (or **PREMIER CRU**): [as *adj.*] *a second-growth wine was added as a bonus for the group.*

sec·ond-guess ▸*v.* [*trans.*] **1** anticipate or predict (someone's actions or thoughts) by guesswork: *he had to second-guess what the environmental regulations would be in five years' time.* **2** judge or criticize (someone) with hindsight: *the prime minister was willing to second-guess senior ministers in public.* **—sec·ond-guess·er** *n.*

sec·ond·hand /'sekən(d)'hand/ (also **sec·ond-hand**) ▸*adj.* **1** (of goods) having had a previous owner; not new: *a secondhand car.* ■ [*attrib.*] denoting a store or shop where such goods can be bought: *a secondhand bookstore.* **2** (of information or experience) accepted on another's authority and not from original investigation: *secondhand knowledge of her country.*
▸*adv.* **1** on the basis that something has had a previous owner: *tips on the pitfalls to avoid when buying secondhand.* **2** on the basis of what others have said; indirectly: *I was discounting anything I heard secondhand.*
▸*PHRASE* □ **at second hand** by hearsay rather than direct observation or experience.

sec·ond hand ▸*n.* an extra hand in some watches and clocks that moves around to indicate the seconds.

sec·ond·hand smoke ▸*n.* smoke inhaled involuntarily from tobacco being smoked by others.

sec·ond·hand speech ▸*n.* conversation on a cellular phone that is overheard by people nearby: *I was alternately amused and annoyed by the secondhand speech in the waiting room.*

sec·ond hon·ey·moon ▸*n.* a romantic vacation taken by a couple who have been married for some time.

sec·ond-in-com·mand ▸*n.* the officer next in authority to the commanding or chief officer.

sec·ond in·ten·tion ▸*n. Medicine* the healing of a wound in which the edges do not meet, and new epithelium must form across granulation tissue: *healing* ***by second intention.***

Sec·ond In·ter·na·tion·al see **INTERNATIONAL** (sense 2 of the *noun*).

Sec·ond I·sa·iah another name for **DEUTERO-ISAIAH**.

sec·ond lieu·ten·ant ▸*n.* a commissioned officer of the lowest rank in the U.S. Army, Air Force, and Marine Corps ranking above chief warrant officer and below first lieutenant.

sec·ond line ▸*n.* anything used or held in reserve as support, replacement, or reinforcement, in particular: ■ [usu. as *adj.*] a medical treatment or therapy used in support of another, or as a more drastic measure if the primary treatment is ineffective. ■ a battle line behind the front line to support it and make good its losses. ■ [as *adj.*] ranking second in strength, effectiveness, ability, or value: *the clutch of second-line U.S. computer manufacturers.*

sec·ond·ly /'sekən(d)lē/ ▸*adv.* in the second place (used to introduce a second point or reason): *he was presented first of all as a hopelessly unqualified candidate and, secondly, as an extremist.*

sec·ond mate ▸*n.* an assistant mate on a merchant ship.

sec·ond mes·sen·ger ▸*n. Physiology* a substance whose release within a cell is promoted by a hormone and that brings about a response by the cell.

sec·ond mort·gage ▸*n.* a mortgage taken out on a property that is already mortgaged.

sec·ond name ▸*n. Brit.* a surname.

sec·ond na·ture ▸*n.* a characteristic or habit in someone that appears to be instinctive because that person has behaved in a particular way so often: *deceit was becoming* ***second nature to*** *her.*

se·con·do /sə'kändō; -'kôn-/ ▸*n.* (*pl.* **-di** /-dē/) *Music* the second or lower part in a duet. ▷Italian.

sec·ond of·fi·cer ▸*n.* another term for **SECOND MATE**.

sec·ond per·son ▸*n.* see **PERSON** (sense 2).

sec·ond po·si·tion ▸*n.* **1** *Ballet* a posture in which the feet form a straight line, being turned out to either side with the heels separated by the distance of a small step. ■ a position of the arms in which they are held out to each side of the body, curving forward and slightly upward. **2** *Music* a position of the left hand on the fingerboard of a stringed instrument nearer to the bridge than the first position, enabling a higher-pitched set of notes to be played.

sec·ond-rate ▸*adj.* of mediocre or inferior quality: *a second-rate theater.* **—sec·ond-rat·ed·ness** *n.* **—sec·ond-rat·er** *n.*

sec·ond read·ing ▸*n.* a second presentation of a bill to a legislative assembly, in the U.S. to debate committee reports and in the UK to approve the bill's general principles.

Sec·ond Reich see **REICH**[1].

Sec·ond Re·pub·lic the republican regime in France from the deposition of King Louis Philippe (1848) to the beginning of the Second Empire (1852).

sec·ond sight ▸*n.* the supposed ability to perceive future or distant events; clairvoyance. **—sec·ond-sight·ed** *adj.*

sec·ond-stor·y man ▸*n.* a burglar who enters through an upper-story window.

sec·ond strike ▸*n.* a retaliatory attack conducted with weapons designed to withstand an initial nuclear attack (a "first strike").

sec·ond string ▸*n.* **1** (in sports) the players who are available to replace or relieve those who start a game: [as *adj.*] *the second-string quarterback.* **2** an alternative resource or course of action in case another one fails. **—sec·ond-string·er** *n.*

sec·ond thoughts (also **sec·ond thought**) ▸*plural n.* a change of opinion or resolve reached after considering something again: ***on second thought,*** *perhaps he was right.*

sec·ond wind /wind/ ▸*n.* [in *sing.*] a person's ability to breathe freely during exercise, after having been out of breath. ■ a new strength or energy to continue something that is an effort: *she gained a second wind during the campaign and turned the opinion polls around.*

Sec·ond World ▸*n.* the former communist block consisting of the Soviet Union and some countries in eastern Europe.

Sec·ond World War another term for **WORLD WAR II**.

se·cre·cy /'sēkrəsē/ ▸*n.* the action of keeping something secret or the state of being kept secret: *the bidding is conducted* ***in secrecy.*** ▷late Middle English: from **SECRET**, probably on the pattern of *privacy.*

se·cret /'sēkrit/ ▸*adj.* not known or seen or not meant to be known or seen by others: *how did you guess I had a secret plan?* | *the resupply effort was probably* ***kept secret from*** *Congress.* ■ [*attrib.*] not meant to be known as such by others: *a secret drinker.* ■ fond of or good at keeping things about oneself unknown: *he can be the most secret man.* ■ (of information or documents) given the security classification above confidential and below top secret.
▸*n.* something that is kept or meant to be kept unknown or unseen by others: *a state secret* | *at first I tried to* ***keep it a secret from*** *my wife.* ■ something that is not properly understood; a mystery: *I'm not trying to explain the secrets of the universe in this book.* ■ a valid but not commonly known or recognized method of achieving or maintaining something: *the secret of a happy marriage is compromise.* ■ formerly, the name of a prayer said by the priest in a low voice after the offertory in a Roman Catholic Mass. ▷late Middle English: from Old French, from Latin *secretus* (adjective) 'separate, set apart,' from the verb *secernere*, from *se-* 'apart' + *cernere* 'sift.' **—se·cret·ly** *adv.*
▸*PHRASES* □ **be in on the secret** be among the few people who know something. □ **in secret** without others knowing. □ **make no secret of something** make something perfectly clear.

THE RIGHT WORD **clandestine, covert, furtive, secret, stealthy, surreptitious, underhanded**

While all of these adjectives describe an attempt to do something without attracting attention or observation, **secret** is the most general term, implying that something is being concealed or kept from the knowledge of others (*a secret pact; a secret passageway*).

Covert suggests that something is being done under cover, or concealed as if with a veil or disguise (*a covert attack; a covert threat*), while **clandestine** suggests that something illicit or immoral is being concealed (*a clandestine meeting between the two lovers*).

Someone who is deliberately sneaking around and trying to do something without attracting notice is best described as **stealthy** (*the cat moved toward the bird with a slow, stealthy pace*), and **furtive** connotes even more slyness and watchfulness, as revealed not only by movements but by facial expressions (*a furtive glance; a furtive movement toward the door*).

Surreptitious connotes guilt on the part of the person who is acting in a stealthy or furtive manner (*a surreptitious attempt to hide the book before it was noticed*).

Underhanded is the strongest of these words, implying fraud, deceit, or unfairness (*underhanded business dealings*).

se·cret a·gent ▸*n.* a spy acting for a country.

se·cre·ta·gogue /si'krētə,gôg; -,gäg/ ▸*n. Physiology* a substance that promotes secretion. ▷early 20th cent.: from **SECRETE**[1] + Greek *agōgos* 'leading.'

sec·re·taire /,sekri'te(ə)r/ ▸*n.* a small writing desk; an escritoire. ▷late 18th cent.: from French *secrétaire*, literally 'secretary.'

sec·re·tar·i·at /,sekri'te(ə)rēət/ ▸*n.* a permanent administrative office or department, esp. a governmental one. ■ [treated as *sing.* or *pl.*] the staff working in such an office. ▷early 19th cent.: from French *secrétariat*, from medieval Latin *secretariatus*, from *secretarius* (see **SECRETARY**).

sec·re·tar·y /'sekri,terē/ ▸*n.* (*pl.* **-tar·ies**) a person employed by an individual or in an office to assist with correspondence, keep records, make appointments, and carry out similar tasks. ■ an official of a society or other organization who conducts its correspondence and keeps its records. ■ an official in charge of a government department: [as *title*] *Secretary of the Treasury.* ■ a writing desk with shelves on top of it. ▷late Middle English (originally in the sense 'person entrusted with a secret'): from late Latin *secretarius* 'confidential officer,' from Latin *secretum* 'secret,' neuter of *secretus* (see **SECRET**). **—sec·re·tar·i·al** /-'te(ə)rēəl/ *adj.* **—sec·re·tar·y·ship** /-,SHip/ *n.*

sec·re·tar·y bird ▸*n.* a slender, long-legged African bird of prey that feeds on snakes, having a crest likened to a quill pen stuck behind the ear. • *Sagittarius serpentarius*, the only member of the family Sagittariidae.

sec·re·tar·y-gen·er·al ▸*n.* (*pl.* **sec·re·tar·ies-gen·er·al**) a title given to the principal administrator of some organizations, most notably the United Nations.

sec·re·tar·y of state ▸*n.* **1** (in the U.S.) the head of the State Department, responsible for foreign affairs. **2** (in the UK) the head of a major government

S

department. **3** (in Canada) a government minister responsible for a specific area within a department.

se·cret bal·lot ▸*n.* a ballot in which votes are cast in secret.

se·crete[1] /si'krēt/ ▸*v.* [*trans.*] (of a cell, gland, or organ) produce and discharge (a substance): *insulin is secreted in response to rising levels of glucose in the blood.* ▷early 18th cent.: back-formation from SECRETION. **—se·cre·tor** /-tər/ *n.* **—se·cre·to·ry** /-tərē/ *adj.*

se·crete[2] ▸*v.* [*trans.*] conceal; hide: *the assets had been secreted in Swiss bank accounts.* ▷mid 18th cent.: alteration of the obsolete verb *secret* 'keep secret.'

se·cre·tin /si'krētn/ ▸*n. Biochemistry* a hormone released into the bloodstream by the duodenum (esp. in response to acidity) to stimulate secretion by the liver and pancreas. ▷early 20th cent.: from SECRETION + -IN[1].

Se·cret In·tel·li·gence Serv·ice (abbr.: **SIS**) official name for **MI6**.

se·cre·tion /si'krēsʜən/ ▸*n.* a process by which substances are produced and discharged from a cell, gland, or organ for a particular function in the organism or for excretion. ■ a substance discharged in such a way. ▷mid 17th cent.: from French *sécrétion* or Latin *secretio(n-)* 'separation,' from *secret-* 'moved apart,' from the verb *secernere.*

se·cre·tive /'sēkritiv/ ▸*adj.* (of a person or an organization) inclined to conceal feelings and intentions or not to disclose information: *she was very secretive about her past.* ■ (of a state or activity) characterized by the concealment of intentions and information: *secretive deals.* ■ (of a person's expression or manner) having an enigmatic or conspiratorial quality: *a secretive smile.* ▷mid 19th cent.: back-formation from *secretiveness*, suggested by French *secrétivité*, from *secret* 'secret.' **—se·cre·tive·ly** *adv.* **—se·cre·tive·ness** *n.*

se·cret po·lice ▸*n.* [treated as *pl.*] a police force working in secret against a government's political opponents.

se·cret serv·ice ▸*n.* **1** a government department concerned with espionage. **2** (**Secret Service**) (in the U.S.) a branch of the Treasury Department dealing with counterfeiting and providing protection for the president.

se·cret shop·per ▸*n.* a person employed by a manufacturer or retailer to pose as a shopper in order to evaluate the quality of customer service. Also called MYSTERY SHOPPER.

se·cret so·ci·e·ty ▸*n.* an organization whose members are sworn to secrecy about its activities.

sect /sekt/ ▸*n.* a group of people with somewhat different religious beliefs (typically regarded as heretical) from those of a larger group to which they belong. ■ *often derogatory* a group that has separated from an established church; a nonconformist church. ■ a philosophical or political group, esp. one regarded as extreme or dangerous. ▷Middle English: from Old French *secte* or Latin *secta*, literally 'following,' hence 'faction, party,' from the stem of *sequi* 'follow.'

sect. ▸*abbr.* section.

sec·tar·i·an /sek'te(ə)rēən/ ▸*adj.* denoting or concerning a sect or sects: *among the sectarian offshoots of Ismailism were the Druze of Lebanon.* ■ (of an action) carried out on the grounds of membership of a sect, denomination, or other group: *they are believed to be responsible for the recent sectarian killings of Catholics.* ■ rigidly following the doctrines of a sect or other group: *the sectarian Bolshevism advocated by Moscow.*

▸*n.* a member of a sect. ■ a person who rigidly follows the doctrines of a sect or other group. ▷mid 17th cent.: from SECTARY + -AN, reinforced by SECT. **—sec·tar·i·an·ism** /-ˌnizəm/ *n.* **—sec·tar·i·an·ize** /-ˌnīz/ *v.*

sec·ta·ry /'sektərē/ ▸*n.* (*pl.* **-ries**) a member of a religious or political sect. ▷mid 16th cent.: from modern Latin *sectarius* 'schismatic,' from medieval Latin *sectarius* 'adherent,' from Latin *secta* (see SECT).

sec·tion /'seksʜən/ ▸*n.* **1** any of the more or less distinct parts into which something is or may be divided or from which it is made up: *arrange orange sections on a platter.* See note at FRAGMENT. ■ a relatively distinct part of a book, newspaper, statute, or other document. ■ a measure of land, equal to one square mile. ■ a particular district of a town. **2** a distinct group within a larger body of people or things: *the children's section of the library.* ■ a group of players of a family of instruments within an orchestra: *the brass section.* ■ a small class of students who are part of a larger course but are taught separately: *graduate students lead discussion sections for professors' lecture courses.* ■ [in *names*] a specified military unit: *a camouflage section was added to the army.* ■ a subdivision of an army platoon. ■ *Biology* a secondary taxonomic category, esp. a subgenus. **3** the cutting of a solid by or along a plane. ■ the shape resulting from cutting a solid along a plane. ■ a representation of the internal structure of something as if it has been cut through vertically or horizontally. ■ *Surgery* a separation by cutting. ■ *Biology* a thin slice of plant or animal tissue prepared for microscopic examination.

▸*v.* [*trans.*] divide into sections: *she began to section the grapefruit.* ■ (**section something off**) separate an area from a larger one: *parts of the curved balcony had been sectioned off with wrought-iron grilles.* ■ *Biology* cut (animal or plant tissue) into thin slices for microscopic examination. ■ *Surgery* divide by cutting: *it is common veterinary practice to section the nerves to the hoof of a limping horse.* ▷late Middle English (as a noun): from French *section* or Latin *sectio(n-)*, from *secare* 'to cut.' The verb dates from the early 19th cent. **—sec·tioned** *adj.* [often in *combination*] *a square-sectioned iron peg.*

sec·tion·al /'seksʜənl/ ▸*adj.* of or relating to a section or subdivision of a larger whole: *a sectional championship.* ■ of or relating to a section or group within a community: *the chairman of the commission looked on sectional interests as a danger to the common good.* ■ of or relating to a view of the structure of an object in section: *sectional drawings.* ■ made or supplied in sections: *sectional sills, made from more than one piece of timber.*

▸*n.* a sofa made in sections that can be used separately as chairs. **—sec·tion·al·ize** /-ˌīz/ *v.* **—sec·tion·al·ly** *adv.*

sec·tion·al·ism /'seksʜənlˌizəm/ ▸*n.* restriction of interest to a narrow sphere; undue concern with local interests or petty distinctions at the expense of general well-being. **—sec·tion·al·ist** *n.* & *adj.*

sec·tion gang ▸*n.* a crew of railroad workers responsible for maintaining a particular section of track.

sec·tion hand ▸*n.* a member of a section gang.

sec·tion mark ▸*n.* the sign (§) used as a reference mark or to indicate a section of a book.

sec·tor /'sektər/ ▸*n.* **1** an area or portion that is distinct from others. ■ a distinct part or branch of a nation's economy or society or of a sphere of activity such as education: *the industrial and commercial sector | the Muslim sector of the village.* ■ *Military* a subdivision of an area for military operations. ■ *Computing* a subdivision of a track on a magnetic disk. **2** the plane figure enclosed by two radii of a circle or ellipse and the arc between them. **3** a mathematical instrument consisting of two arms hinged at one end and marked with sines, tangents, etc., for making diagrams. ▷late 16th cent. (in senses 2 and 3): from late Latin, a technical use of Latin *sector* 'cutter,' from *sect-* 'cut off,' from the verb *secare.* **—sec·tor·al** /-rəl/ *adj.*

sec·to·ri·al /sek'tôrēəl/ ▸*adj.* **1** of or like a sector: *sectorial boundaries.* **2** *Zoology* denoting a carnassial tooth, or a similar cutting tooth in mammals other than carnivores.

sec·u·lar /'sekyələr/ ▸*adj.* **1** denoting attitudes, activities, or other things that have no religious or spiritual basis: *secular buildings | secular moral theory.* Contrasted with SACRED. **2** *Christian Church* (of clergy) not subject to or bound by religious rule; not belonging to or living in a monastic or other order. Contrasted with REGULAR. **3** *Astronomy* of or denoting slow changes in the motion of the sun or planets. **4** *Economics* (of a fluctuation or trend) occurring or persisting over an indefinitely long period: *there is evidence that the slump is not cyclical but secular.* **5** occurring once every century or similarly long period (used esp. in reference to celebratory games in ancient Rome).

▸*n.* a secular priest. ▷Middle English: senses 1 and 2 from Old French *seculer*, from Latin *saecularis*, from *saeculum* 'generation, age,' used in Christian Latin to mean 'the world' (as opposed to the Church); senses 3, 4, and 5 (early 19th cent.) from Latin *saecularis* 'relating to an age or period.' **—sec·u·lar·ism** /-ˌrizəm/ *n.* **—sec·u·lar·ist** /-rist/ *n.* **—sec·u·lar·i·ty** /ˌsekyə'laritē/ *n.* **—sec·u·lar·i·za·tion** /ˌsekyələrə'zāsʜən/ *n.* **—sec·u·lar·ize** /-ˌrīz/ *v.* **—sec·u·lar·ly** *adv.*

sec·u·lar arm ▸*n.* (**the secular arm**) the legal authority of the civil power as invoked by the church to punish offenders.

sec·u·lar hu·man·ism ▸*n.* humanism, with regard in particular to the belief that humanity is capable of morality and self-fulfillment without belief in God. **—sec·u·lar hu·man·ist** *n.*

se·cund /'sēˌkənd; si'kənd/ ▸*adj. Botany* arranged on one side only (such as the flowers of lily of the valley). ▷late 18th cent.: from Latin *secundus* (see SECOND[1]). **—se·cund·ly** *adv.*

se·cure /si'kyo͝or/ ▸*adj.* fixed or fastened so as not to give way, become loose, or be lost: *check to ensure that all nuts and bolts are secure.* ■ not subject to threat; certain to remain or continue safe and unharmed: *they are working to ensure that their market share remains **secure against** competition.* ■ protected against attack or other criminal activity: *the official said that no airport could be totally secure.* ■ (of a place of detention) having provisions against the escape of inmates: *a secure unit for youthful offenders.* ■ feeling safe, stable, and free from fear or anxiety: *everyone needs to have a home and to feel secure and wanted.* ■ [*predic.*] (**secure of**) *dated* feeling no doubts about attaining; certain to achieve: *she remained poised and complacent, secure of admiration.*

▸*v.* [*trans.*] fix or attach (something) firmly so that it cannot be moved or lost: *pins **secure** the handle **to** the main body.* ■ make (a door or container) hard to open; fasten or lock: *doors are likely to be well secured at night.* ■ protect against threats; make safe: *the government is concerned to **secure** the economy **against** too much foreign ownership.* ■ capture (a person or animal): *the suspect is secured and in the back of a patrol car.* ■ succeed in obtaining (something), esp. with difficulty: *the division secured a major contract.* See note at GET. ■ seek to guarantee repayment of (a loan) by having a right to take possession of an asset in the event of nonpayment: *a loan **secured on** your home.* ▷mid 16th cent. (in the sense 'feeling no apprehension'): from Latin *securus*, from *se-* 'without' + *cura* 'care.' **—se·cur·a·ble** *adj.* **—se·cure·ly** *adv.* **—se·cure·ment** *n.*

se·cure serv·er ▸*n.* an Internet server that encrypts confidential information supplied by visitors to Web pages, thus protecting the confidentiality.

Se·cu·ri·ta·te /siˌkyo͝ori'tätā/ the internal security force of Romania, set up in 1948 and officially disbanded during the revolution of December 1989. ▷Romanian, 'Security.'

se·cu·ri·tize /sə'kyo͝oriˌtīz/ ▸*v.* [*trans.*] [often as *adj.*] (**securitized**) convert (an asset, esp. a loan) into marketable securities, typically for the purpose of raising cash by selling them to other investors: *the use of securitized debt as a major source of corporate finance.* **—se·cu·ri·ti·za·tion** /-itə'zāsʜən/ *n.*

se·cu·ri·ty /si'kyo͝oritē/ ▸*n.* (*pl.* **-ties**) **1** the state of being free from danger or threat: *the system is designed to provide maximum **security against** toxic spills | job security.* ■ the safety of a state or organization against criminal activity such as terrorism, theft, or espionage: *a matter of national security.* ■ procedures followed or measures taken to ensure such safety: *amid tight security the presidents met in the Colombian resort.* ■ the state of feeling safe, stable, and free from fear or anxiety: *this man could give the emotional security she needed.* **2** a private police force that guards a building, campus, park, etc. **3** a thing deposited or pledged as a guarantee of the fulfillment of an undertaking or the repayment of a loan, to be forfeited in case of default. **4** (often **securities**) a certificate attesting credit, the ownership of stocks or bonds, or the right to ownership connected with tradable derivatives. ▷late Middle English: from Old French *securite* or Latin *securitas*, from *securus* 'free from care' (see SECURE).

▸*PHRASE* □ **on security of something** using something as a guarantee.

se·cu·ri·ty blan·ket ▸*n.* a blanket or other familiar object that is a comfort to someone, typically a child.

se·cu·ri·ty check ▸*n.* a verification of the identity and trustworthiness of someone such as a government employee, in order to maintain security. ■ a search of an area or of a person and their baggage for concealed weapons or bombs.

Se·cu·ri·ty Coun·cil a permanent body of the United Nations seeking to maintain peace and security. It consists of fifteen members, of which five (China, France, Russia, the UK, and the U.S.) are permanent and have the power of veto. The other members are elected for two-year terms.

se·cu·ri·ty guard ▸*n.* a person employed to protect something, esp. a building, against intruders or damage.

se·cu·ri·ty patch ▸*n.* a software or operating-system patch that is intended to correct a vulnerability to hacking or viral infection: *an e-mail purporting to be a security patch from Microsoft support.*

se·cu·ri·ty risk ▸*n.* a person or situation that poses a possible threat to the security of something.

Se·cu·ri·ty Serv·ice official name for **MI5**.

secy. (also **sec'y**) ▸*abbr.* secretary.

sed. ▸*abbr.* ■ sediment. ■ sedimentation.

Se·dak·a /sə'dakə/, Neil (1939–), U.S. singer and songwriter. He became popular during the 1960s and 1970s with hits such as "Breaking Up Is Hard to Do" (1962) and "Laughter in the Rain" (1974).

Se·da·lia /si'dālyə/ an industrial and commercial city in west central Missouri; pop. 19,800.

Se·dan, Bat·tle of a battle fought in 1870 near the town of Sedan in northeastern France, in which the Prussian army defeated a smaller French army under Napoleon III, opening the way for a Prussian advance on Paris and marking the end of the French Second Empire.

se·dan /si'dan/ ▸*n.* **1** (also **se·dan chair**) *chiefly historical* an enclosed chair for conveying one person, carried between horizontal poles by two or more porters. **2** an enclosed automobile for four or more people, having two or four doors. ▷perhaps an alteration of an Italian dialect word, based on Latin *sella* 'saddle,' from *sedere* 'sit.'

sedan chair

se·date[1] /si'dāt/ ▸*adj.* calm, dignified, and unhurried: *in the old days, business was carried on at a rather more sedate pace.* ■ quiet and rather dull: *sedate suburban domesticity.* ▷late Middle English (originally as a medical term meaning 'not sore or painful,' also 'calm, tranquil'): from Latin *sedatus*, past participle of *sedare* 'settle,' from *sedere* 'sit.' **—se·date·ly** *adv.* **—se·date·ness** *n.*

se·date[2] ▸*v.* [*trans.*] calm (someone) or make them sleep by administering a sedative drug: *she was heavily sedated.* ▷1960s: back-formation from **SEDATION**.

se·da·tion /si'dāsʜən/ ▸*n.* the administering of a sedative drug to produce a state of calm or sleep: *he was distraught with grief and* ***under sedation.*** ▷mid 16th cent.: from French *sédation* or Latin *sedatio(n-)*, from *sedare* 'settle' (see **SEDATE**[1]).

sed·a·tive /'sedətiv/ ▸*adj.* promoting calm or inducing sleep: *the seeds have a sedative effect.*

▸*n.* a drug taken for its calming or sleep-inducing effect. ▷late Middle English: from Old French *sedatif* or medieval Latin *sedativus*, from Latin *sedat-* 'settled,' from the verb *sedare* (see **SEDATE**[1]).

sed·en·tar·y /'sedn,terē/ ▸*adj.* (of a person) tending to spend much time seated; somewhat inactive. ■ (of work or a way of life) characterized by much sitting and little physical exercise. ■ (of a position) sitting; seated. ■ *Zoology & Anthropology* inhabiting the same locality throughout life; not migratory or nomadic. ■ *Zoology* (of an animal) sessile. ▷late 16th cent. (in the sense 'not migratory'): from French *sédentaire* or Latin *sedentarius*, from *sedere* 'sit.' **—sed·en·tar·i·ly** /-,te(ə)rəlē/ *adv.* **—sed·en·tar·i·ness** *n.*

Se·der /'sādər/ ▸*n.* a Jewish ritual service and ceremonial dinner for the first night or first two nights of Passover. ▷from Hebrew *sēḏer* 'order, procedure.'

sedge /sej/ ▸*n.* a grasslike plant with triangular stems and inconspicuous flowers, growing typically in wet ground. Sedges are widely distributed throughout temperate and cold regions. • Family Cyperaceae: *Carex* and other genera. ▷Old English *secg*, of Germanic origin, from an Indo-European root shared by Latin *secare* 'to cut.' **—sedg·y** /'sejē/ *adj.*

Sedge·moor, Bat·tle of a battle fought in 1685 on the plain of Sedgemoor in Somerset, England. The forces of the rebel Duke of Monmouth, who had landed in Dorset as champion of the Protestant cause and pretender to the throne, were decisively defeated by James II's troops.

sedge war·bler ▸*n.* a common migratory Eurasian songbird with streaky brown plumage, frequenting marshes and reed beds. • *Acrocephalus schoenobaenus*, family Sylviidae.

Sedg·wick /'sejwik/, Adam (1785–1873), English geologist. He specialized in the fossil record of rocks from North Wales, assigning the oldest of these to a period that he named the Cambrian.

se·dil·i·a /sə'dilēə/ ▸*plural n.* (*sing.* **-di·le** /-'dīlē/) a group of stone seats for clergy in the south chancel wall of a church, usually three in number and often canopied and decorated. ▷late 18th cent.: from Latin, 'seat,' from *sedere* 'sit.'

sed·i·ment /'sedəmənt/ ▸*n.* matter that settles to the bottom of a liquid; dregs. ■ *Geology* particulate matter that is carried by water or wind and deposited on the surface of the land or the bottom of a body of water, and may in time become consolidated into rock.

▸*v.* [*intrans.*] settle as sediment. ■ (of a liquid) deposit a sediment. ■ [*trans.*] deposit (something) as a sediment: *the DNA was sedimented by centrifugation* | [as *adj.*] (**sedimented**) *sedimented waste.* ▷mid 16th cent.: from French *sédiment* or Latin *sedimentum* 'settling,' from *sedere* 'sit.' **—sed·i·men·ta·tion** /,sedəmən'tāsʜən/ *n.*

sed·i·men·ta·ry /,sedə'mentərē/ ▸*adj.* of or relating to sediment. ■ *Geology* (of rock) that has formed from sediment deposited by water or air.

sed·i·men·ta·tion co·ef·fi·cient /,sedəmən'tāsʜən/ (also **sed·i·men·ta·tion con·stant**) ▸*n. Biochemistry* a quantity related to the size of a microscopic particle, equal to the terminal outward velocity of the particle when centrifuged in a fluid medium divided by the centrifugal force acting on it, expressed in units of time.

se·di·tion /si'disʜən/ ▸*n.* conduct or speech inciting people to rebel against the authority of a state or monarch. ▷late Middle English (in the sense 'violent strife'): from Old French, or from Latin *seditio(n-)*, from *sed-* 'apart' + *itio(n-)* 'going' (from the verb *ire*).

se·di·tious /si'disʜəs/ ▸*adj.* inciting or causing people to rebel against the authority of a state or monarch: *the letter was declared seditious.* ▷late Middle English: from Old French *seditieux* or Latin *seditiosus*, from *seditio* 'mutinous separation' (see **SEDITION**). **—se·di·tious·ly** *adv.*

se·di·tious li·bel ▸*n. Law* a published statement that is seditious. ■ the action or crime of publishing such a statement.

Sed·na /'sednə/ ▸*Astronomy* a reddish celestial body about half the size of earth's moon. It is the most distant known object in the solar system and orbits the sun every 10,500 years.

Se·do·na /si'dōnə/ a resort city in north central Arizona, a popular New Age center; pop. 7,720.

se·duce /si'd(y)o͞os/ ▸*v.* [*trans.*] attract (someone) to a belief or into a course of action that is inadvisable or foolhardy: *they should not be* ***seduced into*** *thinking that their success ruled out the possibility of a relapse.* See note at **TEMPT**. ■ entice into sexual activity. ■ attract powerfully: *the melody seduces the ear with warm string tones.* ▷late 15th cent. (originally in the sense 'persuade (someone) to abandon their duty'): from Latin *seducere*, from *se-* 'away, apart' + *ducere* 'to lead.' **—se·duc·er** *n.* **—se·duc·i·ble** *adj.*

se·duc·tion /si'dəksʜən/ ▸*n.* the action of seducing someone: *if seduction doesn't work, she can play on his sympathy* | *she was planning a seduction.* ■ (often **seductions**) a tempting or attractive thing: *the seductions of the mainland.* ▷early 16th cent.: from French *séduction* or Latin *seductio(n-)*, from *seducere* 'draw aside' (see **SEDUCE**).

se·duc·tive /si'dəktiv/ ▸*adj.* tempting and attractive; enticing: *a seductive voice.* ▷mid 18th cent.: from **SEDUCTION**, on the pattern of pairs such as *induction, inductive.* **—se·duc·tive·ly** *adv.* **—se·duc·tive·ness** *n.*

se·duc·tress /si'dəktris/ ▸*n.* a woman who seduces someone, esp. one who entices a man into sexual activity. ▷early 19th cent.: from obsolete *seductor* 'male seducer,' from *seducere* (see **SEDUCE**).

sed·u·lous /'sejələs/ ▸*adj.* (of a person or action) showing dedication and diligence: *he watched himself with the most sedulous care.* See note at **BUSY**. ▷mid 16th cent.: from Latin *sedulus* 'zealous' + **-OUS**. **—se·du·li·ty** /sə'jo͞olitē/ *n.* **—sed·u·lous·ly** *adv.* **—sed·u·lous·ness** *n.*

se·dum /'sēdəm/ ▸*n.* a widely distributed fleshy-leaved plant with small star-shaped yellow, pink, or white flowers, grown as an ornamental. • Genus *Sedum*, family Crassulaceae: many species, including the stonecrops. ▷from modern Latin, denoting a houseleek.

see[1] /sē/ ▸*v.* (**sees** /sēz/, **see·ing** /sē-iɴɢ/; *past* **saw** /sô/; *past part.* **seen** /sēn/) [*trans.*] **1** perceive with the eyes; discern visually: *in the distance she could see the blue sea* | [*intrans.*] *Andrew couldn't see out of his left eye* *figurative I can't* ***see into*** *the future.* ■ [with *clause*] be or become aware of something from observation or from a written or other visual source: *I see from your appraisal report that you have asked for training.* ■ be a spectator of (a film, game, or other entertainment); watch: *I went to see King Lear at the Old Vic.* ■ visit (a place) for the first time: *see Alaska in style.* ■ [in *imperative*] refer to (a specified source) for further information (used as a direction in a text): *elements are usually classified as metals or nonmetals (see chapter 11).* ■ experience or witness (an event or situation): *I shall not live to see it* | [*trans.*] *I can't bear to see you so unhappy.* ■ be the time or setting of (something): *the 1970s saw the beginning of a technological revolution.* ■ observe without being able to affect: *they see their rights being taken away.* ■ (**see something in**) find good or attractive qualities in (someone): *I don't know what I see in you.* **2** discern or deduce mentally after reflection or from information; understand: *I can't see any other way to treat it* | [with *clause*] *I saw that perhaps he was right* | *she could see what Rhoda meant.* ■ [with *clause*] ascertain after inquiring, considering, or discovering an outcome: *I'll go along to the club and see if I can get a game.* ■ [*trans.*] regard in a specified way: *he saw himself as a good teacher* | *you and I see things differently.* ■ foresee; view or predict as a possibility: *I can't see him earning any more anywhere else.* ■ used to ascertain or express comprehension, agreement, or continued attention, or to emphasize that an earlier prediction was correct: *it has to be the answer, don't you see?* | *see, I told you I'd come.* **3** meet (someone one knows) socially or by chance: *I went to see Caroline* | *I saw Colin last night.* ■ meet regularly as a boyfriend or girlfriend: *some guy she was seeing was messing her around.* ■ consult (a specialist or professional): *you may need to see a solicitor.* ■ give an interview or consultation to (someone): *the doctor will see you now.* **4** [*trans.*] escort or conduct (someone) to a specified place: *don't bother seeing me out.* ■ [*intrans.*] (**see to**) attend to; provide for the wants of: *I'll see to Dad's tea.* ■ [*intrans.*] ensure: *Lucy* ***saw to it that*** *everyone got enough to eat and drink* | [with *clause*] ***see that*** *no harm comes to him.* **5** (in poker or brag) equal the bet of (an opponent).

▸*phrasal v.* □ **see about** attend to; deal with: *he had gone to see about a job he had heard of.* □ **see after** take care of; look after. □ **see something of** spend a specified amount of time with (someone) socially: *we saw a lot of the Bakers.* ■ spend some time in (a place): *I want to see something of those countries.* □ **see someone off 1** accompany a person who is leaving to their point of departure: *they came to the station to see him off.* **2** *Brit.* repel an invader or intruder: *the dogs saw them off in no time.* ■ *informal* deal with the threat posed by; get the better of: *they saw off Cambridge in the FA Cup.* □ **see someone out** *Brit.* (of an article) last longer than the remainder of someone's life: *no point in fixing the gate, it'll see me out.* □ **see something out** *Brit.* come to the end of a period of time or undertaking: *I could well see out my career in Italy.* □ **see over** *Brit.* tour and examine (a building or site): *Bridget asked if he'd like to see over the house.* □ **see through** not be deceived by; detect the true nature of: *he can see through her lies and deceptions.* □ **see someone through** support a person for the duration of a difficult time. □ **see something through** persist with an undertaking until it is completed. ▷Old English *sēon*, of Germanic origin; related to Dutch *zien* and German *sehen*, perhaps from an Indo-European root shared by Latin *sequi* 'follow.' **—see·a·ble** *adj.*

▸*PHRASES* □ **as far as I can see** to the best of my understanding or belief. □ **as I see it** in my opinion. □ **be seeing things** see **THING**. □ **(I'll) be seeing you** another way of saying **SEE YOU**. □ **have seen better days** have declined from former prosperity or good condition: *this part of South London has seen better days.* □ **have seen it all before** be very worldly or very familiar with a particular situation. □ **let me see** said as an appeal for time to think before speaking: *Let me see, how old is he now?* □ **see a man about a dog** *humorous* said euphemistically when leaving to go to the toilet or keep an undisclosed appointment. □ **see eye to eye, see fit**, etc. see **EYE, FIT**[1], etc. □ **see here!** said to give emphasis to a statement or command or to express a protest: *now see here, you're going* *to get it back for me!* □ **see one's way clear to do** (or **doing**) **something** find that it is possible or convenient to do something (often used in polite requests). □ **see someone coming** recognize a person who can be fooled or deceived. □ **see something coming** foresee or be prepared for an event, typically an unpleasant one. □ **see someone damned first** *Brit., informal* said when refusing categorically and with hostility to do what a person wants. □ **see someone right** *Brit., informal* make sure that a person is appropriately rewarded or looked after. □ **see sense** (or **reason**) realize that one is wrong and start acting sensibly. □ **see the back of** *Brit., informal* be rid of (an unwanted person or thing): *we were always glad to see the back of her.* □ **see you** (**later**) *informal* said when parting from someone. □ **we'll see about that** said when angrily contradicting or challenging a claim or assertion: *Oh, you think it's funny, do you? We'll see about that!*

see[2] ▸*n.* the place in which a cathedral church stands, identified as the seat of authority of a bishop or archbishop. ▷Middle English: from Anglo-Norman French *sed,* from Latin *sedes* 'seat,' from *sedere* 'sit.'

seed /sēd/ ▸*n.* **1** a flowering plant's unit of reproduction, capable of developing into another such plant. ■ a quantity of these: *grass seed | you can grow artichokes from seed.* ■ *figurative* the cause or latent beginning of a feeling, process, or condition: *the conversation sowed a tiny seed of doubt in his mind.* ■ *archaic* (chiefly in biblical use) a person's offspring or descendants. ■ a man's semen. ■ (also **seed crystal**) a small crystal introduced into a liquid to act as a nucleus for crystallization. ■ a small container for radioactive material placed in body tissue during radiotherapy. **2** any of a number of stronger competitors in a sports tournament who have been assigned a specified position in an ordered list with the aim of ensuring that they do not play each other in the early rounds: *he knocked the top seed out of the championships.*
▸*v.* **1** [*trans.*] sow (land) with seeds: *the shoreline is seeded with a special grass.* ■ sow (a particular kind of seed) on or in the ground. ■ *figurative* cause (something) to begin to develop or grow: *severance payouts that help seed their new businesses.* ■ place a crystal or crystalline substance in (something) in order to cause crystallization or condensation (esp. in a cloud to produce rain). **2** [*intrans.*] (of a plant) produce or drop seeds: *mulches encourage many plants to seed freely.* ■ (**seed itself**) (of a plant) reproduce itself by means of its own seeds: *feverfew will seed itself readily.* **3** [*trans.*] remove the seeds from (vegetables or fruit): *stem and seed the chilies.* **4** [*trans.*] give (a competitor) the status of seed in a tournament: [*with complement*] *Jeff Tarango, seeded five, was defeated by fellow American Todd Witsken.* ▷Old English *sǣd,* of Germanic origin; related to Dutch *zaad,* German *Saat,* also to the verb **sow**[1].
▸*PHRASE* □ **go** (or **run**) **to seed** (of a plant) cease flowering as the seeds develop. ■ deteriorate in condition, strength, or efficiency: *Mark knows he has allowed himself to go to seed.*

seed·bed /ˈsēd,bed/ ▸*n.* a bed of fine soil in which seedlings are germinated.

seed cake ▸*n.* cake containing caraway seeds as flavoring.

seed cap·i·tal ▸*n.* see **SEED MONEY.**

seed coat ▸*n. Botany* the protective outer coat of a seed.

seed corn ▸*n.* good-quality corn kept for seed.

seed·eat·er /ˈsēd,ētər/ ▸*n.* a finch or related songbird that feeds mainly on seeds, in particular: • a small American bunting (genus *Sporophila,* subfamily Emberizinae, family Emberizidae). • an African finch related to the canary (genus *Serinus,* family Fringillidae).

seed·ed /ˈsēdid/ ▸*adj.* **1** [*in combination*] (of a plant or fruit) having a seed or seeds of a specified kind or number: *a single-seeded fruit.* ■ (of land or an area of ground) having been sown with seed: *seeded lawns.* ■ *Heraldry* (of a flower) having seeds of a specified tincture. **2** (of a fruit or vegetable) having had the seeds removed: *seeded, chopped tomatoes.* **3** given the status of seed in a sports tournament: *Italy is one of the eight seeded teams.*

seed·er /ˈsēdər/ ▸*n.* **1** a machine for sowing seed mechanically. **2** a plant that produces seeds in a particular way or under particular conditions: [*in combination*] *a beautiful, hardy annual self-seeder.*

seed fern ▸*n.* another term for **PTERIDOSPERM.**

seed head ▸*n.* a flowerhead in seed.

seed leaf ▸*n. Botany* a cotyledon.

seed·less /ˈsēdlis/ ▸*adj.* denoting a fruit that has no seeds: *seedless grapes.*

seed·ling /ˈsēdliNG/ ▸*n.* a young plant, esp. one raised from seed and not from a cutting.

seed-lip ▸*n. chiefly historical* a basket for holding seed, used when sowing by hand.

seed mon·ey ▸*n.* money allocated to initiate a project.

seed pearl ▸*n.* a very small pearl.

seed·pod /ˈsēd,päd/ ▸*n.* see **POD**[1] (sense 1).

seed po·ta·to ▸*n.* a potato that is planted and used for the production of seeds.

seeds·man /ˈsēdzmən/ ▸*n.* (*pl.* **-men**) a person who deals in seeds as a profession.

seed-snipe ▸*n.* a South American bird resembling a small partridge, with mainly brown plumage. • Family Thinocoridae: two genera and four species.

seed time ▸*n.* the sowing season.

seed·y /ˈsēdē/ ▸*adj.* (**seed·i·er, seed·i·est**) **1** sordid and disreputable: *his seedy affair with a soft-porn starlet.* ■ shabby and squalid: *an increasingly seedy and dilapidated property.* **2** *dated* unwell: *she felt weak and seedy.* **—seed·i·ly** /ˈsēdl-ē/ *adv.* **—seed·i·ness** *n.*

See·ger /ˈsēgər/, Pete (1919–), U.S. folk musician and songwriter. Seeger was a prominent figure in the revival of American folk music. He was also concerned with environmental issues, esp. on the Hudson River. Notable songs: "If I Had a Hammer" (*c.*1949) and "Where Have All the Flowers Gone?" (1956).

see·ing /ˈsē-iNG/ ▸*conj.* because; since: ***seeing as*** *Stuart's an old friend, I thought I might help him out.*
▸*n.* the action of seeing someone or something. ■ *Astronomy* the quality of observed images as determined by atmospheric conditions.
▸*PHRASE* □ **seeing is believing** *proverb* you need to see something before you can accept that it really exists or occurs.

See·ing Eye dog ▸*n. trademark* a guide dog trained to lead the blind.

seek /sēk/ ▸*v.* (*past* **sought** /sôt/) [*trans.*] attempt to find (something): *they came here to seek shelter from biting winter winds.* ■ attempt or desire to obtain or achieve (something): *the new regime sought his extradition | [intrans.] her parents had never sought to interfere with her freedom.* ■ ask for (something) from someone: *he* ***sought*** *help* ***from*** *the police.* ■ (**seek someone/something out**) search for and find someone or something: *it's his job to seek out new customers.* ■ *archaic* go to (a place): *I sought my bedroom each night to brood over it.* ▷Old English *sēcan,* of Germanic origin; related to Dutch *zieken* and German *suchen,* from an Indo-European root shared by Latin *sagire* 'perceive by scent.' **—seek·er** *n.* [*often in combination*] *a pleasure-seeker | a job-seeker.*
▸*PHRASES* □ **seek one's fortune** travel somewhere in the hope of achieving wealth and success. □ **to seek** *archaic* lacking; not yet found: *the end she knew, the means were to seek.* ■ (**far to seek**) out of reach; a long way off.

seek time ▸*n. Computing* the time taken for a disk drive to locate the area on the disk where the data to be read is stored.

seel /sēl/ ▸*v.* [*trans.*] *archaic* close (a person's eyes); prevent (someone) from seeing: *the wise Gods seel our eyes in our own filth.* ▷late 15th cent. (originally a term in falconry meaning 'stitch shut the eyelids of (a hawk)'): from French *ciller,* or medieval Latin *ciliare,* from Latin *cilium* 'eyelid.'

seem /sēm/ ▸*v.* [*intrans.*] give the impression or sensation of being something or having a particular quality: [*with complement*] *Dawn seemed annoyed* | [*with infinitive*] *there seems to be plenty to eat* | [*with clause*] *it seemed that he was determined to oppose her.* ■ [*with infinitive*] used to make a statement or description of one's thoughts, feelings, or actions less assertive or forceful: *I seem to remember giving you very precise instructions.* ■ (**cannot seem to do something**) be unable to do something, despite having tried: *he couldn't seem to remember his lines.* ■ [*with clause*] (**it seems** or **it would seem**) used to suggest in a cautious, guarded, or polite way that something is true or a fact: *it would seem that he has been fooling us all.* ▷Middle English (also in the sense 'suit, befit, be appropriate'): from Old Norse *sœma* 'to honor,' from *sœmr* 'fitting.'

seem·ing /ˈsēmiNG/ ▸*adj.* appearing to be real or true, but not necessarily being so; apparent: *Ellen's seeming indifference to the woman's fate.* See note at **OSTENSIBLE.** ■ [*in combination*] giving the impression of having a specified quality: *an angry-seeming man.*
▸*n. poetic/literary* the outward appearance or aspect of someone or something, esp. when considered as deceptive or as distinguished from reality: *that dissidence between inward reality and outward seeming.*

seem·ing·ly /ˈsēmiNGlē/ ▸*adv.* so as to give the impression of having a certain quality; apparently: *a seemingly competent and well-organized person.* ■ [*sentence adverb*] according to the facts as one knows them; as far as one knows: *it's touch and go, seemingly, and she's asking for you.*

seem·ly /ˈsēmlē/ ▸*adj.* conforming to accepted notions of propriety or good taste; decorous: *I felt it was not seemly to observe too closely.* ▷Middle English: from Old Norse *sœmiligr,* from *sœmr* 'fitting' (see **SEEM**). **—seem·li·ness** *n.*

seen /sēn/ ▸ past participle of **SEE**[1].

See of Rome ▸*n.* another term for **HOLY SEE.**

seep /sēp/ ▸*v.* [*intrans.*] (of a liquid) flow or leak slowly through porous material or small holes: *water began to seep through the soles of his boots.*
▸*n.* a place where petroleum or water oozes slowly out of the ground. ▷late 18th cent.: perhaps a dialect form of Old English *sīpian* 'to soak.'

seep·age /ˈsēpij/ ▸*n.* the slow escape of a liquid or gas through porous material or small holes. ■ the quantity of liquid or gas that seeps out.

seer[1] /ˈsēər; si(ə)r/ ▸*n.* **1** a person who is supposed to be able, through supernatural insight, to see what the future holds. ■ an expert who provides forecasts of the economic or political future: *our seers have grown gloomier about prospects for growth.* **2** [*usu. in combination*] *chiefly archaic* a person who sees something specified: *a seer of the future | ghost-seers.* ▷Middle English: from **SEE**[1] + **-ER**[1].

seer[2] /si(ə)r/ ▸*n.* (in the Indian subcontinent) a varying unit of weight (about one kilogram) or liquid measure (about one liter). ▷from Hindi *ser.*

seer·suck·er /ˈsi(ə)r,səkər/ ▸*n.* a printed cotton or synthetic fabric that has a surface consisting of puckered and flat sections, typically in a striped pattern. ▷early 18th cent.: from Persian *šīr o šakar,* literally 'milk and sugar,' (by transference) 'striped cotton garment.'

see·saw /ˈsē,sô/ (also **see-saw**) ▸*n.* a long plank balanced in the middle on a fixed support, on each end of which children sit and swing up and down by pushing the ground alternately with their feet. ■ *figurative* a situation characterized by rapid, repeated changes from one state or condition to another: *the emotional seesaw of a first love affair* | [*as adj.*] *seesaw interest rates.*
▸*v.* [*intrans.*] change rapidly and repeatedly from one position, situation, or condition to another and back again: *the market seesawed as rumors spread of an imminent cabinet reshuffle.* ■ [*trans.*] cause (something) to move back and forth or up and down rapidly and repeatedly: *Sybil seesawed the car back and forth.* ▷mid 17th cent. (originally used by sawyers as a rhythmical refrain): reduplication of the verb **SAW**[1] (symbolic of the sawing motion).

seethe /sēTH/ ▸*v.* [*intrans.*] (of a liquid) bubble up as a result of being boiled: *the brew foamed and seethed.* ■ [*trans.*] *archaic* cook (food) by boiling it in a liquid: *others were cut into joints and seethed in cauldrons made of the animal's own skins.* ■ (of a river or the sea) foam as if it were boiling; be turbulent: *the gray ocean seethed.* ■ [*intrans.*] (of a person) be filled with intense but unexpressed anger: *inwardly he was seething at the slight to his authority.* ■ (of a place) be crowded with people or things moving about in a rapid or hectic way: *the entire cellar was* ***seething with*** *spiders | the village* ***seethed with*** *life.* ■ [*with adverbial of direction*] (of a crowd of people) move in a rapid or hectic way: *we cascaded down the stairs and seethed across the station* | [*as adj.*] (**seething**) *the seething mass of commuters.* ▷Old English *sēothan* 'make or keep boiling,' of Germanic origin; related to Dutch *zieden.*

see-through ▸*adj.* (esp. of clothing) translucent: *this shirt's a bit see-through when it's wet.*

Se·fer /ˈsāfər; ˈsefer/ ▸*n.* (*pl.* **Si·frei** /ˈsifrā; siˈfrā/) *Judaism* a book of Hebrew religious literature. ■ (usu. **Se·fer To·rah**) a scroll containing the Torah or Pentateuch. ▷from Hebrew *sēper tōrāh* 'book of (the) Law.'

seg·ment ▸*n.* /ˈsegmənt/ **1** each of the parts into which something is or may be divided. See note at **FRAGMENT.** ■ a portion of time allocated to a particular broadcast item on radio or television. ■ a separate broadcast item, typically one of a number that make up a particular program. ■ *Phonetics* the smallest distinct part of a spoken utterance, in particular the vowels and consonants as opposed to stress and intonation. ■ *Zoology* each of the series of similar anatomical units of which the body and appendages of some animals are composed, such as the visible rings of an earthworm's body. **2** *Geometry* a part of a figure cut off by a line or plane intersecting it, in particular: ■ the part of a circle enclosed between an arc and a chord. ■ the part of a line included between two points. ■ the part of a sphere cut off by any plane not passing through the center.

▸*v.* /'seg,ment; seg'ment/ [*trans.*] divide (something) into separate parts or sections: *the unemployed are segmented into two groups.* ■ [*intrans.*] divide into separate parts or sections: *the market is beginning to segment into a number of well-defined categories.* ■ [*intrans.*] *Embryology* (of a cell) undergo cleavage; divide into many cells. ▷late 16th cent. (as a term in geometry): from Latin *segmentum*, from *secare* 'to cut.' The verb dates from the mid 19th cent. **—seg·men·tar·y** /-,terē/ *adj.* **—seg·men·ta·tion** /,segmən'tāsʜən/ *n.*

seg·men·tal /seg'men(t)l/ ▸*adj.* **1** composed of separate parts or sections. ■ *Phonetics* denoting or relating to the division of speech into segments. **2** *Architecture* denoting or of the form of an arch the curved part of which forms a shallow arc of a circle, less than a semicircle. **—seg·men·tal·i·za·tion** /-,men(t)li'zāsʜən/ *n.* **—seg·men·tal·ize** /-,īz/ *v.* **—seg·men·tal·ly** *adv.*

seg·men·ta·tion cav·i·ty ▸*n.* another term for BLASTOCOEL.

seg·men·ted /'seg,men(t)id/ ▸*adj.* consisting of or divided into segments: *segmented labor markets.* ■ *Zoology* (of an animal's body or appendage) formed of a longitudinal series of similar parts.

se·go /'sēgō/ (in full **sego lily**) ▸*n.* (*pl.* **-gos**) a plant of the lily family, with green and white bell-shaped flowers, native to the western U.S. Closely related to the MARIPOSA LILY. • *Calochortus nuttalli*, family Liliaceae. ▷mid 19th cent. Western Shoshone *sikoo.*

sego

Se·go·vi·a /si'gōvēə/, Andrés (1893–1987), Spanish guitarist and composer. Largely responsible for the revival of the classical guitar, he elevated its status to that of concert instrument and made a large number of transcriptions of classical music to increase the repertoire of the instrument.

seg·re·gate[1] /'segri,gāt/ ▸*v.* [*trans.*] (usu. **be segregated**) set apart from the rest or from each other; isolate or divide: *handicapped people should not be segregated from the rest of society.* ■ separate or divide (people, activities, or institutions) along racial, sexual, or religious lines: *blacks were segregated in churches, schools, and colleges* | [as *adj.*] (**segregated**) *segregated education systems.* ■ [*intrans.*] *Genetics* (of pairs of alleles) be separated at meiosis and transmitted independently via separate gametes. ▷mid 16th cent.: from Latin *segregat-* 'separated from the flock,' from the verb *segregare*, from *se-* 'apart' + *grex, greg-* 'flock.' **—seg·re·ga·ble** /-gəbəl/ *adj.* **—seg·re·ga·tive** /-,gātiv/ *adj.*

seg·re·gate[2] /'segrəgit; -,gāt/ ▸*n.* **1** *Genetics* an allele that has undergone segregation. **2** *Botany* a species within an aggregate. ▷late 19th cent.: from Latin *segregatus* 'separate, isolated,' past participle of *segregare* (see SEGREGATE[1]).

seg·re·ga·tion /,segri'gāsʜən/ ▸*n.* the action or state of setting someone or something apart from other people or things or being set apart: *the segregation of pupils with learning difficulties.* ■ the enforced separation of different racial groups in a country, community, or establishment: *an official policy of racial segregation.* ■ *Genetics* the separation of pairs of alleles at meiosis and their independent transmission via separate gametes. **—seg·re·ga·tion·al** /-sʜənl/ *adj.* **—seg·re·ga·tion·ist** /-ist/ *adj.* & *n.* (IN THE RACIAL SENSE).

se·gue /'segwā; 'sā-/ ▸*v.* (**se·gues**, **se·gued** /'segwād; 'sā-/, **se·gue·ing** /'segwā-iɴɢ; 'sā-/) [*intrans.*] (in music and film) move without interruption from one song, melody, or scene to another: *allowing one song to segue into the next.*

▸*n.* an uninterrupted transition from one piece of music or film scene to another. ▷Italian, literally 'follows.'

se·gui·dil·la /,segē'dēə/ ▸*n.* a Spanish dance in triple time. ▷mid 18th cent.: Spanish, from *seguida* 'sequence,' from *seguir* 'follow.'

Se·gur·i·dad /sə,go͝ori'däd/ ▸*n.* the Spanish security service. ▷Spanish, literally 'Security.'

Seg·way /'seg,wā/ ▸*n.* *trademark* a two-wheeled motorized personal vehicle consisting of a platform for the feet mounted above an axle and an upright post surmounted by handles. ▷an invented word based on *segue.*

Sehn·sucht /'zān,zo͞okʜt/ ▸*n.* *poetic/literary* yearning; wistful longing. ▷German.

sei /sā/ ▸*n.* another term for SEI WHALE.

sei·cen·to /sā'cʜen,tō/ ▸*n.* [often as *adj.*] the style of Italian art and literature of the 17th century: *Florentine seicento painting.* ▷Italian, '600,' shortened from *mille seicento* '1600,' used with reference to the years 1600–99. **—sei·cen·tist** /-tist/ *n.*

seiche /sāsʜ/ ▸*n.* a temporary disturbance or oscillation in the water level of a lake or partially enclosed body of water, esp. one caused by changes in atmospheric pressure. ▷mid 19th cent.: from Swiss French, perhaps from German *Seiche* 'sinking (of water).'

sei·del /'sīdl; 'zīdl/ ▸*n.* *dated* a beer mug or glass. ■ the contents of such a vessel: *I drank* **a seidel of** *beer.* ▷early 20th cent.: from German *Seidel*, originally denoting a measure between a third and a half of a liter.

Seid·litz pow·der /'sedlits/ ▸*n.* a laxative preparation that contains tartaric acid, sodium potassium tartrate, and sodium bicarbonate, and that effervesces when mixed with water. ▷late 18th cent.: named with reference to the mineral water of *Seidlitz*, a village in Bohemia.

seif /sāf; sēf/ (in full **seif dune**) ▸*n.* a sand dune in the form of a long narrow ridge. ▷early 20th cent.: from Arabic *sayf* 'sword' (because of the shape).

sei·gneur /sān'yər/ (also **sei·gnior** /sān'yôr; 'sān,yôr/) ▸*n.* *chiefly historical* a feudal lord; the lord of a manor. ▷late 16th cent.: from Old French, from Latin *senior* 'older, elder.' **—sei·gneu·ri·al** /-'yərēəl/ *adj.*

seign·ior·age /'sānyərij/ (also **seign·or·age**) ▸*n.* profit made by a government by issuing currency, esp. the difference between the face value of coins and their production costs. ■ *historical* the Crown's right to a percentage on bullion brought to a mint for coining. ■ *historical* a thing claimed by a sovereign or feudal superior as a prerogative. ▷late Middle English: from Old French *seignorage*, from *seigneur* (see SEIGNEUR).

seign·ior·y /'sānyərē/ (also **seign·eur·y**) ▸*n.* (*pl.* **-ior·ies**) a feudal lordship; the position, authority, or domain of a feudal lord. ▷Middle English: from Old French *seignorie*, from *seigneur* (see SEIGNEUR).

Seine /sān; sen/ a river in northern France. Rising north of Dijon, it flows northwest for 473 miles (761 km) through the cities of Troyes and Paris to the English Channel near Le Havre.

seine /sān/ ▸*n.* (also **seine net**) a fishing net that hangs vertically in the water with floats at the top and weights at the bottom edge, the ends being drawn together to encircle the fish.

▸*v.* [*trans.*] fish (an area) with a seine: *the fishermen then seine the weir.* ■ catch (fish) with a seine: *they seine whitefish and salmon.* ▷Old English *segne*, via Latin from Greek *sagēnē*; reinforced in Middle English by Old French *saine.* **—sein·er** *n.*

Sein·feld /'sīn,feld/, Jerry (1955–) U.S. comedian and actor. He starred in the highly successful television situation comedy "Seinfeld" (1990–98).

seise /sēz/ ▸*v.* see SEIZE (sense 3).

sei·sin /'sēzən/ (also **sei·zin**) ▸*n.* *Law* possession of land by freehold. ■ *Brit., historical* possession, esp. of land: *Richard Fitzhugh did not take* **seisin of** *his lands until 1480.* ▷Middle English: from Old French *seisine*, from *saisir* 'seize.'

seis·mic /'sīzmik/ ▸*adj.* of or relating to earthquakes or other vibrations of the earth and its crust. ■ relating to or denoting geological surveying methods involving vibrations produced artificially by explosions. ■ *figurative* of enormous proportions or effect: *there are seismic pressures threatening American society.* ▷mid 19th cent.: from Greek *seismos* 'earthquake' (from *seien* 'to shake') + -IC. **—seis·mi·cal** *adj.* **—seis·mi·cal·ly** /-ik(ə)lē/ *adv.*

seis·mic·i·ty /sīz'misitē/ ▸*n.* *Geology* the occurrence or frequency of earthquakes in a region: *the high seismicity of the area.*

seis·mic re·flec·tion ▸*n.* *Geology* the reflection of elastic waves at boundaries between bodies of rock of different physical properties, esp. as a technique for prospecting or research.

seis·mic re·frac·tion ▸*n.* *Geology* the refraction of elastic waves on passing between bodies of rock having different seismic velocities.

seis·mic ve·loc·i·ty ▸*n.* *Geology* the velocity of propagation of elastic waves in a particular rock.

seis·mic wave ▸*n.* *Geology* an elastic wave in the earth produced by an earthquake or other means.

seismo- ▸*comb. form* of an earthquake; relating to earthquakes: *seismograph.* ▷from Greek *seismos* 'earthquake.'

seis·mo·gram /'sīzmə,gram/ ▸*n.* a record produced by a seismograph.

seis·mo·graph /'sīzmə,graf/ ▸*n.* an instrument that measures and records details of earthquakes, such as force and duration. **—seis·mo·graph·ic** /,sīzmə'grafik/ *adj.* **—seis·mo·graph·i·cal** /,sīzmə'grafikəl/ *adj.*

seis·mol·o·gy /sīz'mäləjē/ ▸*n.* the branch of science concerned with earthquakes and related phenomena. **—seis·mo·log·i·cal** /,sīzmə'läjikəl/ *adj.* **—seis·mo·log·i·cal·ly** /,sīzmə'läjik(ə)lē/ *adv.* **—seis·mol·o·gist** /-jist/ *n.*

seis·mom·e·ter /sīz'mämitər/ ▸*n.* another term for SEISMOGRAPH.

seis·mo·sau·rus /,sīzmə'sôrəs/ ▸*n.* a huge late Jurassic dinosaur known from only a few bones, probably the longest ever animal with a length of up to 115–150 feet (35–45 m), and one of the heaviest at up to 110 tons. • Genus *Seismosaurus*, infraorder Sauropoda, order Saurischia. ▷modern Latin, from SEISMO- 'of an earthquake' + *sauros* 'lizard.'

sei·tan /'sā,tan/ ▸*n.* a high-protein vegetarian food made from cooked wheat gluten: ▷Japanese: literally, 'is protein.'

sei whale /sā/ ▸*n.* a small rorqual with dark steely-gray skin and white grooves on the belly. • *Balaenoptera borealis*, family Balaenopteridae. ▷early 20th cent.: from Norwegian *sejhval.*

sei·za /'sāzə/ ▸*n.* [in *sing.*] an upright kneeling position that is traditionally used in Japan in meditation and as part of the preparation in martial arts. ▷Japanese, from *sei* 'correct' + *za* 'sitting.'

seize /sēz/ ▸*v.* **1** [*trans.*] take hold of suddenly and forcibly: *she jumped up and seized his arm* | *she* **seized hold of** *the door handle.* ■ capture (a place) using force: *army rebels seized an air force base.* ■ assume (power or control) by force: *the current president seized power in a coup.* ■ (of the police or another authority) take possession of (something) by warrant or legal right; confiscate; impound: *police have seized 726 lb of cocaine.* ■ take (an opportunity or initiative) eagerly and decisively: *he seized his chance to attack as Delaney hesitated.* ■ (of a feeling or pain) affect (someone) suddenly or acutely: *he was seized by the most dreadful fear.* ■ strongly appeal to or attract (the imagination or attention): *the story of the king's escape seized the public imagination.* ■ *formal* understand (something) quickly or clearly: *he always strains to seize the most somber truths.* **2** [*intrans.*] (of a machine with moving parts or a moving part in a machine) become stuck or jammed: *the engine* **seized up** *after only three weeks.* **3** (also **seise**) (**be seized of**) *English Law* be in legal possession of: *the court is currently seized of custody applications.* ■ *historical* have or receive freehold possession of (property): *any person who is seized of land has a protected interest in that land.* ■ be aware or informed of: *the judge was fully seized of the point.* **4** *archaic, Nautical* fasten or attach (someone or something) to something by binding with turns of rope.

▸*phrasal v.* □ **seize on/upon** take eager advantage of (something); exploit for one's own purposes: *the government has eagerly seized on the evidence to deny any link between deprivation and crime.* ▷Middle English: from Old French *seizir* 'give seisin,' from medieval Latin *sacire*, in the phrase *ad proprium sacire* 'claim as one's own,' from a Germanic base meaning 'procedure.' **—seiz·a·ble** *adj.* **—seiz·er** *n.*

▸*PHRASE* □ **seize the day** make the most of the present moment. [see CARPE DIEM.]

sei·zin ▸*n.* variant spelling of SEISIN.

Pronunciation Key ə ago; ər over; 'ə or ,ə up; 'ər or ,ər fur; a hat; ā rate; ä car; cʜ chew; e let; ē see; e(ə)r air; i fit; ī by; i(ə)r ear; ɴɢ sing; ō go; ô for; oi boy; o͝o good; o͞o goo; ou out; sʜ she; тʜ thin; ᴛʜ then; (h)w why; zʜ vision

S

seiz·ing /'sēziNG/ ▶*n. archaic Nautical* a length of cord or rope used for fastening or tying.

sei·zure /'sēzHər/ ▶*n.* **1** the action of capturing someone or something using force: *the seizure of the Assembly building | the Nazi seizure of power.* ■ the action of confiscating or impounding property by warrant of legal right. **2** a sudden attack of illness, esp. a stroke or an epileptic fit: *the patient* ***had a seizure.***

se·jant /'sējənt/ ▶*adj.* [usu. *postpositive*] *Heraldry* (of an animal) sitting upright. ▷late 15th cent.: alteration of an Old French variant of *seant* 'sitting,' from the verb *seoir*, from Latin *sedere* 'sit.'

Sejm /sām/ (also **Seym**) ▶*n.* the lower house of parliament in Poland. ▷Polish.

Sekh·met /'sekmet/ *Egyptian Mythology* a ferocious lioness-goddess, counterpart of the gentle cat-goddess Bastet and wife of Ptah at Memphis.

Sekt /zekt/ ▶*n.* a German sparkling white wine. ▷German.

sel. ▶*abbr.* ■ select. ■ selected. ■ selection; selections.

se·la·chi·an /sə'lākēən/ *Zoology* ▶*n.* an elasmobranch fish of a group that comprises the sharks and dogfishes. • The former group Selachii, subclass Elasmobranchii: now treated as one, two, or three superorders.
▶*adj.* of or relating to the selachians. ▷mid 19th cent.: from modern Latin *Selachii* (from Greek *selakhos* 'shark') + **-AN.**

se·la·dang /sə'lädäNG/ ▶*n.* another term for **GAUR.** ▷early 19th cent.: from Malay.

se·lag·i·nel·la /sə,lajə'nelə/ ▶*n.* a creeping mosslike plant of a genus that includes the lesser club mosses. • Genus *Selaginella*, family Selaginellaceae. ▷modern Latin, diminutive of Latin *selago* 'club moss.'

se·lah /'sēlə; 'sel-/ ▶*exclam.* (in the Bible) occurring frequently at the end of a verse in Psalms and Habakkuk, probably as a musical direction. ▷from Hebrew *selāh*.

Sel·craig /'sel,krāg/ see **SELKIRK.**

sel·dom /'seldəm/ ▶*adv.* not often; rarely: *Islay is seldom visited by tourists | he was seldom absent |* [in *combination*] *an old seldom-used church.*
▶*adj.* [*attrib.*] *dated* not common; infrequent: *a great but seldom pleasure.* ▷Old English *seldan*, of Germanic origin; related to Dutch *zelden* and German *selten*, from a base meaning 'strange, wonderful.'

se·lect /sə'lekt/ ▶*v.* [*trans.*] carefully choose as being the best or most suitable: *students must select their own program |* [*trans.*] *he has been selected to take part |* [*intrans.*] *you can* ***select from*** *a range of quality products.* ■ [*intrans.*] (**select for/against**) *Biology* (in terms of evolution) determine whether (a characteristic or organism) will survive: *a phenotype can be selected against.* ■ use a mouse or keystrokes to mark (something) on a computer screen for a particular operation.
▶*adj.* (of a group of people or things) carefully chosen from a larger number as being the best or most valuable: *he joined his select team of young Intelligence operatives.* ■ (of a place or group of people) only used by or consisting of a wealthy or sophisticated elite; exclusive: *the opera was seen by a small and highly select audience.* ▷mid 16th cent.: from Latin *select-* 'chosen,' from the verb *seligere*, from *se-* 'apart' + *legere* 'choose.' **—se·lect·a·ble** *adj.* **—se·lect·ness** *n.*

se·lect com·mit·tee ▶*n.* a small legislative committee appointed for a special purpose: [in *titles*] *the House Permanent Select Committee on Intelligence.*

se·lect·ee /sə,lek'tē/ ▶*n.* a person who is selected. ■ a conscript.

se·lec·tion /sə'leksHən/ ▶*n.* **1** the action or fact of carefully choosing someone or something as being the best or most suitable: *such men decided the selection of candidates | they objected to his selection.* ■ a number of carefully chosen things: *the publication of a selection of his poems.* ■ a range of things from which a choice may be made: *the restaurant offers a wide selection of hot and cold dishes.* ■ a horse or horses tipped as worth bets in a race or meeting. **2** *Computing* data highlighted on a computer screen that is a target for various manipulations: *your selection may not contain two different data types.* ■ the action or capability of selecting data in this way. **3** *Biology* a process in which environmental or genetic influences determine which types of organism thrive better than others, regarded as a factor in evolution. See also **ATURAL SELECTION.** ▷early 17th cent.: from Latin *se-io(n-)*, from *seligere* 'select by separating off' (see **CT**).

tion·al /sə'leksHənl/ ▶*adj. Linguistics* denoting or relating to the process by which only certain words or structures can occur naturally, normally, or correctly in the context of other words. **—se·lec·tion·al·ly** *adv.*

se·lec·tion pres·sure ▶*n. Biology* an agent of differential mortality or fertility that tends to make a population change genetically.

se·lec·tion rule ▶*n. Physics* a rule that describes whether particular quantum transitions in an atom or molecule are allowed or forbidden.

se·lec·tive /sə'lektiv/ ▶*adj.* relating to or involving the selection of the most suitable or best qualified: *the mini-cow is the result of generations of selective breeding.* ■ (of a person) tending to choose carefully: *he is very* ***selective in*** *his reading.* ■ (of a process or agent) affecting some things and not others: *modern pesticides are more selective in effect.* ■ *chiefly Electronics* operating at or responding to a particular frequency. **—se·lec·tive·ly** *adv.*

se·lec·tive at·ten·tion ▶*n. Psychology* the capacity for or process of reacting to certain stimuli selectively when several occur simultaneously.

se·lec·tive·ness /sə'lektivnis/ ▶*n.* another term for **SELECTIVITY.**

se·lec·tive serv·ice ▶*n.* service in the armed forces under conscription.

se·lec·tiv·i·ty /səlek'tivitē/ ▶*n.* the quality of carefully choosing someone or something as the best or most suitable: *provision is organized on the principle of selectivity.* ■ the property of affecting some things and not others. ■ *Electronics* the ability of a device to respond to a particular frequency without interference from others.

se·lect·man /sə'lektmən/ ▶*n.* (*pl.* **-men**) a member of the local government board of a New England town.

se·lec·tor /sə'lektər/ ▶*n.* a person or thing that selects something, in particular: ■ a device for selecting a particular gear or other setting of a machine or device.

Se·le·ne /sə'lēnē/ *Greek Mythology* the goddess of the moon who fell in love with Endymion. ▷from Greek *selēnē* 'moon.'

se·le·nic ac·id /sə'lenik; -'lē-/ ▶*n. Chemistry* a crystalline acid analogous to sulfuric acid, made by oxidizing certain selenium compounds. • Chem. formula: H_2SeO_4. **—sel·e·nate** /'selə,nāt/ *n.*

sel·e·nite /'selə,nīt/ ▶*n.* a form of gypsum occurring as transparent crystals, sometimes in thin plates. ▷mid 17th cent.: via Latin from Greek *selēnitēs lithos* 'moonstone,' from *selēnē* 'moon' + *lithos* 'stone.'

se·le·ni·um /sə'lēnēəm/ ▶*n.* the chemical element of atomic number 34, a gray crystalline nonmetal with semiconducting properties. (Symbol: **Se**) ▷early 19th cent.: modern Latin, from Greek *selēnē* 'moon.' **—sel·e·nide** /'selə,nīd; -nid/ *n.*

se·le·ni·um cell ▶*n.* a photoelectric device containing a piece of selenium.

seleno- ▶*comb. form* of, relating to, or shaped like the moon: *selenography.* ▷from Greek *selēnē* 'moon.'

se·le·no·dont /sə'lēnə,dänt/ ▶*adj. Zoology* (of molar teeth) having crescent-shaped ridges on the grinding surfaces, characteristic of the ruminants. ■ (of an ungulate) having such teeth. ▷late 19th cent.: from **SELENO-** 'moon-shaped' + Greek *odous, odont-* 'tooth.'

sel·e·nog·ra·phy /,selə'nägrəfē/ ▶*n.* the scientific mapping of the moon; lunar geography. **—sel·e·nog·ra·pher** /-fər/ *n.* **—se·le·no·graph·ic** /,selənə'grafik/ *adj.* **—se·le·no·graph·i·cal** /,selənə'grafikəl/ *adj.*

sel·e·nol·o·gy /,selə'näləjē/ ▶*n.* the scientific study of the moon. **—sel·e·nol·o·gist** /-jist/ *n.*

Sel·es /'seləs/, Monica (1973–), U.S. tennis player, born in Yugoslavia. She was the youngest woman to win a grand slam singles title (French Open 1990). She went on to win there again and at the U.S. Open in 1991 and 1992 and at the Australian Open 1991–93 and 1996. Stabbed on the court by a fan of Steffi Graf in 1993, she returned to play in 1995.

Se·leu·cid /sə'l(y)ōōsid/ ▶*adj.* relating to or denoting a dynasty ruling over Syria and a great part of western Asia from 311 to 65 BC. Its capital was at Antioch.
▶*n.* a member of this dynasty. ▷from *Seleucus* Nicator (the name of the founder, one of Alexander the Great's generals) + **-ID**3.

self /self/ ▶*n.* (*pl.* **selves** /selvz/) a person's essential being that distinguishes them from others, esp. considered as the object of introspection or reflexive action: *our alienation from our true selves |* [in *sing.*] *guilt can be turned against the self | language is an aspect of a person's sense of self.* ■ [with *adj.*] a person's particular nature or personality; the qualities that make a person individual or unique: *by the end of the round he was* ***back to his old self*** *| Paula seemed to be her usual cheerful self.* ■ one's own interests or pleasure: *to love in an unpossessive way implies the total surrender of self.*
▶*pron.* (*pl.* **selves**) oneself, in particular: ■ [with *adj.*] (**one's self**) used ironically to refer in specified glowing terms to oneself or someone else: *the only side worth supporting is your own sweet self.*
▶*adj.* [*attrib.*] (of a trimming or cover) of the same material and color as the rest of the item: *a dress with self belt.*
▶*v.* [*trans.*] *chiefly Botany* self-pollinate; self-fertilize: [as *n.*] (**selfing**) *the flowers never open and pollination is normally by selfing.* ■ [usu. as *adj.*] (**selfed**) *Genetics* cause (an animal or plant) to breed with or fertilize one of the same hybrid origin or strain: *progeny were derived from selfed crosses.* ▷Old English, of Germanic origin; related to Dutch *zelf* and German *selbe*. Early use was emphatic, expressing the sense '(I) myself,' '(he) himself,' etc. The verb dates from the early 20th cent.

self- ▶*comb. form* of or directed toward oneself or itself: *self-hatred.* ■ by one's own efforts; by its own action: *self-acting.* ■ on, in, for, or relating to oneself or itself: *self-adhesive.*

self-a·ban·don·ment (also **self-a·ban·don**) ▶*n.* the action of completely surrendering oneself to a desire or impulse. **—self-a·ban·doned** *adj.*

self-a·base·ment ▶*n.* the belittling or humiliation of oneself: *he began to apologize with copious tears and self-abasement.*

self-ab·ne·ga·tion ▶*n.* the denial or abasement of oneself: *she turned the letter into a groveling form of self-abnegation.*

self-ab·sorp·tion ▶*n.* **1** preoccupation with one's own emotions, interests, or situation. **2** *Physics* the absorption by a body of radiation which it has itself emitted. **—self-ab·sorbed** *adj.*

self-a·buse /ə'byōōs/ ▶*n.* behavior that causes damage or harm to oneself. ■ used euphemistically to refer to masturbation.

self-ac·cu·sa·tion ▶*n.* the action of accusing oneself, stemming from feelings of guilt. **—self-ac·cu·sa·to·ry** *adj.*

self-act·ing ▶*adj. archaic* (of a machine or operation) acting without external influence or control; automatic.

self-ac·tu·al·i·za·tion ▶*n.* the realization or fulfillment of one's talents and potentialities, esp. considered as a drive or need present in everyone.

self-ad·dressed ▶*adj.* (esp. of an envelope) bearing one's own address: *enclose a self-addressed stamped envelope.*

self-ad·he·sive ▶*adj.* coated with a sticky substance; adhering without requiring moistening.

self-ad·just·ing ▶*adj.* (chiefly of machinery) adjusting itself to meet varying requirements. **—self-ad·just·ment** *n.*

self-ad·mi·ra·tion ▶*n.* the admiration of oneself; pride. **—self-ad·mir·ing** *adj.*

self-ad·vance·ment ▶*n.* the advancement or promotion of oneself or one's interests: *a positive step in women's self-advancement.*

self-ad·ver·tise·ment ▶*n.* the active publicization of oneself: *he turned the group into a vehicle for self-advertisement.* **—self-ad·ver·tis·er** *n.* **—self-advertis·ing** *adj.*

self-ad·vo·ca·cy ▶*n.* the action of representing oneself or one's views or interests.

self-af·fir·ma·tion ▶*n.* the recognition and assertion of the existence and value of one's individual self.

self-ag·gran·dize·ment ▶*n.* the action or process of promoting oneself as being powerful or important. **—self-ag·gran·diz·ing** *adj.*

self-al·ien·a·tion ▶*n.* the process of distancing oneself from one's own feelings or activities, such as may occur in mental illness or as a symptom of emotional distress.

self-a·lign·ing ▶*adj.* (of a bearing or machine part) capable of aligning itself automatically.

self-a·nal·y·sis ▶*n.* the analysis of oneself, in particular one's motives and character. **—self-an·a·lyz·ing** *adj.*

self-an·ni·hi·la·tion ▶*n.* the annihilation or obliteration of self, esp. as a process of mystical contemplation.

self-ap·point·ed ▶*adj.* [*attrib.*] having assumed a position or role without the endorsement of others: *self-appointed experts.*

self-ap·pro·ba·tion ▸*n.* another term for SELF-APPROVAL.

self-ap·prov·al ▸*n.* approval or appreciation of oneself. **—self-ap·prov·ing** *adj.* **—self-ap·prov·ing·ly** *adv.*

self-as·sem·bly ▸*n.* **1** *Biology* the spontaneous formation of a ribosome, virus, or other body in a medium containing the appropriate components. ■ a manufacturing process in which atoms, molecules, and components arrange themselves into ordered, functioning entities with no active human involvement **2** *Brit.* the construction of an object, esp. a piece of furniture, from materials sold in kit form: [as *adj.*] *self-assembly furniture.* **—self-as·sem·ble** *v.*

self-as·ser·tion ▸*n.* the confident and forceful expression or promotion of oneself, one's views, or one's desires. **—self-as·sert·ing** *adj.* (*dated*) **—self-as·ser·tive** *adj.* **—self-as·ser·tive·ness** *n.*

self-as·sess·ment ▸*n.* assessment or evaluation of oneself or one's actions and attitudes, in particular, of one's performance at a job or learning task considered in relation to an objective standard.

self-as·sur·ance ▸*n.* confidence in one's own abilities or character. **—self-as·sured** *adj.* **—self-as·sur·ed·ly** *adv.*

self-a·ware·ness ▸*n.* conscious knowledge of one's own character, feelings, motives, and desires: *the process can be painful but it leads to greater self-awareness.* **—self-a·ware** *adj.*

self-be·tray·al ▸*n.* the intentional or inadvertent revelation of the truth about one's actions or thoughts.

self-can·cel·ing ▸*adj.* **1** having elements that contradict or negate one another: *some of the speculation had been self-canceling, with newspapers predicting that the government would take quite opposite courses.* **2** (of a mechanical device) designed to stop working automatically when no longer required.

self-cen·sor·ship ▸*n.* the exercising of control over what one says and does, esp. to avoid castigation: *a climate of self-censorship, fear, and hypocrisy.*

self-cen·tered ▸*adj.* preoccupied with oneself and one's affairs: *he's far too self-centered to care what you do.* **—self-cen·tered·ly** *adv.* **—self-cen·tered·ness** *n.*

self-clean·ing ▸*adj.* (of an object or apparatus) able to clean itself: *a self-cleaning oven.*

self-clos·ing ▸*adj.* (esp. of a door or valve) closing automatically.

self-col·ored ▸*adj.* of a single uniform color: *a self-colored carpet.* ■ of the natural color of something.

self-com·pat·i·ble ▸*adj.* *Botany* (of a plant or species) able to be fertilized by its own pollen.

self-con·ceit ▸*n.* another term for SELF-CONGRATULATION. **—self-con·ceit·ed** *adj.*

self-con·cept ▸*n.* *Psychology* an idea of the self constructed from the beliefs one holds about oneself and the responses of others.

self-con·dem·na·tion ▸*n.* the blaming of oneself: *guilt and self-condemnation were riding her hard.* ■ the inadvertent revelation of one's wrongdoing. **—self-con·demned** *adj.* **—self-con·demn·ing** *adj.*

self-con·fessed ▸*adj.* [*attrib.*] having openly admitted to being a person with certain characteristics: *a self-confessed chocoholic.* **—self-con·fess·ed·ly** /-'fesidlē/ *adv.* **—self-con·fes·sion** *n.* **—self-con·fes·sion·al** *adj.*

self-con·fi·dence ▸*n.* a feeling of trust in one's abilities, qualities, and judgment. **—self-con·fi·dent** *adj.* **—self-con·fi·dent·ly** *adv.*

self-con·grat·u·la·tion ▸*n.* undue complacency or pride regarding one's personal achievements or qualities; self-satisfaction: *a hefty dose of self-congratulation about how noble we are.* **—self-con·grat·u·la·to·ry** *adj.*

self-con·scious ▸*adj.* feeling undue awareness of oneself, one's appearance, or one's actions: *I feel a bit self-conscious parking my scruffy old car | a self-conscious laugh.* ■ *Philosophy & Psychology* having knowledge of one's own existence, esp. the knowledge of oneself as a conscious being. ■ (esp. of an action or intention) deliberate and with full awareness, esp. affectedly so: *her self-conscious identification with the upper classes.* **—self-con·scious·ly** *adv.* **—self-con·scious·ness** *n.*

self-con·sis·tent ▸*adj.* not having parts or aspects that are in conflict or contradiction with each other; consistent: *the theory is both rigorous and self-consistent.* **—self-con·sis·ten·cy** *n.*

self-con·tained ▸*adj.* **1** (of a thing) complete, or having all that is needed, in itself. **2** (of a person) quiet and independent; not depending on or influenced by others. **—self-con·tain·ment** *n.* (in sense 2).

self-con·tempt ▸*n.* contempt or loathing for oneself or one's actions: *they expressed self-contempt for having wasted so many hours in front of the idiot box.* **—self-con·temp·tu·ous** *adj.*

self-con·tra·dic·tion ▸*n.* inconsistency between aspects or parts of a whole: *deconstruction is interested in exploring language and revealing self-contradiction and instability | a puzzling self-contradiction in masochism.* **—self-con·tra·dict·ing** *adj.* **—self-con·tra·dic·to·ry** *adj.*

self-con·trol ▸*n.* the ability to control oneself, in particular one's emotions and desires or the expression of them in one's behavior, esp. in difficult situations: *Lucy silently struggled for self-control.* **—self-con·trolled** *adj.*

self-cor·rect·ing ▸*adj.* correcting oneself or itself without external help: *the scientific process is self-correcting | a self-correcting optical finder.* **—self-cor·rect** *v.* **—self-cor·rec·tion** *n.*

self-cre·at·ed ▸*adj.* created by oneself or itself: *his self-created role as the bad boy of the music scene.* **—self-cre·at·ing** *adj.* **—self-cre·a·tion** *n.*

self-crit·i·cal ▸*adj.* critical of oneself, one's abilities, or one's actions in a self-aware or unduly disapproving manner: *she felt miserably self-critical for her reluctance to go.* ■ able to criticize oneself objectively: *a capacity for self-critical awareness.* **—self-crit·i·cism** *n.*

self-de·ceit ▸*n.* another term for SELF-DECEPTION.

self-de·ceiv·ing ▸*adj.* allowing oneself to believe that a false or unvalidated feeling, idea, or situation is true: *I prefer my cynicism to your self-deceiving optimism.* **—self-de·ceiv·er** *n.*

self-de·cep·tion ▸*n.* the action or practice of allowing oneself to believe that a false or unvalidated feeling, idea, or situation is true: *Jane remarked on men's capacity for self-deception.* **—self-de·cep·tive** *adj.*

self-de·feat·ing ▸*adj.* (of an action or policy) unable, because of its inherent qualities, to achieve the end it is designed to bring about.

self-de·fense ▸*n.* the defense of one's person or interests, esp. through the use of physical force, which is permitted in certain cases as an answer to a charge of violent crime: *he claimed self-defense in the attempted murder charge | [as adj.] self-defense classes.* **—self-de·fen·sive** *adj.*

self-def·i·ni·tion ▸*n.* definition of one's individuality and one's role in life; such definition of a group by its members: *the struggle for national self-definition.*

self-de·light ▸*n.* delight in oneself or one's existence.

self-de·lu·sion ▸*n.* the action of deluding oneself; failure to recognize reality: *he retreats into a world of fantasy and self-delusion.*

self-de·ni·al ▸*n.* the denial of one's own interests and needs; self-sacrifice. **—self-de·ny·ing** *adj.*

self-de·pend·ence ▸*n.* reliance on one's own strengths rather than on others; independence. **—self-de·pend·ent** *adj.*

self-dep·re·cat·ing ▸*adj.* modest about or critical of oneself, esp. humorously so: *self-deprecating jokes.* **—self-dep·re·cat·ing·ly** *adv.* **—self-dep·re·ca·tion** *n.* **—self-dep·re·ca·to·ry** *adj.*

USAGE Of the two combinations **self-depreciating** (which dates from the mid 19th century) and **self-deprecating** (which dates from the mid 20th century), **self-depreciating** better reflects the long-established usage of **depreciate** in the sense of 'disparage, belittle.' **Self-deprecating**, however, reflects the relatively recent use of **deprecate** for **depreciate**, and **self-deprecating**, meaning 'belittling or disparaging oneself,' is now somewhat more common than **self-depreciating**.

self-de·pre·ci·a·tion ▸*n.* another term for SELF-DEPRECATION (see SELF-DEPRECATING). **—self-de·pre·ci·at·ing** *adj.* **—self-de·pre·ci·a·to·ry** *adj.*

USAGE See usage at SELF-DEPRECATING.

self-de·spair ▸*n.* despair or dismay about oneself or one's actions.

self-de·stroy·ing ▸*adj.* destroying or capable of destroying oneself or itself; self-destructive.

self-de·struct ▸*v.* [*intrans.*] (of a thing) destroy itself by exploding or disintegrating automatically, having been preset to do so: *the tape would automatically self-destruct after twenty minutes.* ■ [as *adj.*] denoting a device that enables or causes something to destroy itself in such a way: *the self-destruct button.* **—self-de·struc·tion** *n.* **—self-de·struc·tive** *adj.* **—self-de·struc·tive·ly** *adv.*

self-de·ter·mi·na·tion ▸*n.* the process by which a country determines its own statehood and forms its own allegiances and government: *the changes cannot be made until the country's right to self-determination is recognized.* ■ the process by which a person controls their own life.

self-de·vel·op·ment ▸*n.* the process by which a person's character or abilities are gradually developed: *graduates have stressed the value of their courses for self-development.*

self-de·vo·tion ▸*n.* the devotion of oneself to a person or cause.

self-dif·fu·sion ▸*n.* *Chemistry* the migration of constituent atoms or molecules within the bulk of a substance, esp. in a crystalline solid.

self-di·rect·ed ▸*adj.* (of an emotion, statement, or activity) directed at oneself: *she grimaces with a bitter self-directed humor.* ■ (of an activity) under one's own control: *self-directed learning.* ■ (of a person) showing initiative and the ability to organize oneself. **—self-di·rec·tion** *n.*

self-dis·ci·pline ▸*n.* the ability to control one's feelings and overcome one's weaknesses; the ability to pursue what one thinks is right despite temptations to abandon it. **—self-dis·ci·plined** *adj.*

self-dis·cov·er·y ▸*n.* the process of acquiring insight into one's own character.

self-dis·gust ▸*n.* profound revulsion at one's own character or actions: *his descent into drunkenness filled him with self-disgust.*

self-doubt ▸*n.* lack of confidence in oneself and one's abilities: *his later years were plagued by self-doubt.*

self-dram·a·ti·za·tion ▸*n.* dramatization of one's own situation or feelings for effect.

self-ed·u·cat·ed ▸*adj.* educated largely through one's own efforts, rather than by formal instruction: *he was a self-made and almost self-educated businessman.* **—self-ed·u·ca·tion** *n.*

self-ef·fac·ing ▸*adj.* not claiming attention for oneself; retiring and modest: *his demeanor was self-effacing, gracious, and polite.* **—self-ef·face·ment** *n.* **—self-ef·fac·ing·ly** *adv.*

self-em·ployed ▸*adj.* working for oneself as a freelancer or the owner of a business rather than for an employer: *a self-employed builder.* ■ relating to or designed for people working for themselves: *the rules for self-employed pension plans have been altered.* **—self-em·ploy·ment** *n.*

self-en·closed ▸*adj.* (of a person, community, or system) not choosing to or able to communicate with others or with external systems: *the family is a self-enclosed unit.*

self-es·teem ▸*n.* confidence in one's own worth or abilities; self-respect: *assertiveness training for those with low self-esteem.* See note at PRIDE.

self-e·val·u·a·tion ▸*n.* another term for SELF-ASSESSMENT.

self-ev·i·dent ▸*adj.* not needing to be demonstrated or explained; obvious: *self-evident truths | [with clause] it is self-evident that you cannot work 14 hours a day and have time left over for a child.* **—self-ev·i·dence** *n.* **—self-ev·i·dent·ly** *adv.*

self-ex·am·i·na·tion ▸*n.* the study of one's own behavior and motivations: *a period of considerable self-doubt and self-examination.* ■ the action of examining one's own body for signs of illness.

self-ex·cit·ed ▸*adj.* *Physics* relating to or denoting a dynamo-electric machine or analogous system that generates or excites its own magnetic field.

self-ex·ist·ent ▸*adj.* existing independently of other beings or causes.

self-ex·plan·a·to·ry ▸*adj.* easily understood; not needing explanation: *the film's title is fairly self-explanatory.*

self-ex·pres·sion ▸*n.* the expression of one's feelings, thoughts, or ideas, esp. in writing, art, music, or dance. **—self-ex·pres·sive** *adj.*

self-faced ▸*adj.* (of stone) having an undressed surface.

self-feed·er ▸*n.* **1** a furnace or machine that renews its own fuel or material automatically. **2** a device for supplying food to farm animals automatically. **—self-feed·ing** *adj.*

self-fer·tile ▸*adj.* *Botany* (of a plant) capable of self-fertilization. —**self-fer·til·i·ty** *n.*

self-fer·ti·li·za·tion ▸*n.* *Biology* the fertilization of plants and some invertebrate animals by their own pollen or sperm rather than that of another individual. —**self-fer·ti·lized** *adj.* —**self-fer·ti·liz·ing** *adj.*

self-fi·nanc·ing ▸*adj.* (of an organization or enterprise) having or generating enough income to finance itself. —**self-fi·nanced** *adj.*

self-flag·el·la·tion ▸*n.* the action of flogging oneself, esp. as a form of religious discipline. ■ *figurative* excessive criticism of oneself.

self-flat·ter·y ▸*n.* the holding of an unjustifiably high opinion of oneself or one's actions. —**self-flat·ter·ing** *adj.*

self-for·get·ful ▸*adj.* forgetful of oneself or one's needs. —**self-for·get·ful·ness** *n.*

self-ful·fill·ing ▸*adj.* (of an opinion or prediction) bound to be proved correct or to come true as a result of behavior caused by its being expressed: *expecting something to be bad can turn out to be a self-fulfilling prophecy.*

self-ful·fill·ment (*Brit.* **self-ful·fil·ment**) ▸*n.* the fulfillment of one's hopes and ambitions: *it is the striving for self-fulfillment which guides our lives.*

self-gen·er·at·ing ▸*adj.* generated by itself, rather than by some external force: *the strident activity of the industrial scene seems to be self-generating.*

self-glo·ri·fi·ca·tion ▸*n.* exaltation of oneself and one's abilities: *they fought not merely for self-glorification but for the common good.*

self-gov·ern·ment ▸*n.* **1** government of a country by its own people, esp. after having been a colony. **2** another term for SELF-CONTROL. —**self-gov·erned** *adj.* —**self-gov·ern·ing** *adj.*

self-grav·i·ta·tion ▸*n.* *Astronomy* the gravitational forces acting among the components of a massive body.

self-guid·ed ▸*adj.* (of a walk or visit to a tourist attraction) undertaken without the supervision of a tour guide.

self-ha·tred (also **self-hate**) ▸*n.* intense dislike of oneself.

self-heal (also **self·heal**) ▸*n.* a purple-flowered plant of the mint family that was formerly widely used for healing wounds. Native to Eurasia, it is now widespread throughout North America. • *Prunella vulgaris*, family Labiatae.

self-help ▸*n.* the use of one's own efforts and resources to achieve things without relying on others: *what government does is not a substitute for what people can do with encouragement and self-help.* ■ [as *adj.*] designed to assist people in achieving things for themselves: *a self-help group for drug abusers.*

self·hood /ˈself,ho͝od/ ▸*n.* the quality that constitutes one's individuality; the state of having an individual identity.

self-i·den·ti·fi·ca·tion ▸*n.* the attribution of certain characteristics or qualities to oneself: *self-identification by the old person as sick or inadequate.*

self-i·den·ti·ty ▸*n.* the recognition of one's potential and qualities as an individual, esp. in relation to social context: *caring can become the defining characteristic of women's self-identity.*

self-im·age ▸*n.* the idea one has of one's abilities, appearance, and personality: *sickness is an affront to one's self-image and dignity.*

self-im·mo·la·tion ▸*n.* the offering of oneself as a sacrifice, esp. by burning; such suicidal action in the name of a cause or strongly held belief.

self-im·por·tance ▸*n.* an exaggerated sense of one's own value or importance: *he was a big, blustering, opinionated cop, full of self-importance.* —**self-im·por·tant** *adj.* —**self-im·por·tant·ly** *adv.*

self-im·posed ▸*adj.* (of a task or circumstance) imposed on oneself, not by an external force: *he went into self-imposed exile.*

self-im·prove·ment ▸*n.* the improvement of one's knowledge, status, or character by one's own efforts.

self-in·com·pat·i·ble ▸*adj.* *Botany* (of a plant or species) unable to be fertilized by its own pollen. —**self-in·com·pat·i·bil·i·ty** *n.*

self-in·duced ▸*adj.* **1** brought about by oneself: *self-induced vomiting.* **2** produced by electrical self-induction.

elf-in·duct·ance ▸*n.* *Physics* a measure or coeffi- ent of self-induction in a circuit, usually measured henries. ■ the property of an electric circuit that its self-induction.

·duc·tion ▸*n.* *Physics* the induction of an electromotive force in a circuit when the current in that circuit is varied. Compare with MUTUAL INDUCTION. —**self-in·duc·tive** *adj.*

self-in·dul·gence ▸*n.* the quality of being self-indulgent. ■ something done in a self-indulgent way: *Sunday's simpleminded pleasures and self-indulgences.*

self-in·dul·gent ▸*adj.* characterized by doing or tending to do exactly what one wants, esp. when this involves pleasure or idleness: *a self-indulgent extra hour of sleep.* ■ (of a creative work) lacking economy and control. —**self-in·dul·gent·ly** *adv.*

self-in·flict·ed ▸*adj.* (of a wound or other harm) inflicted on oneself.

self-in·sur·ance ▸*n.* insurance of oneself or one's interests by maintaining a fund to cover possible losses rather than by purchasing an insurance policy.

self-in·ter·est ▸*n.* one's personal interest or advantage, esp. when pursued without regard for others.

self-in·ter·est·ed ▸*adj.* motivated by one's personal interest or advantage, esp. without regard for others: *many groups pursue self-interested aims.*

self-in·volved ▸*adj.* wrapped up in oneself or one's own thoughts. —**self-in·volve·ment** *n.*

self·ish /ˈselfisн/ ▸*adj.* (of a person, action, or motive) lacking consideration for others; concerned chiefly with one's own personal profit or pleasure: *I joined them for selfish reasons.* —**self·ish·ly** *adv.* —**self·ish·ness** *n.*

self·ism /ˈselfizəm/ ▸*n.* concentration on one's own interests; self-centeredness or self-absorption. —**self·ist** *n.*

self-jus·ti·fi·ca·tion ▸*n.* the justification or excusing of oneself or one's actions. —**self-jus·tif·i·ca·to·ry** *adj.* —**self-jus·ti·fy·ing** *adj.*

self-knowl·edge ▸*n.* understanding of oneself or one's own motives or character. —**self-know·ing** *adj.*

self·less /ˈselfləs/ ▸*adj.* concerned more with the needs and wishes of others than with one's own; unselfish: *an act of selfless devotion.* —**self·less·ly** *adv.* —**self·less·ness** *n.*

self-lim·it·ing ▸*adj.* relating to or denoting something that limits itself, in particular: ■ (also **self-lim·it·ed**) *Medicine* (of a condition) ultimately resolving itself without treatment. ■ (in psychology) preventing the development or expression of the self.

self-liq·ui·dat·ing ▸*adj.* denoting an asset that earns back its original cost out of income over a fixed period. ■ denoting a loan used to finance a project that will bring a sufficient return to pay back the loan and its interest and leave a profit. ■ denoting a sales promotion offer that pays for itself by generating increased sales.

self-load·ing ▸*adj.* (esp. of a gun) loading automatically: *a self-loading pistol.* —**self-load·er** *n.*

self-lock·ing ▸*adj.* locking itself shut or in a fixed position: *self-locking screws.*

self-love ▸*n.* regard for one's own well-being and happiness (chiefly considered as a desirable rather than narcissistic characteristic). —**self-lov·ing** *adj.*

self-made ▸*adj.* having become successful or rich by one's own efforts: *a self-made millionaire.* ■ made by oneself: *his self-made fortune | a self-made kite.*

self-man·age·ment ▸*n.* management of or by oneself; the taking of responsibility for one's own behavior and well-being. ■ the distribution of political control to individual regions of a state, esp. as a form of socialism practiced by its own members. ■ management of an organization. —**self-man·ag·ing** *adj.*

self-mas·ter·y ▸*n.* self-control.

self·mate /ˈself,māt/ ▸*n.* *Chess* a problem in which the solver's task is to force the opponent to deliver checkmate.

self-med·i·cate ▸*v.* [*intrans.*] choose and take medicines oneself, rather than by prescription or on expert advice. ■ take addictive or habituating drugs to relieve stress or other conditions: *whenever he hits a period of depression, he has a tendency to self-medicate with any pill or liquid that's in the house.* —**self-med·i·ca·tion** *n.*

self-mock·ing ▸*adj.* mocking oneself: *a wry, self-mocking smile.* —**self-mock·er·y** *n.* —**self-mock·ing·ly** *adv.*

self-mor·ti·fi·ca·tion ▸*n.* the subjugation of appetites or desires by self-denial or self-discipline as an aspect of religious devotion: *voluntary self-mortification such as fasting.*

self-mo·tion ▸*n.* movement caused by oneself or itself, not by an external action or agent. —**self-mov·ing** *adj.*

self-mo·ti·vat·ed ▸*adj.* motivated to do or achieve something because of one's own enthusiasm or interest, without needing pressure from others: *she's a very independent, self-motivated individual.* —**self-mo·ti·vat·ing** *adj.* —**self-mo·ti·va·tion** *n.*

self-mur·der ▸*n.* another term for SUICIDE (sense 1 of the *noun*). —**self-mur·der·er** *n.*

self-mu·ti·la·tion ▸*n.* the mutilation of oneself, esp. as a symptom of mental or emotional disturbance.

self-ne·glect ▸*n.* neglect of oneself, esp. one's physical well-being.

self·ness /ˈselfnəs/ ▸*n.* a person's essential individuality. ■ *archaic* selfishness; self-regard.

self-o·pin·ion·at·ed ▸*adj.* having an arrogantly high regard for oneself or one's own opinions: *a pompous, self-opinionated bully.* —**self-o·pin·ion** *n.*

self-pa·rod·ic ▸*adj.* another term for SELF-PARODYING.

self-par·o·dy ▸*n.* the intentional or inadvertent parodying or exaggeration of one's usual behavior or speech: *they are soft-spoken and clean-cut to the point of self-parody.*

self-par·o·dy·ing ▸*adj.* appearing to parody one's usual behavior or speech, esp. inadvertently: *pathetic, self-parodying former beauty queens propped up by surgery and cosmetics.*

self-per·pet·u·at·ing ▸*adj.* perpetuating itself or oneself without external agency or intervention: *the self-perpetuating power of the bureaucracy.* —**self-per·pet·u·a·tion** *n.*

self-pit·y ▸*n.* excessive, self-absorbed unhappiness over one's own troubles.

self-pit·y·ing ▸*adj.* characterized by self-pity: *he was in one of his self-pitying moods.* —**self-pit·y·ing·ly** *adv.*

self-po·lic·ing ▸*n.* the process of keeping order or maintaining control within a community without accountability or reference to an external authority. ▸*adj.* (of a community) independently responsible for keeping and maintaining order: *as long as the Internet community was relatively small, it could be self-policing.*

self-pol·li·na·tion ▸*n.* *Botany* the pollination of a flower by pollen from the same flower or from another flower on the same plant. —**self-pol·li·nat·ed** *adj.* —**self-pol·li·nat·ing** *adj.* —**self-pol·li·na·tor** *n.*

self-por·trait ▸*n.* a portrait of an artist produced or created by that artist. —**self-por·trai·ture** *n.*

self-pos·sessed ▸*adj.* calm, confident, and in control of one's feelings; composed. —**self-pos·ses·sion** *n.*

self-praise ▸*n.* praise of oneself; boasting.

self-pres·er·va·tion ▸*n.* the protection of oneself from harm or death, esp. regarded as a basic instinct in human beings and animals.

self-pro·claimed ▸*adj.* [*attrib.*] described as or proclaimed to be such by oneself, without endorsement by others: *exercise books written by self-proclaimed experts.*

self-prop·a·gat·ing ▸*adj.* (esp. of a plant) able to propagate itself. —**self-prop·a·ga·tion** *n.*

self-pro·pelled ▸*adj.* moving or able to move without external propulsion or agency: *a self-propelled weapon.* —**self-pro·pel·ling** *adj.*

self-pro·tec·tion ▸*n.* protection of oneself or itself. —**self-pro·tec·tive** *adj.*

self-prov·ing ▸*adj.* *Law* (of a will) accompanied by a witnesses' affidavit for which no oral testimony is needed to be admitted to probate: *we recommend that all wills be self-proving.* ■ of or relating to an affidavit that makes a will self-proving: *attached to the will offered for probate was a self-proving affidavit and certificate executed by the testatrix, the two witnesses to the will, and a notary public.*

self-re·al·i·za·tion ▸*n.* fulfillment of one's own potential.

self-ref·er·en·tial ▸*adj.* making reference to itself or oneself. ■ (of a literary or other creative work) making reference to itself, its author or creator, or their other work: *self-referential elements in Donne's poems.* —**self-ref·er·ence** *n.* —**self-ref·er·en·ti·al·i·ty** *n.* —**self-ref·er·en·tial·ly** *adv.*

self-re·flec·tion ▸*n.* meditation or serious thought about one's character, actions, and motives. —**self-re·flec·tive** *adj.*

self-re·flex·ive ▸*adj.* containing a reflection or image of itself; self-referential: *sociology's self-reflexive critique.*

self-re·gard ▸*n.* regard or consideration for oneself; self-respect. ■ conceit; vanity. —**self-re·gard·ing** *adj.*

self-reg·u·lat·ing ▸*adj.* regulating itself without intervention from external bodies: *advertising is governed by a self-regulating system.* —**self-reg·u·la·tion** *n.* —**self-reg·u·la·to·ry** *adj.*

self-re·li·ance ▶*n.* reliance on one's own powers and resources rather than those of others. —**self-re·li·ant** *adj.* —**self-re·li·ant·ly** *adv.*

self-re·new·al ▶*n.* the process of renewing oneself or itself. —**self-re·new·ing** *adj.*

self-re·nun·ci·a·tion ▶*n.* renunciation of one's own will; self-sacrifice; unselfishness.

self-re·proach ▶*n.* reproach or blame directed at oneself: *the bitter tears of self-reproach.* —**self-re·proach·ful** *adj.*

self-re·spect ▶*n.* pride and confidence in oneself; a feeling that one is behaving with honor and dignity.

self-re·spect·ing ▶*adj.* having self-respect: *proud, self-respecting mountain villagers.* ■ [*attrib.*] *often humorous* a person who merits a particular role or name: *no self-respecting editor would run such an article.*

self-re·straint ▶*n.* restraint imposed by oneself on one's own actions; self-control. —**self-re·strained** *adj.*

self-re·veal·ing ▶*adj.* revealing one's character or motives, esp. inadvertently: *his most intimate and self-revealing book.* —**self-rev·e·la·tion** *n.* —**self-re·vel·a·to·ry** *adj.*

self-right·eous ▶*adj.* having or characterized by a certainty, esp. an unfounded one, that one is totally correct or morally superior: *self-righteous indignation and complacency.* —**self-right·eous·ly** *adv.* —**self-right·eous·ness** *n.*

self-right·ing ▶*adj.* (of a boat) designed to right itself when capsized.

self-ris·ing flour ▶*n.* flour that has a leavening agent already added.

self-rule ▶*n.* another term for **SELF-GOVERNMENT** (sense 1).

self-sac·ri·fice ▶*n.* the giving up of one's own interests or wishes in order to help others or to advance a cause. —**self-sac·ri·fi·cial** *adj.* —**self-sac·ri·fic·ing** *adj.*

self·same /ˈself,sām/ ▶*adj.* [*attrib.*] (usu. **the selfsame**) exactly the same: *he was standing in the selfsame spot you're filling now.*

self-sat·is·fied ▶*adj.* excessively and unwarrantedly satisfied with oneself or one's achievements; smugly complacent: *a pompous, self-satisfied fool* | *a self-satisfied smirk* | *a self-satisfied air.* —**self-sat·is·fac·tion** *n.*

self-seal·ing ▶*adj.* sealing itself without the usual process or procedure, in particular: ■ (of a tire, fuel tank, etc.) able to seal small punctures automatically. ■ (of an envelope) self-adhesive.

self-seed ▶*v.* [*intrans.*] (of a plant) propagate itself by seed: [as *adj.*] (**self-seeding**) *the early-blooming, self-seeding primula.* —**self-seed·er** *n.*

self-seek·ing ▶*adj.* & *n.* another term for **SELF-SERVING**. —**self-seek·er** *n.*

self-se·lect ▶*v.* **1** choose for oneself: [*trans.*] *participants were asked to self-select their titles, which were divided into executive and non-executive.* **2** [*intrans.*] determine one's own status with regard to membership in a group: *the crowd self-selects because this isn't a club for the passing trade.*
▶*adj.* allowing users to select: *the chain decided to move condoms from the pharmacy counter to self-select stands.*

self-se·lec·tion ▶*n.* the action of putting oneself forward for something. —**self-se·lect·ing** *adj.*

self-serv·ice ▶*adj.* denoting a store, restaurant, or service station where customers select goods for themselves or service their car for themselves and pay a cashier: *a self-service cafeteria.*
▶*n.* the system whereby customers select goods for themselves or service their car for themselves and pay a cashier: *providing quick self-service.*

self-serv·ing ▶*adj.* having concern for one's own welfare and interests before those of others: *public accountability is replaced by self-serving propaganda.*
▶*n.* concern for oneself before others.

self-sim·i·lar ▶*adj.* *Mathematics* (of an object or set of objects) similar to itself at a different time, or to a copy of itself on a different scale. —**self-sim·i·lar·i·ty** *n.*

self-slaugh·ter ▶*n.* poetic/literary term for **SUICIDE** (sense 1 of the *noun*).

self-sow /ˈsō/ ▶*v.* [*intrans.*] (of a plant) propagate itself by seed: [as *adj.*] (**self-sown**) *a batch of self-sown seedlings.*

self-start·er ▶*n.* **1** a person who is sufficiently motivated or ambitious to start a new career or business or to pursue further education without the help of others: *he was the self-starter who worked his way up from messenger boy to account executive.* **2** *dated* the starter of a motor-vehicle engine. —**self-start·ing** *adj.*

self-ster·ile ▶*adj.* *Biology* incapable of self-fertilization. —**self-ste·ril·i·ty** *n.*

self-stick ▶*adj.* coated with an adhesive on one side for ready application to a surface: *peel off self-stick backing and attach to either side.*

self-stim·u·la·tion ▶*n.* **1** used euphemistically to refer to masturbation. **2** *Physiology* a phenomenon that occurs in the hypothalamus and other areas of the brain, in which the propagation of electrical stimulation has positive reinforcing properties that act to maintain and perpetuate the impulses.

self-styled ▶*adj.* [*attrib.*] using a description or title that one has given oneself: *self-styled experts* | *the self-styled president of Bougainville.*

self-sub·sist·ent ▶*adj.* subsistent without dependence on or support from external agencies: *this colony was virtually self-subsistent, in management methods as in food.*

self-suf·fi·cient ▶*adj.* needing no outside help in satisfying one's basic needs, esp. with regard to the production of food: *I don't think Botswana, due to the climate, could ever be self-sufficient in food.* ■ emotionally and intellectually independent: *their son was a little bit of a loner and very self-sufficient.* —**self-suf·fi·cien·cy** *n.* —**self-suf·fi·cient·ly** *adv.*

self-sug·ges·tion ▶*n.* another term for **AUTOSUGGESTION**.

self-sup·port·ing ▶*adj.* **1** having the resources to be able to survive without outside assistance. **2** staying up or upright without being supported by something else: *arches were originally self-supporting structures.* —**self-sup·port** *n.*

self-sur·ren·der ▶*n.* the surrender of oneself or one's will to an external influence, an emotion, or another person.

self-sus·tain·ing ▶*adj.* able to continue in a healthy state without outside assistance: *his puny farms were years from being self-sustaining.* —**self-sus·tained** *adj.*

self-sys·tem ▶*n.* *Psychology* the complex of drives and responses relating to the self; the set of potentialities that develop in an individual's character in response to parental and other external influences.

self-tap·ping ▶*adj.* (of a screw) able to cut thread in the material into which it is inserted.

self-taught ▶*adj.* having acquired knowledge or skill on one's own initiative rather than through formal instruction or training: *a self-taught graphic artist.*

self-tim·er ▶*n.* a mechanism in a camera that introduces a delay between the operation of the shutter release and the opening of the shutter, so that the photographer can be included in the photograph.

self-tor·ture ▶*n.* the inflicting of pain, esp. mental pain, on oneself.

self-tran·scend·ence ▶*n.* the overcoming of the limits of the individual self and its desires in spiritual contemplation and realization.

self-un·der·stand·ing ▶*n.* awareness of and ability to understand one's own actions and reactions.

self-willed ▶*adj.* obstinately doing what one wants in spite of the wishes or orders of others: *the child may be very obstinate and self-willed.* —**self-will** *n.*

self-wind·ing /ˈwīndiNG/ ▶*adj.* (chiefly of a watch) wound by some automatic means, such as an electric motor or the movement of the wearer, rather than by hand.

self-worth ▶*n.* another term for **SELF-ESTEEM**.

Sel·juk /selˈjo͞ok; ˈsel,jo͞ok/ ▶*n.* a member of any of the Turkish dynasties that ruled Asia Minor in the 11th to 13th centuries, successfully invading the Byzantine Empire and defending the Holy Land against the Crusaders.
▶*adj.* of or relating to the Seljuks. ▷from Turkish *seljūq*, the name of the reputed ancestor of the dynasty. —**Sel·juk·i·an** /-ˈjo͞okēən/ *adj.* & *n.*

sel·kie /ˈselkē/ (also **sel·ky** or **sil·kie** /ˈsil-/) ▶*n.* (*pl.* **-kies**) *Scottish* a mythical creature that resembles a seal in the water but assumes human form on land. ▷from *selch*, variant of **SEAL**[2], + **-IE**.

Sel·kirk /ˈsel,kərk/, Alexander (1676–1721), Scottish sailor; also called *Alexander Selcraig*. His experiences on one of the uninhabited Juan Fernandez Islands formed the basis of Daniel Defoe's novel *Robinson Crusoe* (1719).

sell /sel/ ▶*v.* (*past* and *past part.* **sold** /sōld/) [*trans.*] **1** give or hand over (something) in exchange for money: *they had sold the car* | *the family business had been **sold off*** | [with *two objs.*] *I was trying to sell him my butterfly collection.* ■ have a stock of (something) available for sale: *the store sells hi-fis, TVs, videos, and other electrical goods.* ■ [*intrans.*] (of a thing) be purchased: *this magazine of yours won't sell.* ■ (of a publication or recording) attain sales of (a specified number of copies): *the album sold 6 million copies in the U.S.* ■ [*intrans.*] (**sell for/at**) be available for sale at (a specified price): *these antiques sell for about $375.* ■ [*intrans.*] (**sell out**) sell all of one's stock of something: *they had nearly **sold out of** the initial run of 75,000 copies.* ■ [*intrans.*] (**sell out**) be all sold: *it was clear that the performances would not sell out.* ■ [*intrans.*] (**sell through**) (of a product) be purchased by a customer from a retail outlet. ■ [*intrans.*] (**sell up**) sell all of one's property, possessions, or assets: *Ernest sold up and retired.* ■ (**sell oneself**) have sex in exchange for money: *if she was going to sell herself then it would be as well not to come too cheap.* ■ *archaic* offer (something) dishonorably for money or other reward; make a matter of corrupt bargaining: *do not your lawyers sell all their practice, as your priests their prayers?* ■ (**sell someone out**) betray someone for one's own financial or material benefit: *the clansmen became tenants and the chiefs sold them out.* ■ [*intrans.*] (**sell out**) abandon one's principles for reasons of expedience: *the prime minister has come under fire for **selling out to** the U.S.* **2** persuade someone of the merits of: *he sold the idea of making a film about Tchaikovsky* | *he could get work but he just won't sell himself.* ■ be the reason for (something) being bought: *what sells CDs to most people is convenience.* ■ cause (someone) to become enthusiastic about: [as *adj.*] (**sold**) *I'm just not **sold on** the idea.* **3** *archaic* trick or deceive (someone): *what we want is to go out of here quiet, and talk this show up, and sell the rest of the town.*
▶*n.* *informal* **1** an act of selling or attempting to sell something: *the excitement of scientific achievement is too subtle a sell to stir the public.* **2** a disappointment, typically one arising from being deceived as to the merits of something: *actually, Hawaii's a bit of a sell.* ▷Old English *sellan* (verb), of Germanic origin; related to Old Norse *selja* 'give up, sell.' Early use included the sense 'give, hand (something) over voluntarily in response to a request.' —**sell·a·ble** *adj.*
▶*PHRASES* □ **sell someone a bill of goods** see **BILL OF GOODS**. □ **sell someone down the river** see **RIVER**. □ **sell someone a** (or **the**) **dummy** see **DUMMY**. □ **sell someone a pup** see **PUP**. □ **sell someone/something short** fail to recognize or state the true value of: *don't sell yourself short—you've got what it takes.* □ **sell one's soul** (**to the devil**) do or be willing to do anything, no matter how wrong it is, in order to achieve one's objective: *universities are selling their souls for commercial success.*

sel·la /ˈselə/ (in full **sel·la tur·ci·ca** /ˈtərkikə; -sikə/) ▶*n.* (*pl.* **sel·lae** /ˈselē; -lī/ or **sel·lae tur·ci·cae** /ˈselē ˈtərsi,kē; ˈselī ˈtərki,kī/) *Anatomy* a depression in the sphenoid bone, containing the pituitary gland. ▷late 17th cent.: from Latin, 'saddle,' (in full) 'Turkish saddle.'

sell-by date ▶*n.* a date marked on a perishable product indicating the recommended time by which it should be sold: *milk past its sell-by date.* ■ *informal, chiefly Brit.* a time after which something or someone is no longer considered desirable or effective: *do broadcasters have a sell-by date?*

sell·down /ˈsel,doun/ ▶*n.* widespread selling of futures, securities, or commodities, triggered by or resulting in falling prices: *a selldown of banking stocks which, in turn, would further depress the market.*

sell·er /ˈselər/ ▶*n.* **1** a person who sells something: *street sellers of newspapers, flowers, etc.* ■ (**the seller**) the party in a legal transaction who is selling: *the seller may accept the buyer's offer.* **2** [with *adj.*] a product that sells in some specified way: *the game will undoubtedly be the biggest seller of the year.*
▶*PHRASE* □ **seller's** (or **sellers'**) **market** an economic situation in which goods or shares are scarce and sellers can keep prices high.

Sel·lers /ˈselərz/, Peter (1925–80), English comic actor. He established his reputation on *The Goon Show*, a radio series of the 1950s, but he is best known for the "Pink Panther" series of movies of the 1960s and 1970s, in which he played French detective Inspector Clouseau. Other notable movies: *The Lady Killers* (1955) and *Dr. Strangelove* (1964).

sell-in ▶*n.* the sale of goods to retail traders prior to public retailing.

sell·ing point ▶*n.* a feature of a product for sale that makes it attractive to customers.

sell·ing race ▶*n.* a horse race after which the winning horse must be auctioned.

S

sell-off ▸*n.* a sale of assets, typically at a low price, carried out in order to dispose of them rather than as normal trade. ■ a sale of shares, bonds, or commodities, esp. one that causes a fall in price.

sell·out /ˈselˌout/ ▸*n.* **1** the selling of an entire stock of something, esp. tickets for an entertainment or sports event. ■ an event for which all tickets are sold: *the game is sure to be a sellout.* **2** a sale of a business or company. ■ a betrayal of one's principles for reasons of expedience: *the sellout of socialist economic policy.*

sell-through ▸*n.* the ratio of the quantity of goods sold by a retail outlet to the quantity distributed to it wholesale: *the sell-through was amazing, 60 percent.* ■ the retail sale of something, typically a prerecorded videocassette, as opposed to its rental: [as *adj.*] *the burgeoning sell-through market.*

Sel·ma /ˈselmə/ an industrial city in south central Alabama, on the Alabama River; pop. 23,755.

selt·zer /ˈseltsər/ (also **selt·zer wa·ter**) ▸*n.* soda water. ■ medicinal mineral water from Niederselters in Germany. ▷mid 18th cent.: alteration of German *Selterser*, from *(Nieder)selters* (see above).

sel·va /ˈselvə/ ▸*n.* a tract of land covered by dense equatorial forest, esp. in the Amazon basin. ▷mid 19th cent.: from Spanish or Portuguese, from Latin *silva* 'woods.'

sel·vage /ˈselvij/ ▸*n.* an edge produced on woven fabric during manufacture that prevents it from unraveling. ■ *Geology* a zone of altered rock, esp. volcanic glass, at the edge of a rock mass. ▷late Middle English: from an alteration of **SELF + EDGE**, on the pattern of early modern Dutch *selfegghe*. The geological term dates from the 1930s.

selves /selvz/ ▸ plural form of **SELF**.

Sel·ye /ˈselyā/, Hans Hugo Bruno (1907–82), Canadian physician, born in Austria. He showed that environmental stress and anxiety could result in the release of hormones that, over a long period, could produce biochemical and physiological disorders.

Selz·nick /ˈselznik/, David O. (1902–65), U.S. movie producer; full name *David Oliver Selznick*. He made *King Kong* (1933) for RKO and *Anna Karenina* (1935) for MGM before establishing his own production company in 1936, where he produced such screen classics as *Gone with the Wind* (1939) and *Rebecca* (1940).

SEM ▸*abbr.* scanning electron microscope.

Sem. ▸*abbr.* ■ seminary. ■ (also **Sem**) Semitic.

sem. ▸*abbr.* semicolon.

se·man·tic /səˈmantik/ ▸*adj.* relating to meaning in language or logic. ▷mid 17th cent.: from French *sémantique*, from Greek *sēmantikos* 'significant,' from *sēmainein* 'signify,' from *sēma* 'sign.' **—se·man·ti·cal·ly** /-ik(ə)lē/ *adv.*

se·man·tic field ▸*n. Linguistics* a lexical set of semantically related items, e.g., verbs of perception.

se·man·tic·i·ty /ˌsimanˈtisitē/ ▸*n.* the quality that a linguistic system has of being able to convey meanings, in particular by reference to the world of physical reality.

se·man·tics /səˈmantiks/ ▸*plural n.* [usu. treated as *sing.*] the branch of linguistics and logic concerned with meaning. There are a number of branches and subbranches of semantics, including **formal semantics**, which studies the logical aspects of meaning, such as sense, reference, implication, and logical form, **lexical semantics**, which studies word meanings and word relations, and **conceptual semantics**, which studies the cognitive structure of meaning. ■ the meaning of a word, phrase, sentence, or text: *such quibbling over semantics may seem petty stuff.* **—se·man·ti·cian** /ˌsēmanˈtisHən/ *n.* **—se·man·ti·cist** *n.*

sem·a·phore /ˈseməˌfôr/ ▸*n.* **1** a system of sending messages by holding the arms or two flags or poles in certain positions according to an alphabetic code. ■ a signal sent by semaphore. **2** an apparatus for signaling in this way, consisting of an upright with movable parts.

▸*v.* [*trans.*] send (a message) by semaphore or by signals resembling semaphore: *Josh stands facing the rear and semaphoring the driver's intentions.* ▷early 19th cent. (denoting a signaling apparatus): from French *sémaphore*, formed irregularly from Greek *sēma* 'sign' + **-PHORE**. **—sem·a·phor·ic** /ˌseməˈfôrik/ *adj.* **—sem·a·phor·i·cal·ly** /ˌseməˈfôrik(ə)lē/ *adv.*

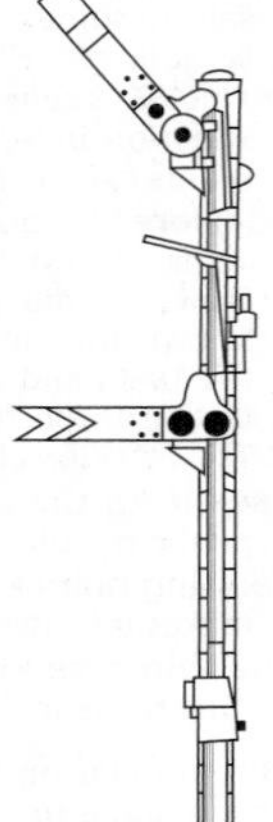
semaphore 2

Se·ma·rang /səˈmäˌräNG/ a port in Indonesia, on the northern coast of Java; pop. 1,249,000.

se·ma·si·ol·o·gy /səˌmāsēˈäləjē; -zē-/ ▸*n.* the branch of knowledge that deals with concepts and the terms that represent them. Compare with **ONOMASIOLOGY**. ▷mid 19th cent.: from German *Semasiologie*, from Greek *sēmasia* 'meaning,' from *sēmainein* 'signify.' **—se·ma·si·o·log·i·cal** /-əˈläjikəl/ *adj.*

sem·bla·ble /ˈsembləbəl/ ▸*n. poetic/literary* a counterpart or equal to someone: *this person is our brother, our semblable, our very self.* ▷Middle English (as an adjective meaning 'like, similar'): from Old French, from *sembler* 'seem.'

sem·blance /ˈsembləns/ ▸*n.* the outward appearance or apparent form of something, esp. when the reality is different: *she tried to force her thoughts back into* **some semblance of** *order.* ■ *archaic* resemblance; similarity: *it bears some* **semblance to** *the thing I have in mind.* ▷Middle English: from Old French, from *sembler* 'seem,' from Latin *similare, simulare* 'simulate.'

se·mé /səˈmā/ (also **se·mée**) ▸*adj. Heraldry* covered with small bearings of indefinite number (e.g., stars, fleurs-de-lis) arranged all over the field. ▷late Middle English: French, literally 'sown,' past participle of *semer*.

Se·mei /ˈsemā/ (also **Se·mey**) an industrial city and river port in eastern Kazakhstan, on the Irtysh River, close to the border with Russia; pop. 339,000. Founded in the 18th century, it was known as Semipalatinsk until 1991.

Sem·e·le /ˈseməlē/ *Greek Mythology* the mother, by Zeus, of Dionysus. The fire of Zeus's thunderbolts killed her but made her child immortal.

se·men /ˈsēmən/ ▸*n.* the male reproductive fluid, containing spermatozoa in suspension. ▷late Middle English: from Latin, literally 'seed,' from *serere* 'to sow.'

se·mes·ter /səˈmestər/ ▸*n.* a half-year term in a school or college, typically lasting fifteen to eighteen weeks. ▷early 19th cent.: from German *Semester*, from Latin *semestris* 'six-monthly,' from *sex* 'six' + *mensis* 'month.'

se·mes·ter·ly /səˈmestərlē/ ▸*adj.* happening or appearing once per academic semester: *fines may be added onto semesterly expenses.*

Se·mey variant spelling of **SEMEI**.

sem·i /ˈsemī/ ▸*n.* (*pl.* **sem·is**) *informal* **1** a tractor-trailer: *she pulled into the path of a semi.* **2** a semifinal: *they defeated them in the semi.* **3** *Brit.* a semidetached house: *a three-bedroom semi.* ▷early 20th cent.: abbreviation.

semi- ▸*prefix* **1** half: *semicircular.* ■ occurring or appearing twice in a specified period: *semiannual.* **2** partly; in some degree or particular: *semiconscious.* ■ almost: *semidarkness.* ▷from Latin; related to Greek *hemi-*.

sem·i·a·cous·tic /ˌsemēəˈko͞ostik; ˌsemˌī-/ ▸*adj.* (of a guitar) having both one or more pickups and a hollow body, typically with f-holes.

▸*n.* a semi-acoustic guitar.

sem·i·an·nu·al /ˌsemēˈanyo͞oəl; ˌsemˌī-/ ▸*adj.* occurring twice a year; half-yearly: *their semiannual meetings.* ■ (of a plant) living for half a year only.

▸*n.* a semiannual plant. **—sem·i·an·nu·al·ly** *adv.*

sem·i·a·quat·ic /ˌsemēəˈkwätik; ˌsemˌī-; -ˈkwatik/ ▸*adj.* (of an animal) living partly on land and partly in water: *semiaquatic crocodiles.* ■ (of a plant) growing in very wet or waterlogged ground.

sem·i·au·to·mat·ic /ˌsemēˌôtəˈmatik; ˌsemˌī-/ ▸*adj.* partially automatic: *a semiautomatic climate-control system.* ■ (of a firearm) having a mechanism for self-loading but not for continuous firing: *semiautomatic rifles.*

▸*n.* a semiautomatic firearm.

sem·i·au·ton·o·mous /ˌsemēôˈtänəməs; ˌsemˌī-/ ▸*adj.* **1** (of a country, state, or community) having a degree of, but not complete, self-government: *Russia's semiautonomous republics.* **2** acting independently to some degree: *semiautonomous working groups.*

sem·i·base·ment /ˈsemēˌbāsmənt; ˈsemˌī-/ ▸*n.* a story of a building partly below ground level.

sem·i·bold /ˈsemēˈbōld; ˈsemˌī-/ ▸*adj. Printing* printed in a typeface with thick strokes but not as thick as bold.

sem·i·breve /ˈsemēˌbrēv; ˈsemˌī-/ ▸*n. Music, chiefly Brit.* a whole note.

sem·i·cir·cle /ˈsemēˌsərkəl; ˈsemˌī-/ ▸*n.* a half of a circle or of its circumference. ■ a set of objects arranged in a semicircle: *chairs were in a semicircle around the hearth.* ▷early 16th cent.: from Latin *semicirculus* (see **SEMI-**, **CIRCLE**). **—sem·i·cir·cu·lar** *adj.*

sem·i·cir·cu·lar ca·nals ▸*plural n.* three fluid-filled bony channels in the inner ear. They are situated at right angles to each other and provide information about orientation to the brain to help maintain balance.

sem·i·civ·i·lized /ˌsemēˈsivəˌlīzd; ˌsemˌī-/ ▸*adj.* partially civilized.

sem·i·clas·si·cal /ˌsemēˈklasikəl; ˌsemˌī-/ ▸*adj.* **1** (of music) having elements both of classical music and of other more popular genres. **2** *Physics* (of a theory or method) intermediate between a classical or Newtonian description and one based on quantum mechanics or relativity.

sem·i·co·lon /ˈsemiˌkōlən; ˈsemˌī-/ ▸*n.* a punctuation mark (;) indicating a pause, typically between two main clauses, that is more pronounced than that indicated by a comma.

sem·i·con·duct·ing /ˈsemēkənˌdəktiNG; ˌsemˌī-/ ▸*adj.* (of a material or device) having the properties of a semiconductor.

sem·i·con·duc·tor /ˈsemēkənˌdəktər; ˈsemˌī-/ ▸*n.* a solid substance that has a conductivity between that of an insulator and that of most metals, either due to the addition of an impurity or because of temperature effects. Devices made of semiconductors, notably silicon, are essential components of most electronic circuits.

sem·i·con·scious /ˌsemēˈkänsHəs; ˌsemˌī-/ ▸*adj.* (of a person) only partially conscious: *he dragged out the semiconscious pilot.* ■ (of a feeling or memory) of which the person experiencing it is only vaguely or partially aware: *semiconscious obsessions.*

sem·i·con·serv·a·tive /ˌsemēkənˈsərvətiv; ˌsemˌī-/ ▸*adj. Biochemistry* relating to or denoting replication of a nucleic acid in which one complete strand of each double helix is directly derived from the parent molecule. **—sem·i·con·serv·a·tive·ly** *adv.*

sem·i·crys·tal·line /ˌsemēˈkristələn; ˌsemˌī-; -ˌlīn/ ▸*adj. Chemistry* (of a solid) possessing crystalline character to some degree.

sem·i·cyl·in·der /ˌsemēˈsiləndər; ˌsemˌī-/ ▸*n. Geometry* half of a cylinder cut longitudinally. **—sem·i·cy·lin·dri·cal** /ˌsemēˌsəˈlindrikəl; ˌsemˌī-/ *adj.*

sem·i·dark·ness /ˌsemēˈdärknəs; ˌsemˌī-/ ▸*n.* a light level in which it is possible to see, but not clearly.

sem·i·dem·i·sem·i·qua·ver /ˌsemēˌdemēˈsemēˌkwāvər/ ▸*n. Music, chiefly Brit.* another term for **HEMIDEMISEMIQUAVER**.

sem·i·der·e·lict /ˌsemēˈderəlikt; ˌsemī-/ ▸*adj.* in a partially derelict state: *a semiderelict farmhouse.*

sem·i·de·tached /ˌsemēdiˈtacHt; ˌsemˌī-/ ▸*adj.* (of a house) joined to another house on one side only by a common wall.

▸*n. Brit.* a semidetached house.

sem·i·di·am·e·ter /ˌsemēdīˈamitər; ˌsemˌī-/ ▸*n. Astronomy & Geometry* half of a diameter; radius. ▷late Middle English: from late Latin.

sem·i·doc·u·men·ta·ry /ˌsemēˌdäkyəˈment(ə)rē; ˌsemˌī-/ ▸*adj.* (of a movie) having a factual background and a fictitious story.

▸*n.* a semidocumentary movie.

sem·i·dome /ˈsemēˌdōm; ˌsemˌī-/ ▸*n. Architecture* a half-dome formed by vertical section.

sem·i·dou·ble /ˌsemēˈdəbəl; ˌsemˌī-/ ▸*adj.* (of a flower) intermediate between single and double in having only the outer stamens converted to petals.

sem·i·el·lip·ti·cal /ˌsemē-iˈliptikəl; ˌsemˌī-/ ▸*adj.* having the shape of half of an ellipse bisected by one of its diameters, esp. the major axis.

sem·i·ev·er·green /ˌsemēˈevərˌgrēn/ ▸*adj.* (of a tree or shrub) retaining foliage part way through a season in which the leaves would normally be lost.

sem·i·fi·nal /ˌsemēˈfīnl; ˌsemˌī-/ ▸*n.* a game or round immediately preceding the final, the winner of which goes on to the final. **—sem·i·fi·nal·ist** *n.*

sem·i·fin·ished /ˌsemēˈfinisHt; ˌsemˌī-/ ▸*adj.* prepared for the final stage of manufacture: *crude steel and semifinished metal products.*

sem·i·fit·ted /ˌsemēˈfitid; ˌsemˌī-/ ▸*adj.* (of a garment) shaped to the body but not closely fitted: *a single-breasted semifitted jacket.*

sem·i·flu·id /ˌsemēˈflo͞o-id; ˌsemˌī-/ ▸*adj.* having a thick consistency between solid and liquid.

▸*n.* a semifluid substance.

sem·i·for·mal /ˌsemēˈfôrməl; ˌsemˌī-/ ▸*adj.* combining formal and informal elements: *in the semiformal atmosphere irritations can be aired.* ■ used to describe clothing that is neither formal nor casual and that is typically worn for a dance, wedding, or other

event: *the casino has a semiformal dress code (men must wear a tie and jacket).*
▶*n.* an event at which semiformal attire is expected: *it had organized its own spring semiformal at a nearby hotel.*

sem·i·gloss /ˈsemē,gläs; ˈsem,ī-; -,glôs/ (also **sem·i-gloss**) ▶*n.* a paint that dries to a moderately glossy sheen.

sem·i-in·de·pend·ent ▶*adj.* partially free from outside control; not wholly depending on another's authority: *detachments are semi-independent units that are armed differently from their regiment.* ■ (of a country or region) partially self-governing. ■ (of an institution) not wholly supported by public funds.

sem·i·in·va·lid /,semē ˈinvəlid; ,sem,ī-/ ▶*n.* a partially disabled or somewhat infirm person.

sem·i·le·thal /,semēˈlēTHəl; ,sem,ī-/ ▶*adj. Genetics* relating to or denoting an allele or chromosomal abnormality that impairs the viability of most of the individuals homozygous for it.

sem·i·liq·uid /,semēˈlikwid; ,sem,ī-/ ▶*adj.* & *n.* another term for SEMIFLUID.

sem·i·lit·er·ate /,semēˈlitərit; ,sem,ī-/ ▶*adj.* unable to read or write with ease or fluency; poorly educated: *a high proportion of the population is still relatively poor and semiliterate.* ■ (of a text) poorly written: *the semiliterate glossies.*
▶*n.* a person who is poorly educated or unable to read or write with ease or fluency. **—sem·i·lit·er·a·cy** /-əsē/ *n.*

Sé·mil·lon /sāmē(l)ˈyôN/ ▶*n.* a variety of white wine grape grown in France and elsewhere. ■ a white wine made from this grape. ▷French dialect, based on Latin *semen* 'seed.'

sem·i·lu·nar /,semēˈlo͞onər; ,sem,ī-/ ▶*adj. chiefly Anatomy* shaped like a half-moon or crescent. ▷late Middle English: from medieval Latin *semilunaris* (see SEMI-, LUNAR).

sem·i·lu·nar bone ▶*n.* another term for LUNATE BONE (see LUNATE).

sem·i·lu·nar car·ti·lage ▶*n.* a crescent-shaped cartilage in the knee.

sem·i·lu·nar valve ▶*n. Anatomy* each of a pair of valves in the heart, at the bases of the aorta and the pulmonary artery, consisting of three cusps or flaps that prevent the flow of blood back into the heart.

sem·i·ma·jor ax·is /ˈsemēˈmājər; ˈsem,ī-/ ▶*n. Geometry* either of the halves of the major axis of an ellipse.

sem·i·mi·nor ax·is /ˈsemēˈmīnər; ˈsem,ī-/ ▶*n. Geometry* either of the halves of the minor axis of an ellipse.

sem·i·mon·o·coque /,semēˈmänə,kōk; -,käk; ,sem,ī-/ ▶*adj.* relating to or denoting aircraft or vehicle structures combining a load-bearing shell with integral frames.

sem·i·month·ly /,semēˈmənTHlē; ,sem,ī-/ ▶*adj.* occurring or published twice a month: *semimonthly paydays.*

sem·i·nal /ˈsemənl/ ▶*adj.* **1** (of a work, event, moment, or figure) strongly influencing later developments: *his seminal work on chaos theory.* **2** of, relating to, or denoting semen. ■ *Botany* of, relating to, or derived from the seed of a plant. ▷late Middle English (sense 2): from Old French *seminal* or Latin *seminalis*, from *semen* 'seed.' Sense 1 dates from the mid 17th cent. **—sem·i·nal·ly** *adv.*

sem·i·nal ves·i·cle ▶*n. Anatomy* each of a pair of glands that open into the vas deferens near its junction with the urethra and secrete many of the components of semen.

sem·i·nar /ˈsemə,när/ ▶*n.* a conference or other meeting for discussion or training. ■ a class at a college or university in which a topic is discussed by a teacher and a small group of students. ▷late 19th cent.: from German *Seminar*, from Latin *seminarium* (see SEMINARY).

sem·i·nar·y /ˈsemə,nerē/ ▶*n.* (*pl.* **-nar·ies**) a college that prepares students to be priests, ministers, or rabbis. ■ *archaic, figurative* a place or thing in which something is developed or cultivated: *a seminary of sedition.* ■ *archaic* a private school or college, esp. one for young women. ▷late Middle English (denoting a seed plot): from Latin *seminarium* 'seed plot,' neuter of *seminarius* 'of seed,' from *semen* 'seed.' **—sem·i·nar·i·an** /,seməˈne(ə)rēən/ *n.* **—sem·i·na·rist** /-nərist/ *n.*

sem·i·nif·er·ous /,seməˈnif(ə)rəs/ ▶*adj.* producing or conveying semen. ▷late 17th cent.: from Latin *semen, semin-* 'seed' + -FEROUS.

Sem·i·nole /ˈsemə,nōl/ ▶*n.* (*pl.* same or **-noles**) **1** a member of an American Indian people of the Creek confederacy and their descendants, noted for resistance in the 19th century to encroachment on their land in Georgia and Florida. Many were resettled in Oklahoma. **2** either of the Muskogean languages, usually Creek, spoken by the Seminole.
▶*adj.* of or relating to the Seminole or their language. ▷from Creek *simanóli, simalóni*, from American Spanish *cimarrón* 'wild,'(as a noun) 'escaped slave'; compare with MAROON.

sem·i·o·chem·i·cal /,semē-ōˈkemikəl; ,sēmē-/ ▶*n. Biochemistry* a pheromone or other chemical that conveys a signal from one organism to another so as to modify the behavior of the recipient organism.

sem·i·of·fi·cial /,semēəˈfiSHəl; ,sem,ī-/ ▶*adj.* having some, but not full, official authority or recognition: *a semiofficial visit.* **—sem·i·of·fi·cial·ly** *adv.*

se·mi·ol·o·gy /,sēmēˈäləjē; ,semē-; ,sēm,ī- / ▶*n.* another term for SEMIOTICS. ▷early 20th cent.: from Greek *sēmeion* 'sign' (from *sēma* 'mark') + -LOGY. **—se·mi·o·log·i·cal** /-əˈläjikəl/ *adj.* **—se·mi·ol·o·gist** /-jist/ *n.*

sem·i·o·paque /,semē-ōˈpāk; ,sem,ī-/ ▶*adj.* not fully clear or transparent.

sem·i·op·er·a /,se,mēˈäp(ə)rə; ,sem,ī-/ ▶*n.* a drama or similar entertainment with a substantial proportion of vocal music in addition to instrumental movements.

sem·i·o·sis /,sēmēˈōsis; ,semē-; ,sem,ī-/ ▶*n. Linguistics* the process of signification in language or literature. ▷early 20th cent.: from Greek *sēmeiōsis* '(inference from) a sign.'

se·mi·ot·ics /,sēmēˈätiks; ,semē-; ,sem,ī-/ ▶*plural n.* [treated as *sing.*] the study of signs and symbols and their use or interpretation. ▷late 19th cent.: from Greek *sēmeiōtikos* 'of signs,' from *sēmeioun* 'interpret as a sign.' **—se·mi·ot·ic** *adj.* **—se·mi·ot·i·cal·ly** /-ik(ə)lē/ *adv.* **—se·mi·o·ti·cian** /,semēəˈtiSHən; ,sēmēə-/ *n.*

Se·mi·pa·la·tinsk /,semipəˈlätinsk; syimipəˈlätyinsk/ former name (until 1991) for SEMEI.

sem·i·pal·mat·ed /,semēˈpal,mātid; -ˈpä(l)-; ,sem,ī-/ ▶*adj.* used in names of wading birds that have toes webbed for part of their length, e.g., **semipalmated sandpiper**.

sem·i·per·ma·nent /,semēˈpərmənənt; ,sem,ī-/ ▶*adj.* less than permanent, but with some stability or endurance: *the company employs him on a semipermanent basis.* **—sem·i·per·ma·nent·ly** *adv.*

sem·i·per·me·a·ble /,semēˈpərmēəbəl; ,sem,ī-/ ▶*adj.* (of a material or membrane) allowing certain substances to pass through it but not others, esp. allowing the passage of a solvent but not of certain solutes.

sem·i·pre·cious /,semēˈpreSHəs; ,sem,ī-/ ▶*adj.* denoting minerals that can be used as gems but are considered to be less valuable than precious stones.

sem·i·pri·vate /,semēˈprīvit; ,sem,ī-/ ▶*adj.* combining public and private elements: *the design gives every unit its own façade and a semiprivate balcony.* ■ (of a hospital room) accommodating two patients.

sem·i·pro ▶*adj.* /,semēˈprō; ,semī-/ & *n.* /ˈsemē,prō; ˈsemī-/ (*pl.* **-pros**) *informal* short for SEMIPROFESSIONAL.

sem·i·pro·fes·sion·al /,semēprəˈfeSHənl; ,sem,ī-/ ▶*adj.* receiving payment for an activity but not relying entirely on it for a living: *a semiprofessional musician.* ■ involving or suitable for people engaged in an activity on such a basis: *training at the semiprofessional level.*
▶*n.* a person who is engaged in an activity on such a basis.

sem·i·qua·ver /,semēˈkwāvər/ ▶*n. Music, chiefly Brit.* a sixteenth note.

Se·mir·a·mis /səˈmirəməs/ *Greek Mythology* the daughter of an Assyrian goddess who married an Assyrian king. After his death she ruled for many years and became one of the founders of Babylon. She is thought to have been based on the historical queen Sammuramat (*c.*800 BC).

sem·i·re·tired /,semēriˈtī(ə)rd; ,semī-/ ▶*adj.* having retired or withdrawn from employment or an occupation but continuing to work part-time or occasionally. **—sem·i·re·tire·ment** /-ˈtī(ə)rmənt/ *n.*

sem·i·rig·id /,semēˈrijid; ,sem,ī-/ ▶*adj.* stiff and solid, but not inflexible: *a semirigid polyethylene hose.* ■ (of an airship) having a stiffened keel attached to a flexible gas container.

sem·i·skilled /,semēˈskild; ,sem,ī-/ ▶*adj.* (of work or a worker) having or needing some, but not extensive, training: *assembly lines of semiskilled workers.*

sem·i·sol·id /,semēˈsälid; ,sem,ī-/ ▶*adj.* highly viscous; slightly thicker than semifluid.

sem·i·sub·mers·i·ble /,semēsəbˈmərsəbəl; ,sem,ī-/ ▶*adj.* denoting an oil or gas drilling platform or barge with submerged pontoons able to be flooded with water when the vessel is anchored on site in order to provide stability.
▶*n.* an oil rig of this type.

sem·i·sweet /,semēˈswēt; ,sem,ī-/ ▶*adj.* (of food) slightly sweetened, but less so than normal: *semisweet chocolates.* ■ (of wine) neither dry nor sweet; slightly sweeter than medium dry.

sem·i·syn·thet·ic /,semēsinˈTHetik; ,sem,ī-/ ▶*adj. Chemistry* (of a substance) made by synthesis from a naturally occurring material.

Sem·ite /ˈsemīt/ ▶*n.* a member of any of the peoples who speak or spoke a Semitic language, including in particular the Jews and Arabs. ▷from modern Latin *Semita*, via late Latin from Greek *Sēm* 'Shem,' son of Noah in the Bible, from whom these people were traditionally supposed to be descended.

Se·mit·ic /səˈmitik/ ▶*adj.* **1** relating to or denoting a family of languages that includes Hebrew, Arabic, and Aramaic and certain ancient languages such as Phoenician and Akkadian, constituting the main subgroup of the Afro-Asiatic family. **2** of or relating to the peoples who speak these languages, esp. Hebrew and Arabic.

sem·i·tone /ˈsemē,tōn; ˈsem,ī-/ ▶*n. Music* the smallest interval used in classical Western music, equal to a twelfth of an octave or half a tone; a half step.

sem·i·trail·er /ˈsemē,trālər; ˈsem,ī-/ ▶*n.* a trailer having wheels at the back but supported at the front by a towing vehicle. ■ a tractor-trailer.

sem·i·trans·par·ent /,semētransˈpe(ə)rənt; ,sem,ī-; -ˈpar-/ ▶*adj.* partially or imperfectly transparent.

sem·i·trop·ics /,semēˈträpiks; ,sem,ī-/ ▶*plural n.* another term for SUBTROPICS. **—sem·i·trop·i·cal** /-ˈträpikəl/ *adj.*

sem·i·vow·el /ˈsemē,vouəl; ˈsem,ī-/ ▶*n.* a speech sound intermediate between a vowel and a consonant, e.g., *w* or *y*. ▷mid 16th cent.: from SEMI- + VOWEL, on the pattern of Latin *semivocalis*.

sem·i·week·ly /,semēˈwēklē; ,sem,ī-/ ▶*adj.* occurring twice a week.

Sem·mel·weis /ˈseməl,vīs/, Ignaz Philipp (1818–65), Hungarian obstetrician; Hungarian name *Ignác Fülöp Semmelweis*. He discovered the infectious character of puerperal fever and advocated rigorous cleanliness and the use of antiseptics by doctors examining patients.

sem·o·li·na /,seməˈlēnə/ ▶*n.* the hard grains left after the milling of flour, used in puddings and in pasta. ▷late 18th cent.: from Italian *semolino*, diminutive of *semola* 'bran,' from Latin *simila* 'flour.'

sem·per fi·de·lis /ˈsempər fiˈdālis/ (also **sem·per fi** ˈsempər ˈfī) ▶*adj.* always faithful (the motto of the U.S. Marine Corps). ▷Latin.

sem·per·vi·vum /,sempərˈvīvəm/ ▶*n.* a plant of a genus that includes the houseleek. • Genus *Sempervivum*, family Crassulaceae. ▷modern Latin, from Latin *semper* 'always' + *vivus* 'living.'

sem·pi·ter·nal /,sempəˈtərnl/ ▶*adj.* eternal and unchanging; everlasting: *his writings have the sempiternal youth of poetry.* ▷late Middle English: from Old French *sempiternel* or late Latin *sempiternalis*, from Latin *sempiternus*, from *semper* 'always' + *aeternus* 'eternal.' **—sem·pi·ter·nal·ly** *adv.* **—sem·pi·ter·ni·ty** /-ˈtərnitē/ *n.*

sem·pli·ce /ˈsempli,CHā/ ▶*adv. Music* (as a direction) in a simple style of performance. ▷Italian, literally 'simple.'

sem·pre /ˈsem,prā/ ▶*adv. Music* (in directions) throughout; always: *sempre forte.* ▷Italian.

semp·stress /ˈsem(p)stris/ ▶*n.* another term for SEAMSTRESS.

Sem·tex /ˈsem,teks/ ▶*n.* a very pliable, odorless plastic explosive. ▷1980s: probably a blend of *Semtin* (the name of a village in the Czech Republic near the place of production) and EXPLOSIVE.

sen /sen/ ▶*n.* (*pl.* same) a monetary unit of Brunei, Cambodia, Indonesia, and Malaysia, equal to one hundredth of a dollar in Brunei, one hundredth of a riel in Cambodia, one hundredth of a rupiah in Indonesia, and one hundredth of a ringgit in Malaysia.

[representing CENT.] ■ a former monetary unit in Japan, equal to one hundredth of a yen. [Japanese.]

Sen. ▸*abbr.* ■ Senate. ■ Senator. ■ Senior.

Se·na·na·ya·ke /ˌsäˌnänəˈyäkā/, Don Stephen (1884–1952), Sinhalese statesman; prime minister of Ceylon 1947–52. As prime minister he presided over Ceylon's achievement of full dominion status within the Commonwealth.

se·nar·ius /səˈne(ə)rēəs/ ▸*n.* (*pl.* **-nar·i·i** /-ˈne(ə)rēˌī; -ˈne(ə)rēˌē/) *Prosody* a Latin verse of six iambic feet. ▷mid 16th cent.: from Latin (see SENARY).

sen·a·ry /ˈsenərē/ ▸*adj. rare* relating to or based on the number six. ▷late 16th cent.: from Latin *senarius* 'containing six,' based on *sex* 'six.'

sen·ate /ˈsenit/ ▸*n.* any of various legislative or governing bodies, in particular: ■ the smaller upper assembly in the U.S. Congress, most U.S. states, France, and other countries. ■ the state council of the ancient Roman republic and empire, which shared legislative power with the popular assemblies, administration with the magistrates, and judicial power with the knights. ■ the governing body of a university or college. ▷Middle English: from Old French *senat*, from Latin *senatus*, from *senex* 'old man.'

sen·a·tor /ˈsenitər/ ▸*n.* a member of a senate. ▷Middle English (denoting a member of the ancient Roman senate): from Old French *senateur*, from Latin *senator* (see SENATE). **—sen·a·to·ri·al** /ˌsenəˈtôrēəl/ *adj.* **—sen·a·tor·ship** /-ˌSHip/ *n.*

sen·a·tor·i·al cour·tes·y /ˌsenəˈtôrēəl/ ▸*n.* a custom whereby presidential appointments are confirmed only if there is no objection to them by the senators from the appointee's state, esp. from the senior senator of the president's party from that state.

sen·a·tor·i·al dis·trict ▸*n.* an electoral division of a state that is represented by a senator in the state's senate.

S

send[1] /send/ ▸*v.* (*past* **sent** /sent/) **1** [*trans.*] cause to go or be taken to a particular destination; arrange for the delivery of, esp. by mail: *we sent a reminder letter but received no reply* | [with *two objs.*] *he sent her a nice little note.* ■ order or instruct to go to a particular destination or in a particular direction: *Clemons sent me to Bangkok for R&R.* ■ [*intrans.*] send a message or letter: *he sent to invite her to supper.* ■ [*trans.*] cause to move sharply or quickly; propel: *the volcano sent clouds of ash up four miles into the air.* ■ (**send someone to**) arrange for someone to go to (an institution) and stay there for a particular purpose: *many parents prefer to send their children to single-sex schools.* **2** [*trans.*] *informal* affect with powerful emotion; put into ecstasy: *it's the spectacle and music that send us, not the words.*

▸*phrasal v.* □ **send away for** order or request that (something) be sent to one: *you can send away for the recipe.* □ **send someone down** *Brit.* **1** expel a student from a university. **2** *informal* sentence someone to imprisonment: *you're going to get sent down for possessing drugs.* □ **send for** order or instruct (someone) to come to one; summon: *if you don't go I shall send for the police.* ■ order by mail: *send for our mail order catalog.* □ **send something in** submit material to be considered for a competition or possible publication: *don't forget to send in your entries for our summer competition.* □ **send off for** another way of saying SEND AWAY FOR above. □ **send someone off** instruct someone to go; arrange for someone's departure: *she sent him off to a lecturing engagement.* ■ (of a referee, esp. in soccer or rugby) order a player to leave the field and take no further part in the game: *the player was sent off for rough play.* □ **send something off** dispatch something by mail: *please take a moment or two to send off a check to a good cause.* □ **send something on** transmit mail or luggage to a further destination or in advance of one's own arrival: *I've got your catalog—would you like me to send it on?* □ **send out for something** order delivery of something: *we sent out for pizza.* □ **send something out 1** produce or give out something; emit something: *radar signals were sent out in powerful pulses.* **2** dispatch items to a number of people; distribute something widely: *the company sent out written information about the stock.* □ **send someone up** sentence someone to imprisonment: *he was sent up for arson.* □ **send someone/something up** *informal* give an exaggerated imitation of someone or something in order to ridicule them: *the humorist who sent up sacred cows like school spirit.* ▷Old English *sendan*, of Germanic origin; related to Dutch *zenden* and German *senden*. **—send·a·ble** *adj.* **—send·er** *n.*

▸PHRASES □ **send someone flying** cause someone to be knocked violently off balance or to the ground. □ **send someone packing** see PACK[1]. □ **send someone to the showers** see SHOWER. □ **send word** send a message: *he sent word that he was busy.*

send[2] ▸*n.* & *v.* variant spelling of SCEND.

Sen·dai /ˈsenˌdī/ a city in Japan, located near the northeastern coast of the island of Honshu; pop. 918,000.

Sen·dai vi·rus /ˈsenˌdī/ ▸*n. Biology* a parainfluenza virus that causes disease of the upper respiratory tract in mice and is used in the laboratory to produce cell fusion.

Sen·dak /ˈsenˌdak/, Maurice (Bernard) (1928–), U.S. writer and illustrator of children's books. He is best known for his award-winning *Where the Wild Things Are* (1963). He also wrote and illustrated *In the Night Kitchen* (1970) and *Outside Over There* (1981).

sen·dal /ˈsendl/ ▸*n. historical* a fine, rich silk material, chiefly used to make ceremonial robes and banners. ▷Middle English: from Old French *cendal*, ultimately from Greek *sindōn*.

Sen·de·ro Lu·mi·no·so /senˈderō ˌlo͞omiˈnōsō/ Spanish name for SHINING PATH.

send·ing /ˈsendiNG/ ▸*n.* an unpleasant or evil thing or creature supposedly sent by someone with paranormal or magical powers to warn, punish, or take revenge on a person. ▷mid 19th cent.: from Old Norse.

send-off ▸*n.* a celebratory demonstration of goodwill at a person's departure: *I got an affectionate send-off from my colleagues.*

send·up /ˈsendˌəp/ ▸*n. informal* an act of imitating someone or something in order to ridicule them; a parody: *a delicious sendup of a speech given by a trendy academic.*

se·ne /ˈsānā/ ▸*n.* (*pl.* same or **se·nes**) a monetary unit of Samoa, equal to one hundredth of a tala. ▷Samoan.

Sen·e·ca[1] /ˈsenəkə/, Lucius Annaeus (*c.*4 BC–AD 65), Roman statesman, philosopher, and playwright; known as **Seneca the Younger**. Son of Seneca the Elder, he became tutor to Nero in 49 and was appointed consul in 57. His *Epistulae Morales* is a notable Stoic work.

Sen·e·ca[2], Marcus (or Lucius) Annaeus (*c.*55 BC–*c.*AD 39), Roman rhetorician, born in Spain; known as **Seneca the Elder**. Father of Seneca the Younger, he is best known for his works on rhetoric, only parts of which survive.

Sen·e·ca[3] ▸*n.* (*pl.* same or **-cas**) **1** a member of an American Indian people that was one of the Five Nations. **2** the Iroquoian language of this people.

▸*adj.* of or relating to this people or their language. ▷via Dutch from Algonquian.

Sen·e·ca Falls a town in west central New York, west of Cayuga Lake, the site in 1848 of the first women's rights convention in the U.S.; pop. 9,384.

Sen·e·ca Lake the largest of the Finger Lakes in west central New York, south of Geneva, north of Watkins Glen.

se·ne·ci·o /sēˈnēsēō; -SHēō/ ▸*n.* (*pl.* **-ci·os**) a plant of a genus that includes the ragworts and groundsels. Many kinds are cultivated as ornamentals and some are poisonous weeds of grassland. • Genus *Senecio*, family Compositae. ▷modern Latin, from Latin, literally 'old man, groundsel,' with reference to the hairy white fruits.

Sen·e·gal /ˈsenəˌgôl; -ˌgäl/ a country on the coast of West Africa; pop. 10,852,000; capital, Dakar; languages, French (official), Wolof, and other West African languages. **—Sen·e·ga·lese** /ˌsenəgəˈlēz; -ˈlēs/ *adj.* & *n.*

Part of the Mali empire in the 14th and 15th centuries, the area was colonized by the French and became part of French West Africa in 1895. Briefly a partner in the Federation of Mali in 1959, Senegal withdrew and became a fully independent republic in 1960. The Gambia forms an enclave within Senegal.

Sen·e·gal Riv·er (also **Sénégal**) a river in western Africa that flows for 680 miles (1,088 km) from the Fouta Djallon of northern Guinea, through Mali and then along the Senegal-Mauritania border, to the Atlantic Ocean at St.-Louis in Senegal.

Sen·e·gam·bi·a /ˌseniˈgambēə; -ˈgäm-/ a region in West Africa that consists of the Senegal and Gambia rivers and the area between them. It lies mostly in Senegal and western Mali.

se·nesce /səˈnes/ ▸*v.* [*intrans.*] *Biology* (of a living organism) deteriorate with age. ▷mid 17th cent.: from Latin *senescere*, from *senex* 'old.'

se·nes·cence /səˈnesəns/ ▸*n. Biology* the condition or process of deterioration with age. ■ loss of a cell's power of division and growth. **—se·nes·cent** *adj.*

sen·e·schal /ˈsenəSHəl/ ▸*n.* **1** *historical* the steward or major-domo of a medieval great house. **2** *chiefly historical* a governor or other administrative or judicial officer. ▷Middle English: from Old French, from medieval Latin *seniscalus*, from a Germanic compound of words meaning 'old' and 'servant.'

sen·ex /ˈsenˌeks/ ▸*n.* (*pl.* **sen·es** /ˈsenˌēz/) (in literature, esp. comedy) an old man as a stock figure. ▷late 19th cent.: from Latin, 'old man.'

se·nhor /sēnˈyôr; sin-/ ▸*n.* (in Portuguese-speaking regions) a man (often used as a title or polite form of address): *Senhor Emílio Sofia Rosa.* ▷Portuguese, from Latin *senior* (see SENIOR).

se·nho·ra /sēnˈyôrə; sin-/ ▸*n.* (in Portuguese-speaking regions) a woman, esp. a married woman (often used as a title or polite form of address): *I look forward to hearing what Senhora Rocha decides.* ▷Portuguese, feminine of SENHOR.

se·nho·ri·ta /ˌsēnyəˈrētə/ ▸*n.* (in Portuguese-speaking regions) a young woman, esp. an unmarried one (often used as a title or polite form of address). ▷Portuguese, diminutive of SENHORA.

se·nile /ˈsēˌnīl; ˈsen-/ ▸*adj.* (of a person) having or showing the weaknesses or diseases of old age, esp. a loss of mental faculties: *she couldn't cope with her senile husband.* ■ (of a condition) characteristic of or caused by old age: *senile decay.* ■ *Geology* approaching the end of a cycle of erosion.

▸*n.* a senile person: *you never know where you stand with these so-called seniles.* ▷mid 17th cent.: from French *sénile* or Latin *senilis*, from *senex* 'old man.' **—se·nil·i·ty** /siˈnilitē/ *n.*

se·nile de·men·tia ▸*n.* severe mental deterioration in old age, characterized by loss of memory and control of bodily functions.

se·nile plaque ▸*n. Medicine* a microscopic mass of fragmented and decaying nerve terminals around an amyloid core, numbers of which occur in the brains of people with Alzheimer's disease.

sen·ior /ˈsēnyər/ ▸*adj.* **1** of a more advanced age: *he is 20 years senior to Leonard.* ■ of or for students in the final year of college or high school. ■ relating to or denoting competitors of above a certain age or of the highest status in a particular sport. ■ *Brit.* of, for, or denoting schoolchildren above a certain age, typically eleven. ■ (often **Senior**) [*postpositive*] (in names) denoting the elder of two who have the same name in a family, esp. a father as distinct from his son: *Henry James senior.* **2** holding a high and authoritative position: *he is a senior Finance Ministry official.* ■ [*predic.*] (**senior to**) holding a higher position than: *the people senior to me in my department.*

▸*n.* a person who is a specified number of years older than someone else: *she was only two years his senior.* ■ an elderly person, esp. one who is retired and living on a pension. ■ a student in the final year of college or high school. ■ *Brit.* a student in a school for older children, esp. those eleven and over. ■ a competitor of above a certain age or of the highest status in a particular sport: *at fourteen you move up to the seniors.* ▷late Middle English: from Latin, literally 'older, older man,' comparative of *senex*, *sen-* 'old man, old.' **—sen·ior·i·ty** /sēnˈyôritē; -ˈyär-/ *n.*

sen·ior chief pet·ty of·fi·cer ▸*n.* a noncommissioned officer in the U.S. Navy or Coast Guard ranking above chief petty officer and below master chief petty officer.

sen·ior cit·i·zen ▸*n.* an elderly person, esp. one who is retired and living on a pension.

sen·ior com·mon room ▸*n. Brit.* a room used for social purposes by fellows, lecturers, and other senior members of a college. ■ [treated as *sing.* or *pl.*] the senior members of a college regarded collectively.

sen·ior high school ▸*n.* a secondary school typically comprising the three highest grades.

sen·ior mas·ter ser·geant ▸*n.* a noncommissioned

officer in the U.S. Air Force ranking above master sergeant and below chief master sergeant.

sen·i·ti /ˈsenitē/ ▶*n.* (*pl.* same) a monetary unit of Tonga, equal to one hundredth of a pa'anga. ▷Tongan.

sen·na /ˈsenə/ ▶*n.* the cassia tree. ■ a laxative prepared from the dried pods of this tree. ▷mid 16th cent.: from medieval Latin *sena*, from Arabic *sanā*.

Sen·nach·er·ib /səˈnakəˌrib/ (died 681 BC) king of Assyria 705–681; son of Sargon II. In 701, he put down a Jewish rebellion and laid siege to Jerusalem but spared it from destruction (according to 2 Kings 19:35). He also rebuilt the city of Nineveh and made it his capital.

sen·net /ˈsenit/ ▶*n.* (in the stage directions of Elizabethan plays) a call on a trumpet or cornet to signal the ceremonial entrance or exit of an actor. ▷late 16th cent.: perhaps a variant of **SIGNET**.

Senn·ett /ˈsenit/, Mack (1880–1960), U.S. movie director, producer, and actor; born in Canada; born *Michael Sinnott*. He produced more than 1,000 slapstick comedy shorts and created the Keystone Kops. Although he graduated to longer and sometimes more serious movies, he was presented with a special Academy Award in 1938 that honored his accomplishments in comedy technique.

sen·night /ˈsenīt/ ▶*n. archaic* a week. ▷Old English *seofon nihta* 'seven nights.'

sen·nit /ˈsenit/ (also **sin·net**) ▶*n.* plaited straw, hemp, or similar fibrous material used in making hats. ■ *Nautical* braided cordage in flat, round, or square form, used for making mats, lashings, etc. ▷early 17th cent.: of unknown origin.

se·ñor /sānˈyôr; sen-/ ▶*n.* (*pl.* **se·ño·res** /sānˈyôrāz; senˈyôres/ or **se·ñors**) a title or form of address used of or to a Spanish-speaking man, corresponding to *Mr.* or *sir*: *he is certain his information is correct, señor.* ▷Spanish, from Latin *senior* (see **SENIOR**).

se·ño·ra /sānˈyôrə; sen-/ ▶*n.* a title or form of address used of or to a Spanish-speaking woman, corresponding to *Mrs.* or *madam*: *Señora Dolores.* ▷Spanish, feminine of **SEÑOR**.

se·ño·ri·ta /ˌsānyəˈrētə; ˌsen-/ ▶*n.* a title or form of address used of or to a Spanish-speaking unmarried woman, corresponding to *Miss*: *a beautiful señorita.* ▷Spanish, diminutive of **SEÑORA**.

Senr. ▶*abbr.* Senior.

sen·sate /ˈsenˌsāt/ ▶*adj. poetic/literary* able to perceive with the senses; sensing: *the infant stretches, sensate, wakening.* ■ perceived by the senses: *you are immersed in an illusory, yet sensate, world.* ▷mid 17th cent.: from late Latin *sensatus* 'having senses,' from *sensus* (see **SENSE**).

sen·sa·tion /senˈsāsʜən/ ▶*n.* **1** a physical feeling or perception resulting from something that happens to or comes into contact with the body: *a burning sensation in the middle of the chest.* ■ the capacity to have such feelings or perceptions: *they had lost sensation in one or both forearms.* ■ an inexplicable awareness or impression: [with *clause*] *she had the eerie* ***sensation that*** *she was being watched.* **2** a widespread reaction of interest and excitement: *his arrest for poisoning* ***caused a sensation.*** ■ a person, object, or event that arouses such interest and excitement: *she was a sensation, the talk of the evening.* ▷early 17th cent.: from medieval Latin *sensatio(n-)*, from Latin *sensus* (see **SENSE**).

sen·sa·tion·al /senˈsāsʜənl/ ▶*adj.* (of an event, a person, or a piece of information) causing great public interest and excitement: *a sensational murder trial.* ■ (of an account or a publication) presenting information in a way that is intended to provoke public interest and excitement, at the expense of accuracy: *cheap sensational periodicals.* ■ *informal* very good indeed; very impressive or attractive: *you look sensational | a sensational view.* **—sen·sa·tion·al·ly** *adv.*

sen·sa·tion·al·ism /senˈsāsʜənlˌizəm/ ▶*n.* **1** (esp. in journalism) the use of exciting or shocking stories or language at the expense of accuracy, in order to provoke public interest or excitement: *media sensationalism.* **2** *Philosophy* another term for **PHENOMENALISM**. **—sen·sa·tion·al·ist** *n.* & *adj.* **—sen·sa·tion·al·is·tic** /senˌsāsʜənlˈistik/ *adj.*

sen·sa·tion·al·ize /senˈsāsʜənlˌīz/ ▶*v.* [*trans.*] (esp. of a newspaper) present information about (something) in a way that provokes public interest and excitement, at the expense of accuracy: *the papers want to sensationalize the tragedy that my family has suffered.*

sense /sens/ ▶*n.* **1** a faculty by which the body perceives an external stimulus; one of the faculties of sight, smell, hearing, taste, and touch: *the bear has a keen sense of smell that enables it to hunt at dusk.* **2** a feeling that something is the case: *she had the sense of being a political outsider.* ■ an awareness or feeling that one is in a specified state: *you can improve your general health and sense of well-being.* ■ (**sense of**) a keen intuitive awareness of or sensitivity to the presence or importance of something: *she had a fine sense of comic timing.* **3** a sane and realistic attitude to situations and problems: *he earned respect by the good sense he showed at meetings.* ■ a reasonable or comprehensible rationale: *I can't* ***see the sense*** *in leaving all the work to you.* **4** a way in which an expression or a situation can be interpreted; a meaning: *it is not clear which sense of the word "characters" is intended in this passage.* **5** *chiefly Mathematics Physics* a property, e.g., direction of motion, distinguishing a pair of objects, quantities, effects, etc., that differ only in that each is the reverse of the other. ■ [as *adj.*] *Genetics* relating to or denoting a coding sequence of nucleotides, complementary to an antisense sequence.

▶*v.* [*trans.*] perceive by a sense or senses: *with the first frost, they could sense a change in the days.* ■ be aware of: *she could sense her father's anger rising.* ■ [with *clause*] be aware that something is the case without being able to define exactly how one knows: *he could sense that he wasn't liked.* ■ (of a machine or similar device) detect: *an optical fiber senses a current flowing in a conductor.* ▷late Middle English (as a noun in the sense 'meaning'): from Latin *sensus* 'faculty of feeling, thought, meaning,' from *sentire* 'feel.' The verb dates from the mid 16th cent.

▶*PHRASES* □ **bring someone to their** (or **come to one's**) **senses** restore someone to (or regain) consciousness. ■ cause someone to (or start to) think and behave reasonably after a period of folly or irrationality. □ **in a** (or **one**) **sense** used to indicate a particular interpretation of a statement or situation: *in a sense, behavior cannot develop independently of the environment.* □ **in one's senses** fully aware and in control of one's thoughts and words; sane: *would any man in his senses invent so absurd a story?* □ **make sense** be intelligible, justifiable, or practicable. □ **make sense of** find meaning or coherence in: *she must try to make sense of what was going on.* □ **out of one's senses** in or into a state of insanity. □ **a sense of direction** a person's ability to know without explicit guidance the direction in which they are or should be moving. □ **take leave of one's senses** (in hyperbolic use) go insane.

sense da·tum ▶*n. Philosophy* an immediate object of perception, which is not a material object; a sense impression.

sen·sei /ˈsenˌsā; senˈsā/ ▶*n.* (*pl.* same) (in martial arts) a teacher: [as *title*] *Sensei Ritchie began work.* ▷Japanese, from *sen* 'previous' + *sei* 'birth.'

sense·less /ˈsensləs/ ▶*adj.* **1** [often as *complement*] (of a person) unconscious: *the attack left a policeman beaten senseless.* ■ incapable of sensation: *she knocked the glass from the girl's senseless fingers.* **2** (esp. of violent or wasteful action) without discernible meaning or purpose: *in Vietnam, I saw the senseless waste of human beings.* ■ lacking common sense; wildly foolish: *it was as senseless as crossing Death Valley on foot.* **—sense·less·ly** *adv.* **—sense·less·ness** *n.*

sense or·gan ▶*n.* an organ of the body that responds to external stimuli by conveying impulses to the sensory nervous system.

sen·si·bil·i·ty /ˌsensəˈbilitē/ ▶*n.* (*pl.* **-ties**) the ability to appreciate and respond to complex emotional or aesthetic influences; sensitivity: *the study of literature leads to a growth of intelligence and sensibility.* ■ (**sensibilities**) a person's delicate sensitivity that makes them readily offended or shocked: *the scale of the poverty revealed by the survey shocked people's sensibilities.* ■ *dated Zoology* sensitivity to sensory stimuli. ▷late Middle English (denoting the power of sensation): from late Latin *sensibilitas*, from *sensibilis* 'that can be perceived by the senses' (see **SENSIBLE**).

sen·si·ble /ˈsensəbəl/ ▶*adj.* **1** (of a statement or course of action) chosen in accordance with wisdom or prudence; likely to be of benefit: *I cannot believe that it is sensible to spend so much | a sensible diet.* ■ (of a person) possessing or displaying prudence: *he was a sensible and capable boy.* ■ (of an object) practical and functional rather than decorative: *Mom always made me have sensible shoes.* **2** *archaic* readily perceived; appreciable: *it will effect a sensible reduction in these figures.* See note at **TANGIBLE**. ■ [*predic.*] (**sensible of/to**) able to notice or appreciate; not unaware of: *we are sensible of the difficulties he faces.* ▷late Middle English (also in the sense 'perceptible by the senses'): from Old French, or from Latin *sensibilis*, from *sensus* (see **SENSE**). **—sen·si·ble·ness** *n.* **—sen·si·bly** /-blē/ *adv.*

THE RIGHT WORD **lucid, rational, sagacious, sane, sensible**

A **sensible** person brings an umbrella when rain is forecast. A **rational** one studies the weather map, observes the movement of the clouds across the sky, listens to the forecast on the radio, and then decides whether or not an umbrella is necessary.

Sensible implies the use of common sense and an appreciation of the value of experience (*a sensible decision not to travel until his injuries had healed*), while *rational* suggests the ability to reason logically and to draw conclusions from inferences (*a rational explanation for why she failed the exam*).

Lucid and **sane**, like *rational*, are associated with coherent thinking. *Lucid* suggests a mind free of internal pressures or distortions (*lucid intervals during which he was able to recognize his wife and children*), while *sane* indicates freedom from psychosis or mental derangement (*judged to have been sane when she committed the crime*). *Sane* also has a meaning very close to that of *sensible* (*a sane approach to disciplining problem teenagers*).

A **sagacious** person is an extremely shrewd one who is both discerning and practical. He or she can look out the window and tell whether it's going to rain by studying the facial expressions of passersby as they glance nervously at the sky.

sen·sil·lum /senˈsiləm/ ▶*n.* (*pl.* **-sil·la** /-ˈsilə/) *Zoology* (in arthropods and some other invertebrates) a simple sensory receptor consisting of a modified cell or small group of cells of the cuticle or epidermis, typically hair- or rod-shaped. ▷early 20th cent.: modern Latin, diminutive of Latin *sensus* 'sense.'

sen·si·tive /ˈsensitiv/ ▶*adj.* **1** quick to detect or respond to slight changes, signals, or influences: *the new method of protein detection was more sensitive than earlier ones | spiders are* ***sensitive to*** *vibrations on their web.* ■ easily damaged, injured, or distressed by slight changes: *the committee called for improved protection of wildlife in environmentally sensitive areas.* ■ (of photographic materials) prepared so as to respond rapidly to the action of light. ■ (of a market) unstable and liable to quick changes of price because of outside influences. **2** (of a person or a person's behavior) having or displaying a quick and delicate appreciation of others' feelings: *I pay tribute to the Minister for his sensitive handling of the bill.* ■ easily offended or upset: *I suppose I shouldn't be so sensitive.* **3** kept secret or with restrictions on disclosure to avoid endangering security: *he was suspected of passing sensitive information to other countries.*

▶*n.* a person who is believed to respond to occult influences. ▷late Middle English (in the sense 'sensory'): from Old French *sensitif, -ive* or medieval Latin *sensitivus*, formed irregularly from Latin *sentire* 'feel.' The current senses date from the early 19th cent. **—sen·si·tive·ly** *adv.* **—sen·si·tive·ness** *n.*

sen·si·tive pe·ri·od ▶*n. Psychology* a time or stage in a person's development when they are more responsive to certain stimuli and quicker to learn particular skills.

sen·si·tive plant ▶*n.* **1** a tropical American plant of the pea family, whose leaflets fold together and leaves bend down when touched. A common weed of sugar cane, it has become naturalized throughout the tropics. • *Mimosa pudica*, family Leguminosae. **2** *figurative* a delicate or sensitive person.

sen·si·tiv·i·ty /ˌsensiˈtivitē/ ▶*n.* (*pl.* **-ties**) the quality or condition of being sensitive: *a total lack of common decency and sensitivity | he has* ***a sensitivity to*** *cow's milk.* ■ (**sensitivities**) a person's feelings which might be easily offended or hurt; sensibilities: *the only rules that matter are practical ones that respect local sensitivities.*

sen·si·tiv·i·ty train·ing ▶*n.* training intended to sensitize people to their attitudes and behaviors that may unwittingly cause offense to others, esp. members of various minorities.

sen·si·tize /ˈsensiˌtīz/ ▶*v.* [*trans.*] cause (someone or something) to respond to certain stimuli; make sensitive: *the introductory section aims to* ***sensitize*** *students* ***to*** *the methodology of the course.* ■ make (photographic film) sensitive to light: *the kit sensitizes any 35 mm film in hours.* ■ (often **be sensitized to**) make (an organism) abnormally sensitive to a foreign substance: *the workers had been immunologically sensitized to the* *enzyme.* —**sen·si·ti·za·tion** /ˌsensitiˈzāsʜən/ *n.* —**sen·si·tiz·er** *n.*

sen·si·tom·e·ter /ˌsensiˈtämitər/ ▸*n. Photography* a device for measuring the sensitivity of photographic equipment to light.

sen·sor /ˈsensər/ ▸*n.* a device that detects or measures a physical property and records, indicates, or otherwise responds to it. ▷1950s: from **SENSORY**, on the pattern of *motor.*

sen·so·ri·mo·tor /ˌsensərēˈmōtər/ ▸*adj.* [*attrib.*] *Physiology* (of nerves or their actions) having or involving both sensory and motor functions or pathways.

sen·so·ri·neu·ral /ˌsensərēˈn(y)o͝orəl/ ▸*adj. Medicine* (of hearing loss) caused by a lesion or disease of the inner ear or the auditory nerve.

sen·so·ri·um /senˈsôrēəm/ ▸*n.* (*pl.* **-so·ri·a** /-ˈsôrēə/ or **-so·ri·ums**) the sensory apparatus or faculties considered as a whole: *virtual reality technology directed at recreating the human sensorium.* ▷mid 17th cent.: from late Latin, from Latin *sens-* 'perceived,' from the verb *sentire.* —**sen·so·ri·al** /-ˈsôrēəl/ *adj.* —**sen·so·ri·al·ly** /-ˈsôrēəlē/ *adv.*

sen·so·ry /ˈsensərē/ ▸*adj.* of or relating to sensation or the physical senses; transmitted or perceived by the senses: *sensory input.* ▷mid 18th cent.: from Latin *sens-* 'perceived' (from the verb *sentire*) or from the noun **SENSE** + **-ORY**[2]. —**sen·so·ri·ly** /-rəlē/ *adv.*

sen·so·ry dep·ri·va·tion ▸*n.* a process by which someone is deprived of normal external stimuli such as sight and sound for an extended period of time, esp. as an experimental technique in psychology.

sen·su·al /ˈsensʜo͞oəl/ ▸*adj.* of or arousing gratification of the senses and physical, esp. sexual, pleasure: *the production of the ballet is sensual and passionate.* See note at **SENSUOUS**. ▷late Middle English (in the sense 'sensory'): from late Latin *sensualis*, from *sensus* (see **SENSE**). —**sen·su·al·ism** /-ˌlizəm/ *n.* —**sen·su·al·ist** /-ist/ *n.* —**sen·su·al·ize** /-ˌlīz/ *v.* —**sen·su·al·ly** *adv.*

S

USAGE The words **sensual** and **sensuous** are frequently used interchangeably to mean 'gratifying the senses,' esp. in a sexual sense. Strictly speaking, this goes against a traditional distinction, by which **sensuous** is a more neutral term, meaning 'relating to the senses rather than the intellect' (*swimming is a beautiful, **sensuous** experience*), while **sensual** relates to gratification of the senses, esp. sexually (*a **sensual** massage*). In fact, the word **sensuous** is thought to have been invented by John Milton (1641) in a deliberate attempt to avoid the sexual overtones of **sensual**. In practice the connotations are such that it is difficult to use **sensuous** in Milton's sense. While traditionalists struggle to maintain a distinction, the evidence suggests that the neutral use of **sensuous** is rare in modern English. If a neutral use is intended, it is advisable to use alternative wording.

sen·su·al·i·ty /ˌsensʜo͞oˈalitē/ ▸*n.* the enjoyment, expression, or pursuit of physical, esp. sexual, pleasure: *he ate the grapes with surprising sensuality.* ■ the condition of being pleasing or fulfilling to the senses: *life can dazzle with its sensuality, its color.* ▷Middle English (denoting the animal side of human nature): from Old French *sensualite*, from late Latin *sensualitas*, from *sensualis* (see **SENSUAL**).

sen·su la·to /ˈsenso͞o ˈlätō/ ▸*adv. formal* in the broad sense. ▷Latin.

sen·sum /ˈsensəm/ ▸*n.* (*pl.* **-sa** /-sə/) *Philosophy* a sense datum. ▷mid 19th cent.: modern Latin, 'something sensed,' neuter past participle of Latin *sentire* 'feel.'

sen·su·ous /ˈsensʜo͞oəs/ ▸*adj.* **1** relating to or affecting the senses rather than the intellect: *the work showed a deliberate disregard of the more sensuous and immediately appealing aspects of painting.* **2** attractive or gratifying physically, esp. sexually: *her voice was rather deep but very sensuous.* ▷mid 17th cent.: from Latin *sensus* 'sense' + **-OUS**. —**sen·su·ous·ly** *adv.* —**sen·su·ous·ness** *n.*

USAGE On the use of the words **sensuous** and **sensual**, see **usage** at **SENSUAL**.

THE RIGHT WORD **epicurean, luxurious, sensuous, sybaritic, voluptuous**

Sensuous implies gratification of the senses for the sake of aesthetic pleasure, or delight in the color, sound, or form of something (*a dress made from a soft, sensuous fabric*).

Luxurious implies indulgence in sensuous pleasures, especially those that induce a feeling of physical comfort or satisfaction (*a luxurious satin coverlet*), while **epicurean** refers to taking delight in the pleasures of eating and drinking (*the epicurean life of a king and his courtiers*).

To be **voluptuous** is to give oneself up to the pleasures of the senses (*the symphony is voluptuous in its scoring*), but it carries a suggestion of physical pleasure and can refer to a curvaceous and sexually attractive woman (*he was seen with a voluptuous blonde*).

Sybaritic implies an overrefined luxuriousness, also suggesting indulgence in good food and drink and the presence of things designed to soothe and charm the senses (*he lived alone, in sybaritic splendor*).

sen·su stric·to /ˈsenso͞o ˈstriktō/ ▸*adv. formal* strictly speaking; in the narrow sense: *the process was one of substitution rather than change sensu stricto.* ▷Latin, 'in the restricted sense.'

sent[1] /sent/ ▸ past and past participle of **SEND**[1].

sent[2] ▸*n.* (*pl.* **sent·i** /ˈsentē/) a monetary unit of Estonia, equal to one hundredth of a kroon. ▷respelling of **CENT**.

sen·te /ˈsenˌtē/ ▸*n.* (*pl.* **li·sen·te** /liˈsentē/) a monetary unit of Lesotho, equal to one hundredth of a loti. ▷Sesotho.

sen·tence /ˈsentns/ ▸*n.* **1** a set of words that is complete in itself, typically containing a subject and predicate, conveying a statement, question, exclamation, or command, and consisting of a main clause and sometimes one or more subordinate clauses. ■ *Logic* a series of signs or symbols expressing a proposition in an artificial or logical language. **2** the punishment assigned to a defendant found guilty by a court: *her husband is **serving** a three-year **sentence for** fraud.* ■ the punishment fixed by law for a particular offense: *slander of an official carried an eight-year prison sentence.*
▸*v.* [*trans.*] declare the punishment decided for (an offender): *ten army officers were **sentenced to** death.* ▷Middle English (in the senses 'way of thinking, opinion,' 'court's declaration of punishment,' and 'gist (of a piece of writing)'): via Old French from Latin *sententia* 'opinion,' from *sentire* 'feel, be of the opinion.'
▸*PHRASE* □ **under sentence of** having been condemned to: *he was under sentence of death.*

sen·tence ad·verb ▸*n. Grammar* an adverb or adverbial phrase that expresses a writer's or speaker's attitude to the content of the sentence in which it occurs (such as *frankly, obviously*), or places the sentence in a particular context (such as *technically, politically*).

USAGE The traditional definition of an adverb is that it is a word that modifies the meaning of a verb, an adjective, or another adverb, as in, for example, *he shook his head **sadly***. However, another important function of some adverbs is to comment on a whole sentence. For example, in the sentence ***sadly**, he is rather overbearing*, **sadly** expresses the speaker's attitude to what is being stated. Traditionalists take the view that the use of sentence adverbs is inherently suspect and that they should always be paraphrased, using wording such as ***it is sad that** he is rather overbearing.* A particular objection is raised to the sentence adverbs **hopefully** and **thankfully**, since they cannot be paraphrased in the usual way (see **usage** at **HOPEFULLY** and **THANKFULLY**). However, there is overwhelming evidence that such usages are well established and widely accepted in everyday speech and writing.

sen·ten·tial /senˈtenᴄʜəl/ ▸*adj. Grammar & Logic* of or relating to a sentence: *sentential meaning.*

sen·ten·tious /senˈtenᴄʜəs/ ▸*adj.* given to moralizing in a pompous or affected manner: *he tried to encourage his men with sententious rhetoric.* ▷late Middle English: from Latin *sententiosus*, from *sententia* 'opinion' (see **SENTENCE**). The original sense was 'full of meaning or wisdom,' later becoming depreciatory. —**sen·ten·tious·ly** *adv.* —**sen·ten·tious·ness** *n.*

sen·tient /ˈsenᴄʜ(ē)ənt/ ▸*adj.* able to perceive or feel things: *she had been instructed from birth in the equality of all sentient life forms.* ▷early 17th cent.: from Latin *sentient-* 'feeling,' from the verb *sentire.* —**sen·tience** *n.* —**sen·tient·ly** *adv.*

sen·ti·ment /ˈsen(t)əmənt/ ▸*n.* **1** a view of or attitude toward a situation or event; an opinion: *I agree with your sentiments regarding the road bridge.* ■ general feeling or opinion: *the council sought steps to control the rise of racist sentiment.* See note at **OPINION**. ■ *archaic* the expression of a view or desire esp. as formulated for a toast. **2** a feeling or emotion: *an intense sentiment of horror.* See note at **EMOTION**. ■ exaggerated and self-indulgent feelings of tenderness, sadness, or nostalgia: *many of the appeals rely on treacly sentiment.* ▷late Middle English (in the senses 'personal experience' and 'physical feeling, sensation'): from Old French *sentement*, from medieval Latin *sentimentum*, from Latin *sentire* 'feel.'

sen·ti·men·tal /ˌsen(t)əˈmen(t)l/ ▸*adj.* of or prompted by feelings of tenderness, sadness, or nostalgia: *she felt a sentimental attachment to the place creep over her.* ■ (of a work of literature, music, or art) dealing with feelings of tenderness, sadness, or nostalgia in an exaggerated and self-indulgent way: *a sentimental ballad.* ■ (of a person) excessively prone to feelings of tenderness, sadness, or nostalgia: *I'm a sentimental old fool.* —**sen·ti·men·tal·ly** *adv.*
▸*PHRASE* □ **sentimental value** the value of something to someone because of personal or emotional associations rather than material worth.

THE RIGHT WORD **effusive, maudlin, mawkish, mushy, romantic, sentimental**

If you are moved to tears by a situation that does not necessarily warrant such a response, you're likely to be called **sentimental**, an adjective used to describe a willingness to get emotional at the slightest prompting (*a sentimental man who kept his dog's ashes in an urn on the mantel*).

Effusive applies to excessive or insincere displays of emotion, although it may be used in an approving sense (*effusive in her gratitude for the help she had received*).

Maudlin derives from the name Mary Magdalene, who was often shown with her eyes swollen from weeping. It implies a lack of self-restraint, particularly in the form of excessive tearfulness.

Mawkish carries sentimentality a step further, implying emotion so excessive that it provokes loathing or disgust (*mawkish attempts to win the audience over*).

Although **romantic** at one time referred to an expression of deep feeling, nowadays it is often used disapprovingly to describe emotion that has little to do with the way things actually are and that is linked to an idealized vision of the way they should be (*she had a romantic notion of what it meant to be a "starving artist"*).

Mushy suggests both excessive emotion or sentimentality and a contempt for romantic love (*a mushy love story*).

sen·ti·men·tal·ism /ˌsen(t)əˈmen(t)lˌizəm/ ▸*n.* the excessive expression of feelings of tenderness, sadness, or nostalgia in behavior, writing, or speech: *the author blends realism with surrealism, journalism with sentimentalism.* —**sen·ti·men·tal·ist** *n.*

sen·ti·men·tal·i·ty /ˌsen(t)əmenˈtalitē; -mən-/ ▸*n.* (*pl.* **-ties**) excessive tenderness, sadness, or nostalgia: *there are passages which verge on sentimentality | sentimentalities of this kind seem reserved, in her, for people she does not know.*

sen·ti·men·tal·ize /ˌsen(t)əˈmen(t)lˌīz/ ▸*v.* [*trans.*] treat (someone or something) with exaggerated and self-indulgent feelings of tenderness, sadness, or nostalgia: [as *adj.*] (**sentimentalized**) *the impossibly sentimentalized and saintly ideal of the Virgin Mother.* —**sen·ti·men·tal·i·za·tion** /-ˌmen(t)liˈzāsʜən/ *n.*

sen·ti·nel /ˈsentn-əl/ ▸*n.* a soldier or guard whose job is to stand and keep watch. ■ *figurative* something that appears to be standing guard or keeping watch. ■ *Medicine* a thing that acts as an indicator of the presence of disease: [as *adj.*] *the first national HIV sentinel surveillance program in the developing world.*
▸*v.* (**-neled**, **-nel·ing**; *chiefly Brit.* **-nelled**, **-nel·ling**) [*trans.*] station a soldier or guard by (a place) to keep watch: *a wide course had been roped off and **sentineled with** police | figurative trees sentineled the trenches.* ▷late 16th cent.: from French *sentinelle*, from Italian *sentinella*, of unknown origin.
▸*PHRASE* □ **stand sentinel** (of a soldier) keep watch: *soldiers stood sentinel with their muskets | figurative a tall round tower standing sentinel over the river.*

sen·try /ˈsentrē/ ▸*n.* (*pl.* **-tries**) a soldier stationed to keep guard or to control access to a place. ▷early 17th cent.: perhaps from obsolete *centrinel*, variant of **SENTINEL**.
▸*PHRASE* □ **stand sentry** keep guard or control access to a place.

sen·try box ▸*n.* a structure providing shelter for a standing sentry.

sen·try-go ▸*n. Military* the duty of being a sentry.

Se·nu·fo /səˈno͞ofō/ ▸*n.* **1** (*pl.* same) a member of a people inhabiting parts of the Ivory Coast, Mali, and Burkina Faso. **2** the Gur language of this people.

▸*adj.* of or relating to this people or their language. ▷Akan.

Se·nus·si /sə'nōōsē/ ▸*n.* (*pl.* same or **-sis**) a member of a North African Muslim religious fraternity founded in 1837 by Sidi Muhammad ibn Ali es-Senussi (d.1859).

Seoul /sōl/ the capital of South Korea, located in the northwestern part of the country, on the Han River; pop. 10,628,000. It was the capital of the Korean Yi dynasty from the late 14th century until 1910, when Korea was annexed by the Japanese. Extensively developed under Japanese rule, it became the capital of South Korea after the partition of 1945.

sep. ▸*abbr.* ■ sepal. ■ separable. ■ separate. ■ separated. ■ separation.

se·pal /'sēpəl/ ▸*n. Botany* each of the parts of the calyx of a flower, enclosing the petals and typically green and leaflike. ▷early 19th cent.: from French *sépale*, modern Latin *sepalum*, from Greek *skepē* 'covering,' influenced by French *pétale* 'petal.'

sep·a·ra·ble /'sep(ə)rəbəl/ ▸*adj.* able to be separated or treated separately: *body and soul are not separable.* ■ *Grammar* (of a German prefix) separated from the base verb when inflected. ■ *Grammar* (of a German verb) consisting of a prefix and a base verb that are separated when inflected, e.g., *einführen.* ■ *Grammar* (of an English phrasal verb) allowing the insertion of the direct object between the base verb and the particle, e.g., *look it over* as opposed to *go over it.* ▷late Middle English: from Latin *separabilis*, from *separare* 'disjoin, divide' (see SEPARATE). **—sep·a·ra·bil·i·ty** /,sep(ə)rə'bilitē/ *n.* **—sep·a·ra·ble·ness** *n.* **—sep·a·ra·bly** /-blē/ *adv.*

sep·a·rate ▸*adj.* /'sep(ə)rit/ forming or viewed as a unit apart or by itself: *this raises two separate issues | he regards the study of literature as quite* ***separate from*** *life.* ■ not joined or touching physically: *hostels with separate quarters for men and women.* ■ different; distinct: *melt the white and dark chocolate in separate bowls.*

▸*v.* /'sepə,rāt/ **1** [*trans.*] cause to move or be apart: *police were trying to separate two rioting mobs | they were separated by the war.* ■ form a distinction or boundary between (people, places, or things): *only a footpath separated their garden from the shore | six years separated the two brothers.* ■ [*intrans.*] become detached or disconnected: *the second stage of the rocket failed to separate.* ■ [*intrans.*] leave another person's company: *they separated at the corner, agreeing to meet within two hours.* ■ [*intrans.*] stop living together as a couple: *after her parents separated, she was brought up by her mother* | [as *adj.*] (**separated**) *her parents are separated.* ■ (often **be separated**) discharge or dismiss (someone) from service or employment: *this year one million veterans will be separated from the service.* **2** divide or cause to divide into constituent or distinct elements: [*intrans.*] *the milk had* ***separated into*** *curds and whey* | [*trans.*] *separate the eggs and beat the yolks.* ■ [*trans.*] extract or remove for use or rejection: *the skins are separated from the juice before fermentation* | *figurative we need to separate fact from speculation.* ■ [*trans.*] distinguish between; consider individually: *we cannot separate his thinking from his activity.* ■ (of a factor or quality) distinguish (someone or something) from others: *his position separates him from those who might share his interests.* ■ [*trans.*] (**separate something off**) make something form, or view something as, a unit apart or by itself: *the organ loft separating off the choir.*

▸*n.* (**separates**) things forming units by themselves, in particular: ■ individual items of clothing, such as skirts, jackets, or pants, suitable for wearing in different combinations. ■ the self-contained, free-standing components of a sound-reproduction system. ■ portions into which a soil, sediment, etc., can be sorted according to particle size, mineral composition, or other criteria. ▷late Middle English: from Latin *separat-* 'disjoined, divided,' from the verb *separare*, from *se-* 'apart' + *parare* 'prepare.' **—sep·a·rate·ly** *adv.* **—sep·a·rate·ness** *n.*

▸*PHRASES* □ **go one's separate ways** leave in a different direction from someone with whom one has just traveled or spent time. ■ end a romantic, professional, or other relationship. □ **separate but equal** *historical* racially segregated but ostensibly ensuring equal opportunities to all races. □ **separate the men from the boys** see MAN. □ **separate the sheep from the goats** divide people or things into superior and inferior groups. [with biblical allusion to Matt. 25:33.] □ **separate the wheat from the chaff** see CHAFF[1].

sep·a·rate school ▸*n. Canadian* a school receiving students from a particular religious group.

sep·a·ra·tion /,sepə'rāSHən/ ▸*n.* **1** the action or state of moving or being moved apart: *the damage that might arise from the separation of parents and children.* ■ the state in which a husband and wife remain married but live apart: *legal grounds for divorce or separation | she and her husband have agreed to a* ***trial separation.*** See also LEGAL SEPARATION (sense 1). **2** the division of something into constituent or distinct elements: *prose structured into short sentences with meaningful* ***separation into*** *paragraphs.* ■ the process of distinguishing between two or more things: *religion involved the separation of the sacred and the profane | the constitution imposed a clear* ***separation between*** *church and state.* ■ the process of sorting and then extracting or removing a specified substance for use or rejection. ■ short for COLOR SEPARATION. ■ (also **stereo separation**) distinction or difference between the signals carried by the two channels of a stereophonic system. ■ *Physics & Aeronautics* the generation of a turbulent boundary layer between the surface of a body and a moving fluid, or between two fluids moving at different speeds. ▷late Middle English: via Old French from Latin *separatio(n-)*, from *separare* 'disjoin, divide' (see SEPARATE).

▸*PHRASE* □ **separation of powers** an act of vesting the legislative, executive, and judicial powers of government in separate bodies.

sep·a·ra·tion anx·i·e·ty ▸*n. Psychiatry* anxiety provoked in a young child by separation or the threat of separation from their mother.

sep·a·ra·tism /'sep(ə)rə,tizəm/ ▸*n.* the advocacy or practice of separation of a certain group of people from a larger body on the basis of ethnicity, religion, or gender: *Kurdish separatism.*

sep·a·ra·tist /'sep(ə)rətist/ ▸*n.* a person who supports the separation of a particular group of people from a larger body on the basis of ethnicity, religion, or gender: *religious separatists.*

▸*adj.* of or relating to such separation or those supporting it: *a separatist rebellion.*

sep·a·ra·tive /'sep(ə)rətiv/ ▸*adj. technical* tending to cause division into constituent or individual elements.

sep·a·ra·tor /'sepə,rātər/ ▸*n.* a machine or device that separates something into its constituent or distinct elements: *a magnetic separator.* ■ something that keeps two or more things apart: *most mail daemons use commas as separators between addresses.*

sepd. ▸*abbr.* separated.

Seph·a·dex /'sefə,deks/ ▸*n. trademark Biochemistry* a preparation of dextran used as a gel in chromatography, electrophoresis, and other separation techniques. ▷1950s: of unknown origin.

Se·phar·di /sə'färdē/ ▸*n.* (*pl.* **-phar·dim** /-'färdim; -,fär'dēm/) a Jew of Spanish or Portuguese descent. They retain their own distinctive customs and rituals, preserving Babylonian Jewish traditions rather than the Palestinian ones of the Ashkenazim. Compare with ASHKENAZI. ■ any Jew of the Middle East or North Africa. ▷modern Hebrew, from *sĕpāraḏ*, a country mentioned in Obad. 20 and taken to be Spain. **—Se·phar·dic** /-dik/ *adj.*

Seph·a·rose /'sefə,rōs; -,rōz/ ▸*n. Biochemistry, trademark* a preparation of agarose used as a gel in chromatography, electrophoresis, and other separation techniques. ▷1960s: of unknown origin.

se·phi·ra /sə'fi(ə)rə/ ▸*n.* (*pl.* **-phi·roth** /-'fi(ə)r,ōt; -,ōs/) (in cabalism) each of the ten attributes or emanations surrounding the Infinite and by means of which it relates to the finite. They are represented as spheres on the Tree of Life. ▷from Hebrew *sĕpīrāh.*

se·pi·a /'sēpēə/ ▸*n.* a reddish-brown color associated particularly with monochrome photographs of the 19th and early 20th centuries. ■ a brown pigment prepared from a black fluid secreted by cuttlefish, used in monochrome drawing and in watercolors. ■ a drawing done with this pigment. ■ a blackish fluid secreted by a cuttlefish as a defensive screen.

▸*adj.* of a reddish-brown color: *old sepia photographs.* ▷late Middle English (denoting a cuttlefish): via Latin from Greek *sēpia* 'cuttlefish.' The current senses date from the early 19th cent.

se·poy /'sē,poi/ ▸*n. historical* an Indian soldier serving under British or other European orders. ■ (in the Indian subcontinent) a police constable. ▷from Urdu and Persian *sipāhī* 'soldier,' from *sipāh* 'army.'

Se·poy Mu·ti·ny another term for INDIAN MUTINY.

sep·pu·ku /'sepōō,kōō; sə'pōōkōō/ ▸*n.* another term for HARA-KIRI. ▷Japanese, from *setsu* 'to cut' + *fuku* 'abdomen.'

seps /seps/ ▸*n.* an African lizard with a snakelike body and very short or nonexistent legs. • Genera *Tetradactylus*, family Gerrhosauridae: several species, formerly regarded as skinks. ▷mid 16th cent. (denoting a venomous serpent described by classical authors): via Latin from Greek *sēps*, from the base of *sēpein* 'make rotten.'

sep·sis /'sepsis/ ▸*n. Medicine* the presence in tissues of harmful bacteria and their toxins, typically through infection of a wound. ▷late 19th cent.: modern Latin, from Greek *sēpsis*, from *sēpein* 'make rotten.'

sept /sept/ ▸*n.* a clan, originally one in Ireland. ▷early 16th cent.: probably an alteration of SECT.

Sept. ▸*abbr.* ■ September. ■ Septuagint.

sept- ▸*comb. form* variant spelling of SEPTI- (as in *septcentenary*).

sep·ta /'septə/ ▸ plural form of SEPTUM.

sep·tage /'septij/ ▸*n.* excrement and other waste material contained in or removed from a septic tank. ▷1970s: from SEPTIC, on the pattern of *sewage.*

sep·tal /'septl/ ▸*adj.* relating to or acting as a partition, in particular: ■ *Anatomy & Biology* relating to a septum or septa.

sep·tar·i·um /sep'te(ə)rēəm/ ▸*n.* (*pl.* **-tar·i·a** /-'te(ə)rēə/) *Geology* a concretionary nodule, typically of ironstone, having radial cracks filled with calcite or another mineral. ▷late 18th cent.: modern Latin, from Latin *septum* 'enclosure.' **—sep·tar·i·an** /-'te(ə)rēən/ *adj.*

sep·tate /'sep,tāt/ ▸*adj. Anatomy & Biology* having or partitioned by a septum or septa. **—sep·ta·tion** /sep'tāSHən/ *n.*

sept·cen·ten·ary /,sep(t)sen'tenərē; -'sentn,erē/ ▸*n.* (*pl.* **-ar·ies**) the seven-hundredth anniversary of a significant event.

▸*adj.* of or relating to a seven-hundredth anniversary.

Sep·tem·ber /sep'tembər/ ▸*n.* the ninth month of the year, in the northern hemisphere usually considered the first month of autumn: *sow the plants in early September* | [as *adj.*] *a warm September evening.* ▷late Old English, from Latin, from *septem* 'seven' (being originally the seventh month of the Roman year).

sep·te·nar·i·us /,septə'ne(ə)rēəs/ ▸*n.* (*pl.* **-nar·i·i** /-'ne(ə)rē,ī/) *Prosody* a Latin verse line of seven feet, esp. a trochaic or iambic tetrameter catalectic, used only in comedy. ▷early 19th cent.: from Latin, from *septeni* 'in sevens,' from *septem* 'seven.'

sep·te·nar·y /'septə,nerē/ ▸*adj.* of, relating to, or divided into seven.

▸*n.* (*pl.* **-nar·ies**) a group or set of seven, in particular: ■ a period of seven years. ■ *Music* the seven notes of the diatonic scale. ▷late Middle English: from Latin *septenarius* (see SEPTENARIUS).

sep·ten·ni·al /sep'tenēəl/ ▸*adj.* recurring every seven years. ■ lasting for or relating to a period of seven years. ▷mid 17th cent.: from late Latin *septennis* (from Latin *septem* 'seven' + *annus* 'year') + -AL.

sep·ten·ni·um /sep'tenēəm/ ▸*n.* (*pl.* **-ten·ni·a** /-'tenēə/ or **-ten·ni·ums**) *rare* a specified period of seven years. ▷mid 19th cent.: from late Latin, from Latin *septem* 'seven' + *annus* 'year.'

sep·tet /sep'tet/ (also **sep·tette**) ▸*n.* a group of seven people playing music or singing together. ■ a composition for such a group. ▷early 19th cent.: from German *Septett*, from Latin *septem* 'seven.'

septi- (also **sept-**) ▸*comb. form* seven; having seven: *septivalent.* ▷from Latin *septem* 'seven.'

sep·tic /'septik/ ▸*adj.* **1** (chiefly of a wound or a part of the body) infected with bacteria. **2** [*attrib.*] denoting a drainage system incorporating a septic tank.

▸*n.* a drainage system incorporating a septic tank. ▷early 17th cent.: via Latin from Greek *sēptikos*, 'rotten.' **—sep·ti·cal·ly** /-ik(ə)lē/ *adv.* **—sep·tic·i·ty** /sep'tisitē/ *n.*

sep·ti·ce·mi·a /,septi'sēmēə/ (*Brit.* **sep·ti·cae·mi·a**) ▸*n.* blood poisoning, esp. that caused by bacteria or their toxins. ▷mid 19th cent.: modern Latin, from Greek *sēptikos* + *haima* 'blood.' **—sep·ti·ce·mic** /-mik/ *adj.*

sep·tic tank ▸*n.* a tank, typically underground, in which sewage is collected and allowed to decompose through bacterial activity before draining by means of a leaching field.

sep·til·lion /sep'tilyən/ ▸*cardinal number* (*pl.* **-lions** or (with numeral) same) a thousand raised to the eighth power (10^{24}). Compare with QUADRILLION. ■ *dated, chiefly Brit.* a million raised to the seventh power (10^{42}). ▷late 17th cent.: from French, from

S

Pronunciation Key ə *ago*; ər *over*; 'ə *or* ,ə *up*; 'ər *or* ,ər *fur*; a *hat*; ā *rate*; ä *car*; CH *chew*; e *let*; ē *see*; e(ə)r *air*; i *fit*; ī *by*; i(ə)r *ear*; NG *sing*; ō *go*; ô *for*; oi *boy*; ŏŏ *good*; ōō *goo*; ou *out*; SH *she*; TH *thin*; TH *then*; (h)w *why*; ZH *vision*

million, by substitution of the prefix *septi-* 'seven' (from Latin *septimus* 'seventh') for the initial letters.

sep·ti·mal /'septəməl/ ▶*adj.* of or relating to the number seven. ▷mid 19th cent.: from Latin *septimus* 'seventh' (from *septem* 'seven') + **-AL.**

sep·time /'sep,tēm/ ▶*n. Fencing* the seventh of eight standard parrying positions. ▷late 19th cent.: from Latin *septimus* 'seventh.'

sep·ti·va·lent /,septə'vālənt/ ▶*adj. Chemistry* another term for **HEPTAVALENT.**

sep·to·ria /sep'tôrēə/ ▶*n.* a fungus of a genus that includes many kinds that cause diseases in plants. • Genus *Septoria,* subdivision Deuteromycotina. ■ leaf spot disease caused by such a fungus. ▷modern Latin, from Latin *septum* (see **SEPTUM**).

sep·tu·a·ge·nar·i·an /,sepCHōōəjə'ne(ə)rēən/ ▶*n.* a person who is from 70 to 79 years old. ▷late 18th cent.: from Latin *septuagenarius* (based on *septuaginta* 'seventy') + **-AN.**

Sep·tu·a·ges·i·ma /,sepCHōōə'jesəmə/ (also **Septuagesima Sunday**) *n.* the Sunday before Sexagesima. ▷late Middle English: from Latin, 'seventieth (day),' probably named by analogy with **QUINQUAGESIMA.**

Sep·tu·a·gint /'sepCHōōə,jint/ *n.* a Greek version of the Hebrew Bible (or Old Testament), including the Apocrypha, made for Greek-speaking Jews in Egypt in the 3rd and 2nd centuries BC and adopted by the early Christian Churches. ▷mid 16th cent. (originally denoting the translators themselves): from Latin *septuaginta* 'seventy,' because of the tradition that it was produced, under divine inspiration, by seventy-two translators working independently.

sep·tum /'septəm/ ▶*n.* (*pl.* **-ta** /-tə/) *chiefly Anatomy Biology* a partition separating two chambers, such as that between the nostrils or the chambers of the heart. ▷mid 17th cent.: from Latin *septum,* from *sepire* 'enclose,' from *sepes* 'hedge.'

sep·tu·ple /'septəpəl; sep't(y)ōōpəl; -'təp-/ *rare* ▶*adj.* [*attrib.*] consisting of seven parts or elements. ■ consisting of seven times as much or as many as usual. ■ (of time in music) having seven beats in a bar.
▶*v.* [*trans.*] multiply (something) by seven; increase sevenfold. ▷early 17th cent. (as a verb): from late Latin *septuplus,* from Latin *septem* 'seven.'

sep·tup·let /sep'təplit; sep't(y)ōō-/ ▶*n.* **1** (usu. **septuplets**) each of seven children born at one birth. **2** *Music* a group of seven notes to be performed in the time of four or six. ▷late 19th cent.: from Latin *septuplus* (see **SEPTUPLE**), on the pattern of words such as *triplet.*

sep·ul·cher /'sepəlkər/ (*Brit.* **sep·ul·chre**) ▶*n.* a small room or monument, cut in rock or built of stone, in which a dead person is laid or buried.
▶*v.* [*trans.*] *chiefly poetic/literary* lay or bury in or as if in a sepulcher: *tomes are soon out of print and sepulchered in the dust of libraries.* ■ serve as a burial place for: *when ocean shrouds and sepulchers our dead.* ▷Middle English: via Old French from Latin *sepulcrum* 'burial place,' from *sepelire* 'bury.'

se·pul·chral /sə'pəlkrəl/ ▶*adj.* of or relating to a tomb or interment: *sepulchral monuments.* ■ gloomy; dismal: *a speech delivered in sepulchral tones.* ▷early 17th cent.: from French *sépulchral* or Latin *sepulchralis,* from *sepulcrum* (see **SEPULCHER**). **—se·pul·chral·ly** *adv.*

sep·ul·ture /'sepəlCHər/ ▶*n. archaic* burial; interment: *the rites of sepulture.* ▷Middle English: via Old French from Latin *sepultura,* from *sepelire* 'bury.'

seq. (also **seqq.**) ▶*adv.* short for **ET SEQ.**

se·qua·cious /si'kwāSHəs/ ▶*adj. formal* (of a person) lacking independence or originality of thought. ▷mid 17th cent.: from Latin *sequax, sequac-* 'following' (from *sequi* 'follow') + **-IOUS.** **—se·qua·cious·ly** *adv.* **—se·quac·i·ty** /-'kwasitē/ *n.*

se·quel /'sēkwəl/ ▶*n.* a published, broadcast, or recorded work that continues the story or develops the theme of an earlier one. ■ something that takes place after or as a result of an earlier event: *this encouragement to grow potatoes had a disastrous sequel some fifty years later.* ▷late Middle English (in the senses 'body of followers,' 'descendants' and 'consequence'): from Old French *sequelle* or Latin *sequella,* from *sequi* 'follow.'

se·que·la /si'kwelə/ ▶*n.* (*pl.* **-que·lae** /-'kwelē; -'kwelī/) (usu. **sequelae**) *Medicine* a condition that is the consequence of a previous disease or injury: *the long-term sequelae of infection.* ▷late 18th cent.: from Latin, from *sequi* 'follow.'

se·quence /'sēkwəns/ ▶*n.* **1** a particular order in which related events, movements, or things follow each other: *the content of the program should follow a logical sequence.* ■ *Music* a repetition of a phrase or melody at a higher or lower pitch. ■ *Biochemistry* the order in which amino acid or nucleotide residues are arranged in a protein, DNA, etc. **2** a set of related events, movements, or things that follow each other in a particular order: *a grueling* ***sequence of*** *exercises | a sonnet sequence.* ■ a set of three or more playing cards of the same suit next to each other in value, for example 10, 9, 8. ■ *Mathematics* an infinite ordered series of numerical quantities. **3** a part of a film dealing with one particular event or topic: *the famous underwater sequence.* **4** (in the Eucharist) a hymn said or sung after the Gradual or Alleluia that precedes the Gospel.
▶*v.* [*trans.*] **1** arrange in a particular order: *trainee librarians decide how a set of misfiled cards could be sequenced.* ■ *Biochemistry* ascertain the sequence of amino acid or nucleotide residues in (a protein, DNA, etc.). **2** play or record (music) with a sequencer. ▷late Middle English (sense 4): from late Latin *sequentia,* from Latin *sequent-* 'following,' from the verb *sequi* 'follow.'
▶*PHRASE* □ **in sequence** in a given order.

se·quence danc·ing ▶*n.* a type of ballroom dancing in which the couples all perform the same steps and movements simultaneously.

se·quence of tens·es ▶*n. Grammar* the dependence of the tense of a subordinate verb on the tense of the verb in the main clause (e.g., *I think that you* are *wrong; I thought that you* were *wrong*).

se·quenc·er /'sēkwənsər/ ▶*n.* **1** a programmable electronic device for storing sequences of musical notes, chords, or rhythms and transmitting them when required to an electronic musical instrument. **2** *Biochemistry* an apparatus for determining the sequence of amino acids or other monomers in a biological polymer.

se·quent /'sēkwənt/ ▶*adj. archaic* following in a sequence or as a logical conclusion. ▷mid 16th cent.: from Old French, or from Latin *sequent-* 'following' (see **SEQUENCE**). **—se·quent·ly** *adv.*

se·quen·tial /si'kwenCHəl/ ▶*adj.* forming or following in a logical order or sequence: *a series of sequential steps.* ■ *chiefly Computing* performed or used in sequence: *sequential processing of data files.* ▷early 19th cent. (as a medical term in the sense 'following as a secondary condition'): from **SEQUENCE,** on the pattern of *consequential.* **—se·quen·ti·al·i·ty** /si,kwenCHē'alitē/ *n.* **—se·quen·tial·ly** *adv.*

se·quen·tial ac·cess ▶*n.* access to a computer data file that requires the user to read through the file from the beginning in the order in which it is stored. Compare with **DIRECT ACCESS.**

se·quen·tial cir·cuit ▶*n. Electronics* a circuit whose output depends on the order or timing of the inputs. Compare with **COMBINATIONAL CIRCUIT.**

se·ques·ter /sə'kwestər/ ▶*v.* [*trans.*] **1** isolate or hide away (someone or something): *Tiberius was sequestered on an island | the artist* ***sequestered himself*** *in his studio for two years.* ■ isolate (a jury) from outside influences during a trial: *the jurors had been sequestered since Monday.* ■ *Chemistry* [*intrans.*] form a chelate or other stable compound with (an ion, atom, or molecule) so that it is no longer available for reactions. **2** take legal possession of (assets) until a debt has been paid or other claims have been met: *the power of courts to sequester the assets of unions.* ■ take forcible possession of (something); confiscate: *compensation for Jewish property sequestered by the Libyan regime.* ■ legally place (the property of a bankrupt) in the hands of a trustee for division among the creditors: [as *adj.*] (**sequestered**) *a trustee in a sequestered estate.* ▷late Middle English: from Old French *sequestrer* or late Latin *sequestrare* 'commit for safekeeping,' from Latin *sequester* 'trustee.' **—se·ques·tra·ble** /si'kwestrəbəl/ *adj.* **—se·ques·tra·tor** /'sēkwi,strātər; 'sek-; si'kwes,trātər/ *n.*

se·ques·tered /sə'kwestərd/ ▶*adj.* (of a place) isolated and hidden away: *a wild sequestered spot.*

se·ques·trate /'sēkwi,strāt; 'sek-; sə'kwes,trāt/ ▶*v.* another term for **SEQUESTER.** ▷late Middle English (in the sense 'separate from general access'): from late Latin *sequestrat-* 'given up for safekeeping,' from the verb *sequestrare* (see **SEQUESTER**).

se·ques·tra·tion /,sēkwi'strāSHən; ,sek-/ ▶*n.* **1** the action of taking legal possession of assets until a debt has been paid or other claims have been met: *if such court injunctions are ignored, sequestration of trade union assets will follow.* ■ the action of taking forcible possession of something; confiscation: *they demanded the sequestration of the incriminating correspondence.* ■ an act of declaring someone bankrupt. ■ the action of making a general cut in government spending: *the measure brings the federal budget closer to sequestration.* ■ *Chemistry* the action of sequestering a substance. **2** the action of isolating a jury during a trial.

se·ques·trum /si'kwestrəm/ ▶*n.* (*pl.* **-tra** /-trə/) *Medicine* a piece of dead bone tissue occurring within a diseased or injured bone, typically in chronic osteomyelitis. ▷mid 19th cent.: modern Latin, neuter of Latin *sequester* 'standing apart.' **—se·ques·tral** /-trəl/ *adj.* **—se·ques·trec·to·my** /,sēkwe'strektəmē/ *n.* (*pl.* **-mies**).

se·quin /'sēkwin/ ▶*n.* **1** a small, shiny disk sewn as one of many onto clothing for decoration. **2** *historical* a Venetian gold coin. ▷late 16th cent. (sense 2): from French, from Italian *zecchino,* from *zecca* 'a mint,' from Arabic *sikka* 'a die for coining.' Sense 1 dates from the late 19th cent. **—se·quined** (also **sequinned**) *adj.*

se·quoi·a /sə'k(w)oi-ə/ ▶*n.* a redwood tree, esp. the California redwood. ▷from modern Latin *Sequoia* (genus name), from *Sequoya.*

Se·quoi·a Na·tion·al Park a national park in the Sierra Nevada of California, east of Fresno. It was established in 1890 to protect groves of giant sequoia trees, of which the largest, the General Sherman Tree, is thought to be between 3,000 and 4,000 years old.

Se·quoy·a /sə'kwoi-ə/ (*c.*1770–1843), Cherokee Indian scholar; also spelled *Sequoyah* or *Sequoia;* Cherokee name *Sogwali;* also known as **George Guess** or **Gist.** He invented a writing system (the Cherokee syllabary) 1809–21 for the Cherokee language and with it taught thousands of Cherokee Indians to read and write. The giant sequoia trees of California are named for him.

ser. ▶*abbr.* ■ serial. ■ series. ■ sermon.

se·ra /'si(ə)rə/ ▶ plural form of **SERUM.**

se·rac /sə'rak/ ▶*n.* a pinnacle or ridge of ice on the surface of a glacier. ▷mid 19th cent.: from Swiss French *sérac,* originally the name of a compact white cheese.

se·ragl·io /sə'rälyō/ ▶*n.* (*pl.* **-ios**) **1** the women's apartments (harem) in a Muslim palace. ■ another term for **HAREM** (sense 2). **2** (**the Seraglio**) *historical* a Turkish palace, esp. the Sultan's court and government offices at Constantinople. ▷late 16th cent.: from Italian *serraglio,* via Turkish from Persian *sarāy* 'palace'; compare with **SERAI.**

se·ra·i /sə'rī/ ▶*n.* another term for **CARAVANSARY** (sense 1).

Se·raing /sə'raN/ an industrial town in Belgium, on the Meuse River, southwest of Liège; pop. 61,000.

se·ra·pe /sə'räpē/ (also **sa·ra·pe**) ▶*n.* a shawl or blanket worn as a cloak in Latin America. ▷Mexican Spanish.

ser·aph /'serəf/ ▶*n.* (*pl.* **ser·a·phim** /'serə,fim/ or **seraphs**) an angelic being, regarded in traditional Christian angelology as belonging to the highest order of the ninefold celestial hierarchy, associated with light, ardor, and purity. ▷Old English, back-formation from *seraphim* (plural), via late Latin and Greek from Hebrew *śĕrāpīm.* Compare with **CHERUB.**

se·raph·ic /sə'rafik/ ▶*adj.* characteristic of or resembling a seraph or seraphim: *a seraphic smile.* ▷mid 17th cent.: from medieval Latin *seraphicus,* from late Latin *seraphim* (see **SERAPH**). **—se·raph·i·cal·ly** /-ik(ə)lē/ *adv.*

Se·raph·ic Doc·tor the nickname of St. Bonaventura.

Se·ra·pis /sə'rāpis/ *Egyptian Mythology* a god whose cult was developed by Ptolemy I at Memphis as a combination of Apis and Osiris, to unite Greeks and Egyptians in a common worship.

ser·a·skier /,serə'ski(ə)r/ ▶*n. historical* the commander in chief and minister of war of the Ottoman Empire. ▷Turkish, from Persian *sar'askar* 'head (of the) army.'

Serb /sərb/ ▶*n.* a native or national of Serbia. ■ a person of Serbian descent.
▶*adj.* of or relating to Serbia, the Serbs, or their language. ▷from Serbo-Croat *Srb.*

Ser·bi·a /'sərbēə/ a republic in the Balkans, part of Serbia and Montenegro; pop. 9,660,000; official language, Serbo-Croat; capital, Belgrade. Serbia was conquered by the Turks in the 14th century and regained independence in 1878. Serbian rivalry with the Austro-Hungarian empire contributed to the outbreak of World War I, after which Serbia was absorbed into the kingdom of Serbs, Croats, and Slovenes (named Yugoslavia from 1929). In 1991–92 four out of the six Yugoslav republics seceded;

Serbia became involved in armed conflict with neighboring Croatia and in the civil war in Bosnia. Serbia and Montenegro formed the Federal Republic of Yugoslavia in April 1992. In February 2003, the two republics formed a loose federation called Serbia and Montenegro.

Ser·bi·a and Mon·te·ne·gro a federation of republics in southeastern Europe, in the Balkans, on the Adriatic Sea; pop. 10,826,000; capital, Belgrade; judicial capital, Podgorica; languages, Serbian and Albanian.

Serbia and Montenegro was formed in February 2003 as a loose federation of the two republics. They were part of the federation of Yugoslavia from 1929 until 1992 and constituted the Federal Republic of Yugoslavia from 1992 to 2003. A referendum on full independence is to be held in each republic in 2006.

Ser·bi·an /ˈsərbēən/ ▸*n.* **1** the dialect of Serbo-Croat used by the Serbs. See **SERBO-CROAT**. **2** another term for **SERB**.
▸*adj.* of or relating to Serbia, the Serbs, or their language.

Serbo- ▸*comb. form* Serbian; Serbian and . . . : *Serbo-Croat.* ■ relating to Serbia.

Ser·bo-Cro·at /ˈsərbō ˈkrō,ät; ˈkrōt/ (also **Ser·bo-Cro·a·tian** /krōˈāshən/) ▸*n.* the South Slavic language spoken in Serbia, Croatia, and elsewhere in the former Yugoslavia. Serbo-Croat is generally classed as one language, but comprises two closely similar forms: Serbian, written in the Cyrillic alphabet, and Croat, written in the Roman alphabet.
▸*adj.* of or relating to this language.

Ser·cial /ˈsərsēəl; sərsˈyäl/ ▸*n.* a variety of wine grape grown chiefly in Madeira. ■ a dry, light Madeira made from this grape. ▷Portuguese.

sere[1] /si(ə)r/ (also **sear**) ▸*adj.* dry; arid: *a harsh life on the sere granite ledges of those remote offshore islands.* See note at **DRY**. ■ (esp. of plants) withered.

sere[2] ▸*n. Ecology* a natural succession of plant (or animal) communities, esp. a full series from uncolonized habitat to the appropriate climax vegetation. Compare with **SUCCESSION**. ▷early 20th cent.: from Latin *serere* 'join in a series.'

Se·rem·ban /səˈrembən/ a town in southwestern Malaysia; pop. 136,000.

ser·e·nade /,serəˈnād/ ▸*n.* a piece of music sung or played in the open air, typically by a man at night under the window of his lover. ■ another term for **SERENATA**.
▸*v.* [*trans.*] entertain (someone) with a serenade: *a strolling guitarist serenades the diners.* ▷mid 17th cent.: from French *sérénade*, from Italian *serenata*, from *sereno* 'serene.' **—ser·e·nad·er** *n.*

ser·e·na·ta /,serəˈnätə/ ▸*n. Music* a cantata with a pastoral subject. ■ a simple form of suite for orchestra or wind band. ▷Italian, 'serenade' (see **SERENADE**).

ser·en·dip·i·ty /,serənˈdipitē/ ▸*n.* the occurrence and development of events by chance in a happy or beneficial way: *a fortunate stroke of serendipity* | *a series of small serendipities.* ▷1754: coined by Horace Walpole, suggested by *The Three Princes of Serendip*, the title of a fairy tale in which the heroes "were always making discoveries, by accidents and sagacity, of things they were not in quest of." **—ser·en·dip·i·tous** /-ˈdipitəs/ *adj.* **—ser·en·dip·i·tous·ly** *adv.*

se·rene /səˈrēn/ ▸*adj.* **1** calm, peaceful, and untroubled; tranquil: *her eyes were closed and she looked very serene* | *serene certainty.* See note at **CALM**. **2** (**Serene**) (in a title) used as a term of respect for members of some European royal families: *His Serene Highness.*
▸*n.* (usu. **the serene**) *archaic* an expanse of clear sky or calm sea: *not a cloud obscured the deep serene.* ▷late Middle English (describing the weather or sky as 'clear, fine, and calm'): from Latin *serenus.* **—se·rene·ly** *adv.*

Ser·en·get·i /,serənˈgetē/ a vast plain in Tanzania, west of the Great Rift Valley. In 1951 the Serengeti National Park was created to protect the area's large numbers of wildebeest, zebra, and Thomson's gazelle.

Se·re·nis·si·ma /,serəˈnisəmə/ ▸*n.* (**La Serenissima, the Serenissima**) Venice: *the ghost-fleets of the Serenissima's seafaring past.* ▷Italian, feminine of *serenissimo* 'most serene.'

se·ren·i·ty /səˈrenitē/ ▸*n.* (*pl.* **-ties**) the state of being calm, peaceful, and untroubled: *an oasis of serenity amidst the bustling city.* ■ (**His/Your,** etc., **Serenity**) a title given to a reigning prince or similar dignitary. ▷late Middle English: from Old French *serenite*, from Latin *serenitas*, from *serenus* 'clear, fair' (see **SERENE**).

serf /sərf/ ▸*n.* an agricultural laborer bound under the feudal system to work on his lord's estate. ▷late 15th cent. (in the sense 'slave'): from Old French, from Latin *servus* 'slave.' **—serf·age** /-fij/ *n.* **—serf·dom** /-dəm/ *n.*

serge /sərj/ ▸*n.* a durable twilled woolen or worsted fabric.
▸*v.* [*trans.*] overcast (the edge of a piece of material) to prevent fraying. ▷late Middle English: from Old French *sarge*, from a variant of Latin *serica (lana)* 'silken (wool),' from *sericus* (see **SILK**).

ser·geant /ˈsärjənt/ ▸*n.* a noncommissioned officer in the armed forces, in particular (in the U.S. Army or Marine Corps) an NCO ranking above corporal and below staff sergeant, or (in the U.S. Air Force) an NCO ranking above airman and below staff sergeant. ■ *Brit.* a police officer ranking below an inspector. ■ a police officer ranking below a lieutenant. ▷Middle English: from Old French *sergent*, from Latin *servient-* 'serving,' from the verb *servire*. Early use was as a general term meaning 'attendant, servant' and 'common soldier'; the term was later applied to specific official roles. **—ser·gean·cy** /-jənsē/ *n.* (*pl.* **-cies**).

ser·geant-at-arms (*Brit.* **ser·jeant-at-arms**) ▸*n.* (*pl.* **ser·geants-at-arms**) an official of a legislative or other assembly whose duty includes maintaining order and security. ■ *Brit., historical* a knight or armed officer in the service of the monarch or a lord.

Ser·geant Ba·ker ▸*n. Austral.* a brightly colored edible marine fish with two elongated dorsal fin rays, occurring in warm Australian coastal waters. • *Aulopus purpurissatus*, family Aulopidae. ▷late 19th cent.: of unknown origin.

ser·geant first class ▸*n.* a noncommissioned officer in the U.S. Army of a rank above staff sergeant and below master sergeant.

ser·geant fish ▸*n.* another term for **COBIA**.

ser·geant ma·jor ▸*n.* **1** an noncommissioned officer in the U.S. Army or Marine Corps of the highest rank, above master sergeant and below warrant officer. **2** a warrant officer in the British army. **3** a fish with boldly striped sides that lives in warm seas, typically on coral reefs. • *Abudefduf saxatilis*, family Pomacentridae.

serg·er /ˈsərjər/ ▸*n.* a sewing machine used for overcasting to prevent material from fraying at the edge.

Ser·gi·us, St. /ˈsərjēəs/ (1314–92), Russian monastic reformer and mystic; Russian name *Svyatoi Sergi Radonezhsky*. He reestablished the monasticism that had been lost through the Tartar invasion and inspired the resistance that saved Russia from the Tartars in 1380. Feast day, September 25.

se·ri·al /ˈsi(ə)rēəl/ ▸*adj.* **1** consisting of, forming part of, or taking place in a series: *a serial publication.* ■ *Music* using transformations of a fixed series of notes. ■ *Computing* (of a device) involving the transfer of data as a single sequence of bits. See also **SERIAL PORT**. ■ *Computing* (of a processor) running only a single task, as opposed to multitasking. ■ *Linguistics* (of verbs) used in sequence to form a construction, as in *they wanted, needed, longed for peace.* **2** [*attrib.*] (of a criminal) repeatedly committing the same offense and typically following a characteristic, predictable behavior pattern: *a suspected serial rapist.* ■ (of a person) repeatedly following the same behavior pattern: *he was a serial adulterer.* ■ denoting an action or behavior pattern that is committed or followed repeatedly: *serial killings* | *serial monogamy.*
▸*n.* a story or play appearing in regular installments on television or radio or in a magazine or newspaper: *a new three-part drama serial.* ■ (usu. **serials**) (in a library) a periodical. ▷mid 19th cent.: from **SERIES** + **-AL**, perhaps suggested by French *sérial*. **—se·ri·al·i·ty** /,si(ə)rēˈalitē/ *n.* **—se·ri·al·ly** *adv.*

se·ri·al·ism /ˈsi(ə)rēə,lizəm/ ▸*n. Music* a compositional technique in which a fixed series of notes, esp. the twelve notes of the chromatic scale, are used to generate the harmonic and melodic basis of a piece and are subject to change only in specific ways. The first fully serial movements appeared in 1923 in works by Arnold Schoenberg. See also **TWELVE-TONE**. **—se·ri·al·ist** *adj.* & *n.*

se·ri·al·ize /ˈsi(ə)rēə,līz/ ▸*v.* [*trans.*] **1** publish or broadcast (a story or play) in regular installments: *sections of the book were serialized in the* New Yorker. **2** arrange (something) in a series. ■ *Music* compose according to the techniques of serialism. **—se·ri·al·i·za·tion** /,si(ə)rēələˈzāshən/ *n.*

se·ri·al num·ber ▸*n.* a number showing the position of an item in a series, esp. one printed on paper currency or on a manufactured article for the purposes of identification.

se·ri·al port ▸*n. Computing* a connector by which a device that sends data one bit at a time may be connected to a computer. Compare with **PARALLEL PORT**.

se·ri·al sec·tion ▸*n. Biology* each of a series of thin sections through tissue cut in successive parallel planes, esp. for mounting on microscope slides. **—se·ri·al sec·tion·ing** *n.*

se·ri·ate /ˈsi(ə)rē,āt/ *technical* ▸*adj.* arranged or occurring in one or more series.
▸*v.* [*trans.*] arrange (items) in a sequence according to prescribed criteria. ▷mid 19th cent.: back-formation from *seriation*, from **SERIES**. **—se·ri·a·tion** /,si(ə)rēˈāshən/ *n.*

se·ri·a·tim /,si(ə)rēˈātəm; -ˈatəm/ ▸*adv. formal* taking one subject after another in regular order; point by point: *it is proposed to deal with these matters seriatim.* ▷late 15th cent.: from medieval Latin, from Latin *series*, on the pattern of Latin *gradatim* and *literatim*.

ser·i·cite /ˈserə,sīt/ ▸*n.* a fine-grained fibrous variety of muscovite formed by the alteration of feldspar, found chiefly in schist and in hydrothermally altered rock. ▷mid 19th cent.: from Latin *sericum* 'silk' + **-ITE**[1].

ser·i·cul·ture /ˈseri,kəlchər/ ▸*n.* the production of silk and the rearing of silkworms for this purpose. ▷mid 19th cent.: abbreviation of French *sériciculture*, from late Latin *sericum* 'silk' + French *culture* 'cultivation.' **—ser·i·cul·tur·al** /,seriˈkəlchərəl/ *adj.* **—ser·i·cul·tur·ist** /,seriˈkəlchərist/ *n.*

ser·i·e·ma /,serēˈēmə; -ˈāmə/ (also **car·i·a·ma** /,karēˈāmə/) ▸*n.* a large, ground-dwelling South American bird related to the bustards, with a long neck and legs and a crest above the bill. • Family Cariamidae: two genera and species. ▷mid 19th cent.: modern Latin, from Tupi *siriema* 'crested.'

se·ries /ˈsi(ə)rēz/ ▸*n.* (*pl.* same) a number of things, events, or people of a similar kind or related nature coming one after another: *the explosion was the latest in* ***a series of*** *accidents* | *he gave* ***a series of*** *lectures on modern art.* ■ [usu. with *adj.*] a set of related television or radio programs, esp. of a specified kind: *a new drama series.* ■ a set of books, maps, periodicals, or other documents published in a common format or under a common title. ■ a set of games played between two teams: *a playoff series against Portland.* See also **WORLD SERIES**. ■ a line of products, esp. vehicles or machines, sharing features of design or assembly and marketed with a separate number from other lines: [as *adj.*] *a series III SWB Land Rover.* ■ a set of stamps, banknotes, or coins issued at a particular time or having a common design or theme. ■ [as *adj.*] denoting electrical circuits or components arranged so that the current passes through each successively. The opposite of **PARALLEL**. ■ *Geology* (in chronostratigraphy) a range of strata corresponding to an epoch in time, being a subdivision of a system and itself subdivided into stages: *the Pliocene series.* ■ *Chemistry* a set of elements with common properties or of compounds related in composition or

Pronunciation Key ə *ago*; ər *over*; ˈə *or* ,ə *up*; ˈər *or* ,ər *fur*; a *hat*; ā *rate*; ä *car*; CH *chew*; e *let*; ē *see*; e(ə)r *air*; i *fit*; ī *by*; i(ə)r *ear*; NG *sing*; ō *go*; ô *for*; oi *boy*; o͝o *good*; o͞o *goo*; ou *out*; SH *she*; TH *thin*; T͟H *then*; (h)w *why*; ZH *vision*

S

structure: *the metals of the lanthanide series.* Compare with **PERIOD** sense 5. ■ *Mathematics* a set of quantities constituting a progression or having the several values determined by a common relation. ■ *Phonetics* a group of speech sounds having at least one phonetic feature in common but distinguished in other respects. ■ *Music* another term for **TONE ROW.** ▷early 17th cent.: from Latin, literally 'row, chain,' from *serere* 'join, connect.'

▸*PHRASE* □ **in series** (of a set of batteries or electrical components) arranged so that the current passes through each successively.

ser·if /'serəf/ ▸*n.* a slight projection finishing off a stroke of a letter, as in T contrasted with T. ▷mid 19th cent.: perhaps from Dutch *schreef* 'dash, line,' of Germanic origin. **—ser·iffed** *adj.*

ser·i·graph /'seri,graf/ ▸*n.* a printed design produced by means of a silkscreen. ▷late 19th cent.: formed irregularly from Latin *sericum* 'silk' + **-GRAPH.** **—se·rig·ra·pher** /sə'rigrəfər/ *n.* **—se·rig·ra·phy** /sə'rigrəfē/ *n.*

ser·in /'serən/ ▸*n.* a small Eurasian and North African finch related to the canary, with a short bill and typically streaky plumage. • Genus *Serinus*, family Fringillidae: several species, in particular the **European serin** (*S. serinus*). ▷mid 16th cent. (denoting a canary): from French, 'canary,' of unknown ultimate origin.

ser·ine /'serēn; 'si(ə)r-; -in/ ▸*n. Biochemistry* a hydrophilic amino acid that is a constituent of most proteins. • Chem. formula: $CH_2OHCHNH_2COOH$. ▷late 19th cent.: from Latin *sericum* 'silk' + **-INE**[4].

se·ri·o·com·ic /,si(ə)rē-ō'kämik/ ▸*adj.* combining the serious and the comic; serious in intention but jocular in manner or vice versa: *a telling seriocomic critique.* **—se·ri·o·com·i·cal·ly** *adv.*

se·ri·ous /'si(ə)rēəs/ ▸*adj.* **1** (of a person) solemn or thoughtful in character or manner: *her face grew serious.* ■ (of a subject, state, or activity) demanding careful consideration or application: *marriage is a serious matter.* ■ (of thought or discussion) careful or profound: *we give serious consideration to safety recommendations.* ■ (of music, literature, or other art forms) requiring deep reflection and inviting a considered response: *he bridges the gap between serious and popular music.* **2** acting or speaking sincerely and in earnest, rather than in a joking or halfhearted manner: *suddenly he wasn't teasing any more—he was deadly serious | actors who are* ***serious about*** *their work.* **3** significant or worrying because of possible danger or risk; not slight or negligible: *she escaped serious injury | Haydn was Mozart's only serious rival.* **4** [*attrib.*] *informal* substantial in terms of size, number, or quality: *he suddenly had serious money to spend | a serious chocolate cheesecake.* ▷late Middle English: from Old French *serieux* or late Latin *seriosus*, from Latin *serius* 'earnest, serious.' **—se·ri·ous·ness** *n.*

se·ri·ous·ly /'si(ə)rēəslē/ ▸*adv.* **1** in a solemn or considered manner: *the doctor looked seriously at him.* **2** with earnest intent; not lightly or superficially: *I seriously considered canceling my subscription.* ■ really or sincerely (used esp. to indicate a response of surprise or shock): *do you seriously believe that I would jeopardize my career by such acts?* ■ [*sentence adverb*] used to add sincerity to a statement that is to follow, esp. after a facetious exchange of remarks: ***seriously though****, shortcuts rarely work.* ■ *informal* used to indicate surprise at what someone has said and to check whether they really meant it: *"I'm dying to know." "Seriously?" "Of course."* **3** to a degree that is significant or worrying because of possible danger or risk: *the amount of fat you eat can seriously affect your health |* [as *submodifier*] *three men are seriously ill in the hospital.* **4** [as *submodifier*] *informal* very: *he was seriously rich | I drove to the station in a seriously bad mood.*

▸*PHRASE* □ **take someone/something seriously** regard someone or something as important and worthy of attention.

ser·jeant-at-arms ▸*n.* British spelling of **SERGEANT-AT-ARMS.**

ser·jeant-at-law ▸*n.* (*pl.* **ser·jeants-at-law**) *Brit., historical* a barrister of the highest rank.

ser·jeant·y /'särjəntē/ ▸*n.* (*pl.* **-jeant·ies**) *Brit., historical* a form of feudal tenure conditional on rendering some specified personal service to the monarch.

Ser·ling /'sərliNG/, Rod(man Edward) (1924–75), U.S. writer and television producer. He created, directed, and hosted the television series "The Twilight Zone" (1959–64). He followed this with "Night Gallery" (1970–73). He also wrote many award-winning scripts for television plays such as *Requiem for a Heavyweight* (1957).

ser·mon /'sərmən/ ▸*n.* a talk on a religious or moral subject, esp. one given during a church service and based on a passage from the Bible. ■ a printed transcript of such a talk: *a volume of sermons.* ■ *informal* a long or tedious piece of admonition or reproof; a lecture. ▷Middle English (also in the sense 'speech, discourse'): from Old French, from Latin *sermo(n-)* 'discourse, talk.' **—ser·mon·ic** /sər'mänik/ *adj.*

ser·mon·ette /,sərmə'net/ ▸*n.* a short sermon.

ser·mon·ize /'sərmə,nīz/ ▸*v.* [*intrans.*] compose or deliver a sermon. ■ deliver an opinionated and dogmatic talk to someone: *they confidently sermonize on the fixed nature of identity |* [*trans.*] *I just don't like being sermonized.* **—ser·mon·iz·er** *n.*

Ser·mon on the Mount ▸*n.* the discourse of Jesus recorded in Matt. 5–7, including the Beatitudes and the Lord's Prayer.

sero- ▸*comb. form* relating to serum: *serotype.* ■ involving a serous membrane: *serositis.* ▷representing **SERUM.**

se·ro·con·vert /,si(ə)rōkən'vərt/ ▸*v.* [*intrans.*] *Medicine* (of a person) undergo a change from a seronegative to a seropositive condition. **—se·ro·con·ver·sion** /-'vərZHən/ *n.*

se·ro·di·ag·no·sis /,si(ə)rō,dīəg'nōsis/ ▸*n. Medicine* diagnosis based on the study of blood sera. **—se·ro·di·ag·nos·tic** /-'nästik/ *adj.*

se·rol·o·gy /si'räləjē/ ▸*n.* the scientific study or diagnostic examination of blood serum, esp. with regard to the response of the immune system to pathogens or introduced substances. **—se·ro·log·ic** /,si(ə)rə'läjik/ *adj.* **—se·ro·log·i·cal** *adj.* **—se·ro·log·i·cal·ly** *adv.* **—se·rol·o·gist** /-jist/ *n.*

se·ro·neg·a·tive /,si(ə)rō'negətiv/ ▸*adj. Medicine* giving a negative result in a test of blood serum, e.g., for the presence of a virus. **—se·ro·neg·a·tiv·i·ty** /-,negə'tivitē/ *n.*

se·ro·pos·i·tive /,si(ə)rō'päzitiv/ ▸*adj. Medicine* giving a positive result in a test of blood serum, e.g., for the presence of a virus. **—se·ro·pos·i·tiv·i·ty** /-,päzi'tivitē/ *n.*

se·ro·prev·a·lence /,si(ə)rō'prevələns/ ▸*n. Medicine* the level of a pathogen in a population, as measured in blood serum.

se·ro·sa /sə'rōsə/ ▸*n. Physiology* the tissue of a serous membrane. ▷modern Latin, feminine of medieval Latin *serosus* 'serous.' **—se·ro·sal** *adj.*

se·ro·si·tis /,sirō'sītis/ ▸*n. Medicine* inflammation of a serous membrane.

ser·o·tine /'serətin; -,tīn/ ▸*n.* a medium-sized insectivorous bat found in Eurasia and Africa: • a chiefly Eurasian bat (genus *Eptesicus*, family Vespertilionidae, in particular the widespread *E. serotinus*). • an African bat (genus *Pipistrellus*, family Vespertilionidae). ▷late 18th cent.: from French *sérotine*, from Latin *serotinus* 'of the evening, late,' from *serus* 'late.'

ser·o·to·nin /,serə'tōnən; ,si(ə)r-/ ▸*n. Biochemistry* a compound present in blood platelets and serum that constricts the blood vessels and acts as a neurotransmitter. • Alternative name: **5-hydroxytryptamine**; chem. formula: $C_{10}H_{12}N_2O$. ▷1940s: from **SERUM + TONIC + -IN**[1].

se·ro·type /'si(ə)rə,tīp; 'serə-/ *Microbiology* ▸*n.* a serologically distinguishable strain of a microorganism.

▸*v.* [*trans.*] assign (a microorganism) to a particular serotype. **—se·ro·typ·ic** /,si(ə)rə'tipik; ,serə-/ *adj.*

se·rous /'si(ə)rəs/ ▸*adj. Physiology* of, resembling, or producing serum. ▷late Middle English: from French *séreux* or medieval Latin *serosus*, from *serum* (see **SERUM**). **—se·ros·i·ty** /si'räsitē/ *n.*

se·rous mem·brane ▸*n.* a mesothelial tissue that lines certain internal cavities of the body, forming a smooth, transparent, two-layered membrane lubricated by a fluid derived from serum. The peritoneum, pericardium, and pleura are serous membranes.

se·row /sə'rō; 'serō/ ▸*n.* a goat-antelope with short sharp horns, long coarse hair, and a beard, native to forested mountain slopes of Southeast Asia, Taiwan, and Japan. • Genus *Capricornis*, family Bovidae: two species. ▷mid 19th cent.: probably from Lepcha *sā-ro.*

Ser·pens /'sərpənz/ *Astronomy* a large constellation (the Serpent) on the celestial equator, said to represent the snake coiled around Ophiuchus. It is divided into two parts by Ophiuchus, **Serpens Caput** (the "head") and **Serpens Cauda** (the "tail"). ■ [as *genitive*] (**Serpentis** /sər'pentis/) used with a preceding letter or numeral to designate a star in this constellation: *the star Beta Serpentis.* ▷Latin.

ser·pent /'sərpənt/ ▸*n.* **1** *chiefly poetic/literary* a large snake. ■ (**the Serpent**) a biblical name for Satan (see Gen. 3, Rev. 20). ■ a dragon or other mythical snakelike reptile. ■ *figurative* a sly or treacherous person, esp. one who exploits a position of trust in order to betray it. **2** *historical* a bass wind instrument made of leather-covered wood in three U-shaped turns, with a cup-shaped mouthpiece and few keys. It was played in military and church bands from the 17th to 19th centuries. ▷Middle English: via Old French from Latin *serpent-* 'creeping,' from the verb *serpere.*

Ser·pen·tes /sər'pentēz/ *Zoology* another term for **OPHIDIA.** ▷Latin, 'reptiles.'

ser·pen·tine /'sərpən,tēn; -,tīn/ ▸*adj.* of or like a serpent or snake: *serpentine coils.* ■ winding and twisting like a snake: *serpentine country lanes.* ■ complex, cunning, or treacherous: *his charm was too subtle and serpentine for me.*

▸*n.* **1** a dark green mineral consisting of hydrated magnesium silicate, sometimes mottled or spotted like a snake's skin. **2** a thing in the shape of a winding curve or line, in particular: ■ a riding exercise consisting of a series of half-circles made alternately to right and left. **3** *historical* a kind of cannon, used esp. in the 15th and 16th centuries.

▸*v.* [*intrans.*] move or lie in a winding path or line: *fresh tire tracks serpentined back toward the hopper.* ▷late Middle English: via Old French from late Latin *serpentinus* (see **SERPENT**).

ser·pen·tin·ite /,sərpən'tēnīt; -'tī-/ ▸*n. Geology* a dark, typically greenish metamorphic rock, consisting largely of serpentine or related minerals, formed when mafic igneous rocks are altered by water. ▷1930s: from **SERPENTINE + -ITE**[1].

ser·pen·tin·ize /,sərpən'tēnīz/ ▸*v.* [*trans.*] *Geology* convert into serpentine. **—ser·pen·tin·i·za·tion** /-,tēni'zāSHən/ *n.*

ser·pig·i·nous /sər'pijənəs/ ▸*adj. Medicine* (of a skin lesion or ulcerated region) having a wavy margin. ▷late Middle English: from medieval Latin *serpigo, serpigin-* 'ringworm' (from Latin *serpere* 'to creep') + **-OUS.**

SERPS /sərps/ ▸*abbr.* (in the UK) state earnings-related pension scheme.

ser·ra·nid /'serənid/ ▸*n. Zoology* a fish of the sea bass family (Serranidae), whose members are predatory marine fish with a spiny dorsal fin. ▷mid 20th cent.: from modern Latin *Serranidae*, from the genus name *Serranus*, from Latin *serra* 'saw.'

ser·ra·no /sə'ränō/ ▸*n.* a small, red or yellow, very hot chile that is used fresh or dried in Mexican cooking.

ser·rate /'ser,āt; -it/ ▸*adj. chiefly Botany* serrated: *serrate leaves.* ▷mid 17th cent.: from late Latin *serratus*, from Latin *serra* 'saw.'

ser·rat·ed /'ser,ātid; sə'rātid/ ▸*adj.* having or denoting a jagged edge; sawlike: *a knife with a serrated edge.*

ser·ra·tion /sə'rāSHən/ ▸*n.* (usu. **serrations**) a tooth or point of a serrated edge or surface: *a heavy-duty knife with sawtooth serrations.*

ser·ried /'serēd/ ▸*adj.* [*attrib.*] (of rows of people or things) standing close together: *serried ranks of soldiers | the serried rows of vines.* ▷mid 17th cent.: past participle of *serry* 'press close,' probably from French *serré* 'close together,' based on Latin *sera* 'lock.'

ser·tão /sir'äNōō/ ▸*n.* (*pl.* **-tãos**) (in Brazil) an arid region of scrub. ▷early 19th cent.: Portuguese.

Ser·to·li cell /sər'tōlē/ ▸*n. Anatomy* a type of somatic cell around which spermatids develop in the tubules of the testis. ▷late 19th cent.: named after Enrico *Sertoli* (1842–1910), Italian histologist.

se·rum /'si(ə)rəm/ ▸*n.* (*pl.* **se·ra** /'si(ə)rə/ or **se·rums**) an amber-colored, protein-rich liquid that separates out when blood coagulates. ■ the blood serum of an animal, used esp. to provide immunity to a pathogen or toxin by inoculation or as a diagnostic agent. ▷late 17th cent.: from Latin, literally 'whey.'

se·rum hep·a·ti·tis ▸*n.* a viral form of hepatitis transmitted through infected blood products, causing fever, debility, and jaundice.

se·rum sick·ness ▸*n.* an allergic reaction to an injection of serum, typically mild and characterized by skin rashes, joint stiffness, and fever.

serv. ▸*abbr.* service.

ser·val /'sərvəl; sər'val/ ▸*n.* a slender African wildcat with long legs, large ears, and a black-spotted orange-brown coat. • *Felis serval*, family Felidae. ▷late 18th cent.: from French, from Portuguese *cerval* 'deerlike,' from *cervo* 'deer,' from Latin *cervus.*

serv·ant /'sərvənt/ ▸*n.* a person who performs duties for others, esp. a person employed in a house on domestic duties or as a personal attendant. ■ a person employed in the service of a government. See also **CIVIL SERVANT, PUBLIC SERVANT.** ■ a devoted and helpful follower or supporter: *a tireless servant of God.* ▷Middle English: from Old French, literally '(person) serving,' present participle (used as a noun) of *servir* 'to serve.' **—serv·ant·hood** /-ˌho͝od/ *n.*

serve /sərv/ ▸*v.* [*trans.*] **1** perform duties or services for (another person or an organization): *Malcolm has served the church very faithfully.* ■ provide (an area or group of people) with a product or service: *a telecommunications company that serves southern New England.* ■ [*intrans.*] be employed as a member of the armed forces: *a military engineer who served with the army.* ■ spend (a period) in office, in an apprenticeship, or in prison: *he is serving a ten-year jail sentence.* **2** present (food or drink) to someone: *they serve wine instead of beer* | [*trans.*] *serve white wines chilled.* ■ present (someone) with food or drink: *I'll* **serve** *you* **with** *coffee and cake* | [with *two objs.*] *Peter served them generous portions of soup.* ■ (of food or drink) be enough for: *the recipe serves four people.* ■ attend to (a customer in a store): *she turned to serve the impatient customer.* ■ supply (goods) to a customer. ■ [*intrans.*] *Christian Church* act as a server at the celebration of the Eucharist. ■ [with *two objs.*] *archaic* play (a trick) on (someone): *I remember the trick you served me.* **3** *Law* deliver (a document such as a summons or writ) in a formal manner to the person to whom it is addressed: *a warrant was* **served on** *Jack Sherman.* ■ deliver a document to (someone) in such a way: *they were just about to* **serve** *him* **with** *a writ.* **4** be of use in achieving or satisfying: *this book will serve a useful purpose* | *the union came into existence to serve the interests of musicians.* ■ [*intrans.*] be of some specified use: *the island's one pub* **serves as** *a café by day* | [with *infinitive*] *sweat serves to cool down the body.* ■ [*trans.*] function for or treat (someone) in a specified way: *the strategy served him well.* ■ (of a male breeding-animal) copulate with (a female). **5** [*intrans.*] (in tennis and other racket sports) hit the ball or shuttlecock to begin play: *he tossed the ball up to serve* | [*trans.*] *serve the ball onto the front wall.* ■ [*trans.*] (in tennis and other racket sports) begin play for each point in (a game). **6** *Nautical* bind (a rope) with thin cord to protect or strengthen it. **7** *Military* operate (a gun): *before long Lodge was the only man in his section able to serve the guns.*
▸*phrasal v.* □ **serve out** *Tennis* win the final game of a set or match while serving: *Fitzgerald then* **served out** *for the set.*
▸*n.* (in tennis and other racket sports) an act or turn of hitting the ball or shuttlecock to start play: *he was let down by an erratic serve.* ▷Middle English: from Old French *servir,* from Latin *servire,* from *servus* 'slave.'
▸**PHRASES** □ **if my memory serves me** if I remember correctly. □ **serve at table** act as a waiter. □ **serve someone right** be someone's deserved punishment or misfortune: *it would serve you right if Jeff walked out on you.* □ **serve one's time** (also **serve out one's time**) hold office for the normal period. ■ (also **serve time**) spend time in office, in an apprenticeship, or in prison. □ **serve two masters** take orders from two superiors or follow two conflicting or opposing principles or policies at the same time. [with biblical allusion to Matt. 6:24.]

serve-and-vol·ley ▸*adj. Tennis* [*attrib.*] denoting a style of play in which the server moves close to the net after serving, ready to play an attacking volley off the return. **—serve-and-vol·ley·er** *n.*

serv·er /ˈsərvər/ ▸*n.* a person or thing that provides a service or commodity, in particular: ■ a computer or computer program that manages access to a centralized resource or service in a network. ■ (in tennis and other racket sports) the player who serves. ■ a waiter or waitress. ■ *Christian Church* a person assisting the celebrant at the celebration of the Eucharist. ■ a large utensil for serving food: [with *adj.*] *a silver pie server.*

serv·er·y /ˈsərvərē/ ▸*n.* (*pl.* **-er·ies**) *Brit.* a counter, service hatch, or room from which meals are served.

Ser·vi·an[1] /ˈsərvēən/ ▸*adj.* of or relating to Servius Tullius, the semilegendary sixth king of ancient Rome (*fl.* 6th century BC).

Ser·vi·an[2] ▸*n.* & *adj.* archaic variant of **SERBIAN.**

Ser·vi·an wall a wall encircling the ancient city of Rome, said to have been built by Servius Tullius. See **SERVIAN** 1.

serv·ice /ˈsərvis/ ▸*n.* **1** the action of helping or doing work for someone: *millions are involved in voluntary service.* ■ an act of assistance: *he has done us a great service* | *he volunteered his services as a driver.* ■ assistance or advice given to customers during and after the sale of goods: *they aim to provide better quality of service.* ■ short for **SERVICE INDUSTRY**: *a private security service.* ■ work done for a customer other than manufacturing: *scheduled commercial airline service* | *highly customized goods and services.* ■ the action or process of serving food and drinks to customers: *they complained of poor bar service.* ■ short for **SERVICE CHARGE**: *service is included in the final bill.* ■ a period of employment with a company or organization: *he retired after 40 years' service.* ■ employment as a servant: *the pitifully low wages gained from domestic service.* See also **IN SERVICE** below. ■ the use that can be made of a machine: *the computer should provide good service for years.* ■ the provision of the necessary maintenance work for a machine: *they phoned for service on their air conditioning.* ■ a periodic routine inspection and maintenance of a vehicle or other machine: *he took his car in for service.* ■ (**the services**) the armed forces: *troops from all branches of the services* | [as *adj.*] (**service**) *service personnel.* ■ (**services**) *chiefly Brit.* an area with parking beside a major road supplying gasoline, refreshments, and other amenities to motorists. **2** a system supplying a public need such as transport, communications, or utilities such as electricity and water: *a regular bus service.* ■ a public department or organization run by the government: *the U.S. Fish and Wildlife Service.* **3** a ceremony of religious worship according to a prescribed form; the prescribed form for such a ceremony: *a funeral service.* **4** [with *adj.*] a set of matching dishes and utensils used for serving a particular meal: *a dinner service.* **5** (in tennis and other racket sports) the action or right of serving to begin play. ■ a serve. **6** *Law* the formal delivery of a document such as a writ or summons.
▸*v.* [*trans.*] **1** (usu. **be serviced**) perform routine maintenance or repair work on (a vehicle or machine): *have your car serviced regularly.* ■ supply and maintain systems for public utilities and transportation and communications in (an area): *the town is small but well serviced.* ■ perform a service or services for (someone): *the state's biggest health maintenance organization servicing the poor.* ■ pay interest on (a debt): *taxpayers are paying $250 million just to service that debt.* **2** (of a male animal) mate with (a female animal). ■ *vulgar slang* (of a man) have sexual intercourse with (a woman). ▷Old English (denoting religious devotion or a form of liturgy), from Old French *servise* or Latin *servitium* 'slavery,' from *servus* 'slave.' The early sense of the verb (mid 19th cent.) was 'be of service to, provide with a service.'
▸**PHRASES** □ **be at someone's service** be ready to assist someone whenever possible. □ **be of service** be available to assist someone. □ **in service 1** in or available for use. **2** *dated* employed as a servant. □ **out of service** not available for use. □ **see service** serve in the armed forces: *he saw service in both world wars.* ■ be used: *the building later saw service as a blacksmith's shop.*

serv·ice·a·ble /ˈsərvəsəbəl/ ▸*adj.* fulfilling its function adequately; usable: *an aging but still serviceable water supply system.* ■ functional and durable rather than attractive. ■ in working order: *only twelve aircraft were fully serviceable this morning.* ▷Middle English (in the sense 'willing to be of service'): from Old French *servisable,* from *servise* (see **SERVICE**). **—serv·ice·a·bil·i·ty** /ˌsərvəsəˈbilitē/ *n.* **—serv·ice·a·bly** /-blē/ *adv.*

serv·ice ar·e·a ▸*n.* **1** a roadside area where services are available to motorists. **2** the area covered by the signal of a broadcasting station.

serv·ice·ber·ry /ˈsərvisˌberē/ ▸*n.* **1** the fruit of the service tree. **2** another term for **JUNEBERRY.**

serv·ice book ▸*n.* a book of authorized forms of worship used in a church.

serv·ice bu·reau ▸*n. Computing* an organization providing services such as scanning, prepress, and color printing.

serv·ice cap ▸*n.* a round, flat-topped cap with a visor that is part of the U.S. Army and U.S. Air Force service uniform.

serv·ice ceil·ing ▸*n.* the maximum height at which an aircraft can sustain a specified rate of climb dependent on engine type.

serv·ice charge (also **serv·ice fee**) ▸*n.* an extra charge assessed for a service.

serv·ice club ▸*n.* an association of business or professional people with the aims of promoting community welfare and goodwill.

serv·ice con·tract ▸*n.* a business agreement between a contractor and customer covering the maintenance and servicing of equipment over a specified period.

serv·ice dress ▸*n. Brit.* military uniform worn on formal but not ceremonial occasions.

serv·ice e·con·o·my ▸*n.* an economy or the sector of an economy that is based on trade in services.

serv·ice game ▸*n.* (in tennis and other racket sports) a game in which a particular player serves. ■ a player's skill or style in serving.

serv·ice in·dus·try ▸*n.* a business that does work for a customer, and occasionally provides goods, but is not involved in manufacturing.

serv·ice line ▸*n.* (in tennis, badminton, and other sports) a line on a court marking the limit of the area into which the ball must be served. ■ (esp. in handball and paddleball) a line on a court marking the boundary of the area in which the server must be standing when serving.

serv·ice·man /ˈsərvəsˌmən; -ˌman/ ▸*n.* (*pl.* **-men**) **1** a man serving in the armed forces. **2** a person providing maintenance on machinery, esp. domestic machinery.

serv·ice mark ▸*n.* a legally registered name or designation used in the manner of a trademark to distinguish an organization's services from those of its competitors.

serv·ice mod·ule ▸*n.* a detachable compartment of a spacecraft carrying fuel and supplies.

serv·ice pack ▸*n.* (abbr. **SP**) a periodically released update to software from a manufacturer, consisting of requested enhancements and fixes for known bugs.

serv·ice pro·vid·er ▸*n. Computing* a company that provides its subscribers access to the Internet.

serv·ice road ▸*n.* another term for **FRONTAGE ROAD.**

ser·vice star ▸*n. Military* a star awarded to indicate service in a specific battle or campaign.

serv·ice sta·tion ▸*n.* an establishment selling gasoline and oil and typically having the facilities to provide automotive repairs and maintenance.

serv·ice stripe ▸*n. Military* a stripe worn on the left sleeve of an enlisted person's tunic, indicating the number of years in service.

serv·ice tree ▸*n.* a Eurasian tree of the rose family, closely related to the rowan. • Genus *Sorbus,* family Rosaceae: the southern European **true service tree** (*S. domestica*), with compound leaves and green-brown fruits that are edible when overripe, and the **wild service tree** (*S. torminalis*), with lobed leaves and brown berries. ▷mid 16th cent.: *service* from an alteration of the plural of obsolete *serve,* from Old English *syrfe,* based on Latin *sorbus.*

serv·ice·wom·an /ˈsərvəsˌwo͝omən/ ▸*n.* (*pl.* **-wom·en**) a woman serving in the armed forces.

ser·vi·ette /ˌsərvēˈet/ ▸*n. Brit.* & *Canadian* a table napkin. ▷late 15th cent.: from Old French, from *servir* 'to serve.'

ser·vile /ˈsərvəl; -ˌvīl/ ▸*adj.* **1** having or showing an excessive willingness to serve or please others: *bowing his head in a servile manner.* See note at **OBSEQUIOUS.** **2** of or characteristic of a slave or slaves. ▷late Middle English (in the sense 'suitable for a slave or for the working class'): from Latin *servilis,* from *servus* 'slave.' **—ser·vile·ly** *adv.* **—ser·vil·i·ty** /sərˈvilitē/ *n.*

serv·ing /ˈsərviNG/ ▸*n.* a quantity of food suitable for or served to one person: *a large* **serving of** *spaghetti.*

serv·ing·man /ˈsərviNGˌman/ ▸*n.* (*pl.* **-men**) *archaic* a male servant or attendant.

serv·ing·wom·an /ˈsərviNGˌwo͝omən/ ▸*n.* (*pl.* **-wom·en**) *archaic* a female servant or attendant.

Ser·vite /ˈsərˌvīt/ ▸*n.* a friar or nun of the Catholic religious order of the Servants of Blessed Mary, founded in 1233.
▸*adj.* of or relating to this order. ▷from medieval Latin *Servitae* (plural), from Latin, from *Servi Beatae Mariae,* the formal title of the order (see above).

ser·vi·tor /ˈsərvitər; -ˌtôr/ ▸*n. archaic* a person who serves or attends on a social superior. ■ *historical* an Oxford University undergraduate performing menial duties in exchange for assistance from college funds. ▷Middle English: via Old French from late Latin, from *servit-* 'served,' from the verb *servire* (see **SERVE**). **—ser·vi·tor·ship** /-ˌSHip/ *n.*

ser·vi·tude /ˈsərviˌt(y)o͞od/ ▸*n.* the state of being a slave or completely subject to someone more powerful. ■ *archaic Law* the subjection of property to an easement. ▷late Middle English: via Old French from Latin *servitudo*, from *servus* 'slave.'

serv·let /'sərvlit/ ▶*n. Computing* a small, server-resident program that typically runs automatically in response to user input: *students will build servlets that generate Web pages and communicate with other Java servers.*

ser·vo /'sərvō/ ▶*n.* (*pl.* **-vos**) short for SERVOMECHANISM or SERVOMOTOR. ■ [as *adj.*] relating to or involving a servomechanism: *hydraulic and electrical servo systems.* ▷late 19th cent.: from Latin *servus* 'slave.'

ser·vo·mech·an·ism /'sərvō,mekə,nizəm/ ▶*n.* a powered mechanism producing motion or forces at a higher level of energy than the input level, e.g., in the brakes and steering of large motor vehicles, esp. where feedback is employed to make the control automatic.

ser·vo·mo·tor /'sərvō,mōtər/ ▶*n.* the motive element in a servomechanism.

SES ▶*abbr.* socioeconomic status.

ses·a·me /'sesəmē/ ▶*n.* a tall annual herbaceous plant of tropical and subtropical areas of the Old World, cultivated for its oil-rich seeds. • *Sesamum indicum*, family Pedaliaceae. ■ (**sesame seed**) the edible seeds of this plant, which are used whole or have the oil extracted. ▷late Middle English: via Latin from Greek *sēsamon, sēsamē*, probably of Semitic origin; compare with Arabic *simsim*.

ses·a·moid /'sesə,moid/ (also **sesamoid bone**) ▶*n.* a small independent bone or bony nodule developed in a tendon where it passes over an angular structure, typically in the hands and feet. The kneecap is a particularly large sesamoid bone. ▷late 17th cent.: from SESAME (with reference to the similarity in shape of a sesame seed) + -OID.

Se·so·tho /sə'sōōtōō/ ▶*n.* the Sotho language of the Basotho people, an official language in Lesotho and South Africa.
▶*adj.* of or relating to this language. ▷the name in Sesotho.

sesqui- ▶*comb. form* denoting one and a half: *sesquicentenary.* ■ *Chemistry* (of a compound) in which a particular element or group is present in a ratio of 3:2 compared with another: *sesquioxide.* ▷from Latin *semi-* (see SEMI-) + *-que* 'and.'

ses·qui·al·tera /,seskwi'altərə/ ▶*adj.* [*attrib.*] *Music* relating to or denoting a ratio of 3:2, as in an interval of a fifth. ■ denoting a mixture stop in an organ, typically consisting of two ranks of narrow-scaled open flue pipes. ▷late Middle English: from Latin, feminine of *sesquialter*, from *sesqui* (see SESQUI-) + *alter* 'second.'

ses·qui·cen·ten·ar·y /,seskwisen'tenərē/ ▶*chiefly Brit. n.* (*pl.* **-ar·ies**) a sesquicentennial.
▶*adj.* of or relating to a sesquicentennial.

ses·qui·cen·ten·ni·al /,seskwisen'tenēəl/ ▶*adj.* of or relating to the one-hundred-and-fiftieth anniversary of a significant event.
▶*n.* a one-hundred-and-fiftieth anniversary.

ses·qui·ox·ide /,seskwē'äk,sīd/ ▶*n. Chemistry* an oxide in which oxygen is present in the ratio of three atoms to two of another element.

ses·qui·pe·da·li·an /,seskwəpə'dālyən/ ▶*adj. formal* (of a word) polysyllabic; long: *sesquipedalian surnames.* ■ characterized by long words; long-winded: *the sesquipedalian prose of scientific journals.* ▷mid 17th cent.: from Latin *sesquipedalis* 'a foot and a half long,' from *sesqui-* (see SESQUI-) + *pes, ped-* 'foot.'

ses·qui·ter·pene /,seskwi'tər,pēn/ ▶*n. Chemistry* a terpene with the formula $C_{15}H_{24}$, or a simple derivative of such a compound.

ses·sile /'sesəl; -īl/ ▶*adj. Biology* (of an organism, e.g., a barnacle) fixed in one place; immobile. ■ (of a plant or animal structure) attached directly by its base without a stalk or peduncle: *sporangia may be stalked or sessile.* ▷early 18th cent.: from Latin *sessilis*, from *sess-* 'seated,' from the verb *sedere*.

ses·sile oak ▶*n.* another term for DURMAST OAK.

ses·sion /'sesHən/ ▶*n.* **1** a meeting of a deliberative or judicial body to conduct its business. ■ a period during which such meetings are regularly held: *legislation to curb wildcat strikes will be introduced during the coming parliamentary session.* ■ the governing body of a Presbyterian Church. **2** [often with *adj.*] a period devoted to a particular activity: *gym is followed by a training session.* ■ *informal* a period of heavy or sustained drinking. ■ a period of recording music in a studio, esp. by a session musician: *he did the sessions for a Great Country Hits album.* ■ an academic year. ■ the period during which a school has classes. ▷late Middle English: from Old French, or from Latin *sessio(n-)*, from *sess-* 'seated' (see SESSILE). —**ses·sion·al** /-sHənl/ *adj.*
▶*PHRASE* □ **in session** assembled for or proceeding with business.

ses·sion clerk ▶*n.* a chief lay official in the session of a Presbyterian Church.

ses·sion mu·si·cian ▶*n.* a freelance musician hired to play on recording sessions.

Ses·sions /'sesHənz/, Roger (Huntington) (1896–1985), U.S. composer. He composed eight symphonies, as well as operas such as *Montezuma* (1959–63), the cantata " When Lilacs Last in the Dooryard Bloom'd" (1970), and "Concerto for Orchestra" (1981).

ses·terce /'sestərs/ (also **ses·ter·ti·us** /se'stərsH(ē)əs/) ▶*n.* (*pl.* **ses·terc·es** /'sestərsəz/ or **ses·ter·ti·i** /ses'tərsHē,ī/) an ancient Roman coin and monetary unit equal to one quarter of a denarius. ▷from Latin *sestertius (nummus)* '(coin) that is two and a half (asses).'

ses·tet /ses'tet/ ▶*n. Prosody* the last six lines of a sonnet. ■ *rare Music* a sextet. ▷early 19th cent.: from Italian *sestetto*, from *sesto*, from Latin *sextus* 'a sixth.'

ses·ti·na /se'stēnə/ ▶*n. Prosody* a poem with six stanzas of six lines and a final triplet, all stanzas having the same six words at the line-ends in six different sequences that follow a fixed pattern, and with all six words appearing in the closing three-line envoi. ▷mid 19th cent.: from Italian, from *sesto* (see SESTET).

Set /set/ variant spelling of SETH.

set[1] /set/ ▶*v.* (**set·ting**; *past* **set**) **1** [*trans.*] put, lay, or stand (something) in a specified place or position: *Dana set the mug of tea down | Catherine set a chair by the bed.* ■ (**be set**) be situated or fixed in a specified place or position: *the village was set among olive groves on a hill.* ■ represent (a story, play, movie, or scene) as happening at a specified time or in a specified place: *a spy novel set in Berlin.* ■ mount a precious stone in (something, typically a piece of jewelry): *a bracelet set with emeralds.* ■ mount (a precious stone) in something. ■ *Printing* arrange (type) as required. ■ *Printing* arrange the type for (a piece of text): *article headings will be set in Times fourteen point.* ■ prepare (a table) for a meal by placing cutlery, dishes, etc., on it in their proper places. ■ (**set something to**) provide (music) so that a written work can be produced in a musical form: *she set his poem to music.* ■ [*intrans.*] (of a dancer) acknowledge another dancer, typically one's partner, using the steps prescribed: *the gentleman sets to and turns with the lady on his left hand.* ■ cause (a hen) to sit on eggs. ■ place (eggs) for a hen to sit on. ■ put (a seed or plant) in the ground to grow. ■ give the teeth of (a saw) alternating outward inclinations. ■ *Sailing* put (a sail) up in position to catch the wind: *a safe distance from shore all sails were set.* See also SET SAIL below. **2** [*trans.*] put or bring into a specified state: *plunging oil prices set in motion an economic collapse in Houston | [trans.] the hostages were set free.* ■ [*trans.*] cause (someone or something) to start doing something: *the incident set me thinking.* ■ [*trans.*] instruct (someone) to do something: *he'll set a man to watch you.* ■ give someone (a task): [with *two objs.*] *the problem we have been set.* ■ devise (a test) and give it to someone to do. ■ establish as (an example) for others to follow, copy, or try to achieve: *the scheme sets a precedent for other companies.* ■ establish (a record): *his time in the 25-meter freestyle set a national record.* ■ decide on: *they set a date for a full hearing at the end of February.* ■ fix (a price, value, or limit) on something: *the unions had set a limit on the size of the temporary workforce.* **3** [*trans.*] adjust the hands of (a clock or watch), typically to show the right time. ■ adjust (an alarm clock) to sound at the required time. ■ adjust (a device or its controls) so that it performs a particular operation: *you have to be careful not to set the volume too high.* ■ *Electronics* cause (a binary device) to enter the state representing the numeral 1. **4** [*intrans.*] harden into a solid or semisolid state: *cook for a further thirty-five minutes until the filling has set.* ■ [*trans.*] arrange (the hair) while damp so that it dries in the required style: *she had set her hair on small rollers.* ■ [*trans.*] put parts of (a broken or dislocated bone or limb) into the correct position for healing. ■ [*trans.*] deal with (a fracture or dislocation) in this way. ■ (of a bone) be restored to its normal condition by knitting together again after being broken: *dogs' bones soon set.* ■ (with reference to a person's face) assume or cause to assume a fixed or rigid expression: [*intrans.*] *her features never set into a civil parade of attention* | [*trans.*] *Travis's face was set as he looked up.* ■ (of the eyes) become fixed in position or in the feeling they are expressing: *his bright eyes set in an expression of mocking amusement.* ■ (of a hunting dog) adopt a rigid attitude indicating the presence of game. **5** [*intrans.*] (of the sun, moon, or another celestial body) appear to move toward and below the earth's horizon as the earth rotates: *the sun was setting and a warm, red glow filled the sky.* **6** [*intrans.*] (of a tide or current) take or have a specified direction or course: *a fair tide can be carried well past Lands End before the stream sets to the north.* **7** [*trans.*] start (a fire). **8** [*trans.*] (of blossom or a tree) develop into or produce (fruit). ■ [*intrans.*] (of fruit) develop from blossom. ■ (of a plant) produce (seed): *the herb has flowered and started to set seed.* **9** *informal dialect* sit: *a perfect lady—just set in her seat and stared.*
▶*phrasal v.* □ **set about 1** start doing something with vigor or determination: *it would be far better to admit the problem openly and set about tackling it.* **2** *Brit., informal* attack (someone). □ **set someone against** cause someone to be in opposition or conflict with: *he hadn't meant any harm, but his few words had set her against him.* □ **set something against** offset something against: *wives' allowances can henceforth be set against investment income.* □ **set someone apart** give someone an air of unusual superiority: *his blunt views set him apart.* □ **set something apart** separate something and keep it for a special purpose: *there were books and rooms set apart as libraries.* □ **set something aside 1** save or keep something, typically money or time, for a particular purpose: *the bank expected to set aside about $700 million for restructuring.* ■ remove land from agricultural production. **2** annul a legal decision or process. □ **set someone/something back 1** delay or impede the progress of someone or something: *this incident undoubtedly set back research.* **2** *informal* (of a purchase) cost someone a particular amount of money: *that must have set you back a bit.* □ **set something by** *dated* save something for future use. □ **set someone down** stop and allow someone to alight from a vehicle. □ **set something down** record something in writing. ■ establish something authoritatively as a rule or principle to be followed: *the Association set down codes of practice for all members to comply with.* □ **set forth** begin a journey or trip. □ **set something forth** state or describe something in writing or speech: *the principles and aims set forth in the Charter.* □ **set forward** *archaic* start on a journey. □ **set in** (of something unpleasant or unwelcome) begin and seem likely to continue: *less hardy plants should be brought inside before cold weather sets in.* □ **set something in** insert something, esp. a sleeve, into a garment. □ **set off** begin a journey. □ **set someone off** cause someone to start doing something, esp. laughing or talking: *anything will set him off laughing.* □ **set something off 1** detonate a bomb. ■ cause an alarm to go off. ■ cause a series of things to occur: *the fear is that this could set off a chain reaction in other financial markets.* **2** serve as decorative embellishment to: *a pink carnation set off nicely by a red bow tie and cream shirt.* □ **set something off against** another way of saying SET SOMETHING AGAINST above. □ **set on** (or **upon**) attack (someone) violently. □ **set someone/something on** (or **upon**) cause or urge a person or animal to attack: *I was asked to leave and threatened with having dogs set upon me.* □ **set out** begin a journey. ■ aim or intend to do something: *she drew up a plan of what her organization should set out to achieve.* □ **set something out** arrange or display something in a particular order or position. ■ present information or ideas in a well-ordered way in writing or speech: *this chapter sets out the debate surrounding pluralism.* □ **set to** begin doing something vigorously: *she set to with bleach and scouring pads to render the vases spotless.* □ **set someone up 1** establish someone in a particular capacity or role: *his father set him up in business.* **2** restore or enhance the health of someone: *after my operation, the doctor recommended a cruise to set me up again.* **3** *informal* make an innocent person appear guilty of something: *suppose Zielinski had set him up for Ingram's murder?* □ **set something up 1** place or erect something in position: *police set up a roadblock on Tenth Street.* **2** establish a business, institution, or other organization. ■ make the arrangements necessary for something: *he asked if I would like him to set up a meeting with the president.* **3** begin making a loud sound. □ **set oneself up as** establish oneself in (a particular occupation): *he set himself up as an attorney in St. Louis.* ■ claim to be or act like a specified kind of person (used to indicate skepticism as to someone's right or ability to do so): *he set himself up as a crusader for higher press and broadcasting standards.* ▷Old English *settan*, of Germanic origin; related to Dutch *zetten*, German *setzen*, also to SIT.

▸*PHRASES* □ **set one's heart** (or **hopes**) **on** have a strong desire for or to do: *she **had her heart set on** going to college.* □ **set sail** hoist the sails of a vessel. ■ begin a voyage: *tomorrow we set sail for France.* □ **set one's teeth** clench one's teeth together. ■ become resolute: *they have set their teeth against a change which would undermine their prospects of forming a government.* □ **set up shop** see **SHOP**. □ **set someone straight** inform someone of the truth of a situation. □ **set the wheels in motion** do something to begin a process or put a plan into action.

USAGE **Set**, meaning 'place or put,' is mainly a transitive verb and takes a direct object: *set the flowers on top of the piano.* **Sit**, meaning 'be seated,' is mainly intransitive and does not take a direct object: *sit in this chair while I check the light meter.*

set[2] ▸*n.* **1** a group or collection of things that belong together, resemble one another, or are usually found together: *a set of false teeth | a new cell with two sets of chromosomes | a spare set of clothes.* ■ a collection of implements, containers, or other objects customarily used together for a specific purpose: *an electric fondue set.* ■ a group of people with common interests or occupations or of similar social status: *it was a fashionable haunt of the literary set.* ■ (in tennis, darts, and other games) a group of games counting as a unit toward a match, only the player or side that wins a defined number or proportion of the games being awarded a point toward the final score: *he took the first set 6-3.* ■ (in jazz or popular music) a sequence of songs or pieces performed together and constituting or forming part of a live show or recording: *a short four-song set.* ■ a group of people making up the required number for a square dance or similar country dance. ■ a fixed number of repetitions of a particular bodybuilding exercise; compare with **REP**[5]. ■ *Mathematics & Logic* a collection of distinct entities regarded as a unit, being either individually specified or (more usually) satisfying specified conditions: *the set of all positive integers.* **2** [in *sing.*] the way in which something is set, disposed, or positioned: *the shape and set of the eyes.* ■ the posture or attitude of a part of the body, typically in relation to the impression this gives of a person's feelings or intentions: *the determined set of her upper torso.* ■ the flow of a current or tide in a particular direction: *the rudder kept the dinghy straight against the set of the tide.* ■ an arrangement of the hair when damp so that it dries in the required style: *a shampoo and set.* ■ (also **dead set**) a setter's pointing in the presence of game. ■ the alternating outward inclinations of the teeth of a saw. ■ a warp or bend in wood, metal, or another material caused by continued strain or pressure. **3** a radio or television receiver: *a TV set.* **4** a collection of scenery, stage furniture, and other articles used for a particular scene in a play or film. ■ the place or area in which filming is taking place or a play is performed: *the magazine has interviews **on set** with top directors.* **5** a cutting, young plant, or bulb used in the propagation of new plants. ■ a young fruit that has just formed. **6** the last coat of plaster on a wall. **7** *Printing* the amount of spacing in type controlling the distance between letters. ■ the width of a piece of type. **8** variant spelling of **SETT**. ▷late Middle English: partly from Old French *sette*, from Latin *secta* 'sect,' partly from **SET**[1].

set[3] ▸*adj.* **1** fixed or arranged in advance: *there is no set procedure.* ■ (of a view or habit) unlikely to change: *I've been on my own a long time and I'm rather **set in my ways**.* ■ (of a person's expression) held for an unnaturally long time without changing, typically as a reflection of determination. ■ (of a meal or menu in a restaurant) offered at a fixed price with a limited choice of dishes. ■ having a conventional or predetermined wording; formulaic: *witnesses often delivered their testimony according to a set speech.* See also **SET PHRASE**. **2** [*predic.*] ready, prepared, or likely to do something: *"All **set for** tonight?" he asked |* [with *infinitive*] *water costs look set to increase.* ■ (**set against**) firmly opposed to: *an approach set against tradition and authority.* ■ (**set on**) determined to do (something): *he's set on marrying that girl.* ▷late Old English, past participle of **SET**[1].

se·ta /'sētə/ ▸*n.* (*pl.* **-tae** /-tē/) *chiefly Zoology* a stiff hairlike or bristlelike structure, esp. in an invertebrate. ■ *Botany* (in a moss or liverwort) the stalk supporting the capsule. ▷late 18th cent.: from Latin, 'bristle.' —**se·ta·ceous** /si'tāshəs/ *adj.* —**se·tal** *adj.*

set-a·side ▸*n.* **1** the policy of taking land out of production to reduce crop surpluses. ■ land taken out of production in this way: *he has fifty acres of set-aside.* **2** a government contract awarded without competition to a minority-owned business. **3** a portion of funds or other resources reserved for a particular purpose: *a set-aside for library services for Native Americans.*

set·back /'set,bak/ ▸*n.* **1** a reversal or check in progress: *a serious setback for the peace process.* **2** *Architecture* a plain, flat offset in a wall. **3** the distance by which a building or part of a building is set back from the property line.

se·ten·ant /sə 'tenənt; sə tə'näN/ ▸*adj. Philately* (of stamps of different designs) joined together side by side when printed: *a se-tenant block of four stamps.* ▷early 20th cent.: from French, literally 'holding together.'

Seth /seTH/ (also **Set**) *Egyptian Mythology* an evil god who murdered his brother Osiris and wounded Osiris's son Horus. Seth is represented as having the head of an animal with a long pointed snout.

SETI /'setē/ ▸*abbr.* Search for Extra-Terrestrial Intelligence, the designation of a series of projects based mainly on attempts to detect artificial radio transmissions from outer space.

set-in ▸*adj.* [*attrib.*] (of a sleeve) made separately and inset into a garment.

set-net ▸*n.* a fishing net fastened in fixed position. —**set-net·ter** *n.*

set-off ▸*n.* **1** an item or amount that is or may be set off against another in the settlement of accounts. ■ *Law* a counterbalancing debt pleaded by the defendant in an action to recover money due. ■ *dated* a counterbalancing or compensating circumstance or condition: *as a set-off against such discussions there had come an improvement in their pecuniary position.* **2** a step or shoulder at which the thickness of part of a building or machine is reduced. **3** *Printing* the unwanted transference of ink from one printed sheet or page to another before it has set.

Se·ton /'sētn/, St. Elizabeth Ann (Bayley) (1774–1821), U.S. religious leader, educator, and social reformer. The widowed mother of five children, she converted to Roman Catholicism in 1805. She became a nun in 1809 and by 1813 had founded the Sisters of Charity, a religious order. In 1975, she became the first native-born American to be canonized as a saint.

se·ton /'sētn/ ▸*n. historical Medicine* a skein of cotton or other absorbent material passed below the skin and left with the ends protruding, to promote drainage of fluid or to act as a counterirritant. ▷late Middle English: from medieval Latin *seto(n-)*, apparently from Latin *seta* 'bristle.'

se·tose /'sē,tōs/ ▸*adj. chiefly Zoology* bearing bristles or setae; bristly. ▷mid 17th cent.: from Latin *seta* 'bristle' + **-OSE**[1].

set phrase ▸*n.* an unvarying phrase having a specific meaning, such as "raining cats and dogs," or being the only context in which a word appears, e.g., "aback" in "take aback."

set piece ▸*n.* a thing that has been carefully or elaborately planned or composed, in particular: ■ a self-contained passage or section of a novel, play, film, or piece of music arranged in an elaborate or conventional pattern for maximum effect: *the film lurches from one comic set piece to another.* ■ a formal and carefully structured speech. ■ a carefully organized and practiced move in a team game by which the ball is returned to play, as at a scrum in rugby or a free kick in soccer. ■ an arrangement of fireworks forming a picture or design.

set play ▸*n. Sports* a prearranged maneuver carried out from a restart or after a timeout by the team that has the advantage: *the Germans scored the deciding goal on a set play, off a corner kick in the 15th minute.*

set point ▸*n.* (in tennis and other sports) a point that, if won by a contestant, will also win the set.

set screw ▸*n.* a screw for adjusting or clamping parts of a machine.

set shot ▸*n. Basketball* a shot made while standing still.

set square ▸*n.* a right-angled triangular plate for drawing lines, esp. at 90°, 45°, 60°, or 30°. ■ a form of T-square with an additional arm turning on a pivot for drawing lines at fixed angles to the head.

Sets·wa·na /set'swänə/ ▸*n.* the Bantu language of the Tswana people, related to the Sotho languages and spoken by over 3 million people in southern Africa. ▸*adj.* of or relating to this language. ▷the name in Setswana.

sett /set/ (also **set**) ▸*n.* **1** the lair or burrow of a badger. **2** the particular pattern of stripes in a tartan. ▷Middle English: variant of **SET**[2], the spelling with *-tt* prevailing in technical senses.

set·tee /se'tē/ ▸*n.* a long upholstered seat for more than one person, typically with a back and arms. ▷early 18th cent.: perhaps a fanciful variant of **SETTLE**[2].

set·ter /'setər/ ▸*n.* **1** a dog of a large, long-haired breed trained to stand rigid when scenting game. See **ENGLISH SETTER, GORDON SETTER, IRISH SETTER.** **2** [usu. in *combination*] a person or thing that sets something: *trend-setters in Hollywood.*

set the·o·ry ▸*n.* the branch of mathematics that deals with the formal properties of sets as units (without regard to the nature of their individual constituents) and the expression of other branches of mathematics in terms of sets. —**set-the·o·ret·ic** *adj.* —**set-the·o·ret·i·cal** *adj.*

set·ting /'setiNG/ ▸*n.* **1** the place or type of surroundings where something is positioned or where an event takes place: *cozy waterfront cottage in a peaceful country setting.* ■ the place and time at which a play, novel, or film is represented as happening: *short stories with a contemporary setting.* ■ a piece of metal in which a precious stone or gem is fixed to form a piece of jewelry. ■ a piece of vocal or choral music composed for particular words: *a setting of Yevtushenko's bleak poem.* ■ short for **PLACE SETTING**. **2** a speed, height, or temperature at which a machine or device can be adjusted to operate: *if you find the room getting too hot, check the thermostat setting.*

set·ting lo·tion ▸*n.* lotion applied to damp hair before it is set, enabling it to keep its shape longer.

set·tle[1] /'setl/ ▸*v.* **1** [*trans.*] resolve or reach an agreement about (an argument or problem): *every effort was made to settle the dispute.* ■ end (a legal dispute) by mutual agreement: *the matter was settled out of court |* [*intrans.*] *he sued for libel and then settled out of court.* ■ determine; decide on: *exactly what goes into the legislation has not been settled |* [*intrans.*] *they had not yet **settled on** a date for the wedding.* ■ pay (a debt or account): *his bill was settled by charge card |* [*intrans.*] *I **settled up with** your brother for my board and lodging.* ■ complete the administration and distribution of a decedent's estate. ■ (**settle something on**) give money or property to (someone) through a deed of settlement or a will. ■ [*intrans.*] (**settle for**) accept or agree to (something that one considers to be less than satisfactory): *it was too cold for champagne so they settled for a cup of tea.* ■ *dated* silence (someone considered a nuisance) by some means: *he told me to hold my tongue or he would find a way to settle me.* **2** [*intrans.*] adopt a more steady or secure style of life, esp. in a permanent job and home: *one day I will **settle down** and raise a family.* ■ [with *adverbial of place*] make one's permanent home somewhere: *in 1863 the family settled in London.* ■ begin to feel comfortable or established in a new home, situation, or job: *she **settled in** happily with a foster family | he had **settled into** his new job.* ■ [*trans.*] establish a colony in: *European immigrants settled much of Australia.* ■ (**settle down to**) turn one's attention to; apply oneself to: *Catherine settled down to her studies.* ■ become or make calmer or quieter: [*intrans.*] *after a few months the controversy settled down |* [*trans.*] *try to settle your puppy down before going to bed.* **3** [*intrans.*] sit or come to rest in a comfortable position: *he settled into an armchair.* ■ [*trans.*] make (someone) comfortable in a particular place or position: *she allowed him to settle her in the taxi.* ■ [*trans.*] move or adjust (something) so that it rests securely: *she settled her bag on her shoulder.* ■ fall or come down on to a surface: *dust from the mill had settled on the roof.* ■ [*intrans.*] (of suspended particles) sink slowly in a liquid to form sediment; (of a liquid) become clear or still through this process: *sediment settles near the bottom of the tank | he pours a glass and leaves it on the bar to settle.* ■ [*intrans.*] (of an object or objects) gradually sink down under its or their own weight: *they listened to the soft ticking and creaking as the house settled.* ■ [*intrans.*] (of a ship or boat) sink gradually. ▷Old English *setlan* 'to seat, place,' from **SETTLE**[2]. —**set·tle·a·ble** *adj.* —**set·tled·ness** *n.*

▸*PHRASES* □ **settle one's affairs** make any necessary arrangements, such as writing a will, before one's death. □ **settle someone's hash** see **HASH**[1].

set·tle[2] ▸*n.* a wooden bench with a high back and arms, typically incorporating a box under the seat.

S

▷Old English *setl* 'a place to sit,' of Germanic origin; related to German *Sessel* and Latin *sella* 'seat,' also to SIT.

set·tle·ment /ˈsetlmənt/ ▶*n.* **1** an official agreement intended to resolve a dispute or conflict: *unions succeeded in reaching a pay settlement | the settlement of the Palestinian problem.* ■ a formal arrangement made between the parties to a lawsuit in order to resolve it, esp. out of court: *the owner reached an out-of-court settlement with the plaintiffs.* **2** a place, typically one that has hitherto been uninhabited, where people establish a community: *the little settlement of Buttermere.* ■ the process of settling in such a place: *the early settlement of Queensland.* ■ the action of allowing or helping people to do this: *Israel's settlement of immigrants in the occupied territories.* **3** *Law* an arrangement whereby property passes to a succession of people as dictated by the settlor. ■ the amount or property given. **4** the action or process of settling an account. **5** subsidence of the ground or a structure built on it: *a boundary wall, which has cracked due to settlement, is to be replaced.*

set·tle·ment house ▶*n.* an institution in an inner-city area providing educational, recreational, and other social services to the community.

set·tler /ˈsetl-ər; ˈsetlər/ ▶*n.* a person who settles in an area, typically one with no or few previous inhabitants.

set·tling time ▶*n. technical* the time taken for a measuring or control instrument to get within a certain distance of a new equilibrium value without subsequently deviating from it by that amount.

set·tlor /ˈsetl-ər; ˈsetlər/ ▶*n. Law* a person who makes a settlement, esp. of a property.

set-to ▶*n.* (*pl.* **-tos**) *informal* a fight or argument: *we had a little set-to about her piano practicing.*

set-top box ▶*n.* a device which converts a digital television signal to analog for viewing on a conventional set.

set·up /ˈsetˌəp/ ▶*n.* [usu. in *sing.*] *informal* **1** the way in which something, esp. an organization or equipment, is organized, planned, or arranged: *would you feel comfortable in a team-teaching setup?* ■ an organization or arrangement: *Moses and Jesus came from strange family setups.* ■ a set of equipment needed for a particular activity or purpose: *I have a recording setup in my house.* ■ (in a ball game) a pass or play intended to provide an opportunity for another player to score. **2** a scheme or trick intended to incriminate or deceive someone: *"Listen. He didn't die. It was a setup."* ■ a contest with a prearranged outcome.

Seu·rat /səˈrä/, Georges Pierre (1859–91), French painter. The founder of neo-Impressionism, he is chiefly associated with pointillism, which he developed during the 1880s. Among his major paintings using this technique is *Sunday Afternoon on the Island of La Grande Jatte* (1884–86).

Seuss /so͞os/, Dr., see GEISEL.

sev /säv; sev/ ▶*n.* an Indian snack consisting of long, thin strands of gram flour, deep-fried and spiced. ▷Hindi.

Sev·a·reid /ˈsevəˌrīd/, Eric (Arnold) (1912–92), U.S. broadcast journalist. Working as a correspondent for CBS News 1939–77, he covered stories that ranged from the European theater during World War II to presidential elections.

Se·vas·to·pol /səˈvastəˌpōl; ˌsevəˈstōpəl/ Ukrainian and Russian name for SEBASTOPOL.

sev·en /ˈsevən/ ▶*cardinal number* equivalent to the sum of three and four; one more than six, or three less than ten; 7: *two sevens are fourteen | the remaining seven were sentenced to terms of imprisonment.* (Roman numeral: **vii**, **VII**.) ■ a group or unit of seven people or things: *animals were offered for sacrifice in sevens.* ■ seven years old: *my mother died when I was seven.* ■ seven o'clock: *the meeting doesn't finish until seven.* ■ a size of garment or other merchandise denoted by seven. ■ a playing card with seven pips. ▷Old English *seofon*, of Germanic origin; related to Dutch *zeven* and German *sieben*, from an Indo-European root shared by Latin *septem* and Greek *hepta*.

sev·en dead·ly sins ▶*plural n.* (**the seven deadly sins**) (in Christian tradition) the sins of pride, covetousness, lust, anger, gluttony, envy, and sloth.

sev·en·fold /ˈsevənˌfōld/ ▶*adj.* seven times as great or as numerous: *stock fund sales were up sevenfold from December.* ■ having seven parts or elements: *the sevenfold purpose of religious education.*
▶*adv.* by seven times; to seven times the number or amount: *his rent had gone up sevenfold.*

Sev·en Sag·es seven wise Greeks of the 6th century BC, to each of whom a moral saying is attributed. The seven, named in a traditional list found in Plato, are Bias, Chilon, Cleobulus, Periander, Pittacus, Solon, and Thales.

sev·en seas ▶*plural n.* (**the seven seas**) all the oceans of the world (conventionally listed as the Arctic, Antarctic, North Pacific, South Pacific, North Atlantic, South Atlantic, and Indian Oceans).

Sev·en Sis·ters (**the Seven Sisters**) **1** *Astronomy* the star cluster of the Pleiades. **2** a group of women's (or formerly women's) colleges in the eastern U.S. having high academic and social prestige. It includes Barnard, Bryn Mawr, Mount Holyoke, Radcliffe, Smith, Vassar, and Wellesley.

Sev·en Sleep·ers (in early Christian legend) seven noble Christian youths of Ephesus who fell asleep in a cave while fleeing from persecution by the Roman emperor Decius (c.250 AD) and awoke 187 years later.

sev·en·teen /ˌsevənˈtēn; ˈsevənˌtēn/ ▶*cardinal number* one more than sixteen, or seven more than ten; 17: *seventeen years later | a list of names, seventeen in all.* (Roman numeral: **xvii**, **XVII**) ■ seventeen years old: *he joined the Marines at seventeen.* ■ a set or team of seventeen individuals. ▷Old English *seofontiene*, from the Germanic base of SEVEN. **—sev·en·teenth** /ˌsevənˈtēnTH; ˈsevənˌtēnTH/ *adj.* & *n.*

sev·en·teen-year lo·cust ▶*n.* the nymph of the northern species of the periodical cicada. See PERIODICAL CICADA.

sev·enth /ˈsevənTH/ ▶*ordinal number* constituting number seven in a sequence; 7th: *his seventh goal of the season | the seventh of June | he was the seventh of eight children.* ■ (**a seventh/one seventh**) each of seven equal parts into which something is or may be divided. ■ the seventh finisher or position in a race or competition: *he finished seventh in the tournament.* ■ seventhly (used to introduce a seventh point or reason). ■ the seventh grade of a school. ■ *Music* an interval spanning seven consecutive notes in a diatonic scale. ■ *Music* the note that is higher by this interval than the tonic of a diatonic scale or root of a chord. ■ *Music* a chord in which the seventh note of the scale forms an important component. **—sev·enth·ly** *adv.*
▶*PHRASE* □ **in seventh heaven** see HEAVEN.

Sev·enth-Day Ad·vent·ist ▶*n.* a member of a Protestant sect that preaches the imminent return of Christ to Earth (originally expecting the Second Coming in 1844) and observes Saturday as the sabbath. See also ADVENTIST.

sev·en·ty /ˈseventē/ ▶*cardinal number* (*pl.* **-ties**) the number equivalent to the product of seven and ten; ten less than eighty; 70: *about seventy people attended | seventy were arrested.* (Roman numeral: **lxx**, **LXX**) ■ (**seventies**) the numbers from seventy to seventy-nine, esp. the years of a century or of a person's life: *Dad was now in his seventies.* ■ seventy years old: *she was nearly seventy.* ■ seventy miles an hour: *doing about seventy.* ▷Old English *hundseofontig*, from *hund-* (of uncertain origin) + *seofon* 'seven.' **—sev·en·ti·eth** /-tēəTH/ *ordinal number* **—sev·en·ty·fold** /-ˌfōld/ *adj.* & *adv.*

sev·en·ty-eight (usu. **78**) ▶*n.* an old phonograph record designed to be played at 78 rpm.

sev·en-up ▶*n. chiefly historical* a variety of the card game "all fours" in which the winner is the first to score seven points.

Sev·en Won·ders of the World the seven most spectacular man-made structures of the ancient world.

Traditionally they comprise (1) the pyramids of Egypt, especially those at Giza; (2) the Hanging Gardens of Babylon; (3) the Mausoleum of Halicarnassus; (4) the temple of Artemis at Ephesus in Asia Minor; (5) the Colossus of Rhodes; (6) the huge ivory and gold statue of Zeus at Olympia in Peloponnesus, made by Phidias *c.*430 BC; (7) the Pharos of Alexandria (or in some lists, the walls of Babylon).

sev·en-year itch ▶*n.* [in *sing.*] a supposed tendency to infidelity after seven years of marriage.

Sev·en Years' War a war (1756–63) that set Britain, Prussia, and Hanover against Austria, France, Russia, Saxony, Sweden, and Spain.

Its main issues were the struggle between Britain and France for supremacy overseas, and that between Prussia and Austria for the domination of Germany. The British made substantial gains over France abroad, capturing French Canada and undermining French influence in India.The war was ended by the Treaties of Paris and Hubertusburg in 1763, leaving Britain the supreme European naval and colonial power and Prussia in an appreciably stronger position than before in central Europe.

sev·er /ˈsevər/ ▶*v.* [*trans.*] divide by cutting or slicing, esp. suddenly and forcibly: *the head was* **severed from** *the body |* [as *adj.*] (**severed**) *severed limbs.* ■ put an end to (a connection or relationship); break off: *he severed his relations with Lawrence.* ▷Middle English: from Anglo-Norman French *severer*, from Latin *separare* 'disjoin, divide.' **—sev·er·a·ble** *adj.*

sev·er·al /ˈsev(ə)rəl/ ▶*adj.* & *pron.* more than two but not many: [as *adj.*] *the author of several books |* [as *pron.*] *Van Gogh was just one of several artists who gathered at Auvers |* **several of** *his friends attended.*
▶*adj.* separate or respective: *the two levels of government sort out their several responsibilities.* ■ *Law* applied or regarded separately. Often contrasted with JOINT. ▷late Middle English: from Anglo-Norman French, from medieval Latin *separalis*, from Latin *separ* 'separate, different.' **—sev·er·al·ly** *adv.*

USAGE See usage at VARIOUS.

sev·er·al·ty /ˈsev(ə)rəltē/ ▶*n. archaic* the condition of being separate. ▷late Middle English: from Anglo-Norman French *severalte*, from *several* (see SEVERAL).

sev·er·ance /ˈsev(ə)rəns/ ▶*n.* the action of ending a connection or relationship: *the severance and disestablishment of the Irish Church | a complete* **severance of** *links with the Republic.* ■ the state of being separated or cut off: *she works on the feeling of severance, of being deprived of her mother.* ■ dismissal or discharge from employment: [as *adj.*] *employees were offered severance terms.* ■ short for SEVERANCE PAY. ▷late Middle English: from Anglo-Norman French, based on Latin *separare* (see SEVER).

sev·er·ance pay ▶*n.* an amount paid to an employee upon dismissal or discharge from employment.

se·vere /səˈvi(ə)r/ ▶*adj.* **1** (of something bad or undesirable) very great; intense: *a severe shortage of technicians | a severe attack of asthma | damage is not too severe.* ■ demanding great ability, skill, or resilience: *a severe test of stamina.* **2** strict or harsh: *the charges would have warranted a severe sentence | he is unusually* **severe on** *what he regards as tendentious pseudo-learning.* **3** very plain in style or appearance: *she wore another severe suit, gray this time.* ▷mid 16th cent. (sense 2): from French *sévère* or Latin *severus.* **—se·vere·ly** *adv.* **—se·ver·i·ty** /-ˈveritē/ *n.*

THE RIGHT WORD **ascetic, austere, severe, stern, strict, unmitigated**

A storm, a hairdo, and a punishment may all be described as **severe**, which means harsh or uncompromising, without a hint of softness, mildness, levity, or indulgence.

Austere, on the other hand, primarily applies to people, their habits, their way of life, and the environments they create; it implies coldness, stark simplicity, and restraint (*an austere room with only a table and chair*).

Ascetic implies extreme self-denial and self-discipline, in some cases to the point of choosing what is painful or disagreeable (*he had an ascetic approach to life and rejected all creature comforts*).

Strict literally means bound or stretched tight; in extended use, it means strenuously exact (*a strict curfew; strict obedience*).

Stern combines harshness and authority with strictness or severity (*a stern judge*).

Unmitigated means unmodified and unsoftened in any way (*a streak of unmitigated bad luck*).

Sev·ern /ˈsevərn/ a river of southwestern Britain. Rising in central Wales, it flows northeast and then south in a broad curve for about 180 miles (290 km) to its mouth on the Bristol Channel.

Se·ver·na·ya Zem·lya /ˈsevərnäˌyä ˌzemlēˈä; syivirnäˈyä zemˈlyä/ a group of uninhabited islands in the Arctic Ocean off the northern coast of Russia, to the north of the Taimyr Peninsula.

Se·ve·ro·dvinsk /ˌseverədˈvinsk; syivyirədˈvyinsk/ a port in northwestern Russia, on the White Sea coast, west of Archangel; pop. 250,000.

Se·ve·rus /səˈvi(ə)rəs/, Septimius (146–211), Roman emperor 193–211; full name *Lucius Septimius Severus Pertinax.* In 208, he led an army to Britain to suppress a rebellion in the north and later died at York.

sev·er·y /ˈsev(ə)rē/ ▶*n.* (*pl.* **-er·ies**) *Architecture* a bay or compartment in a vaulted ceiling. ▷late Middle English: from Old French *civoire* 'ciborium' (see CIBORIUM).

se·vi·che ▶*n.* variant spelling of CEVICHE.

Se·vier Riv·er /sə'vi(ə)r/ a river that flows for 325 miles (525 km) through central Utah, irrigating the eastern edge of the Great Basin.

Se·ville /sə'vil/ a city in southern Spain, the capital of Andalusia, located on the Guadalquivir River; pop. 683,000. Spanish name SEVILLA .

Se·ville or·ange ▶*n.* a bitter-tasting orange used for marmalade.

Se·vin /'sevin/ ▶*n.* trademark for CARBARYL. ▷1950s: of unknown origin.

Sè·vres /'sevrə/ ▶*n.* a type of fine porcelain characterized by elaborate decoration on backgrounds of intense color, made at Sèvres in the suburbs of Paris.

sev·ru·ga /sə'vrōōgə/ ▶*n.* a migratory sturgeon found only in the basins of the Caspian and Black Seas, much fished for its caviar. • *Acipenser stellatus*, family Acipenseridae. ■ caviar obtained from this fish. ▷late 16th cent.: from Russian *sevryuga*.

sew /sō/ ▶*v.* (*past part.* **sewn** /sōn/ or **sewed** /sōd/) [*trans.*] join, fasten, or repair (something) by making stitches with a needle and thread or a sewing machine: *she sewed the seams and hemmed the border* | [*intrans.*] *I don't even sew very well.* ■ [*trans.*] attach (something) to something else by sewing: *she could sew the veil on properly in the morning.* ■ make (a garment) by sewing.
▶*phrasal v.* □ **sew something up** *informal* bring something to a favorable conclusion: *he sank a 3-pointer to sew up a 120-118 victory.* ■ achieve exclusive control over something: *the U.S. courier market has been more or less sewn up by two companies.* ▷Old English *siwan*, of Germanic origin, from an Indo-European root shared by Latin *suere* and Greek *suein.*

sew·age /'sōōij/ ▶*n.* waste water and excrement conveyed in sewers. ▷mid 19th cent.: from SEWER[1], by substitution of the suffix -AGE.

sew·age sludge ▶*n.* semiliquid waste obtained from the processing of municipal sewage, often used as a fertilizer.

Sew·ard /'sōō(w)ərd/, William Henry (1801–72), U.S. statesman and politician. An outspoken anti-slavery politician, he was governor of New York 1839–43, U.S. senator 1849–61, and U.S. secretary of state 1861–69. In 1867, he negotiated the purchase of Alaska from Russia, a purchase that was widely mocked as "Seward's Icebox" and "Seward's Folly."

Sew·ard Pen·in·su·la /'sōōərd/ a region in northwestern Alaska on the Bering Strait and the Chukchi Sea. Nome lies on its southern coast.

se·wel·lel /sə'weləl/ ▶*n.* another term for MOUNTAIN BEAVER. ▷early 19th cent.: from Chinook Jargon *šwalál* 'robe of mountain-beaver skin.'

sew·er[1] /'sōōər/ ▶*n.* an underground conduit for carrying off drainage water and waste matter. ▷Middle English (denoting a watercourse to drain marshy land): from Old Northern French *seuwiere* 'channel to drain the overflow from a fishpond,' based on Latin *ex-* 'out of' + *aqua* 'water.'

sew·er[2] /'sōər/ ▶*n.* a person who sews.

sew·er·age /'sōōərij/ ▶*n.* the provision of drainage by sewers. ■ another term for SEWAGE.

sew·er rat /'sōōər/ ▶*n.* another term for BROWN RAT.

sew·ing /'sō-ING/ ▶*n.* the action or activity of sewing. ■ work that is to be or is being sewn: *she put down her sewing.*

sew·ing ma·chine ▶*n.* a machine with a mechanically driven needle for sewing or stitching cloth.

sewn /sōn/ ▶ past participle of SEW.

sex /seks/ ▶*n.* **1** (chiefly with reference to people) sexual activity, including specifically sexual intercourse: *he enjoyed talking about sex* | *she didn't want to **have sex with** him.* ■ [in *sing.*] a person's genitals (used in novels to avoid more vulgar or anatomically explicit terms). **2** either of the two main categories (male and female) into which humans and most other living things are divided on the basis of their reproductive functions: *adults of both sexes.* ■ the fact of belonging to one of these categories: *direct discrimination involves treating someone less favorably on the grounds of their sex.* ■ the group of all members of either of these categories: *she was well known for her efforts to improve the social condition of her sex.*
▶*v.* [*trans.*] **1** determine the sex of: *sexing chickens.* **2** (**sex someone up**) *informal* arouse or attempt to arouse someone sexually. ▷late Middle English (denoting the two categories, male and female): from Old French *sexe* or Latin *sexus.* —**sex·er** *n.*

> ***USAGE*** On the difference in use between the words **sex** (in sense 2 above) and **gender**, see **usage** at GENDER.

sex- ▶*comb. form* variant spelling of SEXI-, shortened before a vowel (as in *sexennial*), or shortened before a consonant (as in *sexfoil*).

sex act ▶*n.* any sexual act. ■ (**the sex act**) the act of sexual intercourse.

sex·a·ge·nar·i·an /,seksəjə'ne(ə)rēən/ ▶*n.* a person who is from 60 to 69 years old. ▷mid 18th cent.: from Latin *sexagenarius* (based on *sexaginta* 'sixty') + -AN.

Sex·a·ges·i·ma /,seksə'jesəmə/ (also **Sexagesima Sunday**) *n.* the Sunday before Quinquagesima. ▷late Middle English: from ecclesiastical Latin, literally 'sixtieth (day),' probably named by analogy with QUINQUAGESIMA.

sex·a·ges·i·mal /,seksə'jesəməl/ ▶*adj.* **1** of, relating to, or reckoning by sixtieths. **2** of or relating to the number sixty.
▶*n.* (also **sexagesimal fraction**) a fraction based on sixtieths (i.e., with a denominator equal to a power of sixty), as in the divisions of the degree and hour. ▷late 17th cent.: from Latin *sexagesimus* 'sixtieth' + -AL. —**sex·a·ges·i·mal·ly** *adv.*

sex ap·peal ▶*n.* the quality of being attractive in a sexual way: *she just oozes sex appeal.*

sex bomb ▶*n. informal* a woman who is very sexually attractive.

sex·ca·pade /'sekskə,pād/ ▶*n. informal* a sexual escapade; an illicit affair. ▷1960s: blend of SEX and ESCAPADE.

sex·cen·ten·ar·y /,seksen'tenərē/ ▶*n.* (*pl.* **-ar·ies**) the six-hundredth anniversary of a significant event.
▶*adj.* of or relating to a six-hundredth anniversary.

sex change ▶*n.* a change in a person's physical sexual characteristics, typically by surgery and hormone treatment.

sex chro·ma·tin ▶*n. Biology* material found only in the nuclei of female cells (esp. as the Barr body) and believed to represent the inactivated X chromosome.

sex chro·mo·some ▶*n.* a chromosome involved with determining the sex of an organism, typically one of two kinds. Also called HETEROCHROMOSOME.

> In humans and other mammals females have two similar sex chromosomes (XX) while males have dissimilar ones (XY). In birds and some other animals, females have dissimilar sex chromosomes (ZW) and males similar ones (WW). Some other organisms have a sex chromosome present only in one sex.

sex crime ▶*n. informal* a crime involving sexual assault or having a sexual motive.

sex dis·crim·i·na·tion (also **sex·u·al dis·crim·i·na·tion**) ▶*n.* discrimination in employment and opportunity against a person (typically a woman) on grounds of sex.

sex drive ▶*n.* the urge to seek satisfaction of sexual needs.

sexed /sekst/ ▶*adj.* **1** [with *submodifier*] having specified sexual appetites: *highly sexed heterosexual males.* **2** [*attrib.*] having sexual characteristics: *the effects of family and kinship relations on the construction of sexed individuals.*

sex·en·ni·al /sek'senēəl/ ▶*adj.* recurring every six years. ■ lasting for or relating to a period of six years. ▷mid 17th cent.: from SEXENNIUM + -AL.

sex·en·ni·um /sek'senēəm/ ▶*n.* (*pl.* **sex·en·ni·a** /sek'senēə/ or **sex·en·ni·ums**) *rare* a specified period of six years. ▷1950s: from Latin, from *sex* 'six' + *annus* 'year.'

sex·foil /'seks,foil/ ▶*n.* (esp. in architecture) an ornamental design having six leaves or petals radiating from a common center. ▷late 17th cent.: from SEXI- 'six,' on the pattern of words such as *trefoil.*

sex hor·mone ▶*n.* a hormone, such as estrogen or testosterone, affecting sexual development or reproduction.

sexi- (also **sex-** before a vowel) ▶*comb. form* six; having six: *sexivalent.* ▷from Latin *sex* 'six.'

sex in·dus·try ▶*n.* (**the sex industry**) used euphemistically to refer to prostitution.

sex·ism /'sek,sizəm/ ▶*n.* prejudice, stereotyping, or discrimination, typically against women, on the basis of sex. —**sex·ist** *adj.* & *n.*

sex·i·va·lent /'seksə,vālənt/ ▶*adj. Chemistry* another term for HEXAVALENT.

sex kit·ten ▶*n. informal* a young woman who asserts or exploits her sexual attractiveness.

sex·less /'seksləs/ ▶*adj.* **1** lacking in sexual desire, interest, activity, or attractiveness: *I've no patience with pious, sexless females.* **2** neither male nor female: *the stylized and sexless falsetto.* —**sex·less·ly** *adv.* —**sex·less·ness** *n.*

sex life ▶*n.* a person's sexual activity and relationships considered as a whole.

sex-linked ▶*adj. chiefly Biology* tending to be associated with one sex or the other. ■ (of a gene or heritable characteristic) carried by a sex chromosome.

sex ma·ni·ac ▶*n. informal* a person whose need for sexual gratification is excessive or obsessive.

sex ob·ject ▶*n.* a person regarded by another only in terms of their sexual attractiveness or availability: *we're now in a period when it is permissible for women to make men into sex objects.*

sex of·fend·er ▶*n.* a person who commits a crime involving a sexual act.

sex·ol·o·gy /sek'säləjē/ ▶*n.* the study of human sexual life or relationships. —**sex·o·log·i·cal** /,seksə'läjikəl/ *adj.* —**sex·ol·o·gist** /-jist/ *n.*

sex·par·tite /seks'pär,tīt/ ▶*adj.* divided or involving division into six parts: *the sexpartite vault is of 12th-century construction.* ▷mid 18th cent.: from SEXI- 'six' + PARTITE, on the pattern of words such as *bipartite.*

sex·pert /'sekspərt/ ▶*n. informal* an expert in sexual matters.

sex·ploi·ta·tion /,seksploi'tāSHən/ ▶*n. informal* the commercial exploitation of sex, sexual attractiveness, or sexually explicit material. ▷1940s: blend of SEX and *exploitation* (see EXPLOIT).

sex·pot /'seks,pät/ ▶*n. informal* a sexy person.

sex role ▶*n.* the role or behavior learned by a person as appropriate to their sex, determined by the prevailing cultural norms.

sex-starved ▶*adj.* lacking and strongly desiring sexual gratification.

sex sym·bol ▶*n.* a person widely noted for their sexual attractiveness.

sext /sekst/ ▶*n.* a service forming part of the Divine Office of the Western Christian Church, traditionally said (or chanted) at the sixth hour of the day (i.e., noon). ▷late Middle English: from Latin *sexta (hora)* 'sixth (hour),' from *sextus* 'sixth.'

Sex·tans /'sekstənz/ *Astronomy* a faint constellation (the Sextant), lying on the celestial equator between Leo and Hydra. ■ [as *genitive*] (**Sextantis** /sek'stantəs/) used with a preceding letter or numeral to designate a star in this constellation: *the star Alpha Sextantis.* ▷Latin.

sex·tant /'sekstənt/ ▶*n.* an instrument with a graduated arc of 60° and a sighting mechanism, used for measuring the angular distances between objects and esp. for taking altitudes in navigation. ▷late 16th cent. (denoting the sixth part of a circle): from Latin *sextans, sextant-* 'sixth part,' from *sextus* 'sixth.'

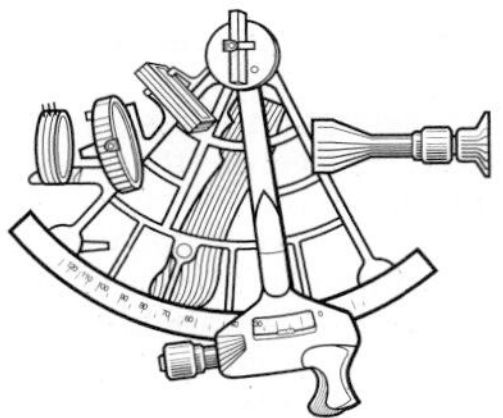

sextant

sex·tet /sek'stet/ (also **sex·tette**) ▶*n.* a group of six people playing music or singing together. ■ a composition for such a group. ■ a set of six people or things: *a sextet of new releases.* ▷mid 19th cent.: alteration of SESTET, suggested by Latin *sex* 'six.'

sex ther·a·py ▶*n.* counseling or other therapy that addresses a person's psychological or physical sexual problems. —**sex ther·a·pist** *n.*

sex·tile /'sek,stīl; -stəl/ ▶*n. Astrology* an aspect of 60° (one sixth of a circle): *the Jupiter–Saturn cycle is now **in sextile to** its most difficult period.* ▷late Middle English: from Latin *sextilis*, from *sextus* 'sixth.'

sex·til·lion /sek'stilyən/ ▶*cardinal number* (*pl.* **-lions** or (with numeral) same) a thousand raised to the seventh power (10^{21}). ■ *dated, chiefly Brit.* a million raised to the sixth power (10^{36}). ▷late 17th cent.: from French, from *million*, by substitution of the prefix *sexti-* 'six' (from Latin *sextus* 'sixth') for the initial letters. —**sex·til·lionth** /sek'stilyənTH/ *ordinal number.*

Pronunciation Key ə *ago;* ər *over;* 'ə or ,ə *up;* 'ər or ,ər *fur;* a *hat;* ā *rate;* ä *car;* CH *chew;* e *let;* ē *see;* e(ə)r *air;* i *fit;* ī *by;* i(ə)r *ear;* NG *sing;* ō *go;* ô *for;* oi *boy;* ōō *good;* ōō *goo;* ou *out;* SH *she;* TH *thin;* TH *then;* (h)w *why;* ZH *vision*

sex·to·dec·i·mo /ˌsekstəˈdesəˌmō/ (abbr.: **16mo**) ▸*n.* (*pl.* **-mos**) a size of book page that results from folding each printed sheet into sixteen leaves (thirty-two pages). ■ a book of this size. ▷late 17th cent.: from Latin *sexto decimo*, ablative of *sextus decimus* 'sixteenth.'

Sex·ton /ˈsekstən/, Anne (1928–74), U.S. poet; born *Anne Harvey*. Plagued by mental illness, she wrote very emotional poems, many of which are collected in the volumes *To Bedlam and Part Way Back* (1960) and *Live or Die* (1966).

sex·ton /ˈsekstən/ ▸*n.* a person who looks after a church and churchyard, sometimes acting as bell-ringer and formerly as a gravedigger. ▷Middle English: from Anglo-Norman French *segrestein*, from medieval Latin *sacristanus* (see SACRISTAN).

sex·ton bee·tle ▸*n.* another term for BURYING BEETLE.

sex tour·ism ▸*n.* the organization of vacations with the purpose of taking advantage of the lack of restrictions imposed on prostitution and other sexual activities by some foreign countries. —**sex tour** *n.* —**sex tour·ist** *n.*

sex·tu·ple /sekˈst(y)o͞opəl; -ˈtəpəl/ ▸*adj.* [*attrib.*] consisting of six parts or things. ■ six times as much or as many.
▸*n.* a sixfold number or amount.
▸*v.* [*trans.*] multiply by six; increase sixfold. ▷early 17th cent.: from medieval Latin *sextuplus*, formed irregularly from Latin *sex* 'six,' on the pattern of late Latin *quintuplus* 'quintuple.' —**sex·tu·ply** /-plē/ *adv.*

sex·tu·plet /sekˈstəplit; -ˈst(y)o͞oplət/ ▸*n.* **1** each of six children born at one birth. **2** *Music* a group of six notes to be performed in the time of four. ▷mid 19th cent.: from SEXTUPLE, on the pattern of words such as *triplet*.

sex typ·ing ▸*n.* **1** *Psychology & Sociology* the stereotypical categorization of people, or their appearance or behavior, according to conventional perceptions of what is typical of each sex. **2** *Biology* the process of determining the sex of a person or other organism, esp. in difficult cases where special tests are necessary. —**sex-typed** *adj.*

sex·u·al /ˈseksʜo͞oəl/ ▸*adj.* **1** relating to the instincts, physiological processes, and activities connected with physical attraction or intimate physical contact between individuals: *she had felt the thrill of a sexual attraction.* **2** of or relating to the two sexes or to gender: *sensitivity about sexual stereotypes.* ■ of or characteristic of one sex or the other: *the hormones which control the secondary sexual characteristics.* ■ *Biology* being of one sex or the other; capable of sexual reproduction. ▷mid 17th cent.: from late Latin *sexualis*, from Latin *sexus* 'sex.' —**sex·u·al·ly** *adv.*

sex·u·al di·mor·phism ▸*n.* *Zoology* distinct difference in size or appearance between the sexes of an animal in addition to difference between the sexual organs themselves.

sex·u·al ha·rass·ment ▸*n.* harassment (typically of a woman) in a workplace, or other professional or social situation, involving the making of unwanted sexual advances or obscene remarks.

sex·u·al in·ter·course ▸*n.* sexual contact between individuals involving penetration, esp. the insertion of a man's erect penis into a woman's vagina, typically culminating in orgasm and the ejaculation of semen.

sex·u·al in·ver·sion ▸*n.* see INVERSION (sense 4).

sex·u·al·i·ty /ˌseksʜo͞oˈalitē/ ▸*n.* (*pl.* **-ties**) capacity for sexual feelings: *she began to understand the power of her sexuality.* ■ a person's sexual orientation or preference: *people with proscribed sexualities.* ■ sexual activity.

sex·u·al·ize /ˈseksʜo͞oəˌlīz/ ▸*v.* [*trans.*] make sexual; attribute sex or a sex role to: [as *adj.*] (**sexualized**) *sexualized images of women.* —**sex·u·al·i·za·tion** /ˌseksʜo͞oələˈzāsʜən/ *n.*

sex·u·al o·ri·en·ta·tion ▸n. a person's sexual attraction toward members of the same, opposite, or both genders: *a draft ordinance that would prohibit discrimination on the basis of sexual orientation.*

sex·u·al pol·i·tics ▸*plural n.* [treated as *sing.*] the principles determining the relationship of the sexes; relations between the sexes regarded in terms of power.

sex·u·al re·la·tions ▸*plural n.* sexual behavior between individuals, esp. sexual intercourse.

sex·u·al re·pro·duc·tion ▸*n.* *Biology* the production of new living organisms by combining genetic information from two individuals of different types (sexes). In most higher organisms, one sex (male) produces a small motile gamete that travels to fuse with a larger stationary gamete produced by the other (female).

sex·u·al rev·o·lu·tion ▸*n.* the liberalization of established social and moral attitudes toward sex, particularly that occurring in western countries during the 1960s, as the women's liberation movement and developments in contraception instigated greater experimentation with sex, esp. outside of marriage.

sex·u·al se·lec·tion ▸*n.* *Biology* natural selection arising through preference by one sex for certain characteristics in individuals of the other sex.

sex work·er ▸*n.* used euphemistically to refer to a prostitute.

sex·y /ˈseksē/ ▸*adj.* (**sex·i·er**, **sex·i·est**) sexually attractive or exciting: *sexy French underwear.* ■ sexually aroused: *neither of them was feeling sexy.* ■ *informal* exciting; appealing: *I've climbed most of the really sexy west coast mountains.* —**sex·i·ly** /-səlē/ *adv.* —**sex·i·ness** *n.*

Sey·chelles /sāˈsʜel(z)/ (also **the Seychelles**) a country that consists of a group of about 90 islands in the Indian Ocean, about 600 miles (1,000 km) northeast of Madagascar; pop. 80,000; capital, Victoria; languages, French (official), English, and Creole. —**Sey·chel·lois** /ˌsāsʜelˈwä/ *adj.* & *n.* (*pl.* same).

The islands were uninhabited until the mid 18th century, when the French annexed them. The Seychelles were captured by Britain during the Napoleonic Wars and administered from Mauritius before becoming a separate colony in 1903 and an independent republic within the Commonwealth of Nations in 1976.

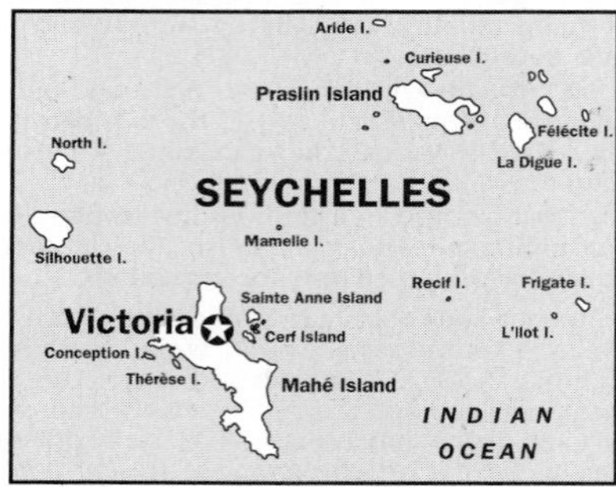

Sey·fert gal·ax·y /ˈsēfərt/ ▸*n.* *Astronomy* a galaxy of a type characterized by a bright compact core that shows strong infrared emission. ▷named after Carl K. *Seyfert* (1911–60), American astronomer.

Seym /sām/ ▸*n.* variant spelling of SEJM.

Sey·mour /ˈsēˌmôr/, Jane (*c.*1509–37), third wife of Henry VIII and mother of Edward VI. She married Henry in 1536 and finally provided the king with the male heir he wanted, although she died twelve days afterward.

sez /sez/ ▸*v.* nonstandard spelling of "says," used in representing uneducated speech: *"Oh Lordy!" sez de man.*

Se·zes·sion /ˌzetˌsesēˈōn/ (also **Se·ces·sion**) ▸*n.* (**the Sezession**) a radical movement involving groups of avant-garde German and Austrian artists who, from 1892, organized exhibitions independently of the traditional academies. The **Vienna Secession** founded by Gustav Klimt in 1897 helped to launch the Jugendstil. ▷German, literally 'secession.'

SF ▸*abbr.* ■ science fiction. ■ Sinn Fein. ■ *Military* Special Forces.

sf *Music* ▸*abbr.* sforzando.

SFA ▸*abbr.* ■ Scottish Football Association. ■ (in the UK) Securities and Futures Authority.

Sfax /sfaks; sfäks/ (also **Sa·fa·qis** /säˈfäkis/) a port on the eastern coast of Tunisia; pop. 231,000.

SFC ▸*abbr.* Sergeant First Class.

sfor·zan·do /sfôrtˈsändō/ (also **sfor·za·to** /sfôrtˈsätō/) *Music* ▸*adv.* & *adj.* (esp. as a direction) with sudden emphasis.
▸*n.* (*pl.* **-dos** or **-di** /-dē/) a sudden or marked emphasis. ▷Italian, literally 'using force.'

SFSR ▸*abbr.* Soviet Federated Socialist Republic.

sfu·ma·to /sfo͞oˈmätō/ ▸*n.* *Art* the technique of allowing tones and colors to shade gradually into one another, producing softened outlines or hazy forms. ▷mid 19th cent.: Italian, literally 'shaded off,' past participle of *sfumare*.

SFX ▸*abbr.* special effects. ▷*FX* representing a pronunciation of *effects*.

sfz *Music* ▸*abbr.* sforzando.

SG ▸*abbr.* ■ *Law* solicitor general. ■ *Physics* specific gravity.

Sg ▸*symbol* the chemical element seaborgium.

sgd ▸*abbr.* signed.

SGM ▸*abbr.* sergeant major.

SGML *Computing* ▸*abbr.* Standard Generalized Markup Language, an international standard for defining methods of encoding electronic texts to describe layout, structure, syntax, etc., which can then be used for analysis or to display the text in any desired format.

sgraf·fi·to /zgräˈfētō; skrä-/ ▸*n.* (*pl.* **-ti** /-tē /) a form of decoration made by scratching through a surface to reveal a lower layer of a contrasting color, typically done in plaster or stucco on walls, or in slip on ceramics before firing. ▷mid 18th cent.: Italian, literally 'scratched away,' past participle of *sgraffiare*.

's-Gra·ven·ha·ge /ˌsᴋʜrävənˈhäᴋʜə/ Dutch name for HAGUE.

Sgt (also **SGT**) ▸*abbr.* sergeant.

Sgt. Maj. ▸*abbr.* Sergeant Major.

sh. *Brit.* ▸*abbr.* shilling(s).

Shaan·xi /ˈsʜänˈsʜē/ (also **Shen·si**) a mountainous province in central China; capital, Xian. It is the site of the earliest known settlements of the ancient Chinese civilizations.

Sha·ba /ˈsʜäbə/ a copper-mining region of southeastern Democratic Republic of the Congo (formerly Zaire); capital, Lubumbashi. Former name (until 1972) KATANGA.

Sha·ba·ka /ˈsʜabəkə/ (died 698 BC), Egyptian pharaoh; founder of the 25th dynasty; reigned 712–698 BC; known as **Sabacon**. He promoted the cult of Amun and revived the custom of pyramid burial in his own death arrangements.

Shab·bat /sʜäˈbät/ ▸*n.* the Jewish Sabbath. ▷from Hebrew *šabbāṯ*.

Shab·bos /ˈsʜäbəs/ (also **Shab·bas** or **Shab·bes**) ▸*n.* the Yiddish term for the Jewish Sabbath. ▷Yiddish, from Hebrew *šabbāṯ*.

shab·by /ˈsʜabē/ ▸*adj.* (**-bi·er**, **-bi·est**) in poor condition through long or hard use or lack of care: *a conscript in a shabby uniform saluted the car.* ■ dressed in old or worn clothes. ■ (of behavior) mean and shameful: *shabby, disrespectful treatment.* ■ inferior in performance or quality: *The gain jumps to 67 percent. Not too shabby.* ▷mid 17th cent.: from dialect *shab* 'scab' (from a Germanic base meaning 'itch') + -Y[1]. —**shab·bi·ly** /-əlē/ *adv.* —**shab·bi·ness** *n.*

shab·rack /ˈsʜabˌrak/ ▸*n.* *historical* a cavalry saddlecloth used in European armies. ▷early 19th cent.: from German *Schabracke*, of eastern European origin; compare with Russian *shabrak*.

sha·bu-sha·bu /ˈsʜäbo͞o ˈsʜäbo͞o/ ▸*n.* a Japanese dish of pieces of thinly sliced beef or pork cooked quickly with vegetables in boiling water and then dipped in sauce. ▷Japanese.

shack /sʜak/ ▸*n.* a roughly built hut or cabin.
▸*v.* [*intrans.*] (**shack up**) *informal* move in or live with someone as a lover. ▷late 19th cent.: perhaps from Mexican *jacal*; see JACAL. The early sense of the verb was 'live in a shack' (originally a U.S. usage).

shack·le /ˈsʜakəl/ ▸*n.* **1** (**shackles**) a pair of fetters connected together by a chain, used to fasten a prisoner's wrists or ankles together. ■ *figurative* used in reference to something that restrains or impedes: *society is going to throw off* **the shackles of** *racism and colonialism.* **2** a metal link, typically U-shaped, closed by a bolt, used to secure a chain or rope to something. ■ a pivoted link connecting a spring in a vehicle's suspension to the body of the vehicle.
▸*v.* [*trans.*] chain with shackles. ■ *figurative* restrain; limit: *they seek to shackle the oil and gas companies by imposing new controls.* ▷Old English *sc(e)acul* 'fetter,' of Germanic origin; related to Dutch *schakel* 'link, coupling.'

Shack·le·ton /ˈsʜakəltən/, Sir Ernest Henry (1874–1922), British explorer. During one of his Antarctic expeditions (1914–16), Shackleton's ship *Endurance* was crushed in the ice. He and his crew eventually reached Elephant Island, from where he and five others made an 800-mile (1,300-km) open-boat voyage to South Georgia to get help.

shack·y /ˈsʜakē/ ▸*adj.* *informal* (of a building) dilapidated or ramshackle.

shad /sʜad/ ▸*n.* (*pl.* same or **shads**) a herringlike fish that spends much of its life in the sea, typically entering rivers to spawn. It is an important food fish in many regions. • Genera *Alosa* and *Caspialosa*, family Clupeidae: several species. See TWAITE SHAD. ▷Old English *sceadd*, of unknown origin.

shad·blow /ˈshad,blō/ ▶*n.* another term for **JUNEBERRY.** ▷mid 19th cent.: from **SHAD** + **BLOW**[3] (because its flowering is associated with the presence of spawning shad in the rivers).

shad·bush /ˈshad,bo͝osh/ (also **shad·blow** /-,blō/) ▶*n.* another term for **JUNEBERRY.** ▷early 19th cent.: so named because it flowers at the same time as shad are found in the rivers.

shad·chan ▶*n.* variant spelling of **SHADKHAN.**

Shad·dai /shäˈdī/ ▶*n.* one of the names given to God in the Hebrew Bible. ▷Hebrew, translated as 'Almighty' in English versions of the Bible, but of uncertain meaning.

shad·dock /ˈshadək/ ▶*n.* another term for **POMELO.** ▷late 17th cent.: named after Captain *Shaddock*, who introduced it to the West Indies in the 17th cent.

shadd·up /,shətˈəp/ ▶*exclam. informal* be quiet!: *"Shaddup! If he wants to confess, let him."* ▷1950s: representing a pronunciation of *shut up*.

shade /shād/ ▶*n.* **1** comparative darkness and coolness caused by shelter from direct sunlight: *sitting in the shade | this area will be* ***in shade*** *for much of the day.* ■ the darker part of a picture. ■ (usu. **shades**) *poetic/literary* a shadow or area of darkness: *the shades of evening drew on.* ■ *figurative* a position of relative inferiority or obscurity: *her elegant pink and black ensemble would* ***put*** *most outfits* ***in the shade.*** ■ *historical* a portrait in silhouette. **2** a color, esp. with regard to how light or dark it is or as distinguished from one nearly like it: *various shades of blue | Maria's eyes darkened* ***in shade.*** ■ *Art* a slight degree of difference between colors. ■ a slightly differing variety of something: *politicians of all shades of opinion.* ■ [in *sing.*] a slight amount of something: *there is* ***a shade*** *of wistfulness in his rejection.* **3** a lampshade. ■ (often **shades**) a screen or blind on a window. ■ an eyeshade. ■ (**shades**) *informal* sunglasses. **4** *poetic/literary* a ghost. ■ (**the Shades**) the underworld; Hades.
▶*v.* [*trans.*] **1** screen from direct light: *she shaded her eyes against the sun.* ■ cover, moderate, or exclude the light of: *he shaded the flashlight with his hand.* **2** darken or color (an illustration or diagram) with parallel pencil lines or a block of color: *she* ***shaded in*** *the outline of a chimney.* ■ [*intrans.*] (of a color or something colored) gradually change into another color: *the sky shaded from turquoise to night blue.* **3** make a slight reduction in the amount, rate, or price of: *banks may shade the margin over base rate they charge customers.* ▷Old English *sc(e)adu*, of Germanic origin. Compare with **SHADOW.** —**shade·less** *adj.* —**shad·er** *n.*
▶*PHRASES* □ **a shade** —— a little ——: *he was a shade hung over.* □ **shades of** —— used to suggest reminiscence of or comparison with someone or something specified: *colleges were conducting campaigns to ban Jewish societies—shades of Nazi Germany.*

shad·ing /ˈshādiNG/ ▶*n.* **1** the darkening or coloring of an illustration or diagram with parallel lines or a block of color. ■ a very slight variation, typically in color or meaning: *the shadings of opinion even among those who are in broad agreement.* **2** a layer of paint or material used to provide shade, esp. for plants: *liquid greenhouse shading.*

shad·khan ▶*n.* /ˈshätKHən; shädˈKHän/ (also **shad·chan**) *n.* (*pl.* same, **shad·kha·nim** /,shädKHäˈnēm/, or **shad·khans**) a Jewish professional matchmaker or marriage broker. ▷from Yiddish *shadkhn*, based on Hebrew *šiddēḵ* 'negotiate.'

sha·doof /shäˈdo͞of/ ▶*n.* a pole with a bucket and counterweight used esp. in Egypt for raising water. ▷mid 19th cent.: from Egyptian Arabic *šādūf*.

shadoof

shad·ow /ˈshadō/ ▶*n.* **1** a dark area or shape produced by a body coming between rays of light and a surface: *trees cast long shadows.* ■ partial or complete darkness, esp. as produced in this way: *the north side of the cathedral was deep in shadow |* (**shadows**) *a stranger slowly approached from the shadows.* ■ the shaded part of a picture. ■ a dark patch or area on a surface: *there are dark shadows beneath your eyes.* ■ a region of opacity on a radiograph: *shadows on his lungs.* ■ short for **EYESHADOW. 2** *figurative* used in reference to proximity, ominous oppressiveness, or sadness and gloom: *the shadow of war fell across Europe | only one shadow lay over Sally's life.* ■ used in reference to something insubstantial or fleeting: *a freedom that was more shadow than substance.* ■ used in reference to a position of relative inferiority or obscurity: *he* ***lived in the shadow of*** *his father.* ■ [with *negative*] the slightest trace of something: *she knew* ***without a shadow of a doubt*** *that he was lying.* ■ a weak or inferior remnant or version of something: *this fine-looking, commanding man had become* ***a shadow of*** *his former self.* ■ an expression of perplexity or sadness: *a shadow crossed Maria's face.* **3** an inseparable attendant or companion: *her faithful shadow, a Yorkshire terrier called Heathcliffe.* ■ a person secretly following and observing another. ■ a person who accompanies someone in their daily activities at work in order to gain experience at or insight into a job. ■ [usu. as *adj.*] *Brit.* the opposition counterpart of a government minister: *the shadow Chancellor.* ■ [as *adj.*] unofficial or alternative: *the Committee of Twenty-Five, a shadow government of unelected businessmen.*
▶*v.* [*trans.*] **1** (often **be shadowed**) envelop in shadow; cast a shadow over: *the market is shadowed by St. Margaret's church | a hood shadowed her face.* **2** follow and observe (someone) closely and typically secretly: *he had been up all night shadowing a team of poachers.* ■ *Brit.* (of an opposition politician) be the counterpart of (a government minister or a ministry). ■ accompany (someone) in their daily activities at work in order to gain experience or insight into a job. ▷Old English *scead(u)we* (noun), oblique case of *sceadu* (see **SHADE**), *sceadwian* 'screen or shield from attack,' of Germanic origin; related to Dutch *schaduw* and German *Schatten* (nouns), from an Indo-European root shared by Greek *skotos* 'darkness.' —**shad·ow·er** *n.* —**shad·ow·less** *adj.*
▶*PHRASE* □ **be frightened of one's shadow** be very timid or nervous.

shad·ow·box /ˈshadō,bäks/ ▶*v.* [*intrans.*] spar with an imaginary opponent as a form of training.
▶*n.* (**shadow box**) a case with a protective transparent front, used for displaying jewelry, coins, or other small objects.

shad·ow e·con·o·my ▶*n.* illicit economic activity (such as black market transactions and undeclared work) existing alongside a country's official economy.

shad·ow·graph /ˈshadō,graf/ ▶*n.* an image formed by the shadow of an object on a surface. ■ an image formed when light shone through a fluid is refracted differently by regions of different density. ■ a radiograph.

shad·ow·land /ˈshadō,land/ ▶*n. poetic/literary* a place in shadow. ■ (usu. **shadowlands**) an indeterminate borderland between places or states, typically represented as an abode of ghosts and spirits: *voices laughing in the shadowlands of my recall.*

shad·ow mask ▶*n.* a perforated metal screen situated directly behind the phosphor screen in certain types of color television tubes, having a pattern of precisely located holes through which the electron beams pass so as to strike the correct dots on the phosphor screen.

shad·ow play ▶*n.* a display in which the shadows of flat jointed puppets are cast on a screen that is viewed by the audience from the other side. Such shows originated in the Far East, and were popular in London and Paris in the 18th and 19th centuries; they survive in traditional form in Java and Bali.

shad·ow price ▶*n. Economics* the estimated price of a good or service for which no market price exists.

shad·ow stitch ▶*n.* a crisscross embroidery stitch used on sheer materials for filling in spaces, worked on the reverse side so as to show through in a shadowy way with an outline resembling a backstitch.

shad·ow work ▶*n.* embroidery done in shadow stitch.

shad·ow·y /ˈshadōē/ ▶*adj.* (**-ow·i·er, -ow·i·est**) full of shadows: *the shadowy back streets of Stringtown.* ■ of uncertain identity or nature: *a shadowy figure appeared through the mist | the shadowy world of covert operations.* ■ insubstantial; unreal: *they were attacked by a swarm of shadowy, ethereal forms.* —**shad·ow·i·ness** *n.*

shad·y /ˈshādē/ ▶*adj.* (**shad·i·er, shad·i·est**) situated in or full of shade: *shady woods.* ■ giving shade from sunlight: *they sprawled under a shady carob tree.* ■ *informal* of doubtful honesty or legality: *he was involved in his grandmother's shady deals.* —**shad·i·ly** *adv.* —**shad·i·ness** *n.*

shaft /shaft/ ▶*n.* **1** a long, narrow part or section forming the handle of a tool or club, the body of a spear or arrow, or a similar implement: *the shaft of a golf club | the shaft of a feather.* ■ an arrow or spear. ■ a column, esp. the main part between the base and capital. ■ a long cylindrical rotating rod for the transmission of motive power in a machine. ■ each of the pair of poles between which a horse is harnessed to a vehicle. ■ a ray of light or bolt of lightning: ***a shaft of*** *sunlight.* ■ a sudden flash of a quality or feeling: ***a shaft of*** *inspiration.* ■ a remark intended to be witty, wounding, or provoking: *he directs his shafts against her.* ■ *vulgar slang* a penis. ■ (**the shaft**) *informal* harsh or unfair treatment: *the executives continue to raise their pay while the workers* ***get the shaft.*** **2** a long, narrow, typically vertical hole that gives access to a mine, accommodates an elevator in a building, or provides ventilation.
▶*v.* **1** [*intrans.*] (of light) shine in beams: *brilliant sunshine shafted through the skylight.* **2** [*trans.*] *vulgar slang* (of a man) have sexual intercourse with (a woman). ■ *informal* treat (someone) harshly or unfairly: *I suppose she'll get a lawyer and I'll be shafted.* ▷Old English *scæft, sceaft* 'handle, pole,' of Germanic origin; related to Dutch *schaft*, German *Schaft*, and perhaps also to **SCEPTER.** Early senses of the verb (late Middle English) were 'fit with a handle' and 'send out shafts of light.' —**shaft·ed** *adj.* [in *combination*] *a long-shafted harpoon.*

shaft drive ▶*n.* a mechanism in which power is transmitted from an engine by means of a driveshaft, esp. to the wheels of a vehicle or a boat's propeller. —**shaft-driv·en** *adj.*

Shaftes·bur·y /ˈshaf(t)s,berē; -b(ə)rē/, Anthony Ashley Cooper, 7th Earl of (1801–85), English philanthropist and social reformer. He inspired much of the legislation designed to improve conditions for the large working class created as a result of the Industrial Revolution.

shaft horse·pow·er ▶*n.* the power delivered to a propeller or turbine shaft.

shaft·ing /ˈshaftiNG/ ▶*n.* a system of connected shafts for transmitting motive power in a machine.

shag[1] /shag/ ▶*n.* **1** [usu. as *adj.*] a carpet or rug with a long, rough pile: *wall-to-wall shag carpet.* ■ [as *adj.*] (of a pile) long and rough: *a shag pile.* ■ cloth with a velvet nap on one side. **2** a thick, tangled hairstyle or mass of hair: *her hair was cut short in a boyish shag |* [as *adj.*] *a shag cut.* **3** (also **shag tobacco**) a coarse kind of cut tobacco. ▷late Old English *sceacga* 'rough matted hair,' of Germanic origin; related to Old Norse *skegg* 'beard' and **SHAW**[2].

shag[2] ▶*n.* a western European and Mediterranean cormorant with greenish-black plumage and a long curly crest in the breeding season. • *Phalacrocorax aristotelis*, family Phalacrocoracidae. ■ *chiefly NZ* any cormorant. ▷mid 16th cent.: perhaps a use of **SHAG**[1], with reference to the bird's "shaggy" crest.

shag[3] ▶*n.* a dance originating in the U.S. in the 1930s and 1940s, characterized by vigorous hopping from one foot to the other. ▷of obscure derivation; perhaps from obsolete *shag* 'waggle.'

shag[4] ▶*v.* [*trans.*] *Baseball* chase or catch (fly balls) for practice. ▷early 20th cent.: of unknown origin.

shag[5] *Brit., vulgar slang* ▶*v.* (**shagged, shag·ging**) [*trans.*] have sexual intercourse with (someone).
▶*n.* an act of sexual intercourse. ■ [with *adj.*] a sexual partner of a specified ability. ▷late 18th cent.: of unknown origin. —**shag·ger** *n.*

shag·bark hick·o·ry /ˈshag,bärk/ ▶*n.* see **HICKORY.**

shagged /shagd/ ▶*adj. Brit., informal* exhausted: *they were too shagged to do any cleaning.* ■ damaged, ruined, or useless: *I thought my hearing was shagged because I play the drums.*

shag·gy /ˈshagē/ ▶*adj.* (**-gi·er, -gi·est**) (of hair or fur) long, thick, and unkempt: *the mountain goat has a long, shaggy coat.* ■ having long, thick, unkempt hair or fur: *a huge shaggy English sheepdog.* ■ of or having a covering resembling rough, thick hair. —**shag·gi·ly** /-əlē/ *adv.* —**shag·gi·ness** *n.*
▶*PHRASE* □ **shaggy-dog story** a long, rambling story or joke, typically one that is amusing only because it is absurdly inconsequential or pointless. [originally an anecdote of this type, about a shaggy-haired dog (1945).]

Pronunciation Key ə ago; ər over; ˈə or ,ə up; ˈər or ,ər fur; a hat; ā rate; ä car; CH chew; e let; ē see; e(ə)r air; i fit; ī by; i(ə)r ear; NG sing; ō go; ô for; oi boy; o͝o good; o͞o goo; ou out; SH she; TH thin; TH then; (h)w why; ZH vision

S

shag·gy mane ▸*n.* a common mushroom that has a tall, narrow white cap covered with shaggy scales, occurring worldwide and edible when young. • *Coprinus comatus,* family Coprinaceae, class Hymenomycetes.

sha·green /shə'grēn/ ▸*n.* **1** sharkskin used as a decorative material or, for its natural rough surface of pointed scales, as an abrasive. **2** a kind of untanned leather with a rough granulated surface. ▷late 17th cent.: variant of **CHAGRIN** in the literal sense 'rough skin.'

Shah /shä/, Reza, see **PAHLAVI**[1].

shah /shä/ ▸*n. historical* a title of the former monarch of Iran. ▷mid 16th cent.: from Persian *šāh,* from Old Persian *ḵšāyaṯiya* 'king.' **—shah·dom** /-dəm/ *n.*

sha·ha·da /shä'hädə/ (also **sha·ha·dah**) ▸*n.* the Muslim profession of faith ("there is no god but Allah, and Muhammad is the messenger of Allah"). ▷from Arabic *šahāda* 'testimony, evidence.'

sha·hid /shä'hēd/ (also **sha·heed**) ▸*n.* a Muslim martyr. ▷late 19th cent.: from Arabic *šhīd* 'witness, martyr.'

Shahn /shän/, Ben(jamin) (1898–1989), U.S. artist and photographer; born in Lithuania. His paintings such as "The Passion of Sacco and Vanzetti" (1931–32) are devoted to political and social themes. He was also a photographer for the U.S. Farm Security Administration during the 1930s.

shah·toosh /shä'to͞osh/ ▸*n.* high-quality wool from the neck hair of the Himalayan ibex. ■ fabric woven from this. ▷mid 19th cent.: via Punjabi from Persian *šāh* 'king' + Kashmiri *tośa* 'fine shawl material.'

shaikh /shēk; shāk/ ▸*n.* variant spelling of **SHEIKH**.

Shai·tan /shī'tän/ ▸*n.* (in Muslim countries) the Devil, Satan, or an evil spirit. ■ (**shaitan**) an evilly disposed, vicious, or cunning person or animal. ▷from Arabic *šayṭān.*

Shai·va /'shīvə/ (also **Sai·va** /'sīvə/) ▸*n.* a member of one of the main branches of modern Hinduism, devoted to the worship of the god Shiva as the supreme being. Compare with **VAISHNAVA**. ▷from Sanskrit *śaiva* 'sacred to Shiva.' **—Shai·vite** /-vīt/ *n. & adj.*

Sha·ka /'shäkə/ (also **Cha·ka**) (*c.*1787–1828), Zulu chief 1816–28. He reorganized his forces and waged war against the Nguni clans, subjugating them and forming a Zulu empire in southeastern Africa.

shake /shāk/ ▸*v.* (*past* **shook** /sho͝ok/; *past part.* **shak·en** /'shākən/) **1** [*intrans.*] (of a structure or area of land) tremble or vibrate: *buildings shook in Sacramento and tremors were felt in Reno.* ■ [*trans.*] cause to tremble or vibrate: *a severe earthquake shook the area.* ■ (of a person, a part of the body, or the voice) tremble uncontrollably from a strong emotion such as fear or anger: *Luke was* ***shaking with*** *rage | her voice* ***shook with*** *passion.* **2** [*trans.*] move (an object) up and down or from side to side with rapid, forceful, jerky movements: *she stood in the hall and shook her umbrella.* ■ [*trans.*] remove (an object or substance) from something by movements of this kind: *they shook the sand out of their shoes.* ■ *informal* get rid of or put an end to (something unwanted): *he was unable to* ***shake off*** *the memories of the trenches.* ■ grasp (someone) and move them roughly to and fro, either in anger or to rouse them from sleep: [*trans.*] *he gently shook the driver awake and they set off.* ■ brandish in anger or as a warning; make a threatening gesture with: *men shook their fists and shouted.* **3** [*trans.*] upset the composure of; shock or astonish: *rumors of a further loss shook the market | the fall* ***shook*** *him* ***up*** *quite badly |* [as *adj.*] (**shaken**) *she was visibly shaken and upset when she returned.* ■ [*trans.*] cause a change of mood or attitude by shocking or disturbing (someone): *he had to shake himself out of his lethargy.* ■ weaken or impair (confidence, a belief, etc.), esp. by shocking or disturbing: *the escalation in costs is certain to shake the confidence of private investors.*

▸*phrasal v.* □ **shake down** become established in a new place or situation; settle down: *it was disruptive to the industry as it was shaking down after deregulation.* □ **shake someone down** *informal* extort money from someone. □ **shake something down** cause something to fall or settle by shaking. □ **shake someone off** get away from someone by shaking their grip loose. ■ manage to evade or outmaneuver someone who is following or pestering one: *he thought he had shaken off his pursuer.* ■ (in sports, esp. a race) outdistance another competitor: *in the final lap she looked as though she had shaken off the Dutch girl.* □ **shake something off** successfully deal with or recover from an illness or injury: *she has shaken off a virus.* □ **shake on** *informal* confirm (an agreement) by shaking hands: *they shook on the deal.* □ **shake out** eventually prove to happen: *we'll see what shakes out.* □ **shake something out 1** empty something out by shaking a container: *he shook out a handful of painkillers.* **2** spread or open something such as a cloth or garment by shaking it: *she shook out the newspaper.* ■ restore something crumpled to its natural shape by shaking: *she undid her helmet and shook out her frizzled hair.* ■ *Sailing* unwind or untie a reef to increase the area of a sail. □ **shake someone up** rouse someone from lethargy, apathy, or complacency: *he had to do something to shake the team up—we lacked spark.* □ **shake something up 1** mix ingredients by shaking: *use soap flakes shaken up in the water to make bubbles.* **2** make radical changes to the organization or structure of an institution or system: *he presented plans to shake up the legal profession.*

▸*n.* **1** an act of shaking: *with a shake of its magnificent antlers the stag charged down the slope | camera shake causes the image to become blurred.* ■ *informal* an earth tremor. ■ an amount of something that is sprinkled by shaking a container: *add a few* ***shakes of*** *sea salt and black pepper.* ■ short for **MILK SHAKE**. ■ (**the shakes**) *informal* a fit of trembling or shivering: *I wouldn't go in there, it gives me the shakes.* **2** *Music* a trill. ▷Old English *sc(e)acan* (verb), of Germanic origin.

▸*PHRASES* □ **get** (or **give someone**) **a fair shake** *informal* get (or give someone) just treatment or a fair chance: *I do not believe he gave the industry a fair shake.* □ **in two shakes** (**of a lamb's tail**) *informal* very quickly: *I'll be back to you in two shakes.* □ **more —— than one can shake a stick at** *informal* used to emphasize the largeness of an amount: *a team with more experience than you can shake a stick at.* □ **no great shakes** *informal* not very good or significant: *it is no great shakes as a piece of cinema.* □ **shake the dust off one's feet** leave indignantly or disdainfully. □ **shake hands** (**with someone**) (or **shake someone by the hand** or **shake someone's hand**) clasp someone's right hand in one's own at meeting or parting, in reconciliation or congratulation, or as a sign of agreement. □ **shake one's head** turn one's head from side to side in order to indicate refusal, denial, disapproval, or incredulity: *she shook her head in disbelief.* □ **shake** (or **quake**) **in one's shoes** (or **boots**) tremble with apprehension. □ **shake a leg** *informal* make a start; rouse oneself: *come on, shake a leg.*

THE RIGHT WORD **quake, quiver, shake, shiver, shudder, tremble**

Does a cool breeze make you **shiver, quiver, shudder,** or **tremble?** All of these verbs describe vibrating, wavering, or oscillating movements that, in living creatures, are often involuntary expressions of strain or discomfort.

Shake, which refers to abrupt forward-and-backward, side-to-side, or up-and-down movements, is different from the others in that it can be done to a person or object as well as by one (*shake a can of paint; shake visibly while lifting a heavy load*).

Tremble applies specifically to the slight and rapid shaking motion the human body makes when it is nervous, frightened, or uneasy (*his hands trembled when he picked up the phone*).

To *shiver* is to make a similar movement with the entire body, but the cause is usually a sensation of cold or fear (*shiver in the draft from an open door*).

Quiver suggests a rapid and almost imperceptible vibration resulting from disturbed or irregular surface tension; it refers more often to things (*the leaves quivered in the breeze*), although people may quiver when they're under emotional tension (*her lower lip quivered and her eyes were downcast*).

Shudder suggests a more intense shaking, usually in response to something horrible or revolting (*shudder at the thought of eating uncooked meat*).

Quake implies a violent upheaval or shaking, similar to what occurs during an earthquake (*the boy's heart quaked at his father's approach*).

shake·down /'shāk,doun/ ▸*n. informal* **1** a radical change or restructuring, particularly in a hierarchical organization or group: *after the collapse of the Soviet Union, a shakedown of the Russian press was inevitable.* ■ a thorough search of a person or place: *harassment and shakedowns by persons in police uniforms.* ■ a swindle; a piece of extortion: *he wants to eliminate bribery, shakedowns, and bid-rigging in New York City's construction industry.* ■ a test of a new product or model, esp. a vehicle or ship: *the high-orbit shakedown of the lunar module had its merits |* [as *adj.*] *the software is expected to enter its final shakedown phase by the middle of September.* **2** a makeshift bed.

shak·en /'shākən/ ▸ past participle of **SHAKE**.

sha·ken ba·by syn·drome ▸*n.* injury to a baby caused by being shaken violently and repeatedly. Shaking can cause swelling of the brain, internal bleeding, detached retinas leading to blindness, mental retardation, and death.

shake-out /'shāk,out/ ▸*n. informal* an upheaval or reorganization of a business, market, or organization due to competition and typically involving streamlining and layoffs.

shak·er /'shākər/ ▸*n.* **1** [with *adj.*] a container used for mixing ingredients by shaking: *a cocktail shaker.* ■ a container with a pierced top from which a powdered substance such as flour or salt is poured by shaking. **2** (**Shaker**) a member of an American religious sect, the United Society of Believers in Christ's Second Coming, established in England *c.*1750 and living simply in celibate mixed communities. [so named from the wild, ecstatic movements engaged in during worship.] ■ [as *adj.*] denoting a style of elegantly functional furniture traditionally produced by Shaker communities. **—Shak·er·ism** /-,rizəm/ *n.* (in sense 2).

Shak·er·ess /'shāk(ə)ris/ ▸*n.* a female Shaker.

Shak·er Heights /'shākər/ a city in northeastern Ohio, an affluent suburb east of Cleveland; pop. 30,831.

Shake·speare /'shāk,spi(ə)r/, William (1564–1616), English playwright. His plays are written mostly in blank verse and include comedies, historical plays, the Greek and Roman plays, enigmatic comedies, the great tragedies, and the group of tragicomedies with which he ended his career. He also wrote more than 150 sonnets, which were published in 1609, as well as narrative poems. **—Shake·spear·e·an** /shāk'spi(ə)rēən/ (also **Shake·spear·i·an**) *n. & adj.*

William Shakespeare

Shake·spear·e·an son·net ▸*n.* another term for **ELIZABETHAN SONNET**.

shake-up (also **shake·up**) ▸*n. informal* a radical reorganization.

Shakh·ty /'shäkhtē/ a coal-mining city in southwestern Russia, in the Donets Basin, northeast of Rostov; pop. 227,000.

shak·o /'shakō; 'shā-/ ▸*n.* (*pl.* **-os**) a cylindrical or conical military hat with a brim and a plume or pom-pom. ▷early 19th cent.: via French from Hungarian *csákó (süveg)* 'peaked (cap),' from *csák* 'peak,' from German *Zacken* 'spike.'

shako

Shak·ti /'shəktē/ ▸*n. Hinduism* the female principle of divine energy, esp. when personified as the supreme deity. See also **DEVI** and **PARVATI**. ▷from Sanskrit *śakti* 'power, divine energy.'

sha·ku·do /shä'ko͞odō/ ▸*n.* a Japanese alloy of copper and gold, typically having a blue patina. ▷mid 19th cent.: Japanese, from *shaku* 'red' + *dō* 'copper.'

sha·ku·ha·chi /'shäko͞o'häche/ ▸*n.* (*pl.* **-chis**) a Japanese bamboo flute, held vertically when played. ▷late 19th cent.: Japanese, from *shaku,* a measure of length (approx. 0.33 meter) + *hachi* 'eight (tenths).'

shak·y /'shākē/ ▸*adj.* (**shak·i·er, shak·i·est**) shaking or trembling: *she managed a shaky laugh.* ■ unstable because of poor construction or heavy use: *a cracked,* *dangerously shaky table.* ■ not safe or reliable; liable to fail or falter: *thoroughly shaky evidence | Burns overcame a shaky start to beat the Red Sox.* —**shak·i·ly** /-kilē/ *adv.* —**shak·i·ness** *n.*

shale /SHāl/ ▶*n.* soft, finely stratified sedimentary rock that formed from consolidated mud or clay and can be split easily into fragile slabs. ▷mid 18th cent.: probably from German *Schale*; related to English dialect *shale* 'dish' (see SCALE[2]). —**shal·y** (also **shal·ey**) *adj.*

shale oil ▶*n.* oil obtained from bituminous shale.

shall /SHal/ ▶*modal verb* (*3rd sing. present* **shall**) **1** (in the first person) expressing the future tense: *this time next week I shall be in Scotland | we shan't be gone long.* **2** expressing a strong assertion or intention: *they shall succeed | you shall not frighten me out of this.* **3** expressing an instruction or command: *you shall not steal.* **4** used in questions indicating offers or suggestions: *shall I send you the book? | shall we go?* ▷Old English *sceal*, of Germanic origin; related to Dutch *zal* and German *soll*, from a base meaning 'owe.'

USAGE There is considerable confusion about when to use **shall** and **will**. The traditional rule in standard English is that **shall** is used with first person pronouns (*I* and *we*) to form the future tense, while **will** is used with second and third persons (*you, he, she, it, they*): ***I shall** be late; **she will** not be there.* When expressing a strong determination to do something, the traditional rule is that **will** is used with the first person, and **shall** with the second and third persons: ***I will** not tolerate this; **you shall** go to school.*

In practice, however, **shall** and **will** are today used more or less interchangeably in statements (although not in questions). Given that the forms are frequently contracted (**we'll**, **she'll**, etc.), there is often no need to make a choice between **shall** and **will**, another factor no doubt instrumental in weakening the distinction. In modern English, the interchangeable use of **shall** and **will** is an acceptable part of standard U.S. and British English.

shal·lop /'SHaləp/ ▶*n. chiefly historical* a light sailboat used mainly for coastal fishing or as a tender. ■ a large heavy boat with one or more masts and carrying fore-and-aft or lug sails and sometimes equipped with guns. ▷late 16th cent.: from French *chaloupe*, from Dutch *sloep* 'sloop.'

shal·lot /SHə'lät; 'SHalət/ ▶*n.* **1** a small bulb that resembles an onion and is used for pickling or as a substitute for onion. **2** the plant that produces these bulbs, each mature bulb producing a cluster of smaller bulbs. • *Allium ascalonicum*, family Liliaceae (or Alliaceae). ▷mid 17th cent.: shortening of *eschalot*, from French *eschalotte*, alteration of Old French *eschaloigne* (in Anglo-Norman French *scaloun*: see SCALLION).

shal·low /'SHalō/ ▶*adj.* of little depth: *serve the noodles in a shallow bowl | being fairly shallow, the water was warm.* ■ situated at no great depth: *the shallow bed of the North Sea.* ■ varying only slightly from a specified or understood line or direction, esp. the horizontal: *a shallow roof.* ■ not exhibiting, requiring, or capable of serious thought: *a shallow analysis of contemporary society.* See note at SUPERFICIAL. ■ (of breathing) taking in little air.

▶*n.* (**shallows**) an area of the sea, a lake, or a river where the water is not very deep.

▶*v.* [*intrans.*] (of the sea, a lake, or a river) become less deep over time or in a particular place: *the boat ground to a halt where the water shallowed.* ▷late Middle English: obscurely related to SHOAL[2]. —**shal·low·ly** *adv.* —**shal·low·ness** *n.*

Shal·ma·ne·ser III /,SHalmə'nēzər/ (died 824 BC), king of Assyria 859–824. Most of his reign was devoted to the expansion of his kingdom and the conquest of neighboring lands. According to Assyrian records, he defeated an alliance of Syrian kings and the king of Israel in a battle at Qarqar on the Orontes in 853 BC. ▷from *Salmanasar*, the Latin form of the name in the Vulgate (2 Kings 17–19).

sha·lom /SHä'lōm; SHə-/ ▶*exclam.* used as salutation by Jews at meeting or parting, meaning "peace." Compare with SALAAM. ▷from Hebrew *šālōm*.

shalt /SHalt/ ▶ archaic second person singular of SHALL.

shal·war /'SHəl,wär/ ▶*n.* variant spelling of SALWAR.

sham /SHam/ ▶*n.* **1** a thing that is not what it is purported to be: *the proposed legislation is a farce and a sham.* ■ pretense: *it all turned out to be sham and hypocrisy.* ■ a person who pretends to be someone or something they are not: *he was a sham, totally unqualified for his job as a senior doctor.* **2** short for PILLOW SHAM.

▶*adj.* bogus; false: *a clergyman who arranged a sham marriage.*

▶*v.* (**shammed, sham·ming**) [*intrans.*] falsely present something as the truth: *was he ill or was he shamming?* ■ [*trans.*] pretend to be or to be experiencing: *she shams indifference.* ▷late 17th cent.: perhaps a northern English dialect variant of the noun SHAME. —**sham·mer** *n.*

sha·mal /SHə'mäl/ ▶*n.* a hot, dry northwesterly wind blowing across the Persian Gulf in summer, typically causing sandstorms. ▷late 17th cent.: from Arabic *šamāl* 'north (wind).'

sha·man /'SHämən; 'SHā-/ ▶*n.* (*pl.* **-mans**) a person regarded as having access to, and influence in, the world of good and evil spirits, esp. among some peoples of northern Asia and North America. Typically such people enter a trance state during a ritual, and practice divination and healing. ▷late 17th cent.: from German *Schamane* and Russian *shaman*, from Tungus *šaman*. —**sha·man·ic** /SHə'manik/ *adj.* —**sha·man·ism** /-,nizəm/ *n.* —**sha·man·ist** /-nist/ *n.* & *adj.* —**sha·man·is·tic** /,SHämə'nistik; ,SHā-/ *adj.* —**sha·man·ize** /-,nīz/ *v.*

sha·ma·teur /'SHamətər; -,tər; -,CHo͝or; -CHər/ ▶*n. derogatory* a sports player who makes money from sports though classified as amateur. ▷late 19th cent.: blend of SHAM and AMATEUR. —**sha·ma·teur·ism** /-,rizəm/ *n.*

sham·ba /'SHämbə/ ▶*n.* (in East Africa) a cultivated plot of ground; a farm or plantation. ▷Kiswahili.

sham·ble /'SHambəl/ ▶*v.* [*intrans.*] (of a person) move with a slow, shuffling, awkward gait: *he shambled off down the corridor* | [as *adj.*] (**shambling**) *a big, shambling, shy man.*

▶*n.* [in *sing.*] a slow, shuffling, awkward gait. ▷late 16th cent.: probably from dialect *shamble* 'ungainly,' perhaps from the phrase *shamble legs*, with reference to the legs of trestle tables (such as would be used in a meat market: see SHAMBLES).

sham·bles /'SHambəlz/ ▶*plural n.* [treated as *sing.*] **1** *informal* a state of total disorder: *my career was* ***in a shambles.*** **2** a butcher's slaughterhouse (archaic except in place names). ■ a scene of carnage: *the room was a shambles—their throats had been cut and they lay in a waste of blood.* ▷late Middle English (in the sense 'meat market'): plural of earlier *shamble* 'stool, stall,' from Latin *scamellum*, diminutive of *scamnum* 'bench.'

sham·bly /'SHamblē/ ▶*adj. informal* (of a building) ramshackle; rickety. ■ (of a person) awkward; ungainly.

sham·bo·lic /SHam'bälik/ ▶*adj. informal, chiefly Brit.* chaotic, disorganized, or mismanaged: *the department's shambolic accounting.* ▷1970s: from SHAMBLES, probably on the pattern of *symbolic*.

shame /SHām/ ▶*n.* a painful feeling of humiliation or distress caused by the consciousness of wrong or foolish behavior: *she was hot with shame | he felt a pang of shame at telling Alice a lie.* ■ a loss of respect or esteem; dishonor: *the incident had brought shame on his family.* ■ used to reprove someone for something of which they should be ashamed: ***shame on you*** *for hitting a woman |* ***for shame****, brother!* ■ [in *sing.*] a regrettable or unfortunate situation or action: *it is a shame that they are not better known.* ■ a person, action, or situation that brings a loss of respect or honor: *ignorance of Latin would be a disgrace and* ***a shame to*** *any public man.*

▶*v.* [*trans.*] (of a person, action, or situation) make (someone) feel ashamed: *I tried to* ***shame*** *him* ***into*** *giving some away.* ■ cause (someone) to feel ashamed or inadequate by outdoing or surpassing them: *she shames me with her eighty-year-old energy.* ▷Old English *sc(e)amu* (noun), *sc(e)amian* 'feel shame,' of Germanic origin; related to Dutch *schamen* (verb) and German *Scham* (noun), *schämen* (verb).

▶*PHRASE* □ **put someone to shame** disgrace or embarrass someone by outdoing or surpassing them: *she puts me to shame, she's so capable.*

shame cul·ture ▶*n. Anthropology* a culture in which conformity of behavior is maintained through the individual's fear of being shamed.

shame·faced /'SHām,fāst/ ▶*adj.* feeling or expressing shame or embarrassment: *all the boys looked shamefaced.* ▷mid 16th cent. (in the sense 'modest, shy'): alteration of archaic *shamefast*, by association with FACE. —**shame·fac·ed·ly** /-,fāsidlē; -,fāstlē/ *adv.* —**shame·fac·ed·ness** /-,fāsidnis/ *n.*

shame·ful /'SHāmfəl/ ▶*adj.* worthy of or causing shame or disgrace: *a shameful accusation.* ▷Old English *sc(e)amful* 'modest, shamefaced' (see SHAME, -FUL). —**shame·ful·ly** *adv.* [as *submodifier*] *record companies are shamefully slow in fulfilling orders.* —**shame·ful·ness** *n.*

shame·less /'SHāmlis/ ▶*adj.* (of a person or their conduct) characterized by or showing a lack of shame: *his shameless hypocrisy.* ▷Old English *sc(e)amlēas* (see SHAME, -LESS). —**shame·less·ly** *adv.* —**shame·less·ness** *n.*

Sha·mir /SHə'mi(ə)r/, Yitzhak (1915–), Israeli statesman, born in Poland; prime minister 1983–84 and 1986–92; Polish name *Yitzhak Jazernicki*. Under his leadership Israel did not retaliate when attacked by Iraqi missiles during the Gulf War and possibly averted an escalation of the conflict.

sha·mi·sen /'SHami,sen/ ▶*n.* variant spelling of SAMISEN.

sham·mes /'SHäməs/ ▶*n.* **1** a sexton in a synagogue. **2** the candle that is used to light the others in a menorah for Hanukkah.

sham·my /'SHamē/ (also **sham·my leath·er**) ▶*n.* (*pl.* **-mies**) informal term for CHAMOIS (sense 2). ▷early 18th cent.: a phonetic spelling.

sham·poo /SHam'po͞o/ ▶*n.* a liquid preparation containing detergent or soap for washing the hair: *he smelt clean, of soap and shampoo | an anti-dandruff shampoo.* ■ a similar substance for cleaning a carpet, soft furnishings, or a car. ■ an act of washing or cleaning something, esp. the hair, with shampoo: *a shampoo and set.*

▶*v.* (**-poos, -pooed** /-'po͞od/) [*trans.*] wash or clean (something, esp. the hair) with shampoo: *Dolly was sitting in the bath shampooing her hair.* ■ (**shampoo something in/out**) wash something in or out of the hair using shampoo: *apply oil to wet hair, otherwise it will be difficult to shampoo it out.* ▷mid 18th cent. (in the sense 'massage (as part of a Turkish bath process)'): from Hindi *cāmpo!* 'press!,' imperative of *cāmpnā*.

sham·rock /'SHam,räk/ ▶*n.* a low-growing, cloverlike plant with three-lobed leaves, used as the national emblem of Ireland. • The shamrock of legend has been identified with a number of different plants in the family Leguminosae, in particular the lesser yellow trefoil (*Trifolium minus*). ■ a spray or leaf of this plant. ▷late 16th cent.: from Irish *seamróg* 'trefoil' (diminutive of *seamar* 'clover').

sha·mus /'SHāməs/ ▶*n. informal* a private detective. ▷1920s: of unknown origin.

Shan /SHan/ ▶*n.* (*pl.* same or **Shans**) **1** a member of a people living mainly in northern Myanmar (Burma) and adjacent parts of southern China. **2** the Tai language of this people.

▶*adj.* of or relating to this people or their language. ▷Burmese.

Shan·dong /'SHän'dôNG/ (also **Shan·tung** /-'to͞oNG/) a coastal province in eastern China; capital, Jinan. It occupies the Shandong Peninsula that separates southern Bo Hai from the Yellow Sea.

shan·dy /'SHandē/ ▶*n.* (*pl.* **-dies**) beer mixed with a nonalcoholic drink (typically lemonade). ▷late 19th cent.: abbreviation of *shandygaff*, in the same sense, of unknown origin.

Shang /SHANG/ a dynasty that ruled China during part of the 2nd millennium BC, probably the 16th–11th centuries. The period encompassed the invention of Chinese ideographic script and the discovery and development of bronze casting.

Shang·hai /'SHANG'hī/ a city on the eastern coast of China, a port on the estuary of the Yangtze River; pop. 7,780,000. Until World War II, Shanghai contained areas of British, French, and American settlement. It was the site in 1921 of the founding of the Chinese Communist Party.

shang·hai /'SHANG,hī/ ▶*v.* (**-hais, -haied** /-,hīd/, **-hai·ing** /-,hī-iNG/) [*trans.*] *historical* force (someone) to join a ship lacking a full crew by drugging them or using other underhanded means. ■ *informal* coerce or trick (someone) into a place or position or into doing something: *Brady shanghaied her into his Jaguar and roared off.* ▷late 19th cent.: from SHANGHAI.

Shan·go /'SHänggō/ ▶*n.* a religious cult originating in western Nigeria and now practiced chiefly in parts of the Caribbean. ■ (also **Shan·gor**) an African god of thunder significant to this cult. ■ a dance associated with this cult. ▷1950s: from Yoruba.

Shan·gri-La /'SHANGgri 'lä/ a Tibetan utopia in James

Hilton's novel *Lost Horizon* (1933). ■ [as *n.*] (**a Shangri-La**) a place regarded as an earthly paradise, esp. when involving a retreat from the pressures of modern civilization. ▷from *Shangri* (an invented name) + Tibetan *la* 'mountain pass.'

shank /SHANGK/ ▶*n.* **1** (often **shanks**) a person's leg, esp. the part from the knee to the ankle: *the old man's thin, bony shanks showed through his trousers.* ■ the lower part of an animal's foreleg. ■ this part of an animal's leg as a cut of meat. **2** the shaft or stem of a tool or implement, in particular: ■ a long narrow part of a tool connecting the handle to the operational end. ■ the cylindrical part of a bit by which it is held in a drill. ■ the long stem of a key, spoon, anchor, etc. ■ the straight part of a nail or fishhook. **3** a part or appendage by which something is attached to something else, esp. a wire loop attached to the back of a button. ■ the band of a ring rather than the setting or gemstone. **4** the narrow middle of the sole of a shoe. **5** *informal* a dagger made by a prison inmate from available materials.
▶*v.* [*trans.*] *Golf* strike (the ball) with the heel of the club: *I shanked a shot and hit a person on a shoulder.* ▷Old English *sceanca*; related to Dutch *schenk* 'leg bone' and High German *Schenkel* 'thigh.' The use of the verb as a golfing term dates from the 1920s. **—shanked** *adj.* [usu. in *combination*] *a long-shanked hook.*

Shan·kar /ˈSHANG,kär/, Ravi (1920–), Indian sitar player and composer. From the mid 1950s, he toured Europe and the U.S. giving sitar recitals and doing much to stimulate Western interest in Indian music.

shank·ing /ˈSHANGKiNG/ ▶*n.* **1** *Golf* the action of striking the ball with the heel of the club. **2** any of a number of plant diseases resulting in the darkening and shriveling of a plant or fruit from the base of a stem or stalk.

shanks' mare (also **shanks' pony**) ▶*n.* used to refer to one's own legs and the action of walking as a means of conveyance. ▷late 18th cent.: first recorded as *shanks-nag* in R. Fergusson's *Poems* (1785).

Shan·non[1] /ˈSHanən/ the longest river in Ireland. It rises in County Leitrim near Lough Allen and flows 240 miles (390 km) south and then west to its estuary on the Atlantic Ocean. ■ an international airport in the Republic of Ireland, situated on the Shannon River west of Limerick.

Shan·non[2], Claude Elwood (1916–2001), U.S. engineer. The pioneer of mathematical communication theory, he also investigated digital circuits and was the first to use the term *bit* to denote a unit of information.

Shan·non's the·o·rem (also **Shannon's information theorem**) a theorem defining the maximum capacity of a communication channel to carry information with no more than an arbitrary error rate, given the bandwidth and signal-to-noise ratio. ▷mid 20th cent.: named after C. E. Shannon (see **SHANNON**[2]).

shan·ny /ˈSHanē/ ▶*n.* (*pl.* **-nies**) a small, greenish-brown European blenny (fish) of the shoreline and intertidal waters. • *Blennius pholis*, family Blenniidae. ▷mid 19th cent.: of unknown origin; compare with earlier *shan*, in the same sense.

shan't /SHant/ ▶*contraction of* shall not.

shan·ti /ˈSHäntē/ ▶*n. Indian* peace: [as *exclam.*] *"Shanti! Shanti! you must not let anger possess you like that."* ▷from Sanskrit *śānti* 'peace, tranquility.'

Shan·tou /ˈSHänˈtō/ a port in the province of Guangdong in southeastern China, situated on the South China Sea at the mouth of the Han River; pop. 860,000. It was one of the ports opened up to foreign trade in 1869. Former name **SWATOW**.

shan·tung /SHanˈtəNG/ ▶*n.* a dress fabric spun from tussore silk with random irregularities in the surface texture. ▷late 19th cent.: from **SHANTUNG** (see **SHANDONG**, where it was originally made.

shan·ty[1] /ˈSHantē/ ▶*n.* (*pl.* **-ties**) a small, crudely built shack. ▷early 19th cent. (originally a North American usage): perhaps from Canadian French *chantier* 'lumberjack's cabin, logging camp.'

shan·ty[2] ▶*n.* (*pl.* **-ties**) variant spelling of **CHANTEY**.

shan·ty·man /ˈSHantē,man/ ▶*n.* (*pl.* **-men**) a lumberjack.

shan·ty·town /ˈSHantē,toun/ ▶*n.* a deprived area on the outskirts of a town consisting of large numbers of crude dwellings.

Shan·xi /ˈSHänˈSHē/ (also **Shan·si** /-ˈsē/) a province in north central China, south of Inner Mongolia; capital, Taiyuan.

SHAPE /SHāp/ ▶*abbr.* Supreme Headquarters Allied Powers Europe.

shape /SHāp/ ▶*n.* **1** the external form or appearance characteristic of someone or something; the outline of an area or figure: *she liked the shape of his nose | houseplants come in all shapes and sizes | chest freezers are square or rectangular in shape.* ■ a person or thing that is difficult to see and identify clearly: *he saw a shape through the mist.* ■ [usu. with *adj.*] a specific form or guise assumed by someone or something: *a fiend in human shape.* ■ a piece of material, paper, etc., made or cut in a particular form: *stick paper shapes on for the puppet's eyes and nose.* **2** [with *adj.*] the particular condition or state of someone or something: *he was in no shape to drive | the building was in poor shape.* ■ the distinctive nature or qualities of something: *the future shape and direction of the country.* ■ definite or orderly arrangement: *check that your structure will* **give shape to** *your essay.*
▶*v.* [*trans.*] (often **be shaped**) give a particular shape or form to: *most caves are shaped by the flow of water through limestone | shape the dough into two-inch balls.* ■ make (something) fit the form of something else: [*trans.*] *suits have been shaped to fit so snugly that no curve is undefined.* ■ determine the nature of; have a great influence on: *his childhood was shaped by a loving relationship with his elder brother.* ■ [*intrans.*] develop in a particular way; progress: *the yacht was shaping well in trials.* ■ form or produce (a sound or words).
▶*phrasal v.* □ **shape up** develop or happen in a particular way: *it was shaping up to be another bleak year.* ■ *informal* improve performance or behavior: *we have never been afraid to tell our children to shape up* ■ become physically fit: *I need to shape up.* ▷Old English *gesceap* 'external form,' also 'creation,' *sceppan* 'create,' of Germanic origin. **—shap·a·ble** (also **shape·a·ble**) *adj.* **—shaped** *adj.* [usu. in *combination*] *egg-shaped | X-shaped.* **—shap·er** *n.*
▶*PHRASES* □ **get into shape** (or **get someone into shape**) become (or make someone) physically fitter by exercise: *if you're thinking of getting into shape, take it easy and build up slowly.* □ **in any (way,) shape or form** in any manner or under any circumstances (used for emphasis): *96 percent of the electorate voted against Europeanization in any shape or form.* □ **in (good) shape** in good physical condition. □ **in the shape of** represented or embodied by: *retribution arrived in the shape of my irate father.* □ **whip** (or **knock** or **lick**) **someone/something into shape** act forcefully to bring someone or something into a fitter, more efficient, or better organized state: *a man who whips a chamber orchestra into shape.* □ **out of shape 1** (of an object) not having its usual or original shape, esp. after being bent or knocked: *check that the pipe end and compression nut are not bent out of shape.* **2** (of a person) in poor physical condition; unfit. □ **the shape of things to come** the way the future is likely to develop. [the title of a novel by H. G. Wells (1933).] □ **shape up or ship out** *informal* used as an ultimatum to someone to improve their performance or behavior or face being made to leave. □ **take shape** assume a distinct form; develop into something definite or tangible: *the past few months have seen the state's health insurance legislation begin to take shape.*

shaped charge ▶*n.* an explosive charge with a cavity that focuses the blast into a small area.

shape·less /ˈSHāplis/ ▶*adj.* (esp. of a garment) lacking a distinctive or attractive shape: *women in shapeless cotton dresses.* **—shape·less·ly** *adv.* **—shape·less·ness** *n.*

shape·ly /ˈSHāplē/ ▶*adj.* (**-li·er**, **-li·est**) (esp. of a woman or part of her body) having an attractive or well-proportioned shape: *however much she ate made no difference to her shapely figure.* **—shape·li·ness** *n.*

shape mem·o·ry ▶*n. Metallurgy* a property exhibited by certain alloys of recovering their initial shape when they are heated after having been plastically deformed.

shape·shift·er /ˈSHāp,SHiftər/ ▶*n.* (chiefly in fiction) a person or being with the ability to change their physical form at will. **—shape·shift·ing** /-,SHiftiNG/ *n.* & *adj.*

Sha·pir·o /SHəˈpi(ə)rō/, Karl (Jay) (1913–2000), U.S. poet. His poems, such as "Elegy for a Dead Soldier" (1944), were collected in volumes such as *V-Letter and Other Poems* (1944), *Adult Book Store* (1976), and *New and Selected Poems 1940–1986* (1987).

shap·ka /ˈSHäpkə/ ▶*n.* a brimless Russian hat of fur or sheepskin. ▷1940s: Russian, literally 'hat.'

Shap·ley /ˈSHaplē/, Harlow (1885–1972), U.S. astronomer. He carried out an extensive survey of galaxies and used his studies on the distribution of globular star clusters to locate the likely center of the galaxy and to infer its structure and dimensions. He found that the solar system is located on the galaxy's edge and not at its center.

sha·ra·ra /SHəˈrärə/ ▶*n.* a pair of loose, pleated trousers worn by women from the Indian subcontinent, typically with a kameez and dupatta. ▷from Urdu.

shard /SHärd/ ▶*n.* a piece of broken ceramic, metal, glass, or rock, typically having sharp edges: *shards of glass flew in all directions.* ▷Old English *sceard* 'gap, notch, potsherd,' of Germanic origin: related to Dutch *schaarde* 'notch,' also to **SHEAR**.

share[1] /SHe(ə)r/ ▶*n.* a part or portion of a larger amount that is divided among a number of people, or to which a number of people contribute: *under the proposals, investors would pay a greater share of the annual fees required | we gave them all the chance to have a share in the profits.* ■ one of the equal parts into which a company's capital is divided, entitling the holder to a proportion of the profits: *bought 33 shares of American Standard.* ■ part proprietorship of property held by joint owners: *Jake had a share in a large seagoing vessel.* ■ [in *sing.*] the allotted or due amount of something that a person expects to have or to do, or that is expected to be accepted or done by them: *she's done more than her* **fair share of** *globe-trotting.*
▶*v.* [*trans.*] have a portion of (something) with another or others: *he* **shared** *the pie* **with** *her | all members of the band equally share the band's profits.* ■ [*trans.*] give a portion of (something) to another or others: *money raised will be shared between the two charities.* ■ use, occupy, or enjoy (something) jointly with another or others: *they once shared a house in the Hamptons |* [*intrans.*] *there weren't enough plates, so we had to share |* [as *adj.*] (**shared**) *a shared bottle of wine.* ■ possess (a view or quality) in common with others: *other countries don't share our reluctance to eat goat meat.* ■ [*intrans.*] (**share in**) (of a number of people or organizations) have a part in (something, esp. an activity): *the companies would share in the development of three oil platforms.* ■ tell someone about (something), esp. something personal: *she had never* **shared** *the secret* **with** *anyone before.* ▷Old English *scearu* 'division, part into which something may be divided,' of Germanic origin; related to Dutch *schare* and German *Schar* 'troop, multitude,' also to **SHEAR**. The verb dates from the late 16th cent. **—share·a·ble** (also **shar·a·ble**) *adj.* **—shar·er** *n.*
▶*PHRASE* □ **share and share alike** having or receiving an equal share: *their representatives shared the inheritance share and share alike.*

share[2] ▶*n.* short for **PLOWSHARE**.

share·crop·per /ˈSHe(ə)r,kräpər/ ▶*n.* a tenant farmer who gives a part of each crop as rent. **—share·crop** *v.* (**-cropped**, **-crop·ping**).

share·hold·er /ˈSHe(ə)r,hōldər/ ▶*n.* an owner of shares in a company. **—share·hold·ing** /-,hōldiNG/ *n.*

share op·tion ▶*n.* British term for **STOCK OPTION**.

share·ware /ˈSHe(ə)r,we(ə)r/ ▶*n. Computing* software that is available free of charge and often distributed informally for evaluation, after which a fee may be requested for continued use.

sha·ri·a /SHäˈrēə/ (also **sha·ri·ah** or **sha·ri·at** /-ät/) ▶*n.* Islamic canonical law based on the teachings of the Koran and the traditions of the Prophet (Hadith and Sunna), prescribing both religious and secular duties and sometimes retributive penalties for lawbreaking. It has generally been supplemented by legislation adapted to the conditions of the day, though the manner in which it should be applied in modern states is a subject of dispute between Islamic fundamentalists and modernists. ▷from Arabic *šarī'a*; the variant *shariat* from Urdu and Persian.

sha·rif /SHəˈrēf/ (also **she·reef** or **she·rif**) ▶*n.* **1** a descendant of Muhammad through his daughter Fatima, entitled to wear a green turban or veil. **2** a Muslim ruler, magistrate, or religious leader. ▷from Arabic *šarīf* 'noble,' from *šarafa* 'be exalted.' **—sha·rif·i·an** *adj.*

Shar·jah /ˈSHärzHə; -jə/ one of the seven member states of the United Arab Emirates; pop. 400,000. Arabic name **ASH SHARIQAH**. ■ its capital city, on the Persian Gulf; pop. 125,000.

shark[1] /SHärk/ ▶*n.* **1** a long-bodied chiefly marine fish with a cartilaginous skeleton, a prominent dorsal fin, and toothlike scales. Most sharks are predatory, although the largest kinds feed on plankton. • Several orders (or superorders) of the subclass Elasmobranchii: many families. **2** a small

Southeast Asian freshwater fish with a sharklike tail, popular in aquariums. • Two species in the family Cyprinidae: the small **red-tailed black shark** (*Labeo bicolor*), and the larger **black shark** (*Morulius chrysophekadion*). **3** a light grayish-brown European moth, the male of which has pale silvery hind wings. • Genus *Cucullia*, family Noctuidae: several species, including *C. umbratica*. ▷late Middle English: of unknown origin.

shark[2] ▸*n. informal* **1** a person who unscrupulously exploits or swindles others: *Coleby was a shark, not the sort of man to pay more when he could pay less* [with *adj.*] *property sharks want to develop 200 acres around the site.* See also **LOAN SHARK. 2** an expert in a specified field: *a pool shark.* ▷late 16th cent.: perhaps from German *Schurke* 'worthless rogue,' influenced by **SHARK**[1].

shark·skin /ˈsʜärkˌskin/ ▸*n.* the rough scaly skin of a shark, sometimes used as shagreen. ■ a stiff, slightly lustrous synthetic fabric.

shark·suck·er ▸*n.* a remora, esp. *Echeneis naucrates*, the most abundant remora of warm waters.

sharksucker

Shar·on /ˈsʜarən; ˈsʜe(ə)r-/ a fertile coastal plain in Israel that lies between the Mediterranean Sea and the hills of Samaria.

shar·on fruit /ˈsʜarən; ˈsʜe(ə)r-/ ▸*n.* a persimmon, esp. one of an early fruiting orange variety grown in Israel. ▷from **SHARON.**

sharp /sʜärp/ ▸*adj.* **1** (of an object) having an edge or point that is able to cut or pierce something: *cut the cake with a very sharp knife* | *keep tools sharp.* See note at **KEEN.** ■ producing a sudden, piercing physical sensation or effect: *I suddenly felt a sharp pain in my back.* ■ (of a food, taste, or smell) acidic and intense: *sharp goats' milk cheese.* ■ (of a sound) sudden and penetrating: *there was a sharp crack of thunder.* ■ (of words or a speaker) intended or intending to criticize or hurt: *she feared his sharp tongue.* ■ (of an emotion or experience) felt acutely or intensely; painful: *her sharp disappointment was tinged with embarrassment.* **2** tapering to a point or edge: *a sharp pencil* | *her face was thin and her nose sharp.* ■ distinct in outline or detail; clearly defined: *the job was a sharp contrast from her past life* | *the scene was as sharp and clear in his mind as a film.* ■ *informal* (of clothes or their wearer) neat and stylish: *they were greeted by a young man in a sharp suit.* **3** (of an action or change) sudden and marked: *there was a sharp increase in interest rates* | *he heard her sharp intake of breath.* ■ (of a bend, angle, or turn) making a sudden change of direction: *a sharp turn in the river.* ■ having or showing speed of perception, comprehension, or response: *her sharp eyes missed nothing* | *his old mind was not so sharp as it once was* | *he had a sharp sense of humor.* ■ quick to take advantage, esp. in an unscrupulous or dishonest way: *Paul's a sharp operator.* **4** (of musical sound) above true or normal pitch. ■ [*postpositive*, in *combination*] (of a note) a semitone higher than a specified note: *the song sits on E and F-sharp* | *the quartet in C-sharp minor.* ■ (of a key) having a sharp or sharps in the key signature: *recorder players are most comfortable in sharp keys.*
▸*adv.* **1** precisely (used after an expression of time): *the meeting starts at 7:30 sharp.* **2** in a sudden or abrupt way: *the creek bent sharp left* | *he was brought up sharp by Helen's voice.* **3** above the true or normal pitch of musical sound: *he heard him playing a little sharp on the high notes.*
▸*n.* **1** a musical note raised a semitone above natural pitch. ■ the sign (♯) indicating this. **2** a long, sharply pointed needle used for general sewing. ■ (usu. **sharps**) a thing with a sharp edge or point, such as a hypodermic needle, a blade, or a fragment of glass: *the safe disposal of sharps and clinical waste.* **3** *informal* a swindler or cheat. See also **CARD SHARP.**
▸*v.* [*trans.*] **1** [usu. as *adj.*] (**sharped**) *Music* raise the pitch of (a note). **2** *archaic* cheat or swindle (someone), esp. at cards: *the fellow is drunk, let's sharp him.* [late 17th cent.: from **SHARPER**; compare with **SHARK**[2].] ▷Old English *sc(e)arp*, of Germanic origin; related to Dutch *scherp* and German *scharf.* —**sharp·ly** *adv.* —**sharp·ness** *n.*
▸*PHRASE* □ **sharp as a tack** extremely clever or astute.

Shar-Pei /ˈsʜär ˈpā/ (also **shar-pei**) ▸*n.* (*pl.* **-Peis**) a compact, squarely built dog of a breed of Chinese origin, with a characteristic wrinkly skin and short bristly coat of a beige, cream, black, or red color. ▷1970s: from Chinese *shā pí*, literally 'sand skin.'

Shar-Pei

sharp·en /ˈsʜärpən/ ▸*v.* make or become sharp: [*trans.*] *she sharpened her pencil* | [*intrans.*] *her tone sharpened to exasperation.* ■ improve or cause to improve: [*intrans.*] *they must **sharpen up** or risk losing half their business* | [*trans.*] *students will **sharpen up** their reading skills.* —**shar·pen·er** *n.*

sharp·er /ˈsʜärpər/ ▸*n. informal* a swindler, esp. at cards.

Sharpe ra·ti·o /sʜärp/ ▸*n. Finance* a measure that indicates the average return minus the risk-free return divided by the standard deviation of return on an investment.

Sharpe·ville mas·sa·cre /ˈsʜärpvəl; -ˌvil/ the killing of sixty-seven anti-apartheid demonstrators by security forces at Sharpeville, a black township south of Johannesburg, on March 21, 1960. Following the massacre, the South African government banned the African National Congress and the Pan-Africanist Congress.

sharp-fea·tured ▸*adj.* (of a person) having well-defined facial features.

sharp·ie /ˈsʜärpē/ ▸*n.* (*pl.* **-ies**) **1** a sharp-prowed, flat-bottomed New England sailboat, with one or two masts each rigged with a triangular sail. **2** *informal* a dishonest and cunning person, esp. a cheat.

sharp prac·tice ▸*n. dated* dishonest or barely honest dealings.

sharp-set ▸*adj. dated* very hungry.

sharp·shoot·er /ˈsʜärpˌsʜo͞otər/ ▸*n.* a person who is very skilled in shooting. —**sharp·shoot·ing** /-ˌsʜo͞otiNG/ *n.* & *adj.*

sharp-tongued ▸*adj.* (of a person) given to using cutting, harsh, or critical language.

sharp-wit·ted ▸*adj.* (of a person) quick to notice and understand things. —**sharp-wit·ted·ly** *adv.* —**sharp-wit·ted·ness** *n.*

shash·lik /ˈsʜäsʜˌlik; sʜäsʜˈlik/ ▸*n.* (*pl.* same or **-liks**) (in Asia and eastern Europe) a mutton kebab. ▷from Russian *shashlyk*, based on Turkish *şiş* 'spit, skewer'; compare with **SHISH KEBAB.**

Shas·ta, Mount /ˈsʜastə/ a peak in northern California, the highest point (14,162 feet; 4,317 m) in the Cascade Range within the state. Shasta Lake lies on its south.

Shas·ta dai·sy /ˈsʜästə/ ▸*n.* a tall, widely cultivated plant of the daisy family that bears large white daisylike flowers. • *Chrysanthemum superbum* or its hybrids, family Compositae. ▷mid 19th cent.: named after Mount *Shasta* in California.

shas·tra /ˈsʜästrə/ (also **sas·tra**) ▸*n.* (in Hinduism) the totality of sacred scripture. ■ (in Hinduism and Buddhism) a treatise or commentary. ▷from Sanskrit *śāstra.*

shat /sʜat/ ▸ past and past participle of **SHIT.**

Shatt al-A·rab /ˌsʜat al ˈarəb; sʜät äl ˈärəb/ a river in southwestern Asia that is formed by the confluence of the Tigris and Euphrates rivers and flows 120 miles (195 km) through southeastern Iraq to the Persian Gulf. Its lower course forms the border between Iraq and Iran. ▷from Arabic, literally 'Arab shore'.

shat·ter /ˈsʜatər/ ▸*v.* break or cause to break suddenly and violently into pieces: [*intrans.*] *bullets riddled the bar top, glasses shattered, bottles exploded* | [*trans.*] *the window was shattered by a stone.* ■ [*trans.*] damage or destroy (something abstract): *the crisis will shatter their confidence.* ■ [*trans.*] upset (someone) greatly: *everyone was shattered by the news* | [as *adj.*] (**shattering**) *he found it a shattering experience.* ▷Middle English (in the sense 'scatter, disperse'): perhaps imitative; compare with **SCATTER.** —**shat·ter·er** *n.* —**shat·ter·ing·ly** *adv.* —**shat·ter·proof** /-ˌpro͞of/ *adj.*

shat·ter cone ▸*n. Geology* a fluted conical structure produced in rock by intense mechanical shock, such as that associated with meteoritic impact.

shau·ri /ˈsʜourē/ ▸*n.* (*pl.* **-ris** or **-ries**) (in East Africa) a debate, argument, or problematic issue. ▷Kiswahili.

shave /sʜāv/ ▸*v.* **1** [*intrans.*] cut the hair off one's face with a razor: *he washed, shaved, and had breakfast.* ■ [*trans.*] cut the hair off (a part of the body) with a razor: *she shaved her legs.* ■ [*trans.*] cut the hair off the face or another part of the body of (someone) with a razor: *his wife washed and shaved him.* ■ cut (hair) off with a razor: *professional male swimmers **shave off** their body hair.* **2** [*trans.*] cut (a thin slice or slices) from the surface of something: *scrape a large, sharp knife across the surface, **shaving off** rolls of very fine chocolate.* ■ reduce by a small amount: *they shaved profit margins.* ■ remove (a small amount) from something: *she **shaved** 0.5 seconds **off** the record.* **3** [*trans.*] pass or send something close to (something else), missing it narrowly: *Scott shaved the post in the 29th minute.*
▸*n.* **1** an act of shaving hair from the face or a part of the body: *he always needed a shave.* **2** a tool used for shaving very thin slices or layers from wood or other material. ▷Old English *sc(e)afan* 'scrape away the surface of (something) by paring,' of Germanic origin; related to Dutch *schaven* and German *schaben.*

shave·ling /ˈsʜāvliNG/ ▸*n. archaic, derogatory* a man of the church with a tonsured head.

shav·en /ˈsʜāvən/ ▸*adj.* shaved: *a boy with a shaven head* | [in *combination*] *shaven-headed monks.*

shav·er /ˈsʜāvər/ ▸*n.* **1** an electric razor. **2** *informal* a young lad: *little shavers and their older brothers.*

shave·tail /ˈsʜāvˌtāl/ ▸*n. military slang, often derogatory* a newly commissioned officer, esp. a second lieutenant. ■ *informal* an inexperienced person: [as *adj.*] *the shavetail Assistant District Attorney.* ▷figuratively, from the early sense 'untrained pack animal' (identified by a shaved tail).

Sha·vi·an /ˈsʜāvēən/ ▸*adj.* of, relating to, or in the manner of G. B. Shaw, his writings, or ideas.
▸*n.* an admirer of Shaw or his work. ▷from *Shavius* (Latinized form of *Shaw*) + **-AN.**

shav·ing /ˈsʜāviNG/ ▸*n.* **1** a thin strip cut off a surface: *she brushed wood shavings from her knees.* **2** the action of shaving.

Sha·vu·oth /sʜəˈvo͞oˌōt; ˌsʜävo͞oˈōt; sʜəˈvo͞oəs/ (also **Sha·vu·ot**) ▸*n.* a major Jewish festival held on the 6th (and usually the 7th) of Sivan, fifty days after the second day of Passover. It was originally a harvest festival, but now also commemorates the giving of the Law (the Torah). Also called **PENTECOST, FEAST OF WEEKS.** ▷from Hebrew *šāḇūʿōṯ* 'weeks,' with reference to the weeks between Passover and Pentecost.

Shaw[1] /sʜô/, George Bernard (1856–1950), Irish playwright and writer. His best-known plays combine comedy with a questioning of conventional morality and thought; they include *Candida* (1897), *Man and Superman* (1903), *Major Barbara* (1905), *Pygmalion* (1913), and *St. Joan* (1923). Nobel Prize for Literature (1925).

Shaw[2], Irwin (1913–84), U.S. writer. He wrote the novels *The Young Lions* (1948), *Rich Man, Poor Man* (1970), and *Acceptable Losses* (1982).

shaw /sʜô/ ▸*n. archaic, chiefly Scottish* a small group of trees; a thicket. ▷Old English *sceaga*, of Germanic origin; related to **SHAG**[1].

shawl /sʜôl/ ▸*n.* a piece of fabric worn by women over the shoulders or head or wrapped around a baby. ▷from Urdu and Persian *šāl*, probably from *Shāliāt*, the name of a town in India. —**shawled** *adj.*

shawl col·lar ▸*n.* a rounded turned-down collar, without lapel notches, that extends down the front of a garment.

shawm /sʜôm/ ▸*n.* a medieval and Renaissance wind instrument, forerunner of the oboe, with a double reed enclosed in a wooden mouthpiece, and having a penetrating tone. ▷Middle English: from Old French *chalemel*, via Latin from Greek *kalamos* 'reed.'

Shaw·nee[1] /sʜôˈnē/ **1** a city in northeastern Kansas, southwest of Kansas City; pop. 47,996. **2** an industrial city in central Oklahoma; pop. 28,692.

Shaw·nee[2] ▸*n.* (*pl.* same or **-nees**) **1** a member of an American Indian people living formerly in the

eastern U.S. and now chiefly in Oklahoma. **2** the Algonquian language of this people.
▸*adj.* of or relating to the Shawnee or their language. ▷Delaware *šắwanōw* (singular), from the Shawnee self-designation *šắwanōki* (plural), literally 'southern people.'

shay /SHā/ ▸*n.* informal term for CHAISE (sense 1). ▷early 18th cent.: back-formation from CHAISE, interpreted as plural.

shaykh /SHāk; SHēk/ ▸*n.* variant spelling of SHEIKH.

sha·zam /SHə'zam/ ▸*exclam.* used to introduce an extraordinary deed, story, or transformation: *She prayed for his arrival and shazam! There he was.* ▷1940s: an invented word, used by conjurors.

Shcher·ba·kov /'SHerbə,kôf; -,käf; ,SHCHi(ə)rbə'kôf/ former name (1946–57) of RYBINSK.

shchi /'SHCHē/ ▸*n.* a type of Russian cabbage soup. ▷Russian.

she /SHē/ ▸*pron.* [*third person singular*] used to refer to a woman, girl, or female animal previously mentioned or easily identified: *my sister told me that she was not happy.* ■ used to refer to a ship, vehicle, country, or other inanimate thing regarded as female: *I was aboard the St. Roch shortly before she sailed for the Northwest Passage.* ■ used to refer to a person or animal of unspecified sex: *only include your child if you know she won't distract you.* ■ any female person: *she who rocks the cradle rules the world.*
▸*n.* [in *sing.*] a female; a woman: *society would label him a slut if he were a she.* ■ [in *combination*] female: *a she-bear* | *a she-wolf.* ▷Middle English: probably a phonetic development of the Old English feminine personal pronoun *hēo, hīe.*

USAGE 1 For a discussion of whether to say *I am older than* **she** or *I am older than* **her**, see **usage** at PERSONAL PRONOUN and THAN.
2 The use of the pronoun **he** to refer to a person of unspecified sex, once quite acceptable, has become problematic in recent years and is now usually regarded as old-fashioned or sexist. One of the responses to this has been to use **she** in the way that **he** has been used, as in *only include your* **child** *if you know* **she** *won't distract you.* In some types of writing, such as books on child care or child psychology, use of **she** has become quite common. In most contexts, however, it is likely to be distracting in the same way that **he** now is, and alternatives such as **he or she** or **they** are preferable. In some contexts where alternation would not distract, writers seeking 'balanced representation' vary the gender of the personal pronoun by using **she** or **her** in one paragraph, and **he** or **him** in the next, and so on. This method should be used with restraint, however, as it may confuse or annoy the reader.
See also **usage** at HE and THEY.

s/he /'SHē ər 'hē; 'SHē'hē/ ▸*pron.* a written representation of "he or she" used as a neutral alternative to indicate someone of either sex.

shea /SHē; SHā/ (also **shea tree**) ▸*n.* a small tropical African tree that bears oily nuts from which shea butter is obtained. • *Vitellaria paradoxa* (or *Butyrospermum parkii*), family Sapotaceae. ▷late 18th cent.: from Mande *sye.*

shea but·ter ▸*n.* a fatty substance obtained from the nuts of the shea tree, used chiefly in cosmetic skin preparations.

shead·ing /'SHēdiNG/ ▸*n.* each of the six administrative divisions of the Isle of Man. ▷late 16th cent.: variant of *shedding* (see SHED²).

sheaf /SHēf/ ▸*n.* (*pl.* **sheaves** /SHēvz/) a bundle of grain stalks laid lengthwise and tied together after reaping. ■ a bundle of objects of one kind, esp. papers: *he waved* **a sheaf of** *papers in the air.*
▸*v.* [*trans.*] bundle into sheaves. ▷Old English *scēaf*, of Germanic origin; related to Dutch *schoof* 'sheaf' and German *Schaub* 'wisp of straw,' also to the verb SHOVE.

sheal·ing /'SHēliNG/ ▸*n.* variant spelling of SHIELING.

shear /SHi(ə)r/ ▸*v.* (*past part.* **shorn** /SHôrn/ or **sheared**) **1** [*trans.*] cut the wool off (a sheep or other animal). ■ cut off (something such as hair, wool, or grass), with scissors or shears: *I'll* **shear off** *all that fleece.* ■ (**be shorn of**) have something cut off: *they were shorn of their hair* | *figurative the richest man in the U.S. was shorn of nearly $2 billion.* **2** break off or cause to break off, owing to a structural strain: [*intrans.*] *the derailleur sheared and jammed in the rear wheel* | [*trans.*] *the left wing had been almost completely* **sheared off.**
▸*n.* a strain in the structure of a substance produced by pressure, when its layers are laterally shifted in relation to each other. See also WIND SHEAR. ▷Old English *sceran* (originally in the sense 'cut through with a weapon'), of Germanic origin; related to Dutch and German *scheren*, from a base meaning 'divide, shear, shave.' —**shear·er** *n.*

USAGE The two verbs **shear** and **sheer** are sometimes confused: see **usage** at SHEER².

Shear·er¹ /'SHi(ə)rər/, (Edith) Norma (1902–83), U.S. actress; born in Canada. She made a successful transition from silent to talking movies, appearing in such movies as *A Lady of Chance* (1928), *The Divorcee* (Academy Award, 1930), and *Her Cardboard Lover* (1942).

Shear·er², Moira (1926–), Scottish ballet dancer and actress; full name *Moira Shearer King.* A ballerina with Sadler's Wells from 1942, she is noted for her portrayal of a dedicated ballerina in the movie *The Red Shoes* (1948).

shear·ling /'SHi(ə)rliNG/ ▸*n.* a sheep that has been shorn once: [as *adj.*] *a group of shearling rams.* ■ wool or fleece from such a sheep. ■ a coat made from or lined with such wool.

shears /SHi(ə)rz/ (also **a pair of shears**) ▸*plural n.* a cutting instrument in which two blades move past each other, like scissors but typically larger: *garden shears.* ▷Old English *scēara* (plural) 'scissors, cutting instrument,' of Germanic origin; related to Dutch *schaar* and German *Schere*, also to SHEAR.

shear·wa·ter /'SHi(ə)r,wôtər; -,wätər/ ▸*n.* **1** a long-winged seabird related to the petrels, often flying low over the surface of the water far from land. • Family Procellariidae: three genera, in particular *Puffinus*, and many species. **2** North American term for SKIMMER (sense 2).

sheat·fish /'SHēt,fiSH/ ▸*n.* (*pl.* same or **-fish·es**) ▷late 16th cent.: from an alteration of SHEATH + FISH¹.

sheath /SHēTH/ ▸*n.* (*pl.* **sheaths** /SHēTHz; SHēTHs/) a close-fitting cover for something, esp. something that is elongated in shape, in particular: ■ a cover for the blade of a knife or sword. ■ a structure in living tissue that closely envelops another: *the fatty sheath around nerve fibers.* ■ (also **sheath dress**) a woman's close-fitting dress: *a tight sheath of black and gold lurex.* ■ a protective covering around an electric cable. ■ a condom. ▷Old English *scǣth, scēath* 'scabbard,' of Germanic origin; related to Dutch *schede*, German *Scheide*, also to the verb SHED². —**sheath·less** *adj.*

sheath·bill /'SHēTH,bil/ ▸*n.* a mainly white pigeonlike bird with a horny sheath around the base of the bill, breeding on the coasts of sub-Antarctic islands and feeding by scavenging. • Family Chionididae and genus *Chionis*: two species.

sheathe /SHēTH/ ▸*v.* [*trans.*] put (a weapon such as a knife or sword) into a sheath. ■ (often **be sheathed in**) encase (something) in a close-fitting or protective covering: *her legs were sheathed in black stockings.* ▷late Middle English: from SHEATH.

sheath·ing /'SHēTHiNG/ ▸*n.* protective casing or covering. ■ sheets of rigid material (often plywood) attached to the framework of a building to strengthen it and to underlie siding or roofing.

sheath knife ▸*n.* a short knife similar to a dagger, carried in a sheath.

sheave /SHēv; SHiv/ ▸*n.* a wheel with a groove for a rope to run on, as in a pulley block. ▷Middle English: from a Germanic base meaning 'wheel, pulley.'

sheaves /SHēvz/ ▸ plural form of SHEAF.

She·ba /'SHēbə/ the biblical name of Saba in southwestern Arabia. The queen of Sheba visited King Solomon in Jerusalem (1 Kings 10). ▷from Hebrew *šəḇā'.*

she·bang /SHə'baNG/ ▸*n.* **1** [in *sing.*] *informal* a matter, operation, or set of circumstances: *the Mafia boss who's running* **the whole shebang.** **2** *archaic* a rough hut or shelter. ▷mid 19th cent.: of unknown origin.

She·bat /SHə'bät/ ▸*n.* variant spelling of SHEVAT.

she·been /SHə'bēn/ ▸*n.* (esp. in Ireland, Scotland, and South Africa) an unlicensed establishment or private house selling alcoholic liquor and typically regarded as slightly disreputable. ▷late 18th cent.: from Anglo-Irish *síbín*, from *séibe* 'mugful.'

She·boy·gan /SHi'boigən/ an industrial city in eastern Wisconsin, a port on Lake Michigan; pop. 50,792.

shed¹ /SHed/ ▸*n.* a simple roofed structure, typically made of wood or metal, used as a storage space, a shelter for animals, or a workshop. ■ a larger structure, typically with one or more sides open, for storing or maintaining vehicles or other machinery: *a shed is required for the three shunt engines.*
▸*v.* (**shed·ded, shed·ding**) [*trans.*] (usu. **be shedded**) park (a vehicle) in a depot. ▷late 15th cent.: apparently a variant of the noun SHADE.

shed² ▸*v.* (**shed·ding**; *past* and *past part.* **shed**) [*trans.*] (of a tree or other plant) allow (leaves or fruit) to fall to the ground: *both varieties shed leaves in winter.* ■ (of a reptile, insect, etc.) allow (its skin or shell) to come off, to be replaced by another one that has grown underneath. ■ (of a mammal) lose (hair) as a result of molting, disease, or age. ■ take off (clothes). ■ discard (something undesirable, superfluous, or outdated): *what they lacked was a willingness to shed the arrogance of the past.* ■ have the property of preventing (something) from being absorbed: *this leather has a superior ability to shed water, sweat, and salt.* ■ eliminate part of (an electrical power load) by disconnecting circuits. ▷Old English *sc(e)ādan* 'separate out (one selected group), divide,' also 'scatter,' of Germanic origin; related to Dutch and German *scheiden.* Compare with SHEATH.
▸*PHRASES* □ **shed (someone's) blood** be injured or killed (or kill or injure someone). □ **shed light on** see LIGHT¹. □ **shed tears** weep; cry.

she'd /SHēd/ ▸*contraction of* she had; she would.

shed·der /'SHedər/ ▸*n.* a person or thing that sheds something. ■ a female salmon after spawning.

she-dev·il ▸*n.* a malicious or spiteful woman.

shed·load /'SHed,lōd/ ▸*n. Brit. informal* a large amount or number: *had she decided to join a rival, she would doubtless be earning a shedload of money.* ▷1990s: from *shed* + *load*; perhaps euphemistic after *shitload.*

Shee·la-na-gig /,SHēlənə'gēg/ ▸*n.* a medieval stone figure of a naked female with the legs wide apart and the hands emphasizing the genitals, found in Britain and Ireland. ▷from Irish *Síle na gcíoch* 'Julia of the breasts.'

sheen /SHēn/ ▸*n.* [in *sing.*] a soft luster on a surface: *black crushed velvet with a slight sheen* | *figurative the sheen of outward party support in China.* See note at POLISH.
▸*v. poetic/literary* shine or cause to shine softly: [*trans.*] *men entered with rain sheening their steel helms* | [*intrans.*] *her black hair sheened in the sun.* ▷early 17th cent.: from obsolete *sheen* 'beautiful, resplendent'; apparently related to the verb SHINE.

sheen·y /'SHēnē/ ▸*adj.* (of an object) having a sheen on its surface; lustrous: *a sheeny gold tie.*
▸*n. informal, offensive* a contemptuous term for a Jewish person.

sheep /SHēp/ ▸*n.* (*pl.* same) **1** a domesticated ruminant animal with a thick woolly coat and (typically only in the male) curving horns. It is kept in flocks for its wool or meat, and is proverbial for its tendency to follow others in the flock. • *Ovis aries*, family Bovidae, descended from the wild mouflon. ■ a wild mammal related to this, such as the argali, bighorn, and urial. **2** a person who is too easily influenced or led: *the party members had become sheep, and she refused to be taken in.* **3** a person regarded as a protected follower of God. [with biblical allusion to Luke 15:6.] ■ *informal* a member of a minister's congregation. ▷Old English *scēp, scǣp, scēap*; related to Dutch *schaap* and German *Schaf.* —**sheep·like** /-,līk/ *adj.*
▸*PHRASES* □ **count sheep** count imaginary sheep jumping over a fence one by one in an attempt to put oneself to sleep. □ **make sheep's eyes at someone** look at someone in a foolishly amorous way.

sheep 1

sheep dip ▸*n.* a liquid preparation for cleansing sheep of parasites or preserving their wool. ■ a place where sheep are dipped in such a preparation.

sheep·dog /'SHēp,dôg; -,däg/ ▸*n.* a dog trained to guard and herd sheep. ■ a dog of a breed suitable for this.

sheep·dog tri·als ▸*plural n.* a public competitive display of the skills of sheepdogs.

sheep·fold /'SHēp,fōld/ ▸*n.* a sheep pen.

sheep·ish /'SHēpiSH/ ▸*adj.* (of a person or expression) showing embarrassment from shame or a lack of self-confidence: *a sheepish grin.* **—sheep·ish·ly** *adv.* **—sheep·ish·ness** *n.*

sheep lau·rel ▶*n.* a North American kalmia that is sometimes cultivated as an ornamental. • *Kalmia angustifolia*, family Ericaceae.

sheep·man /ˈSHēpmən/ ▶*n.* (*pl.* **-men**) a sheep rancher.

sheep run (also **sheep station**) ▶*n.* (esp. in Australia) an extensive tract of land on which sheep are pastured.

sheep scab ▶*n.* an intensely itching skin disease of sheep caused by a parasitic mite. • The mite is *Psoroptes communis*, family Psoroptidae.

sheep·shank /ˈSHēp,SHANGK/ ▶*n.* a kind of knot used to shorten a rope temporarily.

sheeps·head /ˈSHēps,hed/ ▶*n.* (*pl.* same) any of a number of boldly marked edible game fishes that live in warm American waters. • a black and silver striped porgy of Atlantic coastal and brackish waters (*Archosargus probatocephalus*, family Sparidae). • (**California sheepshead**) a black and red wrasse of Californian coastal waters (*Semicossyphus pulcher*, family Labridae).

sheep·skin /ˈSHēp,skin/ ▶*n.* a sheep's skin with the wool on, esp. when made into a garment or rug: [as *adj.*] *a sheepskin coat.* ■ leather from a sheep's skin used in bookbinding. ■ *informal* a diploma.

sheep sor·rel ▶*n.* a sorrel that is common on acid soils in north temperate regions. • *Rumex acetosella*, family Polygonaceae.

sheep tick ▶*n.* a large tick that infests many mammals, including humans, and frequently transmits diseases. • *Ixodes ricinus*, family Ixodidae.

sheep walk ▶*n. Brit.* a tract of land on which sheep are pastured.

sheer[1] /SHi(ə)r/ ▶*adj.* **1** [*attrib.*] nothing other than; unmitigated (used for emphasis): *she giggled with sheer delight | marriage is sheer hard work.* **2** (esp. of a cliff or wall) perpendicular or nearly so: *the sheer ice walls.* **3** (of a fabric) very thin; diaphanous: *sheer white silk chiffon.*

▶*adv.* **1** perpendicularly: *the ridge fell sheer, in steep crags.* **2** *archaic* completely; right: *she went sheer forward when the door was open.*

▶*n.* a very fine or diaphanous fabric or article. ▷Middle English (in the sense 'exempt, cleared'): probably an alteration of dialect *shire* 'pure, clear,' from the Germanic base of the verb **SHINE**. In the mid 16th cent. the word was used to describe clear, pure water, and also in sense 3. **—sheer·ly** *adv.* **—sheer·ness** *n.*

sheer[2] ▶*v.* [*intrans.*] (typically of a boat or ship) swerve or change course quickly: *the boat sheered off to beach further up the coast.* ■ *figurative* avoid or move away from an unpleasant topic: *her mind* **sheered away** *from images she didn't want to dwell on.*

▶*n.* a sudden deviation from a course, esp. by a boat. ▷early 17th cent.: perhaps from Middle Low German *scheren* 'to shear.'

> ***USAGE*** The two verbs **sheer** and **shear** have a similar origin but do not have identical meanings. **Sheer**, the less common verb, means 'swerve or change course quickly': *the boat* **sheers off** *the bank.* **Shear**, on the other hand, usually means 'cut the wool off (a sheep)' and can also mean 'break off (usually as a result of structural strain)': *the pins broke and the wing part* **sheared off**.

sheer[3] ▶*n.* the upward slope of a ship's lines toward the bow and stern. ▷late 17th cent.: probably from the noun **SHEAR**.

sheer·legs /ˈSHi(ə)r,legz/ ▶*plural n.* [treated as *sing.*] a hoisting apparatus made from poles joined at or near the top and separated at the bottom, used for masting ships, installing engines, and lifting other heavy objects.

sheesh /SHēSH/ ▶*exclam.* used to express disbelief or exasperation: *sheesh! what fun is it to mock people when they don't even get it?*

sheet[1] /SHēt/ ▶*n.* **1** a large rectangular piece of cotton or other fabric, used on a bed to cover the mattress and as a layer beneath blankets when these are used. ■ used in comparisons to describe the pallor of a person who is ill or has had a shock: *Are you OK? You're* **as white as a sheet.** ■ a broad flat piece of material such as metal or glass: *the small pipe has been formed from a flat sheet of bronze.* **2** a rectangular piece of paper, esp. one of a standard size produced commercially and used for writing and printing on: *a* **sheet of** *unmarked paper.* ■ a quantity of text or other information contained on such a piece of paper: *he produced yet another* **sheet of** *figures.* ■ a flat piece of paper as opposed to a reel of continuous paper, the bound pages of a book, or a folded map. ■ all the postage stamps printed on one piece of paper: *a sheet of stamps.* ■ a map, esp. one part of a series covering a larger area. **3** an extensive unbroken surface area of something: *a* **sheet of** *ice.* ■ a broad moving mass of flames or water: *the rain was still falling in sheets.*

▶*v.* **1** [*trans.*] cover with or wrap in a sheet or sheets: *we sheeted a narrow bed.* **2** [*intrans.*] (of rain) fall in large quantities: *rain sheeted down.* ▷Old English *scēte, sciete*, of Germanic origin; related to the verb **SHOOT** in its primary sense 'to project.'

sheet[2] *Nautical* ▶*n.* **1** a rope attached to the lower corner of a sail for securing or extending the sail or for altering its direction. **2** (**sheets**) the space at the bow or stern of an open boat.

▶*v.* [*trans.*] (**sheet something in/out**) make a sail more or less taut. ■ (**sheet something home**) extend a sail by tightening the sheets so that the sail is set as flat as possible. ▷Old English *scēata* 'lower corner of a sail,' of Germanic origin; related to Old Norse *skauti* 'kerchief' (see also **SHEET**[1]).

▶***PHRASE*** □ **two** (or **three**) **sheets to the wind** *informal* drunk.

sheet an·chor ▶*n. figurative* a person or thing that is very dependable and relied upon in the last resort. ▷late 15th cent. (denoting an additional anchor for use in emergencies): perhaps related to obsolete *shot*, denoting two cables spliced together, later influenced by **SHEET**[2].

sheet bend ▶*n.* a knot used for temporarily fastening one rope through the loop of another.

sheet·ed /ˈSHētid/ ▶*adj.* **1** covered with or enveloped in a sheet of cloth: *the sheeted body.* **2** *Geology* (of rock) fissured or divided into layers, esp. by faulting.

sheet feed·er ▶*n. Computing* a device for feeding paper into a printer a sheet at a time.

sheet·ing /ˈSHētiNG/ ▶*n.* material formed into or used as a sheet: *a window covered with plastic sheeting.*

sheet·let /ˈSHētlit/ ▶*n.* a small unseparated sheet of postage stamps.

sheet light·ning ▶*n.* lightning with its brightness diffused by reflection within clouds.

sheet met·al ▶*n.* metal formed into thin sheets, typically by rolling or hammering.

sheet mu·sic ▶*n.* printed music, as opposed to performed or recorded music. ■ music published in single or interleaved sheets, not bound.

sheet pile ▶*n.* a pile that is pressed or molded from sheet metal or vinyl so as to interlock with other such piles to form a retaining wall or other piling installation. **—sheet-piling** *n.*

Sheet·rock /ˈSHēt,räk/ ▶*n. trademark* a plasterboard made of gypsum layered between sheets of heavy paper.

Shef·field /ˈSHefēld/ an industrial city in northern England; pop. 500,000. It is noted for the manufacture of cutlery and silverware and for the production of steel.

Shef·field plate ▶*n.* copper plated with silver by rolling and edging with silver film and ribbon, esp. as produced in Sheffield, England, between 1760 and 1840.

sheikh /SHēk; SHāk/ (also **sheik, shaikh,** or **shaykh**) ▶*n.* **1** an Arab leader, in particular the chief or head of an Arab tribe, family, or village. **2** a leader in a Muslim community or organization. ▷late 16th cent.: based on Arabic *šayk* 'old man, sheikh,' from *šāka* 'be or grow old.' **—sheikh·dom** /-dəm/ *n.*

shei·tel /ˈSHātl; ˈSHītl/ ▶*n.* (among Orthodox Ashkenazic Jews) a wig worn by a married woman. ▷late 19th cent.: from Yiddish *sheytl*, from a Germanic base meaning 'crown of the head.'

shek·el /ˈSHekəl/ ▶*n.* the basic monetary unit of modern Israel, equal to 100 agora. ■ *historical* a silver coin and unit of weight used in ancient Israel and the Middle East. ■ (**shekels**) *informal* money; wealth. ▷from Hebrew *šeqel*, from *šāqal* 'weigh.'

She·ki·nah /SHəKHēˈnä; -ˈKHēnə; SHiˈkēnə; -ˈkī-/ (also **She·khi·nah**) ▶*n. Jewish & Christian Theology* the glory of the divine presence, conventionally represented as light or interpreted symbolically (in Kabbalism as a divine feminine aspect). ▷mid 17th cent.: from late Hebrew, from *šākan* 'dwell, rest.'

shel·drake /ˈSHel,drāk/ ▶*n.* another name for **SHELDUCK** (specifically a male).

shel·duck /ˈSHel,dək/ ▶*n.* (*pl.* same or **-ducks**) a large gooselike Old World duck with brightly colored plumage, typically showing black and white wings in flight. • Genus *Tadorna*, family Anatidae: several species, in particular *T. tadorna* of Eurasian coasts, with white, greenish-black, and chestnut plumage. ▷early 18th cent.: probably from dialect *sheld* 'pied' (related to Middle Dutch *schillede* 'variegated') + **DUCK**[1].

shelf /SHelf/ ▶*n.* (*pl.* **shelves** /SHelvz/) a flat length of wood or rigid material, attached to a wall or forming part of a piece of furniture, that provides a surface for the storage or display of objects. ■ a ledge of rock or protruding strip of land. ■ a submarine bank, or a part of the continental shelf. ▷Middle English: from Middle Low German *schelf*; related to Old English *scylfe* 'partition,' *scylf* 'crag.' **—shelf·ful** /-,fo͝ol/ *n.* (*pl.* **-fuls**) **—shelf-like** /-,līk/ *adj.*

▶***PHRASES*** □ **off the shelf** not designed or made to order but taken from existing stock or supplies: *off-the-shelf software packages.* □ **on the shelf** (of people or things) no longer useful or desirable: *an injury that has kept him on the shelf.*

shelf life ▶*n.* the length of time for which an item remains usable, fit for consumption, or saleable.

shelf mark ▶*n.* a notation on a book showing its place in a library.

shelf space ▶*n.* the amount of available space on a shelf.

shelf-sta·ble ▶*adj.* able to survive long periods on store or home shelves without spoiling: *a growing number of dairy-based beverages are shelf-stable and can be stored in the pantry rather than the refrigerator.*

shell /SHel/ ▶*n.* **1** the hard protective outer case of a mollusk or crustacean: *cowrie shells | the technique of carving shell.* ■ the thin outer covering of an animal's egg, which is hard and fragile in that of a bird but leathery in that of a reptile. ■ the outer case of a nut kernel or seed. ■ the carapace of a tortoise, turtle, or terrapin. ■ the wing cases of a beetle. ■ the integument of an insect pupa or chrysalis. ■ (**one's shell**) *figurative* used with reference to a state of shyness or introversion: *she'll soon* **come out of her shell** *with the right encouragement.* **2** something resembling or likened to a shell because of its shape or its function as an outer case: *pasta shells | baked pastry shells filled with cheese.* ■ the walls of an unfinished or gutted building or other structure: *the hotel was a shell, the roof having collapsed completely.* ■ *figurative* an outer form without substance: *he was a shell of the man he had been previously.* ■ a light racing boat used in the sport of crew. ■ a woman's sleeveless sweater or blouse. ■ the metal framework of a vehicle body. ■ an inner or roughly made coffin. ■ the handguard of a sword. ■ *Physics* each of a set of orbitals around the nucleus of an atom, occupied or able to be occupied by electrons of similar energies. **3** an explosive artillery projectile or bomb: *the sound of the shell passing over, followed by the explosion |* [as *adj.*] *shell holes.* ■ a hollow metal or paper case used as a container for fireworks, explosives, or cartridges. ■ a cartridge. **4** *Computing* short for **SHELL PROGRAM**.

▶*v.* **1** [*trans.*] bombard with shells: *the guns started shelling their positions.* **2** [*trans.*] remove the shell or pod from (a nut or seed): *they were shelling peas |* [as *adj.*] (**shelled**) *shelled Brazil nuts.* **3** [*intrans.*] gather seashells: *there was nothing to do except swim or go shelling on the beaches.*

▶*phrasal v.* □ **shell something out** (or **shell out**) *informal* pay a specified amount of money, esp. an amount that is resented as being excessive: *it doesn't make sense to shell out $8.50 for an elevator ride.* ▷Old English *scell* (noun), of Germanic origin; related to Dutch *schel* 'scale, shell,' also to **SCALE**[1]. The verb dates from the mid 16th cent. in sense 2. **—shelled** *adj.* [in *combination*] : *a soft-shelled clam.* **—shell-less** *adj.* **—shell-like** /-,līk/ *adj.* **—shell·y** /ˈSHelē/ *adj.*

she'll /SHēl/ ▶*contraction of* she shall; she will.

shel·lac /SHəˈlak/ ▶*n.* lac resin melted into thin flakes, used for making varnish. ■ a thin varnish containing this resin.

▶*v.* (**-lacked** /-ˈlakt/, **-lack·ing** /-ˈlakiNG/) [*trans.*] **1** [often as *adj.*] (**shellacked**) varnish (something) with shellac. **2** (usu. **be shellacked**) *informal* defeat or beat (someone) decisively: *they were shellacked in the 1982 election.* ▷mid 17th cent.: from **SHELL** + **LAC**[1], translating French *laque en écailles* 'lac in thin plates.'

shell·back /ˈSHel,bak/ ▶*n. informal* an old or experienced sailor, esp. one who has crossed the equator.

shell bit ▶*n.* a gouge-shaped boring bit.

shell com·pa·ny ▸*n.* an inactive company used as a vehicle for various financial maneuvers or kept dormant for future use in some other capacity.

Shel·ley[1] /ˈSHelē/, Mary (Wollstonecraft) (1797–1851), English writer; daughter of William Godwin and Mary Wollstonecraft. She eloped with Percy Bysshe Shelley in 1814 and married him in 1816. She is chiefly remembered as the author of the Gothic novel *Frankenstein, or the Modern Prometheus* (1818).

Shel·ley[2], Percy Bysshe (1792–1822), English poet. A leading figure of the romantic movement with radical political views, his works include *Queen Mab* (1813), *Prometheus Unbound* (1820), and *Adonais* (1821), an elegy on the death of Keats. He was the husband of Mary Shelley.

shell·fire /ˈSHel,fir/ ▸*n.* bombardment by artillery shells.

shell·fish /ˈSHel,fiSH/ ▸*n.* (*pl.* same) an aquatic shelled mollusk (e.g., an oyster or cockle) or a crustacean (e.g., a crab or shrimp), esp. one that is edible. ■ such mollusks or crustaceans as food.

shell game ▸*n.* a game involving sleight of hand, in which three inverted cups or nutshells are moved about, and contestants must spot which is the one with a pea or other object underneath. ■ a deceptive and evasive action or ploy, esp. a political one: *officials **played a shell game** by loading prisoners onto buses during population counts at the jail.*

shell jack·et ▸*n.* an army officer's tight-fitting undress jacket reaching to the waist.

shell lime ▸*n.* fine-quality lime produced by roasting seashells.

shell pink ▸*n.* a delicate pale pink.

shell pro·gram ▸*n. Computing* a program that provides an interface between the user and the operating system.

shell shock ▸*n.* see COMBAT FATIGUE (sense 1). and compare with POST-TRAUMATIC STRESS SYNDROME. ▹World War I: with reference to exposure to shellfire. **—shell-shocked** *adj.*

shell·work /ˈSHel,wərk/ ▸*n.* ornamentation consisting of shells cemented on to a surface.

Shel·ta /ˈSHeltə/ ▸*n.* an ancient secret language used by Irish and Welsh tinkers and gypsies, and based largely on altered Irish or Gaelic words. ▹late 19th cent.: of unknown origin.

shel·ter /ˈSHeltər/ ▸*n.* a place giving temporary protection from bad weather or danger. ■ a place providing food and accommodations for the homeless. ■ an animal sanctuary. ■ a shielded or safe condition; protection: *he hung back in the shelter of a rock | you're welcome to **take shelter** from the storm.*
▸*v.* [*trans.*] protect or shield from something harmful, esp. bad weather: *the hut **sheltered** him **from** the cold wind* | [as *adj.*] (**sheltered**) *the plants need a shady, sheltered spot in the garden.* ■ [*intrans.*] find refuge or take cover from bad weather or danger: *people were sheltering under store canopies and trees.* ■ prevent (someone) from having to do or face something difficult or unpleasant: [as *adj.*] (**sheltered**) *she led a **sheltered life** until her mother and father went through a bitter divorce.* ■ protect (income) from taxation: *only your rental income can be sheltered.* ▹late 16th cent.: perhaps an alteration of obsolete *sheltron* 'phalanx,' from Old English *scieldtruma*, literally 'shield troop.' **—shel·ter·er** *n.* **—shel·ter·less** *adj.*

shel·ter belt ▸*n.* a line of trees or shrubs planted to protect an area, esp. a farm field, from strong winds and the erosion they cause.

shel·tered work·shop ▸*n.* a supervised workplace for physically disabled or mentally handicapped adults.

shel·ter·wood /ˈSHeltər,wo͝od/ ▸*n.* mature trees left standing to provide shelter in which saplings can grow.

shel·tie /ˈSHeltē/ (also **shel·ty**) ▸*n.* (*pl.* **-ties**) a Shetland pony or sheepdog. ▹early 17th cent.: probably representing an Orkney pronunciation of Old Norse *Hjalti* 'Shetlander.'

Shel·ton /ˈSHeltn/ an industrial city in southwestern Connecticut; pop. 35,418.

shelve[1] /SHelv/ ▸*v.* [*trans.*] **1** place or arrange (items, esp. books) on a shelf. ■ *figurative* decide not to proceed with (a project or plan), either temporarily or permanently: *plans to reopen the school have been shelved.* **2** fit with shelves: *one whole long wall was shelved.* ▹late 16th cent. (in the sense 'project like a shelf' (Shakespearean usage)): from *shelves*, plural of SHELF. **—shelv·er** *n.*

shelve[2] ▸*v.* [*intrans.*] (of ground) slope downward in a specified manner or direction: *the ground shelved gently down to the water.* ▹late Middle English: origin uncertain; perhaps from SHELF.

shelves /SHelvz/ ▸ plural form of SHELF.

shelv·ing /ˈSHelviNG/ ▸*n.* shelves collectively: *a lack of shelving and cupboards.* ■ the action of shelving something.

Shem /SHem/ (in the Bible) a son of Noah (Gen. 10:21), traditional ancestor of the Semites.

She·ma /SHəˈmä/ a Hebrew text consisting of three passages from the Pentateuch (Deuteronomy 6:4, 11:13–21; Numbers 15:37–41) and beginning "Hear, O Israel, the Lord is our God, the Lord is one." It forms an important part of Jewish evening and morning prayer and is used as a Jewish confession of faith. ▹Hebrew, literally 'hear,' the first word of Deut. 6:4.

she-male (also **she·male**) ▸*n. informal* a transvestite. ■ a passive male homosexual. ■ a hermaphrodite.

she·moz·zle /SHəˈmäzəl/ (also **sche·moz·zle**) ▸*n. informal* a state of chaos and confusion; a muddle. ▹late 19th cent.: Yiddish, suggested by late Hebrew *šel-lō'-mazzāl* 'of no luck.'

shen /SHen/ ▸*n.* (*pl.* same) (in Chinese thought) the spiritual element of a person's psyche. ▹from Chinese *shén.*

Shen·an·do·ah /,SHenənˈdōə/ a river in Virginia. Rising in two headstreams, one on each side of the Blue Ridge Mountains, it flows about 150 miles (240 km) north to join the Potomac River at Harpers Ferry.

Shen·an·do·ah Na·tion·al Park a national park in the Blue Ridge Mountains of northern Virginia, southeast of the Shenandoah River. It was established in 1935.

she·nan·i·gans /SHəˈnanəgənz/ ▸*plural n. informal* secret or dishonest activity or maneuvering: *widespread financial shenanigans had ruined the fortunes of many.* ■ silly or high-spirited behavior; mischief. ▹mid 19th cent.: of unknown origin.

Shen·yang /ˈSHenˈyaNG; ˈSHənˈyäNG/ a city in northeastern China; pop. 4,500,000. It is the capital of the province of Liaoning. Former name **MUKDEN**.

Shen·zhen /ˈSHenˈZHen; -ˈzen; ˈSHənˈjən/ an industrial city in southern China, north of Hong Kong; pop. 875,000.

She·ol /ˈSHē,ōl; SHēˈōl/ the Hebrew underworld, abode of the dead. ▹Hebrew.

Shep·herd /ˈSHepərd/, Michael, see **LUDLUM**.

shep·herd /ˈSHepərd/ ▸*n.* a person who tends and rears sheep. ■ *figurative* a member of the clergy who provides spiritual care and guidance for a congregation. ■ short for **GERMAN SHEPHERD**.
▸*v.* [*trans.*] [usu. as *n.*] (**shepherding**) tend (sheep) as a shepherd. ■ [*trans.*] guide or direct in a particular direction: *we were shepherded around with great ceremony.* ■ give guidance to (someone), esp. on spiritual matters: *she had to submit the control of her career and money to a group who shepherded her.* ▹Old English *scēaphierde*, from *scēap* 'sheep' + *hierde* 'herder;' see SHEEP and compare with HERD.

shep·herd dog ▸*n.* a sheepdog.

shep·herd·ess /ˈSHepərdis/ ▸*n.* a female shepherd. ■ an idealized or romanticized rustic maiden in pastoral literature.

shep·herd sat·el·lite (also **shepherd moon**) ▸*n. Astronomy* a small moon orbiting close to a planetary ring, esp. of Saturn, and whose gravitational field confines the ring within a narrow band.

shep·herd's crook ▸*n.* a staff with a hook at one end used by shepherds.

shep·herd's nee·dle ▸*n.* a white-flowered Eurasian plant of the parsley family, with long, needle-shaped fruit. • *Scandix pecten-veneris*, family Umbelliferae.

shep·herd's pie ▸*n.* a dish of ground meat under a layer of mashed potato.

shep·herd's plaid (also **shepherd's check**) ▸*n.* a small black-and-white check pattern. ■ woolen cloth with this pattern.

shep·herd's purse ▸*n.* a widely distributed white-flowered weed of the cabbage family, with triangular or heart-shaped seedpods. • *Capsella bursa-pastoris*, family Brassicaceae.

sher·ard·ize /ˈSHerər,dīz/ ▸*v.* [*trans.*] coat (iron or steel) with zinc by heating it in contact with zinc dust. ▹early 20th cent.: from the name of *Sherard* Cowper-Coles (1867–1936), English inventor, + -IZE.

Sher·a·ton /ˈSHerətn/ ▸*adj.* [*attrib.*] (of furniture) designed, made by, or in the simple, delicate, and graceful style of the English furniture maker Thomas Sheraton (1751–1806).

sher·bet /ˈSHərbit/ ▸*n.* a frozen dessert made with fruit juice added to milk or cream, egg white, or gelatin. ■ a frozen fruit juice and sugar mixture served as a dessert or between courses of a meal to cleanse the palate. ■ (esp. in Arab countries) a cooling drink of sweet diluted fruit juices. ■ *Brit.* a flavored sweet effervescent powder eaten alone or made into a drink. ▹early 17th cent.: from Turkish *şerbet*, Persian *šerbet*, from Arabic *šarba* 'drink,' from *šariba* 'to drink.' Compare with **SYRUP**.

USAGE The tendency to insert an *r* into the second syllable of **sherbet** is very common. Frequency of misuse has not changed the fact that the spelling **sherbert** and the pronunciation /ˈSHərbərt/ are wrong and should not be considered acceptable variants.

sherd /SHərd/ ▸*n.* another term for **POTSHERD**.

she·reef /SHəˈrēf/ (also **she·rif**) ▸*n.* variant spelling of **SHARIF**.

Sher·i·dan[1] /ˈSHerədn/ a city in north central Wyoming; pop. 15,804.

Sher·i·dan[2] /ˈSHeridn/, Philip Henry (1831–88) U.S. army officer. A severe and effective Union cavalry commander in the Civil War, he was noted for his decisive victories and plundering raids. In April 1865, he cut off the Confederate retreat at Appomattox, forcing the surrender of General Lee. In 1884, he became commander in chief of the U.S. army.

Sher·i·dan[3], Richard Brinsley (1751–1816), Irish playwright and politician. His plays are comedies of manners and include *The Rivals* (1775) and *The School for Scandal* (1777). In 1780, he entered Parliament, became a celebrated orator, and held senior government posts.

sher·iff /ˈSHerif/ ▸*n.* (in the U.S.) an elected officer in a county who is responsible for keeping the peace. ■ (also **high sheriff**) (in England and Wales) the chief executive officer of the Crown in a county, having various administrative and judicial functions. ■ an honorary officer elected annually in some English towns. ■ (in Scotland) a judge. ▹Old English *scīrgerēfa* (see **SHIRE**, **REEVE**[1]). **—sher·iff·dom** /-dəm/ *n.*

sher·iff clerk ▸*n.* (in Scotland) the clerk of a sheriff's court.

Sher·lock /ˈSHər,läk/ ▸*n. informal* a person who investigates mysteries or shows great perceptiveness: *it doesn't take a Sherlock to figure out that she's lying to me.* ▹early 20th cent.: from *Sherlock* Holmes (see **HOLMES**[2]).

Sher·man[1] /ˈSHərmən/ a commercial and industrial city in northeastern Texas; pop. 31,601.

Sher·man[2], Roger (1721–93), American politician. A Connecticut legislator and jurist, he was an avid proponent of American independence. He held the distinction of having signed all of the following: the Articles of Association 1774, the Declaration of Independence 1776, the Articles of Confederation 1777, and the Constitution 1787. He served as a U.S. senator 1791–93.

Sher·man[3], William Tecumseh (1820–91), U.S. general. In 1864, during the Civil War, he was appointed commander of Union forces in the West. He set out with 60,000 men on a "March to the Sea" through Georgia, during which he crushed Confederate forces and broke civilian morale by his policy of deliberate destruction of the territory through which he passed. He served as commander of the army 1869–84.

William Tecumseh Sherman

Sher·man tank ▸*n.* an American type of medium tank, used in large numbers during World War II.

Sher·pa /ˈsHərpə/ ▸*n.* (*pl.* same or **-pas**) a member of a Himalayan people living on the borders of Nepal and Tibet, renowned for their skill in mountaineering. ■ a civil servant or diplomat who undertakes preparatory political work prior to a summit conference. ▷from Tibetan *sharpa* 'inhabitant of an eastern country.'

Sher·ring·ton /ˈsHəriNGtən/, Sir Charles Scott (1857–1952), English physiologist. He contributed greatly to the understanding of the nervous system and introduced the concept of reflex actions and the reflex arc. Nobel Prize for Physiology or Medicine (1932).

sher·ry /ˈsHerē/ ▸*n.* (*pl.* **-ries**) a fortified wine originally and mainly from southern Spain, often drunk as an aperitif. ▷late 16th cent.: alteration of archaic *sherris*, interpreted as plural, from Spanish *(vino de) Xeres* 'Xeres (wine)' (Xeres being the former name of **JEREZ**).

sher·wa·ni /sHərˈwänē/ ▸*n.* (*pl.* **-nis**) a knee-length coat buttoning to the neck, worn by men from the Indian subcontinent. ▷from Urdu and Persian *širwānī* 'from Shirvan' (referring to a town in northeastern Persia).

she's /sHēz/ ▸*contraction of* she is; she has.

Shet·land Is·lands /ˈsHetlənd/ (also **Shet·land** or **the Shet·lands**) a group of about 100 islands off the north coast of Scotland, northeast of the Orkneys, that constitute the administrative region of Shetland; pop. 22,000; chief town, Lerwick. Together with the Orkney Islands, the Shetland Islands became a part of Scotland in 1472. **—Shet·land·er** *n.*

Shet·land po·ny ▸*n.* a pony of a small, hardy, rough-coated breed.

Shet·land sheep ▸*n.* a sheep of a hardy, short-tailed breed native to Shetland and bred esp. for its fine wool.

Shet·land sheep·dog ▸*n.* a small dog of a collielike breed.

Shet·land wool ▸*n.* a type of fine loosely twisted wool from Shetland sheep.

Shev·ard·na·dze /ˌsHevərdˈnädzə/, Eduard (Amvrosievich) (1928–), Soviet statesman and head of state of Georgia 1992– 2003.

She·vat /sHəˈvät/ (also **She·bat**) ▸*n.* (in the Jewish calendar) the fifth month of the civil and eleventh of the religious year, usually coinciding with parts of January and February. ▷from Hebrew *šᵉḇaṭ*.

shew /sHō/ ▸*v.* old-fashioned variant spelling of **SHOW**.

shew·bread (also **show·bread**) /ˈsHōˌbred/ ▸*n.* twelve loaves placed every Sabbath in the Jewish Temple and eaten by the priests at the end of the week. ▷mid 16th cent.: suggested by German *Schaubrot*, representing Hebrew *leḥem pānīm*, literally 'bread of the face (of God).'

shf (also **SHF**) ▸*abbr.* superhigh frequency.

shh /sH/ (also **sh**) ▸*exclam.* used to call for silence: *"Shh! Keep your voice down!"* ▷mid 19th cent.: variant of **HUSH**.

Shi·a /ˈsHēˌä/ (also **Shi'a**) ▸*n.* (*pl.* same or **Shi·as**) one of the two main branches of Islam, followed esp. in Iran, that rejects the first three Sunni caliphs and regards Ali, the fourth caliph, as Muhammad's first true successor. Compare with **SUNNI**. ■ a Muslim who adheres to this branch of Islam. ▷from Arabic *šī'a* 'party (of Ali).'

shi·at·su /sHēˈätsōō/ ▸*n.* a form of therapy of Japanese origin based on the same principles as acupuncture, in which pressure is applied to certain points on the body using the hands. ▷1960s: Japanese, literally 'finger pressure.'

shib·bo·leth /ˈsHibəliTH; -ˌleTH/ ▸*n.* a custom, principle, or belief distinguishing a particular class or group of people, esp. a long-standing one regarded as outmoded or no longer important: *the party began to break with the shibboleths of the left.* ▷mid 17th cent.: from Hebrew *šibbōleṯ* 'ear of corn,' used as a test of nationality by its difficult pronunciation (Judg. 12:6).

shick·er /ˈsHikər/ (also **shik·ker**) *informal* ▸*adj.* (also **shick·ered** /-ərd/, **shik·kered**) [*predic.*] drunk: *they got shickered, talked cars and deals.*
▸*n.* a drunk. ▷late 19th cent.: from Yiddish *shiker*, from Hebrew *šikkōr*, from *šākar* 'be drunk.'

shid·duch /ˈsHidəKH; sHiˈdōōKH/ ▸*n.* (*pl.* **shid·du·chim** /ˌsHidōōˈKHēm/) a Jewish arranged marriage. ▷late 19th cent.: Yiddish, from Hebrew *šiddūḵ* 'negotiation (of a marriage).'

shied /sHīd/ ▸ past and past participle of **SHY**².

shield /sHēld/ ▸*n.* **1** a broad piece of metal or another suitable material, held by straps or a handle attached on one side, used as a protection against blows or missiles. **2** something shaped like a shield, in particular: ■ a police officer's badge. ■ *Heraldry* a stylized representation of a shield used for displaying a coat of arms. ■ *Geology* a large rigid area of the earth's crust, typically of Precambrian rock, that has been unaffected by later orogenic episodes, e.g., the Canadian Shield. **3** a person or thing providing protection: *a protective coating of grease provides a shield against abrasive dirt.* ■ a protective plate or screen on machinery or equipment. ■ a device or material that prevents or reduces the emission of light or other radiation. ■ short for **DRESS SHIELD**. ■ a hard flat or convex part of an animal, esp. a shell.
▸*v.* [*trans.*] protect (someone or something) from a danger, risk, or unpleasant experience: *he pulled the cap lower to shield his eyes from the glare | these people have been completely shielded from economic forces.* ■ prevent from being seen: *the rocks she sat behind shielded her from the lodge.* ■ enclose or screen (a piece of machinery) to protect the user. ■ prevent or reduce the escape of sound, light, or other radiation from (something): *uranium shutters shield the cobalt radioactive source.* ▷Old English *scild* (noun), *scildan* (verb), of Germanic origin; related to Dutch *schild* and German *Schild*, from a base meaning 'divide, separate.' **—shield·less** *adj.*

shield bug ▸*n.* another term for **STINK BUG**.

shield fern ▸*n.* any of a number of ferns that have circular shieldlike scales protecting the spore cases: • a European fern of damp woodland (genus *Polystichum*, family Dryopteridaceae). • an evergreen fern (genus *Thelypteris*, family Thelypteridaceae). • *Austral.* a fern of forested country (family Aspidiaceae).

shield law ▸*n.* a law that protects witnesses from revealing certain information, esp. in court. ■ a law that protects journalists from having to reveal confidential sources. ■ a law that protects rape victims from having to reveal details of their sexual history.

shield·tail snake /ˈsHēl(d)ˌtāl/ (also **shield-tailed snake**) ▸*n.* a burrowing snake that has a flat disk formed from an enlarged scale on the upper surface of the tail, native to the rain forests of southern India and Sri Lanka. • *Rhinophis, Uropeltis*, and other genera, family Uropeltidae: numerous species.

shield vol·ca·no ▸*n.* *Geology* a broad, domed volcano with gently sloping sides, characteristic of the eruption of fluid, basaltic lava.

shiel·ing /ˈsHēliNG/ (also **sheal·ing**) ▸*n.* *Scottish* a roughly constructed hut used while pasturing animals. ■ an area of pasture. ▷mid 16th cent.: from Scots *shiel* 'hut' (of unknown origin) + **-ING**¹.

shift /sHift/ ▸*v.* move or cause to move from one place to another, esp. over a small distance: [*trans.*] *I shift the weight back to the other leg* | [*intrans.*] *the roof cracked and shifted.* ■ [*intrans.*] change the position of one's body, esp. because one is nervous or uncomfortable: *he shifted a little in his chair.* ■ [*trans.*] change the emphasis, direction, or focus of: *she's shifting the blame onto me.* ■ [*intrans.*] change in emphasis, direction, or focus: *the wind had shifted to the east | the balance of power shifted abruptly.* ■ [*trans.*] *Computing* move (data) one or more places to the right or left in a register: *the partial remainder is shifted left.* ■ [*intrans.*] press the shift key on a typewriter or computer keyboard. ■ [*trans.*] *informal* sell (something): *a lot of high-priced product you simply don't know how to shift.* ■ [*intrans.*] change gear in a vehicle: *she shifted down to fourth.* ■ [*intrans.*] *archaic* be evasive or indirect: *they know not how to shift and rob as the old ones do.*
▸*n.* **1** a slight change in position, direction, or tendency: *a shift of wind took us by surprise | a* **shift in** *public opinion.* ■ *Astronomy* the displacement of spectral lines. See also **REDSHIFT**. ■ (also **shift key**) a key on a typewriter or computer keyboard used to switch between two sets of characters or functions, principally between lower- and upper-case letters. ■ short for **SOUND SHIFT**. ■ the gearshift or gear-changing mechanism in a motor vehicle. ■ *Building* the positioning of successive rows of bricks so that their ends do not coincide. ■ *Computing* a movement of the digits of a word in a register one or more places to left or right, equivalent to multiplying or dividing the corresponding number by a power of whatever number is the base. ■ *Football* a change of position by two or more players before the ball is put into play. **2** one of two or more recurring periods in which different groups of workers do the same jobs in relay: *the night shift.* ■ a group of workers who work in this way. **3** (also **shift dress**) a woman's straight, unwaisted dress. ■ *historical* a long, loose-fitting undergarment. **4** *archaic* an ingenious or devious device or stratagem: *the thousand shifts and devices of which Hannibal was a master.* ▷Old English *sciftan* 'arrange, divide, apportion,' of Germanic origin; related to German *schichten* 'to layer, stratify.' A common Middle English sense 'change, replace' gave rise to the noun sense 3 (via the notion of changing one's clothes) and sense 2 (via the concept of relays of workers). **—shift·a·ble** /ˈsHiftəbəl/ *adj.*
▸*PHRASES* □ **make shift** do what one wants to do in spite of not having ideal conditions. □ **shift for oneself** manage as best one can without help. □ **shift one's ground** say or write something that contradicts something one has previously written or said. □ **shifting sands** something that is constantly changing, esp. unpredictably: *whether something is accepted depends upon* **the shifting sands of** *taste.*

shift·er /ˈsHiftər/ ▸*n.* [usu. in *combination*] a person or thing that shifts something: *each morning the rock-shifters travel by donkey cart to start work.* ■ a gearbox of a motor vehicle or a set of gear levers on a bicycle: *a new, improved five-speed shifter.*

shift·ing cul·ti·va·tion (also **shifting agriculture**) ▸*n.* a form of agriculture, used esp. in tropical Africa, in which an area of ground is cleared of vegetation and cultivated for a few years and then abandoned for a new area until its fertility has been naturally restored.

shift·less /ˈsHiftlis/ ▸*adj.* (of a person or action) characterized by laziness, indolence, and a lack of ambition: *a shiftless lot of good-for-nothings.* **—shift·less·ly** *adv.* **—shift·less·ness** *n.*

shift lev·er ▸*n.* another term for **GEARSHIFT**.

shift reg·is·ter ▸*n.* *Computing* a register that is designed to allow the bits of its contents to be moved to left or right.

shift work ▸*n.* work comprising recurring periods in which different groups of workers do the same jobs in rotation.

shift·y /ˈsHiftē/ ▸*adj.* (**shift·i·er**, **shift·i·est**) *informal* (of a person or their manner) appearing deceitful or evasive: *a shifty, fast-talking lawyer.* **—shift·i·ly** /-əlē/ *adv.* **—shift·i·ness** *n.*

Shi·ga tox·in /ˈsHēgə/ ▸*n.* a toxin produced by certain strains of the bacterium *E. coli* that is pathogenic in humans: *during infection there are changes of cytokine levels that can be ascribed to an effect of Shiga toxin on different cell types.* ▷*c.* 2000: the name arose when it was discovered that the toxin was virtually indistinguishable in both structure and function from the toxin produced by *Shigella dysenteriae*, which was in turn named for Kiyoshi *Shiga*; see **SHIGELLA**.

shi·gel·la /sHəˈgelə/ ▸*n.* a bacterium that is an intestinal pathogen of humans and other primates, some kinds of which cause dysentery. • Genus *Shigella*; Gram-negative rods. ▷modern Latin, from the name of Kiyoshi *Shiga* (1870–1957), Japanese bacteriologist, + the diminutive suffix *-ella*.

Shih Tzu /ˈsHē ˈdzōō/ ▸*n.* a dog of a breed with long, silky, erect hair and short legs. ▷1920s: from Chinese *shizi* 'lion.'

shi·i·ta·ke /sHēˈtäkē; sHē-ēˈtäkē/ (also **shiitake mushroom**) ▸*n.* an edible mushroom that grows on fallen timber, cultivated in Japan and China. • *Lentinus edodes*, family Pleurotaceae, class Hymenomycetes. ▷late 19th cent.: from Japanese, from *shii*, denoting a kind of oak, + *take* 'mushroom.'

Shi·ite /ˈsHēˌit/ (also **Shi'ite**) ▸*n.* an adherent of the Shia branch of Islam.
▸*adj.* of or relating to Shia. **—Shi·ism** /ˈsHēˌizəm/ (also **Shi'ism**) *n.*

Shi·jia·zhuang /ˈsHœˈjyäˈjwäNG/ a city in northeast central China, capital of Hebei province; pop. 1,320,000.

shi·kar /sHiˈkär/ ▸*n.* *Indian* hunting as a sport. ▷from Urdu and Persian *šikār*.

shi·ka·ra /sHiˈkärə/ ▸*n.* *Indian* **1** (in Kashmir) a houseboat. ■ variant spelling of **SHIKARI** (sense 2). **2** a spire on a Hindu temple. ▷via Kashmiri from Persian *šikārī* 'of hunting.'

shi·ka·ri /sHiˈkärē/ ▸*n.* (*pl.* **-ris**) *Indian* **1** a hunter. ■ a guide on hunting expeditions. **2** (also **shi·ka·ra**) (in Kashmir) a light, flat-bottomed boat. ▷via Urdu from Persian *šikārī* 'of hunting.'

shik·ker /ˈsHikər/ ▸*adj.* & *n.* variant spelling of **SHICKER**.

Shi·ko·ku /SHi'kō,ko͞o/ the smallest of the four main islands of Japan, an administrative region; pop. 4,195,000; capital, Matsuyama. The Inland Sea separates it from Kyushu on the west and Honshu on the north.

shik·ra /'SHikrə/ ▸*n.* a small, stocky sparrow hawk found in Africa and Central and South Asia. • Genus *Accipiter*, family Accipitridae: two species, in particular the widespread *A. badius*. ▷mid 19th cent.: from Persian and Urdu *šikara*.

shik·sa /'SHiksə/ ▸*n. often derogatory* (used esp. by Jews) a gentile girl or woman. ▷late 19th cent.: from Yiddish *shikse*, from Hebrew *šiqṣāh* (from *šeqeṣ* 'detested thing' + the feminine suffix *-āh*).

shill /SHil/ *informal* ▸*n.* an accomplice of a hawker, gambler, or swindler who acts as an enthusiastic customer to entice or encourage others.
▸*v.* [*intrans.*] act or work as such a person. ▷early 20th cent.: probably from earlier *shillaber*, of unknown origin.

shil·le·lagh /SHə'lālē/ ▸*n.* a thick stick of blackthorn or oak used in Ireland, typically as a weapon. ▷late 18th cent.: from the name of the town *Shillelagh*, in County Wicklow, Ireland.

shil·ling /'SHiliNG/ ▸*n.* **1** a former British coin and monetary unit equal to one twentieth of a pound or twelve pence. **2** the basic monetary unit in Kenya, Tanzania, and Uganda, equal to 100 cents. ▷Old English *scilling*, of Germanic origin; related to Dutch *schelling* and German *Schilling*.

Shil·long /SHi'lôNG/ a city in northeastern India, capital of the state of Meghalaya; pop. 131,000.

Shil·luk /SHə'lo͝ok/ ▸*n.* (*pl.* same or **-luks**) **1** a member of a Sudanese people living mainly on the west bank of the Nile. **2** the Nilotic language of this people.
▸*adj.* of or relating to this people or their language. ▷the name in Shilluk.

shil·ly-shal·ly /'SHilē ,SHalē/ ▸*v.* (**-lies, -lied**) [*intrans.*] fail to act resolutely or decisively: *the government shilly-shallied about the matter.*
▸*n.* indecisive behavior. ▷mid 18th cent.: originally as *shill I, shall I*, reduplication of *shall I?* **—shil·ly-shal·ly·er** /,SHalēər/ (also **-shal·li·er**) *n.*

Shi·loh /'SHīlō/ a historic site in southwestern Tennessee, near Pittsburg Landing on the Tennessee River, site of a major Civil War battle in April 1862.

shim /SHim/ ▸*n.* a washer or thin strip of material used to align parts, make them fit, or reduce wear.
▸*v.* (**shimmed, shim·ming**) [*trans.*] wedge (something) or fill up (a space) with a shim. ▷early 18th cent.: of unknown origin.

shim·mer /'SHimər/ ▸*v.* [*intrans.*] shine with a soft tremulous light: *the sea shimmered in the sunlight.*
▸*n.* [in *sing.*] a light with such qualities: *a pale shimmer of moonlight.* ▷late Old English *scymrian*, of Germanic origin; related to German *schimmern*, also to **SHINE**. The noun dates from the early 19th cent. **—shim·mer·ing·ly** *adv.* **—shim·mer·y** *adj.*

shim·my /'SHimē/ ▸*n.* (*pl.* **-mies**) **1** a kind of ragtime dance in which the whole body shakes or sways. ▪ shaking, esp. abnormal vibration of the wheels of a motor vehicle: *steering stabilizers reduce shimmy even from oversized tires.* **2** *archaic* informal term for **CHEMISE**.
▸*v.* (**-mies, -mied**) [*intrans.*] dance the shimmy. ▪ shake or vibrate abnormally: *he braked hard and felt the car shimmy dangerously.* ▪ move with a graceful swaying motion: *her hair swung in waves as she shimmied down the catwalk.* ▪ [with *adverbial of direction*] move swiftly and effortlessly: *he shimmied right to the top of one of the chimneys.* ▷early 20th cent.: of unknown origin.

shin /SHin/ ▸*n.* the front of the leg below the knee. ▪ a cut of beef from the lower part of a cow's leg.
▸*v.* (**shinned, shin·ning**) [*intrans.*] (**shin up/down**) climb quickly up or down by gripping with one's arms and legs: *he shinned up a tree.* ▷Old English *scinu*, probably from a Germanic base meaning 'narrow or thin piece'; related to German *Schiene* 'thin plate' and Dutch *scheen*. The verb was originally in nautical use (early 19th cent.).

Shin Bet /,SHin ,bet/ (also **Shin Beth**) the principal security service of Israel, concerned primarily with counter-espionage. ▷modern Hebrew, the initial letters of the first two words of *šērūṯ biṭṭāhōn kĕlālī* '(general) security service.'

shin·bone /'SHin,bōn/ ▸*n.* the tibia.

shin·dig /'SHin,dig/ ▸*n. informal* a large, lively party, esp. one celebrating something. ▷mid 19th cent.: probably from the nouns **SHIN** and **DIG**, influenced later by **SHINDY**.

shin·dy /'SHindē/ ▸*n.* (*pl.* **-dies**) *informal* a noisy disturbance or quarrel: *there were plenty of gulls* **kicking up a shindy**. ▪ a large, lively party. ▷early 19th cent.: perhaps an alteration of **SHINTY**.

shine /SHīn/ ▸*v.* (*past* **shone** /SHōn/ or **shined**) **1** [*intrans.*] (of the sun or another source of light) give out a bright light: *the sun shone through the window.* ▪ glow or be bright with reflected light: *I could see his eyes shining in the light of the fire.* ▪ [*trans.*] direct (a flashlight or other light) somewhere in order to see something in the dark: *an usher shines his flashlight into the boys' faces.* ▪ (of something with a smooth surface) reflect light because clean or polished: *my shoes were polished until they shone like glass.* ▪ (of a person's eyes) be bright with the expression of a particular emotion: *his eyes* **shone with** *excitement.* ▪ [often as *adj.*] (**shining**) *figurative* be brilliant or excellent at something: *he has set a* **shining example** *with his model behavior | she* **shines at** *comedy.* ▪ (**shine through**) *figurative* (of a quality or skill) be clearly evident: *at Regis his talent shone through.* **2** (*past* **shined**) [*trans.*] make (an object made of leather, metal, or wood) bright by rubbing it; polish: *his shoes were shined to perfection.*
▸*n.* [in *sing.*] a quality of brightness, esp. through reflecting light: *a shine of saliva on his chin.* ▪ a high polish or sheen; a luster: *use shoe polish to try and get a shine | my hair has lost its shine.* ▪ an act of rubbing something to give it a shiny surface: *Tom's shoes got a quick shine from a boy with a buffing cloth.* ▪ *offensive* a contemptuous term for a black or dark-skinned person. ▷Old English *scīnan*, of Germanic origin; related to Dutch *schijnen* and German *scheinen*. **—shin·ing·ly** /-niNGlē/ *adv.*
▸*PHRASES* □ **take the shine off** spoil the brilliance or excitement of: *the absence of new jobs has taken some of the shine off his stellar popularity ratings.* □ **take a shine to** *informal* develop a liking for.

shin·er /'SHīnər/ ▸*n.* **1** a thing that shines or reflects light: *moonlight blanked the weakest shiners, but the more powerful stars were gleaming.* ▪ [in *combination*] a person or thing that polishes something: *shoeshiners.* **2** *informal* a black eye. **3** a small silvery North American freshwater fish of the minnow family that typically has colorful markings. • *Notropis* and other genera, family Cyprinidae: several species.

shin·gle[1] /'SHiNGgəl/ ▸*n.* a mass of small rounded pebbles, esp. on a seashore. ▷late Middle English: of unknown origin. **—shin·gly** /-g(ə)lē/ *adj.*

shin·gle[2] ▸*n.* **1** a rectangular tile of asphalt composite, wood, metal, or slate used on walls or roofs. **2** *dated* a woman's short haircut in which the hair tapers from the back of the head to the nape of the neck. [so named because of the layering.] **3** a small signboard, esp. one found outside a doctor's or lawyer's office.
▸*v.* [*trans.*] **1** roof or clad with shingles: [as *adj.*] (**shingled**) *a tower surmounted by a shingled spire.* **2** *dated* cut (a woman's hair) in a shingle. ▷Middle English (as a noun): apparently from Latin *scindula*, earlier *scandula* 'a split piece of wood.'
▸*PHRASE* □ **hang out one's shingle** begin to practice a profession.

shin·gle·back /'SHiNGgəl,bak/ (also **shingleback lizard**) ▸*n.* a slow-moving, heavily built lizard with scales resembling those of pine cones, occurring in arid regions of Australia. • *Trachydosaurus rugosus*, family Scincidae.

shin·gles /'SHiNGgəlz/ ▸*plural n.* [treated as *sing.*] *Medicine* an acute, painful inflammation of the nerve ganglia, with a skin eruption often forming a girdle around the middle of the body. It is caused by the same virus as chicken pox. Also called **HERPES ZOSTER**. ▷late Middle English: representing medieval Latin *cingulus*, variant of Latin *cingulum* 'girdle,' from *cingere* 'gird.'

shin guard ▸*n.* a pad worn to protect the shins when playing soccer, hockey, and other sports.

Shin·ing Path a Peruvian Maoist revolutionary movement and terrorist organization, founded in 1970 and led by Abimael Guzmán (1934–) until his capture and imprisonment in 1992. At first the movement operated in rural areas, but in the 1980s it began to launch terrorist attacks in Peruvian towns and cities. ▷translating Spanish **SENDERO LUMINOSO**.

Shin·kan·sen /'SHinkän,sen/ ▸*n.* (*pl.* same) (in Japan) a railroad system carrying high-speed passenger trains. ▪ (also **shin·kan·sen**) a train operating on such a system. ▷Japanese, from *shin* 'new' + *kansen* 'main line.'

shin·ny[1] /'SHinē/ ▸*v.* (**-nies, -nied**) another term for **SHIN**: *he loved to shinny up that tree.* ▷late 19th cent.: from the noun **SHIN** + **-Y**[2].

shin·ny[2] (also **shinny hockey**) ▸*n.* an informal form of ice hockey played esp. by children, on the street or on ice, often with a ball or other object in place of a puck: *we used to play shinny on the canal with tin cans.* ▷variant of **SHINTY**.

Shi·no·la /SHī'nōlə/ ▸*n. trademark* a brand of boot polish. ▪ *informal* used as a euphemism for "shit": *there'll be the same old Shinola on television.* ▷early 20th cent.: from **SHINE** + *-ola*.
▸*PHRASE* □ **not know shit from Shinola** *vulgar slang* used to indicate that someone is ignorant or innocent.

shin pad ▸*n.* another term for **SHIN GUARD**.

shin·plas·ter /'SHin,plastər/ ▸*n. informal historical* **1** a piece of paper currency or a promissory note regarded as having little or no value. **2** *Canadian* a twenty-five cent bill. ▷so named because of the resemblance to a square piece of paper soaked in vinegar and used to bandage the shin.

shin splints ▸*plural n.* [treated as *sing.* or *pl.*] acute pain in the shin and lower leg caused by prolonged running, typically on hard surfaces.

Shin·to /'SHin,tō/ ▸*n.* a Japanese religion dating from the early 8th century and incorporating the worship of ancestors and nature spirits and a belief in sacred power (**kami**) in both animate and inanimate things. It was the state religion of Japan until 1945. See also **AMATERASU**. ▷Japanese, from Chinese *shen dao* 'way of the gods.' **—Shin·to·ism** /-izəm/ *n.* **—Shin·to·ist** /-ist/ *n.*

shin·ty /'SHin(t)ē/ ▸*n.* (*pl.* **-ties**) a Scottish game resembling field hockey, played by two teams of twelve with curved sticks and a leather-covered cork ball. ▷mid 18th cent. (earlier as *shinny*): apparently from the cry *shin ye, shin you, shin t' ye*, used in the game, of unknown origin.

shin·y /'SHīnē/ ▸*adj.* (**shin·i·er, shin·i·est**) (of a smooth surface) reflecting light, typically because very clean or polished: *shiny hair | shiny black shoes.* **—shin·i·ly** /-əlē/ *adv.* **—shin·i·ness** *n.*

ship /SHip/ ▸*n.* a vessel larger than a boat for transporting people or goods by sea. ▪ a sailing vessel with a bowsprit and three or more square-rigged masts. ▪ *informal* any boat, esp. a racing boat. ▪ a spaceship. ▪ an aircraft.
▸*v.* (**shipped, ship·ping**) **1** [*trans.*] (often **be shipped**) transport (goods or people) on a ship: *the wounded soldiers were shipped home.* ▪ transport by some other means: *the freight would be shipped by rail.* ▪ [*trans.*] send (a package) somewhere via the mail service or a private company: *his papers have already been shipped to the University of Kansas.* ▪ [*trans.*] *Electronics* make (a product) available for purchase. ▪ [*intrans.*] *dated* embark on a ship: *people wishing to get from London to New York ship at Liverpool.* ▪ (of a sailor) serve on a ship: *Jack, you shipped with the Admiral once, didn't you?* **2** [*trans.*] (of a boat) take in (water) over the side. **3** [*trans.*] take (oars) from the oarlocks and lay them inside a boat. ▪ fix (something such as a rudder or mast) in its place on a ship. ▷Old English *scip* (noun), late Old English *scipian* (verb), of Germanic origin; related to Dutch *schip* and German *Schiff*. **—ship·less** *adj.* **—ship·pa·ble** *adj.*
▸*PHRASES* □ **a sinking ship** used in various phrases to describe an organization or endeavor that is failing, usually in the context of criticizing someone for leaving it: *they have fled like rats from a sinking ship.* □ **ship out** (of a naval force or one of its members) go to sea from a home port: *Bob got sick a week before we shipped out.* □ **ship something out** send (goods) to a distributor or customer, esp. by ship: *spare parts were quickly shipped out.* □ **take ship** set off on a voyage by ship; embark: *finally, he took ship for Boston.* □ **when someone's ship comes in** when someone's fortune is made.

-ship ▸*suffix* forming nouns: **1** denoting a quality or condition: *companionship | friendship.* **2** denoting status, office, or honor: *ambassadorship | citizenship.* ▪ denoting a tenure of office: *chairmanship.* **3** denoting a skill in a certain capacity: *entrepreneurship.* **4** denoting the collective individuals of a group: *membership.* ▷Old English *-scipe, scype*, of Germanic origin.

ship·board /'SHip,bôrd/ ▸*n.* [as *adj.*] used or occurring on board a ship: *playing in a shipboard jazz orchestra.*
▸*PHRASE* □ **on shipboard** on board a ship.

ship·break·er /'SHip,brākər/ ▸*n.* a contractor who breaks up old ships for scrap.

ship·bro·ker /'SHip,brōkər/ ▸*n.* a broker who

specializes in arranging charters, cargo space, and passenger bookings on ships.

ship·build·er /ˈSHipˌbildər/ ▸*n.* a person or company whose job or business is the design and construction of ships. —**ship·build·ing** /-ˌbildiNG/ *n.*

ship ca·nal ▸*n.* a canal wide and deep enough for ships to transit it.

ship chan·dler ▸*n.* see **CHANDLER**.

ship-fe·ver ▸*n.* typhus.

ship fit·ter ▸*n.* a person employed to manufacture or assemble the structural parts of a ship.

ship·lap /ˈSHipˌlap/ ▸*v.* [*trans.*] fit (boards) together by halving so that each overlaps the one below: [as *adj.*] (**shiplapped**) *shiplapped pine used as facing for the first floor.*

▸*n.* boards that have been fitted together in this way, typically used for cladding. ■ [usu. as *adj.*] a joint between boards made by halving: *a shiplap joint.*

Ship·ley /ˈSHiplē/, Jenny (1952–), New Zealand stateswoman; prime minister 1997–1999; full name *Jennifer Mary Shipley.*

ship·load /ˈSHipˌlōd/ ▸*n.* as much cargo or as many people as a ship can carry.

ship·mas·ter /ˈSHipˌmastər/ ▸*n.* a ship's captain.

ship·mate /ˈSHipˌmāt/ ▸*n.* a fellow member of a ship's crew.

ship·ment /ˈSHipmənt/ ▸*n.* the action of shipping goods: *logs waiting for shipment | shipments begin this month.* ■ a quantity of goods shipped; a consignment: *coal and oil shipments.*

ship of the des·ert ▸*n. poetic/literary* a camel.

ship of the line ▸*n. historical* a sailing warship of the largest size, used in the line of battle.

ship·own·er /ˈSHipˌōnər/ ▸*n.* a person or company owning a ship or a share in a ship.

ship·per /ˈSHipər/ ▸*n.* a person or company that sends or transports goods by sea, land, or air. ▷late Old English *scipere* 'sailor.' Current senses date from the mid 18th cent.

ship·ping /ˈSHipiNG/ ▸*n.* ships considered collectively, esp. those in a particular area or belonging to a particular country: *the volume of shipping using these ports.* ■ the transport of goods by sea or some other means. ■ a charge imposed by a retail company to send merchandise to a customer: *statues were available at $20 plus $4 for* **shipping and handling**.

ship·ping a·gent ▸*n.* a licensed agent in a port who transacts or supervises a ship's business, such as customs and immigration procedures, insurance, or documentation, on behalf of the owner.

ship-rigged ▸*adj.* (of a sailing ship) square-rigged.

Ship·rock /ˈSHipˌräk/ an eroded volcanic feature that stands above the desert in northwestern New Mexico near the Four Corners. Sacred to the Navajo, it served as a landmark for travelers.

ship's ar·ti·cles ▸*plural n.* the terms on which seamen take service on a ship. ■ a signed contract stipulating such terms.

ship's bis·cuit ▸*n.* British term for **HARDTACK**.

ship's boat ▸*n.* a small boat carried on board a ship.

ship's com·pa·ny ▸*n.* the crew of a ship.

ship·shape /ˈSHipˌSHāp/ ▸*adj.* in good order; trim and neat: *he checked that everything was shipshape.*

ship's hus·band ▸*n.* an agent who is responsible for providing maintenance and supplies for a ship in port. —**ship's hus·band·ry** *n.*

ship's pa·pers ▸*plural n.* documents establishing the details of a ship, including ownership, nationality, and the nature of the cargo.

ship-to-shore ▸*adj.* from a ship to land: *ship-to-shore phone calls.*

▸*n.* a radiotelephone connecting a ship to land, or connecting a train or other vehicle to a control center.

ship·way /ˈSHipˌwā/ ▸*n.* a slope on which a ship is built and down which it slides to be launched.

ship·worm /ˈSHipˌwərm/ ▸*n.* another term for **TEREDO**.

ship·wreck /ˈSHipˌrek/ ▸*n.* the destruction of a ship at sea by sinking or breaking up, e.g., in a storm or after running aground. ■ a ship so destroyed: *the detritus of a forgotten shipwreck in an Arctic sea.*

▸*v.* (**be shipwrecked**) (of a person or ship) suffer a shipwreck: *he was shipwrecked off the coast of Sardinia and nearly drowned | figurative her right to a fair trial might be shipwrecked by prosecutorial misconduct.*

ship·wright /ˈSHipˌrīt/ ▸*n.* a shipbuilder.

ship·yard /ˈSHipˌyärd/ ▸*n.* a place where ships are built and repaired.

Shi·ras /ˈSHīrəs/, George, Jr. (1832–1924), U.S. Supreme Court associate justice 1892–1903. He was appointed to the Court by President Benjamin Harrison.

Shi·raz[1] /SHiˈräz/ a city in southwest central Iran; pop. 965,000.

Shi·raz[2] /SH(i)əˈräz/ ▸*n.* a variety of black wine grape. ■ a red wine made from this grape. ▷from **SHIRAZ**[1], apparently an alteration of French *syrah*, influenced by the belief that the vine was brought from Iran by the Crusades.

shire /SHī(ə)r/ ▸*n. Brit.* a county, esp. in England. ■ (**the Shires**) used in reference to parts of England regarded as strongholds of traditional rural culture, esp. the rural Midlands. ▷Old English *scīr* 'care, official charge, county,' of Germanic origin.

-shire ▸*comb. form* forming the names of counties: *Oxfordshire | Yorkshire.*

shire coun·ty ▸*n.* (in the UK) a nonmetropolitan county (in existence since 1974).

shire horse ▸*n.* a heavy powerful horse of a draft breed, originally from the English Midlands.

shirk /SHərk/ ▸*v.* [*trans.*] avoid or neglect (a duty or responsibility): *their sole motive is to shirk responsibility and rip off the company.*

▸*n. archaic* a person who shirks. ▷mid 17th cent. (in the sense 'practice fraud or trickery'): from obsolete *shirk* 'sponger,' perhaps from German *Schurke* 'scoundrel.' —**shirk·er** *n.*

shirr /SHər/ ▸*v.* [*trans.*] **1** gather (an area of fabric or part of a garment) by means of drawn or elasticized threads in parallel rows: [as *adj.*] (**shirred**) *a swimsuit with a shirred front* | [as *n.*] (**shirring**) *shirring is flattering to all figure types.* **2** bake (an egg without its shell). ▷mid 19th cent.: of unknown origin.

shirt /SHərt/ ▸*n.* a garment for the upper body made of cotton or a similar fabric, with a collar, sleeves, and buttons down the front. ■ [usu. with *adj.*] a similar garment of stretchable material with few or no buttons, typically worn as casual wear or for sports: *a rugby shirt.* ▷Old English *scyrte*, of Germanic origin; related to Old Norse *skyrta* (compare with **SKIRT**), Dutch *schort*, German *Schürze* 'apron,' also to **SHORT**; probably from a base meaning 'short garment.' —**shirt·ed** *adj.* [often in *combination*] *the black-shirted balladeer.* —**shirt·less** *adj.*

▸*PHRASES* □ **keep your shirt on** *informal* don't lose your temper; stay calm. □ **lose one's shirt** *informal* lose all one's possessions. □ **the shirt off one's back** *informal* one's last remaining possessions: *we share things—we'd give our shirt off our back to another.*

shirt·dress /ˈSHərtˌdres/ ▸*n.* a dress with a collar and buttons in the style of a shirt, typically cut without a seam at the waist.

shirt·front /ˈSHərtˌfrənt/ ▸*n.* the breast of a shirt, in particular the part that shows when a suit is worn.

shirt·ing /ˈSHərtiNG/ ▸*n.* a material for making shirts, esp. a fine cotton in plain colors or incorporating a traditional woven stripe.

shirt·sleeve /ˈSHərtˌslēv/ ▸*n.* (usu. **shirtsleeves**) the sleeve of a shirt: *he rolled up his shirtsleeves.*

▸*adj.* **1** (of weather) warm enough to wear a shirt with no jacket: *the shirtsleeve November days before the hard cold set in.* **2** (of work or an atmosphere) straightforward and unpretentious, with hard work being done: *thousands have used this shirtsleeve workshop to improve their company profits.* —**shirt·sleeved** *adj.*

▸*PHRASE* □ **in (one's) shirtsleeves** wearing a shirt with nothing over it.

shirt·tail /ˈSHərˌtāl/ ▸*n.* (also **shirt·tails**) the lower, typically curved, part of a shirt that comes below the waist.

▸*adj.* (of relatives) distantly related: *if you checked back far enough, they were shirttail cousins of Curly's parents.*

shirt·waist /ˈSHərtˌwāst/ ▸*n.* a woman's blouse that resembles a shirt. ■ (also **shirt·waist dress** or **shirt·waist·er**) a woman's dress with a seam at the waist, its bodice incorporating a collar and buttons in the style of a shirt.

shirt·y /ˈSHərtē/ ▸*adj.* (**shirt·i·er**, **shirt·i·est**) *informal* irritable; querulous: *don't get annoyed or shirty on the phone.* —**shirt·i·ly** /-əlē/ *adv.* —**shirt·i·ness** *n.*

shish ke·bab /ˈSHiSH kəˌbäb/ ▸*n.* a dish of pieces of marinated meat and vegetables cooked and served on skewers. ▷from Turkish *şiş kebap*, from *şiş* 'skewer' + *kebāp* 'roast meat.'

shi·so /ˈSHēsō/ ▸*n.* (*pl.* **-sos**) an Asian plant of the mint family used as a culinary herb.

shit /SHit/ *vulgar slang* ▸*v.* (**shit·ting**; *past* and *past part.* **shit·ted** or **shit** or **shat** /SHat/) [*intrans.*] expel feces from the body. ■ (**shit oneself**) soil one's clothes as a result of expelling feces accidentally. ■ (**shit oneself**) *figurative* be very frightened.

▸*n.* feces. ■ [in *sing.*] an act of defecating. ■ a contemptible or worthless person. ■ something worthless; garbage; nonsense. ■ unpleasant experiences or treatment. ■ personal belongings; stuff. ■ any psychoactive drug, e.g., marijuana.

▸*exclam.* an exclamation of disgust, anger, or annoyance. ▷Old English *scitte* 'diarrhea,' of Germanic origin; related to Dutch *schijten*, German *scheissen* (verb). The term was originally neutral and used without vulgar connotation.

▸*PHRASES* □ **beat the shit out of** see **BEAT**. □ **be shitting bricks** be extremely nervous or frightened. □ **eat shit** an exclamation expressing anger or contempt for, or rejection of, someone. □ **get one's shit together** organize oneself so as to be able to deal with or achieve something. □ **in deep shit** (or **in the shit**) in trouble; in a difficult situation. □ **no shit** used to seek confirmation of the truth of a statement or to confirm the truth of a statement. □ **not give a shit** not care at all. □ **not know shit** not know anything. □ **not worth a shit** worthless. □ **shit for brains** a stupid person. □ **shit on someone** show contempt or disregard for someone. □ **be up shit creek (without a paddle)** be in an awkward predicament. □ **when the shit hits the fan** when the disastrous consequences of something become public.

shit·bag /ˈSHitˌbag/ ▸*n. vulgar slang* a contemptible or worthless person.

shit·can /ˈSHitˌkan/ ▸*v.* (**-canned**, **-can·ning**) *vulgar slang* [*trans.*] throw (something) away: *rip up those pictures and shitcan the negatives.* ■ discard or reject (someone or something): *it's hard to shitcan someone who keeps winning writing awards.*

shite /SHīt/ ▸*n.* & *exclam. Brit., vulgar slang* another term for **SHIT**.

shit-eat·ing ▸*adj. vulgar slang* smug; self-satisfied.

shite·poke /ˈSHītˌpōk/ ▸*n. informal* any of a number of birds of the heron family. • Several species in the family Ardeidae, in particular the green-backed *Butorides striatus.* ▷late 18th cent.: from **SHITE** (because of the bird's habit of defecating when disturbed) + the noun **POKE**[1].

shit·face /ˈSHitˌfās/ ▸*n. vulgar slang* an obnoxious person.

shit-faced (also **shit·faced**) ▸*adj.* [*predic.*] *vulgar slang* drunk or under the influence of drugs.

shit·head /ˈSHitˌhed/ ▸*n. vulgar slang* a contemptible person.

shit·hole /ˈSHitˌhōl/ ▸*n. vulgar slang* an extremely dirty, shabby, or otherwise unpleasant place.

shit·house /ˈSHitˌhous/ ▸*n. vulgar slang* a toilet. ■ *figurative* an extremely unpleasant place.

▸*PHRASE* □ **be built like a brick shithouse** **1** (of a person) having a very solid physique. **2** (of a woman) having a very attractive figure.

shit·kick·er /ˈSHitˌkikər/ ▸*n. vulgar slang* **1** an unsophisticated or oafish person, esp. one from a rural area. **2** a person who listens to or performs country music. **3** (**shitkickers**) substantially made boots with thick soles and typically with reinforced toes. —**shit-kick·ing** /-ˌkikiNG/ *adj.*

shit·less /ˈSHitlis/ ▸*adj.* (in phrase **be scared** (or **bored**) **shitless**) *vulgar slang* be extremely frightened (or bored).

shit list (also **shit·list**) ▸*n. vulgar slang* a list of those whom one dislikes or plans to harm.

shit·load /ˈSHitˌlōd/ ▸*n. vulgar slang* a large amount or number: *I have a shitload of work to do this week.* ▷1960s: from *shit* + *load.*

shit-scared ▸*adj. vulgar slang* terrified.

shit stir·rer ▸*n. vulgar slang* a person who takes pleasure in causing trouble or discord. —**shit stir·ring** *n.*

shit·ty /ˈSHitē/ ▸*adj.* (**-ti·er**, **-ti·est**) *vulgar slang* **1** (of a person or action) contemptible; worthless. ■ (of an experience or situation) unpleasant; awful. **2** covered with excrement.

shit·work /ˈSHitˌwərk/ ▸*n. vulgar slang* work considered to be menial or routine.

shi·ur /SHēˈo͝or/ ▸*n.* (*pl.* **shi·u·rim** /SHēˈo͝orim; SHēo͞oˈrēm/) *Judaism* a Talmudic study session, usually led by a rabbi.

shiv /SHiv/ ▸*n. informal* a knife or razor used as a weapon. ▷probably from Romany *chiv* 'blade.'

Shi·va /ˈsʜēvə/ (also **Si·va**) (in Indian religion) a god associated with the powers of reproduction and dissolution. ▷from Sanskrit *Śva*, literally 'the auspicious one.'

Shiva is regarded by some as the supreme being and by others as forming a triad with Brahma and Vishnu. He is worshiped in many aspects: as destroyer, ascetic, lord of the cosmic dance, and lord of beasts, and through the symbolic lingam. His wife is Parvati.

Shiva

shi·va /ˈsʜivə/ (also **shi·vah**) ▸*n.* *Judaism* a period of seven days' formal mourning for the dead, beginning immediately after the funeral: *she went to her sister's funeral and* ***sat shiva***. ▷from Hebrew *šiḇ'āh* 'seven.'

Shi·va·ji /ˈsʜivəjē/ (also **Si·va·ji**) (1627–80), Indian raja of the Marathas 1674–80. He raised a successful Hindu revolt against Muslim rule in 1659 and expanded Maratha territory.

shiv·a·ree ▸*n.* variant spelling of **CHARIVARI**.

shive /sʜīv/ ▸*n.* a broad plug hammered into a hole in the top of a cask when the cask has been filled. ▷Middle English: related to **SHEAVE**[2]. The original sense was 'slice (of bread),' later 'piece of split wood'; the current sense dates from the mid 19th cent.

shiv·er[1] /ˈsʜivər/ ▸*v.* [*intrans.*] (of a person or animal) shake slightly and uncontrollably as a result of being cold, frightened, or excited: *they shivered in the damp foggy cold.* See note at **SHAKE**.
▸*n.* a momentary trembling movement: *she gave a little shiver as the wind flicked at her bare arms | the way he looked at her sent* ***shivers down her spine***. ■ (**the shivers**) a spell or an attack of trembling, typically as a result of fear or horror: *a look that gave him the shivers.* ▷Middle English *chivere*, perhaps an alteration of dialect *chavele* 'to chatter,' from Old English *ceafl* 'jaw.' **—shiv·er·er** *n.* **—shiv·er·ing·ly** *adv.* **—shiv·er·y** /ˈsʜiv(ə)rē/ *adj.*

shiv·er[2] ▸*n.* (usu. **shivers**) each of the small fragments into which something such as glass is shattered when broken; a splinter.
▸*v.* [*intrans.*] *rare* break into such splinters or fragments: *the world seemed to shiver into a million splinters of prismatic color.* ▷Middle English: from a Germanic base meaning 'to split'; related to German *Schiefer* 'slate.'
▸*PHRASE* □ **shiver my** (or **me**) **timbers** a mock oath attributed to sailors.

Shiv Se·na /sʜiv ˈsānə/ ▸*n.* a Hindu nationalist organization centered in Maharashtra. ▷from Sanskrit *śiva* 'auspicious' + *sena* 'army.'

Shi·zu·o·ka /ˌsʜēzo͞oˈōkä/ a port on the southern coast of the island of Honshu in Japan; pop. 472,000.

shlub /sʜləb/ ▸*n.* variant spelling of **SCHLUB**.

shm ▸*abbr.* simple harmonic motion.

shmat·te /ˈsʜmätə/ ▸*n.* variant spelling of **SCHMATTE**.

shmear /sʜmi(ə)r/ (also **shmeer**) ▸*n.* & *v.* variant spelling of **SCHMEAR**.

shmo /sʜmō/ ▸*n.* (*pl.* **shmoes**) variant spelling of **SCHMO**.

sho /sʜō/ ▸*adv.* nonstandard spelling of **SURE**, representing its pronunciation in the southern U.S.: *I sho is glad to see ya.*
▸*PHRASE* □ **sho nuff** nonstandard spelling of **SURE ENOUGH** (see **SURE**): *you sho nuff got some foxes in this here town!*

Sho·ah /ˈsʜōə; sʜōˈä/ ▸*n.* (**the Shoah**) another term for **THE HOLOCAUST** (see **HOLOCAUST** sense 1). ▷modern Hebrew, literally 'catastrophe.'

shoal[1] /sʜōl/ ▸*n.* a large number of fish swimming together: *a shoal of bream.* Compare with **SCHOOL**[2]. ■ *informal* a large number of people: *a rock star's entrance, first proceeding with his shoal of attendants.*
▸*v.* [*intrans.*] (of fish) form shoals. ▷late 16th cent.: probably from Middle Dutch *schōle* 'troop.' Compare with **SCHOOL**[2].

shoal[2] ▸*n.* an area of shallow water, esp. as a navigational hazard. ■ a submerged sandbank visible at low water. ■ (usu. **shoals**) *figurative* a hidden danger or difficulty: *he alone could safely guide them through Hollywood's treacherous shoals.*
▸*v.* [*intrans.*] (of water) become shallower.
▸*adj.* (of water) shallow. ▷Old English *sceald* (adjective), of Germanic origin; related to **SHALLOW**. **—shoal·y** *adj.*

shoat /sʜōt/ (also **shote**) ▸*n.* a young pig, esp. one that is newly weaned. ▷late Middle English: of unknown origin; compare with West Flemish *schote*.

sho·chet /ˈsʜōkʜät; -kʜit; ˈsʜoi-; sʜōˈkʜet/ ▸*n.* (*pl.* **sho·che·tim** /sʜōkʜˈtēm/) a person officially certified as competent to kill cattle and poultry in the manner prescribed by Jewish law. ▷late 19th cent.: from Hebrew *šōḥēṭ* 'slaughtering.'

sho·chu /ˈsʜōcʜo͞o/ ▸*n.* a rough Japanese liquor distilled from any of various ingredients, including sake dregs. ▷from Japanese *shōchū*.

shock[1] /sʜäk/ ▸*n.* **1** a sudden upsetting or surprising event or experience: *it was a shock to face such hostile attitudes when I arrived.* ■ a feeling of disturbed surprise resulting from such an event: *her death gave us all a terrible shock | her eyes opened wide* ***in shock***. ■ an acute medical condition associated with a fall in blood pressure, caused by such events as loss of blood, severe burns, bacterial infection, allergic reaction, or sudden emotional stress, and marked by cold, pallid skin, irregular breathing, rapid pulse, and dilated pupils: *he died of shock due to massive abdominal hemorrhage.* ■ a disturbance causing instability in an economy: *trading imbalances caused by the two oil shocks.* ■ short for **ELECTRIC SHOCK**. **2** a violent shaking movement caused by an impact, explosion, or tremor: *earthquake shocks | rackets today don't bend or absorb shock the way wooden rackets do.* ■ short for **SHOCK ABSORBER**.
▸*v.* **1** [*trans.*] (often **be shocked**) cause (someone) to feel surprised and upset: *she was shocked at the state of his injuries.* ■ offend the moral feelings of; outrage: *the revelations shocked the nation.* ■ [*intrans.*] experience such feelings: *he shocked so easily.* ■ (usu. **be shocked**) affect with physiological shock, or with an electric shock. **2** [*intrans.*] *archaic* collide violently: *carriage after carriage shocked fiercely against the engine.* ▷mid 16th cent.: from French *choc* (noun), *choquer* (verb), of unknown origin. The original senses were 'throw (troops) into confusion by charging at them' and 'an encounter between charging forces,' giving rise to the notion of 'sudden violent blow or impact.' **—shock·a·bil·i·ty** /-əˈbilitē/ *n.* **—shock·a·ble** *adj.*

shock[2] ▸*n.* a group of twelve sheaves of grain placed upright and supporting each other to allow the grain to dry and ripen.
▸*v.* [*trans.*] arrange (sheaves of grain) in such a group. ▷Middle English: perhaps from Middle Dutch, Middle Low German *schok*, of unknown origin.

shock[3] ▸*n.* an unkempt or thick mass of hair: *a slender man with an untamable shock of black hair.* ▷mid 17th cent.: origin uncertain; compare with obsolete *shough*, denoting a breed of lapdog. The word originally denoted a dog with long shaggy hair, and was then used as an adjective meaning 'unkempt, shaggy.' The current sense dates from the early 19th cent.

shock ab·sorb·er ▸*n.* a device for absorbing jolts and vibrations, esp. on a motor vehicle.

shock cord ▸*n.* heavy elasticized cord; bungee cord.

shock·er /ˈsʜäkər/ ▸*n.* *informal* **1** something that shocks, esp. through being unacceptable or sensational: *the play's penultimate sequence is a shocker.* ■ a person who behaves badly or acts in a sensational manner: *I was a shocker when I was younger.* **2** *Brit.* a shock absorber.

shock·head·ed /ˈsʜäkˌhedid/ ▸*adj.* having thick, shaggy, and unkempt hair.

shock·ing /ˈsʜäkiɴɢ/ ▸*adj.* causing indignation or disgust; offensive: *shocking behavior.* ■ causing a feeling of surprise and dismay: *she brought shocking news.* **—shock·ing·ly** *adv.* **—shock·ing·ness** *n.*

shock·ing pink ▸*n.* a vibrant shade of pink.

shock jock ▸*n.* a disc jockey on a talk-radio show who expresses opinions in a deliberately offensive or provocative way.

Shock·ley /ˈsʜäklē/, William (Bradford) (1910–89), U.S. physicist. Shockley and his researchers at Bell Laboratories developed the transistor in 1948. He later became a controversial figure because of his views on race and intelligence. Nobel Prize for Physics (1956, shared with John Bardeen and Walter Brattain).

shock·proof /ˈsʜäkˌpro͞of/ ▸*adj.* **1** designed to resist damage when dropped or knocked: *a shockproof watch.* **2** not easily shocked: *the teacher puts them at ease by her shockproof attitude toward ignorance.*

shock stall ▸*n.* a marked increase in drag and a loss of lift and control on an aircraft approaching the speed of sound.

shock tac·tics ▸*plural n.* a strategy using sudden violent or extreme action to shock someone into doing something.

shock ther·a·py (also **shock treatment**) ▸*n.* treatment of chronic mental conditions by electroconvulsive therapy or by inducing physiological shock. ■ *figurative* sudden and drastic measures taken to solve an intractable problem.

shock troops ▸*plural n.* a group of soldiers trained specially for carrying out a sudden assault. ■ a group of people likened to such soldiers: *the volunteers became the shock troops in his upset victory over Oregon's senator.*

shock wave ▸*n.* a sharp change of pressure in a narrow region traveling through a medium, esp. air, caused by explosion or by a body moving faster than sound: *charting the shock waves of the explosion | figurative the oil embargo sent shock waves through the American economy.*

shock work·er ▸*n.* (in the former USSR) a worker whose group exceeded production quotas and was assigned to an especially urgent or arduous task.

shod /sʜäd/ ▸ past and past participle of **SHOE**.

shod·dy /ˈsʜädē/ ▸*adj.* (**-di·er**, **-di·est**) badly made or done: *we're not paying good money for shoddy goods.* ■ *figurative* lacking moral principle; sordid: *a shoddy misuse of the honor system.*
▸*n.* an inferior quality yarn or fabric made from the shredded fiber of waste woolen cloth or clippings. ▷mid 19th cent.: of unknown origin. **—shod·di·ly** /-əlē/ *adv.* **—shod·di·ness** *n.*

shoe /sʜo͞o/ ▸*n.* **1** a covering for the foot, typically made of leather, with a sturdy sole and not reaching above the ankle. ■ a horseshoe. **2** something resembling a shoe in shape or use, in particular: ■ a drag for a wheel. ■ short for **BRAKE SHOE**. ■ a socket, esp. on a camera, for fitting a flash unit or other accessory. ■ a metal rim or ferrule, esp. on the runner of a sled. ■ a box from which cards are dealt in casinos at baccarat or some other card games.
▸*v.* (**shoes**, **shoe·ing** /sʜo͞oiɴɢ/; *past* and *past part.* **shod** /sʜäd/) [*trans.*] (often **be shod**) fit (a horse) with a shoe or shoes. ■ (**be shod**) [with *adverbial*] (of a person) be wearing shoes of a specified kind: *his large feet were shod in sneakers* ■ protect (the end of an object such as a pole) with a metal shoe: *the four wooden balks were each shod with heavy iron heads.* ■ fit a tire to (a wheel). ▷Old English *scōh* (noun), *scōg(e)an* (verb), of Germanic origin; related to Dutch *schoen* and German *Schuh*. **—shoe·less** *adj.*
▸*PHRASES* □ **be** (or **put oneself**) **in another person's shoes** be (or put oneself) in another person's situation or predicament: *if I'd been in your shoes I'd have walked out on him.* □ **dead men's shoes** property or a position coveted by a prospective successor but available only on a person's death. □ **if the shoe fits, wear it** used as a way of suggesting that someone should accept a generalized remark or criticism as applying to themselves. □ **the shoe** (or *Brit.* **boot**) **is on the other foot** the situation, in particular the holding of advantage, has reversed. □ **shoe leather** *informal* used in reference to the wear on shoes through walking: *you can save on shoe leather by giving us your instructions over the telephone.* □ **wait for the other shoe to drop** *informal* be prepared for a further or consequential event or complication to occur.

shoe·bill /ˈsʜo͞oˌbil/ ▸*n.* an African stork with gray plumage and a very large bill shaped like a wooden shoe. • *Balaeniceps rex*, the only member of the family Balaenicipitidae.

shoe·black /ˈsʜo͞oˌblak/ ▸*n.* *dated, chiefly Brit.* a person who shines the shoes of passersby for payment.

shoe·box /ˈsʜo͞oˌbäks/ ▸*n.* a box in which a pair of shoes is delivered or sold. ■ used in references to small or uniform rooms or spaces: *a shoebox of a room.*

shoe·horn /ˈsʜo͞oˌhôrn/ ▸*n.* a curved instrument used to ease one's heel into a shoe.
▸*v.* [*trans.*] force into an inadequate space: *people were shoehorned into cramped corners.*

shoe·lace /ˈsHo͞oˌlās/ ▸*n.* a cord or leather strip passed through eyelets or hooks on opposite sides of a shoe and pulled tight and fastened.

Shoe·mak·er /ˈsHo͞oˌmākər/, Willie (1931–), U.S. jockey; full name *William Lee Shoemaker*. He held the record in horse racing for all-time career wins (8,833) from 1970 until 1999. He won the Kentucky Derby four times (1955, 1959, 1965, 1986), the Belmont Stakes five times (1957, 1959, 1962, 1967, 1975), and the Preakness twice (1963, 1967).

shoe·mak·er /ˈsHo͞oˌmākər/ ▸*n.* a person who makes shoes and other footwear as a profession. **—shoe·mak·ing** /-ˌmākiNG/ *n.*

Shoe·mak·er–Le·vy 9 /ˈsHo͞oˌmākər ˈlēvē ˈnīn/ a comet discovered in March 1993, when it had just broken up as a result of passing very close to Jupiter. In July 1994 more than twenty separate fragments impacted successively on Jupiter, causing large explosions in its atmosphere. ▹named after Carolyn (1929–) and Eugene *Shoemaker* (1928–97), U.S. astronomers, and David *Levy* (1948–), Canadian astronomer, discoverers of the comet.

shoe·pac /ˈsHo͞oˌpak/ (also **shoe·pack**) ▸*n.* a commercially manufactured oiled leather boot, typically having a rubber sole. ▹mid 18th cent.: from Delaware (Unami) *sippack* 'shoes,' from *čipahkpo* 'moccasins,' later assimilated to **SHOE**.

shoe·shine /ˈsHo͞oˌsHīn/ ▸*n.* an act of polishing someone's shoes, esp. for payment: [as *adj.*] *a shoeshine boy.* **—shoe·shin·er** *n.*

shoe·string /ˈsHo͞oˌstriNG/ ▸*n.* **1** *informal* a small or inadequate budget: *they proved capable of producing high-quality material* ***on a shoestring*** | [as *adj.*] *a shoestring budget.* **2** a shoelace.
▸*adj.* [*attrib.*] (of a save or tackle in sports) near or around the ankles or feet, or just above the ground.

shoe·string po·ta·toes ▸*plural n.* potatoes cut into long thin strips and deep-fried.

shoe tree ▸*n.* a shaped block inserted into a shoe when it is not being worn, to keep the shoe in shape.

sho·far /ˈsHōfər; sHōˈfär/ ▸*n.* (*pl.* **sho·fars** or **sho·froth** /sHōˈfrōt; -ˈfrōs/) a ram's-horn trumpet used by ancient Jews in religious ceremonies and as a battle signal, now sounded at Rosh Hashanah and Yom Kippur. ▹from Hebrew *šōpār*, (plural) *šōpārōṯ*.

sho·gun /ˈsHōgən/ ▸*n.* a hereditary commander-in-chief in feudal Japan. Because of the military power concentrated in his hands and the consequent weakness of the nominal head of state (the mikado or emperor), the shogun was generally the real ruler of the country until feudalism was abolished in 1867. ▹Japanese, from Chinese *jiāng jūn* 'general.' **—sho·gun·ate** /-gənit; -gəˌnāt/ *n.*

sho·ji /ˈsHōjē/ (also **sho·ji screen**) ▸*n.* (*pl.* same or **-jis**) (in Japan) a sliding outer or inner door made of a latticed screen covered with white paper. ▹from Japanese *shōji*.

sho·jo /ˈsHōˌjō/ ▸*n.* manga intended for a primarily female audience: *a very familiar scenario to those who read shojo centering on high school drama.* ▹from Japanese *shojo manga* 'girls' comics.'

Sho·la·pur /ˈsHōləˌpo͝or/ a city in western India, on the Deccan plateau in the state of Maharashtra; pop. 604,000.

Sho·lom A·leich·em /ˈsHōləm əˈlākəm/ (1859–1916), U.S. Yiddish writer; born in Ukraine; born *Solomon J. Rabinowitz*. He wrote about common Russian Jews who lived in small towns. His stories, esp. *Tevye's Daughters* (1894) formed the basis for the musical *Fiddler on the Roof* (1964).

Sho·na /ˈsHōnə/ ▸*n.* (*pl.* same or **-nas**) **1** a member of a group of peoples inhabiting parts of southern Africa. See also **MASHONA**. **2** any of the Bantu languages spoken by these peoples.
▸*adj.* of or relating to the Shona or their languages. ▹a local name.

shone /sHōn/ ▸ past and past participle of **SHINE**.

shoo /sHo͞o/ ▸*exclam.* a word said to frighten or drive away a person or animal.
▸*v.* (**shoos, shooed** /sHo͞od/) [*trans.*] make (a person or animal) go away by waving one's arms at them, saying "shoo," or otherwise acting in a discouraging manner: *I went to comfort her but she shooed me away.* ▹a natural exclamation: first recorded in late Middle English. The verb use dates from the early 17th cent.

shoo-fly pie (also **shoo·fly pie**) ▸*n.* a rich pie made with molasses and topped with crumbs. ▹from the U.S. interjection *shoo-fly* (referring to the need to wave flies away from the sweet treacle).

shoo-in ▸*n.* a person or thing that is certain to succeed, esp. someone who is certain to win a competition: *he was* ***a shoo-in for*** *reelection.* ▹1930s: from the earlier use of the term denoting the winner of a rigged horse race.

shook[1] /sHo͝ok/ past of **SHAKE**. ▸*adj.* [*predic.*] (**shook up**) *informal* emotionally or physically disturbed; upset: *she looks pretty shook up from the letter.*

shook[2] ▸*n.* a set of components ready for assembly into a box or cask. ▹late 18th cent.: of unknown origin.

shoot /sHo͞ot/ ▸*v.* (*past* **shot** /sHät/) **1** [*trans.*] kill or wound (a person or animal) with a bullet or arrow: *he was shot in the leg during an armed robbery* | [*trans.*] *troops* ***shot dead*** *29 people.* ■ [*intrans.*] fire a bullet from a gun or discharge an arrow from a bow: *he shot at me twice* | *the troops were ordered to* ***shoot to kill*** | [*trans.*] *they shot a volley of arrows into the village.* ■ cause (a gun) to fire. ■ [*trans.*] damage or remove (something) with a bullet or missile: *Guy, shoot their hats off.* ■ [*intrans.*] hunt game with a gun: *we go to Scotland to shoot every autumn.* ■ [*intrans.*] (**shoot over**) shoot game over (an estate or other area of countryside). ■ shoot game in or on (an estate, cover, etc.). **2** [*intrans.*] move suddenly and rapidly in a particular direction: *the car shot forward* | *Ward's hand shot out, grabbing his arm.* ■ [*trans.*] cause to move suddenly and rapidly in a particular direction: *he would have fallen if Marc hadn't shot out a hand to stop him* | *Beauchamp shot United into the lead.* ■ [*trans.*] direct (a glance, question, or remark) at someone: [with *two objs.*] *Luke shot her a quick glance* | [with *direct speech*] *"I can't believe what I'm hearing," she* ***shot back.*** ■ [*intrans.*] used to invite a comment or question: *"May I just ask you one more question?" "Shoot."* ■ (of a pain) move with a sharp stabbing sensation: *Claudia felt a shaft of pain shoot through her chest* | *figurative a pang of regret shot through her.* ■ [*trans.*] (of a boat) sweep swiftly down or under (rapids, a waterfall, or a bridge). ■ [*trans.*] *informal* (of a motor vehicle) pass (a traffic light at red). ■ extend sharply in a particular direction: *a road that seemed to just shoot upward at a terrifying angle.* ■ [*trans.*] move (a door bolt) to fasten or unfasten a door. **3** [*intrans.*] (in soccer, hockey, basketball, etc.) kick, hit, or throw the ball or puck in an attempt to score a goal: *Williams twice shot wide* | [*trans.*] *after school, we'd go straight out in the alley to shoot baskets.* ■ [*trans.*] *informal* make (a specified score) for a round of golf: *in the second round he shot a 65.* ■ [*trans.*] *informal* play a game of (pool or dice). **4** [*trans.*] film or photograph (a scene, film, etc.): *she has just been commissioned to shoot a video* | [*intrans.*] *point the camera and just shoot—nothing could be easier.* **5** [*intrans.*] (of a plant or seed) send out buds or shoots; germinate. ■ (of a bud or shoot) appear; sprout. **6** [*trans.*] *informal* inject oneself or another person with (a narcotic drug): *he shot dope into his arm.* **7** [*trans.*] plane (the edge of a board) accurately.
▸*phrasal v.* □ **shoot someone/something down** kill or wound someone by shooting them, esp. in a ruthless way: *troops shot down 28 demonstrators.* ■ bring down an aircraft, missile, or pilot by shooting at it. ■ *figurative* crush someone or their opinions by forceful criticism or argument: *she tried to argue and got* ***shot down in flames*** *for her trouble.* □ **shoot through** *Austral./NZ, informal* leave, typically to escape from or avoid someone or something: *me wife's shot through and I can't pay the rent.* [1940s: from *shoot through like a Bondi tram* (Bondi being the name of a Sydney suburb).] □ **shoot up 1** (esp. of a child) grow taller rapidly: *when she hit thirteen she shot up to a startling 5 foot 9.* ■ (of a price or amount) rise suddenly. **2** see **SHOOT SOMEONE/SOMETHING UP** (sense 2) below. □ **shoot someone/something up 1** cause great damage to something by shooting; kill or wound someone by shooting: *the police shot up our building.* **2** (also **shoot up**) *informal* inject a narcotic drug; inject someone with a narcotic drug: *she went home and shot up alone in her room* | *I was shooting up cocaine.* | *shoot people up with the new chemical and see what happens.*
▸*n.* **1** a young branch or sucker springing from the main stock of a tree or other plant: *he nipped off the new shoots that grew where the leaves joined the stems.* **2** an occasion when a group of people hunt and shoot game for sport: *a grouse shoot.* ■ *Brit.* land used for shooting game. ■ a shooting match or contest: *activities include a weekly rifle shoot.* **3** an occasion when a professional photographer takes photographs or when a film or video is being made: *a photo shoot* | *a fashion shoot.* **4** variant spelling of **CHUTE**[1]. **5** a rapid in a stream: *follow the portages that skirt all nine shoots of whitewater.*
▸*exclam. informal* used as a euphemism for 'shit': *shoot, it was a great day to be alive.* ▹Old English *scēotan*, of Germanic origin; related to Dutch *scieten* and German *schiessen*, also to **SHEET**[1], **SHOT**[1], and **SHUT**. **—shoot·a·ble** *adj.*
▸*PHRASES* □ **have shot one's bolt** see **BOLT**[1]. □ **shoot the breeze** (or **the bull**) *informal* have a casual conversation. □ **shoot one's cuffs** pull one's shirt cuffs out to project beyond the cuffs of one's jacket or coat. □ **shoot from the hip** *informal* react suddenly or without careful consideration of one's words or actions. □ **shoot oneself in the foot** *informal* inadvertently make a situation worse for oneself. □ **shoot it out** *informal* engage in a decisive confrontation, typically a gun battle. □ **shoot a line** *Brit., informal* describe something in an exaggerated, untruthful, or boastful way: *he never shot a line about his escapades.* □ **shoot one's mouth off** *informal* talk boastfully or indiscreetly.

shoot-'em-up ▸*n. informal* a fast-moving story or movie, of which gunfire is a dominant feature. ■ a simple computer game in which the sole objective is to kill as many enemies as possible to achieve a high score.

shoot·er /ˈsHo͞otər/ ▸*n.* **1** a person who uses a gun either regularly or on a particular occasion. ■ *informal* a gun. **2** a member of a team in games such as basketball whose role is to attempt to score goals. ■ a person who throws a die or dice. **3** a marble used to shoot at other marbles. **4** *informal* a small alcoholic drink, esp. of distilled liquor: *geez, he could use a shooter of whiskey.*

shoot·ing /ˈsHo͞otiNG/ ▸*n.* the action or practice of shooting: *the unprovoked shooting of civilians by soldiers* | *20,000 fatal shootings a year.* ■ the sport or pastime of shooting with a gun. ■ the right of shooting game over an area of land. ■ an estate or other area rented to shoot over.
▸*adj.* moving or growing quickly: *shooting beams of light played over the sea.* ■ (of a pain) sudden and piercing.
▸*PHRASE* □ **the whole shooting match** *informal* everything: *the whole shooting match is being computerized.*

shoot·ing board ▸*n.* a board with a step-shaped profile used to guide the motion of a plane relative to a workpiece to ensure accurate planing.

shoot·ing brake ▸*n. Brit., dated* a station wagon.

shoot·ing coat ▸*n.* a padded waterproof coat with large pockets, worn when shooting game. ■ archaic term for **MORNING COAT**.

shoot·ing gal·ler·y ▸*n.* a room or fairground booth used for recreational shooting at targets with guns or air guns. ■ *informal* a place used for taking drugs, esp. injecting heroin.

shoot·ing i·ron ▸*n. informal* a firearm.

shoot·ing range ▸*n.* an area provided with targets for the controlled practice of shooting.

shoot·ing script ▸*n.* a final movie or television script with scenes arranged in the order in which they will be filmed.

shoot·ing star[1] ▸*n.* a small, rapidly moving meteor burning up on entering the earth's atmosphere.

shoot·ing star[2] ▸*n.* a North American plant of the primrose family, with white, pink, or purple hanging flowers with backward curving petals. The flowers are carried above the leaves on slender stems and turn to face up following fertilization. • Genus *Dodecatheon*, family Primulaceae: several species, esp. *D. meadia*.

shooting star[2]

shoot·ing stick ▸*n.* a walking stick with a handle that unfolds to form a seat and a sharpened end that can be stuck firmly in the ground.

shoot·ing war ▸*n.* a war in which there is armed conflict, as opposed to a cold war or war of nerves, for example.

shoot·ist /ˈsHo͞otist/ ▸*n. informal* a person who shoots, especially one skilled in shooting, as a marksman. ▹mid 19th cent.: from *shoot* + *-ist*.

shoot-out ▸*n. informal* a decisive gun battle. ■ (also **penalty shoot-out**) *Soccer* a tiebreaker decided by

Pronunciation Key ə *ago;* ər *over;* ˈə or ˌə *up;* ˈər or ˌər *fur;* a *hat;* ā *rate;* ä *car;* CH *chew;* e *let;* ē *see;* e(ə)r *air;* i *fit;* ī *by;* i(ə)r *ear;* NG *sing;* ō *go;* ô *for;* oi *boy;* o͝o *good;* o͞o *goo;* ou *out;* SH *she;* TH *thin;* T͟H *then;* (h)w *why;* ZH *vision*

each side taking a specified number of penalty kicks.

shoot-the-chute (also **shoot-the-chutes**) ▸*n.* another term for **CHUTE-THE-CHUTE.**
▸*v.* (**shoot the chute** or **shoot the chutes**) another term for **CHUTE THE CHUTE** (see **CHUTE-THE-CHUTE**).

shop /SHäp/ ▸*n.* **1** a building or part of a building where goods or services are sold; a store: *a card shop | a barber shop.* ■ [in *sing.*] *informal* an act of going shopping: *she slogged her way around the supermarket doing the weekly shop.* **2** [usu. with *adj.*] a place where things are manufactured or repaired; a workshop: *an auto repair shop.* ■ a room or department in a factory where a particular stage of production is carried out: *the machine shop.* ■ short for **SHOP CLASS**: *I got an A in shop last year.* ■ a profession, trade, business, etc., esp. as a subject of conversation: *when mathematicians* ***talk shop****, they do it at the blackboard.*
▸*v.* (**shopped, shop·ping**) **1** [*intrans.*] go to a store or stores to buy goods: *she* ***shopped for*** *groceries twice a week.* ■ (**shop around**) look for the best available price or rate for something: *they shopped around for cheaper food.* ■ short for **WINDOW-SHOP. 2** [*trans.*] *informal, chiefly Brit.* inform on (someone): *a concerned member of the public had shopped him—wrongly—for accepting monetary reward.* ▷Middle English: shortening of Old French *eschoppe* 'lean-to booth,' of West Germanic origin; related to German *Schopf* 'porch' and English dialect *shippon* 'cattle shed.' The verb is first recorded (mid 16th cent.) in the sense 'imprison' (from an obsolete slang use of the noun for 'prison'), hence sense 2.
▸*PHRASES* □ **close** (or **shut**) **up shop** cease business or operation, either temporarily or permanently: *the cafes must shut up shop by July 22.* ■ *informal* stop some activity: *rather than close up shop, the team has returned to fighting trim.* □ **set up shop** establish oneself in a business: *he set up shop as a hairdresser in Soho.*

shop·a·hol·ic /ˌSHäpəˈhôlik; -ˈhälik/ ▸*n. informal* a compulsive shopper. ▷1980s: blend of **SHOP** and **ALCOHOLIC.**

shop class ▸*n.* a class in which practical skills such as carpentry or engineering are taught: *back in high school I made a wooden dummy in shop class.*

shop floor ▸*n.* [in *sing.*] the part of a workshop or factory where production as distinct from administrative work is carried out: *working conditions on the shop floor.*

shop·front /ˈSHäpˌfrənt/ ▸*n. chiefly Brit.* another term for **STOREFRONT** (sense 1).

shop·girl (also **shop girl**) ▸*n. dated* a female salesclerk.

shop·house /ˈSHäpˌhous/ ▸*n.* (in Southeast Asia) a store opening onto the sidewalk and also used as the owner's residence.

shop·keep·er /ˈSHäpˌkēpər/ ▸*n.* the owner and manager of a shop. **—shop·keep·ing** /-ˌkēpiNG/ *n.*

shop·lift·ing /ˈSHäpˌliftiNG/ ▸*n.* the criminal action of stealing goods from a shop while pretending to be a customer. **—shop·lift** *v.* **—shop·lift·er** /-ˌliftər/ *n.*

shop·man /ˈSHäpmən/ ▸*n.* (*pl.* **-men**) *Brit., dated* a male salesclerk or shopkeeper.

shoppe ▸*n.* a deliberately archaic spelling of **SHOP**, used in the hopes of imbuing a store with old-fashioned charm or quaintness: *the mishmash of the usual Tourist Gift Shoppe.*

shop·per /ˈSHäpər/ ▸*n.* a person who is shopping.

shop·ping /ˈSHäpiNG/ ▸*n.* [often as *adj.*] the purchasing of goods from stores: *a busy shopping area.* ■ goods bought from stores, esp. food and household goods: *I unloaded all the shopping.*

shop·ping cart ▸*n.* a bag or basket on wheels for carrying shopping purchases, in particular one on wheels provided for the use of supermarket customers.

shop·ping cen·ter ▸*n.* an area or complex of stores with adjacent parking.

shop·ping list ▸*n.* a list of purchases to be made. ■ a list of items to be considered or acted on: *a lengthy shopping list of detailed proposals.*

shop·ping mall ▸*n.* see **MALL** (sense 1).

shop·ping trol·ley ▸*n.* British term for **SHOPPING CART.**

shop-soiled ▸*adj.* British term for **SHOPWORN.**

shop stew·ard ▸*n.* a person elected by workers, for example in a factory, to represent them in dealings with management.

shop·talk /ˈSHäpˌtôk/ (also **shop talk**) ▸*n.* conversation about one's occupation or business at an informal or social occasion.

shop·walk·er /ˈSHäpˌwôkər/ ▸*n.* British term for **FLOORWALKER.**

shop win·dow (also **shop·win·dow**) ▸*n.* a window of a store, in which goods are displayed.

shop·worn /ˈSHäpˌwôrn/ ▸*adj.* (of an article) made dirty or imperfect by being displayed or handled in a store: *he brought out some shopworn lettuce | figurative he appraised his brown but slightly shopworn body in the mirror.*

Shore /SHôr/, Dinah (1921–93), U.S. singer; born *Frances Rose Shore.* She was most noted for her years on television, appearing on "The Dinah Shore Chevy Show" (1956–63), "Dinah's Place" (1970–74), "Dinah!" (1974–80), and "A Conversation with Dinah" (1989–91). She also hosted the Dinah Shore Classic golf tournament from 1972.

shore[1] /SHôr/ ▸*n.* the land along the edge of a sea, lake, or other large body of water: *I took the tiller and made for the shore.* ■ *Law* the land between ordinary high- and low-water marks. ■ (usu. **shores**) a country or other geographic area bounded by a coast: *the ripples of Soviet "new thinking" had reached the distant shores of Africa.* ▷Middle English: from Middle Dutch, Middle Low German *schōre*; perhaps related to the verb **SHEAR. —shore·less** *adj.* **—shore·ward** /-wərd/ *adj. & adv.* **—shore·wards** /-wərdz/ *adv.*
▸*PHRASE* □ **on shore** ashore; on land: *are any of the crew left on shore?*

shore[2] ▸*n.* a prop or beam set obliquely against something weak or unstable as a support.
▸*v.* [*trans.*] support or hold up (something) with such props or beams: *rescue workers had to* ***shore up*** *the building, which was in danger of collapse | figurative tax relief to help shore up the ailing airline industry.* ▷Middle English: from Middle Dutch, Middle Low German *schōre* 'prop,' of unknown origin.

shore[3] ▸ archaic past of **SHEAR.**

shore-based ▸*adj.* operating from or based on a shore: *shore-based guns.*

shore·bird /ˈSHôrˌbərd/ ▸*n.* a wader of the order Charadriiformes, such as a sandpiper. ■ any bird that frequents the shore.

shore crab ▸*n.* a crab that inhabits the seashore and shallow waters. • Several species, in particular the dark green **common shore crab** (*Carcinus maenas*, family Carcinidae) of Europe.

shore·lark /ˈSHôrˌlärk/ ▸*n.* British term for **HORNED LARK.**

shore leave ▸*n.* leisure time spent ashore by a sailor: *the hall was full of sailors* ***on shore leave.***

Shore·line /ˈSHôrˌlīn/ a city in northwestern Washington, north of Seattle; pop. 53,025.

shore·line /ˈSHôrˌlīn/ ▸*n.* the line along which a large body of water meets the land: *he walked along the shoreline.*

shore·side /ˈSHôrˌsīd/ ▸*n.* the edge of a shore: [as *adj.*] *a shoreside restaurant.*

shor·ing /ˈSHôriNG/ ▸*n.* shores or props used to support or hold up something weak or unstable.

shorn /SHôrn/ ▸ past participle of **SHEAR.**

short /SHôrt/ ▸*adj.* **1** measuring a small distance from end to end: *short, dark hair | a short flight of steps | the bed was too short for him.* ■ (of a journey) covering a small distance: *the hotel is a short walk from the sea.* ■ (of a garment or sleeves on a garment) only covering the top part of a person's arms or legs: *a short skirt.* ■ (of a person) small in height: *he is short and tubby.* ■ (of a ball in cricket, a shot in tennis, etc.) traveling only a small distance before bouncing: *he uses his opportunities to attack every short ball.* ■ short for **SHORTSTOP. 2** lasting or taking a small amount of time: *visiting London for a short break | a short conversation.* ■ [*attrib.*] seeming to last less time than is the case; passing quickly: *in 10 short years all this changed.* ■ (of a person's memory) retaining things for only a small amount of time: *he has a short memory for past misdeeds.* ■ *Stock Market* (of stocks or other securities or commodities) sold in advance of being acquired, with reliance on the price falling so that a profit can be made. ■ *Stock Market* (of a broker, position in the market, etc.) buying or based on such stocks or other securities or commodities. ■ denoting or having a relatively early date for the maturing of a bill of exchange. **3** relatively small in extent: *a short speech | he wrote a short book.* ■ [*predic.*] (**short of/on**) not having enough of (something); lacking or deficient in: *they were short of provisions | I know you're short on cash.* ■ [*predic.*] in insufficient supply: *food is short.* ■ [*predic.*] (of a person) terse; uncivil: *he was often sharp and rather* ***short with*** *her.* **4** *Phonetics* (of a vowel) categorized as short with regard to quality and length (e.g., in standard British English the vowel in *good* is short as distinct from the long vowel in *food*). ■ *Prosody* (of a vowel or syllable) having the lesser of the two recognized durations. **5** (of odds or a chance) reflecting or representing a high level of probability: *they have been backed at short odds to win thousands.* **6** (of pastry) containing a high proportion of fat to flour and therefore crumbly. ■ (of clay) having poor plasticity.
▸*adv.* (chiefly in sports) at, to, or over a relatively small distance: *you go deep and you go short.* ■ not as far as the point aimed at; not far enough: *all too often you pitch the ball short.*
▸*n.* **1** *Brit., informal* a strong alcoholic drink, esp. spirits, served in small measures. **2** a short film as opposed to a feature film. ■ a short sound such as a short signal in Morse code or a short vowel or syllable: *her call was two longs and a short.* ■ a short circuit. **3** *Stock Market* a person who sells short. ■ (**shorts**) *Stock Market* short-dated stocks. **4** (**shorts**) a mixture of bran and coarse flour.
▸*v.* short-circuit or cause to short-circuit: [*intrans.*] *the electrical circuit had* ***shorted out*** *| [trans.] if the contact terminals are shorted, the battery quickly overheats.* [early 20th cent.: abbreviation.] ▷Old English *sceort*, of Germanic origin; related to **SHIRT** and **SKIRT. —short·ish** *adj.* **—short·ness** *n.*
▸*PHRASES* □ **be caught** (or *Brit.* **taken**) **short** be put at a disadvantage: *the troubled company has been caught short by price competition in a recession-stricken market.* ■ *Brit., informal* urgently need to urinate or defecate. □ **two bricks short of a load, an oar short of a pair,** etc. *informal* (of a person) stupid; crazy: *she's two bricks short of a load.* □ **bring** (or **pull**) **someone up short** make someone check or pause abruptly: *he was entering the office when he was brought up short by the sight of John.* □ **come short** fail to reach a goal or standard: *we're so close to getting the job done, but we keep* ***coming up*** *short.* ■ *S. African* get into trouble: *if you try to trick him you'll come short.* □ **for short** as an abbreviation or nickname: *the File Transfer Protocol, or ftp for short.* □ **get** (or **have**) **someone by the short hairs** (or *Brit.* **short and curlies**) *informal* have complete control of a person. [from military slang, referring to pubic hair.] □ **go short** not have enough of something, esp. food: *you won't go short when I die.* □ **in short** to sum up; briefly: *he was a faithful, orthodox party member; a Stalinist in short.* □ **in short order** immediately; rapidly: *after the killing the camp had been shut down in short order.* □ **in the short run** in the near future. □ **in short supply** scarce. □ **in the short term** in the near future. □ **little** (or **nothing**) **short of** almost (or equal to); little (or nothing) less than: *he regarded the cost of living as little short of scandalous.* □ **make short work of** accomplish, consume, or destroy quickly: *we made short work of our huge portions.* □ **short and sweet** brief and pleasant: *his comments were short and sweet.* □ **the short end of the stick** an outcome in which one has less advantage than others. □ **short for** an abbreviation or nickname for: *I'm Robbie—short for Roberta.* □ **short of** less than: *he died at sixty-one, four years short of his pensionable age.* ■ not reaching as far as: *a rocket failure left a satellite tumbling in an orbit far short of its proper position.* ■ without going so far as (some extreme action): *short of putting out an all-persons alert, there's little else we can do.* □ **short of breath** panting; short-winded. □ **short, sharp shock** see **SHOCK**[1]. □ **stop short** stop suddenly or abruptly. □ **stop short of** not go as far as (some extreme action): *the measures stopped short of establishing direct trade links.*

short-act·ing ▸*adj.* (chiefly of a drug) having effects that only last for a short time.

short·age /ˈSHôrtij/ ▸*n.* a state or situation in which something needed cannot be obtained in sufficient amounts: *a* ***shortage of*** *hard cash | food shortages.* See note at **LACK.**

short-arm ▸*adj.* denoting a blow or throw executed with the arm not fully extended or with motion from the elbow only.

short·bread /ˈSHôrtˌbred/ ▸*n.* a crisp, rich, crumbly type of cookie made with butter, flour, and sugar. ▷early 19th cent.: *short* from **SHORT** in the sense 'easily crumbled.'

short·cake /ˈSHôrtˌkāk/ ▸*n.* **1** a small cake made of biscuit dough and typically served with fruit and whipped cream as a dessert. ■ a small circular sponge cake used in the same way. **2** a dessert made from shortcake topped with fruit, typically strawberries, and whipped cream. ▷late 16th cent.: see **SHORTBREAD**.

short·change /ˈSHôrtˈCHānj/ (also **short-change**) ▸*v.* [*trans.*] cheat by giving insufficient money as change: *I'm sure I was shortchanged at the bar.* ■ treat unfairly by withholding something of value: *residents perennially complain about their own children's needs being shortchanged.*

short cir·cuit ▸*n.* in a device, an electrical circuit of lower resistance than that of a normal circuit, typically resulting from the unintended contact of components and consequent accidental diversion of the current.
▸*v.* (**short-cir·cuit**) (with reference to an electrical device) malfunction or fail, or cause to do this, as a result of a short circuit across it: [*intrans.*] *the birds caused the electricity supply to short-circuit* | [*trans.*] *water had leaked into the washing machine's motor, short-circuiting it.* ■ [*trans.*] *figurative* shorten (a process or activity) by using a more direct (but often improper) method: *the normal processes of a democracy should not be short-circuited.*

short·com·ing /ˈSHôrt,kəmiNG/ ▸*n.* (usu. **shortcomings**) a fault or failure to meet a certain standard, typically in a person's character, a plan, or a system: *he is so forthright about his shortcomings, it's hard to chastise him.* See note at **FAULT**.

short com·mons ▸*plural n.* see **COMMONS**.

short cov·er·ing ▸*n.* the buying in of stocks or other securities or commodities that have been sold short, typically to avoid loss when prices move upward.

short·cut /ˈSHôrt,kət/ ▸*n.* an shorter alternative route. ■ *figurative* an accelerated way of doing or achieving something: *the promise of* **a shortcut to** *optimum health and fitness is a tantalizing one.*

short-dat·ed ▸*adj.* (of a stock or bond) due for early payment or redemption.

short-day ▸*adj.* [*attrib.*] (of a plant) needing a daily period of darkness of more than a certain length to initiate flowering, which therefore happens naturally as the days shorten in the autumn.

short di·vi·sion ▸*n.* arithmetical division in which the quotient is written directly without a succession of intermediate calculations.

short-eared owl ▸*n.* a migratory day-flying owl that frequents open country, found in northern Eurasia and North and South America. • *Asio flammeus*, family Strigidae.

short·en /ˈSHôrtn/ ▸*v.* make or become shorter: [*trans.*] *he shortened his stride* | [*intrans.*] *around mid-September, days shorten and temperatures dip.* ■ [*trans.*] *Sailing* reduce the amount of (sail) exposed to the wind. ■ (with reference to gambling odds) make or become shorter; decrease: [*intrans.*] *the odds had shortened to 14-1.* ■ [*trans.*] *Prosody & Phonetics* make (a vowel or syllable) short.

short·en·ing /ˈSHôrtniNG; ˈSHôrtn-iNG/ ▸*n.* butter or other fat used for making pastry or bread.

short·fall /ˈSHôrt,fôl/ ▸*n.* a deficit of something required or expected: *they are facing an expected $10 billion* **shortfall in** *revenue.*

short-fused ▸*adj. informal* likely to lose one's temper.

short game ▸*n.* the part of golf concerned with approach shots and putting: *two tips to improve your short game.*

short·hair /ˈSHôrt,he(ə)r/ ▸*n.* a cat of a short-haired breed.

short·hand /ˈSHôrt,hand/ ▸*n.* a method of rapid writing by means of abbreviations and symbols, used esp. for taking dictation.The major systems of shorthand are those devised in 1837 by Sir Isaac Pitman and in 1888 by **John R. Gregg** (1867–1948). ■ [in *sing.*] a short and simple way of expressing or referring to something: *poetry for him is simply a* **shorthand for** *literature that has aesthetic value.*

short-hand·ed ▸*adj.* **1** not having enough or the usual number of staff or crew: *the kitchen was a bit short-handed.* **2** *Ice Hockey* (of a goal) scored by a team playing with fewer players on the ice than their opponent. ■ (of a situation) occurring while or because a team has fewer than six players on the ice.
▸*adv.*

short haul ▸*n.* a relatively short distance in terms of travel or the transport of goods: *it is only a short haul over the mountains to Los Angeles* | [as *adj.*] *short-haul routes.*

short hop ▸*n.* *Baseball* a batted or thrown ball that hits the ground and is caught low just as it makes a bounce: *he got that one* **on the short hop**.
▸*v.* [*trans.*] (**short-hop**) (of a fielder) catch a ball just as it bounces from the ground: *Boggs short-hopped it and threw to first.*

short·horn /ˈSHôrt,hôrn/ ▸*n.* an animal of a breed of cattle with short horns.

short hun·dred·weight ▸*n.* see **HUNDREDWEIGHT**.

short·ie /ˈSHôrtē/ ▸*n.* variant spelling of **SHORTY**.

short list (also **short-list**) ▸*n.* a list of selected candidates from which a final choice is made: *a short list of four companies.*
▸*v.* [*trans.*] (**short-list**) put (someone or something) on a short list: *the novel was* **short-listed for** *the Booker Prize.*

short-lived /ˈlivd; ˈlīvd/ ▸*adj.* lasting only a short time: *a short-lived romance* | *these benefits are likely to be short-lived.*

short·ly /ˈSHôrtlē/ ▸*adv.* **1** in a short time; soon: *the new database will shortly be available for consultation* | *the flight was hijacked* **shortly after** *takeoff.* **2** in a few words; briefly: *they received a letter shortly outlining the proposals.* ■ abruptly, sharply, or curtly: *"Do you like football?" "I do not," she said shortly.* ▷Old English *scortlīce* (see **SHORT**, **-LY**2).

short or·der ▸*n.* an order or dish of food that can be quickly prepared and served: *a short order of souvlaki* | [as *adj.*] *I'm a short-order cook.*
▸*PHRASE* □ **in short order** see **SHORT**.

short-range ▸*adj.* [*attrib.*] **1** (esp. of a vehicle or missile) only able to be used or be effective over short distances: *short-range nuclear weapons.* **2** of or over a short period of future time: *short-range forecasting.*

short ribs ▸*n.* a narrow cut of beef containing the ends of the ribs near the breastbone.

short-run ▸*adj.* taken or considered over a short time period; short-term: *the short-run impact appears to be positive.* ■ *Printing* produced in or relating to a print run of relatively few copies.

shorts /SHôrts/ ▸*plural n.* short pants that reach only to the thighs or knees: *cycling shorts.* ■ men's underpants.

short score ▸*n.* *Music* a score in which the parts are condensed onto a small number of staves.

short-sheet ▸*v.* [*trans.*] fold and arrange the sheet on (a bed) in such a way that anyone getting into the bed will be unable to stretch their legs out beyond the middle of the bed, as a practical joke.

short shrift ▸*n.* rapid and unsympathetic dismissal; curt treatment: *the judge* **gave short shrift to** *an argument based on the right to free speech.* ■ *archaic* little time between condemnation and execution or punishment.

short·sight·ed /ˈSHôrtˈsītid/ (also **short-sight·ed**) ▸*adj.* British term for **NEARSIGHTED**. ■ *figurative* lacking imagination or foresight: *expedient, shortsighted solutions to problems.* —**short·sight·ed·ly** *adv.* —**short·sight·ed·ness** *n.*

short-sleeved ▸*adj.* having sleeves that do not reach below the elbow: *a short-sleeved silk top.*

short-stay ▸*adj.* [*attrib.*] denoting a place in which someone or something stays or remains for only a short period: *short-stay accommodations.* ■ denoting a person staying somewhere for only a short period of time: *short-stay patients.*

short·stop /ˈSHôrt,stäp/ ▸*n.* *Baseball* a fielder positioned in the infield between second and third base, or the position itself.

short sto·ry ▸*n.* a story with a fully developed theme but significantly shorter and less elaborate than a novel.

short sub·ject ▸*n.* a short movie, typically one shown before the screening of a feature film.

short suit ▸*n.* (in bridge or whist) a holding of only one or two cards of one suit in a hand.

short-tailed wea·sel ▸*n.* another term for **STOAT**.

short tem·per ▸*n.* a tendency to lose one's temper quickly. —**short-tem·pered** *adj.*

short ten·nis ▸*n.* tennis played on a small court with a small racket and a soft ball, used esp. as an introduction to the game for children.

short-term ▸*adj.* occurring in or relating to a relatively short period of time: *it might be a wise short-term investment.*

short-term·ism /ˈtərmizəm/ ▸*n.* concentration on short-term projects or objectives for immediate profit at the expense of long-term security.

short-tim·er ▸*n.* *military slang* a person nearing the end of their period of military service.

short ti·tle ▸*n.* an abbreviated form of a title of a book or document.

short ton ▸*n.* see **TON**1.

short waist ▸*n.* **1** a short upper body, with a high waist. **2** *archaic* a woman's dress with a high waist.

short·wave /ˈSHôrtˈwāv/ ▸*n.* a radio wave of a wavelength between about 10 and 100 m (and a frequency of about 3 to 30 MHz): [as *adj.*] *a shortwave transmitter.* ■ broadcasting using radio waves of this wavelength: [as *adj.*] *shortwave radio.*

short weight ▸*n.* weight that is less than that declared: *unscrupulous retailers give short weight by including an excessive amount of packaging.*

short-wind·ed /ˈwindid/ ▸*adj.* (of a person) out of breath or quickly becoming so.

short·y /ˈSHôrtē/ (also **short·ie**) ▸*n.* (*pl.* **short·ies**) *informal* a person who is shorter than average (often used as a nickname). ■ [often as *adj.*] a short garment, esp. a short dress or nightgown: *she pulled on a shorty nightshirt.*

Sho·sho·ne /SHōˈSHōnē/ ▸*n.* (*pl.* same or **-nes**) **1** a member of an American Indian people living chiefly in Wyoming, Idaho, and Nevada. **2** the Uto-Aztecan language of this people.
▸*adj.* of or relating to the Shoshone or their language. ▷of unknown origin.

Sho·sta·ko·vich /,SHästəˈkōviCH; ,SHôstəˈkōviCH/, Dmitri (Dmitrievich) (1906–75), Russian composer. Although he experimented with atonality and 12-note techniques, his music always returned to a basic tonality.

shot1 /SHät/ ▸*n.* **1** the firing of a gun or cannon: *he brought down a caribou with a single shot to the neck* | *figurative the opening shots have been fired in a legal battle over repairs.* ■ an attempt to hit a target by shooting: *he asked me if I would like to* **have a shot** *at a pheasant.* ■ [with *adj.*] the range of a gun or cannon: *six more desperadoes came galloping up and halted just out of rifle shot.* ■ *figurative* a critical or aggressive remark: *Paul tried one last shot—"You realize what you want will cost more money?"* ■ [with *adj.*] a person with a specified level of ability in shooting: *he was an excellent shot at short and long distances.* **2** a hit, stroke, or kick of the ball in sports such as basketball, tennis, or golf: *his partner pulled off a winning backhand shot.* ■ an attempt to drive a ball into a goal; an attempt to score: *he* **took a shot** *that the goalie stopped.* ■ *informal* an attempt to do something: *several of the competitors will* **have a shot** *at the title.* **3** (*pl.* same) a ball of stone or metal used as a missile fired from a large gun or cannon. ■ (also **lead shot**) tiny lead pellets used in quantity in a single charge or cartridge in a shotgun. ■ a heavy ball thrown by a shot-putter. **4** a photograph: *she* **took a shot** *of me holding a lamp near my face.* ■ a film sequence photographed continuously by one camera: *the movie's opening shot is of a character walking across a featureless landscape.* ■ the range of a camera's view: *a prop man was standing just* **out of shot**. **5** *informal* a small drink, esp. of distilled liquor: *he took a shot of whiskey.* ■ an injection of a drug or vaccine: *Jerry gave the monkey a shot of a sedative.* **6** [usu. with *adj.*] the launch of a space rocket: *a moon shot.* ▷Old English *sc(e)ot*, *gesc(e)ot*, of Germanic origin; related to German *Geschoss*, from the base of the verb **SHOOT**.
▸*PHRASES* □ **give it one's best shot** *informal* do the best that one can. □ **like a shot** *informal* without hesitation; willingly: *"Would you go back?" "Like a shot."* □ **a shot across the bows** see **BOW**3. □ **a shot in the arm** *informal* an encouraging stimulus: *the movie was a real shot in the arm for our crew.* □ **a shot in the dark** see **DARK**.

shot2 past and past participle of **SHOOT**. ▸*adj.* **1** (of colored cloth) woven with a warp and weft of different colors, giving a contrasting iridescent effect when looked at from different angles: *a dress of shot silk.* ■ interspersed with a different color: *dark hair* **shot with** *silver.* **2** *informal* ruined or worn out: *a completely shot engine will put you out of the race* | *my nerves are shot.* ■ [*predic.*] drunk.
▸*PHRASES* □ **get** (or **be**) **shot of** *Brit., informal* get (or be) rid of. □ **shot through with** suffused with (a particular feature or quality): *the mist was shot through with orange spokes of light.* □ **shot to pieces** (or **to hell**) *informal* ruined.

shot-blast ▸*v.* [*trans.*] clean or strip (a metal or other surface) by directing a high-speed stream of steel particles at it.

shot·crete /ˈSHätkrēt/ ▸*n.* another term for **GUNITE**. ▷1950s: from **SHOT**2 + **CONCRETE**.

shote /SHōt/ ▸*n.* variant spelling of **SHOAT**.

shot glass ▸*n.* a small glass used for serving liquor.

Pronunciation Key ə *ago*; ər *over*; ˈə *or* ,ə *up*; ˈər *or* ,ər *fur*; a *hat*; ā *rate*; ä *car*; CH *chew*; e *let*; ē *see*; e(ə)r *air*; i *fit*; ī *by*; i(ə)r *ear*; NG *sing*; ō *go*; ô *for*; oi *boy*; o͝o *good*; o͞o *goo*; ou *out*; SH *she*; TH *thin*; T͟H *then*; (h)w *why*; ZH *vision*

shot·gun /ˈSHät,gən/ ▶*n.* **1** a smoothbore gun for firing small shot at short range. **2** (also **shotgun formation**) *Football* an offensive formation in which the quarterback receives the snap while standing several yards behind the line of scrimmage.
▶*adj.* **1** aimed at a wide range of things; with no specific target: *many companies use the shotgun approach, aiming advertising at the widest possible audience.* **2** (of a house or other structure) with the rooms lined up one behind another, forming a long narrow whole: *his family lived in a shotgun shack in South Memphis.*
▶*PHRASE* □ **ride shotgun** see RIDE.

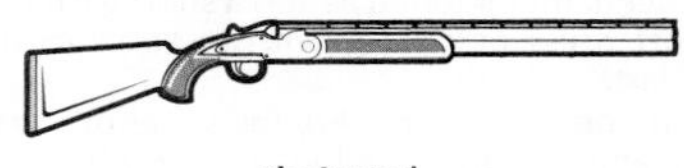

shotgun 1

shot·gun mar·riage (also **shot·gun wed·ding**) ▶*n. informal* an enforced or hurried wedding, esp. because the bride is pregnant.
shot·gun mi·cro·phone ▶*n.* another term for GUN MICROPHONE.
shot hole ▶*n.* **1** a hole made by the passage of a shot. **2** a hole bored in rock for the insertion of a blasting charge. **3** a small round hole made in a leaf by a fungus or bacterium, esp. in a fruit tree following an attack of leaf spot. ■ a small hole made in wood by a boring beetle.
shot·mak·ing /ˈSHät,mākiNG/ ▶*n.* the playing of aggressive or decisive strokes in tennis, golf, and other games. **—shot·mak·er** /-,mākər/ *n.*
Sho·to·kan /SHōˈtōkən/ ▶*n.* [usu. as *adj.*] a style of karate that is popular in many countries. ▷Japanese, from *shō* 'right, true' + *to* 'way' + *kan* 'mansion.'
shot-peen ▶*v.* [*trans.*] shape (sheet metal) by bombarding it with a stream of metal shot.
shot put ▶*n.* an athletic contest in which a very heavy round ball is thrown as far as possible. **—shot-put·ter** *n.* **—shot-put·ting** *n.*
shot·ted /ˈSHätid/ ▶*adj.* filled or weighted with shot.
shot·ten her·ring /ˈSHätn/ ▶*n.* a herring that has spawned. ■ *archaic* a weakened or dispirited person. ▷Middle English: *shotten*, archaic past participle of SHOOT, in the specialized sense 'discharge (spawn).'
shot tow·er ▶*n. historical* a tower in which shot was made from molten lead poured through sieves at the top and falling into water at the bottom.
should /SHo͝od/ ▶*modal verb* (*3rd sing.* **should**) **1** used to indicate obligation, duty, or correctness, typically when criticizing someone's actions: *he should have been careful | I think we should trust our people more | you shouldn't have gone.* ■ indicating a desirable or expected state: *by now students should be able to read with a large degree of independence.* ■ used to give or ask advice or suggestions: *you should go back to bed | what should I wear?* ■ (**I should**) used to give advice: *I should hold out if I were you.* **2** used to indicate what is probable: *$348 million should be enough to buy him out | the bus should arrive in a few minutes.* **3** *formal* expressing the conditional mood: ■ (in the first person) indicating the consequence of an imagined event: *if I were to obey my first impulse, I should spend my days writing letters.* ■ referring to a possible event or situation: *if you should change your mind, I'll be at the hotel | should anyone arrive late, admission is likely to be refused.* **4** used in a clause with "that" after a main clause describing feelings: *it is astonishing that we should find violence here.* **5** used in a clause with "that" expressing purpose: *in order that training should be effective it must be planned systematically.* **6** (in the first person) expressing a polite request or acceptance: *we should be grateful for your advice.* **7** (in the first person) expressing a conjecture or hope: *he'll have a sore head, I should imagine | "It won't happen again." "I should hope not."* **8** used to emphasize to a listener how striking an event is or was: *you should have seen Marge's face.* ■ (**who/what should —— but**) emphasizing how surprising an event was: *I was in this store when who should I see across the street but Toby.* ▷Old English *sceolde*: past of SHALL.

USAGE As with **shall** and **will**, there is confusion about when to use **should** and **would**. The traditional rule is that **should** is used with first person pronouns (*I* and *we*), as in *I said I **should** be late*, and **would** is used with second and third persons (*you, he, she, it, they*), as in *you didn't say you **would** be late.* In practice, however, **would** is normally used instead of **should** in reported speech and conditional clauses: *I said I **would** be late; if we had known, we **would** have invited her.* In spoken and informal contexts, the issue rarely arises, since the distinction is obscured by the use of the contracted forms **I'd**, **we'd**, etc.
In modern English, uses of **should** are dominated by the senses relating to obligation (for which **would** cannot be substituted), as in *you **should** go out more often*, and for related emphatic uses, as in *you **should** have seen her face!*

shoul·der /ˈSHōldər/ ▶*n.* **1** the upper joint of the human arm and the part of the body between this and the neck. ■ (in quadrupeds) the joint of the upper forelimb and the adjacent part of the back. ■ the part of a bird or insect at which the wing is attached. ■ a large cut of meat from the upper foreleg and shoulder blade of an animal: *a shoulder of lamb.* ■ a part of a garment covering the shoulder: *a jacket with padded shoulders.* ■ (**shoulders**) the upper part of the back and arms: *a tall youth with broad shoulders.* ■ (**shoulders**) *figurative* this part of the body regarded as bearing responsibility or hardship or providing strength: *all accounts place the blame squarely on his shoulders.* **2** a part of something resembling a shoulder in shape, position, or function: *the shoulder of a pulley.* ■ a point at which a steep slope descends from a plateau or highland area: *the shoulder of the hill sloped down.* **3** a paved strip alongside a road for stopping on in an emergency.
▶*v.* **1** [*trans.*] put (something heavy) over one's shoulder or shoulders to carry: *we shouldered our crippling backpacks and set off slowly up the hill.* ■ *figurative* take on (a burden or responsibility): *she shouldered the blame for the incident.* **2** [*trans.*] push (someone or something) out of one's way with one's shoulder: *she shouldered him brusquely aside.* ■ [*intrans.*] move in this way: *he shouldered past a woman with a baby | he **shouldered his way** through the seething mass of children.* ▷Old English *sculdor*; related to Dutch *schouder* and German *Schulter*. **—shoul·dered** /ˈSHōldərd/ *adj.* [in *combination*] *broad-shouldered.*
▶*PHRASES* □ **be looking over one's shoulder** be anxious or insecure about a possible danger: *takeovers are the thing that keeps suppliers looking over their shoulders.* □ **put one's shoulder to the wheel** set to work vigorously. □ **shoulder arms** hold a rifle against the side of the body, barrel upward. □ **a shoulder to cry on** someone who listens sympathetically to one's problems. □ **shoulder to shoulder** side by side: *everyone is bunched together shoulder to shoulder.* ■ acting together toward a common aim; with united effort: *we fought shoulder to shoulder with the rest of the country.*
shoul·der bag ▶*n.* a bag with a long strap that is hung over the shoulder.
shoul·der belt ▶*n.* a seat belt that passes over the shoulder and across the chest. ■ a bandolier or other strap passing over one shoulder and under the opposite arm.
shoul·der blade ▶*n.* either of the large, flat, triangular bones that lie against the ribs in the upper back and provide attachments for the bone and muscles of the upper arm. Also called SCAPULA.
should·er har·ness ▶*n.* a strap worn around or across the shoulder, specifically: ■ the part of a seat belt that lies diagonally across the chest. ■ (also **shoulder holster**) a strap worn around the shoulder and under one arm with a holster for carrying a firearm.
shoul·der-high ▶*adj.* & *adv.* up to or at the height of the shoulders: [as *adj.*] *a glade of shoulder-high grass* | [as *adv.*] *he was lifted shoulder-high.*
shoul·der hol·ster ▶*n.* a gun holster worn under the armpit.
shoul·der-in ▶*n.* (in dressage) a movement in which the horse moves parallel to the side of the arena, with its hindquarters carried closer to the wall than its shoulders and its body curved toward the center.
shoul·der joint ▶*n.* the joint connecting an upper limb or forelimb to the body. It is a ball-and-socket joint in which the head of the humerus fits into the socket of the scapula.
shoul·der knot ▶*n.* a knot of ribbon, metal, or lace worn as part of ceremonial dress.
shoul·der pad ▶*n.* a spongy, shaped pad sewn into the shoulder of a garment to provide bulk and shape. ■ a hard protective pad for the shoulders used in certain sports, such as ice hockey and football.
shoul·der sea·son (also **shoul·der per·i·od**) ▶*n.* a travel period between peak and off-peak seasons.
shoul·der stand ▶*n.* a gymnastic movement in which, starting from a supine position, the torso and legs are raised vertically over the head and supported on the shoulders and arms.
shoul·der strap ▶*n.* a narrow strip of material going over the shoulder from the front to the back of a garment. ■ a long strap attached to a bag for carrying it over the shoulder. ■ a strip of cloth from shoulder to collar on a military uniform bearing a symbol of rank. ■ a similar strip on a raincoat.
should·n't /ˈSHo͝odnt/ ▶*contraction of* should not.
shout /SHout/ ▶*v.* **1** [*intrans.*] (of a person) utter a loud call or cry, typically as an expression of a strong emotion: *she shouted for joy.* ■ [*reporting verb*] say something very loudly; call out: [*trans.*] *he leaned out of his window and shouted abuse at them | I **shouted out** a warning* | [with *direct speech*] *"Come back!" she shouted.* ■ (**shout at**) speak loudly and angrily to; insult or scold loudly: *he apologized because he had shouted at her in front of them all.* ■ [*trans.*] (**shout someone down**) prevent someone from speaking or being heard by shouting: *he was shouted down as he tried to explain the decision.* ■ [*trans.*] *figurative* indicate or express (a particular quality or characteristic) unequivocally or powerfully: *from crocodile handbag to gold-trimmed shoes she shouted money.* **2** [with *two objs.*] *Austral./NZ, informal* treat (someone) to (something, esp. a drink): *I'll shout you a beer.* ■ [*intrans.*] buy a round of drinks: *anyone shooting a hole in one must shout for all players present on the course.*
▶*n.* **1** a loud cry expressing a strong emotion or calling attention: *his words were interrupted by warning shouts.* **2** (**one's shout**) *Brit., informal* one's turn to buy a round of drinks: *"Do you want another drink? My shout."* ▷late Middle English: perhaps related to SHOOT; compare with Old Norse *skúta* 'a taunt,' also with the verb SCOUT[2]. **—shout·er** *n.* **—shout·y** *adj.* (*informal*).
▶*PHRASES* □ **give someone a shout** *informal* call for someone's attention. ■ call on or get in touch with someone. □ **in with a shout** *Brit., informal* having a good chance: *they were definitely in with a shout of bringing off a victory.* □ **shout something from the rooftops** talk about something openly and jubilantly, esp. something that is personal or has previously been kept secret. □ **shout the odds** *chiefly Brit.* talk loudly and opinionatedly.
shout·ing match ▶*n.* a loud quarrel.
shove /SHəv/ ▶*v.* [*trans.*] push (someone or something) roughly: *police started **pushing and shoving** people down the street* | [*intrans.*] *kids pushed, kicked, and shoved.* ■ [*intrans.*] make one's way by pushing someone or something: *Woody shoved past him.* ■ [*trans.*] put (something) somewhere carelessly or roughly: *she shoved the books into her briefcase.* ■ (**shove it**) *informal* used to express angry dismissal of something: *I should have told the boss to shove it.*
▶*phrasal v.* □ **shove off 1** [usu. in *imperative*] *informal* go away: *shove off—you're bothering the customers.* **2** push away from the shore or another vessel in a boat.
▶*n.* [usu. in *sing.*] a strong push: *she gave him a hefty shove and he nearly fell.* ▷Old English *scūfan* (verb), of Germanic origin; related to Dutch *schuiven* and German *schieben*, also to SHUFFLE.
shove-half·pen·ny /ˈSHəv ˈhāp(ə)nē/ ▶*n.* a game in which coins are struck so that they slide across a marked board on a table.
shov·el /ˈSHəvəl/ ▶*n.* a tool with a broad flat blade and typically upturned sides, used for moving coal, earth, snow or other material. ■ a machine or part of a machine having a similar shape or function. ■ an amount of something carried or moved with shovel: *a few **shovels of** earth.*
▶*v.* (**-eled, -el·ing**; *Brit.* **-elled, -el·ling**) [*trans.*] move (coal, earth, snow, or similar material) with a shovel: *she shoveled coal on the fire.* ■ [*trans.*] remove snow from (an area) with a shovel: *I'll clean the basement and shovel the walk.* ■ *informal* put or push (something, typically food) somewhere quickly and in large quantities: *Dave was shoveling pasta into his mouth.* ▷Old English *scofl*, of Germanic origin; related to Dutch *schoffel*, German *Schaufel*, also to the verb SHOVE. **—shov·el·ful** /-,fo͝ol/ *n.* (*pl.* **-fuls**).
shov·el·board /ˈSHəvəl,bôrd/ ▶*n.* British term for SHUFFLEBOARD. ▷mid 16th cent.: alteration of obsolete *shoveboard*, from SHOVE + BOARD.
shov·el·er /ˈSHəv(ə)lər/ (*chiefly Brit.* **shov·el·ler**) ▶*n.* **1** a person or thing that shovels something. **2** a dabbling duck with a long broad bill. • Genus *Anas*, family Anatidae: four species, in particular *A. clypeata* of Eurasia and North America. [late Middle English (denoting a spoonbill): alteration of earlier *shovelard*, from SHOVEL, perhaps influenced by *mallard*.]

shov·el hat ▶*n.* a black felt hat with a low round crown and a broad brim turned up at the sides, formerly worn esp. by clergymen.

show /SHō/ ▶*v.* (*past part.* **shown** /SHōn/ or **showed**) **1** be or allow or cause to be visible: [*intrans.*] *wrinkles were starting to show on her face* | [*intrans.*] *the muscles of her jaws showed white through the skin* | [*trans.*] *a white blouse will show the blood.* ■ [*trans.*] offer, exhibit, or produce (something) for scrutiny or inspection: *an alarm salesperson should show an ID card* | [with *two objs.*] *he wants to show you all his woodwork stuff.* ■ [*trans.*] put on display in an exhibition or competition: *he ceased early in his career to show his work* | [*intrans.*] *other artists who showed there included Robert Motherwell.* ■ [*trans.*] present (a movie or television program) on a screen for public viewing. ■ [*intrans.*] (of a movie) be presented in this way: *a movie showing at the Venice Film Festival.* ■ [*trans.*] indicate (a particular time, measurement, etc.): *a travel clock showing the time in different cities.* ■ [*trans.*] represent or depict in art: *a postcard showing the Wicklow Mountains.* ■ (**show oneself**) allow oneself to be seen; appear in public: *he was amazed that she would have the gall to show herself.* ■ [*intrans.*] *informal* arrive or turn up for an appointment or at a gathering: *her date failed to show.* ■ [*intrans.*] finish third or in the first three in a race. ■ [*intrans.*] *informal* (of a woman) be visibly pregnant: *Shirley was four months pregnant and just starting to show.* **2** [*trans.*] display or allow to be perceived (a quality, emotion, or characteristic): *it was Frank's turn to show his frustration* | *his sangfroid showed signs of cracking.* ■ accord or treat someone with (a specified quality): *he urged his soldiers to fight them and show no mercy* | [with *two objs.*] *he has learned to show women some respect.* ■ [*intrans.*] (of an emotion) be noticeable: *he tried not to let his relief show.* **3** [*trans.*] demonstrate or prove: *experts say this shows the benefit of regular inspections* | [with *clause*] *the figures show that the underlying rate of inflation continues to fall.* ■ (**show oneself**) prove or demonstrate oneself to be: [with *infinitive*] *she showed herself to be a harsh critic* | [with *complement*] *he showed himself to be an old-fashioned Baptist separatist.* ■ cause to understand or be capable of doing something by explanation or demonstration: *he showed the boy how to operate the machine.* ■ [*trans.*] conduct or lead: *show them in, please.*

▶*phrasal v.* □ **show something forth** *archaic* exhibit: *the heavens show forth the glory of God.* □ **show off** *informal* make a deliberate or pretentious display of one's abilities or accomplishments. □ **show someone/something off** display or cause others to take notice of someone or something that is a source of pride: *his jeans were tight-fitting, showing off his compact figure.* □ **show out** *Bridge* reveal that one has no cards of a particular suit. □ **show someone around** act as a guide for someone to points of interest in a place or building. □ **show through** (of one's real feelings) be revealed inadvertently. □ **show up 1** be conspicuous or clearly visible. **2** *informal* arrive or turn up for an appointment or gathering. □ **show someone/something up** make someone or something conspicuous or clearly visible: *a rising moon showed up the wild seascape.* ■ expose someone or something as being bad or faulty in some way: *it's a pity they haven't* **showed up** *the authorities* **for** *what they are.* ■ (**show someone up**) *informal* embarrass or humiliate someone: *she says I showed her up in front of her friends.*

▶*n.* **1** a spectacle or display of something, typically an impressive one: *spectacular shows of bluebells.* **2** a public entertainment, in particular: ■ a play or other stage performance, esp. a musical. ■ a program on television or radio. ■ [usu. with *adj.*] an event or competition involving the public display or exhibition of animals, plants, or products: *the annual agricultural show.* ■ *informal* an undertaking, project, or organization: *I man a desk in a little office. I don't run the show.* ■ *informal* an opportunity for doing something; a chance: *I didn't have a show.* **3** an outward appearance or display of a quality or feeling: *Joanie was frightened of any* **show of** *affection.* ■ an outward display intended to give a particular, false impression: *Drew* **made a show of** *looking around for firewood* | *they are all show and no go.* **4** *Medicine* a discharge of blood and mucus from the vagina at the onset of labor or menstruation. ▷Old English *scēawian* 'look at, inspect,' from a West Germanic base meaning 'look'; related to Dutch *schouwen* and German *schauen.*

▶**PHRASES** □ **for show** for the sake of appearance rather than for use. □ **get** (or **keep**) **the show on the road** *informal* begin (or succeed in continuing with) an undertaking or enterprise: *"Let's get this show on the road—we're late already."* □ **good** (or **bad** or **poor**) **show!** *Brit., informal, dated* used to express approval (or disapproval or dissatisfaction). □ **have something** (or **nothing**) **to show for** have a (or no) visible result of (one's work or experience): *a year later, he had nothing to show for his efforts.* □ **on show** being exhibited. □ **show one's cards** another way of saying SHOW ONE'S HAND below. □ **show cause** *Law* produce satisfactory grounds for application of (or exemption from) a procedure or penalty. □ **show someone the door** dismiss or eject someone from a place. □ **show one's face** appear in public: *she had been up in court and was so ashamed she could hardly show her face.* □ **show the flag** see FLAG[1]. □ **show one's hand** (in a card game) reveal one's cards. ■ *figurative* disclose one's plans: *he needed hard evidence, and to get it he would have to show his hand.* □ **show of force** a demonstration of the forces at one's command and of one's readiness to use them. □ **show of hands** the raising of hands among a group of people to indicate a vote for or against something, with numbers typically being estimated rather than counted. □ **show the way** indicate the direction to be followed to a particular place. ■ indicate what can or should be done by doing it first: *Morgan showed the way by becoming Deputy Governor of Jamaica.*

Sho·wa /ˈSHōwä/ ▶*n.* [usu. as *adj.*] the period when Japan was ruled by the emperor Hirohito. ▷Japanese, from *shō* 'bright, clear' + *wa* 'harmony.'

show-and-tell ▶*n.* a teaching method, used esp. in teaching young children, in which students are encouraged to bring items they have selected to class and describe them to their classmates.

show band ▶*n.* a band that plays cover versions of popular songs. ■ a band, esp. a jazz band, that performs with theatrical extravagance.

show bill ▶*n.* an advertising poster, esp. for a theater performance. ■ a listing of events at a horse show: *Horse & Pony Association show bill.*

show biz ▶*n.* informal term for SHOW BUSINESS. **—show·biz·zy** /ˈSHō,bizē/ *adj.*

show·boat /ˈSHō,bōt/ ▶*n.* a river steamboat on which theatrical performances are given. ■ *informal* a show-off; an exhibitionist.

▶*v.* [*intrans.*] *informal* show off: [as *adj.*] (**showboating**) *a lot of showboating politicians.* **—show·boat·er** *n.*

show busi·ness ▶*n.* the theater, movies, television, and pop music as a profession or industry.

show·card /ˈSHō,kärd/ ▶*n.* a large card bearing a conspicuous design, used esp. in advertising, market research, and teaching.

show·case /ˈSHō,kās/ ▶*n.* a glass case used for displaying articles in a store or museum. ■ a place or occasion for presenting something favorably to general attention: *the gallery will provide* **a showcase for** *Atlanta's young photographers.*

▶*v.* [*trans.*] exhibit; display: *the albums showcase his production skills.*

show·down /ˈSHō,doun/ ▶*n.* a final test or confrontation intended to settle a dispute. ■ (in poker) the requirement at the end of a round that the players who remain in must show their cards to determine which is the strongest hand.

show·er /ˈSHou(-ə)r/ ▶*n.* **1** a brief and usually light fall of rain, hail, sleet, or snow. ■ a mass of small things falling or moving at the same time: *a* **shower of** *dust sprinkled his face.* ■ *figurative* a large number of things happening or given to someone at the same time: *he was pleased by the shower of awards.* ■ a group of particles produced by a cosmic-ray particle in the earth's atmosphere. **2** an enclosure in which a person stands under a spray of water to wash. ■ the apparatus that produces such a spray of water. ■ (also **shower bath**) an act of washing oneself in a shower. **3** [often with *adj.*] a party at which presents are given to someone, typically a woman who is about to get married or have a baby: *she loved going to baby showers.*

▶*v.* **1** [*intrans.*] (of a mass of small things) fall or be thrown in a shower: *bits of broken glass showered over me.* ■ [*trans.*] cause (a mass of small things) to fall in a shower: *his hooves showered sparks across the concrete floor.* ■ [*trans.*] (**shower someone with**) throw (a number of small things) all at once toward someone: *hooligans showered him with rotten eggs.* ■ [*trans.*] (**shower someone with**) give someone a great number of (things): *he showered her with kisses.* ■ [*trans.*] (**shower something on/upon**) give a great number of things to (someone): *senior officers showered praise on their young cadet.* **2** [*intrans.*] wash oneself in a shower. ▷Old English *scūr* 'light fall of rain, hail, etc.,' of Germanic origin; related to Dutch *schoer* and German *Schauer.*

▶**PHRASE** □ **send someone to the showers** *informal* cause someone to fail early on in a race or contest.

show·er·proof /ˈSHou(-ə)r,proof/ ▶*adj.* (of a garment) resistant to light rain.

▶*v.* [*trans.*] make showerproof.

show·er·y /ˈSHou(-ə)rē/ ▶*adj.* (of weather or a period of time) characterized by frequent showers of rain.

show·girl /ˈSHō,gərl/ ▶*n.* an actress who sings and dances in musicals, variety acts, and similar shows.

show house (also **show home**) ▶*n.* British term for MODEL HOME.

show·ing /ˈSHō-iNG/ ▶*n.* the action of showing something or the fact of being shown: *German shepherd, championship quality, excellent results in showing.* ■ a presentation of a movie or television program: *another showing of the three-part series.* ■ [with *adj.*] a performance of a specified quality: *a strong second-place showing in a recent Florida straw poll.* ▷Old English *scēawung.*

show jump·ing ▶*n.* the competitive sport of riding horses over a course of fences and other obstacles in an arena, with penalty points for errors. **—show jump** *n.* **—show jumper** *n.*

show·man /ˈSHōmən/ ▶*n.* (*pl.* **-men**) a person who produces or presents shows as a profession, esp. the proprietor, manager, or MC of a circus, fair, or other variety show. ■ a person skilled in dramatic or entertaining presentation, performance, or publicity. **—show·man·ship** /-,SHip/ *n.*

Show Me State a nickname for the state of MISSOURI.

shown /SHōn/ ▶ past participle of SHOW.

show-off ▶*n.* *informal* a person who acts pretentiously or who publicly parades themselves, their possessions, or their accomplishments.

show·piece /ˈSHō,pēs/ ▶*n.* something that attracts attention or admiration as an outstanding example of its type: *the factory has expanded and become a showpiece of American industry.* ■ something that offers a particular opportunity for a display of skill: *the serenade was a showpiece for the wind section.* ■ an item of work presented for exhibition or display.

show·place /ˈSHō,plās/ ▶*n.* a place of beauty or interest attracting many visitors.

show·reel /ˈSHō,rēl/ ▶*n.* a short videotape containing examples of an actor's or director's work for showing to potential employers.

show·room /ˈSHō,rōōm; -,rōōm/ ▶*n.* a room used to display goods for sale, such as appliances, cars, or furniture.

show-stop·per ▶*n.* *informal* a performance or item receiving prolonged applause. ■ something that is striking or has great popular appeal: *a show-stopper of a smile.* **—show-stop·ping** *adj.*

show tri·al ▶*n.* a judicial trial held in public with the intention of influencing or satisfying public opinion, rather than of ensuring justice.

show win·dow ▶*n.* a store window looking on to a street, used for exhibiting goods.

show·y /ˈSHō-ē/ ▶*adj.* (**show·i·er, show·i·est**) having a striking appearance or style, typically by being excessively bright, colorful, or ostentatious: *showy flowers* | *she wore a great deal of showy costume jewelry.* **—show·i·ly** /-əlē/ *adv.* **—show·i·ness** *n.*

sho·yu /ˈSHōyōō/ ▶*n.* a type of Japanese soy sauce. ▷from Japanese *shōyu.*

s.h.p. ▶*abbr.* shaft horsepower.

shpt. ▶*abbr.* shipment.

shr. ▶*abbr.* share; shares.

shrank /SHraNGk/ ▶ past of SHRINK.

shrap·nel /ˈSHrapnəl/ ▶*n.* fragments of a bomb, shell, or other object thrown out by an explosion. ▷early 19th cent.: named after General Henry *Shrapnel* (1761–1842), the British soldier who invented the shell.

shred /SHred/ ▶*n.* (usu. **shreds**) a strip of some material, such as paper, cloth, or food, that has been torn, cut, or scraped from something larger: *her beautiful dress was* **torn to shreds** *figurative my reputation will be* **in shreds.** ■ [often with *negative*] a very small amount: *there was not* **a shred of** *evidence that linked him to the fire.*

▶*v.* (**shredded, shredding**) [*trans.*] tear or cut into shreds: [as *adj.*] (**shredded**) *shredded cabbage.* ▷late

Pronunciation Key ə *ago*; ər *over*; ˈə or ,ə *up*; ˈər or ,ər *fur*; a *hat*; ā *rate*; ä *car*; CH *chew*; e *let*; ē *see*; e(ə)r *air*; i *fit*; ī *by*; i(ə)r *ear*; NG *sing*; ō *go*; ô *for*; oi *boy*; ŏŏ *good*; ōō *goo*; ou *out*; SH *she*; TH *thin*; TH *then*; (h)w *why*; ZH *vision*

Old English *scrēad* 'piece cut off,' *scrēadian* 'trim, prune'; related to **SHROUD**.

shred·ded wheat ▶*n.* a breakfast cereal made of cooked wheat in long brittle shreds that are pressed into compact pieces.

shred·der /ˈSHredər/ ▶*n.* **1** a machine or other device for shredding something, esp. documents. **2** *informal* a snowboarder. [from the notion that snowboarders tear up snow, making it bad for skiing.]

Shreve·port /ˈSHrēvˌpôrt/ an industrial city in northwestern Louisiana, on the Red River, near the border with Texas; pop. 200,145.

shrew /SHro͞o/ ▶*n.* a small mouselike insectivorous mammal with a long pointed snout and tiny eyes. • Family Soricidae: many genera, in particular *Sorex* and *Crocidura*, and numerous species. ■ a bad-tempered or aggressively assertive woman. ▷Old English *scrēawa, scrǣwa*, of Germanic origin; related words in Germanic languages have senses such as 'dwarf,' 'devil,' or 'fox.' **—shrew·ish** *adj.* **—shrew·ish·ly** *adv.* **—shrew·ish·ness** *n.*

shrewd /SHro͞od/ ▶*adj.* **1** having or showing sharp powers of judgment; astute: *she was shrewd enough to guess the motive behind his gesture* | *a shrewd career move.* See note at **KEEN**. **2** *archaic* (esp. of weather) piercingly cold: *a shrewd east wind.* ■ (of a blow) severe: *a bayonet's shrewd thrust.* ■ mischievous; malicious. ▷Middle English (in the sense 'evil in nature or character'): from **SHREW** in the sense 'evil person or thing,' or as the past participle of obsolete *shrew* 'to curse.' The word developed the sense 'cunning,' and gradually gained a favorable connotation during the 17th cent. **—shrewd·ly** *adv.* **—shrewd·ness** *n.*

shrew-mole ▶*n.* a small shrewlike mole with a long tail, native to Asia and North America. • *Neurotrichus* and other genera, family Talpidae: five species, including *N. gibbsii* of the western U.S.

Shri /SHrē/ ▶*n.* *Indian* variant spelling of **SRI**.

shriek /SHrēk/ ▶*v.* [*intrans.*] utter a high-pitched piercing sound or words, esp. as an expression of terror, pain, or excitement: *the audience* ***shrieked with laughter*** | [with *direct speech*] *"There it is!" she shrieked* | [*trans.*] *she was shrieking abuse at a taxi driver.* ■ (of something inanimate) make a high-pitched screeching sound: *the wheels shrieked as the car sped away.* ■ *figurative* be very obvious or strikingly discordant: *the patterned carpets shrieked at Betsy from the shabby store.*
▶*n.* a high-pitched piercing cry or sound; a scream: *shrieks of laughter.* ▷late 15th cent. (as a verb): imitative; compare with dialect *screak*, Old Norse *skrækja*, also with **SCREECH**. **—shriek·er** *n.*

shriev·al /ˈSHrēvəl/ ▶*adj.* *chiefly historical* of or relating to a sheriff. ▷late 17th cent.: from *shrieve*, obsolete variant of **SHERIFF**.

shriev·al·ty /ˈSHrēvəltē/ ▶*n.* (*pl.* **-ties**) *chiefly historical* the office, jurisdiction, or tenure of a sheriff.

shrift /SHrift/ ▶*n.* *archaic* confession, esp. to a priest: *go to shrift.* See also **SHORT SHRIFT**. ■ absolution by a priest. ▷Old English *scrift* 'penance imposed after confession,' from **SHRIVE**.

shrike /SHrīk/ ▶*n.* a songbird with a strong sharply hooked bill, often impaling its prey of small birds, lizards, and insects on thorns. Also called **BUTCHERBIRD**. • Family Laniidae: several genera and numerous species, esp. in Africa, e.g., the **northern shrike** (*Lanius excubitor*), of both Eurasia and North America. ■ used in names of similar birds of other families, e.g., **peppershrike**. ▷mid 16th cent.: perhaps related to Old English *scrīc* 'thrush' and Middle Low German *schrīk* 'corn crake,' of imitative origin.

shrill /SHril/ ▶*adj.* (of a voice or sound) high-pitched and piercing: *a shrill laugh.* ■ *derogatory* (esp. of a complaint or demand) loud and forceful: *a concession to their shrill demands.*
▶*v.* [*intrans.*] make a shrill noise: *a piercing whistle shrilled through the night air.* ■ speak or cry with a shrill voice: [with *direct speech*] *"For God's sake!" shrilled Jan.*
▶*n.* [in *sing.*] a shrill sound or cry: *the rising shrill of women's voices.* ▷late Middle English: of Germanic origin; related to Low German *schrell* 'sharp in tone or taste.' **—shrill·ness** *n.* **—shril·ly** /ˈSHri(l)lē/ *adv.*

shrimp /SHrimp/ ▶*n.* (*pl.* same or **shrimps**) a small free-swimming crustacean with an elongated body, typically marine and frequently harvested for food. • *Pandalus, Penaeus, Crangon*, and other genera, order Decapoda: numerous species, including the commercially important **pink shrimp** (*Penaeus duorarum*). ■ *informal, derogatory* a small, physically weak person.
▶*v.* [*intrans.*] fish for shrimp: [as *adj.*] (**shrimping**) *a shrimping net.* ▷Middle English: probably related to Middle Low German *schrempen* 'to wrinkle,' Middle High German *schrimpfen* 'to contract,' also to **SCRIMP**. **—shrimp·y** *adj.*

shrimp·er /ˈSHrimpər/ ▶*n.* **1** a boat designed or used for catching shrimp. **2** a person who fishes for shrimp.

shrimp plant ▶*n.* an evergreen Mexican shrub with clusters of small flowers in pinkish-brown or pale yellow bracts that are said to resemble shrimp, widely grown as a houseplant. • *Justicia brandegeana*, family Acanthaceae.

shrine /SHrīn/ ▶*n.* a place regarded as holy because of its associations with a divinity or a sacred person or relic, typically marked by a building or other construction. ■ a place associated with or containing memorabilia of a particular revered person or thing: *her grave has become a shrine for fans from all over the world.* ■ a casket containing sacred relics; a reliquary. ■ a niche or enclosure containing a religious statue or other object.
▶*v.* [*trans.*] *poetic/literary* enshrine. ▷Old English *scrīn* 'cabinet, chest, reliquary,' of Germanic origin; related to Dutch *schrijn* and German *Schrein*, from Latin *scrinium* 'chest for books.'

Shrin·er /ˈSHrīnər/ ▶*n.* a member of the Ancient Arabic Order of Nobles of the Mystic Shrine, a charitable society founded in the U.S. in 1872.

shrink /SHriNGk/ ▶*v.* (*past* **shrank** /SHraNGk/; *past part.* **shrunk** /SHrəNGk/ or (esp. as *adj.*) **shrunk·en** /ˈSHrəNGkən/) **1** become or make smaller in size or amount; contract or cause to contract: [*intrans.*] *the workforce has shrunk to less than a thousand* [*trans.*] *the summer sun had shrunk and dried the wood.* ■ [*intrans.*] (of clothes or material) become smaller as a result of being immersed in water. ■ [as *adj.*] (**shrunken**) (esp. of a person's face or other part of the body) withered, wrinkled, or shriveled through old age or illness: *a tiny shrunken face and enormous eyes.* ■ [*intrans.*] (**shrink into oneself**) become withdrawn. ■ [*trans.*] (**shrink something on**) slip a metal tire or other fitting on to (something) while it is expanded with heat and allow it to tighten in place: *the metal is unsuitable for shrinking onto wooden staves.* **2** [*intrans.*] move back or away, esp. because of fear or disgust: *she shrank away from him, covering her face* | *he shrank back against the wall.* ■ [often with *negative*] (**shrink from**) be averse to or unwilling to do (something difficult or unappealing): *I don't shrink from my responsibilities.*
▶*n.* *informal* a clinical psychologist, psychiatrist, or psychotherapist: *you should see a shrink.* [from *headshrinker*.] ▷Old English *scrincan*, of Germanic origin; related to Swedish *skrynka* 'to wrinkle.' **—shrink·a·ble** *adj.* **—shrink·er** *n.* **—shrink·ing·ly** *adv.*

shrink·age /ˈSHriNGkij/ ▶*n.* the process, fact, or amount of shrinking: *give long curtains good hems to allow for shrinkage.* ■ an allowance made for reduction in the earnings of a business due to wastage or theft.

shrink-fit ▶*adj.* designed to fit perfectly after anticipated shrinkage: *a shrink-fit chuck.*
▶*n.* a system that uses shrink-fit parts or fittings.

shrink·ing vi·o·let ▶*n.* *informal* an exaggeratedly shy person: *Dorothy is no shrinking violet when it comes to expressing her views.*

shrink-re·sist·ant ▶*adj.* (of textiles or garments) resistant to shrinkage.

shrink-wrap ▶*v.* [*trans.*] package (an article) by enclosing it in clinging transparent plastic film that shrinks tightly onto it: [as *adj.*] (**shrink-wrapped**) *shrink-wrapped blocks of cheese.* ■ [as *adj.*] (**shrink-wrapped**) *Computing* (of a product) sold commercially as a ready-made software package.
▶*n.* clinging transparent plastic film used to enclose an article as packaging.

shrive /SHrīv/ ▶*v.* (*past* **shrove** /SHrōv/; *past part.* **shriv·en** /ˈSHrivən/) [*trans.*] *archaic* (of a priest) hear the confession of, assign penance to, and absolve (someone). ■ (**shrive oneself**) present oneself to a priest for confession, penance, and absolution. ▷Old English *scrīfan* 'impose as a penance,' of Germanic origin; related to Dutch *schrijven* and German *schreiben* 'write,' from Latin *scribere* 'write.'

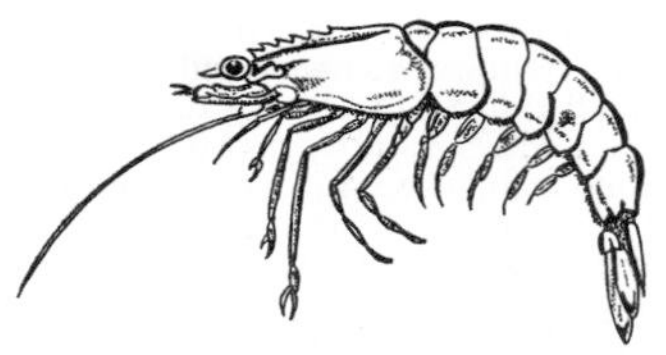
pink shrimp

shriv·el /ˈSHrivəl/ ▶*v.* (**-eled, -el·ing**; *Brit.* **-elled, -el·ling**) wrinkle and contract or cause to wrinkle and contract, esp. due to loss of moisture: [*intrans.*] *the flowers simply* ***shriveled up*** | [*trans.*] *a heat wave so intense that it shriveled the grapes in every vineyard.* ■ [*intrans.*] *figurative* lose momentum, will, or desire; become insignificant or ineffectual: *under the reign of the Nazis, German universities shriveled as centers of learning.* ■ [*trans.*] *figurative* cause to feel worthless or insignificant: *she shriveled him with one glance.* ▷mid 16th cent.: perhaps of Scandinavian origin; compare with Swedish dialect *skryvla* 'to wrinkle.'

shriv·en /ˈSHrivən/ ▶ past participle of **SHRIVE**.

shroud /SHroud/ ▶*n.* **1** a length of cloth or an enveloping garment in which a dead person is wrapped for burial: *he was buried in a linen shroud.* ■ *figurative* a thing that envelops or obscures something: ***a shroud of*** *mist* | *they operate behind a shroud of secrecy.* ■ *technical* a protective casing or cover. **2** (**shrouds**) a set of ropes forming part of the standing rigging of a sailing vessel and supporting the mast from the sides. ■ (also **shroud line**) each of the lines joining the canopy of a parachute to the harness.
▶*v.* [*trans.*] wrap or dress (a body) in a shroud for burial. ■ *figurative* cover or envelop so as to conceal from view: *mountains shrouded by cloud* | *the mystery that shrouds the origins of the universe.* ▷late Old English *scrūd* 'garment, clothing,' of Germanic origin, from a base meaning 'cut'; related to **SHRED**. An early sense of the verb (Middle English) was 'cover so as to protect.'

shroud-laid ▶*adj.* (of rope) made of four strands laid right-handed, typically around a core, used esp. on yachts.

shrove /SHrōv/ ▶ past of **SHRIVE**.

Shrove·tide /ˈSHrōvˌtīd/ ▶*n.* Shrove Tuesday and the two days preceding it, when it was formerly customary to attend confession. ▷late Middle English: of obscure origin; the first element related to **SHRIVE**.

Shrove Tues·day /SHrōv/ ▶*n.* the day before Ash Wednesday. Though named for its former religious significance, it is chiefly marked by feasting and celebration, which traditionally preceded the observance of the Lenten fast. Compare with **MARDI GRAS**.

shrub[1] /SHrəb/ ▶*n.* a woody plant that is smaller than a tree and has several main stems arising at or near the ground. ▷Old English *scrubb, scrybb* 'shrubbery'; compare with West Flemish *schrobbe* 'vetch,' Norwegian *skrubba* 'dwarf cornel,' also with **SCRUB**[2]. **—shrub·by** *adj.*

shrub[2] ▶*n.* **1** a drink made of sweetened fruit juice and liquor, typically rum or brandy. **2** a slightly acid cordial made from fruit juice and water. ▷early 18th cent.: from Arabic *šurb, šarāb*, from *šariba* 'to drink'; compare with **SHERBET** and **SYRUP**.

shrub·ber·y /ˈSHrəb(ə)rē/ ▶*n.* shrubs collectively. ■ (*pl.* **-ber·ies**) an area planted with shrubs.

shrug /SHrəg/ ▶*v.* (**shrugged, shrug·ging**) [*trans.*] raise (one's shoulders) slightly and momentarily to express doubt, ignorance, or indifference: *Jimmy looked inquiringly at Pete, who shrugged his shoulders* | [*intrans.*] *he just shrugged and didn't look interested.* ■ (**shrug something off**) dismiss something as unimportant: *the managing director shrugged off the criticism.*
▶*n.* **1** an act or instance of shrugging one's shoulders: *she gave him a dismissive shrug.* **2** a woman's close-fitting cardigan or jacket, cut short at the front and back so that only the arms and shoulders are covered. ▷late Middle English (in the sense 'fidget'): of unknown origin.

shrunk /SHrəNGk/ (also **shrunk·en**) ▶ past participle of **SHRINK**.

shtetl /ˈSHtetl; ˈSHtātl/ ▶*n.* (*pl.* **shtet·lach** /ˈSHtetläKH; ˈSHtätläKH/ or **shtetls**) *historical* a small Jewish town or village in eastern Europe. ▷1940s: Yiddish, 'little town.'

shtick /SHtik/ ▶*n.* *informal* an attention-getting or theatrical routine, gimmick, or talent. ▷1960s: Yiddish, from German *Stück* 'piece.'

shtup /SHto͝op/ (also **schtup**) *vulgar slang* ▶*v.* (**shtupped, shtup·ping**) [*trans.*] have sexual intercourse with (someone).
▶*n.* an act of sexual intercourse. ▷1960s: Yiddish.

shu·bun·kin /SHo͞oˈbəNGkin; ˈSHo͞obənˌkin/ ▶*n.* a goldfish of an ornamental variety, having black spots, red patches, and long fins and tail. ▷early 20th cent.: from Japanese.

shuck /SHək/ ▸*n.* **1** an outer covering such as a husk or pod, esp. the husk of an ear of corn. ■ the shell of an oyster or clam. ■ the integument of certain insect pupae or larvae. **2** *informal* a person or thing regarded as worthless or contemptible: *William didn't dig the idea at all and said it was a shuck.*

▸*exclam.* (**shucks**) *informal* used to express surprise, regret, irritation, or, in response to praise, self-deprecation: *"Thank you for getting it." "Oh, shucks, it was nothing."* See also AW-SHUCKS.

▸*v.* [*trans.*] **1** remove the shucks from corn or shellfish: *shuck and drain the oysters.* ■ *informal* take off (a garment): *she shucked off her nightdress and started dressing.* ■ *informal* abandon; get rid of: *the regime's ability to* ***shuck off*** *its totalitarian characteristics.* **2** *informal* cause (someone) to believe something that is not true; fool or tease. ▷late 17th cent.: of unknown origin. —**shuck·er** *n.*

shud·der /ˈSHədər/ ▸*v.* [*intrans.*] (of a person) tremble convulsively, typically as a result of fear or repugnance: *he shuddered with revulsion* | [with *infinitive*] *figurative I* ***shudder to think*** *of retirement.* See note at SHAKE. ■ (esp. of a vehicle, machine, or building) shake or vibrate deeply: *the train shuddered and edged forward.* ■ [usu. as *adj.*] (**shuddering**) (of a person's breathing) be unsteady, esp. as a result of emotional disturbance: *he drew a deep, shuddering breath.*

▸*n.* an act of shuddering: *the elevator rose with a shudder* | *figurative the peso's devaluation* ***sent shudders through*** *the market.* ▷Middle English (as a verb): from Middle Dutch *schûderen*, from a Germanic base meaning 'shake.' —**shud·der·ing·ly** *adv.* —**shud·der·y** *adj.*

▸*PHRASE* □ **give someone the shudders** *informal* cause someone to feel repugnance or fear: *it gives me the shudders to hear you use words like that.*

Shu·dra (also **Su·dra**) /ˈsōōdrə/ ▸*n.* a member of the worker caste, lowest of the four Hindu castes. ▷from Sanskrit *śūdra*.

shuf·fle /ˈSHəfəl/ ▸*v.* **1** [*intrans.*] walk by dragging one's feet along or without lifting them fully from the ground: *I stepped into my skis and shuffled to the edge of the steep slope* | [as *adj.*] (**shuffling**) *she heard Grandma's shuffling steps.* ■ shift one's position while sitting or move one's feet while standing, typically because of boredom, nervousness, or embarrassment: *Christine shuffled uneasily in her chair* | [*trans.*] *Ben shuffled his feet in the awkward silence.* **2** [*trans.*] rearrange (a deck of cards) by sliding the cards over each other quickly. ■ move (people or things) around so as to occupy different positions or to be in a different order: *she shuffled her papers into a neat pile.* ■ [*intrans.*] (**shuffle through**) sort or look through (a number of things) hurriedly: *he shuffled through the papers on his desk.* **3** [*trans.*] (**shuffle something into**) put part of one's body into (an item of clothing), typically in a clumsy way: *shuffling her feet into a pair of shoes, she tiptoed out of the room.* ■ (**shuffle something off**) get out of or avoid a responsibility or obligation: *some hospitals can shuffle off their responsibilities by claiming to have no suitable facilities.* ■ [*intrans.*] *archaic* behave in a shifty or evasive manner: *Mr. Mills did not frankly own it, but seemed to shuffle about it.* ■ [*intrans.*] (**shuffle out of**) *archaic* get out of (a difficult situation) in an underhanded or evasive manner: *he shuffles out of the consequences by vague charges of undue influence.*

▸*n.* **1** [in *sing.*] a shuffling movement, walk, or sound: *there was a shuffle of approaching feet.* ■ a quick dragging or scraping movement of the feet in dancing. ■ a dance performed with such steps. ■ a piece of music for or in the style of such a dance. ■ a rhythmic motif based on such a dance step and typical of early jazz, consisting of alternating quarter notes and eighth notes in a triplet pattern. **2** an act of shuffling a deck of cards. ■ a change of order or relative positions; a reshuffle: *the president will deliver a speech short on economic details Cabinet shuffles but long on fight.* ■ a facility on a CD player for playing tracks in an arbitrary order: [as *adj.*] *a fully programmable CD changer with shuffle play.* **3** *archaic* a piece of equivocation or subterfuge. ▷mid 16th cent.: perhaps from Low German *schuffeln* 'walk clumsily,' also 'deal dishonestly, shuffle (cards),' of Germanic origin; related to SHOVE and SCUFFLE. —**shuf·fler** /ˈSHəf(ə)lər/ *n.*

▸*PHRASES* □ **be** (or **get**) **lost in the shuffle** *informal* be overlooked or missed in a confused or crowded situation. □ **shuffle off this mortal coil** see COIL[2].

shuf·fle·board /ˈSHəfəlˌbôrd/ ▸*n.* a game played by pushing disks with a long-handled cue over a marked surface. ▷see SHOVELBOARD.

shuf·ti /ˈSHōōftē/ ▸*n.* (*pl.* **-tis** /-tēz/) *Brit., informal* a look or reconnoiter, esp. a quick one: *I'll take a shufti round the wood while I'm about it.* ▷1940s (originally military slang): from Arabic *šāfa* 'try to see.'

shul /SHōōl; SHŏŏl/ ▸*n.* a synagogue: *on High Holidays he attended shul.* ▷late 19th cent.: Yiddish, from German *Schule* 'school.'

Shu·la /ˈSHōōlə/, Don(ald Francis) (1930–), U.S. football coach and player. After seven seasons of playing professional football, he coached the Baltimore Colts 1963–69 and then the Miami Dolphins 1970–95. Upon his retirement in 1995, he had achieved a record 347 regular season and playoff games won. Football Hall of Fame (1997).

shu·mai /ˈSHōōˌmī/ ▸*plural n.* small steamed dumplings, typically stuffed with seafood and vegetables. ▷Japanese, ultimately from Chinese.

Shu·men /ˈSHōōˌmen/ an industrial city in northeastern Bulgaria; pop. 126,000.

shun /SHən/ ▸*v.* (**shunned**, **shun·ning**) [*trans.*] persistently avoid, ignore, or reject (someone or something) through antipathy or caution: *he shunned fashionable society.* ▷Old English *scunian* 'abhor, shrink back with fear, seek safety from an enemy,' of unknown origin.

shunt /SHənt/ ▸*v.* **1** [*trans.*] push or pull (a train or part of a train) from the main line to a siding or from one track to another: *their train had been shunted into a siding.* ■ (usu. **be shunted**) push or shove (someone or something): *chairs were being shunted back and forth.* ■ direct or divert (someone or something) to a less important place or position: *amateurs were gradually being shunted to filing jobs.* **2** [*trans.*] provide (an electrical current) with a conductor joining two points of a circuit, through which more or less of the current may be diverted.

▸*n.* **1** an act of pushing or shoving something. **2** an electrical conductor joining two points of a circuit, through which more or less of a current may be diverted. ■ *Surgery* an alternative path for the passage of the blood or other body fluid: [as *adj.*] *shunt surgery.* ▷Middle English (in the sense 'move suddenly aside'): perhaps from SHUN.

shunt·er /ˈSHəntər/ ▸*n.* a small locomotive used for shunting. ■ a railroad worker engaged in such work, esp. to couple and uncouple wagons.

shun·ya·ta /ˈSHōōnyəˌtä/ (also **sun·ya·ta**) ▸*n.* *Buddhism* the doctrine that phenomena are devoid of an immutable or determinate intrinsic nature. Compare with TATHATA. ▷from Sanskrit *śūnyatā* 'emptiness.'

shu·ra /ˈSHŏŏrə/ ▸*n.* *Islam* the principle of consultation, in particular as applied to government. ■ a consultative council. ▷from Arabic *šūrā* 'consultation.'

shu·ri·ken /ˈSHŏŏriˌken/ ▸*n.* a weapon in the form of a star with projecting blades or points, used as a missile in some martial arts. ▷Japanese, literally 'dagger in the hand.'

shush /SHŏŏSH; SHəSH/ ▸*exclam.* be quiet: *"Shush! Do you want to wake everyone?"*

▸*n.* **1** an utterance of "shush": *the thumps were followed by shushes from the aunts.* **2** *chiefly Brit.* a soft swishing or rustling sound.

▸*v.* **1** [*trans.*] tell or signal (someone) to be silent: *she shushed him with a wave.* ■ [*intrans.*] become or remain silent: *Beth told her to shush.* **2** [*intrans.*] *chiefly Brit.* move with or make a soft swishing or rustling sound: *I stood to watch a big liner shushing slowly past* | [as *n.*] (**shushing**) *she could hear the gentle shushing of the waves.* ▷1920s: imitative.

Shu·swap /ˈSHōōˌswäp/ ▸*n.* (*pl.* same or **-swaps**) **1** a member of an American Indian people of southern British Columbia. **2** the Salishan language of this people.

▸*adj.* of or relating to this people or their language. ▷from the Shuswap self-designation *sexwépemc*.

shut /SHət/ ▸*v.* (**shut·ting**; *past* **shut**) [*trans.*] move (something) into position so that it blocks an opening: *shut the window, please* | *she shut her lips tight* | [as *adj.*] (**shut**) *she slammed the door shut.* ■ [*intrans.*] (of something that can block an opening) move or be moved into position: *the door shut behind him.* ■ block an opening into (something) by moving something into position: *he shut the box and locked it.* ■ (**shut it**) [in *imperative*] *Brit., informal* stop talking; be quiet. ■ [*trans.*] keep (someone or something) in a place by closing something such as a door: *it was his own dog that he had accidentally shut outside.* ■ fold or bring together the sides of (something) so as to close it: *he shut his book.* ■ prevent access to or along: *they ought to shut the path up to that terrible cliff.* ■ make or become unavailable for business or service, either permanently or until due to be open again; close: [*trans.*] *we shut the shop for lunch* | [*intrans.*] *the accident and emergency departments will shut.*

▸*phrasal v.* □ **shut down** (or **shut something down**) cease (or cause something to cease) business or operation: *the plant's operators decided to shut down the reactor.* □ **shut someone/something in** keep someone or something inside a place by closing something such as a door: *her parents shut her in an upstairs room.* ■ enclose or surround a place: *the village is shut in by the mountains on either side.* ■ trap something by shutting a door or drawer on it: *you shut your finger in the door.* □ **shut off** (or **shut something off**) (used esp. in relation to water, electricity, or gas) stop (or cause something to stop) flowing: *he was about to shut off the power.* ■ stop (or cause something to stop) working: *the engines shut off automatically.* ■ (**shut something off**) block the entrances and exits of something: *the six compartments were being shut off from each other.* □ **shut oneself off** isolate oneself from other people. □ **shut someone/something out** keep someone or something out of a place or situation: *the door swung closed behind them, shutting out some of the noise* ■ prevent an opponent from scoring in a game. ■ screen someone or something from view: *clouds shut out the stars.* ■ prevent something from occurring: *there was a high-mindedness that shut out any consideration of alternatives.* ■ block something such as a painful memory from the mind: *anything he didn't like he shut out.* □ **shut up** (or **shut someone up**) [often in *imperative*] *informal* stop (or cause someone to stop) talking: *just shut up and listen* | *I lifted a finger slightly to shut him up.* □ **shut something up** close all doors and windows of a building or room, typically because it will be unoccupied for some time. ▷Old English *scyttan* 'put (a bolt) in position to hold fast'; related to Dutch *schutten* 'shut up, obstruct,' also to SHOOT.

▸*PHRASES* □ **be** (or **get**) **shut of** *informal* be (or get) rid of: *I'd be glad to be shut of him.* □ **shut the door on** (or **to**) see DOOR. □ **shut one's eyes to** see EYE. □ **shut one's mind to** see MIND. □ **shut the stable door after the horse has bolted** try to avoid or prevent something bad or unwelcome when it is already too late to do so. □ **shut up shop** see SHOP. □ **shut your face** (or **mouth** or **trap**) ! *informal* used as a rude or angry way of telling someone to be quiet.

shut·down /ˈSHətˌdoun/ ▸*n.* a closure of a factory or system, typically a temporary closure due to a malfunction or for maintenance. ■ a turning off of a computer or computer system.

Shute /SHōōt/, Nevil (1899–1960), English novelist; pseudonym of *Nevil Shute Norway*. After World War II he settled in Australia, which provides the setting for his later novels. Notable works: *A Town Like Alice* (1950) and *On the Beach* (1957).

shut-eye ▸*n.* *informal* sleep: *we'd better get some shut-eye.*

shut-in ▸*n.* **1** a person confined indoors, esp. as a result of physical or mental disability. **2** a state or period in which an oil or gas well has available but unused capacity.

shut-off (also **shut-off**) ▸*n.* [usu. as *adj.*] a device used for stopping a supply or operation: *a shutoff valve.* ■ the cessation of flow, supply, or activity.

shut·out /ˈSHətˌout/ ▸*n.* a competition or game in which the losing side fails to score.

shut·out bid ▸*n.* *Bridge* a high bid intended to end the auction; a preemptive bid.

shut·ter /ˈSHətər/ ▸*n.* **1** each of a pair of hinged panels, often louvered, fixed inside or outside a window that can be closed for security or privacy or to keep out light. **2** *Photography* a device that opens and closes to expose the film in a camera. **3** *Music* the blind enclosing the swell box in an organ, used for controlling the volume of sound.

▸*v.* [*trans.*] close the shutters of (a window or building): *the windows were shuttered against the afternoon heat* | [as *adj.*] (**shuttered**) *barred and shuttered stores.* ■ close (a business): *the city was gripped by economic forces that were squeezing its tax base and shuttering its factories.* —**shut·ter·less** *adj.*

shut·ter·bug /ˈSHətərˌbəg/ ▸*n.* *informal* an enthusiastic amateur photographer.

shut·ter·ing /ˈSHətəriNG/ ▸*n.* wood in planks or strips used as a temporary structure for fencing to contain setting concrete, to support the sides of dirt trenches, or for similar purposes. ■ a temporary structure of this kind.

shut·ter pri·or·i·ty ▸*n. Photography* a system used in some automatic cameras in which the shutter speed is selected by the user and the appropriate aperture is then set by the camera. Compare with **APERTURE PRIORITY**.

shut·ter re·lease ▸*n.* the button on a camera that is pressed to make the shutter open.

shut·ter speed ▸*n. Photography* the time for which a shutter is open at a given setting.

shut·tle /ˈsHətl/ ▸*n.* **1** a form of transportation that travels regularly between two places: *the nine o'clock shuttle from Boston* | [as *adj.*] *a shuttle bus service from the city center.* ■ short for **SPACE SHUTTLE**. **2** a wooden device with two pointed ends holding a bobbin, used for carrying the weft thread between the warp threads in weaving. ■ a bobbin carrying the lower thread in a sewing machine. **3** short for **SHUTTLECOCK**.
▸*v.* [*intrans.*] travel regularly between two or more places: *a container ship that shuttled between Rotterdam and the Persian Gulf.* ■ [*trans.*] transport in a shuttle: *the river taxi shuttled employees between the newspaper's offices and the capital.* ▷Old English *scytel* 'dart, missile,' of Germanic origin; compare with Old Norse *skutill* 'harpoon'; related to **SHOOT**. Sense 1 and the verb are from the movement of the bobbin from one side of the loom to the other and back.

shut·tle·cock /ˈsHətl,käk/ ▸*n.* a cork to which feathers are attached to form a cone shape, or a similar object of plastic, struck with rackets in the games of badminton and battledore.

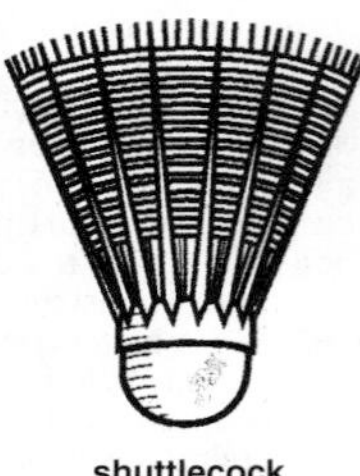
shuttlecock

shut·tle·craft /ˈsHətl,kraft/ ▸*n.* (in science fiction) a space shuttle, typically one used for traveling between a larger spaceship and a planet or between planets in a solar system.

shut·tle di·plo·ma·cy ▸*n.* negotiations conducted by a mediator who travels between two or more parties that are reluctant to hold direct discussions.

shy[1] /sHī/ ▸*adj.* (**shy·er**, **shy·est**) **1** being reserved or having or showing nervousness or timidity in the company of other people: *I was pretty shy at school* | *a shy smile.* ■ [*predic.*] (**shy about**) slow or reluctant to do (something): *she has never been shy about discussing her efforts to raise aesthetic standards.* ■ [in *combination*] having a dislike of or aversion to a specified thing: *they were a little camera-shy.* ■ (of a wild mammal or bird) reluctant to remain in sight of humans. **2** [*predic.*] (**shy of**) *informal* less than; short of: *he won the championship with a score three points shy of a world record.* ■ before: *he left school just shy of his fourteenth birthday.* **3** (of a plant) not bearing flowers or fruit well or prolifically.
▸*v.* (**shies**, **shied**) [*intrans.*] (esp. of a horse) start suddenly aside in fright at an object, noise, or movement. ■ (**shy from**) avoid doing or becoming involved in (something) due to nervousness or a lack of confidence: *don't* **shy away from** *saying what you think.*
▸*n.* a sudden startled movement, esp. of a frightened horse. ▷Old English *scēoh* '(of a horse) easily frightened,' of Germanic origin; related to German *scheuen* 'shun,' *scheuchen* 'scare'; compare with **ESCHEW**. The verb dates from the mid 17th cent. —**shy·er** /ˈsHī(ə)r/ *n.* —**shy·ly** *adv.* —**shy·ness** *n.*

shy[2] *dated* ▸*v.* (**shies**, **shied**) [*trans.*] fling or throw (something) at a target: *he tore the glasses off and shied them at her.*
▸*n.* (*pl.* **shies**) an act of flinging or throwing something at a target. ▷late 18th cent.: of unknown origin.
▸*PHRASE* □ **have a shy at** try to hit something, esp. with a ball or stone. ■ *archaic* attempt to do or obtain something. ■ *archaic* jeer at: *you are always having a shy at Lady Ann and her relations.*

Shy·lock /ˈsHī,läk/ a Jewish moneylender in Shakespeare's *Merchant of Venice*, who lends money to Antonio but demands in return a pound of Antonio's own flesh should the debt not be repaid on time. ■ [as *n.*] (**a Shylock**) a moneylender who charges extremely high rates of interest.

shy·ster /ˈsHīstər/ ▸*n. informal* a person, esp. a lawyer, who uses unscrupulous, fraudulent, or deceptive methods in business. ▷mid 19th cent.: origin uncertain; perhaps related to German *Scheisser* 'worthless person.'

SI ▸*abbr.* ■ the international system of units of measurement. [from French *Système International*.] ■ *Law* statutory instrument.

Si ▸*symbol* the chemical element silicon.

si /sē/ ▸*n. Music* another term for **TI**. ▷early 18th cent.: from the initial letters of *Sancte Iohannes*, the closing words of a Latin hymn (see **SOLMIZATION**).

Sia·chen Glac·ier /ˈsyäcHən/ a glacier in the Karakoram mountains in northwestern India, at an altitude of about 17,800 feet (5,500 m). Extending over 44 miles (70 km), it is one of the world's longest glaciers.

si·al /ˈsī,al/ ▸*n. Geology* the material of the upper or continental part of the earth's crust, characterized as being of relatively low density and rich in silica and alumina. Contrasted with **SIMA**. ▷1920s: from the initial letters of **SILICA** and **ALUMINA**.

si·al·a·gogue /sīˈalə,gäg/ ▸*n. Medicine* a drug that promotes the secretion of saliva. ▷late 18th cent.: from French, from Greek *sialon* 'saliva' + *agōgos* 'leading.'

si·al·ic ac·id /sīˈalik/ ▸*n. Biochemistry* a substance present in saliva that consists of acyl derivatives of neuraminic acid. ▷1950s: *sialic* from Greek *sialon* 'saliva' + **-IC**.

si·al·i·dase /sīˈälidās/ ▸*n.* another term for **NEURAMINIDASE**. ▷1950s: from Greek *sialon* 'saliva' + **-IDE** + **-ASE**.

Si·al·kot /sēˈälkōt/ an industrial city in the province of Punjab, in Pakistan; pop. 296,000.

Si·am /sīˈam/ former name (until 1939) of **THAILAND**.

Si·am, Gulf of former name of the Gulf of Thailand (see **THAILAND, GULF OF**).

si·a·mang /ˈsēə,mäNG/ ▸*n.* a large black gibbon native to Sumatra and the Malay peninsula. • *Hylobates syndactylus*, family Hylobatidae. ▷early 19th cent.: from Malay.

Si·a·mese /,sīəˈmēz/ ▸*n.* (*pl.* same) **1** *dated* a native of Siam (now Thailand). **2** old-fashioned term for **THAI** (the language). **3** (also **Siamese cat**) a cat of a lightly built short-haired breed characterized by slanting blue eyes and typically pale fur with darker points.
▸*adj. dated* of or concerning Siam, its people, or language.

Si·a·mese fight·ing fish ▸*n.* see **FIGHTING FISH**.

Si·a·mese twins ▸*plural n.* twins that are physically joined at birth, sometimes sharing organs, and sometimes separable by surgery (depending on the degree of fusion). ▷with reference to the *Siamese* men Chang and Eng (1811–74), who, despite being joined at the waist, led an active life.

USAGE See usage at **CONJOINED TWIN**.

SIB ▸*abbr. Brit.* Securities and Investment Board, a regulatory body that oversees London's financial markets.

sib /sib/ ▸*n.* **1** *chiefly Zoology* a brother or sister; a sibling. **2** *Anthropology* a group of people recognized by an individual as his or her kindred. ▷Old English, 'related by birth or descent,' of unknown origin. Sense 1 dates from the early 20th cent.

Si·be·li·us /sīˈbälēəs/, Jean (1865–1957), Finnish composer; born *Johan Julius Christian Sibelius*. His affinity for his country's landscape and legends, esp. the epic *Kalevala*, is expressed in a series of symphonic poems including *The Swan of Tuonela* (1893), *Finlandia* (1899), and *Tapiola* (1925).

Ši·be·nik /sHēˈbenik/ an industrial city and port in Croatia, on the Adriatic coast; pop. 41,000.

Si·be·ri·a /sīˈbi(ə)rēə/ a vast region of Russia that extends from the Ural Mountains to the Pacific Ocean and from the Arctic coast to the northern borders of Kazakhstan, Mongolia, and China. Noted for the severity of its winters, it was traditionally used as a place of exile; it is now a major source of minerals and hydroelectric power. —**Si·be·ri·an** *adj.* & *n.*

Si·be·ri·an ti·ger ▸*n.* a tiger of a large and threatened race with a long thick coat, found in southeastern Siberia and northeastern China.

sib·i·lant /ˈsibələnt/ ▸*adj. Phonetics* (of a speech sound) sounded with a hissing effect, for example *s*, *sh*. ■ making or characterized by a hissing sound: *his sibilant whisper.*
▸*n. Phonetics* a sibilant speech sound. ▷mid 17th cent.: from Latin *sibilant-* 'hissing,' from the verb *sibilare*. —**sib·i·lance** *n.*

sib·i·late /ˈsibə,lāt/ ▸*v.* [*trans.*] utter with a hissing sound. ▷mid 17th cent.: from Latin *sibilat-* 'hissed, whistled,' from the verb *sibilare*. —**sib·i·la·tion** /,sibəˈlāsHən/ *n.*

Si·biu /sēˈbyo͞o/ an industrial city in central Romania; pop. 188,000.

sib·li·cide /ˈsibli,sīd/ ▸*n. Zoology* the killing of a sibling or siblings, as a behavior pattern typical in various animal groups.

sib·ling /ˈsibliNG/ ▸*n.* each of two or more children or offspring having one or both parents in common; a brother or sister. ▷Old English in the sense 'relative' (see **SIB**, **-LING**). The current sense dates from the early 20th cent.

sib·ship /ˈsibsHip/ ▸*n. chiefly Zoology* a group of offspring having the same two parents. ■ *Anthropology* the state of belonging to a sib or the same sib.

sib·yl /ˈsibəl/ ▸*n.* a woman in ancient times supposed to utter the oracles and prophecies of a god. ■ *poetic/literary* a woman able to foretell the future. ▷from Old French *Sibile* or medieval Latin *Sibilla*, via Latin from Greek *Sibulla*. —**sib·yl·line** /ˈsibə,līn; -,lēn/ *adj.*

sic[1] /sik/ ▸*adv.* used in brackets after a copied or quoted word that appears odd or erroneous to show that the word is quoted exactly as it stands in the original, as in *a story must hold a child's interest and "enrich his [sic] life."* ▷Latin, literally 'so, thus.'

sic[2] (also **sick**) ▸*v.* (**sicced**, **sic·cing** or **sicked**, **sick·ing**) [*trans.*] (**sic something on**) set a dog or other animal on (someone or something): *the plan was to surprise the heck out of the grizzly by sicking the dog on him.* ■ (**sic someone on**) *informal* set someone to pursue, keep watch on, or accompany (another). ▷mid 19th cent.: dialect variant of **SEEK**.

Sic. ▸*abbr.* ■ Sicilian. ■ Sicily.

sic·ca·tive /ˈsikətiv/ ▸*n.* a drying agent used as a component of paint. ▷late Middle English: from late Latin *siccativus*, from *siccare* 'to dry.'

Si·chuan /ˈsicHˈwän; ˈsœcH-/ (also **Sze·chuan** or **Sze·chwan** /ˈsecH-/) a province in west central China; capital, Chengdu.

Si·ci·lia /siˈsilyə; sēˈcHēlyä/ Italian name for **SICILY**.

si·cil·i·a·no /sə,silēˈänō/ (also **si·cil·i·a·na**) ▸*n.* (*pl.* **-nos**) a dance, song, or instrumental piece in 6/8 or 12/8 time and evoking a pastoral mood. ▷Italian, literally 'Sicilian.'

Si·cil·ian Ves·pers /səˈsilēən; -yən ˈvespərz/ a massacre of French inhabitants of Sicily that began near Palermo at the time of vespers on Easter Monday in 1282. The ensuing war resulted in the replacement of the unpopular French Angevin dynasty by the Spanish House of Aragon.

Sic·i·ly /ˈsisəlē/ a large Italian island in the Mediterranean Sea, off the southwestern tip of Italy; capital, Palermo. It is separated from the Italian mainland by the Strait of Messina. Its highest point is Mount Etna. Italian name **SICILIA**. —**Si·cil·ian** /siˈsilyən/ *adj.* & *n.*

sick[1] /sik/ ▸*adj.* **1** affected by physical or mental illness: *nursing very sick children* | *we were* **sick with** *bronchitis* [as *plural n.*] (**the sick**) *visiting the sick and the elderly.* ■ of or relating to those who are ill: *the company organized a sick fund for its workers.* ■ *figurative* (of an organization, system, or society) suffering from serious problems, esp. of a financial nature: *their economy remains sick.* ■ *archaic* pining or longing for someone or something: *he was* **sick for** *a sight of her.* **2** [*predic.*] feeling nauseous and wanting to vomit: *he was starting to feel sick* | *Mark felt sick with fear.* ■ [*attrib.*] (of an emotion) so intense as to cause one to feel unwell or nauseous: *he had a sick fear of returning.* ■ *informal* disappointed, mortified, or miserable: *he looked pretty sick at that, but he eventually agreed.* **3** [*predic.*] (**sick of**) intensely annoyed with or bored by (someone or something) as a result of having had too much of them: *I'm absolutely sick of your moods.* **4** *informal* (esp. of humor) having something unpleasant such as death, illness, or misfortune as its subject and dealing with it in an offensive way: *this was someone's idea of a sick joke.* ■ (of a person) having abnormal or unnatural tendencies; perverted: *he is a deeply sick man from whom society needs to be protected.*
▸*n. Brit., informal* vomit.
▸*v.* [*trans.*] (**sick something up**) *informal* bring something up by vomiting. ▷Old English *sēoc* 'affected by illness,' of Germanic origin; related to Dutch *ziek* and German *siech*. —**sick·ish** *adj.*
▸*PHRASES* □ **be sick 1** be ill. **2** vomit. □ **fall** (or **take**) **sick** become ill. □ **get sick 1** become ill. **2** vomit. □ **make someone sick** cause someone to vomit or feel nauseous or unwell: *sherry makes me sick and so do cigars.* ■ cause someone to feel intense annoyance or disgust: *you're so damned self-righteous you make me sick!* □ **—— oneself sick** do something to such an extent that one feels nauseous or unwell (often used for emphasis): *she was* **worrying herself sick about** *Mike.* □ **sick and tired of** *informal* annoyed about or bored with (something) and unwilling to put up with it any longer: *I am sick and tired of all the criticism.* □ (**as**)

sick as a dog *informal* extremely ill. □ **(as) sick as a parrot** *Brit., informal* extremely disappointed. □ **the sick man of ——** a country that is politically or economically unsound, esp. in comparison with its neighbors in the region specified: *the country had been the sick man of Europe for too long.* [from a use of *sick man*, frequently applied in the late 19th cent. to the Sultan of Turkey, later extended to Turkey and other countries.] □ **sick to death of** *informal* another way of saying SICK AND TIRED OF above. □ **sick to one's stomach** nauseous. ■ disgusted.

sick[2] ▶*v.* variant of SIC[2].

sick·bay /ˈsikˌbā/ (also **sick bay**) ▶*n.* a room or building set aside for the treatment or accommodation of the sick, esp. within a military base or on board a ship.

sick·bed /ˈsikˌbed/ ▶*n.* an invalid's bed (often used to refer to the state or condition of being an invalid): *he had climbed from his sickbed to help the club.*

sick-build·ing syn·drome ▶*n.* a condition affecting office workers, typically marked by headaches and respiratory problems, attributed to unhealthy or stressful factors in the working environment such as poor ventilation.

sick call ▶*n.* **1** a visit to a sick person, typically one made by a doctor or priest. **2** *Military* a summons for those reporting sick to attend for treatment.

sick day ▶*n.* a day taken off from work because of illness.

sick·en /ˈsikən/ ▶*v.* **1** [*trans.*] (often **be sickened**) make (someone) feel disgusted or appalled: *she was sickened by the bomb attack.* ■ [*intrans.*] *archaic* feel disgust or horror: *he* **sickened at** *the thought.* **2** [*intrans.*] become ill: *Dawson sickened unexpectedly and died in 1916.*

sick·en·er /ˈsikənər/ ▶*n.* **1** *informal* something that causes disgust or severe disappointment. **2** (**the sickener**) a poisonous toadstool with a red cap and a white or cream-colored stem and gills, found commonly in both Eurasia and North America. • Genus *Russula*, family Russulaceae, class Hymenomycetes, in particular *R. emetica.*

sick·en·ing /ˈsikəniNG/ ▶*adj.* causing or liable to cause a feeling of nausea or disgust: *a sickening stench of blood | she hit the ground with a sickening thud.* ■ *informal* causing irritation or annoyance. —**sick·en·ing·ly** *adv.*

sick head·ache ▶*n.* a headache accompanied by nausea, particularly a migraine.

sick·ie /ˈsikē/ ▶*n.* *informal* another term for SICKO.

sick·le /ˈsikəl/ ▶*n.* a short-handled farming tool with a semicircular blade, used for cutting grain, lopping, or trimming. ▷Old English *sicol, sicel*, of Germanic origin; related to Dutch *sikkel* and German *Sichel*, based on Latin *secula*, from *secare* 'to cut.'

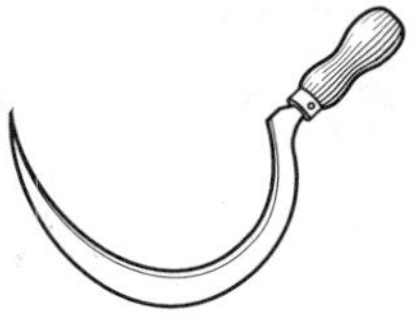
sickle

sick leave ▶*n.* leave of absence granted because of illness.

sick·le·bill /ˈsikəlˌbil/ ▶*n.* any of a number of birds with a long narrow down-curved bill: • a tropical American hummingbird (genus *Eutoxeres*, family Trochilidae: two species). • a New Guinea bird of paradise (two genera in the family Paradisaeidae).

sick·le cell a·ne·mi·a /ˈsikəl sel əˈnēmēə/ (also **sick·le cell dis·ease**) ▶*n.* a severe hereditary form of anemia in which a mutated form of hemoglobin distorts the red blood cells into a crescent shape at low oxygen levels. It is commonest among those of African descent.

sick·le cell trait ▶*n.* a relatively mild condition caused by the presence of a single gene for sickle cell anemia, producing a smaller amount of abnormal hemoglobin and conferring some resistance to malaria.

sick·le feath·er ▶*n.* each of the long middle feathers of a rooster's tail.

sick list ▶*n.* a list, esp. in the military, of people who are ill and unable to work.

sick·ly /ˈsiklē/ ▶*adj.* (**-li·er, -li·est**) **1** often ill; in poor health: *she was a thin, sickly child.* ■ (of a person's complexion or expression) indicative of poor health: *his usual sickly pallor.* ■ *poetic/literary* (of a place, climate, or time) causing or characterized by unhealthiness: *a deep sickly vaporous swamp.* **2** (of a flavor, smell, color, or light) so unpleasant as to induce discomfort or nausea: *the walls were painted a sickly green | she liked her coffee sweet and sickly.* ■ excessively sentimental or mawkish: *a sickly fable of delicate young lovers.* ▷late Middle English: probably suggested by Old Norse *sjúkligr.* —**sick·li·ness** *n.*

sick-mak·ing ▶*adj.* *informal* nauseatingly unpleasant or shocking: *a sick-making stench.* ■ overly sentimental, coy, or trite.

sick·ness /ˈsiknis/ ▶*n.* **1** the state of being ill: *she was absent through sickness.* ■ [often with *adj.*] a particular type of illness or disease: *botulism causes fodder sickness of horses | a woman suffering an incurable sickness.* **2** the feeling or fact of being affected with nausea or vomiting: *she felt a wave of sickness wash over her | travel sickness.* ▷Old English *sēocnesse* (see SICK[1], -NESS).

sick·o /ˈsikō/ ▶*n.* (*pl.* **-os**) *informal* a mentally ill or perverted person, esp. one who is sadistic.

sick·out /ˈsik ˌout/ (also **sick-out**) ▶*n.* *informal* an organized period of unwarranted sick leave taken as a form of group protest, usually as a measure to avoid a formal strike.

sick·room /ˈsikˌro͞om/ ▶*n.* a room in a school or place of work occupied by or set apart for people who are unwell. ■ a room occupied by an ill person.

sick tick·et ▶*n.* *informal, chiefly humorous* a person with an affinity for sick humor: *you'd have to be a sick ticket to eat candy called "gummy rats."*

si·dal·cea /sīˈdalsHēə/ ▶*n.* a herbaceous North American plant of the mallow family, several kinds of which are cultivated as ornamentals. • Genus *Sidalcea*, family Malvaceae. ▷modern Latin, from *Sida* + *Alcea*, names of related genera.

sid·dha /ˈsidə/ ▶*n.* *Hinduism* one who has achieved spiritual realization and supernatural power. ▷Sanskrit.

Sid·dhar·tha Gau·ta·ma /siˈdärtə ˈgôtəmə; siˈdärTHə-/ see BUDDHA.

sid·dhi /ˈsidē/ ▶*n.* *Hinduism & Buddhism* **1** complete understanding and enlightenment possessed by a siddha. **2** (*pl.* **-dhis**) a paranormal power possessed by a siddha. ▷Sanskrit.

Sid·dons /ˈsidnz/, Mrs. Sarah (1755–1831), English actress; born *Sarah Kemble*. She was noted particularly for her role as Lady Macbeth.

side /sīd/ ▶*n.* **1** a position to the left or right of an object, place, or central point: *a town on the other side of the river | on either side of the entrance was a garden | Rachel tilted her head to one side.* ■ either of the two halves of an object, surface, or place regarded as divided by an imaginary central line: *she lay on her side of the bed | the left side of the brain.* ■ the right or the left part of a person's or animal's body, esp. of the human torso: *he has been paralyzed on his right side since birth.* ■ [in *sing.*] a place or position closely adjacent to someone: *his wife stood* **at his side**. ■ either of the lateral halves of the body of a butchered animal, or an animal or fish prepared for eating: *a side of beef.* **2** an upright or sloping surface of a structure or object that is not the top or bottom and generally not the front or back: *a car crashed into the side of the house | line the sides of the cake pan |* [as *adj.*] *a side entrance.* ■ each of the flat surfaces of a solid object. ■ either of the two surfaces of something flat and thin, such as paper or cloth. ■ the amount of writing needed to fill one side of a sheet of paper: *she told us not to write more than three sides.* ■ either of the two faces of a record or of the two separate tracks on a length of recording tape. **3** a part or region near the edge and away from the middle of something: *a minivan was parked at the side of the road | cabins on the south side of the clearing.* ■ [as *adj.*] subsidiary to or less important than something: *a side dish of fresh vegetables.* ■ a dish served as subsidiary to the main one: *sides of German potato salad and red cabbage.* ■ each of the lines forming the boundary of a plane rectilinear figure: *the farm buildings formed three sides of a square.* **4** a person or group opposing another or others in a dispute, contest, or debate: *the two sides agreed to resume border trade | whose side are you on?* ■ *chiefly Brit.* a sports team. ■ the position, interests, or attitude of one person or group, esp. when regarded as being in opposition to another or others: *Mrs. Burt hasn't kept her side of the bargain | the conservationists are on the city's side of the case.* ■ a particular aspect of something, esp. a situation or a person's character: *her ability to put up with his disagreeable side.* ■ a person's kinship or line of descent as traced through either their father or mother: *Richard was of French descent on his mother's side.* **5** (also **side·spin**) horizontal spinning motion given to a ball. ■ *Billiards* another term for ENGLISH (sense 3).

▶*v.* **1** [*intrans.*] (**side with/against**) support or oppose in a conflict, dispute, or debate: *he felt that Max had betrayed him by siding with Beatrice.* **2** [*trans.*] provide with a side or sides; form the side of: *the hills that side a long valley.* ▷Old English *sīde* 'left or right part of the body,' of Germanic origin; related to Dutch *zijde* and German *Seite*, probably from a base meaning 'extending lengthwise.' —**side·less** *adj.*

▶*PHRASES* □ **by** (or **at**) **someone's side** close to someone, esp. so as to give them comfort or moral support: *a stepson who stayed by your side when your own son deserted you.* □ **by the side of** close to: *a house by the side of the road.* □ **from side to side 1** alternately left and right from a central point: *I shook my head frantically from side to side.* **2** across the entire width; right across: *the fleet stretched four miles from side to side.* □ **have something on one's side** (or **something is on one's side**) something is operating to one's advantage: *now that he had time on his side, Tom relaxed a little.* □ **on** (or **to**) **one side** out of one's way; aside. ■ to be dealt with or considered later, esp. because tending to distract one from something more important: *before the kickoff a player has to set his disappointments and frustrations to one side.* □ **on the —— side** tending toward being ——; rather —— (used to qualify an adjective): *these shoes are a bit on the tight side.* □ **on the side 1** in addition to one's regular job or as a subsidiary source of income: *no one lived in the property, but the caretaker made a little on the side by renting rooms out.* **2** secretly, esp. with regard to a relationship in addition to one's legal or regular partner: *Brian had a mistress on the side.* **3** served separately from the main dish: *a club sandwich with french fries on the side.* □ **side by side** (of two or more people or things) close together and facing the same way: *on we jogged, side by side, for a mile.* ■ together: *we have been using both systems, side by side, for two years.* ■ (of people or groups) supporting each other; in cooperation: *the two institutions worked side by side in complete harmony.* □ **side of the fence** see FENCE. □ **take sides** support one person or cause against another or others in a dispute, conflict, or contest: *I do not want to take sides in this matter.* □ **take** (or **draw**) **someone to one side** speak to someone in private, esp. so as to advise or warn them about something. □ **this side of 1** before (a particular time, date, or event): *this side of midnight.* ■ yet to reach (a particular age): *I'm this side of forty-five.* **2** *informal* used in superlative expressions to denote that something is comparable with a paragon or model of its kind: *the finest coffee this side of Brazil.*

side·arm[1] /ˈsīdˌärm/ ▶*adj.* [*attrib.*] (of a throw, pitch, or cast) performed or delivered with a sweeping motion of the arm at or below shoulder level. ■ (of a person, typically a baseball pitcher) using such a sweeping motion of the arm.

▶*adv.* in a sidearm manner: *I could throw sidearm.*

▶*v.* [*trans.*] *chiefly Baseball* throw or pitch a ball to (someone) with such a motion of the arm. ■ throw or pitch (a ball or other object) in this way. —**side·arm·er** *n.*

side·arm[2] (also **side arm**) ▶*n.* a weapon worn at a person's side, such as a pistol or other small firearm (or, formerly, a sword or bayonet).

side·band /ˈsīdˌband/ ▶*n.* *Telecommunications* one of two frequency bands on either side of the carrier wave, containing the modulated signal.

side·bar /ˈsīdˌbär/ ▶*n.* a short article in a newspaper or magazine, typically boxed, placed alongside a main article, and containing additional or explanatory material. ■ a secondary, additional, or incidental thing; a side issue. ■ (also **sidebar conference**) (in a court of law) a discussion between the lawyers and the judge held out of earshot of the jury.

side bet ▶*n.* a bet over and above the main bet, esp. on a subsidiary issue.

side·board /ˈsīdˌbôrd/ ▶*n.* **1** a flat-topped piece of furniture with cupboards and drawers, placed along a wall and used for storing dishes, glasses, and table linen. **2** (usu. **sideboards**) *Brit.* sideburns. **3** a board forming the side, or a part of the side, of a structure, esp. a removable board at the side of a truck or trailer.

side·burn /ˈsīdˌbərn/ ▶*n.* (usu. **sideburns**) a strip of hair grown by a man down each side of the face in front of his ears. ▷late 19th cent.: originally *burnside*, from the name of General *Burnside* (1824–81), who affected this style.

side·car /ˈsīdˌkär/ ▶*n.* **1** a small, low vehicle attached to the side of a motorcycle for carrying passengers.

2 a cocktail of brandy and lemon juice with orange liqueur.

side chain ▸*n.* *Chemistry* a group of atoms attached to the main part of a molecule and having a ring or chain structure.

side chair ▸*n.* an upright wooden chair without arms.

side chap·el ▸*n.* a subsidiary chapel opening off the side aisle in a large church.

side·cut /ˈsīdˌkət/ ▸*n.* a curve in the side of a ski or snowboard that allows it to turn more smoothly.

sid·ed /ˈsīdid/ ▸*adj.* [in *combination*] having sides of a specified number or type: *narrow, steep-sided canyons.* —**sid·ed·ly** *adv.* [in *combination*]. —**sid·ed·ness** *n.*

side dish ▸*n.* a dish served as subsidiary to the main one: *both were served with an excellent side dish of fresh vegetables.*

side door ▸*n.* a door in or at the side of a building. ■ *figurative* an indirect means of access.

side drum ▸*n.* another term for **SNARE DRUM**. ▷late 18th cent.: so named because it was originally played, suspended from the drummer's side.

side ef·fect ▸*n.* a secondary, typically undesirable effect of a drug or medical treatment: *many anticancer drugs now in use have toxic side effects.*

side-glance ▸*n.* a sideways or brief glance.

side·hill /ˈsīdˌhil/ ▸*n.* a hillside.

side is·sue ▸*n.* a point or topic connected to or raised by some other issue, but not as important, esp. one that distracts attention from the more important issue.

side·kick /ˈsīdˌkik/ ▸*n.* *informal* a person's assistant or close associate, esp. one who has less authority than that person.

side·light /ˈsīdˌlīt/ ▸*n.* **1** a light placed at the side of something. ■ (**sidelights**) a ship's port (red) and starboard (green) navigation lights. ■ *figurative* a piece of incidental information that helps to clarify or enliven a subject. ■ natural light coming from the side. **2** a narrow window or pane of glass set alongside a door or larger window.

side·line /ˈsīdˌlīn/ ▸*n.* **1** an activity done in addition to one's main job, esp. to earn extra income: [as *adj.*] *a sideline career as a stand-up comic.* ■ an auxiliary line of goods or business: *electronic handbooks are a lucrative sideline for the firm.* **2** (usu. **sidelines**) either of the two lines bounding the longer sides of a football field, basketball court, tennis court, or similar playing area. ■ the area immediately outside such lines as a place for nonplayers, substitutes, or spectators: *his son watched from the sidelines.* See also **ON THE SIDELINES** below.
▸*v.* [*trans.*] (often **be sidelined**) cause (a player) to be unable to play on a team or in a game: *he has been sidelined for the last six weeks with a fractured wrist.* ■ *figurative* remove from the center of activity or attention; place in a less influential position: *a respected lawyer will be sidelined by alcohol abuse.*
▸*PHRASE* □ **on** (or **from**) **the sidelines** in (or from) a position where one is observing a situation but is unable or unwilling to be directly involved in it.

side·long /ˈsīdˌlôNG/ ▸*adj.* & *adv.* directed to or from one side; sideways: [as *adj.*] *Steve gave her a sidelong glance* | [as *adv.*] *he looked sidelong at her with a quick smile.* ▷late Middle English: alteration of earlier *sideling*, from **SIDE** + the adverbial suffix *-ling*.

side·man /ˈsīdˌman/ ▸*n.* (*pl.* **-men**) a supporting musician in a jazz band or rock group.

side·meat /ˈsīdˌmēt/ ▸*n.* salt pork or bacon, typically cut from the side of the pig.

side-necked tur·tle ▸*n.* a freshwater turtle with a relatively long head and neck that is retracted sideways into the shell for defense. • Suborder Pleurodira: families Chelidae (South America and Australasia) and Pelomedusidae (South America and southern Africa), and several genera.

side note ▸*n.* a marginal note in a text.

side-on ▸*adv.* with the side of someone or something toward something else: *the ship was wallowing side-on to the swell.*
▸*adj.* directed from or toward a side: *a shot of the crowd from the side-on camera.* ■ (of a collision) involving the side of a vehicle.

side plate ▸*n.* a plate smaller than a dinner plate, used for bread or other accompaniments to a meal.

si·de·re·al /sīˈdi(ə)rēəl/ ▸*adj.* of or with respect to the distant stars (i.e., the constellations or fixed stars, not the sun or planets). ▷mid 17th cent.: from Latin *sidereus* (from *sidus, sider-* 'star') + **-AL**.

si·de·re·al clock ▸*n.* *Astronomy* a clock measuring sidereal time in terms of 24 equal divisions of a sidereal day.

si·de·re·al day ▸*n.* *Astronomy* the time between two consecutive transits of the First Point of Aries. It represents the time taken by the earth to rotate on its axis relative to the stars, and is almost four minutes shorter than the solar day because of the earth's orbital motion.

si·de·re·al month ▸*n.* *Astronomy* the time it takes the moon to orbit once around the earth with respect to the stars (approximately 27¼ days).

si·de·re·al pe·ri·od ▸*n.* *Astronomy* the period of revolution of one body around another with respect to the distant stars.

si·de·re·al time ▸*n.* *Astronomy* time reckoned from the motion of the earth (or a planet) relative to the distant stars (rather than with respect to the sun).

si·de·re·al year ▸*n.* *Astronomy* the orbital period of the earth around the sun, taking the stars as a reference frame, being 20 minutes longer than the tropical year because of precession.

sid·er·ite /ˈsīdəˌrīt/ ▸*n.* **1** a brown mineral consisting of ferrous carbonate, occurring as the main component of some kinds of ironstone or as rhombohedral crystals in mineral veins. **2** a meteorite consisting mainly of nickel and iron. ▷late 16th cent. (denoting lodestone): from Greek *sidēros* 'iron' + **-ITE**[1]. —**sid·er·it·ic** /ˌsīdəˈritik/ *adj.*

sidero-[1] ▸*comb. form* of or relating to the stars: *siderostat.* ▷from Latin *sidus, sider-* 'star.'

sidero-[2] ▸*comb. form* of or relating to iron: *siderophore.* ▷from Greek *sidēros* 'iron.'

side road ▸*n.* a minor or subsidiary road, esp. one joining or diverging from a main road.

sid·er·o·phore /ˈsidərəˌfôr/ ▸*n.* *Biochemistry* a molecule that binds and transports iron in microorganisms.

sid·er·o·stat /ˈsidərəˌstat/ ▸*n.* *Astronomy* an instrument used for keeping the image of a celestial object in a fixed position.

side·sad·dle /ˈsīdˌsadl/ (also **side-sad·dle**) ▸*n.* a saddle in which the rider has both feet on the same side of the horse. It is typically used by a woman rider wearing a skirt.
▸*adv.* sitting in this position on a horse.

side shoot ▸*n.* a shoot growing from the side of a plant's stem.

side·show /ˈsīdˌSHō/ ▸*n.* a small show or stall at an exhibition, fair, or circus. ■ *figurative* a minor or diverting incident or issue, esp. one that distracts attention from something more important.

side·slip /ˈsīdˌslip/ (also **side-slip**) ▸*n.* a sideways skid or slip. ■ *Aeronautics* a sideways movement of an aircraft, esp. downward toward the inside of a turn. ■ (in skiing and surfing) an act of traveling down a slope or wave in a direction not in line with one's skis or board.
▸*v.* [*intrans.*] skid or slip sideways: *the weight counteracts the tire's tendency to sideslip.* ■ *Aeronautics* move in a sideslip. ■ (in skiing and surfing) travel sideways or in any direction not in line with one's skis or board.

side·spin /ˈsīdˌspin/ ▸*n.* see **SIDE** (sense 5).

side split ▸*n.* *Canadian* a split-level house with fewer stories on one side than the other.

side·split·ting /ˈsīdˌspliting/ ▸*adj.* *informal* extremely amusing; causing violent laughter: *sidesplitting anecdotes.*

side·step /ˈsīdˌstep/ ▸*v.* (**-stepped, -step·ping**) [*trans.*] avoid (someone or something) by stepping sideways: *as she walked she sidestepped the many cracks in the pavement.* ■ *figurative* avoid dealing with or discussing (something problematic or disagreeable): *he neatly sidestepped the questions about riots.* ■ [*intrans.*] *Skiing* climb or descend by lifting alternate skis while sideways on the slope.
▸*n.* a step taken sideways, typically to avoid someone or something. —**side·step·per** *n.*

side·stream smoke /ˈsīdˌstrēm/ ▸*n.* smoke that passes from a cigarette into the surrounding air, rather than into the smoker's lungs.

side street ▸*n.* a minor or subsidiary street.

side·stroke /ˈsīdˌstrōk/ ▸*n.* [in *sing.*] a swimming stroke similar to the breaststroke in which the swimmer lies on their side.

side suit ▸*n.* *Bridge* a suit other than the trump suit.

side·swipe /ˈsīdˌswīp/ ▸*n.* **1** a glancing blow from or on the side of something, esp. a motor vehicle. **2** a passing critical remark about someone or something.
▸*v.* [*trans.*] strike (someone or something) with or as if with a glancing blow: *Curtis jerked the wheel hard over and sideswiped the other car.*

side ta·ble ▸*n.* a table placed at the side of a room or apart from the main table.

side tone ▸*n.* feedback in a telephone receiver, in particular the reproduction of the user's own voice.

side·track /ˈsīdˌtrak/ ▸*v.* [*trans.*] (usu. **be/get sidetracked**) **1** cause (someone) to be distracted from an immediate or important issue: *he does not let himself get sidetracked by fads and trends.* ■ divert (a project or debate) away from a central issue or previously determined plan: *the effort at reform has been sidetracked for years.* **2** direct (a train) into a branch line or siding. ■ divert (a well or borehole) to reach a productive deposit or to avoid an obstruction.
▸*n.* a minor path or track. ■ a railroad branch line or siding. ■ a well or borehole that runs partly to one side of the original line of drilling.

side trip ▸*n.* a minor excursion during a voyage or trip.

side view ▸*n.* a view from the side.

side·walk /ˈsīdˌwôk/ ▸*n.* a paved path for pedestrians at the side of a road.

side·wall /ˈsīdˌwôl/ ▸*n.* **1** (often **side wall**) a wall forming the side of a structure or room. **2** the side of a tire, typically untreaded and marked or colored distinctively. ■ a tire with distinctively colored sidewalls: *the white sidewalls crunched over gravel.*

side·ward /ˈsīdwərd/ ▸*adj.* another term for **SIDEWAYS**.
▸*adv.* (also **side·wards** /-wərdz/) another term for **SIDEWAYS**.

side·ways /ˈsīdˌwāz/ ▸*adv.* & *adj.* to, toward, or from the side: [as *adv.*] *she tilted her body sideways* | [as *adj.*] *he hurried toward his office without a sideways glance.* ■ [as *adv.*] with one side facing forward: *the truck slid sideways across the road.* ■ so as to occupy a job or position at the same level as one previously held rather than be promoted or demoted: [as *adj.*] *after the reshuffle there were sideways moves for managers.* ■ by an indirect way: [as *adv.*] *he came into politics sideways, as campaign manager for the president.* ■ [as *adj.*] from an unconventional or unorthodox viewpoint: *take a* **sideways look at** *daily life.*
▸*PHRASE* □ **knock someone sideways** see **KNOCK**.

side-wheel·er ▸*n.* a steamboat with paddle wheels on either side. —**side-wheel** *adj.*

side whisk·ers ▸*plural n.* whiskers or sideburns on a man's cheeks.

side·wind /ˈsīdˌwīnd/ ▸*v.* [*intrans.*] [often as *n.*] (**sidewinding**) (of a sidewinder or other snake) move sideways in a series of S-shaped curves.

side wind /sīd wind/ ▸*n.* a wind blowing predominantly from one side. ■ *figurative* an indirect agency or influence.

side·wind·er[1] /ˈsīdˌwīndər/ ▸*n.* a pale-colored, nocturnal, burrowing rattlesnake that moves sideways over sand by throwing its body into S-shaped curves. It is found in the deserts of North America. • *Crotalus cerastes*, family Viperidae.

side·wind·er[2] ▸*n.* a heavy blow with the fist delivered from or on the side.

side·wise /ˈsīdˌwīz/ ▸*adv.* & *adj.* another term for **SIDEWAYS**.

Sidhe /SHē/ ▸*plural n.* the fairy people of Irish folklore, said to live beneath the hills and often identified as the remnant of the ancient Tuatha Dé Danann. ▷from Irish *aos sídhe* 'people of the fairy mound.'

Si·di bel Ab·bès /ˈsēdē bel əˈbes/ a town in northern Algeria, south of Oran; pop. 186,000.

sid·ing /ˈsīdiNG/ ▸*n.* **1** a short track at the side of and opening onto a railroad line, used chiefly for shunting or stabling trains. ■ a loop line. **2** cladding material for the outside of a building.

si·dle /ˈsīdl/ ▸*v.* [*intrans.*] walk in a furtive, unobtrusive, or timid manner, esp. sideways or obliquely: *I* **sidled up to** *her.*
▸*n.* [in *sing.*] an instance of walking in this way. ▷late 17th cent.: back-formation from *sideling* (see **SIDELONG**).

Si·don /ˈsīdn/ a city in Lebanon, on the Mediterranean coast, south of Beirut; pop. 38,000. Founded in the 3rd millennium BC, it was a Phoenician seaport and city-state. Arabic name **SAIDA**.

Sid·ra, Gulf of /ˈsidrə/ (also **Gulf of Sir·te**) a broad inlet of the Mediterranean Sea on the coast of Libya, between the towns of Benghazi and Misratah.

SIDS /sidz/ ▸*abbr.* sudden infant death syndrome.

Sie·ben·ge·bir·ge /ˈzēbəngəˌbirgə/ a range of hills in western Germany, on the right bank of the Rhine River, southeast of Bonn.

siege /sēj/ ▸*n.* a military operation in which enemy forces surround a town or building, cutting off essential supplies, with the aim of compelling the surrender of those inside: *Verdun had withstood a siege of ten weeks* | [as *adj.*] *siege warfare.* ■ a similar operation by a police or other force to compel the surrender of an armed person. ■ a prolonged period of misfortune: *I've been having a siege of headaches.* ▷Middle English: from Old French *sege*, from *asegier* 'besiege.'

▸*PHRASES* □ **lay siege to** conduct a siege of (a place): *government forces laid siege to the building figurative the press laid siege to her apartment.* □ **under siege** (of a place) undergoing a siege.

siege e·con·o·my ▸*n.* an economy in which import controls are imposed and the export of capital is curtailed.

siege gun ▸*n.* a heavy gun used in attacking a place under siege.

siege men·tal·i·ty ▸*n.* a defensive or paranoid attitude based on the belief that others are hostile toward one.

Sieg·fried /'sēg,frēd/ the hero of the first part of the Nibelungenlied. A prince of the Netherlands, Siegfried obtains a hoard of treasure by killing the dragon Fafner. He marries Kriemhild, and helps Gunther to win Brunhild before being killed by Hagen.

Sieg·fried Line /'sēg,frēd/ the line of defense constructed by the Germans along the western frontier of Germany before World War II. ■ another term for **HINDENBURG LINE.**

Sieg Heil /,sēg 'hīl/ ▸*exclam.* a victory salute used originally by Nazis at political rallies. ▷German, literally 'hail victory!' **—Sieg-Heil·ing** *adj.*

Sie·mens /'zēmənz; 'sē-/ a German family of scientific entrepreneurs and engineers. **Ernst Werner von Siemens** (1816–92) was an electrical engineer who developed the process of electroplating, devised an electric generator that used an electromagnet, and pioneered electrical traction. His brother **Karl Wilhelm** (1823–83) (also known as *Sir Charles William Siemens*) moved to England, where he developed the open-hearth steel furnace and designed the cable-laying steamship *Faraday.*Their brother **Friedrich** (1826–1904) applied the principles of the open-hearth furnace to glassmaking.

sie·mens /'sēmənz/ (abbr.: **S**) ▸*n. Physics* the SI unit of conductance, equal to one reciprocal ohm. ▷1930s: named after K. W. von **SIEMENS.**

Sie·na /sē'enə/ a city in west central Italy, in Tuscany; pop. 58,000. In the 13th and 14th centuries, it was the center of a flourishing school of art. **—Si·en·ese** /,sēə'nēz; -'nēs/ *adj.* & *n.*

si·en·na /sē'enə/ ▸*n.* a kind of ferruginous earth used as a pigment in painting, normally yellowish-brown in color (**raw sienna**) or deep reddish-brown when roasted (**burnt sienna**). ■ the color of this pigment. ▷late 18th cent.: from Italian *(terra di) Sienna* '(earth of) Siena.'

Sier·pin·ski tri·an·gle /SHi(ə)r'pinskē/ (also **Sierpinski gasket**) ▸*n. Mathematics* a fractal based on a triangle with four equal triangles inscribed in it. The central triangle is removed and each of the other three treated as the original was, and so on, creating an infinite regression in a finite space. ▷1970s: named after Waclaw *Sierpiński* (1882–1969), Polish mathematician.

si·er·ra /sē'erə/ ▸*n.* **1** a long jagged mountain chain. **2** a code word representing the letter S, used in radio communication. ▷mid 16th cent.: Spanish, from Latin *serra* 'saw.'

Si·er·ra Le·one /sē,erə lē'ōn/ a country on the coast of West Africa; pop. 5,883,000; capital, Freetown; languages, English (official), English Creole, Temne, and other West African languages. **—Si·er·ra Le·o·ne·an** /lē'ōnēən/ *adj.* & *n.*

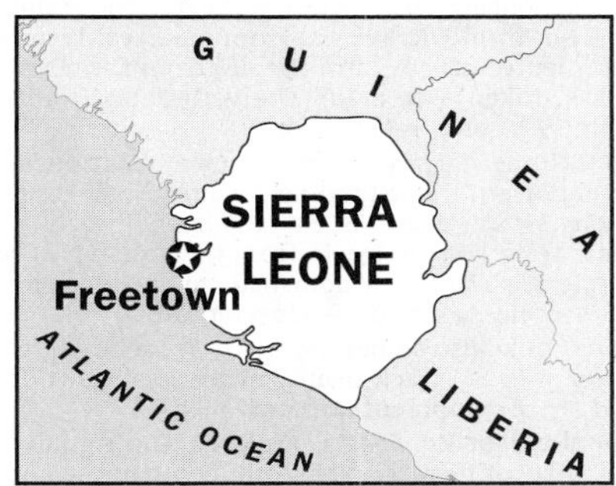

An area of British influence from the late 18th century, the district around Freetown on the coast became a colony in 1807, serving as a center for operations against slave traders. The large inland territory was not declared a protectorate until 1896. Sierra Leone achieved independence within the Commonwealth of Nations in 1961 but was suspended from the organization in 1997 following military coups in 1992 and 1997. National elections were held in 2002, and UN peacekeepers withdrew in 2004, but the situation remained unstable.

Si·er·ra Ma·dre /'mä,drā/ a mountain system in Mexico that extends from the border with the U.S. on the north to the southern border with Guatemala.

Si·er·ra Ne·va·da **1** a mountain range in southern Spain, in Andalusia, southeast of Granada. **2** a mountain range in eastern California. Rising sharply from the Great Basin on the east, it descends more gently to California's Central Valley on the west.

Si·er·ra Vis·ta /sē'erə 'vistə/ a city in the southeastern corner of Arizona, just north of the Mexican border; pop. 37,775.

si·es·ta /sē'estə/ ▸*n.* an afternoon rest or nap, esp. one taken during the hottest hours of the day in a hot climate. ▷mid 17th cent.: Spanish, from Latin *sexta (hora)* 'sixth hour.'

sieve /siv/ ▸*n.* a utensil consisting of a wire or plastic mesh held in a frame, used for straining solids from liquids, for separating coarser from finer particles, or for reducing soft solids to a pulp. ■ used figuratively with reference to the fact that a sieve does not hold all its contents: *she's forgotten all the details already—she's got* ***a mind like a sieve.***

▸*v.* [*trans.*] put (a food substance or other material) through a sieve. ■ [*intrans.*] (**sieve through**) *figurative* examine in detail: *lawyers had sieved through her contract.* ▷Old English *sife* (noun); related to Dutch *zeef* and German *Sieb.* **—sieve·like** /-,līk/ *adj.*

sieve cell ▸*n. Botany* a sieve element of a primitive type present in ferns and gymnosperms, with narrow pores and no sieve plate.

sieve el·e·ment ▸*n. Botany* an elongated cell in the phloem of a vascular plant, in which the primary wall is perforated by pores through which water is conducted.

sieve plate ▸*n. Botany* an area of relatively large pores present in the common end walls of sieve tube elements. ■ *Zoology* a perforated plate in the integument of an invertebrate, esp. the madreporite of an echinoderm.

sie·vert /'sēvərt/ (abbr.: **Sv**) ▸*n. Physics* the SI unit of dose equivalent (the biological effect of ionizing radiation), defined as that which delivers a joule of energy per kilogram of recipient mass. ▷1940s: named after Rolf M. *Sievert* (1896–1966), Swedish radiologist.

sieve tube ▸*n. Botany* a series of sieve tube elements placed end to end to form a continuous tube.

sieve tube el·e·ment (also **sieve tube member**) ▸*n. Botany* a sieve element of a type present in angiosperms, a series of which are joined end to end to form sieve tubes, with sieve plates between the elements.

si·fa·ka /sə'fakə; -'fäkə/ ▸*n.* a large gregarious lemur that leaps from tree to tree in an upright position. • Genus *Propithecus*, family Indriidae: two species. ▷mid 19th cent.: from Malagasy.

sift /sift/ ▸*v.* [*trans.*] put (a fine, loose, or powdery substance) through a sieve so as to remove lumps or large particles: *sift the flour into a large bowl.* ■ *figurative* examine (something) thoroughly so as to isolate that which is most important or useful: *until we sift the evidence ourselves, we can't comment objectively* | [*intrans.*] *the fourth stage involves* ***sifting through*** *the data and evaluating it.* ■ (**sift something out**) separate something, esp. something to be discarded, from something else: *he asked for streamlined procedures to sift out frivolous applications.* ■ cause to flow or pass as through a sieve: *Melanie sifted the warm sand through her fingers.* ■ [*intrans.*] (of snow, ash, light, or something similar) descend or float down lightly or sparsely as if sprinkled from a sieve: *ash began to sift down around them.*

▸*n.* [usu. in *sing.*] an act of sifting something, esp. so as to isolate that which is most important or useful: *a careful archaeological sift must be made through the debris.* ■ an amount of sifted material: *the floor was dusted with a fine* ***sift of*** *flour.* ▷Old English *siftan*; related to Dutch *ziften*, also to **SIEVE. —sift·er** *n.*

SIG *Computing* ▸*abbr.* special interest group, a type of newsgroup.

sig /sig/ ▸*n. informal Computing* a short personalized message at the end of an e-mail. ▷1990s: abbreviation of **SIGNATURE.**

Sig. ▸*abbr.* Signor.

Sig·a·to·ka /,sigə'tōkə/ ▸*n.* a fungal disease of banana plants characterized by elongated spots on the leaves, which then rot completely. • The fungus is *Mycosphaerella musicola*, subdivision Ascomycotina. ▷1920s: named after a district in Fiji.

sigh /sī/ ▸*v.* [*intrans.*] emit a long, deep, audible breath expressing sadness, relief, tiredness, or a similar feeling: *Harry sank into a chair and sighed with relief* | [with *direct speech*] *"I'm in a bit of a mess," Elaine sighed.* ■ *figurative* (of the wind or something through which the wind blows) make a sound resembling this: *a breeze made the treetops sigh.* ■ (**sigh for**) *poetic/literary* feel a deep yearning for (someone or something lost, unattainable, or distant): *he sighed for days gone by.*

▸*n.* a long, deep, audible exhalation expressing sadness, relief, tiredness, or a similar feeling: *she let out a long sigh of despair* | *figurative when the aircraft touched down I breathed* ***a sigh of relief.*** ■ *figurative* a gentle sound resembling this, esp. one made by the wind. ▷Middle English (as a verb): probably a back-formation from *sighte*, past tense of *siche, sike*, from Old English *sīcan*.

sight /sīt/ ▸*n.* **1** the faculty or power of seeing: *Joseph lost his sight as a baby* | [as *adj.*] *a sight test.* ■ the action or fact of seeing someone or something: *I've always been scared of the sight of blood.* ■ the area or distance within which someone can see or something can be seen: *he now refused to let Rose out of his sight.* ■ *dated* a person's view or consideration: *we are all equal* ***in the sight of God.*** **2** a thing that one sees or that can be seen: *John was a familiar sight in the bar for many years* | *he was getting used to seeing unpleasant sights.* ■ (**sights**) places of interest to tourists and visitors in a city, town, or other place: *she offered to show me the sights.* ■ (**a sight**) *informal* a person or thing having a ridiculous, repulsive, or disheveled appearance: *"I must look a frightful sight," she said.* **3** (usu. **sights**) a device on a gun or optical instrument used for assisting a person's precise aim or observation.

▸*v.* **1** [*trans.*] manage to see or observe (someone or something); catch an initial glimpse of: *tell me when you sight London Bridge* | [as *n.*] (**sighting**) *the unseasonal sighting of a cuckoo.* **2** [*intrans.*] take aim by looking through the sights of a gun: *she sighted down the barrel.* ■ take a detailed visual measurement of something with or as with a sight. ■ [*trans.*] adjust the sight of (a firearm or optical instrument). ▷Old English *(ge)sihth* 'something seen'; related to Dutch *zicht* and German *Gesicht* 'sight, face, appearance.' The verb dates from the mid 16th cent. (sense 2). **—sight·er** *n.*

▸*PHRASES* □ **at first sight** on first seeing or meeting someone: *it was* ***love at first sight.*** ■ after an initial impression (which is then found to be different from what is actually the case): *the debate is more complex than it seems at first sight.* □ **catch** (or **get a**) **sight of** glimpse for a moment; suddenly notice: *when she caught sight of him she smiled.* □ **in sight** visible: *no other vehicle was in sight.* ■ near at hand; close to being achieved or realized: *the minister insisted that agreement was in sight.* □ **in** (or **within**) **sight of** so as to see or be seen from: *I climbed the hill and came in sight of the house.* ■ within reach of; close to attaining: *he was safe for the moment and in sight of victory.* □ **in** (or **within**) **one's sights** visible, esp. through the sights of one's gun. ■ within the scope of one's ambitions or expectations: *he had the prize firmly in his sights.* □ **lose sight of** be no longer able to see. ■ fail to consider, be aware of, or remember: *we should not lose sight of the fact that the issues involved are moral ones.* □ **not a pretty sight** *informal* not a pleasant spectacle or situation. □ **on** (or **at**) **sight** as soon as someone or something has been seen: *in Africa, paramilitary game wardens shoot poachers on sight.* □ **out of sight 1** not visible: *she saw them off, waving until the car was out of sight.* **2** (also **out·a·sight**) [often as *exclam.*] *informal* extremely good; excellent: [as *adj.*] *these stereophones are an out-of-sight choice.* □ **out of sight, out of mind** *proverb* you soon forget people or things that are no longer visible or present. □ (**get**) **out of my sight!** go away at once! □ **raise** (or **lower**) **one's**

sights become more (or less) ambitious; increase (or lower) one's expectations. □ **set one's sights on** have as an ambition; hope strongly to achieve or reach: *Katherine set her sights on college.* □ **a sight ——** *informal* or *dialect* used to indicate that something is so described to a considerable extent: *the old lady is a sight cleverer than Sarah | he's a sight too full of himself.* □ **a sight for sore eyes** *informal* a person or thing that one is extremely pleased or relieved to see. □ **a sight to behold** a person or thing that is particularly impressive or worth seeing.

sight de·pos·it ▸*n. Finance* a bank deposit that can be withdrawn immediately without notice or penalty.

sight·ed /ˈsītid/ ▸*adj.* (of a person) having the ability to see; not blind: *a sighted guide is needed* | [as *plural n.*] **(the sighted)** *the blind leading the sighted, I thought.* ■ [in *combination*] having a specified kind of sight: *the keen-sighted watcher may catch a glimpse.*

sight gag ▸*n. informal* a visual joke.

sight glass ▸*n.* a transparent tube or window through which the level of liquid in a reservoir or supply line can be checked visually.

sight·hound /ˈsītˌhound/ ▸*n.* a hound originally bred to hunt independently from humans, such as a greyhound or a whippet.

sight·ing shot ▸*n.* an experimental shot to guide shooters in adjusting their sights.

sight·less /ˈsītlis/ ▸*adj.* unable to see; blind: *blank, sightless eyes.* ■ *poetic/literary* invisible. **—sight·less·ly** *adv.* **—sight·less·ness** *n.*

sight line (also **sight·line**) ▸*n.* a hypothetical line from someone's eye to what is seen (used esp. with reference to good or bad visibility): *the theater has great acoustics and splendid sight lines | the authorities require good sight lines at road junctions.*

sight·ly /ˈsītlē/ ▸*adj.* pleasing to the eye: *metal guards can also be used but are less sightly.* **—sight·li·ness** *n.*

sight-read ▸*v.* [*trans.*] read and perform (music) at sight, without preparation. **—sight-read·er** *n.* **—sight-read·ing** *n.*

sight rhyme ▸*n.* another term for **EYE RHYME**.

sight·see·ing /ˈsītˌsēiNG/ ▸*n.* the activity of visiting places of interest in a particular location: *our two-week trip combines spectacular sightseeing and superb hospitality.* **—sight·see** *v.* **—sight·se·er** /ˈsītˌsiər/ *n.*

sight-sing ▸*v.* [*trans.*] sing (music) at sight, without preparation.

sight un·seen ▸*adv.* without the opportunity to look at the object in question beforehand: *they bought their computers sight unseen through the mail.* ■ without being seen: *what other treasures remain sight unseen?*

sight·wor·thy /ˈsītˌwərT͟Hē/ ▸*adj. rare* worth seeing or visiting.

sig·il /ˈsijəl/ ▸*n.* an inscribed or painted symbol considered to have magical power. ■ *archaic* a seal: *the supply wains bore the High King's sigil.* ■ *poetic/literary* a sign or symbol. ▷late Middle English: from late Latin *sigillum* 'sign.'

SIGINT /ˈsigint/ ▸*abbr.* signals intelligence.

sig·lum /ˈsigləm/ ▸*n.* (*pl.* **sig·la** /ˈsiglə/) a letter (esp. an initial) or other symbol used to denote a word in a book, esp. to refer to a particular text. ▷early 18th cent.: from late Latin *sigla* (plural), perhaps from *singula*, neuter plural of *singulus* 'single.'

sig·ma /ˈsigmə/ ▸*n.* the eighteenth letter of the Greek alphabet (Σ, σ), transliterated as 's.' • The form ς is used instead of σ at the end of a word. The uncial form, called **lunate sigma** and resembling the letter *C*, is also sometimes used. ■ **(Sigma)** [followed by Latin genitive] *Astronomy* the eighteenth star in a constellation: *Sigma Octantis.* ■ *Chemistry & Physics* relating to or denoting an electron or orbital with zero angular momentum around an internuclear axis.

▸*symbol* ■ (Σ) mathematical sum. ■ (σ) standard deviation.

sig·mate /ˈsigmāt; -mit/ ▸*adj.* having the shape of a Σ or a letter S.

sig·moid /ˈsigmoid/ ▸*adj.* **1** curved like the uncial sigma (C); crescent-shaped. **2** S-shaped.

▸*n. Anatomy* short for **SIGMOID COLON**. ▷late 17th cent.: from Greek *sigmoeidēs*, from *sigma* (see **SIGMA**). **—sig·moi·dal** /sigˈmoidəl/ *adj.*

sig·moid co·lon ▸*n. Anatomy* the S-shaped last part of the large intestine, leading into the rectum.

sig·moid·os·co·py /ˌsigmoiˈdäskəpē/ ▸*n.* examination of the sigmoid colon by means of a flexible tube inserted through the anus. **—sig·moid·o·scope** /sigˈmoidəˌskōp/ *n.* **—sig·moid·o·scop·ic** /sigˌmoidəˈskäpik/ *adj.*

sign /sīn/ ▸*n.* **1** an object, quality, or event whose presence or occurrence indicates the probable presence or occurrence of something else: *flowers are often given as a sign of affection* | [with *clause*] *the stores are full, which is a sign that the recession is past its worst.* ■ something regarded as an indication or evidence of what is happening or going to happen: ***the signs are** that counterfeiting is growing at an alarming rate.* ■ [with *negative*] used to indicate that someone or something is not present where they should be or are expected to be: *there was still no sign of her.* ■ *Medicine* an indication of a disease detectable by a medical practitioner even if not apparent to the patient. Compare with **SYMPTOM**. ■ a miracle regarded as evidence of supernatural power (chiefly in biblical and literary use). ■ any trace of a wild animal, esp. its tracks or droppings: *wolverine sign.* **2** a gesture or action used to convey information or instructions: *she gave him the thumbs-up sign.* ■ a notice that is publicly displayed giving information or instructions in a written or symbolic form: *I didn't see the stop sign.* See note at **EMBLEM**. ■ an action or reaction that conveys something about someone's state or experiences: *she gave no sign of having seen him.* ■ a gesture used in a system of sign language. ■ short for **SIGN LANGUAGE**. ■ a symbol or word used to represent an operation, instruction, concept, or object in algebra, music, or other subjects. ■ a word or gesture given according to prior arrangement as a means of identification; a password. **3** (also **zodiacal sign**) *Astrology* each of the twelve equal sections into which the zodiac is divided, named from the constellations formerly situated in each, and associated with successive periods of the year according to the position of the sun on the ecliptic: *a person born **under the sign** of Virgo.* **4** *Mathematics* the positiveness or negativeness of a quantity.

▸*v.* **1** [*trans.*] write one's name on (a letter, card, or similar item) to identify oneself as the writer or sender: *the card was signed by the whole class.* ■ indicate agreement with or authorization of the contents of (a document or other written or printed material) by attaching a signature: *the two countries signed a nonaggression treaty.* ■ write (one's name) for purposes of identification or authorization: *she signed her name in the book* | [*trans.*] *she **signed herself** Ingrid* | [*intrans.*] *he signed on the dotted line.* ■ engage (someone, typically a sports player or a musician) to work for one by signing a contract with them: *the company signed 30 bands.* ■ [*intrans.*] sign a contract committing oneself to work for a particular person or organization: *Sherman has **signed for** another two seasons.* **2** [*intrans.*] use gestures to convey information or instructions: [with *infinitive*] *she signed to her husband to leave the room.* ■ communicate in sign language: *she was learning to sign.* ■ [*trans.*] express or perform (something) in sign language: [as *adj.*] **(signed)** *the theater routinely puts on signed performances.* ■ *archaic* [*trans.*] mark or consecrate with the sign of the cross.

▸*phrasal v.* □ **sign something away/over** officially relinquish rights or property by signing a deed: *I have no intention of signing away my inheritance.* □ **sign for** sign a receipt to confirm that one has received (something delivered or handed over). □ **sign in** sign a register on arrival, typically in a hotel. □ **sign someone in** record someone's arrival in a register. □ **sign off** conclude a letter, broadcast, or other message: *he signed off with a few words of advice.* ■ sign to record that one is leaving work for the day. ■ *Bridge* indicate by a conventional bid that one is seeking to end the bidding. □ **sign someone off** record that someone is entitled to miss work, typically because of illness. □ **sign off on** *informal* assent or give one's approval to: *it was hard to get celebrities to sign off on those issues.* □ **sign on** *chiefly Brit.* commit oneself to employment, membership in a society, or some other undertaking: *I'll **sign on with** an advertising agency.* □ **sign someone on** take someone into one's employment. □ **sign out** sign a register to record one's departure, typically from a hotel. □ **sign someone out** authorize someone's release or record their departure by signing a register. □ **sign something out** sign to indicate that one has borrowed or hired something: *I signed out the keys.* □ **sign up** commit oneself to a period of employment or education or to some other undertaking: *he **signed up for** a ten-week course.* ■ enlist in the armed forces. ■ (also **sign something up**) conclude a business deal: *the company has already signed up a few orders.* □ **sign someone up** formally engage someone in employment. ▷Middle English: from Old French *signe* (noun), *signer* (verb), from Latin *signum* 'mark, token.' **—sign·er** *n.*

▸*PHRASES* □ **sign of the cross** a Christian sign made in blessing or prayer by tracing a cross from the forehead to the chest and to each shoulder, or in the air. □ **sign of the times** something judged to exemplify or indicate the nature or quality of a particular period, typically something unwelcome or unpleasant: *the theft was a sign of the times.* □ **signed, sealed, and delivered** (or **signed and sealed**) formally and officially agreed and in effect.

THE RIGHT WORD **augury, indication, manifestation, omen, sign, signal, symptom, token**

What's the difference between a **sign** and a **signal**? The former (in this sense) is a general term for anything that gives evidence of an event, a mood, a quality of character, a mental or physical state, or a trace of something (*a sign of approaching rain; a sign of good breeding; a sign that someone has entered the house*).

While a sign may be involuntary or even unconscious, a *signal* is always voluntary and is usually deliberate. A ship that shows signs of distress may or may not be in trouble; but one that sends a distress *signal* is definitely in need of help.

Indication, like *sign*, is a comprehensive term for anything that serves to indicate or point out (*he gave no indication that he was lying*).

A **manifestation** is an outward or perceptible indication of something (*the letter was a manifestation of his guilt*), and a **symptom** is an indication of a diseased condition (*a symptom of pneumonia*).

An object that proves the existence of something abstract is called a **token** (*she gave him a locket as a token of her love*).

Omen and **augury** both pertain to foretelling future events, with *augury* being the general term for a prediction of the future and *omen* being a definite sign foretelling good or evil (*they regarded the stormy weather as a bad omen*).

Si·gnac /sēˈnyäk/, Paul (1863–1935), French neo-Impressionist painter. A pointillist painter, his technique was characterized by the use of small dashes and patches of pure color rather than dots.

sign·age /ˈsīnij/ ▸*n.* signs collectively, esp. commercial or public display signs.

sig·nal[1] /ˈsignəl/ ▸*n.* **1** a gesture, action, or sound that is used to convey information or instructions, typically by prearrangement between the parties concerned: *the firing of the gun was the **signal for** a chain of beacons to be lit* | [with *infinitive*] *the policeman raised his hand as a signal to stop.* See note at **SIGN**. ■ an indication of a state of affairs: *the markets are waiting for a clear signal about the direction of policy.* ■ an event or statement that provides the impulse or occasion for something specified to happen: *the champion's announcement that he was retiring was the **signal for** scores of journalists to gather at his last match.* ■ an apparatus on a railroad, typically a colored light or a semaphore, giving indications to train engineers of whether or not the line is clear. ■ *Bridge* a prearranged convention of bidding or play intended to convey information to one's partner. **2** an electrical impulse or radio wave transmitted or received: *equipment for receiving TV signals.*

▸*v.* (**-naled**, **-nal·ing**; *chiefly Brit.* **-nalled**, **-nal·ling**) [*intrans.*] transmit information or instructions by means of a gesture, action, or sound: *hold your fire until I signal.* ■ [*trans.*] instruct (someone) to do something by means of gestures or signs rather than explicit orders: *she signaled Charlotte to be silent.* ■ (of a cyclist, motorist, or vehicle) indicate an intention to turn in a specified direction using an extended arm or flashing indicator: [with *complement*] *Stone signaled right* | [with *infinitive*] *the truck signaled to turn left.* ■ [*trans.*] indicate the existence or occurrence of (something) by actions or sounds: *they could signal displeasure by refusing to cooperate.* ■ [with *clause*] give an indication of a state of affairs: *she gave a glance that signaled that her father was being secretive.* ▷late Middle English: from Old French, from medieval Latin *signale*, neuter of late Latin *signalis*, from Latin *signum* 'mark, token' (see **SIGN**). The verb dates from the early 19th cent. **—sig·nal·er** *n.*

sig·nal[2] ▸*adj.* [*attrib.*] striking in extent, seriousness, or importance; outstanding: *he attacked the administration for its signal failure of leadership.* ▷early 17th cent.: from French *signalé*, from the Italian past participle *segnalato* 'distinguished, made illustrious,' from *segnale* 'a signal.' **—sig·nal·ly** *adv.*

sig·nal box (also **signal tower**) ▸*n. Brit.* a building beside a railroad track from which signals, switches, and other equipment are controlled.

sig·nal-call·er ▸*n. Football* a player who signals the next play or formation to team members.

S

sig·nal·ize /ˈsignəˌlīz/ ▸*v.* [*trans.*] **1** mark or indicate (something), esp. in a striking or conspicuous manner: *people seek to change their name to signalize a change in status that has taken place.* ■ *archaic* make (something) noteworthy or remarkable: *a little flower with not much to signalize it.* **2** provide (an intersection) with traffic signals.

sig·nal·man /ˈsignəlmən/ ▸*n.* (*pl.* **-men**) a railroad worker responsible for operating signals and switches. ■ a person responsible for sending and receiving naval or military signals.

sig·nals in·tel·li·gence ▸*n.* the branch of military intelligence concerned with the monitoring, interception, and interpretation of radio signals, radar signals, and telemetry.

sig·nal-to-noise ra·tio ▸*n.* the ratio of the strength of an electrical or other signal carrying information to that of interference, generally expressed in decibels. ■ *informal* a measure of how much useful information there is in a system, such as the Internet, as a proportion of the entire contents.

sig·na·to·ry /ˈsignəˌtôrē/ ▸*n.* (*pl.* **-ries**) a party that has signed an agreement, esp. a country that has signed a treaty: *Bulgaria is a* **signatory to** *a variety of international human rights conventions* | [as *adj.*] *the signatory states.* ▷late 19th cent.: from Latin *signatorius* 'of sealing,' from *signat-* 'marked (with a cross),' from the verb *signare.*

sig·na·ture /ˈsignəCHər; -ˌCHŏŏr/ ▸*n.* **1** a person's name written in a distinctive way as a form of identification in authorizing a check or document or concluding a letter. ■ the action of signing a document: *the license was sent to the customer for signature.* ■ a distinctive pattern, product, or characteristic by which someone or something can be identified: *the chef produced the pâté that was his signature* | [as *adj.*] *his signature dish.* **2** *Music* short for **KEY SIGNATURE** or **TIME SIGNATURE.** **3** *Printing* a letter or figure printed at the foot of one or more pages of each sheet of a book as a guide in binding. ■ a printed sheet after being folded to form a group of pages. **4** the part of a medical prescription that gives instructions about the use of the medicine or drug prescribed. ▷mid 16th cent. from medieval Latin *signatura* 'signature of a sovereign on an official document,' from Latin *signare* 'to sign, mark.'

sig·na·ture tune ▸*n. chiefly Brit.* a distinctive piece of music associated with a particular program or performer on television or radio; a theme song.

sign·board /ˈsīnˌbôrd/ ▸*n.* a board displaying the name or logo of a business or product. ■ a board displaying a sign to direct traffic or travelers.

sign·ee /sīˈnē; ˈsīnē/ ▸*n.* a person who has signed a contract or other official document.

sig·net /ˈsignit/ ▸*n. historical* a small seal, esp. one set in a ring, used instead of or with a signature to give authentication to an official document. ▷late Middle English: from Old French, or from medieval Latin *signetum*, diminutive of *signum* 'token, seal.'

sig·net ring ▸*n.* a ring with letters, usually one's initials, or a design carved into it.

sig·ni·fiant /ˈsignəˌfiənt/ ▸*n.* another term for **SIGNIFIER.**

sig·nif·i·cance /sigˈnifikəns/ ▸*n.* **1** the quality of being worthy of attention; importance: *adolescent education was felt to be a social issue of some significance.* **2** the meaning to be found in words or events: *the significance of what was happening was clearer to me than to her.* **3** (also **statistical significance**) the extent to which a result deviates from that expected to arise simply from random variation or errors in sampling. ▷late Middle English (denoting unstated meaning): from Old French, or from Latin *significantia*, from *significare* 'indicate, portend.'

sig·nif·i·cant /sigˈnifikənt/ ▸*adj.* **1** sufficiently great or important to be worthy of attention; noteworthy: *a significant increase in sales.* **2** having a particular meaning; indicative of something: *in times of stress her dreams seemed to her especially significant.* ■ suggesting a meaning or message that is not explicitly stated: *she gave him a significant look.* **3** *Statistics* of, relating to, or having significance. ▷late 16th cent. (sense 2): from Latin *significant-* 'indicating,' from the verb *significare* (see **SIGNIFY**). **—sig·nif·i·cant·ly** *adv.*

sig·nif·i·cant fig·ure (also **significant digit**) ▸*n. Mathematics* each of the digits of a number that are used to express it to the required degree of accuracy, starting from the first nonzero digit: *this text will round numbers to three significant figures.*

sig·nif·i·cant oth·er ▸*n.* a person with whom someone has an established romantic or sexual relationship.

sig·ni·fi·ca·tion /ˌsignəfiˈkāSHən/ ▸*n.* the representation or conveying of meaning. ■ an exact meaning or sense. ▷Middle English: via Old French from Latin *significatio(n-)*, from *significare* 'indicate' (see **SIGNIFY**).

sig·nif·i·ca·tive /sigˈnifikātiv/ ▸*adj. rare* being a symbol or sign of something; having a meaning.

sig·nif·i·ca·tor /sigˈnifikātər/ ▸*n. Astrology* (in a horary chart) the planet that signifies the inquirer, or the subject of the question. ■ a card chosen to represent the inquirer in a tarot reading.

sig·ni·fied /ˈsignəˌfīd/ ▸*n. Linguistics* the meaning or idea expressed by a sign, as distinct from the physical form in which it is expressed. Compare with **SIGNIFIER.**

sig·ni·fi·er /ˈsignəˌfīər/ ▸*n. Linguistics* a sign's physical form (such as a sound, printed word, or image) as distinct from its meaning. Compare with **SIGNIFIED.**

sig·ni·fy /ˈsignəˌfī/ ▸*v.* (**-fies, -fied**) **1** [*trans.*] be an indication of: *this decision signified a fundamental change in their priorities.* ■ be a symbol of; have as meaning: *the church used this image to signify the Holy Trinity.* ■ (of a person) indicate or declare (a feeling or intention): *signify your agreement by signing the letter below.* ■ [*intrans.*] [with *negative*] be of importance: *the locked door doesn't necessarily signify.* **2** [*intrans.*] *informal* (among black Americans) exchange boasts or insults as a game or ritual. ▷Middle English: from Old French *signifier*, from Latin *significare* 'indicate, portend,' from *signum* 'token.'

sign·ing /ˈsīniNG/ ▸*n.* **1** the action of writing one's signature on an official document: *he plans to oversee the signing of modest agreements on energy, education, and the environment.* ■ the action of recruiting someone, esp. to a professional sports team or record company: *the signing of overseas players* | [as *adj.*] *a signing bonus.* ■ *Brit.* a person who has recently been recruited, esp. to join a professional sports team or record company: *Manchester United's latest signing.* ■ an event in a bookstore or other place at which an author signs a number of books to gain publicity and sales. **2** sign language. **3** the provision of signs in a street or other place.

sign lan·guage ▸*n.* a system of communication using visual gestures and signs, as used by deaf people.

sign-off ▸*n.* **1** the conclusion of a letter, broadcast, or other message: *that was their daily sign-off on the TV show.* **2** *Bridge* a bid indicating that the bidder wishes to end bidding.

si·gnor /sēnˈyôr/ (also **si·gnore**) ▸*n.* (*pl.* **si·gno·ri** /sēnˈyôrē/) a title or form of address used of or to an Italian-speaking man, corresponding to *Mr.* or *sir*: *Signor Ugolotti* | *I am a man of honor, Signor.* ▷Italian, from Latin *senior* (see **SENIOR**).

si·gno·ra /sēnˈyôrə/ ▸*n.* a title or form of address used of or to an Italian-speaking married woman, corresponding to *Mrs.* or *madam*: *good night, Signora.* ▷Italian, feminine of *signor* (see **SIGNOR**).

si·gno·ri·na /ˌsēnyəˈrēnə/ ▸*n.* a title or form of address used of or to an Italian-speaking unmarried woman, corresponding to *Miss*: *Signorina Rosalba.* ▷Italian, diminutive of *signora* (see **SIGNORA**).

sig·no·ry /ˈsēnyərē/ ▸*n.* (*pl.* **-ries**) another term for **SEIGNIORY.**

sign·post /ˈsīnˌpōst/ ▸*n.* a sign giving information such as the direction and distance to a nearby town, typically found at a crossroads. ■ *figurative* something that acts as guidance or a clue to an unclear or complicated issue: *there are few unambiguous signposts for doctors facing ethical issues.*
▸*v.* [*trans.*] provide (an area) with a signpost or signposts: *most of the walks were well signposted.* ■ *chiefly Brit.* indicate (a place or feature) with a signpost: *Battle is clearly signposted off all the main roads.*

sign-up ▸*n.* [usu. as *adj.*] the action of enrolling for something or of enrolling or employing someone: *a sign-up fee of $29.95.*

Sig·urd /ˈsigərd/ (in Norse legend) the Norse equivalent of Siegfried, husband of Gudrun.

Si·ha·nouk /ˈsēəˌnŏŏk/, Norodom (1922–2004), Cambodian king 1941–55 and 1993–; prime minister 1955–60; head of state 1960–70 and 1975–76.

si·ka /ˈsēkə/ (also **si·ka deer**) ▸*n.* a forest-dwelling deer with a grayish winter coat that turns yellowish-brown with white spots in summer. It is native to Japan and Southeast Asia and naturalized elsewhere. • *Cervus nippon*, family Cervidae. ▷late 19th cent.: from Japanese *shika.*

Sikh /sēk/ ▸*n.* an adherent of Sikhism.
▸*adj.* of or relating to Sikhs or Sikhism. ▷from Punjabi, 'disciple,' from Sanskrit *śiṣya.*

Sikh·ism /ˈsēkizəm/ ▸*n.* a monotheistic religion founded in Punjab in the 15th century by Guru Nanak.

Sikh teaching centers on spiritual liberation and social justice and harmony, though the community took on a militant aspect during early conflicts. The last guru, Gobind Singh (1666–1708), passed his authority to the scripture, the Adi Granth, and to the Khalsa, the body of initiated Sikhs.

Si·king /ˈSHēˈjiNG/ former name of **XIAN.**

Sik·kim /ˈsikim/ a state in northeastern India, in the eastern Himalayas, between Bhutan and Nepal, on the border with Tibet; capital, Gangtok. After British rule, it became an Indian protectorate and then, in 1975, a state of India. **—Sik·kim·ese** /ˌsikiˈmēz; -ˈmēs/ *adj.* & *n.*

Si·kor·sky /siˈkôrskē/, Igor (Ivanovich) (1889–1972), U.S. aircraft designer, born in Russia. He built the Grand, the first large four-engined aircraft, in 1913. He went on to establish the Sikorsky company in the U.S. and, in 1939, developed the first mass-produced helicopter.

si·lage /ˈsīlij/ ▸*n.* grass or other green fodder compacted and stored in airtight conditions, typically in a silo, without first being dried, and used as animal feed in the winter.
▸*v.* [*intrans.*] [often as *n.*] (**silaging**) make silage. ■ [*trans.*] preserve (grass and other green fodder) as silage. ▷late 19th cent.: alteration of **ENSILAGE**, influenced by **SILO.**

sil·ane /ˈsilān/ ▸*n. Chemistry* a colorless gaseous compound of silicon and hydrogen that has strong reducing properties and is spontaneously flammable in air. • Chem. formula: SiH_4. ■ any of the large class of hydrides of silicon analogous to the alkanes. ▷early 20th cent.: from **SILICON** + **-ANE**[2].

si·las·tic /siˈlastik/ ▸*n. trademark* silicone rubber. ▷1940s: blend of **SILICON** and **ELASTIC.**

Si·lat /siˈlat/ ▸*n.* the Malay art of self-defense, practiced as a martial art or accompanied by drums as a ceremonial display or dance. ▷Malay.

Sil·ber·man /ˈsilbərmən/, Jerome, see **WILDER.**

sild /sild/ ▸*n.* (*pl.* same) a small immature herring, esp. one caught in northern European seas. ▷1920s: from Danish and Norwegian.

sil·den·a·fil cit·rate /silˈdenəˌfil/ ▸*n.* an off-white crystalline compound that works by inhibiting the breakdown of enzymes that leads to loss of erection. Also called **VIAGRA** (*trademark*). • Chem. formula: $C_{22}H_{30}N_6O_4S$.

si·lence /ˈsīləns/ ▸*n.* complete absence of sound: *sirens pierce the silence of the night* | *an eerie silence descended over the house.* ■ the fact or state of abstaining from speech: *Karen had withdrawn into sullen silence* | *she was* **reduced to silence** *for a moment.* ■ the avoidance of mentioning or discussing something: *politicians keep their silence on the big questions.* ■ the state of standing still and not speaking as a sign of respect for someone deceased or in an opportunity for prayer: *a* **moment of silence** *presided over by a local minister.*
▸*v.* [*trans.*] (often **be silenced**) cause to become silent; prohibit or prevent from speaking: *the team's performance silenced their critics* | *freedom of the press cannot be silenced by tanks.* ■ [usu. as *adj.*] (**silenced**) fit (a gun or other loud mechanism) with a silencer: *a silenced .22 rifle.* ▷Middle English: from Old French, from Latin *silentium*, from *silere* 'be silent.'
▸*PHRASE* □ **in silence** without speech or other sound: *we finished our meal in silence.*

si·lenc·er /ˈsīlənsər/ ▸*n.* a device for reducing the noise emitted by a gun or other loud mechanism. ■ British term for **MUFFLER** (sense 2).

si·lent /ˈsīlənt/ ▸*adj.* not making or accompanied by any sound: *the woods were still and silent.* ■ (of a person) not speaking: *she fell silent for a moment.* ■ not expressed aloud: *a silent prayer.* ■ (of a letter) written but not pronounced, e.g., *b* in *doubt.* ■ (of a movie) without an accompanying soundtrack. ■ saying or recording nothing on a particular subject: *the poems are silent on the question of marriage.* ■ (of a person) not prone to speak much; taciturn: *I'm the strong, silent type.* ▷late 15th cent. (in the sense 'not speaking'):

Pronunciation Key ə *ago*; ər *over*; ˈə or ˌə *up*; ˈər or ˌər *fur*; a *hat*; ā *rate*; ä *car*; CH *chew*; e *let*; ē *see*; e(ə)r *air*; i *fit*; ī *by*; i(ə)r *ear*; NG *sing*; ō *go*; ô *for*; oi *boy*; ŏŏ *good*; ōō *goo*; ou *out*; SH *she*; TH *thin*; T͟H *then*; (h)w *why*; ZH *vision*

from Latin *silent-* 'being silent,' from the verb *silere*. **—si·lent·ly** *adv.*

▸*PHRASES* □ **(as) silent as the grave** see GRAVE[1]. □ **the silent majority** the majority of people, regarded as holding moderate opinions but rarely expressing them. □ **the silent treatment** a stubborn refusal to talk to someone, esp. after a recent argument or disagreement.

si·lent but·ler ▸*n.* a container with a handle and a hinged cover, used for collecting table crumbs or emptying ashtrays.

si·lent com·merce ▸*n.* a group of technologies based on wireless communications and sensing devices that permit various business and marketing activities to proceed without direct human intervention, on the basis of communications between tagged products and controlling software.

si·lent part·ner ▸*n.* a partner not sharing in the actual work of a firm.

Si·le·nus /sī'lēnəs/ *Greek Mythology* an aged woodland deity, one of the sileni, who was entrusted with the education of Dionysus. He is depicted either as dignified and musical, or as an old drunkard. ■ [as *n.*] **(a silenus)** (*pl.* **-le·ni** /-'lē,nī/) a woodland spirit, usually depicted in art as old and having ears like those of a horse.

Si·le·sia /sī'lēzʜə; -sʜə/ a region of central Europe that is centered on the upper Oder valley, now largely in southwestern Poland. It was partitioned at various times among the states of Prussia, Austria–Hungary, Poland, and Czechoslovakia. **—Si·le·sian** *adj.* & *n.*

si·lex /'sīleks/ ▸*n.* silica, esp. quartz or flint. ▷late 16th cent.: from Latin, 'flint.'

sil·hou·ette /,siloo'et/ ▸*n.* the dark shape and outline of someone or something visible against a lighter background, esp. in dim light. ■ a representation of someone or something showing the shape and outline only, typically colored in solid black.
▸*v.* [*trans.*] (usu. **be silhouetted**) cast or show (someone or something) as a dark shape and outline against a lighter background: *the castle was silhouetted against the sky.* ▷late 18th cent.: named (although the reason remains obscure) after Étienne de *Silhouette* (1709–67), French author and politician.

silhouette

▸*PHRASE* □ **in silhouette** seen or placed as a silhouette.

sil·i·ca /'silikə/ ▸*n.* a hard, unreactive, colorless compound that occurs as the mineral quartz and as a principal constituent of sandstone and other rocks. • Alternative name: **silicon dioxide**; chem. formula: SiO_2. ▷early 19th cent.: from Latin *silex, silic-* 'flint,' on the pattern of words such as *alumina*. **—si·li·ceous** /sə'lisʜəs/ (also **si·li·cious**) *adj.*

sil·i·ca gel ▸*n.* hydrated silica in a hard granular hygroscopic form used as a desiccant.

sil·i·cate /'silə,kāt; -kit/ ▸*n. Chemistry* a salt in which the anion contains both silicon and oxygen, esp. one of the anion SiO_4^{2-}. ■ any of the many minerals consisting primarily of SiO_4^{2-} combined with metal ions, forming a major component of the rocks of the earth's crust.

si·lic·ic /sə'lisik/ ▸*adj. Geology* (of rocks) rich in silica.

si·lic·ic ac·id ▸*n. Chemistry* a weakly acidic colloidal hydrated form of silica made by acidifying solutions of alkali metal silicates.

si·lic·i·clas·tic /si,lisə'klastik/ ▸*adj. Geology* relating to or denoting clastic rocks consisting largely of silica or silicates.

sil·i·cide /'silə,sīd/ ▸*n. Chemistry* a binary compound of silicon with another element or group.

si·lic·i·fy /sə'lisə,fī/ ▸*v.* **(-fies, -fied)** [*trans.*] (usu. **be silicified**) convert into or impregnate with silica. **—si·lic·i·fi·ca·tion** /sə,lisəfi'kāsʜən/ *n.*

si·li·co·fla·gel·late /,silәkō'flajә,lāt/ ▸*n. Zoology* a marine flagellate of the order Silicoflagellida, distinguished by a siliceous skeleton and radiating spines.

sil·i·con /'silə,kän; -kən/ ▸*n.* the chemical element of atomic number 14, a nonmetal with semiconducting properties, used in making electronic circuits. Pure silicon exists in a shiny dark gray crystalline form and as an amorphous powder. (Symbol: **Si**) ▷early 19th cent.: alteration of earlier *silicium*, from Latin *silex, silic-* 'flint,' on the pattern of *carbon* and *boron*.

sil·i·con car·bide ▸*n.* a hard refractory crystalline compound of silicon and carbon; carborundum. • Chem. formula: SiC.

sil·i·con chip ▸*n.* a microchip.

sil·i·cone /'silə,kōn/ ▸*n.* any of a class of synthetic materials that are polymers with a chemical structure based on chains of alternate silicon and oxygen atoms, with organic groups attached to the silicon atoms. Such compounds are typically resistant to chemical attack and insensitive to temperature changes and are used to make rubber, plastics, polishes, and lubricants.
▸*v.* [*trans.*] (usu. **be siliconed**) join or otherwise treat (something) with a silicone.

sil·i·con·ize /'silikə,nīz/ ▸*v.* [*trans.*] [often as *adj.*] **(siliconized)** coat or otherwise treat (something) with silicone.

Sil·i·con Val·ley a name given to an area between San Jose and Palo Alto in Santa Clara County, California, noted for its computing and electronics industries.

sil·i·co·sis /,silə'kōsis/ ▸*n. Medicine* lung fibrosis caused by the inhalation of dust containing silica. **—sil·i·cot·ic** /,silə'kätik/ *adj.*

sil·i·qua /'silikwə/ (also **sil·ique** /sə'lēk/) ▸*n.* (*pl.* **sil·i·quae** /'silə,kwē/ or **si·liques** /sə'lēks; 'siliks/) *Botany* the long, narrow seedpod of many plants of the cabbage family, splitting open when mature. ▷Latin, literally 'pod.' **—sil·i·quose** /-,kwōs/ *adj.*

silk /silk/ ▸*n.* a fine, strong, soft, lustrous fiber produced by silkworms in making cocoons and collected to make thread and fabric. ■ a similar fiber spun by some other insect larvae and by most spiders. ■ [often as *adj.*] thread or fabric made from the fiber produced by the silkworm: *a silk shirt.* ■ **(silks)** garments made from such fabric, esp. as worn by a jockey in the colors of a particular horse owner. ■ *Riding* a cover worn over a riding hat made from a silklike fabric. ■ *Brit., informal* a Queen's (or King's) Counsel. [so named because of the right accorded to wear a gown made of this cloth.] ■ any silklike threads that grow in plants, such as at the end of an ear of corn or in a milkweed pod. ▷Old English *sioloc, seolec*, from late Latin *sericum*, neuter of Latin *sericus*, based on Greek *Sēres*, the name given to the inhabitants of the Far Eastern countries from which silk first came overland to Europe. **—silk·like** /'silk-,līk/ *adj.*

silk cot·ton ▸*n.* another term for KAPOK.

silk-cot·ton tree ▸*n.* a tree that produces silk cotton (kapok). • Two species in the family Bombacaceae: the **Indian silk-cotton tree** (*Bombax ceiba*) and the ceiba.

silk du·pi·on ▸*n.* see DUPION.

silk·en /'silkən/ ▸*adj.* made of silk: *a silken ribbon.* ■ soft or lustrous like silk: *silken hair.* ▷Old English *seolcen* (see SILK, -EN[2]).

silk gland ▸*n.* a gland in a silkworm, spider, or other arthropod that secretes the substance that hardens as threads of silk or web.

silk hat ▸*n.* a man's tall, cylindrical hat covered with black silk plush.

sil·kie /'silkē/ ▸*n.* (*pl.* **-kies**) **1** a small chicken of a breed characterized by long soft plumage. **2** variant spelling of SELKIE.

silk moth ▸*n.* see SILKWORM MOTH.

silk oak (also **silk·y oak**) ▸*n.* a tall Australian tree that yields silky-textured timber similar to oak. • Several species in the family Proteaceae, in particular *Cardwellia sublimis* and the frequently cultivated *Grevillea robusta*.

Silk Road (also **Silk Route**) an ancient caravan route that linked Xian in central China with the eastern Mediterranean. It was established during the period of Roman rule in Europe and took its name from the silk that was brought to the west from China.

silk·screen /'silk,skrēn/ (also **silk screen**) ▸*n.* a screen of fine mesh used in screen-printing. ■ a print made by screen-printing.
▸*v.* [*trans.*] print, decorate, or reproduce using a silkscreen.

silk-stock·ing ▸*adj.* wealthy; aristocratic: *a silk-stocking crowd.*

silk tree ▸*n.* an ornamental tree of the pea family with fernlike leaves and showy pink plumelike flowers that open in midsummer. It is naturalized in most of the eastern U.S. • *Albizia julibrissin*, family Fabaceae.

silk·worm /'silk,wərm/ ▸*n.* the commercially bred caterpillar of the domesticated silkworm moth (*Bombyx mori*), which spins a silk cocoon that is processed to yield silk fiber. ■ [with *adj.*] a commercial silk-yielding caterpillar of a saturniid moth. See TUSSORE, TUSSORE MOTH. ▷Old English *seolcwyrm* (see SILK, WORM).

silk·worm moth ▸*n.* a large moth with a caterpillar that spins a protective silken cocoon: • (also **the silk moth**) a domesticated Asian moth whose larva is the chief commercial silkworm (*Bombyx mori*, family Bombycidae). • (also **giant silk moth**) a saturniid moth.

silk·y /'silkē/ ▸*adj.* **(silk·i·er, silk·i·est)** of or resembling silk, esp. in being soft, fine, and lustrous: *the fur felt silky and soft.* ■ (of a person or their speech or manner) suave and smooth, esp. in a way intended to be persuasive: *a silky, seductive voice.* **—silk·i·ly** /'silkəlē/ *adv.* **—silk·i·ness** *n.*

sill /sil/ ▸*n.* a shelf or slab of stone, wood, or metal at the foot of a window or doorway. ■ a strong horizontal member at the base of any structure, e.g., in the frame of a motor or rail vehicle. ■ *Geology* a tabular sheet of igneous rock intruded between and parallel with the existing strata. Compare with DIKE[1]. ■ an underwater ridge or rock ledge extending across the bed of a body of water. ▷Old English *syll, sylle* 'horizontal beam forming a foundation,' of Germanic origin; related to German *Schwelle* 'threshold.'

sil·la·bub ▸*n.* archaic spelling of SYLLABUB.

sil·li·man·ite /'silәmә,nīt/ ▸*n.* an aluminosilicate mineral typically occurring as fibrous masses, commonly in schist or gneiss. ▷mid 19th cent.: from the name of Benjamin *Silliman* (1779–1864), American chemist + -ITE[1].

Sil·li·toe /'silə,tō/, Alan (1928–), English writer. He is noted for his novels about working-class provincial life. Notable works: *Saturday Night and Sunday Morning* (1958) and *The Loneliness of the Long-Distance Runner* (1959).

Sills /silz/, Beverly (1929–), U.S. opera singer; born *Belle Miriam Silverman*. Her association with the New York City Opera included a career as a soprano 1955–80 and the positions of general director 1979–88 and president 1989–90. In 1993, she became the first woman chairperson of the Lincoln Center for the Performing Arts.

sil·ly /'silē/ ▸*adj.* **(-li·er, -li·est)** having or showing a lack of common sense or judgment; absurd and foolish: *another of his silly jokes | "Don't be silly!" she said.* ■ ridiculously trivial or frivolous: *he would brood about silly things.* ■ [as *complement*] used to convey that an activity or process has been engaged in to such a degree that someone is no longer capable of thinking or acting sensibly: *he often drank himself silly | his mother worried herself silly over him.* ■ *archaic* (esp. of a woman, child, or animal) helpless; defenseless.
▸*n.* (*pl.* **-lies**) *informal* a foolish person (often used as a form of address): *Come on, silly.* ▷late Middle English (in the sense 'deserving of pity or sympathy'): alteration of dialect *seely* 'happy,' later 'innocent, feeble,' from a West Germanic base meaning 'luck, happiness.' The sense 'foolish' developed via the stages 'feeble' and 'unsophisticated, ignorant.' **—sil·li·ly** /'siləlē/ *adv.* **—sil·li·ness** *n.*

▸*PHRASE* □ **the silly season** high summer, regarded as the season when newspapers often publish trivial material because of a lack of important news.

sil·ly bil·ly ▸*n. informal, chiefly Brit.* a stupid or foolish person.

Sil·ly Put·ty ▸*n. trademark* a moldable silicone-based substance, sold chiefly as a toy, with remarkable properties of stretching and bouncing.

si·lo /'sīlō/ ▸*n.* (*pl.* **-los**) **1** a tower or pit on a farm used to store grain. ■ a pit or other airtight structure in which green crops are compressed and stored as silage. **2** an underground chamber in which a guided missile is kept ready for firing. ▷mid 19th cent.: from Spanish, via Latin from Greek *siros* 'cornpit.'

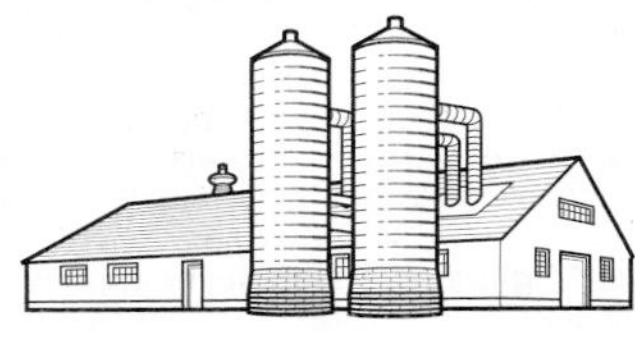

silo 1

Si·lo·am /sī'lōəm; si-/ (in the New Testament) a spring and pool of water near Jerusalem, where a man born blind was told by Jesus to wash, thereby gaining sight (John 9:7).

si·lox·ane /si'läksān/ ▸*n. Chemistry* a compound having a molecular structure based on a chain of alternate silicon and oxygen atoms, esp. (as in silicone) with organic groups attached to the silicon atoms. ▷early 20th cent.: blend of SILICON and OXYGEN + -ANE[2].

silt /silt/ ▸*n.* fine sand, clay, or other material carried by running water and deposited as a sediment, esp. in a channel or harbor. ■ a bed or layer of such material. ■ *technical* sediment whose particles are between clay and sand in size (typically 0.002–0.06 mm).
▸*v.* [*intrans.*] become filled or blocked with silt: *the river's mouth had* **silted up** | [as *n.*] (**silting**) *the silting of the river estuary.* ■ [*trans.*] fill or block with silt. ▷late Middle English: probably originally denoting a salty deposit and of Scandinavian origin, related to Danish and Norwegian *sylt* 'salt marsh,' also to SALT. **—sil·ta·tion** /sil'tāsʜən/ *n.* **—silt·y** *adj.*

silt·stone /'silt,stōn/ ▸*n. Geology* fine-grained sedimentary rock consisting of consolidated silt.

Si·lu·ri·an /si'lo͝orēən; sī-/ ▸*adj. Geology* of, relating to, or denoting the third period of the Paleozoic era, between the Ordovician and Devonian periods. ■ [as *n.*] (**the Silurian**) the Silurian period or the system of rocks deposited during it.

> The Silurian lasted from about 439 million to 409 million years ago. The first true fish and land plants appeared during the period, and the end of the period is marked by the climax of the Caledonian orogeny.

▷early 18th cent.: from Latin *Silures* (denoting a people of ancient southeastern Wales) + -IAN.

sil·van ▸*adj.* variant spelling of SYLVAN.

Sil·va·nus /sil'vānəs/ *Roman Mythology* an Italian woodland deity identified with Pan.

sil·ver /'silvər/ ▸*n.* **1** a precious shiny grayish-white metal, the chemical element of atomic number 47. (Symbol: **Ag**)

> A transition metal, silver is found in nature as the native metal as well as in combined form in ore minerals. It is valued for use in jewelry and other ornaments and formerly in coins, and the decomposition of silver salts by the action of light (depositing metallic silver) is the basis of photography.

2 a shiny gray-white color or appearance like that of silver: *the dark hair was now highlighted with silver.* **3** silver dishes, containers, or cutlery: *thieves stole $5,000 worth of silver* | *the family silver.* ■ household cutlery of any material: *it is important to wash table silver in hot soapy water immediately after each meal.* **4** coins made from silver or from a metal that resembles silver. ■ *chiefly Scottish* money. **5** short for SILVER MEDAL.
▸*adj.* made wholly or chiefly of silver: *silver jewelry.* ■ colored like silver: *a silver Mercedes.* ■ [*attrib.*] denoting a twenty-fifth anniversary.
▸*v.* [*trans.*] [often as *adj.*] (**silvered**) coat or plate with silver: *large silvered candlesticks.* ■ provide (mirror glass) with a backing of a silver-colored material in order to make it reflective. ■ *poetic/literary* (esp. of the moon) give a silvery appearance to: *the brilliant moon silvered the turf.* ■ turn (a person's hair) gray or white. ■ [*intrans.*] (of a person's hair) turn gray or white. ▷Old English *seolfor*, of Germanic origin; related to Dutch *zilver* and German *Silber.*
▸*PHRASES* □ **be born with a silver spoon in one's mouth** be born into a wealthy family of high social standing. □ **every cloud has a silver lining** *proverb* every difficult or sad situation has a comforting or more hopeful aspect even though this may not be immediately apparent. □ **the silver screen** the movie industry; movies collectively: *stars of the silver screen.*

sil·ver age ▸*n.* a period regarded as notable but inferior to a golden age: *the age may in hindsight be seen as not entirely contemptible, perhaps even as a silver age.*

sil·ver·back /'silvər,bak/ ▸*n.* a mature male mountain gorilla, distinguished by an area of white or silvery hair across the back and acting as the dominant member of its social group.

sil·ver·ber·ry /'silvər,berē/ ▸*n.* (*pl.* **-ries**) a North American shrub related to the oleaster, with red-brown stems and silvery leaves, flowers, and berries. • *Elaeagnus commutata*, family Elaeagnaceae.

sil·ver birch ▸*n.* a European birch with silver-gray bark, common on poorer soils to the northern limit of tree growth. • *Betula pendula*, family Betulaceae. ■ another term for PAPER BIRCH.

sil·ver bul·let ▸*n.* a bullet made of silver, used in fiction as a supposedly magical method of killing werewolves. ■ a simple and seemingly magical solution to a complicated problem: *the Internet, like TQM and Reengineering, proved to be no silver bullet* | *an interesting characteristic of silver bullet productivity solutions is their tendency to be recycled every 10 to 20 years.*

sil·ver chlo·ride ▸*n.* a white insoluble powder that darkens on exposure to light, owing to the production of metallic silver. It is used in making photographic emulsions and papers.

sil·ver-eye /'silvər,ī/ ▸*n.* an Australasian songbird of the white-eye family, with mainly greenish plumage and a white ring around the eye. • Genus *Zosterops*, family Zosteropidae: two or three species.

sil·ver fir ▸*n.* a fir tree with foliage that appears silvery or bluish because of whitish lines on the undersides of the needles. • Genus *Abies*, family Pinaceae: several species, in particular the European *A. alba* and the North American *A. amabilis*, a coastal tree found from southern Alaska to northern California.

sil·ver·fish /'silvər,fisʜ/ ▸*n.* (*pl.* same or **-fish·es**) **1** a chiefly nocturnal silvery bristletail that frequents houses and other buildings, feeding on starchy materials. • *Lepisma saccharina*, family Lepismatidae. **2** a silver-colored fish, esp. a goldfish of an unpigmented variety.

sil·ver fox ▸*n.* a red fox of a North American variety that has black fur with white tips. ■ the fur of this animal.

sil·ver gilt ▸*n.* gilded silver. ■ an imitation gilding of yellow lacquer over silver leaf.

sil·ver·ing /'silvəriɴɢ/ ▸*n.* silver-colored material used to coat glass in order to make it reflective.

sil·ver i·o·dide ▸*n.* a yellow insoluble powder that darkens on exposure to light. It is used in photography and artificial rainmaking. • Chem. formula: AgI.

sil·ver ju·bi·lee ▸*n.* the twenty-fifth anniversary of a significant event.

sil·ver leaf ▸*n.* **1** a fungal disease of ornamental and fruit trees, esp. plum trees, resulting in silvery discoloration of the leaves. • The fungus is *Chondrostereum purpureum*, family Stereaceae, class Hymenomycetes. **2** silver that has been beaten into a very thin sheet, suitable for applying to surfaces as a decoration.

Sil·ver·man /'silvərmən/, Belle Miriam, see SILLS.

sil·ver ma·ple ▸*n.* a maple of eastern North America with leaves that are silvery underneath. • *Acer saccharinum*, family Aceraceae.

sil·ver med·al ▸*n.* a medal made of or colored silver, customarily awarded for second place in a race or other competition.

sil·vern /'silvərn/ ▸*adj.* archaic term for SILVER. ▷Old English *seolfren, silfren* (see SILVER, -N[1]).

sil·ver ni·trate ▸*n.* a colorless solid, soluble in water, formerly used in photography. • Chem. formula: $AgNO_3$.

sil·ver pa·per ▸*n.* **1** *chiefly Brit.* foil made of aluminum or other silver-colored metal. **2** *archaic* fine white tissue paper.

sil·ver plate ▸*n.* a thin layer of silver electroplated or otherwise applied as a coating to another metal. ■ objects coated with silver. ■ plates, dishes, etc., made of silver.
▸*v.* (**sil·ver-plate**) [*trans.*] cover (something) with a thin layer of silver.

sil·ver·point /'silvər,point/ ▸*n.* the art of drawing with a silver-pointed instrument on paper prepared with a coating of powdered bone or zinc white, creating a fine durable line composed of metal fragments.

sil·ver salm·on ▸*n.* another term for COHO.

sil·ver serv·ice ▸*n.* a style of serving food at formal meals in which the server uses a silver spoon and fork in one hand to serve the food item by item on to the diner's plate.

sil·ver·side /'silvər,sīd/ ▸*n.* **1** (also **sil·ver·sides**) a small, slender, chiefly marine fish with a bright silver line along its sides. • Family Atherinidae: several genera and species. **2** *Brit.* the upper side of a round of beef from the outside of the leg.

sil·ver·smith /'silvər,smiтʜ/ ▸*n.* a person who makes silver articles. **—sil·ver·smith·ing** *n.*

sil·ver sol·der ▸*n.* a brazing alloy consisting largely of copper and silver.

Sil·ver Spring a residential and commercial suburb in central Maryland, just north of Washington, DC; pop. 76,046.

sil·ver stand·ard ▸*n. historical* a system by which the value of a currency is defined in terms of silver, for which the currency may be exchanged. Compare with GOLD STANDARD.

Sil·ver Star ▸*n.* a decoration bestowed by the U.S. Army upon a soldier for gallantry in action.

Sil·ver State a nickname for the state of NEVADA.

Sil·ver·stein /'silvər,stīn; -,stēn/, Shel(by) (1932–99), U.S. poet, writer, and cartoonist. He is best known for his children's stories and poetry such as in *The Giving Tree* (1964), *Where the Sidewalk Ends* (1974), *The Light in the Attic* (1981), and *Falling Up* (1996).

sil·ver·sword /'silvər,sôrd/ ▸*n.* a Hawaiian plant of the daisy family that has long narrow leaves with silvery hairs and clusters of purplish flowers. • Genus *Argyroxiphium*, family Compositae.

sil·ver thaw ▸*n.* a glassy coating of ice formed on the ground or an exposed surface by freezing rain or the refreezing of thawed ice.

sil·ver tongue ▸*n.* a tendency to be eloquent and persuasive in speaking. **—sil·ver-tongued** *adj.*

sil·ver·ware /'silvər,wer/ ▸*n.* dishes, containers, or cutlery made of or coated with silver. ■ eating and serving utensils made of any material.

sil·ver wed·ding (also **silver wedding anniversary**) ▸*n.* the twenty-fifth anniversary of a wedding.

sil·ver·weed /'silvər,wēd/ ▸*n.* a yellow-flowered herbaceous potentilla with silvery compound leaves, a common grassland weed of north temperate regions. • *Potentilla anserina*, family Rosaceae.

sil·ver·y /'silvərē/ ▸*adj.* like silver in color or appearance; shiny and gray-white: *shoals of silvery fish.* ■ (of a person's hair) gray-white and lustrous. ■ (of a sound) gentle, clear, and melodious: *a little silvery laugh.* **—sil·ver·i·ness** *n.*

sil·vi·cul·ture /'silvi,kəlcʜər/ ▸*n.* the growing and cultivation of trees. ▷late 19th cent.: from French *sylviculture*, from Latin *silva* 'wood' + French *culture* 'cultivation.' **—sil·vi·cul·tur·al** /,silvi'kəlcʜərəl/ *adj.* **—sil·vi·cul·tur·ist** /,silvi'kəlcʜərist/ *n.*

s'il vous plaît /,sēl vo͞o 'ple/ ▸*adv.* French for PLEASE. ▷French, literally 'if it pleases you.'

sim /sim/ ▸*n. informal* a video game that simulates an activity such as flying an aircraft or playing a sport. ▷late 20th cent.: abbreviation of *simulation* (see SIMULATE).

SIM /sim/ (also **SIM card**) ▸*n.* a smart card inside a cellular phone, carrying an identification number unique to the owner, storing personal data, and preventing operation if removed. ▷1980s: acronym from *subscriber identification module.*

si·ma /'sīmə/ ▸*n. Geology* the material of the lower part of the earth's crust, underlying both the ocean and the continents, characterized as relatively dense and rich in silica and magnesia. Contrasted with SIAL. ▷early 20th cent.: blend of SILICA + MAGNESIUM.

si·ma·zine /'sīmə,zēn/ ▸*n.* a synthetic compound derived from triazine and used as a herbicide, esp. to kill broad-leaved weeds and grasses before they emerge. ▷1950s: blend of SYMMETRICAL and TRIAZINE.

Sim·birsk /s(y)im'b(y)irsk/ a city in western Russia, a port on the Volga River, southeast of Nizhni Novgorod; pop. 638,000. Between 1924 and 1992 it was called Ulyanovsk, in honor of Vladimir Ilich Ulyanov Lenin, who was born here in 1870.

sim·cha /'simcʜə/ ▸*n.* a Jewish private party or celebration. ▷from Hebrew *śimḥāh* 'rejoicing.'

Si·me·non /,sēmə'nôɴ/, Georges (Joseph Christian) (1903–89), French novelist, born in Belgium. He is best known for his series of detective novels that feature Commissaire Maigret.

Sim·e·on /'simēən/ (in the Bible) a Hebrew patriarch, second son of Jacob and Leah (Gen. 29:33). ■ the tribe of Israel traditionally descended from him.

Sim·fe·ro·pol /s(y)imfi'rôpəl/ a city in the Crimea, Ukraine; pop. 349,000. It was settled by the Tartars in the 16th century, when it was known as Ak-Mechet, and was seized in 1736 by the Russians.

sim·i·an /'simēən/ ▸*adj.* relating to, resembling, or affecting apes or monkeys: *simian immunodeficiency virus.* Compare with PROSIMIAN.
▸*n.* an ape or monkey. ▷early 17th cent.: from Latin *simia* 'ape,' perhaps via Latin from Greek *simos* 'flat-nosed.'

sim·i·lar /ˈsimələr/ ▸*adj.* resembling without being identical: *a soft cheese* **similar to** *Brie | northern India and similar areas.* ■ *Geometry* (of geometric figures) having the same shape, with the same angles and proportions, though not necessarily of the same size.
▸*n. chiefly archaic* a person or thing similar to another. ■ (usu. **similars**) a substance that produces effects resembling the symptoms of particular diseases (the basis of homeopathic treatment): *the principle of treatment by similars.* ▷late 16th cent. (also as a term in anatomy meaning 'homogeneous'): from French *similaire* or medieval Latin *similaris*, from Latin *similis* 'like.'

sim·i·lar·i·ty /ˌsiməˈlaritē/ ▸*n.* (*pl.* **-ties**) the state or fact of being similar: *the similarity of symptoms makes them hard to diagnose.* See note at **LIKENESS**. ■ (usu. **similarities**) a similar feature or aspect: *the* **similarities between** *people of different nationalities.*

sim·i·lar·ly /ˈsimələrlē/ ▸*adv.* [usu. as *submodifier*] in a similar way: *a similarly priced property.* ■ [*sentence adverb*] used to indicate a similarity between two facts or events: *The diaries of politicians tend to be self-justifying. Similarly, autobiographies may be idealized.*

sim·i·le /ˈsiməlē/ ▸*n.* a figure of speech involving the comparison of one thing with another thing of a different kind, used to make a description more emphatic or vivid (e.g., *as brave as a lion, crazy like a fox*). ■ the use of such a method of comparison. ▷late Middle English: from Latin, neuter of *similis* 'like.'

si·mil·i·tude /siˈmiləˌt(y)o͞od/ ▸*n.* the quality or state of being similar to something. See note at **LIKENESS**. ■ *archaic* a comparison between two things. ■ *archaic* a person or thing resembling someone or something else. ▷late Middle English: from Old French, from Latin *similitudo*, from *similis* 'like.'

Si·mi Val·ley /ˈsēmē; siˈmē/ a city in southwestern California, northwest of Los Angeles; pop. 100,217.

Sim·la /ˈsimlə/ a city in northeastern India, capital of the state of Himachal Pradesh; pop. 110,000.

SIMM /sim/ *Computing* ▸*abbr.* single in-line memory module, containing RAM chips.

Sim·men·tal /ˈzimənˌtäl/ ▸*n.* an animal of a red and white breed of cattle farmed for both meat and milk. ▷1950s: named after a valley in central Switzerland.

sim·mer /ˈsimər/ ▸*v.* [*intrans.*] (of water or food) stay just below the boiling point while being heated: *the goulash was simmering slowly in the oven | figurative the disagreement simmered for years and eventually boiled over.* ■ [*trans.*] keep (something) at such a point when cooking or heating it: *simmer the sauce gently until thickened.* ■ be in a state of suppressed anger or excitement: *she was simmering with resentment.* ■ (**simmer down**) become calmer and quieter.
▸*n.* [in *sing.*] a state or temperature just below the boiling point: *bring the water to a simmer.* ▷mid 17th cent.: alteration of dialect *simper* (in the same sense), perhaps imitative.

sim·nel cake /ˈsimnəl/ ▸*n. chiefly Brit.* a rich fruitcake, typically with a marzipan covering and decoration, eaten esp. at Easter or during Lent. ▷mid 17th cent.: *simnel* from Old French *simenel*, based on Latin *simila* or Greek *semidalis* 'fine flour.'

si·mo·le·on /səˈmōlēən/ ▸*n. informal* a dollar. ▷late 19th cent.: perhaps on the pattern of *napoleon.*

Si·mon[1] /ˈsīmən/, Carly (1945–), U.S. singer and songwriter. Her hits include "Anticipation" (1971), "You're So Vain" (1972), " Nobody Does It Better" (1977), and "Let the River Run" (1988).

Si·mon[2], (Marvin) Neil (1927–), U.S. playwright. Most of his plays are wry comedies that portray aspects of middle-class life. They include *Barefoot in the Park* (1963), *The Odd Couple* (1965), and *Lost in Yonkers* (1991). Many of his plays were made into movies.

Si·mon[3], Paul (1942–), U.S. singer and songwriter. He became known with **Art Garfunkel** (1941–) for the albums *Sounds of Silence* (1966) and *Bridge Over Troubled Water* (1970) and the music for the movie *The Graduate* (1968). The pair split up in 1970 and Simon pursued a successful solo career, recording albums such as *Graceland* (1986).

Si·mon, St., an apostle; known as **Simon the Zealot**. According to one tradition, he preached and was martyred in Persia along with St. Jude. Feast day (with St. Jude), October 28.

Si·mon·i·des /sīˈmänəˌdēz/ (*c.*556–468 BC), Greek lyric poet. Much of his poetry celebrates the heroes of the Persian Wars.

si·mon·ize /ˈsīməˌnīz/ ▸*v.* [*trans.*] polish (a motor vehicle). ▷1930s: from the proprietary name *Simoniz* + **-IZE**.

si·mon-pure /ˈsīmən ˌpyo͝or/ ▸*adj.* completely genuine, authentic, or honest. ▷late 18th cent.: from *(the real) Simon Pure*, a character in Centlivre's *Bold Stroke for a Wife* (1717), who for part of the play is impersonated by another character.

Si·mon Says /ˈsīmən sez/ ▸*n.* a children's game in which players must obey the leader's instructions if (and only if) they are prefaced with the words "Simon says."

si·mo·ny /ˈsīmənē; ˈsi-/ ▸*n. chiefly historical* the buying or selling of ecclesiastical privileges, for example pardons or benefices. ▷Middle English: from Old French *simonie*, from late Latin *simonia*, from *Simon* Magus (Acts 8:18). **—si·mo·ni·ac** /sīˈmōnēˌak; si-/ *adj.* & *n.* **—si·mo·ni·a·cal** /ˌsīməˈnīəkəl; si-/ *adj.*

si·moom /siˈmo͞om/ (also **si·moon** /-ˈmo͞on/) ▸*n.* a hot, dry, dust-laden wind blowing in the desert, esp. in Arabia. ▷late 18th cent.: from Arabic *samūm*, from *samma* 'to poison.'

simp /simp/ ▸*n. informal* a silly or foolish person. ▷early 20th cent.: abbreviation of **SIMPLETON**.

sim·pa·ti·co /simˈpatiˌkō/ ▸*adj.* (of a person) likable and easy to get along with. ■ having or characterized by shared attributes or interests; compatible: *a simpatico relationship.* ▷Italian and Spanish, 'sympathetic'.

sim·per /ˈsimpər/ ▸*v.* [*intrans.*] smile or gesture in an affectedly coquettish, coy, or ingratiating manner: *she simpered, looking pleased with herself.* See note at **SMILE**.
▸*n.* [usu. in *sing.*] an affectedly coquettish, coy, or ingratiating smile or gesture: *an exaggerated simper.* ▷mid 16th cent.: of unknown origin; compare with German *zimpfer* 'elegant, delicate.' **—sim·per·ing·ly** *adv.*

sim·ple /ˈsimpəl/ ▸*adj.* (**-pler**, **-plest**) **1** easily understood or done; presenting no difficulty: *a simple solution | camcorders are now so simple to operate.* ■ plain, basic, or uncomplicated in form, nature, or design; without much decoration or ornamentation: *a simple white blouse | the house is furnished in a simple country style.* ■ [*attrib.*] used to emphasize the fundamental and straightforward nature of something: *the simple truth.* **2** composed of a single element; not compound. ■ *Mathematics* denoting a group that has no proper normal subgroup. ■ *Botany* (of a leaf or stem) not divided or branched. ■ (of a lens, microscope, etc.) consisting of a single lens or component. ■ (in English grammar) denoting a tense formed without an auxiliary, e.g., *sang* as opposed to *was singing.* ■ (of interest) payable on the sum loaned only. Compare with **COMPOUND**[1]. **3** of or characteristic of low rank or status; humble and unpretentious: *a simple Buddhist monk.* **4** of low or abnormally low intelligence.
▸*n. chiefly historical* a medicinal herb, or a medicine made from one: *the gatherers of simples.* ▷Middle English: from Old French, from Latin *simplus.* The noun sense (mid 16th cent.) originally referred to a medicine made from one constituent, esp. from one plant. **—sim·ple·ness** *n.*

sim·ple eye ▸*n.* a small eye of an insect or other arthropod that has only one lens, typically present in one or more pairs. Also called **OCELLUS**. Contrasted with **COMPOUND EYE**.

sim·ple frac·ture ▸*n.* a fracture of the bone only, without damage to the surrounding tissues or breaking of the skin. Compare with **COMPOUND FRACTURE**.

sim·ple har·mon·ic mo·tion ▸*n. Physics* oscillatory motion under a retarding force proportional to the amount of displacement from an equilibrium position.

sim·ple in·ter·val ▸*n. Music* an interval of one octave or less.

sim·ple ma·chine ▸*n. Mechanics* any of the basic mechanical devices for applying a force, such as an inclined plane, wedge, or lever.

sim·ple ma·jor·i·ty ▸*n.* a majority in which the highest number of votes cast for any one candidate, issue, or item exceeds the second-highest number, while not constituting an absolute majority.

sim·ple·mind·ed /ˈsimpəlˈmīndid/ ▸*adj.* having or showing very little intelligence or judgment. **—sim·ple·mind·ed·ly** *adv.* **—sim·ple·mind·ed·ness** *n.*

sim·ple sen·tence ▸*n.* a sentence consisting of only one clause, with a single subject and predicate.

Sim·ple Si·mon ▸*n.* a foolish or gullible person. ▷probably from the name of a character who is featured in various nursery rhymes.

sim·ple time ▸*n.* musical rhythm or meter in which each beat in a measure can be subdivided simply into halves or quarters. Compare with **COMPOUND TIME**.

sim·ple·ton /ˈsimpəltən/ ▸*n.* a foolish or gullible person. ▷mid 17th cent.: from **SIMPLE**, on the pattern of surnames derived from place names ending in *-ton.*

sim·plex /ˈsimpleks/ ▸*adj. technical* composed of or characterized by a single part or structure. ■ (of a communications system, computer circuit, etc.) only allowing transmission of signals in one direction at a time.
▸*n.* a simple or uncompounded word. ▷late 16th cent.: from Latin, literally 'single,' variant of *simplus* 'simple.'

sim·plex meth·od ▸*n. Mathematics* a standard method of maximizing a linear function of several variables under several constraints on other linear functions.

sim·plic·i·ty /simˈplisitē/ ▸*n.* the quality or condition of being easy to understand or do: *for the sake of simplicity, this chapter will concentrate on one theory.* ■ the quality or condition of being plain or natural: *the grandeur and simplicity of Roman architecture.* ■ a thing that is plain, natural, or easy to understand: *the simplicities of pastoral living.* ▷late Middle English: from Old French *simplicite* or Latin *simplicitas*, from *simplex* (see **SIMPLEX**).
▸*PHRASE* □ **be simplicity itself** be extremely easy.

sim·pli·fy /ˈsimpləˌfī/ ▸*v.* (**-fies**, **-fied**) [*trans.*] make (something) simpler or easier to do or understand: *an overhaul of court procedure to simplify litigation.* ▷mid 17th cent.: from French *simplifier*, from medieval Latin *simplificare*, from Latin *simplus* (see **SIMPLE**). **—sim·pli·fi·ca·tion** /ˌsimpləfiˈkāsʜən/ *n.*

sim·plism /ˈsimplizəm/ ▸*n. rare* the oversimplification of an issue.

sim·plis·tic /simˈplistik/ ▸*adj.* treating complex issues and problems as if they were much simpler than they really are: *simplistic solutions.* **—sim·plis·ti·cal·ly** *adv.*

sim·ply /ˈsimplē/ ▸*adv.* **1** in a straightforward or plain manner: *speaking simply and from the heart.* **2** merely; just: *simply complete the application form.* ■ [as *submodifier*] absolutely; completely (used for emphasis): *it makes Terry simply furious.* ■ [*sentence adverb*] used to introduce a short summary of a situation: *quite simply, some things have to be taught.*

Simp·son[1] /ˈsim(p)sən/, Sir James Young (1811–71), Scottish surgeon and obstetrician. He discovered the usefulness of chloroform as an anesthetic.

Simp·son[2], O. J. (1947–), U.S. football player, actor, and celebrity; full name *Orenthal James Simpson.* Following a successful career as a running back for the Buffalo Bills 1969–77 and the San Francisco 49ers 1978–79, he became a television sports commentator. He was arrested in 1994, accused of murdering his wife and her male companion, but acquitted after a lengthy, high-profile trial. In 1997 he lost a civil suit filed by the victims' families.

Simp·son[3], Wallis (1896–1986), wife of Edward, Duke of Windsor (Edward VIII); born *Wallis Warfield.* Her relationship with the king caused a scandal in view of her status as an American divorcee and forced his abdication in 1936.

Simp·son's rule /ˈsimpsənz/ *Mathematics* an arithmetical rule for estimating the area under a curve where the values of an odd number of ordinates, including those at each end, are known. ▷late 19th cent.: named after Thomas *Simpson* (1710–61), English mathematician.

sim·ul /ˈsiməl/ ▸*n. Chess* a display in which a player plays a number of games simultaneously against different opponents. ▷1960s: abbreviation of **SIMULTANEOUS**.

sim·u·la·crum /ˌsimyəˈlākrəm; -ˈlak-/ ▸*n.* (*pl.* **-la·cra** /-ˈlākrə; -ˈlakrə/ or **-la·crums**) an image or representation of someone or something. ■ an unsatisfactory imitation or substitute. ▷late 16th cent.: from Latin, from *simulare* (see **SIMULATE**).

sim·u·lant /ˈsimyələnt/ ▸*n.* a thing that simulates or resembles something else: *jade simulants.* ▷mid 18th cent.: from Latin *simulant-* 'copying, representing,' from the verb *simulare.*

sim·u·late /ˈsimyəˌlāt/ ▸*v.* [*trans.*] imitate the appearance or character of: *red ocher intended to simulate blood |* [as *adj.*] (**simulated**) *a simulated leather handbag.* ■ pretend to have or feel (an emotion): *it was impossible to force a smile, to simulate pleasure.* ■ produce a computer model of: *future population changes were simulated by computer.* ▷mid 17th cent.: from Latin *simulat-* 'copied, represented,' from the verb *simulare*, from *similis* 'like.' —**sim·u·la·tion** /ˌsimyəˈlāsʜən/ *n.* —**sim·u·la·tive** /-ˌlātiv/ *adj.*

sim·u·la·tor /ˈsimyəˌlātər/ ▸*n.* a machine with a similar set of controls designed to provide a realistic imitation of the operation of a vehicle, aircraft, or other complex system, used for training purposes. ■ (also **simulator program**) a program enabling a computer to execute programs written for a different computer.

si·mul·cast /ˈsīməlˌkast/ ▸*n.* a simultaneous transmission of the same program on radio and television, or on two or more channels. ■ a live transmission of a public celebration or sports event: *simulcasts of live races.*
▸*v.* [*trans.*] broadcast (a program) in such a way: *it will be simulcast live to 201 countries.* ▷1940s: blend of **SIMULTANEOUS** and **BROADCAST**.

si·mul·ta·ne·ous /ˌsīməlˈtānēəs/ ▸*adj.* occurring, operating, or done at the same time: *a simultaneous withdrawal of all troops | simultaneous translation.* ▷mid 17th cent.: based on Latin *simul* 'at the same time,' probably influenced by late Latin *momentaneus*. —**si·mul·ta·ne·i·ty** /ˌsīməltəˈnēitē/ *n.* —**si·mul·ta·ne·ous·ly** *adv.* —**si·mul·ta·ne·ous·ness** *n.*

si·mul·ta·ne·ous e·qua·tions ▸*plural n.* equations involving two or more unknowns that are to have the same values in each equation.

si·murg /siˈmərg/ ▸*n.* (in Persian mythology) a large mythical bird of great age, believed to have the power of reasoning and speech. ▷from Persian *sīmurġ*, from Pahlavi *sēn* 'eagle' + *murġ* 'bird.'

sin[1] /sin/ ▸*n.* an immoral act considered to be a transgression against divine law: *a sin in the eyes of God | the human capacity for sin.* ■ an act regarded as a serious or regrettable fault, offense, or omission: *he committed the unforgivable sin of refusing to give interviews | humorous with air like this, it's a sin not to go out.*
▸*v.* (**sinned, sin·ning**) [*intrans.*] commit a sin: *I sinned and brought shame down on us.* ■ (**sin against**) offend against (God, a person, or a principle): *I had sinned against my master.* ▷Old English *synn* (noun), *syngian* (verb); probably related to Latin *sons, sont-* 'guilty.' —**sin·less** *adj.* —**sin·less·ly** *adv.* —**sin·less·ness** *n.*
▸*PHRASES* □ **(as) —— as sin** *informal* having a particular undesirable quality to a high degree: *as ugly as sin.* □ **live in sin** *informal, dated* live together as though married. □ **sin of commission** a sinful action. □ **sin of omission** a sinful failure to perform an action.

THE RIGHT WORD **crime, fault, indiscretion, offense, sin, transgression, vice**

If you've ever driven through a red light or chewed with your mouth open, you've committed an **offense**, which is a broad term covering any violation of the law or of standards of propriety and taste.

A **sin**, on the other hand, is an act that specifically violates a religious, ethical, or moral standard (*to marry someone of another faith was considered a sin*).

Transgression is a weightier and more serious word for *sin*, suggesting any violation of an agreed-upon set of rules (*their behavior was clearly a transgression of the terms set forth in the treaty*).

A **crime** is any act forbidden by law and punishable upon conviction (*a crime for which he was sentenced to death*).

A **vice** has less to do with violating the law and more to do with habits and practices that debase a person's character (*alcohol was her only vice*).

Fault and **indiscretion** are gentler words, although they may be used as euphemisms for *sin* or *crime*.

A *fault* is an unsatisfactory feature in someone's character (*she is exuberant to a fault*), while *indiscretion* refers to an unwise or improper action (*speaking to the media was an indiscretion for which she was chastised*). In recent years, however, *indiscretion* has become a euphemism for such sins as adultery, as if to excuse such behavior by attributing it to a momentary lapse of judgment (*his indiscretions were no secret*).

sin[2] /sīn/ ▸*abbr.* sine.

Si·nai /ˈsīˌnī/ an arid mountainous peninsula in northeastern Egypt that extends into the Red Sea between the Gulf of Suez and the Gulf of Aqaba. It was occupied by Israel between 1967 and 1982. In the south is Mount Sinai, where, according to the Bible, Moses received the Ten Commandments (Exod. 19–34).

Si·na·it·ic /ˌsinēˈitik/ ▸*adj.* of or relating to Mount Sinai or the Sinai peninsula.

Si·na·lo·a /ˌsēnəˈlōə/ a state on the Pacific coast of Mexico; capital, Culiacán Rosales.

Si·nan·thro·pus /sinˈanтнrəpəs; sī-/ ▸*n.* a former genus name applied to some fossilized hominids found in China in 1926. See **PEKING MAN**. ▷modern Latin, from **SINO-** 'Chinese' (because remains were found near Beijing) + Greek *anthrōpos* 'man.'

Si·na·tra /səˈnätrə/, Frank (1915–98), U.S. singer and actor; full name *Francis Albert Sinatra*. He became a star in the 1940s with a large teenage following. His many hits included "Night and Day," "My Way," and "New York, New York." Notable movies: *From Here to Eternity* (Academy Award, 1953), *Ocean's Eleven* (1960), and *The Detective* (1968).

Frank Sinatra

Sin·bad the Sail·or /ˈsinˌbad/ (also **Sind·bad** /ˈsindˌbad/) the hero of one of the tales in the *Arabian Nights*, who relates the fantastic adventures he meets with in his voyages.

since /sins/ ▸*prep., conj., & adv.* **1** in the intervening period between (the time mentioned) and the time under consideration, typically the present: [as *prep.*] *she has suffered from cystic fibrosis since 1984 | the worst property slump since the war |* [as *conj.*] *I've felt better since I've been here |* [as *adv.*] *she ran away on Friday and we haven't seen her since.* **2** [*conj.*] for the reason that: because: *delegates were delighted, since better protection of rhino reserves will help protect other rare species.* **3** [*adv.*] ago: *the settlement had vanished long since.* ▷late Middle English: contraction of obsolete *sithence*, or from dialect *sin* (both from dialect *sithen* 'thereupon, afterward, ever since').

USAGE When using **since** as a causal conjunction to mean 'because' or 'given that,' be aware that in some contexts or constructions the word may be construed as referring to time. For example, in the sentence, *Since Mrs. Jefferson moved to Baltimore in the 1990s, she was not aware of the underlying complexities*, it is not clear, esp. at the beginning, whether **since** means 'because' or 'from the time when.' It is often better to simply say 'because,' if that is the intended meaning.

sin·cere /sinˈsi(ə)r/ ▸*adj.* (**-cer·er, -cer·est**) free from pretense or deceit; proceeding from genuine feelings: *they offer their sincere thanks to Paul.* ■ (of a person) saying what they genuinely feel or believe; not dishonest or hypocritical. ▷mid 16th cent. (also in the sense 'not falsified, unadulterated'): from Latin *sincerus* 'clean, pure.' —**sin·cere·ness** *n.* —**sin·cer·i·ty** /sinˈseritē/ *n.*

sin·cere·ly /sinˈsi(ə)rlē/ ▸*adv.* in a sincere or genuine way: *I sincerely hope that we shall have a change of government |* [as *submodifier*] *sincerely held differences of belief.* ■ (also **sincerely yours** or **yours sincerely**) a formula used to end a letter, typically a formal one in which the recipient is addressed by name.

sin·ci·put /ˈsinsəpət/ ▸*n. Anatomy* the front of the skull from the forehead to the crown. ▷late 16th cent.: from Latin, from *semi-* 'half' + *caput* 'head.' —**sin·cip·i·tal** /sinˈsipitl/ *adj.*

Sin·clair /sinˈkle(ə)r/, Upton (Beall) (1878–1968), U.S. novelist and social reformer. He agitated for social justice in 79 books, including *The Jungle* (1906) and the 11-volume "Lanny Budd" series (1940–53).

Sind /sind/ a province of southeastern Pakistan, traversed by the lower reaches of the Indus River; capital, Karachi.

Sind·hi /ˈsindē/ ▸*n.* (*pl.* **-his**) **1** a native or inhabitant of Sind. **2** the Indic language of Sind, used also in western India.
▸*adj.* of or relating to the province of Sind or its people, or the Sindhi language. ▷from Persian and Urdu *sindī*, from Sanskrit *sindhu* 'river' (specifically the Indus). See **HINDI, INDUS**[1].

sine /sīn/ ▸*n. Mathematics* the trigonometric function that is equal to the ratio of the side opposite a given angle (in a right triangle) to the hypotenuse. ▷late 16th cent.: from Latin *sinus* 'curve,' used in medieval Latin as a translation of Arabic *jayb* 'pocket, sine.'

si·ne·cure /ˈsīnəˌkyo͝or; ˈsi-/ ▸*n.* a position requiring little or no work but giving the holder status or financial benefit. ▷mid 17th cent.: from Latin *sine cura* 'without care.' —**si·ne·cur·ism** /ˈsīnəkyo͝orizəm; si-/ *n.* —**si·ne·cur·ist** /ˈsinəˌkyo͝orist; si-/ *n.*

sine curve /sīn/ (also **sine wave**) ▸*n.* a curve representing periodic oscillations of constant amplitude as given by a sine function. Also called **SINUSOID**.

si·ne di·e /ˈsīnə ˈdīē; ˈsēnā ˈdēā/ ▸*adv.* (with reference to business or proceedings that have been adjourned) with no appointed date for resumption: *the case was adjourned sine die.* ▷Latin, literally 'without a day.'

si·ne qua non /ˌsini ˌkwä ˈnōn; ˌsini ˌkwä ˈnän/ ▸*n.* an essential condition; a thing that is absolutely necessary: *grammar and usage are the sine qua non of language teaching and learning.* ▷Latin, literally '(cause) without which not.'

sin·ew /ˈsinyo͞o/ ▸*n.* a piece of tough fibrous tissue uniting muscle to bone or bone to bone; a tendon or ligament. ■ (usu. **sinews**) *figurative* the parts of a structure, system, or thing that give it strength or bind it together: *the sinews of government.*
▸*v.* [*trans.*] [usu. as *adj.*] (**sinewed**) *poetic/literary* strengthen with or as if with sinews: *the sinewed shape of his back.* ▷Old English *sin(e)we* 'tendon,' of Germanic origin; related to Dutch *zeen* and German *Sehne*. —**sin·ew·less** *adj.* —**sin·ew·y** /-wē/ *adj.*

sin·fo·ni·a /ˌsinfəˈnēə/ ▸*n. Music* a symphony. ■ (in the 17th and 18th centuries) an orchestral piece used as an introduction, interlude, or postlude to an opera, oratorio, cantata, or suite. ▷Italian.

sin·fo·ni·a con·cer·tan·te /ˌsinfəˈnēə ˌkänsərˈtäntā/ ▸*n.* a piece of music for orchestra with more than one soloist, typically from the 18th century. ▷Italian, literally 'harmonizing symphony.'

sin·fo·niet·ta /ˌsinfənˈyetə/ ▸*n. Music* a short or simple symphony. ■ a small symphony orchestra. ▷Italian, diminutive of *sinfonia* (see **SINFONIA**).

sin·ful /ˈsinfəl/ ▸*adj.* wicked and immoral; committing or characterized by the committing of sins: *sinful men | a sinful way of life.* ■ highly reprehensible: *a sinful waste.* ▷Old English *synfull* (see **SIN**[1], **-FUL**). —**sin·ful·ly** *adv.* —**sin·ful·ness** *n.*

sing /siɴɢ/ ▸*v.* (*past* **sang** /saɴɢ/; *past part.* **sung** /səɴɢ/) [*intrans.*] make musical sounds with the voice, esp. words with a set tune: *Bella sang to the baby.* ■ [*trans.*] perform (a song, words, or tune) in this way: *someone started singing "God Bless America" |* [as *n.*] (**singing**) *the singing of hymns in Latin.* ■ (**sing along**) sing in accompaniment to a song or piece of music. ■ (**sing something out**) call something out loudly; shout: *he sang out a greeting.* ■ (of a bird) make characteristic melodious whistling and twittering sounds: *the birds were singing in the chestnut trees.* ■ make a high-pitched whistling or buzzing sound: *the kettle was beginning to sing.* ■ (of a person's ear) be affected with a continuous buzzing sound, esp. as the aftereffect of a blow or loud noise: *a stinging slap that made my ear sing.* ■ *informal* act as an informer to the police: *a leading terrorist was singing like a canary.* ■ [*trans.*] recount or celebrate in a work of literature, esp. poetry: *poetry should sing the strangeness and variety of the human race |* [*intrans.*] *these poets sing of the North American experience.* ■ *archaic* compose poetry.
▸*n.* [in *sing.*] *informal* an act or spell of singing. ■ a meeting for amateur singing. ▷Old English *singan* (verb), of Germanic origin; related to Dutch *zingen* and German *singen*. —**sing·a·ble** *adj.* —**sing·ing·ly** *adv.*
▸*PHRASES* □ **sing a different tune** change one's opinion about or attitude toward someone or something. □ **sing for one's supper** see **SUPPER**. □ **sing the praises of** see **PRAISE**. □ **sing someone to sleep** cause someone to fall asleep by singing gently to them.

sing. ▸*abbr.* singular.

sing-a·long (also **sing·a·long**) ▸*n.* an informal occasion when people sing together in a group. ■ [usu. as *adj.*] a light popular song or tune to which one can

S

easily sing along in accompaniment: *an album featuring simple, sing-along tunes.*

Sin·ga·pore /ˈsiNGə,pôr/ a country in Southeast Asia that consists of the island of Singapore (linked by a causeway to the southern tip of the Malay Peninsula) and about 54 smaller islands; pop. 4,353,000; capital, Singapore City; official languages, Malay, Chinese, Tamil, and English. **—Sin·ga·po·re·an** /,siNGəˈpôrēən/ *adj.* & *n.*

Established as a trading post under the East India Company in 1819, Singapore came under British colonial rule in 1867. Singapore rapidly grew to become the most important commercial center and naval base in Southeast Asia. After World War II, it became first a British Crown Colony in 1946 and then a self-governing state within the Commonwealth of Nations in 1959. Federated with Malaysia in 1963, it declared full independence two years later. In terms of tonnage handled, Singapore's port is the world's busiest.

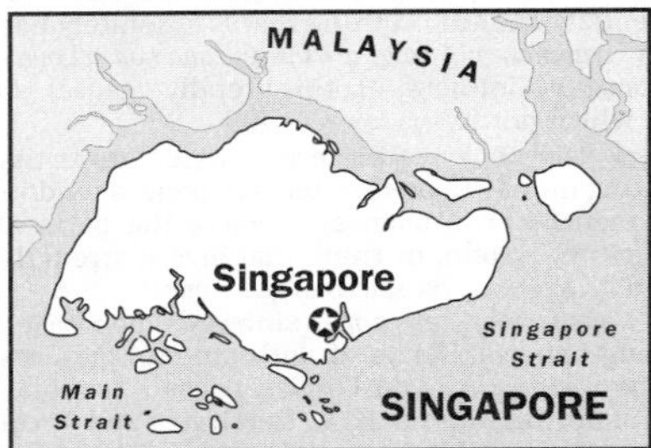

Sin·ga·pore sling ▸*n.* a cocktail made from gin and cherry brandy.

singe /sinj/ ▸*v.* (**singe·ing**) [*trans.*] burn (something) superficially or lightly: *the fire had singed his eyebrows* | [as *adj.*] (**singed**) *a smell of singed feathers.* See note at **BURN**. ■ [*intrans.*] be burned in this way: *the heat was so intense I could feel the hairs on my hands singe.* ■ burn the bristles or down off (the carcass of a pig or fowl) to prepare it for cooking.
▸*n.* a superficial burn. ▷Old English *sencgan*; related to Dutch *zengen*.

Sing·er[1] /ˈsiNGər/, Isaac Bashevis (1904–91), U.S. novelist and short-story writer, born in Poland. His work blends realistic detail and elements of fantasy, mysticism, and magic to portray the lives of Polish Jews during many periods. Notable works: *The Magician of Lublin* (1955), *The Slave* (1962), and *Collected Stories* (1982). Nobel Prize for Literature (1978).

Sing·er[2], Isaac Merrit (1811–75), U.S. inventor. He designed and built the first commercially successful sewing machine in 1852. Singer's company became the world's largest sewing machine manufacturer.

sing·er /ˈsiNGər/ ▸*n.* a person who sings, esp. professionally: *a pop singer.*

sing·er-song·writ·er ▸*n.* a person who sings and writes popular songs, esp. professionally.

Singh /siNG/ ▸*n.* a title or surname adopted by certain warrior castes of northern India, esp. by male members of the Sikh Khalsa. ▷from Punjabi *siṅgh* 'lion,' from Sanskrit *siṃha* 'lion.'

Sin·gha·lese /,siNGgəˈlēz; -ˈlēs/ ▸*n.* & *adj.* variant spelling of **SINHALESE**.

sin·gle /ˈsiNGgəl/ ▸*adj.* **1** [*attrib.*] only one; not one of several: *a single red rose* | *the kingdom was ruled over by a single family.* ■ regarded separately or as distinct from each other or others in a group: *she wrote down every single word* | *it's our single most popular beach.* ■ [with *negative*] even one (used for emphasis): *they didn't receive a single reply.* ■ designed or suitable for one person: *a single bed.* ■ *archaic* not accompanied or supported by others; alone. **2** unmarried or not involved in a stable sexual relationship: *a single mother.* **3** [*attrib.*] consisting of one part: *the studio was a single large room.* ■ *Brit.* (of a ticket) not valid for the return trip; one-way. ■ (of a flower) having only one whorl of petals. ■ denoting an alcoholic drink that consists of one measure of liquor: *a single whiskey.* **4** *archaic* free from duplicity or deceit; ingenuous: *a pure and single heart.*
▸*n.* **1** an individual person or thing rather than part of a pair or a group. ■ a short record with one song on each side. ■ (**singles**) people who are unmarried or not involved in a stable sexual relationship: [as *adj.*] *a singles bar.* ■ *Brit.* a one-way ticket. ■ a bedroom, esp. in a hotel, that is suitable for one person. ■ a single measure of liquor. ■ *informal* a one-dollar bill. **2** *Baseball* a hit that allows the batter to reach first base safely. **3** (**singles**) (esp. in tennis and badminton) a game or competition for individual players, not pairs or teams.
▸*v.* [*trans.*] **1** (**single someone/something out**) choose someone or something from a group for special treatment: *one newspaper was* **singled out for** *criticism.* **2** [*intrans.*] *Baseball* hit a single: *Aaron singled to center.* ■ (**single in**) [*trans.*] cause (a run) to be scored by hitting a single: *they each singled in a run.* ■ [*trans.*] advance (a runner) by hitting a single. ▷Middle English: via Old French from Latin *singulus*, related to *simplus* 'simple.' **—sin·gle·ness** *n.* **—sin·gly** /-glē/ *adv.*

sin·gle-act·ing ▸*adj.* (of an engine) having pressure applied only to one side of the piston.

sin·gle-ac·tion ▸*adj.* (of a gun) needing to be cocked by hand before it can be fired.

sin·gle-blind ▸*adj.* [*attrib.*] denoting a test or experiment in which information that may bias the results is concealed from either tester or subject. Compare with **DOUBLE BLIND**.

sin·gle bond ▸*n.* a chemical bond in which one pair of electrons is shared between two atoms.

sin·gle-breast·ed ▸*adj.* (of a jacket or coat) showing only one row of buttons at the front when fastened.

sin·gle com·bat ▸*n.* fighting between two people: *these two have been engaging* **in single combat** *for years.*

sin·gle-cop·y ▸*adj.* *Genetics* (of a gene or genetic sequence) present in a genome in only one copy.

sin·gle cur·ren·cy ▸*n.* a currency used by all the members of an economic federation. ■ (also **sin·gle Eu·ro·pe·an cur·ren·cy**) the currency (the euro) that replaced the national currencies of twelve member states of the European Union in 2002.

sin·gle-cut ▸*adj.* (of a file) having grooves cut in one direction only, not crossing each other.

sin·gle-end·ed ▸*adj.* (of an electronic device) designed for use with unbalanced signals and therefore having one input and one output terminal grounded.

sin·gle-en·try ▸*adj.* denoting a system of bookkeeping in which each transaction is entered in one account only.

sin·gle file ▸*n.* [in *sing.*] a line of people or things arranged one behind another: *we trooped along* **in single file** | [as *adj.*] *a single-file column.*
▸*adv.* one behind another: *we walked single file.*

sin·gle-foot ▸*v.* [*intrans.*] (of a horse) walk by moving both legs on each side in alternation, each foot falling separately.

sin·gle-hand·ed (also **sin·gle·hand·ed** /ˈsiNGgəlˈhandid/) ▸*adv.* & *adj.* **1** done without help from anyone else: [as *adv.*] *sailing single-handed around the world* | [as *adj.*] *a single-handed crusade.* **2** done or designed to be used with one hand: [as *adv.*] *the tool is easy to use single-handed* | [as *adj.*] *a single-handed ax.* **—sin·gle-hand·ed·ly** (or **sin·gle·hand·ed·ly**) *adv.* **—sin·gle-hand·ed·ness** (or **sin·gle·hand·ed·ness**) *n.*

sin·gle-hand·er ▸*n.* a boat or other craft that can be sailed single-handed. ■ a person who sails a boat or yacht single-handed.

sin·gle-lens re·flex ▸*adj.* denoting a reflex camera in which the lens that forms the image on the film also provides the image in the viewfinder.

sin·gle malt (also **sin·gle-malt whiskey**) ▸*n.* whiskey unblended with any other malt.

sin·gle mar·ket ▸*n.* an association of countries trading with each other without restrictions or tariffs. The European single market came into effect on January 1, 1993.

sin·gle-mind·ed (also **sin·gle·mind·ed** /ˈsiNGgəlˈmīndid/) ▸*adj.* having or concentrating on only one aim or purpose: *the single-minded pursuit of profit.* **—sin·gle-mind·ed·ly** (or **sin·gle·mind·ed·ly**) *adv.* **—sin·gle-mind·ed·ness** (or **sin·gle·mind·ed·ness**) *n.*

sin·gle nu·cle·o·tide pol·y·mor·phism ▸*n.* (abbr. **SNP**.) a variation in a single base pair in a DNA sequence.

sin·gle par·ent ▸*n.* a person bringing up a child or children without a partner.

sin·gles bar ▸*n.* a bar for single people seeking company.

sin·gle seat·er ▸*n.* a vehicle or aircraft for one person: [as *adj.*] *a single-seater glider.*

sin·gle-source ▸*v.* [*trans.*] give a franchise to a single supplier for (a particular product).

sin·gle·stick /ˈsiNGgəl,stik/ (also **sin·gle-stick**) ▸*n.* *Fencing* a wooden stick of about a sword's length. ■ fencing with such a stick.

sin·glet /ˈsiNGlit/ ▸*n.* **1** *chiefly Brit.* a sleeveless garment worn under or instead of a shirt. **2** *Physics* a single unresolvable line in a spectrum, not part of a multiplet. ■ a state or energy level with zero spin, giving a single value for a particular quantum number. ■ *Chemistry* an atomic or molecular state in which all electron spins are paired. ▷mid 18th cent. (originally denoting a man's short jacket): from **SINGLE** (because the garment was unlined) + **-ET**[1], on the pattern of *doublet*.

sin·gle·ton /ˈsiNGgəltən/ ▸*n.* a single person or thing of the kind under consideration: *splitting the clumps of plants into singletons.* ■ [often as *adj.*] a child or animal born singly, rather than one of a multiple birth: *singleton boys.* ■ (in card games, esp. bridge) a card that is the only one of its suit in a hand. ■ *Mathematics* & *Logic* a set that contains exactly one element. ▷late 19th cent.: from **SINGLE**, on the pattern of *simpleton*.

sin·gle·tree /ˈsiNGgəl,trē/ ▸*n.* a crossbar pivoted in the middle, to which the traces are attached in a horse-drawn wagon or plow.

Sing Sing /siNG siNG/ a New York State prison, built in 1825–28 in the town of Ossining (formerly Sing Sing) on the Hudson River, and once notorious for its severe discipline.

sing·song /ˈsiNG,sôNG/ (also **sing-song**) ▸*adj.* (of a person's voice) having a repeated rising and falling rhythm: *the singsong voices of children reciting tables.*
▸*n.* **1** *chiefly Brit., informal* an informal gathering for singing. **2** [in *sing.*] a singsong way of speaking.
▸*v.* (*past* and *past part.* **sing·songed**) [*intrans.*] speak or recite something in a singsong manner.

sing-song girl (also **sing·song girl** /ˈsiNG,sôNG/) ▸*n.* (in China) a female entertainer.

sing·spiel /ˈsiNG,spēl; ˈziNG,SHpēl/ ▸*n.* (*pl.* **sing·spie·le** /-,spēlə; -,SHpēlə/) a form of German light opera, typically with spoken dialogue, popular esp. in the late 18th century. ▷from German *singen* 'sing' + *Spiel* 'play.'

sin·gu·lar /ˈsiNGgyələr/ ▸*adj.* **1** exceptionally good or great; remarkable: *the singular beauty of the desert.* ■ strange or eccentric in some respect: *no explanation accompanied this rather singular statement.* ■ *Mathematics* possessing unique properties. ■ *Mathematics* (of a square matrix) having a zero determinant. ■ *Mathematics* denoting a point that is a singularity. **2** *Grammar* (of a word or form) denoting or referring to just one person or thing. **3** single; unique: *she always thought of herself as singular, as his only daughter.*
▸*n.* (usu. **the singular**) *Grammar* the singular form of a word: *the first person singular.* ▷Middle English (in the sense 'solitary, single,' also 'beyond the average'): from Old French *singuler*, from Latin *singularis*, from *singulus* (see **SINGLE**). **—sin·gu·lar·ly** *adv.*

sin·gu·lar·i·ty /,siNGgyəˈlaritē/ ▸*n.* (*pl.* **-ties**) **1** the state, fact, quality, or condition of being singular: *he believed in the singularity of all cultures.* ■ a peculiarity or odd trait. **2** *Physics* & *Mathematics* a point at which a function takes an infinite value, esp. in space-time when matter is infinitely dense, as at the center of a black hole. ▷Middle English: from Old French *singularite*, from late Latin *singularitas*, from *singularis* 'unique' (see **SINGULAR**).

sin·gu·lar·ize /ˈsiNGgyələ,rīz/ ▸*v.* [*trans.*] *rare* **1** make distinct or conspicuous. **2** give a singular form to (a word). **—sin·gu·lar·i·za·tion** /,siNGgyələrəˈzāSHən; ,siNGgyələ,rīˈzāSHən; ,siNGgyə,lerəˈzāSHən/ *n.*

sinh /sīn; ,sīnˈäCH; sinCH/ *Mathematics* ▸*abbr.* hyperbolic sine. ▷late 19th cent.: from *sin(e)* + *h(yperbolic)*.

Sin·ha·lese /,sinhəˈlēz; -ˈlēs/ (also **Sin·gha·lese**, **Sin·ha·la** /ˈsinhələ/) ▸*n.* (*pl.* same) **1** a member of a people originally from northern India, now forming the majority of the population of Sri Lanka. **2** the Indic language of this people.
▸*adj.* of or relating to this people or language. ▷from Sanskrit *Siṅhala* 'Sri Lanka' + **-ESE**.

sin·is·ter /ˈsinistər/ ▸*adj.* **1** giving the impression that something harmful or evil is happening or will happen: *there was something sinister about that murmuring voice.* ■ wicked or criminal. **2** [*attrib.*] *archaic* & *Heraldry* of, on, or toward the left-hand side (in a coat of arms, from the bearer's point of view, i.e., the right as it is depicted). The opposite of **DEXTER**[1]. ▷late Middle English (in the sense 'malicious, underhanded'): from Old French *sinistre* or Latin *sinister* 'left.' **—sin·is·ter·ly** *adv.* **—sin·is·ter·ness** *n.*

sin·is·tral /ˈsinəstrəl/ ▸*adj.* of or on the left side or the left hand (the opposite of **DEXTRAL**), in particular: ■ left-handed. ■ *Geology* relating to or denoting a strike-slip fault in which the motion of the block on the opposite side of the fault from an observer is toward the left. ■ *Zoology* (of a spiral mollusk shell) with whorls rising to the left and coiling in a clockwise direction. —**sin·is·tral·i·ty** /ˌsinəˈstralitē/ *n.* —**sin·is·tral·ly** *adv.*

sin·is·trorse /ˈsinəˌstrôrs/ ▸*adj.* rising toward the left, esp. of the spiral stem of a plant. ▷mid 19th cent.: from Latin *sinistrorsus*, from *sinister* 'left' + *vertere* 'turn.'

Si·nit·ic /siˈnitik/ ▸*adj.* of, relating to, or denoting the division of the Sino-Tibetan language family that includes the many forms of spoken Chinese.

sink[1] /siNGk/ ▸*v.* (*past* **sank** /saNGk/ or **sunk** /səNGk/; *past part.* **sunk** /səNGk/) **1** [*intrans.*] go down below the surface of something, esp. of a liquid; become submerged: *he saw the coffin sink below the surface of the waves.* ■ (of a ship) go to the bottom of the sea or some other body of water because of damage or a collision: *the trawler sank with the loss of all six crew members.* ■ *figurative* disappear and not be seen or heard of again: *the film* **sank** *virtually* **without trace.** ■ [*trans.*] cause (a ship) to go to the bottom of the sea or other body of water: *a freak wave sank their boat near the shore.* ■ [*trans.*] *figurative* cause to fail: *she apparently wishes to sink the company.* ■ [*trans.*] *figurative* conceal, keep in the background, or ignore: *they agreed to sink their differences.* **2** [*intrans.*] descend; drop: *Sam felt the ground sinking beneath his feet | you can relax on the veranda as the sun sinks.* ■ (of a person) lower oneself or drop gently: *she sank back onto her pillow.* ■ [with *adverbial of direction*] gradually penetrate the surface of something: *her feet sank into the thick pile of the carpet.* ■ (**sink in**) *figurative* (of words or facts) be fully understood or realized: *Peter read the letter twice before its meaning sank in.* ■ [*trans.*] (**sink something into**) cause something sharp to penetrate (a surface): *the dog sank its teeth into her arm.* **3** [*intrans.*] gradually decrease or decline in value, amount, quality, or intensity: *their output sank to a third of the prewar figure | the reputation of the mayor sank to a very low level.* ■ lapse or fall into a particular state or condition, typically one that is unwelcome or unpleasant: *he* **sank into** *a coma after suffering a brain hemorrhage.* ■ be overwhelmed by a darker mood; become depressed: *her heart sank as she thought of Craig.* ■ approach death: *the doctor concluded that Sanders was sinking fast.* **4** [*trans.*] insert beneath a surface by digging or hollowing out: *rails attached with screws sunk below the surface of the wood.* ■ excavate (a well) or bore (a shaft) more or less vertically downward: *they planned to sink a gold mine in Oklahoma.* ■ pocket (a ball) in billiards. ■ *Golf* hit the ball into the hole with (a putt or other shot). ■ [*trans.*] insert into something: *Kelly stood watching, her hands sunk deep into her pockets.* ■ [*intrans.*] (of eyes) appear unusually deep or receded: *her eyes had sunk deep into their sockets.* **5** [*trans.*] (**sink something into**) put money or energy into (something); invest something in: *many investors sank their life savings into the company.* ▷Old English *sincan*, of Germanic origin; related to Dutch *zinken* and German *sinken.* —**sink·a·ble** *adj.* —**sink·age** /ˈsiNGkij/ *n.*

▸***PHRASES*** □ **a** (or **that**) **sinking feeling** an unpleasant feeling caused by the realization that something unpleasant or undesirable has happened or is about to happen. □ **sink or swim** fail or succeed entirely by one's own efforts.

USAGE In modern English, the past tense of **sink** is generally **sank** (less commonly **sunk**), and the past participle is always **sunk**. The form **sunken** now survives only as an adjective: *a* **sunken** *garden;* **sunken** *cheeks.*

sink[2] ▸*n.* a fixed basin with a water supply and a drain. ■ short for SINKHOLE. ■ a pool or marsh in which a river's water disappears by evaporation or percolation. ■ *technical* a body or process that acts to absorb or remove energy or a particular component from a system; the opposite of SOURCE: *a heat sink | the oceans can act as a* **sink** *for CO_2.* ■ *figurative* a place of vice or corruption: *a* **sink** *of unnatural vice, pride, and luxury.* ▷Middle English: from SINK[1].

sink·er /ˈsiNGkər/ ▸*n.* **1** a weight used to sink a fishing line or sounding line. **2** (also **sinker ball**) *Baseball* a pitch that drops markedly as it nears home plate. **3** a type of windsurfing board of insufficient buoyancy to support a person unless moving fast. **4** a doughnut.

sink·hole /ˈsiNGkˌhōl/ ▸*n.* a cavity in the ground, esp. in limestone bedrock, caused by water erosion and providing a route for surface water to disappear underground.

sink·ing fund ▸*n.* a fund formed by periodically setting aside money for the gradual repayment of a debt or replacement of a wasting asset.

sin·ner /ˈsinər/ ▸*n.* a person who transgresses against divine law by committing an immoral act or acts.

sin·net /ˈsinit/ ▸ variant spelling of SENNIT.

Sinn Fein /ˈSHin ˈfān/ a political movement and party seeking a united republican Ireland. ▷from Irish *sinn féin* 'we ourselves.' —**Sinn Fein·er** *n.*

Founded in 1905, Sinn Fein became increasingly committed to Republicanism after the failure of the Home Rule movement. Having won a majority of Irish seats in the 1918 general election, its members refused to go to Westminster and set up their own parliament in Ireland in 1919. After a split in the 1920s, when many of its members joined Fianna Fáil, the party began to function as the political wing of the IRA.

Sin·nott /ˈsinət/, Michael, see SENNETT.

Sino- /ˈsīnō/ ▸*comb. form* Chinese; Chinese and . . . : *Sino-American.* ■ relating to China.

si·no·a·tri·al node /ˌsīnōˈātrēəl/ ▸*n. Anatomy* a small body of specialized muscle tissue in the wall of the right atrium of the heart that acts as a pacemaker by producing a contractile signal at regular intervals. ▷early 20th cent.: from SINUS + *atrial* (see ATRIUM).

sin of·fer·ing ▸*n.* (in traditional or ancient Judaism) an offering made as an atonement for sin.

Si·no-Jap·a·nese Wars two wars (1894–95, 1937–45) fought between China and Japan.

The first war, caused by rivalry over Korea, was ended by a treaty in Japan's favor and led to the eventual overthrow of the Manchus in 1912. In the second war, Japanese expansionism led to trouble in Manchuria in 1931 and to the establishment of a Japanese puppet state (Manchukuo) a year later.

Si·nol·o·gy /sīˈnäləjē/ ▸*n.* the study of Chinese language, history, customs, and politics. —**Si·no·log·i·cal** /ˌsīnlˈäjikəl; ˌsin-/ *adj.* —**Si·nol·o·gist** /-jist/ *n.*

Si·no-Ti·bet·an ▸*adj.* of, relating to, or denoting a large language family of eastern Asia whose branches include Sinitic (Chinese), Tibeto-Burman (Burmese and Tibetan), and, in some classifications, Tai (Thai and Lao). They are tonal languages, but the exact relationships among them are unclear.
▸*n.* this language family.

sin·se·mil·la /ˌsinsəˈmēyə/ ▸*n.* marijuana of a variety that has a particularly high concentration of psychoactive agents. ▷1970s: from American Spanish, literally 'without seed.'

sin tax ▸*n. informal* a tax on items considered undesirable or harmful, such as alcohol or tobacco.

sin·ter /ˈsin(t)ər/ ▸*n.* **1** *Geology* a hard siliceous or calcareous deposit precipitated from mineral springs. **2** solid material that has been sintered, esp. a mixture of iron ore and other materials prepared for smelting.
▸*v.* [*trans.*] make (a powdered material) coalesce into a solid or porous mass by heating it (and usually also compressing it) without liquefaction. ■ [*intrans.*] coalesce in this way. ▷late 18th cent. (as a noun): from German *Sinter*; compare with CINDER.

Sint Maar·ten /sint ˈmärtin/ Dutch name for ST. MARTIN.

sin·u·ate /ˈsinyoōˌāt; -it/ ▸*adj. Botany & Zoology* having a wavy or sinuous margin; with alternate rounded notches and lobes. ▷late 17th cent.: from Latin *sinuatus*, past participle of *sinuare* 'to bend.'

Sin·ui·ju /ˈSHinˈwēˈjoō/ a city and port in North Korea, on the Yalu River near its mouth on the Yellow Sea; pop. 500,000.

sin·u·os·i·ty /ˌsinyoōˈäsitē/ ▸*n.* (*pl.* **-ties**) the ability to curve or bend easily and flexibly. ■ a bend, esp. in a stream or road. ▷late 16th cent.: from French *sinuosité* or medieval Latin *sinuositas*, from *sinuosus* (see SINUOUS).

sin·u·ous /ˈsinyoōəs/ ▸*adj.* having many curves and turns: *the river follows a sinuous trail through the forest.* ■ lithe and supple: *the sinuous grace of a cat.* ▷late 16th cent.: from French *sinueux* or Latin *sinuosus*, from *sinus* 'a bend.' —**sin·u·ous·ly** *adv.* —**sin·u·ous·ness** *n.*

si·nus /ˈsīnəs/ ▸*n.* **1** (often **sinuses**) *Anatomy & Zoology* a cavity within a bone or other tissue, esp. one in the bones of the face or skull connecting with the nasal cavities. ■ an irregular venous or lymphatic cavity, reservoir, or dilated vessel. ■ *Medicine* an infected tract leading from a deep-seated infection and discharging pus to the surface. ■ *Botany* a rounded notch between two lobes on the margin of a leaf or petal. **2** [as *adj.*] *Physiology* relating to or denoting the sinoatrial node of the heart or its function as a pacemaker: *sinus rhythm | sinus tachycardia.* ▷late Middle English (in the medical sense): from Latin, literally 'a recess, bend, bay.'

si·nus·i·tis /ˌsīnəˈsītis/ ▸*n. Medicine* inflammation of a nasal sinus.

si·nus·oid /ˈsīnəˌsoid/ ▸*n.* **1** a curve having the form of a sine wave. **2** *Anatomy* a small irregularly shaped blood vessel found in certain organs, esp. the liver. ▷early 19th cent.: from French *sinusoïde*, from Latin *sinus* (see SINUS). —**si·nus·oi·dal** /ˌsīnəˈsoidl/ *adj.* —**si·nus·oi·dal·ly** /ˌsīnəˈsoidəlē/ *adv.*

si·nus ve·no·sus /vəˈnōsəs/ ▸*n. Zoology* the first chamber of the heart in fish, amphibians, and reptiles, emptying into the right atrium. ▷early 19th cent.: modern Latin, literally 'venous cavity.'

Sion /ˈsīən/ ▸*n.* variant spelling of ZION.

-sion ▸*suffix* forming nouns such as *mansion, persuasion.* ▷from Latin participial stems ending in *-s* + -ION.

Siou·an /ˈsoōən/ ▸*n.* a family of North American Indian languages spoken by the Sioux and related peoples, including Crow, Dakota, Hidatsa, Lakota, Mandan, Omaha, and Yankton.
▸*adj.* of, relating to, or denoting this language family.

Sioux /soō/ ▸*n.* (*pl.* same) another term for the Dakota people or their language. See DAKOTA[2].
▸*adj.* of or relating to this people or their language. ▷North American French, from *Nadouessioux*, from Ojibwa (Ottawa dialect) *nātowēssiwak*, by substitution of the French plural ending *-x* for the Ojibwa plural *-ak.*

Sioux Cit·y a commercial and industrial city in northwestern Iowa, on the Missouri and Big Sioux rivers; pop. 85,013.

Sioux Falls the largest city in South Dakota, a commercial and industrial center in the southeastern part of the state, on the Big Sioux River; pop. 123,975.

Sioux State a nickname for the state of NORTH DAKOTA.

sip /sip/ ▸*v.* (**sipped, sip·ping**) [*trans.*] drink (something) by taking small mouthfuls: *I sat sipping coffee |* [*intrans.*] *she sipped at her tea.*
▸*n.* a small mouthful of liquid: *she* **took a sip of** *the red wine.* ▷late Middle English: perhaps a modification of SUP[1], as symbolic of a less vigorous action. —**sip·per** *n.*

SIPC ▸*abbr.* ■ Securities Investor Protection Corporation. ■ Simply Interactive Personal Computer.

sipe /sīp/ ▸*n.* a groove or channel in the tread of a tire to improve its grip. ▷1950s: from dialect *sipe* 'oozing, trickling,' of unknown origin.

si·phon /ˈsīfən/ (also **sy·phon**) ▸*n.* a pipe or tube used to convey liquid upward from a container and then down to a lower level by gravity, the liquid being made to enter the pipe by atmospheric pressure. ■ *Zoology* a tubular organ in an aquatic animal, esp. a mollusk, through which water is drawn in or expelled.
▸*v.* [*trans.*] draw off or convey (liquid) by means of a siphon. ■ *figurative* draw off or transfer over a period of time, esp. illegally or unfairly: *he's been* **siphoning** *money* **off** *the firm.* ▷late Middle English: from French, or via Latin from Greek *siphōn* 'pipe.' The verb dates from the mid 19th cent. —**si·phon·age** /-nij/ *n.* —**si·phon·al** /-nəl/ *adj.* (*Zoology*) —**si·phon·ic** /sīˈfänik/ *adj.*

Si·phon·ap·ter·a /ˌsīfəˈnaptərə/ *Entomology* an order of insects that comprises the fleas. ▷modern Latin (plural), from Greek *siphōn* 'tube' + *apteros* 'wingless.' —**si·pho·nap·ter·an** /-rən/ *n. & adj.*

Si·pho·noph·o·ra /ˌsīfəˈnäfərə/ *Zoology* an order of colonial marine coelenterates that includes the Portuguese man-of-war, having a float or swimming bell for drifting or swimming on the open sea. ▷modern Latin (plural), from Greek *siphōn* 'tube' + *pherein* 'to bear.' —**si·pho·no·phore** /ˈsīfənəˌfôr; sīˈfänə-/ *n.*

si·phon·o·stele /ˈsīfənəˌstēl; sīˈfänəˌstēl/ ▸*n. Botany* a stele consisting of a core of pith surrounded by concentric layers of xylem and phloem.

si·phun·cle /ˈsīfəNGkəl/ ▸*n. Zoology* (in shelled cephalopods such as nautiloids and ammonoids) a calcareous tube containing living tissue running through all the shell chambers, serving to pump fluid out of vacant chambers in order to adjust buoyancy. ▷mid 18th cent.: from Latin *siphunculus* 'small tube.'

Si·phun·cu·la·ta /sī,fəNGkyə'lātə/ *Entomology* another term for **ANOPLURA**. ▷modern Latin (plural), from Latin *siphunculus* 'little pipe.'

sip·pet /'sipit/ ▶*n.* a small piece of bread or toast, used to dip into soup or sauce or as a garnish. ▷mid 16th cent.: apparently a diminutive of **SOP**.

Si·pun·cu·la /sī'pəNGkyələ/ *Zoology* a small phylum that comprises the peanut worms. Also called **Sipunculida**. ▷modern Latin (plural), from *Sipunculus* (genus name), based on a variant of Latin *siphunculus* 'small tube.' **—si·pun·cu·lan** /-lən/ *n.* & *adj.* **—si·pun·cu·lid** /sī'pəNGkyəlid/ *n.* & *adj.*

Sir. ▶*abbr.* (in biblical references) Sirach (Apocrypha).

sir /sər/ (also **Sir**) ▶*n.* used as a polite or respectful way of addressing a man, esp. one in a position of authority: *excuse me, sir.* ■ used to address a man at the beginning of a formal or business letter: *Dear Sir.* ■ (in Britain) used as a title before the given name of a knight or baronet. ■ another expression for **SIREE**. ▷Middle English: reduced form of **SIRE**.

Si·ra·cu·sa /,sērä'kōōzä/ Italian name for **SYRACUSE** 1.

sir·dar ▶*n.* variant spelling of **SARDAR**.

Sir Dar·yo /sir 'däryə; ,sir där'yä/ a river in central Asia. Rising in two headstreams in the Tien Shan mountains in eastern Uzbekistan, it flows for about 1,380 miles (2,220 km) west and northwest through southern Kazakhstan to the Aral Sea.

sire /sīr/ ▶*n.* **1** the male parent of an animal, esp. a stallion or bull kept for breeding. **2** *archaic* a respectful form of address for someone of high social status, esp. a king. ■ a father or other male forebear.
▶*v.* [*trans.*] be the male parent of (an animal). ■ *poetic/literary* (of a person) be the father of. ▷Middle English (sense 2): from Old French, from an alteration of Latin *senior* (see **SENIOR**). Sense 1 dates from the early 16th cent.

sir·ee /sə'rē/ (also **sir·ree**) ▶*exclam. informal* used for emphasis, esp. after *yes* and *no*: *he's not the type to treat young employees like mud, no siree.* ▷early 19th cent.: from **SIR** + the emphatic suffix *-ee*.

si·ren /'sīrən/ ▶*n.* **1** a device that makes a loud prolonged sound as a signal or warning: *ambulance sirens.* **2** *Greek Mythology* each of a number of women or winged creatures whose singing lured unwary sailors onto rocks. ■ a woman who is considered to be alluring or fascinating but also dangerous in some way. **3** an eel-like American amphibian with tiny forelimbs, no hind limbs, small eyes, and external gills, typically living in muddy pools. • Family Sirenidae: genera *Siren* and *Pseudobranchus*, and three species, including the **greater siren** (*S. lacertina*). ▷Middle English (denoting an imaginary type of snake): from Old French *sirene*, from late Latin *Sirena*, feminine of Latin *Siren*, from Greek *Seirēn*.

Si·re·ni·a /sī'rēnēə/ *Zoology* an order of large aquatic plant-eating mammals that includes the manatees and dugong. They live chiefly in tropical coastal waters and are distinguished by paddlelike forelimbs and a tail flipper replacing hind limbs. • Order Sirenia: two families and four living species. ▷modern Latin (see **SIREN**). **—si·re·ni·an** /-ən/ *n.* & *adj.*

Sir Ga·la·had ▶*n.* see **GALAHAD**.

Sir·i·us /'si(ə)rēəs/ *Astronomy* the brightest star in the sky, south of the celestial equator in the constellation Canis Major. It is a binary star with a dim companion, which is a white dwarf. Also called **Dog Star**. ▷Latin, from Greek *seirios astēr* 'scorching star,' because it rose with the sun in the heat of summer. See **DOG DAYS**.

sir·loin /'sərloin/ ▶*n.* the choicer part of a loin of beef: [as *adj.*] *fresh sirloin steaks.* ▷late Middle English: from Old French (see **SUR-**[1], **LOIN**).

si·roc·co /sə'räkō/ (also **sci·roc·co** /SHə'räkō; sə-/) ▶*n.* (*pl.* **-cos**) a hot wind, often dusty or rainy, blowing from North Africa across the Mediterranean to southern Europe. ▷early 17th cent.: from Italian *scirocco*, from Arabic *šarḳ* 'east wind.'

sir·rah /'sirə/ ▶*n. archaic* used as a term of address for a man or boy, esp. one younger or of lower status than the speaker. ▷early 16th cent.: probably from **SIRE**, when still two syllables in Middle English, with the second syllable assimilated to **AH**.

sir·ta·ki ▶*n.* variant spelling of **SYRTAKI**.

sir·up ▶*n.* variant spelling of **SYRUP**.

sir·up·y ▶*adj.* variant spelling of **SYRUPY**.

SIS ▶*abbr.* (in the UK) Secret Intelligence Service. See **MI6**.

sis /sis/ ▶*n. informal* a person's sister (often used as a form of address): *where are you going, sis?* ▷mid 17th cent.: abbreviation.

si·sal /'sīsəl; 'sī-/ ▶*n.* a Mexican agave with large fleshy leaves, cultivated for fiber production. • *Agave sisalana*, family Agavaceae. ■ the fiber made from this plant, used esp. for ropes or matting. ▷mid 19th cent.: from *Sisal*, the name of a port in Yucatán, Mexico.

sis·kin /'siskin/ ▶*n.* a small songbird related to the goldfinch. • Genus *Carduelis* (and *Serinus*), family Fringillidae: several species, including the **pine siskin** (*C. pinus*) of North America, with darkstreaked plumage, notched tail, and touches of yellow on wings and tail. ▷mid 16th cent.: from Middle Dutch *siseken*, a diminutive related to German *Zeisig*, of Slavic origin.

Sis·ki·you Moun·tains /'siskē,(y)ōō/ a forested range of the Klamath Mountains, in northwestern California and southwestern Oregon.

Sis·ley /sē'slā; 'sizlē/, Alfred (1839–99), French painter, of English descent. He is chiefly remembered for his Impressionist paintings of the countryside around Paris in the 1870s.

sis·sy /'sisē/ *informal* ▶*n.* (*pl.* **-sies**) a person regarded as effeminate or cowardly. ■ *chiefly offensive* an effeminate homosexual.
▶*adj.* (**-si·er, -si·est**) feeble and cowardly. ▷mid 19th cent. (in the sense 'sister'): from **SIS** + **-Y**[2]. **—sis·si·fied** /'sisə,fīd/ *adj.* **—sis·si·ness** *n.* **—sis·sy·ish** *adj.*

sis·ter /'sistər/ ▶*n.* **1** a woman or girl in relation to other daughters and sons of her parents. ■ a half-sister, stepsister, or foster sister. ■ a sister-in-law. ■ a close female friend or associate, esp. a female fellow member of a labor union or other organization. ■ (often **Sister**) a member of a religious order or congregation of women. ■ a fellow woman seen in relation to feminist issues. ■ *informal* a black woman (chiefly used as a term of address by other black people). ■ [usu. as *adj.*] a thing, esp. an organization, that bears a relationship to another of common origin or allegiance or mutual association: *Eastern's sister airline, Continental | a sister ship.* **2** (often **Sister**) *Brit.* a senior female nurse, typically in charge of a ward. ▷Old English, of Germanic origin; related to Dutch *zuster* and German *Schwester*, from an Indo-European root shared by Latin *soror*. **—sis·ter·li·ness** *n.* **—sis·ter·ly** *adj.*

sis·ter cit·y ▶*n.* a city that is linked to another, usually for the purposes of cultural exchange.

sis·ter·hood /'sistər,hŏŏd/ ▶*n.* **1** the relationship between sisters. ■ the feeling of kinship with and closeness to a group of women or all women. **2** (often **Sisterhood**) an association, society, or community of women linked by a common interest, religion, or trade.

sis·ter-in-law ▶*n.* (*pl.* **sis·ters-in-law**) the sister of one's wife or husband. ■ the wife of one's brother or brother-in-law.

Sis·ter of Mer·cy ▶*n.* a member of a Roman Catholic congregation of women founded for educational or charitable purposes, esp. that founded in Dublin in 1827.

Sis·tine /'sistēn/ ▶*adj.* of or relating to any of the popes called Sixtus, esp. Sixtus IV. ▷from Italian *Sistino*, from *Sisto* 'Sixtus.'

Sis·tine Chap·el a chapel in the Vatican, built in the late 15th century by Pope Sixtus IV, containing a painted ceiling and fresco of the Last Judgment by Michelangelo and also frescoes by Botticelli.

sis·trum /'sistrəm/ ▶*n.* (*pl.* **sis·tra** /'sistrə/ or **sis·trums**) a musical instrument of ancient Egypt consisting of a metal frame with transverse metal rods that rattled when the instrument was shaken. ▷late Middle English: via Latin from Greek *seistron*, from *seiein* 'to shake.'

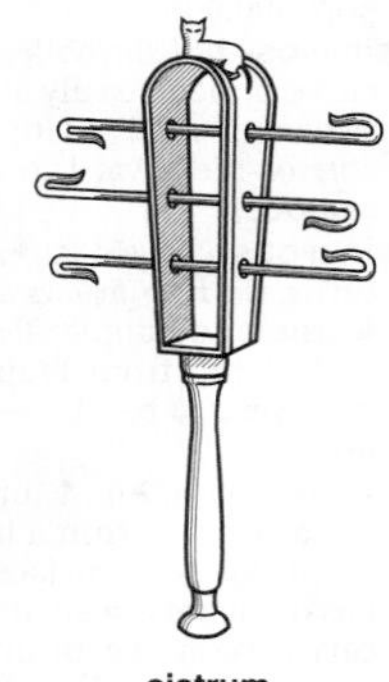
sistrum

Sis·y·phe·an /,sisə'fēən/ ▶*adj.* (of a task) such that it can never be completed. ▷late 16th cent.: from Latin *Sisypheius* (based on Greek *Sisuphos*: see **SISYPHUS**) + **-AN**.

Sis·y·phus /'sisəfəs/ *Greek Mythology* the son of Aeolus, punished in Hades for his misdeeds in life by being condemned to the eternal task of rolling a large stone to the top of a hill, from which it always rolled down again.

sit /sit/ ▶*v.* (**sit·ting**; *past* **sat** /sat/) **1** [*intrans.*] adopt or be in a position in which one's weight is supported by one's buttocks rather than one's feet and one's back is upright: *you'd better* **sit down** *| I sat next to him at dinner.* ■ [*trans.*] cause to adopt or be in such a position: **sit yourself down** *and I'll bring you some coffee.* ■ (of an animal) rest with the hind legs bent and the body close to the ground: *it is important for a dog to sit when instructed.* ■ (of a bird) rest on a branch; perch. ■ (of a bird) remain on its nest to incubate its egg: [as *adj.*] (**sitting**) *a sitting hen.* ■ [*trans.*] ride or keep one's seat on (a horse). ■ [*trans.*] not use (a player) in a game: *the manager must decide who to sit in the World Series.* ■ [*trans.*] (of a table, room, or building) be large enough for (a specified number of seated people): *the cathedral sat about 3,000 people.* ■ (**sit for**) pose, typically in a seated position, for (an artist or photographer): *Walter Deverell asked her to sit for him.* ■ [*intrans.*] be or remain in a particular position or state: *the fridge was sitting in a pool of water.* ■ [with *adverbial*] (of an item of clothing) fit a person well or badly as specified: *the blue uniform sat well on his big frame.* ■ (**sit with**) be harmonious with: *his shyness doesn't sit easily with Hollywood tradition.* **2** [*intrans.*] (of a legislature, committee, court of law, etc.) be engaged in its business: *Congress continued sitting until March 16.* ■ serve as a member of a council, jury, or other official body: *they were determined that women jurists should* **sit on** *the tribunal.* **3** [*trans.*] *chiefly Brit.* take (an examination): *pupils are required to sit nine subjects at GCSE |* [*intrans.*] *he was about to* **sit for** *his Cambridge entrance exam.* **4** [*intrans.*] [usu. in *combination*] stay in someone's house while they are away and look after their house or pet: *Kelly had been cat-sitting for me.* ■ babysit.
▶*phrasal v.* □ **sit back** relax: *sit back and enjoy the music.* ■ take no action; choose not to become involved: *I can't just sit back and let Betsy do all the work.* □ **sit by** take no action in order to prevent something undesirable from occurring: *I'm not going to sit by and let an innocent man go to jail.* □ **sit down** *archaic* encamp outside a city in order to besiege it: *with a large force he* **sat down before** *Ravenna.* □ **sit in** **1** (of a group of people) occupy a place as a form of protest. **2** attend a meeting or discussion without taking an active part in it: *I* **sat in on** *a training session for therapists.* □ **sit in for** temporarily carry out the duties of (another person). □ **sit on** *informal* **1** fail to deal with: *she sat on the article until a deadline galvanized her into putting words to paper.* **2** subdue (someone), typically by saying something intended to discomfit or embarrass them. ■ suppress (something): *tell them to sit on this story until we hear from Quinlan.* □ **sit something out** not take part in a particular event or activity: *he had to sit out the first playoff game.* ■ wait without moving or taking action until a particular unwelcome situation or process is over: *most of the workers seem to be sitting the crisis out, waiting to see what will happen.* □ **sit through** stay until the end of (a tedious or lengthy meeting or performance). □ **sit up** (or **sit someone up**) **1** move (or cause someone to move) from a lying or slouching to a sitting position: *Amy sat up and rubbed her eyes | I'll sit you up on the pillows.* **2** refrain from going to bed until a later time than usual: *we sat up late to watch a horror film.*
▶*n.* [in *sing.*] **1** a period of sitting: *a sit in the shade.* **2** *archaic* the way in which an item of clothing fits someone: *the sit of her gown.* ▷Old English *sittan*, of Germanic origin; related to Dutch *zitten*, German *sitzen*, from an Indo-European root shared by Latin *sedere* and Greek *hezesthai*.
▶*PHRASES* □ **sit at someone's feet** be someone's student or follower. □ **sit in judgment** see **JUDGMENT**. □ **sit on the fence** see **FENCE**. □ **sit on one's ass** *vulgar slang* do nothing; fail to take action. □ **sit on one's hands** take no action. □ **sit** (**heavy**) **on the stomach** (of food) take a long time to be digested. □ **sit tight** *informal* remain firmly in one's place. ■ refrain from taking action or changing one's mind: *we're advising our clients to sit tight and neither to buy nor sell.* □ **sit up** (**and take notice**) *informal* suddenly start paying attention or have one's interest aroused.

USAGE For guidance on the differences between **sit** and **set**, see **usage** at **SET**[1].

Si·ta /'sē,tä/ (in the Ramayana) the wife of Rama. She is the Hindu model of the ideal woman, an incarnation of Lakshmi. ▷from Sanskrit *Sītā*, literally 'furrow.'

si·tar /si'tär/ ▸*n.* a large, long-necked Indian lute with movable frets, played with a wire pick. ▷via Urdu from Persian *sitār*, from *sih* 'three' + *tār* 'string.' —**si·tar·ist** /-ist/ *n.*

sitar

sit·a·tun·ga /ˌsitə'to͞oNGgə/ ▸*n.* a brown or grayish antelope with splayed hoofs and, in the male, spiral horns, inhabiting swampy areas in central and East Africa. • *Tragelaphus spekii*, family Bovidae. ▷late 19th cent.: from Kiswahili.

sit·com /'sitˌkäm/ ▸*n. informal* a situation comedy. ▷1960s: abbreviation.

sit-down ▸*adj.* [*attrib.*] (of a meal) eaten sitting at a table. ■ (of a protest) in which demonstrators occupy their workplace or sit down on the ground in a public place, refusing to leave until their demands are met.
▸*n.* a period of sitting down; a short rest. ■ a sit-down protest.

site /sīt/ ▸*n.* an area of ground on which a town, building, or monument is constructed: *the proposed site of a hydroelectric dam.* ■ a place where a particular event or activity is occurring or has occurred: *the site of the Battle of Antietam | materials for repairs are always* **on site**. ■ short for **BUILDING SITE**. ■ short for **WEB SITE**.
▸*v.* [*trans.*] (usu. **be sited**) fix or build (something) in a particular place: *the rectory is sited behind the church |* [as *n.*] (**siting**) *decisions concerning the siting of nuclear power plants.* ▷late Middle English (as a noun): from Anglo-Norman French, or from Latin *situs* 'local position.' The verb dates from the late 16th cent.

sit-in ▸*n.* a form of protest in which demonstrators occupy a place, refusing to leave until their demands are met.

Sit·ka /'sitkə/ a city in the panhandle of southwestern Alaska, on Baranof Island; pop. 8,835.

Sit·ka spruce /'sitkə spro͞os/ ▸*n.* a fast-growing spruce tree of the northern Pacific coast of North America, widely cultivated in Britain for its strong lightweight timber. • *Picea sitchensis*, family Pinaceae. ▷late 19th cent.: named after *Sitka*, a town in Alaska.

sit-rep /'sitˌrep/ ▸*n. informal* a report on the current military situation in a particular area. ▷1940s: from *sit(uation) rep(ort)*.

Sit·tang /'siˌtäNG/ a river in southern Myanmar (Burma). Rising in the Pegu mountains, it flows about 350 miles (560 km) south into the Bay of Bengal at the Gulf of Martaban.

sit·ter /'sitər/ ▸*n.* **1** a person who sits, esp. for a portrait. ■ a hen sitting on eggs. **2** [usu. in *combination*] a person who looks after children, pets, or a house while the parents or owners are away: *a house-sitter.* ■ a person who provides care and companionship for people who are ill.

sit·ting /'sitiNG/ ▸*n.* a continuous period of being seated, esp. when engaged in a particular activity: *the whole roast was eaten at one sitting.* ■ a period of time spent as a model for an artist or photographer. ■ a scheduled period of time when a group of people are served a meal, esp. in a restaurant: *there will be two sittings for Christmas lunch.* ■ a period of time during which a committee or legislature is engaged in its normal business. ■ *Brit. Law* a period of time when a court of law holds sessions.
▸*adj.* [*attrib.*] **1** denoting a person who has sat down or the position of such a person: *a sitting position.* ■ (of an animal or bird) not running or flying. **2** (of an elected representative) current; present: *the resignation of the sitting congressman.* **3** (of a hen or other bird) settled on eggs for the purpose of incubating them.

Sit·ting Bull (*c.*1831–90), Sioux chief; Sioux name *Tatanka Iyotake*. He led the Sioux in the fight to retain their lands; this resulted in the massacre of Lt. Col. Custer and his men at Little Bighorn. He was killed by reservation police during the Ghost Dance turmoil.

sit·ting duck (also **sitting target**) ▸*n. informal* a person or thing with no protection against an attack or other source of danger.

sit·ting room ▸*n.* a room in a house or hotel in which people can sit down and relax.

sit·u·ate ▸*v.* /'sichoo͞ˌāt/ [*trans.*] (usu. **be situated**) fix or build (something) in a certain place or position: *the pilot light is usually situated at the front of the boiler |* [as *adj.* with *submodifier*] (**situated**) *a conveniently situated hotel.* ■ put in context; describe the circumstances surrounding (something): *it is necessary to situate these ideas in the wider context of the economy.* ■ (**be situated**) [with *adverbial*] be in a specified financial or marital position: *Amy is now comfortably situated.*
▸*adj.* /'sicho͞oit/ *Law* or *archaic* situated. ▷late Middle English: from medieval Latin *situat-* 'placed,' from the verb *situare*, from Latin *situs* 'site.'

sit·u·a·tion /ˌsicho͞o'āshən/ ▸*n.* **1** a set of circumstances in which one finds oneself; a state of affairs: *the situation between her and Jake had come to a head | the political situation in Russia.* **2** the location and surroundings of a place: *the situation of the town is pleasant.* **3** *formal* a position of employment; a job. ▷late Middle English (sense 2): from French, or from medieval Latin *situatio(n-)*, from *situare* 'to place' (see **SITUATE**). Sense 1 dates from the early 18th cent. —**sit·u·a·tion·al** /–shənl/ *adj.* —**sit·u·a·tion·al·ly** *adv.*

sit·u·a·tion com·e·dy ▸*n.* a television or radio series in which the same set of characters are involved in various amusing situations.

sit·u·a·tion eth·ics (also **situational ethics**) ▸*plural n.* [treated as *sing.*] *Philosophy* the doctrine of flexibility in the application of moral laws according to circumstances.

sit·u·a·tion·ism /ˌsicho͞o'āshəˌnizəm/ ▸*n.* the theory that human behavior is determined by surrounding circumstances rather than by personal qualities. —**sit·u·a·tion·ist** *n.* & *adj.*

sit-up ▸*n.* a physical exercise designed to strengthen the abdominal muscles, in which a person sits up from a supine position without using the arms for leverage.

sit-up·on ▸*n. informal, humorous* a person's buttocks.

si·tus /'sītəs; 'sē-/ ▸*n.* situation or position, esp. the normal position of an organ or other part of a living thing. ■ *Law* the place to which, for purposes of legal jurisdiction or taxation, a property belongs.

si·tus in·ver·sus /'sītəs in'vərsəs; 'sē-/ ▸*n. Medicine* an uncommon condition in which the heart and other organs of the body are transposed through the sagittal plane to lie on the opposite (left or right) side from the usual. ▷late 19th cent.: from Latin *situs inversus viscerum* 'inverted placing of the internal organs.'

Sit·well /'sitwəl; -ˌwel/, Dame Edith (Louisa) (1887–1964), English poet and critic. Her early verse, with that of her brothers **Osbert** (1892–1969) and **Sacheverell** (1897–1988), marked a revolt against the prevailing Georgian style of the day.

sitz bath /sits/ ▸*n.* a bath in which only the buttocks and hips are immersed in water. ▷mid 19th cent.: partial translation of German *Sitzbad*, from *sitzen* 'sit' + *Bad* 'bath.'

Sitz·fleisch /'sitsˌflīsh/ (also **sitz·fleisch**) ▸*n. informal* a person's buttocks. ■ power to endure or to persevere in an activity; staying power. ▷from German, from *sitzen* 'sit' + *Fleisch* 'flesh.'

sitz·krieg /'sitsˌkrēg/ ▸*n.* a war, or a phase of a war, in which there is little or no active warfare. ▷1940s: suggested by **BLITZKRIEG**, from German *sitzen* 'sit.'

sitz·mark /'sitsˌmärk/ ▸*n.* an impression made in the snow by a skier falling backward. ▷1930s: from German *sitzen* 'sit' + the noun **MARK**[1].

Si·va /'shēvə; 'sē-/ variant spelling of **SHIVA**.

Si·va·ji variant spelling of **SHIVAJI**.

Si·van /'sivən/ ▸*n.* (in the Jewish calendar) the ninth month of the civil and third of the religious year, usually coinciding with parts of May and June. ▷from Hebrew *sīwān*.

Sitting Bull

Si·wa·lik Hills /si'wälik/ a range of foothills in the southern Himalayas that extend from northeastern India across Nepal to Sikkim.

Si·wash /'sīwäsh; -wôsh/ ▸*n. derogatory* **1** an American Indian of the northern Pacific coast. **2** another term for **CHINOOK JARGON**.
▸*adj. derogatory* of or relating to American Indians of the northern Pacific coast.
▸*v.* [*intrans.*] camp without a tent. ▷Chinook Jargon, from Canadian French *sauvage* 'wild.'

Six, Les see **LES SIX**.

six /siks/ ▸*cardinal number* equivalent to the product of two and three; one more than five, or four less than ten; 6: *she's lived here six months | six of the people arrested have been charged | a six-week tour.* (Roman numeral: **vi**, **VI**.) ■ a group or unit of six people or things. ■ six years old: *a child of six.* ■ six o'clock: *it's half past six.* ■ a size of garment or other merchandise denoted by six. ■ a playing card or domino with six pips. ▷Old English *siex, six, syx*, of Germanic origin; related to Dutch *zes* and German *sechs*, from an Indo-European root shared by Latin *sex* and Greek *hex*.
▸*PHRASES* □ **at sixes and sevens** in a state of total confusion or disarray. □ **knock** (or **hit**) **someone for six** *Brit., informal* utterly surprise or overcome someone. [alluding to the highest-scoring hit in cricket.] □ **six feet under** *informal* dead and buried. □ **six of one and half a dozen of the other** (*Brit.* **six and two threes**) used to convey that there is little real difference between two alternatives.

Six-Day War a war, June 5–10, 1967, in which Israel occupied Sinai, the Old City of Jerusalem, the West Bank, and the Golan Heights and defeated an Egyptian, Jordanian, and Syrian alliance. Arab name **JUNE WAR**.

six·fold /'siksˌfōld/ ▸*adj.* six times as great or as numerous: *a sixfold increase in their overheads.* ■ having six parts or elements: *a sixfold plan of action.*
▸*adv.* by six times; to six times the number or amount: *coal prices have risen sixfold.*

six-gun ▸*n.* another term for **SIX-SHOOTER**.

Six Na·tions ▸*plural n.* (**the Six Nations**) the Five Nations of the original Iroquois confederacy after the Tuscarora joined them in 1722.

six-pack ▸*n.* **1** a pack of six cans of beer or soft drinks typically held together with a plastic fastener. **2** *informal* a set of well-developed abdominal muscles: [as *adj.*] *six-pack abs.*

six·pence /'siksˌpens; -pəns/ ▸*n. Brit.* a coin worth six old pence, withdrawn in 1980. ■ the sum of six pence, esp. before decimalization (1971).

six·pen·ny /'siksˌpenē; -pənē/ ▸*adj.* [*attrib.*] *Brit.* costing or worth six pence, esp. before decimalization (1971).

six-shoot·er ▸*n.* a revolver with six chambers.

sixte /sikst/ ▸*n. Fencing* the sixth of eight standard parrying positions. ▷late 19th cent.: French, from Latin *sextus* 'sixth.'

six·teen /sik'stēn; 'sikˌstēn/ ▸*cardinal number* equivalent to the product of four and four; one more than fifteen, or six more than ten; 16: *sixteen miles east of Detroit | sixteen of our eighteen patients.* (Roman numeral: **xvi**, **XVI**.) ■ a size of garment or other merchandise denoted by sixteen. ■ sixteen years old: *a daughter of sixteen.* ▷Old English *siextīene* (see **SIX**, **-TEEN**). —**six·teenth** /sik'stēnTH; 'sikˌstēnTH/ *ordinal number*.

six·teen·mo /ˌsiks'tēnmō/ ▸*n.* (*pl.* **-mos**) another term for **SEXTODECIMO**.

six·teenth note /ˌsiks'tēnTH/ ▸*n. Music* a note having the time value of a sixteenth of a whole note or half an eighth note, represented by a large dot with a two-hooked stem. Also called **SEMIQUAVER**.

sixth /siksTH/ ▸*ordinal number* constituting number six in a sequence; 6th: *her sixth novel | the sixth of the month | to the original five categories we add a sixth.* ■ (**a sixth/one sixth**) each of six equal parts into which something is or may be divided: *a sixth of the total population.* ■ the sixth finisher or position in a race or other competition: *he could only finish sixth.* ■ the sixth grade of a school. ■ sixthly (used to introduce a sixth point or reason): *sixth, given all the facts there is no logical reason why we can't make a decision.* ■ *Music* an interval spanning six consecutive notes in a diatonic major or minor scale, e.g., C to A (**major sixth**) or A to F (**minor sixth**). ■ *Music* the note that is higher by this interval than the tonic of a scale or root of a chord. **—sixth·ly** *adv.*

sixth sense ▸*n.* [in *sing.*] a supposed intuitive faculty giving awareness not explicable in terms of normal perception: *some sixth sense told him he was not alone.*

six·ty /ˈsikstē/ ▸*cardinal number* (*pl.* **-ties**) the number equivalent to the product of six and ten; ten more than fifty; 60: *a crew of sixty | sixty bedrooms | sixty percent of the children.* (Roman numeral: **lx, LX.**) ■ (**sixties**) the numbers from sixty to sixty-nine, esp. the years of a century or of a person's life: *Morris was in his early sixties | the flower children of the sixties.* ■ sixty miles an hour: *they were doing sixty.* ■ sixty years old: *he retired at sixty.* ▷Old English *siextig* (see **SIX, -TY**2). **—six·ti·eth** /-iTH/ *ordinal number* **—six·ty·fold** /-ˈfōld/ *adj. & adv.*

six·ty-four·mo /ˌsikstē ˈfôrmō/ ▸*n.* (*pl.* **-mos**) a size of book in which each leaf is one sixty-fourth the size of a printing sheet. ■ a book of this size.

six·ty-fourth note ▸*n. Music* a note with the time value of half a thirty-second note, represented by a large dot with a four-flagged stem.

six·ty-four thou·sand dol·lar ques·tion ▸*n. informal* something that is not known and on which a great deal depends. ▷1950s: from a question posed for the top prize in a television quiz show of the same name.

six·ty-nine ▸*n. informal* sexual activity between two people involving mutual oral stimulation of their genitals. ▷from the position of the couple.

siz·a·ble /ˈsīzəbəl/ (also **size·a·ble**) ▸*adj.* fairly large: *a sizable proportion of the population | a sizable apartment.* **—siz·a·bly** /-blē/ *adv.*

siz·ar /ˈsīzər/ ▸*n.* an undergraduate at Cambridge University or at Trinity College, Dublin, receiving financial help from the college and formerly having certain menial duties. ▷late 16th cent.: from obsolete *size* 'ration of bread, beer, etc.' + **-AR**3. **—siz·ar·ship** /-ˌSHip/ *n.*

size1 /sīz/ ▸*n.* **1** the relative extent of something; a thing's overall dimensions or magnitude; how big something is: *the schools varied* **in size** *| a forest* **the size of** *Connecticut | houses of all sizes.* ■ extensive dimensions or magnitude: *she seemed slightly awed by the size of the building.* **2** each of the classes, typically numbered, into which garments or other articles are divided according to how large they are: *I can never find anything in my size.* ■ a person or garment corresponding to such a numbered class: *she's a size 10.*
▸*v.* [*trans.*] alter or sort in terms of size or according to size: *some drills are sized in millimeters.* ■ (**size something up**) estimate or measure something's dimensions: *she was trying to size up a room with a tape measure.* ■ (**size someone/something up**) *informal* form an estimate or rough judgment of someone or something: *the two men sized each other up.*
▸*adj.* [in *combination*] having a specified size; sized: *marble-size chunks of hail.* ▷Middle English (also in the sense 'assize, ordinance fixing a rate of payment'): from Old French *sise*, from *assise* 'ordinance,' or a shortening of **ASSIZE**. **—siz·er** *n.*
▸*PHRASES* □ **of a size** (of two or more people or things) having the same dimensions. □ **of some size** fairly large. □ **that's about the size of it** *informal* said to confirm someone's assessment of a situation, esp. of one regarded as bad. □ **to size** to the dimensions wanted: *the PVC sheet is easily* **cut to size.**

size2 ▸*n.* a gelatinous solution used in gilding paper, stiffening textiles, and preparing plastered walls for decoration.
▸*v.* [*trans.*] treat with size to glaze or stiffen. ▷Middle English: perhaps the same word as **SIZE**1.

size·a·ble ▸*adj.* variant spelling of **SIZABLE**.

sized /sīzd/ ▸*adj.* [in *combination* or with *submodifier*] having a specified size: *sparrow-sized birds | comfortably sized rooms.*

size·ism /ˈsīzˌizəm/ (also **siz·ism**) ▸*n.* prejudice or discrimination on the grounds of a person's size: *requiring large passengers to buy two seats is pure sizeism.* ▷from *size* + *-ism* 'basis for prejudice.' **—size·ist** (also **siz·ist**) *adj. & n.*

siz·zle /ˈsizəl/ ▸*v.* [*intrans.*] (of food) make a hissing sound when frying or cooking: *the bacon began to sizzle in the pan.* ■ [often as *adj.*] (**sizzling**) *informal* be very hot: *the sizzling summer temperatures.* ■ [often as *adj.*] (**sizzling**) *informal* be very exciting or passionate, esp. sexually: *that was the start of a sizzling affair.*
▸*n.* [in *sing.*] a hissing sound, as of food frying or cooking: *the sizzle of hot dogs.* ■ *informal* a state or quality of great excitement or passion: *a dance routine with lots of sizzle.* ▷early 17th cent.: imitative. **—siz·zler** /ˈsiz(ə)lər/ *n.*

SJ ▸*abbr.* Society of Jesus.

Sjæl·land /ˈSHelän/ Danish name for **ZEALAND**.

sjam·bok /SHamˈbäk; -ˈbək; ˈSHambäk; -bək/ ▸*n.* (in South Africa) a long, stiff whip, originally made of rhinoceros hide.
▸*v.* [*trans.*] flog with a sjambok. ▷from South African Dutch *tjambok*, via Malay from Urdu *chābuk*.

SJC ▸*abbr.* (in the U.S.) Supreme Judicial Court.

S.J.D. ▸*abbr.* Doctor of Juridical Science. ▷Latin *Scientiae Juridicae Doctor.*

Sjö·gren's syn·drome /ˈSHəgrənz/ (also **Sjö·gren's dis·ease**) ▸*n. Medicine* a chronic autoimmune condition characterized by degeneration of the salivary and lachrymal glands, causing dryness of the mouth and eyes. ▷1930s: named after Henrik S. C. *Sjögren* (1899–1986), Swedish physician.

SK ▸*abbr.* Saskatchewan (in official postal use).

sk. ▸*abbr.* sack.

ska /skä/ ▸*n.* a style of fast popular music having a strong offbeat and originating in Jamaica in the 1960s, a forerunner of reggae. ▷1960s: of unknown origin.

skag 1 /skag/ (also **scag**) ▸*n. informal* heroin. ▷early 20th cent.: of unknown origin.

skag2 ▸n. variant spelling of **SKEG**.

Skag·er·rak /ˈskagəˌrak; ˈskägəˌräk/ (**the Skagerrak**) a strait that separates southern Norway from the northwest coast of Denmark.

Skag·way /ˈskagˌwā/ a city in southwestern Alaska, in the panhandle; pop. 692. A cruise ship port, it was a gateway to the 1897–98 Klondike gold rush.

skald /skôld; skäld/ (also **scald**) ▸*n. historical* (in ancient Scandinavia) a composer and reciter of poems honoring heroes and their deeds. ▷from Old Norse *skáld*, of unknown origin. **—skald·ic** /-ik/ *adj.*

Skan·da /ˈskəndə/ *Hinduism* the Hindu war god, first son of Shiva and Parvati and brother of Ganesha. He is depicted as a boy or youth, sometimes with six heads and often with his mount, a peacock.

skank /skaNGk/ ▸*n.* **1** *informal* a person perceived to be extremely sleazy or unpleasant. ■ *derogatory* a promiscuous woman. *the office skank.* **2** a steady-paced dance performed to reggae music, characterized by rhythmically bending forward, raising the knees, and extending the hands palms-downward. ■ reggae music suitable for such dancing.
▸*v.* **1** [*trans.*] swindle or deceive: *they made a tidy sum skanking the tourists.* ■ obtain by deception or theft: *I skanked the poster off some wall.* **2** [*intrans.*] [often as *adj.*] (**skanking**) play reggae music or dance in this style. ▷1970s: of unknown origin.

skank·y /ˈskaNGkē/ ▸*adj. informal* very unpleasant; revolting: *along with sandals come a lot of skanky feet.* ■ sleazy; sordid: *his friends were the skanky types who hang around skanky places.*

skarn /skärn/ ▸*n. Geology* lime-bearing siliceous rock produced by the metamorphic alteration of limestone or dolomite. ▷early 20th cent.: from Swedish, literally 'dung, filth.'

skat /skat/ ▸*n.* a three-handed trick-taking card game with bidding, played with 32 cards. ▷mid 19th cent.: from German, from Italian *scarto* 'a discard,' from *scartare* 'discard.'

skate1 /skāt/ ▸*n.* an ice skate or roller skate. ■ a device, typically with wheels on the underside, used to move a heavy or unwieldy object.
▸*v.* [*intrans.*] move on ice skates or roller skates in a gliding fashion: *the boys were skating on the ice.* ■ [*trans.*] perform (a specified figure) on skates: *figure eights skated entirely on one foot.* ■ ride on a skateboard. ■ (**skate over/around**) *figurative* pass over or refer only fleetingly to (a subject or problem): *she seemed to skate over the next part of her story.* ■ (**skate through**) *figurative* make quick and easy progress through: *he admits he had expected to skate through the system.* ▷mid 17th cent. (originally as the plural *scates*): from Dutch *schaats* (singular but interpreted as plural), from Old French *eschasse* 'stilt.' **—skat·er** *n.*

skate2 ▸*n.* (*pl.* same or **skates**) a typically large marine fish of the ray family with a cartilaginous skeleton and a flattened diamond-shaped body. • Family Rajidae: numerous species, in particular the commercially valuable *Raja batis*. ■ the flesh of a skate or thornback used as food. ▷Middle English: from Old Norse *skata*.

skate·board /ˈskātˌbôrd/ ▸*n.* a short narrow board with two small wheels fixed to the bottom of either end, on which (as a recreation or sport) a person can ride in a standing or crouching position, propelling themselves by occasionally pushing one foot against the ground.
▸*v.* [*intrans.*] [often as *n.*] (**skateboarding**) ride on a skateboard. **—skate·board·er** *n.*

skate·park /ˈskātˌpärk/ ▸*n.* an area designated and equipped for skateboarding.

skat·ing /ˈskātiNG/ ▸*n.* the action or activity of skating on ice skates, roller skates, or a skateboard as a sport or pastime.

skat·ing rink ▸*n.* an expanse of ice artificially made for skating, or a floor used for roller skating.

skean dhu /ˌskē(ə)n ˈTHo͞o; ˈdo͞o/ ▸*n.* a dagger worn in the stocking as part of Highland dress. ▷early 19th cent.: from Irish and Scottish Gaelic *sgian* 'knife' + Scottish Gaelic *dubh* 'black.'

sked /sked/ *informal* ▸*n.* short for **SCHEDULE**.

ske·dad·dle /skiˈdadl/ ▸*v.* [*intrans.*] *informal* depart quickly or hurriedly; run away: *when he saw us, he skedaddled.*
▸*n.* a hurried departure or flight. ▷mid 19th cent.: of unknown origin.

skeet /skēt/ (also **skeet shooting**) ▸*n.* a shooting sport in which a clay target is thrown from a trap to simulate the flight of a bird. ▷1920s: apparently a pseudoarchaic alteration of the verb **SHOOT**. **—skeet shoot·er** *n.*

skee·ter /ˈskētər/ ▸*n. informal* a mosquito. ▷mid 19th cent.: shortened form, representing a casual pronunciation.

skeg /skeg/ (also **skag** skag) ▸*n.* a tapering or projecting stern section of a vessel's keel, which protects the propeller and supports the rudder. ■ a fin underneath the rear of a surfboard. ▷early 17th cent.: from Old Norse *skegg* 'beard,' perhaps from Dutch *scheg.*

skein /skān/ ▸*n.* a length of thread or yarn, loosely coiled and knotted. ■ a tangled or complicated arrangement, state, or situation: ***the skeins of*** *her long hair | figurative* ***a skein of*** *lies.* ■ a flock of wild geese or swans in flight, typically in a V-shaped formation. ▷Middle English: shortening of Old French *escaigne*, of unknown origin.

skel·e·tal /ˈskelətl/ ▸*adj.* of, relating to, or functioning as a skeleton: *the skeletal remains of aquatic organisms.* ■ very thin; emaciated: *a small, skeletal boy clothed in rags.* ■ existing only in outline or as a framework of something: *a skeletal plot for a novel | the skeletal leaves of long-faded roses.* **—skel·e·tal·ly** *adv.*

skel·e·tal mus·cle ▸*n.* a muscle that is connected to the skeleton to form part of the mechanical system that moves the limbs and other parts of the body. ■ another term for **STRIATED MUSCLE**.

skel·e·ton /ˈskelitn/ ▸*n.* an internal or external framework of bone, cartilage, or other rigid material supporting or containing the body of an animal or plant. ■ used in exaggerated reference to a very thin or emaciated person or animal: *she was no more than a skeleton at the end.* ■ the remaining part of something after its life or usefulness is gone: *the chapel was stripped to a skeleton of its former self.* ■ the supporting framework, basic structure, or essential part of something: *the concrete skeleton of an unfinished building | the skeleton of a report.* ■ [as *adj.*] denoting the essential or minimum number of people, things, or parts necessary for something: *there was only a skeleton staff on duty.* ▷late 16th cent.: modern Latin, from Greek, neuter of *skeletos* 'dried up,' from *skellein* 'dry up.' **—skel·e·ton·ize** /-ˌīz/ *v.*
▸*PHRASE* □ **skeleton in the closet** a discreditable or embarrassing fact that someone wishes to keep secret.

Skel·e·ton Coast an arid coastal area in Namibia. Comprised of the northern part of the Namib desert, it extends from Walvis Bay in the south to the border with Angola.

skel·e·ton key ▸*n.* a key designed to fit many locks by having the interior of the bit hollowed.

skell /skel/ ▸*n. informal* (in New York) a tramp or homeless person. ▷1980s: perhaps a shortening of *skeleton.*

Skel·ton /ˈskeltn/, Red (1913–97), U.S. comedian; born *Richard Bernard Skelton.* A stage, circus, and movie performer, he starred in the television series "The Red Skelton Show" (1951–71) and brought to life characters such as Clem Kadiddlehopper, Freddie the Freeloader, and Mean Widdle Kid.

skep /skep/ ▸*n.* a straw or wicker beehive. ■ *archaic* a wooden or wicker basket. ▷late Old English *sceppe* 'basket,' from Old Norse *skeppa* 'basket, bushel.'

skep·tic /ˈskeptik/ (*Brit.* **scep·tic**) ▸*n.* **1** a person inclined to question or doubt all accepted opinions. ■ a person who doubts the truth of Christianity and other religions; an atheist or agnostic. **2** *Philosophy* an ancient or modern philosopher who denies the possibility of knowledge, or even rational belief, in some sphere.

The leading ancient skeptic was Pyrrho, whose followers at the Academy vigorously opposed Stoicism. Modern skeptics have held diverse views: the most extreme have doubted whether any knowledge at all of the external world is possible (see SOLIPSISM), while others have questioned the existence of objects beyond our experience of them.

▸*adj.* another term for SKEPTICAL. ▷late 16th cent. (sense 2): from French *sceptique*, or via Latin from Greek *skeptikos*, from *skepsis* 'inquiry, doubt.' **—skep·ti·cism** /ˈskeptəˌsizəm/ (*Brit.* **scep·ti·cism**) *n.*

skep·ti·cal /ˈskeptikəl/ (*Brit.* **scep·ti·cal**) ▸*adj.* **1** not easily convinced; having doubts or reservations: *the public were deeply skeptical about some of the proposals.* **2** *Philosophy* relating to the theory that certain knowledge is impossible. **—skep·ti·cal·ly** /-ik(ə)lē/ (*Brit.* **scep·ti·cal·ly**) *adv.*

sker·ry /ˈskerē/ ▸*n.* (*pl.* **-ries**) *Scottish* a reef or rocky island. ▷early 17th cent.: Orkney dialect, from Old Norse *sker*. Compare with SCAR *n.* 2.

sketch /skeCH/ ▸*n.* **1** a rough or unfinished drawing or painting, often made to assist in making a more finished picture: *a charcoal sketch.* ■ a brief written or spoken account or description of someone or something, giving only basic details: *a biographical sketch of Ernest Hemingway.* ■ a rough or unfinished version of any creative work. **2** a short humorous play or performance, consisting typically of one scene in a comedy program. **3** *informal* a comical or amusing person or thing.

▸*v.* [*trans.*] make a rough drawing of: *as they talked, Modigliani began to sketch her* | [*intrans.*] *Jeanne sketched and painted whenever she had the time.* ■ give a brief account or general outline of: *they* ***sketched out*** *the prosecution case.* ■ perform (a gesture) with one's hands or body: *he sketched a graceful bow in her direction.* ▷mid 17th cent.: from Dutch *schets* or German *Skizze*, from Italian *schizzo*, from *schizzare* 'make a sketch,' based on Greek *skhedios* 'done extempore.' **—sketch·er** *n.*

sketch·book /ˈskeCHˌbo͝ok/ ▸*n.* (also **sketch·pad** /-ˌpad/) a pad or book of drawing paper for sketching on. ■ a book of drawings or literary sketches.

sketch·y /ˈskeCHē/ ▸*adj.* (**sketch·i·er**, **sketch·i·est**) not thorough or detailed: *the information they had was sketchy.* ■ (of a picture) resembling a sketch; consisting of outline without much detail. **—sketch·i·ly** /ˈskeCHəlē/ *adv.* **—sketch·i·ness** *n.*

skew /skyo͞o/ ▸*adj.* **1** neither parallel nor at right angles to a specified or implied line; askew; crooked: *his hat looked slightly skew* | *a skew angle.* ■ *Statistics* (of a statistical distribution) not symmetrical. **2** *Mathematics* (of a pair of lines) neither parallel nor intersecting. ■ (of a curve) not lying in a plane.

▸*n.* an oblique angle; a slant. ■ a bias toward one particular group or subject: *the paper had a working-class skew.* ■ *Statistics* the state of not being symmetrical.

▸*v.* [*intrans.*] suddenly change direction or position: *the car had skewed across the track.* ■ twist or turn or cause to do this: *he skewed around in his saddle* | [*trans.*] *his leg was skewed in and pushed against the other one.* ■ [*trans.*] make biased or distorted in a way that is regarded as inaccurate, unfair, or misleading: *the curriculum is skewed toward the practical subjects.* ■ [*trans.*] *Statistics* cause (a distribution) to be asymmetrical. ▷late Middle English (as a verb in the sense 'move obliquely'): shortening of Old Northern French *eskiuwer*, variant of Old French *eschiver* 'eschew.' The adjective and noun (early 17th cent.) are from the verb. **—skew·ness** *n.*

skew arch (also **skew bridge**) ▸*n.* an arch (or bridge) with the line of the arch not at right angles to the abutment.

skew·back /ˈskyo͞oˌbak/ ▸*n.* the sloping face of the abutment on which an extremity of an arch rests.

skew·bald /ˈskyo͞oˌbôld/ ▸*adj.* (of an animal) with irregular patches of white and another color (properly not black). Compare with PIEBALD.

▸*n.* a skewbald animal, esp. a horse. ▷mid 17th cent.: from obsolete *skewed* 'skewbald' (of uncertain origin), on the pattern of *piebald*.

skew·er /ˈskyo͞oər/ ▸*n.* a long piece of wood or metal used for holding pieces of food, typically meat, together during cooking.

▸*v.* [*trans.*] fasten together or pierce with a pin or skewer: [as *adj.*] (**skewered**) *skewered meat and fish.* ■ *informal* criticize (someone) sharply. ▷late Middle English: of unknown origin.

skew-sym·met·ric ▸*adj. Mathematics* (of a matrix) having all the elements of the principal diagonal equal to zero, and each of the remaining elements equal to the negative of the element in the corresponding position on the other side of the diagonal.

ski /skē/ ▸*n.* (*pl.* **skis**) each of a pair of long narrow pieces of hard flexible material, typically pointed and turned up at the front, fastened under the feet for gliding over snow. ■ a similar device attached beneath a vehicle or aircraft. ■ [as *adj.*] of, relating to, or used for skiing: *a ski instructor* | *ski boots.* ■ another term for WATERSKI.

▸*v.* (**skis**, **skied** /skēd/, **ski·ing** /ˈskē-iNG/) [*intrans.*] travel over snow on skis; take part in the sport or recreation of skiing: *they skied down the mountain.* ■ [*trans.*] ski on (a particular ski run or type of snow): *spring snow is not always easy to ski.* ▷mid 18th cent.: from Norwegian, from Old Norse *skíth* 'stick of wood, snowshoe.' **—ski·a·ble** *adj.*

ski·ag·ra·phy /skīˈagrəfē/ (Brit. **sci·ag·ra·phy**) ▸*n.* the use of shading and the projection of shadows to show perspective in architectural or technical drawing. ▷late 16th cent.: from French *sciagraphie*, via Latin from Greek *skiagraphia*, from *skia* 'shadow.' **—ski·a·gram** /ˈskīəˌgram/ *n.* **—ski·a·graph** /ˈskīəˌgraf/ *n.* & *v.* **—ski·a·graph·ic** /ˌskīəˈgrafik/ *adj.*

Skia·thos /ˈskīəˌTHäs; ˈskēəˌTHôs/ a Greek island in the Aegean Sea, part of the Northern Sporades group. Greek name **Skíathos** .

ski-bob /ˈskē ˌbäb/ ▸*n.* a device resembling a bicycle with skis instead of wheels, used for sliding down snow-covered slopes.

▸*v.* (**-bobbed**, **-bob·bing**) [*intrans.*] ride a ski-bob. **—ski-bob·ber** *n.*

skid /skid/ ▸*v.* (**skid·ded**, **skid·ding**) **1** [*intrans.*] (of a vehicle) slide, typically sideways or obliquely, on slippery ground or as a result of stopping or turning too quickly: *the taxicab skidded to a halt.* ■ slip; slide: *Barbara's foot skidded, and she fell to the floor.* ■ [*trans.*] cause to skid: *he skidded his car.* ■ [*trans.*] move a heavy object on skids: *they skidded the logs down the hill to the waterfront.* ■ *figurative* decline; deteriorate: *its shares have skidded 29% since March.* **2** [*trans.*] fasten a skid to (a wheel) as a brake.

▸*n.* **1** an act of skidding or sliding: *the Volvo went into a skid.* **2** a runner attached to the underside of an aircraft for use when landing on snow or grass. ■ each of a set of wooden rollers used for moving a log or other heavy object. **3** a braking device consisting of a wooden or metal shoe preventing a wheel from revolving. **4** a beam or plank used to support a ship under construction or repair. ▷late 17th cent. (as a noun in the sense 'supporting beam'): perhaps related to Old Norse *skíth* (see SKI).

▸*PHRASES* □ **hit the skids** *informal* begin a rapid decline or deterioration. □ **on the skids** *informal* (of a person or their career) in a bad state; failing. □ **put the skids under** *informal* hasten the decline or failure of.

skid·doo /skəˈdo͞o/ (also **ski·doo**) ▸*v.* (**-doos**, **-dooed**) [*intrans.*] *informal, dated* leave somewhere quickly. ▷early 20th cent.: perhaps from SKEDADDLE. The term is said to have been used originally in reference to male onlookers chased by police from the Flatiron Building, 23rd Street, New York, where the skirts of female passersby were raised by winds intensified by the building's design.

▸*PHRASE* □ **twenty-three skiddoo** a hasty departure. [the origin of *twenty-three* is unknown.]

skid·pad /ˈskidˌpad/ ▸*n.* a road surface used for testing the ability of automobiles to withstand lateral acceleration.

skid road ▸*n.* a road along which logs are hauled. ■ *historical* a part of a town frequented by loggers. ■ another term for SKID ROW.

skid row /rō/ ▸*n. informal* a run-down part of a town frequented by vagrants, alcoholics, and drug addicts. ■ *figurative* a desperately unfortunate or difficult situation: *I don't want to end up* ***on skid row.*** ▷1930s: alteration of SKID ROAD.

ski·er /ˈskēər/ ▸*n.* a person who skis.

skiff /skif/ ▸*n.* a shallow, flat-bottomed open boat with sharp bow and square stern. ▷late 15th cent.: from French *esquif*, from Italian *schifo*, of Germanic origin; related to SHIP.

skif·fle /ˈskifəl/ ▸*n.* **1** (in the U.S.) a style of 1920s and 1930s jazz deriving from blues, ragtime, and folk music, using both improvised and conventional instruments. **2** *Brit.* a kind of folk music with a blues or jazz flavor that was popular in the 1950s, played by a small group and often incorporating improvised instruments such as washboards. ▷1920s: perhaps imitative.

ski-fly·ing ▸*n.* a form of ski jumping incorporating aerodynamic principles to lengthen the jump.

ski·ing /ˈskēiNG/ ▸*n.* the action of traveling over snow on skis, esp. as a sport or recreation. Competitive skiing falls into two categories: **Nordic** (cross-country racing, jumping, and biathlon) and **Alpine** (downhill or straight racing, and slalom racing around a series of markers).

ski·jor·ing /ˌskēˈjôriNG; ˈskēˌjôriNG/ ▸*n.* the action of being pulled over snow or ice on skis by a horse or dog or a motor vehicle, as a sport or recreation activity. ▷1920s: from Norwegian *skikjøring*, from *ski* 'ski' + *kjøre* 'drive.' **—ski·jor·er** /-rər/ *n.*

ski jump ▸*n.* a steep slope leveling off before a drop to a lower slope, used in Nordic skiing to perform jumps. ■ a leap made from such a slope. **—ski jump·er** *n.* **—ski jump·ing** *n.*

skil·full ▸*adj. chiefly Brit.* variant spelling of SKILLFUL.

ski lift ▸*n.* a system used to transport skiers up a slope to the top of a run, typically consisting of moving seats attached to an overhead cable.

skill /skil/ ▸*n.* the ability to do something well; expertise: *difficult work, taking great skill.* ■ a particular ability: *the basic skills of cooking.* ▷late Old English *scele* 'knowledge,' from Old Norse *skil* 'discernment, knowledge.' **—skill·less** *adj.* (*archaic*).

skilled /skild/ ▸*adj.* having or showing the knowledge, ability, or training to perform a certain activity or task well: *a lab technician* ***skilled*** *in electronics* | *skilled draftsmen.* ■ based on such training or experience; showing expertise: *skilled legal advice.* ■ (of work) requiring special abilities or training: *a highly skilled job.*

skil·let /ˈskilit/ ▸*n.* a frying pan. ■ *historical* a small metal cooking pot with a long handle, typically having legs. ▷Middle English: perhaps from Old French *escuelete*, diminutive of *escuele* 'platter,' from late Latin *scutella*.

skill·ful /ˈskilfəl/ (also *chiefly Brit.* **skil·ful**) ▸*adj.* having or showing skill: *a skillful infielder* | *his skillful use of propaganda.* **—skill·ful·ly** *adv.* **—skill·ful·ness** *n.*

skim /skim/ ▸*v.* (**skimmed**, **skim·ming**) **1** [*trans.*] remove (a substance) from the surface of a liquid: *as the scum rises,* ***skim it off.*** ■ remove a substance from the surface of (a liquid): *bring to the boil, then skim it to remove any foam.* ■ *informal* steal or embezzle (money), esp. in small amounts over a period of time: *she was skimming money from the household kitty.* ■ [often as *n.*] (**skimming**) fraudulently copy (credit or debit card details) with a card swipe or other device. **2** [*intrans*, with *adverbial of direction*] go or move quickly and lightly over or on a surface or through the air: *he let his fingers skim across her shoulders.* ■ [*trans.*] pass over (a surface), nearly or lightly touching it in the process: *we stood on the bridge, watching swallows skimming the water.* ■ [*trans.*] throw (a flat stone) low over an expanse of water so that it bounces on the surface several times. ■ [*trans.*] read (something) quickly or cursorily so as to note only the important points: *he sat down and skimmed the report* | [*intrans.*] *she* ***skimmed through*** *the newspaper.* ■ (**skim over**) deal with or treat (a subject) briefly or superficially.

▸*n.* **1** a thin layer of a substance on the surface of a liquid: ***a skim of*** *ice.* **2** an act of reading something quickly or superficially: *a quick skim through the pamphlet.* ▷Middle English (in the sense 'remove scum from (a liquid)'): back-formation from SKIMMER, or from Old French *escumer*, from *escume* 'scum, foam.'

ski mask ▸*n.* a protective covering for the head and face, with holes for the eyes, nose, and mouth.

skim·board /ˈskimˌbôrd/ ▸*n.* a type of surfboard, typically round or short, used for riding shallow water.

skim·mer /ˈskimər/ ▸*n.* **1** a person or thing that skims, in particular: ■ a utensil or device for removing a substance from the surface of a liquid. ■ a device or craft designed to collect oil spilled on water. ■ a hydroplane, hydrofoil, hovercraft, or other vessel that has little or no displacement when traveling. **2** a long-winged seabird related to the terns, feeding by flying low over the water surface with its knifelike extended lower mandible immersed. • Genus *Rynchops*, family Rynchopidae (or Laridae): three species, one each in Africa, Asia, and America. **3** a flat, broad-brimmed straw hat. ■ *informal* a close-fitting dress. **4** a broad-bodied dragonfly commonly found at ponds and swamps. It can rest for long periods on a perch, from which it darts out to grab prey. • Libellulidae and related families: several genera and numerous species, including the **twelve-spotted skimmer** (*Libellula pulchella*). ▷Middle English: from Old French *escumoir*, from *escumer* 'skim,' from *escume* 'scum.'

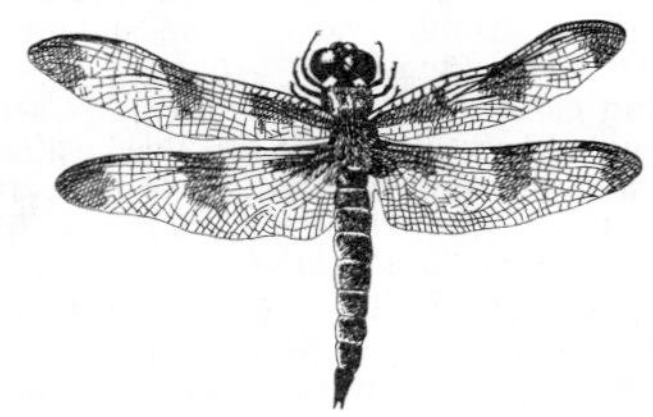

twelve-spotted skimmer

skim milk (also **skimmed milk**) ▸*n.* milk from which the cream has been removed.

skim·ming·ton /ˈskimiNGtən/ ▸*n. historical* a procession made through a village intended to bring ridicule on and make an example of a nagging wife or an unfaithful husband. ▷early 17th cent.: perhaps from *skimming-ladle*, used as a thrashing instrument during the procession.

▸*PHRASE* □ **ride skimmington** hold such a procession.

ski·mo·bile /ˈskēmōˌbēl/ ▸*n.* a snowmobile.

skimp /skimp/ ▸*v.* [*intrans.*] expend or use less time, money, or material on something than is necessary in an attempt to economize: *don't* ***skimp on*** *insurance when you travel overseas.* ▷late 18th cent.: of unknown origin; compare with **SCAMP**2 and **SCRIMP**.

skimp·y /ˈskimpē/ ▸*adj.* (**skimp·i·er**, **skimp·i·est**) (of clothes) short and revealing: *a skimpy dress.* ■ providing or consisting of less than is needed; meager: *my knowledge of music is extremely skimpy.* —**skimp·i·ly** /ˈskimpəlē/ *adv.* —**skimp·i·ness** *n.*

skin /skin/ ▸*n.* **1** the thin layer of tissue forming the natural outer covering of the body of a person or animal: *I use body lotion to keep my skin soft | a flap of skin.* ■ the skin of a dead animal with or without the fur, used as material for clothing or other items: *is this real crocodile skin?* ■ a container made from the skin of an animal such as a goat, used for holding liquids. **2** an outer layer or covering, in particular: ■ the peel or outer layer of certain fruits or vegetables. ■ the thin outer covering of a sausage. ■ a thin layer forming on the surface of certain hot liquids, such as milk, as they cool. ■ the outermost layer of a structure such as a building or aircraft. ■ *Computing* a customized graphic user interface for an application or operating system: *music, reviews, and attitude all wrapped up in the skin of a catalog.* ■ (usu. **skins**) a strip of sealskin or other material attached to the underside of a ski to prevent a skier from slipping backward while climbing. **3** *informal* a skinhead. **4** (usu. **skins**) *informal* (esp. in jazz) a drum or drum head. **5** [as *adj.*] *informal* relating to or denoting pornographic literature or films: *the skin trade.*

▸*v.* (**skinned**, **skin·ning**) **1** [*trans.*] remove the skin from (an animal or a fruit or vegetable). ■ (in hyperbolic use) punish severely: *Dad would* ***skin me alive*** *if I forgot it.* ■ scratch or scrape the skin off (a part of one's body): *he scrambled down from the tree with such haste that he skinned his knees.* ■ *informal* take money from or swindle (someone). **2** [*trans.*] *archaic* cover with skin: *the wound was skinned, but the strength of his leg was not restored.* ■ [*intrans.*] (of a wound) form new skin: *the hole in his skull* ***skinned over.*** ▷late Old English *scinn*, from Old Norse *skinn*; related to Dutch *schinden* 'flay, peel' and German *schinden.* —**skin·less** *adj.*

▸*PHRASES* □ **be skin and bones** (of a person or animal) be very thin. □ **by the skin of one's teeth** by a very narrow margin; barely: *I only got away by the skin of my teeth.* [from a misquotation of Job 19:20: "I am escaped with the skin of my teeth" (i.e., and nothing else). Current use reflects a different sense.] □ **get under someone's skin** *informal* **1** annoy or irritate someone intensely: *it was the sheer effrontery of them that got under my skin.* **2** fill someone's mind in a compelling and persistent way. **3** reach or display a deep understanding of someone: *movies that get under the skin of our national character.* □ **give someone (some) skin** *black slang* shake or slap hands together as a gesture or friendship or solidarity. □ **have a thick** (or **thin**) **skin** be insensitive (or oversensitive) to criticism or insults. □ **it's no skin off my nose** (or **off my back**) *informal* (usually spoken with emphasis on "my") used to indicate that one is not offended or adversely affected by something: *it's no skin off my nose if you don't want dessert.* □ **keep** (or **sleep in**) **a whole skin** *archaic* escape being wounded or injured. □ **make someone's skin** (or **flesh**) **crawl** (or **creep**) cause someone to feel fear, horror, or disgust: *a person dying in a fire—doesn't it make your skin crawl?* □ **save someone's skin** see **SAVE**1. □ **there's more than one way to skin a cat** *proverb* there's more than one way of achieving one's aim. □ **under the skin** in reality, as opposed to superficial appearances: *he still believes that all women are goddesses under the skin.*

skin-deep ▸*adj.* not deep or lasting; superficial: *their left-wing attitudes were only skin-deep.*

skin div·ing ▸*n.* the action or sport of swimming under water without a diving suit, typically in deep water using an aqualung and flippers. —**skin-dive** *v.* —**skin div·er** *n.*

skin ef·fect ▸*n. Physics* the tendency of a high-frequency alternating current to flow through only the outer layer of a conductor.

skin flick (also **skin·flick**) ▸*n. informal* a pornographic film.

skin·flint /ˈskinˌflint/ ▸*n. informal* a person who spends as little money as possible; a miser.

skin fold ▸*n.* a fold of skin and underlying fat formed by pinching, the thickness of which is a measure of nutritional status.

skin·ful /ˈskinfo͝ol/ ▸*n.* [in *sing.*] *informal* enough alcoholic drink to make one drunk: *he had a skinful on New Year's Eve.*

skin game ▸*n. informal* a rigged gambling game; a swindle.

skin graft ▸*n.* a surgical operation in which a piece of healthy skin is transplanted to a new site on the body. ■ a piece of skin transferred in this way.

skin·head /ˈskinˌhed/ ▸*n.* a young person with close-cropped hair, often perceived as aggressive, violent, and racist, and having neo-Nazi tendencies.

skink /skiNGk/ ▸*n.* a smooth-bodied lizard with short or absent limbs, typically burrowing in sandy ground, and occurring throughout tropical and temperate regions. • Family Scincidae: numerous genera and species. ▷late 16th cent.: from French *scinc* or Latin *scincus*, from Greek *skinkos.*

skinned /skind/ ▸*adj.* [in *combination*] having a skin of a specified type: *a fair-skinned woman.*

▸*PHRASE* □ **be thin-skinned** (or **thick-skinned**) be sensitive (or insensitive) to criticism or insults.

Skin·ner /ˈskinər/, B(urrhus) F(rederic) (1904–90), U.S. behaviorist psychologist. He promoted the view that the proper aim of psychology should be to predict behavior and hence be able to control it. He applied the results of his studies to the development of programmed learning and to educational practice.

skin·ner /ˈskinər/ ▸*n.* a person who skins animals or prepares skins. ■ a person who deals in animal skins; a furrier.

Skin·ner box /ˈskinər/ ▸*n. Psychology* an apparatus for studying instrumental conditioning in animals (typically rats or pigeons) in which the animal is isolated and provided with a lever or switch that it learns to use to obtain a reward, such as a food pellet, or to avoid a punishment, such as an electric shock. ▷1940s: named after B. F. **SKINNER**.

skin·ny /ˈskinē/ ▸*adj.* (**-ni·er**, **-ni·est**) *informal* (of a person or part of their body) very thin: *his skinny arms.* See note at **THIN**. ■ (of an article of clothing) tight-fitting: *a skinny black dress.*

▸*n.* (**the skinny**) confidential information on a particular person or topic: *the inside skinny is that he didn't know the deal was in the works.* —**skin·ni·ness** *n.*

skin·ny-dip ▸*v.* [*intrans.*] *informal* swim naked.

▸*n.* a naked swim.

skin-pop *informal* ▸*v.* [*trans.*] inject (a drug, typically a narcotic) subcutaneously.

▸*n.* a subcutaneous injection of a drug, typically a narcotic. —**skin-pop·per** *n.*

skins game ▸*n.* a game of competitive golf in which players make wagers on each hole, the pot carrying over to the next hole whenever two players tie.

skint /skint/ ▸*adj. Brit., informal* (of a person) having little or no money available: *I'm a bit skint just now.* ▷1920s: variant of colloquial *skinned*, in the same sense, past participle of **SKIN**.

skin test ▸*n.* a test for an immune reaction performed by applying a substance topically or injecting it into the skin.

▸*v.* (**skin-test**) [*trans.*] [usu. as *n.*] (**skin-testing**) perform such a test on (someone).

skin·tight /ˈskinˈtīt/ (also **skin-tight**) ▸*adj.* (of a garment) very close-fitting.

skip1 /skip/ ▸*v.* (**skipped**, **skip·ping**) [*intrans.*] move along lightly, stepping from one foot to the other with a hop or bounce: *she began to skip down the path.* ■ [*intrans.*] jump over a rope that is held at both ends by oneself or two other people and turned repeatedly over the head and under the feet, as a game or for exercise. ■ [*trans.*] jump over (a rope) in such a way: *the girls had been skipping rope.* ■ [*trans.*] jump lightly over: *the children used to skip the puddles.* ■ [*trans.*] omit (part of a book that one is reading, or a stage in a sequence that one is following): *the video manual allows the viewer to skip sections he's not interested in* | [*intrans.*] *she disliked him so much that she* ***skipped over*** *any articles that mentioned him.* ■ [*trans.*] fail to attend or deal with as appropriate; miss: *I wanted to skip my English lesson to visit my mother | try not to skip breakfast.* ■ [*intrans.*] move quickly and in an unmethodical way from one point or subject to another: *Marian skipped halfheartedly through the book.* ■ [*trans.*] *informal* depart quickly and secretly from: *she skipped her home amid rumors of a romance.* ■ [*intrans.*] *informal* run away; disappear: *I'm not giving them a chance to* ***skip off*** *again.* ■ (**skip it**) *informal* abandon an undertaking, conversation, or activity: *after several wrong turns in our journey, we almost decided to skip it.* ■ [*trans.*] throw (a stone) so that it ricochets off the surface of water.

▸*n.* a light, bouncing step; a skipping movement: *he moved with a strange, dancing skip.* ■ *Computing* an act of passing over part of a sequence of data or instructions. ■ *informal* a person who defaults or absconds. ▷Middle English: probably of Scandinavian origin.

skip2 ▸*n. Brit.* a dumpster.

skip3 ▸*n.* the captain or director of a team in lawn bowling or curling.

▸*v.* (**skipped**, **skip·ping**) [*trans.*] act as skip of (a side). ▷early 19th cent. (originally Scots): abbreviation of **SKIPPER**1.

ski pants ▸*plural n.* trousers worn for skiing. ■ women's trousers imitating a style of these, made of stretchy fabric with tapering legs and an elastic stirrup under each foot.

skip·jack /ˈskipˌjak/ ▸*n.* **1** (also **skipjack tuna**) a small tuna with dark horizontal stripes, widely distributed throughout tropical and temperate seas. Also called **BONITO** or **OCEAN BONITO**. • *Katsuwonus* (or **Euthynnus**) *pelamis*, family Scombridae. **2** another term for **CLICK BEETLE**. **3** a sloop-rigged sailboat with vertical sides and a flat V-shaped bottom, used chiefly on the east coast of the U.S. ▷early 18th cent.: from the verb **SKIP**1 + **JACK**1. Sense 1 is from the fish's habit of jumping out of the water; senses 2 and 3 arose in the 19th cent.

ski-plane ▸*n.* an airplane fitted with skis for landing on snow or ice.

ski pole ▸*n.* either of two lightweight poles held by a skier to assist in balance or propulsion.

skip·per1 /ˈskipər/ *informal* ▸*n.* the captain of a ship or boat. ■ the captain of a team in a game or sport. ■ the captain of an aircraft.

▸*v.* [*trans.*] act as captain of. ▷late Middle English: from Middle Dutch, Middle Low German *schipper*, from *schip* 'ship.'

skip·per2 ▸*n.* **1** a person or thing that skips. ■ used in names of small insects and crustaceans that skip or hop. **2** a small brownish mothlike butterfly with rapid darting flight. • Family Hesperiidae: numerous genera. **3** the Atlantic saury (see **SAURY**).

skip·pet /ˈskipit/ ▸*n. chiefly historical* a small round wooden box used to preserve documents and seals. ▷late Middle English: of unknown origin.

skirl /skərl/ ▸*n.* a shrill sound, esp. that of bagpipes.

▸*v.* [*intrans.*] (of bagpipes) make such a sound. ▷late Middle English (as a verb): probably of Scandinavian origin; ultimately imitative.

skir·mish /ˈskərmiSH/ ▸*n.* an episode of irregular or unpremeditated fighting, esp. between small or outlying parts of armies or fleets. ■ a short argument: *there was a skirmish over the budget.*

▸*v.* [*intrans.*] [often as *n.*] (**skirmishing**) engage in a skirmish: *reports of skirmishing along the border.* ▷Middle English (as a verb): from Old French *eskirmiss-*, lengthened stem of *eskirmir*, from a Germanic verb meaning 'defend;' related to SCRIMMAGE. —**skir·mish·er** *n.*

skirr /skər/ ▸*v.* [*intrans.*] *rare* move rapidly, esp. with a whirring sound: *five dark birds rose skirring away.* ▷mid 16th cent.: perhaps related to SCOUR[1] or SCOUR[2].

skirt /skərt/ ▸*n.* a woman's outer garment fastened around the waist and hanging down around the legs. ■ the part of a coat or dress that hangs below the waist. ■ *informal, chiefly offensive* a woman or women regarded as objects of sexual desire: *so, Al, off to chase some skirt?* ■ the curtain that hangs around the base of a hovercraft to contain the air cushion. ■ a surface that conceals or protects the wheels or underside of a vehicle or aircraft. ■ a small flap on a saddle, covering the bar from which the stirrup leather hangs. ■ *archaic* an edge, border, or extreme part. Compare with OUTSKIRTS.
▸*v.* [*trans.*] go around or past the edge of: *he did not go through the city but skirted it.* ■ be situated along or around the edge of: *the fields that skirted the highway were full of cattle.* ■ [*intrans.*] (**skirt along/around**) go along or around (something) rather than directly through or across it: *the river valley skirts along the northern slopes of the hills.* ■ attempt to ignore; avoid dealing with: *there was a subject she was always skirting* | [*intrans.*] *the treaty* ***skirted around*** *the question of political cooperation.* ▷Middle English: from Old Norse *skyrta* 'shirt'; compare with synonymous Old English *scyrte*, also with SHORT. The verb dates from the early 17th cent. —**skirt·ed** *adj.* [in *combination*] *a full-skirted dress.*

skirt-chas·er ▸*n. informal* a man who pursues women amorously and is casual in his affections; a womanizer.

skirt·ing /ˈskərtiNG/ (also **skirt·ing board**) ▸*n. chiefly Brit.* a baseboard.

skirt steak ▸*n.* a beefsteak cut from the diaphragm muscle.

ski run ▸*n.* a track on a slope for skiing.

skit /skit/ ▸*n.* a short comedy sketch or piece of humorous writing, esp. a parody: *a skit on daytime magazine programs.* ▷early 18th cent. (in the sense 'satirical comment or attack'): related to the rare verb *skit* 'move lightly and rapidly,' perhaps from Old Norse (compare with *skjóta* 'shoot').

ski tour·ing ▸*n. chiefly Brit.* cross-country skiing. —**ski tour** *n.* —**ski tour·er** *n.*

ski tow ▸*n.* **1** a type of ski lift, with a moving rope or with bars suspended from a moving overhead cable. **2** a tow rope for waterskiers.

skit·ter /ˈskitər/ ▸*v.* [*intrans.*] **1** [*intrans.*] move lightly and quickly or hurriedly: *the girls skittered up the stairs* | *figurative her mind skittered back to that day at the office.* **2** [*trans.*] draw (bait) jerkily across the surface of the water as a technique in fishing. ▷mid 19th cent.: apparently a frequentative of *skite* 'move rapidly,' perhaps of Norse origin.

skit·ter·y /ˈskitərē/ ▸*adj.* restless; skittish: *a skittery horse.*

skit·tish /ˈskitisH/ ▸*adj.* lively and unpredictable; playful: *my skittish and immature mother.* ■ (esp. of a horse) nervous; inclined to shy. ▷late Middle English: perhaps from the rare verb *skit* 'move lightly and rapidly.' —**skit·tish·ly** *adv.* —**skit·tish·ness** *n.*

skit·tle /ˈskitl/ ▸*n.* **1** (**skittles**) [treated as *sing.*] a game played, chiefly in Britain, with wooden pins, typically nine in number, set up at the end of an alley to be bowled down with a wooden ball or disk. **2** a pin used in the game of skittles. ▷mid 17th cent.: of unknown origin. The word *skyttel* exists in Danish and Swedish in the sense 'shuttle, child's marble,' but there is no evidence to connect this with the game of skittles.

skive[1] /skīv/ *Brit., informal* ▸*v.* [*intrans.*] avoid work or a duty by staying away or leaving early; shirk: *I skived off school* | [*trans.*] *she used to skive lessons.*
▸*n.* [in *sing.*] an instance of avoiding work or a duty in this way. ■ an easy option. ▷early 20th cent.: perhaps from French *esquiver* 'slink away.' —**skiv·er** *n.*

skive[2] ▸*v.* [*trans.*] *technical* pare (the edge of a piece of leather or other material) so as to reduce its thickness. ▷early 19th cent.: from Old Norse *skífa*; related to SHIVE.

skiv·vy /ˈskivē/ ▸*n.* (*pl.* **-vies**) **1** (**skivvies**) *trademark* underwear, esp. a set consisting of undershirt and underpants, or just the underpants. [originally a U.S. Navy term.] **2** (also **skiv·vy shirt**) a lightweight high-necked, long-sleeved garment. ■ an undershirt or T-shirt. **3** *Brit., informal* a low-ranking female domestic servant. ■ a person doing work that is poorly paid and considered menial.
▸*v.* (**-vies, -vied**) [*intrans.*] *informal* do menial household tasks; work as a skivvy. ▷early 20th cent.: of unknown origin.

ski·wear /ˈskē,we(ə)r/ ▸*n.* clothing designed or suitable for skiing.

skoal /skōl/ (also **skol**) ▸*exclam.* used to express friendly feelings toward one's companions before drinking. ▷early 17th cent. (a Scots use): from Danish and Norwegian *skaal*, Swedish *skål*, from Old Norse *skál* 'bowl'; perhaps introduced through the visit of James VI to Denmark in 1589. Compare with SCALE[2].

Sko·kie /ˈskōkē/ a residential and industrial village in northeastern Illinois, northwest of Chicago; pop. 59,432.

skoosh /skōōsH/ (also **scoosh**) ▸*Scottish v.* ■ squirt or splash (liquid).
▸*n.* ■ a splash or squirt of liquid. ■ any small amount: *lift that just a skoosh, will you?* ▷imitative.

Skop·je /ˈskôpye/ the capital of the republic of Macedonia, located in the northern part of the country, on the Vardar River; pop. 440,000.

skort /skôrt/ ▸*n.* shorts with full legs and a central flap in front. ▷blend of SKIRT and *short* (see SHORTS).

skosh /skōsH/ ▸*n. informal* a small amount; a little. ▷1950s: from Japanese *sukoshi*.
▸PHRASE □ **a skosh** somewhat; slightly: *it's a skosh more formal than one might like.*

Skr. ▸*abbr.* Sanskrit.

Skrya·bin /skrēˈäbən/ variant spelling of SCRIABIN.

Skt. ▸*abbr.* Sanskrit.

SKU /skyōō/ ▸*abbr.* stock-keeping unit.

sku·a /ˈskyōōə/ ▸*n.* a large brownish predatory seabird related to the gulls, pursuing other birds to make them disgorge fish they have caught. • Family Stercorariidae: genera *Catharacta* (four larger species) and *Stercorarius* (three smaller species). See also JAEGER. ▷late 17th cent.: modern Latin, from Faroese *skúvur*, from Old Norse *skúfr* (apparently imitative).

skul·dug·ger·y /skəlˈdəgərē/ (also **skull·dug·ger·y**) ▸*n.* underhanded or unscrupulous behavior; trickery: *a firm that investigates commercial skulduggery.* ▷mid 19th cent.: alteration of Scots *sculduddery*, of unknown origin.

skulk /skəlk/ ▸*v.* [*intrans.*] keep out of sight, typically with a sinister or cowardly motive: *don't skulk outside the door like a spy!* ■ [with *adverbial of direction*] move stealthily or furtively: *he spent most of his time skulking about the corridors.* ■ shirk duty.
▸*n.* a group of foxes. ▷Middle English: of Scandinavian origin; compare with Norwegian *skulka* 'lurk,' and Danish *skulke*, Swedish *skolka* 'shirk.' —**skulk·er** *n.*

skull /skəl/ ▸*n.* a framework of bone or cartilage enclosing the brain of a vertebrate; the skeleton of a person's or animal's head. ■ *informal* a person's head or brain: *a skull crammed with too many thoughts.*
▸*v.* [*trans.*] hit (someone) on the head. ▷Middle English *scolle*; of unknown origin; compare with Old Norse *skoltr.* —**skulled** *adj.* [in *combination*] *long-skulled.*
▸PHRASES □ **out of one's skull** *informal* **1** out of one's mind; crazy. **2** very drunk. □ **skull and crossbones** a representation of a skull with two thigh bones crossed below it as an emblem of piracy or death.

skull·cap /ˈskəl,kap/ ▸*n.* **1** a small close-fitting cap without a brim. ■ a yarmulke. **2** the top part of the skull. **3** a widely distributed plant of the mint family, whose tubular flowers have a helmet-shaped cup at the base. • Genus *Scutellaria*, family Labiatae.

skullcap 1

skull ses·sion ▸*n. informal* a discussion or conference, esp. to discuss policies, tactics, and maneuvers.

skunk /skəNGk/ ▸*n.* a cat-sized American mammal of the weasel family, with distinctive black-and-white-striped fur. When threatened it squirts a fine spray of foul-smelling irritant liquid from its anal glands toward its attacker. • *Mephitis* and other genera, family Mustelidae: several species, in particular the **striped skunk** (*M. mephitis*). ■ the fur of the skunk. ■ *informal* a contemptible person.
▸*v.* [*trans.*] *informal* **1** (often **be skunked**) defeat (someone) overwhelmingly in a game or contest, esp. by preventing them from scoring at all. **2** *dated* fail to pay (a bill or creditor). ▷mid 17th cent.: from Massachusett *squnck*; cognate forms occur in many other American Indian languages.

skunk cab·bage ▸*n.* a North American plant of the arum family, the flower of which has a distinctive unpleasant smell. • Two species in the family Araceae: the western **yellow skunk cabbage** (*Lysichitum americanum*), with a stalked yellow flower, and the eastern *Symplocarpus foetidus*, with a greenish purple flower.

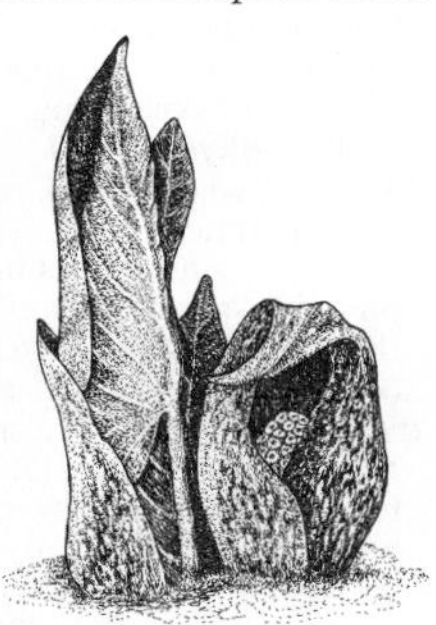
skunk cabbage

skunk·works /ˈskəNGk-,wərks/ (also **skunk works**) ▸*plural n.* [usu. treated as *sing.*] *informal* an experimental laboratory or department of a company or institution, typically smaller than and independent of its main research division.

skunk·y ▸*adj.* **1** like a skunk. **2** disagreeably tainted: *skunky beer.*

skut·te·rud·ite /ˈskətə,rədīt/ ▸*n.* a metallic-gray mineral, typically forming cubic or octahedral crystals, consisting chiefly of an arsenide of cobalt and nickel. ▷mid 19th cent.: from *Skutterud* (now Skotterud), a village in southeastern Norway, + -ITE[1].

sky /skī/ ▸*n.* (*pl.* **skies**) (often **the sky**) the region of the atmosphere and outer space seen from the earth: *hundreds of stars shining in the sky* | *Jillson had never seen so much sky.* ■ *poetic/literary* heaven; heavenly power: *the just vengeance of incensed skies.*
▸*v.* (**skies, skied**) [*trans.*] *informal* hit (a ball) high into the air: *he skied his tee shot.* ■ hang (a picture) very high on a wall, esp. in an exhibition. ▷Middle English (also in the plural denoting clouds): from Old Norse *ský* 'cloud.' The verb dates from the early 19th cent. —**sky·ey** /ˈskīē/ *adj.* —**sky·less** *adj.*
▸PHRASES □ **out of a clear blue sky** see BLUE. □ **the sky's the limit** *informal* there is practically no limit (to something such as a price that can be charged or the opportunities afforded to someone). □ **to the skies** very highly; enthusiastically: *he wrote to his sister praising Lizzie to the skies.*

sky blue ▸*n.* a bright clear blue.

sky·box /ˈskī,bäks/ ▸*n.* a luxurious enclosed seating area located high in a sports arena.

sky·bridge /ˈskī,brij/ ▸*n.* another term for SKYWALK.

sky bur·i·al ▸*n.* a Tibetan funeral ritual involving the exposure of a dismembered corpse to sacred vultures.

sky·cap /ˈskī,kap/ ▸*n.* a porter at an airport.

sky-clad ▸*adj.* naked (used esp. in connection with modern pagan ritual). ▷early 20th cent.: probably a translation of Sanskrit *Digāmbara*, denoting a Jain sect.

sky·div·ing /ˈskī,dīviNG/ ▸*n.* the sport of jumping from an aircraft and performing acrobatic maneuvers in the air during free fall before landing by parachute. —**sky·dive** *v.* —**sky·div·er** *n.*

Skye /skī/ a mountainous island in the Inner Hebrides, linked to the west coast of Scotland by a bridge; chief town, Portree.

Skye ter·ri·er ▸*n.* a small long-haired terrier of a slate-colored or beige-colored Scottish breed.

sky·flow·er /ˈskī,flou(-ə)r/ ▸*n.* a shrub of the verbena family, with clusters of lilac flowers and yellow berries, native to Central and South America. • *Duranta erecta*, family Verbenaceae.

sky·glow /ˈskī,glō/ ▸*n.* brightness of the night sky in a built-up area as a result of light pollution.

sky-high ▸*adv.* & *adj.* as if reaching the sky; very high: [as *adv.*] *they saved a president from being blown sky-high.* ■ at or to a very high level; very great: [as *adj.*] *sky-high premiums.*

sky·hook /ˈskī,ho͝ok/ (also **sky hook** or **sky-hook**) ▸*n.* **1** *dated* an imaginary or fanciful device by which something could be suspended in the air. ■ *figurative* a false hope, or a premise or argument which has no logical grounds. ■ a proposed cable or other

Pronunciation Key ə ago; ər over; ˈə or ,ə up; ˈər or ,ər fur; a hat; ā rate; ä car; CH chew; e let; ē see; e(ə)r air; i fit; ī by; i(ə)r ear; NG sing; ō go; ô for; oi boy; o͝o good; ōō goo; ou out; SH she; TH thin; T͟H then; (h)w why; ZH vision

S

structure reaching from the earth's surface to a satellite, which could be used for transporting spacecraft or other items into space. **2** *Climbing* a small flattened hook, with an eye for attaching a rope, fixed temporarily into a rock face. **3** *Basketball* a very high-arcing hook shot. **4** a helicopter equipped with a steel line and hook for hoisting and transporting heavy objects.

sky·jack /ˈskīˌjak/ ▸*v.* [*trans.*] hijack (an aircraft).
▸*n.* an act of skyjacking. ▷1960s: blend of **SKY** and **HIJACK**. **—sky·jack·er** *n.*

Sky·lab /ˈskīˌlab/ a U.S. orbiting space laboratory. Its three manned missions, all launched in 1973, were used for experiments in zero gravity and for astrophysical studies. Abandoned in 1974, it reentered the earth's atmosphere in 1979, scattering debris in Australia and the Indian Ocean.

sky·lark /ˈskīˌlärk/ ▸*n.* a common Eurasian and North African lark of farmland and open country, noted for its prolonged song during hovering flight. • Genus *Alauda*, family Alaudidae: two species, in particular the widespread *A. arvensis*.
▸*v.* [*intrans.*] pass time by playing tricks or practical jokes; indulge in horseplay: *he was skylarking with a friend when he fell into a pile of boxes.* [late 17th cent. (originally in nautical use): by association with the verb **LARK**[2].]

sky·light /ˈskīˌlīt/ ▸*n.* a window installed in a roof or ceiling. ■ light emanating from the sky.

sky·light·ed /ˈskīˌlītid/ (also **sky·lit** /ˈskīˌlit/) ▸*adj.* fitted with or lit by a skylight or skylights: *skylighted rooms | hunters who sit at the crest of a hill allow the turkey to see them skylighted against the horizon.*

sky·line /ˈskīˌlīn/ ▸*n.* an outline of land and buildings defined against the sky: *the skyline of the city.* ■ the line along which the horizon is visible.

sky pi·lot ▸*n. informal* a member of the clergy, esp. a military chaplain.

skyr /ski(ə)r/ ▸*n.* an Icelandic dish consisting of curdled milk. ▷Icelandic.

sky·rock·et /ˈskīˌräkit/ ▸*n.* a rocket designed to explode high in the air as a signal or firework.
▸*v.* (**-rock·et·ed**, **-rock·et·ing**) [*intrans.*] *informal* (of a price, rate, or amount) increase very steeply or rapidly: *the cost of housing has skyrocketed.*

sky·sail /ˈskīˌsāl/ ▸*n.* a light sail above the royal.

sky·scrap·er /ˈskīˌskrāpər/ ▸*n.* **1** a very tall building of many stories. **2** another term for **SKYSAIL**.

sky·surf·ing /ˈskīˌsərfiNG/ ▸*n.* the sport of jumping from an aircraft and surfing through the air on a board before landing by parachute.

sky·walk /ˈskīˌwôk/ ▸*n.* an enclosed overhead walkway between buildings.

sky·ward /ˈskīwərd/ ▸*adv.* (also **sky·wards**) toward the sky: *flames were now shooting skyward.*
▸*adj.* moving or directed toward the sky: *the city was heavily guarded by skyward laser batteries.*

sky·watch /ˈskīˌwäCH/ ▸*v.* [*intrans.*] *informal* observe or monitor the sky, esp. for heavenly bodies or aircraft. **—sky·watch·er** *n.*

sky wave ▸*n.* a radio wave reflected from the ionosphere.

sky·way /ˈskīˌwā/ ▸*n.* **1** a recognized route followed by aircraft. **2** another term for **SKYWALK**. **3** an elevated highway.

sky·writ·ing /ˈskīˌrītiNG/ ▸*n.* words in the form of smoke trails made by an airplane, esp. for advertising. **—sky·writ·er** /-tər/ *n.*

SL ▸*abbr.* source language.

s.l. ▸*abbr.* ■ salvage loss. ■ (also **sl.**) (in a bibliography) without place (of publication noted). [from Latin *sine loco.*]

slab /slab/ ▸*n.* a large, thick, flat piece of stone, concrete, or wood, typically rectangular: *paving slabs | she settled on **a slab of** rock.* ■ a large, thick slice or piece of cake, bread, chocolate, etc.: ***a slab of** bread and cheese.* ■ *Climbing* a large, smooth, steep body of rock. ■ an outer piece of timber sawn from a log. ■ a table used for laying a body on in a morgue.
▸*v.* (**slabbed**, **slab·bing**) [*trans.*] [often as *n.*] (**slabbing**) remove slabs from (a log or tree) to prepare it for sawing into planks. ▷Middle English: of unknown origin. **—slabbed** *adj.* **—slab·by** *adj.*

slab av·a·lanche ▸*n.* an avalanche formed by a sheet of snow breaking loose.

slab·ber /ˈslabər/ *chiefly Scottish Irish* ▸*v.* [*intrans.*] dribble at the mouth; slaver: *he was slabbering like a child.* ▷mid 16th cent. (in the sense 'dribble on'): related to dialect *slab* 'muddy place, puddle.'

slack[1] /slak/ ▸*adj.* **1** not taut or held tightly in position; loose: *a slack rope | her mouth went slack.* **2** (of business) characterized by a lack of work or activity; quiet: *business was rather slack.* ■ slow or sluggish: *they were working at a slack pace.* ■ having or showing laziness or negligence: *slack accounting procedures.* **3** (of a tide) neither ebbing nor flowing: *soon the water will become slack, and the tide will turn.*
▸*n.* **1** the part of a rope or line that is not held taut; the loose or unused part: *I picked up the rod and wound in the slack.* **2** (**slacks**) casual trousers. **3** *informal* a spell of inactivity or laziness: *he slept deeply, refreshed by a little slack in the daily routine.*
▸*v.* [*trans.*] **1** loosen (something, esp. a rope). ■ reduce the intensity or speed of (something); slacken: *the horse slacked his pace.* ■ [*intrans.*] (**slack off**) decrease in quantity or intensity: *the flow of blood slacked off.* ■ [*intrans.*] *informal* work slowly or lazily: *she reprimanded her girls if they were slacking.* ■ [*intrans.*] (**slack up**) slow down: *the animal doesn't slack up until he reaches the trees.* **2** slake (lime).
▸*adv.* loosely: *their heads were hanging slack in attitudes of despair.* ▷Old English *slæc* 'inclined to be lazy, unhurried,' of Germanic origin; related to Latin *laxus* 'loose.' **—slack·ly** *adv.* **—slack·ness** *n.*
▸*PHRASES* □ **cut someone some slack** *informal* allow someone some leeway in their conduct. □ **take** (or **pick**) **up the slack 1** use up a surplus or improve the use of resources to avoid an undesirable lull in business: *as domestic demand starts to flag, foreign demand will help pick up the slack.* **2** pull on the loose end or part of a rope in order to make it taut.

slack[2] ▸*n.* coal dust or small pieces of coal. ▷late Middle English: probably from Low German or Dutch.

slack·en /ˈslakən/ ▸*v.* make or become slack: [*trans.*] *he slackened his grip | the joints can be tightened and **slackened off** again |* [*intrans.*] *the pace never slackens.*

slack·er /ˈslakər/ ▸*n. informal* a person who avoids work or effort. ■ a person who evades military service. ■ a young person (esp. in the 1990s) of a subculture characterized by apathy and aimlessness.

slack wa·ter ▸*n.* the state of the tide when it is turning, esp. at low tide.

slag /slag/ ▸*n.* **1** stony waste matter separated from metals during the smelting or refining of ore. ■ similar material produced by a volcano; scoria. **2** *Brit., informal, derogatory* a promiscuous woman.
▸*v.* (**slagged**, **slag·ging**) [*intrans.*] [usu. as *n.*] (**slagging**) produce deposits of slag. ▷mid 16th cent.: from Middle Low German *slagge*, perhaps from *slagen* 'strike,' with reference to fragments formed by hammering. **—slag·gy** *adj.* (**-gi·er**, **-gi·est**).

slag heap ▸*n.* a hill or area of refuse from a mine or industrial site.

slain /slān/ ▸ past participle of **SLAY**[1].

slake /slāk/ ▸*v.* [*trans.*] **1** quench or satisfy (one's thirst): *slake your thirst with some lemonade.* ■ *figurative* satisfy (desires): *restaurants worked to slake the Italian obsession with food.* **2** combine (quicklime) with water to produce calcium hydroxide. ▷Old English *slacian* 'become less eager,' also 'slacken,' from the adjective *slæc* 'slack'; compare with Dutch *slaken* 'diminish, relax.'

slaked lime ▸*n.* see **LIME**[1].

sla·lom /ˈsläləm/ ▸*n.* a ski race down a winding course marked by flags or poles. ■ a sporting event on water with a winding course marked by obstacles, typically a canoe or sailing race.
▸*v.* [*intrans.*] move or race in a winding path, avoiding obstacles: *she drove with reckless speed, slaloming in and out of the stalled cars.* ▷1920s: from Norwegian *slalåm*, literally 'sloping track.' **—sla·lom·er** *n.*

slam[1] /slam/ ▸*v.* (**slammed**, **slam·ming**) [*trans.*] shut (a door, window, or lid) forcefully and loudly: *he slams the door behind him as he leaves.* ■ [*intrans.*] be closed forcefully and loudly: *she heard a car door slam.* ■ [*trans.*] push or put somewhere with great force: *Charlie slammed down the phone.* ■ [*intrans.*] (**slam into**) crash into; collide heavily with: *the car mounted the sidewalk, slamming into a lamppost.* ■ [*trans.*] *informal* hit (something) with great force in a particular direction: *he slammed a shot into the net.* ■ put (something) into action suddenly or forcefully: *I slammed on the brakes.* ■ [*intrans.*] move violently or loudly: *he slammed out of the room.* ■ [*trans.*] (usu. **be slammed**) *informal* criticize severely: *his efforts to slam the president destroyed his own campaign.* ■ [*trans.*] *informal* score points against or gain a victory over (someone) easily: *the Blue Devils slammed Kansas to win the title.* ■ [*trans.*] [often as *n.*] (**slamming**) (of a telephone company) take over the account of (a telephone customer) without their permission.
▸*n.* **1** [usu. in *sing.*] a loud bang caused by the forceful shutting of something such as a door: *the back door closed with a slam.* **2** (usu. **the slam**) *informal* prison. [abbr. of **SLAMMER**.] **3** a poetry contest in which competitors recite their entries and are judged by members of the audience, the winner being elected after several elimination rounds. [of unknown origin.] ▷late 17th cent.: probably of Scandinavian origin; compare with Old Norse *slam(b)ra.*

slam[2] ▸*n. Bridge* a grand slam (all thirteen tricks) or small slam (twelve tricks), for which bonus points are scored if bid and made. ▷early 17th cent. (originally the name of a card game): perhaps from obsolete *slampant* 'trickery.'

slam-bang *informal* ▸*adj.* exciting and energetic: *a slam-bang action cartoon.* ■ with no niceties, subtleties, or restraints; direct and forceful: *the slam-bang world of daily journalism.*
▸*adv.* suddenly and forcefully or violently: *I walked slam-bang into this character.*

slam-danc·ing ▸*n.* a form of dancing to rock music in which the dancers deliberately collide with one another. **—slam-dance** *v.* **—slam danc·er** *n.*

slam dunk ▸*n. Basketball* a shot in which a player thrusts the ball forcefully down through the basket. ■ [usu. as *adj.*] *informal* something reliable or unfailing; a foregone conclusion or certainty: *a movie predicted to be the season's one slam-dunk hit.*

Great Pyramid at Giza, Egypt
481 feet
2570 BC

Chartres Cathedral, France
378 / 350 feet
1230

Leaning Tower of Pisa, Italy
181 feet
1372

Statue of Liberty, New York Harbor
301 feet
1884

Washington Monument, Washington, DC
555 feet
1884

Eiffel Tower, Paris
984 feet
1889

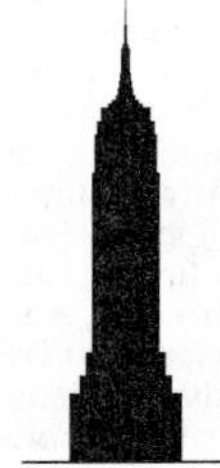
Empire State Building, New York
1,250 feet
1931

skyscrapers and other tall structures

▸*v.* **(slam-dunk)** [*trans.*] thrust (the ball) forcefully down through the basket. ■ *informal* defeat or dismiss decisively: *they continue to slam-dunk every proposal we make.*

slam·mer /ˈslamər/ ▸*n.* **1** (usu. **the slammer**) *informal* prison. **2** a person who deliberately collides with others when slam-dancing. **3** in the game of Pogs, a disk, usually made of plastic or metal, that is thicker and heavier than the standard Pogs.

Slam·min' Sam·my /ˈslamin ˈsamē/ see **SNEAD**.

s.l.a.n. ▸*abbr.* without place, year, or name of publication. [from Latin *sine loco, anno, vel nomine.*]

slan·der /ˈslandər/ ▸*n. Law* the action or crime of making a false spoken statement damaging to a person's reputation: *he is suing the TV network for slander.* Compare with **LIBEL**. ■ a false and malicious spoken statement: *I've had just about all I can stomach of your slanders.*

▸*v.* [*trans.*] make false and damaging statements about (someone): *they were accused of slandering the head of state.* See note at **MALIGN**. ▷Middle English: from Old French *esclandre*, alteration of *escandle*, from late Latin *scandalum* (see **SCANDAL**). **—slan·der·er** *n.* **—slan·der·ous** /-rəs/ *adj.* **—slan·der·ous·ly** /-rəslē/ *adv.*

slang /slaNG/ ▸*n.* a type of language that consists of words and phrases that are regarded as very informal, are more common in speech than writing, and are typically restricted to a particular context or group of people: *grass is slang for marijuana | army slang.* See note at **DIALECT**.

▸*v.* [*trans.*] *informal* attack (someone) using abusive language: *he watched ideological groups slanging one another.* ▷mid 18th cent.: of unknown origin.

slang·y /ˈslaNGē/ ▸*adj.* **(slang·i·er, slang·i·est)** using or denoting slang: *the style is so slangy as to be incomprehensible | a slangy, stand-up comedian.* **—slang·i·ly** /ˈslaNGgəlē/ *adv.* **—slang·i·ness** *n.*

slant /slant/ ▸*v.* [*intrans.*] slope or lean in a particular direction; diverge from the vertical or horizontal: *a plowed field slanted up to the skyline* | [as *adj.*] **(slanting)** *the slanting beams of the roof.* ■ (esp. of light or shadow) fall in an oblique direction: *the early sun slanted across the mountains.* ■ [*trans.*] cause (something) to lean or slope in such a way: *slant your skis as you turn to send up a curtain of water.* ■ [*trans.*] [often as *adj.*] **(slanted)** present or view (information) from a particular angle, esp. in a biased or unfair way: *slanted news coverage.*

▸*n.* **1** [in *sing.*] a sloping position: *the hedge grew **at a slant** | cut flower stems **on the slant**.* **2** a particular point of view from which something is seen or presented: *a new **slant on** science.* **3** *informal, offensive* a contemptuous term for an East Asian or Southeast Asian person.

▸*adj.* [*attrib.*] sloping: *slant pockets.* ▷late Middle English: variant of dialect *slent*, of Scandinavian origin, probably influenced by **ASLANT**.

slant·wise /ˈslant,wīz/ ▸*adj.* & *adv.* at an angle or in a sloping direction: [as *adj.*] *a slantwise glance* | [as *adv.*] *the bird veers and drops slantwise toward the tree.*

slap /slap/ ▸*v.* **(slapped, slap·ping)** [*trans.*] hit (someone or something) with the palm of one's hand or a flat object: *my sister slapped my face.* ■ [*intrans.*] hit against or into something with the sound of such an action: *water **slapped against** the boat.* ■ **(slap someone down)** *informal* reprimand someone forcefully. ■ [*trans.*] put or apply (something) somewhere quickly, carelessly, or forcefully: *slap on a bit of makeup.* ■ **(slap something on)** *informal* impose a fine or other penalty on: *the government had slapped an embargo on imports.*

▸*n.* a blow with the palm of the hand or a flat object: *he gave her a slap across her cheek.* ■ a sound made or as if made by such an action: *she heard the slap of water against the harbor wall.*

▸*adv. informal* suddenly and directly, esp. with great force: *storming out of her room, she ran slap into Luke.* ■ exactly; right: *we passed slap through the middle of an enemy armored unit.* ▷late Middle English (as a verb): probably imitative. The noun dates from the mid 17th cent.

▸*PHRASES* □ **slap in the face** an unexpected rejection or affront. □ **slap on the back** congratulations or commendations: *they deserve a hearty slap on the back for their efforts.* □ **slap someone on the back** congratulate someone. □ **slap on the wrist** a mild reprimand or punishment.

slap and tick·le ▸*n. Brit., informal* physical amorous play.

slap bass /bās/ ▸*n.* a style of playing double bass or bass guitar by pulling and releasing the strings sharply against the fingerboard, used for effect in jazz or popular music. **—slap bass·ist** /-ist/ *n.*

slap·dash /ˈslap,dasH/ ▸*adj.* done too hurriedly and carelessly: *he gave a slapdash performance.* See note at **SUPERFICIAL**.

▸*adv. dated* hurriedly and carelessly.

slap·hap·py /ˈslap,hapē/ (also **slap-hap·py**) ▸*adj. informal* **1** casual or flippant in a cheerful and often irresponsible way: *he possessed slaphappy courage.* ■ (of an action or operation) unmethodical; poorly thought out: *slaphappy surveying methods.* **2** dazed or stupefied from happiness or relief: *she's a bit slaphappy after such a narrow escape.*

slap·jack /ˈslap,jak/ ▸*n.* a pancake.

slap shot ▸*n. Ice Hockey* a hard shot made by raising the stick about waist-high before striking the puck with a sharp slapping motion.

slap·stick /ˈslap,stik/ ▸*n.* comedy based on deliberately clumsy actions and humorously embarrassing events: [as *adj.*] *slapstick humor.* ■ a device consisting of two flexible pieces of wood joined together at one end, used by clowns and in pantomime to produce a loud slapping noise.

slap-up ▸*adj.* [*attrib.*] *informal, chiefly Brit.* (of a meal or celebration) large and sumptuous: *a slap-up dinner.*

slash[1] /slasH/ ▸*v.* [*trans.*] cut (something) with a violent sweeping movement, typically using a knife or sword: *a tire was slashed on my car | they cut and **slashed their way** to the river* | [*intrans.*] *the man **slashed at** him with a sword.* ■ *informal* reduce (a price, quantity, etc.) greatly: *the workforce has been slashed by 2,000.* ■ *archaic* lash, whip, or thrash severely. ■ *archaic* crack (a whip). ■ *archaic* criticize (someone or something) severely.

▸*n.* **1** a cut made with a wide, sweeping stroke: *the man took a mighty slash at his head with a large sword.* ■ a wound or gash made by such an action: *he staggered over with a crimson slash across his temple.* ■ *figurative* a bright patch or flash of color or light: *yellow and gold foliage, with the odd **slash of** red.* **2** an oblique stroke (/) in print or writing, used between alternatives (e.g., *and/or*), in fractions (e.g., *3/4*), in ratios (e.g., *miles/day*), or between separate elements of a text. ■ [as *adj.*] denoting or belonging to a genre of fiction, chiefly published in fanzines, in which any of various male pairings from the popular media is portrayed as having a homosexual relationship. [1980s: from the use of an oblique stroke to link adjoining names or initials (as in *Kirk/Spock* and *K/S*: the latter is also used as an alternative name for the genre, taken from the names of characters in *Star Trek*, a television program).] **3** debris resulting from the felling or destruction of trees. ▷late Middle English: perhaps imitative, or from Old French *esclachier* 'break in pieces.' The noun dates from the late 16th cent.

slash[2] ▸*n.* a tract of swampy ground, esp. in a coastal region.

slash-and-burn ▸*adj.* [*attrib.*] of, relating to, or denoting a method of agriculture in which existing vegetation is cut down and burned off before new seeds are sown, typically used as a method for clearing forest land for farming. ■ *figurative* aggressive and merciless: *her slash-and-burn campaigning style.*

slash·er /ˈslasHər/ ▸*n. informal* **1** a person or thing that slashes. **2** (also **slasher film** or **slasher movie**, etc.) a horror movie, esp. one in which victims (typically women or teenagers) are slashed with knives and razors.

slash·ing /ˈslasHiNG/ ▸*adj.* [*attrib.*] *informal* vigorously incisive or effective: *a slashing magazine attack on her.*

slash pine ▸*n.* a fast-growing, long-needled pine found in low-lying coastal areas (slashes) of the southeastern U.S., commonly harvested for timber. • *Pinus elliottii*, family Pinaceae.

slash pock·et ▸*n.* a pocket set in a garment with a slit for the opening.

slat /slat/ ▸*n.* a thin, narrow piece of wood, plastic, or metal, esp. one of a series that overlap or fit into each other, as in a fence or a Venetian blind. ▷late Middle English (in the sense 'roofing slate'): shortening of Old French *esclat* 'splinter,' from *esclater* 'to split;' related to **ÉCLAT**, **SLAT**. The current sense dates from the mid 18th cent. **—slat·ted** *adj.*

slate /slāt/ ▸*n.* **1** a fine-grained gray, green, or bluish metamorphic rock easily split into smooth, flat pieces. ■ a flat piece of such rock used as roofing material. **2** a flat piece of slate used for writing on, typically framed in wood, formerly used in schools. ■ a list of candidates for election to a post or office, typically a group sharing a set of political views: *another slate of candidates will be picked for the state convention.* ■ a range of something offered: *the company has revealed details of a $60 million slate of film productions.*

Space Needle, Seattle 605 feet
1962

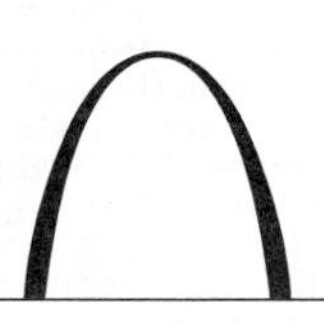
Gateway Arch, St. Louis 630 feet
1965

Transamerica Pyramid, San Francisco 853 feet
1972

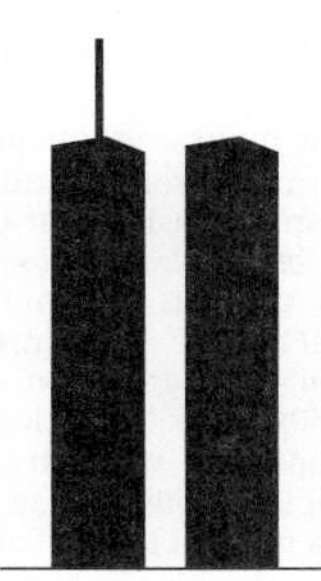
Former World Trade Center, New York 1,368 / 1,362 feet
1972

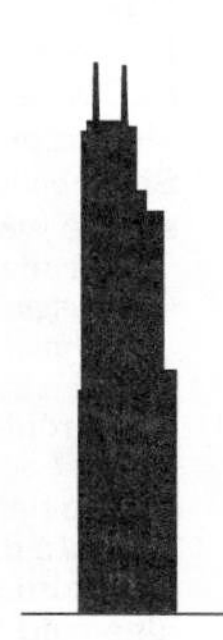
Sears Tower, Chicago 1,454 feet
1974

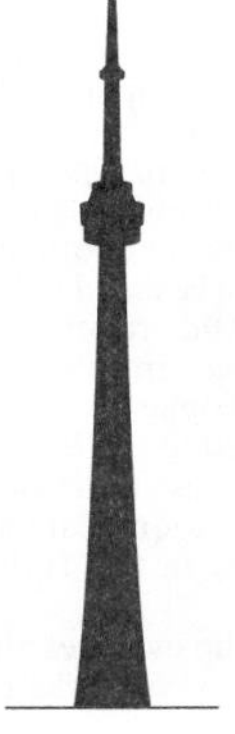
CN Tower, Toronto 1,815 feet
1976

Petronas Towers, Kuala Lumpur 1,482 feet
1997

skyscrapers and other tall structures

■ a board showing the identifying details of a take of a motion picture, which is held in front of the camera at its beginning and end. **3** [usu. as *adj.*] a bluish-gray color: *suits of* ***slate gray.***

▸*v.* [*trans.*] **1** cover (something, esp. a roof) with slates. **2** *Brit., informal* criticize severely: *his work was slated by the critics.* **3** (usu. **be slated**) schedule; plan: *renovations are slated for late June* | [*trans.*] *the former brickyard is slated to be renovated.* ■ (usu. **be slated**) nominate (someone) as a candidate for an office or post: *I understand that I am being slated for promotion.* **4** identify (a movie take) using a slate. ▷Middle English *sclate, sklate*, shortening of Old French *esclate*, feminine, synonymous with *esclat* 'piece broken off' (see **SLAT**). Sense 3 of the verb arose from the practice of noting a name on a writing slate. **—slat·y** *adj.*

▸*PHRASE* □ **wipe the slate clean** see **WIPE**.

Sla·ter /ˈslātər/, Samuel (1768–1835), U.S. inventor and industrialist; born in England. He emigrated from England and, after building a technologically advanced spinning mill from memory in Rhode Island in 1793, he set up his own mills in New England.

slat·er /ˈslātər/ ▸*n.* **1** a person who slates roofs for a living. **2** a wood louse or similar isopod. • Several species in the order Isopoda. See also **SEA SLATER**.

slath·er /ˈslaTHər/ ▸*n.* (often **slathers**) *informal* a large amount.

▸*v.* [*trans.*] *informal* spread or smear (a substance) thickly or liberally: ***slather on*** *some tanning lotion.* | *biscuits* ***slathered with*** *butter.* ▷early 19th cent.: of unknown origin.

slat·tern /ˈslatərn/ ▸*n. dated* a dirty, untidy woman. ▷mid 17th cent.: related to *slattering* 'slovenly,' from dialect *slatter* 'to spill, slop,' frequentative of *slat* 'strike,' of unknown origin. **—slat·tern·li·ness** *n.* **—slat·tern·ly** *adj.*

slaugh·ter /ˈslôtər/ ▸*n.* the killing of animals for food. ■ the killing of a large number of people or animals in a cruel or violent way; massacre: *the slaughter of 20 peaceful demonstrators.* ■ *informal* a thorough defeat: *an absolute slaughter by the Red Sox.*

▸*v.* [*trans.*] (usu. **be slaughtered**) kill (animals) for food. See note at **KILL**. ■ kill (people or animals) in a cruel or violent way, typically in large numbers: *innocent civilians are being slaughtered.* ■ *informal* defeat (an opponent) thoroughly: *our team was slaughtered in the finals.* ▷Middle English (as a noun): from Old Norse *slátr* 'butcher's meat'; related to **SLAY**[1]. The verb dates from the mid 16th cent. **—slaugh·ter·er** *n.* **—slaugh·ter·ous** /-rəs/ *adj.*

slaugh·ter·house /ˈslôtərˌhous/ ▸*n.* a place where animals are slaughtered for food.

Slav /släv/ ▸*n.* a member of a group of peoples in central and eastern Europe speaking Slavic languages.

▸*adj.* another term for **SLAVIC**. ▷from medieval Latin *Sclavus*, late Greek *Sklabos*, later also from medieval Latin *Slavus*.

slave /slāv/ ▸*n. chiefly historical* a person who is the legal property of another and is forced to obey them. ■ a person who works very hard without proper remuneration or appreciation: *by the time I was ten, I had become her slave, doing all the housework.* ■ a person who is excessively dependent upon or controlled by something: *the poorest people of the world are* ***slaves to*** *the banks* | *she was no* ***slave to*** *fashion.* ■ a device, or part of one, directly controlled by another: [as *adj.*] *a slave cassette deck.* Compare with **MASTER**[1]. ■ an ant captured in its pupal state by an ant of another species, for which it becomes a worker.

▸*v.* [*intrans.*] work excessively hard: *after* ***slaving away*** *for fourteen years, all he gets is two thousand.* ■ [*trans.*] subject (a device) to control by another: *should the need arise, the two channels can be slaved together.* ▷Middle English: shortening of Old French *esclave*, equivalent of medieval Latin *sclava* (feminine) 'Slavic (captive)': some South Slavic peoples had been reduced to a servile state by conquest in the 9th cent.

Slave Coast a part of the west coast of Africa, between the Volta River and Mount Cameroon, from which slaves were exported in the 16th–19th centuries.

slave driv·er ▸*n.* a person who oversees and urges on slaves at work. ■ a person who works others very hard. **—slave-drive** *v.*

slave·hold·er /ˈslāvˌhōldər/ ▸*n.* an owner of slaves. **—slave·hold·ing** *n.* & *adj.*

slave la·bor ▸*n.* labor that is coerced and inadequately rewarded, or the people who perform such labor: *most of production is carried out by slave labor* | *they treat us like slave labor.*

slave-mak·ing ant (also **slave-mak·er ant**) ▸*n.* an ant that raids the nests of other ant species and steals the pupae, which later become workers in the new colony. • Several species in the family Formicidae, in particular the European *Formica sanguinea*. See also **AMAZON ANT**.

slav·er[1] /ˈslāvər/ ▸*n. chiefly historical* a person dealing in or owning slaves. ■ a ship used for transporting slaves.

slav·er[2] /ˈslavər/ ▸*n.* saliva running from the mouth. ■ *archaic, figurative* excessive or obsequious flattery.

▸*v.* [*intrans.*] let saliva run from the mouth: *the Labrador was slavering at the mouth.* ■ show excessive desire: *suburbanites* ***slavering over*** *drop-dead models.* ▷Middle English: probably from Low German; compare with **SLOBBER**.

slav·er·y /ˈslāvərē/ ▸*n.* the state of being a slave: *thousands had been sold into slavery.* ■ the practice or system of owning slaves. ■ a condition compared to that of a slave in respect of exhausting labor or restricted freedom: *female domestic slavery.* ■ excessive dependence on or devotion to something: ***slavery to*** *tradition.*

slave ship ▸*n. historical* a ship transporting slaves, esp. one carrying slaves from Africa.

Slave State (also **slave state**) ▸*n. historical* any of the Southern states of the U.S. in which slavery was legal before the Civil War.

slave trade ▸*n. chiefly historical* the procuring, transporting, and selling of human beings as slaves, in particular the former trade in African blacks as slaves by European countries and North America. **—slave trad·er** *n.*

slav·ey /ˈslāvē/ ▸*n.* (*pl.* **-eys**) *Brit., informal, dated* a maidservant, esp. a hard-worked one.

Slav·ic /ˈslävik/ ▸*adj.* of, relating to, or denoting the branch of the Indo-European language family that includes Russian, Ukrainian, and Belorussian (**East Slavic**), Polish, Czech, Slovak, and Sorbian (**West Slavic**), and Bulgarian, Serbo-Croat, Macedonian, and Slovene (**South Slavic**). ■ of, relating to, or denoting the peoples of central and eastern Europe who speak any of these languages.

▸*n.* the Slavic languages collectively. See also **SLAVONIC**.

slav·ish /ˈslāviSH/ ▸*adj.* relating to or characteristic of a slave, typically by behaving in a servile or submissive way: *he noted the slavish, feudal respect they had for her.* See note at **OBSEQUIOUS**. ■ showing no attempt at originality, constructive interpretation, or development: *a slavish adherence to protocol.* **—slav·ish·ly** *adv.* **—slav·ish·ness** *n.*

Sla·von·ic /sləˈvänik/ ▸*adj.* & *n.* another term for **SLAVIC**. See also **CHURCH SLAVIC**. ▷from medieval Latin *S(c)lavonicus*, from *S(c)lavonia* 'country of the Slavs,' from *Sclavus* (see **SLAV**).

slaw /slô/ ▸*n.* coleslaw. ▷late 18th cent.: from Dutch *sla*, shortened from *salade* 'salad.'

slay[1] /slā/ ▸*v.* (*past* **slew** /slo͞o/; *past part.* **slain** /slān/) [*trans.*] *archaic, poetic/literary* kill (a person or animal) in a violent way: *St. George slew the dragon.* See note at **KILL**. ■ (usu. **be slain**) murder (someone) (used chiefly in journalism): *a man was slain with a shotgun* | [as *n.*] (**slaying**) *a gangland slaying.* ■ *informal* greatly impress or amuse (someone): *you slay me, you really do.* ▷Old English *slēan* 'strike, kill,' of Germanic origin; related to Dutch *slaan* and German *schlagen*. **—slay·er** *n.*

slay[2] ▸*n.* variant spelling of **SLEY**.

SLBM ▸*abbr.* submarine-launched ballistic missile.

SLCM ▸*abbr.* sea-launched cruise missile.

sld. ▸*abbr.* ■ sailed. ■ sealed.

SLE ▸*abbr.* systemic lupus erythematosus.

sleaze /slēz/ ▸*n.* immoral, sordid, and corrupt behavior or material, esp. in business or politics: *political campaigns that are long on sleaze and short on substance.* ■ *informal* a sordid, corrupt, or immoral person.

▸*v.* [*intrans.*] *informal* behave in an immoral, corrupt, or sordid way: *you're the last person who has to sleaze around bars.* ▷1960s: back-formation from **SLEAZY**.

sleaze·ball /ˈslēzˌbôl/ (also **sleaze·bag** /-ˌbag/) ▸*n. informal* a disreputable, disgusting, or despicable person (also used as a general term of abuse).

slea·zoid /ˈslēˌzoid/ (also **slea·zo** /-ˌzō/ (*pl.* **-zos**)) *informal* ▸*adj.* sleazy, sordid, or despicable: *a sleazoid lawyer.*

▸*n.* a sleazy, sordid, or despicable person.

slea·zy /ˈslēzē/ ▸*adj.* (**-zi·er**, **-zi·est**) **1** (of a person or situation) sordid, corrupt, or immoral. ■ (of a place) squalid and seedy: *a sleazy all-night cafe.* **2** *dated* (of textiles and clothing) flimsy. ▷mid 17th cent.: of unknown origin. **—slea·zi·ly** /ˈslēzəlē/ *adv.* **—slea·zi·ness** *n.*

sled /sled/ ▸*n.* a vehicle on runners for traveling over snow or ice, either pushed or pulled, drawn by horses, dogs, or a motor vehicle, or allowed to slide downhill. ■ another term for **SLEDGE**[1]. ■ another term for **SNOWMOBILE**.

▸*v.* (**sled·ded**, **sled·ding**) [*intrans.*] ride on a sled: *they sledded down the slopes in the frozen snow* | [as *n.*] (**sledding**) *the sledding has been excellent this year.* ▷Middle English: from Middle Low German *sledde*; related to the verb **SLIDE**.

sled dog ▸*n.* a dog trained to pull a sled, esp. as one of a team.

sledge[1] /slej/ ▸*n.* a vehicle on runners for conveying loads or passengers esp. over snow or ice, often pulled by draft animals. ■ British term for **SLED**.

▸*v.* [*trans.*] carry (a load or passengers) on a sledge: *the task of sledging lifeboats across tundra.* ▷late 16th cent. (as a noun): from Middle Dutch *sleedse*; related to **SLED**. The verb dates from the early 18th cent.

sledge[2] ▸*n.* a sledgehammer. ▷Old English *slecg*, from a Germanic base meaning 'to strike,' related to **SLAY**[1].

sledge·ham·mer /ˈslejˌhamər/ ▸*n.* a large, heavy hammer used for such jobs as breaking rocks and driving in fence posts. ■ [as *adj.*] powerful; forceful: *sledgehammer blows.* ■ [as *adj.*] *figurative* ruthless, insensitive, or using unnecessary force: *under his sledgehammer direction, anything of subtlety is swamped.*

▸*v.* [*trans.*] hit with a sledgehammer.

sleek /slēk/ ▸*adj.* (of hair, fur, or skin) smooth and glossy: *he was tall, with sleek, dark hair.* ■ (of a person or animal) having smooth, glossy skin, hair, or fur, often taken as a sign of physical fitness: *a sleek black cat.* ■ (of a person) having a wealthy and well-groomed appearance: *his sleek and elegant sisters.* ■ (of an object) having an elegant, streamlined shape or design: *his sleek black car slid through the traffic.* ■ ingratiating; unctuous: *she gave Guy a sleek smile to underline her words.*

▸*v.* [*trans.*] make (the hair) smooth and glossy, typically by applying pressure or moisture to it: *her black hair was sleeked down.*

▸*adv. poetic/literary* in a smooth manner: *the hiss of water sliding sleek against the hull.* ▷late Middle English: a later variant of **SLICK** (adjective and verb). **—sleek·ly** *adv.* **—sleek·ness** *n.* **—sleek·y** *adj.*

sleep /slēp/ ▸*n.* a condition of body and mind such as that which typically recurs for several hours every night, in which the nervous system is relatively inactive, the eyes closed, the postural muscles relaxed, and consciousness practically suspended: *I was on the verge of sleep* | [in *sing.*] *a good night's sleep.* ■ *chiefly poetic/literary* a state compared to or resembling this, such as death or complete silence or stillness: *a photograph of the poet in his last sleep.* ■ a gummy or gritty secretion found in the corners of the eyes after sleep: *she sat up, rubbing the sleep from her eyes.*

▸*v.* (*past* and *past part.* **slept** /slept/) [*intrans.*] rest in such a condition; be asleep: *she slept for half an hour* | [as *adj.*] (**sleeping**) *he looked at the sleeping child.* ■ (**sleep through**) fail to be woken by: *he was so tired he slept through the alarm.* ■ [with *adverbial*] have sexual intercourse or be involved in a sexual relationship: *I won't* ***sleep with*** *a man who doesn't respect me.* ■ [*trans.*] (**sleep something off/away**) dispel the effects of or recover from something by going to sleep: *she thought it wise to let him sleep off his hangover.* ■ [*trans.*] provide (a specified number of people) with beds, rooms, or places to stay the night: *studios sleeping two people cost $70 a night.* ■ *figurative* be inactive or dormant: *Copenhagen likes to be known as the city that never sleeps.* ■ *poetic/literary* be at peace in death; lie buried: *he sleeps beneath the silver birches.*

▸*phrasal v.* □ **sleep around** *informal* have many casual sexual partners. □ **sleep in** remain asleep or in bed later than usual in the morning. ■ sleep by night at one's place of work. □ **sleep out** sleep outdoors. □ **sleep over** spend the night at a place other than one's own home: *Katie was asked to sleep over with Jenny.* ▷Old English *slēp, slǣp* (noun), *slēpan, slǣpan* (verb), of Germanic origin; related to Dutch *slapen* and German *schlafen*.

▸*PHRASES* □ **one could do something in one's sleep** *informal* one regards something as so easy that it will require no effort or conscious thought to accomplish: *she knew the music perfectly, could sing it in her sleep.* □ **get to sleep** manage to fall asleep. □ **go to sleep** fall asleep. ■ (of a limb) become numb as a result of prolonged pressure. □ **let sleeping dogs lie**

S

proverb avoid interfering in a situation that is currently causing no problems but might do so as a result of such interference. □ **lose sleep** see **LOSE**. □ **put someone to sleep** make someone unconscious by the use of drugs, alcohol, or an anesthetic. ■ (also **send someone to sleep**) bore someone greatly. □ **put something to sleep** kill an animal, esp. an old, sick, or badly injured one, painlessly (used euphemistically). ■ *Computing* put a computer on standby while it is not being used, esp. in order to reduce power consumption. □ **sleep easy** see **EASY**. □ **sleep like a log** (or **top**) sleep very soundly. □ **sleep on it** *informal* delay making a decision on something until the following day so as to have more time to consider it. □ **the sleep of the just** a deep, untroubled sleep. □ **sleep rough** see **ROUGH**. □ **sleep tight** [usu. in *imperative*] sleep well (said to someone when parting from them at night). □ **sleep with one eye open** sleep very lightly, aware of what is happening around one.

sleep·er /ˈslēpər/ ▸*n.* **1** a person or animal who is asleep. ■ [with *adj.*] a person with a specified sleep pattern: *he was a light sleeper, for long periods an insomniac.* **2** a thing used for or connected with sleeping, in particular: ■ a train carrying sleeping cars. ■ a sleeping car. ■ a berth in a sleeping car. ■ (often **sleepers**) one-piece coverall pajamas for a baby or small child. ■ a sofa or chair that converts into a bed. **3** a movie, book, play, etc., that achieves sudden unexpected success after initially attracting little attention, typically one that proves popular without much promotion or expenditure. ■ an antique whose true value goes unrecognized for some time. ■ (also **sleeper agent**) a secret agent who remains inactive for a long period while establishing a secure position. **4** *Brit.* a railroad tie. **5** a stocky fish with mottled coloration that occurs widely in warm seas and fresh water. • *Dormitator* and other genera, family Gobiidae (or Eleotridae): many species.

sleep·er cell ▸*n.* a secretive group with suspected links to a terrorist organization that is planning or believed capable of carrying out an attack.

sleep-in ▸*adj.* [*attrib.*] (of a domestic employee) resident in an employer's house: *a sleep-in babysitter.*
▸*n.* **1** a person who resides at the premises of their employment. **2** a form of protest in which the participants sleep overnight in premises that they have occupied: *a student sleep-in began last night.*

sleep·ing bag ▸*n.* a warm lined padded bag to sleep in, esp. when camping.

Sleep·ing Beau·ty a fairy-tale heroine who slept for a hundred years until awakened by the kiss of a prince.

sleep·ing car ▸*n.* a railroad car provided with beds or berths.

sleep·ing part·ner ▸*n.* British term for **SILENT PARTNER**.

sleep·ing pill ▸*n.* a tablet of a drug that helps to induce sleep.

sleep·ing sick·ness ▸*n.* **1** a tropical disease caused by a parasitic protozoan (trypanosome) that is transmitted by the bite of the tsetse fly. It causes fever, chills, pain in the limbs, and anemia, and eventually affects the nervous system causing extreme lethargy and death. See also **TRYPANOSOMIASIS**. **2** another term for **ENCEPHALITIS LETHARGICA**.

sleep-learn·ing ▸*n.* learning by hearing while asleep, typically by playing a tape recording of what is to be learned.

sleep·less /ˈslēplis/ ▸*adj.* characterized by or experiencing lack of sleep: *another sleepless night | Lisa lay sleepless.* ■ *chiefly poetic/literary* continually active or moving: *the sleepless river.* **—sleep·less·ly** *adv.* **—sleep·less·ness** *n.*

sleep mode ▸*n.* *Electronics* a power-saving mode of operation in which devices or parts of devices are switched off until needed.

sleep-out ▸*n.* an occasion of sleeping outdoors.

sleep·o·ver /ˈslēpˌōvər/ ▸*n.* an occasion of spending the night away from home, or of having a guest or guests spend the night in one's home, esp. as a party for children.

sleep·walk /ˈslēpˌwôk/ ▸*v.* [*intrans.*] walk around and sometimes perform other actions while asleep.
▸*n.* an instance of such activity. **—sleep·walk·er** *n.* **—sleep·walk·ing** *n.*

sleep·wear /ˈslēpˌwe(ə)r/ ▸*n.* pajamas or other clothing suitable for wearing in bed.

sleep·y /ˈslēpē/ ▸*adj.* (**sleep·i·er**, **sleep·i·est**) needing or ready for sleep: *the wine had made her sleepy.* ■ showing the effects of sleep: *she rubbed her sleepy eyes.* ■ inducing sleep; soporific: *the sleepy heat of the afternoon.* ■ (of a place) without much activity: *he turned off the road into a sleepy little town.* ■ (of a business, organization, or industry) lacking the ability or will to respond to change; not dynamic: *it was once a sleepy subsidiary of Foster & Sykes.* **—sleep·i·ly** /ˈslēpəlē/ *adv.* **—sleep·i·ness** *n.*

sleep·y·head /ˈslēpēˌhed/ ▸*n.* a sleepy or inattentive person (usually as a form of address): *come on, sleepyhead, time to get up.*

Sleep·y Hol·low a town in southeastern New York, east of the Hudson River and north of Tarrytown. It is associated with the writings of Washington Irving.

sleet /slēt/ ▸*n.* a form of precipitation consisting of ice pellets, often mixed with rain or snow. ■ a thin coating of ice formed by sleet or rain freezing on contact with a cold surface.
▸*v.* [*intrans.*] (**it sleets, it is sleeting**, etc.) sleet falls: *it was sleeting so hard we could barely see.* ▷Middle English: of Germanic origin; probably related to Middle Low German *slōten* (plural) 'hail' and German *Schlosse* 'hailstone.' **—sleet·y** *adj.*

sleeve /slēv/ ▸*n.* the part of a garment that wholly or partly covers a person's arm: *a shirt with the sleeves rolled up.* ■ (also **record sleeve** or **album sleeve**) a protective paper or cardboard cover for a record. ■ a protective or connecting tube fitting over or enclosing a rod, spindle, or smaller tube. ▷Old English *slēfe, slīef(e), slȳf*; related to Middle Dutch *sloove* 'covering.' **—sleeved** *adj.* [often in *combination*] *a capsleeved shirt.* **—sleeve·less** *adj.*
▸*PHRASES* □ **up one's sleeve** (of a strategy, idea, or resource) kept secret and in reserve for use when needed: *he was new to the game but had a few tricks up his sleeve.* □ **wear one's heart on one's sleeve** see **HEART**.

sleeve board (also **sleeve·board**) ▸*n.* a small ironing board over which a sleeve is pulled for pressing.

sleeve valve ▸*n.* a valve in the form of a cylinder that slides to cover and uncover an inlet or outlet.

sleigh /slā/ ▸*n.* a sled drawn by horses or reindeer, esp. one used for passengers.
▸*v.* [*intrans.*] [usu. as *n.*] (**sleighing**) ride on a sleigh. ▷early 17th cent. (originally a North American usage): from Dutch *slee*; related to **SLED**.

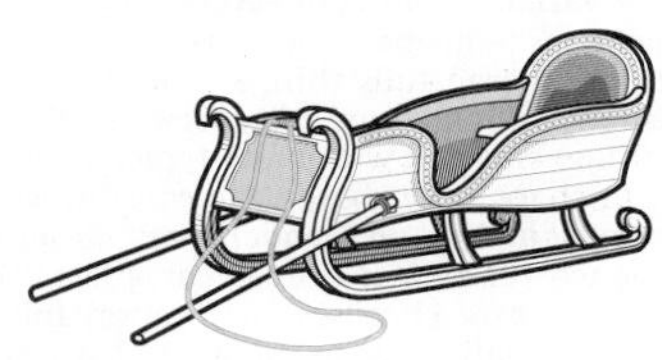

sleigh

sleigh bed ▸*n.* a bed resembling a sleigh, with an outward curving headboard and footboard.

sleigh bell ▸*n.* a tinkling bell attached to the harness of a sleigh horse.

sleight /slīt/ ▸*n.* *poetic/literary* the use of dexterity or cunning, esp. so as to deceive: *except by* **sleight of** *logic, the two positions cannot be harmonized.* ▷Middle English *sleghth* 'cunning, skill,' from Old Norse *slœgth*, from *slœgr* 'sly.'
▸*PHRASE* □ **sleight of hand** manual dexterity, typically in performing tricks: *a nifty bit of sleight of hand got the ashtray into the correct position.* ■ skillful deception: *this is financial sleight of hand of the worst sort.*

slen·der /ˈslendər/ ▸*adj.* (**-der·er**, **-der·est**) **1** (of a person or part of the body) gracefully thin: *her slender neck.* See note at **THIN**. ■ (esp. of a rod or stem) of small girth or breadth: *slender iron railings.* **2** (of something abstract) barely sufficient in amount or basis: *a slender majority of four.* ▷late Middle English: of unknown origin. **—slen·der·ly** *adv.* **—slen·der·ness** *n.*

slen·der·ize /ˈslendəˌrīz/ ▸*v.* [*trans.*] [usu. as *adj.*] (**slenderizing**) make (a person or a part of their body) appear more slender: *my mother has always held that dark colors are slenderizing.* ■ [*intrans.*] (of a person) lose weight; become slim. ■ *figurative* reduce the size of (something): *a campaign promise that he would slenderize the executive branch.*

slen·der lo·ris ▸*n.* see **LORIS**.

slept /slept/ ▸ past and past participle of **SLEEP**.

sleuth /slo͞oTH/ *informal* ▸*n.* a detective.
▸*v.* [*intrans.*] [often as *n.*] (**sleuthing**) carry out a search or investigation in the manner of a detective: *scientists began their genetic sleuthing for honey mushrooms four years ago.* ■ [*trans.*] *dated* investigate (someone or something). ▷Middle English (originally in the sense 'track,' in **SLEUTH-HOUND**): from Old Norse *slóth*; compare with **SLOT**[2]. Current senses date from the late 19th cent.

sleuth-hound ▸*n.* *dated* a bloodhound. ■ *informal* an eager investigator; a detective.

S lev·el ▸*n.* (in the UK except Scotland) an examination, or a pass of one, typically taken together with an A level in the same subject, but having a more advanced syllabus. ▷abbreviation of *Special level* or (formerly) *Scholarship level.*

slew[1] /slo͞o/ (also **slue**) ▸*v.* **1** [*intrans.*] (of a vehicle or person) turn or slide violently or uncontrollably in a particular direction: *the Chevy slewed from side to side in the snow.* ■ [*trans.*] turn or slide (something, esp. a vehicle) in such a way: *he managed to slew the aircraft around before it settled on the runway.* **2** [*intrans.*] (of an electronic device) undergo slewing.
▸*n.* [in *sing.*] a violent or uncontrollable sliding movement: *I was assaulted by the thump and slew of the van.* ▷mid 18th cent. (originally in nautical use): of unknown origin.

slew[2] ▸ past of **SLAY**[1].

slew[3] ▸*n.* *informal* a large number or quantity of something: *he asked me* **a slew of** *questions.* ▷mid 19th cent.: from Irish *sluagh.*

slew·ing /ˈslo͞oiNG/ ▸*n.* *Electronics* the response of an electronic device to a sudden large increase in input, esp. one that causes the device to respond at its maximum rate.

slew rate ▸*n.* *Electronics* the maximum rate at which an amplifier can respond to an abrupt change of input level.

sley /slā/ (also **slay**) ▸*n.* a tool used in weaving to force the weft into place. ▷Old English *slege*; related to **SLAY**[1].

slice /slīs/ ▸*n.* **1** a thin, broad piece of food, such as bread, meat, or cake, cut from a larger portion: *four* **slices of** *bread | potato slices.* ■ a portion or share of something: *local authorities control a huge slice of public spending.* **2** *Golf* a stroke that makes the ball curve away to the right (for a left-handed player, the left), typically inadvertently. Compare with **HOOK**. ■ (in other sports) a shot or stroke made with glancing contact to impart spin. **3** a utensil with a broad, flat blade for lifting foods such as cake and fish.
▸*v.* [*trans.*] **1** cut (something, esp. food) into slices: *slice the onion into rings |* [as *adj.*] (**sliced**) *a sliced loaf.* ■ (**slice something off/from**) cut something or a piece of something off or from (something larger), typically with one clean cut: *he sliced a corner from a fried egg | figurative he sliced 70 seconds off the record.* ■ cut with or as if with a sharp implement: *the bomber's wings were slicing the air with some efficiency |* [*intrans.*] *the blade sliced into his palm.* ■ [*intrans.*] move easily and quickly: *Senna then sliced past Berger to take third place.* **2** *Golf* strike (the ball) or play (a stroke) so that the ball curves away to the right (for a left-handed player, the left), typically inadvertently. ■ (in other sports) propel (the ball) with a glancing contact to impart spin: *Evans went and sliced a corner into his own net.* ▷Middle English (in the sense 'fragment, splinter'): shortening of Old French *esclice* 'splinter,' from the verb *esclicier*, of Germanic origin; related to German *schleissen* 'to slice,' also to **SLIT**. **—slice·a·ble** *adj.* **—slic·er** *n.* [often in *combination*] *a cheese-slicer.*
▸*PHRASE* □ **slice of life** a realistic representation of everyday experience in a movie, play, or book.

slice-and-dice ▸*adj.* involving the quick rearrangement of elements; able to be analyzed in a number of different ways: *each network has analysis teams that slice and dice the exit poll information to find a conclusion.*

slick /slik/ ▸*adj.* **1** (of an action or thing) done or operating in an impressively smooth, efficient, and apparently effortless way: *a slick piece of software.* ■ (of a thing) superficially impressive or efficient in presentation: *the brands are backed by slick advertising.* ■ (of a person or their behavior) adroit or clever; glibly assured: *he's a slick con man.* **2** (of skin or hair) smooth and glossy: *a dandy-looking dude with a slick black ponytail.* ■ (of a surface) smooth, wet, and slippery: *she tumbled back against the slick, damp wall.*
▸*n.* **1** an oil slick. ■ a small smear or patch of a glossy or wet substance, esp. a cosmetic: *a slick of lip balm.*

Pronunciation Key ə *ago*; ər *over*; ˈə or ˌə *up*; ˈər or ˌər *fur*; a *hat*; ā *rate*; ä *car*; CH *chew*; e *let*; ē *see*; e(ə)r *air*; i *fit*; ī *by*; i(ə)r *ear*; NG *sing*; ō *go*; ô *for*; oi *boy*; o͝o *good*; o͞o *goo*; ou *out*; SH *she*; TH *thin*; T͟H *then*; (h)w *why*; ZH *vision*

2 (usu. **slicks**) a race car or bicycle tire without a tread, for use in dry weather conditions. **3** *informal* a glossy magazine.

▸*v.* **1** [*trans.*] make (one's hair) flat, smooth, and glossy by applying water, oil, or cream to it: *his damp hair was slicked back* | [as *adj.* in *combination*] (**slicked**) *his slicked-down hair.* ■ cover with a film of liquid; make wet or slippery: *she woke to find her body slicked with sweat* | [as *adj.* in *combination*] (**-slicked**) *a rain-slicked road.* **2** (**slick someone/something up**) make someone or something smart, tidy, or stylish. ▷Middle English (in the senses 'glossy' and 'make smooth or glossy'): probably from Old English and related to Old Norse *slíkr* 'smooth'; compare with **SLEEK**. **—slick·ly** *adv.* **—slick·ness** *n.*

slick·en·side /ˈslikən,sīd/ ▸*n.* (usu. **slickensides**) *Geology* a polished and striated rock surface that results from friction along a fault or bedding plane. ▷mid 18th cent.: from a dialect variant of the adjective **SLICK** + **SIDE**.

slick·er /ˈslikər/ ▸*n.* **1** *informal* a crook or swindler. ■ short for **CITY SLICKER**. **2** a raincoat made of smooth material.

slide /slīd/ ▸*v.* (*past* **slid** /slid/) [*intrans.*] move along a smooth surface while maintaining continuous contact with it: *she slid down the bank into the water* | [as *adj.*] (**sliding**) *the tank should have a sliding glass cover.* ■ [*trans.*] move (something) along a surface in such a way: *she slid the keys over the table.* ■ move smoothly, quickly, or unobtrusively: *I quickly slid into a seat at the back of the hall.* ■ [*trans.*] move (something) in such a way: *she slid the bottle into her pocket.* ■ change gradually to a worse condition or lower level: *the country faces the prospect of sliding from recession into slump.*

▸*n.* **1** a structure with a smooth sloping surface for children to slide down. ■ a smooth stretch or slope of ice or packed snow for sledding on. ■ an act of moving along a smooth surface while maintaining continuous contact with it: *use an ice ax to halt a slide on ice and snow.* ■ *Baseball* a sliding approach to a base along the ground. ■ a decline in value or quality: *the current slide in house prices.* **2** a part of a machine or musical instrument that slides. ■ the place on a machine or instrument where a sliding part operates. ■ slide guitar: *I'd been playing slide for years.* **3** (also **microscope slide**) a rectangular piece of glass on which an object is mounted or placed for examination under a microscope. ■ a mounted transparency, typically one placed in a projector for viewing on a screen: [as *adj.*] *a slide show.* ▷Old English *slīdan* (verb); related to **SLED** and **SLEDGE**[1]. The noun, first in the sense 'act of sliding,' is recorded from the late 16th cent. **—slid·a·ble** *adj.*

▸*PHRASE* □ **let something slide** negligently allow something to deteriorate: *Papa had let the business slide after Mama's death.*

slide fas·ten·er ▸*n.* *dated* a zipper.

slide gui·tar ▸*n.* a style of guitar playing in which a glissando effect is produced by moving a bottleneck or similar device over the strings, used esp. in blues.

Sli·dell /slīˈdel/ a city in southeastern Louisiana, northeast of New Orleans; pop. 25,695.

slide pro·jec·tor ▸*n.* a piece of equipment used for displaying photographic slides on a screen.

slid·er /ˈslīdər/ ▸*n.* **1** a North American freshwater turtle with a red or yellow patch on the side of the head. • Genus *Trachemys* (or *Pseudemys*), family Emydidae: several species, in particular the **red-eared** (or **pond**) **slider** (*T. scripta*). **2** *Baseball* a pitch that moves laterally as it nears home plate. **3** (usu. **sliders**) a sliding door, esp. one with a glass panel. **4** *Electronics* a knob or lever that is moved horizontally or vertically to control a variable, such as the volume of a radio. ■ *Computing* an icon mimicking such a knob or lever.

slider 1

slide rule ▸*n.* a ruler with a sliding central strip, marked with logarithmic scales and used for making rapid calculations, esp. multiplication and division.

slide show ▸*n.* a presentation supplemented by or based on a series of projected photographic slides.

slide valve ▸*n.* a piece that opens and closes an aperture by sliding across it.

slid·ing door ▸*n.* a door drawn across an aperture on a groove or suspended from a track, rather than turning on hinges.

slid·ing scale ▸*n.* a scale of fees, taxes, wages, etc., that varies in accordance with variation of some standard.

slid·ing seat ▸*n.* a seat able to slide back and forth on runners, esp. one in a racing rowboat used to adjust the length of a stroke.

slight /slīt/ ▸*adj.* **1** small in degree; inconsiderable: *a slight increase* | *a slight ankle injury* | *the chance of success is very slight.* ■ (esp. of a creative work) not profound or substantial; somewhat trivial or superficial: *a slight plot.* **2** (of a person or their build) not sturdy and strongly built: *she was slight and delicate-looking.*

▸*v.* [*trans.*] **1** insult (someone) by treating or speaking of them without proper respect or attention: *he was careful not to slight a guest* | [as *adj.*] (**slighting**) *slighting references to Irish Catholics.* See note at **NEGLECT**. **2** *archaic* raze or destroy (a fortification).

▸*n.* an insult caused by a failure to show someone proper respect or attention: *an unintended slight can create grudges* | *he was seething at the* **slight to** *his authority.* ▷Middle English; the adjective from Old Norse *sléttr* 'smooth' (an early sense in English), of Germanic origin; related to Dutch *slechts* 'merely' and German *schlicht* 'simple,' *schlecht* 'bad'; the verb (originally in the sense 'make smooth or level'), from Old Norse *slétta*. The sense 'treat with disrespect' dates from the late 16th cent. **—slight·ing·ly** *adv.* **—slight·ish** *adj.* **—slight·ness** *n.*

▸*PHRASES* □ **not in the slightest** not at all: *he didn't mind in the slightest.* □ **the slightest ——** [usu. with *negative*] any —— whatsoever: *I don't have the slightest idea.*

slight·ly /ˈslītlē/ ▸*adv.* **1** to a small degree; inconsiderably: *he lowered his voice slightly* | [as *submodifier*] *they are all slightly different.* **2** (with reference to a person's build) in a slender way: *a slightly built girl.*

Sli·go /ˈslīgō/ a county in the Republic of Ireland, in the western part of the province of Connacht. ■ its county town, a seaport on Sligo Bay, an inlet of the Atlantic Ocean; pop. 17,000.

sli·ly ▸*adv.* variant spelling of **SLYLY** (see **SLY**).

slim /slim/ ▸*adj.* (**slim·mer**, **slim·mest**) **1** (of a person or their build) gracefully thin; slenderly built (used approvingly): *her slim figure* | *the girls were tall and slim.* ■ (of a thing) small in width and typically long and narrow in shape: *a slim gold band encircled her wrist.* ■ (of a garment) cut on slender lines; designed to make the wearer appear slim: *a pair of slim, immaculately cut slacks.* ■ (of a business or other organization) reduced to a smaller size in the hope that it will become more efficient. **2** (of something abstract, esp. a chance or margin) very small: *there was just a slim chance of success* | *the evidence is slim.*

▸*v.* (**slimmed**, **slim·ming**) [*intrans.*] make oneself thinner by dieting and sometimes exercising: *I need to* **slim down** *a bit* | [as *n.*] (**slimming**) *an aid to slimming.* ■ [*trans.*] make (a person or a bodily part) thinner in such a way: *how can I* **slim down** *my hips?* ■ [*trans.*] reduce (a business or other organization) to a smaller size in the hope of making it more efficient: *restructuring and* **slimming down** *the organization.*

▸*n.* (also **slim disease**) African term for **AIDS**. ▷mid 17th cent.: from Low German or Dutch (from a base meaning 'slanting, cross, bad'), of Germanic origin. The pejorative sense found in Dutch and German existed originally in the English noun *slim* 'lazy or worthless person.' **—slim·ly** *adv.* **—slim·ness** *n.*

slime /slīm/ ▸*n.* a moist, soft, and slippery substance, typically regarded as repulsive: *the cold stone was wet with slime.* ■ *informal* a slimeball.

▸*v.* [*trans.*] cover with slime: *what grass remained was slimed over with pale brown mud.* ▷Old English *slīm*, of Germanic origin; related to Dutch *slijm* and German *Schleim* 'mucus, slime,' Latin *limus* 'mud,' and Greek *limnē* 'marsh.'

slime·ball /ˈslīm,bôl/ ▸*n.* *informal* a repulsive or despicable person.

slime mold ▸*n.* a simple organism that consists of an acellular mass of creeping jellylike protoplasm containing nuclei, or a mass of ameboid cells. When it reaches a certain size it forms a large number of spore cases. • Division Myxomycota, kingdom Fungi, in particular the class Myxomycetes; also treated as protozoan (phylum Gymnomyxa, kingdom Protista).

slim jim ▸*n.* *informal* a very slim person or thing, in particular: ■ (**slim jims**) a pair of long narrow trousers. ■ (also **Slim Jim**) *(trademark)* a long thin variety of smoked sausage. ■ a long flexible metal strip with a hooked end, used by car thieves and others for entering a locked vehicle.

slim·line /ˈslim,līn/ ▸*adj.* (of a person or article) slender in design or build: *a slimline phone.*

slim vol·ume ▸*n.* a book, typically of verse, by a little-known author.

slim·y /ˈslīmē/ ▸*adj.* (**slim·i·er**, **slim·i·est**) covered by or having the feel or consistency of slime: *the thick, slimy mud* | *the walls were slimy with lichens.* ■ *informal* disgustingly immoral, dishonest, or obsequious: *he was a slimy people-pleaser.* **—slim·i·ly** /-məlē/ *adv.* **—slim·i·ness** *n.*

sling[1] /sliNG/ ▸*n.* **1** a flexible strap or belt used in the form of a loop to support or raise a weight: *the horse had to be supported by a sling fixed to the roof.* ■ a bandage or soft strap looped around the neck to support an injured arm: *she had her arm in a sling.* ■ a pouch or frame for carrying a baby, supported by a strap around the neck or shoulders. ■ a short length of rope used to provide additional support for the body in rappelling or climbing. **2** a simple weapon in the form of a strap or loop, used to hurl stones or other small missiles.

▸*v.* (*past* **slung** /sləNG/) **1** [*trans.*] suspend or arrange (something), esp. with a strap or straps, so that it hangs loosely in a particular position: *a hammock was slung between two trees.* ■ carry (something, esp. a garment) loosely and casually: *he had his jacket* **slung over** *one shoulder.* **2** [*trans.*] *informal* throw; fling (often used to express the speaker's casual attitude): *sling a few things into your knapsack.* ■ hurl (a stone or other missile) from a sling or similar weapon. ■ hoist or transfer (something) with a sling: *horse after horse was slung up from the barges.* ▷Middle English: probably from Low German, of symbolic origin; compare with German *Schlinge* 'noose, snare.' Sense 2 of the verb is from Old Norse *slyngva*. **—sling·er** *n.*

▸*PHRASES* □ **put someone's** (or **have one's**) **ass in a sling** *vulgar slang* cause someone to be (or be) in trouble. □ **sling hash** *informal* serve food in a cafe or diner. □ **slings and arrows** used with reference to adverse factors or circumstances: *the slings and arrows of outrageous critics.* [with reference to Shakespeare's *Hamlet* III. i. 58.]

sling[2] ▸*n.* a sweetened drink of liquor, esp. gin, and water. See also **SINGAPORE SLING**. ▷mid 18th cent.: of unknown origin.

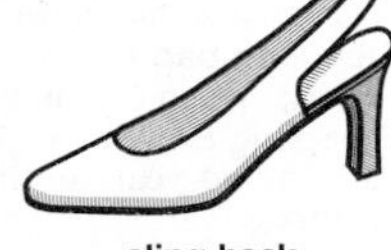

sling-back

sling·back (also **sling·back**) ▸*n.* a shoe held in place by a strap around the back of the ankle: [as *adj.*] *a pair of red sling-back pumps.*

sling·shot /ˈsliNG,shät/ ▸*n.* a forked stick, to which an elastic strap (or a pair of elastic bands connected by a small sling) is fastened to the two prongs, typically used for shooting small stones. ■ [often as *adj.*] the effect of the gravitational pull of a celestial body in accelerating and changing the course of another body or a spacecraft.

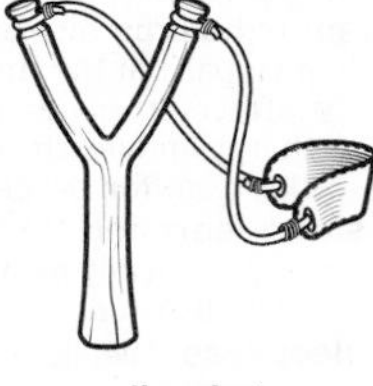

slingshot

▸*v.* (**-shot·ting**; *past* and *past part.* **-shot** or **-shot·ted**) forcefully accelerate or cause to accelerate through use of gravity: [*intrans.*] *the car would hit the first dip, then slingshot off the second rise* | [*trans.*] *Jupiter's gravity slingshots the fragments toward Earth.*

slink /sliNGk/ ▸*v.* (*past* **slunk** /sləNGk/) [*intrans.*] move smoothly and quietly with gliding steps, in a stealthy or sensuous manner: *the fox came slinking through the woods.* ■ come or go unobtrusively or furtively: *all his so-called friends have* **slunk off**.

▸*n.* [in *sing.*] an act of moving in this way: *she moved with a sensuous slink.* ▷Old English *slincan* 'crawl, creep'; compare with Middle Dutch and Middle Low German *slinken* 'subside, sink.'

slink·y /ˈsliNGkē/ ▸*adj.* (**slink·i·er**, **slink·i·est**) *informal* graceful and sinuous in movement, line, or figure: *a slinky black evening dress.*

▸*n.* (**Slinky**) *trademark* a toy consisting of a flexible helical spring that can be made to somersault down steps. **—slink·i·ly** /ˈsliNGkəlē/ *adv.* **—slink·i·ness** *n.*

slip[1] /slip/ ▸*v.* (**slipped**, **slip·ping**) **1** [*intrans.*] (of a person or animal) slide unintentionally for a short distance, typically losing one's balance or footing: *I slipped on the ice | he kept slipping in the mud.* ■ [with *adverbial of direction*] (of a thing) accidentally slide or move out of position or from someone's grasp: *the envelope slipped through Luke's fingers | a wisp of hair had slipped down over her face.* ■ fail to grip or make proper contact with a surface: *the front wheels began to slip* | [as *adj.*] (**slipping**) *a badly slipping clutch.* ■ [with *adverbial of direction*] go or move quietly or quickly, without attracting notice: *we slipped out by a back door.* ■ pass or change to a lower, worse, or different condition, typically in a gradual or imperceptible way: *many people feel standards have slipped* | [with *complement*] *profits slipped 31 percent.* ■ (**be slipping**) *informal* be behaving in a way that is not up to one's usual level of performance: *you're slipping, Joe—you need a vacation.* ■ (**slip away/by**) (of time) elapse: *the night was slipping away.* ■ [*trans.*] put (something) in a particular place or position quietly, quickly, or stealthily: *she slipped the map into her pocket* | [with *two objs.*] *I slipped him a ten-spot to keep quiet.* ■ (**slip into/out of**) put on or take off (a garment) quickly and easily. ■ (**slip something in**) insert a remark smoothly or adroitly into a conversation. **2** [*trans.*] escape or get loose from (a means of restraint): *the giant balloon slipped its moorings.* ■ [*intrans.*] (**slip out**) (of a remark) be uttered inadvertently. ■ (of a thought or fact) fail to be remembered by (one's mind or memory); elude (one's notice): *a beautiful woman's address was never likely to slip his mind.* ■ release (an animal, typically a hunting dog) from restraint. ■ *Knitting* move (a stitch) to the other needle without knitting it. ■ release (the clutch of a motor vehicle) slightly or for a moment. ■ (of an animal) produce (dead young) prematurely; abort.

▸*phrasal v.* □ **slip away** depart without saying goodbye; leave quietly or surreptitiously. ■ slowly disappear; recede or dwindle: *his ability to concentrate is slipping away.* ■ die peacefully (used euphemistically): *he lay there and quietly slipped away.* □ **slip something over on** *informal* take advantage of (someone) by trickery. □ **slip up** *informal* make a careless error: *they often slipped up when it came to spelling.*

▸*n.* **1** an act of sliding unintentionally for a short distance: *a single slip could send them plummeting down the mountainside.* ■ a fall to a lower level or standard: *a continued slip in house prices.* ■ relative movement of an object or surface and a solid surface in contact with it. ■ a reduction in the movement of a pulley or other mechanism due to slipping of the belt, rope, etc. ■ a sideways movement of an aircraft in flight, typically downward toward the center of curvature of a turn. ■ *Geology* the extent of relative horizontal displacement of corresponding points on either side of a fault plane. **2** a minor or careless mistake: *the judge made a slip in his summing up.* See note at MISTAKE. **3** a woman's loose-fitting, dress- or skirt-length undergarment, suspended by shoulder straps (**full slip**) or by an elasticized waistband (**half slip**): *a silk slip.* **4** a slope built leading into water, used for launching and landing boats and ships or for building and repairing them. ■ a space in which to dock a boat or ship, esp. between two wharves or piers. **5** (also **slip leash**) a leash that enables a dog to be released quickly. **6** *Knitting* short for SLIP STITCH: *one color at a time should be knitted in striped slip.* ▷Middle English (in the sense 'move quickly and softly'): probably from Middle Low German *slippen* (verb); compare with SLIPPERY.

▸*PHRASES* □ **give someone the slip** *informal* evade or escape from someone. □ **let something slip 1** reveal something inadvertently in the course of a conversation: [with *clause*] *Alex had let slip he was married.* **2** *archaic* release a hound from the leash so as to begin the chase: *let slip the dogs of war.* □ **let something slip through one's fingers** (or **grasp**) lose hold or possession of something. □ **slip of the pen** (or **the tongue**) a minor mistake in writing (or speech). □ **there's many a slip 'twixt cup and lip** *proverb* many things can go wrong between the start of a project and its completion; nothing is certain until it has happened.

slip[2] ▸*n.* **1** a small piece of paper, typically a form for writing on or one giving printed information: *his monthly salary slip | complete the tear-off slip below.* ■ a long, narrow strip of a thin material such as wood. **2** a cutting taken from a plant for grafting or planting; a scion. ▷late Middle English: probably from Middle Dutch, Middle Low German *slippe* 'cut, strip.'

▸*PHRASE* □ **a slip of a ——** used to denote a small, slim person: *you are little more than a slip of a girl.*

slip[3] ▸*n.* a creamy mixture of clay, water, and typically a pigment, used esp. for decorating earthenware. ▷mid 17th cent.: of obscure origin; compare with Norwegian *slip(a)* 'slime.'

slip·case /ˈslipˌkās/ ▸*n.* a close-fitting case open at one side or end for an object such as a book.

slip cast·ing ▸*n.* the manufacture of ceramics by allowing slip to solidify in a mold. —**slip-cast** *adj.*

slip·cov·er /ˈslipˌkəvər/ ▸*n.* a removable fitted cloth cover for a chair or sofa. ■ a jacket or slipcase for a book.

slip·form /ˈslipˌfôrm/ ▸*n.* a mold in which a concrete structure of uniform cross section is cast by filling the mold with liquid concrete and then continuously moving and refilling it at a sufficiently slow rate for the emerging part to have partially set.

slip-joint pli·ers ▸*plural n.* pliers with a slot in one jaw through which the other jaw slides, permitting an adjustable span.

slip knot ▸*n.* **1** a knot that can be undone by a pull. **2** a running knot.

slip-on ▸*adj.* (esp. of shoes or clothes) having no (or few) fasteners and therefore able to be put on and taken off quickly.

▸*n.* a shoe or garment that can be easily slipped on and off.

slip·o·ver /ˈslipˌōvər/ ▸*n.* a pullover, typically one without sleeves.

▸*adj.* [*attrib.*] (of a garment) designed to be put on over the head: *a slipover sweater.*

slip·page /ˈslipij/ ▸*n.* the action or process of something slipping or subsiding; the amount or extent of this: *$16 million has been spent on cracks and slippage.* ■ failure to meet a standard or deadline; the extent of this: *slippage on any job will entail slippage on the overall project.*

slipped /slipt/ ▸*adj. Heraldry* (of a flower or leaf) depicted with a stalk.

slipped disc (also **slipped disk**) ▸*n.* a vertebral disc that is displaced or partly protruding, pressing on nearby nerves and causing back pain or sciatica. See DISK *noun* sense 2.

slip·per /ˈslipər/ ▸*n.* a comfortable slip-on shoe that is worn indoors. ■ a light slip-on shoe, esp. one used for dancing. —**slip·pered** *adj.*

slip·per·ette /ˌslipəˈret/ ▸*n. trademark* a disposable slipper or similar foot covering, esp. of a kind distributed to airline passengers.

slip·per sock ▸*n.* a thick sock, typically with a leather or vinyl sole, for use as a slipper.

slip·per·y /ˈslipərē/ ▸*adj.* (of a surface or object) difficult to hold firmly or stand on because it is smooth, wet, or slimy: *slippery ice | her hand was slippery with sweat.* ■ (of a person) evasive and unpredictable; not to be relied on: *Martin's a slippery customer.* ■ (of a word or concept) elusive in meaning because changing according to one's point of view: *the word "intended" is a decidedly slippery one.* ▷late 15th cent.: from dialect *slipper* 'slippery.' —**slip·per·i·ly** /ˈslipərəlē/ *adv.* —**slip·per·i·ness** *n.*

▸*PHRASE* □ **slippery slope** an idea or course of action which will lead to something unacceptable, wrong, or disastrous: *he is on the slippery slope toward a life of crime.*

slip·per·y elm ▸*n.* a North American elm with coarsely textured leaves and rough outer bark. • *Ulmus rubra* (or *fulva*), family Ulmaceae. ■ the mucilaginous inner bark of this tree, used medicinally.

slip·py /ˈslipē/ ▸*adj.* (**slip·pi·er**, **slip·pi·est**) *informal* slippery: *the path was slippy with mud | slippy tires.* —**slip·pi·ness** *n.*

slip ring ▸*n.* a ring in a dynamo or electric motor that is attached to and rotates with the shaft, passing an electric current to a circuit via a fixed brush pressing against it.

slip·sheet /ˈslipˌsHēt/ ▸*n. Printing* a sheet of paper placed between newly printed sheets to prevent offset or smudging.

slip·shod /ˈslipˌsHäd/ ▸*adj.* (typically of a person or method of work) characterized by a lack of care, thought, or organization: *he'd caused many problems with his slipshod management.* ■ *archaic* (of shoes) worn down at the heel. ▷late 16th cent. (originally in the sense 'wearing slippers or loose shoes'): from the verb SLIP[1] + SHOD.

slip stitch ▸*n.* **1** (in sewing) a loose stitch joining layers of fabric and not visible externally. **2** [often as *adj.*] *Knitting* a type of stitch in which the stitches are moved from one needle to the other without being knitted: *a slip-stitch pattern.*

▸*v.* (**slip-stitch**) [*trans.*] sew or knit with such stitches.

slip·stone /ˈslipˌstōn/ (also **slip stone**) ▸*n.* a small rounded or tapered whetstone used to sharpen woodworking tools.

slip·stream /ˈslipˌstrēm/ ▸*n.* a current of air or water driven back by a revolving propeller or jet engine. ■ the partial vacuum created in the wake of a moving vehicle, often used by other vehicles in a race to assist in passing. ■ *figurative* an assisting force regarded as drawing something along behind something else: *when the U.S. economy booms, the rest of the world is pulled along in the slipstream.*

▸*v.* [*intrans.*] (esp. in auto racing) another term for DRAFT (sense 4). ■ [*trans.*] travel in the slipstream of (someone), esp. in order to overtake them.

slip-up ▸*n. informal* a mistake or blunder.

slip·ware /ˈslipˌwe(ə)r/ ▸*n.* pottery decorated with slip (see SLIP[3]).

slip·way /ˈslipˌwā/ ▸*n.* another term for SLIP[1] (sense 4).

slit /slit/ ▸*n.* a long, narrow cut or opening: *make a slit in the stem under a bud | arrow slits.*

▸*v.* (**slit·ting**; *past* **slit**) [*trans.*] make a long, narrow cut in (something): *give me the truth or I will slit your throat* | [*trans.*] *he slit open the envelope.* ■ cut (something) into strips: *a wide recording head magnetizes the tape before it is slit to domestic size.* ■ (*past* **slit·ted**) form (one's eyes) into slits; squint. ▷late Old English *slite* (noun); related to Old English *slītan* 'split, rend' (of Germanic origin). —**slit·ter** *n.*

slith·er /ˈsliTHər/ ▸*v.* [*intrans.*] move smoothly over a surface with a twisting or oscillating motion: *I spied a baby adder slithering away.* ■ slide or slip unsteadily on a loose or slippery surface: *we slithered down a snowy mountain track.*

▸*n.* [in *sing.*] a movement in such a manner: *a snakelike slither across the grass.* ▷Middle English: alteration of the dialect verb *slidder*, frequentative from the base of SLIDE. —**slith·er·y** *adj.*

slit lamp ▸*n. Medicine* a lamp that emits a narrow but intense beam of light, used for examining the interior of the eye.

slit trench ▸*n.* a narrow trench for a soldier or a small group of soldiers and their equipment.

Sli·ven /ˈslivən/ a commercial city in east central Bulgaria, in the foothills of the Balkan Mountains; pop. 150,000.

sliv·er /ˈslivər/ ▸*n.* a small, thin, narrow piece of something cut or split off a larger piece: *a sliver of cheese* | *figurative there was a sliver of light under his door.* ■ a strip of loose untwisted textile fibers produced by carding.

▸*v.* [*trans.*] [usu. as *adj.*] (**slivered**) cut or break (something) into small, thin, narrow pieces: *slivered almonds.* ■ convert (textile fibers) into slivers. ▷late Middle English: from dialect *slive* 'cleave.'

sliv·o·vitz /ˈslivəˌvits/ ▸*n.* a type of plum brandy made chiefly in eastern Europe. ▷from Serbo-Croat *šljivovica*, from *šljiva* 'plum;' compare with SLOE.

Sloan /slōn/, John French (1871–1951), U.S. artist. A member of the Ashcan School, he painted scenes of New York City such as in "Backyards, Greenwich Village" (1914).

slob /släb/ ▸*n. informal* a lazy and slovenly person. ▷late 18th cent.: from Irish *slab* 'mud,' from Anglo-Irish *slab* 'ooze, sludge,' probably of Scandinavian origin. —**slob·bish** *adj.* —**slob·by** *adj.*

slob·ber /ˈsläbər/ ▸*v.* [*intrans.*] have saliva dripping copiously from the mouth: *Fido tended to slobber* | [as *adj.*] (**slobbering**) *big slobbering kisses.* ■ (**slobber over**) *figurative* be excessively sentimental; show excessive enthusiasm for: *news executives slobbered over him for autographs | they took turns slobbering all over the new baby.*

▸*n.* saliva dripping copiously from the mouth. ▷late Middle English: probably from Middle Dutch *slobberen* 'walk through mud,' also 'feed noisily,' of imitative origin. —**slob·ber·y** *adj.*

sloe /slō/ ▸*n.* another term for BLACKTHORN. ■ the small bluish-black fruit of the blackthorn, with a sharp sour taste. ▷Old English *slā(h)*, of Germanic origin; related to Dutch *slee* and German *Schlehe*, from an Indo-European root probably shared by Latin *livere* 'be blue' and Serbo-Croat *šljiva* 'plum;' compare with SLIVOVITZ.

S

sloe-eyed ▸*adj.* having attractive dark, typically almond-shaped eyes.

sloe gin ▸*n.* a liqueur made by steeping sloes in gin.

slog /släg/ ▸*v.* (**slogged, slog·ging**) **1** [*intrans.*] work hard over a period of time: *they were slogging away to meet a deadline.* ■ [with *adverbial of direction*] walk or move with difficulty or effort: *he slogged home through the gray slush.* **2** [*intrans.*] hit forcefully and typically wildly, esp. in boxing: *the fighters were slogging away.* ■ (**slog it out**) fight or compete at length or fiercely. ▸*n.* [usu. in *sing.*] a spell of difficult, tiring work or traveling: *it would be* ***a hard slog*** *back to the camp.* ▷early 19th cent.: of unknown origin; compare with SLUG[2]. —**slog·ger** *n.*

slo·gan /ˈslōgən/ ▸*n.* a short and striking or memorable phrase used in advertising. ■ a motto associated with a political party or movement or other group. ■ *historical* a Scottish Highland war cry. ▷early 16th cent.: from Scottish Gaelic *sluagh-ghairm*, from *sluagh* 'army' + *gairm* 'shout.'

slo·gan·eer /ˌslōgəˈnir/ ▸*v.* [usu. as *n.*] (**sloganeering**) [*intrans.*] employ or invent slogans, typically in a political context.
▸*n.* a person who does this: *as the sloganeers put it: "peace through strength."*

slo·ka /ˈslōkə/ ▸*n.* a couplet of Sanskrit verse, esp. one in which each line contains sixteen syllables. ▷from Sanskrit *śloka* 'noise, praise.'

slo-mo /ˈslō ˈmō/ (also **slo·mo**) ▸*n. informal* short for SLOW MOTION.

sloop /slo͞op/ ▸*n.* a one-masted sailboat with a fore-and-aft mainsail and a jib. ■ (also **sloop of war**) *historical* a small square-rigged sailing warship with two or three masts. ■ *historical* a small antisubmarine warship used for convoy escort in World War II. ▷early 17th cent.: from Dutch *sloep(e)*, of unknown origin.

sloop-rigged ▸*adj.* rigged as a sloop.

slop[1] /släp/ ▸*v.* (**slopped, slop·ping**) **1** [*intrans.*] (of a liquid) spill or flow over the edge of a container, typically as a result of careless handling: *water slopped over the edge of the sink.* ■ [*trans.*] cause (a liquid) to spill or overflow in such a way: *in spite of his care he slopped some water.* ■ [*trans.*] apply or put (something) somewhere in a casual or careless manner: *they spent their weekend slopping on paint.* ■ (**slop through**) wade through (a wet or muddy area): *they were slopping through paddy fields.* **2** [*trans.*] feed slops to (an animal, esp. a pig). **3** [*intrans.*] speak or write in a sentimentally effusive manner; gush: *she* ***slopped over*** *her dog.*
▸*n.* **1** (usu. **slops**) waste water from a kitchen, bathroom, or chamber pot that has to be emptied by hand: *sink slops.* ■ (usu. **slops**) semiliquid kitchen refuse, often used as animal food. ■ unappetizing weak, semiliquid food: *they fed us some slop in a bowl.* **2** sentimental language or material: *country music is not all commercial slop.* ▷mid 16th cent. (in the sense 'to spill, splash'): probably related to SLIP[3]. Early use of the noun denoted 'watery mud,' the first of the current senses ('unappetizing food') dating from the mid 17th cent.

slop[2] ▸*n. archaic* **1** a workman's loose outer garment. **2** (**slops**) wide, baggy pants common in the 16th and early 17th centuries, esp. as worn by sailors. ■ clothes and bedding supplied to sailors by the navy. ▷late Middle English (sense 1): from the second element of Old English *oferslop* 'surplice,' literally '(something) slipped over.'

slope /slōp/ ▸*n.* **1** a surface of which one end or side is at a higher level than another; a rising or falling surface: *he slithered helplessly down the slope.* ■ a difference in level or sideways position between the two ends or sides of a thing: *the roof should have a slope sufficient for proper drainage | the backward slope of the chair.* ■ (often **slopes**) a part of the side of a hill or mountain, esp. as a place for skiing: *a ten-minute cable-car ride delivers you to the slopes.* ■ the gradient of a graph at any point. ■ *Electronics* the transconductance of a valve, numerically equal to the gradient of one of the characteristic curves of the valve. **2** *informal, offensive* an Asian person, esp. a Vietnamese or other Southeast Asian. [from the apparent slope of the eyes due to epicanthic folds; compare with SLANT *n.* sense 3.]
▸*v.* [*intrans.*] (of a surface or line) be inclined from a horizontal or vertical line; slant up or down: *the garden* ***sloped down*** *to a stream | the ceiling sloped* | [as *adj.*] (**sloping**) *a sloping floor.* ■ [*trans.*] place or arrange in such a position or inclination: *Poole sloped his shoulders* | [as *adj.*] (**sloped**) *a sloped leather writing surface.* ▷late 16th cent. (as a verb): from the obsolete adverb *slope*, a shortening of ASLOPE.

slop·py /ˈsläpē/ ▸*adj.* (**slop·pi·er, slop·pi·est**) **1** (of semifluid matter) containing too much liquid; watery and disagreeable or unsatisfactory: *do not make the concrete too sloppy.* **2** careless and unsystematic; excessively casual: *your speech has always been sloppy.* ■ (of a garment) casual and loose-fitting: *wearing a sloppy sweater and jeans.* **3** (of literature or behavior) weakly or foolishly sentimental: *lovers of sloppy romance.* —**slop·pi·ly** /ˈsläpəlē/ *adv.* —**slop·pi·ness** *n.*

slop·py joe ▸*n. informal* a sandwich with a filling of ground beef that has been seasoned with a sauce of tomatoes and spices.

slosh /släsн/ ▸*v.* [*intrans.*] (of liquid in a container) move irregularly with a splashing sound: *water in the boat sloshed around under our feet | figurative there is so much money now sloshing around in professional tennis.* ■ (of a person) move through liquid with a splashing sound: *they sloshed up the tracks in the dank woods.* ■ [*trans.*] pour (liquid) clumsily: *she sloshed coffee into a cracked cup.*
▸*n.* an act or sound of splashing: *the distant slosh of the washing machine in the basement.* ▷early 19th cent.: variant of the noun SLUSH.

sloshed /släsнt/ ▸*adj. informal* drunk: *I drank a lot of wine and got sloshed.*

slosh·y /ˈsläsнē/ ▸*adj.* (**slosh·i·er, slosh·i·est**) **1** wet and sticky; slushy: *the hoofprints are sloshy depressions.* **2** excessively sentimental; sloppy: *the program is a sloshy and patronizing affair.*

Slot /slät/ (**the Slot**) name given in World War II by U.S. forces to New Georgia Sound, in the central Solomon Islands. Japanese forces trying to defend Guadalcanal were seen as coming consistently down this passage from the northwest.

slot[1] /slät/ ▸*n.* **1** a long, narrow aperture or slit in a machine for something to be inserted: *he slid a coin into the slot of the jukebox.* ■ a groove or channel into which something fits or in which something works, such as one in the head of a screw. **2** an allotted place in an arrangement or plan such as a broadcasting schedule: *a late-night television slot | landing slots at O'Hare.*
▸*v.* (**slot·ted, slot·ting**) [*trans.*] place (something) into a long, narrow aperture: *he slotted a cassette into the tape machine | the plates come in sections that can be* ***slotted together.*** ■ [*intrans.*] be placed or able to be placed into such an aperture: *the processors will slot into a personal computer.* ▷late Middle English (in the sense 'slight depression running down the middle of the chest,' surviving as a Scots term): from Old French *esclot*, of obscure origin. —**slot·ted** *adj.*

slot[2] ▸*n.* (usu. **slots**) the track of a deer, visible as slotted footprints in soft ground. ▷late 16th cent.: from Old French *esclot* 'hoofprint of a horse,' probably from Old Norse *slóth* 'trail'; compare with SLEUTH.

slot·back /ˈslätˌbak/ ▸*n. Football* an offensive back who is positioned between the tackle and the split end.

slot car ▸*n.* an electrically driven miniature race car that travels in a slot in a track.

sloth /slôтн; släтн; slōтн/ ▸*n.* **1** reluctance to work or make an effort; laziness: *he should overcome his natural sloth and complacency.* **2** a slow-moving tropical American mammal that hangs upside down from the branches of trees using its long limbs and hooked claws. • Families Bradypodidae (three species of **three-toed sloth** in genus *Bradypus*) and Megalonychidae (two species of **two-toed sloth** in genus *Choloepus*), order Xenarthra (or Edentata). ▷Old English: from SLOW + -TH[2].

three-toed sloth

sloth bear ▸*n.* a shaggy-coated nocturnal Indian bear that uses its long curved claws for hanging upside down like a sloth and for opening termite mounds to feed on the insects. • *Melursus ursinus*, family Ursidae.

sloth·ful /ˈslôтнfəl; släтн-; ˈslōтн-/ ▸*adj.* lazy: *fatigue made him slothful.* —**sloth·ful·ly** *adv.* —**sloth·ful·ness** *n.*

slot ma·chine ▸*n.* a machine worked by the insertion of a coin, in particular: ■ a gaming machine that generates random combinations of symbols on a dial, certain combinations winning varying amounts of money for the player. ■ *chiefly Brit.* a vending machine selling small items.

slot·ted spoon ▸*n.* a large spoon with slots or holes for draining liquid from food.

slouch /slouсн/ ▸*v.* **1** [*intrans.*] stand, move, or sit in a lazy, drooping way: *he slouched against the wall* | (**be slouched**) *he was slouched in his chair.* **2** [*trans.*] *dated* bend one side of the brim of (a hat) downward.
▸*n.* [in *sing.*] **1** a lazy, drooping posture or movement: *his stance was a round-shouldered slouch.* **2** [usu. with *negative*] *informal* an incompetent person: *my brother was no slouch at making a buck.* **3** a downward bend of a hat brim. ▷early 16th cent. (in the sense 'lazy, slovenly person'): of unknown origin. *Slouching* was used to mean 'hanging down, drooping' (specifically describing a hat with a brim hanging over the face), and 'having an awkward posture' from the 17th cent. —**slouch·y** *adj.*

slouch hat ▸*n.* a hat with a wide flexible brim.

slough[1] /slou; slo͞o/ ▸*n.* a swamp. ■ *figurative* a situation characterized by lack of progress or activity: *the economic slough of the interwar years.* ■ a muddy side channel or inlet. ▷Old English *slōh, slō(g)*, of unknown origin. —**slough·y** *adj.*

slough[2] /sləf/ ▸*v.* [*trans.*] (of an animal, esp. a snake, or a person) cast off or shed (an old skin or dead skin): *a snake* ***sloughs off*** *its old skin | figurative he is concerned to* ***slough off*** *the country's bad environmental image.* ■ [*intrans.*] (**slough off**) (of dead skin) drop off; be shed. ■ [*intrans.*] (**slough away/down**) (of soil or rock) collapse or slide into a hole or depression.
▸*n.* the dropping off of dead tissue from living flesh: *the drugs can cause blistering and slough.* ▷Middle English (as a noun denoting a skin, esp. the outer skin shed by a snake): perhaps related to Low German *slu(we)* 'husk, peel.' The verb dates from the early 18th cent. —**slough·y** *adj.*

Slough of De·spond (also **slough of despond**) /ˈslou əv dəˈspänd/ ▸*n.* a state of hopeless depression: *while everyone is having a blast I am sinking into the Slough of Despond.* ▷the name of a deep boggy place in John Bunyan's *The Pilgrim's Progress* between the City of Destruction and the gate at the beginning of Christian's journey.

Slo·vak /ˈslōväk; -vak/ ▸*n.* **1** a native or national of Slovakia, or a person of Slovak descent. **2** the West Slavic language of Slovakia, closely related to Czech.
▸*adj.* of or relating to this people or their language. ▷the name in Slovak, from a Slavic root shared with SLOVENE and perhaps related to *slovo* 'word.'

Slo·va·ki·a /slōˈväkēə/ a country in central Europe; pop. 5,432,000; capital, Bratislava; languages, Slovak (official) and Hungarian. —**Slo·va·ki·an** *adj.* & *n.*

Slovakia was dominated by Hungary until it declared independence in 1918 and united with the Czech-speaking areas of Bohemia and Moravia to form Czechoslovakia. The eastern of the two constituent republics of Czechoslovakia, Slovakia became independent on the partition of that country on January 1, 1993. It joined NATO and the EU in 2004.

slov·en /ˈsləvən/ ▸*n. dated* a person who is habitually messy or careless. ▷late 15th cent. (in the sense 'person with base manners'): perhaps from Flemish *sloef* 'dirty' or Dutch *slof* 'careless, negligent.'

Slo·vene /'slōvēn/ ▶*n.* **1** a native or national of Slovenia, or a person of Slovene descent. **2** the South Slavic language of this people.
▶*adj.* of or relating to Slovenia, its people, or their language. ▷from Slovene *Slovenec*, from a Slavic root shared with **SLOVAK** and perhaps related to *slovo* 'word.'

Slo·ve·ni·a /slō'vēnēə/ a country in southeastern Europe; pop. 2,011,000; capital, Ljubljana; official language, Slovene.

Slovenia formed part of the Austrian empire and in 1919 was ceded to the kingdom of Serbs, Croats, and Slovenes (named Yugoslavia from 1929) of which it remained a constituent republic until it declared its independence in 1991. It joined NATO and the EU in 2004.

Slo·ve·ni·an /slō'vēnēən/ ▶*n.* & *adj.* another term for **SLOVENE**.

slov·en·ly /'sləvənlē; 'slä-/ ▶*adj.* (esp. of a person or their appearance) messy and dirty: *he was upbraided for his slovenly appearance.* ■ (esp. of a person or action) careless; excessively casual: *slovenly speech.* **—slov·en·li·ness** *n.*

slow /slō/ ▶*adj.* **1** moving or operating, or designed to do so, only at a low speed; not quick or fast: *a time when diesel cars were slow and noisy* | *a slow dot-matrix printer.* ■ taking a long time to perform a specified action: *she was a slow reader* | [with *infinitive*] *large organizations can be slow to change.* ■ lasting or taking a long time: *a slow process* | *the journey home was slow.* ■ [*attrib.*] not allowing or intended for fast travel: *the slow lane.* ■ (of a playing field) likely to make the ball bounce or run slowly or to prevent competitors from traveling fast. **2** [*predic.* or as *complement*] (of a clock or watch) showing a time earlier than the correct time: *the clock was five minutes slow.* **3** not prompt to understand, think, or learn: *he's so slow, so unimaginative.* See note at **STUPID**. **4** uneventful and rather dull: *a slow and mostly aimless narrative.* ■ (of business) with little activity; slack: *sales were slow.* **5** *Photography* (of a film) needing long exposure. ■ (of a lens) having a small aperture. **6** (of a fire or oven) burning or giving off heat gently: *bake the dish in a preheated slow oven.*
▶*adv.* at a slow pace; slowly: *the train went slower and slower* | [in *combination*] *a slow-moving river.*
▶*v.* [*intrans.*] reduce one's speed or the speed of a vehicle or process: *the train slowed to a halt* | *investment has* **slowed down** | [*trans.*] *he slowed the car.* ■ (**slow down/up**) live or work less actively or intensely: *I wasn't feeling well and had to slow down.* ▷Old English *slāw* 'slow-witted, sluggish,' of Germanic origin. **—slow·ish** *adj.* **—slow·ness** *n.*
▶*PHRASE* □ **slow but sure** not quick but achieving the required result eventually: *a slow but sure increase in the price of gold.*

USAGE The word **slow** is normally used as an adjective (*a* **slow** *learner; the journey was* **slow**). It is also used as an adverb in certain specific contexts, including compounds such as *slow-acting* and *slow-moving* and in the expression *go slow.*
Other adverbial use is informal and usually regarded as nonstandard, as in *he drives too* **slow** and *go as* **slow** *as you can.* In such contexts, standard English uses **slowly** instead. The use of **slow** and **slowly** in this respect contrasts with the use of **fast**, which is completely standard in use as both an adjective and an adverb; there is no word *'fastly.'*

slow·coach /'slō,kōCH/ ▶*n. informal* British term for **SLOWPOKE**.

slow cook·er ▶*n.* a large electric pot used for cooking food, esp. stews, very slowly.

slow·down /'slō,doun/ ▶*n.* an act of slowing down: *a traffic slowdown in the passing lane.* ■ a decline in economic activity.

slow drag ▶*n.* a slow blues rhythm or piece of music.
▶*v.* (**slow-drag**) [*intrans.*] dance to such a rhythm.

slow lo·ris ▶*n.* see **LORIS**.

slow·ly /'slōlē/ ▶*adv.* at a slow speed; not quickly: *they moved forward slowly.*
▶*PHRASE* □ **slowly but surely** achieving the desired results gradually and reliably rather than quickly and spectacularly: *the new church began, slowly but surely, to grow.*

USAGE See usage at **SLOW**.

slow march ▶*n.* [in *sing.*] a military marching pace approximately half the speed of the quick march.

slow match ▶*n. historical* a slow-burning wick or cord for lighting explosives.

slow mo·tion ▶*n.* the action of showing film or playing back video more slowly than it was made or recorded, so that the action appears slower than in real life: *the scene was shown* **in slow motion** | [as *adj.*] *a slow-motion sequence.*

slow neu·tron ▶*n.* a neutron with low kinetic energy, esp. after moderation.

slow·poke /'slō,pōk/ ▶*n. informal* a person who acts or moves slowly: *we were yelling for the slowpokes to catch up.*

slow-scan ▶*adj.* [*attrib.*] *Telecommunications* scanning at a much slower rate than usual, so that the resulting signal has a much smaller bandwidth: *a slow-scan transmission.*

slow track ▶*n.* a route or method that results in slow progress: *a slow track to economic and monetary union.* Compare with **FAST TRACK**.

slow-twitch ▶*adj.* [*attrib.*] *Physiology* (of a muscle fiber) contracting slowly, providing endurance rather than strength.

slow vi·rus ▶*n.* a virus or viruslike organism that multiplies slowly in the host organism and has a long incubation period.

slow-worm ▶*n.* a small snakelike Eurasian legless lizard that is typically brownish or copper-colored and that gives birth to live young. Also called **BLINDWORM**. • *Anguis fragilis*, family Anguidae. ▷Old English *slāwyrm*, from *slā-* (of uncertain origin) + *wyrm* 'snake.'

SLR ▶*abbr.* ■ self-loading rifle. ■ single-lens reflex.

slub[1] /sləb/ ▶*n.* a lump or thick place in yarn or thread. ■ fabric woven from yarn with such a texture.
▶*adj.* [*attrib.*] (of fabric) having an irregular appearance caused by uneven thickness of the warp. ▷early 19th cent.: of unknown origin. **—slubbed** *adj.*

slub[2] ▶*n.* wool that has been slightly twisted in preparation for spinning.
▶*v.* (**slubbed, slub·bing**) [*trans.*] twist (wool) in this way. ▷mid 19th cent.: of unknown origin.

sludge /sləj/ ▶*n.* thick, soft, wet mud or a similar viscous mixture of liquid and solid components, esp. the product of an industrial or refining process. ■ dirty oil, esp. in the sump of an internal combustion engine. ■ sea ice newly formed in small pieces. ▷early 17th cent.: of uncertain origin; compare with **SLUSH**. **—sludg·y** *adj.*

slue ▶*v.* & *n.* variant spelling of **SLEW**[1].

slug[1] /sləg/ ▶*n.* **1** a tough-skinned terrestrial mollusk that typically lacks a shell and secretes a film of mucus for protection. It can be a serious plant pest. See also **SEA SLUG**. • Order Stylommatophora, class Gastropoda. **2** a slow, lazy person; a sluggard. **3** an amount of an alcoholic drink, typically liquor, that is gulped or poured: *he took* **a slug of** *whiskey.* [mid 18th cent.: figuratively from sense 4.] **4** an elongated, typically rounded piece or metal: *the reactor uses embedded* **slugs of** *uranium.* ■ a counterfeit coin; a token. ■ a bullet, esp. one of lead. ■ a missile for an air gun. ■ a line of type in Linotype printing. ■ *Printing* a metal bar used in spacing.
▶*v.* (**slugged, slug·ging**) [*trans.*] drink (something, typically alcohol) in a large draft; swig: *she picked up her drink and slugged it straight back.* ▷late Middle English (in sense 2): probably of Scandinavian origin; compare with Norwegian dialect *slugg* 'large heavy body.' Sense 1 dates from the early 18th cent.

slug[2] *informal* ▶*v.* (**slugged, slug·ging**) [*trans.*] strike (someone) with a hard blow: *he was the one who'd get slugged.* ■ (**slug it out**) settle a dispute or contest by fighting or competing fiercely: *they went outside to slug it out.*
▶*n.* a hard blow. ▷mid 19th cent.: of unknown origin; compare with the verb **SLOG**.

slug·a·bed /'sləgə,bed/ ▶*n.* a lazy person who stays in bed late. ▷late 16th cent.: from the rare verb *slug* 'be lazy or slow' + **ABED**.

slug·fest /'sləg,fest/ ▶*n. informal* a tough and challenging contest, esp. in sports such as boxing and baseball. ▷early 20th cent.: from **SLUG**[2] + **-FEST**.

slug·gard /'sləgərd/ ▶*n.* a lazy, sluggish person. ▷Middle English: from the rare verb *slug* 'be lazy or slow' + **-ARD**. **—slug·gard·li·ness** *n.* **—slug·gard·ly** *adj.*

slug·ger /'sləgər/ ▶*n.* person who throws hard punches. ■ *Baseball* a player who consistently hits for power, esp. home runs and doubles.

slug·gish /'sləgisH/ ▶*adj.* slow-moving or inactive: *a sluggish stream.* ■ lacking energy or alertness: *Alex woke late feeling tired and sluggish.* ■ slow to respond or make progress: *the car had been sluggish all morning.* ▷late Middle English: from the noun **SLUG**[1] or the verb *slug* (see **SLUGGARD**) + **-ISH**[1]. **—slug·gish·ly** *adv.* **—slug·gish·ness** *n.*

sluice /sloōs/ ▶*n.* **1** (also **sluice gate**) a sliding gate or other device for controlling the flow of water, esp. one in a lock gate. ■ (also **sluice·way**) an artificial water channel for carrying off overflow or surplus water. ■ (in gold mining) a channel or trough constructed with grooves into which a current of water is directed in order to separate gold from the sand or gravel containing it. **2** an act of rinsing or showering with water: *a sluice with cold water.*
▶*v.* [*trans.*] wash or rinse freely with a stream or shower of water: *she sluiced her face in cold water* | *crews* **sluiced down** *the decks of their ship.* ■ [*intrans.*] (of water) pour, flow, or shower freely: *the waves sluiced over them.* ▷Middle English (as a noun): from Old French *escluse* 'sluice gate,' based on Latin *excludere* 'exclude.' The verb dates from the late 16th cent.

slum /sləm/ ▶*n.* a squalid and overcrowded urban street or district inhabited by very poor people. ■ a house or building unfit for human habitation.
▶*v.* (**slummed, slum·ming**) [*intrans.*] *informal* spend time at a lower social level than one's own through curiosity or for charitable purposes: *rich tourists slumming among the quaintly dangerous natives.* ■ (**slum it**) put up with conditions that are less comfortable or of a lower quality than one is used to: *businessmen are having to slum it in aircraft economy class seats.* ▷early 19th cent. (originally slang, in the sense 'room'): of unknown origin. **—slum·mer** *n.* **—slum·mi·ness** *n.* **—slum·my** *adj.*

slum·ber /'sləmbər/ *poetic/literary* ▶*v.* [*intrans.*] sleep: *Sleeping Beauty slumbered in her forest castle* | *figurative the village street slumbered under the afternoon sun.*
▶*n.* (often **slumbers**) a sleep: *scaring folk from their slumbers.* ▷Middle English: alteration of Scots and northern English *sloom*, in the same sense. The *-b-* was added for ease of pronunciation. **—slum·ber·er** *n.* **—slum·brous** /-brəs/ (also **slum·ber·ous** /-bərəs/) *adj.*

slum·ber·land /'sləmbər,land/ ▶*n. poetic/literary* or *humorous* the state of being asleep.

slum·ber par·ty ▶*n.* a party, typically for preteen or teenage girls, in which all the guests spend the night at the house where the party is held.

slum·gul·lion /,sləm'gəlyən/ ▶*n. informal* cheap or insubstantial stew.

slum·lord /'sləm,lôrd/ ▶*n. informal* a landlord of slum property, esp. one who profiteers.

slump /sləmp/ ▶*v.* [*intrans.*] **1** [with *adverbial*] sit, lean, or fall heavily and limply, esp. with a bent back: *she slumped against the cushions* | (**be slumped**) *Denis was slumped in his seat.* **2** undergo a sudden severe or prolonged fall in price, value, or amount: *land prices slumped.* ■ fail or decline substantially: *the Giants* **slumped to** *an 8–8 record.*
▶*n.* a sudden severe or prolonged fall in the price, value, or amount of something: *a slump in annual profits.* ■ a prolonged period of abnormally low economic activity, typically bringing widespread unemployment. ■ a period of substantial failure or decline: *the organization's recent slump.* ▷late 17th cent. (in the sense 'fall into a bog'): probably imitative and related to Norwegian *slumpe* 'to fall.' **—slump·y** *adj.*

slung /sləNG/ ▶ past and past participle of **SLING**[1].

slung shot ▶*n.* a hard object, such as a metal ball, attached by a strap or thong to the wrist and used as a weapon.

Pronunciation Key ə *ago*; ər *over*; 'ə or ,ə *up*; 'ər or ,ər *fur*; a *hat*; ā *rate*; ä *car*; CH *chew*; e *let*; ē *see*; e(ə)r *air*; i *fit*; ī *by*; i(ə)r *ear*; NG *sing*; ō *go*; ô *for*; oi *boy*; o͝o *good*; o͞o *goo*; ou *out*; SH *she*; TH *thin*; T͟H *then*; (h)w *why*; ZH *vision*

slunk /sləNGk/ ▸ past and past participle of SLINK.

slur /slər/ ▸v. (**slurred**, **slur·ring**) [trans.] **1** speak (words or speech) indistinctly so that the sounds run into one another: *he was slurring his words like a drunk.* ■ [intrans.] (of words or speech) be spoken in this way: *his speech was beginning to slur.* ■ pass over (a fact or aspect) so as to conceal or minimize it: *essential attributes are being* **slurred over** *or ignored.* **2** *Music* perform (a group of two or more notes) legato: [as adj.] (**slurred**) *a group of slurred notes.* ■ mark (notes) with a slur. **3** make damaging or insulting insinuations or allegations about: *try and slur the integrity of the police to secure an acquittal.*
▸n. **1** an insinuation or allegation about someone that is likely to insult them or damage their reputation: *the comments were a* **slur on** *the staff | a racial slur.* **2** an act of speaking indistinctly so that sounds or words run into one another or a tendency to speak in such a way: *there was a mean slur in his voice.* **3** *Music* a curved line used to show that a group of two or more notes is to be sung to one syllable or played or sung legato. ▷early 17th cent.: of unknown origin. The Middle English noun *slur* 'thin, fluid mud' gave rise to the early verb senses 'smear, smirch' and 'disparage (a person),' later 'gloss over (a fault),' whence current usage.

slurp /slərp/ ▸v. [trans.] eat or drink (something) with a loud sloppy sucking noise: *she slurped her coffee* | [intrans.] *he slurped noisily from a wine cup.*
▸n. a loud sucking sound made while eating or drinking: *she drank it down with a loud slurp.* ▷mid 17th cent.: from Dutch *slurpen.* —**slurp·y** adj.

slur·ry /'slərē/ ▸n. (pl. **-ries**) a semiliquid mixture, typically of fine particles of manure, cement, or coal suspended in water. ▷late Middle English: related to dialect *slur* 'thin mud,' of unknown origin.

slush /sləsH/ ▸n. **1** partially melted snow or ice: *the snow was turning into brown slush in the gutters.* ■ watery mud. **2** *informal* excessive sentiment: *the slush of Hollywood's romantic fifties films.*
▸v. [intrans.] make a squelching or splashing sound: *there was water slushing around in the galley.* ▷mid 17th cent.: probably imitative; compare with SLOSH.

slush fund ▸n. a reserve of money used for illicit purposes, esp. political bribery. ▷mid 19th cent.: originally nautical slang denoting money collected to buy luxuries, from the sale of *slush,* the refuse grease from the meat cooked aboard ship.

slush·y /'sləsHē/ ▸adj. (**slush·i·er**, **slush·i·est**) **1** resembling, consisting of, or covered with slush: *slushy snow.* **2** *informal* excessively sentimental: *slushy novels.* —**slush·i·ness** n.

slut /slət/ ▸n. a slovenly or promiscuous woman. ▷Middle English: of unknown origin. —**slut·tish** adj. —**slut·tish·ness** n.

SLV ▸abbr. standard launch vehicle.

Sly /slī/ see STALLONE.

sly /slī/ ▸adj. (**sly·er**, **sly·est**) having or showing a cunning and deceitful nature: *she had a sly personality.* ■ (of a remark, glance, or facial expression) showing in an insinuating way that one has some secret knowledge that may be harmful or embarrassing: *he gave a sly grin.* ■ (of an action) surreptitious: *a sly sip of water.* ▷Middle English (also in the sense 'dexterous'): from Old Norse *slœgr* 'cunning,' originally 'able to strike,' from the verb *slá*; compare with SLEIGHT. —**sly·ly** (also **sli·ly**) adv. —**sly·ness** n.
▸PHRASE □ **on the sly** in a secretive fashion: *she was drinking on the sly.*

sly·boots /'slī,bo͞ots/ ▸n. *informal* a sly person.

Slye /slī/, Leonard Franklin, see ROGERS[5].

slype /slīp/ ▸n. a covered way or passage between a cathedral transept and the chapter house or deanery. ▷mid 19th cent.: perhaps a variant of dialect *slipe* 'long narrow piece of ground.'

SM ▸abbr. ■ service mark. ■ sadomasochism. ■ sergeant major. ■ short meter.

Sm ▸symbol the chemical element samarium.

sm. ▸abbr. small.

S-M (also **s-m**, **S/M**, **s/m**) ▸abbr. ■ (also **S&M**) sadomasochism. ■ sadomasochistic.

SMA ▸abbr. Surplus Marketing Administration.

smack[1] /smak/ ▸n. a sharp slap or blow, typically one given with the palm of the hand: *she gave Mark a smack across the face.* ■ a loud, sharp sound made by such a blow or a similar action: *she closed the ledger with a smack.* ■ a loud kiss: *I was saluted with two hearty smacks on my cheeks.*
▸v. [trans.] strike (someone or something), typically with the palm of the hand and as a punishment: *Jessica smacked his face quite hard.* ■ [trans.] smash, drive, or put forcefully into or onto something: *he smacked a fist into the palm of a black-gloved hand.* ■ part (one's lips) noisily in eager anticipation or enjoyment of food, drink, or other pleasures. ■ *archaic* crack (a whip).
▸adv. *informal* **1** in a sudden and violent way: *I ran smack into the back of a parked truck.* **2** exactly; precisely: *our mother's house was smack in the middle of the city.* ▷mid 16th cent. (in the sense 'part (one's lips) noisily'): from Middle Dutch *smacken,* of imitative origin; compare with German *schmatzen* 'eat or kiss noisily.'

smack[2] ▸v. [intrans.] (**smack of**) have a flavor of; taste of: *the tea smacked of peppermint.* ■ suggest the presence or effects of (something wrong or unpleasant): *the whole thing smacks of a cover-up.*
▸n. (**a smack of**) a flavor or taste of: *anything with even a modest smack of hops dries the palate.* ■ a trace or suggestion of: *I hear the smack of collusion between them.* ▷Old English *smæc* 'flavor, smell,' of Germanic origin; related to Dutch *smaak* and German *Geschmack.*

smack[3] ▸n. a fishing boat, often one equipped with a well for keeping the caught fish alive. ■ *chiefly Brit.* a single-masted sailboat used for fishing or coastal commerce. ▷early 17th cent.: from Dutch *smak,* of unknown ultimate origin.

smack[4] ▸n. *informal* heroin. ▷1940s: probably an alteration of Yiddish *shmek* 'a sniff.'

smack dab ▸adv. *informal* exactly; precisely: *here I am in Bolivia, smack dab in the heart of South America.*

smack·er /'smakər/ (also **smack·er·oo** /,smakə'ro͞o/) ▸n. *informal* **1** a dollar: *it set me back fifteen smackers.* **2** a loud kiss.

small /smôl/ ▸adj. of a size that is less than normal or usual: *the room was small and quiet | the small hill that sheltered the house.* ■ not great in amount, number, strength, or power: *a small amount of money.* ■ not fully grown or developed; young: *as a small boy, he spent his days either reading or watching TV.* ■ used as the first letter of a word that has both a general and a specific use to show that in this case the general use is intended: *I meant "catholic" with a small c.* ■ insignificant; unimportant: *these are small points.* ■ (of a voice) lacking strength and confidence: *"I'm scared," she said in a small voice.* ■ [attrib.] little; hardly any: *the captain had been paying small attention.* ■ [attrib.] (of a business or its owner) operating on a modest scale: *a small farmer.* ■ *archaic* low or inferior in rank or position; socially undistinguished: *at dinner, some of the smaller neighbors were invited.*
▸n. (**smalls**) *Brit., informal* small items of clothing, esp. underwear.
▸adv. into small pieces: *the okra cut up small.* ■ in a small size: *you shouldn't write so small.* ▷Old English *smæl,* of Germanic origin; related to Dutch *smal* and German *schmal.* —**small·ish** adj. —**small·ness** n.
▸PHRASES □ **feel** (or **look**) **small** feel (or look) contemptibly weak or insignificant. □ **it's a small world** used to express surprise at meeting an acquaintance or discovering a personal connection in a distant place or an unexpected context. □ **no small ——** a good deal of ——: *a matter of no small consequence.* □ **the small of the back** the part of a person's back where the spine curves in at the level of the waist. □ **small potatoes** *informal* something insignificant or unimportant: *her business was small potatoes.* □ **small wonder** not very surprising: *it's small wonder that her emotions had seesawed.*

THE RIGHT WORD **diminutive, little, miniature, minute, petite, small, tiny**

Why do we call a house **small** and a woman **petite**?

Small and **little** are used interchangeably to describe people or things of reduced dimensions, but *small* is preferred when describing something concrete that is of less than the usual size, quantity, value, or importance (*a small matter to discuss; a small room; a small price to pay*).

Little more often refers to concepts (*through little fault of his own; an issue of little importance*) or to a more drastic reduction in scale (*a little shopping cart just like the one her mother used*).

Diminutive and *petite* intensify the meaning of *small,* particularly with reference to women's figures that are very trim and compact (*with her diminutive figure, she had to shop in stores that specialized in petite sizes*).

Tiny is used to describe what is extremely small, often to the point where it can be seen only by looking closely (*a tiny flaw in the material; a tiny insect*), while **minute** not only describes what is seen with difficulty but may also refer to a very small amount of something (*minute traces of gunpowder on his glove*).

Miniature applies specifically to a copy, a model, or a representation of something on a very small scale (*a child's mobile consisting of miniature farm animals*).

small arms ▸plural n. portable firearms, esp. rifles, pistols, and light machine guns.

small beer ▸n. **1** *chiefly Brit.* a thing that is considered unimportant: *even with $10,000 to invest, you are still small beer for most stockbrokers.* **2** *archaic* weak beer.

small-bore ▸adj. denoting a firearm with a narrow bore, in international and Olympic shooting generally .22 inch caliber. ■ *informal* trivial; unimportant: *small-bore economic issues.*

small cal·o·rie ▸n. see CALORIE.

small-cap ▸adj. [attrib.] *Finance* denoting or relating to the stock of a company with a small capitalization.

small cap·i·tal ▸n. a capital letter that is of the same height as a lowercase x in the same typeface, as THIS.

small change ▸n. coins of low value. ■ *figurative* a thing that is considered trivial: *his wrongdoings were small change compared to a lot of happenings in the city.*

small-claims court ▸n. a local court in which claims for small sums of money can be heard and decided quickly and cheaply, without legal representation.

small craft ▸n. a small boat or fishing vessel.

small for·ward ▸n. *Basketball* a forward who is typically smaller than a power forward, and is often more agile and a better shot.

small fry ▸plural n. young fish, animals, or children. ■ insignificant people or things: *high-ranking officials escaped prosecution while numerous small fry were imprisoned.*

small hold·ing (also **small-hold·ing**) ▸n. *chiefly Brit.* an agricultural holding smaller than a farm. ■ the practice of farming such a piece of land: *cooperation with neighbors is the key to successful small holding.* —**small·hold·er** n.

small hours ▸plural n. (**the small hours**) another way of saying THE WEE HOURS (see WEE).

small in·tes·tine ▸n. the part of the intestine that runs between the stomach and the large intestine; the duodenum, jejunum, and ileum collectively.

small let·ter ▸n. a lowercase letter, as distinct from a capital letter.

small-mind·ed ▸adj. having or showing rigid opinions or a narrow outlook; petty. —**small-mind·ed·ly** adv. —**small-mind·ed·ness** n.

small·mouth /'smôl,mouTH/ ▸n. the smallmouth bass. See BLACK BASS.

small·pox /'smôl,päks/ ▸n. an acute contagious viral disease, with fever and pustules usually leaving permanent scars. It was effectively eradicated through vaccination by 1979. Also called VARIOLA.

small print ▸n. another term for FINE PRINT.

small-scale ▸adj. of limited size or extent: *a small-scale research project | small-scale manufacturing.*

small screen ▸n. (**the small screen**) television as a medium: *transplanting the timeless values of good literature to the small screen.*

small slam ▸n. *Bridge* the bidding and winning of twelve of the thirteen tricks.

small-sword ▸n. *chiefly historical* a light, tapering thrusting sword used for fencing or dueling.

small talk ▸n. polite conversation about unimportant or uncontroversial matters, esp. as engaged in on social occasions: *propriety required that he face these people and* **make small talk**.

small-time ▸adj. *informal* unimportant; minor: *a small-time gangster.* —**small-tim·er** n.

small-town ▸adj. of, relating to, or characteristic of a small town, esp. as considered to be unsophisticated or petty: *small-town gossip.*

smalt /smôlt/ ▸n. *chiefly historical* glass colored blue with cobalt oxide. ■ a pigment made by pulverizing such glass. ▷mid 16th cent.: from French, from Italian *smalto,* of Germanic origin; related to SMELT[1].

smalt·ite /'smôl,tīt/ ▸n. a metallic-gray mineral consisting chiefly of cobalt arsenide, typically occurring as cubic or octahedral crystals. ▷mid 19th cent.: from *smaltine* (a rare word with the same sense) + -ITE[1].

smarm /smärm/ *informal* ▸v. **1** [intrans.] *chiefly Brit.* behave in an ingratiating way in order to gain favor: *I* **smarmed my way** *into the air force.* **2** [trans.] smooth down (one's hair), esp. with water, oil, or gel: *he had* **smarmed** *his hair* **down**.

▸*n.* ingratiating behavior: *it takes a combination of smarm and confidence to persuade them.* ▷mid 19th cent. (originally dialect in the sense 'smear, bedaub'): of unknown origin.

smarm·y /ˈsmärmē/ ▸*adj.* (**smarm·i·er, smarm·i·est**) *informal* ingratiating and wheedling in a way that is perceived as insincere or excessive: *a smarmy, unctuous reply.* **—smarm·i·ly** /-məlē/ *adv.* **—smarm·i·ness** *n.*

smart /smärt/ ▸*adj.* **1** *informal* having or showing a quick-witted intelligence: *if he was that smart he would never have been tricked.* ■ (of a device) capable of independent and seemingly intelligent action: *hi-tech smart weapons.* ■ showing impertinence by making clever or sarcastic remarks: *don't get smart or I'll whack you one.* **2** (of a person) clean, neat, and well-dressed: *you look very smart.* ■ (of clothes) attractively neat and stylish: *a smart blue skirt.* ■ (of a thing) bright and fresh in appearance: *a smart green van.* ■ (of a person or place) fashionable and upscale: *a smart restaurant.* **3** quick; brisk: *I gave him a smart salute.* ■ painfully severe: *a dog that snaps is given a smart blow.*

▸*v.* [*intrans.*] (of a wound or part of the body) cause a sharp, stinging pain: *the wound was smarting* | [as *adj.*] (**smarting**) *Susan rubbed her smarting eyes.* ■ (of a person) feel upset and annoyed: *chiefs of staff are still smarting from the government's cuts.*

▸*n.* **1** (**smarts**) *informal* intelligence; acumen: *I don't think I have the smarts for it.* **2** sharp stinging pain: *the smart of the recent blood-raw cuts.* ■ *archaic* mental pain or suffering: *sorrow is the effect of smart, and smart the effect of faith.*

▸*adv. archaic* in a quick or brisk manner: *it is better for tenants to be compelled to pay up smart.* ▷Old English *smeortan* (verb); related to German *schmerzen*; the adjective is related to the verb, the original sense (late Old English) being 'causing sharp pain'; from this arose 'keen, brisk,' whence the current senses of 'mentally sharp' and 'neat in a brisk, sharp style.' **—smart·ing·ly** *adv.* **—smart·ly** *adv.* **—smart·ness** *n.*

smart al·eck (also **smart al·ec**) *informal* ▸*n.* a person considered irritating because they know a great deal or always have a clever answer to a question.

▸*adj.* having or showing an irritating, know-it-all attitude: *a smart-aleck answer.* ▷mid 19th cent.: from SMART + *Aleck*, diminutive of the given name *Alexander.* **—smart-al·eck·y** *adj.*

smart-ass ▸*n. informal* another term for SMART ALECK.

smart bomb ▸*n.* a radio-controlled or laser-guided bomb, often with a built-in computer.

smart card ▸*n.* a plastic card with a built-in microprocessor, used typically for electronic processes such as financial transactions and personal identification.

smart dust ▸*n.* a collection of microelectromechanical systems forming a simple computer in a container light enough to remain suspended in air, used mainly for information gathering in environments that are hostile to life.

smart·en /ˈsmärtn/ ▸*v.* [*trans.*] make (something) smarter in appearance: *he spent part of the proceeds on* ***smartening up*** *his office.* ■ [*intrans.*] (**smarten up**) acquire more common sense; behave more wisely: *if you don't smarten up soon, you'll find yourself out on the street.* ■ [*intrans.*] (**smarten up**) make one's appearance smarter: *I'd like to smarten up and shave.*

smart growth ▸*n.* planned economic and community development that attempts to curb urban sprawl and worsening environmental conditions.

smart mob ▸*n.* a group of people who assemble, move, or act collectively by using cellular phones or other wireless devices to communicate: *smart mobs, moving from party to party with each new reported celebrity sighting.*

smart mon·ey ▸*n.* money bet or invested by people with expert knowledge: *the smart money in entertainment is invested in copyright.* ■ knowledgeable people collectively: *the smart money in music programming is abandoning pop.*

smart mouth *informal* ▸*n.* an ability or tendency to make impertinent retorts; impudence: *why do you hide behind that smart mouth all the time?*

▸*v.* (**smart-mouth**) [*intrans.*] make impudent remarks. ■ [*trans.*] make impudent remarks to. **—smart-mouthed** *adj.*

Smart·phone /ˈsmärt,fōn/ (also **smart·phone**) ▸*n. trademark* a mobile phone that incorporates a PDA.

smart quotes ▸*plural n. Computing* quotation marks that, although all keyed the same, are automatically interpreted and set as opening or closing marks rather than vertical lines.

smart set ▸*n.* (**the smart set**) fashionable people considered as a group.

smart·weed /ˈsmärt,wēd/ ▸*n.* a plant of the dock family, typically having slender leaves and a short spike of tiny compact flowers. • Genus *Polygonum*, family Polygonaceae: several species.

smart·y /ˈsmärtē/ ▸*n.* (*pl.* **smart·ies**) *informal* **1** a know-it-all or a smart aleck. **2** *dated* a smartly dressed person; a member of thesmart set.

smart·y-pants ▸*n.* another term for SMARTY (sense 1).

smash /smash/ ▸*v.* **1** [*trans.*] violently break (something) into pieces: *the thief smashed a window to get into the car* | *gone are the days when he* ***smashed up*** *hotels.* ■ [*intrans.*] be violently broken into pieces; shatter: *the glass ball smashed instantly on the pavement.* ■ violently knock down or crush inward: *soldiers* ***smashed down*** *doors.* ■ crash and severely damage (a vehicle): *my Volvo's been* ***smashed up.*** ■ hit or attack (someone) very violently: *Donald smashed him over the head.* ■ easily or comprehensively beat (a record): *he smashed the course record.* ■ completely defeat, destroy, or foil (something regarded as hostile or dangerous): *a deliberate attempt to smash the union movement.* **2** [*intrans.*] move so as to hit or collide with something with great force and impact: *their plane smashed into a mountainside.* ■ [*trans.*] (in sports) strike (the ball) or score (a goal, run, etc.) with great force: *he smashed that one into the bleachers for another two-run homer.* ■ [*trans.*] (in tennis, badminton, and similar sports) strike (the ball or shuttlecock) downward with a hard overhand stroke.

▸*n.* **1** an act or sound of something smashing: *he heard the smash of glass.* ■ a violent collision or impact between vehicles: *a car smash.* ■ a violent blow: *a forearm smash.* ■ a stroke in tennis, badminton, and similar sports in which the ball is hit downward with a hard overhand volley. ■ *informal, dated* a bankruptcy or financial failure. **2** (also **smash hit**) *informal* a very successful song, film, show, or performer: *a box-office smash.* **3** a mixture of liquors (typically brandy) with flavored water and ice. ▷early 18th cent. (as a noun): probably imitative, representing a blend of words such as *smack, smite* with *bash, mash,* etc.

smashed /smasht/ ▸*adj.* **1** violently or badly broken or shattered: *a smashed collarbone.* **2** [*predic.*] *informal* very drunk: *when they go back to the barracks, the single men get smashed.*

smash·er /ˈsmashər/ ▸*n.* **1** *Brit., informal* a very attractive or impressive person or thing: *his wife is a smasher.* **2** [usu. in *combination*] a person or device that breaks something up: *riot police had clashed with window smashers.*

smash·ing /ˈsmashiNG/ ▸*adj. informal, chiefly Brit.* excellent; wonderful: *you look smashing!* **—smash·ing·ly** *adv.*

smash-mouth ▸*adj.* & *adv. Sports* (of a style of play) aggressive and confrontational: *we're coming into this game ready to play smash-mouth because we know that's the type of game it's going to be.*

smash-up ▸*n. informal* a violent collision, esp. of cars.

smat·ter·ing /ˈsmatəriNG/ (also **smat·ter**) ▸*n.* a slight superficial knowledge of a language or subject: *Edward had only* ***a smattering of*** *Spanish.* ■ a small amount of something: ***a smattering of*** *snow.* ▷mid 16th cent.: from *smatter* 'talk ignorantly, prate' (surviving in Scots), of unknown origin.

smaze /smāz/ ▸*n.* a mixture of smoke and haze.

SME ▸*abbr.* small to medium-sized enterprise, a company with no more than 500 employees.

smear /smi(ə)r/ ▸*v.* [*trans.*] coat or mark (something) messily or carelessly with a greasy or sticky substance: *his face was* ***smeared with*** *dirt.* ■ [*trans.*] spread (a greasy, oily, or sticky substance) over something: *Barbara smeared peanut butter on a slice of bread.* ■ *figurative* damage the reputation of (someone) by false accusations; slander: *someone was trying to smear her by faking letters.* ■ messily blur the outline of (something such as writing or paint); smudge: *her lipstick was smeared.*

▸*n.* **1** a mark or streak of a greasy or sticky substance: *there was an oil smear on his jacket.* ■ *figurative* a false accusation intended to damage someone's reputation: *the media were indulging in unwarranted smears.* ■ a sample of material spread thinly on a microscope slide for examination, typically for medical diagnosis: *the smears were stained for cryptosporidium.* **2** *Climbing* an insecure foothold. ▷Old English *smierwan* (verb), *smeoru* 'ointment, grease,' of Germanic origin; related to German *schmieren* (verb), *Schmer* (noun). **—smear·y** *adj.* **—smear·er** *n.*

smear cam·paign ▸*n.* a plan to discredit a public figure by making false or dubious accusations.

smec·tic /ˈsmektik/ ▸*adj.* denoting or involving a state of a liquid crystal in which the molecules are oriented in parallel and arranged in well-defined planes. Compare with NEMATIC.

▸*n.* a substance of this type. ▷late 17th cent.: via Latin from Greek *smēktikos* 'cleansing' (because of the soaplike consistency).

smec·tite /ˈsmek,tīt/ ▸*n.* a type of clay mineral (e.g., montmorillonite) that undergoes reversible expansion on absorbing water. ▷early 19th cent.: from Greek *smēktis* 'fuller's earth' + -ITE[1].

smeg·ma /ˈsmegmə/ ▸*n.* a sebaceous secretion in the folds of the skin, esp. under a man's foreskin. ▷early 19th cent.: via Latin from Greek *smēgma* 'soap,' from *smēkhein* 'cleanse.'

smell /smel/ ▸*n.* the faculty or power of perceiving odors or scents by means of the organs in the nose: *a highly developed sense of smell* | *dogs locate the bait by smell.* ■ a quality in something that is perceived by this faculty; an odor or scent: *lingering kitchen smells* | *a smell of coffee.* ■ an unpleasant odor: *twenty-seven cats lived there—you can imagine the smell!* ■ [in *sing.*] an act of inhaling in order to ascertain an odor or scent: *have a smell of this.*

▸*v.* (*past* and *past part.* **smelled** or **smelt** /smelt/) **1** [*trans.*] perceive or detect the odor or scent of (something): *I think I can smell something burning.* ■ sniff at (something) in order to perceive or detect its odor or scent: *the dogs smell each other.* ■ [*intrans.*] have or use a sense of smell: *becoming deaf or blind or unable to smell.* ■ (**smell something out**) detect or discover something by the faculty of smell: *his nose can smell out an animal from ten miles away.* ■ detect or suspect (something) by means of instinct or intuition: *he can smell trouble long before it gets serious* | *he can* ***smell out*** *weakness in others.* **2** [*intrans.*] emit an odor or scent of a specified kind: *it* ***smelled like*** *cough medicine* | [with *complement*] *the food smelled and tasted good* | [as *adj.*, in *combination*] (**-smelling**) *pungent-smelling food.* ■ have a strong or unpleasant odor: *if I don't get a bath soon I'll start to smell* | ***it smells*** *in here.* ■ appear in a certain way; be suggestive of something: *it* ***smells like*** *a hoax to me.* ▷Middle English: of unknown origin. **—smell·a·ble** *adj.* **—smell·er** *n.*

▸*PHRASES* □ **smell blood** discern weakness or vulnerability in an opponent. □ **smell a rat** *informal* suspect trickery or deception. □ **smell the roses** *informal* enjoy or appreciate what is often ignored. □ **smell something up** permeate an area with a bad smell: *he smelled up the whole house.*

THE RIGHT WORD **aroma, bouquet, fragrance, odor, perfume, scent, smell, stench, stink**

Everyone appreciates the **fragrance** of fresh-cut flowers, but the **stench** from the paper mill across town is usually unwelcome.

Both have a distinctive **smell**, which is the most general of these words for what is perceived through the nose, but there is a big difference between a pleasant smell and a foul one.

An **odor** may be either pleasant or unpleasant, but it suggests a smell that is clearly recognizable and can usually be traced to a single source (*the pungent odor of onions*).

An **aroma** is a pleasing and distinctive odor that is usually penetrating or pervasive (*the aroma of fresh-ground coffee*), while **bouquet** refers to a delicate aroma, such as that of a fine wine (*after swirling the wine around in her glass, she sniffed the bouquet*).

A **scent** is usually delicate and pleasing, with an emphasis on the source rather than on an olfactory impression (*the scent of balsam associated with Christmas*).

Fragrance and **perfume** are both associated with flowers, but *fragrance* is more delicate. A *perfume* may be so rich and strong that it is repulsive or overpowering (*the air was so dense with the perfume of lilacs that I had to go indoors*).

Stench and **stink** are reserved for smells that are foul, strong, and pervasive, although *stink* implies a sharper sensation, while *stench* refers to a more sickening one (*the stink of sweaty gym clothes; the stench of a rotting carcass*).

smell·ing salts ▸*plural n. chiefly historical* a pungent substance sniffed as a restorative in cases of faintness or headache, typically consisting of ammonium carbonate mixed with perfume.

smell·y /ˈsmelē/ ▶*adj.* (**smell·i·er**, **smell·i·est**) having a strong or unpleasant smell: *smelly feet.* —**smell·i·ness** *n.*

smelt[1] /smelt/ ▶*v.* [*trans.*] [often as *n.*] (**smelting**) extract (metal) from its ore by a process involving heating and melting: *tin smelting.* ■ extract a metal from (ore) in this way. ▷mid 16th cent.: from Middle Dutch, Middle Low German *smelten*; related to the verb **MELT**.

smelt[2] ▶ past and past participle of **SMELL**.

smelt[3] ▶*n.* (*pl.* same or **smelts** /smelts/) a small silvery fish that lives in both marine and fresh water and is sometimes fished commercially, in particular: • a fish of the northern hemisphere (family Osmeridae: *Osmerus* and other genera). • a fish of Australasian waters (family Retropinnidae: several genera). ▷Old English; obscurely related to various European names of fish; compare with **SMOLT**.

smelt·er /ˈsmeltər/ ▶*n.* an installation or factory for smelting a metal from its ore. ■ a person engaged in the business of smelting.

Smersh /smərsʜ/ the popular name for the Russian counterespionage organization responsible for maintaining security within the Soviet armed and intelligence services. ▷abbreviation of Russian *Smert' shpionam*, literally 'death to spies.'

Sme·ta·na /ˈsmetn-ə/, Bedřich (1824–84), Czech composer. He was dedicated to the cause of Czech nationalism, as is apparent in his operas such as *The Bartered Bride* (1866), and in his cycle of symphonic poems *Ma Vlast* (*"My Country"* 1874–79).

sme·ta·na /ˈsmetn-ə/ ▶*n.* sour cream. ▷Russian, from *smetat* 'sweep off.'

smew /smyo͞o/ ▶*n.* a small migratory merganser of northern Eurasia, the male of which has white plumage with a crest and fine black markings. • *Mergus albellus*, family Anatidae. ▷late 17th cent.: obscurely related to Dutch *smient* 'wigeon' and German *Schmeiente* 'small wild duck.'

smidge /smij/ ▶*n. informal* another term for **SMIDGEN**: *a smidge over five foot two.*

smid·gen /ˈsmijin/ (also **smid·geon** or **smid·gin**) ▶*n. informal* a small amount of something: *add* ***a smidgen of*** *cayenne.* ▷mid 19th cent.: perhaps from Scots *smitch* in the same sense.

smi·lax /ˈsmīlaks/ ▶*n.* **1** a widely distributed climbing shrub with hooks and tendrils. Several South American species yield sarsaparilla from their roots, and some are cultivated as ornamentals. • Genus *Smilax*, family Liliaceae. **2** a climbing asparagus, the decorative foliage of which is used by florists. • *Asparagus* (or **Myrsiphyllum**) *asparagoides*, family Liliaceae. ▷late 16th cent.: via Latin from Greek.

smile /smīl/ ▶*v.* [*intrans.*] form one's features into a pleased, kind, or amused expression, typically with the corners of the mouth turned up and the front teeth exposed: *she was smiling* | *he* ***smiled at*** *Shelley* | [as *adj.*] (**smiling**) *smiling faces.* ■ [*trans.*] express (a feeling) with such an expression: *he smiled his admiration of the great stone circle.* ■ [*trans.*] give (a smile) of a specified kind: *Guy smiled a grim smile.* ■ (**smile at/on/upon**) regard favorably or indulgently: *at first fortune smiled on him.* ■ [often as *adj.*] (**smiling**) *poetic/literary* (esp. of a landscape) have a bright or pleasing aspect: *smiling groves and terraces.*

▶*n.* a pleased, kind, or amused facial expression, typically with the corners of the mouth turned up and the front teeth exposed: *he flashed his most winning smile* | *she greeted us all with a smile.* ▷Middle English: perhaps of Scandinavian origin; related to **SMIRK**. —**smil·er** *n.* —**smil·ing·ly** *adv.*

▶*PHRASES* □ **be all smiles** *informal* (of a person) look very cheerful and pleased, esp. in contrast to a previous mood. □ **come up smiling** *informal* recover from adversity and cheerfully face what is to come.

THE RIGHT WORD **grin, simper, smile, smirk**

The facial expression created by turning the corners of the mouth upward is commonly known as a **smile**. It can convey a wide range of emotion, from pleasure, approval, or amusement to insincerity and disinterest (*his complaint was met with a blank smile*).

A **grin** is a wide smile that suggests spontaneous cheerfulness, warmth, pleasure, or amusement (*her teasing provoked an affectionate grin*).

But *grin* may also describe a ferocious baring of the teeth or an angry grimace (*the grin of a skeleton*).

A **simper**, on the other hand, is an expression of smugness and self-righteousness (*her simper of superiority*) as well as a silly or affected smile (*she curtsied with a girlish simper*).

Smirk also implies an affected or self-conscious smile, but one that expresses derision or hostility (*after he tricked them, he smirked and made a fool of himself*).

Smi·ley /ˈsmīlē/, Jane Graves (1949–), U.S. writer. She wrote the award-winning novel *A Thousand Acres* (Pulitzer Prize, 1991), as well as *Moo* (1995), *The All-True Travels and Adventures of Lidie Newton* (1998), and *Horse Heaven* (2000).

smil·ey /ˈsmīlē/ ▶*adj. informal* smiling; cheerful: *he drew a smiley face.*

▶*n.* a symbol that, when viewed sideways, represents a smiling face, formed by the characters :-) and used in electronic communications to indicate that the writer is pleased or joking.

smirch /smərcʜ/ ▶*v.* [*trans.*] make (something) dirty; soil: *the window was smirched by heat and smoke.* ■ *figurative* discredit (a person or their reputation); taint: *I am not accustomed to having my honor smirched.*

▶*n.* a dirty mark or stain. ■ *figurative* a blot on someone's character; a flaw. ▷late 15th cent.

smirk /smərk/ ▶*v.* [*intrans.*] smile in an irritatingly smug, conceited, or silly way: *Dr. Ali smirked in triumph.* See note at **SMILE**.

▶*n.* a smug, conceited, or silly smile: *Gloria pursed her mouth in a self-satisfied smirk.* ▷Old English *sme(a)rcian*, from a base shared by **SMILE**. The early sense was 'to smile'; it later gained a notion of smugness or silliness. —**smirk·er** *n.* —**smirk·i·ly** /-kəlē/ *adv.* —**smirk·ing·ly** *adv.* —**smirk·y** *adj.*

smit /smit/ *archaic* ▶ past participle of **SMITE**.

smite /smīt/ ▶*v.* (*past* **smote** /smōt/; *past part.* **smit·ten** /ˈsmitn/) [*trans.*] *poetic/literary* strike with a firm blow: *he smites the water with his sword.* ■ *archaic* defeat or conquer (a people or land): *he may smite our enemies.* ■ (usu. **be smitten**) *figurative* (esp. of disease) attack or affect severely: *various people had been* ***smitten with*** *untimely summer flu.* ■ (**be smitten**) be strongly attracted to someone or something: *she was so* ***smitten with*** *the boy.*

▶*n. archaic* a heavy blow or stroke with a weapon or the hand. ▷Old English *smītan* 'to smear, blemish,' of Germanic origin; related to Dutch *smijten* and German *schmeissen* 'to fling.' —**smit·er** *n.*

Smith[1] /smiтн/, Adam (1723–90), Scottish economist and philosopher. Often regarded as the founder of modern economics, he advocated minimal state interference in economic matters and discredited mercantilism. His works include *Inquiry into the Nature and Causes of the Wealth of Nations* (1776).

Smith[2], Alfred Emanuel (1873–1944), U.S. politician. He served as governor of New York 1919–20, 1923–28 and was a Democratic presidential candidate in 1928, losing to Republican Herbert Hoover.

Smith[3], Bessie (1894–1937), U.S. blues singer. She became a leading artist in the 1920s and made over 150 recordings, including some with Benny Goodman and Louis Armstrong. She was involved in a car accident and died after being refused admission to a "whites only" hospital.

Smith[4], David (Roland) (1906–65), U.S. sculptor. His early works were marked by recurring motifs of human violence and greed. These later gave way to a calmer, more monumental style, as in the *Cubi* series.

Smith[5], Dean (Edwards) (1931–), U.S. college basketball coach. He coached the University of North Carolina team from 1961 until 1997, establishing a career record of 874 wins and 254 losses. He also coached the 1976 U.S. Olympic basketball team to a gold medal.

Smith[6], Ian (Douglas) (1919–), Rhodesian statesman; prime minister 1964–79. In 1965 he issued a unilateral declaration of independence from Britain (UDI) because he would not agree to black majority rule. He eventually resigned in 1979.

Smith[7], John (c.1580–1631), American colonist; born in England. One of the leading promoters of English colonization in America, he helped to found the colony of Jamestown in 1607 and served as its president 1608–09. When captured by Indians from Powhatan's tribe, he was rescued by Pocahontas, Powhatan's daughter.

Smith[8], Joseph (1805–44), U.S. religious leader and founder of the Church of Jesus Christ of Latter-Day Saints (the Mormons). In 1827, according to his own account, he was led by divine revelation to find the sacred texts written by the prophet Mormon, which he published as *The Book of Mormon* in 1830. He founded the Mormon Church in the same year and later established a large community in Illinois, where he was arrested and murdered by a mob.

Smith[9], Kate (1909–86), U.S. singer; full name *Kathryn Elizabeth Smith*. She began "The Kate Smith Show" on radio in 1931 with her theme song "When the Moon Comes Over the Mountain." In 1938, she introduced Irving Berlin's "God Bless America," which also became her trademark song.

Smith[10], Dame Maggie (1934–), British stage and film actress; born *Margaret Natalie Cross*. Her films include *The Prime of Miss Jean Brodie* (Academy Award, 1969), *California Suite* (Academy Award, 1978), *A Room with a View* (1986), *Gosford Park* (2001), and the Harry Potter films.

Smith[11], Margaret Chase (1897–1995), U.S. politician. A Republican from Maine, she was a member of the U.S. House of Representatives 1940–1949 and a U.S. senator 1949–73, making her the first woman to serve in both houses of Congress.

smith /smiтн/ ▶*n.* a worker in metal. ■ short for **BLACKSMITH**.

▶*v.* [*trans.*] treat (metal) by heating, hammering, and forging it: *tin-bronze was cast into ingots before being smithed into bracelets.* ▷Old English, of Germanic origin; related to Dutch *smid* and German *Schmied*.

-smith ▶*comb. form* denoting a person skilled in creating something with a specified material: *goldsmith* | *wordsmith*.

Smith & Wes·son /ˌsmiтн and ˈwesən/ ▶*n. trademark* a type of firearm, in particular a type of revolver. ▷mid 19th cent.: named after Horace *Smith* (1808–93) and Daniel B. *Wesson* (1825–1906), founders of an American firm of gunsmiths.

smith·er·eens /ˌsmiтнəˈrēnz/ ▶*plural n. informal* small pieces: *a grenade blew him* ***to smithereens.*** ▷early 19th cent.: probably from Irish *smidirín*.

smith·er·y /ˈsmiтнərē/ ▶*n.* the work of or goods made by a smith.

Smith·field /ˈsmiтн,fēld/ a town in southern Virginia, in the Tidewater, known for its ham production; pop. 4,686.

Smith·field ham ▶*n.* a dry-cured ham produced near Smithfield, Virginia, from hogs that have fed on hickory nuts, acorns, and peanuts.

Smith·so·ni·an In·sti·tu·tion /ˌsmiтнˈsōnēən/ a foundation for scientific research, established in 1836 and based in Washington, D.C. It operates more than a dozen museums and institutes in Washington and other cities. It originated with a bequest in the will of English chemist and mineralogist James Smithson (1765–1829).

smith·son·ite /ˈsmiтнsə,nīt/ ▶*n.* a yellow, gray, or green mineral consisting of zinc carbonate typically occurring as crusts or rounded masses. ▷mid 19th cent.: from the name *Smithson* (see **SMITHSONIAN INSTITUTION**) + **-ITE**[1].

Smith·town /ˈsmiтн,toun/ a residential town on the northern shore of Long Island in New York; pop. 113,406.

smith·y /ˈsmiтнē/ ▶*n.* (*pl.* **smith·ies**) a blacksmith's workshop; a forge. ■ a blacksmith. ▷Middle English, from Old Norse *smithja*.

smit·ten /ˈsmitn/ ▶ past participle of **SMITE**.

SMN ▶*abbr.* seaman.

smock /smäk/ ▶*n.* a loose dress or blouse, with the upper part closely gathered in smocking. ■ a loose garment worn over one's clothes to protect them: *an artist's smock.* ■ (also **smock-frock**) *historical* a smocked linen overgarment worn by an agricultural worker.

▶*v.* [*trans.*] [usu. as *adj.*] (**smocked**) decorate (something) with smocking: *smocked dresses.* ▷Old English *smoc* 'woman's loose-fitting undergarment'; probably related to Old English *smūgan* 'to creep' and Old Norse *smjúga* 'put on a garment, creep into.' The use of the verb as a needlework term dates from the late 19th cent.

smock·ing /ˈsmäkiɴɢ/ ▶*n.* decoration on a garment created by gathering a section of the material into tight pleats and holding them together with parallel stitches in an ornamental pattern.

smog / smäg/ ▶*n.* fog or haze combined with smoke and other atmospheric pollutants. ▷early 20th cent.: blend of **SMOKE** and **FOG**[1]. —**smog·gy** *adj.*

smoke /smōk/ ▶*n.* a visible suspension of carbon or other particles in air, typically one emitted from a burning substance: *bonfire smoke.* ■ an act of smoking tobacco: *I'm dying for a smoke.* ■ *informal* a cigarette or cigar.

▶*v.* **1** [*intrans.*] emit smoke or visible vapor: *heat the oil* *until it just smokes* | [as *adj.*] (**smoking**) *they huddled around his smoking fire in the winter damp.* ■ inhale and exhale the smoke of tobacco or a drug: *Janine was sitting at the kitchen table smoking* | [as *n.*] (**smoking**) *the effect of smoking on health* | [*trans.*] *he smoked forty cigarettes a day.* **2** [*trans.*] [often as *adj.*] (**smoked**) cure or preserve (meat or fish) by exposure to smoke: *smoked salmon.* ■ treat (glass) so as to darken it: *the smoked glass of his lenses.* ■ fumigate, cleanse, or purify by exposure to smoke. ■ subdue (insects, esp. bees) by exposing them to smoke. ■ (**smoke someone/something out**) drive someone or something out of a place by using smoke: *we will fire the roof and smoke him out.* ■ (**smoke someone out**) *figurative* force someone to make something known: *as the press smokes him out on other human rights issues, he will be revealed as a social conservative.* **3** [*intrans.*] be aggressive or energetic: [as *adj.*] (**smoking**) *the band responds with a smoking first set.* ■ [*trans.*] *informal* kill (someone) by shooting. ■ defeat overwhelmingly in a fight or contest. **4** [*trans.*] *archaic* make fun of (someone): *we baited her and smoked her.* ▷Old English *smoca* (noun), *smocian* (verb), from the Germanic base of *smēocan* 'emit smoke'; related to Dutch *smook* and German *Schmauch.* —**smok·a·ble** (also **smoke·a·ble**) *adj.*

▸*PHRASES* □ **blow smoke** try to mislead or threaten someone by giving false or exaggerated information: *the coach has been blowing smoke for the past three years about our program.* □ **go up in smoke** *informal* be destroyed by fire. ■ *figurative* (of a plan) come to nothing: *more than one dream is about to go up in smoke.* □ **where there's smoke there's fire** *proverb* there's always some reason for a rumor. □ **smoke and mirrors** the obscuring or embellishing of the truth of a situation with misleading or irrelevant information: *the budget process is an exercise in smoke and mirrors.* [with reference to illusion created by magic tricks.] □ **smoke like a chimney** smoke tobacco incessantly.

smoke bomb ▸*n.* a bomb that emits dense smoke as it explodes, used to produce a smoke screen.

smoke·box /ˈsmōkˌbäks/ ▸*n.* a device for catching or producing and containing smoke, in particular: ■ an oven for smoking food. ■ the chamber in a steam engine or boiler between the flues and the funnel or chimney stack. ■ another term for SMOKER (sense 4).

smoke·bush /ˈsmōkˌbo͝osн/ (also **smoke bush**) ▸*n.* another term for SMOKE TREE.

smoke de·tec·tor (also **smoke alarm**) ▸*n.* a fire-protection device that automatically detects and gives a warning of the presence of smoke.

smoke-dry ▸*v.* [*trans.*] cure (meat or fish) by exposing it to smoke.

smoke·eas·y /ˈsmōkˌēzē/ (also **smoke·eas·y**) ▸*n.* (*pl.* **-eas·ies**) a private club, bar, or other place where smokers gather to avoid anti-smoking laws: *after work we sometimes light up at a smokeeasy in the neighborhood.* ▷late 20th cent.: on the pattern of *speakeasy.*

smoke-free ▸*adj.* without smoke: *a smoke-free environment.* ■ where smoking is not permitted: *a smoke-free train.*

smoke·house /ˈsmōkˌhous/ ▸*n.* a shed or room for curing food by exposure to smoke.

smoke·jump·er /ˈsmōkˌjəmpər/ (also **smoke jump·er**) ▸*n.* a firefighter who parachutes in to the site of a forest fire.

smoke·less /ˈsmōkləs/ ▸*adj.* producing or emitting little or no smoke: *smokeless fuel.*

smoke·less to·bac·co ▸*n.* tobacco that is chewed or snuffed rather than smoked by the user.

smok·er /ˈsmōkər/ ▸*n.* **1** a person who smokes tobacco regularly. ■ (also **smok·ing car**) a train compartment in which smoking is allowed. **2** a person or device that smokes fish or meat. **3** *dated* an informal social gathering for men. **4** a device that emits smoke for subduing bees in a hive.

smoke ring ▸*n.* a ring-shaped puff of smoke exhaled by a smoker.

smok·er's cough ▸*n.* a persistent cough caused by smoking.

smoke screen (also **smoke·screen**) ▸*n.* a cloud of smoke created to conceal military operations. ■ *figurative* a ruse designed to disguise someone's real intentions or activities: *he tried to create a smokescreen by quibbling about the statistics.*

smoke shop ▸*n.* a store selling tobacco products and smoking equipment.

smoke sig·nal ▸*n.* a column of smoke used as a way of conveying a message to a distant person. ■ *figurative* an indication of someone's intentions or views: *the Iowa caucuses might have given a small smoke signal of the Democrats' likely choice.*

smoke·stack /ˈsmōkˌstak/ ▸*n.* a chimney or funnel for discharging smoke from a locomotive, ship, factory, etc. and helping to induce a draft. ■ [as *adj.*] pertaining to heavy industry: *America's smokestack cities and blue-collar suburbs.*

smoke tree ▸*n.* a shrub or small tree of the cashew family that bears long feathery plumes of flowers, giving it a smoky appearance. • Genus *Cotinus*, family Anacardiaceae: two species, the European *C. coggygria*, grown in North America as an ornamental, and the rare American *C. obovatus.*

smok·ie /ˈsmōkē/ ▸*n. Scottish* a smoked haddock.

smok·ing gun ▸*n. figurative* a piece of incontrovertible incriminating evidence.

smok·ing jack·et ▸*n.* a man's comfortable jacket, typically made of velvet, formerly worn while smoking after dinner.

smok·ing room ▸*n.* a room set aside for smoking in a hotel or other public building.

smok·o /ˈsmōkō/ (also **smoke-ho**) ▸*n.* (*pl.* **-os**) *Austral./NZ, informal* a rest from work for a smoke; a tea break.

smok·y /ˈsmōkē/ ▸*adj.* (**smok·i·er**, **smok·i·est**) filled with or smelling of smoke: *a smoky office.* ■ producing or obscured by a great deal of smoke: *smoky factory chimneys.* ■ having the taste or aroma of smoked food: *smoky bacon.* ■ like smoke in color or appearance: *smoky eyes.* —**smok·i·ly** /-kəlē/ *adv.* —**smok·i·ness** *n.*

Smok·y Hill Riv·er a river that flows for 540 miles (870 km) from Colorado across Kansas.

smok·y quartz ▸*n.* a semiprecious variety of quartz ranging in color from light grayish-brown to nearly black.

smol·der /ˈsmōldər/ ▸*v.* [*intrans.*] burn slowly with smoke but no flame: *the bonfire still smoldered, the smoke drifting over the paddock.* ■ show or feel barely suppressed anger, hatred, or another powerful emotion: *Anna* **smoldered with** *indignation* | [as *adj.*] (**smoldering**) *he met her smoldering eyes.* ■ exist in a suppressed or concealed state: *the controversy smoldered on for several years* | [as *adj.*] (**smoldering**) *smoldering rage.*

▸*n.* smoke coming from a fire that is burning slowly without a flame: *the last acrid smolder of his cigarette.* ▷late Middle English: related to Dutch *smeulen.* —**smol·der·ing·ly** *adv.*

Smo·lensk /smōˈlensk; sməˈlyensk/ a city in western Russia, on the Dnieper River, close to the border with Belarus; pop. 346,000.

smolt /smōlt/ ▸*n.* a young salmon (or trout) after the parr stage, when it becomes silvery and migrates to the sea for the first time. ▷late Middle English (originally Scots and northern English): of unknown origin; compare with SMELT[3].

smooch /smo͞ocн/ *informal* ▸*v.* [*intrans.*] kiss and cuddle amorously: *the young lovers smooched in their car.* ■ *Brit.* dance slowly in a close embrace.

▸*n.* a kiss or a spell of amorous kissing and cuddling: *a slurpy smooch on the ear.* ■ *Brit.* a period of slow dancing in a close embrace: *they suggest a dance but it turns into a smooch.* ▷1930s: from dialect *smouch*, of imitative origin. —**smooch·er** *n.* —**smooch·y** *adj.* (**smooch·i·er**, **smooch·i·est**).

smooth /smo͞o*th*/ ▸*adj.* **1** having an even and regular surface or consistency; free from perceptible projections, lumps, or indentations: *smooth flat rocks.* ■ (of a person's face or skin) not wrinkled, pitted, or hairy: *a smooth skin tans more easily.* ■ (of a liquid) with an even consistency; without lumps: *cook gently until the sauce is smooth.* ■ (of the sea or another body of water) without heavy waves; calm: *the smooth summer sea.* ■ (of movement) without jerks: *the trucks gave a smooth ride* | *graphics are excellent, with fast, smooth scrolling.* ■ (of an action, event, or process) without problems or difficulties: *the group's expansion into the U.S. market was not quite so smooth.* ■ denoting the face of a tennis or squash racket without the projecting loops from the stringing process (used as a call when the racket is spun to decide the right to serve first or to choose ends); the opposite of ROUGH (in sense 1). **2** (of food or drink) without harshness or bitterness: *a lovely, smooth, very fruity wine.* ■ (of a person or their manner, actions, or words) suavely charming in a way considered to be unctuous: *his voice was infuriatingly smooth.*

▸*v.* [*trans.*] give (something) a flat, regular surface or appearance by running one's hand over it: *she* **smoothed out** *the newspaper.* ■ rub off the rough edges of (something): *you can use sandpaper to smooth the joint.* ■ deal successfully with (a problem, difficulty, or perceived fault): *these doctrinal disputes were* **smoothed over.** ■ free (a course of action) from difficulties or problems: *a conference would be held to smooth the way for the establishment of the provisional government.* ■ modify (a graph, curve, etc.) so as to lessen irregularities: *values are collected over a long period of time so that fluctuations are* **smoothed out.**

▸*adv. archaic* in a way that is without difficulties: *the course of true love never did run smooth.* ▷Old English *smōth*, probably of Germanic origin, though no cognates are known. The verb dates from Middle English. —**smooth·a·ble** *adj.* —**smooth·er** *n.* —**smooth·ish** *adj.* —**smooth·ly** *adv.* —**smooth·ness** *n.*

▸*PHRASE* □ **smooth someone's ruffled feathers** see RUFFLE.

smooth·bore /ˈsmo͞o*th*ˌbôr/ ▸*n.* [often as *adj.*] a gun with an unrifled barrel: *smoothbore muskets.*

smooth breath·ing ▸*n.* see BREATHING (sense 2).

smooth-faced ▸*adj.* **1** concealing one's true feelings by a show of friendliness. **2** clean-shaven.

smooth hound ▸*n.* a small European shark that typically lives close to the bottom in shallow waters. • Genus *Mustelus*, family Triakidae: two species.

smooth·ie /ˈsmo͞o*th*ē/ ▸*n.* **1** *informal* a man with a smooth, suave manner: *a smoothie with an eye for a pretty girl.* **2** a thick, smooth drink of fresh fruit puréed with milk, yogurt, or ice cream.

smooth mus·cle ▸*n. Physiology* muscle tissue in which the contractile fibrils are not highly ordered, occurring in the gut and other internal organs and not under voluntary control. Often contrasted with STRIATED MUSCLE.

smooth newt ▸*n.* a small yellowish-brown smooth-skinned newt that is widely distributed throughout Europe and western Asia. • *Triturus vulgaris*, family Salamandridae.

smooth snake ▸*n.* a harmless Eurasian snake that is gray to reddish in color, typically living in heathy country where it feeds on lizards. • *Coronella austriaca*, family Colubridae.

smooth talk ▸*n.* charming or flattering language, esp. when used to persuade someone to do something.

▸*v.* (**smooth-talk**) [*trans.*] use such language to (someone), esp. to persuade them to do something: *don't try to smooth-talk me* | [as *adj.*] (**smooth-talking**) *a smooth-talking salesman.* —**smooth talk·er** *n.*

smooth tongue ▸*n.* [in *sing.*] the ability or tendency to use insincere flattery or persuasion: *your smooth tongue could even turn your mistakes to your advantage.* —**smooth-tongued** *adj.*

smor·gas·bord /ˈsmôrgəsˌbôrd/ ▸*n.* a buffet offering a variety of hot and cold meats, salads, hors d'oeuvres, etc. ■ *figurative* a wide range of something; a variety: *the album is a smorgasbord of different musical styles.* ▷Swedish, from *smörgås* '(slice of) bread and butter' (from *smör* 'butter' + *gås* 'goose, lump of butter') + *bord* 'table.'

smor·zan·do /smôrtˈsändō/ *Music* ▸*adv.* & *adj.* (esp. as a direction) dying away. ▷Italian, literally 'extinguishing.'

smote /smōt/ ▸ past of SMITE.

smoth·er /ˈsmə*th*ər/ ▸*v.* [*trans.*] kill (someone) by covering their nose and mouth so that they suffocate. ■ extinguish (a fire) by covering it. ■ (**smother someone/something in/with**) cover someone or something entirely with: *rich orange sorbets smothered in fluffy whipped cream* | *figurative he smothered her with kisses.* ■ make (someone) feel trapped and oppressed by acting in an overly protective manner toward them: *it's time for you to leave the house—she'll smother you if you remain.* ■ suppress (a feeling or an action): *she smothered a sigh.* ■ (in sports) stop the motion of (the ball or a shot) by falling on it and covering it: *the goalkeeper was able to smother the ball.* ■ cook in a covered container, typically with a sauce and vegetables on top: [as *adj.*] (**smothered**) *smothered fried chicken.*

▸*n.* a mass of something that stifles or obscures: *all this vanished in a smother of foam.* ▷Middle English (as a noun in the sense 'stifling smoke'): from the base of Old English *smorian* 'suffocate.' —**smoth·er·y** *adj.*

smoth·ered mate ▸*n. Chess* checkmate in which the king has no vacant square to move to and is checkmated by a knight.

smoul·der /ˈsmōldər/ ▸*v.* British spelling of SMOLDER.

S

SMPTE ▸*abbr.* Society of Television and Motion Picture Engineers (used to denote a time coding system for synchronizing video and audiotapes).

smrit·i /ˈsmritē/ ▸*n.* (*pl.* **smrit·is**) a Hindu religious text containing traditional teachings on religion, such as the Mahābharata. ▷from Sanskrit *smṛti* 'remembrance.'

SMS ▸*abbr.* short message (or messaging) service, a system that enables cellular phone users to send and receive text messages.

SMSA ▸*abbr.* Standard Metropolitan Statistical Area.

SMSgt (also **SMSGT**) ▸*abbr.* senior master sergeant.

SMTP ▸*abbr.* *Computing* simple mail transfer protocol, a data transmission format used to send and receive e-mail.

smudge[1] /sməj/ ▸*n.* a blurred or smeared mark on the surface of something: *a smudge of blood on the floor.* ■ an indistinct or blurred view or image: *the low smudge of hills on the horizon.*
▸*v.* [*trans.*] cause (something) to become messily smeared by rubbing it: *she dabbed her eyes, careful not to smudge her makeup.* ■ [*intrans.*] become smeared when rubbed: *mascaras that smudge or flake around the eyes.* ■ make blurred or indistinct: *the photograph had been smudged by the photocopier and was by no means as clear as the original.* ▷late Middle English (as a verb in the sense 'soil, stain'): of unknown origin. The noun dates from the late 18th cent. **—smudge·less** *adj.*

smudge[2] ▸*n.* a smoky outdoor fire that is lit to keep off insects or protect plants against frost. ▷mid 18th cent. (in the sense 'suffocating smoke'): of unknown origin; related to obsolete *smudge* 'cure (herring) by smoking,' of obscure origin.

smudge pot ▸*n.* a container for a smudge (see **SMUDGE**[2]).

smudg·y /ˈsməjē/ ▸*adj.* (**smudg·i·er**, **smudg·i·est**) smeared or blurred from being smudged: *a smudgy photograph.* **—smudg·i·ly** /-jəlē/ *adv.* **—smudg·i·ness** *n.*

smug /sməg/ ▸*adj.* (**smug·ger**, **smug·gest**) having or showing an excessive pride in oneself or one's achievements: *he was feeling smug after his win.* ▷mid 16th cent. (originally in the sense 'neat, spruce'): from Low German *smuk* 'pretty.' **—smug·ly** *adv.* **—smug·ness** *n.*

smug·gle /ˈsməgəl/ ▸*v.* [*trans.*] move (goods) illegally into or out of a country: *he's been smuggling cigarettes from Gibraltar into Spain* | [as *n.*] (**smuggling**) *cocaine smuggling has increased alarmingly.* ■ [*trans.*] convey (someone or something) somewhere secretly and illicitly: *he smuggled out a message.* ▷late 17th cent.: from Low German *smuggelen*, of unknown ultimate origin. **—smug·gler** /ˈsməg(ə)lər/ *n.*

smush /sməsh; smo͝osh/ ▸*v.* [*trans.*] *informal* crush; smash: *they smushed marshmallows in their mouths.* ▷early 19th cent.: alteration of **MUSH**[1].

smut /smət/ ▸*n.* **1** a small flake of soot or other dirt: *all those black smuts from the engine.* ■ a mark or smudge made by such a flake: *the curtains were gray with city smuts.* **2** a fungal disease of grains in which parts of the ear change to black powder. • The fungi belong to *Ustilago* and other genera, order Ustilaginales, class Teliomycetes. **3** obscene or lascivious talk, writing, or pictures: *porn, in this view, is far from being harmless smut.*
▸*v.* (**smut·ted**, **smut·ting**) [*trans.*] [often as *adj.*] (**smutted**) **1** mark with flakes or soot or other dirt: *the smutted sky.* **2** infect (a plant) with smut: *smutted wheat.* ▷late Middle English (in the sense 'defile, corrupt, make obscene'): related to German *schmutzen*; compare with **SMUDGE**[1]. The noun dates from the mid 17th cent. **—smut·ti·ly** /-təlē/ *adv.* **—smut·ti·ness** *n.* **—smut·ty** *adj.* (**smut·ti·er**, **smut·ti·est**).

Smuts /sməts; smyts/, Jan (Christiaan) (1870–1950), South African statesman and soldier; prime minister 1919–24 and 1939–48. He led Boer forces during the Second Boer War and later commanded Allied troops against German East Africa in 1916. He helped to found the League of Nations.

SMV ▸*abbr.* slow-moving vehicle.

Smyr·na /ˈsmərnə/ **1** an ancient city on the western coast of Asia Minor, on the site of modern Izmir in Turkey. **2** a city in northwestern Georgia, northwest of Atlanta; pop. 40,999.

Sn ▸*symbol* the chemical element tin. ▷from late Latin *stannum* 'tin.'

s.n. ▸*abbr.* without name. [from Latin *sine nomine*.]

snack /snak/ ▸*n.* a small amount of food eaten between meals. ■ a light meal that is eaten in a hurry or in a casual manner.
▸*v.* [*intrans.*] eat a snack: *she likes to* **snack on** *yogurt.* ▷Middle English (originally in the sense 'snap, bite'): from Middle Dutch *snac(k)*, from *snacken* 'to bite,' variant of *snappen*. Senses relating to food date from the late 17th cent.

snack bar ▸*n.* a place where snacks are sold.

snack·ette /ˌsnaˈket/ ▸*n.* *W. Indian* a small store selling snacks, cigarettes, and minor groceries.

snaf·fle /ˈsnafəl/ ▸*n.* (also **snaffle bit**) (on a bridle) a simple bit, typically a jointed one, used with a single set of reins. ■ (also **snaffle bridle**) a bridle with such a bit.
▸*v.* [*trans.*] *informal, chiefly Brit.* take (something) for oneself, typically quickly or without permission: *shall we snaffle some of Bernard's sherry?* ▷mid 16th cent. (denoting a bridle bit): probably from Low German or Dutch; compare with Middle Low German, Middle Dutch *snavel* 'beak, mouth.' The verb (mid 19th cent.) is perhaps a different word.

sna·fu /snaˈfo͞o/ *informal* ▸*n.* a confused or chaotic state; a mess: *an enormous amount of my time was devoted to untangling snafus.*
▸*adj.* in utter confusion or chaos: *our refrigeration plant is snafu.*
▸*v.* [*trans.*] throw (a situation) into chaos: *you ignored his orders and snafued everything.* ▷1940s: acronym from *situation normal: all fouled (or fucked) up.*

snag /snag/ ▸*n.* **1** an unexpected or hidden obstacle or drawback: *the picture's U.S. release* **hit a snag**. **2** a sharp, angular, or jagged projection: *keep an emery board handy in case of nail snags.* ■ a rent or tear in fabric caused by such a projection. **3** a dead tree.
▸*v.* (**snagged**, **snag·ging**) [*trans.*] catch or tear (something) on a projection: *thorns snagged his sweater.* ■ [*intrans.*] become caught on a projection: *radio aerials snagged on bushes and branches.* ■ *informal* catch or obtain (someone or something): *it's the first time they've snagged the star for a photo.* ▷late 16th cent. (sense 2): probably of Scandinavian origin. The early sense 'stump sticking out from a tree trunk' gave rise to a U.S. sense 'submerged piece of timber obstructing navigation,' of which sense 1 is originally a figurative use. Current verb senses arose in the 19th cent. **—snag·gy** *adj.* (in sense 2).

snag·gle /ˈsnagəl/ ▸*n.* a tangled or knotted mass: *figurative a snaggle of import restrictions.*
▸*v.* [*intrans.*] become knotted or tangled: *the column of smoke snaggled for a moment.* ▷early 20th cent.: from the noun **SNAG** + **-LE**[2].

snag·gle·tooth /ˈsnagəlˌto͞oth/ ▸*n.* **1** (*pl.* **-teeth** /-ˌtēth/) an irregular or projecting tooth. **2** (*pl.* **-tooths**) a small deep-sea fish with large fangs at the front of the jaws and a number of light organs on the body. • Family Astronesthidae: several genera and species. **—snag·gle·toothed** *adj.*

snail /snāl/ ▸*n.* a mollusk with a single spiral shell into which the whole body can be withdrawn. • Most orders in the class Gastropoda. ■ (in metaphorical use) any person or thing that moves exceedingly slowly: *a tedious and complicated process enough to exasperate a snail.* ▷Old English *snæg(e)l*, of Germanic origin; related to German *Schnecke*. **—snail·like** /-ˌlīk/ *adj.*

snail

snail dart·er ▸*n.* a small percoid freshwater fish of a type found in U.S. rivers, now nearly extinct.

snail·fish /ˈsnālˌfish/ ▸*n.* (*pl.* same or **-fish·es**) a small fish of cool or cold seas, with loose jellylike skin and typically a ventral sucker. Also called **SEA SNAIL**. • *Liparis* and other genera, family Cyclopteridae: several species, including *L. liparis* of the North Atlantic.

snail mail ▸*n.* *informal* the ordinary postal system as opposed to electronic mail. ■ correspondence sent using the postal system.

snail's pace ▸*n.* [in *sing.*] an extremely slow speed: *he drove at a snail's pace.* **—snail-paced** *adj.*

snake /snāk/ ▸*n.* **1** a long limbless reptile that has no eyelids, a short tail, and jaws that are capable of considerable extension. Some snakes have a venomous bite. • Suborder Ophidia (or Serpentes), order Squamata: many families. ■ (in general use) a limbless lizard or amphibian. **2** (also **snake in the grass**) a treacherous or deceitful person: *that man is a cold-blooded snake.* **3** (in full **plumber's snake**) a long flexible wire for clearing obstacles in piping. **4** (**the snake**) a former system of interconnected exchange rates for the currencies of EC countries.
▸*v.* [*intrans.*] move or extend with the twisting motion of a snake: *a rope snaked down.* ▷Old English *snaca*, of Germanic origin. **—snake·like** /-ˌlīk/ *adj.*

snake·bark ma·ple /ˈsnākˌbärk/ ▸*n.* a maple tree with longitudinal pale stripes on the bark. • Genus *Acer*, family Aceraceae: several species, in particular *A. davidii* of eastern Asia and the striped maple of North America.

snake·bird /ˈsnākˌbərd/ ▸*n.* another term for **ANHINGA**.

snake·bite /ˈsnākˌbīt/ ▸*n.* **1** the bite of a snake, esp. a venomous one. ■ the medical condition resulting from a snakebite. **2** *Brit.* a drink consisting of draft cider and lager in equal proportions.

snake·bit·ten /ˈsnākˌbitn/ ▸*adj.* *informal* doomed to misfortune; unlucky: *the snakebitten space shuttle chalked up a fourth launch delay.*

Snake·board /ˈsnākˌbôrd/ ▸*n.* *trademark* a type of skateboard consisting of two footplates joined by a bar, allowing for greater speed and maneuverability than with a standard skateboard. ▷1990s: blend of *snake* and *skateboard*. **—snake·board·er** *n.* **—snake·board·ing** *n.*

snake charm·er ▸*n.* an entertainer who appears to make snakes move by playing music.

snake dance ▸*n.* a dance in which the performers handle live snakes, imitate the motions of snakes, or form a line that moves in a zigzag fashion, in particular a ritual dance of the Hopi Indians involving the handling of live rattlesnakes.
▸*v.* (**snake-dance**) [*intrans.*] dance in any of these ways.

snake eyes ▸*plural n.* [treated as *sing.*] a throw of two ones with a pair of dice. ■ *figurative* the worst possible result; a complete lack of success: *his elegant, amusing book sadly* **came up snake eyes**.

snake fence (also **snake-rail fence**) ▸*n.* a fence made of roughly split rails or poles joined in a zigzag pattern with their ends crossing.

snake·fish /ˈsnākˌfish/ ▸*n.* (*pl.* same or **-fish·es**) see **CUTLASSFISH**, **LIZARDFISH**.

snake fly ▸*n.* a slender woodland insect with transparent wings and a long "neck" that allows the head to be raised above the body. • Family Raphidiidae, order Neuroptera: *Raphidia* and other genera.

snake·head /snākˌhed/ ▸*n.* a freshwater fish with a broad, heavily scaled head and a long cylindrical body, native to tropical Africa and Asia. • Family Channidae: several genera and species.

snake mack·er·el ▸*n.* another term for **ESCOLAR**.

snake oil ▸*n.* *informal* a substance with no real medicinal value sold as a remedy for all diseases: *some kelp products are snake oil, but the good ones promote plant growth* | *figurative the president's foreign policy is snake oil.*

snake pit ▸*n.* a pit containing poisonous snakes. ■ *figurative* a scene of vicious behavior or ruthless competition: *the literary snake pits of New York.* ■ *figurative* a place of overcrowded squalor, esp. a poorly run mental hospital: *the clinic opened in 1949, when most drug and alcohol sanitariums were still snake pits.* [1946: from the title of a novel by Mary Jane Ward.]

snake-rail fence ▸*n.* another term for **SNAKE FENCE**.

Snake Riv·er a river in northwestern U.S. Rising in Yellowstone National Park in Wyoming, it flows for 1,038 miles (1,670 km) through Idaho into the state of Washington, where it joins the Columbia River.

snake·root /ˈsnakˌro͞ot; -ˌro͝ot/ ▸*n.* **1** any of a number of North American plants reputed to contain an antidote to snake poison, in particular: • (**Virginia snakeroot**) a birthwort with long heart-shaped leaves and curved tubular flowers (*Aristolochia serpentaria*, family Aristolochiaceae). • (**white snakeroot**) a poisonous plant that causes milk sickness in livestock (*Eupatorium rugosum*, family Compositae). **2** any of a number of plants thought to resemble a snake in shape, in particular **Indian snakeroot** (see **RAUWOLFIA**).

snake·skin /ˈsnākˌskin/ ▸*n.* [often as *adj.*] the skin of a snake: *snakeskin boots.*

snake·weed /ˈsnākˌwēd/ ▸*n.* **1** another term for **SNAKEROOT**. **2** old-fashioned term for **BISTORT**.

snake·wood /ˈsnākˌwo͝od/ ▸*n.* **1** a tree or shrub that has wood from which a snakebite antidote or other medicinal extract is obtained. • Several species, in particular the tree *Strychnos minor* (or **colubrina**) (family Loganiaceae), of the Indian subcontinent. **2** a tropical American tree that has timber with a snakeskin pattern, used for decorative work. • *Brosimum rubescens*, family Moraceae.

snak·y /ˈsnākē/ ▸*adj.* (**snak·i·er**, **snak·i·est**) like a snake in appearance; long and sinuous: *a long snaky whip.* ■ of the supposed nature of a snake in showing coldness, venom, or cunning: *a snaky friend.* ■ infested with snakes. —**snak·i·ly** /-kəlē/ *adv.* —**snak·i·ness** *n.*

snap /snap/ ▸*v.* (**snapped**, **snap·ping**) **1** break or cause to break suddenly and completely, typically with a sharp cracking sound: [*intrans.*] *guitar strings kept snapping* | [*trans.*] *dead twigs can be* ***snapped off.*** ■ [*intrans.*] emit a sudden, sharp cracking sound: *banners snapping in the breeze.* ■ [*intrans.*] (of an animal) make a sudden audible bite: *a dog was* ***snapping at*** *his heels.* ■ [*trans.* or *adverbial*] cause to move or alter in a specified way with a brisk movement and typically a sharp sound: *Rosa snapped her bag shut.* ■ [*intrans.*] move or alter in this way: *his mouth snapped into a tight, straight line.* ■ [*intrans.*] *figurative* suddenly lose one's self-control: *she claims she snapped after years of violence.* ■ [*reporting verb*] say something quickly and irritably to someone: [*intrans.*] *McIlvanney* ***snapped at*** *her* | [with *direct speech*] *"I really don't much care," she snapped.* **2** [*trans.*] take a snapshot of: *he planned to spend the time snapping rare wildlife* | [*intrans.*] *photographers were* ***snapping away at*** *her.* **3** [*trans.*] *Football* put (the ball) into play by a quick backward movement from the ground. **4** [*trans.*] fasten with snaps: *he pulled a white rubber swim hat over his head and snapped it under his chin.*

▸*phrasal v.* □ **snap back** recover quickly and easily from an illness or period of difficulty: *our bodies can snap back pretty well from short-term bouts of stress.* □ **snap out of** [often in *imperative*] *informal* get out of (a bad or unhappy mood) by a sudden effort: *come on, Fran—snap out of it!* □ **snap something up** quickly and eagerly buy or secure something that is in short supply or being sold cheaply: *all the tickets have been snapped up.*

▸*n.* **1** a sudden, sharp cracking sound or movement: *she closed her purse with a snap.* ■ [in *sing.*] a hurried, irritable tone or manner: *"I'm still waiting," he said with a snap.* ■ vigor or liveliness of style or action; zest: *the snap of the dialogue.* **2** (usu. **snaps**) a small fastener on clothing, engaged by pressing its two halves together. **3** [in *sing.*] *informal* an easy task: *a control panel that makes operation a snap.* **4** *Football* a quick backward movement of the ball from the ground that begins a play. **5** a snapshot. **6** *Brit.* a card game in which cards from two piles are turned over simultaneously and players call "snap" as quickly as possible when two similar cards are exposed.

▸*adj.* [*attrib.*] done or taken on the spur of the moment, unexpectedly, or without notice: *a snap judgment* | *he could call a snap election.* ▷late 15th cent. (in the senses 'make a sudden audible bite' and 'quick sharp biting sound'): probably from Middle Dutch or Middle Low German *snappen* 'seize'; partly imitative. —**snap·ping·ly** *adv.*

▸*PHRASES* □ **in a snap** *informal* in a moment; almost immediately: *gourmet-quality meals are ready in a snap.* □ **snap one's fingers** make a sharp clicking sound by bending the last joint of the middle finger against the thumb and suddenly releasing it, typically in order to attract attention in a peremptory way or to accompany the beat of music. □ **snap someone's head off** see **HEAD**.

snap-ac·tion ▸*adj.* [*attrib.*] **1** denoting a switch or relay that makes and breaks contact rapidly, whatever the speed of the activating mechanism. **2** denoting a gun whose hinged barrel is secured by a spring catch.

▸*n.* (**snap action**) the operation of such a switch, relay, or gun.

snap bean ▸*n.* a bean of a variety grown for its edible pods. ▷late 18th cent.: so named because the pods are broken into pieces to be eaten.

snap-brim ▸*adj.* (of a hat) with a brim that can be turned up and down at opposite sides.

snap·drag·on /ˈsnapˌdragən/ ▸*n.* a plant of the figwort family, bearing spikes of brightly colored two-lobed flowers that gape like a mouth when a bee lands on the curved lip. • Genus *Antirrhinum*, family Scrophulariaceae: several species, in particular the widely cultivated *A. majus*.

snap hook ▸*n.* a hook with a spring allowing the entrance but preventing the escape of a cord, key ring, etc.

snap lock ▸*n.* a feature of a device or component that allows it to be fastened automatically when pushed into position: [as *adj.*] *the top is secured by snap-lock buckles.*

snap-on (also **snap-in**) ▸*adj.* [*attrib.*] denoting a cover or attachment that is attached or secured with a snap.

snap pea ▸*n.* another term for **SUGAR SNAP**.

snap·per /ˈsnapər/ ▸*n.* **1** a marine fish that is typically reddish and is valued as food: • a fish of a widespread tropical family (Lutjanidae, the **snapper family**) that snaps its toothed jaws. See also **RED SNAPPER**. **2** another term for **SNAPPING TURTLE**. **3** *chiefly Brit.* a paper cracker, or the part of a cracker that makes a bang. **4** *Brit., informal* a photographer.

snap·ping tur·tle ▸*n.* a large American freshwater turtle with a long neck and strong hooked jaws. • Family Chelydridae: two North American species, the **common snapping turtle** (*Chelydra serpentina*) and the larger **alligator snapping turtle** (*Macroclemys temminckii*).

common snapping turtle

snap·pish /ˈsnapish/ ▸*adj.* (of a dog) irritable and inclined to bite. ■ irritable and curt: *she was often snappish with the children.* —**snap·pish·ly** *adv.* —**snap·pish·ness** *n.*

snap·py /ˈsnapē/ ▸*adj.* (**snap·pi·er**, **snap·pi·est**) *informal* **1** irritable and inclined to speak sharply; snappish: *anything unusual made her snappy and nervous.* **2** cleverly concise; neat: *snappy catchphrases.* ■ neat and elegant: *a snappy dresser.* —**snap·pi·ly** /-pəlē/ *adv.* —**snap·pi·ness** *n.*

▸*PHRASE* □ **make it snappy** be quick about it: *into bed and make it snappy!*

snap roll ▸*n.* a maneuver in which an aircraft makes a single quick revolution about its longitudinal axis while flying horizontally.

snap·shot /ˈsnapˌshät/ ▸*n.* **1** an informal photograph taken quickly, typically with a small handheld camera. ■ a brief look or summary: *this excellent book can only be a snapshot of a complex industry.* ■ *Computing* a record of the contents of a storage location or data file at a given time. **2** (**snap shot**) a shot taken quickly by a hunter.

snare /sne(ə)r/ ▸*n.* **1** a trap for catching birds or animals, typically one having a noose of wire or cord. ■ *figurative* a thing likely to lure or tempt someone into harm or error: *the wickedness and snares of the Devil.* ■ *Surgery* a wire loop for severing polyps or other growths. **2** a length of wire, gut, or hide stretched across a drumhead to produce a rattling sound. ■ short for **SNARE DRUM**.

▸*v.* [*trans.*] catch (a bird or mammal) in a snare. ■ *figurative* catch or trap (someone): *I snared a passing waiter.* ▷late Old English *sneare*, from Old Norse *snara*. —**snar·er** *n.*

snare drum ▸*n.* a small drum in the form of a short cylinder with a membrane at each end, the upper one being struck with hard sticks and the lower one fitted with snares. It originated in military use. ▷probably from Middle Low German, Middle Dutch *snare* 'harp string.'

snarf /snärf/ ▸*v.* [*trans.*] *informal* eat or drink quickly or greedily: *they* ***snarfed up*** *frozen yogurt.* ▷1950s: perhaps imitative.

snark /snärk/ ▸*n.* an imaginary animal (used to refer to someone or something that is difficult to track down). ▷1876: nonsense word coined by Lewis Carroll in *The Hunting of the Snark.*

snark·y /ˈsnärkē/ ▸*adj.* (**snark·i·er**, **snark·i·est**) *informal* (of a person, words, or a mood) sharply critical; cutting; snide: *the kid who makes snarky remarks in class.* ■ cranky; irritable: *Bobby's always a bit snarky before his nap.*

snarl[1] /snärl/ ▸*v.* [*intrans.*] (of an animal such as a dog) make an aggressive growl with bared teeth: [as *adj.*] (**snarling**) *snarling Dobermans.* ■ [*reporting verb*] (of a person) say something in an angry, bad-tempered voice: *I used to* ***snarl at*** *anyone I disliked* | [with *direct speech*] *"Shut your mouth!" he snarled* | [*trans.*] *he snarled a few choice remarks at them.*

▸*n.* an act or sound of snarling: *the cat drew its mouth back in a snarl.* ▷late 16th cent.: extension of obsolete *snar*, of Germanic origin; related to German *schnarren* 'rattle, snarl,' probably imitative. —**snarl·er** *n.* —**snarl·ing·ly** *adv.* —**snarl·y** *adj.*

snarl[2] ▸*v.* [*trans.*] **1** entangle or impede (something): *the bus got* ***snarled up*** *in the downtown traffic.* ■ [*intrans.*] become entangled or impeded: *the promising opening soon snarls up in a mess of motives.* **2** decorate (metalwork) with raised shapes by hammering the underside.

▸*n.* a knot or tangle: *snarls of wild raspberry plants* | *our hair hung in damp snarls.* ▷late Middle English (in the senses 'snare, noose' and 'catch in a snare'): from **SNARE**.

snarl-up ▸*n.* *informal* a traffic jam. ■ a muddle or mistake: *there's a snarl-up in editing.*

snatch /snach/ ▸*v.* [*trans.*] quickly seize (something) in a rude or eager way: *she snatched a cookie from the plate* | *figurative a victory snatched from the jaws of defeat.* ■ *informal* steal (something) or kidnap (someone), typically by seizing or grabbing suddenly: *a mission to snatch Winston Churchill.* ■ [*intrans.*] (**snatch at**) hastily or ineffectually attempt to seize (something): *she snatched at the handle.* ■ quickly secure or obtain (something) when a chance presents itself: *snatching a few hours' sleep.* ■ [*intrans.*] (**snatch at**) eagerly take or accept (an offer or opportunity): *I snatched at the chance.*

▸*n.* **1** an act of snatching or quickly seizing something: *a quick snatch of breath.* ■ a short spell of doing something: *brief snatches of sleep.* ■ a fragment of song or talk: *picking up snatches of conversation.* ■ *informal* a kidnapping or theft. **2** *Weightlifting* the rapid raising of a weight from the floor to above the head in one movement. **3** *vulgar slang* a woman's genitals. ▷Middle English *sna(c)che* (verb) 'suddenly snap at,' (noun) 'a snare'; perhaps related to **SNACK**. —**snatch·er** *n.* —**snatch·y** *adj.*

snaz·zy /ˈsnazē/ ▸*adj.* (**snaz·zi·er**, **snaz·zi·est**) *informal* stylish and attractive: *snazzy little silk dresses.* ▷1960s: of unknown origin. —**snaz·zi·ly** /-zəlē/ *adv.* —**snaz·zi·ness** *n.*

SNCC ▸*abbr.* Student Nonviolent Coordinating Committee, a U.S. civil-rights student organization active in the 1960s.

Snead /snēd/, Sam(uel Jackson) (1912–2002), U.S. golfer; nickname **Slammin' Sammy**. He won a record 81 tournaments of the PGA Tour, including the Masters (1949, 1952, 1954), the PGA (1942, 1949, 1951), and the British Open (1946).

sneak /snēk/ ▸*v.* (*past* **sneaked** or *informal* **snuck** /ˈsnək/) [*intrans.*] move or go in a furtive or stealthy manner: *I sneaked out by the back exit.* ■ [*trans.*] convey (someone or something) in such a way: *someone sneaked a camera inside.* ■ [*trans.*] do or obtain (something) in a stealthy or furtive way: *she sneaked a glance at her watch.* ■ (**sneak up on**) creep up on (someone) without being detected: *he sneaks up on us slyly.*

▸*n.* *informal* **1** a furtive and contemptible person: *he was branded a prying sneak for eavesdropping on intimate conversation.* **2** (usu. **sneaks**) short for **SNEAKER**.

▸*adj.* [*attrib.*] acting or done surreptitiously, unofficially, or without warning: *a sneak thief* | *a sneak preview.* ▷late 16th cent.: probably dialect; perhaps related to obsolete *snike* 'to creep.'

USAGE The traditional standard past form of **sneak** is **sneaked** (*she sneaked around the corner*). An alternative past form, **snuck** (*she snuck past me*), arose in the U.S. in the 19th century. Until very recently, **snuck** was confined to U.S. dialect use and was regarded as nonstandard, but in the last few decades its use has spread, particularly in the U.S., where it is now generally regarded as a standard alternative to **sneaked**. In formal contexts, however, **sneaked** remains the preferred form.

sneak·box /ˈsnēkˌbäks/ ▸*n.* a small, flat boat masked with brush or weeds, used in wildfowl hunting.

sneak·er /ˈsnēkər/ ▸*n.* a soft shoe with a rubber sole worn for sports or casual occasions.

sneak·ing /ˈsnēking/ ▸*adj.* [*attrib.*] **1** (of a feeling) persistent in one's mind but reluctantly held or not fully recognized; nagging: *I've a sneaking suspicion*

S

they'll do well. **2** *informal* furtive and contemptible: *an unpleasant, sneaking habit.* **—sneak·ing·ly** *adv.*

sneak·y /ˈsnēkē/ ▸*adj.* (**sneak·i·er**, **sneak·i·est**) furtive; sly: *sneaky, underhanded tactics.* ■ (of a feeling) secret; reluctant: *I developed a sneaky fondness for the old lady.* **—sneak·i·ly** /-kəlē/ *adv.* **—sneak·i·ness** *n.*

sneck /snek/ *Scottish N. English* ▸*n. Scottish & N. English* a latch on a door or window.
▸*v.* [*trans.*] *Scottish & N. English* close or fasten (a door or window) with a latch. ▷Middle English: obscurely related to **SNATCH**.

sneer /sni(ə)r/ ▸*n.* a contemptuous or mocking smile, remark, or tone: *he acknowledged their presence with a condescending sneer.*
▸*v.* [*intrans.*] smile or speak in a contemptuous or mocking manner: *she had* **sneered at** *their bad taste* | [with *direct speech*] *"I see you're conservative in your ways," David sneered.* ▷late Middle English: probably of imitative origin. **—sneer·er** *n.* **—sneer·ing·ly** *adv.*

sneeze /snēz/ ▸*v.* [*intrans.*] make a sudden involuntary expulsion of air from the nose and mouth due to irritation of one's nostrils: *the smoke made her sneeze.*
▸*n.* an act or the sound of expelling air from the nose in such a way: *he stopped a sudden sneeze.* ▷Middle English: apparently an alteration of Middle English *fnese* due to misreading or misprinting (after initial *fn-* had become unfamiliar), later adopted because it sounded appropriate. **—sneez·er** *n.* **—sneez·y** *adj.*
▸*PHRASE* □ **not to be sneezed at** *informal* not to be rejected without careful consideration; worth having or taking into account: *a saving of $550 was not to be sneezed at.*

sneeze·weed /ˈsnēz,wēd/ ▸*n.* a yellow-flowered North American plant of the daisy family, with turned-back rays and a globular disk. Some kinds are toxic to grazing animals and some are used medicinally, esp. by American Indians, in the treatment of colds. • Genus *Helenium*, family Compositae: several species, including *H. autumnale*.

sneeze·wort /ˈsnēzwərt; -wôrt/ (also **sneezewort yarrow**) ▸*n.* a Eurasian yarrow, naturalized in North America, whose dried leaves induce sneezing. • *Achillea ptarmica*, family Compositae.

snell /snel/ ▸*n.* a short line of gut or horsehair by which a fishhook is attached to a longer line.
▸*v.* [*trans.*] tie or fasten (a hook) to a line: [as *adj.*] (**snelled**) *a snelled or long-shanked hook.* ▷mid 19th cent.: of unknown origin.

Snel·len test /ˈsnelən/ ▸*n.* a test of visual acuity using rows of letters printed in successively decreasing sizes (the **Snellen scale**). ▷mid 19th cent.: named after Hermann *Snellen* (1834–1908), Dutch ophthalmologist.

Snell's law /snelz/ *Physics* a law stating that the ratio of the sines of the angles of incidence and refraction of a wave are constant when it passes between two given media. ▷late 19th cent.: named after Willebrord Van Roijen *Snell* (1591–1626), Dutch mathematician.

snert /snərt/ ▸*n. informal Computing* a participant in an Internet chat room who acts in a rude, annoying, or juvenile manner: *I could tell he was a snert from his sarcastic comments.* ■ a person whose online posts or e-mails are annoying to others: *do you ever get unsolicited messages from snerts?* ▷of uncertain origin, possibly an acronym from *snot-nosed egotistical rude twit* (or *teenager*).

SNG ▸*abbr.* synthetic natural gas.

snick /snik/ ▸*v.* [*trans.*] **1** cut a small notch or incision in (something): *the stem can be carefully snicked to allow the bud to swell.* **2** cause (something) to make a sharp clicking sound: [*trans.*] *he placed the pen in the briefcase and snicked it shut.* ■ [*intrans.*] make such a sound: *the bolt snicked into place.*
▸*n.* **1** a small notch or cut: *he had several shaving snicks.* **2** a sharp click: *he heard the snick of the latch.* ▷late 17th cent.: probably from obsolete *snick or snee* 'fight with knives.'

snick·er /ˈsnikər/ ▸*v.* [*intrans.*] give a smothered or half-suppressed laugh; snigger. ■ (of a horse) whinny.
▸*n.* a smothered laugh; a snigger. ■ a whinny. ▷late 17th cent.: imitative. **—snick·er·ing·ly** *adv.*

snide /snīd/ ▸*adj.* **1** derogatory or mocking in an indirect way: *snide remarks about my mother.* ■ (of a person) devious and underhanded: *a snide divorce lawyer.* **2** *chiefly Brit.* counterfeit; inferior: *snide Rolex watches.*
▸*n.* an unpleasant or underhanded person or remark. ▷mid 19th cent. (originally slang in sense 2): of unknown origin. **—snide·ly** *adv.* **—snide·ness** *n.* **—snid·ey** *adj.*

sniff /snif/ ▸*v.* [*intrans.*] draw in air audibly through the nose to detect a smell, to stop it from running, or to express contempt: *his dog* **sniffed at** *my trousers* | [with *direct speech*] *"You're behaving in an unladylike fashion," sniffed Mother.* ■ [*trans.*] draw in (a scent, substance, or air) through the nose. ■ [usu. with *negative*] (**sniff at**) show contempt or dislike for: *the price is not to be sniffed at.* ■ (**sniff around**) *informal* investigate covertly, esp. to find out confidential or incriminating information about someone. ■ [*trans.*] (**sniff something out**) *informal* discover something by investigation: *he made millions upon millions sniffing out tax loopholes for companies.*
▸*n.* an act or sound of drawing air through the nose: *he gave a sniff of disapproval.* ■ an amount of air or other substance taken up in such a way: *his drug use was confined to a* **sniff of** *amyl nitrite.* ■ [in *sing.*] *informal* a trace, hint, or small amount: *they're off at the first* **sniff of** *trouble.* ■ [in *sing.*] *Brit., informal* a small chance: *the Olympic hosts will at least get a sniff at a medal.* ▷Middle English: imitative.

sniff·er /ˈsnifər/ ▸*n.* **1** a person who sniffs, esp. one who sniffs a drug or toxic substance: [with *adj.*] *a glue sniffer.* ■ *informal* a device for detecting an invisible and dangerous substance, such as gas or radiation: *electronic sniffers are used to detect the presence of a nuclear mass.* **2** *informal* a person's nose. **3** (also **sniffer program**) a computer program that detects and records a variety of restricted information, esp. the secret passwords needed to gain access to files or networks.

sniff·er dog ▸*n. informal* a dog trained to find drugs or explosives by smell.

snif·fle /ˈsnifəl/ ▸*v.* [*intrans.*] sniff slightly or repeatedly, typically because of a cold or fit of crying.
▸*n.* an act of sniffing in such a way: *he was restraining his sniffles rather well.* ■ a head cold causing a running nose and sniffing: *she had a slight cough and a sniffle* | *they may get damp and catch* **the sniffles**. ▷mid 17th cent.: imitative; compare with **SNIVEL**. **—snif·fler** /ˈsnif(ə)lər/ *n.* **—snif·fly** /ˈsnif(ə)lē/ *adj.*

snif·fy /ˈsnifē/ ▸*adj.* (**snif·fi·er**, **snif·fi·est**) *informal* scornful; contemptuous: *some people are sniffy about tea bags.* **—sniff·i·ly** /-fəlē/ *adv.* **—sniff·i·ness** *n.*

snif·ter /ˈsniftər/ ▸*n.* a footed glass that is wide at the bottom and tapers to the top, used for brandy and other drinks. ■ *informal* a small quantity of an alcoholic drink: *care to join me for a snifter?* ▷mid 19th cent.: imitative; compare with dialect *snift* 'to snort.'

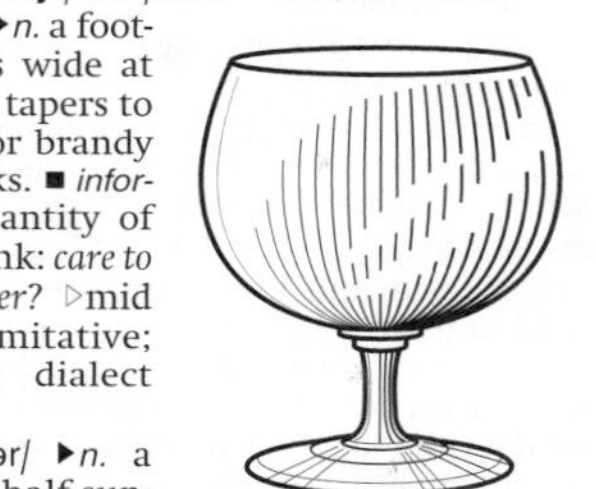
snifter

snig·ger /ˈsnigər/ ▸*n.* a smothered or half-suppressed laugh.
▸*v.* [*intrans.*] give such a laugh: *the boys at school were sure to snigger at him behind his back* | [with *direct speech*] *"Doesn't he look like a fool?" they sniggered.* ▷early 18th cent.: later variant of **SNICKER**. **—snig·ger·er** *n.* **—snig·ger·ing·ly** *adv.*

snig·ger·y /ˈsnigərē/ ▸*adj. informal* characterized by or liable to cause sniggering: *sniggery jokes.*

snig·gle /ˈsnigəl/ ▸*v.* [*intrans.*] fish for eels by pushing a baited hook into holes in which they are hiding. ▷mid 17th cent.: frequentative, based on earlier *snig* 'small eel,' of unknown origin.

snip /snip/ ▸*v.* (**snipped**, **snip·ping**) [*trans.*] cut (something) with scissors or shears, typically with small quick strokes: *she snipped layers into the hair around her face* | [*intrans.*] *she inspected the embroidery,* **snipping at** *loose threads.*
▸*n.* **1** an act of cutting something in such a way: *he took a snip at a dandelion on the grass.* ■ a small piece of something that has been cut off: *the collage consists of snips of wallpaper.* **2** *informal* a small or insignificant person: *imagine that little snip telling me I was wrong!* **3** (**snips**) hand shears, esp. for cutting metal: *use tin snips.* **4** [in *sing.*] *Brit., informal* a surprisingly cheap item; a bargain: *the wine is a snip at £2.65.* ■ *dated* a thing that is easily achieved. ▷mid 16th cent. (in the sense 'a shred'): from Low German *snip* 'small piece,' of imitative origin.

snipe /snīp/ ▸*n.* (*pl.* same or **snipes**) a wading bird of marshes and wet meadows, with brown camouflaged plumage, a long straight bill, and typically a drumming display flight. See also **PAINTED SNIPE**, **SEED-SNIPE**. • *Gallinago* and other genera, family Scolopacidae: several species, e.g., the **common snipe** (*G. gallinago*).
▸*v.* [*intrans.*] shoot at someone from a hiding place, esp. accurately and at long range: *the soldiers in the trench* **sniped at** *us.* ■ make a sly or petty verbal attack: *the state governor constantly* **sniped at** *the president* | [as *n.*] (**sniping**) *there has been some sniping about inept leadership.* ▷Middle English: probably of Scandinavian origin; compare with Icelandic *mýrisnípa*; obscurely related to Dutch *snip* and German *Schnepfe*. **—snip·er** *n.*

snipe eel ▸*n.* a slender marine eel with a long, thin, beaklike snout, typically occurring in deep water. • Family Nemichthyidae: several genera and species.

snipe fly ▸*n.* a slender, long-legged predatory fly that catches insect prey on the wing. • Family Rhagionidae: many genera and species.

snip·pet /ˈsnipit/ ▸*n.* a small piece or brief extract: *snippets of information about the war.* **—snip·pet·y** *adj.*

snip·py /ˈsnipē/ ▸*adj.* (**snip·pi·er**, **snip·pi·est**) *informal* curt or sharp, esp. in a condescending way: *a snippy note from our landlord.* **—snip·pi·ly** /-pəlē/ *adv.* **—snip·pi·ness** *n.*

snit /snit/ ▸*n. informal* a fit of irritation; a sulk: *the ambassador and delegation had withdrawn* **in a snit**. ▷1930s: of unknown origin.

snitch /snicн/ *informal* ▸*v.* **1** [*trans.*] steal. **2** [*intrans.*] inform on someone: *she wouldn't tell who* **snitched on** *me.*
▸*n.* an informer. ▷late 17th cent.: of unknown origin.

sniv·el /ˈsnivəl/ ▸*v.* (**sniv·eled**, **sniv·el·ing**; *Brit.* **snivelled**, **sniv·el·ling**) [*intrans.*] cry and sniffle: *Kate started to snivel, looking sad and stunned.* ■ complain in a whining or tearful way: *he shouldn't snivel about his punishment* | [as *adj.*] (**sniveling**) *you sniveling little brat!*
▸*n.* a slight sniff indicating suppressed emotion or crying: *Lucy's torrent of howls weakened to a snivel.* ▷late Old English (recorded only in the verbal noun *snyflung* 'mucus'), from *snofl*, in the same sense; compare with **SNUFFLE**. **—sniv·el·er** *n.* **—sniv·el·ing·ly** *adv.*

sniv·el gear ▸*n.* the items carried by a soldier for personal comfort in inclement weather.

snob /snäb/ ▸*n.* a person with an exaggerated respect for high social position or wealth who seeks to associate with social superiors and dislikes people or activities regarded as lower-class. ■ [with *adj.*] a person who believes that their tastes in a particular area are superior to those of other people: *a musical snob.* ▷late 18th cent. (originally dialect in the sense 'cobbler'): of unknown origin; early senses conveyed a notion of 'lower status or rank,' later denoting a person seeking to imitate those of superior social standing or wealth. Folk etymology connects the word with Latin *sine nobilitate* 'without nobility' but the earliest recorded sense has no connection with this. **—snob·ber·y** /-bərē/ *n.* (*pl.* **-ber·ies**) **—snob·bism** /-,bizəm/ *n.* **—snob·by** *adj.* (**-bi·er**, **-bi·est**).

snob·bish /ˈsnäbisн/ ▸*adj.* of, characteristic of, or like a snob: *the writer takes a rather snobbish tone.* **—snob·bish·ly** *adv.* **—snob·bish·ness** *n.*

SNOBOL /ˈsnō,bôl/ ▸*n.* a high-level computer programming language used esp. in manipulating textual data. ▷1960s: formed from letters taken from *string-oriented symbolic language*, on the pattern of *COBOL*.

snob val·ue ▸*n.* value attached to something for its power to indicate supposed social superiority; cachet: *the coffin was more expensive and carried snob value.*

sno-cone ▸*n.* variant spelling of **SNOW CONE**.

snog /snäg/ *Brit., informal* ▸*v.* (**snogged**, **snog·ging**) [*trans.*] kiss and caress amorously.
▸*n.* an act or spell of amorous kissing and caressing. ▷1940s: of unknown origin. **—snog·ger** *n.*

snood /sno͝od/ ▸*n.* **1** an ornamental hairnet or fabric bag worn over the hair at the back of a woman's head. ■ *historical* a ribbon or band worn by unmarried women in Scotland to confine their hair. **2** a wide ring of knitted material worn as a hood or scarf. **3** a short line attaching a hook to a main line in sea fishing. ▷Old English *snōd*, of unknown origin.

snook[1] /sno͝ok/ ▸*n.* a large edible game fish of the Caribbean that is sometimes found in brackish water. • *Centropomus undecimalis*, family Centropomidae. ▷late 17th cent.: from Dutch *snoek* 'pike.'

snook[2] ▸*n.* (in phrase **cock a snook**) *informal, chiefly Brit.* place one's hand so that the thumb touches one's nose and the fingers are spread out, in order to express contempt: *you wouldn't be so quick to cock a snook if she were actually looking at you.* ■ *figurative* openly show contempt or a lack of respect for someone or something; thumb one's nose: *he spent a lifetime cocking a snook at the art world.* ▷late 18th cent.: of unknown origin.

snook·er /ˈsno͝okər/ ▶*n.* a game played with cues on a billiard table in which the players use a cue ball (white) to pocket the other balls (fifteen red and six colored) in a set order. ■ a position in a game of snooker or pool in which a player cannot make a direct shot at any permitted ball; a shot placing an opponent in such a position: *he needed a snooker to have a chance of winning the frame.*
▶*v.* [*trans.*] subject (oneself or one's opponent) to a snooker. ■ *figurative* leave (someone) in a difficult position; thwart: *I managed to lose my car keys—that was me snookered.* ■ *figurative* trick, entice, or trap: *they were* ***snookered into*** *buying books at prices that were too high.* ▷late 19th cent.: of unknown origin.

snoop /sno͞op/ *informal* ▶*v.* [*intrans.*] investigate or look around furtively in an attempt to find out something, esp. information about someone's private affairs: *your sister might find the ring if she goes* ***snooping around*** | [as *adj.*] (**snooping**) *snooping neighbors.*
▶*n.* [in *sing.*] an act of looking around in such a way: *I could go back to her cottage and have another snoop.* ■ a person who investigates in such a way; a detective. ▷mid 19th cent.: from Dutch *snæpen* 'eat on the sly.' —**snoop·er** *n.* —**snoop·y** *adj.*

snoop·er·scope /ˈsno͞opər,skōp/ ▶*n.* a device that converts infrared radiation into a visible image, used for seeing in the dark.

snoot /sno͞ot/ ▶*n.* **1** *informal* a person's nose. **2** *informal* a person who shows contempt for those considered to be of a lower social class: *the snoots complain that the paper has lowered its standards.* **3** a tubular or conical attachment used to produce a narrow beam from a spotlight. ▷mid 19th cent.: variant of SNOUT.

snoot·ful /ˈsno͞otfo͝ol/ ▶*n.* enough alcoholic drink to make one drunk: *they're tongue-tied until they've* ***had a snootful.*** ■ as much as one can take of something: *he decided he'd had a snootful of playing the role.*

snoot·y /ˈsno͞otē/ ▶*adj.* (**snoot·i·er, snoot·i·est**) *informal* showing disapproval or contempt toward others, esp. those considered to belong to a lower social class: *snooty neighbors.* ▷early 20th cent.: from SNOOT + -Y[1]; compare with SNOTTY. —**snoot·i·ly** /-təlē/ *adv.* —**snoot·i·ness** *n.*

snooze /sno͞oz/ *informal* ▶*n.* a short, light sleep, esp. during the day: *he settled in the grass for a snooze.* ■ a boring event or person: *months go by and the job's a snooze.*
▶*v.* [*intrans.*] have a short, light sleep: *the children play beach games while the adults snooze in the sun.* ▷late 18th cent.: of unknown origin. —**snooz·er** /ˈsno͞ozər/ *n.* —**snooz·y** /ˈsno͞ozē/ *adj.* (**snooz·i·er, snooz·i·est**).

snooze but·ton ▶*n.* a control on a clock that sets an alarm to repeat after a short interval, allowing time for a little more sleep.

snore /snôr/ ▶*n.* a snorting or grunting sound in a person's breathing while asleep: *she lay on the mattress listening to Sally's snores.* ■ *informal* a thing that is extremely boring: *she sings a version of "Passionate Kisses" that's a certified snore.*
▶*v.* [*intrans.*] breathe with a snorting or grunting sound while asleep: *he was snoring loudly* | [as *n.*] (**snoring**) *you keep me awake all night with your snoring.* ▷Middle English (in the sense 'a snort, snorting'): probably imitative; compare with SNORT. —**snor·er** *n.*

snor·kel /ˈsnôrkəl/ ▶*n.* **1** a short curved tube for a swimmer to breathe through while keeping the face under water. **2** (**Snorkel**) *trademark* a type of hydraulically elevated platform for fire-fighting.
▶*v.* (**-keled, -kel·ing**; *Brit.* **-kelled, -kel·ling**) [*intrans.*] [often as *n.*] (**snorkeling**) swim using a snorkel: *the sea is incredibly clear, which is ideal for snorkeling* | *snorkel around the unspoiled coral reefs.* ▷1940s: from German *Schnorchel.* —**snor·kel·er** *n.*

snorkel 1

Snor·ri Stur·lu·son /ˈsnôrē ˈstərləsən/ (1178–1241), Icelandic historian and poet. A leading figure of medieval Icelandic literature, he wrote the *Younger Edda* or *Prose Edda* and the *Heimskringla*, a history of the kings of Norway from mythical times to 1177.

snort /snôrt/ ▶*n.* an explosive sound made by the sudden forcing of breath through a person's nose, used to express indignation, derision, or incredulity: *he gave a snort of disgust.* ■ a similar sound made by an animal, typically when excited or frightened. ■ *informal* an inhaled dose of an illegal powdered drug, esp. cocaine: *they were high on a few snorts.* ■ *informal* a measure of an alcoholic drink: *a bottle of rum was opened and they took a good long snort.*
▶*v.* [*intrans.*] make a sudden sound through one's nose, esp. to express indignation or derision: *she snorted with laughter* | [with *direct speech*] *"How perfectly ridiculous!" he snorted.* ■ (of an animal) make such a sound, esp. when excited or frightened. ■ [*trans.*] *informal* inhale (an illegal drug). ▷late Middle English (as a verb, also in the sense 'snore'): probably imitative; compare with SNORE. The noun dates from the early 19th cent.

snort·er /ˈsnôrtər/ ▶*n.* *informal* **1** a person or thing that snorts, esp. someone who inhales cocaine. **2** *Brit., dated* a thing that is an extreme or remarkable example of its kind, esp. for its strength or severity: *the opening batsman fended off a snorter.*

snot /snät/ ▶*n.* *informal* nasal mucus. ■ an arrogant or conceited person. ■ a contemptible or worthless person. ▷late Middle English: probably from Middle Dutch, Middle Low German; related to SNOUT.

snot-nosed ▶*adj.* *informal* childish and inexperienced (used as a general term of abuse): *a boy at thirteen is a* ***snot-nosed kid.*** ■ (of a person) considering oneself superior; conceited: *a snot-nosed snob.*

snot rag ▶*n.* *informal* a handkerchief.

snot·ter /ˈsnä tər/ ▶*n.* *Nautical* a fitting that holds the heel of a sprit close to the mast. ■ a length of rope with an eye spliced in each end. ▷mid 18th cent.: of unknown origin.

snot·ty /ˈsnätē/ ▶*adj.* (**-ti·er, -ti·est**) *informal* **1** full of or covered with nasal mucus: *a snotty nose.* **2** having or showing a superior or conceited attitude: *a snotty letter.* —**snot·ti·ly** /-təlē/ *adv.* —**snot·ti·ness** *n.*

snot·ty-nosed ▶*adj.* *informal* another term for SNOT-NOSED.

snout /snout/ ▶*n.* **1** the projecting nose and mouth of an animal, esp. a mammal. ■ *derogatory* a person's nose. ■ the projecting front or end of something such as a pistol. **2** *Brit., informal* a cigarette. ■ tobacco. [late 19th cent.: of unknown origin.] **3** *Brit., informal* a police informer. ▷Middle English: from Middle Dutch, Middle Low German *snūt*; related to SNOT. —**snout·ed** *adj.* [often in *combination*] *long-snouted baboons.* —**snout·y** *adj.*

snout bee·tle ▶*n.* another term for WEEVIL.

Snow /snō/, C. P., 1st Baron Snow of Leicester (1905–80), English novelist and scientist; full name *Charles Percy Snow.* He is best known for his sequence of 11 novels, starting with *Strangers and Brothers* (1940), that deals with moral dilemmas in the academic world and for his lecture *Two Cultures* (1959).

snow /snō/ ▶*n.* **1** atmospheric water vapor frozen into ice crystals and falling in light white flakes or lying on the ground as a white layer: *we were trudging through deep snow* | *the first snow of the season.* **2** something that resembles snow in color or texture, in particular: ■ a mass of flickering white spots on a television or radar screen, caused by interference or a poor signal. ■ *informal* cocaine. ■ a dessert or other dish resembling snow: *vanilla snow.* ■ [with *adj.*] a frozen gas resembling snow: *carbon dioxide snow.*
▶*v.* **1** [*intrans.*] (**it snows, it is snowing,** etc.) snow falls: *it's not snowing so heavily now.* ■ (**be snowed in**) be confined or blocked by a large quantity of snow: *I was snowed in for a week.* ■ [*trans.*] *figurative* used to describe the arrival of an overwhelming quantity of something: *in the last week it had snowed letters and business.* ■ [*trans.*] sprinkle or scatter (something), causing it to fall like snow: *the ceiling is snowing green flakes of paint onto the seats.* **2** [*trans.*] *informal* mislead or charm (someone) with elaborate and insincere words: *they would snow the public into believing that all was well.*
▶*phrasal v.* □ **snow someone under** (usu. **be snowed under**) overwhelm someone with a large quantity of something, esp. work: *he's been snowed under with urgent cases.* ▷Old English *snāw,* of Germanic origin; related to Dutch *sneeuw* and German *Schnee,* from an Indo-European root shared by Latin *niv-* and Greek *nipha.* —**snow·less** *adj.* —**snow·like** /-,līk/ *adj.*

snow·ball /ˈsnō,bôl/ ▶*n.* **1** a ball of packed snow, esp. one made for throwing at other people for fun. ■ *figurative* a thing that grows rapidly in intensity or importance: *the small speculator jumps in for a quick profit, adding his weight to the snowball, and the price goes up.* ■ a dessert resembling a ball of snow, esp. one containing or covered in ice cream. **2** a cocktail containing gin, anisette, and cream.
▶*v.* **1** [*trans.*] throw snowballs at: *I made sure the other kids stopped snowballing Celia.* **2** [*intrans.*] increase rapidly in size, intensity, or importance: *the campaign was snowballing.*
▶*PHRASE* □ **a snowball's chance (in hell)** *informal* no chance at all: *the plan has a snowball's chance in hell of being accepted.*

snow·ball bush (also **snow·ball tree**) ▶*n.* a guelder rose, esp. one of a sterile variety that produces large globular white flowerheads.

snow·bell /ˈsnō,bel/ ▶*n.* an Asian tree related to the storax, bearing clusters of fragrant white hanging flowers at midsummer, widely cultivated as an ornamental. • *Styrax japonica,* family Styracaceae.

snow·ber·ry /ˈsnō,berē/ ▶*n.* a North American shrub of the honeysuckle family, bearing white berries and often cultivated as an ornamental or for hedging. • *Symphoricarpos albus,* family Caprifoliaceae.

snow·bird /ˈsnō,bərd/ ▶*n.* **1** *informal* a northerner who moves to a warmer southern state in the winter. **2** a widespread and variable junco with gray or brown upper parts and a white belly. • *Junco hyemalis,* family Emberizidae (subfamily Emberizinae). Alternative names: **northern junco, dark-eyed junco, slate-colored junco.** ■ the snow bunting.

snow-blind ▶*adj.* temporarily blinded by the glare of light reflected by a large expanse of snow. —**snow blind·ness** *n.*

snow·blink /ˈsnō,blingk/ ▶*n.* a white reflection in the sky of snow or ice on the ground.

snow·blow·er /ˈsnō,blōwər/ ▶*n.* a machine that clears fallen snow by blowing it to the side.

snow·board /ˈsnō,bôrd/ ▶*n.* a board resembling a short, broad ski, used for sliding downhill on snow.
▶*v.* [*intrans.*] slide downhill on such a board: [as *n.*] (**snowboarding**) *the thrills of snowboarding.* —**snow·board·er** *n.*

snow boot ▶*n.* a warm waterproof boot worn in the snow.

snow·bound /ˈsnō,bound/ ▶*adj.* prevented from traveling or going out by snow or snowy weather: *he was snowbound in the nearby mountains.* ■ covered in snow or inaccessible because of it: *a snowbound Alpine village.*

snow bunt·ing ▶*n.* a northern bunting that breeds mainly in the Arctic, the male having white plumage with a black back in the breeding season. • *Plectrophenax nivalis,* family Emberizidae (subfamily Emberizinae).

snow·cap /ˈsnō,kap/ ▶*n.* **1** a covering of snow on the top of a mountain. **2** a small Central American hummingbird with mainly purple plumage and a white crown. • *Microchera albocoronata,* family Trochilidae. —**snow-capped** *adj.* (in sense 1).

snow·cat /ˈsnō,kat/ ▶*n.* another term for SNOWMOBILE. ▷1940s: from SNOW + CATERPILLAR.

snow chains ▶*plural n.* a pair or set of meshes of metal chain, fitted around a vehicle's tires to give extra traction in snow.

snow cone (also **sno-cone**) ▶*n.* a paper cup filled with fruit-flavored crushed ice.

snow crab ▶*n.* an edible spider crab found off the eastern seaboard of Canada. • *Chionoecetes opilio,* section Oxyrhyncha.

snow·drift /ˈsnō,drift/ ▶*n.* a bank of deep snow heaped up by the wind.

snow·drop /ˈsnō,dräp/ ▶*n.* a widely cultivated bulbous European plant that bears drooping white flowers during the late winter. • *Galanthus nivalis,* family Liliaceae (or Amaryllidaceae).

snow·fall /ˈsnō,fôl/ ▶*n.* a fall of snow: *heavy snowfalls made travel absolutely impossible.* ■ the quantity of snow falling within a given area in a given time: *winters with above-average snowfall.*

snow fence ▶*n.* a fence erected to prevent hazardous snowdrifts, typically by the side of a road.

snow·field /ˈsnō,fēld/ ▶*n.* a permanent wide expanse of snow in mountainous or polar regions.

snow·flake /ˈsnō,flāk/ ▶*n.* **1** a flake of snow, esp. a feathery ice crystal, typically displaying delicate

S

sixfold symmetry. **2** a white-flowered Eurasian plant related to and resembling the snowdrop, typically blooming in the summer or autumn. • Genus *Leucojum*, family Liliaceae (or Amaryllidaceae).

snow flea ▸*n.* either of two small insects that appear on or near snow in northern regions or on mountains: • a springtail that often swarms on snow, making it appear black (family Isotomidae, including the Alpine *Isotoma saltans* and the North American *Hypogastrura nivicola*). • a small flightless scorpionfly that feeds on mosses (family Boreidae, including the Eurasian *Boreus hyemalis*).

snow globe ▸*n.* a toy or ornament consisting of a model of a scene in a liquid containing white particles that, when shaken, mimic a snowstorm.

snow goose ▸*n.* a gregarious goose that breeds in Arctic Canada and Greenland, typically having white plumage with black wing tips. • *Anser caerulescens*, family Anatidae.

snow gun ▸*n.* a machine that makes artificial snow and blows it onto ski slopes.

snow job ▸*n. informal* a deception or concealment of one's real motive in an attempt to flatter or persuade: *we need to* ***do a snow job on*** *him.*

snow leop·ard ▸*n.* a rare large cat that has pale gray fur patterned with dark blotches and rings, living in the Altai mountains, Hindu Kush, and Himalayas. Also called OUNCE[2]. • *Panthera uncia*, family Felidae.

snow line ▸*n.* (usu. **the snow line**) the altitude above which some snow remains on the ground in a particular place throughout the year. ■ the altitude above which there is snow on the ground in a particular place at a given time.

snow ma·chine ▸*n.* another term for SNOWMOBILE.

snow·making /ˈsnō,mākiNG/ ▸*n.* [often as *adj.*] the production of artificial snow, esp. for ski slopes: *snowmaking machines.*

snow·man /ˈsnō,man/ ▸*n.* (*pl.* **-men**) a representation of a human figure created with compressed snow.

snow·melt /ˈsnō,melt/ ▸*n.* the melting of fallen snow: *heavy rains combine with rapid snowmelt.* ■ water that results from this: *the day was springlike and the snowmelt shone in blue and gold.*

snow·mo·bile /ˈsnōmō,bēl/ ▸*n.* a motor vehicle, esp. one with runners in the front and caterpillar tracks in the rear, for traveling over snow.
▸*v.* [*intrans.*] travel by snowmobile: [as *n.*] (**snowmobiling**) *the county offers snowmobiling, ice fishing, kayaking, and rafting.* —**snow·mo·bil·er** *n.*

snowmobile

snow·pack /ˈsnō,pak/ ▸*n.* a mass of snow on the ground that is compressed and hardened by its own weight.

snow pea ▸*n.* a pea of a variety with an edible pod, eaten when the pod is young and flat. Compare with SUGAR SNAP.

snow·plow /ˈsnō,plou/ (*Brit.* **snow·plough**) ▸*n.* **1** an implement or vehicle for clearing roads of snow by pushing it aside. **2** *Skiing* an act of turning the points of one's skis inward in order to slow down or turn.
▸*v.* [*intrans.*] ski with the tips of one's skis pointing inward in order to slow down or turn.

snow·scape /ˈsnō,skāp/ ▸*n.* a landscape covered in snow. ■ a picture of such a landscape.

snow·shoe /ˈsnō,SHo͞o/ ▸*n.* a flat device resembling a racket that is attached to the sole of a boot and used for walking on snow.
▸*v.* [*intrans.*] travel wearing snowshoes: *we snowshoed down into the next valley.* —**snow·sho·er** /-ər/ *n.* —**snow·shoe·ing** /-iNG/ *n.*

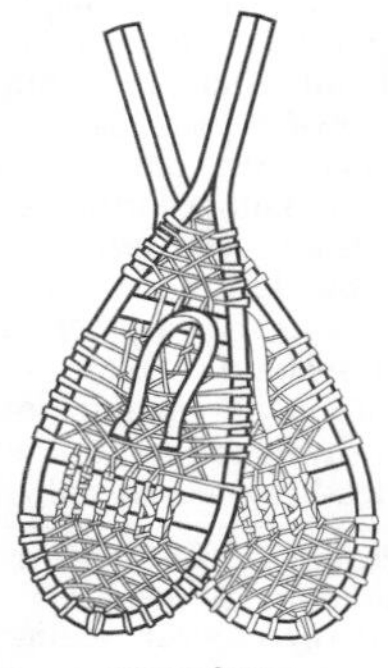

snowshoes

snow·shoe hare (also **snow·shoe rab·bit**) ▸*n.* a North American hare with large hairy hind feet, fairly small ears, and a white winter coat. • *Lepus americanus*, family Leporidae.

snow·storm /ˈsnō,stôrm/ ▸*n.* a heavy fall of snow, esp. with a high wind. ■ *figurative* a shower or large quantity of something: *it swam away in a flurry of wings and flippers, raising a snowstorm of foam.* ■ chiefly British term for SNOW GLOBE.

snow·suit /ˈsnō,so͞ot/ ▸*n.* a child's one- or two-piece coverall with a warm lining for protection against cold and often with a water-repellent outer material.

snow throw·er ▸*n.* another term for SNOWBLOWER.

snow tire ▸*n.* a tire with a tread that gives extra traction on snow or ice.

snow-white ▸*adj.* of a pure white color: *perfect spotless utensils on a snow-white tablecloth.*

snow·y /ˈsnōē/ ▸*adj.* (**snow·i·er**, **snow·i·est**) covered with snow: *snowy mountains.* ■ (of weather or a period of time) characterized by snowfall: *a snowy January day.* ■ of or like snow, esp. in being pure white: *snowy hair.* —**snow·i·ly** /ˈsnōəlē/ *adv.* —**snow·i·ness** *n.*

snow·y e·gret ▸*n.* a North American egret with all-white plumage, black legs, and yellow feet. • *Egretta thula*, family Ardeidae.

snow·y owl ▸*n.* a large northern owl that breeds mainly in the Arctic tundra, the male being entirely white and the female having darker markings. • *Nyctea scandiaca*, family Strigidae.

snow·y plov·er ▸*n.* a small white-breasted plover related to the ringed plover, found on most continents. • *Charadrius alexandrinus*, family Charadriidae.

SNP /snip/ ▸*abbr.* single nucleotide polymorphism.

Snr. ▸*abbr. chiefly Brit.* Senior: *John Hammond Snr.*

snub /snəb/ ▸*v.* (**snubbed**, **snub·bing**) [*trans.*] **1** rebuff, ignore, or spurn disdainfully: *he snubbed faculty members and students alike* | *he snubbed her request to wind up the debate.* **2** check the movement of (a horse or boat), esp. by a rope wound around a post: *a horse snubbed to a tree.*
▸*n.* an act of showing disdain or a lack of cordiality by rebuffing or ignoring someone or something: *he couldn't help thinking that the whole thing was meant to be taken as a snub.*
▸*adj.* (of a person's or animal's nose) short and turned up at the end: [in *combination*] *snub-nosed.* ▷Middle English (as a verb, originally in the sense 'rebuke with sharp words'): from Old Norse *snubba* 'chide, check the growth of.' The adjective dates from the early 18th cent.

snub·ber /ˈsnəbər/ ▸*n.* **1** a simple kind of shock absorber. **2** an electric circuit intended to suppress voltage spikes.

snuck /snək/ *informal* ▸ past and past participle of SNEAK.

snuff[1] /snəf/ ▸*v.* [*trans.*] extinguish (a candle): *a breeze* ***snuffed out*** *the candle.* ■ *informal* put an end to (something) in a brutal manner: *his life was snuffed out by a sniper's bullet.* ■ *informal* kill: *I lost track of the number of people he snuffed who were wearing bulletproof fabric.* ■ (**snuff it**) *Brit., informal* die. ■ *dated* trim the charred wick from (a candle).
▸*n.* the charred part of a candle wick. ▷late Middle English: of unknown origin.

snuff[2] ▸*n.* powdered tobacco that is sniffed up the nostril rather than smoked: *a pinch of snuff.*
▸*v.* [*trans.*] inhale or sniff at (something): *they stood* ***snuffing up*** *the keen cold air.* ■ [*intrans.*] *archaic* sniff up powdered tobacco. ▷late Middle English (as a verb): from Middle Dutch *snuffen* 'to snuffle.' The noun dates from the late 17th cent. and is probably an abbreviation of Dutch *snuftabak.*
▸*PHRASE* □ **up to snuff** *informal* **1** meeting the required standard: *they need a million dollars to get their facilities up to snuff.* ■ in good health: *he hadn't felt up to snuff all summer.* **2** *Brit., archaic* not easily deceived; knowing: *an up-to-snuff old vagabond.*

snuff·box /ˈsnəf,bäks/ ▸*n.* a small ornamental box for holding snuff.

snuff·er /ˈsnəfər/ (also **can·dle·snuff·er**) ▸*n.* a small hollow metal cone on the end of a handle, used to extinguish a candle by smothering the flame. ■ (usu. **snuffers** or **candlesnuffers**) an implement resembling scissors with an inverted metal cup attached to one blade, used to extinguish a candle or trim its wick.

snuff film (also **snuff movie**) ▸*n. informal* a pornographic movie of an actual murder.

snuf·fle /ˈsnəfəl/ ▸*v.* [*intrans.*] breathe noisily through the nose due to a cold or crying: *Alice was weeping quietly, snuffling a little.* ■ (esp. of an animal) make repeated sniffing sounds as though smelling at something: *the collie snuffled around his boots* | [as *n.*] (**snuffling**) *she heard a strange, persistent snuffling.*
▸*n.* a sniff or sniffing sound: *a silence broken only by the faint snuffles of the dogs.* ■ (usu. **the snuffles**) *informal* a cold or other infection that causes sniffing: *he went down with the snuffles.* ▷late 16th cent.: probably from Low German and Dutch *snuffelen*; compare with SNUFF[2] and SNIVEL. —**snuf·fler** *n.* —**snuf·fly** *adj.*

snuff·y[1] /ˈsnəfē/ ▸*adj.* (**snuff·i·er**, **snuff·i·est**) *archaic* supercilious or contemptuous: *some snuffy old stockbroker.* ■ easily offended; annoyed.

snuff·y[2] ▸*adj. archaic* resembling powdered tobacco in color or substance.

snug /snəg/ ▸*adj.* (**snug·ger**, **snug·gest**) **1** comfortable, warm, and cozy; well protected from the weather or cold: *she was safe and snug in Ruth's arms* | *a snug cottage.* ■ *archaic* (of an income or employment) allowing one to live in comfort and comparative ease. **2** (esp. of clothing) very tight or close-fitting: *a well-shaped hood for a snug fit.*
▸*n. Brit.* a small, comfortable public room in a pub or inn.
▸*v.* [*trans.*] place (something) safely or cozily: *she tucks him in, snugging the blanket up to his chin.* ■ [*intrans.*] settle comfortably and cozily: *the passengers snugged down among the cargo.* ▷late 16th cent. (originally in nautical use in the sense 'shipshape, compact, prepared for bad weather'): probably of Low German or Dutch origin. —**snug·ly** *adv.* —**snug·ness** *n.*
▸*PHRASE* □ **snug as a bug (in a rug)** *humorous* in an extremely comfortable position or situation.

snug·ger·y /ˈsnəgərē/ ▸*n.* (*pl.* **-ger·ies**) a cozy or comfortable place, esp. someone's private room or den. ■ *Brit., archaic* another term for SNUG.

snug·gle /ˈsnəgəl/ ▸*v.* settle or move into a warm, comfortable position: [*intrans.*] *I* ***snuggled down*** *in my sleeping bag* | [*trans.*] *she snuggled her head into his shoulder.* ▷late 17th cent.: frequentative of the verb SNUG.

so[1] /sō/ ▸*adv.* **1** [as *submodifier*] to such a great extent: *the words tumbled out* ***so*** *fast* ***that*** *I could barely hear them* | *don't look so worried* | *I'm not* ***so*** *foolish* ***as to*** *say that.* ■ extremely; very much (used for emphasis): *she looked so pretty* | *I do love it so.* ■ *informal* used to emphasize a clause or negative statement: *that's so not fair* | *you are so going to regret this.* ■ *informal* used with a gesture to indicate size: *the bird was about so long.* **2** [as *submodifier*] [with *negative*] to the same extent (used in comparisons): *he isn't* ***so*** *bad* ***as*** *you'd think* | *without his parents' support, he would not have done so well.* **3** referring back to something previously mentioned: ■ that is the case: *"Is it going to rain?" "I think so."* | *if she notices, she never says so.* ■ the truth: *I hear that you're a writer—is that so?* ■ similarly; and also: *times have changed and so have I.* ■ expressing agreement: *"It's cold in here." "So it is."* ■ *informal* used to emphatically contradict a negative statement: *it is so!* **4** in the way described or demonstrated; thus: *hold your arms so* | ***so it was that*** *he was still a bachelor.*
▸*conj.* **1** and for this reason; therefore: *it was still painful, so I went to see a specialist* | *you know I'm telling the truth, so don't interrupt.* ■ (**so that**) with the result that: *it was overgrown with brambles, so that I had difficulty making any progress.* **2** (**so that**) with the aim that; in order that: *they whisper to each other so that no one else can hear.* **3** and then; as the next step: *and so to the finals.* **4** introducing a question: *so, what did you do today?* ■ introducing a question following on from what was said previously: *so what did he do about it?* ■ (also **so what?**) *informal* why should that be considered significant?: *"Marv is wearing a suit." "So?"* | ***so what if*** *he failed?* **5** introducing a statement that is followed by a defensive comment: *so I like anchovies—what's wrong with that?* **6** introducing a concluding statement: *so that's that.* **7** in the same way; correspondingly: ***just as*** *bad money drives out good,* ***so*** *does bad art drive out the good.* ▷Old English *swā*, of Germanic origin; related to Dutch *zo* and German *so.*
▸*PHRASES* □ **and so on** (or **forth**) and similar things; et cetera: *these snacks include cheeses, cold meats, and so on.* □ **just so much** *chiefly derogatory* emphasizing a large amount of something: *it's just so much ideological cant.* □ **not so much —— as ——** not —— but rather ——: *the novel was not so much unfinished as unfinishable.* □ **only so much** a limited amount: *there is only so much you can do to protect yourself.* □ **or so** see OR[1]. □ **so as to do something** in order to do something: *she had put her hair up so as to look older.* □ **so be it** an expression of acceptance or resignation. □ **so far** see FAR. □ **so far, so good** see FAR. □ **so long!** *informal* goodbye until we meet again. □ **so long as** see LONG[1]. □ **so many** (or **much**) indicating a particular

but unspecified quantity: *so many hours at such-and-such a speed.* □ **so much as** [with *negative*] even: *he sat down without so much as a word to anyone.* □ **so much for 1** indicating that one has finished talking about something: *So much for the melodic line. We now turn our attention to the accompaniment.* **2** suggesting that something has not been successful or useful: *so much for that idea!* □ **so much so that** to such an extent that: *I was fascinated by the company, so much so that I wrote a book about it.* □ **so to speak** (or **say**) used to highlight the fact that one is describing something in an unusual or metaphorical way: *delving into the body's secrets, I looked death in the face, so to speak.*

so[2] ▸*n.* alternate spelling of **SOL**[1].

So. ▸*abbr.* South.

s.o. ▸*abbr.* ■ seller's option. ■ shipping order.

-so ▸*comb. form* equivalent to **-SOEVER**.

soak /sōk/ ▸*v.* [*trans.*] **1** make or allow (something) to become thoroughly wet by immersing it in liquid: *soak the beans overnight in water.* ■ [*intrans.*] be immersed in water or another liquid: *she spent some time soaking in a hot bath.* ■ (of a liquid) cause (something or someone) to become extremely wet: *the rain poured down, soaking their hair.* ■ [*intrans.*] (of a liquid) penetrate or permeate completely: *cold water was soaking into my shoes.* ■ (**soak something off/out**) remove something by immersing it in water for a period of time: *don't disturb the wound—soak the dressing off if necessary.* ■ (**soak oneself in**) immerse oneself in (a particular experience, activity, or interest): *he soaked himself in the music of Mozart.* **2** *informal* impose heavy charges or taxation on: *few of us common people care how much tax Congress soaks on racing motorboats.* **3** [*intrans.*] *archaic, informal* drink heavily: *you keep soaking in taverns.*
▸*phrasal v.* □ **soak something up** absorb a liquid: *use clean tissues to soak up any droplets of water.* ■ *figurative* expose oneself to or experience (something beneficial or enjoyable): *lie back and soak up the Mediterranean sun | he spends his time painting and soaking up the culture.* ■ *informal* cost or use up money: *the project had soaked up over $1 billion.*
▸*n.* **1** [in *sing.*] an act of immersing someone or something in liquid for a period of time: *I'm looking forward to a long soak in the tub.* **2** *informal* a heavy drinker: *his daughter stayed up to put the* **old soak** *to bed.* ▷Old English *socian* 'become saturated with a liquid by immersion'; related to *sūcan* 'to suck.' **—soak·age** /ˈsōkij/ *n.* **—soak·er** *n.*

soaked /sōkt/ ▸*adj.* extremely wet; saturated: *my shirt is soaked through | she was soaked to the skin |* [in *combination*] *figurative a sun-soaked beach.*

soak·ing /ˈsōkiNG/ ▸*adj.* extremely wet; wet through: *his jacket was soaking.*
▸*n.* an act of wetting something thoroughly: *in spring, give the soil a good soaking.*

so-and-so ▸*n.* (*pl.* **-sos**) a person or thing whose name the speaker does not need to specify or does not know or remember. ■ *informal* a person who is disliked or is considered to have a particular characteristic, typically an unfavorable one: *nosy old so-and-so!*

soap /sōp/ ▸*n.* **1** a substance used with water for washing and cleaning, made of a compound of natural oils or fats with sodium hydroxide or another strong alkali, and typically having perfume and coloring added: *a bar of soap.* **2** *informal* a soap opera: *the soaps are at the top of the ratings.*
▸*v.* [*trans.*] wash with soap: *she soaped her face.* ▷Old English *sāpe*; related to Dutch *zeep* and German *Seife*. The verb dates from the mid 16th cent. **—soap·less** *adj.*
▸*PHRASE* □ **no soap** *informal* used to convey that there is no chance of something happening or occurring: *They needed a writer with some enthusiasm. No soap.*

soap·ber·ry /ˈsōpˌberē/ ▸*n.* a tree or shrub with berries that produce a soapy froth when crushed, in particular: • a plant with saponin-rich berries that are used as a soap substitute (genus *Sapindus*, family Sapindaceae). • another term for **BUFFALO BERRY**. ■ the berry of any of these plants.

soap·box /ˈsōpˌbäks/ ▸*n.* a box or crate used as a makeshift stand by a public speaker: [as *adj.*] *a soapbox orator.* ■ *figurative* a thing that provides an opportunity for someone to air their views publicly: *fanzines are soapboxes for critical sports fans.* ■ *chiefly historical* a box or crate in which soap is packed and transported.

soap·box der·by (also **Soap Box Derby** *trademark*) ▸*n.* a race for children driving motorless, improvised vehicles made from crates and crudely resembling race cars.

soap bub·ble ▸*n.* an iridescent bubble consisting of air in a thin film of soapy water.

soap·fish /ˈsōpˌfisH/ ▸*n.* (*pl.* same or **-fish·es**) a stout-bodied fish of tropical seas that produces large amounts of toxic mucus from the skin, giving it a soapy feel when handled. • Family Grammistidae, several genera and species.

soap flakes ▸*plural n. dated* soap in the form of thin flakes, typically used for washing clothes.

soap op·er·a ▸*n.* a television or radio drama series dealing typically with daily events in the lives of the same group of characters. ▷1930s: so named because such serials were originally sponsored by soap manufacturers.

soap plant ▸*n.* a plant of the lily family with white flowers, found in dry habitats of California. The fiber-covered bulbs were used as soap by American Indians. • Genus *Chlorogalum*, family Liliaceae: two species, the wavy-leaved *C. pomeridianum* and the narrow-leaved *C. angustifolium*.

soap pow·der ▸*n.* detergent in the form of a powder, typically used for washing clothes.

soap·stone /ˈsōpˌstōn/ ▸*n.* a soft rock consisting largely of talc. Compare with **STEATITE**.

soap·suds /ˈsōpˌsədz/ ▸*plural n.* froth made from soap and water.

soap·wort /ˈsōpwərt; -ˌwôrt/ ▸*n.* a plant of the pink family, with fragrant pink or white flowers and leaves that were formerly used to make soap. • *Saponaria officinalis*, family Caryophyllaceae.

soap·y /ˈsōpē/ ▸*adj.* (**soap·i·er**, **soap·i·est**) **1** containing or covered with soap: *hot soapy water.* ■ of or like soap: *his hands smelled soapy.* ■ (of a person or behavior) unpleasantly flattering and ingratiating: *a soapy, worshipful look.* **2** *informal* characteristic of a soap opera: *soapy little turns of plot.* **—soap·i·ly** /-pəlē/ *adv.* **—soap·i·ness** *n.*

soar /sôr/ ▸*v.* [*intrans.*] fly or rise high in the air: *the bird spread its wings and soared into the air | figurative when she heard his voice, her spirits soared.* ■ maintain height in the air without flapping wings or using engine power: *the gulls soared on the summery winds.* ■ increase rapidly above the usual level: *the cost of living continued to soar |* [as *adj.*] (**soaring**) *the soaring crime rate.* ▷late Middle English: shortening of Old French *essorer*, based on Latin *ex-* 'out of' + *aura* 'breeze.' **—soar·er** *n.* **—soar·ing·ly** *adv.*

soar·a·way /ˈsôrəˌwā/ ▸*adj.* [*attrib.*] *Brit.* making or characterized by rapid or impressive progress: *a soaraway success.*

So·a·ve /ˈswävā/ ▸*n.* a dry white wine produced in the region of northern Italy around Soave.

SOB ▸*abbr.* son of a bitch.

sob /säb/ ▸*v.* (**sobbed**, **sob·bing**) [*intrans.*] cry noisily, making loud, convulsive gasps: *he broke down and sobbed like a child* [*trans.*] *he sobbed himself to sleep.* ■ [*trans.*] say while crying noisily: [with *direct speech*] *"I thought they'd killed you," he sobbed weakly.*
▸*n.* an act or sound of sobbing: *with a sob of despair she threw herself onto the bed.* ▷Middle English: perhaps of Dutch or Low German origin; compare with Dutch dialect *sabben* 'to suck.' **—sob·bing·ly** *adv.*

so·ba /ˈsōbə/ ▸*n.* Japanese noodles made from buckwheat flour. ▷Japanese.

so·ber /ˈsōbər/ ▸*adj.* (**-ber·er**, **-ber·est**) not affected by alcohol; not drunk. ■ serious, sensible, and solemn: *a sober view of life | his expression became sober.* ■ free from alcoholism; not habitually drinking alcohol: *I've been clean and sober for five years.* ■ muted in color: *a sober gray suit.*
▸*v.* make or become sober after drinking alcohol: [*trans.*] *that coffee* **sobered** *him* **up** | [*intrans.*] *I ought to* **sober up** *a bit.* ■ make or become more serious, sensible, and solemn: [*intrans.*] *his expression sobered her |* [as *adj.*] (**sobering**) *a sobering thought.* ▷Middle English: from Old French *sobre*, from Latin *sobrius*. **—so·ber·ing·ly** *adv.* **—so·ber·ly** *adv.*

so·ber·sides /ˈsōbərˌsīdz/ ▸*n. informal* a sedate and serious person. **—so·ber·sid·ed** /-ˈsīdid/ *adj.*

So·bies·ki /sôbˈyäskē/, John, see **JOHN III**.

so·bri·e·ty /səˈbrīətē; sō-/ ▸*n.* the state of being sober: *the price of beer compelled me to maintain a certain level of sobriety.* ■ the quality of being staid or solemn. ▷late Middle English: from Old French *sobriete* or Latin *sobrietas*, from *sobrius* (see **SOBER**).

so·bri·quet /ˈsōbriˌkā; -ˌket/ (also **sou·bri·quet** /ˈsōōbri-/) ▸*n.* a person's nickname. ▷mid 17th cent.: French, originally in the sense 'tap under the chin,' of unknown origin.

sob sis·ter ▸*n. informal* a female journalist who writes articles with sentimental appeal or answers readers' problems. ■ an overly sentimental woman.

sob sto·ry ▸*n. informal* a story or explanation intended to make someone feel sympathy for the person relating it.

soc /sōsH/ ▸*n. informal* (esp. among academics) sociology: [as *adj.*] *she's a soc major.*

Soc. ▸*abbr.* ■ Socialist. ■ Society.

so·ca /ˈsōkə/ ▸*n.* calypso music with elements of soul, originally from Trinidad. ▷1970s: blend of **SOUL** and **CALYPSO**.

soc·age /ˈsäkij/ (also **soc·cage**) ▸*n. historical* a feudal tenure of land involving payment of rent or other nonmilitary service to a superior. ▷Middle English: from Anglo-Norman French, from *soc*, variant of **SOKE**.

so-called ▸*adj.* [*attrib.*] used to show that something or someone is commonly designated by the name or term specified: *at the foundation of the Korean economy are the so-called chaebols or conglomerates.* ■ used to express one's view that such a name or term is inappropriate: *she could trust him more than any of her so-called friends.*

soc·cer /ˈsäkər/ ▸*n.* a game played by two teams of eleven players with a round ball that may not be touched with the hands or arms during play except by the goalkeepers. The object of the game is to score goals by kicking or heading the ball into the opponents' goal. ▷late 19th cent.: from a shortening of **ASSOCIATION FOOTBALL** + an extended use of **-ER**[1].

soc·cer mom ▸*n. informal* a middle-class suburban mother who is actively involved in her children's participation in soccer (and other sports) by providing transportation, attending games, etc.

So·chi /ˈsōCHē/ a port and resort in southwestern Russia, located in the western foothills of the Caucasus, on the Black Sea coast, close to the border with Georgia; pop. 339,000.

so·cia·ble /ˈsōsHəbəl/ ▸*adj.* willing to talk and engage in activities with other people; friendly: *being a sociable person, Eva loved entertaining.* ■ (of a place, occasion, or activity) marked by friendliness: *a very sociable little village.*
▸*n.* **1** *historical* an open carriage with facing side seats. **2** *dated* an informal social gathering: *a church sociable.* ▷mid 16th cent.: from French, or from Latin *sociabilis*, from *sociare* 'unite,' from *socius* 'companion.' **—so·cia·bil·i·ty** /ˌsōsHəˈbilitē/ *n.* **—so·cia·ble·ness** *n.* **—so·cia·bly** /-blē/ *adv.*

so·cial /ˈsōsHəl/ ▸*adj.* **1** [*attrib.*] of or relating to society or its organization: *alcoholism is recognized as a major social problem | a traditional Japanese social structure.* ■ of or relating to rank and status in society: *a recent analysis of social class in Britain | her mother is a lady of the highest social standing.* ■ needing companionship and therefore best suited to living in communities: *we are social beings as well as individuals.* ■ relating to or designed for activities in which people meet each other for pleasure: *Guy led a full social life.* **2** *Zoology* (of a bird) gregarious; breeding or nesting in colonies. ■ (of an insect) living together in organized communities, typically with different castes, as ants, bees, wasps, and termites do. ■ (of a mammal) living together in groups, typically in a hierarchical system with complex communication.
▸*n.* an informal social gathering, esp. one organized by the members of a particular club or group: *a church social.* ▷late Middle English: from Old French, or from Latin *socialis* 'allied,' from *socius* 'friend.' **—so·ci·al·i·ty** /ˌsōsHēˈalədē/ *n.* **—so·cial·ly** /ˈsōsHəlē/ *adv. families who are socially disadvantaged.*

so·cial an·thro·pol·o·gy ▸*n.* see **ANTHROPOLOGY**.

so·cial as·sis·tance ▸*n.* Canadian term for **SOCIAL SECURITY**.

so·cial ben·e·fit ▸*n.* a benefit payable under a social security system.

so·cial climb·er ▸*n. derogatory* a person who is eager to gain a higher social status. Also called **CLIMBER**. **—so·cial climb·ing** *n.*

so·cial con·science ▸*n.* a sense of responsibility or concern for the problems and injustices of society.

so·cial con·tract (also **social compact**) ▸*n.* an implicit agreement among the members of a society to cooperate for social benefits, for example by sacrificing some individual freedom for state protection. Theories of a social contract became popular in the

Pronunciation Key ə ago; ər over; ˈə or ˌə up; ˈər or ˌər fur; a hat; ā rate; ä car; CH chew; e let; ē see; e(ə)r air; i fit; ī by; i(ə)r ear; NG sing; ō go; ô for; oi boy; ŏŏ good; ōō goo; ou out; SH she; TH thin; TH then; (h)w why; ZH vision

16th, 17th, and 18th centuries among theorists such as Thomas Hobbes, John Locke, and Jean-Jacques Rousseau, as a means of explaining the origin of government and the obligations of subjects.

so·cial cred·it ▸*n.* the economic theory that consumer purchasing power should be increased either by subsidizing producers so that they can lower prices or by distributing the profits of industry to consumers.

so·cial Dar·win·ism ▸*n.* the theory that individuals, groups, and peoples are subject to the same Darwinian laws of natural selection as plants and animals. Now largely discredited, social Darwinism was advocated by Herbert Spencer and others in the late 19th and early 20th centuries and was used to justify political conservatism, imperialism, and racism and to discourage intervention and reform.

so·cial de·moc·ra·cy ▸*n.* a socialist system of government achieved by democratic means. **—so·cial dem·o·crat** *n.*

so·cial dis·ease ▸*n. informal* a venereal disease.

so·cial dis·tance ▸*n.* the perceived or desired degree of remoteness between a member of one social group and the members of another, as evidenced in the level of intimacy tolerated between them.

so·cial en·gi·neer·ing ▸*n.* the application of sociological principles to specific social problems. **—so·cial en·gi·neer** *n.*

so·cial fact ▸*n.* a thing originating in the institutions or culture of a society that affects the behavior or attitudes of an individual member of that society.

so·cial ge·og·ra·phy ▸*n.* the study of people and their environment with particular emphasis on social factors.

so·cial gos·pel ▸*n.* Christian faith practiced as a call not just to personal conversion but to social reform. **—so·cial gos·pel·er** *n.*

so·cial in·sur·ance ▸*n.* a system of compulsory contribution to provide government assistance in sickness, unemployment, etc.

so·cial·ism /ˈsōsHə,lizəm/ ▸*n.* a political and economic theory of social organization that advocates that the means of production, distribution, and exchange should be owned or regulated by the community as a whole. ■ policy or practice based on this theory. ■ (in Marxist theory) a transitional social state between the overthrow of capitalism and the realization of communism.

The term "socialism" has been used to describe positions as far apart as anarchism, Soviet state communism, and social democracy; however, it necessarily implies an opposition to the untrammeled workings of the economic market.The socialist parties that have arisen in most European countries from the late 19th century have generally tended toward social democracy.

▷early 19th cent.: from French *socialisme*, from *social* (see **SOCIAL**). **—so·cial·ist** *n.* & *adj.* **—so·cial·is·tic** /,sōsHəˈlistik/ *adj.* **—so·cial·is·ti·cal·ly** /,sōsHəˈlistik(ə)lē/ *adv.*

so·cial·ist re·al·ism ▸*n.* the theory of art, literature, and music officially sanctioned by the state in some communist countries (esp. in the Soviet Union under Stalin), by which artistic work was supposed to reflect and promote the ideals of a socialist society.

so·cial·ite /ˈsōsHə,līt/ ▸*n.* a person who is well known in fashionable society and is fond of social activities and entertainment.

so·cial·ize /ˈsōsHə,līz/ ▸*v.* **1** [*intrans.*] mix socially with others: *he didn't mind* ***socializing with*** *his staff.* **2** [*trans.*] make (someone) behave in a way that is acceptable to their society: *newcomers are* ***socialized into*** *orthodox ways* | [as *adj.*] (**socializing**) *a socializing effect.* **3** [*trans.*] organize according to the principles of socialism: [as *adj.*] (**socialized**) *socialized economies.* **—so·cial·i·za·tion** /,sōsHələˈzāsHən/ *n.* (in senses 2 and 3).

so·cial·ized med·i·cine ▸*n.* the provision of medical and hospital care for all by means of public funds.

so·cial lad·der (also **social scale**) ▸*n.* (usu. **the social ladder**) the hierarchical structure of society or of a society: *it would be a step up the social ladder for him when the marriage came off.*

so·cial mar·ket e·con·o·my (also **social market**) ▸*n.* an economic system based on a free market operated in conjunction with state provision for those unable to sell their labor, such as the elderly or unemployed.

so·cial proc·ess ▸*n.* the pattern of growth and change in a society over the years.

so·cial pro·mo·tion ▸*n.* the practice promoting a child to the next grade level regardless of skill mastery in the belief that it will promote self-esteem.

so·cial psy·chol·o·gy ▸*n.* the branch of psychology that deals with social interactions, including their origins and their effects on the individual. **—so·cial psy·chol·o·gist** *n.*

so·cial re·al·ism ▸*n.* the realistic depiction in art of contemporary life, as a means of social or political comment.

so·cial scale ▸*n.* another term for **SOCIAL LADDER**.

so·cial sci·ence ▸*n.* the scientific study of human society and social relationships. ■ a subject within this field, such as economics or politics. **—so·cial sci·en·tist** *n.*

so·cial sec·re·tar·y ▸*n.* a person who arranges the social activities of a person or organization.

so·cial se·cu·ri·ty ▸*n.* any government system that provides monetary assistance to people with an inadequate or no income. ■ (**Social Security**) (in the U.S.) a federal insurance program that provides benefits to retired persons, the unemployed, and the disabled.

So·cial Se·cur·i·ty num·ber (abbr.: **SSN**) ▸*n.* (in the U.S.) a number in the format 000-00-0000, unique for each individual, used to track Social Security benefits and for other identification purposes.

so·cial serv·ice ▸*n.* (**social services**) government services provided for the benefit of the community, such as education, medical care, and housing. ■ activity aiming to promote the welfare of others.

so·cial stud·ies ▸*plural n.* [treated as *sing.*] various aspects or branches of the study of human society, considered as an educational discipline.

so·cial u·nit ▸*n.* an individual, or a group or community, considered as a discrete constituent of a society or larger group.

so·cial work ▸*n.* work carried out by trained personnel with the aim of alleviating the conditions of those in need of help or welfare. **—so·cial work·er** *n.*

so·ci·e·tal /səˈsīitl/ ▸*adj.* of or relating to society or social relations: *societal change.* **—so·ci·e·tal·ly** *adv.*

so·ci·e·ty /səˈsīətē/ ▸*n.* (*pl.* **-ties**) **1** the aggregate of people living together in a more or less ordered community: *drugs, crime, and other dangers to society.* ■ the community of people living in a particular country or region and having shared customs, laws, and organizations: *the high incidence of violence in American society* | *modern industrial societies.* ■ [with *adj.*] a specified section of such a community: *no one in polite society uttered the word.* ■ (also **high society**) the aggregate of people who are fashionable, wealthy, and influential, regarded as forming a distinct group in a community: [as *adj.*] *a society wedding.* ■ a plant or animal community. **2** an organization or club formed for a particular purpose or activity: [in *names*] *the American Society for the Prevention of Cruelty to Animals.* **3** the situation of being in the company of other people: *she shunned the society of others.* ▷mid 16th cent. (in the sense 'companionship, friendly association with others'): from French *société*, from Latin *societas*, from *socius* 'companion.'

So·ci·e·ty Is·lands a group of islands in the South Pacific Ocean that form part of French Polynesia. ▷named in honor of the Royal Society by Captain Cook, who visited the islands in 1769.

So·ci·e·ty of Je·sus official name of the Jesuits (see **JESUIT**).

socio- ▸*comb. form* **1** relating to society; society and . . . : *socioeconomic.* **2** relating to sociology; sociology and . . . : *sociolinguistics.* ▷from Latin *socius* 'companion.'

so·ci·o·bi·ol·o·gy /,sōsēō,bīˈäləjē/ ▸*n.* the scientific study of the biological (esp. ecological and evolutionary) aspects of social behavior in animals and humans. **—so·ci·o·bi·o·log·i·cal** /-,bīəˈläjikəl/ *adj.* **—so·ci·o·bi·o·log·i·cal·ly** /-,bīəˈläjik(ə)lē/ *adv.* **—so·ci·o·bi·ol·o·gist** /-jist/ *n.*

so·ci·o·cul·tur·al /,sōsēōˈkəlcHərəl/ ▸*adj.* combining social and cultural factors. **—so·ci·o·cul·tur·al·ly** *adv.*

so·ci·o·e·col·o·gy /,sōsēō,ēˈkäləjē; -eˈkä-/ ▸*n.* the branch of science that deals with the interactions among the members of a species, and between them and the environment. **—so·ci·o·ec·o·log·i·cal** /-kəˈlsHjikəl/ *adj.* **—so·ci·o·e·col·o·gist** /-jist/ *n.*

so·ci·o·ec·o·nom·ic /,sōsēō,ēkəˈnämik; -ekə-/ ▸*adj.* relating to or concerned with the interaction of social and economic factors. **—so·ci·o·ec·o·nom·i·cal·ly** *adv.*

so·ci·o·ge·no·mics /,sōsēōjēˈnämiks; -ji-; -ˈnōmiks/ ▸*plural n.* [treated as *singular*] a scientific discipline that attempts to find the genetic basis of social behavior and its evolution.

so·ci·o·lect /ˈsōsēō,lekt/ ▸*n.* the dialect of a particular social class. ▷1970s: from **SOCIO-** + *-lect* as in **DIALECT**.

so·ci·o·lin·guis·tics /,sōsēōliNGˈgwistiks/ ▸*plural n.* [treated as *sing.*] the study of language in relation to social factors, including differences of regional, class, and occupational dialect, gender differences, and bilingualism. **—so·ci·o·lin·guist** /-ˈliNGgwist/ *n.* **—so·ci·o·lin·guis·tic** *adj.* **—so·ci·o·lin·guis·ti·cal·ly** /-ik(ə)lē/ *adv.*

so·ci·ol·o·gy /,sōsēˈäləjē/ ▸*n.* the study of the development, structure, and functioning of human society. ■ the study of social problems. ▷mid 19th cent.: from French *sociologie* (see **SOCIO-**, **-LOGY**). **—so·ci·o·log·i·cal** /,sōsēōˈläjikəl/ *adj.* **—so·ci·o·log·i·cal·ly** /,sōsēōˈläjik(ə)lē/ *adv.* **—so·ci·ol·o·gist** /-jist/ *n.*

so·ci·om·e·try /,sōsēˈämətrē/ ▸*n.* the quantitative study and measurement of relationships within a group of people. **—so·ci·o·met·ric** /,sōsēōˈmetrik/ *adj.* **—so·ci·o·met·ri·cal·ly** /,sōsēōˈmetrik(ə)lē/ *adv.* **—so·ci·om·e·trist** /-trist/ *n.*

so·ci·o·path /ˈsōsēō,paTH/ ▸*n.* a person with a personality disorder manifesting itself in extreme antisocial attitudes and behavior and a lack of conscience. **—so·ci·o·path·ic** /,sōsēōˈpaTHik/ *adj.* **—so·ci·op·a·thy** /,sōsēˈäpəTHē/ *n.*

so·ci·o·po·lit·i·cal /,sōsēōpəˈlitikəl/ ▸*adj.* combining social and political factors.

sock /säk/ ▸*n.* **1** a garment for the foot and lower part of the leg, typically knitted from wool, cotton, or nylon. ■ a removable inner sole placed inside a shoe or boot for added warmth or to improve the fit. ■ a white marking on the lower part of a horse's leg, not extending as far as the knee or hock. Compare with **STOCKING**. **2** *informal* a hard blow: *a sock on the jaw.* ■ force or emphasis: *we have enough speed and sock in our lineup to score runs.*

▸*v. informal* [*trans.*] hit forcefully: *Jess socked his father across the face.* ■ (often **be socked with**) affect disadvantageously: *consumers have been socked with huge price increases.*

▸*phrasal v.* □ **sock something away** put money aside as savings: *you'll need to sock away about $900 a month.* □ **sock something in** (or **sock in**) (of weather) envelop: *the beach was* ***socked in with*** *fog.* ▷Old English *socc* 'light shoe,' of Germanic origin, from Latin *soccus* 'comic actor's shoe, light low-heeled slipper,' from Greek *sukkhos.*

▸*PHRASES* □ **knock** (or **blow**) **someone's socks off** *informal* amaze or impress someone. □ **knock the socks off** *informal* surpass or beat: *it will knock the socks off the opposition.* □ **—— one's socks off** *informal* do something with great energy and enthusiasm: *she acted her socks off.* □ **put a sock in it** [usu. in *imperative*] *Brit., informal* stop talking. □ **sock and buskin** *archaic* the theatrical profession; drama. □ **sock it to someone** *informal* attack or make a forceful impression on someone.

sock·et /ˈsäkit/ ▸*n.* **1** a natural or artificial hollow into which something fits or in which something revolves: *the eye socket.* ■ the part of the head of a golf club into which the shaft is fitted. **2** an electrical device receiving a plug or light bulb to make a connection.

▸*v.* (**-et·ed, -et·ing**) [*trans.*] **1** place in or fit with a socket. **2** *Golf* old-fashioned term for **SHANK**. ▷Middle English (in the sense 'head of a spear, resembling a plowshare'): from an Anglo-Norman French diminutive of Old French *soc* 'plowshare,' probably of Celtic origin.

sock·et set ▸*n.* a number of detachable sockets of different sizes for use with a socket wrench.

sock·et wrench ▸*n.* a ratchet tool with a series of detachable sockets for tightening and loosening nuts of different sizes.

sock·eye /ˈsäk,ī/ (also **sock·eye sal·mon**) ▸*n.* a commercially valuable salmon of the North Pacific and rivers draining into it. Also called **RED SALMON**. • *Oncorhynchus nerka*, family Salmonidae. See also **KOKANEE**. ▷late 19th cent.: by folk etymology from Salish *sukai*, literally 'fish of fishes.'

sock hop ▸*n. dated* a dance for young teenagers at which they may dance in stocking feet.

sock·ing /ˈsäkiNG/ ▸*adv.* [as *submodifier*] *Brit., informal* used for emphasis: *a brooch with a* ***socking great*** *diamond in the middle.*

sock·o /ˈsäkō/ ▸*adj. informal* stunningly effective or successful: *a sellout, socko performance.* ▷1920s: from **SOCK** in the sense 'forceful blow' + **-O**.

so·cle /ˈsäkəl/ ▸*n. Architecture* a plain low block or plinth serving as a support for a column, urn, statue, etc., or as the foundation of a wall. ▷early 18th cent.: from French, from Italian *zoccolo*, literally 'wooden shoe,' from Latin *socculus*, from *soccus* (see **SOCK**).

Soc·ra·tes /ˈsäkrəˌtēz/ (469–399 BC), ancient Athenian philosopher. As represented in the writings of his disciple Plato, he engaged in dialogue with others in an attempt to reach understanding and ethical concepts by exposing and dispelling error (the **Socratic method**). Charged with introducing strange gods and corrupting the young, he committed suicide as required.

So·crat·ic /səˈkratik/ ▸*adj.* of or relating to Socrates or his philosophy.
▸*n.* a follower of Socrates. **—So·crat·i·cal·ly** /-ik(ə)lē/ *adv.*

So·crat·ic e·len·chus /səˈkratik iˈlengkəs/ ▸*n.* see **ELENCHUS**.

So·crat·ic i·ro·ny ▸*n.* a pose of ignorance assumed in order to entice others into making statements that can then be challenged.

sod[1] /säd/ ▸*n.* **(the sod)** the surface of the ground, with the grass growing on it. ■ a piece of this, usually sold in rolls and used to start a new lawn, athletic field, etc.
▸*v.* **(sod·ded, sod·ding)** [*trans.*] cover with sod or pieces of turf: *the stadium has been sodded.* ▷late Middle English: from Middle Dutch, Middle Low German *sode*, of unknown ultimate origin.
▸*PHRASES* □ **the old sod** one's native country. □ **under the sod** dead and buried in a grave.

sod[2] *chiefly Brit., vulgar slang* ▸*n.* an unpleasant or obnoxious person. ■ [with *adj.*] a person of a specified kind. ■ something that is difficult or causes problems.
▸*v.* **(sod·ded, sod·ding)** [*trans.*] used to express one's anger or annoyance at someone or something. ■ [*intrans.*] **(sod off)** [in *imperative*] go away. ■ [as *adj.*] **(sodding)** used as a general term of contempt. ▷early 19th cent.: abbreviation of **SODOMITE**.
▸*PHRASE* □ **sod all** absolutely nothing.

so·da /ˈsōdə/ ▸*n.* **1** (also **soda water** or **club soda**) carbonated water (originally made with sodium bicarbonate) drunk alone or with liquor or wine: *a whiskey and soda.* ■ (also **soda pop**) a carbonated soft drink: *a can of soda.* **2** sodium carbonate, esp. as a natural mineral or as an industrial chemical. ■ sodium in chemical combination: *nitrate of soda.* ▷late Middle English (in sense 2): from medieval Latin, from Arabic *suwwad* 'saltwort.'

so·da ash ▸*n.* commercially manufactured anhydrous sodium carbonate.

so·da bread ▸*n.* bread leavened with baking soda.

so·da crack·er ▸*n.* a thin, crisp cracker leavened with baking soda.

so·da foun·tain ▸*n.* a device that dispenses soda water or soft drinks. ■ a shop or counter selling drinks from such a device.

so·da jerk (also **so·da jerk·er**) ▸*n. informal, dated* a person who serves and sells soft drinks and ice cream at a soda fountain.

so·da lake ▸*n.* a salt lake with a high content of sodium salts.

so·da lime ▸*n.* a mixture of calcium oxide and sodium hydroxide.

so·da·lite /ˈsōdlˌīt/ ▸*n.* a blue mineral consisting mainly of an aluminosilicate and chloride of sodium, occurring chiefly in alkaline igneous rocks. ▷early 19th cent.: from **SODA** + **-LITE**.

so·dal·i·ty /sōˈdalitē/ ▸*n.* (*pl.* **-ties**) a confraternity or association, esp. a Roman Catholic religious guild or brotherhood. ■ fraternity; friendship. ▷early 17th cent.: from French *sodalité* or Latin *sodalitas*, from *sodalis* 'comrade.'

so·da pop ▸*n. n.* see **SODA** (sense 1).

so·da wa·ter ▸*n.* see **SODA** (sense 1).

sod·bust·er /ˈsädˌbəstər/ ▸*n. informal* a farmer or farm worker who plows the land.

sod·den /ˈsädn/ ▸*adj.* saturated with liquid, esp. water; soaked through: *his clothes were sodden.* ■ [in *combination*] having drunk an excessive amount of a particular alcoholic drink: *a whiskey-sodden criminal.*
▸*v.* [*trans.*] *archaic* saturate (something) with water. ▷Middle English (in the sense 'boiled, cooked by boiling'): archaic past participle of **SEETHE**. **—sod·den·ly** *adv.* **—sod·den·ness** *n.*

Sod·dy /ˈsädē/, Frederick (1877–1956), English physicist. He assisted William Ramsay in the discovery of helium, formulated a theory of isotopes, and coined the word *isotope* in 1913 after working on radioactive decay. Nobel Prize for Chemistry (1921).

so·dger /ˈsōjər/ ▸*n.* nonstandard spelling of **SOLDIER**, used to represent regional pronunciation.

so·dic /ˈsōdik/ ▸*adj.* of or containing sodium.■ *Mineralogy* (of mineral, rock, or soil) containing a higher proportion of sodium than usual.

so·di·um /ˈsōdēəm/ ▸*n.* the chemical element of atomic number 11, a soft silver-white reactive metal of the alkali metal group. (Symbol: **Na**) ▷early 19th cent.: from **SODA** + **-IUM**.

so·di·um am·y·tal ▸*n.* see **AMYTAL**.

so·di·um bi·car·bon·ate ▸*n.* a soluble white powder used in fire extinguishers and effervescent drinks and as a leavening agent in baking. Also called **BAKING SODA**. • Chem. formula: $NaHCO_3$.

so·di·um car·bon·ate ▸*n.* a white alkaline compound with many commercial applications including the manufacture of soap and glass. Also called **WASHING SODA**. • Chem. formula: Na_2CO_3.

so·di·um chlo·ride ▸*n.* a colorless crystalline compound occurring naturally in seawater and halite; common salt. • Chem. formula: NaCl.

so·di·um cy·a·nide ▸*n.* a white odorless crystalline soluble compound that has, when damp, an odor of hydrogen cyanide. It is used for extracting gold and silver from their ores and for case-hardening steel. • Chem. formula: NaCN.

so·di·um hy·drox·ide ▸*n.* a strongly alkaline white deliquescent compound used in many industrial processes, e.g., the manufacture of soap and paper. • Chem. formula: NaOH.

so·di·um ni·trate ▸*n.* a white powdery compound used mainly in the manufacture of fertilizers. • Chem. formula: $NaNO_3$.

so·di·um thi·o·sul·phate /ˌTHīōˈsəlfāt/ ▸*n.* a white soluble compound used in photography as a fixer to dissolve unchanged silver halides. Also called **HYPO**[1]. • Chem. formula: $Na_2S_2O_3$.

so·di·um-va·por lamp (also **so·di·um lamp**) ▸*n.* a lamp in which an electrical discharge in sodium vapor gives a yellow light, typically used in street lighting.

Sod·om /ˈsädəm/ a town in ancient Palestine, probably south of the Dead Sea. According to Gen. 19:24 it was destroyed by fire from heaven, together with Gomorrah, for the wickedness of its inhabitants. ■ [as *n.*] **(a Sodom)** a wicked or depraved place.

sod·om·ite /ˈsädəˌmīt/ ▸*n.* a person who engages in sodomy. ▷Middle English (in the sense 'sodomy'): via Old French from late Latin *Sodomita*, from Greek *Sodomitēs* 'inhabitant of Sodom.' **—sod·o·mit·ic** /ˌsädəˈmitik/ *adj.* **—sod·o·mit·i·cal** /ˌsädəˈmitikəl/ *adj.*

sod·om·y /ˈsädəmē/ ▸*n.* sexual intercourse involving anal or oral copulation. ▷Middle English: from medieval Latin *sodomia*, from late Latin *peccatum Sodomiticum* 'sin of Sodom' (after Gen. 19:5, which implies that the men of Sodom practiced homosexual rape) (see **SODOM**). **—sod·om·ize** /ˈsädəˌmīz/ *v.*

Sod's Law /sädz/ another name for **MURPHY'S LAW**.

SOE ▸*abbr.* Special Operations Executive.

so·ev·er /sōˈevər/ ▸*adv. archaic* or *poetic/literary* of any kind; to any extent: *how great soever the assurance is.*

-soever ▸*comb. form* of any kind; to any extent: *whatsoever | whosoever.* ▷Middle English: originally as the phrase *so ever.*

so·fa /ˈsōfə/ ▸*n.* a long upholstered seat with a back and arms, for two or more people. ▷early 17th cent.: from French, based on Arabic *ṣuffa.*

so·fa bed ▸*n.* a sofa that can be converted into a bed, typically for occasional use.

SOFAR /ˈsōfär/ (also **sofar**) ▸*n.* a system in which the sound waves from an underwater explosion are detected and located by three or more listening stations, useful in determining the position at sea of survivors of a disaster. ▷1940s: from *So(und) f(ixing) a(nd) r(anging).*

sof·fit /ˈsäfit/ ▸*n.* the underside of an architectural structure, such as an arch, a balcony, or overhanging eaves. ▷early 17th cent.: from French *soffite* or Italian *soffitto*, based on Latin *suffixus* 'fastened below.'

So·fi·a /sōˈfēə; ˈsōfēə/ the capital of Bulgaria, in the western part of the country; pop. 1,221,000.

so·fri·to /sōˈfrētō/ ▸*n.* a Caribbean and Latin American sauce of tomatoes, onions, peppers, garlic, and herbs. ▷American Spanish, from past participle of Spanish *sofreír* 'to fry.'

S. of S. ▸*abbr. Bible* Song of Songs (or Song of Solomon).

S. of Sol. ▸*abbr. Bible* Song of Solomon.

soft /sôft/ ▸*adj.* **1** easy to mold, cut, compress, or fold; not hard or firm to the touch: *soft margarine | the ground was soft beneath their feet.* ■ having a smooth surface or texture that is pleasant to touch; not rough or coarse: *soft crushed velvet | her hair felt very soft.* ■ rounded; not angular: *the soft edges of their adobe home.* **2** having a pleasing quality involving a subtle effect or contrast rather than sharp definition: *the soft glow of the lamps | the moon's pale light cast soft shadows.* ■ (of a voice or sound) quiet and gentle: *they spoke in soft whispers.* ■ (of rain, wind, or other natural force) not strong or violent: *a soft breeze rustled the trees.* ■ (of a consonant) pronounced as a fricative (as *c* in *ice*). ■ (of a market, currency, or commodity) falling or likely to fall in value. **3** sympathetic, lenient, or compassionate, esp. to a degree perceived as excessive; not strict or sufficiently strict: *the administration is not becoming* ***soft on*** *crime | Julia's soft heart was touched by his grief.* ■ (of words or language) not harsh or angry; conciliatory; soothing: *he was no good with soft words, gentle phrases.* ■ not strong or robust: *soft, out-of-shape executives in a computer company.* ■ *informal* (of a job or way of life) requiring little effort. ■ (of news or other journalism) regarded more as entertainment than as basic news: *fashion is regarded as soft news.* ■ willing to compromise in political matters; moderate: *candidates ranging from far right to soft left.* ■ *informal* foolish; silly: *he must be going soft in the head.* ■ [*predic.*] **(soft on)** *informal* infatuated with: *was Brendan soft on her?* ■ *chiefly Brit.* willing to compromise in political matters; moderate: *candidates ranging from far right to soft left.* **4** (of a drink) not alcoholic: *all they had was ginger ale and a few other soft drinks.* ■ (of a drug) not likely to cause addiction. ■ (of water) free from mineral salts that make lathering difficult. ■ (of radiation) having little penetrating power. ■ (of a detergent) biodegradable. ■ (also **soft-core**) (of pornography) suggestive or erotic but not explicit.
▸*adv.* softly: *I can just speak soft and she'll hear me.* ■ in a weak or foolish way: *don't talk soft.* ▷Old English *sōfte* 'agreeable, calm, gentle'; related to Dutch *zacht* and German *sanft.* **—soft·ish** *adj.* **—soft·ness** *n.*
▸*PHRASES* □ **have a soft spot for** be fond of or affectionate toward. □ **soft option** an easier alternative: *probation should in no sense be seen as a soft option by the judiciary.* □ **soft touch** (also **easy touch**) *informal* a person who readily gives or does something if asked.

sof·ta /ˈsôftə/ ▸*n.* a Muslim student of sacred law and theology. ▷Turkish, from Persian *sūḵta* 'burned, on fire.'

soft·ball /ˈsôf(t)ˌbôl/ ▸*n.* a modified form of baseball played on a smaller field with a larger ball, seven rather than nine innings, and underarm pitching. The game evolved in the U.S. during the late 19th century from a form of indoor baseball. ■ the ball used in this game.

soft-boiled ▸*adj.* (of an egg) boiled for a short time, leaving the yolk soft or liquid. ■ *figurative* gentle or sentimental: *she's perfected the soft-boiled New York type she's played in most of her movies.*

soft chan·cre /ˈSHangkər/ ▸*n.* another term for **CHANCROID**.

soft clam ▸*n.* another term for **SOFT-SHELL CLAM**.

soft coal ▸*n.* bituminous coal.

soft cop·y ▸*n. Computing* a legible version of a piece of data that is not printed on a physical medium, esp. as stored or displayed on a computer.

soft cor·al ▸*n.* see **CORAL** (sense 2).

soft-core ▸*adj.* another term for **SOFT** (sense 4).

soft·cov·er /ˈsôf(t)ˌkəvər/ ▸*adj.* & *n.* another term for **PAPERBACK**.

soft crab ▸*n.* another term for **SOFT-SHELL CRAB**.

soft drink ▸*n.* a nonalcoholic drink, esp. one that is carbonated.

soft·en /ˈsôfən/ ▸*v.* make or become less hard: [*trans.*] *plant extracts to soften and moisturize the skin* | [*intrans.*] *let the vegetables soften over a low heat.* ■ make or become less severe: [*intrans.*] *her expression softened at the sight of Diane's white face.* ■ [*trans.*] undermine the resistance of (someone): *the blockade appears a better weapon with which to* ***soften*** *them* ***up*** *for eventual surrender.* ■ [*trans.*] remove mineral salts from (water).

soft·en·er /ˈsôf(ə)nər/ ▸*n.* a substance or device that softens something, esp. a fabric softener.

Pronunciation Key ə ago; ər over; ˈə or ˌə up; ˈər or ˌər fur; a hat; ā rate; ä car; CH chew; e let; ē see; e(ə)r air; i fit; ī by; i(ə)r ear; NG sing; ō go; ô for; oi boy; o͝o good; o͞o goo; ou out; SH she; TH thin; T͟H then; (h)w why; ZH vision

soft·en·ing of the brain ▸*n. informal* or *archaic* mental deterioration, esp. senile dementia, supposedly resulting from degeneration of the brain tissue.

soft fo·cus ▸*n.* deliberate slight blurring or lack of definition in a photograph or movie.
▸*adj.* (**soft-focus**) characterized by or producing such a lack of definition. ■ denoting a point of view or style of presentation that obscures or avoids sharp definition in order to be more widely acceptable: *soft-focus, nonpolitical essays about American life.*

soft fruit ▸*n. Brit.* a small stoneless fruit, such as a strawberry or a black currant.

soft goods ▸*plural n.* textiles.

soft-head·ed (also **soft·head·ed**) ▸*adj.* lacking wisdom or intelligence. —**soft-head·ed·ness** *n.*

soft-heart·ed /ˈsôftˈhärtid/ ▸*adj.* kind and compassionate. —**soft-heart·ed·ness** *n.*

soft hy·phen ▸*n.* a hyphen inserted into a word in word processing, to be displayed or typeset only if it falls at the end of a line of text.

soft·ie /ˈsôftē/ (also **soft·y**) ▸*n.* (*pl.* **soft·ies**) *informal* a softhearted, weak, or sentimental person.

soft i·ron ▸*n.* iron that has a low carbon content and is easily magnetized and demagnetized, used to make the cores of solenoids and other electrical equipment.

soft land·ing ▸*n.* a controlled landing of a spacecraft during which no serious damage is incurred. —**soft-land** *v.*

soft line ▸*n.* a flexible and moderate attitude or policy: *the chancellor is taking a soft line on inflation.*

soft loan ▸*n.* a loan, typically one to a developing country, made on terms very favorable to the borrower.

soft·ly /ˈsôf(t)lē/ ▸*adv.* in a quiet voice or manner: *"Can't you sleep?" she asked softly | the door opened softly.* ■ with a gentle or slow movement: *he touched her cheek softly.* ■ in a pleasantly subdued manner: *the room was softly lit by a lamp.*

soft mon·ey ▸*n.* a contribution to a political party that is not accounted as going to a particular candidate, thus avoiding various legal limitations.

soft-nosed ▸*adj.* (of a bullet) expanding on impact.

soft pal·ate /ˈpalit/ ▸*n.* the fleshy, flexible part toward the back of the roof of the mouth.

soft-paste ▸*adj.* denoting artificial porcelain, typically made with white clay and ground glass and fired at a comparatively low temperature.

soft ped·al ▸*n.* a pedal on a piano that can be pressed to make the tone softer. See also **UNA CORDA**.
▸*v.* (**soft-ped·al**) [*trans.*] *Music* play with the soft pedal down. ■ refrain from emphasizing the more unpleasant aspects of; play down: *the administration's decision to soft-pedal the missile program.*

soft rock ▸*n.* rock music with a less persistent beat and more emphasis on lyrics and melody than hard rock has.

soft roe ▸*n.* see **ROE**[1].

soft rot ▸*n.* any of a number of bacterial and fungal diseases of fruit and vegetables in which the tissue becomes soft and slimy. ■ any of a number of fungal conditions affecting timber, which becomes soft and friable.

soft sell ▸*n.* [in *sing.*] subtly persuasive selling.
▸*v.* (**soft-sell**) [*trans.*] sell (something) by using such a method.

soft-shell clam (also **soft·shell clam**) ▸*n.* a marine bivalve mollusk with a thin shell and a long siphon, valued as food on the east coast of North America. Also called **SOFT CLAM, STEAMER.** • Genus *Mya*, family Myidae, esp. *M. arenaria*.

soft-shell crab (also **soft·shell crab**) ▸*n.* a crab, esp. a blue crab, that has recently molted and has a new shell that is still soft and edible. Also called **SOFT CRAB.**

soft-shelled tur·tle (also **soft-shell tur·tle**) ▸*n.* a freshwater turtle with a flattened leathery shell, native to Asia, Africa, and North America. • Family Trionychidae: several genera and many species, including the **spiny soft-shelled turtle** (*Apalone* (or *Trionyx*) *spinifera*) of North America.

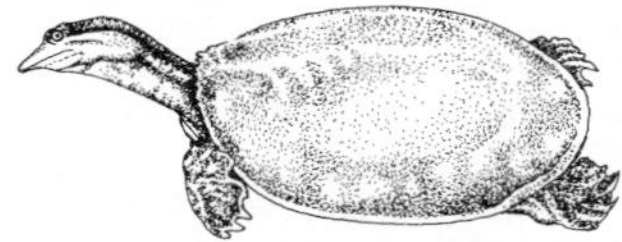

spiny soft-shelled turtle

soft-shoe ▸*n.* a kind of tap dance performed in soft-soled shoes: *he could dance a jig or a soft-shoe* | [as *adj.*] *a soft-shoe shuffle.*
▸*v.* [*intrans.*] perform a dance of this kind. ■ [*intrans.*] move quietly and carefully so as not to draw attention to oneself: *I soft-shoed after him* | *figurative he soft-shoed into a safer topic of conversation.*

soft shoul·der ▸*n.* an unpaved strip of land at the side of a road.

soft soap ▸*n.* **1** a semifluid soap, esp. one made with potassium rather than sodium salts. **2** *informal* persuasive flattery.
▸*v.* (**soft-soap**) [*trans.*] *informal* use flattery in order to persuade or cajole (someone) to do something.

soft-spo·ken ▸*adj.* speaking or said with a gentle, quiet voice.

soft tar·get ▸*n.* a person or thing that is relatively unprotected or vulnerable, esp. to military or terrorist attack.

soft-top ▸*n.* another term for **CONVERTIBLE** (sense 1). ■ (**soft top**) the roof of a convertible.

soft·ware /ˈsôftˌwe(ə)r/ ▸*n.* the programs and other operating information used by a computer. Compare with **HARDWARE.**

soft wheat ▸*n.* wheat of a variety having a soft grain rich in starch.

soft·wood /ˈsôftˌwo͝od/ ▸*n.* **1** the wood from a conifer (such as pine, fir, or spruce) as distinguished from that of broad-leaved trees. ■ a tree producing such wood. **2** (in gardening) young pliable growth on shrubs and other plants from which cuttings can be taken.

soft·y ▸*n.* variant spelling of **SOFTIE.**

SOG ▸*abbr.* Special Operations Group.

sog·gy /ˈsägē/ ▸*adj.* (**-gi·er**, **-gi·est**) wet and soft: *the sandbags were soggy and split open* | *figurative the chorus sings powerfully but the interpretation is ultimately soggy.* ▷early 18th cent. (in the sense 'boggy'): from dialect *sog* 'a swamp' + **-Y**[1]. —**sog·gi·ly** /ˈsägəlē/ *adv.* —**sog·gi·ness** *n.*

Sogne Fiord /ˈsôngnə/ a fiord on the western coast of Norway. The longest and deepest fiord in the country, it extends inland for about 125 miles (200 km), with a maximum depth of 4,291 feet (1,308 m). Norwegian name **SOGNAFJORDEN** .

so·go sho·sha /ˈsōgō ˈshōshə/ ▸*n.* (*pl.* same) a very large Japanese company that trades internationally in a wide range of goods and services. ▷Japanese, from *sōgō* 'comprehensive' + *shōsha* 'mercantile society.'

So·gwa·li /səˈgwälē/ see **SEQUOYA.**

SOHO /ˈsōˌhō/ ▸*adj.* relating to a market for relatively inexpensive consumer electronics used by individuals and small companies. ▷1990s: acronym from *small office home office.*

So·Ho /ˈsōˌhō/ a district in southern Manhattan in New York City, known for its artist-occupied industrial lofts and galleries. Its name is derived from South of Houston Street.

soi-di·sant /ˌswä dēˈzän(t)/ ▸*adj.* self-styled; so-called: *a soi-disant novelist.* ▷French, from *soi* 'oneself' + *disant* 'saying.'

soi·gné /swänˈyā/ ▸*adj.* (*fem.* **-gnée** *pronunc.* same) dressed very elegantly; well groomed: *she was dark, petite, and soignée.* ▷past participle of French *soigner* 'take care of,' from *soin* 'care.'

soil[1] /soil/ ▸*n.* the upper layer of earth in which plants grow, a black or dark brown material typically consisting of a mixture of organic remains, clay, and rock particles: *blueberries need very acid soil* | *figurative the Garden State has provided fertile soil for the specialty beer market.* ■ the territory of a particular nation: *the stationing of U.S. troops on Japanese soil.* ▷late Middle English: from Anglo-Norman French, perhaps representing Latin *solium* 'seat,' by association with *solum* 'ground.' —**soil·less** *adj.*

soil[2] ▸*v.* [*trans.*] make dirty: *he might soil his expensive suit* | [as *adj.*] (**soiled**) *a soiled T-shirt.* ■ (esp. of a child, patient, or pet) make (something) dirty by defecating in or on it. ■ *figurative* bring discredit to; tarnish: *what good is there in soiling your daughter's reputation?*
▸*n.* waste matter, esp. sewage containing excrement. See also **NIGHT SOIL.** ■ *archaic* a stain or discoloring mark. ▷Middle English (as a verb): from Old French *soiller*, based on Latin *sucula*, diminutive of *sus* 'pig.' The earliest use of the noun (late Middle English) was 'muddy wallow for wild boar'; current noun senses date from the early 16th cent.

soil[3] ▸*v.* [*trans.*] *rare* feed (cattle) on fresh-cut green fodder (originally for the purpose of purging them). ▷early 17th cent.: perhaps from **SOIL**[2].

soil me·chan·ics ▸*plural n.* [usu. treated as *sing.*] the branch of science concerned with the properties and behavior of soil as they affect its use in civil engineering.

soil pipe ▸*n.* a sewage or waste water pipe.

soil sci·ence ▸*n.* the branch of science concerned with the formation, nature, ecology, and classification of soils.

soil stack ▸*n.* the pipe that takes all the waste water from the upstairs plumbing system of a building.

soi·rée /swäˈrā/ ▸*n.* an evening party or gathering, typically in a private house, for conversation or music. ▷French, from *soir* 'evening.'

soi·xante-neuf /ˌswäsän(t) ˈnəf; -zän(t)-/ ▸*n.* another term for **SIXTY-NINE.** ▷French, literally 'sixty-nine,' from the position of the couple.

so·journ /ˈsōjərn/ *formal* ▸*n.* a temporary stay: *her sojourn in Rome.*
▸*v.* [*intrans.*] stay somewhere temporarily: *she had sojourned once in Egypt.* ▷Middle English: from Old French *sojourner*, based on Latin *sub-* 'under' + late Latin *diurnum* 'day.' —**so·journ·er** *n.*

So·ka Gak·kai /ˌsōkə ˈgäkī/ a political and lay religious organization founded in Japan in 1930, based on the teachings of the Nichiren Buddhist sect. ▷Japanese, from *sō* 'create' + *ka* 'value' + *gakkai* '(learned) society.'

so·kai·ya /ˌsōˈkīyə/ ▸*n.* (*pl.* same) a holder of shares in a Japanese company who tries to extort money from it by threatening to cause trouble for executives at a general meeting of the shareholders. ▷Japanese, from *sōkai* 'general meeting' + *-ya* 'dealer.'

soke /sōk/ ▸*n. Brit., historical* a right of local jurisdiction. ■ a district under a particular jurisdiction; a minor administrative district. ▷late Old English, back-formation from obsolete *soken* 'habitual visiting of a place.'

So·kol /ˈsäkäl/ ▸*n.* a Slavic gymnastic society aiming to promote a communal spirit and physical fitness, originating in Prague in 1862. ▷Czech, literally 'falcon' (the emblem of the society).

SOL ▸*abbr. vulgar slang* shit out of luck.

Sol /säl; sōl/ *Roman Mythology* the sun, esp. when personified as a god. ▷Latin.

sol[1] /sōl/ (also **so**) ▸*n. Music* (in solmization) the fifth note of a major scale. ■ the note G in the fixed-do system. ▷Middle English *sol*: representing (as an arbitrary name for the note) the first syllable of *solve*, taken from a Latin hymn (see **SOLMIZATION**).

sol[2] /säl; sôl/ ▸*n. Chemistry* a fluid suspension of a colloidal solid in a liquid. ▷late 19th cent.: abbreviation of **SOLUTION.**

sol[3] /sōl; sôl/ (also **nue·vo sol** /ˈnwāvō/) ▸*n.* (*pl.* **so·les** /ˈsōlāz; ˈsôles/) the basic monetary unit of Peru, equal to 100 centavos. It replaced the inti in 1991. ▷Spanish, literally 'sun.'

sol. ▸*abbr.* ■ soluble. ■ solution.

-sol ▸*comb. form* in nouns denoting different kinds and states of soil: *histosol* | *vertisol.* ▷from Latin *solum* 'soil.'

so·la[1] /ˈsōlə/ ▸*n.* an Indian swamp plant of the pea family, with stems that yield the pith that is used to make sola topis. • *Aeschynomene indica*, family Leguminosae. ▷mid 19th cent.: from Bengali *solā*, Hindi *śolā*.

so·la[2] ▸*n.* feminine form of **SOLUS.**

sol·ace /ˈsälis/ ▸*n.* comfort or consolation in a time of distress or sadness: *she sought solace in her religion.*
▸*v.* [*trans.*] give solace to. ▷Middle English: from Old French *solas* (noun), *solacier* (verb), based on Latin *solari* 'to console.'

so·lan /ˈsōlən/ (also **so·lan goose**) ▸*n.* the northern gannet. See **GANNET** (sense 1). ▷late Middle English: probably from Old Norse *súla* 'gannet' + *and-* 'duck.'

sol·a·na·ceous /ˌsäləˈnāshəs/ ▸*adj. Botany* of, relating to, or denoting plants of the nightshade family (Solanaceae). ▷early 19th cent.: from modern Latin *Solanaceae* (plural), based on Latin *solanum* 'nightshade,' + **-OUS.**

so·lan·der /səˈlandər/ (also **so·lan·der box**) ▸*n.* a protective box made in the form of a book, for holding such items as botanical specimens, maps, and color plates. ▷late 18th cent.: named after Daniel C. *Solander* (1736–82), Swedish botanist.

so·la·nine /ˈsōləˌnēn; -nin/ ▸*n. Chemistry* a poisonous compound that is present in green potatoes and in related plants. It is a steroid glycoside of the saponin group. ▷mid 19th cent.: from French, from the genus name *Solanum* + **-INE**[4].

so·la·num /sōˈlānəm/ ▸*n.* a plant of a genus that

includes the potato and woody nightshade. • Genus *Solanum*, family Solanaceae. ▷Latin.

so·lar[1] /ˈsōlər/ ▸*adj.* of, relating to, or determined by the sun: *solar radiation.* ■ relating to or denoting energy derived from the sun's rays: *solar heating.* ▷late Middle English: from Latin *solaris*, from *sol* 'sun.'

so·lar[2] ▸*n. Brit.* an upper chamber in a medieval house. ▷Middle English: from Anglo-Norman French *soler*, from Latin *solarium* 'gallery, terrace.'

so·lar bat·ter·y (also **so·lar cell**) ▸*n.* a device converting solar radiation into electricity.

so·lar con·stant ▸*n. Physics* the rate at which energy reaches the earth's surface from the sun, usually taken to be 1,388 watts per square meter.

so·lar day ▸*n.* the time between successive meridian transits of the sun at a particular place.

so·lar e·clipse ▸*n.* an eclipse in which the sun is obscured by the moon.

so·lar en·er·gy ▸*n.* radiant energy emitted by the sun. ■ another term for SOLAR POWER.

so·lar flare ▸*n. Astronomy* a brief eruption of intense high-energy radiation from the sun's surface, associated with sunspots and causing electromagnetic disturbances on the earth, as with radio frequency communications and power line transmissions.

so·lar·i·um /səˈle(ə)rēəm; sō-/ ▸*n.* (*pl.* **-lar·i·ums** or **-lar·i·a** /-ˈle(ə)rēə/) a room fitted with extensive areas of glass to admit sunlight. ■ a room equipped with sunlamps or tanning beds that can be used to acquire an artificial suntan. ▷mid 19th cent.: from Latin, literally 'sundial, place for sunning oneself,' from *sol* 'sun.'

so·lar·ize /ˈsōləˌrīz/ ▸*v.* [*trans.*] *Photography* change the relative darkness of (a part of an image) by overexposure to light. —**so·lar·i·za·tion** /ˌsōləriˈzāsʜən/ *n.*

so·lar mass ▸*n. Astronomy* the mass of the sun used as a unit of mass, equal to 1.989×10^{30} kg.

so·lar myth ▸*n.* a myth ascribing the sun's course or attributes to a particular god or hero.

so·lar neu·tri·no u·nit /n(y)o͞oˈtrēnō/ (abbr.: **SNU**) ▸*n. Astronomy* a unit used in expressing the detected flux of neutrinos from the sun, equal to 10^{-36} neutrino captures per target atom per second.

so·lar pan·el ▸*n.* a panel designed to absorb the sun's rays as a source of energy for generating electricity or heating.

so·lar plex·us /ˈpleksəs/ ▸*n.* a complex of ganglia and radiating nerves of the sympathetic system at the pit of the stomach. ■ the area of the body near the base of the sternum: *she felt as if someone had punched her in the solar plexus.*

so·lar pond ▸*n.* a pool of very salty water in which convection is inhibited, allowing accumulation of energy from solar radiation in the lower layers.

so·lar pow·er ▸*n.* power obtained by harnessing the energy of the sun's rays.

so·lar sys·tem ▸*n. Astronomy* the collection of nine planets and their moons in orbit around the sun, together with smaller bodies in the form of asteroids, meteoroids, and comets.

so·lar wind ▸*n.* the continuous flow of charged particles from the sun that permeates the solar system.

so·lar year ▸*n.* see YEAR (sense 1).

SOLAS /ˈsōləs/ ▸*n.* [usu. as *adj.*] the provisions made during a series of international conventions governing maritime safety. ▷1960s: acronym from *safety of life at sea.*

so·la·ti·um /səˈlāsʜēəm/ ▸*n.* (*pl.* **-ti·a** /-sʜēə/) *informal* a thing given to someone as a compensation or consolation: *a suitable solatium in the form of an apology was offered to him.* ▷early 19th cent.: from Latin, literally 'solace.'

so·la to·pi /ˈsōlə ˈtōpē/ ▸*n.* (*pl.* **so·la to·pis**) an Indian sun hat made from the pith of the stems of sola plants.

sold /sōld/ ▸ past and past participle of SELL.

sol·der /ˈsädər/ ▸*n.* a low-melting alloy, esp. one based on lead and tin or (for higher temperatures) on brass or silver, used for joining less fusible metals.

▸*v.* [*trans.*] join with solder. ▷Middle English: from Old French *soudure*, from the verb *souder*, from Latin *solidare* 'fasten together,' from *solidus* 'solid.' —**sol·der·a·ble** *adj.* —**sol·der·er** *n.*

sol·der·ing i·ron ▸*n.* a tool used for melting solder and applying it to metals that are to be joined.

sol·di /ˈsäldē/ ▸ plural form of SOLDO.

sol·dier /ˈsōljər/ ▸*n.* **1** a person who serves in an army. ■ (also **common soldier** or **private soldier**) a private in an army. **2** *Entomology* a wingless caste of ant or termite with a large specially modified head and jaws, involved chiefly in defense. **3** *Brit., informal* a strip of bread or toast, used for dipping into a soft-boiled egg. ■ [usu. as *adj.*] an upright brick, timber, or other building element.

▸*v.* [*intrans.*] serve as a soldier: [as *n.*] (**soldiering**) *soldiering was what the colonel understood.* ■ (**soldier on**) *informal* carry on doggedly; persevere: *Gary wasn't enjoying this, but he soldiered on.* ■ *informal* work more slowly than one's capacity; loaf or malinger: *is it the reason you've been soldiering on the job?* ▷Middle English: from Old French *soldier*, from *soulde* '(soldier's) pay,' from Latin *solidus* (see SOLIDUS). The verb dates from the early 17th cent. —**sol·dier·ly** *adj.* —**sol·dier·ship** /-ˌsʜip/ *n.* (*archaic*).

sol·dier bee·tle ▸*n.* an elongated flying beetle with soft downy wing cases, typically found on flowers where it hunts other insects. • Family Cantharidae: several genera.

sol·dier·fish /ˈsōljərˌfisʜ/ ▸*n.* (*pl.* same or **-fish·es**) a squirrelfish that is typically bright red in color. • Several genera and species in the family Holocentridae.

sol·dier fly ▸*n.* a bright metallic fly with a flattened body, frequently basking in the sun with its wings folded flat over the body. • Family Stratiomyidae: many genera.

sol·dier of for·tune ▸*n.* a person who works as a soldier for any country or group that will pay them; a mercenary.

sol·dier·y /ˈsōljərē/ ▸*n.* (*pl.* **-dier·ies**) soldiers collectively: *the town was filled with disbanded soldiery.* ■ military training or knowledge: *the arts of soldiery.*

sol·do /ˈsäldō/ ▸*n.* (*pl.* **sol·di** /ˈsäldē/) a former Italian coin and monetary unit worth the twentieth part of a lira. ▷Italian, from Latin *solidus* (see SOLIDUS).

sole[1] /sōl/ ▸*n.* the undersurface of a person's foot: *the soles of their feet were nearly black with dirt.* ■ the section forming the underside of a piece of footwear (typically excluding the heel when this forms a distinct part). ■ the part of the undersurface of a person's foot between the toes and the instep. ■ the undersurface of a tool or implement such as a plane or the head of a golf club. ■ the floor of a ship's cabin or cockpit.

▸*v.* [*trans.*] (usu. **be soled**) put a new sole onto (a shoe). ▷Middle English: from Old French, from Latin *solea* 'sandal, sill,' from *solum* 'bottom, pavement, sole'; compare with Dutch *zool* and German *Sohle.* —**soled** *adj.* [in *combination*] *rubber-soled shoes.*

sole[2] ▸*n.* a marine flatfish of almost worldwide distribution, important as a food fish. • Several species in the families Soleidae, Pleuronectidae, and Bothidae. See DOVER SOLE, LEMON SOLE. ▷Middle English: from Old French, from Provençal *sola*, from Latin *solea* (see SOLE[1]), named from its shape.

sole[3] ▸*adj.* [*attrib.*] one and only: *my sole aim was to contribute to the national team.* ■ belonging or restricted to one person or group of people: *loans can be in sole or joint names | the health club is for the sole use of our guests.* ■ *archaic* (esp. of a woman) unmarried. ■ *archaic* alone; unaccompanied. ▷late Middle English (also in the senses 'secluded' and 'unrivaled'): from Old French *soule*, from Latin *sola*, feminine of *solus* 'alone.'

sol·e·cism /ˈsäləˌsizəm; ˈsō-/ ▸*n.* a grammatical mistake in speech or writing. ■ a breach of good manners; a piece of incorrect behavior. ▷mid 16th cent.: from French *solécisme*, or via Latin from Greek *soloikismos*, from *soloikos* 'speaking incorrectly.' —**sol·e·cis·tic** /ˌsäləˈsistik; ˌsō-/ *adj.*

So·le·dad /ˈsōliˌdad/ a city in the Salinas Valley of west central California, home to a well-known state prison; pop. 7,146.

sole·ly /ˈsō(l)lē/ ▸*adv.* not involving anyone or anything else; only: *he is solely responsible for any debts the company may incur | people are appointed solely on the basis of merit.*

sol·emn /ˈsäləm/ ▸*adj.* formal and dignified: *a solemn procession.* ■ not cheerful or smiling; serious: *Tim looked very solemn.* ■ characterized by deep sincerity: *he swore a solemn oath to keep faith.* ▷Middle English (in the sense 'associated with religious rites'): from Old French *solemne*, from Latin *sollemnis* 'customary, celebrated at a fixed date,' from *sollus* 'entire.' —**sol·emn·ly** *adv.* —**sol·emn·ness** *n.*

so·lem·ni·ty /səˈlemnitē/ ▸*n.* (*pl.* **-ties**) the state or quality of being serious and dignified: *his ashes were laid to rest with great solemnity.* ■ (usu. **solemnities**) a formal, dignified rite or ceremony: *the ritual of the church was observed in all its solemnities.* ▷Middle English (in the sense 'observance of formality and ceremony,' frequently in the phrases *in solemnity*, *with solemnity*): from Old French *solemnite*, from Latin *sollemnitas*, from *sollemnis* (see SOLEMN).

sol·em·nize /ˈsäləmˌnīz/ ▸*v.* [*trans.*] duly perform (a ceremony, esp. that of marriage). ■ mark with a formal ceremony. ▷late Middle English: from Old French *solemniser*, from medieval Latin *solemnizare*, from Latin *sollemnis* (see SOLEMN). —**sol·em·ni·za·tion** /ˌsäləmniˈzāsʜən/ *n.*

Sol·emn League and Cov·e·nant an agreement made in 1643 between the English Parliament and the Scottish Covenanters during the English Civil War, by which the Scots would provide military aid in return for the establishment of a Presbyterian system in England, Scotland, and Ireland. Although the Scottish support proved crucial in the Parliamentary victory, the principal Presbyterian leaders were expelled from Parliament in 1647 and the covenant was never honored.

Sol·emn Mass ▸*n.* another term for HIGH MASS.

so·le·no·don /səˈlēnəˌdän; -ˈlenə-/ ▸*n.* a forest-dwelling mammal with a long flexible snout and a stiff muscular tail, occurring only in Cuba and Hispaniola. • Family Solenodontidae and genus *Solenodon*: two species. ▷modern Latin, from Greek *sōlēn* 'channel, pipe' + *odō* (variant of *odous, odont-*) 'tooth.'

so·le·noid /ˈsōləˌnoid/ ▸*n.* a cylindrical coil of wire acting as a magnet when carrying electric current. ▷early 19th cent.: from French *solénoïde*, from Greek *sōlēn* 'channel, pipe.' —**so·le·noi·dal** /ˌsōləˈnoidl/ *adj.*

So·lent /ˈsōlənt/ (**the Solent**) a channel between the northwestern coast of the Isle of Wight and the mainland of southern England.

sole·plate /ˈsōlˌplāt/ ▸*n.* **1** a metal plate forming the base of an electric iron, machine saw, or other machine. **2** a horizontal timber at the base of a wall frame.

so·le·ra /səˈle(ə)rə/ ▸*n.* (also **so·le·ra sys·tem**) a Spanish method of producing wine, esp. sherry and Madeira, whereby small amounts of younger wines stored in an upper tier of casks are systematically blended with the more mature wine in the casks below. ■ (also **so·le·ra wine**) a blend of sherry or Malaga wine produced by the solera system. ■ a wine cask, typically one with a capacity of four hogsheads, on the bottom tier of the solera system and containing the oldest wine. ▷Spanish, literally 'crossbeam, stone base.'

S

So·leure /sôˈlœr/ French name for SOLOTHURN.

so·le·us /ˈsōlēəs/ (also **so·le·us mus·cle**) ▸*n. Anatomy* a broad muscle in the lower calf, below the gastrocnemius, that flexes the foot to point the toes downward. ▷late 17th cent.: modern Latin, from Latin *solea* 'sole.'

sol-fa /ˌsōl ˈfä/ ▸*n.* short for TONIC SOL-FA.

▸*v.* (**-fas, -faed** /-ˈfäd/, **-fa·ing**) [*trans.*] sing using the sol-fa syllables.

sol·fa·ta·ra /ˌsälfəˈtärə; ˌsōl-/ ▸*n. Geology* a volcanic crater emitting only sulfurous and other gases. ▷late 18th cent.: from the name of a volcano near Naples, from Italian *solfo* 'sulfur.'

sol·fège /sälˈfezʜ/ ▸*n. Music* **1** solmization. ■ an exercise in singing using solmization syllables. **2** the study of singing and musicianship using solmization syllables. ▷early 20th cent.: French, from Italian *solfeggio.*

sol·feg·gio /sälˈfejēˌō/ ▸*n.* (*pl.* **-gi** /-jē/) another term for SOLFÈGE, esp. sense 1. ▷late 18th cent.: Italian.

so·li /ˈsōlē/ ▸ plural form of SOLO.

so·lic·it /səˈlisit/ ▸*v.* (**-it·ed, -it·ing**) [*trans.*] ask for or try to obtain (something) from someone: *he called a meeting to solicit their views.* See note at BEG. ■ ask (someone) for something: *historians and critics are solicited for opinions by the auction houses.* ■ [*intrans.*] accost someone and offer one's or someone else's services as a prostitute: [as *n.*] (**soliciting**) *although prostitution was not itself an offense, soliciting was.* ▷late Middle English: from Old French *solliciter*, from Latin *sollicitare* 'agitate,' from *sollicitus* 'anxious,' from *sollus* 'entire' + *citus* (past participle of *ciere* 'set in motion'). —**so·lic·i·ta·tion** /səˌlisəˈtāsʜən/ *n.*

so·lic·i·tor /səˈlisitər/ ▸*n.* **1** a person who tries to obtain business orders, advertising, etc.; a canvasser. **2** the chief law officer of a city, town, or government department. ■ *Brit.* a member of the legal profession qualified to deal with conveyancing, the drawing up of wills, and other legal matters. ▷late

Middle English (denoting an agent or deputy): from Old French *solliciteur*, from *solliciter* (see SOLICIT).

so·lic·i·tor gen·er·al ▶*n.* (*pl.* **so·lic·i·tors gen·er·al**) the law officer directly below the attorney general in the U.S. Department of Justice, responsible for arguing cases before the U.S. Supreme Court. ■ a similar position in some U.S. states.

so·lic·i·tous /sə'lisitəs/ ▶*adj.* characterized by or showing interest or concern: *she was always solicitous about the welfare of her students | a solicitous inquiry.* ■ *archaic* eager or anxious to do something: *he was solicitous to cultivate her mamma's good opinion.* ▷mid 16th cent.: from Latin *sollicitus* (see SOLICIT) + -OUS. —**so·lic·i·tous·ly** *adv.* —**so·lic·i·tous·ness** *n.*

so·lic·i·tude /sə'lisi,t(y)o͞od/ ▶*n.* care or concern for someone or something: *I was touched by his solicitude.* ▷late Middle English: from Old French *sollicitude*, from Latin *sollicitudo*, from *sollicitus* (see SOLICITOUS).

sol·id /'sälid/ ▶*adj.* (**-id·er**, **-id·est**) **1** firm and stable in shape; not liquid or fluid: *the stream was frozen solid | solid fuels.* ■ strongly built or made of strong materials; not flimsy or slender: *a solid door with good, secure locks.* ■ having three dimensions: *a solid figure with six plane faces.* ■ [*attrib.*] concerned with objects having three dimensions: *solid geometry.* **2** not hollow or containing spaces or gaps: *a sculpture made out of solid rock | a solid mass of flowers | the stores were packed solid.* ■ consisting of the same substance throughout: *solid silver cutlery.* ■ (of typesetting) without extra space between the lines of characters. ■ (of a line or surface) without spaces; unbroken: *the solid outline encloses the area within which we measured.* ■ (of time) uninterrupted; continuous: *a solid day of meetings | [postpositive] it poured for two hours solid.* **3** dependable; reliable: *the defense is solid | there is solid evidence of lower inflation.* ■ sound but without any special qualities or flair: *the rest of the acting is solid.* ■ unanimous or undivided: *they received solid support from their teammates.* ■ financially sound: *the company is very solid and will come through the current recession.* ■ [*predic.*] (**solid with**) *informal* on good terms with: *he thought he could put himself* **in solid with** *you by criticizing her.*
▶*n.* a substance or object that is solid rather than liquid or fluid. ■ (**solids**) food that is not liquid: *she drinks only milk and rarely eats solids.* ■ *Geometry* a body or geometric figure having three dimensions. ▷late Middle English: from Latin *solidus*; related to *salvus* 'safe' and *sollus* 'entire.' —**sol·id·ly** *adv.* —**sol·id·ness** *n.*

sol·i·da·go /,sälə'dāgō/ ▶*n.* (*pl.* **-gos**) a plant of the genus *Solidago* in the daisy family, esp. (in gardening) goldenrod. ▷modern Latin, from a medieval Latin alteration of late Latin *consolida* 'comfrey.'

sol·id an·gle ▶*n.* a three-dimensional analog of an angle, such as that subtended by a cone or formed by planes meeting at a point. It is measured in steradians.

sol·i·dar·i·ty /,sälə'de(ə)ritē/ ▶*n.* **1** unity or agreement of feeling or action, esp. among individuals with a common interest; mutual support within a group: *factory workers voiced solidarity with the striking students.* **2** (**Solidarity**) an independent trade union movement in Poland that developed into a mass campaign for political change and inspired popular opposition to communist regimes across eastern Europe during the 1980s. [translating Polish *Solidarność*.] ▷mid 19th cent.: from French *solidarité*, from *solidaire* 'solidary.'

sol·i·dar·y /'sälə,derē/ ▶*adj.* (of a group or community) characterized by solidarity or coincidence of interests. ▷early 19th cent.: from French *solidaire*, from *solide* 'solid.'

sol·id-bod·y ▶*adj.* denoting or relating to an electric guitar without a sound box, the strings being mounted on a solid shaped block forming the guitar body.

sol·id-drawn ▶*adj.* (of a tube) pressed or drawn out from a solid bar of metal.

sol·i·di /'säli,dī/ ▶ plural form of SOLIDUS.

so·lid·i·fy /sə'lidə,fī/ ▶*v.* (**-fies**, **-fied**) make or become hard or solid: [*intrans.*] *the magma slowly solidifies and forms crystals.* ■ [*trans.*] *figurative* make stronger; reinforce: *social and political pressures helped to solidify national identities.* —**so·lid·i·fi·ca·tion** /sə,lidəfi'kāshən/ *n.* —**so·lid·i·fi·er** /-,fīər/ *n.*

so·lid·i·ty /sə'liditē/ ▶*n.* the quality or state of being firm or strong in structure: *the sheer strength and solidity of Romanesque architecture.* ■ the quality of being substantial or reliable in character: *he exuded an aura of reassuring solidity.*

sol·id so·lu·tion ▶*n.* *Chemistry* a solid mixture containing a minor component uniformly distributed within the crystal lattice of the major component.

sol·id South ▶*n.* (**the solid South**) *chiefly historical* the politically united southern states of America, traditionally regarded as giving unanimous electoral support to the Democratic Party.

sol·id state ▶*n.* the state of matter in which materials are not fluid but retain their boundaries without support, the atoms or molecules occupying fixed positions with respect to one another and unable to move freely.
▶*adj.* (**sol·id-state**) (of a device) making use of the electronic properties of solid semiconductors (as opposed to electron tubes).

sol·i·dus /'sälidəs/ ▶*n.* (*pl.* **-di** /-,dī/) **1** another term for SLASH[1] (sense 2). **2** (also **sol·i·dus curve**) *Chemistry* a curve in a graph of the temperature and composition of a mixture, below which the substance is entirely solid. **3** *historical* a gold coin of the later Roman Empire. [from Latin *solidus (nummus)*.] ▷Latin, literally 'solid.'

so·li·fluc·tion /,sälə'fləkshən; ,sō-/ ▶*n.* *Geology* the gradual movement of wet soil or other material down a slope, esp. where frozen subsoil acts as a barrier to the percolation of water. ▷early 20th cent.: from Latin *solum* 'soil' + *fluctio(n-)* 'flowing,' from the verb *fluere.*

so·lil·o·quy /sə'liləkwē/ ▶*n.* (*pl.* **-quies**) an act of speaking one's thoughts aloud when by oneself or regardless of any hearers, esp. by a character in a play. ■ a part of a play involving such an act. ▷Middle English: from late Latin *soliloquium*, from Latin *solus* 'alone' + *loqui* 'speak.' —**so·lil·o·quist** /-kwist/ *n.* —**so·lil·o·quize** /-,kwīz/ *v.*

sol·ip·sism /'sälip,sizəm/ ▶*n.* the view or theory that the self is all that can be known to exist. ▷late 19th cent.: from Latin *solus* 'alone' + *ipse* 'self' + -ISM. —**sol·ip·sist** *n.* —**sol·ip·sis·tic** /,sälip'sistik/ *adj.* —**sol·ip·sis·ti·cal·ly** /,sälip'sistik(ə)lē/ *adv.*

sol·i·taire /'sälə,te(ə)r/ ▶*n.* **1** any of various card games played by one person, the object of which is to use up all one's cards by forming particular arrangements and sequences. **2** a diamond or other gem set in a piece of jewelry by itself. ■ a ring set with such a gem. **3** either of two large extinct flightless birds related to the dodo, found on two of the Mascarene Islands until they were exterminated in the 18th century. • Family Raphidae: the **Rodriguez solitaire** (*Pezophaps solitaria*), and the poorly known **Réunion solitaire** (*Ornithaptera solitaria*). **4** a large American thrush with mainly gray plumage and a short bill. • Genus *Myadestes*, subfamily Turdinae, family Muscicapidae: several species. ▷early 18th cent.: from French, from Latin *solitarius* (see SOLITARY).

sol·i·tar·y /'sälə,terē/ ▶*adj.* done or existing alone: *I live a pretty solitary life | tigers are essentially solitary.* ■ (of a place) secluded or isolated: *solitary farmsteads.* ■ [*attrib.*] [often with *negative*] single; only: *we have not a solitary shred of evidence to go on.* ■ (of a bird, mammal, or insect) living alone or in pairs, esp. in contrast to related social forms: *a solitary wasp.* ■ (of a flower or other part) borne singly.
▶*n.* (*pl.* **-tar·ies**) **1** a recluse or hermit. **2** *informal* short for SOLITARY CONFINEMENT. ▷Middle English: from Latin *solitarius*, from *solus* 'alone.' —**sol·i·tar·i·ly** /-rəlē/ *adv.* —**sol·i·tar·i·ness** *n.*

sol·i·tar·y con·fine·ment ▶*n.* the isolation of a prisoner in a separate cell as a punishment.

sol·i·tar·y wave ▶*n.* another term for SOLITON.

sol·i·ton /'säli,tän/ ▶*n.* *Physics* a quantum or quasiparticle propagated as a traveling nondissipative wave that is neither preceded nor followed by another such disturbance. ▷1960s: from SOLITARY + -ON.

sol·i·tude /'sälə,t(y)o͞od/ ▶*n.* the state or situation of being alone: *she savored her few hours of freedom and solitude.* ■ a lonely or uninhabited place. ▷Middle English: from Old French, or from Latin *solitudo*, from *solus* 'alone.'

THE RIGHT WORD **alienation, desolation, disaffection, estrangement, lonesomeness, solitude**

Loneliness, which refers to a lack of companionship and is often associated with unhappiness, should not be confused with **solitude**, which is the state of being alone or cut off from all human contact (*the solitude of the lighthouse keeper*).

You can be in the midst of a crowd of people and still experience *loneliness*, but not *solitude*, since you are not physically alone. Similarly, if you enjoy being alone, you can have *solitude* without *loneliness*.

Lonesomeness is more intense than *loneliness*, suggesting the downheartedness you may experience when a loved one is absent (*she experienced lonesomeness following the death of her dog*).

Desolation is more intense still, referring to a state of being utterly alone or forsaken (*the widow's desolation*). *Desolation* can also indicate a state of ruin or barrenness (*the desolation of the volcanic islands*).

Alienation, **disaffection**, and **estrangement** have less to do with being or feeling alone and more to do with emotions that change over time.

Alienation is a word that suggests a feeling of unrelatedness, especially a feeling of distance from your social or intellectual environment (*alienation from society*).

Disaffection suggests that you now feel indifference or even distaste toward someone you were once fond of (*a wife's growing disaffection for her husband*), while *estrangement* is a voluntary disaffection that can result in complete separation and strong feelings of dislike or hatred (*a daughter's estrangement from her parents*).

sol·mi·za·tion /,sälmi'zāshən; sōl-/ ▶*n.* *Music* a system of associating each note of a scale with a particular syllable, esp. to teach singing.

The commonest European system, still in use, originally named the notes *ut, re, mi, fa, sol, la* in groups of six (hexachords) beginning on G, C, or F, using syllables from a Latin hymn for St. John the Baptist's Day in which each phrase begins on the next note in the scale: "*Ut* queant laxis *re*sonare fibris *Mi*ra gestorum *fa*muli tuorum, *Sol*ve polluti *la*bii reatum, Sancte Iohannes." A seventh note *si* was added later (from the initials of Sancte Iohannes). Modern systems typically use the sequence as arbitrarily adapted in the 19th century: *do, re, mi, fa, sol, la, ti*, with do being C in the fixed-do system and the keynote in the movable-do or tonic sol-fa system.

▷mid 18th cent.: from French *solmisation*, based on *sol* 'sol' + *mi*.

soln. ▶*abbr.* solution.

Soln·ho·fen /'zōln'hōfən/ a village in Bavaria, Germany, near which there are extensive, thinly stratified beds of lithographic limestone dating from the Upper Jurassic period. These beds are noted as the chief source of archaeopteryx fossils.

so·lo /'sōlō/ ▶*n.* (*pl.* **-los**) **1** a thing done by one person unaccompanied, in particular: ■ (*pl.* **so·los** or **so·li** /'sōlē/) a piece of vocal or instrumental music or a dance, or a part or passage in one, for one performer. ■ an unaccompanied flight by a pilot in an aircraft. **2** a card game in which one player plays against the others in an attempt to win a specified number of tricks.
▶*adj.* & *adv.* for or done by one person alone; unaccompanied: [as *adj.*] *a solo album* | [as *adv.*] *she'd spent most of her life flying solo.*
▶*v.* (**so·loes**, **so·loed**) [*intrans.*] perform something unaccompanied, in particular: ■ perform an unaccompanied piece of music or a part or passage in one. ■ fly an aircraft unaccompanied. ■ undertake solo climbing. ▷late 17th cent. (as a musical term): from Italian, from Latin *solus* 'alone.'

so·lo climb·ing ▶*n.* the sport of climbing unaided by ropes and other equipment, and without the assistance of other people. —**so·lo climb·er** *n.*

so·lo·ist /'sōlōist/ ▶*n.* a singer or other musician who performs a solo.

Sol·o·mon /'säləmən/, son of David; king of Israel *c.*970–*c.*930 BC. In the Bible he is traditionally associated with the Song of Solomon, Ecclesiastes, and Proverbs, while his wisdom is illustrated by the Judgment of Solomon. ■ [as *n.*] (usu. **a Solomon**) a very wise person. —**Sol·o·mon·ic** /,sälə'mänik/ *adj.*

Sol·o·mon Is·lands (also **the Sol·o·mons**) a country that consists of a group of islands in the southwestern Pacific, to the east of New Guinea; pop. 523,000;

capital, Honiara; languages, English (official), Pidgin, and local Austronesian languages. —**Sol·o·mon Is·land·er** *n.*

The islands were divided between Britain and Germany in the late 19th century; the southern islands became a British protectorate in 1893 while the north remained German until mandated to Australia in 1920.With the exception of the northern part of the chain (now part of Papua New Guinea), the Solomons became self-governing in 1976 and fully independent within the Commonwealth of Nations two years later.

Sol·o·mon's seal ▶*n.* **1** a figure similar to the Star of David. **2** a widely distributed plant of the lily family, having arching stems that bear a double row of broad leaves with drooping flowers in their axils. • Genus *Polygonatum*, family Liliaceae: many species, including *P. biflorum*, which has greenish-yellow paired flowers and is common in the woods of the eastern U.S.

Solomon's seal 1

So·lon /ˈsōlən; ˈsō,län/ (*c.*630–*c.*560 BC), Athenian statesman and lawgiver. One of the Seven Sages, he revised the code of laws established by Draco. His division of the citizens into four classes based on wealth rather than birth was the basis for Athenian democracy.

So·lo·thurn /ˈzôlə,tərn/ a canton in northwestern Switzerland, in the Jura mountains. French name **SOLEURE**. ■ its capital, a town on the Aare River; pop. 15,000.

sol·stice /ˈsōlstis/ ▶*n.* either of the two times in the year, the **summer solstice** and the **winter solstice**, when the sun reaches its highest or lowest point in the sky at noon, marked by the longest and shortest days. ▷Middle English: from Old French, from Latin *solstitium*, from *sol* 'sun' + *stit-* 'stopped, stationary' (from the verb *sistere*). —**sol·sti·tial** /sōlˈstisHəl/ *adj.*

Sol·ti /ˈSHōltē/, Sir Georg (1912–97), British conductor, born in Hungary. He was conductor of the Chicago Symphony Orchestra 1969–91 and the London Philharmonic Orchestra 1979–83.

sol·u·bi·lize /ˈsälyəbə,līz/ ▶*v.* [*trans.*] *technical* make (a substance) soluble or more soluble. —**sol·u·bi·li·za·tion** /,sälyəbəliˈzāsHən/ *n.*

sol·u·ble /ˈsälyəbəl/ ▶*adj.* **1** (of a substance) able to be dissolved, esp. in water: *the poison is* **soluble in** *alcohol.* **2** (of a problem) able to be solved. ▷late Middle English: from Old French, from late Latin *solubilis*, from *solvere* (see **SOLVE**). —**sol·u·bil·i·ty** /,sälyəˈbilitē/ *n.*

sol·u·ble glass ▶*n.* another term for **WATER GLASS** (sense 1).

so·lu·nar /sōˈlo͞onər/ ▶*adj.* of or relating to the combined influence or conjunction of the sun and moon. ▷late 18th cent.: blend of **SOL** and **LUNAR**.

so·lus /ˈsōləs/ ▶*adj.* (*fem.* **so·la** /ˈsōlə/) alone or unaccompanied (used esp. as a stage direction). ▷Latin.

sol·ute /ˈsäl,yo͞ot/ ▶*n.* the minor component in a solution, dissolved in the solvent. ▷late 19th cent.: from Latin *solutum*, neuter of *solutus* 'loosened,' past participle of the verb *solvere*.

so·lu·tion /səˈlo͞osHən/ ▶*n.* **1** a means of solving a problem or dealing with a difficult situation: *there are no easy solutions to financial and marital problems.* ■ the correct answer to a puzzle: *the solution to this month's crossword.* **2** a liquid mixture in which the minor component (the solute) is uniformly distributed within the major component (the solvent). ■ the process or state of being dissolved in a solvent. **3** *archaic* the action of separating or breaking down; dissolution: *the solution of British supremacy in South Africa.* ▷late Middle English: from Old French, from Latin *solutio(n-)*, from *solvere* 'loosen' (see **SOLVE**).

so·lu·tion set ▶*n. Mathematics* the set of all the solutions of an equation or condition.

So·lu·tre·an /səˈlo͞otrēən/ ▶*adj. Archaeology* of, relating to, or denoting an Upper Paleolithic culture of central and southwestern France and parts of Iberia. It is dated to about 21,000–18,000 years ago, following the Aurignacian and preceding the Magdalenian. ■ [as *n.*] (**the Solutrean**) the Solutrean culture or period. ▷late 19th cent.: from *Solutré*, the site of a cave in eastern France, where objects from this culture were found, + **-AN**.

solv·ate /ˈsälvāt/ ▶*v.* [*trans.*] *Chemistry* (of a solvent) enter into reversible chemical combination with (a dissolved molecule, ion, etc.).
▶*n.* a more or less loosely bonded complex formed between a solvent and a dissolved species. ▷early 20th cent.: formed irregularly from **SOLVE** + **-ATE**[1]. —**solv·a·tion** /sälˈvāsHən/ *n.*

Sol·vay proc·ess /ˈsälvā/ ▶*n. Chemistry* an industrial process for obtaining sodium carbonate from limestone, ammonia, and brine. ▷late 19th cent.: named after Ernest *Solvay* (1838–1922), Belgian chemist.

solve /sälv; sôlv/ ▶*v.* [*trans.*] find an answer to, explanation for, or means of effectively dealing with (a problem or mystery): *the policy could solve the town's housing crisis* | *a murder investigation that has never been solved.* ▷late Middle English (in the sense 'loosen, dissolve, untie'): from Latin *solvere* 'loosen, unfasten.' —**solv·a·ble** *adj.* —**solv·er** *n.*

sol·vent /ˈsälvənt/ ▶*adj.* **1** having assets in excess of liabilities; able to pay one's debts: *interest rate rises have very severe effects on normally solvent companies.* **2** [*attrib.*] able to dissolve other substances: *osmotic, chemical, or solvent action.*
▶*n.* the liquid in which a solute is dissolved to form a solution. ■ a liquid, typically one other than water, used for dissolving other substances. ■ *figurative* something that acts to weaken or dispel a particular attitude or situation: *an unrivaled* **solvent of** *social prejudices.* ▷mid 17th cent.: from Latin *solvent-* 'loosening, unfastening, paying,' from the verb *solvere*. —**sol·ven·cy** *n.* (in sense 1 of the *adjective*).

sol·vent a·buse ▶*n.* the use of certain volatile organic solvents as intoxicants by inhalation, e.g., glue sniffing.

Sol·way Firth /,sôlwā/ an inlet of the Irish Sea that separates northwestern England from Dumfries and Galloway in Scotland.

Sol·zhe·ni·tsyn /,sōlzHəˈnētsən; ,sôl-/, Alexander (1918–), Russian novelist; Russian name *Aleksandr Isaevich Solzhenitsyn*. After spending eight years in a labor camp, he began writing. He was exiled in 1974 and eventually returned in 1994. Notable works: *One Day in the Life of Ivan Denisovich* (1962), *Cancer Ward* (1968), and *The Gulag Archipelago* (1973). Nobel Prize for Literature (1970).

som /sōm/ ▶*n.* (*pl.* same) the basic monetary unit of Kyrgyzstan, equal to 100 tiyin.

so·ma[1] /ˈsōmə/ ▶*n.* [usu. in *sing.*] *Biology* the parts of an organism other than the reproductive cells. ■ the body as distinct from the soul, mind, or psyche. ▷late 19th cent.: from Greek *sōma* 'body.'

so·ma[2] ▶*n. Hinduism* an intoxicating drink prepared from a plant and used in Vedic ritual, believed to be the drink of the gods. ■ (also **soma plant**) the plant from which this drink is prepared. See **HOM**. ▷from Sanskrit *sōma*.

som·aes·thet·ic ▶*adj.* British spelling of **SOMESTHETIC**.

So·ma·li /səˈmälē; sō-/ ▶*n.* (*pl.* same or **-lis**) a member of a mainly Muslim people of Somalia. ■ the Cushitic language that is the official language of Somalia, also spoken in Djibouti and parts of Kenya and Ethiopia. ■ a native or national of Somalia.
▶*adj.* of or relating to Somalia, the Somalis, or their language. ▷the name in Somali. —**So·ma·li·an** /-lēən/ *adj.* & *n.*

So·ma·li·a /səˈmälēə; sōˈmälyə/ a country in northeastern Africa, on the peninsula known as the Horn of Africa; pop. 8,304,000; capital, Mogadishu; languages, Somali and Arabic (both official).

The area of the Horn of Africa was divided between British and Italian spheres of influence in the late 19th century, and the modern republic of Somalia became independent in 1960 following the unification of the former British Somaliland and Italian Somalia. Civil war broke out in Somalia in 1988 and led to the overthrow of the government in 1991; the U.S. intervened militarily 1992–94. In 1991, northern Somalia declared independence as the Somaliland Republic. Several factions continue to fight for control of southern areas.

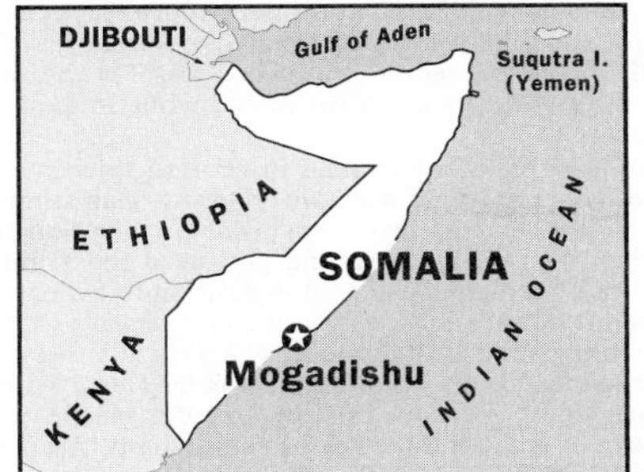

So·ma·li Pen·in·su·la another name for **HORN OF AFRICA**.

so·man /ˈsōmən/ (also **So·man**) ▶*n.* a lethal organophosphorus nerve gas, developed in Germany during World War II. ▷1950s: from German, of unknown origin.

so·mat·ic /səˈmatik; sō-/ ▶*adj.* of or relating to the body, esp. as distinct from the mind. ■ *Biology* of or relating to the soma. ■ *Anatomy* of or relating to the outer wall of the body, as opposed to the viscera. ▷late 18th cent.: from Greek *sōmatikos*, from *sōma* 'body.' —**so·mat·i·cal·ly** *adv.*

so·mat·ic cell ▶*n. Biology* any cell of a living organism other than the reproductive cells.

so·mat·i·za·tion /sə,matəˈzāsHən; ˈsōmə-/ ▶*n. Psychiatry* the production of recurrent and multiple medical symptoms with no discernible organic cause.

somato- ▶*comb. form* of or relating to the human or animal body: *somatotype.* ▷from Greek *sōma, sōmat-* 'body.'

so·mat·o·me·din /sə,matəˈmēdn; ,sōmə-/ ▶*n. Biochemistry* a hormone that acts as an intermediate in the stimulation of tissue growth by growth hormone. ▷1970s: from **SOMATO-** 'of the body' + *(inter)med(iary)* + **-IN**[1].

so·mat·o·pleure /səˈmatə,plo͝o(ə)r; ˈsōmətə-/ ▶*n. Embryology* a layer of tissue in a vertebrate embryo comprising the ectoderm and the outer layer of mesoderm, and giving rise to the amnion, the chorion, and part of the body wall. Often contrasted with **SPLANCHNOPLEURE**. ▷late 19th cent.: from **SOMATO-** 'of the body' + Greek *pleura* 'side.'

so·mat·o·sen·so·ry /sə,matəˈsensərē; ,sōmətə-/ ▶*adj. Physiology* relating to or denoting a sensation (such as pressure, pain, or warmth) that can occur anywhere in the body, in contrast to one localized at a sense organ (such as sight, balance, or taste). Also called **SOMESTHETIC**.

so·mat·o·stat·in /sə,matəˈstatn; ,sōmə-/ ▶*n. Biochemistry* a hormone secreted in the pancreas and pituitary gland that inhibits gastric secretion and somatotropin release.

so·mat·o·tro·pin /sə,matəˈtrōpən/ (also **so·mat·o·tro·phin**) ▶*n. Biochemistry* a growth hormone secreted by the anterior pituitary gland.

so·mat·o·type /səˈmatə,tīp; ,sōmə-/ ▶*n.* a category to which people are assigned according to the extent to which their bodily physique conforms to a basic type (usually endomorphic, mesomorphic, or ectomorphic). ▷1940s: coined by W. H. Sheldon in *Varieties of Human Physique*. —**so·mat·o·typ·ing** *n.*

som·ber /ˈsämbər/ (*Brit.* also **som·bre**) ▶*adj.* dark or dull in color or tone; gloomy: *the night skies were somber and starless.* ■ oppressively solemn or sober in mood; grave: *he looked at her with a somber expression.* ▷mid 18th cent.: from French, based on Latin *sub* 'under' + *umbra* 'shade.' —**som·ber·ly** *adv.* —**som·ber·ness** *n.*

som·bre·ro /sämˈbre(ə)rō/ ▶*n.* (*pl.* **-ros**) a broad-brimmed felt or straw hat, typically worn in Mexico and the southwestern U.S. ▷Spanish, from *sombra* 'shade' (see **SOMBER**).

sombrero

some /səm/ ▶*adj.* **1** an unspecified amount or number of: *I made some money running errands* | *he played some records for me.* **2** used to refer to someone or something that is unknown or unspecified: *she married some newspaper magnate twice her age* | *there must be some mistake* | *he's in* **some kind of** *trouble.* **3** (used with a number) approximately: *some thirty different languages are spoken.* **4** a considerable amount or number of: *he went to some trouble* | *I've known you for some*

Pronunciation Key ə *ago*; ər *over*; ˈə or ,ə *up*; ˈər or ,ər *fur*; a *hat*; ā *rate*; ä *car*; CH *chew*; e *let*; ē *see*; e(ə)r *air*; i *fit*; ī *by*; i(ə)r *ear*; NG *sing*; ō *go*; ô *for*; oi *boy*; o͝o *good*; o͞o *goo*; ou *out*; SH *she*; TH *thin*; T͟H *then*; (h)w *why*; ZH *vision*

years now. **5** at least a small amount or number of: *he liked some music but generally wasn't musical.* **6** expressing admiration of something notable: *that was some goal.* ■ used ironically to express disapproval or disbelief: *Mr. Power gave his stock reply. Some help.*
▸*pron.* **1** an unspecified number or amount of people or things: *here are* **some of** *our suggestions | if you want whiskey I'll give you some.* **2** at least a small amount or number of people or things: *surely some have noticed.*
▸*adv. informal* to some extent; somewhat: *when you get to the majors, the rules change some.* ▷Old English *sum,* of Germanic origin, from an Indo-European root shared by Greek *hamōs* 'somehow' and Sanskrit *sama* 'any, every.'
▸*PHRASES* □ **and then some** *informal* and plenty more than that: *we got our money's worth and then some.* □ **some few** see FEW. □ **some little** a considerable amount of: *we are going to be working together for some little time yet.*

-some[1] ▸*suffix* forming adjectives meaning: **1** productive of: *loathsome.* **2** characterized by being: *wholesome.* ■ apt to: *tiresome.* ▷Old English *-sum.*

-some[2] ▸*suffix* (forming nouns) denoting a group of a specified number: *foursome.* ▷Old English *sum* 'some.'

-some[3] ▸*comb. form* denoting a portion of a body, esp. a particle of a cell: *chromosome.* ▷from Greek *sōma* 'body.'

some·bod·y /ˈsəmˌbädē/ ▸*pron.* **1** some person; someone. **2** a person of importance or authority: *I'd like to be somebody* | [as *n.*] *nobodies who want to become somebodies.*

some·day /ˈsəmˌdā/ ▸*adv.* at some time in the future: *I know someday my whole family will be together and happy.*

some·how /ˈsəmˌhou/ ▸*adv.* in some way; by some means: *somehow I managed to get the job done.* ■ for a reason that is not known or specified: *he looked different somehow.*

some·one /ˈsəmˌwən/ ▸*pron.* **1** an unknown or unspecified person; some person: *there's someone at the door | someone from the audience shouted out.* **2** a person of importance or authority: *a small-time lawyer keen to be someone.*

some·place /ˈsəmˌplās/ ▸*adv. & pron. informal* another term for SOMEWHERE.

som·er·sault /ˈsəmərˌsôlt/ ▸*n.* an acrobatic movement in which a person turns head over heels in the air or on the ground and lands or finishes on their feet: *a backward somersault* | *figurative Paula's stomach* **turned** *a* **somersault.** ■ *figurative* a dramatic upset or reversal of policy or opinion: *those who perform doctrinal somersaults almost overnight.*
▸*v.* [*intrans.*] perform such an acrobatic feat, or make a similar movement accidentally: *his car somersaulted into a ditch.* ▷mid 16th cent. (as a noun): from Old French *sombresault,* from Provençal *sobresaut,* from *sobre* 'above' + *saut* 'leap.'

Som·er·ville /ˈsəmərˌvil/ an industrial and residential city in eastern Massachusetts, northwest of Boston; pop. 77,478.

som·es·thet·ic /ˌsōmesˈᴛʜetik/ (*Brit.* **som·aes·thet·ic**) ▸*adj.* another term for SOMATOSENSORY. ▷late 19th cent.: from Greek *sōma* 'body' + AESTHETIC.

some·thing /ˈsəmˌᴛʜiNG/ ▸*pron.* **1** a thing that is unspecified or unknown: *we stopped for something to eat | I knew something terrible had happened | something about her frightened me.* **2** used in various expressions indicating that a description or amount being stated is not exact: *a wry look,* **something between** *amusement and regret | grassland totaling* **something over** *three hundred acres | there were* **something like** *fifty applications.*
▸*adv.* [as *submodifier*] **1** *informal* used for emphasis with a following adjective functioning as an adverb: *my back hurts something terrible.* **2** *archaic* or *dialect* to some extent; somewhat: *the people were something scared.* ▷Old English *sum thing* (see SOME, THING).
▸*PHRASES* □ **or something** *informal* added as a reference to an unspecified alternative similar to the thing mentioned: *you look like you just climbed a mountain or something.* □ **really** (or **quite**) **something** *informal* something considered impressive or notable: *Want to see the library? It's really something.* □ **something else** *informal* an exceptional person or thing: *the reaction from the crowd was something else.* □ **something of** to some degree: *Richard was something of an expert at the game.* □ **something or other** see OTHER. □ **there is something in/to —— ——** is worth considering; there is some truth in ——: *perhaps there is something to his theory | I think there's something in this alien business.* □ **thirty-something** (**forty-something,** etc.) *informal* an unspecified age between thirty and forty (forty and fifty, etc.): *I'm guessing she's forty-something.* ■ of or relating to a person between thirty and forty (forty and fifty, etc.): *this music appeals more to your thirty-something crowd.*

some·time /ˈsəmˌtīm/ ▸*adv.* at some unspecified or unknown time: *you must come and have supper sometime | sometime after six everybody left.* ■ *archaic* at one time; formerly: *the Emperor Constantine used this speech sometime unto his bishops.*
▸*adj.* **1** former: *the sometime editor of the paper.* **2** occasional: *a sometime contributor.*

some·times /ˈsəmˌtīmz/ ▸*adv.* occasionally, rather than all of the time: *sometimes I want to do things on my own.*

some·way /ˈsəmˌwā/ ▸*adv.* (often **someways**) *informal* in some way or manner; by some means: *we've got to make money someway.*

some·what /ˈsəmˌ(h)wät/ ▸*adv.* to a moderate extent or by a moderate amount: *matters have improved somewhat since then* | [as *submodifier*] *a somewhat thicker book.*
▸*PHRASE* □ **somewhat of** something of: *it was* **somewhat of a** *disappointment.*

some·when /ˈsəmˌ(h)wen/ ▸*adv. informal* at some time: *somewhen between 1918 and 1930.*

some·where /ˈsəmˌ(h)we(ə)r/ ▸*adv.* in or to some place: *I've seen you somewhere before | can we go somewhere warm?* ■ used to indicate an approximate amount: *it cost* **somewhere around** *two thousand dollars.*
▸*pron.* some unspecified place: *in search of somewhere to live.*
▸*PHRASE* □ **get somewhere** *informal* make progress; achieve success.

so·mite /ˈsōmīt/ ▸*n. Zoology* each of a number of body segments containing the same internal structures, clearly visible in invertebrates such as earthworms but also present in the embryonic stages of vertebrates. Also called METAMERE. ▷mid 19th cent.: from Greek *sōma* 'body' + -ITE[1].

Somme /sôm; säm/ a river in northern France. Rising east of Saint-Quentin, it flows 153 miles (245 km) through Amiens to the English Channel northeast of the port of Dieppe. The area around it was the scene of heavy fighting in World War I.

Somme, Battle of the a major battle of World War I between the British and the Germans, on the Western Front in northern France July–November 1916. More than a million men on both sides were killed or wounded.

som·me·lier /ˌsəməlˈyā/ ▸*n.* a wine steward. ▷early 19th cent.: French, literally 'butler.'

som·nam·bu·lism /sämˈnambyəˌlizəm/ ▸*n.* sleepwalking. ▷late 18th cent.: from French *somnambulisme,* from Latin *somnus* 'sleep' + *ambulare* 'to walk.' **—som·nam·bu·lant** /-lənt/ *adj.* **—som·nam·bu·lant·ly** /-ləntlē/ *adv.* **—som·nam·bu·list** *n.* **—som·nam·bu·lis·tic** /-ˌnambyəˈlistik/ *adj.* **—som·nam·bu·lis·ti·cal·ly** /-ˌnambyəˈlistik(ə)lē/ *adv.*

som·nif·er·ous /sämˈnifərəs/ ▸*adj.* tending to induce sleep; soporific. ▷early 17th cent.: from Latin *somnifer* (from *somnium* 'dream') + -OUS.

som·no·lent /ˈsämnələnt/ ▸*adj.* sleepy; drowsy. ■ causing or suggestive of drowsiness: *a somnolent summer day.* ■ *Medicine* abnormally drowsy. ▷late Middle English (in the sense 'causing sleepiness'): from Old French *sompnolent* or Latin *somnolentus,* from *somnus* 'sleep.' **—som·no·lence** *n.* **—som·no·len·cy** *n.* **—som·no·lent·ly** *adv.*

So·mo·za /səˈmōsə; -zə/ the name of a family of Nicaraguan statesmen: ■ **Anastasio** (1896–1956), president 1937–47 and 1951–56; full name *Anastasio Somoza García.* He took presidential office following a military coup in 1936 and ruled Nicaragua as a virtual dictator. ■ **Luis** (1922–67), president 1957–63; son of Anastasio; full name *Luis Somoza Debayle.* ■ **Anastasio** (1925–80), president 1967–79; younger brother of Luis; full name *Anastasio Somoza Debayle.* His dictatorial regime was overthrown by the Sandinistas, and he was assassinated while in exile in Paraguay.

son /sən/ ▸*n.* a boy or man in relation to either or both of his parents. ■ a male offspring of an animal. ■ a male descendant: *the sons of Adam.* ■ (**the Son**) (in Christian belief) the second person of the Trinity; Christ. ■ a man considered in relation to his native country or area: *one of Nevada's most famous sons.* ■ a man regarded as the product of a particular person, influence, or environment: *sons of the French Revolution.* ■ (also **my son**) used by an elder person as a form of address for a boy or young man: *"You're on private land, son."* ▷Old English *sunu,* of Germanic origin; related to Dutch *zoon* and German *Sohn,* from an Indo-European root shared by Greek *huios.* **—son·ship** /ˈsənˌSHip/ *n.*
▸*PHRASES* □ **son of a bitch** (*pl.* **sons of bitch·es**) used as a general term of contempt or abuse. □ **son of a gun** (*pl.* **sons of guns**) *informal* a jocular or affectionate way of addressing or referring to someone: *he's a pretentious son of a gun, but he's got a heart of gold.* [with reference to the guns carried aboard ships: the epithet is said to have been applied originally to babies born at sea to women allowed to accompany their husbands.]

so·nar /ˈsōˌnär/ ▸*n.* a system for the detection of objects under water and for measuring the water's depth by emitting sound pulses and detecting or measuring their return after being reflected. ■ an apparatus used in this system. ■ the method of echolocation used in air or water by animals such as whales and bats. ▷1940s: from *so(und) na(vigation and) r(anging),* on the pattern of *radar.*

so·na·ta /səˈnätə/ ▸*n.* a classical composition for an instrumental soloist, often with a piano accompaniment. It is typically in several movements with one (esp. the first) or more in sonata form. ▷late 17th cent.: Italian, literally 'sounded' (originally as distinct from 'sung'), feminine past participle of *sonare.*

so·na·ta form (also **so·na·ta·al·le·gro form**) ▸*n. Music* a type of composition in three sections (exposition, development, and recapitulation) in which two themes or subjects are explored according to set key relationships. It forms the basis for much classical music, including the sonata, symphony, and concerto.

son·a·ti·na /ˌsänəˈtēnə/ ▸*n.* a simple or short sonata. ▷mid 18th cent.: Italian, diminutive of SONATA.

sonde /sänd/ ▸*n.* an instrument probe that automatically transmits information about its surroundings underground, under water, in the atmosphere, etc. ▷early 20th cent.: from French, literally 'sounding (line).'

Sond·heim /ˈsändˌhīm/, Stephen (Joshua) (1930–), U.S. composer and lyricist. He became known for his lyrics for *West Side Story* (1957) and has since written a number of musicals, including *A Little Night Music* (1973), *Sweeney Todd* (1979), and *Sunday in the Park with George* (1984).

sone /sōn/ ▸*n.* a unit of subjective loudness, equal to 40 phons. ▷1930s: from Latin *sonus* 'a sound.'

son et lu·mière /ˈsôɴ nā lo͞omˈyer; lʏˈmyer/ ▸*n.* an entertainment held by night at a historic monument or building, telling its history by the use of lighting effects and recorded sound. ▷French, literally 'sound and light.'

Song variant spelling of SUNG.

song /sôNG/ ▸*n.* a short poem or other set of words set to music or meant to be sung. ■ singing or vocal music: *the young airmen* **broke into song.** ■ a musical composition suggestive of a song. ■ the musical phrases uttered by some birds, whales, and insects, typically forming a recognizable and repeated sequence and used chiefly for territorial defense or for attracting mates. ■ a poem, esp. one in rhymed stanzas: *The Song of Hiawatha.* ■ *archaic* poetry. ▷Old English *sang,* of Germanic origin; related to Dutch *zang* and German *Sang,* also to SING.
▸*PHRASES* □ **for a song** *informal* very cheaply: *the place was going for a song.* □ **on song** *Brit., informal* performing well: *when he is on song, no one can stop him.* □ **a song and dance** *informal* a long explanation that is pointless or deliberately evasive: *Don't give me a song and dance, Sandy. Yes or no?* ■ *chiefly Brit.* a fuss or commotion: *she would be sure to* **make a song and dance about** *her aching feet.*

song·bird /ˈsôNGˌbərd/ ▸*n.* **1** a bird with a musical song. **2** *Ornithology* a perching bird of an advanced group distinguished by having the muscles of the syrinx attached to the bronchial semirings; an oscine passerine. • Suborder Oscines, order Passeriformes; in Europe 'songbird' is effectively synonymous with 'passerine' or 'perching bird.' **3** *figurative* a woman singer.

song·book /ˈsôNGˌbo͝ok/ ▸*n.* a book containing a collection of songs with music.

song cy·cle ▸*n.* a set of related songs, often on a romantic theme, intended to form a single musical entity.

song form ▸*n.* a form used in the composition of a song, in particular a simple melody and accompaniment or a three-part work in which the third part is a repetition of the first.

Son·ghai /säNGˈgī/ ▸*n.* (*pl.* same or **-ghais**) **1** a

member of a people living mainly in Niger and Mali. **2** ■ the Nilo-Saharan language of this people.
▸*adj.* of or relating to this people or their language. ▷the name in Songhai.

Song Hong Vietnamese name for **Red River** (sense 1).

Song·nam /'səNG'näm/ a city in northwestern South Korea, southeast of Seoul; pop. 869,000.

Song of Songs (also **Song of Sol·o·mon**) a book of the Bible containing an anthology of Hebrew love poems traditionally ascribed to Solomon but in fact dating from a much later period. Jewish and Christian writers have interpreted the book allegorically as representing God's relationship with his people, or with the soul.

song·smith /'sôNG,smiTH/ ▸*n. informal* a person who writes popular songs.

song spar·row ▸*n.* a sparrowlike North American bird related to the buntings, noted for its constant and characteristic song. • *Melospiza melodia*, family Emberizidae (subfamily Emberizinae).

song·ster /'sôNGstər/ ▸*n.* a person who sings, esp. fluently and skillfully. ■ a person who writes songs or verse. ■ a songbird. ▷Old English *sangestre* (see **song, -ster**).

song·stress /'sôNGstris/ ▸*n.* a female songster.

song thrush ▸*n.* a common European and central Asian thrush with a buff spotted breast, having a loud song in which each phrase is repeated two or three times. • *Turdus philomelos*, subfamily Turdinae, family Muscicapidae.

song·writ·er /'sôNG,rītər/ ▸*n.* a person who writes popular songs or the music for them. —**song·writ·ing** *n.*

son·ic /'sänik/ ▸*adj.* relating to or using sound waves. ■ denoting or having a speed equal to that of sound. ▷1920s: from Latin *sonus* 'sound' + **-ic**. —**son·i·cal·ly** /-ik(ə)lē/ *adv.*

son·i·cate /'sänikāt/ *Biochemistry* ▸*v.* [*trans.*] (usu. **be sonicated**) subject (a biological sample) to ultrasonic vibration so as to fragment the cells, macromolecules, and membranes.
▸*n.* a biological sample that has been subjected to such treatment. ▷1950s: from **sonic** + **-ate**[2].

son·ic bar·ri·er ▸*n.* another term for **sound barrier**.

son·ic boom ▸*n.* a loud explosive noise caused by the shock wave from an aircraft traveling faster than the speed of sound.

son·ics /'säniks/ ▸*plural n.* musical sounds artificially produced or reproduced.

So·nin·ke /sä'nenGkā/ ▸*n.* (*pl.* same or **-kes**) **1** a member of a people living in Mali and Senegal. **2** the Mande language of this people.
▸*adj.* of or relating to this people or their language. ▷the name in Soninke.

son-in-law ▸*n.* (*pl.* **sons-in-law**) the husband of one's daughter.

son·net /'sänit/ ▸*n.* a poem of fourteen lines using any of a number of formal rhyme schemes, in English typically having ten syllables per line.
▸*v.* (**-net·ed, -net·ing**) [*intrans.*] *archaic* compose sonnets. ■ [*trans.*] celebrate in a sonnet. ▷mid 16th cent.: from French, or from Italian *sonetto*, diminutive of *suono* 'a sound.'

son·net·eer /,säni'ti(ə)r/ ▸*n.* a writer of sonnets.

son·ny /'sənē/ ▸*n. informal* used by an older person as a familiar form of address to a young boy. ■ (*Brit.* also **Sonny Jim**) used as a humorous or patronizing way of addressing a man: *look, sonny, that's all I can tell you.*

sono- ▸*comb. form* of or relating to sound: *sonometer.* ▷from Latin *sonus* 'sound.'

son·o·bu·oy /'sänə,bōōē; -,boi/ ▸*n.* a buoy equipped to detect underwater sounds and transmit them by radio.

son·o·gram /'sänə,gram/ ▸*n.* **1** a graph representing a sound, showing the distribution of energy at different frequencies. **2** a visual image produced from an ultrasound examination.

so·nog·ra·phy /sə'nägrəfē/ ▸*n.* **1** the analysis of sound using an instrument that produces a graphical representation of its component frequencies. **2** another term for **ultrasonography**. —**son·o·graph** /'sänə,graf/ *n.* —**son·o·graph·ic** /,sänə'grafik/ *adj.*

son·o·lu·mi·nes·cence /,sänō,lōōmə'nesəns/ ▸*n. Physics* luminescence excited in a substance by the passage of sound waves through it. —**son·o·lu·mi·nes·cent** *adj.*

So·no·ma Coun·ty /sə'nōmə/ a county in northwestern California, known for its wineries; pop. 388,222.

So·no·ra /sə'nôrə/ a state of northwestern Mexico, on the Gulf of California; capital, Hermosillo.

So·no·ra Des·ert an arid region in North America, in southeastern California and southwestern Arizona in the U.S. and much of Baja California and the western part of Sonora in Mexico.

So·no·ran /sə'nôrən/ ▸*adj.* relating to, denoting, or characteristic of a biogeographical region including desert areas of the southwestern U.S. and central Mexico. ▷late 19th cent.: from **Sonora** + **-an**.

so·no·rant /'sänərənt/ ▸*n. Phonetics* a sound produced with the vocal cords so positioned that spontaneous voicing is possible; a vowel, a glide, or a liquid or nasal consonant. ▷1930s: from **sonorous** + **-ant**.

so·nor·i·ty /sə'nôritē/ ▸*n.* the quality or fact of being sonorous. ■ *Phonetics* the relative loudness of a speech sound.

so·no·rous /'sänərəs/ ▸*adj.* (of a person's voice or other sound) imposingly deep and full. ■ capable of producing a deep or ringing sound: *the alloy is sonorous and useful in making bells.* ■ (of a speech or style) using imposing language: *they had expected the lawyers to deliver sonorous lamentations.* ■ having a pleasing sound: *she used the misleadingly sonorous name "melanoma" to describe it.* ▷early 17th cent.: from Latin *sonorus* (from *sonor* 'sound') + **-ous**. —**so·no·rous·ly** *adv.* —**so·no·rous·ness** *n.*

son·sy /'sänsē/ (also **son·sie**) ▸*adj.* (**-si·er, -si·est**) *Scottish poetic/literary* having an attractive and healthy appearance. ▷mid 16th cent. (also in the sense 'lucky'): from Irish and Scottish Gaelic *sonas* 'good fortune' (from *sona* 'fortunate') + **-y**[1].

Son·tag /'sän,tag/, Susan (1933–2004), U.S. writer and critic. She established her reputation as a radical intellectual with *Against Interpretation* (essays, 1966). Other notable works: *On Photography* (1976) and *Illness as Metaphor* (1979).

sook[1] /sŏŏk; sək/ ▸*n.* a female crab. ▷1950s: of unknown origin.

sook[2] ▸*n. informal, chiefly Austral./NZ Canadian* a person lacking spirit or self-confidence; a coward. ■ a hand-reared calf. ▷mid 19th cent.: dialect variant of the noun **suck**.

soon /sōōn/ ▸*adv.* **1** in or after a short time: *everyone will soon know the truth | he'll be home soon | they arrived soon after 7:30.* ■ early: *it's a pity you have to leave so soon | I wish you'd told me sooner | it was too soon to know.* **2** used to indicate one's preference in a particular matter: ***I'd just as soon*** *Tim did it | I would sooner resign than transfer to Toronto.* ▷Old English *sōna* 'immediately.' —**soon·ish** *adv.*
▸*PHRASES* □ **no sooner —— than** used to convey that the second event mentioned happens immediately after the first: *she had no sooner spoken than the telephone rang.* □ **sooner or later** at some future time; eventually: *you'll have to tell him sooner or later.*

USAGE 1 In standard English, the phrase **no sooner** is followed by **than**, as in *we had **no sooner** arrived **than** we had to leave.* This is because **sooner** is a comparative, and comparatives are followed by **than** (*earlier **than**; better **than**,* etc.). It is incorrect to follow **no sooner** with **when** rather than **than**, as in *we had **no sooner** arrived **when** we had to leave.*
2 Careful writers avoid the often-used phrase *sooner rather than later.* Besides being redundant, it fails to make a complete comparison (*sooner rather than later?* *later* than what?). The simple word **soon** is clear enough.

Soon·er State /'sōōnər/ a nickname for the state of **Oklahoma**. ▷*Sooner* in the sense "one who acts prematurely," i.e., a person who tried to get into the frontier territory of Oklahoma before the U.S. government opened it to settlers in 1889.

soot /sŏŏt/ ▸*n.* a black powdery or flaky substance consisting largely of amorphous carbon, produced by the incomplete burning of organic matter.
▸*v.* [*trans.*] cover or clog (something) with soot. ▷Old English *sōt*, of Germanic origin; related to German dialect *Sott*, from an Indo-European root shared by the verb **sit**.
▸*PHRASE* □ (**as**) **black as soot** intensely black.

sooth /sōōTH/ ▸*n. archaic* truth. ▷Old English *sōth* (originally as an adjective in the sense 'genuine, true'), of Germanic origin.
▸*PHRASE* □ **in sooth** in truth; really.

soothe /sōōTH/ ▸*v.* [*trans.*] gently calm (a person or their feelings): *a shot of brandy might soothe his nerves |* [as *adj.*] (**soothing**) *she put on some soothing music.* ■ reduce pain or discomfort in (a part of the body): *to soothe the skin try chamomile or thyme.* ■ relieve or ease (pain): *it contains a mild anesthetic to soothe the pain.* ▷Old English *sōthian* 'verify, show to be true,' from *sōth* 'true' (see **sooth**). In the 16th cent. the verb passed through the senses 'corroborate (a statement),' 'humor (a person) by expressing assent' and 'flatter by one's assent,' whence 'mollify, appease' (late 17th cent.). —**sooth·er** *n.* —**sooth·ing·ly** *adv.*

sooth·say·er /'sōōTH,sāər/ ▸*n.* a person supposed to be able to foresee the future. ▷Middle English (in the sense 'person who speaks the truth'): see **sooth**. —**sooth·say·ing** *n.*

soot·y /'sŏŏtē/ ▸*adj.* (**soot·i·er, soot·i·est**) covered with or colored like soot: *the front of the fireplace was blackened and sooty | his olive skin and sooty eyes.* ■ used in names of birds and other animals that are mainly blackish or brownish black, e.g., **sooty tern**. —**soot·i·ly** /'sŏŏtəlē/ *adv.* —**soot·i·ness** *n.*

soot·y mold ▸*n.* a black velvety mold that grows on the surfaces of leaves and stems affected by honeydew. • Family Capnodiaceae, subdivision Ascomycotina.

soot·y tern ▸*n.* a large oceanic tern that is blackish above and white below, and breeds throughout the tropical oceans. • *Sterna fuscata*.

SOP ▸*abbr.* ■ Standard Operating Procedure. ■ Standing Operating Procedure.

sop /säp/ ▸*n.* **1** a thing given or done as a concession of no great value to appease someone whose main concerns or demands are not being met: *my agent telephones as a sop but never finds me work.* **2** a piece of bread dipped in gravy, soup, or sauce.
▸*v.* (**sopped, sop·ping**) [*trans.*] (**sop something up**) soak up liquid using an absorbent substance: *he used some bread to sop up the sauce.* ■ wet thoroughly; soak. ▷Old English *soppian* 'dip (bread) in liquid,' *sopp* (noun), probably from the base of Old English *sūpan* 'sup.' Sense 1 (mid 17th cent.) alludes to the sop used by Aeneas on his visit to Hades to appease Cerberus.

sop. ▸*abbr.* soprano.

so·pai·pil·la /,sōpī'pēyə/ (also **so·pa·pil·la** /,sōpə-/) ▸*n.* (esp. in New Mexico) a deep-fried pastry, typically square, eaten with honey or sugar or as a bread. ▷American Spanish.

soph. ▸*abbr.* sophomore.

soph säf ▸*n. informal* sophomore: *the sophs get their assignments tomorrow.*

soph·ism /'säfizəm/ ▸*n.* a fallacious argument, esp. one used deliberately to deceive. ▷late Middle English: from Old French *sophime*, via Latin from Greek *sophisma* 'clever device,' from *sophizesthai* 'become wise' (see **sophist**).

soph·ist /'säfist/ ▸*n.* a paid teacher of philosophy and rhetoric in ancient Greece, associated in popular thought with moral skepticism and specious reasoning. ■ a person who reasons with clever but fallacious arguments. ▷mid 16th cent.: via Latin from Greek *sophistēs*, from *sophizesthai* 'devise, become wise,' from *sophos* 'wise.' —**so·phis·tic** /sə'fistik/ *adj.* —**so·phis·ti·cal** /sə'fistikəl/ *adj.* —**so·phis·ti·cal·ly** /sə'fistik(ə)lē/ *adv.*

so·phis·ti·cate ▸*v.* /sə'fistə,kāt/ [*trans.*] cause (a person or their thoughts, attitudes, and expectations) to become less simple or straightforward through education or experience: *readers who have been sophisticated by modern literary practice.* ■ develop (something such as a piece of equipment or a technique) into a more complex form: *functions that other software applications have sophisticated.* ■ [*intrans.*] *archaic* talk or reason in an impressively complex and educated manner. ■ *archaic* mislead or corrupt (a person, an argument, the mind, etc.) by sophistry: *books of casuistry, which sophisticate the understanding and defile the heart.*
▸*adj.* /sə'fistə,kāt; -kit/ *archaic* sophisticated.
▸*n.* /sə'fistə,kāt; -kit/ a person with much worldly experience and knowledge of fashion and culture: *he is still the butt of jokes made by New York sophisticates.* ▷late Middle English (as an adjective in the sense 'adulterated,' and as a verb in the sense 'mix with a foreign substance'): from medieval Latin *sophisticatus* 'tampered with,' past participle of the verb *sophisticare*, from *sophisticus* 'sophistic.' The shift of sense probably occurred first in the adjective *unsophisticated*, from 'uncorrupted' via 'innocent' to 'inexperienced, uncultured.' The noun dates from the early 20th cent. —**so·phis·ti·ca·tion** /sə,fisti'kāsHən/ *n.*

Pronunciation Key ə *ago*; ər *over*; 'ə or ,ə *up*; 'ər or ,ər *fur*; a *hat*; ā *rate*; ä *car*; CH *chew*; e *let*; ē *see*; e(ə)r *air*; i *fit*; ī *by*; i(ə)r *ear*; NG *sing*; ō *go*; ô *for*; oi *boy*; ŏŏ *good*; ōō *goo*; ou *out*; SH *she*; TH *thin*; TH *then*; (h)w *why*; ZH *vision*

S

so·phis·ti·cat·ed /sə'fisti,kātid/ ▶*adj.* (of a machine, system, or technique) developed to a high degree of complexity: *highly sophisticated computer systems.* ■ (of a person or their thoughts, reactions, and understanding) aware of and able to interpret complex issues; subtle: *discussion and reflection are necessary for a sophisticated response to a text.* ■ having, revealing, or proceeding from a great deal of worldly experience and knowledge of fashion and culture: *a chic, sophisticated woman | a young man with sophisticated tastes.* See note at **URBANE**. ■ appealing to people with such knowledge of experience: *a sophisticated restaurant.* **—so·phis·ti·cat·ed·ly** *adv.*

soph·ist·ry /'säfəstrē/ ▶*n.* (*pl.* **-ries**) the use of fallacious arguments, esp. with the intention of deceiving. ■ a fallacious argument.

Soph·o·cles /'säfə,klēz/ (*c.*496–406 BC), Greek playwright. His seven surviving plays are notable for their complexity of plot and depth of characterization and for their examination of the relationship between mortals and the divine order. Notable plays: *Antigone* and *Oedipus Rex* (also called *Oedipus Tyrannus*).

soph·o·more /'säf(ə),môr/ ▶*n.* a second-year college or high school student. ▷mid 17th cent.: perhaps from earlier *sophumer*, from *sophum*, *sophom* (obsolete variants of **SOPHISM**) + **-ER**[1].

soph·o·mor·ic /,säf(ə)'môrik/ ▶*adj.* of, relating to, or characteristic of a sophomore: *my sophomoric years.* ■ pretentious or juvenile: *sophomoric double entendres.*

So·phy /'sōfē; 'sä-/ ▶*n.* (*pl.* **-phies**) *historical* a former title for the ruler of Persia associated esp. with the Safavid dynasty. ▷from Arabic *Ṣafi-al-dīn* 'pure of religion.'

sop·o·rif·ic /,säpə'rifik/ ▶*adj.* tending to induce drowsiness or sleep: *the motion of the train had a somewhat soporific effect.* ■ sleepy or drowsy: *some medicine made her soporific.* ■ tediously boring or monotonous: *a libel trial is in large parts intensely soporific.*
▶*n.* a drug or other agent of this kind. ▷mid 17th cent.: from Latin *sopor* 'sleep' + **-IFIC**. **—sop·o·rif·i·cal·ly** /-ik(ə)lē/ *adv.*

sop·ping /'säpiNG/ ▶*adj.* saturated with liquid; wet through: *get those sopping clothes off* | [as *submodifier*] *the handkerchief was sopping wet.* ▷mid 19th cent.: present participle of **SOP**.

sop·py /'säpē/ ▶*adj.* (**-pi·er**, **-pi·est**) *informal* self-indulgently sentimental: *I look at babies with a soppy smile on my face | an enjoyably soppy story.* ■ *Brit.* lacking spirit and common sense; feeble: *my little sisters were too soppy for our adventurous games.* ▷early 19th cent. (in the sense 'soaked with water'): from **SOP** + **-Y**[1]. **—sop·pi·ly** /'säpəlē/ *adv.* **—sop·pi·ness** *n.*

so·pra·ni·no /,säprə'nēnō/ ▶*n. Music* (*pl.* **-ni·nos**) an instrument, esp. a recorder or saxophone, higher than soprano. ▷early 20th cent.: Italian, diminutive of **SOPRANO**.

so·pran·o /sə'pranō/ ▶*n.* (*pl.* **-pran·os**) the highest of the four standard singing voices: *a piece composed for soprano, flute, and continuo* | [as *adj.*] *a good soprano voice.* ■ a female or boy singer with such a voice. ■ a part written for such a voice. ■ [usu. as *adj.*] an instrument of a high or the highest pitch in its family: *a soprano saxophone.* ▷mid 18th cent.: Italian, from *sopra* 'above,' from Latin *supra*.

so·pran·o clef /klef/ ▶*n. Music* an obsolete clef placing middle C on the lowest line of the staff.

so·pran·o re·cord·er ▶*n. Music* the most common size of recorder, with a range of two octaves from the C above middle C upward.

so·ra /'sôrə/ (also **so·ra crake** or **rail**) ▶*n.* a common small brown and gray American rail, frequenting marshes. • *Porzana carolina*, family Rallidae. ▷early 18th cent.: probably from an American Indian language.

Sorb /sôrb/ ▶*n.* a member of a Slavic people living in parts of southeastern Brandenburg and eastern Saxony. Also called **WEND**. ▷from German *Sorbe*.

sorb /sôrb/ ▶*n.* the fruit of the true service tree. ▷early 16th cent.: from French *sorbe* or Latin *sorbus* 'service tree,' *sorbum* 'serviceberry.'

sor·bent /'sôrbənt/ ▶*n. Chemistry* a substance that has the property of collecting molecules of another substance by sorption. ▷early 20th cent.: from *sorb* 'take up by sorption,' on the pattern of *absorbent*.

sor·bet /sôr'bā; 'sôrbit/ ▶*n.* a dessert consisting of frozen fruit juice or flavored water and sugar. ■ *archaic* an Arabian sherbet. ▷late 16th cent.: from French, from Italian *sorbetto*, from Turkish *şerbet*, based on Arabic *šariba* 'to drink'; compare with **SHERBET**.

Sorb·i·an /'sôrbēən/ ▶*adj.* of or relating to the Sorbs or their language.
▶*n.* the West Slavic language of the Sorbs, which has been revived from near extinction and has around 70,000 speakers. Also called **WENDISH** or **LUSATIAN**.

sor·bi·tan /'sôrbə,tan/ ▶*n.* [usu. as *adj.*] *Chemistry* any of a group of compounds that are cyclic ethers derived from sorbitol or its derivatives. ▷1930s: blend of **SORBITOL** and **ANHYDRIDE**.

sor·bi·tol /'sôrbi,tôl; -,täl/ ▶*n. Chemistry* a sweet-tasting crystalline compound found in some fruit. • A hexahydric alcohol; chem. formula: $CH_2OH(CHOH)_4CH_2OH$. ▷late 19th cent.: from **SORB** + **-ITE**[1] + **-OL**.

Sor·bonne /sôr'bən/ the seat of the faculties of science and literature of the University of Paris. ▷originally a theological college founded by Robert de Sorbon, chaplain to Louis IX, *c.*1257.

sor·cer·er /'sôrsərər/ ▶*n.* a person who claims or is believed to have magic powers; a wizard. ▷late Middle English: from *sorser* (from Old French *sorcier*, based on Latin *sors, sort-* 'lot') + **-ER**[1].

sor·cer·er's ap·pren·tice ▶*n.* a person who instigates a process or project which they are then unable to control. ▷translating French *l'apprenti sorcier*, a symphonic poem (1897) by Paul Dukas, suggested by German *der Zauberlehrling* (1797), a poem by Goethe.

sor·cer·ess /'sôrsəris/ ▶*n.* a female sorcerer; a witch.

sor·cer·y /'sôrsərē/ ▶*n.* the use of magic, esp. black magic. **—sor·cer·ous** /-rəs/ *adj.*

sor·did /'sôrdid/ ▶*adj.* involving ignoble actions and motives; arousing moral distaste and contempt: *the story paints a sordid picture of bribes and scams.* ■ dirty or squalid: *the overcrowded housing conditions were sordid and degrading.* ▷late Middle English (as a medical term in the sense 'purulent'): from French *sordide* or Latin *sordidus*, from *sordere* 'be dirty.' The current senses date from the early 17th cent. **—sor·did·ly** *adv.* **—sor·did·ness** *n.*

sor·di·no /sôr'dēnō/ ▶*n.* (*pl.* **-ni** /-nē/) *Music* a mute. ■ (**sordini**) (on a piano) the dampers. ▷late 16th cent.: from Italian, from *sordo* 'mute,' from Latin *surdus*.

sor·dor /'sôrdər/ ▶*n. chiefly poetic/literary* physical or moral sordidness. ▷early 19th cent.: from **SORDID**, on the pattern of the pair *squalid, squalor*.

sore /sôr/ ▶*adj.* (of a part of one's body) painful or aching: *my feet were sore and my head ached.* ■ [*predic.*] suffering pain from a part of one's body: *he was sore from the long ride.* ■ [*predic.*] *informal* upset and angry: *I didn't even know they were* **sore at us**. ■ [*attrib.*] severe; urgent: *we're in sore need of him.*
▶*n.* a raw or painful place on the body: *we had sores on our hands.* ■ a cause or source of distress or annoyance: *there's no point raking over the past and opening old sores.*
▶*adv. archaic* extremely; severely: *they were sore afraid.* ▷Old English *sār* (noun and adjective), *sāre* (adverb), of Germanic origin; related to Dutch *zeer* 'sore' and German *sehr* 'very.' The original sense was 'causing intense pain, grievous,' whence the adverbial use. **—sore·ness** *n.*
▶*PHRASES* □ **sore point** a subject or issue about which someone feels distressed or annoyed: *the glamorous image of their paramilitary rivals was always a sore point with the police.* □ **stand** (or **stick**) **out like a sore thumb** be obviously different from the surrounding people or things.

sore·head /'sôr,hed/ ▶*n. informal* a person who is in a bad temper or easily irritated.

sore·ly /'sôrlē/ ▶*adv.* to a very high degree or level of intensity (esp. of an unwelcome or unpleasant state or emotion): *she would sorely miss his company | help was sorely needed.* ▷Old English *sārlīce* (see **SORE**, **-LY**[2]).

sor·ghum /'sôrgəm/ ▶*n.* a widely cultivated cereal native to warm regions of the Old World. It is a major source of grain and of feed for livestock. • Genus *Sorghum*, family Gramineae: many species, in particular *S. bicolor* and its cultivars. ■ a syrupy sweetener made from a type of this cereal. ▷late 16th cent.: modern Latin, from Italian *sorgo*, perhaps based on a variant of Latin *syricum* 'Syrian.'

so·ri /'sô,rī/ ▶ plural form of **SORUS**.

so·ro·ral /sə'rôrəl/ ▶*adj. formal* of or like a sister or sisters. ▷mid 17th cent.: from Latin *soror* 'sister' + **-AL**.

so·ror·i·ty /sə'rôritē; -'rä-/ ▶*n.* (*pl.* **-ties**) a society for female students in a university or college, typically for social purposes. ▷mid 16th cent.: from medieval Latin *sororitas*, or from Latin *soror* 'sister' (on the pattern of *fraternity*).

so·ro·sis /sə'rōsis/ ▶*n.* (*pl.* **-ses** /-,sēz/) *Botany* a fleshy multiple fruit, e.g., a pineapple or mulberry, derived from the ovaries of several flowers. ▷mid 19th cent.: modern Latin, from Greek *sōros* 'heap.'

sorp·tion /'sôrpSHən/ ▶*n. Chemistry* absorption and adsorption considered as a single process. ▷early 20th cent.: back-formation from **ABSORPTION** and **ADSORPTION** (see **ADSORB**).

sor·rel[1] /'sôrəl/ ▶*n.* a European plant of the dock family, with arrow-shaped leaves that are used in salads and cooking for their acidic flavor. See also **WOOD SORREL**. • Genus *Rumex*, family Polygonaceae: several species, including the **English sorrel** (*R. acetosa*) and the more slender-leaved **French sorrel** (*R. scutatus*). ▷late Middle English: from Old French *sorele*, of Germanic origin; related to **SOUR**.

sor·rel[2] ▶*n.* a horse with a light reddish-brown coat. ■ [usu. as *adj.*] a light reddish-brown color: *a sorrel mare with four white socks.* ▷Middle English: from Old French *sorel*, from *sor* 'yellowish,' from a Germanic adjective meaning 'dry.'

sor·rel tree ▶*n.* another term for **SOURWOOD**.

sor·row /'särō/ ▶*n.* a feeling of deep distress caused by loss, disappointment, or other misfortune suffered by oneself or others: *he understood the sorrow and discontent underlying his brother's sigh.* ■ an event or circumstance that causes such a feeling: *it was a great sorrow to her when they separated.* ■ the outward expression of grief; lamentation.
▶*v.* [*intrans.*] feel or display deep distress: [as *adj.*] (**sorrowing**) *the sorrowing widower found it hard to relate to his sons.* See note at **MOURN**. ▷Old English *sorh, sorg* (noun), *sorgian* (verb), of Germanic origin; related to Dutch *zorg* and German *Sorge*.

sor·row·ful /'särəfəl/ ▶*adj.* feeling or showing grief: *she looked at him with sorrowful eyes.* ■ causing grief: *the sorrowful news of his father's death.* ▷Old English *sorhful* (see **SORROW**, **-FUL**). **—sor·row·ful·ly** *adv.* **—sor·row·ful·ness** *n.*

sor·ry /'särē; 'sô-/ ▶*adj.* (**-ri·er**, **-ri·est**) **1** [*predic.*] feeling distress, esp. through sympathy with someone else's misfortune: *I was sorry to hear about what happened to your family.* ■ (**sorry for**) filled with compassion for: *he couldn't help feeling sorry for her when he heard how she'd been treated.* ■ feeling regret or penitence: *he said he was sorry he had upset me | I'm sorry if I was a bit brusque.* ■ used as an expression of apology: *sorry—I was trying not to make a noise.* ■ used as a polite request that someone should repeat something that one has failed to hear or understand: *Sorry? In case I what?* **2** [*attrib.*] in a poor or pitiful state or condition: *he looks a sorry sight with his broken jaw.* ■ unpleasant and regrettable, esp. on account of incompetence or misbehavior: *we feel so ashamed that we keep quiet about the whole sorry business.* ▷Old English *sārig* 'pained, distressed,' from the base of the noun **SORE**. The shortening of the root vowel has given the word an apparent connection with the unrelated **SORROW**. **—sor·ri·ly** /'särəlē; sô-/ *adv.* **—sor·ri·ness** *n.*
▶*PHRASE* □ **sorry for oneself** sad and self-pitying.

sort /sôrt/ ▶*n.* **1** a category of things or people having some common feature; a type: *if only we knew the sort of people she was mixing with | a radical change poses* ***all sorts of*** *questions.* ■ [with *adj.*] *informal* a person of a specified character or nature: *Frank was a genuinely friendly sort.* ■ *archaic* a manner or way: *in law also the judge is* ***in a sort*** *superior to his king.* **2** *Computing* the arrangement of data in a prescribed sequence. **3** *Printing* a letter or piece in a font of type.
▶*v.* [*trans.*] **1** arrange systematically in groups; separate according to type, class, etc.: *she* ***sorted out*** *the clothes, some to be kept, some to be thrown away.* ■ (**sort through**) look at (a group of things) one after another in order to classify them or make a selection: *she sat down and sorted through her mail.* **2** resolve (a problem or difficulty): *the teacher helps the children to* ***sort out*** *their problems.* ■ resolve the problems or difficulties of (oneself): *I need time to* ***sort myself out***.
▶*phrasal v.* □ **sort someone out** *informal* deal with someone who is causing trouble, typically by restraining, reprimanding, or punishing them: *if he can't pay you, I'll sort him out.* □ **sort something out** **1** separate something from a mixed group: *she started* ***sorting out*** *the lettuce* ***from*** *the spinach.* **2** arrange; prepare: *they are anxious to sort out traveling arrangements.* ▷late Middle English: from Old French *sorte*, from an alteration of Latin *sors, sort-* 'lot, condition.' **—sort·a·ble** *adj.* **—sort·er** *n.*
▶*PHRASES* □ **after a sort** *dated* after a fashion. □ **in some sort** to a certain extent: *I am in some sort indebted to you.* □ **nothing of the sort** used as an emphatic way of denying permission or refuting an earlier statement or assumption: *"I'll pay." "You'll do*

nothing of the sort." □ **of a sort** (or **of sorts**) *informal* of an atypical and typically inferior type: *the training camp actually became a tourist attraction of sorts.* □ **out of sorts** slightly unwell: *feeling nauseous and generally out of sorts.* ■ in low spirits; irritable: *the trying events of the day had put him out of sorts.* □ **sort of** *informal* to some extent; in some way or other (used to convey inexactness or vagueness): *"Do you see what I mean?" "Sort of," answered Jean cautiously.* □ **the —— sort** the kind of person likely to do or be involved with the thing specified: *she'd never imagined Steve to be the marrying sort.*

USAGE The construction **these sort of**, as in *I don't want to answer **these sort of** questions*, is technically ungrammatical because **these** is plural and needs to agree with a plural noun (**sorts**). The construction is undoubtedly common, however, and has been used for hundreds of years. There are some grammarians who analyze the construction differently, seeing the words "these sort of" as a single invariable unit.
For more details, see **usage** at KIND[1].

sor·tal /ˈsôrtl/ *Linguistics & Philosophy* ▸*adj.* denoting or relating to a term representing a semantic feature that applies to an entity, classifying it as being of a particular kind.
▸*n.* a term of this kind, for example *human* as opposed to *engineer*.

sor·ta·tion /sôrˈtāsʜən/ ▸*n.* (especially in data processing) the process of sorting or its result. ▷mid 19th cent.: from *sort* (verb) + *-ation*.

sort·ed /sôrdid/ ▸*adj. Brit., informal* organized; arranged; fixed up: *"And your social commitments?" "They're well sorted."* ■ (of a person) having obtained illegal drugs. ■ (of a person) confident, organized, and emotionally well balanced: *a pretty sorted kind of fellow.*

sor·tes /ˈsôrˌtēz; -ˌtāz/ ▸*plural n.* [treated as *sing.*] divination, or the seeking of guidance, by chance selection of a passage in the Bible or another text regarded as authoritative. ▷Latin, 'chance selections (of the Bible).'

sort·ie /ˌsôrˈtē; ˈsôrtē/ ▸*n.* an attack made by troops coming out from a position of defense. ■ an operational flight by a single military aircraft. ■ a short trip or journey: *I went on a shopping sortie.*
▸*v.* (**-ies, -ied, -ie·ing**) [*intrans.*] come out from a defensive position to make an attack. ▷late 18th cent.: from French, feminine past participle of *sortir* 'go out.'

sor·ti·lege /ˈsôrdl-ij/ ▸*n. chiefly historical* the practice of foretelling the future from a card or other item drawn at random from a collection. ▷late Middle English: via Old French from medieval Latin *sortilegium* 'sorcery,' from Latin *sortilegus* 'sorcerer,' from *sors, sort-* 'lot, chance' + *legere* 'choose.'

sor·ti·tion /sôrˈtisʜən/ ▸*n.* the action of selecting or determining something by the casting or drawing of lots. ▷late 16th cent.: from Latin *sortitio(n-)*, from *sortire* 'divide or obtain by lot.'

so·rus /ˈsôrəs/ ▸*n.* (*pl.* **so·ri** /ˈsôrī/) *Botany* a cluster of spore-producing receptacles on the underside of a fern frond. ■ a gamete-producing or fruiting body in certain algae and fungi. ▷mid 19th cent.: modern Latin, from Greek *sōros* 'heap.'

SOS ▸*n.* (*pl.* **SOSs**) an international code signal of extreme distress, used esp. by ships at sea. ■ an urgent appeal for help. ■ *Brit.* a message broadcast to an untraceable person in an emergency: *here is an SOS message for Mr. Arthur Brown about his brother, who is dangerously ill.* ▷early 20th cent.: letters chosen as being easily transmitted and recognized in Morse code; by folk etymology an abbreviation of *save our souls*.

So·sa /ˈsōsə/, Sammy (1968–), U.S. baseball player; born in Dominican Republic; full name *Samuel Sosa*. An outfielder for the Chicago Cubs from 1989 (and a brief stint with the Texas Rangers in 1989), he is best known for his home-run totals, hitting at least 50 each year for 4 consecutive years 1998, 1999, 2000, 2001.

Sos·no·wiec /sôsˈnôvyets/ an industrial mining town in southwestern Poland, west of Cracow; pop. 259,000.

so-so ▸*adj.* neither very good nor very bad: *a happy ending to a so-so season* | *"How are you?" "So-so."*

sos·te·nu·to /ˌsästəˈnōōtō/ *Music* ▸*adj.* (of a passage of music) to be played in a sustained or prolonged manner.
▸*n.* (*pl.* **-tos**) a passage to be played in a sustained and prolonged manner. ■ performance in this manner. ▷Italian, 'sustained.'

sot /sät/ ▸*n.* a habitual drunkard.
▸*v.* (**sot·ted, sot·ting**) [*intrans.*] *archaic* drink habitually. ▷late Old English *sott* 'foolish person,' from medieval Latin *sottus*, reinforced by Old French *sot* 'foolish.' The current sense of the noun dates from the late 16th cent. —**sot·tish** *adj.*

so·te·ri·ol·o·gy /səˌti(ə)rēˈäləjē/ ▸*n. Theology* the doctrine of salvation. ▷mid 19th cent.: from Greek *sōtēria* 'salvation' + -LOGY. —**so·te·ri·o·log·i·cal** /-ēəˈläjikəl/ *adj.*

So·thic /ˈsōTHik; ˈsä-/ ▸*adj.* of or relating to Sirius (the Dog Star), esp. with reference to the ancient Egyptian year fixed by its heliacal rising. ▷early 19th cent.: from Greek *Sōthis* (from an Egyptian name of the Dog Star) + -IC.

So·tho /ˈsōtō/ ▸*n.* (*pl.* same or **-thos**) **1** a member of a group of peoples living chiefly in Botswana, Lesotho, and northern South Africa. **2** the group of Bantu languages spoken by these peoples.
▸*adj.* of or relating to this people or their languages. ▷the stem of BASOTHO and SESOTHO.

so·tol /ˈsōˌtōl/ ▸*n.* a North American desert plant of the agave family, with spiny-edged leaves and small white flowers. • Genus *Dasylirion*, family Agavaceae: several species, including **smooth-leaf sotol** (*D. leiophyllum*). ■ an alcoholic drink made from the sap of this plant. ▷late 19th cent.: via American Spanish from Nahuatl *tzotolli*.

sot·to vo·ce /ˈsätō ˈvōCHē/ ▸*adv. & adj.* (of singing or a spoken remark) in a quiet voice, as if not to be overheard: [as *adv.*] *"It won't be cheap," he added sotto voce* | [as *adj.*] *a sotto voce remark.* ▷from Italian *sotto* 'under' + *voce* 'voice.'

sou /sōō/ ▸*n. historical* a former French coin of low value. ■ [usu. with *negative*] *informal* a very small amount of money: *he didn't have a sou.* ▷French, originally as *sous* (plural), from Old French *sout*, from Latin *solidus* (see SOLIDUS).

sou·bise /sōōˈbēz/ ▸*n.* a thick white sauce made with onion purée and often served with fish or eggs. ▷named after Charles de Rohan *Soubise* (1715–87), French general and courtier.

sou·bre·saut /ˌsōōbrəˈsō/ ▸*n.* (*pl. pronunc.* same) *Ballet* a straight-legged jump from both feet with the toes pointed and feet together, one behind the other. ▷French.

sou·brette /sōōˈbret/ ▸*n.* a minor female role in a comedy, typically that of a pert maidservant. ▷mid 18th cent.: French, from Provençal *soubreto*, feminine of *soubret* 'coy,' from *sobrar*, from Latin *superare* 'be above.'

sou·bri·quet ▸*n.* variant spelling of SOBRIQUET.

sou·chong /ˈsōōˈCHông; ˈSHông/ ▸*n.* a fine black variety of China tea. ▷mid 18th cent.: from Chinese *siú* 'small' + *chúng* 'sort.'

sou·cou·yant /ˌsōōkōōˈyän(t)/ ▸*n.* (in eastern Caribbean folklore) a malignant witch believed to shed her skin by night and suck the blood of her victims. ▷West Indian Creole.

souf·fle /ˈsōōfəl/ ▸*n. Medicine* a low murmuring or blowing sound heard through a stethoscope. ▷late 19th cent.: from French, from *souffler* 'to blow,' from Latin *sufflare*.

souf·flé /sōōˈflā/ ▸*n.* a light, spongy baked dish made typically by adding flavored egg yolks to stiffly beaten egg whites. ■ any of various light dishes made with beaten egg whites. ▷French, literally 'blown,' past participle of *souffler* (see SOUFFLE).

Sou·fri·ère /sōōˈfryer/ **1** a dormant volcano on the French island of Guadeloupe in the Caribbean Sea. Rising to 4,813 feet (1,468 m), it is the highest peak in the Lesser Antilles. **2** an active volcanic peak on the island of St. Vincent in the Caribbean. It rises to a height of 4,006 feet (1,234 m). ▷French, from *soufre* 'sulfur.'

sough /səf; sou/ ▸*v.* [*intrans.*] (of the wind in trees, the sea, etc.) make a moaning, whistling, or rushing sound.
▸*n.* [in *sing.*] a sound of this type. ▷Old English *swōgan*, of Germanic origin.

sought /sôt/ ▸ past and past participle of SEEK.

sought af·ter ▸*adj.* in demand; generally desired: *this print will be much sought after by collectors* | *the most expensive and sought-after perfume.*

souk /sōōk/ (also **suk, sukh,** or **suq**) ▸*n.* an Arab market or marketplace; a bazaar. ▷from Arabic *sūk*.

sou·kous /ˈsōōˈkōōs/ ▸*n.* a style of African popular music characterized by syncopated rhythms and intricate contrasting guitar melodies, originating in the Democratic Republic of the Congo (formerly Zaire). ▷perhaps from French *secouer* 'to shake.'

soul /sōl/ ▸*n.* **1** the spiritual or immaterial part of a human being or animal, regarded as immortal. ■ a person's moral or emotional nature or sense of identity: *in the depths of her soul, she knew he would betray her.* ■ the essence of something: *integrity is the soul of intellectual life.* ■ emotional or intellectual energy or intensity, esp. as revealed in a work of art or an artistic performance: *their interpretation lacked soul.* **2** a person regarded as the embodiment of a specified quality: *he was **the soul of** discretion.* ■ an individual person: *I'll never tell a soul.* ■ a person regarded with affection or pity: *she's a nice old soul.* **3** African-American culture or ethnic pride. ■ short for SOUL MUSIC. ▷Old English *sāwol, sāw(e)l*, of Germanic origin; related to Dutch *ziel* and German *Seele*. —**souled** *adj.* [in *combination*] *she was a great-souled character.*

▸*PHRASES* □ **bare one's soul** see BARE. □ **the life and soul of the party** see LIFE. □ **lost soul** a soul that is damned. ■ *chiefly humorous* a person who seems unable to cope with everyday life. □ **sell one's soul (to the devil)** see SELL. □ **upon my soul** *dated* an exclamation of surprise.

soul broth·er ▸*n. informal* used as a term of address or reference between African-American men. ■ a man whose thoughts, feelings, and attitudes closely match those of another; a kindred spirit.

soul food ▸*n.* traditional southern African-American food.

soul·ful /ˈsōlfəl/ ▸*adj.* expressing or appearing to express deep and often sorrowful feeling: *she gave him a soulful glance.* —**soul·ful·ly** *adv.* —**soul·ful·ness** *n.*

soul kiss ▸*n.* another term for FRENCH KISS.

soul·less /ˈsōlˌlis/ ▸*adj.* (of a building, room, or other place) lacking character and individuality: *she found the apartment beautiful but soulless.* ■ (of an activity) tedious and uninspiring: *soulless, nonproductive work.* ■ lacking or suggesting the lack of human feelings and qualities: *two soulless black eyes were watching her.* —**soul·less·ly** *adv.* —**soul·less·ness** *n.*

soul mate (also **soul·mate**) ▸*n.* a person ideally suited to another as a close friend or romantic partner.

soul mu·sic ▸*n.* a kind of music incorporating elements of rhythm and blues and gospel music, popularized by African-Americans. Characterized by an emphasis on vocals and an impassioned improvisatory delivery, it is associated with performers such as Marvin Gaye, Aretha Franklin, James Brown, and Otis Redding.

soul-search·ing ▸*n.* deep and anxious consideration of one's emotions and motives or of the correctness of a course of action.
▸*adj.* involving or expressing such consideration: *long, soul-searching conversations about religion.*

soul sis·ter ▸*n. informal* used as a term of address or reference between African-American women. ■ a woman whose thoughts, feelings, and attitudes closely match those of another; a kindred spirit.

soul·ster /ˈsōlstər/ ▸*n. informal* a singer of soul music.

Sound /sound/ (**the Sound**) another name for ØRESUND.

sound[1] /sound/ ▸*n.* vibrations that travel through the air or another medium and can be heard when they reach a person's or animal's ear: *light travels faster than sound.* ■ a group of vibrations of this kind; a thing that can be heard: *she heard the sound of voices in the hall* | *don't make a sound.* ■ the area or distance within which something can be heard: *we were always **within sound of** the train whistles.* ■ short for SPEECH SOUND. ■ the ideas or impressions conveyed by words: *you've had a hard day, **by the sound of it**.* ■ (also **musical sound**) sound produced by continuous and regular vibrations, as opposed to noise. ■ music, speech, and sound effects when recorded, used to accompany a film or video production, or broadcast: [as *adj.*] *a sound studio.* ■ broadcasting by radio as distinct from television. ■ the distinctive quality of the music of a particular composer or performer or of the sound produced by a particular musical instrument: *the sound of the Beatles.* ■ (**sounds**) *informal* music, esp. popular music: *sounds of the sixties.*
▸*v.* [*intrans.*] emit sound: *a loud buzzer sounded.* ■ [*trans.*] cause (something) to emit sound: *she sounded the horn.* ■ [*trans.*] give an audible signal to warn of or indicate (something): *a different bell begins to sound midnight.* ■ [*trans.*] say (something); utter: *he*

sounded a warning that a coup was imminent. ■ convey a specified impression when heard: [with *complement*] *he sounded worried.* ■ (of something or someone that has been described to one) convey a specified impression: ***it sounds as though*** *you really do believe that* | [with *complement*] *the house sounds lovely.* ■ [*trans.*] test (the lungs or another body cavity) by noting the sound they produce: *the doctor sounded her chest.*

▸*phrasal v.* □ **sound off** express one's opinions in a loud or forceful manner. ▷Middle English *soun,* from Anglo-Norman French *soun* (noun), *suner* (verb), from Latin *sonus.* The form with *-d* was established in the 16th cent. **—sound·less** *adj.* **—sound·less·ly** *adv.* **—sound·less·ness** *n.*

sound2 ▸*adj.* **1** in good condition; not damaged, injured, or diseased: *they returned* ***safe and sound*** | *he was not of sound mind.* ■ based on reason, sense, or judgment: *sound advice for healthy living* | *the scientific content is sound.* ■ competent, reliable, or holding acceptable views: *he's a bit stuffy, but he's very sound on his law.* ■ financially secure: *she could get her business on a sound footing for the first time.* **2** (of sleep) deep and undisturbed. ■ (of a person) tending to sleep deeply: *I am a sound sleeper.* **3** severe: *such people should be given a sound thrashing.*

▸*adv.* soundly: *he was sound asleep.* ▷Middle English: from Old English *gesund;* related to Dutch *gezond* and German *gesund.* **—sound·ly** *adv.* **—sound·ness** *n.*

▸*PHRASE* □ **(as) sound as a bell** in perfect condition.

sound3 ▸*v.* **1** [*trans.*] ascertain (the depth of water), typically by means of a line or pole or using sound echoes. ■ *Medicine* examine (a person's bladder or other internal cavity) with a long surgical probe. **2** [*trans.*] question (someone), typically in a cautious or discreet way, as to their opinions or feelings on a subject: *we'll* ***sound out*** *our representatives first.* ■ inquire into (someone's opinions of feelings) in this way: *officials arrived to* ***sound out*** *public opinion at meetings in factories.* **3** [*intrans.*] (esp. of a whale) dive down steeply to a great depth.

▸*n.* a long surgical probe, typically with a curved, blunt end. ▷late Middle English: from Old French *sonder,* based on Latin *sub-* 'below' + *unda* 'wave.' **—sound·er** *n.*

sound4 ▸*n.* a narrow stretch of water forming an inlet or connecting two wider areas of water such as two seas or a sea and a lake. ▷Middle English: from Old Norse *sund* 'swimming, strait'; related to **SWIM**.

sound·a·like /'soundə,līk/ ▸*n.* a person or thing that closely resembles another in sound, esp. someone whose voice or style of speaking or singing is very similar to that of a famous person.

sound bar·ri·er ▸*n.* (**the sound barrier**) the increased drag, reduced controllability, and other effects that occur when an aircraft approaches the speed of sound, formerly regarded as an obstacle to supersonic flight.

sound bite ▸*n.* a short extract from a recorded interview, chosen for its pungency or appropriateness.

sound·board /'soun(d),bôrd/ (also **sound·ing board**) ▸*n.* a thin sheet of wood over which the strings of a piano or similar instrument are positioned to increase the sound produced.

sound box (also **sound·box** /'soun(d),bäks/) ▸*n.* the hollow chamber that forms the body of a stringed musical instrument and provides resonance.

sound card ▸*n.* a device that can be slotted into a computer to allow the use of audio components for multimedia applications.

sound check (also **sound·check** /'soun(d),CHek/) ▸*n.* a test of sound equipment before a musical performance or recording to check that the desired sound is being produced.

sound con·di·tion·er ▸*n.* a device designed to mask or block out undesirable sounds by generating white noise or some other continuous, unobtrusive sound.

sound ef·fect ▸*n.* a sound other than speech or music made artificially for use in a play, movie, or other broadcast production: *the play used sound effects of galley oars and blood-curdling yells.*

sound en·gi·neer ▸*n.* a technician dealing with acoustics for a broadcast or musical performance.

Sound·ex /'soundeks/ ▸*n. Computing* a phonetic coding system intended to suppress spelling variations, used esp. to encode surnames for the linkage of medical and other records. ▷1950s: from **SOUND**1 + the arbitrary ending *-ex.*

sound hole ▸*n.* an aperture in the belly of a stringed instrument.

sound·ing1 /'soundiNG/ ▸*n.* the action or process of measuring the depth of the sea or other body of water. ■ a measurement taken by sounding. ■ the determination of any physical property at a depth in the sea or at a height in the atmosphere. ■ (**soundings**) *figurative* information or evidence ascertained as a preliminary step before deciding on a course of action: *he's been* ***taking soundings*** *about the possibility of moving his offices.* ■ (**soundings**) *archaic* the area of sea close to the shore that is shallow enough for the bottom to be reached by means of a sounding line.

sound·ing2 ▸*adj.* [*attrib.*] *archaic* giving forth sound, esp. loud or resonant sound: *he went in with a sounding plunge.* ■ having an imposing sound but little substance: *the orator has been apt to deal in sounding commonplaces.*

sound·ing board ▸*n.* **1** a board or screen placed over or behind a pulpit or stage to reflect a speaker's voice forward. ■ another term for **SOUNDBOARD**. **2** a person or group whose reactions to suggested ideas are used as a test of their validity or likely success before they are made public: *I considered him mainly as a sounding board for my impressions.* ■ a channel through which ideas are disseminated.

sound·ing line ▸*n.* a weighted line with distances marked off at regular intervals, used to measure the depth of water under a boat.

sound·ing rod ▸*n.* a rod used to measure the depth of water under a boat or in a ship's hold or other container.

sound post ▸*n.* a small wooden rod wedged between the front and back surfaces of a violin or similar instrument and modifying its vibrations.

sound pres·sure ▸*n. Physics* the difference between the instantaneous pressure at a point in the presence of a sound wave and the static pressure of the medium.

sound·proof /'soun(d),prōōf/ ▸*adj.* preventing, or constructed of material that prevents, the passage of sound: *there was a soundproof, state-of-the-art recording studio.*

▸*v.* [*trans.*] make (a room or building) resistant to the passage of sound. **—sound·proof·ing** *n.*

sound·scape /'soun(d),skāp/ ▸*n.* a piece of music considered in terms of its component sounds: *his lush keyboard soundscapes.* ■ the sounds heard in a particular location, considered as a whole: *institutions concerned with the world soundscape as an ecologically balanced entity.*

sound shift ▸*n. Linguistics* a systematic change in the pronunciation of a set of speech sounds as a language evolves.

sound spec·tro·graph ▸*n.* an instrument for analyzing sound into its frequency components.

sound·stage /'soun(d),stāj/ (also **sound stage**) ▸*n.* an area of a movie studio with acoustic properties suitable for the recording of sound, typically used to record dialogue.

sound sym·bol·ism ▸*n.* the partial representation of the sense of a word by its sound, as in *bang, fizz,* and *slide.* See also **ONOMATOPOEIA**.

sound sys·tem ▸*n.* a set of equipment for the reproduction and amplification of sound.

sound·track /'soun(d),trak/ ▸*n.* a recording of the musical accompaniment to a movie: *she has requested a collaboration for the soundtrack to her forthcoming movie.* ■ a strip on the edge of a film on which the sound component is recorded.

▸*v.* [*trans.*] provide (a movie) with a soundtrack: *it is soundtracked by the great Ennio Morricone.*

sound wave ▸*n. Physics* a wave of compression and rarefaction, by which sound is propagated in an elastic medium such as air.

soup /sōōp/ ▸*n.* **1** a liquid dish, typically made by boiling meat, fish, or vegetables, etc., in stock or water: *a bowl of tomato soup.* ■ *figurative* a substance or mixture perceived to resemble soup in appearance or consistency: *the waves and the water beyond have become a thick brown soup.* **2** *informal* nitroglycerine or gelignite, esp. as used for safecracking. **3** *informal* the chemicals in which film is developed. ▷Middle English: from Old French *soupe* 'sop, broth (poured on slices of bread),' from late Latin *suppa,* of Germanic origin. **—soup·like** *adj.*

▸*phrasal v.* □ **soup something up** *informal* increase the power and efficiency of an engine or other machine. ■ make something more elaborate or impressive: *we had to soup up the show for the new venue.* [1930s, perhaps influenced by **SUPER-**.]

▸*PHRASES* □ **from soup to nuts** *informal* from beginning to end; completely: *I know all about that game from soup to nuts.* [from the courses of a dinner.] □ **in the soup** *informal* in trouble.

soup-and-fish ▸*n. Brit., informal, dated* men's evening dress. ▷so named from the traditional first two courses of a formal dinner.

soup·çon /sōōp'sôN/ ▸*n.* [in *sing.*] a very small quantity of something: *a soupçon of mustard.* ▷mid 18th cent.: French, from Old French *souspeçon,* from medieval Latin *suspectio* (see **SUSPICION**).

soup kitch·en ▸*n.* a place where free food is served to those who are homeless or destitute.

soup plate ▸*n.* a deep, wide-rimmed plate in which soup is served.

soup·spoon /'sōōp,spōōn/ (also **soup spoon**) ▸*n.* a large spoon with a round bowl, used for eating soup.

soup·y /'sōōpē/ ▸*adj.* (**soup·i·er, soup·i·est**) having the appearance or consistency of soup: *a soupy stew.* ■ (of the air or climate) humid. ■ *informal* mawkishly sentimental: *soupy nostalgia.* **—soup·i·ly** /'sōōpəlē/ *adv.* **—soup·i·ness** *n.*

sour /'sou(ə)r/ ▸*adj.* having an acid taste like lemon or vinegar: *she sampled the wine and found it was sour.* ■ (of food, esp. milk) spoiled because of fermentation. ■ having a rancid smell: *her breath was always sour.* ■ *figurative* feeling or expressing resentment, disappointment, or anger: *she was quite a different woman from the sour, bored creature I had known.* ■ (of soil) deficient in lime and usually dank. ■ (of petroleum or natural gas) containing a relatively high sulfur content.

▸*n.* [with *adj.*] a drink made by mixing an alcoholic beverage with lemon juice or lime juice: *a rum sour.*

▸*v.* make or become sour: [*trans.*] *water soured with tamarind* | [as *adj.*] (**soured**) *soured cream* | [*intrans.*] *a bowl of milk was souring in the sun.* ■ make or become unpleasant, acrimonious, or difficult: [*trans.*] *a dispute soured relations between the two countries for over a year* | [*intrans.*] *many friendships have soured over borrowed money.* ▷Old English *sūr,* of Germanic origin; related to Dutch *zuur* and German *sauer.* **—sour·ish** *adj.* **—sour·ly** *adv.* **—sour·ness** *n.*

▸*PHRASES* □ **go** (or **turn**) **sour** become less pleasant or attractive; turn out badly: *the case concerns a property deal that turned sour.* □ **sour grapes** an attitude in which someone disparages or affects to despise something because they cannot have it themselves: *government officials dismissed many of the complaints as sour grapes.* [with allusion to Aesop's fable *The Fox and the Grapes.*]

sour ball ▸*n.* a hard candy, esp. a jawbreaker, with a sour flavor.

source /sôrs/ ▸*n.* a place, person, or thing from which something comes or can be obtained: *mackerel is a good source of fish oil.* See note at **ORIGIN**. ■ a spring or fountainhead from which a river or stream issues: *the source of the Nile.* ■ a person who provides information: *military sources announced a reduction in strategic nuclear weapons.* ■ a book or document used to provide evidence in research. ■ *technical* a body or process by which energy or a particular component enters a system. The opposite of **SINK**2. ■ *Electronics* a part of a field-effect transistor from which carriers flow into the interelectrode channel.

▸*v.* [*trans.*] (often **be sourced**) obtain from a particular source: *each type of coffee is sourced from one country.* ■ find out where (something) can be obtained: *she was called upon to source a supply of carpet.* ▷late Middle English: from Old French *sours(e),* past participle of *sourdre* 'to rise,' from Latin *surgere.* **—source·less** *adj.*

▸*PHRASE* □ **at source** *chiefly Brit.* at the point of origin or issue: *reduction of pollution at source.* ■ used to show that an amount is deducted from earnings or other payments before they are made: *your pension contribution will be deducted at source.*

source·book /'sôrs,bŏŏk/ ▸*n.* a collection of writings and articles on a particular subject, esp. one used as a basic introduction to that subject.

source code ▸*n. Computing* a text listing of commands to be compiled or assembled into an executable computer program.

source crit·i·cism ▸*n.* the analysis and study of the sources used by biblical authors.

source pro·gram ▸*n. Computing* a program written in a language other than machine code, typically a high-level language.

source rock ▸*n. Geology* a rock from which later sediments are derived or in which a particular mineral originates. ■ a sediment containing sufficient organic matter to be a future source of hydrocarbons.

sour cher·ry ▸*n.* a jawbreaker candy with a sour flavor.
▸*n.* another term for **MORELLO**.

sour cream ▸*n.* cream that has been deliberately fermented by the addition of certain bacteria.

sour·dough /ˈsou(ə)rˌdō/ ▸*n.* **1** leaven for making bread, consisting of fermenting dough, typically that left over from a previous batch. ■ bread made using such leaven. **2** an experienced prospector in the western U.S. or Canada; an old-timer.

Sour·dough State a nickname for the state of **ALASKA**.

sour·gum /ˈsou(ə)rˌgəm/ (also **sour gum**) ▸*n.* a tupelo of eastern North America, with dark bark that has a deeply checkered pattern. Its bitter blue fruits are eaten by black bears and numerous species of birds. Also called **BLACK GUM**, **BLACK TUPELO**, **PEPPERIDGE**. • *Nyssa sylvatica*, family Nyssaceae.

sour mash ▸*n.* a mash used in distilling certain malt whiskeys. ■ whiskey distilled from this.

sour·puss /ˈsou(ə)rˌpo͝os/ ▸*n. informal* a bad-tempered or habitually sullen person. ▷1930s (originally U.S.): from **SOUR** + **PUSS**².

sour·sop /ˈsou(ə)rˌsäp/ ▸*n.* **1** a large acidic fruit with white fibrous flesh. **2** the evergreen tropical American tree that bears this fruit. • *Annona muricata*, family Annonaceae.

sour·wood /ˈsou(ə)rˌwo͝od/ ▸*n.* a North American tree of the heath family with sour-tasting leaves. Most common in the southeastern U.S., it has drooping clusters of white bell-like flowers in early summer and bright red foliage in autumn. Also called **SORREL TREE**. • *Oxydendrum arboreum*, family Ericaceae.

sous- ▸*prefix* (in words adopted from French) subordinate: *sous-chef.* ▷from French *sous* 'under.'

Sou·sa /ˈso͞ozə/, John Philip (1854–1932), U.S. composer and conductor; known as the **March King**. His works include more than a hundred marches, for example *The Stars and Stripes Forever*, *King Cotton*, and *Hands Across the Sea*. The sousaphone, invented in 1898, was named in his honor.

sou·sa·phone /ˈso͞ozəˌfōn/ ▸*n.* a form of tuba with a wide bell pointing forward above the player's head and circular coils resting on the player's left shoulder and right hip, used in marching bands. ▷1920s: named after J. P. **SOUSA**, on the pattern of *saxophone*. —**sou·sa·phon·ist** /-ist/ *n.*

souse /sous/ ▸*v.* [*trans.*] soak in or drench with liquid: *souse the quilts in warm suds until thoroughly clean.* ■ [often as *adj.*] (**soused**) put (gherkins, fish, etc.) in a pickling solution or a marinade: *soused herring.* ■ [as *adj.*] (**soused**) *informal* drunk: *I was soused to the eyeballs.*
▸*n.* **1** liquid, typically salted, used for pickling. ■ pickled food, esp. a pig's head. **2** *informal* a drunkard. ■ *dated* a drinking bout. ▷late Middle English (as a noun denoting pickled meat): from Old French *sous* 'pickle,' of Germanic origin; related to **SALT**.

sous·lik /ˈso͞oslik/ (also **sus·lik** /ˈsəsˌlik/) ▸*n.* a short-tailed ground squirrel native to Eurasia and the Arctic. • Genus *Spermophilus*, family Sciuridae: several species, in particular the **European souslik** (*S. citellus*). ▷late 18th cent.: from Russian.

Sousse /so͞os/ (also **Su·sah**, **Su·sa** /ˈso͞ozə/) a port and resort on the east coast of Tunisia; pop. 125,000.

sous vide /so͞oz ˈvēd/ ▸*n.* a method of treating food by partial cooking followed by vacuum-sealing and chilling.
▸*adj.* & *adv.* (of food or cooking) involving such preparation: [as *adj.*] *a convection oven can be used in sous vide operations* | [as *adv.*] *cooking cuisine sous vide.* ▷French, literally 'under vacuum.'

sou·tache /so͞oˈtasH/ ▸*n.* a narrow, flat, ornamental braid used to trim garments. ▷mid 19th cent.: from French, from Hungarian *sujtás*.

sou·tane /so͞oˈtän/ ▸*n.* a type of cassock worn by Roman Catholic priests. ▷mid 19th cent.: from French, from Italian *sottana*, from *sotto* 'under,' from Latin *subtus*.

sou·te·neur /ˌso͞otnˈər/ ▸*n.* a pimp. ▷French, literally 'protector.'

Sou·ter /ˈso͞otər/, David (Hackett) (1939–) U.S. Supreme Court associate justice 1990– . Considered a moderate conservative, he worked for the justice system in New Hampshire 1971–90 before being appointed to the Supreme Court by President George H. W. Bush.

sou·ter /ˈso͞otər/ (also **sou·tar**) ▸*n. Scottish* & *N. English* a shoemaker. ▷Old English *sūtere*, from Latin *sutor*, from *suere* 'sew.'

South /sousH/ (**the South**) in the U.S., a term with several definitions, most commonly the 11 states of the 1861–65 Confederacy: Alabama, Arkansas, Florida, Georgia, Louisiana, Mississippi, North Carolina, South Carolina, Tennessee, Texas, and Virginia. —**South·ern** *adj.*

south /sousH/ ▸*n.* (usu. **the south**) **1** the direction toward the point of the horizon 90° clockwise from east, or the point on the horizon itself: *the breeze came from the south* | *they trade with the countries* **to the south**. ■ the compass point corresponding to this. **2** the southern part of the world or of a specified country, region, or town: *he was staying in the south of France.* ■ (usu. **the South**) the southern states of the U.S. **3** [as *name*] (**South**) *Bridge* the player sitting opposite and partnering North.
▸*adj.* [*attrib.*] **1** lying toward, near, or facing the south: *the south coast.* ■ (of a wind) blowing from the south. **2** of or denoting the southern part of a specified area, city, or country or its inhabitants: *Telegraph Hill in South Boston.*
▸*adv.* to or toward the south: *they journeyed south along the valley* | *it is handily located ten miles* **south of** *Baltimore.*
▸*v.* [*intrans.*] move toward the south: *the wind southed a point or two.* ■ (of a celestial body) cross the meridian. ▷Old English *sūth*, of Germanic origin; related to Low German *sud*.
▸*PHRASES* □ **down south** *informal* to or in the south of a country. □ **south by east** (or **west**) between south and south-southeast (or south-southwest).

South Af·ri·ca a country that occupies the most southern part of Africa; pop. 42,718,000; administrative capital, Pretoria; legislative capital, Cape Town; judicial capital, Bloemfontein; languages, English, Afrikaans, Zulu, Xhosa, and others. —**South Af·ri·can** *adj.* & *n.*

Settled by the Dutch in the 17th century, the area of the cape came under British administration in 1806. There followed inland expansion and British dominance of local populations, culminating in victory in the Zulu and Boer Wars at the end of the 19th century. The colonies of Natal, the Cape, Transvaal, and Orange Free State joined to form the self-governing Union of South Africa in 1910. In 1961 South Africa became a republic and left the Commonwealth of Nations. From 1948, it pursued a policy of white minority rule (apartheid), which led to international diplomatic isolation. A gradual dismantling of apartheid began in 1990 following the release of the African National Congress leader Nelson Mandela. Majority rule was achieved after the country's first democratic elections in April 1994, won by the ANC. South Africa rejoined the Commonwealth in 1994.

South Af·ri·can Dutch ▸*n.* the Afrikaans language from the 17th to the 19th centuries, during its development from Dutch.

South A·mer·i·ca a continent that comprises the southern half of the American landmass, connected to North America by the Isthmus of Panama. It includes the Falkland Islands, the Galapagos Islands, and Tierra del Fuego. (See also **AMERICA**.) See map on page 1622. —**South A·mer·i·can** *adj.* & *n.*

South·amp·ton /sousHˈ(h)am(p)tən/ **1** an industrial city and seaport on the southern coast of England; pop. 194,000. **2** a resort and residential town in southeastern New York, at the eastern end of Long Island; pop. 44,976.

South At·lan·tic O·cean see **ATLANTIC OCEAN**.

South Aus·tral·ia a state in south central Australia; capital, Adelaide.

South·a·ven /ˈsouˌTHāvən/ a city in northeastern Mississippi, just south of the Tennessee border and of Memphis in Tennessee; pop. 28,977.

South Bend an industrial city in northern Indiana; pop. 107,789. The University of Notre Dame is nearby to the north.

South Bos·ton a residential district of eastern Boston in Massachusetts, noted for its Irish working-class community. Familiarly, **Southie**.

south·bound /ˈsousHˌbound/ ▸*adj.* traveling or leading toward the south: *southbound traffic* | *the southbound two-lane road.*

South Car·o·li·na /ˌkarəˈlīnə/ a state in the southeastern U.S., on the coast of the Atlantic Ocean; pop. 4,012,012; capital, Columbia; statehood, May 23, 1788 (8).The region was permanently settled by the English from 1663. Separated from North Carolina in 1729, it became one of the original thirteen states. In 1860, it was the first state to secede from the Union, precipitating the Civil War. —**South Car·o·lin·i·an** -ˈlinēən *n.* & *adj.*

South Chi·na Sea see **CHINA SEA**.

South Da·ko·ta a state in the northern central U.S.; pop. 754,844; capital, Pierre; statehood, Nov. 2, 1889 (40). Acquired partly by the Louisiana Purchase in 1803, it became a part of the former Dakota Territory in 1861. The scene of a gold rush in 1874, it separated from North Dakota in 1889. —**South Da·ko·tan** *n.* & *adj.*

South·down /ˈsousHˌdoun/ ▸*n.* a sheep of a breed raised esp. for mutton, originally on the South Downs of southern England.

south·east /ˌsousHˈēst/ ▸*n.* **1** (usu. **the southeast**) the direction toward the point of the horizon midway between south and east, or the point on the horizon itself: *a ship was coming in from the southeast.* ■ the compass point corresponding to this. **2** (also **the Southeast**) the southeastern part of a country, region, or town: *most "Mexican" foods in the southeast are actually Texan.*
▸*adj.* [*attrib.*] **1** lying toward, near, or facing the southeast: *a table stood in the southeast corner.* ■ (of a wind) blowing from the southeast. **2** of or denoting the southeastern part of a specified country, region, or town or its inhabitants: *Southeast Asia.*
▸*adv.* to or toward the southeast: *turn southeast to return to your starting point.* —**south·east·ern** /-ərn/ *adj.*

South·east A·sia an area in southeastern Asia that includes the countries of Cambodia, Indonesia, Laos, Malaysia, Myanmar, Philippines, Singapore, Thailand, and Vietnam.

South·east A·sia Trea·ty Or·gan·i·za·tion (abbr.: **SEATO**) a defense alliance that existed between 1954 and 1977 for countries of Southeast Asia and part of the southwestern Pacific, to further a U.S. policy of containing communism. Its members were Australia, Britain, France, New Zealand, Pakistan, the Philippines, Thailand, and the U.S.

south·east·er /ˌsousHˈēstər/ ▸*n.* a wind blowing from the southeast.

south·east·er·ly /ˌsousHˈēstərlē/ ▸*adj.* & *adv.* another term for **SOUTHEAST**: [as *adj.*] *southeasterly winds* | [as *adv.*] *the route turns southeasterly.*
▸*n.* another term for **SOUTHEASTER**.

south·east·ward /ˌsousHˈēstwərd/ ▸*adv.* (also **south·east·wards**) toward the southeast: *he walked southeastward from the river.*
▸*adj.* situated in, directed toward, or facing the southeast.

South·end-on-Sea /ˈsousHˌend/ a resort town on the Thames estuary, east of London; pop. 153,000.

South E·qua·to·ri·al Cur·rent an ocean current that flows west across the Pacific Ocean just south of the equator.

south·er·ly /ˈsəTHərlē/ ▸*adj.* & *adv.* in a southward position or direction: [as *adj.*] *the most southerly of the Greek islands* | [as *adv.*] *they made off southerly.* ■ (of a wind) blowing from the south: [as *adj.*] *a southerly gale* | [as *adv.*] *the wind had backed southerly.*
▸*n.* (often **southerlies**) a wind blowing from the south.

south·ern /ˈsəTHərn/ ▸*adj.* **1** [*attrib.*] situated in the south or directed toward or facing the south: *the southern hemisphere.* ■ (of a wind) blowing from the south. **2** living in or originating from the south: *the southern rural poor.* ■ of, relating to, or characteristic of the south or its inhabitants: *a faintly southern accent.* ▷Old English *sūtherne* (see **SOUTH**, **-ERN**). —**south·ern·most** /-ˌmōst/ *adj.*

South·ern Alps a mountain range on South Island,

Pronunciation Key ə *ago*; ər *over*; ˈə or ˌə *up*; ˈər or ˌər *fur*; a *hat*; ā *rate*; ä *car*; CH *chew*; e *let*; ē *see*; e(ə)r *air*; i *fit*; ī *by*; i(ə)r *ear*; NG *sing*; ō *go*; ô *for*; oi *boy*; o͝o *good*; o͞o *goo*; ou *out*; SH *she*; TH *thin*; TH *then*; (h)w *why*; ZH *vision*

SOUTH AMERICA
Caribbean Sea
Aruba I. (Netherlands)
Netherland Antilles (Netherlands)
Margarita I. (Venezuela)
TRINIDAD AND TOBAGO
PANAMA
Lake Maracaibo
Caracas
VENEZUELA
Orinoco R.
Georgetown
Paramaribo
GUYANA
SURINAME
Cayenne
French Guiana
ATLANTIC OCEAN
Bogota
COLOMBIA
Galapagos Islands (Ecuador)
Marajo I.
Caquetá R.
Negro R.
Quito
Putumayo R.
Japurá R.
ECUADOR
Napa R.
Amazon R.
Puna I.
Gulf of Guayaquil
B R A Z I L
Tapajos R.
Juruá R.
Purus R.
Madeira R.
Teles Pires R.
Xingu R.
Araguaia R.
Tocantins R.
São Francisco R.
PERU
Ucayali R.
Lima
Madre de Dios R.
Brasilia
La Paz
Lake Titicaca
BOLIVIA
Sucre
Paraná R.
PARAGUAY
São Paulo
Rio de Janeiro
San Felix I. (Chile)
CHILE
San Ambrosia I. (Chile)
Asunción
Iguaçu Falls
SOUTH PACIFIC OCEAN
Uruguay R.
URUGUAY
ARGENTINA
Santiago
Buenos Aires
Montevideo
SOUTH ATLANTIC OCEAN
Gulf of San Matias
Gulf of San Jorge
Patagonia
Strait of Magellan
Falkland Islands (UK)
Port Stanley
Tierra del Fuego
South Georgia Island (UK)
Drake Passage
Scotia Sea

New Zealand. Running roughly parallel to the west coast, it extends for almost the entire length of the island. Mount Cook, its highest peak, rises to 12,349 feet (3,764 m).

South·ern Bap·tist ▶*n.* a member of a large convention of Baptist churches established in the U.S. in 1845, typically having a fundamentalist and evangelistic approach to Christianity.

South·ern blot ▶*n. Biology* a procedure for identifying specific sequences of DNA, in which fragments separated on a gel are transferred directly to a second medium on which detection by hybridization may be carried out. ▷late 20th cent.: named after Edwin M. *Southern* (born 1938), British biochemist.

South·ern Cone ▶*n.* the region of South America comprising the countries of Brazil, Paraguay, Uruguay, Argentina, and Chile.

South·ern Cross *Astronomy* the smallest constellation (the Crux or Cross), but the most familiar one to observers in the southern hemisphere. It contains the bright star Acrux, the "Jewel Box" star cluster, and most of the Coalsack nebula.

South·ern·er (also **south·ern·er**) /'səT͟Hərnər/ ▶*n.* a native or inhabitant of the south, esp. of the southern U.S.

south·ern-fried ▶*adj.* (of food, esp. chicken) coated in flour, egg, and breadcrumbs and then deep-fried.

south·ern hem·i·sphere the half of the earth that is south of the equator.

south·ern lights another name for the aurora australis. See **AURORA**.

South·ern O·cean the expanse of ocean that surrounds Antarctica.

South·ern Pines a resort town in south central North Carolina, noted for its golf courses; pop. 9,129.

South·ern Rho·de·sia see **ZIMBABWE**.

south·ern·wood /'səT͟Hərn,wo͝od/ ▶*n.* a bushy artemisia native to southern Europe. Also called **LAD'S LOVE, OLD MAN.** • *Artemisia abrotanum*, family Compositae.

Sou·they /'souT͟Hē; 'səT͟Hē/, Robert (1774–1843), English poet. Associated with the Lake Poets, he was best known for his shorter poems, such as the "Battle of Blenheim" (1798). He was made England's poet laureate in 1813.

South·field /'souTH'fēld/ a residential and industrial city in southeastern Michigan, northwest of Detroit; pop. 78,296.

South Gate an industrial city in southwestern California, southeast of Los Angeles; pop. 86,284.

South Geor·gia a barren island in the South Atlantic Ocean, 700 miles (1,120 km) east of the Falkland Islands, of which it is a dependency. It was first explored in 1775 by Captain James Cook, who named the island after George III.

South Had·ley /'hadlē/ a town in western Massachusetts, on the Connecticut River, north of Springfield, home to Mount Holyoke College; pop. 16,685.

south·ing /'souT͟HiNG/ ▶*n.* distance traveled or measured southward, esp. at sea. ■ a figure or line representing southward distance on a map. ■ *Astronomy* the transit of a celestial object, esp. the sun, across the meridian due south of the observer. ■ *Astronomy* the angular distance of a star or other object south of the celestial equator.

South Is·land the larger and more southern of the two main islands of New Zealand, separated from North Island by Cook Strait.

South Jor·dan a city in northern Utah, a southern suburb of Salt Lake City; pop. 29,437.

South Kings·town /'kiNGstən; 'kiNGz,toun/ a town in southern Rhode Island; pop. 27,971.

South Ko·re·a a country in the Far East, occupying the southern part of the peninsula of Korea; pop. 48,598,000; official language, Korean; capital, Seoul. Official name **KOREA, REPUBLIC OF.** —**South Ko·re·an** *adj.* & *n.*

South Korea was formed in 1948 when Korea was partitioned along the 38th parallel; the Korean War (1950–53) has been followed by decades of hostility between North and South Korea. An emerging industrial power, South Korea has had one of the world's fastest-growing economies since the 1960s.

South Ork·ney Is·lands a group of uninhabited islands in the South Atlantic Ocean, northeast of the Antarctic Peninsula. Discovered in 1821, they are administered as part of the British Antarctic Territory.

South Os·se·tia an autonomous region of Georgia, situated in the Caucasus on the border with Russia; capital, Tskhinvali. (See also **OSSETIA**.)

South Pass a valley in the Wind River Mountains of southwestern Wyoming that was a major route for settlers moving west through the Rocky Mountains during the 19th century.

south·paw /'souTH,pô/ ▶*n.* a left-handed person, esp. a boxer who leads with the right hand or a baseball pitcher . ▷mid 19th cent. (denoting the left hand or a punch with the left hand): the usage in baseball is perhaps from the orientation of early baseball fields to the same points of the compass, such that the pitcher's left arm was on the "south" side of his body.

South Platte Riv·er a river that flows for 425 miles (685 km) from the Rocky Mountains in Colorado through Denver and across Colorado to Nebraska, where it joins the North Platte River to form the Platte River.

South Pole ▶*n.* see **POLE**².

South Port·land a city in southern Maine, a southwestern suburb of Portland; pop. 23,324.

South Sand·wich Is·lands a group of uninhabited volcanic islands in the South Atlantic Ocean, 300 miles (480 km) southeast of South Georgia. They are administered from the Falkland Islands.

South Sea (also **South Seas**) *archaic* the southern Pacific Ocean.

South Sea Bub·ble a speculative boom in the shares of the South Sea Company in 1720 that ended with the failure of the company and a general financial collapse.

South Shet·land Is·lands a group of uninhabited islands in the South Atlantic Ocean, north of the Antarctic Peninsula. Discovered in 1819, they are administered as part of the British Antarctic Territory.

south-south·east ▶*n.* the compass point or direction midway between south and southeast.

south-south·west ▶*n.* the compass point or direction midway between south and southwest.

South Uist see **UIST**.

south·ward /'souTHwərd/ *Nautical* ▶*adj.* in a southerly direction: *employment and people began a southward drift.*
▶*adv.* (also **south·wards**) toward the south: *he took a train that carried him southward.*
▶*n.* (**the southward**) the direction or region to the south: *cool air from the ocean to the southward.* —**south·ward·ly** *adv.*

south·west /,souTH'west/ ▶*n.* **1** (usu. **the southwest**) the direction toward the point of the horizon midway between south and west, or the point of the horizon itself: *clouds uncoiled from the southwest.* ■ the compass point corresponding to this. **2** the southwestern part of a country, region, or town: *the beach is in the southwest of the island.* ■ (usu. **the Southwest**) the southwestern part of the U.S.: *the desert turtle population in the Southwest.*
▶*adj.* [*attrib.*] **1** lying toward, near, or facing the southwest: *the southwest tower collapsed in a storm.* ■ (of a wind) blowing from the southwest. **2** of or denoting the southwestern part of a specified country, region, or town or its inhabitants: *fishing in southwest Alaska's Bristol Bay area.*
▶*adv.* to or toward the southwest: *they drove directly southwest.* —**south·west·ern** /-ərn/ *adj.*

South West Af·ri·ca former name of **NAMIBIA**.

South West Af·ri·ca Peo·ple's Or·gan·i·za·tion (abbr.: **SWAPO**) a nationalist organization formed in Namibia in 1964–66 to oppose the illegitimate South African rule over the region. It waged a guerrilla campaign, operating largely from Angola; it eventually gained UN recognition, and won elections in 1989.

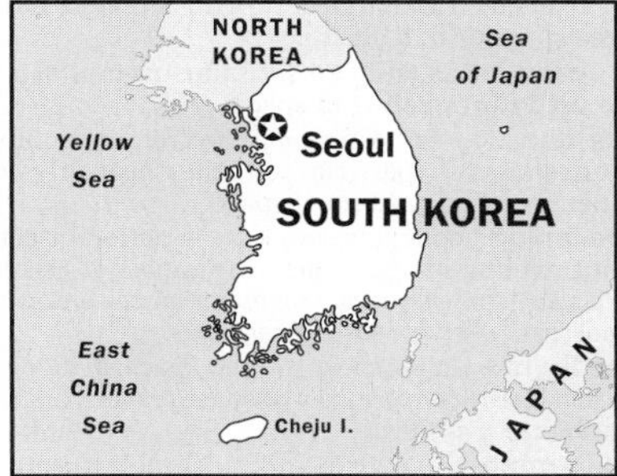

south·west·er /,souTH'westər/ ▶*n.* a wind blowing from the southwest.

south·west·er·ly /,souTH'westərlē/ ▶*adj.* & *adv.* another term for **SOUTHWEST**.
▶*n.* another term for **SOUTHWESTER**.

south·west·ward /,souTH'westwərd/ ▶*adv.* (also **south·west·wards**) toward the southwest: *the governor sent two companies of foot soldiers southwestward.*
▶*adj.* situated in, directed toward, or facing the southwest: *the southwestward extension of the valley.*

Sou·tine /so͞o'tēn/, Chaim (1893–1943), French painter, born in Lithuania. A major exponent of expressionism, his early pictures were of grotesque figures, while his later pictures tended to be still lifes.

sou·ve·nir /,so͞ovə'nir/ ▶*n.* a thing that is kept as a reminder of a person, place, or event.
▶*v.* [*trans.*] *informal* take as a memento: *many parts of the aircraft have been souvenired.* ▷late 18th cent.: from French, from *souvenir* 'remember,' from Latin *subvenire* 'occur to the mind.'

souv·la·ki /so͞ov'läkē/ ▶*n.* (*pl.* **-la·kia** /-'läkyä/ or **-la·kis**) a Greek dish of pieces of meat grilled on a skewer: *a generous plate of souvlaki | souvlakia in pita.* ▷modern Greek.

sou'·west·er /,sou'westər/ ▶*n.* a waterproof hat with a broad flap covering the neck.

sou'wester

sov·er·eign /'säv(ə)rən/ ▶*n.* **1** a supreme ruler, esp. a monarch. **2** a former British gold coin worth one pound sterling, now only minted for commemorative purposes.
▶*adj.* possessing supreme or ultimate power: *in modern democracies the people's will is in theory sovereign.* ■ [*attrib.*] (of a nation or state) fully independent and determining its own affairs: *a sovereign, democratic republic.* ■ [*attrib.*] (of affairs) subject to a specified state's control without outside interference: *criticism was seen as interference in China's sovereign affairs.* ■ [*attrib.*] *archaic* or *poetic/literary* possessing royal power and status: *our most sovereign lord the King.* ■ [*attrib.*] *dated* very good or effective: *a **sovereign remedy** for all ills.* ▷Middle English: from Old French *soverain*, based on Latin *super* 'above.' The change in the ending was due to association with **REIGN**. —**sov·er·eign·ly** *adv.*

sov·er·eign pon·tiff ▶*n.* see **PONTIFF**.

sov·er·eign·ty /'säv(ə)rəntē/ ▶*n.* (*pl.* **-ties**) supreme power or authority: *how can we hope to wrest sovereignty away from the oligarchy and back to the people?* ■ the authority of a state to govern itself or another state: *national sovereignty.* See note at **JURISDICTION**. ■ a self-governing state. ▷late Middle English: from Old French *sovereinete*, from *soverain* (see **SOVEREIGN**).

so·vi·et /'sōvēit; -,et/ ▶*n.* **1** an elected local, district, or national council in the former USSR. ■ a revolutionary council of workers or peasants in Russia before 1917. **2** (**Soviet**) a citizen of the former USSR.
▶*adj.* (**So·vi·et**) of or concerning the former Soviet Union: *the Soviet leader.* ▷early 20th cent.: from Russian *sovet* 'council.' —**So·vi·et·i·za·tion** /,sōvēiti'zāSHən/ *n.* —**So·vi·et·ize** /-,tīz/ *v.*

So·vi·et·ol·o·gist /,sōvēi'täləjist/ ▶*n.* a person who studies the former Soviet Union. —**So·vi·et·o·log·i·cal** /-tə'läjikəl/ *adj.* —**So·vi·et·ol·o·gy** /-jē/ *n.*

So·vi·et Un·ion a former federation of communist republics that occupied the northern half of Asia and part of eastern Europe; capital, Moscow. Created from the Russian empire in the aftermath of the 1917 Russian Revolution, the Soviet Union was the largest country in the world. After World War II, it emerged as a superpower that rivaled the U.S. and led to the Cold War. After decades of repression and economic failure, the Soviet Union was formally dissolved in 1991. Some of its constituents joined a looser confederation, the Commonwealth of Independent States. Full name **UNION OF SOVIET SOCIALIST REPUBLICS**.

sov·khoz /'säv,kôz/ ▶*n.* (*pl.* same, **-khoz·es**, or **-kho·zy** /-,kôzē/) a state-owned farm in the former USSR. ▷Russian, from *sov(etskoe) khoz(yaĭstvo)* 'Soviet farm.'

sow[1] /sō/ ▶*v.* (*past* **sowed**; *past part.* **sown** /sōn/ or **sowed**) [*trans.*] plant (seed) by scattering it on or in

S

the earth: *fill a pot with compost and sow a thin layer of seeds on top.* ■ plant the seeds of (a plant or crop): *the corn had just been sown.* ■ plant (a piece of land) with seed: *the field used to be sown with oats.* ■ (**be sown with**) be thickly covered with: *we walked through a valley sown with boulders.* ■ cause to appear or spread: *the new policy has sown confusion and doubt.* ▷Old English *sāwan*, of Germanic origin; related to Dutch *zaaien* and German *säen*. —**sow·er** *n.*

▸*PHRASE* □ **sow the seeds** (or **seed**) **of** do something that will eventually bring about (a particular result, esp. a disastrous one): *the seeds of dissension had been sown.*

sow[2] /sou/ ▸*n.* **1** an adult female pig, esp. one that has farrowed. ■ the female of certain other mammals, e.g., the guinea pig. **2** a large block of metal (larger than a "pig") made by smelting. ▷Old English *sugu*; related to Dutch *zeug*, German *Sau*, from an Indo-European root shared by Latin *sus* and Greek *hus* 'pig.'

sow·back /ˈsouˌbak/ ▸*n.* a low ridge of sand.

sow·bug /ˈsouˌbəg/ (also **sow bug**) ▸*n.* another term for WOOD LOUSE.

So·we·to /səˈwetō; -ˈwātō/ a large urban area, consisting of several townships, in South Africa, southwest of Johannesburg. In 1976, demonstrations against the compulsory use of Afrikaans in schools resulted in violent police activity and the deaths of hundreds of people. ▷from *So(uth) We(stern) To(wnships)*. —**So·we·tan** /-ˈwetn; -ˈwātn/ *n.* & *adj.*

sown /sōn/ ▸ past participle of SOW[1].

sow this·tle /ˈsou ˈTHisəl/ (also **sow-this·tle**) ▸*n.* a Eurasian plant with yellow flowers, thistlelike leaves, and milky sap. Also called MILK THISTLE. • Genus *Sonchus*, family Compositae.

sox /säks/ ▸*n.* nonstandard plural spelling of SOCK (sense 1).

Soxh·let /ˈsäkslət/ ▸*n.* [as *adj.*] *Chemistry* denoting a form of condensing apparatus used for the continuous solvent extraction of a solid. ▷late 19th cent.: named after Franz *Soxhlet* (1848–1926), Belgian chemist.

soy /soi/ ▸*n.* another term for SOYBEAN. ▷from Japanese *shō-yu*, from Chinese *shi-yu*, from *shi* 'salted beans' + *yu* 'oil.'

soy·a /ˈsoiə/ (also **soy·a bean**) ▸*n.* British term for SOY or SOYBEAN. ▷late 17th cent.: from Dutch *soja*, from Malay *soi* (see SOY).

soy·bean /ˈsoiˌbēn/ ▸*n.* a leguminous plant native to Asia, *Glycine max*, widely cultivated for its edible seeds. ■ the fruit of this plant, used in a variety of foods and fodder, esp. as a replacement for animal protein.

So·yin·ka /soiˈiNGkə/, Wole (1934–), Nigerian playwright, novelist, and critic. His writing often uses satire to explore the contrast between traditional and modern society in Africa. Notable works: *The Lion and the Jewel* (1959) and *The Interpreters* (1965). Nobel Prize for Literature (1986).

soy·meal /ˈsoiˌmēl/ ▸*n.* a high-protein foodstuff made by cracking, heating, flaking, cooking, and grinding soybeans. It is used in livestock feeds and as a raw ingredient in some processed foods. Also called SOYBEAN MEAL.

soy milk (also **soy·bean milk**) ▸*n.* the liquid obtained by suspending soybean flour in water, used as a fat-free substitute for milk, particularly by vegans and by those unable to tolerate milk products.

soy sauce (also *chiefly Brit.* **soya sauce**) ▸*n.* a sauce made with fermented soybeans, used in Chinese and Japanese cooking.

So·yuz /ˈsôˌyo͞oz/ a series of manned Soviet orbiting spacecraft, used to investigate the operation of orbiting space stations. ▷from Russian *Soyúz*, literally 'union.'

soz·zled /ˈsäzəld/ ▸*adj. informal* very drunk: *Uncle Brian's sozzled!* ▷late 19th cent.: past participle of dialect *sozzle* 'mix sloppily,' probably of imitative origin.

SP ▸*abbr.* ■ starting price. ■ service pack (usually followed by a number): *Windows 2000 SP3 and SP4.*

Sp. ▸*abbr.* ■ Spain. ■ Spaniard. ■ (also **Sp**) Spanish.

sp. ▸*abbr.* species (usually singular).

s.p. ▸*abbr.* without issue; childless. [from Latin *sine prole.*]

Spa /spä/ a small town in eastern Belgium, southeast of Liège; pop. 10,140. It has been celebrated since medieval times for the curative properties of its mineral springs.

spa /spä/ ▸*n.* a mineral spring considered to have health-giving properties. ■ a place or resort with such a spring. ■ a commercial establishment offering health and beauty treatment through such means as steam baths, exercise equipment, and massage. ■ a bath or small pool containing hot aerated water. ▷early 17th cent.: from SPA.

Spaatz /späts/, Carl (1891–1974), U.S. Air Force officer; born *Carl Spatz*. He directed the U.S. bombing force in Germany in 1944 and in Japan in 1945, including the dropping of atomic bombs on Hiroshima and Nagasaki. In 1947–48, he served as the first chief of staff of the newly independent U.S. Air Force.

space /spās/ ▸*n.* **1** a continuous area or expanse that is free, available, or unoccupied: *a table took up much of the space | we shall all be living together in a small space | he backed out of the parking space.* ■ an area of land that is not occupied by buildings: *she had a love of open spaces.* ■ an empty area left between one-, two-, or three-dimensional points or objects: *the space between a wall and a utility pipe.* ■ a blank between printed, typed, or written words, characters, numbers, etc. ■ *Music* each of the four gaps between the five lines of a staff. ■ an interval of time (often used to suggest that the time is short, considering what has happened or been achieved in it): *both their cars were stolen* ***in the space of*** *three days.* ■ pages in a newspaper, or time between television or radio programs, available for advertising. ■ (also **commercial space**) an area rented or sold as business premises. ■ the amount of paper used or needed to write about a subject: *there is no space to give further details.* ■ the freedom and scope to live, think, and develop in a way that suits one: *a teenager needing her own space.* ■ *Telecommunications* one of two possible states of a signal in certain systems. The opposite of MARK[1] (sense 2). **2** the dimensions of height, depth, and width within which all things exist and move: *the work gives the sense of a journey in space and time.* ■ (also **outer space**) the physical universe beyond the earth's atmosphere. ■ the near vacuum extending between the planets and stars, containing small amounts of gas and dust. ■ *Mathematics* a mathematical concept generally regarded as a set of points having some specified structure.

▸*v.* **1** [*trans.*] (usu. **be spaced**) position (two or more items) at a distance from one another: *the houses are* ***spaced out.*** ■ (in printing or writing) put blanks between (words, letters, or lines): [as *n.*] (**spacing**) *the default setting is single line spacing.* **2** (usu. **be spaced out** or **space out**) *informal* be or become distracted, euphoric, or disoriented, esp. from taking drugs; cease to be aware of one's surroundings: *I was so tired that I began to feel totally spaced out | I kind of space out for a few minutes.* ▷Middle English: shortening of Old French *espace*, from Latin *spatium*. Current verb senses date from the late 17th cent. —**spac·er** *n.*

▸*PHRASE* □ **watch this space** *informal* further developments are expected and more information will be given later.

space age ▸*n.* (**the space age** or **the Space Age**) the era starting when the exploration of space became possible: *as the Space Age evolved, massive amounts of data gushed in.*

▸*adj.* (**space-age**) very modern; technologically advanced: *a space-age control room.*

space bar ▸*n.* a long key on a typewriter or computer keyboard for making a space between words.

space blan·ket ▸*n.* a light metal-coated sheet designed to retain heat.

space ca·det ▸*n.* a trainee astronaut. ■ an enthusiast for space travel, typically a young person. ■ *informal* a person perceived as out of touch with reality, as though high on drugs.

space cap·sule ▸*n.* a small spacecraft or the part of a larger one that contains the instruments or crew.

space charge ▸*n. Physics* a collection of particles with a net electric charge occupying a region, either in free space or in a device.

space·craft /ˈspāsˌkraft/ ▸*n.* (*pl.* same or **-crafts**) a vehicle used for traveling in space.

space den·si·ty ▸*n. Astronomy* the frequency of occurrence of stars, particles, or other heavenly bodies, per specified volume of space.

space·far·ing /ˈspāsˌfe(ə)riNG/ ▸*n.* the action or activity of traveling in space: *the complications in spacefaring |* [as *adj.*] *spacefaring nations are racing to develop new technologies.* —**space·far·er** /-rer/ *n.*

space flight ▸*n.* a journey through space: *the 30th anniversary of the first space flight.* ■ space travel: *the stresses involved in space flight.*

space frame ▸*n.* a three-dimensional structural framework that is designed to behave as an integral unit and to withstand loads applied at any point.

space heat·er ▸*n.* a self-contained appliance, usually electric, for heating an enclosed room. —**space-heat·ed** *adj.* —**space heat·ing** *n.*

space lat·tice /ˈlatis/ ▸*n. Crystallography* a regular, indefinitely repeated array of points in three dimensions in which the points lie at the intersections of three sets of parallel equidistant planes.

space·man /ˈspāsˌman; -mən/ ▸*n.* (*pl.* **-men**) a male astronaut.

space op·er·a ▸*n. informal* a novel, movie, or television program set in outer space, typically of a simplistic and melodramatic nature.

space·plane /ˈspāsˌplān/ ▸*n.* an aircraft that takes off and lands conventionally but is capable of entry into orbit or travel through space.

space·port /ˈspāsˌpôrt/ ▸*n.* a base from which spacecraft are launched.

space probe ▸*n.* see PROBE.

space race ▸*n.* (**the space race**) the competition between nations regarding achievements in the field of space exploration.

space rock·et ▸*n.* a rocket designed to travel through space or to launch a spacecraft.

space·ship /ˈspā(s)ˌSHip/ ▸*n.* a spacecraft, esp. one controlled by a crew.

Space·ship Earth ▸*n.* [in *sing.*] the world considered as possessing finite resources common to all humankind. ▷1966: first appeared in the title of a work by B. Ward.

space shot ▸*n.* the launch of a spacecraft and its subsequent progress in space.

space shut·tle ▸*n.* a rocket-launched spacecraft, able to land like an unpowered aircraft, used to make repeated journeys between the earth and earth orbit.

space sta·tion ▸*n.* a large artificial satellite used as a long-term base for manned operations in space.

space·suit /ˈspāsˌso͞ot/ ▸*n.* a garment designed to allow an astronaut to survive in space.

space tel·e·scope ▸*n.* an astronomical telescope that operates in space by remote control, to avoid interference by the earth's atmosphere.

space-time ▸*n. Physics* the concepts of time and three-dimensional space regarded as fused in a four-dimensional continuum.

space trav·el ▸*n.* travel through outer space. —**space trav·el·er** *n.*

space ve·hi·cle ▸*n.* a spacecraft.

space·walk /ˈspāsˌwôk/ ▸*n.* a period of physical activity engaged in by an astronaut in space outside a spacecraft. —**space·walk·er** *n.*

space warp ▸*n.* an imaginary or hypothetical distortion of space-time that enables space travelers to travel faster than light or otherwise make journeys contrary to the commonly accepted laws of physics.

space weath·er ▸*n.* natural processes in space that can affect the near-earth environment, satellites, and space travel, such as magnetospheric disturbances solar coronal events.

space·wom·an /ˈspāsˌwo͝omən/ ▸*n.* (*pl.* **-wom·en**) a female astronaut.

spac·ey /ˈspāsē/ (also **spac·y**) ▸*adj.* (**spac·i·er, spac·i·est**) *informal* out of touch with reality, as though high on drugs: *I remember babbling, high and spacey.* ■ (of popular, esp. electronic music) drifting and ethereal.

spa·cial ▸*adj.* variant spelling of SPATIAL.

spa·cious /ˈspāSHəs/ ▸*adj.* (esp. of a room or building) having ample space. ▷late Middle English: from Old French *spacios* or Latin *spatiosus*, from *spatium* (see SPACE). —**spa·cious·ly** *adv.* —**spa·cious·ness** *n.*

Spack·le /ˈspakəl/ ▸*n.* (**spackle**) *trademark* a compound used to fill cracks in plaster and produce a smooth surface.

▸*v.* [*trans.*] (**spackle**) repair (a surface) or fill (a hole or crack) with Spackle. ▷1920s: perhaps a blend of SPARKLE and German *Spachtel* 'putty knife, mastic.'

spade[1] /spād/ ▸*n.* a tool with a sharp-edged, typically rectangular, metal blade and a long handle, used for digging or cutting earth, sand, turf, etc. ■ a tool of a similar shape for another purpose, esp. one for removing the blubber from a whale. ■ the part of the trail of a gun carriage that digs into the earth to brace the gun during recoil.

▸*v.* [*trans.*] dig in (ground) with a spade: *while spading the soil, I think of the flowers.* ■ [*trans.*] move (soil) with a spade: *earth is spaded into the grave.* ▷Old English *spadu*, *spada*, of Germanic origin; related to Dutch

spade, German *Spaten*, also to Greek *spathē* 'blade, paddle.' —**spade·ful** /-ˌfo͝ol/ *n.* (*pl.* **-fuls**).
▸*PHRASE* □ **call a spade a spade** speak plainly without avoiding unpleasant or embarrassing issues.

spade2 ▸*n.* **1** (**spades**) one of the four suits in a conventional deck of playing cards, denoted by a black inverted heart-shaped figure with a small stalk. ■ (**a spade**) a card of this suit. **2** *informal, offensive* a black person. ▷late 16th cent.: from Italian *spade*, plural of *spada* 'sword,' via Latin from Greek *spathē*; compare with SPADE1.
▸*PHRASE* □ **in spades** *informal* to a very high degree: *he got his revenge now in spades.*

spade·fish /ˈspādˌfisʜ/ ▸*n.* (*pl.* same or **-fish·es**) a marine fish with an almost disk-shaped body. It lives in tropical inshore waters, where it often forms schools. • *Chaetodipterus* and other genera, family Ephippidae: several species, including the western Atlantic *C. faber*.

spade foot ▸*n.* a square enlargement at the end of a chair leg.

spade·foot toad /ˈspādˌfo͝ot/ ▸*n.* a plump, short-legged burrowing toad with a prominent sharp-edged tubercle on the hind feet, native to North America and Europe. • Family Pelobatidae: several genera, including *Scaphiophus* (of America) and *Pelobates* (of Europe), and several species, in particular *P. fuscus*.

spade·work /ˈspādˌwərk/ ▸*n.* routine or difficult preparatory work.

spa·dille /spəˈdil/ ▸*n.* (in the card games ombre and quadrille) the ace of spades. ▷late 17th cent.: from French, from Spanish *espadilla*, diminutive of *espada* 'sword' (see SPADE2).

spa·dix /ˈspādiks/ ▸*n.* (*pl.* **-di·ces** /-dəsēz/) **1** *Botany* a spike of minute flowers closely arranged around a fleshy axis and typically enclosed in a spathe, characteristic of the arums. **2** *Zoology* (in certain invertebrates) a part or organ that is more or less conical in shape, e.g., a group of connected tentacles in a nautiloid. ▷mid 18th cent.: via Latin from Greek, literally 'palm branch.'

spaetz·le /ˈsʜpetslə; -səl; -slē/ (also **spätz·le**) ▸*plural n.* [treated as *sing.* or *pl.*] small dumplings of a type made in southern Germany and Alsace, consisting of seasoned dough poached in boiling water. ▷from German dialect *Spätzle*, literally 'little sparrows.'

spag bol /ˈspag ˈbōl/ *informal, chiefly Brit.* ▸*abbr.* spaghetti bolognese.

spa·ghet·ti /spəˈgetē/ ▸ *n.* pasta made in long, slender, solid strings. ■ an Italian dish consisting largely of this, typically with a sauce. ■ *figurative* a tangle of stringlike objects, resembling a plate of cooked spaghetti: *a clumsy spaghetti of coils and wires.* ■ *Electronics* a type of narrow tubing that encases and insulates wire. ▷Italian, plural of the diminutive of *spago* 'string.'

spa·ghet·ti bo·lo·gnese /ˌbōlənˈyēz; -ˈyāz/ ▸*n.* spaghetti served with a sauce of ground beef, tomato, onion, and herbs. ▷Italian, literally 'spaghetti of Bologna.'

spa·ghet·ti·ni /ˌspagəˈtēnē/ ▸ *n.* pasta in the form of strings of thin spaghetti. ▷Italian, diminutive of *spaghetti* 'little strings' (see SPAGHETTI).

spa·ghet·ti squash ▸*n.* an edible squash of a variety with slightly stringy flesh which when cooked has a texture and appearance like that of spaghetti. Also called VEGETABLE SPAGHETTI.

spa·ghet·ti strap ▸*n.* a thin shoulder strap on an item of women's clothing.

spa·ghet·ti west·ern ▸*n.* *informal* a western movie made cheaply in Europe by an Italian director.

spa·hi /ˈspähē/ ▸*n.* *historical* **1** a member of the Turkish irregular cavalry. **2** a member of the Algerian cavalry in French service. ▷mid 16th cent.: from Turkish *sipahi*, from Persian *sipāhī* (see SEPOY).

Spahn /spän/, Warren (Edward) (1921–2003), U.S. baseball player. He played for the Boston (later Milwaukee) Braves 1942–65 and held the record for the most games won (363) by a left-handed pitcher. Baseball Hall of Fame (1973).

Spain /spān/ a country in southwestern Europe that occupies the greater part of the Iberian peninsula; pop. 40,280,000; capital, Madrid; languages, Spanish (official) and Catalan. Spanish name **España**.

Spain was dominated by the Moors between 711 and 718 until the rise of independent Christian kingdoms, notably Aragon and Castile, in the medieval period; the last Moorish stronghold, Granada, was won back in the late 15th century. Under the Habsburg kings of the 16th-century, Spain became the dominant European power, building up a huge empire in America and elsewhere; most of this was lost in the early 19th century.The Spanish Civil War (1936–39) was followed by the establishment of a Fascist dictatorship under General Franco; after his death in 1975 a constitutional monarchy was reestablished. Spain became a member of the EC (now the EU) in 1986.

spake /spāk/ *archaic poetic/literary* ▸ past of SPEAK.

spall /spôl/ ▸*v.* [*trans.*] break (ore, rock, stone, or concrete) into smaller pieces, esp. in preparation for sorting. ■ [*intrans.*] (of ore, rock, or stone) break off in fragments: *cracks below the surface cause slabs of material to* **spall off**.
▸*n.* a splinter or chip, esp. of rock. ▷late Middle English (as a noun): of unknown origin. The verb dates from the mid 18th cent.

spall·a·tion /spôˈlāsʜən/ ▸*n.* **1** *Physics* the breakup of a bombarded nucleus into several parts. **2** *Geology* separation of fragments from the surface of a rock, esp. by interaction with a compression wave.

spal·peen /spalˈpēn/ ▸*n.* *Irish* a rascal. ▷late 18th cent. (denoting a migratory farm worker): from Irish *spailpín*, of unknown origin.

spalt·ed /ˈspôltid/ ▸*adj.* (of wood) containing blackish irregular lines as a result of fungal decay, and sometimes used to produce a decorative surface. ▷1970s: from dialect *spalt* 'to split, splinter' + -ED1.

spam /spam/ ▸*n.* **1** (**Spam**) *trademark* a canned meat product made mainly from ham. **2** irrelevant or inappropriate messages sent on the Internet to a large number of recipients.
▸*v.* [*trans.*] send the same message indiscriminately to (large numbers of recipients) on the Internet. ▷1930s: apparently from *sp(iced h)am*. —**spam·mer** *n.*

span1 /span/ ▸*n.* the full extent of something from end to end; the amount of space that something covers: *a warehouse with a clear span of 28 feet.* ■ the length of time for which something lasts: *a short concentration span.* ■ the wingspan of an aircraft or a bird. ■ an arch or part of a bridge between piers or supports. ■ the maximum distance between the tips of the thumb and little finger, taken as the basis of a measurement equal to 9 inches. ■ *archaic* a short distance or time.
▸*v.* (**spanned, span·ning**) [*trans.*] (of a bridge, arch, etc.) extend from side to side of: *the stream was spanned by a narrow bridge.* ■ extend across (a period of time or a range of subjects): *their interests span almost all the conventional disciplines.* ■ cover or enclose with the length of one's hand: *her waist was slender enough for him to span with his hands.* ▷Old English, 'distance between the tips of the thumb and little finger,' of Germanic origin; reinforced in Middle English by Old French *espan*.

span2 ▸*n.* **1** *Nautical* a rope with its ends fastened at different points to a spar or other object in order to provide a purchase. **2** a team of people or animals, in particular: ■ a matched pair of horses, mules, or oxen. ▷mid 16th cent. (as a verb meaning 'harness or yoke (an animal)'): from Dutch or Low German *spannen*. The noun (originally in nautical use) dates from the mid 18th cent.

span3 ▸*adj.* see SPICK-AND-SPAN.

span4 *chiefly archaic* ▸ past of SPIN.

Span. ▸*abbr.* ■ Spaniard. ■ Spanish.

spa·na·ko·pi·ta /ˌspanəˈkäpitə/ ▸*n.* (in Greek cooking) a phyllo pastry stuffed with spinach and feta cheese. ▷modern Greek, literally 'spinach pie.'

span·dex /ˈspandeks/ ▸*n.* a type of stretchy polyurethane fabric. ▷1950s: an arbitrary formation from EXPAND.

span·drel /ˈspandrəl/ ▸*n.* *Architecture* the almost triangular space between one side of the outer curve of an arch, a wall, and the ceiling or framework. ■ the space between the shoulders of adjoining arches and the ceiling or molding above. ▷late Middle English: perhaps from Anglo-Norman French *spaund(e)re*, or from *espaundre* 'expand.'

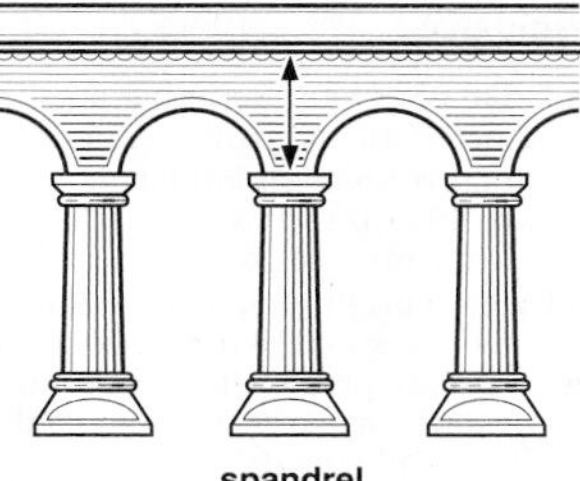
spandrel

span·drel wall ▸*n.* a wall built on the curve of an arch, filling in the spandrel.

spang /spaɴɢ/ ▸*adv.* *informal* directly; completely: *looking the general right spang in the eye.* ▷mid 19th cent.: of unknown origin.

span·gle /ˈspaɴɢɢəl/ ▸*n.* a small thin piece of glittering material, typically used in quantity to ornament a dress; a sequin. ■ a small sparkling object; a spot of bright color or light.
▸*v.* [*trans.*] [usu. as *adj.*] (**spangled**) cover with spangles or other small sparkling objects: *a spangled Christmas doll.* ▷late Middle English: diminutive from obsolete *spang* 'glittering ornament,' from Middle Dutch *spange* 'buckle.' —**span·gly** *adj.*

span·gle gall ▸*n.* a reddish disk-shaped gall that forms on the undersides of oak leaves in response to the developing larva of a gall wasp. It results from eggs laid in the summer and alternates with the currant gall.

Spang·lish /ˈspaɴɢɢlisʜ/ ▸*n.* a hybrid language combining words and idioms from both Spanish and English, esp. Spanish speech that uses many English words and expressions.

span·iel /ˈspanyəl/ ▸*n.* a dog of a breed with a long silky coat and drooping ears. ■ used in similes and metaphors as a symbol of devotion or obsequiousness: *I followed my uncles around as faithfully as any spaniel.* ▷Middle English: from Old French *espaigneul* 'Spanish (dog),' from Latin *Hispaniolus* 'Spanish.'

Span·ish /ˈspanisʜ/ ▸*adj.* of or relating to Spain, its people, or its language.
▸*n.* **1** [as *plural n.*] (**the Spanish**) the people of Spain. **2** the Romance language of most of Spain and of much of Central and South America and several other countries. ▷Middle English: from SPAIN + -ISH1, with later shortening of the first vowel. —**Span·ish·ness** *n.*

Span·ish A·mer·i·ca the parts of America once colonized by Spaniards and in which Spanish is still generally spoken. This includes most of Central and South America (except Brazil) and part of the Caribbean.

Span·ish-A·mer·i·can War a war between Spain and the U.S. in the Caribbean and the Philippines in 1898. American public opinion having been aroused by Spanish atrocities in Cuba and the destruction of the warship *Maine* in Santiago harbor, the U.S. declared war and successfully invaded Cuba, Puerto Rico, and the Philippines, all of which Spain gave up by the Treaty of Paris (1898).

Span·ish Ar·ma·da see ARMADA.

Span·ish bay·o·net (also **Span·ish dag·ger**) ▸*n.* a yucca native to the southern U.S. and the American tropics. • Genus *Yucca*, family Agavaceae: several species, in particular *Y. aloifolia*.

Span·ish broom ▸*n.* a Mediterranean broom with fragrant yellow flowers and almost leafless stems that were formerly used in basketry. • *Spartium junceum*, family Leguminosae.

Span·ish chest·nut ▸*n.* see CHESTNUT (sense 2).

Span·ish Civ·il War the conflict (1936–39) between Nationalist forces (including monarchists and members of the Falange Party) and Republicans (including socialists, communists, and Catalan and Basque separatists) in Spain.

It began with a military uprising against the leftist, Republican Popular Front government in July 1936. In bitter fighting the Nationalists, led by General Franco, gradually gained control of the countryside but failed to capture the capital, Madrid. After periods of prolonged stalemate, Franco finally succeeded in capturing Barcelona and Madrid in early 1939. He established a Fascist dictatorship that lasted until his death in 1975.

Span·ish-Co·lo·ni·al ▸*adj.* denoting a style of architecture characteristic of Spanish America.

Span·ish flu (also **Spanish influenza**) ▸*n.* influenza caused by an influenza virus of type A, in particular that of the pandemic that began in 1918.

Span·ish fly ▸*n.* a bright green European blister beetle with a mousy smell. • *Lytta vesicatoria*, family Meloidae. ■ a toxic preparation of the dried bodies of these beetles, formerly used in medicine as a counterirritant and sometimes taken as an aphrodisiac. Also called CANTHARIDES.

Span·ish gui·tar ▸*n.* the standard six-stringed acoustic guitar, used esp. for classical and folk music.

Span·ish i·bex (also **Spanish goat**) ▸*n.* see IBEX.

Span·ish In·qui·si·tion /ˌiNGkwiˈziSHən/ an ecclesiastical court established in Roman Catholic Spain in 1478 and directed originally against converts from Judaism and Islam but later also against Protestants. It operated with great severity until suppressed in the early 19th century.

Span·ish mack·er·el ▸*n.* a large edible game fish related to the mackerel. • Genus *Scomberomorus*, family Scombridae: several species, in particular *S. maculatus* of the tropical Atlantic, and *S. commerson* of the Indo-Pacific.

Span·ish Main /mān/ the former name for the northwestern coast of South America between the Orinoco River and Panama and adjoining parts of the Caribbean Sea when they were under Spanish control.

Span·ish Mis·sion ▸*n.* [as *adj.*] denoting a style of architecture characteristic of the Catholic missions in Spanish America.

Span·ish moss ▸*n.* a tropical American plant that grows as silvery-green festoons on trees, obtaining water and nutrients directly through its surface. • *Tillandsia usneoides*, family Bromeliaceae. See also AIR PLANT.

Span·ish nee·dles ▸*n.* an American beggar ticks with rayless flowers that develop into a cluster of barbed achenes. • *Bidens bipinnata*, family Compositae.

Span·ish om·e·let ▸*n.* an omelet containing chopped vegetables, often served open rather than folded.

Span·ish on·ion ▸*n.* a large cultivated onion with a mild flavor.

Span·ish rice ▸*n.* a dish of rice with onions, peppers, tomatoes, and other vegetables, often colored and flavored with saffron.

Span·ish Sa·har·a former name (1958–75) of WESTERN SAHARA.

Span·ish Suc·ces·sion, War of the a European war (1701–14), provoked by the death of the Spanish king Charles II without issue. The Grand Alliance of Britain, the Netherlands, and the Holy Roman Emperor threw back a French invasion of the Low Countries and prevented Spain and France from being united under one crown.

Span·ish Town a town in Jamaica, west of Kingston, the second largest town in Jamaica, a former capital; pop. 110,000.

Span·ish wind·lass ▸*n.* a device for tightening a rope or cable by twisting it using a stick as a lever.

spank /spaNGk/ ▸*v.* [*trans.*] slap with one's open hand or a flat object, esp. on the buttocks as a punishment: *she was spanked for spilling ink on the carpet.*
▸*n.* a slap of this type. ▷early 18th cent.: perhaps imitative.

spank·er /ˈspaNGkər/ ▸*n.* **1** a fore-and-aft sail set on the after side of a ship's mast, esp. the mizzenmast. **2** *informal, dated* a very fine person or thing.

spank·ing /ˈspaNGkiNG/ ▸*adj.* **1** (esp. of a horse or its gait) lively; brisk: *a spanking trot.* **2** *informal* very good: *we had a spanking time.* ■ fine and impressive: *a spanking white Rolls Royce* | [as *submodifier*] *a* ***spanking new*** *conference center.*
▸*n.* [in *sing.*] an act of slapping, esp. on the buttocks as a punishment for children: *you deserve a good spanking.*

span·ner /ˈspanər/ ▸*n. chiefly Brit.* a wrench. ▷late 18th cent.: from German *spannen* 'draw tight' + -ER[1].

span of con·trol ▸*n.* the area of activity or number of functions, people, or things for which an individual or organization is responsible.

span·sule /ˈspansoōl/ ▸*n. trademark* a capsule that when swallowed releases one or more medicinal drugs over a set period. ▷mid 20th cent.: blend of the noun SPAN[1] and CAPSULE.

span·worm /ˈspanˌwərm/ ▸*n.* another term for INCHWORM.

spar[1] /spär/ ▸*n.* a thick, strong pole such as is used for a mast or yard on a ship. ■ the main longitudinal beam of an airplane wing. ▷Middle English: shortening of Old French *esparre*, or from Old Norse *sperra*; related to Dutch *spar* and German *Sparren*.

spar[2] ▸*v.* (**sparred, spar·ring**) [*intrans.*] make the motions of boxing without landing heavy blows, as a form of training: *one contestant broke his nose while sparring.* ■ engage in argument, typically of a kind that is prolonged or repeated but not violent: *mother and daughter spar regularly over drink, drugs, and career.* ■ (of a gamecock) fight with the feet or spurs.
▸*n.* **1** a period or bout of sparring. **2** *informal, chiefly Brit.* a close friend. ▷Old English *sperran, spyrran* 'strike out,' of unknown origin; compare with Old Norse *sperrask* 'kick out.'

spar[3] ▸*n.* [usu. in *combination* or with *adj.*] a crystalline, easily cleavable, light-colored mineral. ▷late 16th cent.: from Middle Low German; related to Old English *spærstān* 'gypsum.' **—spar·ry** *adj.*

spar·a·ble /ˈsparəbəl/ ▸*n.* a headless nail used for the soles and heels of shoes. ▷early 17th cent.: contraction of *sparrow-bill*, in the same sense.

spar bu·oy ▸*n.* a buoy made of a spar with one end moored so that the other stands up.

spar deck ▸*n.* an upper deck of a ship or other vessel.

spare /spe(ə)r/ ▸*adj.* **1** additional to what is required for ordinary use: *few people had spare cash for inessentials.* ■ not currently in use or occupied: *the spare bedroom.* **2** with no excess fat; thin: *a spare, bearded figure.* See note at THIN. ■ elegantly simple: *her clothes are smart and spare in style.* ■ meager; nearly inadequate: *the furnishings were spare and unadorned.*
▸*n.* **1** an item kept in case another item of the same type is lost, broken, or worn out. ■ a spare tire: *make sure there are no problems with any of the tires, including the spare.* **2** (in tenpin bowling) an act of knocking down all the pins with two consecutive rolls of the ball.
▸*v.* **1** [with *two objs.*] give (something of which one has enough) to (someone); afford to give to: *she asked if I could spare her a dollar or two.* ■ make free or available: *I'm sure you can spare me a moment.* ■ [*intrans.*] *archaic* be frugal: *but some will spend, and some will spare.* **2** [*trans.*] refrain from killing, injuring, or distressing: *there was no way the men would spare her.* ■ [with *two objs.*] refrain from inflicting (something) on (someone): *the country had until now been spared the violence occurring elsewhere.* ■ (**spare oneself**) [with *negative*] try to ensure or satisfy one's own comfort or needs: *in her concern to help others, she has never spared herself.* ▷Old English *spær* 'not plentiful, meager,' *sparian* 'refrain from injuring,' 'refrain from using,' of Germanic origin; related to Dutch and German *sparen* 'to spare.' **—spare·ly** *adv.* **—spare·ness** *n.* **—spar·er** *n.* (*rare*).
▸*PHRASES* □ **go spare** *Brit., informal* **1** become extremely angry or distraught: *he'd go spare if he lost the money.* **2** be unwanted or not needed and therefore available for use: *I didn't have much money going spare.* □ **spare no expense** (or **no expense spared**) be prepared to pay any amount (used to indicate the importance of achieving something). □ **spare the rod and spoil the child** see ROD. □ **spare a thought for** *chiefly Brit.* remember: *spare a thought for our volunteer group at Christmas.* □ **to spare** left over: *that turkey will feed ten people with some to spare.*

spare part ▸*n.* a duplicate part to replace a lost or damaged part of a machine.

spare·ribs / ˈspe(ə)rˌribz/ (also **spare ribs**) ▸*plural n.* closely trimmed ribs of pork or sometimes beef. ▷late 16th cent.: probably from Middle Low German *ribbesper* (by transposition of the syllables), and associated with the adjective SPARE.

spare time ▸*n.* time that is not taken up by one's usual activities; leisure time.

spare tire ▸*n.* an extra tire carried in a motor vehicle for emergencies. ■ *informal* a roll of fat around a person's waist.

sparge /spärj/ *chiefly technical* ▸*v.* [*trans.*] moisten by sprinkling, esp. with water in brewing.
▸*n.* the action of sprinkling or splashing. ■ a spray of hot water, esp. water sprinkled over malt when brewing. ▷late 16th cent. (as a verb in the sense 'sprinkle (water) around'): apparently from Latin *spargere* 'to sprinkle.' The current senses date from the early 19th cent. **—sparg·er** *n.*

spar·id /ˈsparid/ ▸*n. Zoology* a fish of the sea bream family (Sparidae), whose members are marine and have deep bodies with long spiny dorsal fins. ▷1960s: from modern Latin *Sparidae* (plural), via Latin from Greek *sparos* 'sea bream.'

spar·ing /ˈspe(ə)riNG/ ▸*adj.* moderate; economical: *physicians advised sparing use of the ointment.* See note at ECONOMICAL. **—spar·ing·ly** *adv.* **—spar·ing·ness** *n.*

Spark /spärk/, Dame Muriel (1918–), Scottish novelist. Notable works:*The Prime of Miss Jean Brodie* (1961), *The Mandelbaum Gate* (1965), and *Symposium* (1990).

spark[1] /spärk/ ▸*n.* a small fiery particle thrown off from a fire, alight in ashes, or produced by striking together two hard surfaces such as stone or metal. ■ a light produced by a sudden disruptive electrical discharge through the air. ■ a discharge such as this serving to ignite the explosive mixture in an internal combustion engine. ■ a small bright object or point: *there was a spark of light.* ■ a trace of a specified quality or intense feeling: *a tiny spark of anger flared within her.* ■ a sense of liveliness and excitement: *there was a spark between them at their first meeting.*
▸*v.* **1** [*intrans.*] emit sparks of fire or electricity: *the ignition sparks as soon as the gas is turned on.* ■ produce sparks at the point where an electric circuit is interrupted. **2** [*trans.*] ignite: *the explosion sparked a fire.* ■ *figurative* provide the stimulus for (a dramatic event or process): *the severity of the plan* ***sparked off*** *street protests.* ▷Old English *spærca, spearca*, of unknown origin. **—spark·er** *n.* **—spark·less** *adj.* **—spark·y** *adj.*
▸*PHRASES* □ **spark out** *Brit., informal* completely unconscious: *I think he would knock Bowe spark out.* □ **sparks fly** an encounter becomes heated or lively: *sparks always fly when you two get together.*

spark[2] *archaic* ▸*n.* a lively young fellow.
▸*v.* [*intrans.*] engage in courtship. ▷early 16th cent.: probably a figurative use of SPARK[1]. **—spark·ish** *adj.*

spark cham·ber ▸*n. Physics* an apparatus designed to show ionizing particles.

spark gap ▸*n.* a space between electrical terminals across which a transient discharge passes.

spark·ing plug ▸*n. Brit.* another term for SPARK PLUG.

spar·kle /ˈspärkəl/ ▸*v.* [*intrans.*] shine brightly with flashes of light: *her earrings sparkled as she turned her head* | [as *adj.*] (**sparkling**) *her sparkling blue eyes.* ■ be vivacious and witty: *after a glass of wine, she began to sparkle.* ■ [as *adj.*] (**sparkling**) (of wine and similar drinks) effervescent; compare with STILL[1].
▸*n.* a glittering flash of light: *there was a sparkle in his eyes.* ■ vivacity and wit: *she's got a kind of sparkle.* ▷Middle English: frequentative (verb) or diminutive (noun) of SPARK[1]. **—spar·kling·ly** *adv.* **—spar·kly** *adj.*

spar·kler /ˈspärk(ə)lər/ ▸*n.* **1** a thing that sparkles, in particular: ■ a hand-held firework that emits sparks. ■ *informal* a gemstone, esp. a diamond. ■ *informal* a sparkling wine. **2** a nozzle attached to the spout on a beer pump to give the beer a frothy head.

spark plug ▸*n.* a device for firing the explosive mixture in an internal combustion engine.

Sparks /spärks/ a city in western Nevada, just east of Reno; pop. 66,346.

spar·ling /ˈspärliNG/ ▸*n.* an edible European smelt (fish) that migrates into fresh water to spawn. • *Osmerus eperlanus*, family Osmeridae. ▷Middle English: shortening of Old French *esperlinge*, of Germanic origin.

spar·ring part·ner ▸*n.* a boxer employed to engage in sparring with another as training. ■ a person with whom one continually argues or contends.

spar·row /ˈsparō/ ▸*n.* **1** a small finchlike Old World bird related to the weaverbirds, typically with brown and gray plumage. • Family Passeridae (or Ploceidae): four genera, in particular *Passer*, and many species, e.g., the cosmopolitan **house sparrow** (*P. domesticus*). **2** [usu. with *adj.*] any of a number of birds that resemble true sparrows in size or color: • an American bunting (many genera in the subfamily Emberizinae, family Emberizidae). • a waxbill, in particular the Java sparrow. • see HEDGE SPARROW. ▷Old English *spearwa*, of Germanic origin.

spar·row·grass /ˈsparō,gras/ ▶*n.* dialect term for ASPARAGUS. ▷mid 17th cent.: corruption (by folk etymology) of obsolete *sparagus* 'asparagus.'

spar·row hawk ▶*n.* a small Old World woodland hawk that preys on small birds. • Genus *Accipiter*, family Accipitridae: many species, in particular the widespread **northern sparrow hawk** (*A. nisus*). ■ the American kestrel (see KESTREL).

sparse /spärs/ ▶*adj.* thinly dispersed or scattered: *areas of sparse population.* ■ austere; meager: *an elegantly sparse chamber.* ▷early 18th cent. (used to describe writing in the sense 'widely spaced'): from Latin *sparsus*, past participle of *spargere* 'scatter.' **—sparse·ly** *adv.* **—sparse·ness** *n.* **—spar·si·ty** /ˈspärsitē/ *n.*

Spar·ta /ˈspärtə/ a city in the southern Peloponnese in Greece, capital of the department of Laconia; pop. 13,000. It was a powerful city-state in the 5th century BC and defeated its rival Athens in the Peloponnesian War to become the leading city of Greece.

Spar·ta·cist /ˈspärtəsist/ ▶*n.* a member of the Spartacus League.

Spar·ta·cus /ˈspärtəkəs/ (died *c.*71 BC), Thracian slave and gladiator. He led a revolt against Rome in 73, but eventually was defeated by Crassus in 71 and crucified.

Spar·ta·cus League a German revolutionary socialist group founded in 1916 by Rosa Luxemburg and Karl Liebknecht (1871–1919). At the end of 1918 the group became the German Communist Party, which in 1919 organized an uprising in Berlin that was brutally crushed. ▷*Spartacus* was adopted as a pseudonym by Karl Liebknecht.

Spar·tan /ˈspärtn/ ▶*adj.* of or relating to Sparta in ancient Greece. ■ (usu. **spartan**) showing the indifference to comfort or luxury traditionally associated with ancient Sparta: *spartan but adequate rooms.*
▶*n.* a citizen of Sparta.

Spar·tan·burg /ˈspärtn,bərg/ an industrial and commercial city in northwestern South Carolina; pop. 39,673.

spar·ti·na /ˈspärtn-ə/ (also **spar·ti·na grass**) ▶*n.* a plant of a genus that comprises the cordgrasses. • Genus *Spartina*, family Gramineae. ▷modern Latin, from Greek *spartinē* 'rope.'

spar tree ▶*n.* *Forestry* a tree or other tall structure to which cables are attached for hauling logs.

spasm /ˈspazəm/ ▶*n.* a sudden involuntary muscular contraction or convulsive movement. ■ a sudden and brief spell of an activity or sensation: *a spasm of coughing woke him.* ■ prolonged involuntary muscle contraction: *the airways in the lungs go **into spasm**.* ▷late Middle English: from Old French *spasme*, or via Latin from Greek *spasmos*, *spasma*, from *span* 'pull.'

spas·mod·ic /spazˈmädik/ ▶*adj.* occurring or done in brief, irregular bursts: *spasmodic fighting continued.* ■ caused by, subject to, or in the nature of a spasm or spasms: *a spasmodic cough.* ▷late 17th cent.: from modern Latin *spasmodicus*, from Greek *spasmōdēs*, from *spasma* (see SPASM). **—spas·mod·i·cal·ly** /-ik(ə)lē/ *adv.*

spas·mo·lyt·ic /,spazməˈlitik/ *Medicine* ▶*adj.* (of a drug or treatment) able to relieve spasm of smooth muscle.
▶*n.* a drug of this kind.

spas·mo·phil·i·a /,spazməˈfilēə/ ▶*n.* *Medicine* undue tendency of the muscles to contract, caused by ionic imbalance in the blood, or associated with anxiety disorders. **—spas·mo·phile** /ˈspazmə,fil/ *n.*

Spas·sky /ˈspaskē; ˈspäs-/, Boris (Vasilevich) (1937–), Russian chess player; world champion 1969–72. He was defeated by Bobby Fischer in 1972 and moved to Paris in 1975. In 1992, he had a rematch with Fischer, played in Montenegro and Serbia; Fischer won again.

spas·tic /ˈspastik/ ▶*adj.* relating to or affected by muscle spasm. ■ relating to or denoting a form of muscular weakness (**spastic paralysis**) typical of cerebral palsy, caused by damage to the brain or spinal cord and involving reflex resistance to passive movement of the limbs and difficulty in initiating and controlling muscular movement. ■ (of a person) affected with cerebral palsy. ■ *informal, offensive* incompetent or uncoordinated.
▶*n.* a person with cerebral palsy. ■ *informal, offensive* an incompetent or uncoordinated person. ▷mid 18th cent.: via Latin from Greek *spastikos* 'pulling,' from *span* 'pull.' **—spas·ti·cal·ly** *adv.* **—spas·tic·i·ty** /spaˈstisitē/ *n.*

> *USAGE* **Spastic**, usually used as an adjective, has been used in medical senses since the 18th century and is still a neutral term for conditions like *spastic colon* or *spastic paraplegia*. In the 1970s and 1980s, **spastic**, usually used as a noun, became a term of abuse and was directed toward anyone regarded as incompetent or physically uncoordinated. Nowadays, this latter use of **spastic**, whether as a noun or as an adjective, is likely to cause offense, and even in medical use it is preferable to use phrasing such as *person with cerebral palsy* instead of the noun **spastic**.

spat[1] /spat/ ▶ past and past participle of SPIT[1].

spat[2] ▶*n.* **1** (usu. **spats**) *historical* a short cloth gaiter covering the instep and ankle. **2** a cover for the upper part of an aircraft wheel. ▷early 19th cent.: abbreviation of SPATTERDASH.

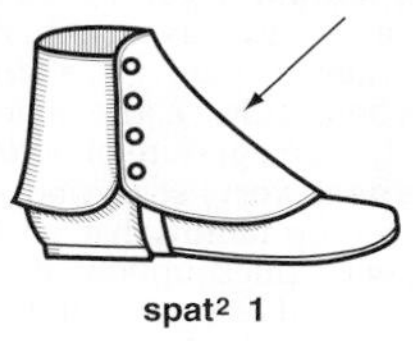

spat[2] 1

spat[3] *informal* ▶*n.* a petty quarrel.
▶*v.* (**spat·ted**, **spat·ting**) [*intrans.*] quarrel pettily. ■ [*trans.*] slap lightly: *I spatted your hands when you were naughty.* ▷early 19th cent. (originally a U.S. colloquial usage): probably imitative.

spat[4] ▶*n.* the spawn or larvae of shellfish, esp. oysters. ▷mid 17th cent.: from Anglo-Norman French, of unknown ultimate origin.

spatch·cock /ˈspacн,käk/ ▶*n.* a chicken or game bird split open and grilled.
▶*v.* [*trans.*] split open (a poultry or game bird) to prepare it for grilling. ■ *informal, chiefly Brit.* add (a phrase, sentence, clause, etc.) in a context where it is inappropriate: *a new clause has been spatchcocked into the bill.* ▷late 18th cent. (originally an Irish usage): perhaps related to the noun DISPATCH + COCK[1], but compare with SPITCHCOCK.

spate /spāt/ ▶*n.* **1** [usu. in *sing.*] a large number of similar things or events appearing or occurring in quick succession: *a spate of attacks on travelers.* **2** *chiefly Brit.* a sudden flood in a river, esp. one caused by heavy rains or melting snow. ▷late Middle English (originally Scots and northern English in the sense 'flood, inundation'): of unknown origin.
▶*PHRASE* □ **in (full) spate** (of a river) overflowing due to a sudden flood. ■ *figurative* (of a person or action) at the height of activity: *work was in full spate.*

spathe /spā*TH*/ ▶*n.* *Botany* a large sheathing bract enclosing the flower cluster of certain plants, esp. the spadix of arums and palms. ▷late 18th cent.: via Latin from Greek *spathē* 'broad blade.'

spath·u·late /ˈspaтнyəlit; -,lāt/ ▶*adj.* *Botany* & *Zoology* variant spelling of SPATULATE.

spa·tial /ˈspāsнəl/ (also **spa·cial**) ▶*adj.* of or relating to space: *the spatial distribution of population* | *a mouse's spatial memory.* ▷mid 19th cent.: from Latin *spatium* 'space' + -AL. **—spa·ti·al·i·ty** /,spāsнēˈalitē/ *n.* **—spa·tial·i·za·tion** /,spāsнələˈzāsнən/ *n.* **—spa·tial·ize** /ˈspāsнə,līz/ *v.* **—spa·tial·ly** *adv.*

spa·ti·o·tem·po·ral /,spāsнēōˈtempərəl/ ▶*adj.* *Physics* & *Philosophy* belonging to both space and time or to space-time. **—spa·ti·o·tem·po·ral·ly** *adv.*

Spät·le·se /ˈsнpāt,lāzə/ ▶*n.* (*pl.* **-ses** or **-sen** /-zən/,) a white wine of German origin or style made from grapes harvested late in the season. ▷from German, from *spät* 'late' + *Lese* 'picking, vintage.'

spat·ter /ˈspatər/ ▶*v.* [*trans.*] cover with drops or spots of something: *passing vehicles **spattered** his shoes and pants **with** mud.* ■ scatter or splash (liquid, mud, etc.) over a surface: *he spatters grease all over the stove.* ■ [*intrans.*] fall so as to be scattered over an area: *she watched the raindrops spatter down.*
▶*n.* a spray or splash of something. ■ a sprinkling: *there was a spatter of freckles over her nose.* ■ a short outburst of sound: *the sharp spatter of shots.* ▷mid 16th cent. (in the sense 'splutter while speaking'): frequentative, from a base shared by Dutch, Low German *spatten* 'burst, spout.'

spat·ter·dash /ˈspatər,dasн/ ▶*n.* (usu. **spatterdashes**) *historical* a long gaiter or legging worn to keep stockings or pants clean, esp. when riding.

spat·ter·dock /ˈspatər,däk/ ▶*n.* a yellow-flowered water lily. • Genus *Nuphar*, family Nymphaeaceae: several species, in particular *N. advena*.

spat·ter·ware /ˈspatər,wer/ ▶*n.* pottery decorated by sponging with color; sponged ware.

spat·u·la /ˈspacнələ/ ▶*n.* an implement with a broad, flat, blunt blade, used for mixing and spreading things, esp. in cooking and painting. ■ British term for TONGUE DEPRESSOR. ▷early 16th cent.: from Latin, variant of *spathula*, diminutive of *spatha* (see SPATHE).

spat·u·late /ˈspacнələt/ ▶*adj.* having a broad, rounded end: *his thick, spatulate fingers.* ■ (also **spath·u·late**) *Botany* & *Zoology* broad at the apex and tapered to the base: *large spatulate leaves.*

Spatz /späts/, Carl see SPAATZ.

spätz·le ▶*plural n.* variant spelling of SPAETZLE.

spav·in /ˈspavin/ ▶*n.* a disorder of a horse's hock. See BONE SPAVIN. ▷late Middle English: shortening of Old French *espavin*, variant of *esparvain*, of Germanic origin. **—spav·ined** *adj.*

spawn /spôn/ ▶*v.* [*intrans.*] (of a fish, frog, mollusk, crustacean, etc.) release or deposit eggs: *the fish spawn among fine-leaved plants* | [*trans.*] *a large brood is spawned.* ■ (**be spawned**) (of a fish, frog, etc.) be laid as eggs. ■ [*trans.*] (of a person) produce (offspring, typically offspring regarded as undesirable): *why had she married a man who could spawn a boy like that?* ■ [*trans.*] produce or generate, esp. in large numbers: *the decade spawned a bewildering variety of books on the forces.* ■ *Computing* [*trans.*] generate (a dependent or subordinate computer process): *from time to time it spawns two copies of the ip-up program, other times only one.*
▶*n.* the eggs of fish, frogs, etc.: *the fish covers its spawn with gravel.* ■ the process of producing such eggs. ■ the product or offspring of a person or place (used to express distaste or disgust): *the spawn of chaos: demons and sorcerers.* ■ the mycelium of a fungus, esp. a cultivated mushroom. ▷late Middle English: shortening of Anglo-Norman French *espaundre* 'to shed roe,' variant of Old French *espandre* 'pour out,' from Latin *expandere* 'expand.' **—spawn·er** *n.*

spay /spā/ ▶*v.* [*trans.*] (usu. **be spayed**) sterilize (a female animal) by removing the ovaries: *the animals must be spayed or neutered before they are given up for adoption.* ▷late Middle English: shortening of Old French *espeer* 'cut with a sword,' from *espee* 'sword,' from Latin *spatha* (see SPATHE).

spaz /spaz/ (also **spazz**) *informal* ▶*n.* (*pl.* **spaz·zes**) *offensive* short for SPASTIC.
▶*v.* [*intrans.*] (**spaz out**) lose physical or emotional control: *he offered a post-game assessment: "I spazzed out real bad."* ▷1960s: abbreviation of SPASTIC.

SPCA ▶*abbr.* Society for the Prevention of Cruelty to Animals.

SPCC ▶*abbr.* Society for the Prevention of Cruelty to Children.

SPCK ▶*abbr.* Society for Promoting Christian Knowledge.

speak /spēk/ ▶*v.* (*past* **spoke** /spōk/; *past part.* **spo·ken** /ˈspōkən/) [*intrans.*] **1** say something in order to convey information, an opinion, or a feeling: *in his agitation he was unable to speak* | *she refused to speak about the incident.* ■ have a conversation: *I wish to **speak** privately **with** you* | *I'll **speak to** him if he calls.* ■ [*trans.*] utter (a word, message, speech, etc.): *patients copy words spoken by the therapist.* ■ [*trans.*] communicate in or be able to communicate in (a specified language): *my mother spoke Russian.* ■ make a speech before an audience, or make a contribution to a debate: *twenty thousand people attended to hear him speak.* ■ (**speak for**) express the views or position of (another person or group): *he claimed to speak for the majority of local people.* ■ convey one's views or position indirectly: ***speaking through** his attorney, he refused to join the debate.* ■ (**speak of**) mention or discuss in speech or writing: *the books speak of betrayal.* ■ (of behavior, a quality, an event, etc.) serve as evidence for something: *her harping on him **spoke** strongly **of** a crush* | [*trans.*] *his frame spoke tiredness.* ■ (of an object that typically makes a sound when it functions) make a characteristic sound: *the gun spoke again.* ■ [*trans.* or *adverbial*] *archaic* show or manifest (someone or something) to be in a particular state or to possess a certain quality: *she had seen nothing that spoke him of immoral habits.* ■ (of an organ pipe or other musical instrument) make a sound: *insufficient air circulates for the pipes to speak.* ■ (of a dog) bark. ■ [*trans.*] *archaic Nautical* hail and hold communication with (a ship) at sea. **2** (**speak to**) talk to in order to reprove or advise: *she tried to speak to Seth about his drinking.* ■ talk to in order to give or extract information: *he had spoken to the police.* ■ discuss or comment on formally:

the Church wants to speak to real issues. ■ appeal or relate to: *the story spoke to him directly.*

▸*phrasal v.* □ **speak out** (or **up**) express one's feelings or opinions frankly and publicly: *the administration will be forthright in speaking out against human rights abuses.* □ **speak up** **1** speak more loudly: *We can't hear you. Speak up!* **2** see SPEAK OUT above. □ **speak up for** speak in defense or support of: *there was no independent body to speak up for press freedoms.* ▷Old English *sprecan*, later *specan*; related to Dutch *spreken* and German *sprechen*. —**speak·a·ble** *adj.*

▸*PHRASES* □ **not to speak of** used in introducing a further factor to be considered: *the rent had to be paid, not to speak of school tuition.* □ **nothing** (or **no** —— or **none**) **to speak of** used to indicate that there is some but very little of something: *I've no capital—well, none to speak of.* □ **so to speak** see SO¹. □ **something speaks for itself** something's implications are so clear that it needs no supporting evidence or comments: *the figures speak for themselves.* □ **speak for oneself** give one's own opinions. ■ [in *imperative*] used to tell someone that what they have said may apply to them but does not apply to others: *"This is such a boring place." "Speak for yourself—I like it."* □ **speak in tongues** see TONGUE. □ **speaking of** used to introduce a statement or question about a topic recently alluded to: *speaking of cost, can I afford to buy it?* □ **speak one's mind** express one's feelings or opinions frankly. □ **speak volumes** (of a gesture, circumstance, or object) convey a great deal: *a look that spoke volumes.* ■ be good evidence for: *his record* ***speaks volumes for*** *his determination.* □ **speak well** (or **ill**) **of** praise (or criticize).

-speak ▸*comb. form* forming nouns denoting a manner of speaking, characteristic of a specified field or group: *technospeak.* ▷on the pattern of *(New)speak.*

speak·eas·y /ˈspēkˌēzē/ ▸*n.* (*pl.* **-eas·ies**) *informal* (during Prohibition) an illicit liquor store or nightclub.

speak·er /ˈspēkər/ ▸*n.* **1** a person who speaks. ■ a person who delivers a speech or lecture. ■ [usu. with *adj.* or in *combination*] a person who speaks a specified language: *he is a fluent English and French speaker.* **2** (**Speaker**) the presiding officer in a legislative assembly, esp. the House of Representatives. **3** short for LOUDSPEAKER: *a cassette player with two speakers.* —**speak·er·ship** /-ˌSHip/ *n.* (in sense 2).

speak·er·phone /ˈspēkərˌfōn/ ▸*n.* a telephone with a loudspeaker and microphone, allowing it to be used without picking up the handset.

speak·ing /ˈspēkiNG/ ▸*n.* the action of conveying information or expressing one's thoughts and feelings in spoken language. ■ the activity of delivering speeches or lectures: *public speaking.*

▸*adj.* [*attrib.*] used for or engaged in speech: *you have a clear speaking voice.* ■ conveying meaning as though in words: *she gave him a speaking look.* ■ (of a portrait) so like the subject as to seem to be alive and capable of speech: *a speaking likeness.* ■ [in *combination*] able to communicate in a specified language: *an English-speaking guide.*

▸*PHRASES* □ **on speaking terms** **1** slightly acquainted. **2** sufficiently friendly to talk to each other: *she parted from her mother barely on speaking terms.* □ —— **speaking** used to indicate the degree of accuracy intended in a statement or the point of view from which it is made: *broadly speaking, there are three major models for local-central relations.* □ **speaking in tongues** another term for GLOSSOLALIA.

speak·ing trum·pet ▸*n. historical* an instrument for making the voice carry, esp. at sea.

speak·ing tube ▸*n.* a pipe for conveying a person's voice from one room or building to another.

spear /spi(ə)r/ ▸*n.* a weapon with a long shaft and a pointed tip, typically of metal, used for thrusting or throwing. ■ a similar barbed instrument used for catching fish. ■ *archaic* a spearman. ■ a plant shoot, esp. a pointed stem of asparagus or broccoli.

▸*v.* [*trans.*] pierce or strike with a spear or other pointed object: *she speared her last French fry with her fork.* ■ quickly extend the arm to catch (a fast-moving ball or other object): *he hit a line drive that Bogar speared backhanded.* ▷Old English *spere*, of Germanic origin; compare with Dutch *speer* and German *Speer.*

spear car·ri·er (also **spear-car·rier**) ▸*n.* an actor with a walk-on part. ■ an unimportant participant in something.

spear·fish /ˈspi(ə)rˌfiSH/ ▸*n.* (*pl.* same or **-fish·es**) a billfish that resembles the marlin. • Genus *Tetrapturus*, family Istiophoridae: several species.

▸*v.* [*intrans.*] fish using a spear: *resort owners do not allow tourists to spearfish* | [as *n.*] (**spearfishing**) *spearfishing is strictly illegal in the marine parks.*

spear grass (also **spear·grass**) ▸*n.* any of a number of grasses with hard pointed seed heads, some of which are sharp enough to harm livestock. • *Heteropogon, Stipa*, and other genera, family Gramineae.

spear·gun /ˈspi(ə)rˌgən/ ▸*n.* a gun used to propel a spear in underwater fishing.

spear·head /ˈspi(ə)rˌhed/ ▸*n.* the point of a spear. ■ an individual or group chosen to lead an attack or movement: *she became the* ***spearhead of*** *a health education program.*

▸*v.* [*trans.*] lead (an attack or movement): *he's spearheading a campaign to reduce the number of accidents at work.*

spear·man /ˈspi(ə)rmən/ ▸*n.* (*pl.* **-men**) *chiefly historical* a man, esp. a soldier, who uses a spear.

spear·mint /ˈspi(ə)rˌmint/ ▸*n.* the common garden mint, used as a culinary herb and to flavor candy, chewing gum, etc. • *Mentha spicata*, family Labiatae.

spear side ▸*n.* the male side or members of a family. The opposite of DISTAFF SIDE.

spear·wort /ˈspi(ə)rwərt; -ˌwôrt/ ▸*n.* a plant of the buttercup family that grows in marshes and ditches, with thick hollow stems and long narrow spear-shaped leaves. • Genus *Ranunculus*, family Ranunculaceae: the **lesser spearwort** (*R. flammula*) and the less common **greater spearwort** (*R. lingua*).

spec¹ /spek/ ▸*n.* (in phrase **on spec**) *informal* in the hope of success but without any specific commission or instructions: *he built the factory on spec and hoped someone would buy it.* ▷late 18th cent.: abbreviation of SPECULATION (see SPECULATE).

spec² ▸*n. informal* a detailed working description: *I'll have to look at the specs on the equipment* | [as *adj.*] *our spec chart indicates a transmission speed of 9 seconds.* ▷1950s: abbreviation of SPECIFICATION.

spe·cial /ˈspeSHəl/ ▸*adj.* better, greater, or otherwise different from what is usual: *they always made a special effort at Christmas.* ■ exceptionally good or precious: *she's a very special person.* ■ belonging specifically to a particular person or place: *we want to preserve our town's special character.* ■ designed or organized for a particular person, purpose, or occasion: *we will return by special coaches.* ■ (of a subject) studied in particular depth. ■ used to denote education for children with particular needs, esp. those with learning difficulties. ■ *Mathematics* denoting a group consisting of matrices of unit determinant.

▸*n.* a thing, such as an event, product, or broadcast, that is designed or organized for a particular occasion or purpose: *television's election night specials.* ■ a dish not on the regular menu at a restaurant but served on a particular day. ■ *informal* a product or service offered at a temporarily reduced price. ▷Middle English: shortening of Old French *especial* 'especial' or Latin *specialis*, from *species* 'appearance' (see SPECIES). —**spe·cial·ness** *n.*

▸*PHRASE* □ **on special** available for sale at a reduced price: *they have hamburger buns on special today.*

Spe·cial Branch (in the UK) the police department dealing with political security.

spe·cial case ▸*n.* **1** a situation or person that has unusual qualities or needs. **2** *Law* a written statement of fact presented by litigants to a court.

spe·cial cor·re·spond·ent ▸*n.* a journalist writing for a newspaper on special events or a special area of interest.

spe·cial de·liv·er·y ▸*n.* a former express mail service of the U.S. Postal Service that involved expedited delivery of mail, often by special courier. ■ any mail service that involves special handling or expedited delivery. ■ a letter or parcel sent by a special-delivery service.

spe·cial draw·ing rights (abbr.: **SDR**) ▸*plural n.* a form of international money, created by the International Monetary Fund, and defined as a weighted average of various convertible currencies.

spe·cial e·di·tion ▸*n.* an edition of a newspaper, magazine, television program, etc., that differs from the usual format, esp. in concentrating on one particularly important story.

spe·cial ef·fects ▸*plural n.* illusions created for movies and television by props, camerawork, computer graphics, etc.

Spe·cial For·ces ▸*n.* an elite force within the U.S. Army specializing in guerrilla warfare and counterinsurgency.

spe·cial in·ten·tion ▸*n.* (in the Roman Catholic Church) a special aim or purpose for which a Mass is celebrated or prayers are said.

spe·cial in·ter·est (also **special interest group**) ▸*n.* a group of people or an organization seeking or receiving special advantages, typically through political lobbying.

spe·cial·ist /ˈspeSHəlist/ ▸*n.* a person who concentrates primarily on a particular subject or activity; a person highly skilled in a specific and restricted field. ■ a physician highly trained in a particular branch of medicine. ■ (in the U.S. Army) an enlisted person of one of four grades (**specialist 4**, equivalent to the rank of corporal, being the most junior, **specialist 7**, equivalent to sergeant first class, being the most senior) who has technical or administrative duties but does not exercise command.

▸*adj.* possessing or involving detailed knowledge or study of a restricted topic: *the project may involve people with specialist knowledge.* ■ [*attrib.*] concentrating on a restricted field, market, or area of activity: *a specialist electrical shop.* —**spe·cial·ism** /-ˌlizəm/ *n.*

spe·ci·al·i·ty /ˌspeSHēˈalitē/ ▸*n.* (*pl.* **-ties**) British term for SPECIALTY. ▷late Middle English (denoting the quality of being special or distinctive): from Old French *especialite* or late Latin *specialitas*, from Latin *specialis* (see SPECIAL).

spe·cial·ize /ˈspeSHəˌlīz/ ▸*v.* [*intrans.*] concentrate on and become expert in a particular subject or skill: *he could* ***specialize in*** *tropical medicine.* ■ confine oneself to providing a particular product or service: *the company* ***specialized in*** *commercial brochures.* ■ make a habit of engaging in a particular activity: *a group of writers has* ***specialized in*** *attacking the society they live in.* ■ [*trans.*] (often **be specialized**) *Biology* adapt or set apart (an organ or part) to serve a special function or to suit a particular way of life: *zooids specialized for different functions.* ▷early 17th cent.: from French *spécialiser*, from *spécial* 'special.' —**spe·cial·i·za·tion** /ˌspeSHəliˈzāSHən/ *n.*

spe·cial·ized /ˈspeSHəˌlīzd/ ▸*adj.* requiring or involving detailed and specific knowledge or training: *skilled treatment for these patients is very specialized.* ■ concentrating on a small area of a subject: *periodicals have become more and more specialized.* ■ designed for a particular purpose: *specialized software.*

spe·cial·ly /ˈspeSHəlē/ ▸*adv.* for a special purpose: *they have been fabricated specially for this boat* | [as *submodifier*] *a specially commissioned report.*

USAGE On the differences between **specially** and **especially**, see **usage** at ESPECIALLY.

spe·cial needs ▸*plural n.* (in the context of children at school) particular educational requirements resulting from learning difficulties, physical disability, or emotional and behavioral difficulties.

Spe·cial O·lym·pics ▸*n.* an international competition, modeled on the Olympic Games, in which mentally and physically handicapped athletes compete.

Spe·cial Op·er·a·tions Ex·ec·u·tive (abbr.: **SOE**) a secret British military service during World War II, set up in 1940 to carry out clandestine operations and coordinate with resistance movements in Europe and later the Far East.

spe·cial plead·ing ▸*n.* argument in which the speaker deliberately ignores aspects that are unfavorable to their point of view. ■ appeals to give a particular interest group special treatment: *we heard his special pleading for his constituency.*

spe·cial sort ▸*n. Printing* a character, such as an accented letter or a symbol, that is not normally included in any font.

spe·cial team ▸*n. Football* a squad that is used for kickoffs, punts, or other special plays.

spe·cial·ty /ˈspeSHəltē/ (*Brit.* also **spe·ci·al·i·ty** /ˌspeSHēˈalitē/) ▸*n.* (*pl.* **-ties**) **1** a pursuit, area of study, or skill to which someone has devoted much time and effort and in which they are expert: *his specialty was watercolors.* ■ a particular branch of medicine or surgery. ■ a product, esp. a type of food, that a person or region is famous for making well: *the local specialties are all seafood.* ■ [as *adj.*] meeting particular tastes or needs: *specialty potatoes for salads.* **2** *Law* a contract under seal. ▷Middle English (denoting special affection or attachment): shortening of Old French *especialte*, from *especial* (see SPECIAL).

spe·cial ver·dict ▸*n. Law* a verdict that requires an answer to a specific detailed question. ■ a verdict that an accused is not guilty by reason of insanity.

spe·ci·a·tion /ˌspēSHēˈāSHən; ˌspēsē-/ ▸*n. Biology* the formation of new and distinct species in the course of evolution. —**spe·ci·ate** /ˈspēSHēˌāt; spēsē-/ *v.*

spe·cie /ˈspēSHē; -sē/ ▸*n.* money in the form of coins rather than notes. ▷mid 16th cent. (sense 2): from Latin, ablative of *species* 'form, kind,' in the phrase *in specie* 'in the actual form.'

▸PHRASE □ **in specie** 1 in coin. 2 *Law* in the real, precise, or actual form specified: *the plaintiff could not be sure of recovering his goods in specie.*

spe·cies /ˈspēsēz; -sHēz/ ▸n. (pl. same) 1 (abbr.: **sp.**, **spp.**) *Biology* a group of living organisms consisting of similar individuals capable of exchanging genes or interbreeding. The species is the principal natural taxonomic unit, ranking below a genus and denoted by a Latin binomial, e.g., *Homo sapiens.* ■ *Logic* a group subordinate to a genus and containing individuals agreeing in some common attributes and called by a common name. ■ a kind or sort: *a species of invective at once tough and suave.* ■ used humorously to refer to people who share a characteristic or occupation: *a political species that is becoming more common, the environmental statesman.* ■ *Chemistry & Physics* a particular kind of atom, molecule, ion, or particle: *a new molecular species.* 2 *Christian Church* the visible form of each of the elements of consecrated bread and wine in the Eucharist. ▷late Middle English: from Latin, literally 'appearance, form, beauty,' from *specere* 'to look.'

spe·cies·ism /ˈspēsHē,zizəm; spēsē-/ ▸n. the assumption of human superiority leading to the exploitation of animals. **—spe·cies·ist** *adj.* & *n.*

spe·cies rose ▸n. a rose belonging to a distinct species and not to one of the many varieties produced by hybridization.

specif. ▸*abbr.* ■ specific; specifically.

spe·cif·ic /spəˈsifik/ ▸*adj.* 1 clearly defined or identified: *increasing the electricity supply only until it met specific development needs.* ■ precise and clear in making statements or issuing instructions: *when ordering goods be specific.* ■ belonging or relating uniquely to a particular subject: *information needs are often very* **specific to** *companies and individuals.* 2 *Biology* of, relating to, or connected with species or a species. 3 (of a duty or a tax) levied at a fixed rate per physical unit of the thing taxed, regardless of its price. 4 *Physics* of or denoting a number equal to the ratio of the value of some property of a given substance to the value of the same property of some other substance used as a reference, such as water, or of a vacuum, under equivalent conditions. ■ of or denoting a physical quantity expressed in terms of a unit mass, volume, or other measure, in order to give a value independent of the properties or scale of the particular system studied.
▸n. 1 *dated* a medicine or remedy effective in treating a particular disease or part of the body. 2 (usu. **specifics**) a precise detail: *he worked through the specifics of the contract.* ▷mid 17th cent. (originally in the sense 'having a special determining quality'): from late Latin *specificus*, from Latin *species* (see **SPECIES**). **—spe·cif·i·cal·ly** *adv.* **—spec·i·fic·i·ty** /,spesəˈfisitē/ *n.*

spe·cif·ic ac·tiv·i·ty ▸n. *Physics* the activity of a given radioisotope per unit mass.

spec·i·fi·ca·tion /,spesəfiˈkāsHən/ ▸n. an act of describing or identifying something precisely or of stating a precise requirement: *give a full specification of the job advertised | there was no clear specification of objectives.* ■ (usu. **specifications**) a detailed description of the design and materials used to make something. ■ a standard of workmanship, materials, etc., required to be met in a piece of work: *everything was built to a higher specification.* ■ a description of an invention accompanying an application for a patent. ▷late 16th cent.: from medieval Latin *specificatio(n-)*, from late Latin *specificare* (see **SPECIFY**).

spe·cif·ic charge ▸n. *Physics* the ratio of the charge of an ion or subatomic particle to its mass.

spe·cif·ic dis·ease ▸n. a disease caused by a particular and characteristic organism.

spe·cif·ic ep·i·thet /spəˈsifik ˈepə,THet/ ▸n. *chiefly Botany Microbiology* the second element in the Latin binomial name of a species, which follows the generic name and distinguishes the species from others in the same genus. Compare with **SPECIFIC NAME, TRIVIAL NAME.**

spe·cif·ic grav·i·ty ▸n. *Chemistry* the ratio of the density of a substance to the density of a standard, usually water for a liquid or solid, and air for a gas.

spe·cif·ic heat ▸n. *Physics* the heat required to raise the temperature of the unit mass of a given substance by a given amount (usually one degree).

spe·cif·ic name ▸n. *chiefly Botany Microbiology* the Latin binomial name of a species, consisting of the generic name followed by the specific epithet. ■ *chiefly Zoology* another term for **SPECIFIC EPITHET.**

spe·cif·ic per·for·mance ▸n. *Law* the performance of a contractual duty, as ordered in cases where damages would not be adequate remedy.

spec·i·fy /ˈspesə,fi/ ▸v. (**-fies, -fied**) [*trans.*] identify clearly and definitely: *the coup leader promised an election but did not specify a date.* ■ [with *clause*] state a fact or requirement clearly and precisely: *the agency failed to* **specify that** *the workers were not their employees.* ■ include in an architect's or engineer's specifications: *naval architects specified circular portholes.* ▷Middle English: from Old French *specifier* or late Latin *specificare* (see **SPECIFIC**). **—spec·i·fi·a·ble** /,spesəˈfīəbəl/ *adj.* **—spec·i·fi·er** *n.*

spec·i·men /ˈspesəmən/ ▸n. an individual animal, plant, piece of a mineral, etc., used as an example of its species or type for scientific study or display. ■ an example of something such as a product or piece of work, regarded as typical of its class or group. ■ a sample for medical testing, esp. of urine. ■ *informal* used to refer humorously to a person or animal: *in her he found himself confronted by a sorrier specimen than himself.* ▷early 17th cent. (in the sense 'pattern, model'): from Latin, from *specere* 'to look.'

spec·i·men plant ▸n. an unusual or impressive plant grown as a focus of interest in a garden.

spe·cious /ˈspēsHəs/ ▸*adj.* superficially plausible, but actually wrong: *a specious argument.* ■ misleading in appearance, esp. misleadingly attractive: *the music trade gives Golden Oldies a specious appearance of novelty.* ▷late Middle English (in the sense 'beautiful'): from Latin *speciosus* 'fair,' from *species* (see **SPECIES**). **—spe·cious·ly** *adv.* **—spe·cious·ness** *n.*

speck /spek/ ▸n. a tiny spot: *the figure in the distance had become a mere speck.* ■ a small particle of a substance: **specks of** *dust.*
▸v. [*trans.*] (usu. **be specked**) mark with small spots: *their skin was specked with goose pimples.* ▷Old English *specca*; compare with the noun **SPECKLE.** **—speck·less** *adj.*

speck·le /ˈspekəl/ ▸n. (usu. **speckles**) a small spot or patch of color.
▸v. [*trans.*] [often as *adj.*] (**speckled**) mark with a large number of small spots or patches of color: *a large speckled brown egg.* ▷late Middle English (as a noun): from Middle Dutch *spekkel*; the verb (late 16th cent.) from the noun or a back-formation from *speckled*.

speck·led trout ▸n. the brook trout. See **CHAR**[4].

speck·led wood ▸n. a brown Eurasian butterfly with cream or orange markings, favoring light woodland habitats. • *Pararge aegeria*, subfamily Satyrinae, family Nymphalidae.

specs /ˈspeks/ ▸*plural n. informal* 1 a pair of spectacles. 2 plural form of **SPEC**[2]. ▷early 19th cent.: abbreviation.

spect /spekt/ ▸v. nonstandard form of **EXPECT**: *I spect they've been to a party.*

spec·ta·cle /ˈspektəkəl/ ▸n. a visually striking performance or display: *the acrobatic feats make a good spectacle | the show is pure spectacle.* ■ an event or scene regarded in terms of its visual impact: *the spectacle of a city's mass grief.* ▷Middle English: via Old French from Latin *spectaculum* 'public show,' from *spectare*, frequentative of *specere* 'to look.'
▸PHRASE □ **make a spectacle of oneself** draw attention to oneself by behaving in a ridiculous way in public.

spec·ta·cled /ˈspektəkəld/ ▸*adj.* wearing spectacles. ■ used in names of animals with markings that resemble spectacles.

spec·ta·cled bear ▸n. a South American bear with a black or dark brown coat and white markings around the eyes. • *Tremarctos ornatus*, family Ursidae.

spec·ta·cled cai·man /ˈkāmən/ ▸n. a small South American caiman with a bony ridge between the eyes that gives the appearance of spectacles. • *Caiman sclerops*, family Alligatoridae.

spec·ta·cled co·bra ▸n. an Asian cobra with a marking on the hood that resembles spectacles. Also called **INDIAN COBRA, ASIAN COBRA.** • *Naja naja*, family Elapidae.

spec·ta·cles /ˈspektəkəlz/ ▸*plural n.* another term for **GLASSES.**

spec·tac·u·lar /spekˈtakyələr/ ▸*adj.* beautiful in a dramatic and eye-catching way: *spectacular mountain scenery.* ■ strikingly large or obvious: *the party suffered a spectacular loss in the election.*
▸n. an event such as a pageant or musical, produced on a large scale and with striking effects. ▷late 17th cent.: from **SPECTACLE**, on the pattern of words such as *oracular.* **—spec·tac·u·lar·ly** *adv.*

spec·tate /spekˈtāt/ ▸v. [*intrans.*] be a spectator, esp. at a sporting event: *an entire defense starts to spectate like fans in the stands.* ▷early 18th cent.: back-formation from **SPECTATOR.**

spec·ta·tor /ˈspek,tātər/ ▸n. a person who watches at a show, game, or other event. ▷late 16th cent.: from French *spectateur* or Latin *spectator*, from *spectare* 'gaze at, observe' (see **SPECTACLE**). **—spec·ta·to·ri·al** /,spektəˈtôrēəl/ *adj.* (*rare*).

spec·ta·tor sport ▸n. a sport that many people find entertaining to watch.

spec·ter /ˈspektər/ (*Brit.* **spec·tre**) ▸n. a ghost. ■ something widely feared as a possible unpleasant or dangerous occurrence: **the specter of** *nuclear holocaust.* ▷early 17th cent.: from French *spectre* or Latin *spectrum* (see **SPECTRUM**).

spec·ti·no·my·cin /,spektənəˈmīsin/ ▸n. *Medicine* a bacterial antibiotic used as an alternative to penicillin. • The drug is obtained from the bacterium *Streptomyces spectabilis.* ▷1960s: from the specific epithet *spectabilis* (see above), literally 'visible, remarkable' + **-MYCIN.**

Spec·tor /ˈspektər/, Phil (1940–), U.S. record producer and songwriter. He pioneered a "wall of sound" style, using echo and tape loops, and had a succession of hit recordings in the 1960s with groups such as the Ronettes and the Crystals.

spec·tra /ˈspektrə/ ▸ plural form of **SPECTRUM.**

spec·tral /ˈspektrəl/ ▸*adj.* 1 of or like a ghost. [early 18th cent.: from **SPECTER** + **-AL.**] 2 of or concerning spectra or the spectrum. [mid 19th cent.: from **SPECTRUM** + **-AL.**] **—spec·tral·ly** *adv.*

spec·tral in·dex ▸n. an exponential factor relating the flux density of a radio source to its frequency.

spec·tral tar·si·er /ˈtärsēər/ ▸n. a tarsier that has a tail with a long bushy tuft and a scaly base, native to Sulawesi. • *Tarsius spectrum*, family Tarsiidae.

spec·tral type (also **spectral class**) ▸n. *Astronomy* the group in which a star is classified according to its spectrum, esp. using the Harvard classification.

spec·tre ▸n. British spelling of **SPECTER.**

spectro- ▸*comb. form* representing **SPECTRUM.**

spec·tro·gram /ˈspektrə,gram/ ▸n. a photographic or other visual or electronic representation of a spectrum.

spec·tro·graph /ˈspektrə,graf/ ▸n. an apparatus for photographing or otherwise recording spectra. **—spec·tro·graph·ic** /,spektrəˈgrafik/ *adj.* **—spec·tro·graph·i·cal·ly** /,spektrəˈgrafik(ə)lē/ *adv.* **—spec·trog·ra·phy** /spekˈträgrəfē/ *n.*

spec·tro·he·li·o·graph /,spektrōˈhēlēə,graf/ ▸n. an instrument for taking photographs of the sun in light of one wavelength only.

spec·tro·he·li·o·scope /,spektrōˈhēlēə,skōp/ ▸n. a device similar to a spectroheliograph that produces a directly observable monochromatic image of the sun.

spec·trom·e·ter /spekˈträmitər/ ▸n. an apparatus used for recording and measuring spectra, esp. as a method of analysis. **—spec·tro·met·ric** /,spektrəˈmetrik/ *adj.* **—spec·trom·e·try** /spekˈträmətrē/ *n.*

spec·tro·pho·tom·e·ter /,spektrōfōˈtämitər/ ▸n. an apparatus for measuring the intensity of light in a part of the spectrum, esp. as transmitted or emitted by particular substances. **—spec·tro·pho·to·met·ric** /,spektrə,fōtəˈmetrik/ *adj.* **—spec·tro·pho·to·met·ri·cal·ly** /,spektrə,fōtəˈmetrik(ə)lē/ *adv.* **—spec·tro·pho·tom·e·try** /-mətrē/ *n.*

spec·tro·scope /ˈspektrə,skōp/ ▸n. an apparatus for producing and recording spectra for examination.

spec·tros·co·py /spekˈträskəpē/ ▸n. the branch of science concerned with the investigation and measurement of spectra produced when matter

spectacled cobra

Pronunciation Key ə *ago*; ər *over*; ˈə or ,ə *up*; ˈər or ,ər *fur*; a *hat*; ā *rate*; ä *car*; CH *chew*; e *let*; ē *see*; e(ə)r *air*; i *fit*; ī *by*; i(ə)r *ear*; NG *sing*; ō *go*; ô *for*; oi *boy*; o͝o *good*; o͞o *goo*; ou *out*; SH *she*; TH *thin*; T͟H *then*; (h)w *why*; ZH *vision*

interacts with or emits electromagnetic radiation. —**spec·tro·scop·ic** /ˌspektrəˈskäpik/ *adj.* —**spec·tro·scop·i·cal·ly** /ˌspektrəˈskäpik(ə)lē/ *adv.* —**spec·tros·co·pist** /-pist/ *n.*

spec·trum /ˈspektrəm/ ▶*n.* (*pl.* **-tra** /-trə/) **1** a band of colors, as seen in a rainbow, produced by separation of the components of light by their different degrees of refraction according to wavelength. ■ (**the spectrum**) the entire range of wavelengths of electromagnetic radiation. ■ an image or distribution of components of any electromagnetic radiation arranged in a progressive series according to wavelength. ■ a similar image or distribution of components of sound, particles, etc., arranged according to such characteristics as frequency, charge, and energy. **2** used to classify something, or suggest that it can be classified, in terms of its position on a scale between two extreme or opposite points: *the left or the right of the political spectrum.* ■ a wide range: *self-help books are covering a broader and broader spectrum.* ▷early 17th cent. (in the sense 'specter'): from Latin, literally 'image, apparition,' from *specere* 'to look.'

spec·trum an·a·lyz·er ▶*n.* a device for analyzing a system of oscillations, esp. sound, into its separate components.

spec·u·la /ˈspekyələ/ ▶ plural form of **SPECULUM**.

spec·u·lar /ˈspekyələr/ ▶*adj.* of, relating to, or having the properties of a mirror. ▷late 16th cent. (in *specular stone*, a substance formerly used as glass): from Latin *specularis*, from *speculum* (see **SPECULUM**).

spec·u·lar i·ron ore ▶*n.* hematite with a metallic luster.

spec·u·late /ˈspekyəˌlāt/ ▶*v.* [*intrans.*] **1** form a theory or conjecture about a subject without firm evidence: *my colleagues speculate about my private life* | [with *clause*] *observers* ***speculated that*** *the authorities wished to improve their image.* **2** invest in stocks, property, or other ventures in the hope of gain but with the risk of loss: *he didn't look as though he had the money to* ***speculate in*** *stocks.* ▷late 16th cent.: from Latin *speculat-* 'observed from a vantage point,' from the verb *speculari*, from *specula* 'watchtower,' from *specere* 'to look.' —**spec·u·la·tion** /ˌspekyəˈlāsHən/ *n.* —**spec·u·la·tor** /-ˌlātər/ *n.*

spec·u·la·tive /ˈspekyəˌlātiv; -lətiv/ ▶*adj.* **1** engaged in, expressing, or based on conjecture rather than knowledge: *discussion of the question is largely speculative.* **2** (of an investment) involving a high risk of loss. ■ (of a business venture) undertaken on the chance of success, without a preexisting contract. —**spec·u·la·tive·ly** *adv.* —**spec·u·la·tive·ness** *n.*

spec·u·la·tive build·er ▶*n.* a person who has houses constructed without securing buyers in advance.

spec·u·lum /ˈspekyələm/ ▶*n.* (*pl.* **-la** /-lə/) **1** *Medicine* a metal or plastic instrument that is used to dilate an orifice or canal in the body to allow inspection. **2** *Ornithology* a bright patch of plumage on the wings of certain birds, esp. a strip of metallic sheen on the secondary flight feathers of many ducks. **3** a mirror or reflector of glass or metal, esp. (formerly) a metallic mirror in a reflecting telescope. ■ short for **SPECULUM METAL**. ▷late Middle English: from Latin, literally 'mirror,' from *specere* 'to look.'

spec·u·lum met·al ▶*n.* an alloy of copper and tin used to make mirrors, esp. formerly for telescopes.

sped /sped/ ▶ past and past participle of **SPEED**.

speech /spēcH/ ▶*n.* **1** the expression of or the ability to express thoughts and feelings by articulate sounds: *he was born deaf and without the power of speech.* ■ a person's style of speaking: *she wouldn't accept his correction of her speech.* ■ the language of a nation, region, or group: *the distinctive rhythms of their speech.* **2** a formal address or discourse delivered to an audience: *the headmistress made a speech about how much they would miss her.* ■ a sequence of lines written for one character in a play. ▷Old English *sprǣc*, *sprēc*, later *spēc*: related to Dutch *spraak*, German *Sprache*, also to **SPEAK**.

speech act ▶*n. Linguistics & Philosophy* an utterance considered as an action, particularly with regard to its intention, purpose, or effect.

speech cen·ter (also **speech area**) ▶*n.* a region of the brain involved in the comprehension or production of speech.

speech com·mu·ni·ty ▶*n.* a group of people sharing a common language or dialect.

speech·i·fy /ˈspēcHəˌfī/ ▶*v.* (**-fies**, **-fied**) [*intrans.*] deliver a speech, esp. in a tedious or pompous way: *writers should write, not speechify* | [as *n.*] (**speechifying**) *the after-dinner speechifying begins.* —**speech·i·fi·ca·tion** /ˌspēcHəfiˈkāsHən/ *n.* —**speech·i·fi·er** *n.*

speech·less /ˈspēcHlis/ ▶*adj.* unable to speak, esp. as the temporary result of shock or some strong emotion: *he was* ***speechless with*** *rage.* ■ unable to be expressed in words: *surges of speechless passion.* ▷Old English *spǣclēas* (see **SPEECH**, **-LESS**). —**speech·less·ly** *adv.* —**speech·less·ness** *n.*

speech pa·thol·o·gy /pəˈTHäləjē/ ▶*n.* the study and treatment of speech and language problems. —**speech pa·thol·o·gist** /-jist/ *n.*

speech·read·ing /ˈspēcHˌrēdiNG/ ▶*n.* lip-reading.

speech rec·og·ni·tion ▶*n. Computing* the ability of a computer to identify and respond to the sounds produced in human speech: [as *adj.*] *speech recognition technologies.*

speech sound ▶*n.* a phonetically distinct unit of speech.

speech syn·the·siz·er /ˈsinTHəˌsīzər/ ▶*n.* a machine that generates spoken language on the basis of written input. —**speech syn·the·sis** /ˈsinTHəsis/ *n.*

speech ther·a·py ▶*n.* training to help people with speech and language problems to speak more clearly. —**speech ther·a·pist** *n.*

speech·writ·er /ˈspēcHˌrītər/ ▶*n.* a person employed to write speeches for others to deliver.

speed /spēd/ ▶*n.* **1** rapidity of movement or action: *the accident was due to excessive speed* | *figurative they were bemused by the speed of events.* ■ the rate at which someone or something is able to move or operate: *the car has a top speed of 147 mph.* ■ each of the possible gear ratios of a bicycle or motor vehicle. ■ the sensitivity of photographic film to light. ■ the light-gathering power or f-number of a camera lens. ■ the duration of a photographic exposure. **2** *informal* an amphetamine drug, esp. methamphetamine. **3** *informal* something that matches one's tastes or inclinations: *oak tables and chairs are more his speed.* **4** *archaic* success; prosperity: *wish me good speed.*

▶*v.* (*past* **sped** /sped/ or **speed·ed**) **1** [*intrans.*] move quickly: *I got into the car and home we sped.* ■ [*intrans.*] (of a motorist) travel at a speed that is greater than the legal limit: *the car that crashed was speeding.* ■ (**speed up**) move or work more quickly: *you force yourself to speed up because you don't want to keep others waiting.* ■ [*trans.*] cause to move, act, or happen more quickly: *recent initiatives have sought to* ***speed up*** *decision-making.* **2** [*trans.*] *archaic* make prosperous or successful: *may God speed you.* **3** [*intrans.*] *informal* take or be under the influence of an amphetamine drug: *more kids than ever are speeding, tripping, and getting stoned.* ▷Old English *spēd* (noun), *spēdan* (verb), from the Germanic base of Old English *spōwan* 'prosper, succeed,' a sense reflected in early usage. —**speed·er** *n.*

▶*PHRASES* □ **at speed** quickly: *a car flashed past them at speed.* □ **up to speed** operating at full speed. ■ (of a person or company) performing at an anticipated rate or level. ■ (of a person) fully informed or up to date: *that reminds me to bring you up to speed on the soap opera.*

speed bag ▶*n.* a small punching bag used by boxers for practicing quick punches.

speed·ball /ˈspēdˌbôl/ ▶*n. informal* a mixture of cocaine and heroin.

speed·boat /ˈspēdˌbōt/ ▶*n.* a motorboat designed for high speed. —**speed·boat·ing** *n.*

speed bump (*Brit.* also **speed hump**) ▶*n.* a ridge set in a road surface, typically at intervals, to control the speed of vehicles.

speed dat·ing ▶*n.* a social activity in which equal complements of potential partners spend a few minutes in short interviews with all other participants in order to determine whether there is interest.

speed di·al ▶*n.* a function on some telephones that allows numbers to be entered into a memory and dialed using fewer buttons.

▶*v.* (**speed-dial**) [*trans.*] dial (a telephone number) by using the speed dial function.

speed lim·it ▶*n.* the maximum speed at which a vehicle may legally travel on a particular stretch of road.

speed mer·chant ▶*n. informal* **1** a motorist who enjoys driving fast. **2** *Baseball* a player noted for speed, such as a very fast base runner or a fastball pitcher.

speed·o /ˈspēdō/ ▶*n.* (*pl.* **-os**) **1** *informal* short for **SPEEDOMETER**. **2** (**Speedo**) *trademark* a bathing suit.

speed·om·e·ter /spəˈdämitər/ ▶*n.* an instrument on a vehicle's dashboard indicating its speed.

speed-read /rēd/ ▶*v.* read rapidly by assimilating several phrases or sentences at once. —**speed-read·er** *n.*

speed skat·ing ▶*n.* the sport of competitive racing on specially designed skates, typically around an oval track.

speed·ster /ˈspēdstər/ ▶*n. informal* a person who drives or runs fast. ■ a thing that operates well at high speed, for example a fast car.

speed trap ▶*n.* an area of road in which hidden police detect vehicles exceeding a speed limit, typically by radar.

speed-up ▶*n.* an increase in speed, esp. in a person's or machine's rate of working.

speed·way /ˈspēdˌwā/ ▶*n.* a stadium or track used for automobile or motorcycle racing. ■ a highway for fast motor traffic. ■ *Brit.* a form of motorcycle racing on an oval dirt track, typically in a stadium.

speed·well /ˈspēdˌwel/ ▶*n.* a small creeping herbaceous plant of north temperate regions, with small blue or pink flowers. • Genus *Veronica*, family Scrophulariaceae: several species, including the **germander speedwell**.

speed·writ·ing /ˈspēdˌrītiNG/ ▶*n. trademark* a form of shorthand using the letters of the alphabet. —**speed·writ·er** /-tər/ *n.*

speed·y /ˈspēdē/ ▶*adj.* (**speed·i·er**, **speed·i·est**) **1** done or occurring quickly: *a speedy recovery.* **2** moving quickly: *a speedy center fielder.* —**speed·i·ly** /ˈspēdəlē/ *adv.* —**speed·i·ness** *n.*

speed·y tri·al ▶*n. chiefly Law* a criminal trial held after minimal delay, as considered to be a citizen's constitutional right.

Speer /spi(ə)r/, Albert (1905–81), German architect and Nazi government official; designer of the Nuremberg stadium for the 1934 Nazi Party congress. He was also minister for armaments and munitions. Following the Nuremberg trials, he served 20 years in Spandau prison.

speiss /spīs/ ▶*n.* a mixture of impure arsenides and antimonides of nickel, cobalt, iron, and other metals, produced in the smelting of cobalt and other ores. ▷late 18th cent.: from German *Speise* 'food, amalgam.'

Speke /spēk/, John Hanning (1827–64), English explorer. With Sir Richard Burton, he was the first European to visit Lake Tanganyika (1858). He also explored Lake Victoria, naming it in honor of the queen.

spe·le·ol·o·gy /ˌspēlēˈäləjē/ ▶*n.* the study or exploration of caves. ▷late 19th cent.: from French *spéléologie*, via Latin from Greek *spēlaion* 'cave.' —**spe·le·o·log·i·cal** /ˌspēlēəˈläjikəl/ *adj.* —**spe·le·ol·o·gist** /-jist/ *n.*

spe·le·o·them /ˈspēlēəˌTHem/ ▶*n. Geology* a structure formed in a cave by the deposition of minerals from water, e.g., a stalactite or stalagmite. ▷1950s: from Greek *spēlaion* 'cave' + *thema* 'deposit.'

spell[1] /spel/ ▶*v.* (*past* and *past part.* **spelled** /speld/ or *chiefly Brit.* **spelt** /spelt/) [*trans.*] write or name the letters that form (a word) in correct sequence: *Dolly spelled her name* | [*intrans.*] *journals have a house style about how to spell.* ■ (of letters) make up or form (a word): *the letters spell the word "how."* ■ be recognizable as a sign or characteristic of: *she had the chic, efficient look that spells Milan.* ■ lead to: *the plans would spell disaster for the economy.*

▶*phrasal v.* □ **spell something out** speak the letters that form a word in sequence. ■ explain something in detail: *I'll spell out the problem again.* ▷Middle English: shortening of Old French *espeller*, from the Germanic base of **SPELL**[2].

spell[2] ▶*n.* a form of words used as a magical charm or incantation. ■ a state of enchantment caused by such a form of words: *the magician may* ***cast a spell on*** *himself.* ■ an ability to control or influence people as though one had magical power over them: *she is afraid that you are waking from her spell.* ▷Old English *spel(l)* 'narration,' of Germanic origin.

▶*PHRASES* □ **under a spell** not fully in control of one's thoughts and actions, as though in a state of enchantment. □ **under someone's spell** so devoted to someone that they seem to have magic power over one.

spell[3] ▶*n.* a short period: *I want to get away from racing for a spell.* ■ a period spent in an activity: *a spell of greenhouse work.* ■ a period of a specified kind of weather: *an early cold spell in autumn.* ■ a period of suffering from a specified kind of illness: *she plunges off a yacht and suffers a spell of amnesia.* ■ *Austral.* a period of rest from work.

▶*v.* [*trans.*] allow (someone) to rest briefly by taking

their place in some activity: *I got sleepy and needed her to spell me for a while at the wheel.* ■ [*intrans.*] *Austral.* take a brief rest: *I'll spell for a bit.* ▷late 16th cent.: variant of dialect *spele* 'take the place of,' of unknown origin. The early sense of the noun was 'shift of relief workers.'

spell·bind /ˈspelˌbīnd/ ▶*v.* (*past* and *past part.* **-bound**) [*trans.*] hold the complete attention of (someone) as though by magic; fascinate: [as *adj.*] (**spellbinding**) *she told the spellbinding story of her life* | [as *adj.*] (**spellbound**) *the killer whale gave the spellbound audience a good soaking.* —**spell·bind·er** *n.* —**spell·bind·ing·ly** *adv.*

spell-check (also **spell check**) *Computing* ▶*v.* [*trans.*] check the spelling in (a text) using a spell-checker. ▶*n.* a check of the spelling in a file of text using a spell-checker: *prerecorded macros for starting a spell-check or saving a file.* ■ a spell-checker.

spell-check·er (also **spell checker**) ▶*n.* a computer program that checks the spelling of words in files of text, typically by comparison with a stored list of words.

spell·er /ˈspelər/ ▶*n.* [with *adj.*] a person who spells with a specified ability: *a very weak speller.* ■ a book for teaching spelling. ■ another term for **SPELL-CHECKER**.

spell·ing /ˈspeliNG/ ▶*n.* the process or activity of writing or naming the letters of a word. ■ the way a word is spelled: *the spelling of his name was influenced by French.* ■ a person's ability to spell words: *her spelling was deplorable.* ■ a school subject.

spell·ing bee ▶*n.* a spelling competition.

spell·ing check·er ▶*n.* another term for **SPELL-CHECKER**.

spelt[1] ▶*chiefly Brit.* past and past participle of **SPELL**[1].

spelt[2] /spelt/ ▶*n.* an old kind of wheat with bearded ears and spikelets that each contain two narrow grains, not widely grown but favored as a health food. Compare with **EINKORN**, **EMMER**. • *Triticum spelta*, family Gramineae. ▷late Old English, from Old Saxon *spelta*. The word was rare until the 16th cent., when it was readopted from Middle Dutch.

spel·ter /ˈspeltər/ ▶*n.* commercial crude smelted zinc. ■ a solder or other alloy in which zinc is the main constituent. ▷mid 17th cent.: compare with Old French *espeautre*, Middle Dutch *speauter*; related to **PEWTER**.

spe·lunk·ing /spiˈləNGkiNG/ ▶*n.* the exploration of caves, esp. as a hobby. ▷1940s: from obsolete *spelunk* 'cave' (from Latin *spelunca*) + **-ING**[1]. —**spe·lunk·er** /-kər/ *n.*

spence /spens/ ▶*n.* *archaic* a larder. ▷late Middle English: shortening of Old French *despense*, from Latin *dispensa*, feminine past participle of *dispendere* (see **DISPENSE**).

Spen·cer /ˈspensər/, Herbert (1820–1903), English philosopher and sociologist. He sought to apply the theory of natural selection to human societies, developing social Darwinism and coining the phrase the "survival of the fittest" in 1864.

spen·cer[1] /ˈspensər/ ▶*n.* a short, close-fitting jacket, worn by women and children in the early 19th century. ■ a thin woolen vest, worn by women for extra warmth in winter. ▷probably named after the second Earl *Spencer* (1758–1834), English politician.

spen·cer[2] ▶*n.* *Sailing* a boomless gaff sail on a square-rigged ship's foremast or mainmast (replaced in the mid 19th cent. by staysails). ▷mid 19th cent.: of unknown origin.

Spen·ce·ri·an /spenˈsi(ə)rēən/ ▶*adj.* of or relating to a style of sloping handwriting widely taught in American schools from around 1850. ▷mid 19th cent.: named after the U.S. calligrapher Platt Rogers *Spencer* (1800–64) who developed it.

spend /spend/ ▶*v.* (*past* and *past part.* **spent** /spent/) [*trans.*] pay out (money) in buying or hiring goods or services: *the firm has* **spent** *$100,000* **on** *hardware and software.* ■ pay out (money) for a particular person's benefit or for the improvement of something: *the college* **spent** *$140* **on** *each of its students.* ■ used to show the activity in which someone is engaged or the place where they are living over a period of time: *she spent a lot of time traveling.* ■ use or give out the whole of; exhaust: *she couldn't buy any more because she had already spent her money* | *the initial surge of interest had* **spent itself**.
▶*n.* *informal* an amount of money paid for a particular purpose or over a particular period of time: *the average spend at the cafe is about $10 a head.* ▷Old English *spendan*, from Latin *expendere* 'pay out'; partly also a shortening of obsolete *dispend*, from Latin *dispendere* 'pay out.' —**spend·a·ble** *adj.* —**spend·er** *n.*
▶**PHRASE** □ **spend a penny** *Brit., informal* urinate (used euphemistically). [with reference to the coin-operated locks of public toilets.]

Spen·der /ˈspendər/, Sir Stephen (1909–95), English poet and critic. In his critical work *The Destructive Element* (1935) he defended the importance of political subject matter in literature.

spend·ing mon·ey ▶*n.* money available to be spent on pleasures and entertainment.

spend·thrift /ˈspen(d)ˌTHrift/ ▶*n.* a person who spends money in an extravagant, irresponsible way.

Speng·ler /ˈspeNGglər; ˈSHpeNG-/, Oswald (1880–1936), German philosopher. In his book *The Decline of the West* (1918–22) he argued that civilizations undergo a seasonal cycle of a thousand years and are subject to growth and decay analogous to biological species.

Spen·ser /ˈspensər/, Edmund (*c.*1552–99), English poet. He is best known for his allegorical romance the *Faerie Queene* (1590; 1596) that celebrated Queen Elizabeth I and was written in the Spenserian stanza. —**Spen·se·ri·an** /spenˈsi(ə)rēən/ *adj.*

Spen·se·ri·an stan·za ▶*n.* the stanza used by Spenser in the *Faerie Queene*, consisting of eight iambic pentameters and an alexandrine, with the rhyming scheme *ababbcbcc*.

spent /spent/ ▶ past and past participle of **SPEND**.
▶*adj.* having been used and unable to be used again: *a spent matchstick.* ■ having no power or energy left: *the movement has become a spent force.*

spent tan ▶*n.* see **TAN**[1] (sense 2).

sperm /spərm/ ▶*n.* (*pl.* same or **sperms**) **1** short for **SPERMATOZOON**. ■ *informal* semen. [late Middle English: via late Latin from Greek *sperma* 'seed,' from *speirein* 'to sow.'] **2** short for **SPERM WHALE**. ■ short for **SPERMACETI** or **SPERM OIL**.

sper·ma·cet·i /ˌspərməˈsetē/ ▶*n.* a white waxy substance produced by the sperm whale, formerly used in candles and ointments. It is present in a rounded organ in the head, where it focuses acoustic signals and aids in the control of buoyancy. ▷late 15th cent.: from medieval Latin, from late Latin *sperma* 'sperm' + *ceti* 'of a whale' (genitive of *cetus*, from Greek *kētos* 'whale'), from the belief that it was whale spawn.

sper·ma·the·ca /ˌspərməˈTHēkə/ ▶*n.* (*pl.* **-cae** /-kē/) *Zoology* (in a female or hermaphrodite invertebrate) a receptacle in which sperm is stored after mating. ▷early 19th cent.: from late Latin *sperma* 'sperm' + **THECA**.

sper·mat·ic /spərˈmatik/ ▶*adj.* [*attrib.*] of or relating to sperm or semen. ▷late Middle English: via late Latin from Greek *spermatikos*, from *sperma* (see **SPERM**). —**sper·mat·i·cal·ly** *adv.*

sper·mat·ic cord ▶*n.* a bundle of nerves, ducts, and blood vessels connecting the testicles to the abdominal cavity.

sper·ma·tid /ˈspərməˌtid/ ▶*n.* *Biology* an immature male sex cell formed from a spermatocyte that can develop into a spermatozoon without further division. —**sper·ma·ti·dal** /ˌspərməˈtīdl/ *adj.*

spermato- ▶*comb. form* *Biology* relating to sperm or seeds: *spermatophore* | *spermatozoid.* ▷from Greek *sperma, spermat-* 'sperm.'

sper·mat·o·cyte /spərˈmatəˌsīt/ ▶*n.* *Biology* a cell produced at the second stage in the formation of spermatozoa, formed from a spermatogonium and dividing by meiosis into spermatids.

sper·mat·o·gen·e·sis /ˌspərmətəˈjenəsis; spərˌma-/ ▶*n.* *Biology* the production or development of mature spermatozoa.

sper·mat·o·go·ni·um /spərˌmatəˈgōnēəm; ˌspərmə-/ ▶*n.* (*pl.* **-go·ni·a** /-ˈgōnēə/) *Biology* a cell produced at an early stage in the formation of spermatozoa, formed in the wall of a seminiferous tubule and giving rise by mitosis to spermatocytes. ▷late 19th cent.: from **SPERM** + modern Latin *gonium* (from Greek *gonos* 'offspring, seed'). —**sper·mat·o·go·ni·al** /-nēəl/ *adj.*

sper·mat·o·phore /spərˈmatəˌfôr/ ▶*n.* *Zoology* a protein capsule containing a mass of spermatozoa, transferred during mating in various insects, arthropods, cephalopod mollusks, etc.

sper·mat·o·phyte /spərˈmatəˌfīt/ ▶*n.* *Botany* a plant of a large division that comprises those that bear seeds, including the gymnosperms and angiosperms. • Division Spermatophyta.

sper·ma·to·zo·id /ˌspərmətəˈzoid; spərˌma-/ ▶*n.* *Botany* a motile male gamete produced by a lower plant or a gymnosperm. Also called **ANTHEROZOID**.

sper·ma·to·zo·on /ˌspərmətəˈzōən; spərˌma-/ ▶*n.* (*pl.* **-zo·a** /-ˈzōə/) *Biology* the mature motile male sex cell of an animal, by which the ovum is fertilized, typically having a compact head and one or more long flagella for swimming. ▷mid 19th cent.: from Greek *sperma, spermat-* 'seed' + *zōion* 'animal.' —**sper·ma·to·zo·al** /-zōəl/ *adj.* —**sper·ma·to·zo·an** /-ˈzōən/ *adj.*

sperm bank ▶*n.* a place where semen is kept in cold storage for use in artificial insemination.

sperm count ▶*n.* a measure of the number of spermatozoa per ejaculation or per measured amount of semen, used as an indication of a man's fertility.

sper·mi·cide /ˈspərməˌsīd/ ▶*n.* a substance that kills spermatozoa, used as a contraceptive. —**sper·mi·cid·al** /ˌspərməˈsīdl/ *adj.*

sper·mi·dine /ˈspərməˌdēn/ ▶*n.* *Biochemistry* a colorless compound with a similar distribution and effect to spermine. • A polyamine; chem. formula: $H_2N(CH_2)_3NH(CH_2)_4NH_2$. ▷1920s: from **SPERM** + **-IDE** + **-INE**[4].

sper·mine /ˈspərˌmēn/ ▶*n.* *Biochemistry* a deliquescent compound that acts to stabilize various components of living cells and is widely distributed in living and decaying tissues. • A polyamine; chem. formula: $(H_2N(CH_2)_3NH(CH_2)_2)_2$. ▷so called because first found in sperm.

spermo- ▶*comb. form* equivalent to **SPERMATO-**.

sperm oil ▶*n.* an oil found with spermaceti in the head of the sperm whale, used formerly as a lubricant.

sperm whale ▶*n.* a toothed whale with a massive head, typically feeding at great depths on squid, formerly valued for the spermaceti and sperm oil in its head and the ambergris in its intestines. • Family Physeteridae: two genera and three species, in particular the very large *Physeter macrocephalus* (also called **CACHALOT**). ▷mid 19th cent.: *sperm*, abbreviation of **SPERMACETI**.

S

spes·sart·ine /ˈspesərˌtēn/ ▶*n.* a form of garnet containing manganese and aluminum, occurring as orange-red to dark brown crystals. ▷mid 19th cent.: from French, from *Spessart*, the name of a district in northwestern Bavaria, Germany, + **-INE**[4].

spew /spyo͞o/ ▶*v.* [*trans.*] expel large quantities of (something) rapidly and forcibly: *buses were* **spewing out** *black clouds of exhaust.* ■ [*intrans.*] be poured or forced out in large quantities: *oil spewed out of the damaged tanker.* ■ [*intrans.*] *informal* vomit. ▷Old English *spīwan, spēowan*, of Germanic origin; related to German *speien*. —**spew·er** *n.*

Spey /spā/ a river in east central Scotland. Rising in the Grampian Mountains east of the Great Glen, it flows 108 mi. (171 km.) northeast to the North Sea.

SPF ▶*abbr.* sun protection factor (indicating the effectiveness of protective skin preparations).

sphag·num /ˈsfagnəm; ˈspag-/ ▶*n.* a plant of a genus that comprises the peat mosses. • Genus *Sphagnum*, family Sphagnaceae. ▷mid 18th cent.: modern Latin, from Greek *sphagnos*, denoting a kind of moss.

sphal·er·ite /ˈsfaləˌrīt/ ▶*n.* a shiny mineral, yellow to dark brown or black in color, consisting of zinc sulfide. ▷mid 19th cent.: from Greek *sphaleros* 'deceptive' + **-ITE**[1]. Compare with **BLENDE**.

sphene /sfēn/ ▶*n.* a greenish-yellow or brown mineral consisting of a silicate of calcium and titanium, occurring in granitic and metamorphic rocks in wedge-shaped crystals. ▷early 19th cent.: from French *sphène*, from Greek *sphēn* 'wedge.'

sphe·noid /ˈsfēnoid/ *Anatomy* ▶*n.* (also **sphe·noid bone**) a compound bone that forms the base of the cranium, behind the eye and below the front part of the brain. It has two pairs of broad lateral "wings" and a number of other projections, and contains two air-filled sinuses.
▶*adj.* of or relating to this bone. ▷mid 18th cent.: from modern Latin *sphenoides*, from Greek *sphēnoeidēs*, from *sphēn* 'wedge.' —**sphe·noi·dal** /sfēˈnoidl/ *adj.*

Sphe·nop·si·da /sfiˈnäpsidə/ *Botany* a class of pteridophyte plants that comprises the horsetails and their extinct relatives. ▷modern Latin (plural), from Greek *sphēn* 'wedge' + *opsis* 'appearance.' —**sphe·nop·sid** /-sid/ *n.* & *adj.*

sphere /sfi(ə)r/ ▶*n.* **1** a round solid figure, or its surface, with every point on its surface equidistant

from its center. ■ an object having this shape; a ball or globe. ■ a globe representing the earth. ■ *chiefly poetic/literary* a celestial body. ■ *poetic/literary* the sky perceived as a vault upon or in which celestial bodies are represented as lying. ■ each of a series of revolving concentrically arranged spherical shells in which celestial bodies were formerly thought to be set in a fixed relationship. **2** an area of activity, interest, or expertise: *his new wife's skill in the domestic sphere.* ■ a section of society or an aspect of life distinguished and unified by a particular characteristic: *political reforms to match those in the economic sphere.*
▸*v.* [*trans.*] *archaic* enclose in or as if in a sphere. ■ form into a rounded or perfect whole. ▷Middle English: from Old French *espere*, from late Latin *sphera*, earlier *sphaera*, from Greek *sphaira* 'ball.' **—spher·al** /-əl/ *adj.* (*archaic*).
▸*PHRASES* □ **music** (or **harmony**) **of the spheres** the natural harmonic tones supposedly produced by the movement of the celestial spheres or the bodies fixed in them. □ **sphere of influence** (or **interest**) a country or area in which another country has power to affect developments although it has no formal authority. ■ a field or area in which an individual or organization has power to affect events and developments.

-sphere ▸*comb. form* denoting a structure or region of spherical form, esp. a region around the earth: *ionosphere.* ▷from SPHERE, on the pattern of *(atmo)sphere.*

spher·ic /'sfi(ə)rik; 'sfer-/ ▸*adj.* spherical. **—sphe·ric·i·ty** /sfi'risitē/ *n.*

spher·i·cal /'sfi(ə)rikəl; 'sfer-/ ▸*adj.* shaped like a sphere. See note at ROUND. ■ of or relating to the properties of spheres. ■ formed inside or on the surface of a sphere. ▷late 15th cent.: via late Latin from Greek *sphairikos*, from *sphaira* (see SPHERE). **—spher·i·cal·ly** *adv.*

spher·i·cal ab·er·ra·tion /ˌabə'rāsнən/ ▸*n.* a loss of definition in the image arising from the surface geometry of a spherical mirror or lens.

spher·i·cal an·gle ▸*n.* an angle formed by the intersection of two great circles of a sphere.

spher·i·cal co·or·di·nates (also **spherical polar coordinates**) ▸*plural n.* three coordinates that define the location of a point in three-dimensional space. They are the length of its radius vector *r*, the angle ϑ between the vertical plane containing this vector and the *x*-axis, and the angle ϕ between this vector and the horizontal *x–y* plane. • Usually written (r, ϑ, ϕ).

spher·i·cal tri·an·gle ▸*n.* a triangle formed by three arcs of great circles on a sphere.

spher·i·cal trig·o·nom·e·try ▸*n.* the branch of trigonometry concerned with the measurement of the angles and sides of spherical triangles.

sphe·roid /'sfi(ə)rˌoid/ ▸*n.* a spherelike but not perfectly spherical body. ■ a solid generated by a half-revolution of an ellipse about its major axis (**prolate spheroid**) or minor axis (**oblate spheroid**). **—sphe·roi·dal** /sfi'roidl/ *adj.* **—sphe·roi·dic·i·ty** /ˌsfi(ə)roi'disitē/ *n.*

sphe·ro·plast /'sfi(ə)rəˌplast; 'sfer-/ ▸*n. Biology* a bacterium or plant cell bound by its plasma membrane, the cell wall being deficient or lacking and the whole having a spherical form.

spher·ule /'sfi(ə)r(y)o͞ol; 'sfer-/ ▸*n.* a small sphere. ▷mid 17th cent.: from late Latin *sphaerula*, diminutive of Latin *sphaera* (see SPHERE). **—spher·u·lar** /-yo͝olər/ *adj.*

spher·u·lite /'sfi(ə)r(y)əˌlīt; 'sfer-/ ▸*n. chiefly Geology* a small spheroidal mass of crystals (esp. of a mineral) grouped radially around a point. ▷early 19th cent.: from SPHERULE + -ITE[1]. **—spher·u·lit·ic** /ˌsfi(ə)r(y)ə'litik; ˌsfer-/ *adj.*

sphinc·ter /'sfiNGktər/ ▸*n. Anatomy* a ring of muscle surrounding and serving to guard or close an opening or tube, such as the anus or the openings of the stomach. ▷late 16th cent.: via Latin from Greek *sphinktēr*, from *sphingein* 'bind tight.' **—sphinc·ter·al** /-əl/ *adj.* **—sphinc·ter·ic** /ˌsfiNGk'terik/ *adj.*

sphin·gid /'sfinjid/ ▸*n. Entomology* a moth of the hawk moth family (Sphingidae). ▷early 20th cent.: from modern Latin *Sphingidae* (plural), from Greek *Sphinx* (see SPHINX).

sphingo- ▸*comb. form* used in the names of various related compounds isolated from the brain and nervous tissue: *sphingomyelin.* ▷from Greek *Sphinx*, *Sphing-* 'Sphinx,' originally in *sphingosine*, with reference to the enigmatic nature of the compound.

sphin·go·lip·id /ˌsfiNGgō'lipid/ ▸*n. Biochemistry* any of a class of compounds that are fatty acid derivatives of sphingosine and occur chiefly in the cell membranes of the brain and nervous tissue.

sphin·go·my·e·lin /ˌsfiNGgō'mīəlin/ ▸*n. Biochemistry* a substance that occurs widely in brain and nervous tissue, consisting of complex phosphoryl derivatives of sphingosine and choline.

sphin·go·sine /'sfiNGgəˌsēn/ ▸*n. Biochemistry* a basic compound that is a constituent of a number of substances important in the metabolism of nerve cells, esp. sphingomyelins. • A crystalline alcohol; chem. formula: $C_{18}H_{37}NO_2$.

sphinx /sfiNGks/ ▸*n.* **1** (**Sphinx**) *Greek Mythology* a winged monster of Thebes, having a woman's head and a lion's body. It propounded a riddle about the three ages of man, killing those who failed to solve it, until Oedipus was successful, whereupon the Sphinx committed suicide. ■ (**the Sphinx**) an ancient Egyptian stone figure having a lion's body and a human or animal head, esp. the huge statue near the Pyramids at Giza. ■ (usu. **sphinx**) an enigmatic or inscrutable person. **2** (also **sphinx moth**) another term for HAWK MOTH. ▷late Middle English: via Latin from Greek *Sphinx*, apparently from *sphingein* 'draw tight.'

the Sphinx at Giza

sp ht ▸*abbr.* specific heat.

sphygmo- ▸*comb. form Physiology* of or relating to the pulse or pulsation: *sphygmograph.* ▷from Greek *sphugmos* 'pulse.'

sphyg·mo·graph /'sfigməˌgraf/ ▸*n.* an instrument that produces a line recording the strength and rate of a person's pulse.

sphyg·mo·ma·nom·e·ter /ˌsfigmōmə'nämitər/ ▸*n.* an instrument for measuring blood pressure, typically consisting of an inflatable rubber cuff that is applied to the arm and connected to a column of mercury next to a graduated scale, enabling the determination of systolic and diastolic blood pressure by increasing and gradually releasing the pressure in the cuff. **—sphyg·mo·ma·nom·e·try** /-mətrē/ *n.*

Sphynx /sfinNGsk/ ▸*n.* a cat of a hairless breed, originally from North America.

spic /spik/ ▸*n. informal, offensive* a contemptuous term for a Spanish-speaking person from Central or South America or the Caribbean. ▷early 20th cent.: abbreviation of U.S. slang *spiggoty*, in the same sense, of uncertain origin: perhaps an alteration of *speak the* in 'no speak the English.'

Spi·ca /'spīkə/ *Astronomy* the brightest star in the constellation Virgo. ▷Latin, literally 'ear of wheat (in the hand of the goddess).'

spi·ca /'spīkə/ ▸*n. Medicine* a bandage folded into a spiral arrangement resembling an ear of wheat or barley. ▷late 17th cent.: from Latin, literally 'spike, ear of corn'; related to *spina* 'spine.' The current sense is influenced by Greek *stakhus* 'ear of wheat.'

spic-and-span ▸*adj.* variant spelling of SPICK-AND-SPAN.

spic·ca·to /spi'kätō/ *Music* ▸*n.* a style of staccato playing on stringed instruments involving bouncing the bow on the strings.
▸*adj.* & *adv.* to be performed in this style. ▷Italian, literally 'detailed, distinct.'

spice /spīs/ ▸*n.* **1** an aromatic or pungent vegetable substance used to flavor food, e.g., cloves, pepper, or mace: *enjoy the taste and aroma of freshly ground spices.* ■ an element providing interest and excitement: *healthy rivalry adds spice to the game.* **2** a russet color.
▸*v.* [*trans.*] [often as *adj.*] (**spiced**) flavor with spice: *turbot with a spiced sauce.* ■ add an interesting or piquant quality to; make more exciting: *she was probably adding details to* **spice up** *the story.* ▷Middle English: shortening of Old French *espice*, from Latin *species* 'sort, kind,' in late Latin 'wares.'

spice·bush /'spīsˌbo͝osн/ ▸*n.* a North American shrub with aromatic leaves, bark, and fruit. The leaves were formerly used for a tea and the fruit as an allspice substitute. • *Lindera benzoin*, family Lauraceae.

Spice Is·lands former name of MOLUCCA ISLANDS.

spick-and-span /'spik ən 'span/ (also **spic-and-span**) ▸*adj.* spotlessly clean and well looked after: *spick-and-span shining bathrooms.* ▷late 16th cent. (in the sense 'brand new'): from *spick and span new*, emphatic extension of dialect *span new*, from Old Norse *spán-nýr*, from *spánn* 'chip' + *nýr* 'new'; *spick* influenced by Dutch *spiksplinternieuw*, literally 'splinter new.'

spic·ule /'spikˌyo͞ol/ ▸*n.* **1** *technical* a minute sharp-pointed object or structure that is typically present in large numbers, such as a fine particle of ice. ■ *Zoology* each of the small needlelike or sharp-pointed structures of calcite or silica that make up the skeleton of a sponge. **2** *Astronomy* a short-lived, relatively small radial jet of gas in the chromosphere or lower corona of the sun. ▷late 18th cent.: from modern Latin *spicula*, *spiculum*, diminutives of *spica* 'ear of grain.' **—spic·u·lar** /-yələr/ *adj.* **—spic·u·late** /-yəlit; -yəˌlāt/ *adj.* **—spic·u·la·tion** *n.*

spic·y /'spīsē/ ▸*adj.* (**spic·i·er**, **spic·i·est**) flavored with or fragrant with spice: *pasta in a spicy tomato sauce.*

spi·der /'spīdər/ ▸*n.* an eight-legged predatory arachnid with an unsegmented body consisting of a fused head and thorax and a rounded abdomen. Spiders have fangs that inject poison into their prey, and most kinds spin webs in which to capture insects. • Order Araneae, class Arachnida. ■ used in names of similar or related arachnids, e.g., **sea spider**, **sun spider**. ■ any object resembling a spider, esp. one having numerous or prominent legs or radiating spokes. ■ a cast-iron iron frying pan, originally made with legs for cooking on coals in a hearth. ■ a long-legged rest for a billiard cue that can be placed over a ball without touching it.
▸*v.* [*intrans.*] move in a scuttling manner suggestive of a spider: *a treecreeper spidered head first down the tree trunk.* ■ form a pattern suggestive of a spider or its web. ▷late Old English *spīthra*, from *spinnan* (see SPIN). **—spi·der·ish** *adj.*

spi·der crab ▸*n.* a crab with long thin legs and a compact pear-shaped body, which is camouflaged in some kinds by attached sponges and seaweed. • Majidae and other families, order Decapoda: *Macropodia* and other genera.

spi·der flow·er ▸*n.* a plant with clusters of flowers that have long protruding stamens or styles, giving the flowerhead a spiderlike appearance. • a South American plant (genus *Cleome*, family Capparidaceae, in particular *C. hassleriana*). • an Australian grevillea.

spi·der hole ▸*n.* a trench or indentation used by a spider for rest or ambush. ■ a small, rough excavation for concealing a person, as from an enemy.

spi·der lil·y ▸*n.* a lily that typically has long slender petals or elongated petallike parts around the flower. • *Hymenocallis* and other genera, family Liliaceae (or Amaryllidaceae).

spi·der·man /'spīdərˌman/ ▸*n.* (*pl.* **-men**) *Brit., informal* a person who works at great heights in building work.

spi·der mite ▸*n.* an active plant-eating mite that resembles a minute spider and is frequently a serious garden and greenhouse pest. • Family Tetranychidae: many species, in particular the **red spider mite** (*Tetranychus urticae*).

spi·der mon·key ▸*n.* a South American monkey with very long limbs and a long prehensile tail. • Genus *Ateles*, family Cebidae: four species.

spi·der ne·vus /'nēvəs/ ▸*n.* a cluster of minute red blood vessels visible under the skin, occurring typically during pregnancy or as a symptom of certain diseases (e.g., cirrhosis or acne rosacea).

spi·der plant ▸*n.* a plant of the lily family that has long narrow leaves with a central yellow or white stripe, native to southern Africa and popular as a houseplant. • *Chlorophytum comosum*, family Liliaceae.

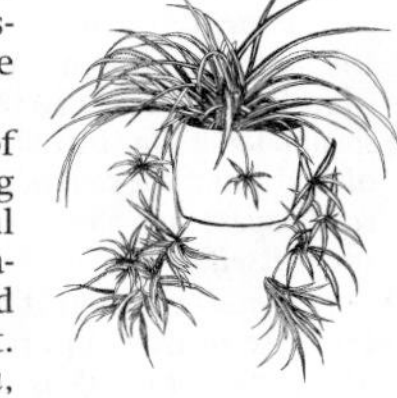

spider plant

spi·der veins ▸*plural n.* dilated capillaries on the skin, resembling spider legs, and common among children and pregnant women.

spi·der·web /ˈspīdərweb/ ▸*n.* a web made by a spider. ■ a thing resembling such a web: *the spiderweb of overhead transmission lines.* ■ a type of turquoise crisscrossed with fine dark lines.
▸*v.* **(-webbed, -web·bing)** [*trans.*] cover with a pattern resembling a spiderweb: *a glass block spiderwebbed with cracks.*

spi·der·wort /ˈspīdərwərt; -wôrt/ ▸*n.* an American plant whose flowers bear long hairy stamens. • Genus *Tradescantia*, family Commelinaceae: several species, including the blue-flowered North American *T. virginiana*, from which many cultivars have been derived.

spi·der·y /ˈspīdərē/ ▸*adj.* resembling a spider, esp. having long, thin, angular lines like a spider's legs: *the letters were written in a spidery hand.*

spie·gel·ei·sen /ˈspēgəˌlīzən/ ▸*n.* an alloy of iron and manganese, used in steelmaking. ▹mid 19th cent.: from German, from *Spiegel* 'mirror' + *Eisen* 'iron.'

spiel /spēl; SHpēl/ *informal* ▸*n.* a long or fast speech or story, typically one intended as a means of persuasion or as an excuse but regarded with skepticism or contempt by those who hear it: *he delivers a breathless and effortless spiel in promotion of his new novel.*
▸*v.* [*trans.*] reel off; recite: *he solemnly spieled all he knew.* ■ [*intrans.*] speak glibly or at length. ▹late 19th cent.: from German *Spiel* 'a game.'

Spiel·berg /ˈspēlˌbərg/, Steven (1947–), U.S. movie director and producer. His science-fiction and adventure movies such as *ET* (1982), *Jaws* (1985), *Jurassic Park* (1992), and *Saving Private Ryan* (1998) broke box-office records, while *Schindler's List* (1993) won seven Academy Awards.

spiel·er /ˈspēlər/ *informal* ▸*n.* **1** a glib or voluble speaker. **2** *Austral./NZ* a gambler or swindler. **3** *chiefly Brit.* a gambling club. ▹mid 19th cent.: from German *Spieler* 'player' (see **SPIEL**).

spiff /spif/ ▸*v.* [*trans.*] **(spiff someone/something up)** *informal* make someone or something attractive, tidy, or stylish: *he arrived all spiffed up in a dinner jacket.* ▹late 19th cent.: perhaps from dialect *spiff* 'well-dressed.'

spif·fing /ˈspifiNG/ ▸*adj. Brit., informal, dated* excellent; splendid: *how spiffing you look!* ▹late 19th cent.: of unknown origin.

spif·fli·cate /ˈspifliˌkāt/ (also **spif·li·cate**) ▸*v.* [*trans.*] *informal, humorous* treat roughly or severely; destroy: *the mosquito was spifflicated.* ▹mid 18th cent.: a fanciful formation. —**spif·fli·ca·tion** /ˌspifliˈkāSHən/ *n.*

spiff·y /ˈspifē/ ▸*adj.* **(spiff·i·er, spiff·i·est)** *informal* smart in appearance: *a spiffy new outfit.* ▹mid 19th cent.: of unknown origin. —**spif·fi·ly** /ˈspifəlē/ *adv.*

spig·ot /ˈspigət/ ▸*n.* **1** a small peg or plug, esp. for insertion into the vent of a cask. **2** a faucet. ■ a device for controlling the flow of liquid in a faucet. **3** the plain end of a section of a pipe fitting into the socket of the next one. ▹Middle English: perhaps an alteration of Provençal *espigou(n)*, from Latin *spiculum*, diminutive of *spicum*, variant of *spica* (see **SPICA**).

spike[1] /spīk/ ▸*n.* **1** a thin, pointed piece of metal, wood, or another rigid material. ■ a large stout nail, esp. one used to fasten a rail to a railroad tie. ■ each of several metal points set into the sole of an athletic shoe to prevent slipping. ■ **(spikes)** a pair of athletic shoes with such metal points. ■ short for **SPIKE HEEL**. ■ *informal* a hypodermic needle. **2** a sharp increase in the magnitude or concentration of something: *the oil price spike.* ■ *Electronics* a pulse of very short duration in which a rapid increase in voltage is followed by a rapid decrease.
▸*v.* [*trans.*] **1** impale on or pierce with a sharp point: *she spiked another oyster.* ■ *Baseball* injure (a player) with the spikes on one's shoes. ■ (of a newspaper editor) reject (a story) by or as if by filing it on a spike: *the editors deemed the article in bad taste and spiked it.* ■ stop the progress of (a plan or undertaking); put an end to: *he doubted they would spike the entire effort over this one negotiation.* ■ *historical* render (a gun) useless by plugging up the vent with a spike. **2** form into or cover with sharp points: *his hair was matted and spiked with blood.* ■ [*intrans.*] take on a sharp, pointed shape: *lightning spiked across the sky.* ■ [*intrans.*] increase and then decrease sharply; reach a peak: *oil prices would spike and fall again.* **3** *informal* add alcohol or a drug to contaminate (drink or food) surreptitiously: *she bought me an orange juice and spiked it with vodka.* ■ add sharp or pungent flavoring to (food or drink): *spike the liquid with lime or lemon juice.* ■ enrich (a nuclear reactor or its fuel) with a particular isotope. **4** (in volleyball) hit (the ball) forcefully from a position near the net so that it moves downward into the opposite court. ■ *Football* fling (the ball) forcefully to the ground, typically in celebration of a touchdown. ▹Middle English: perhaps from Middle Low German, Middle Dutch *spiker*, related to **SPOKE**[1]. The verb dates from the early 17th cent.

spike[2] ▸*n. Botany* a flower cluster formed of many flowerheads attached directly to a long stem. Compare with **CYME**, **RACEME**. ▹late Middle English (denoting an ear of corn): from Latin *spica* (see **SPICA**).

spike heel ▸*n.* a high tapering heel on a woman's shoe.

spike·let /ˈspīklit/ ▸*n. Botany* the basic unit of a grass flower, consisting of two glumes or outer bracts at the base and one or more florets above.

spike·nard /ˈspīkˌnärd/ ▸*n.* **1** *historical* a costly perfumed ointment much valued in ancient times. **2** the Himalayan plant of the valerian family that produces the rhizome from which this ointment was prepared. • *Nardostachys grandiflora*, family Valerianaceae. ■ a plant resembling spikenard in fragrance. ▹Middle English: from medieval Latin *spica nardi* (see **SPIKE**[2], **NARD**), translating Greek *nardostakhus*.

spik·y /ˈspīkē/ ▸*adj.* **(spik·i·er, spik·i·est)** like a spike or spikes or having many spikes: *he has short spiky hair.* ■ *informal* easily offended or annoyed. —**spik·i·ly** /-kəlē/ *adv.* —**spik·i·ness** *n.*

spile /spīl/ ▸*n.* **1** a small wooden peg or spigot for stopping a cask. ■ a small wooden or metal spout for tapping the sap from a sugar maple. **2** a large, heavy timber driven into the ground to support a superstructure.
▸*v.* [*trans.*] broach (a cask) with a peg in order to draw off liquid. ▹early 16th cent.: from Middle Dutch, Middle Low German, 'wooden peg'; in sense 2 apparently an alteration of **PILE**[2].

spi·lite /ˈspīˌlīt/ ▸*n. Geology* an altered form of basalt, rich in albite and commonly amygdaloidal in texture, typical of basaltic lava solidified under water. ▹mid 19th cent.: from French *spillite*, from Greek *spilos* 'spot, stain.' —**spi·lit·ic** /spīˈlitik/ *adj.*

spill[1] /spil/ ▸*v.* (*past* **spilled** or **spilt** /spilt/) [*trans.*] cause or allow (liquid) to flow over the edge of its container, esp. unintentionally: *you'll spill that coffee if you're not careful* | *figurative azaleas spilled cascades of flowers over the pathways.* ■ [*intrans.*] (of liquid) flow over the edge of its container: *some of the wine spilled onto the floor* | *figurative years of frustration* ***spilled over*** *into violence.* ■ [*intrans.*] (of the contents of something) be emptied out onto a surface: *passengers' baggage had* ***spilled out*** *of the hold.* ■ cause or allow (the contents of something) to be emptied out: *injured cells tend to swell up and burst, spilling their contents.* ■ [*intrans.*] (of a number of people) move out of somewhere quickly: *students began to spill out of the building.* ■ *informal* reveal (confidential information) to someone: *he was reluctant to spill her address.* ■ cause (someone) to fall off a horse or bicycle: *the horse was wrenched off course, spilling his rider.* ■ *Sailing* let (wind) out of a sail, typically by slackening the sheets. ■ *Brit.* (in the context of ball games) drop (the ball).
▸*n.* **1** a quantity of liquid that has spilled or been spilled: *a 25-ton oil spill* | *wipe up spills immediately* | *figurative their shifting spill of lantern-light.* ■ an instance of a liquid spilling or being spilled: *he was absolved from any blame for the oil spill.* **2** a fall from a horse or bicycle: *Granddad took a spill while riding the bay mare.* ▹Old English *spillan* 'kill, destroy, waste, shed (blood)'; of unknown origin. —**spill·er** *n.*
▸*PHRASES* □ **spill the beans** *informal* reveal secret information unintentionally or indiscreetly. □ **spill (someone's) blood** kill or wound people. □ **spill one's guts** *informal* reveal copious information to someone in an uninhibited way.

spill[2] ▸*n.* a thin strip of wood or paper used for lighting a fire, candle, pipe, etc. ▹Middle English (in the sense 'sharp fragment of wood'): obscurely related to **SPILE**. The current sense dates from the early 19th cent.

spill·age /ˈspilij/ ▸*n.* the action of causing or allowing a liquid to spill, or liquid spilled in this way: *accidents involving chemical spillage* | *oil spillages at sea.*

Spil·lane /spəˈlān/, Mickey (1918–), U.S. writer; pseudonym of *Frank Morrison Spillane*. His popular detective novels, many of which feature private detective Mike Hammer, include *My Gun Is Quick* (1950) and *The Big Kill* (1951).

spil·li·kin /ˈspilikin/ ▸*n.* **1** **(spillikins)** another term for **JACKSTRAW**. **2** a splinter or fragment. ▹mid 18th cent.: from **SPILL**[2] + **-KIN**.

spill·o·ver /ˈspilˌōvər/ ▸*n.* an instance of overflowing or spreading into another area: *there has been a spillover into public schools of the ethos of private schools.* ■ a thing that spreads or has spread into another area: *the village was a spillover from a neighboring, larger village.* ■ [usu. as *adj.*] an unexpected consequence, repercussion, or byproduct: *the spillover effect of the quarrel.*

spill·way /ˈspilˌwā/ ▸*n.* a passage for surplus water from a dam. ■ a natural drainage channel cut by water from melting glaciers or ice fields.

spilt /spilt/ ▸ past and past participle of **SPILL**[1].

spilth /spilTH/ ▸*n. archaic* the action of spilling; material that is spilled.

spin /spin/ ▸*v.* **(spin·ning;** *past* and *past part.* **spun** /spən/) **1** turn or cause to turn or whirl around quickly: [*intrans.*] *the girl* ***spun around*** *in alarm* | *the rear wheels spun violently* | [*trans.*] *he fiddled with the radio, spinning the dial.* ■ [*intrans.*] (of a person's head) give a sensation of dizziness: *the figures were enough to make her head spin.* ■ [*trans.*] *chiefly Cricket* impart a revolving motion to (a ball) when bowling. ■ [*intrans.*] (of a ball) move through the air with such a revolving motion. ■ [*trans.*] give (a news story or other information) a particular interpretation, esp. a favorable one. ■ [*trans.*] shape (sheet metal) by pressure applied during rotation on a lathe: [as *adj.*] **(spun)** *spun metal components.* **2** [*trans.*] draw out (wool, cotton, or other material) and convert it into threads, either by hand or with machinery: *they* ***spin*** *wool* ***into*** *the yarn for weaving* | [as *adj.*] **(spun)** *spun glass.* ■ make (threads) in this way: *this method is used to spin filaments from syrups.* ■ (of a spider or a silkworm or other insect) produce (gossamer or silk) or construct (a web or cocoon) by extruding a fine viscous thread from a special gland. **3** [*intrans.*] fish with a spinner: *they were spinning for salmon in the lake.*
▸*phrasal v.* □ **spin something off** (of a parent company) turn a subsidiary into a new and separate company. □ **spin out** (of a driver or car) lose control, esp. in a skid. □ **spin something out** make something last as long as possible: *they seem keen to spin out the debate through their speeches and interventions.* ■ spend or occupy time aimlessly or without profit: *Shane and Mary played games to spin out the afternoon.*
▸*n.* **1** a rapid turning or whirling motion: *he concluded the dance with a double spin.* ■ revolving motion imparted to a ball in a game such as baseball, cricket, tennis, or billiards: *this racket enables the player to impart more spin to the ball* ■ [in *sing.*] a particular bias, interpretation, or point of view, intended to create a favorable (or sometimes, unfavorable) impression when presented to the public: *he tried to put a positive spin on the president's campaign.* ■ [usu. in *sing.*] a fast revolving motion of an aircraft as it descends rapidly: *he tried to stop the plane from* ***going into a spin.*** ■ *Physics* the intrinsic angular momentum of a subatomic particle. **2** [in *sing.*] *informal* a brief trip in a vehicle for pleasure: *a spin around town.* ▹Old English *spinnan* 'draw out and twist (fiber)'; related to German *spinnen*. The noun dates from the mid 19th cent.
▸*PHRASES* □ **spin one's wheels** *informal* waste one's time or efforts. □ **spin a yarn** tell a long, far-fetched story.

spi·na bif·i·da /ˈspīnə ˈbifidə/ ▸*n.* a congenital defect of the spine in which part of the spinal cord and its meninges are exposed through a gap in the backbone. It often causes paralysis of the lower limbs, and sometimes mental handicap. ▹early 18th cent.: modern Latin (see **SPINE**, **BIFID**).

spin·ach /ˈspiniCH/ ▸*n.* a widely cultivated edible Asian plant of the goosefoot family, with large, dark green leaves that are eaten raw or cooked as a vegetable. • *Spinacia oleracea*, family Chenopodiaceae. ▹Middle English: probably from Old French *espinache*, via Arabic from Persian *aspānāk*. —**spin·ach·y** *adj.*

spi·nal /ˈspīnl/ ▸*adj.* of or relating to the spine: *spinal injuries.* ■ relating to or forming the central axis or backbone of something: *the building of a new spinal road.* ▹late 16th cent.: from late Latin *spinalis*, from Latin *spina* (see **SPINE**). —**spi·nal·ly** *adv.*

spi·nal ca·nal ▸*n.* a cavity that runs successively

S

through each of the vertebrae and contains the spinal cord.

spi·nal col·umn ▸*n.* the spine; the backbone.

spi·nal cord ▸*n.* the cylindrical bundle of nerve fibers and associated tissue that is enclosed in the spine and connects nearly all parts of the body to the brain, with which it forms the central nervous system.

spi·nal tap ▸*n.* another term for LUMBAR PUNCTURE.

spin·dle /ˈspindl/ ▸*n.* **1** a slender rounded rod with tapered ends used in hand spinning to twist and wind thread from a mass of wool or flax held on a distaff. ■ a pin or rod used on a spinning wheel to twist and wind the thread. ■ a pin bearing the bobbin of a spinning machine. ■ a measure of length for yarn, equal to 15,120 yards (13,826 m) for cotton or 14,400 yards (13,167 m) for linen. ■ a pointed metal rod on a base, used to impale paper items for temporary filing. ■ a turned piece of wood used as a banister or chair leg. **2** a rod or pin serving as an axis that revolves or on which something revolves. ■ the vertical rod at the center of a record turntable that keeps the record in place during play. **3** *Biology* a slender mass of microtubules formed when a cell divides. At metaphase, the chromosomes become attached to it by their centromeres before being pulled toward its ends. **4** (also **spindle tree**) a shrub or small tree with slender toothed leaves and pink capsules containing bright orange seeds. The hard timber was formerly used for making spindles. • Genus *Euonymus*, family Celastraceae: several species, in particular the Eurasian *E. europaeus*.
▸*v.* [*trans.*] impale (a piece of paper) on a metal spindle for temporary filing purposes: *do not fold, spindle, or mutilate.* ▷Old English *spinel*, from the base of the verb SPIN.

spin·dle cell ▸*n.* a narrow, elongated cell, in particular: ■ *Medicine* a cell of this shape indicating the presence of a type of sarcoma. ■ *Zoology* a cell of this shape present in the blood of most nonmammalian vertebrates, functioning as a platelet.

S

spin·dle legs (also **spin·dle·shanks** /ˈspindl-ˌSHANGks/) ▸*plural n.* long thin legs. ■ [treated as *sing.*] a person with long thin legs. —**spin·dle-leg·ged** *adj.*

spin·dle-shaped ▸*adj.* having a circular cross section and tapering toward each end.

spin·dle tree ▸*n.* see SPINDLE (sense 4).

spin·dly /ˈspin(d)lē/ ▸*adj.* (of a person or limb) long or tall and thin: *spindly arms and legs.* ■ (of a thing) thin and weak or insubstantial in construction: *spindly chairs.*

spin doc·tor ▸*n. informal* a spokesperson employed to give a favorable interpretation of events to the media, esp. on behalf of a political party.

spin-down ▸*n.* a decrease in the speed of rotation of a spinning object, in particular a heavenly body or a computer disk.

spin·drift /ˈspinˌdrift/ ▸*n.* spray blown from the crests of waves by the wind. ■ driving snow or sand. ▷early 17th cent. (originally Scots): variant of *spoondrift*, from archaic *spoon* 'run before wind or sea' + the noun DRIFT.

spin dry·er ▸*n.* a machine for drying wet clothes by spinning them in a revolving perforated drum. —**spin-dry** *v.*

spine /spīn/ ▸*n.* **1** a series of vertebrae extending from the skull to the small of the back, enclosing the spinal cord and providing support for the thorax and abdomen; the backbone. ■ *figurative* a thing's central feature or main source of strength: *players who will form the spine of our team.* ■ *figurative* resolution or strength of character. ■ the part of a book's jacket or cover that encloses the inner edges of the pages, facing outward when the book is on a shelf and typically bearing the title and the author's name. **2** *Zoology* & *Botany* any hard pointed defensive projection or structure, such as a prickle of a hedgehog, a spikelike projection on a sea urchin, a sharp ray in a fish's fin, or a spike on the stem of a plant. ■ *Geology* a tall mass of viscous lava extruded from a volcano. ▷late Middle English: shortening of Old French *espine*, or from Latin *spina* 'thorn, prickle, backbone.' —**spined** *adj.* [in *combination*] *broken-spined paperbacks.*

spine-chill·er ▸*n.* a story or movie that inspires terror and excitement.

spine-chill·ing ▸*adj.* inspiring terror or terrified excitement: *a spine-chilling silence.*

spi·nel /spiˈnel/ ▸*n.* a hard glassy mineral occurring as octahedral crystals of variable color and consisting chiefly of magnesium and aluminum oxides. ■ *Chemistry* any of a class of oxides including this, containing aluminum and another metal and having the general formula MAl_2O_4. ▷early 16th cent.: from French *spinelle*, from Italian *spinella*, diminutive of *spina* 'thorn.'

spine·less /ˈspīnlis/ ▸*adj.* **1** having no spine or backbone; invertebrate. ■ *figurative* (of a person) lacking resolution; weak and purposeless: *a spineless coward.* **2** (of an animal or plant) lacking spines: *spineless forms of prickly pear have been selected.* —**spine·less·ly** *adv.* —**spine·less·ness** *n.*

spi·nel ru·by ▸*n.* a deep red variety of spinel, often of gem quality.

spin·et /ˈspinit/ ▸*n.* **1** *historical* a small harpsichord with the strings set obliquely to the keyboard, popular in the 18th century. **2** a type of small upright piano. ▷mid 17th cent.: shortening of obsolete French *espinette*, from Italian *spinetta* 'virginal, spinet,' diminutive of *spina* 'thorn' (see SPINE), the strings being plucked by quills.

spine-tin·gling ▸*adj. informal* thrilling or pleasurably frightening: *a spine-tingling adventure.*

Spin·garn /ˈspinˌgärn/, Joel Elias (1875–1939), U.S. writer, critic, and social reformer. A founder of the National Association for the Advancement of Colored People (NAACP) in 1909, he established the Spingarn Medal, given annually to an African American for exceptional achievement, in 1913. He was also a founder of Harcourt, Brace & Co. in 1919 and worked as its literary adviser until 1924.

spin·mei·ster /ˈspinˌmīstər/ ▸*n. informal* another term for SPIN DOCTOR. ▷1990s: from *spin* + *-meister*.

spin·na·ker /ˈspinəkər/ ▸*n.* a large three-cornered sail, typically bulging when full, set forward of the mainsail of a yacht when running before the wind. ▷mid 19th cent.: apparently a fanciful formation from *Sphinx*, the name of the yacht first using it, perhaps influenced by SPANKER.

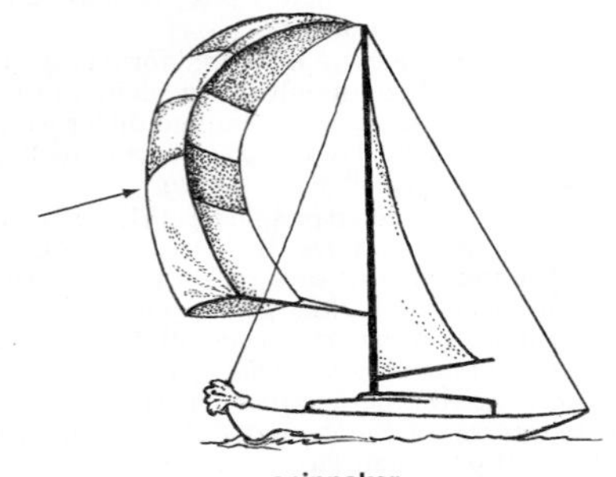
spinnaker

spin·ner /ˈspinər/ ▸*n.* **1** a person occupied in making thread by spinning. **2** a person or thing that spins. **3** (also **spin·ner·bait**) *Fishing* a lure designed to revolve when pulled through the water. ■ a type of fishing fly, used chiefly for trout. **4** a metal fairing that is attached to and revolves with the propeller boss of an aircraft in order to streamline it.

spin·ner dol·phin ▸*n.* a dolphin of warm seas that has a long slender beak and is noted for rotating several times while leaping into the air. • Genus *Stenella*, family Delphinidae: two species, in particular *S. longirostris*.

spin·ner·et /ˌspinəˈret/ ▸*n. Zoology* any of a number of different organs through which the silk, gossamer, or thread of spiders, silkworms, and certain other insects is produced. ■ (in the production of manmade fibers) a cap or plate with a number of small holes through which a fiber-forming solution is forced.

spin·ney /ˈspinē/ ▸*n.* (*pl.* **-neys**) *Brit.* a small area of trees and bushes. ▷late 16th cent.: shortening of Old French *espinei*, from an alteration of Latin *spinetum* 'thicket,' from *spina* 'thorn.'

spin·ning /ˈspiniNG/ ▸*n.* **1** the action or process of converting fibers into thread or yarn. **2** a form of exercise that involves fast pedaling on an exercise bike.

spin·ning jen·ny ▸*n. historical* a machine for spinning with more than one spindle at a time, patented by James Hargreaves in 1770.

spin·ning mule ▸*n.* see MULE[1] (sense 3).

spin·ning top ▸*n.* see TOP[2].

spin·ning wheel ▸*n.* an apparatus for spinning yarn or thread, with a spindle driven by a wheel attached to a crank or treadle.

spin-off (also **spin·off**) ▸*n.* a byproduct or incidental result of a larger project: *the commercial spin-off from defense research.* ■ a product marketed by its association with a popular television program, movie, personality, etc.: [as *adj.*] *spin-off merchandising.* ■ a business or organization developed out of or by members of another organization, in particular a subsidiary of a parent company that has been sold off, creating a new company.

Spi·no·ne /spiˈnōnē/ ▸*n.* (*pl.* **-no·ni** *pronunc.* same) a wire-haired gun dog of an Italian breed, typically white with brown markings, drooping ears, and a docked tail. ▷1940s: Italian.

spi·nose /ˈspīnōs/ (also **spi·nous** /-nəs/) ▸*adj. chiefly Botany Zoology* having spines; spiny: *spinose forms will need care in collecting.*

spin-out ▸*n. informal* **1** another term for SPIN-OFF. **2** a skidding spin by a vehicle out of control.

Spi·no·za /spiˈnōzə/, Baruch (or Benedict) de (1632–77), Dutch philosopher. Spinoza espoused a pantheistic system, seeing "God or nature" as a single infinite substance, with mind and matter being two incommensurable ways of conceiving the one reality. —**Spi·no·zism** /-ˌzizəm/ *n.* —**Spi·no·zist** /-zist/ *n.* & *adj.* —**Spi·no·zis·tic** /ˌspinəˈzistik/ *adj.*

spin-sta·bi·lized ▸*adj.* (of a satellite or spacecraft) stabilized in a desired orientation by being made to rotate about an axis. —**spin-sta·bi·li·za·tion** *n.*

spin·ster /ˈspinstər/ ▸*n. derogatory* an unmarried woman, typically an older woman beyond the usual age for marriage. ▷late Middle English (in the sense 'woman who spins'): from the verb SPIN + -STER; in early use the term was appended to names of women to denote their occupation. The current sense dates from the early 18th cent. —**spin·ster·hood** /-ˌhŏŏd/ *n.* —**spin·ster·ish** *adj.*

USAGE The development of the word **spinster** is a good example of the way in which a word acquires strong connotations to the extent that it can no longer be used in a neutral sense. From the 17th century, the word was appended to names as the official legal description of an unmarried woman: *Elizabeth Harris of Boston, Spinster.* This type of use survives today in some legal and religious contexts. In modern everyday English, however, **spinster** cannot be used to mean simply 'unmarried woman'; it is now always a derogatory term, referring or alluding to a stereotype of an older woman who is unmarried, childless, prissy, and repressed.

spin·thar·i·scope /spinˈTHarəˌskōp/ ▸*n. Physics* an instrument that shows the incidence of alpha particles by flashes on a fluorescent screen. ▷early 20th cent.: formed irregularly from Greek *spintharis* 'spark' + -SCOPE.

spin-the-bot·tle ▸*n.* a party game in which players take turns spinning a bottle lying flat, and then kiss the person to whom the bottle neck points on stopping.

spin·to /ˈspintō/ ▸*n.* (*pl.* **-tos**) a lyric soprano or tenor voice of powerful dramatic quality. ■ a singer with such a voice. ▷1950s: Italian, literally 'pushed,' past participle of *spingere* 'push.'

spin·tron·ics /ˌspinˈträniks/ ▸*plural n.* [treated as *sing.*] a field of electronics in which electron spin is manipulated to yield a desired outcome. —**spin·tron·ic** *adj. a spintronic transistor that could play a major role in the quest for quantum computing.*

spin·u·lose /ˈspinyəˌlōs/ ▸*adj. Botany* & *Zoology* having small spines. ▷early 19th cent.: from modern Latin *spinulosus*, from *spinula*, diminutive of *spina* 'thorn, spine.'

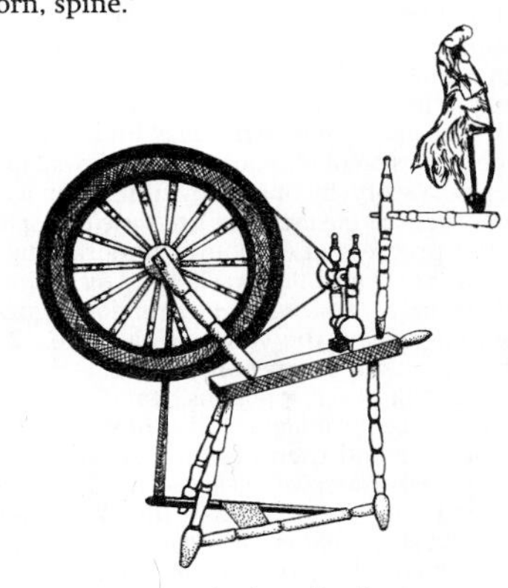
spinning wheel

spin·y /ˈspīnē/ ▸*adj.* (**spin·i·er, spin·i·est**) full of or covered with prickles: *a spiny cactus.* ■ *informal* difficult to understand or handle: *a spiny problem.* —**spin·i·ness** *n.*

spin·y ant·eat·er ▸*n.* another term for ECHIDNA.

spin·y dog·fish ▸*n.* a large white-spotted gray dogfish with venomous spines in front of the dorsal fins. It occurs in the North Atlantic and the Mediterranean, often in large shoals. • *Squalus acanthias*, family Squalidae.

spin·y lob·ster ▸*n.* a large edible crustacean with a spiny shell and long heavy antennae, but lacking the large claws of true lobsters. • Family Palinuridae: several genera and species, in particular *Palinuris vulgaris* of European waters, and the **California spiny lobster** (*Panulirus interruptus*).

spin·y mouse ▸*n.* a mouse that has spines mixed with the hair on its back, native to Africa and southwestern Asia. • Genus *Acomys*, family Muridae: several species.

spi·ra·cle /ˈspirəkəl; ˈspī-/ ▸*n. Zoology* an external respiratory opening, esp. each of a number of pores on the body of an insect, or each of a pair of vestigial gill slits behind the eye of a cartilaginous fish. ▷late 18th cent.: from Latin *spiraculum*, from *spirare* 'breathe.' —**spi·rac·u·lar** /spiˈrakyələr; spī-/ *adj.*

spi·rae·a ▸*n.* variant spelling of SPIREA.

spi·ral /ˈspīrəl/ ▸*adj.* winding in a continuous and gradually widening (or tightening) curve, either around a central point on a flat plane or about an axis so as to form a cone: *a spiral pattern.* ■ winding in a continuous curve of constant diameter about a central axis, as though along a cylinder; helical. ■ (of a staircase) constantly turning in one direction as it rises, around a solid or open center. ■ *Medicine* (of a fracture) curving around a long bone lengthwise. ■ short for SPIRAL-BOUND: *a spiral notebook.*

▸*n.* **1** a spiral curve, shape, or pattern: *he spotted a spiral of smoke.* ■ a spiral spring. ■ *Astronomy* short for SPIRAL GALAXY. **2** a progressive rise or fall of prices, wages, etc., each responding to an upward or downward stimulus provided by a previous one: *an inflationary spiral.* ■ a process of deterioration through the continuous increase or decrease of a specified feature: *a downward spiral of sex and drink.* **3** *Football* a pass or kick that moves smoothly through the air while spinning on its long axis.

▸*v.* (**-raled, -ral·ing**; *Brit.* **-ralled, -ral·ling**) **1** [*intrans.*] move in a spiral course: *a wisp of smoke spiraled up from the trees.* ■ [*trans.*] cause to have a spiral shape or follow a spiral course: *spiral the bandage around the injured limb.* **2** [*intrans.*] show a continuous and dramatic increase: *inflation continued to spiral* | [as *adj.*] (**spiraling**) *he needed to relax after the spiraling tensions of the day.* ■ (**spiral down/downward**) decrease or deteriorate continuously: *he expects the figures to spiral down further.* ▷mid 16th cent. (as an adjective): from medieval Latin *spiralis*, from Latin *spira* 'coil' (see SPIRE2). —**spi·ral·ly** *adv.*

spi·ral-bound ▸*adj.* (of a book or notepad) bound with a wire or plastic spiral threaded through a row of holes along one edge.

spi·ral gal·ax·y ▸*n.* a galaxy in which the stars and gas clouds are concentrated mainly in one or more spiral arms.

spi·rant /ˈspīrənt/ ▸*adj. Phonetics* (of a consonant) uttered with a continuous expulsion of breath.

▸*n.* such a consonant; a fricative. ▷mid 19th cent.: from Latin *spirant-* 'breathing,' from the verb *spirare.* —**spi·rant·i·za·tion** /ˌspīrəntəˈzāsʜən/ *n.* —**spi·rant·ize** /-ˌtīz/ *v.*

spire1 /spī(ə)r/ ▸*n.* a tapering conical or pyramidal structure on the top of a building, typically a church tower. ■ the continuation of a tree trunk above the point where branching begins, esp. in a tree of a tapering form. ■ a long tapering object: *spires of delphiniums.* ▷Old English *spīr* 'tall slender stem of a plant'; related to German *Spier* 'tip of a blade of grass.' —**spired** *adj.* —**spir·y** *adj.*

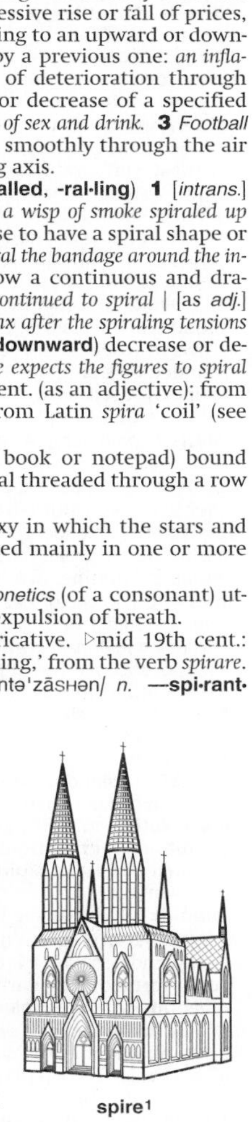

spire1

spire2 ▸*n. Zoology* the upper tapering part of the spiral shell of a gastropod mollusk, comprising all but the whorl containing the body. ▷mid 16th cent. (in the general sense 'a spiral'): from French, or via Latin from Greek *speira* 'a coil.'

spi·re·a /spīˈrēə/ (also **spi·rae·a**) ▸*n.* a shrub of the rose family, with clusters of small white or pink flowers. Found throughout the northern hemisphere, it is widely cultivated as a garden ornamental. • Genus *Spiraea*, family Rosaceae. ▷modern Latin, from Greek *speiraia*, from *speira* 'a coil.'

spire shell ▸*n.* a marine or freshwater mollusk with a long conical spiral shell. • Hydrobiidae and related families, class Gastropoda.

spi·ril·lum /spīˈriləm/ ▸*n.* (*pl.* **-la** /-lə/) a bacterium with a rigid spiral structure, found in stagnant water and sometimes causing disease. • Genus *Spirillum*; Gram-negative. ▷modern Latin, irregular diminutive of Latin *spira* 'a coil.'

spir·it /ˈspirit/ ▸*n.* **1** the nonphysical part of a person that is the seat of emotions and character; the soul: *we seek a harmony between body and spirit.* ■ such a part regarded as a person's true self and as capable of surviving physical death or separation: *a year after he left, his spirit is still present.* ■ such a part manifested as an apparition after their death; a ghost. ■ a supernatural being: *shrines to nature spirits.* ■ (**the Spirit**) short for HOLY SPIRIT. ■ *archaic* a highly refined substance or fluid thought to govern vital phenomena. **2** [in *sing.*] those qualities regarded as forming the definitive or typical elements in the character of a person, nation, or group or in the thought and attitudes of a particular period: *the university is a symbol of the nation's egalitarian spirit.* ■ [with *adj.*] a person identified with their most prominent mental or moral characteristics or with their role in a group or movement: *he was a leading spirit in the conference.* ■ a specified emotion or mood, esp. one prevailing at a particular time: *I hope the team will build on this* ***spirit of*** *confidence.* ■ (**spirits**) a person's mood: *the warm weather lifted everyone's spirits after the winter.* ■ the quality of courage, energy, and determination or assertiveness: *his visitors admired his spirit and good temper.* ■ the attitude or intentions with which someone undertakes or regards something: *he confessed in a spirit of self-respect, not defiance.* ■ the real meaning or the intention behind something as opposed to its strict verbal interpretation: *the rule had been broken in spirit if not in letter.* **3** (usu. **spirits**) strong distilled liquor such as brandy, whiskey, gin, or rum. ■ [with *adj.*] a volatile liquid, esp. a fuel, prepared by distillation: *aviation spirit.* ■ *archaic* a solution of volatile components extracted from something, typically by distillation or by solution in alcohol: ***spirits of*** *turpentine.*

▸*v.* (**-it·ed, -it·ing**) [*trans.*] convey rapidly and secretly: *stolen cows were* ***spirited away*** *some distance to prevent detection.*

▸*phrasal v.* □ **spirit someone up** *archaic* stimulate, animate, or cheer up someone. ▷Middle English: from Anglo-Norman French, from Latin *spiritus* 'breath, spirit,' from *spirare* 'breathe.'

▸*PHRASES* □ **enter into the spirit** join wholeheartedly in an event, esp. one of celebration and festivity: *he* ***entered into the spirit*** *of the occasion by dressing as a Pierrot.* □ **in** (or **in the**) **spirit** in thought or intention though not physically: *he couldn't be here in person, but he is with us in spirit.* □ **out of spirits** sad; discouraged: *I was too tired and out of spirits to eat or drink much.* □ **the spirit is willing but the flesh is weak** *proverb* someone has good intentions but fails to live up to them. [with biblical allusion to Matt. 26:41.] □ **when the spirit moves someone** when someone feels inclined to do something: *he can be quite candid when the spirit moves him.* [a phrase originally in Quaker use, with reference to the Holy Spirit.] □ **the spirit world** (in animistic and occult belief) the nonphysical realm in which disembodied spirits have their existence.

spir·it·ed /ˈspiritid/ ▸*adj.* **1** full of energy, enthusiasm, and determination: *a spirited campaigner for women's rights.* **2** [in *combination*] having a specified character, outlook on life, or mood: *he was a warmhearted, generous-spirited man.* —**spir·it·ed·ly** *adv.* —**spir·it·ed·ness** *n.*

spir·it gum ▸*n.* a quick-drying solution of gum, chiefly used by actors to attach false hair to their faces.

spir·it·ism /ˈspiriˌtizəm/ ▸*n.* another term for SPIRITUALISM (sense 1). —**spir·it·ist** /ˈspiritist/ *adj.* & *n.* —**spir·it·is·tic** /-ˌtistik/ *adj.*

spir·it lamp ▸*n.* a lamp burning volatile spirits, esp. methylated spirits, instead of oil.

spir·it·less /ˈspiritlis/ ▸*adj.* lacking courage, vigor, or vivacity: *Ruth and I played a spiritless game of Scrabble.* —**spir·it·less·ly** *adv.* —**spir·it·less·ness** *n.*

spir·it lev·el ▸*n.* a device consisting of a sealed glass tube partially filled with alcohol or other liquid, containing an air bubble whose position reveals whether a surface is perfectly level. Also called LEVEL.

spir·it of harts·horn /ˈhärtsˌhôrn/ ▸*n.* see HARTSHORN.

spir·it of wine (also **spir·its of wine**) ▸*n. archaic* purified alcohol.

spir·i·tous /ˈspiritəs/ ▸*adj.* another term for SPIRITUOUS.

spir·its of salt ▸*n.* archaic term for HYDROCHLORIC ACID.

spir·it·u·al /ˈspiricʜo͞oəl/ ▸*adj.* **1** of, relating to, or affecting the human spirit or soul as opposed to material or physical things: *I'm responsible for his spiritual welfare* | *the spiritual values of life.* ■ (of a person) not concerned with material values or pursuits. **2** of or relating to religion or religious belief: *Iran's spiritual leader.*

▸*n.* (also **Negro spiritual**) a religious song of a kind associated with black Christians of the southern U.S., and thought to derive from the combination of European hymns and African musical elements by black slaves. ▷Middle English: from Old French *spirituel*, from Latin *spiritualis*, from *spiritus* (see SPIRIT). —**spir·it·u·al·i·ty** /ˌspiricʜo͞oˈalitē/ *n.* —**spir·it·u·al·ly** *adv.*

▸*PHRASE* □ **one's spiritual home** a place in which one feels a profound sense of belonging: *I had always thought of Italy as my spiritual home.*

spir·it·u·al·ism /ˈspiricʜo͞oəˌlizəm/ ▸*n.* **1** a system of belief or religious practice based on supposed communication with the spirits of the dead, esp. through mediums. **2** *Philosophy* the doctrine that the spirit exists as distinct from matter, or that spirit is the only reality. —**spir·it·u·al·ist** *n.* —**spir·it·u·al·is·tic** /ˌspiricʜo͞oəˈlistik/ *adj.*

spir·it·u·al·ize /ˈspiricʜo͞oəˌlīz/ ▸*v.* [*trans.*] elevate to a spiritual level. —**spir·it·u·al·i·za·tion** /ˌspiricʜo͞oələˈzāsʜən/ *n.*

spir·it·u·ous /ˈspiricʜo͞oəs/ ▸*adj. formal* or *archaic* containing much alcohol; distilled: *spirituous beverages.* ▷late 16th cent. (in the sense 'spirited, lively'): from Latin *spiritus* 'spirit' + -OUS, or from French *spiritueux.*

spir·i·tus /ˈspiritəs/ ▸*n.* Latin term for BREATH, often used figuratively to mean spirit.

spir·i·tus rec·tor /ˈspiritus ˈrektər/ ▸*n.* a ruling or directing spirit. ▷Latin.

spiro-1 ▸*comb. form* **1** spiral; in a spiral: *spirochete.* **2** *Chemistry* denoting a molecule with two rings with one atom common to both: *spironolactone.* ▷from Latin *spira*, Greek *speira* 'a coil.'

spiro-2 ▸*comb. form* relating to breathing: *spirometer.* ▷formed irregularly from Latin *spirare* 'breathe.'

spi·ro·chete /ˈspīrəˌkēt/ (*Brit.* **spi·ro·chaete**) ▸*n.* a flexible spirally twisted bacterium, esp. one that causes syphilis. • *Treponema* and other genera, order Spirochaetales; Gram-negative. ▷late 19th cent.: from SPIRO-1 'in a spiral' + Greek *khaitē* 'long hair.'

spi·ro·graph /ˈspīrəˌgraf/ ▸*n.* an instrument for recording breathing movements. —**spi·ro·graph·ic** /ˌspīrəˈgrafik/ *adj.*

spi·ro·gy·ra /ˌspīrəˈjīrə/ ▸*n. Botany* a filamentous freshwater green alga containing spiral bands of chloroplasts. • Genus *Spirogyra*, division Chlorophyta. ▷modern Latin, from SPIRO-1 'spiral' + Greek *guros, gura* 'round.'

spi·rom·e·ter /spīˈrämitər/ ▸*n.* an instrument for measuring the air capacity of the lungs. —**spi·rom·e·try** /-mitrē/ *n.*

spi·ro·no·lac·tone /ˌspīrənōˈlaktōn/ ▸*n. Medicine* a steroid drug that promotes sodium excretion and is used in the treatment of certain types of edema and hypertension. ▷1960s: from SPIRO-1 (sense 2) + LACTONE, with the insertion of -ONE.

spirt /spərt/ ▸*v.* & *n.* old-fashioned spelling of SPURT.

spi·ru·li·na /ˌspīrəˈlīnə/ ▸*n.* filamentous cyanobacteria that form tangled masses in warm alkaline lakes in Africa and Central and South America. • Genus *Spirulina*, division Cyanobacteria. ■ (usu. **Spirulina**) the substance of such growths dried and prepared as a food or food additive, which is a rich source of many vitamins and minerals. ▷modern Latin, from *spirula* 'small spiral (shell).'

spit[1] /spit/ ▸v. (**spit·ting**; *past* and *past part.* **spit** or **spat** /spat/) [*intrans.*] **1** eject saliva forcibly from one's mouth, sometimes as a gesture of contempt or anger: *Todd spit in Hugh's face.* ■ [*trans.*] forcibly eject (food or liquid) from one's mouth: *he **spits out** his piece of coconut* | *figurative ATMs that spit out $20 bills.* ■ (**spit up**) (esp. of a baby) vomit or regurgitate food. ■ [*trans.*] utter in a hostile or aggressive way: *she spat abuse at the jury* | [with *direct speech*] *"Go to hell!" she spat.* ■ be extremely angry or frustrated: *he was spitting with sudden fury.* ■ (of a fire or something being cooked) emit small bursts of sparks or hot fat with a series of short, explosive noises. ■ (of a cat) make a hissing noise as a sign of anger or hostility. **2** (**it spits, it is spitting**, etc.) *Brit.* light rain falls: *it began to spit.*
▸n. **1** saliva, typically that which has been ejected from a person's mouth. ■ short for CUCKOO SPIT. **2** an act of spitting. ▷Old English *spittan*, of imitative origin.
▸PHRASES □ **spit in the eye** (or **face**) **of** show contempt or scorn for. □ **spit it out** *informal* used to urge someone to say or confess something quickly: *spit it out, man, I haven't got all day.*

spit[2] ▸n. **1** a long, thin metal rod pushed through meat in order to hold and turn it while it is roasted over an open fire: *chicken cooked on a spit.* **2** a narrow point of land projecting into the sea: *a narrow spit of land shelters the bay.*
▸v. (**spit·ted, spit·ting**) [*trans.*] put a spit through (meat) in order to roast it over an open fire: *I spitted the squirrel meat and turned it over the flames.* ▷Old English *spitu*; related to Dutch *spit* and German *Spiess.*

spit[3] ▸n. (*pl.* same or **spits**) a layer of earth whose depth is equal to the length of the blade of a spade: *break up the top spit with a fork.* ▷early 16th cent.: from Middle Dutch and Middle Low German; probably related to SPIT[2].

spit and pol·ish ▸n. thorough or exaggerated cleaning and polishing, esp. by a soldier: *they gave the dining room some extra spit and polish.*

spit·ball /'spit,bôl/ ▸n. **1** a piece of paper that has been chewed and shaped into a ball for use as a missile. **2** *Baseball* an illegal pitch made with a ball moistened with saliva or another substance to make it move erratically.
▸v. [*trans.*] *informal* throw out (a suggestion) for discussion: *I'm just spitballing a few ideas.* —**spit·ball·er** n.

spitch·cock /'spicH,käk/ ▸n. an eel that has been split and grilled or fried.
▸v. [*intrans.*] prepare (an eel or other fish) in this way. ▷late 15th cent.: of unknown origin; compare with SPATCHCOCK.

spit curl ▸n. a small curl of hair trained to lie flat on the forehead, at the nape of the neck, or in front of the ear.

spite /spīt/ ▸n. a desire to hurt, annoy, or offend someone: *he'd think I was saying it out of spite.* ■ *archaic* an instance of such a desire; a grudge: *it seemed as if the wind **had a spite at** her.*
▸v. [*trans.*] deliberately hurt, annoy, or offend (someone): *he put the house up for sale to spite his family.* ▷Middle English: shortening of Old French *despit* 'contempt,' *despiter* 'show contempt for.'
▸PHRASES □ **in spite of** without being affected by the particular factor mentioned: *he was suddenly cold in spite of the sun.* □ **in spite of oneself** although one did not want or expect to do so: *Oliver smiled in spite of himself.*

spite·ful /'spītfəl/ ▸adj. showing or caused by malice: *the teachers made spiteful little jokes about me.* See note at VINDICTIVE. —**spite·ful·ly** *adv.* —**spite·ful·ness** *n.*

spit·fire /'spit,fīr/ ▸n. a person with a fierce temper.

Spit·head /,spit'hed/ a channel between the northeastern coast of the Isle of Wight and the mainland of southern England. It offers sheltered access to Southampton Water and deep anchorage.

spit-roast ▸v. [*trans.*] [usu. as *adj.*] (**spit-roasted**) cook (a piece of meat) on a spit: *spit-roasted lamb.*

Spits·ber·gen /'spits,bərgən/ a Norwegian island in the Svalbard archipelago, in the Arctic Ocean north of Norway; principal settlement, Longyearbyen.

spit·ter /'spitər/ ▸n. **1** a person who spits. **2** another term for SPITBALL (sense 2).

spit·ting co·bra ▸n. an African cobra that defends itself by spitting venom from the fangs, typically at the aggressor's eyes. • Genera *Naja* and *Hemachatus*, family Elapidae: three species, in particular the **black-necked spitting cobra** (*N. nigricollis*).

spit·ting im·age ▸n. (**the spitting image of**) *informal* the exact double of (another person or thing): *she's the spitting image of her mum.*

spit·tle /'spitl/ ▸n. saliva, esp. as ejected from the mouth. ▷late 15th cent.: alteration of dialect *spattle*, by association with SPIT[1]. —**spit·tly** *adj.*

spit·tle·bug /'spitl,bəg/ ▸n. another term for FROGHOPPER.

spit·toon /spi'to͞on/ ▸n. a metal or earthenware pot typically having a funnel-shaped top, used for spitting into.

Spitz /spits/, Mark (Andrew) (1950–), U.S. swimmer. He won 7 gold medals in the 1972 Olympic Games at Munich and set 27 world records for free style and butterfly between 1967 and 1972.

spitz /spits/ ▸n. a dog of a small breed with a pointed muzzle, esp. a Pomeranian. ▷mid 19th cent.: from German *Spitz(hund)*, from *spitz* 'pointed' + *Hund* 'dog.'

spiv /spiv/ ▸n. *Brit., informal* a man, typically characterized by flashy dress, who makes a living by disreputable dealings. ▷1930s: perhaps related to SPIFFY. —**spiv·vish** *adj.* —**spiv·vy** *adj.*

splake /splāk/ ▸n. a hybrid trout of North American lakes. • Produced by crossing the speckled trout (*Salvelinus fontinalis*) with the lake trout (*S. namaycush*). ▷1950s: blend of *speckled* and LAKE[1].

splanch·nic /'splaNGknik/ ▸adj. of or relating to the viscera or internal organs, esp. those of the abdomen. ▷late 17th cent.: from modern Latin *splanchnicus*, from Greek *splankhnikos*, from *splankhna* 'entrails.'

splanch·no·pleure /'splaNGknə,plo͝or/ ▸n. *Embryology* a layer of tissue in a vertebrate embryo comprising the endoderm and the inner layer of mesoderm, and giving rise to the gut, lungs, and yolk sac. Often contrasted with SOMATOPLEURE. ▷late 19th cent.: from Greek *splankhna* 'entrails' + *pleura* 'side.'

splash /splasH/ ▸n. a sound made by something striking or falling into liquid: *we hit the water with a mighty splash.* ■ a spell of moving about in water energetically: *the girls joined them for a final splash in the pool.* ■ a small quantity of liquid that has fallen or been dashed against a surface: ***a splash of** gravy.* ■ a small quantity of liquid added to a drink: ***a splash of** lemonade.* ■ a bright patch of color: *add a red scarf to give **a splash of** color.* ■ *informal* a prominent or sensational news feature or story: *a front-page splash.* ■ *informal* a striking, ostentatious, or exciting effect or event: *there's going to be a big splash when Mike returns to the ring.*
▸v. [*trans.*] cause (liquid) to strike or fall on something in irregular drops: *she splashed cold water onto her face.* ■ [*trans.*] make wet by doing this: *they splashed each other with water.* ■ [*intrans.*] (of a liquid) fall or be scattered in irregular drops: *a tear fell and splashed onto the pillow.* ■ [*intrans.*] strike or move around in a body of water, causing it to fly about noisily: *some stones splashed into the water* | *wheels splashed through a puddle.* ■ (**be splashed with**) be decorated with scattered patches of: *a field splashed with purple clover.* ■ [*trans.*] print (a story or photograph, esp. a sensational one) in a prominent place in a newspaper or magazine: *the story was **splashed across** the front pages.*
▸phrasal v. □ **splash down** (of a spacecraft) land on water. □ **splash out** (or **splash money out**) *Brit., informal* spend money freely: *she **splashed out on** a Mercedes.* ▷early 18th cent. (as a verb): alteration of PLASH[1].
▸PHRASE □ **make a splash** *informal* attract a great deal of attention.

splash·board /'splasH,bôrd/ ▸n. a screen designed to protect the passengers of a vehicle or boat from splashes.

splash·down /'splasH,doun/ ▸n. the alighting of a returning spacecraft on the sea, with the assistance of parachutes.

splash·y /'splasHē/ ▸adj. (**splash·i·er, splash·i·est**) **1** characterized by water flying about noisily in irregular drops: *a splashy waterfall.* ■ characterized by irregular patches of bright color: *splashy floral silks.* **2** *informal* attracting a great deal of attention; elaborately or ostentatiously impressive: *I don't care for splashy Hollywood parties.*

splat[1] /splat/ ▸n. a piece of thin wood in the center of a chair back. ▷mid 19th cent.: from obsolete *splat* 'split up'; related to SPLIT.

splat[2] *informal* ▸n. a sound of something soft and wet or heavy striking a surface: *the goblin makes a huge splat as he hits the ground.*
▸adv. with a sound of this type: *he lands splat on his right elbow.*
▸v. (**splat·ted, splat·ting**) [*trans.*] crush or squash (something) with a sound of this type: *he was splatting a bug.* ■ [*intrans.*] land or be squashed with a sound of this type. ▷late 19th cent.: abbreviation of SPLATTER.

splat·ter /'splatər/ ▸v. [*trans.*] splash with a sticky or viscous liquid: *a passing cart rolled by, splattering him with mud.* ■ splash (such a liquid) over a surface or object. ■ [*intrans.*] (of such a liquid) splash: *heavy droplets of rain splatter onto the windshield.* ■ *informal* prominently or sensationally publish (a story) in a newspaper: *the story is **splattered over** pages two and three.*
▸n. **1** a spot or trail of a sticky or viscous liquid splashed over a surface or object: *each puddle we crossed threw **a splatter of** mud on the windshield.* **2** [as *adj.*] *informal* denoting or referring to films featuring many violent and gruesome deaths: *a splatter movie.* ▷late 18th cent.: imitative.

splat·ter·punk /'splatər,pəNGk/ ▸n. *informal* a literary genre characterized by the explicit description of horrific, violent, and often pornographic scenes.

splay /splā/ ▸v. [*trans.*] thrust or spread (things, esp. limbs or fingers) out and apart: *her hands were splayed across his broad shoulders* | *he stood with his legs and arms **splayed out.*** ■ [*intrans.*] (esp. of limbs or fingers) be thrust or spread out and apart: *his legs **splayed out** in front of him.* ■ [*intrans.*] (of a thing) diverge in shape or position; become wider or more separated: *the river **splayed out**, deepening to become an estuary.* ■ [usu. as *adj.*] (**splayed**) construct (a window, doorway, or aperture) so that it diverges or is wider at one side of the wall than the other: *the walls are pierced by splayed window openings.*
▸n. **1** a widening or outward tapering of something, in particular: ■ a tapered widening of a road at an intersection to increase visibility. ■ a splayed window aperture or other opening. **2** a surface making an oblique angle with another, such as the splayed side of a window or embrasure. ■ the degree of bevel or slant of a surface.
▸adj. [usu. in *combination*] turned outward or widened: *the girls were sitting splay-legged.* ▷Middle English (in the sense 'unfold to view, display'): shortening of the verb DISPLAY.

splay-foot ▸n. a broad flat foot turned outward. —**splay-foot·ed** *adj.*

spleen /splēn/ ▸n. **1** *Anatomy* an abdominal organ involved in the production and removal of blood cells in most vertebrates and forming part of the immune system. **2** bad temper; spite: *he could **vent his spleen** on the institutions that had duped him.* [from the earlier belief that the spleen was the seat of such emotions.] ▷Middle English: shortening of Old French *esplen*, via Latin from Greek *splēn.* —**spleen·ful** /-fəl/ *adj.* (in sense 2).

spleen·wort /'splēnwərt; -,wôrt/ ▸n. a small fern that grows in rosettes on rocks and walls, typically with rounded or triangular lobes on a slender stem and formerly used as a remedy for disorders of the spleen. • Genus *Asplenium*, family Aspleniaceae.

splen- ▸*comb. form Anatomy* of or relating to the spleen: *splenectomy.* ▷from Greek *splēn* 'spleen.'

Splen·da /'splendə/ ▸n. *trademark* an artificial sweetener used as a calorie-free sugar substitute.

splen·dent /'splendənt/ ▸adj. *archaic* shining brightly. ■ illustrious; great. ▷late 15th cent.: from Latin *splendent-* 'shining,' from the verb *splendere.*

splen·did /'splendid/ ▸adj. magnificent; very impressive: *a splendid view of Windsor Castle* | *his robes were splendid.* ■ *informal* excellent; very good: *a splendid fellow* | [as *exclam.*] *"Is your family well? Splendid!"* ▷early 17th cent.: from French *splendide* or Latin *splendidus*, from *splendere* 'shine, be bright.' —**splen·did·ly** *adv.* [as *submodifier*] *a splendidly ornate style.* —**splen·did·ness** *n.*
▸PHRASE □ **splendid isolation** used to emphasize the isolation of a person or thing: *the stone stands **in splendid isolation** near the moorland road.* [1896: first applied to the period from 1890 to 1907 when Britain pursued a policy of diplomatic and commercial noninvolvement.]

Splen·did Splint·er see WILLIAMS 4.

splen·dif·er·ous /splen'difərəs/ ▸adj. *informal, humorous* splendid: *a splendiferous Sunday dinner.* ▷mid 19th cent.: formed irregularly from SPLENDOR. —**splen·dif·er·ous·ly** *adv.* —**splen·dif·er·ous·ness** *n.*

splen·dor /'splendər/ (*Brit.* **splen·dour**) ▸n. magnificent and splendid appearance; grandeur: *the splendor of the Florida Keys.* ■ (**splendors**) magnificent features or qualities: *the splendors of the imperial court.* ▷late Middle English: from Anglo-Norman French *splendur* or Latin *splendor*, from *splendere* 'shine, be bright.'

sple·nec·to·my /splə'nektəmē/ ▸n. (*pl.* **-mies**) a surgical operation involving removal of the spleen.

sple·net·ic /splə'netik/ ▶*adj.* **1** bad-tempered; spiteful: *a splenetic outburst.* **2** archaic term for **SPLENIC**. ▷late Middle English (as a noun denoting a person with a diseased spleen): from late Latin *spleneticus*, from Greek *splēn* (see **SPLEEN**). **—sple·net·i·cal·ly** *adv.* (in sense 1).

splen·ic /'splēnik; 'sple-/ ▶*adj.* of or relating to the spleen: *the splenic artery.* ▷early 17th cent.: from French *splénique*, or via Latin from Greek *splēnikos*, from *splēn* (see **SPLEEN**).

sple·ni·tis /splē'nītis; sple-/ ▶*n.* *Medicine* inflammation of the spleen.

sple·ni·um /'splēnēəm/ ▶*n.* *Anatomy* the thick posterior part of the corpus callosum of the brain. ▷mid 19th cent.: from Latin. **—sple·ni·al** /'splēnēəl/ *adj.*

sple·ni·us /'splēnēəs/ (also **sple·ni·us mus·cle**) ▶*n.* (*pl.* **-ni·i** /-nē,ī/) *Anatomy* any of two pairs of muscles attached to the vertebrae in the neck and upper back that draw back the head. ▷mid 18th cent.: modern Latin, from Greek *splēnion* 'bandage.'

sple·no·meg·a·ly /,splēnə'megəlē; ,sple-/ ▶*n.* abnormal enlargement of the spleen. ▷early 20th cent.: from **SPLEN-** 'spleen' + Greek *megas, megal-* 'great.'

splice /splīs/ ▶*v.* [*trans.*] join or connect (a rope or ropes) by interweaving the strands: *we learned how to weave and splice ropes* | *a cord was* **spliced on** | *figurative the work splices detail and generalization.* ■ join (pieces of timber, film, or tape) at the ends: *commercials can be* **spliced in** *later* | *I was* **splicing together** *a video from the footage on opium-growing.* ■ *Genetics* join or insert (a gene or gene fragment).

▶*n.* a union of two ropes, pieces of timber, or similar materials spliced together at the ends. ▷early 16th cent.: probably from Middle Dutch *splissen*, of unknown origin. **—splic·er** *n.*

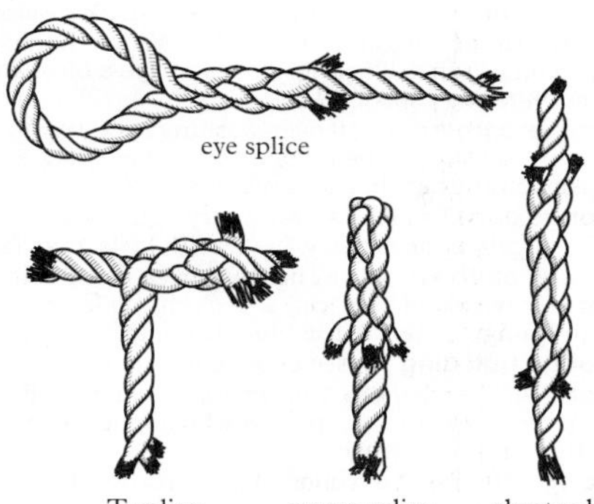

rope splices

spliff /splif/ ▶*n.* *Brit., informal* a marijuana cigarette. ▷1930s: of unknown origin.

spline /splīn/ ▶*n.* **1** a rectangular key fitting into grooves in the hub and shaft of a wheel, esp. one formed integrally with the shaft that allows movement of the wheel on the shaft. ■ a corresponding groove in a hub along which the key may slide. **2** a slat. ■ a flexible wood or rubber strip used esp. in drawing large curves. **3** (also **spline curve**) *Mathematics* a continuous curve constructed so as to pass through a given set of points and have a certain number of continuous derivatives.

▶*v.* [*trans.*] secure (a part) by means of a spline. ■ [usu. as *adj.*] (**splined**) fit with a spline: *splined freewheels.* ▷mid 18th cent. (originally East Anglian dialect): perhaps related to **SPLINTER**.

splint /splint/ ▶*n.* **1** a strip of rigid material used for supporting and immobilizing a broken bone when it has been set: *she had to wear splints on her legs.* **2** a long, thin strip of wood used to light a fire. ■ a rigid or flexible strip, esp. of wood, used in basketwork. **3** a bony enlargement on the inside of a horse's leg, on the splint bone.

▶*v.* [*trans.*] secure (a broken limb) with a splint or splints: *his leg was splinted.* ▷Middle English (sense 2; also denoting a section of armor): from Middle Dutch, Middle Low German *splinte* 'metal plate or pin'; related to **SPLINTER**.

splint bone ▶*n.* either of two small bones in the foreleg of a horse or other large quadruped, lying behind and close to the cannon bone.

splin·ter /'splin(t)ər/ ▶*n.* a small, thin, sharp piece of wood, glass, or similar material broken off from a larger piece: *a splinter of ice.*

▶*v.* break or cause to break into small sharp fragments: [*intrans.*] *the soap box splintered* | *figurative the party had begun to splinter into factions* | [*trans.*] *he crashed into a fence, splintering the wooden barricade.* ▷Middle English: from Middle Dutch *splinter, splenter*; related to **SPLINT**. **—splin·ter·y** *adj.*

splin·ter group (also **splinter party**) ▶*n.* a small organization, typically a political party, that has broken away from a larger one.

splin·ter-proof ▶*adj.* **1** capable of withstanding splinters from bursting shells or bombs: *splinter-proof shutters.* **2** not producing splinters when broken: *splinter-proof glass.*

Split /split/ a seaport on the coast of southern Croatia; pop. 189,000. It contains the ruins of the palace of the emperor Diocletian, built in about AD 300.

split /split/ ▶*v.* (**split·ting**; *past* and *past part.* **split**) **1** break or cause to break forcibly into parts, esp. into halves or along the grain: [*intrans.*] *the ice cracked and heaved and split* | [*trans.*] *split and toast the muffins.* ■ remove or be removed by breaking, separating, or dividing: [*trans.*] *the point was pressed against the edge of the flint to* **split off** *flakes* | [*intrans.*] *an incentive for regions to* **split away** *from countries.* ■ divide or cause to divide into parts or elements: [*intrans.*] *the river had* **split into** *a number of channels* | [*trans.*] **splitting** *water* **into** *oxygen and hydrogen.* ■ [*trans.*] divide and share (something, esp. resources or responsibilities): *they met up and split the booty.* ■ [*trans.*] cause the fission of (an atom). ■ [*trans.*] issue new shares of (stock) to existing stockholders in proportion to their current holdings. **2** (with reference to a group of people) divide into two or more groups: [*intrans.*] *let's* **split up** *and find the other two* | [*trans.*] *once again the family was* **split up**. ■ [*intrans.*] end a marriage or an emotional or working relationship: *I* **split up** *with my boyfriend a year ago.* ■ [*trans.*] (often **be split**) (of an issue) cause (a group) to be divided because of opposing views: *the party was deeply* **split over** *its future direction.* **3** [*intrans.*] *informal* (of one's head) suffer great pain from a headache: *my head is splitting* | [as *adj.*] (**splitting**) *a splitting headache.* **4** [*intrans.*] *informal* leave a place, esp. suddenly: *"Let's split," Harvey said.* **5** [*intrans.*] *Brit., informal* betray the secrets of or inform on someone: *I told him I wouldn't* **split on** *him.*

▶*n.* **1** a tear, crack, or fissure in something, esp. down the middle or along the grain: *light squeezed through a small split in the curtain.* ■ an instance or act of splitting or being split; a division: *the split between the rich and the poor.* ■ a separation into parties or within a party; a schism: *the accusations caused a split in the party.* ■ an ending of a marriage or an emotional or working relationship: *a much-publicized split with his wife.* ■ short for **STOCK SPLIT**. **2** (**a split** or **the splits**) (in gymnastics and dance) an act of leaping in the air or sitting down with the legs straight and at right angles to the upright body, one in front and the other behind, or one at each side: *I could never* **do a split** *before.* **3** a thing that is divided or split, in particular: ■ a bun, roll, or cake that is split or cut in half. ■ a split osier used in basketwork. ■ each strip of steel or cane that makes up the reed in a loom. ■ half a bottle or glass of champagne or other liquor. ■ a single thickness of split hide. ■ (in bowling) a formation of standing pins after the first ball in which there is a gap between two pins or groups of pins, making a spare unlikely. ■ a drawn game or series. ■ a split-level house. **4** the time taken to complete a recognized part of a race, or the point in the race where such a time is measured. ▷late 16th cent. (originally in the sense 'break up (a ship),' describing the force of a storm or rock): from Middle Dutch *splitten*, of unknown ultimate origin.

▶*PHRASES* □ **split the difference** take the average of two proposed amounts. □ **split hairs** see **HAIR**. □ **split one's sides** (also **split a gut**) *informal* be convulsed with laughter: *the dynamic comedy duo will have you splitting your sides with laughter.* □ **split the ticket** (or **one's vote**) vote for candidates of more than one party. □ **split the vote** (of a candidate or minority party) attract votes from another candidate or party with the result that both are defeated by a third.

split-brain ▶*adj.* [*attrib.*] *Psychiatry* (of a person or animal) having the corpus callosum severed or absent, so as to eliminate the main connection between the two hemispheres of the brain.

split de·ci·sion ▶*n.* a decision based on a majority verdict rather than on a unanimous one, esp. on a court panel or among referees judging the winner of a boxing match.

split end ▶*n.* **1** (usu. **split ends**) a tip of a person's hair that has split from dryness or ill-treatment. **2** *Football* an offensive end positioned on the line of scrimmage but several yards away from the other linemen.

split-half ▶*adj.* [*attrib.*] *Statistics* relating to or denoting a technique of splitting a body of supposedly homogeneous data into two halves and calculating the results separately for each to assess their reliability.

split im·age ▶*n.* an image in a rangefinder or camera focusing system that has been bisected by optical means, the halves being aligned only when the system is in focus.

split in·fin·i·tive ▶*n.* a construction consisting of an infinitive with an adverb or other word inserted between *to* and the verb, e.g., *she seems to really like it.*

USAGE Is it wrong to use a **split infinitive**, separating the infinitive marker **to** from the verb? If so, then these statements are grammatically incorrect: *you have* **to really watch** *him;* **to boldly go** *where no one has gone before.*Writers who long ago insisted that English could be modeled on Latin created the "rule" that the English infinitive must not be split: *to clearly state* violates this rule; one must say *to state clearly*. But the Latin infinitive is one word (e.g., *amare*, 'to love') and cannot be split, so the rule is not firmly grounded, and treating two English words as one can lead to awkward, stilted sentences. In particular, the placing of an adverb in English is extremely important in giving the appropriate emphasis. Consider, for example, the "corrected" forms of the previous examples: *you really have* **to watch** *him;* **to go** *boldly where no one has gone before.* The original, intended emphasis of each statement has been changed, and for no other reason than to satisfy an essentially unreasonable rule. Some traditionalists may continue to hold up the split infinitive as an error, but in standard English, the principle of allowing split infinitives is broadly accepted as both normal and useful.

split-lev·el ▶*adj.* (of a building) having a room or rooms higher than others by less than a whole story: *a large split-level house.* ■ (of a room) having its floor on two levels.

▶*n.* a split-level building.

split pea ▶*n.* a pea dried and split in half for cooking.

split per·son·al·i·ty ▶*n.* less common term for **MULTIPLE PERSONALITY**. ■ archaic term for **SCHIZOPHRENIA**.

split-phase ▶*adj.* denoting or relating to an induction motor or other device utilizing two or more voltages at different phases produced from a single-phase supply.

split-rail ▶*adj.* denoting a fence or enclosure made from pieces of wood split lengthwise from a log.

split run ▶*n.* a print run of a newspaper during which some articles or advertisements are changed so as to produce different editions.

split screen ▶*n.* a movie, television, or computer screen on which two or more separate images are displayed.

split sec·ond ▶*n.* a very brief moment of time: *for a split second, I hesitated.*

▶*adj.* very rapid or accurate: *split-second timing is crucial.*

split shift ▶*n.* a working shift comprising two or more separate periods of duty in a day.

split shot ▶*n.* **1** (also **split-shot**) small pellets used to weight a fishing line. **2** *Croquet* a stroke driving two touching balls in different directions.

split·ter /'splitər/ ▶*n.* a person or thing occupied in or designed for splitting something: *a log splitter.* ■ a person, esp. a taxonomist, who attaches more importance to differences than to similarities in classification. Contrasted with **LUMPER**.

split·tism /'splitizəm/ ▶*n.* (among communists, or in communist countries) the pursuance of factional interests in opposition to official Communist Party policy. **—split·tist** *n.*

splodge /spläj/ ▶*n.* & *v.* *Brit.* another term for **SPLOTCH**. **—splodgy** *adj.*

splosh /spläsh/ *informal* ▶*v.* [*intrans.*] make a soft splashing sound as one moves: *he sploshed across the road.*

▶*n.* a soft splashing sound: *a quiet splosh.* ■ a splash of liquid: **sploshes** *of wine.* ▷mid 19th cent.: imitative.

splotch /spläch/ *informal* ▶*n.* a daub, blot, or smear of something, typically a liquid: **a splotch of** *red in a larger area of yellow.*

▶*v.* [*trans.*] (usu. **be splotched**) make such a daub, blot,

Pronunciation Key ə *ago*; ər *over*; 'ə *or* ,ə *up*; 'ər *or* ,ər *fur*; a *hat*; ā *rate*; ä *car*; CH *chew*; e *let*; ē *see*; e(ə)r *air*; i *fit*; ī *by*; i(ə)r *ear*; NG *sing*; ō *go*; ô *for*; oi *boy*; o͝o *good*; o͞o *goo*; ou *out*; SH *she*; TH *thin*; T͟H *then*; (h)w *why*; ZH *vision*

or smear on: *a rag splotched with grease.* ▷early 17th cent.: perhaps a blend of SPOT and obsolete *plotch* 'blotch.' —**splotch·y** *adj.*

splurge /splərj/ *informal* ▶*n.* an act of spending money freely or extravagantly: *the annual pre-Christmas splurge.* ■ a large or excessive amount of something: *there has recently been a splurge of teach-yourself books.*
▶*v.* [*trans.*] spend (money) freely or extravagantly: *I'd* ***splurged*** *about $2,500* ***on*** *clothes* | [*intrans.*] *we* ***splurged on*** *T-bone steaks.* ▷early 19th cent. (originally U.S.): probably imitative.

splurt /splərt/ *informal* ▶*n.* a sudden gush, esp. of saliva. ■ a sudden brief outburst of something: *I let out* ***a splurt of*** *laughter.*
▶*v.* [*trans.*] push out with force; spit out: *the rear wheels splurted gravel.* ▷late 18th cent.: imitative.

splut·ter /ˈsplətər/ ▶*v.* [*intrans.*] make a series of short explosive spitting or choking sounds: *she coughed and spluttered, tears coursing down her face.* ■ [*reporting verb*] say something rapidly, indistinctly, and with a spitting sound, as a result of anger, embarrassment, or another strong emotion: [*trans.*] *he began to splutter excuses* | [with *direct speech*] *"How dare you?" she spluttered.* ■ [*trans.*] spit (something) out from one's mouth noisily and in small splashes: *spluttering brackish water, he struggled to regain his feet.*
▶*n.* a short explosive spitting or choking noise. ▷late 17th cent.: imitative; compare with SPUTTER. —**splut·ter·er** *n.* —**splut·ter·ing·ly** *adv.*

Spock /späk/, Benjamin McLane (1903–98), U.S. pediatrician and writer; known as **Dr. Spock**. His influential manual *The Common Sense Book of Baby and Child Care,* first published in 1946, challenged traditional ideas in child-rearing in favor of a psychological approach.

Benjamin Spock

Spode /ˈspōd/ ▶*n. trademark* fine pottery or porcelain made at the factories of the English potter Josiah Spode (1755–1827) or his successors, characteristically consisting of ornately decorated and gilded services and large vases.

spod·o·sol /ˈspädəˌsäl; -ˌsôl/ ▶*n. Soil Science* a soil of an order rich in aluminum oxide and organic matter, typically characterized by low fertility, and including most podzols. ▷1960s: from Greek *spodos* 'ashes, embers' + -SOL + Latin *solum* 'soil.'

spod·u·mene /ˈspäjo͞oˌmēn/ ▶*n.* a translucent, typically grayish-white aluminosilicate mineral that is an important source of lithium. ▷early 19th cent.: from French *spodumène,* from Greek *spodoumenos* 'burning to ashes,' present participle of *spodousthai,* from *spodos* 'ashes.'

spoil /spoil/ ▶*v.* (*past* and *past part.* **spoiled** or *chiefly Brit.* **spoilt** /spoilt/) [*trans.*] **1** diminish or destroy the value or quality of: *I wouldn't want to spoil your fun* | *a series of political blunders spoiled their chances of being reelected.* ■ prevent someone from enjoying (an occasion or event): *she was afraid of spoiling Christmas for the rest of the family.* ■ [*intrans.*] (of food) become unfit for eating: *I've got some ham that'll spoil if we don't eat it tonight.* **2** harm the character of (a child) by being too lenient or indulgent: *the last thing I want to do is spoil Thomas* | [as *adj.*] (**spoiled**) *a spoiled child.* ■ treat with great or excessive kindness, consideration, or generosity: *breakfast in bed—you're spoiling me!* **3** [*intrans.*] (**be spoiling for**) be extremely or aggressively eager for: *Cooper was spoiling for a fight.* **4** *archaic* rob (a person or a place) of goods or possessions by force or violence.
▶*n.* **1** (usu. **spoils**) goods stolen or taken forcibly from a person or place: *the looters carried their spoils away.* **2** waste material brought up during the course of an excavation or a dredging or mining operation. ▷Middle English (in the sense 'to plunder'): shortening of Old French *espoille* (noun), *espoillier* (verb), from Latin *spoliare,* from *spolium* 'plunder, skin stripped from an animal,' or a shortening of DESPOIL.

spoil·age /ˈspoilij/ ▶*n.* **1** the action of spoiling, esp. the deterioration of food and perishable goods. **2** waste produced by material being spoiled, esp. paper that is spoiled in printing.

spoil·er /ˈspoilər/ ▶*n.* **1** a person or thing that spoils. ■ (esp. in a political context) a person who obstructs or prevents an opponent's success while having no chance of winning a contest themselves. ■ an electronic device for preventing unauthorized copying of sound recordings by means of a disruptive signal inaudible on the original. **2** a flap on an aircraft or glider that can be projected from the surface of a wing in order to create drag and so reduce speed. ■ a similar device on a motor vehicle intended to prevent it from being lifted off the road when traveling at very high speeds.

spoils·man /ˈspoilzmən/ ▶*n.* (*pl.* **-men**) a person who seeks to profit by the spoils system; a person who supports this system.

spoil·sport /ˈspoilˌspôrt/ ▶*n.* a person who behaves in a way that spoils others' pleasure, esp. by not joining in an activity.

spoils sys·tem ▶*n.* the practice of a successful political party giving public office to its supporters.

spoilt /spoilt/ *chiefly Brit.* ▶ past and past participle of SPOIL.

Spo·kane /spōˈkan/ a city in eastern Washington, at the falls of the Spokane River, near the border with Idaho; pop. 195,629.

spoke[1] /spōk/ ▶*n.* each of the bars or wire rods connecting the center of a wheel to its outer edge. ■ each of a set of radial handles projecting from a ship's wheel. ■ each of the metal rods in an umbrella to which the material is attached. ▷Old English *spāca*; related to Dutch *speek,* German *Speiche,* from the base of SPIKE[1]. —**spoked** *adj.* [in *combination*] *a wire-spoked wheel.*

spoke[2] ▶ past of SPEAK.

spo·ken /ˈspōkən/ ▶ past participle of SPEAK.
▶*adj.* [in *combination*] speaking in a specified way: *a blunt-spoken man.*
▶*PHRASE* □ **be spoken for** be already claimed, owned, or reserved. ■ (of a person) already have a romantic commitment: *he knows Claudine is spoken for.*

spoke·shave /ˈspōkˌshāv/ ▶*n.* a small plane with a handle on each side of its blade, used for shaping curved surfaces (originally wheel spokes).
▶*v.* [*trans.*] shape with a plane of this type.

spokes·man /ˈspōksmən/ ▶*n.* (*pl.* **-men**) a person, esp. a man, who makes statements on behalf of another individual or a group: *a spokesman for Greenpeace.* ▷early 16th cent.: formed irregularly from SPOKE[2], on the pattern of words such as *craftsman.*

spokes·mod·el /ˈspōksˌmädl/ ▶*n. informal* an attractive, elegant, and stylishly dressed spokesperson. ▷blend of *spokesperson* and *model.*

spokes·per·son /ˈspōksˌpərsən/ ▶*n.* (*pl.* **-per·sons** or **-peo·ple** /-ˌpēpəl/) a spokesman or spokeswoman (used as a neutral alternative).

spokes·wom·an /ˈspōksˌwo͝omən/ ▶*n.* (*pl.* **-wom·en**) a woman who makes statements on behalf of another individual or a group.

spo·li·a·tion /ˌspōlēˈāshən/ ▶*n.* **1** the action of ruining or destroying something: *the spoliation of the countryside.* **2** the action of taking goods or property from somewhere by illegal or unethical means: *the spoliation of the Church.* ▷late Middle English (denoting pillaging): from Latin *spoliatio(n-),* from the verb *spoliare* 'strip, deprive' (see SPOIL). —**spo·li·a·tor** /ˈspōlēˌātər/ *n.*

spon·da·ic /spänˈdāik/ ▶*adj. Prosody* of or concerning spondees. ■ (of a hexameter) having a spondee as its fifth foot. ▷late 16th cent.: via French or late Latin from Greek *spondeiakos,* from *spondeios* (see SPONDEE).

spon·dee /ˈspändē/ ▶*n. Prosody* a foot consisting of two long (or stressed) syllables. ▷late Middle English: from Old French, or via Latin from Greek *spondeios (pous)* '(foot) of a libation,' from *spondē* 'libation' (being characteristic of music accompanying libations).

spon·dy·li·tis /ˌspändəˈlītis/ ▶*n. Medicine* inflammation of the joints of the backbone. See also ANKYLOSING SPONDYLITIS. ▷mid 19th cent.: from Latin *spondylus* 'vertebra' (from Greek *spondulos*) + -ITIS.

spon·dy·lo·sis /ˌspändəˈlōsis/ ▶*n. Medicine* a painful condition of the spine resulting from the degeneration of the intervertebral disks. ▷early 20th cent.: from Greek *spondulos* 'vertebra' + -OSIS.

sponge /spənj/ ▶*n.* **1** a primitive sedentary aquatic invertebrate with a soft porous body that is typically supported by a framework of fibers or calcareous or glassy spicules. Sponges draw in a current of water to extract nutrients and oxygen. • Phylum Porifera: several classes. **2** a piece of a soft, light, porous substance originally consisting of the fibrous skeleton of such an invertebrate but now usually made of synthetic material. Sponges absorb liquid and are used for washing and cleaning. ■ [in *sing.*] an act of wiping or cleaning with a sponge: *they gave him a quick* ***sponge down.*** ■ such a substance used as padding or insulating material: *the headguard is padded with sponge.* ■ a piece of such a substance impregnated with spermicide and inserted into a woman's vagina as a form of barrier contraceptive. ■ *informal* a heavy drinker. ■ [with *adj.*] metal in a porous form, typically prepared by reduction without fusion or by electrolysis: *platinum sponge.* **3** *Brit.* (also **sponge pudding**) a steamed or baked pudding of fat, flour, and eggs. ■ short for SPONGE CAKE. **4** *informal* a person who lives at someone else's expense.
▶*v.* (**sponging** or **spongeing**) **1** [*trans.*] wipe, rub, or clean with a wet sponge or cloth: *she* ***sponged*** *him* ***down*** *in an attempt to cool his fever.* ■ remove or wipe away (liquid or a mark) in such a way: *I'll go and* ***sponge*** *this orange juice* ***off*** *my dress.* ■ give a decorative mottled or textured effect to (a painted wall or surface) by applying a different shade of paint with a sponge. **2** [*intrans.*] *informal* obtain or accept money or food from other people without doing or intending to do anything in return: *they found they could earn a perfectly good living by* ***sponging off*** *others.* ■ [*trans.*] obtain (something) in such a way: *he edged closer, clearly intending to sponge money from her.* ▷Old English (sense 2 of the *noun*), via Latin from Greek *spongia,* later form of *spongos,* reinforced in Middle English by Old French *esponge.* —**sponge·a·ble** *adj.* —**sponge·like** /ˈspənjˌlīk/ *adj.*

sponge bath ▶*n.* an all-over washing, as given to a person confined to bed, done with a wet sponge or washcloth rather than in a tub or shower.

sponge cake /ˈspənj ˌkāk/ ▶*n.* a very light sweet cake of spongelike consistency, made with little or no fat.

sponge cloth ▶*n.* **1** soft, lightly woven cloth with a slightly wrinkled surface. **2** a cloth made from a thin spongy material, used for cleaning.

sponge pud·ding ▶*n.* see SPONGE (sense 3).

spong·er /ˈspənjər/ ▶*n.* **1** *informal* a person who lives at others' expense. **2** a person who applies paint to pottery using a sponge.

sponge rub·ber ▶*n.* rubber latex processed into a spongelike substance.

sponge tree ▶*n.* another term for HUISACHE.

spon·gi·form /ˈspənjiˌfôrm/ ▶*adj. chiefly Veterinary Medicine* having, relating to, or denoting a porous structure or consistency resembling that of a sponge.

spon·gin /ˈspənjin/ ▶*n. Biochemistry* the horny or fibrous substance found in the skeleton of many sponges.

spon·gy /ˈspənjē/ ▶*adj.* (**-gi·er**, **-gi·est**) like a sponge, esp. in being porous, compressible, elastic, or absorbent: *a soft, spongy blanket of moss.* ■ (of metal) having an open, porous structure: *spongy platinum.* ■ (chiefly of a motor vehicle's braking system) lacking firmness. —**spon·gi·ly** /ˈspənjəlē/ *adv.* —**spon·gi·ness** *n.*

spon·son /ˈspänsən/ ▶*n.* a projection on the side of a boat, ship, or seaplane. ■ a gun platform standing out from a warship's side. ■ a short subsidiary wing that serves to stabilize a seaplane. ■ a buoyancy chamber fitted to a boat's hull, esp. on a canoe. ■ a triangular platform supporting the wheel on a paddle steamer. ▷mid 19th cent.: of unknown origin.

spon·sor /ˈspänsər/ ▶*n.* **1** a person or organization that provides funds for a project or activity carried out by another, in particular: ■ an individual or organization that pays some or all of the costs involved in staging a sporting or artistic event in return for advertising. ■ a person who pledges to donate a certain amount of money to another person after they have participated in a fund-raising event organized on behalf of a charity. ■ a business or organization that pays for or contributes to the costs of a radio or television program in return for advertising. **2** a person who introduces and supports a proposal for legislation: *a leading sponsor of the bill.* ■ a person taking official responsibility for the actions of another: *they act as informants, sponsors, and contacts for new immigrants.* ■ a godparent at a child's

baptism. ■ (esp. in the Roman Catholic Church) a person presenting a candidate for confirmation.
▸*v.* [*trans.*] **1** provide funds for (a project or activity or the person carrying it out): *Joe is being sponsored by his church.* ■ pay some or all of the costs involved in staging (a sporting or artistic event) in return for advertising. ■ pledge to donate a certain sum of money to (someone) after they have participated in a fund-raising event organized on behalf of a charity. ■ [often as *adj.*] (**sponsored**) pledge to donate money because someone is taking part in (such an event): *they raised $70 by a sponsored walk.* **2** introduce and support (a proposal) in a legislative assembly: *Senator Hardin sponsored the bill.* ■ propose and organize (negotiations or talks) between other people or groups: *the U.S. sponsored negotiations between the two sides.* ▷mid 17th cent. (as a noun): from Latin, from *spondere* 'promise solemnly'. The verb dates from the late 19th cent. —**spon·sor·ship** /-,SHip/ *n.*

spon·ta·ne·ous /spän'tānēəs/ ▸*adj.* performed or occurring as a result of a sudden inner impulse or inclination and without premeditation or external stimulus: *the audience broke into spontaneous applause | a spontaneous display of affection.* ■ (of a person) having an open, natural, and uninhibited manner. ■ (of a process or event) occurring without apparent external cause: *spontaneous miscarriages.* ■ *archaic* (of a plant) growing naturally and without being tended or cultivated. ■ *Biology* (of movement or activity in an organism) instinctive or involuntary: *the spontaneous mechanical activity of circular smooth muscle.* ▷mid 17th cent.: from late Latin *spontaneus* (from *(sua) sponte* 'of (one's) own accord') + **-ous**. —**spon·ta·ne·i·ty** /,späntə'nēitē; -'nā-/ *n.* —**spon·ta·ne·ous·ly** *adv.*

THE RIGHT WORD **impromptu, improvised, impulsive, offhand, spontaneous, unpremeditated**

If you're the kind of person who acts first and thinks about it later, your friends are likely to describe you as **spontaneous**, which means that you behave in a very natural way, without prompting or premeditation (*a spontaneous embrace; a spontaneous burst of applause*).

Or they may call you **impulsive**, which has somewhat less positive connotations, suggesting someone who is governed by his or her own moods and whims without regard for others. Although *impulsive* behavior may be admirable (*his impulsive generosity prompted him to empty his pockets*), it is just as likely to be ugly or disruptive (*impulsive buying; an impulsive temper*).

Offhand also has negative overtones, implying behavior that is spontaneous to the point of being cavalier or brusque (*her offhand remarks offended them*).

Unpremeditated is a more formal term, often used in a legal context to describe an impulsive crime committed without forethought (*unpremeditated murder*).

In the world of public speaking, an **extemporaneous** speech is one that is delivered without referring to a written text, although the speaker may have been aware that he or she would be called upon to speak, while an **impromptu** speech is one that the speaker was not expecting to give.

Improvised is often used in the context of a musical or theatrical performance, suggesting a basic structure within which the performers are free to play in a spontaneous manner (*by its very nature, jazz is improvised*). But it has broader applications as well; in fact, anything that is devised on the spur of the moment may be described as *improvised*.

spon·ta·ne·ous com·bus·tion ▸*n.* the ignition of organic matter (e.g., hay or coal) without apparent cause, typically through heat generated internally by rapid oxidation.

spon·ta·ne·ous gen·er·a·tion ▸*n.* *historical* the supposed production of living organisms from nonliving matter, as inferred from the apparent appearance of life in some infusions.

spoof /spo͞of/ *informal* ▸*n.* **1** a humorous imitation of something, typically a film or a particular genre of film, in which its characteristic features are exaggerated for comic effect: *a Robin Hood spoof.* **2** a trick played on someone as a joke.
▸*v.* [*trans.*] **1** imitate (something) while exaggerating its characteristic features for comic effect: *it is a movie that spoofs other movies.* **2** hoax or trick (someone): *they proceeded to spoof Western intelligence with false information.* ■ interfere with (radio or radar signals) so as to make them useless. ▷late 19th cent.: coined by Arthur Roberts (1852–1933), English comedian. —**spoof·er** *n.* —**spoof·er·y** /'spo͞ofərē/ *n.*

spook /spo͝ok/ *informal* ▸*n.* **1** a ghost. **2** a spy: *a CIA spook.* **3** *dated, offensive* a contemptuous term for a black person.
▸*v.* [*trans.*] frighten; unnerve: *they spooked a couple of grizzly bears.* ■ [*intrans.*] (esp. of an animal) take fright suddenly: *he'll spook if we make any noise.* ▷early 19th cent.: from Dutch, of unknown origin.

spook·y /'spo͝okē/ ▸*adj.* (**spook·i·er**, **spook·i·est**) *informal* **1** sinister or ghostly in a way that causes fear and unease: *I bet this place is really spooky late at night.* **2** (of a person or animal) easily frightened; nervous. —**spook·i·ly** /'spo͝okəlē/ *adv.* —**spook·i·ness** *n.*

spool[1] /spo͞ol/ ▸*n.* a cylindrical device on which film, magnetic tape, thread, or other flexible materials can be wound; a reel: *spools of electrical cable.* ■ a cylindrical device attached to a fishing rod and used for winding and unwinding the line as required. ■ [as *adj.*] denoting furniture of a style popular in England in the 17th century and North America in the 19th century, typically ornamented with a series of small knobs resembling spools: *a narrow spool bed.*
▸*v.* **1** [*trans.*] wind (magnetic tape or thread) on to a spool: *he was trying to spool his tapes back into the cassettes with a pencil eraser.* ■ [*intrans.*] be wound on or off a spool: *the plastic reel allows the line to run free as it spools out.* **2** [*intrans.*] (of an engine) increase its speed of rotation, typically to that required for operation: *a jet engine can take up to six seconds to* **spool up**. ▷Middle English (denoting a cylinder on to which spun thread is wound): shortening of Old French *espole* or from Middle Low German *spōle*, of West Germanic origin; related to Dutch *spoel* and German *Spule*. The verb dates from the early 17th cent.

spool[2] ▸*v.* [*trans.*] *Computing* send (data that is intended for printing or processing on a peripheral device) to an intermediate store: *users can set which folder they wish to spool files to.* ▷acronym from *simultaneous peripheral operation online*.

spoon /spo͞on/ ▸*n.* **1** an implement consisting of a small, shallow oval or round bowl on a long handle, used for eating, stirring, and serving food. ■ the contents of such an implement: *three spoons of sugar.* ■ (**spoons**) a pair of spoons held in the hand and beaten together rhythmically as a percussion instrument. **2** a thing resembling a spoon in shape, in particular: ■ (also **spoon bait**) a fishing lure designed to wobble when pulled through the water. ■ an oar with a broad curved blade. ■ *dated Golf* a club with a slightly concave wooden head.
▸*v.* **1** [*trans.*] convey (food) somewhere by using a spoon: *Rosie spooned sugar into her mug.* ■ hit (a ball) up into the air with a soft or weak stroke: *he spooned his shot high over the bar.* **2** [*intrans.*] *informal, dated* (of two people) behave in an amorous way; kiss and cuddle: *I saw them spooning on the beach.* ■ (of two people) lie close together sideways and front to back with bent knees, so as to fit together like spoons. ▷Old English *spōn* 'chip of wood,' of Germanic origin; related to German *Span* 'shaving.' Sense 1 is of Scandinavian origin. The verb dates from the early 18th cent. —**spoon·er** *n.* (in sense 2 of the verb). —**spoon·ful** /-,fo͝ol/ *n.* (*pl.* **-fuls** /-,fo͝olz/).

spoon·bill /'spo͞on,bil/ ▸*n.* a tall mainly white or pinkish wading bird related to ibises, having a long bill with a very broad flat tip. • Genera *Platalea* and *Ajaia*, family Threskiornithidae: several species.

spoon bread ▸*n.* soft cornbread served with a spoon.

spoon·er·ism /'spo͞onə,rizəm/ ▸*n.* a verbal error in which a speaker accidentally transposes the initial sounds or letters of two or more words, often to humorous effect, as in the sentence *you have hissed the mystery lectures*, accidentally spoken instead of the intended sentence *you have missed the history lectures.* ▷early 20th cent.: named after the Rev. W. A. *Spooner* (1844–1930), an English scholar who reputedly made such errors in speaking.

spoon-feed ▸*v.* [*trans.*] feed (someone) by using a spoon. ■ *figurative* provide (someone) with so much help or information that they do not need to think for themselves.

Spoon Riv·er a river that flows for 160 miles (260 km) through central Illinois, associated with the verse of Edgar Lee Masters.

spoon·worm /'spo͞on,wərm/ ▸*n.* an unsegmented wormlike marine invertebrate that lives in burrows, crevices, or discarded shells. Spoonworms typically have a sausage-shaped body with a long proboscis that can be extended over the seabed. • Phylum Echiura.

spoon·y /'spo͞onē/ *informal* ▸*adj.* (**spoon·i·er**, **spoon·i·est**) *dated* sentimentally or foolishly amorous: *I was spoony over Miss Talmadge to the point of idolatry.* ■ *archaic* foolish; silly.
▸*n.* (*pl.* **spoon·ies**) *archaic* a simple, silly, or foolish person. —**spoon·i·ly** /'spo͞onəlē/ *adv.* —**spoon·i·ness** *n.*

spoor /spo͝or; spô(ə)r/ ▸*n.* the track or scent of an animal: *they searched around the hut for a spoor | the trail is marked by wolf spoor.*
▸*v.* [*trans.*] follow the track or scent of (an animal or person): *taking the spear, he set off to spoor the man.* ▷early 19th cent.: from Afrikaans, from Middle Dutch *spor*, of Germanic origin. —**spoor·er** *n.*

Spor·a·des /'spôrə,dēz/ two groups of Greek islands in the Aegean Sea. The **Northern Sporades**, which lie close to the eastern coast of mainland Greece, include the islands of Euboea, Skiros, Skiathos, and Skopelos. The **Southern Sporades**, situated off the western coast of Turkey, include Rhodes and the other islands of the Dodecanese.

spo·rad·ic /spə'radik/ ▸*adj.* occurring at irregular intervals or only in a few places; scattered or isolated: *sporadic fighting broke out.* ▷late 17th cent.: via medieval Latin from Greek *sporadikos*, from *sporas, sporad-* 'scattered'; related to *speirein* 'to sow.' —**spo·rad·i·cal·ly** /-ik(ə)lē/ *adv.*

spo·ran·gi·o·phore /spə'ranjēə,fôr/ ▸*n.* *Botany* (in a fungus) a specialized hypha bearing sporangia.

spo·ran·gi·um /spə'ranjēəm/ ▸*n.* (*pl.* **-gi·a** /-jēə/) *Botany* (in ferns and lower plants) a receptacle in which asexual spores are formed. ▷early 19th cent.: modern Latin, from Greek *spora* 'spore' + *angeion* 'vessel.' —**spo·ran·gi·al** /-jēəl/ *adj.*

spore /spôr/ ▸*n.* *Biology* a minute, typically one-celled, reproductive unit capable of giving rise to a new individual without sexual fusion, characteristic of lower plants, fungi, and protozoans. ■ *Botany* (in a plant exhibiting alternation of generations) a haploid reproductive cell that gives rise to a gametophyte. ■ *Microbiology* (in bacteria) a rounded resistant form adopted by a bacterial cell in adverse conditions. ▷mid 19th cent.: from modern Latin *spora*, from Greek *spora* 'sowing, seed,' from *speirein* 'to sow.'

spork /spôrk/ ▸*n.* a spoon-shaped eating utensil with short tines at the tip. ▷blend of *spoon* and *fork*.

sporo- ▸*comb. form Biology* of or relating to spores: *sporogenesis.* ▷from Greek *spora* 'spore.'

spo·ro·cyst /'spôrə,sist/ ▸*n.* *Zoology* a parasitic fluke in the initial stage of infection in a snail host, developed from a miracidium. ■ (in parasitic sporozoans) an encysted zygote in an invertebrate host.

spo·ro·gen·e·sis /,spôrə'jenəsis/ ▸*n.* *chiefly Botany* the process of spore formation.

spo·rog·e·nous /spə'räjənəs/ ▸*adj.* *chiefly Botany* (of an organism or tissue) producing spores.

spo·rog·o·ny /spə'rägənē/ ▸*n.* *Zoology* the asexual process of spore formation in parasitic sporozoans.

spo·ro·phore /'spôrə,fôr/ ▸*n.* *Botany* the spore-bearing structure of a fungus.

spo·ro·phyte /'spôrə,fīt/ ▸*n.* *Botany* (in the life cycle of plants with alternating generations) the asexual and usually diploid phase, producing spores from which the gametophyte arises. It is the dominant form in vascular plants, e.g., the frond of a fern. —**spo·ro·phyt·ic** /,spôrə'fitik/ *adj.*

spo·ro·tri·cho·sis /,spôrətri'kōsis/ ▸*n.* *Medicine* a chronic fungal infection producing nodules and ulcers in the lymph nodes and skin. • The disease is caused by the fungus *Sporothrix schenckii*.

Spo·ro·zo·a /,spôrə'zōə/ *Zoology & Medicine* a phylum of mainly parasitic spore-forming protozoans that have a complex life cycle with sexual and asexual generations. They include the organisms that cause malaria, babesiosis, coccidiosis, and toxoplasmosis. Also called **Apicomplexa**. ▷modern Latin (plural), from **spore** + Greek *zōia* 'animals.' —**spo·ro·zo·an** /-ən/ *n.* & *adj.*

spo·ro·zo·ite /,spôrə'zō,īt/ ▸*n.* *Zoology & Medicine* a motile sporelike stage in the life cycle of some parasitic sporozoans (e.g., the malaria organism) that is typically the infective agent introduced into a host. ▷late 19th cent.: from **sporo-** 'relating to spores' + Greek *zoion* 'animal' + **-ite**[1].

spor·ran /'spärən/ ▸*n.* a small pouch worn around the waist so as to hang in front of the kilt as part of

S

men's Scottish Highland dress. ▷mid 18th cent.: from Scottish Gaelic *sporan*.

sport /spôrt/ ▶*n.* **1** an activity involving physical exertion and skill in which an individual or team competes against another or others for entertainment: *team sports such as baseball and soccer* | [as *adj.*] (**sports**) *a sports center.* ■ *dated* entertainment; fun: *it was considered great sport to trip him up.* ■ *archaic* a source of amusement or entertainment: *I do not wish to show myself the sport of a man like Williams.* **2** *informal* a person who behaves in a good or specified way in response to teasing, defeat, or a similarly trying situation: *go on, be a sport!* | *Angela's a bad sport.* **3** *Biology* an animal or plant showing abnormal or striking variation from the parent type, esp. in form or color, as a result of spontaneous mutation.
▶*v.* **1** [*trans.*] wear or display (a distinctive or noticeable item): *he was sporting a huge handlebar mustache.* **2** [*intrans.*] amuse oneself or play in a lively, energetic way: *the children sported in the water.* ▷late Middle English (in the sense 'pastime, entertainment'): shortening of DISPORT. —**sport·er** *n.*
▶PHRASES □ **in sport** for fun: *I have assumed the name was given more or less in sport.* □ **make sport of** *dated* make fun of. □ **the sport of kings** horse racing.

sport coat (also **sports coat** or **sport jack·et** or **sports jack·et**) ▶*n.* a man's jacket resembling a suit jacket, for informal wear.

spor·tif /spôr'tēf/ ▶*adj.* (of a person) active or interested in athletic sports: *he was sportif and ready for action.* ■ (of an action or event) intended in fun or as a joke. ■ (of a garment or style of dress) suitable for sport or informal wear; casual.
▶*n.* a person who is active or interested in sport. ▷French.

sport·ing /spôrtiNG/ ▶*adj.* **1** [*attrib.*] connected with or interested in sports: *a major sporting event.* **2** fair and generous in one's behavior or treatment of others, esp. in a game or contest: *it was not very sporting of Smith to hit Gonzales with that pitch.* —**sport·ing·ly** *adv.* (in sense 2).

sport·ing chance ▶*n.* [in *sing.*] a reasonable chance of winning or succeeding: *I'll give you a sporting chance.*

spor·tive /'spôrtiv/ ▶*adj.* playful; lighthearted. ■ *archaic* amorous or lustful. —**spor·tive·ly** *adv.* —**spor·tive·ness** *n.*

sports bar ▶*n.* a bar where televised sporting events are shown continuously.

sports car ▶*n.* a low-built car designed for performance at high speeds.

sports·cast /'spôrts,kast/ ▶*n.* a broadcast of sports news or a sports event. —**sports·cast·er** *n.* —**sports·cast·ing** *n.*

sports·find·er /'spôrts,fīndər/ ▶*n.* *Photography* a direct-vision viewfinder typically consisting of a simple frame that allows action outside the field of view of the camera to be seen. This is often fitted to twin-lens reflex cameras.

sports·man /'spôrtsmən/ ▶*n.* (*pl.* **-men**) a man who takes part in a sport, esp. as a professional. ■ a person who behaves sportingly. ■ *dated* a man who hunts or shoots wild animals as a pastime. —**sports·man·like** /-,līk/ *adj.* —**sports·man·ship** /-,SHip/ *n.*

sports·per·son /'spôrts,pərsən/ ▶*n.* (*pl.* **-per·sons** or **-peo·ple** /-,pēpəl/) a sportsman or sportswoman (used as a neutral alternative).

sport·ster /'spôrtstər/ ▶*n.* *informal* a sports car.

sports·wear /'spôrts,we(ə)r/ ▶*n.* clothes worn for casual outdoor use or for such sports activities as jogging, cycling, tennis, sailing, etc.

sports·wom·an /'spôrts,wo͝omən/ ▶*n.* (*pl.* **-wom·en**) a woman who takes part in sports, esp. professionally. —**sports·wom·an·ship** /-,SHip/ *n.*

sports·writ·er /'spôrts,rītər/ ▶*n.* a journalist who writes about sports. —**sports·writ·ing** /-tiNG/ *n.*

sport u·til·i·ty ve·hi·cle (abbr.: **SUV**) ▶*n.* a high-performance four-wheel-drive vehicle.

sport·y /'spôrtē/ ▶*adj.* (**sport·i·er**, **sport·i·est**) *informal* flashy or showy in dress or behavior. ■ (of clothing) casual yet attractively stylish: *a sporty outfit.* ■ (of a car) compact and with fast acceleration: *a sporty red coupe.* ■ fond of or good at sports. —**sport·i·ly** /'spôrtəlē/ *adv.* —**sport·i·ness** *n.*

spor·u·late /'spôryə,lāt/ ▶*v.* [*intrans.*] *Biology* produce or form a spore or spores. —**spor·u·la·tion** /,spôryə'lāSHən/ *n.*

spor·ule /'spôryo͞ol/ ▶*n.* *Biology* a small spore. —**spor·u·lar** /-yələr/ *adj.*

s'pose /s(ə)'pōz/ ▶*v.* nonstandard spelling of SUPPOSE, representing informal speech.

spot /spät/ ▶*n.* **1** a small round or roundish mark, differing in color or texture from the surface around it: *ladybugs have black spots on their red wing covers.* ■ a small mark or stain: *a spot of mildew on the wall.* ■ a pimple. ■ *archaic* a moral blemish or stain. ■ a pip on a domino, playing card, or die. ■ [in *combination*] *informal* a banknote of a specified value: *a ten-spot.* **2** a particular place or point: *a nice secluded spot* | *an ideal picnic spot.* ■ [with *adj.*] a small feature or part of something with a particular quality: *his bald spot* | *there was one bright spot in a night of dismal failure.* ■ a position within a listing; a ranking: *the runner-up spot.* ■ *Sports* an advantage allowed to a player as a handicap. ■ a place for an individual item within a show: *she couldn't do her usual singing spot in the club.* **3** *informal, chiefly Brit.* a small amount of something: *a spot of rain.* **4** [as *adj.*] denoting a system of trading in which commodities or currencies are delivered and paid for immediately after a sale: *trading in the spot markets* | *the current spot price.* **5** short for SPOTLIGHT.
▶*v.* (**spot·ted**, **spot·ting**) **1** [*trans.*] see, notice, or recognize (someone or something) that is difficult to detect or that one is searching for: *Andrew spotted the ad in the paper* | *the men were spotted by police.* ■ (usu. **be spotted**) recognize that (someone) has a particular talent, esp. for sports or show business: *we were spotted by a talent scout.* ■ [*intrans.*] *Military* locate an enemy's position, typically from the air: *they were* **spotting for** *enemy aircraft.* **2** [*trans.*] (usu. **be spotted**) mark with spots: *the velvet was spotted with stains.* ■ [*intrans.*] become marked with spots: *a damp atmosphere causes the flowers to spot.* ■ cover (a surface or area) thinly: *thorn trees spotted the land.* ■ *archaic* stain or sully the moral character or qualities of. **3** [*trans.*] place (a billiard ball or football) on its designated starting point. **4** [with *two objs.*] *informal* give or lend (money) to (someone): *I'll spot you $300.* ■ allow (an advantage) to (someone) in a game or sport: *the higher-rated team spots the lower-rated team the difference in their handicaps.* **5** [*trans.*] observe or assist (a gymnast) during a performance in order to minimize the chance of injury to the gymnast. ▷Middle English: perhaps from Middle Dutch *spotte*. The sense 'notice, recognize' arose from the early 19th-cent. slang use 'note as a suspect or criminal.'
▶PHRASES □ **hit the spot** *informal* be exactly what is required: *the cup of coffee hit the spot.* □ **in a spot** *informal* in a difficult situation. □ **on the spot 1** without any delay; immediately: *he offered me the job on the spot.* **2** at the scene of an action or event: *journalists on the spot reported no progress.* □ **put someone on the spot** *informal* force someone into a situation in which they must make a difficult decision or answer a difficult question.

spot check ▶*n.* a test made without warning on a randomly selected subject.
▶*v.* (**spot-check**) [*trans.*] subject (someone or something) to such a test.

spot·less /'spätlis/ ▶*adj.* absolutely clean or pure; immaculate: *a spotless white apron.* —**spot·less·ly** *adv.* —**spot·less·ness** *n.*

spot·light /'spät,līt/ ▶*n.* a lamp projecting a narrow, intense beam of light directly onto a place or person, esp. a performer on stage. ■ a beam of light from a lamp of this kind: *the knife flashed in the spotlight.* ■ (**the spotlight**) *figurative* intense scrutiny or public attention: *she was constantly* **in the** *media* **spotlight**.
▶*v.* (*past* and *past part.* **-light·ed** or **-lit** /-lit/) [*trans.*] illuminate with a spotlight: *the dancers are spotlighted from time to time throughout the evening.* ■ *figurative* direct attention to (a particular problem or situation): *the protest spotlighted the overcrowding in federal prisons.*

spot me·ter ▶*n.* *Photography* a photometer that measures the intensity of light received within a cone of small angle, usually 2° or less.

spot news ▶*n.* news reported of events as they occur.

Spot·syl·va·nia Coun·ty /,spätsəl'vānēə/ a rural county in northeastern Virginia, site of Civil War battles including those at Fredericksburg and Spotsylvania Court House; pop. 90,395.

spot·ted /'spätid/ ▶*adj.* marked or decorated with spots. —**spot·ted·ness** *n.*

spot·ted ca·vy ▶*n.* another term for PACA.

spot·ted deer ▶*n.* another term for AXIS DEER.

spot·ted dick ▶*n.* *Brit.* a suet pudding containing currants.

spot·ted fe·ver ▶*n.* any of a number of diseases characterized by fever and skin spots: ■ cerebrospinal meningitis. ■ typhus. ■ see ROCKY MOUNTAIN SPOTTED FEVER.

spot·ted hy·e·na /hī'ēnə/ ▶*n.* a southern African hyena that has a grayish-yellow to reddish coat with irregular dark spots, and a loud laughing call. Also called LAUGHING HYENA. • *Crocuta crocuta*, family Hyaenidae.

spotted hyena

spot·ted knap·weed ▶*n.* a biennial herb of European origin with pink flowers on prickly stems. It is established across most of North America and is regarded as a noxious weed nearly everywhere. • *Centaurea biebersteinii*, family Compositae.

spot·ted tur·tle ▶*n.* a North American freshwater turtle with few or numerous yellow spots on the carapace. Once abundant, esp. along the east coast of the U.S., the spotted turtle is protected in many areas. • *Clemmys guttata*, family Emydidae.

spotted turtle

spot·ter /'spätər/ ▶*n.* *informal* a person employed by a company or business to keep watch on employees or customers. ■ an aviator or aircraft employed in locating or observing enemy positions: [as *adj.*] *spotter planes.* ■ a person who observes or assists a gymnast or weightlifter during a performance or practice in order to minimize the chance of injury to the gymnast or weightlifter.

spot·ty /'spätē/ ▶*adj.* (**-ti·er**, **-ti·est**) marked with spots: *a spotty purple flower.* ■ of uneven quality; patchy: *his spotty record on the environment.* —**spot·ti·ly** /'spätəlē/ *adv.* —**spot·ti·ness** *n.*

spot-weld ▶*v.* [*trans.*] join by welding at a number of separate points: *the wire was spot-welded in place.*
▶*n.* (**spot weld**) each of the welds so made. —**spot weld·er** *n.* —**spot weld·ing** *n.*

spous·al /'spouzəl/ ▶*adj.* [*attrib.*] *Law* of or relating to marriage or to a husband or wife: *the spousal benefits of married couples.*

spouse /spous/ ▶*n.* a husband or wife, considered in relation to their partner. ▷Middle English: from Old French *spous(e)*, variant of *espous(e)*, from Latin *sponsus* (masculine), *sponsa* (feminine), past participles of *spondere* 'betroth.'

spout /spout/ ▶*n.* **1** a tube or lip projecting from a container, through which liquid can be poured: *a teapot with a chipped spout.* ■ a pipe or trough through which water may be carried away or from which it can flow out. ■ a sloping trough for conveying something to a lower level; a chute. ■ *historical* a lift in a pawnshop used to convey pawned items up for storage. **2** a stream of liquid issuing from somewhere with great force: *the tall spouts of geysers.* ■ the plume of water vapor ejected from the blowhole of a whale: *the spout of an occasional whale.*
▶*v.* [*trans.*] **1** send out (liquid) forcibly in a stream: *volcanoes spouted ash and lava.* ■ [*intrans.*] (of a liquid) flow out of somewhere in such a way: *blood was spouting from the cuts on my hand.* ■ (of a whale or dolphin) eject (water vapor and air) through its blowhole. **2** express (one's views or ideas) in a lengthy, declamatory, and unreflecting way: *he was spouting platitudes about animal rights* | [*intrans.*] *they like to* **spout off** *at each other.* ▷Middle English (as a verb): from Middle Dutch *spouten*, from an imitative base shared by Old

Norse *spýta* 'to spit.' —**spout·ed** *adj.* —**spout·er** *n.* —**spout·less** *adj.*

▸*PHRASE* □ **up the spout** *Brit., informal* **1** no longer working, or unlikely to be useful or successful. **2** (of a woman) pregnant. **3** pawned: *by Friday, half his belongings were up the spout.*

spp. ▸*abbr.* species (plural).

SPQR ▸*abbr.* ■ *historical* the Senate and people of Rome. ▷from Latin *Senatus Populusque Romanus.*

spr. ▸*abbr.* spring.

Sprach·ge·fühl /'SHpräkgə,fo͝ol/ ▸*n.* intuitive feeling for the natural idiom of a language. ■ the essential character of a language. ▷German, from *Sprache* 'speech, a language' + *Gefühl* 'feeling.'

sprad·dle /'spradl/ ▸*v.* [*trans.*] [usu. as *adj.*] (**spraddled**) spread (one's legs) far apart: *the cat's spraddled hind legs.* ▷mid 17th cent. (in the sense 'sprawl'): probably from *sprad*, dialect past participle of **SPREAD**.

sprag /sprag/ ▸*n.* **1** a simple brake on a vehicle, esp. a stout stick or bar inserted between the spokes of a wheel to check its motion. ■ a one-way clutch that keeps a vehicle from rolling backwards. **2** *Mining* a prop used to support a roof, wall, or seam. ▷mid 19th cent: of unknown origin.

sprain /sprān/ ▸*v.* [*trans.*] wrench or twist the ligaments of (an ankle, wrist, or other joint) violently so as to cause pain and swelling but not dislocation: *he left in a wheelchair after spraining an ankle.*

▸*n.* the result of such a wrench or twist of a joint. ▷early 17th cent.: of unknown origin.

sprang /spraNG/ ▸ past of **SPRING**.

USAGE See usage at **SPRING**.

sprat /sprat/ ▸*n.* a small marine fish of the herring family, widely caught for food and fish products. • *Sprattus* and other genera, family Clupeidae: several species, in particular *S. sprattus* of European inshore waters. ■ any of a number of small fishes that resemble the true sprats, e.g., the sand eel. ▷late 16th cent.: variant of Old English *sprot*, of unknown origin.

Sprat·ly Is·lands /'spratlē/ a group of small islands and coral reefs in the South China Sea, between Vietnam and Borneo. Dispersed over a distance of about 600 miles (965 km), the islands are variously claimed by China, Taiwan, Vietnam, the Philippines, and Malaysia.

sprawl /sprôl/ ▸*v.* [*intrans.*] sit, lie, or fall with one's arms and legs spread out in an ungainly or awkward way: *the door shot open, sending him sprawling across the pavement | she lay sprawled on the bed.* ■ spread out over a large area in an untidy or irregular way: *the town sprawled along several miles of cliff top.* | [as *adj.*] (**sprawling**) *the sprawling suburbs.*

▸*n.* [usu. in *sing.*] an ungainly or carelessly relaxed position in which one's arms and legs are spread out: *she fell into a sort of luxurious sprawl.* ■ a group or mass of something that has spread out in an untidy or irregular way: *a sprawl of buildings.* ■ the expansion of an urban or industrial area into the adjoining countryside in a way perceived to be disorganized and unattractive: *the growth of urban sprawl.* ■ such an area: *Washington's suburban sprawl.* ▷Old English *spreawlian* 'move the limbs convulsively'; related to Danish *sprælle* 'kick or splash around.' The noun dates from the early 18th cent. —**sprawl·ing·ly** *adv.*

spray[1] /sprā/ ▸*n.* liquid that is blown or driven through the air in the form of tiny drops: *a torrent of white foam and spray | a fine spray of mud.* ■ a liquid preparation that can be forced out of a can or other container in such a form: *a can of insect spray.* ■ a can or container holding such a preparation. ■ an act of applying such a preparation: *refresh your flowers with a quick spray.*

▸*v.* [*trans.*] apply (liquid) to someone or something in the form of a shower of tiny drops: *the product can be sprayed on to wet or dry hair.* ■ [*trans.*] sprinkle or cover (someone or something) with a shower of tiny drops of liquid: *she sprayed herself with perfume.* ■ [*intrans.*] (of liquid) be driven through the air or forced out of something in such a form: *water sprayed into the air.* ■ [*trans.*] treat (a plant) with insecticide or herbicide in such a way: *avoid spraying your plants with pesticides.* ■ scatter (something) somewhere with great force: *the truck shuddered to a halt, spraying gravel from under its wheels.* ■ [*trans.*] fire a rapid succession of bullets at: *enemy gunners sprayed the decks of the warships.* ■ [*trans.*] (of a male cat) direct a stream of urine over (an object or area) to mark a territory. ■ [*trans.*] (in a sporting context) kick, hit, or throw (the ball) in an unpredictable or inaccurate direction: *he began his round by spraying his fairway shots.* ▷early 17th cent. (earlier as *spry*): related to Middle Dutch *spra(e)yen* 'sprinkle.' —**spray·a·ble** *adj.* —**spray·er** *n.*

spray[2] ▸*n.* a stem or small branch of a tree or plant, bearing flowers and foliage: ***a spray of** honeysuckle.* ■ a bunch of cut flowers arranged in an attractive way. ■ a brooch in the form of a bouquet of flowers. ▷Middle English: representing late Old English *(e)sprei*, recorded in personal and place names, of unknown origin.

spray·deck /'sprā,dek/ ▸*n.* a flexible cover that is fitted to the opening in the top of a kayak to form a waterproof seal around the kayaker's body.

spray-dry ▸*v.* [*trans.*] dry (a foodstuff or a ceramic material) by spraying particles of it into a current of hot air, the water in the particles being rapidly evaporated. —**spray dry·er** *n.*

spray gun ▸*n.* a device resembling a gun that is used to spray a liquid such as paint or pesticide under pressure.

spray-paint ▸*v.* [*trans.*] (often **be spray-painted**) paint (an image or message) onto a surface with a spray. ■ paint (a surface) with a spray: *they were spray-painting the chairs.*

▸*n.* (**spray paint**) paint that is contained in an aerosol can for the purpose of spraying onto a surface.

spray·skirt /'sprā,skərt/ ▸*n.* another term for **SPRAY-DECK**.

spread /spred/ ▸*v.* (*past* and *past part.* **spread**) **1** [*trans.*] open out (something) so as to extend its surface area, width, or length: *I spread a towel on the sand and sat down | she helped Chris to **spread out** the map.* ■ stretch out (arms, legs, hands, fingers, or wings) so that they are far apart: *the swan spread its wings.* **2** [no *obj.*, with *adverbial*] extend over a large or increasing area: *she stood at the window looking at the town spread out below.* ■ (**spread out**) (of a group of people) move apart so as to cover a wider area: *the Marines spread out across the docks.* ■ [with *obj.* and *adverbial*] distribute or disperse (something) over a certain area: *volcanic eruptions spread dust high into the stratosphere.* ■ gradually reach or cause to reach a larger and larger area or more and more people: [*intrans.*] *the violence spread from the city to the suburbs |* [*trans.*] *she's always spreading rumors about other people.* ■ (of people, animals, or plants) become distributed over a large or larger area: *the owls have spread as far north as Yellowknife.* ■ [with *obj.* and *adverbial*] distribute (something) in a specified way: *you can **spread** the payments **over** as long a period as you like.* **3** [with *obj.* and *adverbial*] apply (a substance) to an object or surface in an even layer: *he sighed, spreading jam on a croissant.* ■ cover (a surface) with a substance in such a way: *spread each slice thinly with mayonnaise.* ■ [no *obj.*, with *adverbial*] be able to be applied in such a way: *the whipped butter spreads easily.* **4** [*trans.*] *archaic* lay (a table) for a meal.

▸*n.* **1** the fact or process of spreading over an area: *the spread of AIDS | the spread of the urban population into rural areas.* **2** the extent, width, or area covered by something: *the male's antlers can attain a spread of six feet.* ■ the wingspan of a bird. ■ an expanse or amount of something: *the green spread of the park.* ■ a large farm or ranch. **3** the range or variety of something: *a wide spread of ages.* ■ the difference between two rates or prices: *the very narrow spread between borrowing and deposit rates.* ■ short for **POINT SPREAD**. **4** a soft paste that can be applied in a layer to bread or other food. **5** an article or advertisement covering several columns or pages of a newspaper or magazine, esp. one on two facing pages: *a double-page spread.* ■ a bedspread. **6** *informal* a large and impressively elaborate meal. ▷Old English *-sprǣdan* (used in combinations); related to Dutch *spreiden* and German *spreiten.* —**spread·a·ble** *adj.* (usu. in sense 3).

▸*PHRASES* □ **spread like wildfire** see **WILDFIRE**. □ **spread oneself too thin** be involved in so many different activities or projects that one's time and energy are not used to good effect. □ **spread one's wings** see **WING**.

spread-ea·gle ▸*v.* [*trans.*] (usu. **be spread-eagled**) stretch (someone) out with their arms and legs extended: *he lay spread-eagled in the road.* ■ [*intrans.*] *Skating* perform a spread eagle.

▸*n.* (**spread ea·gle**) an emblematic representation of an eagle with its legs and wings extended. ■ *Figure Skating* a straight glide made with the feet in a line, with the heels touching, and the arms stretched out to either side.

▸*adj.* **1** stretched out with one's arms and legs extended: *prisoners are chained to their beds, spread-eagle, for days at a time.* **2** loudly or aggressively patriotic about the U.S.: *spread-eagle oratory.*

spread·er /'spredər/ ▸*n.* a device used for spreading or scattering a substance over a wide area. ■ a person who spreads or disseminates something: *they were spreaders of terror.* ■ [often in *combination*] a device that spreads apart one thing from another: *rubber toe-spreaders used for pedicures.* ■ a bar attached to the mast of a yacht in order to spread the angle of the upper shrouds.

spread·sheet /'spred,SHēt/ ▸*n.* a computer program used chiefly for accounting, in which figures arranged in the rows and columns of a grid can be manipulated and used in calculations.

▸*v.* [*intrans.*] [usu. as *n.*] (**spreadsheeting**) use such a computer program.

Sprech·ge·sang /'SHprekgə,zäNG/ (also **sprech·ge·sang**) ▸*n.* *Music* a style of dramatic vocalization intermediate between speech and song. ▷German, literally 'speech song.'

Sprech·stim·me /'SHprek,SHtimə/ (also **sprech·stim·me**) ▸*n.* *Music* another term for **SPRECHGESANG**. ■ the kind of voice used in Sprechgesang. ▷German, literally 'speech voice.'

spree /sprē/ ▸*n.* a spell or sustained period of unrestrained activity of a particular kind: *he went on a six-month crime spree | a shopping spree.* ■ a spell of unrestrained drinking.

▸*v.* (**sprees, spreed, spree·ing**) [*intrans.*] *dated* take part in a spree. ▷late 18th cent.: of unknown origin.

sprei·te /sprīt; 'SHprītə/ ▸*n.* (*pl.* **sprei·ten** /'sprītn; 'SHprī-/ or **spreites**) *Paleontology* a banded pattern of uncertain origin found in the infill of the burrows of certain fossil invertebrates. ▷1960s: from German *Spreite* 'layer, lamina.'

sprez·za·tu·ra /,spretsə't(y)o͝orə/ ▸*n.* studied carelessness, esp. as a characteristic quality or style of art or literature. ▷Italian.

sprig[1] /sprig/ ▸*n.* a small stem bearing leaves or flowers, taken from a bush or plant: *a sprig of holly.* ■ a descendant or younger member of a family or social class: *a sprig of the French nobility.* ■ *archaic, chiefly derogatory* a young man. ■ a small molded decoration applied to a piece of pottery before firing.

▸*v.* [*trans.*] decorate (pottery) with small, separately molded designs. ▷Middle English: from or related to Low German *sprick.* —**sprig·gy** *adj.*

sprig[2] ▸*n.* another term for **GLAZIER'S POINT**. ▷Middle English: of unknown origin.

sprigged /sprigd/ ▸*adj.* (chiefly of fabric or paper) decorated with a design of sprigs of leaves or flowers.

spright·ly /'sprītlē/ (also **sprite·ly**) ▸*adj.* (**-li·er, -li·est**) (esp. of an old person) lively; full of energy: *she was quite sprightly for her age.* ▷late 16th cent.: from *spright* (rare variant of **SPRITE**) + **-LY**[1]. —**spright·li·ness** *n.*

spring /spriNG/ ▸*v.* (*past* **sprang** /spraNG/ or **sprung** /sprəNG/; *past part.* **sprung**) **1** [*intrans.*] move or jump suddenly or rapidly upward or forward: *I sprang out of bed | figurative they sprang to her defense.* ■ [*intrans.*] move rapidly or suddenly from a constrained position by or as if by the action of a spring: *the drawer sprang open.* ■ operate or cause to operate by means of a mechanism: [*trans.*] *he prepared to spring his trap |* [*intrans.*] *the engine sprang into life.* ■ [*trans.*] cause (a game bird) to rise from cover. ■ [*trans.*] *informal* bring about the escape or release of (a prisoner): *the president sought to spring the hostages.* **2** [*intrans.*] (**spring from**) originate or arise from: *madness and creativity could spring from the same source.* ■ appear suddenly or unexpectedly from: *tears sprang from his eyes.* ■ (**spring up**) suddenly develop or appear: *a terrible storm sprang up.* ■ [*trans.*] (**spring something on**) present or propose something suddenly or unexpectedly to (someone): *we decided to spring a surprise on them.* **3** [*trans.*] [usu. as *adj.*] (**sprung**) cushion or fit (a vehicle or item of furniture) with springs: *a fully sprung mattress.* **4** [*intrans.*] (esp. of wood) become warped or split. ■ [*trans.*] (of a boat) suffer splitting of (a mast or other part). **5** [*intrans.*] (**spring for**) *informal* pay for, esp. as a treat for someone else: *he's never offered to spring for dinner.* ■ [*trans.*] *archaic* spend (money): *he might spring a few pennies more.*

▸*n.* **1** the season after winter and before summer, in which vegetation begins to appear, in the northern hemisphere from March to May and in the southern hemisphere from September to November: *in spring the garden is a feast of blossom |* [as *adj.*] *spring* rain | *figurative he was in the spring of his years.* ■ *Astronomy* the period from the vernal equinox to the summer solstice. ■ short for SPRING TIDE. **2** a resilient device, typically a helical metal coil, that can be pressed or pulled but returns to its former shape when released, used chiefly to exert constant tension or absorb movement. ■ the ability to spring back strongly; elasticity: *the mattress has lost its spring.* **3** [in *sing.*] a sudden jump upward or forward: *with a sudden spring, he leapt onto the table.* ■ *informal, dated* an escape or release from prison. **4** a place where water or oil wells up from an underground source, or the basin or flow formed in such a way: [as *adj.*] *spring water.* ■ *figurative* the origin or a source of something: *the place was a spring of musical talent.* **5** an upward curvature of a ship's deck planking from the horizontal. ■ a split in a wooden plank or spar under strain. ▷Old English *spring* (noun), *springan* (verb), of Germanic origin; related to Dutch and German *springen.* Early use in the senses 'head of a well' and 'rush out in a stream' gave rise to the figurative use 'originate.' **—spring·less** *adj.* **—spring·like** /-ˌlīk/ *adj.*

▸PHRASE □ **spring a leak** (of a boat or container) develop a leak. [originally a phrase in nautical use, referring to timbers springing out of position.]

USAGE The past tense of **spring** is **sprang**, although occasionally one hears, and even reads, **sprung**. The past participle is **sprung**: *"Not only might the hose spring a leak," said Crawford, "but it sprang two yesterday and has sprung yet again!"*

spring 2

spring beau·ty ▸*n.* a spring-flowering succulent plant of the purslane family. • Genus *Claytonia*, family Portulacaceae: several species, in particular the white- or pink-flowered *C. virginica*, found in moist woods in North America.

spring·board /ˈspriNGˌbôrd/ ▸*n.* a strong, flexible board from which someone can jump in order to gain added impetus when performing a dive or a gymnastic movement. ■ *figurative* a thing that lends impetus or assistance to a particular action, enterprise, or development: *an economic plan that may be the springboard for recovery.*

spring·bok /ˈspriNGˌbäk/ ▸*n.* a gazelle with a characteristic habit of leaping (pronking) when disturbed, forming large herds on arid plains in southern Africa. • *Antidorcas marsupialis*, family Bovidae. ▷late 18th cent.: from Afrikaans, from Dutch *springen* 'to spring' + *bok* 'antelope.'

spring chick·en ▸*n.* **1** [usu. with *negative*] *informal* a young person: *you're no spring chicken yourself anymore.* **2** a young chicken for eating (originally available only in spring).

spring clean·ing ▸*n.* a thorough cleaning of a house or room, typically undertaken in spring.

▸*v.* **(spring-clean)** [*trans.*] clean (a home or room) thoroughly: *it was Veronica who spring-cleaned the apartment.*

Spring·dale /ˈspriNGˌdāl/ a commercial and agricultural city in northwestern Arkansas; pop. 45,798.

springe /sprinj/ ▸*n.* a noose or snare for catching small game. ▷Middle English: from the base of SPRING.

spring e·qui·nox ▸*n.* another term for VERNAL EQUINOX.

spring·er /ˈspriNGər/ ▸*n.* **1** (usu. **spring·er span·iel**) a small spaniel of a breed originally used to spring game. There are two main breeds, the **English springer spaniel**, typically black and white or brown and white, and the less common red and white **Welsh springer spaniel**. **2** *Architecture* the lowest stone in an arch, where the curve begins. **3** a cow or heifer near to calving.

spring·er·le /SHpriNGərlə/ ▸*n.* a German anise-flavored Christmas cookie with an embossed design on top made with a special rolling pin. ▷German dialect *Springerle*, literally 'little jumping horses.'

spring fe·ver ▸*n.* a feeling of restlessness and excitement felt at the beginning of spring.

Spring·field[1] /ˈspriNGˌfēld/ **1** the state capital of Illinois; pop. 111,454. It was the home and burial place of Abraham Lincoln. **2** a city in southwestern Massachusetts, on the Connecticut River; pop. 152,082. It was first settled in 1636. **3** a city in southwestern Missouri, on the northern edge of the Ozark Mountains; pop. 151,580. **4** a city in west central Ohio, west of Columbus and northeast of Dayton; pop. 65,358. **5** a city in western Oregon, on the Willamette River, an eastern suburb of Eugene; pop. 52,864.

Spring·field[2], Dusty (1939–99), British pop-rock singer; born *Mary O'Brien*. Her hits include "You Don't Have to Say You Love Me" (1966) and "What Have I Done to Deserve This" (1987). Among her albums are *Dusty in Memphis* (1969), *Reputation* (1990), and *A Very Fine Love* (1995).

spring·form pan /ˈspriNGˌfôrm/ ▸*n.* a round cake pan with a removable bottom that is held in place by a sprung collar forming the sides.

spring·hare /ˈspriNGˌhe(ə)r/ (also **spring·haas** /ˈspriNGˌhäs/) ▸*n.* (*pl.* **-hares** also **-haas**) a large nocturnal burrowing rodent resembling a miniature kangaroo, with a rabbitlike head, a long bushy tail, and long hind limbs, native to southern Africa. • *Pedetes capensis*, the only member of the family Pedetidae.

spring line ▸*n.* a hawser laid out diagonally aft from a ship's bow or forward from a ship's stern and secured to a fixed point in order to prevent movement or assist maneuvering.

spring-load·ed ▸*adj.* containing a compressed or stretched spring pressing one part against another: *a spring-loaded clothespin.*

spring lock ▸*n.* a type of lock with a spring-loaded bolt that requires a key to open it, as distinct from a deadbolt.

spring on·ion ▸*n.* British term for GREEN ONION.

spring peep·er ▸*n.* see PEEPER[2].

spring roll ▸*n.* an Asian snack consisting of rice paper filled with minced vegetables and usually meat, rolled into a cylinder and fried.

Spring·steen /ˈspriNGˌstēn/, Bruce (Frederick Joseph) (1949–), U.S. rock singer, songwriter, and guitarist; noted for his songs about working-class life in the U.S. Notable albums: *Born to Run* (1975) and *Born in the U.S.A.* (1984).

spring·tail /ˈspriNGˌtāl/ ▸*n.* a minute primitive wingless insect that has a springlike organ under the abdomen that enables it to leap when disturbed. Springtails are abundant in the soil and leaf litter. • Order Collembola: many families.

spring·tide ▸*n.* *poetic/literary* term for SPRINGTIME.

spring tide /ˈspriNG ˌtīd/ ▸*n.* a tide just after a new or full moon, when there is the greatest difference between high and low water.

spring·time /ˈspriNGˌtīm/ ▸*n.* the season of spring. ■ *figurative* or *poetic/literary* the early part or first stage of something: *the springtime of their marriage.*

spring train·ing ▸*n.* *Baseball* the preseason period, esp. in February and March, when baseball players prepare for the upcoming season.

spring·y /ˈspriNGē/ ▸*adj.* (**spring·i·er**, **spring·i·est**) springing back quickly when squeezed or stretched; elastic: *the springy turf.* ■ (of movements) light and confident: *he left the room with a springy step.* **—spring·i·ly** /ˈspriNGəlē/ *adv.* **—spring·i·ness** *n.*

sprin·kle /ˈspriNGkəl/ ▸*v.* **1** [*trans.*] scatter or pour small drops or particles of a substance over (an object or surface): *I sprinkled the floor with water.* ■ scatter or pour (small drops or particles of a substance) over an object or surface: *sprinkle sesame seeds over the top.* ■ *figurative* distribute or disperse something randomly or irregularly throughout (something): *he sprinkled his conversation with quotations.* ■ *figurative* place or attach (a number of things) at irregularly spaced intervals: *a dress with little daisies sprinkled all over it.* **2** [*intrans.*] **(it sprinkles, it is sprinkling**, etc.) rain very lightly: *it began to sprinkle.*

▸*n.* **1** a small quantity or amount of something scattered over an object or surface: ***a generous sprinkle of** pepper* | *figurative fiction with **a sprinkle of** fact.* **2** [in *sing.*] a light rain. **3** (**sprinkles**) tiny sugar shapes, typically strands and balls, used for decorating cakes and desserts. ▷late Middle English: perhaps from Middle Dutch *sprenkelen.*

sprin·kler /ˈspriNGk(ə)lər/ ▸*n.* a device that sprays water. ■ a device used for watering lawns. ■ an automatic fire extinguisher installed in the ceilings of a building.

sprin·kling /ˈspriNGk(ə)liNG/ ▸*n.* a small thinly distributed amount of something: ***a sprinkling of** gray in his hair.*

sprint /sprint/ ▸*v.* [*intrans.*] run at full speed over a short distance: *I saw Charlie sprinting through the traffic toward me.*

▸*n.* an act or short spell of running at full speed. ■ a short, fast race in which the competitors run a distance of 400 meters or less: *the 100 meters sprint.* ■ a short, fast race or exercise in cycling, swimming, horse racing, etc. ▷late 18th cent. (as a dialect term meaning 'a bound or spring'): related to Swedish *spritta.* **—sprint·er** *n.*

sprint·ing /ˈsprintiNG/ ▸*n.* the competitive athletic sport of running distances of 400 meters or less.

sprit /sprit/ ▸*n.* *Sailing* a small spar reaching diagonally from low on a mast to the upper outer corner of a sail. ▷Old English *sprēot* '(punting) pole'; related to SPROUT.

sprite /sprīt/ ▸*n.* **1** an elf or fairy. **2** a computer graphic that may be moved on-screen and otherwise manipulated as a single entity. **3** a faint flash, typically red, sometimes emitted in the upper atmosphere over a thunderstorm owing to the collision of high-energy electrons with air molecules. ▷Middle English: alteration of *sprit*, a contraction of SPIRIT.

sprite·ly ▸*adj.* variant spelling of SPRIGHTLY.

sprit·sail /ˈspritˌsāl; -səl/ ▸*n.* a sail extended by a sprit. ■ *historical* a sail extended by a yard set under a ship's bowsprit.

spritz /sprits/ ▸*v.* [*trans.*] squirt or spray something at or onto (something) in quick short bursts: *she spritzed her neck with cologne.*

▸*n.* an act or an instance of squirting or spraying in quick short bursts. ▷early 20th cent.: from German *spritzen* 'to squirt.'

spritz·er /ˈspritsər/ ▸*n.* a mixture of wine and soda water. ▷1960s: from German *Spritzer* 'a splash.'

sprock·et /ˈspräkit/ ▸*n.* each of several projections on the rim of a wheel that engage with the links of a chain or with holes in film, tape, or paper. ■ (also **sprock·et wheel**) a wheel with teeth of this kind. ▷mid 16th cent. (denoting a triangular piece of timber used in a roof): of unknown origin.

sprocket

sprout /sprout/ ▸*v.* [*intrans.*] (of a plant) put forth shoots: *the weeds begin to sprout.* ■ [*trans.*] grow (plant shoots or hair): *many black cats sprout a few white hairs.* ■ [*intrans.*] (of a plant, flower, or hair) start to grow; spring up: *crocuses sprouted up from the grass* | *figurative forms of nationalism sprouted as the system collapsed.*

▸*n.* **1** a shoot of a plant. ■ (**sprouts**) young shoots eaten as a vegetable, esp. the shoots of alfalfa, mung beans, or soybeans. **2** short for BRUSSELS SPROUT. ▷Middle English: related to Dutch *spruiten* and German *spriessen.*

Spru·ance /ˈsprōōəns/, Raymond Ames (1886–1969), U.S. admiral. After commanding in various areas in the Pacific during World War II, he was made commander in chief of the U.S. Pacific fleet 1945–46. He later served as the U.S. ambassador to the Philippines 1952–55.

spruce[1] /sprōōs/ ▸*n.* a widespread coniferous tree that has a distinctive conical shape and hanging cones, widely grown for timber, pulp, and Christmas trees. • Genus *Picea*, family Pinaceae: many species. ▷late Middle English (denoting Prussia or something originating in Prussia): alteration of obsolete *Pruce* 'Prussia.' The application to the tree dates from the early 17th cent.

spruce[2] ▸*adj.* neat in dress and appearance: *he looked as spruce as if he were getting married.*

▸*v.* [*trans.*] (**spruce someone/something up**) make a person or place smarter or tidier: *the fund will be used to spruce up historic buildings.* ▷late 16th cent.: perhaps from SPRUCE[1] in the obsolete sense 'Prussian,' in the phrase *spruce (leather) jerkin.* **—spruce·ly** *adv.* **—spruce·ness** *n.*

spruce beer ▸*n.* a fermented drink using spruce twigs and needles as flavoring.

spruce bud·worm ▸*n.* the brown caterpillar of a small North American moth that is a serious pest of spruce and other conifers. • *Choristoneura fumiferana*, family Tortricidae.

sprue[1] /sprōō/ ▸*n.* a channel through which metal or plastic is poured into a mold. ■ a piece of metal or plastic that has solidified in a sprue, esp. one joining a number of small molded plastic items. ▷early 19th cent.: of unknown origin.

sprue[2] ▸*n.* disease of the small intestine causing malabsorption of food, in particular: ■ (also **tropical sprue**) a disease characterized by ulceration of the mouth and chronic enteritis, suffered by visitors to tropical regions from temperate countries. ■ (also **nontropical sprue**) another term for CELIAC DISEASE. ▷late 19th cent.: from Dutch *spruw* 'thrush'; perhaps related to Flemish *spruwen* 'sprinkle.'

sprung /sprəNG/ ▸ past and past participle of SPRING.

USAGE See usage at SPRING.

sprung rhythm ▸*n.* a poetic meter approximating speech, each foot having one stressed syllable followed by a varying number of unstressed ones. ▷late 19th cent.: coined by G. M. Hopkins, who used the meter.

spry /sprī/ ▸*adj.* (**spry·er, spry·est** or **spri·er, spri·est**) (esp. of an old person) active; lively: *he continued to look spry and active well into his eighties.* ▷mid 18th cent.: of unknown origin. —**spry·ly** *adv.* —**spry·ness** *n.*

s.p.s. ▸*abbr.* without surviving issue. [from Latin *sine prole superstite.*]

spt. ▸*abbr.* seaport.

spud /spəd/ ▸*n.* **1** *informal* a potato. **2** a small, narrow spade for cutting the roots of plants, esp. weeds. **3** [often as *adj.*] a short length of pipe that is used to connect two components or that takes the form of a projection from a fitting to which a pipe may be screwed: *a spud washer.* **4** a chisel-like tool, as for removing bark or digging into ice.
▸*v.* (**spud·ded, spud·ding**) [*trans.*] **1** dig up or cut (plants, esp. weeds) with a spud. **2** make the initial drilling for (an oil well). ▷late Middle English (denoting a short knife): of unknown origin. The sense 'potato' (dating from the mid 19th cent.) was originally slang and dialect.

spud wrench ▸*n.* a long bar with a socket on the end for tightening bolts.

spue /spyōō/ ▸*v.* archaic spelling of SPEW.

spu·man·te /spə'mäntē; spyə-/ ▸*n.* an Italian sparkling white wine. ▷Italian, literally 'sparkling.'

spume /spyōōm/ *poetic/literary* ▸*n.* froth or foam, esp. that found on waves.
▸*v.* [*intrans.*] form or produce a mass of froth or foam: *water was spuming under the mill.* ▷late Middle English: from Old French *(e)spume* or Latin *spuma.* —**spu·mous** /-məs/ *adj.* —**spum·y** *adj.*

spu·mo·ni /spōō'mōnē/ (also **spu·mo·ne**) ▸*n.* a kind of ice cream with different colors and flavors in layers, and often made with bits of fruit and nuts. ▷from Italian *spumone,* from *spuma* 'foam.'

spun /spən/ ▸ past and past participle of SPIN.

spunk /spəNGk/ ▸*n.* **1** *informal* courage and determination. **2** tinder; touchwood. **3** *Brit., vulgar slang* semen. ▷mid 16th cent. (in the sense 'a spark, vestige'): of unknown origin; perhaps a blend of SPARK[1] and obsolete *funk* 'spark.'

spunk·y /'spəNGkē/ ▸*adj.* (**spunk·i·er, spunk·i·est**) *informal* courageous and determined: *a spunky performance.* —**spunk·i·ly** /'spəNGkəlē/ *adv.* —**spunk·i·ness** *n.*

spun silk ▸*n.* yarn made of short-fibered and waste silk. ■ fabric made from this yarn.

spun sug·ar ▸*n.* hardened sugar syrup drawn out into long filaments and used to make cotton candy or as a decoration for sweet dishes.

spun yarn ▸*n.* *Nautical* cord made by twisting together from two to four untwisted yarns of tarred hemp.

spur /spər/ ▸*n.* **1** a device with a small spike or a spiked wheel that is worn on a rider's heel and used for urging a horse forward. ■ *figurative* a thing that prompts or encourages someone; an incentive: *profit was both the spur and the reward of enterprise.* ■ a hard spike on the back of the leg of a cock or male game bird, used in fighting. ■ a steel point fastened to the leg of a gamecock. ■ a climbing iron. **2** a thing that projects or branches off from a main body, in particular: ■ a projection from a mountain or mountain range. ■ a short branch road or rail line. ■ *Botany* a slender tubular projection from the base of a flower, e.g., a honeysuckle or orchid, typically containing nectar. ■ a short fruit-bearing side shoot.

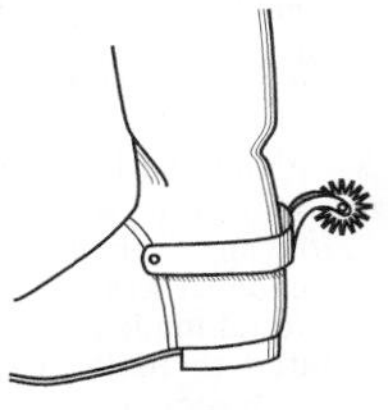

spur 1

▸*v.* (**spurred, spur·ring**) [*trans.*] urge (a horse) forward by digging one's spurs into its sides: *she spurred her horse toward the hedge.* ■ give an incentive or encouragement to (someone): *her sons' passion for computer games* **spurred** *her* **on** *to set up a software store.* ■ cause or promote the development of; stimulate: *governments cut interest rates to spur demand.* ▷Old English *spora, spura,* of Germanic origin; related to Dutch *spoor* and German *Sporn,* also to SPURN. —**spur·less** *adj.* —**spurred** *adj.*

▸*PHRASE* □ **on the spur of the moment** on a momentary impulse; without premeditation.

spurge /spərj/ ▸*n.* a herbaceous plant or shrub with milky latex and very small typically greenish flowers. Many kinds are cultivated as ornamentals and some are of commercial importance. • Genus *Euphorbia,* family Euphorbiaceae: numerous species. ▷late Middle English: shortening of Old French *espurge,* from *espurgier,* from Latin *expurgare* 'cleanse' (because of the purgative properties of the milky latex).

spur gear ▸*n.* a gearwheel with teeth projecting parallel to the wheel's axis.

spurge lau·rel ▸*n.* a low-growing evergreen Eurasian shrub with leathery leaves, small green flowers, and black poisonous berries. • *Daphne laureola,* family Thymelaeaceae.

spu·ri·ous /'spyŏŏrēəs/ ▸*adj.* not being what it purports to be; false or fake: *separating authentic and spurious claims.* ■ (of a line of reasoning) apparently but not actually valid: *this spurious reasoning results in nonsense.* ■ *archaic* (of offspring) illegitimate. ▷late 16th cent. (in the sense 'born out of wedlock'): from Latin *spurius* 'false' + -OUS. —**spu·ri·ous·ly** *adv.* —**spu·ri·ous·ness** *n.*

THE RIGHT WORD **apocryphal, artificial, counterfeit, ersatz, spurious, synthetic**

These adjectives pertain to what is false or not what it appears to be, although not all have negative connotations.

Artificial implies man-made, especially in imitation of something natural (*artificial flowers; artificial turf*).

A **synthetic** substance or material is one produced by a chemical process and used as a substitute for the natural substance it resembles (*boots made from synthetic rubber*).

Something that is **counterfeit** is an imitation of something else—usually something rarer, finer, or more valuable—and is intended to deceive or defraud (*counterfeit bills*).

Spurious also means false rather than true or genuine, but it carries no strong implication of being an imitation (*spurious letters falsely attributed to Winston Churchill*).

Ersatz refers to an artificial substitute that is usually inferior (*ersatz tea made from tree bark and herbs*).

The meaning of **apocryphal,** however, is much more restricted. It applies to accounts of the past that are widely circulated but whose truth or accuracy are doubtful (*an apocryphal story about George Washington as a boy*).

spurn /spərn/ ▸*v.* [*trans.*] reject with disdain or contempt: *he spoke gruffly, as if afraid that his invitation would be spurned.* ■ *archaic* strike, tread, or push away with the foot: *with one touch of my feet, I spurn the solid Earth.*
▸*n.* *archaic* an act of spurning. ▷Old English *spurnan, spornan;* related to Latin *spernere* 'to scorn'; compare with SPUR. —**spurn·er** *n.*

spur·rey /'spərē; 'spə-rē/ (also **spur·ry**) ▸*n.* (*pl.* **-reys** or **-ries**) a small widely distributed plant of the pink family, with pink or white flowers. • Genera *Spergula* and *Spergularia,* family Caryophyllaceae: several species, in particular **corn spurrey** (*Spergula arvensis*), a spindly weed of cornfields, and **sand spurrey** (*Spergularia rubra*), of sandy and gravelly soils. ▷late 16th cent.: from Dutch *spurrie;* probably related to medieval Latin *spergula.*

spur·ri·er /'spərēər/ ▸*n.* *rare* a person who makes spurs.

spurt /spərt/ ▸*v.* [*intrans.*] gush out in a sudden and forceful stream: *he cut his finger, and blood spurted over the sliced potatoes.* ■ [*trans.*] cause to gush out suddenly: *the kettle boiled and spurted scalding water everywhere.* ■ move with a sudden burst of speed: *the other car had spurted to the top of the ramp | figurative automobile sales spurted 2.1 percent in May.*
▸*n.* a sudden gushing stream: *a sudden spurt of blood gushed into her eyes.* ■ a sudden marked burst or increase of activity or speed: *late in the race he* **put on a spurt** *and reached second place | a growth spurt.* ▷mid 16th cent.: of unknown origin.

spur wheel ▸*n.* another term for SPUR GEAR.

Sput·nik /'spətnik; 'spŏŏt-/ ▸*n.* each of a series of Soviet artificial satellites, the first of which (launched on October 4, 1957) was the first satellite to be placed in orbit. ▷Russian, literally 'fellow-traveler.'

sput·ter /'spətər/ ▸*v.* **1** [*intrans.*] make a series of soft explosive sounds, typically when being heated or as a symptom of a fault: *the engine sputtered and stopped.* ■ [*reporting verb*] speak in a series of incoherent bursts as a result of indignation or some other strong emotion: [with *direct speech*] *"But . . . but . . . " she sputtered.* ■ [*trans.*] emit with a spitting sound: *the goose is in the oven, sputtering fat.* ■ [with *adverbial*] *figurative* proceed or develop in a spasmodic and feeble way: *strikes in the public services sputtered on.* **2** [*trans.*] *Physics* deposit (metal) on a surface by using fast ions to eject particles of it from a target. ■ cover (a surface) with metal by this method.
▸*n.* a series of soft explosive sounds, typically produced by an engine or by something heating or burning: *the sputter of the motor died away.* ▷late 16th cent. (as a verb): from Dutch *sputteren,* of imitative origin. —**sput·ter·er** *n.*

spu·tum /'spyōōtəm/ ▸*n.* a mixture of saliva and mucus coughed up from the respiratory tract, typically as a result of infection or other disease and often examined microscopically to aid medical diagnosis. ▷late 17th cent.: from Latin, neuter past participle of *spuere* 'to spit.'

spy /spī/ ▸*n.* (*pl.* **spies**) a person who secretly collects and reports information on the activities, movements, and plans of an enemy or competitor. ■ a person who keeps watch on others secretly: [as *adj.*] *a spy camera.*
▸*v.* (**spies, spied, spy·ing**) [*intrans.*] work for a government or other organization by secretly collecting information about enemies or competitors: *he agreed to spy for the West.* ■ (**spy on**) observe (someone) furtively: *the couple were spied on by reporters.* ■ [*trans.*] discern or make out, esp. by careful observation: *he could spy a figure in the distance.* ■ [*trans.*] (**spy something out**) collect information about something to use in deciding how to act: *he would go and spy out the land.* ▷Middle English: shortening of Old French *espie* 'espying,' *espier* 'espy,' of Germanic origin, from an Indo-European root shared by Latin *specere* 'behold, look.'

spy·glass /'spī,glas/ ▸*n.* a small hand-held telescope.

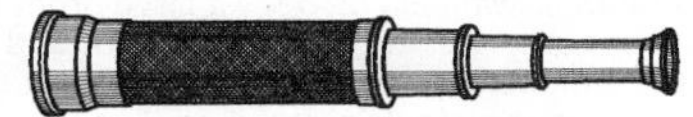

spyglass

spy·mas·ter /'spī,mastər/ ▸*n.* the head of an organization of spies.

spy·ware /'spī,we(ə)r/ ▸*n.* software that self-installs on computers and tracks the user's Internet use, mainly for marketing purposes.

sq ▸*abbr.* square: *51,100 sq km.*

SQL *Computing* ▸*abbr.* Structured Query Language, an international standard for database manipulation.

squab /skwäb/ ▸*n.* **1** a young unfledged pigeon. ■ the flesh of such a bird as food: *roast squab.* **2** a thick stuffed cushion, esp. one covering the seat of a chair or sofa.
▸*adj.* *archaic* (of a person) short and fat. ▷mid 17th cent. (in the sense 'inexperienced person'): of unknown origin; compare with obsolete *quab* 'shapeless thing' and Swedish dialect *skvabba* 'fat woman.'

squab·ble /'skwäbəl/ ▸*n.* a noisy quarrel about something petty or trivial: *family squabbles.* See note at QUARREL.
▸*v.* [*intrans.*] quarrel noisily over a trivial matter: *the boys were squabbling over a ball.* ▷early 17th cent.: probably imitative; compare with Swedish dialect *skvabbel* 'a dispute.' —**squab·bler** /'skwäb(ə)lər/ *n.*

squad /skwäd/ ▸*n.* [treated as *sing.* or *pl.*] a small group of people having a particular task: *an assassination squad.* ■ a small number of soldiers assembled for drill or assigned to some special task, esp. an infantry unit forming part of a platoon. ■ a group of sports players or competitors from which a team is chosen: *eleven first-string players on the Nebraska squad.* ■ a division of a police force dealing with a particular crime or type of crime: *the narcotics crime squad.* ▷mid 17th cent.: shortening of French *escouade*, variant of *escadre*, from Italian *squadra* 'square.'

squad car ▶*n.* a police patrol car.

squad·ron /ˈskwädrən/ ▶*n.* an operational unit in an air force consisting of two or more flights of aircraft and the personnel required to fly them. ■ a principal division of an armored or cavalry regiment, consisting of two or more troops. ■ a group of warships detached on a particular duty or under the command of a flag officer. ■ *informal* a large group of people or things: *he immediately commissioned a squadron of architects.* ▷mid 16th cent. (originally denoting a group of soldiers in square formation): from Italian *squadrone*, from *squadra* 'square.'

squal·a·mine /ˈskwāləˌmēn/ ▶*n. Biochemistry* a compound of the steroid type that is found in sharks and that has antibiotic properties. ▷late 20th cent.: from Latin *squalus* (denoting a kind of marine fish and used as a rare term in English for 'shark') + **AMINE.**

squa·lene /ˈskwālēn/ ▶*n. Biochemistry* an oily liquid hydrocarbon that occurs in shark liver oil and human sebum, and is a metabolic precursor of sterols. • A triterpenoid; chem. formula: $C_{30}H_{50}$. ▷early 20th cent.: from Latin *squalus* (see **SQUALAMINE**) + **-ENE.**

squal·id /ˈskwälid/ ▶*adj.* (of a place) extremely dirty and unpleasant, esp. as a result of poverty or neglect: *the squalid, overcrowded prison.* ■ showing or involving a contemptible lack of moral standards: *a squalid attempt to save themselves from electoral embarrassment.* ▷late 16th cent.: from Latin *squalidus*, from *squalere* 'be rough or dirty.' **—squal·id·ly** *adv.* **—squal·id·ness** *n.*

squall /skwôl/ ▶*n.* a sudden violent gust of wind or a localized storm, esp. one bringing rain, snow, or sleet: *low clouds and squalls of driving rain.* ■ a loud cry: *he emitted a short mournful squall.*
▶*v.* [*intrans.*] (of a baby or small child) cry noisily and continuously: *Sarah was squalling in her crib.* ▷mid 17th cent.: probably an alteration of **SQUEAL**, influenced by **BAWL.** **—squal·ly** *adj.*

squall line ▶*n. Meteorology* a narrow band of high winds and storms associated with a cold front.

squal·or /ˈskwälər/ ▶*n.* a state of being extremely dirty and unpleasant, esp. as a result of poverty or neglect: *they lived in squalor and disease.* ▷early 17th cent.: from Latin, from *squalere* 'be dirty.'

Squa·ma·ta /skwāˈmätə/ *Zoology* a large order of reptiles that comprises the snakes, lizards, and worm lizards. ▷modern Latin (plural), from Latin *squama* 'scale.' **—squa·mate** /ˈskwāmāt/ *adj.* & *n.*

Squa·mish /ˈskwämisн/ ▶*n.* (*pl.* same) **1** a member of an American Indian people of southwestern British Columbia. **2** the Salishan language of this people.
▶*adj.* of or relating to this people or their language. ▷alteration of the Squamish name.

squa·mo·sal /skwəˈmōsəl/ ▶*n. Zoology* the squamous portion of the temporal bone, esp. when this forms a separate bone that, in mammals, articulates with the lower jaw. ▷mid 19th cent.: from Latin *squamosus* (from *squama* 'scale') + **-AL.**

squa·mous /ˈskwāməs/ (also **squa·mose**) ▶*adj.* covered with or characterized by scales: *a squamous black hide.* ■ *Anatomy* relating to, consisting of, or denoting a layer of epithelium that consists of very thin flattened cells: *squamous cell carcinoma.* ■ [*attrib.*] *Anatomy* denoting the flat portion of the temporal bone that forms part of the side of the skull. ▷late Middle English: from Latin *squamosus*, from *squama* 'scale.'

squan·der /ˈskwändər/ ▶*v.* [*trans.*] waste (something, esp. money or time) in a reckless and foolish manner: *entrepreneurs squander their profits on expensive cars.* ■ allow (an opportunity) to pass or be lost: *the team squandered several good scoring chances.* ▷late 16th cent.: of unknown origin. **—squand·er·er** *n.*

Squan·to /ˈskwäntō/ (c.1585–1622), Pawtuxet Indian, later of the Wampanoag tribe in what is now Massachusetts. He was captured by an English sea captain and taken to Spain to be sold into slavery. He escaped, made his way to England, and from there returned to North America. He befriended the Pilgrims in Plymouth Colony in 1621 and acted as their interpreter and adviser on planting and fishing.

square /skwe(ə)r/ ▶*n.* **1** a plane figure with four equal straight sides and four right angles. ■ a thing having such a shape or approximately such a shape: *she tore a bit of cloth into a four-inch square.* ■ a thing having the shape or approximate shape of a cube: *a small square of chocolate.* ■ an open (typically four-sided) area surrounded by buildings in a town, village, or city: *a market square* | [in *place names*] *Herald Square.* ■ an open area at the meeting of streets. ■ a small square area on the board used in a game. ■ a block of buildings bounded by four streets. ■ *historical* a body of infantry drawn up in rectangular form. ■ a unit of 100 square ft. used as a measure of flooring, roofing, etc. **2** the product of a number multiplied by itself: *a circle's area is proportional to the square of its radius.* **3** an L-shaped or T-shaped instrument used for obtaining or testing right angles: *a carpenter's square.* ■ *Astrology* an aspect of 90° (one quarter of a circle): *Venus* ***in square to*** *Jupiter.* **4** *informal* a person considered to be old-fashioned or boringly conventional in attitude or behavior. **5** *informal* a square meal: *three squares a day.*
▶*adj.* **1** having the shape or approximate shape of a square: *a square table.* ■ having the shape or approximate shape of a cube: *a square box.* ■ having or in the form of two right angles: *a suitable length of wood with square ends.* ■ having an outline resembling two corners of a square: *his square jaw.* ■ broad and solid in shape: *he was short and square.* **2** denoting a unit of measurement equal to the area of a square whose side is of the unit specified: *30,000 square feet of new gallery space.* ■ [*postpositive*] denoting the length of each side of a square shape or object: *the office was fifteen feet square.* **3** at right angles; perpendicular: *these lines must be* ***square to*** *the top and bottom marked edges.* ■ *Astrology* having or denoting an aspect of 90°: *Jupiter is square to the Sun.* **4** level or parallel: *place one piece of wood on top of the other, ensuring that they are exactly square.* ■ properly arranged; in good order: *we should get everything square before we leave.* ■ compatible or in agreement: *he wanted to make sure we were* ***square with*** *the court's decision and not subject to a lawsuit.* ■ fair and honest: *she'd been as square with him as anybody could be.* **5** (of two people) owing nothing to each other: *an acknowledgment that we are square.* ■ with both players or sides having equal scores in a game: *the goal brought the match* ***all square*** *once again.* **6** *informal* old-fashioned or boringly conventional: *Elvis was anything but square.* **7** (of rhythm) simple and straightforward.
▶*adv.* directly; straight: *it hit me square in the forehead* ■ *informal* fairly; honestly: *I'd acted square and on the level with him.*
▶*v.* [*trans.*] **1** make square or rectangular; give a square or rectangular cross section to: *you can* ***square off*** *the other edge.* ■ [usu. as *adj.*] (**squared**) mark out in squares. **2** multiply (a number) by itself: *5 squared equals 25.* ■ [usu. as *postpositive adj.*] (**squared**) convert (a linear unit of measurement) to a unit of area equal to a square whose side is of the unit specified: *there were only three people per kilometer squared.* **3** make compatible; reconcile: *I'm able to* ***square*** *my profession* ***with*** *my religious beliefs.* ■ [*intrans.*] be compatible: *do those announcements really* ***square with*** *the facts?* **4** balance (an account): *they're anxious to square their books before the audit.* ■ make the score of (a match or game) even: [*trans.*] *his goal squared the match 1-1.* ■ *informal* secure the help, acquiescence, or silence of (someone), esp. by offering an inducement: *trying to square the press.* **5** bring (one's shoulders) into a position in which they appear square and broad, typically to prepare oneself for a difficult task or event: *chin up, shoulders squared, she stepped into the room.* ■ (**square oneself**) adopt a posture of defense. **6** *Sailing* set (a yard or other part of a ship) approximately at right angles to the keel or other point of reference. **7** *Astrology* (of a planet) have a square aspect with (another planet or position): *Saturn squares the Sun on the 17th.*
▶*phrasal v.* □ **square something away** arrange or deal with something in a satisfactory way: *don't you worry, we'll get things squared away.* □ **square off** assume the attitude of a person about to fight: *the two men squared off* | *figurative a debate gives the candidates an opportunity to square off.* □ **square up** settle or pay an account: *would you square up the bill?* ■ settle a dispute or misunderstanding: *I want to square up whatever's wrong between us.* ▷Middle English: shortening of Old French *esquare* (noun), *esquarre* (past participle, used as an adjective), *esquarrer* (verb), based on Latin *quadra* 'square.' **—square·ness** *n.* **—squar·er** *n.* **—squar·ish** *adj.*
▶*PHRASES* □ **back to** (or **at**) **square one** *informal* back to where one started, with no progress having been made. □ **on the square 1** *informal* honest; straightforward. **2** *informal* honestly; fairly. **3** at right angles. □ **out of square** not at right angles. □ **square accounts with** see **ACCOUNT.** □ **square the circle** construct a square equal in area to a given circle (a problem incapable of a purely geometric solution). ■ do something that is considered to be impossible. □ **a square peg in a round hole** see **PEG.**

square brack·et ▶*n.* see **BRACKET** (sense 1).

square dance ▶*n.* a country dance that starts with four couples facing one another in a square, with the steps and movements shouted out by a caller.
▶*v.* (**square dance**) [*intrans.*] [often as *n.*] (**square dancing**) participate in a square dance. **—square danc·er** *n.*

square deal ▶*n.* [usu. in *sing.*] a fair bargain or treatment: *the workers feel they are not getting a square deal.*

square·head /ˈskwe(ə)rˌhed/ ▶*n. informal* **1** a stupid or inept person. **2** *offensive* a person of German, Dutch, or Scandinavian, esp. Swedish, origin.

square knot ▶*n.* a type of double knot that is made symmetrically to hold securely and to be easy to untie.

square law ▶*n. Physics* a law relating two variables, one of which varies (directly or inversely) as the square of the other. See also **INVERSE SQUARE LAW.**

square·ly /ˈskwe(ə)rlē/ ▶*adv.* directly, without deviating to one side: *Ashley looked at him squarely.* ■ in a direct and uncompromising manner; without equivocation: *they placed the blame squarely on the president.*

square meal ▶*n.* a substantial, satisfying, and balanced meal: *three square meals a day.* ▷said to derive from nautical use, with reference to the square platters on which meals were served on board ship.

square meas·ure ▶*n.* a unit of measurement relating to area.

square-rigged ▶*adj.* (of a sailing ship) having the principal sails at right angles to the length of the ship, supported by horizontal yards attached to the mast or masts.

square-rig·ger ▶*n.* a square-rigged sailing ship.

square rod ▶*n.* see **ROD** (sense 3).

square root ▶*n.* a number that produces a specified quantity when multiplied by itself: *7 is a square root of 49.*

square sail ▶*n.* a four-cornered sail supported by a yard attached to a mast.

square-should·ered ▶*adj.* (of a person) having broad shoulders that do not slope.

square·tail /ˈskwe(ə)rˌtāl/ ▶*n.* a fish of warm seas that has a slender cylindrical body and long tail, the base of which is square in cross section. • Family Tetragonuridae and genus *Tetragonurus*: several species.

square-toed ▶*adj.* (of shoes or boots) having broad, square toes. ■ *archaic* old-fashioned or formal.

square wave ▶*n. Electronics* a periodic wave that varies abruptly in amplitude between two fixed values, spending equal times at each.

squark /skwärk/ ▶*n. Physics* the supersymmetric counterpart of a quark, with spin 0 instead of $1/2$. ▷1980s: from *s(uper)* + **QUARK.**

squash[1] /skwäsн; skwôsн/ ▶*v.* [*trans.*] crush or squeeze (something) with force so that it becomes flat, soft, or out of shape: *wash and squash the cans for the recycling bin* | [as *adj.*] (**squashed**) *a squashed banana.* ■ [*trans.*] squeeze or force (someone or something) into a small or restricted space: *she squashed some of her clothes inside the bag.* ■ [*intrans.*] make one's way into a small or restricted space: *I squashed into the middle of the crowd.* ■ suppress, stifle, or subdue (a feeling, conjecture, or action): *the mournful sound did nothing to squash her high spirits.* ■ firmly reject (an idea or suggestion): *the proposal was immediately squashed by the Historical Society.*
▶*n.* **1** [in *sing.*] a state of being squeezed or forced into a small or restricted space: *it was a tight squash but he didn't seem to mind.* **2** *chiefly Brit.* a concentrated liquid made from fruit juice and sugar, which is diluted to make a drink: *orange squash.* **3** (also **squash racquets**) a game in which two players use rackets to hit a small, soft rubber ball against the walls of a closed court. **4** *Biology* a preparation of softened tissue that has been made thin for microscopic examination by gently compressing or tapping it. ▷mid 16th cent. (as a verb): alteration of **QUASH.**

squash[2] ▶*n.* (*pl.* same or **squash·es**) **1** an edible gourd, the flesh of which may be cooked and eaten as a vegetable. **2** the trailing plant of the gourd family that produces this fruit. • Genus *Cucurbita*, family

Cucurbitaceae: many species and varieties, including the **winter squashes** and **summer squashes**. ▷mid 17th cent.: abbreviation of Narragansett *asquutasquash*.

squash·ber·ry /ˈskwäsh,berē; ˈskwôsh-/ ▸*n.* (*pl.* **-ries**) a North American viburnum which bears edible berries. • *Viburnum edule*, family Caprifoliaceae.

squash blos·som ▸*n.* [as *adj.*] denoting a type of silver jewelry made by Navajos characterized by designs resembling the flower of the squash plant.

squash bug ▸*n.* a dark-colored bug with forewings marked by many veins. • Family Coreidae, suborder Heteroptera: many species, in particular the North American *Anasa tristis*, a serious pest of squashes and similar fruit.

squash·y /ˈskwäshē; ˈskwôshē/ ▸*adj.* (**squash·i·er, squash·i·est**) easily crushed or squeezed into a different shape; having a soft consistency: *a big, squashy leather chair.* **—squash·i·ly** /ˈskwäshəlē; ˈskwôshəlē/ *adv.* **—squash·i·ness** *n.*

squat /skwät/ ▸*v.* (**squat·ted, squat·ting**) **1** [*intrans.*] crouch or sit with one's knees bent and one's heels close to or touching one's buttocks or the back of one's thighs: *I squatted down in front of him.* ■ [*trans.*] *Weightlifting* crouch down in such a way and rise again while holding (a specified weight) at one's shoulders: *he can squat 850 pounds.* **2** [*intrans.*] unlawfully occupy an uninhabited building or settle on a piece of land: *eight families are squatting in the house.* ■ [*trans.*] occupy (an uninhabited building) in such a way.

▸*adj.* (**squat·ter, squat·test**) short and thickset; disproportionately broad or wide: *he was muscular and squat | a squat gray house.*

▸*n.* **1** [in *sing.*] a position in which one's knees are bent and one's heels are close to or touching one's buttocks or the back of one's thighs. ■ *Weightlifting* an exercise in which a person squats down and rises again while holding a barbell at shoulder level. ■ (in gymnastics) an exercise involving a squatting movement or action. **2** *informal* short for DIDDLY-SQUAT: *I didn't know squat about writing plays.* **3** *chiefly Brit.* a building occupied by people living in it without the legal right to do so. ■ an unlawful occupation of an uninhabited building. ▷Middle English (in the sense 'thrust down with force'): from Old French *esquatir* 'flatten,' based on Latin *coactus*, past participle of *cogere* 'compel' (see COGENT). The current sense of the adjective dates from the mid 17th cent. **—squat·ly** *adv.* **—squat·ness** *n.*

squat·ter /ˈskwätər/ ▸*n.* a person who unlawfully occupies an uninhabited building or unused land. ■ *historical* a settler with no legal title to the land occupied, typically one on land not yet allocated by a government.

squat thrust ▸*n.* an exercise in which the legs are thrust backward to their full extent from a squatting position with the hands on the floor.

squaw /skwô/ ▸*n.* *offensive* an American Indian woman or wife. ■ a woman or wife. ▷mid 17th cent.: from Narragansett *squaws* 'woman,' with related forms in many Algonquian dialects.

USAGE Until relatively recently, the word **squaw**, derived from an Algonquian language, was used neutrally in anthropological and other contexts to mean 'an American Indian woman or wife.' With changes in the political climate in the second half of the 20th century, however, the derogatory attitudes of the past toward American Indian women have meant that, in modern American English, the word cannot be used in any sense without being offensive.

squaw·fish /ˈskwô,fish/ ▸*n.* (*pl.* same or **-fish·es**) a large predatory freshwater fish of the minnow family, with a slender body and large mouth, found in western North America. • Genus *Ptychocheilus*, family Cyprinidae: several species, in particular the **northern squawfish** (*P. oregonensis*). ▷late 19th cent.: the word derives from the former importance to American Indians of such fish, as food.

squawk /skwôk/ ▸*v.* [*intrans.*] (of a bird) make a loud, harsh noise: *the geese flew upriver, squawking.* ■ [with *direct speech*] (of a person) say something in a loud, discordant tone: *"What are you doing?" she squawked.* ■ complain or protest about something.

▸*n.* a loud, harsh or discordant noise made by a bird or a person. ■ a complaint or protest: *her plan provoked a loud squawk from her friends.* ▷early 19th cent.: imitative. **—squawk·er** *n.*

squawk box ▸*n.* *informal* a loudspeaker, in particular one that is part of an intercom system.

squaw man ▸*n.* *offensive* a white or black man married to an American Indian woman.

squaw·root /ˈskwô,ro͞ot/ ▸*n.* either of two North American plants: • a yellow-brown parasitic plant related to the broomrape (*Conopholis americana*, family Orobanchaceae). • the blue cohosh. See COHOSH.

Squaw Val·ley /ˈskwô/ a resort in northeastern California, on Lake Tahoe, site of the 1960 Winter Olympic games.

squeak /skwēk/ ▸*n.* a short, high-pitched sound or cry: *the door opened with a slight squeak.* ■ [with *negative*] a single remark, statement, or communication: *I didn't hear a squeak from him for months.*

▸*v.* [*intrans.*] **1** make a high-pitched sound or cry: *he oiled the hinges to stop them from squeaking.* ■ [with *direct speech*] say something in a nervous or excited high-pitched tone: *"You're scaring me," she squeaked.* ■ *informal* inform on someone. **2** [with *adverbial*] *informal* succeed in achieving something by a very narrow margin: *the bill squeaked through with just six votes to spare.* ■ (**squeak by**) make or have just enough money for basic necessities: *she was squeaking by on her minimum-wage job.* ▷late Middle English (as a verb): imitative; compare with Swedish *skväka* 'croak,' also with SQUEAL and SHRIEK. The noun dates from the early 17th cent.

squeak·er /ˈskwēkər/ ▸*n.* a person or thing that squeaks. ■ *informal* a competition or election won or likely to be won by a narrow margin.

squeak·y /ˈskwēkē/ ▸*adj.* (**squeak·i·er, squeak·i·est**) having or making a high-pitched sound or cry: *a high, squeaky voice.* **—squeak·i·ly** /-kəlē/ *adv.* **—squeak·i·ness** *n.*

squeak·y-clean (also **squeak·y clean**) ▸*adj.* *informal* completely clean: *squeaky-clean restrooms.* ■ beyond reproach; without vice: *politicians who are less than squeaky clean.*

squeal /skwēl/ ▸*n.* a long, high-pitched cry or noise: *we heard a splash and a squeal.*

▸*v.* [*intrans.*] **1** make such a cry or noise: *the girls squealed with delight.* ■ [with *direct speech*] say something in a high-pitched, excited tone: *"Don't you dare!" she squealed.* ■ complain or protest about something: *the bookies only squealed because we beat them.* **2** *informal* inform on someone to the police or a person in authority: *she feared they would victimize her for squealing on their pals.* ▷Middle English (as a verb): imitative. The noun dates from the mid 18th cent. **—squeal·er** *n.* (esp. in sense 2).

squeam·ish /ˈskwēmish/ ▸*adj.* (of a person) easily made to feel sick, faint, or disgusted, esp. by unpleasant images, such as the sight of blood: *he was a bit squeamish at the sight of the giant needles.* ■ (of a person) having strong moral views; scrupulous: *she was not squeamish about using her social influence in support of her son.* ▷late Middle English: alteration of dialect *squeamous*, from Anglo-Norman French *escoymos*, of unknown origin. **—squeam·ish·ly** *adv.* **—squeam·ish·ness** *n.*

squee·gee /ˈskwē,jē/ ▸*n.* a scraping implement with a rubber-edged blade set on a handle, typically used for cleaning windows. ■ a similar small instrument or roller used esp. in photography for squeezing water out of prints. ■ [usu. as *adj.*] *informal* a person who cleans the windshield of a car stopped in traffic and then demands payment from the driver: *squeegee guys at every corner | the squeegees wait at busy intersections.*

▸*v.* (**-gees, -geed, -gee·ing**) [*trans.*] clean or scrape (something) with a squeegee: *squeegee the shower doors while the surfaces are still wet.* ▷mid 19th cent.: from archaic *squeege* 'to press,' strengthened form of SQUEEZE.

squeeze /skwēz/ ▸*v.* **1** [*trans.*] firmly press (something soft or yielding), typically with one's fingers: *Kate squeezed his hand affectionately* | [*intrans.*] *he squeezed with all his strength.* ■ [*trans.*] extract (liquid or a soft substance) from something by compressing or twisting it firmly: ***squeeze out** as much juice as you can* | [as *adj.* with *submodifier*] (**squeezed**) *freshly squeezed orange juice.* ■ [*trans.*] obtain (something) from someone with difficulty: *a governor who wants to **squeeze** as much money **out of** taxpayers as he can.* ■ *informal* pressure (someone) in order to obtain something from them: *she used the opportunity to squeeze him for information.* ■ (esp. in a financial or commercial context) have a damaging or restricting effect on: *the economy is being squeezed by foreign debt repayments.* ■ (**squeeze off**) *informal* shoot a round or shot from a gun: *squeeze off a few well-aimed shots.* ■ (**squeeze off**) *informal* take a photograph: *he squeezed off a half-dozen Polaroids.* ■ *Bridge* force (an opponent) to discard a guarding or potentially winning card. **2** [*intrans.*] manage to get into or through a narrow or restricted space: *Sarah squeezed in beside her | he found a hole in the hedge and **squeezed his way** through.* ■ [*trans.*] manage to force into or through such a space: *she squeezed herself into her tightest pair of jeans.* ■ [*intrans.*] (**squeeze up**) move closer to someone or something so that one is pressed tightly against them or it: *he guided her toward a seat, motioning for everyone to squeeze up and make room.* ■ [*trans.*] (**squeeze someone/something in**) manage to find time for someone or something: *the doctor can squeeze you in at noon.* ■ [*trans.*] (**squeeze someone/something out**) force someone or something out of a domain or activity: *workers have been squeezed out of their jobs.*

▸*n.* **1** an act of pressing something with one's fingers: *a gentle squeeze of the trigger.* ■ a hug. ■ a state of forcing oneself or being forced into a small or restricted space: *it was **a tight squeeze** in the tiny hall.* ■ *dated* a crowded social gathering. ■ a small amount of liquid extracted from something by pressing it firmly with one's fingers: *a **squeeze of** lemon juice.* ■ a strong financial demand or pressure, typically a restriction on borrowing, spending, or investment in a financial crisis: *industry faced higher costs and a **squeeze on** profits.* ■ a molding or cast of an object, or an impression or copy of a design, obtained by pressing a pliable substance around or over it. ■ *informal* money illegally extorted or exacted from someone: *he was out to extract some squeeze from her.* ■ *Bridge* a tactic that forces an opponent to discard an important card. ■ (also **squeeze play** or **suicide squeeze**) *Baseball* an act of bunting a ball in order to enable a runner on third base to start for home as soon as the ball is pitched. **2** *informal* a person's girlfriend or boyfriend: *the poor guy just lost his **main squeeze**.* ▷mid 16th cent.: from earlier *squise*, from obsolete *queise*, of unknown origin. **—squeez·a·ble** *adj.* **—squeez·er** *n.*

▸*PHRASE* □ **put the squeeze on** *informal* coerce or pressure (someone).

squeeze bot·tle ▸*n.* a container made of flexible plastic that is squeezed to extract the contents.

squeeze·box /ˈskwēz,bäks/ (also **squeeze box**) ▸*n.* *informal* an accordion or concertina.

squelch /skwelch/ ▸*v.* [*intrans.*] make a soft sucking sound such as that made by walking heavily through mud: *bedraggled guests squelched across the lawn to seek shelter.* ■ [*trans.*] *informal* forcefully silence or suppress: *property developers tried to squelch public protest.*

▸*n.* **1** a soft sucking sound made when pressure is applied to liquid or mud: *the squelch of their feet.* **2** (also **squelch circuit**) *Electronics* a circuit that suppresses the output of a radio receiver if the signal strength falls below a certain level. ▷early 17th cent. (originally denoting a heavy crushing fall on to something soft): imitative. **—squelch·er** *n.* **—squelch·y** *adj.*

squib /skwib/ ▸*n.* **1** a small firework that burns with a hissing sound before exploding. ■ a short piece of satirical writing. ■ a short news item or filler in a newspaper. **2** a small, slight, or weak person, esp. a child. **3** *Football* a short kick on a kickoff. ■ *Baseball* (also **squib·ber**) a blooper or infield grounder that becomes a base hit.

▸*v.* (**squibbed, squib·bing**) **1** [*trans.*] *Football* kick (the ball) a comparatively short distance on a kickoff; execute (a kick) in this way. ■ *Baseball* hit (the ball) with little force, usually with the end of the bat, the typical result being a blooper or infield grounder. **2** [*intrans.*] *archaic* utter, write, or publish a satirical or sarcastic attack. ■ [*trans.*] lampoon: *the mendicant parson, whom I am so fond of squibbing.* ▷early 16th cent. (sense 1): of unknown origin; perhaps imitative of a small explosion. The verb was first recorded in sense 2 (late 16th cent.).

SQUID /skwid/ ▸*n.* *Physics* a device used in particular in sensitive magnetometers, which consists of a superconducting ring containing one or more Josephson junctions. A change by one flux quantum in the ring's magnetic flux linkage produces a sharp change in its impedance. ▷1960s: acronym from *superconducting quantum interference device*.

squid /skwid/ ▸*n.* (*pl.* same or **squids**) an elongated, fast-swimming cephalopod mollusk with ten arms

S

(technically, eight arms and two long tentacles), typically able to change color. • Order Teuthoidea and Vampyromorpha, class Cephalopoda, in particular the common genus *Loligo*. See also **GIANT SQUID.** ■ this mollusk used as food. ■ an artificial bait for fish imitating a squid in form. ■ *military slang* a sailor.

▸*v.* (**squid·ded, squid·ding**) [*intrans.*] fish using squid as bait. ▷late 16th cent.: of unknown origin.

squid

squiffed /skwift/ ▸*adj. informal* slightly drunk. ▷late 19th cent.: variant of **SQUIFFY.**

squif·fy /ˈskwifē/ ▸*adj.* (**-fi·er, -fi·est**) *informal chiefly Brit.* slightly drunk: *he's squiffy from the rum.* ▷mid 19th cent.: of unknown origin.

squig·gle /ˈskwigəl/ ▸*n.* a short line that curls and loops in an irregular way: *some prescriptions are a series of meaningless squiggles.*

▸*v.* [*intrans.*] wriggle; squirm: *a worm that squiggled in his palm.* ■ [*trans.*] squeeze (something) from a tube so as to make irregular, curly lines on a surface. ▷early 19th cent.: perhaps a blend of **SQUIRM** and **WIGGLE** or **WRIGGLE.** **—squig·gly** /ˈskwig(ə)lē/ *adj.*

squill /skwil/ ▸*n.* **1** (also **sea squill**) a coastal Mediterranean plant of the lily family, with broad leaves, white flowers, and a very large bulb. • *Drimia* (or **Urginea**) *maritima*, family Liliaceae. ■ (also **squills**) an extract of the bulb of this plant, which is poisonous and has medicinal and other uses. **2** [usu. with *adj.*] a small plant of the lily family that resembles a hyacinth and has slender straplike leaves and small clusters of violet-blue or blue-striped flowers. • Several species in the family Liliaceae, including the **spring squill** (*Scilla verna*), and the **striped squill** (*Puschkinia scilloides*). ▷late Middle English: via Latin from Greek *skilla.*

squinch¹ /skwinCH/ ▸*n.* a straight or arched structure across an interior angle of a square tower to carry a superstructure such as a dome. ▷late 15th cent.: alteration of obsolete *scunch,* abbreviation of **SCUNCHEON.**

squinch² ▸*v.* [*trans.*] tense up the muscles of (one's eyes or face): *Gina **squinched** her face **up.*** ■ [*intrans.*] (of a person's eyes) narrow so as to be almost closed, typically in reaction to strong light: *he flicked on the light, which made my eyes **squinch up.*** ■ [*intrans.*] crouch down in order to make oneself seem smaller or to occupy less space: *I squinched down under the sheet.* ▷early 19th cent.: perhaps a blend of the verbs **SQUEEZE** and **PINCH.**

squint /skwint/ ▸*v.* **1** [*intrans.*] look at someone or something with one or both eyes partly closed in an attempt to see more clearly or as a reaction to strong light: *the bright sun made them squint.* ■ [*trans.*] partly close (one's eyes) for such reasons. **2** [*intrans.*] have eyes that look in different directions: *Melanie did not squint.* ■ (of a person's eye) have a deviation in the direction of its gaze: *her left eye squinted slightly.*

▸*n.* **1** [in *sing.*] a permanent deviation in the direction of the gaze of one eye: *I had a bad squint.* **2** [in *sing.*] *informal* a quick or casual look: *let me have a squint.* **3** an oblique opening through a wall in a church permitting a view of the altar from an aisle or side chapel. ▷mid 16th cent. (in the sense 'squinting,' as in **SQUINT-EYED**): shortening of **ASQUINT.** **—squint·er** *n.* **—squint·y** *adj.* [often in *combination*] *squinty-eyed.*

squint-eyed ▸*adj. derogatory* **1** (of a person) having a squint. **2** *archaic* spiteful.

squire /ˈskwīr/ ▸*n.* **1** a man of high social standing who owns and lives on an estate in a rural area, esp. the chief landowner in such an area: *the squire of Radbourne Hall* | [as *title*] *Squire Hughes.* ■ *Brit., informal* used by a man as a friendly or humorous form of address to another man. ■ *archaic* a title given to a magistrate, lawyer, or judge in some rural districts. **2** *historical* a young nobleman acting as an attendant to a knight before becoming a knight himself.

▸*v.* [*trans.*] (of a man) accompany or escort (a woman): *she was squired around Rome by a reporter.* ■ *dated* (of a man) have a romantic relationship with (a woman). ▷Middle English (sense 2): shortening of Old French *esquier* 'esquire.' **—squire·dom** /-dəm/ *n.* **—squire·ship** /-ˌSHip/ *n.*

squire·arch /ˈskwīrärk/ ▸*n.* a member of the squirearchy. ▷mid 19th cent.: back-formation from **SQUIREARCHY,** on the pattern of words such as *monarch.* **—squire·ar·chi·cal** /ˌskwīˈrärkikəl/ *adj.*

squire·ar·chy /ˈskwīrärkē/ ▸*n.* (*pl.* **-chies**) landowners collectively, esp. when considered as a class having political or social influence. ▷late 18th cent.: from **SQUIRE,** on the pattern of words such as *hierarchy.*

squirl /skwərl/ ▸*n. informal* an ornamental flourish or curve, esp. in handwriting. ▷mid 19th cent.: perhaps a blend of **SQUIGGLE** and **TWIRL** or **WHIRL.**

squirm /skwərm/ ▸*v.* [*intrans.*] wriggle or twist the body from side to side, esp. as a result of nervousness or discomfort: *all my efforts to squirm out of his grasp were useless.* ■ show or feel embarrassment or shame.

▸*n.* [in *sing.*] a wriggling movement. ▷late 17th cent.: symbolic of writhing movement; probably associated with **WORM.** **—squirm·er** *n.* **—squirm·y** *adj.*

squir·rel /ˈskwər(ə)l/ ▸*n.* an agile tree-dwelling rodent with a bushy tail, typically feeding on nuts and seeds. • Family Sciuridae: several genera, in particular *Sciurus,* and numerous species. ■ a related rodent of this family (see **GROUND SQUIRREL, FLYING SQUIRREL**). ■ the fur of the squirrel.

▸*v.* (**-reled, -rel·ing**) **1** [*trans.*] (**squirrel something away**) hide money or something of value in a safe place: *the money was squirreled away in foreign bank accounts.* **2** [*intrans.*] move in an inquisitive and restless manner: *they were squirreling around in the woods in search of something.* ▷Middle English: shortening of Old French *esquireul,* from a diminutive of Latin *sciurus,* from Greek *skiouros,* from *skia* 'shade' + *oura* 'tail.' Current verb senses date from the early 20th cent.

squir·rel cage ▸*n.* a rotating cylindrical cage in which a small captive animal can exercise as on a treadmill. ■ a monotonous or repetitive activity or way of life: *running madly about in a squirrel cage of activity.* ■ a form of rotor used in small electric motors, resembling a cylindrical cage.

squir·rel·fish /ˈskwərlˌfiSH/ ▸*n.* (*pl.* same or **-fish·es**) a chiefly nocturnal large-eyed marine fish that is typically brightly colored and lives around rocks or coral reefs in warm seas. • Family Holocentridae: several genera and species.

squir·rel·ly /ˈskwər(ə)lē/ ▸*adj.* **1** relating to or resembling a squirrel: *the chipmunks were little squirrelly things.* **2** *informal* restless, nervous, or unpredictable. ■ eccentric or insane.

squir·rel mon·key ▸*n.* a small South American monkey with a nonprehensile tail, typically moving through trees by leaping. • Genus *Saimiri,* family Cebidae: five species, in particular *S. sciureus.*

squir·rel·tail /ˈskwərlˌtāl/ (also **squir·rel·tail grass**) ▸*n.* a kind of barley with bushy spikelets, sometimes cultivated as an ornamental grass. • *Hordeum jubatum,* family Gramineae.

squirt /skwərt/ ▸*v.* [*trans.*] cause (a liquid) to be ejected from a small opening in something in a thin, fast stream or jet: *she squirted soda into a glass.* ■ cause (a container of liquid) to eject its contents in this way: *some youngsters squirted a water pistol in her face.* ■ [*trans.*] wet (someone or something) with a jet or stream of liquid in this way: *she squirted me with the juice from her lemon wedge.* ■ [*intrans.*] (of a liquid) be ejected from something in this way. ■ [*intrans.*] (of an object) move suddenly and unpredictably: *he got his glove on the ball but it squirted away.* ■ transmit (information) in highly compressed or speeded-up form.

▸*n.* **1** a thin stream or small quantity of liquid ejected from something: ***a quick squirt of** perfume.* ■ a small device from which a liquid may be ejected in a thin, fast stream. ■ a compressed radio signal transmitted at high speed. **2** *informal* a person perceived to be insignificant, impudent, or presumptuous: *what did he see in this patronizing little squirt?* ▷Middle English (first recorded as a verb): imitative. **—squirt·er** *n.*

squirt boat ▸*n.* a small, highly maneuverable kayak.

squirt gun ▸*n.* a water pistol.

squish /skwiSH/ ▸*v.* [*intrans.*] make a soft squelching sound when walked on or in: *the mud squished under my shoes.* ■ yield easily to pressure when squeezed or squashed: *strawberries so ripe that they squished if picked too firmly.* ■ [*trans.*] *informal* squash (something): *Naomi was furiously squishing her ice cream in her bowl.* ■ [with *adverbial of direction*] squeeze oneself into somewhere: *she squished in among them on the couch.*

▸*n.* [in *sing.*] a soft squelching sound. ▷mid 17th cent.: imitative. **—squish·y** *adj.* (**squish·i·er, squish·i·est**).

Sr ▸*symbol* the chemical element strontium.

sr ▸*abbr.* steradian(s).

Sr. ▸*abbr.* ■ senior (in names): *E. T. Krebs, Sr.* ■ Señor. ■ Signor. ■ Sister (in a religious order): [as a *title*] *Sr. Agatha.*

Sra. ▸*abbr.* ■ Senhora. ■ Señora.

SRAM /ˈesˌram/ ▸*n. Electronics* a type of memory chip that is faster and requires less power than dynamic memory. ▷acronym from *static random-access memory.*

Sra·nan /ˈsränən/ ▸*n.* another term for **TAKI-TAKI.** ▷from Taki-Taki *Sranan tongo,* literally 'Surinam tongue.'

Sri /srē/ (also **Shri**) ▸*n. Indian* a title of respect used before the name of a man, a god, or a sacred book: *Sri Chaudhuri.* ▷from Sanskrit *Śrī* 'beauty, fortune,' used as an honorific title.

Sri Lan·ka /ˌsrē ˈläNGkə; ˌSHrē; ˈlaNGkə/ an island country off the southeastern coast of India; pop. 19,905,000; capital, Colombo; languages, Sinhalese (official) and Tamil. Former name (until 1972) **CEYLON.** **—Sri Lan·kan** *adj.* & *n.*

The island was ruled by a strong native dynasty from the 12th century but was successively dominated by the Portuguese, Dutch, and British from the 16th century; it was finally annexed by the British in 1815. A Commonwealth of Nations state from 1948, the country became an independent republic in 1972. From 1981 to 2001, there was fighting between government forces and Tamil separatist guerrillas.

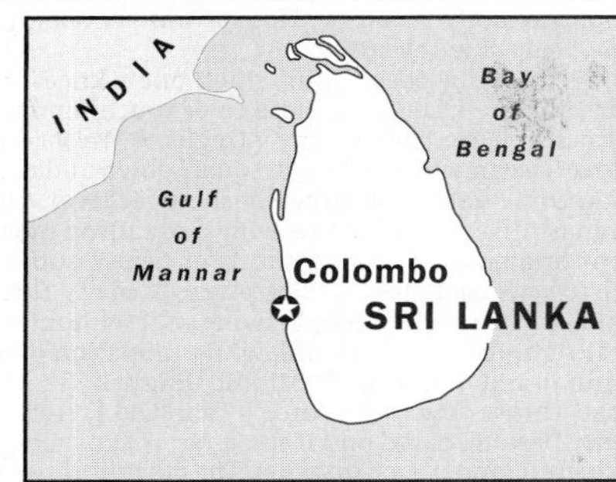

Sri·na·gar /srēˈnəgər; SHrē-/ a city in northwestern India, on the Jhelum River, in the foothills of the Himalayas; pop. 595,000.

SRN ▸*abbr.* State Registered Nurse.

sRNA ▸*abbr.* soluble RNA.

SRO ▸*abbr.* ■ (in the UK) self-regulatory organization, a body that regulates the activities of investment businesses. ■ single room occupancy. ■ standing room only.

Srta. ▸*abbr.* ■ Senhorita. ■ Señorita.

SS¹ ▸*abbr.* ■ Saints: *the Church of SS Peter and Paul.* ■ *Baseball* shortstop. ■ social security. ■ (in prescriptions) in the strict sense. [from Latin *sensu stricto.*] ■ steamship: *the SS Canberra.* ■ Sunday School.

SS² the Nazi special police force. Founded in 1925 by Hitler as a personal bodyguard, the SS provided security forces (including the Gestapo) and administered the concentration camps. ▷abbreviation of German *Schutzstaffel* 'defense squadron.'

ss. ▸*abbr.* ■ *Law* to wit; that is to say; namely (used on legal documents). [from Latin *scilicet.*] ■ sections. ■ *Baseball* shortstop.

s/s ▸*abbr.* same size.

SSA ▸*abbr.* ■ Social Security Act. ■ Social Security Administration.

SSB ▸*abbr.* single sideband transmission, a type of amplitude modulation in which the carrier wave and one sideband are suppressed in order to occupy less bandwidth.

SSC ▸*abbr.* (in Scotland) Solicitor in the Supreme Court. ■ *Physics* superconducting super collider.

SSE ▸*abbr.* south-south-east.

S.Sgt. (or **SSGT**) ▸*abbr.* staff sergeant.

SSI ▸*abbr.* ■ *Electronics* small-scale integration, the process of concentrating semiconductor devices in a single integrated circuit. ■ Supplemental Security Income.

SSL ▸*abbr.* Secure Sockets Layer, a computing protocol that ensures the security of data sent via the Internet by using encryption.

SSN ▸*abbr.* Social Security Number.

ssp. ▸*abbr.* subspecies (usually singular).

sspp. ▸*abbr.* subspecies (plural).

SSR *abbr.* *historical* Soviet Socialist Republic.

SSRC ▸*abbr.* (in the UK) Social Science Research Council.

SSRI ▸*abbr.* selective serotonin reuptake inhibitor, the designation for a class of antidepressants that work by increasing levels of serotonin in the brain.

SSS ▸*abbr.* Selective Service System.

SSSI ▸*abbr.* (in the UK) Site of Special Scientific Interest.

SST ▸*abbr.* supersonic transport.

SSW ▸*abbr.* south-southwest.

ST ▸*abbr.* stokes.

st ▸*abbr.* stone (in weight).

St. ▸*abbr.* ■ Saint: *St. George.* ■ *Physics* stokes.

-st ▸*suffix* variant spelling of **-EST**2.

Sta. ▸*abbr.* station (in particular, a railroad station).

stab /stab/ ▸*v.* (**stabbed, stab·bing**) [*trans.*] (of a person) thrust a knife or other pointed weapon into (someone) so as to wound or kill: *he stabbed him in the stomach* | [as *n.*] (**stabbing**) *the fatal stabbings of four rival gang members.* ■ [*intrans.*] make a thrusting gesture or movement at something with a pointed object: *she stabbed at the earth with the fork* | [*trans.*] *she stabbed the air with her forefinger* ■ [*intrans.*] (**stab into/through**) (of a sharp or pointed object) violently pierce: *a sharp end of wicker stabbed into his sole.* ■ [*intrans.*] (**stab at**) (of a pain or painful thing) cause a sudden sharp sensation: [as *adj.*] (**stabbing**) *I felt a stabbing pain in my chest.*

▸*n.* **1** a thrust with a knife or other pointed weapon: [as *adj.*] *multiple stab wounds.* ■ a wound made in such a way: *she had a deep stab in the back.* ■ a thrusting movement with a finger or other pointed object: *impatient stabs of his finger.* ■ *Tennis* a shot made with a thrusting motion. ■ a sudden sharp feeling or pain: *she felt a stab of jealousy.* **2** (**stab at**) *informal* an attempt to do (something): *Meredith made a feeble stab at joining in.* ▷late Middle English: of unknown origin. **—stab·ber** *n.*

▸*PHRASES* □ **a stab in the back** a treacherous act or statement. □ **stab someone in the back** betray someone. □ **a stab in the dark** see **DARK**.

Sta·bat Ma·ter /'stäbät 'mätər; 'stābat 'mātər/ ▸*n.* a medieval Latin hymn on the suffering of the Virgin Mary at the Crucifixion. ▷from the opening words *Stabat mater dolorosa* 'Stood the mother, full of grief.'

sta·bi·la·tor /'stābə,lātər/ ▸*n.* a combined stabilizer and elevator at the tail of an aircraft.

sta·bile /'stā,bēl/ ▸*n.* *Art* a freestanding abstract sculpture or structure, typically of wire or sheet metal, in the style of a mobile but rigid and stationary. ▷1940s: from Latin *stabilis* 'stable,' influenced by **MOBILE**.

sta·bil·i·ty /stə'bilitē/ ▸*n.* the state of being stable: *there are fears for the political stability of the area.* ▷Middle English: from Old French *stablete*, from Latin *stabilitas*, from *stabilis* 'stable.'

sta·bi·lize /'stābə,līz/ ▸*v.* make or become stable: [*intrans.*] *his condition appears to have stabilized* | [*trans.*] *an emergency program designed to stabilize the economy.* ■ [*trans.*] cause (an object or structure) to be unlikely to overturn: *the craft was stabilized by throwing out the remaining ballast.* **—sta·bi·li·za·tion** /,stābəli'zāsʜən/ *n.*

sta·bi·liz·er /'stābə,līzər/ ▸*n.* a thing used to keep something steady or stable, in particular: ■ another term for **HORIZONTAL STABILIZER**. ■ a gyroscopically controlled system used to reduce the rolling of a ship. ■ a substance that prevents the breakdown of emulsions, esp. in foods and paints. ■ a financial mechanism that prevents unsettling fluctuation in an economic system.

sta·ble1 /'stābəl/ ▸*adj.* (**-bler, -blest**) not likely to change or fail; firmly established: *a stable relationship* | *prices have remained relatively stable.* ■ (of a patient or a medical condition) not deteriorating in health after an injury or operation: *he is now in a stable condition in the hospital.* ■ (of a person) sane and sensible; not easily upset or disturbed: *the officer concerned is mentally and emotionally stable.* ■ (of an object or structure) not likely to give way or overturn; firmly fixed: *specially designed dinghies that are very stable.* ■ not liable to undergo chemical decomposition, radioactive decay, or other physical change. ▷Middle English: from Anglo-Norman French, from Latin *stabilis*, from the base of *stare* 'to stand.' **—sta·bly** /-b(ə)lē/ *adv.*

sta·ble2 ▸*n.* a building set apart and adapted for keeping horses. ■ an establishment where racehorses are kept and trained. ■ the racehorses of a particular training establishment. ■ an organization or establishment providing the same background or training for its members: *the player comes from the same stable as Agassi.* ■ a group of people trained by the same person or under one management: *the agent looked after a big stable of European golfers.*

▸*v.* [*trans.*] put or keep (a horse) in a specially adapted building. ■ put or base (a train) in a depot. ▷Middle English: shortening of Old French *estable* 'stable, pigpen,' from Latin *stabulum*, from the base of *stare* 'to stand.' **—sta·ble·ful** /'stābəl,fōōl/ *n.* (*pl.* **-fuls**).

sta·ble boy ▸*n.* a boy or man employed in a stable.

sta·ble e·qui·lib·ri·um ▸*n.* a state in which a body tends to return to its original position after being disturbed.

sta·ble fly ▸*n.* a bloodsucking fly related to the housefly, biting large mammals including humans. • *Stomoxis calcitrans*, family Muscidae.

sta·ble girl ▸*n.* a girl or woman employed in a stable.

sta·ble·man /'stābəl,mən/ ▸*n.* (*pl.* **-men**) a person employed in a stable.

sta·ble·mate /'stābəl,māt/ ▸*n.* a horse, esp. a racehorse, from the same establishment as another. ■ a person or product from the same organization or background as another: *it is a marketing challenge for Fiat and its stablemate, Alfa Romeo.*

sta·bling /'stāb(ə)liɴɢ/ ▸*n.* accommodations for horses.

stab·lish /'stablisʜ/ ▸*v.* archaic form of **ESTABLISH**.

stac·ca·to /stə'kätō/ *chiefly Music* ▸*adv.* & *adj.* with each sound or note sharply detached or separated from the others: [as *adj.*] *a staccato rhythm.* Compare with **LEGATO, MARCATO**.

▸*n.* (*pl.* **-tos**) performance in this manner. ■ a noise or speech resembling a series of short, detached musical notes: *her heels made a rapid staccato on the polished boards.* ▷Italian, literally 'detached.'

stack /stak/ ▸*n.* **1** a pile of objects, typically one that is neatly arranged: *a **stack of** boxes.* ■ (**a stack of/stacks of**) *informal* a large quantity of something: *there's stacks of work for me now.* ■ a rectangular or cylindrical pile of hay or straw or of grain in sheaf. ■ a vertical arrangement of stereo or guitar amplification equipment. ■ a number of aircraft flying in circles at different altitudes around the same point while waiting for permission to land at an airport. ■ a pyramidal group of rifles. ■ (**the stacks**) units of shelving in part of a library, used to store books compactly. ■ *Computing* a set of storage locations that store data in such a way that the most recently stored item is the first to be retrieved. **2** a chimney, esp. one on a factory, or a vertical exhaust pipe on a vehicle. ■ (also **sea stack**) a column of rock standing in the sea, remaining after erosion of cliffs.

▸*v.* [*trans.*] **1** arrange (a number of things) in a pile, typically a neat one: *the books had been **stacked up** in three piles* | *she stood up, beginning to stack the plates.* ■ fill or cover (a place or surface) with piles of things, typically neat ones: *he spent most of the time stacking shelves.* ■ cause (an aircraft) to fly in circles while waiting for permission to land at an airport: *I hope we aren't stacked for hours over Kennedy.* **2** shuffle or arrange (a deck of cards) dishonestly so as to gain an unfair advantage. ■ (**be stacked against/in favor of**) used to refer to a situation that is such that an unfavorable or a favorable outcome is overwhelmingly likely: *the odds were stacked against Fiji in the World Cup* | *they found the courts stacked in favor of timber interests.* **3** [*intrans.*] (in snowboarding) fall over.

▸*phrasal v.* □ **stack up 1** (or **stack something up**) form or cause to form a large quantity; build up: *cars stack up behind every bus, while passengers stand in line to pay fares.* **2** *informal* measure up; compare: *our rural schools stack up well against their urban counterparts.* ■ [usu. with *negative*] make sense; correspond to reality: *to blame the debacle on the antics of a rogue trader is not credible—it doesn't stack up.* ▷Middle English: from Old Norse *stakkr* 'haystack,' of Germanic origin. **—stack·a·ble** *adj.* **—stack·er** *n.*

▸*PHRASE* □ **stack arms** place a number of rifles with their butts on the ground and the muzzles together.

stacked /stakt/ ▸*adj.* **1** (of a number of things) put or arranged in a stack or stacks: *the stacked chairs.* ■ (of a place or surface) filled or covered with goods: *the stacked shelves.* ■ (of a machine) having sections that are arranged vertically: *full-sized washer-dryers are replacing stacked units.* ■ (of a heel) made from thin layers of wood, plastic, or another material glued one on top of the other. **2** (of a deck of cards) shuffled or arranged dishonestly so as to gain an unfair advantage. **3** *informal* (of a woman) having large breasts. **4** *Computing* (of a task) placed in a queue for subsequent processing. ■ (of a stream of data) stored in such a way that the most recently stored item is the first to be retrieved.

stad·dle /'stadl/ ▸*n.* a platform or framework supporting a stack or rick. ■ (also **staddle stone**) a stone, esp. one resembling a mushroom in shape, supporting a framework or rick. ▷Old English *stathol* 'base, support,' of Germanic origin; related to the verb **STAND**.

sta·di·a rod /'stādēə/ ▸*n.* another term for **LEVELING ROD**.

sta·di·um /'stādēəm/ ▸*n.* (*pl.* **-di·ums** or **-di·a** /-dēə/) **1** a sports arena with tiers of seats for spectators. ■ (in ancient Rome or Greece) a track for a foot race or chariot race. **2** (*pl.* **-di·a**) an ancient Roman or Greek measure of length, about 185 meters. [originally denoting the length of a stadium.] ▷late Middle English (sense 2): via Latin from Greek *stadion*. Sense 1 dates from the mid 19th cent.

stadt·hold·er /'stat,hōldər/ (also **stad·hold·er**) ▸*n.* (from the 15th century to the late 18th century) the chief magistrate of the United Provinces of the Netherlands. ▷mid 16th cent.: from Dutch *stadhouder* 'deputy,' from *stad* 'place' + *houder* 'holder,' translating medieval Latin *locum tenens*. **—stadt·hold·er·ship** /-,sʜip/ *n.*

Staël /stäl/, Mme de, see **DE STAËL**.

staff1 /staf/ ▸*n.* **1** [treated as *sing.* or *pl.*] all the people employed by a particular organization: *a staff of 600* | *hospital staff were not to blame.* ■ the teachers in a school or college: [as *adj.*] *a staff meeting.* **2** [treated as *sing.* or *pl.*] a group of officers assisting an officer in command of an army formation or administration headquarters. ■ (usu. **Staff**) short for **STAFF SERGEANT**. **3** a long stick used as a support when walking or climbing or as a weapon. ■ a rod or scepter held as a sign of office or authority. ■ short for **FLAGSTAFF**. ■ *Surveying* a rod for measuring distances or heights. **4** (*pl.* **staves** /stāvz/) (also **stave**) *Music* a set of five parallel lines and the spaces between them, on which notes are written to indicate their pitch.

▸*v.* [*trans.*] (usu. **be staffed**) provide (an organization, business, etc.) with staff: *legal advice centers are staffed by volunteer lawyers* [as *adj.*, with *submodifier*] (**staffed**) *all units are fully staffed.* ▷Old English *stæf* (sense 3), of Germanic origin; related to Dutch *staf* and German *Stab*.

▸*PHRASE* □ **the staff of life** a staple food, esp. bread.

staff2 ▸*n.* a mixture of plaster of Paris, cement, or a similar material, used for temporary building work. ▷late 19th cent.: of unknown origin.

Staf·fa /'stafə/ a small uninhabited island in the Inner Hebrides, west of Mull.

staf·fage /'stafij/ ▸*n.* accessory items in a painting, esp. figures or animals in a landscape picture. ▷late 19th cent.: from German, from *staffieren* 'decorate,' perhaps from Old French *estoffer*, from *estoffe* 'stuff.'

staff·er /'stafər/ ▸*n.* a member of the staff of an organization, esp. of a newspaper.

staff no·ta·tion ▸*n.* *Music* notation by means of a stave, esp. as distinct from the tonic sol-fa.

staff of·fi·cer ▸*n.* *Military* an officer serving on the staff of a military headquarters or government department.

Staf·ford·shire bull ter·ri·er /'stafərd,sʜi(ə)r/ ▸*n.* a dog of a small stocky breed of short-haired terrier, with a short, broad head and wide-set forelegs.

staff ser·geant ▸*n.* a noncommissioned officer in the armed forces, in particular: ■ a noncommissioned officer in the U.S. Army ranking above sergeant and below sergeant first class. ■ a noncommissioned officer in the U.S. Air Force ranking above sergeant and below technical sergeant. ■ a noncommissioned officer in the U.S. Marine Corps ranking above sergeant and below gunnery sergeant.

stag /stag/ ▸*n.* **1** a male deer. ■ [usu. as *adj.*] a social gathering attended by men only: *a stag event.* ■ a person who attends a social gathering unaccompanied by a partner. **2** *Brit.* *Stock Market* a person who applies for shares in a new issue with a view to selling at once for a profit.

▸*adv.* without a partner at a social gathering: *a lot of boys **went stag**.* ▷Middle English (as a noun): related to Old Norse *steggr* 'male bird,' Icelandic *steggi* 'tomcat.'

stag bee·tle ▶*n.* a large dark beetle, the male of which has large branched jaws that resemble a stag's antlers. • Family Lucanidae: several species, including the European *Lucanus cervus.*

stage /stāj/ ▶*n.* **1** a point, period, or step in a process or development: *there is no need at this stage to give explicit details | I was in the early stages of pregnancy.* ■ a section of a journey or race: *the final stage of the journey is made by taxi.* ■ each of two or more sections of a rocket or spacecraft that have their own engines and are jettisoned in turn when their propellant is exhausted. ■ [with *adj.*] *Electronics* a specified part of a circuit, typically one consisting of a single amplifying transistor or valve with the associated equipment. **2** a raised floor or platform, typically in a theater, on which actors, entertainers, or speakers perform: *there are only two characters* ***on stage.*** ■ **(the stage)** the acting or theatrical profession: *I've always wanted to* ***go on the stage.*** ■ [in *sing.*] a scene of action or forum of debate, esp. in a particular political context: *Argentina is playing a leading role on the international stage.* **3** a floor or level of a building or structure: *the upper stage was added in the 17th century.* ■ (on a microscope) a raised and usually movable plate on which a slide or object is placed for examination. **4** *Geology* (in chronostratigraphy) a range of strata corresponding to an age in time, forming a subdivision of a series. ■ (in paleoclimatology) a period of time marked by a characteristic climate: *the Boreal stage.* **5** archaic term for STAGECOACH.
▶*v.* [*trans.*] **1** present a performance of (a play or other show): *the show is being staged at the Goodspeed Opera House.* ■ (of a person or group) organize and participate in (a public event): *UDF supporters staged a demonstration in Sofia.* ■ cause (something dramatic or unexpected) to happen: *the president's attempt to stage a comeback | the dollar staged a partial recovery.* **2** *Medicine* diagnose or classify (a disease or patient) as having reached a particular stage in the expected progression of the disease. ▷Middle English (denoting a floor of a building, a platform, or a stopping place): shortening of Old French *estage* 'dwelling,' based on Latin *stare* 'to stand.' Current senses of the verb date from the early 17th cent. **—stage·a·bil·i·ty** /ˌstājəˈbilitē/ *n.* **—stage·a·ble** *adj.*
▶***PHRASES*** □ **hold the stage** dominate a scene of action or forum of debate. □ **set the stage for** prepare the conditions for (the occurrence or beginning of something): *these churchmen helped to set the stage for popular reform.* □ **stage left** (or **right**) on the left (or right) side of a stage from the point of view of a performer facing the audience.

stage·coach /ˈstājˌkōCH/ ▶*n.* a large, closed horse-drawn vehicle formerly used to carry passengers and often mail along a regular route between two places.

stagecoach

stage·craft /ˈstājˌkraft/ ▶*n.* skill or experience in writing or staging plays.

stage di·rec·tion ▶*n.* an instruction in the text of a play, esp. one indicating the movement, position, or tone of an actor, or the sound effects and lighting.

stage-div·ing ▶*n.* the practice (typically among audience members) of jumping from the stage at a rock concert or other event to be caught and carried aloft by the crowd below. **—stage-dive** *v.* [*intrans.*] **—stage-div·er** *n.*

stage door ▶*n.* an actors' and workers' entrance from the street to the area of a theater behind the stage.

stage ef·fect ▶*n.* an effect produced by the lighting, sound, or scenery in a play, movie, etc.: *there are some great stage effects.*

stage fright ▶*n.* nervousness before or during an appearance before an audience.

stage·hand /ˈstājˌhand/ ▶*n.* a person who moves scenery or props before or during the performance of a play.

stage-man·age ▶*v.* [*trans.*] be responsible for the lighting and other technical arrangements for (a stage play). ■ arrange and control (something) carefully in order to create a certain effect: *he stage-managed his image with astounding success.* **—stage man·age·ment** *n.*

stage man·ag·er ▶*n.* the person responsible for the lighting and other technical arrangements for a stage play.

stage name ▶*n.* a name assumed for professional purposes by an actor or other performer.

stage play (also **stage production**) ▶*n.* a play performed on stage rather than broadcast or made into a movie.

stage pres·ence ▶*n.* the ability to command the attention of a theater audience by the impressiveness of one's manner or appearance.

stag·er /ˈstājər/ ▶*n. archaic* an actor.

stage-struck ▶*adj.* having a passionate desire to become an actor.

stage whis·per ▶*n.* a loud whisper uttered by an actor on stage, intended to be heard by the audience but supposedly unheard by other characters in the play. ■ any loud whisper intended to be overheard.

stage·y ▶*adj.* variant spelling of STAGY.

stag·fla·tion /ˌstagˈflāSHən/ ▶*n. Economics* persistent high inflation combined with high unemployment and stagnant demand in a country's economy. ▷1960s: blend of *stagnation* (see STAGNATE) and INFLATION.

stag·ger /ˈstagər/ ▶*v.* **1** [*intrans.*] walk or move unsteadily, as if about to fall: *he staggered to his feet, swaying a little.* ■ [with *adverbial of direction*] *figurative* continue in existence or operation uncertainly or precariously: *the council staggered from one crisis to the next.* ■ *archaic* waver in purpose; hesitate. ■ *archaic* [*trans.*] (of a blow) cause (someone) to walk or move unsteadily, as if about to fall: *the collision staggered her and she fell.* **2** [*trans.*] astonish or deeply shock: *I was staggered to find it was six o'clock | [as adj.]* **(staggering)** *the staggering bills for maintenance and repair.* **3** [*trans.*] arrange (events, payments, hours, etc.) so that they do not occur at the same time; spread over a period of time: *meetings are staggered throughout the day.* ■ arrange (objects or parts of an object) in a zigzag order or so that they are not in line: *stagger the screws at each joint.*
▶*n.* [in *sing.*] **1** an unsteady walk or movement: *she walked with a stagger.* **2** an arrangement of things in a zigzag order or so that they are not in line. ▷late Middle English (as a verb): alteration of dialect *stacker*, from Old Norse *stakra*, frequentative of *staka* 'push, stagger.' The noun dates from the late 16th cent. **—stag·ger·er** *n.* **—stag·ger·ing·ly** *adv.* [as *submodifier*] *a staggeringly unjust society.*

stag·gers /ˈstagərz/ ▶*plural n.* [usu. treated as *sing.*] any of several parasitic or acute deficiency diseases of farm animals characterized by staggering or loss of balance. ■ the inability to stand or walk steadily, esp. as a result of giddiness.

stag·horn cor·al /ˈstagˌhôrn/ ▶*n.* a large stony coral with antlerlike branches. • Genus *Acropora*, order Scleractinia, in particular *A. cervicornis.*

stag·horn fern ▶*n.* a fern with fronds that resemble antlers, occurring in tropical rain forests where it typically grows as an epiphyte. • Genus *Platycerium*, family Polypodiaceae.

stag·horn su·mac /ˈstagˌhôrn/ ▶*n.* see SUMAC.

stag·hound /ˈstagˌhound/ ▶*n.* a large dog of a breed used for hunting deer by sight or scent.

stag·ing /ˈstājiNG/ ▶*n.* **1** an instance or method of presenting a play or other dramatic performance: *one of the better stagings of this Shakespearean classic | the quality of staging and design.* ■ an instance of organizing a public event or protest: *the fourteenth staging of the championships.* **2** a stage or set of stages or temporary platforms arranged as a support for performers or between different levels of scaffolding. **3** *Medicine* diagnosis or classification of the particular stage reached by a progressive disease. **4** the arrangement of stages in a rocket or spacecraft. ■ the separation and jettisoning of a stage from the remainder of a rocket when its propellant is spent.

stag·ing ar·e·a (also **staging point** or **staging post**) ▶*n.* a stopping place or assembly point en route to a destination: *a vast staging area for guerrilla attacks | the geese's major staging area on the St. Lawrence River.*

stag·nant /ˈstagnənt/ ▶*adj.* (of a body of water or the atmosphere of a confined space) having no current or flow and often having an unpleasant smell as a consequence: *a stagnant ditch.* ■ *figurative* showing no activity; dull and sluggish: *a stagnant economy.* ▷mid 17th cent.: from Latin *stagnant-* 'forming a pool of standing water,' from the verb *stagnare*, from *stagnum* 'pool.' **—stag·nan·cy** /-nənsē/ *n.* **—stag·nant·ly** *adv.*

stag·nate /ˈstagˌnāt/ ▶*v.* [*intrans.*] (of water or air) cease to flow or move; become stagnant. ■ *figurative* cease developing; become inactive or dull: *teaching can easily stagnate into a set of routines |* [as *adj.*] **(stagnating)** *stagnating consumer confidence.* ▷mid 17th cent.: from Latin *stagnat-* 'settled as a still pool,' from the verb *stagnare*, from *stagnum* 'pool.' **—stag·na·tion** /stagˈnāSHən/ *n.*

stag par·ty ▶*n.* a celebration held for a man shortly before his wedding, attended by his male friends only. ■ any party attended by men only.

stag·y /ˈstājē/ (also **stag·ey**) ▶*adj.* (**stag·i·er**, **stag·i·est**) excessively theatrical; exaggerated: *a stagy melodramatic voice.* **—stag·i·ly** /-jilē/ *adv.* **—stag·i·ness** *n.*

staid /stād/ ▶*adj.* sedate, respectable, and unadventurous: *staid law firms.* ▷mid 16th cent.: archaic past participle of STAY[1]. **—staid·ly** *adv.* **—staid·ness** *n.*

stain /stān/ ▶*v.* [*trans.*] **1** mark (something) with colored patches or dirty marks that are not easily removed: *her clothing was stained with blood |* [as *adj.*] **(stained)** *a stained placemat |* [*intrans.*] *red ink can stain.* ■ [*intrans.*] be marked or be liable to be marked with such patches. ■ *figurative* damage or bring disgrace to (the reputation or image of someone or something): *the awful events would unfairly stain the city's reputation.* **2** color (a material or object) by applying a penetrative dye or chemical: *wood can always be stained to a darker shade.*
▶*n.* **1** a colored patch or dirty mark that is difficult to remove: *there were mud stains on my shoes.* ■ a thing that damages or brings disgrace to someone or something's reputation: *he regarded his time in jail as a* ***stain on*** *his character.* ■ a patch of brighter or deeper color that suffuses something: *the sun left a red stain behind as it retreated.* **2** a penetrative dye or chemical used in coloring a material or object. ■ *Biology* a special dye used to color organic tissue so as to make the structure visible for microscopic examination. ■ *Heraldry* any of the minor colors used in blazoning and liveries, esp. tenné and sanguine. ▷late Middle English (as a verb): shortening of archaic *distain*, from Old French *desteindre* 'tinge with a color different from the natural one.' The noun was first recorded (mid 16th cent.) in the sense 'defilement, disgrace.' **—stain·a·ble** *adj.* **—stain·er** *n.* (both in sense 2 of the *verb*).

stained glass ▶*n.* colored glass used to form decorative or pictorial designs, notably for church windows, both by painting and esp. by setting contrasting pieces in a lead framework like a mosaic.

stain·less /ˈstānlis/ ▶*adj.* unmarked by or resistant to stains or discoloration. ■ *figurative* (of a person or their reputation) free from wrongdoing or disgrace: *her supposedly stainless past.*

stain·less steel ▶*n.* a form of steel containing chromium, resistant to tarnishing and rust.

stair /ste(ə)r/ ▶*n.* (usu. **stairs**) a set of steps leading from one floor of a building to another, typically inside the building: *he came up the stairs.* ■ single step in such a set: *the bottom stair.* ▷Old English *stǣger*, of Germanic origin; related to Dutch *steiger* 'scaffolding,' from a base meaning 'climb.'

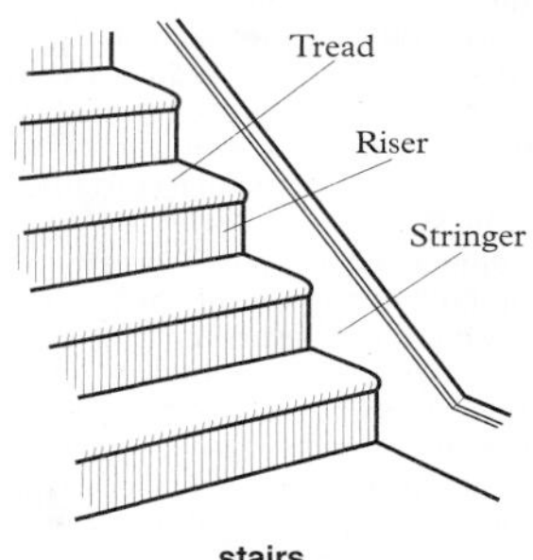

stairs

stair·case /ˈste(ə)rˌkās/ ▶*n.* a set of stairs and its surrounding walls or structure.

stair·climb·er /ˈste(ə)rˌklīmər/ ▶*n.* an exercise machine on which the user simulates the action of climbing a staircase.

stair·head /ˈste(ə)rˌhed/ ▶*n. chiefly Brit.* a landing at the top of a set of stairs.

stair·lift /ˈste(ə)rˌlift/ ▶*n.* a lift in the form of a chair that can be raised or lowered at the edge of a domestic staircase, used for carrying a person who is unable to go up or down the stairs.

stair·way /ˈste(ə)rˌwā/ ▸*n.* a set of steps or stairs and its surrounding walls or structure.

stair·well /ˈste(ə)rˌwel/ ▸*n.* a shaft in a building in which a staircase is built.

stake[1] /stāk/ ▸*n.* **1** a strong wooden or metal post with a point at one end, driven into the ground to support a tree, form part of a fence, act as a boundary mark, etc. ■ a long vertical rod used in basketmaking. ■ a metalworker's small anvil, typically with a projection for fitting into a socket on a bench. **2** (**the stake**) *historical* a wooden post to which a person was tied before being burned alive as a punishment. **3** a territorial division of the Mormon Church under the jurisdiction of a president.
▸*v.* [*trans.*] **1** support (a tree or plant) with a stake or stakes. **2** (**stake something out**) mark an area with stakes so as to claim ownership of it: *the boundary between the two ranches was properly staked out* | *figurative the local dog staked out his territory.* ■ be assertive in defining and defending a position or policy: *Elena was staking out a role for herself as a formidable political force.*
▸*phrasal v.* □ **stake someone/something out** *informal* continuously watch a place or person in secret: *they'd staked out Culley's house for half a day.* ▷Old English *staca;* related to Dutch *staak,* also to STICK[2].
▸*PHRASES* □ **pull up stakes** move or go to live elsewhere. □ **stake a claim** assert one's right to something.

stake[2] ▸*n.* (usu. **stakes**) a sum of money or something else of value gambled on the outcome of a risky game or venture: *playing dice for high stakes* | *figurative the mayor* **raised the stakes** *in the battle for power.* ■ a share or interest in a business, situation, or system: *GM acquired a 50 percent stake in Saab.* ■ (**stakes**) prize money, esp. in horse racing. ■ [in *names*] (**stakes**) a horse race in which all the owners of the racehorses running contribute to the prize money: *the horse is to run in the Lexington Stakes.* ■ [with *adj.*] (**stakes**) a situation involving competition in a specified area: *we will keep you one step ahead in the fashion stakes.*
▸*v.* [*trans.*] **1** gamble (money or something else of value) on the outcome of a game or race: *one gambler staked everything he'd got and lost* | *figurative it was risky to* **stake** *his reputation* **on** *one big success.* **2** *informal* give financial or other support to: *he* **staked** *him* **to** *an education at the École des Beaux-Arts.* ▷late Middle English: perhaps a specialized usage of STAKE[1], from the notion of an object being placed as a wager on a post or stake.
▸*PHRASE* □ **at stake** **1** to be won or lost; at risk: *people's lives could be at stake.* **2** at issue or in question: *the logical response is to give up, but there's more at stake than logic.*

stake bod·y ▸*n.* a body for a truck having a flat open platform with removable posts along the sides.

stake·hold·er /ˈstākˌhōldər/ ▸*n.* **1** (in gambling) an independent party with whom each of those who make a wager deposits the money or counters wagered. **2** a person with an interest or concern in something, esp. a business. ■ [as *adj.*] denoting a type of organization or system in which all the members or participants are seen as having an interest in its success: *a stakeholder economy.*

stake·out /ˈstākˌout/ ▸*n.* *informal* a period of secret surveillance of a building or an area by police in order to observe someone's activities.

Sta·kha·nov·ite /stəˈkänəˌvīt/ ▸*n.* a worker in the former USSR who was exceptionally hardworking and productive. ■ an exceptionally hardworking or zealous person. ▷1930s: from the name of Aleksei Grigorevich *Stakhanov* (1906–1977), Russian coal miner. —**Sta·kha·nov·ism** /-ˌvizəm/ *n.* —**Sta·kha·nov·ist** /-vist/ *n.* & *adj.*

sta·lac·tite /stəˈlakˌtīt/ ▸*n.* a tapering structure hanging like an icicle from the roof of a cave, formed of calcium salts deposited by dripping water. Compare with STALAGMITE. ▷late 17th cent.: from modern Latin *stalactites,* from Greek *stalaktos* 'dripping,' based on *stalassein* 'to drip.' —**sta·lac·tit·ic** /ˌstaləkˈtitik/ *adj.*

stalactites and stalagmites

Sta·lag /ˈstäˌläg/ (also **sta·lag**) ▸*n.* (in World War II) a German prison camp, esp. for noncommissioned officers and privates. ▷German, contraction of *Stammlager,* from *Stamm* 'base, main stock' + *Lager* 'camp.'

sta·lag·mite /stəˈlagˌmīt/ ▸*n.* a mound or tapering column rising from the floor of a cave, formed of calcium salts deposited by dripping water and often uniting with a stalactite. ▷late 17th cent.: from modern Latin *stalagmites,* from Greek *stalagma* 'a drop,' based on *stalassein* (see STALACTITE). —**stal·ag·mit·ic** /ˌstaləgˈmitik/ *adj.*

stale[1] /stāl/ ▸*adj.* (**stal·er, stal·est**) (of food) no longer fresh and pleasant to eat; hard, musty, or dry: *stale bread.* ■ no longer new and interesting or exciting: *their marriage had gone stale.* ■ [*predic.*] (of a person) no longer able to perform well or creatively because of having done something for too long: *a top executive tends to get stale.* ■ (of a check or legal claim) invalid because out of date.
▸*v.* make or become stale. ▷Middle English (describing beer in the sense 'clear from long standing, strong'): probably from Anglo-Norman French and Old French, from *estaler* 'to halt'; compare with the verb STALL. —**stale·ly** /ˈstā(l)lē/ *adv.* —**stale·ness** *n.*

stale[2] ▸*v.* [*intrans.*] (of an animal, esp. a horse) urinate. ▷late Middle English: perhaps from Old French *estaler* 'come to a stop, halt' (compare with STALE[1]).

stale·mate /ˈstālˌmāt/ ▸*n.* *Chess* a position counting as a draw, in which a player is not in check but cannot move except into check. ■ a situation in which further action or progress by opposing or competing parties seems impossible: *the war had again reached stalemate.*
▸*v.* [*trans.*] bring to or cause to reach stalemate: [as *adj.*] (**stalemated**) *the currently stalemated peace talks.* ▷mid 18th cent.: from obsolete *stale* (from Anglo-Norman French *estale* 'position,' from *estaler* 'be placed') + MATE[2].

Sta·lin /ˈstälin/, Joseph (1879–1953), Soviet statesman; general secretary of the Communist Party of the Soviet Union 1922–53; born *Iosif Vissarionovich Dzhugashvili.* In 1928, he launched a succession of five-year plans for rapid industrialization and the enforced collectivization of agriculture. His large-scale purges of the intelligentsia in the 1930s were equally ruthless.

Joseph Stalin

Sta·lin·a·bad /ˌstälənəˈbäd/ former name (1929–61) for **DUSHANBE**.

Sta·lin·grad /ˈstälənˌgrad; -ˌgräd/ former name (1925–61) of **VOLGOGRAD**.

Sta·lin·ism /ˈstäləˌnizəm/ ▸*n.* the ideology and policies adopted by Stalin, based on centralization, totalitarianism, and the pursuit of communism. ■ any rigid centralized authoritarian form of communism. —**Sta·lin·ist** *n.* & *adj.*

Sta·lin Peak former name (1933-1962) of **COMMUNISM PEAK**.

stalk[1] /stôk/ ▸*n.* the main stem of a herbaceous plant: *he chewed a stalk of grass.* ■ the slender attachment or support of a leaf, flower, or fruit: *the acorns grow on stalks.* ■ a similar support for a sessile animal, or for an organ in an animal. ■ a slender support or stem of something: *drinking glasses with long stalks.* ▷Middle English: probably a diminutive of dialect *stale* 'rung of a ladder, long handle.' —**stalked** *adj.* [in *combination*] *rough-stalked meadow grass.* —**stalk·less** *adj.* —**stalk·like** /-ˌlīk/ *adj.* —**stalk·y** *adj.*

stalk[2] ▸*v.* **1** [*trans.*] pursue or approach stealthily: *a cat stalking a bird.* ■ harass or persecute (someone) with unwanted and obsessive attention: *for five years she was stalked by a man who would taunt and threaten her.* ■ *chiefly poetic/literary* move silently or threateningly through (a place): *the tiger stalks the jungle* | *figurative fear stalked the camp.* **2** [*intrans.*] stride somewhere in a proud, stiff, or angry manner: *without another word she turned and stalked out.*
▸*n.* **1** a stealthy pursuit of someone or something. **2** a stiff, striding gait. ▷late Old English *-stealcian* (in *bistealcian* 'walk cautiously or stealthily'), of Germanic origin; related to STEAL.

stalk·er /ˈstôkər/ ▸*n.* a person who stealthily hunts or pursues an animal or another person. ■ a person who harasses or persecutes someone with unwanted and obsessive attention.

stalk·er·az·zi /ˌstôkəˈrätsē/ ▸*plural n.* *informal* photojournalists who follow celebrities closely and persistently with the intention of obtaining sensational pictures. ▷from *stalker* + *-azzi,* on the pattern of *paparazzi.*

stalk-eyed ▸*adj.* (of a crustacean) having eyes mounted on stalks.

stalk·ing horse ▸*n.* a screen traditionally made in the shape of a horse behind which a hunter can stay concealed when stalking prey. ■ a false pretext concealing someone's real intentions. ■ a political candidate who runs only in order to provoke the election and thus allow a stronger candidate to come forward. ▷early 16th cent.: from the former practice of using a horse trained to allow a fowler to hide behind it, or under its coverings, until within easy range of prey.

stall /stôl/ ▸*n.* **1** a stand, booth, or compartment for the sale of goods in a market or large covered area: *fruit and vegetable stalls.* **2** an individual compartment for an animal in a stable or barn, enclosed on three sides. ■ a stable. ■ a marked-out parking space for a vehicle. ■ a compartment for one person in a shower room, toilet, or similar facility. **3** a fixed seat in the choir or chancel of a church, more or less enclosed at the back and sides and often canopied, typically reserved for a particular member of the clergy. **4** (**stalls**) *Brit.* the seats on the ground floor in a theater. **5** an instance of an engine, vehicle, aircraft, or boat stalling: *speed must be maintained to avoid a stall and loss of control.*
▸*v.* **1** [*intrans.*] (of a motor vehicle or its engine) stop running, typically because of an overload on the engine: *her car stalled at the crossroads.* ■ (of an aircraft or its pilot) reach a condition where the speed is too low to allow effective operation of the controls. ■ *Sailing* have insufficient wind power in the sails to give controlled motion. ■ [*trans.*] cause (an engine, vehicle, aircraft, or boat) to stall. **2** [*intrans.*] (of a situation or process) stop making progress: *his career had stalled, hers taken off.* ■ [*trans.*] delay, obstruct, or block the progress of (something): *the government has stalled the much-needed project.* ■ speak or act in a deliberately vague way in order to gain more time to deal with a question or issue; prevaricate: *she was* **stalling for time.** ■ [*trans.*] delay or divert (someone) by acting in such a way: *stall him until I've had time to take a look.* **3** [*trans.*] put or keep (an animal) in a stall, esp. in order to fatten it. ▷Old English *steall* 'stable or cattle shed,' of Germanic origin; related to Dutch *stal,* also to STAND. Early senses of the verb included 'reside, dwell' and 'bring to a halt.'

stal·lion /ˈstalyən/ ▸*n.* an uncastrated adult male horse. ▷Middle English: from an Anglo-Norman French variant of Old French *estalon,* from a derivative of a Germanic base shared by STALL.

Stal·lone /stəˈlōn/, Sylvester Enzio (1946–), U.S. actor, writer, and director; nickname **Sly**. He is best known for writing and starring in five *Rocky* movies (1976, 1979 1982, 1985, 1990) and three *Rambo* movies (1982, 1985, 1988). He also directed *Rocky II, Rocky III,* and *Rocky IV.*

stal·wart /ˈstôlwərt/ ▸*adj.* loyal, reliable, and hardworking: *he remained a stalwart supporter of the cause.* ■ *dated* strongly built and sturdy: *he was of stalwart build.*
▸*n.* a loyal, reliable, and hardworking supporter or participant in an organization or team: *the stalwarts of the Ladies' Auxiliary.* ▷late Middle English: Scots variant of obsolete *stalworth,* from Old English *stǣl* 'place' + *weorth* 'worth.' —**stal·wart·ly** *adv.* —**stal·wart·ness** *n.*

Stam·boul /stam'bo͞ol; stäm-/ archaic name for **ISTANBUL.**

sta·men /'stāmin/ ▶*n. Botany* the male fertilizing organ of a flower, typically consisting of a pollen-containing anther and a filament. ▷mid 17th cent.: from Latin, literally 'warp in an upright loom, thread.'

Stam·ford /'stamfərd/ a commercial city in southwestern Connecticut, on Long Island Sound; pop. 117,083.

stam·i·na /'stamənə/ ▶*n.* the ability to sustain prolonged physical or mental effort: *their secret is stamina rather than speed.* ▷late 17th cent. (in the sense 'rudiments, essential elements of something'): from Latin, plural of **STAMEN** in the sense 'threads spun by the Fates.'

stam·i·nate /'stamə,nāt/ ▶*adj. Botany* (of a plant or flower) having stamens but no pistils. Compare with **PISTILLATE.**

stam·i·node /'stamə,nōd/ ▶*n. Botany* a sterile or abortive stamen, frequently resembling a stamen without its anther.

stam·mer /'stamər/ ▶*v.* [*intrans.*] speak with sudden involuntary pauses and a tendency to repeat the initial letters of words. ■ [*trans.*] utter (words) in such a way: *I **stammered out** my history* | [with *direct speech*] *"I . . . I can't," Isabel stammered.*
▶*n.* [in *sing.*] a tendency to stammer: *as a young man, he had a dreadful stammer.* ▷late Old English *stamerian*; related to **STUMBLE.** The noun dates from the late 18th cent. **—stam·mer·er** *n.* **—stam·mer·ing·ly** *adv.*

stamp /stamp/ ▶*v.* [*trans.*] **1** bring down (one's foot) heavily on the ground or on something on the ground: *he stamped his foot in frustration* | [*intrans.*] *he threw his cigarette down and stamped on it* | *figurative Robertson stamped on all these suggestions.* ■ [*trans.*] crush, flatten, or remove with a heavy blow from one's feet: *he stamped out the flames before they could grow.* ■ (**stamp something out**) suppress or put an end to something by taking decisive action: *urgent action is required to stamp out corruption.* ■ [*intrans.*] walk with heavy, forceful steps: *John stamped off, muttering.* **2** impress a pattern or mark, esp. an official one, on (a surface, object, or document) using an engraved or inked block or die or other instrument: *the woman stamped my passport.* ■ impress (a pattern or mark) on something in such a way: *a key with a number **stamped on** the shaft* | *figurative he must be able to **stamp** his authority **on** his team.* ■ make (something) by cutting it out with a die or mold: *the knives are **stamped out from** a flat strip of steel.* ■ *figurative* reveal or mark out as having a particular character, quality, or ability: *his style **stamps** him **as** a player to watch.* **3** affix a postage stamp or stamps onto (a letter or package): *Annie stamped the envelope for her.* **4** crush or pulverize (ore).
▶*n.* **1** an instrument for stamping a pattern or mark, in particular an engraved or inked block or die. ■ a mark or pattern made by such an instrument, esp. one indicating official validation or certification: *passports with visa stamps* | *figurative the emperor gave them his stamp of approval.* ■ *figurative* a characteristic or distinctive impression or quality: *the whole project has the stamp of authority.* ■ a particular class or type or person or thing: *empiricism of this stamp has been esp. influential in British philosophy.* **2** a small adhesive piece of paper stuck to something to show that an amount of money has been paid, in particular a postage stamp: *a first-class stamp.* **3** an act or sound of stamping with the foot: *the stamp of boots on the bare floor.* **4** a block for crushing ore in a stamp mill. ▷Middle English (in the sense 'crush to a powder'): of Germanic origin; related to German *stampfen* 'stamp with the foot'; reinforced by Old French *estamper* 'to stamp.' Compare with **STOMP.** **—stamp·er** *n.*

Stamp Act ▶*n.* an act of the British Parliament in 1756 that exacted revenue from the American colonies by imposing a stamp duty on newspapers and legal and commercial documents. Colonial opposition led to the act's repeal in 1766 and helped encourage the revolutionary movement against the British Crown.

stam·pede /stam'pēd/ ▶*n.* a sudden panicked rush of a number of horses, cattle, or other animals. ■ a sudden rapid movement or reaction of a mass of people in response to a particular circumstance or stimulus: *a stampede of bargain hunters.* ■ [often in *titles*] a rodeo: *the Calgary Stampede.*
▶*v.* [*intrans.*] (of horses, cattle, or other animals) rush wildly in a sudden mass panic: *the nearby sheep stampeded as if they sensed impending danger.* ■ [*intrans.*] (of people) move rapidly in a mass: *the children stampeded through the kitchen, playing tag or hide-and-seek.* ■ [*trans.*] cause (people or animals) to move in such a way: *the raiders stampeded 200 mules* | *figurative don't let them **stampede** us **into** anything.* ▷early 19th cent.: Mexican Spanish use of Spanish *estampida* 'crash, uproar,' of Germanic origin; related to the verb **STAMP.** **—stam·ped·er** *n.*

stamp·ing ground ▶*n.* another term for **STOMPING GROUND.**

stamp mill ▶*n.* a mill for crushing ore.

stance /stans/ ▶*n.* **1** the way in which someone stands, esp. when deliberately adopted (as in baseball, golf, and other sports); a person's posture: *she altered her stance, resting all her weight on one leg.* ■ the attitude of a person or organization toward something; a standpoint: *the party is changing its **stance on** the draft.* **2** *Climbing* a ledge or foothold on which a belay can be secured. ▷Middle English (denoting a standing place): from French, from Italian *stanza.*

stanch[1] /stônch; stänch/ (also **staunch**) ▶*v.* [*trans.*] stop or restrict (a flow of blood) from a wound: *colleagues may have saved her life by stanching the flow* | *figurative the company did nothing to stanch the tide of rumors.* ■ stop the flow of blood from (a wound). ▷Middle English: from Old French *estanchier,* from the base of **STAUNCH**[1].

stanch[2] ▶*adj.* variant spelling of **STAUNCH**[1] (sense 2).

stan·chion /'stanchən/ ▶*n.* an upright bar, post, or frame forming a support or barrier. ▷Middle English: from Anglo-Norman French *stanchon,* from Old French *estanchon,* from *estance* 'a support,' probably based on Latin *stant-* 'standing,' from the verb *stare.* **—stan·chioned** *adj.*

stand /stand/ ▶*v.* (*past* **stood** /sto͝od/) **1** [*intrans.*] have or maintain an upright position, supported by one's feet: *Lionel stood in the doorway* | *she stood still, heart hammering.* ■ rise to one's feet: *the two men **stood up** and shook hands.* ■ [*intrans.*] move to and remain in a specified position: *she stood aside to let them enter.* ■ [*trans.*] place or set in an upright or specified position: *don't stand the plant in direct sunlight.* ■ [*trans.*] *Bell-ringing* bring (a bell) to rest in the mouth upward position ready for ringing. **2** [*intrans.*] (of an object, building, or settlement) be situated in a particular place or position: *the town stood on a hill* | *the hotel stands in three acres of gardens.* ■ (of a building or other vertical structure) remain upright and entire rather than fall into ruin or be destroyed: *after the heavy storms, only one house was left standing.* ■ remain valid or unaltered: *my decision stands* | *his strikeout record stood for 38 years.* ■ (esp. of a vehicle) remain stationary: *the train now standing on track 3.* ■ (of a liquid) collect and remain motionless: *avoid planting in soil where water stands in winter.* ■ (of food, a mixture, or liquid) rest without disturbance, typically so as to infuse or marinate: *pour boiling water over the fruit and leave it to stand for 5 minutes.* ■ [*intrans.*] (of a ship) remain on a specified course: *the ship was standing north.* **3** [*intrans.*] be in a specified state or condition: *since mother's death, the house had stood empty* | *sorry, darling—I stand corrected.* ■ adopt a particular attitude toward a matter or issue: *students should consider where they stand on this issue.* ■ be of a specified height: *Sampson was a small man, standing 5 ft. 4 in. tall.* ■ (**stand at**) be at (a particular level or value): *the budget stood at $14 million per annum.* ■ [*intrans.*] be in a situation where one is likely to do something: *investors stood to lose heavily.* ■ act in a specified capacity: *he stood watch all night.* ■ (also **stand at stud**) [*intrans.*] (of a stallion) be available for breeding. **4** [*trans.* often *modal*] withstand (an experience or test) without being damaged: *small boats that could stand the punishment of heavy seas.* ■ [usu. with *negative*] *informal* be able to endure or tolerate: *I can't stand the way Mom talks to him.* ■ [with *modal negative*] *informal* strongly dislike: *I can't stand brandy.* **5** [*intrans.*] *Brit.* be a candidate in an election: *he **stood for** Parliament in 1968.* **6** [usu. with *two objs.*] provide (food or drink) for someone at one's own expense: *somebody in the bar would stand him a beer.*
▶*phrasal v.* □ **stand alone** be unequaled: *when it came to fun, Julia stood alone.* □ **stand aside** take no action to prevent, or not involve oneself in, something that is happening: *the army had stood aside as the monarchy fell.* ■ another way of saying **STAND DOWN** (sense 1) below. □ **stand back** withdraw from a situation emotionally in order to view it more objectively. ■ another way of saying **STAND ASIDE** above. □ **stand by 1** be present while something bad is happening but fail to take any action to stop it: *he was beaten to the ground as onlookers stood by.* **2** support or remain loyal to (someone), typically in a time of need: *she had stood by him during his years in prison.* ■ adhere to or abide by (something promised, stated, or decided): *the government must stand by its pledges.* **3** be ready to deal or assist with something: *two battalions were on their way, and a third was standing by.* □ **stand down 1** withdraw or resign from a position or office: *he stood down as leader of the party.* **2** (**stand down** or **stand someone down**) relax or cause to relax after a state of readiness: *if something doesn't happen soon, I guess they'll stand us down.* **3** (of a witness) leave the witness stand after giving evidence. □ **stand for 1** be an abbreviation of or symbol for: *NASA stands for National Aeronautics and Space Administration.* **2** [with *negative*] *informal* refuse to endure or tolerate: *I won't stand for any nonsense.* **3** support (a cause or principle): *we stand for animal welfare.* □ **stand in 1** deputize: *Brown **stood in for** the injured Simpson.* **2** *Nautical* sail closer to the shore. □ **stand off** move or keep away: *the women stood off at a slight distance.* ■ *Nautical* sail further away from the shore. □ **stand someone off** keep someone away: repel someone. □ **stand on 1** be scrupulous in the observance of: *call me Alex—let's not stand on formality.* **2** *Nautical* continue on the same course. □ **stand out 1** project from a surface: *the veins in his neck stood out.* ■ be easily noticeable: *he was one of those men who stood out in a crowd.* ■ be clearly better or more significant than someone or something: *four issues stand out as being of crucial importance.* **2** persist in opposition or support of something: *she **stood out against** public opinion* | *the company **stood out for** the product it wanted.* □ **stand over 1** stand close to (someone) so as to watch, supervise, or intimidate them. **2** (**stand over** or **stand something over**) be postponed or postpone to be dealt with at a later date: *a number of points were stood over to a further meeting.* □ **stand to** [often in *imperative*] *Military* stand ready for an attack, esp. one before dawn or after dark. □ **stand up** (of an argument, claim, evidence, etc.) remain valid after close scrutiny or analysis: *but will your story stand up in court?* □ **stand someone up** *informal* fail to keep an appointment with a boyfriend or girlfriend. □ **stand up for** speak or act in support of: *she learned to **stand up for herself.*** ■ act as best man for in a wedding. □ **stand up to 1** make a spirited defense against: *giving workers the confidence to stand up to their employers.* **2** be resistant to the harmful effects of (prolonged wear or use).
▶*n.* **1** [usu. in *sing.*] an attitude toward a particular issue; a position taken in an argument: *the party's tough stand on welfare* | *his traditionalist stand.* ■ a determined effort to resist or fight for something: *this was not the moment to **make a stand for** independence* | *we have to **take a stand against** racism.* ■ an act of holding one's ground against or halting to resist an opposing force: *Custer's legendary last stand.* **2** a place where, or an object on which, someone or something stands, sits, or rests, in particular: ■ a large raised tiered structure for spectators, typically at a sports arena: *her parents watched from the stands.* ■ a rack, base, or piece of furniture for holding, supporting, or displaying something: *a microphone stand.* ■ a small stall or booth in a street, market, or public building from which goods are sold: *a hot-dog stand.* ■ a raised platform for a band, orchestra, or speaker. ■ (**the stand**) (also **witness stand**) a witness box: *Sergeant Harris took the stand.* ■ the place where someone typically stands or sits: *she took her stand in front of the desks.* ■ a place where vehicles, typically taxicabs, wait for passengers. **3** [usu. in *sing.*] a cessation from motion or progress: *the train drew to a stand by the signal box.* ■ each halt made on a touring theatrical production to give one or more performances. **4** a group of growing plants of a specified kind, esp. trees: *a stand of poplars.* ▷Old English *standan* (verb), *stand* (noun), of Germanic origin, from an Indo-European root shared by Latin *stare* and Greek *histanai,* also by the noun **STEAD.** **—stand·er** *n.*
▶*PHRASES* □ **as it stands** in its present condition: *there are no merits in the proposal as it stands.* ■ (also **as things stand**) in the present circumstances: *the country would struggle, as it stands, to host the next Winter Olympic Games.* □ **it stands to reason** see **REASON.** □ **stand a chance** see **CHANCE.** □ **stand one's ground** maintain one's position, typically in the face of opposition: *she stood her ground, refusing to let him intimidate her.* □ **stand someone in good stead** see **STEAD.** □ **stand on one's own (two) feet** be or become self-reliant or independent. □ **stand out a mile** see **MILE.** □ **stand out like a sore thumb** see **SORE.** □ **stand pat** see **PAT**[2]. □ **stand trial** be tried in a court of law. □ **stand up and be counted** state publicly one's

support for someone or something. □ **will the real —— please stand up** *informal* used rhetorically to indicate that the specified person should clarify their position or reveal their true character: *he was so different from the unhappy man of a week ago—would the real Jack Lawrence please stand up?*

stand-a·lone (also **stand·a·lone** /ˈstandə,lōn/) ▸*adj.* (of computer hardware or software) able to operate independently of other hardware or software.

stand·ard /ˈstandərd/ ▸*n.* **1** a level of quality or attainment: *their restaurant offers a high standard of service | the governor's ambition to raise standards in schools.* ■ a required or agreed level of quality or attainment: *half of the beaches fail to comply with EPA standards | their tap water was not* ***up to standard.*** **2** an idea or thing used as a measure, norm, or model in comparative evaluations: *the wages are low by today's standards | the system had become an industry standard.* ■ (**standards**) principles of conduct informed by notions of honor and decency: *a decline in moral standards.* ■ a form of language that is widely accepted as the correct form. ■ the prescribed weight of fine metal in gold or silver coins: *the sterling standard for silver.* ■ a system by which the value of a currency is defined in terms of gold or silver or both. **3** an object that is supported in an upright position, in particular: ■ a military or ceremonial flag carried on a pole or hoisted on a rope. ■ a tree or shrub that grows on an erect stem of full height. ■ a shrub grafted on an erect stem and trained in tree form. ■ *Botany* the large frequently erect uppermost petal of a papilionaceous flower. Also called **VEXILLUM**. ■ *Botany* one of the inner petals of an iris flower, frequently erect. ■ an upright water or gas pipe. **4** a tune or song of established popularity.
▸*adj.* **1** used or accepted as normal or average: *the standard rate of income tax | it is standard practice in museums to register objects as they are acquired.* ■ (of a size, measure, design, etc.) such as is regularly used or produced; not special or exceptional: *all these doors come in a range of standard sizes.* ■ (of a work, repertoire, or writer) viewed as authoritative or of permanent value and so widely read or performed: *his essays on the interpretation of reality became a standard text.* ■ denoting or relating to the spoken or written form of a language widely accepted as usual and correct: *speakers of standard English.* **2** [*attrib.*] (of a tree or shrub) growing on an erect stem of full height. ■ (of a shrub) grafted on an erect stem and trained in tree form: *standard roses.* ▹Middle English (denoting a flag raised on a pole as a rallying point, the authorized exemplar of a unit of measurement, or an upright timber): shortening of Old French *estendart,* from *estendre* 'extend'; in sense 3, influenced by the verb **STAND**. —**stand·ard·ly** *adv.*
▸*PHRASE* □ **raise one's** (or **the**) **standard** *chiefly figurative* take up arms: *he is the only one who has dared raise his standard against her.*

Stand·ard & Poor's 500 /ˈstandərd ən ˈpo͝orz/ (abbr.: **S&P 500**) ▸*n. Finance* a group of 500 companies whose average daily share prices are used to calculate an index of the day's security prices.

stand·ard-bear·er ▸*n.* a soldier who is responsible for carrying the distinctive flag of a unit, regiment, or army. ■ a leading figure in a cause or movement: *the announcement made her a standard-bearer for gay rights.*

Stand·ard·bred /ˈstandərd,bred/ (also **stand·ard·bred**) ▸*n.* a horse of a breed able to attain a specified speed, developed esp. for trotting.

stand·ard de·vi·a·tion ▸*n. Statistics* a quantity calculated to indicate the extent of deviation for a group as a whole.

stand·ard er·ror ▸*n. Statistics* a measure of the statistical accuracy of an estimate, equal to the standard deviation of the theoretical distribution of a large population of such estimates.

stand·ard gauge ▸*n.* a railroad gauge of 56.5 inches (1.435 m), standard in the U.S., Britain, and many other parts of the world.

stand·ard·ize /ˈstandər,dīz/ ▸*v.* [*trans.*] cause (something) to conform to a standard: *Jones's effort to standardize oriental spelling.* ■ [*intrans.*] (**standardize on**) adopt (something) as one's standard: *we could standardize on U.S. equipment.* ■ determine the properties of by comparison with a standard. —**stand·ard·iz·a·ble** *adj.* —**stand·ard·i·za·tion** /,standərdiˈzāsнən/ *n.* —**stand·ard·iz·er** *n.*

stand·ard mod·el ▸*n.* (**the standard model**) *Physics* a mathematical description of the elementary particles of matter and the electromagnetic, weak, and strong forces by which they interact.

stand·ard of liv·ing ▸*n.* the degree of wealth and material comfort available to a person or community.

stand·ard time ▸*n.* a uniform time for places in approximately the same longitude, established in a country or region by law or custom.

stand·by /ˈstan(d),bī/ ▸*n.* (*pl.* **-bys**) readiness for duty or immediate deployment: *buses were placed* ***on standby*** *for the trip to Washington.* ■ the state of waiting to secure an unreserved place for a journey or performance, allocated on the basis of earliest availability: *passengers were obliged to go* ***on standby.*** ■ a person waiting to secure such a place. ■ a person or thing ready to be deployed immediately, esp. if needed as backup in an emergency: *a generator was kept as a standby in case of power failure |* [as *adj.*] *a standby rescue vessel.* ■ an operational mode of an electrical appliance in which the power is switched on but the appliance is not actually functioning.

stand-down ▸*n. chiefly Military* a period of relaxation after a state of alert. ■ an off-duty period.

stand·ee /stanˈdē/ ▸*n.* a person who stands, esp. in a passenger vehicle when all the seats are occupied or at a performance or sporting event.

stand-in ▸*n.* a person who stands in for another, esp. in a performance; a substitute: *his stand-in does all the dancing sequences.*

stand·ing /ˈstandiNG/ ▸*n.* **1** position, status, or reputation: *their standing in the community | a man of high social standing.* ■ (**standings**) the table of scores indicating the relative positions of competitors in a sports contest: *she heads the world championship standings.* **2** used to specify the length of time that something has lasted or that someone has fulfilled a particular role: *an interdepartmental squabble* ***of long standing.***
▸*adj.* [*attrib.*] **1** (of a jump or a start in a running race) performed from rest or an upright position, without a run-up or the use of starting blocks. **2** remaining in force or use; permanent: *he has a standing invitation to visit them | a standing army.* **3** (of water) stagnant or still. **4** (of grain) not yet reaped and so still erect. **5** *Printing* (of metal type) kept set up after use.
▸*PHRASES* □ **all standing** *Sailing* (chiefly with reference to a boat's stopping) without time to lower the sails. □ **in good standing** in favor or on good terms with someone: *the companies wanted to stay* ***in good standing with*** *the government.* □ **leave someone/something standing** *informal* be much better or make much faster progress than someone or something else.

stand·ing com·mit·tee ▸*n.* a permanent committee that meets regularly.

stand·ing count (also **standing eight count**) ▸*n. Boxing* a count of eight taken on a boxer who has not been knocked down but who appears temporarily unfit to continue fighting.

stand·ing crop ▸*n.* a growing crop, esp. of a grain. ■ *Ecology* the total biomass of an ecosystem or any of its components at a given time.

stand·ing joke ▸*n.* something that regularly causes amusement or provokes ridicule.

stand·ing or·der ▸*n.* **1** an order or ruling governing the procedures of a society, council, or other deliberative body. **2** a military order or ruling that is retained irrespective of changing conditions.

stand·ing o·va·tion ▸*n.* a period of prolonged applause during which those in the crowd or audience rise to their feet.

stand·ing part ▸*n.* the end of a rope in a ship's rigging that is made fast, as distinct from the end to be hauled on. ■ (in knot-tying) the main part of the rope as opposed to the free end.

stand·ing rig·ging ▸*n.* see **RIGGING** (sense 1).

Stand·ing Rock a Sioux Indian reservation that straddles the North Dakota–South Dakota border, west of the Missouri River.

stand·ing room ▸*n.* space available for people to stand rather than sit in a vehicle, building, or stadium.

stand·ing stone ▸*n.* another term for **MENHIR**.

stand·ing wave ▸*n. Physics* a vibration of a system in which some particular points remain fixed while others between them vibrate with the maximum amplitude. Compare with **TRAVELING WAVE**.

Stan·dish /ˈstandisн/, Miles (*c.* 1584–1656), American colonist; born in England. He accompanied the Pilgrims to America in 1620 and became the military leader of Plymouth Colony. He was a cofounder of Duxbury, Massachusetts, in 1631. He is romanticized as the lovelorn suitor in Longfellow's fictional poem "The Courtship of Miles Standish" (1858).

stand·ish /ˈstandisн/ ▸*n. chiefly historical* a stand for holding pens, ink, and other writing equipment. ▹Middle English: commonly held to be from the verb **STAND + DISH**, but evidence of such a use of *dish* is lacking.

stand·off /ˈstand,ôf; -,äf/ ▸*n.* a stalemate or deadlock between two equally matched opponents in a dispute or conflict: *the 16-day-old standoff was no closer to being resolved.*

stand·off·ish /,standˈôfisн; -ˈäfisн/ ▸*adj. informal* distant and cold in manner; unfriendly. —**stand·off·ish·ly** *adv.* —**stand·off·ish·ness** *n.*

stand·out /ˈstand,out/ *informal* ▸*n.* a person or thing of exceptional ability or high quality: *standouts include the homemade ravioli and the pizzas.*
▸*adj.* [*attrib.*] exceptionally good: *he became a standout quarterback in the NFL.*

stand·pipe /ˈstan(d),pīp/ ▸*n.* a vertical pipe extending from a water supply, esp. one connecting a temporary tap to the main.

stand·point /ˈstan(d),point/ ▸*n.* an attitude to or outlook on issues, typically arising from one's circumstances or beliefs: *she writes on religion* ***from the standpoint of*** *a believer.* ■ the position from which someone is able to view a scene or an object.

St. An·drews a town in eastern Scotland, on the North Sea; pop. 14,000. It is noted for its university that was founded in 1410 and for its historic, championship golf courses.

St. An·drew's Cross *n. Heraldry* an X-shaped cross, esp. white on a blue background (as a national emblem of Scotland). Also called **SALTIRE**.

stand·still /ˈstan(d),stil/ ▸*n.* [in *sing.*] a situation or condition in which there is no movement or activity at all: *the traffic* ***came to a standstill.***

stand·still a·gree·ment ▸*n. Finance* an agreement between two countries in which a debt owed by one to the other is held in abeyance for a specified period. ■ an agreement between a company and a bidder for the company in which the bidder agrees to buy no more shares for a specified period.

stand-to ▸*n. Military* the state of readiness for action or attack. ■ the formal start to a day of military operations.

stand-up (also **stand·up** /ˈstand,əp/) ▸*adj.* [*attrib.*] **1** involving, done by, or engaged in by people standing up: *a stand-up party.* ■ such that people have to stand rather than sit: *a stand-up bar.* ■ (of a comedian) performing by standing in front of an audience and telling jokes. ■ (of comedy) performed in such a way: *his stand-up routine depends on improvised observations.* **2** *informal* courageous and loyal in a combative way: *he was a stand-up kind of guy* **3** designed to stay upright or erect.
▸*n.* a comedian who performs by standing in front of an audience and telling jokes. ■ comedy performed in such a way: *he began doing stand-up when he was fifteen.* ■ a brief monologue by a television news reporter.

Stan·ford /ˈstanfərd/, A(masa) Leland (1824–93), U.S. railroad official and philanthropist. He was governor of California 1861–63; a member of the U.S. Senate 1885–93; promoter, financier, and director of two railroads, the Central Pacific and the Southern Pacific; and founder of Stanford University in 1885.

Stan·ford-Bi·net test /ˈstanfərd bəˈnā/ ▸*n.* an intelligence test based on the Binet-Simon scale, commonly administered to children.

stan·hope /ˈstan,hōp; ˈstanəp/ ▸*n. historical* a light open horse-drawn carriage for one person, with two or four wheels. ▹early 19th cent.: named after Fitzroy *Stanhope* (1787–1864), an English clergyman for whom the first one was made.

Stan·is·laus, St. /ˈstanə,slôs; -,släs/ (1030–79), patron saint of Poland; Polish name *Stanisław*; known as **St. Stanislaus of Cracow**. As bishop of Cracow 1072–79, he excommunicated King Boleslaus II. According to tradition, Stanislaus was murdered by Boleslaus while attending Mass. Feast day, April 11 (formerly May 7).

Stan·i·slav·sky /,stanəˈsläfskē/, Konstantin (Sergeevich) (1863–1938), Russian theater director and actor; born *Konstantin Sergeevich Alekseev.* He trained actors to take a psychological approach and to use latent powers of self-expression when taking on roles; his theory and technique were later developed into method acting.

S

stank /stanGk/ ▶ past of STINK.

Stan·ley[1] /ˈstanlē/ (also **Port Stan·ley**) the chief port and town in the Falkland Islands, on the island of East Falkland; pop. 1,557.

Stan·ley[2], Sir Henry Morton (1841–1904), Welsh explorer; born *John Rowlands*. In 1871, he found David Livingstone (1813–73) at Lake Tanganyika in Africa. After Livingstone's death, Stanley continued his explorations in Africa, charting Lake Victoria (1874), tracing the course of the Congo (1874–77), and mapping Lake Albert (1889). In 1889, he was the first European to visit Lake Edward.

Stan·ley, Mount a mountain in the Ruwenzori range in central Africa, on the border between the Democratic Republic of the Congo (formerly Zaire) and Uganda. Margherita Peak, which rises to 16,765 feet (5,110 m), is the third-highest mountain in Africa. African name **NGALIEMA, MOUNT**. ▷named after Sir Henry M. *Stanley*, the first European to reach it (1889).

Stan·ley crane ▶*n.* another term for BLUE CRANE.

Stan·ley Cup a trophy awarded annually to the ice hockey team that wins the championship in the National Hockey League. ▷named after Lord *Stanley* of Preston (1841–1908), the governor general of Canada who donated the trophy in 1893.

Stan·ley·ville /ˈstanlē,vil/ former name (1882–1966) for **KISANGANI**.

stan·na·ry /ˈstanərē/ ▶*n.* (*pl.* **-ries**) (usu. **the stannaries**) *Brit., chiefly historical* a tin-mining district in Cornwall or Devon, England. ▷late Middle English: from medieval Latin *stannaria* (plural), from late Latin *stannum* 'tin.'

stan·nic /ˈstanik/ ▶*adj. Chemistry* of tin with a valence of four; of tin(IV). Compare with STANNOUS. ▷late 18th cent.: from late Latin *stannum* 'tin' + -IC.

stan·nous /ˈstanəs/ ▶*adj. Chemistry* of tin with a valence of two; of tin(II). Compare with STANNIC. ▷mid 19th cent.: from late Latin *stannum* 'tin' + -OUS.

St. An·tho·ny's Cross (also **St. An·tho·ny Cross**) ▶*n.* a T-shaped cross.

St. An·tho·ny's Fire *n.* **1** another term for ERYSIPELAS. **2** another term for ERGOTISM.

Stan·ton[1] /ˈstantən/, Edwin McMasters (1814–69), U.S. lawyer and public official. As secretary of war 1862–67 and briefly during 1868, he served under President Lincoln and played a pivotal role in the impeachment proceedings against President Andrew Johnson. In 1869, he was appointed to the U.S. Supreme Court but died before taking office.

Stan·ton[2], Elizabeth Cady (1815–1902), U.S. social reformer. With Lucretia Mott, she organized the first U.S. women's rights convention, in Seneca Falls, New York, in 1848. From 1852, she led the women's rights movement with Susan B. Anthony. She was president of the National Woman Suffrage Association 1869–90 and an editor of the radical feminist magazine *Revolution* 1868–70.

Elizabeth Cady Stanton

stan·za /ˈstanzə/ ▶*n.* a group of lines forming the basic recurring metrical unit in a poem; a verse. ■ a group of four lines in some Greek and Latin meters. ▷late 16th cent.: from Italian, literally 'standing place,' also 'stanza.' **—stan·zaed** (also **stan·za'd**) *adj.* **—stan·za·ic** /stanˈzā-ik/ *adj.*

sta·pe·di·al /stəˈpēdēəl/ ▶*adj.* [*attrib.*] *Anatomy & Zoology* of or relating to the stapes. ▷late 19th cent.: from modern Latin *stapedius* (denoting the muscle attached to the neck of the stapes) + -AL.

sta·pe·li·a /stəˈpēlyə/ ▶*n.* a succulent African plant with large star-shaped fleshy flowers that have bold markings and a fetid carrionlike smell that attracts pollinating flies. Also called CARRION FLOWER. • Genus *Stapelia*, family Asclepiadaceae. ▷modern Latin, named after Jan Bode von *Stapel* (died 1636), Dutch botanist.

sta·pes /ˈstāpēz/ ▶*n.* (*pl.* same) *Anatomy* a small stirrup-shaped bone in the middle ear, transmitting vibrations from the incus to the inner ear. Also called STIRRUP. ▷mid 17th cent.: modern Latin, from medieval Latin *stapes* 'stirrup.'

staph /staf/ ▶*n. informal* **1** *Medicine* short for STAPHYLOCOCCUS. **2** *Entomology* short for STAPHYLINID.

staph·y·lin·id /,stafəˈlinid/ ▶*n. Entomology* a beetle of a family (Staphylinidae) that comprises the rove beetles. ▷late 19th cent.: from modern Latin *Staphylinidae* (plural), from the genus name *Staphylinus*, from Greek *staphulinos*, denoting a kind of insect.

staph·y·lo·coc·cus /,staf(ə)lōˈkäkəs/ ▶*n.* (*pl.* **-coc·ci** /-ˈkäk,sī; -,sē/) a bacterium of a genus that includes many pathogenic kinds that cause pus formation, esp. in the skin and mucous membranes. • Genus *Staphylococcus*; Gram-positive cocci in clusters. ▷modern Latin, from Greek *staphulē* 'bunch of grapes' + *kokkos* 'berry.' **—staph·y·lo·coc·cal** /-ˈkäkəl/ *adj.*

sta·ple[1] /ˈstāpəl/ ▶*n.* a piece of bent metal or wire pushed through something or clipped over it as a fastening, in particular: ■ a piece of thin wire with a long center portion and two short end pieces that are driven by a stapler through sheets of paper to fasten them together. ■ a small U-shaped metal bar with pointed ends for driving into wood to hold attachments such as electric wires, battens, or sheets of cloth in place.

▶*v.* [*trans.*] attach or secure with a staple or staples: *Mark stapled a batch of papers together.* ▷Old English *stapol*, of Germanic origin; related to Dutch *stapel* 'pillar' (a sense reflected in English in early use).

sta·ple[2] ▶*n.* **1** a main or important element of something, esp. of a diet: *bread, milk, and other staples* | *Greek legend was the staple of classical tragedy.* ■ a main item of trade or production: *rubber became the staple of the Malayan economy.* **2** the fiber of cotton or wool considered with regard to its length and degree of fineness: [*in combination*] *jackets made from* **long-staple** *Egyptian cotton.* **3** [often with *adj.*] *historical* a center of trade, esp. in a specified commodity: *proposals were made for a wool staple at Pisa.*

▶*adj.* [*attrib.*] main or important, esp. in terms of consumption: *the staple foods of the poor* | *figurative violence is the staple diet of the video generation.* ■ most important in terms of trade or production: *rice was the staple crop grown in most villages.*

▶*v.* [*trans.*] sort or classify (wool, etc.) according to fiber. ▷Middle English (sense 3): from Old French *estaple* 'market,' from Middle Low German, Middle Dutch *stapel* 'pillar, emporium'; related to STAPLE[1]. **—stapled** *adj.* [*in combination*] *a long-stapled type of fiber.*

sta·ple gun ▶*n.* a hand-held mechanical tool for driving staples into a hard surface.

sta·pler /ˈstāp(ə)lər/ ▶*n.* a device for fastening together sheets of paper with a staple or staples.

star /stär/ ▶*n.* **1** a fixed luminous point in the night sky that is a large, remote incandescent body like the sun.

True stars were formerly known as the **fixed stars**, to distinguish them from the planets or **wandering stars**. They are gaseous spheres consisting primarily of hydrogen and helium, there being an equilibrium between the compressional force of gravity and the outward pressure of radiation resulting from internal thermonuclear fusion reactions. Some six thousand stars are visible to the naked eye, but there are actually more than a hundred billion in our own Galaxy, while billions of other galaxies are known.

2 a conventional or stylized representation of a star, typically one having five or more points: *the walls were painted with silver moons and stars.* ■ a symbol of this shape used to indicate a category of excellence: *the hotel has three stars.* ■ an asterisk. ■ a white patch on the forehead of a horse or other animal. ■ (also **star network**) [usu. as *adj.*] a data or communication network in which all nodes are independently connected to one central unit: *computers in a star layout.* **3** a famous or exceptionally talented performer in the world of entertainment or sports: *a pop star* | [as *adj.*] *singers of* **star quality**. ■ an outstandingly good or successful person or thing in a group: *a* **rising star** *in the party* | [as *adj.*] *Ellen was a star student.* **4** *Astrology* a planet, constellation, or configuration regarded as influencing someone's fortunes or personality: *his golf destiny was written in the stars.* ■ (**stars**) a horoscope published in a newspaper or magazine: *what do my stars say?*

▶*v.* (**starred, star·ring**) [*trans.*] **1** (of a movie, play, or other show) have (someone) as a principal performer: *a film starring Liza Minnelli.* ■ [*intrans.*] (of a performer) have a principal role in a movie, play, or other show: *McQueen had* **starred in** *such epics as* The Magnificent Seven | [as *adj.*] (**starring**) *his first starring role.* ■ [*intrans.*] (of a person) perform brilliantly or prominently in a particular endeavor or event: *Vitt starred at third base for the Detroit Tigers.* **2** decorate or cover with star-shaped marks or objects: *thick grass* **starred with** *flowers.* ■ mark (something) for special notice or recommendation with an asterisk or other star-shaped symbol: *the activities listed below are starred according to their fitness ratings* | [as *adj.*, in *combination*] (**-starred**) *Michelin-starred restaurants.* ▷Old English *steorra*, of Germanic origin; related to Dutch *ster*, German *Stern*, from an Indo-European root shared by Latin *stella* and Greek *astēr*. **—star·less** *adj.* **—star·like** /-,līk/ *adj.*

▶*PHRASES* □ **my stars!** *informal, dated* an expression of astonishment. □ **reach for the stars** have high or ambitious aims. □ **see stars** see flashes of light, esp. as a result of being hit on the head. □ **someone's star is rising** see RISE. □ **stars in one's eyes** used to describe someone who is idealistically hopeful or enthusiastic about their future: *a singer selected from hundreds of applicants with stars in their eyes.*

star an·ise ▶*n.* **1** a small star-shaped fruit with one seed in each arm. It has an aniseed flavor and is used unripe as a spice in Asian cooking. **2** the small Chinese evergreen tree from which this spice is obtained. Also called **CHINESE ANISE**. • *Illicium verum*, family Illiciaceae.

star ap·ple ▶*n.* an edible purple fruit with a star-shaped cross section. • This is produced by the evergreen tropical American tree *Chrysophyllum cainito* (family Sapotaceae).

Sta·ra Za·go·ra /ˈstärə zəˈgôrə/ a city in east central Bulgaria; pop. 188,000.

star·board /ˈstär,bôrd/ ▶*n.* the side of a ship or aircraft that is on the right when one is facing forward. The opposite of PORT[3].

▶*v.* [*trans.*] turn (a ship or its helm) to starboard. ▷Old English *stēorbord* 'rudder side' (see STEER[1], BOARD), because early Teutonic sailing vessels were steered with a paddle over the right side.

star·board watch ▶*n.* see WATCH (sense 2).

star·burst /ˈstär,bərst/ ▶*n.* a pattern of lines or rays radiating from a central object or source of light: [as *adj.*] *a starburst pattern.* ■ an explosion producing such an effect. ■ a camera lens attachment that produces a pattern of rays around the image of a source of light. ■ a period of intense activity in a galaxy involving the formation of stars.

starch /stärCH/ ▶*n.* an odorless tasteless white substance occurring widely in plant tissue and obtained chiefly from cereals and potatoes. It is a polysaccharide that functions as a carbohydrate store and is an important constituent of the human diet. ■ food containing this substance. ■ powder or spray made from this substance and used before ironing to stiffen fabric or clothing. ■ *figurative* stiffness of manner or character: *the starch in her voice.*

▶*v.* [*trans.*] stiffen (fabric or clothing) with starch: [as *adj.*] (**starched**) *his immaculately starched shirt.* ■ *informal* (of a boxer) defeat (an opponent) by a knockout: *Domenge starched Geddami in the first.* ▷Old English (recorded only in the past participle *sterced* 'stiffened'), of Germanic origin; related to Dutch *sterken*, German *stärken* 'strengthen,' also to STARK. **—starch·er** *n.*

▶*PHRASE* □ **take the starch out of someone** deflate or humiliate someone.

Star Cham·ber an English court of civil and criminal jurisdiction that developed in the late 15th century, trying esp. those cases affecting the interests of the Crown. It was noted for its arbitrary and oppressive judgments and was abolished in 1641.

starch·y /ˈstärCHē/ ▶*adj.* (**starch·i·er, starch·i·est**) **1** (of food or diet) containing a relatively high amount of starch. **2** (of clothing) stiff with starch. ■ *informal* very stiff, formal, or prim in manner or character: *the manager is usually a bit starchy.* **—starch·i·ly** /-CHəlē/ *adv.* **—starch·i·ness** *n.*

star cloud ▶*n.* a region where stars appear to be especially numerous and close together.

star-crossed ▶*adj. poetic/literary* (of a person or a plan) thwarted by bad luck.

star·dom /ˈstärdəm/ ▶*n.* the state or status of being a famous or exceptionally talented performer in the world of entertainment or sports.

star·dust /ˈstär,dəst/ ▶*n.* (esp. in the context of success in the world of entertainment or sports) a magical or charismatic quality or feeling: *a gang of Hollywood stars anointing us with sparkling stardust.*

stare /ste(ə)r/ ▶*v.* [*intrans.*] look fixedly or vacantly at someone or something with one's eyes wide open: *he stared at her in amazement | Robin sat staring into space, her mind numb.* ■ (of a person's eyes) be wide open, with a fixed or vacant expression: *her gray eyes stared back at him.* ■ [*intrans.*] (of a thing) be unpleasantly prominent or striking: *the obituaries stared out at us.* ■ [*trans.*] (**stare someone into**) reduce someone to (a specified condition) by looking fixedly at them: *Sandra stared him into silence.*
▶*phrasal v.* □ **stare someone down** look fixedly at someone until they feel forced to lower their eyes or turn away.
▶*n.* a long fixed or vacant look: *she gave him a cold stare.* ▷Old English *starian*, of Germanic origin, from a base meaning 'be rigid.' —**star·er** *n.*
▶**PHRASES** □ **be staring something in the face** be on the verge of something inevitable or inescapable: *our team was staring defeat in the face.* □ **stare someone in the eye** (or **face**) look fixedly or boldly at someone. □ **stare someone in the face** be glaringly apparent or obvious: *the answer had been staring him in the face.*

sta·re de·ci·sis /ˈste(ə)rē diˈsīsis/ ▶*n.* *Law* the legal principle of determining points in litigation according to precedent. ▷Latin, literally 'stand by things decided.'

star·fish /ˈstär,fisн/ ▶*n.* (*pl.* same or **-fish·es**) a marine echinoderm with five or more radiating arms. The undersides of the arms bear tube feet for locomotion and, in predatory species, for opening the shells of mollusks. • Class Asteroidea.

star·flow·er /ˈstär,flou(-ə)r/ ▶*n.* a plant with starlike flowers, in particular: • a small North American woodland plant (*Trientalis borealis*, family Primulaceae). • a star-of-Bethlehem.

star fruit (also **star·fruit**) ▶*n.* another term for CARAMBOLA.

star·gaz·er /ˈstär,gāzər/ ▶*n.* **1** *informal* an astronomer or astrologer. ■ a daydreamer. **2** a fish of warm seas that normally lies buried in the sand with only its eyes, which are on top of the head, protruding: • a widely distributed fish that has electric organs (family Uranoscopidae: several genera). • (**sand stargazer**) a western Atlantic fish (family Dactyloscopidae: several genera). —**star·gaze** *v.*

Star·gell /ˈstärjəl/, Willie (1940–2001), U.S. baseball player; full name *Wilver Dornell Stargell.* With the Pittsburgh Pirates 1962–82, he was noted for his hitting ability. Baseball Hall of Fame (1988).

stark /stärk/ ▶*adj.* **1** severe or bare in appearance or outline: *the ridge formed a stark silhouette against the sky.* ■ unpleasantly or sharply clear; impossible to avoid: *his position on civil rights is **in stark contrast to** that of his liberal opponent | **the stark reality** of life for deprived minorities.* **2** [*attrib.*] complete; sheer: *he came running back in stark terror.* ■ *rare* completely naked. **3** *archaic* or *poetic/literary* stiff, rigid, or incapable of movement: *a human body lying stiff and stark by the stream.* ■ physically strong or powerful: *the dragoons were stark fellows.* ▷Old English *stearc* 'unyielding, severe,' of Germanic origin; related to Dutch *sterk* and German *stark* 'strong.' —**stark·ly** *adv.* [as *submodifier*] *the reality is starkly different.* —**stark·ness** *n.*
▶**PHRASES** □ **stark naked** completely naked. □ **stark raving mad** *informal* completely crazy.

Stark ef·fect /stärk/ ▶*n.* *Physics* the splitting of a spectrum line into several components by the application of an electric field. ▷early 20th cent.: named after Johannes Stark (1874–1957), German physicist.

stark·ers /ˈstärkərz/ ▶*adj.* [*predic.*] *informal, chiefly Brit.* **1** completely naked: *they ran starkers across the stage!* **2** mad; crazy: *his lifestyle would **drive me starkers**.*

Stark·ville /ˈstärk,vil; -vəl/ a city in east central Mississippi; pop. 21,869.

star·let /ˈstärlit/ ▶*n.* *informal* a young actress with aspirations to become a star: *a Hollywood starlet.*

star·light /ˈstär,līt/ ▶*n.* the light that comes from the stars.

Star·ling /ˈstärliNG/, Ernest Henry (1866–1927), English physiologist and founder of the science of endocrinology. He demonstrated the existence of peristalsis and coined the term *hormone* for the substance secreted by the pancreas that stimulates the secretion of digestive juices.

star·ling[1] /ˈstärliNG/ ▶*n.* a gregarious Old World songbird with a straight bill, typically with dark lustrous or iridescent plumage but sometimes brightly colored. • Family Sturnidae (the **starling family**): many genera and numerous species, in particular the speckled **common** (or **European**) **starling** (*Sturnus vulgaris*), widely introduced elsewhere. The starling family also includes the mynahs, grackles, and (usually) the oxpeckers. ▷Old English *stærlinc*, from *stær* 'starling' (of Germanic origin) + -LING.

star·ling[2] ▶*n.* a wooden pile erected with others around or just upstream of a bridge or pier to protect it from the current or floating objects. ▷late 17th cent.: perhaps a corruption of dialect *staddling* 'staddle.'

star·lit /ˈstär,lit/ ▶*adj.* lit or made brighter by stars: *a clear starlit night.*

star net·work ▶*n.* another term for STAR (sense 2).

star-nosed mole ▶*n.* a mole with a number of fleshy radiating tentacles around its nostrils, native to northeastern North America. • *Condylura cristata*, family Talpidae.

Star of Beth·le·hem ▶*n.* a resplendent star that is said to have guided the Magi to the birthplace of the infant Jesus.

star-of-Beth·le·hem ▶*n.* a plant of the lily family with star-shaped flowers that typically have green stripes on the outer surface, native to the temperate regions of the Old World. • Genera *Ornithogalum* and *Gagea*, family Liliaceae: several species, including the white-flowered *O. umbellatum* and the yellow-flowered *G. luteum*.

Star of Da·vid ▶*n.* a six-pointed figure consisting of two interlaced equilateral triangles, used as a Jewish and Israeli symbol. Also called MAGEN DAVID.

Star of David

Starr[1] /stär/, Bart (1934–), U.S. football player; full name *Bryan Bartlett Starr.* A quarterback with the Greenbay Packers 1956–72, he led them to NFL championships 1965–68 and to Super Bowl wins in 1967 and 1968. Football Hall of Fame (1977).

Starr[2], Ringo (1940–), English rock and pop drummer; born *Richard Starkey.* He was the drummer for the Beatles, and occasionally a singer. After the band split up in 1970, he pursued a solo career as a musician, singer, and actor, starring in such movies as *Caveman* (1981) and in the television series *Shining Time Station* (1990–91). See photograph at LENNON.

star route ▶*n.* a postal delivery route served by a private contractor. ▷from the use of a star or asterisk to mark the routes in postal records.

star ru·by ▶*n.* a cabochon ruby reflecting an opalescent starlike image owing to its regular internal structure.

star·ry /ˈstärē/ ▶*adj.* (**-ri·er**, **-ri·est**) full of or lit by stars: *a starry sky.* ■ resembling a star in brightness or shape: *tiny white starry flowers.* —**star·ri·ness** *n.*

star·ry-eyed ▶*adj.* naively enthusiastic or idealistic; failing to recognize the practical realities of a situation.

Stars and Bars ▶*plural n.* [treated as *sing.*] *historical* the flag of the Confederate States of America. It had a horizontal white stripe between two red stripes, and in the upper left corner was a blue field with a circle of seven white stars, one for each of the original seven seceded states.

Stars and Stripes ▶*plural n.* [treated as *sing.*] the national flag of the U.S. It has 13 horizontal stripes, alternating red and white, which represent the original Thirteen Colonies. In the upper left corner is a field of blue with 50 white stars, which represent the 50 states.

star sap·phire ▶*n.* a cabochon sapphire that reflects a starlike image resulting from its regular internal structure.

star shell ▶*n.* an explosive projectile designed to burst in the air and light up an enemy's position.

star·ship /ˈstär,sнip/ ▶*n.* (in science fiction) a large manned spaceship used for interstellar travel.

star-span·gled ▶*adj.* *poetic/literary* covered, glittering, or decorated with stars: *the star-spangled horizon.* ■ *figurative* glitteringly successful: *a star-spangled career.* ■ used humorously with reference to the U.S. national flag and a perceived American identity: *star-spangled decency.*

Star-Span·gled Ban·ner the U.S. national anthem, officially adopted in 1931. The words were written in 1814 by Francis Scott Key as a poem originally titled "Defence of Fort M'Henry" and were later put to a tune adapted from a popular English drinking song, "To Anacreon in Heaven."

star stream ▶*n.* *Astronomy* a systematic drift of stars in the same general direction within a galaxy.

star-struck ▶*adj.* fascinated or greatly impressed by famous people, esp. those connected with the entertainment industry: *I was a star-struck teenager.*

star-stud·ded ▶*adj.* **1** (of the night sky) filled with stars. **2** *informal* featuring a number of famous people, esp. actors or sports players: *a star-studded cast.*

star sys·tem ▶*n.* **1** a large number of stars with a perceptible structure; a galaxy. **2** the practice of promoting or otherwise favoring individuals who have become famous and popular, in particular in the motion-picture industry.

START /stärt/ ▶*abbr.* Strategic Arms Reduction Talks.

start /stärt/ ▶*v.* **1** [*intrans.*] come into being; begin or be reckoned from a particular point in time or space: *the season starts in September | we ate before the show started | below Roaring Springs the real desert starts.* ■ [with *infinitive* or *present participle*] embark on a continuing action or a new venture: *I started to chat to him | we plan to start building in the fall.* ■ use a particular point, action, or circumstance as an opening for a course of action: *the teacher can **start by** capitalizing on children's curiosity | I shall **start with** the case you mention first.* ■ [*intrans.*] begin to move or travel: *we started out into the snow | he started for the door.* ■ [*trans.*] begin to attend (an educational establishment) or engage in (an occupation, esp. a profession): *she will start school today | he started work at a travel agency.* ■ begin one's working life: *he started as a typesetter | she **started off** as a general practitioner.* ■ [*trans.*] begin to live through (a period distinguished by a specified characteristic): *they started their married life.* ■ cost at least a specified amount: *fees **start at** around $300.* **2** [*trans.*] cause (an event or process) to happen: *two men started the blaze that caused the explosion | those women started all the trouble.* ■ bring (a project or an institution) into being; cause to take effect or begin to work or operate: *I'm starting a campaign to get the law changed.* ■ cause (a machine) to begin to work: *we had trouble starting the car | he **starts up** his van.* ■ [*intrans.*] (of a machine or device) begin operating or being used: *the noise of a tractor **starting up** | there was a moment of silence before the organ started.* ■ cause or enable (someone or something) to begin doing or pursuing something: *his father **started** him **off** in business | [trans.] what he said started me thinking.* ■ give a signal to (competitors) to start in a race. **3** [*intrans.*] give a small jump or make a sudden jerking movement from surprise or alarm: *"Oh my!" she said, starting.* ■ [*intrans.*] *poetic/literary* move or appear suddenly: *she had seen Meg start suddenly from a thicket.* ■ (of eyes) bulge so as to appear to burst out of their sockets: *his eyes **started out of** his head like a hare's.* ■ be displaced or displace by pressure or shrinkage: [*intrans.*] *the mortar in the joints had started.* ■ [*trans.*] rouse (game) from its lair.
▶*phrasal v.* □ **start in** *informal* begin doing something, esp. talking: *people groan when she starts in about her acting ambitions.* ■ (**start in on**) begin to do or deal with: *you vacuum the stairs and I'll start in on the laundry.* ■ (**start in on**) attack verbally; begin to criticize: *before you start in on me, let me explain.* □ **start off** (or **start someone/something off**) begin (or cause someone or something to begin) working, operating, or dealing with something: *treatment should start off with attention to diet | what started you off on this search?* ■ (**start off**) begin a meal: *she **started off with** soup.* □ **start on 1** begin to work on or deal with: *I'm starting on a new book.* **2** *informal* begin to talk to someone, esp. in a critical or hostile way: *she started on about my not having nice furniture.* □ **start out** (or **up**) embark on a venture or undertaking, esp. a commercial one: *the company will start out with a hundred employees.* □ **start over** make a new beginning: *could you face going back to school and starting over?*
▶*n.* [in *sing.*] **1** the point in time or space at which something has its origin; the beginning of something: *he takes over as chief executive at the start of next year | the event was a shambles from start to finish | his bicycle was found close to the start of a forest trail.* ■ the point or moment at which a race begins. ■ an act of

Pronunciation Key ə *ago*; ər *over*; ˈə or ˌə *up*; ˈər or ˌər *fur*; a *hat*; ā *rate*; ä *car*; CH *chew*; e *let*; ē *see*; e(ə)r *air*; i *fit*; ī *by*; i(ə)r *ear*; NG *sing*; ō *go*; ô *for*; oi *boy*; o͝o *good*; o͞o *goo*; ou *out*; SH *she*; TH *thin*; T͟H *then*; (h)w *why*; ZH *vision*

S

beginning to do or deal with something: *I can* ***make a start on*** *cleaning up* | *an early start enabled us to avoid the traffic.* ■ used to indicate that a useful initial contribution has been made but that more remains to be done: *if he would tell her who had put him up to it, it would be a start.* ■ a person's position or circumstances at the beginning of their life, esp. a position of advantage: *she's anxious to give her baby the best* ***start in life.*** ■ an advantage consisting in having set out in a race or on journey earlier than one's rivals or opponents: *he would have a ninety-minute* ***start on*** *them.* **2** a sudden movement of surprise or alarm: *she awoke* ***with a start*** | *the woman* ***gave*** *a nervous* ***start.*** ▷Old English *styrtan* 'to caper, leap,' of Germanic origin; related to Dutch *storten* 'push' and German *stürzen* 'fall headlong, fling.' From the sense 'sudden movement' arose the sense 'initiation of movement, setting out on a journey' and hence 'beginning (of a process, etc.).'

▸*PHRASES* □ **don't start** (or **don't you start**) *informal* used to tell someone not to grumble or criticize: *don't start—I do my fair share.* □ **for a start** *informal* used to introduce or emphasize the first or most important of a number of considerations: *this side is at an advantage—for a start, there are more of them.* □ **get the start of** *dated* gain an advantage over. □ **start a family** conceive one's first child. □ **start something** *informal* cause trouble. □ **to start with** at the beginning of a series of events or period of time: *she wasn't very keen on the idea to start with.* ■ as the first thing to be taken into account: *to start with, I was feeling down.*

start·er /ˈstärtər/ ▸*n.* a person or thing that starts an event, activity, or process, in particular: ■ *chiefly Brit.* the first course of a meal; an appetizer. ■ an automatic device for starting a machine, esp. the engine of a vehicle. ■ a person who gives the signal for the start of a race. ■ [with *adj.*] a horse, competitor, or player taking part in a race or game at the start: *the trainer has confirmed Cool Ground as a definite starter.* ■ *Baseball* the pitcher who starts the game. ■ *Baseball* a pitcher who normally starts games, and seldom is used as a relief pitcher. ■ [with *adj.*] a person or thing that starts in a specified way, esp. with reference to time or speed: *he was a* ***late starter*** *in photography* | *I'm just a* ***slow starter.*** ■ a topic, question, or other item with which to start a group discussion or course of study: *material to act as a* ***starter for*** *discussion.* ■ (also **starter culture**) a bacterial culture used to initiate souring in making yogurt, cheese, or butter. ■ a preparation of chemicals to initiate the breakdown of vegetable matter in making compost.

▸*PHRASE* □ **for starters** *informal* first of all; to start with.

start·er home ▸*n.* a relatively small, economical house or condominium that meets the requirements of young people buying their first home.

start·er mar·riage ▸*n.* a short-lived first marriage between young people that produces no offspring.

start·ing block ▸*n.* (usu. **starting blocks**) a shaped rigid block for bracing the feet of a runner at the start of a race.

start·ing gate ▸*n.* (usu. **the starting gate**) a restraining structure incorporating a barrier that is raised at the start of a race, typically in horse racing and skiing, to ensure a simultaneous start.

start·ing pis·tol ▸*n.* a pistol used to give the signal for the start of a race.

star·tle /ˈstärtl/ ▸*v.* [*trans.*] cause (a person or animal) to feel sudden shock or alarm: *a sudden sound in the doorway startled her* | [with *infinitive*] *he was startled to see a column of smoke.* ▷Old English *steartlian* 'kick, struggle,' from the base of START. The early sense gave rise to 'move quickly, caper' (typically said of cattle), whence '(cause to) react with fear' (late 16th cent.). **—star·tler** *n.*

star·tling /ˈstärtl-iNG/ ▸*adj.* very surprising, astonishing, or remarkable: *he bore a startling likeness to their father* | *she had startling blue eyes.* **—star·tling·ly** *adv.* [as *submodifier*] *a startlingly good memory.*

start-up (also **start·up** /ˈstär,təp/) ▸*n.* the action or process of setting something in motion: *the start-up of marketing in Europe* | [as *adj.*] *start-up costs.* ■ a newly established business: *problems facing start-ups and small firms in rural areas.*

star turn ▸*n.* the person or act that gives the most heralded or impressive performance in a program.

starve /stärv/ ▸*v.* [*intrans.*] **1** (of a person or animal) suffer severely or die from hunger: *she left her animals to starve* | *seven million* ***starved to death*** | [as *adj.*] (**starving**) *the world's starving children.* ■ [*trans.*] cause (a person or animal) to suffer severely or die from hunger: *for a while she had considered starving herself.* ■ (**be starving** or **starved**) *informal* feel very hungry: *I don't know about you, but I'm starving.* ■ (**starve someone out** or **into**) force someone out of a place or into a specified state by stopping supplies of food: *the Royalists were starved out after eleven days* | *German U-boats hoping to starve Britain into submission.* ■ [*trans.*] (usu. **be starved of** or **for**) deprive of something necessary: *the arts are being starved of funds.* **2** *archaic* be freezing cold: *pull down that window for we are perfectly starving here.* ▷Old English *steorfan* 'to die,' of Germanic origin, probably from a base meaning 'be rigid' (compare with STARE); related to Dutch *sterven* and German *sterben.* **—star·va·tion** /-ˈvāSHən/ *n.*

starve·ling /ˈstärvliNG/ *archaic* ▸*n.* an undernourished or emaciated person or animal.

▸*adj.* (of a person or animal) lacking enough food; emaciated: *a starveling child.*

star·wort /ˈstärwərt; -,wôrt/ ▸*n.* any of a number of plants with starlike flowers or leaves. • *Stellaria* (family Caryophyllaceae), *Callitriche* (family Callitrichaceae), and other genera: several species, including the **lesser stitchwort** (*S. graminea*).

stash1 /staSH/ *informal* ▸*v.* [*trans.*] store (something) safely and secretly in a specified place: *their wealth had been* ***stashed away*** *in Swiss banks.*

▸*n.* **1** a secret store of something: *the man grudgingly handed over* ***a stash of*** *notes.* ■ a quantity of an illegal drug, esp. one kept for personal use: *one prisoner tried to swallow his stash.* **2** *dated* a hiding place or hideout. ▷late 18th cent.: of unknown origin.

stash2 ▸*n.* *informal* a mustache. ▷1940s: shortened form.

Sta·si /ˈstäzē/ the internal security force of the former German Democratic Republic, abolished in 1989. ▷German, from *Sta(ats)si(cherheitsdienst)* 'state security service.'

sta·sis /ˈstāsis/ ▸*n.* *formal* or *technical* a period or state of inactivity or equilibrium. ■ *Medicine* a stoppage of flow of a body fluid. ▷mid 18th cent.: modern Latin, from Greek, literally 'standing, stoppage,' from *sta-*, base of *histanai* 'to stand.'

-stasis ▸*comb. form* (*pl.* **-stas·es**) *Physiology* slowing down; stopping: *hemostasis.* ▷from Greek *stasis* 'standing, stoppage.'

stat1 /stat/ *informal* ▸*abbr.* ■ photostat. ■ statistic. ■ statistics: [as *adj.*] *a stat sheet.* ■ thermostat.

stat2 ▸*adv.* (in a medical direction or prescription) immediately. ▷late 19th cent.: abbreviation of Latin *statim.*

stat. ▸*abbr.* ■ (in prescriptions) immediately. [from Latin *statim.*] ■ statuary. ■ statue. ■ statute.

-stat ▸*comb. form* denoting instruments, substances, etc., maintaining a controlled state: *thermostat* | *hemostat.* ▷partly from *(helio)stat,* partly a back-formation from STATIC.

sta·tant /ˈstātnt/ ▸*adj.* [usu. *postpositive*] *Heraldry* (of an animal) standing with all four paws on the ground. ▷late 15th cent.: formed irregularly from Latin *stat-* 'fixed, stationary' (from the verb *stare* 'to stand)' + -ANT.

state /stāt/ ▸*n.* **1** the particular condition that someone or something is in at a specific time: *the state of the company's finances* | *we're worried about her* ***state of mind.*** ■ a physical condition as regards internal or molecular form or structure: *water in a liquid state.* ■ [in *sing.*] (**a state**) *informal* an agitated or anxious condition: *don't* ***get into a state.*** ■ [in *sing.*] *informal* a dirty or untidy condition: *look at the state of you—what a mess!* ■ *Physics* short for QUANTUM STATE. **2** a nation or territory considered as an organized political community under one government: *the state of Israel.* ■ an organized political community or area forming part of a federal republic: *the German state of Bavaria.* ■ (**the States**) informal term for UNITED STATES. **3** the civil government of a country: *services provided by the state* | [in *combination*] *state-owned companies* | *King Fahd appointed a council to advise him on* ***affairs of state.*** ■ (**the States**) the legislative body in Jersey, Guernsey, and Alderney. **4** pomp and ceremony associated with monarchy or high levels of government: *he was buried* ***in state.*** **5** [usu. with *adj.*] an impression taken from an etched or engraved plate at a particular stage. ■ a particular printed version of the first edition of a book, distinguished from others by prepublication changes.

▸*adj.* [*attrib.*] **1** of, provided by, or concerned with the civil government of a country: *the future of state education* | *a state secret.* **2** used or done on ceremonial occasions; involving the ceremony associated with a head of state: *a state visit to Hungary by Queen Elizabeth.*

▸*v.* **1** [*reporting verb*] express something definitely or clearly in speech or writing: [with *clause*] *the report stated that more than 51 percent of voters failed to participate* | [with *direct speech*] *"Money hasn't changed me," she stated firmly* | [*trans.*] *people will be invited to state their views.* ■ [*trans.*] *chiefly Law* specify the facts of (a case) for consideration: *judges must give both sides an equal opportunity to state their case.* **2** [*trans.*] *Music* present or introduce (a theme or melody) in a composition. ▷Middle English (as a noun): partly a shortening of ESTATE, partly from Latin *status* 'manner of standing, condition' (see STATUS). The current verb senses date from the mid 17th cent. **—stat·a·ble** *adj.*

▸*PHRASES* □ **state of affairs** (or **things**) a situation or set of circumstances: *the survey revealed a sorry state of affairs in schools.* □ **state of the art** the most recent stage in the development of a product, incorporating the newest ideas and the most up-to-date features. ■ [as *adj.*] incorporating the newest ideas and the most up-to-date features: *a new state-of-the-art hospital.* □ **state of emergency** a situation of national danger or disaster in which a government suspends normal constitutional procedures in order to regain control: *the government has declared a state of emergency.* □ **state of grace** a condition of being free from sin. □ **state of life** (in religious contexts) a person's occupation, calling, or status. □ **state of war** a situation when war has been declared or is in progress.

state cap·i·tal·ism ▸*n.* a political system in which the state has control of production and the use of capital.

State Col·lege a borough in central Pennsylvania, in the Nittany Valley, home to Pennsylvania State University; pop. 38,923.

state·craft /ˈstāt,kraft/ ▸*n.* the skillful management of state affairs; statesmanship: *issues of statecraft require great deliberation.*

State De·part·ment the department in the U.S. government dealing with foreign affairs.

state·hood /ˈstāt,ho͝od/ ▸*n.* the status of being a recognized independent nation: *the Jewish struggle for statehood.* ■ the status of being a state of the U.S.: *a proposed referendum on statehood for Puerto Rico.*

state house (also **state·house**) ▸*n.* the building where a state legislature meets.

state·less /ˈstātlis/ ▸*adj.* (of a person) not recognized as a citizen of any country. **—state·less·ness** /ˈstātlᵊsnᵊs/ *n.*

state·let /ˈstātlit/ ▸*n.* a small state, esp. one that is closely affiliated with or has emerged from the breakup of a larger state.

state·ly /ˈstātlē/ ▸*adj.* (**-li·er**, **-li·est**) having a dignified, unhurried, and grand manner; majestic in manner and appearance: *a stately procession* | *his tall and stately wife.* **—state·li·ness** *n.*

state·ly home ▸*n.* *Brit.* a large and fine house that is occupied or was formerly occupied by an aristocratic family.

state ma·chine ▸*n.* *Electronics* a device that can be in one of a set number of stable conditions depending on its previous condition and on the present values of its inputs.

state·ment /ˈstātmənt/ ▸*n.* a definite or clear expression of something in speech or writing: *do you agree with this statement?* | *this is correct as a* ***statement of fact.*** ■ an official account of facts, views, or plans, esp. one for release to the media: *the officials issued a joint statement calling for negotiations.* ■ a formal account of events given by a witness, defendant, or other party to the police or in a court of law: *she* ***made a statement*** *to the police.* ■ a document setting out items of debit and credit between a bank or other organization and a customer. ■ the expression of an idea or opinion through something other than words: *their humorous kitschiness makes a statement of serious wealth.* ■ *Music* the occurrence of a musical idea or motive within a composition: *a carefully structured musical and dramatic progression from the first statement of this theme.*

Stat·en Is·land /ˈstatn/ an island borough of New York City, in the southwestern part of the city; pop. 378,977. ▷named after the Staten or States General of the Netherlands.

State of the Un·ion mes·sage (also **State of the Union address**) ▸*n.* a yearly address delivered in January by the president of the U.S. to Congress, giving the administration's view of the state of the nation and plans for legislation.

stat·er /ˈstātər/ ▸*n.* *historical* an ancient Greek gold or silver coin. ▷via late Latin from Greek *statēr,* from a base meaning 'weigh.'

state·room /ˈstātˌro͞om; -ˌro͝om/ ▶*n.* a private compartment on a ship. ■ a captain's or superior officer's room on a ship. ■ a private compartment on a train. ■ a large room in a palace or public building, for use on formal occasions.

state's at·tor·ney ▶*n.* a lawyer representing a state in court.

state school ▶*n.* another term for STATE UNIVERSITY. ■ *Brit.* a school that is funded and controlled by the government and for which no fees are charged.

state se·cret ▶*n.* a sensitive issue or piece of information that is kept secret by the government, usually to protect the public. ■ *humorous* a piece of information, usually of a trivial or personal nature, that is closely guarded and desired to be kept private: *she thought her affair with the boss was a state secret, but we all giggled about it behind her back.*

state's ev·i·dence ▶*n. Law* evidence for the prosecution given by a participant in or accomplice to the crime being tried.
▶*PHRASE* □ **turn state's evidence** give such evidence: *persuading one-time gang members to turn state's evidence.*

States-Gen·er·al ▶*n.* **1** the bicameral legislative body in the Netherlands. **2** (also **Es·tates Gen·er·al**) *historical* the legislative body in France until 1789, representing the three estates of the realm (i.e., the clergy, the nobility, and the commons).

state·side /ˈstātˌsīd/ ▶*adj.* & *adv. informal* of, in, or toward the U.S. (used in reference to the U.S. from elsewhere or from the geographically separate states of Alaska and Hawaii): [as *adj.*] *stateside police departments* | [as *adv.*] *they were headed stateside.*

states·man /ˈstātsmən/ ▶*n.* (*pl.* **-men**) a skilled, experienced, and respected political leader or figure. ▷late 16th cent.: from *state's man*, translating French *homme d'état*. —**states·man·like** /-ˌlīk/ *adj.* —**states·man·ship** /-ˌSHip/ *n.*

state so·cial·ism ▶*n.* a political system in which the state has control of industries and services.

states' rights ▶*plural n.* the rights and powers held by individual U.S. states rather than by the federal government.

States' Rights Dem·o·crat·ic Party ▶*n.* a political party formed in 1948 advocating states' rights and opposing the presidential candidacy of Harry S Truman.

states·wom·an /ˈstātsˌwo͝omən/ ▶*n.* (*pl.* **-wom·en**) a skilled, experienced, and respected female political leader.

state u·ni·ver·si·ty ▶*n.* a university managed by the public authorities of a particular U.S. state.

state vec·tor ▶*n. Physics* a vector in a space whose dimensions correspond to all the independent wave functions of a system, the instantaneous value of the vector conveying all possible information about the state of the system at that instant.

state vis·it ▶*n.* a ceremonial visit to a foreign country by a head of state.

state·wide /ˈstātˈwīd/ ▶*adj.* & *adv.* extending throughout a particular U.S. state: [as *adj.*] *a statewide health system* | [as *adv.*] *two stations will broadcast the final statewide.*

stat·ic /ˈstatik/ ▶*adj.* **1** lacking in movement, action, or change, esp. in a way viewed as undesirable or uninteresting: *demand has grown in what was a fairly static market* | *the whole ballet appeared too static.* ■ *Computing* (of a process or variable) not able to be changed during a set period, for example, while a program is running. **2** *Physics* concerned with bodies at rest or forces in equilibrium. Often contrasted with DYNAMIC. ■ (of an electric charge) having gathered on or in an object that cannot conduct a current. ■ acting as weight but not moving. ■ of statics. **3** *Computing* (of a memory or store) not needing to be periodically refreshed by an applied voltage.
▶*n.* crackling or hissing noises on a telephone, radio, or other telecommunications system. ■ short for STATIC ELECTRICITY. ■ *informal* angry or critical talk or behavior: *the reception was going sour, breaking up into static.* ▷late 16th cent. (denoting the science of weight and its effects): via modern Latin from Greek *statikē (tekhnē)* 'science of weighing'; the adjective from modern Latin *staticus*, from Greek *statikos* 'causing to stand,' from the verb *histanai*. Sense 1 of the adjective dates from the mid 19th cent. —**stat·i·cal·ly** /-ik(ə)lē/ *adv.* —**stat·ick·y** /-ikē/ *adj.*

-static ▶*comb. form* in adjectives corresponding to nouns ending in *-stasis* (such as *hemostatic* corresponding to *hemostasis*).

stat·ic cling ▶*n.* the adhering of a garment to the wearer's body or to another garment, caused by a buildup of static electricity.

stat·ice /ˈstatisē; ˈstatis/ ▶*n.* another term for SEA LAVENDER, esp. when cultivated as a garden plant. ▷mid 18th cent.: from modern Latin *statice* (former genus name), based on Greek, feminine of *statikos* 'causing to stand still' (with reference to medicinal use of the plant to stanch blood).

stat·ic e·lec·tric·i·ty ▶*n.* a stationary electric charge, typically produced by friction, that causes sparks or crackling or the attraction of dust or hair.

stat·ic line ▶*n.* a length of cord used instead of a ripcord for opening a parachute, attached at one end to the aircraft and temporarily snapped to the parachute at the other.

stat·ic pres·sure ▶*n. Physics* the pressure of a fluid on a body when the body is at rest relative to the fluid.

stat·ics /ˈstatiks/ ▶*plural n.* **1** [usu. treated as *sing.*] the branch of mechanics concerned with bodies at rest and forces in equilibrium. Compare with DYNAMICS (sense 1). **2** another term for STATIC.

stat·in /ˈstatn/ ▶*n. Medicine* any of a group of drugs that act to reduce levels of fats, including triglycerides and cholesterol, in the blood.

sta·tion /ˈstāSHən/ ▶*n.* **1** a regular stopping place on a public transportation route, esp. one on a railroad line with a platform and often one or more buildings. **2** [usu. with *adj.*] a place or building where a specified activity or service is based: *a research station in the rain forest* | *coastal radar stations.* ■ a small military base, esp. of a specified kind: *a naval station.* ■ a police station. ■ a subsidiary post office. ■ *Austral./NZ* a large sheep or cattle farm. **3** [with *adj.*] a company involved in broadcasting of a specified kind: *a radio station.* **4** the place where someone or something stands or is placed on military or other duty: *the lookout resumed his station in the bow.* ■ *dated* one's social rank or position: *Karen was getting ideas* **above her station**. **5** *Botany* a particular site at which an interesting or rare plant grows. **6** short for STATION OF THE CROSS.
▶*v.* [*trans.*] put in or assign to a specified place for a particular purpose, esp. a military one: *troops* **were stationed in** *the town* | *a young girl had* **stationed herself by** *the door.* ▷Middle English (as a noun): via Old French from Latin *statio(n-)*, from *stare* 'to stand.' Early use referred generally to 'position,' esp. 'position in life, status,' and specifically, in ecclesiastical use, to 'a holy place of pilgrimage (visited as one of a succession).' The verb dates from the late 16th cent.

sta·tion·ar·y /ˈstāSHəˌnerē/ ▶*adj.* not moving or not intended to be moved: *a car collided with a stationary vehicle.* ■ *Astronomy* (of a planet) having no apparent motion in longitude. ■ not changing in quantity or condition: *a stationary population.* ▷late Middle English: from Latin *stationarius* (originally in the sense 'belonging to a military station'), from *station-* 'standing' (see STATION).

USAGE Be careful to distinguish **stationary** ('not moving, fixed') from **stationery** ('writing paper and other supplies').

sta·tion·ar·y bi·cy·cle (also **sta·tion·ar·y bike**) ▶*n.* an exercise bike.

sta·tion·ar·y en·gine ▶*n.* an engine that remains in a fixed position, esp. one that drives generators or other machinery in a building.

sta·tion·ar·y state ▶*n.* an unvarying condition in a physical process.

sta·tion·ar·y wave ▶*n. Physics* another term for STANDING WAVE.

sta·tion bill ▶*n.* a list showing the prescribed stations of a ship's crew in specified emergencies.

sta·tion break ▶*n.* a pause between broadcast programs for an announcement of the identity of the station transmitting them, typically also containing commercials.

sta·tion·er /ˈstāSH(ə)nər/ ▶*n.* a person or store selling paper, pens, and other writing and office materials. ▷Middle English (in the sense 'bookseller'): from medieval Latin *stationarius* 'tradesman (at a fixed location, i.e., not itinerant).' Compare with STATIONARY.

sta·tion·er·y /ˈstāSHəˌnerē/ ▶*n.* writing paper, esp. with matching envelopes. ■ writing and other office materials.

USAGE See usage at STATIONARY.

sta·tion house ▶*n.* a police or fire station.

sta·tion·keep·ing /ˈstāSHənˌkēpiNG/ ▶*n.* the maintenance of a ship's proper position relative to others in a fleet.

sta·tion·mas·ter /ˈstāSHənˌmastər/ ▶*n.* an official in charge of a railroad station.

Sta·tion of the Cross ▶*n.* (usu. **Stations of the Cross**) one of a series of fourteen pictures or carvings representing successive incidents during Jesus' progress from Pilate's house to his crucifixion at Calvary, before which devotions are performed in some churches.

sta·tion wag·on ▶*n.* a car with a longer body than usual, incorporating a large carrying area behind the seats and having an extra door at the rear for easy loading.

stat·ism /ˈstātˌizəm/ ▶*n.* a political system in which the state has substantial centralized control over social and economic affairs: *the rise of authoritarian statism.* —**stat·ist** *n.* & *adj.*

sta·tis·tic /stəˈtistik/ ▶*n.* a fact or piece of data from a study of a large quantity of numerical data: *the statistics show that the crime rate has increased.* ■ an event or person regarded as no more than such a piece of data (used to suggest an inappropriately impersonal approach): *he was just another statistic.*
▶*adj.* another term for STATISTICAL. ▷late 18th cent.: from German *statistisch* (adjective), *Statistik* (noun).

sta·tis·ti·cal /stəˈtistikəl/ ▶*adj.* of or relating to the use of statistics: *a statistical comparison.* —**sta·tis·ti·cal·ly** /-ik(ə)lē/ *adv.* [*sentence adverb*] *these differences were not statistically significant.*

sta·tis·ti·cal in·fer·ence ▶*n.* the theory, methods, and practice of forming judgments about the parameters of a population and the reliability of statistical relationships, typically on the basis of random sampling.

sta·tis·ti·cal me·chan·ics ▶*plural n.* [treated as *sing.*] the description of physical phenomena in terms of a statistical treatment of the behavior of large numbers of atoms or molecules, esp. with regard to the distribution of energy among them.

sta·tis·ti·cal phys·ics ▶*plural n.* [treated as *sing.*] a branch of physics concerned with large numbers of particles to which statistics can be applied.

sta·tis·ti·cal sig·nif·i·cance ▶*n.* see SIGNIFICANCE.

sta·tis·ti·cal ta·bles ▶*plural n.* the values of the cumulative distribution functions, probability functions, or probability density functions of certain common distributions presented as reference tables for different values of their parameters.

stat·is·ti·cian /ˌstatiˈstiSHən/ ▶*n.* an expert in the preparation and analysis of statistics.

sta·tis·tics /stəˈtistiks/ ▶*plural n.* [treated as *sing.*] the practice or science of collecting and analyzing numerical data in large quantities, esp. for the purpose of inferring proportions in a whole from those in a representative sample.

Sta·ti·us /ˈstāSH(ē)əs/, Publius Papinius (c.AD 45–96), Roman poet. He is best known for the *Silvae*, a miscellany of poems addressed to friends, and for the *Thebais*, an epic concerning the bloody quarrel between the sons of Oedipus.

sta·tive /ˈstātiv/ *Linguistics* ▶*adj.* (of a verb) expressing a state or condition rather than an activity or event, such as *be* or *know*, as opposed to *run* or *grow*. Contrasted with DYNAMIC.
▶*n.* a stative verb. ▷mid 17th cent.: from Latin *stativus*, from *stat-* 'stopped, standing,' from the verb *stare*.

stato- ▶*comb. form* relating to statics: *statocyst.* ▷from Greek *statos* 'standing.'

stat·o·blast /ˈstatəˌblast/ ▶*n. Zoology* (in bryozoans) a resistant reproductive body produced asexually.

stat·o·cyst /ˈstatəˌsist/ ▶*n. Zoology* a small organ of balance and orientation in some aquatic invertebrates, consisting of a sensory vesicle or cell containing statoliths. Also called OTOCYST.

stat·o·lith /ˈstatəˌliTH/ ▶*n. Zoology* a calcareous particle in the statocysts of invertebrates that stimulates sensory receptors in response to gravity, so enabling balance and orientation. ■ another term for OTOLITH.

sta·tor /ˈstātər/ ▶*n.* the stationary portion of an electric generator or motor, esp. of an induction motor. ■ a row of small stationary airfoils attached to the casing of an axial-flow turbine, positioned between the rotors. ▷late 19th cent.: from STATIONARY, on the pattern of *rotor*.

stat·o·scope /ˈstatəˌskōp/ ▶*n.* a form of aneroid

Pronunciation Key ə *ago*; ər *over*; ˈə *or* ˌə *up*; ˈər *or* ˌər *fur*; a *hat*; ā *rate*; ä *car*; CH *chew*; e *let*; ē *see*; e(ə)r *air*; i *fit*; ī *by*; i(ə)r *ear*; NG *sing*; ō *go*; ô *for*; oi *boy*; o͝o *good*; o͞o *goo*; ou *out*; SH *she*; TH *thin*; T͟H *then*; (h)w *why*; ZH *vision*

barometer for measuring minute variations of pressure, used esp. to indicate the altitude of an aircraft. ▷early 20th cent.: from Greek *statos* 'standing' + **-SCOPE**.

stats /stats/ ▶*plural n. informal* short for **STATISTICS**.

stat·u·ar·y /ˈstaCHo͞oˌerē/ ▶*n.* sculpture consisting of statues; statues regarded collectively: *fragments of broken statuary | classical statuary.* ■ *archaic* the art or practice of making statues. ■ *archaic* a sculptor. ▷mid 16th cent.: from Latin *statuarius*, from *statua* (see **STATUE**).

stat·ue /ˈstaCHo͞o/ ▶*n.* a carved or cast figure of a person or animal, esp. one that is life-size or larger. ▷Middle English: from Old French, from Latin *statua*, from *stare* 'to stand.' **—stat·ued** *adj.*

Stat·ue of Lib·er·ty a statue at the entrance to New York Harbor, a symbol of welcome to immigrants, representing a draped female figure carrying a book of laws in her left hand and holding aloft a torch in her right. Dedicated in 1886, it was designed by Frédéric-Auguste Bartholdi and was the gift of the French, commemorating the alliance of France and the U.S. during the American Revolution.

Statue of Liberty

Stat·ue of Li·ber·ty play ▶*n. Football* a trick play in which a ballcarrier takes the ball from the quarterback, who is poised as if to make a forward pass.

stat·u·esque /ˌstaCHo͞oˈesk/ ▶*adj.* (esp. of a woman) attractively tall and dignified: *her statuesque beauty.* ▷late 18th cent.: from **STATUE**, on the pattern of *picturesque*. **—stat·u·esque·ly** *adv.* **—stat·u·esque·ness** *n.*

stat·u·ette /ˌstaCHo͞oˈet/ ▶*n.* a small statue or figurine, esp. one that is smaller than life-size. ▷mid 19th cent.: from French, diminutive of *statue*.

stat·ure /ˈstaCHər/ ▶*n.* a person's natural height: *a man of short stature | she was small in stature.* ■ importance or reputation gained by ability or achievement: *an architect of international stature.* ▷Middle English: via Old French from Latin *statura*, from *stare* 'to stand.' The sense 'importance' dates from the mid 19th cent. **—stat·ured** *adj.* [in combination] *a short-statured fourteen-year-old.*

sta·tus /ˈstātəs; ˈstatəs/ ▶*n.* **1** the relative social, professional, or other standing of someone or something: *an improvement in the status of women.* ■ high rank or social standing: *those who enjoy wealth and status.* ■ the official classification given to a person, country, or organization, determining their rights or responsibilities: *the duchy had been elevated to the status of a principality.* **2** the position of affairs at a particular time, esp. in political or commercial contexts: *an update on the status of the bill.* ▷late 18th cent. (as a legal term meaning 'legal standing'): from Latin, literally 'standing,' from *stare* 'to stand.'

sta·tus asth·mat·i·cus /ˈstātəs azˈmatikəs; ˈstatəs/ ▶*n. Medicine* a severe condition in which asthma attacks follow one another without pause. ▷modern Latin.

sta·tus bar ▶*n. Computing* a horizontal bar, typically at the bottom of the screen or window, showing information about a document being edited or a program running.

sta·tus ep·i·lep·ti·cus /ˈstātəs ˌepəˈleptikəs; ˈstatəs/ ▶*n. Medicine* a dangerous condition in which epileptic seizures follow one another without recovery of consciousness between them. ▷modern Latin.

sta·tus quo /ˈstātəs ˈkwō; ˈstatəs/ ▶*n.* (usu. **the status quo**) the existing state of affairs, esp. regarding social or political issues: *they have a vested interest in maintaining the status quo.* ▷Latin, literally 'the state in which.'

sta·tus quo an·te /ˈstātəs kwō ˈantē; statəs/ ▶*n.* (usu. **the status quo rate**) the previously existing state of affairs. ▷Latin, literally 'the state in which before.'

sta·tus sym·bol ▶*n.* a possession that is taken to indicate a person's wealth or high social or professional status.

stat·ute /ˈstaCHo͞ot/ ▶*n.* a written law passed by a legislative body: *violation of the hate crimes statute | the tax is not specifically disallowed* **by statute**. ■ a rule of an organization or institution: *the appointment will be subject to the statutes of the university.* ■ *archaic* (in biblical use) a law or decree made by a sovereign, or by God. ▷Middle English: from Old French *statut*, from late Latin *statutum*, neuter past participle of Latin *statuere* 'set up,' from *status* 'standing' (see **STATUS**).

stat·ute book ▶*n.* a book in which laws are written.

stat·ute law ▶*n.* the body of principles and rules of law laid down in statutes. Compare with **COMMON LAW, CASE LAW**.

stat·ute mile ▶*n.* see **MILE**.

stat·ute of lim·i·ta·tions ▶*n. Law* a statute prescribing a period of limitation for the bringing of certain kinds of legal action.

stat·utes at large ▶*plural n.* a country's statutes in their original version, regardless of later modifications.

stat·u·to·ry /ˈstaCHəˌtôrē/ ▶*adj.* required, permitted, or enacted by statute: *the courts did award statutory damages to each of the plaintiffs.* ■ (of a criminal offense) carrying a penalty prescribed by statute: *statutory theft.* ■ of or relating to statutes: *constitutional and statutory interpretation.* **—stat·u·to·ri·ly** /-ˌtôrəlē/ *adv.*

stat·u·to·ry in·stru·ment ▶*n. Law* a government or executive order of subordinate legislation.

stat·u·to·ry rape ▶*n. Law* sexual intercourse with a minor.

Stau·back /ˈstôˌbăk; ˈstou-; -ˌbak/, Roger (Thomas) (1942–), U.S. football player. A quarterback for the Dallas Cowboys 1969–79, he led them to Super Bowl wins in 1972 and 1978. He was a four-time passing leader in the NFL. Football Hall of Fame (1985).

staunch[1] /stônCH; stänCH/ ▶*adj.* **1** loyal and committed in attitude: *a staunch supporter of the antinuclear lobby | a staunch Catholic.* See note at **RESOLUTE**. **2** (of a wall) of strong or firm construction. ■ (also **stanch**) *archaic* (of a ship) watertight. ▷late Middle English (in the sense 'watertight'): from Old French *estanche*, feminine of *estanc*, from a Romance base meaning 'dried up, weary.' Sense 1 dates from the early 17th cent. **—staunch·ly** *adv.* **—staunch·ness** *n.*

staunch[2] ▶*v.* variant spelling of **STANCH**[1].

Staun·ton /ˈstantn/ a city in north central Virginia, in the Shenandoah Valley; pop. 24,461.

stau·ro·lite /ˈstôrəˌlīt/ ▶*n.* a brown glassy mineral that occurs as hexagonal prisms often twinned in the shape of a cross. It consists of a silicate of aluminum and iron. ▷early 19th cent.: from Greek *stauros* 'cross' + **-LITE**.

stave /stāv/ ▶*n.* **1** a vertical wooden post or plank in a building or other structure. ■ any of the lengths of wood attached side by side to make a barrel, bucket, or other container. ■ a strong wooden stick or iron pole used as a weapon. **2** *Music* another term for **STAFF**[1] (sense 4). **3** a verse or stanza of a poem.

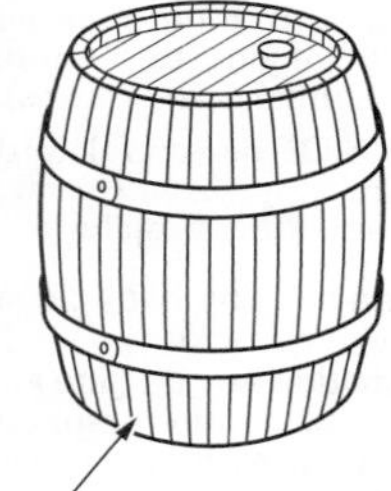
barrel stave

▶*v.* [*trans.*] **1** (*past* and *past part.* **staved** or **stove** /stōv/) (**stave something in**) break something by forcing it inward or piercing it roughly: *the door was staved in.* **2** (*past* and *past part.* **staved**) (**stave something off**) avert or delay something bad or dangerous: *a reassuring presence can stave off a panic attack.* ▷Middle English: back-formation from *staves*. Current senses of the verb date from the early 17th cent.

stave church ▶*n.* a church of a type built in Norway from the 11th to the 13th century, the walls of which were constructed of upright planks or staves.

staves·a·cre /ˈstāvzˌākər/ ▶*n.* a southern European larkspur whose seeds were formerly used as an insecticide. • *Delphinium staphisagria*, family Ranunculaceae. ▷late Middle English: via Latin from Greek *staphis agria* 'wild raisin.'

Stav·ro·pol /ˈstävrəpəl; stavˈrōpəl/ **1** an administrative territory in southern Russia, in the northern Caucasus. ■ its capital city; pop. 324,000. **2** former name (until 1964) for **TOGLIATTI**.

stay[1] /stā/ ▶*v.* **1** [*intrans.*] remain in the same place: *you stay here and I'll be back soon | Jenny decided to stay at home with their young child | he stayed with the firm as a consultant.* ■ (**stay for/to**) delay leaving so as to join in (an activity): *why not stay for lunch?* ■ (**stay down**) (of food) remain in the stomach, rather than be thrown up as vomit. ■ (**stay with**) remain in the mind or memory of (someone): *Gary's words stayed with her all evening.* **2** [*intrans.*] remain in a specified state or position: *her ability to stay calm | tactics used to stay in power | I managed to stay out of trouble.* ■ (**stay with**) continue or persevere with (an activity or task): *the incentive needed to stay with a healthy diet.* ■ (**stay with**) (of a competitor or player) keep up with (another) during a race or match. **3** [*intrans.*] (of a person) live somewhere temporarily as a visitor or guest: *the girls had gone to stay with friends | Minton invited him to* **stay the night**. ■ *Scottish* & *S. African* live permanently: *where do you stay?* **4** [*trans.*] stop, delay, or prevent (something), in particular suspend or postpone (judicial proceedings) or refrain from pressing (charges). ■ assuage (hunger) for a short time: *I grabbed something to stay the pangs of hunger.* ■ *poetic/literary* curb; check: *he tries to stay the destructive course of barbarism.* ■ [*intrans.*] *archaic* wait a moment in order to allow someone time to think or speak: *stay, stand apart, I know not which is which.* **5** [*trans.*] (usu. **be stayed**) *poetic/literary* support or prop up.

▶*phrasal v.* □ **stay on** continue to study, work, or be somewhere after others have left: *75 percent of sixteen-year-olds stay on in full-time education.* □ **stay over** (of a guest or visitor) sleep somewhere, esp. at someone's home, for the night. □ **stay up** not go to bed: *they stayed up all night.*

▶*n.* **1** a period of staying somewhere, in particular of living somewhere temporarily as a visitor or guest: *an overnight stay at a luxury hotel.* **2** *poetic/literary* a curb or check: *there is likely to be a good public library as a stay against boredom.* ■ *Law* a suspension or postponement of judicial proceedings: *a stay of prosecution.* **3** a device used as a brace or support. ■ (**stays**) *historical* a corset made of two pieces laced together and stiffened by strips of whalebone. **4** *archaic* power of endurance. ▷late Middle English (as a verb): from Anglo-Norman French *estai-*, stem of Old French *ester*, from Latin *stare* 'to stand'; in the sense 'support' (senses 5 of the *verb* and 3 of the *noun*), partly from Old French *estaye* (noun), *estayer* (verb), of Germanic origin.

▶*PHRASES* □ **be here** (or **have come**) **to stay** *informal* be permanent or widely accepted: *the Internet is here to stay.* □ **stay the course** (or **distance**) keep going strongly to the end of a race or contest. ■ pursue a difficult task or activity to the end. □ **a stay of execution** a delay in carrying out a court order. □ **stay put** (of a person or object) remain somewhere without moving or being moved.

stay[2] ▶*n.* a large rope, wire, or rod used to support a ship's mast, leading from the masthead to another mast or spar or down to the deck. ■ a guy or rope supporting a flagpole or other upright pole. ■ a supporting wire or cable on an aircraft.

▶*v.* [*trans.*] secure or steady (a mast) by means of stays. ▷Old English *stæg*, of Germanic origin; related to Dutch *stag*, from a base meaning 'be firm.'

▶*PHRASE* □ **be in stays** (of a sailing ship) be head to the wind while tacking.

stay-at-home *informal* ▶*adj.* [*attrib.*] preferring to be at home rather than to travel, socialize, or go out to work: *a stay-at-home family man.*

▶*n.* a person who lives in such a way.

stay·er /ˈstāər/ ▶*n.* **1** a tenacious person or thing, esp. a horse able to hold out to the end of a race. **2** a person who lives somewhere temporarily as a visitor or guest.

stay·ing pow·er ▶*n. informal* the ability to maintain an activity or commitment despite fatigue or difficulty; stamina: *do you have the staying power to study alone at home?* ■ long-term popularity of a product or trend: *what needs to be acknowledged about hip-hop is its remarkable staying power.*

stay-in strike ▶*n. Brit.* a sit-down strike.

Stay·man /ˈstāmən/ (also **Stay·man Wine·sap** /ˈwīnˌsap/) ▶*n.* an apple of a deep red variety with a mildly tart flavor, originating in the U.S.

stay·sail /ˈstāsəl; -ˌsāl/ ▶*n.* a triangular fore-and-aft sail extended on a stay.

stay stitch·ing ▶*n.* stitching placed along a bias or curved seam to prevent the fabric of a garment from stretching while the garment is being made. **—stay stitch** *v.*

St. Bas·il's Ca·the·dral /ˈbazəlz/ a cathedral on the south side of Red Square in Moscow, commissioned by Ivan the Terrible to commemorate his capture of Kazan from the Tartars in 1552 and built between 1555 and 1560. The official name of the cathedral is the *Cathedral of the Intercession of the Virgin*, for Kazan was taken on October 1, the Orthodox feast of the Intercession of the Virgin. The more common name *St. Basil's Cathedral* is from *St. Basil the Blessed*, a 'holy fool' who was buried near the site of the cathedral.

St. Basil's Cathedral

stbd. ▸*abbr.* starboard.

St. Ber·nard /bərˈnärd/ (also **St. Bernard dog**) ▸*n.* a large dog of a breed originally kept to rescue travelers by the monks of the Hospice on the Great St. Bernard Pass in the Swiss Alps.

St. Bernard

St. Ber·nard Pass either of two passes across the Alps in southern Europe. The **Great St. Bernard Pass**, on the border between southwestern Switzerland and Italy, rises to 8,100 feet (2,469 m). The **Little St. Bernard Pass**, on the French–Italian border southeast of Mont Blanc, rises to 7,178 feet (2,188 m). ▹named after the hospices founded on their summits in the 11th century by the French monk *St. Bernard*.

St. Chris·to·pher and Ne·vis, Federation of official name of **St. Kitts and Nevis**.

St. Croix /kroi/ an island in the Caribbean Sea, the largest of the U.S. Virgin Islands; chief town, Christiansted. Purchased by Denmark in 1753, it was sold to the U.S. in 1917.

STD ▸*abbr.* ■ Doctor of Sacred Theology. [from Latin *Sanctae Theologiae Doctor*.] ■ sexually transmitted disease. ■ *Brit.* subscriber trunk dialing.

std. ▸*abbr.* standard.

Ste. ▸*abbr.* Saint (referring to a woman). ▹from French *Sainte*.

stead /sted/ ▸*n.* the place or role that someone or something should have or fill (used in referring to a substitute): *you wish to have him superseded and to be appointed* **in his stead**. ▹Old English *stede* 'place,' of Germanic origin; related to Dutch *stad* 'town,' German *Statt* 'place,' *Stadt* 'town,' from an Indo-European root shared by the verb **stand**.

▸*PHRASE* □ **stand someone in good stead** be advantageous or useful to someone over time or in the future: *his early training stood him in good stead.*

stead·fast /ˈsted,fast/ ▸*adj.* resolutely or dutifully firm and unwavering: *steadfast loyalty.* ▹Old English *stedefæst* 'standing firm' (see **stead, fast**[1]). **—stead·fast·ly** *adv.* **—stead·fast·ness** *n.*

Stead·i·cam /ˈstedē,kam/ ▸*n. trademark* a lightweight mounting for a movie camera that keeps it steady for filming when hand-held or moving.

stead·ing /ˈstediNG/ ▸*n. Scottish & N. English* a farm and its buildings; a farmstead.

stead·y /ˈstedē/ ▸*adj.* (**stead·i·er, stead·i·est**) **1** firmly fixed, supported, or balanced; not shaking or moving: *the lighter the camera, the harder it is to hold steady* | *he refilled her glass with a steady hand.* ■ not faltering or wavering; controlled: *a steady gaze* | *she tried to keep her voice steady.* ■ (of a person) sensible, reliable, and self-restrained: *a solid, steady young man.* **2** regular, even, and continuous in development, frequency, or intensity: *a steady decline in the national birth rate* | *sales remain steady.* ■ not changing; regular and established: *I thought I'd better get a steady job* | *a steady boyfriend.* ■ (of a ship) moving without deviation from its course.

▸*v.* (**stead·ies, stead·ied**) make or become steady: [*trans.*] *I took a deep breath to steady my nerves* [as *adj.*] (**steadying**) *she's the one steadying influence in his life* | [*intrans.*] *by the beginning of May prices had steadied.*

▸*exclam.* used as a warning to someone to keep calm or take care: *Steady now! We don't want you hurting yourself.*

▸*n.* (*pl.* **stead·ies**) *informal* a person's regular boyfriend or girlfriend: *his steady chucked him two weeks ago.* ▹Middle English (in the sense 'unwavering, without deviation'): from **stead** + **-y**[1]. The verb dates from the mid 16th cent. **—stead·i·er** *n.* **—stead·i·ly** /ˈstedəlē/ *adv.* **—stead·i·ness** *n.*

▸*PHRASES* □ **go steady** *informal* have a regular romantic or sexual relationship with a particular person. □ **steady on!** *Brit.* used as a way of exhorting someone to calm down or be more reasonable in what they are saying or doing.

stead·y-go·ing ▸*adj.* (of a person) moderate and sensible in behavior; levelheaded.

stead·y state ▸*n.* an unvarying condition in a physical process, esp. as in the theory that the universe is eternal and maintained by constant creation of matter.

The steady state theory postulates that the universe maintains a constant average density, with more matter continuously created to fill the void left by galaxies that are receding from one another. The theory has now largely been abandoned in favor of the big bang theory and an evolving universe.

steak /stāk/ ▸*n.* high-quality beef taken from the hindquarters of the animal, typically cut into thick slices that are cooked by broiling or frying: *he liked his steak rare.* ■ a thick slice of such beef or other high-quality meat or fish: *a salmon steak.* ■ poorer-quality beef that is cubed or ground and cooked more slowly by braising or stewing. ▹Middle English: from Old Norse *steik*; related to *steikja* 'roast on a spit' and *stikna* 'be roasted.'

steak au poivre /ō ˈpwävrə; ˈpwäv/ ▸*n.* steak coated liberally with crushed peppercorns before cooking. ▹French, literally 'steak with pepper.'

steak Di·ane /dīˈan/ ▸*n.* a dish consisting of thin slices of steak fried with seasonings, esp. Worcestershire sauce.

steak·house /ˈstāk,hous/ ▸*n.* a restaurant that specializes in serving steaks.

steak knife ▸*n.* a knife with a serrated blade for use when eating steak.

steak tar·tare /tä(r)ˈtär/ ▸*n.* a dish consisting of raw ground steak mixed with raw egg, onion, and seasonings.

steal /stēl/ ▸*v.* (*past* **stole** /stōl/; *past part.* **sto·len** /ˈstōlən/) **1** [*trans.*] take (another person's property) without permission or legal right and without intending to return it: *thieves stole her bicycle* | [*intrans.*] *she was found guilty of stealing from her employers* | [as *adj.*] (**stolen**) *stolen goods.* ■ dishonestly pass off (another person's ideas) as one's own: *accusations that one group had stolen ideas from the other were soon flying.* ■ take the opportunity to give or share (a kiss) when it is not expected or when people are not watching: *he was allowed to steal a kiss in the darkness.* ■ (in various sports) gain (an advantage, a run, or possession of the ball) unexpectedly or by exploiting the temporary distraction of an opponent. ■ *Baseball* (of a base runner) advance safely to (the next base) by running to it as the pitcher begins the delivery: *Rickey stole third base.* ■ attract the most notice in (a scene or a theatrical production) while not being the featured performer: *why not be a big ham, and steal as many scenes as possible.* **2** [*intrans.*] move somewhere quietly or surreptitiously: *he stole down to the kitchen* | *figurative a delicious languor was stealing over her.* ■ [*trans.*] direct (a look) quickly and unobtrusively: *he stole a furtive glance at her.*

▸*n.* [in *sing.*] **1** *informal* a bargain: *for $5 it was a steal.* **2** an act of stealing something: *New York's biggest art steal.* ■ an idea taken from another work. ■ *Baseball* an act of stealing a base. ▹Old English *stelan* (verb), of Germanic origin; related to Dutch *stelen* and German *stehlen.* **—steal·er** *n.* [in *combination*] *a sheep-stealer.*

▸*PHRASES* □ **steal someone blind** see **blind**. □ **steal a march on** gain an advantage over (someone), typically by acting before they do: *stores that open on Sunday are stealing a march on their competitors.* □ **steal someone's heart** win someone's love. □ **steal the show** attract the most attention and praise. □ **steal someone's thunder** win praise for oneself by pre-empting someone else's attempt to impress.

stealth /stelTH/ ▸*n.* cautious and surreptitious action or movement: *the silence and stealth of a hungry cat* | *why did you slip away* **by stealth** *like this?*

▸*adj.* (chiefly of aircraft) designed in accordance with technology that makes detection by radar or sonar difficult: *a stealth bomber.* ■ secretive; trying to avoid notice: *she has been ducking the press as befits a stealth candidate.* ▹Middle English (in the sense 'theft'): probably representing an Old English word related to **steal**, + **-th**[2].

stealth·y /ˈstelTHē/ ▸*adj.* (**stealth·i·er, stealth·i·est**) behaving, done, or made in a cautious and surreptitious manner, so as not to be seen or heard: *stealthy footsteps.* See note at **secret**. **—stealth·i·ly** /-THəlē/ *adv.* **—stealth·i·ness** *n.*

steam /stēm/ ▸*n.* the vapor into which water is converted when heated, forming a white mist of minute water droplets in the air. ■ the invisible gaseous form of water, formed by boiling, from which this vapor condenses. ■ the expansive force of this vapor used as a source of power for machines: *the equipment was originally powered by steam* | [as *adj.*] *a steam train.* ■ locomotives and railroad systems powered in this way: *the last years of steam.* ■ *figurative* energy and momentum or impetus: *the anti-corruption drive* **gathered steam**.

▸*v.* **1** [*intrans.*] give off or produce steam: *a mug of coffee was steaming at her elbow.* ■ (**steam up** or **steam something up**) become or cause to become covered or misted over with steam: [*intrans.*] *the glass keeps steaming up* | [*trans.*] *the warm air had begun to steam up the windows.* ■ (often **be/get steamed up**) *informal* be or become extremely agitated or angry: *you got all steamed up over nothing!* | *after steaming behind the closed door in his office, he came out and screamed at her.* **2** [*trans.*] cook (food) by heating it in steam from boiling water: *steam the vegetables until just tender.* ■ [*intrans.*] (of food) cook in this way: *add the mussels and leave them to steam.* ■ clean or otherwise treat with steam: *he steamed his shirts in the bathroom to remove the wrinkles.* ■ [with *obj.* and *complement* or *adverbial*] apply steam to (something fixed with adhesive) so as to open or loosen it: *he'd steamed the letter open and then resealed it.* ■ operate (a steam locomotive). **3** [no *obj.*, with *adverbial of direction*] (of a ship or train) travel somewhere under steam power: *the 11:54 steamed into the station.* ■ *informal* come, go, or move somewhere rapidly or in a forceful way: *Jerry steamed in ten minutes late* | *figurative the company has steamed ahead with its investment program.* ■ [*intrans.*] (**steam in**) *Brit., informal* start or join a fight. ■ [*intrans.*] [often as *n.*] (**steaming**) *Brit., informal* (of a gang of thieves) move rapidly through a public place, stealing things or robbing people on the way. ▹Old English *stēam* 'vapor,' *stēman* 'emit a scent, be exhaled,' of Germanic origin; related to Dutch *stoom* 'steam.'

▸*PHRASES* □ **pick up** (or **get up**) **steam 1** generate enough pressure to drive a steam engine. **2** (of a project in its early stages) gradually gain more impetus and driving force: *his campaign steadily picked up steam.* □ **have steam coming out of one's ears** *informal* be extremely angry or irritated. □ **in steam** (of a steam locomotive) ready for work, with steam in the boiler. □ **let** (or **blow**) **off steam** *informal* (of a person) get rid of pent-up energy or strong emotion. □ **run out of** (or **lose**) **steam** *informal* lose impetus or enthusiasm: *a rebellion that had run out of steam.* □ **under one's own steam** (with reference to travel) without assistance from others: *we're going to have to get there under our own steam.* □ **under steam** (of a machine) being operated by steam.

steam age ▸*n.* the time when trains were drawn by steam locomotives.

S

steam bath ▸*n.* a room that is filled with hot steam for the purpose of cleaning and refreshing the body and for relaxation. ■ a session in such a bath.

steam beer ▸*n. trademark* an effervescent beer brewed chiefly in the western U.S.

steam·boat /ˈstēmˌbōt/ ▸*n.* a boat that is propelled by a steam engine, esp. a paddle-wheel craft of a type used widely on rivers in the 19th century.

Steam·boat Springs a resort city in northwestern Colorado, a well-known skiing center; pop. 6,695.

steam boil·er ▸*n.* a container such as that in a steam engine in which water is boiled to generate steam.

steam dis·til·la·tion ▸*n. Chemistry* distillation of a liquid in a current of steam, used esp. to purify liquids that are not very volatile and are immiscible with water.

steamed /stēmd/ ▸*adj.* **1** having been cooked by steaming: *a cornucopia of steamed dumplings.* **2** [*predic.*] *informal* extremely angry: *you're simply steamed about some editor's bad treatment of you.* ■ *Brit., informal* extremely drunk: *we went out and got steamed.*

steam en·gine ▸*n.* an engine that uses the expansion or rapid condensation of steam to generate power. ■ a steam locomotive.

steam·er /ˈstēmər/ ▸*n.* **1** a ship or boat powered by steam. ■ *informal* a steam locomotive. **2** a type of saucepan in which food can be steamed. ■ a device used to direct a jet of hot steam onto a garment in order to remove creases. **3** (in full **steamer clam**) another term for SOFT-SHELL CLAM. **4** *informal* a wetsuit.

steam·er duck ▸*n.* a sturdily built grayish duck that churns the water with its wings when fleeing danger, typically flightless and native to southern South America. • Genus *Tachyeres*, family Anatidae: several species, including the flightless *T. brachypterus* of the Falkland Islands.

steam·er rug ▸*n.* a lap robe, esp. for use on board a passenger ship for keeping warm on deck.

steam·er trunk ▸*n.* a sturdy trunk designed or intended for use on board a steamship.

steam gauge ▸*n.* a pressure gauge attached to a steam boiler.

steam ham·mer ▸*n.* a large steam-powered hammer used in forging.

steam heat ▸*n.* heat produced by steam, esp. by a central heating system in a building or on a train or ship that uses steam.
▸*v.* [*trans.*] (**steam-heat**) heat (something) by passing hot steam through it, esp. at high pressure.

steam·ing ▸*adj.* /stēmiNG/ **1** giving off steam: *a basin of steaming water.* **2** *informal* very angry. **3** *Brit., informal* extremely drunk.
▸*adv.* /ˈstēmiNG/ [as *submodifier*] (**steaming hot**) extremely hot.

steam i·ron ▸*n.* an electric iron that emits steam from holes in its flat surface.

steam jack·et ▸*n.* a steam-filled casing that is fitted around a cylinder in order to heat its contents.

steam or·gan ▸*n.* a pipe organ that is driven by a steam engine and played by means of a keyboard or a system of punched cards.

steam·roll /ˈstēmˌrōl/ ▸*v.* another term for STEAMROLLER.

steam·roll·er /ˈstēmˌrōlər/ ▸*n.* a heavy, slow-moving vehicle with a roller, used to flatten the surfaces of roads during construction. ■ *figurative* an oppressive and relentless power or force: *victims of an ideological steamroller.*
▸*v.* (also **steam·roll**) [*trans.*] (of a government or other authority) forcibly pass (a measure) by restricting debate or otherwise overriding opposition: *they would have to work together to steamroller the necessary bills past the smaller parties.* ■ force (someone) into doing or accepting something: *an attempt to* **steamroller** *the country* **into** *political reforms.* ■ [*intrans.*] proceed forcefully and seemingly invincibly: *they steamrolled through the playoffs undefeated.*

steam·ship /ˈstēmˌSHip/ ▸*n.* a ship that is propelled by a steam engine.

steam shov·el ▸*n.* an excavator that is powered by steam.

steam ta·ble ▸*n.* (in a cafeteria or restaurant) a table with slots to hold food containers that are kept hot by steam circulating beneath them.

steam·tight /ˈstēmˌtīt/ ▸*adj.* not allowing steam to pass through: *steamtight joints.*

steam tur·bine ▸*n.* a turbine in which a high-velocity jet of steam rotates a bladed disk or drum.

steam·y /ˈstēmē/ ▸*adj.* (**steam·i·er**, **steam·i·est**) producing, filled with, or clouded with steam: *a small steamy kitchen.* ■ (of a place or its atmosphere) hot and humid: *the hot, steamy jungle.* ■ *informal* depicting or involving erotic sexual activity: *steamy sex scenes* | *a steamy affair.* —**steam·i·ly** /-məlē/ *adv.* —**steam·i·ness** /-ēnis/ *n.*

ste·ar·ic ac·id /stēˈarik; ˈsti(ə)r-/ ▸*n. Chemistry* a solid saturated fatty acid obtained from animal or vegetable fats. • Chem. formula: $CH_3(CH_2)_{16}COOH$. ▷mid 19th cent.: *stearic* from French *stéarique*, from Greek *stear* 'tallow.' —**ste·a·rate** /ˈstē-əˌrāt; ˈsti(ə)r-ˌāt/ *n.*

ste·a·rin /ˈstēərin; ˈsti(ə)rin/ ▸*n.* a white crystalline substance that is the main constituent of tallow and suet. It is a glyceryl ester of stearic acid. ■ a mixture of fatty acids used in candlemaking. ▷early 19th cent.: from French *stéarine*, from Greek *stear* 'tallow.'

ste·a·tite /ˈstēəˌtīt/ ▸*n.* the mineral talc occurring in consolidated form, esp. as soapstone. ▷mid 18th cent.: via Latin from Greek *steatītēs*, from *stear*, *steat-* 'tallow.' —**ste·a·tit·ic** /ˌstēəˈtitik/ *adj.*

steato- ▸*comb. form* relating to fatty matter or tissue: *steatosis.* ▷from Greek *stear*, *steat-* 'tallow, fat.'

ste·at·o·py·gi·a /ˌstēətəˈpijēə; stēˌatə-/ ▸*n.* accumulation of large amounts of fat on the buttocks, esp. as a normal condition in the Khoikhoi and other peoples of arid parts of southern Africa. ▷early 19th cent.: modern Latin, from Greek *stear*, *steat-* 'tallow' + *pugē* 'rump.' —**ste·at·o·py·gous** /ˌstēətəˈpīgəs; ˌstēˈtāpəgəs/ *adj.*

ste·at·or·rhe·a /ˌstēətəˈrēə; stēˌatə-/ (*Brit.* **ste·at·or·rhoe·a**) ▸*n. Medicine* the excretion of abnormal quantities of fat with the feces owing to reduced absorption of fat by the intestine.

ste·a·to·sis /ˌstēəˈtōsis/ ▸*n. Medicine* infiltration of liver cells with fat, associated with disturbance of the metabolism by, for example, alcoholism, malnutrition, pregnancy, or drug therapy.

steed /stēd/ ▸*n. archaic* or *poetic/literary* a horse being ridden or available for riding. ▷Old English *stēda* 'stallion'; related to STUD².

Steel /stēl/, Danielle (1947–), U.S. writer. A prolific romance novelist, her works include *Changes* (1983), *Zoya* (1988), *The Ranch* (1997), *The Wedding* (2000), and *The House on Hope Street* (2000).

steel /stēl/ ▸*n.* a hard, strong, gray or bluish-gray alloy of iron with carbon and usually other elements, used extensively as a structural and fabricating material. ■ used as a symbol or embodiment of strength and firmness: *nerves of steel* | [as *adj.*] *a steel will.* ■ a rod of roughened steel on which knives are sharpened.
▸*v.* [*trans.*] mentally prepare (oneself) to do or face something difficult: *I speak quickly,* **steeling myself** *for a mean reply.* ▷Old English *stȳle*, *stēli*, of Germanic origin; related to Dutch *staal*, German *Stahl*, also to STAY². The verb dates from the late 16th cent.

steel band ▸*n.* a band that plays music on steel drums.

steel blue ▸*n.* a dark bluish-gray color.

steel drum ▸*n.* a percussion instrument originating in Trinidad, made out of an oil drum with one end beaten down and divided by grooves into sections to give different notes. Also called PAN¹ (esp. by players).

Steele /stēl/, Sir Richard (1672–1729), Irish essayist and playwright. He founded and wrote for the *Tatler* (1709–11) and the *Spectator* (1711–12), both periodicals, the latter in collaboration with Joseph Addison. Both had an important influence on the manners, morals, and literature of the time.

steel en·grav·ing ▸*n.* the process or action of engraving a design into a steel plate. ■ a print made from an engraved steel plate.

steel gray ▸*n.* a dark purplish-gray color: [as *adj.*] *the steel-gray November sky.*

steel·head /ˈstēlˌhed/ (also **steel·head trout**) ▸*n.* a rainbow trout of a large migratory variety.

steel pan ▸*n.* another term for STEEL DRUM.

steel wool ▸*n.* fine strands of steel matted together into a mass, used as an abrasive.

steel·work /ˈstēlˌwərk/ ▸*n.* articles of steel.

steel·works /ˈstēlˌwərks/ ▸*plural n.* [usu. treated as *sing.*] a factory where steel is manufactured. —**steel·work·er** /-ˌwərkər/ *n.*

steel·y /ˈstēlē/ ▸*adj.* (**steel·i·er**, **steel·i·est**) resembling steel in color, brightness, or strength: *a steely blue.* ■ *figurative* coldly determined; hard: *there was a steely edge to his questions.* —**steel·i·ness** *n.*

steel·yard /ˈstēlˌyärd/ ▸*n.* an apparatus for weighing that has a short arm taking the item to be weighed and a long graduated arm along which a weight is moved until it balances.

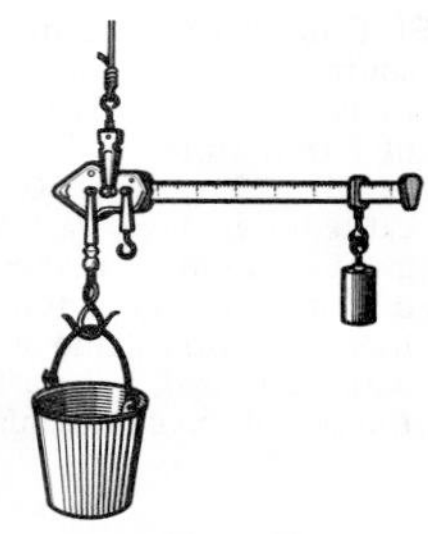

steelyard

steen·bok /ˈstēnˌbäk/ (also **stein·bok** or **steen·buck**) ▸*n.* a small African antelope with large ears, a small tail, and smooth upright horns. • *Raphiceros campestris*, family Bovidae. ▷late 18th cent.: from Dutch, from *steen* 'stone' + *bok* 'buck.'

steep¹ /stēp/ ▸*adj.* **1** (of a slope, flight of stairs, angle, ascent, etc.) rising or falling sharply; nearly perpendicular: *she pushed the bike up the steep hill.* ■ (of a rise or fall in an amount) large or rapid: *the steep rise in unemployment.* **2** *informal* (of a price or demand) not reasonable; excessive: *a steep membership fee.* ■ *dated* (of a claim or account) exaggerated or incredible: *this is a rather steep statement.*
▸*n. chiefly Skiing* or *poetic/literary* a steep mountain slope: *hair-raising steeps.* ▷Old English *stēap* 'extending to a great height'; related to STEEPLE and STOOP¹. —**steep·ish** *adj.* —**steep·ly** *adv.* —**steep·ness** *n.*

steep² ▸*v.* [*trans.*] soak (food or tea) in water or other liquid so as to extract its flavor or to soften it: *the chilies are steeped in olive oil* | [*intrans.*] *the noodles should be left to steep for 3–4 minutes.* ■ soak or saturate (cloth) in water or other liquid. ■ (usu. **be steeped in**) *figurative* surround or fill with a quality or influence: *a city steeped in history.* ▷Middle English: of Germanic origin; related to STOUP.

steep·en /ˈstēpən/ ▸*v.* become or cause to become steeper: [*intrans.*] *the snow improved as the slope steepened.*

stee·ple /ˈstēpəl/ ▸*n.* a church tower and spire. ■ a spire on the top of a church tower or roof. ■ *archaic* a tall tower of a church or other building. ▷Old English *stēpel*, of Germanic origin; related to STEEP¹. —**stee·pled** *adj.*

stee·ple·chase /ˈstēpəlˌCHās/ ▸*n.* a horse race run on a racecourse having ditches and hedges as jumps. ■ a running race in which runners must clear hurdles and water jumps. ▷late 18th cent.: from STEEPLE (because originally a steeple marked the finishing point across country) + CHASE¹. —**stee·ple·chas·er** *n.* —**stee·ple·chas·ing** *n.*

stee·ple·jack /ˈstēpəlˌjak/ ▸*n.* a person who climbs tall structures such as chimneys and steeples in order to carry out repairs.

steer¹ /sti(ə)r/ ▸*v.* [*trans.*] (of a person) guide or control the movement of (a vehicle, vessel, or aircraft), for example by turning a wheel or operating a rudder: *he steered the boat slowly toward the busy quay* | [*intrans.*] *he let Lily steer.* ■ [*intrans.*] (of a vehicle, vessel, or aircraft) be guided in a specified direction in such a way: *the ship* **steered into** *port.* ■ [*trans.*] follow (a course) in a specified direction: *the fishermen were steering a direct course for Kodiak* | [*intrans.*] *figurative try to steer away from foods based on sugar.* ■ [*trans.*] guide the movement or course of (someone or something): *he had steered her to a chair* | *figurative he made an attempt to steer the conversation back to Heather.*
▸*n. informal* a piece of advice or information concerning the development of a situation: *the need for the school to be given a clear steer as to its future direction.* ▷Old English *stīeran*, of Germanic origin; related to Dutch *sturen* and German *steuern.* —**steer·a·ble** /ˈsti(ə)rəbəl/ *adj.*
▸*PHRASES* □ **steer clear of** take care to avoid or keep away from: *his program steers clear of prickly local issues.* □ **steer a middle course** see MIDDLE.

steer² ▸*n.* a male domestic bovine animal that has been castrated and is raised for beef. ▷Old English *stēor*, of Germanic origin; related to Dutch *stier* and German *Stier.*

steer·age /ˈsti(ə)rij/ ▸*n.* **1** *historical* the part of a ship providing accommodations for passengers with the cheapest tickets: *poor emigrants in steerage.* **2** *archaic* or *poetic/literary* the action of steering a boat.

steer·age·way /ˈsti(ə)rijˌwā/ (also **steer·age-way**) ▸*n.* (of a vessel) the minimum speed required for proper response to the helm.

steer·er /ˈsti(ə)rər/ ▸*n.* a person or mechanism that steers a vehicle or vessel. ■ *informal* a person who takes or entices someone to meet a racketeer or swindler.

steer·ing /ˈsti(ə)riNG/ ▸*n.* the action of steering a vehicle, vessel, or aircraft. ■ the mechanism in a vehicle, vessel, or aircraft that makes it possible to steer it in different directions.

steer·ing col·umn ▸*n.* a shaft that connects the steering wheel of a vehicle to the rest of the steering mechanism.

steer·ing com·mit·tee (*Brit.* also **steer·ing group**) ▸*n.* a committee that decides on the priorities or order of business of an organization and manages the general course of its operations.

steer·ing wheel ▸*n.* a wheel that a driver rotates in order to steer a vehicle.

steers·man /ˈsti(ə)rzmən/ ▸*n.* (*pl.* **-men**) a person who is steering a boat or ship.

steeve /stēv/ ▸*n.* (in a sailing ship) the angle of the bowsprit in relation to a horizontal plane.
▸*v.* [*trans.*] (usu. **be steeved**) give (the bowsprit) a specified inclination. ▷mid 17th cent.: of unknown origin.

Ste·fan–Boltz·mann law /ˈstefən ˈbōltsmən/ *Physics* a law stating that the total radiation emitted by a black body is proportional to the fourth power of its absolute temperature. ▷late 19th cent.: named after Josef *Stefan* (1835–93), Austrian physicist, and L. **BOLTZMANN**.

Stef·fens /ˈstefənz/, (Joseph) Lincoln (1866–1936) U.S. journalist. A leader of the muckraking movement, he was editor of *McClure's* magazine 1902–06 and, as an associate editor, contributed articles to *American* and *Everybody's* magazines 1906–11.

Steg·ner /ˈstegnər/, Wallace (Earle) (1909–93) U.S. writer, teacher, and environmentalist. He taught at Stanford University 1945–71 and was chairman of the National Parks Advisory Board 1965–66. His novels include *The Big Rock Candy Mountain* (1943), *The Spectator Bird* (1976), *Recapitulation* (1979), and *Crossing to Safety* (1987).

steg·o·saur /ˈstegəˌsôr/ (also **steg·o·sau·rus** /ˌstegəˈsôrəs/) ▸*n.* a small-headed quadrupedal herbivorous dinosaur of the Jurassic and early Cretaceous periods, with a double row of large bony plates or spines along the back. • Infraorder Stegosauria, order Ornithischia: several genera, including *Stegosaurus*. ▷modern Latin, from Greek *stegē* 'covering' + *sauros* 'lizard.'

Stei·chen /ˈstīkən/, Edward Jean (1879–1973) U.S. photographer; born in Luxembourg; first name originally *Edouard*. He is credited with transforming photography to an art form. He worked with Stieglitz in the early 1900s and then was chief photographer for *Vogue* and *Vanity Fair* 1923–38 and, from 1947, the director of photography for New York City's Museum of Modern Art.

Steig·er /ˈstīgər/, Rod (1925–2002), U.S. actor; born *Rodney Stephen Steiger*. His many movies include *On the Waterfront* (1954), *The Longest Day* (1962), *In the Heat of the Night* (Academy Award, 1967), *The Hurricane* (1999), and *Crazy in Alabama* (1999).

Stein /stīn/, Gertrude (1874–1946), U.S. writer. She developed an esoteric stream-of-consciousness style, notably in *The Autobiography of Alice B. Toklas* (1933). Her home in Paris became a focus for the avant-garde during the 1920s and 1930s.

stein /stīn/ ▸*n.* a large earthenware beer mug. ▷mid 19th cent.: from German *Stein*, literally 'stone.'

Stein·beck /ˈstīnˌbek/, John (Ernst) (1902–68), U.S. novelist. His work, such as *Of Mice and Men* (1937) and *The Grapes of Wrath* (1939), is noted for its sympathetic and realistic portrayal of migrant agricultural workers in California. His later novels include *Cannery Row* (1945) and *East of Eden* (1952). Nobel Prize for Literature (1962).

stein·bok /ˈstīnˌbäk/ ▸*n.* variant spelling of **STEENBOK**.

Stein·bren·ner /ˈstīnˌbrenər/, George (Michael, III) (1930–), U.S. businessman. The principal owner of the New York Yankees baseball team from 1973, he was also chairman of the board of the American Ship Building Co. from 1978.

Stein·em /ˈstīnəm/, Gloria (1934–), U.S. social reformer and journalist. A women's rights activist, she cofounded the National Women's Political Caucus 1971 and cofounded *Ms.* magazine in 1972 and served as its editor until 1987. Her works include *Outrageous Acts and Everyday Rebellions* (1983) and *Revolution from Within* (1992).

Stei·ner /ˈstīnər; ˈSHtī-/, Rudolf (1861–1925), Austrian philosopher; founder of anthroposophy. He founded the Anthroposophical Society in 1912, aiming to integrate the practical and psychological in education. The society has contributed to child-centered education, esp. with its Steiner schools.

Stein·way /ˈstīnˌwā; ˈSHtīn-/, Henry (Engelhard) (1797–1871), German piano-maker; resident in the U.S. from 1849; born *Heinrich Engelhard Steinweg*. He founded his piano-making firm in New York City in 1853.

ste·la /ˈstēlə/ ▸*n.* (*pl.* **-lae** /-ˌlē/) *Archaeology* an upright stone slab or column typically bearing a commemorative inscription or relief design, often serving as a gravestone. ▷late 18th cent.: via Latin from Greek (see **STELE**).

ste·le /stēl; ˈstēlē/ ▸*n.* **1** *Botany* the central core of the stem and root of a vascular plant, consisting of the vascular tissue (xylem and phloem) and associated supporting tissue. Also called **VASCULAR CYLINDER**. **2** *Archaeology* another term for **STELA**. ▷early 19th cent.: from Greek *stēlē* 'standing block.' **—ste·lar** /ˈstēlər/ *adj.* (in sense 1).

Stel·la /ˈstelə/, Frank (Philip) (1936–), U.S. painter, an important figure in minimalism known for his series of all-black paintings. He later experimented with shaped canvases and cut-out shapes in relief.

Stel·la Mar·is /ˈstelə ˈmaris/ ▸*n.* *chiefly poetic/literary* a female protector or guiding spirit at sea (a title sometimes given to the Virgin Mary). ▷Latin, literally 'star of the sea.'

stel·lar /ˈstelər/ ▸*adj.* of or relating to a star or stars: *stellar structure and evolution.* ■ *informal* featuring or having the quality of a star performer or performers: *a stellar cast had been assembled.* ■ *informal* exceptionally good; outstanding: *his restaurant has received stellar ratings in the guides.* ▷mid 17th cent.: from late Latin *stellaris*, from Latin *stella* 'star.' **—stel·li·form** /ˈsteləˌfôrm/ *adj.*

stel·lar·a·tor /ˈsteləˌrātər/ ▸*n.* *Physics* a toroidal apparatus for producing controlled fusion reactions in hot plasma, where all the controlling magnetic fields inside it are produced by external windings. ▷1950s: from **STELLAR** (with reference to the fusion processes in stars), on the pattern of *generator*.

stel·lar wind /wind/ ▸*n.* *Astronomy* a continuous flow of charged particles from a star.

stel·late /ˈstelit; -ˌāt/ ▸*adj.* *technical* arranged in a radiating pattern like that of a star. ▷mid 17th cent.: from Latin *stellatus*, from *stella* 'star.' **—stel·lat·ed** *adj.*

Stel·ler's jay /ˈstelərz ˈjā/ ▸*n.* a blue jay with a dark crest, found in western North America. • *Cyanocitta stelleri*.

Stel·ler's sea cow ▸*n.* a very large relative of the dugong that was formerly found in the area of the Bering Sea and Kamchatka Peninsula, discovered and exterminated in the 18th century. • *Hydrodamalis gigas*, family Dugongidae.

stel·li·um /ˈstelēəm/ ▸*n.* *Astrology* another term for **SATELLITIUM**.

St. El·mo's fire /ˈelmōz/ ▸*n.* a phenomenon in which a luminous electrical discharge appears on a ship or aircraft during a storm. ▷regarded as a sign of protection given by St. Elmo, the patron saint of sailors.

stem[1] /stem/ ▸*n.* **1** the main body or stalk of a plant or shrub, typically rising above ground but occasionally subterranean. ■ the stalk supporting a fruit, flower, or leaf, and attaching it to a larger branch, twig, or stalk. **2** a long and thin supportive or main section of something: *the main stem of the wing feathers.* ■ the slender part of a wineglass between the base and the bowl. ■ the tube of a tobacco pipe. ■ a rod or cylinder in a mechanism, for example the sliding shaft of a bolt or the winding pin of a watch. ■ a vertical stroke in a letter or musical note. **3** *Grammar* the root or main part of a noun, adjective, or other word, to which inflections or formative elements are added. ■ *archaic* or *poetic/literary* the main line of descent of a family or nation: *the Hellenic tribes were derived from the Aryan stem.* **4** the main upright timber or metal piece at the bow of a ship, to which the ship's sides are joined. **5** *informal* a pipe used for smoking crack or opium.
▸*v.* (**stemmed**, **stem·ming**) **1** [*intrans.*] (**stem from**) originate in or be caused by: *many of the universities' problems stem from rapid expansion.* **2** [*trans.*] remove the stems from (fruit or tobacco leaves). **3** [*trans.*] (of a boat) make headway against (the tide or current). ▷Old English *stemn*, *stefn*, of Germanic origin; related to Dutch *stam* and German *Stamm*. Sense 4 is related to Dutch *steven*, German *Steven*. **—stem·less** *adj.* **—stem·like** /-ˌlīk/ *adj.*
▸PHRASE □ **from stem to stern** from the front to the back, esp. of a ship: *surges of water rocked their boats from stem to stern.* ■ along the entire length of something; throughout: *the album is a joy from stem to stern.*

Gloria Steinem

stem[2] ▸*v.* (**stemmed**, **stem·ming**) **1** [*trans.*] stop or restrict (the flow of something): *a nurse did her best to stem the bleeding* | *figurative an attempt to stem the rising tide of unemployment.* **2** [*intrans.*] *Skiing* slide the tail of one ski or both skis outward in order to turn or slow down. ▷Middle English (in the sense 'to stop, delay'): from Old Norse *stemma*, of Germanic origin. The skiing term (early 20th cent.) is from the German verb *stemmen*.

stem cell ▸*n.* *Biology* an undifferentiated cell of a multicellular organism that is capable of giving rise to indefinitely more cells of the same type, and from which certain other kinds of cell arise by differentiation.

stem chris·tie /ˈkristē/ ▸*n.* *Skiing* a turn made by stemming with the upper ski and then lifting the other one parallel to it for most of the turn.

stem·ma /ˈstemə/ ▸*n.* (*pl.* **-ma·ta**) a recorded genealogy of a family; a family tree. ■ a diagram showing the relationship between a text and its various manuscript versions. ▷mid 17th cent.: via Latin from Greek *stemma* 'wreath,' from *stephein* 'wreathe, crown.'

stem·ma·tics /stemˈatiks/ ▸*plural n.* [treated as *sing.*] the branch of study concerned with analyzing the relationship of surviving variant versions of a text to each other, esp. so as to reconstruct a lost original.

stemmed /stemd/ ▸*adj.* [*attrib.*] **1** [in *combination*] having a stem of a specified length or kind: *red-stemmed alder bushes.* **2** (of a glass, cup, or dish) having a slender supportive section between the base and bowl: *a stemmed goblet.* **3** (of fruit or leaves) having had the stems removed.

stem stitch ▸*n.* an embroidery stitch forming a continuous line of long, overlapped stitches, typically used to represent narrow stems.

stem turn ▸*n.* *Skiing* a turn made by stemming with the upper ski and lifting the lower one parallel to it toward the end of the turn.

stem·ware /ˈstemˌwe(ə)r/ ▸*n.* goblets and stemmed glasses regarded collectively.

stem-wind·er /ˌwīndər/ (also **stem·wind·er**) ▸*n.* **1** *informal* an entertaining and rousing speech: *the speech was a classic stem-winder in the best southern tradition.* **2** *dated* a watch wound by turning a knob on the end of a stem. ▷sense 1 from the notion of "winding up" or causing a lively reaction from those listening.

sten. ▸*abbr.* ■ stenographer. ■ stenography.

stench /stenCH/ ▸*n.* a strong and very unpleasant smell: *the stench of rotting fish.* See note at **SMELL**. ▷Old English *stenc* 'smell,' of Germanic origin; related to Dutch *stank*, German *Gestank*, also to the verb **STINK**.

stench war·fare ▸*n.* the use of highly offensive odors to sicken, immobilize, or drive away an enemy: *they are hoping to win a big contract for their innovations in stench warfare.* ▷on the pattern of *trench warfare*.

sten·cil /ˈstensəl/ ▸*n.* a thin sheet of cardboard, plastic, or metal with a pattern or letters cut out of it, used to produce the cut design on the surface below by the application of ink or paint through the holes. ■ a design produced by such a sheet: *a floral stencil around the top of the room.*
▸*v.* (**-ciled**, **-cil·ing**; *Brit.* **-cilled**, **-cil·ling**) [*trans.*]

S

Pronunciation Key ə *ago*; ər *over*; ˈə or ˌə *up*; ˈər or ˌər *fur*; a *hat*; ā *rate*; ä *car*; CH *chew*; e *let*; ē *see*; e(ə)r *air*; i *fit*; ī *by*; i(ə)r *ear*; NG *sing*; ō *go*; ô *for*; oi *boy*; o͝o *good*; o͞o *goo*; ou *out*; SH *she*; TH *thin*; T͟H *then*; (h)w *why*; ZH *vision*

decorate (a surface) with such a design: *the walls had been* ***stenciled with*** *designs* | [as *n.*] (**stenciling**) *the art of stenciling.* ■ produce (a design) with a stencil: *stencil a border around the door* | [as *adj.*] (**stenciled**) *the stenciled letters.* ▷early 18th cent.: from earlier *stansel* 'ornament with various colors' (based on Latin *scintilla* 'spark').

STENCIL

stenciled lettering

Sten·dhal /sten'däl; sten-/ (1783–1842), French novelist; pseudonym of *Marie Henri Beyle*. His two best-known novels are *Le Rouge et le noir* (1830), relating the rise and fall of a young man from the provinces, and *La Chartreuse de Parme* (1839).

Sten·gel /'steNGgəl/, Casey (*c.*1890–1975) U.S. baseball player and manager; full name *Charles Dillon Stengel*. An outfielder 1910–31 and a manager 1931–48 for various minor and major league teams, he managed the New York Yankees 1949–60, guiding them to ten American League pennants and seven World Series. He also managed the New York Mets 1962–65. Baseball Hall of Fame (1966).

Casey Stengel

Sten gun /'sten/ ▸*n.* a type of lightweight British submachine gun. ▷1940s: from the initials of the inventors' surnames, Shepherd and Turpin, suggested by **Bren**.

Ste·no /'stänō/, Nicolaus (1638–86), Danish anatomist and geologist; Danish name *Niels Steensen*. His ideas are now regarded as fundamental—that fossils are the petrified remains of living organisms, that many rocks arise from consolidation of sediments and occur in layers in the order in which they were laid down.

ste·no /'stenō/ ▸*n.* (*pl.* **-os**) *informal* a stenographer: *it was written by the steno herself.* ■ [as *adj.*] short for **stenography**: *the steno pool* | *I carry a steno pad and two pens.*

stenog. ▸*abbr.* ■ stenographer. ■ stenographic. ■ stenography.

ste·nog·ra·phy /stə'nägrəfē/ ▸*n.* the action or process of writing in shorthand and taking dictation. ▷early 17th cent.: from Greek *stenos* 'narrow' + **-graphy**. —**ste·nog·ra·pher** /-fər/ *n.* —**sten·o·graph·ic** /ˌstenə'grafik/ *adj.*

ste·no·ha·line /ˌstenə'hālīn; -halīn/ ▸*adj. Ecology* (of an aquatic organism) able to tolerate only a narrow range of salinity. Often contrasted with **euryhaline**. ▷1930s: from Greek *stenos* 'narrow' + *halinos* 'of salt.'

ste·no·sis /stə'nōsis/ ▸*n.* (*pl.* **-ses** /-ˌsēz/) *Medicine* the abnormal narrowing of a passage in the body. ▷late 19th cent.: modern Latin, from Greek *stenōsis* 'narrowing,' from *stenoun* 'make narrow,' from *stenos* 'narrow.' —**ste·nosed** /stə'nōst; -nōzd/ *adj.* —**ste·nos·ing** /-'nōsiNG; -'nōz-/ *adj.* —**ste·not·ic** /stə'nätik/ *adj.*

sten·o·ther·mal /ˌstenə'THərməl/ ▸*adj. Ecology* (of an organism) able to tolerate only a small range of temperature. Often contrasted with **eurythermal**. ▷late 19th cent.: from Greek *stenos* 'narrow' + **thermal**.

sten·o·top·ic /ˌstenə'täpik/ ▸*adj. Ecology* (of an organism) able to tolerate only a restricted range of habitats or ecological conditions. Often contrasted with **eurytopic**. ▷1940s: from Greek *stenos* 'narrow' + *topos* 'place' + **-ic**.

sten·o·type /'stenəˌtīp/ ▸*n.* a machine resembling a typewriter that is used for recording speech in syllables or phonemes. ▷late 19th cent.: from **stenography** + **type**. —**sten·o·typ·ist** /-ˌtīpist/ *n.* —**sten·o·typ·y** /-ˌtīpē/ *n.*

stent /stent/ ▸*n. Medicine* a tubular support placed temporarily inside a blood vessel, canal, or duct to aid healing or relieve an obstruction. ■ an impression or cast of a part or body cavity, used to maintain pressure so as to promote healing, esp. of a skin graft. ▷late 19th cent.: from the name of Charles T. Stent (1807–85), English dentist. The sense 'tubular support' dates from the 1960s.

sten·tor /'stenˌtôr; 'stentər/ ▸*n.* **1** *poetic/literary* a person with a powerful voice. **2** *Zoology* a sedentary trumpet-shaped single-celled animal that is widespread in fresh water. • Genus *Stentor*, phylum Ciliophora, kingdom Protista. ▷early 17th cent.: from Greek *Stentōr*, the name of a herald in the Trojan War.

sten·to·ri·an /sten'tôrēən/ ▸*adj.* (of a person's voice) loud and powerful: *he introduced me to the staff with a stentorian announcement.*

step /step/ ▸*n.* **1** an act or movement of putting one leg in front of the other in walking or running: *Ron took a step back* | *she turned and retraced her steps.* ■ the distance covered by such a movement: *Richard came a couple of steps nearer.* ■ [usu. in *sing.*] a person's particular way of walking: *she left the room with a springy step.* ■ one of the sequences of movement of the feet that make up a dance. ■ a short or easily walked distance: *the market is only a short step from the end of the lake.* **2** a flat surface, esp. one in a series, on which to place one's foot when moving from one level to another: *the bottom step of the staircase* | *a flight of marble steps.* ■ a doorstep: *there was a pint of milk on the step.* ■ a rung of a ladder. ■ (**steps**) (or **a pair of steps**) *Brit.* a stepladder. ■ *Climbing* a foothold cut in a slope of ice. ■ a block, typically fixed to the vessel's keel, on which the base of a mast is seated. ■ *Physics* an abrupt change in the value of a quantity, esp. voltage. **3** a measure or action, esp. one of a series taken in order to deal with or achieve a particular thing: *the government must* ***take steps*** *to discourage age discrimination* | *a major step forward in the fight against terrorism.* ■ a stage in a gradual process: *sales are up, which is a step in the right direction.* ■ a particular position or grade on an ascending or hierarchical scale: *the first step on the managerial ladder.* **4** *Music* an interval in a scale; a tone (whole step) or semitone (half step). **5** step aerobics: [as *adj.*] *a step class.*

▸*v.* (**stepped**, **step·ping**) **1** [*intrans.*] lift and set down one's foot or one foot after the other in order to walk somewhere or move to a new position: *Claudia tried to step back* | *I accidentally stepped on his foot.* ■ [as *imperative*] used as a polite or deferential way of asking someone to walk a short distance for a particular purpose: *please step this way.* ■ (**step it**) *dated* perform a dance: *they stepped it down the room between the lines of dancers.* ■ take a particular course of action: *young men have temporarily stepped out of the labor market.* **2** [*trans.*] *Nautical* set up (a mast) in its step.

▸*phrasal v.* □ **step aside** another way of saying **step down** below. □ **step back** mentally withdraw from a situation in order to consider it objectively. □ **step down** withdraw or resign from an important position or office: *Mr. Krenz stepped down as party leader a week ago.* □ **step something down** decrease voltage by using a transformer. □ **step forward** offer one's help or services: *a company has stepped forward to sponsor the team.* □ **step in** become involved in a difficult or problematic situation, esp. in order to help or prevent something from happening. ■ act as a substitute for someone: *Lucy stepped in at very short notice to take Joan's place.* □ **step out 1** leave a room or building, typically for a short time. **2** *informal* go out to have a good time: *he was* ***stepping out with*** *a red-headed waitress.* **3** walk with long or vigorous steps: *she enjoyed the outing, stepping out manfully.* □ **step something up** increase the amount, speed, or intensity of something: *police decided to step up security plans for the game.* ■ increase voltage using a transformer. ▷Old English *stæpe*, *stepe* (noun), *stæppan*, *steppan* (verb), of Germanic origin; related to Dutch *steppen* and German *stapfen*. —**step·like** /-ˌlīk/ *adj.*

▸*PHRASES* □ **break step** stop walking or marching in step with others. □ **fall into step** change the way one is walking so that one is walking in step with another person. □ **in** (or **out of**) **step** putting (or not putting) one's feet forward alternately in the same rhythm as the people one is walking, marching, or dancing with. ■ *figurative* conforming (or not conforming) to what others are doing or thinking: *the party is clearly* ***out of step with*** *voters.* ■ *Physics* (of two or more oscillations or other cyclic phenomena) having (or not having) the same frequency and always in the same phase. □ **keep step** remain walking, marching, or dancing in step. □ **one step ahead** managing to avoid competition or danger from someone or something: *I try to keep one step ahead of the rest of the staff.* □ **step by step** so as to progress gradually and carefully from one stage to the next: *I'll explain it to you step by step* | [as *adj.*] *a step-by-step guide.* □ **step into the breach** see **breach**. □ **step into someone's shoes** take control of a task or job from another person. □ **step on it** (or **step on the gas**) *informal* go faster, typically in a motor vehicle. □ **step** (or **tread**) **on someone's toes** offend someone by encroaching on their area of responsibility. □ **step out of line** behave inappropriately or disobediently.

step- ▸*comb. form* denoting a relationship resulting from a remarriage: *stepmother.* ▷Old English *stēop-*, from a Germanic base meaning 'bereaved, orphaned.'

step aer·o·bics ▸*plural n.* [often treated as *sing.*] a type of aerobics that involves stepping up onto and down from a portable block.

Ste·pa·na·kert /ˌstepənə'kert; sti,pänə-/ Russian name for **Xankändi**.

step·broth·er /'stepˌbrəTHər/ ▸*n.* a son of one's stepparent, by a marriage other than that with one's own father or mother.

step·child /'stepˌCHīld/ ▸*n.* (*pl.* **-chil·dren**) a child of one's husband or wife by a previous marriage. ▷Old English *stēopcild* (see **step-**, **child**).

step cut ▸*n.* a cut for gemstones in the form of straight facets around the center.

step·dad /'stepˌdad/ ▸*n.* informal term for **stepfather**.

step·daugh·ter /'stepˌdôtər; 'stepˌdätər/ ▸*n.* a daughter of one's husband or wife by a previous marriage.

step·fam·i·ly /'stepˌfam(ə)lē/ ▸*n.* (*pl.* **-lies**) a family that is formed on the remarriage of a divorced or widowed person and that includes one or more children.

step·fa·ther /'stepˌfäTHər/ ▸*n.* a man who is married to one's mother after the divorce of one's parents or the death of one's father.

step func·tion ▸*n. Mathematics & Electronics* a function that increases or decreases abruptly from one constant value to another.

steph·a·no·tis /ˌstefə'nōtis/ ▸*n.* a Madagascan climbing plant that is cultivated for its fragrant waxy white flowers. • Genus *Stephanotis*, family Asclepiadaceae. ▷modern Latin, from Greek, literally 'fit for a wreath,' from *stephanos* 'wreath.'

Ste·phen /'stēvən/ (*c.*1097–1154), grandson of William the Conqueror; king of England 1135–54. He seized the throne from Matilda a few months after the death of Henry I. Civil war followed until Matilda was defeated and forced to leave England in 1148.

Ste·phen, St.[1] (died *c.*35), Christian martyr. One of the original seven deacons in Jerusalem appointed by the Apostles, he was charged with blasphemy and stoned, thus becoming the first Christian martyr. Feast day (Western Church) December 26; (Eastern Church) December 27.

Ste·phen, St.[2] (*c.*977–1038), king and patron saint of Hungary; reigned 1000–38. The first king of Hungary, he took steps to Christianize the country. Feast day, September 2 or (in Hungary) August 20.

Ste·phen·son /'stēvənsən/, George (1781–1848), British engineer; a pioneer of steam locomotives and railroads. With his son **Robert** (1803–59) he built the *Rocket* (1829), the prototype for all future steam locomotives.

step-in ▸*adj.* [*attrib.*] denoting a garment or pair of shoes that is put on by being stepped into and has no need for fasteners.

▸*n.* (**step-ins**) **1** a pair of such shoes; slip-ons. **2** *dated* a pair of women's panties.

step·lad·der /'stepˌladər/ ▸*n.* a short folding ladder with flat steps and a small platform.

step·mom /'stepˌmäm/ ▸*n.* informal term for **stepmother**.

step·moth·er /'stepˌməTHər/ ▸*n.* a woman who is married to one's father after the divorce of one's parents or the death of one's mother.

step·par·ent /ˈste(p)ˌparənt; -ˌpe(ə)r-/ ▸*n.* a stepfather or stepmother.

steppe /step/ ▸*n.* (often **steppes**) a large area of flat unforested grassland in southeastern Europe or Siberia. ▷late 17th cent.: from Russian *step′*.

stepped /stept/ ▸*adj.* having or formed into a step or series of steps: *a building with stepped access.* ■ carried out or occurring in stages or with pauses rather than continuously: *a stepped scale of discounts.*

step·per /ˈstepər/ ▸*n.* **1** an electric motor or other device that moves or rotates in a series of small discrete steps. **2** a portable block used in step aerobics. **3** *dated* a horse with a brisk, attractive walking gait: *choosing a showy gray stepper for May's brougham.* ■ a person who steps, esp. a dancer.

step·ping·stone /ˈstepiNGˌstōn/ ▸*n.* a raised stone used singly or in a series as a place on which to step when crossing a stream or muddy area. ■ *figurative* an undertaking or event that helps one to make progress toward a specified goal: *the school championships are a* ***steppingstone to*** *international competition.*

step re·sponse ▸*n. Electronics* the output of a device in response to an abrupt change in voltage.

step·sis·ter /ˈstepˌsistər/ ▸*n.* a daughter of one's stepparent by a marriage other than with one's own father or mother.

step·son /ˈstepˌsən/ ▸*n.* a son of one's husband or wife by a previous marriage. ▷Old English *stēopsunu* (see **STEP-**, **SON**).

step wedge ▸*n. Photography* a series of contiguous, uniformly shaded rectangles growing progressively darker, from white (or light gray) at one end to black (or dark gray) at the other.

step·wise /ˈstepˌwīz/ ▸*adv.* & *adj.* **1** in a series of distinct stages; not continuously: [as *adv.*] *concentrations of the acid tend to decrease stepwise.* **2** *Music* (of melodic motion) moving by adjacent scale steps rather than leaps: *crackling solos and juicy, stepwise guitar counterpoints.*

-ster ▸*suffix* **1** denoting a person engaged in or associated with a particular activity or thing: *gangster* | *songster.* **2** denoting a person having a particular quality: *youngster.* ▷Old English *-estre, -istre*, etc., of Germanic origin.

ste·ra·di·an /stəˈrādēən/ (abbr.: **sr**) ▸*n.* the SI unit of solid angle, equal to the angle at the center of a sphere subtended by a part of the surface equal in area to the square of the radius. ▷late 19th cent.: from Greek *stereos* 'solid' + **RADIAN**.

ster·ane /ˈsterˌān; ˈsti(ə)r-/ ▸*n. Chemistry* any of a class of saturated polycyclic hydrocarbons that are found in crude oils and are derived from the sterols of ancient organisms. ▷1950s: from **STEROID** + **-ANE**[2].

ster·co·ra·ceous /ˌstərkəˈrāSHəs/ ▸*adj. technical* consisting of or resembling dung or feces. ■ (of an insect) living in dung. ▷mid 18th cent.: from Latin *stercus, stercor-* 'dung' + **-ACEOUS**.

stere /sti(ə)r/ ▸*n.* a unit of volume equal to one cubic meter. ▷late 18th cent.: from French *stère*, from Greek *stereos* 'solid.'

ster·e·o /ˈsterēˌō; ˈsti(ə)r-/ ▸*n.* (*pl.* **-os**) **1** sound that is directed through two or more speakers so that it seems to surround the listener and to come from more than one source; stereophonic sound. ■ a sound system, typically including a CD, tape, or record player, that has two or more speakers and produces stereo sound. **2** *Photography* another term for **STEREOSCOPE**. **3** *Printing* short for **STEREOTYPE**.
▸*adj.* **1** short for **STEREOPHONIC**: *stereo equipment* | *stereo sound.* **2** *Photography* short for **STEREOSCOPIC** (see **STEREOSCOPE**).

stereo- ▸*comb. form* relating to solid forms having three dimensions: *stereography.* ■ relating to a three-dimensional effect, arrangement, etc.: *stereochemistry* | *stereophonic* | *stereoscope.* ▷from Greek *stereos* 'solid.'

ster·e·o·bate /ˈsterēəˌbāt; ˈsti(ə)r-/ ▸*n. Architecture* a solid mass of masonry serving as a foundation for a wall or row of columns. ▷mid 19th cent.: from French *stéréobate*, via Latin from Greek *stereobatēs*, from *stereos* 'solid' + *batēs* 'base' (from *bainein* 'to walk').

ster·e·o·cam·e·ra /ˈsterēōˌkam(ə)rə; ˈsti(ə)r-/ ▸*n. Photography* a camera for simultaneously taking two photographs of the same thing from adjacent viewpoints, so that they will form a stereoscopic pair.

ster·e·o·chem·is·try /ˌsterēōˈkeməstrē; ˌsti(ə)r-/ ▸*n.* the branch of chemistry concerned with the three-dimensional arrangement of atoms and molecules and the effect of this on chemical reactions. **—ster·e·o·chem·i·cal** /-ˈkemikəl/ *adj.* **—ster·e·o·chem·i·cal·ly** *adv.*

ster·e·og·no·sis /ˌsterē-ägˈnōsis; ˌsti(ə)r-/ ▸*n. Psychology* the mental perception of depth or three-dimensionality by the senses, usually in reference to the ability to perceive the form of solid objects by touch. ▷early 20th cent.: from Greek *stereos* 'solid' + *gnōsis* 'knowledge.' **—ster·e·og·nos·tic** /-ˈnästik/ *adj.*

ster·e·o·gram /ˈsterēəˌgram; ˈsti(ə)r-/ ▸*n.* **1** a diagram or computer-generated image giving a three-dimensional representation of a solid object or surface. **2** another term for **STEREOGRAPH** (see **STEREOGRAPHY**).

ster·e·o·graph·ic pro·jec·tion /ˌsterēəˈgrafik; ˌsti(ə)r-/ ▸*n. Mathematics* mathematical projection in which the angular relationships of lines and planes of the object represented are drawn in terms of their relationship to the great circle formed by the intersection of the equatorial plane with the surface of an imaginary sphere containing the object. This technique has applications in cartography and astronomy.

ster·e·og·ra·phy /ˌsterēˈägrəfē; ˌsti(ə)r-/ ▸*n.* the depiction or representation of three-dimensional things by projection onto a two-dimensional surface, e.g., in cartography. **—ster·e·o·graph** /ˈsterēəˌgraf; ˈsti(ə)r-/ *n.* **—ster·e·o·graph·ic** /ˌsterēəˈgrafik; ˌsti(ə)r-/ *adj.*

ster·e·o·i·so·mer /ˌsterē-ōˈīsəmər; ˌsti(ə)r-/ ▸*n. Chemistry* each of two or more compounds differing only in the spatial arrangement of their atoms. **—ster·e·o·i·so·mer·ic** /-ˌīsəˈmerik/ *adj.* **—ster·e·o·i·som·er·ism** /-īˈsäməˌrizəm/ *n.*

ster·e·o·li·thog·ra·phy /ˌsterē-ōliˈTHägrəfē; ˌsti(ə)r-/ ▸*n.* a technique or process for creating three-dimensional objects, in which a computer-controlled moving laser beam is used to build up the required structure, layer by layer, from a liquid polymer that hardens on contact with laser light. **—ster·e·o·lith·o·graph·ic** /-ˌliTHəˈgrafik/ *adj.*

ster·e·om·e·try /ˌsterēˈämitrē; ˌsti(ə)r-/ ▸*n. Geometry* the measurement of solid bodies.

ster·e·o·mi·cro·scope /ˌsterē-ōˈmīkrəˌskōp; ˌsti(ə)r-/ ▸*n.* a binocular microscope that gives a relatively low-power stereoscopic view of the subject.

ster·e·o·phon·ic /ˌsterēəˈfänik; ˌsti(ə)r-/ ▸*adj.* (of sound recording and reproduction) using two or more channels of transmission and reproduction so that the reproduced sound seems to surround the listener and to come from more than one source. **—ster·e·o·phon·i·cal·ly** *adv.* **—ster·e·oph·o·ny** /-ˈäfənē/ *n.*

ster·e·op·sis /ˌsterēˈäpsis/ ▸*n.* the perception of depth produced by the reception in the brain of visual stimuli from both eyes in combination; binocular vision. ▷early 20th cent.: from **STEREO-** 'three-dimensional' + Greek *opsis* 'sight.' **—ster·e·op·tic** /-ˈäptik/ *adj.*

ster·e·op·ti·con /ˌsterēˈäptiˌkän; ˌsti(ə)r-/ ▸*n.* a slide projector that combines two images to create a three-dimensional effect, or makes one image dissolve into another. ▷mid 19th cent.: from **STEREO-** 'three-dimensional' + Greek *optikon*, neuter of *optikos* 'relating to vision.'

ster·e·o·scope /ˈsterēəˌskōp; ˈsti(ə)r-/ ▸*n.* a device by which two photographs of the same object taken at slightly different angles are viewed together, creating an impression of depth and solidity. **—ster·e·o·scop·ic** /ˌsterēəˈskäpik; ˌsti(ə)r-/ *adj.* **—ster·e·o·scop·i·cal·ly** *adv.* **—ster·e·os·co·py** /ˌsterēˈäskəpē; ˌsti(ə)r-/ *n.*

ster·e·o·se·lec·tive /ˌsterē-ōsəˈlektiv; ˌsti(ə)r-/ ▸*adj. Chemistry* another term for **STEREOSPECIFIC**. **—ster·e·o·se·lec·tiv·i·ty** /-səlekˈtivitē/ *n.*

ster·e·o sep·a·ra·tion ▸*n.* see **SEPARATION** (sense 2).

ster·e·o·spe·cif·ic /ˌsterē-ōspəˈsifik; ˌsti(ə)r-/ ▸*adj. Chemistry* (of a reaction) preferentially producing a particular stereoisomeric form of the product, irrespective of the configuration of the reactant. **—ster·e·o·spe·cif·i·cal·ly** *adv.* **—ster·e·o·spec·i·fic·i·ty** /-ˌspesəˈfisitē/ *n.*

ster·e·o·spon·dyl /ˌsterēəˈspändl; ˌsti(ə)r-/ ▸*n.* an extinct amphibian with a broad flat head, occurring in the Permian and Triassic periods. • Suborder Stereospondyli, order Temnospondyli: several families. ▷early 20th cent.: from modern Latin *Stereospondyli* (plural), from Greek *stereos* 'solid' + *spondulos* 'vertebra.'

ster·e·o·tac·tic /ˌsterēəˈtaktik; ˌsti(ə)r-/ (also **ster·e·o·tax·ic** /-ˈtaksik/) ▸*adj.* relating to or denoting techniques for surgical treatment or scientific investigation that permit the accurate positioning of probes inside the brain or other parts of the body, based on three-dimensional diagrams. **—ster·e·o·tac·ti·cal·ly** *adv.*

ster·e·o·tax·is /ˌsterēəˈtaksis; ˌsti(ə)r-/ (also **ster·e·o·tax·y** /ˈsterēəˌtaksē; ˈstir-/) ▸*n.* the use of stereotactic instruments or devices in surgery or research. ▷late 19th cent.: from **STEREO-** 'three-dimensional' + Greek *taxis* 'orientation.'

ster·e·o·type /ˈsterēəˌtīp; ˈsti(ə)r-/ ▸*n.* **1** a widely held but fixed and oversimplified image or idea of a particular type of person or thing: *the stereotype of the woman as the carer* | *sexual and racial stereotypes.* ■ a person or thing that conforms to such an image: *don't treat anyone as a stereotype.* **2** a relief printing plate cast in a mold made from composed type or an original plate.
▸*v.* [*trans.*] view or represent as a stereotype: *the city is too easily stereotyped as an industrial wasteland* | [as *adj.*] (**stereotyped**) *the film is weakened by its stereotyped characters.* ▷late 18th cent.: from French *stéréotype* (adjective). **—ster·e·o·typ·ic** /ˌsterēəˈtipik/ *adj.* **—ster·e·o·typ·i·cal** *adj.* **—ster·e·o·typ·i·cal·ly** *adv.*

ster·e·o·typ·y /ˈsterēəˌtīpē; ˈsti(ə)r-/ ▸*n.* the persistent repetition of an act, esp. by an animal, for no obvious purpose.

ster·ic /ˈsterik; ˈsti(ə)r-/ ▸*adj. Chemistry* of or relating to the spatial arrangement of atoms in a molecule, esp. as it affects chemical reactions. ▷late 19th cent.: formed irregularly from Greek *stereos* 'solid' + **-IC**. **—ster·i·cal·ly** *adv.*

ste·rig·ma /stəˈrigmə/ ▸*n.* (*pl.* **-ma·ta** /-mətə/) *Botany* (in some fungi) a spore-bearing projection from a cell. ▷mid 19th cent.: modern Latin, from Greek *stērigma* 'a support,' from *stērizein* 'to support.'

ster·i·lant /ˈsterələnt/ ▸*n.* an agent used to destroy microorganisms; a disinfectant. ■ a chemical agent used to destroy pests and diseases in the soil, esp. fungi and nematodes.

ster·ile /ˈsterəl/ ▸*adj.* **1** not able to produce children or young: *the disease had made him sterile.* ■ (of a plant) not able to produce fruit or seeds. ■ (of land or soil) too poor in quality to produce crops. ■ lacking in imagination, creativity, or excitement; uninspiring or unproductive: *he found the fraternity's teachings sterile.* **2** free from bacteria or other living microorganisms; totally clean: *a sterile needle and syringes.* See note at **SANITARY**. ▷late Middle English: from Old French, or from Latin *sterilis*; related to Greek *steira* 'barren cow.' Sense 2 dates from the late 19th cent. **—ster·ile·ly** /ˈsterə(l)lē/ *adv.* **—ste·ril·i·ty** /stəˈrilitē/ *n.*

ster·i·lize /ˈsterəˌlīz/ ▸*v.* [*trans.*] **1** make (something) free from bacteria or other living microorganisms: *babies' feeding equipment can be cleaned and sterilized* | [as *adj.*] (**sterilized**) *sterilized jars.* **2** (usu. **be sterilized**) deprive (a person or animal) of the ability to produce offspring, typically by removing or blocking the sex organs. ■ make (land or water) unable to produce crops or support life. **—ster·i·liz·a·ble** *adj.* **—ster·i·li·za·tion** /ˌsterəl(ə)ˈzāSHən/ *n.* **—ster·i·liz·er** *n.*

ster·let /ˈstərlit/ ▸*n.* a small sturgeon of the Danube basin and Caspian Sea area, farmed and commercially fished for its flesh and caviar. • *Acipenser ruthenus*, family Acipenseridae. ▷late 16th cent.: from Russian *sterlyad′*.

ster·ling /ˈstərliNG/ ▸*n.* British money: *prices in sterling are shown* | [as *adj.*] *issues of sterling bonds.* ■ short for **STERLING SILVER**: [as *adj.*] *a sterling spoon.*
▸*adj.* (of a person or their work, efforts, or qualities) excellent or valuable: *this organization does sterling work for youngsters.* ▷Middle English: probably from *steorra* 'star' + **-LING** (because some early Norman pennies bore a small star). Until recently one popular theory was that the coin was originally made by *Easterling* moneyers (from the "eastern" Hansa towns), but the stressed first syllable would not have been dropped.

ster·ling ar·e·a a group of countries, most belonging to the Commonwealth of Nations, that formerly pegged their exchange rates to sterling or kept their reserves in sterling rather than gold or dollars. Also called **sterling bloc**.

Ster·ling Heights /ˈstərliNG/ a city in southeastern Michigan, north of Detroit; pop. 124,471.

ster·ling sil·ver ▸*n.* silver of 92$\frac{1}{4}$ percent purity.

Ster·li·ta·mak /ˌsterlitəˈmäk/ an industrial city in southern Russia, on the Belaya River, north of Orenburg; pop. 250,000.

Stern /stərn/, Isaac (1920–2001), U.S. violinist; born in Russia. He made his New York debut in 1937 at Carnegie Hall. In 1956, he was the first American to perform in Russia after World War II, and he was invited to China in 1979. He served as president of Carnegie Hall from 1960.

stern[1] /stərn/ ▶*adj.* (of a person or their manner) serious and unrelenting, esp. in the assertion of authority and exercise of discipline: *a smile transformed his stern face | Mama looked stern.* ■ (of an act or statement) strict and severe; using extreme measures or terms: *stern measures to restrict growth of traffic.* See note at **SEVERE**. ■ (of competition or opposition) putting someone or something under extreme pressure: *the past year has been a stern test of the ability of local industry.* ▷Old English *styrne*, probably from the West Germanic base of the verb **STARE**. —**stern·ly** *adv.* —**stern·ness** *n.*

▶*PHRASES* □ **be made of sterner stuff** have a stronger character and be more able to overcome problems than others: *whereas James was deeply wounded by the failure, George was made of sterner stuff.* [from Shakespeare's *Julius Caesar* (III. 2. 93).] □ **the sterner sex** *archaic* men regarded collectively and in contrast to women.

stern[2] ▶*n.* the rearmost part of a ship or boat: *he stood at the stern of the yacht.* ■ *humorous* a person's bottom: *my stern can't take too much sun.* ▷Middle English: probably from Old Norse *stjórn* 'steering,' from *stýra* 'to steer.' —**sterned** /stərnd/ *adj.* [in *combination*] *a square-sterned vessel.* —**stern·most** /-ˌmōst/ *adj.* —**stern·ward** /-wərd/ *adv.*

ster·nal /ˈstərnl/ ▶*adj.* of or relating to the sternum: *the sternal area | sternal muscles.*

ster·nal rib ▶*n.* another term for **TRUE RIB**.

stern·drive /ˈstərnˌdrīv/ ▶*n.* an inboard engine connected to an outboard drive unit at the rear of a powerboat.

Stern Gang /ˈstərn/ a militant Zionist group that campaigned in Palestine during the 1940s for the creation of a Jewish state. Founded by Avraham Stern (1907–42) as an offshoot of Irgun, the group assassinated the British Minister for the Middle East, Lord Moyne, and Count Folke Bernadotte (1895–1948), the UN mediator for Palestine.

ster·nite /ˈstərˌnīt/ ▶*n. Entomology* (in an insect) a sclerotized plate forming the sternum of a segment. Compare with **TERGITE**.

Sterno /ˈstərnō/ ▶*n. trademark* flammable hydrocarbon jelly supplied in cans for use as fuel for cooking stoves or chafing dishes. ▷early 20th cent.: from the name of *Sternau* and Co., New York, + **-O**.

ster·no·clei·do·mas·toid /ˌstərnōˌklīdəˈmastoid/ (also **sternocleidomastoid muscle**) ▶*n. Anatomy* each of a pair of long muscles that connect the sternum, clavicle, and mastoid process of the temporal bone and serve to turn and nod the head.

ster·no·mas·toid /ˌstərnōˈmastoid/ ▶*n.* another term for **STERNOCLEIDOMASTOID**.

stern·post /ˈstərnˌpōst/ ▶*n.* the central upright structure at the stern of a vessel, typically bearing the rudder.

stern·sheets /ˈstərnˌSHēts/ ▶*plural n.* the flooring planks in a boat's after section, or the seating in this section of an open boat.

ster·num /ˈstərnəm/ ▶*n.* (*pl.* **-nums** or **-na** /-nə/) the breastbone. ■ *Zoology* a thickened ventral plate on each segment of the body of an arthropod. ▷mid 17th cent.: modern Latin, from Greek *sternon* 'chest.'

ster·nu·ta·tion /ˌstərnyəˈtāSHən/ ▶*n. formal* the action of sneezing. ▷late Middle English: from Latin *sternutatio(n-)*, from the verb *sternutare*, frequentative of *sternuere* 'to sneeze.'

ster·nu·ta·tor /ˈstərnyəˌtātər/ ▶*n. technical* an agent that causes sneezing. ■ an agent used in chemical warfare that causes irritation to the nose and eyes, pain in the chest, and nausea. —**ster·nu·ta·to·ry** /stərˈnyōōtəˌtôrē/ *adj.* & *n.* (*pl.* **-ries**).

stern·way /ˈstərnˌwā/ ▶*n.* backward movement of a ship: *we begin* ***making sternway*** *toward the shoal.*

stern·wheel·er /ˈstərnˌ(h)wēlər/ ▶*n.* a steamer propelled by a paddle wheel positioned at the stern.

ste·roid /ˈsterˌoid; ˈsti(ə)r-/ ▶*n. Biochemistry* any of a large class of organic compounds with a characteristic molecular structure containing four rings of carbon atoms (three six-membered and one five). They include many hormones, alkaloids, and vitamins. ■ short for **ANABOLIC STEROID**. ▷1930s: from **STEROL** + **-OID**. —**ste·roi·dal** /steˈroidl; sti-/ *adj.*

▶*PHRASE* □ **on steroids** used to suggest a highly exaggerated, enhanced, or accelerated version of something: *high-protein gelatin squares, available in bright red or bright green, sort of like Jell-O on steroids.*

ste·rol /ˈsterôl; -äl; ˈsti(ə)r-/ ▶*n. Biochemistry* any of a group of naturally occurring unsaturated steroid alcohols, typically waxy solids. ▷early 20th cent.: independent usage of the ending of words such as **CHOLESTEROL** and **ERGOSTEROL**.

ster·to·rous /ˈstərtərəs/ ▶*adj.* (of breathing) noisy and labored. ▷early 19th cent.: from modern Latin *stertor* 'snoring sound' (from Latin *stertere* 'to snore') + **-OUS**. —**ster·to·rous·ly** *adv.*

stet /stet/ ▶*v.* (**stet·ted**, **stet·ting**) [*intrans.*] let it stand (used as an instruction on a printed proof to indicate that a correction or alteration should be ignored). ■ [*trans.*] write such an instruction against (something corrected or deleted).
▶*n.* such an instruction made on a printed proof. ▷Latin, 'let it stand,' from *stare* 'to stand.'

steth·o·scope /ˈsteTHəˌskōp/ ▶*n.* a medical instrument for listening to the action of someone's heart or breathing, typically having a small disk-shaped resonator that is placed against the chest and two tubes connected to earpieces. ▷early 19th cent.: from French *stéthoscope*, from Greek *stēthos* 'breast' + *skopein* 'look at.' —**steth·o·scop·ic** /ˌsteTHəˈskäpik/ *adj.*

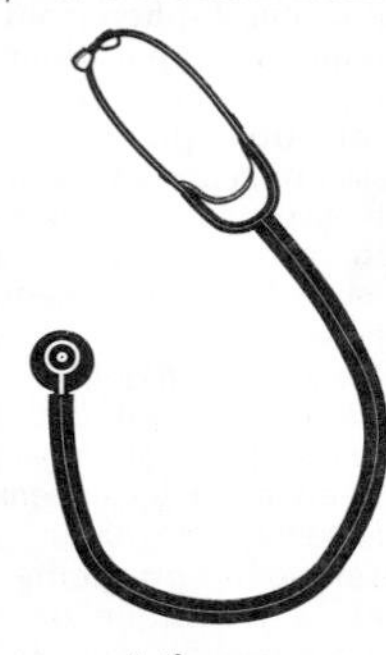
stethoscope

St.-É·tienne /saNt āˈtyen/ an industrial city in southeastern central France, southwest of Lyons; pop. 202,000.

Stet·son /ˈstetsən/ ▶*n. trademark* a hat with a high crown and a wide brim, traditionally worn by cowboys and ranchers in the U.S. ▷late 19th cent.: named after John B. *Stetson* (1830–1906), American hat manufacturer.

Stet·tin /SHteˈtēn/ German name for **SZCZECIN**.

Steu·ben /ˈSHtoibən; ˈst(y)ōōbən/, Friedrich (Wilhelm Ludolf Gerhard Augustin) von (1730–94), American army officer; born in Prussia. He came to America in December 1777 and joined Washington at Valley Forge, where he introduced European methods of training and discipline. Appointed inspector general of the Continental Army 1778, he was instrumental in shaping American forces into a legitimate military force.

Steu·ben·ville /ˈst(y)ōōbənˌvil/ an industrial city in eastern Ohio, on the Ohio River; pop. 22,125.

St. Eu·sta·ti·us /yoo'stāsH(ē)əs/ a small volcanic island in the Caribbean Sea, in the Netherlands Antilles; pop. 2,000 (1992).

ste·ve·dore /ˈstēvəˌdôr/ ▶*n.* a person employed, or a contractor engaged, at a dock to load and unload cargo from ships. ▷late 18th cent.: from Spanish *estivador*, from *estivar* 'stow a cargo,' from Latin *stipare*.

Ste·ven·graph /ˈstēvənˌgraf/ ▶*n.* a type of small picture made from brightly colored woven silk, produced during the late 19th century. ▷named after Thomas *Stevens* (1828–88), English weaver, whose firm made them.

Ste·vens[1] /ˈstēvənz/, John Paul (1920–), U.S. Supreme Court associate justice 1975– . Appointed to the Court by President Ford, he was considered a moderate conservative.

Ste·vens[2], Wallace (1879–1955), U.S. poet. He developed an original and colorful style, writing his poetry privately and mostly in isolation from the literary community. His *Collected Poems* (1954) won a Pulitzer Prize.

Ste·ven·son[1] /ˈstēvənsən/, Adlai Ewing (1900–1965), U.S. statesman and politician. A popular supporter of social reform and internationalism, he was governor of Illinois 1949–53 and was the unsuccessful Democratic candidate for the presidency 1952 and 1956. He later served as U.S. ambassador to the UN 1960–65.

Ste·ven·son[2], Robert Louis (Balfour) (1850–94), Scottish novelist, poet, and travel writer. Stevenson, who wrote *Treasure Island* (1883), is also known for *A Child's Garden of Verses*, a collection of poetry first published as *Penny Whistles* in 1885. Oher notable works: *The Strange Case of Dr. Jekyll and Mr. Hyde* and *Kidnapped* (both 1886).

Ste·vens Point /ˈstēvənz/ an industrial and commercial city in central Wisconsin, on the Wisconsin River; pop. 23,006.

ste·vi·a /ˈstēvēə; ˈstev-/ ▶*n.* a composite herb native to South America (Genus *Stevia*, especially *S. rebaudiana*, native to Paraguay) whose leaves are the source of a noncaloric sweetener. ■ a food supplement prepared from this, used as a sweetener. ▷from modern Latin *Stevia*, from the name of the 16th-cent. Spanish botanist Pedro Jaime *Esteve*.

ste·vi·o·side /ˈstēvēəˌsīd; ˈstev-/ ▶*n.* a sweet compound of the glycoside class obtained from the leaves of a Paraguayan shrub and used as a food sweetener. • The shrub is *Stevia rebaudiana* (family Compositae). ▷1930s: from the genus name *Stevia* (from the name of P. J. *Esteve* (died 1566), Spanish botanist) + **-OSE**[2] + **-IDE**.

stew[1] /st(y)ōō/ ▶*n.* **1** a dish of meat and vegetables cooked slowly in liquid in a closed dish or pan: *lamb stew | add to casseroles, stews, and sauces.* **2** [in *sing.*] *informal* a state of great anxiety or agitation: *I suppose he's all* ***in a stew.*** **3** *archaic* a heated public room used for hot steam baths. ■ a brothel.
▶*v.* [*trans.*] cook (meat, fruit, or other food) slowly in liquid in a closed dish or pan: *a new way to stew rhubarb.* ■ [*intrans.*] (of meat, fruit, or other food) be cooked in such a way. ■ [*intrans.*] *informal* remain in a heated or stifling atmosphere: *sweaty clothes left to stew in a plastic bag.* ■ [*intrans.*] *informal* worry about something, esp. on one's own: *James will be expecting us, so we will let him stew a bit.* ■ [*intrans.*] *Brit.* (of tea) become strong and bitter with prolonged brewing. ■ (**be stewed in**) *poetic/literary* be steeped in or imbued with: *politics there are stewed in sexual prejudice and privilege.* ▷Middle English (in the sense 'cauldron'): from Old French *estuve* (related to *estuver* 'heat in steam'), probably based on Greek *tuphos* 'smoke, steam.' Sense 1 (mid 18th cent.) is directly from the verb (dating from late Middle English).

▶*PHRASE* □ **stew in one's own juice** *informal* suffer anxiety or the unpleasant consequences of one's own actions without the consoling intervention of others.

stew[2] ▶*n. Brit.* a pond or large tank for keeping fish for eating. ■ an artificial oyster bed. ▷Middle English: from Old French *estui*, from *estoier* 'confine.'

stew[3] ▶*n. informal* an air steward or stewardess. ▷1970s: abbreviation.

stew·ard /ˈst(y)ōōərd/ ▶*n.* **1** a person who looks after the passengers on a ship, aircraft, or train and brings them meals. ■ a person responsible for supplies of food to a college, club, or other institution. **2** an official appointed to supervise arrangements or keep order at a large public event, for example a sporting event. ■ short for **SHOP STEWARD**. **3** a person employed to manage another's property, esp. a large house or estate. ■ a person whose responsibility it is to take care of something: *farmers pride themselves on being stewards of the countryside.*
▶*v.* [*trans.*] **1** (of an official) supervise arrangements or keep order at (a large public event): *the event was organized and stewarded properly.* **2** manage or look after (another's property). ▷Old English *stīweard*, from *stig* (probably in the sense 'house, hall') + *weard* 'ward.' The verb dates from the early 17th cent. —**stew·ard·ship** *n.*

stew·ard·ess /ˈst(y)ōōərdis/ ▶*n.* a woman who is employed to provide meals for and otherwise look after the passengers on a ship or aircraft.

Stew·art[1] *adj.* & *n.* variant spelling of **STUART**[5].

Stew·art[2], Jackie (1939–), British race car driver; born *John Young Stewart*. He was the world champion three times—1969, 1971, and 1973.

Stew·art[3], Jimmy (1908–97), U.S. actor; full name *James Maitland Stewart*; famous for roles in which the all-American hero was embodied. His movies

James Stewart

include *Mr. Smith Goes to Washington* (1939), *The Philadelphia Story* (Academy Award, 1940), *It's a Wonderful Life* (1946), *The Man from Laramie* (1955), and *Vertigo* (1958).

Stew·art[4], Martha (1941–), U.S. businesswoman; born *Martha Kostyra*. She turned her home decorating and cooking ideas into an industry, including a radio talk show, a "Martha Stewart Living" television program and a magazine, a syndicated newspaper column, an Internet site, and a signature line of housewares. In 2004 she was convicted of lying to investigators about a 2001 stock sale and was sentenced to five months in prison.

Stew·art[5], (William) Payne (1957–1999), U.S. golfer. His championship titles include the PGA (1989), and the U.S. Open (1991, 1999). He owned a clothing line that featured his familiar plus fours (baggy knickers worn as traditional golfing attire). Stewart died in an airplane crash.

Stew·art[6], Potter (1915–85) U.S. Supreme Court associate justice 1958–81. Appointed to the Court by President Eisenhower, he was noted for his 1964 opinion on pornography, ". . . I know it when I see it." He upheld the First Amendment claim in the Pentagon Papers case in 1971.

Stew·art[7], Rod (1945–), English pop singer and songwriter; full name *Roderick David Stewart*. In 1971 his single "Maggie May" and its album *Every Picture Tells a Story* topped the singles and album charts in both Britain and the U.S. Later hits include "Sailing" (1976) and "Do You Think I'm Sexy" (1978).

stew·bum /ˈst(y)o͞oˌbəm/ ▸*n. informal* an alcoholic, esp. one who has become vagrant.

stewed /st(y)o͞od/ ▸*adj.* (of food) cooked slowly in liquid in a closed dish or pan: *stewed apples.* ■ [*predic.*] *informal* drunk: *we got* **stewed** *at their party.* ■ *Brit.* (of tea) tasting strong and bitter because of prolonged brewing.

stew·ing /ˈst(y)o͞oiNG/ ▸*adj.* [*attrib.*] (of meat or other food) suitable for stewing: *a stewing chicken.*

stew·pot /ˈst(y)o͞oˌpät/ ▸*n.* a large pot in which stews are cooked.

St. Ex. ▸*abbr.* Stock Exchange.

stg ▸*abbr.* sterling.

stge. ▸*abbr.* storage.

St. George's the capital of Grenada in the Caribbean Sea, a port in the southwestern part of the island; pop. 36,000.

St. George's Chan·nel a channel between Wales and Ireland that links the Irish Sea with the Celtic Sea.

St. George's Cross ▸*n.* a cross shaped like a plus sign, red on a white background (esp. as a national emblem of England).

Sth ▸*abbr.* south.

St. He·le·na /həˈlēnə/ a solitary island in the South Atlantic, a British dependency; pop. 6,000; capital, Jamestown. The islands of Ascension, Tristan da Cunha, and Gough Island are dependencies of St. Helena. It is known as the place of Napoleon's exile 1815–21 and death. ▷so named when it was discovered by the Portuguese on the feast day of *St. Helena*, May 21, 1502. **—St. He·le·ni·an** /-nēən/ *adj.* & *n.*

St. Hel·ens /ˈhelənz/ an industrial town in northwestern England, northeast of Liverpool; pop. 175,000.

St. Hel·ens, Mount an active volcano in southwestern Washington, in the Cascade Range, that rises to 8,312 feet (2,560 m). A dramatic eruption in May 1980 reduced its height by more than a thousand feet and spread volcanic ash and debris over a vast area. In late 2004, a massive extrusion of lava had geologists monitoring the possibility of another explosive eruption.

sthen·ic /ˈsTHenik/ ▸*adj. dated Medicine* of or having a high or excessive level of strength and energy. ▷late 18th cent.: from Greek *sthenos* 'strength,' on the pattern of *asthenic*.

stib·nite /ˈstibnīt/ ▸*n.* a lead-gray mineral, typically occurring as striated prismatic crystals, that consists of antimony sulfide and is the chief ore of antimony. ▷mid 19th cent.: from Latin *stibium* 'black antimony' + **-INE**[4] + **-ITE**[1].

sti·cho·myth·i·a /ˌstikəˈmiTHēə/ ▸*n.* dialogue in which two characters speak alternate lines of verse, used as a stylistic device in ancient Greek drama. ▷mid 19th cent.: modern Latin, from Greek *stikhomuthia*, from *stikhos* 'row, line of verse' + *muthos* 'speech, talk.'

stick[1] /stik/ ▸*n.* **1** a thin piece of wood that has fallen or been cut from a tree. **2** a thin piece of wood that has been trimmed for a particular purpose, in particular: ■ a long piece of wood used for support in walking or as a weapon with which to hit someone or something. ■ (in hockey, polo, and other games) a long implement, typically made of wood, with a head or blade of varying form that is used to hit or direct the ball or puck. ■ [usu. with *adj.*] a short piece of wood used to impale food: *Popsicle sticks.* ■ *figurative* a piece of basic furniture: *every* **stick of** *furniture just vanished.* ■ (**sticks**) (in field hockey) the foul play of raising the stick above the shoulder. ■ *archaic Nautical* a mast or spar. ■ (**the sticks**) *Brit., informal* goalposts. **3** something resembling or likened to a stick, in particular: ■ a long, thin piece of something: **a stick of** *dynamite* | *cinnamon sticks.* ■ a quarter-pound rectangular block of butter or margarine. ■ a conductor's baton. ■ a gear or control lever. ■ (in extended and metaphorical use) a very thin person or limb: *the girl was a stick* | *her arms were* **like sticks.** ■ a number of bombs or paratroopers dropped rapidly from an aircraft. ■ a small group of soldiers assigned to a particular duty: **a stick of** *heavily armed guards.* ■ *informal* a marijuana cigarette. **4** a threat of punishment or unwelcome measures (often contrasted with the offer of reward as a means of persuasion): *training that relies more on the carrot than on the stick.* ■ *Brit., informal* severe criticism or treatment: *I took a lot of stick from the press.* **5** (**the sticks**) *informal, derogatory* rural areas far from cities: *a small, dusty town* **out in the sticks.** **6** [with *adj.*] *informal, dated* a person of a specified kind: *Janet's not such a bad* **old stick** *sometimes.* ▷Old English *sticca* 'peg, stick, spoon'; related to Dutch *stek* 'cutting from a plant' and German *Stecken* 'staff, stick.' **—stick-like** /-ˌlīk/ *adj.*

▸*PHRASES* □ **up the stick** *Brit., informal* pregnant. □ **up sticks** *Brit., informal* go to live elsewhere. [from nautical slang *to up sticks* 'set up a boat's mast' (ready for departure).]

stick[2] ▸*v.* (*past* **stuck** /stək/) **1** [*trans.*] (**stick something in/into/through**) push a sharp or pointed object into or through (something): *he stuck his fork into the sausage* | *the candle was stuck in a straw-covered bottle.* ■ (**stick something on**) fix something on (a point or pointed object): *stick the balls of wool on knitting needles.* ■ [*intrans.*] (**stick in/into/through**) (of a pointed object) be or remain fixed with its point embedded in (something): *there was a slim rod sticking into the ground beside me.* ■ [*trans.*] insert, thrust, or push: *a youth with a cigarette stuck behind one ear* | *she stuck out her tongue at him.* ■ [*intrans.*] protrude or extend in a certain direction: *his front teeth* **stick out** | *Sue's hair was* **sticking up** *at all angles.* ■ [*trans.*] put somewhere, typically in a quick or careless way: *just stick that sandwich on my desk.* ■ *informal* used to express angry dismissal of a particular thing: *he told them they could stick the job—he didn't want it anyway.* ■ *informal* cause to incur an expense or loss: *she stuck me for all of last month's rent.* ■ stab or pierce with a sharp object: [as *adj.*] (**stuck**) *he screamed like a stuck pig.* **2** [*intrans.*] adhere or cling to a substance or surface: *the plastic seats* **stuck to** *my skin.* ■ [*trans.*] fasten or cause to adhere to an object or surface: *she stuck the stamp on the envelope.* ■ be or become fixed or jammed in one place as a result of an obstruction: *he drove into a bog, where his wheels stuck fast.* ■ remain in a static condition; fail to progress: *he lost a lot of weight but had stuck at 210 pounds.* ■ (of a feeling or thought) remain persistently in one's mind: *one particular incident sticks in my mind.* ■ *informal* be or become convincing, established, or regarded as valid: *the authorities couldn't make the charges stick* | *the name stuck and Anastasia she remained.* ■ (in blackjack and similar card games) decline to add to one's hand. **3** (**be stuck**) be fixed in a particular position or unable to move or be moved: *Sara tried to open the window but it was stuck* | *we got stuck in a traffic jam* | *the cat's stuck up a tree.* ■ be unable to progress with a task or find the answer or solution to something: *I'm doing the crossword and I'm stuck.* ■ [with *adverbial of place*] *informal* be or remain in a specified place or situation, typically one perceived as tedious or unpleasant: *I don't want to be stuck in an office all my life.* ■ (**be stuck for**) be at a loss for or in need of: *I'm not usually stuck for words.* ■ (**be stuck with**) *informal* be unable to get rid of or escape from: *like it or not, she and Grant were stuck with each other.* ■ (**be stuck on**) *informal* be infatuated with: *he's too good for Jenny, even though she's so stuck on him.* **4** [often with *negative*] *Brit., informal* accept or tolerate (an unpleasant or unwelcome person or situation): *I can't stick Geoffrey—he's a real old misery.* ■ (**stick it out**) *informal* put up with or persevere with something difficult or disagreeable.

▸*phrasal v.* □ **stick around** *informal* remain in or near a place: *I'd like to stick around and watch the game.* □ **stick at** *informal* persevere with (a task or endeavor) in a steady and determined way. □ **stick by 1** continue to support or be loyal to (someone), typically during difficult times: *I love him and whatever happens, I'll stick by him.* **2** another way of saying **STICK TO** in sense 2 below. □ **stick something on** *informal* place the blame for a mistake or wrongdoing on (someone). □ **stick out** be extremely noticeable: *many important things had happened to him, but one stuck out.* □ **stick out for** refuse to accept less than (what one has asked for); persist in demanding (something): *they offered him a Rover but Vic stuck out for a Jaguar.* □ **stick to 1** continue or confine oneself to doing or using (a particular thing): *I'll stick to bitter lemon, thanks.* ■ not move or digress from (a path or a subject). **2** adhere to (a commitment, belief, or rule): *the government stuck to its election pledges.* □ **stick together** *informal* remain united or mutually loyal: *we Europeans must stick together.* □ **stick someone/something up** *informal* rob someone at gunpoint. □ **stick up for** support or defend (a person or cause). □ **stick with** *informal* **1** persevere or continue with: *I'm happy to stick with the present team.* **2** another way of saying **STICK BY** above. ▷Old English *stician*, of Germanic origin; related to German *sticken* 'embroider,' from an Indo-European root shared by Greek *stizein* 'to prick,' *stigma* 'a mark' and Latin *instigare* 'spur on.' Early senses included 'pierce' and 'remain fixed (by its embedded pointed end).'

▸*PHRASES* □ **get stuck in** (or **into**) *Brit., informal* start doing (something) enthusiastically or with determination: *we got stuck into the decorating.* □ **stick at nothing** allow nothing to deter one from achieving one's aim, however wrong or dishonest: *he would stick at nothing to preserve his privileges.* □ **stick 'em up!** *informal* hands up! (spoken typically by a person threatening someone else with a gun). □ **stick in one's throat** (or **craw**) be difficult or impossible to accept; be a source of continuing annoyance. ■ (of words) be difficult or impossible to say: *she couldn't say "Thank you"—the words stuck in her throat.* □ **stick it to** *informal* treat (someone) harshly or severely. □ **stick one** (or **it**) **on** *Brit., informal* hit (someone). □ **stick one's neck out** *informal* risk incurring criticism or anger by acting or speaking boldly. □ **stick out a mile** see **MILE.** □ **stick out like a sore thumb** see **SORE.** □ **stick to one's guns** see **GUN.** □ **stick to one's ribs** (of food) be filling and nourishing: *a bowl of soup that will stick to your ribs.*

stick·a·bil·i·ty /ˌstikəˈbilitē/ ▸*n. informal* a person's ability to persevere with something; staying power: *the secret of success is stickability.*

stick·ball /ˈstikˌbôl/ ▸*n.* an informal game resembling baseball, played with a stick and a (usually rubber) ball.

stick·built /ˈstikˌbilt/ (also **stick-built**) ▸*adj.* (of houses or other buildings) built piece-by-piece on the premises, rather than constructed from prefabricated units.

stick·er /ˈstikər/ ▸*n.* an adhesive label or notice, generally printed or illustrated. ■ short for **STICKER PRICE.**

stick·er price ▸*n.* the advertised retail price of an item, esp. the price listed on a sticker attached to the window of a new automobile.

stick·er shock ▸*n. informal* shock or dismay experienced by the potential buyers of a particular product on discovering its high or increased price: *drugstore consumers are feeling the pain of sticker shock as never before.*

stick·han·dle /ˈstikˌhandl/ ▸*v.* [*intrans.*] [as *n.*] (**stickhandling**) (in hockey and other games) control the puck or ball with one's stick. **—stick·han·dler** *n.*

stick·ie /ˈstikē/ ▸*n.* (*pl.* **-ies**) informal term for **POST-IT.**

stick·ing plas·ter ▸*n. chiefly Brit.* an adhesive bandage, available in a roll or as individual patches.

stick·ing point ▸*n.* a point at which an obstacle arises in progress toward an agreement or goal: *Jerusalem emerged as a key sticking point in Israeli–Palestinian negotiations.*

stick in·sect ▸*n.* another term for **WALKING STICK** (sense 2).

stick-in-the-mud ▸*n. informal* a person who is dull and unadventurous and who resists change.

stick·le·back /ˈstikəl,bak/ ▸*n.* a small fish with sharp spines along its back, able to live in both salt and fresh water and found in both Eurasia and North America. • Family Gasterosteidae: several genera and species, including the common and widespread **three-spined stickleback** (*Gasterosteus aculeatus*). ▷late Middle English: from Old English *sticel* 'thorn, sting' + *bæc* 'back.'

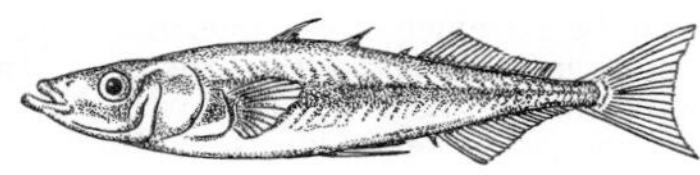

three-spined stickleback

stick·ler /ˈstik(ə)lər/ ▸*n.* **1** a person who insists on a certain quality or type of behavior: ***a stickler for** accuracy| a stickler when it comes to timekeeping.* **2** a difficult problem; a conundrum. ▷mid 16th cent. (in the sense 'umpire'): from obsolete *stickle* 'be umpire,' alteration of obsolete *stightle* 'to control,' frequentative of Old English *stiht(i)an* 'set in order.'

stick-nest rat ▸*n.* a fluffy-haired gregarious Australian rat that builds nests of interwoven sticks. • Genus *Leporillus*, family Muridae: two species, in particular *L. conditor*.

stick·pin /ˈstik,pin/ ▸*n.* a straight pin with an ornamental head, worn to keep a tie in place or as a brooch.

stick·seed /ˈstik,sēd/ ▸*n.* a plant of the borage family that bears small barbed seeds. • Genera *Hackelia* and *Lappula*, family Boraginaceae: several species, in particular *H. floribunda*, which resembles a forget-me-not.

stick shift ▸*n.* a manual transmission.

stick-to-it·ive·ness /stik ˈto͞oitivnis/ ▸*n. informal* perseverance; persistence.

stick·um /ˈstikəm/ ▸*n. informal* a sticky or adhesive substance; gum or paste. ▷early 20th cent.: from the verb STICK[2] + *-um* (representing the pronoun *them*).

stick·up /ˈstik,əp/ ▸*n. informal* an armed robbery in which a gun is used to threaten people.

stick·weed /ˈstik,wēd/ ▸*n.* any of a number of North American plants with hooked or barbed seeds, e.g., ragweed.

stick·y /ˈstikē/ ▸*adj.* (**stick·i·er, stick·i·est**) **1** tending or designed to stick to things on contact or covered with something that sticks: *her sticky bubblegum | sticky tape.* ■ (of a substance) glutinous; viscous: *the dough should be moist but not sticky.* ■ (of prices, interest rates, or wages) slow to change or react to change. **2** (of the weather) hot and damp; muggy: *it was an unusually hot and sticky summer.* ■ damp with sweat: *she felt hot and sticky and changed her clothes.* **3** *informal* involving problems; difficult or awkward: *the relationship is going through a sticky patch.* **—stick·i·ly** /ˈstikəlē/ *adv.* **—stick·i·ness** *n.*

▸*PHRASES* □ **sticky fingers** *informal* a propensity to steal. □ **sticky wicket** see WICKET.

stick·y·beak /ˈstikē,bēk/ *Austral./NZ, informal* ▸*n.* an inquisitive and prying person.

▸*v.* [*intrans.*] pry into other people's affairs: *I don't mean to stickybeak, but where is he going to leave?*

stick·y end ▸*n. Biochemistry* an end of a DNA double helix at which a few unpaired nucleotides of one strand extend beyond the other.

stick·y-fin·gered ▸*adj. informal* given to stealing: *a sticky-fingered con artist.*

stic·tion /ˈstikSHən/ ▸*n. Physics* the friction that tends to prevent stationary surfaces from being set in motion.

Stieg·litz /ˈstēglits/, Alfred (1864–1946), U.S. photographer; husband of Georgia O'Keeffe. He pioneered the establishment of photography as a fine art in the U.S. He gained an international reputation in the 1890s when he experimented with such innovations as night-time photography.

sti·fa·do /stiˈfädō/ ▸*n.* a Greek dish of meat stewed with onions and sometimes tomatoes. ▷from modern Greek *stiphado*.

stiff /stif/ ▸*adj.* **1** not easily bent or changed in shape; rigid: *a stiff black collar | stiff cardboard.* ■ not moving as freely as is usual or desirable; difficult to turn or operate: *a stiff drawer | the faucet in the shower is a little stiff.* ■ (of a person or part of the body) unable to move easily and without pain: *he was stiff from sitting on the desk | a stiff back.* ■ (of a person or their manner) not relaxed or friendly; constrained: *she greeted him with stiff politeness.* ■ viscous; thick: *add wheat until the mixture is quite stiff.* **2** severe or strong: *they face stiff fines and a possible jail sentence | a stiff increase in taxes.* ■ (of a wind) blowing strongly: *a stiff breeze stirring the lake.* ■ requiring strength or effort; difficult: *a long stiff climb up the bare hillside.* ■ (of an alcoholic drink) strong: *a stiff measure of brandy.* **3** [*predic.*] (**stiff with**) *informal* full of: *the place is stiff with alarm systems.* **4** (**—— stiff**) *informal* having a specified unpleasant feeling to an extreme extent: *she was scared stiff | I was bored stiff with my project.* **5** *Bridge* a card that is the only one of its suit in a hand: *two red aces and a stiff club.*

▸*n. informal* **1** a dead body. **2** a boring, conventional person: *ordinary working stiffs in respectable offices.* ■ *informal* a fellow: *the lucky stiff!*

▸*v.* [*trans.*] *informal* **1** (often **be stiffed**) cheat (someone) out of something, esp. money: *several workers were stiffed out of their pay.* ■ fail to leave (someone) a tip. **2** ignore deliberately; snub. ■ fail to appear for a promised engagement or appointment: *he stiffed us and didn't show up.* **3** kill: *I want to get those pigs who stiffed your doctor.* ■ [*intrans.*] be unsuccessful: *as soon as he began singing about the wife and kids, his albums stiffed.* ▷Old English *stīf*, of Germanic origin; related to Dutch *stijf*. **—stiff·ish** *adj.* **—stiff·ly** *adv.* **—stiff·ness** *n.*

▸*PHRASES* □ **stiff as a board** *informal* (of a person or part of the body) extremely stiff. □ **a stiff upper lip** a quality of uncomplaining stoicism: *senior managers had to keep a stiff upper lip and remain optimistic.*

stiff-arm ▸*v.* [*trans.*] tackle or fend off (a person) by extending an arm rigidly.

stiff·en /ˈstifən/ ▸*v.* make or become stiff or rigid: [*trans.*] *he stiffened his knees in an effort to prevent them from trembling* | [*intrans.*] *my back* ***stiffens up*** *and I can't bend.* ■ [*trans.*] support or strengthen (a garment or fabric), typically by adding tape or an adhesive layer. ■ *figurative* make or become stronger or more steadfast: [*trans.*] *outrage over the murders stiffened the government's resolve to confront the Mafia* | [*intrans.*] *the regime's resistance stiffened.* **—stiff·en·er** /ˈstif(ə)nər/ *n.*

stiff·en·ing /ˈstif(ə)niNG/ ▸*n.* material used to stiffen a garment, fabric, or other object.

stiff-necked ▸*adj.* (of a person or their behavior) haughty and stubborn.

stiff·tail /ˈstif,tāl/ (also **stiff-tailed duck**) ▸*n.* a diving duck with a stiff tail of pointed feathers, often held up at an angle. • Family Anatidae: four genera, in particular *Oxyura*, and several species, e.g., the ruddy duck.

stif·fy /ˈstifē/ (also **stif·fie**) ▸*n.* (*pl.* **-fies**) *chiefly Brit. vulgar slang* an erection of a man's penis.

sti·fle[1] /ˈstīfəl/ ▸*v.* [*trans.*] **1** make (someone) unable to breathe properly; suffocate: *those in the streets were stifled by the fumes* | [as *adj.*] (**stifling**) *stifling heat.* **2** restrain (a reaction) or stop oneself acting on (an emotion): *she stifled a giggle | she stifled a desire to turn and flee* | [as *adj.*] (**stifled**) *she gave a stifled cry of disappointment.* ■ prevent or constrain (an activity or idea): *high taxes were stifling private enterprise.* ▷late Middle English: perhaps from a frequentative of Old French *estouffer* 'smother, stifle.' **—sti·fler** /-f(ə)lər/ *n.* **—sti·fling·ly** /-f(ə)liNGlē/ *adv.* [as *submodifier*] *a stiflingly hot day.*

sti·fle[2] (also **sti·fle joint**) ▸*n.* a joint in the legs of horses, dogs, and other animals, equivalent to the knee in humans. ▷Middle English: of unknown origin.

sti·fle bone ▸*n.* the bone in front of a stifle.

stig·ma /ˈstigmə/ ▸*n.* (*pl.* **stig·mas** or esp. in sense 2 **stig·ma·ta** /stigˈmätə; ˈstigmətə/) **1** a mark of disgrace associated with a particular circumstance, quality, or person: *the stigma of mental disorder | to be a nonreader carries a social stigma.* **2** (**stigmata**) (in Christian tradition) marks corresponding to those left on Jesus' body by the Crucifixion, said to have been impressed by divine favor on the bodies of St. Francis of Assisi and others. **3** *Medicine* a visible sign or characteristic of a disease. ■ a mark or spot on the skin. **4** *Botany* (in a flower) the part of a pistil that receives the pollen during pollination. ▷late 16th cent. (denoting a mark made by pricking or branding): via Latin from Greek *stigma* 'a mark made by a pointed instrument, a dot'; related to STICK[1].

stig·mar·i·a /stigˈme(ə)rēə/ ▸*n.* (*pl.* **-mar·i·ae** /-ˈme(ə)rē-ē/) *Paleontology* a fossilized root of a giant lycopod, common in Carboniferous coal measures. • Class Lycopsida, in particular the genera *Lepidodendron* and *Sigillaria*. ▷mid 19th cent.: modern Latin, from Greek *stigma*, with reference to the scars where rootlets were attached, covering the fossils. **—stig·mar·i·an** *adj.*

stig·mat·ic /stigˈmatik/ ▸*adj.* **1** of or relating to a stigma or stigmas, in particular constituting or conveying a mark of disgrace. **2** another term for ANASTIGMATIC.

▸*n.* a person bearing stigmata. ▷late 16th cent. (in the sense '(person) marked with a blemish or deformity'): from Latin *stigma*, *stigmat-* + -IC. **—stig·mat·i·cal·ly** /-ik(ə)lē/ *adv.*

stig·ma·tist /ˈstigmətist/ ▸*n.* another term for STIGMATIC.

stig·ma·tize /ˈstigmə,tīz/ ▸*v.* [*trans.*] **1** (usu. **be stigmatized**) describe or regard as worthy of disgrace or great disapproval: *the institution* ***was stigmatized as*** *a last resort for the destitute.* **2** mark with stigmata. ▷late 16th cent. (in the sense 'mark with a brand'): from French *stigmatiser* or medieval Latin *stigmatizare*, from Greek *stigmatizein*, from *stigma* (see STIGMA). **—stig·ma·ti·za·tion** /,stigmətiˈzāSHən/ *n.*

Stijl /stīl/ see DE STIJL.

stilb /stilb/ ▸*n.* a unit of luminance equal to one candela per square centimeter. ▷1940s: from French, from Greek *stilbein* 'to glitter.'

stil·bene /ˈstil,bēn/ ▸*n. Chemistry* a synthetic aromatic hydrocarbon that forms phosphorescent crystals and is used in dye manufacture. • Alternative name: ***trans*-1,2-diphenylethene**; chem. formula: $C_6H_5CH{=}CHC_6H_5$. ▷mid 19th cent.: from Greek *stilbein* 'to glitter' + -ENE.

stil·bes·trol /stilˈbes,trôl; -,träl/ (*Brit.* **stil·boes·trol**) ▸*n. Biochemistry* a powerful synthetic estrogen used in hormone therapy, as a postcoital contraceptive, and as a growth-promoting agent for livestock. ▷1930s: from STILBENE + ESTRUS + -OL.

stile[1] /stīl/ ▸*n.* an arrangement of steps that allows people but not animals to climb over a fence or wall. ▷Old English *stigel*, from a Germanic root meaning 'to climb.'

stile[2] ▸*n.* a vertical piece in the frame of a paneled door or sash window. Compare with RAIL[1] (sense 3). ▷late 17th cent.: probably from Dutch *stijl* 'pillar, doorpost.'

Stiles /stīlz/, Ezra (1727–95), U.S. scholar, teacher, lawyer, and minister. A Congregational minister in Newport, Rhode Island 1755–86, he was a president of Yale College 1778–95 and founder of Rhode Island College (later Brown University) in 1764.

sti·let·to /stəˈletō/ ▸*n.* (*pl.* **-tos**) **1** a short dagger with a tapering blade. ■ a sharp-pointed tool for making eyelet holes. **2** (also **sti·let·to heel**) a thin, high, tapering heel on a woman's shoe: [as *adj.*] *the rapid click of stiletto heels on pavement.* ■ a shoe with such a heel. ▷early 17th cent.: from Italian, diminutive of *stilo* 'dagger.'

still[1] /stil/ ▸*adj.* not moving or making a sound: *the still body of the young man.* ■ (of air or water) undisturbed by wind, sound, or current; calm and tranquil: *her voice carried on the still air | a still autumn day.* ■ (of a drink such as wine) not effervescent; compare with SPARKLE.

▸*n.* **1** deep silence and calm; stillness: *the still of the night.* **2** an ordinary static photograph as opposed to a motion picture, esp. a single shot from a movie.

▸*adv.* **1** without moving: *the sheriff commanded him to stand still and drop the gun.* **2** up to and including the present or the time mentioned; even now (or then) as formerly: *he still lives with his mother | it was still raining.* ■ referring to something that will or may happen in the future: *we could still win.* **3** nevertheless; all the same: *I'm afraid he's crazy. Still, he's harmless.* **4** even (used with comparatives for emphasis): *write, or better still, type, captions for the pictures | Hank, already sweltering, began to sweat still more profusely.*

▸*v.* make or become still; quieten: [*trans.*] *she raised her hand, stilling Erica's protests* | [*intrans.*] *the din in the hall stilled.* ▷Old English *stille* (adjective and adverb), *stillan* (verb), from a base meaning 'be fixed, stand.' **—still·ness** *n.*

▸*PHRASES* □ **still and all** *informal* nevertheless; even so. □ **still small voice** the voice of one's conscience (with reference to 1 Kings 19:12). □ **still waters run deep** *proverb* a quiet or placid manner may conceal a more passionate nature.

still[2] ▸*n.* an apparatus for distilling alcoholic drinks such as whiskey. ▷mid 16th cent.: from the rare verb *still* 'extract by distillation,' shortening of DISTILL.

stil·lage /ˈstilij/ ▸*n.* a wooden rack or pallet for holding stored goods off the floor or separating goods in transit. ▷late 16th cent. (originally denoting a stand for casks): apparently from Dutch *stellagie* 'scaffold,' from *stellen* 'to place.'

still·birth /ˈstil,bərTH/ ▶*n.* the birth of an infant that has died in the womb (strictly, after having survived through at least the first 28 weeks of pregnancy, earlier instances being regarded as abortion or miscarriage).

still·born /ˈstil,bôrn/ ▶*adj.* (of an infant) born dead. ■ *figurative* (of a proposal or plan) having failed to develop or succeed; unrealized: *the proposed wealth tax was stillborn.*

still-hunt ▶*v.* [*intrans.*] [often as *n.*] (**still-hunting**) hunt game stealthily; stalk.
▶*n.* (**still hunt**) a stealthy hunt for game.

still life ▶*n.* (*pl.* **still lifes** /,līfs/) a painting or drawing of an arrangement of objects, typically including fruit and flowers and objects contrasting with these in texture, such as bowls and glassware. ■ this type or genre of painting or drawing.

still·room /ˈstil,ro͞om; -,ro͝om/ ▶*n. Brit., historical* a room in a large house used by the housekeeper for the storage of preserves, cakes, and liqueurs and the preparation of tea and coffee. ▷early 18th cent.: a term used earlier for a room in a house where a still was kept for the distillation of perfumes and cordials.

Still·son /ˈstilsən/ (also **Still·son wrench**) ▶*n.* a large wrench with jaws that tighten as pressure is increased. ▷early 20th cent.: named after Daniel C. *Stillson* (1830–99), its American inventor.

Still·wa·ter /ˈstil,wätər; -,wätər/ a city in north central Oklahoma, home to Oklahoma State University; pop. 39,065.

stil·ly /ˈstil-lē/ *poetic/literary* ▶*adv.* quietly and with little movement: *the birds rested stilly.*
▶*adj.* still and quiet: *the stilly night.*

stilt /stilt/ ▶*n.* **1** either of a pair of upright poles with supports for the feet enabling the user to walk at a distance above the ground. ■ each of a set of posts or piles supporting a building above the ground. ■ a small, flat, three-pointed support for ceramic ware in a kiln. **2** a long-billed wading bird with predominantly black and white plumage and long slender reddish legs. • Family Recurvirostridae: two genera, in particular *Himantopus*, and several species. ▷Middle English: of Germanic origin; related to Dutch *stelt* and German *Stelze*. Sense 2 dates from the late 18th cent.
▶*PHRASE* □ **on stilts 1** supported by stilts. **2** (of language) bombastic or stilted: *he is talking nonsense on stilts, and he knows it.*

stilt bug ▶*n.* a plant bug with very long slender legs. • Family Berytidae, suborder Heteroptera: many genera.

stilt·ed /ˈstiltid/ ▶*adj.* **1** (of a manner of talking or writing) stiff and self-conscious or unnatural: *we made stilted conversation.* **2** standing on stilts: *villages of stilted houses.* ■ *Architecture* (of an arch) with pieces of upright masonry between the imposts and the springers. **—stilt·ed·ly** *adv.* **—stilt·ed·ness** *n.*

Stil·ton /ˈstiltn/ ▶*n. trademark* a kind of strong rich cheese, often with blue veins, originally made at various places in Leicestershire, England. ▷so named because it was formerly sold to travelers at a coaching inn in Stilton, England.

Stil·well /ˈstil,wel/, Joseph Warren (1883–1946), U.S. army officer; known as **Uncle Joe** or **Vinegar Joe**. He commanded U.S. troops in the China-Burma-India theater 1942–44, U.S. army ground forces under Douglas MacArthur in 1945, and the U.S. 10th Army in the Pacific 1945–46.

Stim·son /ˈstimsən/, Henry Lewis (1867–1950), U.S. lawyer and statesman. He served five presidents—as secretary of war under President Taft 1911–13, as governor-general of the Philippines under President Coolidge 1927–29, as secretary of state under President Hoover 1929–33, as secretary of war under President Franklin D. Roosevelt 1940–45, and as chief adviser on atomic policy under Presidents Roosevelt and Truman.

stim·u·lant /ˈstimyələnt/ ▶*n.* a substance that raises levels of physiological or nervous activity in the body. ■ something that increases activity, interest, or enthusiasm in a specified field: *population growth is a major stimulant to industrial development.*
▶*adj.* raising levels of physiological or nervous activity in the body: *caffeine has stimulant effects on the heart.* ▷early 18th cent.: from Latin *stimulant-* 'urging, goading,' from the verb *stimulare.*

stim·u·late /ˈstimyə,lāt/ ▶*v.* [*trans.*] raise levels of physiological or nervous activity in (the body or any biological system): *the women are given fertility drugs to stimulate their ovaries.* See note at QUICKEN. ■ encourage interest or activity in (a person or animal): *the reader could not fail to be stimulated by the ideas presented* | [as *adj.*] (**stimulating**) *a rich and stimulating working environment.* See note at ENCOURAGE. ■ encourage development of or increased activity in (a state or process): *the courses stimulate a passion for learning* | *tax changes designed to stimulate economic growth.* ▷mid 16th cent. (in the sense 'sting, afflict'): from Latin *stimulat-* 'urged, goaded,' from the verb *stimulare.* **—stim·u·la·ble** /-ləbəl/ *adj.* **—stim·u·lat·ing·ly** *adv.* **—stim·u·la·tion** /,stimyəˈlāSHən/ *n.* **—stim·u·la·tive** /-,lātiv; -lətiv/ *adj.* **—stim·u·la·tor** /-,lātər/ *n.* **—stim·u·la·to·ry** /-lə,tôrē/ *adj.*

stim·u·lus /ˈstimyələs/ ▶*n.* (*pl.* **-li** /-,lī/) a thing or event that evokes a specific functional reaction in an organ or tissue: *areas of the brain which respond to auditory stimuli.* ■ a thing that rouses activity or energy in someone or something; a spur or incentive: *if the tax were abolished, it would act as a stimulus to exports.* ■ an interesting and exciting quality: *she loved the stimulus of the job.* ▷late 17th cent.: from Latin, 'goad, spur, incentive.'

sting /stiNG/ ▶*n.* **1** a small sharp-pointed organ at the end of the abdomen of bees, wasps, ants, and scorpions, capable of inflicting a painful or dangerous wound by injecting poison. ■ any of a number of minute hairs or other organs of plants, jellyfishes, etc., that inject a poisonous or irritating fluid when touched. ■ a wound from such an animal or plant organ: *a wasp or bee sting.* ■ a sharp tingling or burning pain or sensation: *I felt **the sting of** the cold, bitter air.* ■ [in *sing.*] *figurative* a hurtful quality or effect: *she smiled to take the sting out of her words.* **2** *informal* a carefully planned operation, typically one involving deception: *five blackmailers were jailed last week after they were snared in a police sting.*
▶*v.* (*past* and *past part.* **stung** /stəNG/) **1** [*trans.*] wound or pierce with a sting: *he was stung by a jellyfish* | [*intrans.*] *a nettle stings if you brush it lightly.* **2** feel or cause to feel a sharp tingling or burning pain or sensation: [*intrans.*] *her eyes stung* | [*trans.*] *the brandy stung his throat* | [as *adj.*] (**stinging**) *a stinging pain.* ■ [*trans.*] *figurative* (typically of something said) hurt or upset (someone): *stung by her mockery, Frank hung his head.* ■ (**sting someone into**) provoke someone to do (something) by causing annoyance or offense: *he was stung into action by an article in the paper.* **3** [*trans.*] *informal* swindle or exorbitantly overcharge (someone): *an elaborate fraud that **stung** a bank **for** thousands.* ▷Old English *sting* (noun), *stingan* (verb), of Germanic origin. **—sting·ing·ly** *adv.* **—sting·less** *adj.*
▶*PHRASE* □ **sting in the tail** an unexpected, typically unpleasant or problematic end to something: *the Budget comes with a sting in the tail—future tax increases.*

sting·a·ree /,stiNGəˈrē/ ▶*n.* a cinnamon-brown stingray occurring on sand flats in shallow Australian waters. • *Urolophus testaceus*, family Urolophidae. ■ *informal* any stingray. ▷mid 19th cent.: alteration of STINGRAY.

stinge /stinj/ ▶*n. informal* a mean or ungenerous person. ▷early 20th cent.: back-formation from STINGY.

sting·er /ˈstiNGər/ ▶*n.* **1** an insect or animal that stings, such as a bee or jellyfish. ■ the part of an insect or animal that holds a sting. ■ *informal* a painful blow: *he suffered a stinger on his right shoulder.* **2** a cocktail including crème de menthe and brandy. **3** (**Stinger**) a heat-seeking ground-to-air missile that is launched from the shoulder.

sting·ing net·tle ▶*n.* a Eurasian nettle covered in minute hairs that inject irritants when they are touched. These include histamine, which causes itching, and acetylcholine, which causes a burning sensation. • Genus *Urtica*, family Urticaceae: several species, in particular *U. dioica*, well established in North America.

sting·ray /ˈstiNG,rā/ ▶*n.* a bottom-dwelling marine ray with a flattened diamond-shaped body and a long poisonous serrated spine at the base of the tail. • Families Dasyatidae (the **long-tailed stingrays**) and Urolophidae (the **short-tailed stingrays**): several species, including the long-tailed **common stingray** (*Dasyatis centrourus*).

stin·gy /ˈstinjē/ ▶*adj.* (**-gi·er**, **-gi·est**) unwilling to give or spend; ungenerous: *his employer is stingy and idle* | *he was **stingy with** his information.* ■ insufficient in quantity; scanty: *the crabmeat is stingy and the black bean soup is not quite hot enough.* ▷mid 17th cent.: perhaps a dialect variant of the noun STING + -Y[1]. **—stin·gi·ly** /-lē/ *adv.* **—stin·gi·ness** *n.*

stink /stiNGk/ ▶*v.* (*past* **stank** /staNGk/ or **stunk** /stəNGk/; *past part.* **stunk**) [*intrans.*] **1** have a strong unpleasant smell: *the place stank like a sewer* | *his breath **stank of** drink.* See note at SMELL. ■ [*trans.*] (**stink a place up**) fill a place with such a smell: *I hope they are not going to stink up the house with curry.* **2** *informal* be very unpleasant, contemptible, or scandalous: *the industry's reputation stinks.* ■ (**stink of**) be highly suggestive of (something regarded with disapproval): *the whole affair stinks of a setup.* ■ (**stink of**) have or appear to have a scandalously large amount of (something, esp. money): *the whole place was luxurious and stank of money.*
▶*n.* [in *sing.*] **1** a strong unpleasant smell; a stench: *the stink of the place hit me as I went in.* **2** *informal* a commotion or fuss: *we go to the Four Seasons where Brad makes a big stink about getting a fountainside table.* ▷Old English *stincan*; related to Dutch and German *stinken*, also to STENCH.
▶*PHRASE* □ **like stink** *informal, chiefly Brit.* extremely hard or intensely: *she's working like stink to get everything ready.*

stink·ard /ˈstiNGkərd/ ▶*n.* **1** *archaic* a smelly or despicable person. **2** a member of a lower social order in some American Indian communities.

stink bomb ▶*n.* a small bomb that emits a strong and unpleasant smell when exploded.

stink bug ▶*n.* a broad shield-shaped bug that is typically brightly colored or boldly marked. It emits a foul smell when handled or molested. • Pentatomidae and other families, suborder Heteroptera.

stink·er /ˈstiNGkər/ ▶*n. informal* a person or thing that smells very bad. ■ a very bad or unpleasant person or thing: *have those little stinkers been bullying you?* ■ a difficult task: *Tackled the crossword yet? It's a stinker.*

stink·horn /ˈstiNGk,hôrn/ ▶*n.* a widely distributed fungus that has a tall whitish stem with a rounded greenish-brown gelatinous head that turns into a foul-smelling slime containing the spores. • Family Phallaceae, class Gasteromycetes: many species, including the common European *Phallus impudicus.*

stink·ing /ˈstiNGkiNG/ ▶*adj.* foul-smelling: *he was locked in a stinking cell.* ■ *informal* very bad or unpleasant: *a stinking cold.*
▶*adv.* [as *submodifier*] *informal* extremely: *she is obviously stinking rich* | *I want to get stinking drunk and forget.* **—stink·ing·ly** *adv.*

stink·ing ce·dar ▶*n.* a tree of the yew family found only in Florida, with fetid leaves, branches, and timber. Also called FLORIDA TORREYA. • *Torreya taxifolia*, family Taxaceae.

stink·ing smut ▶*n.* another term for BUNT[2].

stink·o /ˈstiNGkō/ ▶*adj. informal* **1** extremely drunk: *they took three-hour lunches and came back stinko.* **2** worthless or contemptible: *the plot and cast of characters are just plain stinko.*

stink·pot /ˈstiNGk,pät/ ▶*n.* **1** *informal* an unpleasant person (used as a term of abuse). ■ a vehicle that emits foul-smelling exhaust fumes, esp. a motorboat as opposed to a sailboat. **2** another term for MUSK TURTLE.

stink·weed /ˈstiNGk,wēd/ ▶*n.* any of a number of plants with a strong or fetid smell, e.g., jimson weed.

stink·wood /ˈstiNGk,wo͝od/ ▶*n.* any of a number of trees that yield timber with an unpleasant odor, in particular: • (**black stinkwood**) a South African tree (*Ocotea bullata*, family Lauraceae). • a New Zealand tree (*Coprosoma foetidissima*, family Rubiaceae).

stink·y /ˈstiNGkē/ ▶*adj.* (**stink·i·er**, **stink·i·est**) *informal* having a strong or unpleasant smell: *stinky cigarette smoke.* ■ very disagreeable and unpleasant: *a stinky job.*

stint[1] /stint/ ▶*v.* [*trans.*] [often with *negative*] supply an

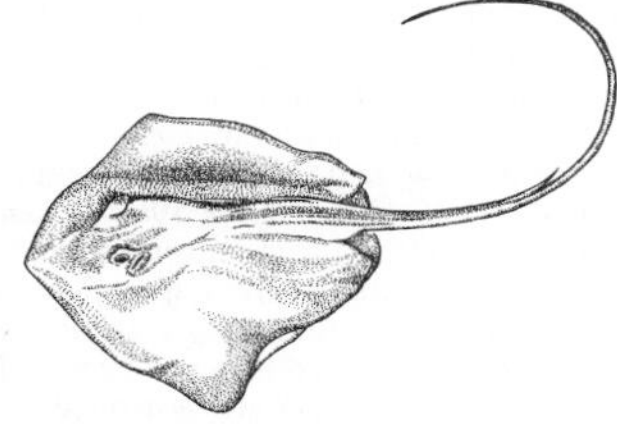

common stingray

Pronunciation Key ə *ago*; ər *over*; ˈə or ,ə *up*; ˈər or ,ər *fur*; a *hat*; ā *rate*; ä *car*; CH *chew*; e *let*; ē *see*; e(ə)r *air*; i *fit*; ī *by*; i(ə)r *ear*; NG *sing*; ō *go*; ô *for*; oi *boy*; o͝o *good*; o͞o *goo*; ou *out*; SH *she*; TH *thin*; T͟H *then*; (h)w *why*; ZH *vision*

ungenerous or inadequate amount of (something): *stowage room hasn't been stinted.* ■ [*intrans.*] be economical or frugal about spending or providing something: *he doesn't* **stint on** *wining and dining.* ■ restrict (someone) in the amount of something (esp. money) given or permitted: *to avoid having to stint yourself, budget in advance.*
▸*n.* **1** a person's fixed or allotted period of work: *his varied career included a stint as a magician.* **2** limitation of supply or effort: *a collector with an eye for quality and the means to indulge it* **without stint**. ▷Old English *styntan* 'make blunt,' of Germanic origin; related to STUNT[1].

stint[2] ▸*n.* a small short-legged sandpiper of northern Eurasia and Alaska, with a brownish back and white underparts. • Genus *Calidris*, family Scolopacidae: four species. ▷Middle English: of unknown origin.

stip. ▸*abbr.* ■ stipend. ■ stipulation.

stipe /stīp/ ▸*n. Botany* a stalk or stem, esp. the stem of a seaweed or fungus or the stalk of a fern frond. ▷late 18th cent.: from French, from Latin *stipes* (see STIPES).

sti·pend /ˈstīˌpend; -pənd/ ▸*n.* a fixed regular sum paid as a salary or allowance. ▷late Middle English: from Old French *stipendie* or Latin *stipendium*, from *stips* 'wages' + *pendere* 'to pay.'

sti·pen·di·ar·y /stīˈpendēˌerē/ ▸*adj.* receiving a stipend; working for payment rather than on a voluntary, unpaid basis: *stipendiary clergy.* ■ of, relating to, or of the nature of a stipend: *stipendiary obligations.*
▸*n.* (*pl.* **-ar·ies**) a person receiving a stipend. ▷late Middle English (as a noun): from Latin *stipendiarius*, from *stipendium* (see STIPEND).

sti·pes /ˈstīˌpēz/ ▸*n.* (*pl.* **sti·pi·tes** /ˈstipəˌtēz/) *Zoology* a part or organ resembling a stalk, esp. the second joint of the maxilla of an insect. ■ *Botany* more technical term for STIPE. ▷mid 18th cent.: from Latin, literally 'log, tree trunk.'

stip·i·tate /ˈstipiˌtāt/ ▸*adj. chiefly Botany* (esp. of a fungus) having a stipe or a stipes.

stip·ple /ˈstipəl/ ▸*v.* [*trans.*] (in drawing, painting, and engraving) mark (a surface) with numerous small dots or specks: [as *n.*] (**stippling**) *the miniaturist's use of stippling.* ■ produce a decorative effect on (paint or other material) by roughening its surface when it is wet.
▸*n.* the process or technique of stippling a surface, or the effect so created. ▷mid 17th cent.: from Dutch *stippelen*, frequentative of *stippen* 'to prick,' from *stip* 'a point.' —**stip·pler** /ˈstip(ə)lər/ *n.*

stip·u·late[1] /ˈstēpyəˌlāt/ ▸*v.* [*trans.*] demand or specify (a requirement), typically as part of a bargain or agreement: *he stipulated certain conditions before their marriage* | [as *adj.*] (**stipulated**) *the stipulated time has elapsed.* ▷early 17th cent.: from Latin *stipulat-* 'demanded as a formal promise,' from the verb *stipulari*. —**stip·u·la·tion** /ˌstipyəˈlāsHən/ *n.* —**stip·u·la·tor** /-ˌlātər/ *n.*

stip·u·late[2] ▸*adj. Botany* (of a leaf or plant) having stipules. ▷late 18th cent.: from Latin *stipula* (see STIPULE) + -ATE[2].

stip·ule /ˈstipyo͞ol/ ▸*n. Botany* a small leaflike appendage to a leaf, typically borne in pairs at the base of the leaf stalk. ▷late 18th cent.: from French *stipule* or Latin *stipula* 'straw.' —**stip·u·lar** /-yələr/ *adj.*

stir[1] /stər/ ▸*v.* (**stirred**, **stir·ring**) **1** [*trans.*] move a spoon or other implement around in (a liquid or other substance) in order to mix it thoroughly: *stir the batter until it is just combined.* ■ (**stir something in/into**) add an ingredient to (a liquid or other substance) in such a way: *stir in the flour and cook gently for two minutes.* **2** [*intrans.*] move or begin to move slightly: *nothing stirred except the wind.* ■ [*trans.*] cause to move or be disturbed slightly: *a gentle breeze stirred the leaves* | *cloudiness is caused by the fish* **stirring up** *mud.* ■ (of a person or animal) rise or wake from sleep: *no one else had stirred yet.* ■ (**stir from**) (of a person) leave or go out of (a place): *as he grew older, he seldom stirred from his apartment.* ■ begin or cause to begin to be active or to develop: [*intrans.*] *the 1960s, when the civil rights movement stirred* | [*trans.*] *a voice* **stirred** *her* **from** *her reverie* | *he even* **stirred himself** *to play an encore.* **3** [*trans.*] arouse strong feelings in (someone); move or excite: *they will be* **stirred to** *action by what is written* | *he* **stirred up** *the sweating crowd.* ■ arouse or prompt (a feeling or memory) or inspire (the imagination): *the story stirred many memories of my childhood* | *the rumors had* **stirred up** *his anger.*
▸*phrasal v.* □ **stir something up** cause or provoke trouble or bad feeling: *he accused me of trying to stir up trouble.*
▸*n.* [in *sing.*] **1** a slight physical movement: *I stood, straining eyes and ears for the faintest stir.* ■ a commotion: *the event caused quite a stir.* ■ an initial sign of a specified feeling: *Caroline felt a stir of anger deep within her breast.* **2** an act of mixing food or drink with a spoon or other implement: *he gives his chocolate milk a stir.* ▷Old English *styrian*, of Germanic origin; related to German *stören* 'disturb.'
▸*PHRASES* □ **stir someone's blood** make someone excited or enthusiastic. □ **stir one's stumps** [often in *imperative*] *Brit., informal, dated* (of a person) begin to move or act.

stir[2] ▸*n. informal* prison: *I've spent twenty-eight years* **in stir.** ▷mid 19th cent.: perhaps from Romany *sturbin* 'jail.'

stir·a·bout /ˈstərəˌbout/ ▸*n. chiefly Irish* porridge made by stirring oatmeal in boiling water or milk.

stir-cra·zy ▸*adj. informal* psychologically disturbed, esp. as a result of being confined or imprisoned.

stir-fry ▸*v.* [*trans.*] fry (meat, fish, or vegetables) rapidly over a high heat while stirring briskly: [as *adj.*] (**stir-fried**) *stir-fried beef.*
▸*n.* a dish cooked by such a method.

stirk /stərk/ ▸*n. Brit.* a yearling bullock or heifer. ▷Old English *stirc*, perhaps from *stēor* 'steer' + *-oc* (see -OCK).

Stir·ling en·gine /ˈstərliNG/ ▸*n.* a machine used to provide power or refrigeration, operating on a closed cycle in which a working fluid is cyclically compressed and expanded at different temperatures.

stir·rer /ˈstərər/ ▸*n.* an object or mechanical device used for stirring something. ■ *Brit., informal* a person who deliberately causes trouble between others by spreading rumors or gossip.

stir·ring /ˈstəriNG/ ▸*adj.* **1** causing great excitement or strong emotion; rousing: *stirring songs.* **2** *archaic* moving briskly; active.
▸*n.* an initial sign of activity, movement, or emotion: *the first stirrings of anger.* —**stir·ring·ly** *adv.*

stir·rup /ˈstərəp; ˈstə-rəp; ˈstir-/ ▸*n.* **1** each of a pair of devices attached to each side of a horse's saddle, in the form of a loop with a flat base to support the rider's foot. **2** (**stir·rups**) a pair of metal supports in which a woman's heels may be placed during gynecological examinations and childbirth, to hold her legs in a position that will facilitate medical examination or intervention. **3** (also **stir·rup bone**) another term for STAPES. **4** (**stirrups**) short for STIRRUP PANTS. ▷Old English *stigrāp*, from the Germanic base of obsolete *sty* 'climb' + ROPE.

stirrup 1

stir·rup cup ▸*n.* a cup of wine or other alcoholic drink offered to a person on horseback who is about to depart on a journey.

stir·rup i·ron ▸*n.* the metal loop of a stirrup, in which the rider's foot rests.

stir·rup leath·er ▸*n.* the strap attaching a stirrup iron to a saddle.

stir·rup pants ▸*plural n.* a pair of women's or girls' stretch pants with a band of elastic at the bottom of each leg that passes under the arch of the foot.

stir·rup pump ▸*n. chiefly historical* a portable hand-operated water pump with a footrest resembling a stirrup, used to extinguish small fires.

stish·ov·ite /ˈstisHəˌvīt/ ▸*n.* a mineral that is a dense polymorph of silica and is formed at very high pressures, esp. in meteorite craters. ▷1960s: from the name of Sergei M. *Stishov*, 20th-cent. Russian chemist, + -ITE[1].

stitch /sticH/ ▸*n.* **1** a loop of thread or yarn resulting from a single pass or movement of the needle in sewing, knitting, or crocheting. ■ a loop of thread used to join the edges of a wound or surgical incision: *a neck wound requiring forty stitches.* ■ [usu. with *adj.*] a method of sewing, knitting, or crocheting producing a particular pattern or design: *basic embroidery stitches.* ■ [in *sing.*, usu. with *negative*] *informal* the smallest item of clothing: *a man answered the door without a stitch on.* **2** a sudden sharp pain in the side of the body, caused by strenuous exercise: *she ran with a stitch in her side.*
▸*v.* [*trans.*] make, mend, or join (something) with stitches: *stitch a plain seam with right sides together* | *they stitched the cut on her face* | [as *adj.*], [in *combination*] (**stitched**) *hand-stitched English dresses.* ▷Old English *stice* 'a puncture, stabbing pain,' of Germanic origin; related to German *Stich* 'a sting, prick,' also to STICK[2]. The sense 'loop' (in sewing, etc.) arose in Middle English. —**stitch·er** *n.* —**stitch·er·y** *n.*
▸*PHRASES* □ **in stitches** *informal* laughing uncontrollably: *his unique brand of droll self-mockery* **had** *his audiences* **in stitches**. □ **a stitch in time saves nine** *proverb* if you sort out a problem immediately it may save a lot of extra work later.

stitch·bird /ˈsticHˌbərd/ ▸*n.* a rare New Zealand honeyeater with mainly dark brown or blackish plumage and a sharp call that resembles the word "stitch." • *Notiomystis cincta*, family Meliphagidae.

stitch·ing /ˈsticHiNG/ ▸*n.* a row of stitches sewn onto cloth: *the gloves were white with black stitching.* ■ the action or work of stitching or sewing: *one of the mares cut her leg and it required stitching.*

stitch-up ▸*n. Brit., informal* an act of placing someone in a position in which they will be wrongly blamed for something, or of manipulating a situation to one's advantage.

stitch·wort /ˈsticHwərt; -ˌwôrt/ ▸*n.* a straggling plant of the pink family with a slender stem and white starry flowers. It was formerly thought to cure a stitch in the side. • Genus *Stellaria*, family Caryophyllaceae: several species, in particular **greater stitchwort** (*S. holostea*) and **lesser stitchwort** (*S. graminea*).

sti·ver /ˈstīvər/ ▸*n.* a small coin formerly used in the Netherlands, equal to one twentieth of a guilder. ■ *archaic* any coin of low value. ■ [with *negative*] *archaic* a very small or insignificant amount: *they didn't care a stiver.* ▷from Dutch *stuiver*, denoting a small coin; probably related to the noun STUB.

St. John 1 an island in the Caribbean Sea, one of the three principal islands of the U.S. Virgin Islands. **2** (usu. **Saint John**) a city in New Brunswick, in eastern Canada, a port on the Bay of Fundy, at the mouth of the St. John River; pop. 74,969.

St. John's 1 the capital of Antigua and Barbuda, situated on the northwestern coast of Antigua; pop. 36,000. **2** the capital of Newfoundland, a port on the southeastern coast of the island; pop. 95,770.

St. John's wort (also **St. Johns wort**) ▸*n.* a herbaceous plant or shrub with distinctive yellow five-petaled flowers and paired oval leaves, used in medicinal preparations to treat various disorders, including depression. • Genus *Hypericum*, family Guttiferae: many species, in particular *H. perforatum*. ▷so named because some species come into flower near the feast day of St. John the Baptist (June 24).

stk. ▸*abbr.* stock.

St. Kil·da /ˈkildə/ a small group of uninhabited islands in the Outer Hebrides.

St. Kitts and Ne·vis /ˈkits and ˈnēvis; ˈnevis/ a country that consists of two adjoining islands in the Leeward Islands in the Caribbean Sea; pop. 44,000; capital, Basseterre (on St. Kitts); languages, English (official) and Creole. Official name ST. CHRISTOPHER AND NEVIS, FEDERATION OF. ▷*St. Kitts*, alteration (by settlers) of *St. Christopher*, a name given to the island by Columbus; *Nevis* from Spanish *las nieves* 'the snows' (because of the "snowy" clouds surrounding the peak).

St. Kitts was visited in 1493 by Christopher Columbus. The islands were colonized by English settlers from 1623 and became the first successful English colony in the West Indies. A self-governing union between St. Kitts and Nevis (and briefly Anguilla) was created in 1967 and became a fully independent member of the Commonwealth of Nations in 1983.

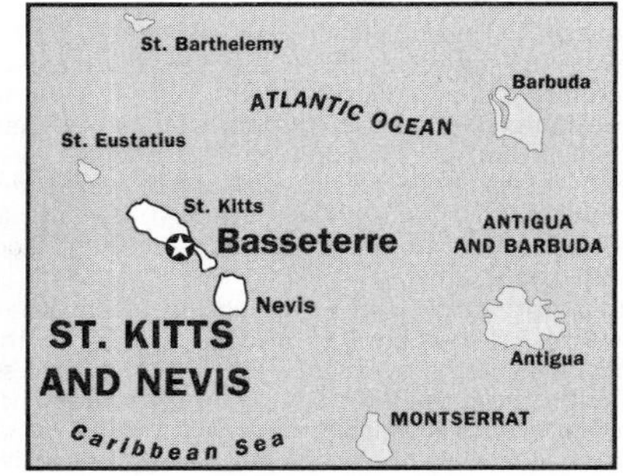

St. Law·rence Riv·er a river in North America that flows for about 750 miles (1,200 km) from Lake Ontario along the border between Canada and the U.S. to the Gulf of St. Lawrence on the Atlantic coast.

St. Law·rence Sea·way a waterway in North America that flows for 2,342 miles (3,768 km) through the Great Lakes and along the course of the St. Lawrence River to the Atlantic Ocean. Consisting of channels connecting the lakes and a number of artificial sections that bypass the rapids in the river, it is open along its entire length to oceangoing vessels. It was inaugurated in 1959.

St. Lou·is /'lo͞o-is; 'lo͞o-ē/ a city and port in eastern Missouri, on the Mississippi River just south of its confluence with the Missouri River; pop. 348,189. Founded as a French fur-trading post in the 1760s, it passed to the Spanish, the French again, and finally in 1803 to the U.S. as part of the Louisiana Purchase.

St. Lou·is en·ceph·a·li·tis /'lo͞ois/ ▸*n.* a form of viral encephalitis that can be fatal and is transmitted by mosquitoes.

St. Lu·cia /'lo͞oSHə; lo͞o'sēə/ a country in the Caribbean Sea, one of the Windward Islands; pop. 164,200; capital, Castries; languages, English (official) and French Creole. **—St. Lu·cian** *adj.* & *n.*

First encountered by Europeans around 1500, St. Lucia was settled by both French and British in the 17th century. Possession of the island was long disputed until France ceded it to Britain in 1814. Since 1979, it has been an independent state within the Commonwealth of Nations.

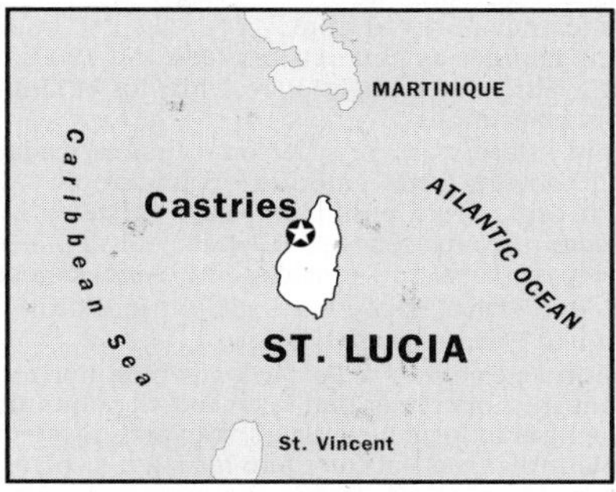

STM ▸*abbr.* scanning tunneling microscope.

St. Mark's Ca·the·dral the cathedral church of Venice since 1807. It was built in the 9th century to house relics of St. Mark, and rebuilt in the 11th century.

St. Mar·tin /sānt 'märtn; saN mär'taN/ a small island in the Caribbean, one of the Leeward Islands; pop. 32,000. The southern section of the island forms part of the Netherlands Antilles; the larger northern part of the island is part of the French overseas department of Guadeloupe. Dutch name **SINT MAARTEN.**

St. Mo·ritz /sānt mə'rits; saN mô'rēts/ a resort and winter-sports center in southeastern Switzerland.

sto·a /'stōə/ ▸*n.* a classical portico or roofed colonnade. ■ **(the Stoa)** the great hall in Athens in which the ancient Greek philosopher Zeno gave the founding lectures of the Stoic school of philosophy. ▷Greek.

stoat /stōt/ ▸*n.* a small carnivorous mammal of the weasel family that has chestnut fur with white underparts and a black-tipped tail. It is native to both Eurasia and North America and in northern areas the coat turns white in winter. Also called **SHORT-TAILED WEASEL.** Compare with **ERMINE, WEASEL.** • *Mustela erminea*, family Mustelidae. ▷late Middle English: of unknown origin.

stob /stäb/ ▸*n.* *dialect* a broken branch or a stump. ■ a stake used for fencing. ▷Middle English: variant of **STUB.**

sto·chas·tic /stə'kastik/ ▸*adj.* randomly determined; having a random probability distribution or pattern that may be analyzed statistically but may not be predicted precisely. ▷mid 17th cent.: from Greek *stokhastikos*, from *stokhazesthai* 'aim at, guess,' from *stokhos* 'aim.' **—sto·chas·ti·cal·ly** /-ik(ə)lē/ *adv.*

stock /stäk/ ▸*n.* **1** the goods or merchandise kept on the premises of a business or warehouse and available for sale or distribution: *the store has a very low turnover of stock | buy now, while stocks last!* | [as *adj.*] *stock shortages.* ■ a supply or quantity of something accumulated or available for future use: *I need to replenish my* **stock of** *wine | fish stocks are being dangerously depleted.* ■ farm animals such as cattle, pigs, and sheep, bred and kept for their meat or milk; livestock. ■ short for **ROLLING STOCK.** ■ (also **film stock**) photographic film that has not been exposed or processed. ■ the undealt cards of the deck, left on the table to be drawn from in some card games. **2** the capital raised by a business or corporation through the issue and subscription of shares: *between 1982 and 1986, the value of the company's stock rose by 86%.* ■ (also **stocks**) a portion of this as held by an individual or group as an investment: *she owned $3000 worth of stock.* ■ (also **stocks**) the shares of a particular company, type of company, or industry: *blue-chip stocks.* ■ securities issued by the government in fixed units with a fixed rate of interest: *government gilt-edged stock.* ■ *figurative* a person's reputation or popularity: *I felt I was right, but my stock was low with this establishment.* **3** liquid made by cooking bones, meat, fish, or vegetables slowly in water, used as a basis for the preparation of soup, gravy, or sauces: *a pint of chicken stock.* ■ [with *adj.*] the raw material from which a specified commodity can be manufactured: *the fat can be used as soap stock.* **4** [usu. with *adj.*] a person's ancestry or line of descent: *her mother was of French stock | both of them came from peasant stock.* ■ a breed, variety, or population of an animal or plant. **5** the trunk or woody stem of a living tree or shrub, esp. one into which a graft (scion) is inserted. ■ the perennial part of a herbaceous plant, esp. a rhizome. **6** a herbaceous European plant that is widely cultivated for its fragrant flowers, which are typically lilac, pink, or white. [mid 17th cent.: from *stock-gillyflower*.] • Genus *Matthiola*, family Brassicaceae: several species. **7 (the stocks)** [treated as *sing.* or *pl.*] *historical* an instrument of punishment consisting of an adjustable wooden structure with holes for securing a person's feet and hands, in which criminals were locked and exposed to public ridicule or assault. **8** the part of a rifle or other firearm to which the barrel and firing mechanism are attached, held against one's shoulder when firing the gun. ■ the crosspiece of an anchor. ■ the handle of something such as a whip or fishing rod. ■ short for **HEADSTOCK** (sense 1). ■ short for **TAILSTOCK. 9** a band of white material tied like a cravat and worn as a part of formal horse-riding dress. ■ a piece of black material worn under a clerical collar. **10 (stocks)** a frame used to support a ship or boat out of water, esp. when under construction.

▸*adj.* [*attrib.*] **1** (of a product or type of product) usually kept in stock and thus regularly available for sale: *25 percent off stock items.* **2** (of a phrase or expression) so regularly used as to be automatic or hackneyed: *their stock response to the refugee crisis was "We can't take everyone."* ■ denoting a conventional character type or situation that recurs in a particular genre of literature, theater, or film: *the stock characters in every cowboy movie.* ■ denoting or relating to cinematic footage that can be regularly used in different productions, typically that of outdoor scenes used to add realism to a production shot in an indoor set.

▸*v.* [*trans.*] **1** have or keep a supply of (a particular product or type or product) available for sale: *most supermarkets now stock a range of organic produce.* ■ provide or fill with goods, items, or a supply of something: *I must* **stock up** *the fridge* | [as *adj.*, with *submodifier* or in *combination*] **(stocked)** *a well-stocked store.* ■ [*intrans.*] **(stock up)** amass supplies of something, typically for a particular occasion or purpose: *I'm stocking up for Christmas | you'd better* **stock up with** *fuel.* **2** fit (a rifle or other firearm) with a stock. ▷Old English *stoc(c)* 'trunk, block of wood, post,' of Germanic origin; related to Dutch *stok* and German *Stock* 'stick.' The notion 'store, fund' (senses 1 and 2) arose in late Middle English and is of obscure origin, perhaps expressing 'growth from a central stem' or 'firm foundation.' **—stock·less** *adj.*

▸*PHRASES* □ **in** (or **out of**) **stock** (of goods) available (or unavailable) for immediate sale in a store. □ **on the stocks** in construction or preparation: *also on the stocks is a bill to bring about tax relief for these businesses.* □ **put stock in** [often with *negative*] have a specified amount of belief or faith in: *I don't put much stock in modern medicine.* □ **take stock** review or make an overall assessment of a particular situation, typically as a prelude to making a decision: *he needed a period of peace and quiet in order to* **take stock of** *his life.*

stock·ade /stä'kād/ ▸*n.* a barrier formed from upright wooden posts or stakes, esp. as a defense against attack or as a means of confining animals. ■ an enclosure bound by such a barrier: *we got ashore and into the stockade.* ■ a military prison.

▸*v.* [*trans.*] [usu. as *adj.*] **(stockaded)** enclose (an area) by erecting such a barrier. ▷early 17th cent.: shortening of obsolete French *estocade*, alteration of *estacade*, from Spanish *estacada*, from the Germanic base of the noun **STAKE**[1].

stock·breed·er /'stäk,brēdər/ ▸*n.* a farmer who breeds livestock. **—stock·breed·ing** /-,brēdiNG/ *n.*

stock brick ▸*n.* a hard solid brick pressed in a mold.

Stock·bridge /'stäk,brij/ a resort town in western Massachusetts, in the Berkshire Hills; pop. 2,408. Tanglewood estate, site of a noted summer music festival, is here.

stock·brok·er /'stäk,brōkər/ ▸*n.* a broker who buys and sells securities on a stock exchange on behalf of clients. **—stock·brok·er·age** /-,brōk(ə)rij/ *n.* **—stock·brok·ing** /-,brōkiNG/ *n.*

stock·brok·er belt ▸*n.* *Brit.* an affluent residential area outside a large city.

stock car ▸*n.* **1** an ordinary car that has been modified for racing. **2** a railroad car for transporting livestock.

stock com·pa·ny ▸*n.* a repertory company that is largely based in one theater.

stock dove /dəv/ ▸*n.* a gray Eurasian and North African pigeon that resembles a small wood pigeon and nests in holes in trees. • *Columba oenas*, family Columbidae.

stock·er /'stäkər/ ▸*n.* **1** a farm animal, typically a young steer or heifer, destined for slaughter but kept until matured or fattened. **2** a person whose job is to fill the shelves of a store or supermarket with merchandise. **3** *informal* a stock car.

stock ex·change ▸*n.* a market in which securities are bought and sold: *the company was floated* **on the Stock Exchange.** ■ **(the Stock Exchange)** the level of prices in such a market: *a plunge in the Stock Exchange during the election campaign.*

stock·feed /'stäk,fēd/ ▸*n.* food for livestock: *meat and bonemeal stockfeed has been banned for all livestock.*

stock·fish /'stäk,fiSH/ ▸*n.* (*pl.* same or **-fish·es**) **1** cod or a similar fish split and dried in the open air without salt. **2** a commercially valuable hake of coastal waters of southern Africa. • *Merluccius capensis*, family Merlucciidae. ▷Middle English (sense 1): from Middle Low German, Middle Dutch *stokvisch*, of unknown origin; sense 2 (early 19th cent.) from South African Dutch.

stock·hold·er /'stäk,hōldər/ ▸*n.* a shareholder. **—stock·hold·ing** /-,hōldiNG/ *n.*

Stock·holm /'stäk,hō(l)m/ the capital of Sweden, a seaport on the eastern coast, on the mainland and on numerous adjacent islands; pop. 674,000.

Stock·holm syn·drome ▸*n.* feelings of trust or affection felt in certain cases of kidnapping or hostage-taking by a victim toward a captor. ▷1970s: with reference to a bank robbery in Stockholm, Sweden.

Stock·holm tar ▸*n.* a kind of tar prepared from resinous pinewood and used esp. in shipbuilding and as an ingredient of ointments.

stock horse ▸*n.* a horse that is trained to herd livestock.

stock in·dex fu·tures ▸*plural n.* contracts to buy a range of shares at an agreed price but delivered and paid for later.

stock·i·nette /,stäkə'net/ (also **stock·i·net**) ▸*n.* **1** a soft, loosely knitted stretch fabric, formerly used for making underwear and now used for cleaning, wrapping, or bandaging. **2** (also **stockinette stitch**) a knitting stitch consisting of alternate rows of knit (plain) and purl stitch. ▷late 18th cent.: probably an alteration of *stocking-net*.

stock·ing /'stäkiNG/ ▸*n.* a women's garment, typically made of translucent nylon or silk, that fits closely over the foot and is held up by garters or an elasticized strip at the upper thigh. ■ short for **CHRISTMAS STOCKING.** ■ a long sock worn by men. ■ [usu. with *adj.*] a cylindrical bandage or other medical covering for the leg resembling a stocking, esp. an elasticized support used in the treatment of disorders of the veins. ■ a white marking of the lower part of a horse's leg, extending as far as, or just beyond, the knee or hock. ▷late 16th cent.: from **STOCK** in the dialect sense 'stocking' + **-ING**[1]. **—stock·inged** /'stäkiNGd/ *adj.* [in *combination*] *her black-stockinged legs.* **—stock·ing·less** *adj.*

▸*PHRASE* □ **in (one's) stocking feet** without shoes: *she stood five feet ten in her stocking feet.*

Pronunciation Key ə *ago*; ər *over*; 'ə or ,ə *up*; 'ər or ,ər *fur*; a *hat*; ā *rate*; ä *car*; CH *chew*; e *let*; ē *see*; e(ə)r *air*; i *fit*; ī *by*; i(ə)r *ear*; NG *sing*; ō *go*; ô *for*; oi *boy*; o͝o *good*; o͞o *goo*; ou *out*; SH *she*; TH *thin*; TH *then*; (h)w *why*; ZH *vision*

stock·ing cap ▸*n.* a knitted conical hat with a long tapered end, often bearing a tassle, that hangs down.

stock·ing mask ▸*n.* a nylon stocking pulled over the face to disguise the features, used by criminals.

stock·ing stitch ▸*n.* another term for STOCKINETTE (sense 2).

stock·ing stuff·er (*Brit.* **stocking filler**) ▸*n.* a small present suitable for putting in a Christmas stocking.

stock-in-trade ▸*n.* the typical subject or commodity a person, company, or profession uses or deals in: *information is our stock-in-trade.* ■ qualities, ideas, or behavior characteristic of a person or their work: *flippancy is his stock-in-trade.* ■ the goods kept on hand by a business for the purposes of its trade.

stock·ist /ˈstäkist/ ▸*n. Brit.* a retailer that stocks goods of a particular type for sale: *one of the country's largest stockists of Italian designer labels.*

stock·job·ber /ˈstäkˌjäbər/ ▸*n. derogatory* a stockbroker. **—stock·job·bing** /-ˌjäbiNG/ *n.*

stock·man /ˈstäkmən; -ˌman/ ▸*n.* (*pl.* **-men**) **1** a person who looks after livestock. ■ an owner of livestock. **2** a person who looks after a stockroom or warehouse.

stock mar·ket ▸*n.* (usu. **the stock market**) a stock exchange.

stock op·tion ▸*n.* a benefit in the form of an option given by a company to an employee to buy stock in the company at a discount or at a stated fixed price.

stock·out /ˈstäkˌout/ ▸*n.* a situation in which an item is out of stock.

stock·pile /ˈstäkˌpīl/ ▸*n.* a large accumulated stock of goods or materials, esp. one held in reserve for use at a time of shortage or other emergency.
▸*v.* [*trans.*] accumulate a large stock of (goods or materials): *he claimed that the weapons were being stockpiled.* **—stock·pil·er** *n.*

Stock·port /ˈstäkˌpôrt/ an industrial town in northwestern England, near Manchester; pop. 130,000.

stock·pot /ˈstäkˌpät/ ▸*n.* a pot in which stock for soup is prepared by long, slow cooking.

stock·room /ˈstäkˌro͞om; -ˌro͝om/ ▸*n.* a room in which quantities of goods are stored.

stock split ▸*n.* an issue of new shares in a company to existing shareholders in proportion to their current holdings.

stock-still ▸*adv.* without any movement; completely still: *he stood stock-still.*

stock swap ▸*n.* **1** acquisition of a company in which payment consists of stock in the buying company. **2** a means of exercising stock options in which shares already owned are traded for a greater number of shares at the exercise price.

stock·tak·ing /ˈstäkˌtākiNG/ ▸*n.* the action or process of recording the amount of stock held by a business: *the store is closed for stocktaking.* ■ the action of reviewing and assessing one's situation and options: *she had some mental stocktaking to do.* **—stock·take** *n.* **—stock·tak·er** /-ˌtākər/ *n.*

Stock·ton /ˈstäktən/ an industrial city in north central California, a port on the San Joaquin River; pop. 243,771.

Stock·ton-on-Tees /ˈstäktən än ˈtēz; ôn/ an industrial town in northeastern England, a port on the Tees River near its mouth on the North Sea; pop. 170,000.

stock whip ▸*n.* a whip used for driving cattle.

stock·y /ˈstäkē/ ▸*adj.* (**stock·i·er**, **stock·i·est**) (of a person) broad and sturdily built. **—stock·i·ly** /ˈstäkəlē/ *adv.* **—stock·i·ness** *n.*

stock·yard /ˈstäkˌyärd/ ▸*n.* a large yard containing pens and sheds, typically adjacent to a slaughterhouse, in which livestock is kept and sorted.

stodge /stäj/ ▸*n. informal, chiefly Brit.* food that is heavy, filling, and high in carbohydrates: *she ate her way through a plateful of stodge.* ■ *figurative* dull and uninspired material or work. ▷late 17th cent. (as a verb in the sense 'stuff to stretching point'): symbolic, suggested by STUFF and PODGE.

stodg·y /ˈstäjē/ ▸*adj.* (**stodg·i·er**, **stodg·i·est**) **1** dull and uninspired: *some of the material is rather stodgy and top-heavy with facts.* **2** *Brit.* (of food) heavy, filling, and high in carbohydrates. ■ bulky or heavy in appearance: *this stodgy three-story building.* **—stodg·i·ly** /ˈstäjəlē/ *adv.* **—stodg·i·ness** *n.*

stoep /sto͞op/ ▸*n. S. African* a terraced porch in front of a house. ▷Afrikaans, from Dutch; related to STEP.

stog /stäg/ ▸*v.* (**be stogged**) *dialect* be stuck or bogged down: *people are stogged in their misery.* ▷early 19th cent.: perhaps symbolic and suggested by STICK[2] and BOG.

sto·gie /ˈstōgē/ (also **sto·gy**) ▸*n.* (*pl.* **-gies**) a long, thin, inexpensive cigar. ▷mid 19th cent. (originally as *stoga*): from *Conestoga*, because the cigars are thought to have been smoked by the drivers of Conestoga wagons.

sto·ic /ˈstō-ik/ ▸*n.* **1** a person who can endure pain or hardship without showing their feelings or complaining. **2** (**Stoic**) a member of the ancient philosophical school of Stoicism.
▸*adj.* **1** another term for STOICAL. **2** (**Stoic**) of or belonging to the Stoics or their school of philosophy. ▷late Middle English: via Latin from Greek *stōikos*, from STOA (with reference to Zeno's teaching in the *Stoa Poikilē* or Painted Porch, at Athens).

sto·i·cal /ˈstō-ikəl/ ▸*adj.* enduring pain and hardship without showing one's feelings or complaining: *he taught a stoical acceptance of suffering.* **—sto·i·cal·ly** /-ik(ə)lē/ *adv.*

stoi·chi·o·met·ric /ˌstoikē-ōˈmetrik/ ▸*adj. Chemistry* of or relating to stoichiometry. ■ relating to or denoting quantities of reactants in simple integral ratios, as prescribed by an equation or formula. **—stoi·chi·o·met·ri·cal·ly** /-ik(ə)lē/ *adv.*

stoi·chi·om·e·try /ˌstoikēˈämitrē/ ▸*n. Chemistry* the relationship between the relative quantities of substances taking part in a reaction or forming a compound, typically a ratio of whole integers. ▷early 19th cent.: from Greek *stoikheion* 'element' + -METRY.

sto·i·cism /ˈstō-iˌsizəm/ ▸*n.* **1** the endurance of pain or hardship without a display of feelings and without complaint. **2** (**Stoicism**) an ancient Greek school of philosophy founded at Athens by Zeno of Citium. The school taught that virtue, the highest good, is based on knowledge, and that the wise live in harmony with the divine Reason (also identified with Fate and Providence) that governs nature, and are indifferent to the vicissitudes of fortune and to pleasure and pain.

stoke /stōk/ ▸*v.* [*trans.*] add coal or other solid fuel to (a fire, furnace, or boiler). ■ encourage or incite (a strong emotion or tendency): *his composure had the effect of stoking her anger.* ■ [often as *adj.*] (**stoked**) *informal* excite or thrill: *when they told me I was on the team, I was stoked.* ■ [*intrans.*] *informal* consume a large quantity of food or drink to give one energy: *Carol was at the coffee machine,* ***stoking up*** *for the day.* ▷mid 17th cent.: back-formation from STOKER.

stoke·hold /ˈstōkˌhōld/ ▸*n.* a compartment in a steamship from which the boiler fires are stoked.

stoke·hole /ˈstōkˌhōl/ ▸*n.* a space in front of a furnace in which a stoker works.

Stoke-on-Trent /ˈstōk än ˈtrent; ôn/ a city on the River Trent; pop. 245,000.

Stok·er /ˈstōkər/, Bram (1847–1912), Irish novelist and theater manager; full name *Abraham Stoker*. He is chiefly remembered as the author of the vampire story, *Dracula* (1897).

stok·er /ˈstōkər/ ▸*n.* a person who tends the furnace on a steamship or steam locomotive. ■ a mechanical device for supplying fuel to a firebox or furnace, esp. on a steam locomotive. ▷mid 17th cent.: from Dutch, from *stoken* 'stoke (a furnace),' from Middle Dutch *stoken* 'push, poke'; related to STICK[1].

Stokes /stōks/, Carl (1927–96), U.S. politician. He was the first African-American mayor of a major U.S. city (Cleveland 1967–72). After serving as mayor, he was a newscaster and a municipal court judge before being appointed as U.S. ambassador to the Seychelles 1993–96.

stokes /stōks/ (abbr.: **ST**) ▸*n.* (*pl.* same) *Physics* the cgs unit of kinematic viscosity, corresponding to a dynamic viscosity of 1 poise and a density of 1 gram per cubic centimeter, equivalent to 10^{-4} square meters per second. ▷mid 20th cent.: from the name of Sir G. *Stokes* (see STOKES' LAW).

Stokes' law /stōks/ *Physics* **1** a law stating that in fluorescence the wavelength of the emitted radiation is longer than that of the radiation causing it. This is not true in all cases. **2** an expression describing the resisting force on a particle moving through a viscous fluid and showing that a maximum velocity is reached in such cases, e.g., for an object falling under gravity through a fluid. ▷late 19th cent.: named after Sir George *Stokes* (1819–1903), British physicist.

Stokes' the·o·rem *Mathematics* a theorem proposing that the surface integral of the curl of a function over any surface bounded by a closed path is equal to the line integral of a particular vector function around that path. ▷late 19th cent.: named after Sir G. *Stokes* (see STOKES' LAW).

Sto·kow·ski /stəˈkôfskē; -ˈkou-/, Leopold (1882–1977), U.S. conductor, born in Britain. He is best known for arranging and conducting the music for Walt Disney's movie *Fantasia* (1940), which sought to bring classical music to movie audiences by means of cartoons.

STOL /ˈestôl; stôl/ ▸*abbr. Aeronautics* short takeoff and landing.

stole[1] /stōl/ ▸*n.* a woman's long scarf or shawl, esp. fur or similar material, worn loosely over the shoulders. ■ of a strip of fabric used as an ecclesiastical vestment, worn over the shoulders and hanging down to the knee or below. ▷Old English (in the senses 'long robe' and 'priest's vestment'), via Latin from Greek *stolē* 'clothing,' from *stellein* 'array.'

ecclesiastical stole

stole[2] ▸ past of STEAL.

sto·len /ˈstōlən/ ▸ past participle of STEAL.

sto·len gen·er·a·tion ▸*n. Austral.* the Aboriginal people forcibly removed from their families as children between the 1900s and the 1960s, to be brought up by white foster families or in institutions.

stol·id /ˈstälid/ ▸*adj.* (of a person) calm, dependable, and showing little emotion or animation. ▷late 16th cent.: from obsolete French *stolide* or Latin *stolidus* (perhaps related to *stultus* 'foolish'). **—sto·lid·i·ty** /stəˈliditē/ *n.* **—stol·id·ly** *adv.* **—stol·id·ness** *n.*

stol·len /ˈstōlən; ˈsHtô-/ ▸*n.* a rich German fruit and nut loaf. ▷from German *Stollen.*

sto·lon /ˈstōlən/ ▸*n.* **1** *Botany* a creeping horizontal plant stem or runner that takes root at points along its length to form new plants. ■ an arching stem of a plant that roots at the tip to form a new plant, as in the bramble. **2** *Zoology* the branched stemlike structure of some colonial hydroid coelenterates, attaching the colony to the substrate. ▷early 17th cent.: from Latin *stolo, stolon-* 'shoot, scion.' **—sto·lon·ate** /-nit; -ˌnāt/ *adj.* **—sto·lo·nif·er·ous** /ˌstōləˈnif(ə)rəs/ *adj.*

sto·ma /ˈstōmə/ ▸*n.* (*pl.* **sto·mas** or **sto·ma·ta** /-mətə; ˌstōˈmätə/) *Botany* any of the minute pores in the epidermis of the leaf or stem of a plant, forming a slit of variable width that allows movement of gases in and out of the intercellular spaces. Also called STOMATE. ■ *Zoology* a small mouthlike opening in some lower animals. ■ *Medicine* an artificial opening made into a hollow organ, esp. one on the surface of the body leading to the gut or trachea. ▷late 17th cent.: modern Latin, from Greek *stoma* 'mouth.' **—sto·mal** *adj.* (*Medicine*).

stom·ach /ˈstəmək/ ▸*n.* **1** the internal organ in which the first part of digestion occurs, being (in humans and many mammals) a pear-shaped enlargement of the alimentary canal linking the esophagus to the small intestine. ■ each of four such organs in a ruminant (the rumen, reticulum, omasum, and abomasum). ■ any of a number of analogous organs in lower animals. ■ the front part of the body between the chest and thighs; the belly: *Blake hit him in the stomach.* ■ [in *sing.*] the stomach viewed as the seat of hunger, nausea, anxiety, or other unsettling feelings: *Virginia had a sick feeling in her stomach.* **2** [in *sing.*] [usu. with *negative*] an appetite for food or drink: *she doesn't have the stomach to eat anything.* ■ a desire or inclination for something involving conflict, difficulty, or unpleasantness: *the teams proved to have* ***no stomach for*** *a fight* | [with *infinitive*] *frankly, I don't have the stomach to find out.*
▸*v.* [*trans.*] (usu. **cannot stomach**) consume (food or drink) without feeling or being sick: *if you cannot stomach orange juice, try apple juice.* ■ endure or accept (an obnoxious thing or person): *I can't stomach the self-righteous attitude of some managers.* ▷Middle English: from Old French *estomac, stomaque*, via Latin from Greek *stomakhos* 'gullet,' from *stoma* 'mouth.' The early sense of the verb was 'be offended at, resent' (early 16th cent.). **—stom·ach·ful** /-ˌfo͝ol/ *n.* (*pl.* **-fuls**).
▸*PHRASES* □ **an army marches on its stomach** a group of soldiers or workers can only fight or function effectively if they have been well fed. [translating French *c'est la soupe qui fait le soldat*, a maxim of Napoleon.] □ **on a full** (or **an empty**) **stomach** after

having eaten (or having not eaten): *I think better on a full stomach.* □ **a strong stomach** an ability to see or do unpleasant things without feeling sick or squeamish.

stom·ach·ache /ˈstəmək,āk/ ▶*n.* a pain in a person's belly: *most childhood stomachaches aren't serious.*

stom·ach·er /ˈstəməkər/ ▶*n. historical* a V-shaped piece of decorative cloth, worn over the chest and stomach by men and women in the 16th century, later only by women. ▷late Middle English: probably a shortening of Old French *estomachier*, from *estomac* (see STOMACH).

stom·ach flu ▶*n.* a short-lived stomach disorder of unknown cause, popularly attributed to a virus.

sto·mach·ic /stəˈmakik/ *dated* ▶*adj.* promoting the appetite or assisting digestion. ■ of or relating to the stomach.

▶*n.* a medicine or tonic that promotes the appetite or assists digestion.

sto·mach mus·cles ▶*plural n.* the muscles constituting the front wall of the abdomen.

sto·mach pump ▶*n.* a syringe attached to a long tube, used for extracting the contents of a person's stomach (for example, if they have swallowed poison).

sto·ma·ta /ˈstōmətə; stōˈmätə/ ▶ plural form of STOMA.

stom·a·tal /ˈstōmətl; ˈstäm-/ ▶*adj. chiefly Botany* of or relating to a stoma or stomata.

sto·mate /ˈstō,māt/ ▶*n. Botany* another term for STOMA. ▷mid 19th cent.: apparently an English singular of STOMATA.

sto·ma·ti·tis /,stōməˈtītis/ ▶*n. Medicine* inflammation of the mucous membrane of the mouth. ▷mid 19th cent.: modern Latin, from *stoma, stomat-* 'mouth' + -ITIS.

sto·ma·to·gas·tric /stō,matəˈgastrik; ,stōmətə-/ ▶*adj. chiefly Zoology* relating to or connected with the mouth and stomach, particularly denoting a system of visceral nerves in invertebrates. ▷mid 19th cent.: from Greek *stoma, stomat-* 'mouth' + GASTRIC.

stomp /stämp; stômp/ ▶*v.* [*intrans.*] tread heavily and noisily, typically in order to show anger: *Martin stomped off to the spare room.* ■ [*intrans.*] (**stomp on**) tread heavily or stamp on: *I stomped on the accelerator.* ■ [*trans.*] deliberately trample or tread heavily on: *Cobb proceeded to kick and stomp him viciously.* ■ [*trans.*] stamp (one's feet). ■ [*intrans.*] dance with heavy stamping steps.

▶*n. informal* (in jazz or popular music) a tune or song with a fast tempo and a heavy beat. ■ a lively dance performed to such music, involving heavy stamping. ▷early 19th cent. (originally U.S. dialect): variant of the verb STAMP. —**stomp·er** *n.* —**stomp·y** *adj.*

stomp·ing /ˈstämpiNG; ˈstôm-/ ▶*adj.* (of music) having a lively stamping rhythm.

stomp·ing ground (also **stamp·ing ground**) ▶*n.* a place where someone regularly spends time; a favorite haunt.

Stone[1] /stōn/, Edward Durell (1902–78), U.S. architect. His notable designs include the Museum of Modern Art in New York City 1937–39; the U.S. embassy in New Delhi, India 1954–58; and the John F. Kennedy Center for the Performing Arts in Washington, D.C. 1964–69.

Stone[2], Harlan Fiske (1872–1946), U.S. chief justice 1941–46. He was the dean of the Columbia Law School 1910–24 and, briefly, U.S. attorney general 1924 in President Coolidge's cabinet before he was appointed to the U.S. Supreme Court as an associate justice 1925–41. He was named chief justice by President Franklin D. Roosevelt.

Stone[3], Lucy (1818–93), U.S. feminist and abolitionist. The first woman in Massachusetts to earn a college degree (Oberlin College 1847), she traveled widely during the 1850s lecturing on women's rights. In 1869, she founded the American Woman Suffrage Association, which merged with the National Woman Suffrage Association in 1890 to form the National American Woman Suffrage Association.

Stone[4] /stōn/, Oliver (1946–), U.S. movie director, screenwriter, and producer. He won Academy Awards for his adaptation of the novel *Midnight Express* (1978) and for his direction of *Platoon* (1986) and *Born on the Fourth of July* (1989), both of which indict U.S. involvement in the Vietnam War. Other notable movies: *JFK* (1991) and *Natural Born Killers* (1994).

stone /stōn/ ▶*n.* **1** the hard, solid, nonmetallic mineral matter of which rock is made, esp. as a building material: *the houses are built of stone* | [as *adj.*] *high stone walls.* ■ a small piece of rock found on the ground. ■ (in metaphorical use) weight or lack of feeling, expression, or movement: *Isabel stood as if* ***turned to stone*** | *her face became* ***as hard as stone*** | *the elevator* ***dropped like a stone.*** ■ *Astronomy* a meteorite made of rock, as opposed to metal. ■ *Medicine* a calculus; a gallstone or kidney stone. **2** a piece of stone shaped for a purpose, esp. one of commemoration, ceremony, or demarcation: *a memorial stone* | *boundary stones.* ■ a gem or jewel. ■ short for CURLING STONE. ■ a round piece or counter, originally made of stone, used in various board games such as backgammon. ■ a large flat table or sheet, originally made of stone and later usually of metal, on which pages of type were made up. **3** a hard seed in a cherry, plum, peach, and some other fruits. **4** (*pl.* same) *Brit.* a unit of weight equal to 14 pounds (6.35 kg): *I weighed 10 stone.* **5** a natural shade of whitish-gray or brownish-gray: [as *adj.*] *stone stretch trousers.*

▶*v.* [*trans.*] **1** throw stones at: *policemen were stoned by the crowd.* ■ *chiefly historical* execute (someone) by throwing stones at them: *Stephen* ***was stoned to death*** *in Jerusalem.* **2** remove the stone from (a fruit): *halve, stone, and peel the avocados.* **3** build, face, or pave with stone. ▷Old English *stān* (noun), of Germanic origin; related to Dutch *steen* and German *Stein*. The verb dates from Middle English (first recorded in sense 1). —**stone·less** *adj.*

▶*PHRASES* □ **be written** (or **engraved** or **set**) **in stone** used to emphasize that something is fixed and unchangeable: *anything can change—nothing is written in stone.* □ **cast** (or **throw**) **the first stone** be the first to make an accusation (used to emphasize that a potential critic is not wholly blameless). [with biblical allusion to John 8:7.] □ **leave no stone unturned** try every possible course of action in order to achieve something. □ **stone me!** (or **stone the crows!**) *Brit., informal* an exclamation of surprise or shock. □ **a stone's throw** a short distance: *wild whales blowing a stone's throw from the boat.*

Stone Age a prehistoric period when weapons and tools were made of stone or of organic materials such as bone, wood, or horn.

The Stone Age covers a period of about 2.5 million years, from the first use of tools by the ancestors of man (*Australopithecus*) to the introduction of agriculture and the first towns. It is subdivided into the Paleolithic, Mesolithic, and Neolithic periods, and is succeeded in Europe by the Bronze Age (or, sometimes, the Copper Age) about 5,000–4,000 years ago.

stone boat ▶*n.* a flat-bottomed sled used for transporting stones and other heavy objects.

stone-broke ▶*adj. informal* entirely without money.

stone·chat /ˈstōn,CHat/ ▶*n.* a small Old World songbird of the thrush subfamily, having bold markings and a call that sounds like two stones being knocked together. • Genus *Saxicola*, subfamily Turdinae, family Muscicapidae: three or four species, in particular the widespread *S. torquata*, the male of which has a black head and orange breast.

stone chi·na ▶*n.* a kind of very hard earthenware resembling porcelain.

stone cold ▶*adj.* completely cold.

▶*adv.* (**stone-cold**) [as *submodifier*] completely: *stone-cold sober.*

stone crab ▶*n.* a large, heavy, edible crab of the Gulf of Mexico and Caribbean area. • *Menippe mercenaria*, family Xanthidae.

stone·crop /ˈstōn,kräp/ ▶*n.* a small fleshy-leaved plant that typically has star-shaped yellow or white flowers and grows among rocks or on walls. • Genus *Sedum*, family Crassulaceae: many species, including the **mossy stonecrop** (*S. acre*), whose tiny, thick leaves have a bitter, peppery taste.

stone cur·lew ▶*n.* another term for THICK-KNEE.

stone·cut·ter /ˈstōn,kətər/ ▶*n.* a person who cuts stone from a quarry or who shapes and carves it for use.

stoned /stōnd/ ▶*adj. informal* under the influence of drugs, esp. marijuana: *he was up in the deck chair* ***getting stoned.*** ■ very drunk.

stone dead ▶*adj.* [*predic.*] completely dead.

stone deaf ▶*adj.* completely deaf: *the racket drove out any deer not stone deaf* | *the stone-deaf person relies entirely on sight.*

stone face ▶*n. informal* a face that reveals no emotions. —**stone-faced** *adj.*

stone·fish /ˈstōn,fiSH/ ▶*n.* (*pl.* same or **-fish·es**) a chiefly marine fish of bizarre appearance that lives in the tropical Indo-Pacific. It rests motionless in the sand with its venomous dorsal spines projecting and is a frequent cause of injury to swimmers. • Family Synanceiidae: several genera and species, including *Synanceia verrucosa* (also called DEVILFISH.)

stone·fly /ˈstōn,flī/ ▶*n.* (*pl.* **-flies**) a slender insect with transparent membranous wings, the larvae of which live in clean running water. The adults are used as bait by fly fishermen. • Order Plecoptera: many families.

stone fruit ▶*n.* a fruit with flesh or pulp enclosing a stone, such as a peach, plum, or cherry.

stone-ground /ˈstōnˈground/ ▶*adj.* (of flour) ground with millstones.

Stone·henge /ˈstōn,henj/ a megalithic monument on Salisbury Plain in Wiltshire, England. Completed in several constructional phases from *c.*2950 BC, it was probably used for ritual purposes. ▷from Old English *stān* 'stone' + an element related to *hengan* 'to hang.'

Stonehenge

stone lil·y ▶*n.* (*pl.* **-lil·ies**) *dated* a fossilized sea lily.

stone mar·ten ▶*n.* a Eurasian marten that has chocolate-brown fur with a white throat. Also called BEECH MARTEN. • *Martes foina*, family Mustelidae.

stone·ma·son /ˈstōn,māsən/ ▶*n.* a person who cuts, prepares, and builds with stone. —**stone·ma·son·ry** /-,māsənrē/ *n.*

Stone Moun·tain a granite mass east of Atlanta in Georgia, site of the Confederate National Monument that was designed by Gutzon Borglum and created (1917–67).

stone pine ▶*n.* an umbrella-shaped southern European pine tree with large needles, very large glossy brown cones, and edible seeds ("pine nuts"). Also called UMBRELLA PINE. • *Pinus pinea*, family Pinaceae.

ston·er /ˈstōnər/ ▶*n.* **1** *informal* a person who regularly takes drugs, esp. marijuana: *I was a real stoner when I was a teenager.* **2** [in *combination*] *Brit.* a person or thing that weighs a specified number of stone: *a couple of 16-stoners.*

stone·roll·er ▶*n.* a small freshwater fish of the minnow family that uses the hard ridge on its lower jaw to scrape food, esp. algae, from rocks. • Genus *Campostoma*, family Cyprinidae: several species, including the **central stoneroller** (*C. anomalum*) of the eastern and central U.S., and the **Mexican stoneroller** (*C. ornatum*) of the southwestern U.S. and northern Mexico.

stone·wall /ˈstōn,wôl/ ▶*v.* [*trans.*] delay or block (a request, process, or person) by refusing to answer questions or by giving evasive replies, esp. in politics: *the highest level of bureaucracy stonewalled us* | [as *n.*] (**stonewalling**) *the art of stonewalling and political intimidation.* —**stone·wall·er** *n.*

Stone·wall Jack·son see JACKSON[9].

stoneware /ˈstōn,we(ə)r/ ▶*n.* a type of pottery that is impermeable and partly vitrified but opaque.

stone·washed /ˈstōn,wôSHt; -,wäSHt/ (also **stone·wash**) ▶*adj.* (of a garment or fabric, esp. denim) washed with abrasives to produce a worn or faded appearance.

stone·work /ˈstōn,wərk/ ▶*n.* the parts of a building that are made of stone. ■ the work of a mason: *a masterpiece of clever stonework.* —**stone·work·er** *n.*

stone·wort /ˈstōnwərt; -,wôrt/ ▶*n.* a freshwater plant with whorls of slender leaves, related to green algae. Many kinds become encrusted with chalky deposits, giving them a stony feel. • *Chara* and other genera in the class Charophyceae, division Chlorophyta; sometimes placed in its own division (Charophyta).

stonk /stäNGk/ *military slang* ▶*n.* a concentrated artillery bombardment.
▶*v.* [*trans.*] bombard with concentrated artillery fire. ▷1940s: said to be formed from elements of the artillery term *Standard Regimental Concentration.*

stonk·er /ˈstäNGkər; ˈstôNG-/ ▶*n. Brit., informal* something that is very large or impressive of its kind: *it's a real stonker of a plan.*

stonk·ing /ˈstäNGkiNG; ˈstôNG-/ ▶*adj. Brit., informal* used to emphasize something remarkable or exciting: *a stonking 207 mph maximum speed.* ▷1980s: from the verb **STONK**.

ston·y /ˈstōnē/ ▶*adj.* (**ston·i·er**, **ston·i·est**) covered with or full of small pieces of rock: *rough stony paths.* ■ made of or resembling stone: *stony steps.* ■ not having or showing feeling or sympathy: *Lorenzo's hard, stony eyes* | [in *combination*] *he walked away, stony-faced.* ■ *Astronomy* (of a meteorite) consisting mostly of rock, as opposed to metal. ▷Old English *stānig* (see **STONE**, **-Y**[1]). **—ston·i·ly** /-nəlē/ *adv.* **—ston·i·ness** *n.*
▶*PHRASE* □ **fall on stony ground** (of words or a suggestion) be ignored or badly received. [with biblical reference to the parable of the sower (Matt. 13:5).]

ston·y cor·al ▶*n.* see **CORAL** (sense 2).

ston·y-heart·ed ▶*adj.* cruel or unfeeling.

ston·y-i·ron *Astronomy* ▶*adj.* (of a meteorite) containing appreciable quantities of both rock and iron.
▶*n.* a stony-iron meteorite.

stood /sto͝od/ ▶ past and past participle of **STAND**.

stooge /sto͞oj/ ▶*n.* **1** *derogatory* a person who serves merely to support or assist others, particularly in doing unpleasant work: *you fell for that helpless-female act and let her make you a stooge.* ■ a person who is employed to assume a particular role while keeping their true identity hidden: *a police stooge.* **2** a performer whose act involves being the butt of a comedian's jokes.
▶*v.* [*intrans.*] **1** move around aimlessly; drift or cruise: *she* **stooged around** *in the bathroom for a while.* **2** perform a role that involves being the butt of a comedian's jokes. ▷early 20th cent.: of unknown origin.

stook /sto͞ok; sto͝ok/ *Brit.* ▶*n.* a group of sheaves of grain stood on end in a field.
▶*v.* [*trans.*] arrange in stooks. ▷Middle English (as a noun): from or related to Middle Low German *stūke*.

stool /sto͞ol/ ▶*n.* **1** a seat without a back or arms, typically resting on three or four legs or on a single pedestal. ■ a support on which to stand in order to reach high objects. ■ short for **FOOTSTOOL**. **2** a piece of feces. **3** a root or stump of a tree or plant from which shoots spring. **4** a decoy bird in hunting.
▶*v.* [*intrans.*] (of a plant) throw up shoots from the root. ■ [*trans.*] cut back (a plant) to or near ground level in order to induce new growth. ▷Old English, of Germanic origin; related to Dutch *stoel*, German *Stuhl*, also to **STAND**. Current senses of the verb date from the late 18th cent.
▶*PHRASE* □ **at stool** *Medicine* when defecating.

stool·ie /ˈsto͞olē/ ▶*n. informal* short for **STOOL PIGEON**.

stool pi·geon ▶*n.* a police informer. ■ a person acting as a decoy. ▷late 19th cent.: so named from the original use of a pigeon fixed to a stool as a decoy.

stoop[1] /sto͞op/ ▶*v.* [*intrans.*] **1** bend one's head or body forward and downward: *he* **stooped down** *and reached toward the coin* | *Linda stooped to pick up the bottles* | [*trans.*] *the man stoops his head.* ■ have the head and shoulders habitually bent forward: *he tends to stoop when he walks* | [as *adj.*] (**stooping**) *a thin, stooping figure.* ■ (of a bird of prey) swoop down on a quarry. **2** lower one's moral standards so far as to do something reprehensible: *Craig wouldn't* **stoop to** *thieving* | *she was unwilling to believe that anyone could* **stoop so low** *as to steal from a dead woman.* ■ [with *infinitive*] condescend to do something.
▶*n.* **1** [in *sing.*] a posture in which the head and shoulders are habitually bent forward: *a tall, thin man with a stoop.* **2** the downward swoop of a bird of prey. ▷Old English *stūpian* (verb), of Germanic origin; related to the adjective **STEEP**[1]. Both senses of the noun date from the late 16th cent.

stoop[2] ▶*n.* a porch with steps in front of a house or other building. ▷mid 18th cent.: from Dutch *stoep* (see **STOEP**).

stoop ball ▶*n.* a ball game resembling baseball in which the ball is thrown against a building or the steps of a stoop rather than to a batter.

stooped /sto͞opt/ ▶*adj.* (of a person) having the head and shoulders habitually bent forward: *a thin, stooped figure.* ■ (of the shoulders or another part of the body) habitually bent forward: *the man was slight, with stooped shoulders.*

stoop la·bor ▶*n.* agricultural labor performed in a stooping or squatting position.

stop /stäp/ ▶*v.* (**stopped**, **stop·ping**) **1** [*intrans.*] (of an event, action, or process) come to an end; cease to happen: *his laughter stopped as quickly as it had begun* | *the rain had stopped and the clouds had cleared.* ■ [with *present participle*] cease to perform a specified action or have a specified experience: *she stopped giggling* | [*trans.*] *he stopped work for tea.* ■ [with *present participle*] abandon a specified practice or habit: *I've stopped eating meat.* ■ stop moving or operating: *he stopped to look at the view* | *my watch has stopped.* ■ (of a bus or train) call at a designated place to pick up or let off passengers: *main-line trains stop at platform 7.* ■ *Brit., informal* stay somewhere for a short time: *you'll have to* **stop the night**. **2** [*trans.*] cause (an action, process, or event) to come to an end: *this harassment has got to be stopped.* ■ prevent (an action or event) from happening: *a security guard was killed trying to stop a raid.* ■ prevent or dissuade (someone) from continuing in an activity or achieving an aim: *a campaign is under way to stop the bombers.* ■ [*trans.*] prevent (someone or something) from performing a specified action or undergoing a specified experience: *you can't* **stop** *me* **from** *getting what I want.* ■ cause or order to cease moving or operating: *he stopped his car by the house* | *police were given powers to stop and search suspects.* ■ *informal* be hit by (a bullet). ■ instruct a bank to withhold payment on (a check). ■ refuse to supply as usual; withhold or deduct: *the union has threatened to stop the supply of minerals.* ■ *Boxing* defeat (an opponent) by a knockout: *he was stopped in the sixth by Tyson.* **3** [*trans.*] block or close up (a hole or leak): *he tried to stop the hole with the heel of his boot* | *the drain has been* **stopped up**. ■ block the mouth of (a fox's earth) prior to a hunt. ■ plug the upper end of (an organ pipe), giving a note an octave lower. ■ obtain the required pitch from (the string of a violin or similar instrument) by pressing at the appropriate point with the finger. ■ make (a rope) fast with a stopper.
▶*phrasal v.* □ **stop by** (or **in**) call briefly and informally as a visitor. □ **stop something down** *Photography* reduce the aperture of a lens with a diaphragm. □ **stop off** (or **over**) pay a short visit en route to one's ultimate destination when traveling: *I stopped off to visit him and his wife* | *he decided to stop over in Paris.* □ **stop something out** cover an area that is not to be printed or etched when making a print or etching.
▶*n.* **1** a cessation of movement or operation: *all business* **came to a stop** | *there were constant stops and changes of pace.* ■ a break or halt during a journey: *allow an hour or so for driving and as long as you like for stops* | *the flight landed for a refueling stop.* ■ a place designated for a bus or train to halt and pick up or drop off passengers: *the bus was pulling up at her stop.* ■ an object or part of a mechanism that is used to prevent something from moving: *the shelves have special stops to prevent them from being pulled out too far.* ■ *Brit., dated* a punctuation mark, esp. a period. ■ used in telegrams to indicate a period: *MEET YOU AT THE AIRPORT STOP.* ■ *Phonetics* a consonant produced with complete closure of the vocal tract. ■ *Bridge* a high card that prevents the opponents from establishing a particular suit; a control. ■ *Nautical* a short length of cord used to secure something. **2** a set of organ pipes of a particular tone and range of pitch. ■ (also **stop knob**) a knob, lever, or similar device in an organ or harpsichord that brings into play a set of pipes or strings of a particular tone and range of pitch. **3** *Photography* the effective diameter of a lens. ■ a device for reducing this. ■ a unit of change of relative aperture or exposure (with a reduction of one stop equivalent to halving it). ▷Old English *(for)stoppian* 'block up (an aperture)'; related to German *stopfen*, from late Latin *stuppare* 'to stuff.' **—stop·pa·ble** *adj.*
▶*PHRASES* □ **pull out all the stops** make a very great effort to achieve something: *the director pulled out all the stops to meet the impossible deadline.* ■ do something very elaborately or on a grand scale: *they gave a Christmas party and pulled out all the stops.* [with reference to the stops of an organ.] □ **put a stop to** cause (an activity) to end: *she would have to put a stop to all this nonsense.* □ **stop at nothing** be utterly ruthless or determined in one's attempt to achieve something: *he would stop at nothing to retain his position of power.* □ **stop dead** (or **short**) suddenly cease moving, speaking, or acting. □ **stop one's ears** put one's fingers in one's ears to avoid hearing something. □ **stop someone's mouth** induce someone to keep silent about something. □ **stop the show** (of a performer) provoke prolonged applause or laughter, causing an interruption.

stop-and-go ▶*n.* [usu. as *adj.*] alternate stopping and restarting of progress: *stop-and-go driving.*

stop·band /ˈstäp,band/ ▶*n. Electronics* a band of frequencies that are attenuated by a filter.

stop·bank /ˈstäp,baNGk/ ▶*n. Austral./NZ* an embankment built to prevent a river from flooding.

stop bath ▶*n. Photography* a bath for stopping the action of a preceding bath by neutralizing any of its chemical still present.

stop bit ▶*n. Telecommunications* (in asynchronous data transfers) one of a pattern of bits that indicate the end of a character or of the whole transmission.

stop·cock /ˈstäp,käk/ ▶*n.* an externally operated valve regulating the flow of a liquid or gas through a pipe.

stope /stōp/ ▶*n.* (usu. **stopes**) a steplike part of a mine where minerals are being extracted.
▶*v.* [*intrans.*] [usu. as *n.*] (**stoping**) (in mining) excavate a series of steps or layers in (the ground or rock). ■ [as *n.*] (**stoping**) *Geology* the process by which country rock is broken up and removed by the upward movement of magma. ▷mid 18th cent.: apparently related to the noun **STEP**.

stop·gap /ˈstäp,gap/ ▶*n.* a temporary way of dealing with a problem or satisfying a need: *transplants are only a stopgap until more sophisticated alternatives can work.*

stop knob ▶*n.* the knob controlling a stop on an organ or harpsichord.

stop·light /ˈstäp,līt/ ▶*n.* **1** another term for **TRAFFIC LIGHT**. ■ a red traffic light. **2** another term for **BRAKE LIGHT**.

stop list ▶*n.* a list of words automatically omitted from a computer-generated concordance or index, typically the most frequent words, which would slow down processing unacceptably.

stop-loss ▶*adj. Finance* **1** denoting or relating to an order to sell a security or commodity at a specified price in order to limit a loss. **2** denoting or relating to a policy of the armed forces to forcibly retain members on active duty beyond their original agreed period of enlistment.

stop-mo·tion ▶*n.* [usu. as *adj.*] a cinematographic technique whereby the camera is repeatedly stopped and started, for example to give animated figures the impression of movement.

stop-off ▶*n.* another term for **STOPOVER**.

stop-out ▶*n. Brit., informal* a person who stays out late at night.

stop·o·ver /ˈstäp,ōvər/ ▶*n.* a break in a journey: *the one-day stopover in Honolulu.* ■ a place where a journey is broken: *an inviting stopover between Quebec City and Montreal.*

stop·page /ˈstäpij/ ▶*n.* an instance of movement, activity, or supply stopping or being stopped: *the result of the air raid was complete stoppage of production.* ■ a blockage in a narrow passage, such as the barrel of a gun. ■ a cessation of work by employees protesting the terms set by their employers. ■ *Boxing* a knockout.

stop·page time ▶*n.* another term for **INJURY TIME**.

Stop·pard /ˈstäpərd; ˈstäp,ärd/, Sir Tom (1937–), British playwright, born in Czechoslovakia; born *Thomas Straussler*. His best-known plays are comedies, often dealing with metaphysical and ethical questions; for example, *Rosencrantz and Guildenstern Are Dead* (1966) is based on the characters in *Hamlet*.

stop pay·ment ▶*n.* an authorized withholding of payment on a check: *call the bank tomorrow and get a stop payment on that check.* ▷the usage as a noun derives from the verb phrase *stop payment*, meaning "instruct a bank to withhold payment on a check."

stop·per /ˈstäpər/ ▶*n.* **1** a plug for sealing a hole, esp. in the neck of a bottle or other container. **2** a person or thing that halts or obstructs a specified thing: [in *combination*] *a crime-stopper.* ■ (in soccer and other sports) a player whose function is to block attacks on goal from the middle of the field. ■ *Baseball* a starting pitcher depended on to win a game or stop a losing streak, or a relief pitcher used to prevent the opposing team from scoring. ■ (in sailing or climbing) a rope or clamp for preventing a rope or cable from running out. ■ *Bridge* another term for **CONTROL**.
▶*v.* [usu. as *adj.*] (**stoppered**) use a stopper to seal (a bottle or other container): *a small stoppered jar.*
▶*PHRASE* □ **put a** (or **the**) **stopper on** *informal* prevent from happening or continuing.

stop·ping point ▸*n.* a point or place at which it is convenient to stop during a journey or activity.

stop·ple /ˈstäpəl/ ▸*n.* a stopper or plug.
▸*v.* [*trans.*] seal with a stopper. ▷Middle English: partly a shortening of Old French *estouppail* 'bung,' reinforced by the verb STOP.

stop-start (also **stop-and-start**) ▸*adj. informal* alternately stopping and starting; progressing interruptedly: *a $150 stop-start taxi ride.*

stop time ▸*n.* (in jazz) a rhythmic device whereby a chord or accent is played only on the first beat of every bar or every other bar, typically accompanying a solo.

stop valve ▸*n.* a valve used to stop the flow of liquid in a pipe.

stop vol·ley ▸*n. Tennis* a volley played close to the net in which the player stops the ball without a forceful stroke, sending it just barely back over the net.

stop·watch /ˈstäp,wäCH/ ▸*n.* a special watch with buttons that start, stop, and then zero the hands, used to time races.

stor·age /ˈstôrij/ ▸*n.* the action or method of storing something for future use: *the chair can be folded flat for easy storage* | [as *adj.*] *the room lacked storage space.* ■ the retention of retrievable data on a computer or other electronic system; memory. ■ space available for storing something, esp. allocated space in a warehouse: *Cooper had put much of the furniture into storage.* ■ the cost of storing something in a warehouse.

stor·age bat·ter·y (also **stor·age cell**) ▸*n.* a battery (or cell) used for storing electrical energy.

stor·age de·vice ▸*n.* a piece of computer equipment on which information can be stored.

stor·age heat·er ▸*n. Brit.* an electric heater that accumulates heat in water or bricks during the night (when electricity is cheaper) and releases it during the day.

stor·age ring ▸*n. Physics* an approximately circular accelerator in which particles can be effectively stored by being made to circulate continuously at high energy.

sto·rax /ˈstô,raks/ (also **sty·rax** /ˈstī-/) ▸*n.* **1** a rare fragrant gum resin obtained from an eastern Mediterranean tree, sometimes used in medicine, perfumery, and incense. ■ (**liquid storax**) a liquid balsam obtained from the Asian liquidambar tree. **2** a tropical or subtropical tree or shrub with showy white flowers in drooping clusters. • Genus *Styrax*, family Styracaceae: several species, in particular *S. officinalis*, from which the resin storax is obtained. ▷late Middle English: from Latin, from a variant of Greek *sturax*.

store /stôr/ ▸*n.* **1** a retail establishment selling items to the public: *a health-food store.* ■ [as *adj.*] store-bought: *there's a loaf of store bread.* **2** a quantity or supply of something kept for use as needed: *the squirrel has **a store of** food* | *figurative her vast **store of** knowledge.* ■ a place where things are kept for future use or sale: *a grain store.* ■ (**stores**) supplies of equipment and food kept for use by members of an army, navy, or other institution, or the place where they are kept. ■ *Brit.* a computer memory. **3** *chiefly Brit.* a sheep, steer, cow, or pig acquired or kept for fattening.
▸*v.* [*trans.*] keep or accumulate (something) for future use: *a small room used for storing furniture.* ■ retain or enter (information) for future electronic retrieval: *the data is **stored on disk**.* ■ (**be stored with**) have a supply of (something useful): *a mind well stored with esoteric knowledge.* ■ [*intrans.*] remain fresh while being stored: *they do not ship or store well.* ▷Middle English: shortening of Old French *estore* (noun), *estorer* (verb), from Latin *instaurare* 'renew'; compare with RESTORE. —**stor·a·ble** *adj.* —**stor·er** *n.*
▸*PHRASES* □ **in store 1** in a safe place while not being used or displayed: *items **held in store**.* **2** coming in the future; about to happen: *he did not yet know what **lay in store for** him.* □ **set** (or **lay** or **put**) **store by** (or **on**) consider (something) to be of a particular degree of importance or value: *many people set much store by privacy.*

store-and-for·ward ▸*adj.* [*attrib.*] *Telecommunications* relating to or denoting a data network in which messages are routed to one or more intermediate stations where they may be stored before being forwarded to their destinations.

store-bought ▸*adj.* bought ready-made from a store; not homemade.

store·front /ˈstôr,frənt/ ▸*n.* **1** the facade of a store. **2** a room or set of rooms facing the street on the ground floor of a commercial building, typically used as a store: [as *adj.*] *a bright storefront eatery.*

store·house /ˈstôr,hous/ ▸*n.* a building used for storing goods. ■ a large supply of something: *an enormous **storehouse of** facts.*

store·keep·er /ˈstôr,kēpər/ ▸*n.* **1** a person who owns or runs a store. **2** a person responsible for stored goods.

store·room /ˈstôr,ro͞om; -,ro͝om/ ▸*n.* a room in which items are stored.

sto·rey /ˈstôrē/ ▸*n. chiefly Brit.* variant spelling of STORY[2].

sto·ri·at·ed /ˈstôrē,ātid/ ▸*adj. rare* decorated with historical, legendary, or emblematic designs. ▷late 19th cent.: compare with HISTORIATED. —**sto·ri·a·tion** /,stôrēˈāSHən/ *n.*

sto·ried /ˈstôrēd/ ▸*adj.* [*attrib.*] *poetic/literary* celebrated in or associated with stories or legends: *the island's storied past.*

stork /stôrk/ ▸*n.* a tall long-legged wading bird with a long heavy bill and typically with white and black plumage. • Family Ciconiidae: several genera and species, in particular the **white stork** (*Ciconia ciconia*), with black wing tips and a reddish bill and legs, often nesting on tall buildings in Europe. ■ the white stork as the pretended bringer of babies. ▷Old English *storc*, of Germanic origin; probably related to STARK (because of its rigid stance).

storm /stôrm/ ▸*n.* **1** a violent disturbance of the atmosphere with strong winds and usually rain, thunder, lightning, or snow. ■ (also **storm system**) an intense low-pressure weather system; a cyclone. ■ a wind of force 10 on the Beaufort scale (48–55 knots or 55-63 mph). ■ a heavy discharge of missiles or blows: *two men were taken by **a storm of** bullets.* **2** [usu. in *sing.*] a tumultuous reaction; an uproar or controversy: *the book caused a storm in South America* | *she has been at the center of a storm concerning payments.* ■ a violent or noisy outburst of a specified feeling or reaction: *the disclosure raised **a storm of protest**.* **3** (**storms**) storm windows. **4** a direct assault by troops on a fortified place.
▸*v.* **1** [*intrans.*] move angrily or forcefully in a specified direction: *she burst into tears and stormed off* | *he stormed out of the house.* ■ [with *direct speech*] shout (something) angrily; rage: *"Don't patronize me!" she stormed.* ■ move forcefully and decisively to a specified position in a game or contest: *he barged past and stormed to the checkered flag.* **2** [*trans.*] (of troops) suddenly attack and capture (a building or other place) by means of force: *Indian commandos stormed a hijacked plane early today* | [as *n.*] (**storming**) *the storming of the Bastille.* See note at ATTACK. **3** [*intrans.*] (of the weather) be violent, with strong winds and usually rain, thunder, lightning, or snow: *when **it stormed** in the day, I shoveled the drive before Harry came home.* ▷Old English, of Germanic origin; related to Dutch *storm* and German *Sturm*, probably also to the verb STIR[1]. The verb dates from late Middle English in sense 3. —**storm·proof** /-,pro͞of/ *adj.*
▸*PHRASES* □ **go down a storm** *Brit.* be enthusiastically received by an audience. □ **the calm** (or **lull**) **before the storm** a period of unusual tranquility or stability that seems likely to presage difficult times. □ **storm and stress** another term for STURM UND DRANG. □ **a storm in a teacup** British term for A TEMPEST IN A TEAPOT (see TEMPEST). □ **take something by storm** (of troops) capture a place by a sudden and violent attack. ■ have great and rapid success in a particular place or with a particular group of people: *his first collection took the fashion world by storm.* □ **— up a storm** perform the specified action with great enthusiasm and energy: *the band could really **play up a storm**.*

storm beach ▸*n.* an expanse of sand or gravel thrown up on the coast by storms.

storm·bound /ˈstôrm,bound/ ▸*adj.* prevented by storms from starting or continuing a journey.

storm cen·ter ▸*n.* the point to which the wind blows spirally inward in a cyclonic storm. ■ the central point around which controversy or trouble happens.

storm cloud ▸*n.* a heavy, dark rain cloud. ■ (**storm clouds**) used in reference to a threatening or ominous state of affairs: *the beginning of the decade saw **storm clouds gathering** over Europe.*

storm·cock /ˈstôrm,käk/ ▸*n. dialect* the mistle thrush.

storm cuff ▸*n.* a tight-fitting inner cuff, typically an elasticized one, that prevents rain or wind from getting inside a coat.

storm door ▸*n.* an additional outer door for protection in bad weather or winter.

storm drain ▸*n.* another term for STORM SEWER.

storm·er /ˈstôrmər/ ▸*n.* [usu. in *sing.*] *Brit., informal* something particularly impressive or good of its kind: *a stormer of an album* | *the engine is a real stormer.*

storm flap ▸*n.* a piece of material designed to protect an opening or fastener on a tent or coat from the effects of rain.

storm glass ▸*n.* a sealed tube containing a solution whose clarity is thought to change when storms approach.

storm·ing /ˈstôrmiNG/ ▸*adj.* [*attrib.*] *Brit., informal* (of a performance, esp. in sports or music) outstandingly vigorous or impressive: *his storming finish carried him into third place.*

Storm·in' Nor·man /ˈstôrmin/ see SCHWARZKOPF.

storm jib ▸*n. Sailing* a small heavy jib for use in a high wind.

storm pet·rel ▸*n.* a small seabird of the open ocean, typically having blackish plumage and a white rump, and formerly believed to be a harbinger of bad weather. • Family Hydrobatidae: several genera and many species, e.g., *Hydrobates pelagicus* of the northeastern Atlantic and Mediterranean.

storm sail ▸*n.* a sail used in stormy weather, of smaller size and stronger material than the corresponding one used in ordinary weather.

storm sew·er /ˈso͞oər/ ▸*n.* a sewer built to carry away excess water in times of heavy rain.

storm sig·nal ▸*n.* a lamp, flag, or other device used to give a visible warning of an approaching storm.

storm surge ▸*n.* a rising of the sea as a result of atmospheric pressure changes and wind associated with a storm.

storm troops ▸*plural n.* another term for SHOCK TROOPS. ■ (**Storm Troops**) *historical* the Nazi political militia. —**storm troop·er** *n.*

storm wa·ter ▸*n.* surface water in abnormal quantity resulting from heavy falls of rain or snow.

storm win·dow ▸*n.* a window fixed outside a normal window for protection and insulation in bad weather or winter.

storm·y /ˈstôrmē/ ▸*adj.* (**storm·i·er, storm·i·est**) (of weather) characterized by strong winds and usually rain, thunder, lightning, or snow: *a dark and stormy night.* ■ (of the sea or sky) having large waves or dark clouds because of windy or rainy conditions: *gray and stormy skies.* ■ full of angry or violent outbursts of feeling: *a long and stormy debate* | *a stormy relationship.* —**storm·i·ly** /-məlē/ *adv.* —**storm·i·ness** *n.*

storm·y pet·rel ▸*n.* another term for STORM PETREL.

Stor·ting /ˈstôrtiNG/ the Norwegian parliament. ▷Norwegian, from *stor* 'great' + *ting* 'assembly.'

Stor·y /ˈstôrē/, Joseph (1779–1845), U.S. Supreme Court associate justice 1811–45. Appointed to the Court by President Madison, he was the youngest associate justice ever to serve. He established the supremacy of Supreme Court rulings.

sto·ry[1] /ˈstôrē/ ▸*n.* (*pl.* **-ries**) **1** an account of imaginary or real people and events told for entertainment: *an adventure story* | *I'm going to tell you a story.* ■ a plot or story line: *the novel has a good story.* ■ a report of an item of news in a newspaper, magazine, or news broadcast: *stories in the local papers.* ■ a piece of gossip; a rumor: *there have been lots of stories going around, as you can imagine.* ■ *informal* a false statement or explanation; a lie: *Ellie never **told stories**—she had always believed in the truth.* **2** an account of past events in someone's life or in the evolution of something: *the story of modern farming* | *the film is based on a true story.* ■ a particular person's representation of the facts of a matter, esp. as given in self-defense: *during police interviews, Harper changed his story.* ■ [in *sing.*] a situation viewed in terms of the information known about it or its similarity to another: *having such information is useful, but it is not the whole story* | *many children with leukemia now survive—twenty years ago it was a very different story.* ▷Middle English (denoting a historical account or representation): shortening of Anglo-Norman French *estorie*, from Latin *historia* (see HISTORY).
▸*PHRASES* □ **but that's another story** *informal* used after raising a matter to indicate that one does not want to expand on it for now. □ **end of story** *informal* used to emphasize that there is nothing to add on a matter just mentioned: *Men don't cry in public. End of story.* □ **it's a long story** *informal* used to indicate that, for now, one does not want to talk about

S

something that is too involved or painful. □ **it's** (or **that's**) **the story of one's life** *informal* used to lament the fact that a particular misfortune has happened too often in one's experience: *"It's the story of my life," my mother would say when she returned home from a sale empty-handed.* □ **the same old story** used to indicate that a particular bad situation is tediously familiar: *are we not faced with the same old story of a badly managed project?* □ **the story goes** it is said or rumored: *the story goes that he's fallen out with his friends.* □ **to make** (or *Brit.* **cut**) **a long story short** used to end an account of events quickly: *to make a long story short, I married Stephen.*

sto·ry[2] (*Brit.* also **sto·rey**) ▶*n.* a part of a building comprising all the rooms that are on the same level: [in *combination*] *a three-story building.* ▷late Middle English: shortening of Latin *historia* 'history, story,' a special use in Anglo-Latin, perhaps originally denoting a tier of painted windows or sculptures on the front of a building (representing a historical subject). **—sto·ried** (*Brit.* also **sto·reyed**) *adj.* [in *combination*] *four-storied houses.*

sto·ry·board /ˈstôrēˌbôrd/ ▶*n.* a sequence of drawings, typically with some directions and dialogue, representing the shots planned for a movie or television production.

sto·ry·book /ˈstôrēˌbo͝ok/ ▶*n.* a book containing a story or collection of stories intended for children. ■ [as *adj.*] denoting something that is as idyllically perfect as things typically are in storybooks: *it was a storybook finish to an illustrious career.*

sto·ry ed·i·tor ▶*n.* an editor who advises on the content and form of movie or television scripts.

sto·ry line ▶*n.* the plot of a novel, play, movie, or other narrative form.

sto·ry·tell·er /ˈstôrēˌtelər/ ▶*n.* a person who tells stories. **—sto·ry·tell·ing** /-ˌteliNG/ *n.* & *adj.*

Sto·ry·ville /ˈstôrēˌvil/ a former entertainment district in New Orleans in Louisiana, closed in 1917, associated with the early development of jazz music.

stot /stät/ ▶*v.* (**stot·ted, stot·ting**) [*intrans.*] another term for **PRONK**. ▷early 16th cent.: of unknown origin.

sto·tin /stäˈtēn/ ▶*n.* a monetary unit of Slovenia, equal to one hundredth of a tolar. ▷Slovene.

sto·tin·ka /stôˈtiNGkə/ ▶*n.* (*pl.* **-ki** /-kē/) a monetary unit of Bulgaria, equal to one hundredth of a lev. ▷Bulgarian, literally 'one hundredth.'

stoup /sto͞op/ ▶*n.* a basin for holy water, esp. on the wall near the door of a Roman Catholic church for worshipers to dip their fingers in before crossing themselves. ■ *archaic* or *historical* a flagon or beaker for drink. ▷Middle English (in the sense 'pail, small cask'): from Old Norse *staup*, of Germanic origin; related to the verb **STEEP**[2].

stour /sto͝or/ (also **stoor**) ▶*n. Scottish* & *N. English* dust forming a cloud or deposited in a mass. ▷late Middle English: of uncertain origin. **—stour·y** *adj.*

Stout /stout/, Rex (Todhunter) (1886–1975) U.S. writer. He created the portly, food-loving, orchid aficionado Nero Wolfe, a detective that appeared in many of his novels; the first novel was *Fer de Lance* (1934) and the last, *A Family Affair* (1975).

stout /stout/ ▶*adj.* **1** (of a person) somewhat fat or of heavy build: *stout middle-aged men.* ■ (of an object) strong and thick: *Billy had armed himself with a stout stick | stout walking boots.* **2** (of an act, quality, or person) brave and determined: *he put up a stout defense in court.*
▶*n.* a kind of strong, dark beer brewed with roasted malt or barley. ▷Middle English: from Anglo-Norman French and Old French dialect, of West Germanic origin; perhaps related to **STILT**. The noun (late 17th cent.) originally denoted any strong beer and is probably elliptical for *stout ale.* **—stout·ish** *adj.* (in sense 1). **—stout·ly** *adv.* **—stout·ness** *n.* (in sense 1).

stout·heart·ed /ˈstoutˈhärtid/ ▶*adj.* courageous or determined. **—stout·heart·ed·ly** *adv.* **—stout·heart·ed·ness** *n.*

stove[1] /stōv/ ▶*n.* an apparatus for cooking or heating that operates by burning fuel or using electricity. ■ (also **stove house**) *Brit.* a hothouse for plants.
▶*v.* [*trans.*] **1** treat (an object) by heating it in a stove in order to apply a desired surface coating. **2** *Brit.* raise (plants) in a hothouse. ▷Middle English (in the sense 'sweating room'): from Middle Dutch or Middle Low German *stove*; perhaps related to the noun **STEW**[1]. Current verb senses date from the early 17th cent.

stove[2] ▶ past and past participle of **STAVE**.

stoved /stōvd/ ▶*adj.* [*attrib.*] *Brit.* (of vegetables or meat) stewed.

stove e·nam·el *Brit.* ▶*n.* a heatproof enamel produced by heat treatment in a stove, or a paint imitating it.
▶*v.* [*trans.*] [usu. as *adj.*] (**stove-enamelled**) give (something) a finish of this kind.

stove·pipe /ˈstōvˌpīp/ ▶*n.* **1** the pipe taking the smoke and gases from a stove up through a roof or to a chimney. **2** an information conduit that traverses vertical levels effiiciently but does not disperse widely: [as *adj* .] *a computer system that was expected to integrate 40 different stovepipe entities that previously were unable to communicate with one another.*
▶*v.* [*trans.*] transmit (information) directly through levels of a hierarchy: *neocons who stovepiped lies straight up to the White House.*

stove·pipe hat ▶*n.* a silk hat resembling a top hat but much taller.

stove·top /ˈstōvˌtäp/ ▶*n.* the upper surface of a cooking stove, including the burners.
▶*adj.* of or related to a stovetop: *healthy, no-oil stovetop grill pan.* ■ designed to be prepared on a stovetop, rather than in an oven: *beef noodle stovetop casserole.*

stow /stō/ ▶*v.* [*trans.*] pack or store (an object) carefully and neatly in a particular place: *the bathhouse offers baskets in which to stow your clothes | she* **stowed** *the map* **away** *in the glove compartment.*
▶*phrasal v.* □ **stow away** conceal oneself on a ship, aircraft, or other passenger vehicle in order to travel secretly or without paying the fare: *he stowed away on a ship bound for South Africa.* ▷late Middle English: shortening of **BESTOW**.
▶*PHRASE* □ **stow it!** *informal* used as a way of urging someone to be quiet or to stop doing something.

stow·age /ˈstōij/ ▶*n.* the action or manner of stowing something. ■ space for stowing something in: *there is plenty of stowage beneath the berth.*

stow·a·way /ˈstōəˌwā/ ▶*n.* a person who stows away.

Stowe[1] /stō/ a town in north central Vermont, a noted skiing and resort center; pop. 3,433.

Stowe[2], Harriet (Elizabeth) Beecher (1811–96), U.S. novelist. She won fame with her novel *Uncle Tom's Cabin* (1852), which strengthened the contemporary abolitionist cause with its descriptions of the sufferings caused by slavery. She was the sister of Catharine Beecher and Henry Ward Beecher.

STP ▶*abbr.* ■ *Physiology* short-term potentiation. ■ *Chemistry* standard temperature and pressure. ■ Professor of Sacred Theology. [from Latin *Sanctae Theologiae Professor.*]

St. Paul /ˌsānt ˈpôl/ the capital of Minnesota, on the Mississippi River adjacent to Minneapolis with which it forms the Twin Cities metropolitan area; pop. 287,151. First settled in 1838, it prospered as a trading center and became the state capital in 1858.

St. Paul's Ca·the·dral a cathedral on Ludgate Hill, London, designed by Sir Christopher Wren and built between 1675 and 1711.

St. Paul's Cathedral

St. Pe·ters /ˈpētərz/ a city in eastern Missouri, northwest of St. Louis; pop. 51,381.

St. Pe·ter's Ba·sil·i·ca a Roman Catholic basilica in the Vatican City. Built in the 16th century on the site of a structure erected by Constantine on the supposed site of St. Peter's crucifixion, it is the largest Christian church.

St. Pe·ters·burg /ˈpētərzˌbərg/ **1** a city and seaport in northwestern Russia, located on the delta of the Neva River, on the eastern shores of the Gulf of Finland; pop. 5,035,000. Founded in 1703 by Peter the Great, St. Petersburg was the capital of Russia from 1712 until the Russian Revolution. During World War II, it was held under siege by the Germans and Finns 1941–44. Former names **PETROGRAD** (1914–24) and **LENINGRAD** (1924–91). **2** a resort city in western Florida, on the Gulf of Mexico; pop. 248,232.

St. Pierre and Miq·ue·lon /sānt ˈpi(ə)r and ˈmikəˌlän; saN ˈpyer ā mekˈlôN/ a group of eight small islands in the North Atlantic Ocean, off the southern coast of Newfoundland; pop. 6,390. An overseas territory of France, the islands are the last remaining French possession in North America.

STR ▶*abbr.* synchronous transmitter receiver.

str. ▶*abbr.* strait. ■ *Rowing* stroke.

stra·bis·mus /strəˈbizməs/ ▶*n.* abnormal alignment of the eyes; the condition of having a squint. ▷late 17th cent.: modern Latin, from Greek *strabismos*, from *strabizein* 'to squint,' from *strabos* 'squinting.' **—stra·bis·mic** /-mik/ *adj.*

Stra·bo /ˈstrābō/ (*c.*63 BC–*c.*AD 23), historian and geographer. His only extant work, *Geographica*, in 17 volumes, provides a detailed physical and historical geography of the ancient world during the reign of Augustus.

strac·cia·tel·la /ˌsträcHēəˈtelə/ ▶*n.* an Italian soup containing eggs and cheese. ▷Italian.

Stra·chey /ˈsträcHē/, (Giles) Lytton (1880–1932), English biographer. A prominent member of the Bloomsbury Group, he achieved recognition with *Eminent Victorians* (1918).

Strad /strad/ ▶*n. informal* a Stradivarius. ▷late 19th cent.: abbreviation.

strad·dle /ˈstradl/ ▶*v.* [*trans.*] sit or stand with one leg on either side of: *he turned the chair around and straddled it.* ■ place (one's legs) wide apart: *he shifted his legs, straddling them to keep his balance.* ■ [*intrans.*] *archaic* stand, walk, or sit with one's legs wide apart. ■ extend across or be situated on both sides of: *a mountain range straddling the Franco-Swiss border.* ■ take up or maintain an equivocal position with regard to (a political issue): *a man who had straddled the issue of taxes.*
▶*n.* **1** an act of sitting or standing with one's legs wide apart. **2** *Stock Market* a simultaneous purchase of options to buy and to sell a security or commodity at a fixed price, allowing the purchaser to make a profit whether the price of the security or commodity goes up or down. ▷mid 16th cent.: alteration of dialect *striddle*, back-formation from dialect *striddling* 'astride,' from **STRIDE** + the adverbial suffix *-ling*. **—strad·dler** *n.*

Stra·di·va·ri /ˌsträdəˈvärē; ˌstradəˈverē/, Antonio (*c.*1644–1737), Italian violin-maker. He devised the proportions of the modern violin, giving a more powerful and rounded sound than earlier instruments possessed. About 650 of his celebrated violins, violas, and violoncellos are still in existence.

Strad·i·var·i·us /ˌstradəˈve(ə)rēəs/ ▶*n.* a violin or other stringed instrument made by Antonio Stradivari or his followers. ▷mid 19th cent.: Latinized form of **STRADIVARI**.

strafe /strāf/ ▶*v.* [*trans.*] attack repeatedly with bombs or machine-gun fire from low-flying aircraft: *military aircraft strafed the village.*
▶*n.* an attack from low-flying aircraft. ▷early 20th cent.: humorous adaptation of the German World War I catchphrase *Gott strafe England* 'may God punish England.'

strag·gle /ˈstragəl/ ▶*v.* [*intrans.*] move along slowly, typically in a small irregular group, so as to remain some distance behind the person or people in front: *half the men were already straggling back into the building* | [as *adj.*] (**straggling**) *the straggling crowd of refugees.* ■ grow, spread, or be laid out in an irregular, untidy way: *her hair was straggling over her eyes.*
▶*n.* an untidy or irregularly arranged mass or group of something: *a straggle of cottages.* ▷late Middle English: perhaps from dialect *strake* 'go.' **—strag·gler** /ˈstrag(ə)lər/ *n.* **—strag·gly** /ˈstrag(ə)lē/ *adj.*

straight /strāt/ ▶*adj.* **1** extending or moving uniformly in one direction only; without a curve or bend: *a long, straight road.* ■ *Geometry* (of a line) lying on the shortest path between any two of its points. ■ (of an aim, blow, or course) going direct to the intended target: *a straight punch to the face.* ■ (of hair) not curly or wavy. ■ (of a garment) not flared or fitted closely to the body: *a straight skirt.* ■ (of an arch) flat-topped. **2** properly positioned so as to be level, upright, or symmetrical: *he made sure his tie was straight.* ■ [*predic.*] in proper order or condition: *it'll* *take a long time to get the place straight.* **3** not evasive; honest: *a straight answer | thank you for being straight with me.* ■ simple; straightforward: *a straight choice between nuclear power and penury.* ■ (of a look) bold and steady: *he gave her a straight, no-nonsense look.* ■ (of thinking) clear, logical, and unemotional. ■ not addicted to drugs. **4** [*attrib.*] in continuous succession: *he scored his fourth straight win.* ■ supporting all the principles and candidates of one political party: *he generally voted a* **straight ticket**. **5** (of an alcoholic drink) undiluted; neat: *straight brandy.* **6** (esp. of drama) serious as opposed to comic or musical; employing the conventional techniques of its art form: *a straight play.* ■ *informal* (of a person) conventional or respectable: *she looked pretty straight in her school clothes.* ■ *informal* heterosexual.

▸*adv.* **1** in a straight line; directly: *he was gazing straight at her | keep* **straight on**. ■ with no delay or diversion; directly or immediately: *after dinner we went straight back to our hotel | I fell into bed and went straight to sleep.* ■ *archaic* at once; immediately: *I'll fetch up the bath to you straight.* **2** in or into a level, even, or upright position: *he pulled his clothes straight | sit up straight!* **3** correctly; clearly: *I'm so tired I can hardly think straight.* ■ honestly and directly; in a straightforward manner: *I told her straight—the kid's right.* **4** without a break; continuously: *he remembered working sixteen hours straight.*

▸*n.* **1** a part of something that is not curved or bent, esp. the concluding stretch of a racetrack: *he pulled away in the straight to win by half a second.* ■ *archaic* a form or position that is not curved or bent: *the rod flew back to the straight.* **2** *Poker* a continuous sequence of five cards. **3** *informal* a conventional person. ■ a heterosexual. ▷Middle English (as an adjective and adverb): archaic past participle of STRETCH. **—straight·ish** *adj.* **—straight·ly** *adv.* **—straight·ness** *n.*

▸*PHRASES* □ **get something straight** make a situation clear, esp. by reaching an understanding. □ **go straight** live an honest life after being a criminal. □ **a straight face** a blank or serious facial expression, esp. when trying not to laugh: *my father* **kept a straight face** *when he joked.* □ **the straight and narrow** the honest and morally acceptable way of living: *he's making a real effort to get back on the straight and narrow.* □ **straight out** (or **off**) *informal* without hesitation or deliberation: *If you're not going to help me, just say so straight out.* □ **straight up** *informal* **1** unmixed; unadulterated: *a dry Martini served straight up.* **2** *Brit.* truthfully; honestly: *come on, Bert, I won't hurt you—straight up.*

straight-a·head ▸*adj.* (esp. of popular music) straightforward, simple, or unadorned.

straight an·gle ▸*n.* *Mathematics* an angle of 180°.

straight-arm ▸*v.* [*trans.*] *informal* ward off (an opponent) or remove (an obstacle) with the arm unflexed: *I straight-armed the woman leaning in on her.*

straight ar·row ▸*n.* *informal* an honest, morally upright person.

straight·a·way /ˈstrātəˌwā/ ▸*adv.* immediately.
▸*adj.* extending or moving in a straight line.
▸*n.* a straight section of a road or racetrack.

straight chain ▸*n.* *Chemistry* a chain of atoms in a molecule, usually carbon atoms, that is neither branched nor formed into a ring.

straight chair ▸*n.* a straight-backed side chair.

straight·edge /ˈstrātˌej/ ▸*n.* a bar with one accurately straight edge, used for testing whether something else is straight.

straight·en /ˈstrātn/ ▸*v.* make or become straight: [*trans.*] *she helped him straighten his tie* | [*intrans.*] *where the river straightened he took his chance to check the barometer.* ■ [*trans.*] make tidy or put in order again: *he sat down at his desk, straightening his things that Lee had moved | they are asking for help in* **straightening out** *their lives.* ■ [*intrans.*] stand or sit erect after bending: *he* **straightened up**, *using the bedside table for support.* ■ [*intrans.*] (**straighten up**) (of a vehicle, ship, or aircraft) stop turning and move in a straight line. **—straight·en·er** *n.*

straight-faced ▸*adj.* with a blank or serious facial expression.

straight flush ▸*n.* (in poker or brag) a hand of cards all of one suit and in a continuous sequence (for example, the seven, eight, nine, ten, and jack of spades).

straight·for·ward /ˌstrātˈfôrwərd/ ▸*adj.* uncomplicated and easy to do or understand: *in a straightforward case no fees will be charged.* ■ (of a person) honest and frank: *a straightforward young man.* **—straight·for·ward·ly** *adv.* **—straight·for·ward·ness** *n.*

straight·jack·et ▸*n.* & *v.* variant spelling of STRAITJACKET.

straight-laced ▸*adj.* variant spelling of STRAIT-LACED.

straight-line ▸*adj.* containing, characterized by, or relating to straight lines or motion in a straight line: *a straight-line graph | the Porsche's straight-line stability.* ■ *Finance* of or relating to a method of depreciation allocating a given percentage of the cost of an asset each year for a fixed period.

straight man ▸*n.* the person in a comedy duo who speaks lines that give a comedian the opportunity to make jokes.

straight pool ▸*n.* a form of pool in which the players specify the ball they plan to pocket and which pocket the ball will drop into before taking a shot.

straight ra·zor ▸*n.* a razor having a long blade set in a handle, usually folding like a penknife.

straight shoot·er ▸*n.* *informal* an honest and forthright person. **—straight-shoot·ing** *adj.*

straight-six ▸*n.* an internal combustion engine with six cylinders in line. ■ a vehicle with an engine of this type.

straight stitch ▸*n.* a single, short, separate embroidery stitch.

straight time ▸*n.* normal working hours, paid at a regular rate.

straight-up ▸*adj.* *informal* honest; trustworthy: *you sounded like a straight-up guy.*

straight·way /ˈstrātˌwā/ ▸*adv.* archaic form of STRAIGHTAWAY.

strain[1] /strān/ ▸*v.* **1** [*trans.*] force (a part of one's body or oneself) to make a strenuous or unusually great effort: *I stopped and listened, straining my ears for any sound.* ■ injure (a limb, muscle, or organ) by overexerting it or twisting it awkwardly: *on cold days you are more likely to strain a muscle | glare from the screen can strain your eyes.* ■ [*intrans.*] make a strenuous and continuous effort: *his voice was so quiet that I had to strain to hear it.* ■ make severe or excessive demands on: *he strained her tolerance to the limit.* ■ [*intrans.*] pull or push forcibly at something: *the bear* **strained at** *the chain around its neck | his stomach was swollen,* **straining against** *the thin shirt.* ■ stretch (something) tightly: *the barbed wire fence was strained to posts six feet high.* ■ *archaic* embrace (someone) tightly: *she strained the infant to her bosom again.* **2** [*trans.*] pour (a mainly liquid substance) through a porous or perforated device or material in order to separate out any solid matter: *strain the custard into a bowl.* ■ cause liquid to drain off (food that has been boiled, soaked, or canned) by using such a device. ■ drain off (liquid) in this way: **strain off** *the surplus fat.*

▸*n.* **1** a force tending to pull or stretch something to an extreme or damaging degree: *the usual type of chair puts an enormous strain on the spine | aluminum may bend under strain.* ■ *Physics* the magnitude of a deformation, equal to the change in the dimension of a deformed object divided by its original dimension. ■ an injury to a part of the body caused by overexertion or twisting a muscle awkwardly: *he has a slight groin strain.* **2** a severe or excessive demand on the strength, resources, or abilities of someone or something: *the accusations* **put a strain on** *relations between the two countries | she's obviously* **under** *considerable* **strain**. ■ a state of tension or exhaustion resulting from this: *the telltale signs of nervous strain.* **3** (usu. **strains**) the sound of a piece of music as it is played or performed: *through the open windows came the strains of a hurdy-gurdy playing in the street.* ▷Middle English (as a verb): from Old French *estreindre*, from Latin *stringere* 'draw tight.' Current senses of the noun arose in the mid 16th cent. **—strain·a·ble** *adj.*

▸*PHRASES* □ **at** (**full**) **strain** *archaic* using the utmost effort. □ **strain every nerve** see NERVE. □ **strain at the leash** see LEASH.

strain[2] ▸*n.* **1** a breed, stock, or variety of an animal or plant developed by breeding. ■ a natural or cultured variety of a microorganism with a distinct form, biochemistry, or virulence. **2** a particular tendency as part of a person's character: *there was a powerful strain of insanity on her mother's side of the family.* ■ a variety of a particular abstract thing: *a strain of feminist thought.* ▷Old English *strīon* 'acquisition, gain,' of Germanic origin; related to Latin *struere* 'to build up.'

strained /strānd/ ▸*adj.* **1** (of an atmosphere, situation, or relationship) not relaxed or comfortable; tense or uneasy: *there was a strained silence | relations between the two countries were strained.* ■ (of a person) showing signs of tiredness or nervous tension: *Jean's pale, strained face.* ■ (of an appearance or performance) produced by deliberate effort rather than natural impulse; artificial or forced: *I put on my strained smile for the next customer.* ■ (of a statement or representation) labored or far-fetched: *my example may seem a little strained and artificial.* **2** (of a limb or muscle) injured by overexertion or twisting. **3** (of a mainly liquid substance) having been strained to separate out any solid matter.

strain en·er·gy ▸*n.* *Mechanics* energy stored in an elastic body under loading.

strain·er /ˈstrānər/ ▸*n.* a device having holes punched in it or made of crossed wires for separating solid matter from a liquid: *a tea strainer.*

strain gauge ▸*n.* a device for indicating the strain of a material or structure at the point of attachment.

strait /strāt/ ▸*n.* **1** (also **straits**) a narrow passage of water connecting two seas or two large areas of water: [in *place names*] *the Strait of Gibraltar.* **2** (**straits**) used in reference to a situation characterized by a specified degree of trouble or difficulty: *the economy is* **in dire straits** *| a crippling disease could leave anyone in serious financial straits.*

▸*adj.* *archaic* (of a place) of limited spatial capacity; narrow or cramped: *the road was so strait that a handful of men might have defended it.* ■ close, strict, or rigorous: *my captivity was strait as ever.* ▷Middle English: shortening of Old French *estreit* 'tight, narrow,' from Latin *strictus* 'drawn tight' (see STRICT). **—strait·ly** *adv.* **—strait·ness** *n.*

strait·en /ˈstrātn/ ▸*v.* *archaic* make or become narrow: [*trans.*] *the passage was straitened by tables.*

strait·ened /ˈstrātnd/ ▸*adj.* **1** characterized by poverty: *they lived in straitened circumstances.* **2** restricted in range or scope: *their straitened horizons.*

strait·jack·et /ˈstrātˌjakət/ (also **straight·jack·et**) ▸*n.* a strong garment with long sleeves that can be tied together to confine the arms of a violent prisoner or mental patient. ■ used in reference to something that restricts freedom of action, development, or expression: *the government is operating in an economic straitjacket.*

▸*v.* (**-jack·eted**, **-jack·eting**) [*trans.*] restrain with a straitjacket. ■ impose severely restrictive measures on (a person or activity): *the treaty should not be used as a tool to straitjacket international trade.*

strait-laced (also **straight-laced**) ▸*adj.* having or showing very strict moral attitudes.

strake /strāk/ ▸*n.* **1** a continuous line of planking or plates from the stem to the stern of a ship or boat. **2** a protruding ridge fitted to an aircraft or other structure to improve aerodynamic stability. ▷Middle English: from Anglo-Latin *stracus, straca*; probably from the Germanic base of the verb STRETCH.

stra·mo·ni·um /strəˈmōnēəm/ ▸*n.* a preparation of the dried leaves or poisonous seeds of the jimson weed, with medical and other uses. ▷mid 17th cent.: modern Latin (part of the plant's binomial), perhaps an alteration of Tartar *turman* 'horse medicine.'

strand[1] /strand/ ▸*v.* [*trans.*] drive or leave (a boat, sailor, or sea creature) aground on a shore: *the ships were stranded in shallow water*| [as *adj.*] (**stranded**) *a stranded whale.* ■ leave (someone) without the means to move from somewhere: *they were stranded in St. Louis by the blizzard.*

▸*n.* *poetic/literary* the shore of a sea, lake, or large river: *a heron glided to rest on a pebbly strand.* ▷Old English (as a noun), of unknown origin. The verb dates from the early 17th cent.

strand[2] ▸*n.* a single thin length of something such as thread, fiber, or wire, esp. as twisted together with others: *a strand of cotton | strands of grass.* ■ a string of beads or pearls. ■ an element that forms part of a complex whole: *Marxist theories evolved from different strands of social analysis.* ▷late 15th cent.: of unknown origin.

strand·ed /ˈstrandid/ ▸*adj.* [*attrib.*] (of thread, rope, or similar) arranged in single thin lengths twisted together: *stranded cotton* | [in *combination*] *figurative the many-stranded passions of the country.*

strand·wolf /ˈstrandˌwo͝olf/ ▸*n.* *S. African* the brown hyena, which often frequents the shore, where it scavenges dead fish and birds. • *Hyaena brunnea*, family Hyaenidae. ▷late 18th cent.: from South African Dutch, from *strand* 'beach' + *wolf* 'wolf.'

strange /strānj/ ▸*adj.* **1** unusual or surprising in a way that is unsettling or hard to understand: *children have some strange ideas | he's a very strange man* | [with *clause*]

Pronunciation Key ə ago; ər over; ˈə or ˌə up; ˈər or ˌər fur; a hat; ā rate; ä car; CH chew; e let; ē see; e(ə)r air; i fit; ī by; i(ə)r ear; NG sing; ō go; ô for; oi boy; o͝o good; o͞o goo; ou out; SH she; TH thin; TH then; (h)w why; ZH vision

it is strange how things change. **2** not previously visited, seen, or encountered; unfamiliar or alien: *she found herself in bed in a strange place | a harsh accent that was* **strange to** *his ears.* ■ [*predic.*] (**strange to/at/in**) *archaic* unaccustomed to or unfamiliar with: *I am strange to the work.* **3** *Physics* having a nonzero value for strangeness. ▷Middle English: shortening of Old French *estrange*, from Latin *extraneus* 'external, strange.' **—strange·ly** *adv.* [as *submodifier*] *the house was strangely quiet* | [*sentence adverb*] **strangely enough,** *people were able to perform this task without difficulty.*

▸*PHRASES* □ **feel strange** (of a person or part of the body) feel unwell; have unpleasant sensations: *her head still felt strange.* ■ be uncomfortable or ill at ease in a situation: *the family had expected to feel strange in Stephen's company.* □ **strange to say** (or *poetic/literary* **tell**) it is surprising or unusual that: *strange to say, I didn't really like carol singers.*

strange at·trac·tor ▸*n.* *Mathematics* an equation or fractal set representing a complex pattern of behavior in a chaotic system.

strange·ness /'strānjnis/ ▸*n.* **1** the state or fact of being strange. **2** *Physics* one of six flavors of quark.

strange par·ti·cle ▸*n.* *Physics* a subatomic particle classified as having a nonzero value for strangeness.

stran·ger /'strānjər/ ▸*n.* a person whom one does not know or with whom one is not familiar: *don't talk to strangers| she remained* **a stranger to** *him.* ■ a person who does not know, or is not known in, a particular place or community: *I'm a* **stranger in** *these parts | he must have been a* **stranger to** *the village.* ■ (**stranger to**) a person entirely unaccustomed to (a feeling, experience, or situation): *he* **is no stranger to** *controversy.* ▷late Middle English: shortening of Old French *estrangier*, from Latin *extraneus* (see STRANGE).

▸*PHRASE* □ **hello, stranger!** *humorous* used to greet someone whom one has not seen for some time.

stran·gle /'straNGgəl/ ▸*v.* [*trans.*] squeeze or constrict the neck of (a person or animal), esp. so as to cause death: *the victim was strangled with a scarf.* ■ [as *adj.*] (**strangled**) sounding as though the speaker's throat is constricted: *a series of strangled gasps.* ■ suppress (an impulse, action, or sound): *she strangled a sob.* ■ hamper or hinder the development or activity of: *overrestrictive policies that strangle growth.* ▷Middle English: shortening of Old French *estrangler*, from Latin *strangulare*, from Greek *strangalan*, from *strangalē* 'halter,' related to *strangos* 'twisted.' **—stran·gler** /'straNGg(ə)lər/ *n.*

stran·gle·hold /'straNGgəl,hōld/ ▸*n.* [in *sing.*] a grip around the neck of another person that can kill by asphyxiation if held for long enough. ■ complete or overwhelming control: *he broke the union that held a* **stranglehold on** *bus service.*

stran·gles /'straNGgəlz/ ▸*plural n.* [usu. treated as *sing.*] a bacterial infection of the upper respiratory tract of horses, causing enlargement of the lymph nodes in the throat, which may impair breathing. • This disease is caused by the bacterium *Streptococcus equi.* ▷early 17th cent.: plural of obsolete *strangle* 'strangulation,' from STRANGLE.

stran·gu·late /'straNGgyə,lāt/ ▸*v.* [*trans.*] [often as *adj.*] (**strangulated**) **1** *Medicine* prevent circulation of the blood supply through (a part of the body, esp. a hernia) by constriction: *a strangulated hernia.* **2** *informal* strangle; throttle: *the poor woman died strangulated.* ■ [as *adj.*] (**strangulated**) sounding as though the speaker's throat is constricted: *a strangulated cry.* ▷mid 17th cent. (in the sense 'suffocate'): from Latin *strangulat-* 'choked,' from the verb *strangulare* (see STRANGLE).

stran·gu·la·tion /,straNGgyə'lāSHən/ ▸*n.* **1** the action or state of strangling or being strangled: *death due to strangulation.* ■ the process or state of severely restricting the activities or supplies of an area or community or of undergoing such restrictions: *economic strangulation.* **2** *Medicine* the condition in which circulation of blood to a part of the body (esp. a hernia) is cut off by constriction.

stran·gu·ry /'straNGgyərē/ ▸*n.* a condition caused by blockage or irritation at the base of the bladder, resulting in severe pain and a strong desire to urinate. ▷late Middle English: via Latin from Greek *strangouria*, from *stranx, strang-* 'drop squeezed out' + *ouron* 'urine.' **—stran·gu·ri·ous** /-'gyo͝orēəs/ *adj.*

strap /strap/ ▸*n.* a strip of leather, cloth, or other flexible material, often with a buckle, used to fasten, secure, or carry something or to hold on to something: *her bra strap | the strap of his shoulder bag.* ■ a strip of metal, often hinged, used to fasten or secure something. ■ (**the strap**) punishment by beating with a strip of leather. ■ variant form of STROP.

▸*v.* (**strapped, strap·ping**) **1** [*trans.*] fasten or secure in a specified place or position with a strap or seat belt: *I had to strap the bag to my bicycle | the children were strapped into their car seats.* **2** [*trans.*] beat (someone) with a strip of leather: *I expected when my dad walked in that he'd strap him.* ▷late 16th cent. (denoting a trap for birds, also a piece of timber fastening two objects together): dialect form of STROP.

strap·hang·er /'strap,haNGər/ ▸*n.* *informal* a standing passenger in a bus or train. ■ a person who commutes to work by public transportation. **—strap·hang** *v.*

strap hinge ▸*n.* a hinge with long leaves or flaps for screwing onto the surface of a door or gate.

strap·less /'strapləs/ ▸*adj.* (esp. of a dress or bra) without shoulder straps.

strap-on ▸*adj.* able to be attached by a strap or straps.

strap·pa·do /strə'pādō; -'pä-/ ▸*n.* (*pl.* **-dos**) (usu. **the strappado**) *historical* a form of punishment or torture in which the victim was secured to a rope and made to fall from a height almost to the ground before being stopped with an abrupt jerk. ■ the instrument used for inflicting this punishment or torture. ▷mid 16th cent.: from French *(e)strapade*, from Italian *strappata*, from *strappare* 'to snatch.'

strapped /strapt/ ▸*adj.* *informal* short of money: *I'm constantly* **strapped for cash.**

strap·ping[1] /'strapiNG/ ▸*adj.* (esp. of a young person) big and strong: *they had three strapping sons.*

strap·ping[2] ▸*n.* **1** adhesive plaster for binding injured parts of the body. **2** strips of leather or pliable metal used to hold, strengthen, or fasten something.

strap·py /'strapē/ ▸*adj.* (of shoes or clothes) having eye-catching straps: *white strappy sandals.*

Stras·berg /'stras,bərg; 'sträs-/, Lee (1901–82), U.S. actor, director, and drama teacher, born in Austria; born *Israel Strassberg.* As artistic director of the Actors' Studio in New York City (1948–82), he was the leading figure in the development of method acting in the U.S.

Stras·bourg /'sträs,bo͝org; 'sträz-; -,bərg/ a city in northeastern France, in Alsace, close to the border with Germany; pop. 256,000. It is the headquarters of the Council of Europe and of the European Parliament.

stra·ta /'strātə; 'strätə/ ▸ plural form of STRATUM.

strat·a·gem /'stratəjəm/ ▸*n.* a plan or scheme, esp. one used to outwit an opponent or achieve an end: *a series of devious stratagems.* ■ *archaic* skill in devising such plans or schemes; cunning. ▷late 15th cent. (originally denoting a military ploy): from French *stratagème*, via Latin from Greek *stratēgēma*, from *stratēgein* 'be a general,' from *stratēgos*, from *stratos* 'army' + *agein* 'to lead.'

stra·tal /'strātl/ ▸*adj.* relating or belonging to strata or a stratum.

stra·te·gic /strə'tējik/ ▸*adj.* relating to the identification of long-term or overall aims and interests and the means of achieving them: *the company should take strategic actions to cope with fundamental changes in the environment | strategic planning for the organization is the responsibility of top management.* ■ carefully designed or planned to serve a particular purpose or advantage: *alarms are positioned at strategic points around the prison.* ■ relating to the gaining of overall or long-term military advantage: *New Orleans was of strategic importance | a hazard to British strategic and commercial interests.* ■ (of human or material resources) essential in fighting a war: *the strategic forces on Russian territory.* ■ (of bombing or weapons) done or for use against industrial areas and communication centers of enemy territory as a long-term military objective: *strategic nuclear missiles.* Often contrasted with TACTICAL. ▷early 19th cent.: from French *stratégique*, from Greek *stratēgikos*, from *stratēgos* (see STRATAGEM). **—stra·te·gi·cal** *adj.* **—stra·te·gi·cal·ly** /-ik(ə)lē/ *adv.* [as *submodifier*] *a strategically placed mirror.*

Stra·te·gic Arms Lim·i·ta·tion Talks (abbr. **SALT**) a series of negotiations between the U.S. and the Soviet Union aimed at the limitation or reduction of nuclear armaments, which produced the Strategic Arms Limitation Treaty. The talks were organized from 1968 onward and held in stages until superseded by the START negotiations in 1983.

Stra·te·gic Arms Re·duc·tion Talks (abbr.: **START**) a series of arms-reduction negotiations between the U.S. and the Soviet Union begun in 1983. The Intermediate Nuclear Forces (INF) treaty was signed in 1987 and the Strategic Arms Reduction Treaty in 1991.

strat·e·gist /'stratəjist/ ▸*n.* a person skilled in planning action or policy, esp. in war or politics.

strat·e·gize /'stratə,jiz/ ▸*v.* [*intrans.*] devise a strategy or strategies.

strat·e·gy /'stratəjē/ ▸*n.* (*pl.* **-gies**) a plan of action or policy designed to achieve a major or overall aim: *time to develop a coherent economic strategy | shifts in marketing strategy.* ■ the art of planning and directing overall military operations and movements in a war or battle. Often contrasted with TACTICS (see TACTIC). ■ a plan for such military operations and movements: *nonprovocative defense strategies.* ▷early 19th cent.: from French *stratégie*, from Greek *stratēgia* 'generalship,' from *stratēgos* (see STRATAGEM).

Strat·ford /'stratfərd/ **1** an industrial town in southwestern Connecticut, east of Bridgeport, former home to the American Shakespeare Festival; pop. 49,389. **2** a city in southern Ontario in Canada, on the Avon River, noted for its summer Shakespeare Festival; pop. 27,666.

Strat·ford-up·on-A·von /'stratfərd ə,pän 'āvən; ə,pôn; 'ā,vän/ a town in central England, on the Avon River; pop. 20,000. Noted as the birth and burial place of William Shakespeare, it is the site of the Royal Shakespeare Theatre. **—Strat·for·di·an** /strat'fôrdēən/ *n.*

strath /straTH/ ▸*n.* *Scottish* a broad mountain valley. ▷mid 16th cent.: from Scottish Gaelic *srath.*

strath·spey /straTH'spā/ ▸*n.* a slow Scottish dance. ■ a piece of music for such a dance, typically in four-four time. ▷mid 18th cent.: from *Strathspey*, the name of the valley of the Spey River in Scotland.

strat·i·fied sam·ple /'stratə,fīd/ ▸*n.* *Statistics* a sample that is drawn from a number of separate strata of the population, rather than at random from the whole population, in order that it should be representative.

strat·i·form /'stratə,fôrm/ ▸*adj.* *technical* arranged in layers: *stratiform clouds.* ■ *Geology* (of a mineral deposit) formed parallel to the bedding planes of the surrounding rock.

strat·i·fy /'stratə,fī/ ▸*v.* (**-fies, -fied**) [*trans.*] [usu. as *adj.*] (**stratified**) form or arrange into strata: *socially stratified cities* | [*intrans.*] *the residues have begun to stratify.* ■ arrange or classify: *stratifying patients into well-defined risk groups.* ■ place (seeds) close together in layers in moist sand or peat to preserve them or to help them germinate. ■ [*intrans.*] (of seeds) be germinated by this method. **—strat·i·fi·ca·tion** /,stratəfi'kāSHən/ *n.*

stra·tig·ra·phy /strə'tigrəfē/ ▸*n.* the branch of geology concerned with the order and relative position of strata and their relationship to the geological time scale. ■ the analysis of the order and position of layers of archaeological remains. ■ the structure of a particular set of strata. ▷mid 19th cent.: from STRATUM + -GRAPHY. **—stra·tig·ra·pher** /-fər/ *n.* **—strat·i·graph·ic** /,stratə'grafik/ *adj.* **—strat·i·graph·i·cal** /,stratə'grafikəl/ *adj.*

stra·toc·ra·cy /strə'täkrəsē/ ▸*n.* (*pl.* **-cies**) *rare* government by military forces. ■ a military government.

stra·to·cu·mu·lus /,stratō'kyo͞omyələs; ,strā-/ ▸*n.* cloud forming a low layer of clumped or broken gray masses.

stra·to·pause /'stratə,pôz/ ▸*n.* the interface between the stratosphere and the ionosphere. ▷1950s: from STRATOSPHERE, suggested by TROPOPAUSE.

strat·o·sphere /'stratə,sfi(ə)r/ ▸*n.* the layer of the earth's atmosphere above the troposphere, extending to about 50 km above the earth's surface (the lower boundary of the mesosphere). ■ *figurative* the very highest levels of a profession or other sphere, or of prices or other quantities: *her next big campaign launched her into the fashion stratosphere.* **—strat·o·spher·ic** /,stratə'sfi(ə)rik; -'sferik/ *adj.*

strat·o·vol·ca·no /,stratōväl'kānō; ,strä-/ ▸*n.* (*pl.* **-noes**) a volcano built up of alternate layers of lava and ash.

Strat·ton /'stratn/, Charles S. see THUMB.

stra·tum /'strātəm; 'stra-/ ▸*n.* (*pl.* **stra·ta** /'strātə; 'stra-/) **1** a layer or a series of layers of rock in the ground: *a stratum of flint.* ■ a thin layer within any structure: *thin strata of air.* **2** a level or class to which people are assigned according to their social status, education, or income: *members of other social strata.* ■ *Statistics* a group into which members of a population are divided in stratified sampling. ▷late 16th cent. (in the sense 'layer or coat of a substance'): modern Latin, from Latin, literally 'something spread or laid down,' neuter past participle of *sternere* 'strew.'

S

USAGE In Latin, the word **stratum** is singular and its plural form is **strata**. In English, this distinction is maintained. It is therefore incorrect to use **strata** as a singular or to create the form **stratas** as the plural: *a series of overlying* **strata** (not *a series of overlying* **stratas**); *a new* **stratum** *was uncovered* (not *a new* **strata** *was uncovered*).

stra·tum cor·ne·um /ˈstrātəm ˌkôrnēəm; ˈstra-/ ▸*n.* *Anatomy* the horny outer layer of the skin. ▷Latin, literally 'horny layer.'

stra·tus /ˈstrātəs; ˈstra-/ ▸*n.* cloud forming a continuous horizontal gray sheet, often with rain or snow. ▷early 19th cent.: modern Latin, from Latin, literally 'strewn,' past participle of *sternere*.

Strauss[1] /strous; SHtrous/ the name of two Austrian composers: ■ **Johann** (1804–49), a leading composer of waltzes; known as **Strauss the Elder**. His best-known work is the *Radetzky March* (1838). ■ **Johann** (1825–99), son of Strauss the Elder; known as **Strauss the Younger** and as the **waltz king**. He composed many famous waltzes, such as *The Blue Danube* (1867) and *Tales from the Vienna Woods* (1868). He is also noted for the operetta *Die Fledermaus* (1874).

Strauss[2], Levi (c.1829–1902), U.S. manufacturer; born in Germany. He established Levi Strauss & Company in 1850 to sell pants made of tent canvas to gold miners. He eventually switched to denim cloth and made the work pants that became known as blue jeans or "Levi's."

Strauss[3], Richard (1864–1949), German composer. With librettist Hugo von Hofmannsthal he produced operas such as *Der Rosenkavalier* (1911). He is often regarded as the last of the 19th-century romantic composers.

Stra·vin·sky /strəˈvinskē/, Igor (Fyodorovich) (1882–1971), Russian composer, resident of the U.S. from 1939. His ballets *The Firebird* (1910) and *The Rite of Spring* (1913) shocked Paris audiences with their irregular rhythms and frequent dissonances. He later developed a neoclassical style typified by the opera *The Rake's Progress* (1948–51) and experimented with serialism in *Threni*.

straw /strô/ ▸*n.* **1** dried stalks of grain, used esp. as fodder or as material for thatching, packing, or weaving: [as *adj.*] *a straw hat.* ■ a pale yellow color like that of straw: [as *adj.*] *a dull straw color.* ■ used in reference to something insubstantial or worthless: *it seemed as if the words were merely straw.* ■ [with *negative*] anything or at all (used to emphasize how little something is valued): *if he finds you here, my life* ***won't be worth a straw.*** **2** a single dried stalk of grain: *the tramp sat chewing a straw.* ■ a stalk of grain or something similar used in drawing lots: *we had to* ***draw straws*** *for the food we had.* **3** a thin hollow tube of paper or plastic for sucking drink from a glass or bottle. ▷Old English *strēaw*, of Germanic origin; related to Dutch *stroo* and German *Stroh*, also to STREW. **—straw·y** *adj.*

▸PHRASES □ **grasp** (or **clutch** or **catch**) **at straws** (or **a straw**) be in such a desperate situation as to resort to even the most unlikely means of salvation. [from the proverb *a drowning man will clutch at a straw.*] □ **draw the short straw** be the unluckiest of a group of people, esp. in being chosen to perform an unpleasant task. □ **the last** (or **final**) **straw** a further difficulty or annoyance, typically minor in itself but coming on top of a whole series of difficulties, that makes a situation unbearable: *his affair was the last straw.* [from the proverb *the last straw breaks the (laden) camel's back.*] □ **a straw in the wind** a slight hint of future developments.

straw·ber·ry /ˈstrôˌberē; -b(ə)rē/ ▸*n.* **1** a sweet soft red fruit with a seed-studded surface. **2** the low-growing plant that produces this fruit, having white flowers, lobed leaves, and runners, and found throughout north temperate regions. • Genus *Fragaria*, family Rosaceae; the commercial strawberry is usually *F.* × *ananassa*. **3** a deep pinkish-red color. ▷Old English *strēa(w)berige*, *strēowberige* (see STRAW, BERRY).

straw·ber·ry blond (also **strawberry blonde**) ▸*adj.* (of hair) of a light reddish-blond color. ■ (of a person) having hair of such a color.
▸*n.* a light reddish-blond hair color. ■ a person who has hair of such a color.

straw·ber·ry mark ▸*n.* a soft red birthmark.

straw·ber·ry roan ▸*adj.* denoting an animal's coat that is chestnut mixed with white or gray.
▸*n.* a strawberry roan animal.

straw·ber·ry tree ▸*n.* a small evergreen European tree of the heath family that bears clusters of whitish flowers late in the year, often at the same time as the strawberrylike fruit from the previous season's flowers. • *Arbutus unedo*, family Ericaceae.

straw·board /ˈstrôˌbôrd/ ▸*n.* board made of straw pulp, used in building (faced with paper) and in book covers.

straw boss ▸*n.* *informal* a junior supervisor, esp. a worker who has some responsibility but little authority.

straw·flow·er /ˈstrôˌflou(-ə)r/ ▸*n.* an everlasting flower of the daisy family. • Several species in the family Compositae, in particular the Australian *Helichrysum bracteatum* and plants of the genus *Helipterum*.

straw man ▸*n.* a person compared to a straw image; a sham. ■ a sham argument set up to be defeated.

straw poll (also **straw vote**) ▸*n.* an unofficial ballot conducted as a test of opinion: *I* ***took a straw poll*** *among my immediate colleagues.*

stray /strā/ ▸*v.* [*intrans.*] move without a specific purpose or by mistake, esp. so as to get lost or arrive somewhere where one should not be: *I strayed a few blocks in the wrong direction | the military arrested anyone who* ***strayed into*** *the exclusion zone.* ■ move so as to escape from control or leave the place where one should be: *dog owners are urged not to allow their dogs to stray | figurative I appear to have strayed a long way from our original topic.* ■ [*intrans.*] (of the eyes or a hand) move idly or casually in a specified direction: *her eyes strayed to the telephone.* ■ (of a person who is married or in a long-term relationship) be unfaithful: *men who stray are seen as more exciting and desirable.* ■ [*intrans.*] *poetic/literary* wander or roam in a specified direction: *over these mounds the Kurdish shepherd strays.*
▸*adj.* [*attrib.*] **1** not in the right place; not where it should be or where other items of the same kind are: *he pushed a few stray hairs from her face.* ■ appearing somewhere by chance or accident; not part of a general pattern or plan: *she was killed by a stray bullet.* ■ (of a domestic animal) having no home or having wandered away from home: *stray dogs.* **2** *Physics* (of a physical quantity) arising as a consequence of the laws of physics, not by deliberate design, and usually having a detrimental effect on the operation or efficiency of equipment: *stray capacitance.*
▸*n.* **1** a stray person or thing, esp. a domestic animal. **2** (**strays**) electrical phenomena interfering with radio reception. ▷Middle English: shortening of Anglo-Norman French and Old French *estrayer* (verb), Anglo-Norman French *strey* (noun), partly from ASTRAY. **—stray·er** *n.*

streak /strēk/ ▸*n.* **1** a long, thin line or mark of a different substance or color from its surroundings: *a streak of oil.* ■ *Microbiology* a narrow line of bacteria smeared on the surface of a solid culture medium. **2** an element of a specified kind in someone's character: *there's a streak of insanity in the family | Lucy had a ruthless streak.* ■ [usu. with *adj.*] a continuous period of specified success or luck: *the theater is* ***on a winning streak*** *| the team closed the season with an 11-game* ***losing streak.***
▸*v.* **1** [*trans.*] cover (a surface) with streaks: *tears streaking her face, Cynthia looked up | his beard was* ***streaked with*** *gray.* ■ dye (hair) with long, thin lines of a different, typically lighter color than one's natural hair color: [*trans.*] *hair that was* ***streaked blond.*** ■ *Microbiology* smear (a needle, swab, etc.) over the surface of a solid culture medium to initiate a culture. **2** [*intrans.*] move very fast in a specified direction: *the cat leaped free and streaked across the street.* **3** [*intrans.*] *informal* run naked in a public place so as to shock or amuse others. ▷Old English *strica*, of Germanic origin; related to Dutch *streek* and German *Strich*, also to STRIKE. The sense 'run naked' originated in the U.S. in the 1970s. **—streak·er** *n.* (in sense 3 of the *verb*).
▸PHRASES □ **like a streak** *informal* very fast: *he is off like a streak.* □ **streak of lightning** a flash of lightning.

streak·ing /ˈstrēkiNG/ ▸*n.* long, thin lines of a different color from their surroundings, esp. on dyed hair.

streak·y /ˈstrēkē/ ▸*adj.* (**streak·i·er**, **streak·i·est**) having streaks of different colors or textures: *streaky blond hair.* ■ *informal* variable in quality; not predictable or reliable: *King has always been a famously streaky hitter.* **—streak·i·ly** /-lē/ *adv.* **—streak·i·ness** *n.*

stream /strēm/ ▸*n.* **1** a small, narrow river. **2** a continuous flow of liquid, air, or gas: *Frank blew out* ***a stream of*** *smoke | the blood gushed out in scarlet streams.* ■ a current within a larger body of water or in the ocean. ■ (**a stream/streams of**) a mass of people or things moving continuously in the same direction: *there is a steady stream of visitors.* ■ (**a stream/streams of**) a large number of things that happen or come one after the other: *a woman shouted a stream of abuse.* ■ *Computing* a continuous flow of data or instructions, typically one having a constant or predictable rate. **3** British term for TRACK *noun* sense 5.
▸*v.* **1** [*intrans.*] (of liquid) run or flow in a continuous current in a specified direction: *she sat with tears* ***streaming down*** *her face | figurative sunlight* ***streamed through*** *the windows.* ■ (of a mass of people or things) move in a continuous flow in a specified direction: *he was watching the taxis* ***streaming past.*** **2** [*intrans.*] (usu. **be streaming**) (of a person or part of the body) produce a continuous flow of liquid; run with liquid: *my eyes were streaming | I woke up in the night,* ***streaming with*** *sweat |* [*trans.*] *his mouth was streaming blood.* **3** [*intrans.*] (of hair, clothing, etc.) float or wave at full extent in the wind: *her black cloak* ***streamed behind*** *her.* **4** *Computing* [*trans.*] transmit (audio or video data) continuously, so that the parts arriving first can be viewed or listened to while the remainder is downloading. **5** British term for TRACK *verb* sense 4. ▷Old English *strēam* (noun), of Germanic origin; related to Dutch *stroom*, German *Strom*, from an Indo-European root shared by Greek *rhein* 'to flow.'
▸PHRASES □ **against** (or **with**) **the stream** against (or with) the prevailing view or tendency: *a world in which the demand for quality does not run against the stream.* □ **on stream** in or into operation or existence; available: *more jobs are* ***coming on stream.***

stream·er /ˈstrēmər/ ▸*n.* a long, narrow strip of material used as a decoration or symbol: *plastic party streamers | figurative a streamer of smoke.* ■ [usu. as *adj.*] a banner headline in a newspaper: *his appearance was announced with a streamer headline.* ■ [usu. as *adj.*] *Fishing* a fly with feathers attached: *a streamer fly.* ■ *Astronomy* an elongated mass of luminous matter, e.g., in auroras or the sun's corona.

stream·flow /ˈstrēmˌflō/ ▸*n.* the flow of water in a stream or river.

stream·ing /ˈstrēmiNG/ ▸*n.* a method of relaying data (especially video and audio material) over a computer network as a steady continuous stream, allowing playback to proceed while subsequent data is being received.
▸*adj.* [*attrib.*] *Computing* (of data) transmitted in a continuous stream while earlier parts are being used.

stream·let /ˈstrēmlit/ ▸*n.* a small stream.

stream·line /ˈstrēmˌlīn/ ▸*v.* [*trans.*] [usu. as *adj.*] (**streamlined**) design or provide with a form that presents very little resistance to a flow of air or water, increasing speed and ease of movement: *streamlined passenger trains.* ■ *figurative* make (an organization or system) more efficient and effective by employing faster or simpler working methods: *the company streamlined its operations by removing whole layers of management.*
▸*n.* a line along which the flow of a moving fluid is least turbulent.
▸*adj.* **1** (of fluid flow) free from turbulence. **2** *dated* having a streamlined shape: *a streamline airplane.*

stream of con·scious·ness ▸*n.* *Psychology* a person's thoughts and conscious reactions to events, perceived as a continuous flow. The term was introduced by William James in his *Principles of Psychology* (1890). ■ a literary style in which a character's thoughts, feelings, and reactions are depicted in a continuous flow uninterrupted by objective description or conventional dialogue. James Joyce, Virginia Woolf, and Marcel Proust are among its notable early exponents.

Streep /strēp/, Meryl (1949–), U.S. actress; born *Mary Louise Streep*. She won Academy Awards for her performance in *Kramer vs. Kramer* (1980) and *Sophie's Choice* (1982). Other movies include *The French Lieutenant's Woman* (1981), *Out of Africa* (1986), *One True Thing* (1998), *The Hours* (2002), and *The Manchurian Candidate* (2004).

street /strēt/ ▸*n.* a public road in a city or town, typically with houses and buildings on one or both sides: *the narrow, winding streets of Greenwich Village |* [*in place names*] *45 Lake Street.* ■ (**the street**) used to refer to the financial markets and activities on Wall Street. ■ (**the street/streets**) the roads or public areas of a city or town: *every week, fans stop me in the street.* ■ [as *adj.*] of or relating to the outlook, values, or lifestyle of those young people who are perceived as composing a fashionable urban subculture: *New York City street culture.* ■ [as *adj.*] denoting someone who is homeless: *he ministered to street people in storefront missions.* ■ [as *adj.*] performing or being performed on the street: *street theater.* ▷Old English *strǣt*, from late Latin *strāta (via)* 'paved (way),' feminine past participle of *sternere* 'lay down.' —**street·ed** *adj.* [in *combination*] *a many-streeted tangle of low, brick buildings.* —**street·ward** /-wərd/ *adj.* & *adv.*

▸*PHRASES* □ **on the streets** **1** homeless. **2** working as a prostitute. □ **streets ahead** *Brit., informal* greatly superior: *the restaurant is streets ahead of its local rivals.*

street Ar·ab ▸*n. archaic* a raggedly dressed homeless child wandering the streets.

street·car /ˈstrētˌkär/ ▸*n.* another term for TROLLEY CAR.

street clothes ▸*plural n.* clothes suitable for everyday wear in public.

street cred·i·bil·i·ty (also *informal* **street cred**) ▸*n.* acceptability among young black urban residents.

street cries ▸*plural n.* the cries used by street vendors to advertise their wares.

street fur·ni·ture ▸*n.* objects placed or fixed in the street for public use, such as mailboxes, road signs, and benches.

street hock·ey ▸*n.* a form of hockey played on a paved surface using in-line skates.

street-leg·al ▸*adj.* (of a vehicle) meeting all legal requirements for use on ordinary roads.

street·light /ˈstrētˌlīt/ (also **street·lamp**) ▸*n.* a light illuminating a road, typically mounted on a tall post.

street name ▸*n.* the name of a brokerage firm, bank, or dealer in which stock is held on behalf of a purchaser.

street-smart ▸*adj. informal* having the skills and knowledge necessary for dealing with modern urban life, esp. the difficult or criminal aspects of it: *a street-smart hustler on a motorcycle.*

▸*n.* (**street smarts**) these skills and knowledge: *take the advice of somebody who's got a little more street smarts than you.*

street val·ue ▸*n.* the price a commodity, esp. an amount of drugs, would fetch if sold illicitly: *detectives seized drugs with a street value of $300,000.*

street ven·dor ▸*n.* a person who sells something in the street, either from a stall or van or with their goods laid out on the sidewalk.

street·walk·er /ˈstrētˌwôkər/ ▸*n.* a prostitute who seeks customers in the street. —**street·walk·ing** /-ˌwôking/ *n.* & *adj.*

street·wise /ˈstrētˌwīz/ ▸*adj.* another term for STREET SMART. ■ reflective of modern urban life, esp. that of urban youth: *streetwise fashion.*

Stre·ga /ˈstrāgə/ ▸*n. trademark* a kind of orange-flavored Italian liqueur. ▷Italian, literally 'witch.'

Strei·sand /ˈstrīˌzand; -zənd/, Barbra (Joan) (1942–), U.S. singer, actress, and movie director. She won an Academy Award for her performance in *Funny Girl* (1968). She later produced and starred in *A Star is Born* (1976); she also composed the movie's song "Evergreen," which won an Academy Award. Streisand starred in, produced, and directed *Yentl* (1983).

strength /strenG(k)TH; strenTH/ ▸*n.* **1** the quality or state of being strong, in particular: ■ physical power and energy: *cycling can help you build up your strength.* ■ the emotional or mental qualities necessary in dealing with situations or events that are distressing or difficult: *many people find strength in religion | it takes strength of character to admit one needs help.* ■ the capacity of an object or substance to withstand great force or pressure: *they were taking no chances with the strength of the retaining wall.* ■ the influence or power possessed by a person, organization, or country: *the political and military strength of European governments.* ■ the degree of intensity of a feeling or belief: *street protests demonstrated the strength of feeling against the president.* ■ the cogency of an argument or case: *the strength of the argument for property taxation.* ■ the potency, intensity, or speed of a force or natural agency: *the wind had markedly increased in strength.* ■ the potency or degree of concentration of a drug, chemical, or drink: *it's double the strength of your average beer | the solution comes in two strengths.* **2** a good or beneficial quality or attribute of a person or thing: *the strengths and weaknesses of their sales and marketing operation | his strength was his obsessive single-mindedness.* ■ *poetic/literary* a person or thing perceived as a source of mental or emotional support: *he was my closest friend, my strength and shield.* **3** the number of people comprising a group, typically a team or army: *the peacetime strength of the army was 415,000.* ■ a number of people required to make such a group complete: *we are now more than 100 officers **below strength** | some units will be maintained **at full strength** while others will rely on reserves | [in combination] an under-strength side.* ▷Old English *strengthu*, from the Germanic base of STRONG. —**strength·less** *adj.*

▸*PHRASES* □ **from strength** from a secure or advantageous position: *it makes sense to negotiate from strength.* □ **go from strength to strength** develop or progress with increasing success. □ **in strength** in large numbers: *security forces were out in strength.* □ **on the strength of** on the basis or with the justification of: *she got into Princeton on the strength of her essays.* □ **tower** (or **pillar**) **of strength** a person who can be relied upon to give a great deal of support and comfort to others.

strength·en /ˈstrenG(k)THən; ˈstren-/ ▸*v.* make or become stronger: [*trans.*] *he advises an application of fluoride to strengthen the teeth | [intrans.] the wind won't strengthen until after dark.* —**strength·en·er** *n.*

▸*PHRASE* □ **strengthen someone's hand** (or **hands**) enable or encourage a person to act more vigorously or effectively.

stren·u·ous /ˈstrenyo͞oəs/ ▸*adj.* requiring or using great exertion: *Beijing's strenuous efforts to join the World Trade Organization.* ▷early 17th cent.: from Latin *strenuus* 'brisk' + -OUS. —**stren·u·ous·ly** *adv.* —**stren·u·ous·ness** *n.*

strep /strep/ ▸*n. informal Medicine* short for STREPTOCOCCUS.

Strep·sip·ter·a /strepˈsiptərə/ *Entomology* an order of minute parasitic insects that comprises the stylopids. ▷modern Latin (plural), from Greek *strepsi-* (combining form of *strephein* 'to turn') + *pteron* 'wing.' —**strep·sip·ter·an** *n.* & *adj.*

strepto- ▸*comb. form* twisted; in the form of a twisted chain: *streptomycete.* ■ associated with streptococci or streptomycetes: *streptokinase.* ▷from Greek *streptos* 'twisted,' from *strephein* 'to turn.'

strep·to·coc·cus /ˌstreptəˈkäkəs/ ▸*n.* (*pl.* **-coc·ci** /-ˈkäksī; -sē/) a bacterium of a genus that includes the agents of souring of milk and dental decay, and hemolytic pathogens causing various infections such as scarlet fever and pneumonia. • Genus *Streptococcus*; Gram-positive cocci in pairs and chains. —**strep·to·coc·cal** /-ˈkäkəl/ *adj.*

strep·to·ki·nase /ˌstreptəˈkīnās; -ˈkinās; -nāz/ ▸*n. Biochemistry* an enzyme produced by some streptococci that is involved in breaking down red blood cells. It is used to treat inflammation and blood clots.

strep·to·my·cete /ˌstreptəˈmīsēt/ ▸*n.* a bacterium that occurs chiefly in soil as aerobic saprophytes resembling molds, several of which are important sources of antibiotics. • *Streptomyces* and related genera, order Actinomycetales; Gram-positive filaments forming chains of spores. ▷1950s: anglicized singular of modern Latin *Streptomyces*, from STREPTO- 'twisted' + Greek *mukēs, mukēt-* 'fungus.'

strep·to·my·cin /ˌstreptəˈmīsin/ ▸*n. Medicine* an antibiotic that was the first drug to be successful against tuberculosis but is now chiefly used with other drugs because of its toxic side effects. • This antibiotic is produced by the bacterium *Streptomyces griseus.*

STRESS /stres/ ▸*n. Computing* a language designed for use in solving civil engineering structural analysis problems. ▷acronym from *str(uctural) e(ngineering) s(ystems) s(olver).*

stress /stres/ ▸*n.* **1** pressure or tension exerted on a material object: *the distribution of stress is uniform across the bar.* ■ the degree of this measured in units of force per unit area. **2** a state of mental or emotional strain or tension resulting from adverse or very demanding circumstances: *he's obviously **under** a lot of **stress** | [in combination] stress-related illnesses.* ■ something that causes such a state: *the stresses and strains of public life.* **3** particular emphasis or importance: *he has started to **lay** greater **stress on** the government's role in industry.* ■ emphasis given to a particular syllable or word in speech, typically through a combination of relatively greater loudness, higher pitch, and longer duration: *normally, the stress falls on the first syllable.*

▸*v.* **1** [*reporting verb*] give particular emphasis or importance to (a point, statement, or idea) made in speech or writing: [*trans.*] *they stressed the need for reform | [with clause] she was anxious to stress that her daughter's safety was her only concern | [with direct speech] "I want it done very, very neatly," she stressed.* ■ [*trans.*] give emphasis to (a syllable or word) when pronouncing it. **2** [*trans.*] subject to pressure or tension: *this type of workout does stress the shoulder and knee joints.* **3** [*trans.*] cause mental or emotional strain or tension in: *I avoid many of the things that used to stress me before | [as adj.] (**stressed**) she should see a doctor if she is feeling particularly **stressed out**.* ■ [*intrans.*] *informal* become tense or anxious; worry: *don't stress—there's plenty of time to get a grip on the situation.* ▷Middle English (denoting hardship or force exerted on a person for the purpose of compulsion): shortening of DISTRESS, or partly from Old French *estresse* 'narrowness, oppression,' based on Latin *strictus* 'drawn tight' (see STRICT). —**stress·less** *adj.* —**stres·sor** /-ər/ *n.* (in senses 2 and 3 of the *verb*).

stress frac·ture ▸*n.* a fracture of a bone caused by repeated (rather than sudden) mechanical stress.

stress·ful /ˈstresfəl/ ▸*adj.* causing mental or emotional stress: *corporate finance work can be stressful.* —**stress·ful·ly** *adv.* —**stress·ful·ness** *n.*

stress in·con·ti·nence ▸*n.* a condition (found chiefly in women) in which there is involuntary emission of urine when pressure within the abdomen increases suddenly, as in coughing or jumping.

stress-timed ▸*adj.* (of a language) characterized by a rhythm in which primary stresses occur at roughly equal intervals, irrespective of the number of unstressed syllables in between. English is a stress-timed language. Contrasted with SYLLABLE-TIMED.

stretch /strecH/ ▸*v.* [*intrans.*] **1** (of something soft or elastic) be made or be capable of being made longer or wider without tearing or breaking: *my sweater stretched in the wash | rubber will stretch easily when pulled.* ■ [*trans.*] cause to do this: *stretch the elastic.* ■ [*trans.*] pull (something) tightly from one point to another or across a space: *small squares of canvas were stretched over the bamboo frame.* ■ last or cause to last longer than expected: [*intrans.*] *her nap had stretched to two hours | [trans.] stretch your weekend into a mini summer vacation.* ■ [*trans.*] make great demands on the capacity or resources of: *the cost of the court case has **stretched** their finances **to the limit**.* ■ [*trans.*] cause (someone) to make maximum use of their talents or abilities: *it's too easy—it doesn't stretch me.* ■ [*trans.*] adapt or extend the scope of (something) in a way that exceeds a reasonable or acceptable limit: *to describe her as sweet would be stretching it a bit.* **2** straighten or extend one's body or a part of one's body to its full length, typically so as to tighten one's muscles or in order to reach something: *the cat yawned and stretched | [trans.] stretching my cramped legs we lay **stretched out** on the sand.* **3** [*intrans.*] extend or spread over an area or period of time: *the beach stretches for over four miles | the long hours of night stretched ahead of her.*

▸*n.* **1** an act of stretching one's limbs or body: *I got up and had a stretch.* ■ the fact or condition of a muscle being stretched: *she could feel the stretch and pull of the muscles in her legs.* ■ *Baseball* a phase of a pitcher's delivery, during which the arms are raised above and behind the head. ■ *Baseball* a shortened form of a pitcher's windup, typically used to prevent base runners from stealing or gaining a long lead. ■ [usu. as *adj.*] the capacity of a material or garment to stretch or be stretched; elasticity: *stretch jeans.* ■ a difficult or demanding task: *it was a stretch for me sometimes to come up with the rent.* **2** a continuous area or expanse of land or water: *a treacherous stretch of road.* ■ a continuous period of time: *long stretches of time.* ■ *informal* a period of time spent in prison: *a four-year stretch for tax fraud.* ■ a straight part of a racetrack, typically the homestretch: *he made a promising start, but faded down the stretch.* ■ *Sailing* the distance covered on one tack. **3** [usu. as *adj.*] *informal* a motor vehicle or aircraft modified so as to have extended seating or storage capacity: *a black stretch limo.* ▷Old English *streccan*; related to Dutch *strekken* and German *strecken*. The noun dates from the late 16th cent. —**stretch·a·bil·i·ty** /-əˈbilitē/ *n.* —**stretch·a·ble** *adj.*

▸*PHRASES* □ **at a stretch** in one continuous period: *I often had to work for over twenty hours at a stretch.* □ **by no** (or **not by any**) **stretch of the imagination** used to emphasize that something is definitely not the case: *by no stretch of the imagination could Carl ever be called good-looking.* □ **stretch one's legs** go for a short walk, typically after sitting in one place for some time. □ **stretch one's wings** see WING.

stretch·er /ˈstrecHər/ ▸*n.* **1** a framework of two poles with a long piece of canvas slung between them, used for carrying sick, injured, or dead people. ■ a gurney. **2** a thing that stretches something, in particular: ■ a wooden frame over which a canvas is spread and tautened ready for painting. ■ *archaic, informal* an exaggeration or lie. **3** a rod or bar joining and supporting chair legs. ■ a crosspiece in the bottom of a boat on which a rower's feet are braced. **4** a brick or stone laid with its long side along the face of a wall. Compare with HEADER (sense 3).

stretch·er-bear·er ▸*n.* a person who helps to carry the sick or injured on stretchers, esp. in time of war or at the scene of an accident.

stretch marks ▸*plural n.* streaks or stripes on the skin, esp. on the abdomen, caused by distention of the skin from obesity or during pregnancy.

stretch re·cep·tor ▸*n. Physiology* a sensory receptor that responds to the stretching of surrounding muscle tissue and so contributes to the coordination of muscle activity.

stretch·y /ˈstreCHē/ ▸*adj.* (**stretch·i·er, stretch·i·est**) (esp. of material or a garment) able to stretch or be stretched easily: *stretchy miniskirts.* —**stretch·i·ness** *n.*

stret·to /ˈstretō/ *Music* ▸*n.* (*pl.* **stret·ti** /ˈstretē/) a section at the end of a fugue in which successive introductions of the theme follow at shorter intervals than before, increasing the sense of excitement. ■ (also **stret·ta**) a passage, esp. at the end of an aria or movement, to be performed in quicker time.
▸*adv.* (as a direction) in quicker time. ▷Italian, literally 'narrow.'

streu·sel /ˈstroozəl; ˈstroi-/ ▸*n.* a crumbly topping or filling made from fat, flour, sugar, and often cinnamon. ■ a cake or pastry with such a topping. ▷from German *Streusel*, from *streuen* 'sprinkle.'

strew /stroo/ ▸*v.* (*past part.* **strewn** /stroon/ or **strewed**) [*trans.*] (usu. **be strewn**) scatter or spread (things) untidily over a surface or area: *a small room with newspapers* ***strewn all over*** *the floor.* ■ (usu. **be strewn with**) cover (a surface or area) with untidily scattered things: *the table was strewn with books and papers* | [as *adj.*, in *combination*] (**strewn**) *boulder-strewn slopes.* ■ be scattered or spread untidily over (a surface or area): *leaves strewed the path.* ▷Old English *stre(o)wian*, of Germanic origin; related to Dutch *strooien*, German *streuen*, from an Indo-European root shared by Latin *sternere* 'lay flat.' —**strew·er** *n.*

strewn field ▸*n. Geology* a region of the earth's surface over which tektites of a similar age and presumed origin are found.

stri·a /ˈstrīə/ ▸*n.* (*pl.* **stri·ae** /ˈstrī-ē/) *technical* a linear mark, slight ridge, or groove on a surface, often one of a number of similar parallel features. ■ *Anatomy* any of a number of longitudinal collections of nerve fibers in the brain. ▷late 17th cent. (as a scientific term): from Latin, literally 'furrow.'

stri·ate /ˈstrī,āt/ *technical* ▸*adj.* marked with striae: *the striate cortex.*
▸*v.* [*trans.*] [usu. as *adj.*] (**striated**) mark with striae: *striated bark.* —**stri·a·tion** /strīˈāSHən/ *n.*

stri·at·ed mus·cle ▸*n. Physiology* muscle tissue in which the contractile fibrils in the cells are aligned in parallel bundles, so that their different regions form stripes visible in a microscope. Muscles of this type are attached to the skeleton by tendons and are under voluntary control. Also called SKELETAL MUSCLE. Often contrasted with SMOOTH MUSCLE.

stri·a·tum /strīˈātəm/ ▸*n.* (*pl.* **-a·ta** /-ˈātə/) *Anatomy* short for CORPUS STRIATUM. —**stri·a·tal** /-ˈātl/ *adj.*

strick·en /ˈstrikən/ ▸ past participle of STRIKE.
▸*adj.* seriously affected by an undesirable condition or unpleasant feeling: *the pilot landed the stricken aircraft* | *Raymond was* ***stricken with*** *grief* | [in *combination*] *the farms were drought-stricken.* ■ (of a face or look) showing great distress: *she looked at Anne's stricken face, contorted with worry.*
▸*PHRASE* □ **stricken in years** *dated* used euphemistically to describe someone old and feeble.

strick·le /ˈstrikəl/ ▸*n.* **1** a rod used to level off a heaped measure. **2** a whetting tool. ▷Old English *stricel* (sense 1); related to STRIKE. Sense 2 dates from the mid 17th cent.

strict /strikt/ ▸*adj.* demanding that rules concerning behavior are obeyed and observed: *my father was very strict* | *a strict upbringing.* See note at SEVERE. ■ (of a rule or discipline) demanding total obedience or observance; rigidly enforced: *civil servants are bound by strict rules on secrecy.* ■ (of a person) following rules or beliefs exactly: *a strict vegetarian.* ■ exact in correspondence or adherence to something; not allowing or admitting deviation or relaxation: *a strict interpretation of the law.* ▷late Middle English (in the sense 'restricted in space or extent'): from Latin *strictus*, past participle of *stringere* 'tighten, draw tight.' —**strict·ness** *n.*

strict con·struc·tion ▸*n. Law* a literal interpretation of a statute or document by a court. —**strict con·struc·tion·ist** *n.*

strict li·a·bil·i·ty ▸*n. Law* liability that does not depend on actual negligence or intent to harm.

strict·ly /ˈstrik(t)lē/ ▸*adv.* **1** in a way that involves rigid enforcement or that demands obedience: | *he's been brought up strictly.* **2** used to indicate that one is applying words or rules exactly or rigidly: [*sentence adverb*] ***strictly speaking,*** *ham is a cured, cooked leg of pork* | [as *submodifier*] *to be strictly accurate, there are two Wolvertons.* ■ with no exceptions; completely or absolutely: *these foods are strictly forbidden.* ■ no more than; purely: *that visit was strictly business* | *his attitude and manner were strictly professional.*

stric·ture /ˈstrikCHər/ ▸*n.* **1** a restriction on a person or activity: *religious strictures on everyday life.* **2** a sternly critical or censorious remark or instruction: *his strictures on their lack of civic virtue.* **3** *Medicine* abnormal narrowing of a canal or duct in the body: *a colonic stricture* | *jaundice caused by bile duct stricture.* ▷late Middle English (sense 3): from Latin *strictura*, from *stringere* 'draw tight' (see STRICT). Another sense of the Latin verb, 'touch lightly,' gave rise to sense 2 via an earlier meaning 'incidental remark.' —**stric·tured** *adj.*

stride /strīd/ ▸*v.* (*past* **strode** /strōd/; *past part.* **strid·den** /ˈstridn/) **1** [*intrans.*] walk with long, decisive steps in a specified direction: *he strode across the road* | *figurative striding confidently toward the future.* ■ [*trans.*] walk about or along (a street or other place) in this way: *a woman striding the cobbled streets.* **2** [*intrans.*] (**stride across/over**) cross (an obstacle) with one long step: *by giving a little leap she could stride across like a grown-up.* ■ [*trans.*] *poetic/literary* bestride: *new wealth enabled Britain to stride the world once more.*
▸*n.* **1** a long, decisive step: *he crossed the room in a couple of strides.* ■ [in *sing.*] the length of a step or manner of taking steps in walking or running: *the horse shortened its stride* | *he followed her with an easy stride.* **2** (usu. **strides**) a step or stage in progress toward an aim: *great strides have been made toward equality.* ■ (**one's stride**) a good or regular rate of progress, esp. after a slow or hesitant start: *after months of ineffective campaigning, he seems to have* ***hit his stride.*** **3** [as *adj.*] denoting or relating to a rhythmic style of jazz piano playing in which the left hand alternately plays single bass notes on the downbeat and chords an octave higher on the upbeat: *a stride pianist.* ▷Old English *stride* (noun) 'single long step,' *strīdan* (verb) 'stand or walk with the legs wide apart,' probably from a Germanic base meaning 'strive, quarrel'; related to Dutch *strijden* 'fight' and German *streiten* 'quarrel.' —**strid·er** *n.*
▸*PHRASES* □ **break (one's) stride** slow or interrupt the pace at which one walks or moves. □ **match someone stride for stride** manage to keep up with a competitor. □ **take something in (one's) stride** deal with something difficult or unpleasant in a calm and accepting way: *we took each new disease in stride.*

stri·dent /ˈstrīdnt/ ▸*adj.* loud and harsh; grating: *his voice had become increasingly sharp, almost strident.* See note at VOCIFEROUS. ■ presenting a point of view, esp. a controversial one, in an excessively and unpleasantly forceful way: *public pronouncements on the crisis became less strident.* ■ *Phonetics* another term for SIBILANT. ▷mid 17th cent.: from Latin *strident-* 'creaking,' from the verb *stridere.* —**stri·den·cy** *n.* —**stri·dent·ly** *adv.*

stri·dor /ˈstrīdər/ ▸*n.* a harsh or grating sound: *the engines' stridor increased.* ■ *Medicine* a harsh vibrating noise when breathing, caused by obstruction of the windpipe or larynx. ▷mid 17th cent.: from Latin, from *stridere* 'to creak.'

strid·u·late /ˈstrijə,lāt/ ▸*v.* [*intrans.*] (of an insect, esp. a male cricket or grasshopper) make a shrill sound by rubbing the legs, wings, or other parts of the body together. ▷mid 19th cent.: from French *striduler*, from Latin *stridulus* 'creaking,' from the verb *stridere.* —**strid·u·lant** /-lənt/ *adj.* —**strid·u·la·tion** /,strijəˈlāSHən/ *n.* —**strid·u·la·to·ry** /-lə,tôrē/ *adj.*

strife /strīf/ ▸*n.* angry or bitter disagreement over fundamental issues; conflict: *strife within the community* | *ethnic and civil strife.* ▷Middle English: shortening of Old French *estrif* (related to Old French *estriver* 'strive').

strig·il /ˈstrijəl/ ▸*n.* an instrument with a curved blade used, esp. by ancient Greeks and Romans, to scrape sweat and dirt from the skin in a hot-air bath or after exercise; a scraper. ■ *Entomology* a comblike structure on the forelegs of some insects, used chiefly for grooming. ▷from Latin *strigilis*, from *stringere* 'touch lightly.' The term in entomology dates from the late 19th cent.

stri·gose /ˈstrī,gōs/ ▸*adj. Botany* covered with short stiff adpressed hairs. ■ *Entomology* finely grooved or furrowed. ▷late 18th cent.: from Latin *striga* 'swath, furrow' + -OSE[1].

strike /strīk/ ▸*v.* (*past* **struck** /strək/) **1** [*trans.*] hit forcibly and deliberately with one's hand or a weapon or other implement: *he raised his hand, as if to strike me* | *one man was struck on the head with a stick* | [*intrans.*] *Edgar* ***struck out at*** *her.* ■ inflict (a blow): [with *two objs.*] *he struck her two blows on the leg.* ■ accidentally hit (a part of one's body) against something: *she fell, striking her head against the side of the boat.* ■ come into forcible contact or collision with: *he was struck by a car on Whitepark Road.* ■ (of a beam or ray of light or heat) fall on (an object or surface): *the light struck her ring, reflecting off the diamond.* ■ (in sporting contexts) hit or kick (a ball) so as to score a run, point, or goal: *he struck the ball into the back of the net.* ■ [*intrans.*] (of a clock) indicate the time by sounding a chime or stroke: [with *complement*] *the church clock struck twelve.* ■ ignite (a match) by rubbing it briskly against an abrasive surface. ■ produce (fire or a spark) as a result of friction: *his iron stick struck sparks from the pavement.* ■ bring (an electric arc) into being. ■ produce a musical note) by pressing or hitting a key. **2** [*trans.*] (of a disaster, disease, or other unwelcome phenomenon) occur suddenly and have harmful or damaging effects on: *an earthquake struck the island* | [*intrans.*] *tragedy struck when he was killed in a car crash* | [as *adj.* in *combination*] (**struck**) *storm-struck areas.* ■ [*intrans.*] carry out an aggressive or violent action, typically without warning: *it was eight months before the murderer struck again.* ■ (usu. **be struck down**) kill or seriously incapacitate (someone): *he was struck down by a mystery virus.* ■ (**strike something into**) cause or create a particular strong emotion in (someone): *drugs—a subject guaranteed to strike fear into parents' hearts.* ■ [*trans.*] cause (someone) to be in a specified state: *he was struck dumb.* **3** [*trans.*] (of a thought or idea) come into the mind of (someone) suddenly or unexpectedly: *a disturbing thought struck Melissa.* ■ cause (someone) to have a particular impression: [with *clause*] *it struck him that Marjorie was unusually silent the idea* ***struck*** *her* ***as*** *odd.* ■ (**be struck by/with**) find particularly interesting, noticeable, or impressive: *Lucy was struck by the ethereal beauty of the scene.* **4** [*intrans.*] (of employees) refuse to work as a form of organized protest, typically in an attempt to obtain a particular concession or concessions from their employer: *workers may strike over threatened job losses.* ■ [*trans.*] undertake such action against (an employer). **5** [*trans.*] cancel, remove, or cross out with or as if with a pen: ***strike*** *his name* ***from*** *the list* | ***striking*** *words* ***through*** *with a pen.* ■ (**strike someone off**) officially remove someone from membership of a professional group: *he had been struck off as a disgrace to the profession.* ■ (**strike something down**) abolish a law or regulation: *the law was struck down by the Supreme Court.* **6** [*trans.*] make (a coin or medal) by stamping metal. ■ (in cinematography) make (another print) of a film. ■ reach, achieve, or agree to (something involving agreement, balance, or compromise): *the team has* ***struck a deal*** *with a sports marketing agency* | *you have to* ***strike a happy medium.*** ■ (in financial contexts) reach (a figure) by balancing an account: *last year's loss was struck after allowing for depreciation of 67 million dollars.* ■ *Canadian* form (a committee): *the government struck a committee to settle the issue.* **7** [*trans.*] discover (gold, minerals, or oil) by drilling or mining. ■ [*intrans.*] (**strike on/upon**) discover or think of, esp. unexpectedly or by chance: *pondering, she struck upon a brilliant idea.* ■ come to or reach: *several days out of the village, we struck the Gilgit Road.* **8** [*intrans.*] move or proceed vigorously or purposefully: *she* ***struck out*** *into the lake with a practiced crawl* | *he struck off down the track.* ■ (**strike out**) start out on a new or independent course or endeavor: *after two years he was able to strike out on his own.* **9** [*trans.*] take down (a tent or the tents of an encampment): *it took ages to strike camp.* ■ dismantle (theatrical scenery): *the minute we finish this evening, they'll start striking the set.* ■ lower or take down (a flag or sail), esp. as a salute or to signify surrender: *the ship struck her German colors.* **10** [*trans.*] insert (a cutting of a plant) in soil to take root. ■ [*intrans.*] (of a plant or cutting) develop roots: *small conifers will strike from cuttings.* ■ [*intrans.*] (of a young oyster) attach itself to a bed. **11** [*intrans.*] *Fishing* secure a hook in the mouth of a fish by jerking or tightening the line after it has taken the bait or fly.

▸*phrasal v.* □ **strike back 1** retaliate: *he* ***struck back*** *at critics who claim he is too negative.* **2** (of a gas burner) burn from an internal point before the gas has become mixed with air. □ **strike in** *archaic* intervene in a conversation or discussion. □ **strike someone out** (or **strike out**) *Baseball* put a batter out (or be put out) from play as a batter by means of three strikes. ■ (**strike out**) *informal* fail or be unsuccessful: *the company struck out the first time it tried to manufacture personal computers.* □ **strike up** (or **strike something up**) (of a band or orchestra) begin to play a piece of music: *they struck up the "Star-Spangled Banner"* ■ (**strike something up**) begin a friendship or conversation with someone, typically in a casual way.

▸*n.* **1** a refusal to work organized by a body of employees as a form of protest, typically in an attempt to gain a concession or concessions from their employer: *dockers voted for an all-out strike | local government workers* ***went on strike*** | [as *adj.*] *strike action.* ■ [with *adj.*] a refusal to do something expected or required, typically by a body of people, with a similar aim: *a rent strike.* **2** a sudden attack, typically a military one: *the threat of nuclear strikes.* ■ (in bowling) an act of knocking down all the pins with one's first ball. ■ *Fishing* an act or instance of jerking or tightening the line to secure a fish that has already taken the bait or fly. **3** a discovery of gold, minerals, or oil by drilling or mining: *the Lena goldfields strike of 1912.* **4** *Baseball* a pitch that is counted against the batter, in particular one that the batter swings at and misses, or that passes through the strike zone without the batter swinging, or that the batter hits foul (unless two strikes have already been called). A batter accumulating three strikes is out. ■ a pitch that passes through the strike zone and is not hit. ■ something to one's discredit: *when they returned from Vietnam they had* ***two strikes against*** *them.* **5** the horizontal or compass direction of a stratum, fault, or other geological feature. **6** short for FLY STRIKE. ▷Old English *strīcan* 'go, flow' and 'rub lightly'; related to German *streichen* 'to stroke,' also to STROKE. The sense 'deliver a blow' dates from Middle English.

▸*PHRASES* □ **strike a balance** see BALANCE. □ **strike a blow for** (or **at/against**) do something to help (or hinder) a cause, belief, or principle: *just by finishing the race, she hopes to strike a blow for womankind.* □ **strike a chord** see CHORD[2]. □ **strike at the root** (or **roots**) **of** see ROOT[1]. □ **strike hands** *archaic* (of two people) clasp hands to seal a deal or agreement. □ **strike home** see HOME. □ **strike it rich** *informal* acquire a great deal of money, typically in a sudden or unexpected way. □ **strike me pink** *Brit., informal dated* used to express astonishment or indignation. □ **strike a pose** (or **attitude**) hold one's body in a particular position to create an impression: *striking a dramatic pose, Antonia announced that she was leaving.* □ **strike while the iron is hot** make use of an opportunity immediately. [with reference to smithing.]

strike·break·er /ˈstrīkˌbrākər/ ▸*n.* a person who works or is employed in place of others who are on strike, thereby making the strike ineffectual. **—strike·break** *v.* **—strike·break·ing** /-ˌbrākiNG/ *n.*

strike force ▸*n.* [treated as *sing.* or *pl.*] a military force equipped and organized for sudden attack.

strike·out /ˈstrīkˌout/ ▸*n.* *Baseball* an out called when a batter accumulates three strikes.

▸*adj.* *Computing* (of text) having a horizontal line through the middle; crossed out.

strike pay ▸*n.* money paid to strikers by their trade union.

strike price ▸*n.* *Finance* **1** the price fixed by the seller of a security after receiving bids in a tender offer, typically for a sale of bonds or a new stock market issue. **2** the price at which a put or call option can be exercised.

strik·er /ˈstrīkər/ ▸*n.* **1** an employee on strike. **2** the player who is to strike the ball in a game; a player considered in terms of ability to strike the ball: *a gifted striker of the ball.* ■ (chiefly in soccer) a forward or attacker.

strik·er plate ▸*n.* a metal plate attached to a doorjamb or lidded container, against which the end of a spring-lock bolt strikes when the door or lid is closed.

strike-slip fault ▸*n.* *Geology* a fault in which rock strata are displaced mainly in a horizontal direction, parallel to the line of the fault.

strike zone ▸*n.* *Baseball* an area over home plate extending approximately from the armpits to the knees of a batter when in the batting position. The ball must be pitched through this area in order for a strike to be called.

strik·ing /ˈstrīkiNG/ ▸*adj.* **1** attracting attention by reason of being unusual, extreme, or prominent: *the murder bore a striking similarity to an earlier shooting* | [with *clause*] *it is* ***striking that*** *no research into the problem is occurring.* See note at NOTICEABLE. ■ dramatically good-looking or beautiful: *she is naturally striking | a striking landscape.* **2** [*attrib.*] (of an employee) on strike: *striking mine workers.*

▸*n.* the action of striking: *substantial damage was caused by the striking of a submerged object.* **—strik·ing·ly** *adv.* [as *submodifier*] *a strikingly beautiful girl.*

▸*PHRASE* □ **within striking distance** see DISTANCE.

strik·ing price ▸*n.* another term for STRIKE PRICE.

Strind·berg /ˈstrin(d)ˌbərg/, (Johan) August (1849–1912), Swedish playwright and novelist. His satire *The Red Room* (1879) is regarded as Sweden's first modern novel. His later plays are typically tense, psychic dramas, such as *A Dream Play* (1902).

Strine /strīn/ (also **strine**) *informal* ▸*n.* the English language as spoken by Australians; the Australian accent, esp. when considered striking or uneducated. ■ an Australian.

▸*adj.* of or relating to Australians or Australian English: *he spoke with a broad Strine accent.* ▷1960s: representing the pronunciation of *Australian* in Strine.

string /striNG/ ▸*n.* **1** material consisting of threads of cotton, hemp, or other material twisted together to form a thin length. ■ a piece of such material used to tie around or attach to something. ■ a piece of catgut or similar material interwoven with others to form the head of a sports racket. ■ a length of catgut or wire on a musical instrument, producing a note by vibration. ■ (**strings**) the stringed instruments in an orchestra. ■ [as *adj.*] of, relating to, or consisting of stringed instruments: *a string quartet.* **2** a set of things tied or threaded together on a thin cord: *she wore* ***a string of*** *agates around her throat.* ■ a sequence of similar items or events: ***a string of*** *burglaries.* ■ *Computing* a linear sequence of characters, words, or other data. ■ a group of racehorses trained at one stable. ■ a team or player holding a specified position in an order of preference: *Gary was first string on the varsity football team.* **3** a tough piece of fiber in vegetables, meat, or other food, such as a tough elongated piece connecting the two halves of a bean pod. **4** short for STRINGBOARD. **5** a hypothetical one-dimensional subatomic particle having the dynamical properties of a flexible loop. ■ (also **cosmic string**) (in cosmology) a hypothetical threadlike concentration of energy within the structure of space-time.

▸*v.* (*past* **strung** /strəNG/) **1** [*trans.*] hang (something) so that it stretches in a long line: *lights were strung across the promenade.* ■ thread (a series of small objects) on a string: *he collected stones with holes in them and strung them on a strong cord.* ■ (**be strung**) be arranged in a long line: *the houses were strung along the road.* ■ (**string something together**) add items to one another to form a series or coherent whole: *he can't string two sentences together.* **2** [*trans.*] fit a string or strings to (a musical instrument, a racket, or a bow): *the harp had been newly strung.* **3** [*trans.*] remove the strings from (a bean). **4** *Brit., Billiards* another term for LAG[1] (sense 2).

▸*phrasal v.* □ **string along** *informal* stay with or accompany a person or group casually or as long as it is convenient. □ **string someone along** *informal* mislead someone deliberately over a length of time, esp. about one's intentions: *she had no plans to marry him—she was just stringing him along.* □ **string something out** cause something to stretch out; prolong something. ■ (**string out**) stretch out into a long line: *the runners string out in a line across the road.* ■ (**be strung out**) be nervous or tense: *I often felt strung out by daily stresses.* ■ (**be strung out**) be under the influence of alcohol or drugs: *he died,* ***strung out on*** *booze and cocaine.* □ **string someone/something up** hang something up on strings. ■ kill someone by hanging. ▷Old English *streng* (noun), of Germanic origin; related to German *Strang*, also to STRONG. The verb (dating from late Middle English) is first recorded in the senses 'arrange in a row' and 'fit with a string.' **—string·less** *adj.* **—string·like** /-ˌlīk/ *adj.*

▸*PHRASES* □ **no strings attached** *informal* used to show that an offer or opportunity carries no special conditions or restrictions. □ **on a string** under one's control or influence: *I've got the world on a string.*

string bass /bās/ ▸*n.* (esp. among jazz musicians) a double bass.

string bean ▸*n.* **1** any of various beans eaten in their fibrous pods, such as scarlet runners. **2** *informal* a tall thin person.

string bi·ki·ni ▸*n.* a scant bikini with straps of thin cord.

string·board /ˈstriNGˌbôrd/ ▸*n.* a board with which the ends of the steps in a staircase are covered.

string·course /ˈstriNGˌkôrs/ ▸*n.* a raised horizontal band or course of bricks on a building. Also called CORDON.

stringed /striNGd/ ▸*adj.* [*attrib.*] (of a musical instrument) having strings: [in *combination*] *a three-stringed fiddle.*

strin·gen·do /strēnˈjendō; strin-/ *Music* ▸*adv.* & *adj.* (esp. as a direction) with increasing speed.

▸*n.* (*pl.* **-gen·dos** or **-gen·di** /-ˈjendē/) a passage marked to be performed in this way. ▷Italian, literally 'squeezing, binding together.'

strin·gent /ˈstrinjənt/ ▸*adj.* (of regulations, requirements, or conditions) strict, precise, and exacting: *California's air pollution guidelines are stringent.* ▷mid 17th cent. (in the sense 'compelling, convincing'): from Latin *stringent-* 'drawing tight,' from the verb *stringere.* **—strin·gen·cy** *n.* **—strin·gent·ly** *adv.*

string·er /ˈstriNGər/ ▸*n.* **1** a longitudinal structural piece in a framework, esp. that of a ship or aircraft. **2** *informal* a newspaper correspondent not on the regular staff of a newspaper, esp. one retained on a part-time basis to report on events in a particular place. **3** a side of a staircase, which supports the treads and risers. **4** [in *combination*] a sports player holding a specified position in an order of preference: *a third-stringer on the football team.*

string·halt /ˈstriNGˌhôlt/ ▸*n.* a condition affecting one or both of a horse's hind legs, causing exaggerated bending of the hock.

string or·ches·tra ▸*n.* an orchestra consisting only of bowed string instruments of the violin family.

string·piece /ˈstriNGˌpēs/ ▸*n.* a long piece supporting and connecting the parts of a wooden framework.

string quar·tet ▸*n.* a chamber music ensemble consisting of first and second violins, viola, and cello. ■ a piece of music for such an ensemble.

string the·o·ry ▸*n.* a cosmological theory based on the existence of cosmic strings. See also STRING (sense 5).

string tie ▸*n.* a very narrow necktie.

string·y /ˈstriNGē/ ▸*adj.* (**string·i·er**, **string·i·est**) (esp. of hair) resembling string; long, thin, and lusterless. ■ (of a person) tall, wiry, and thin. ■ (of food) containing tough fibers and so hard to eat. ■ (of a liquid) viscous; forming strings. **—string·i·ly** /-lē/ *adv.* **—string·i·ness** *n.*

strip[1] /strip/ ▸*v.* (**stripped**, **strip·ping**) [*trans.*] **1** remove all coverings from: *they stripped the bed.* ■ remove the clothes from (someone): [*trans.*] *the man had been stripped naked.* ■ [*intrans.*] take off one's clothes: *they stripped and showered | she* ***stripped down*** *to her underwear.* ■ pull or tear off (a garment or covering): *she* ***stripped off*** *her shirt | figurative* ***strip away*** *the hype, and you'll find original thought.* ■ remove bark and branches from (a tree). ■ remove paint from (a surface) with solvent. ■ remove (paint) in this way: ***strip off*** *the existing paint.* ■ remove the stems from (tobacco). ■ milk (a cow) to the last drop. **2** leave bare of accessories or fittings: *thieves* ***stripped*** *the room* ***of*** *luggage.* ■ remove the accessory fittings of or take apart (a machine, motor vehicle, etc.) to inspect or adjust it: *the tank was* ***stripped down*** *piece by piece.* **3** (**strip someone of**) deprive someone of (rank, power, or property): *the lieutenant was stripped of his rank.* **4** sell off (the assets of a company) for profit. ■ *Finance* divest (a bond) of its interest coupons so that it and they may be sold separately. **5** tear the thread or teeth from (a screw, gearwheel, etc.). ■ [*intrans.*] (of a screw, gearwheel, etc.) lose its thread or teeth. **6** [*intrans.*] (of a bullet) be fired from a rifled gun without spin owing to a loss of surface.

▸*n.* an act of undressing, esp. in a striptease: *she got drunk and did a strip on top of the piano.* ■ [as *adj.*] used for or involving the performance of stripteases: *a campaigner against strip joints.* ▷Middle English (as a verb): of Germanic origin; related to Dutch *stropen.*

strip[2] ▸*n.* **1** a long, narrow piece of cloth, paper, plastic, or some other material: ***a strip of*** *linen.* ■ a long, narrow area of land. ■ a main road in or leading out of a town, lined with shops, restaurants, and

S

other facilities. ■ steel or other metal in the form of narrow flat bars. **2** a comic strip. ▷late Middle English: from or related to Middle Low German *strippe* 'strap, thong,' probably also to STRIPE.

strip crop·ping ▸*n.* cultivation in which different crops are sown in alternate strips to prevent soil erosion.

stripe /strīp/ ▸*n.* **1** a long narrow band or strip, typically of the same width throughout its length, differing in color or texture from the surface on either side of it: *a pair of blue shorts with pink stripes.* ■ *archaic* a blow with a scourge or lash. **2** a chevron sewn onto a uniform to denote military rank. ■ a type or category: *entrepreneurs **of all stripes** are joining in the offensive.*

▸*v.* [*trans.*] (usu. **be striped**) mark with stripes: *her body was striped with bands of sunlight.* ▷late Middle English: perhaps a back-formation from STRIPED, of Dutch or Low German origin; compare with Middle Dutch and Middle Low German *stripe.*

striped /strīpt/ ▸*adj.* marked with or having stripes: [in *combination*] *a green-striped coat.*

striped bass /bas/ ▸*n.* a large bass of North American coastal waters, with dark horizontal stripes along the upper sides, migrating up streams to breed. • *Morone* (or **Roccus**) *saxatilis,* family Percichthyidae.

striped hy·e·na ▸*n.* a hyena with numerous black stripes on the body and legs, living in steppe and desert areas from northeastern Africa to India. • *Hyaena hyaena,* family Hyaenidae.

striped ma·ple ▸*n.* a compact North American maple with large leaves and vertically striped bark. Also called MOOSEWOOD (so named because moose often feed on the bark during severe winters). • *Acer pennsylvanicum,* family Aceraceae.

striped pole·cat ▸*n.* another term for ZORILLA.

strip·ey /'strīpē/ ▸*adj.* variant spelling of STRIPY.

strip·ling /'stripliNG/ ▸*n. humorous* a young man. ▷Middle English: probably from STRIP[2] (from the notion of "narrowness," i.e., slimness) + -LING.

strip mall ▸*n.* a shopping mall consisting of stores and restaurants typically in one-story buildings located on a busy main road.

strip-mine ▸*v.* [*trans.*] obtain (ore or coal) by open-pit mining: *lignite coal is strip-mined at depths of 45 to 100 feet* | [as *n.*] (**strip-mining**) *protected lands opened up to strip-mining for coal.* ■ subject (an area of land) to open-pit mining.

▸*n.* (**strip mine**) a mine worked by this method.

stripped-down ▸*adj.* [*attrib.*] reduced to essentials: *an interim, stripped-down funding bill.* ■ (of a machine, motor vehicle, etc.) having had all internal parts removed; dismantled.

strip·per /'stripər/ ▸*n.* **1** a device used for stripping something: *plier-style wire strippers.* ■ solvent for removing paint. **2** a striptease performer.

strip pok·er ▸*n.* a form of poker in which a player with a losing hand takes off an item of clothing as a forfeit.

strip-search ▸*v.* [*trans.*] search (someone) for concealed items, typically drugs or weapons, in a way that involves the removal of all their clothes.

▸*n.* (**strip search**) an act of searching someone in such a way.

strip·tease /'strip,tēz/ ▸*n.* a form of entertainment in which a performer gradually undresses to music in a way intended to be sexually exciting. **—strip·teas·er** *n.*

strip·y /'strīpē/ (also **strip·ey**) ▸*adj.* striped: *a stripy T-shirt.*

strive /strīv/ ▸*v.* (*past* **strove** /strōv/ or **strived**; *past part.* **striv·en** /strivən/ or **strived**) [*intrans.*] make great efforts to achieve or obtain something: *national movements were **striving for** independence* | [with *infinitive*] *we must strive to secure steady growth.* ■ struggle or fight vigorously: *scholars must **strive against** bias.* ▷Middle English: shortening of Old French *estriver;* related to *estrif* 'strife.' **—striv·er** *n.*

strobe /strōb/ *informal* ▸*n.* **1** a stroboscope. ■ a stroboscopic lamp: [as *adj.*] *strobe lights dazzled her.* **2** an electronic flash for a camera.

▸*v.* [*intrans.*] **1** flash intermittently: *the light of the fireworks strobed around the room.* ■ [*trans.*] light as if with a stroboscope: *a neon sign strobed the room.* **2** exhibit or give rise to strobing: *he explained that the stripes I was wearing would strobe.* ▷1940s: abbreviation of *stroboscopic* (see STROBOSCOPE).

stro·bi·la /strə'bīlə/ ▸*n.* (*pl.* **-lae** /-lē/) *Zoology* a form of an invertebrate that can divide to form a series of individual organisms. ■ the segmented part of the body of a tapeworm that consists of a long chain of proglottids. ■ a stack of immature larval jellyfish formed on a sessile polyplike form by sequential budding. ▷mid 19th cent.: modern Latin, from Greek *strobilē* 'twisted plug of lint,' from *strephein* 'to twist.' **—strob·i·la·tion** /,strōbə'lāsHən/ *n.*

stro·bi·lus /'strōbələs/ ▸*n.* (*pl.* **-li** /-,lī/) *Botany* the cone of a pine, fir, or other conifer. ■ a conelike structure, such as the flower of the hop. ▷mid 18th cent.: from late Latin, from Greek *strobilos,* from *strephein* 'to twist.'

strob·ing /'strōbiNG/ ▸*n.* **1** irregular movement and loss of continuity sometimes seen in lines and stripes in a television picture. **2** jerkiness in what should be a smooth movement of an image on a screen.

stro·bo·scope /'strōbə,skōp/ ▸*n. Physics* an instrument for studying periodic motion or determining speeds of rotation by shining a momentary bright light at intervals so that a moving object appears stationary. ■ a lamp made to flash intermittently, esp. for this purpose. ▷mid 19th cent.: from Greek *strobos* 'whirling' + -SCOPE. **—stro·bo·scop·ic** /,strōbə'skäpik/ *adj.* **—stro·bo·scop·i·cal·ly** /,strōbə'skäpik(ə)lē/ *adv.*

strode /strōd/ ▸ past of STRIDE.

stro·ga·noff /'strôgə,nôf; 'strō-/ ▸*n.* a dish in which the central ingredient, typically strips of beef, is cooked in a sauce containing sour cream. ▷named after Count Pavel *Stroganov* (1772–1817), Russian diplomat.

stroke /strōk/ ▸*n.* **1** an act of hitting or striking someone or something; a blow: *he received three strokes of the cane.* ■ a method of striking the ball in sports or games. ■ *Golf* an act of hitting the ball with a club, as a unit of scoring: *won by two strokes.* ■ the sound made by a striking clock. **2** an act of moving one's hand or an object across a surface, applying gentle pressure: *massage the cream into your skin using light upward strokes.* ■ a mark made by drawing a pen, pencil, or paintbrush in one direction across paper or canvas: *the paint had been applied in careful, regular strokes.* ■ a line forming part of a written or printed character. ■ a short printed or written diagonal line typically separating characters or figures. **3** a movement, esp. one of a series, in which something moves out of its position and back into it; a beat: *the ray swam with effortless strokes of its huge wings.* ■ the whole motion of a piston in either direction. ■ the rhythm to which a series of repeated movements is performed: *the rowers sing to keep their stroke.* ■ a movement of the arms and legs forming one of a series in swimming. ■ style of moving the arms and legs in swimming: *front crawl is a popular stroke.* ■ (in rowing) the mode or action of moving the oar. ■ (also **stroke oar**) the oar or oarsman nearest the stern of a boat, setting the timing for the other rowers. **4** a sudden disabling attack or loss of consciousness caused by an interruption in the flow of blood to the brain, esp. through thrombosis.

▸*v.* [*trans.*] **1** move one's hand with gentle pressure over (a surface, esp. hair, fur, or skin), typically repeatedly; caress: *he put his hand on her hair and stroked it.* ■ [*trans.*] apply (something) to a surface using a gentle movement: *she strokes blue eyeshadow on her eyelids.* ■ *informal* reassure or flatter (someone), esp. in order to gain their cooperation: *production executives were expert at stroking stars and brokering talent.* **2** act as the stroke of (a boat or crew): *he stroked Penn's rowing eight to victory.* **3** hit or kick (a ball) smoothly and deliberately: *Miller calmly stroked three-pointers throughout the tournament.* ■ score (a run or point) in such a manner: *the senior stroked a two-run single.* ▷Old English *strācian* 'caress lightly,' of Germanic origin; related to Dutch *streek* 'a stroke,' German *streichen* 'to stroke,' also to STRIKE. The earliest noun sense 'blow' is first recorded in Middle English.

▸*PHRASES* □ **at a** (or **one**) **stroke** by a single action having immediate effect: *attitudes cannot be changed at one stroke.* □ **not** (or **never**) **do a stroke of work** do no work at all. □ **on the stroke of ——** precisely at the specified time: *he arrived on the stroke of two.* □ **put someone off their stroke** disconcert someone so that they do not work or perform as well as they might; break the pattern or rhythm of someone's work. □ **stroke of business** a profitable transaction. □ **stroke of genius** an outstandingly brilliant and original idea. □ **stroke of luck** (or **good luck**) a fortunate occurrence that could not have been predicted or expected.

stroke play ▸*n.* a game of golf in which the score is reckoned by counting the number of strokes taken overall, as opposed to the number of holes won. Also called MEDAL PLAY.

stroll /strōl/ ▸*v.* [*intrans.*] walk in a leisurely way: *I strolled around the city.*

▸*n.* a short leisurely walk. ■ *figurative* a victory or objective that is easily achieved. ▷early 17th cent. (in the sense 'roam as a vagrant'): probably from German *strollen, strolchen,* from *Strolch* 'vagabond,' of unknown ultimate origin.

stroll·er /'strōlər/ ▸*n.* **1** a chair on wheels, typically folding, in which a baby or young child can be pushed along. **2** a person taking a leisurely walk: *shady gardens where strollers could relax.*

stroll·ing play·ers ▸*plural n. historical* a troupe of itinerant actors.

stro·ma /'strōmə/ ▸*n.* (*pl.* **-ma·ta** /-mətə/) **1** *Anatomy & Biology* the supportive tissue of an epithelial organ, tumor, gonad, etc., consisting of connective tissues and blood vessels. ■ the spongy framework of protein fibers in a red blood cell or platelet. ■ *Botany* the matrix of a chloroplast, in which the grana are embedded. **2** *Botany* a cushionlike mass of fungal tissue, having spore-bearing structures either embedded in it or on its surface. ▷mid 19th cent.: modern Latin, via late Latin from Greek *strōma* 'coverlet.' **—stro·mal** *adj.* (*chiefly Anatomy*) **—stro·mat·ic** /strō'matik/ *adj.* (*chiefly Botany*).

stro·mat·o·lite /strō'matə,līt/ ▸*n.* a calcareous mound built up of layers of lime-secreting cyanobacteria and trapped sediment, found in Precambrian rocks as the earliest known fossils, and still being formed in lagoons in Australasia. ▷1930s: from modern Latin *stroma, stromat-* 'layer, covering' + -LITE.

stro·ma·top·o·roid /,strōmə'täpə,roid/ ▸*n.* an extinct, sessile, corallike marine organism of uncertain relationship that built up calcareous masses composed of laminae and pillars, occurring from the Cambrian to the Cretaceous. ▷late 19th cent.: from modern Latin *Stromatopora* (genus name), from *stroma, stromat-* 'layer, covering' + *-pora* (on the pattern of *madrepora*).

Strom·bo·li /'strämbəlē/ a volcanic island in the Mediterranean Sea, one of the Lipari Islands.

Strom·bo·li·an /sträm'bōlēən/ ▸*adj. Geology* denoting volcanic activity of the kind typified by Stromboli, with continual mild eruptions in which lava fragments are ejected.

Strong /strôNG; sträNG/, William (1808–95), U.S. Supreme Court associate justice 1870–80. Appointed to the Court by President Grant, he wrote the majority opinion in the Court's 1871 reversal of its decision that declared the Legal Tender Act of 1862 unconstitutional.

strong /strôNG/ ▸*adj.* (**strong·er** /strôNGgər/, **strong·est** /strôNGgist/) **1** having the power to move heavy weights or perform other physically demanding tasks: *she cut through the water with her strong arms.* ■ [*attrib.*] able to perform a specified action well and powerfully: *he was not a strong swimmer.* ■ exerting great force: *a strong current.* ■ (of an argument or case) likely to succeed because of sound reasoning or convincing evidence: *there is a strong argument for decentralization.* ■ possessing skills and qualities that create a likelihood of success: *the competition was too strong.* ■ powerfully affecting the mind, senses, or emotions: *his imagery made a strong impression on the critics.* ■ used after a number to indicate the size of a group: *a hostile crowd several thousand strong.* **2** able to withstand great force or pressure: *cotton is strong, hard-wearing, and easy to handle.* ■ (of a person's constitution) not easily affected by disease or hardship. ■ (of a person's nervous or emotional state) not easily disturbed or upset: *driving on these highways requires strong nerves.* ■ (of a person's character) showing determination, self-control, and good judgment: *only a strong will enabled him to survive.* ■ in a secure financial position: *the company's chip business remains strong.* ■ (of a market) having steadily high or rising prices. ■ offering security and advantage: *the company was in a strong position to negotiate a deal.* ■ (of a belief or feeling) intense and firmly held. ■ (of a relationship) lasting and remaining warm despite difficulties. **3** (of light) very intense. ■ (of something seen or heard) not soft or muted; clear or prominent: *she should wear strong colors.* ■ (of food or its flavor) distinctive and pungent: *strong cheese.* ■ (of

S

a solution or drink) containing a large proportion of a particular substance; concentrated: *a cup of strong coffee.* ■ (of language or actions) forceful and extreme, esp. excessively or unacceptably so: *the government was urged to take strong measures against the perpetrators of violence.* ■ *Chemistry* (of an acid or base) fully ionized into cations and anions in solution; having (respectively) a very low or a very high pH. **4** *Grammar* denoting a class of verbs in Germanic languages that form the past tense and past participle by a change of vowel within the stem rather than by addition of a suffix (e.g., *swim, swam, swum*); contrasted with **WEAK**. **5** *Physics* of, relating to, or denoting the strongest of the known kinds of force between particles, which acts between nucleons and other hadrons when closer than about 10^{-13} cm (so binding protons in a nucleus despite the repulsion due to their charge), and which conserves strangeness, parity, and isospin. ▷Old English, of Germanic origin; related to Dutch and German *streng*, also to **STRING**. **—strong·ish** *adj.* **—strong·ly** *adv.*

▶*PHRASES* □ **come on strong** *informal* **1** behave aggressively or assertively, esp. in making sexual advances to someone. **2** improve one's position considerably: *he came on strong toward the end of the round.* □ **going strong** *informal* continuing to be healthy, vigorous, or successful: *the program is still going strong after twelve episodes.* □ **strong on** good at: *he is strong on comedy.* ■ possessing large quantities of: *our pizza wasn't strong on pepperoni.* □ **one's strong point** something at which one excels: *arithmetic had never been my strong point.*

strong-arm ▶*adj.* [*attrib.*] using or characterized by force or violence: *they were furious at what they said were government strong-arm tactics.*

▶*v.* [*trans.*] use force or violence against: *the culprit shouted before being strong-armed out of the door.*

S

strong·box /ˈstrôNG,bäks/ ▶*n.* a small lockable box, typically made of metal, in which valuables may be kept.

strong breeze ▶*n.* a wind of force 6 on the Beaufort scale (22–27 knots or 25–31 mph).

strong drink ▶*n.* alcohol, esp. liquor.

strong gale ▶*n.* a wind of force 9 on the Beaufort scale (41–47 knots or 47–54 mph).

strong·hold /ˈstrôNG,hōld/ ▶*n.* a place that has been fortified so as to protect it against attack. ■ a place where a particular cause or belief is strongly defended or upheld: *a Republican stronghold.*

strong in·ter·ac·tion ▶*n.* interaction at short distances between certain subatomic particles mediated by the strong force. See **STRONG** (sense 5).

strong·man /ˈstrôNG,man/ ▶*n.* (*pl.* **-men**) a man of great physical strength, esp. one who performs feats of strength as a form of entertainment. ■ a leader who rules by the exercise of threats, force, or violence.

strong-mind·ed ▶*adj.* not easily influenced by others; resolute and determined. **—strong-mind·ed·ness** *n.*

strong·point /ˈstrôNG,point/ ▶*n.* a specially fortified defensive position.

strong·room /ˈstrôNG,ro͞om; -,ro͝om/ ▶*n.* a room, typically one in a bank, designed to protect valuable items against fire and theft.

strong safe·ty ▶*n.* *Football* a defensive back positioned opposite the offensive team's stronger side, who often covers the tight end.

strong side ▶*n.* *Sports* (on teams with an odd number of players) the half of an offensive or defensive alignment that has one player more.

strong suit ▶*n.* (in bridge) a holding of a number of high cards of one suit in a hand. ■ a desirable quality that is particularly prominent in someone's character or an activity at which they excel: *compassion is not Jack's strong suit.*

stron·gyle /ˈsträn,jīl/ ▶*n.* a nematode of a group that includes several common disease-causing parasites of mammals and birds. • Genus *Strongylus* or family Strongylidae, class Phasmida. See also **RED WORM** (sense 2). ▷mid 19th cent.: from modern Latin *Strongylus*, from Greek *strongulos* 'round.'

stron·gy·loi·di·a·sis /,stränjəloiˈdīəsis/ ▶*n.* infestation with threadworms of a type found in tropical and subtropical regions, chiefly affecting the small intestine and causing ulceration and diarrhea. • The worms belong to the genus *Strongyloides*, class Phasmida, in particular *S. stercoralis*.

stron·ti·a /ˈstränSH(ē)ə/ ▶*n.* *Chemistry* strontium oxide, a white solid resembling quicklime. • Chem. formula: SrO. ▷early 19th cent.: from earlier *strontian*, denoting native strontium carbonate from *Strontian*, a parish in the Highland region of Scotland, where it was discovered.

stron·ti·an·ite /ˈstränSH(ē)ə,nīt/ ▶*n.* a rare pale greenish-yellow or white mineral consisting of strontium carbonate. ▷late 18th cent.: from *strontian* (see **STRONTIA**) + **-ITE**[1].

stron·ti·um /ˈstränCHēəm; -tēəm/ ▶*n.* the chemical element of atomic number 38, a soft, silver-white metal of the alkaline earth series. Its salts are used in fireworks and flares because they give a brilliant red light. (Symbol: **Sr**) ▷early 19th cent.: from **STRONTIA** + **-IUM**.

strop /sträp/ ▶*n.* a device, typically a strip of leather, for sharpening straight razors. ■ (also **strap**) *Nautical* a rope sling for handling cargo.

▶*v.* (**stropped**, **strop·ping**) [*trans.*] sharpen on or with a strop: *he stropped a knife razor-sharp on his belt.* ▷late Middle English (in the sense 'thong,' also as a nautical term): probably a West Germanic adoption of Latin *stroppus* 'thong.'

stro·phan·thin /strōˈfanTHən/ ▶*n.* *Medicine* a poisonous substance of the glycoside class, obtained from certain African trees and used as a heart stimulant. • This substance is obtained from trees of the genera *Strophanthus* and *Acokanthera* (family Apocynaceae). ▷late 19th cent.: from modern Latin *strophanthus* (from Greek *strophos* 'twisted cord' + *anthos* 'flower,' referring to the long segments of the corolla) + **-IN**[1].

stro·phe /ˈstrōfē/ ▶*n.* the first section of an ancient Greek choral ode or of one division of it. Compare with **ANTISTROPHE** and **EPODE** (sense 2). ■ a structural division of a poem containing stanzas of varying line-length, especially an ode or free verse poem. ▷early 17th cent.: from Greek *strophē*, literally 'turning,' from *strephein* 'to turn'; the term originally denoted a movement from right to left made by a Greek chorus, or lines of choral song recited during this. **—stroph·ic** /-fik; ˈsträ-/ *adj.*

stroud /stroud/ ▶*n.* coarse woolen fabric, formerly used in the manufacture of blankets for sale to North American Indians.

strove /strōv/ ▶ past of **STRIVE**.

strow /strō/ ▶*v.* (*past part.* **strown** /strōn/ or **strowed**) archaic variant of **STREW**.

struck /strək/ ▶ past and past participle of **STRIKE**.

struck joint ▶*n.* a masonry joint in which the mortar between two courses of bricks is sloped inward so as to be flush with the surface of one but below that of the other.

struc·tur·al /ˈstrəkCHərəl/ ▶*adj.* of, relating to, or forming part of the structure of a building or other item: *the blast left ten buildings with major structural damage.* ■ of or relating to the arrangement of and relations between the parts or elements of a complex whole: *there have been structural changes in the industry.* **—struc·tur·al·ly** *adv.*

struc·tur·al en·gi·neer·ing ▶*n.* the branch of civil engineering that deals with large modern buildings and similar structures. **—struc·tur·al en·gi·neer** *n.*

struc·tur·al for·mu·la ▶*n.* *Chemistry* a formula that shows the arrangement of atoms in the molecule of a compound. Compare with **EMPIRICAL FORMULA**, **MOLECULAR FORMULA**.

struc·tur·al·ism /ˈstrəkCHərə,lizəm/ ▶*n.* a method of interpretation and analysis of aspects of human cognition, behavior, culture, and experience that focuses on relationships of contrast between elements in a conceptual system that reflect patterns underlying a superficial diversity. ■ the doctrine that structure is more important than function.

Originating in the structural linguistics of Ferdinand de Saussure and extended into anthropology by Claude Lévi-Strauss, structuralism was adapted to a wide range of social and cultural studies, esp. in the 1960s, by writers such as Roland Barthes, Louis Althusser, and Jacques Lacan.

—struc·tur·al·ist *n.* & *adj.*

struc·tur·al lin·guis·tics ▶*plural n.* [treated as *sing.*] the branch of linguistics that deals with language as a system of interrelated structures, in particular the theories and methods of Leonard Bloomfield, emphasizing the accurate identification of syntactic and lexical form as opposed to meaning and historical development.

struc·tur·al steel ▶*n.* strong mild steel in shapes suited to construction work.

struc·tur·al un·em·ploy·ment ▶*n.* unemployment resulting from industrial reorganization, typically due to technological change, rather than fluctuations in supply or demand.

struc·tur·a·tion /,strəkCHəˈrāSHən/ ▶*n.* the state or process of organization in a structured form.

struc·ture /ˈstrəkCHər/ ▶*n.* the arrangement of and relations between the parts or elements of something complex: *flint is extremely hard, like diamond, which has a similar structure.* ■ the organization of a society or other group and the relations between its members, determining its working. ■ a building or other object constructed from several parts. ■ the quality of being organized: *we shall use three headings to give some structure to the discussion.*

▶*v.* [*trans.*] (often **be structured**) construct or arrange according to a plan; give a pattern or organization to: *the game is structured so that there are five ways to win.* ▷late Middle English (denoting the process of building): from Old French, or from Latin *structura*, from *struere* 'to build.' The verb is rarely found before the 20th cent. **—struc·ture·less** *adj.*

struc·tured set·tle·ment ▶*n.* a legal settlement paid out as an annuity rather than in a lump sum, usually with certain tax advantages for the recipient and a savings for the payer.

stru·del /ˈstro͞odl/ ▶*n.* a confection of thin pastry rolled up around a fruit filling and baked. ▷from German *Strudel*, literally 'whirlpool.'

strug·gle /ˈstrəgəl/ ▶*v.* [*intrans.*] make forceful or violent efforts to get free of restraint or constriction: *before she could struggle, he lifted her up* | [with *infinitive*] *he struggled to break free.* ■ strive to achieve or attain something in the face of difficulty or resistance: [with *infinitive*] *many families struggle to make ends meet.* ■ (**struggle with**) have difficulty handling or coping with: *passengers struggle with bags and briefcases.* ■ engage in conflict: *politicians continued to struggle over familiar issues.* ■ [*intrans.*] make one's way with difficulty: *he struggled to the summit of the world's highest mountain.* ■ have difficulty in gaining recognition or a living: *new authors are struggling in the present climate.*

▶*n.* a forceful or violent effort to get free of restraint or resist attack. ■ a conflict or contest: *a power struggle for the leadership.* ■ a great physical effort: *with a struggle, she pulled the stroller up the slope.* ■ a determined effort under difficulties: *the center is the result of the scientists' struggle to realize their dream.* ■ a very difficult task: *it was a struggle to make herself understood.* ▷late Middle English: frequentative, perhaps of imitative origin. The noun dates from the late 17th cent. **—strug·gler** /ˈstrəg(ə)lər/ *n.*

▶*PHRASE* □ **the struggle for existence** (or **life**) the competition between organisms, esp. as an element in natural selection, or between people seeking a livelihood.

strum /strəm/ ▶*v.* (**strummed**, **strum·ming**) [*trans.*] play (a guitar or similar instrument) by sweeping the thumb or a plectrum up or down the strings. ■ play (a tune) in such a way: *he strummed a few chords.* ■ [*intrans.*] play casually or unskillfully on a stringed or keyboard instrument.

▶*n.* [in *sing.*] the sound made by strumming: *the brittle strum of acoustic guitars.* ■ an instance or spell of strumming. ▷late 18th cent.: imitative; compare with **THRUM**[1]. **—strum·mer** *n.*

stru·ma /ˈstro͞omə/ ▶*n.* (*pl.* **-mae** /-mē; /) *Medicine* a swelling of the thyroid gland; a goiter. ▷mid 16th cent. (in the Latin sense): modern Latin, from Latin, 'scrofulous tumor.'

stru·mous /ˈstro͞oməs/ ▶*adj.* *archaic* scrofulous. ▷late 16th cent.: from Latin *strumosus*, from *struma* (see **STRUMA**).

strum·pet /ˈstrəmpət/ ▶*n.* *dated* a female prostitute or a promiscuous woman. ▷Middle English: of unknown origin.

strung /strəNG/ ▶ past and past participle of **STRING**.

strut /strət/ ▶*n.* **1** a rod or bar forming part of a framework and designed to resist compression. **2** [in *sing.*] a stiff, erect, and apparently arrogant or conceited gait: *that old confident strut and swagger has returned.*

▶*v.* (**strut·ted**, **strut·ting**) **1** [*intrans.*] walk with a stiff, erect, and apparently arrogant or conceited gait: *peacocks strut through the grounds.* **2** [*trans.*] brace (something) with a strut or struts: *the holes were close-boarded and strutted.* ▷Old English *strūtian* 'protrude stiffly,' of Germanic origin. Current senses date from the late 16th cent. **—strut·ter** *n.* **—strut·ting·ly** *adv.*

▶*PHRASE* □ **strut one's stuff** *informal* dance or behave in a confident and expressive way.

Stru·ve /ˈSHtro͞ovə/, Otto (1897–1963), U.S.

astronomer, born in Russia. In 1938, he discovered the presence of ionized hydrogen in interstellar space.

strych·nine /ˈstrik,nīn; -,nēn/ ▸*n.* a bitter and highly poisonous compound obtained from nux vomica and related plants. An alkaloid, it has occasionally been used as a stimulant. ▷early 19th cent.: from French, via Latin from Greek *strukhnos*, denoting a kind of nightshade.

Stryker (in full **Stryk·er Ar·mored Ve·hi·cle**) ▸*n.* an eight-wheeled armored vehicle used by the Army with defense capabilities similar to those of a tank, but with greater mobility and fewer logistical requirements. ▷named for two different veterans of earlier wars who shared the surname *Stryker*.

Sts. ▸*abbr.* Saints.

St. Thom·as /ˈtäməs/ an island in the Caribbean Sea, the second largest of the U.S. Virgin Islands, east of Puerto Rico; pop. 48,170; chief town, Charlotte Amalie. Settled by the Dutch in 1657, it passed to Denmark in 1666, which sold it to the U.S. in 1917.

Stu·art[1] /ˈst(y)o͞oərt/, Charles Edward (1720–88), son of James Stuart; pretender to the British throne; known as **the Young Pretender** or **Bonnie Prince Charlie**.

Stu·art[2], Gilbert Charles (1755–1828), U.S. artist. Considered the father of American portraiture, he is best known for his portraits of the first five presidents, painted between 1817 and 1821.

Stu·art[3], James (Francis Edward) (1688–1766), son of James II (James VII of Scotland); pretender to the British throne; known as **the Old Pretender**.

Stu·art[4], Jeb (1833–64), U.S. military officer; full name *James Ewell Brown Stuart*. He resigned from the U.S. army in 1861 to join the Confederate army as a brigadier general. Known for his brazen missions of reconnaissance during the Civil War, his raid that surrounded McClellan's army in 1862 is praised as superb military strategy. He was mortally wounded at the Battle of Yellow Tavern in Virginia.

Stu·art[5], Mary, see **MARY, QUEEN OF SCOTS**.

Stu·art[6] (also **Stew·art**) ▸*adj.* of or relating to the royal family ruling Scotland 1371–1714 and Britain 1603–49 and 1660–1714.
▸*n.* a member of this family.

stub /stəb/ ▸*n.* **1** the truncated remnant of a pencil, cigarette, or similar-shaped object after use. ■ a truncated or unusually short thing: *he wagged his little stub of tail.* ■ [as *adj.*] denoting a projection or hole that goes only part of the way through a surface: *a stub tenon.* **2** the part of a check, receipt, ticket, or other document torn off and kept as a record.
▸*v.* (**stubbed, stub·bing**) [*trans.*] **1** accidentally strike (one's toe) against something: *I stubbed my toe, swore, and tripped.* **2** extinguish (a lighted cigarette) by pressing the lighted end against something: *she **stubbed out** her cigarette in the overflowing ashtray.* **3** dig up (a plant) by the roots. ▷Old English *stub(b)* 'stump of a tree,' of Germanic origin. The verb is first recorded (late Middle English) in sense 3; sense 1 of the *verb* (mid 19th cent.) was originally a U.S. usage.

stub ax·le ▸*n.* an axle supporting only one wheel of a pair on opposite sides of a vehicle.

stub·ble /ˈstəbəl/ ▸*n.* the cut stalks of grain plants left sticking out of the ground after the grain is harvested. ■ short, stiff hairs growing on a man's face when he has not shaved for a while. ▷Middle English: from Anglo-Norman French *stuble*, from Latin *stupla*, *stupula*, variants of *stipula* 'straw.' —**stub·bled** *adj.* —**stub·bly** /ˈstəb(ə)lē/ *adj.*

stub·born /ˈstəbərn/ ▸*adj.* having or showing dogged determination not to change one's attitude or position on something, esp. in spite of good arguments or reasons to do so: *he accused her of being a silly, stubborn old woman.* ■ difficult to move, remove, or cure: *the removal of stubborn screws.* ▷Middle English (originally in the sense 'untamable, implacable'): of unknown origin. —**stub·born·ly** *adv.* —**stub·born·ness** *n.*

THE RIGHT WORD **dogged, intractable, obdurate, obstinate, pertinacious, stubborn,**

If you're the kind of person who takes a stand and then refuses to back down, your friends might say you have a **stubborn** disposition, a word that implies an innate resistance to any attempt to change one's purpose, course, or opinion.

People who are *stubborn* by nature exhibit this kind of behavior in most situations, but they might be **obstinate** in a particular instance (*a stubborn child, he was obstinate in his refusal to eat vegetables*). *Obstinate* implies sticking persistently to an opinion, purpose, or course of action, especially in the face of persuasion or attack.

While *obstinate* is usually a negative term, **dogged** can be either positive or negative, implying both tenacious, often sullen, persistence (*dogged pursuit of a college degree, even though he knew he would end up in the family business*) and great determination (*dogged loyalty to a cause*).

Obdurate usually connotes a stubborn resistance marked by harshness and lack of feeling (*obdurate in ignoring their pleas*), while **intractable** means stubborn in a headstrong sense and difficult for others to control or manage (*intractable pain*).

No matter how stubborn you are, you probably don't want to be called **pertinacious**, which implies persistence to the point of being annoying or unreasonable (*a pertinacious panhandler*).

stub·by /ˈstəbē/ ▸*adj.* (**-bi·er, -bi·est**) short and thick: *Bloom pointed with a stubby finger.* —**stub·bi·ly** /-əlē/ *adv.* —**stub·bi·ness** *n.*

stuc·co /ˈstəkō/ ▸*n.* fine plaster used for coating wall surfaces or molding into architectural decorations.
▸*v.* (**-coes, -coed**) [*trans.*] [usu. as *adj.*] (**stuccoed**) coat or decorate with such plaster: *a stuccoed house.* ▷late 16th cent. (as a noun): from Italian, of Germanic origin.

stuck /stək/ ▸ past and past participle of **STICK**[2].

stuck-up ▸*adj. informal* staying aloof from others because one thinks one is superior.

stud[1] /stəd/ ▸*n.* **1** a large-headed piece of metal that pierces and projects from a surface, esp. for decoration. ■ a small, simple piece of jewelry for wearing in pierced ears or nostrils. ■ a fastener consisting of two buttons joined with a bar, used in formal wear to fasten a shirtfront or to fasten a collar to a shirt. ■ (usu. **studs**) a small projection fixed to the base of footwear, esp. athletic shoes, to allow the wearer to grip the ground. ■ (usu. **studs**) a small metal piece set into the tire of a motor vehicle to improve roadholding in slippery conditions. **2** an upright support in the wall of a building to which laths and plasterboard are attached. ■ the height of a room as indicated by the length of this. **3** a rivet or crosspiece in each link of a chain cable.
▸*v.* (**stud·ded, stud·ding**) [*trans.*] (usu. **be studded**) decorate or augment (something) with many studs or similar small objects: *a dagger **studded with** precious diamonds.* ■ strew or cover (something) with a scattering of small objects or features: *the sky was clear and **studded with** stars.* ▷Old English *studu, stuthu* 'post, upright prop'; related to German *stützen* 'to prop.' The sense 'ornamental metal knob' arose in late Middle English.

stud[2] ▸*n.* **1** an establishment where horses or other domesticated animals are kept for breeding: [as *adj.*] *a stud farm* | *the horse was retired **to stud**.* ■ a collection of horses or other domesticated animals belonging to one person. ■ (also **stud horse**) a stallion. ■ *informal* a young man thought to be very active sexually or regarded as a good sexual partner. **2** (also **stud poker**) a form of poker in which the first card of a player's hand is dealt face down and the others face up, with betting after each round of the deal. ▷Old English *stōd*, of Germanic origin; related to German *Stute* 'mare,' also to **STAND**.

stud. ▸*abbr.* student.

stud book ▸*n.* a book containing the pedigrees of horses.

stud·ding /ˈstədiNG/ ▸*n.* studs collectively. See **STUD**[1] (sense 2).

stud·ding·sail /ˈstədiNG,sāl; ˈstənsəl/ ▸*n.* (on a square-rigged sailing ship) an additional sail set at the end of a yard in light winds. ▷mid 16th cent.: *studding* perhaps from Middle Low German, Middle Dutch *stōtinge* 'a thrusting.'

stu·dent /ˈst(y)o͞odnt/ ▸*n.* a person who is studying at a school or college. ■ [as *adj.*] denoting someone who is studying in order to enter a particular profession: *a group of student nurses.* ■ a person who takes an interest in a particular subject: *a **student of** the free market.* ▷late Middle English: from Latin *student-* 'applying oneself to,' from the verb *studere*, related to *studium* 'painstaking application.' —**stu·dent·ship** /-,SHip/ *n. Brit.* —**stu·dent·y** *adj. Brit.* (*informal*).

Stu·dent's t-test ▸*n.* a test for statistical significance that uses tables of a statistical distribution called **Student's *t*-distribution**, which is that of a fraction (t) whose numerator is drawn from a normal distribution with a mean of zero, and whose denominator is the root mean square of k terms drawn from the same normal distribution (where k is the number of degrees of freedom). ▷early 20th cent.: *Student*, the pseudonym of William Sealy Gosset (1876–1937), English brewery employee.

stud horse ▸*n.* see **STUD**[2] (sense 1).

stud·ied /ˈstədēd/ ▸*adj.* (of a quality or result) achieved or maintained by careful and deliberate effort: *he treated them with studied politeness.* —**stud·ied·ly** *adv.* —**stud·ied·ness** *n.*

stu·di·o /ˈst(y)o͞odē,ō/ ▸*n.* (*pl.* **-os**) **1** a room where an artist, photographer, sculptor, etc., works. ■ a place where performers, esp. dancers, practice and exercise. ■ a room where musical or sound recordings can be made. ■ a room from which television or radio programs are broadcast, or in which they are recorded. ■ a place where movies are made or produced. **2** a film or television production company. **3** a studio apartment. ▷early 19th cent.: from Italian, from Latin *studium* (see **STUDY**).

stu·di·o a·part·ment ▸*n.* an apartment containing one main room.

stu·di·o couch ▸*n.* a sofa bed.

stu·di·o por·trait ▸*n.* a large photograph for which the sitter is posed, typically taken in the photographer's studio.

stu·di·o the·a·ter ▸*n.* a small theater where experimental and innovative productions are staged.

stu·di·ous /ˈst(y)o͞odēəs/ ▸*adj.* spending a lot of time studying or reading: *he was quiet and studious.* ■ done deliberately or with a purpose in mind: *his studious absence from public view.* ■ showing great care or attention: *a studious inspection.* ▷Middle English: from Latin *studiosus*, from *studium* 'painstaking application.' —**stu·di·ous·ly** *adv.* —**stu·di·ous·ness** *n.*

stud·muf·fin /ˈstəd,məfin/ ▸*n. informal* a man perceived as sexually attractive, typically one with well-developed muscles.

stud pok·er ▸*n.* see **STUD**[2] (sense 2).

stud·y /ˈstədē/ ▸*n.* (*pl.* **stud·ies**) **1** the devotion of time and attention to acquiring knowledge on an academic subject, esp. by means of books: *the study of English* | *an application to continue full-time study.* ■ (**studies**) activity of this type as pursued by one person: *some students may not be able to resume their studies.* ■ an academic book or article on a particular topic: *a study of Jane Austen's novels.* ■ (**studies**) used in the title of an academic subject: *a major in East Asian studies.* **2** a detailed investigation and analysis of a subject or situation: *a study of a sample of 5,000 children* | *the study of global problems.* ■ a portrayal in literature or another art form of an aspect of behavior or character: *a study of a man devoured by awareness of his own mediocrity.* ■ *archaic* a thing that is or deserves to be investigated; the subject of an individual's study: *I have made it my study to examine the nature and character of the Indians.* ■ *archaic* the object or aim of someone's endeavors: *the acquisition of a fortune is the study of all.* ■ [with *adj.*] a person who learns a skill or acquires knowledge at a specified speed: *I'm a quick study.* [originally theatrical slang, referring to an actor who memorizes a role.] **3** a room used or designed for reading, writing, or academic work. **4** a piece of work, esp. a drawing, done for practice or as an experiment. ■ a musical composition designed to develop a player's technical skill. **5** (**a study in**) a thing or person that is an embodiment or good example of something: *he perched on the edge of the bed, a study in confusion and misery.* ■ *informal* an amusing or remarkable thing or person: *Ira's face was a study as he approached the car.*
▸*v.* (**stud·ies, stud·ied**) [*trans.*] **1** devote time and attention to acquiring knowledge on (an academic subject), esp. by means of books: *she studied biology and botany.* ■ investigate and analyze (a subject or situation) in detail: *he has been studying mink for many years.* ■ [*intrans.*] apply oneself to study: *he spent his time listening to the radio rather than studying.* ■ [*intrans.*] acquire academic knowledge at an educational establishment: *he studied at the Kensington School of Art.* ■ [*intrans.*] (**study up**) learn intensively about something, esp. in preparation for a test of knowledge: *a graduate student studies up for her doctoral exams.* ■ (of an actor) try to learn (the words of one's role). ■ *W. Indian* give serious thought or consideration to: *the people here don't make so much noise, so you will find that the government doesn't have us to study.* **2** look at closely in order to observe or read: *she bent her head to*

study the plans. **3** *archaic* make an effort to achieve (a result) or take into account (a person or their wishes): *with no husband to study, housekeeping is mere play.* ▷Middle English: shortening of Old French *estudie* (noun), *estudier* (verb), both based on Latin *studium* 'zeal, painstaking application.'

▸*PHRASE* □ **in a brown study** absorbed in one's thoughts. [apparently originally from *brown* in the sense 'gloomy.']

stud·y group ▸*n.* a group of people who meet to study a particular subject and then report their findings or recommendations.

stud·y hall ▸*n.* the period of time in a school curriculum set aside for the preparation of schoolwork. ■ a schoolroom used for such work.

stuff /stəf/ ▸*n.* **1** matter, material, articles, or activities of a specified or indeterminate kind that are being referred to, indicated, or implied: *a pickup truck picked the stuff up | a girl who's good at the technical stuff.* ■ a person's belongings, equipment, or baggage: *he took his stuff and went.* ■ *Brit., informal, dated* worthless or foolish ideas, speech, or writing; rubbish: [as *exclam.*] ***stuff and nonsense!*** ■ *informal* drink or drugs. ■ (**one's stuff**) things in which one is knowledgeable and experienced; one's area of expertise: *he **knows his stuff** and can really write.* **2** the basic constituents or characteristics of something or someone: *Healey was made of sterner stuff | such a trip was the stuff of his dreams.* **3** *Brit., dated* woolen fabric, esp. as distinct from silk, cotton, and linen: [as *adj.*] *her dark stuff gown.* **4** (in sports) spin given to a ball to make it vary its course. ■ *Baseball* a pitcher's ability to produce such spin or control the speed of delivery of a pitch.

▸*v.* [*trans.*] **1** fill (a receptacle or space) tightly with something: *an old teapot **stuffed full of** cash | figurative his head has been **stuffed with** myths and taboos.* ■ *informal* force or cram (something) tightly into a receptacle or space: *he stuffed a thick wad of cash into his jacket pocket.* ■ *informal* hastily or clumsily push (something) into a space: *Sadie took the coin and stuffed it in her coat pocket.* ■ fill (the cavity of an item of food) with a savory or sweet mixture, esp. before cooking: *chicken stuffed with mushrooms and breadcrumbs.* ■ (**be stuffed up**) (of a person) have one's nose blocked up with mucus as a result of a cold. ■ *informal* fill (oneself) with large amounts of food: *he **stuffed himself with** potato chips.* ■ fill out the skin of (a dead animal or bird) with material to restore the original shape and appearance: *he took the bird to a taxidermist to be stuffed* | [as *adj.*] (**stuffed**) *a stuffed parrot.* ■ *informal* fill (envelopes) with identical copies of printed matter: *they spent the whole time in a back room stuffing envelopes.* ■ place bogus votes in (a ballot box). **2** *Brit., vulgar slang* (of a man) have sexual intercourse with (someone). **3** *Brit., informal* defeat heavily in sport: *Town got stuffed every week.* **4** [usu. in *imperative*] *Brit., informal* used to express indifference toward or rejection of (something): *stuff the diet!* ▷Middle English (denoting material for making clothes): shortening of Old French *estoffe* 'material, furniture,' *estoffer* 'equip, furnish,' from Greek *stuphein* 'draw together.' —**stuff·er** *n.* [in *combination*] *a sausage-stuffer.*

▸*PHRASES* □ **and stuff** *informal* said in vague reference to additional things of a similar nature to those specified: *all that running and swimming and stuff.* □ **get stuffed** [usu. in *imperative*] *vulgar slang* said in anger to tell someone to go away or as an expression of contempt. □ **stuff it** *informal* said to express indifference, resignation, or rejection: *Stuff it, I'm 61, what do I care?* □ **that's the stuff** *informal* said in approval of what has just been done or said.

stuffed shirt ▸*n. informal* a conservative, pompous person.

stuff·ing /ˈstəfiNG/ ▸*n.* **1** a mixture used to stuff poultry or meat before cooking. **2** padding used to stuff cushions, furniture, or soft toys.

▸*PHRASE* □ **knock** (or **take**) **the stuffing out of** *informal* severely impair the confidence or strength of (someone).

stuff·ing box ▸*n.* a casing in which material such as greased wool is compressed around a shaft or axle to form a seal against gas or liquid, used for instance where the propeller shaft of a boat passes through the hull.

stuff sack ▸*n.* a bag into which a sleeping bag, clothing, and other items can be stuffed or packed for ease of carrying or when not in use.

stuff·y /ˈstəfē/ ▸*adj.* (**stuff·i·er, stuff·i·est**) (of a place) lacking fresh air or ventilation: *a stuffy, overcrowded office.* ■ (of a person's nose) blocked up and making breathing difficult, typically as a result of illness. ■ (of a person) not receptive to new or unusual ideas and behavior; conventional and narrow-minded: *he was steady and rather stuffy.* —**stuff·i·ly** /ˈstəfəlē/ *adv.* —**stuff·i·ness** *n.*

Stu·ka /ˈstōōkə; ˈSHtōō-/ ▸*n.* a type of German military aircraft (the Junkers Ju 87) designed for dive-bombing, much used in World War II. ▷contraction of German *Sturzkampfflugzeug* 'dive-bomber.'

stul·ti·fy /ˈstəltəˌfī/ ▸*v.* (**-fies, -fied**) [*trans.*] **1** [usu. as *adj.*] (**stultifying**) cause to lose enthusiasm and initiative, esp. as a result of a tedious or restrictive routine: *the mentally stultifying effects of a disadvantaged home.* **2** cause (someone) to appear foolish or absurd: *Counsel is not expected to **stultify himself** in an attempt to advance his client's interests.* ▷mid 18th cent.: from late Latin *stultificare*, from Latin *stultus* 'foolish.' —**stul·ti·fi·ca·tion** /ˌstəltəfiˈkāSHən/ *n.* —**stul·ti·fi·er** *n.*

stum /stəm/ ▸*n.* unfermented grape juice.

▸*v.* (**stummed, stum·ming**) [*trans.*] **1** prevent or stop the fermentation of (wine) by fumigating a cask with burning sulfur. **2** renew the fermentation of (wine) by adding stum. ▷mid 17th cent.: from Dutch *stom* (noun), *stommen* (verb), from *stom* 'dumb.'

stum·ble /ˈstəmbəl/ ▸*v.* [*intrans.*] trip or momentarily lose one's balance; almost fall: *her foot caught a shoe and she stumbled.* ■ [with *adverbial of direction*] trip repeatedly as one walks: *his legs still weak, he stumbled after them.* ■ make a mistake or repeated mistakes in speaking: *she **stumbled over** the words.* ■ (**stumble across/on/upon**) find or encounter by chance: *they stumbled across a farmer selling 25 acres.*

▸*n.* an act of stumbling. ■ a stumbling walk: *he parodied my groping stumble across the stage.* ▷Middle English (as a verb): from Old Norse, from the Germanic base of **STAMMER**. —**stum·bler** /-b(ə)lər/ *n.* —**stum·bling·ly** /-b(ə)liNGlē/ *adv.*

stum·ble·bum /ˈstəmbəlˌbəm/ ▸*n. informal* a clumsy or inept person.

stum·bling block ▸*n.* a circumstance that causes difficulty or hesitation: *bashfulness is a great stumbling block to some men.*

stump /stəmp/ ▸*n.* **1** the bottom part of a tree left projecting from the ground after most of the trunk has fallen or been cut down. ■ the small projecting remnant of something that has been cut or broken off or worn away: *the stump of an amputated arm.* **2** *Cricket* each of the three upright pieces of wood that form a wicket. **3** *Art* a cylinder with conical ends made of rolled paper or other soft material, used for softening or blending marks made with a crayon or pencil. **4** [as *adj.*] engaged in or involving political campaigning: *he is an inspiring stump speaker.* [referring to the use of a tree stump, from which an orator would speak.]

▸*v.* [*trans.*] **1** (usu. **be stumped**) (of a question or problem) be too hard for; baffle: *education chiefs were stumped by some of the exam questions.* ■ (**be stumped**) be at a loss; be unable to work out what to do or say: *detectives are **stumped for** a reason for the attack.* **2** [*intrans.*] walk stiffly and noisily: *he stumped away on short thick legs.* **3** travel around (a district) making political speeches: *there is no chance that he will be well enough to stump the country* | [*intrans.*] *the two men had come to the city to stump for the presidential candidate.* **4** use a stump on (a drawing, line, etc.).

▸*phrasal v.* □ **stump something up** *Brit., informal* pay a sum of money: *a buyer would have to stump up at least 8.5 million dollars for the site.* ▷Middle English (denoting a part of a limb remaining after an amputation): from Middle Low German *stump(e)* or Middle Dutch *stomp*. The early sense of the verb was 'stumble.'

▸*PHRASES* □ **on the stump** *informal* engaged in political campaigning. □ **up a stump** *informal* in a situation too difficult for one to manage.

stump·er /ˈstəmpər/ ▸*n. informal* a puzzling question.

stump·nose /ˈstəmpˌnōz/ ▸*n.* (*pl.* same) *chiefly S. African* a southern African sea bream, popular with anglers. • *Rhabdosargus* and other genera, family Sparidae: several species, in particular the **white stumpnose** (*R. globiceps*), which is of commercial importance.

stump work ▸*n.* a type of raised embroidery popular between the 15th and 17th centuries and characterized by elaborate designs padded with wool or hair.

stump·y /ˈstəmpē/ ▸*adj.* (**stump·i·er, stump·i·est**) short and thick; squat: *weak stumpy legs.* —**stump·i·ly** /-pəlē/ *adv.* —**stump·i·ness** *n.*

stun /stən/ ▸*v.* (**stunned, stun·ning**) [*trans.*] knock unconscious or into a dazed or semiconscious state: *the man was strangled after being stunned by a blow to the head.* ■ (usu. **be stunned**) astonish or shock (someone) so that they are temporarily unable to react: *the community was stunned by the tragedy.* ■ (of a sound) deafen temporarily: *a blast like that could stun anybody.* ▷Middle English: shortening of Old French *estoner* 'astonish.'

stung /stəNG/ ▸ past and past participle of **STING**.

stun gre·nade ▸*n.* a grenade that stuns people with its sound and flash, without causing serious injury.

stun gun ▸*n.* a device used to immobilize an attacker without causing serious injury, typically by administering an electric shock.

stunk /stəNGk/ ▸ past and past participle of **STINK**.

stun·ner /ˈstənər/ ▸*n. informal* a strikingly beautiful or impressive person or thing: *the girl was a stunner.* ■ an amazing turn of events.

stun·ning /ˈstəniNG/ ▸*adj.* extremely impressive or attractive: *she looked stunning.* —**stun·ning·ly** *adv.*

stun·sail /ˈstənsəl/ (also **stun·s'l**) ▸*n.* another term for **STUDDINGSAIL**. ▷mid 18th cent.: contraction.

stunt[1] /stənt/ ▸*v.* [*trans.*] [often as *adj.*] (**stunted**) retard the growth or development of: *trees damaged by acid rain had stunted branches.* ■ frustrate and spoil: *she was concerned at the stunted lives of those around her.* ▷late 16th cent. (in the sense 'bring to an abrupt halt'): from dialect *stunt* 'foolish, stubborn,' of Germanic origin; perhaps related to **STUMP**. —**stunt·ed·ness** *n.*

stunt[2] ▸*n.* an action displaying spectacular skill and daring. ■ something unusual done to attract attention: *the story was spread as a publicity stunt to help sell books.*

▸*v.* [*intrans.*] perform stunts, esp. aerobatics: *agile terns are stunting over the water.* ▷late 19th cent. (originally U.S. college slang): of unknown origin.

stunt cast·ing ▸*n.* to cast a notorious or unusual person as a guest star on a TV show, in order to garner publicity or higher ratings.

stunt·man /ˈstəntˌman/ ▸*n.* (*pl.* **-men**) a man employed to take an actor's place in performing dangerous stunts.

stunt·wom·an /ˈstəntˌwŏŏmən/ ▸*n.* (*pl.* **-wom·en**) a woman employed to take an actor's place in performing dangerous stunts.

stu·pa /ˈstōōpə/ ▸*n.* a dome-shaped structure erected as a Buddhist shrine. ▷from Sanskrit *stūpa*.

stupe[1] /st(y)ōōp/ *archaic* ▸*n.* a piece of soft cloth or absorbent cotton dipped in hot water and used to make a poultice.

▸*v.* [*trans.*] treat with such a poultice. ▷late Middle English (as a noun): via Latin from Greek *stupē*.

stupe[2] ▸*n. informal* a stupid person. ▷mid 18th cent.: abbreviation of **STUPID**.

stu·pe·fa·cient /ˌst(y)ōōpəˈfāSHənt/ *Medicine* ▸*adj.* (chiefly of a drug) causing semiconsciousness.

▸*n.* a drug of this type. ▷mid 17th cent.: from Latin *stupefacient-* 'stupefying,' from the verb *stupefacere*.

stu·pe·fy /ˈst(y)ōōpəˌfī/ ▸*v.* (**-fies, -fied**) [*trans.*] make (someone) unable to think or feel properly: *the offense of administering drugs to a woman with intent to stupefy her.* ■ astonish and shock: *the amount they spend on clothes would appall their parents and stupefy their grandparents.* ▷late Middle English: from French *stupéfier*, from Latin *stupefacere*, from *stupere* 'be struck senseless.' —**stu·pe·fac·tion** /ˌst(y)ōōpəˈfakSHən/ *n.* —**stu·pe·fi·er** *n.* —**stu·pe·fy·ing·ly** *adv.* [as *submodifier*] *a stupefyingly tedious task.*

stu·pen·dous /st(y)ōōˈpendəs/ ▸*adj. informal* extremely impressive: *a stupendous display of technique.* ▷mid 16th cent.: from Latin *stupendus* 'to be wondered at' (gerundive of *stupere*) + **-ous**. —**stu·pen·dous·ly** *adv.* —**stu·pen·dous·ness** *n.*

stu·pid /ˈst(y)ōōpid/ ▸*adj.* (**-pid·er, -pid·est**) lacking intelligence or common sense: *I was stupid enough to think she was perfect.* ■ dazed and unable to think clearly: *apprehension was numbing her brain and making her stupid.* ■ *informal* used to express exasperation or boredom: *she told him to stop messing with his stupid painting.*

▸*n. informal* a stupid person (often used as a term of address): *you're not a coward, stupid!* ▷mid 16th cent.: from French *stupide* or Latin *stupidus*, from *stupere* 'be amazed or stunned.' —**stu·pid·i·ty** /st(y)ōōˈpiditē/ *n.* —**stu·pid·ly** *adv.*

THE RIGHT WORD **asinine, dense, dull, dumb, obtuse, slow, stupid, unintelligent**

If you want to impugn someone's intelligence, the options are almost limitless.

You can call the person **stupid**, a term that implies a sluggish, slow-witted lack of intelligence.

Asinine is a harsher word, implying asslike or foolish behavior rather than slow-wittedness (*a woman her age looked asinine in a miniskirt*).

Calling someone **dumb** is risky, because it is not

only an informal word (*you dumb bunny!*), but because it also means mute and is associated with the offensive expression "deaf and dumb," used to describe people who cannot hear or speak.

Dense implies an inability to understand even simple facts or instructions (*too dense to get the joke*), while **dull** suggests a sluggishness of mind unrelieved by any hint of quickness, brightness, or liveliness (*a dull stare*).

Slow also implies a lack of quickness in comprehension or reaction and is often used as a euphemistic substitute for *stupid* (*he was a little slow intellectually*).

Obtuse is a more formal word for slow-wittedness, but with a strong undercurrent of scorn (*it almost seemed as though he were being deliberately obtuse*).

You can't go wrong with a word like **unintelligent**, which is probably the most objective term for low mental ability and the least likely to provoke an angry response (*unintelligent answers to the teacher's questions*).

stu·pid·ness /ˈst(y)o͞opidnis/ ▸*n. W. Indian* foolish or nonsensical talk or behavior: *girl, what stupidness are you talking?*

stu·por /ˈst(y)o͞opər/ ▸*n.* [in *sing.*] a state of near-unconsciousness or insensibility: *a drunken stupor.* ▷late Middle English: from Latin, from *stupere* 'be amazed or stunned.' —**stu·por·ous** /-rəs/ *adj.*

Stur·bridge /ˈstərˌbrij/ a town in south central Massachusetts, noted for its historical recreation of Old Sturbridge Village; pop. 7,775.

stur·dy /ˈstərdē/ ▸*adj.* (**-di·er, -di·est**) (of a person or their body) strongly and solidly built: *he had a sturdy, muscular physique.* ■ strong enough to withstand rough work or treatment: *the bike is sturdy enough to cope with bumpy tracks.* ■ showing confidence and determination: *the townspeople have a sturdy independence.*
▸*n.* vertigo in sheep caused by a tapeworm larva encysted in the brain. ▷Middle English (in the senses 'reckless, violent' and 'intractable, obstinate'): shortening of Old French *esturdi* 'stunned, dazed.' The derivation remains obscure; thought by some to be based on Latin *turdus* 'a thrush' (compare with the French phrase *soûl comme une grive* 'drunk as a thrush'). —**stur·died** *adj.* (from the *noun*) —**stur·di·ly** /-dl-ē/ *adv.* —**stur·di·ness** *n.*

stur·geon /ˈstərjən/ ▸*n.* a very large primitive fish with bony plates on the body. It occurs in temperate seas and rivers of the northern hemisphere, esp. central Eurasia, and is of commercial importance for its caviar and flesh. • Family Acipenseridae: several genera and species. ▷Middle English: from Anglo-Norman French, of Germanic origin; related to Dutch *steur* and German *Stör.*

Sturm·ab·tei·lung /ˌsʜto͝ormˈäpˌtīlo͝onɢ/ (abbr.: **SA**) see **BROWNSHIRT**. ▷German, literally 'storm division.'

Stur·mer /ˈstərmər/ (also **Sturmer pippin**) ▸*n.* an eating apple of a late-ripening variety with a mainly yellowish-green skin and firm yellowish flesh. ▷mid 19th cent.: named after the village of *Sturmer* in eastern England, where it was first grown.

Sturm und Drang /ˈsʜto͝orm o͝on(d) ˈdränɢ/ ▸*n.* a literary and artistic movement in Germany in the late 18th century, influenced by Jean-Jacques Rousseau and characterized by the expression of emotional unrest and a rejection of neoclassical literary norms. ▷German, literally 'storm and stress.'

Sturt's des·ert rose /stərts/ ▸*n.* see **DESERT ROSE** (sense 3).

stut·ter /ˈstətər/ ▸*v.* [*intrans.*] talk with continued involuntary repetition of sounds, esp. initial consonants: *the child was stuttering in fright.* ■ [*trans.*] utter in such a way: *he shyly* **stuttered out** *an invitation to the movies* | [with *direct speech*] *"W-what's happened?" she stuttered.* ■ (of a machine or gun) produce a series of short, sharp sounds: *she flinched as a machine gun stuttered nearby.*
▸*n.* a tendency to stutter while speaking. ■ a series of short, sharp sounds produced by a machine or gun. ▷late 16th cent. (as a verb): frequentative of dialect *stut,* of Germanic origin; related to German *stossen* 'strike against.' —**stut·ter·er** *n.* —**stut·ter·ing·ly** *adv.*

stut·ter tone ▸*n.* a dial tone interrupted by several short gaps, indicating the arrival of new voicemail messages to the user.

Stutt·gart /ˈsʜto͞otˌgärt; ˈsto͞ot-; ˈstət-/ an industrial city in western Germany, the capital of Baden-Württemberg, on the Neckar River; pop. 592,000.

Stuy·ves·ant /ˈstīvəsənt/, Peter (c.1610–72), Dutch administrator in North America. Appointed colonial governor of New Netherland (what are now the states of New York and New Jersey) in 1647, he served until the colony was captured by English forces in 1664. In 1655, he expanded the colony by taking over New Sweden in the Delaware River area.

St. Val·en·tine's Day Mas·sa·cre the shooting on February 14, 1929, of seven members of the rival "Bugsy" Moran's gang by some of Al Capone's men disguised as policemen.

St. Vin·cent and the Gren·a·dines an island state in the Windward Islands in the Caribbean Sea that consists of the mountainous island of St. Vincent and some of the Grenadine islands; pop. 108,000; capital, Kingstown; languages, English (official) and English-based Creole.

The French, Dutch, and British all made attempts at settlements in the 18th century, and the islands finally fell to British possession in 1783.The state obtained full independence with a limited form of membership of the Commonwealth of Nations in 1979.

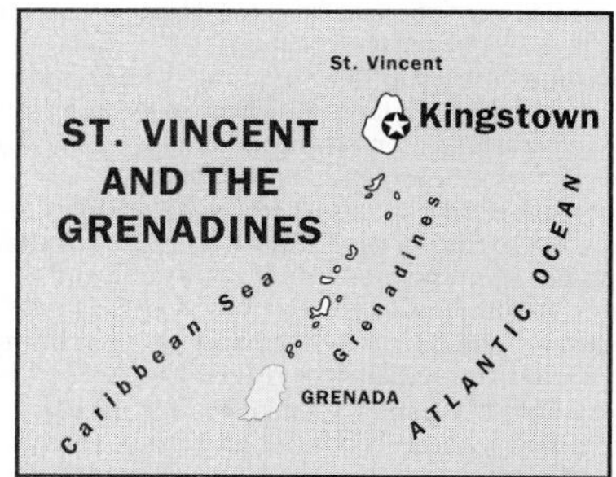

St. Vi·tus's dance ▸*n.* old-fashioned term for **SYDENHAM'S CHOREA**. ▷so named because a visit to *St. Vitus*'s shrine was believed to alleviate the disease.

sty[1] /stī/ ▸*n.* a pigpen.
▸*v.* (**sties, stied**) [*trans.*] *archaic* keep (a pig) in a sty: *the most beggarly place that ever pigs were stied in.* ▷Old English *stī-* (in *stīfearh* 'sty pig'), probably identical with *stig* 'hall' (see **STEWARD**), of Germanic origin.

sty[2] (also **stye**) ▸*n.* (*pl.* **sties** /stīz/ or **styes**) an inflamed swelling on the edge of an eyelid, caused by bacterial infection of the gland at the base of an eyelash. ▷early 17th cent.: from dialect *styany,* from *styan* (from Old English *stīgend* 'riser') + **EYE**.

Styg·i·an /ˈstijēən/ ▸*adj.* of or relating to the Styx River. ■ *poetic/literary* very dark: *the Stygian crypt.*

sty·lar /ˈstīlər/ ▸*adj. Botany* of or relating to the style or styles of a flower.

style /stīl/ ▸*n.* **1** a manner of doing something: *different styles of management.* ■ a way of painting, writing, composing, building, etc., characteristic of a particular period, place, person, or movement. ■ a way of using language: *he never wrote in a journalistic style* | *students should pay attention to style and idiom.* ■ [usu. with *negative*] a way of behaving or approaching a situation that is characteristic of or favored by a particular person: *backing out isn't my style.* ■ an official or legal title: *the partnership traded* **under the style of** *Storr and Mortimer.* **2** a distinctive appearance, typically determined by the principles according to which something is designed: *the pillars are no exception to the general style.* ■ a particular design of clothing. ■ a way of arranging the hair. **3** elegance and sophistication: *a sophisticated nightspot with style and taste.* **4** a rodlike object or part, in particular: ■ archaic term for **STYLUS** (sense 2). ■ *Botany* (in a flower) a narrow, typically elongated extension of the ovary, bearing the stigma. ■ *Zoology* (in an invertebrate) a small slender pointed appendage; a stylet. ■ the gnomon of a sundial.
▸*v.* [*trans.*] **1** design or make in a particular form: *the yacht is well proportioned and conservatively styled.* ■ arrange (hair) in a particular way: *he styled her hair by twisting it up to give it body.* **2** [*trans.*] designate with a particular name, description, or title: *the official is styled principal and vice chancellor of the university.* ▷Middle English (denoting a stylus, also a literary composition, an official title, or a characteristic manner of literary expression): from Old French *stile,* from Latin *stilus.* The verb dates (first in sense 2) from the early 16th cent. —**style·less** /ˈstīl(l)is/ *adj.* —**style·less·ness** /ˈstīl(l)isnis/ *n.* —**styl·er** *n.*
▸*PHRASE* □ **in style** (or **in grand style**) in an impressive, grand, or luxurious way.

-style ▸*suffix* (forming adjectives and adverbs) in a manner characteristic of: *family-style* | *church-style.* ▷from **STYLE**.

style sheet ▸*n. Computing* a type of template file consisting of font and layout settings to give a standardized look to certain documents.

sty·let /stīˈlet; ˈstīlit/ ▸*n.* **1** *Medicine* a slender probe. ■ a wire or piece of plastic run through a catheter or cannula in order to stiffen it or to clear it. **2** *Zoology* (in an invertebrate) a small style, esp. a piercing mouthpart of an insect. ▷late 17th cent.: from French *stilet,* from Italian *stiletto* (see **STILETTO**).

sty·li /ˈstīlī/ ▸ plural form of **STYLUS**.

sty·lish /ˈstīlisʜ/ ▸*adj.* having or displaying a good sense of style: *these are elegant and stylish performances.* ■ fashionably elegant: *a stylish and innovative range of jewelry.* —**styl·ish·ly** *adv.* —**styl·ish·ness** *n.*

styl·ist /ˈstīlist/ ▸*n.* **1** a person who works creatively in the fashion and beauty industry, in particular: ■ a designer of fashionable styles of clothing. ■ a hairdresser. **2** a person noted for elegant work or performance, in particular: ■ a writer noted for taking great pains over the style in which he or she writes. ■ (in sports or music) a person who performs with style.

sty·lis·tic /stīˈlistik/ ▸*adj.* of or concerning style, esp. literary style: *the stylistic conventions of magazine stories.* ▷mid 19th cent.: from **STYLIST**, suggested by German *stilistisch.* —**styl·is·ti·cal·ly** /-ik(ə)lē/ *adv.*

sty·lis·tics /stīˈlistiks/ ▸*plural n.* [treated as *sing.*] the study of the distinctive styles found in particular literary genres and in the works of individual writers.

sty·lite /ˈstīˌlīt/ ▸*n. historical* an ascetic living on top of a pillar, esp. in ancient or medieval Syria, Turkey, and Greece in the 5th century AD. ▷mid 17th cent.: from ecclesiastical Greek *stulitēs,* from *stulos* 'pillar.'

styl·ize /ˈstīˌlīz/ ▸*v.* [*trans.*] [usu. as *adj.*] (**stylized**) depict or treat in a mannered and nonrealistic style: *gracefully shaped vases decorated with stylized but recognizable white lilies.* ▷late 19th cent.: from **STYLE**, suggested by German *stilisiren.* —**styl·i·za·tion** /ˌstīliˈzāsʜən/ *n.*

sty·lo /ˈstīlō/ ▸*n.* (*pl.* **-los**) *informal* short for **STYLOGRAPH**.

sty·lo·bate /ˈstīləˌbāt/ ▸*n.* a continuous base supporting a row of columns in classical Greek architecture. ▷late 17th cent.: via Latin from Greek *stulobatēs,* from *stulos* 'pillar' + *batēs* 'base' (from *bainein* 'to walk').

sty·lo·graph /ˈstīləˌgraf/ ▸*n.* a kind of fountain pen having a fine perforated tube instead of a split nib. ▷mid 19th cent.: from **STYLUS** + **-GRAPH**. —**sty·lo·graph·ic** /ˌstīləˈgrafik/ *adj.*

sty·loid /ˈstīˌloid/ ▸*adj. technical* resembling a stylus or pen.
▸*n.* short for **STYLOID PROCESS**.

sty·loid proc·ess ▸*n. Anatomy* a slender projection of bone, such as that from the lower surface of the temporal bone of the skull, or those at the lower ends of the ulna and radius.

sty·lo·lite /ˈstīləˌlīt/ ▸*n. Geology* an irregular surface or seam within a limestone or other sedimentary rock, characterized by irregular interlocking pegs and sockets around 1 cm in depth and a concentration of insoluble minerals. ■ a grooved peg forming part of such a seam. ▷mid 19th cent.: from Greek *stulos* 'column' + **-LITE**.

sty·lom·e·try /stīˈlämitrē/ ▸*n.* the statistical analysis of variations in literary style between one writer or genre and another. —**sty·lo·met·ric** /-ləˈmetrik/ *adj.*

sty·lo·phone /ˈstīləˌfōn/ ▸*n.* a miniature electronic musical instrument producing a distinctive buzzing sound when a stylus is drawn along its metal keyboard.

sty·lo·pized /ˈstīləˌpēzd; -ˌpīzd/ ▸*adj. Entomology* (of a bee or other insect) parasitized by a stylops.

sty·lops /ˈstīˌläps/ ▸*n.* (*pl.* same) a minute insect that spends part or all of its life as an internal parasite of other insects, esp. bees or wasps. The males are winged and the females typically retain a grublike form and remain parasitic. • Order Strepsiptera, in particular genus *Stylops,* family Stylopidae. ▷late 19th cent.: modern Latin, from Greek *stulos* 'column' + *ōps* 'eye, face.' —**sty·lo·pid** /-ləˌpid/ *n.* & *adj.*

sty·lus /ˈstīləs/ ▸*n.* (*pl.* **-li** /-ˌlī/ or **-lus·es**) **1** a hard point, typically of diamond or sapphire, following a groove in a phonograph record and transmitting

Pronunciation Key ə *ago;* ər *over;* ˈə *or* ˌə *up;* ˈər *or* ˌər *fur;* a *hat;* ā *rate;* ä *car;* ᴄʜ *chew;* e *let;* ē *see;* e(ə)r *air;* i *fit;* ī *by;* i(ə)r *ear;* ɴɢ *sing;* ō *go;* ô *for;* oi *boy;* o͝o *good;* o͞o *goo;* ou *out;* sʜ *she;* ᴛʜ *thin;* T͟H *then;* (h)w *why;* ᴢʜ *vision*

the recorded sound for reproduction. ■ a similar point producing such a groove when recording sound. **2** an ancient writing implement, consisting of a small rod with a pointed end for scratching letters on wax-covered tablets, and a blunt end for obliterating them. ■ an implement of similar shape used esp. for engraving and tracing. ■ *Computing* a penlike device used to input handwritten text or drawings directly into a computer or for input on a touch-sensitive monitor. ▷early 18th cent. (as a modern Latin term in botany: see STYLE): erroneous spelling of Latin *stilus*.

sty·mie /ˈstīmē/ ▸*v.* (**-mies**, **-mied**, **-my·ing** or **-mie·ing**) [*trans.*] *informal* prevent or hinder the progress of: *the changes must not be allowed to stymie new medical treatments.* ▷mid 19th cent. (originally a golfing term, denoting a situation on the green where a ball obstructs the shot of another player): of unknown origin.

styp·tic /ˈstiptik/ *Medicine* ▸*adj.* (of a substance) capable of causing bleeding to stop when it is applied to a wound.

▸*n.* a substance of this kind. ▷late Middle English: via Latin from Greek *stuptikos*, from *stuphein* 'to contract.'

styp·tic pen·cil ▸*n.* a stick of a styptic substance, used to treat small cuts.

sty·rax /ˈstīˌraks/ ▸*n.* variant of STORAX.

sty·rene /ˈstīˌrēn/ ▸*n.* *Chemistry* an unsaturated liquid hydrocarbon obtained as a petroleum byproduct. It is easily polymerized and is used to make plastics and resins. • Chem. formula: $C_6H_5CH{=}CH_2$. ▷late 19th cent.: from STYRAX + -ENE.

sty·ro·foam /ˈstīrəˌfōm/ ▸*n.* *trademark* a kind of expanded polystyrene. ▷1950s: from POLYSTYRENE + FOAM.

Sty·ron /ˈstīrən/, William (Clark, Jr.) (1925–), U.S. writer. His works include *The Confessions of Nat Turner* (1967); *Sophie's Choice* (1979); *Darkness Visible* (1990), about his own battle with depression; and *A Tidewater Morning: Three Tales from Youth* (1993).

Styx /stiks/ *Greek Mythology* one of the rivers in the underworld, over which Charon ferried the souls of the dead. ▷from Greek *Stux*, from *stugnos* 'hateful, gloomy.'

sua·sion /ˈswāzʜən/ ▸*n.* *formal* persuasion as opposed to force or compulsion. ▷late Middle English: from Old French, or from Latin *suasio(n-)*, from *suadere* 'to urge.'

sua·sive /ˈswāsiv/ ▸*adj.* serving to persuade. ■ *Grammar* denoting a class of English verbs, for example, *insist*, whose meaning includes the notion of persuading and that take a subordinate clause whose verb may either be in the subjunctive or take a modal.

suave /swäv/ ▸*adj.* (**suav·er**, **suav·est**) (esp. of a man) charming, confident, and elegant: *all the waiters were suave and deferential.* See note at URBANE. ▷late Middle English (in the sense 'gracious, agreeable'): from Old French, or from Latin *suavis* 'agreeable.' The current sense dates from the mid 19th cent. —**suave·ly** *adv.* —**suave·ness** *n.* —**suav·i·ty** /-itē/ *n.* (*pl.* **-ties**).

sub /səb/ *informal* ▸*n.* **1** a submarine. ■ short for SUBMARINE SANDWICH. **2** a subscription. **3** a substitute.

▸*v.* (**subbed**, **sub·bing**) [*intrans.*] act as a substitute for someone: *he **subbed for** Scott as weatherman.*

sub. ▸*abbr.* ■ subordinated. ■ subscription. ■ substitute. ■ suburb. ■ suburban. ■ subway.

sub- ▸*prefix* **1** at, to, or from a lower level or position: *subalpine* | *sub-basement.* ■ lower in rank: *subdeacon.* ■ of a smaller size; of a subordinate nature: *subculture.* ■ of lesser quality; inferior: *subhuman* | *substandard.* **2** somewhat; nearly; more or less: *subantarctic.* **3** denoting a later or secondary action of the same kind: *sublet* | *subdivision* | *subsequent.* **4** denoting support: *subvention.* **5** *Chemistry* in names of compounds containing a relatively small proportion of a component: *suboxide.* ▷from Latin *sub* 'under, close to.'

USAGE Sub- is also found assimilated in the following forms: **suc-** before *c*; **suf-** before *f*; **sug-** before *g*; **sup-** before *p*; **sur-** before *r*; **sus-** before *c, p, t.*

sub·ac·id /ˌsəbˈasid/ ▸*adj.* (of a fruit) moderately sharp to the taste. ▷mid 17th cent.: from Latin *subacidus* (see SUB-, ACID).

sub·a·cute /ˌsəbəˈkyo͞ot/ ▸*adj.* **1** *Medicine* (of a condition) between acute and chronic. **2** moderately acute in shape or angle.

sub·a·dult /ˌsəbəˈdəlt/ ▸*n.* *Zoology* an animal that is not fully adult.

sub·aer·i·al /ˌsəbˈe(ə)rēəl/ ▸*adj.* *Geology* existing, occurring, or formed in the open air or on the earth's surface, not underwater or underground. —**sub·aer·i·al·ly** *adv.*

sub·a·gen·cy /ˌsəbˈājənsē/ ▸*n.* (*pl.* **-cies**) a subordinate commercial, political, or other agency. —**sub·a·gent** /-ˈājənt/ *n.*

sub·al·pine /ˌsəbˈalpīn/ ▸*adj.* of or situated on the higher slopes of mountains just below the treeline.

sub·al·tern ▸*n.* /səbˈôltərn/ an officer in the British army below the rank of captain, esp. a second lieutenant.

▸*adj.* /səbˈôltərn/ **1** of lower status: *the private tutor was a recognized subaltern part of the bourgeois family.* **2** /ˈsəbəlˌtərn/ *dated Logic* (of a proposition) implied by another proposition (e.g., as a particular affirmative is by a universal one), but not implying it in return. ▷late 16th cent. (as an adjective): from late Latin *subalternus*, from Latin *sub-* 'below' + *alternus* 'every other.'

sub·ant·arc·tic /ˌsəbantˈärktik; -ˈärtik/ ▸*adj.* of or relating to the region immediately north of the Antarctic Circle.

sub·a·quat·ic /ˌsəbəˈkwätik; -ˈkwa-/ ▸*adj.* underwater: *a narrow, subaquatic microclimate.*

sub·a·que·ous /səbˈākwēəs; -ˈak-/ ▸*adj.* existing, formed, or taking place underwater. ■ *figurative* lacking in substance or strength: *the light that filtered through the leaves was pale, subaqueous.*

sub·a·rach·noid /ˌsəbəˈraknoid/ ▸*adj.* *Anatomy* denoting or occurring in the fluid-filled space around the brain between the arachnoid membrane and the pia mater, through which major blood vessels pass.

sub·arc·tic /ˌsəbˈärktik; -ˈärtik/ ▸*adj.* of or relating to the region immediately south of the Arctic Circle.

sub·as·sem·bly /ˌsəbəˈsemblē/ ▸*n.* (*pl.* **-blies**) a unit assembled separately but designed to be incorporated with other units into a larger manufactured product.

Sub-At·lan·tic ▸*adj.* *Geology* of, relating to, or denoting the fifth climatic stage of the postglacial period in northern Europe, following the Sub-Boreal stage (from about 2,800 years ago to the present day). The climate has been cooler and wetter than in the earlier postglacial periods. ■ [as *n.*] (**the Sub-Atlantic**) the Sub-Atlantic climatic stage.

sub·a·tom·ic /ˌsəbəˈtämik/ ▸*adj.* smaller than or occurring within an atom.

sub·a·tom·ic par·ti·cle ▸*n.* a particle smaller than an atom (e.g., a neutron) or a cluster of such particles (e.g., an alpha particle). Compare with ELEMENTARY PARTICLE.

sub·au·di·tion /ˌsəbôˈdisʜən/ ▸*n.* a thing that is not stated, only implied or inferred. ▷late 18th cent.: from late Latin *subauditio(n-)*, from *subaudire* 'understand.'

sub·base·ment ▸*n.* a story below a basement.

Sub-Bo·re·al ▸*adj.* *Geology* of, relating to, or denoting the fourth climatic stage of the postglacial period in northern Europe, between the Atlantic and Sub-Atlantic stages (about 5,000 to 2,800 years ago). The stage corresponds to the Neolithic period and Bronze Age, and the climate was cooler and drier than previously but still warmer than today. ■ [as *n.*] (**the Sub-Boreal**) the Sub-Boreal climatic stage.

sub·branch ▸*n.* a secondary or subordinate branch of anything that has branches, such as a tree, a subject of study, or a bank.

sub·breed ▸*n.* a minor variant of a breed; a secondary breed.

sub·car·ri·er /ˈsəbˌkarēər/ ▸*n.* *Telecommunications* a carrier wave modulated by a signal wave and then used with other subcarriers to modulate the main carrier wave.

sub·cat·e·go·ry /ˈsəbˌkatəˌgôrē/ ▸*n.* (*pl.* **-ries**) a secondary or subordinate category. —**sub·cat·e·go·ri·za·tion** /ˌsəbˌkatəgəriˈzāsʜən/ *n.* —**sub·cat·e·go·rize** /ˌsəbˈkatəgəˌrīz/ *v.*

sub·class /ˈsəbˌklas/ ▸*n.* a secondary or subordinate class. ■ *Biology* a taxonomic category that ranks below class and above order.

sub·cla·vi·an /səbˈklāvēən/ ▸*adj.* *Anatomy* relating to or denoting an artery or vein that serves the neck and arm on the left or right side of the body. ▷mid 17th cent.: from modern Latin *subclavius*, from *sub* 'under' + *clavis* 'key' (see CLAVICLE), + -IAN.

sub·clin·i·cal /ˌsəbˈklinikəl/ ▸*adj.* *Medicine* relating to or denoting a disease that is not severe enough to present definite or readily observable symptoms.

sub·com·mit·tee /ˈsəbkəˌmitē/ ▸*n.* a committee composed of some members of a larger committee, board, or other body and reporting to it.

sub·com·pact /səbˈkämpakt/ ▸*n.* a motor vehicle that is smaller than a compact.

sub·con·i·cal /səbˈkänikəl/ ▸*adj.* approximately conical.

sub·con·scious /səbˈkänsʜəs/ ▸*adj.* of or concerning the part of the mind of which one is not fully aware but which influences one's actions and feelings: *my subconscious fear.*

▸*n.* (**one's/the subconscious**) this part of the mind (not in technical use in psychoanalysis, where *unconscious* is preferred). —**sub·con·scious·ly** *adv.* —**sub·con·scious·ness** *n.*

sub·con·ti·nent /ˌsəbˈkäntə)nənt/ ▸*n.* a large, distinguishable part of a continent, such as North America or southern Africa. See also INDIAN SUBCONTINENT. —**sub·con·ti·nen·tal** /-ˌkäntəˈnen(t)l/ *adj.*

sub·con·tract ▸*v.* /səbkənˈtrakt/ [*trans.*] employ a business or person outside one's company to do (work) as part of a larger project: *we would **subcontract** the translation work **out**.* ■ [*intrans.*] (of a business or person) carry out work for a company as part of a larger project.

▸*n.* /səbˈkäntrakt/ a contract for a company or person to do work for another company as part of a larger project.

sub·con·trac·tor /səbˈkänˌtraktər/ ▸*n.* a business or person that carries out work for a company as part of a larger project.

sub·con·tra·ry /ˌsəbˈkäntrerē/ *dated Logic* ▸*adj.* denoting propositions that can both be true, but cannot both be false (e.g., *some X are Y* and *some X are not Y*).

▸*n.* (*pl.* **-ries**) a proposition of this kind. ▷late 16th cent.: from late Latin *subcontrarius*, translation of Greek *hupenantios*.

sub·cor·ti·cal /səbˈkôrtikəl/ ▸*adj.* below the cortex. ■ *Anatomy* relating to or denoting the region of the brain below the cortex.

sub·cos·tal /səbˈkôstl; -ˈkästl/ ▸*adj.* *Anatomy* beneath a rib; below the ribs.

sub·crit·i·cal /səbˈkritikəl/ ▸*adj.* *Physics* below a critical threshold, in particular: ■ (in nuclear physics) containing or involving less than the critical mass. ■ (of a flow of fluid) slower than the speed at which waves travel in the fluid.

sub·cul·ture /ˈsəbˌkəlcʜər/ ▸*n.* a cultural group within a larger culture, often having beliefs or interests at variance with those of the larger culture. —**sub·cul·tur·al** /ˌsəbˈkəlcʜərəl/ *adj.*

sub·cu·ta·ne·ous /ˌsəbkyo͞oˈtānēəs/ ▸*adj.* *Anatomy & Medicine* situated or applied under the skin: *subcutaneous fat.* —**sub·cu·ta·ne·ous·ly** *adv.*

sub·dea·con /ˈsəbˌdēkən/ ▸*n.* (in some Christian churches) a minister of an order ranking below deacon. Now largely obsolete in the Western church, the liturgical role has been taken by other ministers. —**sub·di·ac·o·nate** /ˌsəbdīˈakənit; -ˌnāt/ *n.*

sub·di·rec·to·ry /ˌsəbdəˈrektərē/ ▸*n.* (*pl.* **-ries**) *Computing* a directory below another directory in a hierarchy.

sub·di·vide /ˈsəbdəˌvīd/ ▸*v.* [*trans.*] divide (something that has already been divided or that is a separate unit): *the heading was **subdivided into** eight separate sections.* ▷late Middle English: from Latin *subdividere* (see SUB-, DIVIDE).

sub·di·vi·sion /ˈsəbdəˌvizʜən/ ▸*n.* the action of subdividing or being subdivided. ■ a secondary or subordinate division. ■ an area of land divided into plots for sale; an area of housing. ■ *Biology* any taxonomic subcategory, esp. (in botany) one that ranks below division and above class.

sub·dom·i·nant /səbˈdämənənt/ ▸*n.* *Music* the fourth note of the diatonic scale of any key.

sub·duc·tion /səbˈdəksʜən/ ▸*n.* *Geology* the sideways and downward movement of the edge of a plate of the earth's crust into the mantle beneath another plate. ▷1970s: via French from Latin *subductio(n-)*, from *subduct-* 'drawn from below,' from the verb *subducere*. —**sub·duct** /-ˈdəkt/ *v.*

sub·due /səbˈd(y)o͞o/ ▸*v.* (**-dues**, **-dued**, **-du·ing**) [*trans.*] overcome, quieten, or bring under control (a feeling or person): *she managed to subdue an instinct to applaud.* ■ bring (a country or people) under control by force: *Charles went on a campaign to subdue the Saxons.* ▷late Middle English: from Anglo-Norman French *suduire*, from Latin *subducere*, literally 'draw from below.' —**sub·du·a·ble** *adj.*

sub·dued /ˌsəbˈd(y)o͞od/ ▸*adj.* **1** (of a person or their manner) quiet and rather reflective or depressed: *I* *felt strangely subdued as I drove home.* **2** (of color or lighting) soft and restrained: *a subdued plaid shirt.*

sub·du·ral /səb'd(y)ŏŏrəl/ ▸*adj. Anatomy* situated or occurring between the dura mater and the arachnoid membrane of the brain and spinal cord.

sub·ed·it /səb'edit/ ▸*v.* (**-ed·it·ed**, **-ed·it·ing**) [*trans.*] *chiefly Brit.* check, correct, and adjust the extent of (the text of a newspaper or magazine before printing), typically also writing headlines and captions. —**sub·ed·i·tor** /-'editər/ *n.*

su·ber·in /'sōōbərən/ ▸*n. Botany* an inert impermeable waxy substance present in the cell walls of corky tissues. ▷mid 19th cent.: from Latin *suber* 'cork' + -IN[1].

su·ber·ize /'sōōbə,rīz/ ▸*v.* [*trans.*] [usu. as *adj.*] (**suberized**) *Botany* impregnate (the wall of a plant cell) with suberin: *suberized cell walls.* —**su·ber·i·za·tion** /,sōōbəri'zāSHən/ *n.*

sub·fam·i·ly /'səb,fam(ə)lē/ ▸*n.* (*pl.* **-lies**) a subdivision of a group. ■ *Biology* a taxonomic category that ranks below family and above tribe or genus, usually ending in *-inae* (in zoology) or *-oideae* (in botany).

sub·floor /'səb,flôr/ ▸*n.* the foundation for a floor in a building.

sub·form /'səb,fôrm/ ▸*n.* a subordinate or secondary form.

sub·frame /'səb,frām/ ▸*n.* a supporting frame, esp. one into which a window or door is set, or one to which the engine or suspension of a car without a true chassis is attached.

sub·fusc /səb'fəsk/ ▸*adj. poetic/literary* dull; gloomy: *the light was subfusc and aqueous.*
▸*n. Brit.* the formal clothing worn for examinations and formal occasions at some universities. ▷early 18th cent.: from Latin *subfuscus*, from *sub-* 'somewhat' + *fuscus* 'dark brown.'

sub·ge·nus /'səb,jēnəs/ ▸*n.* (*pl.* **-gen·er·a** /-,jenərə/) *Biology* a taxonomic category that ranks below genus and above species. —**sub·ge·ner·ic** /,səbjə'nerik/ *adj.*

sub·gla·cial /,səb'glāSHəl/ ▸*adj. Geology* situated or occurring underneath a glacier or ice sheet.

sub·group /'səb,grōōp/ ▸*n.* a subdivision of a group. ■ *Mathematics* a group whose members are all members of another group, both being subject to the same operations.

sub·har·mon·ic /,səbhär'mänik/ ▸*n.* an oscillation with a frequency equal to an integral submultiple of another frequency.
▸*adj.* denoting or involving a subharmonic.

sub·head·ing /'səb,hediNG/ (also **sub·head**) ▸*n.* a heading given to a subsection of a piece of writing.

sub·hu·man /səb'(h)yōōmən/ ▸*adj.* of a lower order of being than the human. ■ *Zoology* (of a primate) closely related to humans. ■ *derogatory* (of people or their behavior) not worthy of a human being; debased or depraved: *he regards all PR people as subhuman.*
▸*n.* a subhuman creature or person.

Su·bic Bay /'sōōbik/ an inlet of the South China Sea in the Philippines, off central Luzon Island. A large U.S. naval facility closed here in 1992.

subj. ▸*abbr.* ■ subject. ■ subjective. ■ subjectively. ■ subjunctive.

sub·ja·cent /səb'jāsənt/ ▸*adj. technical* situated below something else. ▷late 16th cent.: from Latin *subjacent-* 'lying underneath,' from *sub-* 'under' + *jacere* 'to lie.' —**sub·ja·cen·cy** *n.*

sub·ject ▸*n.* /'səbjəkt/ **1** a person or thing that is being discussed, described, or dealt with: *I've said all there is to be said on the subject | he's the subject of a major new biography.* ■ a person or circumstance giving rise to a specified feeling, response, or action: *the incident was the* ***subject of*** *international condemnation.* ■ *Grammar* a noun phrase functioning as one of the main components of a clause, being the element about which the rest of the clause is predicated. ■ *Logic* the part of a proposition about which a statement is made. ■ *Music* a theme of a fugue or of a piece in sonata form; a leading phrase or motif. ■ a person who is the focus of scientific or medical attention or experiment. **2** a branch of knowledge studied or taught in a school, college, or university. **3** a citizen or member of a state other than its supreme ruler. **4** *Philosophy* a thinking or feeling entity; the conscious mind; the ego, esp. as opposed to anything external to the mind. ■ the central substance or core of a thing as opposed to its attributes.
▸*adj.* /'səbjəkt/ [*predic.*] (**subject to**) **1** likely or prone to be affected by (a particular condition or occurrence, typically an unwelcome or unpleasant one): *he was subject to bouts of manic depression.* **2** dependent or conditional upon: *the proposed merger is subject to the approval of the shareholders.* **3** under the authority of: *legislation making Congress subject to the laws it passes.* ■ [*attrib.*] under the control or domination of (another ruler, country, or government): *the Greeks were the first subject people to break free from Ottoman rule.*
▸*adv.* /'səbjəkt/ (**subject to**) conditionally upon: *subject to bankruptcy court approval, the company expects to begin liquidation of its inventory.*
▸*v.* /səb'jekt/ [*trans.*] **1** (**subject someone/something to**) cause or force to undergo (a particular experience of form of treatment): *he'd subjected her to a terrifying ordeal.* **2** bring (a person or country) under one's control or jurisdiction, typically by using force. ▷Middle English (in the sense '(person) owing obedience'): from Old French *suget*, from Latin *subjectus* 'brought under,' past participle of *subicere*, from *sub-* 'under' + *jacere* 'throw.' Senses relating to philosophy, logic, and grammar are derived ultimately from Aristotle's use of *to hupokeimenon* meaning 'material from which things are made' and 'subject of attributes and predicates.' —**sub·jec·tion** /səb'jekSHən/ *n.* —**sub·ject·less** /'səbjək(t)ləs/ *adj.*

sub·ject cat·a·log ▸*n.* a catalog, esp. in a library, that is arranged according to the subjects treated.

sub·jec·tive /səb'jektiv/ ▸*adj.* **1** based on or influenced by personal feelings, tastes, or opinions: *his views are highly subjective | there is always the danger of making a subjective judgment.* Contrasted with OBJECTIVE. ■ dependent on the mind or on an individual's perception for its existence. **2** *Grammar* of, relating to, or denoting a case of nouns and pronouns used for the subject of a sentence.
▸*n.* (**the subjective**) *Grammar* the subjective case. ▷late Middle English (originally in the sense 'characteristic of a political subject, submissive'): from Latin *subjectivus*, from *subject-* 'brought under' (see SUBJECT). —**sub·jec·tive·ly** *adv.* —**sub·jec·tive·ness** *n.* —**sub·jec·tiv·i·ty** /,səbjek'tivitē/ *n.*

sub·jec·tive case ▸*n. Grammar* the nominative.

sub·jec·tiv·ism /səb'jektə,vizəm/ ▸*n. Philosophy* the doctrine that knowledge is merely subjective and that there is no external or objective truth. —**sub·jec·tiv·ist** *n. & adj.*

sub·ject mat·ter ▸*n.* the topic dealt with or the subject represented in a debate, exposition, or work of art.

sub·join /səb'join/ ▸*v.* [*trans.*] *formal* add (comments or supplementary information) at the end of a speech or text. ▷late 16th cent.: from obsolete French *subjoindre*, from Latin *subjungere*, from *sub-* 'in addition' + *jungere* 'to join.'

sub ju·di·ce /,sōōb 'yōōdi,kā; ,səb 'jōōdi,sē/ ▸*adj. Law* under judicial consideration and therefore prohibited from public discussion elsewhere: *the cases were still sub judice.* ▷Latin, literally 'under a judge.'

sub·ju·gate /'səbjə,gāt/ ▸*v.* [*trans.*] bring under domination or control, esp. by conquest: *the invaders had soon subjugated most of the native population.* ■ (**subjugate someone/something to**) make someone or something subordinate to: *the new ruler firmly subjugated the Church to the state.* ▷late Middle English: from late Latin *subjugat-* 'brought under a yoke,' from the verb *subjugare*, based on *jugum* 'yoke.' —**sub·ju·ga·tion** /,səbjə'gāSHən/ *n.* —**sub·ju·ga·tor** /-,gātər/ *n.*

sub·junc·tive /səb'jəNG(k)tiv/ *Grammar* ▸*adj.* relating to or denoting a mood of verbs expressing what is imagined or wished or possible. Compare with INDICATIVE.
▸*n.* a verb in the subjunctive mood. ■ (**the subjunctive**) the subjunctive mood. ▷mid 16th cent.: from French *subjonctif, -ive* or late Latin *subjunctivus*, from *subjungere* (see SUBJOIN), rendering Greek *hupotaktikos* 'subjoined.' —**sub·junc·tive·ly** *adv.*

USAGE These sentences all contain a verb in the **subjunctive mood**; . . . *if I* ***were*** *you; the report recommends that he* ***face*** *the tribunal; it is important that they* ***be*** *aware of the provisions of the act.* The subjunctive is used to express situations that are hypothetical or not yet realized and is typically used for what is imagined, hoped for, demanded, or expected. In English, the subjunctive mood is fairly uncommon (esp. in comparison with other languages such as French and Spanish), mainly because most of the functions of the subjunctive are covered by modal verbs such as **might, could,** and **should.** In fact, in English the subjunctive is often indistinguishable from the ordinary **indicative mood** since its form in most contexts is identical. It is distinctive only in the third person singular, where the normal indicative **-s** ending is absent (*he* ***face*** rather than *he* ***faces*** in the example above), and in the verb 'to be' (*I* ***were*** rather than *I* ***was***, and *they* ***be*** rather than *they* ***are*** in the examples above). In modern English, the subjunctive mood still exists but is regarded in many contexts as optional. Use of the subjunctive tends to convey a more formal tone, but there are few people who would regard its absence as actually wrong. Today, it survives mostly in fixed expressions, as in ***be*** *that as it may; far* ***be*** *it from me; as it* ***were***; *lest we* ***forget***; *God* ***help*** *you;* ***perish*** *the thought*; and ***come*** *what may.*

sub·king·dom /'səb,kiNGdəm/ ▸*n. Biology* a taxonomic category that ranks below kingdom and above phylum or division.

sub·lan·guage /'səb,laNGgwij/ ▸*n.* a specialized language or jargon associated with a specific group or context.

sub·late /sə'blāt/ ▸*v.* [*trans.*] *Philosophy* assimilate (a smaller entity) into a larger one: *fragmented aspects of the self the subject is unable to sublate.* ▷mid 19th cent.: from Latin *sublat-* 'taken away,' from *sub-* 'from below' + *lat-* (from the stem of *tollere* 'take away'). —**sub·la·tion** /-'blāSHən/ *n.*

sub·lat·er·al /'səb,latərəl/ ▸*n.* a side shoot developing from a lateral shoot or branch of a plant.

sub·lease ▸*n.* /'səb,lēs/ a lease of a property by a tenant to a subtenant.
▸*v.* /səb'lēs/ another term for SUBLET.

sub·les·see /,səble'sē/ ▸*n.* a person who holds a sublease.

sub·les·sor /,səble'sôr/ ▸*n.* a person who grants a sublease.

sub·let ▸*v.* /səb'let/ (**-let·ting**; *past* and *past part.* **-let**) [*trans.*] lease (a property) to a subtenant: *I quit my job and sublet my apartment.*
▸*n.* /'səb,let/ another term for SUBLEASE. ■ *informal* a property that has been subleased.

sub·le·thal /səb'lēTHəl/ ▸*adj.* having an effect less than lethal.

sub·li·cense /,səb'līsəns/ ▸*n.* a license granted to a third party by a licensee, extending some rights or privileges that the licensee enjoys.
▸*v.* [*trans.*] grant a sublicense to or for.

sub·lieu·ten·ant /,səb,lōō'tenənt/ ▸*n.* an officer in the British Royal Navy ranking above midshipman and below lieutenant.

sub·li·mate ▸*v.* /'səblə,māt/ **1** [*trans.*] (esp. in psychoanalytic theory) divert or modify (an instinctual impulse) into a culturally higher or socially more acceptable activity: *people who will* ***sublimate*** *sexuality* ***into*** *activities which help to build up and preserve civilization | he sublimates his hurt and anger into humor.* **2** *Chemistry* [*intrans.*] another term for SUBLIME.
▸*n.* /-,mit; -,māt/ *Chemistry* a solid deposit of a substance that has sublimed. ▷late Middle English (in the sense 'raise to a higher status'): from Latin *sublimat-* 'raised up,' from the verb *sublimare.* —**sub·li·ma·tion** /,səblə'māSHən/ *n.*

sub·lime /sə'blīm/ ▸*adj.* (**-lim·er**, **-lim·est**) of such excellence, grandeur, or beauty as to inspire great admiration or awe: *Mozart's sublime piano concertos |* [as *n.*] (**the sublime**) *experiences that ranged* ***from the sublime to the ridiculous.*** ■ used to denote the extreme or unparalleled nature of a person's attitude or behavior: *he had the sublime confidence of youth.*
▸*v.* **1** [*intrans.*] *Chemistry* (of a solid substance) change directly into vapor when heated, typically forming a solid deposit again on cooling. ■ [*trans.*] cause (a substance) to do this: *these crystals could be sublimed under a vacuum.* **2** [*trans.*] *archaic* elevate to a high degree of moral or spiritual purity or excellence. ▷late 16th cent. (in the sense 'dignified, aloof'): from Latin *sublimis*, from *sub-* 'up to' + a second element perhaps related to *limen* 'threshold,' *limus* 'oblique.' —**sub·lime·ly** *adv.* —**sub·lim·i·ty** /-'blimitē/ *n.*

Sub·lime Porte /sə'blīm 'pôrt/ ▸*n.* see PORTE.

sub·lim·i·nal /sə'blimənl/ ▸*adj. Psychology* (of a stimulus or mental process) below the threshold of sensation or consciousness; perceived by or affecting someone's mind without their being aware of it. ▷late 19th cent.: from SUB- 'below' + Latin *limen, limin-* 'threshold' + -AL. —**sub·lim·i·nal·ly** *adv.*

sub·lim·i·nal ad·ver·tis·ing ▸*n.* the use by advertisers of images and sounds to influence consumers' responses without their being conscious of it.

sub·lin·gual /,səb'liNGgwəl/ ▸*adj. Anatomy & Medicine*

S

situated or applied under the tongue. ■ denoting a pair of small salivary glands beneath the tongue. —**sub·lin·gual·ly** *adv.*

sub·lit·to·ral /ˌsəbˈlitərəl/ *chiefly Ecology* ▸*adj.* (of a marine animal, plant, or deposit) living, growing, or accumulating near to or just below the shore. ■ relating to or denoting a biogeographic zone extending (in the sea) from the average line of low tide to the edge of the continental shelf or (in a large lake) beyond the littoral zone but still well lit.
▸*n.* (**the sublittoral**) the sublittoral zone.

Sub-Lt. ▸*abbr.* Sublieutenant.

sub·lu·nar /səbˈlo͞onər/ ▸*adj. Astronomy* within the moon's orbit and subject to its influence.

sub·lu·nar·y /səbˈlo͞onərē/ ▸*adj. poetic/literary* belonging to this world as contrasted with a better or more spiritual one: *the concept was irrational to sublunary minds.* ▹late 16th cent. (in the sense 'terrestrial'): from modern Latin *sublunaris.*

sub·lux·a·tion /ˌsəbləkˈsāSHən/ ▸*n. Medicine* a partial dislocation. ■ a slight misalignment of the vertebrae, regarded in chiropractic theory as the cause of many health problems. ▹late 17th cent.: from modern Latin *subluxatio(n-)* (see **SUB-**, **LUXATE**).

sub·ma·chine gun /ˌsəbməˈSHēn/ ▸*n.* a hand-held, lightweight machine gun.

sub·man·dib·u·lar /ˌsəbmanˈdibyələr/ ▸*adj. Anatomy* situated beneath the jaw or mandible. ■ relating to or affecting a submandibular gland.

sub·man·dib·u·lar gland ▸*n. Anatomy* either of a pair of salivary glands situated below the lower jaw. Also called **SUBMAXILLARY GLAND**.

sub·mar·gin·al /ˌsəbˈmärjənl/ ▸*adj.* (of land) not allowing profitable farming or cultivation.

sub·ma·rine /ˌsəbməˈrēn; ˈsəbməˌrēn/ ▸*n.* a warship with a streamlined hull designed to operate completely submerged in the sea for long periods, equipped with an internal store of air and a periscope and typically armed with torpedoes and/or missiles. ■ a submersible craft of any kind. ■ a submarine sandwich.
▸*adj.* existing, occurring, done, or used under the surface of the sea: *submarine volcanic activity.* —**sub·ma·rin·er** /səbˈmarənər; -məˈrēnər/ *n.*

sub·ma·rine sand·wich ▸*n.* a sandwich made of a long roll typically filled with meat, cheese, and vegetables such as lettuce, tomato, and onions.

sub·max·il·lar·y gland /səbˈmaksəˌlerē/ ▸*n.* another term for **SUBMANDIBULAR GLAND**.

sub·me·di·ant /ˌsəbˈmēdēənt/ ▸*n. Music* the sixth note of the diatonic scale of any key.

sub·men·u /ˈsəbˌmenyo͞o/ ▸*n. Computing* a menu accessed from a more general menu.

sub·merge /səbˈmərj/ ▸*v.* [*trans.*] (usu. **be submerged**) cause to be under water: *houses had been flooded and cars submerged.* ■ [*intrans.*] descend below the surface of an area of water: *the U-boat had had time to submerge.* ■ completely cover or obscure: *the tensions submerged earlier in the campaign now came to the fore.* ▹early 17th cent.: from Latin *submergere,* from *sub-* 'under' + *mergere* 'to dip.' —**sub·mer·gence** /-jəns/ *n.* —**sub·mer·gi·ble** /-jəbəl/ *adj.*

sub·merse /səbˈmərs/ ▸*v.* [*trans.*] submerge: *pellets were then submersed in agar.*
▸*adj.* (**submersed**) *Botany* denoting or characteristic of a plant growing entirely underwater. Contrasted with **EMERSED**. ▹late Middle English: from Latin *submers-* 'plunged below,' from the verb *submergere* (see **SUBMERGE**). —**sub·mer·sion** /-ˈmərZHən; -SHən/ *n.*

sub·mers·i·ble /səbˈmərsəbəl/ ▸*adj.* designed to be completely submerged or to operate while submerged.
▸*n.* a small boat or other craft of this kind, esp. one designed for research and exploration.

sub·mi·cro·scop·ic /ˌsəbmīkrəˈskäpik/ ▸*adj.* too small to be seen by an ordinary light microscope.

sub·min·i·a·ture /səbˈmin(ē)əCHər; -ˌCHo͝or/ ▸*adj.* of greatly reduced size. ■ (of a camera) very small and using 16-mm film.

sub·mis·sion /səbˈmiSHən/ ▸*n.* **1** the action or fact of accepting or yielding to a superior force or to the will or authority of another person: *they were forced into submission.* ■ *Wrestling* an act of surrendering to a hold by one's opponent. ■ *archaic* humility; meekness: *servile flattery and submission.* **2** the action of presenting a proposal, application, or other document for consideration or judgment: *reports should be prepared for submission at partners' meetings.* ■ a proposal, application, or other document presented in this way. ■ *Law* a proposition or argument presented by a lawyer to a judge or jury. ▹late Middle English: from Old French, or from Latin *submissio(n-),* from the verb *submittere* (see **SUBMIT**).

sub·mis·sive /səbˈmisiv/ ▸*adj.* ready to conform to the authority or will of others; meekly obedient or passive. ▹late 16th cent.: from **SUBMISSION**, on the pattern of pairs such as *remission, remissive.* —**sub·mis·sive·ly** *adv.* —**sub·mis·sive·ness** *n.*

sub·mit /səbˈmit/ ▸*v.* (**-mit·ted**, **-mit·ting**) **1** [*intrans.*] accept or yield to a superior force or to the authority or will of another person: *the original settlers were forced to* **submit to** *Bulgarian rule.* ■ (**submit oneself**) consent to undergo a certain treatment: *he* **submitted himself to** *a body search.* ■ [*trans.*] subject to a particular process, treatment, or condition: *samples* **submitted to** *low pressure.* ■ agree to refer a matter to a third party for decision or adjudication: *the U.S. refused to* **submit to** *arbitration.* **2** [*trans.*] present (a proposal, application, or other document) to a person or body for consideration or judgment: *the panel's report was* **submitted to** *a parliamentary committee.* ■ [with *clause*] (esp. in judicial contexts) suggest; argue: *he submitted that such measures were justified.* ▹late Middle English: from Latin *submittere,* from *sub-* 'under' + *mittere* 'send, put.' Sense 2 'present for judgment' dates from the mid 16th cent. —**sub·mit·ter** *n.*

sub·mod·i·fi·er /səbˈmädəˌfīər/ ▸*n. Grammar* an adverb used in front of an adjective or another adverb to modify its meaning, for example *very* in *very cold* or *unusually* in *an unusually large house.* —**sub·mod·i·fi·ca·tion** /səbˌmädəfiˈkāSHən/ *n.* —**sub·mod·i·fy** /-ˌfī/ *v.*

sub·mon·tane /səbˈmäntān/ ▸*adj.* passing under or through mountains. ■ situated in the foothills or lower slopes of a mountain range.

sub·mu·co·sa /ˌsəbmyo͞oˈkōsə/ ▸*n.* (*pl.* **-sae** /-sē/) *Physiology* the layer of areolar connective tissue lying beneath a mucous membrane. ▹late 19th cent.: from modern Latin *submucosa (membrana),* feminine of *submucosus* 'submucous.' —**sub·mu·co·sal** *adj.*

sub·mul·ti·ple /səbˈməltəpəl/ ▸*n.* a number that can be divided exactly into a specified number.
▸*adj.* of or pertaining to such a number.

sub·mu·ni·tion /ˌsəbmyo͞oˈniSHən/ ▸*n.* a small weapon or device that is part of a larger warhead and separates from it prior to impact.

sub·net·work /səbˈnetwərk/ (also **sub·net** /səbˈnet/) ▸*n. Computing* a part of a larger network such as the Internet.

sub·nor·mal /səbˈnôrməl/ ▸*adj.* not meeting standards or reaching a level regarded as usual, esp. with respect to intelligence or development. —**sub·nor·mal·i·ty** /ˌsəbnôrˈmalitē/ *n.*

sub·nu·cle·ar /səbˈn(y)o͞oklēər/ ▸*adj. Physics* occurring in or smaller than an atomic nucleus.

sub·op·ti·mal /səbˈäptəməl/ ▸*adj. technical* of less than the highest standard or quality.

sub·or·bit·al /ˌsəbˈôrbitl/ ▸*adj.* **1** situated below or behind the orbit of the eye. **2** of, relating to, or denoting a trajectory that does not complete a full orbit of the earth or other celestial body.

sub·or·der /ˈsəbˌôrdər/ ▸*n. Biology* a taxonomic category that ranks below order and above family.

sub·or·di·nar·y /ˌsəbˈôrdnˌerē/ ▸*n.* (*pl.* **-nar·ies**) *Heraldry* a simple device or bearing that is less common than the ordinaries (e.g., roundel, orle, lozenge).

sub·or·di·nate ▸*adj.* /səˈbôrdnit/ lower in rank or position: *his subordinate officers.* ■ of less or secondary importance: *in adventure stories, character must be* **subordinate to** *action.*
▸*n.* /səˈbôrdnit/ a person under the authority or control of another within an organization.
▸*v.* /-ˌāt/ [*trans.*] treat or regard as of lesser importance than something else: *practical considerations were* **subordinated to** *political expediency.* ■ make subservient to or dependent on something else. ▹late Middle English: from medieval Latin *subordinatus* 'placed in an inferior rank,' from Latin *sub-* 'below' + *ordinare* 'ordain.' —**sub·or·di·nate·ly** *adv.* —**sub·or·di·na·tion** /-ˌbôrdnˈāSHən/ *n.* —**sub·or·di·na·tive** /-ətiv/ *adj.*

sub·or·di·nate clause ▸*n.* a clause, typically introduced by a conjunction, that forms part of and is dependent on a main clause (e.g., "when it rang" in "she answered the phone when it rang").

sub·or·di·nat·ed debt /səbˈôrdnˌātid/ ▸*n. Finance* a debt owed to an unsecured creditor that can only be paid, in the event of a liquidation, after the claims of secured creditors have been met.

sub·or·di·nat·ing con·junc·tion /səˈbôrdnˌātiNG/ ▸*n.* a conjunction that introduces a subordinate clause, e.g., *although, because.* Contrasted with **COORDINATING CONJUNCTION**.

sub·orn /səˈbôrn/ ▸*v.* [*trans.*] bribe or otherwise induce (someone) to commit an unlawful act such as perjury: *he was accused of conspiring to suborn witnesses.* ▹mid 16th cent.: from Latin *subornare* 'incite secretly,' from *sub-* 'secretly' + *ornare* 'equip.' —**sub·or·na·tion** /ˌsəbôrˈnāSHən/ *n.* —**sub·orn·er** *n.*

sub·os·cine /səbˈäsin; -īn/ *Ornithology* ▸*adj.* of, relating to, or denoting passerine birds of a division that includes those other than songbirds, found chiefly in America. Compare with **OSCINE**. • Suborder Deutero-Oscines, order Passeriformes.
▸*n.* a bird of this division.

sub·ox·ide /səbˈäkˌsīd/ ▸*n. Chemistry* an oxide containing the lowest or an unusually small proportion of oxygen.

sub·par /səbˈpär/ ▸*adj.* below an average level.

sub·par·al·lel /səbˈparəˌlel/ ▸*adj. chiefly Geology* almost parallel.

sub·phy·lum /ˈsəbˌfīləm/ ▸*n.* (*pl.* **-phy·la** /-ˌfīlə/) *Zoology* a taxonomic category that ranks below phylum and above class.

sub·plot /ˈsəbˌplät/ ▸*n.* a subordinate plot in a play, novel, or similar work.

sub·poe·na /səˈpēnə/ *Law* ▸*n.* (in full **subpoena ad testificandum**) a writ ordering a person to attend a court: *a subpoena may be issued to compel their attendance* | *they were all* **under subpoena** *to appear.*
▸*v.* (**-nas**, **-naed** /-nəd/, **-na·ing**) [*trans.*] summon (someone) with a subpoena: *the Queen is above the law and cannot be subpoenaed.* ■ require (a document or other evidence) to be submitted to a court of law: *the decision to subpoena government records.* ▹late Middle English (as a noun): from Latin *sub poena* 'under penalty' (the first words of the writ). Use as a verb dates from the mid 17th cent.

sub·poe·na du·ces te·cum /səˈpēnə ˈdo͞osēz ˈtēkəm/ ▸*n. Law* a writ ordering a person to attend a court and bring relevant documents. ▹Latin, literally 'under penalty you shall bring with you.'

sub·pro·gram /ˈsəbˌprōgram; -grəm/ ▸*n. Computing* another term for **SUBROUTINE**.

sub·re·gion /ˈsəbˌrējən/ ▸*n.* a division of a region. —**sub·re·gion·al** /ˌsəbˈrēj(ə)nəl/ *adj.*

sub·ro·ga·tion /ˌsəbrəˈgāSHən/ ▸*n. Law* the substitution of one person or group by another in respect of a debt or insurance claim, accompanied by the transfer of any associated rights and duties. ▹late Middle English (in the general sense 'substitution'): from late Latin *subrogatio(n-),* from *subrogare* 'choose as substitute,' from *sub-* 'in place of another' + *rogare* 'ask.' —**sub·ro·gate** /ˈsəbrəˌgāt/ *v.*

sub ro·sa /ˌsəb ˈrōzə/ ▸*adj. & adv. formal* happening or done in secret: [as *adv.*] *the committee operates sub rosa* | [as *adj.*] *sub rosa inspections.* ▹Latin, literally 'under the rose,' as an emblem of secrecy.

sub·rou·tine /ˈsəbro͞oˌtēn/ ▸*n. Computing* a set of instructions designed to perform a frequently used operation within a program.

subs. ▸*abbr.* subscription.

sub-Sa·har·an ▸*adj.* [*attrib.*] from or forming part of the African regions south of the Sahara desert.

sub·sam·ple ▸*n.* /ˈsəbˌsampəl/ a sample drawn from a larger sample.
▸*v.* /səbˈsampəl/ [*trans.*] take such a sample from.

sub·scribe /səbˈskrīb/ ▸*v.* **1** [*intrans.*] arrange to receive something regularly, typically a publication, by paying in advance: **subscribe to** *the magazine for twelve months and receive a free T-shirt.* ■ arrange for access to an online service: *I* **subscribe to** *an Internet newsgroup.* ■ *chiefly Brit.* contribute or undertake to contribute a certain sum of money to a particular fund, project, or charitable cause, typically on a regular basis: *he is one of the millions who* **subscribe to** *the NSPCC* | [*trans.*] *he* **subscribed** *£400* **to** *the campaign.* ■ (**subscribe to**) *figurative* express or feel agreement with (an idea or proposal): *we prefer to subscribe to an alternative explanation.* ■ [*trans.*] apply to participate in: *the course has been fully subscribed.* ■ apply for or undertake to pay for an offering of shares of stock: *investors would* **subscribe** *electronically* **to** *the initial stock offerings* | [*trans.*] *yesterday's offering was fully subscribed.* ■ [*trans.*] (of a bookseller) agree before publication to take (a certain number of copies of a book): *most of the first print run of 15,000 copies has been subscribed.* **2** *formal* sign (a will, contract, or other document): *he subscribed the will as a witness.* ■ sign (one's name) on such a document. ■ (**subscribe oneself**) [with *complement*] *archaic* sign oneself as: *he ventured still to subscribe himself her most obedient servant.* ▹late

Middle English (in the sense 'sign at the bottom of a document'): from Latin *subscribere*, from *sub-* 'under' + *scribere* 'write.' **—sub·scrib·er** *n.*

sub·script /'səbˌskript/ ▶*adj.* (of a letter, figure, or symbol) written or printed below the line.
▶*n.* a subscript letter, figure, or symbol. ■ *Computing* a symbol (notionally written as a subscript but in practice usually not) used in a program, alone or with others, to specify one of the elements of an array. ▷early 18th cent.: from Latin *subscript-* 'written below,' from the verb *subscribere* (see SUBSCRIBE).

sub·scrip·tion /səb'skripSHən/ ▶*n.* **1** the action of making or agreeing to make an advance payment in order to receive or participate in something: *the newsletter is available only on subscription | take out a one-year subscription.* ■ an arrangement by which access is granted to an online service. ■ *chiefly Brit.* a payment of such a type: *membership is available at an annual subscription of £300.* ■ a system in which the production of a book is wholly or partly financed by advance orders. **2** *formal* a signature or short piece of writing at the end of a document: *he signed the letter and added a subscription.* ■ *archaic* a signed declaration or agreement. ▷late Middle English (sense 2): from Latin *subscriptio(n-)*, from *subscribere* 'write below' (see SUBSCRIBE).

sub·scrip·tion con·cert ▶*n.* one of a series of concerts for which tickets are sold mainly in advance.

sub·sea /səb'sē/ ▶*adj.* (esp. of processes or equipment used in the oil industry) situated or occurring beneath the surface of the sea.

sub·sec·tion /'səbˌsekSHən/ ▶*n.* a division of a section.

sub·sel·li·um /ˌsəb'selēəm/ ▶*n.* (*pl.* **-sel·li·a** /-'selēə/) another term for MISERICORD (sense 1). ▷Latin, from *sub-* 'secondary' + *sella* 'seat.'

sub·sense /'səbˌsens/ ▶*n.* a subsidiary sense of a word defined in a dictionary.

sub·se·quence[1] /'səbsəkwəns/ ▶*n.* *formal* the state of following something, esp. as a result or effect: *an affair which appeared in due subsequence in the newspapers.*

sub·se·quence[2] /'səbˌsēkwəns/ ▶*n.* a sequence contained in or forming part of another sequence. ■ *Mathematics* a sequence derived from another by the omission of a number of terms.

sub·se·quent /'səbsəkwənt/ ▶*adj.* coming after something in time; following: *the theory was developed* ***subsequent to*** *the earthquake of 1906.* ■ *Geology* (of a stream or valley) having a direction or character determined by the resistance to erosion of the underlying rock, and typically following the strike of the strata. ▷late Middle English: from Old French, or from Latin *subsequent-* 'following after' (from the verb *subsequi*). **—sub·se·quent·ly** *adv.*

sub·serve /səb'sərv/ ▶*v.* [*trans.*] help to further or promote: *officers are appointed to subserve their own profit and convenience.* ▷mid 17th cent.: from Latin *subservire* (see SUB-, SERVE).

sub·ser·vi·ent /səb'sərvēənt/ ▶*adj.* prepared to obey others unquestioningly: *she was* ***subservient to*** *her parents.* See note at OBSEQUIOUS. ■ less important; subordinate: *Marxism makes freedom* ***subservient to*** *control.* ■ serving as a means to an end: *the whole narration is* ***subservient to*** *the moral plan of exemplifying twelve virtues in twelve knights.* ▷mid 17th cent.: from Latin *subservient-* 'subjecting to, complying with,' from the verb *subservire* (see SUBSERVE). **—sub·ser·vi·ence** *n.* **—sub·ser·vi·en·cy** *n.* **—sub·ser·vi·ent·ly** *adv.*

sub·set /'səbˌset/ ▶*n.* a part of a larger group of related things. ■ *Mathematics* a set of which all the elements are contained in another set.

sub·shrub /'səbˌSHrəb/ ▶*n.* *Botany* a dwarf shrub, esp. one that is woody only at the base. **—sub·shrub·by** *adj.*

sub·side /səb'sīd/ ▶*v.* [*intrans.*] **1** become less intense, violent, or severe: *I'll wait a few minutes until the storm subsides.* ■ lapse into silence or inactivity: *Fred opened his mouth to protest again, then subsided.* **2** (of water) go down to a lower or the normal level: *the floods subside almost as quickly as they arise.* ■ (of the ground) cave in; sink: *the island is subsiding.* ■ (of a swelling) reduce until gone: *it took seven days for the swelling to subside completely.* ▷late 17th cent.: from Latin *subsidere*, from *sub-* 'below' + *sidere* 'settle' (related to *sedere* 'sit').

sub·sid·ence /səb'sīdns; 'səbsidns/ ▶*n.* the gradual caving in or sinking of an area of land. ▷mid 17th cent.: from Latin *subsidentia* 'sediment,' from the verb *subsidere* (see SUBSIDE).

sub·sid·i·ar·y /səb'sidēˌerē/ ▶*adj.* less important than but related or supplementary to: *many environmentalists argue that the cause of animal rights is subsidiary to that of protecting the environment.* ■ [*attrib.*] (of a company) controlled by a holding or parent company.
▶*n.* (*pl.* **-ar·ies**) a company controlled by a holding company. ■ *rare* a thing that is of lesser importance than but related to something else. ▷mid 16th cent. (in the sense 'serving to help or supplement'): from Latin *subsidiarius*, from *subsidium* 'support, assistance' (see SUBSIDY). **—sub·sid·i·ar·i·ly** /-ˌsidē'e(ə)rəlē/ *adv.* (*rare*).

sub·si·dize /'səbsəˌdīz/ ▶*v.* [*trans.*] support (an organization or activity) financially: *it was beyond the power of a state to subsidize a business.* ■ pay part of the cost of producing (something) to reduce prices for the buyer: *the government subsidizes basic goods including sugar, petroleum, and wheat.* **—sub·si·di·za·tion** /ˌsəbsədi'zāSHən/ *n.* **—sub·si·diz·er** *n.*

sub·si·dy /'səbsidē/ ▶*n.* (*pl.* **-dies**) **1** a sum of money granted by the government or a public body to assist an industry or business so that the price of a commodity or service may remain low or competitive: *a farm subsidy | they disdain government subsidy.* ■ a sum of money granted to support an arts organization or other undertaking held to be in the public interest. ■ a sum of money paid by one government to another for the preservation of neutrality, the promotion of war, or to repay military aid. ■ a grant or contribution of money. **2** *historical* a parliamentary grant to the sovereign for state needs. ■ a tax levied on a particular occasion. ▷late Middle English: from Anglo-Norman French *subsidie*, from Latin *subsidium* 'assistance.'

sub·sist /səb'sist/ ▶*v.* [*intrans.*] **1** maintain or support oneself, esp. at a minimal level: *thousands of refugees* ***subsist on*** *international handouts.* ■ [*trans.*] *archaic* provide sustenance for: *the problem of subsisting the poor in a period of high bread prices.* **2** *chiefly Law* remain in being, force, or effect. ■ (**subsist in**) be attributable to: *the effect of genetic maldevelopment may subsist in chromosomal mutation.* ▷mid 16th cent. (in the sense 'continue to exist'): from Latin *subsistere* 'stand firm,' from *sub-* 'from below' + *sistere* 'set, stand.' **—sub·sist·ent** /-ənt/ *adj.*

sub·sist·ence /səb'sistəns/ ▶*n.* **1** the action or fact of maintaining or supporting oneself at a minimum level: *the minimum income needed for subsistence.* ■ the means of doing this: *the garden provided not only subsistence but a little cash crop | the agricultural working class were deprived of a subsistence.* ■ [as *adj.*] denoting or relating to production at a level sufficient only for one's own use or consumption, without any surplus for trade: *subsistence agriculture.* **2** *chiefly Law* the state of remaining in force or effect: *rights of occupation normally only continue during the subsistence of the marriage.*

sub·sist·ence lev·el (also **subsistence wage**) ▶*n.* a standard of living (or wage) that provides only the bare necessities of life.

sub·soil /'səbˌsoil/ ▶*n.* the soil lying immediately under the surface soil.
▶*v.* [*trans.*] [usu. as *n.*] (**subsoiling**) plow (land) so as to cut into the subsoil.

sub·soil·er /'səbˌsoilər/ ▶*n.* a kind of plow with no moldboard, used to loosen the soil at some depth below the surface without turning it over.

sub·song /'səbˌsôNG; ˌsäNG/ ▶*n.* *Ornithology* birdsong that is softer and less well defined than the usual territorial song, sometimes heard only at close quarters as a quiet warbling.

sub·son·ic /ˌsəb'sänik/ ▶*adj.* relating to or flying at a speed or speeds less than that of sound. **—sub·son·i·cal·ly** /-ik(ə)lē/ *adv.*

subsp. ▶*abbr.* subspecies.

sub·space /'səbˌspās/ ▶*n.* **1** *Mathematics* a space that is wholly contained in another space, or whose points or elements are all in another space. **2** (in science fiction) a hypothetical space-time continuum used for communication at a speed faster than that of light.

sub spe·cie ae·ter·ni·ta·tis /'səb 'spēSHē ēˌtərni'tätis; 'spēsē/ ▶*adv.* viewed in relation to the eternal; in a universal perspective: *sub specie aeternitatis the authors have got it about right.* ▷Latin, literally 'under the aspect of eternity.'

sub·spe·cies /'səbˌspēSHēz; -sēz/ (abbr.: **subsp.** or **ssp.**) ▶*n.* (*pl.* same) *Biology* a taxonomic category that ranks below species, usually a fairly permanent geographically isolated race. Subspecies are designated by a Latin trinomial, e.g., (in zoology) *Ursus arctos horribilis* or (in botany) *Beta vulgaris* subsp. *crassa.* Compare with FORM (sense 3) and VARIETY (sense 2). **—sub·spe·cif·ic** /'ˌsəbspə'sifik/ *adj.*

subst. ▶*abbr.* ■ substantive. ■ substantively. ■ substitute.

sub·stage /'səbˌstāj/ ▶*n.* [usu. as *adj.*] an apparatus fixed beneath the ordinary stage of a compound microscope to support mirrors and other accessories.

sub·stance /'səbstəns/ ▶*n.* **1** a particular kind of matter with uniform properties: *a steel tube coated with a waxy substance.* ■ an intoxicating, stimulating, or narcotic chemical or drug, esp. an illegal one. **2** the real physical matter of which a person or thing consists and which has a tangible, solid presence: *proteins compose much of the actual substance of the body.* ■ the quality of having a solid basis in reality or fact: *the claim has no substance.* ■ the quality of being dependable or stable: *some were inclined to knock her for her lack of substance.* **3** the quality of being important, valid, or significant: *he had yet to accomplish anything of substance.* ■ the most important or essential part of something; the real or essential meaning: *the substance of the treaty.* ■ the subject matter of a text, speech, or work of art, esp. as contrasted with the form or style in which it is presented. ■ wealth and possessions: *a woman of substance.* ■ *Philosophy* the essential nature underlying phenomena, which is subject to changes and accidents. ▷Middle English (denoting the essential nature of something): from Old French, from Latin *substantia* 'being, essence,' from *substant-* 'standing firm,' from the verb *substare.*
▶*PHRASE* □ **in substance** essentially: *basic rights are equivalent in substance to human rights.*

sub·stance a·buse ▶*n.* overindulgence in or dependence on an addictive substance, esp. alcohol or drugs.

sub·stance P ▶*n.* *Biochemistry* a compound thought to be involved in the synaptic transmission of pain and other nerve impulses. It is a polypeptide with eleven amino-acid residues.

sub·stand·ard /səb'standərd/ ▶*adj.* **1** below the usual or required standard: *substandard housing.* **2** another term for NONSTANDARD.

sub·stan·tial /səb'stanCHəl/ ▶*adj.* **1** of considerable importance, size, or worth: *a substantial amount of cash.* ■ strongly built or made: *a row of substantial Victorian villas.* ■ (of a meal) large and filling. ■ important in material or social terms; wealthy: *a substantial Devon family.* **2** concerning the essentials of something: *there was substantial agreement on changing policies.* **3** real and tangible rather than imaginary: *spirits are shadowy, human beings substantial.* ▷Middle English: from Old French *substantiel* or Christian Latin *substantialis*, from *substantia* 'being, essence' (see SUBSTANCE). **—sub·stan·ti·al·i·ty** /-ˌstanCHē'alitē/ *n.*

sub·stan·tial·ism /səb'stanCHəˌlizəm/ ▶*n.* *Philosophy* the doctrine that behind phenomena there are substantial realities. **—sub·stan·tial·ist** *n.* & *adj.*

sub·stan·tial·ize /səb'stanCHəˌlīz/ ▶*v.* [*trans.*] give (something) substance or actual existence: *the universe is a series of abstract truths, substantialized by their reference to God.*

sub·stan·tial·ly /səb'stanCHəlē/ ▶*adv.* **1** to a great or significant extent: *profits grew substantially | [as submodifier] substantially higher earnings.* **2** for the most part; essentially: *things will remain substantially the same over the next ten years.*

sub·stan·ti·ate /səb'stanCHēˌāt/ ▶*v.* [*trans.*] provide evidence to support or prove the truth of: *they had found nothing to substantiate the allegations.* ▷mid 17th cent.: from medieval Latin *substantiat-* 'given substance,' from the verb *substantiare.* **—sub·stan·ti·a·tion** /-ˌstanCHē'āSHən/ *n.*

sub·stan·tive /'səbstəntiv/ ▶*adj.* **1** having a firm basis in reality and therefore important, meaningful, or considerable: *there is no substantive evidence for the efficacy of these drugs.* **2** having a separate and independent existence. ■ (of a dye) not needing a mordant. **3** (of law) defining rights and duties as opposed to giving the rules by which such things are established.
▶*n.* *Grammar* a noun. ▷late Middle English (in the sense 'having an independent existence'): from Old French *substantif, -ive* or late Latin *substantivus*, from *substantia* 'essence' (see SUBSTANCE). **—sub·stan·ti·val** /ˌsəbstən'tīvəl/ *adj.* **—sub·stan·tive·ly** *adv.*

sub·sta·tion /'səbˌstāSHən/ ▶*n.* **1** a set of equipment reducing the high voltage of electrical power transmission to that suitable for supply to consumers. **2** a subordinate station for the police or fire department. ■ a small post office, for example one situated within a larger store.

sub·stel·lar /'səb,stelər/ ▶*adj. Astronomy* relating to or denoting a body much smaller than a typical star whose mass is not great enough to support main sequence hydrogen burning.

sub·stit·u·ent /səb'stichōōənt/ ▶*n. Chemistry* an atom or group of atoms taking the place of another atom or group or occupying a specified position in a molecule. ▷late 19th cent.: from Latin *substituent-* 'standing in place of,' from the verb *substituere* (see SUBSTITUTE).

sub·sti·tute /'səbsti,t(y)ōōt/ ▶*n.* a person or thing acting or serving in place of another: *soy milk is used as a* ***substitute for*** *dairy milk.* ■ a sports player nominated as eligible to replace another after a game has begun. ■ *Psychology* a person or thing that becomes the object of love or other emotion deprived of its natural outlet: *a father substitute.*

▶*v.* [*trans.*] use or add in place of: *dried rosemary can be* ***substituted for*** *the fresh herb.* ■ [*intrans.*] act or serve as a substitute: *I found someone to* ***substitute for*** *me.* ■ replace (someone or something) with another: *customs officers* ***substituted*** *the drugs* ***with*** *another substance | this was substituted by a new clause.* ■ replace (a sports player) with a substitute during a contest: *he was substituted for Nichols in the fifth inning.* ■ *Chemistry* replace (an atom or group in a molecule, esp. a hydrogen atom) with another. ■ [as *adj.*] (**substituted**) *Chemistry* (of a compound) in which one or more hydrogen atoms have been replaced by other atoms or groups: *a substituted alkaloid.* ▷late Middle English (denoting a deputy or delegate): from Latin *substitutus* 'put in place of,' past participle of *substituere,* based on *statuere* 'set up.' **—sub·sti·tut·a·bil·i·ty** /,səbstə,t(y)ōōtə'bilitē/ *n.* **—sub·sti·tut·a·ble** *adj.* **—sub·sti·tu·tive** /-,t(y)ōōtiv/ *adj.*

USAGE Traditionally, the verb **substitute** is followed by **for** and means 'put (someone or something) in place of another,' as in *she* ***substituted*** *the fake vase* ***for*** *the real one.* From the late 17th century **substitute** has also been used with **with** or **by** to mean 'replace (something) with something else,' as in *she* ***substituted*** *the real vase* ***with*** *the fake one.* This can be confusing, since the two sentences shown above mean the same thing, yet the object of the verb and the object of the preposition have swapped positions. Despite the potential confusion, the second, newer use is well established and, although still disapproved of by traditionalists, is now generally regarded as part of normal standard English.

sub·sti·tu·tion /,səbsti't(y)ōōshən/ ▶*n.* the action of replacing someone or something with another person or thing: *the* ***substitution of*** *pediatricians* ***for*** *grandmothers in guiding baby care | a tactical substitution.* **—sub·sti·tu·tion·al** /-shənl/ *adj.* **—sub·sti·tu·tion·ar·y** /-,nerē/ *adj.*

sub·storm /'səb,stôrm/ ▶*n.* a localized disturbance of the earth's magnetic field in high latitudes, typically manifested as an aurora.

sub·strate /'səb,strāt/ ▶*n.* a substance or layer that underlies something, or on which some process occurs, in particular: ■ the surface or material on or from which an organism lives, grows, or obtains its nourishment. ■ the substance on which an enzyme acts. ■ a material that provides the surface on which something is deposited or inscribed, for example the silicon wafer used to manufacture integrated circuits. ▷early 19th cent.: anglicized form of SUBSTRATUM.

sub·stra·tum /'səb,strātəm; -,stra-/ ▶*n.* (*pl.* **-ta** /-tə/) an underlying layer or substance, in particular, a layer of rock or soil beneath the surface of the ground. ■ a foundation or basis of something: *there is a broad* ***substratum of*** *truth in it.* ▷mid 17th cent.: modern Latin, neuter past participle (used as a noun) of Latin *substernere,* from *sub-* 'below' + *sternere* 'strew.' Compare with STRATUM.

sub·struc·ture /'səb,strəkchər/ ▶*n.* an underlying or supporting structure. **—sub·struc·tur·al** /,səb'strəkchərəl/ *adj.*

sub·sume /səb'sōōm/ ▶*v.* [*trans.*] (often **be subsumed**) include or absorb (something) in something else: *most of these phenomena can be* ***subsumed under*** *two broad categories.* ▷mid 16th cent. (in the sense 'subjoin, add'): from medieval Latin *subsumere,* from *sub-* 'from below' + *sumere* 'take.' The current sense dates from the early 19th cent. **—sub·sum·a·ble** *adj.* **—sub·sump·tion** /-'səm(p)shən/ *n.*

sub·sur·face /'səb,sərfəs/ ▶*n.* the stratum or strata below the earth's surface.

sub·sys·tem /'səb,sistəm/ ▶*n.* a self-contained system within a larger system.

sub·ten·ant /səb'tenənt/ ▶*n.* a person who leases property from a tenant. **—sub·ten·an·cy** /-'tenənsē/ *n.*

sub·tend /səb'tend/ ▶*v.* [*trans.*] **1** (of a line, arc, or figure) form (an angle) at a particular point when straight lines from its extremities are joined at that point. ■ (of an angle or chord) have bounding lines or points that meet or coincide with those of (a line or arc). **2** *Botany* (of a bract) extend under (a flower) so as to support or enfold it. ▷late 16th cent. (sense 1): from Latin *subtendere,* from *sub-* 'under' + *tendere* 'stretch.' Sense 2 dates from the late 19th cent.

sub·tense /səb'tens/ ▶*n. Geometry* a subtending line, esp. the chord of an arc. ■ the angle subtended by a line at a point. ▷early 17th cent.: from modern Latin *subtensa (linea),* feminine past participle of *subtendere* (see SUBTEND).

sub·ter·fuge /'səbtər,fyōōj/ ▶*n.* deceit used in order to achieve one's goal. ■ a statement or action resorted to in order to deceive. ▷late 16th cent.: from French, or from late Latin *subterfugium,* from Latin *subterfugere* 'escape secretly,' from *subter-* 'beneath' + *fugere* 'flee.'

sub·ter·mi·nal /'səb,tərmənl/ ▶*adj. technical* near the end of a chain or other structure.

sub·ter·ra·ne·an /,səbtə'rānēən/ ▶*adj.* existing, occurring, or done under the earth's surface. ■ secret; concealed: *the subterranean world of the behind-the-scenes television powerbrokers.* ▷early 17th cent.: from Latin *subterraneus* (from *sub-* 'below' + *terra* 'earth') + -AN. **—sub·ter·ra·ne·ous·ly** /-'rānēəslē/ *adv.*

sub·text /'səb,tekst/ ▶*n.* an underlying and often distinct theme in a piece of writing or conversation.

sub·til·ize /'sətl,īz/ ▶*v.* [*trans.*] *archaic* make more subtle; refine. **—sub·til·i·za·tion** /,sətl-i'zāshən/ *n.*

sub·ti·tle /'səb,tītl/ ▶*n.* **1** (**subtitles**) captions displayed at the bottom of a movie or television screen that translate or transcribe the dialogue or narrative. **2** a subordinate title of a published work or article giving additional information about its content.

▶*v.* [*trans.*] (usu. **be subtitled**) **1** provide (a movie or program) with subtitles: *much of the film is subtitled.* **2** provide (a published work or article) with a subtitle: *the novel was aptly subtitled.*

sub·tle /'sətl/ ▶*adj.* (**-tler**, **-tlest**) (esp. of a change or distinction) so delicate or precise as to be difficult to analyze or describe: *his language expresses rich and subtle meanings.* ■ (of a mixture or effect) delicately complex and understated: *subtle lighting.* ■ making use of clever and indirect methods to achieve something: *he tried a more subtle approach.* ■ capable of making fine distinctions: *a subtle mind.* ■ arranged in an ingenious and elaborate way. ■ *archaic* crafty; cunning. ▷Middle English (also in the sense 'not easily understood'): from Old French *sotil,* from Latin *subtilis* 'fine, delicate.'. **—sub·tle·ness** *n.* **—sub·tly** *adv.*

sub·tle·ty /'sətltē/ ▶*n.* (*pl.* **-ties**) the quality or state of being subtle: *the textural subtlety of Degas.* ■ a subtle distinction, feature, or argument: *the subtleties of English grammar.* ▷Middle English: from Old French *soutilte,* from Latin *subtilitas,* from *subtilis* 'fine, delicate' (see SUBTLE).

sub·ton·ic /səb'tänik/ ▶*n. Music* the note below the tonic, the seventh note of the diatonic scale of any key.

sub·to·tal /'səb,tōtl/ ▶*n.* the total of one set of a larger group of figures to be added.

▶*v.* (**-taled**, **-tal·ing**; *Brit.* **-talled**, **-tal·ling**) [*trans.*] add (numbers) so as to obtain a subtotal.

▶*adj. Medicine* (of an injury or a surgical operation) partial; not total.

sub·tract /səb'trakt/ ▶*v.* [*trans.*] take away (a number or amount) from another to calculate the difference: *subtract 43 from 60.* ■ take away (something) from something else so as to decrease the size, number, or amount: *programs were added and subtracted as called for.* ▷mid 16th cent.: from Latin *subtract-* 'drawn away,' from *sub-* 'from below' + *trahere* 'to draw.' **—sub·tract·er** *n.* **—sub·trac·tive** /-tiv/ *adj.*

sub·trac·tion /səb'trakshən/ ▶*n.* the process or skill of taking one number or amount away from another: ***subtraction*** *of this figure* ***from*** *the total.* ■ *Mathematics* the process of taking a matrix, vector, or other quantity away from another under specific rules to obtain the difference.

sub·tra·hend /'səbtrə,hend/ ▶*n. Mathematics* a quantity or number to be subtracted from another. ▷late 17th cent.: from Latin *subtrahendus* 'to be taken away,' gerundive of *subtrahere* (see SUBTRACT).

sub·trop·ics /səb'träpiks/ ▶*plural n.* (**the subtropics**) the regions adjacent to or bordering on the tropics. **—sub·trop·i·cal** /-'träpikəl/ *adj.*

sub·type /'səb,tīp/ ▶*n.* a secondary or subordinate type. ■ a subdivision of a type of microorganism: *HIV-1 infections reflect a diverse range of non-B subtypes.*

Su·bud /sōō'bōōd/ a movement, founded in 1947 and led by the Javanese mystic Pak Muhammad Subuh, based on a system of exercises by which the individual seeks to approach a state of perfection through divine power. ▷contraction of Javanese *susila budhi dharma,* from Sanskrit *suśīla* 'good disposition' + *buddhi* 'understanding' + *dharma* 'religious duty.'

su·bu·late /'səbyəlit; -,lāt/ ▶*adj. Botany & Zoology* (of a part) slender and tapering to a point; awl-shaped. ▷mid 18th cent.: from Latin *subula* 'awl' + -ATE[2].

sub·um·brel·la /,səbəm'brelə/ ▶*n. Zoology* the concave inner surface of the umbrella of a jellyfish or other medusa. **—sub·um·brel·lar** *adj.*

sub·un·gu·late /səb'əNGgyəlit; -,lāt/ ▶*n. Zoology* a mammal of a diverse group that probably evolved from primitive ungulates, comprising the elephants, hyraxes, sirenians, and perhaps the aardvark.

sub·u·nit /'səb,yōōnit/ ▶*n.* a distinct component of something: *chemical subunits of human DNA.*

sub·urb /'səbərb/ ▶*n.* an outlying district of a city, esp. a residential one. ▷Middle English: from Old French *suburbe* or Latin *suburbium,* from *sub-* 'near to' + *urbs, urb-* 'city.'

sub·ur·ban /sə'bərbən/ ▶*adj.* of or characteristic of a suburb: *suburban life.* ■ contemptibly dull and ordinary: *Elizabeth despised Ann's house-proudness as deeply suburban.* **—sub·ur·ban·ite** *n.* **—sub·ur·ban·i·za·tion** /sə,bərbənə'zāshən/ *n.* **—sub·ur·ban·ize** *v.*

sub·ur·bi·a /sə'bərbēə/ ▶*n.* the suburbs or their inhabitants viewed collectively.

sub·vent /səb'vent/ ▶*v.* [*trans.*] *formal* support or assist by the payment of a subvention. ▷early 20th cent.: from Latin *subvent-* 'assisted,' from the verb *subvenire* (see SUBVENTION).

sub·ven·tion /səb'venchən/ ▶*n.* a grant of money, esp. from a government. ▷late Middle English (in the sense 'provision of help'): from Old French, from late Latin *subventio(n-),* from Latin *subvenire* 'assist,' from *sub-* 'from below' + *venire* 'come.'

sub·ver·sive /səb'vərsiv/ ▶*adj.* seeking or intended to subvert an established system or institution: *subversive literature.*

▶*n.* a person with such aims. ▷mid 17th cent.: from medieval Latin *subversivus,* from the verb *subvertere* (see SUBVERT). **—sub·ver·sive·ly** *adv.* **—sub·ver·sive·ness** *n.*

sub·vert /səb'vərt/ ▶*v.* [*trans.*] undermine the power and authority of (an established system or institution): *an attempt to subvert democratic government.* ▷late Middle English: from Old French *subvertir* or Latin *subvertere,* from *sub-* 'from below' + *vertere* 'to turn.' **—sub·ver·sion** /-'vərzhən; -shən/ *n.* **—sub·vert·er** *n.*

sub·vo·cal /səb'vōkəl/ ▶*adj.* (of a word or sound) barely audible: *a subvocal sigh.* ■ *Psychology & Philosophy* relating to or denoting an unarticulated level of speech comparable to thought: *almost all of what is called "thinking" is subvocal talk.*

sub·vo·cal·ize /səb'vōkə,līz/ ▶*v.* [*trans.*] utter (words or sounds) with the lips silently or with barely audible sound, esp. when talking to oneself, memorizing something, or reading. **—sub·vo·cal·i·za·tion** /-,vōkəli'zāshən/ *n.*

sub·way /'səb,wā/ ▶*n.* **1** an underground electric railroad. **2** *Brit.* a tunnel under a road for use by pedestrians.

sub·web /'səb,web/ ▶*n.* an isolated part of a Web site, especially one that is password-protected or that is not obviously accessible from the main page.

sub·woof·er /'səb,wōōfər/ ▶*n.* a loudspeaker component designed to reproduce very low bass frequencies.

sub·ze·ro /,səb'zi(ə)rō/ ▶*adj.* below zero on the Fahrenheit scale (−18 Celsius); very cold. ■ below zero on the Celsius scale; below freezing.

suc- ▶*prefix* variant spelling of SUB- assimilated before *c* (as in *succeed, succussion*).

suc·cah /so͞o'kä; 'so͝okə/ (also **suk·kah**) ▶*n.* a temporary shelter covered in natural materials, built near a synagogue or house and used esp. for meals during the Jewish festival of Succoth. ▷late 19th cent.: from Hebrew *sukkāh* 'hut.'

suc·ce·da·ne·um /ˌsəksi'dānēəm/ ▶*n.* (*pl.* **-ne·a** /-nēə/) *dated* or *poetic/literary* a substitute, esp. for a medicine or drug. ▷early 17th cent.: modern Latin, neuter of Latin *succedaneus* 'following after,' from *succedere* 'come close after' (see SUCCEED). **—suc·ce·da·ne·ous** /-nēəs/ *adj.*

suc·ceed /sək'sēd/ ▶*v.* **1** [*intrans.*] achieve what one aims or wants to: *he* ***succeeded in*** *winning a pardon.* ■ (of a plan, request, or undertaking) lead to the desired result: *a mission which could not possibly succeed.* **2** [*trans.*] take over a throne, inheritance, office, or other position from: *he would succeed Hawke as prime minister.* ■ [*intrans.*] become the new rightful holder of an inheritance, office, title, or property: *he* ***succeeded to*** *his father's kingdom.* ■ come after and take the place of: *her embarrassment was succeeded by fear.* ▷late Middle English: from Old French *succeder* or Latin *succedere* 'come close after,' from *sub-* 'close to' + *cedere* 'go.' **—suc·ceed·er** *n.* (*archaic*).

▶*PHRASE* □ **nothing succeeds like success** *proverb* success leads to opportunities for further and greater successes.

suc·cen·tor /sək'sen(t)ər/ ▶*n.* a precentor's deputy in some cathedrals. ▷early 17th cent.: from late Latin, from Latin *succinere* 'sing to, chime in,' from *sub-* 'subordinately' + *canere* 'sing.'

suc·cès de scan·dale /so͞okˌsā də ˌskän'däl/ ▶*n.* a success due to notoriety or a thing's scandalous nature. ▷French, literally 'success of scandal.'

suc·cès d'es·time /so͞okˌsā des'tēm/ ▶*n.* (*pl.* same) a success through critical appreciation, as opposed to popularity or commercial gain. ▷French, literally 'success of opinion.'

suc·cess /sək'ses/ ▶*n.* the accomplishment of an aim or purpose: *the president had some* ***success in*** *restoring confidence.* ■ the attainment of popularity or profit: *the success of his play.* ■ a person or thing that achieves desired aims or attains prosperity: *I must make a success of my business.* ■ *archaic* the outcome of an undertaking, specified as achieving or failing to achieve its aims: *the good or ill success of their maritime enterprises.* ▷mid 16th cent.: from Latin *successus*, from the verb *succedere* 'come close after' (see SUCCEED).

suc·cess·ful /sək'sesfəl/ ▶*adj.* accomplishing an aim or purpose: *a successful attack on the town.* ■ having achieved popularity, profit, or distinction: *a successful actor.* **—suc·cess·ful·ly** *adv.* **—suc·cess·ful·ness** *n.*

Suc·ces·sion, Act of (in English history) each of three Acts of Parliament passed during the reign of Henry VIII regarding the succession of his children.

The first (1534) declared Henry's marriage to Catherine of Aragon to be invalid, fixing the succession on any child born to Henry's new wife Anne Boleyn. The second (1536) canceled this, asserting the rights of Jane Seymour and her issue, while the third (1544) determined the order of succession of Henry's three children, the future Edward VI, Mary I, and Elizabeth I.

suc·ces·sion /sək'seSHən/ ▶*n.* **1** a number of people or things sharing a specified characteristic and following one after the other: *she had been secretary to a succession of board directors.* ■ *Geology* a group of strata representing a single chronological sequence. **2** the action or process of inheriting a title, office, property, etc.: *the new king was already elderly at the time of his succession.* ■ the right or sequence of inheriting a position, title, etc.: *the* ***succession to*** *the Crown was disputed.* ■ *Ecology* the process by which a plant or animal community successively gives way to another until a stable climax is reached. Compare with SERE[2]. ▷Middle English (denoting legal transmission of an estate or the throne to another, also in the sense 'successors, heirs'): from Old French, or from Latin *successio(n-)*, from the verb *succedere* (see SUCCEED). The term in ecology dates from the mid 19th cent. **—suc·ces·sion·al** /-SHənl/ *adj.*

▶*PHRASES* □ **in quick** (or **rapid**) **succession** following one another at short intervals. □ **in succession** following one after the other without interruption: *she won the race for the second year in succession.* □ **in succession to** inheriting or elected to the place of: *he is not first in succession to the presidency.* □ **settle the succession** determine who shall succeed someone.

suc·ces·sive /sək'sesiv/ ▶*adj.* [*attrib.*] following one another or following others: *they were looking for their fifth successive win.* ▷late Middle English: from medieval Latin *successivus*, from *success-* 'followed closely,' from the verb *succedere* (see SUCCEED). **—suc·ces·sive·ly** *adv.* **—suc·ces·sive·ness** *n.*

suc·ces·sor /sək'sesər/ ▶*n.* a person or thing that succeeds another: *Schoenberg saw himself as a natural* ***successor to*** *the German romantic school.*

suc·cess sto·ry ▶*n.* *informal* a successful person or thing.

suc·cinct /sə(k)'siNG(k)t/ ▶*adj.* (esp. of something written or spoken) briefly and clearly expressed: *use short, succinct sentences.* See note at TERSE. ▷late Middle English (in the sense 'encircled'): from Latin *succinctus* 'tucked up,' past participle of *succingere*, from *sub-* 'from below' + *cingere* 'gird.' **—suc·cinct·ly** *adv.* **—suc·cinct·ness** *n.*

suc·cin·ic ac·id /səkˌsinik/ ▶*n.* *Biochemistry* a crystalline organic acid which occurs in living tissue as an intermediate in glucose metabolism. • Chem. formula: HOOC$(CH_2)_2$COOH. ▷late 18th cent.: *succinic* from French *succinique*, from Latin *succinum* 'amber' (from which it was first derived). **—suc·ci·nate** /'səksəˌnāt/ *n.*

suc·ci·nyl·cho·line /ˈsəksənlˈkōlēn/ ▶*n.* *Medicine* a synthetic compound used as a short-acting muscle relaxant and local anesthetic. It is an ester of choline with succinic acid.

suc·cor /'səkər/ (*Brit.* **suc·cour**) ▶*n.* assistance and support in times of hardship and distress. ■ (**succors**) *archaic* reinforcements of troops.

▶*v.* [*trans.*] give assistance or aid to: *prisoners of war were liberated and succored.* ▷Middle English: via Old French from medieval Latin *succursus*, from Latin *succurrere* 'run to the help of,' from *sub-* 'from below' + *currere* 'run.' **—suc·cor·less** *adj.*

suc·co·ry /'səkərē/ ▶*n.* another term for CHICORY (sense 1). ▷mid 16th cent.: alteration of obsolete French *cicorée.*

suc·co·tash /'səkəˌtaSH/ ▶*n.* a dish of corn and lima beans cooked together. ▷mid 18th cent.: from Narragansett *msícquatash* (plural).

Suc·coth /so͞o'kōt; 'so͝okəs/ ▶*n.* a major Jewish festival held in the autumn (beginning on the 15th day of Tishri) to commemorate the sheltering of the Israelites in the wilderness. Also called FEAST OF TABERNACLES. See also SUCCAH. ▷from Hebrew *sukkōṯ*, plural of *sukkāh* 'thicket, hut.'

suc·cour ▶*n.* & *v.* British spelling of SUCCOR.

suc·cu·bous /'səkyəbəs/ ▶*adj.* *Botany* (of a liverwort) having leaves obliquely inserted on the stem so that their upper edges are overlapped by the lower edges of the leaves above. Often contrasted with INCUBOUS. ▷mid 19th cent.: from late Latin *succubare* 'lie under' + -OUS.

suc·cu·bus /'səkyəbəs/ ▶*n.* (*pl.* **-bi** /-ˌbī/) a female demon believed to have sexual intercourse with sleeping men. ▷late Middle English: from medieval Latin *succubus* 'prostitute,' from *succubare*, from *sub-* 'under' + *cubare* 'to lie.'

suc·cu·lent /'səkyələnt/ ▶*adj.* (of food) tender, juicy, and tasty. ■ *Botany* (of a plant, esp. a xerophyte) having thick fleshy leaves or stems adapted to storing water.

▶*n.* *Botany* a succulent plant. ▷early 17th cent.: from Latin *succulentus*, from *succus* 'juice.' **—suc·cu·lence** *n.* **—suc·cu·lent·ly** *adv.*

suc·cumb /sə'kəm/ ▶*v.* [*intrans.*] fail to resist (pressure, temptation, or some other negative force): *he has become the latest to* ***succumb to*** *the strain.* ■ die from the effect of a disease or injury. ▷late 15th cent. (in the sense 'bring low, overwhelm'): from Old French *succomber* or Latin *succumbere*, from *sub-* 'under' + a verb related to *cubare* 'to lie.'

suc·cur·sal /sə'kərsəl/ ▶*adj.* (of a religious establishment such as a monastery) subsidiary to a principal establishment. ▷mid 19th cent.: from French *succursale*, from medieval Latin *succursus*, from the verb *succurrere* (see SUCCOR).

suc·cuss /sə'kəs/ ▶*v.* [*trans.*] (in preparing homeopathic remedies) shake (a solution) vigorously. ▷mid 19th cent.: from Latin *succuss-* 'shaken,' from the verb *succutere*, from *sub-* 'away' + *quatere* 'to shake.' **—suc·cus·sion** /-'kəSHən/ *n.*

such /səCH/ ▶*adj.*, *predeterminer*, & *pron.* **1** of the type previously mentioned: [as *adj.*] *I have been involved in many such courses* | [as *predeterminer*] *I longed to find a kindred spirit, and in him I thought I had found such a person* | [as *pron.*] *we were second-class citizens and they treated us* ***as such.*** **2** (**such —— as/that**) of the type about to be mentioned: [as *adj.*] *there is no such thing as a free lunch* | [as *predeterminer*] *the farm is organized in such a way that it can be run by two adults* | [as *pron.*] *the wound was such that I had to have stitches.* **3** to so high a degree; so great (often used to emphasize a quality): [as *adj.*] *this material is of* ***such*** *importance* ***that*** *it has a powerful bearing on the case* | [as *predeterminer*] *autumn's such a beautiful season* | [as *pron.*] ***such*** *is the elegance of his typeface* ***that*** *it is still a favorite of designers.* ▷Old English *swilc, swylc*; related to Dutch *zulk*, German *solch*, from the Germanic bases of SO[1] and ALIKE.

▶*PHRASES* □ **and such** and similar things: *he had activities like the scouts and Sunday school and such.* □ **as such** [often with *negative*] in the exact sense of the word: *it is possible to stay overnight here although there is no guest house as such.* □ **such and such** (or **such-and-such**) used to refer vaguely to a person or thing that does not need to be specified: *they'll want to know what actor played such-and-such a character.* □ **such as 1** for example: *wildflowers such as daisies and red clover.* **2** of a kind that; like: *an event such as we've shared.* □ **such as it is** (or **they are**) what little there is; for what it's worth: *the law, such as it is, will be respected.* □ **such a one** such a person or thing: *what was the reward for* ***such a one as*** *Fox?* □ **such that** to the extent that: *the linking of sentences such that they constitute a narrative.*

such·like /'səCHˌlīk/ ▶*pron.* things of the type mentioned: *carpets, old chairs, tables, and suchlike.*

▶*adj.* of the type mentioned: *food, drink, clothing, and suchlike provisions.*

suck /sək/ ▶*v.* **1** [*trans.*] draw into the mouth by contracting the muscles of the lip and mouth to make a partial vacuum: *they suck mint juleps through straws.* ■ hold (something) in the mouth and draw at it by contracting the lip and cheek muscles: *she sucked a mint* | [*intrans.*] *the child* ***sucked on*** *her thumb.* ■ draw milk, juice, or other fluid from (something) into the mouth or by suction: *she sucked each segment of the orange carefully.* ■ [*trans.*] draw in a specified direction by creating a vacuum: *he was sucked under the surface of the river.* ■ *figurative* involve (someone) in something without their choosing: *I didn't want to be* ***sucked into*** *the role of dutiful daughter.* ■ [*intrans.*] (of a pump) make a gurgling sound as a result of drawing air. **2** [*intrans.*] *informal* be very bad, disagreeable, or disgusting: *I love your country, but the weather sucks.*

▶*phrasal v.* □ **suck up** *informal* behave obsequiously, esp. for one's own advantage: *he has risen to where he is mainly by* ***sucking up to*** *the president.*

▶*n.* an act of sucking something. ■ the sound made by water retreating and drawing at something: *the soft suck of the sea against the sand.* ▷Old English *sūcan* (verb), from an Indo-European imitative root; related to SOAK.

▶*PHRASES* □ **give suck** *archaic* give milk from the breast or teat; suckle. □ **suck someone dry** exhaust someone's physical, material, or emotional resources. □ **suck someone in** cheat or deceive someone: *we were sucked in by his charm and good looks.* □ **suck someone off** *vulgar slang* perform fellatio on someone. □ **suck it up** *informal* accept a hardship.

suck·er /'səkər/ ▶*n.* **1** a person or thing that sucks, in particular: ■ a flat or concave organ enabling an animal to cling to a surface by suction. ■ the piston of a suction pump. ■ a pipe through which liquid is drawn by suction. **2** *informal* a gullible or easily deceived person. ■ (**a sucker for**) a person especially susceptible to or fond of a specified thing: *I always was a sucker for a good fairy tale.* **3** *informal* a thing or person not specified by name: *he's one strong sucker.* **4** *Botany* a shoot springing from the base of a tree or other plant, esp. one arising from the root below ground level at some distance from the main stem or trunk. ■ a side shoot from an axillary bud, as in tomato plants. **5** a freshwater fish with thick lips that are used to suck up food from the bottom, native to North America and Asia. • Family Catostomidae: many genera and species. **6** *informal* a lollipop.

▶*v.* **1** [*intrans.*] *Botany* (of a plant) produce suckers: *it spread rapidly after being left undisturbed to sucker.* **2** [*trans.*] *informal* fool or trick (someone): *they got suckered into accepting responsibility.*

suck·er·fish /'səkərˌfiSH/ ▶*n.* (*pl.* same or **-fish·es**) another term for REMORA.

suck·er punch ▶*n.* an unexpected punch or blow.

▶*v.* (**suck·er-punch**) [*trans.*] hit (someone) with such a punch or blow: *Joe sucker-punched him and knocked him out.*

suck·le /ˈsəkəl/ ▸*v.* [*trans.*] feed (a baby or young animal) from the breast or teat: *a mother pig suckling a huge litter.* ■ [*intrans.*] (of a baby or young animal) feed by sucking the breast or teat: *the infant's biological need to suckle.* ▷late Middle English: probably a back-formation from SUCKLING.

suck·ler /ˈsək(ə)lər/ ▸*n.* an unweaned animal, esp. a calf. ■ a cow used to breed and suckle calves for beef.

suck·ling /ˈsəkliNG/ ▸*n.* an unweaned child or animal: [as *adj.*] *roast suckling pig.* ▷Middle English: from the verb SUCK + -LING.

suck-up ▸*n. informal* a person who behaves obsequiously, esp. to earn approval or favoritism.

suck·y /ˈsəkē/ ▸*adj.* (**suck·i·er**, **suck·i·est**) *informal* disagreeable; unpleasant: *her sucky job.*

su·cral·fate /ˈso͝okrəlˌfāt/ ▸*n. Medicine* a drug used in the treatment of gastric and duodenal ulcers. It is a complex of aluminum hydroxide and a sulfate derivative of sucrose. ▷1960s: blend of SUCROSE, ALUMINUM, and SULFATE).

su·crase /ˈso͞oˌkrās; -ˌkrāz/ ▸*n.* another term for INVERTASE.

Su·cre[1] /ˈso͞okrā/ the judicial capital and seat of the judiciary of Bolivia; pop. 131,000. Located in the Andes, at an altitude of 8,860 feet (2,700 m), it was named Chuquisaca by the Spanish in 1539. It was renamed in 1825 in honor of Antonio José de Sucre.

Su·cre[2] /ˈso͞oˌkrā/, Antonio José de (1795–1830), Venezuelan revolutionary and statesman; president of Bolivia 1826–28. He served as Simón Bolívar's chief of staff, liberating Ecuador, Peru, and Bolivia from the Spanish. He was the first president of Bolivia.

su·cre /ˈso͞oˌkrā/ ▸*n.* the basic monetary unit of Ecuador, equal to 100 centavos. ▷named after A. J. de *Sucre* (see SUCRE[2]).

S

su·crose /ˈso͞oˌkrōs/ ▸*n. Chemistry* a compound that is the chief component of cane or beet sugar. • A disaccharide containing glucose and fructose units; chem. formula: $C_{12}H_{22}O_{11}$. ▷mid 19th cent.: from French *sucre* 'sugar' + -OSE[2].

suc·tion /ˈsəksHən/ ▸*n.* the production of a partial vacuum by the removal of air in order to force fluid into a vacant space or procure adhesion.
▸*v.* [*trans.*] remove (something) using suction: *physicians used a tube to suction out the gallstones.* ▷early 17th cent.: from late Latin *suctio(n-)*, from Latin *sugere* 'suck.'

suc·tion pump ▸*n.* a pump for drawing liquid through a pipe into a chamber emptied by a piston.

suc·to·ri·al /ˌsəkˈtôrēəl/ ▸*adj. chiefly Zoology* adapted for sucking (descriptive, for example, of the mouthparts of some insects). ■ (of an animal) having a sucker for feeding or adhering to something. ▷mid 19th cent.: from modern Latin *suctorius* (from Latin *sugere* 'suck') + -AL. —**suc·to·ri·al·ly** *adv.*

Su·dan /so͞oˈdan/ (also **the Sudan**) **1** a country in northeastern Africa, south of Egypt, with a coastline on the Red Sea; pop. 39,148,000; capital, Khartoum; languages, Arabic (official), Dinka, Hausa, and others.

Under Arab rule from the 13th century, the country was conquered by Egypt in 1820–22. Sudan was separated from its northern neighbor by the Mahdist revolt of 1881–98 and administered after the reconquest of 1898 as an Anglo-Egyptian condominium. It became an independent republic in 1956, but has suffered severely as a result of protracted civil war between the Islamic government in the north and separatist forces in the south. In 2004 Arab militas attacked villagers in western Darfur, leaving more than 50,000 people dead and displacing more than 1 million.

2 a vast region in North Africa that extends across the width of the continent from the southern edge of the Sahara to the tropical equatorial zone in the south. ▷from Arabic *sūdān*, literally 'country of the blacks.' —**Su·da·nese** /ˌso͞odnˈēz; -ˈēs/ *adj.* & *n.*

su·dan grass /so͞oˈdan/ ▸*n.* a Sudanese sorghum cultivated for fodder in dry regions of the U.S. • *Sorghum sudanense*, family Gramineae.

Sud·bur·y /ˈsədˌberē; -b(ə)rē/ a city in central Ontario; pop. 92,884. It lies at the center of Canada's largest mining region.

sudd /səd/ ▸*n.* (**the sudd**) an area of floating vegetation in a stretch of the White Nile, thick enough to impede navigation. ▷Arabic, literally 'obstruction.'

sud·den /ˈsədn/ ▸*adj.* occurring or done quickly and unexpectedly or without warning: *a sudden bright flash.*
▸*adv. poetic/literary* or *informal* suddenly: *sudden there swooped an eagle downward.* ▷Middle English: from Anglo-Norman French *sudein*, from an alteration of Latin *subitaneus*, from *subitus* 'sudden.' —**sud·den·ness** *n.*
▸PHRASE □ **all of a sudden** suddenly: *I feel really tired all of a sudden.*

sud·den death ▸*n. informal* a means of deciding the winner in a tied contest, in which play continues and the winner is the first side or player to score: [as *adj.*] *a sudden-death playoff.*

sud·den in·fant death syn·drome ▸*n.* the death of a seemingly healthy baby in its sleep, due to an apparent spontaneous cessation of breathing.

sud·den·ly /ˈsədn-lē/ ▸*adv.* quickly and unexpectedly: *the ambassador died suddenly* | [*sentence adverb*] *suddenly I heard a loud scream.*

sud·den oak death ▸*n.* a disease of various oaks and other forest trees, sometimes resulting in sudden death as a result of bark cankers that encircle the trunk. • The infecting organism is the water mold *Phytophthora Ramorum.*

Su·de·ten·land /so͞oˈdātnˌland; -ˌlänt/ an area in the northwestern part of the Czech Republic, on the border with Germany. Allocated to Czechoslovakia after World War I, it became an object of Nazi expansionist policies and was ceded to Germany as a result of the Munich Agreement of September 1938. In 1945, the area was returned to Czechoslovakia. Czech name SUDETY.

su·dor·if·er·ous /ˌso͞odəˈrif(ə)rəs/ ▸*adj.* (of a gland) secreting sweat. ▷late 16th cent. (in the sense 'sudorific'): from late Latin *sudorifer* (from Latin *sudor* 'sweat') + -OUS.

su·dor·if·ic /ˌso͞odəˈrifik/ *Medicine* ▸*adj.* relating to or causing sweating.
▸*n.* a drug that induces sweating. ▷early 17th cent.: from modern Latin *sudorificus*, from Latin *sudor* 'sweat.'

suds /sədz/ ▸*plural n.* short for SOAPSUDS. ■ *informal* beer.
▸*v.* [*trans.*] lather, cover, or wash in soapy water: *Martha sudsed my back.* ■ [*intrans.*] form suds: *soft baby soap that sudsed.* ▷mid 19th cent.: of uncertain sense development but perhaps originally denoting the flood water of the English Fens; compare with Middle Low German *sudde*, Middle Dutch *sudse* 'marsh, bog'; probably related to SEETHE. —**suds·y** *adj.*

suds·er /ˈsədzər/ ▸*n. informal* a soap opera.

sue /so͞o/ ▸*v.* (**sues, sued, su·ing**) **1** [*trans.*] institute legal proceedings against (a person or institution), typically for redress: *she is to sue the baby's father* | [*intrans.*] *I* **sued for** *breach of contract.* **2** [*intrans.*] *formal* appeal formally to a person for something: *the rebels were forced to* **sue for** *peace.* ▷Middle English: from Anglo-Norman French *suer*, based on Latin *sequi* 'follow.' Early senses were very similar to those of the verb *follow.* —**su·er** /ˈso͞oər/ *n.*

suede /swād/ ▸*n.* leather, esp. kidskin, with the flesh side rubbed to make a velvety nap. ▷mid 17th cent.: from French *(gants de) Suède* '(gloves of) Sweden.'

suede·head /ˈswādˌhed/ ▸*n. chiefly Brit.* a person, esp. a youth, whose appearance is similar to that of a skinhead but generally characterized by slightly longer hair and neater, more stylish clothes.

su·et /ˈso͞oit/ ▸*n.* the hard white fat on the kidneys and loins of cattle, sheep, and other animals, used to make foods including puddings, pastry, and mincemeat. ▷Middle English: from Anglo-Norman French, from the synonymous word *su*, from Latin *sebum* 'tallow.' —**su·et·y** *adj.*

Sue·to·ni·us /so͞oəˈtōnēəs; swēˈtō-/ (*c.*69–*c.*150), Roman biographer and historian; full name *Gaius Suetonius Tranquillus.* His surviving works include *Lives of the Caesars.*

Su·ez, Isthmus of /so͞oˈez; ˈso͞oˌez/ an isthmus between the Mediterranean and the Red seas that connects Egypt and Africa to the Sinai Peninsula and Asia. The port of Suez lies in the south, and the isthmus is traversed by the Suez Canal.

Su·ez Ca·nal a shipping canal that connects the Mediterranean Sea at Port Said with the Red Sea. It was constructed between 1859 and 1869 under the direction of Ferdinand de Lesseps. In 1875, it came under British control; its nationalization by Egypt in 1956 prompted the Suez crisis.

suf. ▸*abbr.* suffix.

suf- ▸*prefix* variant spelling of SUB- assimilated before *f* (as in *suffocate, suffuse*).

Suff. ▸*abbr.* ■ Suffolk. ■ suffragan.

suff. ▸*abbr.* ■ sufficient. ■ suffix.

suf·fer /ˈsəfər/ ▸*v.* [*trans.*] **1** experience or be subjected to (something bad or unpleasant): *he'd suffered intense pain* | [*intrans.*] *he'd suffered a great deal since his arrest* | [as *n.*] (**suffering**) *weapons that cause unnecessary suffering.* ■ [*intrans.*] (**suffer from**) be affected by or subject to (an illness or ailment): *his daughter suffered from agoraphobia.* ■ [*intrans.*] become or appear worse in quality: *his relationship with Anne did suffer.* ■ [*intrans.*] *archaic* undergo martyrdom or execution. **2** *dated* tolerate: *France will no longer suffer the existing government.* ■ allow (someone) to do something: *my conscience would not suffer me to accept any more.* ▷Middle English: from Anglo-Norman French *suffrir*, from Latin *sufferre*, from *sub-* 'from below' + *ferre* 'to bear.' —**suf·fer·a·ble** /ˈsəf(ə)rəbəl/ *adj.* —**suf·fer·er** /ˈsəf(ə)rər/ *n.* (in sense 1).
▸PHRASE □ **not suffer fools gladly** be impatient or intolerant toward people one regards as foolish or unintelligent. [with biblical allusion to 2 Cor. 11–19.]

suf·fer·ance /ˈsəf(ə)rəns/ ▸*n.* **1** absence of objection rather than genuine approval; toleration: *Charles was only here* **on sufferance.** ■ *Law* the condition of the holder of an estate who continues to hold it after the title has ceased, without the express permission of the owner: *an estate at sufferance.* ■ *archaic* patient endurance. **2** *archaic* the suffering or undergoing of something bad or unpleasant. ▷Middle English (sense 2): from Anglo-Norman French *suffraunce*, from late Latin *sufferentia*, from *sufferre* (see SUFFER).

suf·fice /səˈfīs/ ▸*v.* [*intrans.*] be enough or adequate: *a quick look should suffice* | [with *infinitive*] *two examples should suffice to prove the contention.* ■ [*trans.*] meet the needs of: *simple mediocrity cannot suffice them.* ▷Middle English: from Old French *suffis-*, stem of *suffire*, from Latin *sufficere* 'put under, meet the need of,' from *sub-* 'under' + *facere* 'make.'
▸PHRASE □ **suffice (it) to say** used to indicate that one is saying enough to make one's meaning clear while withholding something for reasons of discretion or brevity: *suffice it to say that they were not considered suitable for this project.*

suf·fi·cien·cy /səˈfisHənsē/ ▸*n.* (*pl.* **-cies**) the condition or quality of being adequate or sufficient. ■ [in *sing.*] an adequate amount of something, esp. of something essential: ***a sufficiency of** good food.* ■ *archaic* self-sufficiency or independence of character, esp. of an arrogant or imperious sort. ▷late 15th cent. (denoting sufficient means or wealth): from late Latin *sufficientia*, from the verb *sufficere* (see SUFFICE).

suf·fi·cient /səˈfisHənt/ ▸*adj.* enough; adequate: *a small income that was* **sufficient for** *her needs* | *they had sufficient resources to survive.* ▷Middle English (in the sense 'legally satisfactory'): from Old French, or from Latin *sufficient-* 'meeting the need of' (see SUFFICE). —**suf·fi·cient·ly** *adv.*

suf·fix ▸*n.* /ˈsəfiks/ a morpheme added at the end of a word to form a derivative, e.g., *-ation, -fy, -ing, -itis.*
▸*v.* /ˈsəfiks; səˈfiks/ [*trans.*] append, esp. as a suffix. ▷late 18th cent. (as a noun): from modern Latin *suffixum*, neuter past participle (used as a noun) of Latin *suffigere*, from *sub-* 'subordinately' + *figere* 'fasten.' —**suf·fix·a·tion** /ˌsəfikˈsāsHən/ *n.*

suf·fo·cate /ˈsəfəˌkāt/ ▸*v.* die or cause to die from lack of air or inability to breathe: [*intrans.*] *ten detainees suffocated in an airless police cell.* | [*trans.*] *she was suffocated by the fumes.* ■ have or cause to have difficulty in breathing: [*intrans.*] *he was suffocating, his head jammed up against the back of the sofa* | [*trans.*] *you're suffocating me—I can scarcely breathe* | [as *adj.*] (**suffocating**) *the* *suffocating heat.* ■ *figurative* feel or cause to feel trapped and oppressed: [as *adj.*] (**suffocated**) *I felt suffocated by my marriage.* ▷late 15th cent.: from Latin *suffocat-* 'stifled,' from the verb *suffocare*, from *sub-* 'below' + *fauces* 'throat.' —**suf·fo·cat·ing·ly** *adv.* —**suf·fo·ca·tion** /ˌsəfəˈkāSHən/ *n.*

Suf·folk[1] /ˈsəfək/ **1** a county in eastern England, on the coast of East Anglia; county town, Ipswich. **2** a commercial and agricultural city in southern Virginia, in the Hampton Roads area; pop. 63,677.

Suf·folk[2] (also **Suf·folk sheep**) ▶*n.* a sheep of a large black-faced breed with a short fleece.

Suf·folk Coun·ty a suburban, agricultural, and resort county in southeastern New York, on the eastern end of Long Island; pop. 1,419,369.

suf·fra·gan /ˈsəfrəgən/ (also **suffragan bishop** or **bishop suffragan**) ▶*n.* a bishop appointed to help a diocesan bishop. ■ a bishop in relation to his archbishop or metropolitan. ▷late Middle English: from Anglo-Norman French and Old French, representing medieval Latin *suffraganeus* 'assistant (bishop),' from Latin *suffragium* (see **SUFFRAGE**).

suf·frage /ˈsəfrij/ ▶*n.* **1** the right to vote in political elections. ■ *archaic* a vote given in assent to a proposal or in favor of the election of a particular person. **2** (usu. **suffrages**) a series of intercessory prayers or petitions. ▷late Middle English (in the sense 'intercessory prayers,' also 'assistance'): from Latin *suffragium*, reinforced by French *suffrage*. The modern sense of 'right to vote' was originally U.S. (dating from the late 18th cent.).

suf·fra·gette /ˌsəfrəˈjet/ ▶*n.* *historical* a woman seeking the right to vote through organized protest.

suf·fra·gist /ˈsəfrəjist/ ▶*n.* *chiefly historical* a person advocating the extension of suffrage, esp. to women. —**suf·fra·gism** /-ˌjizəm/ *n.*

suf·fuse /səˈfyo͞oz/ ▶*v.* [*trans.*] gradually spread through or over: *her cheeks were suffused with color* | *the first half of the poem is suffused with idealism.* ▷late 16th cent.: from Latin *suffus-* 'poured into,' from *sub-* 'below, from below' + *fundere* 'pour.' —**suf·fu·sion** /-ˈfyo͞oZHən/ *n.* —**suf·fu·sive** /-ˈfyo͞osiv/ *adj.*

Su·fi /ˈso͞ofē/ ▶*n.* (*pl.* **-fis**) a Muslim ascetic and mystic. ▷mid 17th cent.: from Arabic *ṣūfī*, perhaps from *ṣūf* 'wool' (referring to the woolen garment worn). —**Su·fic** /-fik/ *adj.*

Su·fism /ˈso͞oˌfizəm/ ▶*n.* the mystical system of the Sufis.

Sufism is the esoteric dimension of the Islamic faith, the spiritual path to mystical union with God. It is influenced by other faiths, such as Buddhism, and reached its peak in the 13th century. There are many Sufi orders, the best known being the dervishes.

sug /səg/ ▶*v.* (**sugged, sug·ging**) [*intrans.*] *informal, chiefly Brit.* sell or attempt to sell a product under the guise of conducting market research: *a market researcher claims the firm is sugging.* ▷1980s: acronym from *sell under the guise.*

sug- ▶*prefix* variant spelling of **SUB-** assimilated before g (as in *suggest*).

sug·ar /ˈSHo͝ogər/ ▶*n.* **1** a sweet crystalline substance obtained from various plants, esp. sugar cane and sugar beet, consisting essentially of sucrose, and used as a sweetener in food and drink. ■ a lump or teaspoonful of this, used to sweeten tea or coffee: *I'll have mine black with two sugars.* ■ *informal* used as a term of endearment or an affectionate form of address: *what's wrong, sugar?* ■ [as *exclam.*] *informal* used as a euphemism for "shit." ■ *informal* a psychoactive drug in the form of white powder, esp. heroin or cocaine. **2** *Biochemistry* any of the class of soluble, crystalline, typically sweet-tasting carbohydrates found in living tissues and exemplified by glucose and sucrose.

▶*v.* [*trans.*] sweeten, sprinkle, or coat with sugar: *she absentmindedly sugared her tea* | [as *adj.*] (**sugared**) *sugared almonds.* ■ *figurative* make more agreeable or palatable: *the novel was preachy but sugared heavily with jokes.* ▷Middle English: from Old French *sukere*, from Italian *zucchero*, probably via medieval Latin from Arabic *sukkar*. —**sug·ar·less** *adj.*

▶*PHRASE* □ **sugar the pill** see **PILL**[1].

sug·ar ap·ple ▶*n.* another term for **SWEETSOP**.

sug·ar beet ▶*n.* beet of a variety from which sugar is extracted. It provides an important alternative sugar source to cane, and the pulp that remains after processing is used as feed for livestock.

sug·ar·bird /ˈSHo͝ogərˌbərd/ (also **sug·ar bird**) ▶*n.* **1** a southern African songbird with a long fine bill and very long tail, feeding on nectar and insects. • Genus *Promerops*, family Promeropidae (or Meliphagidae): two species. **2** another term for **BANANAQUIT**.

sug·ar bush (also **sug·ar·bush** /ˈSHo͝ogərˌbo͝oSH/) ▶*n.* a plantation of sugar maples.

sug·ar can·dy ▶*n.* another term for **CANDY**, esp. hard candy.

sug·ar cane (also **sug·arcane** /ˈSHo͝ogərˌkān/) ▶*n.* a perennial tropical grass with tall stout jointed stems from which sugar is extracted. The fibrous residue can be used as fuel, in fiberboard, and for a number of other purposes. • Genus *Saccharum*, family Gramineae: several species, in particular *S. officinarum* and its hybrids.

sug·ar·coat /ˈSHo͝ogərˌkōt/ ▶*v.* [*trans.*] coat (an item of food) with sugar: [as *adj.*] (**sugarcoated**) *sugarcoated almonds.* ■ make superficially attractive or acceptable: *you won't see him sugarcoat the truth.* ■ make excessively sentimental: *the filmmakers' proficiency is overpowered by their tendency to sugarcoat the material.*

sug·ar cube ▶*n.* a small cube of compacted sugar used esp. for sweetening hot drinks.

sug·ar dad·dy ▶*n.* *informal* a rich older man who lavishes gifts on a young woman in return for her company or sexual favors.

sug·ar glid·er ▶*n.* a flying phalanger that feeds on wattle gum and eucalyptus sap, native to Australia, New Guinea, and Tasmania. • *Petaurus breviceps*, family Petauridae.

sug·ar·ing /ˈSHo͝ogəriNG/ ▶*n.* **1** (also **sug·ar·ing off**) the boiling down of maple sap until it thickens into syrup or crystallizes into sugar. **2** a method of removing unwanted hair by applying a mixture of lemon juice, sugar, and water to the skin and then peeling it off together with the hair.

sug·ar·loaf /ˈSHo͝ogərˌlōf/ ▶*n.* a conical molded mass of sugar (now used chiefly in similies and metaphors to describe the shape of other objects): [as *adj.*] *a sugarloaf hat.*

Sug·ar Loaf Moun·tain a rocky peak in Brazil, northeast of Rio de Janeiro's Copacabana Beach. It rises to a height of 1,296 feet (390 m).

sug·ar ma·ple ▶*n.* a North American maple, from the sap of which maple sugar and maple syrup are made. Also called **ROCK MAPLE**. • *Acer saccharum*, family Aceraceae.

sug·ar of lead /led/ ▶*n.* *dated Chemistry* lead acetate, a soluble white crystalline salt. • Chem. formula: $Pb(CH_3CO_2)_2$. ▷mid 17th cent.: so named for its sweet taste.

sug·ar pine ▶*n.* a tall pine tree, the heartwood of which exudes a sweet substance, hence its name. Found primarily in California and Oregon, sugar pines have very long cones, some reaching 26 inches in length. • *Pinus lambertiana.*

sug·ar·plum /ˈSHo͝ogərˌpləm/ ▶*n.* a small round candy of flavored boiled sugar.

sug·ar snap (also **sug·ar snap pea**) ▶*n.* a snow pea, esp. of a variety with distinctively thick and rounded pods.

sug·ar·y /ˈSHo͝ogərē/ ▶*adj.* containing much sugar: *energy-restoring, sugary drinks.* ■ resembling or coated in sugar: *a sugary texture.* ■ excessively sentimental: *sugary romance.* —**sug·ar·i·ness** *n.*

sug·gest /sə(g)ˈjest/ ▶*v.* [*reporting verb*] put forward for consideration: [with *clause*] *I suggest that we wait a day or two* | [with *direct speech*] *"Maybe you ought to get an expert," she suggested* | [*trans.*] *Ruth suggested a vacation.* ■ [*trans.*] cause one to think that (something) exists or is the case: *finds of lead coffins suggested a cemetery north of the river* | [with *clause*] *the temperature wasn't as tropical as the bright sunlight may have suggested* ■ state or express indirectly: [with *clause*] *are you suggesting that I should ignore her?* | [*trans.*] *the seduction scenes suggest his guilt and her loneliness.* ■ [*trans.*] evoke: *the theatrical interpretation of weather and water almost suggests El Greco.* ■ (**suggest itself**) (of an idea) come into one's mind. ▷early 16th cent.: from Latin *suggest-* 'suggested, prompted,' from the verb *suggerere*, from *sub-* 'from below' + *gerere* 'bring.' —**sug·gest·er** *n.*

sug·gest·i·ble /sə(g)ˈjestəbəl/ ▶*adj.* open to suggestion; easily swayed: *a suggestible client would comply.* —**sug·gest·i·bil·i·ty** /-ˌjestəˈbilitē/ *n.*

sug·ges·tion /sə(g)ˈjesCHən/ ▶*n.* an idea or plan put forward for consideration. ■ the action of doing this: *at my* **suggestion**, *the museum held an exhibition of his work.* ■ something that implies or indicates a certain fact or situation: *there is no suggestion that he was involved in any wrongdoing.* ■ a slight trace or indication of something: *there was a suggestion of a smile on his lips.* ■ the action or process of calling up an idea or thought in someone's mind by associating it with other things: *the power of suggestion.* ■ *Psychology* the influencing of a person to accept an idea, belief, or impulse uncritically, esp. as a technique in hypnosis or other therapies. ■ *Psychology* a belief or impulse of this type. ▷Middle English (in the sense 'an incitement to evil'): via Old French from Latin *suggestio(n-)*, from the verb *suggerere* (see **SUGGEST**).

sug·ges·tive /sə(g)ˈjestiv/ ▶*adj.* tending to suggest an idea: *there were various suggestive pieces of evidence.* ■ indicative or evocative: *flavors* **suggestive of** *coffee and blackberry.* ■ making someone think of sex and sexual relationships: *a suggestive remark.* —**sug·ges·tive·ly** *adv.* —**sug·ges·tive·ness** *n.*

suh /sə(r)/ ▶*n.* nonstandard spelling of **SIR**, used in representing chiefly southern U.S., black, or British dialect: *my dear suh, we are shocked by your candor* | *I'm not gonna do it, no suh.*

Su·har·to /so͞oˈhärtō/, Raden (1921–), Indonesian president 1968–98. As president, he restored political, social, and economic stability to Indonesia, but after the economy began to falter in 1997 and opposition to his rule spread in 1998, he resigned from office.

Sui /swā/ a dynasty that ruled in China AD 581–618 and reunified the country.

su·i·cid·al /ˌso͞oiˈsīdl/ ▶*adj.* deeply unhappy or depressed and likely to commit suicide: *far from being suicidal, he was clearly enjoying life.* ■ relating to or likely to lead to suicide: *I began to take her suicidal tendencies seriously.* ■ likely to have a disastrously damaging effect on oneself or one's interests: *a suicidal career move.* —**su·i·cid·al·ly** *adv.*

su·i·cide /ˈso͞oiˌsīd/ ▶*n.* the action of killing oneself intentionally: *he* **committed suicide** *at the age of forty* | *gun control laws may reduce suicides.* ■ a person who does this. ■ a course of action that is disastrously damaging to oneself or one's own interests: *it would be political suicide to restrict criteria for unemployment benefits.* ■ [as *adj.*] relating to or denoting a violent act or attack carried out by a person who does not expect to survive it: *a suicide bombing.*

▶*v.* [*intrans.*] intentionally kill oneself: *she suicided in a very ugly manner.* ▷mid 17th cent.: from modern Latin *suicida* 'act of suicide,' *suicidium* 'person who commits suicide,' from Latin *sui* 'of oneself' + *caedere* 'kill.'

su·i·cide gene ▶*n.* an introduced gene that causes a tumor cell to produce an enzyme that will attract a drug lethal to the tumor.

su·i·cide pact ▶*n.* an agreement between two or more people to commit suicide together.

su·i ge·ne·ris /ˌso͞oˌī ˈjenərəs; ˌso͞oē/ ▶*adj.* unique: *the sui generis nature of animals.* ▷Latin, literally 'of its own kind.'

su·i ju·ris /ˌso͞oˌī ˈjo͝oris; ˌso͞oē/ ▶*adj.* *Law* of age; independent: *the beneficiaries are all sui juris.* ▷Latin, literally 'of one's own right.'

su·int /ˈso͞oənt; swint/ ▶*n.* the natural grease in sheep's wool, from which lanolin is obtained. ▷late 18th cent.: from French, from *suer* 'sweat.'

Suisse /swēs/ French name for **SWITZERLAND**.

suit /so͞ot/ ▶*n.* **1** a set of outer clothes made of the same fabric and designed to be worn together, typically consisting of a jacket and trousers or a jacket and skirt. ■ a set of clothes to be worn on a particular occasion or for a particular activity: *a jogging suit.* ■ a complete set of pieces of armor for covering the whole body. ■ a complete set of sails required for a ship or for a set of spars. ■ (usu. **suits**) *informal* an executive in a business or organization, typically one regarded as exercising influence in an impersonal way: *maybe now the suits in Washington will listen.* **2** any of the sets distinguished by their pictorial symbols into which a deck of playing cards is divided, in conventional decks comprising spades, hearts, diamonds, and clubs. **3** short for **LAWSUIT**. ■ the process of trying to win a woman's affection, typically with a view to marriage: *he could not compete with John's charms in Marian's eyes and his suit came to nothing.* ■ *poetic/literary* a petition or entreaty made to a person in authority.

▶*v.* **1** [*trans.*] be convenient for or acceptable to: *he lied whenever it suited him* | [*intrans.*] *the apartment has two bedrooms—if it suits, you can have one of them.* ■ (**suit**

oneself) [often in *imperative*] act entirely according to one's own wishes (often used to express the speaker's annoyance): *"I'm not going to help you." "Suit yourself."* ■ go well with or enhance the features, figure, or character of (someone): *the dress didn't suit her.* ■ (**suit something to**) *archaic* adapt or make appropriate for (something): *they took care to suit their answers to the questions put to them.* **2** [*intrans.*] put on clothes, typically for a particular activity: *I* ***suited up*** *and entered the water.* ▷Middle English: from Anglo-Norman French *siwte*, from a feminine past participle of a Romance verb based on Latin *sequi* 'follow.' Early senses included 'attendance at a court' and 'legal process'; senses 1 and 2 derive from an earlier meaning 'set of things to be used together.' The verb sense 'make appropriate' dates from the late 16th cent.

▸*PHRASE* □ **follow suit** see FOLLOW.

suit·a·ble /'so͞otəbəl/ ▸*adj.* right or appropriate for a particular person, purpose, or situation: *these toys are not* ***suitable for*** *children under five.* ▷late 16th cent.: from the verb SUIT, on the pattern of *agreeable.* **—suit·a·bil·i·ty** /,so͞otə'bilitē/ *n.* **—suit·a·ble·ness** *n.* **—suit·a·bly** /-blē/ *adv.*

suit·case /'so͞ot,kās/ ▸*n.* a case with a handle and a hinged lid, used for carrying clothes and other personal possessions. **—suit·case·ful** /-,fo͝ol/ *n.* (*pl.* **-fuls**).

suite /swēt/ ▸*n.* **1** a set of things belonging together, in particular: ■ a set of rooms designated for one person's or family's use or for a particular purpose. ■ a set of furniture of the same design. ■ *Music* a set of instrumental compositions, originally in dance style, to be played in succession. ■ *Music* a set of selected pieces from an opera or musical, arranged to be played as one instrumental work. ■ *Computing* a set of programs with a uniform design and the ability to share data. ■ *Geology* a group of minerals, rocks, or fossils occurring together and characteristic of a location or period. **2** a group of people in attendance on a monarch or other person of high rank. ▷late 17th cent.: from French, from Anglo-Norman French *siwte* (see SUIT).

suit·ed /'so͞otid/ ▸*adj.* **1** [*predic.*] right or appropriate for a particular person, purpose, or situation: *the task is ideally* ***suited to*** *a computer.* **2** [in *combination*] wearing a suit of clothes of a specified type, fabric, or color: *a dark-suited man | sober-suited lawyers.*

suit·ing /'so͞otiNG/ ▸*n.* fabric of a suitable quality for making suits, trousers, jackets, and skirts. ■ suits collectively.

suit·or /'so͞otər/ ▸*n.* a man who pursues a relationship with a particular woman, with a view to marriage. ■ a prospective buyer of a business or corporation. ▷late Middle English (in the sense 'member of a retinue,'): from Anglo-Norman French *seutor*, from Latin *secutor*, from *sequi* 'follow.'

suk /so͞ok/ (also **sukh**) ▸*n.* variant spelling of SOUK.

Su·kar·no /so͞o'kärnō/, Achmad (1901–70), Indonesian statesman; president 1945–67. He led the struggle for independence, which was formally granted in 1949, but lost power in the 1960s after having been implicated in the abortive communist coup of 1965.

su·ki·ya·ki /so͞okē'yäkē/ ▸*n.* a Japanese dish of sliced meat, esp. beef, fried rapidly with vegetables and sauce. ▷Japanese.

suk·kah ▸*n.* variant spelling of SUCCAH.

Suk·kur /'so͞okər/ a city in southeastern Pakistan, on the Indus River; pop. 350,000. Nearby is the Sukkur Barrage, a dam constructed across the Indus that directs water through irrigation channels to a large area of the Indus valley.

Su·la·we·si /,so͞olə'wāsē/ a mountainous island in the Greater Sunda group in Indonesia, east of Borneo; chief town, Ujung Pandang. Former name **CELEBES**.

Su·lay·ma·ni·yah /,so͞olimä'nē(y)ə/ a town in northeastern Iraq, in the mountainous region of southern Kurdistan; pop. 279,000. It is the capital of a Kurdish governorate of the same name. Full name **As Sulaymaniyah**; also called **Sulaimaniya**.

sul·cate /'səl,kāt/ ▸*adj. Botany & Zoology* marked with parallel grooves. ▷mid 18th cent.: from Latin *sulcatus* 'furrowed,' past participle of *sulcare.*

sul·cus /'səlkəs/ ▸*n.* (*pl.* **sul·ci** /'səl,sī; -,sē/) *Anatomy* a groove or furrow, esp. one on the surface of the brain. ▷mid 17th cent.: from Latin, 'furrow, wrinkle.'

Su·lei·man I /,so͞olā'män/ (also **So·li·man** or **So·ly·man**) (*c.*1494–1566), sultan of the Ottoman Empire 1520–66; also known as **Suleiman the Magnificent** or **Suleiman the Lawgiver**. The Ottoman Empire reached its fullest extent under his rule.

sul·fa /'səlfə/ (*chiefly Brit.* also **sul·pha**) ▸*n.* [usu. as *adj.*] the sulfonamide family of drugs: *a succession of lifesaving sulfa drugs.* ▷1940s: abbreviation (see SULFA-).

sulfa- (*chiefly Brit.* also **sulph-**) ▸*comb. form* in names of drugs derived from sulfanilamide. ▷abbreviation of SULFANILAMIDE.

sul·fa·di·a·zine /,səlfə'dīə,zēn/ (*chiefly Brit.* also **sul·pha·di·a·zine**) ▸*n. Medicine* a sulfonamide antibiotic used to treat meningococcal meningitis.

sul·fa·dim·i·dine /,səlfə'dimi,dēn/ (*chiefly Brit.* also **sul·pha·dim·i·dine**) ▸*n. Medicine* a sulfonamide antibiotic used chiefly to treat human urinary infections and to control respiratory disease in pigs. ▷mid 20th cent.: from SULFA- + DI-[1] + PYRIMIDINE.

sul·fa·meth·ox·a·zole /,səlfəme'THäksə,zōl/ (*chiefly Brit.* also **sul·pha·meth·ox·a·zole**) ▸*n. Medicine* a sulfonamide antibiotic used to treat respiratory and urinary tract infections, and as a component of the preparation co-trimoxazole.

sul·fa·mic ac·id /səl'famik/ (*chiefly Brit.* also **sul·pham·ic ac·id**) ▸*n. Chemistry* a strongly acid crystalline compound used in cleaning agents and to make weed killers. • Chem. formula: $HOSO_2NH_2$. ▷mid 19th cent.: *sulfamic* from SULFUR + AMIDE + -IC. **—sul·fa·mate** /'səlfə,māt/ *n.*

sul·fa·nil·a·mide /,səlfə'nilə,mīd/ (*chiefly Brit.* also **sul·pha·nil·a·mide**) ▸*n. Medicine* a synthetic compound with antibacterial properties that is the basis of the sulfonamide drugs. • Alternative name: ***p*-aminobenzenesulfonamide**; chem. formula: $(H_2N)C_6H_4(SO_2NH_2)$. ▷1930s: from *sulfanilic* (from SULFUR + ANILINE + -IC) + AMIDE.

sul·fa·pyr·i·dine /,səlfə'pirə,dēn/ (*chiefly Brit.* also **sul·pha·pyr·i·dine**) ▸*n. Medicine* a sulfonamide antibiotic used to treat some forms of dermatitis.

sul·fa·sal·a·zine /,səlfə'salə,zēn/ (*chiefly Brit.* also **sul·pha·sal·a·zine**) ▸*n. Medicine* a sulfonamide antibiotic used to treat ulcerative colitis and Crohn's disease. ▷mid 20th cent.: from SULFA- + *sal(icylic acid)* + AZINE.

sul·fate /'səl,fāt/ (*chiefly Brit.* also **sul·phate**) ▸*n. Chemistry* a salt or ester of sulfuric acid, containing the anion SO_4^{2-} or the divalent group $-OSO_2O-$. ▷late 18th cent.: French, from Latin *sulfur* (see SULFUR).

sul·fide /'səl,fīd/ (*chiefly Brit.* also **sul·phide**) ▸*n. Chemistry* a binary compound of sulfur with another element or group.

sul·fite /'səl,fīt/ (*chiefly Brit.* also **sul·phite**) ▸*n. Chemistry* a salt of sulfurous acid, containing the anion SO_3^{2-}. ▷late 18th cent.: French, alteration of *sulfate* (see SULFATE).

sul·fon·a·mide /səl'fänə,mīd/ (*chiefly Brit.* also **sul·phon·a·mide**) ▸*n. Medicine* any of a class of synthetic drugs, derived from sulfanilamide, that are able to prevent the multiplication of some pathogenic bacteria. ▷late 19th cent.: from SULFONE + AMIDE.

sul·fo·nate /'səlfə,nāt/ (*chiefly Brit.* also **sul·pho·nate**) *Chemistry* ▸*n.* a salt or ester of a sulfonic acid.

▸*v.* [*trans.*] convert (a compound) into a sulfonate, typically by reaction with sulfuric acid. **—sul·fo·na·tion** /,səlfə'nāSHən/ *n.*

sul·fone /'səl,fōn/ (*chiefly Brit.* also **sul·phone**) ▸*n. Chemistry* an organic compound containing a sulfonyl group linking two organic groups. ▷late 19th cent.: from German *Sulfon*, from *Sulfur* (see SULFUR).

sul·fon·ic ac·id /səl'fänik/ (*chiefly Brit.* also **sul·phon·ic**) ▸*n. Chemistry* an organic acid containing the group $-SO_2OH$.

sul·fo·nyl /'səlfənil/ (*chiefly Brit.* also **sul·pho·nyl**) ▸*n.* [as *adj.*] *Chemistry* of or denoting a divalent radical, $-SO_2-$, derived from a sulfonic acid group.

sul·fur /'səlfər/ (also *chiefly Brit.* **sul·phur**) ▸*n.* **1** the chemical element of atomic number 16, a yellow combustible nonmetal. (Symbol: **S**) ■ the material of which hellfire and lightning were believed to consist. ■ a pale greenish-yellow color: [as *adj.*] *the bird's* ***sulfur-yellow*** *throat.*

Sulfur occurs uncombined in volcanic and sedimentary deposits, as well as being a constituent of many minerals and petroleum. It is normally a bright yellow crystalline solid, but several other allotropic forms can be made. Sulfur is an ingredient of gunpowder, and is used in making matches and as an antiseptic and fungicide.

2 an American butterfly with predominantly yellow wings that may bear darker patches. • *Colias, Phoebis,* and other genera, family Pieridae.

▸*v.* [*trans.*] disinfect or fumigate with sulfur. ▷Middle English: from Anglo-Norman French *sulfre*, from Latin *sulfur, sulphur.* **—sul·fur·y** *adj.*

USAGE In general use, the standard U.S. spelling is **sulfur** and the standard British spelling is **sulphur**. In chemistry, however, **sulfur** is now the standard form in the field in both U.S. and British contexts.

sul·fu·rate /'səlf(y)ə,rāt/ (*chiefly Brit.* also **sul·phu·rate**) ▸*v.* [*trans.*] impregnate, fumigate, or treat with sulfur, esp. in bleaching. **—sul·fu·ra·tion** /,səlf(y)ə'rāSHən/ *n.* **—sul·fu·ra·tor** /-,rātər/ *n.*

sul·fur di·ox·ide ▸*n. Chemistry* a colorless pungent toxic gas formed by burning sulfur in air. • Chem. formula: SO_2.

sul·fu·re·ous /səl'fyo͝orēəs/ (*chiefly Brit.* also **sul·phu·re·ous**) ▸*adj.* of, like, or containing sulfur. ▷early 16th cent.: from Latin *sulfureus* (from SULFUR) + -OUS.

sul·fu·ret·ed hy·dro·gen ▸*n. Chemistry* archaic term for HYDROGEN SULFIDE.

sul·fu·ric /səl'fyo͝orik/ (*chiefly Brit.* also **sul·phu·ric**) ▸*adj.* containing sulfur or sulfuric acid: *the sulfuric byproducts of wood fires.* ▷late 18th cent.: from French *sulfurique*, from Latin (as SULFUR).

sul·fu·ric ac·id ▸*n.* a strong acid made by oxidizing solutions of sulfur dioxide and used in large quantities as an industrial and laboratory reagent. The concentrated form is an oily, dense, corrosive liquid. • Chem. formula: H_2SO_4.

sul·fu·rize /'səlf(y)ə,rīz/ (also *chiefly Brit.* also **sul·phu·rize**) ▸*v.* another term for SULFURATE. **—sul·fu·ri·za·tion** /,səlf(y)ərə'zāSHən/ *n.*

sul·fur·ous /'səlfərəs/ (*chiefly Brit.* also **sul·phur·ous**) ▸*adj.* (chiefly of vapor or smoke) containing or derived from sulfur: *wafts of sulfurous fumes.* ■ sulfureous. ■ like sulfur in color; pale yellow. ■ marked by bad temper, anger, or profanity: *a sulfurous glance.* ▷late Middle English: from Latin *sulfurosus*, from *sulfur* (see SULFUR).

sul·fur·ous ac·id ▸*n. Chemistry* an unstable weak acid formed when sulfur dioxide dissolves in water. It is used as a reducing and bleaching agent. • Chem. formula: H_2SO_3.

sul·fur spring ▸*n.* a spring of which the water contains sulfur or its compounds.

sulk /səlk/ ▸*v.* [*intrans.*] be silent, morose, and bad-tempered out of annoyance or disappointment: *he was sulking over the breakup of his band.*

▸*n.* a period of gloomy and bad-tempered silence stemming from annoyance and resentment: *she was in a fit of* ***the sulks.*** ▷late 18th cent.: perhaps a back-formation from SULKY. **—sulk·er** *n.*

sulk·y /'səlkē/ ▸*adj.* (**sulk·i·er, sulk·i·est**) morose, bad-tempered, and resentful; refusing to be cooperative or cheerful: *disappointment was making her sulky.* ■ expressing or suggesting gloom and bad temper: *she had a sultry, sulky mouth.* ■ *figurative* not quick to work or respond: *a sulky fire.*

▸*n.* (*pl.* **sulk·ies**) a light two-wheeled horse-drawn vehicle for one person, used chiefly in harness racing. ▷mid 18th cent.: perhaps from obsolete *sulke* 'hard to dispose of,' of unknown origin. **—sulk·i·ly** /-kəlē/ *adv.* **—sulk·i·ness** *n.*

sulky

sull /səl/ ▸*v.* [*intrans.*] *informal* or *dialect* (of an animal) refuse to go on. ■ (of a person) become sullen; sulk: *don't* ***sull up*** *on me, let's get it aired.* ▷mid 19th cent.: back-formation from SULLEN.

Sul·la /'so͝olə/ (138–78 BC), Roman general and politician; full name *Lucius Cornelius Sulla Felix.* After a victorious campaign against Mithridates VI, Sulla invaded Italy in 83. He was elected dictator in 82 and implemented constitutional reforms in favor of the Senate.

sul·lage /'səlij/ ▸*n.* waste from household sinks, showers, and baths, but not toilets. ■ *archaic* refuse, esp. sewage. ▷mid 16th cent.: perhaps from Anglo-Norman French *suillage*, from *suiller* 'to soil.'

sul·len /'sələn/ ▸*adj.* bad-tempered and sulky; gloomy: *a sullen pout | figurative a sullen sunless sky.*

See note at GLUM. ■ (esp. of water) slow-moving: *rivers in sullen, perpetual flood.*
▶*n.* **(the sullens)** *archaic* a sulky or depressed mood. ▷Middle English (in the senses 'solitary, averse to company,' and 'unusual'): from Anglo-Norman French *sulein*, from *sol* 'sole.' **—sul·len·ly** *adv.* **—sul·len·ness** *n.*

Sul·li·van[1] /ˈsələvən/, Sir Arthur (Seymour) (1842–1900), English composer. He is best known for the 14 light operas that he wrote in collaboration with librettist W. S. Gilbert.

Sul·li·van[2], Ed(ward Vincent) (1901–74), U.S. television show host and journalist. As the host of television's "Ed Sullivan Show" 1948–71, he gave national exposure to many performers who at the time were on their way to stardom, including Elvis Presley and the Beatles.

Sul·li·van[3], John L(awrence) (1858–1918), U.S. boxer. Fighting with his bare knuckles, he was proclaimed the world heavyweight champion in 1882. In 1892, when boxing rules changed and padded gloves were used, he fought James J. Corbett for the heavyweight championship and lost, being knocked out in the 21st round.

Sul·li·van[4], Louis Henry (1856–1924), U.S. architect. He developed modern functionalism in architecture by designing skyscrapers. Among his works were the Auditorium (1886–90), the Stock Exchange (1893–94), and the Carson, Pirie, Scott (1899–1904) buildings in Chicago, as well as the Wainwright building in St. Louis (1890–91).

Sul·ly /ˈsəlē/, Thomas (1783–1872), U.S. artist; born in England. Chiefly a portrait painter, his works include portraits of Queen Victoria, the Marquis de Lafayette, Thomas Jefferson, and James Monroe. His other paintings include "The Passage of the Delaware" (1819) and "Mother and Child" (1827).

sul·ly /ˈsəlē/ ▶*v.* **(-lies, -lied)** [*trans.*] *poetic/literary* or *ironic* damage the purity or integrity of; defile: *they were outraged that anyone should sully their good name.* ▷late 16th cent.: perhaps from French *souiller* 'to soil.'

sulpha- ▶*comb. form* chiefly British spelling of SULFA-.

Sul·phur /ˈsəlfər/ a city in southwestern Louisiana, a western suburb of Lake Charles; pop. 20,512.

sul·phur, etc. ▶*n.* chiefly British spelling of SULFUR, etc.

USAGE See usage at SULFUR.

Sul·pi·cian /səlˈpisʜən/ ▶*n.* a member of a congregation of secular Roman Catholic priests founded in 1642 by a priest of St. Sulpice, Paris, mainly to train candidates for holy orders.
▶*adj.* relating to or denoting this congregation.

sul·tan /ˈsəltn/ ▶*n.* a Muslim sovereign. ■ **(the Sultan)** *historical* the sultan of Turkey. ▷mid 16th cent.: from French, or from medieval Latin *sultanus*, from Arabic *sulṭān* 'power, ruler.' **—sul·tan·ate** /-ˌāt/ *n.*

sul·tan·a /səlˈtanə/ ▶*n.* **1** a small, light brown, seedless raisin used in foods such as puddings and cakes. **2** a wife or concubine of a sultan. ■ any other woman in a sultan's family. ▷late 16th cent. (sense 2): from Italian, feminine of *sultano* (see SULTAN). Sense 1 dates from the mid 19th cent.

sul·try /ˈsəltrē/ ▶*adj.* **(-tri·er, -tri·est) 1** (of the air or weather) hot and humid. **2** (of a person, esp. a woman) attractive in a way that suggests a passionate nature. ▷late 16th cent.: from obsolete *sulter* 'swelter.' **—sul·tri·ly** /-trəlē/ *adv.* **—sul·tri·ness** *n.*

su·lu /ˈso͞olo͞o/ ▶*n.* (*pl.* **-lus**) a length of cotton or other light fabric wrapped about the body as a sarong, worn from the waist by men and full-length by women from the Melanesian Islands. ▷Fijian.

Su·lu Sea /ˈso͞olo͞o/ a sea in the Malay Archipelago, surrounded by the northeastern coast of Borneo and the western islands of the Philippines.

Sulz·ber·ger /ˈsəltsˌbərgər/, Arthur Ochs (1926–) U.S. publisher. He worked for *The New York Times* from 1951, serving as its president from 1963 until 1979. He was responsible for modernizing and broadening the newspaper's editorial range and for reorganizing the staff and day-to-day operations.

sum /səm/ ▶*n.* **1** a particular amount of money: *they could not afford such a sum.* **2** **(the sum of)** the total amount resulting from the addition of two or more numbers, amounts, or items: *the sum of two prime numbers.* ■ the total amount of something that exists: *the sum of his own knowledge.* **3** an arithmetical problem, esp. at an elementary level.
▶*v.* **(summed, sum·ming)** [*trans.*] *technical* find the sum of (two or more amounts): *if we sum these equations we obtain x.* ■ [*intrans.*] **(sum to)** (of two or more amounts) add up to a specified total: *these additional probabilities must sum to 1.*
▶*phrasal v.* □ **sum up** give a brief summary of something: *Gerard will open the debate and I will sum up.* ■ *Law* (of a judge) review the evidence at the end of a case, and direct the jury regarding points of law. □ **sum someone/something up** express a concise idea of the nature or character of a person or thing: *selfish—that summed her up.* ▷Middle English: via Old French from Latin *summa* 'main part, sum total,' feminine of *summus* 'highest.'
▶*PHRASE* □ **in sum** to sum up; in summary: *this interpretation does little, in sum, to add to our understanding.*

su·mac /ˈso͞omak; ˈsʜo͞o-/ (also **su·mach**) ▶*n.* a shrub or small tree of the cashew family, with compound leaves, fruits in conical clusters, and bright autumn colors. • Genera *Rhus* and *Cotinus*, family Anacardiaceae: several species, including the North American **staghorn sumac** (*R. typhina*), with densely clustered reddish hairy fruits, and **poison sumac** (*R. vernix*), with loosely clustered greenish-white fruits. Touching any part of the poison sumac can cause severe dermatitis. ▷Middle English (denoting the dried and ground leaves of *R. coriaria* used in tanning and dyeing): from Old French *sumac* or medieval Latin *sumac(h)*, from Arabic *summāḳ*.

Su·ma·tra /səˈmätrə/ a large island in Indonesia, southwest of the Malay Peninsula, from which it is separated by the Strait of Malacca; chief city, Medan. **—Su·ma·tran** *adj.* & *n.*

Su·ma·tran rhi·noc·er·os /səˈmätrən/ ▶*n.* a rare hairy two-horned rhinoceros found in montane rain forests from Malaysia to Borneo. • *Dicerorhinus sumatrensis*, family Rhinocerotidae.

su·ma·trip·tan /ˌso͞oməˈtripˌtan; -tən/ ▶*n.* a serotonin-agonist drug used for the acute treatment of migraines.

Sum·ba /ˈso͞ombə/ an island of the Lesser Sunda group in Indonesia, south of the islands of Flores and Sumbawa; chief town, Waingapu. Also called SANDALWOOD ISLAND.

Sum·ba·wa /so͞omˈbäwə/ an island in the Lesser Sunda group in Indonesia, situated between the islands of Lombok and Flores.

Su·mer /ˈso͞omər/ an ancient region in southwestern Asia, in present-day Iraq, comprising the southern part of Mesopotamia. From the 4th millennium BC it was the site of city-states that became part of ancient Babylonia.

Su·me·ri·an /səˈmerēən; -ˈmiər-/ ▶*adj.* of or relating to Sumer, its ancient language, or the early, non-Semitic element it contributed to Babylonian civilization.
▶*n.* **1** a member of the indigenous non-Semitic people of ancient Babylonia. **2** the Sumerian language.

The Sumerians had the oldest known written language, whose relationship to any other language is unclear. Theirs is the first historically attested civilization, and they invented cuneiform writing, the sexagesimal system of mathematics, and the sociopolitical institution of the city-state. Their art, literature, and theology had a profound influence long after their demise *c.*2000 BC.

▷late 19th cent.: from French *sumérien*, from SUMER.

Sum·ga·it /ˌso͞omgäˈēt/ Russian name for SUMQAYIT.

su·mi /ˈso͞omē/ ▶*n.* a type of black Japanese ink prepared in solid sticks and used for painting and writing. ▷early 20th cent.: Japanese, literally 'ink, blacking.'

su·mi-e /ˈso͞omē e/ ▶*n.* Japanese ink painting using sumi. ▷early 20th cent.: from SUMI + Japanese *e* 'painting.'

sum·ma /ˈsəmə; ˈso͞omə/ ▶*n.* (*pl.* **sum·mae** /ˈsəmē; ˈso͞omi/) *chiefly archaic* a summary of a subject. ▷early 18th cent.: from Latin, literally 'sum total' (a sense reflected in Middle English).

sum·ma cum lau·de /ˈso͞omə ˌko͞om ˈloudə; ˈloudē/ ▶*adv.* & *adj.* with the highest distinction: [as *adv.*] *he graduated summa cum laude* | [as *adj.*] *three scientific degrees, all summa cum laude.* ▷Latin, literally 'with highest praise.'

sum·mand /ˈsəmand; səˈmand/ ▶*n. Mathematics* a quantity to be added to another. ▷mid 19th cent.: from Latin *summandus* 'to be added,' gerundive of *summare*.

sum·ma·rize /ˈsəməˌrīz/ ▶*v.* [*trans.*] give a brief statement of the main points of (something): *these results can be summarized in the following table* | [*intrans.*] *to summarize, there are three main categories.* **—sum·ma·ri·za·tion** /ˌsəmərəˈzāsʜən/ *n.* **—sum·ma·riz·er** *n.*

sum·ma·ry /ˈsəmərē/ ▶*n.* (*pl.* **-ries**) a brief statement or account of the main points of something: *a summary of Chapter Three.*
▶*adj.* **1** dispensing with needless details or formalities; brief: *summary financial statements.* **2** *Law* (of a judicial process) conducted without the customary legal formalities: *summary arrest.* ■ (of a conviction) made by a judge or magistrate without a jury. ▷late Middle English (as an adjective): from Latin *summarius*, from *summa* 'sum total' (see SUM). **—sum·mar·i·ly** /səˈme(ə)rəlē; ˈsəmərəlē/ *adv.* **—sum·mar·i·ness** /səˈmerēnis/ *n.*
▶*PHRASE* □ **in summary** in short: *in summary, there is no clear case for one tax system compared to another.*

sum·ma·tion /səˈmāsʜən/ ▶*n.* **1** the process of adding things together: *the summation of numbers of small pieces of evidence.* ■ a sum total of things added together. **2** the process of summing something up: *these will need summation in a single document.* ■ a summary. ■ *Law* an attorney's closing speech at the conclusion of the giving of evidence. **—sum·ma·tion·al** /-sʜənl/ *adj.* **—sum·ma·tive** /ˈsəmətiv/ *adj.*

sum·mer[1] /ˈsəmər/ ▶*n.* the warmest season of the year, in the northern hemisphere from June to August and in the southern hemisphere from December to February: *the plant flowers in late summer* | *a long hot summer* | [as *adj.*] *summer vacation* | (*figurative*) *the golden summer of her life.* ■ *Astronomy* the period from the summer solstice to the autumnal equinox. ■ **(summers)** *poetic/literary* years, esp. of a person's age: *a girl of sixteen or seventeen summers.*
▶*v.* [*intrans.*] spend the summer in a particular place: *well over 100 birds summered there in 1976.* ■ [*trans.*] pasture (cattle) for the summer. ▷Old English *sumor*, of Germanic origin; related to Dutch *zomer*, German *Sommer*, also to Sanskrit *samā* 'year.' **—sum·mer·y** *adj.*

sum·mer[2] (also **sum·mer·tree** /ˈsəmərˌtrē/) ▶*n.* a horizontal bearing beam, esp. one supporting joists or rafters. ■ a capstone that supports an arch or lintel. ■ a lintel. ▷Middle English: from Old French *somier* 'packhorse,' from late Latin *sagmarius*, from Greek *sagma* 'packsaddle.'

sum·mer camp ▶*n.* a camp providing recreational and athletic facilities for children during the summer vacation period.

sum·mer cy·press ▶*n.* another term for KOCHIA.

sum·mer·house /ˈsəmərˌhous/ (also **sum·mer house**) ▶*n.* a small, typically rustic building in a garden or park, used for sitting in during the summer months. ■ (usu. **summer house**) a cottage or house use as a second residence, esp. during the summer.

Sum·mer Pal·ace a palace (now in ruins) of the former Chinese emperors near Beijing.

sum·mer·sault ▶*n.* & *v.* archaic spelling of SOMERSAULT.

sum·mer sau·sage ▶*n.* a type of hard dried and smoked sausage that is similar to salami in preparation and can be kept without refrigeration.

sum·mer school ▶*n.* courses held during school summer vacations, taken for remedial purposes, as part of an academic program, or for professional or personal purposes.

sum·mer sol·stice ▶*n.* the solstice that marks the onset of summer, at the time of the longest day, about June 21 in the northern hemisphere and December 22 in the southern hemisphere. ■ *Astronomy* the solstice in June.

sum·mer squash ▶*n.* a squash that is eaten before the seeds and rind have hardened. Unlike winter squash, summer squash does not keep well. • Cultivars of *Cucurbita pepo* var. *melopepo*, family Cucurbitaceae.

sum·mer stock ▶*n.* theatrical productions by a repertory company organized for the summer season, esp. at vacation resorts or in a suburban area.

sum·mer tan·a·ger ▶*n.* a tanager, the adult male of which is rosy red, and which is a common summer visitor in the central and southern U.S. • *Piranga rubra.*

sum·mer·time /ˈsəmərˌtīm/ ▶*n.* the season or period of summer: *in summertime trains run every ten minutes.*

sum·mer·tree /ˈsəmərˌtrē/ ▶*n.* see SUMMER[2].

Sum·mer·ville /ˈsəmərˌvil/ a city in southeastern South Carolina, northwest of North Charleston; pop. 27,752.

S

sum·mer-weight ▸*adj.* (of clothes) made of light fabric and therefore cool to wear.

sum·ming-up ▸*n.* a restatement of the main points of an argument, case, etc.

sum·mit /ˈsəmit/ ▸*n.* **1** the highest point of a hill or mountain. ■ *figurative* the highest attainable level of achievement: *the dramas are considered to form one of the summits of world literature.* **2** a meeting between heads of government: [as *adj.*] *a summit conference.* ▷late Middle English (in the general sense 'top part'): from Old French *somete*, from *som* 'top,' from Latin *summum*, neuter of *summus* 'highest.'

sum·mit·eer /ˌsəmiˈti(ə)r/ ▸*n.* a participant in a meeting between heads of government.

sum·mon /ˈsəmən/ ▸*v.* [*trans.*] authoritatively or urgently call on (someone) to be present, esp. as a defendant or witness in a law court: *the pope summoned Anselm to Rome.* ■ urgently demand (help): *she summoned medical assistance.* ■ call people to attend (a meeting): *he summoned a meeting of head delegates.* ■ bring to the surface (a particular quality or reaction) from within oneself: *she managed to* **summon up** *a smile.* ■ (**summon something up**) call an image to mind: *names that summon up images of far-off places.* ▷Middle English: from Old French *somondre*, from Latin *summonere* 'give a hint,' later 'call, summon,' from *sub-* 'secretly' + *monere* 'warn.' **—sum·mon·a·ble** *adj.* **—sum·mon·er** *n.*

sum·mons /ˈsəmənz/ ▸*n.* (*pl.* **-mons·es**) an order to appear before a judge or magistrate, or the writ containing it: *a summons for nonpayment of a parking ticket.* ■ an authoritative or urgent call to someone to be present or to do something: [with *infinitive*] *they might receive a summons to fly to France next day.*
▸*v.* [*trans.*] *chiefly Law* serve (someone) with a summons: [*trans.*] *he has been summonsed to appear in court next month.* ▷Middle English: from Old French *sumunse*, from an alteration of Latin *summonita*, feminine past participle of *summonere* (see SUMMON).

sum·mum bo·num /ˈsōōməm ˈbōnəm/ ▸*n.* the highest good, esp. as the ultimate goal according to which values and priorities are established in an ethical system. ▷Latin.

su·mo /ˈsōōmō/ ▸*n.* (*pl.* **-mos**) a Japanese form of heavyweight wrestling, in which a wrestler wins a bout by forcing his opponent outside a marked circle or by making him touch the ground with any part of his body except the soles of his feet. ■ a sumo wrestler. ▷from Japanese *sūmo*.

sump /səmp/ ▸*n.* a pit or hollow in which liquid collects, in particular: ■ the base of an internal combustion engine, which serves as a reservoir of oil for the lubrication system. ■ a depression in the floor of a mine or basement in which water collects. ■ a cesspool. ▷Middle English (in the sense 'marsh'): from Middle Dutch or Low German *sump*, or (in the mining sense) from German *Sumpf*; related to SWAMP.

sump·ter /ˈsəm(p)tər/ ▸*n.* *archaic* a pack animal. ▷Middle English: from Old French *sommetier*, via late Latin from Greek *sagma*, *sagmat-* 'packsaddle'; compare with SUMMER[2].

sump·tu·ary /ˈsəm(p)CHōōˌerē/ ▸*adj.* [*attrib.*] *chiefly historical* relating to or denoting laws that limit private expenditure on food and personal items. ▷early 17th cent.: from Latin *sumptuarius*, from *sumptus* 'cost, expenditure,' from *sumere* 'take.'

sump·tu·ous /ˈsəm(p)CHōōəs/ ▸*adj.* splendid and expensive-looking: *the banquet was a sumptuous, luxurious meal.* ▷late Middle English (in the sense 'made or produced at great cost'): from Old French *somptueux*, from Latin *sumptuosus*, from *sumptus* 'expenditure' (see SUMPTUARY). **—sump·tu·os·i·ty** /ˌsəm(p)CHōōˈäsitē/ *n.* **—sump·tu·ous·ly** *adv.* **—sump·tu·ous·ness** *n.*

Sum·qay·it /ˌsōōmgäˈ(y)ēt/ an industrial city in eastern Azerbaijan, on the Caspian Sea; pop. 235,000. Russian name **SUMGAIT**.

Sum·ter /ˈsəmtər/ a commercial and industrial city in east central South Carolina; pop. 39,643.

sum to·tal ▸*n.* another term for SUM (sense 2).

Su·my /ˈsōōmē/ an industrial city in northeastern Ukraine, near the border with Russia; pop. 296,000.

sun /sən/ ▸*n.* **1** (also **Sun**) the star around which the earth orbits. ■ any similar star in the universe, with or without planets.

The sun is the central body of the solar system. It provides the light and energy that sustains life on earth, and its position relative to the earth's axis determines the terrestrial seasons. The sun is a star of a type known as a G2 dwarf, a sphere of hydrogen and helium 870,000 miles (1.4 million km) in diameter that obtains its energy from nuclear fusion reactions in its interior, where the temperature is about 15 million °C. The surface is a little under 6,000°C.

2 (usu. **the sun**) the light or warmth received from the earth's sun: *we sat outside in the sun.* ■ *poetic/literary* a person or thing regarded as a source of glory or inspiration or understanding: *the rhetoric faded before the sun of reality.* ■ *poetic/literary* used with reference to someone's success or prosperity: *the sun of the Plantagenets went down in clouds.* **3** *poetic/literary* a day or a year: *after going so many suns without food, I was sleeping.*
▸*v.* (**sunned**, **sun·ning**) (**sun oneself**) sit or lie in the sun: *Buzz could see Clare sunning herself on the terrace below.* ■ [*trans.*] expose (something) to the sun, esp. to warm or dry it: *the birds are sunning their wings.* ▷Old English *sunne*, of Germanic origin; related to Dutch *zon* and German *Sonne*, from an Indo-European root shared by Greek *hēlios* and Latin *sol*. **—sun·less** *adj.* **—sun·less·ness** *n.* **—sun·like** /-ˌlīk/ *adj.* **—sun·ward** /-wərd/ *adj.* & *adv.* **—sun·wards** /-wərdz/ *adv.*
▸*PHRASES* □ **against the sun** *Nautical* against the direction of the sun's apparent movement in the northern hemisphere; from right to left or counterclockwise. □ **catch the sun** see CATCH. □ **make hay while the sun shines** see HAY[1]. □ **on which the sun never sets** (of an empire) worldwide. [applied in the 17th cent. to the Spanish dominions, later to the British Empire.] □ **place in the sun** see PLACE. □ **shoot the sun** *Nautical* ascertain the altitude of the sun with a sextant in order to determine one's latitude. □ **under the sun** on earth; in existence (used in expressions emphasizing the large number of something): *they exchanged views on every subject under the sun.* □ **with the sun** *Nautical* in the direction of the sun's apparent movement in the northern hemisphere; from left to right or clockwise.

Sun. ▸*abbr.* Sunday.

sun-and-plan·et gear ▸*n.* a system of gearwheels consisting of a central wheel (a **sun gear** or **sun wheel**) around which one or more outer wheels (**planet gears** or **planet wheels**) travel.

sun-baked ▸*adj.* (esp. of the ground) exposed to the heat of the sun and therefore dry and hard.

sun·bath /ˈsənˌbaTH/ ▸*n.* a period of sunbathing: *an upstairs deck on which you could* **take a sunbath**.

sun·bathe /ˈsənˌbā<u>TH</u>/ ▸*v.* [*intrans.*] sit or lie in the sun, esp. to tan the skin: [as *n.*] (**sunbathing**) *it was too hot for sunbathing.* **—sun·bath·er** *n.*

sun·beam /ˈsənˌbēm/ ▸*n.* a ray of sunlight.

sun bear (also **Malayan sun bear**) ▸*n.* a small mainly nocturnal bear that has a brownish-black coat with a light-colored mark on the chest, native to Southeast Asia. • *Helarctos malayanus*, family Ursidae.

sun·belt /ˈsənˌbelt/ (also **sun belt**) ▸*n.* a strip of territory receiving a high amount of sunshine, esp.: ■ (**Sunbelt** or **Sun Belt**) the southern U.S. from California to Florida, noted for resort areas and for the movement of businesses and population into these states from the colder northern states.

sun·bird /ˈsənˌbərd/ ▸*n.* a small, brightly colored Old World songbird with a long down-curved bill, feeding on nectar and resembling a hummingbird (but not able to hover). • Family Nectariniidae: four genera, in particular *Nectarinia*, and numerous species.

sun·bit·tern /ˈsənˌbitərn/ (also **sun bit·tern**) ▸*n.* a tropical American wading bird with a long bill, neck, and legs, having mainly grayish plumage but showing chestnut and orange on the wings when they are spread in display. • *Eurypyga helias*, the only member of the family Eurypygidae. ▷late 19th cent.: so named because of the pattern on the spread wings, which resembles a sunset.

sun·block /ˈsənˌbläk/ ▸*n.* a cream or lotion for protecting the skin from the sun and preventing sunburn.

sun·bon·net /ˈsənˌbänit/ ▸*n.* a close-fitting brimmed cotton hat that protects the head and neck from the sun, worn esp. by infants and formerly by women.

sun·burn /ˈsənˌbərn/ ▸*n.* reddening, inflammation, and, in severe cases, blistering and peeling of the skin caused by overexposure to the ultraviolet rays of the sun.
▸*v.* (*past* and *past part.* **-burned** or **-burnt**) (**be sunburned**) (of a person or bodily part) suffer from sunburn: *most of us managed to get sunburnt.* ■ [usu. as *adj.*] (**sunburned** or **sunburnt**) ruddy from exposure to the sun: *a handsome sunburned face.* ■ [*intrans.*] suffer from sunburn: *a complexion that sunburned easily.*

sun·burst /ˈsənˌbərst/ ▸*n.* a sudden brief appearance of the full sun from behind clouds. ■ a decoration or ornament resembling the sun and its rays: [as *adj.*] *a pair of sunburst diamond earrings.* ■ a pattern of irregular concentric bands of color with the brightest at the center.

Sun Cit·y a retirement community in south central Arizona, northwest of Phoenix; pop. 38,126.

sun·dae /ˈsənˌdā/ ▸*n.* a dish of ice cream with added ingredients such as fruit, nuts, syrup, and whipped cream. ▷late 19th cent. (originally U.S.): perhaps an alteration of **SUNDAY**, either because the dish was made with ice cream left over from Sunday and sold cheaply on Monday, or because it was sold only on Sundays, a practice devised (according to some accounts) to circumvent Sunday legislation.

Sun·da Is·lands /ˈsəndə; ˈsōōn-/ a chain of islands in the southwestern part of the Malay Archipelago. They are divided into two groups: the **Greater Sunda Islands**, which include Sumatra, Java, Borneo, and Sulawesi, and the **Lesser Sunda Islands**, which lie to the east of Java and include Bali, Sumbawa, Flores, Sumba, and Timor.

sun dance ▸*n.* a dance performed by North American Plains Indians in honor of the sun and to prove bravery by overcoming pain.

Sun·da·nese /ˌsəndəˈnēz; -ˈnēs/ ▸*n.* (*pl.* same) **1** a member of a mainly Muslim people of western Java. **2** the Indonesian language of this people.
▸*adj.* of or relating to the Sundanese or their language. ▷from Sundanese *Sunda*, the western part of Java, + -ESE.

Sun·day /ˈsənˌdā/ ▸*n.* the day of the week before Monday and following Saturday, observed by Christians as a day of rest and religious worship and (together with Saturday) forming part of the weekend: *they left town* **on Sunday** | *many people work on Sundays* | [as *adj.*] *Sunday evening.*
▸*adv.* on Sunday: *the concert will be held Sunday.* ■ (**Sundays**) on Sundays; each Sunday: *the program is repeated Sundays at 9 p.m.* ▷Old English *Sunnandæg* 'day of the sun,' translation of Latin *dies solis*; compare with Dutch *zondag* and German *Sonntag*.

Sun·day best ▸*n.* (**one's Sunday best**) a person's best clothes, worn to church or on special occasions.

Sun·day driv·er ▸*n.* a person perceived as driving in an inexperienced or unskillful way, esp. one who drives slowly.

Sun·day-go-to-meet·ing ▸*adj.* (of a hat, clothes, etc.) suitable for going to church in.

Sun·day punch ▸*n.* *informal* a powerful or devastating punch or other attacking action.

Sun·day school ▸*n.* a class held on Sundays to teach children about their religion.

sun deck ▸*n.* **1** the deck, or part of a deck, of a yacht or cruise ship that is open to the sky. **2** a terrace or balcony positioned to catch the sun.

sun·der /ˈsəndər/ ▸*v.* [*trans.*] *poetic/literary* split apart: *the crunch of bone when it is sundered.* ▷late Old English *sundrian*; related to German *sondern*.
▸*PHRASE* □ **in sunder** apart or into pieces: *hew their bones in sunder!*

Sun·der·land /ˈsəndərlənd/ an industrial city in northeastern England, a port at the mouth of the Wear River; pop. 287,000.

sun·dew /ˈsənˌd(y)ōō/ ▸*n.* a small carnivorous plant of boggy places, with rosettes of leaves that bear sticky glandular hairs. These trap insects, which are then digested. • Genus *Drosera*, family Droseraceae: many species, including the common European *D. rotundifolia*.

sun·di·al /ˈsənˌdīl/ ▸*n.* **1** an instrument showing the time by the shadow of a pointer cast by the sun onto a plate marked with the hours of the day. **2** (also **sundial shell**) a mollusk with a flattened spiral shell that is typically patterned in shades of brown, living in tropical and subtropical seas. • Family Architectonicidae, class Gastropoda.

sundial 1

sun disk ▸*n.* (esp. in ancient Egypt) a winged disk representing a sun god.

sun dog (also **sun·dog** /ˈsən,dôg/) ▸*n.* another term for **PARHELION**.

sun·down /ˈsən,doun/ ▸*n.* [in *sing.*] the time in the evening when the sun disappears or daylight fades.

sun·down·er /ˈsən,dounər/ ▸*n.* **1** *Brit., informal* an alcoholic drink taken at sunset. **2** *Austral.* a tramp arriving at a sheep station in the evening under the pretense of seeking work, so as to obtain food and shelter.

sun·dress /ˈsən,dres/ ▸*n.* a light, loose, sleeveless dress, typically having a wide neckline and thin shoulder straps.

sun·drops /ˈsən,dräps/ ▸*n.* a day-flowering North American plant with yellow flowers, related to the evening primrose. • Genera *Oenothera* and *Calylophus*, family Onagraceae.

sun·dry /ˈsəndrē/ ▸*adj.* [*attrib.*] of various kinds; several: *lemon rind and sundry herbs.*
▸as *plural n.* (**sundries**) various items not important enough to be mentioned individually: *a drugstore selling magazines, newspapers, and sundries.* ▷Old English *syndrig* 'distinct, separate'; related to **SUNDER**.
▸*PHRASE* □ **all and sundry** see **ALL**.

sun-dry ▸*v.* [*trans.*] [usu. as *adj.*] (**sun-dried**) dry (something, esp. food) in the sun, as opposed to using artificial heat: *sun-dried tomatoes.*

sun·fast /ˈsən,fast/ ▸*adj.* (of a dye or fabric) not prone to fade in sunlight.

sun·fish /ˈsən,fisн/ ▸*n.* (*pl.* same or **-fish·es**) **1** a large deep-bodied marine fish of warm seas, with tall dorsal and anal fins near the rear of the body and a very short tail. Also called **MOLA**. • Family Molidae: three genera and several species, in particular the very large **ocean sunfish** (*Mola mola*), also commonly called **mola mola**. **2** a nest-building freshwater fish that is native to North America and popular in aquariums, e.g., the pumpkinseed. • Several genera and species in the family Centrarchidae (the **sunfish family**). This family also includes sport fish such as the black basses, rock bass, bluegill, and crappies.

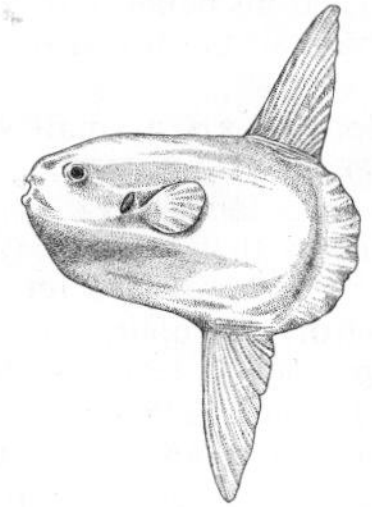
ocean sunfish

sun·flow·er /ˈsən,flou(-ə)r/ ▸*n.* a tall North American plant of the daisy family, with very large golden-rayed flowers. Sunflowers are cultivated for their edible seeds, which are an important source of oil for cooking and margarine. • *Helianthus annus*, family Compositae.

sunflower

sun·flow·er seed ▸*n.* the hard-shelled edible seed of a plant of the daisy family, yielding an oil used in cooking and margarine.

Sun·flow·er State a nickname for the state of **KANSAS**.

Sung /so͝onɢ/ (also **Song**) a dynasty that ruled in China AD 960–1279. The period was marked by the first use of paper money and by advances in printing, firearms, shipbuilding, clockmaking, and medicine.

sung /səɴɢ/ ▸ past participle of **SING**.

sun·glass·es /ˈsən,glasiz/ ▸*plural n.* glasses tinted to protect the eyes from sunlight or glare.

sun hat (also **sun·hat** /ˈsən,hat/) ▸*n.* a broad-brimmed hat that protects the head and neck from the sun.

sunk /səɴɢk/ ▸ past and past participle of **SINK**[1].

USAGE See usage at **SINK**[1].

sunk·en /ˈsəɴɢkən/ ▸*adj.* **1** [*attrib.*] having sunk or been submerged in water: *the wreck of a sunken ship.* **2** having sunk below the usual or expected level: *the inspector looked at his sunken head with compassion.* ■ [*attrib.*] at a lower level than the surrounding area: *a sunken garden.* ■ (of a person's eyes or cheeks) deeply recessed, esp. as a result of illness, hunger, or stress: *her face was white, with sunken cheeks.* ▷late Middle English: past participle of **SINK**[1].

sunk fence ▸*n.* a ditch with one side formed by a wall or with a fence running along the bottom.

Sun King the nickname of Louis XIV of France (see **LOUIS**[1]).

sun-kissed ▸*adj.* made warm or brown by the sun: *the sun-kissed resort of Acapulco | her sun-kissed shoulders.*

sun·lamp /ˈsən,lamp/ ▸*n.* **1** a lamp emitting ultraviolet rays used as a substitute for sunlight, typically to produce an artificial suntan or in therapy. **2** a large lamp with a parabolic reflector used in filmmaking.

sun·light /ˈsən,līt/ ▸*n.* light from the sun: *a shaft of sunlight.*

sun·lit /ˈsən,lit/ ▸*adj.* illuminated by direct light from the sun: *clear sunlit waters.*

sunn /sən/ (also **sunn hemp**) ▸*n.* a hemplike fiber from southern Asia. ▷late 18th cent.: from Urdu and Hindi *san*, from Sanskrit *śaṇá* 'hempen.'

Sun·na /ˈsənə/ ▸*n.* the traditional portion of Muslim law based on Muhammad's words or acts, accepted (together with the Koran) as authoritative by Muslims and followed particularly by Sunni Muslims. ▷Arabic, literally 'form, way, course, rule.'

Sun·ni /ˈso͞onē/ ▸*n.* (*pl.* same or **-nis**) one of the two main branches of Islam, commonly described as orthodox, and differing from Shia in its understanding of the Sunna and in its acceptance of the first three caliphs. Compare with **SHIA**. ■ a Muslim who adheres to this branch of Islam. ▷from the Arabic for 'an adherent of Sunna.' —**Sun·nite** /so͞onīt/ *adj.* & *n.*

Sun·ni Tri·an·gle ▸*n.* an area of Iraq bounded roughly by Baghdad in the southeast, Ramadi in the southwest, and Tikrit in the north. It is predominantly Sunni and has been a focus of opposition to occupation forces.

sun·ny /ˈsənē/ ▸*adj.* (**-ni·er**, **-ni·est**) bright with sunlight: *a sunny day.* ■ (of a place) receiving much sunlight: *find a sunny patch for the dahlia tubers.* ■ (of a person or their temperament) cheery and bright: *he had a sunny disposition.* ■ suggestive of the warmth or brightness of the sun: *the room was done up in nice sunny colors.* —**sun·ni·ly** /ˈsənəlē/ *adv.* —**sun·ni·ness** *n.*

sun·ny side ▸*n.* the side of something that receives the sun for longest: *a well-known hotel on the sunny side of the island.* ■ the more cheerful or pleasant aspect of a state of affairs: *he was fond of the sunny side of life.*
▸*PHRASE* □ **sunny side up** (of an egg) fried on one side only.

Sun·ny·vale /ˈsənē,vāl/ a city in north central California, one of the technological centers of Silicon Valley; pop. 117,229.

sun porch (also **sun·porch** /ˈsən,pôrcн/) ▸*n.* another term for **SUNROOM**.

Sun·rise /ˈsən,rīz/ a city in southeastern Florida, west of Fort Lauderdale; pop. 64,407.

sun·rise /ˈsən,rīz/ ▸*n.* [in *sing.*] the time in the morning when the sun appears or full daylight arrives: *an hour before sunrise.* ■ the colors and light visible in the sky on an occasion of the sun's first appearance in the morning, considered as a view or spectacle: *a spectacular sunrise over the summit of the mountain.*

sun·rise in·dus·try ▸*n.* a new and growing industry, esp. in electronics or telecommunications.

sun·roof /ˈsən,ro͞of; -,ro͝of/ ▸*n.* a panel in the roof of a car that can be opened for extra ventilation.

sun·room /ˈsən,ro͞om; -,ro͝om/ ▸*n.* a room with large windows and sometimes a glass roof, designed to allow in a lot of sunlight.

sun·scald /ˈsən,skôld/ (also **sun scald**) ▸*n.* damage to plant tissue, esp. bark or fruit, caused by exposure to excessive sunlight.

sun·screen /ˈsən,skrēn/ ▸*n.* a cream or lotion rubbed onto the skin to protect it from the sun. ■ an active ingredient of creams and lotions of this kind and other preparations for the skin.

sun·set /ˈsən,set/ ▸*n.* [in *sing.*] the time in the evening when the sun disappears or daylight fades: *sunset was still a couple of hours away.* ■ the colors and light visible in the sky on an occasion of the sun's disappearance in the evening, considered as a view or spectacle: *a blue and gold sunset.* ■ *figurative* a period of decline, esp. the last years of a person's life: *the sunset of his life.*

Sun·set Boul·e·vard a road that links the center of Los Angeles with the Pacific Ocean 30 miles (48 km) to the west. The eastern section between Fairfax Avenue and Beverly Hills is known as Sunset Strip.

sun·set in·dus·try ▸*n.* an old and declining industry.

sun·set law ▸*n.* *Law* a law that automatically terminates a regulatory agency, board, or function of government on a certain date, unless renewed: *in accordance with the state sunset law, the act sets the expiration date for the committee three years after the date of its creation.*

sun·set pro·vi·sion ▸*n.* a stipulation that an agency or program be disbanded or terminated at the end of a fixed period unless it is formally renewed.

sun·shade /ˈsən,sнād/ ▸*n.* a parasol, awning, or other device giving protection from the sun.

sun·shine /ˈsən,sнīn/ ▸*n.* direct sunlight unbroken by cloud, esp. over a comparatively large area: *we walked in the warm sunshine.* ■ *figurative* cheerfulness; happiness: *their colorful music can bring a ray of sunshine.* —**sun·shin·y** *adj.*

sun·shine law ▸*n.* a law requiring certain proceedings of government agencies to be open or available to the public.

Sun·shine State ▸ a nickname for the state of **FLORIDA**.

sun·space /ˈsən,spās/ ▸*n.* a room or area in a building having a glass roof and walls and intended to maximize the power of the sun's rays.

sun spi·der ▸*n.* a fast-moving predatory arachnid with a pair of massive vertical pincers (chelicerae). Sun spiders live chiefly in warm deserts, many are active by day, and some grow to a large size. • Order Solifugae (or Solpugida).

sun·spot /ˈsən,spät/ ▸*n.* *Astronomy* a spot or patch appearing from time to time on the sun's surface, appearing dark by contrast with its surroundings.

Sunspots are regions of lower surface temperature and are believed to form where loops in the sun's magnetic field intersect the surface; an individual spot may persist for several weeks. The number of sunspots on the solar surface fluctuates according to a regular cycle, with times of maximum sunspot activity recurring every eleven years.

sun·star /ˈsən,stär/ ▸*n.* a widely distributed starfish with a large number of arms. • Genus *Solaster*, class Asteroidea.

sun·stone /ˈsən,stōn/ ▸*n.* a chatoyant gem consisting of feldspar, with a red or gold color.

sun·stroke /ˈsən,strōk/ ▸*n.* heatstroke brought about by excessive exposure to the sun.

sun·suit /ˈsən,so͞ot/ ▸*n.* a child's one- or two-piece suit of clothes, typically consisting of shorts and sleeveless top, worn in hot sunny weather.

sun·tan /ˈsən,tan/ ▸*n.* a browning of skin caused by exposure to the sun: *he had acquired quite a suntan.* ■ a light or medium brownish color.
▸*v.* [*trans.*] [usu. as *adj.*] (**suntanned**) expose to the sun in order to achieve such a brown color: *a suntanned face.*

sun·up /ˈsən,əp/ ▸*n.* [in *sing.*] the time in the morning when the sun appears or full daylight arrives: *they worked from sunup to sundown.*

Sun Valley a city in south central Idaho, a well-known winter sports resort; pop. 938.

sun vi·sor ▸*n.* a small screen above a vehicle's windshield, attached by a hinge so that it can be lowered to protect the occupants' eyes from bright sunlight.

sun·ya·ta /ˈsнo͞onyə,tä; ˈso͞on-/ ▸*n.* variant of **SHUNYATA**.

Sun Yat-sen /ˈso͞on ˈyät ˈsen/ (also **Sun Yi·xian** /ˈyēsнēˈän/) (1866–1925), Chinese statesman; provisional president of the Republic of China 1911–12 and president of the Southern Chinese Republic 1923–25. He organized the Kuomintang force and established a secessionist government at Guangzhou.

Sun Yat-sen

Suo·mi /ˈso͞oˌōmē/ Finnish name for **Finland**.

sup[1] /səp/ ▸*v.* **(supped, sup·ping)** [*trans.*] *dated or dialect* take (drink or liquid food) by sips or spoonfuls: *she* ***supped up*** *her soup delightedly* | [*intrans.*] *he was supping straight from the bottle.*
▸*n.* a sip of liquid: *he took another sup of wine.* ▷Old English *sūpan* (verb), *sūpa* (noun), of Germanic origin; related to Dutch *zuipen*, German *saufen* 'to drink.'

sup[2] ▸*v.* **(supped, sup·ping)** [*intrans.*] *dated* eat supper: *you'll* ***sup on*** *seafood delicacies.* ▷Middle English: from Old French *super*, of Germanic origin; related to **sup**[1].

sup. ▸*abbr.* ■ superior. ■ superlative. ■ supine. ■ supplement. ■ supplementary. ■ supply. ■ supra.

sup- ▸*prefix* variant spelling of **sub-** assimilated before *p* (as in *suppurate*).

Sup. Ct. ▸*abbr.* ■ Superior Court. ■ Supreme Court.

su·per /ˈso͞opər/ ▸*adj.* **1** *informal* very good or pleasant; excellent: *Julie was a super girl* | [as *exclam.*] *You're both coming in? Super!* **2** (of a manufactured product) superfine: *a super quality binder.*
▸*adv.* [as *submodifier*] *informal* especially; particularly: *he's been super understanding.*
▸*n. informal* **1** a superintendent. **2** *archaic* an extra, unwanted, or unimportant person; a supernumerary. ■ *theatrical slang, dated* an extra. **3** superphosphate. **4** superfine fabric or manufacture. ▷mid 19th cent.: abbreviation.

super. ▸*abbr.* ■ superintendent. ■ superior.

super- ▸*comb. form* above; over; beyond: *superlunary* | *superstructure.* ■ to a great or extreme degree: *superabundant* | *supercool.* ■ extra large of its kind: *supercontinent.* ■ having greater influence, capacity, etc., than another of its kind: *superbike* | *superpower.* ■ of a higher kind (esp. in names of classificatory divisions): *superfamily.* ▷from Latin *super-*, from *super* 'above, beyond.'

su·per·a·ble /ˈso͞opərəbəl/ ▸*adj.* able to be overcome. ▷early 17th cent.: from Latin *superabilis*, from *superare* 'overcome.'

su·per·a·bound /ˌso͞opərəˈbound/ ▸*v.* [*intrans.*] *archaic* be very or too abundant: *the capitalists do not need to combine when labor superabounds.* ▷late Middle English (in the sense 'be more abundant'): from late Latin *superabundare* (see **super-**, **abound**).

su·per·a·bun·dant /ˌso͞opərəˈbəndənt/ ▸*adj.* excessive in quantity; more than sufficient; overabundant. ▷late Middle English (in the sense 'very plentiful'): from late Latin *superabundant-* 'abounding to excess,' from the verb *superabundare*. **—su·per·a·bun·dance** *n.* **—su·per·a·bun·dant·ly** *adv.*

su·per·ac·id /ˈso͞opərˌasid/ ▸*n. Chemistry* a solution of a strong acid in a very acidic (usually nonaqueous) solvent, functioning as a powerful protonating agent. **—su·per·a·cid·i·ty** /ˌso͞opərəˈsiditē/ *n.*

su·per·add /ˌso͞opərˈad/ ▸*v.* [*trans.*] *rare* add (something) to what has already been added: [as *adj.*] (**superadded**) *the presence of superadded infection by bacteria.* ▷late Middle English: from Latin *superaddere* (see **super-**, **add**). **—su·per·ad·di·tion** /-əˈdisHən/ *n.*

su·per·ad·i·a·bat·ic /ˌso͞opərˌādīəˈbatik; -ˌadēə-/ ▸*adj. chiefly Meteorology* relating to or denoting a temperature gradient which is steeper than that occurring in adiabatic conditions.

su·per·al·loy /ˈso͞opərˌaloi/ ▸*n.* an alloy capable of withstanding high temperatures, high stresses, and often highly oxidizing atmospheres.

su·per·an·nu·ate /ˌso͞opərˈanyo͞oˌāt/ ▸*v.* [*trans.*] (usu. **be superannuated**) retire (someone) with a pension: *his pilot's license was withdrawn and he was superannuated.* ■ [as *adj.*] (**superannuated**) (of a position or employee) belonging to a superannuation plan: *she is not superannuated and has no paid vacation.* ■ [usu. as *adj.*] (**superannuated**) cause to become obsolete through age or new technological or intellectual developments: *superannuated computing equipment.* ▷mid 17th cent.: back-formation from *superannuated*, from medieval Latin *superannuatus*, from Latin *super-* 'over' + *annus* 'year.' **—su·per·an·nu·a·ble** /-ˈanyo͞oəbəl/ *adj.*

su·per·an·nu·a·tion /ˌso͞opərˌanyo͞oˈāsHən/ ▸*n.* [usu. as *adj.*] regular payment made into a fund by an employee toward a future pension: *a superannuation fund.* ■ a pension of this type paid to a retired person. ■ the process of superannuating an employee.

su·perb /so͞oˈpərb; sə-/ ▸*adj.* **1** excellent: *a superb performance.* **2** impressively splendid: *a superb Egyptian statue of Osiris.* ▷mid 16th cent. (sense 2): from Latin *superbus* 'proud, magnificent.' **—su·perb·ly** *adv.* **—su·perb·ness** *n.*

Su·per Bowl ▸*n.* the National Football League championship game, played annually between the champions of the National and the American Football Conferences.

su·per·bug /ˈso͞opərˌbəg/ ▸*n.* **1** a bacterium that is useful in biotechnology, typically one that has been genetically engineered to enhance its usefulness for a particular purpose. **2** a strain of bacteria that has become resistant to antibiotic drugs. ■ an insect that is difficult to control or eradicate, esp. because it has become immune to insecticides.

su·per·cal·en·der /ˈso͞opərˌkaləndər/ ▸*v.* [*trans.*] give a highly glazed finish to (paper) by calendering it more than normally calendered paper: [as *adj.*] (**supercalendered**) *a supercalendered art paper.*

su·per·car·go /ˈso͞opərˌkärgō/ ▸*n.* (*pl.* **-goes** or **-gos**) a representative of the ship's owner on board a merchant ship, responsible for overseeing the cargo and its sale. ▷late 17th cent.: alteration of earlier *supracargo*, from Spanish *sobrecargo*, from *sobre* 'over' + *cargo* 'cargo.'

su·per·cede ▸*v.* variant spelling of **supersede**.

> ***USAGE*** The standard spelling is **supersede**, not **supercede**. The word is derived from the Latin verb *supersedere* but has been influenced by the presence of other words in English spelled with **-cede**, such as **intercede** and **accede**. The spelling **supercede** is recorded as early as the 16th century, but is still regarded as incorrect.

su·per·cell /ˈso͞opərˌsel/ ▸*Meteorology n.* a system producing severe thunderstorms and featuring rotating winds sustained by a prolonged updraft that may result in hail or tornadoes.

su·per·cen·te·nar·i·an /ˌso͞opərˌsentnˈe(ə)rēən/ ▸*n.* a person who is 110 years old or older.

su·per·charge /ˈso͞opərˌCHärj/ ▸*v.* [*trans.*] fit or design (an internal combustion engine) with a supercharger: [as *adj.*] (**supercharged**) *a supercharged 3.8-liter V6.* ■ [usu. as *adj.*] (**supercharged**) supply with extra energy or power: *a supercharged computer.* ■ [as *adj.*] (**supercharged**) having powerful emotional overtones or associations: *appeasement is one of those supercharged words, like terrorism and fascism.*

su·per·charg·er /ˈso͞opərˌCHärjər/ ▸*n.* a device that increases the pressure of the fuel-air mixture in an internal combustion engine, used in order to achieve greater efficiency.

su·per·cil·i·ar·y /ˌso͞opərˈsilēˌerē/ ▸*adj.* [*attrib.*] *Anatomy* of or relating to the eyebrow or the region over the eye. ▷mid 18th cent.: from Latin *supercilium* 'eyebrow' (from *super-* 'above' + *cilium* 'eyelid') + **-ary**[1].

su·per·cil·i·ous /ˌso͞opərˈsilēəs/ ▸*adj.* behaving or looking as though one thinks one is superior to others: *a supercilious lady's maid.* ▷early 16th cent.: from Latin *superciliosus* 'haughty,' from *supercilium* 'eyebrow.' **—su·per·cil·i·ous·ly** *adv.* **—su·per·cil·i·ous·ness** *n.*

su·per·class /ˈso͞opərˌklas/ ▸*n. Biology* a taxonomic category that ranks above class and below phylum.

su·per·clus·ter /ˈso͞opərˌkləstər/ ▸*n. Astronomy* a cluster of galaxies which themselves occur as clusters.

su·per·coil /ˈso͞opərˌkoil/ *Biochemistry* ▸*n.* another term for **superhelix**.
▸*v.* [*trans.*] form (a substance) into a superhelix: [as *adj.*] (**supercoiled**) *a supercoiled circular DNA molecule.*

su·per·col·lid·er /ˈso͞opərkəˌlīdər/ ▸*n. Physics* a collider in which superconducting magnets are used to accelerate particles to energies of millions of megavolts.

su·per·com·put·er /ˈso͞opərkəmˌpyo͞otər/ ▸*n.* a particularly powerful mainframe computer. **—su·per·com·put·ing** /-ˌpyo͞otiNG/ *n.*

su·per·con·duc·tiv·i·ty /ˌso͞opərˌkänˌdəkˈtivitē/ ▸*n. Physics* the property of zero electrical resistance in some substances at very low absolute temperatures. **—su·per·con·duct** /-kənˈdəkt/ *v.* **—su·per·con·duct·ing** /-kənˈdəktiNG/ *adj.* **—su·per·con·duc·tive** /-kənˈdəktiv/ *adj.*

su·per·con·duc·tor /ˈso͞opərkənˌdəktər/ ▸*n. Physics* a substance capable of becoming superconducting at sufficiently low temperatures. ■ a substance in the superconducting state.

su·per·con·scious /ˌso͞opərˈkänsHəs/ ▸*adj.* transcending human or normal consciousness: *the superconscious, universal mind of God.* **—su·per·con·scious·ly** *adv.* **—su·per·con·scious·ness** *n.*

su·per·con·ti·nent /ˈso͞opərˌkäntn-ənt/ ▸*n.* each of several large landmasses (notably Pangaea, Gondwana, and Laurasia) thought to have divided to form the present continents in the geological past.

su·per·cool /ˌso͞opərˈko͞ol/ ▸*v.* [*trans.*] *Chemistry* cool (a liquid) below its freezing point without solidification or crystallization. ■ [*intrans.*] *Biology* (of a living organism) survive body temperatures below the freezing point of water.
▸*adj. informal* extremely attractive, impressive, or calm: *the supercool tracks in this collection.*

su·per·crit·i·cal /ˌso͞opərˈkritikəl/ ▸*adj. Physics* above a critical threshold, in particular: ■ (in nuclear physics) containing or involving more than the critical mass. ■ (of a flow of fluid) faster than the speed at which waves travel in the fluid. ■ denoting an airfoil or aircraft wing designed to tolerate shock-wave formation at transonic speeds. ■ of, relating to, or denoting a fluid at a temperature and pressure greater than its critical temperature and pressure.

su·per-du·per /ˈso͞opər ˈdo͞opər/ ▸*adj. humorous* very good; marvelous: *this new line of toys is super-duper.* ■ tremendous or colossal in size or degree: *a super-duper ice sculpture.*

su·per·e·go /ˌso͞opərˈēgō/ ▸*n.* (*pl.* **-gos**) *Psychoanalysis* the part of a person's mind that acts as a self-critical conscience, reflecting social standards learned from parents and teachers. Compare with **ego** and **id**.

su·per·el·e·va·tion /ˌso͞opərˌeləˈvāsHən/ ▸*n.* the amount by which the outer edge of a curve on a road or railroad is banked above the inner edge.

su·per·em·i·nent /ˌso͞opərˈemənənt/ ▸*adj.* chiefly dated term for **preeminent**. ▷mid 16th cent.: from Latin *supereminent-* 'rising above,' from the verb *supereminere* 'rise above' (see **super-**, **eminent**). **—su·per·em·i·nence** *n.* **—su·per·em·i·nent·ly** *adv.*

su·per·er·o·ga·tion /ˌso͞opərˌerəˈgāsHən/ ▸*n.* the performance of more work than duty requires. ▷early 16th cent.: from late Latin *supererogatio(n-)*, from *supererogare* 'pay in addition,' from *super-* 'over' + *erogare* 'pay out.' **—su·per·e·rog·a·to·ry** /-əˈrägəˌtôrē/ *adj.*
▸*PHRASE* □ **works of supererogation** (in the Roman Catholic Church) actions believed to form a reserve fund of merit that can be drawn on by prayer in favor of sinners.

su·per·ette /ˌso͞opərˈet/ ▸*n.* a small supermarket. ▷1930s: from **supermarket** + **-ette**.

su·per·fam·i·ly /ˈso͞opərˌfam(ə)lē/ ▸*n.* (*pl.* **-lies**) *Biology* a taxonomic category that ranks above family and below order. ■ *Linguistics* another term for **phylum**.

su·per·fe·cun·da·tion /ˌso͞opərˌfekənˈdāsHən/ ▸*n. Medicine & Zoology* another term for **superfetation**.

su·per·fe·ta·tion /ˌso͞opərˌfēˈtāsHən/ ▸*n. Medicine & Zoology* the occurrence of a second conception during pregnancy, giving rise to embryos of different ages in the uterus. ■ *figurative* the accretion of one thing on another: *the superfetation of ideas.* ▷early 17th cent.: from French *superfétation* or modern Latin *superfetatio(n-)*, from Latin *superfetare*, from *super-* 'above' + *fetus* 'fetus.'

su·per·fi·cial /ˌso͞opərˈfisHəl/ ▸*adj.* existing or occurring at or on the surface: *the building suffered only superficial damage.* ■ situated or occurring on the skin or immediately beneath it: *the superficial muscle groups.* ■ appearing to be true or real only until examined more closely: *the resemblance between the breeds is superficial.* ■ not thorough, deep, or complete; cursory: *he had only the most superficial knowledge of foreign countries.* ■ not having or showing any depth of character or understanding: *perhaps I was a superficial person.* ▷late Middle English: from late Latin *superficialis*, from Latin *superficies* (see **superficies**). **—su·per·fi·ci·al·i·ty** /-ˌfisHēˈalitē/ *n.* (*pl.* **-ties**) **—su·per·fi·cial·ly** *adv.* **—su·per·fi·cial·ness** *n.*

> ***THE RIGHT WORD*** **cursory, hasty, shallow, slapdash, superficial**
>
> No one wants to be accused of being **superficial** or **shallow**, two adjectives that literally indicate a lack of depth (*a superficial wound; a shallow grave*).
>
> *Superficial* suggests too much concern with the surface or obvious aspects of something, and it is considered a derogatory term because it connotes a personality that is not genuine or sincere.
>
> *Shallow* is even more derogatory because it implies not only a refusal to explore something deeply but an inability to feel, sympathize, or understand. It is unlikely that a *shallow* person, in other words, will ever have more than superficial relationships with his or her peers.
>
> **Cursory**, which may or may not be a derogatory term, suggests a lack of thoroughness or attention to detail (*a cursory glance at the newspaper*), while **hasty** emphasizes a refusal or inability to spend the

necessary time on something (*a hasty review of the facts*).

If you are **slapdash** in your approach, it means that you are both careless and hasty (*a slapdash job of cleaning up*).

su·per·fi·ci·es /ˌsoōpərˈfisHēz; -ˈfisHē-ēz/ ▸*n.* (*pl.* same) *archaic* a surface: *the superficies of a sphere.* ■ an outward part or appearance: *the superficies of life.* ▷mid 16th cent.: from Latin, from *super-* 'above' + *facies* 'face.'

su·per·fine /ˌsoōpərˈfīn/ ▸*adj.* **1** of especially high quality: *superfine upholstery.* **2** (of fibers or an instrument) very thin: *superfine tweezers.* ■ consisting of especially small particles: *superfine sugar.* ▷late 16th cent. (in the sense 'excessively elegant'): from SUPER- 'to a high degree' + FINE[1].

su·per·fine sug·ar ▸*n.* finely granulated white sugar that dissolves quickly and is used in cold drinks and baking.

su·per·flu·id·i·ty /ˌsoōpərˌfloōˈiditē/ ▸*n. Physics* the property of flowing without friction or viscosity, as in liquid helium below about 2.18 kelvins. **—su·per·flu·id** /ˈsoōpərˌfloō-id/ *n.* & *adj.*

su·per·flu·i·ty /ˌsoōpərˈfloō-itē/ ▸*n.* (*pl.* **-ties**) [in *sing.*] an unnecessarily or excessively large amount or number of something: ***a superfluity of*** *unoccupied time.* ■ an unnecessary thing: *they thought the garrison a superfluity.* ■ the state of being superfluous: *servants who had nothing to do but to display their own superfluity.* ▷late Middle English: from Old French *superfluite*, from late Latin *superfluitas*, from Latin *superfluus* 'running over' (see SUPERFLUOUS).

su·per·flu·ous /soōˈpərfloōwəs/ ▸*adj.* unnecessary, esp. through being more than enough: *the purchaser should avoid asking for superfluous information.* ▷late Middle English: from Latin *superfluus*, from *super-* 'over' + *fluere* 'to flow.' **—su·per·flu·ous·ly** *adv.* **—su·per·flu·ous·ness** *n.*

su·per·food /ˈsoōpərˌfoōd/ ▸*n.* (not in technical use) a natural food regarded as especially beneficial because of its nutrient profile or its health-protecting qualities: *he touts broccoli sprouts and salmon as two of the most perfect superfoods.*

su·per·fund /ˈsoōpərˌfənd/ ▸*n.* a fund established to finance a long-term, expensive project. ■ (**Superfund**) a U.S. federal government program designed to fund the cleanup of toxic wastes: *billions have been spent on Superfund since 1980.*

su·per·gal·ax·y /ˈsoōpərˌgaləksē/ ▸*n.* (*pl.* **-ax·ies**) another term for SUPERCLUSTER.

su·per·gene[1] /ˈsoōpərˌjēn/ ▸*adj.* [*attrib.*] *Geology* relating to or denoting the deposition or enrichment of mineral deposits by solutions moving downward through the rocks.

su·per·gene[2] ▸*n. Genetics* a group of closely linked genes, typically having related functions.

su·per·gi·ant /ˈsoōpərˌjīənt/ ▸*n. Astronomy* a very large star that is even brighter than a giant, often despite being relatively cool.

su·per·glue /ˈsoōpərˌgloō/ ▸*n.* a very strong quick-setting adhesive, based on cyanoacrylates or similar polymers.

▸*v.* (**-glues**, **-glued**, **-glu·ing** or **-glue·ing**) [*trans.*] stick with superglue: *he superglued his hands together.*

su·per·grav·i·ty /ˌsoōpərˈgravitē/ ▸*n. Physics* gravity as described or predicted by a supersymmetric quantum field theory.

su·per·group /ˈsoōpərˌgroōp/ ▸*n.* an exceptionally successful rock group, in particular one formed by musicians already famous from playing in other groups.

su·per·heat /ˌsoōpərˈhēt/ *Physics* ▸*v.* [*trans.*] heat (a liquid) under pressure above its boiling point without vaporization. ■ heat (a vapor) above its temperature of saturation. ■ heat to a very high temperature.

▸*n.* the excess of temperature of a vapor above its temperature of saturation. **—su·per·heat·er** *n.*

su·per·heav·y /ˌsoōpərˈhevē/ ▸*adj. Physics* relating to or denoting an element with an atomic mass or atomic number greater than those of the naturally occurring elements, esp. one belonging to a group above atomic number 110 having proton/neutron ratios that in theory confer relatively long half-lives.

su·per·he·lix /ˈsoōpərˌhēliks/ ▸*n.* (*pl.* **-hel·i·ces** /-ˌheləˌsēz; -ˌhēləˌsēz/ or **-he·lix·es**) *Biochemistry* a helical structure formed from a number of protein or nucleic acid chains that are individually helical. **—su·per·hel·i·cal** /ˌsoōpərˈhelikəl; -ˈhēli-/ *adj.*

su·per·he·ro /ˈsoōpərˌhirō/ ▸*n.* (*pl.* **-roes**) a benevolent fictional character with superhuman powers, such as Superman.

su·per·het /ˈsoōpərˌhet/ ▸*n. informal* short for SUPERHETERODYNE.

su·per·het·er·o·dyne /ˌsoōpərˈhetərəˌdīn/ ▸*adj.* denoting or using a system of radio and television reception in which the receiver produces a tunable signal that is combined with the incoming signal to produce a predetermined intermediate frequency, on which most of the amplification is formed.

▸*n.* a superheterodyne receiver. ▷1920s: from SUPERSONIC + HETERODYNE.

su·per·high·way /ˈsoōpərˌhīwā; ˌsoōpərˈhīˌwā/ ▸*n.* an expressway.

su·per·hu·man /ˌsoōpərˈ(h)yoōmən/ ▸*adj.* having or showing exceptional ability or powers: *the pilot made one last superhuman effort not to come down right on our heads.* ▷mid 17th cent.: from late Latin *superhumanus* (see SUPER-, HUMAN). **—su·per·hu·man·ly** *adv.*

su·per·hy·dro·pho·bic /ˌsoōpərˌhīdrəˈfōbik/ ▸*adj.* repelling water to the degree that droplets do not flatten but roll off instead: *superhydrophobic butterfly wings.* **—su·per·hy·dro·pho·bi·a** /-ˈfōbēə/ *n.*

su·per·im·pose /ˌsoōpərimˈpōz/ ▸*v.* [*trans.*] place or lay (one thing) over another, typically so that both are still evident: *the number will appear on the screen,* ***superimposed on*** *a flashing button* | [as *adj.*] (**superimposed**) *different stone tools were found in superimposed layers.* **—su·per·im·pos·a·ble** *adj.* **—su·per·im·po·si·tion** /-ˌimpəˈzisHən/ *n.*

su·per·in·cum·bent /ˌsoōpərinˈkəmbənt; -iNGˈkəm-/ ▸*adj. poetic/literary* lying on something else: *the crushing effect of the superincumbent masonry.*

su·per·in·duce /ˌsoōpərinˈd(y)oōs/ ▸*v.* [*trans.*] introduce or induce in addition: *both genes are known to be superinduced in fibroblasts by inhibition of protein synthesis.* ▷mid 16th cent.: from Latin *superinducere* 'cover over, bring from outside' (see SUPER-, INDUCE).

su·per·in·fec·tion /ˌsoōpərinˈfeksHən/ ▸*n. Medicine* infection occurring after or on top of an earlier infection, esp. following treatment with broad-spectrum antibiotics.

su·per·in·tend /ˌsoōpərinˈtend/ ▸*v.* [*trans.*] be responsible for the management or arrangement of (an activity or organization); oversee: *he superintended a land reclamation program.* ▷early 17th cent.: from ecclesiastical Latin *superintendere*, translating Greek *episkopein*. **—su·per·in·tend·ence** /-dəns/ *n.* **—su·per·in·tend·en·cy** /-dənsē/ *n.*

su·per·in·tend·ent /ˌsoōpərinˈtendənt/ ▸*n.* a person who manages or superintends an organization or activity: *the construction superintendent* | [as *adj.*] *the superintendent registrar.* ■ a high-ranking official, esp. the head of a large urban police department. ■ the caretaker of a building. ▷mid 16th cent.: from ecclesiastical Latin *superintendent-* 'overseeing,' from the verb *superintendere* (see SUPERINTEND).

Su·pe·ri·or /səˈpi(ə)rēər/ a port city in northwestern Wisconsin, on Lake Superior, adjacent to Duluth in Minnesota; pop. 27,134.

Su·pe·ri·or, Lake the largest of the five Great Lakes of North America, on the border between Canada and the U.S. With an area of 31,800 square miles (82,350 sq km), it is the largest freshwater lake in the world.

su·pe·ri·or /səˈpi(ə)rēər/ ▸*adj.* **1** higher in rank, status, or quality: *a superior officer* | *it is* ***superior to*** *every other car on the road.* ■ of high standard or quality: *superior malt whiskeys.* ■ greater in size or power: *deploying superior force.* ■ [*predic.*] (**superior to**) above yielding to or being influenced by: *I felt superior to any accusation of anti-Semitism.* ■ having or showing an overly high opinion of oneself; supercilious: *that girl was frightfully superior.* **2** *chiefly Anatomy* further above or out; higher in position. ■ (of a letter, figure, or symbol) written or printed above the line. ■ *Astronomy* (of a planet) having an orbit further from the sun than the earth's. ■ *Botany* (of the ovary of a flower) situated above the sepals and petals.

▸*n.* **1** a person or thing superior to another in rank, status, or quality, esp. a colleague in a higher position: *obeying their superiors' orders.* ■ the head of a monastery or other religious institution. **2** *Printing* a superior letter, figure, or symbol. ▷late Middle English: from Old French *superiour*, from Latin *superior*, comparative of *superus* 'that is above,' from *super* 'above.' **—su·pe·ri·or·ly** *adv.* (usu. in sense 2 of the *adjective*).

su·pe·ri·or con·junc·tion ▸*n. Astronomy* a conjunction of Mercury or Venus with the sun, when the planet and the earth are on opposite sides of the sun.

su·pe·ri·or court ▸*n. Law* **1** (in many states of the U.S.) a court of appeals or a court of general jurisdiction. **2** a court with general jurisdiction over other courts; a higher court.

su·pe·ri·or·i·ty /səˌpi(ə)rēˈôritē; -ˈäritē/ ▸*n.* the state of being superior: *an attempt to establish* ***superiority over*** *others* | *the allies have achieved air superiority.* ■ a supercilious manner or attitude: *he attacked the media's smug superiority.*

su·pe·ri·or·i·ty com·plex ▸*n.* an attitude of superiority that conceals actual feelings of inferiority and failure.

su·pe·ri·or plan·et ▸*n. Astronomy* any of the planets (Mars, Jupiter, Saturn, Uranus, Neptune, and Pluto) whose orbits are further from the sun than the Earth's. Compare with INFERIOR PLANET.

su·pe·ri·us /səˈpi(ə)rēəs/ ▸*n.* the highest voice part in early choral music; the cantus. ▷late 18th cent.: from Latin, neuter (used as a noun) of *superior* (see SUPERIOR).

su·per·ja·cent /ˌsoōpərˈjāsənt/ ▸*adj. technical* lying over or above something else; overlying. ▷late 16th cent.: from Latin *superjacent-*, from *super-* 'over' + *jacere* 'to lie.'

su·per·la·tive /səˈpərlətiv/ ▸*adj.* **1** of the highest quality or degree: *a superlative piece of skill.* **2** *Grammar* (of an adjective or adverb) expressing the highest or a very high degree of a quality (e.g., *bravest, most fiercely*). Contrasted with POSITIVE and COMPARATIVE.

▸*n.* **1** *Grammar* a superlative adjective or adverb. ■ (**the superlative**) the highest degree of comparison. **2** (usu. **superlatives**) an exaggerated or hyperbolical expression of praise: *the critics ran out of superlatives to describe him.* **3** something or someone embodying excellence. ▷late Middle English: from Old French *superlatif, -ive*, from late Latin *superlativus*, from Latin *superlatus* 'carried beyond,' past participle of *superferre*. **—su·per·la·tive·ly** *adv.* [as *submodifier*] *he was superlatively fit.* **—su·per·la·tive·ness** *n.*

su·per·lat·tice /ˈsoōpərˌlatis/ ▸*n. Metallurgy* & *Physics* an ordered arrangement of certain atoms that occurs in a solid solution and which is superimposed on the solvent crystal lattice.

su·per·lu·mi·nal /ˌsoōpərˈloōmənl/ ▸*adj. Physics* denoting or having a speed greater than that of light. ▷1950s: from SUPER- 'above' + Latin *lumen, lumin-* 'a light' + -AL.

su·per·lu·na·ry /ˌsoōpərˈloōnərē/ ▸*adj.* belonging to a higher world; celestial. ▷early 17th cent.: from medieval Latin *superlunaris* (see SUPER-, LUNAR).

su·per·ma·jor·i·ty /ˈsoōpərməˌjôritē; -ˌjär-/ ▸*n.* (*pl.* **-ties**) a number that is much more than half of a total, esp. in a vote.

su·per·man /ˈsoōpəˌman/ ▸*n.* (*pl.* **-men**) **1** *chiefly Philosophy* the ideal superior man of the future. See ÜBERMENSCH. **2** (**a superman**) *informal* a man with exceptional physical or mental ability. ▷early 20th cent.: from SUPER- 'exceptional' + MAN, coined by G. B. Shaw in imitation of German *Übermensch* (used by Nietzsche).

su·per·mar·ket /ˈsoōpərˌmärkit/ ▸*n.* a large self-service store selling foods and household goods.

su·per·mas·sive /ˈsoōpərˈmasiv/ ▸*adj. Astronomy* having a mass many times (typically between 10^6 and 10^9 times) that of the sun: *a supermassive star.*

su·per·min·i /ˈsoōpərˌminē/ (also **su·per·min·i·com·put·er**) ▸*n.* (*pl.* **-min·is**) a microcomputer with the speed, power, and capabilities of a mainframe.

su·per·mod·el /ˈsoōpərˌmädl/ ▸*n.* a successful fashion model who has reached the status of a celebrity.

su·per·nal /səˈpərnl/ ▸*adj. chiefly poetic/literary* of or relating to the sky or the heavens; celestial. ■ of exceptional quality or extent: *he is the supernal poet of our age* | *supernal erudition.* ▷late Middle English: from Old French, or from medieval Latin *supernalis*, from Latin *supernus*, from *super* 'above.' **—su·per·nal·ly** *adv.*

su·per·na·tant /ˌsoōpərˈnātnt/ *technical* ▸*adj.* denoting the liquid lying above a solid residue after crystallization, precipitation, centrifugation, or other process.

▸*n.* a volume of supernatant liquid.

S

su·per·nat·u·ral /ˌso͞opərˈnaCH(ə)rəl/ ▸*adj.* (of a manifestation or event) attributed to some force beyond scientific understanding or the laws of nature: *a supernatural being.* ■ unnaturally or extraordinarily great: *a woman of supernatural beauty.*
▸*n.* (**the supernatural**) manifestations or events considered to be of supernatural origin, such as ghosts. —**su·per·nat·u·ral·ism** *n.* —**su·per·nat·u·ral·ist** *n.* —**su·per·nat·u·ral·ly** *adv.* [as *submodifier*] *the monster was supernaturally strong.*

su·per·nor·mal /ˌso͞opərˈnôrməl/ ▸*adj.* exceeding or beyond the normal; exceptional: *a supernormal human.* —**su·per·nor·mal·i·ty** /-ˌnôrˈmalitē/ *n.*

su·per·no·va /ˈso͞opərˌnōvə/ ▸*n.* (*pl.* **-no·vae** /-ˌnōvē/ or **-no·vas**) *Astronomy* a star that suddenly increases greatly in brightness because of a catastrophic explosion that ejects most of its mass.

su·per·nu·mer·ar·y /ˌso͞opərˈn(y)o͞oməˌrerē/ ▸*adj.* present in excess of the normal or requisite number, in particular: ■ (of a person) not belonging to a regular staff but engaged for extra work. ■ not wanted or needed; redundant: *books were obviously supernumerary, and he began jettisoning them.* ■ *Botany & Zoology* denoting a structure or organ occurring in addition to the normal ones: *a pair of supernumerary teats.* ■ (of an actor) appearing on stage but not speaking.
▸*n.* (*pl.* **-ar·ies**) a supernumerary person or thing. ▷early 17th cent.: from late Latin *supernumerarius* '(soldier) added to a legion after it is complete,' from Latin *super numerum* 'beyond the number.'

su·per·or·der /ˈso͞opərˌôrdər/ ▸*n. Biology* a taxonomic category that ranks above order and below class.

su·per·or·di·nate /ˌso͞opərˈôrdn-ət/ ▸*n.* a thing that represents a superior order or category within a system of classification: *a pair of compatibles must have a common superordinate.* ■ a person who has authority over or control of another within an organization. ■ *Linguistics* a word whose meaning includes the meaning of one or more other words: *"bird" is the superordinate of "canary."*
▸*adj.* superior in status: *senior staff's superordinate position.* ▷early 17th cent.: from **SUPER-** 'above,' on the pattern of *subordinate.*

su·per·ox·ide /ˌso͞opərˈäkˌsīd/ ▸*n. Chemistry* an oxide containing the anion O_2^-.

su·per·phos·phate /ˈso͞opərˌfäsˌfāt/ ▸*n.* a fertilizer made by treating phosphate rock with sulfuric or phosphoric acid.

su·per·plas·tic /ˈso͞opərˌplastik/ *Metallurgy* ▸*adj.* (of a metal or alloy) capable of extreme plastic extension under load.
▸*n.* a metal or alloy having this property. —**su·per·plas·tic·i·ty** /ˌso͞opərplasˈtisitē/ *n.*

su·per·pose /ˌso͞opərˈpōz/ ▸*v.* [*trans.*] place (something) on or above something else, esp. so that they coincide: [as *adj.*] (**superposed**) *a border of superposed triangles.* ▷early 19th cent.: from French *superposer,* from *super-* 'above' + *poser* 'to place.' —**su·per·pos·a·ble** *adj.* —**su·per·po·si·tion** /-pəˈzisHən/ *n.*

su·per·pow·er /ˈso͞opərˌpouər/ ▸*n.* a very powerful and influential nation (used esp. with reference to the U.S. and the former USSR when these were perceived as the two most powerful nations in the world). ■ a dominant or preeminent individual or organization, esp. in a particular field: *the network evolved into a sleek superpower.*

su·per·sat·u·rate /ˌso͞opərˈsacHəˌrāt/ ▸*v.* [*trans.*] *Chemistry* increase the concentration of (a solution) beyond saturation point. —**su·per·sat·u·ra·tion** /-ˌsacHəˈrāsHən/ *n.*

su·per·sca·lar /ˌso͞opərˈskālər/ ▸*adj.* denoting a computer architecture where several instructions are loaded at once and, as far as possible, are executed simultaneously, shortening the time taken to run the whole program.

su·per·scribe /ˌso͞opərˈskrīb/ ▸*v.* [*trans.*] write or print (an inscription) at the top of or on the outside of a document: *they had superscribed "Top Secret" across the cover page.* ■ write or print an inscription at the top of or on the outside of (a document): *he invariably will want to superscribe the memo with one of his banal mottoes.* ■ write or print (a letter, word, symbol, or line of writing or printing) above an existing letter, word, or line. ▷late 15th cent.: from Latin *superscribere,* from *super-* 'over' + *scribere* 'write.' —**su·per·scrip·tion** /-ˈskripsHən/ *n.*

su·per·script /ˈso͞opərˌskript/ ▸*adj.* (of a letter, figure, or symbol) written or printed above the line.
▸*n.* a superscript letter, figure, or symbol. ▷late 19th cent. (as an adjective): from Latin *superscriptus* 'written above,' past participle of *superscribere.*

su·per·sede /ˌso͞opərˈsēd/ ▸*v.* [*trans.*] take the place of (a person or thing previously in authority or use); supplant: *the older models have now been superseded.* See note at **REPLACE.** ▷late 15th cent. (in the sense 'postpone, defer'): from Old French *superseder,* from Latin *supersedere* 'be superior to,' from *super-* 'above' + *sedere* 'sit.' The current sense dates from the mid 17th cent. —**su·per·ses·sion** /-ˈsesHən/ *n.*

USAGE See usage at **SUPERCEDE.**

su·per·set /ˈso͞opərˌset/ ▸*n. Mathematics* a set that includes another set or sets.

su·per·size /ˈso͞opərˌsīz/ ▸*v.* [*trans.*] produce or serve something in a larger size: *click here to supersize the picture.*
▸*adj.* larger than normal: *this supersize clock has black 2-inch numbers on white face in a simple lightweight black frame.*

su·per·soap /ˈso͞opərˌsōp/ ▸*n.* a soap that contains a bactericide.

su·per·son·ic /ˌso͞opərˈsänik/ ▸*adj.* involving or denoting a speed greater than that of sound. —**su·per·son·i·cal·ly** /-ik(ə)lē/ *adv.*

su·per·son·ics /ˌso͞opərˈsäniks/ ▸*plural n.* [treated as *sing.*] another term for **ULTRASONICS.**

su·per·son·ic trans·port (abbr.:**SST**) ▸*n.* a commercial jet capable of exceeding the speed of sound.

su·per·space /ˈso͞opərˌspās/ ▸*n. Physics* a concept of space-time in which points are defined by more than four coordinates. ■ a space of infinitely many dimensions postulated to contain actual space-time and all possible spaces.

su·per·star /ˈso͞opərˌstär/ ▸*n.* a high-profile and extremely successful performer or athlete. —**su·per·star·dom** /-dəm/ *n.*

su·per·state /ˈso͞opərˌstāt/ ▸*n.* a large and powerful state or union formed from a federation of nations: *we are not advocates of a European superstate.*

su·per·sta·tion /ˈso͞opərˌstāsHən/ ▸*n.* a television station that broadcasts widely via cable or satellite.

su·per·sti·tion /ˌso͞opərˈstisHən/ ▸*n.* excessively credulous belief in and reverence for supernatural beings: *he dismissed the ghost stories as mere superstition.* ■ a widely held but unjustified belief in supernatural causation leading to certain consequences of an action or event, or a practice based on such a belief: *she touched her locket for luck, a superstition she had had since childhood.* ▷Middle English: from Old French, or from Latin *superstitio(n-),* from *super-* 'over' + *stare* 'to stand' (perhaps from the notion of "standing over" something in awe). —**su·per·sti·tious** /-ˈstisHəs/ *adj.* —**su·per·sti·tious·ly** /-ˈstisHəslē/ *adv.* —**su·per·sti·tious·ness** /-ˈstisHəsnəs/ *n.*

su·per·store /ˈso͞opərˌstôr/ ▸*n.* a retail store, as a grocery store or bookstore, with more than the average amount of space and variety of stock.

su·per·stra·tum /ˈso͞opərˌstrātəm; -ˌstratəm/ ▸*n.* (*pl.* **-ta** /-tə/) an overlying stratum.

su·per·string /ˈso͞opərˌstriNG/ ▸*n. Physics* a subatomic particle in a version of string theory that incorporates supersymmetry.

su·per·struc·ture /ˈso͞opərˌstrəkCHər/ ▸*n.* a structure built on top of something else. ■ the parts of a ship, other than masts and rigging, built above its hull and main deck. ■ the part of a building above its foundations. ■ a concept or idea based on others. ■ (in Marxist theory) the institutions and culture considered to result from or reflect the economic system underlying a society. —**su·per·struc·tur·al** /ˌso͞opərˈstrəkCHərəl/ *adj.*

su·per·sym·me·try /ˈso͞opərˌsimitrē/ ▸*n. Physics* a very general type of mathematical symmetry that relates fermions and bosons. —**su·per·sym·met·ric** /-siˈmetrik/ *adj.*

su·per·tank·er /ˈso͞opərˌtaNGkər/ ▸*n.* a very large oil tanker, specifically one whose dead-weight capacity exceeds 75,000 tons.

su·per·tax /ˈso͞opərˌtaks/ ▸*n.* an additional tax on something already taxed.

su·per·ti·tle /ˈso͞opərˌtītl/ ▸*n.* (usu. **supertitles**) a caption projected on a screen above the stage in an opera, translating the text being sung.
▸*v.* [*trans.*] provide (an opera) with supertitles.

su·per·ton·ic /ˈso͞opərˌtänik/ ▸*n. Music* the second note of the diatonic scale of any key; the note above the tonic.

Su·per Tues·day ▸*n. informal* a day on which several U.S. states hold primary elections.

su·per·vene /ˌso͞opərˈvēn/ ▸*v.* [*intrans.*] occur later than a specified or implied event or action, typically in such a way as to change the situation: [as *adj.*] (**supervening**) *any plan that is made is liable to be disrupted by supervening events.* ■ *Philosophy* (of a fact or property) be entailed by or consequent on the existence or establishment of another: *the view that mental events* **supervene upon** *physical ones.* ▷mid 17th cent.: from Latin *supervenire,* from *super-* 'in addition' + *venire* 'come.' —**su·per·ven·ient** /-ˈvēnyənt/ *adj.* —**su·per·ven·tion** /-ˈvencHən/ *n.*

su·per·vise /ˈso͞opərˌvīz/ ▸*v.* [*trans.*] observe and direct the execution of (a task, project, or activity): *the sergeant left to supervise the loading of the trucks.* ■ observe and direct the work of (someone): *nurses were supervised by a consulting psychiatrist.* ■ keep watch over (someone) in the interest of their or others' security: *prisoners were supervised by two officers.* ▷late 15th cent. (in the sense 'survey, peruse'): from medieval Latin *supervis-* 'surveyed, supervised,' from *supervidere,* from *super-* 'over' + *videre* 'to see.' —**su·per·vi·sion** /ˌso͞opərˈvizHən/ *n.* —**su·per·vi·sor** /-ˌvīzər/ *n.* —**su·per·vi·so·ry** /ˌso͞opərˈvīzərē/ *adj.*

su·per·vol·tage /ˈso͞opərˌvōltij/ ▸*n.* [usu. as *adj.*] *Medicine* a voltage in excess of 200 kV used in X-ray radiotherapy: *supervoltage therapy.*

su·per·wom·an /ˈso͞opərˌwo͝omən/ ▸*n.* (*pl.* **-wom·en**) *informal* a woman with exceptional strength or ability, esp. one who successfully manages a home, brings up children, and has a full-time job.

su·pi·nate /ˈso͞opəˌnāt/ ▸*v.* [*trans.*] *technical* **1** put or hold (a hand, foot, or limb) with the palm or sole turned upward: [as *adj.*] (**supinated**) *a supinated foot.* Compare with **PRONATE. 2** walk or run with most of the weight on the inside of the feet. ▷mid 19th cent.: back-formation from *supination,* from Latin *supinatio(n-),* from *supinare* 'lay backward,' from *supinus* (see **SUPINE**). —**su·pi·na·tion** /ˌso͞opəˈnāsHən/ *n.*

su·pi·na·tor /ˈso͞opəˌnātər/ ▸*n. Anatomy* **1** a muscle whose contraction produces or assists in the supination of a limb or part of a limb. ■ any of several specific muscles in the forearm. **2** one who supinates when walking or running.

su·pine /ˈso͞oˌpīn/ ▸*adj.* **1** (of a person) lying face upward. ■ *technical* having the front or ventral part upward. ■ (of the hand) with the palm upward. **2** failing to act or protest as a result of moral weakness or indolence: *supine in the face of racial injustice.*
▸*n.* a Latin verbal noun used only in the accusative and ablative cases, esp. to denote purpose (e.g., *dictu* in *mirabile dictu* "wonderful to relate"). ▷late Middle English: the adjective from Latin *supinus* 'bent backward' (related to *super* 'above'); the noun from late Latin *supinum,* neuter of *supinus.* —**su·pine·ly** *adv.* —**su·pine·ness** *n.*

supp. ▸*abbr.* ■ supplement. ■ supplementary.

sup·per /ˈsəpər/ ▸*n.* an evening meal, typically a light or informal one: *we had a delicious cold supper | I was sent to bed without any supper.* ■ a late-night dinner. ■ an evening social event at which food is served. ▷Middle English: from Old French *super* 'to sup' (used as a noun) (see **SUP**[2]). —**sup·per·less** *adj.*
▸*PHRASE* □ **sing for one's supper** earn a favor or benefit by providing a service in return: *the cruise lecturers are academics singing for their supper.*

sup·per club ▸*n.* a restaurant or nightclub serving suppers and usually providing entertainment.

suppl. ▸*abbr.* ■ supplement. ■ supplementary.

sup·plant /səˈplant/ ▸*v.* [*trans.*] supersede and replace: *the socialist society that Marx believed would eventually supplant capitalism.* See note at **REPLACE.** ▷Middle English: from Old French *supplanter* or Latin *supplantare* 'trip up,' from *sub-* 'from below' + *planta* 'sole.' —**sup·plant·er** *n.*

sup·ple /ˈsəpəl/ ▸*adj.* (**-pler, -plest**) bending and moving easily and gracefully; flexible: *her supple fingers | figurative my mind is becoming more supple.* See note at **FLEXIBLE.** ■ not stiff or hard; easily manipulated: *this body oil leaves your skin feeling deliciously supple.*
▸*v.* [*trans.*] make more flexible. ▷Middle English: from Old French *souple,* from Latin *supplex, supplic-* 'submissive,' from *sub-* 'under' + *placere* 'propitiate.' —**sup·ple·ly** /ˈsəp(ə)lē/ (also **sup·ply**) *adv.* —**sup·ple·ness** *n.*

sup·ple·jack /ˈsəpəlejak/ ▸*n.* either of two New World twining plants: • a tall North American climber (*Berchemia scandens,* family Rhamnaceae). • a plant of the Caribbean and tropical America (*Paullinia plumieri,* family Sapindaceae).

sup·ple·ment ▸*n.* /ˈsəpləmənt/ **1** something that completes or enhances something else when added to it: *the handout is a* **supplement to** *the official manual.* ■ a substance taken to remedy the deficiencies in a person's diet: *multivitamin supplements.* ■ a part added to a book to provide further or corrected information but separate from the main body of the text. ■ a

separate section, esp. a color magazine, added to a newspaper or periodical. **2** *Geometry* the amount by which an angle is less than 180°.
▶*v.* /ˈsəpləˌment; -mənt/ [*trans.*] add an extra element or amount to: *she took the job to supplement her husband's income.* ▷late Middle English: from Latin *supplementum*, from *supplere* 'fill up, complete' (see SUPPLY[1]). —**sup·ple·men·tal** /ˌsəpləˈmentl/ *adj.* —**sup·ple·men·tal·ly** /ˌsəpləˈmentl-ē/ *adv.* —**sup·ple·men·ta·tion** /ˌsəpləˌmenˈtāsHən/ *n.*

sup·ple·men·ta·ry /ˌsəpləˈmentərē/ ▶*adj.* completing or enhancing something: *the center's work was to be seen as* **supplementary to** *orthodox treatment and not a substitute for it.*
▶*n.* a supplementary person or thing. —**sup·ple·men·tar·i·ly** /-ˌmenˈte(ə)rəlē/ *adv.*

sup·ple·men·ta·ry an·gle ▶*n. Mathematics* either of two angles whose sum is 180°.

sup·ple·tion /səˈplēsHən/ ▶*n. Linguistics* the occurrence of an unrelated form to fill a gap in a conjugation (e.g., *went* as the past tense of *go*). ▷Middle English: from Old French, from medieval Latin *suppletio(n-)*, from *supplere* 'fill up, make full' (see SUPPLY[1]). —**sup·ple·tive** /səˈplētiv; ˈsəplətiv/ *adj.*

Sup·plex /ˈsəpleks/ ▶*n. trademark* a synthetic stretchable fabric which is permeable to air and water vapor, used in sports and outdoor clothing.

sup·pli·ant /ˈsəplēənt/ ▶*n.* a person making a humble plea to someone in power or authority.
▶*adj.* making or expressing a plea, esp. to someone in power or authority: *their faces were suppliant.* ▷late Middle English (as a noun): from French, 'beseeching,' present participle of *supplier*, from Latin *supplicare* (see SUPPLICATE). —**sup·pli·ant·ly** *adv.*

sup·pli·cate /ˈsəpliˌkāt/ ▶*v.* [*intrans.*] ask or beg for something earnestly or humbly: [with *infinitive*] *the plutocracy supplicated to be made peers.* ▷late Middle English: from Latin *supplicat-* 'implored,' from the verb *supplicare*, from *sub-* 'from below' + *placere* 'propitiate.' —**sup·pli·cant** /-kənt/ *adj.* & *n.* —**sup·pli·ca·tion** /ˌsəpliˈkāsHən/ *n.* —**sup·pli·ca·to·ry** /-kəˌtôrē/ *adj.*

sup·ply[1] /səˈplī/ ▶*v.* (**-plies, -plied**) [*trans.*] make (something needed or wanted) available to someone; provide: *the farm supplies apples to cider makers.* ■ provide (someone) with something needed or wanted: *they struggled to* **supply** *the besieged island* **with** *aircraft.* ■ be a source of (something needed): *eat foods that supply a significant amount of dietary fiber.* ■ be adequate to satisfy (a requirement or demand): *the two reservoirs supply about 1% of the city's needs.* ■ *archaic* take over (a place or role left by someone else): *when she died, no one could supply her place.*
▶*n.* (*pl.* **-plies**) a stock of a resource from which a person or place can be provided with the necessary amount of that resource: *there were fears that the drought would limit the exhibition's water supply.* ■ the action of providing what is needed or wanted: *the deal involved the supply of forty fighter aircraft.* ■ *Economics* the amount of a good or service offered for sale. ■ (**supplies**) the provisions and equipment necessary for an army or for people engaged in a particular project or expedition. ■ (**supplies**) *Brit.* a grant of money by Parliament for the costs of government. ■ [usu. as *adj.*] a person acting as a temporary substitute for another. ■ [as *adj.*] providing necessary goods and equipment: *a supply ship.* ▷late Middle English: from Old French *soupleer*, from Latin *supplere* 'fill up,' from *sub-* 'from below' + *plere* 'fill.' The early sense of the noun was 'assistance, relief' (chiefly a Scots use). —**sup·pli·er** *n.*
▶*PHRASES* □ **in short supply** not easily obtainable; scarce: *he meant to go, but time and gas were in short supply.* □ **supply and demand** the amount of a good or service available and the desire of buyers for it, considered as factors regulating its price: *by the law of supply and demand the cost of health care will plummet.*

sup·ply[2] /ˈsəp(ə)lē/ ▶*adv.* variant spelling of SUPPLELY (see SUPPLE).

sup·ply chain ▶*n.* the sequence of processes involved in the production and distribution of a commodity.

sup·ply-side ▶*adj.* [*attrib.*] *Economics* denoting or relating to a policy designed to increase output and employment by changing the conditions under which goods and services are supplied, esp. by measures that reduce government involvement in the economy and allow the free market to operate. —**sup·ply-sid·er** *n.*

sup·port /səˈpôrt/ ▶*v.* [*trans.*] **1** bear all or part of the weight of; hold up: *the dome was supported by a hundred white columns.* ■ produce enough food and water for; be capable of sustaining: *the land had lost its capacity to support life.* ■ be capable of fulfilling (a role) adequately: *tutors gain practical experience that helps them support their tutoring role.* ■ endure; tolerate: *at work during the day I could support the grief.* **2** give assistance to, esp. financially; enable to function or act: *the government gives $2.5 billion a year to support the activities of the voluntary sector.* ■ provide with a home and the necessities of life: *my main concern was to support my family.* ■ give comfort and emotional help to: *I like to visit her to support her.* ■ approve of and encourage: *the proposal was supported by many delegates.* ■ suggest the truth of; corroborate: *the studies support our findings.* ■ be actively interested in and concerned for the success of (a particular sports team). ■ [as *adj.*] (**supporting**) (of an actor or a role) important in a play or film but subordinate to the leading parts. ■ (of a pop or rock group or performer) function as a secondary act to (another) at a concert. **3** *Computing* (of a computer or operating system) allow the use or operation of (a program, language, or device): *the new versions do not support the graphical user interface standard.*
▶*n.* **1** a thing that bears the weight of something or keeps it upright: *the best support for a camera is a tripod.* ■ the action or state of bearing the weight of something or someone or of being so supported: *she clutched the sideboard for support.* **2** material assistance: *he urged that military support be sent to protect humanitarian convoys* | [as *adj.*] *support staff.* ■ comfort and emotional help offered to someone in distress: *she's been through a bad time and needs our support.* ■ approval and encouragement: *the policies of reform enjoy widespread support.* ■ a secondary act at a pop or rock concert. ■ technical help given to the user of a computer or other product. ▷Middle English (originally in the sense 'tolerate, put up with'): from Old French *supporter*, from Latin *supportare*, from *sub-* 'from below' + *portare* 'carry.' —**sup·port·a·bil·i·ty** /səˌpôrtəˈbilitē/ *n.* —**sup·port·a·ble** *adj.*
▶*PHRASE* □ **in support of** giving assistance to: *air operations in support of the land forces.* ■ showing approval of: *the paper printed many letters in support of the government.* ■ attempting to promote or obtain: *a strike in support of an 8.5% pay raise.*

sup·port·er /səˈpôrtər/ ▶*n.* **1** a person who approves of and encourages someone or something (typically a public figure, a movement or party, or a policy): *Reagan supporters* | **supporters of** *the boycott.* ■ a person who is actively interested in and wishes success for a particular sports team. **2** *Heraldry* a representation of an animal or other figure, typically one of a pair, holding up or standing beside an escutcheon. **3** (in full **athletic supporter**) another term for JOCKSTRAP.

sup·port group ▶*n.* **1** a group of people who are available to support one another emotionally, socially, and sometimes financially: *a support group for gay teens.* **2** a system implemented with the aim of providing support for an enterprise, product line, or project: *Unix system support group.*

sup·port·ive /səˈpôrtiv/ ▶*adj.* providing encouragement or emotional help: *the staff are extremely* **supportive of** *each other.* —**sup·port·ive·ly** *adv.* —**sup·port·ive·ness** *n.*

sup·port·ive ther·a·py ▶*n.* treatment designed to improve, reinforce, or sustain a patient's physiological well-being or psychological self-esteem and self-reliance.

sup·pose /səˈpōz/ ▶*v.* **1** [with *clause*] assume that something is the case on the basis of evidence or probability but without proof or certain knowledge: *I suppose I got there about half past eleven.* ■ used to make a reluctant or hesitant admission: *I'm quite a good actress, I suppose.* ■ used to introduce a hypothesis and trace or ask about what follows from it: *suppose he had been murdered—what then?* ■ [in *imperative*] used to introduce a suggestion: *suppose we leave this to the police.* ■ (of a theory or argument) assume or require that something is the case as a precondition: *the procedure supposes that a will has already been proved* | [*trans.*] *the theory supposes a predisposition to interpret utterances.* ■ [*trans.*] believe to exist or to possess a specified characteristic: *he* **supposed** *the girl* **to be** *about twelve* [as *adj.*] (**supposed**) often /səˈpōzid/ *people admire their supposed industriousness.* **2** (**be supposed to do something**) be required to do something because of the position one is in or an agreement one has made: *I'm supposed to be meeting someone at the airport.* ■ [with *negative*] be forbidden to do something: *I shouldn't have been in the kitchen—I'm not supposed to go in there.* ▷Middle English: from Old French *supposer*, from Latin *supponere* (from *sub-* 'from below' + *ponere* 'to place'), but influenced by Latin *suppositus* 'set under' and Old French *poser* 'to place.' —**sup·pos·a·ble** *adj.*
▶*PHRASE* □ **I suppose so** used to express hesitant or reluctant agreement.

sup·pos·ed·ly /səˈpōzidlē/ ▶*adv.* [*sentence adverb*] according to what is generally assumed or believed (often used to indicate that the speaker doubts the truth of the statement): *the ads are aimed at women, supposedly because they do the shopping.*

sup·po·si·tion /ˌsəpəˈzisHən/ ▶*n.* an uncertain belief: *they were working on the supposition that his death was murder* | *their outrage was based on supposition and hearsay.* ▷late Middle English (as a term in scholastic logic): from Old French, or from late Latin *suppositio(n-)* (translating Greek *hupothesis* 'hypothesis'), from the verb *supponere* (see SUPPOSE). —**sup·po·si·tion·al** /-sHənl/ *adj.*

sup·po·si·tious /ˌsəpəˈzisHəs/ ▶*adj.* **1** based on assumption rather than fact: *most of the evidence is purely suppositious.* **2** supposititious. ▷early 17th cent. (in the sense 'supposititious'): partly a contraction of SUPPOSITITIOUS, reinforced by SUPPOSITION. —**sup·po·si·tious·ly** *adv.* —**sup·po·si·tious·ness** *n.*

sup·pos·i·ti·tious /səˌpäzəˈtisHəs/ ▶*adj.* **1** substituted for the real thing; not genuine: *the supposititious heir to the throne.* **2** suppositious. ▷early 17th cent.: from Latin *supposititius* (from *supponere* 'to substitute') + -OUS. —**sup·pos·i·ti·tious·ly** *adv.* —**sup·pos·i·ti·tious·ness** *n.*

sup·pos·i·to·ry /səˈpäzəˌtôrē/ ▶*n.* (*pl.* **-ries**) a solid medical preparation in a roughly conical or cylindrical shape, designed to be inserted into the rectum or vagina to dissolve. ▷late Middle English: from medieval Latin *suppositorium*, neuter (used as a noun) of late Latin *suppositorius* 'placed underneath.'

sup·press /səˈpres/ ▶*v.* [*trans.*] forcibly put an end to: *the uprising was savagely suppressed.* ■ prevent the development, action, or expression of (a feeling, impulse, idea, etc.); restrain: *she could not suppress a rising panic.* ■ prevent the dissemination of (information): *the report had been suppressed.* ■ prevent or inhibit (a process or reaction): *use of the drug suppressed the immune response.* ■ partly or wholly eliminate (electrical interference). ■ *Psychoanalysis* consciously inhibit (an unpleasant idea or memory) to avoid considering it. ▷late Middle English: from Latin *suppress-* 'pressed down,' from the verb *supprimere*, from *sub-* 'down' + *premere* 'to press.' —**sup·press·i·ble** *adj.* —**sup·pres·sive** /-siv/ *adj.* —**sup·pres·sor** /-sər/ *n.*

sup·pres·sant /səˈpresənt/ ▶*n.* a drug or other substance that acts to suppress or restrain something: *an appetite suppressant.*

sup·pres·sion /səˈpresHən/ ▶*n.* the action of suppressing something such as an activity or publication: *the Communist Party's forcible suppression of the opposition in 1948.* ■ *Medicine* stoppage or reduction of a discharge or secretion. ■ *Biology* the absence or nondevelopment of a part or organ that is normally present. ■ *Genetics* the canceling of the effect of one mutation by a second mutation. ■ *Psychology* the restraint or repression of an idea, activity, or reaction by something more powerful. ■ *Psychoanalysis* the conscious inhibition of unacceptable memories, impulses, or desires. ■ prevention of electrical interference.

sup·pres·sor cell /səˈpresər/ (also **suppressor T cell**) ▶*n. Physiology* a lymphocyte that can suppress antibody production by other lymphoid cells.

sup·pu·rate /ˈsəpyəˌrāt/ ▶*v.* [*intrans.*] undergo the formation of pus; fester. ▷late Middle English (in the sense 'cause to form pus'): based on Latin *sub-* 'below' + *pus, pur-* 'pus.' —**sup·pu·ra·tion** /ˌsəpyəˈrāsHən/ *n.* —**sup·pu·ra·tive** /-ˌrātiv/ *adj.*

supr. ▶*abbr.* ■ superior. ■ supreme.

su·pra /ˈso͞oprə/ ▶*adv. formal* used in academic or legal texts to refer to someone or something mentioned above or earlier: *the recent work by McAuslan and others (supra).* ▷Latin.

supra- ▶*prefix* **1** beyond; transcending: *supranational.* **2** above: *suprarenal.* ▷from Latin *supra* 'above, beyond, before in time.'

su·pra·chi·as·mat·ic nu·cle·us /ˈso͞oprəˌkīəzˈmatik/ ▶*n. Anatomy* each of a pair of small nuclei in the hypothalamus of the brain, above the optic chiasma, thought to be concerned with the regulation of physiological circadian rhythms.

su·pra·mo·lec·u·lar /ˌsoōprəməˈlekyələr/ ▸*adj. Biochemistry* relating to or denoting structures composed of several or many molecules.

su·pra·na·tion·al /ˌsoōprəˈnashənl/ ▸*adj.* having power or influence that transcends national boundaries or governments: *supranational law.* **—su·pra·na·tion·al·ism** /-ˌizəm/ *n.* **—su·pra·na·tion·al·i·ty** /-ˌnashəˈnalitē/ *n.*

su·pra·op·tic /ˌsoōprəˈäptik/ ▸*adj. Anatomy* situated above the optic chiasma.

su·pra·or·bit·al /ˌsoōprəˈôrbitl/ ▸*adj. Anatomy* situated above the orbit of the eye.

su·pra·re·nal /ˌsoōprəˈrēnl/ ▸*adj. Anatomy* another term for **ADRENAL**.

su·pra·seg·men·tal /ˌsoōprəˌsegˈmentl/ *Linguistics* ▸*adj.* denoting a feature of an utterance other than the consonantal and vocalic components, e.g., (in English) stress and intonation.
▸*n.* such a feature.

su·prem·a·cist /səˈpreməsist; soō-/ ▸*n.* an advocate of the supremacy of a particular group, esp. one determined by race or sex: *a white supremacist.*
▸*adj.* relating to or advocating such supremacy. **—su·prem·a·cism** /-ˌsizəm/ *n.*

su·prem·a·cy /səˈpreməsē; soō-/ ▸*n.* the state or condition of being superior to all others in authority, power, or status: *the supremacy of the king.*

su·prem·a·tism /səˈpreməˌtizəm; soō-/ ▸*n.* the Russian abstract art movement developed by Kazimir Malevich *c.*1915, characterized by simple geometric shapes and associated with ideas of spiritual purity. **—su·prem·a·tist** *n.*

su·preme /səˈprēm; soō-/ ▸*adj.* (of authority or an office, or someone holding it) superior to all others: *a unified force with a supreme commander.* ■ strongest, most important, or most powerful: *on the racetrack he* ***reigned supreme.*** ■ very great or intense; extreme: *he was nerving himself for a supreme effort.* ■ (of a penalty or sacrifice) involving death: *our comrades who made the supreme sacrifice.* ■ [*postpositive*] used to indicate that someone or something is very good at or well known for a specified activity: *here was the gift supreme.*
▸*n.* (also **su·prême**) a rich cream sauce. ■ a dish served in such a sauce: *chicken supreme.* [from French *suprême.*] ▷late 15th cent. (in the sense 'highest'): from Latin *supremus*, superlative of *superus* 'that is above,' from *super* 'above.' **—su·preme·ly** *adv.*
▸*PHRASE* □ **the Supreme Being** a name for God.

Su·preme Court ▸*n.* the highest judicial court in most U.S. states. ■ (in full **U.S. Supreme Court**) the highest federal court in the U.S., consisting of nine justices and taking judicial precedence over all other courts in the nation.

U.S. Supreme Court Building

su·preme pon·tiff ▸*n.* see **PONTIFF**.

Su·preme So·vi·et ▸*n.* the governing council of the former USSR or one of its constituent republics. That of the USSR was its highest legislative authority and was composed of two equal chambers: the Soviet of Union and the Soviet of Nationalities.

Supt. ▸*abbr.* Superintendent.

supvr. ▸*abbr.* supervisor.

suq ▸*n.* variant spelling of **SOUK**.

Sur, Point /ˈsər/ see **BIG SUR**.

sur. ▸*abbr.* ■ surface. ■ surplus.

sur-[1] ▸*prefix* equivalent to **SUPER-** (as in *surcharge, surmount*). ▷from French.

sur-[2] ▸*prefix* variant spelling of **SUB-** assimilated before *r* (as in *surrogate*).

su·ra /ˈsoōrə/ (also **su·rah**) ▸*n.* a chapter or section of the Koran. ▷from Arabic *sūra.*

Su·ra·ba·ya /ˌsoōrəˈbīə/ a seaport in Indonesia, on the northern coast of Java; pop. 2,473,000. It is Indonesia's principal naval base and its second largest city.

su·rah /ˈsoōrə/ ▸*n.* a soft twilled silk fabric used in dressmaking. ▷late 19th cent.: representing the French pronunciation of **SURAT**, where it was originally made.

su·ral /ˈsoōrəl/ ▸*adj. Anatomy* of or relating to the calf of the leg. ▷early 17th cent.: from modern Latin *suralis*, from Latin *sura* 'calf.'

Su·rat /ˈsoōrˌat; soōˈrat/ a city in the state of Gujarat in western India, a port on the Tapti River near its mouth on the Gulf of Cambay; pop. 1,497,000.

sur·cease /sərˈsēs/ ▸*n.* cessation: *he teased us without surcease.* ■ relief or consolation: *drugs are taken to provide surcease from intolerable psychic pain.*
▸*v.* [*intrans.*] *archaic* cease. ▷late Middle English (as a verb): from Old French *sursis*, past participle of Old French *surseoir* 'refrain, delay,' from Latin *supersedere* (see **SUPERSEDE**). The change in the ending was due to association with **CEASE**; the noun dates from the late 16th cent.

sur·charge /ˈsərˌchärj/ ▸*n.* **1** an additional charge or payment: *we guarantee that no surcharges will be added to the cost of your trip.* ■ a charge made by assessors as a penalty for false returns of taxable property. ■ the showing of an omission in an account for which credit should have been given. **2** a mark printed on a postage stamp changing its value.
▸*v.* [*trans.*] **1** exact an additional charge or payment from: *retailers will be able to surcharge credit-card users.* **2** mark (a postage stamp) with a surcharge. ▷late Middle English (as a verb): from Old French *surcharger* (see **SUR-**[1], **CHARGE**). The early sense of the noun (late 15th cent.) was 'excessive load.'

sur·cin·gle /ˈsərˌsinggəl/ ▸*n.* a wide strap that runs over the back and under the belly of a horse, used to keep a blanket or other equipment in place. ▷Middle English: from Old French *surcengle*, based on *cengle* 'girth,' from Latin *cingula*, from *cingere* 'gird.'

sur·coat /ˈsərˌkōt/ ▸*n. historical* a loose robe worn over armor. ■ a similar sleeveless garment worn as part of the insignia of an order of knighthood. ■ an outer coat of rich material. ▷Middle English: from Old French *surcot*, from *sur* 'over' + *cot* 'coat.'

sur·cu·lose /ˈsərkyəˌlōs; -ˌlōz/ ▸*adj. Botany* producing suckers. ▷mid 19th cent.: from Latin *surculosus*, from *surculus* 'twig.'

surd /sərd/ ▸*adj.* **1** *Mathematics* (of a number) irrational. **2** *Phonetics* (of a speech sound) uttered with the breath and not the voice (e.g., *f, k, p, s, t*).
▸*n.* **1** *Mathematics* a surd number, esp. the irrational root of an integer. **2** *Phonetics* a surd consonant. ▷mid 16th cent.: from Latin *surdus* 'deaf, mute'; as a mathematical term, translating Greek (Euclid) *alogos* 'irrational, speechless,' apparently via Arabic *jiḏr aṣamm*, literally 'deaf root.' The phonetics senses date from the mid 18th cent.

sure /shoōr/ ▸*adj.* [*predic.*] [often with *clause*] confident in what one thinks or knows; having no doubt that one is right: *I'm sure I've seen that dress before | she had to check her diary to be* **sure of** *the day of the week.* ■ (**sure of**) having a certain prospect or confident anticipation of: *Ripken can be sure of a place in the Hall of Fame.* ■ [with *infinitive*] certain to do something: *it's sure to rain before morning.* ■ true beyond any doubt: *what is sure is that learning is a complex business.* ■ [*attrib.*] able to be relied on or trusted: *her neck was red—a sure sign of agitation.* ■ confident; assured: *the drawings impress by their sure sense of rhythm.*
▸*adv. informal* certainly (used for emphasis): *Texas sure was a great place to grow up.* ■ [as an *exclam.*] used to show assent: *"Are you serious?" "Sure."* ▷Middle English: from Old French *sur*, from Latin *securus* 'free from care.' **—sure·ness** *n.*
▸*PHRASES* □ **be sure** [usu. in *imperative*] do not fail (used to emphasize an invitation or instruction): [with *infinitive*] *be sure to drop by* | [with *clause*] *be sure that you know what is required.* □ **for sure** *informal* without doubt: *I can't say for sure what George really wanted.* □ **make sure** [usu. with *clause*] establish that something is definitely so; confirm: *go and make sure she's all right.* ■ ensure that something is done or happens: *he made sure that his sons were well educated.* □ **sure enough** *informal* used to introduce a statement that confirms something previously predicted: *when X-rays were taken, sure enough, there was the needle.* □ **sure of oneself** very confident of one's own abilities or views: *he's very sure of himself.* □ **sure thing** *informal* a certainty. ■ [as *exclam.*] certainly; of course: *"Can I watch?" "Sure thing."* □ **to be sure** used to concede the truth of something that conflicts with another point that one wishes to make: *the ski runs are very limited, to be sure, but excellent for beginners.* ■ used for emphasis: *what an extraordinary woman she was, to be sure.*

USAGE Unless intending an informal effect, do not use **sure** when the adverb **surely** is meant: *I* **surely** *enjoyed the show* (not *I* **sure** *enjoyed the show*).

sure-fire ▸*adj.* [*attrib.*] *informal* certain to succeed: *bad behavior is a sure-fire way of getting attention.*

sure-foot·ed (also **sure·foot·ed**) ▸*adj.* unlikely to stumble or slip: *tough, sure-footed ponies.* ■ confident and competent: *the challenges of the 1990s demand a responsible and sure-footed government.* **—sure-foot·ed·ly** *adv.* **—sure-foot·ed·ness** *n.*

sure·ly /ˈshoōrlē/ ▸*adv.* **1** [*sentence adverb*] used to emphasize the speaker's firm belief that what they are saying is true and often their surprise that there is any doubt of this: *if there is no will, then surely the house goes automatically to you.* ■ without doubt; certainly: *if he did not heed the warning, he would surely die.* ■ [as *exclam.*] *informal* of course; yes: *"You'll wait for me?" "Surely."* **2** with assurance or confidence: *no one knows how to move the economy quickly and surely in that direction.*

USAGE See usage at **SURE**.

Sûre·té /syrˈtā/ (also **Sûreté nationale** /näsyônˈnäl/) the French police department of criminal investigation. ▷French, literally '(National) Security.'

sur·e·ty /ˈshoōritē/ ▸*n.* (*pl.* **-ties**) a person who takes responsibility for another's performance of an undertaking, for example their appearing in court or the payment of a debt. ■ money given to support an undertaking that someone will perform a duty, pay their debts, etc.; a guarantee: *the judge granted bail with a surety of $500.* ■ the state of being sure or certain of something: *I was enmeshed in the surety of my impending fatherhood.* ▷Middle English (in the sense 'something given to support an undertaking that someone will fulfill an obligation'): from Old French *surte*, from Latin *securitas* (see **SECURITY**). **—sur·e·ty·ship** /-ˌship/ *n.*
▸*PHRASE* □ **of** (or **for**) **a surety** *archaic* for certain: *who can tell that for a surety?*

surf /sərf/ ▸*n.* the mass or line of foam formed by waves breaking on a seashore or reef: *the roar of the surf.* ■ [in *sing.*] a spell of surfing: *he went for an early surf.*
▸*v.* [*intrans.*] ride on the crest of a wave, typically toward the shore while riding on a surfboard: *learning to surf.* ■ [*trans.*] ride (a wave) toward the shore in such a way: *he has built a career out of surfing big waves.* ■ *informal* ride on the roof or outside of a fast-moving vehicle, typically a train, for excitement: *he fell to his death while surfing on a 70 mph train.* ■ short for **CHANNEL-SURF**. ■ [*trans.*] move from site to site on (the Internet). ▷late 17th cent.: apparently from obsolete *suff*, of unknown origin, perhaps influenced by the spelling of *surge.* **—surf·er** *n.* **—surf·y** *adj.*

sur·face /ˈsərfis/ ▸*n.* **1** the outside part or uppermost layer of something (often used when describing its texture, form, or extent): *the earth's surface | poor road surfaces.* ■ the level top of something: *roll out the dough on a floured surface.* ■ (also **surface area**) the area of such an outer part or uppermost layer: *the surface area of a cube.* ■ [in *sing.*] the upper limit of a body of liquid: *fish floating on the surface of the water.* ■ [in *sing.*] what is apparent on a casual view or consideration of someone or something, esp. as distinct from feelings or qualities that are not immediately obvious: *Tom was a womanizer, but on the surface he remained respectable* | [as *adj.*] *we need to go beyond surface appearances.* **2** *Geometry* a set of points that has length and breadth but no thickness.
▸*adj.* [*attrib.*] of, relating to, or occurring on the upper or outer part of something: *surface workers at the copper mines.* ■ denoting ships that travel on the surface of the water as distinct from submarines: *the surface fleet.* ■ carried by or denoting transportation by sea or overland as contrasted with by air: *surface mail.*
▸*v.* **1** [*intrans.*] rise or come up to the surface of the water or the ground: *he surfaced from his dive.* ■ come to people's attention; become apparent: *the quarrel first surfaced two years ago.* ■ *informal* (of a person) appear after having been asleep: *it was almost noon before Anthony surfaced.* **2** [*trans.*] (usu. **be surfaced**) provide (something, esp. a road) with a particular upper or outer layer: *a small path surfaced with terra-cotta tiles.* ▷early 17th cent.: from French (see **SUR-**[1], **FACE**), suggested by Latin *superficies.* **—sur·faced** *adj.* [often in *combination*] *a smooth-surfaced cylinder.* **—sur·fac·er** *n.*

sur·face-ac·tive ▸*adj.* (of a substance, such as a detergent) tending to reduce the surface tension of a liquid in which it is dissolved.

sur·face bound·a·ry lay·er ▸*Meteorology n.* the lowest layer of the earth's atmosphere extending to about one kilometer. Winds within it are affected by friction with the earth's surface.

sur·face chem·is·try ▸*n.* the branch of chemistry concerned with the processes occurring at interfaces between phases, esp. that between liquid and gas.

sur·face mount (also **sur·face-mount**) ▸*adj.* (of an electronic component) having leads that are designed to be soldered on the side of a circuit board that the body of the component is mounted on.

sur·face noise ▸*n.* extraneous noise in playing a phonograph record, caused by imperfections in the grooves or in the pickup system.

sur·face struc·ture ▸*n.* (in generative grammar) the structure of a well-formed phrase or sentence in a language, as opposed to its underlying abstract representation. Contrasted with DEEP STRUCTURE.

sur·face ten·sion ▸*n.* the tension of the surface film of a liquid caused by the attraction of the particles in the surface layer by the bulk of the liquid, which tends to minimize surface area.

sur·face-to-air ▸*adj.* [*attrib.*] (of a missile) designed to be fired from the ground or a vessel at an aircraft.

sur·face-to-sur·face ▸*adj.* [*attrib.*] (of a missile) designed to be fired from one point on the ground or a vessel at another such point or vessel.

sur·face wa·ter ▸*n.* **1** water that collects on the surface of the ground. **2** (also **surface waters**) the top layer of a body of water: *the surface water of a pond or lake.*

sur·fac·tant /sərˈfaktənt/ ▸*n.* a substance that tends to reduce the surface tension of a liquid in which it is dissolved. ▷1950s: from *surf(ace)-act(ive)* + -ANT.

surf·bird /ˈsərf,bərd/ ▸*n.* a small migratory wader of the sandpiper family, with mainly dark gray plumage and a short bill and legs, breeding in Alaska. • *Aphriza virgata*, family Scolopacidae.

surf·board /ˈsərf,bôrd/ ▸*n.* a long, narrow streamlined board used in surfing.

surf·cast·ing /ˈsərf,kastiNG/ (also **surf cast·ing** or **surf-cast·ing**) ▸*n.* fishing by casting a line into the sea from the shore or near the shore. —**surf·cast·er** /-,kastər/ *n.*

sur·feit /ˈsərfət/ ▸*n.* [usu. in *sing.*] an excessive amount of something: *a surfeit of food and drink.* ■ *archaic* an illness caused or regarded as being caused by excessive eating or drinking: *he died of a surfeit.*
▸*v.* (**-feit·ed**, **-feit·ing**) [*trans.*] (usu. **be surfeited with**) cause (someone) to desire no more of something as a result of having consumed or done it to excess: *I am surfeited with shopping.* ■ [*intrans.*] *archaic* consume too much of something: *he never* **surfeited on** *rich wine.* ▷Middle English: from Old French *surfeit*, based on Latin *super-* 'above, in excess' + *facere* 'do.'

sur·fi·cial /sərˈfiSHəl/ ▸*adj. Geology* of or relating to the earth's surface: *surficial deposits.* ▷late 19th cent.: from SURFACE, on the pattern of *superficial.* —**sur·fi·cial·ly** *adv.*

surf·ing /ˈsərfiNG/ ▸*n.* the sport or pastime of being carried to the shore on the crest of large waves while standing or lying on a surfboard.

surf mu·sic ▸*n.* a style of popular music originating in the U.S. in the early 1960s, characterized by high harmony vocals and typically having lyrics relating to surfing.

surf 'n' turf /ˈsərf ən ˈtərf/ (also **surf and turf**) ▸*n.* a dish containing both seafood and meat, typically shellfish and steak.

surf·perch /ˈsərf,pərCH/ ▸*n.* (*pl.* same or **-perch·es**) a deep-bodied livebearing fish of the North Pacific, living chiefly in coastal waters. Also called SEA PERCH. • Family Embiotocidae: several genera and species.

surg. ▸*abbr.* ■ surgeon. ■ surgery. ■ surgical.

surge /sərj/ ▸*n.* a sudden powerful forward or upward movement, esp. by a crowd or by a natural force such as the waves or tide: *flooding caused by tidal surges.* ■ a sudden large increase, typically a brief one that happens during an otherwise stable or quiescent period: *the firm predicted a 20% surge in sales.* ■ a powerful rush of an emotion or feeling: *Sophie felt a surge of anger.* ■ a sudden marked increase in voltage or current in an electric circuit.
▸*v.* [*intrans.*] (of a crowd or a natural force) move suddenly and powerfully forward or upward: *the journalists surged forward.* ■ increase suddenly and powerfully, typically during an otherwise stable or quiescent period: *shares surged to a record high.* ■ (of an emotion or feeling) affect someone powerfully and suddenly: *indignation surged up within her.* ■ (of an electric voltage or current) increase suddenly. ■ *Nautical* (of a rope, chain, or windlass) slip back with a jerk. ▷late 15th cent. (in the sense 'fountain, stream'): the noun (in early use) from Old French *sourgeon*; the verb partly from the Old French stem *sourge-*, based on Latin *surgere* 'to rise.' Early senses of the verb included 'rise and fall on the waves' and 'swell with great force.'

surge cham·ber ▸*n.* another term for SURGE TANK.

sur·geon /ˈsərjən/ ▸*n.* a medical practitioner qualified to practice surgery. ▷Middle English: from Anglo-Norman French *surgien*, contraction of Old French *serurgien*, based on Latin *chirurgia*, from Greek *kheirourgia* 'handiwork, surgery,' from *kheir* 'hand' + *ergon* 'work.'

sur·geon·fish /ˈsərjən,fiSH/ ▸*n.* (*pl.* same or **-fish·es**) a deep-bodied and typically brightly colored tropical marine fish with a scalpellike spine on each side of the tail. • Family Acanthuridae: several genera and many species. See also TANG[3].

sur·geon gen·er·al ▸*n.* (*pl.* **sur·geons gen·er·al**) the head of a public health service or of an armed forces medical service.

sur·geon's knot ▸*n.* a square knot with one or more extra turns in the first half knot. ▷from the use of such a knot to tie a ligature in surgery.

sur·ger·y /ˈsərjərē/ ▸*n.* (*pl.* **-ger·ies**) **1** the branch of medicine concerned with treatment of injuries or disorders of the body by incision or manipulation, esp. with instruments: *cardiac surgery.* ■ such treatment, as performed by a surgeon: *he had surgery on his ankle.* **2** *Brit.* a place where a doctor, dentist, or other medical practitioner treats or advises patients. ■ [in *sing.*] an occasion on which such treatment or consultation occurs: *Doctor Bailey had finished his evening surgery.* ▷Middle English: from Old French *surgerie*, contraction of *serurgerie*, from *serurgien* (see SURGEON).

surge tank ▸*n.* a tank connected to a pipe carrying a liquid and intended to neutralize sudden changes of pressure in the flow by filling when the pressure increases and emptying when it drops.

sur·gi·cal /ˈsərjikəl/ ▸*adj.* of, relating to, or used in surgery: *a surgical dressing | a surgical ward.* ■ (of a special garment or appliance) worn to correct or relieve an injury, illness, or deformity: *surgical stockings.* ■ *figurative* denoting something done with great precision, esp. a swift and highly accurate military attack from the air: *surgical bombing.* ▷late 18th cent. (earlier as *chirurgical*): from French *cirurgical*, from Old French *sirurgie* (see SURGERY). —**sur·gi·cal·ly** /-ik(ə)lē/ *adv.*

Su·ri·ba·chi, Mount /,so͝orəˈbäCHē/ a small dormant volcano on Iwo Jima, in the western Pacific Ocean, site of a February 1945 flag-raising by U.S. Marines that was the subject of a well-known World War II photograph and a monument in Arlington National Cemetery in Virginia.

su·ri·cate /ˈso͝ori,kāt/ ▸*n.* a gregarious burrowing meerkat with dark bands on the back and a black-tipped tail, native to southern Africa. • *Suricata suricatta*, family Herpestidae. ▷late 18th cent.: via French from a local African word.

suricate

su·ri·mi /səˈrēmē/ ▸*n.* fish (often pollock) that is minced and rinsed to make a gelatinous paste that is then flavored, reformed into flakes, sticks, or other shapes, and colored. It is used as a crab substitute. ▷from Japanese, 'formed fish.'

Su·ri·na·me /,so͝orəˈnämə; ˈso͝orə,näm; -,nam/ (also **Su·ri·nam** /ˈso͝orə,näm; -,nam/) a country on the northeastern coast of South America; pop. 437,000; capital, Paramaribo; languages, Dutch (official), Creoles, and Hindi. Former name (until 1948) DUTCH GUIANA. —**Su·ri·nam·er** /,so͝orəˈnämər/ *n.* —**Su·ri·na·mese** /,so͝orənəˈmēz; -ˈmēs/ *adj.* & *n.*

Colonized by the Dutch and the English from the 17th century, Suriname became fully independent in 1975. The population is descended largely from African slaves and Asian laborers brought in to work on sugar plantations; there is also a small American Indian population.

Su·ri·nam toad /ˈso͝orə,nam/ ▸*n.* an aquatic South American toad with a flat body and long webbed feet, the female of which carries the eggs and tadpoles in pockets on her back. • *Pipa pipa*, family Pipidae.

sur·ly /ˈsərlē/ ▸*adj.* (**-li·er**, **-li·est**) bad-tempered and unfriendly: *he left with a surly expression.* See note at BRUSQUE. ▷mid 16th cent. (in the sense 'lordly, haughty, arrogant'): alteration of obsolete *sirly* (see SIR, -LY[1]). —**sur·li·ly** /-lәlē/ *adv.* —**sur·li·ness** *n.*

sur·mise ▸*v.* /sərˈmīz/ [*intrans.*] [usu. with *clause*] suppose that something is true without having evidence to confirm it: *he surmised that something must be wrong* | [with *direct speech*] *"I don't think they're locals," she surmised.*
▸*n.* /sərˈmīz; ˈsər,mīz/ a supposition that something may be true, even though there is no evidence to confirm it: *Charles was glad to have his surmise confirmed | all these observations remain surmise.* ▷late Middle English (in the senses 'formal allegation' and 'allege formally'): from Anglo-Norman French and Old French *surmise*, feminine past participle of *surmettre* 'accuse,' from late Latin *supermittere* 'put in afterward,' from *super-* 'over' + *mittere* 'send.'

sur·mount /sərˈmount/ ▸*v.* [*trans.*] **1** overcome (a difficulty or obstacle): *all manner of cultural differences were surmounted.* **2** (usu. **be surmounted**) stand or be placed on top of: *the tomb was surmounted by a sculptured angel.* ▷late Middle English (also in the sense 'surpass, be superior to'): from Old French *surmonter* (see SUR-[1], MOUNT[1]). —**sur·mount·a·ble** *adj.*

sur·mul·let /sərˈməlit/ ▸*n.* a red mullet that is widely distributed in the tropical Indo-Pacific. • *Pseudupeneus fraterculus*, family Mullidae. ▷late 17th cent.: from French *surmulet*, from Old French *sor* 'red' + *mulet* 'mullet.'

sur·name /ˈsər,nām/ ▸*n.* a hereditary name common to all members of a family, as distinct from a given name. ■ *archaic* a name, title, or epithet added to a person's name, esp. one indicating their birthplace or a particular quality or achievement: *by his successes there, he acquired the surname of "the African."*
▸*v.* [*trans.*] (usu. **be surnamed**) give a surname to: *Eddie Penham, so aptly surnamed, had produced a hand-painted sign for us.* ▷Middle English: partial translation of Anglo-Norman French *surnoun*, suggested by medieval Latin *supernomen.*

sur·pass /sərˈpas/ ▸*v.* [*trans.*] exceed; be greater than: *prewar levels of production were surpassed in 1929.* ■ be better than: *he continued to surpass me at all games.* ■ (**surpass oneself**) do or be better than ever before: *the organist was surpassing himself.* ■ [as *adj.*] (**surpassing**) *dated* or *poetic/literary* incomparable or outstanding: *a picture of surpassing beauty.* ▷mid 16th cent.: from French *surpasser*, from *sur-* 'above' + *passer* 'to pass.' —**sur·pass·a·ble** *adj.* —**sur·pass·ing·ly** *adv.*

sur·plice /ˈsərplis/ ▸*n.* a loose white linen vestment varying from hip-length to calf-length, worn over a cassock by clergy, acolytes, and choristers at Christian church services. ▷Middle English: from Old French *sourpelis*, from medieval Latin *superpellicium*, from *super-* 'above' + *pellicia* 'fur garment.' —**sur·pliced** *adj.*

surplice

Pronunciation Key ə *ago*; ər *over*; ˈə or ,ə *up*; ˈər or ,ər *fur*; a *hat*; ā *rate*; ä *car*; CH *chew*; e *let*; ē *see*; e(ə)r *air*; i *fit*; ī *by*; i(ə)r *ear*; NG *sing*; ō *go*; ô *for*; oi *boy*; o͝o *good*; o͞o *goo*; ou *out*; SH *she*; TH *thin*; TH *then*; (h)w *why*; ZH *vision*

sur·plus /ˈsərpləs/ ▶*n.* an amount of something left over when requirements have been met; an excess of production or supply over demand: *exports of food surpluses.* ■ an excess of income or assets over expenditure or liabilities in a given period, typically a fiscal year: *a trade surplus of $1.4 billion.* ■ the excess value of a company's assets over the face value of its stock.
▶*adj.* more than what is needed or used; excess: *make the most of your surplus cash.* ■ denoting a store selling excess or out-of-date military equipment or clothing: *she had picked up her boots in an army surplus store.* ▷late Middle English: from Old French *sourplus*, from medieval Latin *superplus*, from *super-* 'in addition' + *plus* 'more.'

sur·plus val·ue ▶*n. Economics* (in Marxist theory) the excess of value produced by the labor of workers over the wages they are paid.

sur·prise /sə(r)ˈprīz/ ▶*n.* **1** an unexpected or astonishing event, fact, or thing: *the announcement was a complete surprise.* ■ a feeling of mild astonishment or shock caused by something unexpected: *much to her surprise, she'd missed him.* ■ [as *adj.*] denoting something made, done, or happening unexpectedly: *a surprise attack.* **2** [as *adj.*] *Bell-ringing* denoting a class of complex methods of change-ringing: *surprise major.*
▶*v.* [*trans.*] (often **be surprised**) (of something unexpected) cause (someone) to feel mild astonishment or shock: *I* **was surprised at** *his statement* | [*trans.*] *Joe was surprised that he enjoyed the journey* | [with *infinitive*] *she was surprised to learn that he was forty* | [as *adj.*] (**surprising**) *a surprising sequence of events.* ■ capture, attack, or discover suddenly and unexpectedly; catch unawares: *he surprised a gang stealing scrap metal.* ▷late Middle English (in the sense 'unexpected seizure of a place, or attack on troops'): from Old French, feminine past participle of *surprendre*, from medieval Latin *superprehendere* 'seize.' **—sur·pris·ed·ly** /-z(i)dlē/ *adv.* **—sur·pris·ing·ly** *adv.* [as *submodifier*] *the profit margin in advertising is surprisingly low* | [*sentence adverb*] *not surprisingly, his enthusiasm knew no bounds.* **—sur·pris·ing·ness** *n.*
▶*PHRASES* □ **surprise, surprise** *informal* said when giving someone a surprise. ■ said ironically when one believes that something was entirely predictable: *we entrust you with Jason's care and, surprise surprise, you make a mess of it.* □ **take someone/something by surprise** attack or capture someone or something unexpectedly. ■ (**take someone by surprise**) happen when someone is not prepared or is expecting something different: *the question took David by surprise.*

surr. ▶*abbr.* surrender.

sur·ra /ˈso͞orə; ˈsərə/ ▶*n.* a parasitic disease of camels and other mammals caused by trypanosomes, transmitted by biting flies and occurring chiefly in North Africa and Asia. ▷late 19th cent.: from Marathi *sūra* 'air breathed through the nostrils.'

sur·re·al /səˈrēəl/ ▶*adj.* having the qualities of surrealism; bizarre: *a surreal mix of fact and fantasy.* ▷1930s: back-formation from SURREALISM. **—sur·re·al·i·ty** /ˌsərēˈalitē/ *n.* **—sur·re·al·ly** *adv.*

sur·re·al·ism /səˈrēəˌlizəm/ ▶*n.* a 20th-century avant-garde movement in art and literature that sought to release the creative potential of the unconscious mind, for example by the irrational juxtaposition of images.

Launched in 1924 by a manifesto of André Breton and having a strong political content, the movement grew out of symbolism and Dada and was strongly influenced by Sigmund Freud. In the visual arts its most notable exponents were André Masson, Jean Arp, Joan Miró, René Magritte, Salvador Dali, Max Ernst, Man Ray, and Luis Buñuel.

▷early 20th cent.: from French *surréalisme* (see SUR-[1], REALISM). **—sur·re·al·ist** *n. & adj.* **—sur·re·al·is·tic** /səˌrēəˈlistik/ *adj.* **—sur·re·al·is·ti·cal·ly** /səˌrēəˈlistik(ə)lē/ *adv.*

sur·re·but·tal /ˈsərəˌbətl/ ▶*n.* another term for SURREBUTTER.

sur·re·but·ter /ˌsərəˈbətər/ ▶*n. archaic Law* a plaintiff's reply to the defendant's rebutter. ▷late 16th cent.: from SUR-[1] 'in addition' + REBUTTER, on the pattern of *surrejoinder.*

sur·re·join·der /ˌsərəˈjoindər/ ▶*n. archaic Law* a plaintiff's reply to the defendant's rejoinder. ▷mid 16th cent.: from SUR-[1] 'in addition' + REJOINDER.

sur·ren·der /səˈrendər/ ▶*v.* [*intrans.*] cease resistance to an enemy or opponent and submit to their authority: *over 140 rebels surrendered to the authorities.* ■ [*trans.*] give up or hand over (a person, right, or possession), typically on compulsion or demand: *in 1815 Denmark* **surrendered** *Norway* **to** *Sweden* | *they refused to surrender their weapons.* See note at RELINQUISH. ■ [*trans.*] (in a sports contest) lose (a point, game, or advantage): *she surrendered only twenty games in her five qualifying matches.* ■ (**surrender to**) abandon oneself entirely to (a powerful emotion or influence); give in to: *he was surprised that Miriam should surrender to this sort of jealousy* | *he* **surrendered himself** *to the mood of the hills.* ■ [*trans.*] (of an insured person) cancel (a life insurance policy) and receive back a proportion of the premiums paid.
▶*n.* the action of surrendering. ■ the action of surrendering a life insurance policy. ▷late Middle English (chiefly in legal use): from Anglo-Norman French (see SUR-[1], RENDER).

sur·ren·der val·ue ▶*n.* the amount payable to a person who surrenders a life insurance policy.

sur·rep·ti·tious /ˌsərəpˈtisHəs/ ▶*adj.* kept secret, esp. because it would not be approved of: *they carried on a surreptitious affair.* See note at SECRET. ▷late Middle English (in the sense 'obtained by suppression of the truth'): from Latin *surreptitius* (from the verb *surripere*, from *sub-* 'secretly' + *rapere* 'seize') + -OUS. **—sur·rep·ti·tious·ly** *adv.* **—sur·rep·ti·tious·ness** *n.*

Sur·rey /ˈsərē/ a county in southeastern England; county town, Kingston-upon-Thames.

sur·rey /ˈsərē/ ▶*n.* (*pl.* **-reys**) *historical* a light four-wheeled carriage with two seats facing forward. ▷late 19th cent.: originally denoting a *Surrey cart*, first made in SURREY, from which the carriage was later adapted.

surrey

sur·ro·ga·cy /ˈsərəgəsē/ ▶*n.* the action or state of being a surrogate. ■ the process of giving birth as a surrogate mother or of arranging such a birth.

sur·ro·gate /ˈsərəgit; -ˌgāt/ ▶*n.* a substitute, esp. a person deputizing for another in a specific role or office: *she was regarded as the* **surrogate for** *the governor during his final illness.* ■ (in the Christian Church) a bishop's deputy who grants marriage licenses. ■ a judge in charge of probate, inheritance, and guardianship. ▷early 17th cent.: from Latin *surrogatus*, past participle of *surrogare* 'elect as a substitute,' from *super-* 'over' + *rogare* 'ask.'

sur·ro·gate moth·er ▶*n.* **1** a person, animal, or thing that takes on all or part of the role of mother to another person or animal. **2** a woman who bears a child on behalf of another woman, either from her own egg fertilized by the other woman's partner, or from the implantation in her uterus of a fertilized egg from the other woman.

sur·round /səˈround/ ▶*v.* [*trans.*] (usu. **be surrounded**) be all around (someone or something): *the hotel is surrounded by its own gardens* | *figurative he loves to* **surround himself with** *family and friends* | [as *adj.*] (**surrounding**) *the surrounding countryside.* See note at CIRCUMSCRIBE. ■ (of troops, police, etc.) encircle (someone or something) so as to cut off communication or escape: *troops surrounded the parliament building.* ■ be associated with: *the killings were surrounded by controversy.*
▶*n.* a thing that forms a border or edging around an object: *an oak fireplace surround.* ■ (usu. **surrounds**) the area encircling something; surroundings: *the beautiful surrounds of Moosehead Lake.* ▷late Middle English (in the sense 'overflow'): from Old French *souronder*, from late Latin *superundare*, from *super-* 'over' + *undare* 'to flow' (from *unda* 'a wave'); later associated with ROUND. Current senses of the noun date from the late 19th cent.

sur·round·ings /səˈroundiNGz/ ▶*plural n.* the things and conditions around a person or thing: *I took up the time admiring my surroundings.*

sur·round sound ▶*n.* a system of stereophonic sound involving three or more speakers surrounding the listener so as to create a more realistic effect.

sur·tax /ˈsərˌtaks/ ▶*n.* an additional tax on something already taxed, such as a higher rate of tax on incomes above a certain level. ▷late 19th cent.: from French *surtaxe* (see SUR-[1], TAX).

sur·tout /sərˈto͞o(t)/ ▶*n. historical* a man's overcoat of a style similar to a frock coat. ▷late 17th cent.: from French, from *sur* 'over' + *tout* 'everything.'

Surt·sey /ˈsərtsē/ a small island south of Iceland, formed by a volcanic eruption in 1963.

sur·veil·lance /sərˈvāləns/ ▶*n.* close observation, esp. of a suspected spy or criminal: *he found himself put* **under surveillance** *by military intelligence.* ▷early 19th cent.: from French, from *sur-* 'over' + *veiller* 'watch' (from Latin *vigilare* 'keep watch').

sur·vey ▶*v.* /sərˈvā/ [*trans.*] **1** (of a person or their eyes) look carefully and thoroughly at (someone or something), esp. so as to appraise them: *her green eyes surveyed him coolly* | *I surveyed the options.* ■ investigate the opinions or experience of (a group of people) by asking them questions: *95% of patients surveyed were satisfied with the health service.* ■ investigate (behavior or opinions) by questioning a group of people: *the investigator surveyed the attitudes and beliefs held by residents.* **2** examine and record the area and features of (an area of land) so as to construct a map, plan, or description: *he surveyed the coasts of New Zealand.*
▶*n.* /ˈsərˌvā/ **1** a general view, examination, or description of someone or something: *the author provides a survey of the relevant literature.* ■ an investigation of the opinions or experience of a group of people, based on a series of questions. **2** an act of surveying an area of land: *the flight involved a detailed aerial survey of military bases.* ■ a map, plan, or detailed description obtained in such a way. ■ a department carrying out the surveying of land: *the U.S. Geological Survey.* ▷late Middle English (in the sense 'examine and ascertain the condition of'): from Anglo-Norman French *surveier*, from medieval Latin *supervidere*, from *super-* 'over' + *videre* 'to see.' The early sense of the noun (late 15th cent.) was 'supervision.'

Sur·vey·or /sərˈvāər/ a series of unmanned U.S. spacecraft sent to the moon between 1966 and 1968, five of which successfully made soft landings.

sur·vey·or /sərˈvāər/ ▶*n.* a person who surveys, esp. one whose profession is the surveying of land. ■ a person who investigates or examines something, esp. boats for seaworthiness: *a marine surveyor.* ▷late Middle English (denoting a supervisor): from Anglo-Norman French *surveiour*, from the verb *surveier* (see SURVEY). **—sur·vey·or·ship** /-ˌSHip/ *n.*

sur·viv·a·ble /sərˈvīvəbəl/ ▶*adj.* (of an accident or ordeal) able to be survived; not fatal: *air crashes are becoming more survivable.*

sur·viv·al /sərˈvīvəl/ ▶*n.* the state or fact of continuing to live or exist, typically in spite of an accident, ordeal, or difficult circumstances: *the animal's chances of survival were pretty low* | *figurative he was fighting for his political survival.* ■ an object or practice that has continued to exist from an earlier time: *his shorts were a survival from his army days.*
▶*PHRASE* □ **survival of the fittest** *Biology* the continued existence of organisms that are best adapted to their environment, with the extinction of others, as a concept in the Darwinian theory of evolution. Compare with NATURAL SELECTION.

sur·viv·al curve ▶*n.* a graph showing the proportion of a population living after a given age, or at a given time after contracting a serious disease or receiving a radiation dose.

sur·viv·al·ism /sərˈvīvəˌlizəm/ ▶*n.* **1** the policy of trying to ensure one's own survival or that of one's social or national group. **2** the practicing of outdoor survival skills as a sport or hobby. **—sur·viv·al·ist** *n. & adj.*

sur·viv·al kit ▶*n.* a pack of emergency equipment, including food, medical supplies, and tools, esp. as carried by members of the armed forces. ■ a collection of items to help someone in a particular situation: *a substitute teacher survival kit.*

sur·viv·al val·ue ▶*n.* the property of an ability, faculty, or characteristic that makes individuals possessing it more likely to survive, thrive, and reproduce: *everyone knows that a bad smell is of survival value to the skunk.*

sur·vive /sərˈvīv/ ▶*v.* [*intrans.*] continue to live or exist, esp. in spite of danger or hardship: *against all odds the child survived.* ■ [*trans.*] continue to live or exist in spite of (an accident or ordeal): *he has survived several assassination attempts.* ■ [*trans.*] remain alive after the death of (a particular person): *he was survived by his wife and six children* | [as *adj.*] (**surviving**) *there were no surviving relatives.* ■ [*intrans.*] manage to keep going in difficult circumstances: *she had to work day and night and* ***survive on*** *two hours sleep.* ▷late Middle English: from Old French *sourvivre*, from Latin *supervivere*, from *super-* 'in addition' + *vivere* 'live.'

sur·vi·vor /sər'vīvər/ ▶*n.* a person who survives, esp. a person remaining alive after an event in which others have died: *the sole survivor of the massacre.* ■ the remainder of a group of people or things: *a survivor from last year's team.* ■ a person who copes well with difficulties in their life: *she is a born survivor.* ■ *Law* a joint tenant who has the right to the whole estate on the other's death.

sur·vi·vor·ship /sər'vīvər,SHip/ ▶*n.* the state or condition of being a survivor; survival. ■ *Law* a right depending on survival, esp. the right of a survivor of people with a joint interest to take the whole on the death of the others.

Sus. ▶*abbr.* (in biblical references) Susanna (Apocrypha).

sus- ▶*prefix* variant spelling of **SUB-** before *c, p, t* (as in *susceptible, suspend, sustain.*)

Su·sa /'sōōzə; -sə/ **1** an ancient city in southwestern Asia, one of the chief cities of the kingdom of Elam and later capital of the Persian Achaemenid dynasty. **2** another name for **SOUSSE**.

sus·cep·ti·bil·i·ty /sə,septə'bilitē/ ▶*n.* (*pl.* **-ties**) **1** the state or fact of being likely or liable to be influenced or harmed by a particular thing: *lack of exercise increases* ***susceptibility to*** *disease.* ■ (**susceptibilities**) a person's feelings, typically considered as being easily hurt: *I was so careful not to offend their susceptibilities.* **2** *Physics* the ratio of magnetization to a magnetizing force.

sus·cep·ti·ble /sə'septəbəl/ ▶*adj.* **1** likely or liable to be influenced or harmed by a particular thing: *patients with liver disease may be* ***susceptible to*** *infection.* ■ (of a person) easily influenced by feelings or emotions; sensitive: *they only do it to tease him—he's too susceptible.* **2** [*predic.*] (**susceptible of**) capable or admitting of: *the problem is not susceptible of a simple solution.* ▷early 17th cent.: from late Latin *susceptibilis*, from Latin *suscipere* 'take up, sustain,' from *sub-* 'from below' + *capere* 'take.' —**sus·cep·ti·bly** /-blē/ *adv.*

sus·cep·tive /sə'septiv/ ▶*adj. archaic* receptive or sensitive to something; susceptible. ▷late Middle English: from late Latin *susceptivus*, from *suscept-* 'taken up,' from the verb *suscipere* (see **SUSCEPTIBLE**).

su·shi /'sōōSHē/ ▶*n.* a Japanese dish consisting of small balls or rolls of vinegar-flavored cold cooked rice served with a garnish of raw fish, vegetables, or egg. ▷Japanese.

sus·lik /'səs,lik/ ▶*n.* variant spelling of **SOUSLIK**.

sus·pect ▶*v.* /sə'spekt/ [*trans.*] **1** have an idea or impression of the existence, presence, or truth of (something) without certain proof: *if you suspect a gas leak, do not turn on an electric light* | [with *clause*] *she suspected that he might be bluffing* | [as *adj.*] (**suspected**) *a suspected heart condition.* ■ believe or feel that (someone) is guilty of an illegal, dishonest, or unpleasant act, without certain proof: *parents* ***suspected of*** *child abuse.* **2** doubt the genuineness or truth of: *a broker whose honesty he had no reason to suspect.*
▶*n.* /'səs,pekt/ a person thought to be guilty of a crime or offense: *the police have arrested a suspect.*
▶*adj.* /'səs,pekt/ not to be relied on or trusted; possibly dangerous or false: *a suspect package was found on the platform.* ▷Middle English (originally as an adjective): from Latin *suspectus* 'mistrusted,' past participle of *suspicere*, from *sub-* 'from below' + *specere* 'to look.'

sus·pend /sə'spend/ ▶*v.* [*trans.*] (usu. **be suspended**) **1** temporarily prevent from continuing or being in force or effect: *work on the dam was suspended.* ■ officially prohibit (someone) from holding their usual post or carrying out their usual role for a particular length of time: *two officers were* ***suspended from*** *duty pending the outcome of the investigation.* ■ defer or delay (an action, event, or judgment): *the judge suspended judgment until January 15.* See note at **POSTPONE**. ■ *Law* (of a judge or court) cause (an imposed sentence) to be unenforced as long as no further offense is committed within a specified period: *the sentence was suspended for six months* | [as *adj.*] (**suspended**) *a suspended jail sentence.* **2** hang (something) from somewhere: *the light was* ***suspended from*** *the ceiling.* **3** (**be suspended**) (of solid particles) be dispersed throughout the bulk of a fluid: *the paste contains collagen suspended in a salt solution.* ▷Middle English: from Old French *suspendre* or Latin *suspendere*, from *sub-* 'from below' + *pendere* 'hang.'
▶***PHRASES*** □ **suspend disbelief** temporarily allow oneself to believe something that isn't true, esp. in order to enjoy a work of fiction. □ **suspend payment** (of a company) cease to meet its financial obligations as a result of insolvency or insufficient funds.

sus·pend·ed an·i·ma·tion ▶*n.* the temporary cessation of most vital functions without death, as in a dormant seed or a hibernating animal.

sus·pend·ers /sə'spendərz/ ▶*plural n.* a pair of straps that pass over the shoulders and fasten to the waistband of a pair of trousers or a skirt at the front and back to hold it up.

sus·pense /sə'spens/ ▶*n.* **1** a state or feeling of excited or anxious uncertainty about what may happen: *come on, Fran, don't keep me* ***in suspense!*** ■ a quality in a work of fiction that arouses excited expectation or uncertainty about what may happen: *a tale of mystery and suspense* | [as *adj.*] *a suspense novel.* **2** *chiefly Law* the temporary cessation or suspension of something. ▷late Middle English: from Old French *suspens* 'abeyance,' based on Latin *suspensus* 'suspended, hovering, doubtful,' past participle of *suspendere* (see **SUSPEND**). —**sus·pense·ful** /-fəl/ *adj.*

sus·pense ac·count ▶*n.* an account in the books of an organization in which items are entered temporarily before allocation to the correct or final account.

sus·pen·sion /sə'spenSHən/ ▶*n.* **1** the action of suspending someone or something or the condition of being suspended, in particular: ■ the temporary prevention of something from continuing or being in force or effect: *the suspension of military action.* ■ the official prohibition of someone from holding their usual post or carrying out their usual role for a particular length of time: *the investigation led to the suspension of several officers* | *a four-game suspension.* ■ *Music* a discord made by prolonging a note of a chord into the following chord. **2** the system of springs and shock absorbers by which a vehicle is cushioned from road conditions: *the car's rear suspension.* **3** a mixture in which particles are dispersed throughout the bulk of a fluid: *a suspension of corn starch in peanut oil.* ■ the state of being dispersed in such a way: *the agitator in the vat keeps the slurry* ***in suspension.*** ▷late Middle English: from French, or from Latin *suspensio(n-)*, from the verb *suspendere* (see **SUSPEND**).

sus·pen·sion bridge ▶*n.* a bridge in which the weight of the deck is supported by vertical cables suspended from further cables that run between towers and are anchored in abutments at each end.

sus·pen·sive /sə'spensiv/ ▶*adj.* **1** of or relating to the deferral or suspension of an event, action, or legal obligation. **2** causing suspense. —**sus·pen·sive·ly** *adv.* —**sus·pen·sive·ness** *n.*

sus·pen·so·ry /sə'spensərē/ ▶*adj.* **1** holding and supporting an organ or part: *a suspensory ligament.* **2** of or relating to the deferral or suspension of an event, action, or legal obligation: *a suspensory requirement.* ▷late Middle English: from medieval Latin *suspensorius* 'used for hanging something up,' from Latin *suspendere* (see **SUSPEND**).

sus·pi·cion /sə'spiSHən/ ▶*n.* **1** a feeling or thought that something is possible, likely, or true: *she had a sneaking* ***suspicion that*** *he was laughing at her.* ■ a feeling or belief that someone is guilty of an illegal, dishonest, or unpleasant action: *police would not say what aroused their suspicions* | *he was arrested* ***on suspicion of*** *murder.* ■ cautious distrust: *her activities were regarded with suspicion by the headmistress.* **2** a very slight trace of something: ***a suspicion of*** *a smile.* ▷Middle English: from Anglo-Norman French *suspeciun*, from medieval Latin *suspectio(n-)*, from *suspicere* 'mistrust.' The change in the second syllable was due to association with Old French *suspicion* (from Latin *suspicio(n-)* 'suspicion').
▶***PHRASES*** □ **above suspicion** too obviously good or honest to be thought capable of wrongdoing. □ **under suspicion** thought to be guilty of wrongdoing.

sus·pi·cious /sə'spiSHəs/ ▶*adj.* having or showing a cautious distrust of someone or something: *he was* ***suspicious of*** *her motives* | *she gave him a suspicious look.* ■ causing one to have the idea or impression that something or someone is of questionable, dishonest, or dangerous character or condition: *they are not treating the fire as suspicious.* ■ having the belief or impression that someone is involved in an illegal or dishonest activity: *police were called when staff became suspicious.* ▷Middle English: from Old French *suspicious*, from Latin *suspiciosus*, from *suspicio(n-)* (see **SUSPICION**). —**sus·pi·cious·ly** *adv.* [as *submodifier*] *it's suspiciously cheap* —**sus·pi·cious·ness** *n.*

sus·pire /sə'spīr/ ▶*v.* [*intrans.*] *poetic/literary* breathe. ▷late Middle English (in the sense 'yearn after'): from Latin *suspirare*, from *sub-* 'from below' + *spirare* 'breathe.' —**sus·pi·ra·tion** /,səspə'rāSHən/ *n.*

Sus·que·han·na /,səskwə'hanə/ a river in the northeastern U.S. It has two headstreams, one that rises in New York and one in Pennsylvania, both of which meet in central Pennsylvania. The river then flows 150 miles (240 km) south to Chesapeake Bay.

suss /səs/ *chiefly Brit., informal* ▶*v.* (**sussed, sus·sing**) [*trans.*] realize; grasp: *he's sussed it* | [with *clause*] *she* ***sussed out*** *right away that there was something fishy going on.* ▷1930s: abbreviation of **SUSPECT, SUSPICION.**

Sus·sex /'səsəks/ ▶*n.* a speckled or red bird of a domestic English breed of chicken.

sus·tain /sə'stān/ ▶*v.* [*trans.*] **1** strengthen or support physically or mentally: *this thought had sustained him throughout the years* | [as *adj.*] (**sustaining**) *a sustaining breakfast of bacon and eggs.* ■ cause to continue or be prolonged for an extended period or without interruption: *he cannot sustain a normal conversation* | [as *adj.*] (**sustained**) *several years of sustained economic growth.* ■ (of a performer) represent (a part or character) convincingly: *he sustained the role with burly resilience.* ■ bear (the weight of an object) without breaking or falling: *he sagged against her so that she could barely sustain his weight* | *figurative his health will no longer enable him to sustain the heavy burdens of office.* **2** undergo or suffer (something unpleasant, esp. an injury): *he died after sustaining severe head injuries.* **3** uphold, affirm, or confirm the justice or validity of: *the allegations of discrimination were sustained.*
▶*n. Music* an effect or facility on a keyboard or electronic instrument whereby a note can be sustained after the key is released. ▷Middle English: from Old French *soustenir*, from Latin *sustinere*, from *sub-* 'from below' + *tenere* 'hold.' —**sus·tain·ed·ly** /-nidlē/ *adv.* —**sus·tain·er** *n.* —**sus·tain·ment** *n.*

sus·tain·a·ble /sə'stānəbəl/ ▶*adj.* able to be maintained at a certain rate or level: *sustainable fusion reactions.* ■ *Ecology* (esp. of development, exploitation, or agriculture) conserving an ecological balance by avoiding depletion of natural resources. ■ able to be upheld or defended: *sustainable definitions of good educational practice.* —**sus·tain·a·bil·i·ty** /sə,stānə'bilitē/ *n.* —**sus·tain·a·bly** /-blē/ *adv.*

sus·tained-re·lease ▶*adj.* [*attrib.*] *Medicine* denoting a drug preparation in a capsule containing numerous tiny pellets with different coatings that release their contents steadily over a long period.

sus·tained yield ▶*n.* a level of exploitation or crop production that is maintained by restricting the quantity harvested to avoid long-term depletion.

sus·te·nance /'səstənəns/ ▶*n.* food and drink regarded as a source of strength; nourishment: *poor rural economies turned to potatoes for sustenance.* ■ the maintaining of someone or something in life or existence: *he kept two or three cows for the sustenance of his family* | *the sustenance of democracy.* ▷Middle English: from Old French *soustenance*, from the verb *soustenir* (see **SUSTAIN**).

sus·ten·ta·tion /,səst(ə)n'tāSHən/ ▶*n. formal* the support or maintenance of someone or something, esp. through the provision of money: *provision is made for the sustentation of preachers.* ▷late Middle English: from Old French, or from Latin *sustentatio(n-)*, from *sustentare* 'uphold, sustain,' frequentative of *sustinere* (see **SUSTAIN**).

Su·su /'sōō,sōō/ ▶*n.* (*pl.* same) **1** a member of a people of northwestern Sierra Leone and the southern coast of Guinea. **2** the Mande language of this people.
▶*adj.* of or relating to this people or their language. ▷the name in Susu.

su·sur·rus /sōō'sərəs/ (also **su·sur·ra·tion** /,sōōsə'rāSHən/) ▶*n. poetic/literary* whispering, murmuring, or rustling: *the susurrus of the stream.* ▷late Middle English: from late Latin *susurratio(n-)*, from Latin *susurrare* 'to murmur, hum.' —**su·sur·rant** /sōō'sərənt/ *adj.* —**su·sur·rate** /'sōōsə,rāt; sōō'sər,āt/ *v.* —**su·sur·rous** /sōō'sərəs/ *adj.*

Suth·er·land[1] /'səTHərlənd/, Donald (1935–), Canadian actor. He is best known for his role in *M*A*S*H* (1970) and also appeared in *Don't Look Now* (1973), *The Great Train Robbery* (1979), and *Eye of the Needle* (1981).

Pronunciation Key ə ago; ər over; 'ə or ,ə up; 'ər or ,ər fur; a hat; ā rate; ä car; CH chew; e let; ē see; e(ə)r air; i fit; ī by; i(ə)r ear; NG sing; ō go; ô for; oi boy; ŏŏ good; ōō goo; ou out; SH she; TH thin; TH then; (h)w why; ZH vision

S

Suth·er·land[2], George (1862–1942), U.S. Supreme Court associate justice 1922–38. Appointed to the Court by President Harding, he was a conservative and strongly opposed many of President Franklin D. Roosevelt's New Deal programs.

Suth·er·land[3], Graham (Vivian) (1903–80), English painter. During World War II he was an official war artist. His postwar work included the tapestry *Christ in Majesty* (1962) in Coventry cathedral.

Suth·er·land[4], Dame Joan (1926–), Australian opera singer. She is noted for her dramatic coloratura roles, particularly the title role in Donizetti's *Lucia di Lammermoor.*

Sut·lej /ˈsətlij/ a river in northern India and Pakistan that rises in the Himalayas in southwestern Tibet and flows for 900 miles (1,450 km) west through India into Punjab province in Pakistan, where it joins the Chenab River to form the Panjnad River, which eventually joins the Indus River. It is one of the five rivers that gave Punjab its name.

sut·ler /ˈsətlər/ ▸*n. historical* a person who followed an army and sold provisions to the soldiers. ▷late 16th cent.: from obsolete Dutch *soeteler,* from *soetelen* 'perform menial duties.'

su·tra /ˈso͞otrə/ ▸*n.* a rule or aphorism in Sanskrit literature, or a set of these on a technical subject. See also **Kama Sutra**. ■ a Buddhist or Jain scripture. ▷from Sanskrit *sūtra* 'thread, rule,' from *siv* 'sew.'

sut·tee /səˈtē; ˈsə,tē/ (also **sa·ti** *pronunc.* same) ▸*n.* (*pl.* **sut·tees**; also **sa·tis** /səˈtēz; ˈsə,tēz/) the former Hindu practice of a widow immolating herself on her husband's funeral pyre. ■ a widow who committed such an act. ▷Hindi, from Sanskrit *satī* 'faithful wife,' from *sat* 'good.'

su·ture /ˈso͞oCHər/ ▸*n.* **1** a stitch or row of stitches holding together the edges of a wound or surgical incision. ■ a thread or wire used for this. ■ the action of stitching together the edges of a wound or incision. **2** a seamlike immovable junction between two bones, such as those of the skull. ■ *Zoology* a similar junction, such as between the sclerites of an insect's body. ■ *Geology* a line of junction formed by two crustal plates that have collided.
▸*v.* [*trans.*] stitch up (a wound or incision) with a suture: *the small incision was sutured.* ▷late Middle English: from French, or from Latin *sutura,* from *suere* 'sew.' —**su·tur·al** /-CHərəl/ *adj.*

SUV ▸*abbr.* sport utility vehicle.

Su·va /ˈso͞ovə/ the capital of Fiji, on the southeastern coast of the island of Viti Levu; pop. 72,000.

Su·wan·nee /ˈswänē; səˈwänē/ (also **Swa·nee** /ˈswä-/) a river in southeastern U.S. Rising in southeastern Georgia, it flows for about 250 miles (400 km) southwest through northern Florida to the Gulf of Mexico.

su·ze·rain /ˈso͞ozərən; -,rān/ ▸*n.* a sovereign or state having some control over another state that is internally autonomous. ■ *historical* a feudal overlord. ▷early 19th cent.: from French, apparently from *sus* 'above' (from Latin *su(r)sum* 'upward'), suggested by *souverain* 'sovereign.' —**su·ze·rain·ty** /-rəntē; -,rāntē/ *n.*

Su·zhou /ˈso͞oˈjō/ (also **Su·chou** or **Soo·chow** /-ˈCHou; -ˈjō/) a city in eastern China, in the province of Jiangsu, west of Shanghai on the Grand Canal; pop. 840,000.

Su·zu·ki /səˈzo͞okē/ ▸*adj.* relating to or denoting a method of teaching the violin, typically to very young children in large groups, developed by Shin'ichi Suzuki (1898–1998), Japanese educator and violin teacher.

Sv ▸*abbr.* sievert(s).

s.v. ▸*abbr.* used in textual references before a word or heading to indicate that a specified item can be found under it: *the dictionary defines "sweet dreams" (s.v. "sweet").* ▷from Latin *sub voce* or *sub verbo,* literally 'under the word or voice.'

Sval·bard /ˈsväl,bär(d)/ a group of islands in the Arctic Ocean about 400 miles (640 km) north of Norway; pop. 3,700. They came under Norwegian sovereignty in 1925. The chief settlement (on Spitsbergen) is Longyearbyen.

svc (also **svce**) ▸*abbr.* service.

Sved·berg /ˈsfed,bərg; ˈsved-/ (also **Svedberg unit**) (abbr.: **S**) ▸*n. Biochemistry* a unit of time equal to 10^{-13} seconds, used in expressing sedimentation coefficients.

svelte /svelt; sfelt/ ▸*adj.* (of a person) slender and elegant. See note at **thin**. ▷early 19th cent.: from French, from Italian *svelto.*

Sven·ga·li /svenˈgälē; sfen-/ a musician in George du Maurier's novel *Trilby* (1894) who trains Trilby's voice and controls her stage singing hypnotically. ■ [as *n.*] (**a Svengali**) a person who exercises a controlling or mesmeric influence on another, esp. for a sinister purpose.

Sverd·lovsk /sverdˈlôfsk; svərd-/ former name (1924–91) of **Ekaterinburg**.

Sve·ri·ge /ˈsvaryə/ Swedish name for **Sweden**.

Sve·tam·ba·ra /SHveˈtämbərə/ ▸*n.* a member of one of the two principal sects of Jainism, which was formed as a result of doctrinal schism *c.* AD 80 and survives today in parts of India. The sect's adherents practice asceticism and wear white clothing. See also **Digambara**. ▷from Sanskrit *śvetāmbara,* literally 'white-clad.'

SVGA ▸*abbr.* super video graphics array, a high-resolution standard for computer monitors and display screens.

svgs. ▸*abbr.* savings.

S-VHS ▸*abbr.* super video home system, an improved version of VHS using the same tape cassettes as the standard version.

Sviz·ze·ra /ˈzvētsə,rä/ Italian name for **Switzerland**.

SW ▸*abbr.* ■ southwest. ■ southwestern.

Sw. (also **Swed**) ▸*abbr.* ■ Sweden. ■ Swedish.

sw. ▸*abbr.* switch.

swab /swäb/ ▸*n.* **1** an absorbent pad or piece of material used in surgery and medicine for cleaning wounds, applying medication, or taking specimens. ■ a specimen of a secretion taken with a swab for examination: *he had taken throat swabs.* ■ a piece of absorbent material used for cleaning the bore of a firearm, a woodwind instrument, etc. **2** a mop or other absorbent device for cleaning or mopping up a floor or other surface. **3** another term for **swabbie**.
▸*v.* (**swabbed, swab·bing**) [*trans.*] clean (a wound or surface) with a swab: ***swabbing down** the decks | swab a patch of skin with alcohol.* ■ [with *adverbial*] absorb or clear (moisture) with a swab: *the blood was swabbed away.* ▷mid 17th cent. (in the sense 'mop for cleaning the decks'): back-formation from *swabber* 'sailor detailed to swab decks,' from early modern Dutch *zwabber,* from a Germanic base meaning 'splash' or 'sway.'

swab·bie /ˈswäbē/ (also **swab·by**) ▸*n.* (*pl.* **-bies**) *Nautical slang* a member of the navy, typically one who is of low rank.

Swa·bi·a /ˈswäbēə/ a former duchy of medieval Germany, now divided between southwestern Germany, Switzerland, and France. German name **Schwaben**. —**Swa·bi·an** *adj.* & *n.*

swacked /swakt/ ▸*adj. informal* drunk. ▷1930s: past participle of Scots *swack* 'fling, strike heavily.'

swad·dle /ˈswädl/ ▸*v.* [*trans.*] wrap (someone, esp. a baby) in garments or cloth: *she swaddled the baby tightly | figurative they have grown up swaddled in consumer technology.* ▷Middle English: frequentative of **swathe**.

swad·dling clothes /ˈswädliNG/ ▸*plural n.* narrow bands of cloth formerly wrapped around a newborn child to restrain its movements and quiet it.

swag /swag/ ▸*n.* **1** an ornamental festoon of flowers, fruit, and greenery: *ribbon-tied swags of flowers.* ■ a carved or painted representation of such a festoon: *fine plaster swags.* ■ a curtain or piece of fabric fastened so as to hang in a drooping curve. **2** *informal* money or goods taken by a thief or burglar: *garden machinery is the most popular swag.* ■ *informal* a large number, amount, or variety: *a swag of events including fleece competitions, poultry and water fowl competitions, and a tractor pull.* **3** *Austral./NZ* a traveler's or miner's bundle of personal belongings.
▸*v.* (**swagged, swag·ging**) [*trans.*] **1** arrange in or decorate with a swag or swags of fabric: *swag the fabric gracefully over the curtain tie-backs* | [as *adj.*] (**swagged**) *the swagged contours of nomads' tents.* **2** *Austral./NZ* travel with one's personal belongings in a bundle: ***swagging it** in Queensland | **swagging my way** up to the Northern Territory.* **3** [*intrans.*] *chiefly poetic/literary* hang heavily: *the crinkly old hide swags here and there.* ■ sway from side to side: *the stout chief sat swagging from one side of the carriage to the other.* ▷Middle English (in the sense 'bulging bag'): probably of Scandinavian origin. The original sense of the verb (early 16th cent.) was 'cause to sway or sag.'

swage /swāj/ ▸*n.* **1** a shaped tool or die for giving a desired form to metal by hammering or pressure. **2** a groove, ridge, or other molding on an object.
▸*v.* [*trans.*] shape (metal) using a swage, esp. in order to reduce its cross section. ■ [with *adverbial*] join (metal pieces) together by this process. ▷late Middle English (sense 2): from Old French *souage* 'decorative groove,' of unknown origin.

swage block ▸*n.* a grooved or perforated block for shaping metal.

swag·ger /ˈswagər/ ▸*v.* [*intrans.*] walk or behave in a very confident and typically arrogant or aggressive way: *he swaggered along the corridor* | [as *adj.*] (**swaggering**) *a swaggering gait.*
▸*n.* [in *sing.*] a very confident and typically arrogant or aggressive gait or manner: *they strolled around the camp with an exaggerated swagger.*
▸*adj.* [*attrib.*] denoting a coat or jacket cut with a loose flare from the shoulders. ▷early 16th cent.: apparently a frequentative of the verb **swag**. —**swag·ger·er** /ˈswag(ə)rər/ *n.* —**swag·ger·ing·ly** /ˈswag(ə)riNGlē/ *adv.*

swag·ger stick ▸*n.* a short cane carried by a military officer.

swag·man /ˈswagmən/ ▸*n.* (*pl.* **-men**) *Austral./NZ* a person carrying a swag.

Swa·hi·li /swäˈhēlē/ ▸*n.* (*pl.* same) **1** a Bantu language widely used as a lingua franca in East Africa and having official status in several countries. Also called **Kiswahili**. **2** a member of a people of Zanzibar and nearby coastal regions, descendants of the original speakers of Swahili.
▸*adj.* of or relating to this language or to the people who are its native speakers. ▷from Arabic *sawāḥil,* plural of *sāḥil* 'coast.'

swain /swān/ ▸*n. archaic* a country youth. ■ *poetic/literary* a young lover or suitor. ▷late Old English (denoting a young man attendant on a knight), from Old Norse *sveinn* 'lad.'

Swain·son's hawk /ˈswānsənz/ ▸*n.* a dark-colored, narrow-winged buteo of western North America. • *Buteo swainsoni,* family Accipitridae. ▷mid 19th cent.: named after William *Swainson* (1789–1855), English naturalist.

Swainson's hawk

SWAK ▸*abbr.* sealed with a kiss (written on the flap of an envelope).

swale /swāl/ ▸*n.* a low or hollow place, esp. a marshy depression between ridges. ▷early 16th cent.: British, of unknown origin.

swal·low[1] /ˈswälō/ ▸*v.* [*trans.*] cause or allow (something, esp. food or drink) to pass down the throat: *she swallowed a mouthful slowly.* ■ [*intrans.*] perform the muscular movement of the esophagus required to do this, esp. through fear or nervousness: *she swallowed hard, sniffing back her tears.* ■ put up with or meekly accept (something insulting or unwelcome): *he seemed ready to swallow any insult.* ■ believe unquestioningly (a lie or unlikely assertion): *she had swallowed his story hook, line, and sinker.* ■ resist expressing (a feeling) or uttering (words): *he swallowed his pride.* ■ take in and cause to disappear; engulf: *the dark mist **swallowed** her **up**.* ■ completely use up (money or resources): *debts **swallowed up** most of the money he had gotten for the house.*
▸*n.* an act of swallowing something, esp. food or drink: *he downed his drink in one swallow.* ■ an amount of something swallowed in one action: *he said he'd like just **a swallow of** pie.* ▷Old English *swelgan,* of Germanic origin; related to Dutch *zwelgen* and German *schwelgen.* —**swal·low·a·ble** *adj.* —**swal·low·er** *n.*

swal·low[2] ▸*n.* a migratory swift-flying songbird with a forked tail and long pointed wings, feeding on insects in flight. • Family Hirundinidae: several genera, in particular *Hirundo,* and numerous species, including the widespread **barn swallow** (*H. rustica*). ▷Old English *swealwe,* of Germanic origin; related to Dutch *zwaluw* and German *Schwalbe.*

barn swallow

▸*PHRASE* □ **one swallow does not make a summer** *proverb* a single fortunate event does not mean that what follows will also be good.

swal·low dive ▸*n.* British term for **swan dive**.

swal·low·tail /ˈswälō,tāl/ ▸*n.* **1** (also **swallowtail butterfly**) a large brightly colored butterfly with taillike projections (suggestive of a swallow's tail) on the hind wings. • Family Papilionidae: many genera and species, including the **pipevine swallowtail** (*Battus philenor*) of southern North America and the **eastern**

tiger swallowtail (*Papilio glaucus*) of eastern North America. **2** [usu. as *adj.*] a deeply forked tail; a thing resembling such a tail in shape: *swallowtail suits.* **—swal·low-tailed** *adj.*

eastern tiger swallowtail

swal·low·wort /ˈswälōwərt; -ˌwôrt/ ▸*n.* **1** a plant of the milkweed family, the follicles of which suggest a swallow with outstretched wings, often becoming a weed. • Several species in the family Asclepiadaceae, in particular the **black swallowwort** (*Cynanchum* (or **Vincetoxicum**) *nigrum*). **2** *chiefly Brit.* the greater celandine, formerly believed to be used by swallows to restore their sight.

swam /swam/ ▸ past of **SWIM**.

swa·mi /ˈswämē/ ▸*n.* (*pl.* **-mis**) a Hindu male religious teacher: [as *title*] *Swami Satchidananda.* ▷from Hindi *swāmī* 'master, prince,' from Sanskrit *svāmin.*

Swam·mer·dam /ˈsvämərˌdäm/, Jan (1637–80), Dutch naturalist and microscopist. He classified insects into four groups and was the first to observe red blood cells.

swamp /swämp/ ▸*n.* an area of low-lying, uncultivated ground where water collects; a bog or marsh. ■ used to emphasize the degree to which a piece of ground is waterlogged: *the ceaseless deluge had turned the lawn into a swamp.*
▸*v.* [*trans.*] overwhelm or flood with water: *a huge wave swamped the canoes.* ■ *figurative* overwhelm with an excessive amount of something; inundate: *feelings of guilt suddenly swamped her | the country* **was swamped with** *goods from abroad.* ■ [*intrans.*] (of a boat) become overwhelmed with water and sink. ▷early 17th cent.: probably ultimately from a Germanic base meaning 'sponge' or 'fungus.' **—swamp·y** *adj.*

swamp bug·gy ▸*n.* an amphibious vehicle with wheels or a continuous track and an elevated body, used for navigating marshes or swamps.

swamp cab·bage ▸*n.* skunk cabbage, esp. the species of western North America (*Lysichitum americanum*), the leaves of which are sometimes used in cooking.

swamp cy·press ▸*n.* chiefly British term for **BALD CYPRESS**.

swamp·er /ˈswämpər/ ▸*n. informal, dated* **1** a laborer, esp. one employed as a general assistant to a riverboat captain. ■ a worker who trims felled trees and clears a road for lumberers in a forest. **2** a native or inhabitant of a swampy region.

swamp fe·ver ▸*n.* **1** a contagious viral disease of horses that causes anemia and emaciation and is usually fatal. **2** *dated* malaria.

Swamp Fox see **MARION**.

swamp gas ▸*n.* another term for **MARSH GAS**.

swamp·land /ˈswämpˌland/ ▸*n.* (also **swamplands**) land consisting of swamps.

Swan /swän/, Sir Joseph Wilson (1828–1914), English physicist and chemist. He devised an electric light bulb in 1860, and in 1883 he formed a partnership with Thomas Edison to manufacture it.

swan /swän/ ▸*n.* a large waterbird with a long flexible neck, short legs, webbed feet, a broad bill, and typically all-white plumage. • Genus *Cygnus* (and *Coscoroba*): several species.
▸*v.* (**swanned, swan·ning**) [*intrans.*] *informal* move about or go somewhere in a casual, relaxed way, typically perceived as irresponsible or ostentatious by others: *swanning around in a $2,000 sharkskin suit doesn't make you a Renaissance prince.* ▷Old English, of Germanic origin; related to Dutch *zwaan* and German *Schwan.* **—swan·like** /-ˌlīk/ *adj.*

swan dive ▸*n.* a dive performed with one's arms outspread until close to the water.
▸*v.* [*intrans.*] (**swan-dive**) perform a swan drive.

swank /swaNGk/ *informal* ▸*v.* [*intrans.*] display one's wealth, knowledge, or achievements in a way that is intended to impress others: **swanking about,** *playing the dashing young master spy.*
▸*n.* behavior, talk, or display intended to impress others: *a little money will buy you a good deal of swank.*
▸*adj.* another term for **SWANKY**: *coming out of some swank nightclub.* ▷early 19th cent.: of unknown origin.

swank·y /ˈswaNGkē/ ▸*adj.* (**swank·i·er, swank·i·est**) *informal* stylishly luxurious and expensive: *directors with swanky company cars.* ■ using one's wealth, knowledge, or achievements to try to impress others. **—swank·i·ly** /-kəlē/ *adv.* **—swank·i·ness** *n.*

swan neck ▸*n.* a curved structure shaped like a swan's neck: [as *adj.*] *a small swan-neck dispenser.* ■ another term for **GOOSENECK**. **—swan-necked** *adj.*

swan·ner·y /ˈswänərē/ ▸*n.* (*pl.* **-ner·ies**) a place set aside for swans to breed.

Swan Riv·er a river in western Australia. Rising as the Avon River southeast of Perth, it flows north and west through Perth to the Indian Ocean at Fremantle. It was the site of the first free European settlement in the state of Western Australia.

swans·down /ˈswänzˌdoun/ (also **swan's down**) ▸*n.* **1** the fine down of a swan, used for trimmings and powder puffs. **2** a thick cotton fabric with a soft nap on one side, used esp. for baby clothes. ■ a soft, thick fabric made from wool mixed with a little silk or cotton.

Swan·sea /ˈswänzē/ a city in southern Wales, on the Bristol Channel; pop. 182,000. Welsh name **ABERTAWE**.

Swan·son /ˈswänsən/, Gloria (1899–1983), U.S. actress; born *Gloria May Josephine Svensson.* She was a major star of silent movies, such as *Sadie Thompson* (1928), but is chiefly known for her performance as the fading movie star in *Sunset Boulevard* (1950).

swan song ▸*n.* a person's final public performance or professional activity before retirement: *he has decided to make this tour his swan song.* ▷early 19th cent.: suggested by German *Schwanengesang,* a song like that fabled to be sung by a dying swan.

swan-up·ping ▸*n. Brit.* the annual practice of catching the swans on the River Thames and marking them to indicate their ownership.

swap /swäp/ (also **swop**) ▸*v.* (**swapped, swap·ping**) [*trans.*] take part in an exchange of: *we swapped phone numbers | I'd* **swap** *places* **with** *you any day |* [*intrans.*] *I was wondering if you'd like to* **swap with** *me.* ■ give (one thing) and receive something else in exchange: **swap** *one of your sandwiches* **for** *a cheese and pickle?* ■ substitute (one thing) for another: *I* **swapped** *my busy life on Wall Street* **for** *a peaceful mountain retreat.*
▸*n.* an act of exchanging one thing for another: *let's* **do a swap.** ■ a thing that has been or may be given in exchange for something else: *I've got one already, but I'll keep this as a swap.* ■ *Finance* an exchange of liabilities between two borrowers, either so that each acquires access to funds in a currency they need or so that a fixed interest rate is exchanged for a floating rate. ▷Middle English (originally in the sense 'throw forcibly'): probably imitative of a resounding blow. Current senses have arisen from an early use meaning 'clasp hands as a token of agreement.' **—swap·pa·ble** *adj.* **—swap·per** *n.*

swap·file /ˈswäpˌfīl/ ▸*n. Computing* a file on a hard disk used to provide space for programs that have been transferred from the processor's memory.

swap meet ▸*n.* a gathering at which enthusiasts or collectors trade or exchange items of common interest: *a computer swap meet.* ■ a flea market.

SWAPO /ˈswäpō/ (also **Swapo**) ▸*abbr.* South West Africa People's Organization.

swap shop ▸*n. informal* an agency that provides a communication channel for people with articles to exchange or trade: *radio swap shops remain popular ways to exchange goods in farm communities.* ■ an event to which people are invited to bring articles for exchange or trade.

swap·tion /ˈswäpSHən/ ▸*n. Finance* an option giving the right but not the obligation to engage in a swap. ▷1980s: blend of **SWAP** and **OPTION**.

sward /swôrd/ ▸*n.* an expanse of short grass. ■ *Farming* the upper layer of soil, esp. when covered with grass. ▷Old English *sweard* 'skin.' The sense 'upper layer of soil' developed in late Middle English (at first in phrases such as *sward of the earth*). **—sward·ed** *adj.*

sware /swe(ə)r/ ▸ archaic past of **SWEAR**.

swarm /swôrm/ ▸*n.* a large or dense group of insects, esp. flying ones. ■ a large number of honeybees that leave a hive en masse with a newly fertilized queen in order to establish a new colony. ■ **(a swarm/swarms of)** a large number of people or things: *a swarm of journalists.* ■ a series of similar-sized earthquakes occurring together, typically near a volcano. ■ *Astronomy* a large number of minor celestial objects occurring together in space, esp. a dense shower of meteors.
▸*v.* **1** [*intrans.*] (of insects) move in or form a swarm: [as *adj.*] (**swarming**) *swarming locusts.* ■ (of honeybees, ants, or termites) issue from the nest in large numbers with a newly fertilized queen in order to found new colonies: *the bees had swarmed and left the hive.* **2** [*intrans.*] move somewhere in large numbers: *protesters were swarming into the building.* ■ (**swarm with**) (of a place) be crowded or overrun with (moving people or things): *the place was swarming with police.*
▸*phrasal v.* □ **swarm up** climb (something) rapidly by gripping it with one's hands and feet, alternately hauling and pushing oneself upward: *I swarmed up the mast.* [mid 16th cent.: of unknown origin.] ▷Old English *swearm* (noun), of Germanic origin; related to German *Schwarm,* probably also to the base of Sanskrit *svarati* 'it sounds.'

swarm·er /ˈswôrmər/ (also **swarm·er cell**) ▸*n. Biology* another term for **ZOOSPORE**.

swart /swôrt/ ▸*adj. archaic* or *poetic/literary* swarthy. ▷Old English *sweart,* of Germanic origin; related to Dutch *zwart* and German *schwarz.*

swarth·y /ˈswôrT͟Hē/ ▸*adj.* (**swarth·i·er, swarth·i·est**) dark-skinned: *she looked frail standing next to her strong and swarthy brother.* ▷late 16th cent.: alteration of obsolete *swarty* (see **SWART**). **—swarth·i·ly** /-T͟Hələ̄/ *adv.* **—swarth·i·ness** *n.*

swash[1] /swôSH; swäSH/ ▸*v.* [*intrans.*] **1** (of water or an object in water) move with a splashing sound: *the water swashed and rippled around the car wheels.* **2** *archaic* (of a person) flamboyantly swagger about or wield a sword: *he swashed about self-confidently.*
▸*n.* the rush of seawater up the beach after the breaking of a wave. ■ *archaic* the motion or sound of water dashing or washing against something. ▷mid 16th cent. (in the sense 'make a noise like swords clashing or beating on shields'): imitative.

swash[2] ▸*adj. Printing* denoting an ornamental written or printed character, typically a capital letter. ▷late 17th cent.: of unknown origin.

swash·buck·le /ˈswôSHˌbəkəl; ˈswäSH-/ ▸*v.* [*intrans.*] [usu. as *adj.*] (**swashbuckling**) engage in daring and romantic adventures with ostentatious bravado or flamboyance: *a crew of swashbuckling buccaneers.* ▷late 19th cent.: back-formation from **SWASHBUCKLER**.

swash·buck·ler /ˈswôSHˌbəklər; ˈswäSH-/ ▸*n.* a swashbuckling person. ▷mid 16th cent.: from **SWASH**[1] + **BUCKLER**.

swash plate ▸*n.* an inclined disk revolving on an axle and giving reciprocating motion to a part in contact with it.

swas·ti·ka /ˈswästikə/ ▸*n.* an ancient symbol in the form of an equal-armed cross with each arm continued at a right angle, used (in clockwise form) as the emblem of the German Nazi Party. ▷late 19th cent.: from Sanskrit *svastika,* from *svasti* 'well-being,' from *su* 'good' + *asti* 'being.'

swastika

swat /swät/ ▸*v.* (**swat·ted, swat·ting**) [*trans.*] hit or crush (something, esp. an insect) with a sharp blow from a flat object: *I swatted a mosquito that had landed on my wrist |* [*intrans.*] **swatting at** *a fly.* ■ hit (someone) with a sharp blow: *she swatted him over the head with a rolled-up magazine.*
▸*n.* such a sharp blow: *the dog gave the hedgehog a sideways swat.* ▷early 17th cent. (in the sense 'sit down'): northern English dialect and U.S. variant of **SQUAT**.

swatch /swäCH/ ▸*n.* a sample, esp. of fabric. ■ a collection of such samples, esp. in the form of a book. ■ a patch or area of a material or surface: *the sunset had filled the sky with swatches of deep orange.* ▷early 16th cent. (originally Scots and northern English, denoting the counterfoil of a tally, and later a tally fixed to a piece of cloth before dyeing): of unknown origin.

swath /swäTH; swôTH/ (also **swathe** /swäT͟H; swôT͟H; swāT͟H/) ▸*n.* (*pl.* **swaths** /swäTHs; swôTHs/ or **swathes** /swāT͟Hz/) **1** a row or line of grass, grain, or other crop as it lies when mown or reaped. ■ a strip left clear by the passage of a mowing machine or scythe: *the combine had cut a deep swath around the border of the*

Pronunciation Key ə ago; ər over; ˈə or ˌə up; ˈər or ˌər fur; a hat; ā rate; ä car; CH chew; e let; ē see; e(ə)r air; i fit; ī by; i(ə)r ear; NG sing; ō go; ô for; oi boy; o͝o good; o͞o goo; ou out; SH she; TH thin; T͟H then; (h)w why; ZH vision

S

fields. **2** a broad strip or area of something: *vast* **swaths** *of countryside* | *figurative a significant* **swath** *of popular opinion.* ▷Old English *swæth, swathu* 'track, trace'; related to Dutch *zwad(e)* and German *Schwade.* In Middle English the term denoted a measure of the width of grassland, probably reckoned by a sweep of the mower's scythe.

▸*PHRASES* □ **cut a swath through** pass through (something) causing great damage, destruction, or change: *a tornado cut a two-mile long swath through residential neighborhoods.* □ **cut a wide swath** attract a great deal of attention by trying to impress others.

swathe /swäTH; swāTH/ ▸*v.* [*trans.*] (usu. **be swathed in**) wrap in several layers of fabric: *his hands were swathed in bandages.*

▸*n.* a piece or strip of material in which something is wrapped. ▷late Old English *swath-* (noun), *swathian* (verb); compare with SWADDLE.

swath·er /'swäTHər; 'swäTH-/ ▸*n.* a device on a mowing machine for raising uncut fallen grain and marking the line between cut and uncut grain.

Swa·tow /'swä'tou/ former name of **SHANTOU**.

SWAT team /swät/ ▸*n.* a group of elite police marksmen who specialize in high-risk tasks such as hostage rescue. ■ any group of specialists brought in to solve a difficult or urgent problem: *an economic SWAT team that aims to bolster the region's hunting and outdoor recreation industry.* ▷1980s: acronym from *Special Weapons and Tactics.*

sway /swā/ ▸*v.* move or cause to move slowly or rhythmically backward and forward or from side to side: [*intrans.*] *he swayed slightly on his feet* | [as *adj.*] (**swaying**) *swaying palm trees* | [*trans.*] *wind rattled and swayed the trees.* ■ [*trans.*] control or influence (a person or course of action): *he's easily swayed by other people.* ■ *poetic/literary* rule; govern: *now let the Lord forever reign and sway us as he will.*

▸*phrasal v.* □ **sway something up** *Nautical* hoist a mast into position.

▸*n.* **1** a rhythmical movement from side to side: *the easy sway of her hips.* **2** rule; control: *the part of the continent* **under** *Russia's* **sway.** See note at **JURISDICTION**. ▷Middle English: corresponding in sense to Low German *swājen* 'be blown to and fro' and Dutch *zwaaien* 'swing, walk totteringly.'

▸*PHRASE* □ **hold sway** have great power or influence over a particular person, place, or domain.

sway·back /'swā,bak/ ▸*n.* an abnormally hollowed back, esp. in a horse; lordosis. **—sway-backed** *adj.*

Swayne /swān/, Noah Haynes (1804–84), U.S. Supreme Court associate justice 1862–81. Appointed to the Court by President Lincoln, he opposed slavery and advocated expanded federal powers.

Swa·zi /'swäzē/ ▸*n.* (*pl.* same or **-zis**) **1** a member of a people inhabiting Swaziland and parts of eastern Transvaal. ■ a native or national of Swaziland. **2** the Nguni language of this people, an official language in Swaziland and South Africa.

▸*adj.* of or relating to Swaziland, the Swazis, or their language. ▷from the name of *Mswati,* a 19th-century king of the Swazis.

Swa·zi·land /'swäzē,land/ a small landlocked kingdom in southern Africa, bounded by South Africa and Mozambique; pop. 1,169,000; capital, Mbabane; languages, Swazi and English (both official).

Swaziland was a South African protectorate from 1894 and came under British rule in 1902 after the Second Boer War. In 1968 it became a fully independent Commonwealth of Nations state.

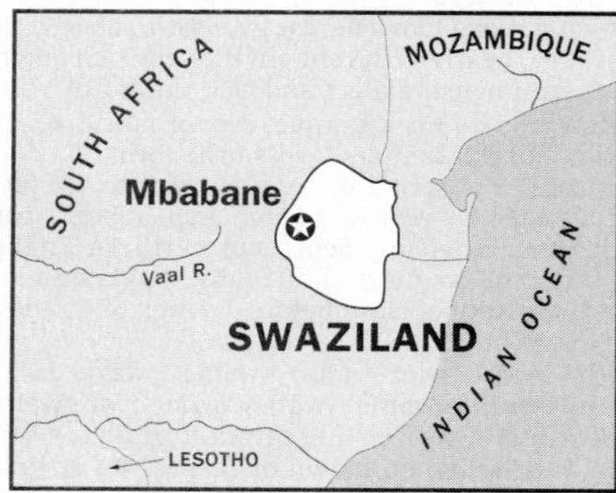

SWB ▸*abbr.* short wheelbase.

swbd. ▸*abbr.* switchboard.

SWbS ▸*abbr.* southwest by south.

SWbW ▸*abbr.* southwest by west.

Swe. ▸*abbr.* ■ Sweden. ■ Swedish.

swear /swe(ə)r/ ▸*v.* (*past* **swore** /swôr/; *past part.* **sworn** /swôrn/) **1** [*reporting verb*] make a solemn statement or promise undertaking to do something or affirming that something is the case: [with *clause*] *Maria made me swear I would never tell anyone* | *I* **swear by** *all I hold dear that I had nothing to do with it* | [with *infinitive*] *he swore to obey the rules* | [with *direct speech*] *"Never again," she swore, "will I be short of money"* | [*trans.*] *they were reluctant to swear allegiance.* ■ [*trans.*] take (an oath): *he forced them to swear an oath of loyalty to him.* ■ [*trans.*] take a solemn oath as to the truth of (a statement): *I asked him if he would swear a statement to this effect.* ■ [*trans.*] (**swear someone in**) admit someone to a particular office or position by directing them to take a formal oath: *he was sworn in as president on July 10.* ■ [*trans.*] make (someone) promise to observe a certain course of action: *I've been* **sworn to** *secrecy.* ■ [*intrans.*] (**swear to**) express one's assurance that something is the case: *I couldn't swear to it, but I'm pretty sure it's his writing.* ■ [*intrans.*] (**swear off**) *informal* promise to abstain from: *I'd sworn off alcohol.* ■ [*intrans.*] (**swear by**) *informal* have or express great confidence in the use, value, or effectiveness of: *Iris swears by her yoga.* **2** [*intrans.*] use offensive language, esp. as an expression of anger: *Peter swore under his breath.*

▸*phrasal v.* □ **swear something out** *Law* obtain the issue of (a warrant for arrest) by making a charge on oath. ▷Old English *swerian,* of Germanic origin; related to Dutch *zweren,* German *schwören,* also to **ANSWER**. **—swear·er** *n.*

▸*PHRASE* □ **swear up and down** *informal* affirm something emphatically: *he swore up and down they'd never get him up on that stage.*

swear word ▸*n.* an offensive word, used esp. as an expression of anger.

sweat /swet/ ▸*n.* **1** moisture exuded through the pores of the skin, typically in profuse quantities as a reaction to heat, physical exertion, fever, or fear. ■ an instance of exuding moisture in this way over a period of time: *even thinking about him made me* **break out in a sweat.** | *we'd all* **worked up a sweat** *in spite of the cold.* ■ *informal* a state of flustered anxiety or distress: *I don't believe he'd* **get into** *such* **a sweat** *about a girl.* ■ *informal* hard work; effort: *computer graphics take a lot of the sweat out of animation.* **2** (**sweats**) informal term for **SWEATSUIT** or **SWEATPANTS**. ■ [as *adj.*] denoting loose casual garments made of thick, fleecy cotton: *sweat tops and bottoms.*

▸*v.* (*past* **sweat·ed** or **sweat**) **1** [*intrans.*] exude sweat: *he was sweating profusely.* ■ [*trans.*] (**sweat something out/off**) get rid of (something) from the body by exuding sweat: *a well-hydrated body sweats out waste products more efficiently.* ■ [*trans.*] cause (a person or animal) to exude sweat by exercise or exertion: *cold as it was, the climb had sweated him.* ■ (of food or an object) ooze or exude beads of moisture onto its surface: *cheese stored at room temperature will quickly begin to sweat.* ■ (of a person) exert a great deal of strenuous effort: *I've* **sweated over** *this for six months.* ■ (of a person) be or remain in a state of extreme anxiety, typically for a prolonged period: *I let her sweat for a while, then I asked her out again.* ■ [*trans.*] *informal* worry about (something): *he's not going to have a lot of time to sweat the details.* **2** [*trans.*] heat (chopped vegetables) slowly in a pan with a small amount of fat, so that they cook in their own juices: *sweat the celery and onions with olive oil and seasoning.* ■ [*intrans.*] (of chopped vegetables) be cooked in this way: *let the chopped onion sweat gently for five minutes.* **3** [*trans.*] subject (metal) to surface melting, esp. to fasten or join by solder without a soldering iron: *the tire is sweated on to the wooden parts.* ▷Old English *swāt* (noun), *swǣtan* (verb), of Germanic origin; related to Dutch *zweet* and German *Schweiss,* from an Indo-European root shared by Latin *sudor.*

▸*PHRASES* □ **break a sweat** *informal* exert oneself physically. □ **by the sweat of one's brow** by one's own hard work, typically manual labor. □ **don't sweat it** used to urge someone not to worry. □ **no sweat** *informal* used to convey that one perceives no difficulty or problem with something: *"We haven't any decaf, I'm afraid." "No sweat."* □ **sweat blood** *informal* make an extraordinarily strenuous effort to do something: *she's sweated blood to support her family.* ■ be extremely anxious: *we've been sweating blood over the question of what is right.* □ **sweat buckets** *informal* sweat profusely. □ **sweat bullets** *informal* be extremely anxious or nervous. □ **sweat it out** *informal* endure an unpleasant experience, typically one involving physical exertion in great heat: *about 1,500 runners are expected to sweat it out in this year's run.* ■ wait in a state of extreme anxiety for something to happen or be resolved: *he sweated it out until the lab report was back.* □ **sweat the small stuff** worry about trivial things.

sweat·band /'swet,band/ ▸*n.* a band of absorbent material worn around the head or wrist to soak up sweat, esp. by participants in sports. ■ a band of absorbent material lining a hat.

sweat eq·ui·ty ▸*n. informal* an interest or increased value in a property earned from labor toward upkeep or restoration.

sweat·er /'swetər/ ▸*n.* **1** a knitted garment typically with long sleeves, worn over the upper body. **2** *dated* an employer who works employees hard in poor conditions for low pay.

sweat·er set ▸*n.* another term for **TWINSET**.

sweat gland ▸*n.* a small gland that secretes sweat, situated in the dermis of the skin. Such glands are found over most of the body, and have a simple coiled tubular structure.

sweat·ing sick·ness ▸*n.* any of various fevers with intense sweating, epidemic in England in the 15th–16th centuries.

sweat lodge ▸*n.* a hut, typically dome-shaped and made with natural materials, used by North American Indians for ritual steam baths as a means of purification.

sweat·pants /'swet,pants/ ▸*plural n.* loose, warm trousers with an elasticized or drawstring waist, worn when exercising or as leisurewear.

sweat·shirt /'swet,SHərt/ ▸*n.* a loose, heavy shirt, typically made of cotton, worn when exercising or as leisurewear.

sweat·shop /'swet,SHäp/ ▸*n.* a factory or workshop, esp. in the clothing industry, where manual workers are employed at very low wages for long hours and under poor conditions.

sweat sock ▸*n.* a thick, absorbent, calf-length sock, often worn with athletic shoes.

sweat·suit /'swet,so͞ot/ ▸*n.* a suit consisting of a sweatshirt and sweatpants, worn when exercising or as leisurewear.

sweat·y /'swetē/ ▸*adj.* (**sweat·i·er, sweat·i·est**) exuding, soaked in, or inducing sweat: *my feet got so hot and sweaty.* **—sweat·i·ly** /'swetəlē/ *adv.* **—sweat·i·ness** *n.*

Swede /swēd/ ▸*n.* a native or national of Sweden, or a person of Swedish descent. ▷from Middle Low German and Middle Dutch *Swēde,* probably from Old Norse *Svíthjóth,* from *Svíar* 'Swedes' + *thjóth* 'people.'

swede /swēd/ ▸*n.* British term for **RUTABAGA**. ▷early 19th cent.: from **SWEDE**, being first introduced into Scotland from Sweden in 1781–82.

Swe·den /'swēdn/ a country that occupies the eastern part of the Scandinavian peninsula; pop. 8,986,000; capital, Stockholm; language, Swedish (official). Swedish name **SVERIGE**.

Originally united in the 12th century, Sweden formed part of the Union of Kalmar with Denmark and Norway from 1397 until its reemergence as an independent kingdom in 1523. Between 1814 and 1905, it was united with Norway. A constitutional monarchy, Sweden has pursued a policy of nonalignment, and it remained neutral in the two world wars. Sweden joined the European Union in 1995.

Swe·den·borg /ˈswēdnˌbôrg/, Emanuel (1688–1772), Swedish scientist, philosopher, and mystic. The spiritual beliefs that he expounded after a series of mystical experiences blended Christianity with pantheism and theosophy. **—Swe·den·bor·gi·an** /ˌswēdənˈbôrgēən/ *adj.* & *n.*

Swede saw ▶*n. chiefly Canadian* a type of saw with a bowlike tubular frame and many cutting teeth. ▷*Swede* in the sense 'Swedish.'

Swed·ish /ˈswēdisн/ ▶*adj.* of or relating to Sweden, its people, or their language.
▶*n.* the North Germanic language of Sweden, also spoken in parts of Finland.

Swed·ish mas·sage ▶*n.* a popular general-purpose system of massage, devised in Sweden.

sweep /swēp/ ▶*v.* (*past* **swept** /swept/) **1** [*trans.*] clean (an area) by brushing away dirt or litter: *I've swept the floor | Greg **swept out** the kitchen.* ■ [*trans.*] move or remove (dirt or litter) in such a way: *she swept the tea leaves into a dustpan.* ■ [*trans.*] move or push (someone or something) with great force: *I was swept along by the crowd.* ■ [*trans.*] brush (hair) back from one's face or upward: *long hair swept up into a high chignon.* ■ search (an area) for something: *the detective swept the room for hair and fingerprints.* ■ examine (a place or thing) for electronic listening devices: *the line is swept every fifteen minutes.* ■ cover (an entire area) with a gun: *they were trying to get the Lewis gun up behind some trees from where they would sweep the trench.* **2** [*intrans.*] move swiftly and smoothly: *a large black car swept past the open windows | figurative a wave of sympathy swept over him.* ■ [*trans.*] cause to move swiftly and smoothly: *he swept his hand around the room.* ■ (of a person) move in a confident and stately manner: *she swept magnificently from the hall.* ■ (of a geographical or natural feature) extend continuously in a particular direction, esp. in a curve: *green forests swept down the hillsides.* ■ [*trans.*] look swiftly over: *her eyes swept the room.* ■ affect (an area or place) swiftly and widely: *violence swept the country | [intrans.] the rebellion had swept through all four of the country's provinces.* ■ [*trans.*] win all the games in (a series); take each of the winning or main places in (a contest or event): *we knew we had to sweep these three home games.*
▶*phrasal v.* □ **sweep something away** (or **aside**) remove, dispel, or abolish something in a swift and sudden way: *Nahum's smile swept away the air of apprehensive gloom.*
▶*n.* **1** an act of sweeping something with a brush: *I was giving the floor a quick sweep.* ■ short for CHIMNEY SWEEP. **2** a long, swift, curving movement: *a grandiose sweep of his hand.* ■ a comprehensive search or survey of a place or area: *the police finished their sweep through the woods.* ■ *Electronics* the movement of a beam across the screen of a cathode-ray tube. ■ (often **sweeps**) a survey of the ratings of broadcast stations, carried out at regular intervals to determine advertising rates. **3** a long, typically curved stretch of road, river, country, etc.: *we could see a wide sweep of country perhaps a hundred miles across.* ■ a curved part of a drive in front of a building: *one fork of the drive continued on to the gravel sweep.* ■ *figurative* the range or scope of something: *the whole sweep of the history of the USSR.* See note at RANGE. **4** *informal* a sweepstake. **5** an instance of winning every event, award, or place in a contest: *a World Series sweep.* **6** a long heavy oar used to row a barge or other vessel: [as *adj.*] *a big, heavy sweep oar.* **7** a sail of a windmill. **8** a long pole mounted as a lever for raising buckets from a well. ▷Old English *swāpan* (verb), of Germanic origin; related to German *schweifen* 'sweep in a curve.'
▶*PHRASES* □ **a clean sweep** see CLEAN. □ **sweep the board** (or **boards**) win every event or prize in a contest. □ **sweep someone off their feet** see FOOT. □ **sweep something under the rug** (or **carpet**) conceal or ignore a problem or difficulty in the hope that it will be forgotten.

sweep·back /ˈswēpˌbak/ ▶*n.* the angle at which an aircraft's wing is set back from a right angle to the body.

sweep·er /ˈswēpər/ ▶*n.* **1** a person or device that cleans a floor or road by sweeping. **2** a small nocturnal shoaling fish of reefs and coastal waters, occurring chiefly in the tropical Indo-Pacific. • Family Pempheridae: several genera and species, including the western Atlantic **glassy sweeper** (*Pempheris schomburgki*), with transparent young.

sweep·ing /ˈswēpiNG/ ▶*adj.* wide in range or effect: *we cannot recommend any sweeping alterations.* ■ extending or performed in a long, continuous curve: *sweeping, desolate moorlands | a smooth sweeping motion.* ■ (of a statement) taking no account of particular cases or exceptions; too general: *a sweeping assertion.*
▶*n.* (**sweepings**) dirt or refuse collected by sweeping: *the sweepings from the house.* **—sweep·ing·ly** *adv.* **—sweep·ing·ness** *n.*

sweep sec·ond hand ▶*n.* a second hand on a clock or watch, moving on the same dial as the other hands.

sweep·stake /ˈswēpˌstāk/ ▶*n.* (also **sweepstakes**) a form of gambling, esp. on horse races, in which all the stakes are divided among the winners: [as *adj.*] *a sweepstake ticket.* ■ a race on which money is bet in this way. ■ a prize or prizes won in a sweepstake.

Sweet /swēt/ , Sarah C., see JEWETT.

sweet /swēt/ ▶*adj.* **1** having the pleasant taste characteristic of sugar or honey; not salty, sour, or bitter: *a cup of hot sweet tea | figurative a sweet taste of success.* ■ (of air, water, or food) fresh, pure, and untainted: *lungfuls of the clean, sweet air.* ■ [often in *combination*] smelling pleasant like flowers or perfume; fragrant: *sweet-smelling flowers.* **2** pleasing in general; delightful: *it was the sweet life he had always craved.* ■ highly satisfying or gratifying: *some sweet, short-lived revenge.* ■ [often as *exclam.*] *informal* used in expressions of assent or approval: *Yeah, I'd like to come to the party. Sweet.* ■ working, moving, or done smoothly or easily: *the sweet handling of this motorcycle.* ■ (of sound) melodious or harmonious: *the sweet notes of the flute.* ■ denoting music, esp. jazz, played at a steady tempo without improvisation. **3** (of a person or action) pleasant and kind or thoughtful: *a very sweet nurse came along.* ■ (esp. of a person or animal) charming and endearing: *a sweet little cat.* ■ [*predic.*] (**sweet on**) *informal, dated* infatuated or in love with: *she seemed quite sweet on him.* ■ dear; beloved: *my sweet love.* ■ *archaic* used as a respectful form of address: *go to thy rest, sweet sir.* **4** used for emphasis in various phrases and exclamations: *What had happened? Sweet nothing.* ■ (**one's own sweet ——**) used to emphasize the unpredictable individuality of someone's actions: *I'd rather carry on in my own sweet way.*
▶*n.* **1** *chiefly Brit.* a small shaped piece of confectionery made with sugar: *a bag of sweets.* **2** (**sweets**) sweet foods, collectively: *Americans eat too many sweets.* ■ *Brit.* a sweet dish forming a course of a meal; a dessert: *she served up a lovely sweet made with whipped chestnuts and almond paste.* **3** used as an affectionate form of address to a person one is very fond of: *hello, my sweet.* **4** (**the sweet**) *archaic* or *poetic/literary* the sweet part or element of something: *you have had the bitter, now comes the sweet.* ■ (**sweets**) the pleasures or delights found in something: *the sweets of office.* ▷Old English *swēte*, of Germanic origin; related to Dutch *zoet*, German *süss*, from an Indo-European root shared by Latin *suavis* and Greek *hēdus*. **—sweet·ish** *adj.* **—sweet·ly** *adv.*
▶*PHRASES* □ **sweet dreams** used to express good wishes to a person going to bed. □ **sweet sixteen** used to refer to the age of sixteen as characterized by prettiness and innocence in a girl.

sweet a·ca·cia ▶*n.* another term for HUISACHE.

sweet alys·sum ▶*n.* see ALYSSUM.

sweet-and-sour ▶*adj.* [*attrib.*] (esp. of Chinese-style food) cooked in a sauce containing sugar and either vinegar or lemon.

sweet balm ▶*n.* see BALM (sense 3).

sweet bas·il ▶*n.* see BASIL.

sweet bay ▶*n.* see BAY[2].

sweet birch ▶*n.* a North American birch, esp. of Appalachian forests, with brown or black bark and smooth twigs that smell of wintergreen when broken or crushed. The leaves and sap of sweet birch yield oil of wintergreen (see WINTERGREEN). Also called BLACK BIRCH. • *Betula lenta*, family Betulaceae.

sweet·bread /ˈswētˌbred/ ▶*n.* the thymus gland (or, rarely, the pancreas) of an animal, esp. as used for food.

sweet·bri·er /ˈswētˌbrīər/ (also **sweet·bri·ar**) ▶*n.* a Eurasian wild rose with fragrant leaves and flowers. • *Rosa eleganteria*, family Rosaceae.

sweet but·ter ▶*n.* a type of unsalted butter made from fresh pasteurized cream.

sweet cher·ry ▶*n.* another term for MAZZARD.

sweet chest·nut ▶*n.* see CHESTNUT.

sweet cic·e·ly ▶*n.* another term for CICELY.

sweet clov·er /swēt ˈklōvər/ ▶*n.* another term for MELILOT.

sweet corn ▶*n.* corn of a variety with kernels that have a high sugar content. It is grown for human consumption and is harvested while slightly immature. ■ the kernels of this plant eaten as a vegetable.

sweet·en /ˈswētn/ ▶*v.* make or become sweet or sweeter, esp. in taste: [*trans.*] *a cup of coffee sweetened with saccharin | [intrans.] her smile sweetened.* ■ [*trans.*] make more agreeable or acceptable: *there is no way to sweeten the statement.* ■ [*trans.*] *informal* induce (someone) to be well disposed or helpful to oneself: *I am in the process of **sweetening** him **up**.*
▶*PHRASES* □ **sweeten the pill** see PILL[1]. □ **sweeten the pot** add to the total sum of bets made in poker. ■ add an inducement, typically in the form of money or a concession: *he is trying to sweeten the pot, offering workers a 50-cent raise.*

sweet·en·er /ˈswētn-ər; ˈswētnər/ ▶*n.* a substance used to sweeten food or drink, esp. one other than sugar. ■ *informal* an inducement, typically in the form of money or a concession: *these sweeteners made rental cars a bargain.*

sweet fen·nel ▶*n.* see FENNEL.

sweet flag (also **sweet-flag**) ▶*n.* an Old World waterside plant of the arum family, with leaves that resemble those of the iris. It is used medicinally and as a flavoring. Also called CALAMUS. • *Acorus calamus*, family Araceae.

sweet gale ▶*n.* a deciduous shrub of boggy places, with short upright catkins and aromatic gray-green leaves. It has insecticidal properties. Also called BOG MYRTLE. • *Myrica gale*, family Myricaceae. ▷mid 17th cent.: *gale* from Old English *gagel*, *gagelle*, of Germanic origin; related to Dutch *gagel*, German *Gagel*.

sweet gal·in·gale ▶*n.* another term for GALINGALE (sense 1).

sweet·grass /ˈswētˌgras/ ▶*n.* any of a number of grasses that possess a sweet flavor, making them attractive to livestock, or a sweet smell, resulting in their former use as herbs for strewing or burning. • *Glyceria*, *Hierochloe*, and other genera, family Gramineae.

sweet gum ▶*n.* the North American liquidambar, which yields a balsam and decorative heartwood that is marketed as satin walnut. • *Liquidambar styraciflua*, family Hamamelidaceae.

sweet·heart /ˈswētˌhärt/ ▶*n.* used as a term of endearment or affectionate form of address: *don't worry, sweetheart, I've got it all worked out.* ■ a person that one is in love with: *the pair were childhood sweethearts.* ■ a particularly lovable or pleasing person or thing: *he is an absolute sweetheart.* ■ [as *adj.*] *informal* denoting an arrangement reached privately by two sides, esp. an employer and a labor union, in their own interests: *a sweetheart agreement.*

sweet·heart neck·line ▶*n.* a neckline on a dress or blouse that is low at the front and shaped like the top of a stylized heart.

sweet·heart rose ▶*n.* a rose with small pink, white, or yellow flowers that are particularly attractive as buds.

sweet·ie /ˈswētē/ *informal* ▶*n.* **1** (also **sweet·ie pie**) used as a term of endearment (esp. as a form of address). **2** a green-skinned grapefruit of a variety noted for its sweet taste.

sweet·ing /ˈswētiNG/ ▶*n.* **1** an apple of a sweet-flavored variety. **2** *archaic* darling.

sweet·lips /ˈswētˌlips/ (also **sweet·lip**) ▶*n.* (*pl.* same) a patterned grunt (fish) that changes its color and markings with age, occurring in the Indo-Pacific. • *Plectorhynchus* and other genera, family Pomadasyidae: several species, including the **oriental sweetlips** (*P. orientalis*).

sweet·meat /ˈswētˌmēt/ ▶*n.* *archaic* an item of confectionery or sweet food.

sweet milk ▶*n.* fresh whole milk, as opposed to buttermilk.

sweet·ness /ˈswētnis/ ▶*n.* the quality of being sweet. ■ used as an affectionate form of address, though often ironically: *I've just got to go, sweetness.*
▶*PHRASE* □ **sweetness and light** social or political harmony: *Khrushchev's next visit to the West was one of sweetness and light.* ■ a reasonable and peaceable person: *when he's around she's all sweetness and light.* [taken

from Swift and used with aesthetic or moral reference, first by Arnold in *Culture and Anarchy* (1869).]

sweet pea ▶*n.* a climbing plant of the pea family, widely cultivated for its colorful fragrant flowers. • Genus *Lathyrus*, family Leguminosae: several species, in particular *L. odoratus*, which originated in southern Italy and Sicily.

sweet pep·per ▶*n.* a large green, yellow, orange, or red variety of capsicum that has a mild or sweet flavor and is often eaten raw. Also called BELL PEPPER. • *Capsicum annuum* var. *annuum*, *'grossum'* group (or var. *grossum*).

sweet po·ta·to ▶*n.* **1** an edible tropical tuber with pinkish orange, slightly sweet flesh. **2** the Central American climbing plant that yields this tuber, widely cultivated in warm countries. • *Ipomoea batatas*, family Convolvulaceae. **3** *informal* another term for OCARINA.

sweet rock·et ▶*n.* a herbaceous plant of the cabbage family, cultivated for its long spikes of mauve or white flowers that are fragrant in the evening. • *Hesperis matronalis*, family Brassicaceae.

sweet·sop /ˈswēt,säp/ ▶*n.* **1** a round or heart-shaped custard apple that has a green scaly rind and a sweet pulp. Also called SUGAR APPLE. **2** the tropical American evergreen shrub that yields this fruit. • *Annona squamosa*, family Annonaceae.

sweet spot ▶*n. informal* the point or area on a bat, club, or racket at which it makes most effective contact with the ball.

sweet sul·tan ▶*n.* a Near Eastern plant of the daisy family, with sweet-scented flowers, slender stems, and narrow gray-green leaves, cultivated for garden plantings. • *Centaurea moschata*, family Compositae.

sweet talk *informal* ▶*v.* (**sweet-talk**) [*trans.*] insincerely praise (someone) in order to persuade them to do something: *detectives* ***sweet-talked them into*** *confessing.*
▶*n.* insincere praise used to persuade someone to do something.

sweet tooth ▶*n.* [usu. in *sing.*] (*pl.* **sweet tooths**) a great liking for sweet-tasting foods. —**sweet-toothed** *adj.*

sweet ver·nal grass ▶*n.* see VERNAL GRASS.

sweet vi·o·let ▶*n.* a sweet-scented Old World violet with heart-shaped leaves, used in perfumery and as a flavoring. • *Viola odorata*, family Violaceae.

sweet wil·liam (also **sweet Wil·liam**) ▶*n.* a fragrant garden pink with flattened clusters of vivid red, pink, or white flowers. • *Dianthus barbatus*, family Caryophyllaceae.

sweet wood·ruff ▶*n.* see WOODRUFF.

swell /swel/ ▶*v.* (*past part.* **swol·len** /ˈswōlən/ or **swelled**) [*intrans.*] (esp. of a part of the body) become larger or rounder in size, typically as a result of an accumulation of fluid: *her bruised knee was already* ***swelling up*** | *figurative the sky was black and swollen with rain* | [as *adj.*] (**swollen**) *swollen glands.* ■ become or make greater in intensity, number, amount, or volume: [*intrans.*] *the murmur swelled to a roar* | [as *adj.*] (**swelling**) *the swelling ranks of Irish singer-songwriters* | [*trans.*] *the population was swollen by refugees.* ■ be intensely affected or filled with a particular emotion: *she felt herself* ***swell with*** *pride.*
▶*n.* **1** [in *sing.*] a full or gently rounded shape or form: *the soft swell of her breast.* ■ a gradual increase in sound, amount, or intensity: *there was a swell of support in favor of him.* ■ a welling up of a feeling: *a swell of pride swept over George.* **2** [usu. in *sing.*] a slow, regular movement of the sea in rolling waves that do not break: *there was a heavy swell.* **3** a mechanism for producing a crescendo or diminuendo in an organ or harmonium. **4** *informal, dated* a person of wealth or high social position, typically one perceived as fashionable or stylish: *a crowd of city swells.*
▶*adj. informal, dated* excellent; very good: *you're looking swell.* ■ *archaic* smart; fashionable: *a swell boulevard.*
▶*adv. informal, dated* excellently; very well: *everything was just going swell.* ▷Old English *swellan* (verb), of Germanic origin; related to German *schwellen*. Current senses of the noun date from the early 16th cent.; the informal adjectival use derives from noun sense 4 (late 18th cent.).
▶*PHRASE* □ **someone's head swells** someone becomes conceited: *I am not saying this to make your head swell* | *if I say this, you'll get* ***swollen-headed.***

swell box ▶*n.* a part of a large organ in which some of the pipes are enclosed, with a movable shutter for controlling the sound level.

swell·ing /ˈsweliNG/ ▶*n.* an abnormal enlargement of a part of the body, typically as a result of an accumulation of fluid. ■ a natural rounded protuberance: *the lobes are prominent swellings on the base of the brain.*

swell or·gan ▶*n.* a section of a large organ consisting of pipes enclosed in a swell box, usually played with an upper keyboard.

swel·ter /ˈsweltər/ ▶*v.* [*intrans.*] (of a person or the atmosphere at a particular time or place) be uncomfortably hot: *Barney sweltered in his doorman's uniform* | [as *adj.*] (**sweltering**) *the sweltering afternoon heat.*
▶*n.* [in *sing.*] an uncomfortably hot atmosphere: *the swelter of an August day.* ▷Middle English: from the base of dialect *swelt* 'perish,' of Germanic origin. —**swel·ter·ing·ly** *adv.*

swept /swept/ ▶ past and past participle of SWEEP.

swept-back ▶*adj.* [*attrib.*] (of an aircraft wing) positioned to point somewhat backward.

swept-up ▶*adj.* another term for UPSWEPT.

swept-wing ▶*adj.* [*attrib.*] (of an aircraft) having swept-back wings.

swerve /swərv/ ▶*v.* change or cause to change direction abruptly: [*intrans.*] *a car swerved around a corner* | [*trans.*] *he swerved the truck, narrowly missing a teenager on a skateboard.*
▶*n.* an abrupt change of direction: *do not make sudden swerves, particularly around parked vehicles.* ▷Old English *sweorfan* 'depart, leave, turn aside,' of Germanic origin; related to Middle Dutch *swerven* 'to stray.' —**swerv·er** *n.*

Sweyn I /sven; svān/ (also **Sven** /sven/) (died 1014), king of Denmark *c.*985–1014; known as **Sweyn Forkbeard**. From 1003, he launched a series of attacks on England, finally causing Ethelred the Unready to flee to Normandy at the end of 1013. Sweyn then became king of England but died five weeks later.

SWF ▶*abbr.* single white female (used in personal ads).

swid·den /ˈswidn/ ▶*n.* an area of land cleared for cultivation by slashing and burning vegetation. ■ the method of clearing land in this way: *the practice of swidden.* ▷late 18th cent. (as a verb, originally dialect): variant of dialect *swithen* 'to burn.'

Swift /swift/, Jonathan (1667–1745), Irish satirist, poet, and Anglican cleric; known as **Dean Swift**. He is best known for *Gulliver's Travels* (1726), a satire on human society in the form of a fantastic tale of travels in imaginary lands.

swift /swift/ ▶*adj.* happening quickly or promptly: *a remarkably swift recovery.* ■ moving or capable of moving at high speed: *the water was very swift* | *the swiftest horse in his stable.*
▶*adv. poetic/literary except in combination* swiftly: *streams that ran swift and clear* | *a swift-acting poison.*
▶*n.* **1** a swift-flying insectivorous bird with long slender wings and a superficial resemblance to a swallow, spending most of its life on the wing. • Family Apodidae: several genera and numerous species, including the common **Eurasian swift** (*Apus apus*). **2** (also **swift moth**) a moth, typically yellow-brown in color, with fast darting flight. The eggs are scattered in flight and the larvae live underground feeding on roots, where they can be a serious pest. • Family Hepialidae: *Hepialus* and other genera. **3** a light, adjustable reel for holding a skein of silk or wool. ▷Old English (as an adjective), from the Germanic base of Old English *swīfan* 'move in a course, sweep.' The bird name dates from the mid 17th cent. —**swift·ly** *adv.* —**swift·ness** *n.*

swift fox ▶*n.* a small fox with a yellowish-buff coat and a black-tipped tail, living on the plains of North America. • *Vulpes velox*, family Canidae.

swift·let /ˈswif(t)lit/ ▶*n.* a small swift found in South Asia and Australasia. • Genera *Aerodramus* and *Collocalia*, family Apodidae: many species.

swig /swig/ *informal* ▶*v.* (**swigged** /swigd/, **swig·ging**) [*trans.*] drink in large gulps: *Dave swigged the wine in five gulps* | [*intrans.*] *old men* ***swigged from*** *bottles of plum brandy.*
▶*n.* a large draft of drink: *he took a swig of tea.* ▷mid 16th cent. (as a noun in the obsolete sense 'liquor'): of unknown origin. —**swig·ger** *n.*

swill /swil/ ▶*v.* **1** [*trans.*] *Brit.* wash or rinse out (an area or container) by pouring large amounts of water or other liquid over or into it: *I* ***swilled out*** *the mug.* ■ cause (liquid) to swirl around in a container or cavity: *she gently* ***swilled*** *her brandy* ***around*** *her glass.* ■ [*intrans.*] (of a liquid) move or splash about over a surface: *the icy water swilled around us.* **2** [*trans.*] drink (something) greedily or in large quantities: *they whiled away their evening swilling pints of beer* | [as *adj.*] (**swilling**) *his beer-swilling pals.* ■ accompany (food) with large quantities of drink: *a feast swilled down with pints of cider.*
▶*n.* **1** kitchen refuse and scraps of waste food mixed with water for feeding to pigs. ■ alcohol of inferior quality: *the beer was just warm swill.* **2** a large mouthful of a drink: *a swill of ale.* ▷Old English *swillan*, *swilian* (verb), of unknown origin. The noun dates from the mid 16th cent. —**swill·er** *n.* [usu. in *combination*] *beer-swillers.*

swim /swim/ ▶*v.* (**swim·ming**; *past* **swam** /swam/; *past part.* **swum** /swəm/) **1** [*intrans.*] propel the body through water by using the limbs, or (in the case of a fish or other aquatic animal) by using fins, tail, or other bodily movement: *they swam ashore* | *Adrian taught her to swim breaststroke.* ■ [*trans.*] cross (a particular stretch of water) in this way: *she swam the Channel.* ■ float on or at the surface of a liquid: *bubbles swam on the surface.* ■ [*trans.*] cause to float or move across water: *the Russians were able to swim their infantry carriers across.* **2** [*intrans.*] be immersed in or covered with liquid: *mashed potatoes* ***swimming in*** *gravy.* **3** [*intrans.*] appear to reel or whirl before one's eyes: *Emily rubbed her eyes as the figures swam before her eyes.* ■ experience a dizzily confusing sensation in one's head: *the drink made his head swim.*
▶*n.* **1** an act or period of swimming: *we went for a swim in the river.* **2** a pool in a river that is a particularly good spot for fishing: *he landed two 5 lb chub from the same swim.* ▷Old English *swimman* (verb), of Germanic origin; related to Dutch *zwemmen* and German *schwimmen*. —**swim·ma·ble** *adj.* —**swim·mer** *n.*
▶*PHRASES* □ **in the swim** involved in or aware of current affairs or events. □ **swim with** (or **against**) **the tide** act in accordance with (or against) the prevailing opinion or tendency.

USAGE In standard English, the past tense of **swim** is **swam** (*she* ***swam*** *to the shore*) and the past participle is **swum** (*she had never* ***swum*** *there before*).

swim blad·der ▶*n. Zoology* a gas-filled sac present in the body of many bony fishes, used to maintain and control buoyancy.

swim·mer·et /ˌswiməˈret/ ▶*n.* another term for PLEOPOD.

swim·ming /ˈswimiNG/ ▶*n.* the sport or activity of propelling oneself through water using the limbs.

swim·ming bath /ˈswimiNG ˌbaTH/ ▶*n.* (also **swimming baths**) *Brit.* a swimming pool, esp. a public indoor one.

swim·ming crab ▶*n.* a coastal crab that has paddlelike rear legs for swimming. • Family Portunidae: many species, including the **velvet swimming crab** (*Macropipus puber*).

swim·ming hole ▶*n.* a deep place for swimming in a stream or river.

swim·ming·ly /ˈswimiNGlē/ ▶*adv.* smoothly and satisfactorily: *things are going swimmingly.*

swim·ming pool ▶*n.* an artificial pool for swimming in.

swim·suit /ˈswim,so͞ot/ ▶*n.* a garment worn for swimming. —**swim·suit·ed** *adj.*

swim trunks (also **swim·ming trunks**) ▶*plural n.* shorts worn by men for swimming.

swim·wear /ˈswim,we(ə)r/ ▶*n.* clothing worn for swimming.

Swin·burne /ˈswin,bərn/, Algernon Charles (1837–1909), English poet and critic. Associated as a poet with the Pre-Raphaelites, he also contributed to the revival of interest in Elizabethan and Jacobean drama and produced influential studies of William Blake and the Brontës.

swin·dle /ˈswindl/ ▶*v.* [*trans.*] use deception to deprive (someone) of money or possessions: *a businessman* ***swindled*** *investors* ***out of*** *millions of dollars.* ■ obtain (money) fraudulently: *he was said to have swindled $62.5 million from the pension fund.*
▶*n.* a fraudulent scheme or action: *he is mixed up in a $10 million insurance swindle.* ▷late 18th cent.: back-formation from *swindler*, from German *Schwindler* 'extravagant maker of schemes, swindler,' from *schwindeln* 'be giddy,' also 'tell lies.' —**swin·dler** *n.*

Swin·don /ˈswindən/ an industrial town in central England; pop. 100,000.

swine /swīn/ ▶*n.* (*pl.* same) **1** a pig. **2** (*pl.* same or **swines**) *informal* a person regarded by the speaker with contempt and disgust: *what an arrogant, unfeeling swine!* ▷Old English *swīn*, of Germanic origin; related to Dutch *zwijn* and German *Schwein*, also to sow². —**swin·ish** *adj.* —**swin·ish·ly** *adv.* —**swin·ish·ness** *n.*

swine fe·ver ▸*n.* an intestinal viral disease of pigs.

swine·herd /ˈswin,hərd/ ▸*n. chiefly historical* a person who tends pigs. ▷Old English, from SWINE + obsolete *herd* 'herdsman.'

swine ve·sic·u·lar dis·ease /vəˈsikyələr/ ▸*n.* an infectious viral disease of pigs causing mild fever and blisters around the mouth and feet.

swing /swiNG/ ▸*v.* (*past* **swung** /swəNG/) **1** move or cause to move back and forth or from side to side while or as if suspended: [*intrans.*] *her long black skirt swung about her legs* | [*trans.*] *a priest began swinging a censer* | [as *adj.*] (**swinging**) *local girls with their castanets and their swinging hips.* ■ [often with *adverbial* or *complement*] move or cause to move in alternate directions or in either direction on an axis: [*intrans.*] *a wooden gate swinging crazily on its hinges* | [*trans.*] *he swung the heavy iron door shut.* ■ [*trans.*] turn (a ship or aircraft) to all compass points in succession, in order to test compass error. ■ [*intrans.*] *informal* be executed by hanging: *now he was going to swing for it.* **2** [*intrans.*] move by grasping a support from below and leaping: *we swung across like two trapeze artists* | (**swing oneself**) *the Irishman swung himself into the saddle.* ■ move quickly around to the opposite direction: *Ronni had swung around to face him.* ■ move with a rhythmic swaying gait: *the riflemen swung along smartly.* **3** [with *adverbial of direction*] move or cause to move in a smooth, curving line: [*trans.*] *he swung her bag up onto the rack* | [*intrans.*] *the cab swung into the parking lot.* ■ [*trans.*] bring down (something held) with a curving movement, typically in order to hit an object: *I swung the club and missed the ball.* ■ [*intrans.*] (**swing at**) attempt to hit or punch, typically with a wide curving movement of the arm: *he swung at me with the tire iron.* ■ [*trans.*] throw (a punch) with such a movement: *she swung a punch at him.* **4** shift or cause to shift from one opinion, mood, or state of affairs to another: [*intrans.*] *opinion swung in the chancellor's favor* | [*trans.*] *the failure to seek a peace could swing sentiment the other way.* ■ [*trans.*] have a decisive influence on (something, esp. a vote or election): *an attempt to swing the vote in their favor.* ■ [*trans.*] *informal* succeed in bringing about: *with us backing you we might be able to swing something.* **5** [*intrans.*] play music with an easy flowing but vigorous rhythm: *the band swung on.* ■ (of music) be played with such a rhythm. **6** [*intrans.*] *informal* (of an event, place, or way of life) be lively, exciting, or fashionable. **7** [*intrans.*] *informal* be promiscuous, typically by engaging in group sex or swapping sexual partners.

▸*n.* **1** a seat suspended by ropes or chains, on which someone may sit and swing back and forth. ■ a spell of swinging on such an apparatus. **2** an act of swinging: *with the swing of her arm, the knife flashed through the air.* ■ the manner in which a golf club or a bat is swung: *improve your golf swing.* ■ the motion of swinging: *this short cut gave her hair new movement and swing.* ■ [in *sing.*] a smooth flowing rhythm or action: *they came with a steady swing up the last reach.* **3** a discernible change in opinion: *the South's swing to the right.* **4** a style of jazz or dance music with an easy flowing but vigorous rhythm. ■ the rhythmic feeling or drive of such music. **5** a swift tour involving a number of stops, esp. one undertaken as part of a political campaign. ▷Old English *swingan* 'to beat, whip,' also 'rush,' *geswing* 'a stroke with a weapon,' of Germanic origin; related to German *schwingen* 'brandish.' —**swing·er** *n.*

▸*PHRASES* □ **get (back) into the swing of things** *informal* get used to (or return to) being easy and relaxed about an activity or routine one is engaged in. □ **in full swing** at the height of activity: *by nine-thirty the dance was in full swing.* □ **swing into action** quickly begin acting or operating.

swing bridge ▸*n.* a bridge over water that can be rotated horizontally to allow ships through.

swing·by /ˈswiNG,bī/ ▸*n.* a change in the flight path of a spacecraft using the gravitational pull of a celestial body. Compare with SLINGSHOT.

swing coat ▸*n.* a coat cut so as to swing when the wearer moves.

swinge /swinj/ ▸*v.* (**swinge·ing**) [*trans.*] *poetic/literary* strike hard; beat. ▷Old English *swengan* 'shake, shatter, move violently,' of Germanic origin.

swinge·ing /ˈswinjiNG/ ▸*adj. chiefly Brit.* severe or otherwise extreme: *swingeing cuts in public expenditure.* —**swinge·ing·ly** *adv.*

swing·ing /ˈswiNGiNG/ ▸*adj. informal* (of a person, place, or way of life) lively, exciting, and fashionable: *a swinging resort* | *the Swinging Sixties.* ■ sexually liberated or promiscuous. —**swing·ing·ly** *adv.*

swing·ing door ▸*n.* a door that can be opened in either direction and is closed by a spring device when released.

swin·gle /ˈswiNGgəl/ ▸*n.* **1** a wooden tool for beating flax and removing the woody parts from it. **2** the swinging part of a flail.

▸*v.* [*trans.*] beat (flax) with such a tool. ▷Middle English: from Middle Dutch *swinghel*, from the base of the verb SWING.

swin·gle·tree /ˈswiNGgəl,trē/ ▸*n.* chiefly British term for SINGLETREE.

swing·man /ˈswiNGmən; -,man/ ▸*n.* (*pl.* **-men**) *Basketball* a player who can play both guard and forward.

swing set ▸*n.* a frame for children to play on, typically including one or more swings and a slide.

swing shift ▸*n.* a work shift from mid-afternoon to around midnight.

swing vote ▸*n.* a vote that has a decisive influence on the result of an election. —**swing vot·er** *n.*

swing-wing ▸*n.* [usu. as *adj.*] an aircraft wing that can move from a right-angled to a swept-back position: *swing-wing fighter bombers.* ■ an aircraft with wings of this design.

swing·y /ˈswiNGē/ ▸*adj.* (**swing·i·er**, **swing·i·est**) **1** (of music) characterized by swing (see SWING (sense 4 of the *noun*)). **2** (of a skirt, coat, or other garment) cut so as to swing as the wearer moves.

swipe /swīp/ *informal* ▸*v.* [*trans.*] **1** hit or try to hit with a swinging blow: *she swiped me right across the nose* | [*intrans.*] *she lifted her hand to* **swipe at** *a cat.* **2** steal: *someone swiped one of his sausages.* **3** pass (a card with a magnetic strip) through an electronic device that reads it.

▸*n.* a sweeping blow: *he missed the ball with his first swipe.* ■ an attack or criticism: *he* **took a swipe at** *his critics.* ▷mid 18th cent.: perhaps a variant of SWEEP. —**swip·er** *n.*

swipe card ▸*n.* a plastic card such as a credit card or ID card bearing magnetically encoded information that is read when the edge of the card is slid through an electronic device.

swip·ple /ˈswipəl/ ▸*n. dialect* the swinging part of a flail. ▷late Middle English: probably based on the verb SWEEP.

swirl /swərl/ ▸*v.* [*intrans.*] move in a twisting or spiraling pattern: *the smoke was swirling around him* | [as *adj.*] (**swirling**) *figurative a flood of swirling emotions.* ■ [*trans.*] cause to move in such a pattern: *swirl a little cream into the soup.*

▸*n.* a quantity of something moving in such a pattern: *swirls of dust swept across the floor.* ■ a twisting or spiraling movement or pattern: *she emerged with a swirl of skirts* | *swirls of color.* ▷late Middle English (originally Scots in the sense 'whirlpool'): perhaps of Low German or Dutch origin; compare with Dutch *zwirrelen* 'to whirl.' —**swirl·y** *adj.*

swish /swisH/ ▸*v.* [*intrans.*] move with a hissing or rushing sound: *a car swished by.* ■ [*trans.*] cause to move with such a sound: *a girl came in, swishing her long skirts.* ■ aim a swinging blow at something: *he* **swished at** *a bramble with a piece of stick.* ■ [*trans.*] *Basketball* sink (a shot) without the ball touching the backboard or rim.

▸*n.* **1** a hissing or rustling sound: *he could hear the swish of a distant car.* ■ a rapid swinging movement: *the cow gave a swish of its tail.* ■ *Basketball, informal* a shot that goes through the basket without touching the backboard or rim. **2** *informal, offensive* an effeminate male homosexual.

▸*adj.* **1** *informal, offensive* effeminate. **2** *Brit., informal* impressively attractive and fashionable: *dinner at a swish hotel.* ▷mid 18th cent.: imitative.

swish·y /ˈswisHē/ ▸*adj.* **1** making a swishing sound or movement. **2** *informal, offensive* effeminate.

Swiss /swis/ ▸*adj.* of or relating to Switzerland or its people. ■ [as *plural n.*] (**the Swiss**) the people of Switzerland.

▸*n.* (*pl.* same) a native or national of Switzerland, or a person of Swiss descent. ▷early 16th cent.: from French *Suisse*, from Middle High German *Swīz* 'Switzerland.'

Swiss ar·my knife ▸*n.* a penknife incorporating several blades and other tools such as scissors and screwdrivers.

Swiss chard ▸*n.* see CHARD.

Swiss cheese ▸*n.* cheese of a style originating in Switzerland, typically containing large holes. ■ used figuratively to refer to something that is full of holes, gaps, or defects: *the team has Swiss cheese for a defense.*

swiss cheese plant ▸*n.* another term for CERIMAN.

Swiss Con·fed·er·a·tion the confederation of cantons that form Switzerland.

Swiss guard ▸*n.* [often treated as *pl.*] Swiss mercenaries employed as a special guard, formerly by sovereigns of France, now only at the Vatican.

Swiss roll ▸*n. Brit.* a jelly roll.

switch /swicH/ ▸*n.* **1** a device for making and breaking the connection in an electric circuit: *the guard hit a switch and the gate swung open.* ■ *Computing* a program variable that activates or deactivates a certain function of a program. **2** an act of adopting one policy or way of life, or choosing one type of item, in place of another; a change, esp. a radical one: *his friends were surprised at his switch from newspaper owner to farmer.* **3** a slender flexible shoot cut from a tree. **4** a junction of two railroad tracks, with a pair of linked tapering rails that can be moved laterally to allow a train to pass from one line to the other. **5** a tress of false or detached hair tied at one end, used in hairdressing to supplement natural hair.

▸*v.* [*trans.*] **1** change the position, direction, or focus of: *the company switched the boats to other routes.* ■ adopt (something different) in place of something else; change: *she's managed to switch careers.* ■ [*intrans.*] adopt a new policy, position, way of life, etc.: *she worked as a librarian and then switched to journalism.* ■ substitute (two items) for each other; exchange: *after ten minutes, listener and speaker switch roles.* **2** *archaic* beat or flick with or as if with a switch.

▸*phrasal v.* □ **switch something off** turn off an electrical device. ■ (**switch off**) *informal* cease to pay attention: *as he waffles on, I switch off.* □ **switch something on** turn on an electrical device. ▷late 16th cent. (denoting a thin tapering riding whip): probably from Low German. —**switch·a·ble** *adj.*

switch·back /ˈswicH,bak/ ▸*n.* **1** a 180° bend in a road or path, esp. one leading up the side of a mountain. **2** *Brit.* a road, path, or railroad with alternate sharp ascents and descents. ■ a roller coaster.

▸*v.* [*intrans.*] (of a road or vehicle) make a series of switchback turns: *a road that switchbacked up blue and distant hills.*

switch·blade /ˈswicH,blād/ ▸*n.* a knife with a blade that springs out from the handle when a button is pressed.

switch·board /ˈswicH,bôrd/ ▸*n.* an installation for the manual control of telephone connections in an office, hotel, or other large building. ■ another term for HELPLINE. ■ an apparatus for varying connections between electric circuits in other applications.

switch·er /ˈswicHər/ ▸*n.* **1** a shunting engine. **2** a piece of electronic equipment used to select or combine different video and audio signals.

switch·er·oo /,swicHəˈro͞o/ ▸*n. informal* a change, reversal, or exchange, esp. a surprising or deceptive one. ▷late 20th cent.: from the noun SWITCH + *-eroo*, a humorous suffix probably imitative of *buckaroo*.

switch·gear /ˈswicH,gi(ə)r/ ▸*n.* **1** switching equipment used in the transmission of electricity. **2** the switches or electrical controls in a motor vehicle.

switch·grass /ˈswicH,gras/ ▸*n.* a tall North American panic grass that forms large clumps. • *Panicum virgatum*, family Gramineae.

switch-hit·ter ▸*n. Baseball* a batter who can hit from either side of home plate. ■ *informal* a bisexual. —**switch-hit** *v.* —**switch-hit·ting** *adj.*

switch·o·ver (also **switch·o·ver**) ▸*n.* an instance of adopting a new policy, position, way of life, etc.: *a product switchover in its mainframe computer line.*

switch·yard /ˈswicH,yärd/ ▸*n.* **1** the part of a railroad yard taken up by junctions, in which trains are made up. **2** an enclosed area of a power system containing the switchgear.

Swith·in, St. /ˈswiT͟Hən/ (also **Swith·un**) (died 862), English ecclesiastic; bishop of Winchester 852–862. The tradition that if it rains on St. Swithin's Day it will do so for the next 40 days may have its origin in the heavy rain said to have occurred when his relics were to be transferred to a shrine in Winchester Cathedral. Feast day, July 15.

Switz·er·land /ˈswitsərlənd/ a mountainous, landlocked country in central Europe; pop. 7,450,000;

S

capital, Berne; languages, French, German, Italian, and Romansh (all official). French name **SUISSE**, German name **SCHWEIZ**, Italian name **SVIZZERA**; also called by its Latin name **HELVETIA**.

Switzerland emerged as an independent country in the 14th and 15th centuries, when the states or cantons formed a confederation to defeat first their Habsburg overlords and then their Burgundian neighbors. After a period of French domination (1798–1815) the Swiss Confederation's neutrality was guaranteed by the other European powers. Neutral in both world wars, Switzerland emerged as an international financial center and as the headquarters of several international organizations such as the Red Cross.

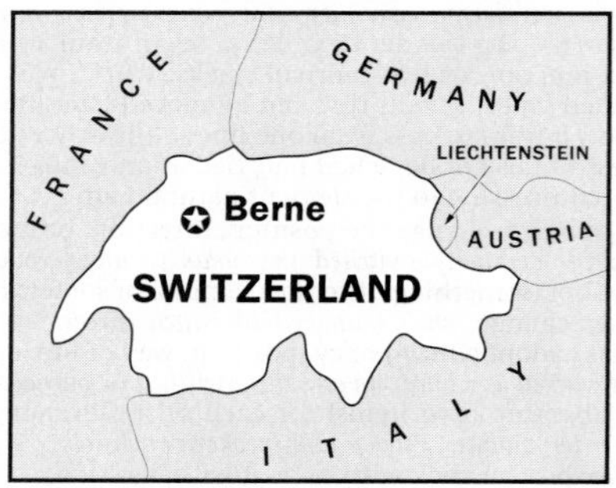

swive /swīv/ ▶*v.* [*trans.*] *archaic* or *humorous* have sexual intercourse with. ▷Middle English: apparently from the Old English verb *swīfan* 'move (along a course), sweep.'

swiv·el /ˈswivəl/ ▶*n.* a coupling between two parts enabling one to revolve without turning the other.
▶*v.* (**-eled**, **-el·ing**; *Brit.* **-elled**, **-el·ling**) [often with *adverbial*] turn around a point or axis or on a swivel: [*intrans.*] *he swiveled in the chair* | [*trans.*] *she swiveled her eyes around.* ▷Middle English, from the base of Old English *swīfan* 'to move (along a course), sweep.'

swiv·el chair ▶*n.* a chair with a seat able to be turned on its base to face in any direction.

swiv·et /ˈswivit/ ▶*n.* [in *sing.*] a fluster or panic: *the incomprehensible did not throw him into a swivet.* ▷late 19th cent.: of unknown origin.

swiz·zle /ˈswizəl/ ▶*n.* a mixed alcoholic drink, esp. a frothy one of rum or gin and bitters.
▶*v.* [*trans.*] stir (a drink) with a swizzle stick. ▷early 19th cent.: of unknown origin.

swiz·zle stick ▶*n.* a stick used for stirring still drinks or taking the fizz out of sparkling ones.

SWM ▶*abbr.* single white male (used in personal ads).

swol·len /ˈswōlən/ ▶ past participle of **SWELL**.

swoon /swo͞on/ ▶*v.* [*intrans.*] faint from extreme emotion: *I don't want a nurse who swoons at the sight of blood.* ■ be emotionally affected by someone or something that one admires; become ecstatic: *teenagers **swoon over** Japanese pop singers.*
▶*n.* an occurrence of fainting: *her strength ebbed away and she fell into a swoon.* ▷Middle English: the verb from obsolete *swown* 'fainting,' the noun from *aswoon* 'in a faint,' both from Old English *geswōgen* 'overcome.'

swoop /swo͞op/ ▶*v.* **1** [*intrans.*] (esp. of a bird) move rapidly downward through the air: *the barn owl can **swoop down on** a mouse in total darkness* | *the aircraft swooped in to land.* ■ carry out a sudden attack, esp. in order to make a capture or arrest: *investigators **swooped on** the Graf family home.* **2** [*trans.*] *informal* seize with a sweeping motion: *she **swooped up** the hen in her arms.*
▶*n.* a swooping or snatching movement or action: *four members were arrested following a swoop by detectives on their homes.* ▷mid 16th cent. (in the sense 'sweep along in a stately manner'): perhaps a dialect variant of Old English *swāpan* (see **SWEEP**). The early sense of the noun was 'a blow, stroke.'
▶*PHRASE* □ **at** (or **in**) **one fell swoop** see **FELL**[4].

swoosh /swo͞osh; swo͝osh/ ▶*n.* the sound produced by a sudden rush of air or liquid: *the swoosh of surf.*
▶*v.* [*intrans.*] move with such a sound: *swooshing down beautiful ski slopes.* ▷mid 19th cent.: imitative.

swop /swäp/ ▶*v.* & *n.* *chiefly Brit.* variant spelling of **SWAP**.

sword /sôrd/ ▶*n.* a weapon with a long metal blade and a hilt with a handguard, used for thrusting or striking and now typically worn as part of ceremonial dress. ■ (**the sword**) *poetic/literary* military power, violence, or destruction: *not many perished by the sword.* ■ (**swords**) one of the suits in a tarot pack. ▷Old English *sw(e)ord*, of Germanic origin; related to Dutch *zwaard* and German *Schwert*. —**sword·like** /-ˌlīk/ *adj.*
▶*PHRASES* □ **beat** (or **turn**) **swords into ploughshares** devote resources to peaceful rather than warlike ends. [with biblical allusion to Is. 2:4 and Mic. 4:3.] □ **he who lives by the sword dies by the sword** *proverb* those who commit violent acts must expect to suffer violence themselves. □ **put to the sword** kill, esp. in war. □ **the sword of justice** judicial authority.

sword-and-sor·cer·y ▶*n.* a genre of fiction characterized by heroic adventures and elements of fantasy.

sword-bear·er ▶*n.* an official who carries a sword for a sovereign or other dignitary on formal occasions.

sword·bill /ˈsôrd,bil/ (also **sword-billed hummingbird**) ▶*n.* a mainly green hummingbird with a very long bill, found in northern South America. • *Ensifera ensifera*, family Trochilidae.

sword dance ▶*n.* a dance in which the performers brandish swords or step around swords laid on the ground, originally as a tribal preparation for war or as a victory celebration.

sword fern ▶*n.* a fern with long slender fronds. • Genera *Polystichum* and *Nephrolepis*, family Dryopteridaceae: several species, including the North American *P. munitum* and the tropical *N. exaltata*.

sword·fish /ˈsôrd,fish/ ▶*n.* (*pl.* same or **-fish·es**) a large edible marine fish with a streamlined body and a long flattened swordlike snout, related to the billfishes and popular as a game fish. • *Xiphias gladius*, the only member of the family Xiphiidae.

swordfish

sword knot ▶*n.* a ribbon or tassel attached to a sword hilt, originally for securing it to the wrist.

sword lil·y ▶*n.* a gladiolus.

sword of Dam·o·cles ▶*n.* see **DAMOCLES**.

sword of state ▶*n.* the sword carried in front of a sovereign on state occasions.

sword·play /ˈsôrd,plā/ ▶*n.* the activity or skill of fencing with swords or foils. ■ *figurative* repartee; skillful debate: *this intellectual swordplay went on for several minutes.*

swords·man /ˈsôrdzmən/ ▶*n.* (*pl.* **-men**) a man who fights with a sword (typically with his level of skill specified): *an expert swordsman.* —**swords·man·ship** /-ˌship/ *n.*

sword swal·low·er ▶*n.* a person who passes (or pretends to pass) a sword blade down the throat and gullet as entertainment.

sword·tail /ˈsôrd,tāl/ ▶*n.* a livebearing freshwater fish of Central America, popular in aquariums. The lower edge of the tail is elongated and brightly marked in the male. • *Xiphophorus helleri*, family Poeciliidae.

swore /swôr/ ▶ past of **SWEAR**.

sworn /swôrn/ ▶ past participle of **SWEAR**.
▶*adj.* [*attrib.*] **1** (of testimony or evidence) given under oath: *he made a sworn statement.* **2** determined to remain in the role or condition specified: *they were sworn enemies.*

swot /swät/ *Brit., informal* ▶*v.* (**swot·ted**, **swot·ting**) [*intrans.*] study assiduously: *kids swotting for exams.*
▶*phrasal v.* □ **swot up on** study (a subject) intensively, esp. in preparation for something: *teachers spend their evenings swotting up on jargon* | (**swot something up**) *I've always been interested in old furniture and I've swotted it up a bit.*
▶*n.* a person who studies hard, esp. one regarded as spending too much time studying. ▷mid 19th cent.: dialect variant of **SWEAT**. —**swot·ty** *adj.*

SWOT a·nal·y·sis /ˈswät/ ▶*n.* a study undertaken by an organization to identify its internal strengths and weaknesses, as well as its external opportunities and threats. ▷acronym from *strengths, weaknesses, opportunities, threats.*

swum /swəm/ ▶ past participle of **SWIM**.

swung /swəng/ ▶ past and past participle of **SWING**.

swung dash ▶*n.* a dash (~) in the form of a reverse *s* on its side.

SY ▶*abbr.* steam yacht: *the SY Morning.*

-sy ▶*suffix* forming diminutive nouns and adjectives such as *folksy*, *mopsy*, also nicknames or hypocoristics such as *Patsy*. ▷variant of **-Y**[2].

syb·a·rite /ˈsibə,rīt/ ▶*n.* a person who is self-indulgent in their fondness for sensuous luxury. ▷mid 16th cent. (originally denoting an inhabitant of Sybaris, an ancient Greek city in southern Italy, noted for luxury): via Latin from Greek *Subaritēs*. —**syb·a·rit·ism** /-rīt,izəm/ *n.*

syb·a·rit·ic /ˌsibəˈritik/ ▶*adj.* fond of sensuous luxury or pleasure; self-indulgent: *their opulent and sybaritic lifestyle.* See note at **SENSUOUS**.

syc·a·mine /ˈsikə,mīn; -min/ ▶*n.* (in biblical use) the black mulberry tree (see Luke 17:6; in modern versions translated as "mulberry tree"). ▷early 16th cent.: via Latin from Greek *sukaminos* 'mulberry tree,' from Hebrew *šiqmāh* 'sycamore,' assimilated to Greek *sukon* 'fig.'

syc·a·more /ˈsikə,môr/ ▶*n.* **1** an American plane tree. • Genus *Platanus*, family Platanaceae: several species, in particular *P. occidentalis* (also called **BUTTONWOOD** or **BUTTONBALL TREE**), which is the largest deciduous tree in the U.S. ■ the timber of this tree. **2** (in full **sycamore maple**) a large Eurasian maple with winged fruits, native to central and southern Europe. • *Acer pseudoplatanus*, family Aceraceae. ■ the timber of this tree. ▷Middle English: from Old French *sic(h)amor*, via Latin from Greek *sukomoros*, from *sukon* 'fig' + *moron* 'mulberry.'

syce /sīs/ ▶*n.* (esp. in India) a groom (taking care of horses). ▷from Persian and Urdu *sā'is*, from Arabic.

sy·con /ˈsī,kän/ ▶*n.* *Zoology* a sponge of intermediate structure, showing some folding of the body wall with choanocytes lining only radial canals. Compare with **ASCON** and **LEUCON**. ▷late 19th cent.: adopted as a genus name from Greek *sukon* 'fig.' —**sy·co·noid** /-kə,noid/ *adj.*

sy·co·ni·um /sīˈkōnēəm/ ▶*n.* (*pl.* **-ni·a** /-nēə/) *Botany* a fleshy hollow receptacle that develops into a multiple fruit, as in the fig. ▷mid 19th cent.: modern Latin, from Greek *sukon* 'fig.'

syc·o·phant /ˈsikəfənt; -ˌfant/ ▶*n.* a person who acts obsequiously toward someone in order to gain advantage; a servile flatterer. ▷mid 16th cent. (denoting an informer): from French *sycophante*, or via Latin from Greek *sukophantēs* 'informer,' from *sukon* 'fig' + *phainein* 'to show'; the association with informing against the illegal exportation of figs from ancient Athens (recorded by Plutarch) is not substantiated. —**syc·o·phan·cy** /-fənsē; -ˌfansē/ *n.* —**syc·o·phan·tic** /ˌsikəˈfantik/ *adj.* —**syc·o·phan·ti·cal·ly** /ˌsikəˈfantik(ə)lē/ *adv.*

sy·co·sis /sīˈkōsis/ ▶*n.* inflammation of the hair follicles in the bearded part of the face, caused by bacterial infection. ▷late 16th cent. (originally denoting any fig-shaped skin ulcer): modern Latin, from Greek *sukōsis*, from *sukon* 'fig.'

Sy·den·ham /ˈsidn-əm; ˈsidnəm/, Thomas (*c.*1624–89), English physician; known as **the English Hippocrates**. He emphasized the healing power of nature, made a study of epidemics, and explained the nature of the type of chorea that is named after him.

Sy·den·ham's cho·rea /ˈsidnəmz kôˈrēə/ ▶*n.* a form of chorea chiefly affecting children, associated with rheumatic fever. Formerly called **ST. VITUS'S DANCE**.

Syd·ney /ˈsidnē/ the capital of New South Wales in southeastern Australia, the country's largest city and chief port; pop. 3,098,000. It has a fine natural harbor, crossed by the Sydney Harbour Bridge (1932), and a striking opera house (1973).

sy·e·nite /ˈsīə,nīt/ ▶*n.* *Geology* a coarse-grained gray igneous rock composed mainly of alkali feldspar and ferromagnesian minerals such as hornblende. ▷late 18th cent.: from French *syénite*, from Latin *Syenites (lapis)* '(stone) of *Syene*' (from Greek *Suēnē* 'Aswan,' a town in Egypt). —**sy·e·nit·ic** /ˌsīəˈnitik/ *adj.*

Syk·tyv·kar /ˌsiktifˈkär/ a city in northwestern Russia, capital of the autonomous republic of Komi; pop. 235,000.

syl. ▶*abbr.* syllable.

syl- ▶*prefix* variant spelling of **SYN-** assimilated before *l* (as in *syllogism*).

syll. ▶*abbr.* ■ syllable. ■ syllabus.

syl·la·bar·y /ˈsilə,berē/ ▶*n.* (*pl.* **-bar·ies**) a set of written characters representing syllables and (in some languages or stages of writing) serving the purpose of an alphabet. ▷mid 19th cent.: from modern Latin *syllabarium*, from Latin *syllaba* (see **SYLLABLE**).

syl·la·bi /ˈsilə,bī/ ▸ plural form of SYLLABUS.

syl·lab·ic /səˈlabik/ ▸*adj.* of, relating to, or based on syllables: *a system of syllabic symbols.* ■ *Prosody* based on the number of syllables in a line: *the recreation of classical syllabic meters.* ■ (of a consonant, esp. a nasal or other continuant) constituting a whole syllable, such as the *m* in *Mbabane* or the *l* in *bottle.* ■ articulated in syllables: *syllabic singing.*
▸*n.* a written character that represents a syllable. *Inuit syllabics.* ▷early 18th cent.: from French *syllabique* or late Latin *syllabicus,* from Greek *sullabikos,* from *sullabē* 'syllable.' —**syl·lab·i·cal·ly** /-ik(ə)lē/ *adv.* —**syl·la·bic·i·ty** /,siləˈbisitē/ *n.*

syl·lab·i·fi·ca·tion /sə,labəfiˈkāsHən/ (also **syl·lab·i·ca·tion** /səˈlabiˈkāsHən/) ▸*n.* the division of words into syllables, either in speech or in writing. —**syl·lab·i·fy** /səˈlabə,fī/ *v.* (**-fies, -fied**).

syl·la·bize /ˈsilə,bīz/ ▸*v.* [*trans.*] divide into or articulate by syllables. ▷late 16th cent.: via medieval Latin from Greek *sullabizein,* from *sullabē* 'syllable.'

syl·la·ble /ˈsiləbəl/ ▸*n.* a unit of pronunciation having one vowel sound, with or without surrounding consonants, forming the whole or a part of a word; e.g., there are two syllables in *water* and three in *inferno.* ■ a character or characters representing a syllable. ■ [usu. with *negative*] the least amount of speech or writing; the least mention of something: *I'd never have breathed a syllable if he'd kept quiet.*
▸*v.* [*trans.*] pronounce (a word or phrase) clearly, syllable by syllable. ▷late Middle English: from an Anglo-Norman French alteration of Old French *sillabe,* via Latin from Greek *sullabē,* from *sun-* 'together' + *lambanein* 'take.' —**syl·la·bled** *adj.* [usu. in *combination*] *poems of few-syllabled lines.*

syl·la·ble-timed ▸*adj.* (of a language) characterized by a rhythm in which syllables occur at roughly equivalent time intervals, irrespective of the stress placed on them. French is a syllable-timed language. Contrasted with STRESS-TIMED.

syl·la·bub /ˈsilə,bəb/ ▸*n.* a whipped cream dessert, typically flavored with white wine or sherry. ▷of unknown origin.

syl·la·bus /ˈsiləbəs/ ▸*n.* (*pl.* **-bus·es** or **-bi** /-,bī/) **1** an outline of the subjects in a course of study or teaching: *there isn't time to cover the syllabus | the history syllabus.* **2** (in the Roman Catholic Church) a summary of points decided by papal decree regarding heretical doctrines or practices. ▷mid 17th cent. (in the sense 'concise table of headings of a discourse'): modern Latin, originally a misreading of Latin *sittybas,* accusative plural of *sittyba,* from Greek *sittuba* 'title slip, label.'

syl·lep·sis /səˈlepsis/ ▸*n.* (*pl.* **-ses** /-sēz/) a figure of speech in which a word is applied to two others in different senses (e.g., *caught the train and a bad cold*) or to two others of which it grammatically suits only one (e.g., *neither they nor it is working*). Compare with ZEUGMA. ▷late Middle English: via late Latin from Greek *sullēpsis* 'taking together.' —**syl·lep·tic** /-tik/ *adj.*

syl·lo·gism /ˈsilə,jizəm/ ▸*n.* an instance of a form of reasoning in which a conclusion is drawn (whether validly or not) from two given or assumed propositions (premises), each of which shares a term with the conclusion, and shares a common or middle term not present in the conclusion (e.g., *all dogs are animals; all animals have four legs; therefore all dogs have four legs*). ■ deductive reasoning as distinct from induction: *logic is rules or syllogism.* ▷late Middle English: via Old French or Latin from Greek *sullogismos,* from *sullogizesthai,* from *sun-* 'with' + *logizesthai* 'to reason' (from *logos* 'reasoning'). —**syl·lo·gis·tic** /,siləˈjistik/ *adj.* —**syl·lo·gis·ti·cal·ly** /,siləˈjistik(ə)lē/ *adv.*

syl·lo·gize /ˈsilə,jīz/ ▸*v.* [*intrans.*] use syllogisms. ■ [*trans.*] put (facts or an argument) in the form of syllogism. ▷late Middle English: via Old French or late Latin from Greek *sullogizesthai* (see SYLLOGISM).

sylph /silf/ ▸*n.* **1** an imaginary spirit of the air. ■ a slender woman or girl. **2** a mainly dark green and blue hummingbird, the male of which has a long forked tail. • Genus *Aglaiocercus* (and *Neolesbia*), family Trochilidae: three species. ▷mid 17th cent.: from modern Latin *sylphes, sylphi* and the German plural *Sylphen,* perhaps based on Latin *sylvestris* 'of the woods' + *nympha* 'nymph.'

sylph·like /ˈsilf,līk/ ▸*adj.* (of a woman or girl) slender and graceful.

syl·van /ˈsilvən/ (also **sil·van**) ▸*adj. chiefly poetic/literary* consisting of or associated with woods; wooded: *trees and contours all add to a sylvan setting.* ■ pleasantly rural or pastoral: *vistas of sylvan charm.* ▷mid 16th cent. (as a noun denoting an inhabitant of the woods): from French *sylvain* or Latin *Silvanus* 'woodland deity,' from *silva* 'a wood.'

Syl·va·ner /silˈvänər; -ˈvanər/ ▸*n.* a variety of wine grape first developed in German-speaking districts, the dominant form being a white grape. ■ a white wine made from this grape. ▷German.

syl·vat·ic /silˈvatik/ ▸*adj. Veterinary Medicine* relating to or denoting certain diseases when contracted by wild animals, and the pathogens causing them: *an epidemic of sylvatic plague among prairie dogs.* ▷1930s: from Latin *silvaticus,* from *silva* 'wood.'

Syl·vi·an fis·sure /ˈsilvēən/ (also **fis·sure of Syl·vi·us** /ˈsilvēəs/) ▸*n. Anatomy* a large diagonal fissure on the lateral surface of the brain that separates off the temporal lobe. ▷mid 19th cent.: named after François de la Boë *Sylvius* (1614–72), Flemish anatomist.

syl·vine ▸*n.* another term for SYLVITE.

syl·vin·ite /ˈsilvə,nīt/ ▸*n.* a mixture of the minerals sylvite and halite, mined as a source of potash. ▷late 19th cent.: from SYLVINE + -ITE[1].

syl·vite /ˈsil,vīt/ ▸*n.* a colorless or white mineral consisting of potassium chloride, occurring typically as cubic crystals. Also called SYLVINE. ▷mid 19th cent.: from modern Latin *(sal digestivus) Sylvii,* the old name of this salt, + -ITE[1].

sym. ▸*abbr.* ■ symbol. ■ *Chemistry* symmetrical. ■ symphony. ■ symptom.

sym- ▸*prefix* variant spelling of SYN- assimilated before *b, m, p* (as in *symbiosis, symmetry, symphysis*).

sym·bi·ont /ˈsimbē,änt; -bī-/ ▸*n. Biology* either of two organisms that live in symbiosis with one another. ▷late 19th cent.: formed irregularly from Greek *sumbiōn* 'living together,' present participle of *sumbioun* (see SYMBIOSIS).

sym·bi·o·sis /,simbēˈōsis; -bī-/ ▸*n.* (*pl.* **-ses** /-,sēz/) *Biology* interaction between two different organisms living in close physical association, typically to the advantage of both. Compare with ANTIBIOSIS. ■ a mutually beneficial relationship between different people or groups: *a perfect mother and daughter symbiosis.* ▷late 19th cent.: modern Latin, from Greek *sumbiōsis* 'a living together,' from *sumbioun* 'live together,' from *sumbios* 'companion.' —**sym·bi·ot·ic** /-ˈätik/ *adj.* —**sym·bi·ot·i·cal·ly** /-ˈätik(ə)lē/ *adv.*

sym·bol /ˈsimbəl/ ▸*n.* a thing that represents or stands for something else, esp. a material object representing something abstract: *the limousine was another symbol of his wealth and authority.* See note at EMBLEM. ■ a mark or character used as a conventional representation of an object, function, or process, e.g., the letter or letters standing for a chemical element or a character in musical notation. ■ a shape or sign used to represent something such as an organization, e.g., a red cross or a Star of David.
▸*v.* (**-boled, -bol·ing;** *Brit.* **-bol·led, -bol·ling**) [*trans.*] *archaic* symbolize. ▷late Middle English (denoting the Apostles' Creed): from Latin *symbolum* 'symbol, Creed (as the mark of a Christian),' from Greek *sumbolon* 'mark, token,' from *sun-* 'with' + *ballein* 'to throw.'

sym·bol·ic /simˈbälik/ ▸*adj.* **1** serving as a symbol: *a repeating design symbolic of eternity.* ■ significant purely in terms of what is being represented or implied: *the release of the dissident was an important symbolic gesture.* **2** involving the use of symbols or symbolism: *the symbolic meaning of motifs and designs.* ▷mid 17th cent.: from French *symbolique* or late Latin *symbolicus,* from Greek *sumbolikos.* The adjective *symbolical* dates from the early 17th cent. —**sym·bol·i·cal** *adj.* —**sym·bol·i·cal·ly** /-ik(ə)lē/ *adv.*

sym·bol·ic in·ter·ac·tion·ism ▸*n. Sociology* the view of social behavior that emphasizes linguistic or gestural communication and its subjective understanding, esp. the role of language in the formation of the child as a social being.

sym·bol·ic log·ic ▸*n.* the use of symbols to denote propositions, terms, and relations in order to assist reasoning.

sym·bol·ism /ˈsimbə,lizəm/ ▸*n.* the use of symbols to represent ideas or qualities: *in China, symbolism in gardens achieved great subtlety.* ■ symbolic meaning attributed to natural objects or facts: *the old-fashioned symbolism of flowers.* ■ (also **Symbolism**) an artistic and poetic movement or style using symbolic images and indirect suggestion to express mystical ideas, emotions, and states of mind. It originated in late 19th century France and Belgium, with important figures including Mallarmé, Maeterlinck, Verlaine, Rimbaud, and Redon. —**sym·bol·ist** *n.* & *adj.*

sym·bol·ize /ˈsimbə,līz/ ▸*v.* [*trans.*] be a symbol of: *the ceremonial dagger symbolizes justice.* ■ represent by means of symbols: *a tendency to symbolize the father as the sun.* —**sym·bol·i·za·tion** /,simbəliˈzāsHən/ *n.*

sym·bol·o·gy /simˈbäləjē/ ▸*n.* the study or use of symbols. ■ symbols collectively: *the use of religious symbology.*

sym·met·ri·cal /səˈmetrikəl/ ▸*adj.* made up of exactly similar parts facing each other or around an axis; showing symmetry. —**sym·met·ric** *adj.* —**sym·met·ri·cal·ly** /-ik(ə)lē/ *adv.*

sym·me·try /ˈsimitrē/ ▸*n.* (*pl.* **-tries**) the quality of being made up of exactly similar parts facing each other or around an axis: *this series has a line of symmetry through its center | a crystal structure with hexagonal symmetry.* ■ correct or pleasing proportion of the parts of a thing: *an overall symmetry making the poem pleasant to the ear.* ■ similarity or exact correspondence between different things: *a lack of* ***symmetry between*** *men and women | history sometimes exhibits weird symmetries between events.* ■ *Physics & Mathematics* a law or operation where a physical property or process has an equivalence in two or more directions. ▷mid 16th cent. (denoting proportion): from French *symétrie* or Latin *symmetria,* from Greek, from *sun-* 'with' + *metron* 'measure.' —**sym·me·trize** /-,trīz/ *v.*

sym·me·try break·ing ▸*n. Physics* the absence or reduction of manifest symmetry in a situation despite its presence in the laws of nature underlying it.

sym·path·ec·to·my /,simpəˈTHektəmē/ ▸*n.* the surgical cutting of a sympathetic nerve or removal of a ganglion to relieve a condition affected by its stimulation.

sym·pa·thet·ic /,simpəˈTHetik/ ▸*adj.* **1** feeling, showing, or expressing sympathy: *he was* ***sympathetic toward*** *staff with family problems | he spoke in a sympathetic tone.* ■ [*predic.*] showing approval of or favor toward an idea or action: *he was* ***sympathetic to*** *evolutionary ideas.* **2** pleasant or agreeable, in particular: ■ (of a person) attracting the liking of others: *Audrey develops as a sympathetic character.* ■ (of a structure) designed in a sensitive or fitting way: *buildings that were* ***sympathetic to*** *their surroundings.* **3** relating to or denoting the part of the autonomic nervous system consisting of nerves arising from ganglia near the middle part of the spinal cord, supplying the internal organs, blood vessels, and glands, and balancing the action of the parasympathetic nerves. **4** relating to, producing, or denoting an effect that arises in response to a similar action elsewhere. ▷mid 17th cent. (in the sense 'relating to an affinity or paranormal influence,' as in SYMPATHETIC MAGIC): from SYMPATHY, on the pattern of *pathetic.* —**sym·pa·thet·i·cal·ly** /-ik(ə)lē/ *adv.*

S

sym·pa·thet·ic mag·ic ▸*n.* primitive or magical ritual using objects or actions resembling or symbolically associated with the event or person over which influence is sought.

sym·pa·thet·ic smok·er ▸*n.* a person who smokes only in the company of another smoker.

sym·pa·thet·ic string ▸*n.* each of a group of additional wire strings fitted to certain stringed instruments to give extra resonance.

sym·pa·thize /ˈsimpə,THīz/ ▸*v.* [*intrans.*] **1** feel or express sympathy: *it is easy to understand and* ***sympathize with*** *his predicament.* **2** agree with a sentiment or opinion: *they* ***sympathize with*** *critiques of traditional theory.* ▷late 16th cent. (in the sense 'suffer with another person'): from French *sympathiser,* from *sympathie* 'sympathy, friendly understanding' (see SYMPATHY). —**sym·pa·thiz·er** *n.*

sym·pa·tho·lyt·ic /,simpəTHōˈlitik/ *Medicine* ▸*adj.* (of a drug) antagonistic to or inhibiting the transmission of nerve impulses in the sympathetic nervous system.
▸*n.* a drug having this effect, often used in the treatment of high blood pressure.

sym·pa·tho·mi·met·ic /,simpəTHōməˈmetik/ *Medicine* ▸*adj.* (of a drug) producing physiological effects characteristic of the sympathetic nervous system by promoting the stimulation of sympathetic nerves.
▸*n.* a drug having this effect, often used in nasal decongestants.

sym·pa·thy /ˈsimpəTHē/ ▸*n.* (*pl.* **-thies**) **1** feelings of pity and sorrow for someone else's misfortune: *they* *had great* ***sympathy for*** *the flood victims.* ■ (**one's sympathies**) formal expression of such feelings; condolences: *all Tony's friends joined in sending their sympathies to his widow Jean.* **2** understanding between people; common feeling: *the special sympathy between the two boys was obvious to all.* ■ (**sympathies**) support in the form of shared feelings or opinions: *his sympathies lay with his constituents.* ■ agreement with or approval of an opinion or aim; a favorable attitude: *I have some* ***sympathy for*** *this view.* ■ (**in sympathy**) relating harmoniously to something else; in keeping: *repairs had to be* ***in sympathy with*** *the original structure.* ■ the state or fact of responding in a way similar or corresponding to an action elsewhere: *the magnetic field oscillates* ***in sympathy.*** ▷late 16th cent. (sense 2): via Latin from Greek *sumpatheia*, from *sumpathēs*, from *sun-* 'with' + *pathos* 'feeling.'

sym·pat·ric /sim'patrik/ ▸*adj. Biology* (of animals or plants, esp. of related species or populations) occurring within the same geographical area; overlapping in distribution. Compare with ALLOPATRIC. ■ (of speciation) taking place without geographical separation. ▷early 20th cent.: from SYM- 'with, together' + Greek *patra* 'fatherland' + -IC. **—sym·pa·try** /'simˌpatrē; -pətrē/ *n.*

sym·pet·al·ous /sim'petl-əs/ ▸*adj. Botany* (of a flower or corolla) having the petals united along their margins to form a tubular shape. **—sym·pet·a·ly** *n.*

sym·phon·ic /sim'fänik/ ▸*adj.* (of music) relating to or having the form or character of a symphony: *Franck's Symphonic Variations.* ■ relating to or written for a symphony orchestra: *symphonic and chamber music.* **—sym·phon·i·cal·ly** /-ik(ə)lē/ *adv.*

sym·phon·ic po·em ▸*n.* another term for TONE POEM.

sym·pho·nist /'simfənist/ ▸*n.* a composer of symphonies.

sym·pho·ny /'simfənē/ ▸*n.* (*pl.* **-nies**) an elaborate musical composition for full orchestra, typically in four movements, at least one of which is traditionally in sonata form. ■ *chiefly historical* an orchestral interlude in a large-scale vocal work. ■ something regarded, typically favorably, as a composition of different elements: *autumn is* ***a symphony of*** *texture and pattern.* ■ (esp. in names of orchestras) short for SYMPHONY ORCHESTRA: *the Boston Symphony.* ■ a concert performed by a symphony orchestra: *tickets to the symphony.* ▷Middle English (denoting any of various instruments such as the dulcimer or the virginal): from Old French *symphonie*, via Latin from Greek *sumphōnia*, from *sumphōnos* 'harmonious,' from *sun-* 'together' + *phōnē* 'sound.'

sym·pho·ny or·ches·tra ▸*n.* a large classical orchestra, including string, wind, brass, and percussion instruments.

Sym·phy·la /'simfələ/ *Zoology* a small class of myriapod invertebrates that resemble the centipedes. They are small eyeless animals with one pair of legs per segment, typically living in soil and leaf mold. ▷modern Latin (plural), from SYM- 'together' + Greek *phulē*, *phulon* 'tribe.' **—sym·phy·lan** *n. & adj.*

sym·phy·sis /'simfəsis/ ▸*n.* (*pl.* **-ses** /-ˌsēz/) **1** the process of growing together. **2** a place where two bones are closely joined, either forming an immovable joint (as between the pubic bones in the center of the pelvis) or completely fused (as at the midline of the lower jaw). ▷late 16th cent. (sense 2): modern Latin, from Greek *sumphusis*, from *sun-* 'together' + *phusis* 'growth.' **—sym·phys·e·al** /sim'fizēəl/ *adj.* **—sym·phys·i·al** /sim'fizēəl/ *adj.*

sym·plasm /'simˌplazəm/ ▸*n. Botany* a symplast, esp. the cytoplasm of which it is composed. **—sym·plas·mic** /sim'plazmik/ *adj.*

sym·plast /'simˌplast/ ▸*n. Botany* a continuous network of interconnected plant cell protoplasts. ▷1930s: from German *Symplast.* **—sym·plas·tic** /sim'plastik/ *adj.*

sym·po·di·um /sim'pōdēəm/ ▸*n.* (*pl.* **-di·a** /-dēə/) *Botany* the apparent main axis or stem of a plant, made up of successive secondary axes due to the death of each season's terminal bud, as in the vine. ▷mid 19th cent.: modern Latin, from Greek *syn-* 'together' + *pous, pod-* 'foot.' **—sym·po·di·al** /-dēəl/ *adj.*

sym·po·si·ast /sim'pōzēəst/ ▸*n.* a participant in a symposium.

sym·po·si·um /sim'pōzēəm/ ▸*n.* (*pl.* **-si·a** /-zēə/ or **-si·ums**) a conference or meeting to discuss a particular subject. ■ a collection of essays or papers on a particular subject by a number of contributors. ■ a drinking party or convivial discussion, esp. as held in ancient Greece after a banquet (and notable as the title of a work by Plato). ▷late 16th cent. (denoting a drinking party): via Latin from Greek *sumposion*, from *sumpotēs* 'fellow drinker,' from *sun-* 'together' + *potēs* 'drinker.'

symp·tom /'sim(p)təm/ ▸*n. Medicine* a physical or mental feature that is regarded as indicating a condition of disease, particularly such a feature that is apparent to the patient: *dental problems may be a symptom of other illness.* Compare with SIGN (sense 1). ■ a sign of the existence of something, esp. of an undesirable situation: *the government was plagued by leaks—a symptom of divisions and poor morale.* See note at SIGN. ▷late Middle English *synthoma*, from medieval Latin, based on Greek *sumptōma* 'chance, symptom,' from *sumpiptein* 'happen'; later influenced by French *symptome.* **—symp·tom·less** *adj.*

symp·to·mat·ic /ˌsim(p)tə'matik/ ▸*adj.* serving as a symptom or sign, esp. of something undesirable: *the closings are symptomatic of a decaying city.* ■ exhibiting or involving symptoms: *patients with symptomatic celiac disease | symptomatic patients.* **—symp·to·mat·i·cal·ly** /-ik(ə)lē/ *adv.*

symp·tom·a·tol·o·gy /ˌsim(p)təmə'täləjē/ ▸*n.* the set of symptoms characteristic of a medical condition or exhibited by a patient.

symp·tom·ize /'simptəˌmīz/ ▸*v.* [*trans.*] be a symptom or sign of: *hypothermia is* ***symptomized by*** *confusion, slurred speech, and stiff muscles.*

syn. ▸*abbr.* ■ synonym. ■ synonymous. ■ synonymy.

syn- ▸*prefix* united; acting or considered together: *synchrony | syncarpous.* ▷from Greek *sun* 'with.'

syn·aes·the·sia ▸*n.* British spelling of SYNESTHESIA.

syn·a·gogue /'sinəˌgäg/ ▸*n.* the building where a Jewish assembly or congregation meets for religious worship and instruction. ■ such a Jewish assembly or congregation. ▷Middle English: via Old French and late Latin from Greek *sunagōgē* 'meeting,' from *sun-* 'together' + *agein* 'bring.' **—syn·a·gog·al** /ˌsinə'gägəl; -'gôgəl/ *adj.* **—syn·a·gog·i·cal** /ˌsinə'gäjikəl/ *adj.*

syn·ap·o·mor·phy /si'napəˌmôrfē/ ▸*n.* (*pl.* **-phies**) *Biology* the possession by two organisms of a characteristic (not necessarily the same in each) that is derived from one characteristic in an organism from which they both evolved. ■ a characteristic derived in this way. ▷1960s: from SYN- 'together' + APO- 'away from' + Greek *morphē* 'form.'

syn·apse /'sinˌaps/ ▸*n.* a junction between two nerve cells, consisting of a minute gap across which impulses pass by diffusion of a neurotransmitter. ▷late 19th cent.: from Greek *sunapsis*, from *sun-* 'together' + *hapsis* 'joining,' from *haptein* 'to join.'

syn·ap·sid /sə'napsid/ ▸*n.* a fossil reptile of a Permian and Triassic group, the members of which show increasingly mammalian characteristics and include the ancestors of mammals. Also called MAMMALLIKE REPTILE. • Subclass Synapsida; includes the pelycosaurs and the therapsids. ▷early 20th cent.: from modern Latin *Synapsida*, from Greek *sun-* 'together' + *apsis, apsid-* 'arch.'

syn·ap·sis /sə'napsis/ ▸*n. Biology* the fusion of chromosome pairs at the start of meiosis. ▷late 19th cent.: modern Latin, from Greek *sunapsis* 'connection, junction.'

syn·ap·tic /sə'naptik/ ▸*adj. Anatomy* of or relating to a synapse or synapses between nerve cells: *the synaptic membrane.* **—syn·ap·ti·cal·ly** /-ik(ə)lē/ *adv.*

syn·ap·to·ne·mal com·plex /səˌnaptə'nēməl/ ▸*n. Biology* a ladderlike series of parallel threads visible in electron microscopy adjacent to and coaxial with pairing chromosomes in meiosis. ▷1950s: from *synapto-* (combining form of SYNAPSIS) + Greek *nēma* 'thread' + -AL.

syn·ar·chy /'sinərkē/ ▸*n.* joint rule or government by two or more individuals or parties. ▷mid 18th cent.: from Greek *sunarkhia*, from *sunarkhein* 'rule jointly.' **—synarchic** /sə'närkik/ *adj.* **—synarchist** /-kist/ *n.*

syn·ar·thro·sis /ˌsinär'THrōsis/ ▸*n.* (*pl.* **-ses** /-ˌsēz/) *Anatomy* an immovably fixed joint between bones connected by fibrous tissue (for example, the sutures of the skull). ▷late 16th cent.: from modern Latin, from Greek *sunarthrōsis*, from *sun-* 'together' + *arthrōsis* 'jointing' (from *arthron* 'joint').

syn·as·try /sə'nastrē; 'sinəstrē/ ▸*n. Astrology* comparison between the horoscopes of two or more people in order to determine their likely compatibility and relationship. ▷mid 17th cent.: via late Latin from Greek *sunastria*, from *sun-* 'together' + *astēr, astr-* 'star.'

sync /siNGk/ (also **synch**) *informal* ▸*n.* synchronization: *images flash onto your screen* ***in sync with*** *the music.* ▸*v.* [*trans.*] synchronize: *the flash needs to be synced to your camera.* ▷1920s: abbreviation.

▸*PHRASE* □ **in** (or **out of**) **sync** working well (or badly) together; in (or out of) agreement: *her eyes and her brain seemed to be seriously out of sync.*

syn·car·pous /sin'kärpəs/ ▸*adj. Botany* (of a flower, fruit, or ovary) having the carpels united. Often contrasted with APOCARPOUS. ▷mid 19th cent.: from SYN- 'together' + Greek *karpos* 'fruit' + -OUS.

syn·chon·dro·sis /ˌsiNGkən'drōsis/ ▸*n.* (*pl.* **-ses** /-ˌsēz/) *Anatomy* an almost immovable joint between bones bound by a layer of cartilage, as in the vertebrae. ▷late 16th cent.: from modern Latin, from Greek *sunkhondrōsis*, from *sun-* 'together' + *khondros* 'cartilage.'

syn·chro /'siNGkrō/ ▸*n.* **1** short for SYNCHROMESH. **2** synchronized or synchronization: *tape editing with synchro start.* **3** short for SYNCHRONIZED SWIMMING.

synchro- ▸*comb. form* synchronous: *synchrotron.*

syn·chro·cy·clo·tron /ˌsiNGkrō'sikləˌträn/ ▸*n. Physics* a cyclotron able to achieve higher energies by decreasing the frequency of the accelerating electric field as the particles increase in energy and mass.

syn·chro·mesh /'siNGkrōˌmesH/ ▸*n.* a system of gear changing, esp. in motor vehicles, in which the driving and driven gearwheels are made to revolve at the same speed during engagement by means of a set of friction clutches, thereby easing the change. ▷1920s: contraction of *synchronized mesh.*

syn·chron·ic /siNG'kränik/ ▸*adj.* concerned with something, esp. a language, as it exists at one point in time: *synchronic linguistics.* Often contrasted with DIACHRONIC. ▷1920s: from late Latin *synchronus* (see SYNCHRONOUS) + -IC. **—syn·chron·i·cal·ly** /-ik(ə)lē/ *adv.*

syn·chro·nic·i·ty /ˌsiNGkrə'nisitē/ ▸*n.* **1** the simultaneous occurrence of events that appear significantly related but have no discernible causal connection: *such synchronicity is quite staggering.* **2** another term for SYNCHRONY (sense 1). ▷1950s: coined (in sense 1) by C. G. Jung.

syn·chro·nism /'siNGkrəˌnizəm/ ▸*n.* another term for SYNCHRONY. ▷late 16th cent.: from Greek *sunkhronismos*, from *sunkhronos* (see SYNCHRONOUS). **—syn·chro·nis·tic** /ˌsiNGkrə'nistik/ *adj.* **—syn·chro·nis·ti·cal·ly** /ˌsiNGkrə'nistik(ə)lē/ *adv.*

syn·chro·nize /'siNGkrəˌnīz/ ▸*v.* [*trans.*] cause to occur or operate at the same time or rate: *soldiers used watches to synchronize movements | synchronize your hand gestures with your main points.* ■ [*intrans.*] occur at the same time or rate: *sometimes converging swells will synchronize to produce a peak.* ■ adjust (a clock or watch) to show the same time as another: *It is now 5:48. Synchronize watches.* ■ [*intrans.*] tally; agree: *their version failed to synchronize with the police view.* ■ coordinate; combine: *both media* ***synchronize*** *national interests* ***with*** *multinational scope.* **—syn·chro·ni·za·tion** /ˌsiNGkrənə'zāsHən/ *n.* **—syn·chro·niz·er** *n.*

syn·chro·nized swim·ming ▸*n.* a sport in which members of a team of swimmers perform coordinated or identical movements in time to music. **—syn·chro·nized swim·mer** *n.*

syn·chro·nous /'siNGkrənəs/ ▸*adj.* **1** existing or occurring at the same time: *glaciations were approximately synchronous in both hemispheres.* **2** (of a satellite or its orbit) making or denoting an orbit around the earth or another celestial body in which one revolution is completed in the period taken for the body to rotate about its axis. ▷mid 17th cent.: from late Latin *synchronus* (from Greek *sunkhronos*, from *sun-* 'together' + *khronos* 'time') + -OUS. **—syn·chro·nous·ly** *adv.*

syn·chro·nous mo·tor ▸*n.* an electric motor having a speed exactly proportional to the current frequency.

syn·chro·ny /'siNGkrənē/ ▸*n.* **1** simultaneous action, development, or occurrence. ■ the state of operating or developing according to the same time scale as something else: *some individuals do not remain* ***in synchrony with*** *the twenty-four-hour day.* **2** synchronic treatment or study: *the structuralist distinction between synchrony and diachrony.* ▷mid 19th cent.: from Greek *sunkhronos* (see SYNCHRONOUS).

syn·chro·tron /'siNGkrəˌträn/ ▸*n. Physics* a cyclotron in which the magnetic field strength increases with the energy of the particles to keep their orbital radius constant.

syn·chro·tron ra·di·a·tion ▸*n. Physics* polarized radiation emitted by a charged particle spinning in a magnetic field.

syn·cline /'sinˌklīn/ ▸*n. Geology* a trough or fold of stratified rock in which the strata slope upward from the axis. Compare with ANTICLINE. ▷late 19th cent.: from **SYN-** 'together' + Greek *klinein* 'to lean,' on the pattern of *incline*. **—syn·cli·nal** /sin'klīnl/ *adj.*

syn·co·pate /'siNGkə,pāt/ ▶*v.* [*trans.*] **1** [usu. as *adj.*] (**syncopated**) displace the beats or accents in (music or a rhythm) so that strong beats become weak and vice versa: *syncopated dance music.* **2** shorten (a word) by dropping sounds or letters in the middle, as in *symbology* for *symbolology*, or *Gloster* for *Gloucester*. ▷early 17th cent.: from late Latin *syncopat-* 'affected with syncope,' from the verb *syncopare* 'to swoon' (see **SYNCOPE**). **—syn·co·pa·tion** /,siNGkə'pāSHən/ *n.* **—syn·co·pa·tor** /-,pātər/ *n.*

syn·co·pe /'siNGkəpē/ ▶*n.* **1** *Medicine* temporary loss of consciousness caused by a fall in blood pressure. **2** *Grammar* the omission of sounds or letters from within a word, e.g., when *probably* is pronounced /'präblē/ . ▷late Middle English: via late Latin from Greek *sunkopē*, from *sun-* 'together' + *koptein* 'strike, cut off.' **—syn·co·pal** /-pəl/ *adj.*

syn·cre·tism /'siNGkrə,tizəm/ ▶*n.* **1** the amalgamation or attempted amalgamation of different religions, cultures, or schools of thought. **2** *Linguistics* the merging of different inflectional varieties of a word during the development of a language. ▷early 17th cent.: from modern Latin *syncretismus*, from Greek *sunkrētismos*, from *sunkrētizein* 'unite against a third party,' from *sun-* 'together' + *krēs* 'Cretan' (originally with reference to ancient Cretan communities). **—syn·cret·ic** /siNG'kretik/ *adj.* **—syn·cre·tist** *n.* & *adj.* **—syn·cre·tis·tic** /,siNGkrə'tistik/ *adj.*

syn·cre·tize /'siNGkri,tīz/ ▶*v.* [*trans.*] attempt to amalgamate or reconcile (differing things, esp. religious beliefs, cultural elements, or schools of thought). **—syn·cre·ti·za·tion** /,siNGkritə'zāSHən/ *n.*

syn·cy·tium /sin'siSHəm/ ▶*n.* (*pl.* **-cy·tia** /-'siSHə/) *Biology* a single cell or cytoplasmic mass containing several nuclei, formed by fusion of cells or by division of nuclei. ■ *Embryology* material of this kind forming the outermost layer of the trophoblast. ▷late 19th cent.: from **SYN-** 'together' + **-CYTE** 'cell' + **-IUM**. **—syn·cy·tial** /-SHəl/ *adj.*

synd. ▶*abbr.* ■ syndicate. ■ syndicated.

syn·dac·tyl·y /sin'daktəlē/ ▶*n. Medicine* & *Zoology* the condition of having some or all of the fingers or toes wholly or partly united, either naturally (as in web-footed animals) or as a malformation. ▷mid 19th cent.: from **SYN-** 'united' + Greek *daktulos* 'finger' + **-Y**[3].

syn·des·mo·sis /,sin,dez'mōsis/ ▶*n.* (*pl.* **-ses** /-,sēz/) *Anatomy* an immovable joint in which bones are joined by connective tissue (e.g., between the fibula and tibia at the ankle). ▷late 16th cent.: modern Latin, from Greek *sundesmos* 'binding, fastening.'

syn·det·ic /sin'detik/ ▶*adj. Grammar* of or using conjunctions. ▷early 17th cent.: from Greek *sundetikos*, from *sundein* 'bind together.'

syn·dic /'sindik/ ▶*n.* **1** a government official in various countries. **2** (in the UK) a business agent of certain universities and corporations. ▷early 17th cent.: from French, via late Latin from Greek *sundikos*, from *sun-* 'together' + *dikē* 'justice.' **—syn·di·cal** *adj.*

syn·di·cal·ism /'sindəkə,lizəm/ ▶*n. historical* a movement for transferring the ownership and control of the means of production and distribution to workers' unions. Influenced by Proudhon and by the French social philosopher Georges Sorel (1847–1922), syndicalism developed in French labor unions during the late 19th century and was at its most vigorous between 1900 and 1914, particularly in France, Italy, Spain, and the U.S. ▷early 20th cent.: from French *syndicalisme*, from *syndical*, from *syndic* 'a delegate' (see **SYNDIC**). **—syn·di·cal·ist** *n.* & *adj.*

syn·di·cate ▶*n.* /'sindikit/ a group of individuals or organizations combined to promote some common interest: *large-scale buyouts involving a syndicate of financial institutions | a crime syndicate.* ■ an association or agency supplying material simultaneously to a number of newspapers or periodicals. ■ a committee of syndics.

▶*v.* /'sindi,kāt/ [*trans.*] (usu. **be syndicated**) control or manage by a syndicate: *the loans are syndicated to a group of banks.* ■ publish or broadcast (material) simultaneously in a number of newspapers, television stations, etc.: *his reports were syndicated to 200 other papers.* ■ sell (a horse) to a syndicate: *the stallion was syndicated for a record $5.4 million.* ▷early 17th cent. (denoting a committee of syndics): from French *syndicat*, from medieval Latin *syndicatus*, from late Latin *syndicus* 'delegate of a corporation' (see **SYNDIC**). Current verb senses date from the late 19th cent. **—syn·di·ca·tion** /,sindi'kāSHən/ *n.* **—syn·di·ca·tor** /-,kātər/ *n.*

syn·di·o·tac·tic /,sindīō'taktik; sin,dī-/ ▶*adj. Chemistry* (of a polymer or polymeric structure) in which the repeating units have alternating stereochemical configurations. ▷1950s: from Greek *sunduo* 'two together' + *taktos* 'arranged' + **-IC**.

syn·drome /'sin,drōm/ ▶*n.* a group of symptoms that consistently occur together or a condition characterized by a set of associated symptoms: *a rare syndrome in which the production of white blood cells is damaged.* ■ a characteristic combination of opinions, emotions, or behavior: *the "Not In My Backyard" syndrome.* ▷mid 16th cent.: modern Latin, from Greek *sundromē*, from *sun-* 'together' + *dramein* 'to run.' **—syn·drom·ic** /sin'drämik/ *adj.*

syne /sīn/ ▶*adv. Scottish* ago. See also **AULD LANG SYNE, LANG SYNE.** ▷Middle English: contraction of dialect *sithen* 'ever since.'

syn·ec·do·che /si'nekdəkē/ ▶*n.* a figure of speech in which a part is made to represent the whole or vice versa, as in *Cleveland won by six runs* (meaning "Cleveland's baseball team"). ▷late Middle English: via Latin from Greek *sunekdokhē*, from *sun-* 'together' + *ekdekhesthai* 'take up.' **—syn·ec·doch·ic** /,sinek'däkik/ *adj.* **—syn·ec·doch·i·cal** /,sinek'däkikəl/ *adj.* **—syn·ec·doch·i·cal·ly** /-'däkik(ə)lē/ *adv.*

syn·e·col·o·gy /,sini'käləjē/ ▶*n.* the ecological study of whole plant or animal communities. Contrasted with **AUTECOLOGY**. ▷early 20th cent.: from **SYN-** 'together' + **ECOLOGY**. **—syn·ec·o·log·i·cal** /sin,ekə'läjikəl; -,ēkə-/ *adj.* **—syn·e·col·o·gist** /-jist/ *n.*

syn·ec·tics /sə'nektiks/ ▶*plural n.* [treated as *sing.*] *trademark* a problem-solving technique that seeks to promote creative thinking, typically among small groups of people of diverse experience and expertise. ▷1960s: from late Latin *synecticus* (based on Greek *sunekhein* 'hold together'), on the pattern of *dialectics*.

syn·er·e·sis /sə'nerəsis/ ▶*n.* (*pl.* **-ses** / -,sēz/) **1** the contraction of two vowels into a diphthong or single vowel. **2** *Chemistry* the contraction of a gel accompanied by the separating out of liquid. ▷late 16th cent.: via late Latin from Greek *sunairesis*, based on *sun-* 'together' + *hairein* 'take.'

syn·er·gist /'sinərjist/ ▶*n.* a substance, organ, or other agent that participates in an effect of synergy. **—syn·er·gis·tic** /,sinər'jistik/ *adj.* **—syn·er·gis·ti·cal·ly** /,sinər'jistik(ə)lē/ *adv.*

syn·er·gy /'sinərjē/ (also **syn·er·gism** /-,jizəm/) ▶*n.* the interaction or cooperation of two or more organizations, substances, or other agents to produce a combined effect greater than the sum of their separate effects: *the synergy between artist and record company.* ▷mid 19th cent.: from Greek *sunergos* 'working together,' from *sun-* 'together' + *ergon* 'work.' **—syn·er·get·ic** /,sinər'jetik/ *adj.* **—syn·er·gic** /sə'nərjik/ *adj.*

syn·es·the·sia /,sinəs'THēZHə/ (*Brit.* **syn·aes·the·sia**) ▶*n. Physiology* & *Psychology* the production of a sense impression relating to one sense or part of the body by stimulation of another sense or part of the body. ■ the poetic description of a sense impression in terms of another sense, as in "a loud perfume" or "an icy voice." ▷late 19th cent.: modern Latin, from **SYN-** 'with,' on the pattern of *anesthesia*. **—syn·es·thete** /'sinis,THēt/ *n.* **—syn·es·thet·ic** /-'THetik/ *adj.*

syn·fu·el /'sin,fyo͞oəl/ ▶*n.* fuel made from coal, corn, etc., as a substitute for a petroleum product.

syn·ga·my /'siNGgəmē/ ▶*n. Biology* the fusion of two cells, or of their nuclei, in reproduction. ▷early 20th cent.: from **SYN-** 'with' + Greek *gamos* 'marriage.'

syn·gas /'sin,gas/ ▶*n.* short for **SYNTHESIS GAS**.

Synge /siNG/, J. M. (1871–1909), Irish playwright; full name *Edmund John Millington Synge*. His *The Playboy of the Western World* (1907) caused riots at the Abbey Theatre, Dublin, because of its explicit language and its implication that Irish peasants would condone a brutal murder.

syn·ge·ne·ic /,sinjə'nēik/ ▶*adj. Medicine* & *Biology* (of organisms or cells) genetically similar or identical and hence immunologically compatible, esp. so closely related that transplantation does not provoke an immune response. ▷1960s: from **SYN-** 'together' + Greek *genea* 'race, stock' + **-IC**.

syn·ge·net·ic /,sinjə'netik/ ▶*adj. Geology* relating to or denoting a mineral deposit or formation produced at the same time as the enclosing or surrounding rock.

syng·na·thid /'siNGnə,THid; 'siNGgnə-/ ▶*n.* any of a family of fish with an elongated snout and no ventral and first dorsal fins. It includes the sea moths, seahorses, and trumpet fish.

syn·od /'sinəd/ ▶*n.* **1** an assembly of the clergy and sometimes also the laity in a diocese or other division of a particular church. **2** a Presbyterian ecclesiastical court above the presbyteries and subject to the General Assembly. ▷late Middle English: via late Latin from Greek *sunodos* 'meeting,' from *sun-* 'together' + *hodos* 'way.'

syn·od·ic /sə'nädik/ ▶*adj. Astronomy* relating to or involving the conjunction of stars, planets, or other celestial objects. ▷mid 17th cent.: via late Latin from Greek *sunodikos*, from *sunodos* (see **SYNOD**).

syn·od·i·cal /sə'nädikəl/ ▶*adj.* **1** *Christian Church* of, relating to, or constituted as a synod: *synodical government.* **2** *Astronomy* another term for **SYNODIC**. **—syn·od·al** /'sinədl/ *adj.* (in sense 1).

syn·od·ic month ▶*n. Astronomy* another term for **LUNAR MONTH**.

syn·od·ic pe·ri·od ▶*n. Astronomy* the time between successive conjunctions of a planet with the sun.

syn·o·nym /'sinə,nim/ ▶*n.* a word or phrase that means exactly or nearly the same as another word or phrase in the same language, for example *shut* is a synonym of *close*. ■ a person or thing so closely associated with a particular quality or idea that the mention of their name calls it to mind: *the Victorian age is a synonym for sexual puritanism.* ■ *Biology* a taxonomic name that has the same application as another, esp. one that has been superseded and is no longer valid. ▷late Middle English: via Latin from Greek *sunōnumon*, neuter (used as a noun) of the adjective *sunōnumos*, from *sun-* 'with' + *onoma* 'name.' **—syn·o·nym·ic** /,sinə'nimik/ *adj.* **—syn·o·nym·i·ty** /,sinə'nimitē/ *n.*

syn·on·y·mous /sə'nänəməs/ ▶*adj.* (of a word or phrase) having the same or nearly the same meaning as another word or phrase in the same language: *aggression is often taken as* **synonymous with** *violence.* ■ closely associated with or suggestive of something: *his deeds had made his name synonymous with victory.* **—syn·on·y·mous·ly** *adv.* **—syn·on·y·mous·ness** *n.*

S

syn·on·y·my /sə'nänəmē/ ▶*n.* the state of being synonymous. ▷mid 16th cent.: via late Latin from Greek *sunōnumia*, from *sunōnumos* (see **SYNONYM**).

syn·op·sis /sə'näpsis/ ▶*n.* (*pl.* **-ses** /-,sēz/) a brief summary or general survey of something: *a synopsis of the accident.* ■ an outline of the plot of a book, play, movie, or episode of a television show. ▷early 17th cent.: via late Latin from Greek, from *sun-* 'together' + *opsis* 'seeing.' **—syn·op·size** /-,sīz/ *v.*

syn·op·tic /sə'näptik/ ▶*adj.* **1** of or forming a general summary or synopsis: *a synoptic outline of the contents.* ■ taking or involving a comprehensive mental view: *a synoptic model of higher education.* **2** of or relating to the Synoptic Gospels.

▶*n.* (**Synoptics**) the Synoptic Gospels. ▷early 17th cent.: from Greek *sunoptikos*, from *sunopsis* (see **SYNOPSIS**). **—syn·op·ti·cal** *adj.* **—syn·op·ti·cal·ly** /-ik(ə)lē/ *adv.*

Syn·op·tic Gos·pels ▶*plural n.* the Gospels of Matthew, Mark, and Luke, which describe events from a similar point of view, as contrasted with that of John.

syn·op·tist /sə'näptist/ ▶*n.* the writer of a Synoptic Gospel.

syn·os·to·sis /,sinä'stōsis/ ▶*n.* (*pl.* **-ses** /-sēz/) *Physiology* & *Medicine* the union or fusion of adjacent bones by the growth of bony substance, either as a normal process during growth or as the result of ankylosis. ▷mid 19th cent.: from **SYN-** 'together' + Greek *osteon* 'bone' + **-OSIS**.

syn·o·vi·al /sə'nōvēəl/ ▶*adj.* relating to or denoting a type of joint that is surrounded by a thick flexible membrane forming a sac into which is secreted a viscous fluid that lubricates the joint. ▷mid 18th cent.: from modern Latin *synovia*, probably formed arbitrarily by Paracelsus.

syn·o·vi·tis /,sinə'vītis/ ▶*n. Medicine* inflammation of a synovial membrane.

syn·sac·rum /sin'sakrəm; -'sā-/ ▶*n.* (*pl.* **-sac·ra** /-'sakrə; -'sākrə/ or **-sac·rums**) *Zoology* an elongated composite sacrum containing a number of fused vertebrae, present in birds and some extinct reptiles.

Pronunciation Key ə *ago*; ər *over*; 'ə or ,ə *up*; 'ər or ,ər *fur*; a *hat*; ā *rate*; ä *car*; CH *chew*; e *let*; ē *see*; e(ə)r *air*; i *fit*; ī *by*; i(ə)r *ear*; NG *sing*; ō *go*; ô *for*; oi *boy*; o͝o *good*; o͞o *goo*; ou *out*; SH *she*; TH *thin*; T͟H *then*; (h)w *why*; ZH *vision*

syn·tac·tic /sin'taktik/ ▸*adj.* of or according to syntax: *syntactic analysis.* ▷early 19th cent.: from Greek *suntaktikos*, from *suntassein* 'arrange together' (see **SYNTAX**). —**syn·tac·ti·cal** *adj.* —**syn·tac·ti·cal·ly** /-ik(ə)lē/ *adv.*

syn·tagm /'sin,tam/ (also **syn·tag·ma** /sin'tagmə/) ▸*n.* (*pl.* **syn·tagms** or **syn·tag·mas** or **syn·tag·ma·ta** /sin'tagmətə/) a linguistic unit consisting of a set of linguistic forms (phonemes, words, or phrases) that are in a sequential relationship to one another. Often contrasted with **PARADIGM**. ■ the relationship between any two such forms. ▷mid 17th cent.: via late Latin from Greek *suntagma*, from *suntassein* 'arrange together.'

syn·tag·mat·ic /,sintag'matik/ ▸*adj.* of or denoting the relationship between two or more linguistic units used sequentially to make well-formed structures. Contrasted with **PARADIGMATIC**. —**syn·tag·mat·i·cal·ly** /-ik(ə)lē/ *adv.* —**syn·tag·mat·ics** *plural n.* [treated as *sing.*]

syn·tax /'sin,taks/ ▸*n.* the arrangement of words and phrases to create well-formed sentences in a language: *the syntax of English.* ■ a set of rules for or an analysis of this: *generative syntax.* ■ the branch of linguistics that deals with this. ▷late 16th cent.: from French *syntaxe*, or via late Latin from Greek *suntaxis*, from *sun-* 'together' + *tassein* 'arrange.'

syn·tax er·ror ▸*n. Computing* a character or string incorrectly placed in a command or instruction that causes a failure in execution.

syn·ten·ic /sin'tenik/ ▸*adj. Genetics* (of genes) occurring on the same chromosome: *syntenic sequences.* ▷1970s: from **SYN-** 'together' + Greek *tainia* 'band, ribbon' + **-IC**. —**syn·te·ny** /'sintənē/ *n.*

synth /sinTH/ ▸*n. informal* short for **SYNTHESIZER**.

synth·ase /'sin,THās; -,THāz/ ▸*n.* [often with *adj.*] *Biochemistry* an enzyme that catalyzes the linking together of two molecules, esp. without the direct involvement of ATP: *nitric oxide synthases.* Compare with **LIGASE**.

syn·the·sis /'sinTHəsis/ ▸*n.* (*pl.* **-ses** /-,sēz/) combination or composition, in particular: ■ the combination of ideas to form a theory or system: *the synthesis of intellect and emotion in his work | the ideology represented a synthesis of certain ideas.* Often contrasted with **ANALYSIS**. ■ the production of chemical compounds by reaction from simpler materials: *the synthesis of methanol from carbon monoxide and hydrogen.* ■ (in Hegelian philosophy) the final stage in the process of dialectical reasoning, in which a new idea resolves the conflict between thesis and antithesis. ■ *Grammar* the process of making compound and derivative words. ■ *Linguistics* the use of inflected forms rather than word order to express grammatical structure. ▷early 17th cent.: via Latin from Greek *sunthesis*, from *suntithenai* 'place together.' —**syn·the·sist** *n.*

syn·the·sis gas ▸*n.* a mixture of carbon monoxide and hydrogen produced industrially, esp. from coal, and used as a feedstock in making synthetic chemicals.

syn·the·size /'sinTHi,sīz/ (also **syn·the·tize** /-,tīz/) ▸*v.* [*trans.*] make (something) by synthesis, esp. chemically: *man synthesizes new chemical poisons and sprays the countryside wholesale.* ■ combine (a number of things) into a coherent whole: *pupils should synthesize the data they have gathered | Darwinian theory has been synthesized with modern genetics.* ■ produce (sound) electronically: *trigger chips that synthesize speech* [as *adj.*] (**synthesized**) *synthesized chords.*

syn·the·siz·er /'sinTHə,sīzər/ ▸*n.* an electronic musical instrument, typically operated by a keyboard, producing a wide variety of sounds by generating and combining signals of different frequencies.

syn·thes·pi·an /sin'THespēən/ ▸*n.* a computer-generated three-dimensional human character, designed to simulate a lifelike performance on film: *her first little-girl crush was on a synthespian, none other than Buzz Lightyear.* ▷blend of *synthetic* and *thespian*.

syn·thet·ic /sin'THetik/ ▸*adj.* relating to or using synthesis. ■ (of a substance) made by chemical synthesis, esp. to imitate a natural product: *synthetic rubber.* ■ (of an emotion or action) not genuine; insincere: *their tears are a bit synthetic.* See note at **SPURIOUS**. ■ *Logic* (of a proposition) having truth or falsity determinable by recourse to experience. Compare with **ANALYTIC**. ■ *Linguistics* (of a language) characterized by the use of inflections rather than word order to express grammatical structure. Contrasted with **AGGLUTINATIVE** and **ANALYTIC**.
▸*n.* (often **synthetics**) a synthetic material or chemical, esp. a textile fiber. ▷late 17th cent.: from French *synthétique* or modern Latin *syntheticus*, from Greek *sunthetikos*, based on *suntithenai* 'place together.' —**syn·thet·i·cal** *adj.* —**syn·thet·i·cal·ly** /-ik(ə)lē/ *adv.*

syn·thet·ic res·in ▸*n.* see **RESIN**.

syn·thon /'sin,THän/ ▸*n. Chemistry* a constituent part of a molecule to be synthesized that is regarded as the basis of a synthetic procedure. ▷1960s: from **SYNTHESIS** + **-ON**.

syn·ton·ic /sin'tänik/ ▸*adj. Psychology* (of a person) responsive to and in harmony with their environment so that affect is appropriate to the given situation: *culturally syntonic.* ■ [in *combination*] (of a psychiatric condition or psychological process) consistent with other aspects of an individual's personality and belief system: *this phobia was ego-syntonic.* ■ *historical* relating to or denoting the lively and responsive type of temperament that was considered liable to manic-depressive psychosis. See also **CYCLOTHYMIA**. ▷late 19th cent.: from German *Syntonie* 'state of being syntonic' + **-IC**. —**syn·tone** /'sin,tōn/ *n.*

syn·type /'sin,tīp/ ▸*n. Botany & Zoology* each of a set of type specimens of equal status, upon which the description and name of a new species is based. Compare with **HOLOTYPE**.

syph·i·lis /'sifəlis/ ▸*n.* a chronic bacterial disease that is contracted chiefly by infection during sexual intercourse, but also congenitally by infection of a developing fetus. • This is caused by the spirochete *Treponema pallidum*. The infection progresses in four successive stages: **primary syphilis**, characterized by a chancre in the part infected; **secondary syphilis**, affecting chiefly the skin, lymph nodes, and mucous membranes; **tertiary syphilis**, involving the spread of tumorlike lesions (gummas) throughout the body, frequently damaging the cardiovascular and central nervous systems; **quaternary syphilis** neurosyphilis. ▷early 18th cent.: modern Latin, from *Syphilis, sive Morbus Gallicus*, the title of a Latin poem (1530), from the name of the character *Syphilus*, the supposed first sufferer of the disease. —**syph·i·lit·ic** /,sifə'litik/ *adj.* & *n.*

sy·phon ▸*n.* & *v.* variant spelling of **SIPHON**.

Syr·a·cuse /'sirə,kyo͞os; -,kyo͞oz/ **1** a port on the eastern coast of Sicily; pop. 125,000. Italian name **SIRACUSA**. **2** a city in New York, southeast of Lake Ontario; pop. 147,306. The site of salt springs, it was an important center of salt production during the 19th century.

Sy·rah /sə'rä; 'sirə/ ▸*n.* another term for **SHIRAZ**[2].

syr·ette /si'ret/ ▸*n. trademark Medicine* a disposable injection unit comprising a collapsible tube with an attached hypodermic needle and a single dose of a drug, commonly morphine. ▷1940s: from **SYRINGE** + **-ETTE**.

Syr·i·a /'si(ə)rēə/ a country in the Middle East, on the eastern Mediterranean Sea; pop. 18,016,000; capital, Damascus; language, Arabic (official). —**Syr·i·an** *adj.* & *n.*

Syria was the site of various early civilizations, most notably that of the Phoenicians. Falling successively within the empires of Persia, Macedon, and Rome, it became a center of Islamic power and civilization from the 7th century and a province of the Ottoman Empire in 1516. After the Turkish defeat in World War I, Syria was mandated to France and became independent with the ejection of Vichy troops by the Allies in 1941. From 1958 to 1961, Syria was united with Egypt as the United Arab Republic. It lost the Golan Heights to Israel in the 1967 war.

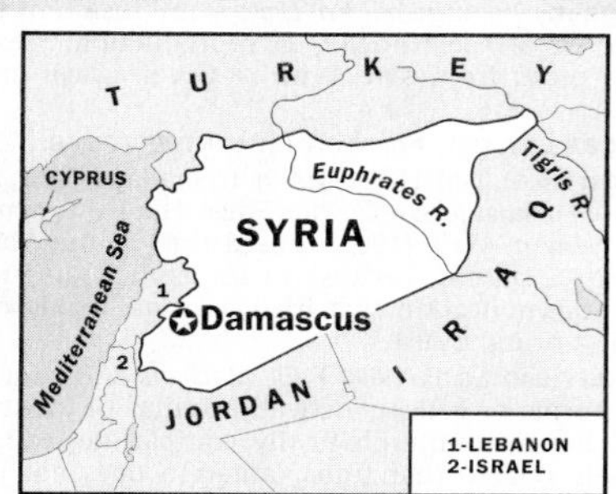

Syr·i·ac /'si(ə)rē,ak/ ▸*n.* the language of ancient Syria, a western dialect of Aramaic in which many important early Christian texts are preserved, and that is still used by Syrian Christians as a liturgical language.
▸*adj.* of or relating to this language.

sy·rin·ga /sə'riNGgə/ ▸*n.* **1** a plant of the genus *Syringa* (family Oleaceae), esp. (in gardening) the lilac. **2** *informal* another term for **MOCK ORANGE**. ▷modern Latin, from Greek *surinx*, *suring-* 'tube' (with reference to the use of its stems as pipe stems).

sy·ringe /sə'rinj; 'sirinj/ ▸*n. Medicine* a tube with a nozzle and piston or bulb for sucking in and ejecting liquid in a thin stream, used for cleaning wounds or body cavities, or fitted with a hollow needle for injecting or withdrawing fluids. ■ any similar device used in gardening or cooking.
▸*v.* (**-ring·ing**) [*trans.*] spray liquid into (the ear or a wound) with a syringe: *I had my ears syringed.* ■ spray liquid over (plants) with a syringe: *syringe the leaves frequently during warm weather.* ▷late Middle English: from medieval Latin *syringa*, from *syrinx* (see **SYRINX**).

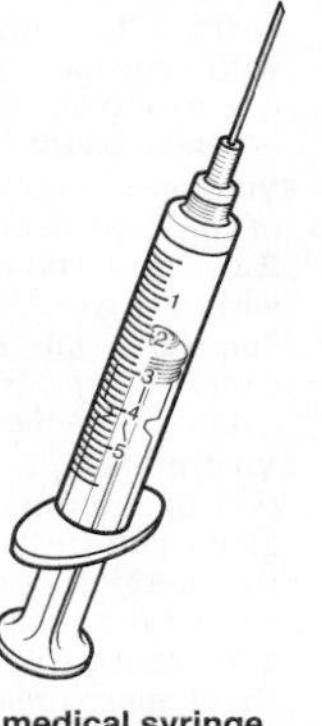
medical syringe

sy·rin·go·my·e·li·a /sə,riNGgō,mī'ēlēə; -'ēlyə/ ▸*n. Medicine* a chronic progressive disease in which longitudinal cavities form in the cervical region of the spinal cord. This characteristically results in wasting of the muscles in the hands and a loss of sensation. ▷late 19th cent.: modern Latin, from Greek *surinx*, *suring-* 'tube, channel' + *muelos* 'marrow.'

syr·inx /'siriNGks/ ▸*n.* (*pl.* **-inx·es**) **1** a set of panpipes. **2** *Ornithology* the lower larynx or voice organ in birds, situated at or near the junction of the trachea and bronchi and well developed in songbirds. ▷early 17th cent.: via Latin from Greek *surinx* 'pipe, channel.'

Syro- ▸*comb. form* Syrian; Syrian and . . . : *Syro-Palestinian.* ■ relating to Syria.

syr·phid /'sərfid/ ▸*n. Entomology* a fly of the hoverfly family (Syrphidae). ▷late 19th cent.: from modern Latin *Syrphidae* (plural), from the genus name *Syrphus*, from Greek *surphos* 'gnat.'

syr·ta·ki /sər'takē; -'täkē/ (also **sir·ta·ki**) ▸*n.* (*pl.* **-kis** or **-kia** /-kyä/) a Greek folk dance in which dancers form a line or chain. ▷modern Greek, from Greek *surtos* 'drawn, led' + the diminutive suffix *-aki*.

syr·up /'sirəp; 'sər-/ (also **sirup**) ▸*n.* a thick sweet liquid made by dissolving sugar in boiling water, often used for preserving fruit. ■ a thick sweet liquid containing medicine or used as a drink: *cough syrup.* ■ a thick sticky liquid derived from a sugar-rich plant, esp. sugar cane, corn, and maple. ■ *figurative* excessive sweetness or sentimentality of style or manner: *Mr. Gurney's poems are almost all of them syrup.* ▷late Middle English: from Old French *sirop* or medieval Latin *siropus*, from Arabic *šarāb* 'beverage'; compare with **SHERBET** and **SHRUB**[2].

syr·up of figs ▸*n.* a laxative syrup made from dried figs, typically with senna and carminatives.

syr·up·y /'sirəpē; 'sər-/ (also **sir·up·y**) ▸*adj.* having the consistency or sweetness of syrup: *syrupy desserts.* ■ *figurative* excessively sentimental: *a particularly syrupy moment from a corny film.*

sys·op /'si,säp/ ▸*n. Computing* a system operator. ▷1980s: abbreviation.

syst. ▸*abbr.* system.

sys·tem /'sistəm/ ▸*n.* **1** a set of connected things or parts forming a complex whole, in particular: ■ a set of things working together as parts of a mechanism or an interconnecting network: *the state railroad system | fluid is pushed through a system of pipes or channels.* ■ *Physiology* a set of organs in the body with a common structure or function: *the digestive system.* ■ the human or animal body as a whole: *you need to get the cholesterol out of your system.* ■ *Computing* a group of related hardware units or programs or both, esp. when dedicated to a single application. ■ *Geology* (in chronostratigraphy) a major range of strata that corresponds to a period in time, subdivided into series. ■ *Astronomy* a group of celestial objects connected by their mutual attractive forces, esp. moving in orbits about a center: *the system of bright stars known as the Gould Belt.* ■ short for **CRYSTAL SYSTEM**. **2** a set of principles or procedures according to which something is done; an organized scheme or method: *a multiparty system of government | the public school system.* ■ orderliness; method: *there was no system at all in the company.* ■ a method of choosing one's procedure in gambling. ■ a set of rules used in measurement or classification: *the metric system.* ■ (**the system**) the prevailing political or social order, esp. when regarded as oppressive and intransigent: *don't try bucking the system.* **3** *Music* a set of staves in a musical score joined by a brace. ▷early 17th cent.: from French *système* or late Latin *systema*, from Greek *sustēma*, from *sun-* 'with' + *histanai* 'set up.' —**sys·tem·less** *adj.*

▶*PHRASE* □ **get something out of one's system** *informal* get rid of a preoccupation or anxiety: *she let her get the crying out of her system.*

sys·tem·at·ic /ˌsistəˈmatik/ ▶*adj.* done or acting according to a fixed plan or system; methodical: *a systematic search of the whole city.* ▷early 18th cent.: from French *systématique*, via late Latin from late Greek *sustēmatikos*, from *sustēma* (see **SYSTEM**). —**sys·tem·at·i·cal·ly** /-ik(ə)lē/ *adv.* —**sys·tem·a·tist** /ˈsistəməˌtist/ *n.*

sys·tem·at·ic de·sen·si·ti·za·tion ▶*n. Psychiatry* a treatment for phobias in which the patient is exposed to progressively more anxiety-provoking stimuli and taught relaxation techniques.

sys·tem·at·ic er·ror ▶*n. Statistics* an error having a nonzero mean, so that its effect is not reduced when observations are averaged.

sys·tem·at·ic name ▶*n. Astronomy, Biology, Chemistry* a standardized name, esp. for a chemical element or compound, a biological taxon, or a star or other astronomical object. Compare with **BINOMIAL NOMENCLATURE, TRINOMIAL, TRIVIAL NAME.**

sys·tem·at·ics /ˌsistəˈmatiks/ ▶*plural n.* [treated as *sing.*] the branch of biology that deals with classification and nomenclature; taxonomy.

sys·tem·at·ic the·ol·o·gy ▶*n.* a form of theology in which the aim is to arrange religious truths in a self-consistent whole. —**sys·tem·at·ic the·o·lo·gian** *n.*

sys·tem·a·tize /ˈsistəməˌtīz/ ▶*v.* [*trans.*] arrange according to an organized system; make systematic: *Galen set about systematizing medical thought* | [as *adj.*] (**systematized**) *systematized reading schemes.* —**sys·tem·a·ti·za·tion** /ˌsistəmətiˈzāshən/ *n.* —**sys·tem·a·tiz·er** *n.*

sys·tem·ic /səˈstemik/ ▶*adj.* **1** of or relating to a system, esp. as opposed to a particular part: *the disease is localized rather than systemic.* ■ (of an insecticide, fungicide, or similar substance) entering the plant via the roots or shoots and passing through the tissues. **2** *Physiology* denoting the part of the circulatory system concerned with the transportation of oxygen to and carbon dioxide from the body in general, esp. as distinct from the pulmonary part concerned with the transportation of oxygen from and carbon dioxide to the lungs. ▷early 19th cent.: formed irregularly from **SYSTEM** + **-IC.** —**sys·tem·i·cal·ly** /-ik(ə)lē/ *adv.*

sys·tem in·te·gra·tor (also **sys·tems in·te·gra·tor**) ▶*n.* see **INTEGRATOR.**

sys·tem·ize /ˈsistəˌmīz/ ▶*v.* another term for **SYSTEMATIZE.** —**sys·tem·i·za·tion** /ˌsistəmiˈzāshən/ *n.* —**sys·tem·iz·er** *n.*

sys·tem op·er·a·tor (also **sys·tems op·er·a·tor**) ▶*n. Computing* a person who manages the operation of a computer system, such as an electronic bulletin board.

sys·tems an·a·lyst ▶*n.* a person who analyzes a complex process or operation in order to improve its efficiency, esp. by applying a computer system. —**sys·tems a·nal·y·sis** *n.*

sys·to·le /ˈsistəlē/ ▶*n. Physiology* the phase of the heartbeat when the heart muscle contracts and pumps blood from the chambers into the arteries. Often contrasted with **DIASTOLE.** ▷late 16th cent.: via late Latin from Greek *sustolē*, from *sustellein* 'to contract.' —**sys·tol·ic** /siˈstälik/ *adj.*

syz·y·gy /ˈsizijē/ ▶*n.* (*pl.* **-gies**) *Astronomy* a conjunction or opposition, esp. of the moon with the sun: *the planets were aligned* **in syzygy**. ■ a pair of connected or corresponding things: *animus and anima represent a supreme pair of opposites, the syzygy.* ▷early 17th cent.: via late Latin from Greek *suzugia*, from *suzugos* 'yoked, paired,' from *sun-* 'with, together' + the stem of *zeugnunai* 'to yoke.'

Szcze·cin /ˈshchechēn/ a city in northwestern Poland, a port on the Oder River, near the border with Germany; pop. 413,000. German name **STETTIN.**

Sze·chuan /ˈsechˈwän/ (also **Sze·chwan**) variant of **SICHUAN.**

Sze·ged /ˈsegˌed/ a city in southern Hungary, a port on the Tisza River, near the border with Serbia; pop. 178,000.

Szent-Györ·gyi /sānt ˈjôrj(ē)/, Albert von (1893–1986), U.S. biochemist, born in Hungary. He discovered ascorbic acid, which was later identified with vitamin C.

Szi·lard /ˈzilˌärd; ˈsil-; -ərd/, Leo (1898–1964), U.S. physicist and molecular biologist, born in Hungary. He fled from Nazi Germany to the U.S., where he became a central figure in the Manhattan Project, which developed the atom bomb.

Tt

T[1] /tē/ (also **t**) ▸*n.* (*pl.* **Ts** or **T's**) **1** the twentieth letter of the alphabet. ■ denoting the next after S in a set of items, categories, etc. **2** (**T**) (also **tee**) a shape like that of a capital T: [in *combination*] *make a T-shaped wound in the rootstock and insert the cut bud.* See also **T-SQUARE**, etc.

▸*PHRASES* □ **cross the T** *historical* (of a naval force) cross in front of an enemy force approximately at right angles, securing a tactical advantage for gunnery. □ **to a T** *informal* exactly; to perfection: *I baked it to a T, and of course it was delicious.*

T[2] ▸*abbr.* ■ [in *combination*] (in units of measurement) tera- (10^{12}): *12 Tbytes of data storage.* ■ tesla. ■ *Brit.* (in names of sports clubs) Town: *Mansfield T.*

▸*symbol* ■ temperature. ■ *Chemistry* the hydrogen isotope tritium.

t ▸*abbr.* long or metric ton(s).

▸*symbol* (*t*) *Statistics* a number characterizing the distribution of a sample taken from a population with a normal distribution (see **STUDENT'S T-TEST**).

't ▸*contraction of* the word "it," attached to the end of a verb, esp. in the transcription of regional spoken use: *I'll never do't again.*

-t[1] ▸*suffix* equivalent to **-ED**[2] (as in *crept, sent, slept*).

-t[2] ▸*suffix* equivalent to **-EST**[2] (as in *shalt*).

T-1 ▸*n.* (also **T-3**) *Computing* a high-speed data transmission line.

Ta ▸*symbol* the chemical element tantalum.

ta /tä/ ▸*exclam. Brit., informal* thank you. ▷late 18th cent.: a child's word.

TAB /tab/ ▸*abbr.* ■ typhoid–paratyphoid A and B vaccine.

tab[1] /tab/ ▸*n.* **1** a small flap or strip of material attached to or projecting from something, used to hold or manipulate it, or for identification and information. ■ a similar piece of material forming part of a garment: [as *adj.*] *shirts with tab collars.* ■ a strip or ring of metal attached to the top of a canned drink and pulled to open the can. **2** *informal* a restaurant or bar bill. **3** *Aeronautics* a part of a control surface, typically hinged, that modifies the action or response of the surface.

▸*v.* (**tabbed, tab·bing**) [*trans.*] mark or identify with a projecting piece of material: *he opened the book at a page tabbed by a cloth bookmark.* ■ *figurative* identify as being of a specified type or suitable for a specified position: *he was tabbed by the president as the next Republican National Committee chairman.* ▷late Middle English: perhaps related to **TAG**[1]. **—tabbed** *adj.*

▸*PHRASES* □ **keep tabs** (or **a tab**) **on** *informal* monitor the activities or development of; keep under observation. □ **pick up the tab** *informal* pay for something: *my company will pick up the tab for all moving expenses.*

tab[2] ▸*n.* a facility in a word-processing program, or a device on a typewriter, used for advancing to a sequence of set positions in tabular work: *set tabs at 1.4 inches and 3.4 inches.*

▸*v.* (**tabbed, tab·bing**) **1** short for **TABULATE**. **2** [*intrans.*] activate the tab feature on a word processor or typewriter: *the user can tab to the phrase and press Enter.*

tab[3] ▸*n. informal* a tablet containing a dose of a drug. ▷1960s: abbreviation.

tab[4] ▸*n. informal* a tabloid newspaper: *she tries to cover up his pecadillos before they make the tabs' front pages.*

tab. ▸*abbr.* ■ tables. ■ (in prescriptions) tablet. [from Latin *tabella*.]

ta·bac /tä'bäk/ ▸*n.* (*pl. pronunc.* same) (in French-speaking regions) a tobacconist's shop. ▷French, literally *tobacco*.

tab·ard /'tābərd/ ▸*n.* a sleeveless jerkin consisting only of front and back pieces with a hole for the head. ■ *historical* a coarse garment of this kind as the outer dress of medieval peasants and clerics, or worn as a surcoat over armor. ■ a herald's official coat emblazoned with the arms of the sovereign. ▷Middle English: from Old French *tabart*, of unknown origin.

tab·a·ret /'tabərit/ ▸*n.* an upholstery fabric of alternate satin and watered silk stripes. ▷late 18th cent.: probably from **TABBY**.

Ta·bas·co[1] /tə'baskō; -'bäs-/ a state in southeastern Mexico, on the Gulf of Mexico; capital, Villahermosa.

Ta·bas·co[2] /tə'baskō/ (also **Ta·bas·co sauce**) ▸*n. trademark* a pungent sauce made from the fruit of a capsicum pepper. • The plant is *Capsicum frutescens* (or *C. anuum*), family Solanaceae. ▷late 19th cent.: named after the state of *Tabasco* (see **TABASCO**[1]).

tab·bou·leh /tə'bōōlē/ (also **ta·bou·li**) ▸*n.* an Arab salad of cracked wheat mixed with finely chopped ingredients such as tomatoes, onions, and parsley. ▷from Arabic *tabbūla*.

tab·by /'tabē/ ▸*n.* (*pl.* **-bies**) **1** (also **tab·by cat**) a cat whose fur is mottled or streaked with dark stripes. [late 17th cent. (as *tabby cat*): said to be so named from its striped coloring.] ■ *informal* any domestic cat. **2** a fabric with a watered pattern, typically silk. **3** a plain weave. **4** a type of concrete made of lime, shells, gravel, and stones that dries very hard. [early 19th cent. (originally *tabby work*): perhaps a different word, or from a resemblance in color to that of a tabby cat.]

▸*adj.* (of a cat) gray or brownish in color and streaked with dark stripes. ▷late 16th cent. (denoting a kind of silk taffeta, originally striped, later with a watered finish: see sense 2): from French *tabis*, based on Arabic *al-'Attābiyya*, the name of the quarter of Baghdad where tabby was manufactured.

tab·er·nac·le /'tabər,nakəl/ ▸*n.* **1** (in biblical use) a fixed or movable habitation, typically of light construction. ■ a tent used as a sanctuary for the Ark of the Covenant by the Israelites during the Exodus and until the building of the Temple. **2** a meeting place for worship used by some Protestants or Mormons. **3** an ornamented receptacle or cabinet in which a pyx or ciborium containing the reserved sacrament may be placed in Catholic churches, usually on or above an altar. ■ *archaic* a canopied niche or recess in the wall of a church. **4** a partly open socket or double post on a sailboat's deck into which a mast is fixed, with a pivot near the top so that the mast can be lowered. ▷Middle English: via French from Latin *tabernaculum* 'tent,' diminutive of *taberna* 'hut, tavern.' **—tab·er·nac·led** *adj.*

ta·bes /'tābēz/ ▸*n. Medicine* emaciation. See also **TABES DORSALIS**. ▷late 16th cent.: from Latin, literally 'wasting away.' **—ta·bet·ic** /tə'betik/ *adj.*

ta·bes·cent /tə'besənt/ ▸*adj.* wasting away. ▷late 19th cent.: from Latin *tabescent-* 'beginning to waste away,' from the verb *tabescere*, from *tabere* 'waste away.'

ta·bes dor·sal·is /'tābēz dôr'salis; -'sālis/ ▸*n. Medicine* loss of coordination of movement, esp. as a result of syphilitic infection of the spinal cord. Also called **LOCOMOTOR ATAXIA**. ▷modern Latin, literally 'wasting of the back.'

ta·bi /'täbē/ ▸*n.* (*pl.* same) a thick-soled Japanese ankle sock with a separate section for the big toe. ▷Japanese.

ta·bla /'täblə/ ▸*n.* a pair of small hand drums attached together, used in Indian music; one is slightly larger than the other and is played using pressure from the heel of the hand to vary the pitch. ▷from Persian and Urdu *tablah*, Hindi *tablā*, from Arabic *ṭabl* 'drum.'

tab·la·ture /'tabləCHər; -,CHōōr/ ▸*n. chiefly historical* a form of musical notation indicating fingering rather than the pitch of notes, written on lines corresponding to, for example, the strings of a lute or the holes on a flute. ▷late 16th cent.: from French, probably from Italian *tavolatura*, from *tavolare* 'set to music.'

ta·ble /'tābəl/ ▸*n.* **1** a piece of furniture with a flat top and one or more legs, providing a level surface on which objects may be placed, and that can be used for such purposes as eating, writing, working, or playing games. ■ [in *sing.*] food provided in a restaurant or household: *he was reputed to have the finest French table of the time.* ■ a group seated at a table for a meal: *the whole table was in gales of laughter.* ■ (**the table**) a meeting place for formal discussions held to settle an issue or dispute: *the negotiating table.* ■ [in *sing.*] *Bridge* the dummy hand (which is exposed on the table): *they made the hand easily with the aid of a club ruff on the table.* **2** a set of facts or figures systematically displayed, esp. in columns: *the population has grown, as shown in table 1 | a table of contents.* ■ *Computing* a collection of data stored in memory as a series of records, each defined by a unique key stored with it. **3** a flat surface, in particular: ■ *Architecture* a flat, typically rectangular, vertical surface. ■ a horizontal molding, esp. a cornice. ■ a slab of wood or stone bearing an inscription. ■ a flat surface of a gem. ■ a cut gem with two flat faces. ■ each half or quarter of a folding board for backgammon.

▸*v.* [*trans.*] **1** postpone consideration of: *I'd like the issue to be tabled for the next few months.* **2** *Brit.* present formally for discussion or consideration at a meeting: *an MP tabled an amendment to the bill.* ▷Old English *tabule* 'flat slab, inscribed tablet,' from Latin *tabula* 'plank, tablet, list,' reinforced in Middle English by Old French *table*. **—ta·ble·ful** /-,fōōl/ *n.* (*pl.* **-fuls**).

▸*PHRASES* □ **at table** seated at a table eating a meal. □ **lay something on the table 1** make something known so that it can be freely and sensibly discussed. **2** postpone something indefinitely. □ **on the table** offered for discussion: *our offer remains on the table.* □ **turn the tables** reverse one's position relative to someone else, esp. by turning a position of disadvantage into one of advantage: *police invited householders to a seminar on how to* ***turn the tables on*** *burglars.* □ **under the table 1** *informal* very drunk: *by 3:30 everybody was under the table.* **2** (esp. of making a payment) secretly or covertly: *he accepted a slew of payoffs under the table.* ■ another term for **UNDER THE COUNTER** (see **COUNTER**[1]).

tab·leau /,ta'blō/ ▸*n.* (*pl.* **tab·leaux** /,ta'blōz/) a group of models or motionless figures representing a scene from a story or from history; a tableau vivant. ▷late 17th cent. (in the sense 'picture,' figuratively 'picturesque description'): from French, literally 'picture,' diminutive of *table* (see **TABLE**).

tab·leau vi·vant /ta'blō vē'vän; -'vänt/ ▸*n.* (*pl.* **tab·leaux vi·vants** *pronunc.* same) *chiefly historical* a silent and motionless group of people arranged to represent a scene or incident. ▷French, literally 'living picture.'

ta·ble·cloth /'tābəl,klôTH; -,kläTH/ ▸*n.* a cloth spread over a table, esp. during meals.

ta·ble d'hôte /,täbəl 'dōt; ,täblə; ,tabəl/ ▸*n.* a restaurant meal offered at a fixed price and with few if any choices. ▷early 17th cent.: French, literally 'host's table.' The term originally denoted a table in a hotel or restaurant where all guests ate together, hence a meal served there at a stated time and for a fixed price.

ta·ble lamp ▸*n.* a small lamp designed to stand on a table.

T

ta·ble·land /ˈtābəl,(l)and/ ▸*n.* a broad, high, level region; a plateau.

ta·ble lin·en ▸*n.* fabric items used at mealtimes, such as tablecloths and napkins, collectively.

ta·ble man·ners ▸*plural n.* a pattern of behavior that is conventionally required of someone while eating.

Ta·ble Moun·tain a flat-topped mountain near the southwestern tip of South Africa that overlooks Cape Town and Table Bay. It is 3,563 feet (1,087 m) high.

ta·ble salt ▸*n.* salt suitable for sprinkling on food at meals.

ta·ble saw ▸*n.* a circular saw mounted under a table or bench so that the blade projects up through a slot.

table saw

ta·ble·spoon /ˈtābəl,spo͞on/ ▸*n.* a large spoon for serving food. ■ (abbr.: **tbsp.** or **tbs.** or **T**) a measurement in cooking, equivalent to 1/2 fluid ounce, three teaspoons, or 15 ml. **—ta·ble·spoon·ful** /-,fo͝ol/ *n.* (*pl.* **-fuls**).

tab·let /ˈtablit/ ▸*n.* a flat slab of stone, clay, or wood, used esp. for an inscription. ■ a small disk or cylinder of a compressed solid substance, typically a measured amount of a medicine or drug; a pill. ■ a writing pad. ■ *Brit.* a small flat piece of soap. ■ *Architecture* another term for TABLE (sense 3). ▷Middle English: from Old French *tablete*, from a diminutive of Latin *tabula* (see TABLE).

ta·ble talk ▸*n.* informal conversation carried on at meals.

ta·ble ten·nis ▸*n.* an indoor game based on tennis, played with small paddles and a ball bounced on a table divided by a net.

ta·ble·top /ˈtābəl,täp/ ▸*n.* the horizontal top part of a table. ■ [as *adj.*] small or portable enough to be placed or used on a table: *a tabletop hockey game.*

tab·let PC ▸*n.* a microcomputer that accepts input directly onto an LCD screen by means of a stylus, savable as image or text.

ta·ble·ware /ˈtābəl,wer/ ▸*n.* dishes, utensils, and glassware used for serving and eating meals at a table.

ta·ble wine ▸*n.* wine of moderate quality considered suitable for drinking with a meal.

ta·blier /täblēˈā/ ▸*n. historical* a part of a woman's dress resembling an apron. ▷mid 19th cent.: from French, based on Latin *tabula* (see TABLE).

tab·loid /ˈtab,loid/ ▸*n.* a newspaper having pages half the size of those of a standard newspaper, typically popular in style and dominated by headlines, photographs, and sensational stories. ■ [as *adj.*] sensational in a lurid or vulgar way: *they argued about who made what allegation on what tabloid TV show.* ▷late 19th cent.: from TABLET + -OID. Originally the proprietary name of a medicine sold in tablets, the term came to denote any small medicinal tablet; the current sense reflects the notion of "concentrated, easily assimilable."

tab·loid·i·za·tion /,tabloidəˈzāsHən/ ▸*n.* a change in emphasis from the factual to the sensational, esp. in television news: *the tabloidization of the nightly news during sweeps week.*

ta·boo /təˈbo͞o; ta-/ (also **ta·bu**) ▸*n.* (*pl.* **-boos** also **-bus** /təˈbo͞oz/) a social or religious custom prohibiting or restricting a particular practice or forbidding association with a particular person, place, or thing.

▸*adj.* prohibited or restricted by social custom: *sex was a taboo subject.* ■ designated as sacred and prohibited: *the burial ground was seen as a taboo place.*

▸*v.* (**-boos**, **-booed** /-ˈbo͞od/ or **-bus**, **-bued**) [*trans.*] place under such prohibition: *traditional societies taboo female handling of food during this period.* ▷late 18th cent.: from Tongan *tabu* 'set apart, forbidden'; introduced into English by Captain Cook.

ta·bor /ˈtābər/ ▸*n. historical* a small drum, esp. one used simultaneously by the player of a simple pipe. ▷Middle English: from Old French *tabour* 'drum'; perhaps related to Persian *tabīra* 'drum.' Compare with TAMBOUR.

tab·o·ret /tabəˈret; ˈtabərit/ (**tab·ou·ret**) ▸*n.* a low stool or small table. ▷mid 17th cent.: from French, 'stool,' diminutive of *tabour* 'drum' (see TABOR).

ta·bou·li ▸*n.* variant spelling of TABBOULEH.

Ta·briz /təˈbrēz/ a city in northwestern Iran; pop. 1,089,000. It lies at about 4,485 feet (1,367 m) above sea level at the center of a volcanic region and has been subject to frequent destructive earthquakes.

Ta·briz rug ▸*n.* a rug made in Tabriz, the older styles of which typically have a rich decorative medallion pattern.

tab·u·lar /ˈtabyələr/ ▸*adj.* **1** (of data) consisting of or presented in columns or tables: *a tabular presentation of running costs.* **2** broad and flat like the top of a table: *a huge tabular iceberg.* ■ (of a crystal) relatively broad and thin, with two well-developed parallel faces. ▷mid 17th cent. (sense 2): from Latin *tabularis*, from *tabula* (see TABLE). **—tab·u·lar·ly** *adv.*

ta·bu·la ra·sa /ˈtäbyo͝olə ˈräsə; ˈräzə/ ▸*n.* (*pl.* **ta·bu·lae ra·sae** /ˈtäbyo͝olē ˈräsē; ˈräzē/) an absence of preconceived ideas or predetermined goals; a clean slate: *the team did not have complete freedom and a tabula rasa from which to work.* ■ the human mind, esp. at birth, viewed as having no innate ideas. ▷Latin, literally 'scraped tablet,' denoting a tablet with the writing erased.

tab·u·late /ˈtabyə,lāt/ ▸*v.* [*trans.*] arrange (data) in tabular form: [as *adj.*] (**tabulated**) *tabulated results.* ▷early 17th cent. (originally Scots in the sense 'enter on a roll'): in modern use from TABLE + -ATE[3]. **—tab·u·la·tion** /,tabyəˈlāsHən/ *n.*

tab·u·la·tor /ˈtabyəlātər/ ▸*n.* **1** a person or thing that arranges data in tabular form. **2** another term for TAB[2].

ta·bun /ˈtäbo͞on/ ▸*n.* an organophosphorus nerve gas, developed in Germany during World War II. ▷German, of unknown origin.

TAC ▸*abbr.* Tactical Air Command.

tac·a·ma·hac /ˈtakəmə,hak/ ▸*n.* another term for BALSAM POPLAR. ▷late 16th cent. (originally denoting the aromatic resin of *Bursera simaruba*: see ELEMI): from obsolete Spanish *tacamahaca*, from Aztec *tecomahiyac*.

tac·an /ˈtakən/ ▸*n.* an electronic ultrahigh-frequency navigational aid system for aircraft that measures bearing and distance from a ground beacon. ▷1950s: from *tac(tical) a(ir) n(avigation)*.

ta·cet /ˈtāsit; ˈtas-; ˈtäket/ ▸*v.* [*intrans.*] *Music* (as a direction) indicating that a voice or instrument is silent. ▷Latin, literally 'is silent,' from *tacere* 'be silent.'

tach /tak/ ▸*n. informal* short for TACHOMETER.

tach·ism /ˈta,sHizəm/ (also **tach·isme**) ▸*n.* a style of painting adopted by some French artists from the 1940s, involving the use of dabs or splotches of color, similar in aims to abstract expressionism. ▷1950s: from French *tachisme*, from *tache* 'a stain.'

ta·chis·to·scope /təˈkistə,skōp/ ▸*n.* an instrument used for exposing objects to the eye for a very brief measured period of time. ▷late 19th cent.: from Greek *takhistos* 'swiftest' + -SCOPE. **—ta·chis·to·scop·ic** /-,kistəˈskäpik/ *adj.* **—ta·chis·to·scop·i·cal·ly** /-ˈskäpik(ə)lē/ *adv.*

tacho- ▸*comb. form* relating to speed: *tachograph.* ▷from Greek *takhos* 'speed.'

tach·o·graph /ˈtakə,graf/ ▸*n.* a tachometer providing a record of engine speed over a period, esp. in a commercial road vehicle.

ta·chom·e·ter /taˈkämitər; tə-/ ▸*n.* an instrument that measures the working speed of an engine (esp. in a road vehicle), typically in revolutions per minute.

tachy- ▸*comb. form* rapid: *tachycardia.* ▷from Greek *takhus* 'swift.'

tach·y·car·di·a /,takiˈkärdēə/ ▸*n.* an abnormally rapid heart rate. ▷late 19th cent.: from TACHY- 'swift' + Greek *kardia* 'heart.'

ta·chyg·ra·phy /taˈkigrəfē; tə-/ ▸*n.* stenography or shorthand, esp. that of ancient or medieval scribes. **—tach·y·graph·ic** /,takiˈgrafik/ *adj.*

tach·y·kin·in /,takəˈkinin/ ▸*n. Biochemistry* any of a class of substances formed in bodily tissue in response to injury and having a rapid stimulant effect on smooth muscle.

ta·chym·e·ter /taˈkimitər; tə-/ ▸*n.* **1** a theodolite for the rapid measurement of distances in surveying. **2** a facility on a watch for measuring speed. **—tach·y·met·ric** / ,takəˈmetrik/ *adj.*

tach·y·on /ˈtakē,än/ ▸*n. Physics* a hypothetical particle that travels faster than light. ▷1960s: from TACHY- 'swift' + -ON.

tach·y·phy·lax·is /,takəfiˈlaksis/ ▸*n. Medicine* rapidly diminishing response to successive doses of a drug, rendering it less effective. The effect is common with drugs acting on the nervous system.

tach·yp·ne·a /,takə(p)ˈnēə/ (*Brit.* **tach·yp·noe·a**) ▸*n. Medicine* abnormally rapid breathing. ▷late 19th cent.: from TACHY- 'swift' + Greek *pnoē* 'breathing.'

tac·it /ˈtasit/ ▸*adj.* understood or implied without being stated: *your silence may be taken to mean tacit agreement.* ▷early 17th cent. (in the sense 'wordless, noiseless'): from Latin *tacitus*, past participle of *tacere* 'be silent.' **—tac·it·ly** *adv.*

tac·i·turn /ˈtasi,tərn/ ▸*adj.* (of a person) reserved or uncommunicative in speech; saying little. ▷late 18th cent.: from Latin *taciturnus*, from *tacitus* (see TACIT). **—tac·i·tur·ni·ty** /,tasiˈtərnitē/ *n.* **—tac·i·turn·ly** *adv.*

Tac·i·tus /ˈtasətəs/ (*c.* 56–120), Roman historian; full name *Publius* (or *Gaius*) *Cornelius Tacitus*. His *Annals* (covering the years 14–68) and *Histories* (69–96) are major works on the history of the Roman Empire.

tack[1] /tak/ ▸*n.* **1** a small, sharp, broad-headed nail. ■ a thumbtack. **2** a long stitch used to fasten fabrics together temporarily, prior to permanent sewing. **3** *Sailing* an act of changing course by turning a vessel's head into and through the wind, so as to bring the wind on the opposite side. ■ a boat's course relative to the direction of the wind: *the brig bowled past on the opposite tack.* ■ a distance sailed between such changes of course. ■ *figurative* a method of dealing with a situation or problem; a course of action or policy: *as she could not stop him from going she tried another tack and insisted on going with him.* **4** *Sailing* a rope for securing the weather clew of a course. ■ the weather clew of a course, or the lower forward corner of a fore-and-aft sail. **5** the quality of being sticky: *cooking the sugar to caramel gives tack to the texture.*

▸*v.* **1** [*trans.*] fasten or fix in place with tacks: *he used the tool to tack down sheets of fiberboard.* ■ fasten (pieces of cloth) together temporarily with long stitches. ■ (**tack something on**) add or append something to something already existing: *long-term savings plans with some life insurance tacked on.* **2** [*intrans.*] *Sailing* change course by turning a boat's head into and through the wind. Compare with WEAR[2]. [from the practice of shifting ropes (see sense 4) to change direction.] ■ [*trans.*] alter the course of (a boat) in such a way. ■ [with *adverbial of direction*] make a series of such changes of course while sailing: *she spent the entire night tacking back and forth.* ■ *figurative* make a change in one's conduct, policy, or direction of attention: *he answered, but she had tacked and was on a new tangent.* ▷Middle English (in the general sense 'something that fastens one thing to another'): probably related to Old French *tache* 'clasp, large nail.' **—tack·er** *n.*

▸*PHRASE* □ **on the port** (or **starboard**) **tack** *Sailing* with the wind coming from the port (or starboard) side of the boat.

tack[2] ▸*n.* equipment used in horseback riding, including the saddle and bridle.

▸*v.* [*trans.*] (usu. **tack up**) put tack on (a horse): *he was cooperative about being tacked up and groomed.* ▷late 18th cent. (originally dialect in the general sense 'apparatus, equipment'): shortening of TACKLE. The noun sense dates from the 1920s.

tack coat ▸*n.* (in roadmaking) a thin coating of tar or asphalt applied before a road is paved to form an adhesive bond.

tack·le /ˈtakəl/ ▸*n.* **1** the equipment required for a task or sport: *fishing tackle.* **2** a mechanism consisting of ropes, pulley blocks, hooks, or other things for lifting heavy objects. ■ the running rigging and gear used to work a boat's sails. **3** *Football* & *Rugby* an act of seizing and stopping a player in possession of the ball by knocking them to the ground. ■ (in soccer and other games) an act of taking the ball, or attempting to take the ball, from an opponent. **4** *Football* a player who lines up inside the end along the line of scrimmage.

▸*v.* [*trans.*] make determined efforts to deal with (a problem or difficult task): *police have launched an initiative to tackle rising crime.* ■ *Football* & *Rugby* stop the forward progress of (the ball carrier) by seizing them and knocking them to the ground. ■ *chiefly Soccer* try to take the ball from (an opponent) by intercepting them. ▷Middle English (denoting equipment for a specific task): probably from Middle Low

Pronunciation Key ə *ago*; ər *over*; ˈə or ,ə *up*; ˈər or ,ər *fur*; a *hat*; ā *rate*; ä *car*; CH *chew*; e *let*; ē *see*; e(ə)r *air*; i *fit*; ī *by*; i(ə)r *ear*; NG *sing*; ō *go*; ô *for*; oi *boy*; o͝o *good*; o͞o *goo*; ou *out*; SH *she*; TH *thin*; T͟H *then*; (h)w *why*; ZH *vision*

German *takel*, from *taken* 'lay hold of.' Early senses of the verb (late Middle English) described the provision and handling of a ship's equipment. **—tack·ler** /ˈtak(ə)lər/ *n.*

tack·le block ▶*n.* a pulley over which a rope runs.

tack·le-fall ▶*n.* a rope for applying force to the blocks of a tackle. See TACKLE (sense 2).

tack room ▶*n.* a room in a stable building where saddles, bridles, and other equipment are kept.

tack·y[1] /ˈtakē/ ▶*adj.* (**tack·i·er**, **tack·i·est**) (of glue, paint, or other substances) retaining a slightly sticky feel; not fully dry: *the paint was still tacky.* **—tack·i·ness** *n.*

tack·y[2] ▶*adj.* (**tack·i·er**, **tack·i·est**) *informal* showing poor taste and quality: *even in her faintly tacky costumes, she won our hearts.* ▷early 19th cent.: of unknown origin. Early use was as a noun denoting a horse of little value, later applied to a poor white in some Southern states, hence 'shabby, cheap, in bad taste' (mid 19th cent.). **—tack·i·ly** /ˈtakəlē/ *adv.* **—tack·i·ness** *n.*

ta·co /ˈtäkō/ ▶*n.* (*pl.* **-cos**) a Mexican dish consisting of a fried tortilla, typically folded, filled with various mixtures, such as seasoned meat, beans, lettuce, and tomatoes. ▷Mexican Spanish, from Spanish, literally 'plug, wad.'

ta·co chip ▶*n.* a fried fragment of a taco, flavored with spices and eaten as a snack.

Ta·co·ma /təˈkōmə/ an industrial port city in west central Washington, on Puget Sound, south of Seattle; pop. 193,556.

Ta·con·ic Moun·tains /təˈkänik/ (also **the Taconics**) a range of the Appalachian system, along the eastern border of New York with three states: Connecticut, Massachusetts, and Vermont.

tac·o·nite /ˈtakəˌnīt/ ▶*n.* a low-grade iron ore consisting largely of chert, occurring in the US chiefly around Lake Superior. ▷early 20th cent.: from the name of the *Taconic* Mountains (in southeastern New York State, western Massachusetts, and southwestern Vermont) + -ITE[1].

tac·rine /ˈtakˌrēn/ ▶*n.* *Medicine* a synthetic drug used in Alzheimer's disease to inhibit the breakdown of acetylcholine by cholinesterase and thereby enhance neurological function. • An acridine derivative; chem. formula: $C_{13}H_{15}N_2Cl$. ▷1960s: from *t(etra-)* + *acr(id)ine.*

tact /takt/ ▶*n.* adroitness and sensitivity in dealing with others or with difficult issues: *the inspector broke the news to me with tact and consideration.* ▷mid 17th cent. (denoting the sense of touch): via French from Latin *tactus* 'touch, sense of touch,' from *tangere* 'to touch.'

Tac·tel /ˈtakˌtel/ ▶*n.* *trademark* a polyamide fabric or fiber with a soft, silky feel.

tact·ful /ˈtak(t)fəl/ ▶*adj.* having or showing tact: *they need a tactful word of advice | they were too tactful to say anything.* **—tact·ful·ly** *adv.* **—tact·ful·ness** *n.*

tac·tic /ˈtaktik/ ▶*n.* an action or strategy carefully planned to achieve a specific end. ■ (**tactics**) [also treated as *sing.*] the art of disposing armed forces in order of battle and of organizing operations, esp. during contact with an enemy. Often contrasted with STRATEGY. ▷mid 18th cent.: from modern Latin *tactica*, from Greek *taktikē (tekhnē)* '(art) of tactics,' feminine of *taktikos*, from *taktos* 'ordered, arranged,' from the base of *tassein* 'arrange.' **—tac·ti·cian** /takˈtisʜən/ *n.*

tac·ti·cal /ˈtaktikəl/ ▶*adj.* of, relating to, or constituting actions carefully planned to gain a specific military end: *as a tactical officer in the field he had no equal.* ■ (of bombing or weapons) done or for use in immediate support of military or naval operations. Often contrasted with STRATEGIC. ■ (of a person or their actions) showing adroit planning; aiming at an end beyond the immediate action: *in a tactical retreat, she moved into a hotel with her daughters.* ▷late 16th cent. (in the sense 'relating to military or naval tactics'): from Greek *taktikos* (see TACTIC) + -AL. **—tac·ti·cal·ly** /-ik(ə)lē/ *adv.*

tac·tile /ˈtaktl; ˈtakˌtīl/ ▶*adj.* of or connected with the sense of touch: *vocal and visual signals become less important as tactile signals intensify.* ■ perceptible by touch or apparently so; tangible: *she had a distinct, almost tactile memory.* ■ designed to be perceived by touch: *tactile exhibitions help blind people enjoy the magic of sculpture.* ■ (of a person) given to touching others, esp. as an unselfconscious expression of sympathy or affection. ▷early 17th cent. (in the sense 'perceptible by touch, tangible'): from Latin *tactilis*, from *tangere* 'to touch.' **—tac·til·i·ty** /takˈtilitē/ *n.*

tact·less /ˈtaktləs/ ▶*adj.* having or showing a lack of adroitness and sensitivity in dealing with others or with difficult issues: *a tactless remark.* **—tact·less·ly** *adv.* **—tact·less·ness** *n.*

tac·tu·al /ˈtakcʜo͞oəl/ ▶*adj.* another term for TACTILE.

tac·tus /ˈtäktōos/ ▶*n.* *Music* a principal accent or rhythmic unit, esp. in 15th- and 16th-century music. ▷Latin.

tad /tad/ *informal* ▶*adv.* (**a tad**) to a small extent; somewhat: *Mark looked a tad embarrassed.*
▶*n.* [in *sing.*] a small amount of something: *biscuits sweetened with* **a tad of** *honey.* ▷late 19th cent. (denoting a small child): origin uncertain, perhaps from TADPOLE. The current usage dates from the 1940s.

ta-da /tä ˈdä/ (also **ta-dah**) ▶*exclam.* an imitation of a fanfare, used typically to call attention to an impressive entrance or a dramatic announcement. ▷late 20th cent.: imitative.

Ta·djik ▶*n.* & *adj.* variant spelling of TAJIK.

tad·pole /ˈtadˌpōl/ ▶*n.* the tailed aquatic larva of an amphibian (frog, toad, newt, or salamander), breathing through gills and lacking legs until its later stages of development. ▷late 15th cent.: from Old English *tāda* 'toad' + POLL (probably because the tadpole seems to consist of a large head and a tail in its early development stage).

Ta·dzhik ▶*n.* & *adj.* variant spelling of TAJIK.

tae-bo /ˈtī ˈbō/ ▶*n.* *trademark* an exercise system combining elements of aerobics and kick-boxing. ▷1990s: from Korean *t'ae* 'foot' + *bo*, short for *boxing.*

tae·di·um vi·tae /ˈtēdēəm ˈvēˌtī; ˈvītē/ ▶*n.* a state of extreme ennui; weariness of life. ▷Latin.

Tae·gu /ˈtaˌgo͞o/ a city in southeastern South Korea; pop. 2,229,000. Nearby is the Haeinsa temple, which was established in AD 802 and contains 80,000 Buddhist printing blocks dating from the 13th century.

Tae·jon /ˈtaˈjən; -ˈjôn/ a city in central South Korea; pop. 1,062,000.

tae kwon do /ˈtī ˈkwän ˈdō/ ▶*n.* a modern Korean martial art similar to karate. ▷Korean, literally 'art of hand and foot fighting,' from *t'ae* 'kick' + *kwon* 'fist' + *do* 'art, method.'

tael /tāl/ ▶*n.* a weight used in China and the Far East, originally of varying amount but later fixed at about 38 grams (1 1/3 oz.). ■ a former Chinese monetary unit based on the value of this weight of standard silver. ▷from Malay *tahil* 'weight.'

tae·ni·a /ˈtēnēə/ (also **te·ni·a**) ▶*n.* (*pl.* **-ni·ae** /-nēˌē; -nēˌī/ or **-ni·as**) **1** *Anatomy* a flat ribbonlike structure in the body. ■ (**tae·ni·ae co·li** /ˈkōlī/) the smooth longitudinal muscles of the colon. **2** *Architecture* a fillet between a Doric architrave and frieze. **3** (in ancient Greece) a band or ribbon worn around a person's head. **4** a large tapeworm that parasitizes mammals. • Genus *Taenia*, class Cestoda: several species, in particular *T. saginata* and *T. soleum.* ▷mid 16th cent. (sense 2): via Latin from Greek *tainia* 'band, ribbon.' **—tae·ni·oid** /-nēˌoid/ *adj.*

taen·ite /ˈtēˌnīt/ ▶*n.* a nickel-iron alloy occurring as lamellae and strips in meteorites. ▷mid 19th cent.: from TAENIA + -ITE[1].

taf·fe·ta /ˈtafitə/ ▶*n.* a fine lustrous silk or similar synthetic fabric with a crisp texture. ▷late Middle English (originally denoting a plain-weave silk): from Old French *taffetas* or medieval Latin *taffata*, based on Persian *tāftan* 'to shine.'

taff·rail /ˈtafˌrāl; -rəl/ ▶*n.* a rail and ornamentation around a ship's stern. ▷early 19th cent.: alteration (by association with RAIL[1]) of obsolete *tafferel* 'panel,' used to denote the flat part of a ship's stern above the transom, from Dutch *tafereel.*

taf·fy /ˈtafē/ ▶*n.* (*pl.* **-fies**) **1** a candy similar to toffee, made from sugar or molasses, boiled with butter and pulled until glossy. **2** *informal* insincere flattery. ▷early 19th cent.: earlier form of TOFFEE.

taf·fy pull ▶*n.* *dated* a social occasion on which young people meet to make taffy.

taf·i·a /ˈtafēə/ ▶*n.* *W. Indian* a drink similar to rum, distilled from molasses or waste from the production of brown sugar. ▷via French from West Indian Creole, alteration of RATAFIA.

Taft /taft/, William Howard (1857–1930), 27th president of the U.S. 1909–13. A Republican, he succeeded Theodore Roosevelt to the presidency. His administration is remembered for its use of dollar diplomacy, enforcement of antitrust laws, and enactment of tariff laws. He later served as chief justice of the U.S. 1921–30.

tag[1] /tag/ ▶*n.* **1** a label attached to someone or something for the purpose of identification or to give other information. ■ an electronic device that can be attached to someone or something for monitoring purposes, e.g., to deter shoplifters. ■ a nickname or description popularly given to someone or something. ■ a license plate of a motor vehicle. ■ *Computing* a character or set of characters appended to or enclosing an item of data in order to identify it. **2** a small piece or part that is attached to a main body. ■ a ragged lock of wool on a sheep. ■ the tip of an animal's tail when it is distinctively colored. ■ a loose or spare end of something; a leftover. ■ a metal or plastic point at the end of a shoelace that stiffens it, making it easier to insert through an eyelet. **3** a frequently repeated quotation or stock phrase. ■ *Theater* a closing speech addressed to the audience. ■ the refrain of a song. ■ a musical phrase added to the end of a piece. ■ *Grammar* a short phrase or clause added to an already complete sentence, as in *I like it, I do.* See also TAG QUESTION.
▶*v.* (**tagged**, **tag·ging**) [*trans.*] **1** attach a label to: *the bears were tagged and released.* ■ [*trans.* or *complement*] give a specified name or description to: *he left because he didn't want to be tagged as a soap star.* ■ attach an electronic tag to: [as *n.*] (**tagging**) *laser tattooing is used in the tagging of cattle.* ■ *Computing* add a character or set of characters to (an item of data) in order to identify it for later retrieval. ■ *Biology & Chemistry* label (something) with a radioactive isotope, fluorescent dye, or other marker: *pieces of DNA tagged with radioactive particles.* **2** [*trans.*] add to something, esp. as an afterthought or with no real connection: *she meant to* **tag** *her question* **on** *at the end of her remarks.* ■ [*intrans.*] follow or accompany someone, esp. without invitation: *that'll teach you not to* **tag along** *where you're not wanted.* **3** shear away ragged locks of wool from (sheep). ▷late Middle English (denoting a narrow hanging section of a decoratively slashed garment): of unknown origin. The verb dates from the early 17th cent.

tag[2] ▶*n.* a children's game in which one chases the rest, and anyone who is touched then becomes the pursuer. ■ *Baseball* the action of tagging out a runner or tagging a base: *he narrowly avoided a sweeping tag by the first baseman.* ■ [as *adj.*] denoting a form of wrestling involving tag teams. See TAG TEAM.
▶*v.* (**tagged**, **tag·ging**) [*trans.*] touch (someone being chased) in a game of tag. ■ (**tag out**) *Baseball* put out (a runner) by touching them with the ball or with the glove holding the ball: *catching their fastest runner in a rundown and tagging him out.* ■ *Baseball* (of a base runner, or a fielder with the ball) touch (a base) with the foot: *the short center fielder could field the ball and tag second base for a force out.* ■ [*intrans.*] (usu. **tag up**) *Baseball* (of a base runner) touch the base one has occupied after a fly ball is caught, before running to the next base: *when the ball was hit, he went back to the bag to tag up.*

Ta·ga·log /təˈgäləg; -lôg/ ▶*n.* **1** a member of a people originally of central Luzon in the Philippine Islands. **2** the Austronesian language of this people. Its vocabulary has been much influenced by Spanish and English, and it is the basis of a standardized national language of the Philippines (Filipino).
▶*adj.* of or relating to this people or their language. ▷the name in Tagalog, from *tagá* 'native' + *ilog* 'river.'

Tag·a·met /ˈtagəˌmet/ ▶*n.* trademark for CIMETIDINE. ▷1970s: an arbitrary formation.

Ta·gan·rog /ˌtəgənˈrôk; ˈtagənˌräg; -ˌrôg/ an industrial port in southwestern Russia on the Gulf of Taganrog, which is an inlet of the Sea of Azov; pop. 293,000. It was founded in 1698 by Peter the Great as a fortress and naval base.

William Howard Taft

tag·board /'tag,bôrd/ ▸*n.* a kind of sturdy cardboard used esp. for making luggage labels and posters. Also called OAKTAG.

tag day ▸*n. dated* a day on which money is collected for a charity in the street and donors are given tags to show that they have contributed.

tag end ▸*n.* the last remaining part of something: *the tag end of the season.*

ta·gine /tə'ZHĒn; tə'jēn / ▸*n.* a North African stew of spiced meat and vegetables prepared by slow cooking in a shallow earthenware cooking dish with a tall, conical lid. ▷from Moroccan Arabic: *ṭažin* from Arabic *ṭājin* 'frying pan.'

ta·gli·a·tel·le /,tälyə'telē/ ▸*n.* pasta in long ribbons. ▷Italian, from *tagliare* 'to cut.'

tag line ▸*n. informal* a catchphrase or slogan, esp. as used in advertising, or the punchline of a joke.

Ta·gore /tə'gôr/, Rabindranath (1861–1941), Indian writer and philosopher. His poetry pioneered the use of colloquial Bengali. Nobel Prize for Literature (1913).

tag ques·tion ▸*n. Grammar* a question converted from a statement by an appended interrogative formula, e.g., *it's nice out, isn't it?*

tag sale ▸*n.* a rummage sale or garage sale.

tag team ▸*n.* a pair of wrestlers who fight as a team, taking the ring alternately. One team member cannot enter the ring until touched or tagged by the one leaving. ■ *informal* a pair of people working together.

ta·gua nut /'tägwə/ ▸*n.* another term for IVORY NUT. ▷mid 19th cent.: *tagua,* via Spanish from Quechua *tawa.*

Ta·gus /'tāgəs/ a river in southwestern Europe, the longest river on the Iberian peninsula. It rises in the mountains of eastern Spain and flows over 625 miles (1,000 km) west into Portugal, where it turns southwest and empties into the Atlantic Ocean near Lisbon. Spanish name **TAJO**, Portuguese name **TEJO**.

tag wres·tling ▸*n.* a form of wrestling involving tag teams.

ta·hi·ni /tə'hēnē/ (also **ta·hi·na** /-nə/) ▸*n.* a Middle Eastern paste or sauce made from ground sesame seeds. ▷from modern Greek *takhini,* based on Arabic *ṭaḥana* 'to crush.'

Ta·hi·ti /tə'hētē; tä-/ an island in the central South Pacific Ocean, one of the Society Islands that forms part of French Polynesia; pop. 116,000; capital, Papeete. One of the largest islands in the South Pacific, it was declared a French colony in 1880.

Ta·hi·tian /tə'hēSHən/ ▸*n.* **1** a native or national of Tahiti, or a person of Tahitian descent. **2** the Polynesian language of Tahiti.
▸*adj.* of or relating to Tahiti, its people, or their language.

Ta·hoe, Lake /'tähō/ a mountain lake on the border of north central California with Nevada.

tahr /tär/ ▸*n.* a goatlike mammal inhabiting cliffs and mountain slopes in Oman, southern India, and the Himalayas. • Genus *Hemitragus,* family Bovidae: three species. ▷mid 19th cent.: a local word in Nepal.

Tai /tī/ ▸*adj.* of, relating to, or denoting a family of tonal Southeast Asian languages, including Thai and Lao, of uncertain affinity to other language groups, but sometimes linked with the Sino-Tibetan family.

tai /tī/ ▸*n.* (*pl.* same) a deep red-brown Pacific sea bream, eaten as a delicacy in Japan. • *Pagrus major,* family Sparidae. ▷early 17th cent.: from Japanese.

Tai-'an /'tī'än/ a city in northeastern China, in Shandong province; pop. 1,370,000.

t'ai chi ch'uan /'tī ,CHē 'CHwän; ,jē/ (also **t'ai chi** /'tī 'CHē/) ▸*n.* **1** a Chinese martial art and system of calisthenics, consisting of sequences of very slow controlled movements. **2** (in Chinese philosophy) the ultimate source and limit of reality, from which spring yin and yang and all of creation. ▷Chinese, literally 'great ultimate boxing,' from *tài* 'extreme' + *jí* 'limit' + *quán* 'fist, boxing.'

Tai·chung /'tī'CHŏŏNG/ a city in west central Taiwan; pop. 774,000.

Ta·'if /'tä-if/ a city in western Saudi Arabia, southeast of Mecca, in the Asir Mountains; pop. 205,000. It is the unofficial seat of government of Saudi Arabia during the summer.

tai·ga /'tīgə/ ▸*n.* (often **the taiga**) the sometimes swampy coniferous forest of high northern latitudes, esp. that between the tundra and steppes of Siberia and North America. ▷late 19th cent.: from Russian *taĭga,* from Mongolian.

tai·ko /'tīkō/ ▸*n.* (*pl.* same or **-kos**) a Japanese barrel-shaped drum. ▷late 19th cent.: Japanese.

tai·ko·naut /'tīkə,nôt/ ▸*n.* the English rendering of the Chinese word for astronaut. ▷early 21st cent.: from Chinese *taikong,* 'space' + *-naut.*

tail[1] /tāl/ ▸*n.* **1** the hindmost part of an animal, esp. when prolonged beyond the rest of the body, such as the flexible extension of the backbone in a vertebrate, the feathers at the hind end of a bird, or a terminal appendage in an insect. ■ a thing resembling an animal's tail in its shape or position, typically something extending downward or outward at the end of something: *the trailed tail of a capital Q | the cars were head to tail.* ■ the rear part of an airplane, with the horizontal stabilizer and rudder. ■ the lower or hanging part of a garment, esp. the back of a shirt or coat. ■ (**tails**) *informal* a tailcoat; a man's formal evening suit with such a coat: *the men looked debonair in white tie and tails.* ■ the luminous trail of particles following a comet. ■ the lower end of a pool or stream. ■ the exposed end of a slate or tile in a roof. **2** the end of a long train or line of people or vehicles: *an armored truck at the tail of the convoy.* ■ [in *sing.*] the final, more distant, or weaker part of something: *the forecast says we're in for the tail of a hurricane.* ■ *informal* a person secretly following another to observe their movements. **3** *informal* a person's buttocks: *fireworks followed when the coach kicked Ryan in his tail.* ■ *vulgar slang* a woman's genitals. ■ *informal, chiefly offensive* women collectively regarded as a means of sexual gratification: *my wife thinks going out with you guys will keep me from chasing tail.* **4** (**tails**) the reverse side of a coin (used when tossing a coin).
▸*v.* [*trans.*] **1** *informal* follow and observe (someone) closely, esp. in secret: *a flock of paparazzi had tailed them all over Paris.* ■ [*intrans.*] follow: *they went to their favorite cafe—Bill and Sally tailed along.* **2** [*intrans.*] (of an object in flight) drift or curve in a particular direction: *the next pitch tailed in on me at the last second.* **3** *rare* provide with a tail: *her calligraphy was topped by banners of black ink and tailed like the haunches of fabulous beasts.* **4** *archaic* join (one thing) to another: *each new row of houses tailed on its drains to those of its neighbors.*
▸*phrasal v.* □ **tail something in** (or **into**) insert the end of a beam, stone, or brick into (a wall). □ **tail off** (or **away**) gradually diminish in amount, strength, or intensity: *the economic boom was beginning to tail off.* ▷Old English *tægl, tægel,* from a Germanic base meaning 'hair, hairy tail'; related to Middle Low German *tagel* 'twisted whip, rope's end.' The early sense of the verb (early 16th cent.) was 'fasten to the back of something.' —**tailed** *adj.* [in *combination*] *a white-tailed deer.* —**tail·less** *adj.* —**tail·less·ness** *n.*
▸*PHRASES* □ **chase one's (own) tail** *informal* rush around ineffectually. □ **on someone's tail** following someone closely: *a police car stayed on his tail for half a mile.* □ **a piece of tail** see PIECE. □ **the tail wags the dog** the less important or subsidiary factor, person, or thing dominates a situation; the usual roles are reversed: *the financing system is becoming the tail that wags the dog.* □ **with one's tail between one's legs** *informal* in a state of dejection or humiliation.

tail[2] ▸*n. Law, chiefly historical* limitation of ownership, esp. of an estate or title limited to a person and their heirs: *the land was held* **in tail** *general.* See also FEE TAIL. ▷Middle English (denoting a tallage): from Old French *taille* 'notch, tax,' from *taillier* 'to cut,' based on Latin *talea* 'twig, cutting.'

tail·back /'tāl,bak/ ▸*n. Football* (in some offensive formations) the back who is positioned farthest from the line of scrimmage.

tail·board /'tāl,bôrd/ ▸*n.* chiefly British term for TAILGATE.

tail·bone /'tāl,bōn/ ▸*n.* less technical term for COCCYX.

tail·coat /'tāl,kōt/ ▸*n.* a man's formal morning or evening coat, with a long skirt divided at the back into tails and cut away in front.

tail cov·ert ▸*n.* (in a bird's tail) each of the smaller feathers covering the bases of the main feathers.

tail·drag·ger /'tāl,dragər/ ▸*n.* an airplane that lands and taxis on a tail wheel or tail skid, its nose off the ground.

tail end ▸*n.* [in *sing.*] the last or hindmost part of something: *the tail end of the 19th century | the tail end of a herd of cattle.*

tail fin ▸*n. Zoology* a fin at the posterior extremity of a fish's body, typically continuous with the tail. Also called CAUDAL FIN. ■ *Aeronautics* a projecting vertical surface on the tail of an aircraft, providing stability and typically housing the rudder. ■ an upswept projection on each rear corner of an automobile, popular in the 1950s.

tail gas ▸*n.* gas produced in a refinery and not required for further processing.

tail·gate /'tāl,gāt/ ▸*n.* a hinged flap at the back of a truck that can be lowered or removed when loading or unloading the vehicle. ■ the door at the back of a station wagon. ■ [as *adj.*] relating to or denoting an informal meal served from the back of a parked vehicle, typically in the parking lot of a sports stadium: *a tailgate lunch | they turned the parking lot into a huge tailgate party.* ■ [as *adj.*] denoting a style of jazz trombone playing characterized by improvisation in the manner of the early New Orleans musicians.
▸*v. informal* **1** [*trans.*] drive too closely behind another vehicle: *he started tailgating the car in front | [intrans.] drivers who will tailgate at 90 mph.* ■ (of a person or vehicle) gain unauthorized entry to a secured area by closely following someone with authority to enter: *a Toyota pickup that tailgated the delivery vehicle into the prison | three boys tailgated a group of tourists into the theater.* **2** [*intrans.*] eat a meal served from the back of a parked vehicle: *Lot 16E is reserved for alumni who wish to tailgate before the game.* —**tail·gat·er** *n.*

tail·ing /'tāliNG/ ▸*n.* **1** (**tailings**) the residue of something, esp. ore. **2** the part of a beam or projecting brick or stone embedded in a wall.

taille /tāl; 'täyə/ ▸*n.* (*pl.* same) **1** (in France before 1789) a tax levied on the common people by the king or an overlord. [compare with TAIL[2].] **2** the juice produced from a second pressing of the grapes during winemaking, generally considered inferior because it contains less sugar and more tannin and has lower acidity than the first pressing. ■ low-quality wine made from this residue. ▷French.

Tail·le·ferre /,tīə'fer/, Germaine (1892–1983), French composer and pianist. A member of Les Six, she composed concertos for unusual combinations of instruments.

tail·leur /tä'yər/ ▸*n.* (*pl.* same) *dated* or *formal* a woman's tailor-made suit. ▷French.

tail·light /'tāl,(l)īt/ (also **tail·lamp**) ▸*n.* a red light at the rear of a motor vehicle, train, or bicycle.

tai·lor /'tālər/ ▸*n.* **1** a person whose occupation is making fitted clothes such as suits, pants, and jackets to fit individual customers. **2** (also **tai·lor·fish**) another term for BLUEFISH.
▸*v.* [*trans.*] (usu. **be tailored**) (of a tailor) make (clothes) to fit individual customers: *he was wearing a sports coat that had obviously been tailored in New York.* ■ make or adapt for a particular purpose or person: *arrangements can be* **tailored to** *meet individual requirements.* ▷Middle English: from Anglo-Norman French *taillour,* literally 'cutter,' based on late Latin *taliare* 'to cut.' The verb dates from the mid 17th cent.

tai·lor·bird /'tālər,bərd/ ▸*n.* a small South Asian warbler that makes a row of holes in one or two large leaves and stitches them together with cottony fibers or silk to form a container for the nest. • Genus *Orthotomus,* family Sylviidae: several species.

tai·lored /'tālərd/ ▸*adj.* **1** (of clothes) smart, fitted, and well cut: *a tailored charcoal-gray suit.* ■ [with *submodifier*] (of clothes) cut in a particular way: *her clothes were well tailored and expensive.* **2** made or adapted for a particular purpose or person: *specially tailored courses can be run on request.*

tai·lor·ing /'tāləriNG/ ▸*n.* the activity or trade of a tailor. ■ the style or cut of a garment or garments.

tai·lor-made ▸*adj.* (of clothes) made by a tailor for a particular customer: *tailor-made suits.* ■ made, adapted, or suited for a particular purpose or person: *he was* **tailor-made for** *the job.*
▸*n.* a garment that has been specially made for a particular customer: *a lady in a red tailor-made.* ■ a cigarette made in a factory, rather than being hand-rolled.

tai·lor's chalk ▸*n.* hard chalk or soapstone used in tailoring and dressmaking for marking fabric.

tail·piece /'tāl,pēs/ ▸*n.* a final or end part of something, in particular: ■ a part added to the end of a story or piece of writing. ■ a small decorative design at the foot of a page or the end of a chapter or book. ■ the piece at the base of a violin or other stringed instrument to which the strings are attached.

tail·pipe /'tāl,pīp/ ▸*n.* the rear section of the exhaust system of a motor vehicle.

tail·plane /'tāl,plān/ ▸*n. Brit.* another term for HORIZONTAL STABILIZER.

tail·race /'tāl,rās/ ▸*n.* a water channel below a dam or water mill.

tail ro·tor ▸*n. Aeronautics* an auxiliary rotor at the tail of a helicopter designed to counterbalance the torque of the main rotor.

tail skid ▸*n.* a support for the tail of an aircraft when on the ground.

tail slide ▸*n.* a backward movement of an aircraft from a vertical stalled position.

tail·spin /ˈtālˌspin/ ▸*n.* an aircraft's diving descent combined with rotation. ■ a state or situation characterized by chaos, panic, or loss of control: *the rise in interest rates sent the stock market into a tailspin.*
▸*v.* (**-spin·ning**; *past* and *past part.* **-spun**) [*intrans.*] become out of control: *an economy tailspinning into chaos.*

tail·stock /ˈtālˌstäk/ ▸*n.* the adjustable part of a lathe holding the fixed spindle.

tail·wa·ter /ˈtālˌwôtər; -ˌwätər/ ▸*n.* the water in a tailrace.

tail·wheel /ˈtālˌ(h)wēl/ ▸*n.* a wheel supporting the tail of an aircraft, designed to ease handling while on the ground.

tail·wind /ˈtālˌwind/ ▸*n.* a wind blowing in the direction of travel of a vehicle or aircraft; a wind blowing from behind.

tai·men /ˈtīmen/ ▸*n.* (*pl.* same) a food fish that is closely related to the huchen, widespread in Siberia and eastern Asia. • *Hucho taimen,* family Salmonidae. ▷1970s: from Russian.

Tai·myr Pen·in·su·la /tīˈmi(ə)r/ (also **Tay·myr**) a vast, almost uninhabited peninsula on the northern coast of central Russia that extends into the Arctic Ocean and separates the Kara Sea from the Laptev Sea. Its northern tip is the northernmost point in Asia.

Tai·nan /ˈtīˈnän/ a city on the southwestern coast of Taiwan; pop. 690,000. Its original name was Taiwan, the name later given to the whole island.

Tai·no /ˈtīnō/ ▸*n.* **1** a member of an extinct Arawak people formerly inhabiting the Greater Antilles and the Bahamas. **2** the extinct Arawakan language of this people. ▷from Taino *taino* 'noble, lord.'

taint /tānt/ ▸*n.* a trace of a bad or undesirable quality or substance: *the taint of corruption that adhered to the regime.* ■ a thing whose influence or effect is perceived as contaminating or undesirable: *the taint that threatens to stain most of the company's other partners.* ■ an unpleasant smell: *the lingering taint of creosote.*
▸*v.* [*trans.*] (often **be tainted**) contaminate or pollute (something): *the air was tainted by fumes from the cars.* See note at POLLUTE. ■ affect with a bad or undesirable quality: *his administration was tainted by scandal.* ■ [*intrans.*] *archaic* (of food or water) become contaminated or polluted. ▷Middle English (as a verb in the sense 'convict, prove guilty'): partly from Old French *teint* 'tinged,' based on Latin *tingere* 'to dye, tinge'; partly a shortening of ATTAINT. **—taint·less** *adj.* (*poetic/literary*).

tai·pan[1] /ˈtīˌpan/ ▸*n.* a foreigner who is head of a business in China or Hong Kong. ▷mid 19th cent.: from Chinese (Cantonese dialect) *daaihbāan.*

tai·pan[2] ▸*n.* a large, brown, highly venomous Australian snake. • Genus *Oxyuranus,* family Elapidae: two species, in particular *O. scutellatus.* ▷1930s: from Wik Munkan (an extinct Aboriginal language of northern Queensland) *dhayban.*

Tai·pei /ˌtīˈpā; -ˈbā/ the capital of Taiwan, in the northern part of the country; pop. 2,718,000.

Tai·wan /ˌtīˈwän/ an island country off the southeastern coast of China; pop. 22,700,000; capital, Taipei; language, Mandarin Chinese (official). Official name CHINA, REPUBLIC OF. Former name FORMOSA. **—Tai·wan·ese** /ˌtīwəˈnēz; -wä-; -ˈnēs/ *adj.* & *n.*

In 1949, toward the end of the war with the communist regime of mainland China, Chiang Kai-shek withdrew here with 500,000 nationalist Kuomintang troops. Taiwan became the headquarters of the Kuomintang, which has held power since then. Taiwan has undergone steady economic growth. In 1971, it lost its seat in the United Nations to the People's Republic of China, which regards Taiwan as one of its provinces. Power was transferred from the Nationalist to the Democratic Progressive Party in 2000.

Tai·yuan /ˈtīyo͞oˈän/ a city in northern China, capital of Shanxi province; pop. 1,900,000.

Tai Yue Shan /ˈtī yo͞oˈä ˈshän/ Chinese name for LANTAU.

Ta·'iz /täˈēz/ a city in southwestern Yemen; pop. 290,000. It was the administrative capital of Yemen 1948–62.

taj /täzh; täj/ ▸*n.* a tall conical cap worn by a dervish. ■ *historical* a crown worn by an Indian prince of high rank. ▷mid 19th cent.: from Persian *tāj* 'crown.'

Ta·jik /täˈjik/ (also **Ta·djik** or **Ta·dzhik**) ▸*n.* **1** a member of a mainly Muslim people inhabiting Tajikistan and parts of neighboring countries. ■ a native or national of the republic of Tajikistan. **2** (also **Ta·ji·ki** /-ˈjikē/) the Iranian language of the Tajiks.
▸*adj.* of or relating to Tajikistan, the Tajiks, or their language. ▷from Persian *tājik* 'a Persian, someone who is neither an Arab nor a Turk.'

Ta·jik·i·stan /təˈjēkəˌstan; tä-; -ˈjikə; -ˌstän/ (also **Ta·dzhi·ki·stan**) a mountainous republic in central Asia, north of Afghanistan; pop. 7,011,000; capital, Dushanbe; languages, Tajik (official) and Russian.

The region was conquered by the Mongols in the 13th century and absorbed into the Russian empire during the 1880s and 1890s. From 1929, Tajikistan formed a constituent republic of the Soviet Union; it became an independent republic within the Commonwealth of Independent States in 1991.

Taj Ma·hal /ˈtäzh məˈhäl; ˈtäj/ a mausoleum at Agra, India, built by the Mogul emperor Shah Jahan (1592–1666) in memory of his favorite wife, completed *c.*1649. Set in formal gardens, the domed building in white marble is reflected in a pool flanked by cypresses. ▷perhaps a corruption of Persian *Mumtaz Mahal,* from *mumtāz* 'chosen one' (the title of the wife of Shah Jahan) and *mahal* 'abode.'

Taj Mahal

Ta·jo /ˈtähō/ Spanish name for TAGUS.

ta·ka /ˈtäkə/ ▸*n.* (*pl.* same) the basic monetary unit of Bangladesh, equal to 100 poisha. ▷from Bengali *ṭākā.*

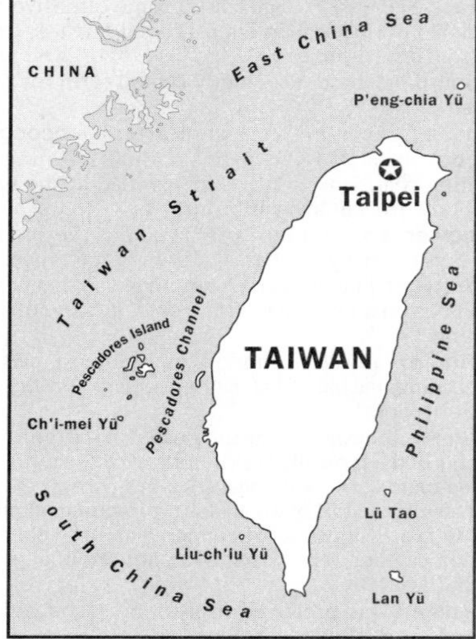

ta·ka·he /təˈkī/ ▸*n.* a large, rare, flightless rail with bluish-black and olive-green plumage and a large red bill, found in mountain grassland in New Zealand. • *Porphyrio mantelli,* family Rallidae. ▷mid 19th cent.: from Maori.

take /tāk/ ▸*v.* (*past* **took** /to͝ok/; *past part.* **tak·en** /ˈtākən/) [*trans.*] **1** lay hold of (something) with one's hands; reach for and hold: *he leaned forward to take her hand.* ■ [*trans.*] remove (someone or something) from a particular place: *he took an envelope from his inside pocket* | *the police took him away.* ■ consume as food, drink, medicine, or drugs: *take an aspirin and lie down.* ■ capture or gain possession of by force or military means: *twenty of their ships were sunk or taken* | *the French took Ghent.* ■ (in bridge, hearts, and similar card games) win (a trick). ■ *Chess* capture (an opposing piece or pawn). ■ dispossess someone of (something); steal or illicitly remove: *someone must have sneaked in here and taken it.* ■ cheat (someone) of something: *can I get taken by buying mutual funds?* ■ subtract: ***take** two **from** ten* | *add the numbers together and **take away** five.* ■ occupy (a place or position): *we found that all the seats were taken.* ■ buy or rent (a house). ■ agree to buy (an item): *I'll take the one on the end.* ■ gain or acquire (possession or ownership of something): *he took possession of a unique Picasso ceramic piece.* ■ (**be taken**) *humorous* (of a person) already be married or in an emotional relationship. ■ [in *imperative*] use or have ready to use: *take half the marzipan and roll out.* ■ [usu. in *imperative*] use as an instance or example in support of an argument: *let's take Napoleon, for instance.* ■ regularly buy or subscribe to (a particular newspaper or periodical). ■ ascertain by measurement or observation: *the nurse takes my blood pressure.* ■ write down: *he was taking notes.* ■ make (a photograph) with a camera. ■ (usu. **be taken**) (esp. of illness) suddenly strike or afflict (someone): *he was taken with a seizure of some kind.* ■ have sexual intercourse with. **2** [*trans.*] carry or bring with one; convey: *he took along a portfolio of his drawings* | *the drive takes you through some wonderful scenery* | [with *two objs.*] *I took him a letter.* ■ accompany or guide (someone) to a specified place: *I'll take you to your room* | *he called to **take** her **out** for a meal.* ■ bring into a specified state: *the invasion took Europe to the brink of war.* ■ use as a route or a means of transportation: *take 95 north to Baltimore* | *we took the night train to Scotland.* **3** accept or receive (someone or something): *she was advised to take any job offered* | *they don't take children.* ■ understand or accept as valid: *I take your point.* ■ acquire or assume (a position, state, or form): *teaching methods will take various forms* | *he took office in September.* ■ achieve or attain (a victory or result): *John Martin took the men's title.* ■ act on (an opportunity): *he took his chance to get out while the house was quiet.* ■ experience or be affected by: *the lad took a savage beating.* ■ tolerate, stand: *I can't take the humidity.* ■ [*trans.*] react to or regard (news or an event) in a specified way: *she took the news well* | *everything you say, he takes it the wrong way.* ■ [*trans.*] deal with (a physical obstacle or course) in a specified way: *he takes the corners with no concern for his own safety.* ■ *Baseball* (of a batter) allow (a pitch) to go by without attempting to hit the ball. ■ regard or view in a specified way: *he somehow **took** it **as** a personal insult* | [*trans.*] *I fell over what I took to be a heavy branch.* ■ (**be taken by/with**) be attracted or charmed by: *Billie was very taken with him.* ■ submit to, tolerate, or endure: *they refused to take it any more* | *some people found her hard to take.* ■ (**take it**) [with *clause*] assume: *I take it that someone is coming to meet you.* **4** make, undertake, or perform (an action or task): *Lucy took a deep breath* | *he took the oath of office.* ■ be taught or examined in (a subject): *some degrees require a student to take a secondary subject.* ■ *Brit.* obtain (an academic degree) after fulfilling the required conditions: *she took a degree in English.* **5** require or use up (a specified amount of time): *the jury took an hour and a half to find McPherson guilty* | [with *two objs.*] *it takes me about a quarter of an hour to walk to work.* ■ (of a task or situation) need or call for (a particular person or thing): *it will take an electronics expert to dismantle it.* ■ hold; accommodate: *an exclusive island hideaway that takes just twenty guests.* ■ wear or require (a particular size of garment or type of complementary article): *he takes size 5 boots.* **6** [*intrans.*] (of a plant or seed) take root or begin to grow; germinate: *the fuchsia cuttings had taken and were looking good.* ■ (of an added substance) become successfully established. **7** *Grammar* have or require as part of the appropriate construction: *verbs that take both the infinitive and the finite clause as their object.*

▸*phrasal v.* □ **take after** resemble (a parent or ancestor): *the rest of us take after our mother.* □ **take something apart** dismantle something. ■ (**take someone/something apart**) *informal* attack, criticize, or defeat someone or something in a vigorous or forceful way. □ **take something away** *Brit.* another way of saying TAKE SOMETHING OUT (sense 2). □ **take away from** detract from: *that shouldn't take away from the achievement of the French.* □ **take someone back** strongly remind someone of a past time: *if "Disco Inferno" doesn't take you back, the bell-bottom pants will.* □ **take something back 1** retract a statement: *I take back nothing of what I said.* **2** return unsatisfactory goods to a store. ■ (of a store) accept such goods. **3** *Printing* transfer text to the previous line. □ **take something down 1** write down spoken words: *I took down the address.* **2** dismantle and remove a structure: *the old Norman church was taken down in 1819.* □ **take from** another way of saying TAKE AWAY FROM. □ **take someone in 1** accommodate someone as a lodger or because they are homeless or in difficulties. **2** cheat, fool, or deceive someone: *she tried to pass this off as an amusing story, but nobody was taken in.* □ **take something in 1** undertake work at home: *she took in laundry on weekends.* **2** make a garment tighter by altering its seams. ■ *Sailing* furl a sail. **3** receive a specified amount of money as payment or earnings: *our club took in nearly $800,000 in its first year.* **4** include or encompass something: *the sweep of his arm took in most of Main Street.* ■ fully understand or absorb something heard or seen: *she took in the scene at a glance.* **5** visit or attend a place or event in a casual way or on the way to another: *he'd maybe take in a movie, or just relax.* □ **take off 1** (of an aircraft or bird) become airborne. ■ (of an enterprise) become successful or popular: *the newly launched electronic newspaper has really taken off.* **2** depart hastily: *the officer took off after his men.* □ **take something off 1** remove clothing from one's or another's body: *she took off her cardigan.* **2** deduct part of an amount. **3** choose to have a period away from work: *I took the next day off.* □ **take someone on 1** hire an employee. **2** be willing or ready to meet an adversary or opponent, esp. a stronger one: *a group of villagers has taken on the planners.* □ **take something on 1** undertake a task or responsibility, esp. a difficult one: *whoever takes on the trout farm will have their work cut out.* **2** acquire a particular meaning or quality: *the subject has taken on a new significance in the past year.* □ **take someone out 1** to escort, as on a date: *I finally get to take her out on Saturday night.* **2** *Bridge* respond to a bid or double by one's partner by bidding a different suit. □ **take someone/something out** *informal* kill, destroy, or disable someone or something. □ **take something out 1** obtain an official document or service: *you can take out a loan for a specific purchase.* ■ get a license or summons issued. **2** buy food at a cafe or restaurant for eating elsewhere: *he ordered a lamb madras to take out.* □ **take something out on** relieve frustration or anger by attacking or mistreating (a person or thing not responsible for such feelings). □ **take something over 1** (also **take over**) assume control of something: *British troops had taken over the German trenches.* ■ (of a company) buy out another. ■ become responsible for a task in succession to another: *he will take over as chief executive in April.* **2** *Printing* transfer text to the next line. □ **take to 1** begin or fall into the habit of: *he took to hiding some secret supplies in his desk.* **2** form a liking for: *Mrs. Brady never took to Moran.* ■ develop an ability for (something), esp. quickly or easily: *I took to pole-vaulting right away.* **3** go to (a place) to escape danger or an enemy: *they took to the hills.* □ **take something up 1** become interested or engaged in a pursuit: *she took up tennis at the age of 11.* ■ begin to hold or fulfill a position or post: *he left to take up an appointment as a missionary.* ■ accept an offer or challenge. **2** occupy time, space, or attention: *I don't want to take up any more of your time.* **3** pursue a matter later or further: *he'll have to* **take it up with** *the bishop.* ■ (also **take up**) resume speaking after an interruption: *I took up where I had left off.* **4** shorten a garment by turning up the hem. □ **take someone up on 1** accept (an offer or challenge) from someone: *I'd like to take you up on that offer.* **2** challenge or question a speaker on (a particular point): *the interviewer did not take him up on his quotation.* □ **take up with** begin to associate with (someone), esp. in a way disapproved of by the speaker: *he's taken up with a divorced woman, I understand.*

▸*n.* **1** a scene or sequence of sound or vision photographed or recorded continuously at one time: *he completed a particularly difficult scene in two takes.* ■ a particular version of or approach to something: *his own whimsical* **take on** *life.* **2** an amount of something gained or acquired from one source or in one session: *the take from commodity taxation.* ■ the money received at a theater, arena, etc., for seats. **3** *Printing* an amount of copy set up at one time or by one compositor. ▷late Old English *tacan* 'get (esp. by force), capture,' from Old Norse *taka* 'grasp, lay hold of,' of unknown ultimate origin. **—tak·a·ble** /ˈtākəbəl/ (also **take·a·ble**) *adj.*

▸*PHRASES* □ **be on the take** *informal* take bribes. □ **be taken ill** become ill suddenly. □ **have what it takes** *informal* have the necessary qualities for success. □ **take a chair** sit down. □ **take advantage of, take advice**, etc. see ADVANTAGE, ADVICE, etc. □ **take something as read** *Brit.* accept something without considering or discussing it; assume something. □ **take the cake** *informal* (of a person or incident) be the most remarkable or foolish of their kind. □ **take five** (or **ten**) take a five (or ten) minute break before resuming work or another activity. □ **take a lot of** (or **some**) —— be difficult to do or effect in the specified way: *he might take some convincing.* □ **take someone in hand** undertake to control or reform someone. □ **take something in hand** start doing or dealing with a task. □ **take the heat** *informal* accept blame or withstand disapproval: *"Don't worry about it," Mulder said, "we'll take the heat. You can tell him we pulled rank."* □ **take something ill** *archaic* resent something done or said: *I did not mean for you to take my comments ill.* □ **take it from me** I can assure you: *take it from me, kid—I've been there.* □ **take it on one** (or **oneself**) **to do something** decide to do something without asking for permission or advice. □ **take it or leave it** [usu. in *imperative*] said to express that the offer one has made is not negotiable and that one is indifferent to another's reaction to it: *that's the deal—take it or leave it.* □ **take it out of** exhaust the strength of (someone): *parties and tours can take it out of you, especially if you are over 65.* □ **take sick** (or **ill**) *informal* become ill, esp. suddenly. □ **take the stand** testify at a trial. □ **take someone out of themselves** make a person forget their worries. □ **take that!** exclaimed when hitting someone or taking decisive action against them. □ **take one's time** not hurry.

take·a·way /ˈtākəˌwā/ ▸*n.* **1** *Sports* (in football and hockey) an act of regaining the ball or puck from the opposing team. **2** *Brit.* a takeout restaurant: *the menu from a Chinese takeaway.* ■ a meal or dish of such food. **3** *Golf* another term for BACKSWING.

take·down /ˈtākˌdoun/ ▸*n.* **1** a wrestling maneuver in which an opponent is swiftly brought to the mat from a standing position. **2** *informal* a police raid or arrest. **3** [as *adj.*] denoting a firearm with the capacity to have the barrel and magazine detached from the stock.

take-home pay ▸*n.* the pay received by an employee after the deduction of taxes and other obligations.

take·off /ˈtākˌôf; -ˌäf/ (also **take-off**) ▸*n.* **1** the action of becoming airborne: *the plane accelerated down the runway for takeoff.* **2** an act of mimicking someone or something: *a pleasant* **takeoff on** *some Everly Brothers routine.*

take·out /ˈtākˌout/ (also **take-out**) ▸*n.* **1** food that is cooked and sold by a restaurant or store to be eaten elsewhere: *cartons of Chinese takeout for late-night dinners* | [as *adj.*] *takeout pizza.* **2** *Bridge* a bid in a different suit made in response to a bid or double by one's partner.

take·out dou·ble ▸*n.* *Bridge* a double that, by convention, requires one's partner to bid, used to convey information rather than to score penalty points. Often contrasted with BUSINESS DOUBLE.

take·o·ver /ˈtākˌōvər/ ▸*n.* an act of assuming control of something, esp. the buying out of one company by another.

tak·er /ˈtākər/ ▸*n.* **1** [in *combination*] a person who takes a specified thing: *a drug-taker* | *a risk-taker.* **2** a person who takes a bet or accepts an offer or challenge: *there were plenty of takers when I offered a small wager.*

Tak·e·shi·ta /ˌtäkəˈSHētə/, Noboru (1924–2000) Japanese politician. He served as Japan's prime minister from 1987 until 1989, when he was forced to resign because of a scandal that involved bribery and many in his cabinet. He remained a powerful force in Japanese politics

take-up ▸*n.* **1** a device for taking up slack or excess: [as *adj.*] *a take-up reel.* **2** the action of taking something up: *automatic bobbin thread take-up.* **3** *chiefly Brit.* the acceptance of something offered: *practices that discourage take-up of legal advice.*

ta·kin /ˈtäˌkēn/ ▸*n.* a large heavily built goat-antelope found in steep, dense woodlands of the eastern Himalayas. • *Budorcas taxicolor*, family Bovidae. ▷mid 19th cent.: a local word.

tak·ing /ˈtākiNG/ ▸*n.* **1** the action or process of taking something: *the taking of life.* **2** (**takings**) the amount of money earned by a business from the sale of goods or services: *box-office takings were scant.*

▸*adj. dated* (of a person) captivating in manner; charming: *he was not a very taking person, she felt.* **—tak·ing·ly** *adv.*

▸*PHRASE* □ **for the taking** ready or available for someone to take advantage of: *the big money is out there for the taking.*

Ta·ki-Ta·ki /ˈtākē ˈtākē/ ▸*n.* an English-based Creole language of Suriname. Also called SRANAN. ▷an alteration and reduplication of TALK.

Ta·kli·ma·kan Des·ert /ˌtäkləməˈkän/ (also **Tak·la Ma·kan**) a desert in the Xinjiang autonomous region of northwestern China that lies between the Kunlun Shan and Tien Shan mountains and forms the greater part of the Tarim Basin.

Ta·ko·ra·di /ˌtäkəˈrädē/ a seaport in western Ghana, on the Gulf of Guinea; pop. 615,000.

ta·la[1] /ˈtälə/ ▸*n.* a traditional rhythmic pattern in classical Indian music. ▷from Sanskrit *tāla* 'handclapping, musical time.'

ta·la[2] ▸*n.* (*pl.* same or **ta·las** /ˈtäləz/) the basic monetary unit of Western Samoa, equal to 100 sene. ▷from Samoan *tālā*.

tal·a·poin /ˈtaləˌpoin/ ▸*n.* a small West African monkey that lives in large groups near watercourses and in swamp forest. • *Miopithecus talapoin*, family Cercopithecidae. ▷late 16th cent.: from Portuguese *talapão*, from Mon *tala pôi*, literally 'lord of merit,' used as a respectful title for a Buddhist monk.

ta·laq /təˈläk/ ▸*n.* (in Islamic law) divorce effected by the husband's threefold repetition of the word "talaq," this constituting a formal repudiation of his wife. ▷from Arabic *ṭalāq*, from *ṭalaqas* 'repudiate.'

ta·lar·i·a /təˈle(ə)rēə/ ▸*plural n.* (in Roman mythology) winged sandals as worn by certain gods and goddesses, esp. Mercury. ▷Latin, neuter plural of *talaris*, from *talus* 'ankle.'

tal·bot /ˈtalbət; ˈtôl-/ ▸*n.* a dog of an extinct light-colored breed of hound with large ears and heavy jaws. ▷late Middle English: probably from the family name *Talbot*; the term was also used to denote the representation of such a dog in the coat of arms of the Talbot family, earls of Shrewsbury (a town in western England).

talc /talk/ ▸*n.* talcum powder. ■ a white, gray, or pale green soft mineral with a greasy feel, occurring as translucent masses or laminae and consisting of magnesium hydroxyl silicate.

▸*v.* (**talced, talc·ing**) [*trans.*] powder or treat (something) with talc. ▷late 16th cent. (denoting the mineral): from medieval Latin *talcum* (see TALCUM). **—talc·ose** /ˈtalkōs/ *adj.* (*Geology*). **—talc·y** /ˈtalkē/ *adj.*

tal·cum /ˈtalkəm/ (also **tal·cum pow·der**) ▸*n.* a cosmetic or toilet preparation consisting of the mineral talc in powdered form, typically perfumed.

▸*v.* (**-cumed, -cum·ing**) [*trans.*] powder (something) with this substance. ▷mid 16th cent.: from medieval Latin, from Arabic *ṭalḳ*, from Persian.

tale /tāl/ ▸*n.* **1** a fictitious or true narrative or story, esp. one that is imaginatively recounted. ■ a lie. **2** *archaic* a number or total: *an exact tale of the dead bodies.* ▷Old English *talu* 'telling, something told,' of Germanic origin; related to Dutch *taal* 'speech' and German *Zahl* 'number,' also to TELL[1]. Sense 2 is probably from Old Norse.

▸*PHRASE* □ **tell tales** see TELL[1].

tale·bear·er /ˈtālˌbe(ə)rər/ ▸*n.* *dated* a person who maliciously gossips or reveals secrets. **—tale·bear·ing** /-ˌbe(ə)riNG/ *n.* & *adj.*

ta·leg·gio /təˈlejēˌō/ ▸*n.* a type of soft Italian cheese made from cows' milk. ▷named after the *Taleggio* valley in Lombardy.

tal·ent /ˈtalənt/ ▸*n.* **1** natural aptitude or skill: *he possesses more talent than any other player* | *she displayed a* **talent for** *garden design.* ■ people possessing such aptitude or skill: *I signed all the talent in Rome* | *Simon is a talent to watch.* ■ *informal* people regarded as sexually attractive or as prospective sexual partners: *most Saturday nights I have this urge to go on the hunt for new talent.* **2** a former weight and unit of currency, used esp. by the ancient Romans and Greeks. ▷Old English *talente, talentan* (as a unit of weight), from Latin *talenta*, plural of *talentum* 'weight, sum of money,' from Greek *talanton*. Sense 1 is a figurative use with biblical allusion to the parable of the talents (Matt. 25:14–30). **—tal·ent·less** *adj.*

tal·ent·ed /'taləntid/ ▸*adj.* having a natural aptitude or skill for something: *a talented young musician.*

tal·ent scout ▸*n.* a person whose job is to search for talented performers who can be employed or promoted, esp. in sports and entertainment.

tales /tālz; 'tālēz/ ▸*n. Law* a writ for summoning substitute jurors when the original jury has become deficient in number. ▷from Latin *tales (de circumstantibus)* 'such (of the bystanders),' the first words of the writ.

tales·man /'tālzmən/ ▸*n.* (*pl.* **-men**) *Law* a person summoned by a tales.

tale-tell·er ▸*n.* a person who tells stories. ■ a person who spreads gossip or reveals secrets. **—tale-tell·ing** *n.*

ta·li /'tā,lī/ ▸ plural form of TALUS[1].

Tal·i·ban /'tali,ban/ a fundamentalist Muslim movement whose militia took control of much of Afghanistan from early 1995, and in 1996 took Kabul and set up a radical Islamic state. The movement provided support for the al Qaeda terrorists and was forcibly removed from power by the U.S. and its allies after the September 11, 2001, attacks. ▷from Pashto or Dari, from Persian, literally 'students, seekers of knowledge.'

ta·lik /'tälik; 'tal-/ ▸*n. Geology* an area of unfrozen ground surrounded by permafrost. ▷1940s: from Russian, from *tayat'* 'melt.'

tal·i·pes /'talə,pēz/ ▸*n. Medicine* technical term for CLUB FOOT. ▷mid 19th cent.: modern Latin, from Latin *talus* 'ankle' + *pes* 'foot.'

tal·i·pot /'talə,pät/ ▸*n.* a tall Indian palm with very large fan-shaped leaves that are used as sunshades and for thatching, and to make the material upon which books were traditionally written. When the talipot matures, at about 40–60 years, it sends up a 25-foot (8-m) stalk bearing millions of flowers, and subsequently the tree dies. • *Corypha umbraculifera*, family Palmae. ▷late 17th cent.: from Malayalam *tālipat*, from Sanskrit *tālīpatra*, from *tālī* 'palm' + *patra* 'leaf.'

tal·is·man /'talismən; -iz-/ ▸*n.* (*pl.* **-mans**) an object, typically an inscribed ring or stone, that is thought to have magic powers and to bring good luck. ▷mid 17th cent.: based on Arabic *ṭilsam*, apparently from an alteration of late Greek *telesma* 'completion, religious rite,' from *telein* 'complete, perform a rite,' from *telos* 'result, end.' **—tal·is·man·ic** /,taliz'manik/ *adj.*

talk /tôk/ ▸*v.* [*intrans.*] speak in order to give information or express ideas or feelings; converse or communicate by spoken words: *the two men talked | we'd sit and* **talk about** *jazz | it was no use* **talking to** *Anthony | [trans.] you're talking rubbish.* ■ have the power of speech: *he can talk as well as you or I can.* ■ discuss personal or intimate feelings: *we need to talk, Maggie.* ■ have formal dealings or discussions; negotiate: *they won't* **talk to** *the regime that killed their families.* ■ **(talk something over/through)** discuss something thoroughly. ■ **(talk at)** address (someone) in a hectoring or self-important way without listening to their replies: *he never talked at you.* ■ **(talk to)** reprimand or scold (someone): *someone will have to talk to Lily.* ■ [*trans.*] **(be talking)** *informal* used to emphasize the seriousness, importance, or extent of the thing one is mentioning or in the process of discussing: *we're talking big money.* ■ [*trans.*] use (a particular language) in speech: *we were talking German.* ■ [*trans.*] persuade or cause (someone) to do something by talking: *don't try to talk me into acting as a go-between.* ■ reveal secret or confidential information; betray secrets. ■ gossip: *you'll have the whole school talking.*

▸*phrasal v.* □ **talk back** reply defiantly or insolently. □ **talk down to** speak patronizingly or condescendingly to. □ **talk something out** *Brit.* (in Parliament) block the course of a bill by prolonging discussion to the time of adjournment. □ **talk someone around** (or *Brit.* **round**) bring someone to a particular point of view by talking. □ **talk someone through** enable someone to perform (a task) by giving them continuous instruction. □ **talk someone/something up** (or **down**) discuss someone or something in a way that makes them seem more (or less) interesting or attractive.

▸*n.* conversation; discussion: *there was a slight but noticeable lull in the talk.* ■ a period of conversation or discussion, esp. a relatively serious one: *my mother had a talk with Louis.* ■ an informal address or lecture. ■ rumor, gossip, or speculation: *there is* **talk of** *an armistice.* ■ empty promises or boasting: *he's all talk.* ■ **(the talk of)** a current subject of widespread gossip or speculation in (a particular place): *within days I was* **the talk of the town.** ■ **(talks)** formal discussions or negotiations over a period: *peace talks.* ▷Middle English: frequentative verb from the Germanic base of TALE or TELL[1]. **—talk·er** *n.*

▸*PHRASES* □ **don't talk to me about ——** *informal* said in protest when someone introduces a subject of which the speaker has had bitter personal experience. □ **know what one is talking about** be expert or authoritative on a specified subject. □ **look who's talking** another way of saying YOU SHOULDN'T TALK. □ **now you're talking** see NOW. □ **you shouldn't** (or **should**) (or *chiefly Brit.* **can't** or **can**) **talk** *informal* used to convey that a criticism made applies equally well to the person who has made it: *"He'd chase anything in a skirt!" "You shouldn't talk!"* □ **talk a blue streak** see BLUE. □ **talk about ——!** *informal* used to emphasize that something is an extreme or striking example of a particular situation, state, or experience: *Talk about hangovers! But aching head or not we were getting ready.* □ **talk big** *informal* talk boastfully or overconfidently. □ **talk dirty** see DIRTY. □ **talk the hind leg off a donkey** *Brit., informal* talk incessantly. □ **talk nineteen to the dozen** see DOZEN. □ **talk of the devil** see DEVIL. □ **talk sense into** persuade (someone) to behave more sensibly. □ **talk shop** see SHOP. □ **talk through one's hat** (or **ass** or **backside** or *Brit.* **arse**) *informal* talk foolishly, wildly, or ignorantly. □ **talk turkey** see TURKEY.

talk·a·thon /'tôkə,THän/ ▸*n. informal* a prolonged discussion or debate. ▷1930s (denoting a debate artificially prolonged to prevent the progress of a bill): blend of TALK and MARATHON.

talk·a·tive /'tôkətiv/ ▸*adj.* fond of or given to talking: *the talkative driver hadn't stopped chatting.* **—talk·a·tive·ly** *adv.* **—talk·a·tive·ness** *n.*

> *THE RIGHT WORD* **garrulous, glib, loquacious, talkative, voluble**
>
> Someone who likes to talk frequently or at length might be described as **talkative** (*he was the most talkative person I'd ever met*).
>
> While *talkative* implies a readiness to engage in talk, **loquacious** implies an inclination to talk incessantly or to keep up a constant flow of chatter (*a loquacious woman who never seemed to tire of hearing her own voice*).
>
> **Glib** and **voluble** pertain to the ease with which someone is able to converse or speak, although *voluble* may be used in either an approving or a critical sense (*a voluble speaker who was in great demand; a voluble neighbor who could not keep a secret*).
>
> *Glib* is almost always negative, referring to a superficial or slick way of speaking (*the glib manner of a used-car salesperson*).
>
> **Garrulous** also has negative overtones, implying a tedious or rambling talkativeness, usually about trivial things (*a garrulous old man who bored everyone with his stories about "the old days"*).

talk·back /'tôk,bak/ ▸*n.* a system of two-way communication by loudspeaker.

talk·fest /'tôk,fest/ ▸*n. informal* a session of lengthy discussion, conversation, or debate.

talk·ie /'tôkē/ ▸*n. informal* a movie with a soundtrack, as distinct from a silent film. ▷early 20th cent. (in the phrase *the talkies*): from TALK, on the pattern of *movie*.

talk·ing /'tôkiNG/ ▸*adj.* [*attrib.*] engaging in speech. ■ (of an animal or object) able to make sounds similar to those of speech: *the world's greatest talking bird.* ■ silently expressive: *he did have talking eyes.*

▸*n.* the action of talking; speech or discussion: *I'll do the talking—you just back me up.*

▸*PHRASE* □ **talking of ——** while we are on the subject of —— (said when one is reminded of something by the present topic of conversation): *talking of cards, you'd better take a couple of my business cards.*

talk·ing blues ▸*plural n.* a style of blues music in which the lyrics are more or less spoken rather than sung.

talk·ing book ▸*n.* a recorded reading of a book, originally designed for use by the blind.

talk·ing cure ▸*n.* a form of psychotherapy that relies on verbal interaction, esp. psychoanalysis.

talk·ing drum ▸*n.* one of a set of West African drums, each having a different pitch, that are beaten to transmit a tonal language.

talk·ing head ▸*n. informal* a commentator or reporter on television who addresses the camera and is viewed in close-up.

talk·ing pic·ture (also **talk·ing film**) ▸*n.* a movie with a soundtrack, as distinct from a silent film.

talk·ing point ▸*n.* a topic that invites discussion or argument.

talk·ing-to ▸*n.* [in *sing.*] *informal* a sharp reprimand in which someone is told that they have done wrong.

talk ra·di·o ▸*n.* a type of radio broadcast in which the presenter talks about topical issues and encourages listeners to call in to air their opinions.

talk show ▸*n.* a television or radio show in which various topics are discussed informally and listeners, viewers, or the studio audience are invited to participate in the discussion.

talk time ▸*n.* the time during which a mobile telephone is in use to handle calls, esp. as a measure of the duration of the telephone's battery.

tall /tôl/ ▸*adj.* **1** of great or more than average height, esp. (with reference to an object) relative to width: *a tall, broad-shouldered man | a tall glass of iced tea.* ■ (after a measurement and in questions) measuring a specified distance from top to bottom: *he was over six feet tall | how tall are you?* ■ [as *adv.*] used in reference to proud and confident movement or behavior: *stop wishing that you were somehow different—start to* **walk tall!** **2** [*attrib.*] *informal* (of an account) fanciful and difficult to believe; unlikely: *sometimes it's hard to tell a legend from a* **tall tale.** ▷late Middle English: probably from Old English *getæl* 'swift, prompt.' Early senses also included 'fine, handsome' and 'bold, strong, good at fighting.' **—tall·ish** *adj.* **—tall·ness** *n.*

▸*PHRASE* □ **a tall order** an unreasonable or difficult demand.

tal·lage /'talij/ ▸*n. historical* a form of arbitrary taxation levied by kings on the towns and lands of the Crown, abolished in the 14th century. ■ a tax levied on feudal dependents by their superiors. ▷Middle English: from Old French *taillage*, from *tailler* 'to cut' (see TAIL[2]).

Tal·la·has·see /,talə'hasē/ the capital of Florida, in the northwestern part of the state; pop. 150,624.

Tal·la·poo·sa Riv·er /,talə'po͞osə/ a river that flows for 268 miles (430 km) from northwestern Georgia to Alabama, where it joins the Coosa River to form the Alabama River.

tall·boy /'tôl,boi/ ▸*n. chiefly Brit.* a tall chest of drawers, typically one mounted on legs and in two sections, one standing on the other. Compare with HIGHBOY.

Tal·ley·rand /'tali,rand; ,tälē'räN/, Charles Maurice de (1754–1838), French statesman; full surname *Talleyrand-Périgord*. He became head of the new government after the fall of Napoleon in 1814 and was later instrumental in the overthrow of Charles X and the accession of Louis Philippe in 1830.

tall hat ▸*n.* another term for TOP HAT.

Tal·linn /'tälən; 'talən/ the capital of Estonia, a port on the Gulf of Finland; pop. 505,000.

tal·lith /'tälis; tä'lēt/ (also **tal·lis**) ▸*n.* a fringed shawl traditionally worn by Jewish men at prayer. ▷from Rabbinical Hebrew *ṭallīt*, from biblical Hebrew *ṭillel* 'to cover.'

tal·low /'talō/ ▸*n.* a hard fatty substance made from rendered animal fat, used in making candles and soap.

▸*v.* [*trans.*] *archaic* smear (something, esp. the bottom of a boat) with such a substance. ▷Middle English: perhaps from Middle Low German; related to Dutch *talk* and German *Talg*. **—tal·low·y** *adj.*

tal·low·wood /'talō,wo͝od/ ▸*n.* see HOG PLUM.

tall pop·py syn·drome ▸*n. informal, chiefly Austral.* a perceived tendency to discredit or disparage those who have achieved notable wealth or prominence in public life.

tall ship ▸*n.* a sailing ship with high masts.

tall tim·ber ▸*n.* dense and uninhabited forest. ■ (usu. **tall timbers**) *informal* a remote or unknown place.

tal·ly /'talē/ ▸*n.* (*pl.* **-lies**) **1** a current score or amount: *that takes his tally to 10 goals in 10 games.* ■ a record of a score or amount: *I* **kept a** *running* **tally** *of David's debt on a note above my desk.* ■ a particular number taken as a group or unit to facilitate counting. ■ a mark registering such a number. ■ (also **tal·ly stick**) *historical* a piece of wood scored across with notches for the items of an account and then split into halves, each party keeping one. ■ an account kept in such a way. ■ *archaic* a counterpart or duplicate of something. **2** a label attached to a plant or tree, or stuck

in the ground beside it, that gives information about it, such as its name and class.
▸*v.* (**-lies**, **-lied**) **1** [*intrans.*] agree or correspond: *their signatures should tally with their names on the register.* **2** [*trans.*] calculate the total number of: *the votes were being tallied with abacuses.* ▷late Middle English (denoting a notched tally stick): from Anglo-Norman French *tallie*, from Latin *talea* 'twig, cutting.' Compare with TAIL[2]. **—tal·li·er** *n.*

tal·ly·ho /ˈtalēˈhō/ (also **tal·ly-ho**) ▸*exclam.* a huntsman's cry to the hounds on sighting a fox.
▸*n.* (*pl.* **-hos**) **1** an utterance of this. **2** *historical* a fast horse-drawn coach.
▸*v.* (**-hoes**, **-hoed**) [*intrans.*] utter a cry of "tallyho." ▷late 18th cent.: apparently an alteration of French *taïaut*, of unknown origin.

tal·ly·man /ˈtalēmən; -ˌman/ ▸*n.* (*pl.* **-men**) **1** a person who keeps a score or record of something. **2** *Brit.* a person who sells merchandise on credit, esp. from door to door.

Tal·mud /ˈtälˌmo͝od; ˈtalməd/ ▸*n.* (**the Talmud**) the body of Jewish civil and ceremonial law and legend comprising the Mishnah and the Gemara. There are two versions of the Talmud: the Babylonian Talmud (which dates from the 5th century AD but includes earlier material) and the earlier Palestinian or Jerusalem Talmud. ▷from late Hebrew *talmūḏ* 'instruction,' from Hebrew *lāmaḏ* 'learn.' **—Tal·mud·ic** /talˈm(y)o͞odik; -ˈmo͝odik/ *adj.* **—Tal·mud·i·cal** /talˈm(y)o͞odikəl; -ˈmo͝od-/ *adj.* **—Tal·mud·ist** /ˈtälmo͝odist; ˈtalməd-/ *n.*

Tal·mud To·rah /ˈtälmo͝od ˈtōrə; ˈtalməd; ˈtôrə; tälˈmo͝od tôˈrä/ ▸*n. Judaism* the field of study that deals with the Jewish law. ■ a communal school where children are instructed in Judaism.

tal·on /ˈtalən/ ▸*n.* **1** a claw, esp. one belonging to a bird of prey. **2** the shoulder of a bolt against which the key presses to slide it in a lock. **3** (in various card games) the cards remaining undealt. ▷late Middle English (denoting any heellike part or object): from Old French, literally 'heel,' from Latin *talus* 'ankle bone, heel.' **—tal·oned** *adj.*

ta·lus[1] /ˈtāləs/ ▸*n.* (*pl.* **ta·li** /ˈtālī/) *Anatomy* the large bone in the ankle that articulates with the tibia of the leg and the calcaneum and navicular bone of the foot. Also called ASTRAGALUS. ▷late 16th cent.: from Latin, literally 'ankle, heel.'

ta·lus[2] ▸*n.* (*pl.* **ta·lus·es**) a sloping mass of rock fragments at the foot of a cliff. ■ the sloping side of an earthwork, or of a wall that tapers to the top. ▷mid 17th cent.: from French, of unknown origin.

TAM ▸*abbr.* television audience measurement.

tam /tam/ ▸*n.* a tam-o'-shanter. ▷late 19th cent.: abbreviation.

ta·ma·got·chi /ˌtäməˈgōchē; ˌtam-; -ˈgächē/ ▸*n.* an electronic toy displaying a digital image of a creature, which has to be looked after and responded to by the "owner" as if it were a pet. ▷Japanese.

ta·ma·le /təˈmälē/ ▸*n.* a Mexican dish of seasoned meat wrapped in cornmeal dough and steamed or baked in corn husks. ▷from Mexican Spanish *tamal*, plural *tamales*, from Nahuatl *tamalli*.

ta·man·du·a /təˈmando͞oə/ ▸*n.* a small nocturnal arboreal anteater with a naked prehensile tail, native to tropical America. • Genus *Tamandua*, family Myrmecophagidae: two species. ▷early 17th cent.: via Portuguese from Tupi *tamanduá*, from *taly* 'ant' + *mondar* 'hunter.'

Tam·a·rac /ˈtaməˌrak/ a city in southeastern Florida, northwest of Fort Lauderdale; pop. 44,822.

tam·a·rack /ˈtaməˌrak/ ▸*n.* a slender North American larch. • *Larix laricina*, family Pinaceae. ▷early 19th cent.: from Canadian French *tamarac*, probably of Algonquian origin.

ta·ma·rau /ˌtaməˈrou/ ▸*n.* a small brownish-black buffalo similar to the anoa, found only on Mindoro in the Philippines. • *Bubalus mindorensis*, family Bovidae. ▷late 19th cent.: from Tagalog.

ta·ma·ri /təˈmärē/ (also **ta·ma·ri sauce**) ▸*n.* a variety of rich, naturally fermented soy sauce. ▷Japanese.

ta·ma·ril·lo /ˌtaməˈrilō; -ˈrē-ō/ ▸*n.* (*pl.* **-los**) a tropical South American plant of the nightshade family that bears edible egg-shaped red fruits. Also called TREE TOMATO. • *Cyphomandra betacea*, family Solanaceae. ■ the fruit of this plant. ▷1960s (originally NZ): an invented name, perhaps suggested by Spanish *tomatillo*, diminutive of *tomate* 'tomato.'

tam·a·rin /ˈtamərin; -ˌran/ ▸*n.* a small forest-dwelling South American monkey of the marmoset family, typically brightly colored and with tufts and crests of hair around the face and neck. • Genera *Saguinus* and *Leontopithecus*, family Callitrichidae (or Callithricidae): several species. ▷late 18th cent.: from French, from Galibi.

tam·a·rind /ˈtaməˌrind/ ▸*n.* **1** sticky brown acidic pulp from the pod of a tree of the pea family, widely used as a flavoring in Asian cooking. ■ the pod from which this pulp is extracted. **2** the tropical African tree that yields these pods, cultivated throughout the tropics and also grown as an ornamental and shade tree. • *Tamarindus indica*, family Leguminosae. ▷late Middle English: from medieval Latin *tamarindus*, from Arabic *tamr hindī* 'Indian date.'

tam·a·risk /ˈtaməˌrisk/ ▸*n.* an Old World shrub or small tree with tiny scalelike leaves borne on slender branches, giving it a feathery appearance. • Genus *Tamarix*, family Tamaricaceae: many species. ▷late Middle English: from late Latin *tamariscus*, variant of Latin *tamarix*, of unknown origin.

ta·mas /ˈtəməs/ ▸*n.* (in Vedanta) the element or mode of prakriti associated with lethargy, darkness, and ignorance.

ta·ma·sha /təˈmäshə/ ▸*n. Indian* a grand show, performance, or celebration, esp. one involving dance. ■ [in *sing.*] a fuss or confusion: *what a tamasha!* ▷via Persian and Urdu from Arabic *tamāšā* 'walk around together.'

Tam·a·shek /ˈtaməˌshek/ ▸*n.* the dialect of Berber spoken by the Tuareg, sometimes regarded as a separate language. ▷the name in Berber.

ta·mas·ic /təˈmasik/ ▸*adj.* (in Ayurveda) denoting a class of foods that are dry, old, foul, or unpalatable, and are thought to promote pessimism, ignorance, laziness, criminal tendencies, and doubt. Compare RAJASIC, SATTVIC.

Ta·mau·li·pas /ˌtämouˈlēpäs/ a state in northeastern Mexico, on the Gulf of Mexico; capital, Ciudad Victoria.

tam·ba·la /tämˈbälə/ ▸*n.* (*pl.* same or **-las**) a monetary unit of Malawi, equal to one hundredth of a kwacha. ▷from Nyanja, literally 'cockerel.'

tam·bour /ˈtamˌbo͝or/ ▸*n.* **1** *historical* a small drum. **2** something resembling a drum in shape or construction, in particular: ■ a circular frame for holding fabric taut while it is being embroidered. ■ *Architecture* a wall of circular plan, such as one supporting a dome or surrounded by a colonnade. ■ *Architecture* each of a sequence of cylindrical stones forming the shaft of a column. ■ a sloping buttress or projection in a court tennis or fives court. ■ [usu. as *adj.*] a sliding flexible shutter or door on a piece of furniture, made of strips of wood attached to a backing of canvas: *a tambour door.*
▸*v.* [*trans.*] [often as *adj.*] (**tamboured**) decorate or embroider on a tambour: *a tamboured waistcoat.* ▷late 15th cent.: from French *tambour* 'drum'; perhaps related to Persian *tabīra* 'drum.' Compare with TABOR.

tam·bou·ra /tamˈbo͝orə/ (also **tam·bu·ra**) ▸*n.* **1** a large four-stringed lute used in Indian music as a drone accompaniment. **2** a long-necked lute or mandolin of Balkan countries. ▷late 16th cent. (denoting a type of long-necked lute): from Arabic *ṭanbūr* or Persian *tunbūra*, both from Persian *dunbara*, literally 'lamb's tail.'

tam·bou·rin /ˈtambo͝orin; tanbo͞oˈran/ ▸*n.* a long narrow drum used in Provence. ■ a dance accompanied by such a drum. ▷French, diminutive of *tambour* (see TAMBOUR).

tam·bou·rine /ˌtambəˈrēn/ ▸*n.* a percussion instrument resembling a shallow drum with small metal disks in slots around the edge, played by being shaken or hit with the hand. ▷late 16th cent.: from French *tambourin* (see TAMBOURIN). **—tam·bou·rin·ist** /-nist/ *n.*

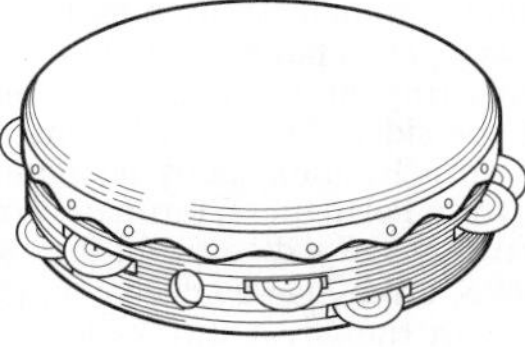
tambourine

Tam·bov /tämˈbôf; -ˈbôv/ an industrial city in southwestern Russia; pop. 307,000.

tam·bu·ra ▸*n.* variant spelling of TAMBOURA.

tam·bu·rit·za /tamˈbo͝oritsə; ˌtambəˈritsə/ ▸*n.* a kind of long-necked mandolin played in Croatia and neighboring countries. ▷Serbo-Croat, diminutive of *tambura* TAMBOURA.

tame /tām/ ▸*adj.* **1** (of an animal) not dangerous or frightened of people; domesticated: *the fish are so tame you have to push them away from your face mask.* ■ not exciting, adventurous, or controversial: *network TV on Saturday night is a pretty tame affair.* ■ *informal* (of a person) willing to cooperate. **2** (of a plant) produced by cultivation. ■ (of land) cultivated.
▸*v.* [*trans.*] (often **be tamed**) domesticate (an animal): *wild rabbits can be kept in captivity and eventually tamed.* ■ make less powerful and easier to control: *the battle to tame inflation.* ■ cultivate (land or wilderness). ▷Old English *tam* (adjective), *temmian* (verb), of Germanic origin; related to Dutch *tam* and German *zahm*, from an Indo-European root shared by Latin *domare* and Greek *daman* 'tame, subdue.' **—tam·a·ble** (also **tame·a·ble**) *adj.* **—tame·ly** *adv.* **—tame·ness** *n.* **—tam·er** *n.*

Tam·er·lane /ˈtamərˌlān-/ (also **Tam·bur·laine** /ˈtambər-/) (1336–1405), Mongol ruler of Samarkand 1369–1405; Tartar name *Timur Lenk* ("lame Timur"). Leading a force of Mongols and Turks, he conquered Persia, northern India, and Syria and established his capital at Samarkand. He was the ancestor of the Mogul dynasty in India.

Tam·il /ˈtaməl/ ▸*n.* **1** a member of a people inhabiting parts of southern India and Sri Lanka. **2** the Dravidian language of the Tamils.
▸*adj.* of or relating to this people or their language. ▷the name in Tamil. **—Tam·il·i·an** /təˈmilēən/ *adj.* & *n.*

Tam·il Na·du /ˈtaməl ˈnädo͞o/ a state in southeastern India, on the Coromandel Coast, with a largely Tamil-speaking Hindu population; capital, Madras. Former name (until 1968) MADRAS.

Tam·il Ti·gers a Sri Lankan guerrilla organization founded in 1972 that seeks the establishment of an independent state (Eelam) in the northeast of the country for the Tamil community. Also called LIBERATION TIGERS OF TAMIL EELAM.

Tam·la Mo·town /ˈtamlə ˈmōˌtoun/ *n.* trade name for MOTOWN (sense 1).

Tam·ma·ny /ˈtamənē/ (also **Tam·ma·ny Hall**) a powerful organization within the Democratic Party that was widely associated with corruption. Founded as a fraternal and benevolent society in 1789, it came to dominate political life in New York City in the 19th and early 20th centuries, before being reduced in power by Franklin D. Roosevelt in the early 1930s. ■ [as *n.*] (**a Tammany**) a corrupt political organization or group. ▷named after an American Indian chief of the late 17th cent., said to have welcomed William Penn, and regarded as "patron saint" of Pennsylvania and other northern colonies. **—Tam·ma·ny·ite** /-nēˌīt/ *n.*

tam·mar wal·la·by /ˈtamər/ ▸*n.* a small grayish-brown wallaby found in southwestern Australia. • *Macropus eugenii*, family Macropodidae. ▷mid 19th cent.: from Gaurna (an Aboriginal language) *tamma*.

Tam·mer·fors /ˌtämərˈfô(r)sh/ Swedish name for TAMPERE.

Tam·muz[1] /ˈtämo͝oz; ˈtaməz/ *Near Eastern Mythology* a Mesopotamian god, lover of Ishtar and similar in some respects to the Greek Adonis. He became the personification of the seasonal death and rebirth of crops. ▷from Ezek. 8:14, from Akkadian *Dumuzi*.

Tam·muz[2] variant spelling of THAMMUZ.

tam-o'-shan·ter /ˈtam əˌshantər/ ▸*n.* a round woolen or cloth cap of Scottish origin, with a pom-pom in the center. ▷mid 19th cent.: named after the hero of Burns's poem *Tam o' Shanter* (1790).

tam-o'-shanter

ta·mox·i·fen /təˈmäksəfən/ ▸*n. Medicine* a synthetic drug used to treat breast cancer and infertility in women. It acts as an estrogen antagonist. ▷1970s: an arbitrary formation based on TRANS-, AMINE, OXY-[2], PHENOL, elements of the drug's chemical name.

tamp /tamp/ ▸*v.* [*trans.*] pack (a blast hole) full of clay or sand to concentrate the force of the explosion: *when the hole was tamped to the top, gunpowder was inserted.* ■ [*trans.*] ram or pack (a substance) down or into something firmly: *he* ***tamped down*** *the tobacco with his thumb.* ▷early 19th cent.: probably a back-formation from *tampin* (interpreted as 'tamping'), variant of TAMPION.

Tam·pa /ˈtampə/ a port and resort on the western coast of Florida; pop. 303,447.

Tam·pa Bay an inlet of the Gulf of Mexico, in southwestern Florida. Tampa and St. Petersburg are among the cities that lie along its shores.

tam·per /ˈtampər/ ▸*v.* **1** [*intrans.*] (**tamper with**) interfere with (something) in order to cause damage or make unauthorized alterations: *someone tampered with the brakes on my car.* **2** [*intrans.*] (**tamper with**) exert a secret or corrupt influence upon (someone).
▸*n.* a person or thing that tamps something down, esp. a machine or tool for tamping down earth or ballast. ▷mid 16th cent. (in the sense 'busy oneself to a particular end, machinate'): alteration of the verb TEMPER. —**tam·per·er** *n.*

Tam·pe·re /ˈtämpəˌrä; ˈtam-; ˈtampərə/ a city in southwestern Finland; pop. 173,000. Swedish name TAMMERFORS.

tam·per-ev·i·dent ▸*adj.* (of packaging) designed to reveal any interference with the contents.

tam·per-proof ▸*adj.* made so that it cannot be interfered with or changed.

Tam·pi·co /tamˈpēkō; täm-/ a principal seaport in Mexico, on the Gulf of Mexico; pop. 272,000.

tam·pi·on /ˈtampēən/ (also **tom·pi·on** /ˈtämpēən/) ▸*n.* a wooden stopper for the muzzle of a gun. ■ a plug for the top of an organ pipe. ▷late Middle English: from French *tampon* 'tampon.'

tam·pon /ˈtamˌpän/ ▸*n.* a plug of soft material inserted into the vagina to absorb menstrual blood. ■ *Medicine* a plug of material used to stop a wound or block an opening in the body and absorb blood or secretions.
▸*v.* (**-poned**, **-pon·ing**) [*trans.*] plug with a tampon. ▷mid 19th cent.: from French, nasalized variant of *tapon* 'plug, stopper,' ultimately of Germanic origin and related to TAP[1].

tam·pon·ade /ˌtampəˈnād/ ▸*n. Medicine* **1** (in full **cardiac tamponade**) compression of the heart by an accumulation of fluid in the pericardial sac. **2** the surgical use of a plug of absorbent material.

tam-tam /ˈtəm ˌtəm; ˈtam ˌtam/ ▸*n.* a large metal gong with indefinite pitch. ▷mid 19th cent.: perhaps from Hindi *ṭam-ṭam* (see TOM-TOM).

Tan /tan/, Amy, (1952–) U.S. writer. Her works include *The Joy Luck Club* (1989), *The Kitchen God's Wife* (1991), *The Hundred Secret Senses* (1995), and *The Bonesetter's Daughter* (2000). She also wrote children's stories, such as *The Moon Lady* (1992) and *The Chinese Siamese Cat* (1994).

tan[1] /tan/ ▸*n.* **1** a yellowish-brown color: *the overall color scheme of tan and cream.* ■ a golden-brown shade of skin developed by pale-skinned people after exposure to the sun. **2** (also **tan·bark** /ˈtanˌbärk/) bark of oak or other trees, bruised and used as a source of tannin for converting hides into leather. ■ (also **spent tan**) such bark from which the tannin has been extracted, used for covering the ground for walking, riding, children's play, etc., and in gardening.
▸*v.* (**tanned**, **tan·ning**) **1** [*intrans.*] (of a pale-skinned person or their skin) become brown or browner after exposure to the sun: *you'll tan very quickly in the pure air.* ■ [*trans.*] [usu. as *adj.*] (**tanned**) (of the sun) cause (a pale-skinned person or their skin) to become brown or browner: *he looked tanned and fit.* **2** [*trans.*] convert (animal skin) into leather by soaking in a liquid containing tannic acid, or by the use of other chemicals. **3** [*trans.*] *informal, dated* beat (someone) repeatedly, esp. as a punishment: *"If Mickey touches a fishing net, I'll* ***tan his hide!****"*
▸*adj.* of a yellowish-brown color: *a tan baseball cap with orange piping.* ■ (of a pale-skinned person) having golden-brown skin after exposure to the sun: *she looks tall, tan, and healthy.* ▷late Old English *tannian* 'convert into leather,' probably from medieval Latin *tannare*, perhaps of Celtic origin; reinforced in Middle English by Old French *tanner*. Early use of the noun (late Middle English) was in sense 2. —**tan·na·ble** *adj.* —**tan·nish** *adj.*

tan[2] ▸*abbr.* tangent.

Ta·na, Lake /ˈtänə/ a lake in northern Ethiopia, the source of the Blue Nile.

tan·a·ger /ˈtanəjər/ ▸*n.* a small American songbird of the bunting family, the male of which typically has brightly colored plumage. • Family Emberizidae (subfamily Thraupinae): many genera, in particular *Tangara*, and numerous species. ▷early 17th cent. (originally as *tangara*): from Tupi *tangará*, later refashioned on the pattern of the modern Latin genus name *Tanagra*.

Ta·na·na·rive /ˌtanənəˈrēv; təˌnanə-/ former name (until 1975) of ANTANANARIVO.

Tan·a·na Riv·er /ˈtanəˌnô/ a river that flows for 600 miles (1,000 km) from Yukon Territory across Alaska, to meet the Yukon River west of Fairbanks.

tan·bark /ˈtanˌbärk/ ▸*n.* see TAN[1] (sense 2).

T & A ▸*abbr.* tits and ass.

tan·dem /ˈtandəm/ ▸*n.* (also **tan·dem bicycle**) a bicycle with seats and pedals for two riders, one behind the other. ■ a carriage driven by two animals harnessed one in front of the other. ■ a group of two people or machines working together. ■ a truck with two rear drive axles.
▸*adv.* with two or more horses harnessed one behind another: *I rode tandem to Paris.* ■ alongside each other; together.
▸*adj.* having two things arranged one in front of the other: *satisfactory steering angles can be maintained with tandem trailers.* ▷late 18th cent.: humorously from Latin, literally 'at length.'
▸PHRASE □ **in tandem** alongside each other; together: *a tight fiscal policy working in tandem with a tight foreign exchange policy.* ■ one behind another.

tan·door /tanˈdo͝or; tän-/ ▸*n.* a clay oven of a type used originally in northern India and Pakistan. ▷from Urdu *tandūr*, from Persian *tanūr*, based on Arabic *tannūr* 'oven.'

tan·door·i /tanˈdo͝orē; tän-/ ▸*adj.* denoting or relating to a style of Indian cooking based on the use of a tandoor: *tandoori chicken.*
▸*n.* food or cooking of this type. ■ a restaurant serving such food. ▷from Urdu and Persian *tandūrī*, from *tandūr* (see TANDOOR).

Tan·dy /ˈtandē/, Jessica, (1909–94) U.S. actress; born in England. She made many stage appearances, some with her husband Hume Cronyn, including *The Gin Game* (1978). Her movies include *Cocoon* (1985), *Driving Miss Daisy* (Academy Award, 1989), and *Fried Green Tomatoes* (1991).

Tan·ey /ˈtônē/, Roger Brooke, (1777–1864) U.S. chief justice 1836–64. He was active in Maryland politics and was the U.S. attorney general 1831–33 before being appointed chief justice. He upheld the principle of federal supremacy over states' rights. In the *Dred Scott* v. *Sandford* case 1857, he expressed the opinion that blacks could not be citizens and that Congress had no control over slavery in the territories.

Tang /täNG/ a dynasty ruling China 618–*c.*906, a period noted for territorial conquest and great wealth and regarded as the golden age of Chinese poetry and art.

tang[1] /taNG/ ▸*n.* **1** [in *sing.*] a strong taste, flavor, or smell: *the clean salty tang of the sea.* ■ a characteristic quality: *the tang of finality hovers throughout Tolstoy's story.* **2** the projection on the blade of a tool such as a knife, by which the blade is held firmly in the handle. ▷Middle English (denoting a snake's tongue, formerly believed to be a stinging organ; also denoting the sting of an insect): from Old Norse *tangi* 'point, tang of a knife.'

tang[2] ▸*v.* [*intrans.*] make a loud ringing or clanging sound: *the bronze bell tangs.*
▸*n.* a tanging sound. ▷mid 16th cent.: imitative.

tang[3] ▸*n.* a surgeonfish that occurs around reefs and rocky areas, where it browses on algae. • Genus *Acanthurus*, family Acanthuridae: several species, in particular the **blue tang** (*A. coeruleus*) of the western Atlantic. ▷mid 18th cent.: from TANG[1].

Tan·ga /ˈtaNGgə; ˈtäNG-/ one of the principal ports in Tanzania, situated in the northeastern part of the country, on the Indian Ocean; pop. 188,000.

tan·ga /ˈtaNGgə/ (also **tan·ga briefs**) ▸*n. Brit.* a pair of briefs consisting of small panels connected by strings at the sides. ▷early 20th cent. (denoting a loincloth worn by indigenous peoples in tropical America): from Portuguese, ultimately of Bantu origin. The current sense dates from the 1970s.

Tan·gan·yi·ka, Lake /ˌtan-gənˈyēkə; ˌtaNG-/ a lake in East Africa, in the Great Rift Valley. The deepest lake in Africa and the longest freshwater lake in the world, it forms most of the border of the Democratic Republic of the Congo (formerly Zaire) with Tanzania and Burundi.

tan·ge·lo /ˈtanjəˌlō/ ▸*n.* (*pl.* **-los**) a hybrid of the tangerine and grapefruit. ▷early 20th cent.: blend of TANGERINE and POMELO.

tan·gent /ˈtanjənt/ ▸*n.* **1** a straight line or plane that touches a curve or curved surface at a point, but if extended does not cross it at that point. ■ *figurative* a completely different line of thought or action: *she* ***went off on a tangent*** *about how she and her husband had driven past a department store window.* **2** *Mathematics* the trigonometric function that is equal to the ratio of the sides (other than the hypotenuse) opposite and adjacent to an angle in a right triangle.

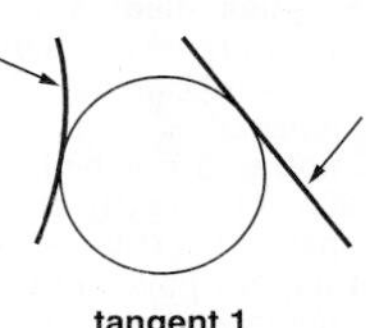
tangent 1

▸*adj.* (of a line or plane) touching, but not intersecting, a curve or curved surface. ▷late 16th cent. (in sense 2 and as an adjective): from Latin *tangent-* 'touching,' from the verb *tangere*. —**tan·gen·cy** /-jənsē/ *n.*

tan·gen·tial /tanˈjenCHəl/ ▸*adj.* of, relating to, or along a tangent: *a tangential line.* ■ diverging from a previous course or line; erratic: *tangential thoughts.* ■ hardly touching a matter; peripheral: *the reforms were tangential to efforts to maintain a basic standard of life.* —**tan·gen·tial·ly** *adv.*

tan·ge·rine /ˌtanjəˈrēn/ ▸*n.* **1** a small citrus fruit with a loose skin, esp. one of a variety with deep orange-red skin. ■ a deep orange-red color. **2** the citrus tree that bears this fruit. • *Citrus reticulata*, family Rutaceae. ▷mid 19th cent.: from *Tanger* (former name of TANGIER) + -INE[1]. The fruit, exported from Tangier, was originally called the *tangerine orange*.

tan·gi·ble /ˈtanjəbəl/ ▸*adj.* perceptible by touch: *the atmosphere of neglect and abandonment was* ***almost tangible.*** ■ clear and definite; real: *the emphasis is now on tangible results.*
▸*n.* (usu. **tangibles**) a thing that is perceptible by touch. ▷late 16th cent.: from French, or from late Latin *tangibilis*, from *tangere* 'to touch.' —**tan·gi·bil·i·ty** /ˌtanjəˈbilitē/ *n.* —**tan·gi·ble·ness** *n.* —**tan·gi·bly** /-blē/ *adv.*

THE RIGHT WORD **appreciable, corporeal, palpable, perceptible, sensible, tangible**

Anything that can be grasped, either with the hand or with the mind, is **tangible** (*tangible assets; tangible objects*).

Palpable, like *tangible*, means capable of being touched or felt (*a palpable mist*), but it is often applied to whatever evokes a tactile response from the body (*a palpable chill in the room*).

Perceptible is used to describe something that just crosses the border between invisibility and visibility or some other sense barrier (*a perceptible change in her tone of voice; a perceptible odor of garlic*).

Sensible (in this sense) describes that which can clearly be perceived through the senses or which makes a strong impression on the mind through the medium of sensations. In contrast to *perceptible*, something that is *sensible* is more obvious or immediately recognized (*a sensible shift in the tenor of the conversation*).

Corporeal means bodily or material, in contrast to things that are immaterial or spiritual (*corporeal goods*).

Something that is **appreciable** is large enough to be measured, valued, estimated, or considered significant.

An *appreciable* change in temperature, for example, can be determined by looking at a thermometer; a *palpable* change in temperature may be slight, but still great enough to be felt; and a *perceptible* change in temperature might be so slight that it almost—but not quite—escapes notice.

Tan·gier /tanˈji(ə)r/ a seaport on the northern coast of Morocco, on the Strait of Gibraltar where it stands guard at the western entrance to the Mediterranean Sea; pop. 307,000.

tan·gle[1] /ˈtaNGgəl/ ▸*v.* [*trans.*] (usu. **be tangled**) twist together into a confused mass: *the broom somehow got* ***tangled up*** *in my long skirt.* ■ [*intrans.*] (**tangle with**) *informal* become involved in a conflict or fight with: *I know there'll be trouble if I try to tangle with him.*
▸*n.* a confused mass of something twisted together: *a tangle of golden hair.* ■ a confused or complicated state; a muddle. ■ *informal* a fight, argument, or disagreement. ▷Middle English (in the sense 'entangle, catch in a tangle'): probably of Scandinavian origin and related to Swedish dialect *taggla* 'disarrange.' —**tan·gly** /-g(ə)lē/ *adj.*
▸PHRASE □ **a tangled web** a complex, difficult, and confusing situation or thing. [from 'O what a tangled

web we weave, When first we practise to deceive' (Scott's *Marmion*).]

tan·gle[2] ▶*n.* any of a number of brown seaweeds, esp. oarweed. ▷mid 16th cent.: probably from Norwegian *tongul.*

tan·gle·foot /'taNGgəl,fo͝ot/ ▶*n.* **1** *trademark* material applied to a tree trunk as a grease band, esp. to prevent infestation by insects. **2** *informal* intoxicating liquor, esp. cheap whiskey.

tan·go /'taNGgō/ ▶*n.* (*pl.* **-gos**) **1** a ballroom dance originating in Buenos Aires, characterized by marked rhythms and postures and abrupt pauses. ■ a piece of music written for or in the style of this dance, typically in a slow dotted duple rhythm. **2** a code word representing the letter T, used in voice communication by radio.
▶*v.* (**-goes, -goed**) [*intrans.*] dance the tango. ▷late 19th cent.: from Latin American Spanish, perhaps of African origin.
▶*PHRASE* □ **it takes two to tango** *informal* both parties involved in a situation or argument are responsible for it.

tan·gram /'taNG,grəm/ ▶*n.* a Chinese geometric puzzle consisting of a square cut into seven pieces that can be arranged to make various other shapes. ▷mid 19th cent.: of unknown origin.

Tang·shan /'täNG'SHän/ an industrial city in Hebei province, northeastern China; pop. 1,500,000. It was rebuilt after an earthquake in 1976.

tang·y /'taNGē/ ▶*adj.* (**tang·i·er, tang·i·est**) having a strong, piquant flavor or smell: *a tangy salad.* **—tang·i·ness** *n.*

tanh *Mathematics* ▶*abbr.* hyperbolic tangent.

tan·ist /'tanist; 'THô-/ ▶*n.* the heir apparent to a Celtic chief, typically the most vigorous adult of his kin, elected during the chief's lifetime. ▷mid 16th cent.: from Irish, Scottish Gaelic *tánaiste*, literally 'second in excellence.' **—tan·ist·ry** /-istrē/ *n.*

Tan·jung·ka·rang /,tänjo͝oNG'käräNG/ see **BANDAR LAMPUNG.**

tank /taNGk/ ▶*n.* **1** a large receptacle or storage chamber, esp. for liquid or gas. ■ the container holding the fuel supply in a motor vehicle. ■ a receptacle with transparent sides in which to keep fish; an aquarium. **2** a heavy armored fighting vehicle carrying guns and moving on a continuous articulated metal track. [from the use of *tank* as a secret code word during manufacture in 1915.] **3** *informal* a cell in a police station or jail.
▶*v.* **1** [*intrans.*] fill the tank of a vehicle with fuel: *the cars stopped to* **tank up.** ■ (**be/get tanked up**) *informal* drink heavily; become drunk: *they get tanked up before the game.* **2** [*intrans.*] *informal* fail completely, esp. at great financial cost. ■ [*trans.*] *informal* (in sports) deliberately lose or fail to finish (a game): *the lackluster performance prompted speculation that he tanked the second set.* ▷early 17th cent.: perhaps from Gujarati *tānkũ* or Marathi *tānkẽ* 'underground cistern,' from Sanskrit *tadāga* 'pond,' probably influenced by Portuguese *tangue* 'pond,' from Latin *stagnum.* **—tank·ful** /-,fo͝ol/ *n.* (*pl.* **-fuls**). **—tank·less** *adj.*

tank 2

tan·ka[1] /'täNGkə/ ▶*n.* (*pl.* same or **-kas**) a Japanese poem consisting of five lines, the first and third of which have five syllables and the other seven, making 31 syllables in all and giving a complete picture of an event or mood. ▷Japanese, from *tan* 'short' + *ka* 'song.'

tan·ka[2] ▶*n.* (*pl.* **-kas**) a Tibetan religious painting on a scroll, hung as a banner in temples and carried in processions. ▷from Tibetan *t'án-ka* 'image, painting.'

tank·age /'taNGkij/ ▶*n.* **1** the storage capacity of a tank. ■ the storage of something in a tank or a charge made for such storage. **2** a fertilizer or animal feed obtained from the residue from tanks in which animal carcasses have been rendered.

tank·ard /'taNGkərd/ ▶*n.* a tall beer mug, typically made of silver or pewter, with a handle and sometimes a hinged lid. ■ the contents of or an amount held by such a mug: *I've downed* **a tankard of** *ale.* ▷Middle English (denoting a large tub for carrying liquid): perhaps related to Dutch *tanckaert.*

tank·er /'taNGkər/ ▶*n.* **1** a ship, road vehicle, or aircraft for carrying liquids, esp. petroleum, in bulk. **2** *Military* member of a tank crew.

tank farm ▶*n.* an area of oil or gas storage tanks.

tank·i·ni /taNG'kēnē/ ▶*n.* a two-piece bathing suit consisting of a tank top and a bikini bottom.

tank kill·er ▶*n.* an aircraft, vehicle, or missile effective against tanks.

tank top ▶*n.* a close-fitting sleeveless top.

tank town ▶*n.* a small unimportant town (used originally of a town at which trains stopped to take on water).

tan·ner[1] /'tanər/ ▶*n.* **1** a person who tans animal hides, esp. to earn a living. **2** a lotion or cream designed to promote the development of a suntan or produce a similar skin color artificially.

tan·ner[2] ▶*n. Brit., informal* a sixpence. ▷early 19th cent.: of unknown origin.

tan·ner·y /'tanərē/ ▶*n.* (*pl.* **-ner·ies**) a place where animal hides are tanned; the workshop of a tanner.

Tann·häu·ser /'tän,hoizər/ (*c.*1200–*c.*1270), German poet. In reality a minnesinger whose works included lyrics and love poetry, he became a legendary figure as a knight who visited Venus's grotto. He spent seven years in debauchery, then repented and sought absolution from the pope.

tan·nic /'tanik/ ▶*adj.* of or related to tannin: *a dry wine with a slightly tannic aftertaste.* ▷mid 19th cent.: from French *tannique*, from *tanin* (see **TANNIN**).

tan·nic ac·id ▶*n.* another term for **TANNIN. —tan·nate** /'tanāt/ *n.*

tan·nin /'tanin/ ▶*n.* a yellowish or brownish bitter-tasting organic substance present in some galls, barks, and other plant tissues, consisting of derivatives of gallic acid, used in leather production and ink manufacture. ▷early 19th cent.: from French *tanin*, from *tan* 'tanbark' (ultimately related to **TAN**[1]) + **-IN**[1].

tan·ning bed ▶*n.* an apparatus used for tanning, consisting of a bank of sunlamp tubes, typically horizontal for lying on, with another above.

Tan·nu-Tu·va /'täno͞o 'to͞ovə/ former name for **TUVA.**

Ta·no·an /'tänōən/ ▶*n.* a small language family comprising a number of Pueblo Indian languages, including Tewa and Tiwa, and related to Kiowa.
▶*adj.* of or relating to this language family. ▷from Spanish *Tano* + **-AN.**

tan·su /'tänso͞o; 'tan-/ ▶*n.* (*pl.* same) a Japanese chest of drawers or cabinet. ▷Japanese.

tan·sy /'tanzē/ ▶*n.* a plant of the daisy family with yellow flat-topped buttonlike flowerheads and aromatic leaves, formerly used in cooking and medicine. • Genus *Tanacetum*, family Compositae: several species, in particular **common tansy** (*T. vulgare*). ▷Middle English: from Old French *tanesie*, probably from medieval Latin *athanasia* 'immortality,' from Greek.

tan·ta·lite /'tantl,īt/ ▶*n.* a rare, dense, black mineral consisting of a mixed oxide of tantalum, of which it is the principal source, and iron. ▷early 19th cent.: from **TANTALUM** + **-ITE**[1].

tan·ta·lize /'tantl,īz/ ▶*v.* [*trans.*] torment or tease (someone) with the sight or promise of something that is unobtainable: *such ambitious questions have long tantalized the world's best thinkers.* ■ excite the senses or desires of (someone): *she still tantalized him* | [as *adj.*] (**tantalizing**) *the tantalizing fragrance of fried bacon.* ▷late 16th cent.: from **TANTALUS** + **-IZE. —tan·ta·li·za·tion** /,tantli'zāSHən/ *n.* **—tan·ta·liz·er** *n.* **—tan·ta·liz·ing·ly** *adv.*

tan·ta·lum /'tantl-əm/ ▶*n.* the chemical element of atomic number 73, a hard silver-gray metal of the transition series. (Symbol: **Ta**) ▷early 19th cent.: from **TANTALUS**, with reference to its frustrating insolubility in acids. **—tan·tal·ic** /tan'talik/ *adj.*

Tan·ta·lus /'tantl-əs/ *Greek Mythology* a Lydian king, son of Zeus and father of Pelops. As punishment for his crimes (which included killing Pelops), he was forced to remain in chin-deep water with fruit-laden branches over his head, both of which receded when he reached for them. His name is the origin of the word *tantalize.*

tan·ta·lus /'tantl-əs/ ▶*n. chiefly Brit.* a stand in which decanters of liquor can be locked up though still visible.

tan·ta·mount /'tantə,mount/ ▶*adj.* [*predic.*] (**tantamount to**) equivalent in seriousness to; virtually the same as: *the resignations were tantamount to an admission of guilt.* See note at **SAME.** ▷mid 17th cent.: from the earlier verb *tantamount* 'amount to as much,' from Italian *tanto montare.*

tante /tänt; 'täntə/ ▶*n.* (esp. among those of French or German origin) a mature or elderly woman who is related or well known to the speaker (often used as a respectful form of address). ▷French, Dutch *tante*, German *Tante* 'aunt.'

tan·tiv·y /tan'tivē/ *archaic* ▶*n.* (*pl.* **-tiv·ies**) a rapid gallop or ride.
▶*exclam.* used as a hunting cry.
▶*adj.* moving or riding swiftly. ▷mid 17th cent.: probably imitative of the sound of galloping.

tant mieux /'täN 'myə/ ▶*exclam.* so much the better. ▷French.

tan·to[1] /'täntō/ ▶*n.* (*pl.* **-tos**) a Japanese short sword or dagger. ▷Japanese.

tan·to[2] ▶*adv.* [usu. with *negative*] *Music* (esp. as a direction after a tempo marking) too much: *allegro non tanto.* ▷Italian.

tant pis /'täN 'pē/ ▶*exclam.* so much the worse; the situation is regrettable but now beyond retrieval. ▷French.

Tan·tra /'təntrə; 'tan-/ ▶*n.* a Hindu or Buddhist mystical or ritual text, dating from the 6th to the 13th centuries. ■ adherence to the doctrines or principles of the tantras, involving mantras, meditation, yoga, and ritual. ▷Sanskrit, literally 'loom, groundwork, doctrine,' from *tan* 'stretch.' **—tan·tric** /-trik/ *adj.* **—tan·trism** /-,trizəm/ *n.* **—tan·trist** /-trist/ *n.*

tan·trum /'tantrəm/ ▶*n.* an uncontrolled outburst of anger and frustration, typically in a young child: *he has* **temper tantrums** *if he can't get his own way.* ▷early 18th cent.: of unknown origin.

Tan·za·ni·a /,tanzə'nēə/ a country in East Africa, on the Indian Ocean; pop. 36,580,000; capital, Dar es Salaam (Dodoma, in central Tanzania, is expected to become the official capital city by 2005); languages, Swahili and English (both official). **—Tan·za·ni·an** *adj. & n.*

Tanzania consists of a mainland area (the former Tanganyika) and the island of Zanzibar. A German colony (German East Africa) from the late 19th century, Tanganyika became a British mandate after World War I and a trust territory, administered by Britain, after World War II, before becoming independent within the Commonwealth of Nations in 1961. It was named Tanzania after its union with Zanzibar in 1964.

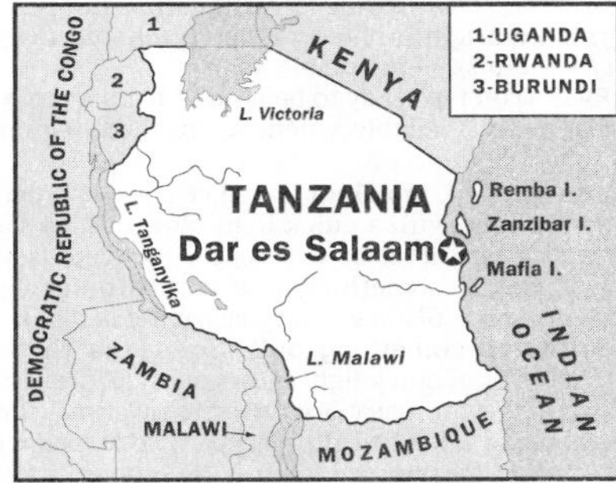

tan·za·nite /'tanzə,nīt/ ▶*n.* a blue or violet gem variety of zoisite, containing vanadium. ▷1960s: from **TANZANIA** + **-ITE**[1].

Tao /dou; tou/ ▶*n.* (in Chinese philosophy) the absolute principle underlying the universe, combining within itself the principles of yin and yang and signifying the way, or code of behavior, that is in harmony with the natural order. The interpretation of Tao in the Tao-te-Ching developed into the philosophical religion of Taoism. ▷Chinese, literally '(right) way.'

Taoi·seach /'tēSHək; -SHəKH; 'THē-/ ▶*n.* the prime minister of the Irish Republic. ▷Irish, literally 'chief, leader.'

Tao·ism /'dou,izəm; 'tou-/ ▶*n.* a Chinese philosophy based on the writings of Lao-tzu (*fl.* 6th century BC), advocating humility and religious piety.

The central concept and goal is the Tao, and its most important text is the Tao-te-Ching. Taoism has both a philosophical and a religious aspect. Philosophical Taoism emphasizes inner contemplation and mystical union with nature; wisdom, learning, and purposive action should be abandoned in favor of simplicity and **wu-wei** (nonaction, or letting things take their natural course). The religious aspect of Taoism developed later, *c.*3rd century AD, incorporating certain Buddhist features and developing a monastic system.

—**Tao·ist** *n.* & *adj.* —**Tao·is·tic** /tou'istik/ *adj.*

Ta·or·mi·na /ˌtour'mēnə/ a resort town on the eastern coast of Sicily; pop. 10,905 (1990). It was founded by Greek colonists in the 4th century BC.

Taos[1] /tous; 'tä-ōs/ a town in northern New Mexico, in the Sangre de Cristo Mountains; pop. 4,065.

Taos[2] ▶*n.* (*pl.* same) a North American people native to New Mexico. ■ a member of this people. ■ the language of this people.

Tao-te-Ching /'dou də 'jiNG/ ▶*n.* the central Taoist text, ascribed to Lao-tzu, the traditional founder of Taoism. Apparently written as a guide for rulers, it defined the Tao, or way, and established the philosophical basis of Taoism. ▷Chinese, literally 'the Book of the Way and its Power.'

tap[1] /tap/ ▶*n.* **1** a device by which a flow of liquid or gas from a pipe or container can be controlled. ■ a device connected to a telephone used for listening secretly to someone's conversations. ■ an act of listening secretly to someone's telephone conversation. ■ (also **tap·ping**) an electrical connection made to some point between the end terminals of a transformer coil or other component. **2** an instrument for cutting a threaded hole in a material. **3** *Brit.* a taproom.
▶*v.* (**tapped, tap·ping**) [*trans.*] **1** draw liquid through the tap or spout of (a cask, barrel, or other container): *hoarse chatter of tests they had aced and kegs they had tapped.* ■ draw (liquid) from a cask, barrel, or other container: *the butlers were tapping new and old ale.* ■ (often **be tapped**) connect a device to (a telephone) so that conversation can be listened to secretly: *the telephones were tapped by the state security police.* ■ *informal* obtain money or information from (someone): *he considered whom he could* **tap for** *information.* ■ exploit or draw a supply from (a resource): *clients from industry seeking to tap Philadelphia's resources of expertise* | [*intrans.*] *these magazines have* **tapped into** *a target market of consumers.* ■ draw sap from (a tree) by cutting into it. **2** cut a thread in (something) to accept a screw. ▷Old English *tæppa* 'peg for the vent hole of a cask,' *tæppian* 'provide (a cask) with a stopper,' of Germanic origin; related to Dutch *tap* and German *Zapfen* (nouns). —**tap·pa·ble** *adj.*
▶*PHRASE* □ **on tap** ready to be poured from a tap. ■ *informal* freely available whenever needed. ■ *informal* on schedule to occur.

tap[2] ▶*v.* (**tapped, tap·ping**) [*trans.*] **1** strike (someone or something) with a quick light blow or blows: *one of my staff tapped me on the shoulder.* ■ strike (something) against something else with a quick light blow or blows: *Gloria was tapping her feet in time to the music.* ■ (**tap something out**) produce (a rhythm) with a series of quick light blows on a surface: *drums that tapped out a rumba beat.* ■ write or enter (something) using a keyboard or keypad: *he* **tapped out** *a few words on the keyboard.* **2** (usu. **be tapped**) *informal* designate or select (someone) for a task or honor, esp. membership in an organization or committee: *he had been tapped earlier to serve in Costa Rica.*
▶*n.* **1** a quick light blow or the sound of such a blow. **2** tap dancing. ■ a piece of metal attached to the toe and heel of a tap dancer's shoe to make a tapping sound. **3** (**taps**) [treated as *sing.* or *pl.*] a bugle call for lights to be put out in army quarters. [so named because the signal was originally sounded on a drum.] ■ a similar call sounded at a military funeral. ▷Middle English: from Old French *taper,* or of imitative origin; compare with CLAP[1] and RAP[1]. —**tap·per** *n.*

ta·pa /'täpə/ ▶*n.* the bark of the paper mulberry tree. ■ (also **ta·pa cloth**) cloth made from such bark, used in the Pacific islands. ▷early 19th cent.: of Polynesian origin.

ta·pas /'täpəs/ ▶*plural n.* small Spanish savory dishes, typically served with drinks at a bar. ▷Spanish, literally 'cover, lid' (because the dishes were given free with the drink, served on a dish balanced on, therefore "covering," the glass).

tap dance ▶*n.* a dance performed wearing shoes fitted with metal taps, characterized by rhythmical tapping of the toes and heels.
▶*v.* [*intrans.*] (**tap-dance**) perform such a dance. —**tap danc·er** *n.* —**tap danc·ing** *n.*

tape /tāp/ ▶*n.* a narrow strip of material, typically used to hold or fasten something: *a roll of tape* | *a dirty apron fastened with thin tapes.* ■ [often with *adj.*] long narrow flexible material with magnetic properties, used for recording sound, pictures, or computer data. ■ a cassette or reel containing such material. ■ a recording on such a cassette or reel. ■ (also **adhesive tape**) a strip of paper or plastic coated with adhesive, used to stick things together. ■ a strip of material stretched across the finish line of a race, to be broken by the winner. ■ a strip of white material at the top of a tennis net. ■ a strip of material used to mark off an area. ■ a tape measure.
▶*v.* [*trans.*] **1** record (sound or pictures) on audio or videotape: *it is not known who taped the conversation.* **2** fasten or attach (something) with adhesive tape. **3** (**tape something off**) seal or mark off an area or thing with tape. ▷Old English *tæppa, tæppe;* perhaps related to Middle Low German *teppen* 'pluck, tear.'
▶*PHRASE* □ **on tape** recorded on magnetic tape.

tape deck ▶*n.* a piece of equipment for playing audiotapes, esp. as part of a stereo system.

tape grass ▶*n.* a submerged aquatic plant of the frog's-bit family, with narrow grasslike leaves. Also called EELGRASS and RIBBON GRASS. • Genus *Vallisneria*, family Hydrocharitaceae: several species.

tape ma·chine ▶*n.* a tape recorder.

tape meas·ure ▶*n.* a length of tape or thin flexible metal, marked at intervals for measuring.

ta·pe·nade /ˌtäpə'näd/ ▶*n.* a Provençal paste or dip, made from black olives, capers, and anchovies. ▷French, from Provençal.

ta·per /'tāpər/ ▶*n.* a slender candle. ■ a wick coated with wax, used for conveying a flame. ■ a gradual narrowing: *the current industry standard taper of 5 degrees.*
▶*v.* diminish or reduce or cause to diminish or reduce in thickness toward one end: [*intrans.*] *the tail tapers to a rounded tip* | [*trans.*] *David asked my dressmaker to taper his trousers.* ■ [*intrans.*] gradually lessen: *the impact of the dollar's depreciation started to* **taper off**. ▷Old English (denoting any wax candle), dissimilated form (by alteration of *p-* to *t-*) of Latin *papyrus* (see PAPYRUS), the pith of which was used for candle wicks.

tape re·cord·er ▶*n.* an apparatus for recording sounds on magnetic tape and later reproducing them. —**tape-re·cord** *v.* —**tape re·cord·ing** *n.*

ta·per pin ▶*n.* a short round metal rod having a small degree of taper that enables it to act as a stop or wedge when driven into a hole.

tap·es·try /'tapistrē/ ▶*n.* (*pl.* **-tries**) a piece of thick textile fabric with pictures or designs formed by weaving colored weft threads or by embroidering on canvas, used as a wall hanging or furniture covering. ■ *figurative* used in reference to an intricate or complex combination of things or sequence of events: *a tapestry of cultures, races, and customs.* ▷late Middle English: from Old French *tapisserie,* from *tapissier* 'tapestry worker' or *tapisser* 'to carpet,' from *tapis* 'carpet, tapis.' —**tap·es·tried** *adj.*

tap·es·try moth ▶*n.* another term for CARPET MOTH.

ta·pe·tum /tə'pētəm/ ▶*n.* *Zoology* a reflective layer of the choroid in the eyes of many animals, causing them to shine in the dark. ▷early 18th cent.: from late Latin, from Latin *tapete* 'carpet.'

tape·worm /'tāpˌwərm/ ▶*n.* a parasitic flatworm, the adult of which lives in the intestine of humans and other vertebrates. It has a long ribbonlike body with many segments that can become independent, and a small head bearing hooks and suckers. • Class Cestoda, phylum Platyhelminthes.

ta·phon·o·my /tə'fänəmē/ ▶*n.* the branch of paleontology that deals with the processes of fossilization. ▷1940s: from Greek *taphos* 'grave' + -NOMY. —**taph·o·nom·ic** /ˌtafə'nämik/ *adj.* —**ta·phon·o·mist** /-mist/ *n.*

tap-in ▶*n.* *chiefly Golf, Soccer, & Basketball* a relatively easy, close-range putt, shot, or tap of the ball into the goal or hole.

tap·i·o·ca /ˌtapē'ōkə/ ▶*n.* a starchy substance in the form of hard white grains, obtained from cassava and used in cooking puddings and other dishes. ▷early 18th cent.: from Tupi-Guarani *tipioca,* from *tipi* 'dregs' + *og, ok* 'squeeze out.'

tap·i·o·ca milk tea ▶*n.* another term for BUBBLE TEA.

ta·pir /'tāpər/ ▶*n.* a nocturnal hoofed mammal with a stout body, sturdy limbs, and a short flexible proboscis, native to the forests of tropical America and Malaysia. • Family Tapiridae and genus *Tapirus*: four species, including the black and white **Malayan tapir** (*T. indicus*) and the reddish-brown or black **mountain tapir** (*T. pinchaque*), which is the smallest tapir. ▷late 18th cent.: via Spanish and Portuguese from Tupi *tapyra.*

tap·is /'tapē; 'tapis; tä'pē/ ▶*n.* (*pl.* same) *archaic* a tapestry or richly decorated cloth, used as a hanging or a covering for something. ▷French, from Old French *tapiz,* via late Latin from Greek *tapētion,* diminutive of *tapēs* 'tapestry.'

ta·pote·ment /tə'pōtmənt/ ▶*n.* rapid and repeated striking of the body as a technique in massage. ▷late 19th cent.: French, from *tapoter* 'to tap.'

tap pants ▶*plural n.* a pair of brief lingerie shorts, usually worn with a camisole top. ▷so named because such shorts were formerly worn for tap dancing.

Tap·pan Zee /'tapən ˌzē/ a broadening of the Hudson River in southeastern New York, near the village of Tarrytown.

tap·pet /'tapit/ ▶*n.* a lever or projecting part on a machine that intermittently makes contact with a cam or other part so as to give or receive motion. ▷mid 18th cent.: apparently an irregular diminutive of TAP[2].

tap·ping /'tapiNG/ ▶*n.* the action of a person or things that taps. ■ a sound made by this.

tap·room /'tapˌro͞om; -ˌro͝om/ ▶*n.* a room in which alcoholic drinks, esp. beer, are available on tap; a bar in a hotel or inn.

tap·root /'tapˌro͞ot; -ˌro͝ot/ ▶*n.* a straight tapering root growing vertically downward and forming the center from which subsidiary rootlets spring.

tap shoe ▶*n.* a shoe with a specially hardened sole or attached metal plates at toe and heel to make a tapping sound in tap dancing.

tap·ster /'tapstər/ ▶*n.* *archaic* a person who draws and serves alcoholic drinks at a bar. ▷Old English *tæppestre,* denoting a woman serving ale (see TAP[1], -STER).

tap wa·ter ▶*n.* water from a piped supply.

ta·que·ri·a /ˌtäkə'rēə; ˌtak-/ ▶*n.* a Mexican restaurant specializing in tacos. ▷Mexican Spanish.

tar[1] /tär/ ▶*n.* a dark, thick, flammable liquid distilled from wood or coal, consisting of a mixture of hydrocarbons, resins, alcohols, and other compounds. It is used in roadmaking and for coating and preserving timber. ■ a similar substance formed by burning tobacco or other material: [in *combination*] *low-tar cigarettes.*
▶*v.* (**tarred, tar·ring**) [*trans.*] [usu. as *adj.*] (**tarred**) cover (something) with tar: *a newly tarred road.* ▷Old English *teru, teoru,* of Germanic origin; related to Dutch *teer,* German *Teer,* and perhaps ultimately to TREE.
▶*PHRASES* □ **beat** (or **whale**) **the tar out of** *informal* beat or thrash severely. □ **tar and feather** smear with tar and then cover with feathers as a punishment. □ **tar people with the same brush** consider specified people to have the same faults.

tar[2] ▶*n.* *informal, dated* a sailor. ▷mid 17th cent.: perhaps an abbreviation of TARPAULIN, also used as a nickname for a sailor at this time.

Ta·rab·u·lus Al-Gharb /tə'räbələs al 'gärb/ Arabic name for TRIPOLI (sense 1).

Ta·rab·u·lus Ash-Sham /tə'räbələs ash 'sham/ Arabic name for TRIPOLI (sense 2).

tar·a·did·dle /'tarəˌdidl/ (also **tar·ra·did·dle**) ▶*n.* *informal, chiefly Brit.* a petty lie. ■ pretentious nonsense. ▷late 18th cent.: perhaps related to DIDDLE.

Ta·ra·hu·ma·ra /ˌtärəho͞o'märə/ ▶*n.* (*pl.* same) **1** a member of a native people of northwestern Mexico. **2** the Uto-Aztecan language of this people.
▶*adj.* of or relating to this people or their language. ▷Spanish from Tarahumara *rarámuri.*

ta·ra·ma·sa·la·ta /ˌtärəməsə'lätə/ (also **ta·ra·ma** /ˌtärə'mä/) ▶*n.* a pinkish paste or dip made from the roe of certain fish, mixed with olive oil and seasoning. ▷from modern Greek *taramas* 'roe' (from Turkish *tarama,* denoting a preparation of soft roe or red caviar) + *salata* 'salad.'

tar·an·tel·la /ˌtarən'telə/ (also **tar·an·telle** /-'tel/) ▶*n.* a

mountain tapir

rapid whirling dance originating in southern Italy. ■ a piece of music written in fast 6/8 time in the style of this dance. ▷late 18th cent.: Italian, from the name of the seaport **TARANTO**; so named because it was thought to be a cure for tarantism, the victim dancing the tarantella until exhausted. See also **TARANTULA**.

Ta·ran·ti·no /ˌtarən'tēnō/, Quentin (Jerome) (1963–), U.S. movie director, screenwriter, and actor. He came to sudden prominence with *Reservoir Dogs* (1992) and followed in 1994 with *Pulp Fiction,* for which he won an Academy Award for best original screenplay. Both films aroused controversy for their amorality and violence but also won admiration for their wit and style.

tar·ant·ism /'tarənˌtizəm/ ▸*n.* a psychological illness characterized by an extreme impulse to dance, prevalent in southern Italy from the 15th to the 17th century, and widely believed at the time to have been caused by the bite of a tarantula. ▷mid 17th cent.: from Italian *tarantismo*, from the name of the seaport **TARANTO**, after which the tarantula is also named. Compare with **TARANTELLA**.

Ta·ran·to /'tärənˌtō; tə'rantō/ a seaport and naval base in southeastern Italy; pop. 244,000.

ta·ran·tu·la /tə'ranCHələ/ ▸*n.* **1** a large hairy spider found chiefly in tropical and subtropical America, some kinds of which are able to catch small lizards, frogs, and birds. • Family Theraphosidae, suborder Mygalomorphae: numerous species. **2** a large black wolf spider of southern Europe whose bite was formerly believed to cause tarantism. • *Lycosa tarentula*, family Lycosidae. ▷mid 16th cent.: from medieval Latin, from Old Italian *tarantola* 'tarantula,' from the name of the seaport **TARANTO**. Compare with **TARANTELLA** and **TARANTISM**.

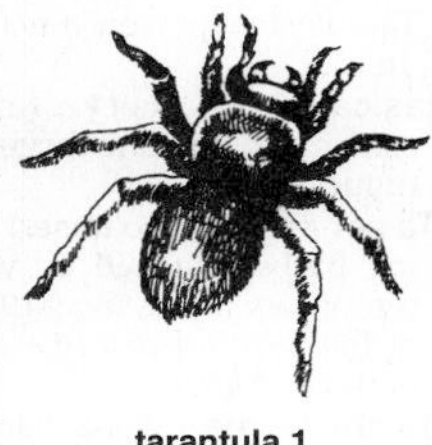

tarantula 1

ta·ran·tu·la hawk ▸*n.* a large spider-hunting wasp of the southwestern U.S. • Genus *Pepsis*, family Pompilidae.

Ta·ras·can /tə'raskən/ ▸*n.* (*pl.* same or **-cans**) **1** a member of an American Indian people of a mountainous area in Michoacán, Mexico. **2** the language of this people.
▸*adj.* of or relating to this people or their language. ▷from Spanish *Tarasco* (a Meso-American Indian language of Mexico) + **AN**.

Ta·ra·wa /tə'räwə; 'tarəˌwä/ an atoll in the South Pacific Ocean, one of the Gilbert Islands in Kiribati; pop. 28,000. Bairiki, Kiribati's capital, is located here.

ta·rax·a·cum /tə'raksəkəm/ ▸*n.* any plant of the genus *Taraxacum* (daisy family), including the dandelion. ■ a preparation of the dried roots of this, used medicinally. ▷early 18th cent.: from medieval Latin *altaraxacon*, via Arabic from Persian *talk̲* 'bitter' + *čakūk̲* 'purslane.'

tar ba·by ▸*n. informal* a difficult problem that is only aggravated by attempts to solve it. ▷with allusion to the doll smeared with tar as a trap for Brer Rabbit, in J. C. Harris's *Uncle Remus*.

Tar·bell /'tärbəl/, Ida M(inerva), (1857–1944), U.S. writer. She was a leader of the muckraking movement and a writer for *McClure's* magazine 1896–1904 and for *American* magazine 1906–15. Her books include the exposé *The History of the Standard Oil Company* (1904) and *The Business of Being a Woman* (1912).

tar·boosh /tär'bo͞osh/ ▸*n.* a man's cap similar to a fez, typically of red felt with a tassel at the top. ▷early 18th cent.: from Egyptian Arabic *ṭarbūš*, based on Persian *sarpūš*, from *sar* 'head' + *pūš* 'cover.'

tar·brush /'tärˌbrəSH/ ▸*n.* (**the tarbrush**) *offensive* black or Indian ancestry.

Tar·di·gra·da /tär'digrədə/ *Zoology* a small phylum that comprises the water bears. ▷modern Latin (plural), from Latin *tardigradus*, from *tardus* 'slow' + *gradi* 'to walk.' —**tar·di·grade** /'tärdəˌgrād/ *n.*

Tar·dis /'tärdis/ ▸*n.* **1** a time machine. **2** a building or container that is larger inside than it appears to be from outside. ▷the name (said to be an acronym from *time and relative dimensions in space*) of a time machine that had the exterior of a police telephone box in the British TV science-fiction series *Doctor Who*, first broadcast in 1963.

tar·dive dys·ki·ne·sia /ˌtärdiv ˌdiskə'nēZH(ē)ə/ ▸*n. Medicine* a neurological disorder characterized by involuntary movements of the face and jaw. ▷1960s: *tardive* from French *tardif, tardive* (see **TARDY**).

tar·dy /'tärdē/ ▸*adj.* (**-di·er**, **-di·est**) delaying or delayed beyond the right or expected time; late: *please forgive this tardy reply.* ■ slow in action or response; sluggish. ▷mid 16th cent.: from French *tardif, -ive*, from Latin *tardus* 'slow.' —**tar·di·ly** /'tärdl-ē/ *adv.* —**tar·di·ness** *n.*

tare[1] /te(ə)r/ ▸*n.* **1** a vetch, esp. the common vetch. **2** (**tares**) (in biblical use) an injurious weed resembling wheat when young (Matt. 13:24–30). ▷Middle English: of unknown origin.

tare[2] ▸*n.* an allowance made for the weight of the packaging in order to determine the net weight of goods. ■ the weight of a motor vehicle, railroad car, or aircraft without its fuel or load. ▷late Middle English: from French, literally 'deficiency, tare,' from medieval Latin *tara*, based on Arabic *ṭaraḥa* 'reject, deduct.'

tar·ga /'tärgə/ ▸*n.* [usu. as *adj.*] a type of convertible sports car with hood or panel that can be removed, esp. leaving a central roll bar for passenger safety: *a targa roof.* ▷Italian, literally 'shield,' given as a name to a model of Porsche with a detachable hood (1965), probably suggested by the *Targa Florio* ('Florio Shield'), a motor time trial held annually in Sicily.

targe /tärj/ ▸*n.* archaic term for **TARGET** (sense 2). ▷Old English *targa, targe*, of Germanic origin; reinforced in Middle English by Old French *targe*.

tar·get /'tärgit/ ▸*n.* **1** a person, object, or place selected as the aim of an attack. ■ a mark or point at which someone fires or aims, esp. a round or rectangular board marked with concentric circles used in archery or shooting. ■ an objective or result toward which efforts are directed: *the car met its sales target in record time.* ■ *Phonetics* an idealization of the articulation of a speech sound, with reference to which actual utterances can be described. ■ a person or thing against whom criticism or abuse is or may be directed. **2** *historical* a small, round shield or buckler.
▸*v.* (**-get·ed**, **-get·ing**) [*trans.*] (usu. **be targeted**) select as an object of attention or attack: *two men were targeted by the attackers.* ■ aim or direct (something): *a significant nuclear capability targeted on the U.S.* ▷late Middle English (sense 2): diminutive of **TARGE**. The noun came to denote various round objects. The verb dates from the early 17th cent. —**tar·get·a·ble** *adj.*
▸*PHRASE* □ **on target** accurately hitting the thing aimed at. ■ proceeding or improving at a good enough rate to achieve an objective: *the new police station is on target for a June opening.*

tar·get cell ▸*n.* **1** *Physiology* a cell that bears receptors for a hormone, drug, or other signaling molecule, or is the focus of contact by a virus, phagocyte, nerve fiber, etc. **2** *Medicine* an abnormal form of red blood cell that appears as a dark ring surrounding a dark central spot, typical of certain kinds of anemia.

tar·get lan·guage ▸*n.* the language into which a text, document, or speech is translated. ■ a foreign language which a person intends to learn.

tar·get of op·por·tu·ni·ty ▸*n.* an object to which effort or study is diverted as soon as it becomes known: *every difference between cancerous and normal cells is a potential target of opportunity for new drug discovery.* ■ a military target that is attacked while in pursuit of another.

tar·get or·gan ▸*n. Physiology & Medicine* a specific organ on which a hormone, drug, or other substance acts.

Tar·gum /'tärˌgo͝om; -ˌgo͞om/ ▸*n.* an ancient Aramaic paraphrase or interpretation of the Hebrew Bible, of a type made from about the 1st century AD when Hebrew was declining as a spoken language. ▷from Aramaic *targūm* 'interpretation.'

Tar Heel State a nickname for the state of **NORTH CAROLINA**.

tar·iff /'tarif/ ▸*n.* a tax or duty to be paid on a particular class of imports or exports. ■ a list of these taxes. ■ a table of the fixed charges made by a business, esp. in a hotel or restaurant.
▸*v.* [*trans.*] fix the price of (something) according to a tariff: *these services are tariffed by volume.* ▷late 16th cent. (also denoting an arithmetical table): via French from Italian *tariffa*, based on Arabic *'arrafa* 'notify.'

Ta·rim /'tä'rēm/ a river in northwestern China, in Xinjiang autonomous region. It rises as the Yarkand in the Kunlun Shan mountains and flows for over 1,250 miles (2,000 km) east through the dry Tarim Basin, petering out in the Lop Nor depression. For much of its course, the river follows no clearly defined bed and is subject to much evaporation.

ta·ri·qa /tə'rēkə/ (also **ta·ri·qat** /-kət/) ▸*n.* the Sufi doctrine or path of spiritual learning. ■ a Sufi missionary. ▷from Arabic *ṭarīka* 'manner, way, creed.'

Tar·king·ton /'tärkiNGtən/, (Newton) Booth, (1869–1946), U.S. writer. His novels include *The Magnificent Ambersons* (1918) and *Alice Adams* (1921). He is equally well known for his young adult novels such as *Penrod* (1914) and *Seventeen* (1916).

Tar·kov·sky /tär'kôfskē/, Andrei (Arsenevich) (1932–86), Russian movie director. Featuring a poetic and impressionistic style, his movies include *Ivan's Childhood* (1962), *Solaris* (1972), and *The Sacrifice* (1986), which won the special grand prize at Cannes.

tar·la·tan /'tärlətn/ ▸*n.* a thin, starched, open-weave muslin fabric, used for stiffening evening gowns. ▷early 18th cent.: from French *tarlatane*, probably of Indian origin.

Tar·mac /'tärˌmak/ ▸*n.* (usu. **tarmac**) *trademark* material used for surfacing roads or other outdoor areas, consisting of crushed rock mixed with tar. ■ (**the tarmac**) a runway or other area surfaced with such material. ▷early 20th cent.: abbreviation of **TARMACADAM**.

tar·mac·ad·am /'tärməˌkadəm/ ▸*n. chiefly Brit.* another term for **TARMAC**. ▷late 19th cent.: from **TAR**[1] + **MACADAM**. —**tar·mac·ad·amed** *adj.*

Tarn /tärn/ a river in southern France that rises in the Cévennes and flows 235 miles (380 km) southwest through deep gorges before meeting the Garonne River northwest of Toulouse.

tarn /tärn/ ▸*n.* a small mountain lake. ▷Middle English (originally northern English dialect): from Old Norse *tjǫrn*.

tar·na·tion /tär'nāSHən/ ▸*n.* & *exclam.* used as a euphemism for "damnation." ▷late 18th cent.: alteration.

tar·nish /'tärniSH/ ▸*v.* lose or cause to lose luster, esp. as a result of exposure to air or moisture: [*intrans.*] *silver tarnishes too easily* | [*trans.*] *lemon juice would tarnish the gilded metal.* ■ *figurative* make or become less valuable or respected: [*trans.*] *his regime had not been tarnished by human rights abuses.*
▸*n.* dullness of color; loss of brightness. ■ a film or stain formed on an exposed surface of a mineral or metal. ■ *figurative* damage or harm done to something. ▷late Middle English (as a verb): from French *terniss-*, lengthened stem of *ternir*, from *terne* 'dark, dull.' —**tar·nish·a·ble** *adj.*

tar·nished plant bug ▸*n.* either of two brownish mirid bugs that are pests of numerous fruits, vegetables, and other crops. • *Lygus lineolaris* (in North America) and *Lygus rugulipennis* (in Europe).

ta·ro /'tarō; 'te(ə)rō/ ▸*n.* a tropical Asian plant of the arum family that has edible starchy corms and edible fleshy leaves, esp. a variety with a large central corm grown as a staple in the Pacific. Also called **DASHEEN**. Compare with **EDDO**. • *Colocasia esculenta* var. *esculenta*, family Araceae. ■ the corm of this plant. ▷mid 18th cent.: of Polynesian origin.

ta·rot /'tarō; 'te(ə)rō; tə'rō/ ▸*n.* (**the Tarot**) playing cards, traditionally a pack of 78 with five suits, used for fortune-telling and (esp. in Europe) in certain games. The suits are typically swords, cups, coins (or pentacles), batons (or wands), and a permanent suit of trump. ■ a card game played with such cards. ■ a card from such a set. ▷late 16th cent.: from French, from Italian *tarocchi*, of unknown origin.

tarp /tärp/ ▸*n. informal* a tarpaulin sheet or cover. ▷early 20th cent.: abbreviation.

tar·pan /'tärˌpan/ ▸*n.* a grayish wild horse that was formerly common in eastern Europe and western Asia, exterminated in 1919. • *Equus caballus gomelini*, family Equidae. ▷Kyrgyz.

tar·pa·per /'tärˌpāpər/ ▸*n.* a heavy paper impregnated with tar and used as a waterproofing material in building.

tar·pau·lin /tär'pôlən; 'tärpə-/ ▸*n.* **1** heavy-duty waterproof cloth, originally of tarred canvas. ■ a sheet or covering of this. **2** *historical* a sailor's tarred or oilskin hat. ■ *archaic* a sailor. ▷early 17th cent.: probably from **TAR**[1] + **PALL**[1] + **-ING**[1].

Pronunciation Key ə *ago*; ər *over*; 'ə or ˌə *up*; 'ər or ˌər *fur*; a *hat*; ā *rate*; ä *car*; CH *chew*; e *let*; ē *see*; e(ə)r *air*; i *fit*; ī *by*; i(ə)r *ear*; NG *sing*; ō *go*; ô *for*; oi *boy*; o͝o *good*; o͞o *goo*; ou *out*; SH *she*; TH *thin*; T̲H̲ *then*; (h)w *why*; ZH *vision*

Tar·pe·ia /tär'pēə/ one of the Vestal Virgins, the daughter of a commander of the Capitol in ancient Rome. According to legend she betrayed the citadel to the Sabines in return for whatever they wore on their arms, hoping to receive their golden bracelets; however, the Sabines killed her by throwing their shields onto her.

tar pit ▸*n.* a hollow in which natural tar accumulates by seepage. ■ *figurative* a complicated or difficult situation or problem: *the tar pit of municipal poverty.*

tar·pon /'tärpən/ ▸*n.* a large tropical marine fish of herringlike appearance. • Two species in the family Megalopidae: *Tarpon atlanticus*, a prized Atlantic game fish, and *Megalops cyprinoides* of the Indo-Pacific. ▷late 17th cent.: probably from Dutch *tarpoen*, perhaps from a Central American language.

Tar·quin·i·us /tär'kwinēəs/ the name of two semilegendary Etruscan kings of ancient Rome; anglicized name *Tarquin*: ■ **Tarquinius Priscus**, reigned *c.*616–*c.*578 BC; full name *Lucius Tarquinius Priscus*. According to tradition he was murdered by the sons of the previous king. ■ **Tarquinius Superbus**, reigned *c.*534–*c.*510 BC; full name *Lucius Tarquinius Superbus*; known as **Tarquin the Proud**. According to tradition he was the son or grandson of Tarquinius Priscus. Noted for his cruelty, he was expelled from the city, and the republic was founded.

tar·ra·did·dle /'tarə,didl/ ▸*n.* variant spelling of TARADIDDLE.

tar·ra·gon /'tarə,gän; -gən/ ▸*n.* a perennial plant of the daisy family, with narrow aromatic leaves that are used as a culinary herb. • *Artemisia dracunculus*, family Compositae. ▷mid 16th cent.: representing medieval Latin *tragonia* and *tarchon*, perhaps from an Arabic alteration of Greek *drakōn* 'dragon' (by association with *drakontion* ' green dragon').

tar·ra·gon vin·e·gar ▸*n.* a culinary seasoning made by steeping the young shoots and leaves of tarragon in wine vinegar.

Tar·ra·sa /tə'räsə/ (also **Ter·ras·sa** /tə'räsə/) an industrial city in Catalonia, in northeastern Spain; pop. 154,000.

tar·ry[1] /'tärē/ ▸*adj.* (**-ri·er, -ri·est**) of, like, or covered with tar: *a length of tarry rope.* —**tar·ri·ness** *n.*

tar·ry[2] /'tarē/ ▸*v.* (**-ries, -ried**) [*intrans.*] *dated* stay longer than intended; delay leaving a place: *she could tarry a bit and not get home until four.* ▷Middle English: of unknown origin. —**tar·ri·er** *n.* (*rare*).

tar·sal /'tärsəl/ *Anatomy Zoology* ▸*adj. Anatomy & Zoology* of or relating to the tarsus: *the tarsal claws of beetles.*
▸*n. Anatomy & Zoology* a bone of the tarsus. ▷early 19th cent.: from TARSUS + -AL.

tar sand ▸*n.* (often **tar sands**) *Geology* a deposit of sand impregnated with bitumen.

tar·si /'tärsī; -sē/ ▸ plural form of TARSUS.

tar·si·er /'tärsēər/ ▸*n.* a small insectivorous, tree-dwelling, nocturnal primate with large eyes, a long tufted tail, and long hind limbs, native to the islands of Southeast Asia. • Family Tarsiidae and genus *Tarsius*, suborder Prosimii: four species. ▷late 18th cent.: from French, from *tarse* 'tarsus,' with reference to the animal's long tarsal bones.

tar·so·met·a·tar·sus /'tärsō,metə'tärsəs/ ▸*n.* (*pl.* **-tar·si** /-'tärsī; -,sē/) *Zoology* a long bone in the lower leg of birds and some reptiles, formed by fusion of tarsal and metatarsal structures. —**tar·so·met·a·tar·sal** /-'tärsəl/ *adj.*

Tar·sus /'tärsəs/ an ancient city in southern Turkey, now a market town. It is the birthplace of St. Paul.

tar·sus /'tärsəs/ ▸*n.* (*pl.* **tar·si** /'tärsī; -sē/) **1** *Anatomy* a group of small bones between the main part of the hind limb and the metatarsus in terrestrial vertebrates. The seven bones of the human tarsus form the ankle and upper part of the foot. They are the talus, calcaneus, navicular, and cuboid and the three cuneiform bones. ■ *Zoology* the shank or tarsometatarsus of the leg of a bird or reptile. ■ *Zoology* the foot or fifth joint of the leg of an insect or other arthropod, typically consisting of several small segments and ending in a claw. **2** *Anatomy* a thin sheet of fibrous connective tissue which supports the edge of each eyelid. ▷late Middle English: modern Latin, from Greek *tarsos* 'flat of the foot, the eyelid.'

tart[1] /tärt/ ▸*n.* an open pastry case containing a filling. ▷late Middle English (denoting a savory pie): from Old French *tarte* or medieval Latin *tarta*, of unknown origin. —**tart·let** /-lit/ *n.*

tart[2] ▸*n. informal, derogatory* a prostitute or a promiscuous woman.
▸*v.* [*trans.*] (**tart oneself up**) *informal, chiefly Brit.* dress or make oneself up in order to look attractive or eye-catching. ■ (**tart something up**) decorate or improve the appearance of something: *the page layouts have been tarted up with cartoons.* ▷mid 19th cent.: probably an abbreviation of SWEETHEART.

tart[3] ▸*adj.* sharp or acid in taste: *a tart apple.* ■ (of a remark or tone of voice) cutting, bitter, or sarcastic: *I bit back a tart reply.* ▷Old English *teart* 'harsh, severe,' of unknown origin. —**tart·ly** *adv.* —**tart·ness** *n.*

tar·tan[1] /'tärtn/ ▸*n.* a woolen cloth woven in one of several patterns of plaid, esp. of a design associated with a particular Scottish clan.
▸*adj.* used allusively in reference to Scotland or the Scots. ▷late 15th cent. (originally Scots): perhaps from Old French *tertaine*, denoting a kind of cloth; compare with *tartarin*, a rich fabric formerly imported from the east through Tartary.

tartan[1]

tar·tan[2] ▸*n. historical* a lateen-rigged, single-masted ship used in the Mediterranean. ▷early 17th cent.: from French *tartane*, from Italian *tartana*, perhaps from Arabic *ṭarīda*.

Tar·tar /'tärtər/ ▸*n. historical* a member of the combined forces of central Asian peoples, including Mongols and Turks, who under the leadership of Genghis Khan conquered much of Asia and eastern Europe in the early 13th century, and under Tamerlane (14th century) established an empire with its capital at Samarkand. See also TATAR. ■ (**tartar**) a harsh, fierce, or intractable person: *"Merciful God! but you're a tartar, miss!" said the sheriff, ruefully.* ▷from Old French *Tartare* or medieval Latin *Tartarus*, alteration (influenced by TARTARUS) of TATAR. —**Tar·tar·i·an** /tär'te(ə)rēən/ *adj.*

tar·tar /'tärtər/ ▸*n.* a hard calcified deposit that forms on the teeth and contributes to their decay. ■ a deposit of impure potassium hydrogen tartrate formed during the fermentation of wine. See also CREAM OF TARTAR. ▷late Middle English: via medieval Latin from medieval Greek *tartaron*, of unknown origin. —**tar·tar·ic** /tär'tarik/ *adj.*

tar·tare /tär'tär; 'tärtər/ ▸*adj.* [*postpositive*] (of fish) served raw, typically seasoned and shaped into small cakes. See also STEAK TARTARE. ▷French, literally 'Tartar.'

tar·tar e·met·ic ▸*n.* a toxic compound used in treating protozoal disease in animals, as a mordant in dyeing, and formerly as an emetic. • Alternative name: **potassium antimony tartrate**; chem. formula: $K(SbO)C_4H_4O_6$.

tar·tar·ic ac·id ▸*n. Chemistry* a crystalline organic acid that is present esp. in unripe grapes and is used in baking powders and as a food additive. • A dibasic acid; chem. formula: $COOH(CHOH)_2COOH$. ▷late 18th cent.: *tartaric* from obsolete French *tartarique*, from medieval Latin *tartarum* (see TARTAR).

tar·tar sauce (also **tar·tare sauce**) ▸*n.* a cold sauce, typically eaten with fish, consisting of mayonnaise mixed with chopped pickles, capers, etc.

Tar·ta·rus /'tärtərəs/ *Greek Mythology* **1** a primeval god, offspring of Chaos. **2** a part of the underworld where the wicked suffered punishment for their misdeeds, esp. those such as Ixion and Tantalus who had committed some outrage against the gods. —**Tar·tar·e·an** /tär'te(ə)rēən/ *adj.*

Tar·ta·ry /'tärtərē/ a historical region of Asia and eastern Europe, esp. the high plateau of central Asia and its northwestern slopes, which formed part of the Tartar empire in the Middle Ages.

tarte Ta·tin /'tärt ta'taN/ ▸*n.* a type of upside-down apple tart consisting of pastry baked over slices of fruit arranged in caramelized sugar, served fruit side up after cooking. ▷French, from *tarte* 'tart' + *Tatin*, the surname of the sisters said to have created the dish.

tar·trate /'tärtrāt/ ▸*n. Chemistry* a salt or ester of tartaric acid. ▷late 18th cent.: from French, from *tartre* 'tartar' + -ATE[1].

tar·tra·zine /'tärtrə,zēn; -zin/ ▸*n. Chemistry* a brilliant yellow synthetic dye derived from tartaric acid and used to color food, drugs, and cosmetics. ▷late 19th cent.: from French *tartre* 'tartar' + AZO- + -INE[4].

Tar·tuffe /tär'tōōf/ ▸*n. poetic/literary* or *humorous* a religious hypocrite, or a hypocritical pretender to excellence of any kind. [from the name of the principal character (a religious hypocrite) in Molière's *Tartuffe* (1664).] —**Tar·tuf·fer·ie** /-'tōōfərē/ (also **Tar·tuf·fer·y**) *n.*

tar·tu·fo /tär'tōōfō/ ▸*n.* **1** an edible fungus, esp. the white truffle. **2** an Italian dessert, containing chocolate, of a creamy mousselike consistency. ▷Italian, literally 'truffle.'

tart·y /'tärtē/ ▸*adj.* (**tart·i·er, tart·i·est**) *informal* (of a woman) dressed in a sexually provocative manner that is considered to be in bad taste. ■ (of clothes) contributing to a sexually provocative appearance. —**tart·i·ly** /'tärtəlē/ *adv.* —**tart·i·ness** *n.*

tar·weed /'tär,wēd/ ▸*n.* any of a number of American plants of the daisy family with sticky leaves and heavy scent. • *Madia, Grindelia, Hemizonia*, and related genera, family Compositae.

Tar·zan /'tärzan; -zən/ a fictitious character created by Edgar Rice Burroughs. Tarzan (Lord Greystoke by birth) is orphaned in West Africa in his infancy and reared by apes in the jungle. ■ [as *n.*] (**a Tarzan**) a man of great agility and powerful physique.

TAS ▸*abbr.* ■ telephone answering system. ■ true airspeed.

Tas. *chiefly Austral.* ▸*abbr.* Tasmania.

Ta·sa·day /'tasə,dā; tə'sädī/ ▸*n.* (*pl.* same or **-days**) a member of a small group of people living on the Philippine island of Mindanao, formerly said to represent a long-isolated Stone Age people discovered only in the 1960s.
▸*adj.* of or relating to this people. ▷apparently from Tasaday *tau* 'person' + *sa* (expressing location) + *dáya* 'inland.'

tas·ca /'täskə; 'tas-/ ▸*n.* (in Spain and Portugal) a tavern or bar, esp. one serving food. ▷Spanish and Portuguese.

Ta·ser /'tāzər/ (also **ta·ser**) ▸*n. trademark* a weapon firing barbs attached by wires to batteries, causing temporary paralysis. ▷1970s: from the initial letters of *Tom Swift's electric rifle* (a fictitious weapon), on the pattern of *laser*.

Ta·shi La·ma /'täshē 'lämə/ ▸*n.* another name for PANCHEN LAMA.

Tash·kent /,tash'kent; ,täsh-/ the capital of Uzbekistan, in the northeast part of the country, in the western foothills of the Tien Shan mountains: pop. 2,094,000. One of the oldest cities in central Asia, it was an important center on the trade route between Europe and the Orient. It became part of the Mongol empire in the 13th century, was captured by the Russians in 1865, and replaced Samarkand as capital of Uzbekistan in 1930.

task /task/ ▸*n.* a piece of work to be done or undertaken.
▸*v.* [*trans.*] (usu. **be tasked**) assign such a piece of work to: *NATO troops are **tasked with** separating the warring parties.* ■ make great demands on (someone's resources or abilities): *it tasked his diplomatic skill to effect his departure in safety.* ▷Middle English: from an Old Northern French variant of Old French *tasche*, from medieval Latin *tasca*, alteration of *taxa*, from Latin *taxare* 'censure, charge' (see TAX). An early sense of the verb was 'impose a tax on.'
▸*PHRASE* □ **take someone to task** reprimand or criticize someone severely for a fault or mistake.

task force ▸*n.* an armed force organized for a special operation. ■ a unit specially organized for a task: *aides say his plans include a task force on hate crimes.*

task·mas·ter /'task,mastər/ ▸*n.* a person who imposes a harsh or onerous workload on someone.

Tas·man /'tazmən/, Abel (Janszoon) (1603–*c.*1659), Dutch navigator. Sent in 1642 by Anthony van Diemen (1593–1645), the governor general of the Dutch East Indies, to explore Australian waters, he reached Tasmania (which he named Van Diemen's Land) and New Zealand. He arrived at Tonga and Fiji in 1643.

Tas·ma·ni·a /taz'mānēə; -'mānyə/ a state in Australia that consists of the mountainous island of Tasmania itself and several smaller islands; separated from the southeast coast of mainland Australia by the Bass Strait; pop. 458,000; capital, Hobart. It was known as Van Diemen's Land until 1855. —**Tas·ma·ni·an** *adj.* & *n.*

Tas·ma·ni·an dev·il /taz'mānēən; -'mānyən/ ▸*n.* a heavily built marsupial with a large head, powerful jaws, and mainly black fur, found only in Tasmania. It is slow-moving and aggressive, feeding mainly on carrion. • *Sarcophilus harrisii*, family Dasyuridae.

Tas·ma·ni·an wolf (also **Tas·ma·ni·an ti·ger**) ▸*n.* another term for THYLACINE.

Tas·man Sea /'tazmən/ an arm of the South Pacific Ocean that lies between Australia and New Zealand.

Tass /täs; tas/ the official news agency of the former Soviet Union, renamed ITAR-Tass in 1992. ▷Russian acronym, from *Telegrafnoe agentstvo Sovetskogo Soyuza* 'Telegraphic Agency of the Soviet Union.'

tas·sel /'tasəl/ ▶*n.* a tuft of loosely hanging threads, cords, or other material knotted at one end and attached for decoration to home furnishings, clothing, or other items. ■ the tufted head of some plants, esp. a flowerhead with prominent stamens at the top of a cornstalk.
▶*v.* (**-seled, -sel·ing**; *Brit.* **-selled, -sel·ling**) **1** [*trans.*] [usu. as *adj.*] (**tasseled**) provide with a tassel or tassels: *a tasseled tablecloth.* **2** [*intrans.*] (of corn or other plants) form tassels. ▷Middle English (also denoting a clasp for a cloak): from Old French *tassel* 'clasp,' of unknown origin.

tas·so /'täsō/ ▶*n.* spicy cured pork cut into strips. [perhaps from Spanish *tasajo* 'slice of dried meat.']

taste /tāst/ ▶*n.* **1** the sensation of flavor perceived in the mouth and throat on contact with a substance: *the wine had a fruity taste.* ■ the faculty of perceiving this quality: *birds do not have a highly developed sense of taste.* ■ a small portion of food or drink taken as a sample: *try a taste of Gorgonzola.* ■ a brief experience of something, conveying its basic character: *it was his first taste of serious action.* **2** a person's liking for particular flavors: *this pudding is too sweet for my taste.* ■ a person's tendency to like and dislike certain things: *he found the aggressive competitiveness of the profession was not* **to his taste**. ■ (**taste for**) a liking for or interest in (something): *have you lost your taste for fancy restaurants?* ■ the ability to discern what is of good quality or of a high aesthetic standard: *she has awful* **taste** *in literature.* ■ conformity or failure to conform with generally held views concerning what is offensive or acceptable: *that's a joke* **in** *very bad* **taste**.
▶*v.* [*trans.*] perceive or experience the flavor of: *she had never tasted ice cream before.* ■ [*intrans.*] have a specified flavor: [with *complement*] *the spinach tastes delicious.* ■ sample or test the flavor of (food or drink) by taking it into the mouth: *the waiter poured some wine for him to taste.* ■ eat or drink a small portion of. ■ have experience of: *the team has not yet tasted victory at home.* ▷Middle English (also in the sense 'touch'): from Old French *tast* (noun), *taster* (verb) 'touch, try, taste,' perhaps based on a blend of Latin *tangere* 'to touch' and *gustare* 'to taste.'
▶*PHRASES* □ **a bad** (or **bitter**) **taste in someone's mouth** *informal* a feeling of distress or disgust following an experience: *this incident has left a bad taste in all our mouths.* □ **taste blood** see BLOOD. □ **to taste** in the amount needed to give a flavor pleasing to someone eating a dish: *add salt and pepper to taste.*

taste bud ▶*n.* (usu. **taste buds**) any of the clusters of bulbous nerve endings on the tongue and in the lining of the mouth that provide the sense of taste.

taste·ful /'tāstfəl/ ▶*adj.* showing good aesthetic judgment or appropriate behavior: *Sarah's modest, tasteful apartment.* —**taste·ful·ly** *adv.* —**taste·ful·ness** *n.*

taste·less /'tāstlis/ ▶*adj.* **1** lacking flavor. **2** considered to be lacking in aesthetic judgment or to offend against what is regarded as appropriate behavior: *a tasteless joke.* —**taste·less·ly** *adv.* —**taste·less·ness** *n.*

taste·mak·er /'tāst,mākər/ ▶*n.* a person who decides or influences what is or will become fashionable.

tast·er /'tāstər/ ▶*n.* **1** a person employed to test food or drink for quality by tasting it: *experienced tasters can tell which plantation coffee beans are from.* ■ a small cup used by a person tasting wine in such a way. ■ an instrument for extracting a small sample from within a cheese. **2** *Brit.* a small quantity or brief experience of something, intended as a sample; a taste: *the song is a taster for the band's new LP.* ▷late Middle English: in early use from Anglo-Norman French *tastour*, from Old French *taster* 'to taste'; later from TASTE + -ER[1].

tas·te·vin /,tastə'vaN/ ▶*n.* (*pl.* same) a small, shallow silver cup for tasting wines, of a type used in France. ▷French, literally 'wine taster.'

tast·ing /'tāstiNG/ ▶*n.* a gathering at which people sample, compare, and evaluate different wines, or other drinks or food: *we did a tasting of over forty of the cheaper champagnes.* See also WINE TASTING.

tast·y /'tāstē/ ▶*adj.* (**tast·i·er, tast·i·est**) (of food) having a pleasant, distinct flavor: *a tasty snack.* ■ *informal, chiefly Brit.* attractive; very appealing: *some tasty acoustic piano licks.* —**tast·i·ly** /-stilē/ *adv.* —**tast·i·ness** *n.*

tat[1] /tat/ ▶*v.* (**tat·ted, tat·ting**) [*trans.*] make (a decorative mat or edging) by tying knots in thread and using a small shuttle to form lace. ▷late 19th cent.: back-formation from TATTING.

tat[2] ▶*n.* (in phrase **tit for tat**) see TIT[3].

tat[3] ▶*n. Brit., informal* tasteless or shoddy clothes, jewelry, or ornaments. ▷mid 19th cent. (in the senses 'rag' and 'person in rags'): probably a back-formation from TATTY.

ta-ta /tä 'tä/ ▶*exclam. informal, chiefly Brit.* goodbye. ▷early 19th cent.: of unknown origin; compare with earlier *da-da.*

ta·ta·mi /tə'tämē/ (also **ta·ta·mi mat**) ▶*n.* (*pl.* same or **-mis**) a rush-covered straw mat forming a traditional Japanese floor covering. ▷Japanese.

Ta·tar /'tätər/ ▶*n.* **1** a member of a Turkic people living in Tatarstan and various other parts of Russia and Ukraine. They are the descendants of the Tartars who ruled central Asia in the 14th century. **2** the Turkic language of this people.
▶*adj.* of or relating to this people or their language. ▷the Turkic name of a Tartar tribe.

Ta·tar·stan /'tätər,stan; -,stän/ an autonomous republic in western Russia, in the valley of the Volga River; pop. 3,658,000; capital, Kazan.

Tate /tāt/, Nahum (1652–1715), Irish playwright and poet, resident in London from the 1670s. He was appointed poet laureate in 1692.

ta·ter /'tātər/ ▶*n. informal* a potato. ▷mid 18th cent.: alteration.

Ta·tha·ga·ta /tə'tägətə/ ▶*n.* an honorific title of a buddha. ▷from Pali *Tathāgata*, from *tathā* 'in that manner' + *gata* 'gone.'

ta·tha·ta /'tətə,tä/ ▶*n. Buddhism* the ultimate inexpressible nature of all things. Compare with SUNYATA. ▷Pali, literally 'true state of things.'

Ta·ti /tä'tē/, Jacques (1908–82), French movie director and actor; born *Jacques Tatischeff.* He introduced the comically inept character Monsieur Hulot in *Monsieur Hulot's Holiday* (1953), seen again in movies that included the Academy Award-winning *Mon oncle* (1958).

Ta·tra Moun·tains /'tätrə/ (also **the Ta·tras**) a range of mountains in eastern Europe on the Polish–Slovak border, the highest range in the Carpathian Mountains, that rise to 8,710 feet (2,655 m) at Mount Gerlachovsky.

tat·tered /'tatərd/ ▶*adj.* torn, old, and in generally poor condition; in tatters: *an old woman in tattered clothes.* ■ *figurative* virtually destroyed; ruined: *the tattered remnants of her dreams.* ▷Middle English (in the sense 'dressed in decoratively slashed or jagged clothing'): apparently originally from the noun *tatter* 'scrap of cloth' + -ED[1]; later treated as a past participle.

tat·ters /'tatərz/ ▶*plural n.* irregularly torn pieces of cloth, paper, or other material. ▷late Middle English (also in the singular meaning 'scrap of cloth'): from Old Norse *tǫtrar* 'rags.'
▶*PHRASE* □ **in tatters** *informal* torn in many places; in shreds: *wallpaper hung in tatters.* ■ *figurative* destroyed; ruined: *the cease-fire was in tatters within hours.*

tat·ter·sall /'tatər,sôl/ (also **tat·ter·sall check**) ▶*n.* a woolen fabric with a pattern of colored checks and intersecting lines, resembling a tartan. ▷late 19th cent.: named after *Tattersalls*, an English firm of horse auctioneers (named after the horseman Richard *Tattersall* (1724–95)), by association with the traditional design of horse blankets.

tat·ting /'tatiNG/ ▶*n.* a kind of knotted lace made by hand with a small shuttle, used chiefly for trimming. ■ the process of making such lace. ▷mid 19th cent.: of unknown origin.

tat·tle /'tatl/ ▶*v.* [*intrans.*] report another's wrongdoing: *he never tattled or told tales | I would* **tattle on** *her whenever I had hard evidence.* ■ gossip idly.
▶*n.* gossip; idle talk. ▷late 15th cent. (in the sense 'falter, stammer,' also 'make meaningless sounds,' referring to a small child): from Middle Flemish *tatelen, tateren*, of imitative origin.

tat·tler /'tatl-ər; 'tatlər/ ▶*n.* **1** a person who tattles. **2** a migratory sandpiper with mainly gray plumage, breeding in northwestern Canada or eastern Siberia. • Genus *Heteroscelus*, family Scolopacidae: two species, in particular the **wandering tattler** (*H. incanus*) of Canada, noted for its loud cry.

tat·tle·tale /'tatl,tāl/ ▶*n.* a person, esp. a child, who reveals secrets or informs on others; a telltale.

tat·too[1] /ta'to͞o/ ▶*n.* (*pl.* **-toos**) an evening drum or bugle signal recalling soldiers to their quarters. ■ an entertainment consisting of music, marching, and the performance of displays and exercises by military personnel. ■ a rhythmic tapping or drumming. ▷mid 17th cent. (originally as *tap-too*): from Dutch *taptoe!*, literally 'close the tap (of the cask)!'

tat·too[2] ▶*v.* (**-toos, -tooed** /-'to͞od/) [*trans.*] mark (a person or a part of the body) with an indelible design by inserting pigment into punctures in the skin: *his cheek was tattooed with a winged fist.* ■ make (a design) in such a way: *he has a heart tattooed on his left hand.*
▶*n.* (*pl.* **-toos**) a design made in such a way. ▷mid 18th cent.: from Tahitian, Tongan, and Samoan *ta-tau* or Marquesan *ta-tu.* —**tat·too·er** *n.* —**tat·too·ist** /ta'to͞oist/ *n.*

tat·ty /'tatē/ ▶*adj.* (**-ti·er, -ti·est**) *informal* worn and shabby; in poor condition: *the room was furnished in slightly tatty upholstered furniture.* ■ of poor quality: *his gap-toothed smile and tatty haircut.* ▷early 16th cent. (originally Scots, in the sense 'tangled, matted, shaggy'): apparently ultimately related to Old English *tættec* 'rag,' of Germanic origin; compare with TATTERED. —**tat·ti·ly** /'tatəlē/ *adv.* —**tat·ti·ness** *n.*

Ta·tum /'tātəm/, Art (1910–56), U.S. jazz pianist; full name *Arthur Tatum.* Almost completely blind, he was known for his solo and trio work in the 1930s.

tau /tou; tô/ ▶*n.* the nineteenth letter of the Greek alphabet (**Τ**, **τ**), transliterated as 't.' ■ (**Tau**) [followed by Latin genitive] *Astronomy* the nineteenth star in a constellation: *Tau Ceti.* ■ (in full **tau particle** or **tau lepton**) *Physics* an unstable subatomic particle of the lepton class, with a charge of −1 and a mass roughly 3,500 times that of the electron.

tau cross ▶*n.* a T-shaped cross.

taught /tôt/ ▶ past and past participle of TEACH.

tau neu·tri·no ▶*n. Physics* a neutrino of the type associated with the tau particle.

taunt /tônt/ ▶*n.* a remark made in order to anger, wound, or provoke someone.
▶*v.* [*trans.*] provoke or challenge (someone) with insulting remarks: *students began taunting her about her weight.* ■ reproach (someone) with something in a contemptuous way: *she had* **taunted** *him* **with** *going to another man.* ▷early 16th cent.: from French *tant pour tant* 'like for like, tit for tat,' from *tant* 'so much,' from Latin *tantum*, neuter of *tantus.* An early use of the verb was 'exchange banter.' —**taunt·er** *n.* —**taunt·ing·ly** *adv.*

Taun·ton /'tôntn/ an industrial city in southeastern Massachusetts; pop. 49,832.

tau par·ti·cle ▶*n.* see TAU.

taupe /tōp/ ▶*n.* gray with a tinge of brown: [as *adj.*] *a taupe overcoat.* ▷early 20th cent.: from French, literally 'mole, moleskin,' from Latin *talpa.*

Tau·po, Lake /'toupō/ the largest lake of New Zealand, in the center of North Island. The town of Taupo is situated on its northern shore. Maori name TAUPOMOANA.

tau·rine[1] /'tô,rēn/ ▶*n. Biochemistry* a sulfur-containing amino acid important in the metabolism of fats. • Chem. formula: $NH_2CH_2CH_2SO_3H$. ▷mid 19th cent.: from Greek *tauros* 'bull' (because it was originally obtained from ox bile) + -INE[4].

tau·rine[2] /'tô,rīn/ ▶*adj.* of or like a bull. ■ of or relating to bullfighting: *taurine skill.* ▷early 17th cent.: from Latin *taurinus*, from *taurus* 'bull.'

tau·ro·cho·lic ac·id /,tôrə'kōlik; -'kälik/ ▶*n. Biochemistry* an acid formed by the combination of taurine with cholic acid, occurring in bile. ▷mid 19th cent.: from Greek *tauros* 'bull' + *kholē* 'bile' + -IC. —**tau·ro·cho·late** /-'kōlāt/ *n.*

tau·rom·a·chy /tô'räməkē/ ▶*n.* (*pl.* **-chies**) *rare* bullfighting. ■ a bullfight. ▷mid 19th cent.: from Greek *tauromakhia*, from *tauros* 'bull' + *makhē* 'battle.' —**tau·ro·ma·chi·an** /,tôrə'mākēən/ *adj.* —**tau·ro·mach·ic** /,tôrə'makik/ *adj.*

Tau·rus /'tôrəs/ **1** *Astronomy* a constellation (the Bull), said to represent a bull with brazen feet that was tamed by Jason. Its many bright stars include Aldebaran (the bull's eye), and it contains the Crab Nebula and the star clusters of the Hyades and the Pleiades. ■ [as *genitive*] (**Tauri** /'tôrī/) used with a preceding letter or numeral to designate a star in this constellation: *the star Beta Tauri.* **2** *Astrology* the second sign of the zodiac, which the sun enters on about April 21. ■ (**a Taurus**) (*pl.* same) a person born when the sun is in this sign. ▷Latin. —**Tau·re·an** /'tôrēən; tô'rēən/ *n.* & *adj.* (in sense 2).

Tau·rus Moun·tains a range of mountains in southern Turkey, parallel to the Mediterranean coast. Rising to 12,250 feet (3,734 m) at Mount Aladaē, the range forms the southern edge of the Anatolian plateau.

taut /tôt/ ▶*adj.* stretched or pulled tight; not slack: *the fabric stays taut without adhesive.* ■ (esp. of muscles or nerves) tense; not relaxed. ■ *figurative* (of writing, music, etc.) concise and controlled: *a taut text of only a hundred and twenty pages.* ■ (of a ship) having a disciplined and efficient crew. ▷Middle English *tought* 'distended,' perhaps originally a variant of TOUGH. **—taut·en** /ˈtôtn/ *v.* **—taut·ly** *adv.* **—taut·ness** *n.*

tauto- ▶*comb. form* same: *tautology.* ▷from Greek *tauto*, contraction of *to auto* 'the same.'

tau·tog /tôˈtôg; tôˈtäg/ ▶*n.* a grayish-olive edible wrasse that occurs off the Atlantic coast of North America. • *Tautoga onitis*, family Labridae. ▷mid 17th cent.: from Narragansett *tautauog*, plural of *taut*.

tau·tol·o·gy /tôˈtäləjē/ ▶*n.* (*pl.* **-gies**) the saying of the same thing twice in different words, generally considered to be a fault of style (e.g., *they arrived one after the other in succession*). ■ a phrase or expression in which the same thing is said twice in different words. ■ *Logic* a statement that is true by necessity or by virtue of its logical form. ▷mid 16th cent.: via late Latin from Greek, from *tautologos* 'repeating what has been said,' from *tauto-* 'same' + *-logos* (see -LOGY). **—tau·to·log·i·cal** /ˌtôtlˈäjikəl/ *adj.* **—tau·to·log·i·cal·ly** /ˌtôtlˈäjik(ə)lē/ *adv.* **—tau·tol·o·gist** /-jist/ *n.* **—tau·tol·o·gize** /-ˌjīz/ *v.* **—tau·tol·o·gous** /-gəs/ *adj.*

tau·to·mer /ˈtôtəmər/ ▶*n. Chemistry* each of two or more isomers of a compound that exist together in equilibrium, and are readily interchanged by migration of an atom or group within the molecule. ▷early 20th cent.: blend of TAUTO- 'same' and ISOMER. **—tau·to·mer·ic** /ˌtôtəˈmerik/ *adj.* **—tau·tom·er·ism** /tôˈtäməˌrizəm/ *n.*

tau·to·nym /ˈtôtəˌnim/ ▶*n. Botany & Zoology* a scientific name in which the same word is used for both genus and species, for example *Vulpes vulpes* (the red fox). ■ *Linguistics* a word that designates different objects or concepts in different dialects (e.g., *corn* is *wheat* in England and *oats* in Scotland). **—tau·ton·y·my** /tôˈtänəmē/ *n.*

Ta·vel /täˈvel/ ▶*n.* a fine rosé wine produced at Tavel in the south of France.

tav·ern /ˈtavərn/ ▶*n.* an establishment for the sale of beer and other drinks to be consumed on the premises, sometimes also serving food. ▷Middle English: from Old French *taverne*, from Latin *taberna* 'hut, tavern.' Compare with TABERNACLE.

ta·ver·na /təˈvərnə/ ▶*n.* a small Greek restaurant or café. ▷modern Greek, from Latin *taberna* (see TAVERN).

taw[1] /tô/ ▶*v.* [*trans.*] make (hide) into leather without the use of tannin, esp. by soaking it in a solution of alum and salt. ▷Old English *tawian* 'prepare raw material for use or further processing,' of Germanic origin; related to TOOL. **—taw·er** *n.*

taw[2] ▶*n.* a large marble. ■ a game of marbles. ■ a line from which players throw marbles. ▷early 18th cent.: of unknown origin.

taw·dry /ˈtôdrē/ ▶*adj.* (**-dri·er**, **-dri·est**) showy but cheap and of poor quality: *tawdry jewelry.* ■ sordid or unpleasant: *the tawdry business of politics.*
▶*n. archaic* cheap and gaudy finery. ▷early 17th cent.: short for *tawdry lace*, a fine silk lace or ribbon worn as a necklace in the 16th–17th centuries, contraction of *St. Audrey's lace*: *Audrey* was a later form of *Etheldrida* (died 679), patron saint of Ely, England, where tawdry laces, along with cheap imitations and other cheap finery, were traditionally sold at a fair. **—taw·dri·ly** /-drəlē/ *adv.* **—taw·dri·ness** *n.*

taw·ny /ˈtônē/ ▶*adj.* (**-ni·er**, **-ni·est**) of an orange-brown or yellowish-brown color: *tawny eyes.*
▶*n.* an orange-brown or yellowish-brown color: *pine needles turning from tawny to amber.* ▷Middle English: from Old French *tane*, from *tan* 'tanbark'; related to TAN[1]. **—taw·ni·ness** *n.*

taw·ny owl ▶*n.* a common Eurasian owl with either reddish-brown or gray plumage and a quavering hoot. • *Strix aluco*, family Strigidae.

taw·ny port ▶*n.* a port wine made from a blend of several vintages matured in wood.

tawse /tôz/ (also **taws**) ▶*n. Scottish* a thong with a slit end, formerly used in schools for punishing children. ▷early 16th cent. (denoting a whip for driving a spinning top): apparently the plural of obsolete *taw* 'tawed leather,' from TAW[1].

tax /taks/ ▶*n.* a compulsory contribution to state revenue, levied by the government on workers' income and business profits or added to the cost of some goods, services, and transactions. ■ [in *sing.*] *figurative* a strain or heavy demand: *a heavy* **tax on** *the reader's attention.*
▶*v.* [*trans.*] **1** impose a tax on (someone or something): *hardware and software is* **taxed at** *7.5 percent.* ■ *figurative* make heavy demands on (someone's powers or resources): *she knew that the ordeal to come would tax all her strength.* **2** confront (someone) with a fault or wrongdoing: *why are you* **taxing** *me* **with** *these preposterous allegations?* **3** *Law* examine and assess (the costs of a case). ▷Middle English (also in the sense 'estimate or determine the amount of a penalty or damages,' surviving in sense 3): from Old French *taxer*, from Latin *taxare* 'to censure, charge, compute,' perhaps from Greek *tassein* 'fix.' **—tax·a·ble** *adj.* **—tax·er** *n.*

tax·a /ˈtaksə/ ▶ plural form of TAXON.

tax-and-spend ▶*n.* a policy, usually associated with the political left, of increasing taxes in order to fund an increase in government spending, especially for social services: [as *adj.*] *they remain committed to their tax-and-spend philosophy.*
▶*v.* [*intrans.*] implement a policy of raising taxes in order to increase spending: *you can't tax-and-spend your way to prosperity.* **—tax-and-spend·er** *n.*

tax·a·tion /takˈsāSHən/ ▶*n.* the levying of tax. ■ money paid as tax. ▷Middle English (in the sense 'the assessment of a penalty or damages'; compare with TAX): via Old French from Latin *taxatio(n-)*, from *taxare* 'to censure, charge.'

tax a·void·ance ▶*n.* the arrangement of one's financial affairs to minimize tax liability within the law. Compare with TAX EVASION.

tax brack·et ▶*n. Economics* a range of incomes taxed at a given rate.

tax break ▶*n. informal* a tax concession or advantage allowed by a government.

tax cred·it ▶*n.* an amount of money that can be offset against a tax liability.

tax-de·duct·i·ble ▶*adj.* able to be deducted from taxable income when calculating income tax due.

tax e·va·sion ▶*n.* the illegal nonpayment or underpayment of tax. Compare with TAX AVOIDANCE.

tax ex·ile ▶*n.* a person with a high income or considerable wealth who chooses to live in a country or area with low tax rates.

tax-free ▶*adj.* & *adv.* (of goods, income, etc.) exempt from tax: [as *adj.*] *a tax-free lump sum* | [as *adv.*] *your return is paid to you tax-free.*

tax ha·ven ▶*n.* a country or independent area where taxes are levied at a low rate.

tax·i /ˈtaksē/ ▶*n.* (*pl.* **tax·is**) short for TAXICAB. ■ a boat or other means of transportation used to convey passengers in return for payment of a fare.
▶*v.* (**tax·is**, **tax·ied**, **tax·i·ing** or **tax·y·ing**) [*intrans.*] **1** (of an aircraft) move slowly along the ground before takeoff or after landing: *the plane taxis up to a waiting limousine.* ■ [*trans.*] (of a pilot) cause (an aircraft) to move in such a way: *he taxied it to the very end of the airstrip.* **2** take a taxi as a means of transport: *I would taxi home and sleep till eight.* ▷early 20th cent.: abbreviation of *taxicab* or *taximeter cab* (see TAXIMETER).

tax·i·cab /ˈtaksēˌkab/ ▶*n.* a car licensed to transport passengers in return for payment of a fare, usually fitted with a taximeter. ▷early 20th cent.: shortened form of *taximeter cab*.

tax·i danc·er ▶*n.* a dancing partner available for a fee.

tax·i·der·mist /ˈtaksəˌdərmist/ ▶*n.* a person who practices taxidermy.

tax·i·der·my /ˈtaksəˌdərmē/ ▶*n.* the art of preparing, stuffing, and mounting the skins of animals with lifelike effect. ▷early 19th cent.: from Greek *taxis* 'arrangement' + *derma* 'skin.' **—tax·i·der·mal** /ˌtaksəˈdərməl/ *adj.* **—tax·i·der·mic** /ˌtaksəˈdərmik/ *adj.* **—tax·i·der·mi·cal·ly** /ˌtaksəˈdərmik(ə)lē/ *adv.*

tax·i·me·ter /ˈtaksēˌmētər/ ▶*n.* a device used in taxicabs that automatically records the distance traveled and the fare payable. ▷late 19th cent.: from French *taximètre*, from *taxe* 'tariff,' from the verb *taxer* 'to tax' + *-mètre* '(instrument) measuring.'

tax·ing /ˈtaksiNG/ ▶*adj.* physically or mentally demanding: *they find the work too taxing.*

tax·is /ˈtaksis/ ▶*n.* (*pl.* **tax·es** /ˈtakˌsēz/) **1** *Surgery* the restoration of displaced bones or organs by manual pressure alone. **2** *Biology* a motion or orientation of a cell, organism, or part in response to an external stimulus. Compare with KINESIS. **3** *Linguistics* the systematic arrangement of linguistic units (phonemes, morphemes, words, phrases, or clauses) in linear sequence. ▷mid 18th cent. (sense 1): from Greek, literally 'arrangement,' from *tassein* 'arrange.' Sense 2 dates from the late 19th cent.

tax·i squad ▶*n. Football* a group of players who take part in practices and may be called on as reserves for the team.

tax·i stand (*Brit.* **tax·i rank**) ▶*n.* a place where taxicabs park while waiting to be engaged.

tax·i·way /ˈtaksēˌwā/ ▶*n.* a route along which an aircraft can taxi when moving to or from a runway.

tax loss ▶*n. Economics* a loss that can be offset against taxable profit earned elsewhere or in a different period.

tax·man /ˈtaksˌman/ ▶*n.* (*pl.* **-men**) *informal, chiefly Brit.* a collector of taxes. ■ (**the taxman**) the government department that collects tax: *he denies conspiracy to cheat the taxman.*

Tax·ol /ˈtaksôl; -säl/ (also **tax·ol**) ▶*n. trademark Medicine* a compound, originally obtained from the bark of the Pacific yew tree, that has been found to inhibit the growth of certain cancers. ▷1970s: from Latin *taxus* 'yew' + -OL.

tax·on /ˈtaksän/ ▶*n.* (*pl.* **tax·a** /ˈtaksə/) *Biology* a taxonomic group of any rank, such as a species, family, or class. ▷1920s: back-formation from TAXONOMY.

tax·on·o·my /takˈsänəmē/ ▶*n. chiefly Biology* the branch of science concerned with classification, esp. of organisms; systematics. ■ the classification of something, esp. organisms: *the taxonomy of these fossils.* ■ a scheme of classification: *a* **taxonomy of** *smells.* ▷early 19th cent.: coined in French from Greek *taxis* 'arrangement' + *-nomia* 'distribution.' **—tax·o·nom·ic** /ˌtaksəˈnämik/ *adj.* **—tax·o·nom·i·cal** /ˌtaksəˈnämikəl/ *adj.* **—tax·o·nom·i·cal·ly** /ˌtaksəˈnämik(ə)lē/ *adv.* **—tax·on·o·mist** /-mist/ *n.*

tax·pay·er /ˈtaksˌpāər/ ▶*n.* a person who pays taxes.

tax re·turn ▶*n.* a form on which a taxpayer makes an annual statement of income and personal circumstances, used by the tax authorities to assess liability for tax.

tax shel·ter ▶*n.* a financial arrangement made to avoid or minimize taxes.

Tay /tā/ the longest river in Scotland that flows 120 miles (192 km) east through Loch Tay and enters the North Sea through the Firth of Tay.

Tay, Firth of the estuary of the Tay River, on the North Sea coast of Scotland.

Tay·lor[1] /ˈtālər/ a city in southeastern Michigan, southwest of Detroit; pop. 70,811.

Tay·lor[2], Elizabeth (1932–), U.S. actress, born in England. Notable movies include *National Velvet* (1944), *Cat on a Hot Tin Roof* (1958), *Butterfield 8* (Academy Award, 1960), *Cleopatra* (1963), and *Who's Afraid of Virginia Woolf?* (Academy Award, 1966). She was married eight times, including twice to actor Richard Burton.

Elizabeth Taylor

Tay·lor[3], James (1948–) U.S. pop singer and songwriter. His hit songs include "You've Got a Friend" and "Fire and Rain." His albums include *Sweet Baby James* (1970), *Greatest Hits* (1988), and *Hour Glass* (1997).

Tay·lor[4], Lawrence, (1959–) U.S. football player. A linebacker for the New York Giants 1981–93, he was voted the NFL's most valuable player in 1986. He played in ten Pro Bowl games. Football Hall of Fame (1999).

Tay·lor[5], Zachary (1784–1850), 12th president of the U.S. 1849–50. Long in the military 1808–49, he became a national hero after his victories in the war with Mexico 1846–48. He negotiated the Clayton-Bulwer Treaty of 1850 with Great Britain that stated that any canal built in Central America would be under the joint control of Great Britain and the U.S.

As the last Whig president, he came into conflict with Congress over his desire to admit California to the Union as a free state (without slavery) and died before the problem was resolved.

Zachary Taylor

Tay·lor·ism /ˈtāləˌrizəm/ ▸*n.* the principles or practice of scientific management. ▷mid 19th cent.: from the name of Frederick W. *Taylor* (1856–1915), the American engineer who expounded the system, + **-ISM**. —**Tay·lor·ist** *n.* & *adj.*

Tay·lor se·ries ▸*n. Mathematics* an infinite sum giving the value of a function $f(z)$ in the neighborhood of a point a in terms of the derivatives of the function evaluated at a. ▷early 19th cent.: named after Brook *Taylor* (1685–1731), English mathematician.

Tay·lors·ville /ˈtālərzˌvil/ a city in northwestern Utah, a southwestern suburb of Salt Lake City; pop. 57,439. It was incorporated as a city in 1995.

tay·ra /ˈtīrə/ ▸*n.* a large, agile, tree-dwelling animal of the weasel family, with a short dark coat, native to Central and South America. • *Eira barbara*, family Mustelidae. ▷mid 19th cent.: from Tupi *taira*.

Tay–Sachs dis·ease /ˈtā ˌsaks/ ▸*n.* an inherited metabolic disorder in which certain lipids accumulate in the brain, causing spasticity and death in childhood. ▷early 20th cent.: from the names of Warren *Tay* (1843–1927), English ophthalmologist, and Bernard *Sachs* (1858–1944), American neurologist, who described it in 1881 and 1887 respectively.

taz·za /ˈtätsə/ ▸*n.* a saucer-shaped cup mounted on a foot. ▷early 19th cent.: from Italian, from Arabic *ṭasa* 'bowl.'

TB ▸*abbr.* ■ terabyte(s). ■ (also **t.b.**) tubercle bacillus. ■ (also **t.b.**) tuberculosis.

Tb ▸*abbr.* ■ terabyte(s). ■ *Bible* Tobit.
▸*symbol* the chemical element terbium.

t.b. ▸*abbr.* ■ trial balance.

t.b.a. ▸*abbr.* to be announced (in notices about events): *7 p.m. party with live band t.b.a.*

T-back ▸*n.* a high-cut undergarment or swimsuit having only a thin strip of material passing between the buttocks. ■ a style of back on a bra or bikini top in which the shoulder straps meet a supporting lateral strap below the shoulder blades.

t-ball ▸*n.* variant spelling of **TEE-BALL**.

T-bar ▸*n.* **1** a beam or bar shaped like the letter T. ■ (also **T-bar lift**) a type of ski lift in the form of a series of inverted T-shaped bars for towing two skiers at a time uphill. **2** the horizontal line of the letter *T*.

Tbi·li·si /ˌtəbəˈlēsē/ the capital of Georgia; pop. 1,267,000. From 1845 until 1936, its name was Tiflis.

T-bill ▸*n. informal* short for **TREASURY BILL**.

T-bond ▸*n. informal* short for **TREASURY BOND**.

T-bone ▸*n.* (also **T-bone steak**) a large choice piece of loin steak containing a T-shaped bone.
▸*v.* [*trans.*] crash head-on into the side of (another vehicle): *his car rolled over and was T-boned by an oncoming vehicle.*

tbsp. (also **tbs.**) (*pl.* same or **tbsps.**) ▸*abbr.* tablespoonful.

Tc ▸*symbol* the chemical element technetium.

TCA ▸*abbr.* **TRICHLORANISOLE**.

TCD ▸*abbr.* Trinity College, Dublin.

TCDD ▸*abbr.* tetrachlorodibenzoparadioxin (see **DIOXIN**).

T cell (also **T-cell**) ▸*n. Physiology* a lymphocyte of a type produced or processed by the thymus gland and actively participating in the immune response. Also called **T LYMPHOCYTE**. Compare with **B CELL**. ▷1970s: from *T* for *thymus*.

tch /CH/ ▸*exclam.* used to express irritation, annoyance, or impatience.

Tchai·kov·sky /CHīˈkôfskē/, Pyotr (Ilich) (1840–93), Russian composer. His music is characterized by melodiousness and depth of expression and is often melancholy. Notable works include the ballets *Swan Lake* (1877) and *The Nutcracker* (1892) and the overture *1812* (1880).

tchotch·ke /ˈCHäCHkə/ (also **tsats·ke**) ▸*n. informal* **1** a small object that is decorative rather than strictly functional; a trinket. **2** a pretty girl or woman. ▷1960s: Yiddish.

tchr. ▸*abbr.* teacher.

TCP/IP *trademark Computing* ▸*abbr.* transmission control protocol/Internet protocol, used to govern the connection of computer systems to the Internet.

TD ▸*abbr.* ■ technical drawing. ■ *Football* touchdown. ■ Treasury Department.

TDD ▸*abbr.* telecommunications device for the deaf.

TDN (also **t.d.n.**) ▸*abbr.* totally digestible nutrients.

TDY ▸*abbr.* temporary duty.

Te ▸*symbol* the chemical element tellurium.

tea /tē/ ▸*n.* **1** a hot drink made by infusing the dried, crushed leaves of the tea plant in boiling water. ■ the dried leaves used to make such a drink. ■ (also **iced tea**) such a drink served cold with ice cubes. ■ [usu. with *adj.*] a hot drink made from the infused leaves, fruits, or flowers of other plants: *herbal tea* | *fruit teas.* **2** (also **tea plant**) the evergreen shrub or small tree that produces these leaves, native to South and eastern Asia and grown as a major cash crop. • *Camellia sinensis*, family Theaceae. **3** *chiefly Brit.* a light afternoon meal consisting typically of tea to drink, sandwiches, and cakes. ■ *Brit.* a cooked evening meal. See also **HIGH TEA**. **4** *informal* another term for **MARIJUANA**. ▷mid 17th cent.: probably via Malay from Chinese (Min dialect) *te*; related to Mandarin *chá*. Compare with **CHAR**[3].

tea bag ▸*n.* a small porous bag containing tea leaves or powdered tea, onto which boiling water is poured in order to make a drink of tea.

tea ball ▸*n.* a hollow ball of perforated metal to hold tea leaves, over which boiling water is poured in order to make a drink of tea.

tea cad·dy ▸*n.* a small container in which tea is kept for daily use.

tea·cake /ˈtēˌkāk/ ▸*n. Brit.* a light yeast-raised sweet bun with dried fruit, typically served toasted and buttered.

tea cer·e·mo·ny ▸*n.* an elaborate Japanese ritual of serving and drinking tea, as an expression of Zen Buddhist philosophy.

Teach /tēCH/, Edward, see **BLACKBEARD**.

teach /tēCH/ ▸*v.* (*past* **taught** /tôt/) [*trans.* or *clause*] show or explain to (someone) how to do something: *she taught him to read* | *he taught me how to ride a bike.* ■ [*trans.*] give information about or instruction in (a subject or skill): *he came one day each week to teach painting* | [with *two objs.*] *she teaches me French.* ■ [*intrans.*] give such instruction professionally: *she teaches at the local high school.* ■ [*trans.*] encourage someone to accept (something) as a fact or principle: *the philosophy teaches self-control.* ■ cause (someone) to learn or understand something: *she'd been taught that it paid to be passive.* ■ induce (someone) by example or punishment to do or not to do something: *my upbringing taught me never to be disrespectful to elders.* ■ *informal* make (someone) less inclined to do something: *"I'll teach you to mess with young girls!"*
▸*n. informal* a teacher. ▷Old English *tǣcan* 'show, present, point out,' of Germanic origin; related to **TOKEN**, from an Indo-European root shared by Greek *deiknunai* 'show,' and Latin *dicere* 'say.'
▸*PHRASES* □ **teach someone a lesson** see **LESSON**. □ **teach school** be a schoolteacher.

teach·a·ble /ˈtēCHəbəl/ ▸*adj.* **1** (of a person) able to learn by being taught. **2** (of a subject) able to be taught. —**teach·a·bil·i·ty** /ˌtēCHəˈbilitē/ *n.* —**teach·a·ble·ness** *n.*

teach·er /ˈtēCHər/ ▸*n.* a person who teaches, esp. in a school. —**teach·er·ly** *adj.*

teach·er·age /ˈtēCHərij/ ▸*n.* a house or accommodations provided for a teacher by a school.

teach·ers col·lege (also **Teach·ers Col·lege**) ▸*n.* a four-year college with a special curriculum for training primary and secondary school teachers.

tea chest ▸*n.* a light metal-lined wooden box in which tea is transported.

teach-in ▸*n. informal* an informal lecture and discussion or series of lectures on a subject of public interest.

teach·ing /ˈtēCHiNG/ ▸*n.* **1** the occupation, profession, or work of a teacher. **2** (**teachings**) ideas or principles taught by an authority: *the teachings of the Koran.*

teach·ing fel·low ▸*n.* a postgraduate student who carries out teaching or laboratory duties in return for accommodations, tuition, or expenses.

teach·ing hos·pi·tal ▸*n.* a hospital that is affiliated with a medical school, in which medical students receive practical training.

teach·ing ma·chine ▸*n.* a machine or computer that gives instruction to a student according to a program, reacting to their responses.

tea co·zy ▸*n.* a thick or padded cover placed over a teapot to keep the tea hot.

tea·cup /ˈtēˌkəp/ ▸*n.* a cup from which tea is drunk. ■ an amount held by this, about 150 ml. —**tea·cup·ful** /-ˌfo͝ol/ *n.* (*pl.* **-fuls**).

tea dance ▸*n.* an afternoon tea with dancing, originating in 19th-century society.

Tea·gar·den /ˈtēˌgärdn/, Jack (1905–64) U.S. jazz trombonist and singer; full name *Weldon John Teagarden.* He had his own big band 1939–46 and then played with Louis Armstrong's All-Stars 1947–51.

tea gar·den ▸*n.* **1** a garden in which tea and other refreshments are served to the public. **2** a tea plantation.

tea gown ▸*n. dated* a long, loose-fitting dress, typically made of fine fabric and lace-trimmed, worn at afternoon tea and popular in the late 19th and early 20th centuries.

tea·head /ˈtēˌhed/ ▸*n. informal, dated* a habitual user of marijuana.

teak /tēk/ ▸*n.* **1** hard durable timber used in shipbuilding and for making furniture. **2** the large deciduous tree native to India and Southeast Asia that yields this timber. • *Tectona grandis*, family Verbenaceae. ▷late 17th cent.: from Portuguese *teca*, from Tamil and Malayalam *tēkku*.

tea·ket·tle /ˈtēˌketl/ ▸*n.* a typically metal container with a lid, spout, and handle, used for boiling water.

teal /tēl/ ▸*n.* (*pl.* same or **teals**) a small freshwater duck, typically with a greenish band on the wing that is most prominent in flight. • Genus *Anas*, family Anatidae: several species, in particular the common Eurasian and Canadian (**green-winged**) **teal** (*A. crecca*). ■ (also **teal blue**) a dark greenish-blue color. ▷Middle English: of unknown origin; related to Dutch *teling*.

tea leaf ▸*n.* a dried leaf of tea. ■ (**tea leaves**) dried leaves of tea after they have been used to make tea or as dregs.

team /tēm/ ▸*n.* [treated as *sing.* or *pl.*] a group of players forming one side in a competitive game or sport. ■ two or more people working together: ***a team of** researchers* | [as *adj.*] *a team effort.* ■ two or more animals, esp. horses, harnessed together to pull a vehicle.
▸*v.* **1** [*intrans.*] (**team up**) come together as a team to achieve a common goal: *he **teamed up with** the band to produce the album.* **2** [*trans.*] (usu. **team something with**) match or coordinate a garment with (another): *a pinstripe suit teamed with a crisp white shirt.* **3** [*trans.*] harness (animals, esp. horses) together to pull a vehicle: *the horses are teamed in pairs.* ▷Old English *tēam* 'team of draft animals,' of Germanic origin; related to German *Zaum* 'bridle,' also to **TEEM**[1] and **TOW**[1], from an Indo-European root shared by Latin *ducere* 'to lead.'

team·mate /ˈtē(m)ˌmāt/ ▸*n.* a fellow member of a team.

team play·er ▸*n.* a person who plays or works well as a member of a team or group.

team spir·it ▸*n.* feelings of camaraderie among the members of a group, enabling them to cooperate and work well together.

team·ster /ˈtēmstər/ ▸*n.* **1** a truck driver. ■ a member of the Teamsters Union, including truck drivers, chauffeurs, and warehouse workers. **2** a driver of a team of animals.

team teach·ing ▸*n.* coordinated teaching by a team of teachers working together.

team·work /ˈtēmˌwərk/ ▸*n.* the combined action of a group of people, esp. when effective and efficient.

Tea·neck /ˈtēˌnek/ a township in northeastern New Jersey; pop. 37,825.

Pronunciation Key ə *ago*; ər *over*; ˈə or ˌə *up*; ˈər or ˌər *fur*; a *hat*; ā *rate*; ä *car*; CH *chew*; e *let*; ē *see*; e(ə)r *air*; i *fit*; ī *by*; i(ə)r *ear*; NG *sing*; ō *go*; ô *for*; oi *boy*; o͝o *good*; o͞o *goo*; ou *out*; SH *she*; TH *thin*; TH *then*; (h)w *why*; ZH *vision*

T

tea oil ▸*n.* an oil resembling olive oil obtained from the seeds of the sasanqua and related plants, used chiefly in China and Japan.

tea par·ty ▸*n.* a social gathering in the afternoon at which tea, cakes, and other light refreshments are served.

tea·pot /ˈtē,pät/ ▸*n.* a pot with a handle, spout, and lid, in which tea is brewed and from which it is poured. ■ a teakettle.

Tea·pot Dome an oil field in southeastern Wyoming that, as a naval reserve, was the focus of a 1920s corruption scandal.

tea·poy /ˈtē,poi/ ▸*n.* a small three-legged table or stand, esp. one that holds a tea caddy. ▷early 19th cent.: from Hindi *tī-* 'three' + Urdu and Persian *pāī* 'foot,' the sense and spelling influenced by TEA.

tear[1] /te(ə)r/ ▸*v.* (*past* **tore** /tôr/; *past part.* **torn** /tôrn/) **1** [*trans.*] pull or rip (something) apart or to pieces with force: *I* **tore up** *the letter.* ■ remove by pulling or ripping forcefully: *he tore up the floorboards* | *he* **tore off** *his belt* | *Joe* **tore** *the sack* **from** *her hand.* ■ (**be torn between**) *figurative* have great difficulty in choosing between: *he was torn between his duty and his better instincts.* ■ [*trans.*] make a hole or split in (something) by ripping or pulling at it: *she was always tearing her clothes.* ■ make (a hole or split) in something by force: *the blast tore a hole in the wall.* ■ [*intrans.*] come apart; rip: *the material wouldn't tear.* ■ [*trans.*] damage (a muscle or ligament) by overstretching it: *he tore a ligament playing squash.* **2** [*intrans.*] *informal* move very quickly, typically in a reckless or excited manner: *she tore along the footpath on her bike.*
▸*phrasal v.* □ **tear someone/something apart 1** destroy something, esp. good relations between people: *a bloody civil war had torn the country apart.* **2** upset someone greatly: *stop crying—it's tearing me apart.* **3** search a place thoroughly: *I'll help you find it; I'll tear your house apart if I have to.* **4** criticize someone or something harshly. □ **tear oneself away** [often with *negative*] leave despite a strong desire to stay: *she couldn't tear herself away from the view.* □ **tear someone/something down 1** demolish something, esp. a building. **2** *informal* criticize or punish someone severely. □ **tear into 1** attack verbally: *she tore into him: "Don't you realize what you've done to me?"* **2** make an energetic or enthusiastic start on: *a jazz trio is tearing into the tune with gusto.*
▸*n.* **1** a hole or split in something caused by it having been pulled apart forcefully. **2** *informal* a spell of great success or excellence in performance: *he went* **on a tear,** *winning three out of every four hands.* ■ a brief spell of erratic behavior; a binge or spree: *every so often she goes* **on a tear,** *walking around town and zapping people with orange spray paint.* ▷Old English *teran,* of Germanic origin; related to Dutch *teren* and German *zehren,* from an Indo-European root shared by Greek *derein* 'flay.' The noun dates from the early 17th cent. —**tear·a·ble** *adj.* —**tear·er** *n.*
▸*PHRASES* □ **tear one's hair out** *informal* act with or show extreme desperation. □ **tear someone/something to shreds** (or **pieces**) *informal* criticize someone or something forcefully or aggressively: *a defense counsel would tear his evidence to shreds.* □ **that's torn it** *Brit., informal* used to express dismay when something unfortunate has happened to disrupt someone's plans: *a friend of her father's arrived. "That's torn it," she said.*

tear[2] /ti(ə)r/ ▸*n.* a drop of clear salty liquid secreted from glands in a person's eye when they cry or when the eye is irritated. ■ a drop of such liquid secreted continuously to lubricate the surface of the eyeball under the eyelid. ■ (**tears**) the state or action of crying: *he was so hurt by her attitude he was nearly* **in tears** | *sock puppets that* **moved** *Jack* **to tears.**
▸*v.* [*intrans.*] (of the eye) produce tears: *she arrived in a fur coat, cheeks red and eyes tearing from the chill.* ▷Old English *tēar,* of Germanic origin; related to German *Zähre,* from an Indo-European root shared by Old Latin *dacruma* (classical Latin *lacrima*) and Greek *dakru.* —**tear·like** /-,līk/ *adj.*

tear·a·way /ˈte(ə)rə,wā/ ▸*n. Brit.* a person who behaves in a wild or reckless manner.

tear·drop /ˈti(ə)r,dräp/ ▸*n.* a single tear. ■ [as *adj.*] shaped like a single tear: *a wardrobe with brass teardrop handles.*

tear duct /ti(ə)r/ ▸*n.* a passage through which tears pass from the lachrymal glands to the eye or from the eye to the nose.

tear·ful /ˈti(ə)rfəl/ ▸*adj.* crying or inclined to cry: *a tearful infant* | *Stephen felt tearful.* ■ causing tears; sad or emotional: *a tearful farewell.* —**tear·ful·ly** *adv.* —**tear·ful·ness** *n.*

tear gas /ti(ə)r/ ▸*n.* gas that causes severe irritation to the eyes, chiefly used in riot control to force crowds to disperse.
▸*v.* (**tear-gas**) [*trans.*] (usu. **be tear-gassed**) attack with tear gas.

tear·ing /ˈte(ə)riNG/ ▸*adj.* [*attrib.*] violent; extreme: *he did seem to be in a tearing hurry* | *the tearing wind.*

tear·jerk·er /ˈti(ə)r,jərkər/ ▸*n. informal* a sentimental story, movie, or song, calculated to evoke sadness or sympathy. —**tear·jerk·ing** /-,jərkiNG/ *n.* & *adj.*

tear·less /ˈti(ə)rlis/ ▸*adj.* not crying: *Mary watched in tearless silence as the coffin was lowered.* —**tear·less·ly** *adv.* —**tear·less·ness** *n.*

tear-off /te(ə)r/ ▸*adj.* denoting something that is removed by being torn off, typically along a perforated line: *please complete the tear-off slip.*

tea·room /ˈtē,ro͞om; -,ro͝om/ (also **tea room**) ▸*n.* **1** a small restaurant or café where tea and other light refreshments are served. **2** *informal* a public restroom used as a meeting place for homosexual encounters.

tea rose ▸*n.* a garden rose with flowers that have a delicate scent said to resemble that of tea. • Numerous cultivars of the Chinese hybrid *Rosa × odorata.*

tear sheet /te(ə)r/ ▸*n.* a page that can be or has been removed from a newspaper, magazine, or book for use separately.

tear-stained /ti(ə)r/ ▸*adj.* wet with tears: *I looked at the man's tear-stained face.*

Teas·dale /ˈtēz,dāl/, Sara, (1884–1933) U.S. poet; born *Sarah Trevor.* Her poetry is collected in *Helen of Troy and Other Poetry* (1911), *River to the Sea* (1915), *Love Songs* (1917), *Flame and Shadow* (1920), and *Strange Victory* (1933).

tease /tēz/ ▸*v.* [*trans.*] **1** make fun of or attempt to provoke (a person or animal) in a playful way: *Brenda teased her father about the powerboat that he bought but seldom used* | [*intrans.*] *she was just teasing* | [with *direct speech*] *"Think you're clever, don't you?" she teased.* ■ tempt (someone) sexually with no intention of satisfying the desire aroused. **2** [*trans.*] gently pull or comb (something tangled, esp. wool or hair) into separate strands: *she was teasing out the curls into her usual hairstyle.* ■ (**tease something out**) *figurative* find something out from a mass of irrelevant information: *a historian who tries to tease out the truth.* ■ comb (hair) in the reverse direction of its natural growth in order to make it appear fuller. ■ *archaic* comb (the surface of woven cloth) to raise a nap.
▸*n. informal* a person who makes fun of someone playfully or unkindly. ■ a person who tempts someone sexually with no intention of satisfying the desire aroused. ■ [in *sing.*] an act of making fun of or tempting someone: *she couldn't resist a gentle tease.* ▷Old English *tǣsan* (sense 2); related to Dutch *teezen* and German dialect *zeisen,* also to TEASEL. Sense 1 is a development of the earlier and more serious 'irritate by annoying actions' (early 17th cent.), a figurative use of the word's original sense. —**teas·ing·ly** *adv.*

tea·sel /ˈtēzəl/ (also **tea·zle** or **tea·zel**) ▸*n.* a tall prickly Eurasian plant with spiny purple flowerheads. • Genus *Dipsacus,* family Dipsacaceae: several species, including **fuller's teasel.** ■ a large, dried, spiny head from such a plant, or a device serving as a substitute for one of these, used in the textile industry to raise a nap on woven cloth.
▸*v.* [*trans.*] [often as *n.*] (**teaseling**) *chiefly archaic* raise a nap on (cloth) with or as if with teasels. ▷Old English *tǣsl, tǣsel;* related to TEASE.

teas·er /ˈtēzər/ ▸*n.* **1** *informal* a difficult or tricky question or task. **2** a person who makes fun of or provokes others in a playful or unkind way. ■ a person who tempts someone sexually with no intention of satisfying the desire aroused. ■ a short introductory advertisement for a product, esp. one that does not mention the name of the thing being advertised. ■ *Fishing* a lure or bait trailed behind a boat to attract fish. ■ an inferior stallion or ram used to excite mares or ewes before they are served by the stud animal.

tea set (also **tea serv·ice**) ▸*n.* a set of dishes, typically of china or silver, used for serving tea.

tea shop ▸*n.* another term for TEAROOM (sense 1).

tea·spoon /ˈtē,spo͞on/ ▸*n.* a small spoon used typically for adding sugar to and stirring hot drinks or for eating some soft foods. ■ (abbr.: **ts.p** or **t**) a measurement used in cooking, equivalent to 1/6 fluid ounce, 1/3 tablespoon, or 4.9 ml. —**tea·spoon·ful** /-,fo͝ol/ *n.* (*pl.* **-fuls**).

tea strain·er ▸*n.* a small device incorporating a fine mesh for straining tea.

teat /tēt/ ▸*n.* a nipple of the mammary gland of a female mammal, from which the milk is sucked by the young. ■ *Brit.* a thing resembling this, esp. a perforated plastic bulb by which an infant or young animal can suck milk from a bottle. ▷Middle English (superseding earlier TIT[2]): from Old French *tete,* probably of Germanic origin.

tea·time /ˈtē,tīm/ ▸*n. chiefly Brit.* the time in the afternoon when tea is traditionally served.

tea tow·el ▸*n.* chiefly British term for DISH TOWEL.

tea tray ▸*n.* a tray from which tea is served.

tea tree ▸*n.* an Australasian flowering shrub or small tree with leaves that are sometimes used for tea. • Genus *Leptospermum,* family Myrtaceae: several species, in particular *L. scoparium.*

tea·zle (also **tea·zel**) ▸*n.* variant spelling of TEASEL.

Te·bet /ˈtāvās; -vāt; teˈvet/ (also **Te·vet**) ▸*n.* (in the Jewish calendar) the fourth month of the civil and tenth of the religious year, usually coinciding with parts of December and January. ▷from Hebrew *ṭēḇēṯ.*

tec. ▸*abbr.* ■ technical. ■ technician.

tech /tek/ (*Brit.* also **tec**) ▸*n. informal* technology. See also HIGH-TECH, LOW-TECH. ■ a technician. ■ *Basketball* a technical.
▸*adj.* technical: *I was in tech school then.* ▷early 20th cent.: abbreviation.

tech. ▸*abbr.* ■ technic. ■ technical. ■ technology.

tech·ie /ˈtekē/ (also **tek·kie** or **tech·y**) ▸*n.* (*pl.* **-ies**) *informal* a person who is expert in or enthusiastic about technology, esp. computing. ▷1960s: from TECH + -IE. First recorded as a U.S. slang term for a technical college student, the word was later used as British service slang, denoting a technician. Sense 1 dates from the 1980s.

tech·ne·ti·um /tekˈnēsH(ē)əm/ ▸*n.* the chemical element of atomic number 43, a radioactive metal. Technetium was the first element to be created artificially, in 1937, by bombarding molybdenum with deuterons. (Symbol: **Tc**) ▷1940s: modern Latin, from Greek *tekhnētos* 'artificial,' from *tekhnasthai* 'make by art,' from *tekhnē* 'art.'

tech·nic /ˈteknik/ ▸*n.* **1** technique. **2** (**technics**) [treated as *sing.* or *pl.*] technical terms, details, and methods; technology. ▷early 17th cent. (as an adjective in the sense 'to do with art or an art'): from Latin *technicus,* from Greek *tekhnikos,* from *tekhnē* 'art.' The noun dates from the 19th cent. —**tech·ni·cist** /-nisist/ *n.*

tech·ni·cal /ˈteknikəl/ ▸*adj.* **1** of or relating to a particular subject, art, or craft, or its techniques: *technical terms* | *a test of an artist's technical skill.* ■ (esp. of a book or article) requiring special knowledge to be understood: *a technical report.* **2** of, involving, or concerned with applied and industrial sciences: *an important technical achievement.* **3** resulting from mechanical failure: *a technical fault.* **4** according to a strict application or interpretation of the law or rules: *the arrest was a technical violation of the treaty.*
▸*n. Basketball* short for TECHNICAL FOUL.

tech·ni·cal col·lege ▸*n.* a college providing courses in a range of practical subjects, such as information technology, applied sciences, engineering, agriculture, and secretarial skills.

tech·ni·cal draw·ing ▸*n.* the practice or skill of delineating objects in a precise way using certain techniques of draftsmanship, as employed in architecture or engineering. ■ a drawing produced in such a way.

tech·ni·cal foul ▸*n. Basketball* a violation of certain rules of the game, not usually involving physical contact, but often involving unsportsmanlike actions.

tech·ni·cal·i·ty /,tekniˈkalitē/ ▸*n.* (*pl.* **-ties**) a point of law or a small detail of a set of rules: *their convictions were overturned* **on a technicality.** ■ (**technicalities**) the specific details or terms belonging to a particular field: *he has great expertise in the technicalities of the game.* ■ the state of being technical; the use of technical terms or methods: *the extreme technicality of the proposed constitution.*

tech·ni·cal knock·out (abbr.: **TKO**) ▸*n. Boxing* the ending of a fight by the referee on the grounds of one contestant's inability to continue, the opponent being declared the winner.

tech·ni·cal·ly /ˈteknik(ə)lē/ ▸*adv.* **1** [usu. *sentence adverb*] according to the facts or exact meaning of something; strictly: *technically, a nut is a single-seeded fruit.* **2** with reference to the technique displayed: *a technically brilliant boxing contest.* **3** involving or regarding the technology available: *technically advanced tools.*

tech·ni·cal ser·geant ▶*n.* a noncommissioned officer in the U.S. Air Force ranking above staff sergeant and below master sergeant.

tech·ni·cal sup·port ▶*n. Computing* a service provided by a hardware or software company that provides registered users with help and advice about their products. ■ a department within an organization that maintains and repairs computers and computer networks.

tech·ni·cian /tek'nisʜən/ ▶*n.* a person employed to look after technical equipment or do practical work in a laboratory. ■ an expert in the practical application of a science. ■ a person skilled in the technique of an art or craft.

Tech·ni·col·or /'tekni,kələr/ ▶*n. trademark* a process of color cinematography using synchronized monochrome films, each of a different color, to produce a movie in color. ■ (**technicolor**) *informal* vivid color: [as *adj.*] *a technicolor bruise.* ▷early 20th cent.: blend of TECHNICAL and COLOR. —**tech·ni·col·ored** *adj.*

tech·ni·col·or yawn ▶*n. informal, humorous* an act of vomiting.

tech·nique /tek'nēk/ ▶*n.* a way of carrying out a particular task, esp. the execution or performance of an artistic work or a scientific procedure. ■ skill or ability in a particular field: *he has excellent technique* | [in *sing.*] *an established athlete with a very good technique.* ■ a skillful or efficient way of doing or achieving something: *tape recording is a good technique for evaluating our own communications.* ▷early 19th cent.: from French, from Latin *technicus* (see TECHNIC).

tech·no /'teknō/ ▶*n.* a style of fast, heavy electronic dance music, typically with few or no vocals. ▷1980s: abbreviation of TECHNOLOGICAL.

techno- ▶*comb. form* relating to technology or its use: *technophobe.* ▷from Greek *tekhnē* 'art, craft.'

tech·no·bab·ble /'teknō,babəl/ ▶*n. informal* incomprehensible technical jargon.

tech·noc·ra·cy /tek'näkrəsē/ ▶*n.* (*pl.* **-cies**) the government or control of society or industry by an elite of technical experts. ■ an instance or application of this. ■ an elite of technical experts. ▷early 20th cent.: from Greek *tekhnē* 'art, craft' + -CRACY.

tech·no·crat /'teknə,krat/ ▶*n.* an exponent or advocate of technocracy. ■ a member of a technically skilled elite. —**tech·no·crat·ic** /,teknə'kratik/ *adj.* —**tech·no·crat·i·cal·ly** /,teknə'kratik(ə)lē/ *adv.*

tech·no·fear /'teknō,fi(ə)r/ ▶*n. informal, chiefly Brit.* fear of using technological equipment, esp. computers.

technol. ▶*abbr.* technology.

tech·no·log·i·cal /,teknə'läjikəl/ ▶*adj.* of, relating to, or using technology: *the quickening pace of technological change.* —**tech·no·log·i·cal·ly** /-ik(ə)lē/ *adv.*

tech·nol·o·gy /tek'näləjē/ ▶*n.* (*pl.* **-gies**) the application of scientific knowledge for practical purposes, esp. in industry: *advances in computer technology* | *recycling technologies.* ■ machinery and equipment developed from such scientific knowledge. ■ the branch of knowledge dealing with engineering or applied sciences. ▷early 17th cent.: from Greek *tekhnologia* 'systematic treatment,' from *tekhnē* 'art, craft' + *-logia* (see -LOGY). —**tech·nol·o·gist** /-jist/ *n.* —**tech·nol·o·gize** /-,jīz/ *v.*

tech·nol·o·gy park ▶*n.* a science park.

tech·nol·o·gy trans·fer ▶*n.* the transfer of new technology from the originator to a secondary user, esp. from developed to less developed countries in an attempt to boost their economies.

tech·no·phile /'teknə,fīl/ ▶*n.* a person who is enthusiastic about new technology. —**tech·no·phil·i·a** /,teknə'filēə/ *n.* —**tech·no·phil·ic** /,teknə'filik/ *adj.*

tech·no·phobe /'teknə,fōb/ ▶*n.* a person who fears, dislikes, or avoids new technology. —**tech·no·pho·bi·a** /,teknə'fōbēə/ *n.* —**tech·no·pho·bic** /,teknə'fōbik/ *adj.*

tech·no·speak /'teknə,spēk/ ▶*n.* another term for TECHNOBABBLE.

tech·no·stress /'teknō,stres/ ▶*n. informal* stress or psychosomatic illness caused by working with computer technology on a daily basis.

tech·no·struc·ture /'teknō,strəkcʜər/ ▶*n.* [treated as *sing.* or *pl.*] a group of technologists or technical experts having considerable control over the workings of industry or government. ▷1960s: coined by J. K. Galbraith.

tech·no-thril·ler /'teknō 'thrilər/ ▶*n.* a novel or movie in which the excitement of the plot depends in large part upon the descriptions of computers, weapons, software, military vehicles, or other machines: *Tom Clancy's best-selling techno-thriller.*

tech·y /'tecʜē/ ▶*n.* variant spelling of TECHIE.

tec·ton·ic /tek'tänik/ ▶*adj.* **1** *Geology* of or relating to the structure of the earth's crust and the large-scale processes that take place within it. **2** of or relating to building or construction. ▷mid 17th cent. (sense 2): via late Latin from Greek *tektonikos,* from *tektōn* 'carpenter, builder.' —**tec·ton·i·cal·ly** /-ik(ə)lē/ *adv.*

tec·ton·ics /tek'täniks/ ▶*plural n.* [treated as *sing.* or *pl.*] *Geology* large-scale processes affecting the structure of the earth's crust.

tec·to·no·phys·ics /tek,tänō'fiziks; ,tektənō-/ ▶*plural n.* [treated as *sing.*] the branch of geophysics that deals with the forces that cause movement and deformation in the earth's crust. ▷1950s: from TECTONICS + PHYSICS. —**tec·to·no·phys·i·cist** /-'fizəsist/ *n.*

tec·to·ri·al /tek'tôrēəl/ ▶*adj. Anatomy* forming a covering. ■ denoting the membrane covering the organ of Corti in the inner ear. ▷late 19th cent.: from Latin *tectorium* 'covering, a cover' (from *tegere* 'to cover') + -AL.

tec·trix /'tek,triks/ ▶*n.* (*Pl.* **-tri·ces** /-,trisēz/) *Ornithology* a covert of a bird. ▷late 19th cent.: modern Latin, from Latin *tect-* 'covered,' from the verb *tegere.*

tec·tum /'tektəm/ ▶*n. Anatomy* the uppermost part of the midbrain, lying to the rear of the cerebral aqueduct. ■ (in full **optic tectum**) a rounded swelling (colliculus) forming part of this and containing cells involved in the visual system. ▷early 20th cent.: from Latin, literally 'roof.'

Te·cum·seh /ti'kəmsə/ (1768–1813) Shawnee Indian chief; also *Tecumtha.* His plan to organize a military confederacy of tribes to resist U.S. encroachment was thwarted by the defeat of his brother, **Tenskwatawa** (c.1768–1834) (also called *the Prophet*), at Tippecanoe 1811. An ally of the British in the War of 1812, Tecumseh fought and died at the Battle of the Thames.

Tecumseh

ted /ted/ ▶*v.* (**ted·ded**, **ted·ding**) [*trans.*] [often as *n.*] (**tedding**) turn over and spread out (grass, hay, or straw) to dry or for bedding. ▷Middle English: from Old Norse *tethja* 'spread manure' (past tense *tadda*), related to *tad* 'dung.' —**ted·der** *n.*

ted·dy /'tedē/ ▶*n.* (*pl.* **-dies**) **1** (also **ted·dy bear**) a soft toy bear. **2** a woman's all-in-one undergarment. ▷early 20th cent.: from *Teddy,* nickname for the given name *Theodore*: in sense 1 alluding to *Theodore* ROOSEVELT[3], an enthusiastic bear hunter.

Ted·dy boy ▶*n. Brit.* (in the 1950s) a young man of a subculture characterized by a style of dress based on Edwardian fashion and a liking for rock and roll music. ▷from *Teddy,* nickname for the given name *Edward* (with reference to Edward VII's reign).

Te De·um /tā 'dāəm; tē 'dēəm/ ▶*n.* a hymn beginning *Te Deum laudamus,* "We praise Thee, O God," sung at matins or on special occasions such as a thanksgiving. ■ a musical setting of this. ■ an expression of thanksgiving or exultation. ▷Latin.

te·di·ous /'tēdēəs/ ▶*adj.* too long, slow, or dull: tiresome or monotonous: *a tedious journey.* ▷late Middle English: from Old French *tedieus* or late Latin *taediosus,* from Latin *taedium* (see TEDIUM). —**te·di·ous·ly** *adv.* —**te·di·ous·ness** *n.*

te·di·um /'tēdēəm/ ▶*n.* the state of being tedious: *cousins and uncles filled the tedium of winter nights with many a tall tale.* ▷mid 17th cent.: from Latin *taedium,* from *taedere* 'be weary of.'

tee[1] /tē/ ▶*n.* see T[1] (sense 2).

tee[2] ▶*n.* **1** a cleared space on a golf course, from which the ball is struck at the beginning of play for each hole. ■ a small peg with a concave head that can be placed in the ground to support a golf ball before it is struck from such an area. ■ *Football* a small stand on which the ball is placed for a placekick. ■ a waist-high or higher stand used in tee-ball to hold a baseball before it is hit with a bat. [late 17th cent. (originally Scots, as *teaz*): of unknown origin.] **2** a mark aimed at in lawn bowling, quoits, curling, and other similar games. [late 18th cent. (originally Scots): perhaps the same word as TEE[1].]

▶*v.* (**tees**, **teed**, **tee·ing**) [*intrans.*] (usu. **tee up**) *Golf* place the ball on a tee ready to make the first stroke of the round or hole: *he had not missed a par as he teed up for the last hole* | [*trans.*] *she fished in her pocket for a ball and teed it.* ■ [*trans.*] place (something) in position, esp. to be struck: *a shining white radar dome was teed up on top of the mountain.*

▶*phrasal v.* □ **tee off** *Golf* play the ball from a tee; begin a round or hole of golf: *we spend ten minutes practicing putting before we tee off.* ■ *informal* make a start on something. □ **tee off on someone/something** *informal* sharply attack someone or something: *he will tee off on conservative politicians* | *Chang teed off on his opponent's serve.* □ **tee someone off** (usu. **be teed off**) *informal* make someone angry or annoyed: *Tommy was really teed off at Ernie.*

tee[3] ▶*n. informal* a T-shirt.

tee-ball (also **t-ball**) ▶*n.* a game for young children, played by the rules of baseball, in which the ball is not pitched but hit from a stationary tee.

tee-hee /,tē 'hē/ ▶*n.* a giggle or titter.

▶*v.* (**-hees**, **-heed**, **-hee·ing**) [*intrans.*] titter or giggle in such a way. ▷Middle English (as a verb): imitative.

teem[1] /tēm/ ▶*v.* [*intrans.*] (**teem with**) be full of or swarming with: *every garden is teeming with wildlife* | [as *adj.*] (**teeming**) *she walked briskly through the teeming streets.* ▷Old English *tēman, tieman,* of Germanic origin; related to TEAM. The original senses included 'give birth to,' also 'be or become pregnant,' giving rise to 'be full of' in the late 16th cent.

teem[2] ▶*v.* [*intrans.*] (of water, esp. rain) pour down; fall heavily: *with the rain* ***teeming down*** *at the manor, Italy seemed a long way off.* ▷Middle English: from Old Norse *tœma* 'to empty,' from *tómr* 'empty.' The original sense was 'to empty,' specifically 'to drain liquid from, pour liquid out'; the current sense (originally dialect) dates from the early 19th cent.

teen /tēn/ *informal* ▶*adj.* [*attrib.*] of or relating to teenagers: *a teen idol.*

▶*n.* a teenager. ▷early 19th cent. (as a noun): abbreviation. The adjective dates from the 1940s.

-teen ▶*suffix* forming the names of numerals from 13 to 19: *fourteen* | *eighteen.* ▷Old English, inflected form of TEN.

teen·age /'tēn,āj/ ▶*adj.* [*attrib.*] denoting a person between 13 and 19 years old: *a teenage girl.* ■ relating to or characteristic of people of this age: *teenage magazines.* —**teen·aged** *adj.*

teen·ag·er /'tēn,ājər/ ▶*n.* a person aged from 13 to 19 years.

teens /tēnz/ ▶*plural n.* the years of a person's age from 13 to 19: *they were both in their late teens.* ▷late 17th cent.: plural of *teen,* independent usage of -TEEN.

teen·sy /'tēnsē/ ▶*adj.* (**-si·er**, **-si·est**) *informal* tiny: *the dress just needs to be altered a teensy bit.* ▷late 19th cent. (originally dialect): probably an extension of TEENY.

teen·sy-ween·sy /'tēnsē 'wēnsē/ ▶*adj. informal* tiny: *do we detect a teensy-weensy bit of animosity?*

tee·ny /'tēnē/ ▶*adj.* (**-ni·er**, **-ni·est**) *informal* tiny: *a teeny bit of criticism.* ▷early 19th cent.: variant of TINY.

tee·ny·bop·per /'tēnē,bäpər/ ▶*n. informal* a young teenager, esp. a girl, who keenly follows the latest fashions in clothes and pop music. —**tee·ny·bop** *adj.*

tee·ny-wee·ny /'tēnē 'wēnē/ ▶*adj. informal* tiny: *doesn't he have a teeny-weeny twinge of conscience?*

tee·pee ▶*n.* variant spelling of TEPEE.

Tees /tēz/ a river in northeastern England that flows southeast for 80 miles (128 km) to the North Sea at Middlesbrough.

tee shirt ▶*n.* variant spelling of T-SHIRT.

tee·ter /'tētər/ ▶*v.* [*intrans.*] move or balance unsteadily; sway back and forth: *she teetered after him in her high-heeled sandals.* ■ (often **teeter between**) *figurative* be unable to decide between different courses; waver: *she teetered between tears and anger.* ▷mid 19th cent.: variant of dialect *titter,* from Old Norse *titra* 'shake, shiver.'

▶*PHRASE* □ **teeter on the brink** (or **edge**) be very close to a difficult or dangerous situation: *the country teetered on the brink of civil war.*

Pronunciation Key ə *ago*; ər *over*; 'ə or ,ə *up*; 'ər or ,ər *fur*; a *hat*; ā *rate*; ä *car*; cʜ *chew*; e *let*; ē *see*; e(ə)r *air*; i *fit*; ī *by*; i(ə)r *ear*; ɴɢ *sing*; ō *go*; ô *for*; oi *boy*; o͝o *good*; o͞o *goo*; ou *out*; sʜ *she*; tʜ *thin*; t͟ʜ *then*; (h)w *why*; zʜ *vision*

T

tee·ter-tot·ter /ˈtētər ˌtätər/ ▸*n.* a seesaw.
▸*v.* [*intrans.*] teeter; waver. ▷late 19th cent.: reduplication of TEETER or TOTTER.

teeth /tēTH/ ▸ plural form of TOOTH.

teethe /tēTH/ ▸*v.* [*intrans.*] grow or cut teeth, esp. milk teeth. ▷late Middle English: from TEETH.

teeth·ing /ˈtēTHiNG/ ▸*n.* the process of growing one's teeth, esp. milk teeth.

teeth·ing ring ▸*n.* a small ring for an infant to bite on while teething.

tee·to·tal /ˈtēˌtōtl/ ▸*adj.* choosing or characterized by abstinence from alcohol: *a teetotal lifestyle.* ▷mid 19th cent.: emphatic extension of TOTAL, apparently first used by Richard Turner, a worker from Preston, England, in a speech (1833) urging total abstinence from all alcohol, rather than mere abstinence from spirits, advocated by some early temperance reformers. —**tee·to·tal·ism** /-ˌizəm/ *n.*

tee·to·tal·er /ˈtēˌtōtl-ər/ (*Brit.* **tee·to·tal·ler**) ▸*n.* a person who never drinks alcohol.

tee·to·tum /tēˈtōtəm/ ▸*n.* a small spinning top spun with the fingers, esp. one with four sides lettered to determine whether the spinner has won or lost. ▷early 18th cent. (as *T totum*): from *T* (representing *totum*, inscribed on the side of the toy) + Latin *totum* 'the whole' (stake). The letters on the sides (representing Latin words) were *T* (= *totum*), *A* (= *auferre* 'take away'), *D* (= *deponere* 'put down'), and *N* (= *nihil* 'nothing').

tee·vee /tēˈvē/ ▸*n.* nonstandard spelling of **TV**.

teff /tef/ ▸*n.* an African cereal that is cultivated almost exclusively in Ethiopia, used mainly to make flour. • *Eragrostis tef*, family Gramineae. ▷late 18th cent.: from Amharic *ṭēf.*

te·fil·lin /təˈfilin; -fēˈlēn/ ▸*plural n.* collective term for Jewish phylacteries. ▷from Aramaic *tĕpillīn* 'prayers.'

TEFL /ˈtefəl/ ▸*abbr.* teaching of English as a foreign language.

Tef·lon /ˈtefˌlän/ ▸*n.* trademark for POLYTETRAFLUOROETHYLENE.
▸*adj.* able to withstand criticism or attack with no apparent effect: *the head of the crime family is known as the Teflon Don because of his acquittals in three previous trials.* ▷1940s: from TETRA- 'four' + FLUORO- + *-on* on the pattern of words such as *nylon* and *rayon.*

teg /teg/ ▸*n.* a sheep in its second year. ▷early 16th cent. (as a contemptuous term for a woman; later applied specifically to a ewe in her second year): perhaps related to Swedish *tacka* 'ewe.'

teg·men /ˈtegmən/ ▸*n.* (*pl.* **-mi·na** /-mənə/) *Biology* a covering structure or roof of an organ, in particular: ■ *Entomology* a sclerotized forewing serving to cover the hind wing in grasshoppers and related insects. ■ *Botany* the delicate inner protective layer of a seed. ■ (also **tegmen tympani**) *Anatomy* a plate of thin bone forming the roof of the middle ear, a part of the temporal bone. ▷early 19th cent.: from Latin, 'covering,' from *tegere* 'to cover.'

teg·men·tum /tegˈmentəm/ ▸*n.* (*pl.* **-men·ta** /-ˈmentə/) *Anatomy* a region of gray matter on either side of the cerebral aqueduct in the midbrain. ▷mid 19th cent.: from Latin, variant of *tegumentum* 'tegument.' —**teg·men·tal** /tegˈmentl/ *adj.*

te·gu /tiˈgoo/ ▸*n.* (*pl.* same or **-gus**) a large stocky lizard that has dark skin with pale bands of small spots, native to the tropical forests of South America. • Genus *Tupinambis*, family Teiidae: several species, in particular the **common tegu** (*T. teguixin*). ▷1950s: abbreviation of *teguexin*, from Aztec *tecoixin* 'lizard.'

Te·gu·ci·gal·pa /təˌgoosəˈgalpə; -sēˈgäl-/ the capital of Honduras; pop. 670,000.

teg·u·la /ˈtegyələ/ ▸*n.* (*pl.* **-lae** /-ˌlē/) **1** *Entomology* a small scalelike sclerite covering the base of the forewing in many insects. **2** *Archaeology* a flat roof tile, used esp. in Roman roofs. ▷early 19th cent.: from Latin, literally 'tile,' from *tegere* 'to cover.'

teg·u·ment /ˈtegyəmənt/ ▸*n.* *chiefly Zoology* the integument of an organism, esp. a parasitic flatworm. ▷late Middle English (in the general sense 'a covering or coating'): from Latin *tegumentum*, from *tegere* 'to cover.' —**teg·u·men·tal** /ˌtegyəˈmentl/ *adj.* —**teg·u·men·ta·ry** /ˌtegyəˈmen(t)ərē/ *adj.*

Te·hach·a·pi Moun·tains /təˈhacHəˌpē/ a range that lies across California, north of the Transverse Ranges, sometimes considered the divider between north and south California.

Teh·ran /ˌte(ə)ˈran; -ˈrän/ (also **Tehe·ran**) the capital of Iran, in the foothills of the Elburz Mountains; pop. 6,750,000. It replaced Isfahan as the capital of Persia in 1788.

tei·cho·ic ac·id /tīˈkō-ik; tā-/ ▸*n.* *Biochemistry* a compound present in the walls of Gram-positive bacteria. It is a polymer of ribitol or glycerol phosphate. ▷1950s: *teichoic* from Greek *teikhos* 'wall' + -IC. —**tei·cho·ate** /-ˈkōˌāt/ *n.*

Teil·hard de Char·din /tāˈyär də sHärˈdaN/, Pierre (1881–1955), French Jesuit philosopher and paleontologist. His theory, which blends science and Christianity, is that man is evolving mentally and socially toward a perfect spiritual state. The Roman Catholic Church declared that his views were unorthodox.

te·in /ˈtā-in/ ▸*n.* (*pl.* same or **-ins**) a monetary unit of Kazakhstan, equal to one hundredth of a tenge.

Te·ja·no /təˈhänō/ ▸*n.* (*pl.* **-nos**) a Mexican-American inhabitant of southern Texas: [as *adj.*] *the Tejano upper classes.* ■ a style of folk or popular music originating among such people, with elements from Mexican-Spanish vocal traditions and Czech and German dance tunes and rhythms, traditionally played by small groups featuring accordion and guitar. ▷American Spanish, alteration of *Texano* 'Texan.'

Te·jo /ˈtāzHoo/ Portuguese name for **TAGUS**.

tek·kie ▸*n.* variant spelling of TECHIE.

tek·tite /ˈtekˌtīt/ ▸*n.* *Geology* a small black glassy object, many of which are found over certain areas of the earth's surface, believed to have been formed as molten debris in meteorite impacts and scattered widely through the air. ▷early 20th cent.: coined in German from Greek *tēktos* 'molten' (from *tēkein* 'melt') + -ITE[1].

tel. (also **Tel.**) ▸*abbr.* telephone.

tel·a·mon /ˈteləˌmän/ ▸*n.* (*pl.* **tel·a·mo·nes** /ˌteləˈmōnēz/) *Architecture* a male figure used as a pillar to support an entablature or other structure. ▷early 17th cent.: via Latin from Greek *telamōnes*, plural of *Telamōn*, the name of a mythical hero.

tel·an·gi·ec·ta·sia /telˌanjē-ekˈtāzHə/ (also **tel·an·gi·ec·ta·sis** /-ˈektəsis/) ▸*n.* *Medicine* a condition characterized by dilation of the capillaries, which causes them to appear as small red or purple clusters, often spidery in appearance, on the skin or the surface of an organ. ▷mid 19th cent.: modern Latin, from Greek *telos* 'end' + *angeion* 'vessel' + *ektasis* 'dilatation.' —**tel·an·gi·ec·tat·ic** /-ˈtatik/ *adj.*

Tel A·viv /ˌtel əˈvēv/ (also **Tel A·viv-Jaf·fa**) a city on the Mediterranean coast of Israel; pop. 355,000 (with Jaffa). It was founded as a suburb of Jaffa by Russian Jewish immigrants in 1909 and named Tel Aviv a year later.

tel·co /ˈtelkō/ ▸*n.* (*pl.* **-cos**) a telecommunications company. ▷late 20th cent.: abbreviation.

tele- ▸*comb. form* **1** to or at a distance: *telekinesis.* ■ used in names of instruments for operating over long distances: *telemeter.* [from Greek *tēle-* 'far off.'] **2** relating to television: *telecine.* [abbreviation.] **3** done by means of the telephone: *telemarketing.* [abbreviation.]

tel·e·cast /ˈteləˌkast/ ▸*n.* a television broadcast.
▸*v.* [*trans.*] (usu. **be telecast**) transmit by television: *the program will be telecast simultaneously to nearly 150 cities.* —**tel·e·cast·er** *n.*

tel·e·cin·e /ˈteləˌsinē/ ▸*n.* the broadcasting of a movie on television. ■ equipment used in such broadcasting.

tel·e·com /ˈteləˌkäm/ (*Brit.* also **tel·e·coms**) ▸*plural n.* [treated as *sing.*] telecommunications. ▷1960s: abbreviation.

tel·e·com·mu·ni·ca·tion /ˌteləkəˌmyooniˈkāsHən/ ▸*n.* communication over a distance by cable, telegraph, telephone, or broadcasting. ■ (**telecommunications**) [treated as *sing.*] the branch of technology concerned with such communication. ■ *formal* a message sent by such means. ▷1930s: from French *télécommunication*, from *télé-* 'at a distance' + *communication* 'communication.'

tel·e·com·mute /ˌteləkəˈmyoot/ ▸*v.* [*intrans.*] [usu. as *n.*] (**telecommuting**) work from home, communicating with the workplace using equipment such as telephones, fax machines, and modems. —**tel·e·com·mut·er** *n.*

tel·e·com·put·er /ˌteləkəmˈpyootər/ ▸*n.* a device that combines the capabilities of a computer with those of a television and a telephone, particularly for multimedia applications. —**tel·e·com·put·ing** /-tiNG/ *n.*

tel·e·con·fer·ence /ˈteləˌkänf(ə)rəns/ ▸*n.* a conference with participants in different locations linked by telecommunications devices.
▸*v.* [*intrans.*] participate in a teleconference: *he teleconferenced with everyone who had been in attendance.* —**tel·e·con·fer·enc·ing** /ˌteləˈkänf(ə)rənsiNG/ *n.*

tel·e·con·nec·tion /ˌteləkəˈneksHən/ ▸*n.* a causal connection or correlation between meteorological or other environmental phenomena that occur a long distance apart.

tel·e·con·vert·er /ˌteləkənˈvərtər/ ▸*n.* *Photography* a camera lens designed to be fitted in front of a standard lens to increase its effective focal length.

Tel·e·cop·i·er /ˈteləˌkäpēər/ ▸*n.* *trademark* a device that transmits and reproduces facsimile copies over a telephone line.

tel·e·du /ˈteləˌdoo/ ▸*n.* a badgerlike animal that has brownish-black fur with a white stripe along the top of the head and back, and anal glands that contain a foul-smelling liquid that can be squirted at an attacker. It is native to Sumatra, Java, and Borneo. • *Mydaus javanensis*, family Mustelidae. ▷early 19th cent.: from Javanese.

tel·e·fac·sim·i·le /ˌteləˌfakˈsiməlē/ ▸*n.* another term for FAX.

tel·e·fax /ˈteləˌfaks/ *trademark* ▸*n.* the transmission of documents by fax: *for more information contact us by telefax.* ■ a document sent in such a way. ■ a fax machine.
▸*v.* [*trans.*] [usu. as *adj.*] (**telefaxed**) send (a message) by fax: *telefaxed bills of lading.* ▷1940s: abbreviation of TELEFACSIMILE.

tel·e·film /ˈteləˌfilm/ ▸*n.* a movie made for or broadcast on television.

teleg. ▸*abbr.* ■ telegram. ■ telegraph. ■ telegraphy.

tel·e·gen·ic /ˌteləˈjenik/ ▸*adj.* having an appearance or manner that is appealing on television: *his telegenic charm appears to be his major asset.* ▷1930s (originally U.S.): from TELE- 'television' + -GENIC 'well suited to,' on the pattern of *photogenic.* —**tel·e·gen·i·cal·ly** /-ik(ə)lē/ *adv.*

tel·e·gram /ˈteləˌgram/ ▸*n.* a message sent by telegraph and then delivered in written or printed form. ▷mid 19th cent.: from TELE- 'at a distance' + -GRAM[1], on the pattern of *telegraph.*

tel·e·graph /ˈteləˌgraf/ ▸*n.* a system for transmitting messages from a distance along a wire, esp. one creating signals by making and breaking an electrical connection: *news came from the outside world* **by telegraph.** ■ a device for transmitting messages in such a way. ■ *historical* a system for the rapid transmission of messages by relayed visual signals: *the London-Portsmouth telegraph line.*
▸*v.* [*trans.*] send (someone) a message by telegraph: *I must go and telegraph Mom.* ■ send (a message) by telegraph: *she would rush off to telegraph news to her magazine.* ■ convey (an intentional or unconscious message), esp. with facial expression or body language: *a tiny movement of her arm telegraphed her intention to strike.* ▷early 18th cent.: from French *télégraphe*, from *télé-* 'at a distance' + *-graphe* (see -GRAPH). —**te·leg·ra·pher** /təˈlegrəfər/ *n.*

tel·e·graph·ese /ˌteləgraˈfēz/ ▸*n.* *informal* the terse, abbreviated style of language used in telegrams.

Tel·e·graph Hill a hill neighborhood in San Francisco in California, named for the signal stations that surmounted it in the 19th century.

tel·e·graph·ic /ˌteləˈgrafik/ ▸*adj.* **1** of or by telegraphs or telegrams: *the telegraphic transfer of the funds.* **2** (esp. of speech) omitting inessential words; concise. —**tel·e·graph·i·cal·ly** /-ik(ə)lē/ *adv.*

te·leg·ra·phist /təˈlegrəfist/ ▸*n.* a person skilled or employed in telegraphy. ■ a person whose job is to operate telegraph equipment.

tel·e·graph key ▸*n.* a button that is pressed to produce a signal when transmitting Morse code.

tel·e·graph plant ▸*n.* a tropical Asian plant of the pea family whose leaves have a spontaneous jerking motion. • *Codariocalyx motorius* (formerly *Desmodium gyrans*), family Leguminosae.

te·leg·ra·phy /təˈlegrəfē/ ▸*n.* the science or practice of using or constructing communications systems for the transmission or reproduction of information.

Tel·e·gu ▸*n.* variant spelling of **TELUGU**.

tel·e·im·mer·sion /ˌtelə iˈmərzHən; -sHən/ ▸*n.* two-way remote communication in which each party gets an audio and three-dimensional visual representation of the other, via high-speed data exchange: *teleimmersion allows users to climb into a computer screen.*

tel·e·ki·ne·sis /ˌteləkiˈnēsis/ ▸*n.* the supposed ability to move objects at a distance by mental power or other nonphysical means. ▷late 19th cent.: from TELE- 'at a distance' + Greek *kinēsis* 'motion' (from *kinein* 'to move'). —**tel·e·ki·net·ic** /-ˈnetik/ *adj.*

Te·lem·a·chus /tə'leməkəs/ *Greek Mythology* the son of Odysseus and Penelope.

Te·le·mann /'tālə,män; 'tel-/, Georg Philipp (1681–1767), German composer and organist. His works include church music, oratorios, and a great deal of instrumental music.

tel·e·mark /'telə,märk/ *Skiing* ▶*n.* a turn in downhill skiing or a landing style in ski jumping with one ski advanced and the knees bent.
▶*v.* [*intrans.*] perform such a turn while skiing: *they went telemarking silently through the trees.* ▷early 20th cent.: named after *Telemark*, the district in Norway, where it originated.

tel·e·mar·ket·ing /,telə'märkitiNG/ ▶*n.* the marketing of goods or services by means of telephone calls, typically unsolicited, to potential customers. **—tel·e·mar·ket·er** /-,märkitər/ *n.*

tel·e·mat·ics /,telə'matiks/ ▶*plural n.* [treated as *sing.*] the branch of information technology that deals with the long-distance transmission of computerized information. ▷1970s: blend of TELECOMMUNICATION and INFORMATICS. **—tel·e·mat·ic** *adj.*

tel·e·med·i·cine /'telə,medisin/ ▶*n.* the remote diagnosis and treatment of patients by means of telecommunications technology.

te·lem·e·ter ▶*n.* /tə'lemitər; 'telə,mētər/ an apparatus for recording the readings of an instrument and transmitting them by radio.
▶*v.* /'telə,mētər/ [*trans.*] transmit (readings) to a distant receiving set or station. **—tel·e·met·ric** /,telə'metrik/ *adj.* **—te·lem·e·try** /tə'lemitrē/ *n.*

tel·en·ceph·a·lon /,telən'sefəlän; -lən/ ▶*n.* *Anatomy* the most highly developed and anterior part of the forebrain, consisting chiefly of the cerebral hemispheres. Compare with DIENCEPHALON. ▷late 19th cent.: from TELE- 'far' + ENCEPHALON.

tel·e·no·vel·a /,telənō'velə/ ▶*n.* (in Latin America) a television soap opera. Also called NOVELA. ▷Spanish.

tel·e·o·log·i·cal ar·gu·ment /,telēə'läjikəl; ,tēlē- / ▶*n.* *Philosophy* the argument for the existence of God from the evidence of order, and hence design, in nature. Compare with ARGUMENT FROM DESIGN, COSMOLOGICAL ARGUMENT, and ONTOLOGICAL ARGUMENT.

tel·e·ol·o·gy /,telē'äləjē; ,tēlē-/ ▶*n.* (*pl.* **-gies**) *Philosophy* the explanation of phenomena by the purpose they serve rather than by postulated causes. ■ *Theology* the doctrine of design and purpose in the material world. ▷mid 18th cent. (denoting the branch of philosophy that deals with ends or final causes): from modern Latin *teleologia*, from Greek *telos* 'end' + *-logia* (see -LOGY). **—tel·e·o·log·ic** /-ə'läjik/ *adj.* **—tel·e·o·log·i·cal** /-ə'läjikəl/ *adj.* **—tel·e·o·log·i·cal·ly** /-ə'läjik(ə)lē/ *adv.* **—tel·e·ol·o·gism** /-,jizəm/ *n.* **—tel·e·ol·o·gist** /-jist/ *n.*

tel·e·op·er·a·tion /,telə,äpə'rāsHən/ ▶*n.* the electronic remote control of machines. **—tel·e·op·er·ate** /-'äpə,rāt/ *v.*

tel·e·op·er·a·tor /,telə'äpə,rātər/ ▶*n.* a machine operated by remote control so as to imitate the movements of its operator.

tel·e·ost /'telē,äst; 'tēlē-/ ▶*n.* *Zoology* a fish of a large group that comprises all ray-finned fishes apart from the primitive bichirs, sturgeons, paddlefishes, freshwater garfishes, and bowfins. • Division (or infraclass) Teleostei, subclass Actinopterygii: many orders. ▷mid 19th cent.: from Greek *teleos* 'complete' + *osteon* 'bone.'

tel·e·path /'teləpaTH/ ▶*n.* a person with the ability to communicate using telepathy. ▷late 19th cent. (as a verb, meaning 'to use telepathy'): back-formation from TELEPATHY.

te·lep·a·thy /tə'lepəTHē/ ▶*n.* the supposed communication of thoughts or ideas by means other than the known senses. **—tel·e·path·ic** /,telə'paTHik/ *adj.* **—tel·e·path·i·cal·ly** /,telə'paTHik(ə)lē/ *adv.* **—te·lep·a·thist** /-THist/ *n.*

tel·e·phone /'telə,fōn/ ▶*n.* **1** a system that converts acoustic vibrations to electrical signals in order to transmit sound, typically voices, over a distance using wire or radio. ■ an instrument used as part of such a system, typically a single unit including a handset with a transmitting microphone and a set of numbered buttons by which a connection can be made to another such instrument. **2** a game in which a message is distorted by being passed around in a whisper. Also called CHINESE WHISPERS.
▶*v.* [*trans.*] call or speak to (someone) using the telephone: *he had just finished telephoning his wife.* ■ [*intrans.*] make a telephone call: *she* **telephoned for** *help.* ■ send (a message) by telephone: *Barbara had telephoned the news.* **—tel·e·phon·er** *n.* **—tel·e·phon·ic** /,telə'fänik/ *adj.* **—tel·e·phon·i·cal·ly** /,telə'fänik(ə)lē/ *adv.*

tel·e·phone bank·ing ▶*n.* a method of banking in which the customer conducts transactions by telephone, typically by means of a computerized system using touch-tone dialing or voice-recognition technology.

tel·e·phone book ▶*n.* a telephone directory.

tel·e·phone booth (*Brit.* also **tel·e·phone box**) ▶*n.* a public booth or enclosure housing a pay phone.

tel·e·phone call ▶*n.* a communication or conversation by telephone.

tel·e·phone card ▶*n.* another term for CALLING CARD (sense 2).

tel·e·phone di·rec·to·ry ▶*n.* a book listing the names, addresses, and telephone numbers of the people in a particular area.

tel·e·phone ex·change ▶*n.* a set of equipment that connects telephone lines during a call.

tel·e·phone num·ber ▶*n.* a number assigned to a particular telephone and used in making connections to it.

tel·e·phone op·er·a·tor ▶*n.* a person who works at the switchboard of a telephone exchange.

tel·e·phone pole /'telə,fōn pōl/ ▶*n.* a tall pole used to carry telephone wires and other utility lines above the ground.

tel·e·phone tag ▶*n.* *informal* the action of two people repeatedly trying unsuccessfully to reach each other by telephone, usually by leaving messages.

te·leph·o·nist /'telə,fōnist; tə'lefə-/ ▶*n.* *Brit.* an operator of a switchboard.

te·leph·o·ny /tə'lefənē; 'telə,fōnē/ ▶*n.* the working or use of telephones.

tel·e·pho·to /'telə,fōtō/ (also **tel·e·pho·to lens**) ▶*n.* (*pl.* **-tos**) a lens with a longer focal length than standard, giving a narrow field of view and a magnified image.

tel·e·pic /'telə,pik/ ▶*n.* *informal* a movie made for television. ▷blend of *television* and *epic.*

tel·e·play /'telə,plā/ ▶*n.* a play written or adapted for television.

tel·e·port /'telə,pôrt/ ▶*v.* (esp. in science fiction) transport or be transported across space and distance instantly.
▶*n.* **1** a center providing interconnections between different forms of telecommunications, esp. one that links satellites to ground-based communications. [1980s: originally the name of such a center in New York.] **2** an act of teleporting. ▷1950s: back-formation from *teleportation* (1930s), from TELE- 'at a distance' + a shortened form of TRANSPORTATION. **—tel·e·por·ta·tion** /,telə,pôr'tāsHən/ *n.*

tel·e·pres·ence /'telə,prezəns/ ▶*n.* the use of virtual reality technology, esp. for remote control of machinery or for apparent participation in distant events. ■ a sensation of being elsewhere, created in such a way.

tel·e·print·er /'telə,prin(t)ər/ ▶*n.* a device for transmitting telegraph messages as they are keyed, and for printing messages received.

Tel·e·Promp·Ter /'telə,präm(p)tər/ ▶*n.* *trademark* a device used in television and moviemaking to project a speaker's script out of sight of the audience.

tel·e·sales /'telə,sālz/ ▶*plural n.* the selling of goods or services over the telephone: *sales personnel work on fully automated telesales systems.*

tel·e·scope /'telə,skōp/ ▶*n.* an optical instrument designed to make distant objects appear nearer, containing an arrangement of lenses, or of curved mirrors and lenses, by which rays of light are collected and focused and the resulting image magnified. ■ short for RADIO TELESCOPE.
▶*v.* [*trans.*] cause (an object made of concentric tubular parts) to slide into itself, so that it becomes smaller. ■ [*intrans.*] be capable of sliding together in this way: *five steel sections that telescope into one another.* ■ crush (a vehicle) by the force of an impact. ■ *figurative* condense or conflate so as to occupy less space or time: *a way of telescoping many events into a relatively brief period.* ▷mid 17th cent.: from Italian *telescopio* or modern Latin *telescopium*, from *tele-* 'at a distance' + *-scopium* (see -SCOPE).

telescope

tel·e·scop·ic /,telə'skäpik/ ▶*adj.* **1** of, relating to, or made with a telescope. ■ capable of viewing and magnifying distant objects. ■ *Astronomy* visible only through a telescope. **2** having or consisting of concentric tubular sections designed to slide into one another: *a telescopic umbrella.* **—tel·e·scop·i·cal·ly** /-ik(ə)lē/ *adv.*

tel·e·scop·ic sight ▶*n.* a small telescope used for sighting, typically mounted on a rifle.

tel·e·shop·ping /'telə,sHäpiNG/ ▶*n.* the ordering of goods by customers using a telephone or direct computer link.

tel·e·the·sia /,teləs'THēzH(ē)ə/ (*Brit.* **tel·aes·the·sia**) ▶*n.* the supposed perception of distant occurrences or objects otherwise than by the recognized senses. ▷late 19th cent.: from TELE- + Greek *aisthēsis* 'perception.' **—tel·es·thet·ic** /-'THetik/ *adj.*

tel·e·sur·ger·y /'telə,sərjərē/ ▶*n.* surgery performed by a doctor considerably distant from the patient, using medical robotics and multimedia image communication. **—tel·e·sur·geon** /'telə,sərjən/ *n.*

tel·e·text /'telə,tekst/ ▶*n.* a news and information service in the form of text and graphics, transmitted using the spare capacity of existing television channels to televisions with appropriate receivers.

tel·e·thon /'telə,THän/ ▶*n.* a very long television program, typically one broadcast to raise money for a charity. ▷1940s (originally U.S.): from TELE- 'at a distance' + *-thon* on the pattern of *marathon.*

Tel·e·type /'telə,tīp/ (often **tel·e·type**) ▶*n.* *trademark* a kind of teleprinter. ■ a message received and printed by a teleprinter.
▶*v.* [*trans.*] send (a message) by means of a teleprinter.

tel·e·type·writ·er /,telə'tīp,rītər/ ▶*n.* a teleprinter.

tel·e·van·ge·list /,telə'vanjəlist/ ▶*n.* an evangelical preacher who appears regularly on television to preach and appeal for funds. **—tel·e·van·gel·i·cal** /,telə,van'jelikəl/ *adj.* **—tel·e·van·ge·lism** /-,lizəm/ *n.*

tel·e·view·er /'telə,vyo͞oər/ ▶*n.* a person who watches television. **—tel·e·view·ing** /-,vyo͞o-iNG/ *n.* & *adj.*

tel·e·vise /'telə,vīz/ ▶*v.* [*trans.*] [usu. as *adj.*] (**televised**) transmit by television: *a live televised debate between the party leaders.* ▷1920s: back-formation from TELEVISION. **—tel·e·vis·a·ble** *adj.*

tel·e·vi·sion /'telə,vizHən/ ▶*n.* **1** a system for transmitting visual images and sound that are reproduced on screens, chiefly used to broadcast programs for entertainment, information, and education. ■ the activity, profession, or medium of broadcasting on television: *neither of my children showed the merest inclination to follow me into television* | [as *adj.*] *television news.* ■ television programs: *Dan was sitting on the sofa watching television.* **2** (also **tel·e·vi·sion set**) a box-shaped device that receives television signals and reproduces them on a screen. ▷early 20th cent.: from TELE- 'at a distance' + VISION.
▶*PHRASE* □ **on (the) television** being broadcast by television; appearing in a television program: *Norman was on television yesterday.*

tel·e·vi·sion·ar·y /,telə'vizHə,nerē/ ▶*n.* (*pl.* **-ar·ies**) *informal, often humorous* an enthusiast for television.
▶*adj.* of, relating to, or induced by television: *televisionary indoctrination in Luanda.*

tel·e·vi·sion sta·tion ▶*n.* an organization transmitting television programs.

tel·e·vis·u·al /,telə'vizHo͞oəl/ ▶*adj.* relating to or suitable for television: *the world of televisual images.* **—tel·e·vi·su·al·ly** *adv.*

tel·e·work /'telə,wərk/ ▶*v.* another term for TELECOMMUTE.
▶*n.* work performed primarily on computers linked to other locations, esp. from home or a remote location. **—tel·e·work·er** *n.* **—tel·e·work·ing** *n.*

tel·ex /'teleks/ ▶*n.* an international system of telegraphy with printed messages transmitted and received by teleprinters using the public telecommunications network. ■ a device used for this. ■ a message sent by this system.
▶*v.* [*trans.*] communicate with (someone) by telex.

T

■ send (a message) by telex. ▷1930s: blend of TELEPRINTER and EXCHANGE.

Tel·ford[1] /ˈtelfərd/ a town in west central England; pop. 115,000.

Tel·ford[2], Thomas (1757–1834), Scottish civil engineer. He built hundreds of miles of roads, more than a thousand bridges, and some canals, including the Caledonian Canal across Scotland that opened in 1822.

tel·ic /ˈtelik; ˈtē-/ ▸*adj.* (of an action or attitude) directed or tending to a definite end. ■ *Linguistics* (of a verb, conjunction, or clause) expressing goal, result, or purpose. ▷mid 19th cent.: from Greek *telikos* 'final,' from *telos* 'end.' **—te·lic·i·ty** /təˈlisitē/ *n.*

Tell /tel/, William, a legendary hero of the liberation of Switzerland from Austrian oppression. He was required to hit with an arrow an apple placed on the head of his son, which he did successfully. The events are placed in the 14th century, but there is no evidence for a historical person of this name, and similar legends are of widespread occurrence.

tell[1] /tel/ ▸*v.* (*past* **told** /tōld/) **1** [*reporting verb*] communicate information, facts, or news to someone in spoken or written words: [*trans.*] *I told her you were coming* | [*trans.*] *"We have nothing in common," she told him* | [*trans.*] *he's telling the truth* | [with *two objs.*] *we must be told the facts.* ■ [*trans.*] order, instruct, or advise (someone) to do something: *tell him to go away.* ■ [*trans.*] narrate or relate (a tale or story). ■ [*trans.*] reveal (information) to someone in a nonverbal way: *the figures tell a different story* | [with *two objs.*] *the smile on her face told him everything.* ■ [*intrans.*] divulge confidential or private information: *promise you won't tell.* ■ [*intrans.*] (**tell on**) *informal* inform someone of the misdemeanors of: *friends don't tell on each other.* **2** [with *clause*] decide or determine correctly or with certainty: *you can tell they're in love.* ■ [*trans.*] distinguish (one person or thing) from another; perceive (the difference) between one person or thing and another: *I can't tell the difference between margarine and butter.* **3** [*intrans.*] (of an experience or period of time) have a noticeable, typically harmful, effect on someone: *the strain of supporting the family was beginning to tell on him.* ■ (of a particular factor) play a part in the success or otherwise of someone or something: *lack of fitness told against him on his first run of the season.* **4** [*trans.*] *archaic* count (the members of a series or group): *the shepherd had told all his sheep.*

▸*phrasal v.* □ **tell someone off** *informal* reprimand or scold someone: *my parents told me off for coming home late.*

▸*n.* (esp. in poker) an unconscious behavior that is thought to betray an attempted deception. ▷Old English *tellan* 'relate, count, estimate,' of Germanic origin; related to German *zählen* 'reckon, count,' *erzählen* 'recount, relate,' also to TALE. **—tell·a·ble** *adj.*

▸*PHRASES* □ **as far as one can tell** judging from the available information. □ **I tell you** (or **I can tell you**) used to emphasize a statement: *that took me by surprise, I can tell you!* □ **I** (or **I'll**) **tell you what** used to introduce a suggestion: *I tell you what, why don't we meet for lunch tomorrow?* □ **I told you** (**so**) used as a way of pointing out that one's warnings, although ignored, have been proved to be well founded. □ **tell one's beads** see BEAD. □ **tell someone's fortune** see FORTUNE. □ **tell it like it is** *informal* describe the facts of a situation no matter how unpleasant they may be. □ **tell its own tale** (or **story**) be significant or revealing, without any further explanation or comment being necessary: *the worried expression on Helen's face told its own tale.* □ **tell me about it** *informal* used as an ironic acknowledgment of one's familiarity with a difficult or unpleasant situation or experience described by someone else. □ **tell me another** *informal* used as an expression of disbelief or incredulity. □ **tell something a mile off** see MILE. □ **tell tales** make known or gossip about another person's secrets, wrongdoings, or faults. □ **tell it to the marines** see MARINE. □ **tell time** be able to ascertain the time from reading the face of a clock or watch. □ **tell someone where to get off** (or **where they get off**) *informal* angrily dismiss or rebuke someone. □ **tell someone where to put** (or **what to do with**) **something** *informal* angrily or emphatically reject something: *I told him what he could do with his diamond.* □ **that would be telling** *informal* used to convey that one is not prepared to divulge secret or confidential information. □ **there is no telling** used to convey the impossibility of knowing what has happened or will happen: *there's no telling how she will react.* □ **to tell** (**you**) **the truth** used as a preface to a confession or admission of something. □ **you're telling me!** *informal* used to emphasize that one is already well aware of something or in complete agreement with a statement.

tell[2] ▸*n. Archaeology* (in the Middle East) an artificial mound formed by the accumulated remains of ancient settlements. ▷mid 19th cent.: from Arabic *tall* 'hillock.'

tell-all ▸*adj.* revealing private or salacious details: *a tell-all article in the tabloids.*

▸*n.* a biography or memoir that reveals intimate details about its subject.

Tell·er /ˈtelər/, Edward, (1908–2003), U.S. physicist, born in Hungary. He worked on the first atomic reactor and the first atom bombs, and work under his guidance led to the detonation of the first hydrogen bomb in 1952.

tell·er /ˈtelər/ ▸*n.* **1** a person employed to deal with customers' transactions in a bank. ■ an automated teller machine. **2** a person who tells something: *a foul-mouthed teller of lies.* **3** a person appointed to count votes, esp. in a legislature. **—tell·er·ship** /-ˌSHip/ *n.* (*chiefly historical*) (in sense 1).

tell·ing /ˈteliNG/ ▸*adj.* having a striking or revealing effect; significant: *a telling argument against this theory.* **—tell·ing·ly** *adv.*

tell·tale /ˈtelˌtāl/ ▸*adj.* [*attrib.*] revealing, indicating, or betraying something: *the telltale bulge of a concealed weapon.*

▸*n.* **1** a person, esp. a child, who reports others' wrongdoings or reveals their secrets. **2** a device or object that automatically gives a visual indication of the state or presence of something. ■ (on a sailboat) a piece of string or fabric that shows the direction and force of the wind.

tel·lu·ri·an /təˈlo͝orēən/ ▸*adj. formal* or *poetic/literary* of or inhabiting the earth.

▸*n. formal* or *poetic/literary* an inhabitant of the earth. ▷mid 19th cent.: from Latin *tellus, tellur-* 'earth' + -IAN.

tel·lu·ric /təˈlo͝orik/ ▸*adj.* of the earth as a planet. ■ of the soil. ▷mid 19th cent.: from Latin *tellus, tellur-* 'earth' + -IC.

tel·lu·ric ac·id ▸*n. Chemistry* a crystalline acid made by oxidizing tellurium dioxide. • Chem. formula: $Te(OH)_6$. **—tel·lu·rate** /ˈtelyəˌrāt/ *n.*

Tel·lu·ride /ˈtelyəˌrīd/ a resort town in southwestern Colorado, a former mining center, now a popular ski resort; pop. 1,309.

tel·lu·ride ▸*n. Chemistry* a compound of tellurium with another more electropositive element or a radical.

tel·lu·rite /ˈtelyəˌrīt/ ▸*n. Chemistry* a salt of the anion TeO_3^{2-}.

tel·lu·ri·um /təˈlo͝orēəm/ ▸*n.* the chemical element of atomic number 52, a brittle, shiny, silvery-white semimetal resembling selenium and occurring mainly in small amounts in metallic sulfide ores. It is a semiconductor and is used in some electrical devices and in specialized alloys. (Symbol: **Te**) ▷early 19th cent.: modern Latin, from Latin *tellus, tellur-* 'earth,' probably named in contrast to URANIUM. **—tel·lu·ride** /ˈtelyəˌrīd/ *n.*

tel·ly /ˈtelē/ ▸*n.* (*pl.* **-lies**) *Brit.* informal term for TELEVISION.

tel·net /ˈtelˌnet/ *Computing* ▸*n.* a network protocol that allows a user on one computer to log on to another computer that is part of the same network. ■ a program that establishes a connection from one computer to another by means of such a protocol. ■ a link established in such a way.

▸*v.* (**-net·ted, -net·ting**) [*intrans.*] *informal* log on to a remote computer using a telnet program. ▷1970s: blend of TELECOMMUNICATION and NETWORK. **—tel·net·ta·ble** *adj.*

tel·o·lec·i·thal /ˌteləˈlesəTHəl; ˌtēlō-/ ▸*adj. Zoology* (of an egg or egg cell) having a large yolk situated at or near one end. ▷late 19th cent.: from Greek *telos* 'end' + *lekithos* 'egg yolk' + -AL.

te·lom·er·ase /təˈläməˌrās; təˈlō; -ˌrāz/ ▸*n.* an enzyme that adds nucleotides to telomeres, especially in cancer cells.

tel·o·mere /ˈtēləˌmi(ə)r; ˈtelə-/ ▸*n. Genetics* a compound structure at the end of a chromosome. ▷1940s: from Greek *telos* 'end' + *meros* 'part.' **—tel·o·mer·ic** /ˌtēləˈmerik; ˌtelə-/ *adj.*

tel·o·phase /ˈtēləˌfāz; ˈtelə-/ ▸*n. Biology* the final phase of cell division, between anaphase and interphase, in which the chromatids or chromosomes move to opposite ends of the cell and two nuclei are formed. ▷late 19th cent.: from Greek *telos* 'end' + PHASE.

te·los /ˈteläs; ˈtē-/ ▸*n.* (*pl.* **te·loi** /ˈteloi; ˈtēloi/) *chiefly Philosophy* or *poetic/literary* an ultimate object or aim. ▷Greek, literally 'end.'

tel·son /ˈtelsən/ ▸*n. Zoology* the last segment in the abdomen, or a terminal appendage to it, in crustaceans, chelicerates, and embryonic insects. ▷mid 19th cent.: from Greek, literally 'limit.'

Tel·star /ˈtelˌstär/ the first of the active communications satellites (i.e., both receiving and retransmitting signals, not merely reflecting signals from the earth). It was launched by the U.S. in 1962 and used in the transmission of television broadcasting and telephone communication.

Tel·u·gu /ˈteləˌgo͞o/ (also **Tel·e·gu**) ▸*n.* (*pl.* same or **-gus**) **1** a member of a people of southeastern India. **2** the Dravidian language of this people, spoken mainly in the state of Andhra Pradesh.

▸*adj.* of or relating to this people or their language. ▷from the name in Telugu, *teluṅgu.*

tem·blor /ˈtemblər; -ˌblôr/ ▸*n.* an earthquake. ▷late 19th cent.: from American Spanish.

tem·er·ar·i·ous /ˌteməˈre(ə)rēəs/ ▸*adj. poetic/literary* reckless; rash. ▷mid 16th cent.: from Latin *temerarius* (from *temere* 'rashly') + -OUS.

te·mer·i·ty /təˈmeritē/ ▸*n.* excessive confidence or boldness; audacity: *no one had the temerity to question his conclusions.* ▷late Middle English: from Latin *temeritas*, from *temere* 'rashly.'

THE RIGHT WORD **audacity, effrontery, foolhardiness, gall, impetuosity, rashness, temerity**

The line that divides boldness from foolishness or stupidity is often a fine one.

Someone who rushes hastily into a situation without thinking about the consequences might be accused of **rashness**, while **temerity** implies exposing oneself needlessly to danger while failing to estimate one's chances of success (*she had the temerity to criticize her teacher in front of the class*).

Audacity describes a different kind of boldness, one that disregards moral standards or social conventions (*he had the audacity to ask her if she would mind paying for the trip*).

Someone who behaves with **foolhardiness** is reckless or downright foolish (*climbing the mountain after dark was foolhardiness and everyone knew it*), while **impetuosity** describes an eager impulsiveness or behavior that is sudden, rash, and sometimes violent (*his impetuosity had landed him in trouble before*).

Gall and **effrontery** are always derogatory terms. *Effrontery* is a more formal word for the flagrant disregard of the rules of propriety and courtesy (*she had the effrontery to call the president by his first name*), while *gall* is more colloquial and suggests outright insolence (*he was the only one with enough gall to tell the boss off*).

Tem·es·vár /ˈtemeSHˌvär/ Hungarian name for TIMIŞOARA.

Tem·ne /ˈtemnē/ ▸*n.* (*pl.* same or **-nes**) **1** a member of a people of Sierra Leone. **2** the Niger–Congo language of this people, the main language of Sierra Leone.

▸*adj.* of or relating to this people or their language. ▷the name in Temne.

tem·no·spon·dyl /ˌtemnōˈspändl/ ▸*n.* an extinct amphibian of a large group that was dominant from the Carboniferous to the Triassic. • Order (or grade) Temnospondyli: many families. ▷early 20th cent.: from modern Latin *Temnospondyli* (plural), from Greek *temnein* 'to cut' + *spondulos* 'vertebra.'

temp[1] /temp/ *informal* ▸*n.* a temporary employee, typically an office worker who finds employment through an agency.

▸*v.* [*intrans.*] work as a temporary employee. ▷1930s: abbreviation.

temp[2] ▸*abbr.* temperature.

temp. ▸*abbr.* in or from the time of: *a Roman aqueduct temp. Augustus.* ▷from Latin *tempore*, ablative of *tempus* 'time.'

Tem·pe /temˈpē; ˈtempē/ a city in south central Arizona, east of Phoenix, home to Arizona State University; pop. 158,625.

tem·peh /ˈtempā/ ▸*n.* an Indonesian dish made by deep-frying fermented soybeans. ▷from Indonesian *tempe.*

tem·per /ˈtempər/ ▸*n.* **1** [in *sing.*] a person's state of mind seen in terms of their being angry or calm: *he rushed out in a very bad temper.* ■ a tendency to become angry easily: *I know my temper gets the better of* *me at times.* ■ an angry state of mind: *Drew had walked out **in a temper** | I only said it **in a fit of temper**.* ■ a character or mode of thought: *the temper of the late sixties.* **2** the degree of hardness and elasticity in steel or other metal: *the blade rapidly heats up and the metal loses its temper.*

▸*v.* [*trans.*] **1** improve the hardness and elasticity of (steel or other metal) by reheating and then cooling it. ■ improve the consistency or resiliency of (a substance) by heating it or adding particular substances to it. **2** (often **be tempered with**) serve as a neutralizing or counterbalancing force to (something): *their idealism is tempered with realism.* See note at ALLEVIATE. **3** tune (a piano or other instrument) so as to adjust the note intervals correctly. ▷Old English *temprian* 'bring something into the required condition by mixing it with something else,' from Latin *temperare* 'mingle, restrain oneself.' Sense development was probably influenced by Old French *temprer* 'to temper, moderate.' The noun originally denoted a proportionate mixture of elements or qualities, also the combination of the four bodily humors, believed in medieval times to be the basis of temperament, hence sense 1 (late Middle English). Compare with TEMPERAMENT. **—tem·per·er** *n.*

▸*PHRASES* □ **keep** (or **lose**) **one's temper** refrain (or fail to refrain) from becoming angry. □ **out of temper** in an irritable mood.

tem·per·a /'tempərə/ ▸*n.* a method of painting with pigments dispersed in an emulsion miscible with water, typically egg yolk. The method was used in Europe for fine painting, mainly on wood panels, from the 12th or early 13th century until the 15th, when it began to give way to oils. ■ emulsion used in this method of painting. ▷mid 19th cent.: from Italian, in the phrase *pingere a tempera* 'paint in distemper.'

tem·per·a·ment /'temp(ə)rəmənt/ ▸*n.* **1** a person's or animal's nature, esp. as it permanently affects their behavior: *she had an artistic temperament.* ■ the tendency to behave angrily or emotionally: *he had begun to show signs of temperament.* **2** the adjustment of intervals in tuning a piano or other musical instrument so as to fit the scale for use in different keys; in **equal temperament**, the octave consists of twelve equal semitones. ▷late Middle English: from Latin *temperamentum* 'correct mixture,' from *temperare* 'mingle.' In early use the word was synonymous with the noun TEMPER.

tem·per·a·men·tal /ˌtemp(ə)rə'mentl/ ▸*adj.* **1** (of a person) liable to unreasonable changes of mood. **2** of or relating to a person's temperament: *they were firm friends in spite of temperamental differences.* **—tem·per·a·men·tal·ly** *adv.*

tem·per·ance /'temp(ə)rəns/ ▸*n.* abstinence from alcoholic drink: [as *adj.*] *the temperance movement.* See note at ABSTINENCE. ■ moderation or self-restraint, esp. in eating and drinking. ▷Middle English: from Anglo-Norman French *temperaunce*, from Latin *temperantia* 'moderation,' from *temperare* 'restrain.'

tem·per·ate /'temp(ə)rət/ ▸*adj.* **1** of, relating to, or denoting a region or climate characterized by mild temperatures. **2** showing moderation or self-restraint: *Charles was temperate in his consumption of both food and drink.* ▷late Middle English (in the sense 'not affected by passion or emotion'): from Latin *temperatus* 'mingled, restrained,' from the verb *temperare.* **—tem·per·ate·ly** *adv.* **—tem·per·ate·ness** *n.*

tem·per·ate zone (also **Tem·per·ate Zone**) ▸*n.* each of the two belts of latitude between the torrid zone and the northern and southern frigid zones.

tem·per·a·ture /'temp(ə)rəCHər; -ˌCHŏŏr/ ▸*n.* the degree or intensity of heat present in a substance or object, esp. as expressed according to a comparative scale and shown by a thermometer or perceived by touch. ■ *Medicine* the degree of internal heat of a person's body: *I'll **take her temperature**.* ■ *informal* a body temperature above the normal; fever: *he was **running a temperature**.* ■ the degree of excitement or tension in a discussion or confrontation: *the temperature of the debate was lower than before.* ▷late Middle English: from French *température* or Latin *temperatura*, from *temperare* 'restrain.' The word originally denoted the state of being tempered or mixed, later becoming synonymous with TEMPERAMENT. The modern sense dates from the late 17th cent.

tem·per·a·ture in·ver·sion ▸*n.* see INVERSION (sense 2).

-tempered ▸*comb. form* having a specified temper or disposition: *ill-tempered.*

-temperedly ▸*comb. form* in adverbs corresponding to adjectives ending in *-tempered* (such as *bad-temperedly* corresponding to *bad-tempered*).

-temperedness ▸*comb. form* in nouns corresponding to adjectives ending in *-tempered* (such as *bad-temperedness* corresponding to *bad-tempered*).

tem·pest /'tempist/ ▸*n.* a violent windy storm. ▷Middle English: from Old French *tempeste*, from Latin *tempestas* 'season, weather, storm,' from *tempus* 'time, season.'

▸*PHRASE* □ **a tempest in a teapot** great anger or excitement about a trivial matter.

tem·pes·tu·ous /tem'pesCHōōəs/ ▸*adj.* **1** characterized by strong and turbulent or conflicting emotion: *he had a reckless and tempestuous streak.* **2** very stormy: *a tempestuous wind.* ▷late Middle English: from late Latin *tempestuosus*, from Latin *tempestas* (see TEMPEST). **—tem·pes·tu·ous·ly** *adv.* **—tem·pes·tu·ous·ness** *n.*

tem·pi /'tempē/ ▸ plural form of TEMPO.

Tem·plar /'templər/ ▸*n. historical* a member of the Knights Templars. ▷Middle English: from Old French *templier*, from medieval Latin *templarius*, from Latin *templum* (see TEMPLE[1]).

tem·plate /'templət/ ▸*n.* **1** a shaped piece of metal, wood, card, plastic, or other material used as a pattern for processes such as painting, cutting out, shaping, or drilling. ■ *figurative* something that serves as a model for others to copy: *the plant was to serve as the template for change throughout the company.* ■ *Computing* a preset format for a document or file, used so that the format does not have to be recreated each time it is used: *a memo template.* ■ *Computing* a guide that fits over all or part of a computer keyboard to describe the functions of each key for a particular software application. ■ *Biochemistry* a nucleic acid molecule that acts as a pattern for the sequence of assembly of a protein, nucleic acid, or other large molecule. **2** a timber or plate used to distribute the weight in a wall or under a support. ▷late 17th cent. (as *templet*): probably from TEMPLE[3] + -ET[1]. The change in the ending in the 19th cent. was due to association with PLATE.

Tem·ple[1] /'tempəl/ an industrial and commercial city in central Texas; pop. 46,109.

Tem·ple[2], Shirley (1928–), U.S. child star; married name *Shirley Temple Black.* In the 1930s, she appeared in movies such as *The Little Colonel* (1935) and *Rebecca of Sunnybrook Farm* (1938). She later became active in Republican politics and represented the U.S. at the UN and as an ambassador.

Shirley Temple

tem·ple[1] /'tempəl/ ▸*n.* a building devoted to the worship, or regarded as the dwelling place, of a god or gods or other objects of religious reverence. ■ (**the Temple**) either of two successive religious buildings of the Jews in Jerusalem. The first (957–586 BC) was built by Solomon and destroyed by Nebuchadnezzar; it contained the Ark of the Covenant. The second (515 BC–AD 70) was enlarged by Herod the Great from 20 BC and destroyed by the Romans during a Jewish revolt; all that remains is the Western Wall. ■ (**the Temple**) a group of buildings in Fleet Street in London that stand on land formerly occupied by the headquarters of the Knights Templars. Located there are the Inner and Outer Temple, two of the Inns of Court. ■ a synagogue. ■ a place of Christian public worship, esp. a Protestant church in France. ▷Old English *templ, tempel*, reinforced in Middle English by Old French *temple*, both from Latin *templum* 'open or consecrated space.'

tem·ple[2] ▸*n.* the flat part of either side of the head between the forehead and the ear. ▷Middle English: from Old French, from an alteration of Latin *tempora*, plural of *tempus* 'temple of the head.'

tem·ple[3] ▸*n.* a device in a loom for keeping the cloth stretched. ▷late Middle English: from Old French, perhaps ultimately the same word as TEMPLE[2].

tem·ple block ▸*n.* a percussion instrument consisting of a hollow block of wood that is struck with a stick.

tem·plet ▸*n.* rare spelling of TEMPLATE.

tem·po /'tempō/ ▸*n.* (*pl.* **-pos** or **-pi** /-pē/) **1** *Music* the speed at which a passage of music is or should be played. **2** the rate or speed of motion or activity; pace: *the tempo of life dictated by a heavy workload.* ▷mid 17th cent. (as a fencing term denoting the timing of an attack): from Italian, from Latin *tempus* 'time.'

tem·po·ral[1] /'temp(ə)rəl/ ▸*adj.* **1** relating to worldly as opposed to spiritual affairs; secular. **2** of or relating to time. ■ *Grammar* relating to or denoting time or tense. ▷Middle English: from Old French *temporel* or Latin *temporalis*, from *tempus, tempor-* 'time.' **—tem·po·ral·ly** *adv.*

tem·po·ral[2] ▸*adj. Anatomy* of or situated in the temples of the head. ▷late Middle English: from late Latin *temporalis*, from *tempora* 'the temples' (see TEMPLE[2]).

tem·po·ral bone ▸*n. Anatomy* either of a pair of bones that form part of the side of the skull on each side and enclose the middle and inner ear.

tem·po·ral·is /ˌtempə'raləs; -'rālis/ ▸*n. Anatomy* a fan-shaped muscle that runs from the side of the skull to the back of the lower jaw and is involved in closing the mouth and chewing. ▷late 17th cent.: from late Latin.

tem·po·ral·i·ty /ˌtempə'ralitē/ ▸*n.* (*pl.* **-ties**) **1** the state of existing within or having some relationship with time. **2** (usu. **temporalities**) a secular possession, esp. the properties and revenues of a religious body or a member of the clergy. ▷late Middle English (denoting temporal matters or secular authority): from late Latin *temporalitas*, from *temporalis* (see TEMPORAL[1]).

tem·po·ral lobe ▸*n.* each of the paired lobes of the brain lying beneath the temples, including areas concerned with the understanding of speech.

tem·po·ral pow·er ▸*n.* the power of a bishop or cleric, esp. the pope, in secular matters.

tem·po·rar·y /'tempəˌrerē/ ▸*adj.* lasting for only a limited period of time; not permanent: *a temporary job.* ▸*n.* (*pl.* **-rar·ies**) a person employed on a temporary basis, typically an office worker who finds employment through an agency. See also TEMP[1]. ▷mid 16th cent.: from Latin *temporarius*, from *tempus, tempor-* 'time.' **—tem·po·rar·i·ly** /ˌtempə're(ə)rəlē; 'tempəˌrer-/ *adv.* **—tem·po·rar·i·ness** *n.*

THE RIGHT WORD **ephemeral, evanescent, fleeting, temporary, transient, transitory**

Things that don't last long are called **temporary**, which emphasizes a measurable but limited duration (*a temporary appointment as chief of staff*).

Something that is **fleeting** passes almost instantaneously and cannot be caught or held (*a fleeting thought; a fleeting glimpse*).

Transient also applies to something that lasts or stays only a short time (*transient house guests*), while **transitory** refers to something that is destined to pass away or come to an end (*the transitory pleasure of eating*).

Evanescent and **ephemeral** describe what is even more short-lived. *Ephemeral* literally means lasting for only a single day, but is often used to describe anything that is slight and perishable (*his fame was ephemeral*). *Evanescent* is a more lyrical word for whatever vanishes almost as soon as it appears.

In other words, a job might be *temporary*, an emotion *fleeting*, a visitor *transient*, a woman's beauty *transitory*, and glory *ephemeral*, but the flash of a bird's wing across the sky would have to be called *evanescent.*

tem·po·rize /'tempəˌrīz/ ▸*v.* **1** [*intrans.*] avoid making a decision or committing oneself in order to gain time: *the opportunity was missed because the mayor still temporized.* **2** temporarily adopt a particular course in order to conform to the circumstances: *their unwillingness to temporize had driven their country straight into conflict with France.* ▷late 16th cent.: from French *temporiser* 'bide one's time,' from medieval Latin *temporizare* 'to delay,' from Latin *tempus, tempor-* 'time.' **—tem·po·ri·za·tion** /ˌtempəri'zāSHən/ *n.* **—tem·po·riz·er** *n.*

tem·po·ro·man·dib·u·lar joint /ˌtempərōˌmanˈdibyələr/ ▸*n. Anatomy* the hinge joint between the temporal bone and the lower jaw.

tem·po ru·ba·to /ˈtempō ro͞oˈbätō/ ▸*n.* fuller term for RUBATO.

Tem·pra·ni·llo /ˌtemprəˈnē(l)yō/ ▸*n.* a variety of wine grape grown in Spain, used to make Rioja wine. ■ a red wine made from this grape. ▷named after a village in northern Spain.

tempt /tem(p)t/ ▸*v.* [*trans.*] entice or attempt to entice (someone) to do or acquire something that they find attractive but know to be wrong or not beneficial: *don't allow impatience to* **tempt** *you* **into** *overexposure and sunburn* | *there'll always be someone tempted by the rich pickings of poaching* | [*trans.*] *jobs that involve entertaining may tempt you to drink more than you intend.* ■ (**be tempted to do something**) have an urge or inclination to do something: *I was tempted to look at my watch, but didn't dare.* ■ attract; allure: *he was tempted out of retirement to save the team.* ■ *archaic* risk provoking (a deity or abstract force), usually with undesirable consequences. ▷Middle English: from Old French *tempter* 'to test,' from Latin *temptare* 'handle, test, try.' **—tempt·a·bil·i·ty** /ˌtem(p)təˈbilitē/ *n.* (*rare*) **—tempt·a·ble** *adj.* (*rare*).

▸*PHRASE* □ **tempt fate** (or **providence**) do something that is risky or dangerous.

THE RIGHT WORD **allure, beguile, entice, inveigle, lure, seduce, tempt**

When we are under the influence of a powerful attraction, particularly to something that is wrong or unwise, we are **tempted**.

Entice implies that a crafty or skillful person has attracted us by offering a reward or pleasure (*she was enticed into joining the group by a personal plea from its handsome leader*), while **inveigle** suggests that we are enticed through the use of deception or cajolery (*inveigled into supporting the plan*).

If someone **lures** us, it suggests that we have been tempted or influenced for fraudulent or destructive purposes or attracted to something harmful or evil (*lured by gang members*).

Allure may also suggest that we have been deliberately tempted against our will, but the connotations here are often sexual (*allured by her dark green eyes*).

Seduce carries heavy sexual connotations (*seduced by an older woman*), although it can simply mean prompted to action against our will (*seduced by a clever sales pitch*).

While **beguile** at one time referred exclusively to the use of deception to lead someone astray, nowadays it can also refer to the use of subtle devices to engage someone's attention (*a local festival designed to beguile the tourists*).

temp·ta·tion /tem(p)ˈtāSHən/ ▸*n.* a desire to do something, esp. something wrong or unwise: *he resisted the temptation to call Celia at the office* | *we almost gave in to temptation.* ■ a thing or course of action that attracts or tempts someone: *the temptations of life in New York.* ■ (**the Temptation**) the tempting of Jesus by the Devil (see Matt. 4). ▷Middle English: from Old French *temptacion*, from Latin *temptatio(n-)*, from *temptare* 'handle, test, try.'

tempt·er /ˈtem(p)tər/ ▸*n.* a person or thing that tempts. ■ (**the Tempter**) the Devil. ▷late Middle English: from Old French *tempteur*, from ecclesiastical Latin *temptator*, from Latin *temptare* 'to handle, test, try.'

tempt·ing /ˈtem(p)tiNG/ ▸*adj.* appealing to or attracting someone, even if wrong or inadvisable: *a tempting financial offer* | [with *infinitive*] *it is often tempting to bring about change rapidly.* **—tempt·ing·ly** *adv.*

tempt·ress /ˈtem(p)tris/ ▸*n.* a woman who tempts someone to do something, typically a sexually attractive woman who sets out to allure or seduce someone.

tem·pu·ra /temˈpo͝orə/ ▸*n.* a Japanese dish of fish, shellfish, or vegetables, fried in batter. ▷Japanese, probably from Portuguese *tempêro* 'seasoning.'

ten /ten/ ▸*cardinal number* equivalent to the product of five and two; one more than nine; 10: *the last ten years* | *the house comfortably sleeps ten* | *a ten-foot shrub.* (Roman numeral: **x**, **X**) ■ a group or unit of ten people or things: *count in tens.* ■ ten years old: *the boy was no more than ten.* ■ ten o'clock: *at about ten at night, I got a call.* ■ a size of garment or other merchandise denoted by ten. ■ a ten-dollar bill: *he took the money in tens.* ■ a playing card with ten pips. ■ (**a ten**) used to indicate that someone has done something well; the highest mark on a scale of one to ten: *I would have to give them a ten for all the work they did.* ▷Old English *tēn, tīen*, of Germanic origin; related to Dutch *tien* and German *zehn*, from an Indo-European root shared by Sanskrit *daśa*, Greek *deka*, and Latin *decem*.

▸*PHRASES* □ **be ten a penny** see PENNY. □ **ten to one** very probably: *ten to one you'll never find out who did this.*

ten. *Music* ▸*abbr.* tenuto.

ten·a·ble /ˈtenəbəl/ ▸*adj.* **1** able to be maintained or defended against attack or objection: *such a simplistic approach is no longer tenable.* **2** (of an office, position, scholarship, etc.) able to be held or used: *the post is tenable for three years.* ▷late 16th cent.: from French, from *tenir* 'to hold,' from Latin *tenere.* **—ten·a·bil·i·ty** /ˌtenəˈbilitē/ *n.*

ten·ace /ˈtenˌās; ˈtenis/ ▸*n.* (in bridge, whist, and similar card games) a pair of cards in one hand that rank immediately above and below a card held by an opponent, e.g., the ace and queen in a suit of which an opponent holds the king. ▷mid 17th cent.: from French, from Spanish *tenaza*, literally 'pincers.'

te·na·cious /təˈnāSHəs/ ▸*adj.* not readily letting go of, giving up, or separated from an object that one holds, a position, or a principle: *a tenacious grip* | *he was the most tenacious politician in South Korea.* ■ not easily dispelled or discouraged; persisting in existence or in a course of action: *a tenacious local legend* | *you're tenacious and you get at the truth.* ▷early 17th cent.: from Latin *tenax, tenac-* (from *tenere* 'to hold') + -IOUS. **—te·na·cious·ly** *adv.* **—te·na·cious·ness** *n.* **—te·nac·i·ty** /-ˈnasitē/ *n.*

te·nac·u·lum /təˈnakyələm/ ▸*n.* (*pl.* **-u·la** /-yələ/) a surgical clamp with sharp hooks at the end, used to hold or pick up small pieces of tissue such as the ends of arteries. ▷late 17th cent.: from Latin, literally 'holder, holding instrument,' from *tenere* 'to hold.'

ten·an·cy /ˈtenənsē/ ▸*n.* (*pl.* **-cies**) possession of land or property as a tenant: *Holding took over the tenancy of the farm.*

ten·an·cy in com·mon ▸*n. Law* a shared tenancy in which each holder has a distinct, separately transferable interest.

ten·ant /ˈtenənt/ ▸*n.* a person who occupies land or property rented from a landlord. ■ *Law* a person holding real property by private ownership.
▸*v.* [*trans.*] (usu. **be tenanted**) occupy (property) as a tenant. ▷Middle English: from Old French, literally 'holding,' present participle of *tenir*, from Latin *tenere.* **—ten·ant·a·ble** *adj.* (*formal*) **—ten·ant·less** *adj.*

ten·ant at will ▸*n.* (*pl.* **ten·ants at will**) *Law* a tenant that can be evicted without notice.

ten·ant farm·er ▸*n.* a person who farms rented land.

ten·ant·ry /ˈtenəntrē/ ▸*n.* **1** [treated as *sing.* or *pl.*] the tenants of an estate. **2** tenancy.

Ten·cel /ˈtensel/ ▸*n. trademark* a cellulosic fiber obtained from wood pulp using recyclable solvents; a fabric made from this. ▷1960s (proprietary name of various yarns and fabrics): an invented word.

tench /tenCH/ ▸*n.* (*pl.* same) a European freshwater fish of the minnow family, popular with anglers and widely introduced elsewhere, including several U.S. states. • *Tinca tinca*, family Cyprinidae. ▷Middle English: from Old French *tenche*, from late Latin *tinca.*

Ten Com·mand·ments (in the Bible) the divine rules of conduct given by God to Moses on Mount Sinai, according to Exod. 20:1–17.

The commandments are generally enumerated as: have no other gods; do not make or worship idols; do not take the name of the Lord in vain; keep the sabbath holy; honor one's father and mother; do not kill; do not commit adultery; do not steal; do not give false evidence; do not covet another's property or wife.

tend[1] /tend/ ▸*v.* [*intrans.*] regularly or frequently behave in a particular way or have a certain characteristic: *written language tends to be formal* | *her hair tended to come loose.* ■ [*intrans.*] (**tend to/toward**) be liable to possess or display (a particular characteristic): *Walter tended toward corpulence.* ■ [*intrans.*] go or move in a particular direction: *the road tends west around small mountains.* ■ [*intrans.*] (**tend to**) *Mathematics* approach (a quantity or limit): *the Fourier coefficients tend to zero.* ▷Middle English (in the sense 'move or be inclined to move in a certain direction'): from Old French *tendre* 'stretch, tend,' from Latin *tendere.*

tend[2] ▸*v.* [*trans.*] care for or look after; give one's attention to: *Viola tended plants on the roof* | [*intrans.*] *for two or three months he* **tended to** *business.* ■ direct or manage; work in: *I've been tending bar at the airport lounge.* ■ *archaic* wait on as an attendant or servant. ▷Middle English: shortening of ATTEND. **—tend·ance** /ˈtendəns/ *n.* (*archaic*).

ten·den·cy /ˈtendənsē/ ▸*n.* (*pl.* **-cies**) an inclination toward a particular characteristic or type of behavior: *for students, there is a* **tendency to** *socialize in the evenings* | *criminal tendencies.* ■ a group within a larger political party or movement: *the dominant tendency in the party remained right-wing.* ▷early 17th cent.: from medieval Latin *tendentia*, from *tendere* 'to stretch' (see TEND[1]).

ten·den·tious /tenˈdenSHəs/ ▸*adj.* expressing or intending to promote a particular cause or point of view, esp. a controversial one: *a tendentious reading of history.* ▷early 20th cent.: suggested by German *tendenziös.* **—ten·den·tious·ly** *adv.* **—ten·den·tious·ness** *n.*

ten·der[1] /ˈtendər/ ▸*adj.* (**-der·er, -der·est**) **1** showing gentleness and concern or sympathy: *he was being so kind and tender.* ■ [*predic.*] (**tender of**) *archaic* solicitous of; concerned for: *be tender of a lady's reputation.* **2** (of food) easy to cut or chew; not tough: *tender green beans.* ■ (of a plant) easily injured by severe weather and therefore needing protection. ■ (of a part of the body) sensitive to pain: *the pale, tender skin of her forearm.* ■ young, immature, and vulnerable: *at* **the tender age of** *five.* ■ requiring tact or careful handling: *the issue of conscription was a particularly tender one.* ■ *Nautical* (of a ship) leaning or readily inclined to roll in response to the wind. ▷Middle English: from Old French *tendre*, from Latin *tener* 'tender, delicate.' **—ten·der·ly** *adv.* **—ten·der·ness** *n.*

▸*PHRASE* □ **tender mercies** used ironically to imply that someone cannot be trusted to look after or treat someone else kindly or well: *they have abandoned their children to the tender mercies of the social services.*

ten·der[2] ▸*v.* [*trans.*] offer or present (something) formally: *he tendered his resignation as leader.* ■ offer (money) as payment: *she tendered her fare.* ■ [*intrans.*] make a formal written offer to carry out work, supply goods, or buy land, shares, or another asset for a stated fixed price: *firms of interior decorators have been* **tendering for** *the work.* ■ [*trans.*] make such an offer giving (a stated fixed price): *what price should we tender for a contract?*
▸*n.* an offer to carry out work, supply goods, or buy land, shares, or another asset at a stated fixed price. ▷mid 16th cent. (as a legal term meaning 'formally offer a plea or evidence, or money to discharge a debt,' also as a noun denoting such an offer): from Old French *tendre*, from Latin *tendere* 'to stretch, hold forth' (see TEND[1]). **—ten·der·er** *n.*

▸*PHRASE* □ **put something out to tender** seek offers to carry out work or supply goods at a stated fixed price.

ten·der[3] ▸*n.* **1** [usu. in *combination* or with *adj.*] a person who looks after someone else or a machine or place: *Alexei signaled to one of the engine tenders.* **2** a boat used to ferry people and supplies to and from a ship. **3** a railcar coupled to a steam locomotive to carry fuel and water. ▷late Middle English (in the sense 'attendant, nurse'): from TEND[2] or shortening of *attender* (see ATTEND).

ten·der-eyed ▸*adj.* **1** having gentle eyes. **2** having sore or weak eyes.

ten·der·foot /ˈtendərˌfo͝ot/ ▸*n.* (*pl.* **-foots** or **-feet**) **1** a newcomer or novice, esp. a person unaccustomed to the hardships of pioneer life. **2** a Boy Scout of the lowest rank.

ten·der·heart·ed /ˈtendərˈhärtid/ ▸*adj.* having a kind, gentle, or sentimental nature. **—ten·der·heart·ed·ness** *n.*

ten·der·ize /ˈtendəˌrīz/ ▸*v.* make (meat) more tender by beating or slow cooking.

ten·der·iz·er /ˈtendəˌrīzər/ ▸*n.* a thing used to make meat tender, in particular: ■ a substance such as papain that is rubbed onto meat or used as a marinade to soften the fibers. ■ a small hammer with teeth on the head, used to beat meat.

ten·der·loin /ˈtendərˌloin/ ▸*n.* **1** the tenderest part of a loin of beef, pork, etc., taken from under the short ribs in the hindquarters. ■ the undercut of a sirloin. **2** *informal* a district of a city where vice and corruption are prominent. [late 19th cent.: originally a term applied to a district of New York, seen as a 'choice' assignment by police because of the bribes offered to them to turn a blind eye.]

ten·di·ni·tis /ˌtendəˈnītis/ (also **ten·do·ni·tis**) ▸*n.* inflammation of a tendon, most commonly from overuse but also from infection or rheumatic disease.

ten·don /ˈtendən/ ▸*n.* a flexible but inelastic cord of strong fibrous collagen tissue attaching a muscle to a bone. ■ the hamstring of a quadruped. ▷late Middle English: from French or medieval Latin *tendo(n-)*, translating Greek *tenōn* 'sinew,' from *teinein* 'to stretch.' —**ten·di·nous** /-dənəs/ *adj.*

ten·don or·gan ▸*n. Anatomy* a sensory receptor within a tendon that responds to tension and relays impulses to the central nervous system.

ten·dril /ˈtendrəl/ ▸*n.* a slender threadlike appendage of a climbing plant, often growing in a spiral form, that stretches out and twines around any suitable support. ■ something resembling a plant tendril, esp. a slender curl or ringlet of hair. ▷mid 16th cent.: probably a diminutive of Old French *tendron* 'young shoot,' from Latin *tener* 'tender.'

ten·du /tänˈdo͞o; tänˈdy/ ▸*adj.* [*postpositive*] *Ballet* (of a position) stretched out or held tautly: *battement tendu.* ▷French.

ten·du leaf ▸*n.* the leaves of an Asian ebony tree, gathered in India as a cheap tobacco substitute. • *Diospyros melanoxylon*, family Ebenaceae. ▷Hindi *tendu.*

Ten·e·brae /ˈtenəˌbrā; -ˌbrē/ ▸*plural n. historical* (in the Roman Catholic Church) matins and lauds for the last three days of Holy Week, at which candles were successively extinguished. Several composers have set parts of the office to music. ▷Latin, literally 'darkness.'

ten·e·brous /ˈtenəbrəs/ ▸*adj. poetic/literary* dark; shadowy or obscure. ▷late Middle English: via Old French from Latin *tenebrosus*, from *tenebrae* 'darkness.'

ten·e·ment /ˈtenəmənt/ ▸*n.* **1** a room or a set of rooms forming a separate residence within a house or block of apartments. ■ (also **ten·e·ment house**) a house divided into and rented in such separate residences, esp. one that is run-down and overcrowded. **2** a piece of land held by an owner. ■ *Law* any kind of permanent property, e.g., lands or rents, held from a superior. ▷Middle English (in the sense 'tenure, property held by tenure'): via Old French from medieval Latin *tenementum*, from *tenere* 'to hold.'

Ten·er·ife /ˌtenəˈrēf; -ˈrif; -ˈrēfā/ a volcanic island in the Atlantic Ocean, the largest of the Canary Islands; pop. 771,000; capital, Santa Cruz.

te·nes·mus /təˈnezməs/ ▸*n. Medicine* a continual or recurrent inclination to evacuate the bowels, caused by disorder of the rectum or other illness. ▷early 16th cent.: via medieval Latin from Greek *teinesmos* 'straining,' from *teinein* 'stretch, strain.'

ten·et /ˈtenit/ ▸*n.* a principle or belief, esp. one of the main principles of a religion or philosophy: *the tenets of classical liberalism.* ▷late 16th cent. (superseding earlier *tenent*): from Latin, literally 'he holds,' from the verb *tenere.*

ten·fold /ˈtenˌfōld/ ▸*adj.* ten times as great or as numerous: *a tenfold increase in the use of insecticides.* ■ having ten parts or elements.
▸*adv.* by ten times; to ten times the number or amount: *production increased tenfold.*

ten-gal·lon hat ▸*n.* a large, broad-brimmed hat, traditionally worn by cowboys.

ten·ge /ˈteNGgā/ ▸*n.* (*pl.* same or **-ges**) **1** the basic monetary unit of Kazakhstan, equal to 100 teins. **2** a monetary unit of Turkmenistan, equal to one hundredth of a manat.

te·ni·a ▸*n.* variant spelling of TAENIA.

Ten·iers /ˈtenyərz; təˈni(ə)rs/, David (1610–90), Flemish painter; known as **David Teniers the Younger**.

Ten Lost Tribes of Is·ra·el see LOST TRIBES.

Tenn. ▸*abbr.* Tennessee.

ten·nant·ite /ˈtenənˌtīt/ ▸*n.* a gray-black mineral consisting of a sulfide of copper, iron, and arsenic. It is an important ore of copper. ▷mid 19th cent.: from the name of Smithson *Tennant* (1761–1815), English chemist, + -ITE1.

ten·né /ˈtenē/ (also **ten·ny**) *Heraldry* ▸*n.* orange-brown, as a stain used in blazoning.
▸*adj.* [usu. *postpositive*] of this color. ▷mid 16th cent.: obsolete French, variant of Old French *tane* (see TAWNY).

ten·ner /ˈtenər/ ▸*n. Brit., informal* a ten-pound note.

Ten·nes·see /ˌtenəˈsē/ **1** a river in the southeastern U.S., flowing in a great loop, generally west and then north, for about 875 miles (1,400 km) to join the Ohio River in western Kentucky. **2** a state in the central southeastern U.S.; pop. 5,689,283; capital, Nashville; statehood, June 1, 1796 (16). It was the site of many Civil War battles, including those at Shiloh and Chattanooga. —**Ten·nes·see·an** /-ˈsēən/ *n.* & *adj.*

Ten·nes·see Val·ley Au·thor·i·ty (abbr.: **TVA**) an independent federal government agency in the U.S., created in 1933 as part of the New Deal proposals. Responsible for the development of the whole Tennessee river basin, it provides one of the world's greatest irrigation and hydroelectric power systems.

Ten·nes·see Walk·ing Horse ▸*n.* a powerful riding horse of a breed with a characteristic fast walking pace.

ten·nies /ˈtenēz/ ▸*plural n. informal* tennis shoes.

ten·nis /ˈtenis/ ▸*n.* a game in which two or four players strike a ball with rackets over a net stretched across a court. The usual form (originally called **lawn tennis**) is played with a felt-covered hollow rubber ball on a grass, clay, or artificial surface. See also COURT TENNIS. ▷late Middle English: from *tenetz, tenes* 'court tennis,' apparently from Old French *tenez* 'take, receive' (called by the server to an opponent), imperative of *tenir.*

ten·nis brace·let ▸*n.* a bracelet containing many small gems, usually diamonds, linked together in a narrow chain.

ten·nis el·bow ▸*n.* inflammation of the tendons of the elbow (epicondylitis) caused by overuse of the muscles of the forearm.

ten·nis shoe ▸*n.* a light canvas or leather soft-soled shoe suitable for tennis or casual wear.

Ten·no /ˈtenō/ ▸*n.* (*pl.* **-nos**) the Emperor of Japan. ▷Japanese.

ten·ny /ˈtenē/ ▸*n.* & *adj.* var. of TENNÉ.

Ten·ny·son /ˈtenəsən/, Alfred, 1st Baron Tennyson of Aldworth and Freshwater (1809–92), English poet; poet laureate from 1850. His reputation was established by *In Memoriam* (1850), a long poem concerned with immortality, change, and evolution. Other notable works: "The Charge of the Light Brigade" (1854) and *Idylls of the King* (1859).

Ten·ny·so·ni·an /ˌteniˈsōnēən/ ▸*adj.* relating to or in the style of Tennyson.
▸*n.* an admirer or student of Tennyson or his work.

Te·noch·ti·tlán /təˌnôCHtētˈlän/ the ancient capital of the Aztec empire, founded *c.*1320. In 1521, the Spanish conquistador Cortés destroyed it and established Mexico City on its site.

ten·on /ˈtenən/ ▸*n.* a projecting piece of wood made for insertion into a mortise in another piece.
▸*v.* [*trans.*] (usu. **be tenoned**) join by means of a tenon. ■ cut as a tenon. ▷late Middle English: from French, from *tenir* 'to hold,' from Latin *tenere.* —**ten·on·er** *n.*

ten·or1 /ˈtenər/ ▸*n.* a singing voice between baritone and alto or countertenor, the highest of the ordinary adult male range. ■ a singer with such a voice. ■ a part written for such a voice. ■ [usu. as *adj.*] an instrument, esp. a saxophone, trombone, tuba, or viol, of the lowest pitch but one in its family: *a tenor sax.* ■ (in full **tenor bell**) the largest and deepest bell of a ring or set. ▷late Middle English: via Old French from medieval Latin, based on *tenere* 'to hold'; so named because the tenor part was allotted (and therefore "held") the melody.

ten·or2 ▸*n.* **1** [in *sing.*] (usu. **the tenor of**) the general meaning, sense, or content of something: *the general tenor of the debate.* ■ the subject to which a metaphor refers, e.g., "a large, difficult challenge" conveyed by *bear* in *this one is going to be a bear.* Often contrasted with VEHICLE (sense 2). **2** [in *sing.*] (usu. **the tenor of**) a settled or prevailing character or direction, esp. the course of a person's life or habits: ***the even tenor of** life in the kitchen was disrupted the following day.* **3** *Law* the actual wording of a document. **4** *Finance* the time that must elapse before a bill of exchange or promissory note becomes due for payment. ▷Middle English: from Old French *tenour*, from Latin *tenor* 'course, substance, import of a law,' from *tenere* 'to hold.'

ten·or clef ▸*n. Music* a clef placing middle C on the second-highest line of the stave, used chiefly for cello and bassoon music.

te·no·ri·no /ˌtenəˈrēnō/ ▸*n.* (*pl.* **-ri·ni** /-ˈrēnē/) a high tenor. ▷Italian, diminutive of *tenore* 'tenor.'

ten·or·ist /ˈtenərist/ ▸*n.* a person who plays a tenor instrument, esp. the tenor saxophone.

ten·o·syn·o·vi·tis /ˌtenōˌsinəˈvītis/ ▸*n. Medicine* inflammation and swelling of a tendon, typically in the wrist, often caused by repetitive movements such as typing. ▷late 19th cent.: from Greek *tenōn* 'tendon' + SYNOVITIS.

te·not·o·my /təˈnätəmē/ ▸*n.* the surgical cutting of a tendon, esp. as a remedy for club foot. ▷mid 19th cent.: coined in French from Greek *tenōn* 'tendon' + *-tomia* (see -TOMY).

ten·pin /ˈtenˌpin/ ▸*n.* a wooden pin used in tenpin bowling. ■ (**tenpins**) [treated as *sing.*] tenpin bowling.

ten·pin bowl·ing ▸*n.* a game in which ten wooden pins are set up at the end of a track (typically one of several in a large, automated alley) and bowled down with hard rubber or plastic balls.

ten·pound·er /ˈtenˈpoundər/ ▸*n.* a large, silvery-blue, herringlike fish of tropical seas that is popular as a game fish. Also called LADYFISH. • *Elops saurus* (or **machnata**) , family Elopidae.

ten·rec /ˈtenˌrek/ ▸*n.* a small, insectivorous mammal native to Madagascar, different kinds of which resemble hedgehogs, shrews, or small otters. • Several genera in the family Tenrecidae: many species, including the **common** (or **tailless**) **tenrec** (*Tenrec ecaudatus*), also found in the Comoro islands. ▷late 18th cent.: from French *tanrec*, from Malagasy *tàndraka.*

TENS /tenz/ ▸*abbr.* transcutaneous electrical nerve stimulation, a technique intended to provide pain relief by applying electrodes to the skin to block impulses in underlying nerves.

tense1 /tens/ ▸*adj.* (esp. of a muscle or someone's body) stretched tight or rigid: *she tried to relax her tense muscles.* ■ (of a person) unable to relax because of nervousness, anxiety, or stimulation: *he was tense with excitement.* ■ (of a situation, event, etc.) causing or showing anxiety and nervousness: *relations between the two neighboring states had been tense in recent years.* ■ *Phonetics* (of a speech sound, esp. a vowel) pronounced with the vocal muscles stretched tight. The opposite of LAX.
▸*v.* [*intrans.*] become tense, typically through anxiety or nervousness: *her body **tensed up**.* ■ [*trans.*] make (a muscle or one's body) tight or rigid: *carefully stretch and then tense your muscles.* ▷late 17th cent.: from Latin *tensus* 'stretched,' from the verb *tendere.* —**tense·ly** *adv.* —**tense·ness** *n.* —**ten·si·ty** /ˈtensitē/ *n.* (*dated*).

tense2 ▸*n. Grammar* a set of forms taken by a verb to indicate the time (and sometimes also the continuance or completeness) of the action in relation to the time of the utterance: *the past tense.* ▷Middle English (in the general sense 'time'): from Old French *tens*, from Latin *tempus* 'time.' —**tense·less** *adj.*

ten·seg·ri·ty /tenˈsegritē/ ▸*n. Architecture* the characteristic property of a stable three-dimensional structure consisting of members under tension that are contiguous and members under compression that are not. ▷1950s: from *tensional integrity.*

ten·sile /ˈtensəl; -ˌsīl/ ▸*adj.* **1** of or relating to tension. **2** capable of being drawn out or stretched. ▷early 17th cent. (sense 2): from medieval Latin *tensilis*, from Latin *tendere* 'to stretch.' —**ten·sil·i·ty** /tenˈsilitē/ *n.*

ten·sile strength ▸*n.* the resistance of a material to breaking under tension. Compare with COMPRESSIVE STRENGTH.

ten·sion /ˈtenSHən/ ▸*n.* **1** the state of being stretched tight: *the parachute keeps the cable under tension as it drops.* ■ the state of having the muscles stretched tight, esp. as causing strain or discomfort: *the elimination of neck tension can relieve headaches.* ■ a strained state or condition resulting from forces acting in opposition to each other. ■ the degree of tightness of stitches in knitting and machine sewing. ■ electromotive force. **2** mental or emotional strain: *a mind that is affected by stress or tension cannot think as clearly.* ■ a strained political or social state or relationship: *the coup followed months of tension between the military and the government | racial tensions.* ■ a relationship between ideas or qualities with conflicting demands or implications: *the basic **tension between** freedom and control.*
▸*v.* [*trans.*] apply a force to (something) that tends to stretch it. ▷mid 16th cent. (as a medical term denoting a condition or feeling of being physically stretched or strained): from French, or from Latin *tensio(n-)*, from *tendere* 'stretch.' —**ten·sion·al** /-SHənl/ *adj.* —**ten·sion·al·ly** /-SHənl-ē/ *adv.* —**ten·sion·er** *n.* —**ten·sion·less** *adj.*

ten·sive /ˈtensiv/ ▸*adj.* causing or expressing tension.

Tens·kwa·ta·wa /ten(t)ˈskwätəˌwä/ see TECUMSEH.

Pronunciation Key ə *ago*; ər *over*; ˈə or ˌə *up*; ˈər or ˌər *fur*; a *hat*; ā *rate*; ä *car*; CH *chew*; e *let*; ē *see*; e(ə)r *air*; i *fit*; ī *by*; i(ə)r *ear*; NG *sing*; ō *go*; ô *for*; oi *boy*; o͝o *good*; o͞o *goo*; ou *out*; SH *she*; TH *thin*; TH *then*; (h)w *why*; ZH *vision*

ten·sor /ˈtensər; ˈtenˌsôr/ ▶*n.* **1** *Mathematics* a mathematical object analogous to but more general than a vector, represented by an array of components that are functions of the coordinates of a space. **2** *Anatomy* a muscle that tightens or stretches a part of the body. ▷early 18th cent.: modern Latin, from Latin *tendere* 'to stretch.' —**ten·so·ri·al** /tenˈsôrēəl/ *adj.*

tent /tent/ ▶*n.* a portable shelter made of cloth, supported by one or more poles and stretched tight by cords or loops attached to pegs driven into the ground. ■ *Medicine* short for OXYGEN TENT.
▶*v.* **1** [*trans.*] cover with or as if with a tent: *the garden had been completely tented over for supper.* ■ arrange in a shape that looks like a tent: *Tim tented his fingers.* ■ [as *adj.*] (**tented**) composed of or provided with tents: *they were living in large tented camps.* **2** [*intrans.*] (esp. of traveling circus people) live in a tent. ▷Middle English: from Old French *tente*, based on Latin *tent-* 'stretched,' from the verb *tendere*. The verb dates from the mid 16th cent.

ten·ta·cle /ˈten(t)əkəl/ ▶*n.* a slender flexible limb or appendage in an animal, esp. around the mouth of an invertebrate, used for grasping, moving about, or bearing sense organs. ■ (in a plant) a tendril or a sensitive glandular hair. ■ something resembling a tentacle in shape or flexibility: *trailing tentacles of vapor.* ■ (usu. **tentacles**) *figurative* an insidious spread of influence and control: *the Party's tentacles reached into every nook and cranny of people's lives.* ▷mid 18th cent.: anglicized from modern Latin *tentaculum*, from Latin *tentare, temptare* 'to feel, try.' —**ten·ta·cled** *adj.* [also in *combination*] —**ten·tac·u·lar** /tenˈtakyələr/ *adj.* —**ten·tac·u·late** /tenˈtakyələt/ *adj.*

ten·ta·tive /ˈtentətiv/ ▶*adj.* not certain or fixed; provisional: *a tentative conclusion.* ■ done without confidence; hesitant: *he eventually tried a few tentative steps round his hospital room.* ▷late 16th cent.: from medieval Latin *tentativus*, from *tentare*, variant of *temptare* 'handle, try.' —**ten·ta·tive·ly** *adv.* —**ten·ta·tive·ness** *n.*

tent cat·er·pil·lar ▶*n.* a chiefly American moth caterpillar that lives in groups inside communal silken webs in a tree, which it often defoliates. • Several species in the family Lasiocampidae, esp. *Malacosoma americana*.

tent dress ▶*n.* a full, loose-fitting dress that is narrow at the shoulders and very wide at the hem, having no waistline or darts.

ten·ter /ˈten(t)ər/ ▶*n.* a framework on which fabric can be held taut for drying or other treatment during manufacture. ▷Middle English: from medieval Latin *tentorium*, from *tent-* 'stretched,' from the verb *tendere*.

ten·ter·hook /ˈten(t)ərˌhŏŏk/ ▶*n.* *historical* a hook used to fasten cloth on a drying frame or tenter.
▶*PHRASE* □ **on tenterhooks** in a state of suspense or agitation because of uncertainty about a future event.

tenth /tenTH/ ▶*n.* constituting number ten in a sequence; 10th: *the tenth century | the tenth of September | the tenth-floor locker room.* ■ (**a tenth/one tenth**) each of ten equal parts into which something is or may be divided: *a tenth of a second.* ■ the tenth grade of a school. ■ *Music* an interval or chord spanning an octave and a third in the diatonic scale, or a note separated from another by this interval. —**tenth·ly** *adv.*

tenth-rate ▶*adj.* *informal* of extremely poor quality.

ten·to·ri·um /tenˈtôrēəm/ ▶*n.* (*pl.* **-to·ria** /-ˈtôrēə/) **1** *Anatomy* a fold of the dura mater forming a partition between the cerebrum and cerebellum. **2** *Entomology* an internal skeletal framework in the head of an insect. ▷early 19th cent.: from Latin, literally 'tent.'

tent peg ▶*n.* see PEG (sense 1).

tent stitch ▶*n.* a series of parallel diagonal stitches.

te·nu·i·ty /teˈn(y)ōōitē; tə-/ ▶*n.* lack of solidity or substance; thinness. ▷late Middle English: from Latin *tenuitas*, from *tenuis* 'thin.'

ten·u·ous /ˈtenyōōəs/ ▶*adj.* very weak or slight: *the tenuous link between interest rates and investment.* ■ very slender or fine; insubstantial: *a tenuous cloud.* ▷late 16th cent.: formed irregularly from Latin *tenuis* 'thin' + -OUS. —**ten·u·ous·ly** *adv.* —**ten·u·ous·ness** *n.*

ten·ure /ˈtenyər; -ˌyŏŏr/ ▶*n.* **1** the conditions under which land or buildings are held or occupied. **2** the holding of an office: *his tenure of the premiership would be threatened.* ■ a period for which an office is held. **3** guaranteed permanent employment, esp. as a teacher or professor, after a probationary period.
▶*v.* [*trans.*] give (someone) a permanent post, esp. as a teacher or professor: *I had recently been tenured and then promoted to full professor.* ■ [as *adj.*] (**tenured**) having or denoting such a post: *a tenured faculty member.* ▷late Middle English: from Old French, from *tenir* 'to hold,' from Latin *tenere*.

ten·ure track ▶*n.* [usu. as *adj.*] an employment structure whereby the holder of a post, typically an academic one, is guaranteed consideration for eventual tenure: *a tenure-track position.*

te·nu·to /teˈnōōtō/ *Music* ▶*adv.* & *adj.* (of a note) held for its full time value or slightly more.
▶*n.* (*pl.* **-nu·tos** or **-nu·ti** /-ˈnōōtē/) a note or chord performed in this way. ▷Italian, literally 'held,' past participle of *tenere*.

Ten·zing Nor·gay /ˈtenziNG ˈnôrˌgā/ (1914–86), Sherpa mountaineer. In 1953, as members of the British expedition, he and Sir Edmund Hillary were the first to reach the summit of Mount Everest.

te·o·cal·li /ˌtē-ōˈkälē; ˌtā-/ ▶*n.* (*pl.* **-lis**) a temple of the Aztecs or other Mexican peoples, typically standing on a truncated pyramid. ▷American Spanish, from Nahuatl *teo:kalli*, from *teo:tl* 'god' + *kalli* 'house.'

te·o·sin·te /ˌtē-ōˈsintē, ˌtā-/ ▶*n.* a Mexican grass that is grown as fodder and is considered to be one of the parent plants of modern corn. • *Zea mays* subsp. *mexicana*, family Gramineae. ▷late 19th cent.: from French *téosinté*, from Nahuatl *teocintli*, apparently from *teo:tl* 'god' + *cintli* 'dried ear of maize.'

Te·o·ti·hua·cán /ˌtēəˌtēwäˈkän/ the largest city in pre-Columbian America, 25 miles (40 km) northeast of Mexico City. Built *c.*300 BC, it reached its zenith *c.*AD 300–600, when it was the center of an influential culture that spread throughout Meso-America. It was sacked by the invading Toltecs *c.*900.

te·pa·che /təˈpäCHē/ ▶*n.* a Mexican drink, typically made with pineapple, water, and brown sugar and partially fermented. ▷Mexican Spanish.

te·pal /ˈtēpəl; ˈtepəl/ ▶*n.* *Botany* a segment of the outer whorl in a flower that has no differentiation between petals and sepals. ▷mid 19th cent.: from French *tépale*, blend of *pétale* 'petal' and *sépal* 'sepal.'

tep·a·ry bean /ˈtepərē/ ▶*n.* a bean plant native to the southwestern U.S., cultivated in Mexico and Arizona for its drought-resistant qualities. • *Phaseolus acutifolius*, family Leguminosae. ▷early 20th cent.: from Spanish *tepari*, from Pima.

te·pee /ˈtēˌpē/ (also **tee·pee** or **ti·pi**) ▶*n.* a portable conical tent made of skins, cloth, or canvas on a frame of poles, used by American Indians of the Plains and Great Lakes regions. ▷mid 18th cent.: from Sioux *tipī* 'dwelling.'

tepee

teph·ra /ˈtefrə/ ▶*n.* *Geology* rock fragments and particles ejected by a volcanic eruption. ▷1940s: from Greek, literally 'ash, ashes.'

Te·pic /teˈpēk/ a city in western Mexico, capital of the state of Nayarit; pop. 238,000.

tep·id /ˈtepid/ ▶*adj.* (esp. of a liquid) only slightly warm; lukewarm. ■ *figurative* showing little enthusiasm: *the applause was tepid.* ▷late Middle English: from Latin *tepidus*, from *tepere* 'be warm.' —**te·pid·i·ty** /təˈpiditē/ *n.* —**tep·id·ly** *adv.* —**tep·id·ness** *n.*

TEPP ▶*abbr.* *Chemistry* tetraethyl pyrophosphate.

tep·pan-ya·ki /ˈtepän ˈyākē/ ▶*n.* a Japanese dish of meat, fish, or both, fried with vegetables on a hot steel plate forming the center of the dining table. ▷Japanese, from *teppan* 'steel plate' + *yaki* 'to fry.'

te·qui·la /təˈkēlə/ ▶*n.* a Mexican liquor made from an agave. ▷Mexican Spanish, named after the town of *Tequila* in Mexico, where the drink was first produced.

te·qui·la sun·rise ▶*n.* a cocktail containing tequila, orange juice, and grenadine.

ter. ▶*abbr.* ■ (in prescriptions) rub. [from Latin *tere.*] ■ terrace. ■ territorial. ■ territory.

ter- ▶*comb. form* three; having three: *tercentenary.* ▷from Latin *ter* 'thrice.'

USAGE The combining-form prefix **ter-** is commonly replaced by **tri-**, as in **tricentenary**.

tera- ▶*comb. form* used in units of measurement: **1** denoting a factor of 10^{12}: *terawatt.* **2** *Computing* denoting a factor of 2^{40}. ▷from Greek *teras* 'monster.'

ter·a·byte /ˈterəˌbīt/ (abbr.: **Tb** or **TB**) ▶*n.* *Computing* a unit of information equal to one million million (10^{12}) or strictly, 2^{40} bytes.

ter·a·flop /ˈterəˌfläp/ ▶*n.* *Computing* a unit of computing speed equal to one million million floating-point operations per second.

te·rai /təˈrī/ (also **te·rai hat**) ▶*n.* a wide-brimmed felt hat, typically with a double crown, worn chiefly by travelers in subtropical regions. ▷late 19th cent.: from *Terai*, the name of a belt of marshy jungle between the Himalayan foothills and plains, from Hindi *tarāī* 'marshy lowlands.'

ter·a·phim /ˈterəˌfim/ ▶*plural n.* [also treated as *sing.*] small images or cult objects used as domestic deities or oracles by ancient Semitic peoples. ▷late Middle English: via late Latin from Greek *theraphin*, from Hebrew *tĕrāpīm*.

terato- ▶*comb. form* relating to monsters or abnormal forms: *teratology.* ▷from Greek *teras, terat-* 'monster.'

te·rat·o·car·ci·no·ma /ˌterətōˌkärsəˈnōmə/ ▶*n.* (*pl.* **-ma·ta** /-mətə/ or **-mas**) *Medicine* a form of malignant teratoma occurring esp. in the testis.

te·rat·o·gen /teˈratəjən; -ˌjen; ˈterətəjən/ ▶*n.* an agent or factor that causes malformation of an embryo. —**te·rat·o·gen·ic** /təˌratəˈjenik; ˌterətə-/ *adj.* —**te·rat·o·ge·nic·i·ty** /təˌratəjəˈnisitē; ˌterəˌtō-/ *n.*

te·rat·o·gen·e·sis /ˌterətōˈjenəsis; təˌratō-/ ▶*n.* the process by which congenital malformations are produced in an embryo or fetus.

ter·a·tol·o·gy /ˌterəˈtäləjē/ ▶*n.* **1** *Medicine* & *Biology* the scientific study of congenital abnormalities and abnormal formations. **2** mythology relating to fantastic creatures and monsters. —**ter·a·to·log·i·cal** /ˌterətəˈläjikəl/ *adj.* —**ter·a·tol·o·gist** /-jist/ *n.*

ter·a·to·ma /ˌterəˈtōmə/ ▶*n.* (*pl.* **-mas** or **-ma·ta** /-mətə/) *Medicine* a tumor composed of tissues not normally present at the site (the site being typically in the gonads).

ter·a·watt /ˈterəˌwät/ ▶*n.* a unit of power equal to 10^{12} watts or a million megawatts.

ter·bi·um /ˈtərbēəm/ ▶*n.* the chemical element of atomic number 65, a silvery-white metal of the lanthanide series. The main use of terbium is in making semiconductors. (Symbol **Tb**) ▷mid 19th cent.: modern Latin, from *Ytterby*, the name of a village in Sweden where it was discovered. Compare with ERBIUM and YTTERBIUM.

ter·bu·ta·line /tərˈbyōōtlˌēn/ ▶*n.* *Medicine* a synthetic compound with bronchodilator properties, used esp. in the treatment of asthma. • Chem. formula: $C_{12}H_{19}NO_3$. ▷1960s: from TER- + BUTYL (elements of the systematic name), on the pattern of words such as *isoprenaline*.

terce /tərs/ ▶*n.* a service forming part of the Divine Office of the Western Christian Church, traditionally said (or chanted) at the third hour of the day (i.e., 9 a.m.). ▷late Middle English: from Old French, from Latin *tertia*, feminine of *tertius* 'third.' Compare with TIERCE.

ter·cel /ˈtərsəl/ ▶*n.* variant spelling of TIERCEL. ▷Middle English: from Old French, based on Latin *tertius* 'third,' perhaps from the belief that the third egg of a clutch produced a male.

ter·cen·ten·ar·y /ˌtərsenˈtenərē; terˈsentnˌerē/ ▶*adj.* & *n.* (*pl.* **-ar·ies**) another term for TRICENTENNIAL.

ter·cen·ten·ni·al /ˌtərsenˈtenēəl/ ▶*adj.* & *n.* another term for TRICENTENNIAL.

ter·cet /ˈtərsit/ ▶*n.* *Prosody* a set or group of three lines of verse rhyming together or connected by rhyme with an adjacent tercet. ▷late 16th cent.: from French, from Italian *terzetto*, diminutive of *terzo* 'third,' from Latin *tertius*.

ter·e·binth /ˈterəˌbinTH/ ▶*n.* a small southern European tree of the cashew family that was formerly a source of turpentine. • *Pistacia terebinthus*, family Anacardiaceae. ▷late Middle English: from Old French *therebinte*, or via Latin from Greek *terebinthos*.

te·re·do /təˈrēdō/ ▶*n.* *Zoology* (*pl.* **-dos**) a wormlike bivalve mollusk with reduced shells that it uses to drill into wood. It can cause substantial damage to wooden structures and vessels. Also called SHIPWORM. • Genus *Teredo*, family Teredinidae: several species, in particular *T. navalis*. ▷late Middle English: via Latin from Greek *terēdōn*; related to *teirein* 'rub hard, wear away.'

Ter·ence /ˈterəns/ (*c.*190–159 BC), Roman comic playwright; Latin name *Publius Terentius Afer*. His six surviving comedies are based on the Greek New Comedy; they are marked by more realism and a greater consistency of plot than are the works of Plautus.

ter·eph·thal·ic ac·id /ˈterefˌTHalik/ ▶*n.* *Chemistry* a crystalline organic acid used in making polyester resins and other polymers. • The *para*-isomer of phthalic acid; chem. formula: $C_6H_4(COOH)_2$. ▷mid 19th cent.: blend of *terebic* 'of or from turpentine' (from TEREBINTH) and PHTHALIC ACID. —**ter·eph·thal·ate** /ˌterəfˈTHalˌāt/ *n.*

te·res /ˈti(ə)rēz; ˈterēz/ ▸*n. Anatomy* either of two muscles passing below the shoulder joint from the scapula to the upper part of the humerus, one (**teres major**) drawing the arm toward the body and rotating it inward, the other (**teres minor**) rotating it outward. ▷early 18th cent.: modern Latin, from Latin, literally 'rounded.'

Te·re·sa, Moth·er /təˈrēsə; təˈrāsə/ (also **The·re·sa**) (1910–97), Roman Catholic nun and missionary, born of Albanian parentage in what is now Macedonia; born *Agnes Gonxha Bojaxhiu*. She became an Indian citizen in 1948. She founded the Order of Missionaries of Charity, noted for its work among the poor in Calcutta. Nobel Peace Prize (1979).

Mother Teresa

Te·re·sa of Á·vi·la, St. /ˈävilə/ (1515–82), Spanish Carmelite nun and mystic. She instituted the "discalced" reform movement with St. John of the Cross. Her writings include *The Way of Perfection* (1583) and *The Interior Castle* (1588). Feast day, October 15.

Te·re·sa of Li·sieux, St. /lēsˈyœ/ (also **Thé·rèse** /teˈrez/) (1873–97), French Carmelite nun; born *Marie-Françoise Thérèse Martin*. In her autobiography *L'Histoire d'une âme* (1898) she taught that sanctity can be attained through continual renunciation in small matters. Feast day, October 3.

Te·resh·ko·va /ˌterəSHˈkôvə; ˌter-/, Valentina (Vladimirovna) (1937–), Russian cosmonaut. In June 1963, she was the first woman to go into space.

Te·re·si·na /ˌterəˈzēnə; -ˈsē-/ a river port in northeastern Brazil, on the Parnaíba River, capital of the state of Piauí; pop. 591,000.

te·rete /təˈrēt; ˈterˌēt/ ▸*adj. chiefly Botany* cylindrical or slightly tapering, and without substantial furrows or ridges. ▷early 17th cent.: from Latin *teres, teret-* 'rounded off.'

ter·gal /ˈtərgəl/ ▸*adj. Zoology* of or relating to a tergum of an arthropod. ▷mid 19th cent.: from Latin *tergum* 'back' + -AL.

ter·gite /ˈterˌjīt/ ▸*n. Entomology* (in an insect) a sclerotized plate forming the tergum of a segment. Compare with STERNITE. ▷late 19th cent.: from TERGUM + -ITE[1].

ter·gi·ver·sate /tərˈjivərˌsāt; ˈtərjivər-/ ▸*v.* [*intrans.*] **1** make conflicting or evasive statements; equivocate: *the more she tergiversated, the greater grew the ardency of the reporters for an interview.* **2** change one's loyalties; be apostate. ▷mid 17th cent.: from Latin *tergiversat-* 'with one's back turned,' from the verb *tergiversari*, from *tergum* 'back' + *vertere* 'to turn.' —**ter·gi·ver·sa·tion** /ˌtərjivərˈsāSHən/ *n.* —**ter·gi·ver·sa·tor** /-ˌsātər/ *n.*

ter·gum /ˈtərgəm/ ▸*n.* (*pl.* **-ga** /-gə/) *Zoology* a thickened dorsal plate on each segment of the body of an arthropod. ▷early 19th cent.: from Latin, literally 'back.'

Ter·hune /tərˈhyo͞on/, Albert Payson, (1872–1942) U.S. writer. His fiction for young readers about dogs, esp. collies, includes *Lad: A Dog* (1919), *Treve* (1924), *My Friend the Dog* (1926), and *Loot* (1940).

-teria ▸*suffix* denoting self-service establishments: *washeteria.* ▷on the pattern of *(cafe)teria*.

ter·i·ya·ki /ˌterēˈyäkē/ ▸*n.* a Japanese dish consisting of fish or meat marinated in soy sauce and grilled. ■ (also **ter·i·ya·ki sauce**) a mixture of soy sauce, sake, ginger, and other flavorings, used in Japanese cooking as a marinade or glaze for such dishes. ▷Japanese.

Ter·kel /ˈtərkəl/, Studs, (1912–), U.S. writer, radio and television journalist, and historian; full name *Louis Terkel*. He had his own television show 1950–53 and radio show 1953–98. Thought of as the voice of the common man, he wrote *Division Street: America* (1967), *The Good War* (1984), *Coming of Age* (1995), and *My American Century* (1997).

term /tərm/ ▸*n.* **1** a word or phrase used to describe a thing or to express a concept, esp. in a particular kind of language or branch of study: *the musical term "leitmotiv" | a term of abuse.* ■ (**terms**) language used on a particular occasion; a way of expressing oneself: *a protest in the strongest possible terms.* ■ *Logic* a word or words that may be the subject or predicate of a proposition. **2** a fixed or limited period for which something, e.g., office, imprisonment, or investment, lasts or is intended to last: *the president is elected for a single four-year term.* ■ *archaic* the duration of a person's life. ■ (also **full term**) the completion of a normal length of pregnancy: *the pregnancy* **went to full term** *| low birthweight* **at term**. ■ (also **term for years** or *Brit.* **term of years**) *Law* a tenancy of a fixed period. ■ *archaic* a boundary or limit, esp. of time. **3** each of the periods in the year, alternating with holidays or vacations, during which instruction is given in a school, college, or university, or during which a court holds sessions: *the summer term | term starts tomorrow.* **4** (**terms**) conditions under which an action may be undertaken or agreement reached; stipulated or agreed-upon requirements: *the union and the company agreed upon the contract's terms | he could only be dealt with* **on his own terms**. ■ conditions with regard to payment for something; stated charges: *loans on favorable terms.* ■ agreed conditions under which a war or other dispute is brought to an end: *a deal in Bosnia that could force the Serbs to* **come to terms**. **5** *Mathematics* each of the quantities in a ratio, series, or mathematical expression. **6** *Architecture* another term for TERMINUS.
▸*v.* [*trans.*] give a descriptive name to; call by a specified name: *he has been termed the father of modern theology.* ▷Middle English (denoting a limit in space or time, or (in the plural) limiting conditions): from Old French *terme*, from Latin *terminus* 'end, boundary, limit.'
▸*PHRASES* □ **come to terms with** come to accept (a new and painful or difficult event or situation); reconcile oneself to: *she had come to terms with the tragedies in her life.* □ **in terms of** (or **in —— terms**) with regard to the particular aspect or subject specified: *replacing the printers is difficult to justify in terms of cost | sales are down by nearly 7 percent in* **real terms**. □ **the long/short/medium term** used to refer to a time that is a specified way into the future. □ **on —— terms** in a specified relation or on a specified footing: *we are all on friendly terms.*

term. ▸*abbr.* ■ terminal. ■ termination.

ter·ma·gant /ˈtərməgənt/ ▸*n.* **1** a harsh-tempered or overbearing woman. **2** (**Termagant**) *historical* an imaginary deity of violent and turbulent character, often appearing in morality plays. ▷Middle English (sense 2): via Old French from Italian *Trivigante*, taken to be from Latin *tri-* 'three' + *vagant-* 'wandering,' and to refer to the moon "wandering" between heaven, earth, and hell under the three names *Selene, Artemis*, and *Persephone*.

term for years ▸*n.* see TERM (sense 2).

ter·mi·na·ble /ˈtərmənəbəl/ ▸*adj.* **1** able to be terminated. **2** coming to an end after a certain time.

ter·mi·nal /ˈtərmənl/ ▸*adj.* **1** [*attrib.*] of, forming, or situated at the end or extremity of something: *a terminal date | the terminal tip of the probe.* ■ of or forming a transportation terminal: *terminal platforms.* ■ *Zoology* situated at, forming, or denoting the end of a part or series of parts furthest from the center of the body. ■ *Botany* (of a flower, inflorescence, etc.) borne at the end of a stem or branch. Often contrasted with AXILLARY. **2** (of a disease) predicted to lead to death, esp. slowly; incurable: *terminal cancer.* ■ [*attrib.*] suffering from or relating to such a disease: *a hospice for terminal cases.* ■ [*attrib.*] (of a condition) forming the last stage of such a disease. ■ *informal* extreme and usually beyond cure or alteration (used to emphasize the extent of something regarded as bad or unfortunate): *you're making a terminal ass of yourself.*
▸*n.* **1** an end or extremity of something, in particular: ■ the end of a railroad or other transport route, or a station at such a point. ■ a departure and arrival building for air passengers at an airport. ■ an installation where oil or gas is stored at the end of a pipeline or at a port. **2** a point of connection for closing an electric circuit. **3** a device at which a user enters data or commands for a computer system and that displays the received output. **4** (also **terminal figure**) another term for TERMINUS (sense 3). ▷early 19th cent.: from Latin *terminalis*, from *terminus* 'end, boundary.' —**ter·mi·nal·ly** *adv.* (in sense 2 of the *adjective*) [as *submodifier*] *a terminally ill woman.*

ter·mi·nal mo·raine ▸*n. Geology* a moraine deposited at the point of furthest advance of a glacier or ice sheet.

ter·mi·nal ve·loc·i·ty ▸*n. Physics* the constant speed that a freely falling object eventually reaches when the resistance of the medium through which it is falling prevents further acceleration.

ter·mi·nate /ˈtərməˌnāt/ ▸*v.* [*trans.*] bring to an end: *he was advised to terminate the contract.* ■ [*intrans.*] (**terminate in**) (of a thing) have its end at (a specified place) or of (a specified form): *the chain terminated in an iron ball covered with spikes.* ■ [*intrans.*] (of a train, bus, or boat service) end its journey: *the train will terminate at Stratford.* ■ end (a pregnancy) before term by artificial means. ■ end the employment of (someone); dismiss: *Adamson's putting pressure on me to terminate you.* ■ assassinate (someone, esp. an intelligence agent): *he was terminated by persons unknown.* ■ *archaic* form the physical end or extremity of (an area). ▷late 16th cent. (in the sense 'direct an action toward a specified end'): from Latin *terminat-* 'limited, ended,' from the verb *terminare*, from *terminus* 'end, boundary.'
▸*PHRASE* □ **terminate someone with extreme prejudice** murder or assassinate someone (used as a euphemism).

ter·mi·na·tion /ˌtərməˈnāSHən/ ▸*n.* **1** the action of bringing something or coming to an end: *the termination of a contract.* ■ an act of dismissing someone from employment. ■ an induced abortion. ■ an assassination, esp. of an intelligence agent. **2** an ending or final point of something, in particular: ■ the final letter or letters or syllable of a word, esp. when constituting an element in inflection or derivation. ■ [with *adj.*] *archaic* an ending or result of a specified kind: *a good result and a happy termination.* ▷late Middle English (in the sense 'determination, decision'): from Old French, or from Latin *terminatio(n-)*, from *terminare* 'to limit, end.' —**ter·mi·na·tion·al** /-SHənl/ *adj.*

ter·mi·na·tor /ˈtərməˌnātər/ ▸*n.* a person or thing that terminates something. ■ *Astronomy* the dividing line between the light and dark part of a planetary body. ■ *Biochemistry* a sequence of polynucleotides that causes transcription to end and the newly synthesized nucleic acid to be released from the template molecule.

ter·mi·ner /ˈtərmənər/ ▸*n.* see OYER AND TERMINER.

ter·mi·ni /ˈtərmənī/ ▸ plural form of TERMINUS.

ter·mi·nol·o·gy /ˌtərməˈnäləjē/ ▸*n.* (*pl.* **-gies**) the body of terms used with a particular technical application in a subject of study, theory, profession, etc.: *the terminology of semiotics | specialized terminologies for higher education.* ▷early 19th cent.: from German *Terminologie*, from medieval Latin *terminus* 'term.' —**ter·mi·no·log·i·cal** /-nəˈläjikəl/ *adj.* —**ter·mi·no·log·i·cal·ly** /-nəˈläjik(ə)lē/ *adv.* —**ter·mi·nol·o·gist** /-jist/ *n.*

ter·mi·nus /ˈtərmənəs/ ▸*n.* (*pl.* **-ni** /-nī/ or **-nus·es**) **1** a final point in space or time; an end or extremity: *the exhibition's terminus is 1962.* ■ *Biochemistry* the end of a polypeptide or polynucleotide chain or similar long molecule. **2** *chiefly Brit.* the end of a railroad or other transportation route, or a station at such a point; a terminal. ■ an oil or gas terminal. **3** *Architecture* a figure of a human bust or an animal ending in a square pillar from which it appears to spring, originally used as a boundary marker in ancient Rome. ▷mid 16th cent. (in the sense 'final point in space or time'): from Latin, 'end, limit, boundary.'

ter·mi·nus ad quem /ˈtərmənəs ädˈkwem/ ▸*n.* the point at which something ends or finishes. ■ an aim or goal. ▷Latin, literally 'end to which.'

ter·mi·nus an·te quem /ˈtərmənəs ˈantē ˈkwem/ ▸*n.* the latest possible date for something. ▷Latin, literally 'end before which.'

ter·mi·nus a quo /ˈtərmənəs ä ˈkwō/ ▸*n.* the earliest possible date for something. ■ a starting point or initial impulse. ▷Latin, literally 'end from which.'

ter·mi·nus post quem /ˈtərmənəs ˈpōst ˈkwem/ ▸*n.* the earliest possible date for something. ▷Latin, literally 'end after which.'

ter·mi·tar·i·um /ˌtərmiˈte(ə)rēəm/ ▸*n.* (*pl.* **-tar·i·a** /-ˈte(ə)rēə/) a colony of termites, typically within a mound of cemented earth. ▷mid 19th cent.: modern Latin, from Latin *termes, termit-* 'termite.'

ter·mi·ta·ry /ˈtərmiˌterē/ ▸*n.* (*pl.* **-ries**) another term for TERMITARIUM.

ter·mite /ˈtərˌmīt/ ▸*n.* a small, pale soft-bodied insect that lives in large colonies with several different castes, typically within a mound of cemented earth. Many kinds feed on wood and can be highly destructive to trees and timber. Also called WHITE ANT. • Order Isoptera: several families. ▷late 18th cent.: from Latin *termes, termit-* 'woodworm,' alteration of Latin *tarmes*, perhaps by association with *terere* 'to rub.'

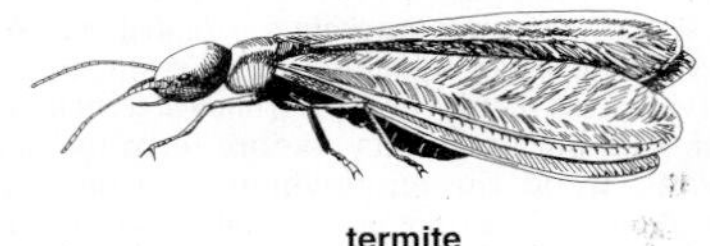

termite

term life in·sur·ance ▸*n.* life insurance that pays a benefit in the event of the death of the insured during a specified term. Compare with WHOLE LIFE INSURANCE.

term of years ▸*n.* see TERM (sense 2).

term pa·per ▸*n.* a student's lengthy essay on a subject drawn from the work done during a school or college term.

terms of trade ▸*plural n. Economics* the ratio of an index of a country's export prices to an index of its import prices.

tern[1] /tərn/ ▸*n.* a seabird related to the gulls, typically smaller and more slender, with long pointed wings and a forked tail. • Family Sternidae (or Laridae): several genera, in particular *Sterna*, and many species. ▷late 17th cent.: of Scandinavian origin; related to Danish *terne* and Swedish *tärna*, both from Old Norse *therna*.

tern[2] ▸*n. rare* a set of three, esp. three lottery numbers that when drawn together win a large prize. ▷late Middle English: apparently from French *terne*, from Latin *terni* 'three at once, three each,' from *ter* 'thrice.'

ter·na·ry /ˈtərnərē/ ▸*adj.* composed of three parts. ■ *Mathematics* using three as a base. ▷late Middle English: from Latin *ternarius*, from *terni* 'three at once.'

ter·na·ry form ▸*n. Music* the form of a movement in which the first subject is repeated after an interposed second subject in a related key.

terne /tərn/ ▸*n.* (also **terne metal**) a lead alloy containing about 20 percent tin and often some antimony. ■ (also **terne·plate**) thin sheet iron or steel coated with this. ▷mid 19th cent. (denoting terneplate): probably from French *terne* 'dull, tarnished.'

ter·pene /ˈtərˌpēn/ ▸*n. Chemistry* any of a large group of volatile unsaturated hydrocarbons found in the essential oils of plants, esp. conifers and citrus trees. They are based on a cyclic molecule having the formula $C_{10}H_{16}$. ▷late 19th cent.: from German *Terpentin* 'turpentine' + -ENE.

ter·pe·noid /ˈtərpəˌnoid/ *Chemistry* ▸*n.* any of a large class of organic compounds including terpenes, diterpenes, and sesquiterpenes. They have unsaturated molecules composed of linked isoprene units, generally having the formula $(C_5H_8)_n$.
▸*adj.* denoting such a compound.

ter·pol·y·mer /tərˈpäləmər/ ▸*n. Chemistry* a polymer synthesized from three different monomers.

Terp·sich·o·re /ˌtərpˈsikərē/ *Greek & Roman Mythology* the Muse of lyric poetry and dance. ▷Greek, literally 'delighting in dancing.'

terp·si·cho·re·an /ˌtərpsikəˈrēən; -ˈkôrēən/ ▸*adj. formal* or *humorous* of or relating to dancing.
▸*n. formal* or *humorous* a dancer. ▷early 19th cent.: from *Terpsichore* (used in the 18th cent. to denote a female dancer or the art of dance) + -AN.

terr. ▸*abbr.* ■ terrace. ■ territorial. ■ territory.

ter·ra /ˈterə/ ▸*n.* **1** (also **Ter·ra**) (in science fiction) the planet earth. **2** [usu. with *adj.*] land or territory. ▷Latin, literally 'earth.'

ter·ra al·ba /ˈterə ˈalbə/ ▸*n.* pulverized gypsum, esp. as an ingredient of medicines. ▷Latin, literally 'white earth.'

ter·race /ˈteris/ ▸*n.* **1** a level paved area or platform next to a building; a patio or veranda. ■ each of a series of flat areas made on a slope, used for cultivation. ■ *Geology* a natural horizontal shelflike formation, such as a raised beach. **2** *chiefly Brit.* a block of row houses. ■ a row house.
▸*v.* [*trans.*] make or form (sloping land) into a number of level flat areas resembling a series of steps. ▷early 16th cent. (denoting an open gallery, later a platform or balcony in a theater): from Old French, literally 'rubble, platform,' based on Latin *terra* 'earth.'

ter·raced /ˈterist/ ▸*adj.* **1** (of land) having been formed into a number of level areas resembling a series of steps. **2** *chiefly Brit.* (of a house) in the style of a row house.

ter·ra cot·ta /ˈterə ˈkätə/ (also **ter·ra·cot·ta**) ▸*n.* unglazed, typically brownish-red earthenware, used chiefly as an ornamental building material and in modeling. ■ a statuette or other object made of such earthenware. ■ a strong brownish-red or brownish-orange color. ▷early 18th cent.: from Italian *terra cotta* 'baked earth,' from Latin *terra cocta*.

ter·ra fir·ma /ˈterə ˈfərmə/ ▸*n.* dry land; the ground as distinct from the sea or air. ▷early 17th cent. (denoting the territories on the Italian mainland that were subject to the state of Venice): from Latin, literally 'firm land.'

ter·ra·form /ˈterəˌfôrm/ ▸*v.* [*trans.*] (esp. in science fiction) transform (a planet) so as to resemble the earth, esp. so that it can support human life. ▷1940s: from Latin *terra* 'earth' + the verb FORM. **—ter·ra·form·er** *n.*

ter·rain /təˈrān/ ▸*n.* **1** a stretch of land, esp. with regard to its physical features: *they were delayed by rough terrain.* **2** *Geology* variant form of TERRANE. ▷early 18th cent. (denoting part of the training ground in a riding school): from French, from a popular Latin variant of Latin *terrenum*, neuter of *terrenus* (see TERRENE).

ter·ra in·cog·ni·ta /ˈterə ˌinkägˈnētə; inˈkägnitə/ ▸*n.* unknown or unexplored territory. ▷Latin, 'unknown land.'

Ter·ra·my·cin /ˌterəˈmīsin/ ▸*n.* trademark for OXYTETRACYCLINE. ▷1950s: from Latin *terra* 'earth' + -MYCIN.

Ter·ran /ˈterən/ ▸*n.* (in science fiction) an inhabitant of the planet Earth.
▸*adj.* (in science fiction) of or relating to the planet Earth or its inhabitants.

ter·rane /təˈrān; ˈterˌān/ (also **ter·rain**) ▸*n. Geology* a fault-bounded area or region with a distinctive stratigraphy, structure, and geological history. ▷early 19th cent: from popular Latin *terranum*. Compare with TERRAIN.

ter·ra·pin /ˈterəˌpin/ ▸*n.* **1** (also **diamondback terrapin**) a small edible turtle with lozenge-shaped markings on its shell, found in coastal marshes of the eastern U.S. • *Malaclemys terrapin*, family Emydidae. **2** a freshwater turtle, esp. one of the smaller kinds of the Old World. Also called TURTLE. • Emydidae and other families, order Chelonia: several genera and species. ▷early 17th cent. (denoting the diamondback terrapin): of Algonquian origin.

diamondback terrapin

ter·ra·que·ous /terˈākwēəs; -ˈak-/ ▸*adj.* consisting of, or formed of, land and water. ▷mid 17th cent.: from Latin *terra* 'land' + AQUEOUS.

ter·rar·i·um /təˈre(ə)rēəm/ ▸*n.* (*pl.* **-rar·i·ums** or **-rar·i·a** /-ˈre(ə)rēə/) a vivarium for smaller land animals, esp. reptiles, amphibians, or terrestrial invertebrates, typically in the form of a glass-fronted case. ■ a sealed transparent globe or similar container in which plants are grown. ▷late 19th cent.: modern Latin, from Latin *terra* 'earth,' on the pattern of *aquarium*.

ter·rasse /teˈräs/ ▸*n.* (*pl.* same) (in France) a flat, paved area outside a cafe where people sit to take refreshments. ▷French, literally 'terrace.'

ter·raz·zo /təˈräzō; tiˈrätsō/ ▸*n.* flooring material consisting of chips of marble or granite set in concrete and polished to give a smooth surface. ▷early 20th cent.: Italian, literally 'terrace,' based on Latin *terra* 'earth.'

Ter·re Haute /ˌter(ə) ˈhōt/ a city in western Indiana, on the Wabash River, near the border with Illinois; pop. 59,614.

ter·rene /təˈrēn; ˈterˌēn/ ▸*adj. archaic* of or like earth; earthy. ■ occurring on or inhabiting dry land. ■ of the world; secular rather than spiritual. ▷Middle English: from Anglo-Norman French, from Latin *terrenus*, from *terra* 'earth.'

terre·plein /ˈterəˌplān/ ▸*n. chiefly historical* a level space where a battery of guns is mounted. ▷late 16th cent. (denoting a sloping bank behind a rampart): from French *terre-plein*, from Italian *terrapieno*, from *terrapienare* 'fill with earth.'

ter·res·tri·al /təˈrestrēəl; -ˈresCHəl/ ▸*adj.* of, on, or relating to the earth: *increased ultraviolet radiation may disrupt terrestrial ecosystems.* ■ denoting television broadcast using equipment situated on the ground rather than by satellite: *terrestrial and cable technology.* ■ of or on dry land: *a submarine eruption will be much more explosive than its terrestrial counterpart.* ■ (of an animal) living on or in the ground; not aquatic, arboreal, or aerial. ■ (of a plant) growing on land or in the soil; not aquatic or epiphytic. ■ *Astronomy* (of a planet) similar in size or composition to the earth, esp. being one of the four inner planets of our solar system. ■ *archaic* of or relating to the earth as opposed to heaven.
▸*n.* an inhabitant of the earth. ▷late Middle English (in the sense 'temporal, worldly, mundane'): from Latin *terrestris* (from *terra* 'earth') + -AL. **—ter·res·tri·al·ly** *adv.*

ter·res·tri·al globe ▸*n.* a spherical representation of the earth with a map on the surface.

ter·res·tri·al mag·net·ism ▸*n.* the magnetic properties of the earth as a whole.

ter·res·tri·al tel·e·scope ▸*n.* a telescope that is used for observing terrestrial objects and gives an uninverted image.

ter·ret /ˈterit/ ▸*n.* each of the loops or rings on a harness pad for the driving reins to pass through. ▷late 15th cent. (denoting either of two rings by which a leash is attached to a hawk's jesses): from Old French *touret*, diminutive of *tour* 'a turn.'

terre verte /ˈter ˈvert/ ▸*n.* a grayish-green pigment made from glauconite and used esp. for watercolors and tempera. Also called GREEN EARTH. ▷mid 17th cent.: French, literally 'green earth.'

ter·ri·bi·li·tà /ˌterəˌbiləˈtä/ ▸*n.* awesomeness or emotional intensity of conception and execution in an artist or work of art, originally as a quality attributed to Michelangelo by his contemporaries. ▷Italian.

ter·ri·ble /ˈterəbəl/ ▸*adj.* extremely and shockingly or distressingly bad or serious: *a terrible crime | terrible pain.* ■ causing or likely to cause terror; sinister: *the stranger gave a terrible smile.* ■ of extremely poor quality: *the terrible conditions in which the ordinary people lived.* ■ [*attrib.*] *informal* used to emphasize the extent of something unpleasant or bad: *what a terrible mess.* ■ extremely incompetent or unskillful: *she is* ***terrible at*** *managing her money.* ■ [as *complement*] feeling or looking extremely unwell: *I was sick all night and felt terrible for two solid days.* ■ [as *complement*] (of a person or their feelings) troubled or guilty: *Maria felt terrible because she had forgotten the woman's name.* ▷late Middle English (in the sense 'causing terror'): via French from Latin *terribilis*, from *terrere* 'frighten.' **—ter·ri·ble·ness** *n.*

ter·ri·bly /ˈterəblē/ ▸*adv.* **1** [usu. as *submodifier*] very; extremely: *I'm terribly sorry | it was all terribly frustrating.* **2** very badly or unpleasantly: *they beat me terribly.* ■ very greatly (used to emphasize something bad, distressing, or unpleasant): *your father misses you terribly.*

ter·ric·o·lous /teˈrikələs/ ▸*adj. Zoology* (of an animal such as an earthworm) living on the ground or in the soil. ■ *Botany* (of a plant, esp. a lichen) growing on soil or on the ground. ▷mid 19th cent.: from Latin *terricola* 'earth dweller' (from *terra* 'earth' + *colere* 'inhabit') + -OUS.

ter·ri·er /ˈterēər/ ▸*n.* a small dog of a breed originally used for turning out foxes and other burrowing animals from their lairs. ■ used in similes to emphasize tenacity or eagerness: *she would fight like a terrier for every penny.* ▷late Middle English: from Old French *(chien) terrier* 'earth (dog),' from medieval Latin *terrarius*, from Latin *terra* 'earth.'

ter·rif·ic /təˈrifik/ ▸*adj.* **1** of great size, amount, or intensity: *there was a terrific bang.* ■ *informal* extremely good; excellent: *it's been such a terrific day | you look terrific.* **2** *archaic* causing terror. ▷mid 17th cent. (sense 2): from Latin *terrificus*, from *terrere* 'frighten.'

—ter·rif·i·cal·ly /-ik(ə)lē/ *adv.* [as *submodifier*] *she's been terrifically busy lately.*

ter·ri·fy /ˈterəˌfī/ ▸*v.* (**-fies, -fied**) [*trans.*] cause to feel extreme fear: *the thought terrifies me* | *he is* **terrified of** *spiders* | [*trans.*] *she was terrified he would drop her* | [as *adj.*] (**terrifying**) *the terrifying events of the past few weeks.* ▷late 16th cent.: from Latin *terrificare*, from *terrificus* 'frightening' (see **TERRIFIC**). **—ter·ri·fi·er** *n.* **—ter·ri·fy·ing·ly** /ˈterəˌfī-iNGlē/ *adv.* [as *submodifier*] *the bombs are terrifyingly accurate.*

ter·rig·e·nous /teˈrijənəs/ ▸*adj. Geology* (of a marine deposit) made of material eroded from the land. ▷late 17th cent. (in the sense 'produced from the earth, earth-born'): from Latin *terrigenus* (from *terra* 'earth' + *-genus* 'born') + **-OUS**.

ter·rine /təˈrēn/ ▸*n.* a meat, fish, or vegetable mixture that has been cooked or otherwise prepared in advance and allowed to cool or set in its container, typically served in slices. ■ a container used for such a dish, typically of an oblong shape and made of earthenware. ▷early 18th cent. (denoting a tureen): from French, literally 'large earthenware pot,' from *terrin* 'earthen.' Compare with **TUREEN**.

ter·ri·to·ri·al /ˌteriˈtôrēəl/ ▸*adj.* **1** of or relating to the ownership of an area of land or sea: *territorial disputes.* ■ *Zoology* (of an animal or species) defending a territory: *these sharks are aggressively territorial.* ■ of or relating to an animal's territory or its defense: *territorial growls.* **2** of or relating to a particular territory, district, or locality: *a bizarre territorial rite.* ■ (usu. **Territorial**) of or relating to a Territory, in the U.S. or Canada.
▸*n.* (**Territorial**) (in the UK) a member of the Territorial Army, a volunteer force locally organized to provide a reserve of trained and disciplined manpower for use in an emergency. ▷early 17th cent.: from late Latin *territorialis*, from Latin *territorium* (see **TERRITORY**). **—ter·ri·to·ri·al·i·ty** /-ˌtôrēˈalitē/ *n.* **—ter·ri·to·ri·al·ly** *adv.*

ter·ri·to·ri·al im·per·a·tive ▸*n.* [usu. in *sing.*] *Zoology & Psychology* the need to claim and defend a territory.

ter·ri·to·ri·al wa·ters ▸*plural n.* the waters under the jurisdiction of a state, esp. the part of the sea within a stated distance of the shore (traditionally three miles from low-water mark).

ter·ri·to·ry /ˈterəˌtôrē/ ▸*n.* (*pl.* **-ries**) **1** an area of land under the jurisdiction of a ruler or state: *the government was prepared to give up the nuclear weapons on its territory* | *sorties into enemy territory.* ■ *Zoology* an area defended by an animal or group of animals against others of the same sex or species. Compare with **HOME RANGE**. ■ an area defended by a team or player in a game or sport. ■ an area in which one has certain rights or for which one has responsibility with regard to a particular type of activity: *a sales rep for a large territory.* ■ *figurative* an area of knowledge, activity, or experience: *the contentious territory of clinical standards* | *the way she felt now—she was in unknown territory.* ■ [with *adj.*] land with a specified characteristic: *woodland territory.* **2** (**Territory**) (esp. in the U.S., Canada, or Australia) an organized division of a country that is not yet admitted to the full rights of a state. ▷late Middle English: from Latin *territorium*, from *terra* 'land.' The word originally denoted the district surrounding and under the jurisdiction of a town or city, specifically a Roman or provincial city.
▸*PHRASE* □ **go** (or **come**) **with the territory** be an unavoidable result of a particular situation.

ter·roir /terˈwär/ ▸*n.* the complete natural environment in which a particular wine is produced, including factors such as the soil, topography, and climate. ■ (also **goût de ter·roir** /go͞o də/) the characteristic taste and flavor imparted to a wine by the environment in which it is produced. ▷1970s: French, from medieval Latin, *terratorium*.

ter·ror /ˈterər/ ▸*n.* **1** extreme fear: *people fled* **in terror** | [in *sing.*] *a terror of darkness.* ■ the use of such fear to intimidate people, esp. for political reasons: *weapons of terror.* ■ [in *sing.*] a person or thing that causes extreme fear: *his unyielding scowl became* **the terror of** *the Chicago mob.* ■ (**the Terror**) the period of the French Revolution between mid 1793 and July 1794 when the ruling Jacobin faction, dominated by Robespierre, ruthlessly executed anyone considered a threat to their regime. Also called **REIGN OF TERROR**. **2** (also **holy terror**) *informal* a person, esp. a child, who causes trouble or annoyance: *placid and obedient in their parents' presence, but holy terrors when left alone.* ▷late Middle English: from Old French *terrour*, from Latin *terror*, from *terrere* 'frighten.'
▸*PHRASE* □ **have** (or **hold**) **no terrors for someone** not frighten or worry someone.

ter·ror·ism /ˈterəˌrizəm/ ▸*n.* the use of violence and intimidation in the pursuit of political aims.

ter·ror·ist /ˈterərist/ ▸*n.* a person who uses terrorism in the pursuit of political aims. ▷late 18th cent.: from French *terroriste*, from Latin *terror* (see **TERROR**). The word was originally applied to supporters of the Jacobins in the French Revolution, who advocated repression and violence in pursuit of the principles of democracy and equality. **—ter·ror·is·tic** /ˌterəˈristik/ *adj.* **—ter·ror·is·ti·cal·ly** *adv.*

ter·ror·ize /ˈterəˌrīz/ ▸*v.* [*trans.*] create and maintain a state of extreme fear and distress in (someone); fill with terror: *he used his private army to terrorize the population* | *the union said staff would not be* **terrorized into** *ending their strike.* **—ter·ror·i·za·tion** /ˌterərəˈzāSHən/ *n.* **—ter·ror·iz·er** *n.*

ter·ror-strick·en (also **terror-struck**) ▸*adj.* feeling or expressing extreme fear.

ter·ry /ˈterē/ (also **ter·ry cloth**) ▸*n.* (*pl.* **-ries**) a fabric with raised uncut loops of thread covering both surfaces, used esp. for towels. ▷late 18th cent.: of unknown origin.

terse /tərs/ ▸*adj.* (**ters·er, ters·est**) sparing in the use of words; abrupt: *a terse statement.* ▷early 17th cent.: from Latin *tersus* 'wiped, polished,' from the verb *tergere*. The original sense was 'polished, trim, spruce,' (relating to language) 'polished, polite,' hence 'concise and to the point' (late 18th cent.). **—terse·ly** *adv.* **—terse·ness** *n.*

THE RIGHT WORD **concise, laconic, pithy, succinct, terse**

If you don't like to mince words, you'll make every effort to be **concise** in both your writing and speaking, which means to remove all superfluous details (*a concise summary of everything that happened*).

Succinct is very close in meaning to *concise*, although it emphasizes compression and compactness in addition to brevity (*succinct instructions for what to do in an emergency*).

If you're **laconic**, you are brief to the point of being curt, brusque, or even uncommunicative (*his laconic reply left many questions unanswered*).

Terse can also mean clipped or abrupt (*a terse command*), but it usually connotes something that is both concise and polished (*a terse style of writing that was much admired*).

A **pithy** statement is not only succinct but full of substance and meaning (*a pithy argument that no one could counter*).

ter·tian /ˈtərSHən/ ▸*adj.* [*attrib.*] *Medicine* denoting a form of malaria causing a fever that recurs every second day: *tertian fever.* • The common benign tertian malaria (or tertian ague) is caused by infection with *Plasmodium vivax* or *P. ovale*, and malignant tertian malaria is caused by *P. falciparum*. Compare with **QUARTAN**. ▷late Middle English (*fever*) *terciane*, from Latin *(febris) tertiana*, from *tertius* 'third' (the fever recurring every third day by inclusive reckoning).

ter·ti·ar·y /ˈtərSHēˌerē; -SHərē/ ▸*adj.* **1** third in order or level: *most of the enterprises were of tertiary importance* | *the tertiary stage of the disease.* ■ *chiefly Brit.* relating to or denoting education at a level beyond that provided by schools, esp. that provided by a college or university. ■ relating to or denoting the medical treatment provided at a specialist institution. **2** (**Tertiary**) *Geology* of, relating to, or denoting the first period of the Cenozoic era, between the Cretaceous and Quaternary periods, and comprising the Paleogene and Neogene subperiods. **3** *Chemistry* (of an organic compound) having its functional group located on a carbon atom that is itself bonded to three other carbon atoms. ■ *Chemistry* (chiefly of amines) derived from ammonia by replacement of three hydrogen atoms by organic groups.
▸*n.* **1** (**the Tertiary**) *Geology* the Tertiary period or the system of rocks deposited during it.

The Tertiary lasted from about 65 million to 1.6 million years ago. The mammals diversified following the demise of the dinosaurs and became dominant, as did the flowering plants.

2 a lay associate of certain Christian monastic organizations: *a Franciscan tertiary.* ▷mid 16th cent. (sense 2 of the *noun*): from Latin *tertiarius* 'of the third part or rank,' from *tertius* 'third.'

ter·ti·ar·y struc·ture ▸*n. Biochemistry* the overall three-dimensional structure resulting from folding and covalent cross-linking of a protein or polynucleotide molecule.

ter·ti·um quid /ˈtərSHēəm ˈkwid; ˈtərtēəm/ ▸*n.* a third thing that is indefinite and undefined but is related to two definite or known things. ▷early 18th cent.: from late Latin, translation of Greek *triton ti* 'some third thing.'

Ter·tul·li·an /tərˈtəlēən; -ˈtəlyən/ (*c.*160–*c.*240), early Christian theologian; Latin name *Quintus Septimius Florens Tertullianus*. His writings include Christian apologetics and attacks on pagan idolatry and Gnosticism.

ter·va·lent /tərˈvālənt/ ▸*adj. Chemistry* another term for **TRIVALENT**.

ter·za ri·ma /ˌtertsə ˈrēmə/ ▸*n. Prosody* an arrangement of triplets, esp. in iambs, that rhyme *aba bcb cdc*, etc., as in Dante's *Divine Comedy*. ▷Italian, literally 'third rhyme.'

TESL /ˈtesəl/ ▸*abbr.* teaching of English as a second language.

Tes·la /ˈteslə/, Nikola (1856–1943), U.S. electrical engineer and inventor, born in what is now Croatia. He developed the first alternating-current induction motor, as well as several forms of oscillators, the tesla coil, and a wireless guidance system for ships.

tes·la /ˈteslə/ (abbr.: **T**) ▸*n. Physics* the SI unit of magnetic flux density. ▷1960s: named after N. **TESLA**.

Tes·la coil ▸*n.* a form of induction coil for producing high-frequency alternating currents.

TESOL /ˈteˌsäl; -ˌsôl; ˈtesəl/ ▸*abbr.* teaching of English to speakers of other languages.

tes·sel·late /ˈtesəˌlāt/ (also **tes·se·late**) ▸*v.* [*trans.*] decorate (a floor) with mosaics. ■ *Mathematics* cover (a plane surface) by repeated use of a single shape, without gaps or overlapping. ▷late 18th cent.: from late Latin *tessellat-*, from the verb *tessellare*, from *tessella*, diminutive of *tessera* (see **TESSERA**). **—tes·sel·la·tion** /ˌtesəˈlāSHən/ (also **tes·se·la·tion**) *n.*

tes·ser·a /ˈtesərə/ ▸*n.* (*pl.* **tes·se·rae** /ˈtesərē/) a small block of stone, tile, glass, or other material used in the construction of a mosaic. ■ (in ancient Greece and Rome) a small tablet of wood or bone used as a token. ▷mid 17th cent.: via Latin from Greek, neuter of *tesseres*, variant of *tessares* 'four.' **—tes·ser·al** /-rəl/ *adj.*

Tes·sin /teˈsaN; teˈsēn/ French and German name for **TICINO**.

tes·si·tu·ra /ˌtesiˈto͝orə/ ▸*n. Music* the range within which most notes of a vocal part fall. ▷Italian, literally 'texture,' from Latin *textura* (see **TEXTURE**).

test[1] /test/ ▸*n.* **1** a procedure intended to establish the quality, performance, or reliability of something, esp. before it is taken into widespread use: *no sparking was visible during the tests.* ■ a short written or spoken examination of a person's proficiency or knowledge: *a spelling test.* ■ an event or situation that reveals the strength or quality of someone or something by putting them under strain: *this is the first serious test of the peace agreement.* ■ an examination of part of the body or a body fluid for medical purposes, esp. by means of a chemical or mechanical procedure rather than simple inspection: *a test for HIV* | *eye tests.* ■ *Chemistry* a procedure employed to identify a substance or to reveal the presence or absence of a constituent within a substance. ■ the result of a medical examination or analytical procedure: *a positive test for protein.* ■ a means of establishing whether an action, item, or situation is an instance of a specified quality, esp. one held to be undesirable: *a statutory test of obscenity.* **2** *Metallurgy* a movable hearth in a reverberating furnace, used for separating gold or silver from lead.
▸*v.* [*trans.*] take measures to check the quality, performance, or reliability of (something), esp. before putting it into widespread use or practice: *this range has not been tested on animals* | [as *n.*] (**testing**) *the testing and developing of prototypes* | *figurative a useful way to* **test out** *ideas before implementation.* ■ reveal the strengths or capabilities of (someone or something) by putting them under strain: *such behavior would severely test any marriage* ■ give (someone) a short written or oral examination of their proficiency or knowledge: *all children are tested at eleven.* ■ judge or measure (someone's proficiency or knowledge) by means of such an examination. ■ carry out a medical test on (a person, a part of the body, or a body fluid). ■ [*intrans.*] produce a specified result in a medical test, esp. a drug test or AIDS test: *he* **tested positive** *for steroids during the race.* ■ *Chemistry* examine (a substance) by means of a reagent. ■ touch or taste

(something) to check that it is acceptable before proceeding further: *she tested the water with the tip of her elbow.* ▷late Middle English (denoting a cupel used to treat gold or silver alloys or ore): via Old French from Latin *testu, testum* 'earthen pot,' variant of *testa* 'jug, shell.' Compare with TEST2. The verb dates from the early 17th cent. **—test·a·bil·i·ty** /ˌtestəˈbilitē/ *n.* **—test·a·ble** *adj.* **—test·ee** /-ˈtē/ *n.*

▶*PHRASES* □ **put someone/something to the test** find out how useful, strong, or effective someone or something is. □ **stand the test of time** last or remain popular for a long time. □ **test the water** judge people's feelings or opinions before taking further action.

test2 ▶*n. Zoology* the shell or integument of some invertebrates and protozoans, esp. the chalky shell of a foraminiferan or the tough outer layer of a tunicate. ▷mid 19th cent.: from Latin *testa* 'tile, jug, shell.' Compare with TEST1.

Test. ▶*abbr.* Testament.

test. ▶*abbr.* ■ testator. ■ testimony.

tes·ta /ˈtestə/ ▶*n.* (*pl.* **-tae** /-tē/) *Botany* the protective outer covering of a seed; the seed coat. ▷late 18th cent.: from Latin, literally 'tile, shell.'

tes·ta·ceous /teˈstāsHəs/ ▶*adj. chiefly Entomology* of a dull brick-red color. ▷mid 17th cent.: from Latin *testaceus* (from *testa* 'tile') + **-OUS**.

tes·ta·ment /ˈtestəmənt/ ▶*n.* **1** a person's will, esp. the part relating to personal property. **2** something that serves as a sign or evidence of a specified fact, event, or quality: *growing attendance figures are a* **testament to** *the event's popularity.* **3** (in biblical use) a covenant or dispensation. ■ (**Testament**) a division of the Bible. See also **OLD TESTAMENT, NEW TESTAMENT.** ■ (**Testament**) a copy of the New Testament. ▷Middle English: from Latin *testamentum* 'a will' (from *testari* 'testify'), in Christian Latin also translating Greek *diathēkē* 'covenant.'

tes·ta·men·ta·ry /ˌtestəˈmen(t)ərē/ ▶*adj.* of, relating to, or bequeathed or appointed through a will. ▷late Middle English: from Latin *testamentarius,* from *testamentum* 'a will,' from *testari* 'testify.'

tes·tate /ˈtesˌtāt/ ▶*adj.* [*predic.*] having made a valid will before one dies.
▶*n.* a person who has died leaving such a will. ▷late Middle English (as a noun): from Latin *testatus* 'testified, witnessed,' past participle of *testari,* from *testis* 'a witness.'

tes·ta·tion /teˈstāsHən/ ▶*n. Law* the disposal of property by will.

tes·ta·tor /ˈtestātər/ ▶*n. Law* a person who has made a will or given a legacy. ▷Middle English: from Anglo-Norman French *testatour,* from Latin *testator,* from the verb *testari* 'testify.'

tes·ta·trix /teˈstātriks/ ▶*n.* (*pl.* **-tri·ces** /-trisēz/ or **-trix·es**) *dated Law* a woman who has made a will or given a legacy. ▷late 16th cent.: from late Latin, feminine of *testator* (see **TESTATOR**).

Test-Ban Trea·ty an international agreement not to test nuclear weapons in the atmosphere, in space, or underwater, signed in 1963 by the U.S., the UK, and the USSR, and later by more than 100 governments.

test bed ▶*n.* a piece of equipment used for testing new machinery, esp. aircraft engines.

test case ▶*n. Law* a case that sets a precedent for other cases involving the same question of law.

test drive ▶*n.* an act of driving a motor vehicle that one is considering buying in order to determine its quality. ■ *figurative* a test of a product before purchase or release.
▶*v.* (**test-drive**) [*trans.*] drive (a vehicle) to determine its qualities with a view to buying it. ■ *figurative* test (a product) before purchase or release.

test·er1 /ˈtestər/ ▶*n.* a person who tests something, esp. a new product. ■ a person who tests another's proficiency. ■ a device that tests the functioning of something: *a cake tester.* ■ a sample of a product provided so that customers can try it before buying it.

test·er2 ▶*n.* a canopy over a four-poster bed. ▷late Middle English: from medieval Latin *testerium, testrum,* from a Romance word meaning 'head,' based on Latin *testa* 'tile.'

tes·tes /ˈtestēz/ ▶ plural form of **TESTIS**.

test flight ▶*n.* a flight during which the performance of an aircraft or its equipment is tested. **—test-fly** *v.*

tes·ti·cle /ˈtestikəl/ ▶*n.* either of the two oval organs that produce sperm in men and other male mammals, enclosed in the scrotum behind the penis. Also called **TESTIS**. ▷late Middle English: from Latin *testiculus,* diminutive of *testis* 'a witness' (i.e., to virility). **—tes·tic·u·lar** /teˈstikyələr/ *adj.*

tes·tic·u·lar fem·i·ni·za·tion ▶*n.* a condition produced in genetically male people by the failure of tissue to respond to male sex hormones, resulting in normal female anatomy but with testes in place of ovaries.

tes·tic·u·late /teˈstikyəlit/ ▶*adj. Botany* (esp. of the twin tubers of some orchids) shaped like a pair of testicles. ▷mid 18th cent.: from late Latin *testiculatus,* from *testiculus* (see **TESTICLE**).

tes·ti·fy /ˈtestəˌfī/ ▶*v.* (**-fies, -fied**) [*intrans.*] give evidence as a witness in a law court: *he testified against his own commander* | [with *clause*] *he testified that he had supplied Barry with crack.* ■ serve as evidence or proof of something's existing or being the case: *the bleak lines* **testify to** *inner torment.* ▷late Middle English: from Latin *testificari,* from *testis* 'a witness.' **—tes·ti·fi·er** *n.*

tes·ti·mo·ni·al /ˌtestəˈmōnēəl/ ▶*n.* a formal statement testifying to someone's character and qualifications. ■ a public tribute to someone and to their achievements. ■ [often as *adj.*] (in sports) a game or event held in honor of a player, who typically receives part of the income generated: *the Yankees held a testimonial day for Gehrig.* ▷late Middle English: from Old French *testimonial* 'testifying, serving as evidence,' from late Latin *testimonialis,* from Latin *testimonium* (see **TESTIMONY**).

tes·ti·mo·ny /ˈtestəˌmōnē/ ▶*n.* (*pl.* **-nies**) a formal written or spoken statement, esp. one given in a court of law. ■ evidence or proof provided by the existence or appearance of something: *his blackened finger was* **testimony to** *the fact that he had played in pain.* ■ a public recounting of a religious conversion or experience. ■ *archaic* a solemn protest or declaration. ▷Middle English: from Latin *testimonium,* from *testis* 'a witness.'

test·ing ground ▶*n.* an area or field of activity used for the testing of a product or an idea, esp. a military site used for the testing of weapons.

tes·tis /ˈtestis/ ▶*n.* (*pl.* **-tes** /-ˌtēz/) *Anatomy & Zoology* an organ that produces spermatozoa (male reproductive cells). Compare with **TESTICLE**. ▷early 18th cent.: from Latin, literally 'a witness' (i.e., to virility). Compare with **TESTICLE**.

test match ▶*n.* an international cricket or rugby match.

test meal ▶*n. Medicine* a portion of food of specified quantity and composition, eaten to stimulate digestive secretions which can then be analyzed.

tes·tos·ter·one /teˈstästəˌrōn/ ▶*n.* a steroid hormone that stimulates development of male secondary sexual characteristics, produced mainly in the testes, but also in the ovaries and adrenal cortex. ▷1930s: from **TESTIS** + *sterone* (blend of **STEROL** and **KETONE**).

test pa·per ▶*n. Chemistry* a paper impregnated with an indicator that changes color under known conditions, used esp. to test for acidity.

test pat·tern ▶*n.* a geometric design broadcast by a television station so that viewers can adjust the quality of their reception.

test pi·lot ▶*n.* a pilot who flies an aircraft to test its performance.

test strip ▶*n.* a strip of material used in testing, esp. (in photography) a strip of sensitized material, sections of which are exposed for varying lengths of time to assess its response.

test tube ▶*n.* a thin glass tube closed at one end, used to hold small amounts of material for laboratory testing or experiments. ■ [as *adj.*] denoting things produced or processes performed in a laboratory: *new forms of test-tube life.*

test-tube ba·by ▶*n. informal* a baby conceived by in vitro fertilization.

Tes·tu·di·nes /teˈst(y)o͞odnˌēz/ *Zoology* an order of reptiles that comprises the turtles, terrapins, and tortoises. They are distinguished by having a shell of bony plates covered with horny scales, and many kinds are aquatic. Also called, esp. formerly, **CHELONIA**. ▷modern Latin (plural), based on Latin *testa* 'shell.'

tes·tu·do /teˈst(y)o͞odō/ ▶*n.* (*pl.* **-dos** or **-di·nes** /-dnˌēz/) (in ancient Rome) a screen on wheels and with an arched roof, used to protect besieging troops. ■ a protective screen formed by a body of troops holding their shields above their heads in such a way that the shields overlap. ▷late Middle English: from Latin, literally 'tortoise,' from *testa* 'tile, shell.'

tes·ty /ˈtestē/ ▶*adj.* easily irritated; impatient and somewhat bad-tempered. ▷late Middle English (in the sense 'headstrong, impetuous'): from Anglo-Norman French *testif,* from Old French *teste* 'head,' from Latin *testa* 'shell.' **—tes·ti·ly** /ˈtestəlē/ *adv.* **—tes·ti·ness** *n.*

te·tan·ic /teˈtanik/ ▶*adj.* relating to or characteristic of tetanus, esp. in connection with tonic muscle spasm. ▷early 18th cent.: via Latin from Greek *tetanikos,* from *tetanos* (see **TETANUS**). **—te·tan·i·cal·ly** /-ik(ə)lē/ *adv.*

tet·a·nus /ˈtetn-əs/ ▶*n.* **1** a bacterial disease marked by rigidity and spasms of the voluntary muscles. See also **TRISMUS**. • This disease is caused by the bacterium *Clostridium tetani*; Gram-positive anaerobic rods. **2** *Physiology* the prolonged contraction of a muscle caused by rapidly repeated stimuli. ▷late Middle English: from Latin, from Greek *tetanos* 'muscular spasm,' from *teinein* 'to stretch.' **—tet·a·nize** /-ˌīz/ *v.* **—tet·a·noid** /-ˌoid/ *adj.*

tet·a·ny /ˈtetn-ē/ ▶*n.* a condition marked by intermittent muscular spasms, caused by malfunction of the parathyroid glands and a consequent deficiency of calcium. ▷late 19th cent.: from French *tétanie,* from Latin *tetanus* (see **TETANUS**).

tetch·y /ˈtecHē/ (also **tech·y**) ▶*adj.* bad-tempered and irritable. ▷late 16th cent.: probably from a variant of Scots *tache* 'blotch, fault,' from Old French *teche.* **—tetch·i·ly** /ˈtecHəlē/ *adv.* **—tetch·i·ness** *n.*

tête-à-tête /ˈtāt ə ˈtāt; ˈtet ə ˈtet/ ▶*n.* **1** a private conversation between two people. See note at **CONVERSATION**. **2** an S-shaped sofa on which two people can sit face to face.
▶*adj. & adv.* involving or happening between two people in private: [as *adj.*] *a tête-à-tête meal* | [as *adv.*] *his business was conducted tête-à-tête.* ▷late 17th cent.: French, literally 'head-to-head.'

tête-bêche /tet ˈbesH/ ▶*adj.* (of a postage stamp) printed upside down or sideways relative to another. ▷French, from *tête* 'head' and *bêche,* contraction of obsolete *béchevet* 'placed with the head of one against the foot of the other.'

teth·er /ˈteT͟Hər/ ▶*n.* a rope or chain with which an animal is tied to restrict its movement.
▶*v.* [*trans.*] tie (an animal) with a rope or chain so as to restrict its movement: *the horse had been tethered to a post.* ▷late Middle English: from Old Norse *tjóthr,* from a Germanic base meaning 'fasten.'
▶*PHRASE* □ **the end of one's tether** see **END**.

teth·er·ball /ˈteT͟Hərˌbôl/ ▶*n.* a game in which two people use their hands or paddles to hit a ball suspended on a cord from an upright post, the winner being the first person to wind the cord completely around the post.

Te·thys /ˈteTHis/ **1** *Greek Mythology* a goddess of the sea, daughter of Uranus (Heaven) and Gaia (Earth). **2** *Astronomy* a satellite of Saturn, the ninth closest to the planet, discovered by Cassini in 1684. It is probably composed mainly of ice and has a diameter of 659 miles (1,060 km). **3** *Geology* an ocean formerly separating the supercontinents of Gondwana and Laurasia, the forerunner of the present-day Mediterranean.

Tet Of·fen·sive /tet/ (in the Vietnam War) an offensive launched in January–February 1968 by the Vietcong and the North Vietnamese army. Timed to coincide with the first day of the Tet (Vietnamese New Year), it was a surprise attack on South Vietnamese cities, notably Saigon. Although repulsed after initial successes, the attack shook U.S. confidence and hastened the withdrawal of its forces.

Te·ton /ˈtēˌtän/ (also **Te·ton Sioux**) ▶*n.* another term for **LAKOTA**. ▷via North American French or directly from the name in Lakota *thíthųwą,* possibly meaning 'dwellers on the prairie.'

Té·touan /tāˈtwän/ a city in northern Morocco; pop. 272,000.

tet·ra /ˈtetrə/ ▶*n.* a small tropical freshwater fish that is typically brightly colored. Native to Africa and America, many tetras are popular in aquariums. • Numerous genera and species in the family Characidae, including the **neon tetra**. ▷mid 20th cent.: abbreviation of modern Latin *Tetragonopterus* (former genus name), literally 'tetragonal-finned.'

tetra- (also **tetr-** before a vowel) ▶*comb. form* **1** four; having four: *tetramerous* | *tetragram* | *tetrode.* **2** *Chemistry* (in names of compounds) containing four atoms or groups of a specified kind: *tetracycline.* ▷from Greek, from *tettares* 'four.'

tet·ra·chord /ˈtetrəˌkôrd/ ▶*n. Music* a scale of four notes, the interval between the first and last being a perfect fourth. ■ *historical* a musical instrument with four strings.

tet·ra·cy·clic /ˌtetrəˈsīklik/ ▶*adj. Chemistry* (of an organic compound) having four fused rings of atoms in its molecule. ▷early 20th cent.: from TETRA- 'four' + Greek *kuklos* 'circle' + -IC.

tet·ra·cy·cline /ˌtetrəˈsīˌklēn; -klin/ ▶*n. Medicine* any of a large group of antibiotics with a molecular structure containing four rings. • These antibiotics are often obtained from bacteria of the genus **Streptomyces**. ▷1950s: from TETRA- + CYCLIC + -INE[4].

tet·rad /ˈteˌtrad/ ▶*n. technical* a group or set of four. ▷mid 17th cent.: from Greek *tetras, tetrad-* 'four, a group of four.'

tet·ra·dac·tyl /ˌtetrəˈdaktl/ ▶*adj. Zoology* (of a vertebrate limb) having four toes or fingers.

tet·ra·eth·yl lead /ˌtetrəˈeTHəl ˈled/ ▶*n. Chemistry* a toxic colorless oily liquid made synthetically and used as an antiknock agent in leaded gasoline. • Chem. formula: $Pb(C_2H_5)_4$.

tet·ra·fluo·ro·eth·yl·ene /ˌtetrəˌflo͝orōˈeTHəˌlēn/ ▶*n. Chemistry* a dense colorless gas that is polymerized to make plastics such as polytetrafluoroethylene. • Chem. formula: $F_2C{=}CF_2$.

te·trag·o·nal /teˈtragənl/ ▶*adj.* of or denoting a crystal system or three-dimensional geometric arrangement having three axes at right angles, two of them equal. ▷late 16th cent.: via late Latin from Greek *tetragōnon* (neuter of *tetragōnos* 'four-angled') + -AL. **—te·trag·o·nal·ly** *adv.*

tet·ra·gram /ˈtetrəˌgram/ ▶*n.* a word consisting of four letters or characters.

Tet·ra·gram·ma·ton /ˌtetrəˈgraməˌtän/ ▶*n.* the Hebrew name of God transliterated in four letters as *YHWH* or *JHVH* and articulated as *Yahweh* or *Jehovah*. ▷Greek, neuter of *tetragrammatos* 'having four letters,' from *tetra-* 'four' + *gramma, grammat-* 'letter.'

tet·ra·he·drite /ˌtetrəˈhēdrīt/ ▶*n.* a gray mineral consisting of a sulfide of antimony, iron, and copper, typically occurring as tetrahedral crystals.

tet·ra·he·dron /ˌtetrəˈhēdrən/ ▶*n.* (*pl.* **-dra** /-drə/ or **-drons**) a solid having four plane triangular faces; a triangular pyramid. ▷late 16th cent.: from late Greek *tetraedron*, neuter (used as a noun) of *tetraedros* 'four-sided.' **—tet·ra·he·dral** /-drəl/ *adj.*

tetrahedron

tet·ra·hy·dro·can·nab·i·nol /ˌtetrəˌhīdrəkəˈnabəˌnôl; -ˌnäl/ ▶*n. Chemistry* a crystalline compound that is the main active ingredient of cannabis. • Chem. formula: $C_{21}H_{30}O_2$.

tet·ra·hy·dro·fu·ran /ˌtetrəˌhīdrōˈfyo͝orˌan/ ▶*n. Chemistry* a colorless liquid used chiefly as a solvent for plastics and as an intermediate in organic syntheses. • A heterocyclic compound; chem. formula: C_4H_8O.

tet·ra·hy·dro·ges·tri·none /ˌtetrəˌhīdrəˈjestrəˌnōn; -ˌhīdrō-/ (abbr.: **THG**) ▶*n.* an artificial anabolic steroid taken for enhancement of athletic performance. It was until recently undetectable in the bloodstream using normal testing techniques.

te·tral·o·gy /teˈträləjē/ ▶*n.* (*pl.* **-gies**) **1** a group of four related literary or operatic works. ■ a series of four ancient Greek dramas, three tragedies and one satyr play, originally presented together. [from Greek *tetralogia*.] **2** *Medicine* a set of four related symptoms or abnormalities frequently occurring together.

te·tral·o·gy of Fal·lot /faˈlō/ ▶*n. Medicine* a congenital heart condition involving four abnormalities occurring together, including a defective septum between the ventricles and narrowing of the pulmonary artery, and accompanied by cyanosis. ▷1920s: named after Etienne L. A. *Fallot* (1850–1911), French physician.

tet·ra·mer /ˈtetrəmər/ ▶*n. Chemistry* a polymer comprising four monomer units. **—tet·ra·mer·ic** /ˌtetrəˈmerik/ *adj.*

te·tram·er·ous /teˈtramərəs/ ▶*adj. Botany & Zoology* having parts arranged in groups of four. ■ consisting of four joints or parts.

te·tram·e·ter /teˈtramitər/ ▶*n. Prosody* a verse of four measures. ▷early 17th cent.: from late Latin *tetrametrus*, from Greek *tetrametros*, from *tetra-* 'four' + *metron* 'measure.'

tet·ra·ple·gi·a /ˌtetrəˈplēj(ē)ə/ ▶*n.* another term for QUADRIPLEGIA. ▷early 20th cent.: from TETRA- 'four' + PARAPLEGIA. **—tet·ra·ple·gic** /-ˈplējik/ *adj. & n.*

tet·ra·ploid /ˈtetrəˌploid/ *Biology* ▶*adj.* (of a cell or nucleus) containing four homologous sets of chromosomes. ■ (of an organism or species) composed of such cells.

▶*n.* an organism, variety, or species of this type. **—tet·ra·ploi·dy** *n.*

tet·ra·pod /ˈtetrəˌpäd/ ▶*n. Zoology* a four-footed animal, esp. a member of a group that includes all vertebrates higher than fishes. • Superclass Tetrapoda: the amphibians, reptiles, birds, and mammals. ■ an object or structure with four feet, legs, or supports. ▷early 19th cent.: from modern Latin *tetrapodus*, from Greek *tetrapous, tetrapod-* 'four-footed,' from *tetra-* 'four' + *pous* 'foot.'

te·trap·ter·ous /teˈtraptərəs/ ▶*adj. Entomology* (of an insect) having two pairs of wings. ▷early 19th cent.: from modern Latin *tetrapterus* (from Greek *tetrapteros*, from *tetra-* 'four' + *pteron* 'wing') + -OUS.

te·trarch /ˈteˌträrk/ ▶*n.* (in the Roman Empire) the governor of one of four divisions of a country or province. ■ one of four joint rulers. ■ *archaic* a subordinate ruler. ▷Old English, from late Latin *tetrarcha*, from Latin *tetrarches*, from Greek *tetrarkhēs*, from *tetra-* 'four' + *arkhein* 'to rule.' **—te·trar·chy** *n.* (*pl.* **-chies**).

tet·ra·spore /ˈtetrəˌspôr/ ▶*n. Botany* a spore occurring in groups of four, in particular (in a red alga) each of four spores produced together, two of which produce male plants and two female.

tet·ra·stich /ˈtetrəˌstik/ ▶*n. Prosody* a group of four lines of verse. ▷late 16th cent.: via Latin from Greek *tetrastikhon* 'having four rows,' from *tetra-* 'four' + *stikhon* 'row, line of verse.'

tet·ra·tom·ic /ˌtetrəˈtämik/ ▶*adj. Chemistry* consisting of four atoms.

tet·ra·va·lent /ˌtetrəˈvālənt/ ▶*adj. Chemistry* having a valence of four.

tet·ra·zole /ˈtetrəˌzōl/ ▶*n. Chemistry* an acidic crystalline compound whose molecule is a five-membered ring of one carbon and four nitrogen atoms. • Chem. formula: CH_2N_4. ▷late 19th cent.: from TETRA- 'four' + AZO- + -OLE.

tet·ra·zo·li·um /ˌtetrəˈzōlēəm/ ▶*n.* [as *adj.*] *Chemistry* a cation derived from tetrazole or one of its derivatives, esp. the triphenyl derivative. ■ (also **ni·tro·blue tet·ra·zo·li·um**) a yellow dye used as a test for viability in biological material.

tet·raz·zi·ni /ˌtetrəˈzēnē/ ▶*adj.* [*postpositive*] served over pasta with mushrooms and almonds in a cream sauce, sprinkled with cheese, and baked in the oven: *turkey tetrazzini*. ▷early 20th cent.: named after *Luisa Tetrazzini* (1871–1940), Italian operatic soprano.

tet·rode /ˈteˌtrōd/ ▶*n.* a thermionic tube having four electrodes. ▷early 20th cent.: from TETRA- 'four' + Greek *hodos* 'way.'

te·tro·do·tox·in /teˌtrōdəˈtäksin/ ▶*n.* a poisonous compound present in the ovaries of certain pufferfishes. It is a powerful neurotoxin. ▷early 20th cent.: from modern Latin *Tetrodon* (former genus name, from Greek *tetra-* 'fourfold' + *odous, odont-* 'tooth') + TOXIN.

tet·rose /ˈtetrōs; -trōz/ ▶*n. Chemistry* any of a group of monosaccharide sugars whose molecules contain four carbon atoms.

te·trox·ide /teˈträkˌsīd/ ▶*n. Chemistry* an oxide containing four atoms of oxygen in its molecule or empirical formula.

tet·ter /ˈtetər/ ▶*n. chiefly archaic* a skin disease in humans or animals causing itchy or pustular patches, such as eczema or ringworm. ▷Old English *teter*, of Germanic origin; from an Indo-European root shared by Sanskrit *dadru* 'skin disease.'

Teut. ▶*abbr.* ■ Teuton. ■ Teutonic.

Teu·ton /ˈt(y)o͞otn/ ▶*n.* a member of a people who lived in Jutland in the 4th century BC and fought the Romans in France in the 2nd century BC. ■ *often derogatory* a German. ▷from Latin *Teutones, Teutoni* (plural), from an Indo-European root meaning 'people' or 'country.'

Teu·ton·ic /t(y)o͞oˈtänik/ ▶*adj.* **1** of or relating to the Teutons. ■ *informal, often derogatory* displaying the characteristics popularly attributed to Germans: *making preparations with Teutonic thoroughness.* **2** *archaic* denoting the Germanic branch of the Indo-European language family.

▶*n. archaic* the language of the Teutons. **—Teu·ton·i·cism** /-ˈtänəˌsizəm/ *n.*

Teu·ton·ic Knights a military and religious order of German knights, priests, and lay brothers, originally enrolled *c.*1191 as the Teutonic Knights of St. Mary of Jerusalem. They became a great sovereign power through conquests made in campaigns against Germany's non-Christian neighbors, such as Prussia and Livonia, from 1225. Abolished by Napoleon in 1809, the order was reestablished in Vienna as an honorary ecclesiastical institution in 1834 and maintains a titular existence.

Te·ve·re /ˈtāvəˌrā/ Italian name for TIBER.

Te·vet ▶*n.* variant spelling of TEBET.

Te·wa /ˈtāwə; ˈtē-/ ▶*n.* (*pl.* same or **-was**) **1** a member of a Pueblo Indian people of the Rio Grande area in the southwestern U.S. **2** the Tanoan language of this people. Do not confuse with TIWA.

▶*adj.* of or relating to this people or their language. ▷from Spanish *Tegua* or directly from the Tewa self-designation *téwa*.

Tewks·bury /ˈt(y)o͞oksb(ə)rē/ a town in northeastern Massachusetts, southeast of Lowell; pop. 27,266.

Tex. ▶*abbr.* Texas.

Tex·ar·kana /ˌteksärˈkanə/ twin cities on the Texas-Arkansas border. The Texas city, in the northeastern part of the state, is home to an army ordnance center; pop. 31,656. The Arkansas city is in the southwestern part of the state; pop. 26,448.

Tex·as /ˈteksəs/ a state in the southern U.S., on the border with Mexico, with a coastline on the Gulf of Mexico; pop. 20,851,820; capital, Austin; statehood, Dec. 29, 1845 (28). The area was part of Mexico until 1836, when it declared independence, became a republic, and began to work for admittance to the U.S. as a state. **—Tex·an** /ˈteksən/ *adj. & n.*

Tex·as Cit·y a port city in southeastern Texas, on Galveston Bay, southeast of Houston; pop. 40,822.

Tex·as fe·ver ▶*n.* the disease babesiosis in cattle.

Tex·as hold·'em /ˈhōldəm/ ▶*n.* a poker game in which players compose their hands from cards dealt to them combined with community cards dealt face up and shared among them.

Tex·as lea·guer ▶*n. Baseball* a pop fly that falls to the ground between the infield and the outfield and results in a base hit.

Tex·as Rang·er ▶*n.* a member of the Texas State police force (formerly, of certain locally mustered regiments in the federal service during the Mexican War).

Tex-Mex /ˈteks ˈmeks/ ▶*adj.* (esp. of cooking and music) having a blend of Mexican and southern American features originally characteristic of the border regions of Texas and Mexico.

▶*n.* **1** music or cooking of such a type. **2** a variety of Mexican Spanish spoken in Texas. ▷1940s: blend of *Texan* and *Mexican*.

text /tekst/ ▶*n.* **1** a book or other written or printed work, regarded in terms of its content rather than its physical form: *a text which explores pain and grief.* ■ a piece of written or printed material regarded as conveying the authentic or primary form of a particular work: *in some passages it is difficult to establish the original text | the text of the lecture was available to guests.* ■ written or printed words, typically forming a connected piece of work: *stylistic features of journalistic text.* ■ *Computing* data in written form, esp. when stored, processed, or displayed in a word processor. ■ a text message. ■ [in *sing.*] the main body of a book or other piece of writing, as distinct from other material such as notes, appendices, and illustrations: *the pictures are clear and relate well to the text.* ■ a script or libretto. ■ a written work chosen or assigned as a subject of study: *the book is intended as a secondary text for religion courses.* ■ a textbook. ■ a passage from the Bible or other religious work, esp. when used as the subject of a sermon. ■ a subject or theme for a discussion or exposition: *he took as his text the fact that Australia is paradise.* **2** (also **text-hand**) fine, large handwriting, used esp. for manuscripts.

▶*v.* to send a text message: *I thought it was fantastic that he took the trouble to text me.* ▷late Middle English: from Old Northern French *texte*, from Latin *textus* 'tissue, literary style' (in medieval Latin, 'Gospel'), from *text-* 'woven,' from the verb *texere*. **—text·less** *adj.*

text·book /ˈteks(t)ˌbo͝ok/ ▶*n.* a book used as a standard work for the study of a particular subject.

▶*adj.* [*attrib.*] conforming to or corresponding to a standard or type that is prescribed or widely held by theorists: *he had the presence of mind to carry out a textbook emergency descent.* **—text·book·ish** *adj.*

text ed·i·tor ▶*n. Computing* a system or program that allows a user to edit text.

tex·tile /ˈtekˌstīl/ ▶*n.* **1** (usu. **textiles**) a type of cloth or woven fabric: *a fascinating range of pottery, jewelry, and textiles.* ■ (**textiles**) the branch of industry involved in the manufacture of cloth. **2** *informal* used by nudists to describe someone wearing clothes, esp. on a beach.
▶*adj.* **1** [*attrib.*] of or relating to fabric or weaving: *the textile industry.* **2** *informal* used by nudists to describe something relating to or restricted to people wearing clothes. ▷early 17th cent.: from Latin *textilis*, from *text-* 'woven,' from the verb *texere*.

text mes·sage ▶*n.* an electronic communication sent and received by cellular phone. **—text mes·sag·ing** *n.*

text·phone /ˈtekstˌfōn/ ▶*n.* a telephone for use by hearing-impaired persons, having a small screen on which a message can be received and a keyboard on which an outgoing message may be typed to another textphone.

text proc·ess·ing ▶*n. Computing* the manipulation of text, esp. the transformation of text from one format to another.

tex·tu·al /ˈteksCHo͞oəl/ ▶*adj.* of or relating to a text or texts: *textual analysis.* ▷late Middle English: from medieval Latin *textualis*, from Latin *textus* (see **TEXT**). **—tex·tu·al·ly** *adv.*

tex·tu·al crit·i·cism ▶*n.* the process of attempting to ascertain the original wording of a text.

tex·tu·al·ist /ˈteksCHo͞oəlist/ ▶*n.* a person who adheres strictly to a text, esp. that of the scriptures. **—tex·tu·al·ism** /-ˌlizəm/ *n.*

tex·tu·al·i·ty /ˌteksCHo͞oˈalitē/ ▶*n.* **1** the quality or use of language characteristic of written works as opposed to spoken usage. **2** strict adherence to a text; textualism.

tex·ture /ˈteksCHər/ ▶*n.* the feel, appearance, or consistency of a surface or a substance: *skin texture and tone* | *the cheese is firm in texture* | *the different colors and textures of bark.* ■ the character or appearance of a textile fabric as determined by the arrangement and thickness of its threads: *a dark shirt of rough texture.* ■ *Art* the tactile quality of the surface of a work of art. ■ the quality created by the combination of the different elements in a work of music or literature: *a closely knit symphonic texture.*
▶*v.* [*trans.*] [usu. as *adj.*] (**textured**) give (a surface, esp. of a fabric or wall covering) a rough or raised texture: *wallcoverings which create a textured finish.* ▷late Middle English (denoting a woven fabric or something resembling this): from Latin *textura* 'weaving,' from *text-* 'woven,' from the verb *texere*. **—tex·tur·al** /-rəl/ *adj.* **—tex·tur·al·ly** /-rəlē/ *adv.* **—tex·ture·less** *adj.*

tex·tured veg·e·ta·ble pro·tein ▶*n.* a type of protein obtained from soybeans and made to resemble minced meat.

tex·ture map·ping ▶*n. Computing* the application of patterns or images to three-dimensional graphics to enhance the realism of their surfaces.

tex·tur·ing /ˈteksCHəriNG/ ▶*n.* the representation or use of texture, esp. in music, fine art, and interior design.

tex·tur·ize /ˈteksCHəˌrīz/ ▶*v.* [*trans.*] impart a particular texture to (a product, esp. a fabric or foodstuff) in order to make it more attractive. ■ cut (hair) in such a way as to remove its weight and create extra fullness.

text wrap ▶*n.* (in word processing) a facility allowing text to surround embedded features such as pictures.

TF ▶*abbr.* Territorial Force.

T-for·ma·tion ▶*n. Football* a T-shaped offensive formation, with the halfbacks and fullback positioned in a line parallel to the line of scrimmage.

tfr. ▶*abbr.* transfer.

TFT *Electronics* ▶*abbr.* thin-film transistor, denoting a technology used to make flat color display screens, usually for high-end portable computers.

TG ▶*abbr.* ■ transformational grammar or transformational-generative grammar.

t.g. ▶*abbr. Biology* type genus.

TGIF ▶*abbr. informal* thank God it's Friday.

T-group ▶*n. Psychology* a group of people undergoing therapy or training in which they observe and seek to improve their own interpersonal relationships or communication skills. ▷1950s: *T* for *training*.

tgt. ▶*abbr.* target.

TGV ▶*n.* a French high-speed electric passenger train. ▷abbreviation of French *train à grande vitesse*.

Th ▶*symbol* the chemical element thorium.

Th. ▶*abbr.* Thursday.

-th[1] (also **-eth**) ▶*suffix* forming ordinal and fractional numbers from *four* onwards: *fifth* | *sixty-sixth.* ▷Old English *-(o)tha, -(o)the*.

-th[2] ▶*suffix* forming nouns: **1** (from verbs) denoting an action or process: *birth* | *growth.* **2** (from adjectives) denoting a state: *filth* | *health* | *width.* ▷Old English *-thu, -tho, -th*.

-th[3] ▶*suffix* variant spelling of **-ETH**[2] (as in *doth*).

Thack·er·ay /ˈTHak(ə)rē; ˈTHakəˌrā/, William Makepeace (1811–63), British novelist, born in Calcutta. He established his reputation with *Vanity Fair* (1847–48), a satire of the upper middle class of early 19th-century society. Other novels included *The History of Henry Esmond* (1852).

Thad·dae·us /ˈTHadēəs/ an apostle named in St. Matthew's gospel, traditionally identified with St. Jude.

Thai /tī/ ▶*adj.* of or relating to Thailand, its people, or their language.
▶*n.* (*pl.* same or **Thais**) **1** a native or national of Thailand. ■ a member of the largest ethnic group in Thailand. ■ a person of Thai descent. **2** the Tai language that is the official language of Thailand. ▷Thai, literally 'free.'

Thai·land /ˈtīˌland/ a kingdom in Southeast Asia, on the Gulf of Thailand; pop. 64,865,000; capital, Bangkok; language, Thai (official). Former name (until 1939) **SIAM**.

A powerful Thai kingdom emerged in the 14th century. In the 19th century, it lost territory in the east to France and in the south to Britain. Thailand was occupied by the Japanese during World War II; it supported the U.S. in the Vietnam War, later experiencing a large influx of refugees from Cambodia, Laos, and Vietnam. Absolute monarchy was abolished in 1932, and the king remains head of state.

Thai·land, Gulf of an inlet of the South China Sea between the Malay Peninsula on the west and Thailand and Cambodia on the east. It was formerly known as the Gulf of Siam.

Thai stick ▶*n.* strong cannabis in leaf form, twisted into a small, tightly packed cylinder ready for smoking.

thal·a·mus /ˈTHaləməs/ ▶*n.* (*pl.* **-mi** /-ˌmī/) *Anatomy* either of two masses of gray matter lying between the cerebral hemispheres on either side of the third ventricle, relaying sensory information and acting as a center for pain perception. ▷late 17th cent. (denoting the part of the brain at which a nerve originates): via Latin from Greek *thalamos*. **—tha·lam·ic** /THəˈlamik/ *adj.*

thal·as·se·mi·a /ˌTHaləˈsēmēə/ (*Brit.* **thal·as·sae·mi·a**) ▶*n. Medicine* any of a group of hereditary hemolytic diseases caused by faulty hemoglobin synthesis, widespread in Mediterranean, African, and Asian countries. ▷1930s: from Greek *thalassa* 'sea' (because the diseases were first known around the Mediterranean) + **-EMIA**.

tha·las·sic /THəˈlasik/ ▶*adj. poetic/literary* or *technical* of or relating to the sea. ▷mid 19th cent.: from French *thalassique*, from Greek *thalassa* 'sea.'

tha·las·so·ther·a·py /THəˌlasōˈTHerəpē; ˌTHaləsō-/ ▶*n.* the use of seawater in cosmetic and health treatment. ▷late 19th cent.: from Greek *thalassa* 'sea' + **THERAPY**.

thale cress /THāl/ ▶*n.* a small white-flowered plant of north temperate regions, widely used in genetics experiments due to its small number of chromosomes and short life cycle. • *Arabidopsis thaliana*, family Brassicaceae. ▷late 18th cent.: named after Johann *Thal* (1542–83), German physician.

tha·ler /ˈtälər/ ▶*n. historical* a German silver coin. ▷German, earlier form of *Taler* (see **DOLLAR**).

Tha·les /ˈTHāˌlēz/ (*c.*624–*c.*545 BC), Greek philosopher, mathematician, and astronomer, living at Miletus. Judged by Aristotle to be the founder of physical science, he is also credited with founding geometry. He proposed that water was the primary substance from which all things were derived.

Tha·li·a /ˈTHālēə/ **1** *Greek & Roman Mythology* the Muse of comedy. **2** *Greek Mythology* one of the Graces. ▷Greek, literally 'rich, plentiful.'

tha·lid·o·mide /THəˈlidəˌmīd/ ▶*n.* a drug formerly used as a sedative, but withdrawn in the early 1960s after it was found to cause congenital malformation or absence of limbs in children whose mothers took the drug during early pregnancy. ▷1950s: from *(ph)thal(ic acid)* + *(im)ido* + *(i)mide*.

thal·li /ˈTHalī/ ▶ plural form of **THALLUS**.

thal·li·um /ˈTHalēəm/ ▶*n.* the chemical element of atomic number 81, a soft silvery-white metal that occurs naturally in small amounts in pyrite, sphalerite, and other ores. Its compounds are very poisonous. (Symbol: **Tl**) ▷mid 19th cent.: modern Latin, from Greek *thallos* 'green shoot,' because of the green line in its spectrum.

thal·lo·phyte /ˈTHaləˌfīt/ ▶*n. Botany* a plant that consists of a thallus. ▷mid 19th cent.: from modern Latin *Thallophyta* (former taxon), from Greek *thallos* (see **THALLUS**) + **-PHYTE**. **—thal·lo·phyt·ic** *adj.*

thal·lus /ˈTHaləs/ ▶*n.* (*pl.* **thal·li** /ˈTHalī/) *Botany* a plant body that is not differentiated into stem and leaves and lacks true roots and a vascular system. Thalli are typical of algae, fungi, lichens, and some liverworts. ▷early 19th cent.: from Greek *thallos* 'green shoot,' from *thallein* 'to bloom.' **—thal·loid** /ˈTHaloid/ *adj.*

thal·weg /ˈtälˌveg/ ▶*n. Geology* a line connecting the lowest points of successive cross-sections along the course of a valley or river. ▷mid 19th cent.: from German, from obsolete *Thal* 'valley, dale' + *Weg* 'way.'

Thames /temz/ **1** a river that flows for 160 miles (260 km) across southern Ontario in Canada. It was the scene of an 1813 battle in which Tecumseh died. **2** a river in southern England that flows 210 miles (338 km) east from the Cotswolds in Gloucestershire through London to the North Sea. **3** /ˈTHāmz; ˈtāmz; ˈtemz/ an estuarial river in southeastern Connecticut that flows from Norwich past New London and Groton to Long Island Sound.

Tham·muz /ˈtämo͝oz; täˈmo͞oz/ (also **Tam·muz** *pronunc.* same) ▶*n.* (in the Jewish calendar) the tenth month of the civil and fourth of the religious year, usually coinciding with parts of June and July. ▷from Hebrew *tammūz*.

than /T͟Han; T͟Hən/ ▶*conj. & prep.* **1** introducing the second element in a comparison: [as *prep.*] *he was much smaller than his son* | [as *conj.*] *Jack doesn't know any more than I do.* **2** used in expressions introducing an exception or contrast: [as *prep.*] *he claims not to own anything* ***other than*** *his home* | [as *conj.*] *they observe* ***rather than*** *act.* **3** [*conj.*] used in expressions indicating one thing happening immediately after another: ***scarcely*** *was the work completed* ***than*** *it was abandoned.* ▷Old English *than(ne), thon(ne), thænne*, originally the same word as **THEN**.

USAGE Traditional grammar holds that personal pronouns following **than** should be in the subjective rather than the objective case: *he is smaller* ***than she*** (rather than *he is smaller* ***than her***). This is based on an analysis of **than** by which **than** is a conjunction and the personal pronoun ('she') is standing in for a full clause: *he is smaller* ***than she is.*** However, it is arguable that **than** in this context is not a conjunction but a preposition, similar grammatically to words like **with**, **between**, or **for**. In this case, the personal pronoun is objective: *he is smaller* ***than her*** is standard in just the same way as, for example, *I work* **with her** is standard (not *I work* **with she**). Whatever the grammatical analysis, the evidence confirms that sentences like *he is smaller* **than she** are uncommon in modern English except in the most formal contexts. Uses involving the objective personal pronoun, on the other hand, are almost universally accepted. For more explanation, see **usage** at PERSONAL PRONOUN and BETWEEN.

than·age /ˈTHānij/ ▸*n. historical* the tenure, land, and rank granted to a thane. ▷late Middle English: from Anglo-Norman French (see THANE, -AGE).

than·a·tol·o·gy /ˌTHanəˈtäləjē/ ▸*n.* the scientific study of death and the practices associated with it, including the study of the needs of the terminally ill and their families. ▷mid 19th cent.: from Greek *thanatos* 'death' + -LOGY. **—than·a·to·log·i·cal** /-ətəˈläjikəl/ *adj.* **—than·a·tol·o·gist** /-jist/ *n.*

Than·a·tos /ˈTHanəˌtōs; -ˌtäs/ (in Freudian theory) the death instinct. Often contrasted with **Eros**. ▷from Greek *thanatos* 'death.'

thane /THān/ ▸*n. historical* (in Anglo-Saxon England) a man who held land granted by the king or by a military nobleman, ranking between an ordinary freeman and a hereditary noble. ■ (in Scotland) a man, often the chief of a clan, who held land from a Scottish king and ranked with an earl's son. ▷Old English *theg(e)n* 'servant, soldier,' of Germanic origin; related to German *Degen* 'warrior,' from an Indo-European root shared by Greek *teknon* 'child,' *tokeus* 'parent.' **—thane·dom** /-dəm/ *n.*

thang /THaNG/ ▸*n. informal* nonstandard spelling of THING representing Southern U.S. pronunciation, and typically used to denote a feeling or tendency: *I'm doing the wild thang now.*

thank /THaNGk/ ▸*v.* [*trans.*] express gratitude to (someone), esp. by saying "Thank you": *Mac* **thanked** *her* **for** *the meal and left.* ■ used ironically to assign blame or responsibility for something: *you have only yourself to thank for the plight you are in.* ▷Old English *thancian*, of Germanic origin; related to Dutch and German *danken*; compare with THANKS.

▸*PHRASES* □ **I will thank you to do something** used to make a request or command and implying a reproach or annoyance: *I'll thank you not to interrupt me again.* □ **thank goodness** (or **God** or **heavens**) an expression of relief: *thank goodness no one was badly injured.* □ **thank one's lucky stars** feel grateful for one's good fortune.

thank·ful /ˈTHaNGkfəl/ ▸*adj.* pleased and relieved: [with *clause*] *they were thankful that the war was finally over* | [with *infinitive*] *I was very thankful to be alive.* ■ expressing gratitude and relief: *an earnest and thankful prayer.* ▷Old English *thancful* (see THANK, -FUL). **—thank·ful·ness** *n.*

thank·ful·ly /ˈTHaNGkfəlē/ ▸*adv.* in a thankful manner: *she thankfully accepted the armchair she was offered.* ■ [*sentence adverb*] used to express pleasure or relief at the situation or outcome that one is reporting; fortunately: *thankfully, everything went smoothly.* ▷Old English *thancfullīce* (see THANKFUL, -LY[2]).

USAGE **Thankfully** has been used for centuries to mean 'in a thankful manner,' as in *she accepted the offer* **thankfully**. Since the 1960s, it has also been used as a sentence adverb to mean 'fortunately,' as in **thankfully**, *we didn't have to wait.* Although this use has not attracted the same amount of attention as **hopefully**, it has been criticized for the same reasons. It is, however, far more common now than is the traditional use. For further explanation, see **usage** at HOPEFULLY and SENTENCE ADVERB.

thank·less /ˈTHaNGklis/ ▸*adj.* (of a job or task) difficult or unpleasant and not likely to bring one pleasure or the appreciation of others. ■ (of a person) not expressing or feeling gratitude. **—thank·less·ly** *adv.* **—thank·less·ness** *n.*

thank-of·fer·ing ▸*n.* an offering made as an act of thanksgiving.

thanks /THaNGks/ ▸*plural n.* an expression of gratitude: *festivals were held to* **give thanks for** *the harvest* | *a letter of thanks.* ■ a feeling of gratitude: *they expressed their thanks and wished her well.* ■ another way of saying THANK YOU: **thanks for** *being so helpful* | *many thanks.* ▷Old English *thancas*, plural of *thanc* '(kindly) thought, gratitude,' of Germanic origin; related to Dutch *dank* and German *Dank*, also to THINK.

▸*PHRASES* □ **no thanks to** used to imply that someone has failed to contribute to, or has hindered, a successful outcome: *we've won, but no thanks to you.* □ **thanks a million** *informal* thank you very much. □ **thanks to** as a result of; due to: *it's thanks to you that he's in this mess.*

thanks·giv·ing /ˌTHaNGksˈgiviNG/ ▸*n.* **1** the expression of gratitude, esp. to God: *he offered prayers* **in thanksgiving for** *his safe arrival* | *he described the service as a thanksgiving.* **2** (**Thanksgiving** or **Thanksgiving Day**) (in North America) an annual national holiday marked by religious observances and a traditional meal including turkey. The holiday commemorates a harvest festival celebrated by the Pilgrims in 1621, and is held in the U.S. on the fourth Thursday in November. A similar holiday is held in Canada, usually on the second Monday in October.

thank you ▸*exclam.* a polite expression used when acknowledging a gift, service, or compliment, or accepting or refusing an offer: **thank you for** *your letter* | *no thank you, I don't believe I will.*

▸*n.* an instance or means of expressing thanks: *Lucy planned a party as a thank you to the nurses* | [as *adj.*] *thank-you letters.*

Thant /THänt; THant/, U, (1909–74), Burmese statesman. He served as Myanmar's (formerly Burma) representative to the UN 1957–61 before becoming UN secretary-general 1961–71. As secretary-general, he worked to settle the 1962 Cuban missile crisis diplomatically, to end the Congolese civil war in 1962, and to keep peace in Cyprus in 1964.

U Thant

Thar Des·ert /tär/ a desert region to the east of the Indus River that lies in the states of Rajasthan and Gujarat in northwestern India and in the Punjab and Sind regions of southeastern Pakistan. Also called GREAT INDIAN DESERT.

Tharp /THärp/, Twyla, (1941–) U.S. dancer and choreographer. She performed with the Paul Taylor Dance Company 1963–65 and then formed her own modern dance troupe 1965–88. She choreographed dances such as "Push Comes to Shove" (1976) and did pieces for movies such as *Hair* (1979), *Ragtime* (1981), and *Amadeus* (1984). She served as an artistic associate for the American Ballet Theater 1988–90.

that /T͟Hat; T͟Hət/ ▸*pron.* (*pl.* **those** /T͟Hōz/) **1** used to identify a specific person or thing observed by the speaker: *that's his wife over there.* ■ referring to the more distant of two things near to the speaker (the other, if specified, being identified by "this"): *this is stronger than that.* **2** referring to a specific thing previously mentioned, known, or understood: *that's a good idea* | *what are we going to do about that?* **3** [often with *clause*] used in singling out someone or something and ascribing a distinctive feature to them: *it is part of human nature to be attracted to* **that which** *is aesthetically pleasing* | *his appearance was* **that of** *an undergrown man* | *they care about the rights of those less privileged than themselves.* **4** (*pl.* **that**) [*relative pron.*] used to introduce a defining or restrictive clause, esp. one essential to identification: ■ instead of "which," "who," or "whom": *the book that I've just written.* ■ instead of "when" after an expression of time: *the year that Anna was born.*

▸*adj.* (*pl.* **those**) **1** used to identify a specific person or thing observed or heard by the speaker: *look at that man there* | *how much are those brushes?* ■ referring to the more distant of two things near to the speaker (the other, if specified, being identified by "this"). **2** referring to a specific thing previously mentioned, known, or understood: *he lived in Mysore at that time* | *seven people died in that incident.* **3** [usu. with *clause*] used in singling out someone or something and ascribing a distinctive feature to them: *I have always envied those people who make their own bread.* **4** referring to a specific person or thing assumed as understood or familiar to the person being addressed: *where is that son of yours?* | *I let him spend all that money on me* | *Dad got that hunted look.*

▸*adv.* [as *submodifier*] to such a degree; so: *I would not go that far.* ■ used with a gesture to indicate size: *it was that big, perhaps even bigger.* ■ [with *negative*] *informal* very: *he wasn't that far away.*

▸*conj.* **1** introducing a subordinate clause expressing a statement or hypothesis: *she said that she was satisfied* | *it is possible that we have misunderstood.* ■ expressing a reason or cause: *he seemed pleased that I wanted to continue.* ■ expressing a result: *she was* **so** *tired* **that** *she couldn't think.* ■ [usu. with *modal*] expressing a purpose, hope, or intention: *we pray that the coming year may be a year of peace* | *I eat that I may live.* **2** [usu. with *modal*] *poetic/literary* expressing a wish or regret: *oh that he could be restored to health.* ▷Old English *thæt*, nominative and accusative singular neuter of *se* 'the,' of Germanic origin; related to Dutch *dat* and German *das*.

▸*PHRASES* □ **and all that** *informal* and that sort of thing; and so on: *other people depend on them for food and clothing and all that.* □ **at that** see AT[1]. □ **like that 1** of that nature or in that manner: *we need more people like that* | *don't talk like that.* **2** *informal* with no preparation or introduction; instantly or effortlessly: *he can't just leave like that.* □ **not all that** —— not very ——: *it was not all that long ago.* □ **that is** (or **that is to say**) a formula introducing or following an explanation or further clarification of a preceding word or words: *androcentric—that is to say, male-dominated—concepts* | *He was a long-haired kid with freckles. Last time I saw him, that is.* □ **that said** even so (introducing a concessive statement): *It's just a gimmick. That said, I'd love to do it.* □ **that's it** see IT. □ **that's that** there is nothing more to do or say about the matter. □ —— **that was** as the specified person or thing was formerly known: *General Dunstaple had married Miss Hughes that was.* □ **that will do** no more is needed or desirable.

USAGE 1 The word **that** can be omitted in standard English where it introduces a *subordinate* clause, as in *she said (that) she was satisfied. That* can also be dropped in a *relative* clause where it is the *object* of the clause, as in *the book (that) I've just written. That*, however, is obligatory when it is the *subject* of the relative clause, as in *the company* **that** *employs Jack.*

2 It is sometimes argued that, in relative clauses, **that** should be used for *nonhuman* references and **who** should be used for *human* references: *a house* **that** *overlooks the park*, but *the woman* **who** *lives next door.* In practice, while it is true to say that *who* is restricted to human references, the function of *that* is flexible. It has been used for both human and nonhuman references since at least the 11th century. In standard English, it is interchangeable with *who* in this context.

3 Is there any difference between the use of **that** and **which** in sentences such as *any book* **that** *gets children reading is worth having*, and *any book* **which** *gets children reading is worth having*? The general rule is that, in *restrictive* relative clauses, where the relative clause serves to define or restrict the reference to the particular one described, *that* is the preferred relative pronoun. However, in *nonrestrictive* relative clauses, where the relative clause serves only to give additional information, *which* must be used: *this book,* **which** *is set in the last century, is very popular with teenagers*, but not *this book,* **that** *is set in the last century, is very popular with teenagers.* For more details, see **usage** at RESTRICTIVE.

that·a·way /ˈT͟Hatəˌwā/ ▸*adv. informal* **1** in that direction. **2** in that way; like that.

thatch /THaCH/ ▸*n.* a roof covering of straw, reeds, palm leaves, or a similar material. ■ straw or a similar material used for such a covering. ■ *informal* the hair on a person's head, esp. if thick or unruly. ■ a matted layer of dead stalks, moss, and other material in a lawn.

▸*v.* [*trans.*] cover (a roof or a building) with straw or a similar material: [as *adj.*] (**thatched**) *thatched cottages* ▷Old English *theccan* 'cover,' of Germanic origin; related to Dutch *dekken* and German *decken.* **—thatch·er** *n.*

Thatch·er /ˈTHaCHər/, Margaret (Hilda), Baroness Thatcher of Kesteven (1925–), British stateswoman; prime minister 1979–90. The country's first woman prime minister and the longest-serving British prime minister of the 20th century, her period in office was marked by an emphasis on monetarist policies, privatization of nationalized industries, and trade union legislation. **—Thatch·er·ism** /-,rizəm/ *n.* **—Thatch·er·ite** /-,rīt/ *n. & adj.*

thau·ma·tin /ˈTHôməˌtēn; -mətn/ ▸*n.* a sweet-tasting protein isolated from a West African fruit (*Thaumatococcus danielli*, family Marantaceae), used as a sweetener in food. ▷1970s: from modern Latin *thaumat-* (from Greek *thauma, thaumat-* 'marvel') + **-IN**[1].

thau·ma·turge /ˈTHôməˌtərj/ ▸*n.* a worker of wonders and performer of miracles; a magician. ▷early 18th cent. (as *thaumaturg*): via medieval Latin from Greek *thaumatourgos*, from *thauma* 'marvel' + *-ergos* '-working.' **—thau·ma·tur·gic** /ˌTHôməˈtərjik/ *adj.* **—thau·ma·tur·gi·cal** *adj.* **—thau·ma·tur·gist** *n.* **—thau·ma·tur·gy** *n.*

thaw /THô/ ▸*v.* [*intrans.*] (of ice, snow, or another frozen substance, such as food) become liquid or soft as a result of warming: *the river thawed and barges of food began to reach the capital* | [as *n.*] (**thawing**) *catastrophic summer floods caused by thawing.* ■ (**it thaws, it is thawing**, etc.) the weather becomes warmer and melts snow and ice. ■ [*trans.*] make (something) warm enough to become liquid or soft: *European exporters simply thawed their beef before unloading.* ■ (of a part of the body) become warm enough to stop feeling numb: *Ryan began to feel his ears and toes* **thaw out**. ■ become friendlier or more cordial: *she* **thawed out** *sufficiently to allow a smile to appear.* ■ [*trans.*] make friendlier or more cordial: *the cast thawed the audience into real pleasure.*
▸*n.* a period of warmer weather that thaws ice and snow: *the thaw came yesterday afternoon.* ■ an increase in friendliness or cordiality: *a thaw in relations between the U.S.A. and Iran.* ▷Old English *thawian* (verb); related to Dutch *dooien*. The noun (first recorded in Middle English) developed its figurative use in the mid 19th cent.

Th.B. ▸*abbr.* Bachelor of Theology. ▷New Latin *Theologicae Baccalaureus*.

THC ▸*abbr.* tetrahydrocannabinol.

Th.D. ▸*abbr.* Doctor of Theology. ▷New Latin *Theologicae Doctor*.

T

the /THē; THə/ [called the *definite article*] ▸*adj.* **1** denoting one or more people or things already mentioned or assumed to be common knowledge: *what's the matter?* | *call the doctor* | *the phone rang.* Compare with **A**. ■ used to refer to a person, place, or thing that is unique: *the Queen* | *the Mona Lisa* | *the Nile.* ■ *informal* denoting a disease or affliction: *I've got the flu.* ■ (with a unit of time) the present; the current: *dish of the day* | *man of the moment.* ■ *informal* used instead of a possessive to refer to someone with whom the speaker or person addressed is associated: *I'm meeting the boss* | *how's the family?* ■ used with a surname to refer to a family or married couple: *the Johnsons were not wealthy.* ■ used before the surname of the chief of a Scottish or Irish clan: *the O'Donoghue.* **2** used to point forward to a following qualifying or defining clause or phrase: *the fuss that he made of her* | *the top of a bus* | *I have done the best I could.* ■ (chiefly with rulers and family members with the same name) used after a name to qualify it: *George the Sixth* | *Edward the Confessor* | *Jack the Ripper.* **3** used to make a generalized reference to something rather than identifying a particular instance: *he taught himself to play the violin* | *worry about the future.* ■ used with a singular noun to indicate that it represents a whole species or class: *they placed the African elephant on their endangered list.* ■ used with an adjective to refer to those people who are of the type described: *the unemployed.* ■ used with an adjective to refer to something of the class or quality described: *they are trying to accomplish the impossible.* ■ used with the name of a unit to state a rate: *they can do 120 miles* **to the** *gallon.* **4** enough of (a particular thing): *he hoped to publish monthly, if only he could find the money.* **5** (pronounced stressing "the") used to indicate that someone or something is the best known or most important of that name or type: *he was* **the** *hot young piano prospect in jazz.* **6** used adverbially with comparatives to indicate how one amount or degree of something varies in relation to another: **the more** *she thought about it,* **the more** *devastating it became.* ■ (usu. **all the** ——) used to emphasize the amount or degree to which something is affected: *commodities made all the more desirable by their rarity.* ▷Old English (Northumbrian and North Mercian dialects) *thē*; related to Dutch *de, dat*, and German *der, die, das*.

USAGE The article **the** is usually pronounced /THə/ before a consonant sound (*please pass the potatoes*) and /THē/ before a vowel sound (*please pass the asparagus*).
Regardless of consonant and vowel sounds, when the desired effect following **the** is to emphasize exclusivity, the pronunciation is /THē/ : *she's not just any expert in vegetation management, she's* **the** *expert.*

the·an·throp·ic /ˌTHēənˈTHräpik/ ▸*adj.* embodying deity in a human form; both divine and human. ▷mid 17th cent.: from ecclesiastical Greek *theanthrōpos* 'god-man' (from *theos* 'god' + *anthrōpos* 'human being') + **-IC**.

the·ar·chy /ˈTHēˌärkē/ ▸*n.* (*pl.* **-chies**) *archaic* rule by a god or gods. ▷mid 17th cent.: from ecclesiastical Greek *thearkhia* 'godhead,' from *theos* 'god' + *arkhein* 'to rule.'

theat. ▸*abbr.* ■ theater. ■ theatrical.

the·a·ter /ˈTHēətər/ (also **the·a·tre**) ▸*n.* a building or outdoor area in which plays and other dramatic performances are given. ■ (often **the theater**) the activity or profession of acting in, producing, directing, or writing plays: *what made you want to go into the theater?* ■ a play or other activity or presentation considered in terms of its dramatic quality: *this is intense, moving, and inspiring theater.* ■ a movie theater. ■ a room or hall for lectures, etc., with seats in tiers. ■ the area in which something happens: *a new* **theater of war** *has been opened up.* ■ [as *adj.*] denoting weapons for use in a particular region between tactical and strategic: *he was working on theater defense missiles.* ▷late Middle English (originally as 'theatre'), from Old French, or from Latin *theatrum*, from Greek *theatron*, from *theasthai* 'behold.'

the·a·ter-in-the-round ▸*n.* a form of theatrical presentation in which the audience is seated in a circle around the stage or on at least three of its sides.

The·a·ter of the Ab·surd ▸*n.* (**the Theater of the Absurd**) drama using the abandonment of conventional dramatic form to portray the futility of human struggle in a senseless world. Major exponents include Samuel Beckett, Eugène Ionesco, and Harold Pinter.

the·at·ric /THēˈatrik/ ▸*adj.* another term for **THEATRICAL**.

the·at·ri·cal /THēˈatrikəl/ ▸*adj.* of, for, or relating to acting, actors, or the theater: *theatrical productions.* ■ exaggerated and excessively dramatic: *Henry looked over his shoulder with theatrical caution.* ▷mid 16th cent.: via late Latin from Greek *theatrikos* (from *theatron* 'theater') + **-AL**. **—the·at·ri·cal·ism** /-ˌlizəm/ *n.* **—the·at·ri·cal·i·ty** /-ˌatriˈkalitē/ *n.* **—the·at·ri·cal·i·za·tion** /-ˌatrikəliˈzāSHən/ *n.* **—the·at·ri·cal·ize** /-ˌlīz/ *v.* **—the·at·ri·cal·ly** /-ik(ə)lē/ *adv.*

the·at·ri·cals /THēˈatrikəlz/ ▸*plural n.* dramatic performances: *I was persuaded to act in some amateur theatricals.*

the·at·rics /THēˈatriks/ ▸*plural n.* excessively emotional and dramatic behavior: *stop your theatrics.* ■ another term for **THEATRICALS**.

the·be /ˈtebe/ ▸*n.* (*pl.* same) a monetary unit of Botswana, equal to one hundredth of a pula. ▷Setswana, literally 'shield.'

Thebes /THēbz/ **1** the Greek name for an ancient city in Upper Egypt, the ruins of which are located on the Nile River about 420 miles (675 km) south of Cairo. The capital of ancient Egypt under the 18th dynasty (*c.*1550–1290 BC), it is the site of the major temples of Luxor and Karnak. **2** a city in Greece, in Boeotia, northwest of Athens. A major military power in Greece following the defeat of the Spartans at the battle of Leuctra in 371 BC, it was destroyed by Alexander the Great in 336 BC. Greek name **Thívai**. **—The·ban** /ˈTHēbən/ *adj. & n.*

the·ca /ˈTHēkə/ ▸*n.* (*pl.* **the·cae** /ˈTHēsē/) a receptacle, sheath, or cell enclosing an organ, part, or structure, in particular: ■ *Anatomy* the loose sheath enclosing the spinal cord. ■ *Zoology* a cuplike or tubular structure containing a coral polyp. ■ *Botany* either of the lobes of an anther, each containing two pollen sacs. ■ (also **the·ca fol·lic·u·li** /fəˈlikyəˌlī/) *Anatomy* the outer layer of cells of a Graafian follicle. ▷early 17th cent.: via Latin from Greek *thēkē* 'case.' **—the·cal** *adj.* **—the·cate** /-ˌkāt/ *adj.*

the·co·dont /ˈTHēkəˌdänt/ ▸*n.* a fossil quadrupedal or partly bipedal reptile of the Triassic period, having teeth fixed in sockets in the jaw. Thecodonts are ancestral to the dinosaurs and other archosaurs. • Order Thecodontia, subdivision Archosauria. ▷mid 19th cent.: from modern Latin *Thecodontia*, from Greek *thēkē* 'case' + *odous, odont-* 'tooth.'

thee /THē/ ▸*pron.* [*second person singular*] archaic or dialect form of **YOU**, as the singular object of a verb or preposition: *we beseech thee O lord.* Compare with **THOU**[1]. ▷Old English *thē*, accusative and dative case of *thū* 'thou.'

USAGE The word **thee** is still used in some traditional dialects (e.g., in northern England) and among certain religious groups (e.g., Quakers), but in standard English it is restricted to archaic or religious contexts. For more details on **thee** and **thou**, see **usage** at **THOU**[1].

theft /THeft/ ▸*n.* the action or crime of stealing: *he was convicted of theft* | *the latest theft happened at a garage.* ▷Old English *thīefth, thēofth*, of Germanic origin; related to **THIEF**.

USAGE See **usage** at **ROB**.

thegn /THān/ ▸*n.* *historical* an English thane. ▷mid 19th cent.: modern representation of Old English *theg(e)n*, adopted to distinguish the Old English use of **THANE** from the Scots use made familiar by Shakespeare.

the·ine /ˈTHē-ēn; -in/ ▸*n.* caffeine, esp. when it occurs in tea. ▷mid 19th cent.: from modern Latin *Thea* (former genus name of the tea plant, from Dutch *thee*) + **-INE**[4].

their /THe(ə)r/ ▸*possessive adj.* **1** belonging to or associated with the people or things previously mentioned or easily identified: *her taunts had lost their power to touch him.* ■ belonging to or associated with a person of unspecified sex: *she heard someone blow their nose loudly.* **2** (**Their**) used in titles: *a double portrait of Their Majesties.* ▷Middle English: from Old Norse *their(r)a* 'of them,' genitive plural of the demonstrative *sá*; related to **THEM** and **THEY**.

USAGE 1 On the use of **their** in the singular to mean 'his or her,' see **usage** at **THEY**.
2 On the differences between **their**, **they're**, and **there**, see **usage** at **THEY**.

theirs /THe(ə)rz/ ▸*possessive pron.* used to refer to a thing or things belonging to or associated with two or more people or things previously mentioned: *they think everything is theirs* | *a favorite game* **of theirs**. ▷Middle English: from **THEIR** + **-'S**[1].

their·selves /THe(ə)rˈselvz/ ▸*pron.* [*third person plural*] dialect form of **THEMSELVES**.

the·ism /ˈTHēˌizəm/ ▸*n.* belief in the existence of a god or gods, esp. belief in one god as creator of the universe, intervening in it and sustaining a personal relation to his creatures. Compare with **DEISM**. ▷late 17th cent.: from Greek *theos* 'god' + **-ISM**. **—the·ist** *n.* **—the·is·tic** /THēˈistik/ *adj.*

The·lon River /ˈTHēˌlän/ a river that rises in the Northwest Territories in Canada and flows for 550 miles (900 km) across Nunavut to Hudson Bay.

them /THem; THəm/ ▸*pron.* [*third person plural*] **1** used as the object of a verb or preposition to refer to two or more people or things previously mentioned or easily identified: *I bathed the kids and read them stories* | *rows of doors, most* **of them** *locked.* Compare with **THEY**. ■ used after the verb "to be" and after "than" or "as": *you think that's them?* | *we're better than them.* ■ [*singular*] referring to a person of unspecified sex: *how well do you have to know someone before you call them a friend?* **2** *archaic* themselves: *they bethought them of a new expedient.*
▸*adj.* *informal* or *dialect* those: *look at them eyes.* ▷Middle English: from Old Norse *theim* 'to those, to them,' dative plural of *sá*; related to **THEIR** and **THEM**.

USAGE On the use of **them** in the singular to mean 'him or her,' see **usage** at **THEY**.

the·mat·ic /THiˈmatik/ ▸*adj.* **1** having or relating to subjects or a particular subject: *the orientation of this anthology is essentially thematic.* ■ *Linguistics* belonging to, relating to, or denoting the theme of a sentence. ■ *Music* of, relating to, or containing melodic subjects: *the concerto relies on the frequent repetition of thematic fragments.* ■ *Philately* British term for **TOPICAL**. **2** *Linguistics* of or relating to the theme of an inflected word. ■ (of a vowel) connecting the theme of a word to its inflections. ■ (of a word) having a vowel connecting its theme to its inflections.
▸*n.* **1** (**thematics**) [treated as *sing.* or *pl.*] a body of topics for study or discussion. **2** *Philately* British term for **TOPICAL**. ▷late 17th cent.: from Greek *thematikos*, from *thema* (see **THEME**). **—the·mat·i·cal·ly** /-ik(ə)lē/ *adv.*

The·mat·ic Ap·per·cep·tion Test ▸*n.* *Psychology* a projective test designed to reveal a person's social drives or needs by their interpretation of a series of pictures of emotionally ambiguous situations.

the·ma·tize /ˈTHēməˌtīz/ ▶*v.* [*trans.*] present or select (a subject) as a theme. ■ *Linguistics* place (a word or phrase) at the start of a sentence in order to focus attention on it. —**the·mat·i·za·tion** /ˌTHēmətiˈzāSHən/ *n.*

theme /THēm/ ▶*n.* **1** the subject of a talk, a piece of writing, a person's thoughts, or an exhibition; a topic: *the theme of the sermon was reverence | a show* ***on the theme of*** *waste and recycling.* ■ *Linguistics* the first major constituent of a clause, indicating the subject-matter, typically being the subject but optionally other constituents, as in "*poor* he is not." Contrasted with **RHEME**. ■ an idea that recurs in or pervades a work of art or literature. ■ *Music* a prominent or frequently recurring melody or group of notes in a composition. ■ [as *adj.*] (of music) frequently recurring in or accompanying the beginning and end of a film, play, or musical: *a theme song.* ■ a setting or ambience given to a leisure venue or activity: *a family fun park with a western theme.* ■ [as *adj.*] denoting a restaurant or bar in which the decor and the food and drink served are intended to suggest a particular foreign country, historical period, or other ambience: *a New Deal theme restaurant.* ■ [in *combination*] (**-themed**) (mainly in journalism) characterized by a theme or pervasive influence: *a golf-themed business park.* ■ an essay written by a student on an assigned subject. **2** *Linguistics* the stem of a noun or verb; the part to which inflections are added, esp. one composed of the root and an added vowel. **3** *historical* any of the twenty-nine provinces in the Byzantine empire.
▶*v.* [*trans.*] give a particular setting or ambience to (a venue or activity): [as *adj.*] (**themed**) *Independence Day was celebrated with special themed menus* | [in *combination*] *a golf-themed business park.* ▷Middle English: via Old French from Latin *thema*, from Greek, literally 'proposition'; related to *tithenai* 'to set or place.'

theme park ▶*n.* an amusement park with a unifying setting or idea.

The·mis /ˈTHēmis/ *Greek Mythology* a goddess, daughter of Uranus (Heaven) and Gaia (Earth). In Homer she was the personification of order and justice, who convened the assembly of the gods.

The·mis·to·cles /THəˈmistəˌklēz/ (*c.*528–462 BC), Athenian statesman. He helped build up the Athenian fleet and defeated the Persian fleet at Salamis in 480.

them·self /THəmˈself; THem-/ ▶*pron.* [*third person singular*] used instead of "himself" or "herself" to refer to a person of unspecified sex: *the casual observer might easily think themself back in 1945.*

> ***USAGE*** The standard reflexive form corresponding to **they** and **them** is **themselves**, as in *they can do it* ***themselves***. The singular form **themself**, first recorded in the 14th century, has reemerged in recent years corresponding to the singular gender-neutral use of **they**, as in *this is the first step in helping someone to help* ***themself***. The form is not widely accepted in standard English, however.
> For more details, see **usage** at **THEY**.

them·selves /THəmˈselvz; THem-/ ▶*pron.* [*third person plural*] **1** [*reflexive*] used as the object of a verb or preposition to refer to a group of people or things previously mentioned as the subject of the clause: *countries unable to look after themselves.* **2** [*emphatic*] used to emphasize a particular group of people or things mentioned: *excellent at organizing others, they may well be disorganized themselves.* **3** [*singular*] used instead of "himself" or "herself" to refer to a person of unspecified sex: *anyone who fancies themselves as a racing driver.*
▶***PHRASES*** □ **(not) be themselves** see **BE ONESELF, NOT BE ONESELF** at **BE**. □ **by themselves** see **BY ONESELF** at **BY**.

> ***USAGE*** On the use of **themselves** in the singular to mean 'himself or herself,' see **usage** at **THEY**.

then /THen/ ▶*adv.* **1** at that time; at the time in question: *I was living in Cairo then* | [after *prep.*] *Phoebe by then was exhausted* | [as *adj.*] *a hotel where the then prime minister, Margaret Thatcher, was staying.* **2** after that; next; afterward: *she won the first and then the second game.* ■ also; in addition: *I'm paid a generous salary, and then there's the money I've made at the races.* **3** in that case; therefore: *if you do what I tell you, then there's nothing to worry about | well, that's okay then.* ■ used at the end of a sentence to emphasize an inference being drawn: *so you're still here, then.* ■ used to finish off a conversation: *see you in an hour, then.* ▷Old English *thænne, thanne, thonne*, of Germanic origin; related to Dutch *dan* and German *dann*, also to **THAT** and **THE**.
▶***PHRASES*** □ **but then (again)** after all; on the other hand (introducing a contrasting comment): *it couldn't help, but then again, it probably couldn't hurt.* □ **then and there** immediately: *she made up her mind then and there.*

the·nar /ˈTHēnär/ *Anatomy* ▶*adj.* of or relating to the rounded fleshy part of the hand at the base of the thumb (the ball of the thumb).
▶*n.* this part of the hand. ▷mid 17th cent.: from Greek, literally 'palm of the hand, sole of the foot.'

the·nard·ite /THəˈnärdīt; tə-/ ▶*n.* a white to brownish translucent crystalline mineral occurring in evaporated salt lakes, consisting of anhydrous sodium sulfate. ▷mid 19th cent.: from the name of Baron Louis-Jacques *Thénard* (1777–1857), French chemist, + **-ITE**[1].

thence /THens/ (also **from thence**) ▶*adv. formal* from a place or source previously mentioned: *they intended to cycle on into France and thence home via Belgium.* ■ as a consequence: *studying maps to assess past latitudes and thence an indication of climate.* ■ from that time: *four months thence I stood once again in the dooryard.* ▷Middle English *thennes*, from earlier *thenne* (from Old English *thanon*) + **-S**[3] (later respelled *-ce* to denote the unvoiced sound).

thence·forth /THensˈfôrTH/ (also **from thence·forth**) ▶*adv. archaic* or *poetic/literary* from that time, place, or point onward: *thenceforth he made his life in England.*

thence·for·ward /THensˈfôrwərd/ ▶*adv.* another term for **THENCEFORTH**.

theo- ▶*comb. form* relating to God or deities: *theocentric | theocracy.* ▷from Greek *theos* 'god.'

the·o·bro·mine /ˌTHēəˈbrōˌmēn; -min/ ▶*n. Chemistry* a bitter, volatile compound obtained from cacao seeds. It is an alkaloid resembling caffeine in its physiological effects. • Chem. formula: $C_7H_8N_4O_2$. ▷mid 19th cent.: from modern Latin *Theobroma* (genus name, from Greek *theos* 'god' and *brōma* 'food') + **-INE**[4].

the·o·cen·tric /ˌTHēōˈsentrik/ ▶*adj.* having God as a central focus: *a theocentric civilization.*

the·oc·ra·cy /THēˈäkrəsē/ ▶*n.* (*pl.* **-cies**) a system of government in which priests rule in the name of God or a god. ■ (**the Theocracy**) the commonwealth of Israel from the time of Moses until the election of Saul as King. ▷early 17th cent.: from Greek *theokratia* (see **THEO-**, **-CRACY**). —**the·o·crat** /ˈTHēəˌkrat/ *n.* —**the·o·crat·ic** /THēəˈkratik/ *adj.* —**the·o·crat·i·cal·ly** /THēəˈkratik(ə)lē/ *adv.*

The·oc·ri·tus /THēˈäkrətəs/ (*c.*310–*c.*250 BC), Greek poet, born in Sicily. He is chiefly known for his *Idylls*, which were hexameter poems presenting the lives of imaginary shepherds and which became the model for Virgil's *Eclogues*.

the·od·i·cy /THēˈädəsē/ ▶*n.* (*pl.* **-cies**) the vindication of divine goodness and providence in view of the existence of evil. ▷late 18th cent.: from French *Théodicée*, the title of a work by Leibniz, from Greek *theos* 'god' + *dikē* 'justice.' —**the·od·i·ce·an** /-ˌädəˈsēən/ *adj.*

the·od·o·lite /THēˈädəˌlīt/ ▶*n.* a surveying instrument with a rotating telescope for measuring horizontal and vertical angles. ▷late 16th cent. (originally denoting an instrument for measuring horizontal angles): from modern Latin *theodelitus*, of unknown origin. —**the·od·o·lit·ic** /-ˌädəˈlitik/ *adj.*

The·o·do·ra /ˌTHēəˈdôrə/ (*c.*500–548), Byzantine empress; wife of Justinian. As Justinian's closest adviser, she exercised considerable influence on political affairs and the theological questions of the time.

The·o·do·ra·kis /ˌTHēədəˈräkis/, Mikis (1925–), Greek composer and politician. He was imprisoned by the military government for his left-wing political activities (1967–70). His compositions include the ballet *Antigone* (1958) and the score for the movie *Zorba the Greek* (1965).

The·o·dore Roo·se·velt Na·tion·al Park /ˈTHēəˌdôr ˈrōzəˌvelt/ a preserve in western North Dakota that incorporates the Roosevelt's ranch home as well as extensive badlands areas.

The·od·o·ric /THēˈädərik/ (*c.*454–526), king of the Ostrogoths 471–526; known as **Theodoric the Great**. At its greatest extent, his empire included Italy, Sicily, Dalmatia, and parts of Germany.

The·o·do·si·us I /ˌTHēəˈdōSH(ē)əs/ (*c.*346–395), Roman emperor 379–395; full name *Flavius Theodosius*; known as **Theodosius the Great**. He took control of the Eastern Empire and ended the war with the Visigoths. A pious Christian, in 391 he banned all forms of pagan worship.

the·og·o·ny /THēˈägənē/ ▶*n.* (*pl.* **-nies**) the genealogy of a group or system of gods. ▷early 17th cent.: from Greek *theogonia*, from *theos* 'god' + *-gonia* '-begetting.'

theol. ▶*abbr.* ■ theologian. ■ theological. ■ theology.

the·o·lo·gian /THēəˈlōjən/ ▶*n.* a person who engages or is an expert in theology. ▷late 15th cent.: from French *théologien*, from *théologie* or Latin *theologia* (see **THEOLOGY**).

the·o·log·i·cal /THēəˈläjikəl/ ▶*adj.* of or relating to the study of theology. ▷late Middle English (in the sense 'relating to the word of God or the Bible'): from medieval Latin *theologicalis*, from late Latin *theologicus*, from Greek *theologikos*, from *theologia* (see **THEOLOGY**). —**the·o·log·i·cal·ly** /-ik(ə)lē/ *adv.* [*sentence adverb*]

the·o·log·i·cal vir·tue ▶*n.* each of the three virtues of faith, hope, and charity as defined by St. Paul. Often contrasted with **CARDINAL VIRTUE**.

the·ol·o·gize /THēˈäləˌjīz/ ▶*v.* **1** [*intrans.*] engage in theological reasoning or speculation. **2** [*trans.*] treat (a person or subject) in theological terms: *he even theologizes writing problems.*

the·ol·o·gy /THēˈäləjē/ ▶*n.* (*pl.* **-gies**) the study of the nature of God and religious belief. ■ religious beliefs and theory when systematically developed: *in Christian theology, God comes to be conceived as Father and Son | a willingness to tolerate new theologies.* ▷late Middle English (originally applying only to Christianity): from French *théologie*, from Latin *theologia*, from Greek, from *theos* 'god' + *-logia* (see **-LOGY**). —**the·ol·o·gist** /-jist/ *n.*

the·om·a·chy /THēˈäməkē/ ▶*n.* (*pl.* **-chies**) a war or struggle against God or among or against the gods. ▷late 16th cent. (denoting fighting against God): from Greek *theomakhia*, from *theos* 'god' + *-makhia* 'fighting.'

the·oph·a·ny /THēˈäfənē/ ▶*n.* (*pl.* **-nies**) a visible manifestation to humankind of God or a god. ▷Old English, via ecclesiastical Latin from Greek *theophaneia*, from *theos* 'god' + *phainein* 'to show.'

the·o·phor·ic /THēəˈfôrik/ (also **the·o·phor·ous** /THēəˈfôrəs/) ▶*adj.* bearing the name of a god.

The·o·phras·tus /ˌTHēəˈfrastəs/ (*c.*370–*c.*287 BC), Greek philosopher and scientist, the student and successor of Aristotle. The most influential of his works was *Characters*, a collection of sketches of psychological types.

the·o·phyl·line /THēˈäfəlin; ˌTHēəˈfilēn/ ▶*n. Chemistry* a bitter crystalline compound present in small quantities in tea leaves, isomeric with theobromine. ▷late 19th cent.: from modern Latin *Thea* (former genus name of the tea plant, from Dutch *thee*) + Greek *phullon* 'leaf' + **-INE**[4].

the·or·bo /THēˈôrbō/ ▶*n.* (*pl.* **-bos**) a large lute with the neck extended to carry several long bass strings, used for accompaniment in 17th- and early 18th-century music. ▷early 17th cent.: from Italian *tiorba*, of unknown origin.

the·o·rem /ˈTHēərəm; ˈTHi(ə)r-/ ▶*n. Physics & Mathematics* a general proposition not self-evident but proved by a chain of reasoning; a truth established by means of accepted truths. ■ a rule in algebra or other branches of mathematics expressed by symbols or formulae. ▷mid 16th cent.: from French *théorème*, or via late Latin from Greek *theōrēma* 'speculation, proposition,' from *theōrein* 'look at,' from *theōros* 'spectator.' —**the·o·re·mat·ic** /ˌTHēərəˈmatik; ˌTHi(ə)rə-/ *adj.*

the·o·ret·ic /THēəˈretik/ ▶*adj.* another term for **THEORETICAL**. ▷early 17th cent. (in the sense 'conjectural'): via late Latin from Greek *theōrētikos*, from *theōrētos* 'that may be seen,' from *theōrein* (see **THEOREM**).

the·o·ret·i·cal /THēəˈretikəl/ ▶*adj.* concerned with or involving the theory of a subject or area of study rather than its practical application: *a theoretical physicist | the training is task-related rather than theoretical.* ■ based on or calculated through theory rather than experience or practice: *the theoretical value of their work.* —**the·o·ret·i·cal·ly** /-ik(ə)lē/ *adv.* [*sentence adverb*] *theoretically we might expect this to be true.*

the·o·re·ti·cian /ˌTHēərəˈtiSHən; ˌTHi(ə)rə-/ ▶*n.* a person who forms, develops, or studies the theoretical framework of a subject.

the·o·rist /ˈTHēərist; ˈTHi(ə)r-/ ▶*n.* a person concerned with the theoretical aspects of a subject; a theoretician.

Pronunciation Key ə *ago*; ər *over*; ˈə or ˌər *up*; ˈər or ˌər *fur*; a *hat*; ā *rate*; ä *car*; CH *chew*; e *let*; ē *see*; e(ə)r *air*; i *fit*; ī *by*; i(ə)r *ear*; NG *sing*; ō *go*; ô *for*; oi *boy*; o͝o *good*; o͞o *goo*; ou *out*; SH *she*; TH *thin*; TH *then*; (h)w *why*; ZH *vision*

the·o·rize /ˈTHēəˌrīz; ˈTHi(ə)rˌīz/ ▸*v.* [*intrans.*] form a theory or set of theories about something: [as *n.*] (**theorizing**) *they are more interested in obtaining results than in political theorizing.* ■ [*trans.*] create a theoretical premise or framework for (something): *women should be doing feminism rather than theorizing it.* —**the·o·ri·za·tion** /ˌTHēərəˈzāSHən; ˌTHi(ə)r-/ *n.* —**the·o·riz·er** *n.*

the·o·ry /ˈTHēərē; ˈTHi(ə)rē/ ▸*n.* (*pl.* **-ries**) a supposition or a system of ideas intended to explain something, esp. one based on general principles independent of the thing to be explained: *Darwin's theory of evolution.* ■ a set of principles on which the practice of an activity is based: *a theory of education | music theory.* ■ an idea used to account for a situation or justify a course of action: *my theory would be that the place has been seriously mismanaged.* ■ *Mathematics* a collection of propositions to illustrate the principles of a subject. ▷late 16th cent. (denoting a mental scheme of something to be done): via late Latin from Greek *theōria* 'contemplation, speculation,' from *theōros* 'spectator.'

▸*PHRASE* □ **in theory** used in describing what is supposed to happen or be possible, usually with the implication that it does not in fact happen: *in theory, things can only get better; in practice, they may well become a lot worse.*

the·o·ry-lad·en ▸*adj.* denoting a term, concept, or statement that has meaning only as part of some theory, so that its use implies the acceptance of that theory.

the·o·ry of games ▸*n.* another term for GAME THEORY.

the·os·o·phy /THēˈäsəfē/ ▸*n.* any of a number of philosophies maintaining that a knowledge of God may be achieved through spiritual ecstasy, direct intuition, or special individual relations, esp. the movement founded in 1875 as the Theosophical Society by Helena Blavatsky and Henry Steel Olcott (1832–1907). ▷mid 17th cent.: from medieval Latin *theosophia*, from late Greek, from *theosophos* 'wise concerning God,' from *theos* 'god' + *sophos* 'wise.' —**the·os·o·pher** /-fər/ *n.* —**the·o·soph·ic** /ˌTHēəˈsäfik/ *adj.* —**the·o·soph·i·cal** /ˌTHēəˈsäfikəl/ *adj.* —**the·o·soph·i·cal·ly** /ˌTHēəˈsäfik(ə)lē/ *adv.* —**the·os·o·phist** /-fist/ *n.*

the·o·ter·ror·ism /ˌTHēōˈterəˌrizəm/ ▸*n.* terrorism that has a religious motive or purpose: *realistic worry about theoterrorism has caused a decline in tourism.* ▷from *theo-* 'relating to God' + *terrorism*.

the·o·ther·a·py /ˌTHēəˈTHerəpē/ ▸*n.* another name for FAITH HEALING.

The·o·to·kos /ˌTHēəˈtäkəs/ ▸*n.* (**the Theotokos**) Mother of God (used in the Eastern Orthodox Church as a title of the Virgin Mary). ▷from ecclesiastical Greek, from *theos* 'god' + *-tokos* 'bringing forth.'

The·ra /ˈTHi(ə)rə/ a Greek island in the southern Cyclades. It suffered a violent volcanic eruption in about 1500 BC; remains of an ancient Minoan civilization have been preserved beneath the volcanic debris. Also called **Santorini**. Greek name **Thíra**.

therap. ▸*abbr.* therapeutic; therapeutics.

ther·a·peu·tic /ˌTHerəˈpyōōtik/ ▸*adj.* of or relating to the healing of disease: *diagnostic and therapeutic facilities.* ■ administered or applied for reasons of health: *a therapeutic shampoo.* ■ having a good effect on the body or mind; contributing to a sense of well-being: *a therapeutic silence.* ▷mid 17th cent.: via modern Latin from Greek *therapeutikos*, from *therapeuein* 'minister to, treat medically.' —**ther·a·peu·ti·cal** *adj.* —**ther·a·peu·ti·cal·ly** /-ik(ə)lē/ *adv.* —**ther·a·peu·tist** /-tist/ *n.* (*archaic*)

ther·a·peu·tics /ˌTHerəˈpyōōtiks/ ▸*plural n.* [treated as *sing.*] the branch of medicine concerned with the treatment of disease and the action of remedial agents. ▷late 17th cent.: plural of earlier *therapeutic* (noun), from French *thérapeutique*, or via late Latin from Greek *therapeutika*, neuter plural (used as a noun) of *therapeutikos* (see THERAPEUTIC).

the·rap·sid /THəˈrapsid/ ▸*n.* an extinct reptile of a Permian and Triassic order, the members of which are related to the ancestors of mammals. • Order Therapsida, Subclass Synapsida: many families and numerous genera, including the cynodonts. ▷early 20th cent.: from modern Latin *Therapsida*, from Greek *thēr* 'beast' + *hapsis, hapsid-* 'arch' (referring to the structure of the skull).

ther·a·py /ˈTHerəpē/ ▸*n.* (*pl.* **-pies**) treatment intended to relieve or heal a disorder: *a course of antibiotic therapy | cancer therapies.* ■ the treatment of mental or psychological disorders by psychological means: *he is currently* **in therapy** | [as *adj.*] *therapy sessions.* ▷mid 19th cent.: from modern Latin *therapia*, from Greek *therapeia* 'healing,' from *therapeuein* 'minister to, treat medically.' —**ther·a·pist** /-pist/ *n.*

Ther·a·va·da /ˌTHerəˈvädə/ (also **Ther·a·va·da Bud·dhism**) ▸*n.* the more conservative of the two major traditions of Buddhism (the other being Mahayana), and a school of Hinayana Buddhism. It is practiced mainly in Sri Lanka, Myanmar (Burma), Thailand, Cambodia, and Laos. ▷from Pali *theravāda*, literally 'doctrine of the elders,' from *thera* 'elder, old' + *vāda* 'speech, doctrine.'

there /T͟He(ə)r/ ▸*adv.* **1** in, at, or to that place or position: *we went on to Paris and stayed there eleven days* | [after *prep.*] *I'm not going in there—it's freezing* | *figurative the opportunity is right there in front of you.* ■ used when pointing or gesturing to indicate the place in mind: *there on the right* | *if anyone wants out,* **there's** *the door!* ■ at that point (in speech, performance, writing, etc.): *"I'm quite—" There she stopped.* ■ in that respect; on that issue: *I don't agree with you there.* ■ [with *infinitive*] used to indicate one's role in a particular situation: *at the end of the day, we are there to make money.* **2** used in attracting someone's attention or calling attention to someone or something: *hello there!* | *there goes the phone.* **3** (usu. **there is/are**) used to indicate the fact or existence of something: *there's a restaurant around the corner* | *there comes a point where you give up.*

▸*exclam.* **1** used to focus attention on something and express satisfaction or annoyance at it: *there, I told you she wouldn't mind!* **2** used to comfort someone: **there, there,** *you must take all of this philosophically.* ▷Old English *thǣr, thēr*, of Germanic origin; related to Dutch *daar* and German *da*, also to THAT and THE.

▸*PHRASES* □ **been there, done that** *informal* used to express past experience of or familiarity with something, esp. something now regarded as boring or unwelcome. □ **be there for someone** be available to provide support or comfort for someone, esp. at a time of adversity. □ **have been there before** *informal* know all about a situation from experience. □ **here and there** see HERE. □ **not all there** (of a person) not fully alert and functioning: *he's not all there. Give him a couple of days to readjust.* □ **so there** *informal* used to express one's defiance or awareness that someone will not like what one has decided or is saying: *you can't share, so there!* □ **there and then** immediately. □ **there goes ——** used to express the destruction or failure of something: *there goes my career.* □ **there it is** that is the situation: *pretty ridiculous, I know, but there it is.* □ **there or thereabouts** in or very near a particular place or position. ■ approximately: *forty years, there or thereabouts, had elapsed.* □ **there you are** (or **go**) *informal* **1** this is what you wanted: *there you are—that'll be $3.80 please.* **2** expressing confirmation, triumph, or resignation: *there you are! I told you the problem was a political one* | *sometimes it is embarrassing, but there you go.* □ **there you go again** used to criticize someone for behaving in a way that is typical of them. □ **there you have it** used to emphasize or draw attention to a particular fact: *so there you have it—the ultimate grand unified theory.* ■ used to draw attention to the simplicity of a process or action: *simply turn the handle three times and there you have it.*

USAGE On the differences between **their, they're,** and **there**, see **usage** at THEY.

there·a·bouts /ˈT͟He(ə)rəˌbouts/ (also **there·a·bout**) ▸*adv.* near that place: *the land is dry in places thereabouts.* ■ used to indicate that a date of figure is approximate: *the notes were written in 1860 or thereabouts.*

there·af·ter /T͟He(ə)rˈaftər/ ▸*adv. formal* after that time: *thereafter their fortunes suffered a steep decline.*

there·at /T͟He(ə)rˈat/ ▸*adv. archaic* or *formal* **1** at that place. **2** on account of or after that.

there·by /T͟He(ə)rˈbī/ ▸*adv.* by that means; as a result of that: *students perform in hospitals, thereby gaining a deeper awareness of the therapeutic power of music.*

▸*PHRASE* □ **thereby hangs a tale** used to indicate that there is more to say about something.

there·for /ˌT͟He(ə)rˈfôr/ ▸*adv. archaic* for that object or purpose.

there·fore /ˈT͟He(ə)rˌfôr/ ▸*adv.* for that reason; consequently: *he was injured and therefore unable to play.*

there·from /T͟He(ə)rˈfrəm/ ▸*adv. archaic* or *formal* from that or that place.

there·in /T͟He(ə)rˈin/ ▸*adv. archaic* or *formal* in that place, document, or respect: *it shall be sufficient evidence of the facts therein contained.*

there·in·af·ter /ˌT͟He(ə)rinˈaftər/ ▸*adv. archaic* or *formal* in a later part of that document.

there·in·be·fore /ˌT͟He(ə)rinbiˈfôr/ ▸*adv. archaic* or *formal* in an earlier part of that document.

there·in·to /T͟He(ə)rˈinˌtōō/ ▸*adv. archaic* or *formal* into that place.

ther·e·min /ˈTHerəˌmin/ ▸*n.* an electronic musical instrument in which the tone is generated by two high-frequency oscillators and the pitch controlled by the movement of the performer's hand toward and away from the circuit. ▷early 20th cent.: named after Lev *Theremin* (1896–1993), its Russian inventor.

there·of /T͟He(ə)rˈəv/ ▸*adv. formal* of the thing just mentioned; of that: *the member state or a part thereof.*

there·on /T͟He(ə)rˈän; -ˈôn/ ▸*adv. formal* on or following from the thing just mentioned: *the order of the court and the taxation consequent thereon.*

there·out /T͟He(ə)rˈout/ ▸*adv. archaic* out of that; from that source.

there's /T͟He(ə)rz/ ▸*contraction of* there is: *there's nothing there.* ■ *informal, chiefly Brit.* used to make a request or express approval of an action in a patronizing manner: *make a cup of tea, there's a good girl.*

The·re·sa, Moth·er see **Teresa, Mother**.

there·through /T͟He(ə)rˈTHrōō/ ▸*adv. archaic* through or by reason of that; thereby.

there·to /T͟He(ə)rˈtōō/ ▸*adv. archaic* or *formal* to that or that place: *the third party assents thereto.*

there·to·fore /ˌT͟He(ə)rtəˈfôr/ ▸*adv. archaic* or *formal* before that time.

there·un·der /T͟He(ə)rˈəndər/ ▸*adv. archaic* or *formal* in accordance with the thing mentioned: *the act and the regulations made thereunder.*

there·un·to /ˌT͟He(ə)rˌənˈtōō/ ▸*adv. archaic* or *formal* to that: *his agent thereunto lawfully authorized in writing or by will.*

there·up·on /ˈT͟He(ə)rəˌpän/ ▸*adv. formal* immediately or shortly after that: *he thereupon returned to Moscow.*

there·with /T͟He(ə)rˈwiTH; -ˈwiTH/ ▸*adv. archaic* or *formal* **1** with or in the thing mentioned: *documents lodged therewith.* **2** soon or immediately after that; forthwith: *therewith he rose.*

there·with·al /ˈT͟He(ə)rwiˌTHôl; -wiTH-/ ▸*adv. archaic* together with that; besides: *he was to make a voyage and his fortune therewithal.*

The·ria /ˈTHi(ə)rēə/ *Zoology* a major group of mammals that comprises the marsupials and placentals. Compare with **Prototheria**. • Subclass Theria, class Mammalia. ▷modern Latin (plural), from Greek *thēria* 'wild animals.' —**the·ri·an** *n.* & *adj.*

the·ri·ac /ˈTHi(ə)rēˌak/ ▸*n. archaic* an ointment or other medicinal compound used as an antidote to snake venom or other poison. ▷late Middle English: from Latin *theriaca* (see TREACLE).

the·ri·an·throp·ic /ˌTHi(ə)rēˌanˈTHräpik/ ▸*adj.* (esp. of a deity) combining the form of an animal with that of a man. ▷late 19th cent.: from Greek *thērion* 'wild animal' + *anthrōpos* 'human being' + **-ic**.

the·ri·o·mor·phic /ˌTHi(ə)rēəˈmôrfik/ ▸*adj.* (esp. of a deity) having an animal form. ▷late 19th cent.: from Greek *thērion* 'wild beast' + **-morph** + **-ic**.

therm /THərm/ ▸*n.* a unit of heat equivalent to 100,000 Btu or 1.055 × 10^8 joules. ▷1920s: from Greek *thermē* 'heat.'

therm. ▸*abbr.* thermometer.

ther·mal /ˈTHərməl/ ▸*adj.* of or relating to heat. ■ another term for GEOTHERMAL. ■ (of a garment) made of a fabric that provides exceptional insulation to keep the body warm: *thermal underwear.*

▸*n.* **1** an upward current of warm air, used by gliders, balloons, and birds to gain height. **2** (usu. **thermals**) a thermal garment, esp. underwear. ▷mid 18th cent. (in the sense 'relating to hot springs'): from French, from Greek *thermē* 'heat.' —**ther·mal·ly** *adv.*

ther·mal de·po·lym·er·i·za·tion ▸*n.* a process of breaking down complex hydrocarbons in an oxygen-deprived, heated and pressurized environment to yield simpler compounds that can be used to produce fuels.

ther·mal ef·fi·cien·cy ▸*n.* the efficiency of a heat engine measured by the ratio of the work done by it to the heat supplied to it.

ther·mal im·ag·ing ▸*n.* the technique of using the heat given off by an object to produce an image of it or locate it.

ther·mal in·ver·sion ▸*n.* see INVERSION (sense 2).

ther·mal·ize /ˈTHərməˌlīz/ ▸*v.* attain or cause to attain thermal equilibrium with the environment. —**ther·mal·i·za·tion** /ˌTHərməliˈzāSHən/ *n.*

ther·mal neu·tron ▸*n.* a neutron in thermal

equilibrium with its surroundings. Compare with SLOW NEUTRON.

ther·mal noise ▸*n. Electronics* electrical fluctuations arising from the random thermal motion of electrons.

ther·mal pa·per ▸*n.* heat-sensitive paper used in thermal printers.

ther·mal print·er ▸*n.* a printer in which small heated pins form characters on heat-sensitive paper.

ther·mal re·ac·tor ▸*n.* a nuclear reactor using thermal neutrons.

ther·mal spring ▸*n.* a spring of naturally hot water.

ther·mal u·nit ▸*n.* a unit for measuring heat.

ther·mic /ˈTHərmik/ ▸*adj.* of or relating to heat. ▷mid 19th cent.: from Greek *thermē* 'heat' + -IC.

Ther·mi·dor /ˈTHərmi,dôr/ ▸*n.* the eleventh month of the French Republican calendar (1793–1805), originally running from July 19 to August 17. ■ a reaction of moderates following a revolution, such as that which occurred in Paris on 9 Thermidor (July 27) 1794 and resulted in the fall of Robespierre. ▷French, from Greek *thermē* 'heat' + *dōron* 'gift.' **—Ther·mi·do·ri·an** /,THərməˈdôrēən/ *adj.*

therm·i·on /ˈTHərm,īən/ ▸*n.* an ion or electron emitted by a substance at high temperature. ▷early 20th cent.: from THERMO- 'of heat' + ION.

therm·i·on·ic /,THərmīˈänik/ ▸*adj.* of or relating to electrons emitted from a substance at very high temperature.

therm·i·on·ic e·mis·sion ▸*n.* the emission of electrons from a heated source.

therm·i·on·ics /,THərmīˈäniks/ ▸*plural n.* [treated as *sing.*] the branch of science and technology concerned with thermionic emission.

therm·i·on·ic tube (*Brit.* **therm·i·on·ic valve**) ▸*n. Electronics* an electron tube giving a unidirectional flow of electrons emitted from a hot cathode, used esp. in the rectification of a current and in radio reception.

therm·is·tor /ˈTHər,mistər/ ▸*n.* an electrical resistor whose resistance is greatly reduced by heating, used for measurement and control. ▷1940s: contraction of *thermal resistor*.

ther·mite /ˈTHər,mīt/ (also *trademark* **Thermit** /-mit/) ▸*n.* a mixture of finely powdered aluminum and iron oxide that produces a very high temperature on combustion, used in welding and for incendiary bombs. ▷early 20th cent.: coined in German from THERMO- 'of heat' + -ITE[1].

thermo- ▸*comb. form* relating to heat: *thermodynamics* | *thermoelectric*. ▷from Greek *thermos* 'hot,' *thermē* 'heat.'

ther·mo·chem·is·try /,THərmōˈkemistrē/ ▸*n.* the branch of chemistry concerned with the quantities of heat evolved or absorbed during chemical reactions. **—ther·mo·chem·i·cal** /-ˈkemikəl/ *adj.*

ther·mo·cline /ˈTHərmō,klīn/ ▸*n.* a steep temperature gradient in a body of water such as a lake, marked by a layer above and below which the water is at different temperatures.

ther·mo·cou·ple /ˈTHərmō,kəpəl/ ▸*n.* a thermoelectric device for measuring temperature, consisting of two wires of different metals connected at two points, a voltage being developed between the two junctions in proportion to the temperature difference.

ther·mo·dy·nam·ics /,THərmōdīˈnamiks/ ▸*plural n.* [treated as *sing.*] the branch of physical science that deals with the relations between heat and other forms of energy (such as mechanical, electrical, or chemical energy), and, by extension, of the relationships and interconvertibility of all forms of energy.

> The **first law of thermodynamics** states the equivalence of heat and work and reaffirms the principle of conservation of energy. The **second law** states that heat does not of itself pass from a cooler to a hotter body. Another, equivalent, formulation of the second law is that the entropy of a closed system can only increase. The **third law** (also called Nernst's heat theorem) states that it is impossible to reduce the temperature of a system to absolute zero in a finite number of operations.

—ther·mo·dy·nam·ic *adj.* **—ther·mo·dy·nam·i·cal** /-ikəl/ *adj.* **—ther·mo·dy·nam·i·cal·ly** /-ik(ə)lē/ *adv.* **—ther·mo·dy·nam·i·cist** /-,dīˈnamisist/ *n.*

ther·mo·e·las·tic /,THərmō-iˈlastik/ ▸*adj.* of or relating to elasticity in connection with heat.

ther·mo·e·lec·tric /,THərmō-iˈlektrik/ ▸*adj.* producing electricity by a difference of temperatures. **—ther·mo·e·lec·tri·cal·ly** *adv.* **—ther·mo·e·lec·tric·i·ty** /-i,lekˈtrisitē; -,ēlek-/ *n.*

ther·mo·form·ing /ˈTHərmō,fôrmiNG/ ▸*n.* the process of heating a thermoplastic material and shaping it in a mold.

ther·mo·gen·e·sis /,THərmōˈjenəsis/ ▸*n.* the production of heat, esp. in a human or animal body. **—ther·mo·gen·ic** /-məˈjenik/ *adj.*

ther·mo·gram /ˈTHərmə,gram/ ▸*n.* a record made by a thermograph.

ther·mo·graph /ˈTHərmə,graf/ ▸*n.* an instrument that produces a trace or image representing a record of the varying temperature or infrared radiation over an area or during a period of time.

ther·mog·ra·phy /THərˈmägrəfē/ ▸*n.* **1** the use of thermograms to study heat distribution in structures or regions, for example in detecting tumors. **2** a printing technique in which a wet ink image is fused by heat or infrared radiation with a resinous powder to produce a raised impression. **—ther·mo·graph·ic** /,THərməˈgrafik/ *adj.*

ther·mo·karst /ˈTHərmə,kärst/ ▸*n. Geology* a form of periglacial topography resembling karst, with hollows produced by the selective melting of permafrost.

ther·mo·la·bile /,THərmōˈlā,bīl; -bəl/ ▸*adj. chiefly Biochemistry* (of a substance) readily destroyed or deactivated by heat.

ther·mo·lu·mi·nes·cence /,THərmō,lo͞oməˈnesəns/ ▸*n.* the property of some materials that have accumulated energy over a long period of becoming luminescent when pretreated and subjected to high temperatures, used as a means of dating ancient ceramics and other artifacts. **—ther·mo·lu·mi·nes·cent** *adj.*

ther·mol·y·sis /THərˈmäləsis/ ▸*n. Chemistry* the breakdown of molecules by the action of heat. **—ther·mo·lyt·ic** /,THərməˈlitik/ *adj.*

ther·mom·e·ter /THərˈmämitər/ ▸*n.* an instrument for measuring and indicating temperature, typically one consisting of a narrow, hermetically sealed glass tube marked with graduations and having at one end a bulb containing mercury or alcohol that expands and contracts in the tube with heating and cooling. ▷mid 17th cent.: from French *thermomètre* or modern Latin *thermometrum*, from THERMO- 'of heat' + *-metrum* 'measure.' **—ther·mo·met·ric** /,THərməˈmetrik/ *adj.* **—ther·mo·met·ri·cal** /,THərməˈmetrikəl/ *adj.* **—ther·mom·e·try** /-trē/ *n.*

ther·mo·nu·cle·ar /,THərmōˈn(y)o͞oklēər; -kli(ə)r/ ▸*adj.* relating to or using nuclear reactions that occur only at very high temperatures. ■ of, relating to, or involving weapons in which explosive force is produced by thermonuclear reactions.

ther·mo·phile /ˈTHərmə,fīl/ ▸*n. Microbiology* a bacterium or other microorganism that grows best at higher than normal temperatures. **—ther·mo·phil·ic** /,THərməˈfilik/ *adj.*

ther·mo·pho·to·vol·ta·ic /,THərmō,fōtōvälˈtā-ik; -vōl-; -vôl-/ ▸*adj.* (abbr. **TPV**) denoting or relating to the capacity to convert infrared radiation (i.e. radiant heat) into electricity.

ther·mo·pile /ˈTHərmə,pīl/ ▸*n.* a set of thermocouples arranged for measuring small quantities of radiant heat.

ther·mo·plas·tic /,THərməˈplastik/ *Chemistry* ▸*adj.* denoting substances (esp. synthetic resins) that become plastic on heating and harden on cooling and are able to repeat these processes. Often contrasted with THERMOSETTING.
▸*n.* (usu. **thermoplastics**) a substance of this kind.

Ther·mop·y·lae /THərˈmäpə,lē; -,lī/ a narrow pass between the mountains and the sea in Greece, about 120 miles (200 km) northwest of Athens, now much widened by the recession of the sea. In 480 BC it was the scene of the defense against the Persian army of Xerxes I by 6,000 Greeks; among them were 300 Spartans, all of whom, including their king Leonidas, were killed.

ther·mo·reg·u·late /,THərmōˈregyə,lāt/ ▸*v.* [*intrans.*] regulate temperature, esp. one's own body temperature. **—ther·mo·reg·u·la·tion** /-,regyəˈlāSHən/ *n.* **—ther·mo·reg·u·la·to·ry** /-lə,tôrē/ *adj.*

ther·mos /ˈTHərməs/ (also **ther·mos bot·tle**) ▸*n.* a container that keeps a drink or other fluid hot or cold by means of a double wall enclosing a vacuum. ▷early 20th cent.: from Greek, literally 'hot.'

ther·mo·set·ting /ˈTHərmō,setiNG/ ▸*adj. Chemistry* denoting substances (esp. synthetic resins) that set permanently when heated. Often contrasted with THERMOPLASTIC. **—ther·mo·set** *adj.* & *n.*

ther·mo·sphere /ˈTHərmō,sfir/ ▸*n.* the region of the atmosphere above the mesosphere and below the height at which the atmosphere ceases to have the properties of a continuous medium. The thermosphere is characterized throughout by an increase in temperature with height.

ther·mo·sta·ble /ˈTHərmō,stābəl/ ▸*adj. chiefly Biochemistry* (of a substance) not readily destroyed or deactivated by heat.

ther·mo·stat /ˈTHərmə,stat/ ▸*n.* a device that automatically regulates temperature, or that activates a device when the temperature reaches a certain point. **—ther·mo·stat·ic** /,THərməˈstatik/ *adj.* **—ther·mo·stat·i·cal·ly** /,THərməˈstatik(ə)lē/ *adv.*

ther·mot·ro·pism /THərˈmätrə,pizəm/ ▸*n. Biology* the turning or bending of a plant or other organism in response to a directional source of heat. **—ther·mo·trop·ic** /,THərməˈtrōpik; -ˈträpik/ *adj.*

the·ro·pod /ˈTHi(ə)rə,päd/ ▸*n.* a carnivorous dinosaur of a group whose members are typically bipedal and range from small and delicately built to very large. • Suborder Theropoda, order Saurischia; includes the carnosaurs, ornithomimosaurs, ceolurosaurs, and dromaeosaurids. ▷1930s: from Greek *thēr* 'beast' + *pous, pod-* 'foot.'

The·roux /THəˈro͞o/, Paul, (1941–) U.S. writer. He wrote fiction that included *The Mosquito Coast* (1982), *My Other Life* (1996), and *Kowloon Tong* (1997) and nonfiction travel books that included *The Great Railway Bazaar* (1975) and *The Pillars of Hercules* (1995).

the·sau·rus /THəˈsôrəs/ ▸*n.* (*pl.* **-sau·ri** /-ˈsôrī/ or **-sau·rus·es**) a book that lists words in groups of synonyms and related concepts. ■ *archaic* a dictionary or encyclopedia. ▷late 16th cent.: via Latin from Greek *thēsauros* 'storehouse, treasure.' The original sense 'dictionary or encyclopedia' was narrowed to the current meaning by the publication of Roget's *Thesaurus of English Words and Phrases* (1852).

these /T͟Hēz/ ▸ plural form of THIS.

The·se·us /ˈTHēsēəs; -syo͞os/ *Greek Mythology* the legendary hero of Athens, son of Poseidon (or, in another account, of Aegeus, king of Athens) and husband of Phaedra. He slew the Cretan Minotaur with the help of Ariadne.

the·sis /ˈTHēsis/ ▸*n.* (*pl.* **-ses** /-sēz/) **1** a statement or theory that is put forward as a premise to be maintained or proved: *his central thesis is that psychological life is not part of the material world.* ■ (in Hegelian philosophy) a proposition forming the first stage in the process of dialectical reasoning. Compare with ANTITHESIS, SYNTHESIS. **2** a long essay or dissertation involving personal research, written by a candidate for a college degree: *a doctoral thesis.* **3** *Prosody* an unstressed syllable or part of a metrical foot in Greek or Latin verse. Often contrasted with ARSIS. ▷late Middle English (sense 3): via late Latin from Greek, literally 'placing, a proposition,' from the root of *tithenai* 'to place.'

thesp *informal* ▸*abbr.* thespian.

thes·pi·an /ˈTHespēən/ *formal humorous* ▸*adj.* of or relating to drama and the theater: *thespian talents.*
▸*n.* an actor or actress. ▷late 17th cent.: from the name THESPIS + -IAN.

Thes·pis /ˈTHespəs/ (6th century BC), Greek dramatic poet. He is regarded as the founder of Greek tragedy.

Thess. ▸*abbr. Bible* Thessalonians.

Thes·sa·lo·ni·ans /,THesəˈlōnēənz/ either of two books of the New Testament, epistles of St. Paul to the new church at Thessalonica.

Thes·sa·lo·ní·ki /,THesəlōˈnēkē/ a seaport in northeastern Greece, the second largest city in Greece and capital of the Greek region of Macedonia; pop. 378,000. Also called SALONICA; Latin name THESSALONICA .

Thes·sa·ly /ˈTHesəlē/ a region of northeastern Greece. Greek name THESSALÍA. **—Thes·sa·li·an** /THeˈsālēən; -ˈsālyən/ *adj.* & *n.*

the·ta /ˈTHātə; ˈTHē-/ ▸*n.* the eighth letter of the Greek alphabet (Θ, ϑ), transliterated as 'th.' ■ (**Theta**) [followed by Latin genitive] *Astronomy* the eighth star in a constellation: *Theta Draconis.* ■ [as *adj.*] *Chemistry* denoting a temperature at which a polymer solution behaves ideally as regards its osmotic pressure. ■ [as *adj.*] denoting electrical activity observed in the brain under certain conditions, consisting of oscillations having a frequency of 4 to 7 hertz: *theta rhythm.*

Pronunciation Key ə *ago*; ər *over*; ˈə *or* ,ə *up*; ˈər *or* ,ər *fur*; a *hat*; ā *rate*; ä *car*; CH *chew*; e *let*; ē *see*; e(ə)r *air*; i *fit*; ī *by*; i(ə)r *ear*; NG *sing*; ō *go*; ô *for*; oi *boy*; o͝o *good*; o͞o *goo*; ou *out*; SH *she*; TH *thin*; T͟H *then*; (h)w *why*; ZH *vision*

▸*symbol* ■ (ϑ) temperature (esp. in degrees Celsius). ■ (ϑ) a plane angle. ■ (ϑ) a polar coordinate. Often coupled with Φ.

The·tis /ˈTHētis/ *Greek Mythology* a sea nymph, mother of Achilles.

the·ur·gy /ˈTHēərjē/ ▸*n.* the operation or effect of a supernatural or divine agency in human affairs. ■ a system of white magic practiced by the early Neoplatonists. ▷mid 16th cent.: via late Latin from Greek *theourgia* 'sorcery,' from *theos* 'god' + *-ergos* 'working.' —**the·ur·gic** /THēˈərjik/ *adj.* —**the·ur·gi·cal** *adj.* —**the·ur·gist** *n.*

thew /TH(y)o͞o/ ▸*n. poetic/literary* muscular strength. ■ (**thews**) muscles and tendons perceived as generating such strength. ▷Old English *thēaw* 'usage, custom,' (plural) '(personal) manner of behaving,' of unknown origin. The sense 'good bodily proportions, muscular development' arose in Middle English. —**thew·y** *adj.*

they /T͟Hā/ ▸*pron.* [*third person plural*] **1** used to refer to two or more people or things previously mentioned or easily identified: *the two men could get life sentences if they are convicted.* ■ people in general: *the rest, as they say, is history.* ■ *informal* a group of people in authority regarded collectively: *they cut my water off.* **2** [*singular*] used to refer to a person of unspecified sex: *ask someone if they could help.* ▷Middle English: from Old Norse *their*, nominative plural masculine of *sá*; related to **THEM** and **THEIR**, also to **THAT** and **THE**.

USAGE **1** The word **they** (with its counterparts **them**, **their**, and **themselves**) as a singular pronoun to refer to a person of unspecified sex has been used since at least the 16th century. In the late 20th century, as the traditional use of **he** to refer to a person of either sex came under scrutiny on the grounds of sexism, this use of **they** has become more common. It is now generally accepted in contexts where it follows an indefinite pronoun such as **anyone, no one, someone,** or **a person**: ***anyone*** *can join if* ***they*** *are a resident;* ***each*** *to* ***their*** *own.* In other contexts, coming after singular nouns, the use of **they** is now common, although less widely accepted, esp. in formal contexts. Sentences such as *ask* ***a friend*** *if* ***they*** *could help* are still criticized for being ungrammatical. Nevertheless, in view of the growing acceptance of **they** and its obvious practical advantages, **they** is used in this dictionary in many cases where **he** would have been used formerly. See also **usage** at **HE** and **SHE**. **2** Don't confuse **their, they're,** and **there. Their** is a possessive pronoun: *I like their new car.* **They're** is a contraction of 'they are': *they're parking the car.* **There** is an adverb meaning 'at that place': *park the car over there.*

they'd /T͟Hād/ ▸*contraction of* ■ they had. ■ they would.

they'll /T͟Hāl/ ▸*contraction of* they shall; they will.

they're /T͟He(ə)r/ ▸*contraction of* they are.

USAGE On the differences between **their, they're,** and **there**, see **usage** at **THEY**.

they've /T͟Hāv/ ▸*contraction of* they have.

THG ▸*abbr.* tetrahydrogestrinone.

THI ▸*abbr.* temperature–humidity index.

thi·a·ben·da·zole /ˌTHīəˈbendəˌzōl/ ▸*n. Medicine* a synthetic compound with anthelmintic properties, derived from thiazole and used chiefly to treat infestation with intestinal nematodes. ▷1960s: from elements from **THIAZOLE** + **BENZENE** + **IMIDAZOLE**.

thi·a·mine /ˈTHīəmin; -mēn/ (also **thi·a·min** /-min/) ▸*n. Biochemistry* a vitamin of the B complex, found in unrefined grains, beans, and liver, a deficiency of which causes beriberi. It is a sulfur-containing derivative of thiazole and pyrimidine. Also called **VITAMIN B$_1$**.

thi·a·zide /ˈTHīəˌzīd/ ▸*n. Medicine* any of a class of sulfur-containing drugs that increase the excretion of sodium and chloride and are used as diuretics and as a method of lowering the blood pressure. ▷1950s: from elements of **THIO-** + **AZINE** + **OXIDE**.

thi·a·zine /ˈTHīəˌzēn/ ▸*n.* any of a class of molecules containing a ring of one nitrogen, one sulfur, and four carbon atoms, used in dyes and more recently in sedatives. ▷late 19th cent.: from *thio-* + *azine.*

thi·a·zole /ˈTHīəˌzōl/ ▸*n. Chemistry* a synthetic foul-smelling liquid whose molecule is a ring of one nitrogen, one sulfur, and three carbon atoms. • Chem. formula: C_3H_3NS.

thick /THik/ ▸*adj.* **1** with opposite sides or surfaces that are a great or relatively great distance apart: *thick slices of bread | the walls are 5 feet thick.* ■ (of a garment or other knitted or woven item) made of heavy material for warmth or comfort: *a thick sweater.* ■ of large diameter: *thick metal cables.* ■ (of script or type) consisting of broad lines: *a headline in thick black type.* **2** made up of a large number of things or people close together: *his hair was long and thick | the road winds through thick forest.* ■ [*predic.*] (**thick with**) densely filled or covered with: *the room was thick with smoke | figurative the air was thick with rumors.* ■ (of air, the atmosphere, or an odor carried by them) heavy or dense: *a thick odor of dust and perfume.* ■ (of darkness or a substance in the air) so black or dense as to be impossible or difficult to see through: *the shore was obscured by thick fog.* **3** (of a liquid or a semiliquid substance) relatively firm in consistency; not flowing freely: *thick mud.* **4** *informal* of low intelligence; stupid: *he's a bit thick | I've got to shout to get it into your thick head.* **5** (of a voice) not clear or distinct; hoarse or husky. ■ (of an accent) very marked and difficult to understand. **6** [*predic.*] *informal* having a very close, friendly relationship: *he's very* ***thick with*** *the new boss.*

▸*n.* (**the thick**) *rare* the busiest or most crowded part of something; the middle of something: *the thick of battle.*

▸*adv.* in or with deep, dense, or heavy mass: *bread spread thick with butter.* ▷Old English *thicce*, of Germanic origin; related to Dutch *dik* and German *dick.* —**thick·ish** *adj.* —**thick·ly** *adv.* [*as submodifier*] *thickly carpeted corridors.*

▸*PHRASES* □ **be thick on the ground** see **GROUND**[1]. □ **a bit thick** *Brit., informal* unfair or unreasonable. □ **have a thick skin** see **SKIN**. □ **thick and fast** rapidly and in great numbers. □ **(as) thick as a brick** very stupid. □ **(as) thick as thieves** *informal* (of two or more people) very close or friendly; sharing secrets. □ **through thick and thin** under all circumstances, no matter how difficult: *they stuck together through thick and thin.*

thick·en /ˈTHikən/ ▸*v.* make or become thick or thicker: [*trans.*] *thicken the sauce with flour* | [*intrans.*] *the fog had thickened.*

▸*PHRASE* □ **the plot thickens** used when a situation is becoming more and more complicated and puzzling.

thick·en·er /ˈTHikənər/ ▸*n.* a substance added to a liquid to make it firmer, esp. in cooking. ■ *Chemistry* an apparatus for the sedimentation of solids from suspension in a liquid.

thick·en·ing /ˈTHikəniNG/ ▸*n.* **1** the process or result of becoming broader, deeper, or denser. ■ a broader, deeper, or denser area of animal or plant tissue. **2** another term for **THICKENER**.

▸*adj.* becoming broader, deeper, or denser: *a hazardous journey through thickening fog.*

thick·et /ˈTHikit/ ▸*n.* a dense group of bushes or trees. ▷Old English *thiccet* (see **THICK**, **-ET**[1]).

thick·head /ˈTHikˌhed/ ▸*n. informal* a stupid person. —**thick·head·ed** *adj.* —**thick·head·ed·ness** *n.*

thick-knee ▸*n.* a large-eyed ploverlike bird with mottled brownish plumage, inhabiting open stony or sandy country. Also called **STONE CURLEW**. • Family Burhinidae: two genera and several species, in particular *Burhinus oedicnemus* of Eurasia and Africa.

thick·ness /ˈTHiknis/ ▸*n.* **1** the distance between opposite sides of something: *the gateway is several feet in thickness | paving slabs can be obtained in varying thicknesses.* ■ the quality of being broad or deep: *the immense thickness of the walls.* ■ a layer of a specified material: *the framework has to support two thicknesses of plasterboard.* ■ [*in sing.*] a broad or deep part of a specified thing: *the beams were set into the thickness of the wall.* **2** the quality of being dense: *he gave his eyes time to adjust to the thickness of the fog.* ■ the state or quality of being made up of many closely packed parts: *the thickness of his hair.* ▷Old English *thicness* (see **THICK**, **-NESS**).

thick·set /ˈTHikˌset/ ▸*adj.* (of a person or animal) heavily or solidly built; stocky.

thick-wit·ted (also **thick-skulled**) ▸*adj.* dull and stupid.

thief /THēf/ ▸*n.* (*pl.* **thieves** /THēvz/) a person who steals another person's property, esp. by stealth and without using force or violence. ▷Old English *thīof, thēof*, of Germanic origin; related to Dutch *dief* and German *Dieb*, also to **THEFT**.

thieve /THēv/ ▸*v.* [*intrans.*] be a thief; steal something: *they began thieving again* | [*as adj.*] (**thieving**) *get lost, you thieving swine.* | [*trans.*] ▷Old English *thēofian*, from *thēof* 'thief.' Transitive uses began in the late 17th cent.

thiev·er·y /ˈTHēv(ə)rē/ ▸*n.* the action of stealing another person's property.

thieves /THēvz/ ▸ plural form of **THIEF**.

thiev·ish /ˈTHēviSH/ ▸*adj.* of, relating to, or given to stealing. —**thiev·ish·ly** *adv.* —**thiev·ish·ness** *n.*

thigh /THī/ ▸*n.* the part of the human leg between the hip and the knee. ■ the corresponding part in other animals. ▷Old English *thēh, thēoh, thīoh*, of Germanic origin; related to Dutch *dij.* —**thighed** *adj.* [*in combination*] .

thigh bone ▸*n.* the femur.

thigh-high ▸*adj.* (of an item of clothing) reaching as far as a person's thigh. ■ at or reaching to the level of a person's thigh: *he waded into the thigh-high river.*

▸*n.* an item of clothing, esp. a garterless stocking, that reaches to a person's thigh.

thigh-slap·per ▸*n. informal* a joke or anecdote considered to be exceptionally funny. —**thigh-slap·ping** *adj.*

thig·mo·tax·is /ˌTHigməˈtaksis/ ▸*n. Biology* the motion or orientation of an organism in response to a touch stimulus. ▷early 20th cent.: from Greek *thigma* 'touch' + **TAXIS**. —**thig·mo·tac·tic** /-ˈtaktik/ *adj.*

thig·mot·ro·pism /THigˈmätrəˌpizəm/ ▸*n. Biology* the turning or bending of a plant or other organism in response to a touch stimulus. ▷early 20th cent.: from Greek *thigma* 'touch' + **TROPISM**. —**thig·mo·trop·ic** /ˌTHigməˈtrōpik; -ˈträpik/ *adj.*

thill /THil/ ▸*n. historical* a shaft, esp. one of a pair, used to attach a cart or carriage to the animal drawing it. ▷Middle English: of unknown origin.

thim·ble /ˈTHimbəl/ ▸*n.* a metal or plastic cap with a closed end, worn to protect the finger and push the needle in sewing. ■ a short metal tube or ferrule. ■ *Nautical* a metal ring, concave on the outside, around which a loop of rope is spliced. ▷Old English *thȳmel* 'finger protector' (see **THUMB**, **-LE**[1].)

thim·ble·ber·ry /ˈTHimbəlˌberē/ ▸*n.* (*pl.* **-ries**) a North American blackberry or raspberry with thimble-shaped fruit. • Genus *Rubus*, family Rosaceae: several species, including *R. parviflorus*, which has white flowers and juicy, somewhat tasteless fruit.

thim·ble·ful /ˈTHimbəlˌfo͝ol/ ▸*n.* (*pl.* **-fuls**) a small quantity of liquid, esp. alcohol: *a* ***thimbleful of*** *brandy.*

thim·ble·rig /ˈTHimbəlˌrig/ ▸*n.* another term for **SHELL GAME**. ▷early 19th cent.: from **THIMBLE** + **RIG**[2] in the sense 'trick, dodge.' —**thim·ble·rig·ger** *n.*

thi·mer·o·sal /THīˈmerəsəl/ ▸*n.* a local antiseptic for abrasions and minor cuts. • Chem. formula: $C_9H_9HgNaO_2S$.

Thim·phu /timˈpo͞o; THim-/ (also **Thim·bu** /-ˈbo͞o/) the capital of Bhutan, in the Himalaya Mountains at an altitude of 8,000 feet (2,450 m); pop. 30,000.

thin /THin/ ▸*adj.* (**thin·ner, thin·nest**) **1** having opposite surfaces or sides close together; of little thickness or depth: *thin slices of bread.* ■ (of a person) having little, or too little, flesh or fat on their body: *she was painfully thin.* ■ (of a garment or other knitted or woven item) made of light material for coolness or elegance. ■ (of a garment) having had a considerable amount of fabric worn away. ■ (of script or type) consisting of narrow lines: *tall, thin lettering.* **2** having few parts or members relative to the area covered or filled; sparse: *a depressingly thin crowd | his hair was going thin.* ■ not dense: *the thin cold air of the mountains.* ■ containing much liquid and not much solid substance: *thin soup.* ■ *Climbing* denoting a route on which the holds are small or scarce. **3** (of a sound) faint and high-pitched: *a thin, reedy little voice.* ■ (of a smile) weak and forced. ■ too weak to justify a result or effect; inadequate: *the evidence is rather thin.*

▸*adv.* [*often in combination*] with little thickness or depth: *thin-sliced ham | cut it as thin as possible.*

▸*v.* (**thinned, thin·ning**) **1** make or become less dense, crowded, or numerous: [*trans.*] *the remorseless fire of archers thinned their ranks* | [*intrans.*] *the trees began to* ***thin out*** | [*as adj.*] (**thinning**) *thinning hair.* ■ [*trans.*] remove some plants from (a row or area) to allow the others more room to grow: ***thin out*** *overwintered rows of peas.* ■ make or become weaker or more watery: [*trans.*] *if the soup is too thick, add a little water to* ***thin*** *it* ***down*** | [*intrans.*] *the blood thins.* **2** make or become smaller in width or thickness: [*trans.*] *their effect in thinning the ozone layer is probably slowing the global warming trend* | [*intrans.*] *the trees have thinned and diminished in size.* **3** [*trans.*] *Golf* hit (a ball) above its center. ▷Old English *thynne*, of Germanic origin; related to Dutch *dun* and German *dünn*, from an Indo-European root shared by Latin *tenuis.* —**thin·ly** *adv.* —**thin·ness** *n.* —**thin·nish** *adj.*

▸*PHRASES* □ **on thin ice** see **ICE**. □ **thin air** used to refer to the state of being invisible or nonexistent: *she just vanished* ***into thin air*** *| they seemed to pluck numbers* ***out of thin air.*** □ **the thin blue line** *informal* used to refer to the police, typically in the context of situations of civil unrest. □ **thin end of the wedge** see WEDGE. □ **thin on top** *informal* balding.

THE RIGHT WORD **gaunt, lean, skinny, slender, spare, svelte, thin**

Like a strict dieter's menu, all of these adjectives are nonfat, but that's not to say that they necessarily describe a healthy ideal.

Thin describes someone whose healthy weight is naturally low in proportion to his or her height, although it may also imply that the person is underweight (*she looked pale and thin after her operation*). **Skinny** is a more blunt and derogatory term for someone who is too thin, and it often implies underdevelopment (*a skinny little boy; a tall, skinny fashion model*).

Most people would rather be called **slender**, which combines thinness with gracefulness and good proportions (*the slender legs of a Queen Anne table*), or better yet, **svelte**, a complimentary term that implies a slim, elegant figure (*after six months of dieting, she looked so svelte I hardly recognized her*).

Lean and **spare** are used to describe people who are naturally thin, although *spare* suggests a more muscular leanness (*a tall, spare man who looked like Abraham Lincoln*).

Gaunt, on the other hand, means so thin that the angularity of the bones can be seen beneath the skin (*looking gaunt after her latest bout with cancer*).

-thin ▸*comb. form* denoting a specified degree of thinness: *gossamer-thin | wafer-thin.*

thine /T͟Hīn/ ▸*possessive pron.* archaic form of YOURS; the thing or things belonging to or associated with thee: *his spirit will take courage from thine.*
▸*possessive adj.* form of THY used before a vowel: *inquire into thine own heart.* ▷Old English *thīn*, of Germanic origin; related to German *dein*, also to THOU[1].

USAGE The use of **thine** is still found in certain religious groups and in some traditional British dialects, but elsewhere it is restricted to archaic contexts. See also **usage** at THOU[1].

thin-film ▸*adj.* (of a process or device) using or involving a very thin solid or liquid film. ■ *Electronics* denoting a miniature circuit or device consisting of a thin layer of metal or semiconductor on a ceramic or glass substrate.

thing /THING/ ▸*n.* **1** an object that one need not, cannot, or does not wish to give a specific name to: *look at that metal rail thing over there | there are lots of things I'd like to buy | she was wearing this pink thing.* ■ (**things**) personal belongings or clothing: *she began to unpack her things.* ■ [with *adj.*] (**things**) objects, equipment, or utensils used for a particular purpose: *they cleared away the last few lunch things.* ■ [with *negative*] (**a thing**) anything (used for emphasis): *she couldn't find a thing to wear.* ■ used to express one's disapproval or contempt for something: *you won't find me smoking those filthy things.* ■ [with *postpositive adj.*] (**things**) all that can be described in the specified way: *his love for all things Italian.* ■ used euphemistically to refer to a man's penis. **2** an inanimate material object as distinct from a living sentient being: *I'm not a thing, not a work of art to be cherished.* ■ [with *adj.*] a living creature or plant: *the sea is the primal source of all living things on earth.* ■ [with *adj.*] used to express and give a reason for one's pity, affection, approval, or contempt for a person or animal: *have a nice weekend in the country, you lucky thing! | the lamb was a puny little thing.* **3** an action, activity, event, thought, or utterance: *she said the first thing that came into her head | the only thing I could do well was cook.* ■ (**things**) circumstances, conditions, or matters that are unspecified: *things haven't gone entirely according to plan | how are things with you?* ■ an abstract entity or concept: *mourning and depression are not the same thing.* ■ a quality or attribute: *they had one thing in common—they were men of action.* ■ a specimen or type of something: *the game is the latest thing in family fun.* ■ (**one's thing**) *informal* one's special interest or concern: *reading isn't my thing.* ■ [with *adj.*] (**a thing**) *informal* a situation or activity of a specified type or quality: *your being here is just a friendship thing, OK?* **4** (**the thing**) *informal* what is needed or required: *you need a tonic–and here's just the thing.* ■ what is socially acceptable or fashionable: *it wouldn't be quite the thing to go to a royal garden party in boots.* ■ used to introduce or draw attention to an important fact or consideration: *the thing is, I am going to sell this house.* ▷Old English, of Germanic origin; related to German *Ding*. Early senses included 'meeting' and 'matter, concern' as well as 'inanimate object.'

▸*PHRASES* □ **be all things to all men** (or **people**) please everyone, typically by regularly altering one's behavior or opinions in order to conform to those of others. ■ be able to be interpreted or used differently by different people to their own satisfaction. □ **be on to a good thing** *informal* have found a job, situation, or lifestyle that is pleasant, profitable, or easy. □ **be hearing** (or **seeing**) **things** imagine that one can hear (or see) something that is not in fact there. □ **a close** (or **near**) **thing** a narrow avoidance of something unpleasant. □ **do one's own thing** *informal* follow one's own interests or inclinations regardless of others. □ **do the —— thing** *informal* engage in the kind of behavior typically associated with someone or something: *a film in which he does the bad-guy thing.* □ **do things to** *informal* have a powerful emotional effect on: *it just does things to me when we kiss.* □ **for one thing** used to introduce one of two or more possible reasons for something, the remainder of which may or may not be stated: *Why hadn't he arranged to see her at the house? For one thing, it would have been warmer.* □ **have a thing about** *informal* have an obsessive interest in or dislike of: *she had a thing about men who wore glasses.* □ **—— is one thing, —— is another** used to indicate that the second item mentioned is much more serious or important than the first, and cannot be compared to it: *physical attraction was one thing, love was quite another.* □ **make a** (**big**) **thing of** (or **about**) *informal* make (something) seem more important than it actually is. □ **of all things** out of all conceivable possibilities (used to express surprise): *What had he been thinking about? A kitten, of all things.* □ (**just**) **one of those things** *informal* used to indicate that one wishes to pass over an unfortunate event or experience by regarding it as unavoidable or to be accepted. □ **one thing leads to another** used to suggest that the exact sequence of events is too obvious to need recounting, the listener or reader being able to guess easily what happened. □ **a thing of the past** a thing that no longer happens or exists. □ **a thing or two** *informal* used to refer to useful information that can be imparted or learned: *Teddy taught me a thing or two about wine.* □ **things that go bump in the night** *informal, humorous* unexplained and frightening noises at night, regarded as being caused by ghosts.

thing·a·ma·jig /ˈTHINGəmə,jig/ (also **thing·u·ma·jig**; **thing·a·ma·bob** or **thing·um·a·bob** /-,bäb/) ▸*n. informal* used to refer to or address a person or thing whose name one has forgotten, does not know, or does not wish to mention: *one of those thingamajigs for keeping all the fireplace tools together.* ▷early 19th cent.: arbitrary extension of earlier *thingum* (from THING + a meaningless suffix). *Thingumabob* dates from the mid 18th cent.

thing·um·my /ˈTHINGəmē/ (also **thing·a·my**) ▸*n.* (*pl.* **-mies**) British term for THINGAMAJIG.

thing·y /ˈTHINGē/ ▸*n.* (*pl.* **thing·ies**) another term for THINGAMAJIG.

think /THiNGk/ ▸*v.* (*past* and *past part.* **thought** /THôt/) **1** [with *clause*] have a particular opinion, belief, or idea about someone or something: *she thought that nothing would be the same again | [intrans.] what would John think of her? |* (**be thought**) *it's thought he may have collapsed from shock |* [with *infinitive*] *up to 300 people were thought to have died.* ■ used in questions to express anger or surprise: *What do you think you're doing?* ■ (**I think**) used in speech to reduce the force of a statement or opinion, or to politely suggest or refuse something: *I thought we could go out for a meal.* **2** [*intrans.*] direct one's mind toward someone or something; use one's mind actively to form connected ideas: *he was thinking about Colin | Jack thought for a moment | [trans.] any writer who so rarely produces a book is not thinking deep thoughts.* ■ (**think of/about**) take into account or consideration when deciding on a possible action: *you can live how you like, but there's the children to think about.* ■ (**think of/about**) consider the possibility or advantages of (a course of action): *he was thinking of becoming a zoologist.* ■ have a particular mental attitude or approach: *he thought like a general |* [with *complement*] *one should always think positive.* ■ (**think of**) have a particular opinion of: *I think of him as a friend | she did not think highly of modern art.* ■ call something to mind; remember: *lemon thyme is a natural pair with any chicken dish you* **can think of** | [with *infinitive*] *I hadn't thought to warn Rachel about him.* ■ imagine (an actual or possible situation): *think of being paid a salary to hunt big game!* ■ [usu. with *clause*] expect: *I never thought we'd raise so much money |* [with *infinitive*] *she said something he'd never thought to have heard said again.* ■ (**think oneself into**) concentrate on imagining what it would be like to be in (a position or role): *she tried to think herself into the part of Peter's fiancée.*

▸*phrasal v.* □ **think back** recall a past event or time: *I keep* **thinking back to** *school.* □ **think on** think of or about. □ **think something out** consider something in all its aspects before taking action: *the plan had not been properly thought out.* □ **think something over** consider something carefully. □ **think something through** consider all the possible effects or implications of something: *they had failed to think the policy through.* □ **think something up** *informal* use one's ingenuity to invent or devise something.

▸*n.* [in *sing.*] *informal* an act of thinking: *I went for a walk to have a think.* ▷Old English *thencan*, of Germanic origin; related to Dutch and German *denken*. —**think·a·ble** /ˈTHINGkəbəl/ *adj.*

▸*PHRASES* □ **have** (**got**) **another think coming** *informal* used to express the speaker's disagreement with or unwillingness to do something suggested by someone else: *if they think I'm going to do physical exercises, they've got another think coming.* □ **think again** reconsider something, typically so as to alter one's intentions or ideas. □ **think out loud** express one's thoughts as soon as they occur. □ **think better of** decide not to do (something) after reconsideration. □ **think big** see BIG. □ **think fit** see FIT[1]. □ **think for oneself** have an independent mind or attitude. □ **think nothing** (or **little**) **of** consider (an activity others regard as odd, wrong, or difficult) as straightforward or normal. □ **think nothing of it** see NOTHING. □ **think on one's feet** see FOOT. □ **think twice** consider a course of action carefully before embarking on it. □ **think the world of** see WORLD.

think·er /ˈTHINGkər/ ▸*n.* a person who thinks deeply and seriously. ■ a person with highly developed intellectual powers, esp. one whose profession involves intellectual activity: *a leading scientific thinker.*

think·ing /ˈTHINGkiNG/ ▸*adj.* [*attrib.*] using thought or rational judgment; intelligent: *he seemed to be a thinking man.*
▸*n.* the process of using one's mind to consider or reason about something: *they have done some thinking about welfare reform.* ■ a person's ideas or opinions: *his thinking is reflected in his later autobiography.* ■ (**thinkings**) *archaic* thoughts; meditations.
▸*PHRASES* □ **good** (or **nice**) **thinking** used as an expression of approval for an ingenious plan, explanation, or observation. □ **put on one's thinking cap** *informal* meditate on a problem.

think piece ▸*n.* an article in a newspaper, magazine, or journal presenting personal opinions, analysis, or discussion, rather than bare facts.

think tank ▸*n.* a body of experts providing advice and ideas on specific political or economic problems. —**think tank·er** *n.*

thin-lay·er chro·ma·tog·ra·phy ▸*n. Chemistry* chromatography in which compounds are separated on a thin layer of adsorbent material, typically a coating of silica gel on a glass plate or plastic sheet.

thin·ner /ˈTHinər/ ▸*n.* a volatile solvent used to make paint or other mixtures less viscous.

thin sec·tion ▸*n.* a thin, flat piece of material prepared for examination with a microscope, in particular a piece of rock about 0.03 millimeters thick, or, for electron microscopy, a piece of tissue about 30 nanometers thick.
▸*v.* (**thin-sec·tion**) [*trans.*] prepare (something) for examination in this way.

Thin·su·late /ˈTHinsəlit/ ▸*n. trademark* a thin, highly insulating fabric made from polypropylene fibers, used to make outdoor clothing and sleeping bags. ▷a blend of THIN + INSULATE.

thio- ▸*comb. form Chemistry* denoting replacement of oxygen by sulfur in a compound: *thiosulphate.* ▷from Greek *theion* 'sulfur.'

thi·o·cy·a·nate /,THī-ōˈsīə,nāt/ ▸*n. Chemistry* a salt containing the anion SCN^-.

thi·ol /ˈTHī,ôl; -,äl/ ▸*n. Chemistry* an organic compound containing the group –SH, i.e., a sulfur-containing analog of an alcohol.

thi·o·nyl /ˈTHīə,nil/ ▸*n.* [as *adj.*] *Chemistry* of or denoting the divalent radical =SO. ▷1857: so named by Hugo Schiff (1834–1915), German chemist.

thi·o·pen·tal /ˌTHī-ō'penˌtal; -tôl/ ▸*n.* *Medicine* a sulfur-containing barbiturate drug used as a general anesthetic and hypnotic, and (reputedly) as a truth serum. ▷1940s: from THIO- + a contraction of PENTOBARBITAL.

thi·o·pen·tone /ˌTHī-ō'penˌtōn/ ▸*n.* British term for PENTOTHAL.

thi·o·rid·a·zine /ˌTHīə'ridəˌzēn; -zin/ ▸*n.* *Medicine* a synthetic compound derived from phenothiazine, used as a tranquilizer, chiefly in the treatment of mental illness. ▷1950s: from THIO- + *(pipe)rid(ine)* + AZINE.

thi·o·sul·fate /ˌTHī-ō'səlˌfāt/ ▸*n.* *Chemistry* a salt containing the anion $S_2O_3^{2-}$, i.e., a sulfate with one oxygen atom replaced by sulfur.

thi·o·u·re·a /ˌTHī-ōyə'rēə/ ▸*n.* *Chemistry* a synthetic crystalline compound used in photography and the manufacture of synthetic resins. • The sulfur analog of urea; chem. formula: $SC(NH_2)_2$.

Thí·ra /'THi(ə)rə/ modern Greek name for THERA.

thi·ram /'THīˌram/ ▸*n.* *Chemistry* a synthetic sulfur-containing compound used as a fungicide and seed protectant. • Chem. formula: $C_6H_{12}N_2S_4$. ▷1950s: from THIO-, *(u)r(ea)*, and *am(ine)*, elements of the systematic name.

third /THərd/ ▸*ordinal number* constituting number three in a sequence; 3rd: *the third century | the third of October | Edward the Third.* ■ **(a third/one third)** each of three equal parts into which something is or may be divided: *a third of a mile.* ■ the third finisher or position in a race or competition: *Hill finished third.* ■ the third in a sequence of a vehicle's gears: *he took the corner in third.* ■ *Baseball* third base. ■ the third grade of a school. ■ thirdly (used to introduce a third point or reason): *second, they are lightly regulated; and third, they do business with nonresident clients.* ■ *Music* an interval spanning three consecutive notes in a diatonic scale, e.g., C to E (**major third**, equal to two tones) or A to C (**minor third**, equal to a tone and a semitone). ■ *Music* the note that is higher by this interval than the tonic of a diatonic scale or root of a chord. ■ *Brit.* a place in the third-highest grade in an examination, esp. that for a degree. ▷Old English *thridda*, of Germanic origin; related to Dutch *derde* and German *dritte*, also to THREE. The spelling *thrid* was dominant until the 16th cent. (but *thirdda* is recorded in Northumbrian dialect as early as the 10th cent.).

▸*PHRASE* □ **third time is a charm** (or *Brit.* **third time lucky**) used to express the hope that, after twice failing to accomplish something, one may succeed in the third attempt.

third class ▸*n.* [in *sing.*] a group of people or things considered together as third best. ■ *Brit.* a university degree or examination result in the third-highest classification. ■ a cheap class of mail for advertising and other printed material that weighs less than 16 ounces and is unsealed. ■ *chiefly historical* the cheapest and least comfortable accommodations in a train or ship.

▸*adj.* & *adv.* of the third-best quality or of lower status: [as *adj.*] *many indigenous groups are still viewed as third-class citizens.* ■ [as *adj.*] *Brit.* of or relating to the third-highest division in a university examination: *he left university with a third-class degree.* ■ of or relating to a cheap class of mail including advertising and other printed material weighing less than 16 ounces: [as *adj.*] *third-class mail.* ■ *chiefly historical* of or relating to the cheapest and least comfortable accommodations in a train or ship: [as *adj.*] *a suffocating third-class compartment* [as *adv.*] *I traveled third class across Europe.*

third coun·try ▸*n.* a Third World country.

third cous·in ▸*n.* see COUSIN.

third-de·gree ▸*adj.* [*attrib.*] **1** denoting burns of the most severe kind, affecting tissue below the skin. **2** *Law* denoting the least serious category of a crime, esp. murder.

▸*n.* **(the third degree)** long and harsh questioning, esp. by police, to obtain information or a confession.

third es·tate ▸*n.* [treated as *sing.* or *pl.*] the commons. [the first two estates were formerly represented by the clergy, and the barons and knights; later the Lords spiritual and the Lords temporal.] ■ **(the Third Estate)** the French bourgeoisie and working class before the French Revolution. [translating French *le tiers état.*]

third eye ▸*n.* **1** *Hinduism* the locus of occult power and wisdom in the forehead of a deity, esp. the god Shiva. ■ the "eye of insight" located in the forehead, which can be activated through the practice of yoga. **2** informal term for PINEAL EYE.

third eye·lid ▸*n.* informal term for NICTITATING MEMBRANE.

third force ▸*n.* [in *sing.*] a political group or party acting as a check on conflict between two extreme or opposing groups.

third-hand (also **third·hand**) ▸*adj.* **1** (of goods) having had two previous owners: *a thirdhand dinner suit.* **2** (of information) acquired from or via several intermediate sources and consequently not authoritative or reliable: *the accounts are third-hand, told years after the event.*

▸*adv.* from or via several intermediate sources: *I heard about the case thirdhand.*

Third In·ter·na·tion·al see INTERNATIONAL (sense 2).

third·ly /'THərdlē/ ▸*adv.* in the third place (used to introduce a third point or reason).

third mar·ket ▸*n.* *Finance* used to refer to over-the-counter trading in listed stocks outside the stock exchange.

third par·ty ▸*n.* a person or group besides the two primarily involved in a situation, esp. a dispute. ■ a political party organized as an alternative to the major parties in a two-party system.

▸*adj.* [*attrib.*] of or relating to a person or group besides the two primarily involved in a situation: *third-party suppliers.*

third per·son ▸*n.* **1** a third party. **2** see PERSON (sense 2).

third po·si·tion ▸*n.* **1** *Ballet* a posture in which the turned-out feet are placed one in front of the other, so that the heel of the front foot fits into the hollow of the instep of the back foot. ■ a position of the arms in which one is held curved in front of the body and the other curved to the side, both at waist level. **2** *Music* a position of the left hand on the fingerboard of a stringed instrument nearer to the bridge than the second position, enabling a higher set of notes to be played.

third rail ▸*n.* an additional rail supplying electric current, used in some electric railroad systems. ■ *Informal* a subject, esp. Social Security, considered by politicians too dangerous to modify or discuss.

third-rate ▸*adj.* of inferior or very poor quality. —**third-rat·er** *n.*

third read·ing ▸*n.* a third presentation of a bill to a legislative assembly, in the U.S. to consider it for the last time, and in the UK to debate committee reports.

Third Reich the Nazi regime, 1933–45.

Third Re·pub·lic the republican regime in France between the fall of Napoleon III in 1870 and the German occupation of 1940.

third ven·tri·cle ▸*n.* *Anatomy* the central cavity of the brain, lying between the thalamus and hypothalamus of the two cerebral hemispheres.

third way (also **Third Way**) ▸*n.* an option regarded as an alternative to two extremes, esp. a political agenda that is centrist and consensus-based rather than left- or right-wing: *the Third Way espoused by Europe's new leaders doesn't challenge the supremacy of the marketplace.*

Third World ▸*n.* (usu. **the Third World**) the developing countries of Asia, Africa, and Latin America. ▷translation of French *tiers monde* first used in the 1950s to distinguish the developing countries from the capitalist and communist blocs.

thirst /THərst/ ▸*n.* a feeling of needing or wanting to drink something: *they quenched their thirst with spring water.* ■ lack of the liquid needed to sustain life: *tens of thousands died of thirst and starvation.* ■ (usu. **thirst for**) *poetic/literary* a strong desire for something: *his thirst for knowledge was mainly academic.*

▸*v.* [*intrans.*] *archaic* (of a person or animal) feel a need to drink something. ■ (usu. **thirst for/after**) *poetic/literary* have a strong desire for something: *an opponent thirsting for revenge.* ▷Old English *thurst* (noun), *thyrstan* (verb), of Germanic origin; related to Dutch *dorst*, *dorsten* and German *Durst*, *dürsten*.

thirst·y /'THərstē/ ▸*adj.* (**thirst·i·er**, **thirst·i·est**) feeling a need to drink something: *the hikers were hot and thirsty.* ■ (of land, plants, or skin) in need of water: dry or parched. ■ (of an engine, plant, or crop) consuming a lot of fuel or water. ■ having or showing a strong desire for something: *Jake was as* **thirsty for** *scandal as anyone else.* ■ [*attrib.*] *informal* (of activity, weather, or a time) causing the feeling of a need to drink something: *modeling is thirsty work.* —**thirst·i·ly** /-stəlē/ *adv.* —**thirst·i·ness** *n.*

thir·teen /ˌTHər'tēn; 'THərˌtēn/ ▸*cardinal number* equivalent to the sum of six and seven; one more than twelve, or seven less than twenty; 13: *thirteen miles away | a rise of 13 percent | thirteen of the bishops voted against the motion.* (Roman numeral: **xiii**, **XIII**.) ■ a size of garment or other merchandise denoted by thirteen. ■ thirteen years old: *two boys aged eleven and thirteen.* ▷Old English *thrēotīene* (see THREE, -TEEN). The spelling with initial *thi-* is recorded in late Middle English. —**thir·teenth** /ˌTHər'tēnTH; 'THərˌtēnTH/ *ordinal number*.

Thir·teen Col·o·nies the British colonies that ratified the Declaration of Independence in 1776 and thereby became founding states of the U.S. The colonies were Virginia, Massachusetts, Maryland, Connecticut, Rhode Island, North Carolina, South Carolina, New York, New Jersey, Delaware, New Hampshire, Pennsylvania, and Georgia.

thir·ty /'THərtē/ ▸*cardinal number* (*pl.* **-ties**) the number equivalent to the product of three and ten; ten less than forty; 30: *thirty or forty years ago | thirty were hurt | thirty of her school friends.* (Roman numeral: **xxx**, **XXX**.) ■ **(thirties)** the numbers from thirty to thirty-nine, esp. the years of a century or of a person's life: *a woman in her thirties | she was a famous actress in the thirties.* ■ thirty years old: *I've got a long way to go before I'm thirty.* ■ thirty miles an hour: *doing about thirty.* ▷Old English *thrītig* (see THREE, -TY[2]). The spelling with initial *thi-* is recorded in the 15th cent., and has been the prevalent form since the 16th cent. —**thir·ti·eth** /-iTH/ *ordinal number* —**thir·ty·fold** /-ˌfōld/ *adj.* & *adv.*

thir·ty-eight ▸*n.* a revolver of .38 caliber.

Thir·ty-nine Ar·ti·cles ▸*plural n.* a series of points of doctrine historically accepted as representing the teaching of the Church of England.

thir·ty-sec·ond note ▸*n.* *Music* a note having the time value of half a sixteenth note, represented by a large dot with a three-hooked stem. Also called DEMISEMIQUAVER.

thir·ty-two-mo /'THərtē 'tōō mō/ ▸*n.* (*pl.* **-mos**) a size of book page that results from folding each printed sheet into thirty-two leaves (sixty-four pages). ■ a book of this size.

Thir·ty Years War a European war of 1618–48 that broke out between the Catholic Holy Roman Emperor and some of his German Protestant states and developed into a struggle for continental hegemony with France, Sweden, Spain, and the Holy Roman Empire as the major protagonists. It was ended by the Treaty of Westphalia.

this /THis/ ▸*pron.* (*pl.* **these** /THēz/) **1** used to identify a specific person or thing close at hand or being indicated or experienced: *is this your bag? | he soon knew that this was not the place for him.* ■ used to introduce someone or something: *this is the captain speaking | listen to this.* ■ referring to the nearer of two things close to the speaker (the other, if specified, being identified by "that"): *this is different from that.* **2** referring to a specific thing or situation just mentioned: *the company was transformed, and Ward had played a vital role in bringing this about.*

▸*adj.* (*pl.* **these**) **1** used to identify a specific person or thing close at hand or being indicated or experienced: *don't listen to this guy | these croissants are delicious.* ■ referring to the nearer of two things close to the speaker (the other, if specified, being identified by "that"): *this one or that one?* **2** referring to a specific thing or situation just mentioned: *there was a court case resulting from this incident.* **3** used with periods of time related to the present: *I thought you were busy all this week | how are you this morning?* ■ referring to a period of time that has just passed: *I haven't left my bed these three days.* **4** *informal* used (chiefly in narrative) to refer to a person or thing previously unspecified: *I turned around, and there was this big mummy standing next to us! | I've got this problem and I need help.*

▸*adv.* [as *submodifier*] to the degree or extent indicated: *they can't handle a job this big | he's not used to this much attention.* ▷Old English, neuter of *thes*; related to THAT and THE.

▸*PHRASES* □ **this and that** (or **this, that, and the other**) *informal* various unspecified things: *they stayed up chatting about this and that.* □ **this here** *informal* used to draw attention emphatically to someone or something: *I've slept in this here bed for forty years.*

This·be /'THizbē/ *Roman Mythology* a Babylonian girl, lover of Pyramus.

this·tle /'THisəl/ ▸*n.* **1** a widely distributed herbaceous plant of the daisy family, which typically has a prickly stem and leaves and rounded heads of

bull thistle

purple flowers. • *Carlina, Cirsium, Carduus,* and other genera, family Compositae: numerous species, including **bull thistle** (*Cirsium vulgare*) and **nodding** (or **musk**) **thistle** (*Carduus nutans*). **2** a plant of this type as the Scottish national emblem. • This is usually identified as the **Scotch** (or **cotton**) **thistle** (*Onopordum acanthium*). ▷Old English *thistel,* of Germanic origin; related to Dutch *distel* and German *Distel.* **—this·tly** /ˈTHis(ə)lē/ *adj.*

this·tle·down /ˈTHisəlˌdoun/ ▸*n.* light fluffy down that is attached to thistle seeds, enabling them to be blown about in the wind.

thith·er /ˈTHiTHər/ ▸*adv. archaic* or *poetic/literary* to or toward that place: *no trickery had been necessary to attract him thither.* ▷Old English *thider,* alteration (by association with HITHER) of *thæder,* of Germanic origin; related to THAT and THE.

Thí·vai /ˈTHēve/ modern Greek name for **THEBES** 2.

thix·ot·ro·py /THikˈsätrəpē/ ▸*n. Chemistry* the property of becoming less viscous when subjected to an applied stress, shown for example by some gels that become temporarily fluid when shaken or stirred. ▷1920s: from Greek *thixis* 'touching' + *tropē* 'turning.' **—thix·o·trop·ic** /ˌTHiksəˈträpik; -ˈtrōpik/ *adj.*

THM ▸*abbr.* TRIHALOMETHANE.

Th.M. ▸*abbr.* Master of Theology.

tho /THō/ (also **tho'**) ▸*conj.* & *adv.* informal spelling of THOUGH.

thole /THōl/ ▸*v.* [*trans.*] *Scottish* or *archaic* endure (something) without complaint or resistance; tolerate. ▷Old English *tholian,* of Germanic origin.

thole pin ▸*n.* a pin, typically one of a pair, fitted to the gunwale of a rowboat to act as the fulcrum for an oar. ▷Old English, of Germanic origin; related to Dutch *dol.*

Thom·as[1] /ˈtäməs/, Clarence, (1948–) U.S. Supreme Court associate justice 1991– . He chaired the Equal Employment Opportunity Commission (EEOC) 1982–90 and was a judge on the U.S. Court of Appeals before being nominated to replace Thurgood Marshall on the Court. His appointment was approved only after a lengthy and controversial Senate hearing in which he had to respond to charges of sexual harassment brought by former colleague Anita Hill (1956–).

Thom·as[2], Danny, (1914–91) U.S. television producer and actor; born *Amos Jacobs.* He starred in the television series "Make Room for Daddy" 1953–64 and "The Danny Thomas Hour" 1967–68. He also was known for his sponsorship of St. Jude's Children's Research Hospital in Memphis, Tennessee.

Thom·as[3], Dylan (Marlais) (1914–53), Welsh poet. In 1953, on radio, he narrated *Under Milk Wood,* a portrait of a small Welsh town, interspersing poetic alliterative prose with songs and ballads. Other notable works: *Portrait of the Artist as a Young Dog* (prose, 1940).

Thom·as[4], Norman (Mattoon), (1884–1968) U.S. social reformer, minister, and politician. A minister 1911–31, he helped found the American Civil Liberties Union 1920 and was a Socialist Party presidential candidate six times between 1928 and 1948.

Thom·as, St. an apostle; known as **Doubting Thomas.** He earned his nickname by saying that he would not believe that Jesus had risen again until he had seen and touched his wounds (John 20:24–29). Feast day, December 21.

Thom·as à Kem·pis /ˈtäməs ə ˈkempəs/ (*c.*1380–1471), German theologian; born *Thomas Hemerken.* He is the probable author of *On the Imitation of Christ* (*c.*1415–24), a manual of spiritual devotion.

Thom·as A·qui·nas, St. /ˈtäməs əˈkwīnəs/, see AQUINAS, ST. THOMAS.

Thom·as More, St. see MORE.

Tho·mism /ˈtōˌmizəm/ ▸*n.* the theology of Thomas Aquinas or of his followers. **—Tho·mist** *n.* & *adj.* **—Tho·mis·tic** /təˈmistik/ *adj.*

Thomp·son[1], Emma (1959–), English actress and screenwriter. Her movies include *Howard's End* (1992), for which she won a best-actress Academy Award, *Much Ado about Nothing* (1993), *Sense and Sensibility* (1995), for which she also wrote the Academy Award-winning screenplay, and *Love Actually* (2003).

Thomp·son[2], Francis (1859–1907), English poet. His work, such as "The Hound of Heaven" (1893), contains powerful imagery to convey intense religious experience.

Thomp·son[3], Smith (1768–1843), U.S. Supreme Court associate justice 1823–43. Appointed to the Court by President Monroe, he was an advocate of states' rights.

Thom·son's ga·zelle ▸*n.* a light brown gazelle with a conspicuous dark band along the flanks, living in large herds on the open plains of East Africa. • *Gazella thomsonii,* family Bovidae. ▷late 19th cent.: named after Joseph *Thomson* (1858–94), Scottish explorer.

thong /THôNG; THäNG/ ▸*n.* **1** a narrow strip of leather or other material, used esp. as a fastening or as the lash of a whip. **2** an item of clothing fastened by or including such a narrow strip, in particular: ■ a skimpy bathing suit or pair of underpants like a G-string. ■ another term for FLIP-FLOP (sense 1).
▸*v.* [*trans.*] *archaic* flog or lash (someone) with a whip. ▷Old English *thwang, thwong,* of Germanic origin; related to German *Zwang* 'compulsion.' Compare with WHANG. **—thonged** *adj.* **—thong·y** *adj.*

Thor /THôr/ *Scandinavian Mythology* the god of thunder, the weather, agriculture, and the home, the son of Odin and Freya (Frigga). Thursday is named after him.

thor·a·ces /ˈTHôrəˌsēz/ ▸ plural form of THORAX.

tho·rac·ic /THəˈrasik/ ▸*adj. Anatomy* & *Zoology* of or relating to the thorax.

tho·rac·ic duct ▸*n. Anatomy* the main vessel of the lymphatic system, passing upward in front of the spine and draining into the left innominate vein near the base of the neck.

tho·rac·ic ver·te·bra ▸*n. Anatomy* each of the twelve bones of the backbone to which the ribs are attached.

tho·ra·co·lum·bar /ˌTHôrəkəˈləmbər/ ▸*adj. Anatomy* of or relating to the thoracic and lumbar regions of the spine. ■ denoting the sympathetic nervous system.

tho·ra·cot·o·my /ˌTHôrəˈkätəmē/ ▸*n.* surgical incision into the chest wall. ▷late 19th cent.: from Greek *thōrax, thorāc-* 'chest' + -TOMY.

tho·rax /ˈTHôrˌaks/ ▸*n.* (*pl.* **tho·rax·es** or **tho·ra·ces** /ˈTHôrəˌsēz/) *Anatomy* & *Zoology* the part of the body of a mammal between the neck and the abdomen, including the cavity enclosed by the ribs, breastbone, and dorsal vertebrae, and containing the chief organs of circulation and respiration; the chest. ■ *Zoology* the corresponding part of a bird, reptile, amphibian, or fish. ■ *Entomology* the middle section of the body of an insect, between the head and the abdomen, bearing the legs and wings. ▷late Middle English: via Latin from Greek *thōrax.*

Tho·ra·zine /ˈTHôrəˌzēn/ ▸*n.* trademark for CHLORPROMAZINE. ▷1950s: formed from elements of the systematic name.

Tho·reau /THəˈrō;THôˈrō; ˈTHôrō/, Henry David (1817–62), U.S. essayist and poet. A key proponent of transcendentalism, he is best known for *Walden, or Life in the Woods* (1854), an account of a two-year experiment in self-sufficiency. His essay on civil disobedience (1849) influenced Mahatma Gandhi's policy of passive resistance.

tho·ri·a /ˈTHôrēə/ ▸*n. Chemistry* thorium dioxide, a white refractory solid used in making gas mantles and other materials for high-temperature applications. • Chem. formula: ThO_2. ▷mid 19th cent.: from THORIUM, on the pattern of words such as *alumina* and *magnesia.*

tho·ri·um /ˈTHôrēəm/ ▸*n.* the chemical element of atomic number 90, a white radioactive metal of the actinide series. (Symbol: **Th**) ▷mid 19th cent.: named after the god **THOR.**

Thorn /tôrn/ German name for **TORUŃ.**

thorn /THôrn/ ▸*n.* **1** a stiff, sharp-pointed, straight or curved woody projection on the stem or other part of a plant. ■ *figurative* a source of discomfort, annoyance, or difficulty; an irritation or an obstacle: *the issue has become a thorn in renewing the peace talks.* See also A THORN IN SOMEONE'S SIDE below. **2** (also **thorn bush** or **thorn tree**) a thorny bush, shrub, or tree, esp. a hawthorn. **3** an Old English and Icelandic runic letter, Þ or þ, representing the dental fricatives /TH/ and /TH/ . In English it was eventually superseded by the digraph *th.* Compare with ETH. [so named from the word of which it was the first letter.] ▷Old English, of Germanic origin; related to Dutch *doorn* and German *Dorn.* **—thorn·less** *adj.* (in sense 1). **—thorn·proof** /-ˌpro͞of/ *adj.* (in sense 1).
▸*PHRASES* □ **there is no rose without a thorn** *proverb* every apparently desirable situation has its share of trouble or difficulty. □ **a thorn in someone's side** (or **flesh**) a source of continual annoyance or trouble: *the pastor has long been a thorn in the side of the regime.*

thorn ap·ple ▸*n. chiefly Brit.* another term for JIMSON WEED.

thorn·back /ˈTHôrnˌbak/ (also **thorn·back ray**) ▸*n.* a ray of shallow inshore waters that has spines on the back and tail, in particular: • a prickly skinned European ray that is often eaten as "skate" (*Raja clavata,* family Rajidae). • a ray that lives in the warm waters of the Pacific (*Platyrhinoidis triseriata,* family Platyrhinidae).

Thorn·ton /ˈTHôrntn/ a city in north central Colorado, south of Denver; pop. 82,384.

thorn·y /ˈTHôrnē/ ▸*adj.* (**thorn·i·er, thorn·i·est**) having many thorns or thorn bushes. ■ *figurative* causing distress, difficulty, or trouble: *a thorny problem for our team to solve.* **—thorn·i·ly** /-nəlē/ *adv.* **—thorn·i·ness** *n.*

thorn·y-head·ed worm ▸*n.* a parasitic worm with a thornlike proboscis for attachment to the gut of vertebrates. • Phylum Acanthocephala.

thorn·y oys·ter ▸*n.* a bivalve mollusk of warm seas, whose pinkish-brown shell is heavily ribbed and bears blunt or flattened spines. • Family Spondylidae: *Spondylus* and other genera.

thor·ough /ˈTHərō/ ▸*adj.* complete with regard to every detail; not superficial or partial: *planners need a thorough understanding of the subject.* ■ performed or written with great care and completeness: *officers have made a thorough examination of the wreckage.* ■ taking pains to do something carefully and completely: *the Canadian authorities are very thorough.* ■ [*attrib.*] absolute (used to emphasize the degree of something, typically something unwelcome or unpleasant): *the child is being a thorough nuisance.* ▷Old English *thuruh,* alteration of *thurh* 'through.' Original use was as an adverb and preposition, in senses of *through.* The adjective dates from the late 15th cent., when it also had the sense 'that goes or extends through something,' surviving in *thoroughfare.* **—thor·ough·ly** *adv.* **—thor·ough·ness** *n.*

thor·ough bass /bās/ ▸*n. Music* basso continuo (see CONTINUO).

thor·ough·bred /ˈTHərəˌbred/ ▸*adj.* (of a horse) of pure breed, esp. of a breed originating from English mares and Arab stallions and widely used as racehorses. ■ *informal* of outstanding quality: *this thoroughbred car affords the luxury of three spoilers.*
▸*n.* a horse of a thoroughbred breed. ■ *informal* an outstanding or first-class person or thing: *this is a real thoroughbred of a record.*

thor·ough·fare /ˈTHərəˌfer/ ▸*n.* a road or path forming a route between two places. ■ a main road in a town.

thor·ough·go·ing /ˈTHərəˌgōiNG/ ▸*adj.* involving or attending to every detail or aspect of something: *a thoroughgoing reform of the whole economy.* ■ [*attrib.*] exemplifying a specified characteristic fully; absolute: *a thoroughgoing chocoholic.*

thor·ough-paced ▸*adj. archaic* highly skilled or trained. ■ absolute (used to emphasize the degree to which someone or something exemplifies a characteristic).

thor·ough·pin /ˈTHərəˌpin/ ▸*n.* a swelling of the tendon sheath above the hock of a horse, which may be pressed from inside to outside and vice versa.

thorp /THôrp/ (also **thorpe**) ▸*n.* [*in place names*] a village or hamlet: *Scunthorpe.* ▷Old English *thorp, throp,* of Germanic origin; related to Dutch *dorp* and German *Dorf.*

Thorpe /THôrp/, Jim, (1888–1953) U.S. athlete; full name *James Francis Thorpe.* After starring as an All-American football player at the Carlisle Indian Industrial School 1911–12, he won Olympic gold medals in the pentathlon and decathlon 1912 and played baseball 1913–19 and football 1917–29 professionally. Although he was required to return his Olympic medals because he had played semi-professional baseball in 1909, they were returned to his family in 1984.

Thor·vald·sen /ˈto͝orˌvälsən/ (also **Thor·wald·sen**), Bertel (*c.*1770–1844), Danish neoclassical sculptor. Major works include a statue of Jason (1803) in Rome and the tomb of Pius VII (1824–31).

Thos ▸*abbr.* Thomas.

those /T͟Hōz/ ▸ plural form of **THAT**.

Thoth /THŌTH; tōt/ *Egyptian Mythology* a moon god, the god of wisdom, justice, and writing, patron of the sciences, and messenger of Ra.

thou[1] /T͟Hou/ ▸*pron.* [*second person singular*] archaic or dialect form of **YOU**, as the singular subject of a verb: *thou art fair, o my beloved.* Compare with **THEE**. ▷Old English *thu*, of Germanic origin; related to German *du*, from an Indo-European root shared by Latin *tu*.

USAGE In modern English, the personal pronoun **you** (together with the possessives **your** and **yours**) covers a number of uses: it is both singular and plural, both objective and subjective, and both formal and familiar. This has not always been the case. In Old English and Middle English, some of these different functions of **you** were supplied by different words. Thus, **thou** was at one time the singular subjective case (*thou art a beast*), while **thee** was the singular objective case (*he cares not for thee*). In addition, the form **thy** (modern equivalent **your**) was the singular possessive determiner, and **thine** (modern equivalent **yours**) the singular possessive pronoun, both corresponding to **thee**. The forms **you** and **ye**, on the other hand, were at one time reserved for plural uses. By the 19th century, these forms were universal in standard English for both singular and plural, polite and familiar. In present day use, **thou**, **thee**, **thy**, and **thine** survive in certain religious groups and in some traditional British dialects, but otherwise are found only in archaic contexts.

thou[2] /THou/ ▸*n.* (*pl.* same or **thous**) *informal* a thousand. ■ one thousandth of an inch. ▷mid 19th cent.: abbreviation.

though /T͟Hō/ ▸*conj.* despite the fact that; although: *though they were speaking in undertones, Philip could hear them.* ■ [with *modal*] even if (introducing a possibility): *you will be informed of its progress, slow though that may be.* ■ however; but (introducing something opposed to or qualifying what has just been said): *her first name was Rose, though no one called her that.*
▸*adv.* however (indicating that a factor qualifies or imposes restrictions on what was said previously): *I was hunting for work. Jobs were scarce though.* ▷Old English *thēah*, of Germanic origin; related to Dutch and German *doch*; superseded in Middle English by forms from Old Norse *thó, thau*.
▸***PHRASES*** □ **as though** see **AS**[1]. □ **even though** see **EVEN**[1].

USAGE On the differences in use between **though** and **although**, see **usage** at **ALTHOUGH**.

thought[1] /THôt/ ▸*n.* **1** an idea or opinion produced by thinking or occurring suddenly in the mind: *Maggie had a sudden thought* | *I asked him if he had any thoughts on how it had happened* | *Mrs. Oliver's first thought was to get help.* See note at **IDEA**. ■ an idea or mental picture, imagined and contemplated: *the mere thought of Peter with Nicole made her see red.* ■ (**one's thoughts**) one's mind or attention: *he's very much **in our thoughts** and prayers.* ■ an act of considering or remembering someone or something: *she hadn't **given a thought to** Max for some time.* ■ (usu. **thought of**) an intention, hope, or idea of doing or receiving something: *he had given up all thoughts of making Manhattan his home.* **2** the action or process of thinking: *Sophie sat deep **in thought**.* ■ the formation of opinions, esp. as a philosophy or system of ideas, or the opinions so formed: *the freedom of thought and action* | *the traditions of Western thought.* ■ careful consideration or attention: *I haven't **given** it much **thought**.* ■ concern for another's well-being or convenience: *he is carrying on the life of a single man, with **no thought for** me.* ▷Old English *thōht*, of Germanic origin; related to Dutch *gedachte*, also to **THINK**.
▸***PHRASES*** □ **don't give it another thought** *informal* used to tell someone not to worry when they have apologized for something. □ **it's the thought that counts** *informal* used to indicate that it is the kindness behind an act that matters, however imperfect or insignificant the act may be. □ **a second thought** [with *negative*] more than the slightest consideration: *not one of them **gave a second thought to** the risks involved.* □ **take thought** *dated* reflect or consider. □ **that's a thought!** *informal* used to express approval of a comment or suggestion.

thought[2] ▸ past and past participle of **THINK**.

thought con·trol ▸*n.* the attempt to restrict ideas and impose opinions through censorship and the control of school curricula.

thought·crime /ˈTHôt,krīm/ (also **thought-crime**) ▸*n.* an instance of unorthodox or controversial thinking, considered as a criminal offense or as socially unacceptable: *academia is pandering to politicized pressure groups with courses on feminism and homosexuality, and persecuting colleagues who are guilty of thought-crimes.*

thought dis·or·der ▸*n.* *Psychiatry* a disorder of cognitive organization, characteristic of psychotic mental illness, in which thoughts and conversation appear illogical and lacking in sequence and may be delusional or bizarre in content.

thought ex·per·i·ment ▸*n.* an experiment carried out only in the imagination.

thought form ▸*n.* (often **thought forms**) (esp. in Christian theology) a combination of presuppositions, imagery, and vocabulary current at a particular time or place and forming the context for thinking on a subject.

thought·ful /ˈTHôtfəl/ ▸*adj.* absorbed in or involving thought: *brows drawn together in thoughtful consideration.* ■ showing consideration for the needs of other people: *he was attentive and thoughtful* | *how very **thoughtful of** you!* ■ showing careful consideration or attention: *her work is thoughtful and provocative.* **—thought·ful·ly** *adv.* **—thought·ful·ness** *n.*

thought lead·er ▸*n.* one whose views on a subject are taken to be authoritative and influential.

thought·less /ˈTHôtləs/ ▸*adj.* (of a person or their behavior) not showing consideration for the needs of other people: *it was **thoughtless of** her to have rushed out and not said where she would be going.* ■ without consideration of the possible consequences: *to think a few minutes of thoughtless pleasure could end in this.* **—thought·less·ly** *adv.* **—thought·less·ness** *n.*

thought pat·tern ▸*n.* a habit of thinking in a particular way, using particular assumptions. ■ a quality characterizing someone's thought processes as expressed in language: *thought patterns such as overgeneralization and illogicality.* ■ another term for **THOUGHT FORM**.

thought po·lice ▸*n.* [treated as *pl.*] a group of people who aim or are seen as aiming to suppress ideas that deviate from the way of thinking that they believe to be correct.

thought-pro·vok·ing ▸*adj.* stimulating careful consideration or attention: *thought-provoking questions.*

thought re·form ▸*n.* the systematic alteration of a person's mode of thinking, esp. (in communist China) a process of individual political indoctrination.

thought trans·fer·ence ▸*n.* another term for **TELEPATHY**.

thought wave ▸*n.* a supposed pattern of energy by which it is claimed that thoughts are transferred from one person to another.

thou·sand /ˈTHouzənd/ ▸*cardinal number* (*pl.* **-sands** /ˈTHouzndz/ or (with numeral or quantifying word) same) (**a/one thousand**) the number equivalent to the product of a hundred and ten; 1,000: *a thousand meters* | *two thousand acres* | *thousands have been killed.* (Roman numeral: **m, M**) ■ (**thousands**) the numbers from one thousand to 9,999: *the cost of repairs could be in the thousands.* ■ (usu. **thousands**) *informal* an unspecified large number: *you'll meet thousands of girls before you find the one you like* | *I have imagined it a thousand times.* ▷Old English *thūsend*, of Germanic origin; related to Dutch *duizend* and German *Tausend*. **—thou·sand·fold** /-ˌfōld/ *adj.* & *adv.* **—thou·sandth** /-zən(t)TH/ *ordinal number*.

Thou·sand and One Nights another name for **ARABIAN NIGHTS**.

Thou·sand Is·land dress·ing ▸*n.* a dressing for salad or seafood consisting of mayonnaise with ketchup and chopped pickles.

Thou·sand Is·lands **1** a group of about 1,500 islands in a widening of the St. Lawrence River, just below Kingston, Ontario, Canada. Some of the islands belong to Canada and some to the U.S. **2** a group of about 100 small islands off the northern coast of Java that form part of Indonesia. Indonesian name **PULAU SERIBU**.

Thou·sand Oaks an industrial city in southwestern California, northwest of Los Angeles; pop. 104,352.

thp (also **t.hp.**) ▸*abbr.* thrust horsepower.

Thrace /THrās/ an ancient country that was west of the Black Sea and north of the Aegean Sea. It is now divided between Turkey, Bulgaria, and Greece. **—Thra·cian** /ˈTHrāSHən/ *adj.* & *n.*

thrall /THrôl/ ▸*n.* *poetic/literary* the state of being in someone's power or having great power over someone: *she was **in thrall to** her abusive husband.* ■ *historical* a slave, servant, or captive. ▷Old English *thrǣl* 'slave,' from Old Norse *þræll*. **—thrall·dom** /-dəm/ (also **thral·dom**) *n.*

thrash /THraSH/ ▸*v.* [*trans.*] beat (a person or animal) repeatedly and violently with a stick or whip: *she thrashed him across the head and shoulders* | [as *n.*] (**thrashing**) *what he needs is a good thrashing.* ■ hit (something) hard and repeatedly: *the wind screeched and the mast thrashed the deck.* ■ [*intrans.*] make a repeated crashing by or as if by hitting something: *the surf thrashed and thundered.* ■ [*intrans.*] move in a violent and convulsive way: *he lay on the ground **thrashing around** in pain* | [*trans.*] *she thrashed her arms, attempting to swim.* ■ [*intrans.*] (**thrash around**) struggle in a wild or desperate way to do something: *two months of thrashing around on my own have produced nothing.* ■ *informal* defeat (someone) heavily in a contest or match: *I thrashed Pete at cards* | [*trans.*] *the Braves were thrashed 8–1 by the Mets.* ■ [*intrans.*] move with brute determination or violent movements: *I wrench the steering wheel back and thrash on up the hill.* ■ rare term for **THRESH** (sense 1).
▸*phrasal v.* □ **thrash something out** discuss something thoroughly and honestly. ■ produce a conclusion by such discussion.
▸*n.* **1** [usu. in *sing.*] a violent or noisy movement, typically involving hitting something repeatedly: *the thrash of the waves.* **2** (also **thrash metal**) a style of fast, loud, harsh-sounding rock music, combining elements of punk and heavy metal. ■ a short, fast, loud piece or passage of rock music. ▷Old English, variant of **THRESH** (an early sense). Current senses of the noun date from the mid 19th cent.

thrash·er[1] /ˈTHraSHər/ ▸*n.* **1** a person or thing that thrashes. **2** archaic spelling of **THRESHER** (sense 1).

thrash·er[2] ▸*n.* a thrushlike American songbird of the mockingbird family, with mainly brown or gray plumage, a long tail, and a down-curved bill. • Family Mimidae: five genera, in particular *Toxostoma*, and several species. ▷early 19th cent.: perhaps from English dialect *thrusher, thresher* 'thrush.'

thrawn /THrôn/ ▸*adj.* *Scottish* perverse; ill-tempered: *your mother's looking a bit thrawn this morning.* ■ twisted; crooked: *a slightly thrawn neck.* ▷late Middle English: Scots form of *thrown* (see **THROW**), in the obsolete sense 'twisted, wrung.'

thread /THred/ ▸*n.* **1** a long, thin strand of cotton, nylon, or other fibers used in sewing or weaving. ■ cotton, nylon, or other fibers spun into long, thin strands and used for sewing. ■ (**threads**) *informal* clothes. **2** a thing resembling a thread in length or thinness, in particular: ■ *chiefly poetic/literary* a long, thin line or piece of something: *the river was a thread of silver below them.* ■ [in *sing.*] something abstract or intangible, regarded as weak or fragile: *keeping the tenuous thread of life attached to a dying body.* ■ a theme or characteristic, typically forming one of several, running throughout a situation or piece of writing: *a **common thread** running through the scandals was the failure to conduct audits.* **3** *Computing* a group of linked messages posted on the Internet that share a common subject or theme. ■ a programming structure or process formed by linking a number of separate elements or subroutines, esp. each of the tasks executed concurrently in multithreading. **4** (also **screw thread**) a helical ridge on the outside of a screw, bolt, etc., or on the inside of a cylindrical hole, to allow two parts to be screwed together.
▸*v.* [*trans.*] **1** pass a thread through the eye of (a needle) or through the needle and guides of (a sewing machine). ■ [*trans.*] pass (a long, thin object or piece of material) through something and into the required position for use: *he threaded the rope through a pulley.* ■ [*intrans.*] move carefully or skillfully in and out of obstacles: *she **threaded her way** through the tables.* ■ interweave or intersperse as if with threads: *his hair had become ill-kempt and **threaded with** gray.* ■ put (beads, chunks of food, or other small objects) together or singly on a thread, chain, or skewer that runs through the center of each one: *Connie sat threading beads.* **2** [usu. as *adj.*] (**threaded**) cut a screw thread in or on (a hole, screw, or other object). ▷Old English *thrǣd* (noun), of Germanic origin; related to Dutch *draad* and German *Draht*, also to the verb **THROW**. The verb dates from late Middle English. **—thread·like** /-ˌlīk/ *adj.*
▸***PHRASES*** □ **hang by a thread** be in a highly precarious state. □ **lose the** (or **one's**) **thread** be unable to follow what someone is saying or remember what one is going to say next.

thread·bare /ˈTHred,ber/ ▸*adj.* (of cloth, clothing, or soft furnishings) becoming thin and tattered with age: *shabby rooms with threadbare carpets* | *figurative the song was a tissue of threadbare clichés.* ■ (of a person, building, or room) poor or shabby in appearance.

thread·er /ˈTHredər/ ▸*n.* **1** a device for passing a thread through the needle and guides of a sewing machine. ■ a factory worker who attaches spools of yarn to a loom. **2** a device for cutting a spiral ridge on the outside of a screw or the inside of a hole.

thread·fin /ˈTHred,fin/ ▸*n.* a tropical marine fish that has long streamers or rays arising from its pectoral fins, locally important as a food fish. • Family Polynemidae: several genera and species.

thread·ing /ˈTHrediNG/ ▸*n.* **1** a process in which unwanted facial hair is removed by using twisted cotton thread to pull the hair from the follicle. **2** *Computing* the system by which consecutive messages relating to a single subject on an electronic bulletin board or newsgroup are stored for retrieval.

thread·worm /ˈTHred,wərm/ ▸*n.* a very slender parasitic nematode worm, esp. a pinworm.

thread·y /ˈTHredē/ ▸*adj.* (**thread·i·er**, **thread·i·est**) **1** of, relating to, or resembling a thread. **2** (of a sound, esp. the voice) scarcely audible: *he managed a thready whisper.* ■ *Medicine* (of a person's pulse) scarcely perceptible.

threat /THret/ ▸*n.* **1** a statement of an intention to inflict pain, injury, damage, or other hostile action on someone in retribution for something done or not done: *members of her family have received* ***death threats.*** ■ *Law* a menace of bodily harm, such as may restrain a person's freedom of action. **2** a person or thing likely to cause damage or danger: *hurricane damage poses a major* ***threat to*** *many coastal communities.* ■ [in *sing.*] the possibility of trouble, danger, or ruin: *the company faces the threat of bankruptcy* | *thousands of railroad jobs came* ***under threat.*** ▷Old English *thrēat* 'oppression,' of Germanic origin; related to Dutch *verdrieten* 'grieve,' German *verdriessen* 'irritate.'

threat·en /ˈTHretn/ ▸*v.* [*reporting verb*] state one's intention to take hostile action against someone in retribution for something done or not done: [*trans.*] *the unions threatened a general strike* | [with *infinitive*] *she made a scene and Tom threatened to leave* | [with *direct speech*] *"I might sue for damages," he threatened.* ■ [*trans.*] express one's intention to harm or kill (someone): *the men* ***threatened*** *the customers* ***with*** *a handgun.* ■ [*trans.*] cause (someone or something) to be vulnerable or at risk; endanger: *a broken finger threatened his career* | *one of four hospitals* ***threatened with*** *closure.* ■ [with *infinitive*] (of a situation or weather conditions) seem likely to produce an unpleasant or unwelcome result: *the dispute threatened to spread to other cities* [*trans.*] *the air was raw and threatened rain.* ■ [*intrans.*] (of something undesirable) seem likely to occur: *unless war threatened, national politics remained the focus of attention.* ▷Old English *thrēatnian* 'urge or induce, esp. by using threats,' from *thrēat* (see THREAT). —**threat·en·er** /ˈTHretn-ər; -nər/ *n.*

threat·en·ing /ˈTHretn-iNG/ ▸*adj.* having a hostile or deliberately frightening quality or manner: *her mother had received a threatening letter.* ■ *Law* (of behavior) showing an intention to cause bodily harm. ■ (of a person or situation) causing someone to feel vulnerable or at risk: *she was a type he found threatening.* ■ (of weather conditions) indicating that bad weather is likely: *black threatening clouds.* —**threat·en·ing·ly** *adv.*

three /THrē/ ▸*cardinal number* equivalent to the sum of one and two; one more than two; 3: *her three children* | *a crew of three* | *a three-bedroom house* | *all three of them are buried there.* (Roman numeral: **iii**, **III**) ■ a group or unit of three people or things: *students clustered in twos or threes.* ■ three years old: *she is only three.* ■ three o'clock: *I'll come at three.* ■ a size of garment or other merchandise denoted by three. ■ a playing card or domino with three pips. ▷Old English *thrīe* (masculine), *thrīo*, *thrēo* (feminine), of Germanic origin; related to Dutch *drie* and German *drei*, from an Indo-European root shared by Latin *tres* and Greek *treis*.

three-card mon·te ▸*n.* a game traditionally associated with con men, in which the dealer shows the player three cards then moves them around face-down, the player being obliged to pick the specified card from among the three.

three cheers ▸*plural n.* see CHEER.

three-col·or proc·ess ▸*n.* *Photography* a means of reproducing natural colors by combining photographic images in the three primary colors.

three-cor·nered ▸*adj.* triangular. ■ (esp. of a contest) between three people or groups.

three-cush·ion bil·liards ▸*plural n.* [usu. treated as *sing.*] a type of billiards in which the cue ball must strike one object ball and three or more cushions before the second object ball.

three-deck·er ▸*n.* a thing with three levels or layers: [as *adj.*] *three-decker sandwiches.* ■ *historical* a sailing warship with three gun decks.

three-di·men·sion·al ▸*adj.* having or appearing to have length, breadth, and depth: *a three-dimensional object.* ■ *figurative* (of a literary or dramatic work) sufficiently full in characterization and representation of events to be believable. —**three-di·men·sion·al·i·ty** /di,menSHəˈnalətē/ *n.* —**three-di·men·sion·al·ly** *adv.*

three·fold /ˈTHrē,fōld/ ▸*adj.* three times as great or as numerous: *a threefold increase in the number of stolen cars.* ■ having three parts or elements: *the differences are threefold.*

▸*adv.* by three times; to three times the number or amount: *the aftershocks intensify threefold each time.*

Three Grac·es see GRACE.

three-leg·ged race /ˈlegəd/ ▸*n.* a race run by pairs of people, one member of each pair having their left leg tied to the right leg of the other.

Three Mile Is·land an island in the Susquehanna River near Harrisburg, Pennsylvania, site of a nuclear power station. In 1979, an accident caused damage to the reactor core, provoking strong reactions against the nuclear industry in the U.S.

three-mile lim·it ▸*n.* *Law* the outer boundary of the area extending 3 miles (4.8 km) out to sea from the coast of a state or country, considered to be within its jurisdiction.

three-par·ent ▸*adj.* **1** *Genetics* containing a chromosomal complement from a mother and father and the mitochondrial DNA from the egg of a donor: *three-parent embryos.* **2** having or regarding three different adults in a parental role: *kids in three-parent homes.*

three-peat (also **three·peat**) ▸*v.* [*intrans.*] win a particular sports championship three times, esp. consecutively: *the Bulls rate as the favorite to three-peat.*

▸*n.* [in *sing.*] a third win of a particular sports championship, esp. the third of three consecutive wins: *all eyes were on the 49ers' bid for a three-peat.* ▷1980s: from THREE + a shortened form of REPEAT.

three·pence /ˈTHrepəns; ˈTHrəp-; ˈTHrē,pens/ ▸*n.* *Brit.* the sum of three pence, esp. before decimalization (1971).

three·pen·ny /ˈTHrip(ə)nē; ˈTHrəp-; ˈTHrē,penē/ ▸*adj.* [*attrib.*] *Brit.* costing or worth three pence, esp. before decimalization (1971). ■ trifling or paltry; of little worth: *a threepenny production.*

three-phase ▸*adj.* (of an electric generator, motor, or other device) designed to supply or use simultaneously three separate alternating currents of the same voltage, but with phases differing by a third of a period.

three-piece ▸*adj.* [*attrib.*] consisting of three separate and complementary items, in particular: ■ (of a set of furniture) consisting of a sofa and two armchairs. ■ (of a set of clothes) consisting of slacks or a skirt with a vest and jacket.

▸*n.* a set of three separate and complementary items. ■ a group consisting of three musicians.

three-ply ▸*adj.* (of material) having three layers or strands.

▸*n.* **1** knitting wool made of three strands. **2** plywood made by gluing together three layers with the grain in different directions.

three-point land·ing ▸*n.* a landing of an aircraft on the two main wheels and the tailwheel or skid simultaneously.

three-point turn ▸*n.* a method of turning a vehicle around in a narrow space by moving forward, backward, and forward again in a sequence of arcs.

three-quar·ter ▸*adj.* [*attrib.*] consisting of three quarters of something (used esp. with reference to size or length): *a three-quarter length cashmere coat.* ■ (of a view or depiction of a person's face) at an angle between full face and profile.

three-ring cir·cus ▸*n.* a circus with three rings for simultaneous performances. ■ a public spectacle, esp. one with little substance: *his attempt at a dignified resignation turned into a three-ring circus.*

three·score /ˈTHrēˈskôr/ ▸*cardinal number poetic/literary* sixty.

Three Sis·ters glacier-covered volcanic peaks in west central Oregon, in the Cascade Range, in a noted wilderness area.

three·some /ˈTHrēsəm/ ▸*n.* a group of three people engaged in the same activity. ■ a game or activity for three people.

three-star ▸*adj.* (esp. of a hotel or restaurant) given three stars in a grading system, typically one in which this denotes a high or average class or quality (four- or five-star denoting the highest standard). ■ (in the U.S. armed services) having or denoting the rank of lieutenant general, distinguished by three stars on the uniform.

Three Stoog·es, U.S. comedy team. Although Shemp Howard (born *Samuel Horwitz*) (1895–1955) was part of the early group and personnel changes were made over the years, the trio basically consisted of brothers Moe Howard (born *Moses Horwitz*) (1897–1975) and Curly Howard (born *Jerome Lester Horwitz*) (1903–52) and of Larry Fine (born *Louis Feinberg*) (1902–75) who replaced Shemp in the early 1930s. The Three Stooges appeared in both full-length movies and, from 1934, short movies.

three strikes ▸*n.* [usu. as *adj.*] legislation providing that an offender's third felony is punishable by life imprisonment or another severe sentence. ▷1990s: from the phrase *three strikes and you're out* (with allusion to baseball).

three-way ▸*adj.* involving three directions, processes, or participants: *a three-way race for the presidency* | *a three-way switch.*

three-wheel·er ▸*n.* a vehicle with three wheels, esp. a child's tricycle.

Three Wise Men another name for MAGI.

threm·ma·tol·o·gy /,THreməˈtäləjē/ ▸*n.* the science of breeding animals and plants. ▷late 19th cent.: from Greek *thremma*, *thremmat-* 'nursling' + -LOGY.

thren·o·dy /ˈTHrenədē/ ▸*n.* (*pl.* **-dies**) a lament. ▷mid 17th cent.: from Greek *thrēnōidia*, from *thrēnos* 'wailing' + *ōidē* 'song.' —**thre·no·di·al** /THrəˈnōdēəl/ *adj.* —**thre·nod·ic** /THrəˈnädik/ *adj.* —**thren·o·dist** /-dist/ *n.*

thre·o·nine /ˈTHrēə,nēn; -nin/ ▸*n.* *Biochemistry* a hydrophilic amino acid that is a constituent of most proteins. It is an essential nutrient in the diet of vertebrates. • Chem. formula: $CH_3CH(OH)CH(NH_2)COOH$. ▷1930s: from *threose* (the name of a tetrose sugar) + -INE[4].

thresh /THresh/ ▸*v.* [*trans.*] **1** separate grain from (a plant), typically with a flail or by the action of a revolving mechanism: *machinery that can reap and thresh corn in the same process* [as *n.*] (**threshing**) *farm workers started the afternoon's threshing.* **2** variant spelling of THRASH (in the sense of violent movement). ▷Old English *therscan*, later *threscan*, of Germanic origin; related to Dutch *dorsen* and German *dreschen*. Compare with THRASH.

thresh·er /ˈTHreshər/ ▸*n.* **1** a person or machine that separates grain from the plants by beating. **2** (also **thresher shark**) a surface-living shark with a long upper lobe to the tail. Threshers often hunt in pairs, lashing the water with their tails to herd fish into a tightly packed shoal. • *Alopias vulpinus*, family Alopiidae.

thresh·ing floor ▸*n.* a hard, level surface on which grain is threshed with a flail.

thresh·ing ma·chine ▸*n.* a power-driven machine for separating the grain from the plants.

thresh·old /ˈTHresh,(h)ōld/ ▸*n.* **1** a strip of wood, metal, or stone forming the bottom of a doorway and crossed in entering a house or room. ■ [in *sing.*] a point of entry or beginning: *she was* ***on the threshold*** *of a dazzling career.* ■ the beginning of an airport runway on which an aircraft is attempting to land. **2** the magnitude or intensity that must be exceeded for a certain reaction, phenomenon, result, or condition to occur or be manifested: *nothing happens until the signal passes the threshold* | [as *adj.*] *a threshold level.* ■ the maximum level of radiation or a concentration of a substance considered to be acceptable or safe: *their water would meet the safety threshold of 50 milligrams of nitrates per liter.* ■ *Physiology & Psychology* a limit below which a stimulus causes no reaction: *everyone has a different pain threshold.* ▷Old English *therscold*, *threscold*; related to German dialect *Drischaufel*; the first element is related to THRESH (in a Germanic sense 'tread'), but the origin of the second element is unknown.

threw /THro͞o/ ▸ past of THROW.

thrice /THrīs/ ▸*adv.* *chiefly formal poetic/literary* three times: *a dose of 25 mg thrice daily.* ■ [as *submodifier*] extremely; very: *I was thrice blessed.* ▷Middle English

Pronunciation Key ə *ago*; ər *over*; ˈə or ˌə *up*; ˈər or ˌər *fur*; a *hat*; ā *rate*; ä *car*; CH *chew*; e *let*; ē *see*; e(ə)r *air*; i *fit*; ī *by*; i(ə)r *ear*; NG *sing*; ō *go*; ô *for*; oi *boy*; o͝o *good*; o͞o *goo*; ou *out*; SH *she*; TH *thin*; T͟H *then*; (h)w *why*; ZH *vision*

thries, from earlier *thrie* (from Old English *thriga*, related to **THREE**) + **-S**3 (later respelled *-ce* to denote the unvoiced sound); compare with **ONCE**.

thrift /THrift/ ▸*n.* **1** the quality of using money and other resources carefully and not wastefully: *the values of thrift and self-reliance.* ■ another term for **SAVINGS AND LOAN**. **2** a European plant that forms low-growing tufts of slender leaves with rounded pink flowerheads, growing chiefly on sea cliffs and mountains. Also called **SEA PINK**. • *Armeria maritima*, family Plumbaginaceae. ▷Middle English (in the sense 'prosperity, acquired wealth, success'): from Old Norse, from *thrífa* 'grasp, get hold of.' Compare with **THRIVE**.

thrift·less /'THriftlis/ ▸*adj.* (of a person or their behavior) spending money in an extravagant and wasteful way. **—thrift·less·ly** *adv.* **—thrift·less·ness** *n.*

thrift shop (also **thrift store**) ▸*n.* a store selling secondhand clothes and other household goods, typically to raise funds for a charitable institution.

thrift·y /'THriftē/ ▸*adj.* (**thrift·i·er, thrift·i·est**) **1** (of a person or their behavior) using money and other resources carefully and not wastefully. See note at **ECONOMICAL**. **2** *chiefly archaic dialect* (of livestock or plants) strong and healthy. ■ *archaic* prosperous. **—thrift·i·ly** /-lē/ *adv.* **—thrift·i·ness** *n.*

thrill /THril/ ▸*n.* a sudden feeling of excitement and pleasure: *the thrill of jumping out of an airplane.* ■ an experience that produces such a feeling. ■ a wave or nervous tremor of emotion or sensation: *a thrill of excitement ran through her.* ■ *archaic* a throb or pulsation. ■ *Medicine* a vibratory movement or resonance heard through a stethoscope.

▸*v.* **1** [*trans.*] cause (someone) to have a sudden feeling of excitement and pleasure: *his kiss thrilled and excited her* | *I'm* **thrilled to death** | *they were* **thrilled to pieces** | [as *adj.*] (**thrilling**) *a thrilling adventure.* ■ [*intrans.*] experience such feeling: **thrill to** *the magic of the world 's greatest guitarist.* **2** [*intrans.*] (of an emotion or sensation) pass with a nervous tremor: *the shock of alarm* **thrilled through** *her.* ■ [*intrans.*] *poetic/literary* quiver or throb. ▷Middle English (as a verb in the sense 'pierce or penetrate'): alteration of dialect *thirl* 'pierce, bore.' **—thrill·ing·ly** *adv.*

▸*PHRASE* □ **thrills and chills** the excitement of dangerous sports or entertainments, as experienced by spectators.

thrill·er /'THrilər/ ▸*n.* a novel, play, or movie with an exciting plot, typically involving crime or espionage. ■ a person, thing, or experience that thrills: *the Rockies could make Game 4 another thriller.*

thrips /THrips/ (also **thrip**) ▸*n.* (*pl.* same) a minute black winged insect that sucks plant sap and can be a serious pest of ornamental and food plants when present in large numbers. • Order Thysanoptera: many species. ▷late 18th cent.: via Latin from Greek, literally 'woodworm.'

thrive /THrīv/ ▸*v.* (*past* **throve** /THrōv/ or **thrived**; *past part.* **thriven** /'THrivən/ or **thrived**) [*intrans.*] (of a child, animal, or plant) grow or develop well or vigorously: *the new baby thrived.* ■ prosper; flourish: *education groups* **thrive on** *organization* | [as *adj.*] (**thriving**) *a thriving economy.* ▷Middle English (originally in the sense 'grow, increase'): from Old Norse *thrífask*, reflexive of *thrífa* 'grasp, get hold of.' Compare with **THRIFT**.

thro' /THro͞o/ (or **thro**) ▸*prep., adv., & adj.* poetic/literary spelling of **THROUGH**.

throat /THrōt/ ▸*n.* the passage that leads from the back of the mouth of a person or animal. ■ the front part of a person's or animal's neck, behind which the esophagus, trachea, and blood vessels serving the head are situated: *a gold pendant gleamed at her throat.* ■ *poetic/literary* a voice of a person or a songbird: *from a hundred throats came the cry "Vive l'Empereur!"* ■ a thing compared to a throat, esp. a narrow passage, entrance, or exit. ■ *Sailing* the forward upper corner of a quadrilateral fore-and-aft sail. ▷Old English *throte, throtu*, of Germanic origin; related to German *Drossel*. Compare with **THROTTLE**. **—throat·ed** *adj.* [in *combination*] *a full-throated baritone* | *a ruby-throated hummingbird.*

▸*PHRASES* □ **be at each other's throats** (of people or organizations) quarrel or fight persistently. □ **cut one's own throat** bring about one's own downfall by one's actions. □ **force** (or **shove** or **ram**) **something down someone's throat** force ideas or material on a person's attention by repeatedly putting them forward. □ **grab** (or **take**) **someone by the throat** put one's hands around someone's throat, typically in an attempt to throttle them. ■ (**grab something by the throat**) seize control of something: *in the second half, the Huskies took the game by the throat.* ■ attract someone's undivided attention: *the movie grabs you by the throat and refuses to let go.* □ **jump down someone's throat** see **JUMP**. □ **stick in one's throat** see **STICK**2.

throat·latch /'THrōt,lach/ (also **throat·lash** /-,lash/) ▸*n.* a strap passing under a horse's throat to help keep the bridle in position.

throat·y /'THrōtē/ ▸*adj.* (**throat·i·er, throat·i·est**) (of a sound such as a person's voice or the noise of an engine) deep and rasping: *rich, throaty laughter.* **—throat·i·ly** /-təlē/ *adv.* **—throat·i·ness** *n.*

throb /THräb/ ▸*v.* (**throbbed, throb·bing**) [*intrans.*] beat or sound with a strong, regular rhythm; pulsate steadily: *the war drums throbbed* | *figurative the crowded streets* **throbbed with** *life.* ■ feel pain in a series of regular beats: *her foot* **throbbed with** *pain* | [as *adj.*] (**throbbing**) *a throbbing headache.*

▸*n.* [usu. in *sing.*] a strong, regular beat or sound; a steady pulsation: *the throb of the ship's engines.* ■ a feeling of pain in a series of regular beats. ▷late Middle English: probably imitative.

throes /THrōz/ ▸*plural n.* intense or violent pain and struggle, esp. accompanying birth, death, or great change: *he convulsed in his* **death throes**. ▷Middle English *throwe* (singular); perhaps related to Old English *thrēa, thrawu* 'calamity,' influenced by *thrōwian* 'suffer.'

▸*PHRASE* □ **in the throes of** in the middle of doing or dealing with something very difficult or painful: *a friend was in the throes of a divorce.*

Throgs Neck /'THrôgz ,nek; 'THrägz/ a peninsula in the southeast Bronx in New York City that gives its name to a major bridge, which crosses Long Island South to Queens on Long Island.

throm·bi /'THräm,bī/ ▸ plural form of **THROMBUS**.

throm·bin /'THrämbin/ ▸*n. Biochemistry* an enzyme in blood plasma that causes the clotting of blood by converting fibrinogen to fibrin. ▷late 19th cent.: from Greek *thrombos* 'blood clot' + **-IN**1.

thrombo- ▸*comb. form* relating to the clotting of blood: *thromboembolism.* ▷from Greek *thrombos* 'blood clot.'

throm·bo·cyte /'THrämbə,sīt/ ▸*n.* another term for **PLATELET**.

throm·bo·cy·to·pe·ni·a /,THrämbō,sītə'pēnēə/ ▸*n. Medicine* deficiency of platelets in the blood. This causes bleeding into the tissues, bruising, and slow blood clotting after injury. ▷1920s: from **THROMBOCYTE** + Greek *penia* 'poverty.'

throm·bo·em·bo·lism /,THrämbō'embə,lizəm/ ▸*n. Medicine* obstruction of a blood vessel by a blood clot that has become dislodged from another site in the circulation. **—throm·bo·em·bol·ic** /-,em'bälik/ *adj.*

throm·bo·phle·bi·tis /,THrämbōflə'bītis/ ▸*n. Medicine* inflammation of the wall of a vein with associated thrombosis, often occurring in the legs during pregnancy.

throm·bo·plas·tin /,THrämbō'plastən/ ▸*n. Biochemistry* an enzyme released from damaged cells, esp. platelets, that converts prothrombin to thrombin during the early stages of blood coagulation.

throm·bo·sis /THräm'bōsis/ ▸*n.* (*pl.* **-ses** /-,sēz/) local coagulation or clotting of the blood in a part of the circulatory system: *increased risk of thrombosis* | *he died of a coronary thrombosis.* ▷early 18th cent.: modern Latin, from Greek *thrombōsis* 'curdling,' from *thrombos* 'blood clot.' **—throm·bot·ic** /-'bätik/ *adj.*

throm·box·ane /THräm'bäksān/ ▸*n. Biochemistry* a hormone of the prostacyclin type released from blood platelets. It induces platelet aggregation and arterial constriction.

throm·bus /'THrämbəs/ ▸*n.* (*pl.* **-bi** /-,bī/) a blood clot formed in situ within the vascular system of the body and impeding blood flow. ▷mid 19th cent.: modern Latin, from Greek *thrombos* 'lump, blood clot.'

throne /THrōn/ ▸*n.* a ceremonial chair for a sovereign, bishop, or similar figure. ■ (**the throne**) used to signify sovereign power: *the heir to the throne.* ■ *humorous* a toilet. ■ (**thrones**) (in traditional Christian angelology) the third-highest order of the ninefold celestial hierarchy.

▸*v.* [*trans.*] (usu. **be throned**) *poetic/literary* place (someone) on a throne: *the king was throned on a rock.* ▷Middle English: from Old French *trone*, via Latin from Greek *thronos* 'elevated seat.'

throng /THrôNG; THräNG/ ▸*n.* a large, densely packed crowd of people or animals: *he pushed his way through the throng* | **a throng of** *birds.*

▸*v.* [*trans.*] (of a crowd) fill or be present in (a place or area): *a crowd thronged the station* | *the streets are* **thronged with** *people.* ■ [*intrans.*] flock or be present in great numbers: *tourists thronged to the picturesque village.* ▷Old English *(ge)thrang* 'crowd, tumult,' of Germanic origin. The early sense of the verb (Middle English) was 'press violently, force one's way.'

thros·tle /'THrôsəl/ ▸*n.* **1** *Brit.* old-fashioned term for **SONG THRUSH**. **2** (also **thros·tle frame**) *historical* a machine for continuously spinning wool or cotton. ▷Old English, of Germanic origin, from an Indo-European root shared by Latin *turdus* 'thrush.' Sense 2 dates from the early 19th cent. and was apparently named from the humming sound of the machine.

throt·tle /'THrätl/ ▸*n.* **1** a device controlling the flow of fuel or power to an engine: *the engines were* **at full throttle**. **2** *archaic* a throat, gullet, or windpipe.

▸*v.* [*trans.*] **1** attack or kill (someone) by choking or strangling them: *she was sorely tempted to throttle him* | *figurative the revolution has throttled the free exchange of information and opinion.* **2** control (an engine or vehicle) with a throttle. ■ [*intrans.*] (**throttle back** or **down**) reduce the power of an engine or vehicle by use of the throttle. ▷late Middle English (as a verb): perhaps a frequentative, from **THROAT**; the noun (dating from the mid 16th cent. in sense 2) is perhaps a diminutive of **THROAT**, but the history of the word is not clear. **—throt·tler** /'THrätl-ər; 'THrätlər/ *n.*

throt·tle·hold /'THrätl,hōld/ ▸*n.* another term for **STRANGLEHOLD**.

through /THro͞o/ ▸*prep. & adv.* **1** moving in one side and out of the other side of (an opening, channel, or location): [as *prep.*] *stepping boldly through the doorway* | [as *adv.*] *as soon as we opened the gate, they came streaming through.* ■ so as to make a hole or opening in (a physical object): [as *prep.*] *the truck smashed through a brick wall* | [as *adv.*] *a cucumber, slit, but not all the way through.* ■ moving around or from one side to the other within (a crowd or group): [as *prep.*] *making my way through the guests.* ■ so as to be perceived from the other side of (an intervening obstacle): [as *prep.*] *the sun was streaming in through the window* | [as *adv.*] *the glass in the front door where the moonlight streamed through.* ■ [*prep.*] expressing the position or location of something beyond or at the far end of (an opening or an obstacle): *the approach to the church is through a gate.* ■ expressing the extent of turning from one orientation to another: [as *prep.*] *each joint can move through an angle within fixed limits.* **2** continuing in time toward completion of (a process or period): [as *prep.*] *he showed up halfway through the second act* | [as *adv.*] *to struggle through until payday.* ■ so as to complete (a particular stage or trial) successfully: [as *prep.*] *she had come through her sternest test* | [as *adv.*] *I will struggle through alone rather than ask for help.* ■ from beginning to end of (an experience or activity, typically a tedious or stressful one): [as *prep.*] *we sat through some very boring speeches* | *she's been through a bad time* | [as *adv.*] *Karl will see you through, Ingrid.* **3** so as to inspect all or part of (a collection, inventory, or publication): [as *prep.*] *flipping through the pages of a notebook* | [as *adv.*] *she read the letter through carefully.* **4** [*prep.*] up to and including (a particular point in an ordered sequence): *they will be in town from March 24 through May 7.* **5** [*prep.*] by means of (a process or intermediate stage): *dioxins get into mothers' milk through contaminated food.* ■ by means of (an intermediary or agent): *seeking justice through the proper channels.* **6** [*adv.*] so as to be connected by telephone: *he put a call through to the senator.*

▸*adj.* **1** [*attrib.*] (of a means of public transportation or a ticket) continuing or valid to the final destination: *a through train from Boston.* **2** [*attrib.*] denoting traffic that passes from one side of a place to another in the course of a longer journey: *neighborhoods from which through traffic would be excluded.* ■ denoting a road that is open at both ends, allowing traffic free passage from one end to the other: *the shopping center is on a busy through road.* **3** [*attrib.*] (of a room) running the whole length of a building. **4** [*predic.*] *informal* having no prospect of any future relationship, dealings, or success: *she told him she was* **through with** *him* | *you and I are through.* ▷Old English *thurh* (preposition and adverb), of Germanic origin; related to Dutch *door* and German *durch*. The spelling change to *thr-* appears *c.*1300, becoming standard from Caxton onward.

▸*PHRASE* □ **through and through** in every aspect; thoroughly or completely: *Harriet was a political animal through and through.*

through-com·posed ▸*adj. Music* (of a composition, esp. a song) not based on repeated sections or verses, esp. having different music for each verse. Also called **DURCHKOMPONIERT**.

through·out /THrōō'out/ ▸*prep. & adv.* all the way through, in particular: ■ in every part of (a place or object): [as *prep.*] *it had repercussions throughout Europe* | [as *adv.*] *the house is in good order throughout.* ■ from beginning to end of (an event or period of time): [as *prep.*] *the Church of which she was a faithful member throughout her life* | [as *adv.*] *both sets of parents retained a smiling dignity throughout.*

through·put /'THrōō,pōōt/ ▸*n.* the amount of material or items passing through a system or process.

through·way ▸*n.* another spelling of THRUWAY.

throve /THrōv/ ▸ past of THRIVE.

throw /THrō/ ▸*v.* (*past* **threw** /THrōō/; *past part.* **thrown** /THrōn/) **1** [*trans.*] propel (something) with force through the air by a movement of the arm and hand: *I threw a brick through the window.* ■ [*trans.* or *complement*] push or force (someone or something) violently and suddenly into a particular physical position or state: *the pilot and one passenger were thrown clear and survived* | *the door was thrown open, and a uniformed guard entered the room.* ■ put in place or erect quickly: *the stewards had thrown a cordon across the fairway.* ■ move (a part of the body) quickly or suddenly in a particular direction: *she threw her head back and laughed.* ■ project or cast (light or shadow) in a particular direction: *a chandelier threw its bright light over the walls.* ■ deliver (a punch). ■ direct (a particular kind of look or facial expression): *she threw a withering glance at him.* ■ project (one's voice) so that it appears to come from someone or something else, as in ventriloquism. ■ (**throw something off/on**) put on or take off a garment hastily: *I threw on my housecoat and went to the door.* ■ move (a switch or lever) so as to operate a device. ■ roll (dice). ■ obtain (a specified number) by rolling dice. ■ *informal* lose (a race or contest) intentionally, esp. in return for a bribe. **2** [*trans.*] cause to enter suddenly a particular state or condition: *he threw all her emotions into turmoil* | *the bond market was thrown into confusion.* ■ put (someone) in a particular place or state, esp. in a rough, abrupt, or summary fashion: *these guys should be thrown in jail.* ■ [*trans.*] disconcert; confuse: *she frowned, thrown by this apparent change of tack.* **3** [*trans.*] send (one's opponent) to the ground in wrestling, judo, or similar activity. ■ (of a horse) unseat (its rider). ■ (of a horse) lose (a shoe). ■ (of an animal) give birth to (young, of a specified kind): *sometimes a completely black calf is thrown.* **4** [*trans.*] form (ceramic ware) on a potter's wheel: *further on, a potter was throwing pots.* ■ turn (wood or other material) on a lathe. ■ twist (silk or other fabrics) into thread or yarn. **5** [*trans.*] have (a fit or tantrum). **6** [*trans.*] give or hold (a party).

▸*phrasal v.* □ **throw money around** spend money freely and ostentatiously. □ **throw oneself at** appear too eager to become the sexual partner of. □ **throw something away 1** discard something as useless or unwanted. ■ waste or fail to make use of an opportunity or advantage: *I've thrown away my chances in life.* ■ discard a playing card in a game. **2** (of an actor) deliver a line with deliberate underemphasis for increased dramatic effect. □ **throw something in 1** include something, typically at no extra cost, with something that is being sold or offered: *they cut the price by $100 and threw in an AC adaptor.* **2** make a remark casually as an interjection in a conversation: *he threw in a sensible remark about funding.* □ **throw oneself into** start to do (something) with enthusiasm and vigor: *Eve threw herself into her work.* □ **throw something off 1** rid oneself of something: *he was struggling to throw off a viral-hepatitis problem.* **2** write or utter in an offhand manner: *Thomas threw off the question lightly.* □ **throw oneself on** (or **upon**) attack (someone) vigorously: *they threw themselves on the enemy.* □ **throw something open** make something accessible: *the market was thrown open to any supplier to compete for contracts.* ■ invite general discussion of or participation in a subject or a debate or other event: *the debate will be thrown open to the audience.* □ **throw someone out 1** expel someone unceremoniously from a place, organization, or activity. **2** *Baseball* put out a runner by a throw to the base being approached, followed by a tag. □ **throw something out 1** discard something as unwanted. **2** (of a court, legislature, or other body) dismiss or reject something brought before it: *the charges were thrown out by the judge.* **3** put forward a suggestion tentatively: *a suggestion that Dunne threw out caught many a reader's fancy.* **4** cause numbers or calculations to become inaccurate: *an undisclosed stock option throws out all your figures.* **5** emit or radiate something: *a big range fire that threw out heat like a furnace.* **6** (of a plant) rapidly develop a side shoot, bud, etc. □ **throw someone over** abandon or reject someone as a lover. □ **throw people together** bring people into contact, esp. by chance. □ **throw something together** make or produce something hastily, without careful planning or arrangement: *the meal was quickly thrown together at news of Rose's arrival.* □ **throw up** vomit. □ **throw something up 1** abandon or give up something, esp. one's job: *why has he thrown up a promising career in politics?* **2** *informal* vomit something one has eaten or drunk. **3** produce something and bring it to notice: *he saw the prayers of the Church as a living and fruitful tradition that threw up new ideas.* **4** erect a building or structure hastily.

▸*n.* **1** an act of throwing something: *Jeter's throw to first base was too late.* ■ an act of throwing one's opponent in wrestling, judo, or similar sport: *a shoulder throw.* **2** a light cover for furniture. ■ short for THROW RUG. **3** short for THROW OF THE DICE (see DICE). **4** *Geology* the extent of vertical displacement between the two sides of a fault. **5** [usu. in *sing.*] the action or motion of a slide valve or of a crank, eccentric wheel, or cam. ■ the extent of such motion. ■ the distance moved by the pointer of an instrument. **6** (**a throw**) *informal* used to indicate how much a single item, turn, or attempt costs: *he was offering to draw on-the-spot portraits at $25 a throw.* ▷Old English *thrāwan* 'to twist, turn'; related to Dutch *draaien* and German *drehen*, from an Indo-European root shared by Latin *terere* 'to rub,' Greek *teirein* 'wear out.' Sense 1, expressing propulsion and sudden action, dates from Middle English. —**throw·a·ble** *adj.* —**throw·er** *n.*

▸*PHRASES* □ **be thrown back on** be forced to rely on (something) because there is no alternative: *we are once again thrown back on the resources of our imagination.* □ **throw away the key** used to suggest that someone who has been put in prison should or will never be released: *the judge should lock up these robbers and throw away the key.* □ **throw the baby out with the bathwater** see BABY. □ **throw something back in someone's face** see FACE. □ **throw the book at** see BOOK. □ **throw cold water on** see COLD. □ **throw down the gauntlet** see GAUNTLET[1]. □ **throw someone for a loop** see LOOP. □ **throw dust in someone's eyes** seek to mislead or deceive someone by misrepresentation or distraction. □ **throw good money after bad** incur further loss in a hopeless attempt to recoup a previous loss. □ **throw one's hand in** withdraw from a card game, poker, because one has a poor hand. ■ withdraw from a contest or activity; give up. □ **throw in one's lot with** see LOT. □ **throw in the towel** (or **sponge**) (of boxers or their seconds) throw a towel (or sponge) into the ring as a token of defeat. ■ abandon a struggle; admit defeat. □ **throw light on** see LIGHT[1]. □ **throw money at something** see MONEY. □ **throw of the dice** see DICE. □ **throw oneself on** (or **upon**) **someone's mercy** abjectly ask someone for help, forgiveness, or leniency. □ **throw up one's hands** raise both hands in the air as an indication of one's exasperation. □ **throw one's weight around** see WEIGHT. □ **throw one's weight behind** see WEIGHT.

throw·a·way /'THrōə,wā/ ▸*adj.* **1** denoting or relating to products that are intended to be discarded after being used once or a few times: *a throwaway camera* | *we live in a throwaway society.* **2** (of a remark) expressed in a casual or understated way: *some people overreacted to a few throwaway lines.*

▸*n.* a thing intended or destined to be discarded after brief use or appeal. ■ a casual or understated remark or idea.

throw·back /'THrō,bak/ ▸*n.* a reversion to an earlier ancestral characteristic: *the eyes could be an ancestral throwback.* ■ a person or thing having the characteristics of a former time: *a lot of his work is* ***a throwback to*** *the fifties.*

throw-in ▸*n.* something or someone that is included as part of an arrangement or transaction, with no additional cost or obligation to the recipient: *the most brilliant acquisition for the Cubs has been their second baseman, who was a throw-in in a trade of shortstops* | *the sunroof and CD player were throw-ins.* ■ *Soccer* the act of throwing the ball from the sideline to restart play after the ball has gone out of bounds.

throw pil·low ▸*n.* a small decorative pillow placed on a chair or couch.

throw rug ▸*n.* a small decorative rug designed to be placed with a casual effect and moved as required.

throw·ster /'THrōstər/ ▸*n.* a person who twists silk fibers into thread.

thru /THrōō/ ▸*prep., adv., & adj.* informal spelling of THROUGH.

thrum[1] /THrəm/ ▸*v.* (**thrummed, thrum·ming**) [*intrans.*] make a continuous rhythmic humming sound: *the boat's huge engines thrummed in his ears.* ■ [*trans.*] strum (the strings of a musical instrument) in a rhythmic way.

▸*n.* [usu. in *sing.*] a continuous rhythmic humming sound: *the steady thrum of rain on the windows.* ▷late 16th cent. (as a verb): imitative.

thrum[2] ▸*n.* (in weaving) an unwoven end of a warp thread, or a fringe of such ends, left in the loom when the finished cloth is cut away. ■ any short loose thread.

▸*v.* (**thrummed, thrum·ming**) [*trans.*] cover or adorn (cloth or clothing) with ends of thread. ▷Old English *thrum* (only in *tungethrum* 'ligament of the tongue'): of Germanic origin; related to Dutch *dreum* 'thrum' and German *Trumm* 'endpiece.' The current sense dates from Middle English. —**thrum·mer** *n.* —**thrum·my** *adj.*

thrush[1] /THrəsh/ ▸*n.* a small or medium-sized songbird, typically having a brown back, spotted breast, and loud song. • Subfamily Turdinae (the **thrush subfamily**), family Muscicapidae: many genera, in particular *Turdus*, and numerous species. The thrush subfamily includes the chats, robins, bluebirds, blackbirds, nightingales, redstarts, and wheatears. ▷Old English *thrysce*, of Germanic origin; related to THROSTLE.

thrush[2] ▸*n.* **1** infection of the mouth and throat by a yeastlike fungus, causing whitish patches. Also called CANDIDIASIS. • The fungus belongs to the genus *Candida*, subdivision Deuteromycotina, in particular *C. albicans*. ■ infection of the female genitals with the same fungus. **2** a chronic condition affecting the frog of a horse's foot, causing the accumulation of a dark, foul-smelling substance. Also called CANKER. ▷mid 17th cent.: origin uncertain; sense 1 possibly related to Swedish *torsk* and Danish *troske*; sense 2 perhaps from dialect *frush* in the same sense, perhaps from Old French *fourchette* 'frog of a horse's hoof.'

thrust /THrəst/ ▸*v.* (*past* **thrust**) [*trans.*] push (something or someone) suddenly or violently in the specified direction: *she thrust her hands into her pockets* | *figurative Howard was thrust into the limelight* | [*intrans.*] *he* ***thrust at*** *his opponent with his sword.* ■ [*intrans.*] (of a person) move or advance forcibly: *she thrust through the bramble canes* | *he tried to* ***thrust his way*** *past her.* ■ [*intrans.*] (of a thing) extend so as to project conspicuously: *beside the boathouse a jetty thrust out into the water.* ■ (**thrust something on/upon**) force (someone) to accept or deal with something: *he felt that fame had been thrust upon him.* ■ [*intrans.*] (of a man) penetrate the vagina or anus of a sexual partner with forceful movements of the penis.

▸*n.* **1** a sudden or violent lunge with a pointed weapon or a bodily part: *he drove the blade upward with one powerful thrust.* ■ a forceful attack or effort: *executives led a new thrust in business development.* ■ [in *sing.*] the principal purpose or theme of a course of action or line of reasoning: *anti-Americanism became* ***the main thrust*** *of their policy.* **2** the propulsive force of a jet or rocket engine. ■ the lateral pressure exerted by an arch or other support in a building. **3** (also **thrust fault**) *Geology* a reverse fault of low angle, with older strata displaced horizontally over younger. ▷Middle English (as a verb): from Old Norse *thrýsta*; perhaps related to Latin *trudere* 'to thrust.' The noun is first recorded (early 16th cent.) in the sense 'act of pressing.'

▸*PHRASE* □ **cut and thrust** see CUT.

thrust·er /'THrəstər/ ▸*n.* a person or thing that thrusts, in particular: ■ a small rocket engine on a spacecraft, used to make alterations in its flight path or altitude. ■ a secondary jet or propeller on a ship or offshore rig, used for accurate maneuvering and maintenance of position.

thrust·ing /'THrəstiNG/ ▸*n.* the motion of pushing or lunging suddenly or violently. ■ *Geology* the pushing upward of the earth's crust.

thrust stage ▸*n.* a stage that extends into the auditorium so that the audience is seated around three sides.

thru·way /'THrōō,wā/ (also **through·way**) ▸*n.* a major road or highway.

Thu·cyd·i·des /THōō'sidē,dēz/ (*c.*455–*c.*400 BC), Greek historian. Remembered for his *History of the Peloponnesian War*, he fought in the conflict on the Athenian side.

thud /THəd/ ▸*n.* a dull, heavy sound, such as that made by an object falling to the ground: *Jean heard the thud of the closing door.*
▸*v.* (**thud·ded, thud·ding**) [*intrans.*] move, fall, or strike something with a dull, heavy sound: *the bullets thudded into the dusty ground.* ▷late Middle English (originally Scots): probably from Old English *thyddan* 'to thrust, push'; related to *thoden* 'violent wind.' The noun is recorded first denoting a sudden blast or gust of wind, later the sound of a thunderclap, whence a dull, heavy sound. The verb dates from the early 16th cent.
▸*PHRASE* □ **with a thud** used to describe a sudden and disillusioning reminder of reality in contrast to someone's dreams or aspirations: *dropouts have now come back down to earth with a thud.*

thud·ding /'THədiNG/ ▸*n.* the action of moving, falling, or striking something with a dull, heavy sound: *he heard the hollow thudding of hooves.*
▸*adj.* [*attrib.*] used to emphasize the clumsiness or awkwardness of something, esp. a remark: *great thudding conversation-stoppers.* —**thud·ding·ly** *adv.*

thug /THəg/ ▸*n.* **1** a violent person, esp. a criminal. [mid 19th cent.: extension of sense 2.] **2** (**Thug**) *historical* a member of a religious organization of robbers and assassins in India. Devotees of the goddess Kali, the Thugs waylaid and strangled their victims, usually travelers, in a ritually prescribed manner. They were suppressed by the British in the 1830s. ▷early 19th cent. (sense 2): from Hindi *ṭhag* 'swindler, thief,' based on Sanskrit *sthagati* 'he covers or conceals.' —**thug·ger·y** /-gərē/ *n.* —**thug·gish** *adj.* —**thug·gish·ly** *adv.* —**thug·gish·ness** *n.*

thug·gee /'THəgē/ ▸*n. historical* the robbery and murder practiced by the Thugs in accordance with their ritual. ▷from Hindi *ṭhagī*, from *ṭhag* (see THUG). —**thug·gism** /-,gizəm/ *n.*

thu·ja /'THōōjə/ (also **thu·ya** /'THōōyə/) ▸*n.* a North American and eastern Asian evergreen coniferous tree of a genus that includes the arbor vitaes. • Genus *Thuja*, family Cupressaceae. ■ the wood from this tree. ▷modern Latin (genus name), from Greek *thuia*, denoting an African tree formerly included in the genus.

Thu·le **1** /'THōōlē; THōōl/ a country described by the ancient Greek explorer Pytheas (*c.*310 BC) as being six days' sail north of Britain, most plausibly identified with Norway. It was regarded by the ancients as the northernmost part of the world. **2** /'tōōlē/ an Eskimo culture existing from Alaska to Greenland c.AD 500–1400. **3** /'tōōlē/ a settlement on the northwestern coast of Greenland, founded in 1910 by Danish explorer Knud Rasmussen (1879–1933).

thu·li·um /'TH(y)ōōlēəm/ ▸*n.* the chemical element of atomic number 69, a soft silvery-white metal of the lanthanide series. (Symbol: **Tm**) ▷late 19th cent.: modern Latin, from Latin *Thule* THULE (sense 1), from Greek *Thoulē*, of unknown origin.

Thumb /THəm/, General Tom, (1838–83) U.S. circus entertainer; born *Charles S. Stratton*. A 40-inch-tall dwarf, he worked as a sideshow attraction in the shows of P. T. Barnum.

thumb /THəm/ ▸*n.* the short, thick first digit of the human hand, set lower and apart from the other four and opposable to them. ■ the corresponding digit of primates or other mammals. ■ the part of a glove intended to cover the thumb.
▸*v.* [*trans.*] press, move, or touch (something) with one's thumb: *as soon as she thumbed the button, the door slid open.* ■ turn over (pages) with or as if with one's thumb: *I've thumbed my address book and found quite a range of smaller hotels* | [*intrans.*] *he was* ***thumbing through*** *that magazine for the umpteenth time.* ■ (usu. **be thumbed**) wear or soil (a book's pages) by repeated handling: *his dictionaries were thumbed and ink-stained.* ■ request or obtain (a free ride in a passing vehicle) by signaling with one's thumb: *three cars passed me and I tried to* ***thumb a ride*** | [*intrans.*] *he was* ***thumbing his way*** *across France.* ▷Old English *thūma*; related to Dutch *duim* and German *Daumen*, from an Indo-European root shared by Latin *tumere* 'to swell.' The verb dates from the late 16th cent., first in the sense 'play (a musical instrument) with the thumbs.' —**thumbed** *adj.* —**thumb·less** *adj.*
▸*PHRASES* □ **be all thumbs** *informal* be clumsy or awkward in one's actions: *I'm all thumbs when it comes to making bows.* □ **thumb one's nose at** *informal* show disdain or contempt for. □ **thumbs up** (or **down**) *informal* an indication of satisfaction or approval (or of rejection or failure): *plans to build a house on the site have been given the thumbs down by the Department of the Environment.* [with reference to the signal of approval or disapproval, used by spectators at a Roman amphitheater; the sense has been reversed, as the Romans used 'thumbs down' to signify that a beaten gladiator had performed well and should be spared, and 'thumbs up' to call for his death.] □ **under someone's thumb** completely under someone's influence or control.

thumb drive ▸*n. Computing* another term for USB FLASH DRIVE.

thumb in·dex ▸*n.* a set of lettered or marked grooves cut down the side of a book, esp. a diary or dictionary, for easy reference. —**thumb-in·dexed** *adj.*

thumb·nail /'THəm,nāl/ ▸*n.* **1** the nail of the thumb. **2** [usu. as *adj.*] a very small or concise description, representation, or summary: *a thumbnail sketch.* ■ *Computing* a small picture of an image or page layout.

thumb pi·an·o ▸*n.* any of various musical instruments, mainly of African origin, made from strips of metal fastened to a resonator and played by plucking with the fingers and thumbs. Also called KALIMBA, MBIRA, or SANSA.

thumb·print /'THəm,print/ ▸*n.* an impression or mark made on a surface by the inner part of the top joint of the thumb, esp. as used for identifying individuals from the unique pattern of whorls and lines. ■ *figurative* a distinctive identifying characteristic: *it has an individuality and thumbprint of its own.*

thumb·screw /'THəm,skrōō/ ▸*n.* **1** a screw with a protruding winged or flattened head for turning with the thumb and forefinger. **2** (usu. **thumbscrews**) an instrument of torture for crushing the thumbs.

thumb·suck·er /'THəm,səkər/ (also **thumb-suck·er**) ▸*n. informal, often derogatory* a serious piece of journalism that concentrates on the background and interpretation of events rather than on the news or action; a think piece. ■ a journalist who writes in this style: *in a few days we'll be inundated with thumbsuckers assessing the first hundred days of the Clinton administration.*

thumb·tack /'THəm,tak/ ▸*n.* a short flat-headed pin, used for fastening paper to a wall or other surface.

thumb·wheel /'THəm,(h)wēl/ ▸*n.* a control device for electrical or mechanical equipment in the form of a wheel operated with the thumb.

Thum·mim ▸*n.* see URIM AND THUMMIM.

thump /THəmp/ ▸*v.* [*trans.*] hit (someone or something) heavily, esp. with the fist or a blunt implement: *Holman thumped the desk with his hand* | [*intrans.*] *she thumped on the door.* ■ [*trans.*] move (something) forcefully, noisily, or decisively: *she picked up the kettle then thumped it down again.* ■ [*intrans.*] move or do something with a heavy deadened sound: *Philip thumped down on the sofa.* ■ [*intrans.*] (of a person's heart or pulse) beat or pulsate strongly, typically because of fear or excitement. ■ (**thump something out**) play a tune enthusiastically but heavy-handedly. ■ *informal* defeat heavily: [*trans.*] *Tampa Bay thumped Toronto 8–0.*
▸*n.* a heavy dull blow with a person's fist or a blunt implement: *I felt a thump on my back.* ■ a loud deadened sound: *his wife put down her iron with a thump.* ■ a strong heartbeat, esp. one caused by fear or excitement. ▷mid 16th cent.: imitative. —**thump·er** *n.*

thump·ing /'THəmpiNG/ ▸*adj.* [*attrib.*] **1** pounding; throbbing: *the thumping beat of her heart.* **2** *informal* of an impressive size, extent, or amount: *a thumping 64 percent majority* | [as *submodifier*] *a thumping great lie.*

thun·der /'THəndər/ ▸*n.* a loud rumbling or crashing noise heard after a lightning flash due to the expansion of rapidly heated air. ■ a resounding loud deep noise: *you can hear the thunder of the falls in the distance.* ■ used in similes and comparisons to refer to an angry facial expression or tone of voice: *"I am Brother Joachim," he announced in a voice like thunder.* ■ [as *exclam.*] *dated* used to express anger, annoyance, or incredulity: *none of this did the remotest good, but,* ***by thunder****, it kept the union activists feeling good.*
▸*v.* [*intrans.*] (**it thunders, it is thundering**, etc.) thunder sounds: *it began to thunder.* ■ make a loud, deep resounding noise: *the motorcycle thundered into life* | *the train thundered through the night.* ■ [*trans.*] strike powerfully: *McGwire thundered that one out of the stadium.* ■ speak loudly and forcefully or angrily, esp. to denounce or criticize: *he* ***thundered against*** *the evils of the age* | [with *direct speech*] *"Sit down!" thundered Morse with immense authority.* ▷Old English *thunor* (noun), *thunrian* (verb), of Germanic origin; related to Dutch *donder* and German *Donner*, from an Indo-European root shared by Latin *tonare* 'to thunder.' —**thun·der·er** *n.* —**thun·der·y** /-d(ə)rē/ *adj.*
▸*PHRASE* □ **steal someone's thunder** see STEAL.

Thun·der Bay a city on a large bay of Lake Superior in western Ontario; pop. 113,946. It is one of Canada's major ports.

thun·der·bird /'THəndər,bərd/ ▸*n.* a mythical bird thought by some North American Indians to bring thunder.

thun·der·bolt /'THəndər,bōlt/ ▸*n. poetic/literary* a flash of lightning with a simultaneous crash of thunder. ■ a supposed bolt or shaft believed to be the destructive agent in a lightning flash, esp. as an attribute of a god such as Jupiter or Thor. ■ used in similes and comparisons to refer to a very sudden or unexpected event or item of news, esp. of an unpleasant nature: *the full force of what she had been told hit her like a thunderbolt.* ■ *informal* a very fast and powerful shot, throw, or stroke.

thun·der·clap /'THəndər,klap/ ▸*n.* a crash of thunder: *the door opened like a thunderclap.* ■ *figurative* something startling or unexpected: *the Argentine invasion of the Falkland Islands came as a thunderclap.*

thun·der·cloud /'THəndər,kloud/ ▸*n.* a cumulus cloud with a towering or spreading top, charged with electricity and producing thunder and lightning. ■ *figurative* something ominous: *mutiny, it was plain, hung over us like a thundercloud.*

thun·der·head /'THəndər,hed/ ▸*n.* a rounded, projecting head of a cumulus cloud, which portends a thunderstorm.

thun·der·ing /'THənd(ə)riNG/ ▸*adj.* [*attrib.*] making a resounding, loud, deep noise: *thundering waterfalls.* ■ *informal* extremely great, severe, or impressive: *a thundering bore* | [as *submodifier*] *a thundering good read.* —**thun·der·ing·ly** *adv.* [as *submodifier*] *it was so thunderingly dull.*

thun·der·ous /'THənd(ə)rəs/ ▸*adj.* of, relating to, or giving warning of thunder: *a thunderous gray cloud.* ■ very loud: *thunderous applause.* ■ very powerful or intense: *thunderous romantic situations and adventures* | *the hockey game against Sweden included several thunderous collisions.* —**thun·der·ous·ly** *adv.* —**thun·der·ous·ness** *n.*

thun·der·storm /'THəndər,stôrm/ ▸*n.* a storm with thunder and lightning and typically also heavy rain or hail.

thun·der·struck /'THəndər,strək/ ▸*adj.* extremely surprised or shocked: *they were thunderstruck by this revelation.*

thun·der thighs ▸*n. informal* large thighs, especially those with a great deal of cellulite.

thunk[1] /THəNGk/ ▸*n.* & *v.* informal term for THUD.

thunk[2] ▸ informal or humorous past and past participle of THINK: *who would've thunk it?*

Thur. ▸*abbr.* Thursday.

Thur·ber /'THərbər/, James (Grover) (1894–1961), U.S. humorist and cartoonist. He published many of his essays, stories, and sketches in the *New Yorker* magazine. His collections of essays, stories, and sketches include *My Life and Hard Times* (1933) and *My World—And Welcome to It* (1942), which contains the story "The Secret Life of Walter Mitty."

thu·ri·ble /'THōōrəbəl/ ▸*n.* a censer. ▷late Middle English: from Old French, or from Latin *thuribulum*, from *thus, thur-* 'incense' (see THURIFER).

thu·ri·fer /'THōōrəfər/ ▸*n.* an acolyte carrying a censer. ▷mid 19th cent.: from late Latin, from Latin *thus, thur-* 'incense' (from Greek *thuos* 'sacrifice') + *-fer* '-bearing.'

Thu·rin·gi·a /THōō'rinj(ē)ə/ a densely forested state of central Germany; capital, Erfurt. German name THÜRINGEN .

Thur·mond /'THərmənd/, (James) Strom, (1902–2003) U.S. politician. He was governor of South Carolina 1947–51 and a member of the U.S. Senate from South Carolina 1954–2003. An ardent segregationist, he ran for president on the States' Rights Party (Dixiecrat) ticket in 1948. Originally a Democrat, he switched to the Republican Party in 1964.

Thurs. ▸*abbr.* Thursday.

Thurs·day /'THərz,dā; -dē/ ▸*n.* the day of the week before Friday and following Wednesday: *the committee met* ***on Thursday*** | *the music program for Thursdays in April* | [as *adj.*] *Thursday morning.*
▸*adv.* on Thursday: *he called her up Thursday.* ■ (**Thursdays**) on Thursdays; each Thursday: *the column is published Thursdays.* ▷Old English *Thu(n)resdæg* 'day of thunder,' translation of late Latin *Jovis dies* 'day of

Jupiter' (god associated with thunder): compare with Dutch *donderdag* and German *Donnerstag.*

thus /T͟Həs/ ▸*adv. poetic/literary* or *formal* **1** as a result or consequence of this; therefore: *Burke knocked out Byrne, thus becoming champion.* **2** in the manner now being indicated or exemplified; in this way: *she phoned Susan, and while she was thus engaged, Charles summoned the doctor.* **3** [as *submodifier*] to this point; so: *the Web site has been cracked three times* ***thus far.*** ▹Old English, of unknown origin.

thus·ly /'T͟Həslē/ ▸*adv. informal* another term for **THUS** (sense 2): *the review was conducted thusly.*

USAGE The expansion of the adverb **thus** to **thusly** is usually considered unnecessary, but it can serve a distinct function, as in introducing a direct quotation: *He answered her thusly: "your evidence is lacking and your conclusions are just plain wrong!"*

thu·ya /'THo͞oyə/ ▸*n.* variant spelling of **THUJA.**

thwack /THwak/ ▸*v.* [*trans.*] strike forcefully with a sharp blow: *she thwacked the back of their knees with a cane.*

▸*n.* a sharp blow: *he hit it with a hefty thwack.* ▹late Middle English: imitative.

thwart /THwôrt/ ▸*v.* [*trans.*] prevent (someone) from accomplishing something: *he never did anything to thwart his father* | *he was* ***thwarted in*** *his desire to punish Uncle Fred.* ■ oppose (a plan, attempt, or ambition) successfully: *the government had been able to thwart all attempts by opposition leaders to form new parties.*

▸*n.* a structural crosspiece sometimes forming a seat for a rower in a boat.

▸*prep. & adv. archaic* or *poetic/literary* from one side to another side of; across: [as *prep.*] *a pink-tinged cloud spread thwart the shore.* ▹Middle English *thwerte*, from the adjective *thwert* 'perverse, obstinate, adverse,' from Old Norse *thvert*, neuter of *thverr* 'transverse,' from an Indo-European root shared by Latin *torquere* 'to twist.'

THE RIGHT WORD **baffle, balk, foil, frustrate, inhibit, thwart**

These verbs refer to the various ways in which we can outwit or overcome opposing forces.

Thwart suggests using cleverness rather than force to bring about the defeat of an enemy or to block progress toward an objective (*thwart a rebellion; have one's goals thwarted by lack of education*).

Balk also emphasizes setting up barriers (*a sudden reversal that balked their hopes for a speedy resolution*), but it is used more often as an intransitive verb meaning to stop at an obstacle and refuse to proceed (*he balked at appearing in front of the angry crowd*).

To **baffle** is to cause defeat by bewildering or confusing (*the police were baffled by the lack of evidence*), while **foil** means to throw off course so as to discourage further effort (*her plan to arrive early was foiled by heavy traffic*).

Frustrate implies rendering all attempts or efforts useless (*frustrated by the increasingly bad weather, they decided to work indoors*), while **inhibit** suggests forcing something into inaction (*to inhibit wage increases by raising corporate taxes*).

Both *frustrate* and *inhibit* are used in a psychological context to suggest barriers that impede normal development or prevent the realization of natural desires (*he was both frustrated by her refusal to acknowledge his presence and inhibited by his own shyness*).

thy /T͟Hī/ (also **thine** before a vowel) ▸*possessive adj.* archaic or dialect form of **YOUR**: *honor thy father and thy mother.* ▹Middle English *thi* (originally before words beginning with any consonant except *h*), reduced from *thin*, from Old English *thīn* (see **THINE**).

USAGE The use of **thy** is still found in certain religious groups and in some traditional British dialects, but elsewhere it is restricted to archaic contexts. See also **usage** at **THOU**[1].

Thy·es·tes /THī'estēz/ *Greek Mythology* the brother of Atreus and father of Aegisthus. **—Thy·es·te·an** /-tēən/ *adj.*

thy·la·cine /'THīlə,sīn; -sin/ ▸*n.* a doglike carnivorous marsupial with stripes across the rump, found only in Tasmania. There have been no confirmed sightings since one was captured in 1933, and it may now be extinct. Also called **TASMANIAN WOLF.** • *Thylacinus cynocephalus*, family Thylacinidae. ▹mid 19th cent.: from modern Latin *Thylacinus* (genus name), from Greek *thulakos* 'pouch.'

thy·la·koid /'THīlə,koid/ ▸*n. Botany* each of a number of flattened sacs inside a chloroplast, bounded by pigmented membranes on which the light reactions of photosynthesis take place, and arranged in stacks or grana. ▹1960s: from German *Thylakoid*, from Greek *thulakoeidēs* 'pouchlike,' from *thulakos* 'pouch.'

thyme /tīm/ ▸*n.* a low-growing aromatic plant of the mint family. The small leaves are used as a culinary herb, and the plant yields a medicinal oil. • Genus *Thymus*, family Labiatae: many species, in particular **common** (or **garden**) **thyme** (*T. vulgaris*). ▹Middle English: from Old French *thym*, via Latin from Greek *thumon*, from *thuein* 'burn, sacrifice.' **—thym·y** /'tīmē/ *adj.*

thy·mec·to·my /THī'mektəmē/ ▸*n.* (*pl.* **-mies**) surgical removal of the thymus gland.

thy·mi /'THīmī/ ▸ plural form of **THYMUS.**

thy·mic /'THīmik/ ▸*adj. Physiology* of or relating to the thymus gland or its functions.

thy·mi·dine /'THīmə,dēn/ ▸*n. Biochemistry* a crystalline nucleoside present in DNA, consisting of thymine linked to deoxyribose. ▹early 20th cent.: from **THYMINE** + **-IDE** + **-INE**[4].

thy·mine /'THī,mēn; -min/ ▸*n. Biochemistry* a compound that is one of the four constituent bases of nucleic acids. A pyrimidine derivative, it is paired with adenine in double-stranded DNA. • Alternative name; **5-methyluracil**; chem. formula: $C_5H_6N_2O_2$. ▹late 19th cent.: from **THYMUS** + **-INE**[4].

thy·mo·cyte /'THīmə,sīt/ ▸*n. Physiology* a lymphocyte within the thymus gland. ▹1920s: from **THYMUS** + **-CYTE.**

thy·mol /'THī,môl; -,mōl/ ▸*n. Chemistry* a white crystalline compound present in oil of thyme and used as a flavoring and preservative. • Alternative name: **2-isopropyl-5-methylphenol**; chem. formula: $C_{10}H_{13}OH$. ▹mid 19th cent.: from Greek *thumon* 'thyme' + **-OL.**

thy·mo·ma /THī'mōmə/ ▸*n.* (*pl.* **-mas** or **-ma·ta** /-mətə/) *Medicine* a rare, usually benign tumor arising from thymus tissue and sometimes associated with myasthenia gravis. ▹early 20th cent.: from **THYMUS** + **-OMA.**

thy·mus /'THīməs/ (also **thy·mus gland**) ▸*n.* (*pl.* **-mus·es** or **-mi** /-mī/) a lymphoid organ situated in the neck of vertebrates that produces T cells for the immune system. The human thymus becomes much smaller at the approach of puberty. ▹late 16th cent. (denoting a growth or tumor resembling a bud): from Greek *thumos* 'excrescence like a thyme bud, thymus gland.'

thy·ris·tor /THī'ristər/ ▸*n. Electronics* a four-layered semiconductor rectifier in which the flow of current between two electrodes is triggered by a signal at a third electrode. ▹1950s: blend of *thyratron*, denoting a kind of thermionic tube (from Greek *thura* 'gate') and **TRANSISTOR.**

thyro- ▸*comb. form* representing **THYROID.**

thy·ro·cal·ci·to·nin /,THīrō,kalsi'tōnin/ ▸*n.* another term for **CALCITONIN**, believed until the late 1960s to denote a different hormone.

thy·ro·glob·u·lin /,THīrō'gläbyəlin/ ▸*n. Biochemistry* a protein present in the thyroid gland, from which thyroid hormones are synthesized.

thy·roid /'THī,roid/ ▸*n.* **1** (also **thyroid gland**) a large ductless gland in the neck that secretes hormones regulating growth and development through the rate of metabolism. ■ an extract prepared from the thyroid gland of animals and used in treating deficiency of thyroid hormones. **2** (also **thyroid cartilage**) a large cartilage of the larynx, a projection of which forms the Adam's apple in humans. ▹early 18th cent. (as an adjective): from Greek *(khondros) thureoeidēs* 'shield-shaped (cartilage),' from *thureos* 'oblong shield.'

thy·roid·ec·to·my /,THīroi'dektəmē/ ▸*n.* (*pl.* **-mies**) removal of the thyroid gland by surgery.

thy·roid·i·tis /,THīroi'dītis/ ▸*n.* inflammation of the thyroid.

thy·roid-stim·u·lat·ing hor·mone ▸*n.* another term for **THYROTROPIN.**

thy·ro·tox·i·co·sis /,THīrō,täksi'kōsis/ ▸*n.* another term for **HYPERTHYROIDISM.**

thy·ro·tro·pin /,THīrō'trōpin; THī'rätrə-/ (also **thy·ro·tro·phin** /-fin/) ▸*n. Biochemistry* a hormone secreted by the pituitary gland that regulates the production of thyroid hormones.

thy·ro·tro·pin-re·leas·ing hor·mone (also **thyrotropin-releasing factor**) ▸*n. Biochemistry* a hormone secreted by the hypothalamus which stimulates release of thyrotropin.

thy·rox·ine /THī'räksēn; -sin/ (also **thy·rox·in** /-sin/) ▸*n. Biochemistry* the main hormone produced by the thyroid gland, acting to increase metabolic rate and so regulating growth and development. • An iodine-containing amino acid; chem. formula: $C_{15}H_{11}NO_4I_4$. ▹early 20th cent.: from **THYROID** + **OX-** 'oxygen' + *in* from **INDOLE** (because of an early misunderstanding of its chemical structure), altered by substitution of **-INE**[4].

thyr·sus /'THərsəs/ ▸*n.* (*pl.* **-si** /-sī/) (in ancient Greece and Rome) a staff or spear tipped with an ornament like a pine cone, carried by Dionysus and his followers. ▹Latin, from Greek *thursos* 'plant stalk, Bacchic staff.'

Thy·sa·nop·ter·a /,THīsə'näptərə; ,THis-/ *Entomology* an order of insects that comprises the thrips. ■ [as *plural n.*] (**thysanoptera**) insects of this order; thrips. ▹modern Latin (plural), from Greek *thusanos* 'tassel' + *pteron* 'wing.' **—thy·sa·nop·ter·an** *n. & adj.*

Thy·sa·nu·ra /,THīsə'n(y)o͝orə/ *Entomology* an order of insects that comprises the true, or three-pronged, bristletails. ■ [as *plural n.*] (**thysanura**) insects of this order; bristletails. ▹modern Latin (plural), from Greek *thusanos* 'tassel' + *oura* 'tail.' **—thy·sa·nu·ran** *n. & adj.*

thy·self /T͟Hī'self/ ▸*pron.* [*second person singular*] archaic or dialect form of **YOURSELF**, corresponding to the subject **THOU**[1] : *thou shalt love thy neighbor as thyself.*

Thz ▸*abbr.* terahertz.

Ti ▸*symbol* the chemical element titanium.

ti /tē/ ▸*n.* (in solmization) the seventh note of a major scale. ■ the note B in the fixed-do system. ▹mid 19th cent.: alteration of **SI**, adopted to avoid having two notes (*sol* and *si*) beginning with the same letter (see **SOLMIZATION**).

TIA *Medicine* ▸*abbr.* transient ischemic attack.

Tia·mat /'tyämät/ *Babylonian Mythology* a monstrous she-dragon who was the mother of the first Babylonian gods. She was slain by Marduk.

tian /tyan/ ▸*n.* (*pl.* same) a dish of finely chopped vegetables cooked in olive oil and then baked au gratin. ■ a large oval earthenware cooking pot traditionally used in Provence. ▹Provençal, based on Greek *tēganon* 'frying pan.'

Tian·an·men Square /tē'enə(n),men; 'tyän'än-/ a square in the center of Beijing adjacent to the Forbidden City, the largest public open space in the world. In spring 1989, government troops opened fire there on unarmed pro-democracy protesters, killing over 2,000. ▹Chinese, literally 'gate of heavenly peace.'

Tiananmen Square

Tian·jin /'tyen'jin/ (also **Tien·tsin** *pronunc.* same or /'tyent'sin/) a port in northeastern China, in Hubei province; pop. 5,700,000.

ti·ar·a /tē'ärə; -'arə; -'e(ə)rə/ ▸*n.* **1** a jeweled ornamental band worn on the front of a woman's hair. **2** a high diadem encircled with three crowns and worn by a pope. ■ *historical* a turban worn by ancient Persian kings. ▹mid 16th cent. (denoting the Persian royal headdress): via Latin from Greek, partly via Italian. Sense 1 dates from the early 18th cent.

ti·a·rel·la /,tēə'relə; ,tī-/ ▸*n.* a small chiefly North American plant of the saxifrage family. • Genus *Tiarella*, family Saxifragaceae, esp. the **foamflower** (*T. cordifolia*). ▹modern Latin, from Latin *tiara* 'turban, tiara' + the diminutive suffix *-ella*.

Tib·bett /'tibit/, Lawrence, (1896–1960) U.S. opera singer. A baritone, he sang with the Metropolitan Opera 1923–50. He also appeared in movies, such as *The Rogue Song* (1930), and sang on the radio.

Ti·ber /'tībər/ a river in central Italy that rises in the Tuscan Apennines and flows southwest for 252 miles (405 km), entering the Tyrrhenian Sea at Ostia. The city of Rome is on its banks. Italian name **TEVERE.**

Pronunciation Key ə *ago*; ər *over*; 'ə *or* ,ə *up*; 'ər *or* ,ər *fur*; a *hat*; ā *rate*; ä *car*; CH *chew*; e *let*; ē *see*; e(ə)r *air*; i *fit*; ī *by*; i(ə)r *ear*; NG *sing*; ō *go*; ô *for*; oi *boy*; o͝o *good*; o͞o *goo*; ou *out*; SH *she*; TH *thin*; T͟H *then*; (h)w *why*; ZH *vision*

Ti·be·ri·as, Lake /tī'bi(ə)rēəs/ another name for Sea of Galilee (see GALILEE, SEA OF).

Ti·be·ri·us /tī'bi(ə)rēəs/ (42 BC–AD 37), Roman emperor AD 14–37; full name *Tiberius Julius Caesar Augustus.*

Ti·bes·ti Moun·tains /tə'bestē/ a mountain range in north central Africa, in the Sahara in northern Chad and southern Libya. It rises to 11,201 feet (3,415 m) at Emi Koussi, the highest point in the Sahara.

Ti·bet /tə'bet/ a mountainous region in Asia on the northern side of the Himalayas, since 1965 forming an autonomous region in the west of China; pop. 2,196,000; official languages, Tibetan and Chinese; capital, Lhasa. Most of Tibet forms a high plateau with an average elevation of over 12,500 feet (4,000 m). Ruled by Buddhist lamas since the 7th century, it was conquered by the Mongols in the 13th century and the Manchus in the 18th. China extended its authority over Tibet in 1951 but gained full control only after crushing a revolt in 1959, during which the country's spiritual leader, the Dalai Lama, escaped to India; he remains in exile and sporadic unrest has continued. Chinese name **XIZANG**.

Ti·bet·an /tə'betn/ ▸*n.* **1** a native of Tibet or a person of Tibetan descent. **2** the Tibeto-Burman language of Tibet, also spoken in neighboring areas of China, India, and Nepal.
▸*adj.* of or relating to Tibet, its people, or its language.

Ti·bet·an an·te·lope ▸*n.* another term for CHIRU.

Ti·bet·an Bud·dhism ▸*n.* the religion of Tibet, a form of Mahayana Buddhism. It was formed in the 8th century AD from a combination of Buddhism and the indigenous Tibetan religion. The head of the religion is the Dalai Lama.

Ti·bet·an mas·tiff ▸*n.* an animal of a breed of large black-and-tan dog with a thick coat and drop ears.

Ti·bet·an span·iel ▸*n.* an animal of a breed of small white, brown, or black dog with a silky coat of medium length.

Ti·bet·an ter·ri·er ▸*n.* an animal of a breed of gray, black, cream, or particolored terrier with a thick shaggy coat.

Ti·bet·o-Bur·man /tə'betō 'bərmən/ ▸*adj.* of, relating to, or denoting a division of the Sino-Tibetan language family that includes Tibetan, Burmese, and a number of other languages spoken in mountainous regions of central southern Asia.

T

tib·i·a /'tibēə/ ▸*n.* (*pl.* **tib·i·ae** /'tibē,ē/ or **tib·i·as**) *Anatomy* the inner and typically larger of the two bones between the knee and the ankle (or the equivalent joints in other terrestrial vertebrates), parallel with the fibula. ■ *Zoology* the tibiotarsus of a bird. ■ *Entomology* the fourth segment of the leg of an insect, between the femur and the tarsus. ▷late Middle English: from Latin, 'shin bone.' —**tib·i·al** *adj.*

tib·i·a·lis /,tibē'alis; -'ālis/ ▸*n. Anatomy* any of several muscles and tendons in the calf of the leg concerned with movements of the foot. ▷late 19th cent.: from Latin, 'relating to the shin bone.'

tib·i·o·tar·sus /,tibēō'tärsəs/ ▸*n.* (*pl.* **-si** /-sī/) *Zoology* the bone in a bird's leg corresponding to the tibia, fused at the lower end with some bones of the tarsus. ▷late 19th cent.: blend of TIBIA and TARSUS.

tic /tik/ ▸*n.* a habitual spasmodic contraction of the muscles, most often in the face. ■ a characteristic or recurrent behavioral trait; idiosyncrasy: *I began with the kind of generalization that was one of my primary tics as a writer.* ▷early 19th cent.: from French, from Italian *ticchio.*

tic dou·lou·reux /'tik ,do͞olə'ro͞o/ ▸*n.* another term for TRIGEMINAL NEURALGIA. ▷early 19th cent.: French, literally 'painful tic.'

Ti·ci·no /ti'CHēnō/ a predominantly Italian-speaking canton in southern Switzerland, on the Italian border; capital, Bellinzona. It joined the Swiss Confederation in 1803. French name **TESSIN**, German name **TESSIN** .

tick[1] /tik/ ▸*n.* **1** a regular short, sharp sound, esp. that made every second by a clock or watch. ■ *Brit. informal* a moment (used esp. to reassure someone that one will return or be ready very soon): *I'll be with you in a tick.* **2** *chiefly Brit.* a check mark. **3** *Stock Market* the smallest recognized amount by which a price of a security or future may fluctuate.
▸*v.* **1** [*intrans.*] (of a clock or other mechanical device) make regular short sharp sounds, typically for every second of time passing: *I could hear the clock ticking.* ■ (**tick away/by/past**) (of time) pass (used esp. when someone is pressed for time or keenly awaiting an event): *the minutes were ticking away till the actor's appearance.* ■ [*trans.*] (**tick something away**) (of a clock or watch) mark the passing of time with regular short sharp sounds: *the little clock ticked the precious minutes away.* ■ proceed or progress: *her book was* **ticking along** *nicely.* **2** *chiefly Brit.* [*trans.*] mark (an item) with a check mark, typically to show that it has been chosen, checked, or approved: *just tick the appropriate box below.* ■ (**tick something off**) list items one by one in one's mind or during a speech: *he ticked the points off on his fingers.*
▸*phrasal v.* □ **tick someone off 1** *informal* make someone annoyed or angry. **2** *Brit. informal* reprimand or rebuke someone: *he was ticked off by Angela* | [as *n.*] (**ticking off**) *he got a ticking off from the boss.* □ **tick over** (of an engine) idle. ■ work or function at a basic or minimum level: *they are keeping things ticking over until their father returns.* ▷Middle English (as a verb in the sense 'pat, touch'): probably of Germanic origin and related to Dutch *tik* (noun), *tikken* (verb) 'pat, touch.' The noun was recorded in late Middle English as 'a light tap'; current senses date from the late 17th cent.
▸*PHRASE* □ **what makes someone tick** *informal* what motivates someone: *people are curious to know what makes these men tick.*

tick[2] ▸*n.* a parasitic arachnid that attaches itself to the skin of a terrestrial vertebrate from which it sucks blood, leaving the host when sated. Some species transmit diseases, including tularemia and Lyme disease. • Suborder Ixodida, order Acarina (or Acari). ■ *informal* a parasitic louse fly. ▷Old English *ticia*, of Germanic origin; related to Dutch *teek* and German *Zecke.*

tick[3] ▸*n.* a fabric case stuffed with feathers or other material to form a mattress or pillow. ■ short for TICKING. ▷late Middle English: probably Middle Low German, Middle Dutch *tēke*, or Middle Dutch *tīke*, via West Germanic from Latin *theca* 'case,' from Greek *thēkē.*

tick[4] ▸*n.* (in phrase **on tick**) *chiefly Brit.* or *dated* on credit. ▷mid 17th cent.: apparently short for TICKET in the phrase *on the ticket*, referring to an IOU or promise to pay.

tick-borne ▸*adj.* transmitted or carried by ticks: *babesiosis is a tick-borne, malaria-like disease.*

Tick·er /'tikər/, Rubin see **TUCKER**.

tick·er /'tikər/ ▸*n.* **1** *informal* a watch. ■ a person's heart. **2** a telegraphic or electronic machine that prints out data on a strip of paper, esp. stock market information or news reports.

tick·er tape ▸*n.* a paper strip on which messages are recorded in a telegraphic tape machine. ■ [as *adj.*] denoting a parade or other event in which this or similar material is thrown from windows.

tick·et /'tikit/ ▸*n.* **1** a piece of paper or small card that gives the holder a certain right, esp. to enter a place, travel by public transport, or participate in an event: *admission is by ticket only.* ■ (**ticket to/out of**) a method of getting into or out of (a specified state or situation): *drugs are seen as the only ticket out of poverty* | *companies that appeared to have a* **one-way ticket** *to profitability.* **2** a certificate or warrant, in particular: ■ an official notice of a traffic offense. ■ a certificate of qualification as a ship's master, pilot, or other crew member. **3** a label attached to a retail product, giving its price, size, and other details. **4** [in *sing.*] a list of candidates put forward by a party in an election: *his presence on the Republican ticket.* ■ a set of principles or policies supported by a party in an election: *he stood for office on a strong right-wing, no-nonsense ticket.* **5** (**the ticket**) *informal, dated* the desirable or correct thing: *a wet spring would be* **just the ticket** *for the garden.*
▸*v.* (**-et·ed, -et·ing**) [*trans.*] **1** issue (someone) with an official notice of a traffic or other offense: *park illegally and you are likely to be ticketed.* **2** (**be ticketed**) (of a passenger) be issued with a travel ticket: *passengers can now get electronically ticketed.* ■ be destined or heading for a specified state or position: *they were sure that Downing was ticketed for greatness.* **3** (**be ticketed**) (of a retail product) be marked with a label giving its price, size, and other details. ▷early 16th cent. (in the general senses 'short written note' and 'a license or permit'): shortening of obsolete French *étiquet*, from Old French *estiquet(te)*, from *estiquier* 'to fix,' from Middle Dutch *steken*. Compare with ETIQUETTE.
▸*PHRASES* □ **punch one's ticket** *informal* deliberately undertake particular assignments that are likely to lead to promotion at work. □ **write one's (own) ticket** *informal* dictate one's own terms.

tick·et·less /'tikitlis/ ▸*adj.* & *adv.* **1** not requiring a paper ticket: [as *adj.*] *all seats are assigned, all travel is ticketless, and all fares are one-way.* **2** not in possession of a valid ticket: [as *adv.*] *activists on Monday traveled ticketless in suburban trains to protest the hike in fares.*

tick·et of·fice ▸*n.* an office or kiosk where tickets are sold, esp. for entertainment events or travel accommodations.

tick·et·y-boo /,tikitē 'bo͞o/ ▸*adj.* [*predic.*] *Brit., informal, dated* in good order; fine: *everything is tickety-boo.* ▷1930s: perhaps from Hindi *ṭhīk hai* 'all right.'

tick fe·ver ▸*n.* any fever transmitted by the bite of a tick.

tick·ing /'tikiNG/ ▸*n.* a strong, durable material, typically striped, used to cover mattresses and pillows. ▷mid 17th cent.: from TICK[3] + -ING[1].

tick·le /'tikəl/ ▸*v.* [*trans.*] **1** lightly touch or prod (a person or a part of the body) in a way that causes itching and often laughter: *she tickled me under the chin.* ■ [*intrans.*] (of a part of the body) give a sensation of mild discomfort similar to that caused by being touched in this way: *his throat had stopped tickling.* ■ touch with light finger movements: [*trans.*] *tickling the safe open took nearly ninety minutes.* **2** appeal to (someone's taste, sense of humor, curiosity, etc.): *here are a couple of anecdotes that might* **tickle your fancy.** ■ (usu. **be tickled**) cause (someone) amusement or pleasure: *he is tickled by the idea.*
▸*n.* [in *sing.*] an act of tickling someone: *Dad gave my chin a little tickle.* ■ a sensation like that of being lightly touched or prodded: *I had a tickle between my shoulder blades.* ▷Middle English (in the sense 'be delighted or thrilled'): perhaps a frequentative of TICK[1], or an alteration of Scots and dialect *kittle* 'to tickle' (compare with KITTLE).
▸*PHRASES* □ **be tickled pink** (or **to death**) *informal* be extremely amused or pleased. □ **tickle the ivories** *informal* play the piano.

tick·ler /'tik(ə)lər/ ▸*n.* a thing that tickles. ■ a memorandum.

tick·lish /'tik(ə)lisH/ ▸*adj.* **1** sensitive to being tickled: *Lhasa apsos are ticklish on their feet.* ■ (of a cough) characterized by persistent irritation in the throat. **2** (of a situation or problem) difficult to deal with; requiring careful handling: *her skill in evading ticklish questions.* ■ (of a person) easily upset. —**tick·lish·ly** *adv.* —**tick·lish·ness** *n.*

tick·ly /'tik(ə)lē/ ▸*adj.* another term for TICKLISH.

tick mark ▸*n. Brit.* another term for CHECK MARK.

tick·seed /'tik,sēd/ ▸*n.* another term for COREOPSIS. ▷mid 16th cent.: so named because of the resemblance of the seed to a parasitic tick.

tick-tack-toe ▸*n.* variant spelling of TIC-TAC-TOE.

tick-tock /'tik ,täk/ ▸*n.* [in *sing.*] the sound of a large clock ticking.
▸*v.* [*intrans.*] make a ticking sound: *the clock on the wall was tick-tocking.* ▷mid 19th cent.: imitative; compare with TICK[1].

tick tre·foil ▸*n.* a tall, spindly leguminous North American plant, the pods of which break up into one-seeded joints that adhere to clothing, animals' fur, etc. • Genus *Desmodium*, family Leguminosae: several species.

tick·y-tack·y /'tikē ,takē/ *informal* ▸*n.* inferior or cheap material, esp. as used in suburban building.
▸*adj.* (esp. of a building or housing development) made of inferior material; cheap or in poor taste: *ticky-tacky little houses.* ▷1960s: probably a reduplication of TACKY[2].

Ti·con·der·o·ga /,tīkändə'rōgə/ an industrial village in northeastern New York, in lowlands between lakes George and Champlain, its nearby fort was fought over repeatedly in the 1750s–80s; pop. 2,770.

tic-tac-toe /'tik ,tak 'tō/ (also **tick-tack-toe**) ▸*n.* a game in which two players seek in alternate turns to complete a row, a column, or a diagonal with either three O's or three X's drawn in the spaces of a grid of nine squares. ▷1960s: imitative; from *tick-tack*, used earlier to denote games in which the pieces made clicking sounds.

t.i.d. ▸*abbr.* (in prescriptions) three times a day. ▷from Latin *ter in die.*

tid·al /'tīdl/ ▸*adj.* of, relating to, or affected by tides: *the river here is not tidal* | *strong tidal currents.* —**tid·al·ly** *adv.*

tid·al ba·sin ▸*n.* a basin for boats that is accessible or navigable only at high tide.

tid·al bore ▸*n.* a large wave caused by the funneling of a flood tide as it enters a long, narrow, shallow inlet.

tid·al farm ▸*n.* an installation of turbines used to generate electricity from tidal forces.

tid·al wave ▸*n.* an exceptionally large ocean wave, esp. one caused by an underwater earthquake or volcanic eruption (used as a nontechnical term for TSUNAMI). ■ *figurative* a widespread or overwhelming manifestation of an emotion or phenomenon: *a tidal wave of crime.*

tid·bit /ˈtidˌbit/ (also *chiefly Brit.* **tit·bit** /ˈtit-/) ▶*n.* a small piece of tasty food. ■ a small and particularly interesting item of gossip or information. ▷mid 17th cent. (as *tyd bit, tid-bit*): from dialect *tid* 'tender' (of unknown origin) + BIT[1].

tid·dle·dy·wink /ˈtidl-dēˌwiNGk/ ▶*n.* variant spelling of TIDDLYWINK.

tid·dly /ˈtidlē/ ▶*adj.* (**-dli·er, -dli·est**) *informal, chiefly Brit.* slightly drunk. ▷mid 19th cent. (as a noun denoting an alcoholic drink, particularly of spirits): perhaps from slang *tiddlywink*, denoting an unlicensed bar. The current sense dates from the early 20th cent.

tid·dly·wink /ˈtidlēˌwiNGk/ (also **tid·dle·dy·wink** /ˈtidl-dē-/) ▶*n.* **1** (**tiddlywinks**) a game in which small plastic counters are flicked into a central receptacle by being pressed on the edge with a larger counter. **2** a counter used in such a game. ▷mid 19th cent.: of unknown origin; perhaps related to TIDDLY. The word originally denoted an unlicensed bar, also a game of dominoes. Current senses date from the late 19th cent.

tide /tīd/ ▶*n.* the alternate rising and falling of the sea, usually twice in each lunar day at a particular place, due to the attraction of the moon and sun: *the changing patterns of the tides | they were driven on by wind and tide.* ■ the water as affected by this: *the rising tide covered the wharf.* ■ *figurative* a powerful surge of feeling or trend of events: *he drifted into sleep on a tide of euphoria | we must reverse the growing tide of racism sweeping the country.*
▶*v.* [*intrans.*] *archaic* drift with or as if with the tide. ■ (of a ship) float or drift in or out of a harbor by taking advantage of favoring tides.
▶*phrasal v.* □ **tide someone over** help someone through a difficult period, esp. with financial assistance: *she needed a small loan to tide her over.* ▷Old English *tīd* 'time, period, era,' of Germanic origin; related to Dutch *tijd* and German *Zeit*, also to TIME. The sense relating to the sea dates from late Middle English. **—tide·less** *adj.*
▶*PHRASE* □ **turn the tide** reverse the trend of events: *the air power that helped to turn the tide of battle.*

-tide ▶*comb. form poetic/literary* denoting a specified time or season: *springtide.* ■ denoting a festival of the Christian Church: *Shrovetide.*

tide·land /ˈtīdˌland/ ▶*n.* (also **tidelands**) land that is submerged at high tide.

tide·line /ˈtīdˌlīn/ (also **tide line**) ▶*n.* a line left or reached by the sea on a shore at the highest point of a tide.

tide·mark /ˈtīdˌmärk/ ▶*n.* a mark left or reached by the sea on a shore at the highest or lowest point of a tide.

tide rip ▶*n.* an area of rough water typically caused by opposing currents or by a rapid current passing over an uneven bottom.

tide ta·ble ▶*n.* a table indicating the times of high and low tides at a particular place.

tide·wait·er /ˈtīdˌwātər/ ▶*n.* *historical* a customs officer who boarded ships on their arrival to enforce the customs regulations.

Tide·wa·ter /ˈtīdˌwôtər; -ˌwätər/ (**the Tidewater**) coastal regions of eastern Virginia where tidal water flows up the Potomac, Rappahannock, York, James, and smaller rivers. Early 17th-century British settlement was focused here.

tide·wa·ter ▶*n.* water brought or affected by tides. ■ an area that is affected by tides: [as *adj.*] *a large area of tidewater country.*

tide·way /ˈtīdˌwā/ ▶*n.* a channel in which a tide runs, esp. the tidal part of a river.

ti·dings /ˈtīdiNGz/ ▶*plural n. poetic/literary* news; information: *the bearer of glad tidings.* ▷late Old English *tīdung* 'announcement, piece of news,' probably from Old Norse *títhindi* 'news of events,' from *títhr* 'occurring.'

ti·dy /ˈtīdē/ ▶*adj.* (**-di·er, -di·est**) **1** arranged neatly and in order: *his scrupulously tidy apartment | figurative the lives they lead don't fit into tidy patterns.* ■ (of a person) inclined to keep things or one's appearance neat and in order: *she was a tidy little girl.* ■ not messy; neat and controlled: *he wrote down her replies in a small, tidy hand.* **2** [*attrib.*] *informal* (of an amount, esp. of money) considerable: *the book will bring in a tidy sum.*
▶*n.* (*pl.* **-dies**) **1** [usu. with *adj.*] a receptacle for holding small objects or waste scraps: *a desk tidy.* **2** another term for ANTIMACASSAR.
▶*v.* (**-dies, -died**) [*trans.*] (often **tidy someone/something up**) bring order to; arrange neatly: *I'd better try to tidy my desk up a bit | figurative the bill is intended to tidy up the law on this matter |* [*intrans.*] *I'll just go and tidy up.* ▷Middle English: from the noun TIDE + -Y[1]. The original meaning was 'timely, opportune'; it later had various senses expressing approval, usually of a person, including 'attractive,' 'healthy,' and 'skillful'; the sense 'orderly, neat' dates from the early 18th cent. **—ti·di·ly** /-dilē/ *adv.* **—ti·di·ness** *n.*

tie /tī/ ▶*v.* (**ty·ing** /ˈtī-iNG/) **1** [*trans.*] attach or fasten (someone or something) with string or similar cord: *they tied Max to a chair | her long hair was tied back in a bow.* ■ fasten (something) to or around someone or something by means of its strings or by forming the ends into a knot or bow: *Lewis tied on his apron.* ■ form (a string, ribbon, or lace) into a knot or bow: *Rick bent to tie his shoelaces.* ■ form (a knot or bow) in this way: *tie a knot in one end of the cotton.* ■ [*intrans.*] be fastened with a knot or bow: *a sarong that ties at the waist.* ■ (often **be tied**) restrict or limit (someone) to a particular situation, occupation, or place: *she didn't want to be like her mother, tied to a feckless man.* **2** [*trans.*] (often **be tied**) connect; link: *self-respect is closely **tied up with** the esteem in which one is held by one's peers.* ■ hold together by a crosspiece or tie: *ceiling joists are used to tie the rafter feet.* ■ *Music* unite (written notes) by a tie. ■ *Music* perform (two notes) as one unbroken note. **3** [*intrans.*] achieve the same score or ranking as another competitor or team: *he **tied for** second in the league |* [*trans.*] *Toronto tied the score in the fourth inning.*
▶*phrasal v.* □ **tie someone down** restrict someone to a particular situation or place: *she didn't want to be tied down by a full-time job.* □ **tie something in** (or **tie in**) cause something to fit or harmonize with something else (or fit or harmonize with something): *her husband is able to **tie in** his shifts **with** hers at the hospital | she may have developed ideas that don't necessarily **tie in with** mine.* □ **tie into** *informal* attack or get to work on vigorously: *tie into breakfast now and let's get a move on.* □ **tie someone up** bind someone's legs and arms together or bind someone to something so that they cannot move or escape: *robbers tied her up and ransacked her home.* ■ (usu. **be tied up**) *informal* occupy someone to the exclusion of any other activity: *she would be tied up at the meeting all day.* □ **tie something up 1** bind or fasten something securely with rope, cord, or string. ■ moor a vessel. ■ (often **be tied up**) invest or reserve capital so that it is not immediately available for use: *money tied up in accounts must be left to grow.* **2** bring something to a satisfactory conclusion; settle: *he said he had a business deal to tie up.*
▶*n.* (*pl.* **ties**) **1** a piece of string, cord, or the like used for fastening or tying something: *he tightened the tie of his robe.* ■ (usu. **ties**) *figurative* a thing that unites or links people: *it is important that we keep family ties strong.* ■ (usu. **ties**) *figurative* a thing that restricts someone's freedom of action: *some cities and merchants were freed from feudal ties.* ■ a rod or beam holding parts of a structure together. ■ a wooden or concrete beam laid transversely under a railroad track to support it. ■ *Music* a curved line above or below two notes of the same pitch indicating that they are to be played for the combined duration of their time values. ■ a shoe tied with a lace. **2** a strip of material worn around the collar and tied in a knot at the front with the ends hanging down, typically forming part of a man's business or formal outfit. **3** a result in a game or other competitive situation in which two or more competitors or teams have the same score or ranking; a draw: *there was a tie for first place.* ▷Old English *tīgan* (verb), *tēah* (noun), of Germanic origin. **—tie·less** *adj.*
▶*PHRASES* □ **fit to be tied** see FIT[1]. □ **tie someone** (**up**) **in knots** see KNOT[1]. □ **tie the knot** see KNOT[1]. □ **tie one on** *informal* get drunk.

tie-back (also **tie·back**) ▶*n.* a decorative strip of fabric or cord, typically used for holding an open curtain off to the side of the window.

tie beam ▶*n.* a horizontal beam connecting two rafters in a roof or roof truss.

tie·break·er /ˈtīˌbrākər/ ▶*n.* a means of deciding a winner from competitors who have tied, in particular (in tennis) a special game to decide the winner of a set when the score is six games all.

tie clasp (also **tie clip**) ▶*n.* an ornamental clip for holding a tie in place.

tie-down ▶*n.* rope, cord, straps, or chains used to attach or secure an item. ■ a stationary ring, post, or the like to which items are secured with tie-downs.

tie-dye ▶*n.* [often as *adj.*] a method of producing textile patterns by tying parts of the fabric to shield it from the dye: *tie-dye T-shirts.*
▶*v.* [*trans.*] dye (a garment or piece of cloth) by such a process.

tie-in ▶*n.* a connection or association: *there's a tie-in to another case I'm working on.* ■ a book, movie, or other product produced to take advantage of a related work in another medium. ■ [as *adj.*] denoting sales made conditional on the purchase of an additional item or items from the same supplier.

tie line ▶*n.* a transmission line connecting parts of a system, esp. a telephone line connecting two private branch exchanges.

Tien Shan /ˈtyen ˈSHän/ (also **Tian Shan**) a range of mountains that lies north of the Tarim Basin in the Xinjiang autonomous region and eastern Kyrgyzstan. Extending for about 1,500 miles (2,500 km), it rises to 24,406 feet (7,439 m) at Pik Pobedy.

tie·pin /ˈtīˌpin/ ▶*n.* an ornamental pin for holding a tie in place.

tier /ti(ə)r/ ▶*n.* a row or level of a structure, typically one of a series of rows placed one above the other and successively receding or diminishing in size: *a tier of seats |* [in *combination*] *the room was full of three-tier metal bunks.* ■ one of a number of successively overlapping ruffles or flounces on a garment. ■ a level or grade within the hierarchy of an organization or system: *companies have taken out a tier of management to save money.* ▷late 15th cent.: from French *tire* 'sequence, order,' from *tirer* 'elongate, draw.' **—tiered** /ti(ə)rd/ *adj.*

tierce /ti(ə)rs/ ▶*n.* **1** another term for TERCE. **2** *Music* an organ stop sounding two octaves and a major third above the pitch of the diapason. **3** (in piquet) a sequence of three cards of the same suit. **4** *Fencing* the third of eight standard parrying positions. **5** a former measure of wine equal to one third of a pipe, usually equivalent to 35 gallons (about 156 liters). ■ *archaic* a cask containing a certain quantity of provisions, the amount varying with the goods. ▷late Middle English: variant of TERCE.

tier·cel /ˈti(ə)rsəl/ (also **ter·cel**) ▶*n.* *Falconry* the male of a hawk, esp. a peregrine or a goshawk. Compare with FALCON.

tie rod ▶*n.* a rod acting as a tie in a building or other structure. ■ a rod in the steering gear of a motor vehicle.

Tier·ra del Fue·go /tēˈerə del ˈfwāgō/ an island off the southern tip of South America, separated from the mainland by the Strait of Magellan. Discovered by Ferdinand Magellan in 1520, it is now divided between Argentina and Chile. ▷Spanish, literally "land of fire."

tie tack (also **tie tac**) ▶*n.* a short pin with an ornamental head, used to attach the ends of a necktie to a shirt front.

tie-up ▶*n.* **1** a link or connection, esp. one between commercial companies: *marketing tie-ups.* ■ a telecommunications link or network. **2** a building where cattle are tied up for the night. ■ a place for mooring a boat. **3** a traffic holdup.

TIFF /tif/ ▶*Computing abbr.* tagged image file format, widely used in desktop publishing.

tiff /tif/ ▶*n.* *informal* a petty quarrel, esp. one between friends or lovers: *Joanna had a tiff with her boyfriend.* ▷early 18th cent. (denoting a slight outburst of temper): probably of dialect origin.

Tif·fa·ny /ˈtifənē/, Louis Comfort (1848–1933), U.S. glassmaker and interior decorator. A leading exponent of art nouveau in the U.S., he established an interior decorating firm in New York City that produced stained glass, vases, lamps, and mosaic.

tif·fa·ny /ˈtifənē/ ▶*n.* thin gauze muslin. ▷early 17th cent.: from Old French *tifanie*, via ecclesiastical Latin from Greek *theophaneia* 'epiphany.' The word is usually taken to be short for *Epiphany silk* or *muslin*, i.e., that worn on Twelfth Night, but may be a humorous allusion to *epiphany* in the sense 'manifestation,' tiffany being semitransparent.

tif·fin /ˈtifin/ ▶*n.* *Indian* or *dated* a light meal, esp. lunch. ▷early 19th cent.: apparently from dialect *tiffing* 'sipping,' of unknown origin.

Tif·lis /ˈtiflis; təˈflēs/ official Russian name (1845–1936) for TBILISI.

Ti·gard /ˈtīgərd/ a city in northwestern Oregon, a southwestern suburb of Portland; pop. 41,223.

ti·ger /ˈtīgər/ ▶*n.* a very large solitary cat with a yellow-brown coat striped with black, native to the forests of Asia but becoming increasingly rare. • *Panthera tigris*, family Felidae. ■ used to refer to someone fierce, determined, or ambitious: *despite his wound, he still fought like a tiger | one of the sport's young tigers.* ■ (also **tiger economy**) a dynamic economy of one of the smaller eastern Asian countries, esp. that of Singapore, Taiwan, or South Korea. ▷Middle English: from Old French *tigre*, from Latin *tigris*, from Greek.

▶*PHRASE* □ **have a tiger by the tail** have embarked on a course of action that proves unexpectedly difficult but that cannot easily or safely be abandoned.

tiger

ti·ger bee·tle ▶*n.* a fast-running predatory beetle that has spotted or striped wing cases and flies in sunshine. The larvae live in tunnels from which they snatch passing insect prey. • Family Cicindelidae: *Cicindela* and other genera.

ti·ger cat ▶*n.* a small forest cat that has a light brown coat with dark stripes and blotches, native to Central and South America. • *Felis tigrina*, family Felidae. ■ any moderate-sized striped cat, such as the ocelot, serval, or margay. ■ a domestic cat with markings like a tiger's.

ti·ger e·con·o·my ▶*n.* see **TIGER**.

ti·ger·ish /ˈtīgərisн/ ▶*adj.* resembling or likened to a tiger, esp. in being fierce and determined: *she was in a tigerish mood.* **—ti·ger·ish·ly** *adv.*

ti·ger lil·y ▶*n.* a tall lily that has orange flowers spotted with black or purple. • *Lilium lancifolium* (or **tigrinum**) , family Liliaceae.

ti·ger ma·ple ▶*n.* the wood from an American maple that contains contrasting light and dark lines.

ti·ger moth ▶*n.* a stout moth that has boldly spotted and streaked wings. • *Arctia* and other genera, family Arctiidae: many species.

ti·ger sal·a·man·der ▶*n.* a large North American salamander that is blackish with yellow patches or stripes. • *Ambystoma tigrinum*, family Ambystomatidae.

ti·ger's eye (also **ti·ger eye**) ▶*n.* a yellowish-brown semiprecious variety of quartz with a silky or chatoyant luster, formed by replacement of crocidolite with chalcedony.

ti·ger shark ▶*n.* an aggressive shark of warm seas, with dark vertical stripes on the body. • *Galeocerdo cuvieri*, family Carcharhinidae.

ti·ger shrimp ▶*n.* a large edible shrimp marked with dark bands, found in the Indian and Pacific oceans. • Genus *Penaeus*, class Malacostraca: several species, in particular the widely farmed *P. monodon*.

tight /tīt/ ▶*adj.* **1** fixed, fastened, or closed firmly; hard to move, undo, or open: *she twisted her handkerchief into a tight knot.* ■ (of clothes or shoes) close-fitting, esp. uncomfortably so: *the dress was too tight for her.* ■ (of a grip) very firm so as not to let go: *she released her tight hold on the dog | figurative presidential advisers* ***keep a tight grip on*** *domestic policy.* ■ (of a ship, building, or object) well sealed against something such as water or air: [in *combination*] *a light-tight container.* ■ (of a formation or a group of people or things) closely or densely packed together: *he levered the bishop out from a tight knot of clerical wives.* ■ (of a community or other group of people) having close relations; secretive: *the tenants were far too tight to let anyone know.* **2** (of a rope, fabric, or surface) stretched so as to leave no slack; not loose: *the drawcord pulls tight.* ■ (of a part of the body or a bodily sensation) feeling painful and constricted, as a result of anxiety or illness: *there was a tight feeling in his gut.* ■ (of appearance or manner) tense, irritated, or angry: *she gave him a tight smile.* ■ (of a rule, policy, or form of control) strictly imposed: *security was tight at yesterday's ceremony.* ■ (of a game or contest) with evenly matched competitors; very close: *he won in a tight finish.* ■ (of a written work or form) concise, condensed, or well structured: *a tight argument.* ■ (of an organization or group of people) disciplined or professional; well coordinated: *the vocalists are strong, and the band is tight.* **3** (of an area or space) having or allowing little room for maneuver: *a tight parking spot | it was a tight squeeze in the tiny vestibule.* ■ (of a bend, turn, or angle) changing direction sharply; having a short radius. ■ (of money or time) limited or restricted: *David was out of work and money was tight | an ability to work to tight deadlines.* ■ *informal* (of a person) not willing to spend or give much money; stingy. **4** [*predic.*] *informal* drunk: *later, at the club, he got tight on brandy.* See note at **DRUNK**.

▶*adv.* very firmly, closely, or tensely: *he went downstairs, holding tight to the banisters.* ▷Middle English (in the sense 'healthy, vigorous,' later 'firm, solid'): probably an alteration of *thight* 'firm, solid,' later 'close-packed, dense,' of Germanic origin; related to German *dicht* 'dense, close.' **—tight·ly** *adv.* **—tight·ness** *n.*

▶*PHRASES* □ **run a tight ship** be very strict in managing an organization or operation. □ **a tight corner** (or **spot** or **place**) a difficult situation: *her talent for talking her way* ***out of tight corners.***

tight-ass ▶*n. informal* an inhibited, repressed, or excessively conventional person. **—tight-assed** *adj.*

tight·en /ˈtītn/ ▶*v.* make or become tight or tighter: [*trans.*] *tighten the bolts* | [*intrans.*] *the revenue laws were tightening up.*

▶*PHRASES* □ **tighten one's belt** see **BELT**. □ **tighten the screw** see **SCREW**.

tight end ▶*n. Football* an offensive end who lines up close to the tackle.

tight-fist·ed /ˈtītˈfistid/ (also **tight-fist·ed**) ▶*adj. informal* not willing to spend or give much money; miserly.

tight-fit·ting ▶*adj.* (of a garment) fitting close to and showing the contours of the body. ■ (of a lid or cover) forming a tight seal when placed on a container.

tight junc·tion ▶*n. Biology* a specialized connection of two adjacent animal cell membranes such that the space usually lying between them is absent.

tight-knit (also **tight·ly knit**) ▶*adj.* (of a group of people) united or bound together by strong relationships and common interests: *tight-knit mining communities.*

tight-lipped ▶*adj.* with the lips firmly closed, esp. as a sign of suppressed emotion or determined reticence: *she stayed tight-lipped and shook her head | figurative a group of tight-lipped air force officers.*

tight mon·ey ▶*n. Finance* money or financing that is available only at high rates of interest.

tight·rope /ˈtītˌrōp/ ▶*n.* a rope or wire stretched tightly high above the ground, on which acrobats perform feats of balancing: [as *adj.*] *a tightrope walker | figurative he continues to* ***walk a tightrope*** *between success and failure.*

▶*v.* [*intrans.*] walk or perform on such a rope.

tights /tīts/ ▶*plural n.* a woman's thin, close-fitting garment, typically made of nylon, cotton, or wool, covering the lower half of the body. ■ a similar garment worn by a dancer or acrobat.

tight·wad /ˈtītˌwäd/ ▶*n. informal* a mean or miserly person.

tigh·ty-whi·ties /ˈtītē ˈ(h)wītēz/ ▶*n. informal* men's white cotton briefs.

Tig·lath-pi·le·ser /ˈtigˌlaтн pīˈlēzər/ the name of three kings of Assyria, notably: ■ **Tiglath-pileser I**, reigned *c.*1115–*c.*1077 BC. He extended Assyrian territory by taking Cappadocia, reaching Syria, and defeating the king of Babylonia. ■ **Tiglath-pileser III**, reigned *c.*745–727 BC. He brought the Assyrian empire to the height of its power by subduing large parts of Syria and Palestine, and he conquered Babylonia.

ti·gnon /ˈtēyôn; tēˈyôn/ ▶*n.* a piece of cloth worn as a turban headdress by Creole women from Louisiana. ▷Louisana French, from French *tigne*, dialect variant of *teigne* 'moth.'

ti·gon /ˈtīgən/ (also **ti·glon** /-glən/) ▶*n.* the hybrid offspring of a male tiger and a lioness. ▷1920s: portmanteau word from **TIGER** and **LION**.

Ti·gray /təˈgrā/ (also **Ti·gre**) a province of Ethiopia, in the north of the country, bordering Eritrea. Tigray engaged in a bitter guerrilla war against the government of Ethiopia 1975–91, during which time the region suffered badly from drought and famine. **—Ti·gray·an** /-ˈgrāən/ (also **Ti·gre·an**) *adj.* & *n.*

Ti·gre /ˈtēgrā/ ▶*n.* a Semitic language spoken in Eritrea and adjoining parts of Sudan. It is not the language of Tigray, which is Tigrinya. ▷the name in Tigre.

ti·gress /ˈtīgris/ ▶*n.* a female tiger. ■ *figurative* a fierce or passionate woman.

Ti·grin·ya /tiˈgrēnyə/ ▶*n.* a Semitic language spoken in Tigray. Compare with **TIGRE**. ▷the name in Tigrinya.

Ti·gris /ˈtīgris/ a river in southwestern Asia. It rises in the mountains of eastern Turkey and flows southeast for 1,150 miles (1,850 km) through Iraq, passing through Baghdad, to join the Euphrates River to form the Shatt al-Arab, which flows into the Persian Gulf.

Ti·hwa /ˈdēˈhwä/ former name (until 1954) for **URUMQI**.

Ti·jua·na /ˌtēəˈwänə; tēˈhwänə/ a town in northwestern Mexico, just south of the U.S. border; pop. 743,000.

Ti·kal /tēˈkäl/ an ancient Mayan city in northern Guatemala. It flourished AD 300–800.

tike ▶*n.* variant spelling of **TYKE**.

ti·ki /ˈtēkē/ ▶*n.* (*pl.* **-kis**) *NZ* a large wooden or small greenstone image of a human figure. ▷Maori, literally 'image.'

tik·ka /ˈtikə; ˈtē-/ ▶*n.* [usu. with *adj.*] an Indian dish of small pieces of meat or vegetables marinated in a spice mixture. ▷from Punjabi *ṭikkā*.

til·ak /ˈtilək/ ▶*n.* a mark worn by a Hindu on the forehead to indicate caste, status, or sect, or as an ornament. ▷from Sanskrit *tilaka*.

ti·la·pi·a /təˈläpēə/ ▶*n.* an African freshwater cichlid fish that has been widely introduced to many areas for food. • *Tilapia* and related genera, family Cichlidae: several species. ▷modern Latin, of unknown origin.

Til·burg /ˈtilˌbərg/ an industrial city in the southern Netherlands, in the province of North Brabant; pop. 159,000.

Til·bur·y /ˈtilbərē; -ˌberē/ the principal container port of London and southeastern England, on the northern bank of the Thames River.

til·bur·y /ˈtilˌberē; -bərē/ ▶*n.* (*pl.* **-bur·ies**) *historical* a light, open two-wheeled carriage. ▷early 19th cent.: named after its inventor.

til·de /ˈtildə/ ▶*n.* an accent (˜) placed over Spanish *n* when pronounced *ny* (as in *señor*) or Portuguese *a* or *o* when nasalized (as in *São Paulo*), or over a vowel in phonetic transcription, indicating nasalization. ■ the same symbol as a part of a URL. ■ a similar symbol used in mathematics to indicate similarity, and in logic to indicate negation. ▷mid 19th cent.: from Spanish, based on Latin *titulus* (see **TITLE**).

Til·den /ˈtildən/, Bill (1893–53), U.S. tennis player; full name *William Tatem Tilden II*. He won the singles at the U.S. Open 1920–25 and 1929, at Wimbledon 1920–21 and 1930, and led the U.S. to seven straight Davis Cup victories 1920–26.

tile /tīl/ ▶*n.* a thin rectangular slab of baked clay, concrete, or other material, used in overlapping rows for covering roofs. ■ a thin square slab of glazed ceramic, cork, linoleum, or other material for covering floors, walls, or other surfaces. ■ a thin, flat piece used in Scrabble, mah-jongg, and certain other games. ■ *Mathematics* a plane shape used in tiling.

▶*v.* [*trans.*] (usu. **be tiled**) cover (something) with tiles: *the lobby was tiled in blue.* ■ *Computing* arrange (two or more windows) on a computer screen so that they do not overlap. ▷Old English *tigele*, from Latin *tegula*, from an Indo-European root meaning 'cover.'

▶*PHRASE* □ **on the tiles** *informal, chiefly Brit.* having a lively night out: *it won't be the first time he's spent* ***a night on the tiles.***

tile·fish /ˈtīlˌfisн/ ▶*n.* (*pl.* same or **-fish·es**) a long, slender bottom-dwelling fish of warm seas. • Several species in the family Malacanthidae (or Branchiostegidae), in particular the large and edible *Lopholatilus chamaeleonticeps* of the Atlantic coast of North America.

til·er /ˈtīlər/ ▶*n.* **1** a person who lays tiles: *a roof tiler.* **2** the doorkeeper of a Masonic lodge, who prevents outsiders from entering.

til·ing /ˈtīliNG/ ▶*n.* the action of laying tiles. ■ a surface covered by tiles: *an area of plain tiling.* ■ tiles collectively, when used to cover a roof, floor, etc. ■ a technique for displaying several nonoverlapping windows on a computer screen. ■ *Mathematics* a way of arranging identical plane shapes so that they completely cover an area without overlapping.

till[1] /til/ ▶*prep.* & *conj.* less formal way of saying **UNTIL**. ▷Old English *til*, of Germanic origin; related to Old Norse *til* 'to,' also ultimately to **TILL**[3].

USAGE In most contexts, **till** and **until** have the same meaning and are interchangeable. The main difference is that **till** is generally considered to be more informal than **until**. **Until** occurs much more frequently than **till** in writing. In addition, **until** tends to be the natural choice at the beginning of a sentence: **until** *very recently, there was still a chance of rescuing the situation.*

Interestingly, while it is commonly assumed that **till** is an abbreviated form of **until** (the spellings **'till** and **'til** reflect this), **till** is in fact the earlier form. **Until** appears to have been formed by the addition of Old Norse *und* ('as far as') several hundred years after the date of the first records for **till**.

till[2] ▸*n.* a cash register or drawer for money in a store, bank, or restaurant. ▷late Middle English (in the general sense 'drawer or compartment for valuables'): of unknown origin.

▸*PHRASE* □ **have** (or **with**) **one's fingers** (or **hand**) **in the till** used in reference to theft from one's place of work: *he was caught with his hand in the till and sacked.*

till[3] ▸*v.* [*trans.*] prepare and cultivate (land) for crops: *no land was being tilled or crops sown.* ▷Old English *tilian* 'strive for, obtain by effort,' of Germanic origin; related to Dutch *telen* 'produce, cultivate' and German *zielen* 'aim, strive,' also ultimately to TILL[1]. The current sense dates from Middle English. —**till·a·ble** *adj.*

till[4] ▸*n. Geology* an unstratified sediment consisting of particles of various sizes and deposited by melting glaciers or ice sheets. ▷late 17th cent. (originally Scots, denoting shale): of unknown origin.

till·age /'tilij/ ▸*n.* the preparation of land for growing crops. ■ land under cultivation: *forty acres of tillage.*

till·er[1] /'tilər/ ▸*n.* a horizontal bar fitted to the head of a boat's rudder post and used as a lever for steering. ▷late Middle English: from Anglo-Norman French *telier* 'weaver's beam, stock of a crossbow,' from medieval Latin *telarium*, from Latin *tela* 'web.'

till·er[2] ▸*n.* an implement or machine for breaking up soil; a plow or cultivator.

till·er[3] ▸*n.* a lateral shoot from the base of the stem, esp. in a grass or cereal.

▸*v.* [*intrans.*] [usu. as *n.*] (**tillering**) develop tillers. ▷mid 17th cent. (denoting a sapling arising from the stool of a felled tree): apparently based on Old English *telga* 'bough,' of Germanic origin.

Til·lich /'tilik/, Paul (Johannes) (1886–1965), U.S. theologian and philosopher, born in Germany. He proposed a form of Christian existentialism, outlining a reconciliation of religion and secular society, as expounded in *Systematic Theology* (1951–63).

till·ite /'tilīt/ ▸*n. Geology* sedimentary rock composed of lithified glacial till.

Til·sit /'tilsit; -zit/ ▸*n.* a semihard mildly flavored cheese. ▷named after the town in East Prussia (now Sovetsk, Russia) where it was first produced.

tilt /tilt/ ▸*v.* **1** move or cause to move into a sloping position: [*intrans.*] *the floor tilted slightly figurative the balance of industrial power tilted toward the workers* | [*trans.*] *he tilted his head to one side.* ■ *figurative* incline or cause to incline toward a particular opinion: [*intrans.*] *he is tilting toward a new economic course.* ■ [*trans.*] move (a camera) in a vertical plane. **2** [*intrans.*] (**tilt at**) *historical* (in jousting) thrust at with a lance or other weapon: *he tilts at his prey* | *figurative the lonely hero tilting at the system.* ■ (**tilt with**) *archaic* engage in a contest with: *I resolved never to tilt with a French lady in compliment.*

▸*n.* **1** a sloping position or movement: *the tilt of her head* | *the coffee cup was on a tilt.* ■ an upward or downward pivoting movement of a camera: *pans and tilts.* ■ an inclination or bias: *the paper's* **tilt toward** *the Republicans.* ■ short for TILT HAMMER. **2** *historical* a combat for exercise or sport between two men on horseback with lances; a joust. ■ (**tilt at**) an attempt at winning (something) or defeating (someone), esp. in sports: *a tilt at the championship.* ▷late Middle English (in the sense 'fall or cause to fall, topple)': perhaps related to Old English *tealt* 'unsteady,' or perhaps of Scandinavian origin and related to Norwegian *tylten* 'unsteady' and Swedish *tulta* 'totter.' —**tilt·er** *n.*

▸*PHRASES* □ (**at**) **full tilt** with maximum energy or force; at top speed. □ **tilt at windmills** attack imaginary enemies or evils. [with allusion to the story of Don Quixote tilting at windmills, believing they were giants.]

tilth /tilTH/ ▸*n.* cultivation of land; tillage. ■ [in *sing.*] the condition of tilled soil, esp. in respect to suitability for sowing seeds: *he could determine whether the soil was of the right tilth.* ■ prepared surface soil. ▷Old English *tilth, tilthe*, from *tilian* (see TILL[3]).

tilt ham·mer ▸*n.* a heavy pivoted hammer used in forging, raised mechanically and allowed to drop on the metal being worked.

tilt yard ▸*n. historical* a place where jousts took place.

Tim. ▸*abbr. Bible* Timothy.

tim·bal /'timbəl/ (also **tym·bal**) ▸*n.* **1** *archaic* a kettledrum. **2** a membrane that forms part of the sound-producing organ in various insects, as the cicada. ▷late 17th cent.: from French *timbale*, alteration (influenced by *cymbale* 'cymbal') of obsolete *tamballe*, from Spanish *atabal*, from Arabic *aṭ-ṭabl* 'the drum.'

tim·bale /'timbəl; tim'bäl/ ▸*n.* **1** a dish of finely minced meat or fish cooked with other ingredients in a pastry shell or in a mold. **2** (**timbales**) paired cylindrical drums played with sticks in Latin American dance music. ▷French, 'drum' (in sense 1 with reference to the shape of the prepared dish; in sense 2 short for *timbales cubains* or *timbales creoles* 'Cuban' or 'creole drums').

tim·ber /'timbər/ ▸*n.* wood prepared for use in building and carpentry: *the exploitation of forests for timber* [as *adj.*] *a small timber building.* ■ trees grown for such wood: *contracts to cut timber.* ■ (usu. **timbers**) a wooden beam or board used in building a house, ship, or other structure. ■ [as *exclam.*] used to warn that a tree is about to fall after being cut: *we cried "Timber!" as our tree fell.* ■ [usu. with *adj.*] personal qualities or character, esp. as seen as suitable for a particular role: *she is frequently hailed as presidential timber.* ▷Old English in the sense 'a building,' also 'building material,' of Germanic origin; related to German *Zimmer* 'room,' from an Indo-European root meaning 'build.'

tim·bered /'timbərd/ ▸*adj.* **1** (of a building) made wholly or partly of timber: *black-and-white timbered buildings.* ■ (of the walls or other surface of a room) covered with wooden panels: *the timbered banqueting hall.* **2** having many trees; wooded.

tim·ber hitch ▸*n.* a knot used to attach a rope to a log or spar. —**tim·ber-hitch** *v.*

tim·ber·ing /'timb(ə)riNG/ ▸*n.* the action of building with wood. ■ wood as a building material, or finished work built from wood.

tim·ber·land /'timbər,land/ ▸*n.* (also **timberlands**) land covered with forest suitable or managed for timber.

tim·ber·line /'timbər,līn/ ▸*n.* (on a mountain) the line or altitude above which no trees grow. Also called TREE LINE. ■ (in high northern (or southern) latitudes) the line north (or south) of which no trees grow.

tim·ber wolf ▸*n.* a wolf of a large variety found mainly in northern North America, with gray brindled fur. Also called GRAY WOLF.

tim·ber yard ▸*n. Brit.* a lumberyard.

tim·bre /'tambər; 'tänbrə/ ▸*n.* the character or quality of a musical sound or voice as distinct from its pitch and intensity: *trumpet mutes with different timbres* | *a voice high in pitch but rich in timbre.* ▷mid 19th cent.: from French, from medieval Greek *timbanon*, from Greek *tumpanon* 'drum.'

tim·brel /'timbrəl/ ▸*n. archaic* a tambourine or similar instrument. ▷early 16th cent.: perhaps a diminutive of obsolete *timbre*, in the same sense, from Old French (see TIMBRE).

Tim·buk·tu /,timbək'to͞o/ (also **Tim·buc·too**) a town in northern Mali; pop. 20,000. Formerly a major trading center for gold and salt on the trans-Saharan trade routes, it reached the height of its prosperity in the 16th century but fell into decline after its capture by the Moroccans in 1591. French name TOMBOUCTOU. ■ used in reference to a remote or extremely distant place: *from here to Timbuktu.*

time /tīm/ ▸*n.* **1** the indefinite continued progress of existence and events in the past, present, and future regarded as a whole: *travel through space and time* | *one of the greatest wits of all time.* ■ the progress of this as affecting people and things: *things were getting better as time passed.* ■ time or an amount of time as reckoned by a conventional standard: *it's eight o'clock Eastern Standard Time.* ■ (**Time** or **Father Time**) the personification of time, typically as an old man with a scythe and hourglass. **2** a point of time as measured in hours and minutes past midnight or noon: *the time is 9:30.* ■ a moment or definite portion of time allotted, used, or suitable for a purpose: *the scheduled departure time* | *should we set a time for the meeting?* ■ (often **time for/to do something**) the favorable or appropriate time to do something; the right moment: *it was time to go* | *it's time for bed.* ■ (**a time**) an indefinite period: *traveling always distorts one's feelings for a time.* ■ (also **times**) a more or less definite portion of time in history or characterized by particular events or circumstances: *Victorian times* | *at the time of Galileo* | *the park is beautiful at this time of year.* ■ (also **times**) the conditions of life during a particular period: *times have changed.* ■ (**the Times**) used in names of newspapers: *The New York Times.* ■ (**one's time**) one's lifetime: *I've known a lot of women in my time.* ■ (**one's time**) the successful, fortunate, or influential part of a person's life or career: *in my time that was unheard of.* ■ (**one's time**) the appropriate or expected time for something, in particular childbirth or death: *he seemed old before his time.* ■ an apprenticeship: *all of our foremen* **served their time** *on the loading dock.* ■ *dated* a period of menstruation or pregnancy. ■ the normal rate of pay for time spent working: *if called out on weekends, they are paid* **time and a half.** ■ the length of time taken to run a race or complete an event or journey: *his time for the mile was 3:49.31.* ■ (in sports) a moment at which play is stopped temporarily within a game, or the act of calling for this: *the umpire* **called time.** ■ *Soccer* the end of the game: *he scored five minutes from time.* **3** time as allotted, available, or used: *we need more time* | *it would be a waste of time.* ■ *informal* a prison sentence: *he was* **doing time for** *fraud.* **4** an instance of something happening or being done; an occasion: *this is the first time I have gotten into debt* | *the nurse came in four times a day.* ■ an event, occasion, or period experienced in a particular way: *we had a good time* | *she was* **having a rough time of it.** **5** (**times**) (following a number) expressing multiplication: *five goes into fifteen three times* | *it burns calories four times faster than walking.* **6** the rhythmic pattern of a piece of music, as expressed by a time signature: *tunes in waltz* **time.** ■ the tempo at which a piece of music is played or marked to be played.

▸*v.* **1** [*trans.* or *infinitive*] plan, schedule, or arrange when (something) should happen or be done: *the first track race is timed for 11:15* | *the bomb had been timed to go off an hour later.* ■ perform (an action) at a particular moment: *Williams timed his pass perfectly from about thirty yards.* **2** [*trans.*] measure the time taken by (a process or activity, or a person doing it): *we were timed and given certificates according to our speed* | [with *clause*] *I timed how long it took to empty that tanker.* **3** [*trans.*] (**time something out**) *Computing* (of a computer or a program) cancel an operation automatically because a predefined interval of time has passed without a certain event happening. ▷Old English *tīma*, of Germanic origin; related to TIDE, which it superseded in temporal senses. The earliest of the current verb senses (dating from late Middle English) is 'do (something) at a particular moment.'

▸*PHRASES* □ **about time** used to convey that something now happening or about to happen should have happened earlier: *it's about time I came clean and admitted it.* □ **against time** with utmost speed, so as to finish by a specified time: *he was working against time.* □ **ahead of time** earlier than expected or required. □ **ahead of one's time** having ideas too enlightened or advanced to be accepted by one's contemporaries. □ **all the time** at all times. ■ very frequently or regularly: *we were in and out of each other's houses all the time.* □ **at one time** in or during a known but unspecified past period: *she was a nurse at one time.* □ **at the same time 1** simultaneously; at once. **2** nevertheless (used to introduce a fact that should be taken into account): *I can't really explain it, but at the same time I'm not convinced.* □ **at a time** separately in the specified groups or numbers: *he took the stairs two at a time.* □ **at times** sometimes; on occasions. □ **before time** before the due or expected time. □ **behind time** late. □ **behind the times** not aware of or using the latest ideas or techniques; out of date. □ **for the time being** for the present; until some other arrangement is made. □ **give someone the time of day** [usu. with *negative*] be pleasantly polite or friendly to someone: *I wouldn't give him the time of day if I could help it.* □ **half the time** as often as not. □ **have no time for** be unable or unwilling to spend time on: *he had no time for anything except essays and projects.* ■ dislike or disapprove of: *he's got no time for airheads.* □ **have the time 1** be able to spend the time needed to do something: *she didn't have the time to look very closely.* **2** know from having a watch what time it is. □ **in** (**less than**) **no time** very quickly or very soon: *the video has sold 30,000 copies in no time.* □ **in one's own time** (also **in one's own good time**) at a time and a rate decided by oneself. □ **in time 1** not late; punctual: *I came back* **in time for** *Molly's party.* **2** eventually: *there is the danger that he might, in time, not be able to withstand temptation.* **3** in accordance with the appropriate musical rhythm or tempo.

□ **keep good** (or **bad**) **time** **1** (of a clock or watch) record time accurately (or inaccurately). **2** (of a person) be habitually punctual (or not punctual). □ **keep time** play or rhythmically accompany music in time. □ **lose no time** do a specified thing immediately or as soon as possible: *the administration* **lost no time in** *trying to regain the initiative.* □ **no time** a very short interval or period: *the renovations were done* **in no time**. □ **on one's own time** outside working hours; without being paid. □ **on time** punctual; punctually: *the train was on time | we paid our bills on time.* □ **out of time** **1** at the wrong time or period: *I felt that I was born out of time.* ■ not following or maintaining the correct rhythm (of music): *every time we get to this part in the song, you are out of time.* **2** with no time remaining to continue or complete something, esp. a task for which a specific amount of time had been allowed: *I knew the answers to all the essay questions, but I* **ran out of time**. □ **pass the time of day** exchange greetings or casual remarks. □ **time after time** (also **time and again** or **time and time again**) on very many occasions; repeatedly. □ **time and tide wait for no man** *proverb* if you don't make use of a favorable opportunity, you may never get the same chance again. □ **time immemorial** used to refer to a point of time in the past that was so long ago that people have no knowledge or memory of it: *markets had been held there* **from time immemorial**. □ **time is money** *proverb* time is a valuable resource, therefore it is better to do things as quickly as possible. □ **the time of one's life** a period or occasion of exceptional enjoyment. □ **time out of mind** another way of saying TIME IMMEMORIAL. □ **time was** there was a time when: *time was, each street had its own specialized trade.* □ (**only**) **time will tell** the truth or correctness of something will (only) be established at some time in the future.

time-and-mo·tion stud·y ▸*n.* a procedure in which the efficiency of an industrial or other operation is evaluated.

time base ▸*n. Electronics* a signal for uniformly and repeatedly deflecting the electron beam of a cathode-ray tube. ■ a line on the display produced in this way and serving as a time axis.

time bomb ▸*n.* a bomb designed to explode at a preset time. ■ *figurative* a process or procedure causing a problem that will eventually become dangerous if not addressed: *an environmental time bomb.*

time cap·sule ▸*n.* a container storing a selection of objects chosen as being typical of the present time, buried for discovery in the future.

time·card /ˈtīmˈkärd/ ▸*n.* a card used to record an employee's starting and quitting times, usually stamped by a time clock.

time clock ▸*n.* a clock with a device for recording employees' times of arrival and departure.

time code ▸*n. Electronics* a coded signal on videotape or film giving information about such things as frame number, time of recording, or exposure.

time con·stant ▸*n. Physics* a time that represents the speed with which a particular system can respond to change, typically equal to the time taken for a specified parameter to vary by a factor of $1-1/e$ (approximately 0.6321).

time-con·sum·ing ▸*adj.* taking a lot of or too much time: *an extremely time-consuming process.*

time de·pos·it ▸*n.* a deposit in a bank account that cannot be withdrawn before a set date or for which notice of withdrawal is required.

time di·vi·sion mul·ti·plex·ing ▸*n. Telecommunications* a technique for transmitting two or more signals over the same telephone line, radio channel, or other medium. Each signal is sent as a series of pulses or packets, which are interleaved with those of the other signal or signals and transmitted as a continuous stream. Compare with FREQUENCY DIVISION MULTIPLEXING.

time do·main ▸*n. Physics* time considered as an independent variable in the analysis or measurement of time-dependent phenomena.

time do·main re·flec·tom·e·ter ▸*n.* see REFLECTOMETER.

time ex·po·sure ▸*n.* the exposure of photographic film for longer than the maximum normal shutter setting.

time frame ▸*n.* a period of time, esp. a specified period in which something occurs or is planned to take place: *the work had to be done in a time frame of fourteen working days.*

time-hon·ored ▸*adj.* [*attrib.*] (of a custom or tradition) respected or valued because it has existed for a long time.

time·keep·er /ˈtīmˌkēpər/ ▸*n.* **1** a person who measures or records the amount of time taken, esp. in a sports competition. **2** [usu. with *adj.*] a person regarded as being punctual or not punctual: *we were good timekeepers.* ■ a watch or clock regarded as recording time accurately or inaccurately: *these watches are accurate timekeepers.* ■ *archaic* a clock. —**time·keep·ing** /-ˌkēpiNG/ *n.*

time lag ▸*n.* see LAG[1] (sense 1).

time-lapse ▸*adj.* denoting the photographic technique of taking a sequence of frames at set intervals to record changes that take place slowly over time. When the frames are shown at normal speed, or in quick succession, the action seems much faster.

time·less /ˈtīmlis/ ▸*adj.* not affected by the passage of time or changes in fashion: *antiques add to the timeless atmosphere of the dining room.* —**time·less·ly** *adv.* —**time·less·ness** *n.*

time lim·it ▸*n.* a limit of time within which something must be done.

time·line /ˈtīmˌlīn/ (also **time line**) ▸*n.* a graphic representation of the passage of time as a line.

time lock ▸*n.* a lock fitted with a device that prevents it from being unlocked until a set time. ■ a device built into a computer program to stop it from operating after a certain time.

▸*v.* (**time-lock**) [*trans.*] secure (a door or other locking mechanism) with a time lock. ■ link (something) inextricably to a certain period of time: *an overdone theme tends to time-lock a setting and stifle imagination.*

time·ly /ˈtīmlē/ ▸*adj.* done or occurring at a favorable or useful time; opportune: *a timely warning.* —**time·li·ness** *n.*

THE RIGHT WORD **opportune, propitious, seasonable, timely**

Some people seem to have a knack for doing or saying the right thing at the right time.

A **timely** act or remark is one that comes at a moment when it is of genuine value or service (*a timely interruption*), while an **opportune** one comes in the nick of time, as if by accident, and exactly meets the needs of the occasion (*a storm came up at an opportune moment, squelching enthusiasm for the fight*).

Seasonable applies to whatever is suited to the season of the year or fits in with the needs of the moment or the character of the occasion (*seasonable weather; a seasonable menu for a cold winter day*).

Propitious means presenting favorable conditions. In other words, while a warm day in December might not be *seasonable*, it might very well be *propitious* for the sailor setting off on a round-the-world cruise.

time ma·chine ▸*n.* (in science fiction) a machine capable of transporting a person backward or forward in time.

time off ▸*n.* time for rest or recreation away from one's usual work or studies: *we're too busy to* **take time off**.

time·ous /ˈtīməs/ ▸*adj. chiefly Scottish* in good time; sufficiently early: *ensure timeous completion and posting of applications.* —**time·ous·ly** *adv.*

time out ▸*n.* **1** time for rest or recreation away from one's usual work or studies: *she is* **taking time out** *from her hectic tour.* ■ (usu. **timeout** or **time-out**) a brief break in play in a game or sport: *he inadvertently called for a timeout with two seconds remaining.* ■ (also **timeout** or **time-out**) an imposed temporary suspension of activities, esp. the separation of a misbehaving child from one or more playmates as a disciplinary measure: *it's the third time this week he's been* **in time-out**. **2** (usu. **timeout**) *Computing* a cancellation or cessation that automatically occurs when a predefined interval of time has passed without a certain event occurring.

time·piece /ˈtīmˌpēs/ ▸*n.* an instrument, such as a clock or watch, for measuring time.

tim·er /ˈtīmər/ ▸*n.* **1** an automatic mechanism for activating a device at a preset time: *a video timer.* ■ a person or device that measures or records the amount of time taken by a process or activity. **2** [in *combination*] used to indicate how many times someone has done something: *for most first-timers the success rate is 45 percent.*

time-re·lease ▸*adj.* denoting something, esp. a medicine, that releases an active substance gradually.

times /tīmz/ ▸*prep.* multiplied by: *eleven times four is forty-four.* ▷see TIME sense 5 of the *noun*

time·sav·ing /ˈtīmˌsāviNG/ ▸*adj.* (of a device, method, etc.) reducing the time spent or required through greater efficiency or a shorter route. —**time·sav·er** /-ˌsāvər/ *n.*

time·scale /ˈtīmˌskāl/ ▸*n.* the time allowed for or taken by a process or sequence of events: *climate changes on a timescale of thousands of years.*

time se·ries ▸*n. Statistics* a series of values of a quantity obtained at successive times, often with equal intervals between them.

time-serv·er ▸*n.* **1** a person who changes their views to suit the prevailing circumstances or fashion. **2** a person who makes very little effort at work because they are waiting to leave or retire. —**time-serv·ing** *adj.*

time·share /ˈtīmˌSHe(ə)r/ ▸*n.* the arrangement whereby several joint owners have the right to use a property as a vacation home under a time-sharing scheme: *a growing interest in timeshare.* ■ a property owned in such a way.

time-shar·ing ▸*n.* **1** the operation of a computer system by several users for different operations at the same time. **2** the use of a property as a vacation home at specified times by several joint owners.

time sheet (also **time·sheet** /ˈtīmˌSHēt/) ▸*n.* a piece of paper for recording the number of hours worked.

time-shift ▸*v.* **1** [*intrans.*] move from one period in time to another. **2** [*trans.*] record (a television program) for later viewing.

▸*n.* (**time shift**) a movement from one period in time to another, esp. in a play or movie.

time sig·na·ture ▸*n. Music* an indication of rhythm following a clef, generally expressed as a fraction with the denominator defining the beat as a division of a whole note and the numerator giving the number of beats in each bar.

time slice ▸*n. Computing* a short interval of time during which a computer or its central processor deals uninterruptedly with one user or program, before switching to another.

Times Square /tīmz/ a focal point of Manhattan in New York City, around the intersection of Broadway and 42nd Street. Its long-held reputation for seediness is giving way to redevelopment.

Times Square

times ta·ble ▸*n.* informal term for MULTIPLICATION TABLE.

time·ta·ble /ˈtīmˌtābəl/ ▸*n.* a chart showing the departure and arrival times of trains, buses, or planes. ■ a plan of times at which events are scheduled to take place, esp. toward a particular end: *the timetable for a military coup.*

▸*v.* [*trans.*] schedule (something) to take place at a particular time: *German lessons were timetabled on Wednesday and Friday.*

time trav·el ▸*n.* (in science fiction) the action of traveling through time into the past or the future. —**time-trav·el** *v.* —**time trav·el·er** *n.*

time tri·al ▸*n.* (in various sports) a test of a competitor's individual speed over a set distance, esp. a cycling race in which competitors are separately timed.

time warp ▸*n.* (esp. in science fiction) an imaginary distortion of space in relation to time whereby people or objects of one period can be moved to another.

time·worn /ˈtīmˌwôrn/ (also **time-worn**) ▸*adj.* damaged or impaired, or made less striking or attractive, as a result of age or much use: *the timeworn faces of the veterans | a timeworn aphorism.*

time zone ▸*n.* see **ZONE** (sense 1).

tim·id /ˈtimid/ ▸*adj.* (**-id·er, -id·est**) showing a lack of courage or confidence; easily frightened: *I was too timid to ask for what I wanted.* ▷mid 16th cent.: from Latin *timidus,* from *timere* 'to fear.' —**ti·mid·i·ty** /təˈmiditē/ *n.* —**tim·id·ly** *adv.* —**tim·id·ness** *n.*

tim·ing /ˈtīmiNG/ ▸*n.* the choice, judgment, or control of when something should be done: *one of the secrets of golf is good timing.* ■ a particular point or period of time when something happens. ■ (in an internal combustion engine) the times when the valves open and close, and the time of the ignition spark, in relation to the movement of the piston in the cylinder.

tim·ing chain ▸*n.* a metal chain or reinforced rubber belt that drives the camshaft of an internal-combustion engine. Also called **timing belt**.

Ti·mi·şoa·ra /ˌtēmēSHˈwärə/ an industrial city in western Romania; pop. 325,000. Formerly part of Hungary, the city has substantial Hungarian- and German-speaking populations. Hungarian name **TEMESVÁR**.

ti·moc·ra·cy /təˈmäkrəsē/ ▸*n.* (*pl.* **-cies**) *chiefly Philosophy* **1** a form of government in which possession of property is required in order to hold office. **2** a form of government in which rulers are motivated by ambition or love of honor. ▷late 15th cent.: from Old French *timocracie,* via medieval Latin from Greek *timokratia,* from *timē* 'honor, worth' + *-kratia* 'power.' Sense 1 reflects Aristotle's usage, sense 2 Plato's. —**ti·mo·crat·ic** /ˌtiməˈkratik/ *adj.*

tim·o·lol /ˈtīməˌlôl; -ˌläl/ ▸*n. Medicine* a synthetic compound that acts as a beta blocker and is used to treat hypertension, migraines, and glaucoma. • Chem. formula: $C_{13}H_{24}N_4O_3S$. ▷1970s: from *tim-* (of unknown origin) + *(propran)olol.*

Ti·mor /ˈtēˌmôr/ the western part of the largest of the Lesser Sunda Islands, in the southern Malay Archipelago; pop. 3,383,000. The island was formerly divided into Dutch West Timor and Portuguese East Timor. In 1950, West Timor was absorbed into the newly formed Republic of Indonesia. In 1975, East Timor declared itself independent but was invaded and occupied by Indonesia; it finally became an independent state in 2002. (see **EAST TIMOR**). —**Ti·mo·rese** /ˌtēməˈrēz; -ˈrēs/ *adj.* & *n.*

tim·or·ous /ˈtimərəs/ ▸*adj.* showing or suffering from nervousness, fear, or a lack of confidence: *a timorous voice.* ▷late Middle English (in the sense 'feeling fear'): from Old French *temereus,* from medieval Latin *timorosus,* from Latin *timor* 'fear,' from *timere* 'to fear.' —**tim·or·ous·ly** *adv.* —**tim·or·ous·ness** *n.*

Ti·mor Sea an arm of the Indian Ocean between Timor and northwestern Australia.

Tim·o·thy /ˈtiməTHē/ either of two books of the New Testament, epistles of St. Paul addressed to St. Timothy.

Tim·o·thy, St. (1st century AD), convert and disciple of St. Paul. Traditionally, he was the first bishop of Ephesus and was martyred in the reign of Roman emperor Nerva. Feast day, January 22 or 26.

tim·o·thy /ˈtiməTHē/ (also **tim·o·thy grass**) ▸*n.* a Eurasian grass that is widely grown for grazing and hay. It is naturalized in North America, where many cultivars have been developed. • *Phleum pratense,* family Gramineae. ▷mid 18th cent.: named after *Timothy* Hanson, the American farmer who introduced it to Carolina from New York (*c.*1720).

tim·pa·ni /ˈtimpənē/ (also **tym·pa·ni**) ▸*plural n.* kettledrums, esp. when played by one musician in an orchestra. ▷late 19th cent.: from Italian, plural of *timpano* 'kettledrum,' from Latin *tympanum* 'drum' (see **TYMPANUM**). —**tim·pa·nist** /-nist/ *n.*

tin /tin/ ▸*n.* **1** a silvery-white metal, the chemical element of atomic number 50. (Symbol: **Sn**) ■ short for **TINPLATE**. ■ *Brit., informal, dated* money.

Tin is quite a rare element, occurring chiefly in the mineral cassiterite. Pure crystalline tin exists in two allotropic modifications, the metallic form (**white tin**), and a semimetallic form (**gray tin**). It is used in various alloys, notably bronze, and for electroplating iron or steel sheets to make tinplate.

2 a metal container, in particular: ■ *chiefly Brit.* another term for **TIN CAN**: *she had opened **a tin of** beans.* ■ a lidded airtight container made of tinplate or aluminum: *Albert got out the cookie tin.* ■ *chiefly Brit.* an open metal container for baking food: *grease a loaf tin.*

▸*v.* (**tinned** /tind/, **tin·ning**) [*trans.*] cover with a thin layer of tin: *the copper pans are tinned inside.* ▷Old English, of Germanic origin; related to Dutch *tin* and German *Zinn.*

▸*PHRASE* □ **have a tin ear** be tone-deaf.

tin·a·mou /ˈtinəˌmo͞o/ ▸*n.* a ground-dwelling tropical American bird that looks somewhat like a grouse. • Family Tinamidae: several genera and many species. ▷late 18th cent.: via French from Galibi *tinamu.*

Tin·ber·gen[1] /ˈtinˌbergə(n)/, Jan (1903–94), Dutch economist. A pioneer in econometrics, he was the brother of zoologist Nikolaas Tinbergen. Nobel Prize for Economics (1969, shared with Ragnar Frisch)

Tin·ber·gen[2], Nikolaas (1907–88), Dutch zoologist. He found that much animal behavior is innate and stereotyped, and he introduced the concept of displacement activity. He was the brother of the economist Jan Tinbergen. Nobel Prize for Physiology or Medicine (1973, shared with Lorentz and Karl von Frisch).

tin can ▸*n.* a tinplate or aluminum container for preserving food, esp. an empty one. ■ *Nautical slang* a destroyer or a submarine.

tinct. ▸*abbr.* tincture.

tinc·to·ri·al /tiNG(k)ˈtôrēəl/ ▸*adj. technical* of or relating to dyeing, coloring, or staining properties. ▷mid 17th cent.: from Latin *tinctorius* (from *tinctor* 'dyer,' from *tingere* 'to dye or color') + **-AL**.

tinc·ture /ˈtiNGkCHər/ ▸*n.* **1** a medicine made by dissolving a drug in alcohol: *the remedies can be administered in the form of tinctures | a bottle containing **tincture of** iodine.* **2** a slight trace of something: *she could not keep **a tincture of** bitterness out of her voice.* **3** *Heraldry* any of the conventional colors (including the metals and stains, and often the furs) used in coats of arms.

▸*v.* (**be tinctured**) be tinged, flavored, or imbued with a slight amount of: *Arthur's affability was tinctured with faint sarcasm.* ▷late Middle English (denoting a dye or pigment): from Latin *tinctura* 'dyeing,' from *tingere* 'to dye or color.' Sense 2 (early 17th cent.) comes from the obsolete sense 'imparted quality,' likened to a tint imparted by a dye.

tin·der /ˈtindər/ ▸*n.* dry, flammable material, such as wood or paper, used for lighting a fire. ▷Old English *tynder, tyndre,* of Germanic origin; related to Dutch *tonder* and German *Zunder.* —**tin·der·y** *adj.*

tin·der·box /ˈtindərˌbäks/ ▸*n. historical* a box containing tinder, flint, a steel, and other items for kindling fires. ■ *figurative* a thing that is readily ignited: *dry winds and no rain have turned parts of the state into a tinderbox.* ■ *figurative* a volatile situation, or a person who is readily aroused, esp. to anger: *the perception of Kosovo as a potential tinderbox within Serbia.*

tin·der-dry ▸*adj.* (of vegetation) extremely dry and flammable.

tine /tīn/ ▸*n.* a prong or sharp point, such as that on a fork or antler. ▷Old English *tind,* of Germanic origin; related to German *Zinne* 'pinnacle.' —**tined** *adj.* [*in combination*] *a three-tined fork.*

tin·e·a /ˈtinēə/ ▸*n.* technical term for **RINGWORM**. ▷late Middle English: from Latin, 'worm.'

tin·foil /ˈtinˌfoil/ (also **tin foil**) ▸*n.* foil made of aluminum or a similar silvery-gray metal, used esp. for covering or wrapping food.

ting /tiNG/ ▸*n.* a sharp, clear ringing sound, such as when a glass is struck by a metal object.

▸*v.* [*intrans.*] emit such a sound. ▷late Middle English (as a verb): imitative. The noun dates from the early 17th cent.

tinge /tinj/ ▸*v.* (**ting·ing** or **tinge·ing**) [*trans.*] (often **be tinged**) color slightly: *a mass of white blossom **tinged with** pink* | [*trans.*] *toward the sun the sky was tinged crimson.* ■ *figurative* have a slight influence on: *this visit will be tinged with sadness.*

▸*n.* a tendency toward or trace of some color: *there was a faint pink tinge to the sky.* ■ *figurative* a slight trace of a feeling or quality. ▷late 15th cent.: from Latin *tingere* 'to dip or color.' The noun dates from the mid 18th cent.

tin·gle /ˈtiNGgəl/ ▸*v.* [*intrans.*] (of a person or a part of their body) experience a slight prickling or stinging sensation: *she was tingling with excitement.* ■ [*trans.*] cause to experience such a sensation: *a standing ovation that tingled your spine.* ■ [*intrans.*] (of such a sensation) be experienced in a part of one's body: *shivers tingled down the length of her spine.*

▸*n.* a slight prickling or stinging sensation: *she felt a tingle in the back of her neck | a tingle of anticipation.* ▷late Middle English: perhaps a variant of **TINKLE**. The original notion was perhaps 'ring in response to a loud noise,' but the term was very early applied to the result of hearing something shocking.

tin·gly /ˈtiNGg(ə)lē/ ▸*adj.* (**-gli·er, -gli·est**) causing or experiencing a slight prickling or stinging sensation: *a tingly sense of excitement.*

tin god ▸*n.* a person, esp. a minor official, who is pompous and self-important. ■ an object of unjustified veneration or respect.

tin·horn /ˈtinˌhôrn/ ▸*n. informal* a contemptible person, esp. one pretending to have money, influence, or ability: *he portrayed Wyatt Earp as a narcissistic tinhorn* | [as *adj.*] *tinhorn politicians.*

tin·ker /ˈtiNGkər/ ▸*n.* **1** (esp. in former times) a person who travels from place to place mending metal utensils as a way of making a living. ■ a person who makes minor mechanical repairs, esp. on a variety of appliances and apparatuses, usually for a living. ■ *Brit., chiefly derogatory* a gypsy or other person living in an itinerant community. **2** an act of attempting to repair something.

▸*v.* [*intrans.*] attempt to repair or improve something in a casual or desultory way, often to no useful effect: *he spent hours **tinkering with** the car.* ■ [*trans.*] *archaic* attempt to mend (something) in such a way. ▷Middle English (first recorded in Anglo-Latin as a surname): of unknown origin. —**tin·ker·er** *n.*

▸*PHRASE* □ **not give a tinker's damn** *informal* not care at all.

Tin·ker·toy /ˈtiNGkərˌtoi/ ▸*n. trademark* a children's building toy consisting of pieces held together by pegs in holes.

tin·kle /ˈtiNGkəl/ ▸*v.* **1** make or cause to make a light, clear ringing sound: [*intrans.*] *cool water tinkled in the stone fountains* | [*trans.*] *the maid tinkled a bell.* **2** [*intrans.*] *informal* urinate.

▸*n.* **1** a light, clear ringing sound: *the distant tinkle of a cow bell.* ■ *Brit., informal* a telephone call: *I'll **give them a tinkle**.* **2** *informal* an act of urinating. ▷late Middle English (also in the sense 'tingle'): frequentative of obsolete *tink* 'to chink or clink,' of imitative origin. —**tin·kly** /-k(ə)lē/ *adj.*

Tin Liz·zie /ˈlizē/ (also **tin liz·zie**) ▸*n. informal, dated* a cheap, old, or run-down automobile (originally used as a nickname for early Ford cars, esp. the Model T). ▷early 20th cent.: *Lizzie,* a nickname for the given name *Elizabeth.*

tinned /tind/ ▸*adj.* **1** [*attrib.*] covered or coated in tin or a tin alloy. **2** *chiefly Brit.* (of food) preserved in a tin can: *tinned fruit.*

tin·ner /ˈtinər/ ▸*n.* a tin miner or tinsmith.

tin·ni·tus /ˈtinitəs; tiˈnī-/ ▸*n. Medicine* ringing or buzzing in the ears. ▷mid 19th cent.: from Latin, from *tinnire* 'to ring, tinkle,' of imitative origin.

tin·ny /ˈtinē/ ▸*adj.* (**-ni·er, -ni·est**) having a displeasingly thin, metallic sound: *tinny music played in the background.* ■ (of an object) made of thin or poor-quality metal: *a tinny little car.* ■ having an unpleasantly metallic taste: *canned artichokes taste somewhat tinny.* —**tin·ni·ly** /ˈtinilē/ *adv.* —**tin·ni·ness** *n.*

Tin Pan Al·ley the name given to a district in New York City (not associated with any particular street, but with the area around 28th Street, between 5th Avenue and Broadway) where many songwriters, arrangers, and music publishers were formerly based. ■ [as *n.*] [usu. as *adj.*] the world of composers and publishers of popular music, particularly with reference to the works of such composers as Irving Berlin, Jerome Kern, George Gershwin, Cole Porter, and Richard Rodgers.

tin·plate /ˈtinˌplāt/ (also **tin plate**) ▸*n.* sheet steel or iron coated with tin.

▸*v.* [*trans.*] [often as *adj.*] (**tinplated** or **tin-plated**) coat (an object) with tin.

tin·pot /ˈtinˌpät/ (also **tin-pot**) ▸*adj.* [*attrib.*] *informal* (esp. of a country or its leader) having or showing poor leadership or organization: *a tinpot dictator.*

tin·sel /ˈtinsəl/ ▸*n.* a form of decoration consisting of thin strips of shiny metal foil. ■ showy or superficial attractiveness or glamour: *his taste for the tinsel of the art world.* ▷late Middle English (denoting fabric either interwoven with metallic thread or spangled): from Old French *estincele* 'spark,' or *estinceler* 'to sparkle,' based on Latin *scintilla* 'a spark.' —**tin·sel·ly** *adj.*

tin·seled /ˈtinsəld/ (also *chiefly Brit.* **tin·selled**) ▸*adj.* decorated or adorned with tinsel. ■ showily or superficially attractive or glamorous: *his tinseled sentiments.*

Tin·sel·town /ˈtinsəlˌtoun/ ▸*n. informal* Hollywood, or the superficially glamorous world it represents.

tin·smith /ˈtinˌsmiTH/ ▸*n.* a person who makes or repairs articles of tin or tinplate.

tin snips (also **tin·snips**) ▸*plural n.* a pair of clippers for cutting sheet metal.

tin sol·dier ▸*n.* a toy soldier made of metal.

tin·stone /ˈtinˌstōn/ ▸*n.* another term for **CASSITERITE**.

tint /tint/ ▸*n.* **1** a shade or variety of color: *the sky was taking on an apricot tint.* ■ *Printing* an area of faint even color printed as a halftone, used for highlighting overprinted text. ■ a set of parallel engraved lines to give uniform shading. ■ a trace of something: ***a tint** of glamour.* **2** an artificial dye for coloring the hair. ■ an application of such a substance: *peering into the mirror to see if any white hair showed after her last tint.*
▸*v.* [*trans.*] (usu. **be tinted**) color (something) slightly; tinge: *her skin was tinted with delicate color* | [as *adj.*] (**tinted**) *a black car with tinted windows.* ■ dye (someone's hair) with a tint. ▷early 18th cent.: alteration (perhaps influenced by Italian *tinta*) of obsolete *tinct* 'to color, tint,' from Latin *tinctus* 'dyeing,' from *tingere* 'to dye or color.' **—tint·er** *n.*

tin·tin·nab·u·la·tion /ˌtintəˌnabyəˈlāSHən/ ▸*n.* a ringing or tinkling sound. ▷mid 19th cent.: from Latin *tintinnabulum* 'tinkling bell' (from *tintinnare*, reduplication of *tinnire* 'to ring, tinkle') + **-ATION**.

Tin·to·ret·to /ˌtintəˈretō/ (1518–94), Italian painter; born *Jacopo Robusti.* His work is typified by a mannerist style, including unusual viewpoints and chiaroscuro effects.

tin·type /ˈtinˌtīp/ ▸*n. historical* a photograph taken as a positive on a thin tin plate.

tin·ware /ˈtinˌwe(ə)r/ ▸*n.* kitchen utensils or other articles made of tin or tinplate.

tin whis·tle ▸*n.* a small flutelike instrument made from a thin metal tube, with six finger holes of varying size on top and no thumb holes.

ti·ny /ˈtīnē/ ▸*adj.* (**-ni·er**, **-ni·est**) very small: *a tiny hummingbird.* See note at **SMALL**. ▷late 16th cent.: extension of obsolete *tine* 'small, diminutive,' of unknown origin. **—ti·ni·ly** /-nəlē/ *adv.* **—ti·ni·ness** *n.*

-tion ▸*suffix* forming nouns of action, condition, etc., such as *completion, relation.* ▷from Latin participial stems ending in *-t* + **-ION**.

tip[1] /tip/ ▸*n.* the pointed or rounded end or extremity of something slender or tapering: *George pressed the tips of his fingers together* | *the northern tip of Maine.* ■ a small piece or part fitted to the end of an object: *the rubber tip of the walking stick.*
▸*v.* (**tipped**, **tip·ping**) [*trans.*] **1** [usu. as *adj.*] (**tipped**) attach to or cover the end or extremity of: *mountains tipped with snow* | [in *combination*] *steel-tipped spears.* ■ color (something) at its end or edge: *velvety red petals tipped with white.* **2** (**tip a page in**) (in bookbinding) paste a single page, typically an illustration, to the neighboring page of a book by a thin line of paste down its inner margin. ▷late Middle English: from Old Norse *typpi* (noun), *typpa* (verb), *typptr* 'tipped'; related to **TOP**[1].
▸*PHRASES* □ **on the tip of one's tongue** used to indicate that someone is almost but not quite able to bring a particular word or name to mind: *his name's on the tip of my tongue!* ■ used to indicate that someone is about to utter a comment or question but thinks better of it: *it was on the tip of his tongue to ask what was the matter.* □ **the tip of the iceberg** see **ICEBERG**.

tip[2] ▸*v.* (**tipped**, **tip·ping**) **1** overbalance or cause to overbalance so as to fall or turn over: [*intrans.*] *the hay caught fire when the candle **tipped over*** | [*trans.*] *a youth sprinted past, **tipping over** her glass.* ■ be or cause to be in a sloping position with one end or side higher than the other: [*trans.*] *I tipped my seat back, preparing myself for sleep* | [*intrans.*] *the car had tipped to one side.* **2** [*trans.*] strike or touch lightly: *I tipped his hoof with the handle of a knife.* ■ [*trans.*] cause (an object) to move somewhere by striking or touching it in this way: *the ball was tipped over the rim by Erving.* **3** [*intrans.*] (**tip off**) *Basketball* put the ball in play by throwing it up between two opponents.
▸*n.* **1** *Brit.* a place where trash is deposited; a dump. **2** *Baseball* a pitched ball that is slightly deflected by the bat. ▷late Middle English: perhaps of Scandinavian origin, influenced later by **TIP**[1] in the sense 'touch with a tip or point.' Current senses of the noun date from the mid 19th cent.
▸*PHRASES* □ **tip one's hand** *informal* reveal one's intentions inadvertently. □ **tip one's hat** (or **cap**) raise or touch one's hat or cap as a way of greeting or acknowledging someone. □ **tip the scales** (or **balance**) (of a circumstance or event) be the deciding factor; make the critical difference: *her proven current form **tips the scales** in her favor.* □ **tip the scales at** have a weight of (a specified amount): *this phone tips the scales at only 5 ounces.*

tip[3] ▸*n.* **1** a sum of money given to someone as a reward for their services. **2** a small but useful piece of practical advice. ■ a prediction or piece of expert information about the likely winner of a race or contest: *Barry had a **hot tip**.*
▸*v.* (**tipped**, **tip·ping**) [*trans.*] **1** give (someone) a sum of money as a way of rewarding them for their services: [with *two objs.*] *I tipped her five dollars* | [*intrans.*] *that sort of person never tips.* **2** (usu. **be tipped**) *Brit.* predict as likely to win or achieve something: *she was widely **tipped to** get the job.* ▷early 17th cent. (in the sense 'give, hand, pass'): probably from **TIP**[1].
▸*PHRASE* □ **tip someone off** *informal* give someone information about something, typically in a discreet or confidential way: *they were arrested after police were tipped off by local residents.*

tip·cat /ˈtipˌkat/ ▸*n. chiefly historical* a game in which a piece of wood tapered at both ends is struck at one end with a stick so as to spring up and is then knocked away by the same player. ■ a tapered piece of wood of this kind.

ti·pi ▸*n.* variant spelling of **TEPEE**.

tip-in ▸*n. Basketball* a score made by tipping a rebound into the basket.

tip-off (also **tip·off**) ▸*n.* **1** *informal* a piece of information, typically one given in a discreet or confidential way. **2** (usu. **tipoff**) a jump ball that begins each period in a basketball game (used esp. in reference to the first tipoff of the game): *the news of his injury came just two hours before tipoff.*

Tip·pe·ca·noe Riv·er /ˌtipikəˈno͞o/ a river that flows for 170 miles (275 km) through Indiana to join the Wabash River. Battle Ground, along the river, is the site of the 1811 Battle of Tippecanoe.

tip·per /ˈtipər/ ▸*n.* [usu. with *adj.*] a person who leaves a specified sort of tip as a reward for services they have received: *he's a big tipper.*

Tip·per·ar·y /ˌtipəˈre(ə)rē/ a county in the Republic of Ireland, in the central part of the country, in the province of Munster; county town, Clonmel.

tip·pet /ˈtipit/ ▸*n.* a woman's long cape or scarf, typically of fur or similar material. ■ a similar ceremonial garment worn esp. by the clergy. ■ *historical* a long, narrow strip of cloth forming part of or attached to a hood or sleeve. ▷Middle English: probably from an Anglo-Norman derivative of the noun **TIP**[1].

Tip·pett /ˈtipit/, Sir Michael (Kemp) (1905–98), English composer. He established his reputation with *A Child of Our Time* (1941), an oratorio that draws on jazz, madrigals, and spirituals as well as on classical sources.

tip·ping point ▸*n.* the point at which a series of small ineffective changes acquires enough pressure or importance to cause a larger, more significant change: *a kind of tipping point in society, where X number of criminal types gets the edge on Y number of honest citizens.* ■ the point at which the buildup of minor incidents reaches a level that causes someone to do something they had formerly resisted.

tip·ple[1] /ˈtipəl/ ▸*v.* [*intrans.*] drink alcohol, esp. habitually: *those who liked to tipple and gamble.*
▸*n. informal* an alcoholic drink. ▷late 15th cent. (in the sense 'sell (alcoholic drink) at retail'): back-formation from **TIPPLER**[1].

tip·ple[2] ▸*n.* a revolving frame or cage in which a truck or freight car is inverted to discharge its load. ■ a place where such loads, esp. from a coal mine, are dumped. ▷early 19th cent.: from dialect *tipple* 'tumble over.'

tip·pler[1] /ˈtip(ə)lər/ ▸*n.* a habitual drinker of alcohol. ▷late Middle English (denoting a retailer of alcoholic liquor): of unknown origin.

tip·pler[2] ▸*n.* a person who operates or works at a tipple, esp. at a mine.

tip·py /ˈtipē/ ▸*adj.* inclined to tilt or overturn; unsteady: *they crossed the water in tippy canoes.*

tip·py-toe ▸*v.* [*intrans.*] *informal* walk on the tips of one's toes; tiptoe: *he tippy-toed around the house.* ▷late 19th cent.: alteration of **TIPTOE**.
▸*PHRASE* □ **on tippy-toe** (or **tippy-toes**) on the tips of one's toes; on tiptoe: *Kurt was mincing around on tippy-toes.*

tip·staff /ˈtipˌstaf/ ▸*n.* a sheriff's officer; a bailiff. ▷mid 16th cent. (first denoting a metal-tipped staff): contraction of *tipped staff* (carried by a bailiff).

tip·ster /ˈtipstər/ ▸*n.* a person who gives tips, esp. about the likely winner of a race or contest, and esp. for a fee.

tip·sy /ˈtipsē/ ▸*adj.* (**-si·er**, **-si·est**) slightly drunk. See note at **DRUNK**. ▷late 16th cent.: from the verb **TIP**[2] + **-SY**. **—tip·si·ly** /-səlē/ *adv.* **—tip·si·ness** *n.*

tip·toe /ˈtipˌtō/ ▸*v.* (**-toes**, **-toed**, **-toe·ing**) [*intrans.*] walk quietly and carefully with one's heels raised and one's weight on the balls of the feet: *Liz tiptoed out of the room.*
▸*PHRASE* □ **on tiptoe** (or **tiptoes**) (also **on one's tiptoes**) with one's heels raised and one's weight on the balls of the feet, esp. in order to move quietly or make oneself taller: *Jane stood on tiptoe to kiss him* | *the children danced on their tiptoes.*

tip-top (also **tip·top**) ▸*adj.* of the very best class or quality; excellent: *an athlete in tip-top condition.*
▸*n.* **1** the highest part or point of excellence. **2** a line guide on a fishing rod.

tip-up ▸*n.* a device used in ice fishing in which a wire attached to the rod is tripped, raising a signal flag, when a fish takes the bait.

ti·rade /ˈtīˌrād; ˌtīˈrād/ ▸*n.* a long, angry speech of criticism or accusation: *a tirade of abuse.* ▷early 19th cent.: from French, literally 'long speech,' from Italian *tirata* 'volley,' from *tirare* 'to pull.'

tir·a·mi·su /ˌtirəmēˈso͞o; -ˈmēso͞o/ (also **tir·a·mi·sù**) ▸*n.* an Italian dessert consisting of layers of sponge cake soaked in coffee and brandy or liqueur with powdered chocolate and mascarpone cheese. ▷Italian, from the phrase *tira mi sù* 'pick me up.'

Ti·ra·na /tiˈränə/ (also **Ti·ra·në**) the capital of Albania, in the central part of the country, on the Ishm River; pop. 210,000.

tire[1] /tīr/ ▸*v.* [*intrans.*] become in need of rest or sleep; grow weary: *soon the ascent grew steeper and he began to tire.* ■ [*trans.*] cause to feel in need of rest or sleep; weary: *the journey had tired her* | *the training **tired us out**.* ■ (**tire of**) lose interest in; become bored with: *she will stay with him until he tires of her.* ■ [*trans.*] exhaust the patience or interest of; bore: *it tired her that Eddie felt important because he was involved behind the scenes.* ▷Old English *tēorian* 'fail, come to an end,' also 'become physically exhausted,' of unknown origin.

tire[2] (*Brit.* **tyre**) ▸*n.* a rubber covering, typically inflated or surrounding an inflated inner tube, placed around a wheel to form a flexible contact with the road. ■ a strengthening band of metal fitted around the rim of a wheel. ▷late 15th cent. (denoting the curved pieces of iron plate with which carriage wheels were formerly shod): perhaps a shortening of **ATTIRE** (because the tire was the "clothing" of the wheel).

tired /tīrd/ ▸*adj.* in need of sleep or rest; weary: *Fisher rubbed his tired eyes* | *she was **tired out** now that the strain was over.* ■ [*predic.*] (**tired of**) bored with: *I have to look after these animals when you get tired of them.* ■ (of a thing) no longer fresh or in good condition: *a few boxes of tired vegetables.* ■ (esp. of a statement or idea) boring or uninteresting because overfamiliar: *tired clichés like the "information revolution."* **—tired·ly** *adv.* **—tired·ness** *n.*

THE RIGHT WORD **exhausted, fatigued, tired, tuckered, weary**

Tired is what you are after you've cleaned the house, spent two hours reading a dull report, or trained for a marathon; it means that your strength and energy are diminished, without giving any indication of degree.

Weary, on the other hand, is how you feel after you've had to interrupt your dinner five or six times to answer the phone. It implies not only a depletion of energy but also the vexation that accompanies having to put up with something that is, or has become, disagreeable.

Exhausted means that you are totally drained of strength and energy, a condition that may even be irreversible (*exhausted by battling a terminal disease*).

Fatigued is a more precise word than either *tired* or *weary*; it implies a loss of energy through strain, illness, or overwork to the point where rest or sleep is essential (*fatigued after working a 24-hour shift*).

Tuckered is an informal word that comes close in meaning to *fatigued* or *exhausted*, but often carries the suggestion of loss of breath (*tuckered out after running up six flights of stairs*).

Ti·ree /tīˈrē/ an island in the Inner Hebrides, west of Mull and Coll.

tire gauge (*Brit.* **tyre gauge**) ▸*n.* a portable gauge for measuring the air pressure in a tire.

tire i·ron (*Brit.* **tyre i·ron**) ▸*n.* a steel lever for removing tires from wheel rims.

tire·less /ˈtīrlis/ ▸*adj.* having or showing great effort or energy: *a tireless campaigner.* **—tire·less·ly** *adv.* **—tire·less·ness** *n.*

Ti·re·si·as /tī'rēsēəs/ (also **Tei·re·si·as**) *Greek Mythology* a blind Theban prophet, so wise that even his ghost had its wits and was not a mere phantom. Legends account variously for his wisdom and blindness; some stories hold also that he spent seven years as a woman.

tire·some /'tīrsəm/ ▸*adj.* causing one to feel bored or annoyed: *weeding is a tiresome but essential job.* **—tire·some·ly** *adv.* [as *submodifier*] *a tiresomely predictable attitude.* **—tire·some·ness** *n.*

Tîr·gu Mu·reş /'tərgo͞o 'mo͞oresh; 'ti(ə)r-/ a city in central Romania, on the Mureş River; pop. 165,000.

Ti·rich Mir /'tirich 'mir/ the highest peak in the Hindu Kush, in northwestern Pakistan. It rises to 25,230 feet (7,690 m).

ti·ro ▸*n.* variant spelling of TYRO.

Tir·ol /tə'rōl; tī'rōl; 'tī,rōl/ German name for TYROL.

Tir·u·chi·ra·pal·li /,tirəchə'räpəlē/ a city in Tamil Nadu, southern India; pop. 387,000. Also called TRICHINOPOLY.

'tis /tiz/ *chiefly poetic/literary* ▸*contraction of* it is.

Ti·sa /'tēsä/ Serbian name for TISZA.

ti·sane /ti'zan; -'zän/ ▸*n.* an herbal tea, consumed esp. for its medicinal properties. ▷1930s: from French.

Tish·ri /'tishrē; -rā/ (also **Tis·ri** /'tiz-/) ▸*n.* (in the Jewish calendar) the first month of the civil and seventh of the religious year, usually coinciding with parts of September and October. ▷from Hebrew *tišrī.*

Ti·siph·o·ne /ti'sifənē/ *Greek Mythology* one of the Furies. ▷Greek, literally 'the avenger of blood.'

tis·sue /'tisho͞o/ ▸*n.* **1** any of the distinct types of material of which animals or plants are made, consisting of specialized cells and their products: *inflammation is a reaction of living tissue to infection or injury* | (**tissues**) *the organs and tissues of the body.* **2** tissue paper. ■ a disposable piece of absorbent paper, used esp. as a handkerchief or for cleaning the skin. ■ rich or fine material of a delicate or gauzy texture: [as *adj.*] *the blue and silver tissue sari.* **3** [in *sing.*] an intricate structure or network made from a number of connected items: *such scandalous stories are* ***a tissue of lies.*** ▷late Middle English: from Old French *tissu* 'woven,' past participle of *tistre,* from Latin *texere* 'to weave.' The word originally denoted a rich material, often interwoven with gold or silver threads, later (mid 16th cent.) any woven fabric, hence the notion of 'intricacy.' **—tis·su·ey** *adj.* (in sense 2).

tis·sue cul·ture ▸*n.* *Biology & Medicine* the growth in an artificial medium of cells derived from living tissue. ■ a cell culture of this kind.

tis·sue flu·id ▸*n.* *Physiology* extracellular fluid that bathes the cells of most tissues, arriving via blood capillaries and being removed via the lymphatic vessels.

tis·sue pa·per ▸*n.* thin, soft paper, typically used for wrapping or protecting fragile or delicate articles.

Ti·sza /'tis,ä/ a river in southeastern Europe, the longest tributary of the Danube River. It rises in the Carpathian Mountains of western Ukraine and flows west for 600 miles (960 km) into Hungary and then south to join the Danube River in Serbia northwest of Belgrade. Serbian name TISA.

tit[1] /tit/ ▸*n.* a titmouse. ■ used in names of similar or related birds, e.g., **New Zealand tit**. ▷mid 16th cent.: probably of Scandinavian origin and related to Icelandic *titlingur* 'sparrow'; compare with TITMOUSE. Earlier senses were 'small horse' and 'girl'; the current sense dates from the early 18th cent.

tit[2] ▸*n.* *vulgar slang chiefly N. Amer.* a woman's breast or nipple. ▷Old English *tit* 'teat, nipple,' of Germanic origin; related to Dutch *tit* and German *Zitze.* The vulgar slang use was originally U.S. and dates from the early 20th cent.

▸*PHRASES* □ **suck the hind tit** *informal* receive less of something than others who are competing for it. □ **tits and ass** *vulgar slang, chiefly N. Amer.* (or *chiefly Brit.* **tits and bums**) used in reference to the use of crudely sexual images of women.

tit[3] ▸*n.* (in phrase **tit for tat**) the infliction of an injury or insult in return for one that one has suffered: [as *adj.*] *the conflict staggered on with tit-for-tat assassinations.* ▷mid 16th cent.: variant of obsolete *tip for tap.*

Tit. ▸*abbr. Bible* Titus.

Ti·tan /'tītn/ **1** *Greek Mythology* any of the older gods who preceded the Olympians and were the children of Uranus (Heaven) and Gaia (Earth). Led by Cronus, they overthrew Uranus; Cronus' son, Zeus, then rebelled against his father and eventually defeated the Titans. ■ [as *n.*] (usu. **a titan**) a person or thing of very great strength, intellect, or importance: *a titan of American industry.* **2** *Astronomy* the largest satellite of Saturn, the fifteenth closest to the planet, discovered by C. Huygens in 1655, and having a diameter of 3,200 miles (5,150 km). It is unique in having a hazy atmosphere of nitrogen, and methane and other hydrocarbons.

ti·tan·ate /'tītn,āt/ ▸*n.* *Chemistry* a salt in which the anion contains both titanium and oxygen, in particular one of the anion TiO_3^{2-}. ▷mid 19th cent.: from TITANIUM + -ATE[1].

Ti·tan·ess /'tītn-is/ ▸*n.* a female Titan. ■ (**titaness**) a female person of very great strength, intellect, or importance.

Ti·ta·ni·a /ti'tānēə/ *Astronomy* the largest satellite of Uranus, the fourteenth closest to the planet, discovered by W. Herschel in 1787. It has an icy surface and a diameter 1,000 miles (1,610 km). ▷the name of the queen of the fairies in Shakespeare's *A Midsummer Night's Dream.*

Ti·tan·ic /tī'tanik/ a British passenger liner, the largest ship in the world when it was built and supposedly unsinkable, that struck an iceberg in the North Atlantic on its maiden voyage in April 1912 and sank with the loss of 1,490 lives.

ti·tan·ic[1] /tī'tanik/ ▸*adj.* of exceptional strength, size, or power: *a series of titanic explosions.* ▷mid 17th cent. (in the sense 'relating to the sun'): from Greek *titanikos,* from *Titan* (see TITAN). **—ti·tan·i·cal·ly** /-ik(ə)lē/ *adv.*

ti·tan·ic[2] ▸*adj.* *Chemistry* of titanium with a valence of four; of titanium(IV). Compare with TITANOUS. ▷early 19th cent.: from TITANIUM + -IC.

ti·tan·if·er·ous /,tītn'ifərəs/ ▸*adj.* (of rocks and minerals) containing or yielding titanium.

ti·tan·ite /'tītn,īt/ ▸*n.* another term for SPHENE. ▷late 18th cent.: from TITANIUM + -ITE[1].

ti·ta·ni·um /tī'tānēəm/ ▸*n.* the chemical element of atomic number 22, a hard silver-gray metal of the transition series, used in strong, light, corrosion-resistant alloys. (Symbol: **Ti**)

> One of the transition metals, titanium is a common element in the earth's crust; the main sources are the minerals ilmenite and rutile. Very large quantities of the dioxide are manufactured for use as a white pigment in paper, paint, etc.

▷late 18th cent.: from TITAN, on the pattern of *uranium.*

ti·ta·ni·um di·ox·ide (also **ti·ta·ni·um ox·ide**) ▸*n.* a white unreactive solid that occurs naturally as the mineral rutile and is used extensively as a white pigment. • Chem. formula: TiO_2.

ti·ta·ni·um white ▸*n.* a white pigment consisting chiefly or wholly of titanium dioxide.

ti·tan·ous /tī'tanəs/ ▸*adj.* *Chemistry* of titanium with a lower valence, usually three. Compare with TITANIC[2]. ▷mid 19th cent.: from TITANIUM, on the pattern of words such as *ferrous.*

tit·bit /'tit,bit/ ▸*n.* chiefly British spelling of TIDBIT.

ti·ter /'tītər/ (*Brit.* **ti·tre**) ▸*n.* *Chemistry* the concentration of a solution as determined by titration. ■ *Medicine* the concentration of an antibody, as determined by finding the highest dilution at which it is still able to cause agglutination of the antigen. ▷mid 19th cent.: from French *titre,* from *titrer* (see TITRATE).

tithe /tī<u>th</u>/ ▸*n.* one tenth of annual produce or earnings, formerly taken as a tax for the support of the church and clergy. ■ (in certain religious denominations) a tenth of an individual's income pledged to the church. ■ [in *sing.*] *archaic* a tenth of a specified thing: *he hadn't said* ***a tithe of*** *the prayers he knew.*

▸*v.* [*trans.*] pay or give as a tithe: *he tithes 10 percent of his income to the church.* ■ *historical* subject to a tax of one tenth of income or produce. ▷Old English *tēotha* (adjective in the ordinal sense 'tenth,' used in a specialized sense as a noun), *tēothian* (verb). **—tith·a·ble** *adj.*

tith·ing /'tī<u>th</u>iNG/ ▸*n.* **1** the practice of taking or paying a tithe. **2** *historical* (in England) a group of ten householders who lived close together and were collectively responsible for each other's behavior. ▷Old English *tēothung* (see TITHE, -ING[1]).

Ti·tho·nus /ti'thōnəs/ *Greek Mythology* a Trojan prince with whom the goddess Aurora fell in love. She asked Zeus to make him immortal but omitted to ask for eternal youth, and he became very old and decrepit although he talked perpetually. Tithonus begged her to remove him from this world, and she changed him into a grasshopper, which chirps ceaselessly.

ti·ti[1] /tē'tē/ (also **ti·ti mon·key**) ▸*n.* (*pl.* **-tis**) a small forest-dwelling monkey of South America. • Genus *Callicebus,* family Cebidae: several species. ▷mid 18th cent.: from Aymara.

ti·ti[2] /'tī,tī; 'tē,tē/ ▸*n.* (*pl.* **-tis**) a shrub or small tree with leathery leaves. • Family Cyrillaceae: three genera, esp. *Cyrilla* and *Cliftonia* of the coastal southeastern U.S., each of which contains a single species: *Cyrilla racemiflora* (**leatherwood**) and *Cliftonia monophylla* (**buckwheat tree** or **titi tree**). ▷early 19th cent.: perhaps of American Indian origin.

Ti·tian[1] /'tishən/ (*c.*1488–1576), Italian painter; Italian name *Tiziano Vecellio.* The most important painter of the Venetian school, he experimented with vivid colors and often broke conventions of composition. He painted many sensual mythological works, including *Bacchus and Ariadne* (*c.*1518–23).

Ti·tian[2] (also **ti·tian**) ▸*adj.* (of hair) bright golden auburn: *a mass of Titian curls.* ▷early 19th cent.: from TITIAN[1], by association with the bright auburn hair portrayed in many of his works.

Ti·ti·ca·ca, Lake /,titē'käkə/ a lake in the Andes, on the border between Peru and Bolivia. At an altitude of 12,497 feet (3,809 m), it is the highest large lake in the world.

tit·il·late /'titl,āt/ ▸*v.* [*trans.*] stimulate or excite (someone), esp. in a sexual way: *these journalists are paid to titillate the public* | [as *adj.*] (**titillating**) *she let slip titillating details about her clients.* ■ *archaic* lightly touch; tickle. ▷early 17th cent.: from Latin *titillat-* 'tickled,' from the verb *titillare.* **—tit·il·lat·ing·ly** *adv.* **—tit·il·la·tion** /,titl'āshən/ *n.*

tit·i·vate /'titə,vāt/ ▸*v.* [*trans.*] *informal* make small enhancing alterations to (something): *she slapped on her warpaint and titivated her hair.* ■ (**titivate oneself**) make oneself look attractive. ▷early 19th cent. (in early use, also as *tidivate*): perhaps from TIDY, on the pattern of *cultivate.* **—tit·i·va·tion** /,titə'vāshən/ *n.*

tit·lark /'tit,lärk/ ▸*n.* *dialect* a pipit.

ti·tle /'tītl/ ▸*n.* **1** the name of a book, composition, or other artistic work: *the author and title of the book.* ■ (usu. as **titles**) a caption or credit in a movie or broadcast. ■ a book, magazine, or newspaper considered as a publication: *the company publishes 400 titles a year.* **2** a name that describes someone's position or job: *Leese assumed the title of director general.* ■ a word such as *Senator* or *Dame* that is used before someone's name, or a form that is used instead of someone's name, to indicate high social or official rank: *he will inherit the title of Duke of Marlborough.* ■ a word such as *Mrs.* or *Dr.* that is used before someone's name to indicate their profession or marital status. ■ a descriptive or distinctive name that is earned or chosen: *Nata's deserved the title of Best Restaurant of the Year.* **3** the position of being the champion of a major sports competition: *Davis won the world title for the first time in 1981.* **4** *Law* a right or claim to the ownership of property or to a rank or throne: *a local family had* ***title to*** *the property* | *the buyer acquires a good title to the merchandise.* **5** (in church use) a fixed sphere of work and source of income as a condition for ordination. ■ a parish church in Rome under a cardinal.

▸*v.* [*trans.*] (usu. **be titled**) give a name to (a book, composition, or other work): *a song titled "You Rascal, You."* ▷Old English *titul,* reinforced by Old French *title,* both from Latin *titulus* 'inscription, title.' The word originally denoted a placard or inscription placed on an object, giving information about it, hence a descriptive heading in a book or other composition.

ti·tle bar ▸*n.* *Computing* a horizontal bar at the top of a window, bearing the name of the program and typically the name of the currently active document.

ti·tled /'tītld/ ▸*adj.* (of a person) having a title indicating high social or official rank.

ti·tle deed ▸*n.* a legal deed or document constituting evidence of a right, esp. to ownership of property.

ti·tle·hold·er /'tītl,hōldər/ (also **ti·tle hold·er**) ▸*n.* a person who holds a title, esp. a sports champion.

ti·tle page ▸*n.* a page at the beginning of a book giving its title, the names of the author and publisher, and other publication information.

ti·tle role ▸*n.* the part in a play, movie, television show, etc., from which the work's title is taken.

tit·mouse /'tit,mous/ ▸*n.* (*pl.* **-mice**) a small songbird that searches acrobatically for insects among foliage and branches. • Family Paridae: three genera, esp. *Parus,* and numerous species, including the

T

chickadees and the **tufted titmouse** (*P. bicolor*). ▷Middle English: from TIT[1] + obsolete *mose* 'titmouse.' The change in the ending in the 16th cent. was due to association with MOUSE, probably because of the bird's size and quick movements.

Ti·to /ˈtētō/ (1892–1980), Yugoslav marshal and statesman; prime minister 1945–53 and president 1953–80; born *Josip Broz*. He organized a communist resistance movement against the German invasion of Yugoslavia in 1941. He became head of the new government at the end of World War II and established Yugoslavia as a nonaligned communist state with a federal constitution.

Ti·to·grad /ˈtētōˌgrad; -ˌgräd/ former name (1946–93) for **Podgorica**.

ti·trate /ˈtīˌtrāt/ ▸*v.* [*trans.*] *Chemistry* ascertain the amount of a constituent in (a solution) by measuring the volume of a known concentration of reagent required to complete a reaction with it, typically using an indicator. ■ *Medicine* continuously measure and adjust the balance of (a physiological function or drug dosage). ▷late 19th cent.: from French *titrer* (from *titre* in the sense 'fineness of alloyed gold or silver') + -ATE[3]. **—ti·trat·a·ble** *adj.* **—ti·tra·tion** /ˌtīˈtrāSHən/ *n.*

ti·tre ▸*n.* British spelling of TITER.

tit·ter /ˈtitər/ ▸*v.* [*intrans.*] give a short, half-suppressed laugh; giggle: *her stutter caused the children to titter.*
▸*n.* a short, half-suppressed laugh. ▷early 17th cent.: imitative. **—tit·ter·er** *n.* **—tit·ter·ing·ly** *adv.*

tit·ti·vate ▸*v.* archaic spelling of TITIVATE.

tit·tle /ˈtitl/ ▸*n.* [in *sing.*] a tiny amount or part of something: *the rules have* **not** *been altered* **one jot or tittle** *since.* ■ *archaic* a small written or printed stroke or dot, indicating omitted letters in a word. ▷late Middle English: from Latin *titulus* (see TITLE), in medieval Latin 'small stroke, accent'; the phrase *jot or tittle* is from Matt. 5:18.

tit·tle-tat·tle ▸*n.* idle talk; gossip.
▸*v.* [*intrans.*] engage in such talk. ▷early 16th cent.: reduplication of TATTLE.

tit·tup /ˈtitəp/ ▸*v.* (**-tuped**, **-tup·ing** or **-tupped**, **-tup·ping**) [*intrans.*] *chiefly Brit.* move with jerky or exaggerated movements: *Nicky came tittupping along in a rakish mood.* ▷late 17th cent. (as a noun): perhaps imitative of hoofbeats.

tit·ty /ˈtitē/ (also **tit·tie**) ▸*n.* (*pl.* **-ties**) another term for TIT[2].

tit·u·ba·tion /ˌtiCHəˈbāSHən/ ▸*n.* *Medicine* nodding movement of the head or body, esp. as caused by a nervous disorder. ▷mid 17th cent.: from Latin *titubatio(n-)*, from *titubare* 'to totter.'

tit·u·lar /ˈtiCHələr/ ▸*adj.* **1** holding or constituting a purely formal position or title without any real authority: *the queen is titular head of the Church of England* | *a titular post.* ■ [*attrib.*] (of a cleric) nominally appointed to serve a diocese, abbey, or other foundation no longer in existence, and typically in fact having authority in another capacity. **2** denoting a person or thing from whom or which the name of an artistic work or similar is taken: *the work's titular song.* ■ [*attrib.*] denoting any of the parish churches in Rome to which cardinals are formally appointed: *the priests of the titular churches.* ▷late 16th cent. (in the sense 'existing only in name'): from French *titulaire* or modern Latin *titularis*, from *titulus* (see TITLE).

tit·u·lar·ly /ˈtiCHələrlē/ ▸*adv.* in name or in name only: *he was titularly a chief petty officer.*

Ti·tus[1] /ˈtītəs/ (AD 39–81), Roman emperor 79–81; son of Vespasian; full name *Titus Vespasianus Augustus*; born *Titus Flavius Vespasianus*. In 70, he ended a revolt in Judaea with the conquest of Jerusalem.

Ti·tus[2] a book of the New Testament, an epistle of St. Paul addressed to St. Titus.

Ti·tus, St. (1st century AD), Greek churchman. A convert and St. Paul's helper, he was traditionally the first bishop of Crete. Feast day (Eastern Church) August 23; (Western Church) February 6.

Ti·tus·ville /ˈtītəsˌvil/ **1** a commercial and resort city in east central Florida, near Cape Canaveral; pop. 39,394. **2** a historic city in northwestern Pennsylvania, on Oil Creek, site of the first operative oil well (1859); pop. 6,434.

Tiv /tiv/ ▸*n.* (*pl.* same or **Tivs**) **1** a member of a people of southeastern Nigeria. **2** the Benue-Congo language of this people.
▸*adj.* of or relating to this people or their language. ▷the name in Tiv.

Ti·wa /ˈtēwə/ ▸*n.* (*pl.* same or **-was**) **1** a member of a Pueblo Indian people living mainly in the region of Taos, New Mexico. **2** the Tanoan language of this people. Do not confuse with **Tewa**.
▸*adj.* of or relating to this people or their language. ▷from Spanish *Tigua*, from a Tanoan name like the Southern Tiwa self-designation *tiwáde*.

ti·yin /tēˈ(y)in/ ▸*n.* (*pl.* same or **-yins**) a monetary unit of Kyrgyzstan, equal to one hundredth of a som.

tiz·zy /ˈtizē/ ▸*n.* (*pl.* **-zies**) [in *sing.*] *informal* a state of nervous excitement or agitation: *he got* **into a tizzy** *and was talking absolute nonsense.* ▷1930s (originally U.S.): of unknown origin.

tk. ▸*abbr.* ■ tank. ■ truck.

TKO *Boxing* ▸*abbr.* technical knockout.

tkt. ▸*abbr.* ticket.

Tl ▸*symbol* the chemical element thallium.

t.l. ▸*abbr.* (in the insurance industry) total loss.

TLA ▸*abbr.* three-letter acronym.

Tlax·ca·la /tläˈskälə/ a state in eastern central Mexico.

TLC *informal* ▸*abbr.* tender loving care.

Tlem·cen /tlemˈsen/ a city in northwestern Algeria; pop. 146,000.

Tlin·git /ˈtliNG(g)it/ ▸*n.* (*pl.* same or **-gits**) **1** a member of an American Indian people of the coasts and islands of southeastern Alaska and adjacent British Columbia. **2** the Na-Dene language of this people.
▸*adj.* of or relating to this people or their language. ▷the name in Tlingit.

t.l.o. ▸*abbr.* (in the insurance industry) total loss only.

tlr. ▸*abbr.* tailor.

T lym·pho·cyte (also **T-lym·pho·cyte**) ▸*n.* another term for **T cell**.

TM *trademark* ▸*abbr.* Transcendental Meditation.

Tm ▸*symbol* the chemical element thulium.

t.m. ▸*abbr.* true mean.

tme·sis /təˈmēsis/ ▸*n.* (*pl.* **-ses** /-sēz/) the separation of parts of a compound word by an intervening word or words, heard mainly in informal speech (e.g., *a whole nother story; shove it back any-old-where in the pile*). ▷mid 16th cent.: from Greek *tmēsis* 'cutting,' from *temnein* 'to cut.'

TMJ ▸*abbr.* temporormandibular joint.

TN ▸*abbr.* ■ Tennessee (in official postal use).

tn ▸*abbr.* ■ ton(s). ■ town. ■ train.

tng. ▸*abbr.* training.

tnpk. ▸*abbr.* turnpike.

TNT ▸*n.* a high explosive formed from toluene by substitution of nitro groups for three hydrogen atoms. It is relatively insensitive to shock and can be conveniently melted. • Alternative name: **trinitrotoluene**; chem. formula: $C_7H_5(NO_2)_3$.

to /to͞o/ ▸*prep.* **1** expressing motion in the direction of (a particular location): *walking down to the mall* | *my first visit to Africa.* ■ expressing location, typically in relation to a specified point of reference: *forty miles to the south of the site* | *place the cursor to the left of the first word.* ■ expressing a point reached at the end of a range or after a period of time: *a drop in profits from $105 million to around $75 million* | *from 1938 to 1945.* ■ (in telling the time) before (the hour specified): *it's five to ten.* ■ approaching or reaching (a particular condition): *Christopher's expression changed from amazement to joy* | *she was close to tears.* ■ expressing the result of a process or action: *smashed to smithereens.* **2** identifying the person or thing affected: *you were terribly unkind to her.* ■ identifying the recipient or intended recipient of something: *he wrote a heart-rending letter to the parents* | *I am deeply grateful to my parents.* **3** identifying a particular relationship between one person and another: *he is married to Jan's cousin* | *economic adviser to the president.* ■ in various phrases indicating how something is related to something else (often followed by a noun without a determiner): *made to order* | *a prelude to disaster.* ■ indicating a rate of return on something, e.g., the distance traveled in exchange for fuel used, or an exchange rate that can be obtained in one currency for another: *it only does ten miles to the gallon.* ■ (**to the**) *Mathematics* indicating the power (exponent) to which a number is raised: *ten to the minus thirty-three.* **4** indicating that two things are attached: *he had left his bike chained to a fence* | *figurative they are inextricably linked to this island.* **5** concerning or likely to concern (something, esp. something abstract): *a threat to world peace* | *a reference to Psalm 22:18.* **6** governing a phrase expressing someone's reaction to something: *to her astonishment, he smiled.* **7** used to introduce the second element in a comparison: *it's nothing to what it once was.*
▸*infinitive marker* **1** used with the base form of a verb to indicate that the verb is in the infinitive, in particular: ■ expressing purpose or intention: *I set out to buy food* | *we tried to help* | *I am* **going to** *tell you a story.* ■ expressing an outcome, result, or consequence: *he was left to die* | *he managed to escape.* ■ expressing a cause: *I'm sorry to hear that.* ■ indicating a desired or advisable action: *I'd love to go to France this summer* | *we asked her to explain* | *the leaflet explains how to start a recycling program.* ■ indicating a proposition that is known, believed, or reported about a specified person or thing: *a house that people believed to be haunted.* ■ (**about to**) forming a future tense with reference to the immediate future: *he was about to sing.* ■ after a noun, indicating its function or purpose: *a chair to sit on* | *something to eat.* ■ after a phrase containing an ordinal number: *the first person to arrive.* **2** used without a verb following when the missing verb is clearly understood: *he asked her to come but she said she didn't want to.*
▸*adv.* so as to be closed or nearly closed: *he pulled the door to behind him.* ▷Old English *tō* (adverb and preposition); related to Dutch *toe* and German *zu*.

t.o. ▸*abbr.* ■ turnover. ■ turn over.

toad /tōd/ ▸*n.* **1** a tailless amphibian with a short stout body and short legs, typically having dry warty skin that can exude poison. • Several families in the order Anura, in particular Bufonidae, which includes the **common toad** (*Bufo bufo*). **2** a contemptible or detestable person (used as a general term of abuse): *you're an arrogant little toad.* ▷Old English *tādde*, *tāda*, abbreviation of *tādige*, of unknown origin. **—toad·ish** *adj.*

toad·fish /ˈtōdˌfiSH/ ▸*n.* (*pl.* same or **-fish·es**) any of a number of fishes with a wide flattened head: • a chiefly bottom-dwelling large-mouthed fish of warm seas that can produce loud grunts (family Batrachoididae: several genera).

toad·flax /ˈtōdˌflaks/ ▸*n.* a Eurasian plant of the figwort family, typically having yellow or purplish snapdragonlike flowers and slender leaves. • *Linaria* and related genera, family Scrophulariaceae: several species, in particular **butter-and-eggs** (*L. vulgaris*), with yellow and orange flowers and found widely as a naturalized North American weed.

toad-in-the-hole ▸*n.* *Brit.* a dish consisting of sausages baked in batter.

toad·stone /ˈtōdˌstōn/ ▸*n.* a gem, fossil tooth, or other stone formerly supposed to have been formed in the body of a toad, and credited with therapeutic or protective properties.

toad·stool /ˈtōdˌsto͞ol/ ▸*n.* the spore-bearing fruiting body of a fungus, typically in the form of a rounded cap on a stalk, esp. one that is believed to be inedible or poisonous. See also MUSHROOM. ▷late Middle English: a fanciful name.

toad·y /ˈtōdē/ ▸*n.* (*pl.* **toad·ies**) a person who behaves obsequiously to someone important.
▸*v.* (**toad·ies**, **toad·ied**) [*intrans.*] act in an obsequious way: *she imagined him* **toadying to** *his rich clients.* ▷early 19th cent.: said to be a contraction of *toad-eater*, a charlatan's assistant who ate toads; toads were regarded as poisonous, and the assistant's survival was thought to be due to the efficacy of the charlatan's remedy. **—toad·y·ish** *adj.* **—toad·y·ism** /-ˌizəm/ *n.*

to and fro (also **to-and-fro**) ▸*adv.* in a constant movement backward and forward or from side to side: *she cradled him, rocking him to and fro.*
▸*v.* [*intrans.*] (**be toing and froing**) move constantly backward and forward: *the ducks were toing and froing.* ■ repeatedly discuss or think about something without making any progress.
▸*n.* [in *sing.*] constant movement backward and forward: *Wilkie watched the to and fro of their dancing.* ■ constant change in action, attitude, or focus.

toast[1] /tōst/ ▸*n.* **1** sliced bread browned on both sides by exposure to radiant heat. **2** a call to a gathering of people to raise their glasses and drink together in honor of a person or thing, or an instance of drinking in this way: *he raised his glass in a toast to his son.* ■ [in *sing.*] a person or thing that is very popular or held in high regard by a particular group of people: *he found himself* **the toast of** *the baseball world.*
▸*v.* [*trans.*] **1** cook or brown (food, esp. bread or cheese) by exposure to a grill, fire, or other source of radiant heat: *he sat by the fire and toasted a piece of bread* | [as *adj.*] (**toasted**) *toasted marshmallows.* ■ [*intrans.*] (of food) cook or become brown in this way: *broil until the nuts have toasted.* ■ warm (oneself or part of one's body) in front of a fire or other source of heat. **2** drink to the health or in honor of (someone or something) by raising one's glass together with

others: *happy families toasting each other's health | figurative he is toasted by the trade as the outstanding dealer in children's books.* ▷late Middle English (as a verb in the sense 'burn as the sun does, parch'): from Old French *toster* 'roast,' from Latin *torrere* 'parch.' The practice of drinking a toast (sense 2) goes back to the late 17th cent., and originated in naming a lady whose health the company was requested to drink, the idea being that the lady's name flavored the drink like the pieces of spiced toast that were formerly placed in drinks such as wine.

▸*PHRASE* □ **be toast** *informal* be or be likely to become finished, defunct, or dead: *one mistake and you're toast.*

toast[2] ▸*v.* [*intrans.*] [usu. as *n.*] (**toasting**) (of a DJ) accompany a reggae backing track or music with improvised rhythmic speech. ▷late 20th cent.: perhaps the same word as TOAST[1]. —**toast·er** *n.*

toast·er /ˈtōstər/ ▸*n.* an electrical device for making toast.

toast·mas·ter /ˈtōs(t),mastər/ ▸*n.* an official responsible for proposing toasts, introducing speakers, and making other formal announcements at a large social event.

toast·mis·tress /ˈtōs(t),mistris/ ▸*n.* a female toastmaster.

toast·y /ˈtōstē/ ▸*adj.* of or resembling toast. ■ comfortably warm: *a roaring fire may make a home seem toasty.*

Tob. ▸*abbr.* (in biblical references) Tobit (Apocrypha).

to·bac·co /təˈbakō/ ▸*n.* (*pl.* **-cos**) **1** a preparation of the nicotine-rich leaves of an American plant, which are cured by a process of drying and fermentation for smoking or chewing. **2** (also **tobacco plant**) the plant of the nightshade family that yields these leaves, native to tropical America. It is widely cultivated in warm regions, esp. in the U.S. and China. • *Nicotiana tabacum*, family Solanaceae. See also NICOTIANA. ▷mid 16th cent.: from Spanish *tabaco.*

to·bac·co mo·sa·ic vi·rus ▸*n.* a virus that causes mosaic disease in tobacco, much used in biochemical research.

to·bac·co·nist /təˈbakənist/ ▸*n.* a dealer in cigarettes, tobacco, cigars, and other items used by smokers.

to·bac·co plant ▸*n.* the plant that yields tobacco. See TOBACCO (sense 2). ■ an ornamental plant related to this. See NICOTIANA.

To·ba·go /təˈbāgō/ see TRINIDAD AND TOBAGO.

To·bit /ˈtōbət/ a pious Israelite living during the Babylonian Captivity, described in the Apocrypha. ■ a book of the Apocrypha telling the story of Tobit.

to·bog·gan /təˈbägən/ ▸*n.* a long narrow sled used for the sport of coasting downhill over snow or ice. It typically is made of a lightweight board that is curved upward and backward at the front.

▸*v.* [*intrans.*] [usu. as *n.*] (**tobogganing**) ride on a toboggan: *he thought he would enjoy the tobogganing.* ▷early 19th cent.: from Canadian French *tabaganne*, from Micmac *topagan* 'sled.' —**to·bog·gan·er** *n.* —**to·bog·gan·ist** /-nist/ *n.*

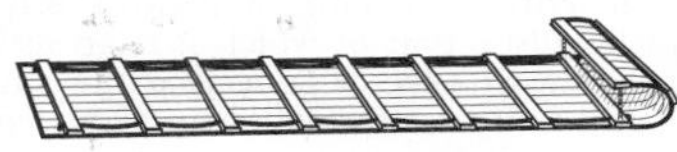

toboggan

to·bra·my·cin /,tōbrəˈmīsin/ ▸*n.* *Medicine* a bacterial antibiotic used chiefly to treat pseudomonas infections. • The drug is obtained from the bacterium *Streptomyces tenebrarius.* ▷1970s: from *to-* (of unknown origin) + Latin *(tene)bra(rius)* 'belonging to darkness' (part of the name of the bacterium) + -MYCIN.

To·bruk /təˈbro͝ok; ˈtō,bro͝ok/ a port on the Mediterranean coast of northeastern Libya; pop. 94,000. It was the scene of fierce fighting during the North African campaign in World War II. Arabic name TUBRUQ.

To·by jug /ˈtōbē/ (also **to·by jug**) ▸*n.* a beer jug or mug in the form of a stout old man wearing a three-cornered hat. ▷mid 19th cent.: nickname for the given name *Tobias*, and said to come from an 18th-cent. poem about *Toby Philpot* (with a pun on *fill pot*), a soldier who liked to drink.

To·can·tins /,tōkənˈtēns/ a river in South America that rises in central Brazil and flows 1,640 miles (2,640 km) north, joining the Pará River to enter the Atlantic Ocean through a large estuary at Belém.

toc·ca·ta /təˈkätə/ ▸*n.* a musical composition for a keyboard instrument designed to exhibit the performer's touch and technique. ▷early 18th cent.: from Italian, feminine past participle of *toccare* 'to touch.'

To·char·i·an /tōˈke(ə)rēən; -ˈkär-/ ▸*n.* **1** a member of a central Asian people who inhabited the Tarim Basin in the 1st millennium AD. **2** ■ either of two extinct languages (**Tocharian A** and **Tocharian B**) spoken by this people, the most easterly of known ancient Indo-European languages, surviving in a few documents and inscriptions and showing affinities to Celtic and Italic languages.

▸*adj.* of or relating to this people or their language. ▷from French *tocharien*, via Latin from Greek *Tokharoi*, the name of a Scythian tribe (almost certainly unrelated to the Tocharians).

to·co /ˈtōkō/ (also **to·co tou·can**) ▸*n.* (*pl.* **-cos**) the largest and most familiar South American toucan, with mainly black plumage, a white throat and breast, and a massive black-tipped orange bill. • *Ramphastos toco*, family Ramphastidae. ▷late 18th cent.: via Portuguese from Tupi; compare with TOUCAN.

toco

to·coph·er·ol /təˈkäfə,rôl; -,räl/ ▸*n.* *Biochemistry* any of several closely related compounds, found in wheat germ oil, egg yolk, and leafy vegetables, that collectively constitute vitamin E. They are fat-soluble alcohols with antioxidant properties, important in the stabilization of cell membranes. ▷1930s: from Greek *tokos* 'offspring' + *pherein* 'to bear' + -OL.

Tocque·ville /ˈtōk,vil/, Alexis de, (1805–59) French politician and historian; full name *Alexis Charles Henri Maurice Clérel de Tocqueville.* He is best known for his classic work of political analysis, *Democracy in America* (1835–40), which he wrote after a visit to the U.S. to study the American penal system.

toc·sin /ˈtäksən/ ▸*n.* an alarm bell or signal. ▷late 16th cent.: from Old French *toquassen*, from Provençal *tocasenh*, from *tocar* 'to touch' + *senh* 'signal bell.'

tod /täd/ ▸*n.* a bushy mass of foliage, esp. ivy.

to·day /təˈdā/ ▸*adv.* on or in the course of this present day: *she's thirty today | he will appear in court today.* ■ at the present period of time; nowadays: *millions of people today cannot afford adequate housing.*

▸*n.* this present day: *today is a day of rest | today's game against the Blue Jays.* ■ the present period of time: *the powerful computers of today | today's society.* ▷Old English *tō dæg* 'on (this) day.' Compare with TOMORROW and TONIGHT.

Todd /täd/, Thomas (1765–1826) U.S. Supreme Court associate justice 1807–26. Appointed to the Court by President Jefferson, he was noted for his expertise in land law.

tod·dle /ˈtädl/ ▸*v.* [*intrans.*] (of a young child) move with short unsteady steps while learning to walk: *William toddled curiously toward the TV crew.* ■ *informal* walk or go somewhere in a casual or leisurely way: *they would go for a drink and then toddle off home.*

▸*n.* [in *sing.*] a young child's unsteady walk. ▷late 16th cent.: of unknown origin.

tod·dler /ˈtädlər/ ▸*n.* a young child who is just beginning to walk. —**tod·dler·hood** /-,ho͝od/ *n.*

tod·dy /ˈtädē/ ▸*n.* (*pl.* **-dies**) **1** a drink made of alcoholic liquor with hot water, sugar, and sometimes spices. **2** the sap of some kinds of palm, fermented to produce arrack. ▷early 17th cent. (sense 2): from Marathi *tāḍī*, Hindi *tāṛī*, from Sanskrit *tāḍī* 'palmyra.'

to-do /tə ˈdo͞o/ ▸*n.* [in *sing.*] *informal* a commotion or fuss: *he ignored the to-do in the hall.* ▷late 16th cent.: from *to do* as in *much to do*, originally meaning 'much needing to be done' but later interpreted as the adjective *much* and a noun; compare with ADO.

to·dy /ˈtōdē/ ▸*n.* (*pl.* **-dies**) a small insectivorous Caribbean bird related to the motmots, with a large head, long bill, bright green upper parts, and a red throat. • Family Todidae and genus *Todus*: five species. ▷late 18th cent.: from French *todier*, from Latin *todus*, the name of a small bird.

toe /tō/ ▸*n.* **1** any of the five digits at the end of the human foot: *he cut his big toe on a sharp stone.* ■ any of the digits of the foot of a quadruped or bird. ■ the part of an item of footwear that covers a person's toes. **2** the lower end, tip, or point of something, in particular: ■ the tip of the head of a golf club, furthest from the shaft. ■ the foot or base of a cliff, slope, or embankment. ■ a flattish portion at the foot of an otherwise steep curve on a graph. ■ a section of a rhizome or similar fleshy root from which a new plant may be propagated.

▸*v.* (**toes, toed, toe·ing**) **1** [*trans.*] push, touch, or kick (something) with one's toe: *he* **toed off** *his shoes and flexed his feet.* ■ *Golf* strike (the ball) with the toe of the club. **2** [*intrans.*] (**toe in/out**) walk with the toes pointed in (or out): *he toes out when he walks.* ■ (of a pair of wheels) converge (or diverge) slightly at the front: *on a turn, the inner wheel toes out more.* ▷Old English *tā*, of Germanic origin; related to Dutch *tee* and German *Zeh, Zehe.* Current senses of the verb date from the mid 19th cent. —**toed** *adj.* [in *combination*] *three-toed feet.* —**toe·less** *adj.*

▸*PHRASES* □ **make someone's toes curl** *informal* bring about an extreme reaction in someone, either of pleasure or of disgust. □ **on one's toes** ready for any eventuality; alert: *he carries out random spot checks to keep everyone on their toes.* □ **toe the line** accept the authority, principles, or policies of a particular group, esp. under pressure. [from the literal sense 'stand with the tips of the toes exactly touching a line.'] □ **toe to toe** (of two people) standing directly in front of one another, esp. in order to fight or argue.

toe·a /ˈtoi-ə/ ▸*n.* (*pl.* same) a monetary unit of Papua New Guinea, equal to one hundredth of a kina. ▷Motu, a Melanesian language, literally 'cone-shaped shell.'

toe cap (also **toe·cap**) ▸*n.* a piece of steel or leather constituting or fitted over the front part of a boot or shoe as protection or reinforcement.

toe clip ▸*n.* a clip on a bicycle pedal to prevent the foot from slipping.

toe·hold /ˈtō,hōld/ ▸*n.* a small place where a person's foot can be lodged to support them, esp. while climbing. ■ a relatively insignificant position from which further progress may be made: *the initiative is helping companies to gain a toehold in the Gulf.* ■ *Wrestling* a hold in which the opponent's toe is seized and the leg forced backward.

toe-in ▸*n.* a slight forward convergence of a pair of wheels so that they are closer together in front than behind.

toe loop ▸*n.* *Figure Skating* a jump, initiated with the help of the supporting foot, in which the skater makes a full turn in the air, taking off from and landing on the outside edge of the same foot.

toe·nail /ˈtō,nāl/ ▸*n.* **1** the nail at the tip of each toe. **2** a nail driven obliquely through a piece of wood to secure it.

▸*v.* [*trans.*] fasten (a piece of wood) in this way.

toe-out ▸*n.* a slight forward divergence of a pair of wheels so that they are closer together behind than in front.

toe-tap·ping ▸*adj.* *informal* (of music) making one want to tap one's feet; lively.

toff /täf/ *Brit., informal, derogatory* ▸*n.* a rich or upper-class person. ▷mid 19th cent.: perhaps an alteration of TUFT, used to denote a gold tassel worn on the cap by titled undergraduates at Oxford and Cambridge.

tof·fee /ˈtôfē; ˈtäfē/ ▸*n.* (*pl.* **-fees**) a kind of firm or hard candy that softens when sucked or chewed, made by boiling together sugar and butter, often with other ingredients or flavorings added. ■ a small shaped piece of such candy. ▷early 19th cent.: alteration of TAFFY.

tof·fee-nosed ▸*adj.* *informal, chiefly Brit.* pretentiously superior; snobbish. —**tof·fee nose** *n.*

Toff·ler /ˈtôflər/, Alvin, (1928–) U.S. futurist and writer. He first gained popularity with the publication of *Future Shock* (1970). *The Third Wave* (1980), and *Powershift* (1991) followed.

to·fu /ˈtōfo͞o/ ▸*n.* curd made from mashed soybeans, used chiefly in Asian and vegetarian cooking. ▷from Japanese *tōfu*, from Chinese *dòufu*, from *dòu* 'beans' + *fǔ* 'rot, turn sour.'

tog /täg/ *informal* ▸*n.* (**togs**) clothes: *running togs.*

▸*v.* (**togged, tog·ging**) (**be/get togged up/out**) be or get dressed for a particular occasion or activity: *we got togged up in our glad rags.* ▷early 18th cent. (as a slang term for a coat or outer garment): apparently an abbreviation of obsolete criminals' slang *togeman(s)* 'a light cloak,' from French *toge* or Latin *toga* (see TOGA).

to·ga /ˈtōgə/ ▸*n.* a loose flowing outer garment worn by the citizens of ancient Rome, made of a single piece of cloth and covering the whole body apart from the right arm. ■ a robe of office; a mantle of responsibility, etc. ▷Latin; related to *tegere* 'to cover.'

toga

to·geth·er /təˈgeT͟Hər/ ▸*adv.* **1** with or in proximity to another person or people: *together they climbed the dark stairs | they stood together in the kitchen.* ■ so as to touch or combine: *she held her hands together as if she were praying | pieces of wood nailed together.* ■ in combination; collectively: *taken together, these measures would significantly improve people's chances of surviving a tornado.* ■ into companionship or close association: *the experience has brought us together.* ■ (of two people) married or in a sexual relationship with each other: *they split up after ten years together.* ■ so as to be united or in agreement: *he won the confidence of the government and the rebels, but could not bring the two sides together.* **2** at the same time: *they both spoke together.* **3** without interruption; continuously: *she sits for hours together in the lotus position.*
▸*adj. informal* self-confident, level-headed, or well organized: *she seems a very together young woman.* ▷Old English *tōgædere*, based on the preposition TO + a West Germanic word related to GATHER. The adjective dates from the 1960s.
▸*PHRASE* □ **together with** as well as; along with: *their meal arrived, together with a carafe of red wine.*

to·geth·er·ness /təˈgeT͟Hərnəs/ ▸*n.* the state of being close to another person or other people: *the sense of family togetherness was strong and excluded neighbors.*

tog·ger·y /ˈtägərē/ ▸*n. informal, humorous* clothes.

tog·gle /ˈtägəl/ ▸*n.* **1** a short rod of wood or plastic sewn to one side of a coat or other garment, pushed through a hole or loop on the other side and twisted so as to act as a fastener. ■ a pin or other crosspiece put through the eye of a rope or a link of a chain to keep it in place. ■ (also **toggle bolt**) a kind of wall fastener for use on hollow walls, having a part that springs open or turns through 90° after it is inserted so as to prevent withdrawal. ■ a movable pivoted crosspiece acting as a barb on a harpoon. **2** (also **toggle switch** or **toggle key**) *Computing* a key or command that is operated the same way but with opposite effect on successive occasions.

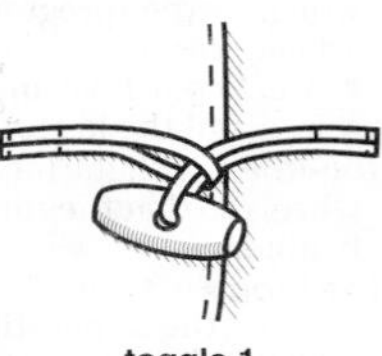

toggle 1

▸*v.* **1** [*intrans.*] *Computing* switch from one effect, feature, or state to another by using a toggle. **2** [*trans.*] provide or fasten with a toggle or toggles. ▷mid 18th cent. (originally in nautical use): of unknown origin.

tog·gle switch ▸*n.* **1** an electric switch operated by means of a projecting lever that is moved up and down. **2** *Computing* another term for TOGGLE.

To·gliat·ti /tôlˈyätē; täl-/ an industrial city and river port in southwestern Russia, on the Volga River; pop. 642,000. Former name (until 1964) **STAVROPOL**. Russian name **TOLYATTI**. ▷renamed in 1964 after Palmiro *Togliatti* (1893–1964), leader of the Italian Communist Party.

To·go /ˈtōgō/ a country in West Africa with a short coastline on the Gulf of Guinea; pop. 5,556,000; capital, Lomé; languages, French (official) and West African languages. Official name **TOGOLESE REPUBLIC**. **—To·go·lese** /ˌtōgōˈlēz; ˌtōgə-; -ˈlēs/ *adj. & n.*

The region formerly known as Togoland lay between the military powers of Ashanti and Dahomey and became a center of the slave trade. It was annexed by Germany in 1884 and divided between France and Britain after World War I. The western, British section joined Ghana when the latter became independent in 1957. The remainder, administered by France under a United Nations mandate after World War II, became an independent republic called Togo in 1960.

to·hu·bo·hu /ˈtōhōōˈbōhōō/ ▸*n. informal* a state of chaos; utter confusion: *a fearful tohubohu.* ▷from Hebrew *tōhū wa-ḇōhū* 'emptiness and desolation,' translated in Gen. 1:2 (Bible of 1611) as 'without form and void.'

toil /toil/ ▸*v.* [*intrans.*] work extremely hard or incessantly: *we toiled away* | [with *infinitive*] *Richard toiled to build his editorial team.* See note at LABOR. ■ [with *adverbial of direction*] move slowly and with difficulty: *she began to toil up the cliff path.*
▸*n.* exhausting physical labor: *a life of toil.* ▷Middle English (in the senses 'contend verbally' and 'strife'): from Anglo-Norman French *toiler* 'strive, dispute,' *toil* 'confusion,' from Latin *tudiculare* 'stir around,' from *tudicula* 'machine for crushing olives,' related to *tundere* 'crush.' **—toil·er** *n.*

toile /twäl/ ▸*n.* **1** an early version of a finished garment made up in cheap material so that the design can be tested and perfected. **2** a translucent linen or cotton fabric, used for making clothes. ■ short for TOILE DE JOUY. ▷late Middle English (denoting cloth or canvas for painting on): from French *toile* 'cloth, web,' from Latin *tela* 'web.'

toile de Jouy /ˌtwäl də ˈZHwē/ ▸*n.* a type of printed calico with a characteristic floral, figure, or landscape design on a light background, typically used for upholstery or curtains. ▷originally made at *Jouy*-en-Josas, near Paris.

toi·let /ˈtoilit/ ▸*n.* **1** a large bowl for urinating or defecating into, typically plumbed into a sewage system and with a flushing mechanism: *Liz heard the toilet flush* | *figurative my tenure was* **down the toilet**. ■ a room, building, or cubicle containing one or more of these. **2** [in *sing.*] the process of washing oneself, dressing, and attending to one's appearance: *her toilet completed, she finally went back downstairs.* ■ [as *adj.*] denoting articles used in this process: *a bathroom cabinet stocked with toilet articles.* ■ the cleansing of part of a person's body as a medical procedure.
▸*v.* (**-let·ed, -let·ing**) [*trans.*] [usu. as *n.*] (**toileting**) assist or supervise (someone, esp. an infant or invalid) in using a toilet. ▷mid 16th cent.: from French *toilette* 'cloth, wrapper,' diminutive of *toile* (see TOILE). The word originally denoted a cloth used as a wrapper for clothes; then (in the 17th cent.) a cloth cover for a dressing table, the articles used in dressing, and the process of dressing, later also of washing oneself (sense 2). In the 19th cent. the word came to denote a dressing room, and, in the U.S., one with washing facilities; hence, a lavatory (early 20th cent.).

toi·let pa·per ▸*n.* paper in sheets or on a roll for wiping oneself clean after urination or defecation.
▸*v.* [*trans.*] (also **t.p.** or **TP**) drape or wind toilet paper around (something) as a prank: *we were toilet papering a coach's house when five county sheriff cars pulled up | my sister-in-law's house got TP'd last Halloween.*

toi·let·ries /ˈtoilitrēz/ ▸*plural n.* articles used in washing and taking care of one's body, such as soap, shampoo, and toothpaste.

toi·lette /twäˈlet/ ▸*n.* [in *sing.*] *dated* the process of washing oneself, dressing, and attending to one's appearance: *Emily got up to begin her morning toilette.* ▷late 17th cent.: French (see TOILET).

toi·let tis·sue ▸*n.* another term for TOILET PAPER.

toi·let-train ▸*v.* [*trans.*] teach (a young child) to use the toilet: *she was toilet-trained by the age of one* | [as *n.*] (**toilet-training**) *books on toilet-training.*

toi·let wa·ter ▸*n.* a dilute form of perfume. Also called EAU DE TOILETTE.

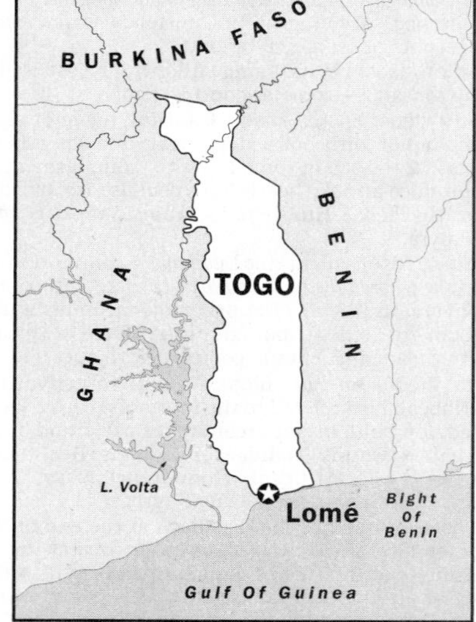

toils /toilz/ ▸*plural n. poetic/literary* used in reference to a situation regarded as a trap: *Henry had become caught in the toils of his own deviousness.* ▷early 16th cent. (denoting a net into which a hunted quarry is driven): plural of *toil*, from Old French *toile* 'net, trap' (see TOILE).

toil·some /ˈtoilsəm/ ▸*adj. archaic* or *poetic/literary* involving hard or tedious work. **—toil·some·ly** *adv.* **—toil·some·ness** *n.*

toil·worn /ˈtoilˌwôrn/ ▸*adj. poetic/literary* exhausted by hard physical labor.

To·jo /ˈtōˈjō/, Hideki (1884–1948), Japanese military leader and statesman; prime minister 1941–44. He initiated the Japanese attack on Pearl Harbor and by 1944 had assumed virtual control of all political and military decision-making. After Japan's surrender, he was tried and hanged as a war criminal.

to·ka·mak /ˈtōkəˌmak; ˈtäk-/ ▸*n. Physics* a toroidal apparatus for producing controlled fusion reactions in hot plasma. ▷1960s: Russian, from *to(roidal'naya) kam(era s) ak(sial'nym magnitnym polem)* 'toroidal chamber with axial magnetic field.'

To·kay /tōˈkā/ ▸*n.* a sweet aromatic wine, originally made near Tokaj in Hungary.

to·kay /tōˈkā/ (also **to·kay geck·o**) ▸*n.* a large gray Southeast Asian gecko with orange and blue spots, having a loud call that resembles its name. • *Gekko gecko*, family Gekkonidae. ▷mid 18th cent.: from Malay dialect *toke&glottalstop;*, from Javanese *tekèk*, imitative of its call.

toke /tōk/ *informal* ▸*n.* the drawing of a puff from a cigarette or pipe, typically one containing marijuana.
▸*v.* [*intrans.*] smoke marijuana or tobacco: *he muses while* **toking on** *a cigarette* | [*trans.*] *we toked some grass.* ▷1950s: of unknown origin. **—tok·er** *n.*

to·ken /ˈtōkən/ ▸*n.* **1** a thing serving as a visible or tangible representation of something abstract: *mistletoe was cut from an oak tree as a token of good fortune.* See notes at EMBLEM, SIGN. ■ a thing given to or done for someone as an expression of one's feelings: *I wanted to offer you a small token of my appreciation.* ■ *archaic* a characteristic or distinctive sign or mark, esp. a badge or favor worn to indicate allegiance to a particular person or party. ■ *archaic* a word or object conferring authority on or serving to authenticate the speaker or holder. ■ *chiefly Brit.* a staff or other object given to a locomotive engineer on a single-track railroad as authority to proceed over a given section of line. ■ *Computing* a sequence of bits used in a certain network architecture in which the ability to transmit information is conferred on a particular node by the arrival there of this sequence, which is passed continuously between nodes in a fixed order. ■ a person chosen by way of tokenism as a nominal representative of a minority or underrepresented group. **2** a voucher that can be exchanged for goods or services, typically one given as a gift or offered as part of a promotional offer: *redeem this token for a free dessert.* ■ a metal or plastic disk used to operate a machine or in exchange for particular goods or services. **3** an individual occurrence of a symbol or string, in particular: ■ *Linguistics* an individual occurrence of a linguistic unit in speech or writing, as contrasted with the type or class of linguistic unit of which it is an instance. Contrasted with TYPE. ■ *Computing* the smallest meaningful unit of information in a sequence of data for a compiler.
▸*adj.* done for the sake of appearances or as a symbolic gesture: *cases like these often bring just token fines from the courts.* ■ [*attrib.*] (of a person) chosen by way of tokenism as a representative of a particular minority or underrepresented group: *she took offense at being called the token woman on the force.* ▷Old English *tāc(e)n*, of Germanic origin; related to Dutch *teken* and German *Zeichen*, also to TEACH.
▸*PHRASES* □ **by the same token** in the same way or for the same reason: *there was little evidence to substantiate the gossip and, by the same token, there was little to disprove it.* □ **in token of** as a sign or symbol of: *we bought each other drinks in token of the holiday season.*

to·ken·ism /ˈtōkəˌnizəm/ ▸*n.* the practice of making only a perfunctory or symbolic effort to do a particular thing, esp. by recruiting a small number of people from underrepresented groups in order to give the appearance of sexual or racial equality within a workforce. **—to·ken·is·tic** /ˌtōkəˈnistik/ *adj.*

to·ken ring ▸*n. Computing* a local area network in which a node can transmit only when in possession of a sequence of bits (called the token) that is passed to each node in turn.

Tok·las /ˈtōkləs/, Alice B(abette), (1877–1967) U.S.

writer. She was a companion and secretary to Gertrude Stein. A collection of her letters, *Staying on Alone* (1973) was published posthumously.

to·ko·no·ma /ˌtōkəˈnōmə/ ▸*n.* (in a Japanese house) a recess or alcove, typically a few inches above floor level, for displaying flowers, pictures, and ornaments. ▷Japanese.

Tok Pis·in /ˌtäk ˈpisin/ ▸*n.* an English-based Creole used as a commercial and administrative language by over 2 million people in Papua New Guinea. Also called **NEO-MELANESIAN**. ▷the name in Tok Pisin, literally 'pidgin talk.'

To·ku·ga·wa /ˌtōkooˈgäwə/ the last shogunate in Japan (1603–1867), founded by Tokugawa Ieyasu (1543–1616).The shogunate was followed by the restoration of imperial power under Meiji Tenno.

To·ky·o /ˈtōkēˌō/ the capital of Japan, located on the northwestern shores of Tokyo Bay, on the southeastern part of the island of Honshu; pop. 8,163,000. Formerly called Edo, it was the center of the military government under the shoguns 1603–1867. Renamed Tokyo in 1868, it replaced Kyoto as the imperial capital.

to·lar /ˈtälär/ ▸*n.* the basic monetary unit of Slovenia, equal to 100 stotins. ▷Slovene; compare with **THALER**.

Tol·bu·khin /tôlˈbookin; -KHin/ former name (1949–91) of **DOBRICH**.

tol·bu·ta·mide /tälˈbyootəˌmīd/ ▸*n.* *Medicine* a synthetic compound used to lower blood sugar levels in the treatment of diabetes. • Alternative name: **1-butyl-3-tosylurea**; chem. formula: $C_{12}H_{18}N_2O_3S$. ▷1950s: from *tol(uene)* + *but(yl)* + **AMIDE**.

told /tōld/ ▸ past and past participle of **TELL**[1].

tole /tōl/ (also **tôle**) ▸*n.* painted, enameled, or lacquered tinplate used to make decorative domestic objects. ▷1940s: French *tôle* 'sheet iron,' from dialect *taule* 'table,' from Latin *tabula* 'flat board.' —**tole·ware** /-ˌwe(ə)r/ *n.*

To·le·do 1 /təˈlādō; -ˈlē-/ a city in central Spain on the Tagus River, capital of Castilla-La Mancha region; pop. 64,000. Toledan steel and sword blades have been well known since the first century BC. **2** /təˈlēdō/ an industrial city and port on Lake Erie, in northwestern Ohio; pop. 313,619. —**To·le·dan** /təˈlēdn/ *adj.* & *n.*

tol·er·a·ble /ˈtälərəbəl/ ▸*adj.* able to be endured: *a stimulant to make life more tolerable.* ■ fairly good; mediocre: *he was fond of music and had a tolerable voice.* ▷late Middle English: via Old French from Latin *tolerabilis*, from *tolerare* (see **TOLERATE**). —**tol·er·a·bil·i·ty** /ˌtäl(ə)rəˈbilitē/ *n.* —**tol·er·a·bly** /-blē/ *adv.* [as *submodifier*] *the welfare state works tolerably well.*

tol·er·ance /ˈtäl(ə)rəns/ ▸*n.* **1** the ability or willingness to tolerate something, in particular the existence of opinions or behavior that one does not necessarily agree with: *the tolerance of corruption | an advocate of religious tolerance.* ■ the capacity to endure continued subjection to something, esp. a drug, transplant, antigen, or environmental conditions, without adverse reaction: *the desert camel shows the greatest tolerance to dehydration | species were grouped according to pollution tolerance | various species of diatoms display different tolerances to acid.* ■ diminution in the body's response to a drug after continued use. **2** an allowable amount of variation of a specified quantity, esp. in the dimensions of a machine or part: *250 parts in his cars were made to tolerances of one thousandth of an inch.* ▷late Middle English (denoting the action of bearing hardship, or the ability to bear pain and hardship): via Old French from Latin *tolerantia*, from *tolerare* (see **TOLERATE**).

tol·er·ance dose ▸*n.* a dose of something toxic, in particular of nuclear radiation, believed to be the maximum that can be taken without harm.

tol·er·ant /ˈtälərənt/ ▸*adj.* **1** showing willingness to allow the existence of opinions or behavior that one does not necessarily agree with: *we must be **tolerant of** others | a more tolerant attitude toward other religions.* **2** (of a plant, animal, or machine) able to endure (specified conditions or treatment): *rye is reasonably **tolerant of** drought* | [in *combination*] *fault-tolerant computer systems.* ▷late 18th cent.: from French *tolérant*, present participle of *tolérer*, from Latin *tolerare* (see **TOLERATE**). Compare with earlier **INTOLERANT**. —**tol·er·ant·ly** *adv.* (in sense 1).

tol·er·ate /ˈtäləˌrāt/ ▸*v.* [*trans.*] allow the existence, occurrence, or practice of (something that one does not necessarily like or agree with) without interference: *a regime unwilling to tolerate dissent.* ■ accept or endure (someone or something unpleasant or disliked) with forbearance: *how was it that she could tolerate such noise?* ■ be capable of continued subjection to (a drug, toxin, or environmental condition) without adverse reaction: *lichens grow in conditions that no other plants tolerate.* ▷early 16th cent. (in the sense 'endure (pain)'): from Latin *tolerat-* 'endured,' from the verb *tolerare.* —**tol·er·a·tor** /-ˌrātər/ *n.*

tol·er·a·tion /ˌtäləˈrāSHən/ ▸*n.* the practice of tolerating something, in particular differences of opinion or behavior: *the king demanded greater religious toleration.* ▷late 15th cent. (denoting the granting of permission by authority): from French *tolération*, from Latin *toleratio(n-)*, from *tolerare* (see **TOLERATE**).

Tol·kien /ˈtōlˌkēn; ˈtäl-/, J. R. R. (1892–1973), British novelist and literary scholar, born in South Africa; full name *John Ronald Reuel Tolkien.* He is known for *The Hobbit* (1937) and *The Lord of the Rings* (1954–55), fantasy adventures set in Middle Earth (films *The Fellowship of the Ring* [2001], *The Two Towers* [2002], and *The Return of the King* [Academy Award, 2003]).

toll[1] /tōl/ ▸*n.* **1** a charge payable for permission to use a particular bridge or road: *turnpike tolls* | [as *adj.*] *a toll bridge.* ■ a charge for a long-distance telephone call. **2** [in *sing.*] the number of deaths, casualties, or injuries arising from particular circumstances, such as a natural disaster, conflict, or accident: *the toll of dead and injured mounted.* ■ the cost or damage resulting from something: *the environmental toll of the policy has been high.*
▸*v.* [*trans.*] [usu. as *n.*] (**tolling**) charge a toll for the use of (a bridge or road): *the report advocates expressway tolling.* ▷Old English (denoting a charge, tax, or duty), from medieval Latin *toloneum*, alteration of late Latin *teloneum*, from Greek *telōnion* 'tollhouse,' from *telos* 'tax.' Sense 2 (late 19th cent.) arose from the notion of paying a toll or tribute in human lives (to an adversary or to death).
▸*PHRASE* □ **take its toll** (or **take a heavy toll**) have an adverse effect, esp. so as to cause damage, suffering, or death: *years of pumping iron have taken their toll on his body.*

toll[2] ▸*v.* [*intrans.*] (of a bell) sound with a slow, uniform succession of strokes, as a signal or announcement: *the bells of the cathedral began to **toll for** evening service.* ■ [*trans.*] cause (a bell) to make such a sound. ■ (of a bell) announce or mark (the time, a service, or a person's death): *the bell of St. Mary's began to toll the curfew.*
▸*n.* [in *sing.*] a single ring of a bell. ▷late Middle English: probably a special use of dialect *toll* 'drag, pull.'

toll·booth /ˈtōlˌbooTH/ ▸*n.* a booth where drivers must pay to use a bridge or road.

toll bridge ▸*n.* a bridge where drivers or pedestrians must pay to cross.

toll·gate /ˈtōlˌgāt/ ▸*n.* a barrier across a road where drivers or pedestrians must pay to go further.

toll·house /ˈtōlˌhous/ ▸*n.* a small house by a tollgate or toll bridge where money is collected from road users.

toll·house cook·ie ▸*n.* a cookie made with flour, brown sugar, chocolate chips, and usually chopped nuts. ▷named after the *Toll House* in Whitman, Massachusetts, source of the original recipe.

toll pla·za ▸*n.* a row of tollbooths on a toll road.

toll road ▸*n.* a road that drivers must pay to use.

toll·way /ˈtōlˌwā/ ▸*n.* a highway for the use of which a charge is made.

Tol·stoy /ˈtōlˌstoi; ˈtōl-/, Count Leo (1828–1910), Russian writer; Russian name *Lev Nikolaevich Tolstoi.* He is noted for the novels *War and Peace* (1863–69), an epic tale of the Napoleonic invasion, and *Anna Karenina* (1873–77).

Leo Tolstoy

Tol·tec /ˈtōlˌtek; ˈtäl-/ ▸*n.* **1** a member of an American Indian people that flourished in Mexico before the Aztecs. **2** the language of this people.
▸*adj.* of or relating to this people. ▷via Spanish from Nahuatl *toltecatl*, literally 'a person from *Tula*' (see **TULA**). —**Tol·tec·an** /tōlˈtekən; täl-/ *adj.*

to·lu /təˈloo/ (also **to·lu bal·sam**) ▸*n.* a fragrant brown balsam obtained from a South American tree, used in perfumery and medicine. • This balsam is obtained mainly from *Myroxylon balsamum*, family Leguminosae. ▷late 17th cent.: named after *Santiago de Tolú* in Colombia, from where it was exported.

To·lu·ca /təˈlookə/ a city in central Mexico, capital of the state of Mexico; pop. 488,000. It lies at the foot of the Nevado de Toluca, an extinct volcano, at an altitude of 8,793 feet (2,680 m). Full name **TOLUCA DE LERDO**.

tol·u·ene /ˈtälyooˌēn/ ▸*n.* *Chemistry* a colorless liquid hydrocarbon present in coal tar and petroleum and used as a solvent and in organic synthesis. • Alternative name: **methylbenzene**; chem. formula: $C_6H_5CH_3$. ▷late 19th cent.: from **TOLU** + **-ENE**.

to·lu·i·dine blue /təˈlooəˌdēn/ ▸*n.* a synthetic blue dye used chiefly as a stain in biology. • A thiazine dye; chem. formula: $C_{15}H_{16}ClN_3S$. ▷late 19th cent.: *toluidine* from **TOLUENE** + **-IDE** + **-INE**[4].

To·lyat·ti /tôlˈyätē; täl-/ Russian name for **TOGLIATTI**.

tom /täm/ ▸*n.* **1** the male of various animals, esp. a turkey or domestic cat. **2** (**Tom**) *informal* short for **UNCLE TOM**.
▸*v.* (**Tom**) (**Tommed, Tom·ming**) [*intrans.*] *informal, derogatory* (of a black person) behave in an excessively obedient or servile way. ▷late Middle English (denoting an ordinary man, surviving in *tomfool*, *tomboy*, and the phrase *Tom, Dick, and Harry*): abbreviation of the given name *Thomas*. Sense 1 dates from the mid 18th cent.

tom·a·hawk /ˈtäməˌhôk/ ▸*n.* a light ax used as a tool or weapon by American Indians.
▸*v.* [*trans.*] strike or cut with or as if with a tomahawk. ▷early 17th cent.: from a Virginia Algonquian language.

tomahawk

tom·al·ley /ˈtämˌalē/ ▸*n.* the digestive gland of a lobster, which turns green when cooked. It is sometimes considered a delicacy. ▷mid 17th cent.: from French *taumalin*, from Carib *taumali*.

Tom and Jer·ry /täm and ˈjerē/ ▸*n.* (*pl.* **-ries**) a kind of hot spiced rum cocktail, made with eggs.

to·ma·til·lo /ˌtōməˈtē(y)ō/ ▸*n.* (*pl.* **-los**) **1** a small edible fruit that is purplish or yellow when ripe, but is most often used when green for salsas and preserves. **2** the Mexican plant, related to the cape gooseberry, that bears this fruit. • *Physalis philadelphica*, family Solanaceae. ▷early 20th cent.: from Spanish, diminutive of *tomate* 'tomato.'

to·ma·to /təˈmātō; -ˈmätō/ ▸*n.* (*pl.* **-toes**) **1** a glossy red, or occasionally yellow, pulpy edible fruit that is typically eaten as a vegetable or in salad. ■ the bright red color of a ripe tomato. **2** the South American plant of the nightshade family that produces this fruit. It is widely grown as a cash crop, and many varieties have been developed. • *Lycopersicon esculentum*, family Solanaceae. ▷early 17th cent.: from French, Spanish, or Portuguese *tomate*, from Nahuatl *tomatl*. —**to·ma·to·ey** /-ˈmātōē; -ˈmätō-ē/ *adj.*

to·ma·to fruit·worm ▸*n.* another term for **CORN EARWORM**.

tomb /toom/ ▸*n.* a large vault, typically an underground one, for burying the dead. ■ an enclosure for a corpse cut in the earth or in rock. ■ a monument to the memory of a dead person, erected over their burial place. ■ used in similes and metaphors to refer to a place or situation that is extremely cold, quiet, or dark, or that forms a confining enclosure: *the house was as quiet as a tomb.* ■ (**the tomb**) *poetic/literary* death: *none escape the tomb.* ▷Middle English: from Old French *tombe*, from late Latin *tumba*, from Greek *tumbos*.

Tom·baugh /ˈtämˌbô/, Clyde William (1906–97), U.S. astronomer. He discovered the planet Pluto on March 13, 1930, and subsequently discovered numerous asteroids.

Tom·big·bee Riv·er /tämˈbigbē/ a river that flows for 400 miles (640 km) from northeastern Mississippi through western Alabama, to the Alabama River. In the 1980s, the **Tennessee-Tombigbee Waterway** connected it with the Tennessee River.

tom·bo·lo /ˈtämbəˌlō/ ▸*n.* (*pl.* **-los**) a bar of sand or shingle joining an island to the mainland. ▷late 19th cent.: from Italian, literally 'sand dune.'

Tom·bouc·tou /ˌtônbo͝okˈto͞o; ˌtämbək-/ French name for **TIMBUKTU**.

tom·boy /ˈtämˌboi/ ▸*n.* a girl who enjoys rough, noisy activities traditionally associated with boys. —**tom·boy·ish** *adj.* —**tom·boy·ish·ness** *n.*

Tomb·stone /ˈto͞omˌstōn/ a historic frontier city in southeastern Arizona, the site of the 1881 gunfight at the O.K. Corral; pop. 1,220.

tomb·stone /ˈto͞omˌstōn/ ▸*n.* **1** a large, flat inscribed stone standing or laid over a grave. **2** (also **tombstone advertisement** or **tombstone ad**) an advertisement listing the underwriters or firms associated with a new issue of securities.

tom·cat /ˈtämˌkat/ ▸*n.* a male domestic cat. ■ *informal* a sexually aggressive man; a womanizer.
▸*v.* (**-cat·ted, -cat·ting**) [*intrans.*] *informal* pursue women promiscuously for sexual gratification: *tomcatting all night and sleeping until afternoon.*

tom·cod /ˈtämˌkäd/ ▸*n.* (*pl.* same or **-cods**) a small edible greenish-brown North American fish of the cod family, popular with anglers. • Genus *Microgradus*, family Gadidae: *M. proximus* of the Pacific coasts, and *M. tomcod* of the Atlantic coasts and fresh water.

Tom Col·lins /täm ˈkälənz/ ▸*n.* a cocktail made from gin mixed with soda water, sugar, and lemon or lime juice. ▷sometimes said to have been named after a 19th-cent. London bartender.

Tom, Dick, and Har·ry /ˈtäm ˈdik and ˈharē/ (also **Tom, Dick, or Harry**) ▸*n.* used to refer to ordinary people in general: *he didn't want every Tom, Dick, and Harry knowing their business.*

tome /tōm/ ▸*n. chiefly humorous* a book, esp. a large, heavy, scholarly one: *a weighty tome.* ▷early 16th cent. (denoting one volume of a larger work): from French, via Latin from Greek *tomos* 'section, roll of papyrus, volume'; related to *temnein* 'to cut.'

-tome ▸*comb. form* **1** denoting an instrument for cutting: *microtome.* **2** denoting a section or segment: *myotome.* ▷sense 1 from Greek *-tomon* (neuter) 'that cuts'; sense 2 from Greek *tomē* 'a cutting,' both from *temnein* 'to cut.'

to·men·tum /tōˈmentəm/ ▸*n.* (*pl.* **-ta** /-tə/) *Botany* a layer of matted woolly down on the surface of a plant. ▷late 17th cent.: from Latin, literally 'cushion stuffing.' —**to·men·tose** /tōˈmentōs; ˈtōmənˌtōs/ *adj.* —**to·men·tous** /-təs/ *adj.*

tom·fool /ˈtämˈfo͞ol/ ▸*n. dated* a foolish person: [as *adj.*] *she was destined to take part in some tomfool caper.*

tom·fool·er·y /tämˈfo͞ol(ə)rē/ ▸*n.* foolish or silly behavior: *he was no longer amused by Ozzie's youthful tomfoolery.*

To·mis /ˈtōməs/ ancient name for **CONSTANŢA**.

Tom·my /ˈtämē/ (also **tom·my**) ▸*n.* (*pl.* **-mies**) *informal* a British private soldier. [nickname for the given name *Thomas*; from a use of the name *Thomas Atkins* in specimens of completed official forms in the British army during the 19th cent.]

tom·my gun /ˈtämē/ ▸*n. informal* a type of submachine gun. ▷1920s: contraction of *Thompson gun*, named by its designer after John T. *Thompson* (1860–1940), the U.S. army officer who conceived the idea for it.

Tom·my John sur·ger·y ▸a surgical procedure in which a healthy tendon extracted from an arm (or sometimes a leg) is used to replace an arm's torn ligament. The healthy tendon is threaded through holes drilled into the bone above and below the elbow. ▷1970s: named after **TOMMY JOHN** (1943–), a U.S. major-league pitcher who, after a debilitating injury, was able to resume his career after undergoing this surgery. The procedure was devised specifically for John by U.S. orthopedic surgeon Dr. Frank Jobe in 1974.

tom·my·rot /ˈtämēˌrät/ ▸*n. informal, dated* nonsense; rubbish: *did you ever hear such awful tommyrot?*

to·mo·gram /ˈtōməˌgram/ ▸*n.* a record obtained by tomography.

to·mog·ra·phy /təˈmägrəfē/ ▸*n.* a technique for displaying a representation of a cross section through a human body or other solid object using X-rays or ultrasound. ▷1930s: from Greek *tomos* 'slice, section' + **-GRAPHY**. —**to·mo·graph·ic** /ˌtōməˈgrafik/ *adj.*

to·mor·row /təˈmôrō; -ˈmärō/ ▸*adv.* on the day after today: *the show opens tomorrow.* ■ in the future, esp. the near future: *East Germany will not disappear tomorrow.*
▸*n.* the day after today: *tomorrow is going to be a special day.* ■ the future, esp. the near future: *today's engineers are tomorrow's buyers.* ▷Middle English (as two words): from the preposition **TO** + **MORROW**. Compare with **TODAY** and **TONIGHT**.
▸*PHRASES* □ **as if there was** (or **as though there were**) **no tomorrow** with no regard for the future consequences: *I ate as if there was no tomorrow.* □ **tomorrow morning** (or **afternoon**, etc.) in the morning (or afternoon, etc.) of tomorrow. □ **tomorrow is another day** used after a bad experience to express one's belief that the future will be better.

Tom·pi·on /ˈtämpēən/, Thomas (*c.*1639–1713), English clock- and watchmaker. He made one of the first balance-spring watches and made two large pendulum clocks for the Royal Greenwich Observatory.

tom·pi·on /ˈtämpēən/ ▸*n.* variant spelling of **TAMPION**.

Tomsk /tämsk; tômsk/ an industrial city in southern Siberia in Russia, a port on the Tom River; pop. 506,000.

Tom Thumb ▸*n.* [usu. as *adj.*] a dwarf variety of a cultivated flower or vegetable: *Tom Thumb lettuce.* ▷late 19th cent.: from the name of the hero of a children's story, a plowman's son who was only as tall as his father's thumb.

tom·tit /tämˈtit/ ▸*n.* a popular name for any of a number of small active songbirds, esp. a tit or a chickadee.

tom-tom ▸*n.* a medium-sized cylindrical drum beaten with the hands and used in jazz bands, etc. ■ an early drum, of Native American or Asian origin, typically played with the hands. ▷late 17th cent.: from Hindi *ṭam ṭam*, Telugu *ṭamaṭama*, of imitative origin.

-tomy ▸*comb. form* cutting, esp. as part of a surgical process: *episiotomy.* ▷from Greek *-tomia* 'cutting,' from *temnein* 'to cut.'

ton[1] /tən/ (abbr.: **t** also **tn**) ▸*n.* **1** (also **short ton**) a unit of weight equal to 2,000 pounds avoirdupois (907.19 kg). ■ (also **long ton**) a unit of weight equal to 2,240 pounds avoirdupois (1016.05 kg). ■ short for **METRIC TON**. ■ (also **displacement ton**) a unit of measurement of a ship's weight representing the weight of water it displaces, equal to 2,240 pounds or 35 cubic feet (0.99 cu m). ■ (also **freight ton**) a unit of weight or volume of sea cargo, equal to a metric ton (1,000kg) or 40 cubic feet. ■ (also **gross ton**) a unit of gross internal capacity, equal to 100 cubic feet (2.83 cu m). ■ (also **net** or **register ton**) an equivalent unit of net internal capacity. ■ a unit of refrigerating power able to freeze 2,000 pounds of water at 0°C in 24 hours. ■ a measure of capacity for various materials, esp. 40 cubic feet of timber. **2** (usu. **a ton of/tons of**) *informal* a large number or amount: *all of a sudden I had tons of friends* | *that bag of yours* ***weighs a ton.*** ▷Middle English: variant of **TUN**, both spellings being used for the container and the weight. The senses were differentiated in the late 17th cent.
▸*PHRASE* □ **like a ton of bricks** see **BRICK**.

ton[2] /tôn/ ▸*n.* fashionable style or distinction. ■ (**the ton**) [treated as *sing.* or *pl.*] fashionable society. ▷French, from Latin *tonus* (see **TONE**).

ton·al /ˈtōnl/ ▸*adj.* of or relating to the tone of music, color, or writing: *his ear for tonal color* | *the poem's tonal lapses.* ■ of or relating to music written using conventional keys and harmony. ■ *Phonetics* (of a language) expressing semantic differences by varying the intonation given to words or syllables of a similar sound. ▷late 18th cent. (designating church music in plainsong mode): from medieval Latin *tonalis*, from Latin *tonus* (see **TONE**). —**ton·al·ly** *adv.*

to·nal·i·ty /tōˈnalitē/ ▸*n.* (*pl.* **-ties**) **1** the character of a piece of music as determined by the key in which it is played or the relations between the notes of a scale or key. ■ the harmonic effect of being in a particular key: *the first bar would seem set to create a tonality of C major.* ■ the use of conventional keys and harmony as the basis of musical composition. **2** the color scheme or range of tones used in a picture.

ton·do /ˈtändō/ ▸*n.* (*pl.* **-di** /-dē/) a circular painting or relief. ▷late 19th cent.: from Italian, literally 'round object,' from *rotondo* 'round,' from Latin *rotundus*.

tone /tōn/ ▸*n.* **1** the overall quality of a musical or vocal sound: *the piano tone appears monochrome or lacking in warmth.* ■ a modulation of the voice expressing a particular feeling or mood: *a firm* ***tone of voice.*** ■ a manner of expression in writing: *there was a general tone of ill-concealed glee in the reporting.* **2** the general character of a group of people or a place or event: *a bell would* ***lower the tone*** *of the place.* ■ *informal* an atmosphere of respectability or class: *they don't feel he gives the place tone.* **3** a musical sound, esp. one of a definite pitch and character. ■ a musical note, warble, or other sound used as a particular signal on a telephone or answering machine. ■ *Phonetics* (in some languages, such as Chinese) a particular pitch pattern on a syllable used to make semantic distinctions. ■ *Phonetics* (in some languages, such as English) intonation on a word or phrase used to add functional meaning. **4** (also **whole tone**) a basic interval in classical Western music, equal to two semitones and separating, for example, the first and second notes of an ordinary scale (such as C and D, or E and F sharp); a major second or whole step. **5** the particular quality of brightness, deepness, or hue of a tint or shade of a color: *an attractive color that is even in tone and texture* | *stained glass in vivid tones of red and blue.* ■ the general effect of color or of light and shade in a picture. ■ a slight degree of difference in the intensity of a color. **6** (also **muscle tone**) the normal level of firmness or slight contraction in a resting muscle. ■ *Physiology* the normal level of activity in a nerve fiber.
▸*v.* [*trans.*] **1** give greater strength or firmness to (the body or a part of it): *exercise* ***tones up*** *the muscles.* ■ [*intrans.*] (**tone up**) (of a muscle or bodily part) became stronger or firmer. **2** [*intrans.*] (**tone with**) harmonize with (something) in terms of color: *the rich orange color of the wood tones beautifully with the yellow roses.* **3** *Photography* give (a monochrome picture) an altered color in finishing by means of a chemical solution.
▸*phrasal v.* □ **tone something down** make something less harsh in sound or color. ■ make something less extreme or intense: *she saw the need to tone down her protests.* ▷Middle English: from Old French *ton*, from Latin *tonus*, from Greek *tonos* 'tension, tone,' from *teinein* 'to stretch.' —**toned** *adj.* [in *combination*] *the fresh-toned singing.* —**tone·less** *adj.* —**tone·less·ly** *adv.*

tone arm (also **tone·arm** /ˈtōnˌärm/) ▸*n.* the movable arm supporting the pickup of a record player.

tone clus·ter ▸*n.* another term for **NOTE CLUSTER**.

tone col·or ▸*n. Music* another term for **TIMBRE**.

tone-deaf ▸*adj.* (of a person) unable to perceive differences of musical pitch accurately. —**tone-deaf·ness** *n.*

tone dialing ▸*n.* a method of telephone dialing in which each digit is transmitted as a different tone. Compare with **PULSE DIALING**.

tone lan·guage ▸*n. Linguistics* a language in which variations in pitch distinguish different words.

ton·eme /ˈtōnēm/ ▸*n. Phonetics* a phoneme distinguished from another only by its tone. ▷1920s: from **TONE**, on the pattern of *phoneme*. —**to·ne·mic** /tōˈnēmik/ *adj.*

tone-on-tone ▸*adj.* (of a fabric or design) dyed with or using different shades of the same color.

tone po·em ▸*n.* a piece of orchestral music, typically in one movement, on a descriptive or rhapsodic theme.

ton·er /ˈtōnər/ ▸*n.* **1** an astringent liquid applied to the skin to reduce oiliness and improve its condition. ■ [with *adj.*] a device or exercise for making a specified part of the body firmer and stronger: *a tummy toner.* **2** a black or colored powder used in xerographic copying processes. ■ [usu. with *adj.*] a chemical bath for changing the color or shade of a photographic print, esp. as specified: *sepia or blue toners.*

tone row ▸*n.* a particular sequence of the twelve notes of the chromatic scale used as a basis for twelve-tone (serial) music.

tong[1] /tông; täng/ ▸*n.* a Chinese association or secret society in the U.S., frequently associated with underworld criminal activity. ▷late 19th cent.: from Chinese (Cantonese dialect) *t'ǒng*, literally 'meeting place.'

tong[2] ▸*v.* [*trans.*] collect, lift, or handle (items such as logs or oysters) using tongs.

Ton·ga /ˈtänggə/ a country in the South Pacific Ocean

that consists of an island group southeast of Fiji; pop. 110,000; capital, Nuku'alofa; languages, Tongan and English (both official). Also called the **Friendly Islands**.

The kingdom of Tonga consists of about 170 volcanic and coral islands, of which 36 are inhabited. Visited by the Dutch in the early 17th century, Tonga became a British protectorate in 1900 and an independent Commonwealth of Nations state in 1970. It has been a constitutional monarchy since 1875.

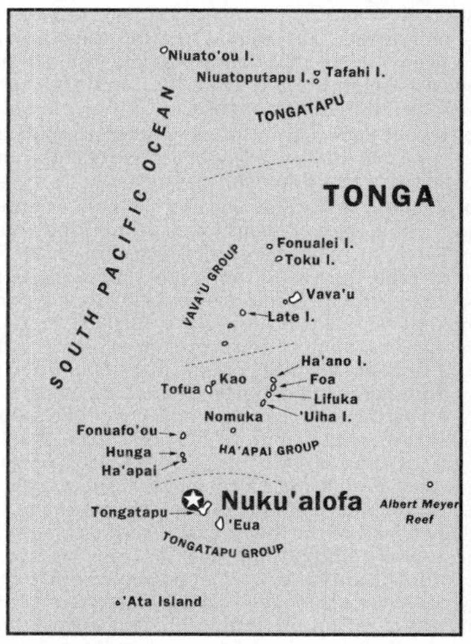

ton·ga /ˈtäNGgə/ ▸*n.* a light horse-drawn two-wheeled vehicle used in India. ▹from Hindi *tāṅgā*.

Ton·gan /ˈtäNGgən/ ▸*adj.* of or relating to Tonga or its people or language.
▸*n.* **1** a native or national of Tonga. **2** the Polynesian language spoken in Tonga.

Ton·gass Na·tion·al For·est /ˈtäNGgəs/ a preserve in southeastern Alaska, the largest U.S. national forest, in the panhandle and on islands in the Alexander Archipelago, the focus of 1990s disputes over logging.

tongs /tôNGz; täNGz/ ▸*plural n.* (also **a pair of tongs**) an instrument with two movable arms that are joined at one end, used for picking up and holding things: *ice tongs.* ▹Old English *tang(e)* (singular), of Germanic origin; related to Dutch *tang* and German *Zange*.

Tong·shan /ˈtŏŏNGˈSHän/ former name (1912–45) of **Xuzhou**.

tongue /təNG/ ▸*n.* **1** the fleshy muscular organ in the mouth of a mammal, used for tasting, licking, swallowing, and (in humans) articulating speech. ■ the equivalent organ in other vertebrates, sometimes used (in snakes) as a scent organ or (in chameleons) for catching food. ■ an analogous organ in insects, formed from some of the mouthparts and used in feeding. ■ the tongue of a hoofed mammal, in particular an ox or lamb, as food. ■ used in reference to a person's style or manner of speaking: *he was a redoubtable debater with a caustic tongue.* ■ a particular language: *the prioress chatted to the peddler in a strange tongue.* ■ **(tongues)** see **the gift of tongues** below. **2** a thing resembling or likened to a tongue, in particular: ■ a long, low promontory of land. ■ a strip of leather or fabric under the laces in a shoe, attached only at the front end. ■ the pin of a buckle. ■ a projecting strip on a wooden board fitting into a groove on another. ■ the vibrating reed of a musical instrument or organ pipe. ■ a jet of flame: *a tongue of flame flashes four feet from the gun.*
▸*v.* (**tongues, ton·gued, ton·guing** /ˈtəNGiNG/) [*trans.*] **1** *Music* sound (a note) distinctly on a wind instrument by interrupting the air flow with the tongue. **2** lick or caress with the tongue: *the other horse tongued every part of the colt's mane.* ▹Old English *tunge*, of Germanic origin; related to Dutch *tong*, German *Zunge* and Latin *lingua*. **—tongue·less** *adj.*
▸*PHRASES* □ **find** (or **lose**) **one's tongue** be able (or unable) to express oneself after a shock. □ **get one's tongue around** pronounce (words): *she found it very difficult to get her tongue around the unfamiliar words.* □ **the gift of tongues** the power of speaking in unknown languages, regarded as one of the gifts of the Holy Spirit (Acts 2). □ **give tongue** (of hounds) bark, esp. on finding a scent. ■ express one's feelings or opinions freely, sometimes objectionably so. □ **keep a civil tongue in one's head** speak politely. □ **speak in tongues** speak in an unknown language during religious worship. □ (**with**) **tongue in cheek** without really meaning what one is saying or writing. □ **someone's tongue is hanging out** someone is very eager for something: *the tabloids have their tongues hanging out for this stuff.*

tongue and groove ▸*n.* wooden planking in which adjacent boards are joined by means of interlocking ridges and grooves down their sides. **—tongued-and-grooved** *adj.*

tongued /təNGd/ ▸*adj.* **1** [*in combination*] having a specified kind of tongue: *the blue-tongued lizard.* ■ (in carpentry) constructed using a tongue. **2** (of a note) played by tonguing.

tongue de·pres·sor ▸*n.* an instrument, typically a small flat piece of wood, used by health practitioners to press down the tongue in order to allow inspection of the mouth or throat.

tongue-in-cheek ▸*adj.* & *adv.* with ironic or flippant intent: [*as adj.*] *her delightful tongue-in-cheek humor* | [*as adv.*] *"I swear there's a female conspiracy against men!" he complained, tongue-in-cheek.*

tongue-lash·ing ▸*n.* [*in sing.*] a loud or severe scolding: *the incensed boss gave him a tongue-lashing.* **—tongue-lash** *v.*

tongue-tie ▸*n.* a malformation that restricts the movement of the tongue and causes a speech impediment.

tongue-tied ▸*adj.* **1** too shy or embarrassed to speak. **2** having a malformation restricting the movement of the tongue.

tongue-twist·er ▸*n.* a sequence of words or sounds, typically of an alliterative kind, that are difficult to pronounce quickly and correctly, as, for example, *tie twine to three tree twigs.* **—tongue-twist·ing** *adj.*

tongue worm ▸*n.* a flattened wormlike parasite that infests vertebrates, esp. reptiles, having a sucking mouth with hooks for attachment to the lining of the respiratory tract. • Subphylum Pentastomida, phylum Arthropoda; sometimes regarded as a class of crustacean.

ton·ic /ˈtänik/ ▸*n.* **1** a medicinal substance taken to give a feeling of vigor or well-being. ■ something with an invigorating effect: *being needed is a tonic for someone at my age.* **2** short for **tonic water**. **3** *Music* the first note in a scale that, in conventional harmony, provides the keynote of a piece of music.
▸*adj.* **1** giving a feeling of vigor or well-being; invigorating. **2** *Music* relating to or denoting the first degree of a scale. **3** *Phonetics* denoting or relating to the syllable within a tone group that has greatest prominence, because it carries the main change of pitch. **4** relating to or restoring normal tone to muscles or other organs. ■ *Physiology* relating to, denoting, or producing continuous muscular contraction. ▹mid 17th cent.: from French *tonique*, from Greek *tonikos* 'of or for stretching,' from *tonos* (see **tone**). **—ton·i·cal·ly** /-ik(ə)lē/ *adv.*

ton·ic–clon·ic /ˌtänik ˈklänik; ˈklōnik/ ▸*adj. Medicine* of or characterized by successive phases of tonic and clonic spasm (as in *grand mal* epilepsy).

to·nic·i·ty /tōˈnisitē/ ▸*n.* **1** muscle tone. **2** *Linguistics* the pattern of tones or stress in speech. **3** *Biology* the state of a solution in respect of osmotic pressure: *the tonicity of the fluid.*

ton·ic sol-fa /ˌsōl ˈfä/ ▸*n.* a system of naming the notes of the scale (usually **do, re, mi, fa, sol, la, ti**) developed in England and used esp. to teach singing, with do as the keynote of all major keys and la as the keynote of all minor keys. See **solmization**.

ton·ic wa·ter ▸*n.* a bitter carbonated soft drink made with quinine, used esp. as a mixer with gin or other liquors (originally used as a stimulant of appetite and digestion).

ton·i·fy /ˈtōnəˌfī; ˈtän-/ ▸*v.* (**-fies, -fied**) [*trans.*] impart tone to (the body or a part of it). ■ (of acupuncture or herbal medicine) increase the available energy of (an organ, part, or system of the body). **—ton·i·fi·ca·tion** /ˌtōnəfiˈkāSHən/ *n.*

to·night /təˈnīt/ ▸*adv.* on the present or approaching evening or night: *are you doing anything tonight?*
▸*n.* the evening or night of the present day: *tonight is a night to remember.* ▹Old English *tō niht*, from the preposition **to** + **night**. Compare with **today** and **tomorrow**.

ton·ka bean /ˈtäNGkə/ ▸*n.* the black seed of a South American tree, which has a vanillalike fragrance. The dried beans are cured in rum or other alcohol and then used in perfumery and for scenting and flavoring tobacco, ice cream, and other products. • The tree is *Dipteryx odorata*, family Leguminosae. ▹late 18th cent.: *tonka*, a local word in Guyana.

Ton·kin /ˈtäNGkən; ˈtänˈkin/ a mountainous region in northern Vietnam, centered on the Red River delta.

Ton·kin, Gulf of an arm of the South China Sea, bounded by the coasts of southern China and northern Vietnam. Its chief port is Haiphong. An incident in 1964 led to increased U.S. military involvement in the area.

Ton·lé Sap /tōnˈlā ˈsap/ a lake in central Cambodia, linked to the Mekong River by the Tonlé Sap River. The ruins of the ancient city Angkor stand on its northwestern shore.

ton-mile /ˈtən ˈmīl/ ▸*n.* one ton of freight carried one mile, as a unit of traffic.

ton·nage /ˈtənij/ ▸*n.* weight in tons, esp. of cargo or freight: *road convoys carry more tonnage.* ■ the size or carrying capacity of a ship measured in tons. ■ shipping considered in terms of total carrying capacity: *the port's total tonnage.* ▹early 17th cent. (denoting a charge per ton on cargo): from **ton**[1] + **-age**.

tonne /tən/ ▸*n.* another term for **metric ton**. ▹late 19th cent.: from French; compare with **ton**[1].

ton·neau /təˈnō; ˈtänō/ ▸*n.* (*pl.* **ton·neaus** or **ton·neaux** /təˈnōz; ˈtänōz/) the part of an automobile, typically an open car, occupied by the back seats. ■ short for **tonneau cover**.

ton·neau cov·er ▸*n.* a protective cover for the seats in an open car or cabin cruiser when they are not in use.

to·nom·e·ter /tōˈnämitər/ ▸*n.* **1** a tuning fork or other instrument for measuring the pitch of musical tones. **2** an instrument for measuring the pressure in a part of the body, such as the eyeball (to test for glaucoma) or a blood vessel. ▹early 18th cent.: from Greek *tonos* (see **tone**) + **-meter**.

ton·o·plast /ˈtänəˌplast; ˈtō-/ ▸*n. Botany* a membrane that bounds the chief vacuole of a plant cell. ▹late 19th cent.: from Greek *tonos* 'tension, tone' + *plastos* 'formed.'

ton·sil /ˈtänsəl/ ▸*n.* either of two small masses of lymphoid tissue in the throat, one on each side of the root of the tongue. ▹late 16th cent.: from French *tonsilles* or Latin *tonsillae* (plural). **—ton·sil·lar** /-sələr/ *adj.*

ton·sil·lec·to·my /ˌtänsəˈlektəmē/ ▸*n.* (*pl.* **-mies**) a surgical operation to remove the tonsils.

ton·sil·li·tis /ˌtänsəˈlītis/ ▸*n.* inflammation of the tonsils.

ton·so·ri·al /tänˈsôrēəl/ ▸*adj. formal* or *humorous* of or relating to hairdressing. ▹early 19th cent.: from Latin *tonsorius* (from *tonsor* 'barber,' from *tondere* 'shear, clip') + **-al**.

ton·sure /ˈtänSHər/ ▸*n.* a part of a monk's or priest's head left bare on top by shaving off the hair. ■ [*in sing.*] an act of shaving the top of a monk's or priest's head as a preparation for entering a religious order.
▸*v.* [*trans.*] [often as *adj.*] (**tonsured**) shave the hair on the crown of. ▹late Middle English: from Old French, or from Latin *tonsura*, from *tondere* 'shear, clip.'

ton·tine /ˈtänˌtēn; tänˈtēn/ ▸*n.* an annuity shared by subscribers to a loan or common fund, the shares increasing as subscribers die until the last survivor enjoys the whole income. ▹mid 18th cent.: from French, named after Lorenzo *Tonti* (1630–95), a Neapolitan banker who started such a program to raise government loans in France (*c.*1653).

Ton·ton Ma·coute /ˈtônˌtôN məˈkōōt/ ▸*n.* (*pl.* **Ton·tons Ma·coutes** *pronunc.* same) a member of a notoriously brutal militia formed by President François Duvalier of Haiti, active from 1961 to 1986. ▹Haitian French, apparently with reference to an ogre of folk tales.

to·nus /ˈtōnəs/ ▸*n.* the constant low-level activity of a body tissue, esp. muscle tone. ▹late 19th cent.: from Latin, from Greek *tonos* 'tension.'

Ton·y /ˈtōnē/ ▸*n.* (*pl.* **Ton·ys**) any of a number of awards given annually in the U.S. for outstanding achievement in the theater in various categories. ▹from the nickname of Antoinette Perry (1888–1946), U.S. actress and director.

Pronunciation Key ə *ago*; ər *over*; ˈə or ˌə *up*; ˈər or ˌər *fur*; a *hat*; ā *rate*; ä *car*; CH *chew*; e *let*; ē *see*; e(ə)r *air*; i *fit*; ī *by*; i(ə)r *ear*; NG *sing*; ō *go*; ô *for*; oi *boy*; ŏŏ *good*; ōō *goo*; ou *out*; SH *she*; TH *thin*; TH *then*; (h)w *why*; ZH *vision*

ton·y /ˈtōnē/ ▸*adj.* (**ton·i·er**, **ton·i·est**) *informal* fashionable among wealthy or stylish people: *a tony restaurant.* ▷late 19th cent.: from the noun TONE + -Y[1].

too /to͞o/ ▸*adv.* **1** [as *submodifier*] to a higher degree than is desirable, permissible, or possible; excessively: *he was driving too fast* | *he wore suits that seemed a size* **too** *small* **for** *him.* ■ *informal* very: *you're too kind.* **2** in addition; also: *is he coming too?* ■ moreover (used when adding a further point): *she is a grown woman, and a strong one too.* ▷Old English, stressed form of TO, spelled *too* from the 16th cent.

▸*PHRASES* □ **all too ——** used to emphasize that something is the case to an extreme or unwelcome extent: *failures are all too common.* □ **none too ——** far from; not very: *her sight's none too good.* □ **only too** see ONLY. □ **too bad** see BAD. □ **too far** see FAR. □ **too much** see MUCH.

too·dle-oo /ˌto͞odl ˈo͞o/ ▸*exclam. informal, dated* goodbye: *we'll see you later, toodle-oo!* ▷early 20th cent.: perhaps an alteration of French *à tout à l'heure* 'see you soon.'

took /to͝ok/ ▸ past of TAKE.

tool /to͞ol/ ▸*n.* **1** a device or implement, esp. one held in the hand, used to carry out a particular function: *gardening tools.* ■ a thing used in an occupation or pursuit: *computers are an essential tool* | *the ability to write clearly is* **a tool of the trade**. ■ a person used or exploited by another: *the beautiful Estella is Miss Havisham's tool.* ■ *Computing* a piece of software that carries out a particular function, typically creating or modifying another program. **2** a distinct design in the tooling of a book. ■ a small stamp or roller used to make such a design. **3** *vulgar slang* a man's penis. ■ *informal* a dull, slow-witted, or socially inept person.

▸*v.* **1** [*trans.*] (usu. **be tooled**) impress a design on (leather, esp. a leather book cover): *volumes bound in green leather and tooled in gold.* ■ dress (stone) with a chisel. **2** equip or be equipped with tools for industrial production: [*trans.*] *the factory must be tooled to produce the models* | [*intrans.*] *they were* **tooling up** *for production.* **3** [*intrans.*] *informal* drive or ride in a casual or leisurely manner: *tooling around town in a pink Rolls-Royce.* ▷Old English *tōl*, from a Germanic base meaning 'prepare'; compare with TAW[1]. The verb dates from the early 19th cent. **—tool·er** *n.*

THE RIGHT WORD **apparatus, appliance, implement, instrument, tool, utensil**

A wrench is a **tool**, meaning that it is a device held in and manipulated by the hand and used by a mechanic, plumber, carpenter, or other laborer to work, shape, move, or transform material (*he couldn't fix the drawer without the right tools*).

An **implement** is a broader term referring to any tool or mechanical device used for a particular purpose (*agricultural implements*).

A washing machine is an **appliance**, which refers to a mechanical or power-driven device, especially for household use (*the newlyweds went shopping for appliances*).

A **utensil** is a hand-held implement for domestic use (*eating utensils*), while an **instrument** is used for scientific or artistic purposes (*musical instrument; surgical instrument*).

Apparatus refers to a collection of distinct instruments, tools, or other devices that are used in connection or combination with one another for a certain purpose (*the gym was open, but the exercise apparatus had not been set up*).

tool·bar /ˈto͞olˌbär/ ▸*n. Computing* (in a program with a graphical user interface) a strip of icons used to perform certain functions.

tool·box /ˈto͞olˌbäks/ ▸*n.* a box or container for keeping tools in. ■ *Computing* a set of software tools. ■ *Computing* the set of programs or functions accessible from a single menu.

tool·ing /ˈto͞oliNG/ ▸*n.* **1** assorted tools, esp. ones required for a mechanized process. ■ the process of making or working something with tools. **2** the ornamentation of a leather book cover with designs impressed by heated tools.

tool kit ▸*n.* a set of tools, esp. one kept in a bag or box and used for a particular purpose. ■ *Computing* a set of software tools.

tool·mak·er /ˈto͞olˌmākər/ ▸*n.* a maker of tools, esp. a person who makes and maintains tools for use in a manufacturing process. **—tool·mak·ing** /-ˌmākiNG/ *n.*

tool push·er (also **tool·push·er**) ▸*n.* a person who directs the drilling on an oil rig.

tool·shed /ˈto͞olˌSHed/ (also **tool shed**) ▸*n.* a one-story structure, typically in a backyard, used for storing tools.

toon /to͞on/ ▸*n. informal* a cartoon film. ■ a character in such a film. ▷1930s: shortening of CARTOON.

too·nie /ˈto͞onē/ (also **twoo·nie**) ▸*n. Canadian informal* the Canadian two-dollar coin. ▷after LOONIE.

toot /to͞ot/ ▸*n.* **1** a short, sharp sound made by a horn, trumpet, or similar instrument. **2** *informal* a snort of a drug, esp. cocaine. ■ cocaine. **3** *informal* a spell of drinking and lively enjoyment; a spree: *a sales manager* **on a toot**.

▸*v.* [*trans.*] **1** sound (a horn or similar instrument) with a short, sharp sound: *behind us an impatient driver tooted a horn.* ■ [*intrans.*] make such a sound: *a car* **tooted at** *us.* **2** *informal* snort (cocaine). ▷early 16th cent.: probably from Middle Low German *tūten*, but possibly an independent imitative formation. **—toot·er** *n.*

tooth /to͞oTH/ ▸*n.* (*pl.* **teeth** /tēTH/) **1** each of a set of hard, bony enamel-coated structures in the jaws of most vertebrates, used for biting and chewing. ■ a similar hard, pointed structure in invertebrate animals, typically functioning in the mechanical breakdown of food. ■ an appetite or liking for a particular thing. ■ roughness given to a surface to allow color or glue to adhere. ■ (**teeth**) *figurative* genuine force or effectiveness of a body or in a law or agreement: *the Charter would be fine if it had teeth and could be enforced.* **2** a projecting part on a tool or other instrument, esp. one of a series that function or engage together, such as a cog on a gearwheel or a point on a saw or comb. ■ a projecting part on an animal or plant, esp. one of a jagged or dentate row on the margin of a leaf or shell. ▷Old English *tōth* (plural *tēth*), of Germanic origin; related to Dutch *tand* and German *Zahn*, from an Indo-European root shared by Latin *dent-*, Greek *odont-*. **—toothed** *adj.* **—tooth·like** /-ˌlīk/ *adj.*

▸*PHRASES* □ **armed to the teeth** formidably armed. □ **fight tooth and nail** fight fiercely. □ **get** (or **sink**) **one's teeth into** work energetically and productively on (a task): *the course gives students something to get their teeth into.* □ **in the teeth of** directly against (the wind). ■ in spite of or contrary to (opposition or difficulty): *we defended it in the teeth of persecution.* □ **set someone's teeth on edge** see EDGE.

tooth·ache /ˈto͞oTHˌāk/ ▸*n.* a pain in a tooth or teeth: *he has a toothache.*

tooth·ache tree ▸*n.* another term for NORTHERN PRICKLY-ASH (see PRICKLY-ASH).

tooth·brush /ˈto͞oTHˌbrəSH/ ▸*n.* a small brush with a long handle, used for cleaning the teeth.

tooth·brush mus·tache ▸*n.* a short bristly mustache trimmed to a rectangular shape.

toothed whale ▸*n.* a predatory whale having teeth rather than baleen plates. Toothed whales include sperm whales, killer whales, beaked whales, narwhals, dolphins, and porpoises. • Suborder Odontoceti, order Cetacea: six families and numerous species.

tooth fair·y ▸*n.* a fairy said to leave a gift, esp. a coin, under a child's pillow in exchange for a baby tooth that has fallen out and been put under the pillow.

tooth·less /ˈto͞oTHlis/ ▸*adj.* having no teeth, typically through old age: *a toothless old man.* ■ *figurative* lacking genuine force or effectiveness: *laws that are well intentioned but toothless.* **—tooth·less·ly** *adv.* **—tooth·less·ness** *n.*

tooth·paste /ˈto͞oTHˌpāst/ ▸*n.* a paste used on a toothbrush for cleaning the teeth.

tooth·pick /ˈto͞oTHˌpik/ ▸*n.* a short pointed piece of wood or plastic used for removing bits of food lodged between the teeth.

tooth pow·der ▸*n.* powder used for cleaning the teeth.

tooth shell ▸*n.* a burrowing mollusk with a slender tusk-shaped shell, which is open at both ends and typically white, and a three-lobed foot. Also called TUSK SHELL. • Class Scaphopoda, in particular the genus *Dentalium*.

tooth·some /ˈto͞oTHsəm/ ▸*adj.* (of food) temptingly tasty: *a toothsome morsel.* ■ *informal* (of a person) good-looking; attractive. **—tooth·some·ly** *adv.* **—tooth·some·ness** *n.*

tooth·y /ˈto͞oTHē/ ▸*adj.* (**tooth·i·er**, **tooth·i·est**) having or showing large, numerous, or prominent teeth: *a toothy smile.* **—tooth·i·ly** /-THəlē/ *adv.*

toot·in' /ˈto͞otn/ ▸*adj. informal* used for emphasis: *he said he was damned tootin' he was right.*

too·tle /ˈto͞otl/ ▸*v.* **1** [*intrans.*] casually make a series of sounds on a horn, trumpet, or similar instrument: *he tootled on the horn.* ■ [*trans.*] play (an instrument) or make (a sound or tune) in such a way: *the video games tootled their tunes.* **2** [*intrans.*] *informal* go or travel in a leisurely way: *they were* **tootling along** *the coast.*

▸*n.* [usu. in *sing.*] **1** an act or sound of casual playing on an instrument such as a horn or trumpet. **2** *informal* a leisurely journey. ▷early 19th cent.: frequentative of TOOT.

too-too ▸*adv.* & *adj. informal, dated* used affectedly to convey that one finds something excessively annoying or fatiguing: [as *adv.*] *it had become too-too tiring* | [as *adj.*] *it is all just too-too.* ▷late 19th cent.: reduplication of TOO.

toot·sie /ˈto͝otsē/ (also **toot·sy**) ▸*n.* (*pl.* **-sies**) *informal* **1** a person's foot. **2** a young woman, esp. one perceived as being sexually available. ▷mid 19th cent.: humorous diminutive of FOOT.

toot sweet ▸*adv. informal* immediately: *hop down here toot sweet and let's have a look at it.* ▷early 20th cent.: anglicized form of French *tout de suite*.

top[1] /täp/ ▸*n.* **1** [usu. in *sing.*] the highest or uppermost point, part, or surface of something: *Eileen stood at the top of the stairs* | *fill the cup almost to the top.* ■ (usu. **tops**) the leaves, stems, and shoots of a plant, esp. those of a vegetable grown for its root. ■ *chiefly Brit.* the end of something that is furthest from the speaker or a point of reference: *the bus shelter at the top of the road.* **2** a thing or part placed on, fitted to, or covering the upper part of something, in particular: ■ a garment covering the upper part of the body and worn with a skirt, pants, or shorts. ■ a lid, cover, or cap for something: *the pen dries out if you leave the top off.* ■ a platform at the head of a ship's mast, esp. (in a sailing ship) a platform around the head of each of the lower masts, serving to extend the topmast shrouds. **3** (**the top**) the highest or most important rank, level, or position: *her talent will take her right to the top* | *the people* **at the top** *must be competent.* ■ a person or thing occupying such a position: *North Korea was top of the agenda.* ■ (**tops**) *informal* a person or thing regarded as particularly good or pleasant: *Davison is tops in its market.* ■ the utmost degree or the highest level: *she shouted at the top of her voice.* ■ *Brit.* the highest gear of a motor vehicle. ■ the high-frequency component of reproduced sound. **4** *Baseball* the first half of an inning: *the top of the eighth.* **5** short for TOPSPIN. **6** (usu. **tops**) a bundle of long wool fibers prepared for spinning. **7** *Physics* one of six flavors of quark. **8** *informal* a male who takes the active role in homosexual intercourse, esp. anal intercourse.

▸*adj.* [*attrib.*] highest in position, rank, or degree: *the top button of his shirt* | *a top executive.*

▸*v.* (**topped**, **top·ping**) [*trans.*] **1** exceed (an amount, level, or number); be more than: *losses are expected to top $100 million this year.* ■ be at the highest place or rank in (a list, poll, chart, or league): *her debut album topped the charts for five weeks.* ■ be taller than: *he topped her by several inches.* ■ surpass (a person or previous achievement or action); outdo: *he was baffled as to how he could top his past work.* ■ appear as the chief performer or attraction at: *Hopper topped a great night of boxing.* ■ reach the top of (a hill or other stretch of rising ground): *they topped a rise and began a slow descent.* **2** (usu. **be topped**) provide with a top or topping: *baked potatoes topped with melted cheese.* ■ complete (an outfit) with an upper garment, hat, or item of jewelry: *a white dress topped by a dark cardigan.* ■ remove the top of (a vegetable or fruit) in preparation for cooking. **3** *Golf* mishit (the ball or a stroke) by hitting above the center of the ball.

▸*phrasal v.* □ **top something off** **1** (often **be topped off**) finish something in a memorable or notable way: *the festivities were topped off with the awarding of prizes.* **2** *informal* fill up a nearly full tank with fuel. □ **top out** reach an upper limit: *collectors whose budgets tend to top out at about $50,000.* □ **top something out** put the highest structural feature on a building, typically as a ceremony to mark the building's completion. □ **top something up** *chiefly Brit.* add to a number or amount to bring it up to a certain level: *a 0.5 percent bonus is offered to top up savings rates.* ■ fill up a glass or other partly full container.

▸*adv.* (**tops**) *informal* at the most: *he makes $28,000 a year, tops.* ▷late Old English *topp* (noun), of Germanic origin; related to Dutch *top* 'summit, crest.' **—top·most** /-ˌmōst/ *adj.* **—topped** *adj.* [in *combination*] *a glass-topped table.*

▸*PHRASES* □ **at the top of one's lungs** as loudly as possible. □ **from top to bottom** completely; thoroughly: *we searched the place from top to bottom.* □ **from top to toe** completely; all over: *she seemed to glow from top to* *toe.* □ **from the top** *informal* from the beginning: *they rehearsed Act One from the top.* □ **off the top of one's head** see **HEAD**. □ **on top** **1** on the highest point or uppermost surface: *a hill with a flat rock on top.* ■ on the upper part of the head: *my hair's thinning on top.* **2** in a leading or the dominant position: *his party came out on top in last month's elections.* □ **on top of** **1** on the highest point or uppermost surface of: *a town perched on top of a hill.* ■ so as to cover; over: *trays stacked one on top of another.* ■ in close proximity to: *we all lived on top of each other.* **2** in command or control of: *he couldn't get on top of his work.* **3** in addition to: *on top of everything else, he's a brilliant linguist.* □ **on top of the world** *informal* happy and elated. □ **over the top** /ˌōvər T͟Hə 'täp/ **1** *informal* to an excessive or exaggerated degree, in particular so as to go beyond reasonable or acceptable limits: *his reactions had been a bit over the top.* **2** *chiefly historical* over the parapet of a trench and into battle. □ **top dollar** *informal* a very high price: *I pay top dollar for my materials.* □ **top forty** (or **ten**, etc.) the first forty (or ten, etc.) records in the pop music charts. □ **to top it all** as a culminating, typically unpleasant, event or action in a series: *her father had a fatal heart attack, and to top it all her mother disowned her.* □ **up top** see **UP**.

top[2] ▸*n.* (also **spinning top**) a conical, spherical, or pear-shaped toy that with a quick or vigorous twist may be set to spin. ▷late Old English, of unknown origin.

to·paz /'tōpaz/ ▸*n.* **1** a precious stone, typically colorless, yellow, or pale blue, consisting of a fluorine-containing aluminum silicate. ■ a dark yellow color. **2** a large tropical American hummingbird with a yellowish throat and a long tail. • Genus *Topaza*, family Trochilidae: two species. ▷Middle English (denoting a yellow sapphire): from Old French *topace*, via Latin from Greek *topazos*.

to·paz·o·lite /tō'pazəˌlīt/ ▸*n.* a yellowish-green variety of andradite (garnet). ▷early 19th cent.: from **TOPAZ** + **-LITE**.

top boot ▸*n. chiefly historical* a high boot with a broad band of a different material or color at the top.

top brass ▸*n.* see **BRASS**.

top·coat /'täpˌkōt/ ▸*n.* **1** an overcoat. **2** an outer coat of paint.

top dead cen·ter ▸*n.* the furthest point of a piston's travel, at which it changes from an upward to a downward stroke.

top dog ▸*n. informal* a person who is successful or dominant in their field: *he was a top dog in the City.*

top-down ▸*adj.* **1** denoting a system of government or management in which actions and policies are initiated at the highest level; hierarchical. **2** proceeding from the general to the particular: *a top-down approach to research.* ■ *Computing* working from the top or root of a treelike system toward the branches.

top draw·er ▸*n.* the uppermost drawer in a chest or desk. ■ (**the top drawer**) *informal* high social position or class: *George and Madge were not out of the top drawer.*
▸*adj.* (**top-draw·er**) *informal* of the highest quality or social class: *a top-drawer performance.*

top-dress·ing (also **top dres·sing**) ▸*n.* an application of manure or fertilizer to the surface layer of soil or a lawn. —**top-dress** *v.*

tope[1] /tōp/ ▸*v.* [*intrans.*] *archaic* or *poetic/literary* drink alcohol to excess, esp. on a regular basis. ▷mid 17th cent.: perhaps an alteration of obsolete *top* 'overbalance'; perhaps from Dutch *toppen* 'slant or tilt a ship's yard.' —**top·er** *n.*

tope[2] ▸*n.* another term for **STUPA**. ▷from Punjabi *thūp, thop* 'barrow, mound,' apparently related to Sanskrit *stūpa.*

tope[3] ▸*n.* a small grayish slender-bodied shark, occurring chiefly in inshore waters. • Genus *Galeorhinus*, family Carcharhinidae: the eastern Atlantic *G. galeus*, and the commercially important *G. australis* of Australia. ▷late 17th cent.: perhaps of Cornish origin.

to·pee ▸*n.* variant spelling of **TOPI**[1].

To·pe·ka /tə'pēkə/ the capital of Kansas, in the east central part of the state; pop. 122,377.

top fer·men·ta·tion ▸*n.* the process by which ale-type beers are fermented, proceeding for a relatively short period at high temperature with the yeast rising to the top.

top flight ▸*n.* (**the top flight**) the highest rank or level.
▸*adj.* [*attrib.*] of the highest rank or level: *a top-flight investment bank.*

Top 40 ▸*plural n.* the forty most popular songs of a given time period.
▸*adj.* made up of, or broadcasting the Top 40: *a Top 40 countdown.*

top·gal·lant /täp'galənt; tə'gal-/ ▸*n.* (also **topgallant mast**) the section of a square-rigged sailing ship's mast immediately above the topmast. ■ (also **topgallant sail**) a sail set on such a mast.

top·ham·per ▸*n. Sailing* sails, rigging, or other things above decks creating top-heaviness or catching too much wind.

top hat ▸*n.* a man's formal hat with a high cylindrical crown.

top hat

top-heav·y ▸*adj.* disproportionately heavy at the top so as to be in danger of toppling. ■ (of an organization) having a disproportionately large number of people in senior administrative positions. ■ *informal* (of a woman) having a disproportionately large bust. —**top-heav·i·ly** *adv.* —**top-heav·i·ness** *n.*

To·phet /'tōfet/ ▸*n.* a term for hell. ▷late Middle English: from Hebrew *tōpet*, the name of a place in the Valley of Hinnom near Jerusalem used for idolatrous worship, including the sacrifice of children (see Jer. 19:6), and later for burning refuse.

top·hole ▸*adj. Brit., informal, dated* excellent; first-rate.

to·phus /'tōfəs/ ▸*n.* (*pl.* **-phi** /-fī/) *Medicine* a deposit of crystalline uric acid and other substances at the surface of joints or in skin or cartilage, typically as a feature of gout. ▷early 17th cent.: from Latin, denoting loose porous stones of various kinds.

to·pi[1] /'tōpē/ (also **to·pee**) ▸*n.* (*pl.* **-pis** also **-pees**) *chiefly Indian* a hat, esp. a sola topi. ▷from Hindi *ṭopī* 'hat.'

to·pi[2] ▸*n.* (*pl.* same or **-pis**) a large African antelope related to the hartebeests, with a pattern of bold black patches on a reddish coat, and thick ridged horns. • *Damaliscus lunatus*, family Bovidae, in particular the race *D. l. topi* of East Africa. Compare with **SASSABY**. ▷late 19th cent.: from Mende.

to·pi·ar·y /'tōpēˌerē/ ▸*n.* (*pl.* **-ar·ies**) the art or practice of clipping shrubs or trees into ornamental shapes. ■ shrubs or trees clipped into ornamental shapes in such a way: *a cottage surrounded by topiary and flowers.* ▷late 16th cent.: from French *topiaire*, from Latin *topiarius* 'ornamental gardener,' from *topia opera* 'fancy gardening,' from a diminutive of Greek *topos* 'place.' —**to·pi·ar·i·an** /ˌtōpē'e(ə)rēən/ *adj.* —**to·pi·a·rist** /-ərist/ *n.*

topiary

top·ic /'täpik/ ▸*n.* a matter dealt with in a text, discourse, or conversation; a subject: *her favorite topic of conversation is her partner.* ■ *Linguistics* that part of a sentence about which something is said, typically the first major constituent. ▷late 15th cent. (originally denoting a set or book of general rules or ideas): from Latin *topica*, from Greek *ta topika*, literally 'matters concerning commonplaces' (the title of a treatise by Aristotle), from *topos* 'a place.'

top·i·cal /'täpikəl/ ▸*adj.* **1** (of a subject) of immediate relevance, interest, or importance owing to its relation to current events: *a wide variety of subjects of topical interest.* ■ relating to a particular subject; classified according to subject: *annotated links to resources in eleven topical categories.* ■ *Philately* relating to the collecting of postage stamps with designs connected with the same subject. **2** *chiefly Medicine* relating or applied directly to a part of the body.
▸*n. Philately* a postage stamp forming part of a set or collection with designs connected with the same subject. ▷late 16th cent.: from Greek *topikos* + **-AL**. Early use was as a term in logic and rhetoric describing a rule or argument as 'applicable in most but not all cases.' —**top·i·cal·i·ty** /ˌtäpə'kalitē/ *n.* —**top·i·cal·ly** /-ik(ə)lē/ *adv.*

top·i·cal·ize /'täpikəˌlīz/ ▸*v.* [*trans.*] *Linguistics* cause (a subject, word, or phrase) to be the topic of a sentence or discourse, typically by placing it first. —**top·i·cal·i·za·tion** /ˌtäpəkəli'zāSHən/ *n.*

top·ic sen·tence ▸*n.* a sentence that expresses the main idea of the paragraph in which it occurs.

top·knot /'täpˌnät/ ▸*n.* a knot of hair arranged on the top of the head. ■ a decorative knot or bow of ribbon worn on the top of the head, popular in the 18th century. ■ (in an animal or bird) a tuft or crest of hair or feathers.

top·less /'täpləs/ ▸*adj.* (of a woman or a woman's item of clothing) having or leaving the breasts uncovered: *a topless dancer | a topless swimsuit.* ■ (of a place such as a bar or beach) where there are women wearing such clothes: *where's the nearest topless beach?* —**top·less·ness** *n.*

top-lev·el ▸*adj.* of the highest level of importance or prestige: *top-level talks.*

top light (also **top·light**) ▸*n.* **1** a skylight: [as *adj.*] (**top-lighted**) *a top-lighted gallery.* **2** *Brit.* a small pane above a main window, typically opening outward and upward.

top-line ▸*adj.* [*attrib.*] of the highest quality or ranking: *a top-line act.*

top·loft·y /'täpˌlôftē/ ▸*adj. informal* haughty and arrogant.

top·mast /'täpˌmast; -məst/ ▸*n.* the second section of a square-rigged sailing ship's mast, immediately above the lower mast.

top·min·now /'täpˌminō/ ▸*n.* a small surface-swimming fish related to the killifishes, found in fresh, brackish, and salt water throughout North America. • Genus *Fundulus*, family Fundulidae: many species, including the **banded topminnow** (*F. cingulatus*) and the **eastern starhead topminnow** (*F. escambiae*).

top-notch ▸*adj. informal* of the highest quality; excellent: *a top-notch hotel.* —**top-notch·er** *n.*

top note ▸*n.* **1** a dominant scent in a perfume: *fragrant musk with a fresh citrus top note.* **2** the highest or a very high note in a piece of music or a singer's vocal range.

top·o /'täpō/ ▸*n.* (*pl.* **top·os**) *informal* a topographic map: *a topo drawn for the Hell Cave area.* ■ *Climbing* a diagram of a mountain with details of routes to the top marked on it.
▸*adj.* short for **TOPOGRAPHICAL**: *the topo map showed a watering hole.* ▷1970s: abbreviation of *topographic* (see **TOPOGRAPHICAL**).

topog. ▸*abbr.* ■ topographical. ■ topography.

top·o·graph·i·cal /ˌtäpə'grafikəl/ ▸*adj.* of or relating to the arrangement or accurate representation of the physical features of an area: *the topographical features of the river valley.* ■ (of a work of art or an artist) dealing with or depicting places (esp. towns), buildings, and natural prospects in a realistic and detailed manner. ■ *Anatomy & Biology* relating to or representing the physical distribution of parts or features on the surface of or within an organ or organism. —**top·o·graph·ic** *adj.* —**top·o·graph·i·cal·ly** /-ik(ə)lē/ *adv.*

to·pog·ra·phy /tə'pägrəfē/ ▸*n.* the arrangement of the natural and artificial physical features of an area: *the topography of the island.* ■ a detailed description or representation on a map of such features. ■ *Anatomy & Biology* the distribution of parts or features on the surface of or within an organ or organism. ▷late Middle English: via late Latin from Greek *topographia*, from *topos* 'place' + *-graphia* (see **-GRAPHY**). —**to·pog·ra·pher** /-fər/ *n.*

to·poi /'tōpoi/ ▸ plural form of **TOPOS**.

top·o·i·so·mer /ˌtäpō'īsəmər/ ▸*n. Biochemistry* a topologically distinct isomer, esp. of DNA.

top·o·i·som·er·ase /ˌtäpōˌī'säməˌrās; -ˌrāz/ ▸*n. Biochemistry* an enzyme that alters the supercoiled form of a DNA molecule. ▷1970s: from Greek *topos* 'place' + **ISOMER** + **-ASE**.

top·o·log·i·cal space /ˌtäpə'läjikəl/ ▸*n. Mathematics* a space that has an associated family of subsets that constitute a topology. The relationships between members of the space are mathematically analogous to those between points in ordinary two- and three-dimensional space.

to·pol·o·gy /tə'päləjē/ ▸*n.* **1** *Mathematics* the study of geometric properties and spatial relations unaffected by the continuous change of shape or size of figures. ■ a family of open subsets of an abstract space such that the union and the intersection of any two of them are members of the family, and that includes the space itself and the empty set. **2** the way in which constituent parts are interrelated or arranged: *the topology of a computer network.* ▷late 19th cent.: via German from Greek *topos* 'place' + **-LOGY**. —**top·o·log·i·cal** /ˌtäpə'läjikəl/ *adj.* —**top·o·log·i·cal·ly** /ˌtäpə'läjik(ə)lē/ *adv.* —**to·pol·o·gist** /-jist/ *n.*

top·o·nym /ˈtäpə,nim/ ▸*n.* a place name, esp. one derived from a topographical feature. ▷1930s: from Greek *topos* 'place' + *onuma* 'a name.'

to·pon·y·my /təˈpänəmē/ ▸*n.* the study of place names. ▷late 19th cent.: from Greek *topos* 'place' + *onuma* 'name.' —**top·o·nym·ic** /,täpəˈnimik/ *adj.*

to·pos /ˈtōpōs/ ▸*n.* (*pl.* **-poi** /-poi/) a traditional theme or formula in literature. ▷1940s: from Greek, literally 'place.'

top·per /ˈtäpər/ ▸*n.* **1** something that goes on top of something else: *slow-moving water toppers, such as spiders.* **2** something that culminates a situation; a clincher: *the topper was a late-evening interview with an old man who ran the place.* **3** a hard protective lightweight cover or shell mounted on the back or bed of a pickup truck. ■ a type of camper mounted on a truck bed. **4** *informal* a top hat. **5** *Brit. informal, dated* an exceptionally good person or thing. **6** a woman's loose, short coat.

top·ping /ˈtäpiNG/ ▸*n.* a layer of food poured or spread over a base of a different type of food to add flavor: *a cake with a marzipan topping.*
▸*adj. Brit., informal, dated* excellent: *that really is a topping dress.*

top·ping lift ▸*n.* a rope or cable on a sailing vessel that supports the weight of a boom or yard and can be used to lift it.

top·ple /ˈtäpəl/ ▸*v.* [*intrans.*] overbalance or become unsteady and fall slowly: *she toppled over when I touched her.* ■ [*trans.*] cause to fall in such a way: *the push almost toppled him to the ground* | *figurative disagreement had threatened to topple the government.* ▷mid 16th cent. (in the sense 'roll around'): frequentative of **TOP**[1].

top quark (abbr.: **t**) ▸*n.* a hypothetical quark with a mass of 360,000 times that of an electron and a charge of +$^2/_3$.

top rope *Climbing* ▸*n.* a rope lowered from above to the lead climber in a group, typically to give assistance at a difficult part of a climb.
▸*v.* (**top-rope**) [*trans.*] climb (a route or part of one) using a top rope.

top round ▸*n.* a cut of meat taken from an inner section of a round of beef.

top·sail /ˈtäpsəl; -,sāl/ ▸*n.* a sail set on a ship's topmast. ■ a fore-and-aft sail set above the gaff.

top se·cret ▸*adj.* of the highest secrecy; highly confidential: *the experiments were top secret* | *a top-secret mission.* ■ (of information or documents) given the highest security classification, above secret.

top·side /ˈtäp,sīd/ ▸*n.* (often **topsides**) the upper part of a ship's side, above the waterline.
▸*adv.* on or toward the upper decks of a ship: *we stayed topside.*

Top-Sid·er ▸*n. trademark* a casual shoe, typically made of leather or canvas with a rubber sole, designed to be worn on boats.

top·soil /ˈtäp,soil/ ▸*n.* the top layer of soil.

top·spin /ˈtäp,spin/ ▸*n.* a fast forward spinning motion imparted to a ball when throwing or hitting it, often resulting in a curved path or a strong forward motion on rebounding. —**top·spin·ner** *n.*

top·stitch /ˈtäp,stiCH/ ▸*v.* [*intrans.*] make a row of continuous stitches on the top or right side of a garment or other article as a decorative feature.

top·sy-tur·vy /ˈtäpsē ˈtərvē/ ▸*adj.* upside down: *the fairground ride turned riders topsy-turvy.* ■ in a state of confusion: *the topsy-turvy months of the invasion.*
▸*n.* [in *sing.*] a state of utter confusion. ▷early 16th cent.: a jingle apparently based on **TOP**[1] and obsolete *terve* 'overturn.' —**top·sy-tur·vi·ly** /ˈtərvəlē/ *adv.* —**top·sy-tur·vi·ness** *n.*

top·wa·ter /ˈtäp,wôtər; -,wätər/ ▸*adj. Fishing* (of a bait) floating on or near the top of the water.

toque /tōk/ ▸*n.* a woman's small hat, typically having a narrow, closely turned-up brim. ■ *historical* a small cap or bonnet of such a type worn by a man or woman. ■ a tall white hat with a full pouched crown, worn by chefs. ▷early 16th cent.: from French, of unknown origin.

to·qui·lla /tōˈkē(y)ə/ ▸*n.* a palmlike tree, *Carludovica palmata*, native to South America. ■ the fiber obtained from this plant, used esp. to make hats. ▷late 19th cent.: from an American Spanish use of Spanish *toquilla* 'small gauze headdress,' diminutive of *toca* 'toque.'

tor /tôr/ ▸*n.* a hill or rocky peak. ▷Old English *torr*, perhaps of Celtic origin and related to Welsh *tor* 'belly' and Scottish Gaelic *tòrr* 'bulging hill.'

To·rah /ˈtôrə; ˈtō-; tôˈrä/ ▸*n.* (usu. **the Torah**) (in Judaism) the law of God as revealed to Moses and recorded in the first five books of the Hebrew scriptures (the Pentateuch). ■ a scroll containing this. ▷from Hebrew *tōrāh* 'instruction, doctrine, law,' from *yārāh* 'show, direct, instruct.'

torc /tôrk/ (also **torque**) ▸*n. historical* a neck ornament consisting of a band of twisted metal, worn esp. by the ancient Gauls and Britons. ▷mid 19th cent.: from French *torque*, from Latin *torques* (see **TORCH**).

torch /tôrCH/ ▸*n. chiefly historical* a portable means of illumination such as a piece of wood or cloth soaked in tallow or an oil lamp on a pole, sometimes carried ceremonially. ■ (usu. **the torch**) *figurative* used to refer to a valuable quality, principle, or cause that needs to be protected and maintained: *mountain warlords carried the torch of Greek independence.* ■ a blowtorch. ■ *informal* an arsonist. ■ British term for **FLASHLIGHT**.
▸*v.* [*trans.*] *informal* set fire to: *the shops had been looted and torched.* ▷Middle English: from Old French *torche*, from Latin *torqua*, variant of *torques* 'necklace, wreath,' from *torquere* 'to twist.' The current verb sense was originally U.S. slang and dates from the 1930s.
▸*PHRASES* □ **carry a torch for** suffer from unrequited love for. □ **put to the torch** (or **put a torch to**) destroy by burning.

torch·bear·er /ˈtôrCH,be(ə)rər/ ▸*n.* a person who carries a ceremonial torch. ■ *figurative* a person who leads or inspires others in working toward a valued goal.

tor·chère /tôrˈSHer/ ▸*n.* a tall ornamental flat-topped stand, traditionally used as a stand for a candlestick. ▷early 20th cent.: French, from *torche* (see **TORCH**).

torch·light /ˈtôrCH,līt/ ▸*n.* the light of a torch or torches. —**torch·lit** /-lit/ *adj.*

tor·chon lace /ˈtôrSHän/ ▸*n.* coarse bobbin lace with geometric designs. ▷mid 19th cent.: from French, literally 'duster, dishcloth,' from *torcher* 'to wipe.'

torch song ▸*n.* a sad or sentimental song of unrequited love. ▷1920s: *torch* from the phrase 'carry a torch for' (see **TORCH**). —**torch sing·er** *n.*

tore[1] /tôr/ ▸ past of **TEAR**[1].

tore[2] ▸*n.* archaic term for **TORUS**. ▷mid 17th cent.: from French.

tor·e·a·dor /ˈtôrēə,dôr/ ▸*n.* a bullfighter. ▷Spanish, from *torear* 'fight bulls,' from *toro* 'bull.'

tor·e·a·dor pants ▸*plural n.* women's tight-fitting calf-length trousers.

to·re·ro /təˈre(ə)rō/ ▸*n.* (*pl.* **-ros**) a bullfighter. ▷Spanish, from *toro* 'bull' (see **TOREADOR**).

to·reu·tics /təˈrōōtiks/ ▸*plural n.* [treated as *sing.*] the art of making designs in relief or intaglio, esp. by chasing, carving, and embossing in metal. ▷mid 19th cent.: from Greek *toreutikos*, from *toreuein* 'to work in relief.' —**to·reu·tic** *adj.*

to·ri /ˈtôrī/ ▸ plural form of **TORUS**.

tor·ic /ˈtôrik/ ▸*adj. Geometry* having the form of a torus or part of a torus. ■ (of a contact lens) having two different curves instead of one, used to correct both astigmatism and near- or farsightedness.

to·ri·i /ˈtôrē,ē/ ▸*n.* (*pl.* same) the gateway of a Shinto shrine, with two uprights and two crosspieces. ▷Japanese, from *tori* 'bird' + *i* 'sit, perch.'

torii

To·ri·no /təˈrēnō/ Italian name for **TURIN**.

tor·ment ▸*n.* /ˈtôrment/ severe physical or mental suffering: *their deaths have left both families in torment.* ■ a cause of such suffering: *the journey must have been a torment for them.*
▸*v.* /tôrˈment/ [*trans.*] cause to experience severe mental or physical suffering: *he was tormented by jealousy.* ■ annoy or provoke in a deliberately unkind way: *every day I have kids tormenting me because they know I live alone.* ▷Middle English (as both noun and verb referring to the infliction or suffering of torture): from Old French *torment* (noun), *tormenter* (verb), from Latin *tormentum* 'instrument of torture,' from *torquere* 'to twist.' —**tor·ment·ed·ly** /tôrˈmentədlē/ *adv.* —**tor·ment·ing·ly** /tôrˈmentiNGlē/ *adv.* —**tor·men·tor** /tôrˈmentər/ *n.*

tor·men·til /ˈtôrmən,til/ ▸*n.* a low-growing Eurasian plant with bright yellow flowers. The root is used in herbal medicine to treat diarrhea. • *Potentilla erecta*, family Rosaceae. ▷late Middle English: from French *tormentille*, from medieval Latin *tormentilla*, of unknown origin.

torn /tôrn/ ▸ past participle of **TEAR**[1].

tor·na·do /tôrˈnādō/ ▸*n.* (*pl.* **-does** or **-dos**) a mobile, destructive vortex of violently rotating winds having the appearance of a funnel-shaped cloud and advancing beneath a large storm system. ■ *figurative* a person or thing characterized by violent or devastating action or emotion: *a tornado of sexual confusion.* ▷mid 16th cent. (denoting a violent thunderstorm of the tropical Atlantic Ocean): perhaps an alteration of Spanish *tronada* 'thunderstorm' (from *tronar* 'to thunder') by association with Spanish *tornar* 'to turn.' —**tor·nad·ic** /-ˈnādik; -ˈnadik/ *adj.*

tor·na·do al·ley ▸*n.* an area of the Great Plains centered on eastern Kansas and Oklahoma and including parts of the surrounding states, where tornadoes are frequent.

Tor·ni·o /ˈtôrnē,ō/ a river that rises in northeastern Sweden and flows south for 356 miles (566 km) to form the border between Sweden and Finland before it empties into the Gulf of Bothnia. Swedish name **TORNE ÄLV**.

to·ro /ˈtôrō/ ▸*n.* a pale, fatty cut of tuna used for sushi and sashimi. ▷Japanese, 'tuna belly.'

to·roid /ˈtôroid/ ▸*n. Geometry* a figure with a shape resembling a torus. ■ *Electronics* a coil shaped like a torus or doughnut.

to·roi·dal /tôˈroidl/ ▸*adj. Geometry* of or resembling a torus. —**to·roi·dal·ly** *adv.*

To·ron·to /təˈräntō/ a city in Canada, capital of Ontario, on the northern shore of Lake Ontario; pop. 635,395. ▷originally named York but renamed *Toronto* in 1834, from an Iroquoian word of uncertain meaning.

tor·pe·do /tôrˈpēdō/ ▸*n.* (*pl.* **-does**) **1** a cigar-shaped self-propelled underwater missile designed to be fired from a ship or submarine or dropped into the water from an aircraft and to explode on reaching a target. ■ a signal placed on a railroad track, exploding as the train passes over it. ■ a firework exploding on impact with a hard surface. ■ *informal* a submarine sandwich. ■ *informal* a gangster hired to commit a murder or other violent act. ■ an explosive device lowered into oil wells to clear obstructions. **2** (also **tor·pe·do ray**) an electric ray.
▸*v.* (**-does, -doed**) [*trans.*] attack or sink (a ship) with a torpedo or torpedoes. ■ *figurative* destroy or ruin (a plan or project): *fighting between the militias torpedoed peace talks.* ▷early 16th cent. (sense 2): from Latin, literally 'stiffness, numbness,' by extension 'electric ray' (which gives a shock causing numbness), from *torpere* 'be numb or sluggish.' Sense 1 dates from the late 18th cent. and first described a timed explosive device for detonation under water. —**tor·pe·do·like** /-,līk/ *adj.*

tor·pe·do boat ▸*n.* a small, fast, light warship armed with torpedoes.

tor·pe·do net ▸*n. historical* a net made of steel wire, hung in the water around an anchored ship to intercept torpedoes.

tor·pe·do tube ▸*n.* a tube in a submarine or other ship from which torpedoes are fired by the use of compressed air or an explosive charge.

tor·pe·fy /ˈtôrpə,fī/ ▸*v.* (**-fies, -fied**) [*trans.*] *formal* make (someone or something) numb, paralyzed, or lifeless. ▷early 19th cent.: from Latin *torpefacere*, from *torpere* 'be numb or sluggish.'

tor·pid /ˈtôrpid/ ▸*adj.* mentally or physically inactive; lethargic: *we sat around in a torpid state.* ■ (of an animal) dormant, esp. during hibernation. ▷late Middle English: from Latin *torpidus*, from *torpere* 'be numb or sluggish.' —**tor·pid·i·ty** /tôrˈpiditē/ *n.* —**tor·pid·ly** *adv.*

tor·por /ˈtôrpər/ ▸*n.* a state of physical or mental inactivity; lethargy: *they veered between apathetic torpor and hysterical fanaticism.* ▷late Middle English: from Latin, from *torpere* 'be numb or sluggish.'

torque /tôrk/ ▸*n.* **1** *Mechanics* a twisting force that tends to cause rotation. **2** variant spelling of **TORC**.
▸*v.* [*trans.*] apply torque or a twisting force to (an object): *he gently torqued the hip joint.* ▷late 19th cent.: from Latin *torquere* 'to twist.' —**tor·quey** *adj.*

torque con·vert·er ▸*n.* a device that transmits or multiplies torque generated by an engine.

Tor·que·ma·da /,tôrkəˈmädə; ,tôrkäˈmäTHä/, Tomás de (*c.*1420–98), Spanish cleric and Grand Inquisitor. A Dominican monk and confessor to Ferdinand and

Isabella, he was the prime mover behind the Inquisition in 1478 and the expulsion of the Jews from Spain beginning in 1492.

torque wrench ▸*n.* a tool for setting and adjusting the tightness of nuts and bolts to a desired value.

torr /tôr/ ▸*n.* (*pl.* same) a unit of pressure used in measuring partial vacuums, equal to 133.32 pascals. ▷1940s: named after E. TORRICELLI.

Tor·rance /ˈtôrəns; ˈtär-/ a commercial and industrial city in southwestern California, south of Los Angeles; pop. 133,107.

Tor·rens sys·tem /ˈtôrənz; ˈtär-/ ▸*n.* *Law* a system of land title registration, adopted originally in Australia and later in some states of the U.S. ▷mid 19th cent.: named after Sir Robert *Torrens* (1814-84), first premier of South Australia.

tor·rent /ˈtôrənt; ˈtär-/ ▸*n.* a strong and fast-moving stream of water or other liquid: *rain poured down in torrents* | *after the winter rains, the stream becomes a raging torrent.* ■ (**a torrent of** or **torrents of**) a sudden, violent, and copious outpouring of (something, typically words or feelings): *she was subjected to a torrent of abuse* | *banks plowed torrents of money into the booming stock and property markets.* ▷late 16th cent.: from French, from Italian *torrente*, from Latin *torrent-* 'boiling, roaring,' from *torrere* 'parch, scorch.'

tor·ren·tial /tôˈrenCHəl; tə-/ ▸*adj.* (of rain) falling rapidly and in copious quantities: *a torrential downpour.* ■ (of water) flowing rapidly and with force. —**tor·ren·tial·ly** *adv.*

Tor·res Strait /ˈtôrˌez; -əs/ a channel that separates the northern tip of Queensland, Australia, from the island of New Guinea and links the Arafura Sea and the Coral Sea. ▷named after Spanish explorer Luis V. de *Torres*, the first European to sail along the southern coast of New Guinea 1606.

Tor·ri·cel·li /ˌtôrəˈCHelē/, Evangelista (1608–47), Italian mathematician and physicist. He invented the mercury barometer, with which he demonstrated that the atmosphere exerts a pressure sufficient to support a column of mercury in an inverted closed tube.

tor·rid /ˈtôrəd; ˈtär-/ ▸*adj.* very hot and dry: *the torrid heat of the afternoon.* ■ full of passionate or highly charged emotions arising from sexual love: *a torrid love affair.* ■ full of difficulty or tribulation: *Wall Street is in for a torrid time in the next few weeks.* ▷late 16th cent.: from French *torride* or Latin *torridus*, from *torrere* 'parch, scorch.' —**tor·rid·i·ty** /təˈriditē/ *n.* —**tor·rid·ly** *adv.*

tor·rid zone (also **Tor·rid Zone**) ▸*n.* the hot central belt of the earth bounded by the tropics of Cancer and Capricorn.

Tor·ring·ton /ˈtôriNGtən; ˈtär-/ a historic industrial and commercial city in northwestern Connecticut, on the Naugatuck River; pop. 33,687.

tor·sade /tôrˈsäd; -ˈsäd/ ▸*n.* a decorative twisted braid, ribbon, or other strand used as trimming. ■ an artificial plait of hair. ▷late 19th cent.: from French, from Latin *tors-* 'twisted,' from *torquere* 'to twist.'

tor·sade de poin·tes /tôrˈsäd də ˈpwänt/ ▸*n.* *Medicine* a form of tachycardia in which the electrical pulse in the heart undergoes a cyclical variation in strength, giving a characteristic electrocardiogram resembling a twisted fringe of spikes. ▷1960s: French, literally 'twist of spikes.'

torse /tôrs/ ▸*n.* *Heraldry* a wreath. ▷late 16th cent.: from obsolete French, from Latin *torta*, feminine past participle of *torquere* 'twist.'

tor·sion /ˈtôrSHən/ ▸*n.* the action of twisting or the state of being twisted, esp. of one end of an object relative to the other. ■ *Mathematics* the extent to which a curve departs from being planar. ■ *Zoology* (in a gastropod mollusk) the spontaneous twisting of the visceral hump through 180° during larval development. ▷late Middle English (as a medical term denoting colic or in the sense 'twisting' (esp. of a loop of the intestine)): via Old French from late Latin *torsio(n-)*, variant of *tortio(n-)* 'twisting, torture,' from Latin *torquere* 'to twist.' —**tor·sion·al** /-SHənl/ *adj.* —**tor·sion·al·ly** /-SHənl-ē/ *adv.* —**tor·sion·less** *adj.*

tor·sion bal·ance ▸*n.* an instrument for measuring very weak forces by their effect on a system of fine twisted wire.

tor·sion bar ▸*n.* a bar forming part of a vehicle suspension, twisting in response to the motion of the wheels and absorbing their vertical movement.

tor·sion pen·du·lum ▸*n.* a pendulum that rotates rather than swings.

torsk /tôrsk/ ▸*n.* a North Atlantic fish of the cod family, occurring in deep water and of some commercial importance. Also called CUSK. • *Brosme brosme*, family Gadidae. ▷early 18th cent.: from Norwegian *torsk*, from Old Norse *thorskr*; probably related to *thurr* 'dry.'

tor·so /ˈtôrsō/ ▸*n.* (*pl.* **-sos** or **-si** /-sē/) the trunk of the human body. ■ the trunk of a statue without, or considered independently of, the head and limbs. ■ *figurative* an unfinished or mutilated thing, esp. a work of art or literature: *the Requiem torso was preceded by the cantata.* ▷late 18th cent.: from Italian, literally 'stalk, stump,' from Latin *thyrsus* (see THYRSUS).

tort /tôrt/ ▸*n.* *Law* a wrongful act or an infringement of a right (other than under contract) leading to legal liability. ▷Middle English (in the general sense 'wrong, injury'): from Old French, from medieval Latin *tortum* 'wrong, injustice,' neuter past participle of Latin *torquere* 'to twist.'

torte /tôrt; ˈtôrtə/ ▸*n.* (*pl.* **tortes** or *German* **tor·ten** /ˈtôrtn/) a sweet cake or tart. ▷from German *Torte*, via Italian from late Latin *torta* 'round loaf, cake.' Compare with TORTILLA.

tor·tel·li /tôrˈtelē/ ▸*n.* small pasta parcels stuffed with a cheese or vegetable mixture. ▷Italian, plural of *tortello* 'small cake, fritter.'

tor·tel·li·ni /ˌtôrtlˈēnē/ ▸*n.* small squares of pasta that are stuffed with meat or cheese and then rolled and formed into small rings. ▷Italian, plural of *tortellino*, diminutive of *tortello* 'small cake, fritter.'

tort·fea·sor /ˈtôrtˌfēzər; -zôr/ ▸*n.* *Law* a person who commits a tort. ▷mid 17th cent.: from Old French *tort-fesor*, from *tort* 'wrong' and *fesor* 'doer.'

tor·ti·col·lis /ˌtôrtiˈkälis/ ▸*n.* *Medicine* a condition in which the head becomes persistently turned to one side, often associated with painful muscle spasms. Also called WRYNECK. ▷early 19th cent.: modern Latin, from Latin *tortus* 'crooked, twisted' + *collum* 'neck.'

tor·til·la /tôrˈtē(y)ə/ ▸*n.* (in Mexican cooking) a thin, flat pancake of cornmeal or flour, eaten hot or cold, typically with a savory filling. ■ (in Spanish cooking) a thick omelet containing potato and other vegetables, typically served cut into wedges. ▷Spanish, diminutive of *torta* 'cake.' Compare with TORTE.

tor·tious /ˈtôrSHəs/ ▸*adj.* *Law* constituting a tort; wrongful. ▷late Middle English: from Anglo-Norman French *torcious*, from the stem of *torcion* 'extortion, violence,' from late Latin *tortio(n-)* (see TORSION). The original sense was 'injurious.' —**tor·tious·ly** *adv.*

tor·toise /ˈtôrtəs/ ▸*n.* **1** a turtle, typically a herbivorous one that lives on land. ■ *informal* anything exceptionally slow-moving: *you are a tortoise on the uptake today.* **2** another term for TESTUDO. ▷late Middle English *tortu*, *tortuce*: from Old French *tortue* and Spanish *tortuga*, both from medieval Latin *tortuca*, of uncertain origin. The current spelling dates from the mid 16th cent. —**tor·toise·like** /-ˌlīk/ *adj.* & *adv.*

tor·toise bee·tle ▸*n.* a small flattened leaf beetle with an enlarged thorax, having wing cases that cover the entire insect and provide camouflage and protection. The larva carries a construction of feces and molted skins for camouflage. • *Cassida* and other genera, family Chrysomelidae.

tor·toise·shell /ˈtôrtə(s)ˌSHel/ ▸*n.* **1** the semitransparent mottled yellow and brown shell of certain turtles, typically used to make jewelry or ornaments. ■ a synthetic substance made in imitation of this. **2** short for TORTOISESHELL CAT. **3** short for TORTOISESHELL BUTTERFLY.

tor·toise·shell but·ter·fly ▸*n.* a butterfly with mottled orange, yellow, and black markings, and wavy wing margins. • Genera *Aglais* and *Nymphalis*, subfamily Nymphalinae, family Nymphalidae: several species.

tor·toise·shell cat ▸*n.* a domestic cat with markings resembling tortoiseshell.

Tor·to·la /tôrˈtōlə/ the principal island of the British Virgin Islands in the Caribbean Sea. Its chief town, Road Town, is the capital of the British Virgin Islands. ▷Spanish, literally 'turtledove.'

tor·to·ni /tôrˈtōnē/ ▸*n.* an Italian ice cream made with eggs and cream, typically served in a small cup and topped with chopped almonds or crumbled macaroons.

tor·trix /ˈtôrtriks/ (also **tor·trix moth**) ▸*n.* (*pl.* **-tri·ces** /-trisēz/) a small moth with typically green caterpillars that live inside rolled leaves and can be a serious pest of fruit and other trees. • Family Tortricidae: many species. ▷late 18th cent.: modern Latin, feminine of Latin *tortor* 'twister,' from *torquere* 'to twist.' —**tor·tri·cid** /-trisid/ *n.* & *adj.*

tor·tu·ous /ˈtôrCHo͞oəs/ ▸*adj.* full of twists and turns: *the route is remote and tortuous.* ■ excessively lengthy and complex: *a tortuous argument.* ▷late Middle English: via Old French from Latin *tortuosus*, from *tortus* 'twisting, a twist,' from Latin *torquere* 'to twist.' —**tor·tu·os·i·ty** /ˌtôrCHo͞oˈäsitē/ *n.* (*pl.* **-ties**) —**tor·tu·ous·ly** *adv.* —**tor·tu·ous·ness** *n.*

> *USAGE* On the difference between **tortuous** and **torturous**, see usage at TORTUROUS.

tor·ture /ˈtôrCHər/ ▸*n.* the action or practice of inflicting severe pain on someone as a punishment or to force them to do or say something, or for the pleasure of the person inflicting the pain. ■ great physical or mental suffering or anxiety: *the torture I've gone through because of loving you so.* ■ a cause of such suffering or anxiety: *dances were absolute torture because I was so small.*
▸*v.* [*trans.*] inflict severe pain on: *most of the victims had been brutally tortured.* ■ cause great mental suffering or anxiety to: *he was tortured by grief.* ▷late Middle English (in the sense 'distortion, twisting,' or a physical disorder characterized by this): via French from late Latin *tortura* 'twisting, torment,' from Latin *torquere* 'to twist.' —**tor·tur·er** *n.*

tor·tur·ous /ˈtôrCHərəs/ ▸*adj.* characterized by, involving, or causing excruciating pain or suffering: *a torturous eight weeks in their prison camp.* ▷late 15th cent.: from Anglo-Norman French, from *torture* 'torture.' —**tor·tur·ous·ly** *adv.*

> *USAGE* **Tortuous** and **torturous** have different core meanings. **Tortuous** means 'full of twists and turns' or 'devious, circuitous': *both paths were tortuous and strewn with boulders.* **Torturous** is derived from *torture* and means 'involving torture or excruciating pain': *the emergency amputation was torturous.* **Torturous** should be reserved for agonized suffering; it is not a fancy word for 'painful' or 'discomforting,' as in *I found the concert torturous because of the music's volume.*

tor·u·la /ˈtôr(y)ələ/ ▸*n.* (*pl.* **-lae** /-lē; -lī/) **1** (also **tor·u·la yeast**) a yeast cultured for use in medicine and as a food additive, esp. as a source of vitamins and protein. • *Candida utilis*, subdivision Deuteromycotina. **2** a yeastlike fungus composed of chains of rounded cells, several kinds growing on dead vegetation and some causing infections. • Genus *Torula* (or formerly this genus), subdivision Deuteromycotina: several species, in particular *T. herbarum*, which grows on dead grasses. ▷modern Latin (genus name), diminutive of Latin *torus* 'swelling, bolster.'

To·ruń /ˈtôrˌo͞on/ an industrial city in northern Poland, on the Vistula River; pop. 201,000. German name **THORN**.

to·rus /ˈtôrəs/ ▸*n.* (*pl.* **to·ri** /ˈtôrī/ or **to·rus·es**) **1** *Geometry* a surface or solid formed by rotating a closed curve, esp. a circle, around a line that lies in the same plane but does not intersect it (e.g., like a ring-shaped doughnut). ■ a thing of this shape, esp. a large ring-shaped chamber used in physical research. **2** *Architecture* a large convex molding, typically semicircular in cross section, esp. as the lowest part of the base of a column. **3** *Anatomy* a ridge of bone or muscle: *the maxillary torus.* **4** *Botany* the receptacle of a flower. ▷mid 16th cent. (sense 2): from Latin, literally 'swelling, bolster, round molding.' The other senses date from the 19th cent.

To·ry /ˈtôrē/ ▸*n.* (*pl.* **-ries**) **1** an American colonist who supported the British side during the American Revolution. **2** (in the UK) a member or supporter of the Conservative Party. ■ a member of the English political party opposing the exclusion of James II from the succession. It remained the name for members of the English, later British, parliamentary party supporting the established religious and political order until the emergence of the Conservative Party in the 1830s. Compare with **WHIG** (sense 1).
▸*adj.* of or relating to the British Conservative Party or its supporters: *Tory voters.* ▷mid 17th cent.: probably from Irish *toraidhe* 'outlaw, highwayman,' from *tóir* 'pursue.' The word was used of Irish peasants dispossessed by English settlers and living as robbers, and extended to other marauders esp. in the

Scottish Highlands. It was then adopted *c.*1679 as an abusive nickname for supporters of the Catholic James II. **—To·ry·ism** /-ˌizəm/ *n.*

to·sa /ˈtōsə/ ▸*n.* a dog of a breed of mastiff originally kept for dogfighting. ▷1940s: from *Tosa*, the name of a former province in Japan.

Tos·ca·na /tôˈskänä/ Italian name for TUSCANY.

Tos·ca·ni·ni /ˌtäskəˈnēnē/, Arturo (1867–1957), Italian conductor. He was musical director at La Scala in Milan 1898–1903 and 1906–08 before becoming a conductor at the Metropolitan Opera in New York City 1908–21 and the New York Philharmonic Orchestra 1928–38. He founded the NBC Symphony Orchestra in 1937.

tosh /täsн/ ▸*n. Brit., informal* rubbish; nonsense: *it's sentimental tosh.* ▷late 19th cent.: of unknown origin.

toss /tôs; täs/ ▸*v.* **1** [*trans.*] throw (something) somewhere lightly, easily, or casually: *Suzy tossed her bag onto the sofa* | [with *two objs.*] *she tossed me a box of matches.* ■ [*trans.*] (of a horse) throw (a rider) off its back. ■ [*trans.*] throw (a coin) into the air in order to make a decision between two alternatives, based on which side of the coin faces up when it lands: *we could just toss a coin.* ■ [*trans.*] settle a matter with (someone) by doing this: *I'll* **toss you for** *it.* ■ move or cause to move from side to side or back and forth: [*intrans.*] *the tops of the olive trees swayed and tossed* | [*trans.*] *the yachts were tossed around in the harbor like toys* [as *adj.* in *combination*] (**-tossed**) *a storm-tossed sea.* ■ [*trans.*] jerk (one's head or hair) sharply backward: *Paula pursed her lips and tossed her head.* ■ [*trans.*] shake or turn (food) in a liquid, so as to coat it lightly: *toss the pasta in the sauce.* **2** [*trans.*] *informal* search (a place): *I could demand her keys and toss her office.*

▸*phrasal v.* □ **toss something off** **1** drink something rapidly or all at once: *Roger tossed off a full glass of Sauternes.* **2** produce something rapidly or without thought or effort: *some of the best letters are tossed off in a burst of inspiration.*

▸*n.* an action or instance of tossing something: *a defiant toss of her head* | *the toss of a coin.* ■ (**the toss**) the action of tossing a coin as a method of deciding which team has the right to make a particular decision at the beginning of a game: *we'd win the toss and keep the ball.* ▷early 16th cent.: of unknown origin. **—toss·er** *n.*

▸*PHRASES* □ **toss one's cookies** *informal* vomit. □ **tossing the caber** see CABER.

toss·pot /ˈtôsˌpät; ˈtäs-/ ▸*n. informal* a habitual drinker (also used as a general term of abuse).

toss-up ▸*n. informal* the tossing of a coin to make a decision between two alternatives. ■ a situation in which all outcomes or options are equally possible or equally attractive: *the choice of restaurant was a toss-up between Indian and Chinese.*

tos·ta·da /tōˈstädə/ (also **tos·ta·do** /-dō/) ▸*n.* (*pl.* **-das** also **-dos**) a Mexican deep-fried tortilla topped with a seasoned mixture of beans, ground meat, and vegetables. ▷Spanish, literally 'toasted,' past participle of *tostar*.

tos·to·ne /täsˈtōnā/ ▸*n.* a Mexican dish of fried plantains, typically served with a dip. ▷Spanish.

tos·yl /ˈtäsəl/ ▸*n.* ■ [as *modifier*] *Chemistry* of or denoting the toluene-4-sulphonyl radical $-SO_2C_6H_4CH_3$, used in organic synthesis. ▷1930s: from German, from *to(luol)* and *s(ulphon)yl*.

tos·yl·ate /ˈtäsəˌlāt/ ▸*n. Chemistry* an ester containing a tosyl group.

tot[1] /tät/ ▸*n.* **1** a very young child. **2** *chiefly Brit.* a small amount of a strong alcoholic drink such as whiskey or brandy: **a tot of** *brandy.* ▷early 18th cent. (originally dialect): of unknown origin.

tot[2] ▸*v.* (**tot·ted, tot·ting**) [*trans.*] *chiefly Brit.* (**tot something up**) add up numbers or amounts. ■ accumulate something over a period of time: *he has already totted up 89 victories.* ▷mid 18th cent.: from archaic *tot* 'set of figures to be added up,' abbreviation of TOTAL or of Latin *totum* 'the whole.'

to·tal /ˈtōtl/ ▸*adj.* **1** [*attrib.*] comprising the whole number or amount: *a total cost of $4,000.* **2** complete; absolute: *a total stranger* | *they drove home in total silence.*

▸*n.* the whole number or amount of something: *he scored a total of thirty-three points* | **in total**, *200 people were interviewed.*

▸*v.* (**-taled, -tal·ing**; *Brit.* **-talled, -tal·ling**) **1** [*trans.*] amount in number to: *they were left with debts totaling $6,260.* ■ add up the full number or amount of: *the scores were totaled.* **2** [*trans.*] *informal* damage (something, typically a vehicle) beyond repair; wreck. ▷late Middle English: via Old French from medieval Latin *totalis*, from *totum* 'the whole,' neuter of Latin *totus* 'whole, entire.' The verb, at first in the sense 'add up,' dates from the late 16th cent.

to·tal de·prav·i·ty ▸*n. Christian Theology* the Calvinist doctrine that human nature is thoroughly corrupt and sinful as a result of the Fall.

to·tal e·clipse ▸*n.* an eclipse in which the whole of the disk of the sun or moon is obscured.

to·tal har·mon·ic dis·tor·tion ▸*n.* the distortion produced by an amplifier, as measured in terms of the harmonics of the sinusoidal components of the signal that it introduces.

to·tal heat ▸*n.* another term for ENTHALPY.

to·tal·i·tar·i·an /tōˌtaliˈte(ə)rēən/ ▸*adj.* of or relating to a system of government that is centralized and dictatorial and requires complete subservience to the state: *a totalitarian regime.*

▸*n.* a person advocating such a system of government. **—to·tal·i·tar·i·an·ism** /-ˌnizəm/ *n.*

to·tal·i·ty /tōˈtalitē/ ▸*n.* the whole of something: *the totality of their current policies.* ■ *Astronomy* the moment or duration of total obscuration of the sun or moon during an eclipse.

▸*PHRASE* □ **in its totality** as a whole: *a deeper exploration of life in its totality.*

to·tal·i·za·tor /ˈtōtl-iˌzātər/ ▸*n.* a device showing the number and amount of bets staked on a race, to facilitate the division of the total among those backing the winner.

to·tal·ize /ˈtōtlˌīz/ ▸*v.* [*trans.*] [usu. as *adj.*] (**totalizing**) comprehend in an all-encompassing way: *grand ideas and totalizing worldviews.* **—to·tal·i·za·tion** /-ˈzāsнən/ *n.*

to·tal·iz·er /ˈtōtlˌīzər/ ▸*n.* another term for TOTALIZATOR.

to·tal·ly /ˈtōtl-ē/ ▸*adv.* completely; absolutely: *the building was totally destroyed by the fire* | [as *submodifier*] *they came from totally different backgrounds.*

To·tal Qual·i·ty Man·age·ment ▸*n.* a system of management based on the principle that every staff member must be committed to maintaining high standards of work in every aspect of a company's operations.

to·tal re·call ▸*n.* the ability to remember with clarity every detail of the events of one's life or of a particular event, object, or experience.

to·tal war ▸*n.* a war that is unrestricted in terms of the weapons used, the territory or combatants involved, or the objectives pursued, esp. one in which the laws of war are disregarded.

tote[1] /tōt/ ▸*v.* [*trans.*] *informal* carry, wield, or convey (something heavy or substantial): *here are books well worth toting home* | [as *adj.*, in *combination*] (**-toting**) *a gun-toting loner.*

▸*n.* short for TOTE BAG. ▷late 17th cent.: probably of dialect origin. **—tot·er** *n.* [in *combination*] *a gun-toter.*

tote[2] ▸*n.* (**the tote**) *informal* a system of betting based on the use of the totalizator, in which dividends are calculated according to the amount staked rather than odds offered. ▷late 19th cent.: abbreviation.

tote bag ▸*n.* a large bag used for carrying a number of items.

to·tem /ˈtōtəm/ ▸*n.* a natural object or animal believed by a particular society to have spiritual significance and adopted by it as an emblem. ▷mid 18th cent.: from Ojibwa *nindoodem* 'my totem.' **—to·tem·ic** /tōˈtemik/ *adj.* **—to·tem·ism** /-ˌmizəm/ *n.* **—to·tem·ist** /-mist/ *n.* **—to·tem·is·tic** /ˌtōdəˈmistik/ *adj.*

totem pole

to·tem pole ▸*n.* a pole on which totems are hung or on which the images of totems are carved. ■ *figurative* a hierarchy: *the social totem pole.*

t'oth·er /ˈtəᴛʜər/ (also **toth·er**) ▸*adj.* & *pron. dialect* or *humorous* the other: [as *adj.*] *I was talking about it t'other day* | [as *pron.*] *we were talking of this, that, and t'other.* ▷Middle English *the tother*, wrong division of *thet other* 'the other' (*thet*, from Old English *thaet*, the obsolete neuter form of *the*).

to·tip·o·tent /tōˈtipətənt/ ▸*adj. Biology* (of an immature or stem cell) capable of giving rise to any cell type or (of a blastomere) a complete embryo. ▷early 20th cent.: from Latin *totus* 'whole' + POTENT[1].

To·to·nac /ˌtōtəˈnäk/ ▸*n.* (*pl.* same or **-nacs**) **1** a member of an American Indian people of east central Mexico. **2** the language of this people.

▸*adj.* of or relating to this people or their language. ▷from Spanish *Totonaca*, from Nahuatl *Totonacatl*.

tot·ter /ˈtätər/ ▸*v.* [*intrans.*] move in a feeble or unsteady way: *a hunched figure tottering down the path.* ■ [usu. as *adj.*] (**tottering**) (of a building) shake or rock as if about to collapse: *tottering, gutted houses.* ■ *figurative* be insecure or about to collapse: *the pharmaceutical industry has tottered from crisis to crisis.*

▸*n.* [in *sing.*] a feeble or unsteady gait. ▷Middle English: from Middle Dutch *touteren* 'to swing' (the original sense in English). **—tot·ter·er** *n.* **—tot·ter·y** *adj.*

tou·can /ˈtōōˌkan; -ˌkän/ ▸*n.* a tropical American fruit-eating bird with a massive bill and typically brightly colored plumage. • Genera *Ramphastos* and *Andigena*, family Ramphastidae: several species. ▷mid 16th cent.: via French and Portuguese from Tupi *tucan*, imitative of its call.

tou·can·et /ˌtōōkəˈnet/ ▸*n.* a small tropical American toucan with mainly green plumage. • Family Ramphastidae: three genera, in particular *Aulacorhynchus* and *Selenidera*, and several species. ▷early 19th cent.: diminutive of TOUCAN.

touch /təcн/ ▸*v.* [*trans.*] **1** come so close to (an object) as to be or come into contact with it: *the dog had one paw outstretched, not quite touching the ground.* ■ bring one's hand or another part of one's body into contact with: *he touched a strand of her hair* | *she lowered her head to touch his fingers with her lips.* ■ (**touch something to**) move a part of one's body to bring it into contact with: *he gently touched his lips to her cheek.* ■ lightly press or strike (a button or key on a device or instrument) to operate or play it: *he touched a button on the control pad.* ■ [*intrans.*] (of two people or two or more things, typically ones of the same kind) come into contact with each other: *for a moment their fingers touched.* ■ cause (two or more things, typically ones of the same kind) to come into contact: *we touched wheels and nearly came off the road.* ■ *Geometry* be tangent to (a curve or surface) at a certain point. ■ *informal* reach (a specified level or amount): *sales touched twenty grand last year.* ■ [usu. with *negative*] *informal* be comparable to in quality or excellence: *there's no one who can touch him at lightweight judo.* **2** handle in order to manipulate, alter, or otherwise affect, esp. in an adverse way: *I didn't play her records or touch any of her stuff.* ■ cause harm to (someone): *I've got friends who'll pull strings—nobody will dare touch me.* ■ take some of (a store, esp. of money) for use: *in three years I haven't touched a cent of the money.* ■ [usu. with *negative*] consume a small amount of (food or drink): *the beer by his right hand was hardly touched.* ■ [with *negative*] used to indicate that something is avoided or rejected: *he was good only for the jobs that nobody else would touch.* ■ (**touch someone for**) *informal* ask someone for (money or some other commodity) as a loan or gift: *he touched me for his fare.* **3** have an effect on; make a difference to: *a tenth of state companies have been touched by privatization.* ■ be relevant to: *some Canadian interests touched European powers.* ■ (usu. **be touched**) (of a quality or feature) be visible or apparent in the appearance or character of (something): *the trees were beginning to be touched by the colors of autumn.* ■ reach and affect the appearance of: *a wry smile touched his lips.* ■ (**touch something in**) *chiefly Art* lightly mark in features or other details with a brush or pencil. ■ (often **be touched**) produce feelings of affection, gratitude, or sympathy in: *she was touched by her friend's loyalty.* ■ [as *adj.*] (**touched**) *informal* slightly insane.

▸*phrasal v.* □ **touch at** (of a ship or someone in it) call briefly at (a port). □ **touch down** (of an aircraft or spacecraft) make contact with the ground in landing. □ **touch something off** cause something to ignite or explode by touching it with a match. ■ cause something to happen, esp. suddenly: *there was concern that the move could touch off a trade war.* □ **touch on** (or **upon**) **1** deal briefly with (a subject) in written or spoken discussion: *he touches upon several themes from the last chapter.* **2** come near to being: *a self-confident manner touching on the arrogant.* □ **touch something up** make small improvements to something: *these paints are handy for touching up small areas on walls or ceilings.* □ **touch wood** see KNOCK ON WOOD at WOOD.

▸*n.* **1** an act of bringing a part of one's body, typically one's hand, into contact with someone or something: *her touch on his shoulder was hesitant* | *expressions of love through words and touch.* ■ [in *sing.*] an act of lightly pressing or striking something in order to move or operate it: *you can manipulate images on the screen* **at the touch of** *a key.* ■ the faculty of perception through physical contact, esp. with the fingers: *reading by touch.* ■ a musician's manner of playing keys or strings. ■ the manner in which a musical instrument's keys or strings respond to being played: *Viennese instruments with their too delicate touch.* ■ a light stroke with a pen, pencil, etc. ■ [in *sing.*] *informal, dated* an act of asking for and getting money or some other commodity from someone as a loan or gift: *I only tolerated him because he was good for a touch now and then.* ■ [in *sing.*] *archaic* a thing or an action that tries out the worth or character of something; a test: *you must **put** your fate **to the touch**.* **2** a small amount; a trace: *add **a touch of** vinegar | he retired to bed with **a touch of** the flu.* ■ a detail or feature, typically one that gives something a distinctive character: *the film's most inventive touch.* ■ [in *sing.*] a distinctive manner or method of dealing with something: *later he showed a surer political touch.* ■ [in *sing.*] an ability to deal with something successfully: *getting caught looks so incompetent, as though we're losing our touch.* **3** *Bell-ringing* a series of changes shorter than a peal. **4** short for TOUCH FOOTBALL. ▷Middle English: the verb from Old French *tochier*, probably from a Romance word of imitative origin; the noun originally from Old French *touche*, later (in certain senses) directly from the verb. **—touch·a·ble** *adj.* **—touch·er** *n.*

▸*PHRASES* □ **a touch** to a slight degree; a little: *the water was a touch too chilly for us.* □ **in touch 1** in or into communication: *she said that you **kept in touch**, that you wrote | ask someone to **put** you **in touch** with other suppliers.* **2** possessing up-to-date knowledge: *we need to keep in touch with the latest developments.* ■ having an intuitive or empathetic awareness: *you need to be in touch with your feelings.* □ **lose touch 1** cease to correspond or be in communication: *I **lost touch with** him when he joined the air force.* **2** cease to be aware or informed: *we cannot **lose touch with** political reality.* □ **out of touch** lacking knowledge or information concerning current events and developments: *he seems surprisingly out of touch with recent economic thinking.* ■ lacking in awareness or sympathy: *we have been betrayed by a government out of touch with our values.* □ **to the touch** used to describe the qualities of something perceived by touching it or the sensations felt by someone who is touched: *the silk was slightly rough to the touch | the ankle was swollen and painful to the touch.* □ **touch base (with)** see BASE[1]. □ **touch bottom** reach the bottom of a body of water with one's feet or a pole. ■ be at the lowest or worst point: *the housing market has touched bottom.* □ **touch a chord** see CHORD[2]. □ **touch wood** see WOOD. □ **would not touch something with a ten-foot pole** *informal* used to express a refusal to have anything to do with someone or something: *relax, I wouldn't touch you with a ten-foot pole!*

touch and go ▸*adj.* (of an outcome, esp. one that is desired) possible but very uncertain: *it was touch and go there for a while whether they would make it.*
▸*n.* (**touch-and-go**) (*pl.* **touch-and-goes**) a maneuver in which an aircraft touches the ground as in landing, and immediately takes off again.

touch·back /ˈtəCH,bak/ ▸*n. Football* a ball one downs deliberately behind one's own goal line or that is kicked through one's end zone. It is taken to the 20-yard line to resume play.

touch·down /ˈtəCH,doun/ ▸*n.* **1** the moment at which an aircraft's wheels or part of a spacecraft make contact with the ground during landing: *two hours until touchdown.* **2** *Football* a six-point score made by carrying or passing the ball into the end zone of the opposing side, or by recovering it there following a fumble or blocked kick. ■ *Rugby* an act of touching the ground with the ball behind the opponents' goal line, scoring a try.

tou·ché /to͞oˈSHā/ ▸*exclam.* (in fencing) used as an acknowledgment of a hit by one's opponent. ■ used as an acknowledgment during a discussion of a good or clever point made at one's expense by another person. ▷French, literally 'touched,' past participle of *toucher*.

touch foot·ball ▸*n.* a form of football in which a ball carrier is downed by touching instead of tackling.

touch·hole /ˈtəCH,hōl/ ▸*n.* a small hole in early firearms through which the charge is ignited.

touch·ing /ˈtəCHiNG/ ▸*adj.* arousing strong feelings of sympathy, appreciation, or gratitude: *your loyalty is very touching | a touching reconciliation scene.* See note at MOVING. [early 16th cent.: from TOUCH + -ING[2].]
▸*prep.* concerning; about: *evidence touching the facts of Roger's case.* [late Middle English: from French *touchant*, present participle of *toucher* 'to touch.'] **—touch·ing·ly** *adv.* **—touch·ing·ness** *n.*

touch·line /ˈtəCH,līn/ ▸*n. Rugby & Soccer* the boundary line on each side of the field.

touch-me-not ▸*n.* a plant of the balsam family whose ripe seed capsules open explosively when touched, scattering seeds over some distance. • Genus *Impatiens*, family Balsaminaceae: several species, in particular the orange-flowered **spotted touch-me-not** (*I. capensis*).

touch·pad /ˈtəCH,pad/ ▸*n.* a computer input device in the form of a small panel containing different touch-sensitive areas.

touch·point /ˈtəCH,point/ ▸*n.* **1** *Commerce* any point of contact between a buyer and a seller. **2** *Computing* on some laptop computers, a device like a miniature joystick with a rubber tip, manipulated with a finger to move the screen pointer. **3** a time, condition, or circumstance that is vulnerable or unstable enough to precipitate a highly unfavorable, possibly devastating outcome: *so much remains to be done to take the fleeting opportunities there may be still in the Middle East to make it a safer and less terrible touchpoint for world conflagration.* ■ *Psychology* the time in a child's development that precedes an appreciable leap in physical, emotional, or cognitive growth. This phase is often associated with outbursts of uncharacteristic behavior. [1990s: from the usage coined in the book *Touchpoints* (1992) by U.S. pediatrician T. Berry Brazelton (1918–) and U.S. child psychiatrist Joshua D. Sparrow.]

touch screen (also **touch·screen**) ▸*n.* a display device that allows a user to interact with a computer by touching areas on the screen.

touch·stone /ˈtəCH,stōn/ ▸*n.* a piece of fine-grained dark schist or jasper formerly used for testing alloys of gold by observing the color of the mark that they made on it. ■ a standard or criterion by which something is judged or recognized: *they tend to regard grammar as the touchstone of all language performance.*

touch-tone (also **Touch-Tone**) ▸*adj.* (of a telephone) having push buttons and generating tones to dial rather than pulses. ■ (of a service) accessed or controlled by the tones generated by these telephones.
▸*n. trademark* a telephone of this type. ■ one of the set of tones generated by these telephones.

touch-type ▸*v.* [*intrans.*] [often as *n.*] (**touch-typing**) type using all one's fingers and without looking at the keys. **—touch-typ·ist** *n.*

touch-up ▸*n.* a quick restoration or improvement made to the appearance or state of something: *the hotels had undergone more than the customary touch-ups and refurbishing.*

touch·wood /ˈtəCH,wo͝od/ ▸*n. archaic* readily flammable wood used as tinder, esp. when made soft by fungi.

touch·y /ˈtəCHē/ ▸*adj.* (**touch·i·er**, **touch·i·est**) (of a person) oversensitive and irritable. ■ (of an issue or situation) requiring careful handling; delicate: *the monarchy has become a touchy topic.* ▷early 17th cent.: perhaps an alteration of TETCHY, influenced by TOUCH. **—touch·i·ly** /ˈtəCHəlē/ *adv.* **—touch·i·ness** *n.*

touch·y-feel·y /ˈfēlē/ ▸*adj. informal, often derogatory* openly expressing affection or other emotions, esp. through physical contact: *touchy-feely guys calling home to talk baby talk to their kids.* ■ characteristic of or relating to such behavior: *such touchy-feely topics as employees' personal values.*

tough /təf/ ▸*adj.* **1** (of a substance or object) strong enough to withstand adverse conditions or rough or careless handling: *tough backpacks for climbers.* ■ (of a person or animal) able to endure hardship or pain; physically robust: *even at this ripe old age, he's still as tough as old boots.* ■ able to protect one's own interests or maintain one's own opinions without being intimidated by opposition; confident and determined: *she's both sensitive and tough.* ■ demonstrating a strict and uncompromising attitude or approach: *police have been getting tough with drivers | tough new laws on tobacco advertising.* ■ (of a person) strong and prone to violence: *tough young teenagers.* ■ (of an area) notorious for violence and crime. ■ (of food, esp. meat) difficult to cut or chew. **2** involving considerable difficulty or hardship; requiring great determination or effort: *the training has been quite tough | he had a tough time getting into a good college.* ■ used to express sympathy with someone in an unpleasant or difficult situation: *Poor kid. It's **tough on** her.* ■ [often as *exclam.*] used to express a lack of sympathy with someone: *I feel the way I feel, and if you don't like it, tough.*
▸*n.* a tough person, esp. a gangster or criminal: *young toughs sporting their state-of-the-art firearms.* ▷Old English *tōh*, of Germanic origin; related to Dutch *taai* and German *zäh*. **—tough·ish** *adj.* **—tough·ly** *adv.* **—tough·ness** *n.*

▸*PHRASES* □ **tough it out** *informal* endure a period of hardship or difficulty. □ **tough shit** (or **titty**) *vulgar slang* used to express a lack of sympathy with someone.

tough·en /ˈtəfən/ ▸*v.* make or become tougher: [*trans.*] *he tried to **toughen** his son **up** by sending him to public school* | [*intrans.*] *if removed from the oven too soon meringues shrink and toughen.* ■ [*trans.*] make (rules or a policy) stricter and more harsh: *new congressional efforts to toughen the laws.* **—tough·en·er** *n.*

tough·ie /ˈtəfē/ ▸*n. informal* **1** a person who is tough, determined, and not easily daunted. **2** a difficult problem or question: *Whom do you admire most? That's a toughie.*

tough love ▸*n.* promotion of a person's welfare, esp. that of an addict, child, or criminal, by enforcing certain constraints on them, or requiring them to take responsibility for their actions. ■ a political policy designed to encourage self-help by restricting state benefits.

tough-mind·ed ▸*adj.* strong, determined, and able to face up to reality. **—tough-mind·ed·ness** *n.*

Tou·lon /to͞oˈlôN/ a port and naval base on the Mediterranean coast of southern France; pop. 170,000.

Tou·louse /to͞oˈlo͞oz/ a city in southwestern France on the Garonne River, principal city of the Midi-Pyrénées region; pop. 366,000.

Tou·louse-Lau·trec /to͞oˈlo͞oz lōˈtrek/, Henri (Marie Raymond) de (1864–1901), French painter and lithographer. His color lithographs depict actors, music-hall singers, prostitutes, and waitresses from the 1890s in Montmartre: the *Moulin Rouge* series (1894) is particularly well known.

tou·pee /to͞oˈpā/ ▸*n.* a small wig or artificial hairpiece worn to cover a bald spot. ▷early 18th cent. (denoting a curl or lock of artificial hair): alteration of French *toupet* 'hair tuft,' diminutive of Old French *toup* 'tuft,' ultimately of Germanic origin and related to TOP[1].

tour /to͝or/ ▸*n.* **1** a journey for pleasure in which several different places are visited: *three couples from Kansas on an airline tour of Alaska.* ■ a short trip to or through a place in order to view or inspect something: *a tour of the White House.* **2** a journey made by performers or an athletic team, in which they perform or play in several different places: *she joined the Royal Shakespeare Company **on tour**.* ■ (**the tour**) (in golf, tennis, and other sports) the annual round of events in which top professionals compete. **3** (also **tour of duty**) a period of duty on military or diplomatic service: *he was haunted by his tour of duty in Vietnam.*
▸*v.* [*trans.*] make a tour of (an area): *he decided to tour France* | [*intrans.*] *they had toured in a little minivan.* ■ take (a performer, production, etc.) on tour. ▷Middle English (sense 3; also denoting a circular movement): from Old French, 'turn,' via Latin from Greek *tornos* 'lathe.' Sense 1 dates from the mid 17th cent.

tou·ra·co /ˈto͝orə,kō/ (also **tu·ra·co**) ▸*n.* (*pl.* **-cos**) a fruit-eating African bird with brightly colored plumage, a prominent crest, and a long tail. • Family Musophagidae (the **touraco family**): three genera, esp. *Musophaga* and *Tauraco*, and several species. The touraco family also includes the plantain-eaters. ▷mid 18th cent.: French, from a West African word.

Tou·rane /to͞oˈrän/ former name of DA NANG.

tour de force /ˈto͝or də ˈfôrs/ ▸*n.* (*pl.* **tours de force** *pronunc.* same or /ˈto͝orz/) an impressive performance or achievement that has been accomplished or managed with great skill: *his novel is a tour de force.* ▷French, literally 'feat of strength.'

Tour de France /ˈto͝or də ˈfrans/ a French race for professional cyclists held annually since 1903, covering approximately 3,000 miles (4,800 km) of roads in about three weeks, renowned for its mountain stages.

tour d'ho·ri·zon /ˈto͝or dôrēˈzôN/ ▸*n.* (*pl.* **tours d'ho·ri·zon** *pronunc.* same) a broad general survey or summary of an argument or event. ▷French, literally 'tour of the horizon.'

tour en l'air /ˈto͝or än ˈle(ə)r/ ▸*n.* (*pl.* **tours en l'air** /ˈto͝orz/) *Ballet* a movement in which a dancer jumps straight upward and completes at least one full revolution in the air before landing. ▷French, literally 'turn in the air.'

tour·er /'to͝orər/ ▸*n.* a car, camper, or bicycle designed for touring. ■ a person touring with such a vehicle.

Tou·rette's syn·drome /to͝o'rets/ ▸*n. Medicine* a neurological disorder characterized by involuntary tics and vocalizations and often the compulsive utterance of obscenities. ▷late 19th cent.: named after Gilles de la *Tourette* (1857–1904), French neurologist.

tour·ing car ▸*n.* a car designed with room for passengers and luggage. ■ a car of this type used in auto racing, as distinct from a specially designed race car.

tour·ism /'to͝or,izəm/ ▸*n.* the commercial organization and operation of vacations and visits to places of interest.

tour·ist /'to͝orist/ ▸*n.* **1** a person who is traveling or visiting a place for pleasure: *the pyramids have drawn tourists to Egypt.* **2** short for TOURIST CLASS.
▸*v.* [*intrans.*] *rare* travel as a tourist: *American families touristing abroad.* —**tour·is·tic** /to͝o'ristik/ *adj.* —**tour·is·ti·cal·ly** /to͝o'ristik(ə)lē/ *adv.*

tour·ist class ▸*n.* the cheapest accommodations or seating for passengers in a ship, aircraft, or hotel.
▸*adj.* & *adv.* of, relating to, or by such accommodations or seating: [as *adj.*] *a tourist-class hotel* | [as *adv.*] *they had come tourist class from Cairo.*

tour·ist·y /'to͝oristē/ ▸*adj. informal* relating to, appealing to, or visited by tourists (often used to suggest tawdriness or lack of authenticity): *a touristy shopping street.*

tour·ma·line /'to͝ormələn; -,lēn/ ▸*n.* a brittle gray or black mineral that occurs as prismatic crystals in granitic and other rocks. It consists of a boron aluminosilicate and has pyroelectric and polarizing properties, and is used in electrical and optical instruments and as a gemstone. ▷mid 18th cent.: from French, based on Sinhalese *tōramalli* 'carnelian.'

tour·na·ment /'tərnəmənt; 'to͝or-/ ▸*n.* **1** (in a sport or game) a series of contests between a number of competitors, who compete for an overall prize. **2** (in the Middle Ages) a sporting event in which two knights (or two groups of knights) jousted on horseback with blunted weapons, each trying to knock the other off, the winner receiving a prize. ▷Middle English (sense 2): from Anglo-Norman French variants of Old French *torneiement*, from *torneier* 'take part in a tourney' (see TOURNEY).

tour·ne·dos /'to͝ornə,dō/ ▸*n.* (*pl.* same) a small round thick cut from a fillet of beef. ▷French, from *tourner* 'to turn' + *dos* 'back.'

tour·ney /'tərnē; 'to͝or-/ ▸*n.* (*pl.* **-neys**) a tournament.
▸*v.* (**-neys, -neyed**) [*intrans.*] take part in a tournament. ▷Middle English: from Old French *tornei* (noun), *torneier* (verb), based on Latin *tornus* 'a turn.'

tour·ni·quet /'tərnikit; 'to͝or-/ ▸*n.* a device for stopping the flow of blood through an artery, typically by compressing a limb with a cord or tight bandage. ▷late 17th cent.: from French, probably from Old French *tournicle* 'coat of mail,' influenced by *tourner* 'to turn.'

tourniquet

tour op·er·a·tor ▸*n.* a travel agent specializing in package vacations.

Tours /to͝or/ an industrial city in western central France, on the Loire River; pop. 133,000.

tour·tière /to͝or'tyer/ ▸*n.* (*pl.* same) a kind of meat pie traditionally eaten at Christmas in Canada. ▷French.

tou·sle /'touzəl/ ▸*v.* [*trans.*] [usu. as *adj.*] (**tousled**) make (something, esp. a person's hair) untidy: *Nathan's tousled head appeared in the hatchway.*
▸*n.* an act of tousling something, esp. hair: *Annie reached up behind his head and gave his hair a tousle.* ■ a tousled mass, esp. of hair: *he'd gently brush back my tousle.* ▷late Middle English (in the sense 'handle roughly or rudely'): frequentative of dialect *touse* 'handle roughly,' of Germanic origin and related to German *zausen*. Compare with TUSSLE.

Tous·saint L'Ou·ver·ture /to͞o'saN ,lo͞over'tʏr/, Pierre Dominique (*c.*1743–1803), Haitian revolutionary leader. One of the leaders of a rebellion that emancipated the island's slaves in 1791, he was appointed governor general in 1797 by the revolutionary government of France. In 1802, Napoleon, wishing to restore slavery, took over the island and Toussaint died in prison in France.

tout[1] /tout/ ▸*v.* **1** [*trans.*] attempt to sell (something), typically by pestering people in an aggressive or bold manner: *Jim was touting his wares.* ■ (often **be touted**) attempt to persuade people of the merits of (someone or something): *the headquarters facility was touted as the best in the country.* ■ *Brit.* scalp (a ticket). **2** [*intrans.*] offer racing tips for a share of any resulting winnings. ■ [*trans.*] *chiefly Brit.* spy out the movements and condition of (a racehorse in training) in order to gain information to be used when betting.
▸*n.* **1** a person soliciting custom or business, typically in an aggressive or bold manner. ■ *Brit.* a person who buys tickets for an event to resell them at a profit; a scalper. **2** a person who offers racing tips for a share of any resulting winnings. **3** *N. Irish* & *Scottish informal* an informer. ▷Middle English *tute* 'look out,' of Germanic origin; related to Dutch *tuit* 'spout, nozzle.' Later senses were 'watch, spy on' (late 17th cent.) and 'solicit business' (mid 18th cent.). The noun was first recorded (early 18th cent.) in the slang use 'thieves' lookout.' —**tout·er** *n.*

tout[2] /to͞o/ ▸*adj.* (often **le tout**) used before the name of a city to refer to its high society or people of importance: *le tout Washington adored him.* ▷French, suggested by *le tout Paris* 'all (of) Paris,' used to refer to Parisian high society.

tout court /,to͞o 'ko͝or/ ▸*adv.* with no addition or qualification; simply: *he saw it as an illusion, tout court.* ▷French, literally 'very short.'

tout de suite /,to͞ot 'swēt/ ▸*adv.* immediately; at once: *she left tout de suite.* ▷French, literally 'quite in sequence.'

tout le monde /,to͞o lə 'mônd/ ▸*n.* [treated as *sing.* or *pl.*] everyone: *he shouted "Bon appetit, tout le monde!"* ▷French.

to·va·rish /tə'värisн/ (also **to·va·rich**) ▸*n.* (in the former USSR) a comrade (often used as a form of address). ▷from Russian *tovarishch*, from Turkic.

TOW /tō/ ▸*abbr.* tube-launched, optically guided, wire-guided (missile).

tow[1] /tō/ ▸*v.* [*trans.*] (of a motor vehicle or boat) pull (another vehicle or boat) along with a rope, chain, or tow bar. ■ (of a person) pull (someone or something) along behind one: *she saw Frank towing Nicky along by the hand.*
▸*n.* [in *sing.*] an act of towing a vehicle or boat. ■ a rope or line used to tow a vehicle or boat. ▷Old English *togian* 'draw, drag,' of Germanic origin; related to TUG. The noun dates from the early 17th cent. —**tow·a·ble** *adj.*
▸*PHRASE* □ **in tow 1** being towed by another vehicle or boat: *his boat was taken in tow by a trawler.* **2** accompanying or following someone: *trying to shop with three children in tow is no joke.*

tow[2] ▸*n.* the coarse and broken part of flax or hemp prepared for spinning. ■ a bundle of untwisted natural or man-made fibers. ▷Old English (recorded in *towcræft* 'spinning'), of Germanic origin. —**tow·y** *adj.*

tow·age /'tō-ij/ ▸*n.* **1** [usu. as *adj.*] the action or process of towing. **2** a charge for towing a boat or vehicle.

to·ward /tôrd; t(ə)'wôrd/ ▸*prep.* (also **to·wards** /tôrdz; t(ə)'wôrdz/) **1** in the direction of: *I walked toward the front door.* ■ getting closer to achieving (a goal): *an irresistible move toward freedom.* ■ close or closer to (a particular time): *toward the end of April.* **2** as regards; in relation to: *he was warm and tender toward her* | *our attitude toward death.* ■ paying homage to, esp. in a superficial or insincere way: *he gave a nod toward the good work done by the fund.* **3** contributing to the cost of (something): *the council provided a grant toward the cost of new buses.*
▸*adj.* [*predic.*] *archaic* going on; in progress: *is something new toward?* ▷Old English *tōweard* (see TO, -WARD).

tow bar ▸*n.* a bar fitted to the back of a vehicle, used in towing a trailer.

tow-col·ored ▸*adj.* (of hair) very light blonde.

tow·el /'toul/ ▸*n.* a piece of thick absorbent cloth or paper used for drying oneself or wiping things dry.
▸*v.* (**-eled, -el·ing**; *Brit.* **-elled, -el·ling**) [*trans.*] wipe or dry (a person or thing) with a towel: [*trans.*] *she toweled her hair* **dry** | [*intrans.*] *quickly we'd* **towel off** *and dress for dinner.* ▷Middle English: from Old French *toaille*, of Germanic origin. The verb, originally meaning 'beat or thrash,' dates from the early 18th cent. The sense 'wipe with a towel' arose in the mid 19th cent.
▸*PHRASE* □ **throw in the towel** see THROW.

tow·el·ette /tou(ə)'let/ ▸*n.* a small paper or cloth towel, usually premoistened in a sealed package, used for cleansing.

tow·el·head /'tou(ə)l ,hed/ ▸*n. informal, offensive* a person who wears a turban.

tow·el·ing /'touliNG/ (*Brit.* **tow·el·ling**) ▸*n.* thick absorbent cloth, typically cotton with uncut loops, used for towels and robes.

tow·er /'tou(-ə)r/ ▸*n.* **1** a tall narrow building, either freestanding or forming part of a building such as a church or castle. ■ [with *adj.*] a tall structure that houses machinery, operators, etc. ■ [with *adj.*] a tall structure used as a receptacle or for storage: *a CD tower.* ■ a tall pile or mass of something: *a titanic* **tower of** *garbage.* ■ (**the Tower**) see TOWER OF LONDON. **2** a place of defense; a protection.
▸*v.* [*intrans.*] **1** rise to or reach a great height: *he seemed to* **tower over** *everyone else.* **2** (of a bird) soar to a great height, esp. (of a falcon) so as to be able to swoop down on the quarry. ▷Old English *torr*, reinforced in Middle English by Old French *tour*, from Latin *turris*, from Greek. —**tow·ered** *adj.* (*chiefly poetic/literary*). —**tow·er·y** *adj.* (*poetic/literary*).
▸*PHRASE* □ **tower of strength** see STRENGTH.

tow·er·ing /'tou(-ə)riNG/ ▸*adj.* [*attrib.*] extremely tall, esp. in comparison with the surroundings: *Hari looked up at the towering buildings.* ■ of exceptional importance or influence: *a majestic, towering album.* ■ of great intensity: *his towering anger.*

Tow·er of Ba·bel /'babəl; 'bā-/ (in the Bible) a tower built in an attempt to reach heaven, which God frustrated by confusing the languages of its builders so that they could not understand one another (Genesis 11:1–9). ▷*Babel* from Hebrew *Bāḇel* 'Babylon,' from Akkadian *bāb ili* 'gate of god.'

Tow·er of Lon·don (also **the Tower**) a fortress by the Thames River just east of the City of London. The oldest part, the White Tower, was begun in 1078. It was later used as a state prison, and is now open to the public as a repository of ancient armor and weapons, and of the Crown jewels.

Tower of London

tow·head /'tō,hed/ ▸*n.* a head of tow-colored or very blond hair. ■ a person with such hair. —**tow·head·ed** *adj.*

tow·hee /'tō,hē; 'tou-/ ▸*n.* a North American songbird of the bunting family, typically with brownish plumage but sometimes black and rufous. • Genus *Pipilo* (and *Chlorurus*), family Emberizidae (subfamily Emberizinae): several species. ▷mid 18th cent.: imitative of the call of *Pipilo erythrophthalmus.*

tow·line /'tō,līn/ ▸*n.* a rope, cable, or other line used in towing.

town /toun/ ▸*n.* an urban area that has a name, defined boundaries, and local government, and that is larger than a village and generally smaller than a city. ■ the particular town under consideration, esp. one's own town: *Carson was* **in town.** ■ the central part of a neighborhood, with its business or shopping area: *Rachel left to drive back* **into town.** ■ *Brit., dated* the chief city or town of a region: *he has moved* **to town.** ■ a densely populated area, esp. as contrasted with the country or suburbs: *the cultural differences between town and country.* ■ [in *sing.*] a town's community: *the whole town is talking about it.* ■ the permanent residents of a college town as distinct from the members of the college: *a rift between the city's* **town and gown** *that resulted in a petition to the college.* Often contrasted with GOWN. ■ another term for TOWNSHIP (sense 3). ▷Old English *tūn* 'enclosed piece of land, homestead, village,' of Germanic origin; related to Dutch *tuin* 'garden' and German *Zaun* 'fence.' —**town·ish** *adj.* —**town·let** /-lit/ *n.* —**town·ward** /-wərd/ *adj.* & *adv.* —**town·wards** /-wərdz/ *adv.*
▸*PHRASES* □ **go to town** *informal* do something thoroughly, enthusiastically, or extravagantly: *I thought I'd* **go to town on** *the redecoration.* □ **on the town**

informal enjoying the entertainments, esp. the nightlife, of a city or town: *a lot of guys out for* ***a night on the town.***

town car ▸*n.* a limousine.

town clerk ▸*n.* a public official in charge of the records of a town.

town coun·cil ▸*n.* an elected governing body in a municipality. —**town coun·ci·lor** *n.*

town cri·er ▸*n. historical* a person employed to make public announcements in the streets or marketplace of a town.

Townes /tounz/, Charles Hard (1915–), U.S. physicist. His development of microwave oscillators and amplifiers led to his invention of the maser in 1954. He later showed that an optical maser (a laser) was possible. Nobel Prize for Physics (1964, shared with Nicolay Basov [1922–2001] and Aleksandr Prokhorov [1916–2002]).

town hall ▸*n.* a building used for the administration of local government.

town·house /ˈtounˌhous/ (also **town house**) ▸*n.* **1** a tall, narrow, traditional row house, generally having three or more floors. ■ a modern two- or three-story house built as one of a group of similar houses. **2** a house in a town or city belonging to someone who has another property in the country.

town·ie /ˈtounē/ ▸*n.* a person who lives in a town (used esp. with reference to their supposed lack of familiarity with rural affairs). ■ a resident in a college town, rather than a student: *any differences there might have been between townies and students.*

town ma·jor ▸*n. historical* the chief executive officer in a garrison town or fortress.

town meet·ing ▸*n.* a meeting of the voters of a town for the transaction of public business.

Town 'n' Coun·try a residential community in western Florida, northwest of Tampa; pop. 60,946.

town plan·ning ▸*n.* another term for CITY PLANNING. —**town plan·ner** *n.*

town·scape /ˈtounˌskāp/ ▸*n.* the visual appearance of a town or urban area; an urban landscape: *the building's contribution to the townscape | an industrial townscape.* ■ a picture of a town.

towns·folk /ˈtounzˌfōk/ ▸*plural n.* another term for TOWNSPEOPLE.

town·ship /ˈtounˌsHip/ ▸*n.* **1** a division of a county with some corporate powers. ■ a district six miles square. **2** (in South Africa) a suburb or city of predominantly black occupation, formerly officially designated for black occupation by apartheid legislation. **3** *Brit., historical* a manor or parish as a territorial division. ■ a small town or village forming part of a large parish. ▷Old English *tūnscipe* 'the inhabitants of a village' (see TOWN, -SHIP).

town·site /ˈtounˌsīt/ ▸*n.* a tract of land set apart by legal authority to be occupied by a town and usually surveyed and laid out with streets.

towns·man /ˈtounzmən/ ▸*n.* (*pl.* **-men**) a man living in a particular town or city.

towns·peo·ple /ˈtounzˌpēpəl/ (also **towns·folk** /-ˌfōk/) ▸*plural n.* the people living in a particular town or city.

Towns·ville /ˈtounzˌvil/ an industrial port and resort on the coast of Queensland, in northeastern Australia; pop. 101,000.

towns·wom·an /ˈtounzˌwŏŏmən/ ▸*n.* (*pl.* **-wom·en**) a woman living in a particular town or city.

tow·path /ˈtōˌpaTH/ ▸*n.* a path beside a river or canal, originally used as a pathway for horses towing barges.

tow·plane /ˈtōˌplān/ ▸*n.* an aircraft that tows gliders.

tow rope ▸*n.* another term for TOWLINE.

Tow·son /ˈtousən/ a suburban community in northern Maryland, north of Baltimore; pop. 49,445.

tow truck /ˈtō ˌtrək/ ▸*n.* a truck used to tow or pick up damaged or disabled vehicles.

tox·a·phene /ˈtäksəˌfēn/ ▸*n.* a synthetic amber waxy solid with an odor of chlorine and camphor, used as an insecticide. It is a chlorinated terpene. ▷1940s: from TOXIN + *(cam)phene*, a related terpene.

tox·e·mi·a /täkˈsēmēə/ (*Brit.* **tox·ae·mi·a**) ▸*n.* blood poisoning by toxins from a local bacterial infection. ■ (also **toxemia of pregnancy**) another term for PREECLAMPSIA. ▷mid 19th cent.: from TOXI- + -EMIA. —**tox·e·mic** /-ˈsēmik/ *adj.*

toxi- ▸*comb. form* representing TOXIC or TOXIN.

tox·ic /ˈtäksik/ ▸*adj.* poisonous: *the dumping of toxic waste | alcohol is toxic to the ovaries.* ■ of or relating to poison: *toxic hazards.* ■ caused by poison: *toxic liver injury.*

▸*n.* (**toxics**) poisonous substances. ▷mid 17th cent.: from medieval Latin *toxicus* 'poisoned,' from Latin *toxicum* 'poison,' from Greek *toxikon (pharmakon)* '(poison for) arrows,' from *toxon* 'bow.' —**tox·i·cal·ly** /-sik(ə)lē/ *adv.* —**tox·ic·i·ty** /täkˈsisitē/ *n.*

tox·i·cant /ˈtäksikənt/ ▸*n.* a toxic substance introduced into the environment, e.g., a pesticide. ▷late 19th cent.: variant of INTOXICANT, differentiated in sense.

toxico- ▸*comb. form* equivalent to TOXI-. ▷from Greek *toxicon* 'poison.'

tox·i·col·o·gy /ˌtäksiˈkäləjē/ ▸*n.* the branch of science concerned with the nature, effects, and detection of poisons. —**tox·i·co·log·ic** /-kəˈläjik/ *adj.* —**tox·i·co·log·i·cal** /-kəˈläjikəl/ *adj.* —**tox·i·co·log·i·cal·ly** *adv.* —**tox·i·col·o·gist** /-ˈkäləjist/ *n.*

tox·ic shock syn·drome (abbr.: **TSS**) ▸*n.* acute septicemia in women, typically caused by bacterial infection from a retained tampon or IUD.

tox·i·drome /ˈtäksiˌdrōm/ ▸*n.* a group of signs and symptoms constituting the basis for a diagnosis of poisoning.

tox·i·gen·ic /ˌtäksiˈjenik/ ▸*adj.* (esp. of a bacterium) producing a toxin or toxic effect. —**tox·i·ge·nic·i·ty** /-jəˈnisitē/ *n.*

tox·in /ˈtäksin/ ▸*n.* an antigenic poison or venom of plant or animal origin, esp. one produced by or derived from microorganisms and causing disease when present at low concentration in the body. ▷late 19th cent.: from TOXIC + -IN[1].

toxo- ▸*comb. form* equivalent to TOXI-.

tox·o·car·a /ˌtäksəˈkarə/ ▸*n.* a parasitic nematode worm, esp. a common worm of dogs or cats that is transmissible to humans. • Genus *Toxocara*, class Phasmida, in particular *T. canis* (in dogs) and *T. cati* (in cats). ▷modern Latin, from TOXO- (see TOXI-) + Greek *kara* 'head.'

tox·o·car·i·a·sis /ˌtäksəkəˈrīəsis/ ▸*n.* infection of a human with the larvae of toxocara worms, causing illness and a risk of blindness from cyst formation in the eye.

tox·oid /ˈtäkˌsoid/ ▸*n. Medicine* a chemically modified toxin from a pathogenic microorganism, that is no longer toxic but is still antigenic and can be used as a vaccine.

tox·oph·i·lite /täkˈsäfəˌlīt/ *rare* ▸*n.* a student or lover of archery.

▸*adj.* of or relating to archers and archery. ▷late 18th cent.: from *Toxophilus* (a name invented by Ascham, used as the title of his treatise on archery (1545), from Greek *toxon* 'bow' + *-philos* 'loving') + -ITE[1]. —**tox·oph·i·ly** /-ˈsäfəlē/ *n.*

tox·o·plas·ma /ˌtäksəˈplazmə/ ▸*n.* a parasitic spore-forming protozoan that can sometimes cause disease in humans. • Genus *Toxoplasma*, phylum Sporozoa, in particular *T. gondii.*

tox·o·plas·mo·sis /ˌtäksōplazˈmōsis/ ▸*n.* a disease caused by toxoplasmas, transmitted chiefly through undercooked meat, or in soil or cat feces. Symptoms generally pass unremarked in adults, but infection can be dangerous to unborn children.

toy /toi/ ▸*n.* **1** an object for a child to play with, typically a model or miniature replica of something: [as *adj.*] *a toy car.* ■ an object, esp. a gadget or machine, regarded as providing amusement for an adult: *in 1914 the car was still a rich man's toy.* ■ a person treated by another as a source of pleasure or amusement rather than with due seriousness: *a man needed a friend, an ally, not an idol or a toy.* **2** [as *adj.*] denoting a diminutive breed or variety of dog: *a toy poodle.*

▸*phrasal v.* □ **toy with 1** consider (an idea, movement, or proposal) casually or indecisively. ■ treat (someone) without due seriousness, esp. in a superficially amorous way. **2** move or handle (an object) absentmindedly or nervously. ■ eat or drink in an unenthusiastic or restrained way. ▷late Middle English: of unknown origin. The word originally denoted a funny story or remark, later an antic or trick, or a frivolous entertainment. The verb dates from the early 16th cent. —**toy·like** /-ˌlīk/ *adj.*

toy·book /ˈtoiˌbŏŏk/ ▸*n.* a children's book with features that enable it to be played with as well as read.

toy boy ▸*n. Brit., informal* a male lover who is much younger than his partner.

Toyn·bee[1] /ˈtoinbē/, Arnold, (1852–83), English economist and social reformer. He taught both undergraduates and workers' adult education classes in Oxford and worked with the poor in London. He is best known for his pioneering work *The Industrial Revolution* (1884).

Toyn·bee[2], Arnold (Joseph) (1889–1975), English historian. He is best known for his 12-volume *Study of History* (1934–61), in which he traced the pattern of growth, maturity, and decay of different civilizations. He was the nephew of the economist Arnold Toynbee.

to·yon /ˈtoi-än/ ▸*n.* an evergreen Californian shrub of the rose family, the fruiting branches of which are used for Christmas decorations. • *Heteromeles arbutifolia*, family Rosaceae. ▷mid 19th cent.: from Mexican Spanish *tollón.*

tp. ▸*abbr.* ■ township. ■ troop.

t.p. ▸*abbr.* ■ title page. ■ toilet paper. ■ (in surveying) turning point.

▸*v.* (also **TP**) short for TOILET PAPER.

TPA ▸*abbr.* tissue plasminogen activator.

tpk. ▸*abbr.* turnpike.

TPV ▸*abbr.* thermophotovoltaic.

TQM ▸*abbr.* Total Quality Management.

tr. ▸*abbr.* ■ tare. ■ tincture. ■ trace. ■ train. ■ transaction. ■ transitive. ■ translated. ■ translation. ■ translator. ■ transpose. ■ transposition. ■ treasurer. ■ *Music* trill. ■ troop. ■ trust. ■ trustee.

tra·be·a·tion /ˌtrābēˈāsHən/ ▸*n.* the use of beams in architectural construction, rather than arches or vaulting. ▷mid 16th cent. (denoting a horizontal beam): formed irregularly from Latin *trabs, trab-* 'beam, timber' + -ATION. —**tra·be·at·ed** /ˈtrābēˌātid/ *adj.*

tra·bec·u·la /trəˈbekyələ/ ▸*n.* (usu. in *pl.* **-lae** /-lē/) **1** *Anatomy* each of a series or group of partitions formed by bands or columns of connective tissue, esp. a plate of the calcareous tissue forming cancellous bone. **2** *Botany* any of a number of rodlike structures in plants, e.g., a strand of sterile tissue dividing the cavity in a sporangium. ▷mid 19th cent.: from Latin, diminutive of *trabs* 'beam, timber.' —**tra·bec·u·lar** *adj.* —**tra·bec·u·late** /-lit/ *adj.*

Trâ·blous Arabic name for TRIPOLI (sense 2).

Trab·zon /trabˈzän/ a port on the Black Sea in northern Turkey; pop. 144,000. Also called TREBIZOND.

trace[1] /trās/ ▸*v.* [*trans.*] **1** find or discover by investigation: *police are trying to trace a white van seen in the area.* ■ find or describe the origin or development of: *Bob's book traces his flying career with the Marines.* ■ follow or mark the course or position of (something) with one's eye, mind, or finger: *through the binoculars, I traced the path I had taken the night before.* ■ take (a particular path or route): *a tear traced a lonely path down her cheek.* **2** copy (a drawing, map, or design) by drawing over its lines on a superimposed piece of transparent paper. ■ draw (a pattern or line), esp. with one's finger or toe. ■ give an outline of: *the article* ***traces out*** *some of the connections between education, qualifications, and the labor market.*

▸*n.* **1** a mark, object, or other indication of the existence or passing of something: *remove all traces of the old adhesive | the aircraft disappeared without trace.* ■ a beaten path or small road; a track. ■ a physical change in the brain presumed to be caused by a process of learning or memory. ■ a procedure to investigate the source of something, such as the place from which a telephone call was made, or the origin of an error in a computer program. **2** a very small quantity, esp. one too small to be accurately measured: *his body contained traces of amphetamines* [as *adj.*] *trace quantities of PCBs.* ■ a slight indication or barely discernible hint of something: *just a trace of a smile.* **3** a line or pattern displayed by an instrument using a moving pen or a luminous spot on a screen to show the existence or nature of something that is being investigated. ■ a line that represents the projection of a curve or surface on a plane or the intersection of a curve or surface with a plane. **4** *Mathematics* the sum of the elements in the principle diagonal of a square matrix. ▷Middle English (first recorded as a noun in the sense 'path that someone or something takes'): from Old French *trace* (noun), *tracier* (verb), based on Latin *tractus* (see TRACT[1]). —**trace·a·bil·i·ty** /ˌtrāsəˈbilitē/ *n.* —**trace·a·ble** *adj.* —**trace·less** *adj.*

THE RIGHT WORD **remnant, trace, track, trail, vestige**

You can follow the **track** of a deer in the snow, the **trace** of a sleigh, or the **trail** of someone who has just cut down a Christmas tree and is dragging it back to the car.

A *track* is a line or a series of marks left by the

Pronunciation Key ə *ago;* ər *over;* ˈə or ˌə *up;* ˈər or ˌər *fur;* a *hat;* ā *rate;* ä *car;* CH *chew;* e *let;* ē(ə)r *air;* i *fit;* ī *by;* i(ə)r *ear;* NG *sing;* ō *go;* ô *for;* oi *boy;* ŏŏ *good;* o͞o *goo;* ou *out;* SH *she;* TH *thin;* T͟H *then;* (h)w *why;* ZH *vision*

passage of something or someone; it often refers specifically to a line of footprints or a path worn into the ground by the feet (*following the track of a grizzly bear*).

Trace may refer to a line or a rut made by someone or something that has been present or passed by; it may also refer to a mark serving as evidence that something has happened or been there (*traces of mud throughout the house; the telephoto shots have a trace of a camera shake*).

Trail may refer to the track created by the passage of animals or people, or to the mark or marks left by something being dragged along a surface (*they followed the trail of the injured dog*).

Vestige and **remnant** come closer in meaning to *trace*, as they refer to what remains after something has passed away.

A *vestige* is always slight when compared to what it recalls (*the last vestiges of a great civilization*), while a *remnant* is a fragment or scrap of something (*all that remained of the historic tapestry after the fire was a few scorched remnants*).

trace[2] ▸*n.* each of the two side straps, chains, or ropes by which a horse is attached to a vehicle that it is pulling. ▷Middle English (denoting a pair of traces): from Old French *trais*, plural of *trait* (see TRAIT).

trace el·e·ment ▸*n.* a chemical element present only in minute amounts in a particular sample or environment. ■ a chemical element required only in minute amounts by living organisms for normal growth.

trace fos·sil ▸*n. Geology* a fossil of a footprint, trail, burrow, or other trace of an animal rather than of the animal itself.

trace min·er·al ▸*n.* a trace element required for nutrition: *selenium and other trace minerals are vital to good health.*

trac·er /ˈtrāsər/ ▸*n.* a person or thing that traces something or by which something may be traced, in particular: ■ a bullet or shell whose course is made visible in flight by a trail of flames or smoke, used to assist in aiming. ■ a substance introduced into a biological organism or other system so that its subsequent distribution can be readily followed from its color, fluorescence, radioactivity, or other distinctive property. ■ a device that transmits a signal and so can be located when attached to a moving vehicle or other object.

trac·er·y /ˈtrāsərē/ ▸*n.* (*pl.* **-er·ies**) *Architecture* ornamental stone openwork, typically in the upper part of a Gothic window. ■ a delicate branching pattern: *a tracery of red veins.* **—trac·er·ied** *adj.*

tra·che·a /ˈtrākēə/ ▸*n.* (*pl.* **-che·ae** /-kē,ē/ or **-che·as**) *Anatomy* a large membranous tube reinforced by rings of cartilage, extending from the larynx to the bronchial tubes and conveying air to and from the lungs; the windpipe. ■ *Entomology* each of a number of fine chitinous tubes in the body of an insect, conveying air directly to the tissues. ■ *Botany* any duct or vessel in a plant, providing support and conveying water and salts. ▷late Middle English: from medieval Latin, from late Latin *trachia*, from Greek *trakheia (artēria)* 'rough (artery),' from *trakhus* 'rough.' **—tra·che·al** *adj.* **—tra·che·ate** /-it; -,āt/ *adj.*

tra·che·id /ˈtrākēid/ ▸*n. Botany* a type of water-conducting cell in the xylem that lacks perforations in the cell wall. ▷late 19th cent.: from German *Tracheïde*, from medieval Latin *trachea* (see TRACHEA).

tra·che·i·tis /,trākēˈītis/ ▸*n. Medicine* inflammation of the trachea, usually secondary to a nose or throat infection.

tracheo- ▸*comb. form* relating to the trachea: *tracheotomy.*

tra·che·ot·o·my /,trākēˈätəmē/ (also **tra·che·os·to·my** /-ˈästəmē/) ▸*n.* (*pl.* **-mies**) *Medicine* an incision in the windpipe made to relieve an obstruction to breathing.

tra·cho·ma /trəˈkōmə/ ▸*n.* a contagious bacterial infection of the eye in which there is inflamed granulation on the inner surface of the lids. • The disease is caused by the chlamydial organism *Chlamydia trachomatis.* ▷late 17th cent.: from Greek *trakhōma* 'roughness,' from *trakhus* 'rough.' **—tra·chom·a·tous** /-mətəs/ *adj.*

tra·chyte /ˈtrak,īt; ˈtrā-/ ▸*n. Geology* a gray fine-grained volcanic rock consisting largely of alkali feldspar. ▷early 19th cent. (denoting a volcanic rock with a rough or gritty surface): from Greek *trakhus* 'rough' or *trakhutēs* 'roughness.'

tra·chyt·ic /trəˈkitik/ ▸*adj. Geology* relating to or denoting a rock texture (characteristic of trachyte) in which crystals show parallel alignment due to flow in the magma.

trac·ing /ˈtrāsiNG/ ▸*n.* a copy of a drawing, map, or design made by tracing it. ■ a faint or delicate mark or pattern: *tracings of apple blossoms against the deep greens of pines.* ■ another term for TRACE[1] (sense 3). ■ *Figure Skating* the marking out of a figure on the ice when skating.

trac·ing pa·per ▸*n.* transparent paper used for tracing maps, drawings, or designs.

track[1] /trak/ ▸*n.* **1** a rough path or minor road, typically one beaten by use rather than constructed: *follow the track to the farm | a forest track.* See note at TRACE. ■ a prepared course or circuit for athletes, horses, motor vehicles, bicycles, or dogs to race on: *a Formula One Grand Prix track.* ■ the sport of running on such a track. ■ (usu. **tracks**) a mark or line of marks left by a person, animal, or vehicle in passing: *he followed the tracks made by the police cars in the snow.* ■ the course or route followed by someone or something (used esp. in talking about their pursuit by others): *I didn't want the Russians on my track.* ■ *figurative* a course of action; a way of proceeding: *defense budgeting and procurement do not move along different tracks from defense policy as a whole.* **2** a continuous line of rails on a railroad. ■ a metal or plastic strip or rail from which a curtain or spotlight may be hung or fitted. ■ a continuous articulated metal band around the wheels of a heavy vehicle such as a tank or bulldozer, intended to facilitate movement over rough or soft ground. ■ *Electronics* a continuous line of copper or other conductive material on a printed circuit board, used to connect parts of a circuit. ■ *Sailing* a strip on the mast, boom, or deck of a yacht along which a slide attached to a sail can be moved, used to adjust the position of the sail. **3** a section of a record, compact disc, or cassette tape containing one song or piece of music: *the CD contains early Elvis Presley tracks.* [originally denoting a groove on a phonograph record.] ■ a lengthwise strip of magnetic tape containing one sequence of signals. ■ the soundtrack of a film or video. **4** the transverse distance between a vehicle's wheels. **5** a group in which schoolchildren of the same age and ability are taught.

▸*v.* [*trans.*] **1** follow the course or trail of (someone or something), typically in order to find them or note their location at various points: *secondary radars that track the aircraft in flight | he tracked Anna to her room.* ■ *figurative* follow and note the course or progress of: *they are tracking the girth and evolution of stars.* ■ [*intrans.*] follow a particular course: *the storm was tracking across the ground at 30 mph.* ■ (of a stylus) follow (a groove in a record). ■ [*intrans.*] (of a film or television camera) move in relation to the subject being filmed: *the camera eventually tracked away.* [with reference to early filming when a camera was mobile by means of a track.] ■ (**track something up**) leave a trail of dirty footprints on a surface. ■ (**track something in**) leave a trail of dirt, debris, or snow from one's feet: *the road salt I'd tracked in from the street.* **2** [*intrans.*] (of wheels) run so that the back ones are exactly in the track of the front ones. **3** [*intrans.*] *Electronics* (of a tunable circuit or component) vary in frequency in the same way as another circuit or component, so that the frequency difference between them remains constant. **4** assign (a student) to a course of study according to ability.

▸*phrasal v.* ◻ **track someone/something down** find someone or something after a thorough or difficult search. ◻ **track up** (of a horse at the trot) create sufficient impulsion in its hindquarters to cause the hind feet to step on to or slightly ahead of the former position of the forefeet. ▷late 15th cent. (in the sense 'trail, marks left behind'): the noun from Old French *trac*, perhaps from Low German or Dutch *trek* 'drawing, pull'; the verb (current senses dating from the mid 16th cent.) from French *traquer* or directly from the noun.

▸*PHRASES* ◻ **in one's tracks** *informal* where one or something is at that moment; suddenly: *Turner immediately **stopped dead in his tracks**.* ◻ **keep** (or **lose**) **track of** keep (or fail to keep) fully aware of or informed about: *she had lost all track of time and had fallen asleep.* ◻ **make tracks (for)** *informal* leave hurriedly (for a place). ◻ **off the beaten track** see BEATEN. ◻ **off the track** departing from the right course of thinking or behavior. ◻ **on the right** (or **wrong**) **track** acting or thinking in a way that is likely to result in success (or failure): *we are on the right track for continued growth.* ◻ **on track** acting or thinking in a way that is likely to achieve what is required: *formulas for keeping the economy on track.* ◻ **the wrong** (or **right**) **side of the tracks** *informal* a poor, less prestigious (or wealthy, prestigious) part of town.

track[2] ▸*v.* [*trans.*] tow (a boat) along a waterway from the bank. ▷early 18th cent.: apparently from Dutch *trekken* 'to draw, pull, or travel.' The change in the vowel was due to association with TRACK[1].

track·age /ˈtrakij/ ▸*n.* the tracks or lines of a railroad system collectively.

track and field ▸*n.* athletic events that take place on a running track and a nearby field; track events and field events.

track·ball /ˈtrak,bôl/ ▸*n.* a small ball set in a holder that can be rotated by hand to move a cursor on a computer screen.

track·bed /ˈtrak,bed/ ▸*n.* a roadbed for a railroad.

track·er /ˈtrakər/ ▸*n.* **1** a person who tracks someone or something by following their trail. **2** *Music* a connecting rod in the mechanism of some organs.

track e·vents ▸*plural n.* track-and-field contests that take place on a running track, as opposed to those involving throwing or other activities. Compare with FIELD EVENTS.

track·ing /ˈtrakiNG/ ▸*n.* **1** the action of tracking someone or something. ■ *Electronics* the maintenance of a constant difference in frequency between two or more connected circuits or components. ■ the alignment of the wheels of a vehicle. ■ the formation of a conducting path for an electric current over the surface of an insulating material. ■ a control in a videocassette recorder that electronically adjusts the manner in which the head receives signals from the videotape, providing a clearer playback. **2** the practice of putting schoolchildren in groups of the same age and ability to be taught together: *Japan allows virtually no tracking or ability grouping before high school.*

track·ing sta·tion ▸*n.* a place from which the movements of missiles, aircraft, or satellites are tracked by radar or radio.

track·lay·er /ˈtrak,lāər/ ▸*n.* **1** a tractor or other vehicle equipped with continuous tracks. **2** another term for TRACKMAN (sense 1).

track·less /ˈtrakləs/ ▸*adj.* **1** (of land) having no paths or tracks on it: *leading travelers into trackless wastelands.* ■ *poetic/literary* not leaving a track or trace. **2** (of a vehicle or component) not running on a track or tracks.

track light·ing ▸*n.* a lighting system in which the lights are fitted on tracks, allowing variable positioning. **—track lights** *plural n.*

track·man /ˈtrakmən; -,man/ ▸ **1** *n.* (*pl.* **-men**) a person employed in laying and maintaining railroad track. **2** an athlete in track events.

track rec·ord ▸*n.* the best recorded performance in a particular track-and-field event at a particular track. ■ the past achievements or performance of a person, organization, or product: *he has an excellent track record as an author.*

track shoe ▸*n.* a running shoe.

track·side /ˈtrak,sīd/ ▸*n.* **1** the area alongside a railroad track. **2** the area alongside a playing field or a racetrack.

track suit ▸*n.* a loose, warm set of clothes consisting of a sweatshirt or light jacket and pants with an elastic or drawstring waist, worn when exercising or as casual wear.

track·way /ˈtrak,wā/ ▸*n.* a path formed by the repeated treading of people or animals. ■ an ancient roadway.

tract[1] /trakt/ ▸*n.* **1** an area of indefinite extent, typically a large one: *large tracts of natural forest.* ■ *poetic/literary* an indefinitely large extent of something: *the vast tracts of time required to account for the deposition of the strata.* **2** a major passage in the body, large bundle of nerve fibers, or other continuous elongated anatomical structure or region: *the digestive tract.* ▷late Middle English (in the sense 'duration or course (of time)'): from Latin *tractus* 'drawing, dragging,' from *trahere* 'draw, pull.'

tract[2] ▸*n.* a short treatise in pamphlet form, typically on a religious subject. ▷late Middle English (denoting a written work treating a particular topic), apparently an abbreviation of Latin *tractatus* (see TRACTATE). The current sense dates from the early 19th cent.

trac·ta·ble /ˈtraktəbəl/ ▸*adj.* (of a person or animal) easy to control or influence: *the tractable dogs that have had some obedience training.* ■ (of a situation or problem) easy to deal with: *trying to make the* *mathematics tractable.* ▷early 16th cent.: from Latin *tractabilis*, from *tractare* 'to handle' (see TRACTATE). **—trac·ta·bil·i·ty** /ˌtraktəˈbilitē/ *n.* **—trac·ta·bly** /-blē/ *adv.*

Trac·tar·i·an·ism /trakˈte(ə)rēəˌnizəm/ ▸*n.* another name for OXFORD MOVEMENT. ▷mid 19th cent.: from *Tracts for the Times*, the title of a series of pamphlets on theological topics started by J. H. Newman and published in Oxford 1833–41, which set out the doctrines on which the movement was based. **—Trac·tar·i·an** *adj.* & *n.*

trac·tate /ˈtrakˌtāt/ ▸*n. formal* a treatise. ■ a book of the Talmud. ▷late 15th cent.: from Latin *tractatus*, from *tractare* 'to handle,' frequentative of *trahere* 'draw.'

trac·tion /ˈtrakSHən/ ▸*n.* **1** the action of drawing or pulling a thing over a surface, esp. a road or track: *a primitive vehicle used in animal traction.* ■ motive power provided for such movement, esp. on a railroad: *the changeover to diesel and electric traction.* ■ locomotives collectively. **2** *Medicine* the application of a sustained pull on a limb or muscle, esp. in order to maintain the position of a fractured bone or to correct a deformity: *his leg is* ***in traction.*** **3** the grip of a tire on a road or a wheel on a rail: *his car hit a patch of ice and lost traction.* ▷late Middle English (denoting contraction, such as that of a muscle): from French, or from medieval Latin *traction-*, from Latin *trahere* 'draw, pull.' Current senses date from the early 19th cent.

trac·tion en·gine ▸*n.* a steam or diesel-powered road vehicle used (esp. formerly) for pulling very heavy loads.

trac·tive /ˈtraktiv/ ▸*adj.* [*attrib.*] relating to or denoting the power exerted in pulling, esp. by a vehicle or other machine.

trac·tor /ˈtraktər/ ▸*n.* a powerful motor vehicle with large rear wheels, used chiefly on farms for hauling equipment and trailers. ■ a short truck consisting of the driver's cab, designed to pull a large trailer. ▷late 18th cent. (in the general sense 'someone or something that pulls'): from Latin, from *tract-* 'pulled,' from the verb *trahere*.

trac·tor beam ▸*n.* (in science fiction) a hypothetical beam of energy that can be used to move objects such as space ships or hold them stationary.

trac·tor-trail·er ▸*n.* a vehicle consisting of a tractor or cab with an engine and a separate, attached trailer in which goods can be transported.

trac·tot·o·my /trakˈtätəmē/ ▸*n.* the surgical severing of nerve tracts esp. in the medulla of the brain, typically to relieve intractable pain or mental illness, or in research.

trac·trix /ˈtraktriks/ ▸*n.* (*pl.* **trac·tri·ces** /ˌtrakˈtrīsēz; ˈtraktrəˌsēz/) *Geometry* a curve whose tangents all intercept the *x*-axis at the same distance from the point of contact, being the involute of a catenary. ■ one of a class of curves similarly traced by one end of a rigid rod, whose other end moves along a fixed line or curve. ▷early 18th cent.: modern Latin, feminine of late Latin *tractor* 'that which pulls' (see TRACTOR).

Tra·cy[1] /ˈtrāsē/ a commercial and industrial city in north central California, in the San Joaquin Valley; pop. 33,558.

Tra·cy[2], Spencer (1900–67), U.S. actor. He is particularly known for his screen partnership with Katharine Hepburn, with whom he co-starred in movies such as *Adam's Rib* (1949) and *Guess Who's Coming to Dinner?* (1967). He won his first Academy Award for his performance in *Captains Courageous* (1937) and his second for *Boys' Town* (1938).

trad /trad/ *informal* ▸*adj.* (esp. of music) traditional: *trad jazz.*
▸*n.* traditional jazz or folk music. ▷1950s: abbreviation.

trade /trād/ ▸*n.* **1** the action of buying and selling goods and services: *a move to ban all* ***trade in*** *ivory | a significant increase in foreign trade | the meat trade.* ■ *dated, chiefly derogatory* the practice of making one's living in business, as opposed to in a profession or from unearned income: *the aristocratic classes were contemptuous of those* ***in trade.*** ■ (in sports) a transfer; an exchange: *players can demand a trade after five years of service.* **2** a skilled job, typically one requiring manual skills and special training: *the fundamentals of the construction trade | a carpenter by trade.* ■ (**the trade**) [treated as *sing.* or *pl.*] the people engaged in a particular area of business: *in the trade this sort of computer is called "a client-based system."* ■ (**the trade**) [treated as *sing.* or *pl.*] *Brit.* people licensed to sell alcoholic drink. ■ *informal* a person in gay male sexual encounters who is not penetrated sexually and usually considers himself to be heterosexual. **3** (usu. **trades**) a trade wind: *the north-east trades.*
▸*v.* [*intrans.*] buy and sell goods and services: *middlemen* ***trading in*** *luxury goods.* ■ [*trans.*] buy or sell (a particular item or product): *she has traded millions of dollars' worth of metals.* ■ (esp. of shares or currency) be bought and sold at a specified price: *the dollar was trading where it was in January.* ■ [*trans.*] exchange (something) for something else, typically as a commercial transaction: *they trade mud-shark livers for fish oil | the hostages were* ***traded for*** *arms.* ■ [*trans.*] *figurative* give and receive (typically insults or blows): *they traded a few punches.* ■ [*trans.*] transfer (a player) to another club or team.
▸*phrasal v.* □ **trade down** (or **up**) sell something in order to buy something similar but less (or more) expensive. □ **trade something in** exchange a used article in part payment for another: *she* ***traded in*** *her Ford* ***for*** *a BMW.* □ **trade something off** exchange something of value, esp. as part of a compromise: *the government* ***traded off*** *economic advantages* ***for*** *political gains.* □ **trade on** take advantage of (something), esp. in an unfair way: *the government is trading on fears of inflation.* ▷late Middle English (as a noun): from Middle Low German, literally 'track'; related to TREAD. Early senses included 'course, way of life,' which gave rise in the 16th cent. to 'habitual practice of an occupation,' 'skilled handicraft.' The current verb senses date from the late 16th cent. **—trad·a·ble** (or **trade·a·ble**) *adj.*
▸*PHRASE* □ **trade places** change places.

trade book ▸*n.* a book published by a commercial publisher and intended for general readership.

trade def·i·cit ▸*n.* the amount by which the cost of a country's imports exceeds the value of its exports.

trade dis·count ▸*n.* a discount on the retail price of something allowed or agreed between traders or to a retailer by a wholesaler.

trad·ed op·tion ▸*n. Finance* an option on a stock exchange or futures exchange which can itself be bought and sold.

trade e·di·tion ▸*n.* an edition of a book intended for general sale rather than for book clubs or specialist suppliers.

trade gap ▸*n.* another term for TRADE DEFICIT.

trade-in ▸*n.* [usu. as *adj.*] a used article accepted by a retailer in partial payment for another: *the trade-in value of the old car.*

trade jour·nal (also **trade magazine**) ▸*n.* a periodical containing news and items of interest concerning a particular trade.

trade-last ▸*n. dated* a compliment from a third person that is relayed to the person complimented in exchange for a similarly relayed compliment.

trade·mark /ˈtrādˌmärk/ ▸*n.* a symbol, word, or words legally registered or established by use as representing a company or product. ■ *figurative* a distinctive characteristic or object: *it had all the trademarks of a Mafia hit.*
▸*v.* [*trans.*] [usu. as *adj.*] (**trademarked**) provide with a trademark: *they are counterfeiting trademarked goods.* ■ *figurative* identify (a habit, quality, or way of life) as typical of someone: *his trademarked grandiose style.*

trade name ▸*n.* **1** a name that has the status of a trademark. **2** a name by which something is known in a particular trade or profession.

trade-off ▸*n.* a balance achieved between two desirable but incompatible features; a compromise: *a trade-off between objectivity and relevance.*

trade pa·per ▸*n.* another term for TRADE JOURNAL.

trad·er /ˈtrādər/ ▸*n.* a person who buys and sells goods, currency, or stocks. ■ a merchant ship.

Trade·scant /trəˈdeskənt; ˈtradəˌskant/, John (1570–1638), English botanist and horticulturalist. He was the earliest known collector of plants and other natural history specimens.

trad·es·can·tia /ˌtradəˈskancH(ē)ə; -tēə/ ▸*n.* an American plant with triangular three-petaled flowers, esp. a tender kind widely grown as a houseplant for its trailing, typically variegated, foliage. Compare with SPIDERWORT. • Genus *Tradescantia*, family Commelinaceae. ▷modern Latin, named in honor of J. TRADESCANT.

trade se·cret ▸*n.* a secret device or technique used by a company in manufacturing its products.

trades·man /ˈtrādzmən/ ▸*n.* (*pl.* **-men**) a person engaged in trading or a trade, typically on a relatively small scale.

trades·peo·ple /ˈtrādzˌpēpəl/ ▸*plural n.* people engaged in trade.

trade sur·plus ▸*n.* the amount by which the value of a country's exports exceeds the cost of its imports.

trade un·ion (*Brit.* also **trades un·ion**) ▸*n.* an organized association of workers in a trade, group of trades, or profession, formed to protect and further their rights and interests.

trade un·ion·ist (*Brit.* also **trades un·ion·ist**) ▸*n.* a member of a trade union or an advocate of trade unions. **—trade un·ion·ism** *n.*

trade-up ▸*n.* a sale of an article in order to buy something similar but more expensive and of higher quality.

trade war ▸*n.* a situation in which countries try to damage each other's trade, typically by the imposition of tariffs or quota restrictions.

trade wind /wind/ ▸*n.* a wind blowing steadily toward the equator from the northeast in the northern hemisphere or the southeast in the southern hemisphere, esp. at sea. Two belts of trade winds encircle the earth, blowing from the tropical high-pressure belts to the low-pressure zone at the equator. ▷mid 17th cent.: from the phrase *blow trade* 'blow steadily in the same direction.' Because of the importance of these winds to navigation, 18th-cent. etymologists were led erroneously to connect the word *trade* with "commerce."

trad·ing /ˈtrādiNG/ ▸*n.* the action of engaging in trade.

trad·ing card ▸*n.* one of a set of cards, such as those depicting professional athletes, that are collected and traded, esp. by children.

trad·ing floor ▸*n.* an area within an exchange or a bank or securities house where dealers trade in stocks or other securities.

trad·ing post ▸*n.* a store or small settlement established for trading, typically in a remote place.

trad·ing stamp ▸*n.* a stamp given by some stores to a customer according to the amount spent, and exchangeable in the appropriate number for various articles.

tra·di·tion /trəˈdiSHən/ ▸*n.* **1** the transmission of customs or beliefs from generation to generation, or the fact of being passed on in this way: *every shade of color is fixed* ***by tradition*** *and governed by religious laws.* ■ a long-established custom or belief that has been passed on in this way: *Japan's unique cultural traditions.* ■ [*in sing.*] an artistic or literary method or style established by an artist, writer, or movement, and subsequently followed by others: *visionary works* ***in the tradition of*** *William Blake.* **2** *Theology* a doctrine believed to have divine authority though not in the scriptures, in particular: ■ (in Christianity) doctrine not explicit in the Bible but held to derive from the oral teaching of Jesus and the Apostles. ■ (in Judaism) an ordinance of the oral law not in the Torah but held to have been given by God to Moses. ■ (in Islam) a saying or act ascribed to the Prophet but not recorded in the Koran. See HADITH. ▷late Middle English: from Old French *tradicion*, or from Latin *traditio(n-)*, from *tradere* 'deliver, betray,' from *trans-* 'across' + *dare* 'give.' **—tra·di·tion·ar·y** /-ˌnerē/ *adj.* **—tra·di·tion·ist** /-nist/ *n.* **—tra·di·tion·less** *adj.*

tra·di·tion·al /trəˈdiSHənl/ ▸*adj.* existing in or as part of a tradition; long-established: *the traditional festivities of the church year.* ■ produced, done, or used in accordance with tradition: *a traditional fish soup.* ■ habitually done, used, or found: *the traditional drinks in the clubhouse.* ■ (of a person or group) adhering to tradition, or to a particular tradition: *traditional Elgarians.* ■ (of jazz) in the style of the early 20th century. **—tra·di·tion·al·ly** *adv.*

tra·di·tion·al·ism /trəˈdiSHənlˌizəm/ ▸*n.* the upholding or maintenance of tradition, esp. so as to resist change. ■ *chiefly historical* the theory that all moral and religious truth comes from divine revelation passed on by tradition, human reason being incapable of attaining it. **—tra·di·tion·al·ist** *n.* & *adj.* **—tra·di·tion·al·is·tic** /trəˌdiSHənlˈistik/ *adj.*

tra·duce /trəˈd(y)o͞os/ ▸*v.* [*trans.*] speak badly of or tell lies about (someone) so as to damage their reputation. ▷mid 16th cent. (in the sense 'transport, transmit'): from Latin *traducere* 'lead in front of others, expose to ridicule,' from *trans-* 'over, across' + *ducere* 'to lead.' **—tra·duce·ment** *n.* **—tra·duc·er** *n.*

Tra·fal·gar, Bat·tle of /trəˈfalgər/ a decisive naval battle fought on October 21, 1805, off the cape of Trafalgar on the south coast of Spain during the Napoleonic Wars. The British fleet under Horatio

Nelson (who was killed in the action) defeated the combined fleets of France and Spain, which were attempting to clear the way for Napoleon's projected invasion of Britain.

traf·fic /ˈtrafik/ ▶*n.* **1** vehicles moving on a road or public highway: *a stream of heavy traffic.* ■ a large number of such vehicles: *we were caught in traffic on the expressway.* ■ the movement of other forms of transportation or of pedestrians: *managing the air traffic was a mammoth task.* ■ the transportation of goods or passengers: *the increased use of railroads for goods traffic.* ■ the messages or signals transmitted through a communications system: *data traffic between remote workstations.* **2** the action of dealing or trading in something illegal: *the **traffic in** stolen cattle.* **3** *archaic* dealings or communication between people.
▶*v.* (**-ficked**, **-fick·ing**) [*intrans.*] deal or trade in something illegal: *the government will vigorously pursue individuals who **traffic in** drugs.* ▷early 16th cent. (denoting commercial transportation of merchandise or passengers): from French *traffique*, Spanish *tráfico*, or Italian *traffico*, of unknown origin. Sense 1 dates from the early 19th cent. **—traf·fick·er** *n.* **—traf·fic·less** *adj.*

traf·fic calm·ing ▶*n.* the deliberate slowing of traffic in residential areas by building speed bumps or other obstructions. ▷1980s: translation of German *Verkehrsberuhigung*.

traf·fic cir·cle ▶*n.* a road junction at which traffic moves in one direction around a central island.

traf·fic is·land ▶*n.* a small raised area in the middle of a road that provides a safe place for pedestrians to stand and marks a division between two opposing streams of traffic.

traf·fic jam ▶*n.* road traffic at or near a standstill because of road construction, an accident, or heavy congestion.

traf·fic light (also **traf·fic sig·nal**) ▶*n.* a set of automatically operated colored lights, typically red, amber, and green, for controlling traffic at road junctions and crosswalks.

traf·fic pat·tern ▶*n.* a pattern in the air above an airport of permitted lanes for aircraft to follow after takeoff or prior to landing. ■ the characteristic distribution of traffic on a route: *the filming had screwed up the traffic patterns in town.*

traf·fic sign ▶*n.* a sign conveying information, an instruction, or a warning to drivers.

trag·a·canth /ˈtragəˌkanTH; ˈtraj-/ (also **gum tragacanth**) ▶*n.* a white or reddish plant gum used in the food, textile, and pharmaceutical industries. • This gum is obtained from plants of the genus *Astragalus*, family Leguminosae, in particular the Eurasian *A. gummifer*. ▷late 16th cent.: from French *tragacante*, via Latin from Greek *tragakantha* 'goat's thorn,' from *tragos* 'goat' (because it is browsed by goats) + *akantha* 'thorn' (referring to the shrub's spines).

tra·ge·di·an /trəˈjēdēən/ ▶*n.* an actor who specializes in tragic roles. ■ a writer of tragedies. ▷late Middle English (denoting a writer of tragedies): from Old French *tragediane*, from *tragedie* (see TRAGEDY).

tra·ge·di·enne /trəˌjēdēˈen/ ▶*n.* an actress who specializes in tragic roles. ▷mid 19th cent.: from French *tragédienne*, feminine of *tragédien*.

trag·e·dy /ˈtrajidē/ ▶*n.* (*pl.* **-dies**) **1** an event causing great suffering, destruction, and distress, such as a serious accident, crime, or natural catastrophe: *a tragedy that killed 95 people | his life had been plagued by tragedy.* **2** a play dealing with tragic events and having an unhappy ending, esp. one concerning the downfall of the main character. ■ the dramatic genre represented by such plays: *Greek tragedy.* Compare with COMEDY. ▷late Middle English: from Old French *tragedie*, via Latin from Greek *tragōidia*, apparently from *tragos* 'goat' (the reason remains unexplained) + *ōidē* 'song, ode.' Compare with TRAGIC.

tra·ghet·to /trəˈgetō/ ▶*n.* (*pl.* **-ghet·ti** /-ˈgetē/) (in Venice) a landing place or jetty for gondolas. ■ a gondola ferry. ▷Italian.

trag·ic /ˈtrajik/ ▶*adj.* causing or characterized by extreme distress or sorrow: *the shooting was a tragic accident.* ■ suffering extreme distress or sorrow: *the tragic parents reached the end of their tether.* ■ of or relating to tragedy in a literary work. ▷mid 16th cent.: from French *tragique*, via Latin from Greek *tragikos*, from *tragos* 'goat,' but associated with *tragōidia* (see TRAGEDY). **—trag·i·cal** *adj.* **—trag·i·cal·ly** /-ik(ə)lē/ *adv.*

trag·ic flaw ▶*n.* less technical term for HAMARTIA.

trag·ic i·ro·ny ▶*n.* see IRONY[1].

trag·i·com·e·dy /ˌtrajəˈkämidē/ ▶*n.* (*pl.* **-dies**) a play or novel containing elements of both comedy and tragedy. ■ such works as a genre. ▷late 16th cent.: from French *tragicomédie* or Italian *tragicomedia*, based on Latin *tragicocomoedia*, from *tragicus* (see TRAGIC) + *comoedia* (see COMEDY). **—trag·i·com·ic** /-ˈkämik/ *adj.* **—trag·i·com·i·cal·ly** /-ˈkämik(ə)lē/ *adv.*

trag·o·pan /ˈtragəˌpan/ ▶*n.* an Asian pheasant of highland forests, the male of which has brightly colored plumage used in courtship. • Genus *Tragopan*, family Phasianidae: five species. ▷modern Latin, from Greek, the name of a horned bird, from *tragos* 'goat' + the name *Pan* (see PAN).

tra·gus /ˈtrāgəs/ ▶*n.* (*pl.* **-gi** /-jī; -gī/) *Anatomy & Zoology* a prominence on the inner side of the external ear, in front of and partly closing the passage to the organs of hearing. ▷late 17th cent.: from late Latin, via Latin from Greek *tragos* 'goat' (with reference to the characteristic tuft of hair that is often present, likened to a goat's beard).

Tra·herne /trəˈhərn/, Thomas (1637–74), English religious writer and metaphysical poet. His major prose work *Centuries* (1699) was rediscovered in 1896 and republished as *Centuries of Meditation* (1908). It consists of brief meditations showing his joy in creation and in divine love and is noted for its description of his childhood.

tra·hi·son des clercs /trä-ēˈzôN dā ˈkler/ ▶*n. poetic/literary* a betrayal of intellectual, artistic, or moral standards by writers, academics, or artists. ▷French, literally 'treason of the scholars,' the title of a book by Julien Benda (1927).

trail /trāl/ ▶*n.* **1** a mark or a series of signs or objects left behind by the passage of someone or something: *a trail of blood on the grass.* ■ a track or scent used in following someone or hunting an animal: *police followed his trail to Atlantic City.* ■ a part, typically long and thin, stretching behind or hanging down from someone or something: *smoke trails | trails of ivy.* ■ a line of people of things following behind each other: *a trail of ants.* **2** a beaten path through rough country such as a forest or moor. ■ a route planned or followed for a particular purpose: *a Democratic candidate on the campaign trail.* ■ (also **ski trail**) a downhill ski run or cross-country ski route. **3** short for TRAILER (sense 2). **4** the rear end of a gun carriage, resting or sliding on the ground when the gun is unlimbered.
▶*v.* **1** [with *adverbial*] draw or be drawn along the ground or other surface behind someone or something: [*trans.*] *Alex trailed a hand through the clear water* | [*intrans.*] *her robe trailed along the ground.* ■ [*intrans.*] (typically of a plant) grow or hang over the edge of something or along the ground: *the roses grew wild, their stems trailing over the banks.* ■ [*trans.*] follow (a person or animal), typically by using marks, signs, or scent left behind. See note at TRACE. ■ [*intrans.*] be losing to an opponent in a game or contest: [with *complement*] *the Packers were trailing 10–6 at halftime.* **2** [*intrans.*] walk or move slowly or wearily: *she trailed behind, whimpering at intervals.* ■ (of the voice or a speaker) fade gradually before stopping: *her voice **trailed away**.* **3** [*trans.*] advertise (something, esp. a film or program) in advance by broadcasting extracts or details. **4** [*trans.*] apply (slip) through a nozzle or spout to decorate ceramic ware. ▷Middle English (as a verb): from Old French *traillier* 'to tow,' or Middle Low German *treilen* 'haul (a boat),' based on Latin *tragula* 'dragnet,' from *trahere* 'to pull.' Compare with TRAWL. The noun originally denoted the train of a robe, later generalized to denote something trailing.

trail bike ▶*n.* a light motorcycle for use in rough terrain.

trail·blaz·er /ˈtrālˌblāzər/ ▶*n.* a person who makes a new track through wild country. ■ a pioneer; an innovator: *he was a trailblazer for many ideas that are now standard fare.* **—trail·blaz·ing** /-ˌblāziNG/ *n.* & *adj.*

trail boss ▶*n.* a foreman in charge of a cattle drive.

trail·er /ˈtrālər/ ▶*n.* **1** an unpowered vehicle towed by another, in particular: ■ the rear section of a tractor-trailer. ■ an open cart. ■ a platform for transporting a boat. ■ an unpowered vehicle equipped for living in, typically used during vacations. **2** an excerpt or series of excerpts from a movie or program used to advertise it in advance; a preview. **3** a thing that trails, esp. a trailing plant.
▶*v.* [*trans.*] **1** advertise (a movie or program) in advance by broadcasting excerpts or details. **2** transport (something) by trailer.

trail·er park (also **trail·er court**) ▶*n.* an area with special amenities where trailers are parked and used for recreation or as permanent homes. ■ [as *adj.*] lacking refinement, taste, or quality; coarse: *her trailer-park bleached perm.*

trail·er trash ▶*n. informal, offensive* lower-class white people, typified as living in trailers: *their parenting style has moved the family from upper-middle-class suburban to trailer trash in one generation.*

trail·er truck ▶*n.* a tractor-trailer.

trail·head /ˈtrālˌhed/ ▶*n.* the place where a trail begins: *we camped amid the pines at the trailhead.*

trail·ing ar·bu·tus ▶*n.* see ARBUTUS.

trail·ing edge ▶*n.* the rear edge of a moving body, esp. an aircraft wing or propeller blade. ■ *Electronics* the part of a pulse in which the amplitude diminishes.

trail mix ▶*n.* a mixture of dried fruit and nuts eaten as a snack food, originally by hikers and campers.

train /trān/ ▶*v.* **1** [*trans.*] teach (a person or animal) a particular skill or type of behavior through practice and instruction over a period of time: *the plan trains people for promotion* | [*trans.*] *the dogs are trained to sniff out illegal stowaways.* ■ [*intrans.*] be taught in such a way: *he trained as a classicist.* ■ [usu. as *adj.*] (**trained**) cause (a mental or physical faculty) to be sharp, discerning, or developed as a result of instruction or practice: *an alert mind and trained eye give astute evaluations.* ■ cause (a plant) to grow in a particular direction or into a required shape: *they trained roses over their houses.* ■ [*intrans.*] undertake a course of exercise and diet in order to reach or maintain a high level of physical fitness, typically in preparation for participating in a specific sport or event: *she trains three times a week.* ■ cause to undertake such a course of exercise: *the horse was trained in Paris.* ■ [*intrans.*] (**train down**) reduce one's weight through diet and exercise in order to be fit for a particular event: *he trained down to heavyweight.* **2** [*trans.*] (**train something on**) point or aim something, typically a gun or camera, at: *the detective trained his gun on the side door.* **3** [*intrans.*] *dated* go by train: *Charles trained to Chicago with Emily.* **4** [*trans.*] *archaic* entice (someone) by offering pleasure or a reward.
▶*n.* **1** a series of railroad cars moved as a unit by a locomotive or by integral motors: *a freight train | the journey took two hours **by train**.* **2** a succession of vehicles or pack animals traveling in the same direction: *a camel train.* ■ a retinue of attendants accompanying an important person. ■ a series of connected events: *you may be setting in motion a train of events that will cause harm.* ■ [usu. with *adj.*] a series of gears or other connected parts in machinery: ***a train of gears.*** **3** a long piece of material attached to the back of a formal dress or robe that trails along the ground. **4** a trail of gunpowder for firing an explosive charge. ▷Middle English (as a noun in the sense 'delay'): from Old French *train* (masculine), *traine* (feminine), from *trahiner* (verb), from Latin *trahere* 'pull, draw.' Early noun senses were 'trailing part of a robe' and 'retinue'; the latter gave rise to 'line of traveling people or vehicles,' later 'a connected series of things.' The early verb sense 'cause (a plant) to grow in a desired shape' was the basis of the sense 'educate, instruct, teach.' **—train·a·bil·i·ty** /ˌtrānəˈbilitē/ *n.* **—train·a·ble** *adj.*
▶***PHRASES*** □ **in train** (of arrangements) well organized or in progress: *an investigation is in train.* □ **in someone/something's train** (or **in the train of**) following behind someone or something. ■ *figurative* as a sequel or consequence: *unemployment brings great difficulties in its train.* □ **train of thought** the way in which someone reaches a conclusion; a line of reasoning: *I failed to follow his train of thought.*

train·band /ˈtrānˌband/ ▶*n. historical* a division of civilian soldiers in London and other areas of England, in particular in the Stuart period.

train·ee /trāˈnē/ ▶*n.* a person undergoing training for a particular job or profession. **—train·ee·ship** /-ˌSHip/ *n.*

train·er /ˈtrānər/ ▶*n.* **1** a person who trains people or animals. ■ *informal* an aircraft or simulator used to train pilots. **2** a person whose job is to provide medical assistance to athletes. **3** *Brit.* a soft shoe, suitable for sports or casual wear.

train·ing /ˈtrāniNG/ ▶*n.* the action of teaching a person or animal a particular skill or type of behavior: *in-service training for staff.* ■ the action of undertaking a course of exercise and diet in preparation for a sporting event: *you'll have to **go into** strict **training**.*
▶***PHRASE*** □ **in** (or **out of**) **training** undergoing (or no longer undergoing) physical training for a sporting event. ■ physically fit (or unfit) as a result of the amount of training one has undertaken.

train·ing ship ▶*n.* a ship on which people are taught sailing and related skills.

train·ing shoe ▶*n.* a soft shoe designed to be used for athletic training.

train·ing ta·ble ▶*n.* a table in a dining hall where athletes in training are served specially prepared meals.

train·ing wheels ▶*plural n.* a pair of small supporting wheels fitted on either side of the rear wheel of a child's bicycle.

train·load /ˈtrānˌlōd/ ▶*n.* a number of people or a quantity of a commodity transported by train.

train·man /ˈtrānmən; -ˌman/ ▶*n.* (*pl.* **-men**) a railroad employee who works on trains.

train oil ▶*n. chiefly historical* oil obtained from the blubber of a whale (and formerly of other sea creatures), esp. the right whale. ▷mid 16th cent.: from obsolete *train* 'train-oil,' from Middle Low German *trān*, Middle Dutch *traen*, literally 'tear' (because it was extracted in droplets).

train set ▶*n.* **1** a set of trains, tracks, and other things making up a child's model railroad. **2** a set of railroad cars, often with a locomotive, coupled together for a particular service.

train shed ▶*n.* a large structure providing a shelter over the tracks and platforms of a railroad station.

train·sick /ˈtrānˌsik/ ▶*adj.* affected with nausea by the motion of a train.

traipse /trāps/ ▶*v.* [*intrans.*] walk or move wearily or reluctantly: *students had to traipse all over Washington to attend lectures.* ■ walk about casually or needlessly: *there's people traipsing in and out all the time.*

▶*n.* **1** [in *sing.*] a tedious or tiring journey on foot. **2** *archaic* a slovenly woman. ▷late 16th cent. (as a verb): of unknown origin. The noun is first recorded in sense 2 in the late 17th cent.

trait /trāt/ ▶*n.* a distinguishing quality or characteristic, typically one belonging to a person: *he was a letter-of-the-law man, a common trait among coaches.* ■ a genetically determined characteristic. ▷mid 16th cent.: from French, from Latin *tractus* 'drawing, pulling' (see TRACT[1]). An early sense was 'stroke of the pen or pencil in a picture,' giving rise to the sense 'a particular feature of mind or character' (mid 18th cent.).

trai·tor /ˈtrātər/ ▶*n.* a person who betrays a friend, country, principle, etc.: *they see me as a traitor, a sell-out to the enemy.* ▷Middle English: from Old French *traitour*, from Latin *traditor*, from *tradere* 'hand over.' **—trai·tor·ous** /-tərəs/ *adj.* **—trai·tor·ous·ly** *adv.*

▶*PHRASE* □ **turn traitor** betray a group or person: *to think of a man like you turning traitor to his class.*

Tra·jan /ˈtrājən/ (*c.*53–117), Roman emperor 98–117; Latin name *Marcus Ulpius Traianus*. His reign is noted for the Dacian wars (101–106), which ended in the annexation of Dacia as a province.

tra·jec·to·ry /trəˈjektərē/ ▶*n.* (*pl.* **-ries**) **1** the path described by a projectile flying or an object moving under the action of given forces. **2** *Geometry* a curve or surface cutting a family of curves or surfaces at a constant angle. ▷late 17th cent.: from modern Latin *trajectoria* (feminine), from Latin *traject-* 'thrown across,' from the verb *traicere*, from *trans-* 'across' + *jacere* 'to throw.'

Tra·keh·ner /träˈkānər/ ▶*n.* **1** a saddle horse of a light breed first developed at the Trakehnen stud farm near Kaliningrad in Russia. **2** a type of fence used in horse trials, consisting of a ditch spanned by center rails. ▷early 20th cent.: from German.

tra la /trä ˈlä/ (also **tra-la** or **tra-la-la**) ▶*exclam. chiefly ironic* expressing joy or gaiety: *off to his life, kids, and wife, tra la.* ▷early 19th cent.: imitative of a fanfare or of the refrain of a song.

Tra·lee /trəˈlē/ a port on the southwestern coast of the Republic of Ireland, the county town of Kerry; pop. 17,200.

tram /tram/ (also **tram·car**) ▶*n.* **1** *Brit.* a trolley car. **2** a cable car. **3** *historical* a low four-wheeled cart or barrow used in coal mines. ▷early 16th cent. (denoting a shaft of a barrow; also in sense 3): from Middle Low German and Middle Dutch *trame* 'beam, barrow shaft.' In the early 19th cent. the word denoted the parallel wheel tracks used in a mine, on which the public streetcar system was modeled; hence sense 1 (late 19th cent.)

Tra·mi·ner /trəˈmēnər/ ▶*n.* a variety of white wine grape grown chiefly in Germany and Alsace. ■ a white wine with a perfumed bouquet made from this grape. ▷named after the Italian village *Termeno*.

tram·lines /ˈtramˌlīnz/ ▶*n. informal* a pair of parallel lines, in particular the long lines at the sides of a tennis court (enclosing the extra width used in doubles play) or at the side or back of a badminton court. ▷late 19th cent.: from the resemblance to the rails for a tram (trolley car).

tram·mel /ˈtraməl/ ▶*n.* **1** (usu. **trammels**) *poetic/literary* a restriction or impediment to someone's freedom of action: *we will forge our own future, free from the trammels of materialism.* **2** (also **tram·mel net**) a set-net consisting of three layers of netting, designed so that a fish entering through one of the large-meshed outer sections will push part of the finer-meshed central section through the large meshes on the further side, forming a pocket in which the fish is trapped. **3** an instrument consisting of a board with two grooves intersecting at right angles, in which the two ends of a beam compass can slide to draw an ellipse. [early 18th cent.: so named because the motion of the beam is 'restricted' by the grooves.] ■ a beam compass. **4** a hook in a fireplace for a kettle.

▶*v.* (**-meled**, **-mel·ing**; *Brit.* **-melled**, **-mel·ling**) [*trans.*] deprive of freedom of action: *those less trammeled by convention than himself.* ▷late Middle English (sense 2): from Old French *tramail*, from a medieval Latin variant of *trimaculum*, perhaps from Latin *tri-* 'three' + *macula* 'mesh.'

tra·mon·ta·na /ˌträmənˈtänə/ ▶*n.* a cold north wind blowing in Italy or the adjoining regions of the Adriatic and Mediterranean. ▷Italian, 'north wind, North Star' (see TRAMONTANE).

tra·mon·tane /trəˈmänˌtān; ˈtramən-/ ▶*adj. rare* traveling to, situated on, or living on the other side of mountains. ■ *archaic* (esp. from the Italian point of view) foreign; barbarous.

▶*n.* **1** another term for TRAMONTANA. **2** *archaic* a person who lives on the other side of mountains (used in particular by Italians to refer to people beyond the Alps). ▷Middle English (as a noun denoting the Pole Star): from Italian *tramontana* 'North Star, north wind,' *tramontani* 'people living beyond the Alps,' from Latin *transmontanus* 'beyond the mountains,' from *trans-* 'across' + *mons, mont-* 'mountain.'

tramp /tramp/ ▶*v.* [*intrans.*] walk heavily or noisily: *he tramped around the room.* ■ walk through or over a place wearily or reluctantly and for long distances: *we have tramped miles over mountain and moorland.* ■ [*trans.*] tread or stamp on: *one of the few wines still tramped by foot.*

▶*n.* **1** a person who travels from place to place on foot in search of work or as a vagrant or beggar. **2** [in *sing.*] the sound of heavy steps, typically of several people: *the tramp of marching feet.* **3** [in *sing.*] a long walk, typically a tiring one: *they start off on a tramp from Roxbury to New York.* **4** [usu. as *adj.*] a cargo vessel that carries goods among many different ports rather than sailing a fixed route: *a tramp steamer.* **5** *informal* a promiscuous woman. **6** a metal plate protecting the sole of a boot. ■ the top of the blade of a spade. ▷late Middle English (as a verb): probably of Low German origin. The noun dates from the mid 17th cent. **—tramp·er** *n.* **—tramp·ish** *adj.*

tram·ple /ˈtrampəl/ ▶*v.* [*trans.*] tread on and crush: *the fence had been trampled down* | [*intrans.*] *her dog* ***trampled on*** *his tulips.* ■ [*intrans.*] (**trample on/over**) *figurative* treat with contempt: *a drug-testing device that doesn't trample on employees' civil liberties.*

▶*n. poetic/literary* an act or the sound of trampling. ▷late Middle English (in the sense 'tread heavily'): frequentative of TRAMP. **—tram·pler** /-p(ə)lər/ *n.*

tram·po·line /ˈtrampəˌlēn/ ▶*n.* a strong fabric sheet connected by springs to a frame, used as a springboard and landing area in doing acrobatic or gymnastic exercises.

▶*v.* [*intrans.*] [usu. as *n.*] (**trampolining**) do acrobatic or gymnastic exercises on a trampoline as a recreation or sport: *his hobby is trampolining.* ■ [*intrans.*] leap or rebound from something with a springy base: *she trampolined across the bed.* ▷late 18th cent.: from Italian *trampolino*, from *trampoli* 'stilts.' **—tram·po·lin·er** *n.* **—tram·po·lin·ist** /-nist/ *n.*

tram road ▶*n. historical* a road with wooden, stone, or metal tracks for wheels, used by wagons in mining districts.

tram·way /ˈtramˌwā/ ▶*n.* **1** *Brit.* a set of rails that forms the route for a streetcar. ■ a streetcar system. **2** another term for CABLE CAR. **3** *historical* another term for TRAM ROAD.

trance /trans/ ▶*n.* a half-conscious state characterized by an absence of response to external stimuli, typically as induced by hypnosis or entered by a medium: *she put him into a light trance.* ■ a state of abstraction: *the kind of trance he went into whenever illness was discussed.* ■ (also **trance music**) a type of electronic dance music characterized by hypnotic rhythms and sounds.

▶*v.* [*trans.*] (often **be tranced**) *poetic/literary* put into a trance: *she's been tranced and may need waking.* ▷Middle English (originally as a verb in the sense 'be in a trance'): from Old French *transir* 'depart, fall into trance,' from Latin *transire* 'go across.' **—tranced·ly** /ˈtranstlē; ˈtransid-/ *adv.* **—trance·like** /-ˌlīk/ *adj.*

tranche /tränsh/ ▶*n.* a portion of something, esp. money: *they released the first* ***tranche of*** *the loan.* ▷late 15th cent.: from Old French, literally 'slice.'

trank /trangk/ (also **tranq**) ▶*n.* informal term for TRANQUILIZER. **—tranked** *adj.*

tran·nie /ˈtranē/ (also **tran·ny**) ▶*n. informal* **1** a transvestite. **2** the transmission in a motor vehicle. **3** a photographic transparency. **4** *chiefly Brit.* a transistor radio. ▷1960s: abbreviation.

tran·quil /ˈtrangkwəl/ ▶*adj.* free from disturbance; calm: *her tranquil gaze* | *the sea was tranquil.* See note at CALM. ▷late Middle English: from French *tranquille* or Latin *tranquillus*. **—tran·quil·i·ty** /ˌtrangˈkwilitē/ (also **tran·quil·li·ty**) *n.* **—tran·quil·ly** *adv.*

tran·quil·ize /ˈtrangkwəˌlīz/ (*Brit.* **tran·quil·lize**) ▶*v.* [*trans.*] [usu. as *adj.*] (**tranquilizing**) (of a drug) have a calming or sedative effect on: *the majority regarded tranquilizing drugs as the chief therapeutic weapon.* ■ administer such a drug to (a person or animal): *the stray elk was tranquilized and relocated.* ■ *poetic/literary* make tranquil: *joys that tranquilize the mind.*

tran·quil·iz·er /ˈtrangkwəˌlīzər/ (*Brit.* **tran·quil·liz·er**) ▶*n.* a medicinal drug taken to reduce tension or anxiety.

trans /tranz; trans/ ▶*adj. Chemistry* denoting or relating to a molecular structure in which two particular atoms or groups lie on opposite sides of a given plane in the molecule, in particular denoting an isomer in which substituents at opposite ends of a carbon–carbon double bond are also on opposite sides of the bond: *the trans isomer of stilbene.* Compare with CIS. ▷independent usage of TRANS-.

trans. ▶*abbr.* ■ transaction; transactions. ■ transfer. ■ transferred. ■ transformer. ■ transit. ■ transitive. ■ translated. ■ translation. ■ translator. ■ transparent. ■ transportation. ■ transpose. ■ transverse.

trans- ▶*prefix* **1** across; beyond: *transcontinental* | *transgress.* ■ on or to the other side of: *transatlantic* | *transalpine.* Often contrasted with CIS-. **2** through: *transonic.* ■ into another state or place: *transform* | *translate.* ■ surpassing; transcending: *transfinite.* **3** *Chemistry* (usu. ***trans-***) denoting molecules with trans arrangements of substituents: trans-*1,2-dichloroethylene.* ■ *Genetics* denoting alleles on different chromosomes. ▷from Latin *trans* 'across.'

trans·act /tranˈsakt; -ˈzakt/ ▶*v.* [*trans.*] conduct or carry out (business). ▷late 16th cent.: from Latin *transact-* 'driven through,' from the verb *transigere*, from *trans-* 'through' + *agere* 'do, lead.' **—trans·ac·tor** /-tər/ *n.*

trans·ac·tion /tranˈsakshən; -ˈzak-/ ▶*n.* an instance of buying or selling something; a business deal: *in an ordinary commercial transaction a delivery date is essential.* ■ the action of conducting business. ■ an exchange or interaction between people: *intellectual transactions in the classroom.* ■ (**transactions**) published reports of proceedings at the meetings of a learned society. ■ an input message to a computer system that must be dealt with as a single unit of work. ▷late Middle English (as a term in Roman law): from late Latin *transactio(n-)*, from *transigere* 'drive through' (see TRANSACT). **—trans·ac·tion·al** /-shənl/ *adj.* **—trans·ac·tion·al·ly** /-shənl-ē/ *adv.*

trans·ac·tion·al a·nal·y·sis ▶*n.* a system of popular psychology based on the idea that one's behavior and social relationships reflect an interchange between parental (critical and nurturing), adult (rational), and childlike (intuitive and dependent) aspects of personality established early in life.

trans·ac·ti·va·tion /tranˌsaktəˈvāshən; -ˌzakt-/ ▶*n. Biochemistry* activation of a gene at one locus by the presence of a particular gene at another locus, typically following infection by a virus.

Trans-A·las·ka Pipe·line /ˈtranzəˈlaskə/ an oil pipeline that extends for 800 miles (1,300 km) from Prudhoe Bay on the North Slope of Alaska to Valdez on Prince William Sound.

trans·al·pine /trans'alpīn; tranz-/ ▸*adj.* of, related to, or situated in the area beyond the Alps, in particular as viewed from Italy. See also **Gaul**[1]. ■ crossing the Alps: *transalpine road freight.* ▷late 16th cent.: from Latin *transalpinus,* from *trans-* 'across' + *alpinus* (see **alpine**).

trans·am·i·nase /trans'amə,nās; tranz-; -,nāz/ ▸*n. Biochemistry* an enzyme that catalyzes a particular transamination reaction.

trans·am·i·na·tion /trans,amə'nāsHən; tranz-/ ▸*n. Biochemistry* the transfer of an amino group from one molecule to another, esp. from an amino acid to a keto acid. **—trans·am·i·nate** /-,nāt/ *v.*

trans·at·lan·tic /,transət'lantik; ,tranz-/ ▸*adj.* crossing the Atlantic: *a transatlantic flight.* ■ concerning countries on both sides of the Atlantic: *the transatlantic relationship.* ■ of, relating to, or situated on the other side of the Atlantic; British or European (from an American point of view). **—trans·at·lan·ti·cal·ly** /-ik(ə)lē/ *adv.*

trans·ax·le /trans'aksəl; tranz-/ ▸*n.* an integral driving axle and differential gear in a motor vehicle.

Trans-Can·a·da High·way /,trans'kanədə; ,tranz-/ a route, 4,860 miles (7,820 km) long, between Victoria in British Columbia and Saint John's in Newfoundland.

Trans·cau·ca·sia /,trans,kô'kāzHə; ,tranz-/ a region that lies to the south of the Caucasus Mountains, between the Black Sea and the Caspian Sea, and that comprises the present-day republics of Georgia, Armenia, and Azerbaijan. It was created as the Transcaucasian Soviet Federated Socialist Republic, a republic of the Soviet Union, in 1922, but was broken up into its constituent republics in 1936. **—Trans·cau·ca·sian** *adj.*

trans·ceiv·er /tran'sēvər/ ▸*n.* a device that can both transmit and receive communications, in particular a combined radio transmitter and receiver. ▷1930s: blend of **transmitter** and **receiver**.

tran·scend /tran'send/ ▸*v.* [*trans.*] be or go beyond the range or limits of (something abstract, typically a conceptual field or division): *this was an issue transcending party politics.* ■ surpass (a person or an achievement). ▷Middle English: from Old French *transcendre* or Latin *transcendere,* from *trans-* 'across' + *scandere* 'climb.'

tran·scend·ent /tran'sendənt/ ▸*adj.* beyond or above the range of normal or merely physical human experience: *the search for a transcendent level of knowledge.* ■ surpassing the ordinary; exceptional: *the conductor was described as a "transcendent genius."* ■ (of God) existing apart from and not subject to the limitations of the material universe. Often contrasted with **immanent**. ■ (in scholastic philosophy) higher than or not included in any of Aristotle's ten categories. ■ (in Kantian philosophy) not realizable in experience. ▷late Middle English: from Latin *transcendent-* 'climbing over,' from the verb *transcendere* (see **transcend**). **—tran·scend·ence** *n.* **—tran·scend·en·cy** *n.* **—tran·scend·ent·ly** *adv.*

tran·scen·den·tal /,transen'dentl/ ▸*adj.* **1** of or relating to a spiritual or nonphysical realm: *the transcendental importance of each person's soul.* ■ (in Kantian philosophy) presupposed in and necessary to experience; a priori. ■ relating to or denoting Transcendentalism. **2** *Mathematics* (of a number, e.g., *e* or *π*) real but not a root of an algebraic equation with rational roots. ■ (of a function) not capable of being produced by the algebraical operations of addition, multiplication, and involution, or the inverse operations. ▷early 17th cent.: from medieval Latin *transcendentalis* (see **transcendent**). **—tran·scen·den·tal·ize** /-,īz/ *v.* **—tran·scen·den·tal·ly** *adv.*

tran·scen·den·tal·ism /,tran,sen'dentl,izəm/ ▸*n.* **1** (**Transcendentalism**) an idealistic philosophical and social movement that developed in New England around 1836 in reaction to rationalism. Influenced by romanticism, Platonism, and Kantian philosophy, it taught that divinity pervades all nature and humanity, and its members held progressive views on feminism and communal living. Ralph Waldo Emerson and Henry David Thoreau were central figures. **2** a system developed by Immanuel Kant, based on the idea that, in order to understand the nature of reality, one must first examine and analyze the reasoning process that governs the nature of experience. **—tran·scen·den·tal·ist** (also **Tran·scen·den·tal·ist**) *n.* & *adj.*

Tran·scen·den·tal Med·i·ta·tion (abbr.: **TM**) ▸*n. trademark* a technique for detaching oneself from anxiety and promoting harmony and self-realization by meditation, repetition of a mantra, and other yogic practices, promulgated by an international organization founded by the Indian guru Maharishi Mahesh Yogi (*c.*1911–).

trans·code /trans'kōd; tranz-/ ▸*v.* [*trans.*] convert (language or information) from one form of coded representation to another.

trans·con·duct·ance /,transkən'dəktəns; ,tranz-/ ▸*n. Electronics* the ratio of the change in current at the output terminal to the change in the voltage at the input terminal of an active device.

trans·con·ti·nen·tal /,transkäntə'nentl; ,tranz-/ ▸*adj.* (esp. of a railroad line) crossing a continent. ■ extending across or relating to two or more continents: *a transcontinental radio audience.*
▸*n. Canadian* a transcontinental railroad or train. **—trans·con·ti·nen·tal·ly** *adv.*

trans·cor·ti·cal /trans'kôrtikəl; tranz-/ ▸*adj. Physiology* of or relating to nerve pathways that cross the cerebral cortex of the brain.

tran·scribe /tran'skrīb/ ▸*v.* [*trans.*] put (thoughts, speech, or data) into written or printed form: *each interview was taped and transcribed.* ■ transliterate (foreign characters) or write or type out (shorthand, notes, or other abbreviated forms) into ordinary characters or full sentences. ■ arrange (a piece of music) for a different instrument, voice, or group of these: *his largest early work was* **transcribed for** *organ.* ■ *Biochemistry* synthesize (a nucleic acid, typically RNA) using an existing nucleic acid, typically DNA, as a template, thus copying the genetic information in the latter. ▷mid 16th cent. (in the sense 'make a copy in writing'): from Latin *transcribere,* from *trans-* 'across' + *scribere* 'write.' **—tran·scrib·er** *n.*

tran·script /'tran,skript/ ▸*n.* a written or printed version of material originally presented in another medium. ■ *Biochemistry* a length of RNA or DNA that has been transcribed respectively from a DNA or RNA template. ■ an official record of a student's work, showing courses taken and grades achieved. ▷Middle English: from Old French *transcrit,* from Latin *transcriptum,* neuter past participle of *transcribere* (see **transcribe**). The spelling change in the 15th cent. was due to association with the Latin. **—tran·scrip·tive** /,tran'skriptiv/ *adj.*

tran·scrip·tase /tran'skrip,tās; -,tāz/ ▸*n. Biochemistry* an enzyme that catalyzes the formation of RNA from a DNA template during transcription. Also called **RNA polymerase**.

tran·scrip·tion /tran'skripsHən/ ▸*n.* a written or printed representation of something. ■ the action or process of transcribing something: *the funding covers transcription of nearly illegible photocopies.* ■ an arrangement of a piece of music for a different instrument, voice, or number of these: *a transcription for voice and lute.* ■ a form in which a speech sound or a foreign character is represented. ■ *Biochemistry* the process by which genetic information represented by a sequence of DNA nucleotides is copied into newly synthesized molecules of RNA, with the DNA serving as a template. ▷late 16th cent.: from French, or from Latin *transcriptio(n-),* from the verb *transcribere* (see **transcribe**). **—tran·scrip·tion·al** /-sHənl/ *adj.* **—tran·scrip·tion·al·ly** /-sHənl-ē/ *adv.* **—tran·scrip·tion·ist** /-nist/ *n.*

trans·cul·tur·al /trans'kəlcHərəl; tranz-/ ▸*adj.* relating to or involving more than one culture; cross-cultural: *the possibility of transcultural understanding.*

trans·cu·ta·ne·ous /,transkyoo'tānēəs; ,tranz-/ ▸*adj.* existing, applied, or measured across the depth of the skin.

trans·der·mal /trans'dərməl; tranz-/ ▸*adj.* relating to or denoting the application of a medicine or drug through the skin, typically by using an adhesive patch, so that it is absorbed slowly into the body.

trans·dif·fer·en·ti·a·tion /tranz,difə,rensHē'āsHən; trans-/ ▸*n. Biology* the rare natural transformation of cells other than stem cells into a different cell type. **—trans·dif·fer·en·ti·ate** /-sHē,āt/ *v.* [*intrans.*]

trans·duc·er /trans'd(y)oosər; tranz-/ ▸*n.* a device that converts variations in a physical quantity, such as pressure or brightness, into an electrical signal, or vice versa. ▷1920s: from Latin *transducere* 'lead across' (from *trans-* 'across' + *ducere* 'lead') + **-er**[1]. **—trans·duce** *v.* **—trans·duc·tion** /-'dəksHən/ *n.*

tran·sect /tran'sekt/ *technical* ▸*v.* [*trans.*] cut across or make a transverse section in.
▸*n.* a straight line or narrow section through an object or natural feature or across the earth's surface, along which observations are made or measurements taken. ▷mid 17th cent. (as a verb): from **trans-** 'through' + Latin *sect-* 'divided by cutting' (from the verb *secare*). **—tran·sec·tion** /-'seksHən/ *n.*

tran·sept /'tran,sept/ ▸*n.* (in a cross-shaped church) either of the two parts forming the arms of the cross shape, projecting at right angles from the nave: *the north transept.* ▷mid 16th cent.: from modern Latin *transeptum* (see **trans-**, **septum**). **—tran·sep·tal** /tran'septl/ *adj.*

transf. ▸*abbr.* ■ transfer. ■ transferred. ■ transformer.

trans-fat /'trans'fat/ ▸*n.* another term for **trans-fatty acid**.

trans-fat·ty ac·id /'trans'fatē/ ▸*n.* an unsaturated fatty acid with a trans arrangement of the carbon atoms adjacent to its double bonds. Such acids occur esp. in margarines and cooking oils as a result of the hydrogenation process.

trans·fect /trans'fekt/ ▸*v.* [*trans.*] *Microbiology* infect (a cell) with free nucleic acid. ■ introduce (genetic material) in this way. ▷1960s: from **trans-** 'across' + **infect**, or a blend of **transfer** and **infect**. **—trans·fec·tant** /-ənt/ *n.* **—trans·fec·tion** /trans'feksHən/ *n.*

trans·fer ▸*v.* /trans'fər; 'transfər/ (**-ferred**, **-fer·ring**) [*trans.*] move (someone or something) from one place to another: *he would have to* **transfer** *money* **to** *his own account.* ■ move or cause to move to another group, occupation, or service: [*intrans.*] *she transferred to the Physics Department* | [*trans.*] *employees have been transferred to the installation team.* ■ [*intrans.*] enroll in a different school or college: *Ron transferred to the University of Idaho.* ■ (in professional sports) move or cause to move to another team: [*intrans.*] *he transferred to the Dodgers* | [*trans.*] *when a player is transferred to the minors by a major league club.* ■ [*intrans.*] change to another place, route, or means of transportation during a journey: *John advised him to transfer from Rome airport to the railroad station.* ■ make over the possession of (property, a right, or a responsibility) to someone else. ■ convey (a drawing or design) from one surface to another. ■ [usu. as *adj.*] (**transferred**) change (the sense of a word or phrase) by extension or metaphor: *a transferred use of the Old English noun.* ■ redirect (a telephone call) to another line or extension.
▸*n.* /'transfər/ an act of moving something or someone to another place: *a transfer of wealth to the poorer nations* | *a patient had died after transfer from the County Hospital to St. Peter's.* ■ a change of employment, typically within an organization or field: *she was going to ask her boss for a transfer to the city.* ■ *Brit.* an act of selling or moving an athlete to another team: *his transfer from Rangers cost £800,000.* ■ a student who has enrolled in a different school or college: [as *adj.*] *the impact of transfer students on enrollment figures.* ■ a conveyance of property, esp. stocks, from one person to another. ■ a small colored picture or design on paper that can be transferred to another surface by being pressed or heated: *T-shirts with iron-on transfers.* ■ a ticket allowing a passenger to change from one public transportation vehicle to another as part of a single journey. ▷late Middle English (as a verb): from French *transférer* or Latin *transferre,* from *trans-* 'across' + *ferre* 'to bear.' The earliest use of the noun (late 17th cent.) was as a legal term in the sense 'conveyance of property.' **—trans·fer·ee** /,transfə'rē/ *n.* **—trans·fer·or** /trans'fərər; 'transfərər/ *n.* (*chiefly Law*) **—trans·fer·rer** *n.*

trans·fer·a·ble /trans'fərəbəl; 'transfərə-/ ▸*adj.* (typically of financial assets, liabilities, or legal rights) able to be transferred or made over to the possession of another person. **—trans·fer·a·bil·i·ty** /,transfərə'bilitē/ *n.*

trans·fer·ase /'transfə,rās; -,rāz/ ▸*n. Biochemistry* an enzyme that catalyzes the transfer of a particular group from one molecule to another.

trans·fer·ence /trans'fərəns; 'transfərəns/ ▸*n.* the action of transferring something or the process of being transferred: *education involves the transference of knowledge.* ■ *Psychoanalysis* the redirection to a substitute, usually a therapist, of emotions that were originally felt in childhood (in a phase of analysis called **transference neurosis**).

trans·fer fac·tor ▸*n. Biology* a substance released by antigen-sensitized lymphocytes and capable of transferring the response of delayed hypersensitivity to a nonsensitized cell or individual into which it is introduced.

trans·fer func·tion ▸*n. Electronics* a mathematical function relating the output or response of a system such as a filter circuit to the input or stimulus.

trans·fer or·bit ▸*n.* a trajectory by which a spacecraft can pass from one orbit to another at a higher altitude, esp. a geostationary orbit.

trans·fer pay·ment ▸*n. Economics* a payment made

or income received in which no goods or services are being paid for, such as a benefit payment or subsidy.

trans·fer·ral /trans'fərəl/ ▶*n.* an act of transferring someone or something.

trans·fer·rin /trans'ferin/ ▶*n. Biochemistry* a protein of the beta globulin group that binds and transports iron in blood serum. ▷1940s: from TRANS- 'across' + Latin *ferrum* 'iron' + -IN[1].

trans·fer RNA ▶*n. Biochemistry* RNA consisting of folded molecules that transport amino acids from the cytoplasm of a cell to a ribosome.

trans·fig·u·ra·tion /trans,figyə'rāsHən/ ▶*n.* a complete change of form or appearance into a more beautiful or spiritual state: *in this light the junk undergoes a transfiguration; it shines.* ■ (**the Transfiguration**) Christ's appearance in radiant glory to three of his disciples (Matthew 17:2, Mark 9:2–3, Luke 9:28-36). ■ the church festival commemorating this, held on August 6. ▷late Middle English (with biblical reference): from Old French, or from Latin *transfiguratio(n-)*, from the verb *transfigurare* (see TRANSFIGURE).

trans·fig·ure /trans'figyər/ ▶*v.* [*trans.*] (usu. **be transfigured**) transform into something more beautiful or elevated: *the world is made luminous and is transfigured.* ▷Middle English: from Old French *transfigurer* or Latin *transfigurare*, from *trans-* 'across' + *figura* 'figure.'

trans·fi·nite /trans'fī,nīt/ ▶*adj.* **1** *Mathematics* relating to or denoting a number corresponding to an infinite set in the way that a natural number denotes or counts members of a finite set. **2** beyond or surpassing the finite.

trans·fix /trans'fiks/ ▶*v.* [*trans.*] **1** (usu. **be transfixed**) cause (someone) to become motionless with horror, wonder, or astonishment: *he was transfixed by the pain in her face* | *she stared at him, transfixed.* **2** pierce with a sharp implement or weapon: *a field mouse is transfixed by the curved talons of an owl.* ▷late 16th cent. (in sense 2): from Latin *transfix-* 'pierced through,' from the verb *transfigere*, from *trans-* 'across' + *figere* 'fix, fasten.' —**trans·fix·ion** /-'fiksHən/ *n.*

trans·form /trans'fôrm/ ▶*v.* [*trans.*] make a thorough or dramatic change in the form, appearance, or character of: *lasers have transformed cardiac surgery* | *he wanted to* **transform** *himself* **into** *a successful businessman.* ■ [*intrans.*] undergo such a change: *an automobile that* **transformed into** *a boat.* ■ change the voltage of (an electric current). ■ *Mathematics* change (a mathematical entity) by transformation.
▶*n.* /'transfôrm/ *Mathematics & Linguistics* the product of a transformation. ■ a rule for making a transformation. ▷Middle English (as a verb): from Old French *transformer* or Latin *transformare* (see TRANS-, FORM). —**trans·form·a·ble** *adj.* —**trans·form·a·tive** /-mətiv/ *adj.*

trans·for·ma·tion /,transfər'māsHən/ ▶*n.* a thorough or dramatic change in form or appearance: *its landscape has undergone a radical transformation.* ■ a metamorphosis during the life cycle of an animal. ■ *Physics* the induced or spontaneous change of one element into another by a nuclear process. ■ *Mathematics & Logic* a process by which one figure, expression, or function is converted into another that is equivalent in some important respect but is differently expressed or represented. ■ *Linguistics* a process by which an element in the underlying deep structure of a sentence is converted to an element in the surface structure. ■ *Biology* the genetic alteration of a cell by introduction of extraneous DNA, esp. by a plasmid. ■ *Biology* the heritable modification of a cell from its normal state to a malignant state. ▷late Middle English: from Old French, or from late Latin *transformatio(n-)*, from the verb *transformare* (see TRANSFORM).

trans·for·ma·tion·al /,transfər'māsHənl/ ▶*adj.* relating to or involving transformation or transformations. ■ of or relating to transformational grammar. —**trans·for·ma·tion·al·ly** *adv.*

trans·for·ma·tion·al gram·mar ▶*n. Linguistics* a type of grammar that describes a language in terms of transformations applied to an underlying deep structure in order to generate the surface structure of sentences that can actually occur. See also GENERATIVE GRAMMAR.

trans·form·er /trans'fôrmər/ ▶*n.* **1** an apparatus for reducing or increasing the voltage of an alternating current. **2** a person or thing that transforms something.

trans·form fault ▶*n. Geology* a strike-slip fault occurring at the boundary between two plates of the earth's crust.

trans·fuse /trans'fyo͞oz/ ▶*v.* [*trans.*] **1** *Medicine* transfer (blood or its components) from one person or animal to another. ■ inject (liquid) into a blood vessel to replace lost fluid. **2** cause (something or someone) to be permeated or infused by something: *we became transfused by a radiance of joy.* ▷late Middle English (in the sense 'cause to pass from one person to another'): from Latin *transfus-* 'poured from one container to another,' from the verb *transfundere*, from *trans-* 'across' + *fundere* 'pour.'

trans·fu·sion /trans'fyo͞ozHən/ ▶*n.* an act of transfusing donated blood, blood products, or other fluid into the circulatory system of a person or animal.

trans·gen·der /tranz'jendər; trans-/ (also **trans·gen·dered**) ▶*adj.* identified with a gender other than the biological one: *a transgender activist and author.*

trans·gen·ic /trans'jenik; tranz-/ ▶*adj. Biology* of, relating to, or denoting an organism that contains genetic material into which DNA from an unrelated organism has been artificially introduced. ▷1980s: from TRANS- 'across' + GENE + -IC.

trans·gen·ics /trans'jeniks; tranz-/ ▶*plural n.* [usu. treated as *sing.*] the branch of biology concerned with transgenic organisms.

trans·glob·al /trans'glōbəl/ ▶*adj.* (of an expedition, enterprise, search, or network) moving or extending across or around the world.

trans·gress /trans'gres; tranz-/ ▶*v.* [*trans.*] infringe or go beyond the bounds of (a moral principle or other established standard of behavior): *she had transgressed an unwritten social law* | [*intrans.*] *they must control the impulses that lead them to transgress.* ■ *Geology* (of the sea) spread over (an area of land). ▷late 15th cent.: from Old French *transgresser* or Latin *transgress-* 'stepped across,' from the verb *transgredi*, from *trans-* 'across' + *gradi* 'go.' —**trans·gres·sion** /-'gresHən/ *n.* —**trans·gres·sor** /-'gresər/ *n.*

trans·gres·sive /trans'gresiv; tranz-/ ▶*adj.* involving a violation of accepted or imposed boundaries, esp. those of social acceptability: *her experiences of transgressive love with both sexes.* ■ of or relating to fiction, cinematography, or art in which orthodox cultural, moral, and artistic boundaries are challenged by the representation of unconventional behavior and the use of experimental forms. ■ *Geology* (of a stratum) overlapping others unconformably, esp. as a result of marine transgression.

tran·ship ▶*v.* variant spelling of TRANSSHIP.

trans·his·tor·i·cal /,trans-hi'stôrikəl; ,tranz-; -'stär-/ ▶*adj.* transcending historical boundaries; eternal: *femininity may not be a transhistorical absolute.*

trans·hu·mance /trans'(h)yo͞oməns; tranz-/ ▶*n.* the action or practice of moving livestock from one grazing ground to another in a seasonal cycle, typically to lowlands in winter and highlands in summer. ▷early 20th cent.: from French, from the verb *transhumer*, based on Latin *trans-* 'across' + *humus* 'ground.' —**trans·hu·mant** /-mənt/ *adj.*

tran·sient /'transHənt; -zHənt; -zēənt/ ▶*adj.* lasting only for a short time; impermanent: *a transient cold spell.* See note at TEMPORARY. ■ staying or working in a place for only a short time: *the transient nature of the labor force in catering.*
▶*n.* **1** a person who is staying or working in a place for only a short time. **2** a momentary variation in current, voltage, or frequency. ▷late 16th cent.: from Latin *transient-* 'going across,' from the verb *transire*, from *trans-* 'across' + *ire* 'go.' —**tran·sience** *n.* —**tran·sien·cy** *n.* —**tran·sient·ly** *adv.*

tran·si·ent is·che·mic at·tack (abbr.: **TIA**) ▶*n.* technical term for MINISTROKE.

trans·il·lu·mi·nate /,transə'lo͞omə,nāt; ,tranz-/ ▶*v.* [*trans.*] pass strong light through (an organ or part of the body) in order to detect disease or abnormality. —**trans·il·lu·mi·na·tion** /-ə,lo͞omə'nāsHən/ *n.*

tran·sis·tor /tran'zistər/ ▶*n.* a semiconductor device with three connections, capable of amplification in addition to rectification. ■ (also **transistor radio**) a portable radio using circuits containing transistors rather than vacuum tubes. ▷1940s: from TRANSCONDUCTANCE, on the pattern of words such as *varistor*.

tran·sis·tor·ize /tran'zistə,rīz/ ▶*v.* [*trans.*] [usu. as *adj.*] (**transistorized**) design or make with transistors rather than vacuum tubes: *a transistorized tape recorder.* —**tran·sis·tor·i·za·tion** /-,zistəri'zāsHən/ *n.*

tran·sit /'tranzit/ ▶*n.* **1** the carrying of people, goods, or materials from one place to another: *a painting was damaged* **in transit**. ■ an act of passing through or across a place: *the first west-to-east transit of the Northwest Passage* | [as *adj.*] *a transit airline passenger.* ■ the conveyance of passengers on public transportation. ■ *Astronomy* the passage of an inferior planet across the face of the sun, or of a moon or its shadow across the face of a planet. ■ *Astronomy* the apparent passage of a celestial body across the meridian of a place. ■ *Astrology* the passage of a celestial body through a specified sign, house, or area of a chart. **2** *informal* (in full **transit theodolite**) a tool used by surveyors to measure horizontal angles.
▶*v.* (**-sit·ed, -sit·ing**) [*trans.*] pass across or through (an area): *the new large ships will be too big to transit the Panama Canal.* ■ *Astronomy* (of a planet or other celestial body) pass across (a meridian or the face of another body). ■ *Astrology* (of a celestial body) pass across (a specified sign, house, or area of a chart). ▷late Middle English (denoting passage from one place to another): from Latin *transitus*, from *transire* 'go across.'

tran·sit camp ▶*n.* a camp for the temporary accommodation of groups of people, e.g., refugees or soldiers, who are traveling through a country or region.

tran·sit cir·cle (also **transit instrument**) ▶*n.* another term for MERIDIAN CIRCLE.

tran·si·tion /tran'zisHən; -'sisHən/ ▶*n.* the process or a period of changing from one state or condition to another: *students* **in transition** *from one program to another* | *a transition to multiparty democracy.* ■ a passage in a piece of writing that smoothly connects two topics or sections to each other. ■ *Music* a momentary modulation from one key to another. ■ *Physics* a change of an atom, nucleus, electron, etc., from one quantum state to another, with emission or absorption of radiation.
▶*v.* undergo or cause to undergo a process or period of transition: [*trans.*] *the network ought to be built by the federal government and then transitioned into private industry* | [*intrans.*] *we have transitioned from a high-intensity combat operation to a support role in the community.* ▷mid 16th cent.: from French, or from Latin *transitio(n-)*, from *transire* 'go across.' —**tran·si·tion·al** /-sHənl/ *adj.* —**tran·si·tion·a·ry** /-,nerē/ *adj.*

tran·si·tion met·al (also **tran·si·tion el·e·ment**) ▶*n. Chemistry* any of the set of metallic elements occupying a central block (Groups IVB–VIII, IB, and IIB, or 4–12) in the periodic table, e.g., iron, manganese, chromium, and copper. Chemically they show variable valence and a strong tendency to form coordination compounds, and many of their compounds are colored.

tran·si·tion point ▶*n. Chemistry* the set of conditions of temperature and pressure at which different phases of the same substance can be in equilibrium.

tran·si·tion prob·a·bil·i·ty ▶*n. Physics* the probability of the occurrence of a transition between two quantum states of an atom, nucleus, electron, etc.

tran·si·tion tem·per·a·ture ▶*n. Physics* the temperature at which a substance acquires or loses some distinctive property, in particular superconductivity.

tran·si·tive /'transitiv; 'tranz-/ ▶*adj.* **1** *Grammar* (of a verb or a sense or use of a verb) able to take a direct object (expressed or implied), e.g., *saw* in *he saw the donkey*. The opposite of INTRANSITIVE. **2** *Logic & Mathematics* (of a relation) such that, if it applies between successive members of a sequence, it must also apply between any two members taken in order. For instance, if A is larger than B, and B is larger than C, then A is larger than C.
▶*n.* a transitive verb. ▷mid 16th cent. (in the sense 'transitory'): from late Latin *transitivus*, from *transit-* 'gone across' (see TRANSIT). —**tran·si·tive·ly** *adv.* —**tran·si·tive·ness** *n.* —**tran·si·tiv·i·ty** /,transə'tivitē; -zə-/ *n.*

tran·sit lounge ▶*n.* a lounge at an airport for passengers waiting between flights.

tran·si·to·ry /'transi,tôrē; 'tranzi-/ ▶*adj.* not permanent: *transitory periods of medieval greatness.* See note at TEMPORARY. ▷late Middle English: from Old French *transitoire*, from Christian Latin *transitorius*, from *transit-* 'gone across' (see TRANSIT). —**tran·si·to·ri·ly** /-rəlē/ *adv.* —**tran·si·to·ri·ness** *n.*

tran·sit vi·sa ▶*n.* a visa allowing its holder to pass through a country but not to stay there.

Trans·jor·dan /trans'jôrdn; tranz-/ former name (until 1949) of the region east of the Jordan River that now forms the main part of Jordan. —**Trans·jor·da·ni·an** /,trans,jôr'dānēən; ,tranz-/ *adj.*

Trans·kei /tran'skī; -'skā/ a former homeland established in South Africa for the Xhosa people, now part of the province of Eastern Cape.

trans·ke·to·lase /tranz'kētl,ās; -,āz/ ▸*n. Biochemistry* an enzyme that catalyzes the transfer of an alcohol group between sugar molecules.

trans·late /trans'lāt; tranz-/ ▸*v.* [*trans.*] **1** express the sense of (words or text) in another language: *the German original has been **translated into** English.* ■ [*intrans.*] be expressed or be capable of being expressed in another language: *shiatsu literally translates as "finger pressure."* ■ (**translate something into/translate into**) convert or be converted into (another form or medium): [*trans.*] *few of Shakespeare's other works have been translated into ballets.* **2** move from one place or condition to another: *she had been translated from familiar surroundings to a foreign court.* ■ *formal* move (a bishop) to another see or pastoral charge. ■ *formal* remove (a saint's relics) to another place. ■ *poetic/literary* convey (someone, typically still alive) to heaven. ■ *Biology* convert (a sequence of nucleotides in messenger RNA) to an amino-acid sequence in a protein or polypeptide during synthesis. **3** *Physics* cause (a body) to move so that all its parts travel in the same direction, without rotation or change of shape. ■ *Mathematics* transform (a geometric figure) in an analogous way. ▷Middle English: from Latin *translatus* 'carried across,' past participle of *transferre* (see TRANSFER). **—trans·lat·a·bil·i·ty** /,trans,lātə'bilətē; ,tranz-/ *n.* **—trans·lat·a·ble** *adj.*

trans·la·tion /trans'lāsʜən; ,tranz-/ ▸*n.* **1** the process of translating words or text from one language into another: *Constantine's translation of Arabic texts into Latin.* ■ a written or spoken rendering of the meaning of a word, speech, book, or other text, in another language: *a German translation of Oscar Wilde's play | a term for which there is no adequate English translation.* ■ the conversion of something from one form or medium into another: *the translation of research findings into clinical practice.* ■ *Biology* the process by which a sequence of nucleotide triplets in a messenger RNA molecule gives rise to a specific sequence of amino acids during synthesis of a polypeptide or protein. **2** *formal* or *technical* the process of moving something from one place to another: *the translation of the relics of St. Thomas of Canterbury.* ■ *Mathematics* movement of a body from one point of space to another such that every point of the body moves in the same direction and over the same distance, without any rotation, reflection, or change in size. ▷Middle English: from Old French, or from Latin *translatio(n-)*, from *translat-* 'carried across' (see TRANSLATE). **—trans·la·tion·al** /-sʜənl/ *adj.* **—trans·la·tion·al·ly** /-sʜənl-ē/ *adv.*

trans·la·tor /'trans,lātər; 'tranz-/ ▸*n.* a person who translates from one language into another, esp. as a profession. ■ a program that translates from one programming language into another.

trans·lit·er·ate /trans'litə,rāt; tranz-/ ▸*v.* [*trans.*] (usu. **be transliterated**) write or print (a letter or word) using the closest corresponding letters of a different alphabet or language: *names from one language are often **transliterated into** another.* ▷mid 19th cent.: from TRANS- 'across' + Latin *littera* 'letter' + -ATE[3]. **—trans·lit·er·a·tion** /trans,litə'rāsʜən; tranz-/ *n.* **—trans·lit·er·a·tor** /-,rātər/ *n.*

trans·lo·cate /trans'lō,kāt; tranz-/ ▸*v.* [*trans.*] *chiefly technical* move from one place to another: *translocating rhinos to other reserves* | [*intrans.*] *the cell bodies translocate into the other side of the brain.* ■ *Physiology & Biochemistry* transport (a dissolved substance) within an organism, esp. in the phloem of a plant, or actively across a cell membrane. ■ *Genetics* move (a portion of a chromosome) to a new position on the same or another chromosome. **—trans·lo·ca·tion** /trans,lō'kāsʜən; tranz-/ *n.*

trans·lu·cent /trans'lo͞osnt; tranz-/ ▸*adj.* (of a substance) allowing light, but not detailed images, to pass through; semitransparent: *fry until the onions become translucent.* ▷late 16th cent. (in the Latin sense): from Latin *translucent-* 'shining through,' from the verb *translucere*, from *trans-* 'through' + *lucere* 'to shine.' **—trans·lu·cence** *n.* **—trans·lu·cen·cy** *n.* **—trans·lu·cent·ly** *adv.*

trans·lu·nar /trans'lo͞onər; tranz-/ ▸*adj.* of, relating to, or denoting the trajectory of a spacecraft traveling between the earth and the moon.

trans·ma·rine /,transmə'rēn; ,tranz-/ ▸*adj. dated* situated or originating on the other side of the sea: *an alien, or a transmarine stranger.* ■ of or involving crossing the sea: *some birds make long transmarine migrations.* ▷late 16th cent.: from Latin *transmarinus*, from *trans-* 'across' + *marinus* 'marine, of the sea.'

trans·mem·brane /trans'mem,brān; tranz-/ ▸*adj. Biology* existing or occurring across a cell membrane: *transmembrane conductance.*

trans·mi·grant /trans'mīgrənt; tranz-/ ▸*n. rare* a person passing through a country or region in the course of emigrating to another region. ▷early 17th cent.: from Latin *transmigrant-* 'migrating across,' from the verb *transmigrare* (see TRANSMIGRATE).

trans·mi·grate /trans'mī,grāt; tranz-/ ▸*v.* [*intrans.*] **1** (of the soul) pass into a different body after death. **2** *rare* migrate. ▷late Middle English (as an adjective in the sense 'transferred'): from Latin *transmigrat-* 'removed from one place to another,' from the verb *transmigrare* (see TRANS-, MIGRATE). **—trans·mi·gra·tion** /,trans,mī'grāsʜən; ,tranz-/ *n.* **—trans·mi·gra·tor** /-,grātər/ *n.* **—trans·mi·gra·to·ry** /-grə,tôrē/ *adj.*

trans·mis·sion /trans'misʜən; tranz-/ ▸*n.* **1** the action or process of transmitting something or the state of being transmitted: *the transmission of the HIV virus.* ■ a program or signal that is broadcast or sent out: *television transmissions.* **2** the mechanism by which power is transmitted from an engine to the wheels of a motor vehicle. ▷early 17th cent.: from Latin *transmissio* (see TRANS-, MISSION).

trans·mis·sion e·lec·tron mi·cro·scope ▸*n.* a form of electron microscope in which an image is derived from electrons that have passed through the specimen, in particular one in which the whole image is formed at once rather than by scanning.

trans·mis·sion line ▸*n.* a conductor or conductors designed to carry electricity or an electrical signal over large distances with minimum losses and distortion.

trans·mis·siv·i·ty /,transmi'sivitē; ,tranz-/ ▸*n.* (*pl.* **-ties**) the degree to which a medium allows something, in particular electromagnetic radiation, to pass through it.

trans·mit /tranz'mit; trans-/ ▸*v.* (**-mit·ted**, **-mit·ting**) [*trans.*] cause (something) to pass on from one place or person to another: *knowledge is transmitted from teacher to student.* ■ broadcast or send out (an electrical signal or a radio or television program): *the program was transmitted on October 7.* ■ pass on (a disease or trait) to another: [as *adj.*] (**transmitted**) *sexually transmitted diseases.* ■ allow (heat, light, sound, electricity, or other energy) to pass through a medium: *the three bones transmit sound waves to the inner ear.* ■ communicate or be a medium for (an idea or emotion): *the theatrical gift of being able to transmit emotion.* ▷late Middle English: from Latin *transmittere*, from *trans-* 'across' + *mittere* 'send.' **—trans·mis·si·bil·i·ty** /-,misə'bilitē/ *n.* (*chiefly Medicine*). **—trans·mis·si·ble** /-'misəbəl/ *adj.* (*chiefly Medicine*). **—trans·mis·sive** /-'misiv/ *adj.* **—trans·mit·ta·ble** *adj.* **—trans·mit·tal** /-'mitl/ *n.*

trans·mit·tance /trans'mitns; tranz-/ ▸*n. Physics* the ratio of the light energy falling on a body to that transmitted through it.

trans·mit·ter /trans'mitər; tranz-/ ▸*n.* a set of equipment used to generate and transmit electromagnetic waves carrying messages or signals, esp. those of radio or television. ■ a person or thing that transmits something: *reggae has established itself as the principal transmitter of the Jamaican language.* ■ short for NEUROTRANSMITTER.

trans·mog·ri·fy /trans'mägrə,fī; tranz-/ ▸*v.* (**-fies**, **-fied**) [*trans.*] (often **be transmogrified**) *chiefly humorous* transform, esp. in a surprising or magical manner: *the cucumbers that were ultimately transmogrified into pickles.* ▷mid 17th cent.: of unknown origin. **—trans·mog·ri·fi·ca·tion** /-,mägrəfi'kāsʜən/ *n.*

trans·mon·tane /trans'män,tān; tranz-/ ▸*adj.* another term for TRAMONTANE.

trans·mu·ral /trans'myo͝orəl; tranz-/ ▸*adj. Medicine* existing or occurring across the entire wall of an organ or blood vessel.

trans·mu·ta·tion /,transmyo͞o'tāsʜən; ,tranz-/ ▸*n.* the action of changing or the state of being changed into another form: *the transmutation of the political economy of the postwar years was complete.* ■ *Physics* the changing of one element into another by radioactive decay, nuclear bombardment, or similar processes. ■ *Biology, chiefly historical* the conversion or transformation of one species into another. ■ the supposed alchemical process of changing base metals into gold. **—trans·mu·ta·tion·al** /-sʜənl/ *adj.* **—trans·mu·ta·tion·ist** /-nist/ *n.*

trans·mute /trans'myo͞ot; tranz-/ ▸*v.* change in form, nature, or substance: [*trans.*] *the raw material of his experience was **transmuted into** stories* | [*intrans.*] *the discovery that elements can transmute by radioactivity.* ■ [*trans.*] subject (base metals) to alchemical transmutation: *the quest to **transmute** lead **into** gold.* ▷late Middle English: from Latin *transmutare*, from *trans-* 'across' + *mutare* 'to change.' **—trans·mut·a·bil·i·ty** /-,myo͞otə'bilitē/ *n.* **—trans·mut·a·ble** *adj.* **—trans·mut·a·tive** /-'myo͞otətiv/ *adj.* **—trans·mut·er** *n.*

trans·na·tion·al /trans'nasʜənl; tranz-/ ▸*adj.* extending or operating across national boundaries: *transnational advertising agencies.*
▸*n.* a large company operating internationally; a multinational. **—trans·na·tion·al·ism** /-,izəm/ *n.* **—trans·na·tion·al·ly** *adv.*

trans·o·ce·an·ic /,transōsʜē'anik; ,tranz-/ ▸*adj.* crossing an ocean: *the transoceanic cable system.* ■ coming from or situated beyond an ocean: *there is a higher rate for letters intended for transoceanic countries.*

tran·som /'transəm/ ▸*n.* the flat surface forming the stern of a vessel. ■ a horizontal beam reinforcing the stern of a vessel. ■ a strengthening crossbar, in particular one set above a window or door. Compare with MULLION. ■ short for TRANSOM WINDOW. ▷late Middle English (earlier as *traversayn*): from Old French *traversin*, from the verb *traverser* 'to cross' (see TRAVERSE). **—tran·somed** *adj.*
▸*PHRASE* □ **over the transom** *informal* offered or sent without prior agreement; unsolicited: *the editors receive about ten manuscripts a week over the transom.*

tran·som win·dow ▸*n.* a window set above the transom of a door or larger window; a fanlight.

tran·son·ic /tran'sänik/ (also **trans·son·ic**) ▸*adj.* denoting or relating to speeds close to that of sound. ▷1940s: from TRANS- 'through, across' + SONIC, on the pattern of words such as *supersonic.*

trans·pa·cif·ic /,transpə'sifik; ,tranz-/ ▸*adj.* crossing the Pacific: *new transpacific routes to India, Korea, and Japan.* ■ of or relating to an area beyond the Pacific.

trans·par·ence /tran'sparəns/ ▸*n.* rare term for TRANSPARENCY (sense 1).

trans·par·en·cy /tran'sparənsē/ ▸*n.* (*pl.* **-cies**) **1** the condition of being transparent: *the transparency of ice.* **2** an image, text, or positive transparent photograph printed on transparent plastic or glass, able to be viewed using a projector. ▷late 16th cent. (as a general term denoting a transparent object): from medieval Latin *transparentia*, from *transparent-* 'shining through' (see TRANSPARENT).

trans·par·ent /tran'spe(ə)rənt; -'spar-/ ▸*adj.* (of a material or article) allowing light to pass through so that objects behind can be distinctly seen: *transparent blue water.* ■ easy to perceive or detect: *the residents will see through any transparent attempt to buy their votes | the meaning of the poem is by no means transparent.* ■ having thoughts, feelings, or motives that are easily perceived: *you'd be no good at poker—you're too transparent.* ■ (of an organization or its activities) open to public scrutiny: *if you had transparent government procurement, corruption would go away.* ■ *Physics* transmitting heat or other electromagnetic rays without distortion. ■ *Computing* (of a process or interface) functioning without the user being aware of its presence. ▷late Middle English: from Old French, from medieval Latin *transparent-* 'shining through,' from Latin *transparere*, from *trans-* 'through' + *parere* 'appear.' **—trans·par·ent·ly** *adv.* [as *submodifier*] *a transparently feeble argument.*

trans·per·son·al /trans'pərsənl; tranz-/ ▸*adj.* of, denoting, or dealing with states or areas of consciousness beyond the limits of personal identity: *transpersonal states of consciousness.*

tran·spic·u·ous /tran'spikyo͞oəs/ ▸*adj. rare* transparent. ■ easily understood; lucid. ▷mid 17th cent.: from modern Latin *transpicuus* (from Latin *transpicere* 'look through') + -OUS.

trans·pierce /trans'pi(ə)rs/ ▸*v.* [*trans.*] *poetic/literary* pierce through (someone or something).

tran·spi·ra·tion stream /,transpə'rāsʜən/ ▸*n. Botany* the flow of water through a plant, from the roots to the leaves, via the xylem vessels.

tran·spire /tran'spī(ə)r/ ▸*v.* [*intrans.*] **1** occur; happen: *I'm going to find out exactly what transpired.* See note at HAPPEN. ■ prove to be the case: *as it transpired, he was right.* ■ [with *clause*] (usu. **it transpires**) (of a secret or something unknown) come to be known; be revealed: *Yaddo, it transpired, had been under FBI surveillance for some time.* **2** *Botany* (of a plant or leaf) give off water vapor through the stomata. ▷late Middle English (in the sense 'emit as vapor through the surface'): from French *transpirer* or medieval Latin *transpirare*, from Latin *trans-* 'through' + *spirare* 'breathe.' The sense 'be revealed' (mid 18th cent.) is a figurative use comparable with 'leak out.' —**tran·spi·ra·tion** /-spəˈrāsHən/ *n.* (in sense 2).

USAGE The common use of **transpire** to mean 'occur, happen' (*I'm going to find out exactly what transpired*) is a loose extension of an earlier meaning, 'come to be known' (*it transpired that Mark had been baptized a Catholic*). This loose sense of 'happen,' which is now more common in American usage than the sense of 'come to be known,' was first recorded in U.S. English toward the end of the 18th century and has been listed in U.S. dictionaries from the 19th century. Careful writers should note, however, that in cases where *occur* or *happen* would do just as well, the use of **transpire** may strike readers as an affectation or as jargon.

trans·plant ▶*v.* /transˈplant/ [*trans.*] move or transfer (something) to another place or situation, typically with some effort or upheaval: *his endeavor to transplant people from Russia to the Argentine* | [as *adj.*] (**transplanted**) *a transplanted Easterner.* ■ replant (a plant) in another place. ■ remove (living tissue or an organ) and implant it in another part of the body or in another body.
▶*n.* /ˈtransˌplant/ an operation in which an organ or tissue is transplanted: *a heart transplant* | *kidneys available for transplant.* ■ an organ or tissue that is transplanted. ■ a plant that has been or is to be transplanted. ■ a person or thing that has been moved to a new place or situation. ▷late Middle English (as a verb describing the repositioning of a plant): from late Latin *transplantare*, from Latin *trans-* 'across' + *plantare* 'to plant.' The noun, first in the sense 'something or someone moved to a new place,' dates from the mid 18th cent. —**trans·plant·a·ble** /transˈplantəbəl/ *adj.* —**trans·plan·ta·tion** /-ˌplanˈtāsHən/ *n.* —**trans·plant·er** *n.*

tran·spon·der /tranˈspändər/ ▶*n.* a device for receiving a radio signal and automatically transmitting a different signal. ▷1940s: blend of TRANSMIT and RESPOND, + -ER[1].

trans·pon·tine /transˈpänˌtīn/ ▶*adj. dated* **1** on or from the other side of an ocean, in particular the Atlantic. [late 19th cent.: from TRANS- 'across' + Latin *pontus* 'sea' + -INE[1].] **2** on or from the other side of a bridge. [mid 19th cent.: from TRANS- 'across' + Latin *pons, pont-* 'bridge' + -INE[1].]

trans·port ▶*v.* /transˈpôrt/ [*trans.*] take or carry (people or goods) from one place to another by means of a vehicle, aircraft, or ship: *the bulk of freight traffic was transported by truck.* ■ *figurative* cause (someone) to feel that they are in another place or time: *for a moment she was transported to a warm summer garden on the night of a ball.* ■ (usu. **be transported**) overwhelm (someone) with a strong emotion, esp. joy: *she was* ***transported with*** *pleasure.* ■ *historical* send (a convict) to a penal colony.
▶*n.* /ˈtransˌpôrt/ **1** a system or means of conveying people or goods from place to place by means of a vehicle, aircraft, or ship: *many possess their own forms of transport* | *air transport.* ■ the action of transporting something or the state of being transported: *the transport of crude oil.* ■ a large vehicle, ship, or aircraft used to carry troops or stores. ■ *historical* a convict who was transported to a penal colony. **2** (usu. **transports**) an overwhelmingly strong emotion: *art can send people into* ***transports of*** *delight.* See note at RAPTURE. ▷late Middle English: from Old French *transporter* or Latin *transportare*, from *trans-* 'across' + *portare* 'carry.'

trans·port·a·ble /transˈpôrtəbəl/ ▶*adj.* **1** able to be carried or moved: *the first transportable phones.* **2** *historical* (of an offender or an offense) punishable by transportation.
▶*n.* a large portable computer or telephone. —**trans·port·a·bil·i·ty** /ˌtransˌpôrtəˈbilitē/ *n.*

trans·por·ta·tion /ˌtranspərˈtāsHən/ ▶*n.* **1** the action of transporting someone or something or the process of being transported: *the era of global mass transportation.* ■ a system or means of transporting people or goods: *transportation on the site includes a monorail.* **2** *historical* the action or practice of transporting convicts to a penal colony.

trans·port·er /transˈpôrtər/ ▶*n.* a person or thing that transports something, in particular: ■ a large vehicle used to carry heavy objects, e.g., cars. ■ (in science fiction) a device that conveys people or things instantaneously from one place to another.

trans·pose /transˈpōz/ ▶*v.* [*trans.*] **1** cause (two or more things) to change places with each other: *the captions describing the two state flowers were accidentally transposed.* **2** transfer to a different place or context: *the problems of civilization are transposed into a rustic setting.* ■ write or play (music) in a different key from the original: *the basses are* ***transposed down*** *an octave.* ■ *Mathematics* transfer (a term), with its sign changed, to the other side of an equation. ■ change into a new form: *he* ***transposed*** *a gaffe by the mayor* ***into*** *a public-relations advantage.*
▶*n. Mathematics* a matrix obtained from a given matrix by interchanging each row and the corresponding column. ▷late Middle English (also in the sense 'transform, convert'): from Old French *transposer*, from *trans-* 'across' + *poser* 'to place.' —**trans·pos·a·ble** *adj.* —**trans·pos·al** /-ˈspōzəl/ *n.* —**trans·pos·er** *n.*

trans·pos·ing in·stru·ment ▶*n.* an orchestral instrument whose notated pitch is different from its sounded pitch, e.g., the clarinet and many brass instruments.

trans·po·si·tion /ˌtranspəˈzisHən/ ▶*n.* the action of transposing something: *transposition of word order* | *a transposition of an old story into a contemporary context.* ■ a thing that has been produced by transposing something: *in China, the dragon is a transposition of the serpent.* ▷mid 16th cent.: from late Latin *transpositio(n-)* (see TRANS-, POSITION). —**trans·po·si·tion·al** /-sHənl/ *adj.*

trans·po·son /transˈpōˌzän/ ▶*n. Genetics* a chromosomal segment that can undergo transposition, esp. a segment of bacterial DNA that can be translocated as a whole between chromosomal, phage, and plasmid DNA in the absence of a complementary sequence in the host DNA. Also called JUMPING GENE. ▷1970s: from TRANSPOSITION + -ON.

trans·put·er /transˈpyo͞otər/ ▶*n.* a microprocessor with integral memory designed for parallel processing. ▷1970s: blend of TRANSISTOR and COMPUTER.

trans·ra·cial /tranzˈrāsHəl; trans-/ ▶*adj.* across or crossing racial boundaries.

trans·sex·u·al /tran(s)ˈseksHo͞oəl/ ▶*n.* a person born with the physical characteristics of one sex who emotionally and psychologically feels that they belong to the opposite sex. ■ a person who has undergone surgery and hormone treatment in order to acquire the physical characteristics of the opposite sex.
▶*adj.* of or relating to such a person. —**trans·sex·u·al·ism** /-ˌlizəm/ *n.* —**trans·sex·u·al·i·ty** /-ˌseksHo͞oˈalitē/ *n.*

trans·ship /tran(s)ˈsHip/ (also **tran·ship**) ▶*v.* (**-shipped, -ship·ping**) [*trans.*] transfer (cargo) from one ship or other form of transport to another. —**trans·ship·ment** *n.*

trans·son·ic ▶*adj.* variant spelling of TRANSONIC.

trans·syn·ap·tic /ˌtran(s)səˈnaptik; ˌtranz-/ ▶*adj. Physiology* occurring or existing across a nerve synapse.

tran·sub·stan·ti·ate /ˌtransəbˈstancHēˌāt/ ▶*v.* [*trans.*] (usu. **be transubstantiated**) *Christian Theology* convert (the substance of the Eucharistic elements) into the body and blood of Christ. ■ *formal* change the form or substance of (something) into something different. ▷late Middle English: from medieval Latin *transubstantiat-* 'changed in substance,' from the verb *transubstantiare*, from Latin *trans-* 'across' + *substantia* 'substance.'

tran·sub·stan·ti·a·tion /ˌtransəbˌstancHēˈāsHən/ ▶*n. Christian Theology* (esp. in the Roman Catholic Church) the conversion of the substance of the Eucharistic elements into the body and blood of Christ at consecration, only the appearances of bread and wine still remaining. ■ *formal* a change in the form or substance of something.

tran·sude /tranˈso͞od/ ▶*v.* [*trans.*] *archaic* discharge (a fluid) gradually through pores in a membrane, esp. within the body. ■ [*intrans.*] (of a fluid) be discharged in such a way. ▷mid 17th cent.: from French *transsuder* (in Old French *tressuer*), from Latin *trans-* 'across' + *sudare* 'to sweat.' —**tran·su·date** /ˈtranso͞oˌdāt/ *n.* —**tran·su·da·tion** /ˌtranso͞oˈdāsHən/ *n.*

trans·u·ran·ic /ˌtransyəˈranik; tranz-/ ▶*adj. Chemistry* (of an element) having a higher atomic number than uranium (92).

trans·u·re·thral /ˌtransyo͞oˈrēTHrəl; ˌtranz-/ ▶*adj.* (of a medical procedure) performed via the urethra.

Trans·vaal /transˈväl; tranz-; -ˈfäl/ (also **the Trans·vaal**) a former province in northeastern South Africa, north of the Vaal River. Resistance to Britain's annexation of Transvaal in 1877 led to the Boer Wars, after which the Transvaal became a Crown Colony. It became a founding province of the Union of South Africa in 1910 and in 1994 was divided into the provinces of Northern Transvaal, Eastern Transvaal, Pretoria-Witwatersrand-Vereeniging, and the eastern part of North-West Province.

Trans·vaal dai·sy ▶*n.* a South African gerbera, grown for its large brightly colored daisylike flowers. • *Gerbera jamesonii*, family Compositae.

trans·val·ue /transˈvalyo͞o; tranz-/ ▶*v.* (**-val·ues, -val·ued, -val·u·ing**) [*trans.*] (often **be transvalued**) represent (something, typically an idea, custom, or quality) in a different way, altering people's judgment of or reaction to it: *survival strategies are aesthetically* ***transvalued into*** *weapons of attack.* —**trans·val·u·a·tion** /ˌtransvalyo͞oˈāsHən; ˌtranz-/ *n.*

trans·ver·sal /transˈvərsəl; tranz-/ *Geometry* ▶*adj.* (of a line) intersecting a system of lines.
▶*n.* a transversal line. ▷late Middle English (as a synonym of TRANSVERSE): from medieval Latin *transversalis*, from Latin *transversus* 'lying across.' —**trans·ver·sal·i·ty** /ˌtransvərˈsalitē; ˌtranz-/ *n.* —**trans·ver·sal·ly** *adv.*

trans·verse /transˈvərs; tranz-/ ▶*adj.* situated or extending across something: *a transverse beam supports the dashboard.* ▷late Middle English: from Latin *transversus* 'turned across,' past participle of *transvertere*, from *trans-* 'across' + *vertere* 'to turn.' —**trans·verse·ly** *adv.*

trans·verse co·lon ▶*n. Anatomy* the middle part of the large intestine, passing across the abdomen from right to left below the stomach.

trans·verse flute ▶*n.* a flute that is held horizontally when played, e.g., the modern flute as opposed to the recorder.

trans·verse mag·net ▶*n.* a magnet with poles at the sides and not the ends.

trans·verse proc·ess ▶*n. Anatomy* a lateral process of a vertebra.

Trans·verse Ranges a term for various mountain ranges that cross southern California and are often considered the divider between north and south. See also TEHACHAPI MOUNTAINS.

trans·verse wave ▶*n. Physics* a wave vibrating at right angles to the direction of its propagation.

trans·ves·tite /transˈvesˌtīt; tranz-/ ▶*n.* a person, typically a man, who derives pleasure from dressing in clothes appropriate to the opposite sex. ▷1920s: from German *Transvestit*, from Latin *trans-* 'across' + *vestire* 'clothe.' —**trans·ves·tism** /-ˌtizəm/ *n.* —**trans·ves·tist** /-tist/ *n.* (*dated*). —**trans·ves·ti·tism** /-tiˌtizəm/ *n.*

T

Tran·syl·va·nia /ˌtransəlˈvānyə; -ˈvānēə/ **1** a large tableland region of northwestern Romania, separated from the rest of the country by the Carpathian Mountains and the Transylvanian Alps. Part of Hungary until it became a principality of the Ottoman Empire in the 16th century, it was returned to Hungary at the end of the 17th century and was incorporated into Romania in 1918. **2** (in U.S. history) an unrecognized fourteenth colony that was proposed in the 1770s in what is now central Kentucky and neighboring Tennessee. ▷based on Latin *trans* 'across, beyond' + *silva* 'forest.' —**Tran·syl·va·ni·an** *adj.*

trap[1] /trap/ ▶*n.* **1** a device or enclosure designed to catch and retain animals, typically by allowing entry but not exit or by catching hold of a part of the body. ■ a curve in the waste pipe from a bathtub, sink, or toilet that is always full of liquid and prevents gases from coming up the pipe into the building. ■ [with *adj.*] a container or device used to collect a specified thing: *one fuel filter and water trap are sufficient on the fuel system.* ■ a bunker or other hollow on a golf course. ■ the compartment from which a greyhound is released at the start of a race. ■ *figurative* a trick by which someone is misled into giving themselves away or otherwise acting contrary to their interests or intentions: *by keeping quiet I was* ***walking into a trap.*** ■ *figurative* an unpleasant situation from which it is hard to escape: *they* ***fell into the trap*** *of relying too little on equity financing.* **2** a device for hurling an object such as a clay pigeon into the air to be

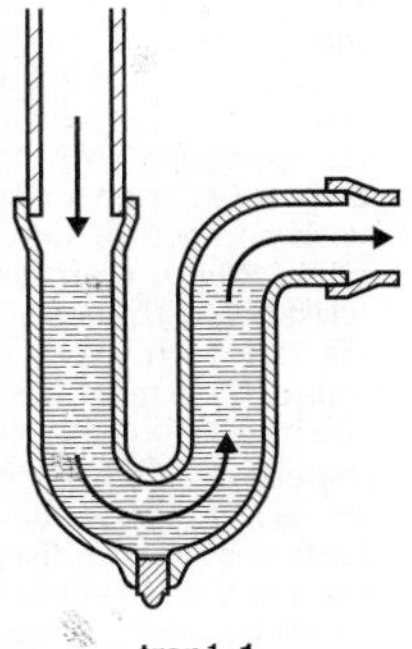

trap[1] **1**

Pronunciation Key ə *ago*; ər *over*; ˈə or ˌə *up*; ˈər or ˌər *fur*; a *hat*; ā *rate*; ä *car*; CH *chew*; e *let*; ē *see*; e(ə)r *air*; i *fit*; ī *by*; i(ə)r *ear*; NG *sing*; ō *go*; ô *for*; oi *boy*; o͝o *good*; o͞o *goo*; ou *out*; SH *she*; TH *thin*; T͟H *then*; (h)w *why*; ZH *vision*

shot at. ■ (in the game of trapball) the shoe-shaped device that is hit with a bat to send the ball into the air. **3** *chiefly historical* a light, two-wheeled carriage pulled by a horse or pony. **4** short for TRAPDOOR. **5** *informal* a person's mouth (used in expressions to do with speaking): *keep your trap shut!* **6** (usu. **traps**) *informal* percussion instruments, typically in a jazz band. **7** *Baseball* & *Football* an act of trapping the ball.

▸*v.* (**trapped, trap·ping**) [*trans.*] catch (an animal) in a trap. ■ (often **be trapped**) prevent (someone) from escaping from a place: *twenty workers were trapped by flames.* ■ have (something, typically a part of the body) held tightly by something so that it cannot move or be freed: *he had trapped his finger in a spring-loaded hinge.* ■ induce (someone), by means of trickery or deception, to do something they would not otherwise want to do: *I hoped to* **trap** *him* **into** *an admission.* ■ *Baseball* & *Football* catch (the ball) after it has briefly touched the ground. ■ *Soccer* bring (the ball) under control with the feet or other part of the body on receiving it. ▷Old English *træppe* (in *coltetræppe* 'Christ's thorn'); related to Middle Dutch *trappe* and medieval Latin *trappa*, of uncertain origin. The verb dates from late Middle English. **—trap·like** /-ˌlīk/ *adj.*

trap[2] ▸*v.* (**trapped, trap·ping**) [*trans.*] [usu. as *adj.*] (**trapped**) *archaic* put trappings on (a horse, etc.): *gaily trapped mules.* ▷late Middle English: from the obsolete noun *trap* 'trappings,' from Old French *drap* 'drape.'

trap[3] (also **trap·rock**) ▸*n.* basalt or a similar dark, fine-grained igneous rock. ▷late 18th cent.: from Swedish *trapp*, from *trappa* 'stair' (because of the often stairlike appearance of its outcroppings).

trap·ball /ˈtrapˌbôl/ ▸*n. historical* a game in which the player uses a bat to hit a trap (see TRAP[1] sense 2) to send a ball into the air and then hits the ball itself. ■ the ball used in this game.

trap crop ▸*n.* a crop planted to attract insect pests from another crop, esp. one in which the pests fail to survive or reproduce.

trap·door /ˈtrapˌdôr/ (also **trap door**) ▸*n.* a hinged or removable panel in a floor, ceiling, or roof. ■ a feature or defect of a computer system that allows surreptitious unauthorized access to data belonging to other users.

trapes ▸*v.* & *n.* archaic spelling of TRAIPSE.

tra·peze /trəˈpēz; tra-/ ▸*n.* **1** (also **flying trapeze**) a horizontal bar hanging by two ropes (usually high in the air) and free to swing, used by acrobats in a circus. **2** *Sailing* a harness attached by a cable to a dinghy's mast, enabling a sailor to balance the boat by leaning backward out over the windward side. ▷mid 19th cent.: from French *trapèze*, from late Latin *trapezium* (see TRAPEZIUM).

Tra·pe·zi·um /trəˈpēzēəm/ (**the Trapezium**) *Astronomy* the multiple star Theta Orionis, which lies within the Great Nebula of Orion and illuminates it. Four stars are visible in a small telescope and two more with a larger telescope.

tra·pe·zi·um /trəˈpēzēəm/ ▸*n.* (*pl.* **-zi·a** /-zēə/ or **-zi·ums**) **1** *Geometry* a type of quadrilateral: ■ a quadrilateral with no sides parallel. Compare with TRAPEZOID. ■ *Brit.* a quadrilateral with one pair of sides parallel. **2** (also **os trapezium**) *Anatomy* a bone in the wrist below the base of the thumb. ▷late 16th cent.: via late Latin from Greek *trapezion*, from *trapeza* 'table.' The term has been used in anatomy since the mid 19th cent.

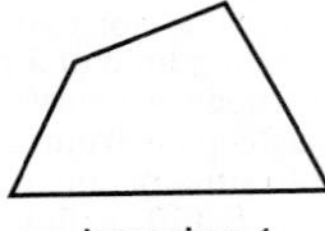
trapezium 1

tra·pe·zi·us /trəˈpēzēəs/ (also **trapezius muscle**) ▸*n.* (*pl.* **-zi·i** /-zēˌī/ or **-zi·us·es**) *Anatomy* either of a pair of large triangular muscles extending over the back of the neck and shoulders and moving the head and shoulder blade. ▷early 18th cent.: from modern Latin, from Greek *trapezion* 'trapezium' (because of the shape formed by the muscles).

tra·pe·zo·he·dron /trəˌpēzōˈhēdrən; ˌtrapizō-/ ▸*n.* (*pl.* **-dra** /-drə/ or **-drons**) a solid figure whose faces are trapeziums or trapezoids. ▷early 19th cent.: from TRAPEZIUM + -HEDRON, on the pattern of words such as *polyhedron.* **—tra·pe·zo·he·dral** /-drəl/ *adj.*

trap·e·zoid /ˈtrapiˌzoid/ ▸*n.* **1** *Geometry* a type of quadrilateral: ■ *N. Amer.* a quadrilateral with only one pair of parallel sides. ■ *Brit.* a quadrilateral with no sides parallel. Compare with TRAPEZIUM. **2** (also **trapezoid bone**) *Anatomy* a small carpal bone in the base of the hand, articulating with the metacarpal of the index finger. ▷early 18th cent.: from modern Latin *trapezoides*, from late Greek *trapezoeidēs*, from *trapeza* 'table' (see TRAPEZIUM). **—trap·e·zoi·dal** /ˌtrapiˈzoidl/ *adj.*

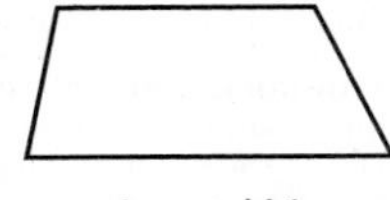
trapezoid 1

trap·line /ˈtrapˌlīn/ ▸*n.* a series of traps for game.

trap·per /ˈtrapər/ ▸*n.* a person who traps wild animals, esp. for their fur.

trap·pings /ˈtrapiNGz/ ▸*plural n.* the outward signs, features, or objects associated with a particular situation, role, or thing: *I had the trappings of success.* ■ a horse's ornamental harness. ▷late Middle English: derivative of TRAP[2].

Trap·pist /ˈtrapist/ ▸*adj.* of, relating to, or denoting a branch of the Cistercian order of monks founded in 1664 and noted for an austere rule including a vow of silence.

▸*n.* a member of this order. ▷early 19th cent.: from French *trappiste*, from *La Trappe* in Normandy.

trap·rock /ˈtrapˌräk/ ▸*n.* see TRAP[3].

traps /traps/ ▸*plural n. informal* personal belongings; baggage: *I was ready to pack my traps and leave.* ▷early 19th cent.: perhaps a contraction of TRAPPINGS.

trap·shoot·ing /ˈtrapˌSHo͞otiNG/ ▸*n.* the sport of shooting at clay pigeons released from a spring trap. **—trap·shoot·er** /-ˌSHo͞otər/ *n.*

trash /traSH/ ▸*n.* discarded matter; refuse. ■ writing, art, or other cultural items of poor quality: *if they read at all, they read trash.* ■ a person or people regarded as being of very low social standing: *she would have been considered trash.* ■ nonsense.

▸*v.* [*trans.*] **1** *informal* damage or wreck: *my apartment's been totally trashed.* ■ discard: *they trashed the tapes and sent her back into the studio.* ■ *Computing* kill (a file or process) or wipe (a disk): *she almost trashed the e-mail window.* ■ criticize severely: *trade associations trashed the legislation as deficient.* ■ [as *adj.*] (**trashed**) intoxicated with alcohol or drugs: *there was pot, there was booze, but nobody really got trashed.* **2** strip (sugar cane) of its outer leaves to ripen it faster. ▷late Middle English: of unknown origin. The verb is first recorded (mid 18th cent.) in sense 2; the other senses have arisen in the 20th cent.

trash can ▸*n.* another term for GARBAGE CAN.

trash talk (also **trash talk·ing**) *informal* ▸*n.* insulting or boastful speech intended to demoralize, intimidate, or humiliate someone, esp. an opponent in an athletic contest: *he heard more trash talk from the Giants before the game than during the game | stop the trash talking and stop the violence.*

▸*v.* [*intrans.*] (**trash-talk**) use insulting or boastful speech for such a purpose: *their players do not swear or tussle or trash-talk |* [as *adj.*] (**trash-talking**) *the worst trash-talking team they had ever encountered.* **—trash talk·er** (also **trash-talk·er**) *n.*

trash·y /ˈtraSHē/ ▸*adj.* (**trash·i·er, trash·i·est**) (esp. of items of popular culture) of poor quality: *trashy novels and formulaic movies.* **—trash·i·ly** /ˈtraSHəlē/ *adv.* **—trash·i·ness** *n.*

trass /tras/ ▸*n.* a light-colored variety of volcanic ash resembling pozzolana, used in making water-resistant cement. ▷late 18th cent.: from Dutch *tras*, German *Trass*, based on Latin *terra* 'earth.'

trat·to·ri·a /ˌträtəˈrēə/ ▸*n.* an Italian restaurant serving simple food. ▷Italian.

trau·ma /ˈtroumə; ˈtrô-/ ▸*n.* (*pl.* **-mas** or **-ma·ta** /-mətə/) a deeply distressing or disturbing experience: *they were reluctant to talk about the traumas of the revolution.* ■ emotional shock following a stressful event or a physical injury, which may be associated with physical shock and sometimes leads to long-term neurosis. ■ *Medicine* physical injury. ▷late 17th cent.: from Greek, literally 'wound.'

trau·mat·ic /trəˈmatik; trou-; trô-/ ▸*adj.* emotionally disturbing or distressing: *she was going through a traumatic divorce.* ■ relating to or causing psychological trauma. ■ *Medicine* relating to or denoting physical injury. ▷mid 19th cent.: via late Latin from Greek *traumatikos*, from *trauma* (see TRAUMA). **—trau·mat·i·cal·ly** /-ik(ə)lē/ *adv.*

trau·ma·tism /ˈtrouməˌtizəm/ ▸*n. chiefly technical* a traumatic effect or condition.

trau·ma·tize /ˈtrouməˌtīz; ˈtrô-/ ▸*v.* [*trans.*] subject to lasting shock as a result of an emotionally disturbing experience or physical injury: *the children were traumatized by separation from their families.* ■ *Medicine* cause physical injury to: *the dressings can be removed without traumatizing newly formed tissue.* **—trau·ma·ti·za·tion** /ˌtroumətiˈzāSHən; ˌtrô-/ *n.*

trav. ▸*abbr.* ■ traveler. ■ travels.

tra·vail /trəˈvāl; ˈtravˌāl/ *poetic/literary* ▸*n.* (also **travails**) painful or laborious effort: *advice for those who wish to save great sorrow and travail.* See note at LABOR. ■ labor pains: *a woman in travail.*

▸*v.* [*intrans.*] engage in painful or laborious effort. ■ (of a woman) be in labor. ▷Middle English: via Old French from medieval Latin *trepalium* 'instrument of torture,' from Latin *tres* 'three' + *palus* 'stake.'

trav·el /ˈtravəl/ ▸*v.* (**-eled, -el·ing**; also *chiefly Brit.* **-elled, -el·ling**) **1** [*intrans.*] make a journey, typically of some length or abroad: *the vessel had been traveling from Libya to Ireland | we traveled thousands of miles.* ■ [*trans.*] journey along (a road) or through (a region): *he traveled the world with the army.* ■ [usu. as *adj.*] (**traveling**) go or be moved from place to place: *a traveling exhibition.* ■ *informal* resist motion sickness, damage, or some other impairment on a journey: *he usually* **travels well**. ■ be enjoyed or successful away from the place of origin: *accordion music travels well.* ■ *dated* go from place to place as a sales representative: *he traveled for a shoe company through Mississippi.* ■ (of an object or radiation) move, typically in a constant or predictable way: *light travels faster than sound.* ■ *informal* (esp. of a vehicle) move quickly. **2** [*intrans.*] *Basketball* take more than the allowed number of steps (typically two) while holding the ball without dribbling it.

▸*n.* the action of traveling, typically abroad: *I have a job that involves a lot of travel.* ■ (**travels**) journeys, esp. long or exotic ones: *perhaps you'll write a book about your travels.* ■ [as *adj.*] (of a device) designed so as to be sufficiently compact for use on a journey: *a travel iron.* ■ the range, rate, or mode of motion of a part of a machine. ▷Middle English: variant of TRAVAIL and originally in the same sense.

trav·el a·gen·cy (also **travel bureau**) ▸*n.* an agency that makes the necessary arrangements for travelers, esp. the booking of airline tickets and hotel rooms. **—trav·el a·gent** *n.*

trav·el·a·tor /ˈtravəˌlātər/ (also **trav·o·la·tor**) ▸*n.* a moving walkway, typically at an airport. ▷1950s: from TRAVEL, suggested by ESCALATOR.

trav·el card ▸*n.* a prepaid card allowing unlimited travel on buses or trains for a specified period of time: *a one-day travel card.*

trav·eled /ˈtravəld/ ▸*adj.* [with *submodifier* or in *combination*] **1** having traveled to many places: *he was widely traveled.* **2** used by people traveling: *a less well-traveled route.*

trav·el·er /ˈtrav(ə)lər/ (*Brit.* **trav·el·ler**) ▸*n.* a person who is traveling or who often travels.

trav·el·er's check ▸*n.* a check for a fixed amount that can be cashed or used in payment after endorsement with the holder's signature.

trav·el·er's joy ▸*n.* a tall scrambling clematis with small fragrant flowers and tufts of gray hairs around the seeds. Native to Eurasia and North Africa, it grows chiefly on calcareous soils. Also called OLD MAN'S BEARD. • *Clematis vitalba*, family Ranunculaceae.

trav·el·er's tale ▸*n.* a story about the unusual characteristics or customs of a foreign country, regarded as probably exaggerated or untrue.

trav·el·ing crane ▸*n.* a crane able to move on rails, esp. along an overhead support.

trav·el·ing peo·ple ▸*plural n.* people whose lifestyle is nomadic, for example gypsies (a term typically used by such people of themselves).

trav·el·ing sales·man ▸*n.* a representative of a company who visits stores and other businesses to show samples and gain orders.

trav·el·ing sales·man prob·lem ▸*n.* a mathematical problem in which one tries to find the shortest route that passes through each of a set of points once and only once.

trav·el·ing wave ▸*n. Physics* a wave in which the medium moves in the direction of propagation.

trav·e·logue /ˈtravəˌlôg; -ˌläg/ ▸*n.* a movie, book, or illustrated lecture about the places visited and experiences encountered by a traveler. ▷early 20th cent.: from TRAVEL, on the pattern of *monologue.*

trav·ers /ˈtravərs; trəˈvərs/ (also **trav·erse**) ▸*n.* a movement performed in dressage, in which the horse moves parallel to the side of the arena, with its shoulders carried closer to the wall than its hindquarters and its body curved toward the center. ▷French, from *pied de travers* 'foot askew.'

tra·verse /trəˈvərs/ ▸*v.* [*trans.*] **1** travel across or through: *he traversed the forest.* ■ extend across or through: *a moving catwalk that traversed a vast* *cavernous space.* ■ [*intrans.*] cross a hill or mountain by means of a series of sideways movements: *I often use this route, eventually traversing around the cliff.* ■ ski diagonally across (a slope), with only a slight descent. ■ *figurative* consider or discuss the whole extent of (a subject): *he would traverse a number of subjects and disciplines.* **2** [*trans.*] move (something) back and forth or sideways: *a probe is traversed along the tunnel.* ■ turn (a large gun or other device on a pivot) to face a different direction. ■ [*intrans.*] (of such a gun or device) be turned in this way. **3** *Law* deny (an allegation) in pleading. ■ *archaic* oppose or thwart (a plan).

▸*n.* **1** an act of traversing something. ■ a sideways movement, or a series of such movements, across a rock face from one line of ascent or descent to another. ■ a place where a movement of this type is necessary: *a narrow traverse made lethal by snow and ice.* ■ a movement following a diagonal course made by a skier descending a slope. ■ a zigzag course followed by a ship because winds or currents prevent it from sailing directly toward its destination. **2** a part of a structure that extends or is fixed across something. ■ a gallery extending from side to side of a church or other building. **3** a mechanism enabling a large gun to be turned to face a different direction. ■ the sideways movement of a part in a machine. **4** a single line of survey, usually plotted from compass bearings and chained or paced distances between angular points. ■ a tract surveyed in this way. **5** *Military* a pair of right-angled bends incorporated in a trench to avoid enfilading fire. **6** variant spelling of TRAVERS.

▸*adj.* (of a curtain rod) allowing the curtain to be opened and closed by sliding it along the rod. ▷Middle English (sense 3 of the *verb*): from Old French *traverser*, from late Latin *traversare*; the noun is from Old French *travers* (masculine), *traverse* (feminine), partly based on *traverser*. **—tra·vers·a·ble** *adj.* **—tra·vers·al** /-səl/ *n.* **—tra·vers·er** *n.*

trav·er·tine /ˈtravərˌtēn; -tin/ ▸*n.* white or light-colored calcareous rock deposited from mineral springs, used in building. ▷late 18th cent.: from Italian *travertino, tivertino*, from Latin *tiburtinus* 'of Tibur' (now Tivoli, a district near Rome).

trav·es·ty /ˈtravistē/ ▸*n.* (*pl.* **-ties**) a false, absurd, or distorted representation of something: *the absurdly lenient sentence is* ***a travesty of*** *justice.* See note at CARICATURE.

▸*v.* (**-ties, -tied**) [*trans.*] represent in such a way: *Michael has betrayed the family by travestying them in his plays.* ▷mid 17th cent. (as an adjective in the sense 'dressed to appear ridiculous'): from French *travesti* 'disguised,' past participle of *travestir*, from Italian *travestire*, from *trans-* 'across' + *vestire* 'clothe.'

tra·vois /trəˈvoi; ˈtravˌoi/ ▸*n.* (*pl.* same) a type of sled formerly used by North American Indians to carry goods, consisting of two joined poles dragged by a horse or dog. ▷mid 19th cent.: alteration of synonymous *travail*, from French.

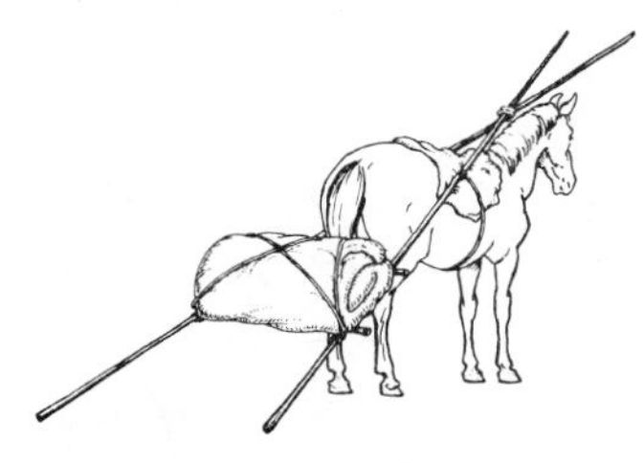

travois

trav·ol·a·tor ▸*n.* variant spelling of TRAVELATOR.

trawl /trôl/ ▸*v.* [*intrans.*] fish with a trawl net or seine: *the boats* ***trawled for*** *flounder* | [as *n.*] (**trawling**) *restrictions on excessive trawling were urgently needed.* ■ [*trans.*] catch with a trawl net. ■ sift through as part of a search: *they* ***trawled through*** *twenty-five-year-old confidential files* | [*trans.*] *he trawled his memory and remembered locking the door.* ■ [*trans.*] drag or trail (something) through water or other liquid: *she trawled a toe to test the temperature.*

▸*n.* **1** an act of fishing with a trawl net: *they had caught two trout on the lazy trawl.* ■ an act of sifting through something as part of a search: *we did a trawl of supermarkets and health-food stores* | *a constant* ***trawl for*** *information.* **2** (also **trawl net**) a large wide-mouthed fishing net dragged by a vessel along the bottom or in the midwater of the sea or a lake. **3** (also **trawl line**) another term for LONG LINE. ▷mid 16th cent. (as a verb): probably from Middle Dutch *traghelen* 'to drag' (related to *traghel* 'dragnet'), perhaps from Latin *tragula* 'dragnet.'

trawl·er /ˈtrôlər/ ▸*n.* a fishing boat used for trawling.

tray /trā/ ▸*n.* a flat, shallow container with a raised rim, typically used for carrying food and drink, or for holding small items. ▷late Old English *trīg*, from the Germanic base of TREE; the primary sense may have been 'wooden container.' **—tray·ful** /-ˌfo͝ol/ *n.* (*pl.* **-fuls**).

trayf /trāf/ (also **treyf** or **trey·fa** /ˈtrāfə/) ▸*adj.* (of food) not satisfying the requirements of Jewish law: *I asked her if she ever ate food that was trayf.* ▷mid 19th cent.: from Hebrew *ṭĕrēpāh* 'the flesh of an animal torn or mauled,' from *ṭārap̄* 'rend.'

treach·er·ous /ˈtreCHərəs/ ▸*adj.* guilty of or involving betrayal or deception: *a treacherous Gestapo agent* | *memory is particularly treacherous.* ■ (of ground, water, conditions, etc.) hazardous because of presenting hidden or unpredictable dangers: *a vacationer was swept away by treacherous currents.* ▷Middle English (in the sense 'involving betrayal'): from Old French *trecherous*, from *trecheor* 'a cheat,' from *trechier* 'to cheat.' **—treach·er·ous·ly** *adv.* **—treach·er·ous·ness** *n.*

treach·er·y /ˈtreCHərē/ ▸*n.* (*pl.* **-er·ies**) betrayal of trust; deceptive action or nature: *his resignation was perceived as an act of treachery* | *the treachery of language.* ▷Middle English: from Old French *trecherie*, from *trechier* 'to cheat.'

trea·cle /ˈtrēkəl/ ▸*n.* British term for MOLASSES. ■ *figurative* cloying sentimentality or flattery: *enough of this treacle—let's get back to business.* ▷Middle English (originally denoting an antidote against venom): from Old French *triacle*, via Latin from Greek *thēriakē* 'antidote against venom,' feminine of *thēriakos* (adjective), from *thērion* 'wild beast.' The sense 'molasses' dates from the late 17th cent.; 'sentimentality' arose in the late 18th cent. **—trea·cly** /ˈtrēk(ə)lē/ *adj.*

tread /tred/ ▸*v.* (*past* **trod** /träd/ /träd/; *past part.* **trod·den** /ˈträdn/ or **trod**) [*intrans.*] walk in a specified way: *he trod lightly, trying to make as little contact with the mud as possible* | *figurative the administration had to* ***tread carefully*** *so as not to offend the judiciary.* ■ (**tread on**) set one's foot down on top of. ■ [*trans.*] walk on or along: *shoppers will soon be treading the floors of the new shopping mall.* ■ [*trans.*] press down into the ground or another surface with the feet: *food and cigarette butts had been* ***trodden into*** *the carpet.* ■ [*trans.*] crush or flatten something with the feet: *the snow had been* ***trodden down*** *by the horses* | [as *adj.*] (**trodden**) *she stood on the floor of trodden earth.*

▸*n.* **1** [in *sing.*] a manner or the sound of someone walking: *I heard the heavy tread of Dad's boots.* **2** the top surface of a step or stair. **3** the thick molded part of a vehicle tire that grips the road. ■ the part of a wheel that touches the ground or rail. ■ the upper surface of a railroad track, in contact with the wheels. ■ the part of the sole of a shoe that rests on the ground. ▷Old English *tredan* (as a verb); related to Dutch *treden* and German *treten*. **—tread·er** *n.*

▸*PHRASES* □ **tread the boards** (or **stage**) see BOARD. □ **tread on someone's toes** see STEP ON SOMEONE'S TOES at STEP. □ **tread water** (*past* **tread·ed**) maintain an upright position in deep water by moving the feet with a walking movement and the hands with a downward circular motion. ■ *figurative* fail to advance or make progress: *men who are treading water in their careers.*

trea·dle /ˈtredl/ ▸*n.* a lever worked by the foot that imparts motion to a machine. ■ any of a row of metal spikes set on an angle on a spring within a plate laid across the entrance or exit of a parking facility, used to prevent drivers from using the facility without paying.

▸*v.* [*trans.*] operate (a machine) using a treadle. ▷Old English *tredel* 'stair, step' (see TREAD).

tread·mill /ˈtredˌmil/ ▸*n.* a device formerly used for driving machinery, consisting of a large wheel with steps fitted into its inner surface. It was turned by the weight of people or animals treading the steps. ■ an exercise machine, typically with a continuous belt, that allows one to walk or run in place. ■ *figurative* a job or situation that is tiring, boring, or unpleasant and from which it is hard to escape: *the soulless treadmill of urban existence.*

treas. ▸*abbr.* ■ treasurer. ■ (also **Treas.**) Treasury.

trea·son /ˈtrēzən/ ▸*n.* (also **high treason**) the crime of betraying one's country, esp. by attempting to kill the sovereign or overthrow the government: *they were convicted of treason.* ■ the action of betraying someone or something: *doubt is the ultimate treason against faith.* ■ (**petty treason**) *historical* the crime of murdering someone to whom the murderer owed allegiance, such as a master or husband. ▷Middle English: from Anglo-Norman French *treisoun*, from Latin *traditio(n-)* 'handing over,' from the verb *tradere*. **—trea·son·ous** /ˈtrēzənəs/ *adj.*

USAGE Formerly, there were two types of crime to which the term **treason** was applied: **petty treason** (the crime of murdering one's master) and **high treason** (the crime of betraying one's country). As a classification of offense, the crime of **petty treason** was abolished in 1828. In modern use, the term **high treason** is now often simply called **treason**.

trea·son·a·ble /ˈtrēzənəbəl/ ▸*adj.* (of an offense or offender) punishable as treason or as committing treason: *there was no evidence of treasonable activity.* **—trea·son·a·bly** /-blē/ *adv.*

treas·ure /ˈtreZHər/ ▸*n.* a quantity of precious metals, gems, or other valuable objects. ■ a very valuable object: *she set out to look at the art treasures.* ■ *informal* a person whom the speaker loves or who is valued for the assistance they can give: *the housekeeper is a real treasure—I don't know what he would do without her.*

▸*v.* [*trans.*] keep carefully (a valuable or valued item). ■ value highly: *the island is treasured by walkers and conservationists* | [as *adj.*] (**treasured**) *his library was his most treasured possession.* ▷Middle English: from Old French *tresor*, based on Greek *thēsauros* (see THESAURUS).

treas·ure hunt ▸*n.* a search for treasure. ■ a game in which players search for hidden objects by following a trail of clues.

treas·ur·er /ˈtreZHərər/ ▸*n.* a person appointed to administer or manage the financial assets and liabilities of a society, company, local authority, or other body. ▷Middle English: from Old French *tresorier*, from *tresor* (see TREASURE), influenced by late Latin *thesaurarius*. **—treas·ur·er·ship** /-ˌSHip/ *n.*

Treas·ure State a nickname for the state of MONTANA[1].

treas·ure trove ▸*n.* valuables of unknown ownership that are found hidden, in some cases declared the property of the finder. ■ a hidden store of valuable or delightful things: *your book is a treasure trove of unspeakable delights.* ▷late Middle English: from Anglo-Norman French *tresor trové*, literally 'found treasure.'

treas·ur·y /ˈtreZHərē/ ▸*n.* (*pl.* **-ur·ies**) **1** the funds or revenue of a government, corporation, or institution: *the country's pledge not to spend more than it has in its treasury.* ■ (**Treasury**) (in some countries) the government department responsible for budgeting for and controlling public expenditure, management of the national debt, and the overall management of the economy. **2** a place or building where treasure is stored. ■ a store or collection of valuable or delightful things: *the old town is a treasury of ancient monuments.* ▷Middle English: from Old French *tresorie* (see TREASURE).

Treas·ur·y bill ▸*n.* a short-dated government security, yielding no interest but issued at a discount on its redemption price.

Treas·ur·y bond ▸*n.* a government bond issued by the U.S. Treasury.

Treas·ur·y note ▸*n.* a note issued by the U.S. Treasury for use as currency.

treat /trēt/ ▸*v.* [*trans.*] **1** behave toward or deal with in a certain way: *she had been brutally treated* | *he* ***treated her with*** *grave courtesy.* ■ (**treat something as**) regard something as being of a specified nature with implications for one's actions concerning it: *the names are being treated as classified information.* ■ give medical care or attention to; try to heal or cure: *the two were* ***treated for*** *cuts and bruises.* ■ apply a process or a substance to (something) to protect or preserve it or to give it particular properties: *linen creases badly unless it is* ***treated with*** *the appropriate finish.* ■ present or discuss (a subject): *the lectures show a striking variation in the level at which subjects are treated.* **2** (**treat someone to**) provide someone with (food, drink, or entertainment) at one's own expense: *the old man had treated him to a drink or two.* ■ give someone (something) as a favor: *he treated her to one of his smiles.* ■ (**treat oneself**) do or have something that gives one great pleasure: *treat yourself—*

Pronunciation Key ə *ago*; ər *over*; ˈə or ˌə *up*; ˈər or ˌər *fur*; a *hat*; ā *rate*; ä *car*; CH *chew*; e *let*; ē *see*; e(ə)r *air*; i *fit*; ī *by*; i(ə)r *ear*; NG *sing*; ō *go*; ô *for*; oi *boy*; o͝o *good*; o͞o *goo*; ou *out*; SH *she*; TH *thin*; TH *then*; (h)w *why*; ZH *vision*

you can diet tomorrow. **3** [*intrans.*] negotiate terms with someone, esp. an opponent: *propagandists claimed that he was* ***treating with*** *the enemy.*

▸*n.* an event or item that is out of the ordinary and gives great pleasure: *he wanted to take her to the movies as a treat.* ■ used with a possessive adjective to indicate that the person specified is paying for food, entertainment, etc., for someone else: *"My treat," he insisted, reaching for the bill.* ▷Middle English (in the senses 'negotiate' and 'discuss (a subject)'): from Old French *traitier*, from Latin *tractare* 'handle,' frequentative of *trahere* 'draw, pull.' The current noun sense dates from the mid 17th cent. **—treat·a·ble** *adj.* **—treat·er** *n.*

▸*PHRASE* □ **—— a treat** *Brit., informal* used to indicate that someone or something does something specified very well or satisfactorily: *their tactics worked a treat.* ■ used to indicate that someone is looking attractive: *I don't know whether she can act, but she* ***looks a treat.***

trea·tise /ˈtrētis/ ▸*n.* a written work dealing formally and systematically with a subject: *a comprehensive* ***treatise on*** *electricity and magnetism.* ▷late Middle English: from Anglo-Norman French *tretis*, from Old French *traitier* (see **TREAT**).

treat·ment /ˈtrētmənt/ ▸*n.* the manner in which someone behaves toward or deals with someone or something: *the directive required equal treatment for men and women.* ■ medical care given to a patient for an illness or injury: *I'm receiving* ***treatment for*** *an injured shoulder.* ■ a session of medical care or the administration of a dose of medicine: *the patient was given repeated treatments as required.* ■ the use of a chemical, physical, or biological agent to preserve or give particular properties to something: *the treatment of hazardous waste is particularly expensive.* ■ the presentation or discussion of a subject: *analysis of the treatment of women in her painting.* ■ (**the full treatment**) *informal* used to indicate that something is done enthusiastically, vigorously, or to an extreme degree: *I gave them the full treatment, and they were just falling over themselves.*

trea·ty /ˈtrētē/ ▸*n.* (*pl.* **-ties**) a formally concluded and ratified agreement between countries. ▷late Middle English: from Old French *traite*, from Latin *tractatus* 'treatise' (see **TRACTATE**).

trea·ty port ▸*n. historical* a port bound by treaty to be open to foreign trade, esp. in 19th- and early 20th-century China and Japan.

Treb·bia·no /trebˈyänō/ ▸*n.* a variety of wine grape widely cultivated in Italy and elsewhere. ■ a wine made from this grape. ▷Italian, from the name of the *Trebbia* River, in northern central Italy.

Treb·i·zond /ˈtrebiˌzänd/ another name for **TRABZON**.

tre·ble[1] /ˈtrebəl/ ▸*adj.* [*attrib.*] consisting of three parts; threefold: *the fish were caught with large treble hooks dragged through the water.* ■ multiplied or occurring three times: *she turned back to make a double and treble check.*

▸*predeterminer* three times as much or as many: *the tip was at least treble what she would normally have given.*

▸*n.* a threefold quantity or thing, in particular: ■ (in show jumping) a fence consisting of three elements. ■ a crochet stitch made with three loops of wool on the hook at a time. ■ a drink of liquor of three times the standard measure.

▸*pron.* a number or amount that is three times as large as a contrasting or usual number or amount: *by virtue of having paid treble, he had a double room to himself.*

▸*v.* make or become three times as large or numerous: [*trans.*] *rents were doubled and probably trebled* | [*intrans.*] *his salary has trebled in a couple of years.* ▷Middle English: via Old French from Latin *triplus* (see **TRIPLE**).

tre·ble[2] ▸*n.* a high-pitched voice, esp. a boy's singing voice. ■ a boy or girl with such a singing voice. ■ a part written for a high voice or an instrument of a high pitch. ■ [as *adj.*] denoting a relatively high-pitched member of a family of similar instruments: *a treble viol.* ■ (also **treble bell**) the smallest and highest-pitched bell of a set. ■ the high-frequency output of an audio system or radio, corresponding to the treble in music. ▷late Middle English: from **TREBLE**[1], because it was the highest part in a three-part contrapuntal composition.

tre·ble clef ▸*n.* a clef placing G above middle C on the second-lowest line of the staff.

Tre·blin·ka /trəˈbliNGkə; tre-/ a Nazi concentration camp in Poland during World War II, where a great many of the Jews of the Warsaw ghetto were murdered.

tre·bly /ˈtreblē/ ▸*adj.* (of sound, esp. recorded music) having much or excessive treble.

▸*adv.* [as *submodifier*] three times as much: *to Katherine, the house was trebly impressive.*

treb·u·chet /ˌtrebyəˈSHet/ ▸*n.* a machine used in medieval siege warfare for hurling large stones or other missiles. ▷Middle English: from Old French, from *trebucher* 'overthrow.'

tre·cen·to /trāˈCHentō/ ▸*n.* (**the trecento**) the 14th century as a period of Italian art, architecture, or literature. ▷Italian, literally '300,' shortened from *milletrecento* '1300,' used with reference to the years 1300–99.

tree /trē/ ▸*n.* **1** a woody perennial plant, typically having a single stem or trunk growing to a considerable height and bearing lateral branches at some distance from the ground. Compare with **SHRUB**[1]. ■ (in general use) any bush, shrub, or herbaceous plant with a tall erect stem, e.g., a banana plant. **2** a wooden structure or part of a structure. ■ *archaic* or *poetic/literary* the cross on which Jesus Christ was crucified. ■ *archaic* a gallows or gibbet. **3** a thing that has a branching structure resembling that of a tree. ■ (also **tree diagram**) a diagram with a structure of branching connecting lines, representing different processes and relationships.

white ash
(*Fraxinus americana*)

quaking aspen
(*Populus tremuloides*)

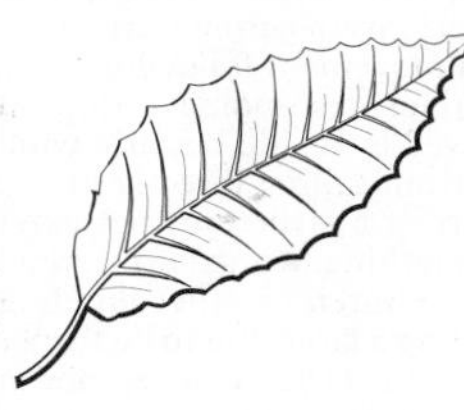
American beech
(*Fagus grandifolia*)

paper birch
(*Betula papyrifera*)

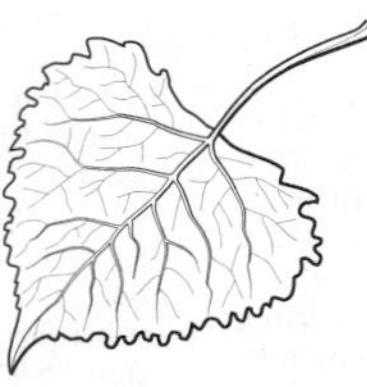
Eastern cottonwood
(*Populus deltoides*)

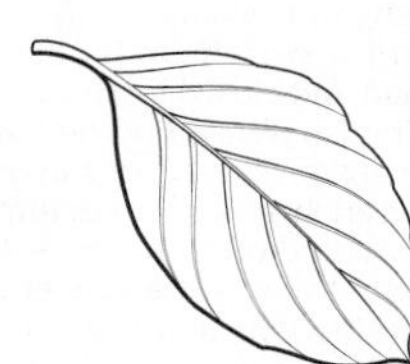
flowering dogwood
(*Cornus florida*)

American holly
(*Ilex opaca*)

horse chestnut
(*Aesculus hippocastanum*)

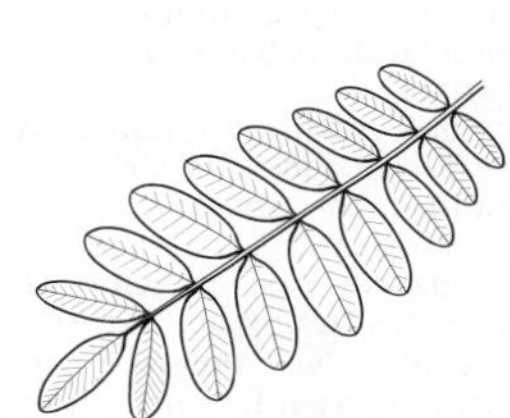
black locust
(*Robinia pseudoacacia*)

silver maple
(*Acer saccharinum*)

sugar maple
(*Acer saccharum*)

pin oak
(*Quercus palustris*)

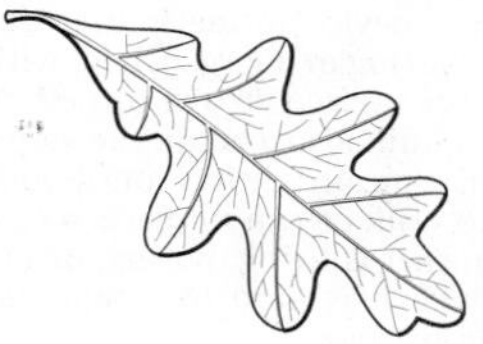
white oak
(*Quercus alba*)

tulip tree (yellow poplar)
(*Liriodendron tulipifera*)

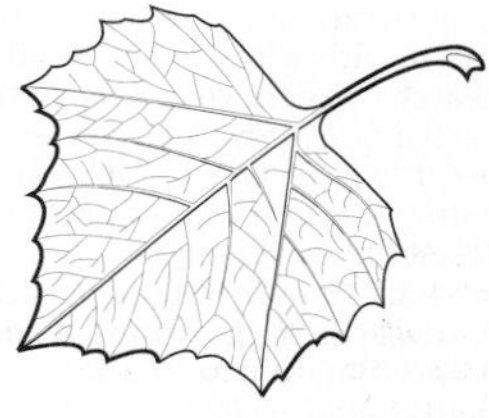
sycamore
(*Platanus occidentalis*)

leaves of familiar trees of North America

▸*v.* (**trees, treed, tree·ing**) [*trans.*] force (a hunted animal) to take refuge in a tree. ■ *informal* force (someone) into a difficult situation. ▷Old English *trēow, trēo*: from a Germanic variant of an Indo-European root shared by Greek *doru* 'wood, spear,' *drus* 'oak.' **—tree·less** *adj.* **—tree·less·ness** *n.* **—tree·like** /-,līk/ *adj.*

▸*PHRASES* □ **out of one's tree** *informal* completely stupid; insane. □ **up a tree** *informal* in a difficult situation without escape; cornered.

tree calf ▸*n.* calfskin stained with a treelike design and used in bookbinding.

tree·creep·er /'trē,krēpər/ ▸*n.* a small songbird with drab plumage and a down-curved bill that creeps around on the trunks of trees to search for insects. Compare with **CREEPER** (sense 2). • a Eurasian and North American bird (*Certhia*, family Certhiidae, in particular the common *C. familiaris*). • an Australasian bird (family Climacteridae and genus *Climacteris*).

tree di·a·gram ▸*n.* see **TREE** (sense 3).

tree duck ▸*n.* another term for **WHISTLING DUCK**.

tree fern ▸*n.* a large palmlike fern with a trunklike stem bearing a crown of large fronds, sometimes reaching a height of 24 m and occurring chiefly in the tropics, particularly the southern hemisphere. • Cyatheaceae and related families, class Filicopsida: seven genera, in particular *Cyathea* and *Dicksonia*.

tree frog ▸*n.* an arboreal frog that has long toes with adhesive disks and is typically small and brightly colored. • Families Hylidae (of Eurasia, America, and Australia) and Rhacophoridae (of Africa and Asia): numerous species, including the common **green tree frog** (*Hyla arborea*) of southern Europe.

tree·hop·per /'trē,häpər/ ▸*n.* a tree-dwelling jumping bug that lives chiefly in the tropics. A tall backward-curving projection of the thorax gives the bug a thornlike appearance for camouflage. • Family Membracidae, suborder Homoptera: species, including the bright green **buffalo treehopper** (*Stictocephalus bisonia*) of North America.

tree house (also **tree·house**) ▸*n.* a structure built in the branches of a tree for children to play in.

tree-hug·ger ▸*n. informal, chiefly derogatory* an environmental campaigner (used in reference to the practice of embracing a tree in an attempt to prevent it from being felled). **—tree-hug·ging** *n.*

tree kan·ga·roo ▸*n.* an agile tree-climbing kangaroo with a long furred tail, and fore- and hind limbs that are of almost equal length, found in the rain forests of Australia and New Guinea. • Genus *Dendrolagus*, family Macropodidae: six species.

tree line ▸*n.* another term for **TIMBERLINE**.

treen /trēn/ ▸*n.* (also **treen·ware** /-,we(ə)r/) [treated as *pl.*] small domestic wooden objects, esp. antiques. ▸*adj. chiefly archaic* wooden. ▷Old English *trēowen* 'wooden' (see **TREE, -EN**[2]).

tree·nail /'trē,nāl; 'trenl/ ▸*n.* a trunnel.

tree of heav·en (also **tree-of-heav·en**) ▸*n.* a fast-growing Chinese ailanthus that is widely cultivated as an ornamental. • *Ailanthus altissima*, family Simaroubaceae.

tree of know·ledge (also **tree of the knowledge of good and evil**) ▸*n.* (in the Bible) the tree in the Garden of Eden bearing the forbidden fruit that Adam and Eve disobediently ate (Gen. 2:9, 3).

tree of life ▸*n.* **1** (**Tree of Life**) (in the Bible) a tree in the Garden of Eden whose fruit imparts eternal life (Gen. 3:22–24). ■ an imaginary branching, treelike structure representing the evolutionary divergence of all living creatures. ■ (in cabalism) a diagram in the form of a tree bearing spheres that represent the sephiroth. **2** the thuja or arbor vitae.

tree pip·it ▸*n.* a widespread Old World pipit that inhabits open country with scattered trees. • *Anthus trivialis*, family Motacillidae.

Tree Plant·ers' State a nickname for the state of **NEBRASKA**.

tree ring ▸*n.* each of a number of concentric rings in the cross section of a tree trunk, representing a single year's growth.

tree shrew ▸*n.* a small squirrellike insectivorous mammal with a pointed snout, native to Southeast Asia, esp. Borneo. • Family Tupaiidae and order Scandentia: several genera, in particular *Tupaia*; tree shrews were formerly placed with either the insectivores or the primates.

tree snake ▸*n.* a harmless arboreal snake, typically very slender and able to mimic a twig. • Several genera in the family Colubridae, e.g., *Dendrelaphis* and *Ahaetulla* (of Asia), and *Leptophis* and *Oxybelis* (of America).

tree spar·row ▸*n.* **1** a Eurasian sparrow with a chocolate-brown cap in both sexes, inhabiting agricultural land. • *Passer montanus*, family Passeridae (or Ploceidae). **2** a migratory sparrowlike songbird of the bunting family, breeding on the edge of the North American tundra. • *Spizella arborea*, family Emberizidae (subfamily Emberizidae).

tree squir·rel ▸*n.* an arboreal squirrel that is typically active in daylight and does not hibernate. • *Sciurus* and other genera, family Sciuridae: numerous species.

tree struc·ture ▸*n. Computing* a structure that has successive branchings or subdivisions.

tree sur·geon ▸*n.* a person who prunes and treats old or damaged trees in order to preserve them. **—tree sur·ger·y** *n.*

tree swal·low ▸*n.* a North American swallow that nests in trees. • *Tachycineta bicolor*.

tree toad ▸*n.* another term for **TREE FROG**.

tree to·ma·to ▸*n.* another term for **TAMARILLO**.

tree·top /'trē,täp/ ▸*n.* (usu. **treetops**) the uppermost part of a tree.

tre·foil /'trē,foil; 'tref,oil/ ▸*n.* a small European plant of the pea family with yellow flowers and three-lobed cloverlike leaves. • Genera *Trifolium* and *Lotus*, family Leguminosae: several species, in particular the **bird's-foot trefoil**. ■ a similar or related plant with three-lobed leaves. ■ an ornamental design of three rounded lobes like a clover leaf, used typically in architectural tracery. ■ a thing having three parts; a set of three: *a trefoil of parachutes lowers the shuttle's used rockets to Earth.* ■ [as *adj.*] denoting something shaped in the form of a trefoil leaf: *trefoil windows.* ▷Middle English: from Anglo-Norman French *trifoil*, from Latin *trifolium*, from *tri-* 'three' + *folium* 'leaf.' **—tre·foiled** *adj.*

trefoil design

tre·ha·lose /trə'hä,lōs/ ▸*n. Chemistry* a sugar of the disaccharide class produced by some fungi, yeasts, and similar organisms. ▷mid 19th cent.: from *trehala* (from Turkish, denoting a sweet substance derived from insect cocoons) + **-OSE**[2].

trek /trek/ ▸*n.* a long arduous journey, esp. one made on foot: *a trek to the South Pole.* ■ a tourist hike.

▸*v.* (**trekked, trek·king**) [*intrans.*] go on a long arduous journey, typically on foot: *we trekked through the jungle.* ■ *chiefly S. African, historical* migrate or journey with one's belongings by ox-wagon. ■ [*intrans.*] *S. African* (of an ox) draw a vehicle or pull a load. ■ *S. African* travel constantly from place to place; lead a nomadic life: *my plan is to trek about seeing the world.* ▷mid 19th cent.: from South African Dutch *trek* (noun), *trekken* (verb) 'pull, travel.' **—trek·ker** *n.*

Trek·kie /'trekē/ ▸*n.* (*pl.* **-kies**) *informal* a fan of the U.S. science-fiction television program *Star Trek*.

trel·lis /'trelis/ ▸*n.* a framework of light wooden or metal bars, chiefly used as a support for fruit trees or climbing plants.

▸*v.* (**-lised, -lis·ing**) [*trans.*] [usu. as *adj.*] (**trellised**) provide with or enclose in a trellis: *a trellised archway.* ■ support (a climbing plant) with a trellis. ▷late Middle English (denoting any latticed screen): from Old French *trelis*, from Latin *trilix* 'three-ply,' from *tri-* 'three' + *licium* 'warp thread.' Current senses date from the early 16th cent.

trellis

trem /trem/ (also **trem arm**) ▸*n. informal* a tremolo arm.

Trem·a·to·da /,tremə'tōdə; ,trē-/ *Zoology* a class of flatworms that comprises those flukes that are internal parasites. The monogenean flukes are sometimes also placed in this class. See **FLUKE**[2] (sense 1) and **DIGENEAN**. ▷modern Latin (plural), from Greek *trēmatōdēs* 'perforated,' from *trēma* 'hole.' **—trem·a·tode** /'tremə,tōd; 'trē-/ *n.*

trem·ble /'trembəl/ ▸*v.* [*intrans.*] shake involuntarily, typically as a result of anxiety, excitement, or frailty: *Isobel was trembling with excitement.* See note at **SHAKE**. ■ be in a state of extreme apprehension: [with *infinitive*] *I* **tremble to think that** *we could ever return to conditions like these.* ■ [usu. as *adj.*] (**trembling**) (of a person's voice) sound unsteady or hesitant. ■ shake or quiver slightly: *the earth trembled beneath their feet.*

▸*n.* **1** a trembling feeling, movement, or sound: *there was a slight tremble in his voice.* **2** (**the trembles**) *informal* a physical or emotional condition marked by trembling. ■ another term for **MILK SICKNESS**. ▷Middle English (as a verb): from Old French *trembler*, from medieval Latin *tremulare*, from Latin *tremulus* (see **TREMULOUS**). **—trem·bling·ly** /-b(ə)liNGlē/ *adv.*

trem·bler /'tremb(ə)lər/ ▸*n.* **1** *informal* an earthquake. **2** a songbird related to the thrashers, found in the Lesser Antilles and named from its habit of violent shaking. • Genera *Cinclocerthia* and *Ramphocinclus*, family Mimidae: three species.

trem·blor /'tremblər; -,blôr/ ▸*n.* an earth tremor. ▷early 20th cent.: alteration of Spanish *temblor* 'shudder,' influenced by **TREMBLER**.

trem·bly /'tremb(ə)lē/ ▸*adj.* (**-bli·er, -bli·est**) *informal* shaking or quivering involuntarily: *her eyes were tearful, her hands trembly | she gave a queer trembly laugh.*

tre·men·dous /trə'mendəs/ ▸*adj.* very great in amount, scale, or intensity: *Penny put in a tremendous amount of time | there was a tremendous explosion.* ■ *informal* extremely good or impressive; excellent: *the crew did a tremendous job.* ▷mid 17th cent.: from Latin *tremendus* (gerundive of *tremere* 'tremble') + **-OUS**. **—tre·men·dous·ly** *adv.* **—tre·men·dous·ness** *n.*

trem·o·lan·do /,tremə'ländō/ *Music* ▸*n.* (*pl.* **-di** /-dē/) another term for **TREMOLO**.

▸*adv.* & *adj.* (esp. as a direction) with tremolo. ▷Italian, literally 'trembling.'

trem·o·lite /'tremə,līt/ ▸*n.* a white to gray amphibole mineral that is characteristic of metamorphosed dolomitic limestones. ▷late 18th cent.: from *Tremola* Valley, Switzerland, + **-ITE**[1].

trem·o·lo /'tremə,lō/ ▸*n.* (*pl.* **-los**) *Music* a wavering effect in a musical tone, typically produced by rapid reiteration of a note, or sometimes by rapid repeated variation in the pitch of a note or by sounding two notes of slightly different pitches to produce prominent overtones. Compare with **VIBRATO**. ■ a mechanism in an organ producing such an effect. ■ (also **tremolo arm**) a lever on an electric guitar, used to produce such an effect. ▷mid 18th cent.: from Italian.

trem·or /'tremər/ ▸*n.* an involuntary quivering movement: *a disorder that causes tremors and muscle rigidity.* ■ (also **earth tremor**) a slight earthquake. ■ a sudden feeling of fear or excitement: *a tremor of unease.* ■ a tremble or quaver in a person's voice. ▷early 17th cent.: from Latin *tremor*, from *tremere* 'to tremble.'

trem·u·lous /'tremyələs/ ▸*adj.* shaking or quivering slightly: *Barbara's voice was tremulous.* ■ timid; nervous: *he gave a tremulous smile.* ▷early 17th cent.: from Latin *tremulus* (from *tremere* 'tremble') + **-OUS**. **—trem·u·lous·ly** *adv.* **—trem·u·lous·ness** *n.*

tre·nail ▸*n.* British term for **TREENAIL**.

trench /trenCH/ ▸*n.* a long, narrow ditch. ■ such a ditch dug by troops to provide a place of shelter from enemy fire. ■ (**trenches**) a connected system of such ditches forming an army's line. ■ (**the trenches**) the battlefields of northern France and Belgium in World War I: *the slaughter in the trenches created a new cynicism | figurative entry-level teachers are taught the latest classroom techniques by colleagues with experience* **in the trenches**. ■ (also **ocean trench**) a long, narrow, deep depression in the ocean floor, typically one running parallel to a plate boundary and marking a subduction zone.

▸*v.* **1** [*trans.*] dig a trench or trenches in (the ground): *she trenched the terrace to a depth of 6 feet.* ■ turn over the earth of (a field or garden) by digging a succession of adjoining ditches. **2** [*intrans.*] (**trench on/upon**) *archaic* border closely on; encroach upon: *this would surely trench very far on the dignity and liberty of citizens.* ▷late Middle English (in the senses 'track cut through a wood' and 'sever by cutting'): from

T

Old French *trenche* (noun), *trenchier* (verb), based on Latin *truncare* (see TRUNCATE).

trench·ant /ˈtrenCHənt/ ▸*adj.* **1** vigorous or incisive in expression or style: *she heard angry voices, not loud, yet certainly trenchant.* **2** *archaic* or *poetic/literary* (of a weapon or tool) having a sharp edge: *a trenchant blade.* ▷Middle English (sense 2): from Old French, literally 'cutting,' present participle of *trenchier* (see TRENCH). **—trench·an·cy** /-CHənsē/ *n.* (in sense 1). **—trench·ant·ly** *adv.* (in sense 1).

trench coat ▸*n.* a loose, belted, double-breasted raincoat in a military style. ■ a lined or padded waterproof coat worn by soldiers.

trench·er[1] /ˈtrenCHər/ ▸*n.* **1** *historical* a wooden plate or platter for food. ■ a thick slice of bread used as a plate or platter. **2** old-fashioned term for MORTARBOARD (sense 1). ▷Middle English: from Anglo-Norman French *trenchour*, from Old French *trenchier* 'to cut' (see TRENCH).

trench·er[2] ▸*n.* a machine or attachment used in digging trenches.

trench·er·man /ˈtrenCHərmən/ ▸*n.* (*pl.* **-men**) [usu. with *adj.*] *humorous* a person who eats in a specified manner, typically heartily: *he is a hearty trencherman, as befits a man of his girth.*

trench fe·ver ▸*n.* a highly contagious rickettsial disease transmitted by lice, that infected soldiers in the trenches in World War I.

trench foot ▸*n.* a painful condition of the feet caused by long immersion in cold water or mud and marked by blackening and death of surface tissue.

trench mor·tar ▸*n.* a light simple mortar designed to propel a bomb into enemy trenches.

trench mouth ▸*n.* ulcerative gingivitis.

trench war·fare ▸*n.* a type of combat in which opposing troops fight from trenches facing each other.

trend /trend/ ▸*n.* a general direction in which something is developing or changing: *an upward trend in sales and profit margins.* ■ a fashion: *the latest trends in modern dance.*
▸*v.* [*intrans.*] (esp. of geographical features) bend or turn away in a specified direction: *the Richelieu River trending southward to Lake Champlain.* ■ change or develop in a general direction: *unemployment has been trending upward.* ▷Old English *trendan* 'revolve, rotate,' of Germanic origin; compare with TRUNDLE. The verb sense 'turn in a specified direction' dates from the late 16th cent. and gave rise to the figurative use 'assume a general tendency' in the mid 19th cent., a development paralleled in the noun.

Tren·de·len·burg po·si·tion /tren'delən,bərg/ ▸*n.* a position, used for pelvic surgery and to treat shock, in which a patient lies face upward on a tilted table or bed with the pelvis higher than the head. ▷late 19th cent.: named after Friedrich *Trendelenburg* (1844–1924), German surgeon.

trend·i·fy /ˈtrendə,fī/ ▸*v.* [*trans.*] *informal, chiefly derogatory* make (something or someone) very fashionable or up to date in style or influence: *the cafe has been trendified to look like a wine bar.*

trend line ▸*n.* a line indicating the general course or tendency of something, e.g., a geographical feature or a set of points on a graph.

trend·oid /ˈtrendoid/ *informal* ▸*n.* a person who follows fashion blindly or excessively.
▸*adj.* following fashion blindly or extravagantly.

trend·set·ter /ˈtren(d),setər/ ▸*n.* a person who leads the way in fashion or ideas. **—trend·set·ting** /-,setiNG/ *adj.*

trend·y /ˈtrendē/ *informal* ▸*adj.* (**trend·i·er**, **trend·i·est**) very fashionable or up to date in style or influence: *I enjoyed being able to go out and buy trendy clothes.*
▸*n.* (*pl.* **trend·ies**) a person who is very fashionable or up to date. **—trend·i·ly** /-dəlē/ *adv.* **—trend·i·ness** *n.*

Treng·ga·nu /treNGˈgänoo/ (also **Ter·eng·ga·nu** /,tereNG-/) a state of Malaysia, on the eastern coast of the Malay Peninsula; capital, Kuala Trengganu.

Trent /trent/ the chief river in central England. It rises in Staffordshire County and flows northeast for 170 miles (275 km) to join the Ouse River 15 miles (25 km) west of Hull to form the Humber estuary.

Trent, Coun·cil of an ecumenical council of the Roman Catholic Church, held in three sessions between 1545 and 1563 in Trento, Italy. Prompted by the opposition of the Reformation, the council clarified and redefined the church's doctrine, abolished many ecclesiastical abuses, and strengthened the authority of the papacy. These measures provided the church with a solid foundation for the Counter-Reformation.

trente et qua·rante /ˈtränt ā kaˈränt/ ▸*n.* a gambling game in which cards are turned up on a table marked with red and black diamonds. ▷French, literally 'thirty and forty,' these being winning and losing numbers respectively in the game.

Tren·to /ˈtrentō/ a city in northern Italy, on the Adige River; pop. 102,000.

Tren·ton /ˈtrentn/ the capital of New Jersey, in the west central part of the state; pop. 85,403.

tre·pan /trəˈpan/ ▸*n. chiefly historical* a trephine (hole saw) used by surgeons for perforating the skull.
▸*v.* (**-panned, -pan·ning**) [*trans.*] perforate (a person's skull) with a trepan. ▷late Middle English: the noun via medieval Latin from Greek *trupanon*, from *trupan* 'to bore,' from *trupē* 'hole'; the verb from Old French *trepaner*. **—trep·a·na·tion** /,trepəˈnāSHən/ *n.*

tre·pang /trəˈpaNG/ ▸*n.* another term for BÊCHE-DE-MER (sense 1). ▷late 18th cent.: from Malay *teripang*.

tre·phine /triˈfīn/ ▸*n.* a hole saw used in surgery to remove a circle of tissue or bone.
▸*v.* [*trans.*] operate on with a trephine. ▷early 17th cent.: from Latin *tres fines* 'three ends,' apparently influenced by TREPAN. **—treph·i·na·tion** /,trefəˈnāSHən/ *n.*

trep·i·da·tion /,trepiˈdāSHən/ ▸*n.* **1** a feeling of fear or agitation about something that may happen: *the men set off in fear and trepidation.* **2** *archaic* trembling motion. ▷late 15th cent.: from Latin *trepidatio(n-)*, from *trepidare* 'be agitated, tremble,' from *trepidus* 'alarmed.' **—trep·i·da·tious** /-SHəs/ *adj.*

trep·o·ne·me /ˈtrepə,nēm/ (also **trep·o·ne·ma** /,trepəˈnēmə/) ▸*n.* a spirochete bacterium that is parasitic or pathogenic in humans and warm-blooded animals, including the causal agents of syphilis and yaws. • Genus *Treponema*, order Spirochaetales; Gram-negative. ▷early 20th cent.: from modern Latin *Treponema*, from Greek *trepein* 'to turn' + *nēma* 'thread.' **—trep·o·ne·mal** /-ˈnēməl/ *adj.*

très /trā/ ▸*adv.* (usually with reference to a fashionable quality) very: *très macho, très chic.* ▷French.

tres·pass /ˈtrespəs; -,pas/ ▸*v.* [*intrans.*] **1** enter the owner's land or property without permission: *there is no excuse for* ***trespassing on*** *railroad property.* ■ (**trespass on**) make unfair claims on or take advantage of (something): *she really must not trespass on his hospitality.* **2** (**trespass against**) *archaic* or *poetic/literary* commit an offense against (a person or a set of rules): *a man who had trespassed against Judaic law.*
▸*n.* **1** *Law* entry to a person's land or property without their permission: *the defendants were guilty of trespass | a mass trespass on the hills.* **2** *archaic* or *poetic/literary* a sin; an offense: *the worst trespass against the goddess Venus is to see her naked and asleep.* ▷Middle English (sense 2): from Old French *trespasser* 'pass over, trespass,' *trespas* 'passing across,' from medieval Latin *transpassare* (see TRANS-, PASS[1]). **—tres·pass·er** *n.*

tress /tres/ ▸*n.* (usu. **tresses**) a long lock of a woman's hair: *she was tugging a comb through her long tresses.*
▸*v.* [*trans.*] *archaic* arrange (a person's hair) into long locks. ▷Middle English: from Old French *tresse*, perhaps based on Greek *trikha* 'threefold.' **—tressed** *adj.* [often in *combination*] *a blonde-tressed sex symbol.* **—tress·y** *adj.*

tres·sure /ˈtreSHər/ ▸*n. Heraldry* a thin border inset from the edge of a shield, narrower than an orle and usually borne double. ■ an ornamental enclosure containing a figure or distinctive device, formerly found on various gold and silver coins. ▷Middle English (denoting a ribbon or band for the hair): from Old French *tressour* (see TRESS).

tres·tle /ˈtresəl/ ▸*n.* a framework consisting of a horizontal beam supported by two pairs of sloping legs, used in pairs to support a flat surface such as a tabletop. ■ (also **tres·tle·work**) an open cross-braced framework used to support an elevated structure such as a bridge. ■ short for TRESTLE TABLE. ■ (also **tres·tle·tree**) each of a pair of horizontal pieces on a sailing ship's lower mast supporting the topmast. ▷Middle English: from Old French *trestel*, based on Latin *transtrum* 'beam.'

tres·tle ta·ble ▸*n.* a table consisting of a board or boards laid on trestles.

tret /tret/ ▸*n. historical* an allowance of extra weight made to purchasers of certain goods to compensate for waste during transportation. ▷late 15th cent: from an Old French variant of *trait* 'act of dragging' (see TRAIT).

tre·tin·o·in /trəˈtinō-in/ ▸*n.* a drug related to retinol (Vitamin A), used as a topical ointment in the treatment of acne and other disorders of the skin.

tre·val·ly /trəˈvalē/ ▸*n.* (*pl.* **-lies**) a marine sporting fish of the Indo-Pacific that is sometimes caught in large quantities for food. • *Caranx* and other genera, family Carangidae: several species. ▷late 19th cent.: probably an alteration of *cavally* 'horse mackerel,' from Spanish *caballo* 'horse.'

Trèves /trev/ French name for TRIER.

Tre·vi Foun·tain /ˈtrevē/ the largest and most famous of the fountains of Rome, situated at the intersection of three roads, built in 1735 by architect Nicola Salvi (1697–1751), and decorated by artists of the Bernini school. ▷from Italian *tri vie* 'three roads.'

Trevi Fountain

Tre·vi·no /trəˈvēnō/, Lee (Buck) (1939–), U.S. golfer; known as **Supermex**. In 1971, he became the first man to win the Canadian, U.S., and British open championships in the same year. His other championship titles include the 1974 and 1984 PGA, the 1968 U.S. Open, and the 1972 British Open.

Trev·i·thick /trəˈviTHik/, Richard (1771–1833), English engineer. He built the world's first railroad locomotive in 1804.

Trev·or /ˈtrevər/, Sarah see TEASDALE.

trews /trooz/ ▸*plural n. chiefly Brit.* trousers. ■ close-fitting tartan trousers worn by certain Scottish regiments. ▷mid 16th cent.: from Irish *triús*, Scottish Gaelic *triubhas* (singular); compare with TROUSERS.

trey /trā/ ▸*n.* (*pl.* **treys**) a thing having three of something, in particular: ■ (in basketball) a shot scoring three points. ■ a playing card or die with three spots. ▷late Middle English: from Old French *trei* 'three,' from Latin *tres*.

trey·fa /ˈtrāfə/ (also **treyf**) /ˈtrāf/ ▸*adj.* another term for TRAYF.

TRH ▸*abbr.* ■ Their Royal Highnesses. ■ *Biochemistry* thyrotropin-releasing hormone.

tri- ▸*comb. form* three; having three: *triathlon.* ■ *Chemistry* (in names of compounds) containing three atoms or groups of a specified kind: *trichloroethane.* ▷from Latin and Greek, from Latin *tres*, Greek *treis* 'three.'

USAGE See usage at TER-.

tri·a·ble /ˈtrīəbəl/ ▸*adj. Law* (of an offense) liable to a judicial trial. ■ (of a case or issue) able to be investigated and decided judicially. ▷late Middle English: from Anglo-Norman French, from Old French *trier* 'sift' (see TRY).

tri·ac /ˈtrīak/ ▸*n. Electronics* a three-electrode semiconductor device that will conduct in either direction when triggered by a positive or negative signal at the gate electrode. ▷1960s: from TRIODE + AC (short for *alternating current*).

tri·ac·e·tate /trīˈasi,tāt/ (also **cellulose triacetate**) ▸*n.* a form of cellulose acetate containing three acetate groups per glucose monomer, used as a basis for man-made fibers.

tri·ad /ˈtrī,ad/ ▸*n.* **1** a group or set of three connected people or things: *the triad of medication, diet, and exercise are necessary in diabetes care.* ■ a chord of three musical notes, consisting of a given note with the third and fifth above it. ■ a Welsh form of literary composition with an arrangement of subjects or statements in groups of three. **2** (also **Triad**) a secret society originating in China, typically involved in organized crime. ■ a member of such a society. ▷mid 16th cent.: from French *triade*, or via late Latin from Greek *trias, triad-*, from *treis* 'three.' **—tri·ad·ic** /trīˈadik/ *adj.* (in sense 1).

tri·age /trēˈäZH; ˈtrē,äZH/ ▸*n.* **1** the action of sorting according to quality. **2** (in medical use) the assignment of degrees of urgency to wounds or illnesses to decide the order of treatment of a large number of patients or casualties.

▸*v.* [*trans.*] assign degrees of urgency to (wounded or ill patients). ▷early 18th cent.: from French, from *trier* 'separate out.' The medical sense dates from the 1930s, from the military system of assessing the wounded on the battlefield.

tri·al /ˈtrī(ə)l/ ▸*n.* **1** a formal examination of evidence by a judge, typically before a jury, in order to decide guilt in a case of criminal or civil proceedings: *the newspaper accounts of the trial | the editor was summoned to* ***stand trial*** *for libel.* **2** a test of the performance, qualities, or suitability of someone or something: *clinical trials must establish whether the new hip replacements are working.* ■ an athletic contest to test the ability of players eligible for selection to a team. ■ (**trials**) an event in which horses, dogs, or other animals compete or perform: *horse trials.* **3** a person, thing, or situation that tests a person's endurance or forbearance: ***the trials and tribulations*** *of married life.*

▸*v.* (**tri·aled**, **tri·al·ing**; *Brit.* **tri·alled**, **tri·al·ling**) **1** [*trans.*] test (something, esp. a new product) to assess its suitability or performance: *all seeds are carefully trialed in a variety of growing conditions.* **2** [*intrans.*] (of a horse, dog, or other animal) compete in trials: *the pup trialed on Saturday.* ▷late Middle English (as a noun): from Anglo-Norman French, or from medieval Latin *triallum*. The verb dates from the 1980s.

▸*PHRASES* □ **on trial** being tried in a court of law. □ **trial and error** the process of experimenting with various methods of doing something until one finds the most successful.

tri·al bal·ance ▸*n.* a statement of all debits and credits in a double-entry account book, with any disagreement indicating an error.

tri·al bal·loon ▸*n.* a tentative measure taken or statement made to see how a new policy will be received. ▷1930s: a translation of French *ballon d'essai*.

tri·al court ▸*n.* a court of law where cases are tried in the first place, as opposed to an appeals court.

tri·al·ist /ˈtrīəlist/ ▸*n.* a person who participates in a trial, in particular: ■ a person who takes part in a sports trial or motorcycle trial. ■ a person who takes part in a clinical or market test of a new product.

tri·al law·yer ▸*n.* a lawyer who practices in a trial court.

tri·a·logue /ˈtrīəˌlôg; -ˌläg/ ▸*n.* a dialogue between three people. ▷mid 16th cent.: formed irregularly from TRI- 'three' + DIALOGUE (*di-* being misinterpreted as 'two').

tri·al run ▸*n.* a test of the operation of a new system or product.

tri·an·gle /ˈtrīˌaNGgəl/ ▸*n.* a plane figure with three straight sides and three angles: *an equilateral triangle.* ■ a thing shaped like such a figure: *a small triangle of grass.* ■ a situation involving three people or things, esp. an emotional relationship involving a couple and a third person with whom one of them is involved. ■ a musical instrument consisting of a steel rod bent into a triangle and sounded by being struck with a small steel rod. ■ a frame used to position the balls in pool and snooker. ■ a drawing instrument in the form of a right triangle. ■ (**triangles**) *historical* a frame of three halberds joined at the top to which a soldier was bound for flogging. ▷late Middle English: from Old French *triangle* or Latin *triangulum*, neuter of *triangulus* 'three-cornered' (see TRI-, ANGLE[1]).

tri·an·gle of forc·es ▸*n. Physics* a triangle whose sides represent in magnitude and direction three forces in equilibrium.

tri·an·gu·lar /trīˈaNGgyələr/ ▸*adj.* shaped like a triangle; having three sides and three corners: *dainty triangular sandwiches.* ■ involving three people or parties: *a triangular relationship.* ■ (of a pyramid) having a three-sided base. ▷mid 16th cent.: from late Latin *triangularis*, from Latin *triangulum* (see TRIANGLE). —**tri·an·gu·lar·i·ty** /trīˌaNGgyəˈlaritē/ *n.* —**tri·an·gu·lar·ly** *adv.*

tri·an·gu·lar num·ber ▸*n.* any of the series of numbers (1, 3, 6, 10, 15, etc.) obtained by continued summation of the natural numbers 1, 2, 3, 4, 5, etc.

tri·an·gu·lar trade ▸*n.* a multilateral system of trading in which a country pays for its imports from one country by its exports to another. ■ used to refer to the trade in the eighteenth and nineteenth centuries that involved shipping goods from Britain to West Africa to be exchanged for slaves, these slaves being shipped to the West Indies and exchanged for sugar, rum, and other commodities, which were in turn shipped back to Britain.

tri·an·gu·late /trīˈaNGgyəˌlāt/ ▸*v.* **1** [*trans.*] divide (an area) into triangles for surveying purposes. ■ measure and map (an area) by the use of triangles with a known base length and base angles. ■ determine (a height, distance, or location) in this way. **2** [*trans.*] form into a triangle or triangles: *the brackets triangulate the frame.* ▷mid 19th cent.: from Latin *triangulum* 'triangle' (see TRIANGLE) + -ATE[3].

tri·an·gu·la·tion /ˌtrīˌaNGgyəˈlāSHən/ ▸*n.* **1** (in surveying) the tracing and measurement of a series or network of triangles in order to determine the distances and relative positions of points spread over a territory or region, esp. by measuring the length of one side of each triangle and deducing its angles and the length of the other two sides by observation from this baseline. **2** formation of or division into triangles.

tri·an·gu·la·tion point ▸*n.* a reference point on high ground used in surveying, typically marked by a small pillar.

Tri·an·gu·lum /trīˈaNGgyələm/ *Astronomy* a small northern constellation (the Triangle), between Andromeda and Aries. ■ [as *genitive*] (**Trianguli** /-gyəˌlī/) used with a preceding letter or numeral to designate a star in this constellation: *the star Beta Trianguli.* ▷Latin.

Tri·an·gu·lum Aus·tra·le /ôˈstrālē/ *Astronomy* a small southern constellation (the Southern Triangle), lying in the Milky Way near the south celestial pole. ■ [as *genitive*] (**Trianguli Australis** /trīˈaNGgyəˌlī ôˈstrālis/) used with a preceding letter or numeral to designate a star in this constellation: *the star Alpha Trianguli Australis.* ▷Latin.

Tri·a·non /ˈtrēəˌnän/ either of two small palaces in the great park at Versailles in France. The larger was built by Louis XIV in 1687; the smaller, built by Louis XV 1762–68, was used first by his mistress Madame du Barry (1743–93) and afterward by Marie Antoinette.

Tri·as·sic /trīˈasik/ ▸*adj. Geology* of, relating to, or denoting the earliest period of the Mesozoic era, between the Permian and Jurassic periods. See also PERMO–TRIASSIC. ■ [as *n.*] (**the Triassic** or **the Trias**) the Triassic period or the system of rocks deposited during it.

> The Triassic lasted from about 245 million to 208 million years ago. Many new organisms appeared following the mass extinctions of the end of the Paleozoic era, including the earliest dinosaurs and ammonites and the first primitive mammals.

▷mid 19th cent.: from late Latin *trias* (see TRIAD), because the strata are divisible into three groups, + -IC.

tri·ath·lon /trīˈaTHlən; -ˌlän/ ▸*n.* an athletic contest consisting of three different events, typically swimming, cycling, and long-distance running. ▷1970s: from TRI- 'three,' on the pattern of *decathlon*. —**tri·ath·lete** /-ˌlēt/ *n.*

tri·a·tom·ic /ˌtrīəˈtämik/ ▸*adj. Chemistry* consisting of three atoms.

tri·ax·i·al /trīˈaksēəl/ ▸*adj.* having or relating to three axes, esp. in mechanical or astronomical contexts.

tri·a·zine /ˈtrīəˌzēn/ ▸*n. Chemistry* any of a group of compounds whose molecules contain an unsaturated ring of three carbon and three nitrogen atoms.

tri·a·zole /ˈtrīəˌzōl; trīˈazôl/ ▸*n.* any compound whose molecule contains a ring of three nitrogen and two carbon atoms, in particular each of five isomeric compounds containing such a ring with two double bonds. • Chem. formula: $C_2H_3N_3$.

trib. ▸*abbr.* tributary.

trib·ade /ˈtribəd/ ▸*n.* a lesbian, esp. one who lies on top of her partner and simulates the movements of the male in heterosexual intercourse. ▷early 17th cent.: from French *tribade*, or via Latin from Greek *tribas*, from *tribein* 'to rub.' —**trib·a·dism** /-ˌdizəm/ *n.*

trib·al /ˈtrībəl/ ▸*adj.* of or characteristic of a tribe or tribes: *tribal people in Malaysia.* ■ *chiefly derogatory* characterized by a tendency to form groups or by strong group loyalty: *British industrial operatives remained locked in primitive tribal attitudes.*

▸*n.* (**tribals**) members of tribal communities, esp. in the Indian subcontinent. —**trib·al·ly** *adv.*

trib·al·ism /ˈtrībəˌlizəm/ ▸*n.* the state or fact of being organized in a tribe or tribes: *black tribalism became the excuse for creating ethnic homelands.* ■ *chiefly derogatory* the behavior and attitudes that stem from strong loyalty to one's own tribe or social group: *an ethnic group demanding the paraphernalia of campus tribalism.*

trib·al·ist /ˈtrībəlist/ ▸*n. chiefly derogatory* an advocate or practitioner of strong loyalty to one's own tribe or social group. —**tri·bal·is·tic** /ˌtrībəˈlistik/ *adj.*

tri·ba·sic /trīˈbāsik/ ▸*adj. Chemistry* (of an acid) having three replaceable hydrogen atoms.

tribe /trīb/ ▸*n.* **1** a social division in a traditional society consisting of families or communities linked by social, economic, religious, or blood ties, with a common culture and dialect, typically having a recognized leader: *indigenous Indian tribes | the Celtic tribes of Europe.* ■ (in ancient Rome) each of several political divisions, originally three, later thirty, ultimately thirty-five. ■ *informal* family: *the entire tribe is coming for Thanksgiving.* ■ *derogatory* a distinctive close-knit social or political group: *she made a stand against the social codes of her English middle-class tribe.* ■ *derogatory* a group or class of people or things: *an outburst against the whole tribe of theoreticians.* ■ (often **tribes**) *informal* large numbers of people or animals: *tribes of children playing under the watchful eyes of nurses.* **2** *Biology* a taxonomic category that ranks above genus and below family or subfamily, usually ending in *-ini* (in zoology) or *-eae* (in botany). ▷Middle English: from Old French *tribu* or Latin *tribus* (singular and plural); perhaps related to *tri-* 'three' and referring to the three divisions of the early people of Rome.

Tri·Be·Ca /trīˈbekə/ a residential and commercial section of southern Manhattan in New York City, noted for its factory lofts converted into apartments. Its name is derived from *Tri*angle *Be*low *Ca*nal Street.

tribes·man /ˈtrībzmən/ ▸*n.* (*pl.* **-men**) a man belonging to a tribe in a traditional society or group.

Tribes of Is·ra·el the twelve divisions of ancient Israel, each traditionally descended from one of the twelve sons of Jacob. Ten of the tribes (Asher, Dan, Gad, Issachar, Levi, Manasseh, Naphtali, Reuben, Simeon, and Zebulun, known as the **Lost Tribes**) were deported to captivity in Assyria *c.*720 BC, leaving only the tribes of Judah and Benjamin. Also called TWELVE TRIBES OF ISRAEL.

tribes·peo·ple /ˈtrībzˌpēpəl/ ▸*plural n.* people belonging to a tribe in a traditional society or group.

tribes·wom·an /ˈtrībzˌwo͝omən/ ▸*n.* (*pl.* **-wom·en**) a woman belonging to a tribe in a traditional society or group.

tribo- ▸*comb. form* relating to friction: *triboelectricity.* ▷from Greek *tribos* 'rubbing.'

tri·bo·e·lec·tric·i·ty /ˌtrībō-iləkˈtrisitē; -ˌēlek-/ ▸*n.* electric charge generated by friction.

tri·bol·o·gy /trīˈbäləjē/ ▸*n.* the study of friction, wear, lubrication, and the design of bearings; the science of interacting surfaces in relative motion. —**tri·bo·log·i·cal** /-bəˈläjikəl/ *adj.* —**tri·bol·o·gist** /-jist/ *n.*

tri·bo·lu·mi·nes·cence /ˌtrībōˌlo͞oməˈnesəns/ ▸*n.* the emission of light from a substance caused by rubbing, scratching, or similar frictional contact. —**tri·bo·lu·mi·nes·cent** *adj.*

tri·bom·e·ter /trīˈbämitər/ ▸*n.* an instrument for measuring friction in sliding.

Tri·bor·ough Bridge /ˈtrībərō/ a bridge complex that opened in 1936 that links the Bronx, Queens, and Manhattan boroughs in New York City.

tri·brach /ˈtrīˌbrak/ ▸*n. Prosody* a metrical foot of three short or unstressed syllables. ▷late 16th cent.: via Latin from Greek *tribrakhus*, from *tri-* 'three' + *brakhus* 'short.' —**tri·brach·ic** /trīˈbrakik/ *adj.*

trib·u·la·tion /ˌtribyəˈlāSHən/ ▸*n.* (usu. **tribulations**) a cause of great trouble or suffering: *the tribulations of being a megastar.* ■ a state of great trouble or suffering: *his time of tribulation was just beginning.* ■ (**the tribulation** or **the Great Tribulation**) *Christian Theology* a period of great suffering expected during the end times. ▷Middle English: via Old French from ecclesiastical Latin *tribulatio(n-)*, from Latin *tribulare* 'press, oppress,' from *tribulum* 'threshing board (constructed of sharp points),' based on *terere* 'rub.'

tri·bu·nal /trīˈbyo͞onl; trə-/ ▸*n.* a court of justice: *an international war crimes tribunal.* ■ a seat or bench for a judge or judges. ▷late Middle English (denoting a seat for judges): from Old French, or from Latin *tribunal* 'raised platform provided for magistrates' seats,' from *tribunus* (see TRIBUNE[1]).

trib·une[1] /ˈtribyo͞on; triˈbyo͞on/ ▸*n.* (also **tribune of the people**) an official in ancient Rome chosen by the plebeians to protect their interests. ■ (also **military tribune**) a Roman legionary officer. ■ *figurative* a popular leader; a champion of the people. ■ used in names of newspapers: *the Chicago Tribune.* ▷late

Middle English: from Latin *tribunus*, literally 'head of a tribe,' from *tribus* 'tribe.' **—trib·u·nate** /'tribyənit; trī'byo͞onit; -ˌnāt/ *n.* **—trib·une·ship** /-ˌSHip/ *n.*

trib·une[2] ▸*n.* **1** an apse in a basilica. **2** a dais or rostrum, esp. in a church. ■ a raised area or gallery with seats, esp. in a church. ▷mid 17th cent. (denoting the principal room in an Italian mansion): via French from Italian, from medieval Latin *tribuna*, alteration of Latin *tribunal* (see TRIBUNAL).

trib·u·tar·y /'tribyəˌterē/ ▸*n.* (*pl.* **-tar·ies**) **1** a river or stream flowing into a larger river or lake: *the Illinois River, a tributary of the Mississippi.* **2** *historical* a person or state that pays tribute to another state or ruler: *tributaries of the Chinese empire.* ▷late Middle English (sense 2): from Latin *tributarius*, from *tributum* (see TRIBUTE). Sense 1 dates from the early 19th cent.

trib·ute /'tribyo͞ot/ ▸*n.* **1** an act, statement, or gift that is intended to show gratitude, respect, or admiration: *the video is a tribute to the musicals of the '40s | a symposium organized to* ***pay tribute to*** *Darwin.* ■ [in *sing.*] something resulting from something else and indicating its worth: *his victory in the championship was* ***a tribute to*** *his persistence.* **2** *historical* payment made periodically by one state or ruler to another, esp. as a sign of dependence: *the king had at his disposal plunder and tribute amassed through warfare.* **3** *historical* a proportion of ore or its equivalent, paid to a miner for his work, or to the owner or lessor of a mine. ▷late Middle English (sense 2): from Latin *tributum*, neuter past participle (used as a noun) of *tribuere* 'assign' (originally 'divide between tribes'), from *tribus* 'tribe.'

tri·cam·er·al /trī'kamərəl/ ▸*adj.* of or relating to the parliamentary system operating in South Africa between 1983 and 1994, in which the legislature consisted of three ethnically based houses.

tri·car·box·yl·ic ac·id cy·cle /ˌtrīkärbäk'silik/ ▸*n.* another term for KREBS CYCLE.

trice /trīs/ ▸*n.* (in phrase **in a trice**) in a moment; very quickly. ▷late Middle English *trice* 'a tug,' figuratively 'an instant,' from Middle Dutch *trīsen* 'pull sharply,' related to *trīse* 'pulley.'

tri·cen·ten·ar·y /trī'sentnˌerē; ˌtrīsen'tenərē/ ▸*n.* (*pl.* **-ar·ies**) another term for TRICENTENNIAL.

tri·cen·ten·ni·al /ˌtrīsen'tenēəl/ ▸*n.* the three-hundredth anniversary of a significant event.
▸*adj.* of or relating to a three-hundredth anniversary: *the tricentennial year.*

tri·ceps /'trīˌseps/ ▸*n.* (*pl.* same) *Anatomy* any of several muscles having three points of attachment at one end, particularly (also **tri·ceps bra·chi·i** /'brākēˌī; -kēˌē; 'brak-/) the large muscle at the back of the upper arm. ▷late 16th cent.: from Latin, literally 'three-headed,' from *tri-* 'three' + *-ceps* (from *caput* 'head').

tri·cer·a·tops /trī'serəˌtäps/ ▸*n.* a large quadrupedal herbivorous dinosaur living at the end of the Cretaceous period, having a massive head with two large horns, a smaller horn on the beaked snout, and a bony frill above the neck. • Genus *Triceratops*, infraorder Ceratopsia, order Ornithischia. ▷modern Latin, from Greek *trikeratos* 'three-horned' + *ōps* 'face.'

tri·chi·a·sis /tri'kīəsis/ ▸*n.* *Medicine* ingrowth or introversion of the eyelashes. ▷mid 17th cent.: via late Latin from Greek *trikhiasis*, from *trikhian* 'be hairy.'

tri·chi·na /tri'kīnə/ ▸*n.* (*pl.* **-nae** /-nē/) a parasitic nematode worm of humans and other mammals, the adults of which live in the small intestine. The larvae form hard cysts in the muscles, where they remain until eaten by the next host. • Genus *Trichinella*, class Aphasmida (or Adenophorea). ▷mid 19th cent.: from modern Latin (former genus name), from Greek *trikhinos* 'of hair.'

Trich·i·nop·o·ly /ˌtrikə'näpəlē; ˌtriCH-/ another name for TIRUCHIRAPALLI.

trich·i·no·sis /ˌtrikə'nōsis/ ▸*n.* a disease caused by trichinae, typically from infected meat, esp. pork, characterized by digestive disturbance, fever, and muscular rigidity. • This disease is typically caused by *Trichinella spiralis*.

tri·chlor·an·i·sole /ˌtrīklôr'anəˌōl/ ▸*n.* a chemical released by a fungus whose smell is detectable in minute concentrations. It is responsible for the musty smell that taints wines bottled with infected corks. (abbr. **TCA**.)

tri·chlo·ro·a·ce·tic ac·id /trīˌklôrōə'sētik/ (also **tri·chlor·a·ce·tic acid** /-ˌklôrə'setik/) ▸*n.* *Chemistry* a toxic deliquescent crystalline solid used as a solvent, analgesic, and anesthetic. • Chem. formula: CCl_3COOH. **—tri·chlo·ro·ac·e·tate** /-'asiˌtāt/ *n.*

tri·chlo·ro·eth·ane /trīˌklôrō'eTHān/ ▸*n.* *Chemistry* a colorless, nonflammable volatile liquid, used as a solvent and cleaner. • Alternative name: **1,1,1-trichloroethane**; chem. formula: CCl_3CH_3.

tri·chlo·ro·eth·yl·ene /trīˌklôrō'eTHəˌlēn/ ▸*n.* *Chemistry* a colorless volatile liquid used as a solvent and formerly as an anesthetic. • Chem. formula: $CCl_2{=}CHCl$.

tri·chlo·ro·phe·nol /trīˌklôrō'fēnôl; -nōl/ ▸*n.* *Chemistry* a synthetic crystalline compound used as an insecticide and preservative and in the synthesis of pesticides. • Chem. formula: $C_6H_2Cl_3(OH)$; six isomers.

tricho- ▸*comb. form* of or relating to hair: *trichology.* ▷from Greek *thrix, trikhos* 'hair.'

trich·o·cyst /'trikəˌsist/ ▸*n.* *Biology* any of numerous minute, rodlike structures, each containing a protrusible filament, found near the surface of ciliates and dinoflagellates.

tri·chol·o·gy /tri'käləjē/ ▸*n.* the branch of medical and cosmetic study and practice concerned with the hair and scalp. **—trich·o·log·i·cal** /ˌtrikə'läjikəl/ *adj.* **—tri·chol·o·gist** /-jist/ *n.*

trich·ome /'trīˌkōm; 'trikōm/ ▸*n.* *Botany* a small hair or other outgrowth from the epidermis of a plant, typically unicellular and glandular. ▷late 19th cent.: from Greek *trikhōma*, from *trikhoun* 'cover with hair.'

trich·o·mon·ad /ˌtrikə'mänad; -'mō-/ ▸*n.* *Zoology* & *Medicine* a parasitic protozoan with four to six flagella and an undulating membrane, infesting the urogenital or digestive system. • Order Trichomonadida, phylum Parabasilia, kingdom Protista. ▷mid 19th cent.: from modern Latin *Trichomonadida* (plural), from Greek *thrix, trikh-* 'hair' + *monas, monad-* 'unit.' **—trich·o·mon·al** /-'mänl; -'mōnl/ *adj.*

trich·o·mo·ni·a·sis /ˌtrikəmə'nīəsis/ ▸*n.* *Medicine* an infection caused by parasitic trichomonads, chiefly affecting the urinary tract, vagina, or digestive system. • Genus *Trichomonas*, in particular *T. vaginalis* (in the reproductive tract) and *T. hominis* (in the large intestine).

Tri·chop·ter·a /trī'käptərə/ *Entomology* an order of insects that comprises the caddisflies. ■ [as *plural n.*] (**trichoptera**) insects of this order. ▷modern Latin (plural), from TRICHO- 'hair' + Greek *pteron* 'wing.' **—tri·chop·ter·an** *n.* & *adj.*

tri·chot·o·my /trī'kätəmē/ ▸*n.* (*pl.* **-mies**) a division into three categories: *the pragmatics–semantics–syntax trichotomy.* ■ the division of the human person into body, soul, and spirit. ▷17th cent.: from Greek *trikha* 'threefold,' from *treis* 'three,' on the pattern of *dichotomy.* **—tri·chot·o·mous** /-məs/ *adj.*

tri·chro·ic /trī'krōik/ ▸*adj.* *Crystallography* (of a crystal) appearing with different colors when viewed along the three crystallographic directions. ▷late 19th cent.: from Greek *trikhroos* (from *tri-* 'three' + *khrōs* 'color') + -IC. **—tri·chro·ism** /'trīkrəˌwizəm/ *n.*

tri·chro·mat·ic /ˌtrīkrō'matik/ ▸*adj.* having or using three colors. ■ having normal color vision, which is sensitive to all three primary colors. **—tri·chro·ma·tism** /-'krōməˌtizəm/ *n.*

tri·chrome /'trīˌkrōm/ ▸*adj.* *Biology* denoting a stain or method of histological staining in which different tissues are stained, each in one of three different colors. ▷early 20th cent.: from TRI- 'three' + Greek *khrōma* 'color.'

trick /trik/ ▸*n.* **1** a cunning or skillful act or scheme intended to deceive or outwit someone: *he's a double-dealer capable of any mean trick.* ■ a mischievous practical joke: *she thought Elaine was* ***playing*** *some* ***trick on*** *her.* ■ a skillful act performed for entertainment or amusement: *he did conjuring tricks for his daughters.* ■ an illusion: *I thought I saw a flicker of emotion, but it was probably* ***a trick of the light.*** ■ a clever or particular way of doing something: *the trick is to put one ski forward and kneel.* **2** a peculiar or characteristic habit or mannerism: *she had a trick of clipping off certain words and phrases.* **3** (in bridge, whist, and similar card games) a sequence of cards forming a single round of play. One card is laid down by each player, the highest card being the winner. **4** *informal* a prostitute's client. **5** a sailor's turn at the helm, usually lasting for two or four hours.
▸*v.* [*trans.*] **1** (often **be tricked**) deceive or outwit (someone) by being cunning or skillful: *buyers can be tricked by savvy sellers.* ■ (**trick someone into**) use deception to make someone do (something): *he tricked her into parting with the money.* ■ (**trick someone out of**) use deception to deprive someone of (something): *the king was tricked out of his land.* **2** *Heraldry* sketch (a coat of arms) in outline, with the colors indicated by letters or signs.
▸*phrasal v.* □ **trick someone/something out** (or **up**) (usu. **be tricked out**) dress or decorate someone or something in an elaborate or showy way: *a Marine* ***tricked out*** *in World War II kit and weaponry.* ▷late 15th cent.: perhaps associated with obsolete French *s'estriquer.*
▸*adj.* [*attrib.*] **1** intended or used to deceive or mystify, or to create an illusion: *a trick question.* **2** liable to fail; defective: *a trick knee.* ▷late Middle English (as a noun): from an Old French dialect variant of *triche*, from *trichier* 'deceive,' of unknown origin. Current senses of the verb date from the mid 16th cent. **—trick·er** *n.* **—trick·ish** *adj.* (*dated*).
▸*PHRASES* □ **do the trick** *informal* achieve the required result. □ **every trick in the book** *informal* every available method of achieving what one wants. □ **how's tricks?** *informal* used as a friendly greeting: *"How's tricks in your neck of the woods?"* □ **not miss a trick** see MISS[1]. □ **the oldest trick in the book** a ruse so hackneyed that it should no longer deceive anyone. □ **trick or treat** a children's custom of calling at houses at Halloween with the threat of pranks if they are not given a small gift (often used as a greeting by children doing this). □ **tricks of the trade** special ingenious techniques used in a profession or craft, esp. those that are little known by outsiders. □ **turn a trick** *informal* (of a prostitute) have a session with a client. □ **up to one's (old) tricks** *informal* misbehaving in a characteristic way.

trick cy·clist ▸*n.* *Brit., informal* used as a humorous euphemism for a psychiatrist.

trick·er·y /'trikərē/ ▸*n.* (*pl.* **-er·ies**) the practice of deception: *the dealer resorted to trickery.*

trick·le /'trikəl/ ▸*v.* [*intrans.*] (of a liquid) flow in a small stream: *a solitary tear trickled down her cheek* | [as *adj.*] (**trickling**) *a trickling brook.* ■ [*trans.*] cause (a liquid) to flow in a small stream: *he trickled the vodka onto the rocks.* ■ come or go slowly or gradually: *the details began to trickle out.*
▸*phrasal v.* □ **trickle down** (of wealth) gradually benefit the poorest as a result of the increasing wealth of the richest.
▸*n.* a small flow of liquid: *a trickle of blood.* ■ a small group or number of people or things moving slowly: *the traffic had dwindled to a trickle.* ▷Middle English (as a verb): imitative.

trick·le charg·er ▸*n.* a battery charger that produces a very small current.

trick·le-down ▸*adj.* (of an economic system) in which the poorest gradually benefit as a result of the increasing wealth of the richest.

trick·le ir·ri·ga·tion ▸*n.* the supply of a controlled flow of water to a number of points in a cultivated area.

trick·ster /'trikstər/ ▸*n.* a person who cheats or deceives people.

trick·sy /'triksē/ ▸*adj.* (**-si·er, -si·est**) clever in an ingenious or deceptive way: *a typically tricksy beginning to his latest venture.* ■ (of a person) playful or mischievous. **—trick·si·ly** /-səlē/ *adv.* **—trick·si·ness** *n.*

trick·y /'trikē/ ▸*adj.* (**trick·i·er, trick·i·est**) (of a task, problem, or situation) requiring care and skill because difficult or awkward: *applying eyeliner can be a tricky business | some things are very tricky to explain.* ■ (of a person or act) deceitful, crafty, or skillful. **—trick·i·ly** /'trikəlē/ *adv.* **—trick·i·ness** *n.*

tri·clad /'trīˌklad/ ▸*n.* *Zoology* a free-living flatworm of an order characterized by having a gut with three branches, including the planarians. • Order Tricladida, class Turbellaria. ▷late 19th cent.: from modern Latin *Tricladida*, from TRI- 'three' + Greek *klados* 'branch.'

tri·clin·ic /trī'klinik/ ▸*adj.* of or denoting a crystal system or three-dimensional geometric arrangement having three unequal oblique axes. ▷mid 19th cent.: from Greek TRI- 'three' + *-clinic*, on the pattern of *monoclinic.*

tri·clin·i·um /trī'klinēəm/ ▸*n.* (*pl.* **-clin·i·a** /-'klinēə/) a dining table with couches along three sides used in ancient Rome. ■ a room containing such a table. ▷Latin, from Greek *triklinion*, from *tri-* 'three' + *klinē* 'couch.'

tri·col·or /'trīˌkələr/ (*Brit.* **tri·col·our**) ▸*n.* a flag with three bands or blocks of different colors, esp. the French national flag with equal upright bands of blue, white, and red.
▸*adj.* (also **tri·col·ored**) having three colors. ▷late 18th cent.: from French *tricolore*, from late Latin *tricolor* (see TRI-, COLOR).

tri·corne /'trīˌkôrn/ (also **tri·corn**) ▸*adj.* [*attrib.*] (of a hat) having a brim turned up on three sides.
▸*n.* a hat of this kind. ▷mid 19th cent.: from French

tricorne or Latin *tricornis*, from *tri-* 'three' + *cornu* 'horn.'

tri·cot /'trēkō/ ▶*n.* a fine knitted fabric made of a natural or man-made fiber. ▷late 18th cent.: from French, literally 'knitting,' from *tricoter* 'to knit,' of unknown origin.

tri·co·teuse /,trēkô'tœz/ ▶*n.* (*pl.* same) a woman who sits and knits (used esp. in reference to a number of women who did this, during the French Revolution, while attending public executions). ▷French, from *tricoter* 'to knit.'

tric-trac /'trik ,trak/ ▶*n. historical* a form of backgammon. ▷late 17th cent.: from French, from the clicking sound made by the game pieces.

tri·cus·pid /trī'kəspid/ ▶*adj.* **1** having three cusps or points, in particular: ■ denoting a tooth with three cusps or points. ■ denoting a valve formed of three triangular segments, particularly that between the right atrium and ventricle of the heart. **2** [*attrib.*] of or relating to the tricuspid valve: *tricuspid atresia.* ▷late 17th cent.: from TRI- 'three' + Latin *cuspis, cuspid-* 'cusp.'

tri·cy·cle /'trīsikəl; -,sikəl/ ▶*n.* a vehicle similar to a bicycle, but having three wheels, two at the back and one at the front.
▶*v.* [*intrans.*] [often as *n.*] (**tricycling**) ride on a tricycle. —**tri·cy·clist** /-ist/ *n.*

tri·cy·clic /trī'sīklik; -'sik-/ ▶*adj. Chemistry* (of an organic compound) having three fused rings of atoms in its molecule.
▶*n.* (usu. **tricyclics**) *Medicine* any of a class of antidepressant drugs having molecules with three fused rings. ▷late 19th cent.: from TRI- 'three' + Greek *kuklos* 'circle' + -IC.

tri·dac·tyl /trī'daktl/ ▶*adj. Zoology* (of a vertebrate limb) having three toes or fingers. ▷early 19th cent.: from TRI- 'three' + Greek *daktulos* 'finger.'

tri·dent /'trīdnt/ ▶*n.* a three-pronged spear, esp. as an attribute of Poseidon (Neptune) or Britannia. ■ (**Trident**) a U.S. design of submarine-launched long-range ballistic missile. ▷late Middle English: from Latin *trident-*, from *tri-* 'three' + *dens, dent-* 'tooth.'

trident

Tri·den·tine /trī'den,tēn; -,tīn/ ▶*adj.* of or relating to the Council of Trent, esp. as the basis of Roman Catholic doctrine. ▷from medieval Latin *Tridentinus*, from *Tridentum* 'Trent.'

Tri·den·tine mass ▶*n.* the Latin Eucharistic liturgy used by the Roman Catholic Church from 1570 to 1964.

trid·y·mite /'tridə,mīt/ ▶*n.* a high-temperature form of quartz found as thin hexagonal crystals in some igneous rocks and stony meteorites. ▷mid 19th cent.: from German *Tridymit*, from Greek *tridumos* 'threefold,' from *tri-* 'three' + *-dumos* (as in *didumos* 'twin'), because of its occurrence in groups of three crystals.

tried /trīd/ ▶ past and past participle of TRY.
▶*adj.* [*attrib.*] used in various phrases to describe something that has proved effective or reliable before: *novel applications of* **tried-and-tested** *methods.*
▶*PHRASE* □ **the tried and true** something that has proved effective or reliable before: *supermarkets generally stick to the tried and true.*

tri·ene /'trī,ēn/ ▶*n. Chemistry* an unsaturated hydrocarbon containing three double bonds between carbon atoms.

tri·en·ni·al /trī'enēəl/ ▶*adj.* recurring every three years: *the triennial meeting of the Association.* ■ lasting for or relating to a period of three years.
▶*n.* a visitation of an Anglican diocese by its bishop every three years. ▷mid 16th cent.: from late Latin *triennis* (from Latin *tri-* 'three' + *annus* 'year') + -AL. —**tri·en·ni·al·ly** *adv.*

tri·en·ni·um /trī'enēəm/ ▶*n.* (*pl.* **-en·ni·a** /-'enēə/ or **-en·ni·ums**) a specified period of three years. ▷mid 19th cent.: from Latin, from *tri-* 'three' + *annus* 'year.'

Tri·er /tri(ə)r/ a city on the Mosel River in Rhineland-Palatinate, in western Germany; pop. 99,000. French name **Trèves**. Established by a Germanic tribe, the Treveri, *c.*400 BC, Trier is one of the oldest cities in Europe.

tri·er /'trīər/ ▶*n.* **1** a person who always makes an effort, however unsuccessful they may be: *Kelly was described by her teachers as a real trier.* **2** a person or body responsible for investigating and deciding a case judicially: *the jury is the* **trier of fact***.*

Tri·este /trē'est; -'estā/ a city in northeastern Italy, the largest port on the Adriatic Sea; pop. 231,000. Formerly held by Austria (1382–1918), Trieste was annexed by Italy after World War I. The Free Territory of Trieste was created after World War II but it was returned to Italy in 1954.

tri·fa·cial nerve /trī'fāshəl/ ▶*n.* another term for TRIGEMINAL NERVE.

tri·fect·a /trī'fektə/ ▶*n.* a bet in which the person betting forecasts the first three finishers in a race in the correct order. ■ [in *sing.*] a run of three wins or grand events: *today is a trifecta of birthdays.* ▷1970s: from TRI- 'three' + PERFECTA.

trif·fid /'trifid/ (also **Trif·fid**) ▶*n.* (in science fiction) one of a race of predatory plants that are capable of growing to a gigantic size and are possessed of locomotor ability and a poisonous sting. ▷coined by John Wyndham in *Day of the Triffids* (1951).

tri·fid /'trīfid/ ▶*adj. chiefly Biology* partly or wholly split into three divisions or lobes. ▷mid 18th cent.: from Latin *trifidus*, from *tri-* 'three' + *fid-* 'split, divided' (from the verb *findere*).

tri·fle /'trīfəl/ ▶*n.* **1** a thing of little value or importance: *we needn't trouble the headmaster over such trifles.* ■ [in *sing.*] a small amount of something: *the thousand yen he'd paid seemed the merest trifle.* **2** *Brit.* a cold dessert of sponge cake and fruit covered with layers of custard, jelly, and cream.
▶*v.* [*intrans.*] **1** (**trifle with**) treat (someone or something) without seriousness or respect: *he is* **not** *a man* **to be trifled with** | *men who trifle with women's affections.* **2** *archaic* talk or act frivolously: *we will not trifle—life is too short.* ■ [*trans.*] (**trifle something away**) waste (something, esp. time) frivolously. ▷Middle English (also denoting an idle story told to deceive or amuse): from Old French *trufle*, by-form of *trufe* 'deceit,' of unknown origin. The verb derives from Old French *truffler* 'mock, deceive.' —**tri·fler** /-f(ə)lər/ *n.*
▶*PHRASE* □ **a trifle** a little; somewhat: *his methods are a trifle eccentric.*

tri·fling /'trīf(ə)liNG/ ▶*adj.* unimportant or trivial: *a trifling sum.* —**tri·fling·ly** *adv.*

tri·flu·o·per·a·zine /trī,flo͞o-ō'perə,zēn/ ▶*n. Medicine* an antipsychotic and sedative drug related to phenothiazine. ▷mid 20th cent.: from TRI- + *fluo(rine)* + *(pi)perazine.*

tri·fo·cal /'trī,fōkəl/ ▶*adj.* (of a pair of glasses) having lenses with three parts with different focal lengths.
▶*n.* (**trifocals**) a pair of glasses with such lenses.

tri·fold /'trī,fōld/ ▶*adj.* triple; threefold: *an ingenious trifold partnership between government, employers, and students.*

tri·fo·li·ate /trī'fōlē-it; -,āt/ ▶*adj.* (of a compound leaf) having three leaflets: *dark green trifoliate leaves.* ■ (of a plant) having such leaves. ■ (of an object or design) having the form of such a leaf: *a bronze trifoliate key handle.*
▶*n.* a plant with such leaves: *poison ivy is a thornless trifoliate.*

tri·fo·ri·um /trī'fôrēəm/ ▶*n.* (*pl.* **-for·i·a** /-'fôrēə/) a gallery or arcade above the arches of the nave, choir, and transepts of a church. ▷early 18th cent.: from Anglo-Latin, of unknown origin.

tri·form /'trī,fôrm/ ▶*adj. technical* composed of three parts: *strawberries nestling among their triform leaves.*

tri·fur·cate ▶*v.* /'trīfər,kāt/ [*intrans.*] divide into three branches or forks.
▶*adj.* (also **tri·fur·cat·ed**) divided into three branches or forks. ▷mid 19th cent.: from Latin *trifurcus* 'three-forked' (from *tri-* 'three' + *furca* 'fork') + -ATE[2]. —**tri·fur·ca·tion** /,trīfər'kāshən/ *n.*

trig[1] /trig/ ▶*n. informal* trigonometry. ▷late 19th cent.: abbreviation.

trig[2] ▶*adj.* neat and smart in appearance: *two trig little boys, each in a gray flannel suit.*
▶*v.* (**trigged, trig·ging**) [*trans.*] make neat and smart in appearance: *he has rigged her and trigged her with paint and spar.* ▷Middle English (in the sense 'faithful, trusty'): from Old Norse *tryggr*; related to TRUE. The current verb sense dates from the late 17th cent.

trig. ▶*abbr.* ■ trigonometric. ■ trigonometrical. ■ trigonometry.

trig·a·mous /'trigəməs/ ▶*adj.* having three wives or husbands at the same time. ▷mid 19th cent.: from Greek *trigamos* (from *tri-* 'three' + *gamos* 'marriage') + -OUS. The nouns *trigamist* and *trigamy* date from the mid 17th cent. —**trig·a·mist** /-mist/ *n.* —**trig·a·my** /-mē/ *n.*

tri·gem·i·nal nerve /trī'jemənl/ ▶*n. Anatomy* each of the fifth and largest pair of cranial nerves, supplying the front part of the head and dividing into the ophthalmic, maxillary, and mandibular nerves.

tri·gem·i·nal neu·ral·gia ▶*n. Medicine* neuralgia involving one or more of the branches of the trigeminal nerves, and often causing severe pain.

tri·gem·i·nus /trī'jemənəs/ ▶*n.* (*pl.* **-ni** /-,nī/) *Anatomy* the trigeminal nerve. ▷late 19th cent.: from Latin, literally 'three born at the same birth,' extended to mean 'threefold.'

trig·ger /'trigər/ ▶*n.* a small device that releases a spring or catch and so sets off a mechanism, esp. in order to fire a gun: *he pulled the trigger of the shotgun.* ■ an event or thing that causes something to happen: *the trigger for the strike was the closure of a mine.*
▶*v.* [*trans.*] (often **be triggered**) cause (an event or situation) to happen or exist: *an allergy can be triggered by stress or overwork.* ■ cause (a device) to function. ▷early 17th cent.: from dialect *tricker*, from Dutch *trekker*, from *trekken* 'to pull.' —**trig·gered** *adj.*
▶*PHRASE* □ **quick on the trigger** quick to respond.

trig·ger fin·ger ▶*n.* **1** the forefinger of the hand, as that with which the trigger of a gun is typically pulled. **2** *Medicine* a defect in a tendon causing a finger to jerk or snap straight when the hand is extended.

trig·ger·fish /'trigər,fish/ ▶*n.* (*pl.* same or **-fish·es**) a marine fish occurring chiefly in tropical inshore waters. It has a large, stout dorsal spine that can be erected and locked into place, allowing the fish to wedge itself into crevices. • Family Balistidae: numerous genera and species.

trig·ger hair ▶*n.* a hairlike structure that triggers a rapid movement when touched, in particular: ■ *Zoology* (in a coelenterate) a filament at the mouth of a nematocyst, triggering the emission of the stinging hair. ■ *Botany* a bristle on the leaf of a Venus flytrap, triggering the closure of the leaf around an insect.

trig·ger-hap·py ▶*adj.* ready to react violently, esp. by shooting, on the slightest provocation: *territory controlled by trigger-happy bandits.*

trig·ger point ▶*n.* a particular circumstance or situation that causes an event to occur: *the army's refusal to withdraw from the territory was the trigger point for military action.* ■ *Physiology* & *Medicine* a sensitive area of the body, stimulation or irritation of which causes a specific effect in another part, esp. a tender area in a muscle that causes generalized musculoskeletal pain when overstimulated.

Tri·glav /'trē,gläf; -,gläv/ a mountain in the Julian Alps, in northwestern Slovenia, near the Italian border. Rising to 9,392 feet (2,863 m), it is the highest peak in the mountains east of the Adriatic Sea.

tri·glyc·er·ide /trī'glisə,rīd/ ▶*n. Chemistry Medicine* an ester formed from glycerol and three fatty acid groups. Triglycerides are the main constituents of natural fats and oils, and high concentrations in the blood indicate an elevated risk of stroke.

tri·glyph /'trī,glif/ ▶*n. Architecture* a tablet in a Doric frieze with three vertical grooves. Triglyphs alternate with metopes. ▷mid 16th cent.: via Latin from Greek *trigluphos*, from *tri-* 'three' + *gluphē* 'carving.' —**tri·glyph·ic** /trī'glifik/ *adj.*

tri·gon /'trī,gän/ ▶*n.* archaic term for TRIANGLE. ■ an ancient triangular lyre or harp. ■ a triangular cutting region formed by three cusps on an upper molar tooth. ▷early 17th cent. (in the sense 'triangle'): via Latin from Greek *trigōnon*, neuter of *trigōnos* 'three-cornered.'

trigon. ▶*abbr.* ■ trigonometric. ■ trigonometrical. ■ trigonometry.

trig·o·nal /'trigənl/ ▶*adj.* triangular: *square or trigonal double-sided inserts.* ■ *chiefly Biology* triangular in cross section: *large trigonal shells.* ■ of or denoting a crystal system or three-dimensional geometric arrangement having three equal axes separated by equal angles that are not right angles. ▷late 16th cent.: from medieval Latin *trigonalis*, from Latin *trigonum* (see TRIGON). —**trig·o·nal·ly** *adv.*

tri·gone /'trī,gōn/ ▶*n. Anatomy* a triangular region or tissue, particularly the area at the base of the urinary bladder, between the openings of the ureters and urethra. ▷mid 19th cent.: from French, from Latin *trigonum* 'triangle.'

trig·o·no·met·ric func·tion ▶*n. Mathematics* a function of an angle, or of an abstract quantity, used in trigonometry, including the sine, cosine, tangent, cotangent, secant, and cosecant, and their hyperbolic counterparts. Also called CIRCULAR FUNCTION.

trig·o·nom·e·try /ˌtrigəˈnämitrē/ ▸*n.* the branch of mathematics dealing with the relations of the sides and angles of triangles and with the relevant functions of any angles. ▷early 17th cent.: from modern Latin *trigonometria* (see TRIGON, -METRY). **—trig·o·no·met·ric** /-nəˈmetrik/ *adj.* **—trig·o·no·met·ri·cal** /-nəˈmetrikəl/ *adj.*

tri·gram /ˈtrīˌgram/ ▸*n.* **1** another term for TRIGRAPH. **2** each of the eight figures formed of three parallel lines, each either whole or broken, combined to form the sixty-four hexagrams of the *I Ching*.

tri·graph /ˈtrīˌgraf/ ▸*n.* a group of three letters representing one sound, for example German *sch-*.

tri·hal·o·meth·ane (abbr.:**THM**) ▸*n.* another term for HALOFORM.

tri·he·dral /trīˈhēdrəl/ ▸*adj.* (of a solid figure or body) having three sides or faces (in addition to the base or ends); triangular in cross section.
▸*n.* a trihedral figure. ▷late 18th cent.: from Greek *tri-* 'three' + *hedra* 'base' + -AL.

tri·he·dron /trīˈhēdrən/ ▸*n.* (*pl.* **-drons** or **-dra** /-drə/) a solid figure having three sides or faces (in addition to the base or ends). ▷early 19th cent.: from TRI- 'three' + -HEDRON, on the pattern of words such as *polyhedron*.

tri·hy·dric /trīˈhīdrik/ ▸*adj. Chemistry* (of an alcohol) containing three hydroxyl groups. ▷mid 19th cent.: from TRI- 'three' + HYDROGEN + -IC.

tri·i·o·do·meth·ane /ˌtrī-īōdōˈmeTHān; -ˌädō-/ ▸*n.* another term for IODOFORM.

tri·i·o·do·thy·ro·nine /ˌtrī-ī,ōdōˈTHīrəˌnēn; -ī,ädō-/ ▸*n. Biochemistry* a thyroid hormone similar to thyroxine but having greater potency.

tri·jet /ˈtrīˌjet/ ▸*n.* an aircraft powered by three jet engines.

trike /trīk/ *informal* ▸*n.* a tricycle. ▷late 19th cent.: abbreviation.

tri·lat·er·al /trīˈlatərəl/ ▸*adj.* shared by or involving three parties: *trilateral negotiations.* ■ *Geometry* of, on, or with three sides.
▸*n.* a triangle.

tril·by /ˈtrilbē/ ▸*n.* (*pl.* **-bies**) *chiefly Brit.* a soft felt hat with a narrow brim and indented crown. ▷late 19th cent.: from the name of the heroine in G. du Maurier's novel *Trilby* (1894), in the stage version of which such a hat was worn. **—tril·bied** *adj.*

tri·lin·e·ar /trīˈlinēər/ ▸*adj. Mathematics* of or having three lines.

tri·lin·gual /trīˈliNGgwəl/ ▸*adj.* (of a person) speaking three languages fluently. ■ (of a text or an activity) written or conducted in three languages: *trilingual magazines in Chinese, Indonesian, and English.* ▷mid 19th cent.: from TRI- 'three' + Latin *lingua* 'tongue' + -AL. **—tri·lin·gual·ism** /-ˌlizəm/ *n.*

trill /tril/ ▸*n.* a quavering or vibratory sound, esp. a rapid alternation of sung or played notes: *they heard the muffled trill of the telephone* | *the caged bird launched into a piercing trill.* ■ the pronunciation of a consonant, esp. *r*, with rapid vibration of the tongue against the hard or soft palate or the uvula.
▸*v.* [*intrans.*] produce a quavering or warbling sound: *a skylark was trilling overhead* | [with *direct speech*] *"Coming sir," they both trilled.* ■ [*trans.*] sing (a note or song) with a warbling or quavering sound: *trilling a love ballad, she led him to her chair.* ■ [*trans.*] pronounce (a consonant) by rapid vibration of the tongue against the hard or soft palate or the uvula. ▷mid 17th cent.: from Italian *trillo* (noun), *trillare* (verb).

trill·er /ˈtrilər/ ▸*n.* an Australasian and Southeast Asian songbird of the cuckoo-shrike family, with mainly black and white plumage. • Family Campephagidae: two genera, in particular *Lalage*, and several species.

Tril·lin /ˈtrilən/, Calvin (1935–), U.S. writer. He became a staff writer for the *New Yorker* magazine in 1963 and had a syndicated newspaper column 1986–95 and a weekly column in *Time* magazine 1995–2001. He was a columnist 1978–85 for *The Nation*, to which he has contributed a weekly satirical verse since 1990. Among his many books are *Remembering Denny* (1993), a story of a college friend, and *Messages from my Father* (1996).

tril·lion /ˈtrilyən/ ▸*cardinal number* (*pl.* **-lions** or (with numeral) same) a million million (1,000,000,000,000 or 10^{12}). ■ (**trillions**) *informal* a very large number or amount: *the yammering of trillions of voices.* ■ *dated, chiefly Brit.* a million million million (1,000,000,000,000,000,000 or 10^{18}). ▷late 17th cent.: from French, from *million*, by substitution of the prefix *tri-* 'three' for the initial letters. **—tril·lionth** /-yənTH/ *ordinal number*.

tril·li·um /ˈtrilēəm/ ▸*n.* a plant with a solitary three-petaled flower above a whorl of three leaves, native to North American and Asia. • Genus *Trillium*, family Liliaceae (or Trilliaceae): several species, in particular **red** (or **purple**) **trillium** (*T. erectum*). ▷modern Latin, apparently an alteration of Swedish *trilling* 'triplet.'

red trillium

tri·lo·bite /ˈtrīləˌbīt/ ▸*n.* an extinct marine arthropod that occurred abundantly during the Paleozoic era, with a carapace over the forepart, and a segmented hindpart divided longitudinally into three lobes. • Subphylum Trilobita, phylum Arthropoda: numerous classes and orders. ▷mid 19th cent.: from modern Latin *Trilobites*, from Greek *tri-* 'three' + *lobos* 'lobe' + -ITE[1].

tril·o·gy /ˈtriləjē/ ▸*n.* (*pl.* **-gies**) a group of three related novels, plays, films, operas, or albums. ■ (in ancient Greece) a series of three tragedies performed one after the other. ■ *figurative* a group or series of three related things: *a trilogy of cases reflected this development.* ▷from Greek *trilogia*, from *tri-* 'three times' + *logos* 'story'.

trim /trim/ ▸*v.* (**trimmed, trim·ming**) [*trans.*] **1** make (something) neat or of the required size or form by cutting away irregular or unwanted parts: *trim the grass using a sharp mower.* ■ [*trans.*] cut off (irregular or unwanted parts): *he was* **trimming** *the fat* **off** *some pork chops.* ■ *figurative* reduce the size, amount, or number of (something, typically expenditure or costs): *Congress had to decide which current defense programs should be trimmed.* ■ [*intrans.*] (**trim down**) (of a person) lose weight; become slimmer: *he works on trimming down and eating right.* ■ firm up or lose weight from (a part of one's body). **2** (usu. **be trimmed**) decorate (something), typically with contrasting items or pieces of material: *a pair of black leather gloves* **trimmed with** *fake fur.* **3** adjust (sails) to take best advantage of the wind. ■ adjust the forward and after drafts of (a vessel) by changing the distribution of weight on board, esp. cargo and ballast. ■ stow (a bulk cargo) properly in a ship's hold by use of manual labor or machinery. ■ keep or adjust the degree to which (an aircraft) can be maintained at a constant altitude without any control forces being present. ■ [*intrans.*] adapt one's views to the prevailing political trends for personal advancement. **4** *informal, dated* get the better of (someone), typically by cheating them out of money. **5** *informal, dated* rebuke (someone) angrily.
▸*n.* **1** additional decoration, typically along the edges of something and in contrasting color or material: *suede sandals with gold trim* | *we painted the buildings off-white with a blue trim.* ■ decorative additions to a vehicle, typically the upholstery or interior lining of a car. **2** [in *sing.*] an act of cutting off part of something in order to neaten it: *his hair needs a trim.* ■ a short piece of film cut out during the final editing stage. **3** the state of being in good order or condition: *no one had been there for months—everything was out of trim.* **4** the degree to which an aircraft can be maintained at a constant altitude without any control forces being present: *the pilot's only problem was the need to constantly readjust the trim.* **5** the difference between a vessel's forward and after drafts, esp. as it affects its navigability.
▸*adj.* (**trim·mer, trim·mest**) neat and smart in appearance; in good order: *she kept her husband's clothes neat and trim* | *a trim little villa.* ■ (of a person or their body) slim and fit: *she has a trim, athletic figure.* ▷Old English *trymman, trymian* 'make firm, arrange,' of which the adjective appears to be a derivative. The word's history is obscure; current verb senses date from the early 16th cent. when usage became frequent and served many purposes: this is possibly explained by spoken or dialect use in the Middle English period not recorded in extant literature. **—trim·ly** *adv.* **—trim·ness** *n.*
▸*PHRASES* □ **in trim** slim and fit. ■ *Nautical* in good order. □ **trim one's sails** (**to the wind**) make changes to suit one's new circumstances.

tri·ma·ran /ˈtrīməˌran/ ▸*n.* a yacht with three hulls in parallel. ▷1940s: from TRI- + CATAMARAN.

Trim·ble /ˈtrimbəl/, Robert (1776–1828), U.S. Supreme Court associate justice 1826–28. Appointed to the Court by President John Quincy Adams, he was an advocate of federal supremacy.

tri·mer /ˈtrīmər/ ▸*n. Chemistry* a polymer comprising three monomer units. **—tri·mer·ic** /trīˈmerik/ *adj.*

trim·er·ous /ˈtrimərəs/ ▸*adj. Botany & Zoology* having parts arranged in groups of three. ■ consisting of three joints or parts.

tri·mes·ter /trīˈmestər; ˈtrīˌmes-/ ▸*n.* a period of three months, esp. as a division of the duration of pregnancy. ■ each of the three terms in an academic year. ▷early 19th cent.: from French *trimestre*, from Latin *trimestris*, from *tri-* 'three' + *mensis* 'month.' **—tri·mes·tral** /trīˈmestrəl/ *adj.* **—tri·mes·tri·al** /trīˈmestrēəl/ *adj.*

trim·e·ter /ˈtrimitər/ ▸*n. Prosody* a line of verse consisting of three metrical feet. ▷mid 16th cent.: via Latin from Greek *trimetros*, from *tri-* 'three' + *metron* 'measure.' **—tri·met·ric** /trīˈmetrik/ *adj.* **—tri·met·ri·cal** /trīˈmetrikəl/ *adj.*

tri·meth·o·prim /trīˈmeTHəˌprim/ ▸*n. Medicine* a synthetic antibiotic used to treat malaria and respiratory and urinary infections (usually in conjunction with a sulfonamide). ▷1960s: from *trimeth(yl)* + *o(xy-)* + *p(y)rim(idine)*.

tri·mix /ˈtrīˌmiks/ ▸*n.* a breathing mixture for deep-sea divers, composed of nitrogen, helium, and oxygen.

trim·mer /ˈtrimər/ ▸*n.* **1** an implement used for trimming off the unwanted or untidy parts of something: *a hedge trimmer.* **2** a person who adapts their views to the prevailing political trends for personal advancement. **3** a person who decorates something: *window trimmers.* **4** (also **trimmer joist**) *Architecture* a crosspiece fixed between full-length joists (and often across the end of truncated joists) to form part of the frame of an opening in a floor or roof. **5** a person responsible for trimming the sails of a yacht. ■ a person employed to arrange cargo or fuel in a ship's hold. **6** a small capacitor or other component used to tune a circuit such as a radio set.

trim·ming /ˈtrimiNG/ ▸*n.* **1** the action of cutting off the unwanted or untidy parts of something: *he keeps his hair short by continual trimming.* ■ (**trimmings**) small pieces cut off in such a way: *hedge trimmings.* **2** decoration, esp. for clothing: *a party dress with lace trimming.* ■ (**the trimmings**) *informal* the traditional accompaniments to something, esp. a meal or special occasion: *roast turkey* **with all the trimmings**.

Tri·mon·ti·um /trīˈmäntēəm/ Roman name for PLOVDIV.

trim·pot /ˈtrimˌpät/ ▸*n.* a small potentiometer used to make small adjustments to the value of resistance or voltage in an electronic circuit.

trim tab (also **trim·ming tab**) ▸*n. Aeronautics* an adjustable tab or airfoil attached to a control surface, used to trim an aircraft in flight.

Tri·mur·ti /triˈmo͝ortē/ *Hinduism* the trinity of Brahma the creator, Vishnu the preserver, and Shiva the destroyer. ▷from Sanskrit *tri* 'three' + *mūrti* 'form.'

trine /trīn/ *Astrology* ▸*n.* an aspect of 120° (one third of a circle): *Venus* **in trine to** *Mars* | [as *adj.*] *a trine aspect.* See also GRAND TRINE.
▸*v.* [*trans.*] (of a planet) be in a trine aspect with (another planet or position): *Jupiter trines Pluto all month.* ▷late Middle English (in the sense 'made up of three parts'): from Old French *trin(e)*, from Latin *trinus* 'threefold,' from *tres* 'three.'

Trin·i /ˈtrinē/ ▸*n. W. Indian* a Trinidadian. ▷abbreviation.

Trin·i·dad and To·ba·go /ˈtrinəˌdad and təˈbāgō/ a country in the Caribbean Sea comprising two islands off the northeastern coast of Venezuela; pop. 1,400,000; capital, Port-of-Spain (on Trinidad); languages, English (official) and Creole. **—Trin·i·da·di·an** /ˌtrinəˈdadēən; -ˈdādē-/ *adj.* & *n.* **—To·ba·gan** /təˈbāgən/ *adj.* & *n.* **—To·ba·go·ni·an** /ˌtōbəˈgōnēən/ *adj.* & *n.*

The larger of the two islands is Trinidad, with Tobago to the northeast. Trinidad, inhabited by

Arawaks, was visited by Columbus in 1498 and settled by the Spanish; Tobago, occupied by Caribs, was colonized by the French and later the British in the 18th century. Trinidad became British during the Napoleonic Wars and was formally amalgamated with Tobago as a Crown Colony in 1888. Trinidad and Tobago became an independent member state of the Commonwealth of Nations in 1962 and finally a republic in 1976.

Trin·i·tar·i·an /ˌtrinəˈte(ə)rēən/ ▸*adj.* of or relating to belief in the doctrine of the Trinity.
▸*n.* a person who believes in the doctrine of the Trinity. **—Trin·i·tar·i·an·ism** /-ˌnizəm/ *n.*

tri·ni·tro·tol·u·ene /trīˌnītrōˈtälyəˌwēn/ ▸*n.* see **TNT**.

trin·i·ty /ˈtrinitē/ ▸*n.* (*pl.* **-ties**) (also **the Trin·i·ty** or **the Ho·ly Trin·i·ty**) the Christian Godhead as one God in three persons: Father, Son, and Holy Spirit. ■ a group of three people or things: *the wine was the first of a trinity of three excellent vintages.* ■ the state of being three: *God is said to be trinity in unity.* ▷Middle English: from Old French *trinite*, from Latin *trinitas* 'triad,' from *trinus* 'threefold' (see **TRINE**).

Trin·i·ty Moun·tains a forested range of the Klamath Mountains in northwestern California.

Trin·i·ty Riv·er a river that flows for 550 miles (900 km) from the Trinity Mountains across Texas to the Gulf of Mexico.

Trin·i·ty Sun·day ▸*n.* the next Sunday after Pentecost, observed in the Western Christian Church as a feast in honor of the Holy Trinity.

Trin·i·ty term ▸*n. Brit.* (in some universities) the term beginning after Easter. ■ a session of the British High Court beginning after Easter.

trin·ket /ˈtriNGkit/ ▸*n.* a small ornament or item of jewelry that is of little value. ▷mid 16th cent.: of unknown origin. **—trin·ket·ry** /-trē/ *n.*

tri·no·mi·al /trīˈnōmēəl/ ▸*adj.* **1** (of an algebraic expression) consisting of three terms. **2** *Biology* a systematic name for a taxon consisting of three terms of which the first is the name of the genus, the second that of the species, and the third that of the subspecies or variety.
▸*n.* **1** an algebraic expression of three terms. **2** *Biology* a trinomial taxonomic name. ▷late 17th cent.: from **TRI-** 'three,' on the pattern of *binomial*.

tri·o /ˈtrē-ō/ ▸*n.* (*pl.* **-os**) a set or group of three people or things: *the hotel was run by a trio of brothers.* ■ a group of three musicians: *a jazz trio.* ■ a composition written for three musicians: *Chopin's G minor Trio.* ■ the central, typically contrastive, section of a minuet, scherzo, or march. ■ (in piquet) a set of three aces, kings, queens, jacks, or tens held in one hand. ▷early 18th cent.: from Italian, from Latin *tres* 'three,' on the pattern of *duo*.

tri·ode /ˈtrīˌōd/ ▸*n.* a vacuum tube having three electrodes. ■ a semiconductor rectifier having three connections. ▷early 20th cent.: from **TRI-** 'three' + **ELECTRODE**.

tri·o·let /ˈtrēəlit; ˈtrī-; ˌtrēəˈlā/ ▸*n.* a poem of eight lines, typically of eight syllables each, rhyming *abaaabab* and so structured that the first line recurs as the fourth and seventh and the second as the eighth. ▷mid 17th cent.: from French.

tri·ose /ˈtrīˌōs/ ▸*n. Chemistry* any of a group of monosaccharide sugars whose molecules contain three carbon atoms.

tri·o so·na·ta ▸*n.* a baroque composition written in three parts, two upper parts and one bass, and usually performed with a keyboard continuo.

tri·ox·ide /trīˈäkˌsīd/ ▸*n. Chemistry* an oxide containing three atoms of oxygen in its molecule or empirical formula.

trip /trip/ ▸*v.* (**tripped**, **trip·ping**) **1** [*intrans.*] catch one's foot on something and stumble or fall: *he tripped over his cat* | *she* **tripped up** *during the penultimate lap.* ■ [*trans.*] cause (someone) to do this: *she shot out her foot to* **trip him up**. ■ (**trip up**) make a mistake: *taxpayers often trip up by not declaring taxable income.* ■ [*trans.*] (**trip someone up**) detect or expose someone in an error, blunder, or inconsistency: *the man was determined to trip him up on his economics.* **2** [*intrans.*] walk, run, or dance with quick light steps: *they tripped up the terrace steps.* ■ (of words) flow lightly and easily: *a name that* **trips off the tongue** | *the guest list tripped from her lips.* **3** [*trans.*] activate (a mechanism), esp. by contact with a switch, catch, or other electrical device: *an intruder trips the alarm.* ■ [*intrans.*] (of part of an electric circuit) disconnect automatically as a safety measure: *the plugs will trip as soon as any change in current is detected.* **4** [*trans.*] *Nautical* release and raise (an anchor) from the seabed by means of a buoyed line attached to the anchor's crown. ■ turn (a yard or other object) from a horizontal to a vertical position for lowering. **5** [*intrans.*] *informal* experience hallucinations induced by taking a psychedelic drug, esp. LSD: *they prance around* **tripping out** *on their hallucinogens.* **6** [*intrans.*] go on a short journey: *when tripping through the Yukon, take some time to explore our museums.*
▸*n.* **1** a journey or excursion, esp. for pleasure: *Sally's gone on a school trip* | *a trip to the North Pole.* See note at **JOURNEY**. ■ an act of going to a place and returning: *a quick trip to the store.* **2** a stumble or fall due to catching one's foot on something. ■ *archaic* a mistake: *an occasional trip in the performance.* **3** *informal* a hallucinatory experience caused by taking a psychedelic drug, esp. LSD: *acid trips.* ■ an exciting or stimulating experience: *it was a trip seeing him again.* ■ a self-indulgent attitude or activity: *politics was a sixties trip.* **4** a device that activates or disconnects a mechanism, circuit, etc. ■ an instance of a device deactivating or the power supply disconnecting as a safety measure. **5** *archaic* a light, lively movement of a person's feet: *yonder comes Dalinda; I know her by her trip.* ▷Middle English: from Old French *triper*, from Middle Dutch *trippen* 'to skip, hop.'
▸*PHRASE* □ **trip the light fantastic** *humorous* dance, in particular engage in ballroom dancing. [from "Trip it as you go On the light fantastic toe" (Milton's *L'Allegro*).]

tri·par·tite /trīˈpärˌtīt/ ▸*adj.* consisting of three parts: *a tripartite classification.* ■ shared by or involving three parties: *a tripartite coalition government.* ▷late Middle English: from Latin *tripartitus*, from *tri-* 'three' + *partitus* 'divided' (past participle of *partiri*). **—tri·par·tite·ly** *adv.* **—tri·par·ti·tion** /ˌtrīpärˈtiSHən/ *n.*

trip com·pu·ter ▸*n.* an electronic odometer, typically with extra capabilities such as the ability to calculate fuel consumption.

tripe /trīp/ ▸*n.* **1** the first or second stomach of a cow or other ruminant used as food. **2** *informal* nonsense; rubbish: *you do talk tripe sometimes.* ▷Middle English: from Old French, of unknown origin.

trip ham·mer ▸*n.* a large, heavy pivoted hammer used in forging, raised by a cam or lever and allowed to drop on the metal being worked.

trip-hop ▸*n.* a style of dance music, usually slow in tempo, that combines elements of hip-hop and dub reggae with softer, more ambient sounds.

triph·thong /ˈtrifˌTHôNG; ˈtrip-/ ▸*n.* a union of three vowels (letters or sounds) pronounced in one syllable (as in some pronunciations of *our*). Contrasted with **DIPHTHONG**, **MONOPHTHONG**. ■ a vowel trigraph (as in *beau*). ▷mid 16th cent.: from French *triphtongue*, from *tri-* 'three,' on the pattern of *diphthong*. **—triph·thong·al** /trifˈTHôNG(g)əl; trip-; -ˈTHäNG(g)əl/ *adj.*

Tri·pi·ta·ka /triˈpitikə/ ▸*n.* (**the Tripitaka**) the discourses of the Buddha, collected in the first century and arranged into the three divisions of sermons, monastic law, and metaphysics. Only the compilation of the Theravada school, written in Pali, survives in its entirety. ▷from Sanskrit *tripiṭaka*, literally 'the three baskets or collections.'

tripl. ▸*abbr.* triplicate.

tri·plane /ˈtrīˌplān/ ▸*n.* an early type of airplane with three pairs of wings, one above the other.

tri·ple /ˈtripəl/ ▸*adj.* [*attrib.*] consisting of or involving three parts, things, or people: *a triple murder* | *triple somersaults.* ■ having three times the usual size, quality, or strength: *a triple dark rum.* ■ (of a person or animal) having done or won something three times: *a triple champion.*
▸*predeterminer* three times as much or as many: *the copper energy cells had triple the efficiency of silicon cells.*
▸*n.* **1** a set of three things or parts. ■ an amount that is three times as large as another: *the triples of numbers.* ■ *Bowling* three consecutive strikes. **2** (**triples**) a sporting contest in which each side has three players. **3** (**Triples**) *Bell-ringing* a system of change ringing using seven bells, with three pairs changing places each time. **4** *Baseball* a hit that enables the batter to reach third base. **5** another term for **TRIFECTA**.
▸*v.* [*intrans.*] **1** become three times as much or as many: *grain prices were expected to triple.* ■ [*trans.*] multiply (something) by three: *the party more than tripled its share of the vote.* **2** *Baseball* hit a triple: *he tripled into right field.* ▷Middle English (as an adjective and adverb): from Old French, or from Latin *triplus*, from Greek *triplous*. **—trip·ly** /ˈtriplē/ *adv.*

tri·ple A (also **AAA**) ▸*n.* **1** [usu. as *adj.*] *Finance* the highest grading available from credit rating agencies. **2** the highest competitive level in minor league baseball. **3** a 1.5 volt dry cell battery size.

Tri·ple Al·li·ance *n.* a union or association between three powers or states, in particular that made in 1668 between England, the Netherlands, and Sweden against France, and that in 1882 between Germany, Austria-Hungary, and Italy against France and Russia.

tri·ple bond ▸*n. Chemistry* a chemical bond in which three pairs of electrons are shared between two atoms.

tri·ple crown ▸*n.* **1** (**Triple Crown**) an award or honor for winning a group of three important events in a sport, in particular victory by one horse in the Kentucky Derby, the Preakness, and the Belmont Stakes. **2** the papal tiara.

Tri·ple En·tente /änˈtänt/ an early 20th-century alliance between Great Britain, France, and Russia. Originally a series of loose agreements, the Triple Entente began to assume the nature of a more formal alliance as the prospect of war with the Central Powers became more likely, and formed the basis of the Allied powers in World War I.

tri·ple jump ▸*n.* **1** (**the triple jump**) a track-and-field event in which competitors attempt to jump as far as possible by performing a hop, a step, and a jump from a running start. **2** *Skating* a jump in which the skater makes three full turns while in the air.
▸*v.* (**tri·ple-jump**) [*intrans.*] (of an athlete) perform a triple jump. **—tri·ple jump·er** *n.*

tri·ple play ▸*n. Baseball* a defensive play in which three runners are put out.

tri·ple point ▸*n. Chemistry* the temperature and pressure at which the solid, liquid, and vapor phases of a pure substance can coexist in equilibrium.

tri·ple rhyme ▸*n.* a feminine rhyme involving one stressed and two unstressed syllables in each rhyming line.

tri·plet /ˈtriplit/ ▸*n.* **1** (usu. **triplets**) one of three children or animals born at the same birth. **2** a set or succession of three similar things. ■ *Music* a group of three equal notes to be performed in the time of two or four. ■ a set of three rhyming lines of verse. **3** *Physics & Chemistry* an atomic or molecular state characterized by two unpaired electrons with parallel spins. ■ a group of three associated lines close together in a spectrum or electrophoretic gel. ▷mid 17th cent.: from **TRIPLE**, on the pattern of *doublet*.

tri·plet code ▸*n. Biology* the standard version of the genetic code, in which a sequence of three nucleotides in a DNA or RNA molecule codes for a specific amino acid in protein synthesis.

tri·ple time ▸*n.* musical time with three beats to the bar.

tri·ple tongu·ing ▸*n. Music* a technique in which alternate movements of the tongue are made (typically as in sounding *ttk*) to facilitate rapid playing of a wind instrument.

tri·plex /ˈtripleks; ˈtrī-/ ▸*n.* **1** a building divided into three self-contained residences. ■ a movie theater with three separate screening rooms. **2** *Biochemistry* a triple-stranded polynucleotide molecule.
▸*adj.* having three parts, in particular: ■ (of a residence) on three floors: *his vast triplex apartment.*
▸*v.* (**be triplexed**) (of electrical equipment or systems) be provided or fitted in triplicate so as to ensure reliability. ▷early 17th cent. (as an adjective in the sense 'threefold'): from Latin, 'threefold,' from *tri-* 'three' + *plicare* 'to fold.' Current specific senses date from the 1920s.

Pronunciation Key ə ago; ər over; ˈə or ˌə up; ˈər or ˌər fur; a hat; ā rate; ä car; CH chew; e let; ē see; e(ə)r air; i fit; ī by; i(ə)r ear; NG sing; ō go; ô for; oi boy; o͝o good; o͞o goo; ou out; SH she; TH thin; TH then; (h)w why; ZH vision

trip·li·cate ▸*adj.* /ˈtriplikit/ [*attrib.*] existing in three copies or examples: *triplicate measurements.*
▸*n.* /ˈtriplikit/ *archaic* a thing that is part of a set of three copies or corresponding parts: *the triplicate of a letter to the Governor.*
▸*v.* /-ˌkāt/ [*trans.*] make three copies of (something); multiply by three. ▷late Middle English: from Latin *triplicat-* 'made three,' from the verb *triplicare*, from *triplex, triplic-* 'threefold' (see TRIPLEX). The verb dates from the early 17th cent. —**trip·li·ca·tion** /ˌtripləˈkāsʜən/ *n.*
▸*PHRASE* □ **in triplicate** three times in exactly the same way: *the procedure was repeated in triplicate.* ■ existing as a set of three exact copies: *this form is in triplicate and must be handed to all employees.*

tri·plic·i·ty /triˈplisitē/ ▸*n.* (*pl.* **-ties**) *rare* a group of three people or things. ■ *archaic* the state of being triple. ▷late Middle English (as a term in astrology): from late Latin *triplicitas*, from Latin *triplex, triplic-* 'threefold' (see TRIPLEX).

trip·lo·blas·tic /ˌtriplōˈblastik/ ▸*adj. Zoology* having a body derived from three embryonic cell layers (ectoderm, mesoderm, and endoderm), as in all multicellular animals except sponges and coelenterates. ▷late 19th cent.: from Greek *triploos* 'threefold' + -BLAST + -IC.

trip·loid /ˈtriploid/ *Genetics* ▸*adj.* (of a cell or nucleus) containing three homologous sets of chromosomes. ■ (of an organism or species) composed of triploid cells.
▸*n.* a triploid organism, variety, or species. —**trip·loi·dy** /ˈtriˌploidē/ *n.*

trip·me·ter /ˈtripˌmētər/ ▸*n.* a vehicle instrument that can be set to record the distance of individual journeys.

tri·pod /ˈtrīpäd/ ▸*n.* **1** a three-legged stand for supporting a camera or other apparatus. **2** *archaic* a stool, table, or cauldron resting on three legs. ■ *historical* the bronze altar at Delphi on which a priestess sat to utter oracles. ▷early 17th cent.: via Latin from Greek *tripous, tripod-*, from *tri-* 'three' + *pous, pod-* 'foot.' —**trip·o·dal** /trīˈpōdl/ *adj.*

Trip·o·li /ˈtripəlē/ **1** the capital and chief port of Libya, on the Mediterranean coast in the northwestern part of the country; pop. 991,000. Founded by Phoenicians in the 7th century BC, its ancient name was Oea. Arabic name TARABULUS AL-GHARB, 'western Tripoli'. **2** a port in northwestern Lebanon; pop. 160,000. It was founded *c.*700 BC and was the capital of the Phoenician triple federation formed by the city-states Sidon, Tyre, and Arvad. Today it is a major port and commercial center. Arabic name TARABULUS ASH-SHAM, 'eastern Tripoli,' TRÂBLOUS.

trip·o·li /ˈtripəlē/ ▸*n.* another term for ROTTENSTONE. ▷early 17th cent.: from French, from TRIPOLI.

Trip·o·li·ta·ni·a /ˌtripələˈtānēə; triˌpälə-; -ˈtānyə/ a coastal region that surrounds Tripoli in North Africa, in what is now northeastern Libya. ▷based on Latin *tripolis* 'three cities,' referring to the Phoenician cities, Oea (now Tripoli), Leptis Magna, and Sabratha, established here in the 7th cent. BC. —**Trip·o·li·ta·ni·an** *adj.* & *n.*

tri·pos /ˈtrīˌpäs/ ▸*n.* [in *sing.*] the final honors examination for a BA degree at Cambridge University. ▷late 16th cent.: alteration of Latin *tripus* 'tripod,' with reference to the stool on which a designated graduate (known as the "Tripos") sat.

trip·pant /ˈtripənt/ ▸*adj.* [usu. *postpositive*] *Heraldry* (of a stag or deer) represented as walking. Compare with PASSANT. ▷mid 17th cent.: from Old French, literally 'walking or springing lightly,' present participle of *tripper.*

trip·per /ˈtripər/ ▸*n. informal* **1** a person who goes on a pleasure trip or excursion. **2** a device that triggers a signal or other operating device.

trip·py /ˈtripē/ ▸*adj.* (**-pi·er**, **-pi·est**) *informal* resembling or inducing the hallucinatory effect produced by taking a psychedelic drug: *trippy house music.*

trip·tych /ˈtriptik/ ▸*n.* a picture or relief carving on three panels, typically hinged together side by side and used as an altarpiece. ■ a set of three associated artistic, literary, or musical works intended to be appreciated together. ▷mid 18th cent. (denoting a set of three writing tablets hinged or tied together): from TRI- 'three,' on the pattern of *diptych.*

trip·tyque /tripˈtēk; ˈtriptik/ ▸*n. dated* a customs permit serving as a passport for a motor vehicle. ▷early 20th cent.: from French, literally 'triptych' (because originally the document had three sections).

Trip·u·ra /ˈtripŏŏrə/ a small state in northeastern India, on the eastern border of Bangladesh; capital, Agartala.

trip·wire /ˈtripˌwīr/ ▸*n.* a wire stretched close to the ground, working a trap, explosion, or alarm when disturbed and serving to detect or prevent people or animals entering an area. ■ a comparatively weak military force employed as a first line of defense, engagement with which will trigger the intervention of strong forces.

tri·que·tra /trīˈkwētrə; -ˈkwetrə/ ▸*n.* (*pl.* **-trae** /-trē/) a symmetrical triangular ornament of three interlaced arcs used on metalwork and stone crosses. ▷late 16th cent. (originally denoting a triangle): from Latin, feminine of *triquetrus* 'three-cornered.'

tri·que·tral /trīˈkwētrəl; -ˈkwetrəl/ (also **tri·que·tral bone**) ▸*n. Anatomy* a carpal bone on the outside of the wrist, articulating with the lunate, hamate, and pisiform bones. ▷mid 17th cent.: from Latin *triquetrus* 'three-cornered' + -AL.

tri·reme /ˈtrīˌrēm/ ▸*n.* an ancient Greek or Roman war galley with three banks of oars. The rowers are believed to have sat in threes on angled benches, rather than in three superimposed banks. ▷from Latin *triremis*, from *tri-* 'three' + *remus* 'oar.'

tris[1] /tris/ (also **tris buff·er**) ▸*n.* a flammable compound that forms a corrosive solution in water and is used as a buffer and emulsifying agent. • Alternative name: **trishydroxymethylaminomethane**; chem. formula: $(HOCH_2)_3CNH_2$. ▷1950s: from *tris-*, the prefix of the systematic name.

tris[2] ▸*n.* an organophosphorus compound, used as a flame retardant. • Alternative name: **tris-2,3-dibromopropylphosphate**; chem. formula: $(Br_2C_3H_5)_3PO_4$. ▷1970s: from *tris-*, the prefix of the systematic name.

tri·sac·cha·ride /trīˈsakəˌrīd/ ▸*n. Chemistry* any of the class of sugars whose molecules contain three monosaccharide molecules.

Tris·agion /trēˈsagēən; -ˈsäyôn/ ▸*n.* a hymn, esp. in the Orthodox Church, with a triple invocation of God as holy. ▷late Middle English: from Greek, neuter of *trisagios*, from *tris* 'three times' + *hagios* 'holy.'

tri·sect /trīˈsekt/ ▸*v.* [*trans.*] divide (something) into three parts, typically three equal parts. ▷late 17th cent.: from TRI- 'three' + Latin *sect-* 'divided, cut' (from the verb *secare*). —**tri·sec·tion** /-ˈseksʜən/ *n.* —**tri·sec·tor** /-tər/ *n.*

tri·shaw /ˈtrīˌsʜô/ ▸*n.* a light three-wheeled vehicle with pedals used in the Far East. ▷1940s: from TRI- 'three' + RICKSHA.

tris·kai·dek·a·pho·bi·a /ˌtriskīˌdekəˈfōbēə; ˌtriskə-/ ▸*n.* extreme superstition regarding the number thirteen. ▷early 20th cent.: from Greek *treiskaideka* 'thirteen' + -PHOBIA.

tris·kel·i·on /trīˈskelēən; tri-/ ▸*n.* a Celtic symbol consisting of three legs or lines radiating from a center. ▷mid 19th cent.: from TRI- 'three' + Greek *skelos* 'leg.'

tris·mus /ˈtrizməs/ ▸*n. Medicine* spasm of the jaw muscles, causing the mouth to remain tightly closed, typically as a symptom of tetanus. Also called LOCKJAW. ▷late 17th cent.: from modern Latin, from Greek *trismos* 'a scream, grinding.'

tri·so·my /trīˈsōmē; ˈtrīsō-/ ▸*n. Medicine* a condition in which an extra copy of a chromosome is present in the cell nuclei, causing developmental abnormalities. ▷1930s: from TRI- 'three' + -SOME[3].

tri·so·my-21 ▸*n. Medicine* the most common form of Down syndrome, caused by an extra copy of chromosome number 21.

Tris·tan /ˈtrisˌtän; -tən/ variant spelling of TRISTRAM.

tris·tesse /trēˈstes/ ▸*n. poetic/literary* a state of melancholy sadness. ▷French.

Tris·tram /ˈtristrəm/ (also **Tris·tan** /ˈtrisˌtän; -tən/) (in medieval legend) a knight who was the lover of Iseult.

tri·syl·la·ble /trīˈsiləbəl/ ▸*n.* a word or metrical foot of three syllables. —**tri·syl·lab·ic** /ˌtrīsəˈlabik/ *adj.*

tri·tag·o·nist /trīˈtagənist/ ▸*n.* the person who is third in importance, after the protagonist and deuteragonist, in an ancient Greek drama. ▷late 19th cent.: from Greek *tritagōnistēs*, from *tritos* 'third' + *agōnistēs* 'actor.'

trit·an·ope /ˈtrītnˌōp/ ▸*n.* a person suffering from tritanopia.

trit·an·o·pi·a /ˌtrītnˈōpēə/ ▸*n.* a rare form of colorblindness resulting from insensitivity to blue light, causing confusion of greens and blues. Compare with PROTANOPIA. ▷early 20th cent.: from TRITO- 'third' (referring to blue as the third color in the spectrum) + AN-[1] 'without' + -OPIA.

trite /trīt/ ▸*adj.* (of a remark, opinion, or idea) overused and consequently of little import; lacking originality or freshness: *this point may now seem obvious and trite.* ▷mid 16th cent.: from Latin *tritus*, past participle of *terere* 'to rub.' —**trite·ly** *adv.* —**trite·ness** *n.*

tri·ter·pene /trīˈtərpēn/ ▸*n. Chemistry* any of a group of terpenes found in plant gums and resins, having unsaturated molecules based on a unit with the formula $C_{30}H_{48}$. —**tri·ter·pe·noid** /-pəˌnoid/ *adj.* & *n.*

tri·the·ism /trīˈтʜēˌizəm/ ▸*n.* (in Christian theology) the doctrine of or belief in the three persons of the Trinity as three distinct gods. —**tri·the·ist** *n.*

tri·ti·at·ed /ˈtritēˌātid; ˈtrisʜ-/ ▸*adj. Chemistry* (of a compound) in which the ordinary isotope of hydrogen has been replaced with tritium. —**tri·ti·a·tion** /ˌtrisʜēˈāsʜən/ *n.*

trit·i·ca·le /ˌtritiˈkālē/ ▸*n.* a hybrid grain produced by crossing wheat and rye, grown as a fodder crop. ▷1950s: modern Latin, from a blend of the genus names *Triticum* 'wheat' and *Secale* 'rye.'

trit·i·um /ˈtritēəm; ˈtrisʜ-/ ▸*n. Chemistry* a radioactive isotope of hydrogen with a mass approximately three times that of the common protium isotope. (Symbol: **T**)

Discovered in 1934, tritium has two neutrons as well as a proton in the nucleus. It occurs in minute traces in nature and can be made artificially from lithium or deuterium in nuclear reactors; it is used as a fuel in thermonuclear bombs.

▷1930s: from modern Latin, from Greek *tritos* 'third.'

trito- ▸*comb. form* third: *tritocerebrum.* ▷from Greek *tritos* 'third.'

tri·to·cer·e·brum /ˌtrītōsəˈrēbrəm; -ˈserə-/ ▸*n.* (*pl.* **-bra** /-brə/) *Entomology* the third and hindmost segment of an insect's brain.

Tri·ton /ˈtrītn/ **1** *Greek Mythology* a minor sea god usually represented as a man with a fish's tail and carrying a trident and shell trumpet. **2** *Astronomy* the largest satellite of Neptune, the seventh closest to the planet, discovered in 1846. It has a retrograde orbit, a thin nitrogen atmosphere, and a diameter of 1,678 miles (2,700 km).

tri·ton[1] /ˈtrītn/ ▸*n.* a large mollusk that has a tall spiral shell with a large aperture, living in tropical and subtropical seas. • Genus *Charonia*, family Cymatiidae, class Gastropoda, in particular *C. tritonis*, which is used as a trumpet shell. ▷late 18th cent.: from TRITON.

tri·ton[2] ▸*n.* a nucleus of a tritium atom, consisting of a proton and two neutrons. ▷1940s: from TRITIUM + -ON.

tri·tone /ˈtrīˌtōn/ ▸*n. Music* an interval of three whole tones (an augmented fourth), as between C and F sharp.

trit·u·rate /ˈtricʜəˌrāt/ ▸*v.* [*trans.*] *technical* grind to a fine powder. ■ chew or grind (food) thoroughly. ▷mid 18th cent.: from Latin *triturat-* '(of corn) threshed,' from *tritura* 'rubbing' (from the verb *terere*). —**trit·u·ra·tion** /ˌtricʜəˈrāsʜən/ *n.* —**trit·u·ra·tor** /-ˌrātər/ *n.*

tri·umph /ˈtrīəmf/ ▸*n.* **1** a great victory or achievement: *a garden built to celebrate Napoleon's many triumphs.* ■ the state of being victorious or successful: *the king returned home **in triumph**.* ■ joy or satisfaction resulting from a success or victory: *"Here it is!" Helen's voice rose **in triumph**.* ■ a highly successful example of something: *the marriage had been **a triumph of** togetherness.* **2** the processional entry of a victorious general into ancient Rome.
▸*v.* [*intrans.*] **1** achieve a victory; be successful: *capitalism seems to have **triumphed over** socialism.* ■ rejoice or exult at a victory or success: *"There!" triumphed Alima.* **2** (of a Roman general) ride into ancient Rome after a victory. ▷late Middle English: from Old French *triumphe* (noun), from Latin *triump(h)us*, probably from Greek *thriambos* 'hymn to Bacchus.' Current senses of the verb date from the early 16th cent.

tri·um·phal /trīˈəmfəl/ ▸*adj.* made, carried out, or used in celebration of a great victory or achievement: *a vast triumphal arch | a triumphal procession.* ▷late Middle English: from Old French *triumphal* or Latin *triumphalis*, from *triump(h)us* (see TRIUMPH).

USAGE On the differences in use of **triumphal** and **triumphant**, see usage at TRIUMPHANT.

tri·um·phal·ism /trīˈəmfəˌlizəm/ ▸*n.* excessive exultation over one's success or achievements (used esp. in a political context): *an air of triumphalism reigns in his administration.* —**tri·um·phal·ist** *adj.* & *n.*

tri·um·phant /trīˈəmfənt/ ▸*adj.* having won a battle or contest; victorious: *the triumphant winner rose from his* seat | [*postpositive*] *a comic fairy tale about innocence triumphant.* ■ feeling or expressing jubilation after having won a victory or mastered a difficulty: *he couldn't suppress a triumphant smile.* ▷late Middle English (in the sense 'victorious'): from Old French, or from Latin *triumphant-* 'celebrating a triumph,' from the verb *triumphare* (see TRIUMPH). —**tri·um·phant·ly** *adv.*

USAGE Of the two words **triumphant** and **triumphal**, the more common is **triumphant**, which means 'victorious' or 'exultant': *she led an arduous campaign to its triumphant conclusion; he returned triumphant with a patent for his device.* **Triumphal** means 'used in or celebrating a triumph': *a triumphal parade.*

tri·um·vir /trī'əmvər/ ▸*n.* (*pl.* **-virs** or **-vi·ri** /-və,rī/) (in ancient Rome) each of three public officers jointly responsible for overseeing any of the administrative departments. ▷Latin, originally as *triumviri* (plural), back-formation from *trium virorum* 'of three men,' genitive of *tres viri.* —**tri·um·vi·ral** /-rəl/ *adj.*

tri·um·vi·rate /trī'əmvərit; -,rāt/ ▸*n.* **1** (in ancient Rome) a group of three men holding power, in particular (**the First Triumvirate**) the unofficial coalition of Julius Caesar, Pompey, and Crassus in 60 BC and (**the Second Triumvirate**) a coalition formed by Antony, Lepidus, and Octavian in 43 BC. ■ a group of three powerful or notable people or things existing in relation to each other: *a triumvirate of three former executive vice presidents.* **2** the office of triumvir in ancient Rome. ▷late 16th cent.: from Latin *triumviratus,* from *triumvir* (see TRIUMVIR).

tri·une /'trī,(y)o͞on/ ▸*adj.* consisting of three in one (used esp. with reference to the Trinity): *the triune Godhead.* ▷early 17th cent.: from TRI- 'three' + Latin *unus* 'one.' —**tri·u·ni·ty** /trī'yo͞onitē/ *n.* (*pl.* **-ties**)

tri·va·lent /trī'vālənt/ ▸*adj. Chemistry* having a valence of three.

Tri·van·drum /trə'vandrəm/ a port on the southwestern coast of India, capital of the state of Kerala; pop. 524,000.

triv·et /'trivit/ ▸*n.* an iron tripod placed over a fire for a cooking pot or kettle to stand on. ■ an iron bracket designed to hook onto bars of a grate for a similar purpose. ■ a small plate placed under a hot serving dish to protect a table. ▷late Middle English: apparently from Latin *tripes, triped-* 'three-legged,' from *tri-* 'three' + *pes, ped-* 'foot.'

triv·i·a /'trivēə/ ▸*plural n.* details, considerations, or pieces of information of little importance or value: *we fill our days with meaningless trivia.* ▷early 20th cent.: from modern Latin, plural of *trivium* 'place where three roads meet,' influenced in sense by TRIVIAL.

triv·i·al /'trivēəl/ ▸*adj.* of little value or importance: *huge fines were imposed for trivial offenses* | *trivial details.* ■ (of a person) concerned only with trifling or unimportant things. ■ *Mathematics* denoting a subgroup that either contains only the identity element or is identical with the given group. ▷late Middle English (in the sense 'belonging to the trivium'): from medieval Latin *trivialis,* from Latin *trivium* (see TRIVIUM). —**triv·i·al·i·ty** /,trivē'alitē/ *n.* (*pl.* **-ties**) —**triv·i·al·ly** *adv.*

triv·i·al·ize /'trivēə,līz/ ▸*v.* [*trans.*] make (something) seem less important, significant, or complex than it really is: *the problem was either trivialized or ignored by teachers.* —**triv·i·al·i·za·tion** /,trivēəli'zāsʜən/ *n.*

triv·i·al name ▸*n. chiefly Chemistry* a name that is in general use although not part of systematic nomenclature: *its common trivial name is citric acid.* Compare with SYSTEMATIC NAME. ■ *chiefly Zoology* another term for SPECIFIC EPITHET.

triv·i·um /'trivēəm/ ▸*n. historical* an introductory curriculum at a medieval university involving the study of grammar, rhetoric, and logic. Compare with QUADRIVIUM. ▷early 19th cent.: from Latin, literally 'place where three roads meet,' from *tri-* 'three' + *via* 'road.'

-trix ▸*suffix* (*pl.* **-trices** or **-trixes**) (chiefly in legal terms) forming feminine agent nouns corresponding to masculine nouns ending in *-tor* (such as *executrix* corresponding to *executor*). ▷from Latin.

tRNA *Biology* ▸*abbr.* transfer RNA.

Tro·ad /'trō,ad/ an ancient region of northwestern Asia Minor. Troy was its chief city.

Tro·bri·and Is·lands /'trōbrē,and; -,änd/ a small group of islands in the southwestern Pacific Ocean, in Papua New Guinea, located off the southeastern tip of the island of New Guinea.

tro·car /'trō,kär/ ▸*n.* a surgical instrument with a three-sided cutting point enclosed in a tube, used for withdrawing fluid from a body cavity. ▷early 18th cent.: from French *trocart, trois-quarts,* from *trois* 'three' + *carre* 'side, face of an instrument.'

tro·cha·ic /trō'kā-ik/ *Prosody* ▸*adj.* consisting of or featuring trochees.
▸*n.* (usu. **trochaics**) a type of verse that consists of or features trochees. ▷late 16th cent.: via Latin from Greek *trokhaikos,* from *trokhaios* (see TROCHEE).

tro·chal disk ▸*n. Zoology* each of two projections below the neck of the femur (thigh bone) to which muscles are attached. ▷mid 19th cent.: *trochal* from Greek *trokhos* 'wheel' + -AL.

tro·chan·ter /trō'kantər/ ▸*n.* **1** *Anatomy* any of two bony protuberances by which muscles are attached to the upper part of the thigh bone. **2** *Entomology* the small second segment of the leg of an insect, between the coxa and the femur. ▷early 17th cent.: from French, from Greek *trokhantēr,* from *trekhein* 'to run.'

tro·chee /'trōkē/ ▸*n. Prosody* a foot consisting of one long or stressed syllable followed by one short or unstressed syllable. ▷late 16th cent.: via Latin from Greek *trokhaios (pous)* 'running (foot),' from *trekhein* 'to run.'

troch·le·a /'träklēə/ ▸*n.* (*pl.* **-le·ae** /-lē,ē/) *Anatomy* a structure resembling or acting like a pulley, such as the groove at the lower end of the humerus forming part of the elbow joint. ▷late 17th cent.: Latin, 'pulley'; compare with Greek *trokhilia* 'sheave of a pulley.'

troch·le·ar /'träklēər/ ▸*adj. Anatomy* of or relating to a part of the body resembling a pulley.

troch·le·ar nerve ▸*n. Anatomy* each of the fourth pair of cranial nerves, supplying the superior oblique muscle of the eyeball.

tro·choid /'trō,koid/ ▸*adj.* **1** *Anatomy* denoting a joint in which one element rotates on its own axis (e.g., the atlas vertebra). **2** *Geometry* denoting a curve traced by a point on a radius of a circle rotating along a straight line or another circle (a cycloid, epicycloid, or hypocycloid). **3** *Zoology* having or denoting a form of mollusk shell that is conical with a flat base, like a top shell.
▸*n.* **1** a trochoid curve. **2** a trochoid joint. ▷early 18th cent.: from Greek *trokhoeidēs* 'wheellike,' from *trokhos* 'wheel.' —**tro·choi·dal** /trō'koidl/ *adj.*

troch·o·phore /'träkə,fôr/ ▸*n. Zoology* the planktonic larva of certain invertebrates, including some mollusks and polychaete worms, having a roughly spherical body, a band of cilia, and a spinning motion. ▷late 19th cent.: from Greek *trokhos* 'wheel' + -PHORE.

Troc·ken·bee·ren·aus·le·se /'träkən,berən,ous,lāzə/ ▸*n.* a sweet German white wine made from selected individual grapes picked later than the general harvest and affected by noble rot. ▷German, from *trocken* 'dry' + BEERENAUSLESE.

troc·to·lite /'träktə,līt/ ▸*n. Geology* gabbro made up mainly of olivine and calcic plagioclase, often having a spotted appearance likened to a trout's back. ▷late 19th cent.: from German *Troklotit,* from Greek *trōktēs,* a marine fish (taken to be 'trout').

trod /träd/ ▸ past and past participle of TREAD.

trod·den /'trädn/ ▸ past participle of TREAD.

Trog·don, William see HEAT-MOON.

trog·lo·dyte /'träglə,dīt/ ▸*n.* (esp. in prehistoric times) a person who lived in a cave. ■ a hermit. ■ a person who is regarded as being deliberately ignorant or old-fashioned. ▷late 15th cent.: via Latin from Greek *trōglodutēs,* alteration of the name of an Ethiopian people, influenced by *trōglē* 'hole.' —**trog·lo·dyt·ic** /,träglə'ditik/ *adj.* —**trog·lo·dyt·ism** /-dī,tizəm/ *n.*

tro·gon /'trō,gän/ ▸*n.* a bird of tropical American forests, with a long tail and brilliantly colored plumage. • Family Trogonidae: several genera, in particular *Trogon,* and many species; the quetzals also belong to this family. ▷late 18th cent.: from modern Latin, from Greek *trōgōn,* from *trōgein* 'gnaw.'

troi·ka /'troikə/ ▸*n.* **1** a Russian vehicle pulled by a team of three horses abreast. ■ a team of three horses for such a vehicle. **2** a group of three people working together, esp. in an administrative or managerial capacity. ▷Russian, from *troe* 'set of three.'

troil·ism /'troi,lizəm/ ▸*n.* sexual activity involving three participants. ▷1950s: perhaps based on French *trois* 'three.'

Troi·lus /'troiləs/ *Greek Mythology* a Trojan prince, the son of Priam and Hecuba, killed by Achilles. In medieval legends of the Trojan War he is portrayed as the forsaken lover of Cressida.

Tro·jan /'trōjən/ ▸*adj.* of or relating to ancient Troy in Asia Minor: *Trojan legends.*
▸*n.* a native or inhabitant of ancient Troy. ▷Middle English: from Latin *Troianus,* from *Troia* 'Troy.'
▸*PHRASE* □ **work like a Trojan** (or **Trojans**) work extremely hard.

Tro·jan as·ter·oid ▸*n.* an asteroid belonging to one of two groups that orbit the sun at the same distance as Jupiter, at the Lagrangian points roughly 60 degrees ahead of it and behind it. ▷early 20th cent.: so named because the first asteroids discovered were named after heroes of the Trojan War.

Tro·jan Horse ▸*n. Greek Mythology* a hollow wooden statue of a horse in which the Greeks concealed themselves in order to enter Troy. ■ (also **Trojan horse**) *figurative* a person or thing intended secretly to undermine or bring about the downfall of an enemy or opponent: *the rebels may use this peace accord as a Trojan horse to try and take over.* ■ (also **Trojan horse**) *Computing* a program designed to breach the security of a computer system while ostensibly performing some innocuous function.

Tro·jan War the legendary ten-year siege of Troy by a coalition of Greeks, described in Homer's *Iliad.*

The Greeks were attempting to recover Helen, wife of Menelaus, who had been abducted by the Trojan prince Paris. The war ended with the capture of the city by a trick: the Greeks ostensibly ended the siege but left behind a group of men concealed in a hollow wooden horse so large that the city walls had to be breached for it to be drawn inside.

troll[1] /trōl/ ▸*n.* a mythical, cave-dwelling being depicted in folklore as either a giant or a dwarf, typically having a very ugly appearance. ▷from Old Norse and Swedish *troll,* Danish *trold;* adopted into English from Scandinavian in the mid 19th cent.

troll[2] ▸*v.* [*intrans.*] **1** fish by trailing a baited line along behind a boat: *we trolled for mackerel.* ■ search for something: *a group of companies trolling for partnership opportunities.* **2** [*trans.*] sing (something) in a happy and carefree way: *troll the ancient Yuletide carol.* **3** [*trans.*] *informal Computing* send (an e-mail message or posting on the Internet) intended to provoke a response from the reader by containing errors. **4** [with *adverbial of direction*] *chiefly Brit.* walk; stroll: *we all trolled into town.*
▸*n.* **1** the action of trolling for fish. ■ a line or bait used in such fishing. **2** *informal Computing* an e-mail message or posting on the Internet intended to provoke an indignant response in the reader. ▷late Middle English (in the sense 'stroll, roll'): origin uncertain; compare with Old French *troller* 'wander here and there (in search of game)' and Middle High German *trollen* 'stroll.' —**troll·er** *n.*

trol·ley /'trälē/ ▸*n.* (*pl.* **-leys**) **1** short for TROLLEY CAR or TROLLEY BUS. **2** (also **trolley wheel**) a wheel attached to a pole, used for collecting current from an overhead electric wire to drive a streetcar or trolley bus. **3** a large metal basket or frame on wheels, resembling a shopping cart and used for transporting luggage at an airport or railroad station; a luggage cart. ■ *Brit.* a shopping cart. ■ *Brit.* a small table on wheels or casters, typically used to convey food and drink. **4** *chiefly Brit.* a low truck, usually without sides or ends, running on a railroad or a track in a factory. ▷early 19th cent.: of dialect origin, perhaps from TROLL[2].
▸*PHRASE* □ **off one's trolley** *informal* mad; insane.

trol·ley bus ▸*n.* a bus powered by electricity obtained from an overhead cable by means of a trolley wheel.

trol·ley car ▸*n.* a passenger vehicle powered by electricity obtained from an overhead cable by means of a trolley wheel. Also called STREETCAR.

trol·ley dol·ly ▸*n. Brit. informal* a flight attendant.

trol·lop /'träləp/ ▸*n. dated* or *humorous* a woman perceived as sexually disreputable or promiscuous. ▷early 17th cent.: perhaps related to TRULL.

Trol·lope /'träləp/, Anthony (1815–82), English novelist. He is noted for the six "Barsetshire" novels, including *The Warden* (1855) and *Barchester Towers* (1857), and for the six political "Palliser" novels.

trom·bone /träm'bōn; trəm-/ ▸*n.* a large brass wind instrument with straight tubing in three sections, ending in a bell over the player's left shoulder, different fundamental notes being made using a forward-pointing extendable slide. ■ an organ stop with the quality of such an instrument. ▷early 18th cent.: from French or Italian, from Italian *tromba* 'trumpet.' —**trom·bon·ist** /-nist/ *n.*

trombone

trom·mel /'träməl/ ▸*n.* *Mining* a rotating cylindrical sieve or screen used for washing and sorting pieces of ore or coal. ▷late 19th cent.: from German, literally 'drum.'

trompe l'oeil /,trômp 'loi/ ▸*n.* (*pl.* **trompe l'oeils** *pronunc.* same) visual illusion in art, esp. as used to trick the eye into perceiving a painted detail as a three-dimensional object. ■ a painting or design intended to create such an illusion. ▷French, literally 'deceives the eye.'

-tron ▸*suffix Physics* **1** denoting a subatomic particle: *positron.* **2** denoting a particle accelerator: *cyclotron.* **3** denoting a vacuum tube: *ignitron.* ▷from (*elec*)*tron.*

tro·na /'trōnə/ ▸*n.* a gray mineral that occurs as an evaporite in salt deposits and consists of a hydrated carbonate and bicarbonate of sodium. ▷late 18th cent.: from Swedish, from Arabic *naṭrūn* (see **NATRON**).

Trond·heim /'trän,hām; 'trôn-/ a fishing port in western central Norway; pop. 138,000. It was the capital of Norway during the Viking period.

troop /trōōp/ ▸*n.* **1** a group of soldiers, esp. a cavalry unit commanded by a captain, or an airborne unit. ■ (**troops**) soldiers or armed forces: *UN peacekeeping troops* | [as *adj.*] (**troop**) *troop withdrawals.* ■ a unit of 18 to 24 Girl Scouts or Boy Scouts organized under a troop leader. **2** a group of people or animals of a particular kind: ***a troop of** musicians.*

▸*v.* [*intrans.*] (of a group of people) come or go together or in large numbers: *the girls **trooped in** for dinner.* ■ (of a lone person) walk at a slow or steady pace: *Caroline trooped wearily home from work.* ▷mid 16th cent.: from French *troupe*, back-formation from *troupeau*, diminutive of medieval Latin *troppus* 'flock,' probably of Germanic origin.

troop car·ri·er ▸*n.* a large aircraft or armored vehicle designed for transporting troops.

troop·er /'trōōpər/ ▸*n.* **1** a state police officer. ■ a mounted police officer. **2** a private soldier in a cavalry, armored, or airborne unit. ■ a cavalry horse. ■ *chiefly Brit.* a ship used for transporting troops.

▸*PHRASE* □ **swear like a trooper** swear a great deal.

troop·ship /'trōōp,SHip/ ▸*n.* a ship designed or used for transporting troops.

trop. ▸*abbr.* ■ tropic. ■ tropical.

trope /trōp/ ▸*n.* a figurative or metaphorical use of a word or expression: *he used the two-Americas trope to explain how a nation free and democratic at home could act wantonly abroad.* ■ a conventional idea or phrase: *her suspicion of ambiguity was more a trope than a fact.*

▸*v.* [*intrans.*] create a trope. ▷mid 16th cent.: via Latin from Greek *tropos* 'turn, way, trope,' from *trepein* 'to turn.'

troph·al·lax·is /,träfə'laksis; ,trō-/ ▸*n.* *Entomology* the mutual exchange of regurgitated liquids between adult social insects or between them and their larvae. ▷early 20th cent.: from **TROPHO-** 'nourishment' + Greek *allaxis* 'exchange.'

troph·ec·to·derm /träf'ektə,dərm; trō-/ ▸*n.* another term for **TROPHOBLAST.**

troph·ic /'trōfik; 'träf-/ ▸*adj.* *Ecology* of or relating to feeding and nutrition. ■ *Physiology* (of a hormone or its effect) stimulating the activity of another endocrine gland. ▷late 19th cent.: from Greek *trophikos*, from *trophē* 'nourishment,' from *trephein* 'nourish.'

-trophic ▸*comb. form* **1** relating to nutrition: *oligotrophic.* **2** relating to maintenance or regulation of a bodily organ or function, esp. by a hormone: *gonadotrophic.* ▷from Greek *trophikos*, from *trophē* 'nourishment.'

troph·ic lev·el ▸*n.* *Ecology* each of several hierarchical levels in an ecosystem, comprising organisms that share the same function in the food chain and the same nutritional relationship to the primary sources of energy.

-trophism ▸*comb. form* in nouns corresponding to adjectives ending in *-trophic* (such as *phototropism* corresponding to *phototrophic*).

tropho- ▸*comb. form* relating to nourishment: *trophoblast.* ▷from Greek *trophē* 'nourishment.'

troph·o·blast /'träfə,blast; 'trō-/ ▸*n.* *Embryology* a layer of tissue on the outside of a mammalian blastula, supplying the embryo with nourishment and later forming the major part of the placenta. —**troph·o·blas·tic** /,träfə'blastik/ *adj.*

troph·o·zo·ite /,träfə'zō,īt; ,trō-/ ▸*n.* *Zoology & Medicine* a growing stage in the life cycle of some sporozoan parasites, when they are absorbing nutrients from the host.

tro·phy /'trōfē/ ▸*n.* (*pl.* **-phies**) **1** a cup or other decorative object awarded as a prize for a victory or success. ■ a souvenir of an achievement, esp. a part of an animal taken when hunting. **2** (in ancient Greece or Rome) the weapons and other spoils of a defeated army set up as a memorial of victory. ■ a representation of such a memorial; an ornamental group of symbolic objects arranged for display. ▷late 15th cent. (sense 2, denoting a display of weapons): from French *trophée*, via Latin from Greek *tropaion*, from *tropē* 'a rout,' from *trepein* 'to turn.'

-trophy ▸*comb. form* in nouns corresponding to adjectives ending in *-trophic* (such as *phototrophy* corresponding to *phototrophic*).

tro·phy child ▸*n.* a child whose birth or achievements are paraded to enhance the parents' status.

tro·phy wife ▸*n.* *informal, derogatory* a young, attractive wife regarded as a status symbol for an older man.

trop·ic[1] /'träpik/ ▸*n.* the parallel of latitude 23°26′ north (**tropic of Cancer**) or south (**tropic of Capricorn**) of the equator. ■ *Astronomy* each of two corresponding circles on the celestial sphere where the sun appears to turn after reaching its greatest declination, marking the northern and southern limits of the ecliptic. ■ (**the tropics**) the region between the tropics of Cancer and Capricorn.

▸*adj.* another term for **TROPICAL** (sense 1). ▷late Middle English (denoting the point on the ecliptic reached by the sun at the solstice): via Latin from Greek *tropikos*, from *tropē* 'turning,' from *trepein* 'to turn.'

trop·ic[2] ▸*adj.* **1** *Biology* relating to, consisting of, or exhibiting tropism. **2** *Physiology* variant spelling of **TROPHIC.**

-tropic ▸*comb. form* **1** turning toward: *heliotropic.* **2** affecting: *psychotropic.* **3** (esp. in names of hormones) equivalent to **-TROPHIC.** ▷from Greek *tropē* 'turn, turning.'

trop·i·cal /'träpəkəl/ ▸*adj.* **1** of, typical of, or peculiar to the tropics: *tropical countries* | *a tropical rain forest.* ■ resembling the tropics, esp. in being very hot and humid: *some plants thrived in last year's tropical summer heat.* **2** *archaic* of or involving a trope; figurative. —**trop·i·cal·ly** /-ik(ə)lē/ *adv.*

trop·i·cal sprue ▸*n.* see **SPRUE**[2].

trop·i·cal storm (also **trop·i·cal cy·clone**) ▸*n.* a localized, very intense low-pressure wind system, forming over tropical oceans and with winds of hurricane force.

trop·i·cal year ▸*n.* see **YEAR** (sense 1).

trop·ic·bird /'träpik,bərd/ ▸*n.* a tropical seabird with mainly white plumage and very long central tail feathers. • Family Phaethontidae and genus *Phaethon*: three species.

trop·ic of Can·cer ▸*n.* see **TROPIC**[1].

trop·ic of Cap·ri·corn ▸*n.* see **TROPIC**[1].

tro·pism /'trō,pizəm/ ▸*n.* *Biology* the turning of all or part of an organism in a particular direction in response to an external stimulus. ▷late 19th cent.: from Greek *tropos* 'turning' (from *trepein* 'to turn') + **-ISM.**

tro·pol·o·gy /trə'päləjē/ ▸*n.* the figurative use of language. ■ *Christian Theology* the figurative interpretation of the scriptures as a source of moral guidance. ▷late Middle English: via late Latin from Greek *tropologia*, from *tropos* (see **TROPE**). —**trop·o·log·i·cal** /,träpə'läjikəl/ *adj.*

trop·o·lone /'träpə,lōn; 'trō-/ ▸*n.* *Chemistry* an organic compound present in various plants, with a molecule based on a seven-membered carbon ring. • An enolic ketone; chem. formula: $C_7H_6O_2$. ▷1940s: from *tropilidine* (a liquid hydrocarbon) + **-OL** + **-ONE.**

trop·o·my·o·sin /,träpō'mīəsən; ,trō-/ ▸*n.* *Biochemistry* a protein involved in muscle contraction. It is related to myosin and occurs together with troponin in the thin filaments of muscle tissue. ▷1940s: from Greek *tropos* 'turning' + **MYOSIN.**

tro·po·nin /'träpənən; 'trō-/ ▸*n.* *Biochemistry* a globular protein complex involved in muscle contraction. It occurs with tropomyosin in the thin filaments of muscle tissue. ▷1960s: from **TROPOMYOSIN** + *-n-* + **-IN**[1].

trop·o·pause /'träpə,pôz; 'trō-/ ▸*n.* the interface between the troposphere and the stratosphere. ▷early 20th cent.: from Greek *tropos* 'turning' + **PAUSE.**

trop·o·sphere /'träpə,sfi(ə)r; 'trō-/ ▸*n.* the lowest region of the atmosphere, extending from the earth's surface to a height of about 6–10 km (the lower boundary of the stratosphere). ▷early 20th cent.: from Greek *tropos* 'turning' + **SPHERE.** —**trop·o·spher·ic** /,träpə'sfi(ə)rik; -'sferik; ,trō-/ *adj.*

trop·po[1] /'träpō/ ▸*adv.* [usu. with *negative*] *Music* (in directions) too much; excessively. ▷Italian.

▸*PHRASE* □ **ma non troppo** /mä ,nôn 'trôpō/ (as a direction) but not too much (used to suggest moderate application of another direction): *allegro ma non troppo.*

trop·po[2] ▸*adj.* *Austral./NZ informal* mentally disturbed, supposedly as a result of spending too much time in a tropical climate: *have you **gone troppo**?* ▷1940s: from **TROPIC**[1] + **-O.**

trot /trät/ ▸*v.* (**trot·ted, trot·ting**) (of a horse or other quadruped) proceed at a pace faster than a walk, lifting each diagonal pair of legs alternately. ■ [*trans.*] cause (a horse) to move at such a pace: *he trotted his horse forward.* ■ [*intrans.*] (of a person) run at a moderate pace, typically with short steps. ■ [*intrans.*] *informal* go or walk briskly: *he trotted over to the bonfire.*

▸*phrasal v.* □ **trot something out** **1** *informal* produce the same information, story, or explanation that has been produced many times before: *everyone trots out the old excuse.* **2** cause a horse to trot to show its paces.

▸*n.* **1** a trotting pace: *our horses slowed to a trot.* **2** (**the trots**) *informal* diarrhea: *a bad case of the trots.* **3** *informal* a literal translation of a foreign language text for use by students, esp. in a surreptitious way: *adult readers who can turn to translations without being penalized for depending on trots.* ▷Middle English: from Old French *trot* (noun), *troter* (verb), from medieval Latin *trottare*, of Germanic origin.

▸*PHRASE* □ **on the trot** *informal* **1** continually busy: *I've been on the trot all day.* **2** *Brit.* in succession: *they lost seven matches on the trot.*

troth /trôTH; trōTH/ ▸*n.* **1** *archaic* or *formal* faith or loyalty when pledged in a solemn agreement or undertaking: *a token of troth.* **2** *archaic* truth. ▷Middle English: variant of **TRUTH.**

▸*PHRASE* □ **pledge** (or **plight**) **one's troth** make a solemn pledge of commitment or loyalty, esp. in marriage.

Trot·sky /'trätskē/, Leon (1879–1940), Russian revolutionary; born *Lev Davidovich Bronshtein.* He helped to organize the October Revolution with Lenin and built up the Red Army. Expelled from the party by Stalin in 1927, he was exiled in 1929. He settled in Mexico in 1937, where he was later murdered by a Stalinist assassin.

Trot·sky·ism /'trätskē,izəm/ ▸*n.* the political or economic principles of Leon Trotsky, esp. the theory that socialism should be established throughout the world by continuing revolution.Trotskyism has generally included elements of anarchism and syndicalism, but the term has come to be used indiscriminately to describe a great many forms of radical socialism. —**Trot·sky·ist** *n.* & *adj.* —**Trot·sky·ite** /-,īt/ *n.* & *adj.* (*derogatory*).

trot·ter /'trätər/ ▸*n.* **1** a horse bred or trained for the sport of harness racing. **2** a pig's foot used as food. ■ *humorous* a human foot.

trot·ting /'trätiNG/ ▸*n.* another term for **HARNESS RACING.**

trou·ba·dour /'trōōbə,dôr; -,dōōr/ ▸*n.* a French medieval lyric poet composing and singing in Provençal in the 11th to 13th centuries, esp. on the theme of courtly love. ■ a poet who writes verse to music. ▷French, from Provençal *trobador*, from *trobar* 'find, invent, compose in verse.'

trou·ble /'trəbəl/ ▸*n.* **1** difficulty or problems: *I had trouble finding somewhere to park* | *the government's policies **ran into trouble*** | *our troubles are just beginning.* ■ the malfunction of something such as a machine or a part of the body: *their helicopter developed engine trouble.* ■ effort or exertion made to do something, esp. when inconvenient: *I wouldn't want to put you to any trouble* | *he's **gone to** a lot of **trouble** to help you.* ■ a cause of worry or inconvenience: *the kid had been **no trouble** up to now.* ■ a particular aspect or quality of something regarded as unsatisfactory or as a source of difficulty: *that's* **the trouble with** *capitalism.* ■ a situation in which one is liable to incur punishment or blame: *he's been* **in trouble with** *the police.* ■ *informal, dated* used to refer to the condition of a pregnant unmarried woman: *she's not the first girl who's* **got** *herself* **into trouble**. **2** public unrest or disorder: *the cops are preparing for trouble by bringing in tear gas.*

▸*v.* [*trans.*] **1** (often **be troubled**) cause distress or anxiety to: *he was not troubled by doubts.* ■ [*intrans.*] (**trouble about/over/with**) be distressed or anxious about: *there is nothing you need trouble about.* ■ cause (someone) pain: *my legs started to trouble me.* ■ cause (someone) inconvenience (typically used as a polite way of asking someone to do or provide something): *sorry to trouble you* | *could I* **trouble** *you* **for** *a receipt?* ■ [*intrans.*] make the effort required to do something: *oh, don't trouble to answer.* **2** disturb or agitate (the surface in a pool or other body of water): *the waters were troubled.* ▷Middle English: from Old French *truble* (noun), *trubler* (verb), based on Latin *turbidus* (see TURBID). **—trou·bler** /-b(ə)lər/ *n.*

▸*PHRASES* □ **ask for trouble** *informal* act in a way that is likely to incur problems or difficulties: *hitching a lift is asking for trouble.* □ **look for trouble** *informal* behave in a way that is likely to provoke an argument or fight: *youths take a cocktail of drink and drugs before going out to look for trouble.* □ **trouble and strife** *Brit., rhyming slang* wife. □ **a trouble shared is a trouble halved** *proverb* talking to someone else about one's problems helps to alleviate them.

trou·bled /ˈtrəbəld/ ▸*adj.* beset by problems or conflict: *his troubled private life.* ■ showing distress or anxiety: *his troubled face.*

▸*PHRASE* □ **troubled waters** a difficult situation or time.

trou·ble·mak·er /ˈtrəbəlˌmākər/ ▸*n.* a person who habitually causes difficulty or problems, esp. by inciting others to defy those in authority. **—trou·ble·mak·ing** /-ˌmākiNG/ *n.* & *adj.*

trou·ble·shoot /ˈtrəbəlˌSHo͞ot/ ▸*v.* [*intrans.*] [usu. as *n.*] (**troubleshooting**) solve serious problems for a company or other organization. ■ trace and correct faults in a mechanical or electronic system. **—trou·ble·shoot·er** *n.*

trou·ble·some /ˈtrəbəlsəm/ ▸*adj.* causing difficulty or annoyance: *a troublesome knee injury.* **—trou·ble·some·ly** *adv.* **—trou·ble·some·ness** *n.*

trou·ble spot ▸*n.* a place where difficulties regularly occur, esp. a country or area where there is a continuous cycle of violence.

trou·blous /ˈtrəbləs/ ▸*adj. archaic* or *poetic/literary* full of difficulty or agitation: *those were troublous times.* ▷late Middle English: from Old French *troubleus*, from *truble* (see TROUBLE).

trough /trôf/ ▸*n.* a long, narrow open container for animals to eat or drink out of: *a water trough.* ■ a container of a similar shape used for a purpose such as growing plants or mixing chemicals. ■ a channel used to convey a liquid. ■ a long hollow in the earth's surface: *a vast glacial trough.* ■ an elongated region of low atmospheric pressure. ■ a hollow between two wave crests in the sea. ■ a low level of economic activity. ■ *Mathematics* a region around the minimum on a curve of variation of a quantity. ■ a point of low achievement or satisfaction: *learning a language is a series of* **peaks and troughs**. ▷Old English *trog*, of Germanic origin; related to Dutch *trog* and German *Trog*, also to TREE.

trough shell ▸*n.* a burrowing marine bivalve mollusk with a thin, smooth shell. • Family Mactridae: *Spisula* and other genera.

trounce /trouns/ ▸*v.* [*trans.*] defeat heavily in a contest: *the Knicks trounced the Rockets on Sunday.* ■ rebuke or punish severely: *some shows were trounced by critics.* ▷mid 16th cent. (also in the sense 'afflict'): of unknown origin. **—trounc·er** *n.*

troupe /tro͞op/ ▸*n.* a group of dancers, actors, or other entertainers who tour to different venues. ▷early 19th cent.: from French, literally 'troop.'

troup·er /ˈtro͞opər/ ▸*n.* an actor or other entertainer, typically one with long experience. ■ a reliable and uncomplaining person: *a* **real trouper**, *Ma concealed her troubles.*

troup·i·al /ˈtro͞opēəl/ ▸*n.* a gregarious songbird of the American oriole family, typically having orange and black plumage and yellow eyes. • Genus *Icterus*, family Icteridae: several species, in particular the tropical American *Icterus icterus.* ▷early 19th cent.: from French *troupiale*, alteration of American Spanish *turpial*, of unknown origin.

trou·ser /ˈtrouzər/ ▸*n.* [as *adj.*] relating to trousers: *his trouser pocket* | *a trouser press.* ■ a trouser leg: *his trouser was torn.*

trou·sers /ˈtrouzərz/ (also **a pair of trousers**) ▸*plural n.* an outer garment covering the body from the waist to the ankles, with a separate part for each leg. ▷early 17th cent.: from archaic *trouse* (singular), from Irish *triús* and Scottish Gaelic *triubhas* (see TREWS), on the pattern of *drawers.* **—trou·sered** /-zərd/ *adj.*

trous·seau /ˈtro͞oˌsō; ˌtro͞oˈsō/ ▸*n.* (*pl.* **-seaux** *pronunc.* same, or **-seaus**) the clothes, household linen, and other belongings collected by a bride for her marriage. ▷mid 19th cent.: from French, diminutive of *trousse* 'bundle' (a sense also found in Middle English).

trout /trout/ ▸*n.* (*pl.* same or **trouts**) a chiefly freshwater fish of the salmon family, found in both Eurasia and North America and highly valued as food and game. • Genera *Salmo* (several species of true trouts, including the European **brown trout** and the **rainbow trout**), and *Salvelinus* (several North American species), family Salmonidae. See also LAKE TROUT, SEA TROUT. ▷late Old English *truht*, from late Latin *tructa*, based on Greek *trōgein* 'gnaw.'

▸*PHRASE* □ **old trout** *informal* an annoying or bad-tempered old person, esp. a woman.

trout·ing /ˈtroutiNG/ ▸*n.* the activity of catching or trying to catch trout, either for food or as a sport.

trout lil·y ▸*n.* a North American dogtooth violet with yellow flowers, so called from its mottled leaves. Also called ADDER'S TONGUE. • *Erythronium americanum*, family Liliaceae.

trou·vaille /tro͞oˈvī/ ▸*n.* a lucky find: *one of numerous trouvailles to be gleaned from his book.* ▷French, from *trouver* 'find.'

trou·vère /tro͞oˈver/ ▸*n.* a medieval epic poet in northern France in the 11th–14th centuries. ▷from Old French *trovere*, from *trover* 'to find'; compare with TROUBADOUR.

trove /trōv/ ▸*n.* a store of valuable or delightful things: *the museum's trove of antique treasure.* ▷late 19th cent.: from TREASURE TROVE.

tro·ver /ˈtrōvər/ ▸*n. Law* common-law action to recover the value of personal property that has been wrongfully disposed of by another person. ▷late 16th cent.: from an Anglo-Norman French noun use of Old French *trover* 'to find.'

trow /trō/ ▸*v.* [*trans.*] *archaic* think or believe: *why, this is strange, I trow!* ▷Old English *trūwian, trēowian* 'to trust'; related to TRUCE.

trow·el /ˈtrouəl/ ▸*n.* **1** a small hand-held tool with a flat, pointed blade, used to apply and spread mortar or plaster. **2** a small hand-held tool with a curved scoop for lifting plants or earth.

▸*v.* (**-eled**, **-el·ing**; *Brit.* **-elled**, **-el·ling**) [*trans.*] apply or spread with or as if with a trowel. ▷Middle English (as a noun): from Old French *truele*, from medieval Latin *truella*, alteration of Latin *trulla* 'scoop,' diminutive of *trua* 'skimmer.'

Troy /troi/ **1** (in Homeric legend) the city of King Priam, besieged for ten years by the Greeks during the Trojan War. It was regarded as having been a purely legendary city until Heinrich Schliemann identified the mound of Hissarlik on the northeast Aegean coast of Turkey as the site of Troy. The city was apparently sacked and destroyed by fire in the mid 13th century BC, a period coinciding with the Mycenaean civilization of Greece. Also called ILIUM. **2** a residential and commercial city in southeastern Michigan; pop. 80,959. **3** an industrial city in eastern New York, on the Hudson and Mohawk rivers, northeast of Albany; pop. 49,170.

troy /troi/ (in full **troy weight**) ▸*n.* a system of weights used mainly for precious metals and gems, with a pound of 12 ounces or 5,760 grains. Compare with AVOIRDUPOIS. ▷late Middle English: from a weight used at the fair of *Troyes.*

Troyes /trwä/, Chrétien de, see CHRÉTIEN DE TROYES.

trp. ▸*abbr.* troop.

tru·ant /ˈtro͞oənt/ ▸*n.* a student who stays away from school without leave or explanation.

▸*adj.* (of a student) being a truant: *truant children.* ■ wandering; straying: *her truant husband.*

▸*v.* [*intrans.*] another way of saying PLAY TRUANT below. ▷Middle English (denoting a person begging through choice rather than necessity): from Old French, probably ultimately of Celtic origin; compare with Welsh *truan*, Scottish Gaelic *truaghan* 'wretched.' **—tru·an·cy** /-ənsē/ *n.*

▸*PHRASE* □ **play truant** stay away from school or work without permission or explanation; play hooky.

truce /tro͞os/ ▸*n.* an agreement between enemies or opponents to stop fighting or arguing for a certain time: *the guerrillas called a three-day truce.* ▷Middle English *trewes, trues* (plural), from Old English *trēowa*, plural of *trēow* 'belief, trust,' of Germanic origin; related to Dutch *trouw* and German *Treue*, also to TRUE.

Tru·cial States /ˈtro͞oSHəl/ former name (until 1971) of UNITED ARAB EMIRATES.

truck[1] /trək/ ▸*n.* **1** a wheeled vehicle, in particular: ■ a large, heavy motor vehicle, used for transporting goods, materials, or troops. ■ *Brit.* a railroad vehicle for carrying freight, esp. a small open one. ■ a low flat-topped cart used for moving heavy items. **2** a undercarriage with four to six wheels pivoted beneath the end of a railroad car. ■ each of two axle units on a skateboard, to which the wheels are attached. **3** a wooden disk at the top of a ship's mast or flagstaff, with sheaves for signal halyards.

▸*v.* [*trans.*] convey by truck: *the food was trucked to St. Petersburg* | [as *n.*] (**trucking**) *industries such as trucking.* ■ [*intrans.*] drive a truck. ■ [*intrans.*] *informal* go or proceed, esp. in a casual or leisurely way: *he walked confidently behind them and trucked on through!* ▷Middle English (denoting a solid wooden wheel): perhaps short for TRUCKLE[1] in the sense 'wheel, pulley.' The sense 'wheeled vehicle' dates from the late 18th cent. **—truck·age** /-kij/ *n.*

truck[2] ▸*n.* **1** *archaic* barter. ■ *chiefly historical* the payment of workers in kind or with vouchers rather than money. **2** *chiefly archaic* small wares. ■ *informal* odds and ends. **3** market-garden produce, esp. vegetables: [as *adj.*] *a truck garden.*

▸*v.* [*trans.*] *archaic* barter or exchange. ▷Middle English (as a verb): probably from Old French, of unknown origin; compare with medieval Latin *trocare.*

▸*PHRASE* □ **have** (or **want**) **no truck with** avoid or wish to avoid dealings or being associated with: *we have no truck with that style of gutter journalism.*

truck·er /ˈtrəkər/ ▸*n.* a long-distance truck driver.

truck farm ▸*n.* a farm that produces vegetables for the market.

truck·le[1] /ˈtrəkəl/ ▸*n.* a small barrel-shaped cheese, esp. cheddar. ▷late Middle English (denoting a wheel or pulley): from Anglo-Norman French *trocle*, from Latin *trochlea* 'sheave of a pulley.' The current sense dates from the early 19th cent. and was originally dialect.

truck·le[2] ▸*v.* [*intrans.*] submit or behave obsequiously: *she despised her husband, who* **truckled to** *her.* ▷mid 17th cent.: figuratively, from TRUCKLE BED; an earlier use of the verb was in the sense *sleep in a truckle bed.* **—truck·ler** /ˈtrək(ə)lər/ *n.*

truck·le bed ▸*n. chiefly Brit.* a trundle bed. ▷late Middle English: from TRUCKLE[1] in the sense 'wheel' + BED.

truck·load /ˈtrəkˌlōd/ ▸*n.* a quantity of goods that can be transported in a truck: *a* **truckload of** *chemicals caught fire.* ■ (**a truckload/truckloads of**) *informal* a large quantity or number of something: *the government had plowed* **truckloads of** *money into this land.*

▸*PHRASE* □ **by the truckload** *informal* in large quantities or numbers: *he had charm by the truckload.*

truck stop ▸*n.* a large roadside service station and restaurant for truck drivers on interstate highways.

truc·u·lent /ˈtrəkyələnt/ ▸*adj.* eager or quick to argue or fight; aggressively defiant: *his days of truculent defiance were over.* ▷mid 16th cent.: from Latin *truculentus*, from *trux, truc-* 'fierce.' **—truc·u·lence** *n.* **—truc·u·lent·ly** *adv.*

Tru·deau[1] /tro͞oˈdō/, Garry (1948–), U.S. editorial cartoonist; full name *Garretson Beekman Trudeau.* He created "Doonesbury", an often controversial comic strip that he began in 1970. He is married to television journalist Jane Pauley (1950–).

Tru·deau[2], Pierre (Elliott) (1919–2000), Canadian statesman; prime minister 1968–79 and 1980–84. Noted for his commitment to federalism, he made both English and French official languages of the Canadian government in 1969, held a provincial referendum in Quebec in 1980 that rejected independence, and saw the transfer of residual constitutional powers from Britain to Canada in 1982.

trudge /trəj/ ▸*v.* [*intrans.*] walk slowly and with heavy steps, typically because of exhaustion or harsh conditions: *I trudged up the stairs* | *she trudged through blinding snow.*

Pronunciation Key ə *ago*; ər *over*; ˈə or ˌə *up*; ˈər or ˌər *fur*; a *hat*; ā *rate*; ä *car*; CH *chew*; e *let*; ē *see*; e(ə)r *air*; i *fit*; ī *by*; i(ə)r *ear*; NG *sing*; ō *go*; ô *for*; oi *boy*; o͝o *good*; o͞o *goo*; ou *out*; SH *she*; TH *thin*; TH *then*; (h)w *why*; ZH *vision*

▸*n.* a difficult or laborious walk: *he began the long trudge back.* ▷mid 16th cent. (as a verb): of unknown origin. —**trudg·er** *n.*

trudg·en /ˈtrəjən/ ▸*n.* [in *sing.*] a swimming stroke like the crawl with a scissors movement of the legs. ▷late 19th cent.: named after John *Trudgen* (1852–1902), English swimmer.

true /tro͞o/ ▸*adj.* (**tru·er**, **tru·est**) **1** in accordance with fact or reality: *a true story | of course it's true | that is not* **true of** *the people I am talking about.* ■ [*attrib.*] rightly or strictly so called; genuine: *people are still willing to pay for true craftsmanship | we believe in true love.* ■ [*attrib.*] real or actual: *he has guessed my true intentions.* ■ said when conceding a point in argument or discussion: *true, it faced north, but you got used to that.* **2** accurate or exact: *it was a true depiction.* ■ (of a note) exactly in tune. ■ (of a compass bearing) measured relative to true north: *steer 085 degrees true.* ■ correctly positioned, balanced, or aligned; upright or level. **3** loyal or faithful: *he was a true friend.* ■ [*predic.*] (**true to**) accurately conforming to (a standard or expectation); faithful to: *this entirely new production remains true to the essence of Lorca's play.* **4** *chiefly archaic* honest: *we appeal to all good men and true to rally to us.*
▸*adv.* **1** *chiefly poetic/literary* truly: *Hobson spoke truer than he knew.* **2** accurately or without variation.
▸*v.* (**trues**, **trued**, **tru·ing** or **true·ing**) [*trans.*] bring (an object, wheel, or other construction) into the exact shape, alignment, or position required. ▷Old English *trēowe*, *trȳwe* 'steadfast, loyal'; related to Dutch *getrouw*, German *treu*, also to TRUCE. —**true·ness** *n.*
▸*PHRASES* □ **come true** actually happen or become the case: *dreams can come true.* □ **out of true** not in the correct or exact shape or alignment: *take care not to pull the frame out of true.* □ **many a true word is spoken in jest** *proverb* a humorous remark not intended to be taken seriously may turn out to be accurate after all. □ **true to form** (or **type**) being or behaving as expected: *true to form, they took it well.* □ **true to life** accurately representing real events or objects: *artworks of the period were often composed in strident colors not true to life.*

true bill ▸*n. Law* a bill of indictment found by a grand jury to be supported by sufficient evidence to justify the hearing of a case.

true-blue ▸*adj.* extremely loyal or orthodox: *I'm a dyed-in-the-wool, true-blue patriot.*

true-born ▸*adj.* [*attrib.*] of a specified kind by birth; genuine: *a true-born criminal.*

true bug ▸*n.* see BUG (sense 2).

true-false test ▸*n.* a test consisting of statements that must be marked as either true or false.

true·heart·ed /ˈtro͞oˈhärtəd/ ▸*adj. poetic/literary* loyal or faithful: *a truehearted paladin.*

true leaf ▸*n. Botany* a foliage leaf of a plant, as opposed to a seed leaf or cotyledon.

true-life ▸*adj.* true to life; realistic: *a story adapted from the true-life confessions of a Bayonne Mafioso.*

true-love knot (also **true-lov·er's knot**) ▸*n.* a kind of knot with interlacing bows on each side, symbolizing the bonds of love.

true north ▸*n.* north according to the earth's axis, not magnetic north.

true rib ▸*n.* a rib that is attached directly to the breastbone. Compare with FLOATING RIB.

Truf·faut /tro͞oˈfō/, François (1932–84), French movie director. His first movie, *The 400 Blows* (1959), established him as a leading director of the *nouvelle vague*. Other movies include *Jules et Jim* (1961) and *The Last Metro* (1980).

truf·fle /ˈtrəfəl/ ▸*n.* **1** a strong-smelling underground fungus that resembles an irregular, rough-skinned potato, growing chiefly in broad-leaved woodland on calcareous soils. It is considered a culinary delicacy and found, esp. in France, with the aid of trained dogs or pigs. • Family Tuberaceae, subdivision Ascomycotina: *Tuber* and other genera. **2** a soft candy made of a chocolate mixture, typically flavored with rum and covered with cocoa. ▷late 16th cent.: probably via Dutch from obsolete French *truffle*, perhaps based on Latin *tubera*, plural of *tuber* 'hump, swelling.' Sense 2 dates from the 1920s.

truf·fled /ˈtrəfəld/ ▸*adj.* (of food) cooked, garnished, or stuffed with truffles: *a truffled turkey.*

truf·fling /ˈtrəf(ə)liNG/ ▸*n.* the activity of hunting or rooting for truffles.

trug /trəg/ (also **trug basket**) ▸*n. Brit.* a shallow oblong basket made of strips of wood, traditionally used for carrying garden flowers and produce. ▷late Middle English (denoting a basin): perhaps a dialect variant of TROUGH.

tru·ism /ˈtro͞oˌizəm/ ▸*n.* a statement that is obviously true and says nothing new or interesting: *the truism that you get what you pay for.* ■ *Logic* a proposition that states nothing beyond what is implied by any of its terms. —**tru·is·tic** /tro͞oˈistik/ *adj.*

truite au bleu /ˌtrwēt ō ˈblœ/ ▸*n.* a dish consisting of trout cooked with vinegar, which turns the fish blue. ▷French, literally 'trout in the blue.'

Tru·ji·llo[1] /tro͞oˈhēyō/ a city on the coast of northwestern Peru; pop. 509,000.

Tru·ji·llo[2], Rafael (1891–1961), Dominican statesman; president of the Dominican Republic 1930–38 and 1942–52; born *Rafael Leónidas Trujillo Molina*; known as **Generalissimo**. Although he was formally president for only two periods, he wielded dictatorial powers from 1930 until his death.

Truk Is·lands /trək; tro͝ok/ a group of 14 volcanic islands and numerous atolls in the western Pacific Ocean, in the Caroline Islands group, that forms part of the Federated States of Micronesia; pop. 54,000. There was a Japanese naval base here during World War II.

trull /trəl/ ▸*n. archaic* a prostitute. ▷early 16th cent.: from German *Trulle*.

tru·ly /ˈtro͞olē/ ▸*adv.* **1** in a truthful way: *he speaks truly.* ■ used to emphasize emotional sincerity or seriousness: *time to reflect on what we truly want | it is truly a privilege to be here |* [as *submodifier*] *I'm truly sorry, but I can't join you today |* [*sentence adverb*] *truly, I don't understand you sometimes.* **2** to the fullest degree; genuinely or properly: *management does not truly understand or care about the residents |* [as *submodifier*] *a truly free press.* ■ [as *submodifier*] absolutely or completely (used to emphasize a description): *a truly dreadful song.* **3** in fact or without doubt; really: *this is truly a miracle.* **4** *archaic* loyally or faithfully: *why cannot all masters be served truly?* ▷Old English *trēowlīce* 'faithfully' (see TRUE, -LY[2]).
▸*PHRASE* □ **yours truly** used as a formula for ending a letter. ■ *humorous* used to refer to oneself: *the demos will be organized by yours truly.*

Tru·man /ˈtro͞omən/, Harry S (1884–1972), 33rd president of the U.S. 1945–53. A Democrat, he served in the U.S. Senate 1934–45. As vice president 1945, he succeeded to the presidency upon the death of Franklin D. Roosevelt during World War II. He authorized the use of the atom bomb against Hiroshima and Nagasaki in 1945, initiated the Truman Doctrine in 1947, introduced the Marshall Plan in 1948, and helped to establish NATO the following year. The U.S. became involved in the Korean War in 1950. Truman's victory over Thomas E. Dewey in the 1948 presidential election was one of the closest in U.S. history.

Harry S Truman

Tru·man Doc·trine the principle that the U.S. should give support to countries or peoples threatened by Soviet forces or communist insurrection. First expressed in 1947 by U.S. President Truman in a speech to Congress seeking aid for Greece and Turkey, the doctrine was seen by the communists as an open declaration of the Cold War.

Trum·bull[1] /ˈtrəmbəl/ a town in southwestern Connecticut, northeast of Bridgeport; pop. 32,016.

Trum·bull[2], John (1756–1843), U.S. artist. He is noted for his large scenes, particularly of the American Revolution, and created paintings for the rotunda of the Capitol building in Washington, D.C. He also painted "The Declaration of Independence" (1796) and several portraits of George Washington.

tru·meau /tro͞oˈmō/ ▸*n.* (*pl.* **-meaux** /-ˈmōz; -ˈmō/) a section of wall or a pillar between two openings, esp. a pillar dividing a large doorway in a church. ▷late 19th cent.: from French, literally 'calf of the leg.'

Trump /trəmp/, Donald John (1946–) U.S. real estate developer. He was noted for building Trump Tower in New York City and the Taj Mahal gambling complex in Atlantic City in New Jersey.

trump[1] /trəmp/ ▸*n.* (in bridge, whist, and similar card games) a playing card of the suit chosen to rank above the others, which can win a trick where a card of a different suit has been led. ■ (**trumps**) the suit having this rank in a particular hand: *the ace of trumps.* ■ (in a tarot pack) any of a special suit of 22 cards depicting symbolic and typical figures and scenes. ■ (also **trump card**) *figurative* a valuable resource that may be used, esp. as a surprise, in order to gain an advantage: *in this month General Haig decided to play his trump card: the tank.* ■ *informal, dated* a helpful or admirable person.
▸*v.* [*trans.*] (in bridge, whist, and similar card games) play a trump on (a card of another suit), having no cards of the suit led. ■ *figurative* beat (someone or something) by saying or doing something better: *if the fetus is human life, that trumps any argument about the freedom of the mother.*
▸*phrasal v.* □ **trump something up** invent a false accusation or excuse: *they've trumped up charges against her.* ▷early 16th cent.: alteration of TRIUMPH, once used in card games in the same sense.

trump[2] ▸*n. archaic* a trumpet or a trumpet blast. ▷Middle English: from Old French *trompe*, of Germanic origin; probably imitative.

trump·er·y /ˈtrəmpərē/ *archaic* ▸*n.* (*pl.* **-er·ies**) attractive articles of little value or use. ■ practices or beliefs that are superficially or visually appealing but have little real value or worth.
▸*adj.* showy but worthless: *trumpery jewelry.* ■ delusive or shallow: *that trumpery hope which lets us dupe ourselves.* ▷late Middle English (denoting trickery): from Old French *tromperie*, from *tromper* 'deceive.'

trum·pet /ˈtrəmpit/ ▸*n.* **1** a brass musical instrument with a flared bell and a bright, penetrating tone. The modern instrument has the tubing looped to form a straight-sided coil, with three valves. ■ an organ reed stop with a quality resembling that of a trumpet. ■ something shaped like a trumpet, esp. the tubular corona of a daffodil flower. ■ a sound resembling that of a trumpet, esp. the loud cry of an elephant. **2** (**trumpets**) a North American pitcher plant. • Genus *Sarracenia*, family Sarraceniaceae: several species, in particular **yellow trumpets** (*S. alata*).
▸*v.* (**-pet·ed**, **-pet·ing**) **1** [*intrans.*] play a trumpet: [as *adj.*] (**trumpeting**) *figures of two trumpeting angels.* ■ make a loud, penetrating sound resembling that of a trumpet: *wild elephants trumpeting in the bush.* **2** [*trans.*] proclaim widely or loudly: *the press trumpeted another defeat for the government.* ▷Middle English: from Old French *trompette*, diminutive of *trompe* (see TRUMP[2]). The verb dates from the mid 16th cent.
▸*PHRASE* □ **blow one's (own) trumpet** talk openly and boastfully about one's achievements: *he refused to* **blow his own trumpet** *and blushingly declined to speak.*

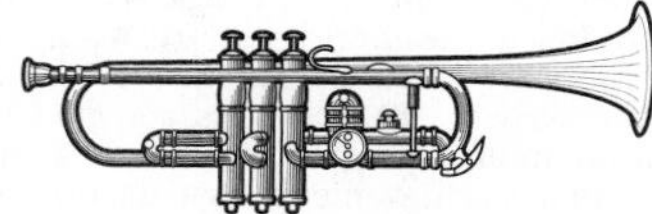

trumpet 1

trum·pet creep·er ▸*n.* another term for TRUMPET VINE.

trum·pet·er /ˈtrəmpitər/ ▸*n.* **1** a person who plays a trumpet. **2** a large gregarious ground-dwelling bird of tropical South American forests, with mainly black plumage and loud trumpeting and booming calls. • Family Psophiidae and genus *Psophia*: three species. **3** a pigeon of a domestic breed that makes a trumpetlike sound. **4** an edible marine fish with a spiny dorsal fin, found chiefly in cool Australasian waters and said to make a grunting or trumpeting sound when taken out of the water. • Family Latrididae: several genera and species, including the **Tasmanian trumpeter** (*Latris lineata*), prized as food.

trum·pet·er swan ▸*n.* a large migratory swan with a black and yellow bill and a honking call, breeding in northern North America. • *Cygnus buccinator*, family Anatidae.

trum·pet·fish /ˈtrəmpitˌfiSH/ ▸*n.* (*pl.* same or **-fish·es**) an elongated marine fish with a long narrow snout, resembling a pipefish. It lives around reefs and rocks in tropical waters and typically hangs in a semivertical position. • Family Aulostomidae and genus *Aulostomus*: several species.

trum·pet ma·jor ▸*n.* the chief trumpeter of a cavalry regiment, typically a principal musician in a regimental band.

trum·pet shell ▸*n.* the shell of a large marine mollusk that can be blown to produce a loud note. • Several species in the class Gastropoda, in particular the triton (*Charonia tritonis*, family Cymatiidae).

trum·pet tree ▸*n.* any of a number of tropical American trees, in particular: • a tree grown in the Caribbean for its numerous trumpet-shaped flowers, which bloom when the tree is leafless (genus *Tabebuia*, family Bignoniaceae). • a cecropia whose hollow branches are used to make wind instruments (*Cecropia peltata*, family Cecropiaceae).

North American trumpet vine

trum·pet vine (also **trum·pet creep·er**) ▸*n.* a climbing shrub with orange or red trumpet-shaped flowers, cultivated as an ornamental. • Genus *Campsis*, family Bignoniaceae: the North American *C. radicans* and the Chinese *C. grandiflora*.

trun·cal /ˈtrəNGkəl/ ▸*adj. Medicine* of or affecting the trunk of the body, or of a nerve.

trun·cate /ˈtrəNG,kāt/ ▸*v.* [*trans.*] [often as *adj.*] (**truncated**) shorten (something) by cutting off the top or the end: *a truncated cone shape* | *discussion was truncated by the arrival of tea.* ■ *Crystallography* replace (an edge or an angle) by a plane, typically so as to make equal angles with the adjacent faces.
▸*adj. Botany & Zoology* (of a leaf, feather, or other part) ending abruptly as if cut off across the base or tip. ▷late 15th cent. (as a verb): from Latin *truncat-* 'maimed,' from the verb *truncare*. **—trun·ca·tion** /,trəNGˈkāSHən/ *n.*

trun·cheon /ˈtrənCHən/ ▸*n. chiefly Brit.* a short, thick stick carried as a weapon by a police officer. ■ a staff or baton acting as a symbol of authority. ▷Middle English (denoting a piece broken off (esp. from a spear), also a cudgel): from Old French *tronchon* 'stump,' based on Latin *truncus* 'trunk.'

trun·dle /ˈtrəndl/ ▸*v.* [*intrans.*] (of a wheeled vehicle or its occupants) move slowly and heavily, typically in a noisy or uneven way: *ten vintage cars trundled past.* ■ (of a person) move in a similar way: *she could hear him coughing as he trundled out.* ■ [*trans.*] cause (something, typically a wheeled vehicle) to roll or move in such a way: *we trundled a wheelbarrow down to the river and collected driftwood.*
▸*n.* [in *sing.*] an act of moving in such a way. ▷mid 16th cent. (denoting a small wheel or roller): a parallel formation to obsolete or dialect *trendle, trindle* '(cause to) revolve'; related to TREND.

trun·dle bed ▸*n.* a low bed on wheels that can be stored under a larger bed.

trunk /trəNGk/ ▸*n.* **1** the main woody stem of a tree as distinct from its branches and roots. ■ the main part of an artery, nerve, or other anatomical structure from which smaller branches arise. ■ short for TRUNK LINE. ■ an enclosed shaft or conduit for cables or ventilation. **2** a person's or animal's body apart from the limbs and head. **3** the elongated, prehensile nose of an elephant. **4** a large box with a hinged lid for storing or transporting clothes and other articles. ■ the space at the back of a car for carrying luggage and other goods. ▷late Middle English: from Old French *tronc*, from Latin *truncus*. **—trunk·ful** /-,fo͝ol/ *n.* (*pl.* **-fuls**) **—trunk·less** *adj.*

trunk call ▸*n. dated, chiefly Brit.* a long-distance telephone call made within the same country.

trunk·fish /ˈtrəNGk,fiSH/ ▸*n.* (*pl.* same or **-fish·es**) another term for BOXFISH.

trunk·ing /ˈtrəNGkiNG/ ▸*n.* **1** a system of shafts or conduits for cables or ventilation. **2** the use or arrangement of trunk lines.

trunk line ▸*n.* a main line of a railroad, telephone system, or other network.

trunk road ▸*n. chiefly Brit.* an important main road used for long-distance travel.

trunks /trəNGks/ ▸*plural n.* men's shorts, worn esp. for swimming or boxing. ▷late 19th cent. (originally U.S.): from an earlier theatrical use denoting short breeches of thin material worn over tights.

trun·nel /ˈtrənl/ ▸*n.* a hard wooden pin used for fastening timbers together.

trun·nion /ˈtrənyən/ ▸*n.* a pin or pivot forming one of a pair on which something is supported. ■ a supporting cylindrical projection on each side of a cannon or mortar. ▷early 17th cent.: from French *trognon* 'core, tree trunk,' of unknown origin.

Tru·ro /ˈtro͝orō/ a resort town in eastern Massachusetts, near the tip of Cape Cod, a well-known arts colony; pop. 1,573.

truss /trəs/ ▸*n.* **1** a framework, typically consisting of rafters, posts, and struts, supporting a roof, bridge, or other structure: *roof trusses.* ■ a surgical appliance worn to support a hernia, typically a padded belt. ■ a large projection of stone or timber, typically one supporting a cornice. **2** *Brit., chiefly historical* a bundle of old hay (56 lb), new hay (60 lb), or straw (36 lb). **3** a compact cluster of flowers or fruit growing on one stalk. **4** *Sailing* a heavy metal ring securing a lower yard to its mast.
▸*v.* [*trans.*] **1** tie up the wings and legs of (a chicken or other bird) before cooking. ■ tie up (someone) with their arms at their sides: *I found him* **trussed up** *in his closet.* **2** [usu. as *adj.*] (**trussed**) support (a roof, bridge, or other structure) with a truss or trusses. ▷Middle English (in the sense 'bundle'): from Old French *trusse* (noun), *trusser* 'pack up, bind in,' based on late Latin *tors-* 'twisted,' from the verb *torquere*. Sense 1 dates from the mid 17th cent. **—truss·er** *n.*

truss 1

trust /trəst/ ▸*n.* **1** firm belief in the reliability, truth, ability, or strength of someone or something: *relations have to be built on trust* | *they have been able to win the trust of the others.* ■ acceptance of the truth of a statement without evidence or investigation: *I used only primary sources,* **taking** *nothing* **on trust.** ■ the state of being responsible for someone or something: *a man in a position of trust.* ■ *poetic/literary* a person or duty for which one has responsibility: *rulership is a trust from God.* ■ *poetic/literary* a hope or expectation: *all the great trusts of womanhood.* **2** *Law* confidence placed in a person by making that person the nominal owner of property to be held or used for the benefit of one or more others. ■ an arrangement whereby property is held in such a way: *a trust was set up* | *the property is to be* **held in trust** *for his son.* **3** a body of trustees. ■ an organization or company managed by trustees: *a charitable trust* | [in *names*] *the National Trust for Historic Preservation.* ■ *dated* a large company that has or attempts to gain monopolistic control of a market. **4** *W. Indian* or *archaic* commercial credit: *my master lived on trust at an alehouse.*
▸*v.* [*trans.*] **1** believe in the reliability, truth, ability, or strength of: *I should never have trusted her* | [*trans.*] *he can be trusted to carry out an impartial investigation* | [as *adj.*] (**trusted**) *a trusted adviser.* ■ (**trust someone with**) allow someone to have, use, or look after (someone or something of importance or value) with confidence: *I'd trust you with my life.* ■ (**trust someone/something to**) commit (someone or something) to the safekeeping of: *they don't like to* **trust** *their money to anyone outside the family.* ■ [with *clause*] have confidence; hope (used as a polite formula in conversation): *I trust that you have enjoyed this book.* ■ [*intrans.*] have faith or confidence: *she* **trusted in** *the powers of justice.* ■ [*intrans.*] (**trust to**) place reliance on (luck, fate, or something else over which one has little control): *trusting to the cover of night, I ventured out.* **2** *chiefly archaic* allow credit to (a customer). ▷Middle English: from Old Norse *traust*, from *traustr* 'strong'; the verb from Old Norse *treysta*, assimilated to the noun. **—trust·a·ble** *adj.* **—trust·er** *n.*
▸*PHRASES* □ **not trust someone as far as one can throw them** *informal* not trust or hardly trust a particular person at all. □ **trust someone to ——** it is characteristic or predictable for someone to act in the specified way: *trust Sam to have all the inside information.*

trust·a·far·i·an /,trəstəˈfe(ə)rēən/ ▸*n. informal* a rich young person who adopts a bohemian lifestyle and lives in a nonaffluent area. ▷1990s: blend of *trust fund* and *Rastafarian*.

trust·bust·er /ˈtrəs(t),bəstər/ ▸*n. informal* a person or agency employed to enforce antitrust legislation.

trust com·pa·ny ▸*n.* a company formed to act as a trustee or to deal with trusts.

trust deed ▸*n. Law* a deed of conveyance creating and setting out the conditions of a trust.

trust·ee /trəˈstē/ ▸*n. Law* an individual person or member of a board given control or powers of administration of property in trust with a legal obligation to administer it solely for the purposes specified. ■ a state made responsible for the government of a trust territory by the United Nations. **—trust·ee·ship** /-,SHip/ *n.*

trust·ee in bank·rupt·cy ▸*n. Law* a person taking administrative responsibility for the financial affairs of a bankrupt and the distribution of assets to creditors.

trust·ful /ˈtrəs(t)fəl/ ▸*adj.* having or marked by a total belief in the reliability, truth, ability, or strength of someone. **—trust·ful·ly** *adv.* **—trust·ful·ness** *n.*

trust fund ▸*n.* a fund consisting of assets belonging to a trust, held by the trustees for the beneficiaries.

trust·ing /ˈtrəstiNG/ ▸*adj.* showing or tending to have a belief in a person's honesty or sincerity; not suspicious: *it is foolish to be too* **trusting of** *other people* | *a shy and trusting child.* See note at GULLIBLE. **—trust·ing·ly** *adv.* **—trust·ing·ness** *n.*

trust ter·ri·to·ry ▸*n.* a territory under the trusteeship of the United Nations or of a country designated by it.

trust·wor·thy /ˈtrəst,wərT͟Hē/ ▸*adj.* able to be relied on as honest or truthful: *leave a spare key with a trustworthy neighbor.* **—trust·wor·thi·ly** /-T͟Hələ̄/ *adv.* **—trust·wor·thi·ness** *n.*

trust·y /ˈtrəstē/ ▸*adj.* (**trust·i·er, trust·i·est**) [*attrib.*] *archaic* or *humorous* having served for a long time and regarded as reliable or faithful: *his trusty Corona typewriter* | *their trusty steeds.*
▸*n.* (*pl.* **trust·ies**) a prisoner who is given special privileges or responsibilities in return for good behavior. **—trust·i·ly** /-təlē/ *adv.* **—trust·i·ness** *n.*

Truth /tro͞oTH/, Sojourner (*c.*1797–1883), U.S. evangelist and reformer; previously *Isabella Van Wagener*. Born into slavery, she was sold to Isaac Van Wagener, who released her in 1827. She became a zealous evangelist and preached in favor of black rights and women's suffrage. In 1864, she was received at the White House by President Lincoln.

truth /tro͞oTH/ ▸*n.* (*pl.* **truths** /tro͞oT͟HZ; tro͞oTHS/) the quality or state of being true: *he had to accept the truth of her accusation.* ■ (also **the truth**) that which is true or in accordance with fact or reality: *tell me the truth* | *she found out the truth about him.* ■ a fact or belief that is accepted as true: *the emergence of scientific truths* | *the fundamental truths about mankind.* ▷Old English *trīewth, trēowth* 'faithfulness, constancy' (see TRUE, -TH[2]).
▸*PHRASES* □ **in truth** really; in fact: *in truth, she was more than a little unhappy.* □ **of a truth** *archaic* certainly: *of a truth, such things used to happen.* □ **to tell the truth** (or **truth to tell** or **if truth be told**) to be frank (used esp. when making an admission or when expressing an unwelcome or controversial opinion): *I think, if truth be told, we were all a little afraid of him.* □ **the truth, the whole truth, and nothing but the truth** used to emphasize the absolute veracity of a statement. [part of a statement sworn by witnesses in court.]

truth con·di·tion ▸*n. Logic* the condition under which a given proposition is true. ■ a statement of this condition, sometimes taken to be the meaning of the proposition.

truth·ful /ˈtro͞oTHfəl/ ▸*adj.* (of a person or statement) telling or expressing the truth; honest: *I think you're confusing being rude with being truthful* | *I want a truthful answer.* ■ (of artistic or literary representation) characterized by accuracy or realism; true to life: *astonishingly truthful acting.* **—truth·ful·ly** *adv.* **—truth·ful·ness** *n.*

truth func·tion ▸*n. Logic* a function whose truth

value is dependent on the truth value of its arguments.

truth se·rum (also **truth drug**) ▶*n.* a drug supposedly able to induce a state in which a person answers questions truthfully.

truth ta·ble ▶*n. Logic* a diagram in rows and columns showing how the truth or falsity of a proposition varies with that of its components. ■ *Electronics* a similar diagram of the outputs from all possible combinations of input.

truth val·ue ▶*n. Logic* the attribute assigned to a proposition in respect of its truth or falsehood, which in classical logic has only two possible values (true or false).

try /trī/ ▶*v.* (**tries, tried**) **1** [*intrans.*] make an attempt or effort to do something: [with *infinitive*] *he* **tried to** *regain his breath* | *I started to* **try and** *untangle the mystery* | *I decided to try writing fiction* | *none of them tried very hard* | [*trans.*] *three times he tried the maneuver and three times he failed.* ■ (**try for**) attempt to achieve or attain: *they decided to try for another baby.* ■ [*trans.*] use, test, or do (something new or different) in order to see if it is suitable, effective, or pleasant: *everyone wanted to know if I'd tried jellied eel* | *these methods are* **tried and tested**. ■ (**try out for**) compete or audition in order to join (a team) or be given (a position): *she tried out for the team.* ■ [*trans.*] go to (a place) or attempt to contact (someone), typically in order to obtain something: *I've tried the apartment, but the number is busy.* ■ [*trans.*] push or pull (a door or window) to determine whether it is locked: *I tried the doors, but they were locked.* ■ [*trans.*] make severe demands on (a person or a quality, typically patience): *Mary tried everyone's patience to the limit.* **2** [*trans.*] (usu. **be tried**) subject (someone) to trial: *he was arrested and tried for the murder.* ■ investigate and decide (a case or issue) in a formal trial: *the most serious criminal cases must be tried by a jury.* **3** [*trans.*] *chiefly Brit.* smooth (roughly planed wood) with a plane to give an accurately flat surface. **4** [*trans.*] extract (oil or fat) by heating: *some of the fat may be* **tried out** *and used.*

▶*phrasal v.* □ **try something on** put on an item of clothing to see if it fits or suits one. □ **try someone/something out** test someone or something new or different to assess their suitability or effectiveness: *I try out new recipes on my daughter.*

▶*n.* (*pl.* **tries**) **1** an effort to accomplish something; an attempt: *Mitterand was elected president on his third try.* ■ an act of doing, using, or testing something new or different to see if it is suitable, effective, or pleasant: *she agreed that they should give the idea a try.* **2** *Rugby* an act of touching the ball down behind the opposing goal line, scoring points and entitling the scoring side to a goal kick. ▷Middle English: from Old French *trier* 'sift,' of unknown origin. Sense 1 of the noun dates from the early 17th cent.

▶**PHRASES** □ **I, he,** etc., **will try anything once** used to indicate willingness to do or experience something new. □ **try something on for size** assess whether something is suitable: *he was trying on the role for size.* □ **try one's hand at** attempt to do (something) for the first time, typically in order to find out if one is good at it: *a chance to try your hand at the ancient art of drystone walling.* □ **try it on** *Brit., informal* attempt to deceive or seduce someone: *he was* **trying it on** *with my wife.* ■ deliberately test someone's patience to see how much one can get away with. □ **try one's luck** see LUCK. □ **try me** used to suggest that one may be willing to do something unexpected or unlikely: *"You won't use a gun up here." "Try me."*

USAGE In practice, there is little discernible difference in meaning between **try to** plus infinitive (*we should* **try to** *help them*) and **try and** plus infinitive (*we should* **try and** *help them*), but there is a difference in formality, with **try to** being regarded as more formal than **try and**. The construction **try and** is grammatically odd, however, in that it cannot be inflected for tense—that is, sentences like *she* **tried and** *fix it* or *they are* **trying and** *renew their visa* are not acceptable, while their equivalents *she* **tried to** *fix it* or *they are* **trying to** *renew their visa* undoubtedly are. For this reason, **try and** is best regarded as a fixed idiom used only in its infinitive and imperative form. See also **usage** at AND.

try·ing /'trī-iNG/ ▶*adj.* difficult or annoying; hard to endure: *it had been a very trying day.* See note at HARD. —**try·ing·ly** *adv.*

try·out /'trī,out/ ▶*n.* a test of the potential of someone or something, esp. in the context of entertainment or sports: *she would be too distraught to compete in cheerleader tryouts.*

try·pan blue /'tripən; trə'pan/ ▶*n.* a diazo dye used as a biological stain due to its absorption by macrophages of the reticuloendothelial system. ▷early 20th cent.: *trypan* from TRYPANOSOME.

try·pan·o·some /trə'panə,sōm; 'tripənə-/ ▶*n. Medicine & Zoology* a single-celled parasitic protozoan with a trailing flagellum, infesting the blood. • Genus *Trypanosoma*, phylum Kinetoplastida, kingdom Protista. ▷early 20th cent.: from Greek *trupanon* 'borer' + -SOME[3].

try·pan·o·so·mi·a·sis /trə,panəsō'mīəsis; 'tripənə-/ ▶*n. Medicine* any tropical disease caused by trypanosomes and typically transmitted by biting insects, esp. sleeping sickness and Chagas' disease.

tryp·sin /'tripsin/ ▶*n. Biochemistry* a digestive enzyme that breaks down proteins in the small intestine. It is secreted by the pancreas in an inactive form, trypsinogen. ▷late 19th cent.: from Greek *tripsis* 'friction,' from *tribein* 'to rub' (because it was first obtained by rubbing down the pancreas with glycerine), + -IN[1]. —**tryp·tic** /-tik/ *adj.*

tryp·sin·o·gen /trip'sinəjən; -,jen/ ▶*n. Biochemistry* an inactive substance secreted by the pancreas, from which the digestive enzyme trypsin is formed in the duodenum.

tryp·ta·mine /'triptə,mēn/ ▶*n. Biochemistry* a compound, of which serotonin is a derivative, produced from tryptophan by decarboxylation. • A heterocyclic amine; chem. formula: $C_8H_6NCH_2CH_2NH$.

tryp·to·phan /'triptə,fan/ ▶*n. Biochemistry* an amino acid that is a constituent of most proteins. It is an essential nutrient in the diet of vertebrates. • An indole derivative; chem. formula: $C_8H_6NCH_2CH(NH_2)COOH$. ▷late 19th cent.: from *tryptic* 'relating to trypsin' + Greek *phainein* 'appear.'

try·sail /'trīsəl; -,sāl/ ▶*n.* a small, strong fore-and-aft sail set on the mast of a sailing vessel in heavy weather.

try square ▶*n.* an implement used to check and mark right angles in construction work.

tryst /trist/ *poetic/literary* ▶*n.* a private, romantic rendezvous between lovers: *a moonlight tryst.*

▶*v.* [*intrans.*] keep a rendezvous of this kind: [as *n.*] (**trysting**) *a trysting place.* ▷late Middle English (originally Scots): variant of obsolete *trist* 'an appointed place in hunting,' from French *triste* or medieval Latin *trista.* —**trys·ter** *n.*

TS ▶*abbr.* tensile strength.

Tsao-chuang /'jou jōō'äNG/ variant of ZAOZHUANG.

tsar /zär/ (also **czar** or **tzar**) ▶*n.* an emperor of Russia before 1917: *Tsar Nicholas II.* ■ a South Slav ruler in former times, esp. one reigning over Serbia in the 14th century. ■ ▷from Russian *tsar'*, representing Latin *Caesar.* —**tsar·dom** /-dəm/ *n.* —**tsar·ism** /-,izəm/ *n.* —**tsar·ist** /-ist/ *n. & adj.*

tsar·e·vich /'zärə,viCH; '(t)sär-/ (also **czar·e·vich** or **tzar·e·vitch**) ▶*n. historical* the eldest son of an emperor of Russia. ▷early 18th cent.: Russian, literally 'son of a tsar.'

tsa·rev·na /zä'revnə; (t)sä-/ ▶*n.* **1** a daughter of a tsar. **2** the wife of a tsarevich.

tsa·ri·na /zä'rēnə; (t)sä-/ (also **cza·ri·na** or **tza·ri·na**) ▶*n. historical* an empress of Russia before 1917.

Tsa·ri·tsyn /(t)sä'rētsin/ former name (until 1925) of VOLGOGRAD.

tsats·ke /'tsätskə/ ▶*n.* variant spelling of TCHOTCHKE.

TSE ▶*abbr.* transmissible spongiform encephalopathy; any spongiform encephalopathy, including BSE and vCJD, that is transmissible between animals, or between animals and humans.

tses·se·bi /'(t)sesəbē/ (also **tses·se·be**) ▶*n.* variant spelling of SASSABY. ▷mid 19th cent.: from Setswana.

tset·se /'(t)sētsē; '(t)set-/ (also **tset·se fly**) ▶*n.* an African bloodsucking fly that bites humans and other mammals, transmitting sleeping sickness and nagana. • Genus *Glossina*, family Tabanidae: several species. ▷mid 19th cent.: from Setswana.

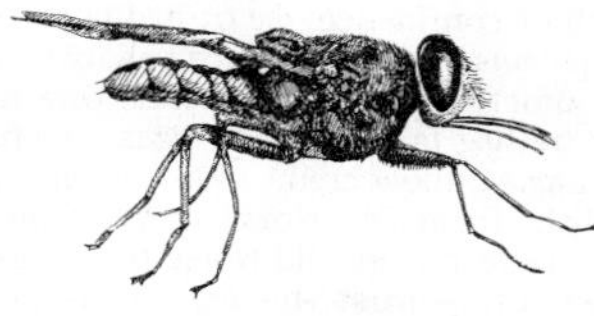

tsetse

TSgt ▶*abbr.* technical sergeant.

TSH ▶*abbr.* thyroid-stimulating hormone.

T-shirt (also **tee shirt**) ▶*n.* a short-sleeved casual top, generally made of cotton, having the shape of a T when spread out flat.

tsim·mes /'tsimis/ (also **tzim·mes** or **tzim·mis**) ▶*n.* (*pl.* same) a Jewish stew of sweetened vegetables or vegetables and fruit, sometimes with meat. ■ *figurative* a fuss or muddle. ▷Yiddish.

Tsim·shi·an /'CHimsHēən; 'tsim-/ ▶*n.* (*pl.* same) **1** a member of an American Indian people of coastal British Columbia. **2** the language of this people.

▶*adj.* of or relating to this people or their language. ▷from the Tsimshian self-designation *c'msyan*, literally 'inside the Skeena River.'

Tsi·nan /'jē'nän/ variant of JINAN.

Tsing·hai /'tsiNG'hī; 'CHiNG/ variant of QINGHAI.

tsk tsk /tisk tisk/ ▶*exclam.* expressing disapproval or annoyance: *you of all people, Goldie—tsk, tsk.*

▶*v.* (**tsk-tsk**) [*intrans.*] make such an exclamation. ▷1940s: imitative.

tsp. ▶*abbr.* (*pl.* same or **tsps.**) teaspoonful.

T-square (also **T square**) ▶*n.* a T-shaped instrument for drawing or testing right angles.

T-square

TSR *Computing* ▶*abbr.* terminate and stay resident, denoting a type of program that remains in the memory of a microcomputer after it has finished running and which can be quickly reactivated.

TSS ▶*abbr.* toxic shock syndrome.

T-storm /'tē,stôrm/ ▶*n. informal* short for THUNDERSTORM.

tsu·ba /'tsōōbə/ ▶*n.* (*pl.* same or **-bas**) a Japanese sword guard, typically elaborately decorated and made of steel. ▷Japanese.

tsu·bo /'tsōōbō/ ▶*n.* (*pl.* same or **-bos**) **1** a Japanese unit of area equal to approximately 3.95 square yards (3.30 sq m). **2** (in complementary medicine) a point on the face or body to which pressure or other stimulation is applied during treatment. ▷Japanese.

tsu·ke·mo·no /'(t)sōōkē'mōnō/ ▶*n.* (*pl.* **-nos**) a Japanese side dish of pickled vegetables, usually served with rice. ▷Japanese, from *tsukeru* 'pickle' + *mono* 'thing.'

tsu·na·mi /(t)sōō'nämē/ ▶*n.* (*pl.* same or **-mis**) a long high sea wave caused by an earthquake, submarine landslide, or other disturbance. ▷late 19th cent.: from Japanese, from *tsu* 'harbor' + *nami* 'wave.'

tsu·ris /'tsōōris; 'tsər/ ▶*n. informal* trouble or woe; aggravation. ▷early 20th cent.: from Hebrew.

Tsu·shi·ma /(t)sōō'sHēmə/ a Japanese island in Korea Strait, between South Korea and Japan. In 1905 it was the scene of a defeat for the Russian navy during the Russo-Japanese War.

tsu·tsu·ga·mu·shi dis·ease /,(t)sōōtsəgə'mōōsHē/ ▶*n.* another term for SCRUB TYPHUS. ▷early 20th cent.: *tsutsugamushi*, from the Japanese name of the mite that transmits the disease.

Tswa·na /'(t)swänə/ ▶*n.* (*pl.* same, **Tswa·nas**, or **Ba·tswa·na** /bät'swänə/) **1** a member of a people living in Botswana, South Africa, and neighboring areas. **2** the Bantu language of this people, also called Setswana.

▶*adj.* of or relating to the Tswana or their language. ▷stem of Setswana *moTswana*, plural *baTswana.*

TT ▶*abbr.* ■ teetotal. ■ teetotaler. ■ tuberculin-tested.

TTL ▶*n. Electronics* a widely used technology for making integrated circuits. [abbreviation of *transistor transistor logic.*]

▶*adj. Photography* (of a camera focusing system) through-the-lens.

T-top /'tē,täp/ ▶*n.* a car roof with removable panels.

TTS ▶*abbr.* text-to-speech, a form of speech synthesis used to create a spoken version of the text in an electronic document.

TTY ▶*abbr.* teletypewriter.

TU ▶*abbr.* Trade Union.

Tu. ▶*abbr.* Tuesday.

Tu·a·mo·tu Ar·chi·pel·a·go /,tōōə'mōtōō/ a group of about 80 coral islands that form part of French Polynesia, in the South Pacific Ocean; pop. 12,000. It is the largest group of coral atolls in the world.

Tua·reg /'twä,reg/ ▶*n.* (*pl.* same or **-regs**) a member of a Berber people of the western and central Sahara, living mainly in Algeria, Mali, Niger, and western Libya, traditionally as nomadic pastoralists.

▶*adj.* of or relating to this people. ▷from Arabic *ṭawāriq.*

tu·a·ta·ra /ˌto͞oəˈtärə/ ▸*n.* a nocturnal burrowing lizardlike reptile with a crest of soft spines along its back, now confined to some small islands off New Zealand. • Order Rhynchocephalia and genus *Sphenodon*: two species, in particular *S. punctatum*. All other members of the order became extinct during the Mesozoic era. ▷late 19th cent.: from Maori, from *tua* 'on the back' + *tara* 'spine.'

Tu·a·tha Dé Da·nann /ˈto͞oəhə dā ˈdänən/ ▸*plural n. Irish Mythology* the members of an ancient race said to have inhabited Ireland before the historical Irish. Formerly believed to have been a real people, they are credited with the possession of magical powers and great wisdom. ▷Irish, literally 'people of the goddess Danann.'

tub /təb/ ▸*n.* **1** a wide, open, deep, typically round container with a flat bottom used for holding liquids, growing plants, etc.: *hydrangeas in a patio tub.* ■ a similar small plastic or cardboard container in which food is bought or stored: *a margarine tub.* ■ the contents of such a container or the amount it can contain: *she ate a tub of yogurt.* ■ a washtub. ■ *informal* a bathtub. ■ *Mining* a container for conveying ore, coal, etc. **2** *informal* an old, awkward, or run-down vessel.
▸*v.* (**tubbed, tub·bing**) [*trans.*] **1** [usu. as *adj.*] (**tubbed**) plant in a tub: *tubbed fruit trees.* **2** *dated* wash or bathe (someone or something) in or as in a tub or bath. ■ [*intrans.*] *Brit., informal* take a bath. ▷Middle English: probably of Low German or Dutch origin; compare with Middle Low German, Middle Dutch *tubbe*. **—tub·ba·ble** *adj.* (*informal*) (sense 2 of the *verb*) **—tub·ful** /-ˌfo͝ol/ *n.* (*pl.* **-fuls**).

tu·ba /ˈt(y)o͞obə/ ▸*n.* a large brass wind instrument of bass pitch, with three to six valves and a broad bell typically facing upward. ■ a powerful reed stop on an organ with the quality of a tuba. ▷mid 19th cent.: via Italian from Latin, 'trumpet.'

tuba

tub·al /ˈt(y)o͞obəl/ ▸*adj.* of, relating to, or occurring in a tube, esp. the fallopian tubes.

tub·al li·ga·tion ▸*n.* a surgical procedure for female sterilization that involves severing and tying the fallopian tubes.

tub·al preg·nan·cy ▸*n. Medicine* an ectopic pregnancy in which the fetus develops in a fallopian tube.

tub·by /ˈtəbē/ ▸*adj.* (**-bi·er, -bi·est**) **1** *informal* (of a person) short and rather fat. [referring to the shape of a tub.] **2** (of a sound) lacking resonance; dull. [referring to the sound of a tub when struck.] **—tub·bi·ness** *n.*

tub chair ▸*n.* a chair with solid arms continuous with a semicircular back.

tube /t(y)o͞ob/ ▸*n.* **1** a long, hollow cylinder of metal, plastic, glass, etc., for holding or transporting something, chiefly liquids or gases. ■ the inner tube of a bicycle tire. ■ material in such a cylindrical form; tubing: *the firm manufactures steel tube for a wide variety of applications.* **2** a thing in the form of or resembling such a cylinder, in particular: ■ a flexible metal or plastic container sealed at one end and having a screw cap at the other, for holding a semiliquid substance ready for use: *a tube of toothpaste.* ■ a rigid cylindrical container: *a tube of lipstick.* ■ [usu. with *adj.*] *Anatomy, Zoology, & Botany* a hollow cylindrical organ or structure in an animal body or in a plant (e.g., a Eustachian tube, a sieve tube). ■ (**tubes**) *informal* a woman's fallopian tubes. ■ a woman's close-fitting garment, typically without darts or other tailoring and made from a single piece of knitted or elasticized fabric: [as *adj.*] *stretchy tube skirts.* ■ (in surfing) the hollow curve under the crest of a breaking wave. **3** (**the tube**) *Brit., informal* the subway system in London. ■ a train running on this system: *I caught the tube home.* **4** a sealed container, typically of glass and either evacuated or filled with gas, containing two electrodes between which an electric current can be made to flow. ■ a cathode-ray tube, esp. in a television set. ■ (**the tube**) *informal* television: *another wasted evening, sitting in front of the tube.* ■ a vacuum tube.
▸*v.* [*trans.*] [usu. as *adj.*] (**tubed**) provide with a tube or tubes: [in *combination*] *a giant eight-tubed hookah.* ▷mid 17th cent.: from French *tube* or Latin *tubus*. **—tube·less** *adj.* **—tube·like** /-ˌlīk/ *adj.*
▸PHRASE □ **go down the tubes** (or **tube**) *informal* be completely lost or wasted; fail utterly: *we watched his political career go down the tubes.*

tu·bec·to·my /t(y)o͞oˈbektəmē/ ▸*n.* (*pl.* **-mies**) another term for **SALPINGECTOMY.**

tube foot ▸*n.* (usu. **tube feet**) *Zoology* (in an echinoderm) each of a large number of small, flexible, hollow appendages protruding through the ambulacra, used either for locomotion or for collecting food and operated by hydraulic pressure within the water-vascular system.

tube·less tire /ˈto͞oblis/ ▸*n.* a rubber tire designed for use without an inner tube.

tube-nosed bat ▸*n.* an Old World bat with tubular nostrils: • a fruit bat found chiefly in New Guinea and Sulawesi (genus *Nyctimene*, family Pteropodidae). • an insectivorous Asian bat (genus *Murina*, family Vespertilionidae).

tube pan ▸*n.* a round cake pan with a hollow, cone-shaped center, used for baking ring-shaped cakes.

tu·ber /ˈt(y)o͞obər/ ▸*n.* **1** a much thickened underground part of a stem or rhizome, e.g., in the potato, serving as a food reserve and bearing buds from which new plants arise. ■ a tuberous root, e.g., of the dahlia. **2** *Anatomy* a rounded swelling or protuberant part. ▷mid 17th cent.: from Latin, literally 'hump, swelling.'

tu·ber ci·ne·re·um /siˈne(ə)rēəm/ ▸*n. Anatomy* the part of the hypothalamus to which the pituitary gland is attached. ▷Latin *cinereum*, neuter of *cinereus* 'ash-colored.'

tu·ber·cle /ˈt(y)o͞obərkəl/ ▸*n.* **1** *Anatomy, Zoology, & Botany* a small rounded projection or protuberance, esp. on a bone or on the surface of an animal or plant. **2** *Medicine* a small nodular lesion in the lungs or other tissues, characteristic of tuberculosis. ▷late 16th cent.: from Latin *tuberculum*, diminutive of *tuber* (see **TUBER**). **—tu·ber·cu·late** /t(y)o͞oˈbərkyəˌlāt; -lit/ *adj.* (in sense 1).

tu·ber·cle ba·cil·lus ▸*n.* a bacterium that causes tuberculosis.

tu·ber·cu·lar /təˈbərkyələr/ ▸*adj. Medicine* of, relating to, or affected with tuberculosis: *a tubercular kidney.* ■ *Biology & Medicine* having or covered with tubercles.
▸*n.* a person with tuberculosis.

tu·ber·cu·la·tion /t(y)o͞oˌbərkyəˈlāsʜən/ ▸*n. chiefly Biology* the formation or presence of tubercles, esp. of a specified type. ▷mid 19th cent.: from Latin *tuberculum* (see **TUBERCLE**) + **-ATION.**

tu·ber·cu·lin /t(y)o͞oˈbərkyəlin/ ▸*n.* a sterile protein extract from cultures of tubercle bacillus, used in a test by hypodermic injection for infection with or immunity to tuberculosis, and also formerly in the treatment of the disease. ▷late 19th cent.: from Latin *tuberculum* (see **TUBERCLE**) + **-IN**[1].

tu·ber·cu·lin-test·ed ▸*adj.* (of cows or their milk) giving, or from cows giving, a negative response to a tuberculin test.

tu·ber·cu·loid /t(y)o͞oˈbərkyəˌloid/ ▸*adj. Medicine* resembling tuberculosis or its symptoms, in particular: ■ relating to or denoting the milder of the two principal forms of leprosy, marked by few, well-defined lesions similar to those of tuberculosis, often with loss of feeling in the affected areas. Compare with **LEPROMATOUS.**

tu·ber·cu·lo·sis /təˌbərkyəˈlōsis; t(y)o͞o-/ (abbr.: **TB**) ▸*n.* an infectious bacterial disease characterized by the growth of nodules (tubercles) in the tissues, esp. the lungs. • The disease is caused by the bacterium *Mycobacterium tuberculosis* or (esp. in animals) a related species; Gram-positive acid-fast rods.

The most common form, **pulmonary tuberculosis** (formerly known as 'consumption'), is caused by inhalation of the bacteria. It was widespread in 19th-century Europe, and still causes 3 million deaths each year in developing countries. The disease can affect other parts of the body, notably the bones and joints and the central nervous system. Its spread is countered by vaccination and by the pasteurization of milk to prevent transmission from cattle. It was once considered incurable, but early X-ray diagnosis permits its arrest by drugs and surgery.

▷mid 19th cent.: modern Latin, from Latin *tuberculum* (see **TUBERCLE**) + **-OSIS.**

tu·ber·cu·lous /təˈbərkyələs; t(y)o͞o-/ ▸*adj.* another term for **TUBERCULAR.**

tu·ber·ose /ˈt(y)o͞obəˌrōs; -ˌrōz/ ▸*n.* **1** a Mexican plant of the agave family, with heavily scented white waxy flowers and a bulblike base. Unknown in the wild, it was formerly cultivated as a flavoring for chocolate; the flower oil is used in perfumery. • *Polianthes tuberosa*, family Agavaceae. **2** variant spelling of **TUBEROUS.** ▷mid 17th cent.: sense 1 from Latin *tuberosa*, feminine of *tuberosus* 'with protuberances'; sense 2 from Latin *tuberosus*.

tu·ber·ous /ˈt(y)o͞obərəs/ (also **tu·ber·ose** /-bəˌrōs/) ▸*adj.* **1** *Botany* of the nature of a tuber. See **TUBEROUS ROOT.** ■ (of a plant) having tubers or a tuberous root. **2** *Medicine* characterized by or affected by rounded swellings: *tuberous sclerosis.* ▷mid 17th cent.: from French *tubéreux* or Latin *tuberosus*, from *tuber* (see **TUBER**). **—tu·ber·os·i·ty** /ˌt(y)o͞obəˈräsitē/ *n.*

tu·ber·ous root ▸*n.* a thick and fleshy root like a tuber but without buds, as in the dahlia.

tube·snout /ˈt(y)o͞obˌsnout/ ▸*n.* a small inshore fish with a very elongated snout, head, and body, living along the Pacific coast of North America. • *Aulorynchus flavidus*, the only member of the family Aulorhynchidae.

tube sock ▸*n.* a sock without a shaped heel.

tube top ▸*n.* a tight-fitting strapless top made of stretchy material and worn by women or girls.

tube well ▸*n. Brit.* another term for **SAND POINT WELL.**

tube worm ▸*n.* a marine bristle worm, esp. a fan worm, that lives in a tube made from sand particles or in a calcareous tube that it secretes. • Families Serpulidae and Sabellidae, phylum Polychaeta. ■ a pogonophoran or vestimentiferan worm.

tu·bic·o·lous /t(y)o͞oˈbikələs/ ▸*adj. Zoology* (of a marine worm) living in a tube.

tu·bi·fex /ˈt(y)o͞obəˌfeks/ ▸*n.* a small red annelid worm that lives in fresh water, partly buried in the mud. Also called **BLOODWORM.** • Genus *Tubifex*, family Tubificidae, class Oligochaeta. ▷modern Latin, from Latin *tubus* 'tube' + *-fex* from *facere* 'make.'

tub·ing /ˈt(y)o͞obiɴɢ/ ▸*n.* **1** a length or lengths of metal, plastic, glass, etc., in tubular form: *use the plastic tubing to siphon the beer into the bottles.* **2** the leisure activity of riding on water or snow on a large inflated inner tube.

Tub·man /ˈtəbmən/, Harriet Ross (*c.* 1820–1913), U.S. abolitionist; born *Araminta Ross*; known as the *Moses of Her People*. She was born a slave in Maryland, but escaped via the Underground Railroad in 1849. Following what she called direct messages from God, she returned to Maryland numerous times to lead about 300 slaves to safety in the North. During the Civil War, she spied and served as a scout for the Union.

Harriet Tubman

tu·bo·cu·ra·rine /ˌt(y)o͞obōk(y)o͞oˈräˌrēn/ ▸*n. Medicine* a compound of the alkaloid class obtained from curare and used to produce relaxation of voluntary muscles before surgery and in tetanus, encephalitis, and poliomyelitis. ▷late 19th cent.: from Latin *tubus* 'tube' + **CURARE** + **-INE**[4].

Tu·bruq /tōˈbro͝ok; to͞o-/ Arabic name for **TOBRUK.**

tub-thump·ing *informal, derogatory* ▸*adj.* [*attrib.*] expressing opinions in a loud and violent or dramatic manner: *a tub-thumping speech.*
▸*n.* the expression of opinions in such a way. **—tub-thump·er** *n.*

Tu·bu·a·i Is·lands /to͞obˈwä-ē/ a group of volcanic islands in the South Pacific Ocean that form part of French Polynesia; pop. 6,500 (1988). The chief town,

Mataura, is on the island of Tubuai. Also called the **AUSTRAL ISLANDS**.

tu·bu·lar /ˈt(y)o͞obyələr/ ▶*adj.* **1** long, round, and hollow like a tube: *tubular flowers of deep crimson.* ■ made from a tube or tubes: *tubular steel chairs.* ■ *Surfing* (of a wave) hollow and well curved. **2** *Medicine* of or involving tubules or other tube-shaped structures.
▶*n.* **1** short for **TUBULAR TIRE**. **2** (**tubulars**) oil-drilling equipment made from tubes. ▷late 17th cent.: from Latin *tubulus* 'small tube' + **-AR**[1].

tu·bu·lar bells ▶*plural n.* an orchestral instrument consisting of a row of vertically suspended metal tubes struck with a mallet.

tu·bu·lar tire ▶*n.* a completely enclosed tire cemented onto the wheel rim, used on racing bicycles.

tu·bule /ˈt(y)o͞o,byo͞ol/ ▶*n.* a minute tube, esp. as an anatomical structure: *kidney tubules.* ▷late 17th cent.: from Latin *tubulus*, diminutive of *tubus* 'tube.'

Tu·bu·li·den·ta·ta /ˌt(y)o͞obyəlidenˈtätə/ *Zoology* an order of mammals that comprises only the aardvark. ▷modern Latin (plural), from **TUBULE** + Greek *odous, odont-* 'tooth.'

tu·bu·lin /ˈt(y)o͞obyəlin/ ▶*n.* *Biochemistry* a protein that is the main constituent of the microtubules of living cells. ▷1960s: from **TUBULE** + **-IN**[1].

Tu·can·a /t(y)o͞oˈkänə; -ˈkanə/ *Astronomy* a southern constellation (the Toucan), south of Grus and Phoenix. It contains the Small Magellanic Cloud. ■ [as *genitive*] (**Tucanae** /-nē/) used with a preceding letter or numeral to designate a star in this constellation: *the star Delta Tucanae.* ▷modern Latin.

Tuch·man /ˈtəkmən/, Barbara (1912–89), U.S. historian and writer. Her many works include *The Guns of August* (1962), *Stilwell and the American Experience in Chain, 1911–45* (1971), *A Distant Mirror* (1978), and *The First Salute* (1988).

tuck /tək/ ▶*v.* **1** [*trans.*] push, fold, or turn (the edges or ends of something, esp. a garment or bedclothes) so as to hide them or hold them in place: *he tucked his shirt into his trousers.* ■ (**tuck someone in**) make someone, esp. a child, comfortable in bed by pulling the edges of the bedclothes firmly under the mattress: *he carried her back to bed and tucked her in.* ■ draw (something, esp. part of one's body) together into a small space: *she tucked her legs under her.* ■ (often **be tucked**) put (something) away in a specified place or way so as to be hidden, safe, comfortable, or tidy: *the colonel was coming toward her, his gun tucked under his arm.* **2** [*trans.*] make a flattened, stitched fold in (a garment or material), typically so as to shorten or tighten it, or for decoration.
▶*phrasal v.* □ **tuck something away 1** store something in a secure place: *employees can tuck away a percentage of their pretax salary.* ■ (usu. **be tucked away**) put or keep someone or something in an inconspicuous or concealed place: *the police station was tucked away in a square behind the main street.* **2** *informal* eat a lot of food. □ **tuck in** (or **into**) *informal* eat food heartily: *I tucked into the bacon and scrambled eggs.*
▶*n.* **1** a flattened, stitched fold in a garment or material, typically one of several parallel folds put in a garment for shortening, tightening, or decoration: *a dress with tucks along the bodice.* ■ [usu. with *adj.*] *informal* a surgical operation to reduce surplus flesh or fat: *a tummy tuck.* **2** *Brit., informal* food, typically cakes and candy, eaten by children at school as a snack: [as *adj.*] *a tuck shop.* **3** (also **tuck position**) (in diving, gymnastics, downhill skiing, etc.) a position with the knees bent and held close to the chest, often with the hands clasped around the shins. ▷Old English *tūcian* 'to punish, ill-treat'; related to **TUG**. Influenced in Middle English by Middle Dutch *tucken* 'pull sharply.'

tuck·a·hoe /ˈtəkə,hō/ ▶*n.* a root or other underground plant part formerly eaten by North American Indians, in particular: • the starchy rhizome of an arum that grows chiefly in marshland (*Peltandra virginica*, family Araceae). • the underground sclerotium of a bracket fungus (*Poria cocos*, class Hymenomycetes). ▷early 17th cent.: from Virginia Algonquian *tockawhoughe.*

Tuck·er[1] /ˈtəkər/, Richard (1913–75) U.S. opera singer; born *Rubin Ticker.* A tenor, he sang with the Metropolitan Opera for 30 seasons, beginning with his debut in 1945.

Tuck·er[2], Tanya (Denise) (1958–) U.S. country and pop singer. At age 13, she became known for her rendition of "Delta Dawn" (1972). Her later albums include *What Do I Do with Me* (1991) and *Complicated* (1997).

tuck·er /ˈtəkər/ ▶*n.* *historical* a piece of lace or linen worn in or around the top of a bodice or as an insert at the front of a low-cut dress. See also **ONE'S BEST BIB AND TUCKER** at **BIB**[1].
▶*v.* [*trans.*] (usu. **be tuckered out**) *informal* exhaust; wear out.

tuck·et /ˈtəkit/ ▶*n.* *archaic* a flourish on a trumpet. ▷late 16th cent.: from obsolete *tuck* 'beat (a drum),' from Old Northern French *toquer*, from the base of **TOUCH**.

tuck-in ▶*n.* *Brit., informal, dated* a large meal.

tuck·ing /ˈtəkiNG/ ▶*n.* a series of stitched tucks in a garment.

tuck-point ▶*v.* [*trans.*] point (brickwork) with colored mortar so as to have a narrow groove that is filled with fine white lime putty allowed to project slightly.

tuck po·si·tion ▶*n.* see **TUCK** (sense 3).

tu·co-tu·co /ˈto͝okō ˈto͝okō/ ▶*n.* (*pl.* **-cos**) a burrowing ratlike rodent native to South America. • Family Ctenomyidae and genus *Ctenomys*: numerous species. ▷mid 19th cent.: imitative of the call of some species.

Tuc·son /ˈto͞o,sän; to͞oˈsän/ a city in southeastern Arizona; pop. 486,699. Its desert climate makes it a tourist resort.

tu·cu·xi /to͞oˈko͞ohē/ ▶*n.* (*pl.* same) a small stout-bodied dolphin with a gray back and pinkish underparts, living along the coasts and rivers from Panama to Brazil and in the Amazon. • *Sotalia fluviatilis*, family Delphinidae.

'tude /t(y)o͞od/ ▶*n.* *informal* short for **ATTITUDE**: *the song bristles with lotsa 'tude.*

-tude ▶*suffix* forming abstract nouns such as *beatitude, solitude.* ▷from French *-tude*, from Latin *-tudo.*

Tu·deh /ˈto͞odā/ (also **Tu·deh Par·ty**) the Communist Party of Iran. ▷Persian, literally 'mass.'

Tu·dor[1] /ˈt(y)o͞odər/ ▶*adj.* of or relating to the English royal dynasty that held the throne from the accession of Henry VII in 1485 until the death of Elizabeth I in 1603. ■ of, denoting, or relating to the prevalent architectural style of the Tudor period, characterized esp. by half-timbering.
▶*n.* a member of this dynasty.

Tu·dor[2], Henry, Henry VII of England (see **HENRY**[1]).

Tu·dor[3], Mary, Mary I of England (see **MARY**[2]).

Tu·dor rose ▶*n.* a conventionalized, typically five-lobed figure of a rose used in architectural and other decoration in the Tudor period, in particular a combination of the red and white roses of Lancaster or York adopted as a badge by Henry VII.

Tues. (also **Tue.**) ▶*abbr.* Tuesday.

Tues·day /ˈt(y)o͞oz,dā/ ▶*n.* the day of the week before Wednesday and following Monday: *come to dinner* **on** *Tuesday* | *the following Tuesday* | [as *adj.*] *Tuesday afternoons.*
▶*adv.* on Tuesday: *they're all leaving Tuesday.* ■ (**Tuesdays**) on Tuesdays; each Tuesday: *she works late Tuesdays.* ▷Old English *Tīwesdæg*, named after the Germanic god *Tīw* (associated with Mars); translation of Latin *dies Marti* 'day of Mars'; compare with Swedish *tisdag.*

tu·fa /ˈt(y)o͞ofə/ ▶*n.* a porous rock composed of calcium carbonate and formed by precipitation from water, e.g., around mineral springs. ■ another term for **TUFF**. ▷late 18th cent.: from Italian, variant of *tufo* (see **TUFF**). —**tu·fa·ceous** /t(y)o͞oˈfāSHəs/ *adj.*

tuff /təf/ ▶*n.* a light, porous rock formed by consolidation of volcanic ash. ▷mid 16th cent.: via French from Italian *tufo*, from late Latin *tofus*, Latin *tophus* (see **TOPHUS**). —**tuff·a·ceous** /təˈfāSHəs/ *adj.*

tuf·fet /ˈtəfit/ ▶*n.* **1** a tuft or clump of something: *grass tuffets.* **2** a footstool or low seat. ▷mid 16th cent.: alteration of **TUFT**.

tuft /təft/ ▶*n.* a bunch or collection of something, typically threads, grass, or hair, held or growing together at the base: *scrubby* **tufts of** *grass.* ■ *Anatomy & Zoology* a bunch of small blood vessels, respiratory tentacles, or other small anatomical structures.
▶*v.* [*trans.*] **1** (usu. **be tufted**) provide (something) with a tuft or tufts. **2** *Needlework* make depressions at regular intervals in (a mattress or cushion) by passing a thread through it. ▷late Middle English: probably from Old French *tofe*, of unknown origin. The final *-t* is typical of phonetic confusion between *-f* and *-ft* at the end of words; compare with **GRAFT**[1]. —**tuft·y** *adj.*

tuft·ed /ˈtəftid/ ▶*adj.* having or growing in a tuft or tufts: *tufted grass.*

tuft·ed duck ▶*n.* a Eurasian freshwater diving duck with a drooping crest, the male having mainly black and white plumage. • *Aythya fuligula*, family Anatidae.

Tu Fu /ˈdo͞o ˈfo͞o/ (also **Du Fu**) (AD 712–770), Chinese poet. He is noted for his bitter satiric poems that attacked social injustice and corruption at court.

tug /təg/ ▶*v.* (**tugged, tug·ging**) [*trans.*] pull (something) hard or suddenly: *she tugged off her boots* | [*intrans.*] *he* **tugged at** *Tom's coat sleeve.*
▶*n.* **1** a hard or sudden pull: *another tug and it came loose* | *figurative an overwhelming tug of attraction.* **2** short for **TUGBOAT**. ■ an aircraft towing a glider. **3** a loop from a horse's saddle that supports a shaft or trace. ▷Middle English: from the base of **TOW**[1]. The noun is first recorded (late Middle English) in sense 3. —**tug·ger** *n.*

tug·boat ▶*n.* a powerful boat used for towing larger vessels, esp. in harbor.

tugboat

tug of war ▶*n.* a contest in which two teams pull at opposite ends of a rope until one drags the other over a central line. ■ *figurative* a situation in which two evenly matched people or factions are striving to keep or obtain the same thing: *a tug of war between builders and environmentalists.*

tu·grik /ˈto͞ogrik/ ▶*n.* (*pl.* same or **-griks**) the basic monetary unit of Mongolia, equal to 100 mongos. ▷Mongolian.

tu·i /ˈto͞oē/ ▶*n.* a large New Zealand honeyeater with glossy blackish plumage and two white tufts at the throat. • *Prosthemadura novaeseelandiae*, family Meliphagidae. ▷mid 19th cent.: from Maori.

tuile /twē/ ▶*n.* (*pl.* same) a thin curved cookie, typically made with almonds. ▷French, literally 'tile.'

Tui·ler·ies /ˈtwēlərē(z)/ (also **Tuileries Gardens**) formal gardens next to the Louvre in Paris. The gardens are all that remain of the Tuileries Palace, a royal residence begun in 1564 and burned down in 1871 during the Commune of Paris. ▷French, literally 'Tile works,' so named because the palace was built on the site of an ancient tile works.

Tu·i·nal /ˈto͞oə,nôl; -,nal/ ▶*n.* *trademark Medicine* a sedative and hypnotic drug consisting of a combination of the barbiturates amobarbital and secobarbital.

tu·i·tion /t(y)o͞oˈiSHən/ ▶*n.* a sum of money charged for teaching or instruction by a school, college, or university: *I'm not paying next year's tuition.* ■ teaching or instruction, esp. of individual pupils or small groups: *private tuition in French.* ▷late Middle English (in the sense 'custody, care'): via Old French from Latin *tuitio(n-)*, from *tueri* 'to watch, guard.' Current senses date from the late 16th cent. —**tu·i·tion·al** /-SHənl/ *adj.*

tuk-tuk /ˈto͝ok ˌto͝ok/ ▶*n.* (in Thailand) a three-wheeled motorized vehicle used as a taxi. ▷imitative.

Tu·la /ˈto͞olə/ **1** an industrial city in western Russia, south of Moscow; pop. 543,000. **2** the ancient capital city of the Toltecs, usually identified with a site near the town of Tula in Hidalgo State, in central Mexico.

Tu·lar·e /to͞oˈle(ə)rē; -le(ə)r/ a commercial city in south central California, in the San Joaquin Valley; pop. 33,249.

tu·la·re·mi·a /ˌt(y)o͞oləˈrēmēə/ (*Brit.* **tu·la·rae·mi·a**) ▶*n.* a severe infectious bacterial disease of animals transmissible to humans, characterized by ulcers at the site of infection, fever, and loss of weight. Compare with **RABBIT FEVER**. • This disease is caused by the bacterium *Francisella tularensis*; Gram-negative rods or cocci. ▷1920s: modern Latin, from *Tulare*, the county in California where it was first observed. —**tu·la·re·mic** /ˈrēmik/ *adj.*

tu·le /ˈto͞olē/ ▶*n.* a large bulrush that is abundant in marshy areas of California. • Genus *Scirpus*, family Cyperaceae: two species, *S. acutus* and *S. validus.* ▷mid 19th cent.: via Spanish from Nahuatl *tullin.*

Tu·le Lake /ˈto͞olē/ a lake in northern California, on the Modoc Plateau, a noted wildfowl refuge and site of fighting during the 1870s Modoc War.

tu·lip /ˈt(y)o͞oləp/ ▶*n.* a bulbous spring-flowering plant of the lily family, with boldly colored cup-shaped flowers. • Genus *Tulipa*, family Liliaceae: numerous complex hybrids. ▷late 16th cent.: from French *tulipe*, via Turkish from Persian *dulband* 'turban,' from the shape of the expanded flower.

tu·lip shell ▸*n.* a predatory marine mollusk with a sculptured spiral shell resembling that of a whelk. • Family Fasciolariidae, class Gastropoda, in particular *Fasciolaria tulipa*, which is common in the Caribbean.

tu·lip tree (also **tu·lip·tree**) ▸*n.* a deciduous North American tree with large distinctively lobed leaves and large green and orange tuliplike flowers. Also called **YELLOW POPLAR.** • *Liriodendron tulipifera*, family Magnoliaceae.

tu·lip·wood /ˈt(y)o͞oləpˌwo͝od/ ▸*n.* **1** an Australian tree of rain forest and scrub, with heavy black and yellow timber that is used mainly for cabinetmaking. • *Harpullia pendula*, family Sapindaceae. **2** the pale timber of the tulip tree.

Tull /təl/, Jethro (1674–1741), English agriculturalist. In 1701, he invented the seed drill, a machine that could sow seeds in accurately spaced rows at a controlled rate, reducing the need for farm laborers.

tulle /to͞ol/ ▸*n.* a soft, fine silk, cotton, or nylon material like net, used for making veils and dresses. ▷early 19th cent.: from *Tulle*, a town in southwestern France, where it was first made.

tul·li·bee /ˈtələˌbē/ ▸*n.* (*pl.* same or **-bees**) a lake cisco (fish) of a deep-bodied race living in the Great Lakes of Canada. • *Coregonus artedii tullibee*, family Salmonidae. ▷late 18th cent.: from Canadian French *toulibi*, *outolouby*, from Ojibwa *otōlipī*.

Tul·sa /ˈtəlsə/ a port on the Arkansas River in northeastern Oklahoma; pop. 393,049.

tul·si /ˈto͝olsē/ ▸*n.* another term for **HOLY BASIL.** ▷from Hindi *tulsī*.

tum /təm/ ▸*n.* *informal* a person's stomach or abdomen. ▷mid 19th cent.: abbreviation of **TUMMY.**

tum·ba·ga /to͞omˈbägə/ ▸*n.* an alloy of gold and copper commonly used in pre-Columbian South and Central America. ▷1930s: from Spanish, from Malay *tembaga* 'copper, brass.'

tum·ble /ˈtəmbəl/ ▸*v.* **1** [*intrans.*] (typically of a person) fall suddenly, clumsily, or headlong: *she pitched forward, tumbling down the remaining stairs.* ■ move or rush in a headlong or uncontrolled way: *police and dogs tumbled from the vehicle.* ■ (of something abstract) fall rapidly in amount or value: *property prices tumbled.* ■ [*trans.*] rumple; disarrange: [as *adj.*] (**tumbled**) *his tumbled bedclothes.* ■ [*trans.*] *informal* have sexual intercourse with (someone). **2** *Brit.* [*intrans.*] (**tumble to**) *informal* understand the meaning or hidden implication of (a situation): *she tumbled to our scam.* **3** [*intrans.*] perform acrobatic or gymnastic exercises, typically handsprings and somersaults in the air. ■ (of tumbler pigeons) repeatedly turn over backward in flight. **4** [*trans.*] clean (castings, gemstones, etc.) in a tumbling barrel.
▸*n.* **1** a sudden or headlong fall: *I took a tumble in the nettles.* ■ a rapid fall in amount or value: *a tumble in share prices.* ■ an untidy or confused arrangement or state: *her hair was a tumble of untamed curls.* ■ *informal* an act of sexual intercourse. ■ a handspring, somersault in the air, or other acrobatic feat. **2** *informal* a friendly sign of recognition, acknowledgment, or interest: *not a soul gave him a tumble.* ▷Middle English (as a verb, also in the sense 'dance with contortions'): from Middle Low German *tummelen*; compare with Old English *tumbian* 'to dance.' The sense was probably influenced by Old French *tomber* 'to fall.' The noun, first in the sense 'tangled mass,' dates from the mid 17th cent.

tum·ble·bug /ˈtəmbəlˌbəg/ ▸*n.* a dung beetle that rolls balls of dung along the ground.

tum·ble·down /ˈtəmbəlˌdoun/ ▸*adj.* (of a building or structure) falling or fallen into ruin; dilapidated.

tum·ble dry ▸*v.* (**dries, dried**) dry washed clothes by spinning them in hot air inside a dryer.

tum·ble·home /ˈtəmbəlˌhōm/ ▸*n.* the inward slope of the upper part of the sides of a boat or ship.

tum·bler /ˈtəmblər/ ▸*n.* **1** a drinking glass with straight sides and no handle or stem. [formerly having a rounded bottom so as not to stand upright.] **2** an acrobat or gymnast, esp. one who performs somersaults. ■ a pigeon of a breed that repeatedly turns over backward in flight. **3** a pivoted piece in a lock that holds the bolt until lifted by a key. ■ a notched pivoted plate in a gunlock. **4** another term for **TUMBLING BARREL.** —**tum·bler·ful** /-ˌfo͝ol/ *n.* (*pl.* **-fuls**).

tum·ble·weed /ˈtəmbəlˌwēd/ ▸*n.* a plant of dry regions that breaks off near the ground in late summer and is tumbled about by the wind, thereby dispersing its seeds. • Genera *Salsola* (family Chenopodiaceae) and *Amaranthus* (family Amaranthaceae).

tum·bling bar·rel /ˈtəmb(ə)liNG/ (also **tum·bling box**) ▸*n.* a revolving device containing an abrasive substance, in which castings, gemstones, or other hard objects can be cleaned and polished by friction.

tum·bril /ˈtəmbrəl/ (also **tum·brel**) ▸*n.* *historical* an open cart that tilted backward to empty out its load, in particular one used to convey condemned prisoners to the guillotine during the French Revolution. ■ a two-wheeled covered cart that carried tools or ammunition for an army. ▷Middle English (originally denoting a type of cucking stool): from Old French *tomberel*, from *tomber* 'to fall.'

tu·me·fy /ˈt(y)o͞oməˌfī/ ▸*v.* (**-fies, -fied**) [*intrans.*] become swollen. ▷late 16th cent. (in the sense 'cause to swell'): from French *tuméfier*, from Latin *tumefacere*, from *tumere* 'to swell.' —**tu·me·fac·tion** /ˌt(y)o͞oməˈfakSHən/ *n.*

tu·mes·cent /t(y)o͞oˈmesənt/ ▸*adj.* swollen or becoming swollen, esp. as a response to sexual arousal. ■ *figurative* (esp. of language or literary style) pompous or pretentious; tumid: *his prose is tumescent, full of orotund language.* ▷mid 19th cent.: from Latin *tumescent-* 'beginning to swell,' from the verb *tumescere*, from *tumere* 'to swell.' —**tu·mes·cence** *n.* —**tu·mes·cent·ly** *adv.*

tu·mid /ˈt(y)o͞omid/ ▸*adj.* (esp. of a part of the body) swollen: *a tumid belly.* ■ *figurative* (esp. of language or literary style) pompous or bombastic: *tumid oratory.* ▷mid 16th cent.: from Latin *tumidus*, from *tumere* 'to swell.' —**tu·mid·i·ty** /t(y)o͞oˈmiditē/ *n.* —**tu·mid·ly** *adv.*

tumm·ler /ˈto͝omlər/ ▸*n.* a person who makes things happen, in particular a professional entertainer whose function is to encourage an audience, guests at a resort, etc., to participate in the entertainments or activities. ■ a professional comedian. ▷1960s: Yiddish, from German *tummeln* 'to stir.'

tum·my /ˈtəmē/ ▸*n.* (*pl.* **-mies**) *informal* a person's stomach or abdomen. ▷mid 19th cent.: child's pronunciation of **STOMACH.**

tum·my tuck ▸*n.* *informal* a surgical operation involving the removal of excess flesh from the abdomen, for cosmetic purposes.

tu·mor /ˈt(y)o͞omər/ (*Brit.* **tu·mour**) ▸*n.* a swelling of a part of the body, generally without inflammation, caused by an abnormal growth of tissue, whether benign or malignant. ■ *archaic* a swelling of any kind. ▷late Middle English: from Latin *tumor*, from *tumere* 'to swell.' —**tu·mor·ous** /-mərəs/ *adj.*

tu·mor·i·gen·e·sis /ˌt(y)o͞oməraˈjenəsis/ ▸*n.* the production or formation of a tumor or tumors.

tu·mor·i·gen·ic /ˌt(y)o͞oməraˈjenik/ ▸*adj.* capable of forming or tending to form tumors. —**tu·mor·i·ge·nic·i·ty** /-jəˈnisitē/ *n.*

tump /təmp/ ▸*n.* *Brit., chiefly dialect* [often in *place names*] **1** a small rounded hill or mound; a tumulus. **2** a clump of trees, shrubs, or grass. ▷late 16th cent.: of unknown origin.

tump·line /ˈtəmpˌlīn/ ▸*n.* a sling for carrying a load on the back, with a strap that passes around the forehead. ■ a strap of this kind. ▷late 18th cent.: based on Algonquian *(mat)tump* + the noun **LINE**[1].

tu·mult /ˈt(y)o͞oˌməlt/ ▸*n.* [usu. in *sing.*] a loud, confused noise, esp. one caused by a large mass of people: *a tumult of shouting and screaming broke out.* ■ confusion or disorder: *the whole neighborhood was in a state of fear and tumult* | *figurative his personal tumult ended when he began writing songs.* ▷late Middle English: from Old French *tumulte* or Latin *tumultus*.

tu·mul·tu·ous /t(y)o͞oˈməlCHo͞oəs; tə-/ ▸*adj.* making a loud, confused noise; uproarious: *tumultuous applause.* ■ excited, confused, or disorderly: *a tumultuous crowd* | *figurative a tumultuous personal life.* ▷mid 16th cent.: from Old French *tumultuous* or Latin *tumultuosus*, from *tumultus* (see **TUMULT**). —**tu·mul·tu·ous·ly** *adv.* —**tu·mul·tu·ous·ness** *n.*

tu·mu·lus /ˈt(y)o͞omyələs/ ▸*n.* (*pl.* **-li** /-ˌlī/) an ancient burial mound; a barrow. ▷late Middle English: from Latin; related to *tumere* 'swell.'

tun /tən/ ▸*n.* **1** a large beer or wine cask. ■ a brewer's fermenting vat. **2** an imperial measure of capacity, equal to 4 hogsheads. **3** (also **tun shell**) a large marine mollusk that has a rounded barrellike shell with broad spirals. • Family Tonnidae, class Gastropoda.
▸*v.* (**tunned, tun·ning**) [*trans.*] *archaic* store (wine or other alcoholic drinks) in a tun. ▷Old English *tunne*, from medieval Latin *tunna*, probably of Gaulish origin.

tu·na[1] /ˈt(y)o͞onə/ ▸*n.* (*pl.* same or **-nas**) a large and active predatory schooling fish of the mackerel family. Found in warm seas, it is extensively fished commercially and is popular as a game fish. • *Thunnus* and other genera, family Scombridae: several species, including the albacore, bigeye, bluefin, skipjack, and yellowfin. ■ (also **tuna fish**) the flesh of this fish as food, usually canned. ▷late 19th cent.: from American Spanish, from Spanish *atún*.

tu·na[2] ▸*n.* **1** the edible fruit of a prickly pear cactus. **2** a cactus that produces such fruit, widely cultivated in Mexico. • Genus *Opuntia*, family Cactaceae: many species, in particular *O. tuna* of Central America and the Caribbean. ▷mid 16th cent.: via Spanish from Taino.

tun·dra /ˈtəndrə/ ▸*n.* a vast, flat, treeless Arctic region of Europe, Asia, and North America in which the subsoil is permanently frozen. ▷late 16th cent.: from Lappish.

tun·dra swan ▸*n.* an Arctic-breeding migratory swan with a yellow and black bill often known by the names of its constituent races, e.g., whistling swan. • *Cygnus columbianus*, family Anatidae.

tune /t(y)o͞on/ ▸*n.* a melody, esp. one that characterizes a certain piece of music: *she left the theater humming a cheerful tune.*
▸*v.* [*trans.*] adjust (a musical instrument) to the correct or uniform pitch: *he tuned the harp for me.* ■ adjust (a receiver circuit such as a radio or television) to the frequency of the required signal: *the radio was* **tuned to** *the CBC* | [*intrans.*] *they* **tuned in** *to watch the game.* ■ (often **tune up**) adjust (an engine) or balance (mechanical parts) so that a vehicle runs smoothly and efficiently: *the suspension was tuned for a softer ride* | *figurative state officials have been tuning up an emergency plan.* ■ (usu. **be tuned**) *figurative* adjust or adapt (something) to a particular purpose or situation: *the animals are finely* **tuned to** *life in the desert.* ■ [*intrans.*] (**tune into**) *figurative* become sensitive to: *you must tune into the needs of loved ones.*
▸*phrasal v.* □ **tune out** *informal* stop listening or paying attention. □ **tune something out** exclude a sound or transmission of a particular frequency. □ **tune up** (of a musician) adjust one's instrument to the correct or uniform pitch. ▷late Middle English: unexplained alteration of **TONE.** The verb is first recorded (late 15th cent.) in the sense 'celebrate in music, sing.' —**tun·a·ble** (also **tune·a·ble**) *adj.* —**tun·ing** *n.*
▸**PHRASES** □ **be tuned in** *informal* be aware of, sensitive to, or able to understand something: *it's important to* **be tuned in to** *your child's needs.* □ **call the tune** see **CALL.** □ **change one's tune** see **CHANGE.** □ **in** (or **out of**) **tune** with correct (or incorrect) pitch or intonation. ■ (of an engine or other machine) properly (or poorly) adjusted. ■ *figurative* in (or not in) agreement or harmony: *he was* **out of tune with** *conventional belief.* □ **to the tune of** *informal* amounting to or involving (a specified considerable sum): *he was in debt to the tune of forty thousand pounds.*

tune·ful /ˈt(y)o͞onfəl/ ▸*adj.* having a pleasing tune; melodious. —**tune·ful·ly** *adv.* —**tune·ful·ness** *n.*

tune·less /ˈt(y)o͞onləs/ ▸*adj.* not pleasing to listen to; unmelodious. —**tune·less·ly** *adv.* —**tune·less·ness** *n.*

tun·er /ˈt(y)o͞onər/ ▸*n.* a person who tunes musical instruments, esp. pianos. ■ an electronic device for tuning a guitar or other instrument. ■ an electronic device for varying the frequency to which a radio or television is tuned. ■ a separate unit for detecting and preamplifying a program signal and supplying it to an audio amplifier.

tune·smith /ˈt(y)o͞onˌsmiTH/ ▸*n.* *informal* a composer of popular music.

tune-up (also **tune·up**) ▸*n.* an act of tuning something up: *take your car in for a tune-up if it's an older model.* ■ a sporting event that serves as a practice for a subsequent event: *a tune-up for the college's fall league.*

tung oil ▸*n.* an oil used as a drying agent in inks, paints, and varnishes. • This oil is obtained from the seeds of trees of the genus *Aleurites*, family Euphorbiaceae. ▷late 19th cent.: *tung*, from Chinese.

tung·state /ˈtəNGˌstāt/ ▸*n.* *Chemistry* a salt in which the anion contains both tungsten and oxygen, esp. one of the anion WO_4^{2-}. ▷early 19th cent.: from **TUNGSTEN** + **-ATE**[1].

tung·sten /ˈtəNGstən/ ▸*n.* the chemical element of atomic number 74, a hard steel-gray metal of the transition series. It has a very high melting point (3410°C) and is used to make electric light filaments.

T

(Symbol: **W**) ▷late 18th cent.: from Swedish, from *tung* 'heavy' + *sten* 'stone.'

tung·sten car·bide ▸*n.* a very hard gray compound made by reaction of tungsten and carbon at high temperatures, used in making engineering dies, cutting and drilling tools, etc. • Chem. formula: WC; some forms also contain W_2C.

tung·stite /ˈtəNGˌstīt/ ▸*n.* a yellow mineral consisting of hydrated tungsten oxide, typically occurring as a powdery coating on tungsten ores. ▷mid 19th cent.: from TUNGSTEN + -ITE[1].

Tun·gus /ˈto͝oNGˈgo͞oz; tən-/ ▸*n.* (*pl.* same) a member of the northern Evenki people of Siberia. ■ older term for EVENKI (the language). ▷Russian, from a Turkic language.

Tun·gus·ic /to͝oNGˈgo͞ozik/ ▸*adj.* of, relating to, or denoting a small family of Altaic languages of Siberia and northern China.
▸*n.* this family of languages collectively.

Tun·gus·ka /to͝oNGˈgo͞oskə; təNG-/ two rivers in Siberia in Russia, the **Lower Tunguska** and the **Stony Tunguska**, that flow west through the forested, sparsely populated Tunguska Basin into the Yenisei River.

tu·nic /ˈt(y)o͞onik/ ▸*n.* **1** a loose garment, typically sleeveless and reaching to the wearer's knees, as worn in ancient Greece and Rome. ■ a loose, thigh-length garment, worn typically by women over a skirt or trousers. **2** a close-fitting short coat as part of a uniform, esp. a police or military uniform. **3** *Biology & Anatomy* an integument or membrane enclosing or lining an organ or part. ■ *Botany* any of the concentric layers of a plant bulb, e.g., an onion. ■ *Zoology* the rubbery outer coat of a sea squirt. ▷Old English, from Old French *tunique* or Latin *tunica*.

tu·ni·ca /ˈt(y)o͞onikə/ ▸*n.* (*pl.* **-ni·cae** /-nəkē; -sē/) **1** *Anatomy* a membranous sheath enveloping or lining an organ. **2** *Botany* the outer layer or layers of cells in an apical meristem, which contribute to surface growth. ▷late 17th cent.: from Latin, literally 'tunic.'

tu·ni·cate /ˈt(y)o͞oniˌkāt/ ▸*n.* *Zoology* a marine invertebrate of a group that includes the sea squirts and salps. They have a rubbery or hard outer coat and two siphons to draw water into and out of the body. • Subphylum Urochordata: three classes.
▸*adj.* (usu. **tunicated**) *Botany* (of a plant bulb, e.g., an onion) having concentric layers. ▷mid 18th cent.: from Latin *tunicatus*, past participle of *tunicare* 'clothe with a tunic,' from *tunica* (see TUNICA).

tu·ni·cle /ˈt(y)o͞onikəl/ ▸*n.* a short liturgical vestment that is traditionally worn over the alb by a subdeacon at celebrations of the Mass. ▷late Middle English: from Old French *tunicle* or Latin *tunicula*, diminutive of *tunica* (see TUNICA).

tun·ing fork ▸*n.* a two-pronged steel device used by musicians, which vibrates when struck to give a note of specific pitch.

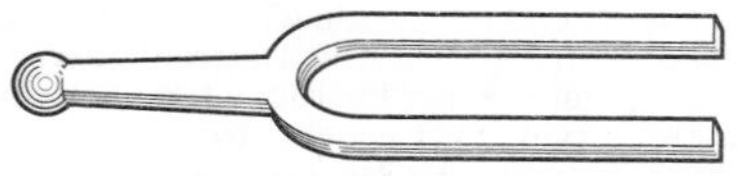

tuning fork

tun·ing pin /ˈt(y)o͞oniNG/ ▸*n.* a pin to which the strings of a piano or harpsichord are attached.

Tu·nis /ˈt(y)o͞onəs/ the capital of Tunisia, a port on the Mediterranean coast of North Africa; pop. 597,000.

Tu·ni·sia /t(y)o͞oˈnēZHə/ a country in North Africa, on the Mediterranean Sea and extending south into the Sahara Desert; pop. 9,974,000; capital, Tunis; language, Arabic (official). **—Tu·ni·sian** *adj.* & *n.*

Phoenician coastal settlements developed into the commercial empire of Carthage (near modern Tunis). The area was conquered by the Arabs in the 7th century and became part of the Ottoman Empire in the 16th century; a French protectorate was established in 1886. The rise of nationalism led to independence and the establishment of a republic in 1956–57.

tun·nel /ˈtənl/ ▸*n.* an artificial underground passage, esp. one built through a hill or under a building, road, or river. ■ an underground passage dug by a burrowing animal. ■ [in *sing.*] a passage in a sports stadium by which players enter or leave the field.
▸*v.* (**-neled, -nel·ing**; *Brit.* **-nelled, -nel·ling**) **1** [*intrans.*] dig or force a passage underground or through something: *he tunneled under the fence* | (**tunnel one's way**) *the insect tunnels its way out of the plant.* **2** [*intrans.*] *Physics* (of a particle) pass through a potential barrier. ▷late Middle English (in the senses 'tunnel net' and 'flue of a chimney'): from Old French *tonel*, diminutive of *tonne* 'cask.' Sense 1 of the noun dates from the mid 18th cent. **—tun·nel·er** *n.*
▸*PHRASE* □ **light at the end of the tunnel** see LIGHT[1].

tun·nel di·ode ▸*n.* *Electronics* a two-terminal semiconductor diode using tunneling electrons to perform high-speed switching operations.

tun·nel kiln ▸*n.* an industrial kiln in which ceramic items being fired are carried on trucks along a continuously heated passage.

tun·nel of love ▸*n.* a fairground amusement for couples involving a train or boat ride through a darkened tunnel.

tun·nel vi·sion ▸*n.* defective sight in which objects cannot be properly seen if not close to the center of the field of view. ■ *informal* the tendency to focus exclusively on a single or limited goal or point of view.

Tun·ney /ˈtənē/, Gene (1898–1978), U.S. boxer; born *James Joseph Tunney*. He became world heavyweight champion in 1926 by defeating Jack Dempsey. After defending his title several times, he retired as the undefeated world heavyweight champion in 1928.

tun·ny /ˈtənē/ (also **tun·ny fish**) ▸*n.* *chiefly Brit.* (*pl.* same or **-nies**) a tuna, esp. the bluefin. ■ tuna as food. ▷mid 16th cent.: from French *thon*, via Latin from Greek *thunnos*.

tun shell ▸*n.* see TUN (sense 3).

Tu·ol·um·ne River /to͞oˈäləmē/ a river that flows from Yosemite National Park in California to the San Joaquin River. It is impounded in the Hetch Hetchy and Don Pedro reservoirs.

tup /təp/ ▸*n.* *chiefly Brit.* a ram.
▸*v.* (**tupped, tup·ping**) [*trans.*] [often as *n.*] (**tup·ping**) *chiefly Brit.* (of a ram) copulate with (a ewe). ■ *vulgar slang* (of a man) have sexual intercourse with (a woman). ▷Middle English: of unknown origin.

Tu·pa·ma·ro /ˌto͞opəˈmäˌrō/ ▸*n.* (*pl.* **-ros**) a member of a Marxist urban guerrilla organization in Uruguay that was active mainly in the late 1960s and early 1970s. ▷1960s: from *Tupac Amarú*, the name of an 18th-cent. Inca leader.

Tu·pe·lo /ˈt(y)o͞opəˌlō/ a city in northeastern Mississippi; pop. 34,211. The site of some Civil War battles, it is also the birthplace of Elvis Presley.

tu·pe·lo /ˈt(y)o͞opəˌlō/ ▸*n.* (*pl.* **-los**) a North American or Asian tree of damp and swampy habitats that yields useful timber. • Genus *Nyssa*, family Nyssaceae: several species, including the **water tupelo** (*N. aquatica*), which grows in the coastal-plain swamps of the southeastern U.S. ▷mid 18th cent.: from Creek, from *ito* 'tree' + *opilwa* 'swamp.'

Tu·pi /ˈto͞opē; to͞oˈpē/ ▸*n.* (*pl.* same or **-pis**) **1** a member of a group of American Indian peoples living in scattered areas throughout the Amazon basin. **2** any of the languages of these peoples, a branch of the Tupi-Guarani language family.
▸*adj.* of or relating to these peoples or their languages. ▷a local name. **—Tu·pi·an** /-pēən/ *adj.*

Tu·pi-Gua·ra·ni /to͞oˈpē ˌgwärəˈnē/ ▸*n.* a South American Indian language family whose principal members are Guarani and the Tupian languages.
▸*adj.* of, relating to, or denoting these languages.

tup·pence ▸*n.* *Brit.* variant spelling of TWOPENCE.

tup·pen·ny /ˈtəp(ə)nē/ ▸*adj.* *Brit.* variant spelling of TWOPENNY.

Tup·per·ware /ˈtəpərˌwer/ ▸*n.* *trademark* a range of plastic containers used chiefly for storing food. ▷1950s: from *Tupper*, the name of the American manufacturer, + WARE[1].

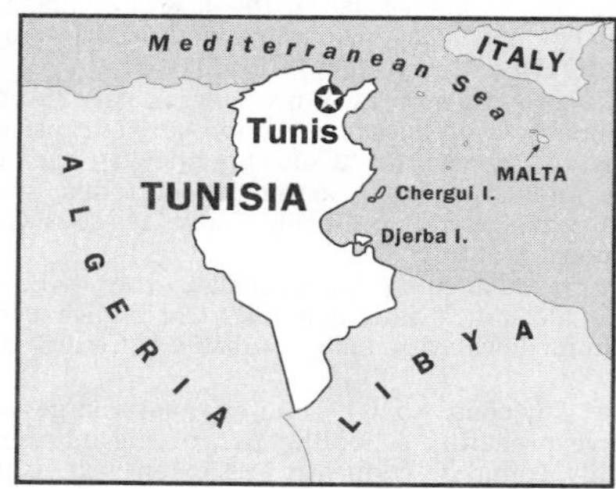

tuque /t(y)o͞ok/ ▸*n.* *Canadian* a close-fitting knitted stocking cap. ▷Canadian French form of TOQUE.

tur /to͝or/ ▸*n.* a wild goat native to the Caucasian mountains. • Genus *Capra*, family Bovidae: two species. ▷late 19th cent.: from Russian.

tu·ra·co ▸*n.* variant spelling of TOURACO.

Tu·ra·ni·an /t(y)o͞oˈrānēən/ ▸*adj.* *dated* of, relating to, or denoting the languages of central Asia, particularly those of the Uralic and Altaic families, or the peoples that speak them. ▷late 18th cent.: from Persian *Tūrān*, the region beyond the Oxus, + -IAN.

tur·ban /ˈtərbən/ ▸*n.* **1** a man's headdress, consisting of a long length of cotton or silk wound around a cap or the head, worn esp. by Muslims and Sikhs. **2** (also **turban shell**) a marine mollusk with a sculptured spiral shell and a distinctive operculum which is smooth on the inside and sculptured and typically patterned on the outside. • Family Turbinidae, class Gastropoda: *Turbo* and other genera. ▷mid 16th cent.: via French from Turkish *tülbent*, from Persian *dulband*. Compare with TULIP. **—tur·baned** *adj.*

turban 1

tur·ban squash ▸*n.* a winter squash with a green and orange rind, shaped somewhat like a turban.

Tur·bel·lar·i·a /ˌtərbəˈle(ə)rēə/ *Zoology* a class of typically free-living flatworms that have a ciliated surface and a simple branched gut with a single opening. ▷modern Latin (plural), from Latin *turbella* 'bustle, stir,' diminutive of *turba* 'crowd.' **—tur·bel·lar·i·an** /ˌtərbəˈle(ə)rēən/ *adj.* & *n.*

tur·bid /ˈtərbid/ ▸*adj.* (of a liquid) cloudy, opaque, or thick with suspended matter: *the turbid estuary* | *figurative a turbid piece of cinéma vérité.* ▷late Middle English (in the figurative sense): from Latin *turbidus*, from *turba* 'a crowd, a disturbance.' **—tur·bid·i·ty** /tərˈbiditē/ *n.* **—tur·bid·ly** *adv.* **—tur·bid·ness** *n.*

USAGE Is it **turbid** or **turgid**? **Turbid** is used of a liquid or color to mean 'muddy, not clear': ***turbid** water.* **Turgid** means 'swollen, inflated, enlarged': ***turgid** veins.* Both **turbid** and **turgid** can also be used to describe language or literary style: as such, **turbid** means 'confused, muddled' (*the **turbid** utterances of Carlyle*), and **turgid** means 'pompous, bombastic' (*a **turgid** and pretentious essay*).

tur·bi·dim·e·ter /ˌtərbiˈdimitər/ ▸*n.* an instrument for measuring the turbidity of a liquid suspension, usually as a means of determining the surface area of the suspended particles. **—tur·bi·di·met·ric** /-dəˈmetrik/ *adj.* **—tur·bi·dim·e·try** /-trē/ *n.*

tur·bi·dite /ˈtərbiˌdīt/ ▸*n.* *Geology* a sediment or rock deposited by a turbidity current. ▷1950s: from *turbid* (see TURBID) + -ITE[1]. **—tur·bi·dit·ic** /ˌtərbiˈditik/ *adj.*

tur·bid·i·ty cur·rent /tərˈbiditē/ ▸*n.* an underwater current flowing swiftly downslope owing to the weight of sediment it carries.

tur·bi·nal /ˈtərbənl/ ▸*n.* (usu. **turbinals**) *Anatomy & Zoology* each of three thin curved shelves of bone in the sides of the nasal cavity in humans and other warm-blooded vertebrates, covered in mucous membrane. ▷late 16th cent. (as an adjective in the sense 'top-shaped'): from Latin *turbo, turbin-* 'spinning top' + -AL.

tur·bi·nate /ˈtərbənit; -ˌnāt/ ▸*adj.* *chiefly Zoology* (esp. of a shell) shaped like a spinning top or inverted cone. ■ *Anatomy* relating to or denoting the turbinals.
▸*n.* (also **turbinate bone**) *Anatomy* another term for TURBINAL. ▷mid 17th cent.: from Latin *turbinatus*, from *turbo, turbin-* (see TURBINE).

tur·bine /ˈtərˌbīn; -bin/ ▸*n.* a machine for producing continuous power in which a wheel or rotor, typically fitted with vanes, is made to revolve by a fast-moving flow of water, steam, gas, air, or other fluid. ▷mid 19th cent.: from French, from Latin *turbo, turbin-* 'spinning top, whirl.'

tur·bit /ˈtərbit/ ▸*n.* a stoutly built pigeon of a domestic breed with a neck frill and short beak. ▷late 17th cent.: apparently from Latin *turbo* 'spinning top,' from its shape.

tur·bo /ˈtərbō/ ▸*n.* (*pl.* **-bos**) short for TURBOCHARGER. ■ a motor vehicle equipped with a turbocharger. ■ a computer program, machine, or other object equipped to operate at high speed.

turbo- ▸*comb. form* having or driven by a turbine: *turboshaft.* ▷from TURBINE.

tur·bo·boost /ˈtərbō,bo͞ost/ ▸*n.* the increase in speed or power produced by turbocharging a car's engine or, specifically, when the turbocharger becomes activated.

tur·bo·charge /ˈtərbō,CHärj/ ▸*v.* [*trans.*] [often as *adj.*] (**turbocharged**) equip (an engine or vehicle) with a turbocharger. ■ add speed or energy to (something): *Asia's turbocharged economies.*

tur·bo·charg·er /ˈtərbō,CHärjər/ ▸*n.* a supercharger driven by a turbine powered by the engine's exhaust gases.

tur·bo die·sel ▸*n.* a turbocharged diesel engine. ■ a vehicle equipped with such an engine.

tur·bo·fan /ˈtərbō,fan/ ▸*n.* a jet engine in which a turbine-driven fan provides additional thrust. ■ an aircraft powered by such an engine.

tur·bo·gen·er·a·tor /,tərbōˈjenə,rātər/ ▸*n.* a large electricity generator driven by a steam turbine.

tur·bo·jet /ˈtərbō,jet/ ▸*n.* a jet engine in which the jet gases also operate a turbine-driven compressor for compressing the air drawn into the engine. ■ an aircraft powered by such an engine.

tur·bo·prop /ˈtərbō,präp/ ▸*n.* a jet engine in which a turbine is used to drive a propeller. ■ an aircraft powered by such an engine.

tur·bo·shaft /ˈtərbō,SHaft/ ▸*n.* a gas turbine engine in which the turbine drives a shaft other than a propeller shaft.

tur·bo·su·per·charg·er /,tərbōˈso͞opər,CHärjər/ ▸*n.* another term for TURBOCHARGER.

tur·bot /ˈtərbət/ ▸*n.* (*pl.* same or **-bots**) a European flatfish of inshore waters that has large bony tubercles on the body and is prized as food. • *Scophthalmus maximus*, family Scophthalmidae (or Bothidae). ■ used in names of similar flatfishes, e.g., **black turbot**. ▷Middle English: from Old French, of Scandinavian origin.

tur·bu·lence /ˈtərbyələns/ ▸*n.* violent or unsteady movement of air or water, or of some other fluid: *the plane shuddered as it entered some turbulence.* ■ *figurative* conflict; confusion: *a time of political turbulence.* ▷late Middle English: from Old French, or from late Latin *turbulentia*, from *turbulentus* 'full of commotion' (see TURBULENT).

tur·bu·lent /ˈtərbyələnt/ ▸*adj.* characterized by conflict, disorder, or confusion; not controlled or calm: *the country's turbulent 20-year history* | *her turbulent emotions.* ■ (of air or water) moving unsteadily or violently: *the turbulent sea.* ■ *technical* of, relating to, or denoting flow of a fluid in which the velocity at any point fluctuates irregularly and there is continual mixing rather than a steady or laminar flow pattern. ▷late Middle English: from Latin *turbulentus* 'full of commotion,' from *turba* 'crowd.' **—tur·bu·lent·ly** *adv.*

Tur·co /ˈtərkō/ ▸*n.* (*pl.* **-cos**) *historical* an Algerian soldier in the French army. ▷mid 19th cent.: from Spanish, Portuguese, and Italian, literally 'Turk.'

Turco- (also **Turko-**) ▸*comb. form* Turkish; Turkish and . . . : *Turco-Tartar.* ■ relating to Turkey.

Tur·co·man ▸*n.* variant spelling of TURKOMAN.

turd /tərd/ ▸*n.* *vulgar slang* a lump of excrement. ■ a person regarded as obnoxious or contemptible. ▷Old English *tord*, of Germanic origin.

tu·reen /t(y)o͞oˈrēn/ ▸*n.* a deep covered dish from which soup is served. ▷mid 18th cent.: alteration of earlier *terrine*, from French *terrine* (see TERRINE), feminine of Old French *terrin* 'earthen,' based on Latin *terra* 'earth.'

turf /tərf/ ▸*n.* (*pl.* **turfs** or **turves** /tərvz/) **1** grass and the surface layer of earth held together by its roots: *they walked across the springy turf.* ■ *Brit.* a piece of such grass and earth cut from the ground. ■ peat used for fuel. **2** (**the turf**) horse racing or racecourses generally: *he spent his money gambling on the turf.* **3** *informal* an area regarded as someone's personal territory; one's home ground: *the team will play Canada on their home turf this summer.* ■ a person's sphere of influence or activity: *we're in similar businesses but we cover different turf.*
▸*v.* **1** [*trans.*] *informal, chiefly Brit.* force (someone) to leave somewhere: *they were* **turfed off** *the bus.* **2** [*trans.*] [often as *adj.*] (**turfed**) cover (a patch of ground) with turf: *a turfed lawn.* ▷Old English, of Germanic origin; related to Dutch *turf* and German *Torf*, from an Indo-European root shared by Sanskrit *darbha* 'tuft of grass.'

turf·man /ˈtərfmən/ ▸*n.* (*pl.* **-men**) a devotee of horse racing, esp. one who owns or trains horses.

turf war (also **turf battle**) ▸*n.* *informal* an acrimonious dispute between rival groups over territory or a particular sphere of influence. ▷1970s: from the notion of a *war* over *turf* in the informal sense 'area regarded as personal territory' (originally the area controlled by, for example, a street gang or criminal).

turf·y /ˈtərfē/ ▸*adj.* (**turf·i·er, turf·i·est**) covered with or consisting of turf; grassy: *a turfy plain.* ■ of or like peat; peaty: *I inhaled the turfy air.*

Tur·ge·nev /to͝orˈgānyəf/, Ivan (Sergeevich) (1818–83), Russian novelist, playwright, and short-story writer. His novels, such as *Fathers and Sons* (1862), examine individual lives to illuminate the social, political, and philosophical issues of the day.

tur·ges·cent /tərˈjesənt/ ▸*adj.* *chiefly technical* becoming or seeming swollen or distended. ▷early 18th cent.: from Latin *turgescent-* 'beginning to swell,' from the verb *turgescere*, from *turgere* 'to swell.' **—tur·ges·cence** *n.*

tur·gid /ˈtərjid/ ▸*adj.* swollen and distended or congested: *a turgid and fast-moving river.* ■ (of language or style) tediously pompous or bombastic: *some turgid verses on the death of Prince Albert.* ▷early 17th cent.: from Latin *turgidus*, from *turgere* 'to swell.' **—tur·gid·i·ty** /tərˈjiditē/ *n.* **—tur·gid·ly** *adv.*

USAGE On the differences in use between **turgid** and **turbid**, see **usage** at TURBID.

tur·gor /ˈtərgər/ ▸*n.* *chiefly Botany* the state of turgidity and resulting rigidity of cells (or tissues), typically due to the absorption of fluid. ▷late 19th cent.: from late Latin, from *turgere* 'to swell.'

Tu·rin /ˈt(y)o͝orən; t(y)o͞oˈrin/ a city in northwestern Italy on the Po River, capital of Piedmont region; pop. 992,000. It was the capital of the kingdom of Sardinia from 1720 and became the first capital of a unified Italy (1861–64). Italian name **TORINO**.

Tu·rin, Shroud of a relic, preserved at Turin since 1578, venerated as the winding sheet in which Christ's body was wrapped for burial. It bears the apparent imprint of the front and back of a human body as well as markings that correspond to the traditional stigmata. Scientific tests carried out in 1988 dated the shroud to the 13th–14th centuries.

Tu·ring /ˈt(y)o͝oriNG/, Alan Mathison (1912–54), English mathematician. He developed the concept of a theoretical computing machine and carried out important code-breaking work during World War II. He also investigated artificial intelligence.

Tu·ring ma·chine ▸*n.* a mathematical model of a hypothetical computing machine that can use a predefined set of rules to determine a result from a set of input variables.

Tu·ring test ▸*n.* a test for intelligence in a computer, requiring that a human being should be unable to distinguish the machine from another human being by using the replies to questions put to both.

tu·ri·on /ˈt(y)o͝orē,än/ ▸*n.* *Botany* (in some aquatic plants) a wintering bud that becomes detached and remains dormant at the bottom of the water. ▷early 18th cent.: from French, from Latin *turio(n-)* 'a shoot.'

tu·ris·ta /to͞oˈrēstə/ ▸*n.* *informal* diarrhea as suffered by travelers when visiting certain foreign countries. ▷Spanish, literally 'tourist.'

Turk /tərk/ ▸*n.* **1** a native or national of Turkey, or a person of Turkish descent. **2** *historical* a member of any of the ancient central Asian peoples who spoke Turkic languages, including the Seljuks and Ottomans. **3** *archaic* a member of the ruling Muslim population of the Ottoman Empire. ▷late Middle English: via Old French from Turkish *türk*.

Tur·ka·na /tərˈkänə/ ▸*n.* (*pl.* same) **1** a member of an East African people living between Lake Turkana and the Nile. **2** the Nilotic language of the Turkana, spoken by about 250,000 people.
▸*adj.* of or relating to the Turkana or their language. ▷a local name.

Tur·ka·na, Lake /tərˈkanə; -ˈkänə/ a salt lake in northwestern Kenya, with no outlet. It was visited in 1888 by Hungarian explorer Count Teleki (1845–1916), who named it Lake Rudolf after the crown prince of Austria. It was given its present name in 1979.

Tur·ke·stan /ˈtərkə,stan; -,stän/ (also **Tur·ki·stan**) a region in central Asia between the Caspian Sea and the Gobi Desert, inhabited mainly by Turkic peoples. It is divided by the Pamir and Tien Shan mountains into eastern Turkestan, now the Xinjiang autonomous region of China, and western Turkestan, which consists of present-day Turkmenistan, Kazakhstan, Uzbekistan, Tajikistan, and Kyrgyzstan.

Tur·key /ˈtərkē/ a country located on the Anatolian peninsula in western Asia, with a small enclave in southeastern Europe west of Istanbul; pop. 68,893,000; capital, Ankara; language, Turkish (official).

The center of the Ottoman Empire before World War I, Turkey became a secular republic in the 1920s. It has a sizable Kurdish minority in the east.

tur·key /ˈtərkē/ ▸*n.* (*pl.* **-keys**) **1** a large mainly domesticated game bird native to North America, having a bald head and (in the male) red wattles. It is prized as food, esp. on festive occasions such as Thanksgiving and Christmas. • *Meleagris gallopavo*, family Meleagridae (or Phasianidae). ■ the flesh of the turkey as food. **2** *informal* something that is extremely or completely unsuccessful, esp. a play or movie. ■ a stupid or inept person. ▷mid 16th cent.: short for TURKEY COCK or *turkey hen*, originally applied to the guinea fowl (which was imported through Turkey), and then erroneously to the American bird.
▸*PHRASE* □ **talk turkey** *informal* discuss something frankly and straightforwardly.

turkey 1

tur·key buz·zard ▸*n.* another term for TURKEY VULTURE.

tur·key call ▸*n.* an instrument used by hunters to decoy the wild turkey by imitating its characteristic gobbling sound.

tur·key cock ▸*n.* a male turkey. ■ a pompous or self-important person.

tur·key oak ▸*n.* a small oak of the coastal plains of the southeastern U.S., with leathery three-lobed leaves shaped like the outline of a turkey track. • *Quercus laevis*, family Fagaceae.

Tur·key red ▸*n.* a scarlet textile dye obtained from madder or alizarin. ■ the color of this dye. ■ cotton cloth dyed with this, popular in the 19th century.

tur·key shoot ▸*n.* *informal* a situation, typically in a war, in which the aggressor has an overwhelming advantage.

tur·key trot ▸*n.* a kind of ballroom dance to ragtime music that was popular in the early 20th century.

tur·key vul·ture ▸*n.* a common American vulture with black plumage and a bare red head. • *Cathartes aura*, family Cathartidae.

Tur·kic /ˈtərkik/ ▸*adj.* of, relating to, or denoting a large group of closely related Altaic languages of western and central Asia, including Turkish, Azerbaijani, Kazakh, Kyrgyz, Uighur, Uzbek, and Tatar.
▸*n.* the Turkic languages collectively. ▷mid 19th cent.: from TURK + -IC.

Turk·ish /ˈtərkiSH/ ▸*adj.* of or relating to Turkey or to the Turks or their language. ■ *historical* relating to or associated with the Ottoman Empire.
▸*n.* the Turkic language that is the official language of Turkey.

Turk·ish bath ▸*n.* a cleansing or relaxing treatment that involves a period of time spent sitting in a room filled with very hot air or steam, generally followed by washing and massage. ■ a building or room where such a treatment is available.

Turk·ish car·pet (also **Turkish rug**) ▸*n.* a rug woven in Turkey in a traditional fashion, typically with a bold colored design and thick wool pile, or made elsewhere in this style.

Turk·ish cof·fee ▸*n.* very strong black coffee served with the fine grounds in it.

Turk·ish de·light ▸*n.* a dessert consisting of flavored gelatin coated in powdered sugar.

Turk·ish slip·per ▸*n.* a soft heelless slipper with a turned-up toe.

Turk·ish tow·el ▸*n.* a towel made of cotton terry toweling.

Turk·ish Van (in full **Turkish Van cat**) ▸*n.* a cat of a long-haired breed, with a white body, auburn markings on the head and tail, and light orange eyes. ▷1960s: named after the town of *Van*, Turkey.

Tur·ki·stan variant spelling of **TURKESTAN**.

Turk·men /ˈtərkmen; -mən/ ▸*n.* (*pl.* same or **-mens**) **1** a member of a group of Turkic peoples inhabiting the region east of the Caspian Sea and south of the Aral Sea, now comprising Turkmenistan and parts of Iran and Afghanistan. **2** the Turkic language of these peoples.
▸*adj.* of or relating to the Turkmens, their language, or the region that they inhabit. ▷from Persian *turkmān*, from Turkish *türkmen*; also influenced by Russian *turkmen*.

Turk·me·ni·stan /tərkˈmenəˌstan; -ˌstän/ a republic in central Asia that lies between the Caspian Sea and Afghanistan; pop. 3,861,000; capital, Ashgabat; languages, Turkoman (official) and Russian. Also called **TURKMENIA**.

Turkmenistan is dominated by the Karakum Desert, which occupies about 90 percent of the country. Previously part of Turkestan, from 1924 it formed a separate constituent republic of the USSR; Turkmenistan became an independent republic within the Commonwealth of Independent States in 1991.

Turko- ▸*comb. form* variant spelling of **TURCO-**.

Tur·ko·man /ˈtərkəmən/ (also **Tur·co·man**) ▸*n.* (*pl.* **-mans**) another term for **TURKMEN**. ▷early 17th cent.: from medieval Latin *Turcomannus*, French *turcoman*, from Persian *turkmān* (see **TURKMEN**).

Turks and Cai·cos Is·lands /ˈtərks and ˈkākəs; ˈkākōs/ a British dependency in the Caribbean Sea that is composed of two island groups between Haiti and the Bahamas; pop. 12,000; capital, Cockburn Town (on the island of Grand Turk).

Turk's-cap lil·y ▸*n.* a lily with orange flowers that resemble turbans due to the almost completely reflexed petals. • *Lilium superbum*, family Liliaceae.

Turk's-cap lily

Turk's head ▸*n.* an ornamental knot resembling a turban in shape, made in the end of a rope to form a stopper.

Turk's-head cac·tus ▸*n.* a barrel-shaped Jamaican cactus that bears red flowers from a terminal part that resembles a fez. Also called **Turk's-cap cactus**. • *Melocactus communis*, family Cactaceae.

Tur·ku /ˈtoŏrkoō/ an industrial port in southwestern Finland; pop. 159,000. It was the capital of Finland until 1812. Swedish name **ÅBO**.

Tur·lock /ˈtərˌläk/ a commercial city in north central California, in the San Joaquin Valley; pop. 42,198.

tur·lough /ˈtərˌlôKH/ ▸*n.* (in Ireland) a low-lying area on limestone that becomes flooded in wet weather through the welling up of groundwater. ▷late 17th cent.: from Irish *turloch*, from *tur* 'dry' + *loch* 'lake.'

tur·mer·ic /ˈtərmərik/ ▸*n.* **1** a bright yellow aromatic powder obtained from the rhizome of a plant of the ginger family, used for flavoring and coloring in Asian cooking and formerly as a fabric dye. **2** the Asian plant from which this rhizome is obtained. • *Curcuma longa*, family Zingiberaceae. ▷late Middle English (earlier as *tarmaret*): perhaps from French *terre mérite* and modern Latin *terra merita*, literally 'deserving earth,' perhaps an alteration of an Asian word.

tur·moil /ˈtərˌmoil/ ▸*n.* a state of great disturbance, confusion, or uncertainty: *the country was* ***in turmoil*** | *he endured years of inner turmoil.* ▷early 16th cent.: of unknown origin.

turn /tərn/ ▸*v.* **1** move or cause to move in a circular direction wholly or partly around an axis or point: [*intrans.*] *the big wheel was turning* | [*trans.*] *I turned the key in the door and crept in.* ■ [*trans.*] move (something) so that it is in a different position in relation to its surroundings or its previous position: *we waited in suspense for him to turn the cards over.* ■ [*trans.*] move (a page) over so that it is flat against the previous or next page: *she turned a page noisily* | [*intrans.*] *turn to page five for the answer.* ■ change or cause to change direction: [*intrans.*] *we turned around and headed back to the house.* ■ [*trans.*] aim, point, or direct (something): *she turned her head toward me* | *the government has now turned its attention to primary schools.* ■ [*intrans.*] change the position of one's body so that one is facing in a different direction: *Charlie turned and looked at his friend.* ■ [*intrans.*] (of the tide) change from flood to ebb or vice versa. ■ [*trans.*] pass around (the flank or defensive lines of an army) so as to attack it from the side or rear. ■ [*trans.*] perform (a somersault or cartwheel). ■ [*trans.*] twist or sprain (an ankle). ■ [*trans.*] fold or unfold (fabric or a piece of a garment) in the specified way: *he turned up the collar of his coat.* ■ [*trans.*] remake (a garment or a sheet), putting the worn outer side on the inside. ■ [*trans.*] [usu. as *adj.*] (**turned**) *Printing* set or print (a type or letter) upside down. ■ [*trans.*] *archaic* bend back (the edge of a blade) so as to make it blunt. **2** [*intrans.*] change in nature, state, form, or color; become: *Emmeline turned pale* | *the slight drizzle turned into a downpour.* ■ [*trans.* or *adverbial*] cause to change in such a way; cause to become: *potatoes are covered with sacking to keep the light from turning them green.* ■ [*intrans.*] (of leaves) change color in the autumn. ■ [*trans.*] pass the age or time of: *I've just turned forty.* ■ (with reference to milk) make or become sour: [*trans.*] *the thunder had turned the milk.* ■ (with reference to the stomach) make or become nauseated: [*trans.*] *the smell was bad enough to turn the strongest stomach.* ■ [*trans.* or *adverbial*] send or put into a specified place or condition: *the dogs were turned loose on the crowd.* **3** [*intrans.*] (**turn to**) start doing or becoming involved with: *in 1939 he turned to films in earnest.* ■ go on to consider next: *we can now turn to another aspect of the problem.* ■ go to for help, advice, or information: *who can she turn to?* ■ have recourse to (something, esp. something dangerous or unhealthy): *he turned to drink and drugs for solace.* **4** [*trans.*] shape (something) on a lathe: *the faceplate is turned rather than cast.* ■ give a graceful or elegant form to: [as *adj.* with *submodifier*] (**turned**) *a production full of so many finely turned words.* ■ make (a profit).
▸*phrasal v.* □ **turn against** (or **turn someone against**) become (or cause someone to become) hostile toward: *public opinion turned against him.* □ **turn around** move so as to face in the opposite direction: *Alice turned around and walked down the corridor.* □ **turn something around** **1** prepare a ship or aircraft for its return journey. **2** reverse the previously poor performance of something, esp. a company, and make it successful. □ **turn someone away** refuse to allow someone to enter or pass through a place. □ **turn back** (or **turn someone/something back**) go (or cause to go) back in the direction in which one has come: *they turned back before reaching the church.* □ **turn someone down** reject an offer or application made by someone: *the Air Force turned him down on medical grounds.* □ **turn something down** **1** reject something offered or proposed: *his novel was turned down by publisher after publisher.* **2** adjust a control on a device to reduce the volume, heat, etc. □ **turn in** *informal* go to bed in the evening. □ **turn someone in** hand someone over to the authorities. □ **turn something in** give something to someone in authority: *I've turned in my resignation.* ■ produce or achieve a particular score or a performance of a specified quality. □ **turn off** leave one road in order to join another. □ **turn someone off** *informal* induce a feeling of boredom or disgust in someone. □ **turn something off** stop the operation or flow of something by means of a valve, switch, or button: *remember to turn off the gas.* ■ operate a valve or switch in order to do this. □ **turn on** **1** suddenly attack (someone) physically or verbally: *he turned on her with cold savagery.* **2** have as the main topic or point of interest: *for most businessmen, the central questions will turn on taxation.* □ **turn someone on** *informal* excite or stimulate the interest of someone, esp. sexually. □ **turn something on** start the flow or operation of something by means of a valve, switch, or button: *she turned on the TV.* ■ operate a valve or switch in order to do this. □ **turn someone on to** *informal* cause someone to become interested or involved in (something, esp. drugs): *he turned her on to heroin.* □ **turn out** **1** prove to be the case: *the job turned out to be beyond his rather limited abilities.* **2** go somewhere in order to do something, esp. to attend a meeting, to play a game, or to vote: *over 75 percent of the electorate turned out to vote.* □ **turn someone out** **1** eject or expel someone from a place. **2** *Military* call a guard from the guardroom. **3** (**be turned out**) be dressed in the manner specified: *she was smartly turned out and as well groomed as always.* □ **turn something out** **1** extinguish a light. **2** produce something: *the plant takes 53 hours to turn out each car.* **3** empty something, esp. one's pockets. **4** tip prepared food from a mold or other container. □ **turn over** (of an engine) start or continue to run properly. □ **turn someone over to** deliver someone to the care or custody of (another person or body, esp. one in authority): *they turned him over to the police.* □ **turn something over** **1** cause an engine to run. **2** transfer control or management of something to someone else: *a plan to* ***turn*** *the bar* ***over*** *to a new manager.* **3** change the function or use of something: *the works was* ***turned over to*** *the production of aircraft parts.* **4** *informal* rob a place. **5** (of a business) have a turnover of a specified amount: *last year the company turned over $12 million.* □ **turn up** **1** be found, esp. by chance, after being lost: *all the missing documents had turned up.* **2** put in an appearance; arrive: *half the guests failed to turn up.* □ **turn something up** **1** increase the volume or strength of sound, heat, etc., by turning a knob or switch on a device. **2** reveal or discover something: *New Yorkers confidently expect the inquiry to turn up nothing.* **3** shorten a garment by raising the hem.
▸*n.* **1** an act of moving something in a circular direction around an axis or point: *a safety lock requiring four turns of the key.* ■ a change of direction when moving: *they made a left turn and picked up speed.* ■ a development or change in circumstances or a course of events: *life has* ***taken a turn for the better.*** ■ a time when one specified period of time ends and another begins: *the turn of the century.* ■ a bend or curve in a road, path, river, etc.: *the twists and turns in the passageways.* ■ a place where a road meets or branches off another. ■ (**the turn**) the beginning of the second nine holes of a round of golf: *he made the turn in one under par.* ■ a change of the tide from ebb to flow or vice versa. ■ one round in a coil of rope or other material. **2** an opportunity or obligation to do something that comes successively to each of a number of people: *it was his turn to speak.* ■ a short performance, esp. one of a number given by different performers in succession: *a comic turn.* ■ a performer giving such a performance. **3** a short walk or ride: *why don't you* ***take a turn*** *around the garden?* **4** *informal* a shock: *you gave us quite a turn!* ■ a brief feeling or experience of illness: *tell me how you feel when you have these funny turns.* **5** the difference between the buying and selling price of stocks or other financial products. ■ a profit made from such a difference. **6** *Music* a melodic ornament consisting of the principal note with those above and below it. ▷Old English *tyrnan*, *turnian* (verb), from Latin *tornare*, from *tornus* 'lathe,' from Greek *tornos* 'lathe, circular movement'; probably reinforced in Middle English by Old French *turner*. The noun (Middle English) is partly from Anglo-Norman French *tourn*, partly from the verb.
▸*PHRASES* □ **at every turn** on every occasion; continually: *her name seemed to come up at every turn.* □ **by turns** one after the other; alternately: *he was by turns amused and mildly annoyed by her.* □ **do someone a good** (or **bad**) **turn** do something that is helpful (or unhelpful) for someone. □ **in turn** in succession; one after the other: *four men prayed in turn.* ■ (also **in one's/its turn**) used to convey that an action, process, or situation is the result or product of a previous one: *he would shout until she, in her turn, lost her temper.* □ **not know which way** (or **where**) **to turn** not know what to do; be completely at a loss. □ **not turn a hair** see **HAIR**. □ **one good turn deserves another** *proverb* if someone does you a favor, you should take the chance to repay it. □ **on the turn** at

a turning point; in a state of change: *my luck is on the turn.* □ **out of turn** at a time when it is not one's turn. □ **speak** (or **talk**) **out of turn** speak in a tactless or foolish way. □ **take turns** (of two or more people) do something alternately or in succession. □ **to a turn** to exactly the right degree (used esp. in relation to cooking): *hamburgers done to a turn.* □ **turn and turn about** *chiefly Brit.* one after another; in succession: *the two men were working in rotation, turn and turn about.* □ **turn one's back on** see **BACK**. □ **turn the corner** pass the critical point and start to improve. □ **turn a deaf ear** see **DEAF**. □ **turn one's hand to something** see **HAND**. □ **turn one's head** see **HEAD**. □ **turn heads** see **HEAD**. □ **turn an honest penny** see **HONEST**. □ **turn in one's grave** see **GRAVE**[1]. □ **turn of mind** a particular way of thinking: *people with a practical turn of mind.* □ **turn of speed** the ability to go fast when necessary. □ **turn on one's heel** see **HEEL**[1]. □ **turn the other cheek** see **CHEEK**. □ **turn over a new leaf** start to act or behave in a better or more responsible way. □ **turn something over in one's mind** think about or consider something thoroughly. □ **turn around and do** (or **say**) **something** *informal* used to convey that someone's actions or words are perceived as unexpected, unwelcome, or confrontational: *then she just turned around and said she wasn't coming after all.* □ **turn the tables** see **TABLE**. □ **turn tail** *informal* turn around and run away. □ **turn the tide** see **TIDE**. □ **turn something to (good) account** see **ACCOUNT**. □ **turn a trick** see **TRICK**. □ **turn turtle** see **TURTLE**. □ **turn up one's nose at** see **NOSE**.

turn·a·bout /ˈtərnəˌbout/ ▸*n.* a sudden and complete change or reversal of policy, opinion, or of a situation: *the move was a significant turnabout for the company.*

turn·a·round /ˈtərnəˌround/ ▸*n.* **1** an abrupt or unexpected change, esp. one that results in a more favorable situation: *it was a remarkable* ***turnaround in*** *his fortunes.* **2** the process of completing or the time needed to complete a task, esp. one involving receiving something, processing it, and sending it out again: *a seven-day turnaround.* ■ the process of or time taken for unloading and reloading a ship, aircraft, or vehicle. **3** a space for vehicles to turn around in, esp. one at the end of a driveway or dead end street.

turn-back /ˈtərnˌbak/ ▸*n.* a part of a garment that is folded back: [as *adj.*] *the jacket has turn-back cuffs.*

turn·buck·le /ˈtərnˌbəkəl/ ▸*n.* a coupling with female screw threads used to connect two rods, lengths of boat rigging, etc., lengthwise and to regulate their length or tension.

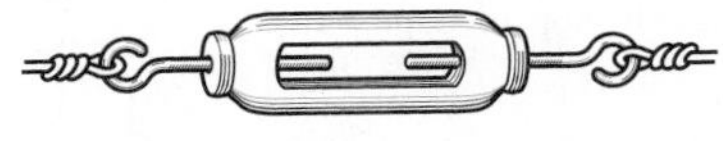

turnbuckle

turn·coat /ˈtərnˌkōt/ ▸*n.* a person who deserts one party or cause in order to join an opposing one.

turn·cock /ˈtərnˌkäk/ ▸*n. historical* a waterworks official responsible for turning on water at the mains.

turn·down /ˈtərnˌdoun/ ▸*n.* **1** a rejection or refusal. **2** a decline in something; a downturn.
▸*adj.* **1** (of a collar) turned down. **2** denoting a hotel service in which the sheets are turned back in preparation for sleeping: *the hotel has nightly turndown service.*

Tur·ner[1] /ˈtərnər/, Frederick Jackson (1861–1932), U.S. historian, educator, and writer. He revolutionized the study of the American frontier with his paper entitled "The Significance of the Frontier in American History" (1893). He also wrote *The Frontier in American History* (1920) and *The Significance of Sections in American History* (1932).

Tur·ner[2], J. M. W. (1775–1851), English painter; full name *Joseph Mallord William Turner.* He painted landscapes and stormy seascapes and became increasingly concerned with depicting the power of light with primary colors, often arranged in a swirling vortex. Notable works: *Rain, Steam, Speed* (1844) and *The Fighting Téméraire* (1838).

Tur·ner[3], Nat (1800–1831), U.S. slave leader. He was convicted of murder and insurrection and hanged for organizing a slave uprising in Southampton, Virginia, in August 1831, in which at least 50 whites were killed.

Tur·ner[4], Ted (1938–), U.S. broadcasting executive; full name *Robert Edward Turner III.* His Turner Broadcasting System (now owned by Time-Warner) included the television networks TBS, CNN, TCM, and the Cartoon Network. He bought the Atlanta Braves baseball team in 1976 and the Atlanta Hawks basketball team in 1977 and started the Atlanta Thrashers hockey team in 1999. An accomplished yachtsman, he won the America's Cup in 1977.

Tur·ner[5], Tina (1939–), U.S. singer; born *Anna Mae Bullock.* With her husband she was part of the duo Ike and Tina Turner, which broke up in 1974. Her hits include "What's Love Got to Do with It" (1984) and "We don't Need Another Hero" (1985). She also was successful with albums such as *Wildest Dreams* (1996) and *Twenty-four Seven* (2000).

turn·er /ˈtərnər/ ▸*n.* **1** a person who is skilled in turning wood on a lathe. **2** an implement that can be used to turn or flip something over: *a pancake turner.* ▷Middle English: from Old French *torneor*, from late Latin *tornator*, from the verb *tornare* (see **TURN**).

Turn·er's syn·drome ▸*n. Medicine* a genetic defect in which affected women have only one X chromosome, causing developmental abnormalities and infertility. ▷named after Henry Hubert *Turner* (1892–1970), the American physician who described it.

turn·er·y /ˈtərnərē/ ▸*n.* the action or skill of making objects on a lathe. ■ objects made on a lathe.

turn·ing /ˈtərniNG/ ▸*n.* **1** a place where a road branches off another: *take the first turning on the right.* **2** the action or skill of using a lathe. ■ (**turnings**) shavings of wood or metal resulting from turning something on a lathe.

turn·ing point ▸*n.* a time at which a decisive change in a situation occurs, esp. one with beneficial results: *this could be the turning point in Nancy's career.*

tur·nip /ˈtərnəp/ ▸*n.* **1** a round root with white or cream flesh that is eaten as a vegetable and also has edible leaves. ■ a similar or related root, esp. a rutabaga. **2** the European plant of the cabbage family that produces this root. • *Brassica rapa*, family Brassicaceae: 'rapifera' group. **3** *informal* a large, thick, old-fashioned pocket watch. ▷mid 16th cent.: first element of unknown origin + **NEEP**. **—tur·nip·y** *adj.*

turn·key /ˈtərnˌkē/ ▸*n.* (*pl.* **-keys**) *archaic* a jailer.
▸*adj.* of or involving the provision of a complete product or service that is ready for immediate use: *turnkey systems for telecommunications customers.*

turn·off /ˈtərnˌôf/ (also **turn-off**) ▸*n.* **1** a junction at which a road branches off from a main road: *Adam missed the turnoff to the village.* **2** [usu. in *sing.*] *informal* a person or thing that causes someone to feel bored, disgusted, or sexually repelled: *he smelled of carbolic soap, a dreadful turnoff.* **3** an instance of turning or switching something off.

turn-on ▸*n.* **1** [usu. in *sing.*] *informal* a person or thing that causes someone to feel excited or sexually aroused: *tight jeans are a real turn-on.* **2** an instance of turning or switching something on.

turn·out /ˈtərnˌout/ ▸*n.* **1** [usu. in *sing.*] the number of people attending or taking part in an event, esp. the number of people voting in an election. **2** a turn in a road. ■ a point at which a railroad track diverges. ■ a widened place in a road for cars to pass each other or park temporarily. **3** a carriage or other horse-drawn vehicle with its horse or horses. **4** [in *sing.*] the way in which a person or thing is equipped or dressed: *his turnout was exceedingly elegant.* **5** *Ballet* the ability to rotate the legs outward at the hips.

turn·o·ver /ˈtərnˌōvər/ ▸*n.* **1** the amount of money taken by a business in a particular period: *a turnover approaching $4 million.* ■ *Stock Market* the volume of shares traded during a particular period, as a percentage of total shares listed. **2** the rate at which employees leave a workforce and are replaced. ■ the rate at which goods are sold and replaced in a store. **3** a small pie made by folding a piece of pastry over on itself to enclose a sweet filling: *an apple turnover.* **4** (in a game) a loss of possession of the ball to the opposing team.

turn·pike /ˈtərnˌpīk/ ▸*n.* **1** an expressway, esp. one on which a toll is charged. ■ *historical* a toll gate. ■ (also **turnpike road**) *historical* a road on which a toll was collected at such a gate. **2** *historical* a spiked barrier fixed in or across a road or passage as a defense against sudden attack.

turn sig·nal ▸*n.* a flashing light on a vehicle to show that it is about to change lanes or turn.

turn·sole /ˈtərnˌsōl/ ▸*n.* a Mediterranean plant of the spurge family, whose flowers are said to turn with the sun. • *Chrozophora tinctoria* (family Euphorbiaceae), from which a blue or purple dye was formerly obtained. ▷late Middle English: from Old French *tournesole*, based on Latin *tornare* (see **TURN**) + *sol* 'sun.'

turn·spit /ˈtərnˌspit/ ▸*n. historical* a servant whose job was to turn a spit on which meat was roasting. ■ a dog kept to perform this task by running on a treadmill connected to the spit.

turns ra·tio ▸*n.* the ratio of the number of turns on the primary coil of an electrical transformer to the number on the secondary, or vice versa.

turn·stile /ˈtərnˌstīl/ ▸*n.* a mechanical gate consisting of revolving horizontal arms fixed to a vertical post, allowing only one person at a time to pass through.

turn·stone /ˈtərnˌstōn/ ▸*n.* a small, short-billed wading bird of the sandpiper family that turns over stones to feed on small animals beneath them. • Genus *Arenaria*, family Scolopacidae: two species, in particular the **ruddy turnstone** (*A. interpres*), breeding in northern Eurasia and northern Canada.

turn·ta·ble /ˈtərnˌtābəl/ ▸*n.* a circular revolving plate supporting a phonograph record as it is played. ■ a circular revolving platform for turning a railroad locomotive or other vehicle.

turn-up ▸*n. Brit.* (usu. **turn-ups**) a pant cuff.

Tur·ow /ˈto͝orō/, Scott F. (1949–), U.S. lawyer and writer. A practicing lawyer, he also writes thrillers such as *Presumed Innocent* (1987), *The Burden of Proof* (1990), *The Laws of Our Fathers* (1996), and *Personal Injuries* (1999).

tur·pen·tine /ˈtərpənˌtīn/ ▸*n.* **1** (also **oil of turpentine**) a volatile pungent oil distilled from gum turpentine or pine wood, used in mixing paints and varnishes and in liniment. • Chem. formula $C_{10}H_{16}$. ■ (also **crude turpentine** or **gum turpentine**) an oleoresin secreted by certain trees, esp. pines, and distilled to make rosin and oil of turpentine. **2** (also **turpentine tree**) any of a number of trees that yield turpentine or a similar resin, in particular: • a coniferous tree of the pine family (*Larix, Pinus*, and other genera, family Pinaceae). • the terebinth.
▸*v.* [*trans.*] apply turpentine to. ▷Middle English: from Old French *ter(e)bentine*, from Latin *ter(e)binthina (resina)* '(resin) of the turpentine tree,' from *terebinthus* (see **TEREBINTH**).

Tur·pin /ˈtərpən/, Dick (1706–39), English robber. He was a cattle and deer thief in Essex before entering into partnership with Tom King, a notorious highway robber. He was hanged for horse-stealing.

tur·pi·tude /ˈtərpiˌt(y)o͞od/ ▸*n. formal* depravity; wickedness: *acts of* ***moral turpitude.*** ▷late 15th cent.: from French, or from Latin *turpitudo*, from *turpis* 'disgraceful, base.'

turps /tərps/ ▸*n. informal* turpentine. ▷early 19th cent.: abbreviation.

tur·quoise /ˈtərˌk(w)oiz/ ▸*n.* **1** a semiprecious stone, typically opaque and of a greenish-blue or sky-blue color, consisting of a hydrated hydroxyl phosphate of copper and aluminum. **2** a greenish-blue color like that of this stone: [as *adj.*] *the turquoise waters of the bay.* ▷late Middle English: from Old French *turqueise* 'Turkish (stone).'

tur·ret /ˈtərit/ ▸*n.* **1** a small tower on top of a larger tower or at the corner of a building or wall, typically of a castle. ■ a low, flat armored gun emplacement, typically one that revolves, in a ship, aircraft, fort, or tank. ■ a rotating holder for tools, esp. on a lathe. **2** (also **turret shell**) a mollusk with a long, slender, pointed spiral shell, typically brightly colored and living in tropical seas. • Family Turitellidae, class Gastropoda: *Turitella* and other genera. ▷Middle English: from Old French *tourete*, diminutive of *tour* 'tower.' **—tur·ret·ed** *adj.*

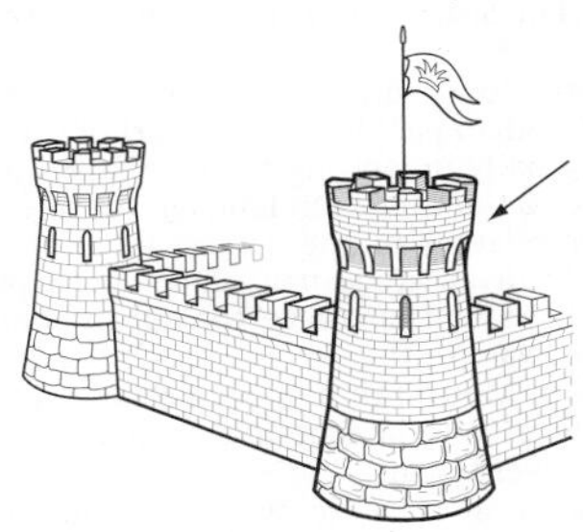

turret 1

tur·ron /tŏŏr'ōn; -'än/ ▸*n.* a kind of Spanish confectionery resembling nougat, made from almonds and honey. ▷from Spanish *turrón.*

tur·tle /'tərtl/ ▸*n.* **1** a slow-moving reptile, enclosed in a scaly or leathery domed shell into which it can retract its head and thick legs. • Family Testudinidae: numerous genera and species, including the **European tortoise** (*Testudo graeca*). **2** (also **sea turtle**) a large marine reptile with a bony or leathery shell and flippers, coming ashore annually on sandy beaches to lay eggs. • Families Cheloniidae (seven species) and Dermochelyidae (the leatherback). ■ the flesh of a sea turtle, esp. the green turtle, used chiefly for soup. **3** a freshwater reptile related to the turtles, typically having a flattened shell. Called **TERRAPIN** in South Africa and India and **TORTOISE** in Australia. • Order Chelonia: several families, in particular Emydidae and Kinosternidae. ■ any reptile of this order, including the terrapins and tortoises. **4** *Computing* a directional cursor in a computer graphics system that can be instructed to move around a screen. **5** short for **TURTLENECK**. ▷mid 16th cent.: apparently an alteration of French *tortue* (see **TORTOISE**).
▸*PHRASE* □ **turn turtle** (chiefly of a boat) capsize.

tur·tle bug ▸*n.* a bug or beetle with a turtlelike carapace, esp. an olive-brown shield bug that frequents grassy places.

tur·tle·dove /'tərdl dōv/ ▸*n.* a small Old World dove with a soft purring call, noted for the apparent affection shown for its mate. • Genus *Streptopelia*, family Columbidae: several species, in particular the migratory European and North African *S. turtur*, with a reddish-brown back and pinkish breast. ▷Middle English: *turtle* from Old English *turtla, turtle* 'turtle dove' (from Latin *turtur*, of imitative origin).

tur·tle grass ▸*n.* a submerged marine flowering plant found in the Caribbean, with long grasslike leaves. • *Thalassia testudinum*, family Hydrocharitaceae.

tur·tle·head /'tərtl,hed/ ▸*n.* a North American plant of the figwort family that produces spikes of pink or white flowers that are said to resemble the head of a turtle. • Genus *Chelone*, family Scrophulariaceae.

tur·tle·neck /'tərtl,nek/ ▸*n.* a high, close-fitting, turned-over collar on a garment, typically a shirt or sweater: [as *adj.*] *a turtleneck sweater.* ■ a shirt or sweater with a neck of this type.

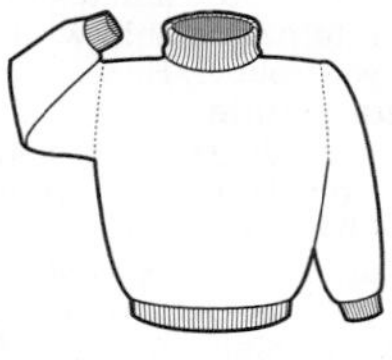

turtleneck

tur·tle·shell /'tərtl,SHel/ ▸*n.* another term for **TORTOISESHELL**.

turves /tərvz/ ▸ plural form of **TURF**.

Tus·ca·loo·sa /,təskə'lōōsə/ an industrial city in west central Alabama, on the Black Warrior River, home to the University of Alabama; pop. 77,906.

Tus·can /'təskən/ ▸*adj.* **1** of or relating to Tuscany, its inhabitants, or the form of Italian spoken there, which is the standard variety taught to foreign learners. **2** relating to or denoting a classical order of architecture resembling the Doric but lacking all ornamentation.
▸*n.* **1** a native or inhabitant of Tuscany. **2** the form of Italian spoken in Tuscany. **3** the Tuscan order of architecture. ▷late Middle English (as a noun denoting an Etruscan): via French from Latin *Tuscanus*, from *Tuscus* 'an Etruscan.'

Tus·ca·ny /'təskənē/ a region in west central Italy, on the Ligurian Sea; capital, Florence. Italian name **TOSCANA**.

Tus·ca·ro·ra /,təskə'rôrə/ ▸*n.* (*pl.* same or **-ras**) **1** an American Indian people forming part of the Six Nations, originally inhabiting the Carolinas and later New York. **2** the Iroquoian language of this people.
▸*adj.* of or relating to the Tuscarora or their language. ▷from an Iroquoian name, perhaps from Catawba (a Siouan language spoken in South Carolina) *taskarudē.*

Tus·ca·ro·ra Moun·tains /,təskə'rôrə/ a range in northeastern Nevada that has been the scene of gold and silver booms.

tusch·e /'tŏŏSH(ə)/ ▸*n.* a greasy black composition, in liquid form or to be mixed with liquids, used as ink for making lithographic drawings. ▷early 20th cent.: from German *tuschen*, from French *toucher* 'to touch'.

tush¹ /təSH/ ▸*exclam. archaic* or *humorous* expressing disapproval, impatience, or dismissal: *tush, these are trifles and mere old wives' tales.* ▷natural utterance: first recorded in late Middle English.

tush² /təSH/ ▸*n.* a long pointed tooth, in particular a canine tooth of a male horse. ■ a stunted tusk of some Indian elephants. ▷Old English *tusc* (see **TUSK**).

tush³ /tŏŏSH/ ▸*n. informal* a person's buttocks. ▷1960s (as *tushie*): from Yiddish *tokhes*, from Hebrew *taḥaṯ* 'beneath.'

tush·y /'tŏŏSHē/ ▸*n.* (*pl.* **tush·ies**) another term for **TUSH**³.

tusk /təsk/ ▸*n.* a long, pointed tooth, esp. one specially developed so as to protrude from the closed mouth, as in the elephant, walrus, or wild boar. ■ a long, tapering object or projection resembling such a tooth. ▷Old English *tux*, variant of *tusc* (see **TUSH**²). **—tusked** *adj.* **—tusk·y** *adj.* (*poetic/literary*).

Tus·ke·gee /tə'skēgē/ a city in east central Alabama, home to Tuskegee Uinversity; pop. 12,257.

tusk·er /'təskər/ ▸*n.* an elephant or wild boar with well-developed tusks.

tusk shell ▸*n.* another term for **TOOTH SHELL**.

tus·sah /'təsə; -sô/ ▸*n.* variant form of **TUSSORE**.

Tus·saud /'tŏŏsō; tə'sôd; tə'sōd/, Madame (1761–1850), French founder of Madame Tussaud's waxworks; resident of Britain from 1802; née *Marie Grosholtz*. She was imprisoned during the French Revolution and compelled to make death masks in wax of prominent victims of the guillotine. In 1835, she founded a permanent waxworks exhibition in Baker Street, London.

tus·sie-mus·sie /'təsē 'məsē/ ▸*n.* (*pl.* **-sies**) a small bunch of flowers or aromatic herbs. ▷late Middle English: of unknown origin.

tus·sive /'təsiv/ ▸*adj. Medicine* relating to coughing. ▷mid 19th cent.: from Latin *tussis* 'a cough' + **-IVE**.

tus·sle /'təsəl/ ▸*n.* a vigorous struggle or scuffle, typically in order to obtain or achieve something: *there was a tussle for the ball.*
▸*v.* [*intrans.*] engage in such a struggle or scuffle: *the demonstrators* **tussled with** *police.* ▷late Middle English (as a verb, originally Scots and northern English): perhaps a diminutive of dialect *touse* 'handle roughly' (see **TOUSLE**).

tus·sock /'təsək/ ▸*n.* **1** a small area of grass that is thicker or longer than the grass growing around it. **2** (also **tussock moth**) a woodland moth whose adults and brightly colored caterpillars both bear tufts of irritant hairs. The caterpillars can be a pest of trees, damaging fruit and stripping leaves. • Family Lymantriidae: many genera. ▷mid 16th cent.: perhaps an alteration of dialect *tusk* 'tuft,' of unknown origin. **—tus·sock·y** *adj.*

tus·sock grass ▸*n.* a grass that grows in tussocks. • Genera *Poa, Nassella,* or *Deschampsia,* family Gramineae: several species, in particular *D. cespitosa*, a coarse fodder grass of the northern hemisphere.

tus·sore /'təsôr/ (also **tus·sah** /'təsə; -sô/) ▸*n.* (also **tussore silk**) coarse silk from the larvae of the tussore moth and related species. ▷late 16th cent.: from Hindi *tasar*, from Sanskrit *tasara* 'shuttle.'

tus·sore moth ▸*n.* a silkworm moth that is sometimes kept in India and China, with caterpillars (**tussore silkworms**) that yield a strong but coarse brown silk. • *Antheraea mylitta*, family Saturniidae.

Tus·tin /'təstin/ a city in southwestern California, southeast of Los Angeles; pop. 50,689.

tut /tət/ ▸*exclam., n.,* & *v.* short for **TUT-TUT**.

Tut·ankh·a·men /,tōō,täNG'kämən; ,tōō,täNG-/ (also **Tut·ankh·a·mun**) (died *c.*1352 BC), Egyptian pharaoh of the 18th dynasty; reigned *c.*1361–*c.*1352 BC. His tomb, which contained a wealth of rich and varied contents, was discovered virtually intact by English archaeologist Howard Carter in 1922.

tu·tee /t(y)ōō'tē/ ▸*n.* a student or pupil of a tutor.

tu·te·lage /'t(y)ōōtl-ij/ ▸*n.* protection of or authority over someone or something; guardianship: *the organizations remained under firm government tutelage.* ■ instruction; tuition: *he felt privileged to be* **under the tutelage of** *an experienced actor.* ▷early 17th cent.: from Latin *tutela* 'keeping' (from *tut-* 'watched,' from the verb *tueri*) + **-AGE**.

tu·te·lar·y /'t(y)ōōtl,erē/ (also **tu·te·lar** /-tl-ər/) ▸*adj.* serving as a protector, guardian, or patron: *the tutelary spirits of these regions.* ■ of or relating to protection or a guardian: *the state maintained a tutelary relation with the security police.* ▷early 17th cent.: from Latin *tutelarius*, from *tutela* 'keeping' (see **TUTELAGE**).

Tuth·mo·sis III /tōōt'mōsəs/ (died *c.*1450 BC), son of Tuthmosis II; Egyptian pharaoh of the 18th dynasty *c.*1504–*c.*1450. His reign was marked by extensive building projects, including Cleopatra's Needles (*c.*1475).

tu·tor /'t(y)ōōtər/ ▸*n.* a private teacher, typically one who teaches a single student or a very small group. ■ *chiefly Brit.* a university or college teacher responsible for the teaching and supervision of assigned students. ■ an assistant lecturer in a college or university.
▸*v.* [*trans.*] act as a tutor to (a single student or a very small group): *his children were privately tutored.* ■ [*intrans.*] work as a tutor. ▷late Middle English: from Old French *tutour* or Latin *tutor*, from *tueri* 'to watch, guard.' **—tu·tor·age** /-rij/ *n.* **—tu·tor·ship** /-,SHip/ *n.*

tu·to·ri·al /t(y)ōō'tôrēəl/ ▸*adj.* of or relating to a tutor or a tutor's instruction: *tutorial sessions.*
▸*n.* a period of instruction given by a university or college tutor to an individual or very small group. ■ an account or explanation of a subject, printed or on a computer screen, intended for private study. ▷early 18th cent.: from Latin *tutorius* (see **TUTOR**) + **-AL**.

Tut·si /'tōōtsē/ ▸*n.* (*pl.* same or **-sis**) a member of a people forming a minority of the population of Rwanda and Burundi, who formerly dominated the Hutu majority. Historical antagonism between the peoples led in 1994 to large-scale ethnic violence, esp. in Rwanda.
▸*adj.* of or relating to this people. ▷a local name. See also **WATUSI**.

tut·ti /'tōōtē/ *Music* ▸*adv.* & *adj.* (esp. as a direction after a solo section) with all voices or instruments together.
▸*n.* (*pl.* **-tis**) a passage to be performed in this way. ▷Italian, plural of *tutto* 'all,' from Latin *totus.*

tut·ti-frut·ti /'tōōtē 'frōōtē/ ▸*n.* (*pl.* **-frut·tis**) a type of ice cream containing or flavored with mixed fruits and sometimes nuts. ▷Italian, literally 'all fruits.'

tut-tut /'tət 'tət/ (also **tut**) ▸*exclam.* expressing disapproval or annoyance: *tut-tut, Robin, you disappoint me.*
▸*n.* such an exclamation: *tut-tuts of disapproval.*
▸*v.* (**tut-tut·ted, tut-tut·ting**) [*intrans.*] make such an exclamation: *Aunt Mary tut-tutted at all the goings-on.* ▷natural utterance (representing a reduplicated clicking sound made by the tongue against the teeth): first recorded in English in the early 16th cent.

Tu·tu /'tōō,tōō/, Desmond (Mpilo) (1931–), South African Anglican clergyman. As general secretary of the South African Council of Churches from 1979 until 1984, he became a leading voice in the struggle against apartheid. He was archbishop of Cape Town 1986–96. Nobel Peace Prize (1984).

tu·tu /'tōō,tōō/ ▸*n.* a female ballet dancer's costume consisting of a bodice and an attached skirt incorporating numerous layers of fabric, this being either short and stiff and projecting horizontally from the waist (the **classical tutu**) or long, soft, and bell-shaped (the **romantic tutu**). ▷early 20th cent.: from French, child's alteration of *cucu*, informal diminutive of *cul* 'buttocks.'

classical tutu

Tu·va /'tōōvə/ an autonomous republic in south central Russia, on the border with Mongolia; pop. 314,000; capital, Kyzyl. Former name **TANNU-TUVA**.

Tutankhamen

Tu·va·lu /to͞o'välo͞o/ a country in the southwestern Pacific Ocean that consists of a group of nine main islands, formerly called the Ellice Islands; pop. 11,400; capital, Funafuti; languages, English and Tuvaluan (both official). **—Tu·va·lu·an** /-lo͞oən/ *adj.* & *n.*

The islands formed part of the British colony of the Gilbert and Ellice Islands but separated from the Gilberts after a referendum in 1975. Tuvalu became independent within the Commonwealth of Nations in 1978.

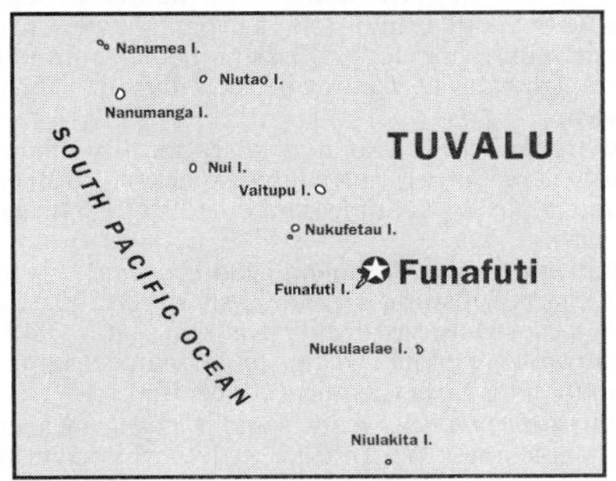

tu-whit tu-whoo /to͞o '(h)wit tə '(h)wo͞o/ ▸*n.* a stylized representation of the cry of the tawny owl. ▷late 16th cent.: imitative.

tux /təks/ ▸*n. informal* a tuxedo.

tux·e·do /tək'sēdō/ ▸*n.* (*pl.* **-dos** or **-does**) a man's dinner jacket. ■ a suit of formal evening clothes including such a jacket. ▷late 19th cent.: from *Tuxedo* Park, the site of a country club in New York, where it was first worn. **—tux·e·doed** *adj.*

Tux·e·do Park /tək'sēdō/ a village in southeastern New York; pop. 706. Developed in the 1880s as a refuge for the rich, it gave its name to the evening jacket.

Tux·tla Gu·tiér·rez /'to͞ostlə go͞o'tyeres/ a city in southeastern Mexico, capital of the state of Chiapas; pop. 296,000.

tu·yère /to͞o'yer; twē-/ ▸*n.* a nozzle through which air is forced into a smelter, furnace, or forge. ▷late 18th cent.: French, from *tuyau* 'pipe.'

Tuz·la /'to͞ozlə/ a town in northeastern Bosnia; pop. 132,000. The town, a Muslim enclave, suffered damage and heavy casualties when besieged by Bosnian Serb forces between 1992 and 1994.

TV ▸*abbr.* ■ television (the system or a set): *anything good on TV tonight?* ■ transvestite.

TVA ▸*abbr.* Tennessee Valley Authority.

TV din·ner ▸*n.* a prepared prepackaged meal that only requires heating before it is ready to eat.

Tver /tver/ an industrial port in western Russia, on the Volga River, northwest of Moscow; pop. 454,000. It was known as Kalinin 1931–91 in honor of President Kalinin.

TVP *trademark* ▸*abbr.* textured vegetable protein.

Twa /twä/ ▸*n.* (*pl.* same or **Twas**) a member of a pygmy people inhabiting parts of Burundi, Rwanda, and the Democratic Republic of the Congo (formerly Zaire).
▸*adj.* of or relating to the Twa. ▷a local word meaning 'foreigner, outsider.'

twad·dle /'twädl/ *informal* ▸*n.* trivial or foolish speech or writing; nonsense: *he dismissed the novel as self-indulgent twaddle.* See note at **NONSENSE**.
▸*v.* [*intrans.*] *archaic* talk or write in a trivial or foolish way: *what is that old fellow twaddling about?* ▷late 18th cent.: alteration of earlier *twattle*, of unknown origin. **—twad·dler** /'twädlər; 'twädl-ər/ *n.*

Twain /twān/, Mark (1835–1910), U.S. novelist and humorist; pseudonym of *Samuel Langhorne Clemens*. After gaining a reputation as a humorist with his early work, he wrote his best-known novels, *The Adventures of Tom Sawyer* (1876) and *The Adventures of Huckleberry Finn* (1885); both give a vivid evocation of Mississippi frontier life.

twain /twān/ ▸*cardinal number* archaic term for **TWO**: *he split it in twain.* ▷Old English *twegen*, masculine of *twā* (see **TWO**).
▸*PHRASE* □ **never the twain shall meet** used to suggest that two things are too different to coexist: *Ulster people are British and Irish people are Irish, and never the twain shall meet.* [from Rudyard Kipling's "Oh, East is East, and West is West, and never the twain shall meet." (*Barrack-room Ballads* (1892).]

twaite shad /'twāt ˌsHad/ ▸*n.* a European shad (fish) with a deep blue back, silvery sides, and some spotting. • *Alosa fallax*, family Clupeidae. ▷early 17th cent. (as *twaite*): of unknown origin.

twang /twaNG/ ▸*n.* a strong ringing sound such as that made by the plucked string of a musical instrument or a released bowstring. ■ a nasal or other distinctive manner of pronunciation or intonation characteristic of the speech of an individual, area, or country: *an American twang.*
▸*v.* make or cause to make such a sound: [*intrans.*] *a spring twanged beneath him.* ■ [*trans.*] play (an instrument) in such a way as to produce such sounds: *some old men were twanging banjos.* ■ [*trans.*] utter (something) with a nasal twang: *the announcer was twanging out all the details.* ▷mid 16th cent.: imitative. **—twang·y** *adj.*

'twas /twəz/ ▸*archaic* or *poetic/literary contraction of* it was.

twat /twät/ ▸*n. vulgar slang* a woman's genitals. ■ a person regarded as stupid or obnoxious. ▷mid 17th cent.: of unknown origin.

tway·blade /'twāˌblād/ ▸*n.* an orchid with a slender spike of greenish or mauvish flowers and a single pair of broad leaves near the base or midway up the stem. • Genera *Listera* and *Liparis*, family Orchidaceae: several species, including the North American **heartleaf twayblade** (*Listera cordata*) and the Eurasian **common twayblade** (*Listera ovata*). ▷late 16th cent.: from *tway* (variant of **TWAIN**) + **BLADE**, translating Latin *bifolium*.

tweak /twēk/ ▸*v.* [*trans.*] **1** twist or pull (something) sharply: *he tweaked the boy's ear.* **2** *informal* improve (a mechanism or system) by making fine adjustments to it: *engineers tweak the car's operating systems during the race.*
▸*n.* **1** a sharp twist or pull. **2** *informal* a fine adjustment to a mechanism or system. ▷early 17th cent.: probably an alteration of dialect *twick* 'pull sharply'; related to **TWITCH**.

twee /twē/ ▸*adj. Brit., chiefly derogatory* excessively or affectedly quaint, pretty, or sentimental: *although the film's a bit twee, it's watchable.* ▷early 20th cent.: representing a child's pronunciation of **SWEET**.

Tweed[1] /twēd/ a river that rises in southeastern Scotland and flows east for 97 miles (155 km) before it crosses into northeastern England and enters the North Sea. Part of its lower course forms the border between Scotland and England.

Tweed[2], William Marcy (1823–78) U.S. politician; known as **Boss Tweed**. As a New York City official and a state senator 1867–71, he became the leader of Tammany Hall, the executive committee of New York City's Democratic Party and a ring of political corruption, that swindled the state treasury out of as much as $200 million. Convicted in 1873, he fled to Cuba and then Spain, but was extradited in 1876 and returned to a New York jail, where he died.

tweed /twēd/ ▸*n.* a rough-surfaced woolen cloth, typically of mixed flecked colors, originally produced in Scotland: [as *adj.*] *a tweed sports jacket.* ■ (**tweeds**) clothes made of this material: *boisterous English-women in tweeds.* ▷mid 19th cent.: originally a misreading of *tweel*, Scots form of **TWILL**, influenced by association with the *Tweed* River.

Twee·dle·dum and Twee·dle·dee /ˌtwēdl'dəm and ˌtwēdl'dē/ ▸*n.* a pair of people or things that are virtually indistinguishable. ▷originally names applied to the composers Bononcini (1670–1747) and Handel, in a 1725 satire by John Byrom (1692–1763); they were later used for two identical characters in Lewis Carroll's *Through the Looking Glass*.

tweed·y /'twēdē/ ▸*adj.* (**tweed·i·er**, **tweed·i·est**) (of a garment) made of tweed cloth: *a tweedy suit.* ■ *informal* (of a person) habitually wearing tweed clothes: *a stout, tweedy woman.* ■ *informal* of a refined, traditional, upscale character: *the tweedy world of books.* **—tweed·i·ly** /-dilē/ *adv.* **—tweed·i·ness** *n.*

Mark Twain

Tween /twēn/ ▸*n. trademark* any of a class of compounds used esp. as emulsifiers and surfactants. They are derivatives of fatty acid esters of sorbitan. ▷1940s: of unknown origin.

tween /twēn/ (also **tween·ie** /'twēnē/) ▸*n.* short for **TWEENAGER**.

'tween /twēn/ ▸*archaic* or *poetic/literary contraction of* between.

tween·ag·er /'twēnˌājər/ ▸*n. informal* a preteen or a young teenager: *the hot Nickelodeon show for tweenagers.*

'tween decks ▸*plural n. Nautical* the space between the decks of a ship, esp. that below the upper deck.

tween·y /'twēnē/ ▸*n.* (*pl.* **tween·ies**) *archaic, informal* a maid who assisted two other members of a domestic staff. ▷late 19th cent.: from *between-maid*, a servant assisting two others.

tweet /twēt/ (also **tweet tweet**) ▸*n.* the chirp of a small or young bird.
▸*v.* [*intrans.*] make a chirping noise: *the birds were tweeting in the branches.* ▷mid 19th cent.: imitative.

tweet·er /'twētər/ ▸*n.* a loudspeaker designed to reproduce high frequencies.

tweeze /twēz/ ▸*v.* [*trans.*] pluck, grasp, or pull with or as if with tweezers: *the brows were tweezed to an almost invisible line.* ▷1930s: back-formation from *tweezer* (see **TWEEZERS**).

tweez·ers /'twēzərz/ ▸*plural n.* (also **a pair of tweezers**) a small instrument like a pair of pincers for plucking out hairs and picking up small objects. ▷mid 17th cent.: extended form of obsolete *tweeze* 'case of surgical instruments,' shortening of *etweese*, plural of **ETUI**.

twelfth /twelfTH/ ▸*ordinal number* constituting number twelve in a sequence; 12th: *the twelfth of November | his twelfth birthday | the twelfth in a series of essays.* ■ (**a twelfth/one twelfth**) each of twelve equal parts into which something is or may be divided. ■ the twelfth grade of a school. ■ *Music* an interval or chord spanning an octave and a fifth in the diatonic scale, or a note separated from another by this interval. ■ (**the Twelfth**) July 12, celebrated by upholders of Protestant supremacy in Ireland as the anniversary of William III's victory over James II at the Battle of the Boyne. **—twelfth·ly** *adv.* **—twelve·fold** /'twel(v)ˌfōld/ *adj.* & *adv.*

Twelfth Day ▸*n.* archaic term for **TWELFTH NIGHT**.

Twelfth Night ▸*n.* January 6, the feast of the Epiphany. ■ strictly, the evening of January 5, the eve of the Epiphany and formerly the twelfth and last day of Christmas festivities.

twelve /twelv/ ▸*cardinal number* equivalent to the product of three and four; two more than ten; 12: *he walked twelve miles | there are just twelve of us in all | a twelve-string guitar.* (Roman numeral: **xii**, **XII**.) ■ a group or unit of twelve people or things. ■ twelve years old: *a small blond girl of about twelve.* ■ twelve o'clock: *it's half past twelve.* ■ a size of garment or other merchandise denoted by twelve. ■ (**the Twelve**) the twelve Apostles. ▷Old English *twelf(e)*, from the base of **TWO** + a second element (probably expressing the sense 'left over'); of Germanic origin and related to Dutch *twaalf* and German *zwölf*. Compare with **ELEVEN**.

twelve-bar ▸*adj.* denoting or relating to a musical structure based on a sequence lasting twelve bars and typically consisting of three chords, the basic unit of much blues and rock and roll music.
▸*n.* a song or piece of music having such a structure.

twelve-bore ▸*n.* British term for **TWELVE-GAUGE**.

twelve-gauge ▸*n.* a shotgun with a gauge corresponding to the diameter of a round bullet of which twelve constitute a pound in weight.

twelve-inch ▸*n.* a phonograph record twelve inches in diameter and played at 45 rpm, esp. one with two or three remixes to a side.

twelve·mo /'twelvˌmō/ ▸*n.* another term for **DUODECIMO**.

twelve·month /'twelvˌmənTH/ ▸*n. archaic* a year.

twelve step ▸*adj.* denoting or relating to a process of recovery from addiction by following a twelve-stage

program, esp. one modeled on that of Alcoholics Anonymous.
▸*v.* (*often as noun* **twelve-stepping**) (of an addict) undergo such a program.

Twelve Ta·bles a set of laws drawn up in ancient Rome in 451 and 450 BC, embodying the most important rules of Roman law.

twelve-tone (also **twelve-note**) ▸*adj.* denoting a system of musical composition using the twelve chromatic notes of the octave on an equal basis without dependence on a key system. Developed by Arnold Schoenberg, the technique is central to serialism and involves the transposition and inversion of a fixed sequence of pitches.

Twelve Tribes of Is·ra·el see TRIBES OF ISRAEL.

Twen·ti·eth Cen·tu·ry Fox /'twentē-ITH/ a U.S. film production company formed in 1935 by the merger of the Fox Company with Twentieth Century. Under production head Darryl F. Zanuck (1902–79) the company pioneered wide-screen film techniques.

twen·ty /'twentē/ ▸*cardinal number* (*pl.* **-ties**) the number equivalent to the product of two and ten; ten less than thirty; 20: *twenty or thirty years ago | twenty of us stood and waited | a twenty-foot aerial.* (Roman numeral: **xx**, **XX.**) ■ (**twenties**) the numbers from twenty to twenty-nine, esp. the years of a century or of a person's life: *he's in his late twenties.* ■ twenty years old: *he's about twenty.* ■ twenty miles an hour. ■ a size of garment or other merchandise denoted by twenty. ■ a twenty-dollar bill. ▷Old English *twentig*, from the base of TWO + -TY². —**twen·ti·eth** /-tēITH/ *ordinal number* —**twen·ty·fold** /-,fōld/ *adj. & adv.*

twen·ty-eight ▸*n. Austral.* a ringneck parrot of a race having a call that resembles the word "twenty-eight." • *Barnardius zonarius semitorquatus*, family Psittacidae; a subspecies of the Port Lincoln parrot.

twen·ty-four-hour clock (also **24-hour clock**) ▸*n.* a method of measuring the time based on the full twenty-four hours of the day, rather than dividing it into two units of twelve hours.

twen·ty-four hours ▸*n. W. Indian* a long-legged arboreal lizard of tropical America, related to the anoles. • *Polychrus marmoratus*, family Iguanidae. ▷so named from the superstition that a person touched by one will die within twenty-four hours.

24/7 /'twentē,fôr 'sevən/ (also **24-7**) ▸*adv. informal* twenty-four hours a day, seven days a week; all the time: *you just can't afford to let things get you down, especially when you are on call 24/7.*

twen·ty-one ▸*n.* the card game blackjack.

twen·ty-twen·ty (also **20/20**) ▸*adj.* denoting vision of normal acuity. ▷the Snellen fraction for normal visual acuity (see SNELLEN TEST).

'twere /twər/ *archaic poetic/literary* ▸*contraction of* it were.

twerp /twərp/ (also **twirp**) ▸*n. informal* a silly or annoying person. ▷late 19th cent.: of unknown origin.

Twi /twē/ ▸*n.* (*pl.* same or **Twis**) **1** a member of an Akan-speaking people of Ghana. **2** another term for AKAN (the language).
▸*adj.* or or relating to this people or their language. ▷the name in Akan.

twi·bill /'twī,bil/ ▸*n. archaic* a double-bladed battle-ax. ▷Old English *twibile* 'ax with two cutting edges,' from *twi-* 'double' + BILL³.

twice /twīs/ ▸*adv.* two times; on two occasions: *she had been married twice | the tablets should be taken twice a day.* ■ double in degree or quantity: *I'm twice your age | an engine **twice as** big as the original.* ▷late Old English *twiges*, from the base of TWO + -S³ (later respelled *-ce* to denote the unvoiced sound); compare with ONCE.
▸*PHRASES* □ **once bitten, twice shy** see BITE. □ **think twice** see THINK.

twice-baked ▸*adj.* (of bread or cookie dough) baked in a loaf and then sliced and returned to the oven to bake again until crisp.

twice-born ▸*adj.* having undergone a renewal of faith or life, in particular: ■ (of a Hindu) belonging to one of the three highest castes, esp. as an initiated Brahman. ■ (of a Christian) born-again.

twid·dle /'twidl/ ▸*v.* [*trans.*] twist, move, or fiddle with (something), typically in a purposeless or nervous way: *she twiddled the dials on the radio* | [*intrans.*] *he began twiddling with the curtain cord.* ■ [*intrans.*] *archaic* turn or move in a twirling way.
▸*n.* an act of twisting or fiddling with something: *one twiddle of a button.* ▷mid 16th cent. (in the sense 'trifle'): apparently imitative, combining the notion *twirl* or *twist* with that of trifling action expressed by *fiddle.* —**twid·dler** /'twidlər; 'twidl-ər/ *n.* —**twid·dly** /'twidlē; 'twidl-ē/ *adj.*
▸*PHRASE* □ **twiddle one's thumbs** rotate one's thumbs around each other with the fingers linked together. ■ be bored or idle because one has nothing to do.

twig¹ /twig/ ▸*n.* a slender woody shoot growing from a branch or stem of a tree or shrub. ■ *Anatomy* a small branch of a blood vessel or nerve. ▷Old English *twigge*, of Germanic origin; related to Dutch *twijg* and German *Zweig*, also to TWAIN and TWO. —**twigged** *adj.* —**twig·gy** *adj.*

twig² ▸*v.* (**twigged**, **twig·ging**) [*intrans.*] *Brit., informal* understand or realize something: *it was amazing that Graham hadn't twigged before.* ■ [*trans.*] *archaic* perceive; observe: *nine days now since my eyes have twigged any terra firma.* ▷mid 18th cent.: of unknown origin.

twig fur·ni·ture ▸*n.* a rustic style of furniture in which the natural state of the wood is retained as an aesthetic feature.

twi·light /'twī,līt/ ▸*n.* the soft glowing light from the sky when the sun is below the horizon, caused by the refraction and scattering of the sun's rays from the atmosphere. ■ the period of the evening during which this takes place, between daylight and darkness: *a pleasant walk in the woods at twilight.* ■ [in *sing.*] *figurative* a period or state of obscurity, ambiguity, or gradual decline: *he was **in the twilight of** his career.* ▷late Middle English: from Old English *twi-* 'two' (used in an obscure sense in this compound) + LIGHT¹.

twi·light of the gods *Scandinavian & Germanic Mythology* the destruction of the gods and the world in a final conflict with the powers of evil. Also called GÖTTERDÄMMERUNG, RAGNARÖK. ▷translating Icelandic *ragna rökr* (see RAGNARÖK).

twi·light sleep ▸*n. Medicine* a state of partial narcosis or stupor without total loss of consciousness, in particular a state induced by an injection of morphine and scopolamine, formerly popular for use during childbirth.

twi·light zone ▸*n.* **1** a conceptual area that is undefined or intermediate: *the twilight zone between the middle and working classes.* ■ a sphere of experience that appears sinister or dangerous because of its uncertainty, unpredictability, or ambiguity: *schizophrenia isolates the individual in a twilight zone of terror.* **2** the lowest level of the ocean to which light can penetrate.

twi·lit /'twī,lit/ ▸*adj.* dimly illuminated by or as if by twilight: *the deserted twilit street.* ■ relating to or denoting the period of twilight: *twilit hours.* ▷mid 19th cent.: past participle of the literary verb *twilight.*

twill /twil/ ▸*n.* a fabric so woven as to have a surface of diagonal parallel ridges.
▸*v.* [*trans.*] [usu. as *adj.*] (**twilled**) weave (fabric) in this way: *twilled cotton.* ▷Middle English: from a Scots and northern English variant of obsolete *twilly*, from Old English *twi-* 'two,' suggested by Latin *bilix* 'two-threaded.'

'twill /twil/ *archaic poetic/literary* ▸*contraction of* it will.

twin /twin/ ▸*n.* **1** one of two children or animals born at the same birth. ■ a person or thing that is exactly like another: *there was a bruise on his cheek, **a twin to** the one on mine.* ■ (**the Twins**) the zodiacal sign or constellation Gemini. **2** something containing or consisting of two matching or corresponding parts, in particular: ■ a twin-bedded room. ■ a twin-engined aircraft. ■ a twinned crystal.
▸*adj.* [*attrib.*] forming, or being one of, a pair born at one birth: *she gave birth to twin boys | her twin sister.* ■ forming a matching, complementary, or closely connected pair: *the twin problems of economic failure and social disintegration.* ■ *Botany* growing in pairs: *twin seed leaves.* ■ (of a bedroom) containing two single beds. ■ (of a crystal) twinned.
▸*v.* (**twinned**, **twin·ning**) [*trans.*] (usu. **be twinned**) link; combine: *the company twinned its core business of brewing with that of distilling.* ▷late Old English *twinn* 'double,' from *twi-* 'two'; related to Old Norse *tvinnr.* Current verb senses date from late Middle English.

twin bed ▸*n.* a bed designed or suitable for one person; a single bed, esp. one of a pair of matching single beds. —**twin-bed·ded** *adj.*

twin-cam ▸*adj.* denoting an engine having two camshafts.

twin cit·y ▸*n.* either of two neighboring cities lying close together. ■ (**the Twin Cities**) Minneapolis and St. Paul in Minnesota.

twine /twīn/ ▸*n.* strong thread or string consisting of two or more strands of hemp, cotton, or nylon twisted together.
▸*v.* [*trans.*] cause to wind or spiral round something: *she **twined** her arms **around** his neck.* ■ [*intrans.*] (of a plant) grow so as to spiral around a support: *runner beans twined around canes.* ■ interlace: *a spray of jasmine was twined in her hair.* ▷Old English *twīn* 'thread, linen,' from the Germanic base of *twi-* 'two'; related to Dutch *twijn.* —**twin·er** *n.*

twin-en·gined (also **twin-en·gine**) ▸*adj.* (chiefly of an aircraft) having two engines.

Twin Falls a commercial and industrial city in south central Idaho, on the Snake River; pop. 34,469.

twin·flow·er /'twin,flou(-ə)r/ ▸*n.* a slender evergreen trailing plant of the honeysuckle family, with pairs of very small trumpet-shaped pink flowers in the leaf axils, native to coniferous woodlands in northern latitudes. • *Linnaea borealis*, family Caprifoliaceae.

twinge /twinj/ ▸*n.* a sudden, sharp localized pain: *he felt a twinge in his knee.* ■ a brief experience of an emotion, typically an unpleasant one: *Kate felt **a twinge of** guilt.*
▸*v.* (**twinge·ing** or **twing·ing** /-JING/) [*intrans.*] (of a part of the body) suffer a sudden, sharp localized pain: *the ankle still twinged, but the pain was slight.* ▷Old English *twengan* 'pinch, wring,' of Germanic origin. The noun dates from the mid 16th cent.

Twin·kie /'twiNGkē/ ▸*n.* (*pl.* **-kies**) **1** *trademark* a small finger-shaped sponge cake with a white synthetic cream filling. **2** (also **twinkie**) *informal, offensive* a gay or effeminate man. ■ a young gay male who is meticulous about his dress, hair, weight, and other aspects of his personal appearance. ▷late 20th cent.: probably related to TWINKLE.

twin·kle /'twiNGkəl/ ▸*v.* [*intrans.*] (of a star or light, or a shiny object) shine with a gleam that varies repeatedly between bright and faint: *the lights twinkled in the distance.* ■ (of a person's eyes) sparkle, esp. with amusement. ■ smile so that one's eyes sparkle: *"Aha!" he said, **twinkling at** her.* ■ [*intrans.*] (of a person's feet) move lightly and rapidly: *his sandaled feet twinkled over the ground.*
▸*n.* a sparkle or gleam in a person's eyes. ■ a light that appears continually to grow brighter and fainter: *the distant twinkle of the lights.* ▷Old English *twinclian* (verb), of Germanic origin. —**twin·kler** /-k(ə)lər/ *n.* —**twin·kly** /-k(ə)lē/ *adj.*
▸*PHRASE* □ **in a twinkling** (or **the twinkling of an eye**) in an instant; very quickly.

twin·kle·toes /'twiNGkəl,tōz/ ▸*n. informal* a person who is nimble and quick on their feet.

twin-lens ▸*adj.* (of a camera) having two identical sets of lenses, either for taking stereoscopic pictures, or with one forming an image for viewing and the other an image to be photographed (**twin-lens reflex**).

twinned /twind/ ▸*adj.* (of a crystal) that is a composite consisting of two (or sometimes more) parts that are reversed in orientation with respect to each other (typically by reflection in a particular plane).

twin·ning /'twiniNG/ ▸*n.* the bearing of twins: *the study showed an increased level of twinning in cattle.* ■ the occurrence or formation of twinned crystals.

twin par·a·dox ▸*n. Physics* the apparent paradox arising from relativity theory that if one of a pair of twins makes a long journey at near the speed of light and then returns, he or she will have aged less than the twin who remains behind.

twin-screw ▸*adj.* (of a ship) having two propellers on separate shafts that rotate in opposite directions.

twin·set /'twin,set/ ▸*n.* a woman's matching cardigan and pullover sweater.

twin·spot /'twin,spät/ ▸*n.* an African waxbill with white-spotted black underparts, the male typically having a reddish face and breast. • *Hypargos* and related genera, family Estrildidae: several species.

twirl /twərl/ ▸*v.* [*intrans.*] spin quickly and lightly around, esp. repeatedly: *she twirled in delight to show off her new dress.* ■ [*trans.*] cause to rotate: *she twirled her fork in the pasta.* ■ [*trans.*] *Baseball* pitch (the ball).
▸*n.* an act of spinning: *Kate did a twirl in front of the mirror.* ■ a spiraling or swirling shape, esp. a flourish made with a pen. ▷late 16th cent.: probably an alteration (by association with WHIRL) of *tirl*, a variant of archaic *trill* 'twiddle, spin.' —**twirl·er** *n.* —**twirl·y** *adj.*

twirp ▸*n.* variant spelling of TWERP.

twist /twist/ ▸*v.* [*trans.*] **1** form into a bent, curling, or distorted shape: *a strip of metal is twisted to form a hollow tube | her pretty features twisted into a fearsome expression.* ■ [*trans.*] form (something) into a particular shape by taking hold of one or both ends and turning them: *she twisted her handkerchief into a knot.* ■ [*trans.*] turn or bend into a specified position or in a specified direction: *he grabbed the man and twisted his arm behind his back.* ■ (**twist something off**) remove something by pulling and rotating it: *beets can be stored once the leaves have been twisted off.* ■ [*intrans.*] move one's body so that the shoulders and hips are facing in different directions: *she twisted in her seat to look at the buildings.* ■ [*intrans.*] move in a wriggling or writhing fashion: *he* **twisted himself** *free.* ■ injure (a joint) by wrenching it: *he twisted his ankle trying to avoid his opponent's lunge.* ■ distort or misrepresent the meaning of (words): *he twisted my words to make it seem that I'd claimed she was a drug addict.* ■ [as *adj.*] (**twisted**) (of a personality or a way of thinking) unpleasantly or unhealthily abnormal: *a man with a twisted mind.* **2** cause to rotate around something that remains stationary; turn: *she twisted her ring around and around on her finger.* ■ [*trans.*] wind around or through something: *she twisted a lock of hair around her finger.* ■ move or cause to move around each other; interlace: [*trans.*] *she twisted her hands together nervously* | *the machine twists together strands to make a double yarn.* ■ make (something) by interlacing or winding strands together. ■ [*intrans.*] take or have a winding course: *the road twisted through a dozen tiny villages.* **3** [*intrans.*] dance the twist. **4** *Brit., informal* cheat; defraud.

▸*n.* **1** an act of turning something so that it moves in relation to something that remains stationary: *the taps needed a single twist to turn them on.* ■ an act of turning one's body or part of one's body: *with a sudden twist, she got away from him.* ■ (**the twist**) a dance with a twisting movement of the body, popular in the 1960s. ■ the extent of twisting of a rod or other object. ■ force producing twisting; torque. ■ forward motion combined with rotation about an axis. ■ the rifling in the bore of a gun: *barrels with a 1:24 inch twist.* **2** a thing with a spiral shape: *a licorice twist.* ■ a curled piece of lemon peel used to flavor a drink. **3** a distorted shape: *he had a cruel twist to his mouth.* ■ an unusual feature of a person's personality, typically an unhealthy one. **4** a point at which something turns or bends: *the car negotiated the twists and turns of the mountain road.* ■ an unexpected development of events: *it was soon time for the next* **twist of fate** *in his extraordinary career.* ■ a new treatment or outlook; a variation: *she takes conventional subjects and gives them a twist.* **5** a fine strong thread consisting of twisted strands of cotton or silk. **6** *Brit.* a drink consisting of two ingredients mixed together. **7** a carpet with a tightly curled pile. ▷Old English (as a noun), of Germanic origin; probably from the base of TWIN and TWINE. Current verb senses date from late Middle English. —**twist·y** *adj.*

▸*PHRASES* □ **twist someone's arm** *informal* persuade someone to do something that they are or might be reluctant to do. □ **twist in the wind** be left in a state of suspense or uncertainty. □ **twist someone around one's little finger** see LITTLE FINGER. □ **twists and turns** intricate or convoluted dealings or circumstances: *the twists and turns of her political career.*

twist drill ▸*n.* a drill with a twisted body like that of an auger.

twist·ed pair ▸*n.* *Electronics* a cable consisting of two wires twisted around each other, used esp. for telephone or computer applications.

twist·ed-stalk ▸*n.* a plant of the lily family with bell-shaped flowers carried on bent or twisted stalks, native to the temperate regions of Russia and North America. • Genus *Streptopus*, family Liliaceae: several species, including the **rosy twisted-stalk** (*S. roseus*), which grows in the coastal mountain regions from British Columbia to Oregon.

twist·er /ˈtwistər/ ▸*n.* a tornado.

twist-grip ▸*n.* a control operated manually by twisting, esp. one serving as a handgrip for operating the throttle on a motorcycle or for changing gear on a bicycle.

twist-lock ▸*n.* a locking device for securing freight containers to the trailers on which they are transported.

twist·or /ˈtwistər/ ▸*n.* *Physics* a complex variable used in some descriptions of space-time.

twist tie ▸*n.* a small piece of paper- or plastic-covered wire, to be twisted around the neck of a plastic bag as a closure.

twit[1] /twit/ ▸*n.* *informal* a silly or foolish person. ▷1930s (earlier dialect, in the sense 'talebearer'): perhaps from TWIT[2]. —**twit·tish** *adj.*

twit[2] ▸*v.* (**twit·ted, twit·ting**) [*trans.*] *dated* tease or taunt (someone), esp. in a good-humored way.

▸*n.* [in *sing.*] a state of nervous excitement: *we're in a twit about your visit.* ▷Old English *ætwītan* 'reproach with,' from *æt* 'at' + *wītan* 'to blame.'

twitch /twiCH/ ▸*v.* **1** give or cause to give a short, sudden jerking or convulsive movement: [*intrans.*] *he saw her lips twitch and her eyelids flutter* | [*trans.*] *the dog twitched his ears.* ■ [*trans.*] cause to move in a specified direction by giving a sharp pull: *he twitched a cigarette out of a packet.* **2** [*trans.*] apply a sudden pull or jerk to (a horse).

▸*n.* **1** a short, sudden jerking or convulsive movement: *his mouth gave a slight twitch.* ■ a sudden pull or jerk: *he gave a twitch at his mustache.* ■ a sudden sharp sensation; a pang: *he felt* **a twitch of** *annoyance.* **2** a stick with a small noose attached to one end. The noose may be twisted around the upper lip or the ear of a horse to subdue it, esp. during veterinary procedures. ▷Middle English: of Germanic origin; related to Old English *twiccian* 'to pluck, pull sharply.'

twitch·er /ˈtwiCHər/ ▸*n.* a person or thing that twitches. ■ *Brit., informal* a birdwatcher whose main aim is to collect sightings of rare birds.

twitch grass ▸*n.* another term for COUCH GRASS. ▷late 16th cent.: *twitch*, alteration of QUITCH.

twitch·y /ˈtwiCHē/ ▸*adj.* (**twitch·i·er, twitch·i·est**) *informal* nervous; anxious: *she felt twitchy about the man hovering in the background.* ■ given to twitching: *a mouse with a twitchy nose.*

twite /twīt/ ▸*n.* a Eurasian moorland finch related to the linnet, having streaky brown plumage and a pink rump. • *Acanthis flavirostris*, family Fringillidae. ▷mid 16th cent.: imitative of its call.

twit·ter /ˈtwitər/ ▸*v.* [*intrans.*] (of a bird) give a call consisting of repeated light tremulous sounds. ■ talk in a light, high-pitched voice: *old ladies in the congregation twittered.* ■ talk rapidly and at length in an idle or trivial way: *he* **twittered on** *about buying a new workshop.*

▸*n.* a series of short, high-pitched calls or sounds: *his words were cut off by a faint electronic twitter.* ■ idle or ignorant talk: *drawing-room twitter.* ▷late Middle English (as a verb): imitative. —**twit·ter·er** *n.* —**twit·ter·y** *adj.*

▸*PHRASE* □ **in** (or **of**) **a twitter** *informal* in a state of agitation or excitement.

'twixt /twikst/ ▸*contraction of* betwixt.

two /to͞o/ ▸*cardinal number* equivalent to the sum of one and one; one less than three; 2: *two years ago* | *a romantic weekend for two in Paris* | *two of Amy's friends.* (Roman numeral: **ii, II.**) ■ a group or unit of two people or things: *they would straggle home in ones and twos.* ■ two years old: *he is only two.* ■ two o'clock: *the bar closed at two.* ■ a size of garment or other merchandise denoted by two. ■ a playing card or domino with two pips. ▷Old English *twā* (feminine and neuter), of Germanic origin; related to Dutch *twee* and German *zwei*, from an Indo-European root shared by Latin and Greek *duo*. Compare with TWAIN.

▸*PHRASES* □ **a —— or two** (or **two or three ——**) used to denote a small but unspecified number: *a minute or two had passed.* □ **be two a penny** see PENNY. □ **in two** in or into two halves or pieces: *he tore the piece of paper in two.* □ **in two shakes** (**of a lamb's tail**) see SHAKE. □ **it takes two to tango** see TANGO. □ **put two and two together** draw an obvious conclusion from what is known or evident. □ **that makes two of us** one is in the same position or holds the same opinion as the previous speaker: *"I haven't a clue!" "That makes two of us."* □ **two by two** side by side in pairs. □ **two can play that game** used to assert that another person's bad behavior can be copied to that person's disadvantage. □ **two's company, three's a crowd** used to indicate that two people, esp. lovers, should be left alone together. □ **two heads are better than one** *proverb* it's helpful to have the advice or opinion of a second person.

two-bit ▸*adj.* [*attrib.*] *informal* insignificant, cheap, or worthless: *some two-bit town.*

two-by-four ▸*n.* a piece of lumber with a rectangular cross section nominally two inches by four inches. ■ [usu. as *adj.*] a small or insignificant thing, typically a building: *they lived in a two-by-four shack of one bedroom.*

two-cy·cle ▸*adj.* another term for TWO-STROKE.

two-di·men·sion·al ▸*adj.* having or appearing to have length and breadth but no depth. ■ lacking depth or substance; superficial: *a nether world of two-dimensional heroes and villains.* —**two-di·men·sion·al·i·ty** *n.* —**two-di·men·sion·al·ly** *adv.*

two-edged ▸*adj.* double-edged.

two-faced ▸*adj.* insincere and deceitful.

two fin·gers ▸*plural n.* [often treated as *sing.*] *Brit.* another term for **V-SIGN** (chiefly in sense 2).

two-fist·ed ▸*adj.* strong, virile, and straightforward.

two·fold /ˈto͞oˌfōld/ ▸*adj.* twice as great or as numerous: *a twofold increase in the risk.* ■ having two parts or elements: *the twofold demands of the business and motherhood.*

▸*adv.* so as to double; to twice the number or amount: *use increased more than twofold from 1979 to 1989.*

two-hand·ed ▸*adj. & adv.* having, using, or requiring the use of two hands. —**two-hand·ed·ly** *adv.*

two-hand·er ▸*n.* **1** a play for two actors. **2** *Tennis* a shot taken with both hands on the racket.

two·ness /ˈto͞onəs/ ▸*n.* the fact or state of being two; duality.

two·pence /ˈtəpəns/ ▸*n.* *Brit.* the sum of two pence, esp. before decimalization (1971). ■ [with *negative*] *informal* a trivial sum; anything at all: *he didn't* **care twopence for** *her.*

two·pen·ny /ˈtəp(ə)nē; ˈto͞oˌpenē/ ▸*adj.* [*attrib.*] *Brit.* costing or worth two pence, esp. before decimalization (1971).

two-phase ▸*adj.* (of an electric generator, motor, or other device) designed to supply or use simultaneously two separate alternating currents of the same voltage, but with phases differing by half a period.

two-piece ▸*adj.* denoting something consisting of two matching items: *a two-piece suit.*

▸*n.* a thing consisting of two matching parts, esp. a suit or swimsuit.

two-ply ▸*adj.* (of a material or yarn) consisting of two layers or strands.

▸*n.* **1** a yarn consisting of two strands. **2** plywood made by gluing together two layers with the grain in different directions.

two-seat·er ▸*n.* a vehicle or piece of furniture with seating for two people.

two shot ▸*n.* a movie or television shot of two people together.

two-sid·ed ▸*adj.* having two sides: *a colorful two-sided leaflet.* ■ having two aspects: *the two-sided nature of the debate.*

two·some /ˈto͞osəm/ ▸*n.* a pair of people considered together. ■ a game or dance for or involving two people.

two-star ▸*adj.* given two stars in a grading system, typically one in which this denotes a low middle standard (four- or five-star denoting the highest standard): *a two-star award in the Michelin guide.* ■ (in the U.S. armed forces) having or denoting the rank of major general, distinguished by two stars on the uniform.

two-step ▸*n.* a round dance with a sliding step in march or polka time.

two-stroke ▸*adj.* denoting an internal combustion engine whose power cycle is completed in one up-and-down movement of the piston. ■ denoting a vehicle having such an engine.

▸*n.* a two-stroke engine or vehicle. Compare with FOUR-STROKE.

two-tailed ▸*adj.* *Statistics* (of a test) testing for deviation from the null hypothesis in both directions.

two-tailed pa·sha ▸*n.* see PASHA.

two-time ▸*v.* [*trans.*] *informal* deceive or be unfaithful to (a lover or spouse): *he was two-timing a fiancé back in England.*

▸*adj.* [*attrib.*] denoting someone who has done or experienced something twice: *a two-time winner of the event.* —**two-tim·er** *n.*

two-tone (also **two-toned**) ▸*adj.* having two different shades or colors: *a two-tone jacket.* ■ emitting or consisting of two different sounds, typically alternately and at intervals: *a two-tone pulse signal.*

'twould /two͝od/ *archaic* ▸*contraction of* it would.

two-way ▸*adj.* allowing or involving movement or communication in opposite directions: *a two-way radio* | *make the interview a two-way process.* ■ involving two participants: *a two-way presidential race.* ■ (of a switch) permitting a current to be switched on or off from either of two points.

▸*PHRASE* □ **two-way street** a situation or relationship involving mutual or reciprocal action or obligation: *trust is a two-way street.*

two-way mir·ror ▸*n.* a panel of glass that can be seen through from one side but is a mirror on the other.

2WD ▸*abbr.* two-wheel drive.

two-wheel drive ▸*n.* a transmission system in a motor vehicle, providing power to either the front or the rear wheels only.

two-wheel·er ▸*n.* a bicycle or motorcycle.

twp. ▸*abbr.* township.

TWX ▸*abbr.* teletypewriter exchange.

TX ▸*abbr.* Texas (in official postal use).

-ty[1] ▸*suffix* forming nouns denoting quality or condition such as *beauty, royalty.* ▷via Old French from Latin *-tas, -tat-*.

-ty[2] ▸*suffix* denoting specified groups of ten: *forty | ninety.* ▷Old English *-tig.*

ty·chism /ˈtīˌkizəm/ ▸*n. Philosophy* the doctrine that account must be taken of the element of chance in reasoning or explanation of the universe. ▷late 19th cent.: from Greek *tukhē* 'chance' + **-ISM**.

ty·coon /tīˈko͞on/ ▸*n.* **1** a wealthy, powerful person in business or industry: *a newspaper tycoon.* **2** a title applied by foreigners to the shogun of Japan in power between 1857 and 1868. ▷mid 19th cent.: from Japanese *taikun* 'great lord.'

ty·ing /ˈtī-iNG/ ▸ present participle of **TIE**.

ty·ing-up ▸*n.* another term for **AZOTURIA** in horses.

tyke /tīk/ (also **tike**) ▸*n.* **1** [usu. with *adj.*] *informal* a small child: *is the little tyke up to his tricks again?* ■ [usu. as *adj.*] *Canadian* an initiation level of sports competition for young children: *tyke hockey.* **2** *dated, chiefly Brit.* an unpleasant or coarse man. **3** a dog, esp. a mongrel. ▷late Middle English (in senses 2 and 3): from Old Norse *tík* 'bitch.'

Ty·le·nol /ˈtīləˌnôl; -ˌnäl/ ▸*n.* trademark for **ACETAMINOPHEN**.

Ty·ler[1] /ˈtīlər/ an industrial city in eastern Texas, noted for its roses; pop. 75,450.

Tyl·er[2], Anne (1941–), U.S. writer. Her novels include *The Accidental Tourist* (1986), *Breathing Lessons* (1988), *Ladder of Years* (1995), and *A Patchwork Planet* (1998).

Ty·ler[3], John (1790–1862), 10th president of the U.S. 1841–45. A Virginia Whig, he served as U.S. congressman 1817–21, governor of Virginia 1825–27, U.S. senator 1827–36, and U.S. vice president 1841. He succeeded to the presidency upon the death of President William H. Harrison. Noted for securing the annexation of Texas (1845), throughout his political career he advocated states' rights. His alliance with Southern Democrats on this issue accentuated the divide between North and South prior to the Civil War.

John Tyler

Ty·ler[4], Wat (died 1381), English leader of the Peasants' Revolt of 1381. He captured Canterbury and went on to take London and secure Richard II's concession to the rebels' demands, which included the lifting of the newly imposed poll tax. He was killed by royal supporters.

ty·lo·pod /ˈtīləˌpäd/ ▸*n. Zoology* an even-toed ungulate mammal of a group that comprises the camels, llamas, and their extinct relatives. They are distinguished by bearing their weight on the sole-pads of the feet rather than on the hoofs, and they do not chew the cud. • Suborder Tylopoda, order Artiodactyla: family Camelidae. ▷late 19th cent.: from modern Latin *Tylopoda*, from Greek *tulos* 'knob' or *tulē* 'callus, cushion' + *pous, pod-* 'foot.'

ty·lo·sin /ˈtīləˌsin/ ▸*n.* an antibiotic that is routinely fed to livestock as a growth promoter and that may contribute to antibiotic resistance in humans.

tym·bal ▸*n.* variant spelling of **TIMBAL**.

tym·pan /ˈtimpən/ ▸*n.* **1** (in letterpress printing) a layer of packing, typically of paper, placed between the platen and the paper to be printed to equalize the pressure over the whole forme. **2** *Architecture* another term for **TYMPANUM**. ▷late 16th cent. (sense 1): from French *tympan* or Latin *tympanum* (see **TYMPANUM**). Sense 2 dates from the early 18th cent.

tym·pa·na /ˈtimpənə/ ▸ plural form of **TYMPANUM**.

tym·pa·ni ▸*plural n.* variant spelling of **TIMPANI**.

tym·pan·ic /timˈpanik/ ▸*adj.* **1** *Anatomy* of, relating to, or having a tympanum. **2** resembling or acting like a drumhead.

tym·pan·ic bone ▸*n. Zoology* a small bone supporting the tympanic membrane in some vertebrates.

tym·pan·ic mem·brane ▸*n.* a membrane forming part of the organ of hearing, which vibrates in response to sound waves. In humans and other higher vertebrates it forms the eardrum, between the outer and middle ear.

tym·pa·ni·tes /ˌtimpəˈnītēz/ ▸*n. Medicine* swelling of the abdomen with air or gas. ▷late Middle English: via late Latin from Greek *tumpanitēs*, from *tumpanon* (see **TYMPANUM**). —**tym·pa·nit·ic** /-ˈnitik/ *adj.*

tym·pa·num /ˈtimpənəm/ ▸*n.* (*pl.* **-nums** or **-na** /-nə/) **1** *Anatomy & Zoology* the tympanic membrane or eardrum. ■ *Entomology* a membrane covering the hearing organ on the leg or body of some insects, sometimes adapted (as in cicadas) for producing sound. ■ *archaic* a drum. **2** *Architecture* a vertical recessed triangular space forming the center of a pediment, typically decorated. ■ a similar space over a door between the lintel and the arch. ▷early 17th cent.: via Latin from Greek *tumpanon* 'drum,' based on *tuptein* 'to strike.'

tym·pa·ny /ˈtimpənē/ ▸*n.* another term for **TYMPANITES** (used esp. in veterinary medicine). ▷early 16th cent.: from Greek *tumpanias*, from *tumpanon* (see **TYMPANUM**).

Tyn·dall /ˈtindəl/, John (1820–93), Irish physicist. He is best known for his work on heat, but he also worked on diamagnetism, the transmission of sound, and the scattering of light by suspended particles. He was the first person to explain why the sky is blue.

Tyne /tīn/ a river in northeastern England, formed by the confluence of two headstreams, the North Tyne, which rises in the Cheviot Hills, and the South Tyne, which rises in the northern Pennines. It flows east and enters the North Sea at Tynemouth.

typ. ▸*abbr.* ■ typographer. ■ typographic. ■ typographical. ■ typography.

type /tīp/ ▸*n.* **1** a category of people or things having common characteristics: *this type of heather grows better in a drier habitat | blood types.* ■ a person, thing, or event considered as a representative of such a category: *it's not the type of car I'd want my daughter to drive | I'm an adventurous type.* ■ [with *adj.*] *informal* a person of a specified character or nature: *professor types in tweed.* ■ (**one's type**) *informal* the sort of person one likes or finds attractive: *she's not really my type.* ■ *Linguistics* an abstract category or class of linguistic item or unit, as distinct from actual occurrences in speech or writing. Contrasted with **TOKEN**. **2** a person or thing symbolizing or exemplifying the ideal or defining characteristics of something: *she characterized his witty sayings as the type of modern wisdom.* See note at **EMBLEM**. ■ an object, conception, or work of art serving as a model for subsequent artists. ■ *Botany & Zoology* an organism or taxon chosen as having the essential characteristics of its group. ■ short for **TYPE SPECIMEN**. **3** printed characters or letters: *bold or italic type.* ■ a piece of metal with a raised letter or character on its upper surface, for use in letterpress printing. ■ such pieces collectively. **4** a design on either side of a medal or coin. **5** *Theology* a foreshadowing in the Old Testament of a person or event of the Christian tradition.

a **a** *a*

roman boldface italic

type 3

▸*v.* [*trans.*] **1** write (something) on a typewriter or computer by pressing the keys: *he* **typed out** *the second draft | [intrans.] I am learning how to type.* **2** *Medicine* determine the type to which (a person or their blood or tissue) belongs: *the kidney was typed.* **3** short for **TYPECAST**. ▷late 15th cent. (in the sense 'symbol, emblem'): from French, or from Latin *typus*, from Greek *tupos* 'impression, figure, type,' from *tuptein* 'to strike.' The use in printing dates from the early 18th cent.; the general sense 'category with common characteristics' arose in the mid 19th cent. —**typ·al** /-pəl/ *adj.* (*rare*).

▸*PHRASE* □ **in type** *Printing* composed and ready for printing.

-type ▸*suffix* (forming adjectives) resembling or having the characteristics of a specified thing: *the dish-type radio telescope | a champagne-type fizzy wine.*

Type A ▸*n.* a personality type characterized by ambition, high energy, and competitiveness, and thought to be susceptible to stress and heart disease.

Type B ▸*n.* a personality type characterized as easygoing and thought to have low susceptibility to stress.

type·cast /ˈtīpˌkast/ ▸*v.* (*past* and *past part.* **-cast**) [*trans.*] (usu. **be typecast**) assign (an actor or actress) repeatedly to the same type of role, as a result of the appropriateness of their appearance or previous success in such roles: *he tends to be typecast as the caring, intelligent male.* ■ represent or regard (a person or their role) as a stereotype: *people are not as likely to be typecast by their accents as they once were.*

type·face /ˈtīpˌfās/ ▸*n. Printing* a particular design of type.

type found·er ▸*n. Printing* a designer and maker of metal type. —**type found·ry** *n.*

type lo·cal·i·ty ▸*n.* **1** *Botany & Zoology* the place in which a type specimen was found. **2** *Geology* a place where deposits regarded as defining the characteristics of a particular geological formation or period occur.

type met·al ▸*n. Printing* an alloy of lead, tin, and antimony, used for casting type.

type·script /ˈtīpˌskript/ ▸*n.* a typed copy of a text.

type·set /ˈtīpˌset/ ▸*v.* (**-set·ting**; *past* and *past part.* **-set**) [*trans.*] arrange or generate the type for (a piece of text to be printed). —**type·set·ting** *n.*

type·set·ter /ˈtīpˌsetər/ ▸*n. Printing* a person who typesets text. ■ a typesetting machine.

type spe·cies ▸*n. Botany & Zoology* the particular species on which the description of a genus is based and with which the genus name remains associated during any taxonomic revision.

type spec·i·men ▸*n. Botany & Zoology* the specimen, or each of a set of specimens, on which the description and name of a new species is based. See also **HOLOTYPE, SYNTYPE**.

type·writ·er /ˈtīpˌrītər/ ▸*n.* an electric, electronic, or manual machine with keys for producing printlike characters one at a time on paper inserted around a roller. —**type·writ·ing** /-ˌrītiNG/ *n.* —**type·writ·ten** /-ˌritn/ *adj.*

typh·li·tis /tifˈlītis/ ▸*n. Medicine* inflammation of the cecum. ▷mid 19th cent.: modern Latin, from Greek *tuphlon* 'cecum or blind gut' (from *tuphlos* 'blind') + **-ITIS**. —**typh·lit·ic** /-ˈlitik/ *adj.*

ty·phoid /ˈtīˌfoid/ (also **ty·phoid fe·ver**) ▸*n.* an infectious bacterial fever with an eruption of red spots on the chest and abdomen and severe intestinal irritation. • Typhoid is caused by the bacterium *Salmonella typhi*; Gram-negative rods. ▷early 19th cent.: from **TYPHUS** + **-OID**. —**ty·phoi·dal** /tīˈfoidl/ *adj.*

Ty·phoid Mar·y ▸*n.* (*pl.* **Ty·phoid Mar·ys**) *informal* a transmitter of undesirable opinions, sentiments, or attitudes. ▷the nickname of *Mary Mallon* (see **MALLON**), an Irish-born cook who transmitted typhoid fever in the U.S.

ty·phoon /tīˈfo͞on/ ▸*n.* a tropical storm in the region of the Indian or western Pacific oceans. ▷late 16th cent.: partly via Portuguese from Arabic *ṭūfān* (perhaps from Greek *tuphōn* 'whirlwind'); reinforced by Chinese dialect *tai fung* 'big wind.' —**ty·phon·ic** /-ˈfänik/ *adj.*

ty·phus /ˈtīfəs/ ▸*n.* an infectious disease caused by rickettsiae, characterized by a purple rash, headaches, fever, and usually delirium, and historically a cause of high mortality during wars and famines. There are several forms, transmitted by vectors such as lice, ticks, mites, and rat fleas. Also called **SPOTTED FEVER**. ▷mid 17th cent.: modern Latin, from Greek *tuphos* 'smoke, stupor,' from *tuphein* 'to smoke.' —**ty·phous** /-fəs/ *adj.*

typ·i·cal /ˈtipikəl/ ▸*adj.* having the distinctive qualities of a particular type of person or thing: *a typical day | a typical example of 1930s art deco | typical symptoms.* See note at **NORMAL**. ■ characteristic of a particular person or thing: *he brushed the incident aside with typical good humor.* ■ *informal* showing the characteristics expected of or popularly associated with a particular person, situation, or thing: *"Typical woman!" John said* *disapprovingly.* ■ representative as a symbol; symbolic: *the pit is typical of hell.* ▷early 17th cent.: from medieval Latin *typicalis*, via Latin from Greek *tupikos*, from *tupos* (see TYPE). —**typ·i·cal·i·ty** /ˌtipiˈkalitē/ *n.* —**typ·i·cal·ly** /-ik(ə)lē/ *adv.* [*sentence adverb*] *typically, she showed no alarm* | [as *submodifier*] *a typically British stiff upper lip.*

typ·i·fy /ˈtipəˌfī/ ▸*v.* (**-fies, -fied**) [*trans.*] be characteristic or a representative example of: *tough, low-lying vegetation typifies this arctic area.* ■ represent; symbolize: *the sun typified the Greeks, and the moon the Persians.* ▷mid 17th cent.: from Latin *typus* (see TYPE) + -FY. —**typ·i·fi·ca·tion** /ˌtipəfiˈkāsʜən/ *n.* —**typ·i·fi·er** *n.*

typ·ing /ˈtīpiɴɢ/ ▸*n.* the action or skill of writing something by means of a typewriter or computer: *they learned shorthand and typing* | [as *adj.*] *typing errors.* ■ writing produced in such a way: *five pages of typing.*

typ·ist /ˈtīpist/ ▸*n.* a person who is skilled in using a typewriter or computer keyboard, esp. one who is employed for this purpose.

ty·po /ˈtīpō/ ▸*n.* (*pl.* **-pos**) *informal* a typographical error. ▷early 19th cent.: abbreviation.

typo. ▸*abbr.* ■ typographer. ■ typographic. ■ typographical. ■ typography.

ty·pog·ra·phy /tīˈpägrəfē/ ▸*n.* the art or process of setting and arranging types and printing from them. ■ the style and appearance of printed matter. ▷early 17th cent.: from French *typographie* or modern Latin *typographia* (see TYPE, -GRAPHY). —**ty·pog·ra·pher** /-fər/ *n.* —**ty·po·graph·ic** /ˌtīpəˈgrafik/ *adj.* —**ty·po·graph·i·cal** /ˌtīpəˈgrafikəl/ *adj.* —**ty·po·graph·i·cal·ly** /ˌtīpəˈgrafik(ə)lē/ *adv.*

ty·pol·o·gy /tīˈpäləjē/ ▸*n.* (*pl.* **-gies**) **1** a classification according to general type, esp. in archaeology, psychology, or the social sciences: *a typology of Saxon cremation vessels.* ■ study or analysis using such classification. **2** the study and interpretation of types and symbols, originally esp. in the Bible. ▷mid 19th cent. (sense 2): from Greek *tupos* 'type' + -LOGY. —**ty·po·log·i·cal** /ˌtīpəˈläjikəl/ *adj.* —**ty·pol·o·gist** /-jist/ *n.*

Tyr /ti(ə)r/ *Scandinavian Mythology* the god of battle, identified with Mars, after whom Tuesday is named.

ty·ra·mine /ˈtīrəˌmēn/ ▸*n.* *Biochemistry* a compound that occurs naturally in cheese and other foods and can cause dangerously high blood pressure in people taking a monoamine oxidase inhibitor. • An amine related to tyrosine; chem. formula: $C_6H_4(OH)CH_2CH_2NH_2$. ▷early 20th cent.: from *tyr(osine)* + AMINE.

ty·ran·ni·cal /təˈranikəl/ ▸*adj.* exercising power in a cruel or arbitrary way: *her father was portrayed as tyrannical and unloving.* ■ characteristic of tyranny; oppressive and controlling: *a momentary quieting of her tyrannical appetite.* ▷mid 16th cent.: from Old French *tyrannique*, via Latin from Greek *turannikos*, from *turannos* (see TYRANT). —**ty·ran·ni·cal·ly** /-ik(ə)lē/ *adv.*

ty·ran·ni·cide /təˈraniˌsīd/ ▸*n.* the killing of a tyrant. ■ the killer of a tyrant. ▷mid 17th cent.: from French, from Latin *tyrannicida* 'killer of a tyrant,' *tyrannicidium* 'killing of a tyrant' (see TYRANT, -CIDE). —**ty·ran·ni·cid·al** /təˌraniˈsīdl/ *adj.*

tyr·an·nize /ˈtirəˌnīz/ ▸*v.* [*trans.*] rule or treat (someone) despotically or cruelly: *she tyrannized her family* | [*intrans.*] *he* **tyrannizes over** *the servants.* ▷late 15th cent.: from French *tyranniser*, from *tyran* 'tyrant.'

ty·ran·no·saur /təˈranəˌsôr/ (also **ty·ran·no·sau·rus** /təˌranəˈsôrəs/) ▸*n.* a very large bipedal carnivorous dinosaur of the late Cretaceous period, with powerful jaws and small clawlike front legs. • Family Tyrannosauridae, infraorder Carnosauria, suborder Theopoda: several species, in particular *Tyrannosaurus rex.* ▷modern Latin, from Greek *turannos* 'tyrant' + *sauros* 'lizard,' on the pattern of *dinosaur.*

ty·ran·nu·let /təˈranyəlit/ ▸*n.* a small tropical American bird of the tyrant flycatcher family, typically with drab grayish or greenish plumage. • Family Tyrannidae: several genera and many species. ▷diminutive based on modern Latin *Tyrannus* (genus name), from Greek *turannos* 'tyrant.'

tyr·an·ny /ˈtirənē/ ▸*n.* (*pl.* **-nies**) cruel and oppressive government or rule: *refugees who managed to escape Nazi tyranny* | *the removal of the regime may be the end of a tyranny.* ■ a nation under such cruel and oppressive government. ■ cruel, unreasonable, or arbitrary use of power or control: *she resented his rages and his tyranny* | *figurative the tyranny of the nine-to-five day* | *his father's tyrannies.* ■ (esp. in ancient Greece) rule by one who has absolute power without legal right. ▷late Middle English: from Old French *tyrannie*, from late Latin *tyrannia*, from Latin *turannus* (see TYRANT). —**tyr·an·nous** /-nəs/ *adj.* —**tyr·an·nous·ly** /-nəslē/ *adv.*

ty·rant /ˈtīrənt/ ▸*n.* **1** a cruel and oppressive ruler: *the tyrant was deposed by popular demonstrations.* ■ a person exercising power or control in a cruel, unreasonable, or arbitrary way: *her father was a tyrant and a bully.* ■ (esp. in ancient Greece) a ruler who seized power without legal right. **2** a tyrant flycatcher. ▷Middle English: from Old French, via Latin from Greek *turannos.*

ty·rant fly·catch·er ▸*n.* a New World perching bird that resembles the Old World flycatchers in behavior, typically with brightly colored plumage. • Family Tyrannidae: many genera and numerous species. ▷mid 18th cent.: so named because of its aggressive behavior toward other birds approaching its nest.

Tyre /tī(ə)r/ a port on the Mediterranean Sea in southern Lebanon; pop. 14,000. Founded in the 2nd millennium BC as a colony of Sidon, it was for centuries a Phoenician port and trading center. —**Tyr·i·an** /ˈtirēən/ *adj.* & *n.*

tyre ▸*n.* British spelling of TIRE[2].

Tyr·i·an pur·ple /ˈtirēən/ ▸*n.* see PURPLE.

ty·ro /ˈtīrō/ (also **ti·ro**) ▸*n.* (*pl.* **-ros**) a beginner or novice. ▷late Middle English: from Latin *tiro*, medieval Latin *tyro* 'recruit.'

Ty·rode's so·lu·tion /ˈtīrōdz/ (also **Ty·rode's**) ▸*n.* *Biology & Medicine* a type of physiological saline solution. ▷1920s: named after Maurice V. *Tyrode* (1878–1930), American pharmacologist.

Ty·rol /təˈrōl; tīˈrōl; ˈtīˌrōl/ an Alpine state in western Austria; capital, Innsbruck. The southern part was ceded to Italy after World War I. German name TIROL. —**Ty·ro·le·an** /təˈrōlēən; tī-/ *adj.* & *n.* —**Tyr·o·lese** /ˌtirəˈlēz; ˌtīrə-; -ˈlēs/ *adj.* & *n.*

Ty·rone /tīˈrōn/ one of the six counties of Northern Ireland, formerly an administrative area; pop. 144,000; chief town, Omagh.

ty·ro·si·nase /tīˈräsəˌnās; -ˌnāz/ ▸*n.* *Biochemistry* a copper-containing enzyme that catalyzes the formation of quinones from phenols and polyphenols (e.g., melanin from tyrosine). ▷late 19th cent.: from TYROSINE + -ASE.

ty·ro·sine /ˈtīrəˌsēn/ ▸*n.* *Biochemistry* a hydrophilic amino acid that is a constituent of most proteins and is important in the synthesis of some hormones. • Chem. formula: $C_6H_4(OH)CH_2CH(NH_2)COOH$. ▷mid 19th cent.: formed irregularly from Greek *turos* 'cheese' + -INE[4].

Tyr·rhe·ni·an /təˈrēnēən/ ▸*adj.* of, relating to, or denoting the Tyrrhenian Sea or the surrounding region. ■ *archaic* Etruscan.
▸*n.* *archaic* an Etruscan.

Tyr·rhe·ni·an Sea a part of the Mediterranean Sea between mainland Italy and the islands of Sicily and Sardinia.

Ty·son /ˈtīsən/, Mike (1966–), U.S. heavyweight boxing champion; full name *Michael Gerald Tyson.*

Tyu·men /tyo͞oˈmen/ a city in west Siberian Russia, in the eastern foothills of the Ural Mountains; pop. 487,000. Founded in 1586, it is thought to be one of the oldest cities in Siberia.

tyu·ya·mu·nite /ˌtyo͞oyəˈmo͞onīt/ ▸*n.* a yellowish earthy mineral that is an ore of uranium. It consists of a hydrated vanadate of calcium and uranium. ▷early 20th cent.: from *Tyuya Muyun*, the name of a Kyrgyz village, + -ITE[1].

tzar ▸*n.* variant spelling of CZAR, etc..

Tza·ra /ˈtsärə/, Tristan (1896–1963), French poet, born in Romania; born *Samuel Rosenstock.* One of the founders of the Dada movement in 1916, he wrote its manifestos. His poetry, with its continuous flow of unconnected images, helped form the basis for surrealism.

tza·ri·na ▸*n.* variant spelling of CZARINA.

tza·tzi·ki /tsäˈtsēkē/ (also **tza·tzi·ki sauce**) ▸*n.* a sauce of Greek origin, made from yogurt, garlic, and cucumbers. ▷mid 20th cent.: modern Greek, from Turkish *cacık.*

tze·da·kah /tsiˈdôkə; tsədäˈkä/ ▸*n.* (among the Jews) charitable giving, typically seen as a moral obligation. ▷from Hebrew *ṣəḏāqāh* 'righteousness.'

Tzel·tal /(t)selˈtäl/ ▸*n.* (*pl.* same or **-tals**) **1** a member of an American Indian people inhabiting parts of southern Mexico. **2** the Mayan language of this people.
▸*adj.* of or relating to this people or their language. ▷Spanish name of one of the three regions of the Mexican state of Chiapas, of uncertain origin.

tzi·gane /(t)siˈgän/ ▸*n.* (*pl.* same or **-ganes**) a Hungarian gypsy. ▷mid 18th cent.: from French, from Hungarian *c(z)igány.*

tzim·mes (also **tzim·mis**) ▸*n.* variant spelling of TSIMMES.

T-zone ▸*n.* the central part of a person's face, including the forehead, nose, and chin, esp. as having oilier skin than the rest of the face. ▷*T* designating the shape of the area defined.

Tzo·tzil /ˈ(t)sōtˈsēl/ ▸*n.* (*pl.* same or **-tzils**) **1** a member of an American Indian people of southern Mexico. **2** the Mayan language of this people.
▸*adj.* of or relating to this people or their language. ▷the name in Tzotzil.

Tzu-po variant of ZIBO.

T

Uu

U[1] /yo͞o/ (also **u**) ▸*n.* (*pl.* **Us** or **U's**) **1** the twenty-first letter of the alphabet. ■ denoting the next after T in a set of items, categories, etc. **2** (**U**) a shape like that of a capital U, esp. a cross section: [in *combination*] *U-shaped glaciated valleys.*

U[2] ▸*symbol* the chemical element uranium.

U[3] ▸*adj. informal, chiefly Brit.* (of language or social behavior) characteristic of or appropriate to the upper social classes: *U manners.* ▷abbreviation of **UPPER CLASS**; coined in 1954 by Alan S. C. Ross, professor of linguistics, the term was popularized by its use in Nancy Mitford's *Noblesse Oblige* (1956).

U[4] /o͞o/ ▸*n.* a Burmese title of respect before a man's name, equivalent to Mr.: *U Thien San.*

u ▸*abbr. Physics* denoting quantum states or wave functions that change sign on inversion through the origin. The opposite of **G**. [from German *ungerade* 'odd.']

▸*symbol* [in *combination*] (in units of measurement) micro- (10^{-6}): *direct readout of concentration in ug or mg/l.* ▷substituted for **MU** (μ).

UAE ▸*abbr.* United Arab Emirates.

U·ban·ghi Sha·ri /(y)o͞o'baNGgē 'SHärē; -'bäNG-/ former name (until 1958) of **CENTRAL AFRICAN REPUBLIC**.

U·ban·gi Riv·er /(y)o͞o'baNGgē/ (French spelling **Oubangui**) a river that flows for 660 miles (1,060 km) from the border of the Central African Republic and the Democratic Republic of the Congo (formerly Zaire), along the border of the latter with the Republic of Congo, to join the Congo River, of which it is the chief northern tributary.

uber- /'o͞obər/ (also **über-** /'Ybər/) ▸*prefix* denoting an outstanding or supreme example of a particular kind of person or thing: *an uberbabe | the uberregulator.* ▷German *über* 'super.'

U

Ü·ber·mensch /'o͞obər,mencH; 'Ybər-/ ▸*n.* (*pl.* **-mensch·en** /-,mencHən/) the ideal superior man of the future who could rise above conventional Christian morality to create and impose his own values, originally described by Nietzsche in *Thus Spake Zarathustra* (1883–85). Also called **SUPERMAN** and **OVERMAN**. ▷German, literally 'superhuman person.'

-ubility ▸*suffix* forming nouns from or corresponding to adjectives ending in *-uble* (such as *solubility* from *soluble*).

u·bi·qui·none /yo͞o'bikwə,nōn/ ▸*n. Biochemistry* any of a class of compounds that occur in all living cells and that act as electron-transfer agents in cell respiration. They are substituted quinones. ▷1950s: blend of **UBIQUITOUS** and **QUINONE**.

u·bi·qui·tin /yo͞o'bikwitin/ ▸*n. Biochemistry* a compound found in living cells that plays a role in the degradation of defective and superfluous proteins. It is a single-chain polypeptide. ▷1970s: from **UBIQUITOUS** + **-IN**[1].

u·biq·ui·tous /yo͞o'bikwətəs/ ▸*adj.* present, appearing, or found everywhere: *his ubiquitous influence was felt by all the family | cowboy hats are ubiquitous among the male singers.* ▷mid 19th cent.: from modern Latin *ubiquitas* (from Latin *ubique* 'everywhere,' from *ubi* 'where') + **-OUS**. —**u·biq·ui·tous·ly** *adv.* —**u·biq·ui·tous·ness** *n.* —**u·biq·ui·ty** /-wətē/ *n.*

-uble ▸*suffix* (forming adjectives) able to: *voluble.* ■ able to be: *soluble.* Compare with **-ABLE**. ▷from French, from Latin *-ubilis.*

-ubly ▸*suffix* forming adverbs corresponding to adjectives ending in *-uble* (such as *volubly* corresponding to *voluble*).

U-boat ▸*n.* a German submarine used in World War I or World War II. ▷from German *U-Boot*, abbreviation of *Unterseeboot* 'undersea boat.'

u·bun·tu /o͞o'bo͝ontoo/ ▸*n.* a quality that includes the essential human virtues; compassion and humanity. ▷Xhosa and Zulu.

u.c. ▸*abbr.* uppercase.

Uca·ya·li River /,o͞okə'yälē/ a river that flows for 1,000 miles (1,600 km) through central and northern Peru to join the Marañón River to form the Amazon River.

UCC ▸*abbr.* Uniform Commercial Code.

ud·der /'ədər/ ▸*n.* the mammary gland of female cattle, sheep, goats, horses, and related ungulates, a baglike organ with two or more teats hanging near the hind legs. ▷Old English *ūder*; related to Dutch *uier* and German *Euter*. —**ud·dered** *adj.* [in *combination*].

Ud·mur·ti·a /o͞od'mo͝orsHə/ an autonomous republic in central Russia; pop. 1,619,000; capital, Izhevsk. Also called **UDMURT REPUBLIC**.

u·don /'o͞o,dän/ ▸*n.* (in Japanese cooking) wheat pasta made in thick strips. ▷Japanese.

UEFA /yo͞o'(w)efə/ ▸*abbr.* Union of European Football Associations, the governing body of soccer in Europe.

U·fa /o͞o'fä/ the capital of Bashkiria, in the Ural Mountains, in southwestern Russia; pop. 1,094,000.

UFO ▸*n.* (*pl.* **UFOs**) a mysterious object seen in the sky for which, it is claimed, no orthodox scientific explanation can be found. ▷1950s: acronym from *unidentified flying object.*

u·fol·o·gy /yo͞o'fäləjē/ ▸*n.* the study of UFOs. —**u·fo·log·i·cal** /,yo͞ofə'läjikəl/ *adj.* —**u·fol·o·gist** /-jist/ *n.*

U·gan·da /yo͞o'gandə/ a landlocked country in East Africa; pop. 26,404,000; capital, Kampala; languages, English (official), Swahili, and other languages. —**U·gan·dan** *adj.* & *n.*

Ethnically and culturally diverse, Uganda became a British protectorate in 1894 and an independent Commonwealth of Nations state in 1962. The country was ruled 1971–79 by dictator Idi Amin, who came to power after an army coup. His overthrow, with Tanzanian military support, was followed by several years of conflict, partly resolved in 1986 by the formation of a government under President Yoweri Museveni.

U·ga·rit /'(y)o͞ogərit; (y)o͞o'gärit/ an ancient port and Bronze Age trading city in northern Syria. Its people spoke a Semitic language written in a distinctive cuneiform alphabet. —**U·ga·rit·ic** /,(y)o͞ogə'ritik/ *adj.* & *n.*

Ugg boot /'əg ,bo͞ot/ (also **Ugh boot**) ▸*n. trademark* a type of soft sheepskin boot originating in Australia: *a music video set in Marrakesh with models dancing in bare midriffs and Ugg boots.* ▷1960s: probably named after *Ugh*, a series of cartoon characters.

ugh /əg; əKH; o͞oKH/ ▸*exclam. informal* used to express disgust or horror: *Ugh! What's this disgusting object?* ▷mid 18th cent.: imitative.

Ug·li fruit /'əglē/ ▸*n.* (*pl.* same) *trademark* a mottled green and yellow citrus fruit that is a hybrid of grapefruit and tangerine. • This fruit is obtained from the tree *Citrus* × *tangelo*, family Rutaceae. ▷1930s: *ugli*, alteration of **UGLY**.

ug·ly /'əglē/ ▸*adj.* (**-li·er**, **-li·est**) unpleasant or repulsive, esp. in appearance: *she thought she was ugly and fat | the ugly sound of a fire alarm* | [as *n.*] (**the ugly**) *he instinctively shrinks from the ugly.* ■ (of a situation or mood) involving or likely to involve violence or other unpleasantness: *the mood in the room turned ugly.* ■ unpleasantly suggestive; causing disquiet: *ugly rumors persisted that there had been a cover-up.* ■ morally repugnant: *racism and its most ugly manifestations, racial attacks and harassment.* ▷Middle English: from Old Norse *uggligr* 'to be dreaded,' from *ugga* 'to dread.' —**ug·li·fi·ca·tion** /,əgləfi'kāsHən/ *n.* —**ug·li·fy** /'əglə,fī/ *v.* —**ug·li·ly** /-ləlē/ *adv.* —**ug·li·ness** *n.*

ug·ly A·mer·i·can ▸*n. informal* an American who behaves offensively when abroad.

ug·ly duck·ling ▸*n.* a person, esp. a child, who turns out to be beautiful or talented against all expectations. ▷from the title of one of Hans Christian Andersen's fairy tales, in which the "ugly duckling" becomes a swan.

U·gri·an /'(y)o͞ogrēən/ ▸*adj.* another term for **UGRIC**.

U·gric /'(y)o͞ogrik/ ▸*adj.* of, relating to, or denoting a branch of the Finno-Ugric language family comprising Hungarian and the Ob-Ugric languages. ▷from Russian *Ugry* (the name of a people dwelling east of the Urals) + **-IC**.

uh[1] /ə; əN/ ▸*exclam.* **1** used to express hesitation: *"I was just, uh, passing by."* **2** another way of saying **HUH**. ▷1960s: imitative.

uh[2] /ə/ ▸*adj.* nonstandard spelling of the indefinite article **A**, used to represent black English: *crabs in uh basket.*

▸*prep.* nonstandard spelling of **OF**, used to represent black English: *a house full uh young 'uns.*

UHF ▸*abbr.* ultrahigh frequency.

uh-huh /ə 'hə; əN 'həN/ ▸*exclam.* used to express assent or as a noncommittal response to a question or remark: *"Do you understand?" "Uh-huh."* ▷1920s: imitative.

uh·lan /o͞o'län; '(y)o͞olən/ ▸*n. historical* a cavalryman armed with a lance as a member of various European armies. ▷mid 18th cent.: via French and German from Polish *(h)ulan*, from Turkish *oğlan* 'youth, servant.'

uh-oh /'ə ,ō/ ▸*exclam.* used to express alarm, dismay, or realization of a difficulty: *"Uh-oh! Take cover!"*

uh-uh /'əN ,əN; 'əN 'əN/ ▸*exclam.* used to express a negative response to a question or remark. ▷1920s: imitative.

Ui·ghur /'wē,go͝or/ (also **Ui·gur**, **Uy·gur**) ▸*n.* **1** a member of a people of northwestern China, particularly the Xinjiang region, and adjoining areas. **2** the Turkic language of this people.

▸*adj.* of or relating to this people or their language. ▷the name in Uighur.

uil·lean pipes /'ilən; 'ilyən/ ▸*plural n.* Irish bagpipes played resting on the knee using bellows worked by the elbow, and having three extra pipes on which chords can be played. ▷early 20th cent.: from Irish *píob uilleann*, literally 'pipe of the elbow.'

u·in·ta·ite /yo͞o'intə,īt/ ▸*n.* a pure form of asphalt mined in the Uinta Mountains and used to soften petroleum products, as well as in manufacturing paints and inks.

U·in·ta Moun·tains /yo͞o'intə/ a range of the Rocky Mountains in northeastern Utah that rises to 13,528 feet (4,123 m) at Kings Peak.

U·ist /'yo͞o-ist/ two islands in the Outer Hebrides, **North Uist** and **South Uist**, that lie to the south of the island of Lewis and Harris.

Uit·land·er /'īt,landər; 'āt-; 'out-/ ▶*n. S. African historical* a British immigrant living in the Transvaal who was denied citizenship by the Boers for cultural and economic reasons. ▷Afrikaans, from Dutch *uit* 'out' + *land* 'land.'

U·ji·ya·ma·da /'o͞ojēyä'mädə/ former name (until 1956) of **ISE**.

Uj·jain /'o͞o,jīn/ a city in west central India, in Madhya Pradesh; pop. 376,000. It is one of the seven holy cities of Hinduism.

U·jung Pan·dang /'o͞o,jo͞ong 'pän,däng/ the chief seaport in the southwest of the island of Sulawesi in Indonesia; pop. 944,300. Former name (until 1973) **MAKASSAR**.

UK ▶*abbr.* United Kingdom.

u·kase /yo͞o'kās; -'kāz/ ▶*n.* an edict of the Russian government: *Tsar Alexander I issued his famous ukase unilaterally decreeing the North Pacific Coast Russian territory.* ■ an arbitrary command: *defying the publisher in the very building from which he had issued his ukase.* ▷from Russian *ukaz* 'ordinance, edict,' from *ukazat'* 'to show, decree.'

uke /yo͞ok/ ▶*n. informal* short for **UKULELE**.

u·ki·yo-e /,o͞okēyō '(y)ā/ ▶*n.* a school of Japanese art depicting subjects from everyday life, dominant in the 17th–19th centuries. ▷Japanese, from *ukiyo* 'fleeting world' + *e* 'picture.'

U·kraine /yo͞o'krān; 'yo͞o,krān/ (also **the U·kraine**) a country in eastern Europe, north of the Black Sea; pop. 47,732,000; capital, Kiev; languages, Ukrainian and Russian. ▷from obsolete Russian *ukraina* 'frontier regions,' from *u* 'at' + *kraĭ* 'edge.'

Ukraine was united with Russia, with the capital at Kiev, in the 9th century. After a period of division between Poland, Russia, and the Ottoman Empire, it was reunited with Russia in 1785. Briefly independent following the 1917 revolution, it became one of the original constituent republics (and the third largest) of the Soviet Union. In 1991, on the breakup of the Soviet Union, Ukraine became an independent republic within the Commonwealth of Independent States.

U·krain·i·an /yo͞o'krānēən/ ▶*n.* **1** a native or national of Ukraine, or a person of Ukrainian descent. **2** the East Slavic language of Ukraine.
▶*adj.* of or relating to Ukraine, its people, or their language.

u·ku·le·le /,yo͞okə'lālē/ ▶*n.* a small four-stringed guitar of Hawaiian origin. ▷late 19th cent.: from Hawaiian, literally 'jumping flea.'

u·la·ma ▶*n.* variant spelling of **ULEMA**.

U·laan·baa·tar /o͞o'län 'bä,tär/ (also **U·lan Ba·tor** /o͞o'län 'bä,tôr; 'o͞o,län/) a city in northeastern Mongolia, the capital of the country; pop. 575,000. Former name (until 1924) **URGA**.

U·lan-U·de /o͞o'län o͞o'dā/ an industrial city in southern Siberia, in southern Russia, capital of the republic of Buryatia; pop. 359,000. Former name (until 1934) **VERKHNEUDINSK**.

-ular ▶*suffix* forming adjectives, sometimes corresponding to nouns ending in *-ule* (such as *pustular* corresponding to *pustule*), but often without diminutive force (as in *angular, granular*). ▷from Latin *-ularis*.

-ularity ▶*suffix* forming nouns corresponding to adjectives ending in *-ular* (such as *modularity* corresponding to *modular*). ▷see **-ULAR**, **-ITY**.

ul·cer /'əlsər/ ▶*n.* an open sore on an external or internal surface of the body, caused by a break in the skin or mucous membrane that fails to heal. ■ *figurative* a moral blemish or corrupting influence: *he's a con man with an incurable ulcer called gambling.* ▷late Middle English: from Latin *ulcus, ulcer-*. **—ul·cered** *adj.* **—ul·cer·ous** /'əls(ə)rəs/ *adj.*

ul·cer·ate /'əlsə,rāt/ ▶*v.* [*intrans.*] develop into or become affected by an ulcer. ▷late Middle English: from Latin *ulcerat-* 'made ulcerous,' from the verb *ulcerare.* **—ul·cer·a·tion** /,əlsə'rāshən/ *n.* **—ul·cer·a·tive** /-rətiv; -,rātiv/ *adj.*

-ule ▶*suffix* forming diminutive nouns such as *capsule* and *pustule.* ▷from Latin *-ulus, -ula, -ulum.*

u·le·ma /'o͞olə,mä/ (also **u·la·ma**) ▶*n.* [treated as *sing.* or *pl.*] a body of Muslim scholars recognized as having specialist knowledge of Islamic sacred law and theology. ■ a member of such a body. ▷from Arabic *'ulamā'*, plural of *'ālim* 'learned,' from *'alima* 'know.'

-ulence ▶*suffix* forming nouns corresponding to adjectives ending in *-ulent* (such as *virulence* corresponding to *virulent*). ▷see **-ULENT**.

-ulent ▶*suffix* (forming adjectives) abounding in; full of: *fraudulent* | *purulent* | *virulent.* Compare with **-LENT**. ▷from Latin *-ulentus.*

u·lex·ite /'yo͞olək,sīt/ ▶*n.* a mineral occurring on alkali flats as rounded masses of small white crystals. It is a hydrated borate of sodium and calcium. ▷mid 19th cent.: from George L. *Ulex* (died 1883), German chemist, + **-ITE**[1].

Ul·has·na·gar /,o͞olhəs'nəgər; -'nägər/ a city in western India, in the state of Maharashtra; pop. 369,000.

U·li·thi /o͞o'lē*th*ē/ an atoll in the western Caroline Islands, in the Federated States of Micronesia, site of a U.S. victory over the Japanese in 1944.

ul·lage /'əlij/ ▶*n.* the amount by which a container falls short of being full. ■ loss of liquid by evaporation or leakage. ▷late Middle English: from Anglo-Norman French *ulliage*, from Old French *euillier* 'fill up,' based on Latin *oculus* 'eye' (with reference to a container's bunghole).

ul·lage rock·et ▶*n.* an auxiliary rocket engine used in weightless conditions to provide sufficient acceleration to maintain the flow of liquid propellant from the fuel tank.

Ulm /o͝olm/ an industrial city on the Danube River in Baden-Württemberg, in southern Germany; pop. 112,000.

ul·na /'əlnə/ ▶*n.* (*pl.* **-nae** /-,nē; -,nī/ or **-nas**) the thinner and longer of the two bones in the human forearm, on the side opposite to the thumb. Compare with **RADIUS** (sense 2). ■ the corresponding bone in a quadruped's foreleg or a bird's wing. ▷late Middle English (denoting the humerus): from Latin; related to **ELL**[1]. **—ul·nar** *adj.*

U-lock ▶*n.* a mechanism used to secure a bicycle when parked, consisting of a U-shaped bar and crosspiece of hardened steel.

-ulous ▶*suffix* forming adjectives such as *incredulous, garrulous.* ▷from Latin *-ulosus, -ulus.*

Ul·san /'o͞ol'sän/ an industrial port on the southern coast of South Korea; pop. 683,000.

Ul·ster /'əlstər/ a former province of Ireland, in the north of the island. The nine counties of Ulster are now divided between Northern Ireland (Antrim, Down, Armagh, Londonderry, Tyrone, and Fermanagh) and the Republic of Ireland (Cavan, Donegal, and Monaghan). ■ (in general use) Northern Ireland. **—Ul·ster·man** /-mən/ *n.* (*pl.* **-men**) **—Ul·ster·wom·an** /-,wo͝omən/ *n.* (*pl.* **-wom·en**).

ul·ster /'əlstər/ ▶*n.* a man's long, loose overcoat of rough cloth, typically with a belt at the back. ▷late 19th cent.: from **ULSTER**, where it was originally sold.

Ul·ster Coun·ty /'əlstər/ a county in southeastern New York, west of the Hudson River, the site of Catskill resorts; pop. 165,304.

ult. ▶*abbr.* ■ ultimate. ■ ultimo.

ul·te·ri·or /,əl'ti(ə)rēər/ ▶*adj.* existing beyond what is obvious or admitted; intentionally hidden: *could there be an ulterior motive behind his request?* ■ beyond what is immediate or present; coming in the future: *ulterior pay promised to the mariners.* ▷mid 17th cent.: from Latin, literally 'further, more distant.'

ul·ti·ma·ta /,əltə'mātə; -'mätə/ ▶ plural form of **ULTIMATUM**.

ul·ti·mate /'əltəmit/ ▶*adj.* being or happening at the end of a process; final: *their ultimate aim was to force his resignation.* ■ being the best or most extreme example of its kind: *the ultimate accolade.* ■ basic or fundamental: *the ultimate constituents of anything that exists are atoms.* ■ *Physics* denoting the maximum possible strength or resistance beyond which an object breaks.
▶*n.* **1** (**the ultimate**) the best achievable or imaginable of its kind: ***the ultimate in*** *decorative luxury.* **2** a final or fundamental fact or principle. ▷mid 17th cent.: from late Latin *ultimatus*, past participle of *ultimare* 'come to an end.' **—ul·ti·ma·cy** /-məsē/ *n.* (*pl.* **-cies**) **—ul·ti·mate·ly** *adv.*

ul·ti·ma Thu·le /'əltəmə '*th*o͞olē; '*th*o͞ol/ ▶*n.* a distant unknown region; the extreme limit of travel and discovery. ▷Latin, literally 'furthest Thule' (see **THULE**).

ul·ti·ma·tum /,əltə'mātəm; -'mät-/ ▶*n.* (*pl.* **-ma·tums** or **-ma·ta** /-'mātə; -'mätə/) a final demand or statement of terms, the rejection of which will result in retaliation or a breakdown in relations: *the UN Security Council ultimatum demanding Iraq's withdrawal from Kuwait* | *a "Marry me or else" ultimatum.* ▷mid 18th cent.: from Latin, neuter past participle of *ultimare* 'come to an end.'

ul·ti·mo /'əltə,mō/ (abbr.: **ult.** or **ulto**) ▶*adj.* [*postpositive*] *dated* of last month: *the 3rd ultimo.* Compare with **INSTANT**, **PROXIMO**. ▷from Latin *ultimo mense* 'in the last month.'

ul·ti·mo·bran·chi·al /,əltəmō'brangkēəl/ ▶*adj. Zoology* relating to or denoting a gland in the neck that in many lower vertebrates regulates the calcium level in the body.

ul·ti·mo·gen·i·ture /,əltəmō'jenichər; -,cho͝or/ ▶*n. Law* a principle of inheritance in which the right of succession belongs to the youngest son. Compare with **PRIMOGENITURE**.

ul·ti·sol /'əltə,säl; -,sôl/ ▶*n. Soil Science* a highly weathered leached red or reddish-yellow acid soil with a clay-rich B horizon (subsoil), occurring in warm, humid climates. ▷1960s: from **ULTIMATE** + Latin *solum* 'soil.'

ul·tra /'əltrə/ *informal* ▶*n.* an extremist.
▶*adv.* [as *submodifier*] very; extremely: *the play was not just boring, it was ultra boring.* ▷early 19th cent.: an independent usage of **ULTRA-**, originally as an abbreviation of French *ultra-royaliste.*

ultra- ▶*prefix* **1** beyond; on the other side of: *ultramontane.* Often contrasted with **CIS-**. **2** extreme; to an extreme degree: *ultramicroscopic* | *ultraradical.* ▷from Latin *ultra* 'beyond.'

ul·tra·ba·sic /,əltrə'bāsik/ ▶*adj. Geology* relating to or denoting igneous rocks having a silica content less than 45 percent by weight, most of which are also ultramafic. Compare with **ULTRAMAFIC**.

ul·tra·cen·tri·fuge /,əltrə'sentrə,fyo͞oj/ ▶*n.* a very fast centrifuge used to precipitate large biological molecules from solution or separate them by their different rates of sedimentation.
▶*v.* [*trans.*] subject to the action of an ultracentrifuge. **—ul·tra·cen·tri·fu·ga·tion** /-,sentrəfyo͞o'gāshən; -sen-,trif(y)ə-/ *n.*

U

ul·tra·con·serv·a·tive /,əltrəkən'sərvətiv; -və,tiv/ ▶*adj.* extremely conservative in politics or in the observance of religion: *an effort by an ultraconservative faction to limit believers' freedom to follow their consciences.*
▶*n.* a person who is extremely conservative in politics or religion: *the literature of the well-organized ultraconservatives is more plentiful.* **—ul·tra·con·serv·a·tism** /-və,tizəm/ *n.*

ul·tra·di·an /əl'trādēən/ ▶*adj. Physiology* (of a rhythm or cycle) having a period of recurrence shorter than a day but longer than an hour. Compare with **INFRADIAN**. ▷1960s: from **ULTRA-** 'beyond' (being of greater frequency than circadian) + **-IAN**.

ul·tra·fil·tra·tion /,əltrəfil'trāshən/ ▶*n.* filtration using a medium fine enough to retain colloidal particles, viruses, or large molecules. **—ul·tra·fil·ter** /'əltrə-,filtər/ *n.* & *v.*

ul·tra·high fre·quen·cy /'əltrə,hī; ,əltrə'hī/ (abbr.: **UHF**) ▶*n.* a radio frequency in the range 300 to 3,000 MHz.

ul·tra·ism /'əltrə,izəm/ ▶*n.* the holding of extreme opinions. **—ul·tra·ist** *n.*

ul·tra·light ▶*adj.* /,əltrə'līt; 'əltrə,līt/ extremely lightweight.
▶*n.* /'əltrə,līt/ a small, light, single-seater aircraft.

ul·tra·maf·ic /,əltrə'mafik/ ▶*adj. Geology* relating to or denoting igneous rocks composed chiefly of mafic minerals. Compare with **ULTRABASIC**.

ul·tra·ma·rine /,əltrəmə'rēn/ ▶*n.* a brilliant deep blue pigment originally obtained from lapis lazuli. ■ an imitation of such a pigment, made from powdered fired clay, sodium carbonate, sulfur, and resin. ■ a brilliant deep blue color. ▷late 16th cent.: from medieval Latin *ultramarinus* 'beyond the sea' with reference to the foreign origin of lapis lazuli.

ul·tra·mi·cro·scope /ˌəltrəˈmīkrəˌskōp/ ▶*n.* an optical microscope used to detect particles smaller than the wavelength of light by illuminating them at an angle and observing the light scattered by the Tyndall effect against a dark background.

ul·tra·mi·cro·scop·ic /ˌəltrəˌmīkrəˈskäpik/ ▶*adj.* too small to be seen by an ordinary optical microscope. ■ of or relating to an ultramicroscope.

ul·tra·mod·ern /ˌəltrəˈmädərn/ ▶*adj.* incorporating ideas, styles, or techniques only recently developed or available: *a wave of ultramodern architecture.*

ul·tra·mon·tane /ˌəltrəˌmänˈtān; -ˈmänˌtān/ ▶*adj.* **1** advocating supreme papal authority in matters of faith and discipline. Compare with **GALLICAN**. **2** situated on the other side of the Alps from the point of view of the speaker.

▶*n.* a person advocating supreme papal authority. ▷late 16th cent. (denoting a representative of the Roman Catholic Church north of the Alps): from medieval Latin *ultramontanus*, from Latin *ultra* 'beyond' + *mons, mont-* 'mountain.' **—ul·tra·mon·ta·nism** /-ˈmäntəˌnizəm/ *n.*

ul·tra·mun·dane /ˌəltrəˈmənˌdān; -ˌmənˈdān/ ▶*adj. poetic/literary* existing outside the known world, the solar system, or the universe. ▷mid 17th cent.: from late Latin *ultramundanus*, from *ultra* 'beyond' + *mundanus* (from *mundus* 'world').

ul·tra·nat·ion·al·ism /ˌəltrəˈnasHənəˌlizəm/ ▶*n.* extreme nationalism that promotes the interest of one state or people above all others: *the Yugoslav president is fanning the flames of ultranationalism.* **—ul·tra·nat·ion·al·ist** *n.* & *adj.* **—ul·tra·nat·ion·al·ist·ic** /-ˌnasHənəˈlistik/ *adj.*

ul·tra·sau·rus /ˈəltrəˌsôrəs; ˌəltrəˈsôrəs/ ▶*n.* a late Jurassic dinosaur related to the brachiosaurus, known from only a few bones but probably the tallest animal ever, and possibly the heaviest at up to 130 tons. • Genus *Ultrasaurus*, infraorder Sauropoda, order Saurischia. ▷modern Latin, from Latin *ultra* 'beyond' + Greek *sauros* 'lizard.'

ul·tra·short /ˌəltrəˈsHôrt/ ▶*adj.* (of radio waves) having a wavelength significantly shorter than that of the usual shortwaves, in particular shorter than 10 meters (i.e., of a VHF frequency above 30 MHz).

ul·tra·son·ic /ˌəltrəˈsänik/ ▶*adj.* of or involving sound waves with a frequency above the upper limit of human hearing. **—ul·tra·son·i·cal·ly** /-ik(ə)lē/ *adv.*

ul·tra·son·ics /ˌəltrəˈsäniks/ ▶*plural n.* [treated as *sing.*] the science and application of ultrasonic waves. ■ [treated as *sing.* or *pl.*] ultrasonic waves; ultrasound.

ul·tra·so·nog·ra·phy /ˌəltrəsəˈnägrəfē/ ▶*n. Medicine* a technique using echoes of ultrasound pulses to delineate objects or areas of different density in the body. **—ul·tra·son·o·graph·ic** /əltrəˌsänəˈgrafik; -ˌsōnə-/ *adj.*

ul·tra·sound /ˈəltrəˌsound/ ▶*n.* sound or other vibrations having an ultrasonic frequency, particularly as used in medical imaging. ■ an ultrasound scan, esp. one of a pregnant woman to examine the fetus.

ul·tra·struc·ture /ˈəltrəˌstrəkCHər/ ▶*n. Biology* a fine structure, esp. within a cell, that can be seen only with the high magnification obtainable with an electron microscope. **—ul·tra·struc·tur·al** /-CHərəl/ *adj.*

ul·tra·vi·o·let /ˌəltrəˈvī(ə)lət/ *Physics* ▶*adj.* (of electromagnetic radiation) having a wavelength shorter than that of the violet end of the visible spectrum but longer than that of X-rays. ■ (of equipment or techniques) using or concerned with this radiation: *an ultraviolet telescope.*

▶*n.* the ultraviolet part of the spectrum; ultraviolet radiation.

Ultraviolet radiation spans wavelengths from about 10 nm to 400 nm and is an important component of sunlight although the ozone layer prevents much of it from reaching the earth's surface. While ultraviolet is necessary for the production of vitamin D_2 in the skin, excessive exposure can be harmful, causing skin cancer and genetic mutation.

ul·tra·vi·o·let lamp ▶*n.* a lamp with a bulb that produces ultraviolet light.

ul·tra vi·res /ˌəltrə ˈvīrēz/ ▶*adj.* & *adv. Law* beyond one's legal power or authority: [as *adj.*] *jurisdictional errors render the decision ultra vires.* ▷Latin, literally 'beyond the powers.'

u·lu /ˈo͞oˌlo͞o/ ▶*n.* (*pl.* **u·lus**) a short-handled knife with a broad crescent-shaped blade, used by Eskimo women. ▷Inuit.

ul·u·late /ˈəlyəˌlāt; ˈyo͞ol-/ ▶*v.* [*intrans.*] howl or wail as an expression of strong emotion, typically grief: *women were ululating as the body was laid out.* ▷early 17th cent.: from Latin *ululat-* 'howled, shrieked,' from the verb *ululare*, of imitative origin. **—ul·u·lant** /-lənt/ *adj.* **—ul·u·la·tion** /ˌəlyəˈlāsHən; ˌyo͞ol-/ *n.*

Ul·u·ru /ˌo͞oləˈro͞o/ Aboriginal name for **AYERS ROCK**.

Ul·ya·nov /o͞olˈyänəf/, Vladimir Ilich, see **LENIN**.

Ul·ya·novsk /o͞olˈyänəfsk; -ˌnôfsk/ former name (1924–92) of **SIMBIRSK**.

U·lys·ses /yo͞oˈlisēz/ *Roman Mythology* Roman name for **ODYSSEUS**.

um /(ə)m/ ▶*exclam.* expressing hesitation or a pause in speech: *anyway, um, where was I?* ▷natural utterance: first recorded in English in the early 17th cent.

-um ▶*suffix* variant spelling of **-IUM** (sense 1).

u·ma·mi /o͞oˈmämē/ ▶*n.* a category of taste in food (besides sweet, sour, salt, and bitter), corresponding to the flavor of glutamates, especially monosodium glutamate. ▷Japanese, literally 'deliciousness.'

U·may·yad /o͞oˈmī(y)əd; -ˌ(y)ad/ (also **O·may·yad** /ō-ˈmī-/) ▶*n.* a member of a Muslim dynasty that ruled the Islamic world from AD 660 (or 661) to 750 and Moorish Spain from 756 to 1031. The dynasty claimed descent from Umayya, a distant relative of Muhammad.

▶*adj.* of or relating to this dynasty.

Um·ban·da /o͝omˈbändə/ ▶*n.* a Brazilian folk religion combining elements of macumba, Roman Catholicism, and South American Indian practices. ▷Portuguese.

um·bel /ˈəmbəl/ ▶*n. Botany* a flower cluster in which stalks of nearly equal length spring from a common center and form a flat or curved surface, characteristic of the parsley family. ▷late 16th cent.: from obsolete French *umbelle* or Latin *umbella* 'sunshade,' diminutive of *umbra* (see **UMBRA**). **—um·bel·late** /ˈəmbəlit; -ˌlāt; ˌəmˈbelit/ *adj.*

um·bel·lif·er /ˌəmˈbeləfər/ ▶*n. Botany* a plant of the parsley family. • Family Umbelliferae: numerous genera and species. ▷early 18th cent.: from obsolete French *umbellifère*, from Latin *umbella* 'parasol' + *-fer* 'bearing.' **—um·bel·lif·er·ous** /-bəˈlif(ə)rəs/ *adj.*

um·ber /ˈəmbər/ ▶*n.* **1** a natural pigment resembling but darker than ocher, normally dark yellowish-brown in color (**raw umber**) or dark brown when roasted (**burnt umber**). ■ the color of this pigment. **2** a brownish-gray moth with coloring that resembles tree bark. • Several species in the family Geometridae. ▷mid 16th cent.: from French (*terre d'*)*ombre* or Italian (*terra di*) *ombra*, literally '(earth of) shadow,' from Latin *umbra* 'shadow' or *Umbra* (feminine) 'Umbrian.'

um·bil·i·cal /ˌəmˈbilikəl/ ▶*adj.* relating to or affecting the navel or umbilical cord: *the umbilical artery.* ■ *figurative* extremely close; inseparable: *their umbilical attachment to the state.* ■ (of a pipe, cable, etc.) connecting someone or something to a source of essential supplies: *our standard dive gear, with 300-foot umbilical hoses.*

▶*n.* short for **UMBILICAL CORD**. ▷mid 16th cent.: from French *ombilical*, or based on Latin *umbilicus* (see **UMBILICUS**). **—um·bil·i·cal·ly** /-ik(ə)lē/ *adv.*

um·bil·i·cal cord ▶*n.* a flexible cordlike structure containing blood vessels and attaching a human or other mammalian fetus to the placenta during gestation. ■ a flexible cable, pipe, or other line carrying essential services or supplies.

um·bil·i·cate /ˌəmˈbilikit; -ˌkāt/ ▶*adj. Botany* & *Zoology* (esp. of the cap of a fungus) having a central depression. ■ (of a shell) having an umbilicus.

um·bil·i·co·plas·ty /ˌəmˈbilikōˌplastē/ ▶*n.* (*pl.* **-ties**) plastic surgery performed on the navel, usu. for cosmetic purposes.

um·bil·i·cus /ˌəmˈbilikəs/ ▶*n.* (*pl.* **-ci** /-ˌkī; ˌ-ˌsī; -ˌkē/ or **-cus·es**) *Anatomy* the navel. ■ *Zoology* a depression or hole at the center of the shell whorls of some gastropod mollusks and many ammonites. ■ *Zoology* a hole at each end of the hollow shaft of a feather. ▷late 17th cent.: from Latin: related to Greek *omphalos*, also to **NAVEL**.

um·bles /ˈəmbəlz/ ▶*plural n.* variant spelling of **NUMBLES**.

um·bo /ˈəmbō/ ▶*n.* (*pl.* **um·bo·nes** /ˌəmˈbōnēz/ or **umbos**) **1** *historical* the central boss of a shield. **2** *Biology* a rounded knob or protuberance. ■ *Zoology* the highest point of each valve of a bivalve shell. ■ *Botany* a central swelling on the cap of a mushroom or toadstool. ▷early 18th cent.: from Latin, 'shield boss.' **—um·bo·nal** /ˈəmbənəl; əmˈbōnəl/ *adj.* (*chiefly Zoology*). **—um·bo·nate** /ˈəmbənit; -ˌnāt/ *adj.* (*chiefly Botany*).

um·bra /ˈəmbrə/ ▶*n.* (*pl.* **-bras** or **-brae** /-ˌbrē; -ˌbrī/) the fully shaded inner region of a shadow cast by an opaque object, esp. the area on the earth or moon experiencing the total phase of an eclipse. Compare with **PENUMBRA**. ■ *Astronomy* the dark central part of a sunspot. ■ *chiefly poetic/literary* shadow or darkness. ▷late 16th cent. (denoting a phantom or ghost): from Latin, literally 'shade.' **—um·bral** *adj.*

um·brage /ˈəmbrij/ ▶*n.* **1** offense or annoyance: *she **took umbrage at** his remarks.* **2** *archaic* shade or shadow, esp. as cast by trees. ▷late Middle English (sense 2): from Old French, from Latin *umbra* 'shadow.' An early sense was 'shadowy outline,' giving rise to 'ground for suspicion,' whence the current notion of 'offense.' **—um·bra·geous** /ˌəmˈbrājəs/ *adj.*

um·brel·la /ˌəmˈbrelə/ ▶*n.* **1** a device consisting of a circular canopy of cloth on a folding metal frame supported by a central rod, used as protection against rain or sometimes sun. ■ *figurative* a protecting force or influence: *the American nuclear umbrella over the west.* ■ a screen of fighter aircraft or antiaircraft artillery. ■ [usu. as *adj.*] a thing that includes or contains many different elements or parts: *an umbrella organization.* **2** *Zoology* the gelatinous disk of a jellyfish, which it contracts and expands to move through the water. ▷early 17th cent.: from Italian *ombrella*, diminutive of *ombra* 'shade,' from Latin *umbra* (see **UMBRA**). **—um·brel·laed** *adj.* **—um·brel·la·like** /-ˌlīk/ *adj.*

um·brel·la bird (also **um·brel·la·bird**) ▶*n.* a large tropical American cotinga with black plumage, a radiating crest, and typically long wattles. • Genus *Cephalopterus*, family Cotingidae: three species.

um·brel·la pine ▶*n.* **1** another term for **STONE PINE**. **2** a tall Japanese evergreen conifer related to the redwoods, with leaves growing in umbrellalike whorls. • *Sciadopitys verticillata*, family Taxodiaceae.

um·brel·la plant ▶*n.* a tropical Old World sedge that has stiff green stems, each terminating in a whorl of arching green leaflike bracts. It is commonly grown as a houseplant. • *Cyperus alternifolius* (or *involucratus*), family Cyperaceae.

um·brel·la tree ▶*n.* either of two small trees or shrubs with leaves or leaflets arranged in umbrellalike whorls: • (also **um·brel·la mag·no·lia**) a North American magnolia (*Magnolia tripetala*, family Magnoliaceae). • an Australian plant that is widely grown elsewhere as a houseplant (*Schefflera actinophylla*, family Araliaceae).

Um·bri·a /ˈəmbrēə/ a region in central Italy, in the valley of the Tiber River; capital, Perugia.

Um·bri·an /ˈəmbrēən/ ▶*adj.* of or relating to Umbria, its people, or their languages.

▶*n.* **1** a native or inhabitant of Umbria, esp. in pre-Roman times. **2** an extinct Italic language of central Italy, related to Oscan and surviving in inscriptions mainly of the 2nd and 1st centuries BC.

Um·bri·el /ˈəmbrēəl/ *Astronomy* a satellite of Uranus, the thirteenth closest to the planet, discovered in 1851, having a diameter of 739 miles (1,190 km). ▷named after a sprite in *The Rape of the Lock* by Alexander Pope.

Um·bun·du /əmˈbo͝onˌdo͞o/ ▶ see **MBUNDU**.

u·mi·ak /ˈo͞omēˌak/ ▶*n.* an Eskimo open boat made with skin stretched over a wooden frame. ▷from Inuit *umiaq*.

um·laut /ˈo͝omˌlout/ *Linguistics* ▶*n.* a mark (¨) used over a vowel, as in German or Hungarian, to indicate a different vowel quality, usually fronting or rounding. ■ (esp. in Germanic languages) the process by which a back vowel becomes front in the context of another front vowel, resulting, e.g., in the differences between modern German *Mann* and *Männer* or (after loss of the inflection) English *man* and *men*.

▶*v.* [*trans.*] modify (a form or a sound) by using an umlaut. ▷mid 19th cent.: from German *Umlaut*, from *um* 'about' + *Laut* 'sound.'

um·ma /ˈo͝omə/ (also **um·mah**) ▶*n.* the whole community of Muslims bound together by ties of religion. ▷Arabic, literally 'people, community.'

Umm al Qai·wain /ˈo͝om äl kīˈwīn; al/ one of the seven member states of the United Arab Emirates; pop. 35,000.

ump /əmp/ ▸*n.* & *v. informal* short for UMPIRE. ▷early 20th cent.: abbreviation.

umph ▸*n.* variant spelling of OOMPH.

um·pire /ˈəmˌpī(ə)r/ ▸*n.* (in some sports) an official who watches a game or match closely to enforce the rules and arbitrate on matters arising from the play. ■ a person chosen to arbitrate between contending parties.
▸*v.* [*intrans.*] act as an umpire. ■ [*trans.*] act as umpire in (a game or match). ▷late Middle English (originally as *noumpere*) (denoting an arbitrator): from Old French *nonper* 'not equal.' The *n* was lost by wrong division of *a noumpere*; compare with ADDER[1]. **—um·pir·age** /-ˌpīrij/ *n.* **—um·pire·ship** /-ˌSHip/ *n.*

ump·teen /ˈəm(p)ˌtēn/ *informal* ▸*cardinal number* indefinitely many; a lot of: *you need umpteen pieces of identification to cash a check.* ▷early 20th cent.: humorous formation based on -TEEN. **—ump·teenth** /-ˌtēnTH/ *ordinal number*.

um·rah /ˈo͝omˌrä/ ▸*n.* the nonmandatory lesser pilgrimage made by Muslims to Mecca, which may be performed at any time of the year. ▷Arabic *ʻumra.*

Um·ta·li /o͝omˈtälē/ former name (until 1982) of MUTARE.

UMTS ▸*abbr.* Universal Mobile Telephone System.

u·mu /ˈo͞omo͞o/ ▸*n.* a Maori oven consisting of a hollow in the earth in which food is cooked on heated stones. ▷Maori.

Um·welt /ˈo͝omˌvelt/ ▸*n.* (*pl.* **-welt·en** /-ˌvelt(ə)n/) (in ethology) the world as it is experienced by a particular organism. ▷German, literally 'environment.'

UN ▸*abbr.* United Nations.

un-[1] ▸*prefix* **1** (added to adjectives, participles, and their derivatives) denoting the absence of a quality or state; not: *unabashed* | *unacademic* | *unrepeatable.* ■ the reverse of (usually with an implication of approval or disapproval, or with another special connotation): *unselfish* | *unprepossessing* | *unworldly.* **2** (added to nouns) a lack of: *unrest* | *untruth.* ▷Old English, of Germanic origin; from an Indo-European root shared by Latin *in-* and Greek *a-*.

USAGE The prefixes **un-** and **non-** both mean 'lacking' or 'not,' but there is a distinction in terms of perspective. The prefix **un-** tends to be stronger and less neutral than **non-**. Consider, for example, the differences between **unacademic** and **nonacademic**,as in *his language was refreshingly unacademic; a nonacademic life suits him.*

un-[2] ▸*prefix* added to verbs: **1** denoting the reversal or cancellation of an action or state: *untie* | *unsettle.* **2** denoting deprivation, separation, or reduction to a lesser state: *unmask* | *unman.* ■ denoting release: *unburden* | *unhand.* ▷Old English *un-*, *on-*, of Germanic origin; related to Dutch *ont-* and German *ent-*.

'un /ən/ *informal* ▸*contraction of* one: *a good 'un* | *a wild 'un.*

un·a·bashed /ˌənəˈbasHt/ ▸*adj.* not embarrassed, disconcerted, or ashamed: *he was unabashed by the furor his words provoked.* **—un·a·bash·ed·ly** /-ˈbasHədlē/ *adv.*

un·a·bat·ed /ˌənəˈbātid/ ▸*adj.* without any reduction in intensity or strength: *the storm was raging unabated.* **—un·a·bat·ed·ly** *adv.*

un·a·ble /ˌənˈābəl/ ▸*adj.* [with *infinitive*] lacking the skill, means, or opportunity to do something: *she was unable to conceal her surprise.*

U·na·bomb·er /ˈyo͞onəˌbämər/ ▸the name given by the FBI to Ted Kaczynski, the elusive perpetrator of a series of bombings (1975–1995) in the U.S. that killed three and wounded 23. The victims were mainly academics in technological disciplines, airline executives, and executives in businesses thought to affect the environment.

un·a·bridged /ˌənəˈbrijd/ ▸*adj.* (of a text) not cut or shortened; complete: *an unabridged edition.*

un·ac·a·dem·ic /ˌənˌakəˈdemik/ ▸*adj.* not adopting or characteristic of a scholarly approach or language: *his language was refreshingly unacademic.* ■ (of a person) not suited or drawn to academic study.

un·ac·cept·a·ble /ˌənəkˈseptəbəl/ ▸*adj.* not satisfactory or allowable: *unacceptable behavior.* **—un·ac·cept·a·bil·i·ty** /-ˌseptəˈbilətē/ *n.* **—un·ac·cept·a·bly** /-blē/ *adv.*

un·ac·com·pa·nied /ˌənəˈkəmp(ə)nēd/ ▸*adj.* having no companion or escort: *no unaccompanied children allowed.* ■ (of a piece of music) sung or played without instrumental accompaniment: *an unaccompanied violin elegy.* ■ (of a state, condition, or event) taking place without something specified taking place at the same time: *the political change was unaccompanied by social change.*

un·ac·com·plished /ˌənəˈkämplisHt/ ▸*adj.* **1** showing little skill. **2** not carried out.

un·ac·count·a·ble /ˌənəˈkountəbəl/ ▸*adj.* **1** unable to be explained: *a strange and unaccountable fact.* ■ (of a person or their behavior) unpredictable and strange. **2** (of a person, organization, or institution) not required or expected to justify actions or decisions; not responsible for results or consequences. **—un·ac·count·a·bil·i·ty** /-ˌkountəˈbilətē/ *n.* **—un·ac·count·a·bly** /-blē/ *adv.*

un·ac·count·ed /ˌənəˈkountid/ ▸*adj.* (**unaccounted for**) not included in (an account or calculation) through being lost or disregarded: *a substantial amount of money is unaccounted for.*

un·ac·cred·it·ed /ˌənəˈkreditid/ ▸*adj.* not recognized as having attained an acceptable standard: *a mail-order degree from an unaccredited correspondence school.*

un·ac·cus·tomed /ˌənəˈkəstəmd/ ▸*adj.* not familiar or usual; out of the ordinary: *they finished their supper with unaccustomed speed.* ■ [*predic.*] (**unaccustomed to**) not familiar with or used to: *the visitors were unaccustomed to country roads.* **—un·ac·cus·tomed·ly** *adv.*

u·na cor·da /ˈo͞onə ˈkôrdə/ *Music* ▸*adv.* & *adj.* (esp. as a direction) using the soft pedal on a piano.
▸*n.* a device in a piano that shifts the mechanism slightly to one side when the soft pedal is depressed, so that the hammers do not strike all of the strings when sounding each note and the tone is therefore quieter. ▷Italian, literally 'one string.'

un·a·dapt·ed /ˌənəˈdaptəd/ ▸*adj.* not adapted: *animals unadapted for surviving shocks.*

un·ad·dressed /ˌənəˈdrest/ ▸*adj.* **1** not considered or dealt with: *wider questions remain unaddressed.* **2** (of a letter or other item sent in the mail) having no address written or printed on it.

un·ad·just·ed /ˌənəˈjəstid/ ▸*adj.* (esp. of figures or statistics) not adjusted or refined: *the unadjusted jobless total increased last month.*

un·a·dorned /ˌənəˈdôrnd/ ▸*adj.* not adorned; plain.

un·a·dul·ter·at·ed /ˌənəˈdəltəˌrātid/ ▸*adj.* not mixed or diluted with any different or extra elements; complete and absolute: *pure, unadulterated jealousy.* ■ (of food or drink) having no inferior added substances; pure: *unadulterated whole-milk yogurt.*

un·ad·ver·tised /ˌənˈadvərˌtīzd/ ▸*adj.* existing or taking place without being made public.

un·ad·vis·a·ble /ˌənədˈvīzəbəl/ ▸*adj.* another term for INADVISABLE.

un·ad·vis·ed·ly /ˌənədˈvīzidlē/ ▸*adv.* in an unwise or rash manner: *they enter into nothing lightly or unadvisedly.*

un·aes·thet·ic /ˌənesˈTHetik/ ▸*adj.* not visually pleasing; unattractive. ■ not motivated by aesthetic principles.

un·af·fect·ed /ˌənəˈfektid/ ▸*adj.* **1** feeling or showing no effects or changes: *the walks are suitable only for people who are unaffected by vertigo.* **2** (of a person) without artificiality or insincerity: *his manner was natural and unaffected.* **—un·af·fect·ed·ly** *adv.* **—un·af·fect·ed·ness** *n.*

un·af·ford·a·ble /ˌənəˈfôrdəbəl/ ▸*adj.* too expensive to be afforded by the average person: *medical care has become unaffordable.*

un·aid·ed /ˌənˈādid/ ▸*adj.* needing or having no assistance; without help: *she can no longer walk unaided.*

un·aired /ˌənˈe(ə)rd/ ▸*adj.* not previously broadcasted: *a rare unaired TV pilot.*

Un·a·las·ka /ˌənəˈlaskə/ an island in the eastern Aleutian Islands of Alaska, on which the naval base of Dutch Harbor and the city of Unalaska (pop. 4,283) are the chief settlements.

un·al·ien·a·ble /ˌənˈālyənəbəl; -ˈālēə-/ ▸*adj.* another term for INALIENABLE.

un·al·le·vi·at·ed /ˌənəˈlēvēˌātid/ ▸*adj.* not alleviated; relentless: *a time of unalleviated misery.*

un·al·loyed /ˌənəˈloid/ ▸*adj.* (of metal) not alloyed; pure: *unalloyed copper.* ■ (chiefly of emotions) complete and unreserved: *unalloyed delight.*

un·al·ter·a·ble /ˌənˈôlt(ə)rəbəl/ ▸*adj.* not able to be changed. **—un·al·ter·a·ble·ness** *n.* **—un·al·ter·a·bly** /-blē/ *adv.*

un·al·tered /ˌənˈôltərd/ ▸*adj.* remaining the same; unchanged: *many buildings survive unaltered.*

un·am·big·u·ous /ˌənamˈbigyəwəs/ ▸*adj.* not open to more than one interpretation: *instructions should be unambiguous.* **—un·am·bi·gu·i·ty** /-ˌambəˈgyo͞oətē/ *n.* **—un·am·big·u·ous·ly** *adv.*

un-A·mer·i·can /ˌənəˈmerikən/ ▸*adj.* not in accordance with American characteristics: *such un-American concepts as subsidized medicine.* ■ *chiefly historical* contrary to the interests of the U.S. and therefore treasonable. **—un-A·mer·i·can·ism** /-ˌnizəm/ *n.*

U·na·mi /o͞oˈnämē/ ▸*n.* see DELAWARE[2] (sense 2). ▷the name in Unami.

un·a·mused /ˌənəˈmyo͞ozd/ ▸*adj.* not responding in a positive way to something intended to be amusing; feeling somewhat annoyed or disapproving: *she was unamused by some of the things written about her.*

un·an·a·lyz·a·ble /ˌənˈanlˌīzəbəl/ (*Brit.* **un·an·a·lys·a·ble**) ▸*adj.* not able to be explained or interpreted through methodical examination: *unanalyzable recorded data.*

un·an·a·lyzed /ˌənˈanlˌīzd/ (*Brit.* **un·an·a·lysed**) ▸*adj.* not revealed, explained, or interpreted through methodical examination.

un·a·neled /ˌənəˈnēld/ ▸*adj. archaic* having died without receiving extreme unction; unanointed.

U·na·ni /yo͞oˈnänē/ ▸*n.* [usu. as *adj.*] a system of medicine practiced in parts of India, thought to be derived via medieval Muslim physicians from Byzantine Greece. It is sometimes contrasted with the Ayurvedic system. ▷from Arabic *Yūnānī* 'Greek.'

u·nan·i·mous /yo͞oˈnanəməs/ ▸*adj.* (of two or more people) fully in agreement: *the doctors were unanimous in their diagnoses.* ■ (of an opinion, decision, or vote) held or carried by everyone involved. ▷early 17th cent.: from Latin *unanimus* (from *unus* 'one' + *animus* 'mind') + -OUS. **—u·na·nim·i·ty** /ˌyo͞onəˈnimətē/ *n.* **—u·nan·i·mous·ly** *adv.*

un·an·nounced /ˌənəˈnounst/ ▸*adj.* not made known; not publicized: *the company has justified its recent unannounced addition of chlorine to its water.* ■ without previous notice or arrangement and therefore unexpected: *he arrived unannounced.*

un·an·swer·a·ble /ˌənˈans(ə)rəbəl/ ▸*adj.* unable to be answered: *unanswerable questions concerning our own mortality.* ■ unable to be disclaimed or proved wrong: *the case for abolishing the fee is unanswerable.* **—un·an·swer·a·bly** /-blē/ *adv.*

un·an·swered /ˌənˈansərd/ ▸*adj.* not answered or responded to: *unanswered letters.* ■ without any scoring in return by the opposition: *the Hornets scored 34 unanswered points in the second half.*

un·an·tic·i·pat·ed /ˌənanˈtisəˌpātid/ ▸*adj.* not expected or predicted.

un·a·pol·o·get·ic /ˌənəˌpäləˈjetik/ ▸*adj.* not acknowledging or expressing regret: *he remained unapologetic about his decision.* **—un·a·pol·o·get·i·cal·ly** /-ik(ə)lē/ *adv.*

un·ap·peal·a·ble /ˌənəˈpēləbəl/ ▸*adj. Law* (of a case or ruling) not able to be referred to a higher court for review.

un·ap·peas·a·ble /ˌənəˈpēzəbəl/ ▸*adj.* not able to be pacified, placated, or satisfied.

un·ap·pe·tiz·ing /ˌənˈapəˌtīziNG/ ▸*adj.* not inviting or attractive; unwholesome. **—un·ap·pe·tiz·ing·ly** *adv.*

un·ap·pre·ci·at·ed /ˌənəˈprēsHēˌātid/ ▸*adj.* not fully understood, recognized, or valued: *she had been brought up in a family where she felt unappreciated and undervalued.*

un·ap·pre·ci·a·tive /ˌənəˈprēsH(ē)ətiv/ ▸*adj.* not fully understanding, recognizing, or valuing something: *one daughter of an unappreciative mother says, "Nothing I ever did for her was enough."*

un·ap·proach·a·ble /ˌənəˈprōCHəbəl/ ▸*adj.* (of a person or institution) not welcoming or friendly. ■ *archaic* (of a place) remote and inaccessible. **—un·ap·proach·a·bil·i·ty** /-ˌprōCHəˈbilətē/ *n.* **—un·ap·proach·a·bly** /-blē/ *adv.*

un·ap·pro·pri·at·ed /ˌənəˈprōprēˌātid/ ▸*adj.* not allocated, assigned, or taken into possession: *vacant and unappropriated land.*

un·ap·proved /ˌənəˈpro͞ovd/ ▸*adj.* not officially accepted or sanctioned: *they deposit waste on unapproved sites.*

un·ar·gu·a·ble /ˌənˈärgyəwəbəl/ ▸*adj.* not open to disagreement; indisputable: *unarguable proof of conspiracy.* ■ not able to be discussed or asserted. **—un·ar·gu·a·bly** /-blē/ *adv.*

un·armed /ˌənˈärmd/ ▸*adj.* not equipped with or carrying weapons: *he was shooting unarmed civilians.*

un·ar·tic·u·lat·ed /ˌənärˈtikyəˌlātid/ ▸*adj.* not mentioned or coherently expressed: *repressed hurt and previously unarticulated anger are explored.*

u·na·ry /ˈyo͞onərē/ ▸*adj.* (esp. of a mathematical operation) consisting of or involving a single component or element.

Pronunciation Key ə *ago*; ər *over*; ˈə or ˌə *up*; ˈər or ˌər *fur*; a *hat*; ā *rate*; ä *car*; CH *chew*; e *let*; ē *see*; e(ə)r *air*; i *fit*; ī *by*; i(ə)r *ear*; NG *sing*; ō *go*; ô *for*; oi *boy*; o͝o *good*; o͞o *goo*; ou *out*; SH *she*; TH *thin*; T͟H *then*; (h)w *why*; ZH *vision*

un·ab·sorbed *adj.*
un·ac·cent·ed *adj.*
un·ac·com·mo·dat·ing *adj.*
un·ac·knowl·edged *adj.*
un·ac·quaint·ed *adj.*
un·a·dapt·a·ble *adj.*
un·a·dapt·ed *adj.*
un·ad·ja·cent *adj.*
un·ad·ven·tur·ous *adj.*
un·ad·ven·tur·ous·ly *adv.*
un·af·fec·tion·ate *adj.*
un·af·fil·i·at·ed *adj.*
un·a·fraid *adj.*
un·ag·gres·sive *adj.*
un·a·ligned *adj.*
un·a·like *adj. & adv.*
un·a·live *adj.*
un·al·lied *adj.*
un·al·low·a·ble *adj.*
un·a·mazed *adj.*
un·am·bi·tious *adj.*
un·am·bi·tious·ly *adv.*
un·am·bi·tious·ness *n.*
un·am·biv·a·lent *adj.*
un·am·biv·a·lent·ly *adv.*
un·a·mi·a·ble *adj.*
un·am·pli·fied *adj.*
un·an·chored *adj.*
un·ap·par·ent *adj.*
un·ap·peal·ing *adj.*
un·ap·peal·ing·ly *adv.*
un·ap·peased *adj.*
un·ap·plied *adj.*
un·ap·pre·hend·ed *adj.*
un·apt *adj.*
un·apt·ly *adv.*
un·apt·ness *n.*
un·ar·rest·ing *adj.*
un·ar·rest·ing·ly *adv.*
un·ar·tis·tic *adj.*
un·ar·tis·ti·cal·ly *adv.*
un·as·cer·tain·a·ble *adj.*
un·as·cer·tained *adj.*
un·as·ser·tive *adj.*
un·as·ser·tive·ly *adv.*
un·as·ser·tive·ness *n.*
un·as·sign·a·ble *adj.*
un·as·signed *adj.*
un·as·so·ci·at·ed *adj.*
un·a·toned *adj.*
un·at·trac·tive *adj.*
un·at·trac·tive·ly *adv.*
un·at·trac·tive·ness *n.*
un·au·dit·ed *adj.*
un·au·then·ti·cat·ed *adj.*
un·au·thor·ized *adj.*
un·a·vail·a·ble *adj.*
un·a·vail·a·bil·i·ty *n.*
un·a·vail·a·ble·ness *n.*
un·a·vowed *adj.*
un·awed *adj.*
un·beau·ti·ful *adj.*
un·beau·ti·ful·ly *adv.*
un·be·fit·ting *adj.*
un·be·fit·ting·ly *adv.*
un·be·fit·ting·ness *n.*
un·be·hold·en *adj.*
un·be·loved *adj.*
un·bid·da·ble *adj.*
un·bleached *adj.*
un·blend·ed *adj.*
un·book·ish *adj.*
un·brand·ed *adj.*
un·breach·a·ble *adj.*
un·break·a·ble *adj.*
un·breath·a·ble *adj.*
un·brib·a·ble *adj.*
un·bridge·a·ble *adj.*
un·bruised *adj.*
un·bur·ied *adj.*
un·burned *adj.*
un·burnt *adj.*
un·busi·ness·like *adj.*
un·caged *adj.*
un·can·did *adj.*
un·ca·non·i·cal *adj.*
un·ca·non·i·cal·ly *adv.*
un·car·pet·ed *adj.*
un·cashed *adj.*
un·catch·a·ble *adj.*
un·caught *adj.*
un·cen·sored *adj.*
un·cen·sured *adj.*
un·change·a·ble *adj. & n.*
un·change·a·bil·i·ty *n.*
un·change·a·ble·ness *n.*
un·change·a·bly *adv.*
un·changed *adj.*
un·chang·ing *adj.*
un·chang·ing·ly *adv.*
un·chap·er·oned *adj.*
un·char·ac·ter·is·tic *adj.*
un·char·ac·ter·is·ti·cal·ly *adv.*
un·char·is·mat·ic *adj.*
un·char·tered *adj.*
un·chiv·al·rous *adj.*
un·chiv·al·rous·ly *adv.*
un·cho·sen *adj.*
un·clas·si·fi·a·ble *adj.*
un·closed *adj.*
un·clut·tered *adj.*
un·coat·ed *adj.*
un·combed *adj.*
un·come·ly *adj.*
un·com·fy *adj.*
un·com·pan·ion·a·ble *adj.*
un·com·plet·ed *adj.*
un·com·plexed *adj.*
un·com·pli·men·ta·ry *adj.*
un·com·pound·ed *adj.*
un·con·clud·ed *adj.*
un·con·fi·dent *adj.*
un·con·fi·dent·ly *adv.*
un·con·gen·ial *adj.*
un·con·jec·tur·a·ble *adj.*
un·con·quered *adj.*
un·con·se·crat·ed *adj.*
un·con·sent·ing *adj.*
un·con·strained *adj.*
un·con·strain·ed·ly *adv.*
un·con·strict·ed *adj.*
un·con·sult·ed *adj.*
un·con·tam·i·nat·ed *adj.*
un·con·ten·tious *adj.*
un·con·tra·dict·ed *adj.*
un·con·trived *adj.*
un·con·trol·la·ble *adj. & n.*
un·con·trol·la·ble·ness *n.*
un·con·trol·la·bly *adv.*
un·con·tro·ver·sial *adj.*
un·con·tro·ver·sial·ly *adv.*
un·cooked *adj.*
un·cop·i·a·ble *adj.*
un·cor·rect·ed *adj.*
un·cor·rob·o·rat·ed *adj.*
un·cor·rupt·ed *adj.*
un·cre·a·tive *adj.*
un·cropped *adj.*
un·crowd·ed *adj.*
un·crush·a·ble *adj.*
un·crushed *adj.*
un·culled *adj.*
un·cul·tured *adj.*
un·curbed *adj.*
un·cured *adj.*
un·cur·tailed *adj.*
un·cur·tained *adj.*
un·dam·aged *adj.*
un·dec·o·rat·ed *adj.*
un·de·feat·ed *adj.*
un·de·fend·ed *adj.*
un·de·liv·ered *adj.*
un·de·liv·er·a·ble *adj.*
un·de·mand·ing *adj.*
un·dem·o·crat·ic *adj.*
un·dem·o·crat·i·cal·ly *adv.*
un·dem·on·strat·ed *adj.*
un·de·nied *adj.*
un·de·nom·i·na·tion·al *adj.*
un·dent·ed *adj.*
un·de·pend·a·ble *adj.*
un·de·signed *adj.*
un·de·sign·ed·ly *adv.*
un·de·sir·ous *adj.*
un·de·tect·a·ble *adj.*
un·de·tect·a·bil·i·ty *n.*
un·de·tect·a·bly *adv.*
un·de·tect·ed *adj.*
un·de·terred *adj.*
un·de·vi·at·ing *adj.*
un·de·vi·at·ing·ly *adv.*
un·di·ag·nosed *adj.*
un·di·gest·ed *adj.*
un·dig·ni·fied *adj.*
un·di·lut·ed *adj.*
un·di·min·ished *adj.*
un·dis·cern·ing *adj.*
un·dis·charged *adj.*
un·dis·ci·plined *adj.*
un·dis·closed *adj.*
un·dis·cov·er·a·ble *adj.*
un·dis·cov·ered *adj.*
un·dis·crim·i·nat·ing *adj.*
un·dis·cussed *adj.*
un·dis·solved *adj.*
un·dis·tort·ed *adj.*
un·dis·trib·ut·ed *adj.*
un·dis·turbed *adj.*
un·do·mes·ti·cat·ed *adj.*
un·drained *adj.*
un·dra·mat·ic *adj.*
un·drawn *adj.*
un·drink·a·ble *adj.*
un·du·ti·ful *adj.*
un·du·ti·ful·ly *adv.*
un·du·ti·ful·ness *n.*
un·dyed *adj.*
un·eat·a·ble *adj.*
un·eat·en *adj.*
un·ed·it·ed *adj.*
un·em·bar·rassed *adj.*
un·em·bel·lished *adj.*
un·em·phat·ic *adj.*
un·em·phat·i·cal·ly *adv.*
un·en·closed *adj.*
un·en·cum·bered *adj.*
un·en·dowed *adj.*
un·en·force·a·ble *adj.*
un·en·gaged *adj.*
un·en·joy·a·ble *adj.*
un·en·light·ened *adj.*
un·en·light·en·ing *adj.*
un·en·light·en·ment *n.*
un·en·ter·pris·ing *adj.*
un·en·thu·si·as·tic *adj.*
un·en·thu·si·as·ti·cal·ly *adv.*
un·en·vied *adj.*
un·e·quipped *adj.*
un·es·tab·lished *adj.*
un·e·van·gel·i·cal *adj.*
un·e·vent·ful *adj.*
un·e·vent·ful·ly *adv.*
un·e·vent·ful·ness *n.*
un·ex·am·ined *adj.*
un·ex·cit·ing *adj.*
un·ex·e·cut·ed *adj.*
un·ex·er·cised *adj.*
un·ex·haust·ed *adj.*
un·ex·plod·ed *adj.*
un·ex·pur·gat·ed *adj.*
un·fad·ing *adj.*
un·fad·ing·ly *adv.*
un·fal·ter·ing *adj.*
un·fal·ter·ing·ly *adv.*
un·fash·ion·a·ble *adj.*
un·fash·ion·a·ble·ness *n.*
un·fash·ion·a·bly *adv.*
un·fa·ther·ly *adj.*
un·fa·ther·li·ness *n.*
un·fath·om·a·ble *adj.*
un·fath·om·a·ble·ness *n.*
un·fath·om·a·bly *adv.*
un·fath·omed *adj.*
un·fazed *adj.*
un·fea·si·ble *adj.*
un·fea·si·bil·i·ty *n.*
un·fea·si·bly *adv.*
un·fed *adj.*
un·fem·i·nine *adj.*
un·fem·i·nin·i·ty *n.*
un·fenced *adj.*
un·fer·ment·ed *adj.*
un·fer·tile *adj.*
un·fer·ti·lized *adj.*
un·filled *adj.*
un·flat·ter·ing *adj.*
un·flat·ter·ing·ly *adv.*
un·ford·a·ble *adj.*
un·fore·see·a·ble *adj.*
un·fore·seen *adj.*
un·for·giv·en *adj.*
un·for·got·ten *adj.*
un·for·mu·lat·ed *adj.*
un·for·ti·fied *adj.*
un·framed *adj.*
un·fund·ed *adj.*
un·fuss·y *adj.*
un·fuss·i·ly *adv.*
un·gain·say·a·ble *adj.*
un·gal·lant *adj.*
un·gal·lant·ly *adv.*
un·gen·er·ous *adj.*
un·gen·er·ous·ly *adv.*
un·gen·er·ous·ness *n.*
un·gen·ial *adj.*
un·gen·tle *adj.*

---

un·a·shamed /ˌənəˈsHāmd/ ▸*adj.* expressed or acting openly and without guilt or embarrassment: *an unashamed emotionalism.* —**un·a·sham·ed·ly** /-ˈsHāmidlē/ *adv.* —**un·a·sham·ed·ness** /-ˈsHām(i)dnis/ *n.*

un·asked /ˌənˈas(k)t/ ▸*adj.* (of a question) not asked. ■ (of an action) not invited or requested: *the memories he had poured unasked into her head.* ■ **(unasked for)** not sought or requested: *unasked-for advice.*

un·as·sail·a·ble /ˌənəˈsāləbəl/ ▸*adj.* unable to be attacked, questioned, or defeated: *an unassailable lead.* —**un·as·sail·a·bil·i·ty** /-ˌsāləˈbilətē/ *n.* —**un·as·sail·a·bly** /-blē/ *adv.*

un·as·signed /ˌənəˈsīnd/ ▸*adj.* not allocated or set aside for a specific purpose: *as cellular phones proliferate, the number of unassigned numbers is being exhausted.*

un·as·sim·i·lat·ed /ˌənəˈsiməˌlātid/ ▸*adj.* (esp. of a people, an idea, or a culture) not absorbed or integrated into a wider society or culture. —**un·as·sim·i·la·ble** /-ləbəl/ *adj.*

un·as·sist·ed /ˌənəˈsistid/ ▸*adj.* not helped by anyone or anything: *medically unassisted births | I could never find the place unassisted.* ■ (of a play in a team sport) done by one player, without an assist from another player: *he made two unassisted tackles.*

un·as·suaged /ˌənəˈswājd/ ▸*adj.* not soothed or relieved: *her unassuaged grief.* —**un·as·suage·a·ble** /-əˈswājəbəl/ *adj.*

un·as·sum·ing /ˌənəˈso͞omiNG/ ▸*adj.* not pretentious or arrogant; modest: *he was an unassuming and kindly man.* —**un·as·sum·ing·ly** *adv.* —**un·as·sum·ing·ness** *n.*

un·at·tached /ˌənəˈtacHt/ ▸*adj.* not working for or belonging to a particular body or organization. ■ not fastened to anything; loose. ■ not married or having an established partner; single.

un·at·tain·a·ble /ˌənəˈtānəbəl/ ▸*adj.* not able to be reached or achieved: *an unattainable goal.* —**un·at·tain·a·ble·ness** *n.* —**un·at·tain·a·bly** /-blē/ *adv.*

un·at·tempt·ed /ˌənəˈtem(p)tid/ ▸*adj.* not previously attempted or embarked upon; untried.

un·at·tend·ed /ˌənəˈtendid/ ▸*adj.* not noticed or dealt with: *her behavior went unnoticed and* ***unattended to.*** ■ not supervised or looked after: *it is not acceptable for parents to leave children unattended at that age.*

un·at·test·ed /ˌənəˈtestid/ ▸*adj.* not existing in any documented form: *if a will contains unattested changes, the changes will be disregarded | although large masonry instruments were not unattested in the world, they were constructed infrequently.* ■ *Linguistics* denoting a form or usage or pronunciation of a word for which there is no evidence: *logically possible but unattested word-formation.*

un·at·trib·ut·ed /ˌənəˈtribyətid/ ▸*adj.* (of a quotation, story, or work of art) not ascribed to any source; of unknown or unpublished provenance. —**un·at·trib·ut·a·ble** /-yətəbəl/ *adj.* —**un·at·trib·ut·a·bly** /-yətəblē/ *adv.*

un·au·then·tic /ˌənôˈTHentik/ ▸*adj.* not made or done in a way that reflects tradition or faithfully resembles an original. —**un·au·then·ti·cal·ly** /-ik(ə)lē/ *adv.*

un·a·vail·ing /ˌənəˈvāliNG/ ▸*adj.* achieving little or nothing; ineffective: *their efforts were unavailing.* —**un·a·vail·ing·ly** *adv.*

un·a·void·a·ble /ˌənəˈvoidəbəl/ ▸*adj.* not able to be avoided, prevented, or ignored; inevitable: *the natural and unavoidable consequences of growing old.* —**un·a·void·a·bil·i·ty** /-ˌvoidəˈbilətē/ *n.* —**un·a·void·a·bly** /-blē/ *adv.*

un·a·wak·ened /ˌənəˈwākənd/ ▸*adj.* not aware of or roused to particular sensations or feelings.

un·a·ware /ˌənəˈwe(ə)r/ ▸*adj.* [*predic.*] having no knowledge of a situation or fact: *they were* ***unaware of*** *his absence.*
▸*adv.* variant of UNAWARES. —**un·a·ware·ness** *n.*

un·a·wares /ˌənəˈwe(ə)rz/ (also **un·a·ware**) ▸*adv.* without being aware of a situation: *it will be flagged so that people don't stumble on it unawares.* ▷mid 16th cent.: from UNAWARE + -S³.
▸*PHRASE* □ **catch** (or **take**) **someone unawares** take someone by surprise: *this morning she caught me unawares before I'd had a single cup of coffee.*

un·backed /ˌənˈbakt/ ▸*adj.* **1** having no financial, material, or moral support. **2** (of a horse) having no backers in a race. **3** having no backing layer: *unbacked hessian.*

un·bal·ance /ˌənˈbaləns/ ▸*v.* [*trans.*] make (someone or something) unsteady so that they tip or fall. ■ upset or disturb the equilibrium of (a state of affairs or someone's state of mind): *this sharing can often unbalance even the closest of relationships.*
▸*n.* a lack of symmetry, balance, or stability.

un·bal·anced /ˌənˈbalənst/ ▸*adj.* not keeping or showing an even balance; not evenly distributed. ■ (of a person) emotionally or mentally disturbed. ■ (of an account) not giving accurate, fair, or equal coverage to all aspects; partial: *this may give an unbalanced impression of the competition.*

un·ban /ˌənˈban/ ▸*v.* (**-banned, -ban·ning**) [*trans.*] remove a ban on (a person, group, or activity).

un·banked /ˌənˈbaNGkt/ ▸*adj.* not served by a bank or similar financial institution.

un·bar /ˌənˈbär/ ▸*v.* (**-barred, -bar·ring**) [*trans.*] remove the bars from (a gate or door); unlock.

un·bear·a·ble /ˌənˈbe(ə)rəbəl/ ▸*adj.* not able to be endured or tolerated: *the heat was getting unbearable.* —**un·bear·a·ble·ness** *n.* —**un·bear·a·bly** /-blē/ *adv.* [as *submodifier*] *it was unbearably hot.*

un·beat·a·ble /ˌənˈbētəbəl/ ▸*adj.* not able to be defeated or exceeded in a contest or commercial market: *the shop sells bikes at unbeatable prices.* ■ extremely good; outstanding: *views from the patio are unbeatable.* —**un·beat·a·bly** /-blē/ *adv.*

un·beat·en /ˌənˈbētn/ ▸*adj.* not defeated or surpassed: *they were the only team to remain unbeaten.* ■ not stirred or whipped: *the white of an unbeaten egg.*

un·be·com·ing /ˌənbiˈkəmiNG/ ▸*adj.* (esp. of clothing or a color) not flattering: *a stout lady in an unbecoming striped sundress.* ■ (of a person's attitude or behavior) not fitting or appropriate; unseemly: *it was* ***unbecoming for*** *a university to do anything so crass as advertising its wares.* —**un·be·com·ing·ly** *adv.* —**un·be·com·ing·ness** *n.*

un·be·got·ten /ˌənbəˈgätn/ ▸*adj. archaic* not brought into existence by the process of reproduction.

un·be·known /ˌənbiˈnōn/ (also **un·be·knownst** /-ˈnōnst/) ▸*adj.* [*predic.*] (**unbeknown to**) without the knowledge of (someone): *unbeknown to me, she made some inquiries.* ▷mid 17th cent.: from UN-¹ 'not' + archaic *beknown* 'known.'

un·be·lief /ˌənbəˈlēf/ ▸*n.* lack of religious belief; an absence of faith. ■ another term for DISBELIEF.

un·gen·tle·ness *n.*
un·gen·tly *adv.*
un·gen·tle·man·ly *adj.*
un·gen·tle·man·li·ness *n.*
un·gift·ed *adj.*
un·glam·or·ous *adj.*
un·grace·ful *adj.*
un·grace·ful·ly *adv.*
un·grace·ful·ness *n.*
un·grudg·ing *adj.*
un·grudg·ing·ly *adv.*
un·guess·a·ble *adj.*
un·ham·pered *adj.*
un·harm·ful *adj.*
un·har·mo·ni·ous *adj.*
un·hatched *adj.*
un·healed *adj.*
un·heat·ed *adj.*
un·heed·ed *adj.*
un·heed·ing *adj.*
un·heed·ing·ly *adv.*
un·help·ful *adj.*
un·help·ful·ly *adv.*
un·help·ful·ness *n.*
un·he·ro·ic *adj.*
un·he·ro·i·cal·ly *adv.*
un·hes·i·tat·ing *adj.*
un·hes·i·tat·ing·ly *adv.*
un·hin·dered *adj.*
un·hon·ored *adj.*
un·housed *adj.*
un·hurt *adj.*
un·hy·gi·en·ic *adj.*
un·hy·gi·en·i·cal·ly *adv.*
un·hy·phen·at·ed *adj.*
un·i·de·al *adj.*
un·i·den·ti·fi·a·ble *adj.*
un·i·den·ti·fied *adj.*
un·il·lu·mi·nat·ed *adj.*
un·il·lus·trat·ed *adj.*
un·im·ag·i·na·tive *adj.*
un·im·ag·i·na·tive·ly *adv.*
un·im·ag·i·na·tive·ness *n.*
un·im·pas·sioned *adj.*
un·im·ped·ed *adj.*
un·im·ped·ed·ly *adv.*
un·im·por·tant *adj.*
un·im·pos·ing *adj.*
un·im·pos·ing·ly *adv.*
un·im·pres·sion·a·ble *adj.*
un·im·pres·sive *adj.*
un·im·pres·sive·ly *adv.*
un·im·pres·sive·ness *n.*
un·in·fect·ed *adj.*
un·in·flamed *adj.*
un·in·flu·enced *adj.*
un·in·flu·en·tial *adj.*
un·in·form·a·tive *adj.*
un·in·formed *adj.*
un·in·hab·it·ed *adj.*
un·in·jured *adj.*
un·in·spir·ing *adj.*
un·in·spir·ing·ly *adv.*
un·in·su·lat·ed *adj.*
un·in·sured *adj.*
un·in·tend·ed *adj.*
un·in·ten·tion·al
un·in·ten·tion·al·ly *adv.*
un·in·ter·est·ing *adj.*
un·in·ter·est·ing·ly *adv.*
un·in·ter·est·ing·ness *n.*
un·in·ven·tive *adj.*
un·in·ven·tive·ly *adv.*
un·in·ven·tive·ness *n.*
un·in·ves·ti·gat·ed *adj.*
un·in·vit·ing *adj.*
un·in·vit·ing·ly *adv.*
un·in·volved *adj.*
un·i·roned *adj.*
un·joined *adj.*
un·joint·ed *adj.*
un·jus·ti·fied *adj.*
un·kill·a·ble *adj.*
un·la·beled *adj.*
un·la·bored *adj.*
un·lib·er·at·ed *adj.*
un·locked *adj.*
un·loved *adj.*
un·lov·ing *adj.*
un·lov·ing·ly *adv.*
un·lov·ing·ness *n.*
un·mar·ket·a·ble *adj.*
un·mar·ried *adj. & n.*
un·ma·tured *adj.*
un·meant *adj.*
un·me·lo·di·ous *adj.*
un·me·lo·di·ous·ly *adv.*
un·mem·o·ra·ble *adj.*
un·mem·o·ra·bly *adv.*
un·mer·chant·a·ble *adj.*
un·me·thod·i·cal *adj.*
un·me·thod·i·cal·ly *adv.*
un·mod·ern·ized *adj.*
un·mod·i·fied *adj.*
un·mount·ed *adj.*
un·mown *adj.*
un·mu·ti·lat·ed *adj.*
un·neigh·bor·ly *adj.*
un·neigh·bor·li·ness *n.*
un·ob·scured *adj.*
un·ob·serv·a·ble *adj.*
un·ob·serv·ant *adj.*
un·ob·serv·ant·ly *adv.*
un·ob·struct·ed *adj.*
un·ob·served *adj.*
un·ob·tain·a·ble *adj.*
un·of·fend·ed *adj.*
un·of·fend·ing *adj.*
un·of·fi·cial *adj.*
un·of·fi·cial·ly *adv.*
un·oiled *adj.*
un·o·pened *adj.*
un·op·posed *adj.*
un·or·di·nar·y *adj.*
un·or·na·men·tal *adj.*
un·or·na·ment·ed *adj.*
un·os·ten·ta·tious *adj.*
un·os·ten·ta·tious·ly *adv.*
un·os·ten·ta·tious·ness *n.*
un·paint·ed *adj.*
un·pas·teur·ized *adj.*
un·pat·ent·ed *adj.*
un·pa·tri·ot·ic *adj.*
un·pa·tri·ot·i·cal·ly *adv.*
un·pa·tron·iz·ing *adj.*
un·pa·tron·iz·ing·ly *adv.*
un·paved *adj.*
un·peeled *adj.*
un·pen·i·tent *adj.*
un·per·cep·tive *adj.*
un·per·cep·tive·ly *adv.*
un·per·cep·tive·ness *n.*
un·per·fect·ed *adj.*
un·per·fo·rat·ed *adj.*
un·per·formed *adj.*
un·per·fumed *adj.*
un·per·suad·a·ble *adj.*
un·per·suad·ed *adj.*
un·per·sua·sive *adj.*
un·per·sua·sive·ly *adv.*
un·pic·tur·esque *adj.*
un·pit·ied *adj.*
un·plucked *adj.*
un·pol·lut·ed *adj.*
un·pre·scribed *adj.*
un·pre·sump·tu·ous *adj.*
un·priced *adj.*
un·pro·claimed *adj.*
un·pro·cur·a·ble *adj.*
un·proud *adj.*
un·pub·li·cized *adj.*
un·pun·ish·a·ble *adj.*
un·pu·ri·fied *adj.*
un·quench·a·ble *adj.*
un·quench·a·bly *adv.*
un·quenched *adj.*
un·quot·a·ble *adj.*
un·reach·a·ble *adj.*
un·reach·a·ble·ness *n.*
un·reach·a·bly *adv.*
un·reached *adj.*
un·re·al·ism *n.*
un·re·al·is·tic *adj.*
un·re·al·is·ti·cal·ly *adv.*
un·rec·og·niz·a·ble *adj.*
un·rec·og·niz·a·bly *adv.*
un·rec·om·pensed *adj.*
un·rec·on·ciled *adj.*
un·re·cord·ed *adj.*
un·re·cord·a·ble *adj.*
un·rec·ti·fied *adj.*
un·rec·ti·fi·a·ble *adj.*
un·re·deem·a·ble *adj.*
un·re·deem·a·bly *adv.*
un·re·deemed *adj.*
un·re·dressed *adj.*
un·re·formed *adj.*
un·re·lat·ed *adj.*
un·re·lat·ed·ness *n.*
un·re·laxed *adj.*
un·re·li·a·ble *adj.*
un·re·li·a·bil·i·ty *n.*
un·re·li·a·bly *adv.*
un·re·li·a·ble·ness *n.*
un·re·mem·bered *adj.*
un·re·morse·ful *adj.*
un·re·morse·ful·ly *adv.*
un·re·mov·a·ble *adj.*
un·re·new·a·ble *adj.*
un·re·newed *adj.*
un·re·pealed *adj.*
un·rep·re·sent·ed *adj.*
un·re·proved *adj.*
un·re·quest·ed *adj.*
un·re·sist·ed *adj.*
un·re·sist·ing *adj.*
un·re·sist·ing·ly *adv.*
un·re·solv·a·ble *adj.*
un·re·spon·sive *adj.*
un·re·spon·sive·ly *adv.*
un·re·spon·sive·ness *n.*
un·rest·ful *adj.*
un·re·vealed *adj.*
un·re·veal·ing *adj.*
un·re·voked *adj.*
un·re·ward·ed *adj.*
un·re·ward·ing *adj.*
un·rhymed *adj.*
un·rhyth·mic *adj.*
un·rhyth·mi·cal *adj.*
un·rhyth·mi·cal·ly *adv.*
un·ripe *adj.*
un·ripe·ness *n.*
un·ris·en *adj.*
un·ro·man·tic *adj.*
un·ro·man·ti·cal·ly *adv.*
un·roy·al *adj.*
un·safe *adj.*
un·safe·ly *adv.*
un·safe·ness *n.*
un·salt·ed *adj.*
un·sanc·ti·fied *adj.*
un·sanc·tioned *adj.*
un·san·i·tar·y *adj.*
un·sat·is·fied *adj.*
un·sat·is·fy·ing *adj.*
un·sat·is·fy·ing·ly *adv.*
un·scent·ed *adj.*
un·sched·uled *adj.*
un·searched *adj.*
un·seg·re·gat·ed *adj.*
un·se·lect *adj.*
un·se·lec·tive *adj.*
un·se·lec·tive·ly *adv.*
un·sep·a·rat·ed *adj.*
un·sewn *v.*
un·shape·ly *adj.*
un·shape·li·ness *n.*
un·shel·tered *adj.*
un·shield·ed *adj.*
un·shock·a·ble *adj.*
un·shock·a·bil·i·ty *n.*
un·solv·a·ble *adj.*
un·solv·a·bil·i·ty *n.*
un·solved *adj.*
un·sort·ed *adj.*
un·soured *adj.*
un·spe·cial·ized *adj.*
un·spot·ted *adj.*
un·stained *adj.*
un·stead·fast *adj.*
un·sub·dued *adj.*
un·sub·ju·gat·ed *adj.*
un·suc·cess *n.*
un·suc·cess·ful *adj.*
un·suc·cess·ful·ly *adv.*
un·suc·cess·ful·ness *n.*
un·sug·ges·tive *adj.*
un·sum·moned *adj.*
un·tal·ent·ed *adj.*
un·trans·port·a·ble *adj.*
un·trimmed *adj.*
un·twist·ed *adj.*
un·ver·i·fi·a·ble *adj.*
un·ver·i·fied *adj.*
un·war·like *adj.*
un·warmed *adj.*
un·watched *adj.*
un·watch·ful *adj.*
un·wea·ry *adj.*
un·wet·ted *adj.*
un·whipped *adj.*
un·win·na·ble *adj.*
un·with·ered *adj.*
un·wound·ed *adj.*
un·writ·a·ble *adj.*

—**un·be·liev·er** /-ˈlēvər/ *n.* —**un·be·liev·ing** /-ˈlēviNG/ *adj.* —**un·be·liev·ing·ly** /-ˈlēviNGlē/ *adv.*

un·be·liev·a·ble /ˌənbəˈlēvəbəl/ ▸*adj.* not able to be believed; unlikely to be true: *unbelievable or not, it happened.* ■ so great or extreme as to be difficult to believe; extraordinary: *your audacity is unbelievable.* —**un·be·liev·a·bil·i·ty** /-ˌlēvəˈbilətē/ *n.* —**un·be·liev·a·bly** /-ˈlēvəblē/ *adv.* [as *submodifier*] *he worked unbelievably long hours.*

un·belt /ˌənˈbelt/ ▸*v.* [*trans.*] remove or undo the belt of (a garment): *he unbelted his kimono.*

un·belt·ed /ˌənˈbeltid/ ▸*adj.* (of a garment) without a belt. ■ (of a person) not wearing a belt, in particular a vehicle seat belt.

un·bend /ˌənˈbend/ ▸*v.* (*past* and *past part.* **-bent**) **1** make or become straight from a bent or twisted form or position: [*trans.*] *I had trouble unbending my cramped knees* | [*intrans.*] *he unbent from the cockpit as she passed.* ■ [*intrans.*] become less reserved, formal, or strict: *you could be fun too, you know, if you'd only unbend a little.* **2** [*trans.*] *Sailing* unfasten (sails) from yards or stays. ■ cast (a cable) loose. ■ untie (a rope).

un·bend·ing /ˌənˈbendiNG/ ▸*adj.* stiff; inflexible: *an ugly branch, ugly and ungraceful, sticking out unbending from a tree.* ■ strict and austere in one's behavior or attitudes: *they were unbending in their demands* | *his unbending iron will.* —**un·bend·ing·ly** *adv.* —**un·bend·ing·ness** *n.*

un·bi·ased /ˌənˈbīəst/ (also *chiefly Brit.* **un·bi·assed**) ▸*adj.* showing no prejudice for or against something; impartial.

un·bib·li·cal /ˌənˈbiblikəl/ ▸*adj.* not found in, authorized by, or based on the Bible.

un·bid·den /ˌənˈbidn/ ▸*adj.* without having been commanded or invited: *unbidden guests.* ■ (esp. of a thought or feeling) arising without conscious effort: *unbidden tears came to his eyes.*

un·bind /ˌənˈbīnd/ ▸*v.* (*past* and *past part.* **-bound**) [*trans.*] release from bonds or restraints.

un·birth·day /ˌənˈbərTHˌdā/ ▸*n. humorous* any day except one's birthday: [as *adj.*] *an unbirthday present.* ▷1871: coined by Lewis Carroll in *Through the Looking Glass.*

un·blem·ished /ˌənˈblemisHt/ ▸*adj.* not damaged or marked in any way; perfect.

un·blessed /ˌənˈblest/ (also **un·blest**) ▸*adj.* not made holy; not consecrated: *unblessed food.* ■ unfortunate; wretched: *a desolate and unblest extent of buffalo-grass.* ■ (**unblessed with**) not endowed with (a particular quality or attribute): *to us, unblessed by our own children, he was almost a son.*

un·blind /ˌənˈblīnd/ ▸*v.* [*trans.*] conduct (a test or experiment) in such a way that it is not blind.

un·blink·ing /ˌənˈbliNGkiNG/ ▸*adj.* (of a person or their gaze or eyes) not blinking. ■ (of a portrayal or scrutiny) direct, thorough, and honest: *they have helped him paint an unblinking portrait of the man and the writer.* —**un·blink·ing·ly** *adv.*

un·block /ˌənˈbläk/ ▸*v.* [*trans.*] remove an obstruction from (something, esp. a pipe or drain): *balloon catheters are used to unblock occluded arteries.*

un·blush·ing /ˌənˈbləsHiNG/ ▸*adj.* not feeling or showing embarrassment or shame. —**un·blush·ing·ly** *adv.*

un·bolt /ˌənˈbōlt/ ▸*v.* [*trans.*] open (a door or window) by drawing back a bolt.

un·bolt·ed /ˌənˈbōltid/ ▸*adj.* **1** (of a door or window) not bolted. **2** (of flour, etc.) not sifted.

un·born /ˌənˈbôrn/ ▸*adj.* (of a baby) not yet born: *the sound of an unborn baby's heartbeat* | *figurative without training, your full talent remains unborn* | [as *plural n.*] *the side with the most power will determine how America treats its unborn.*

un·bos·om /ˌənˈbo͝ozəm/ ▸*v.* [*trans.*] *archaic* disclose (one's thoughts or secrets): *she* ***unbosomed herself*** *to a trusty female friend.*

un·both·ered /ˌənˈbäT͟Hərd/ ▸*adj.* showing or feeling a lack of concern about or interest in something: *she was unbothered by the mess in the sink.*

un·bound[1] /ˌənˈbound/ ▸*adj.* not bound or tied up: *her hair was unbound* | *figurative they were unbound by convention.* ■ (of printed sheets) not bound together. ■ (of a book) not provided with a proper or permanent cover. ■ *Chemistry & Physics* not held by a chemical bond, gravity, or other physical force: *unbound electrons.*

un·bound[2] ▸ past and past participle of **UNBIND**.

un·bound·ed /ˌənˈboundid/ ▸*adj.* having or appearing to have no limits: *the possibilities are unbounded.* —**un·bound·ed·ly** *adv.* —**un·bound·ed·ness** *n.*

un·bowed /ˌənˈboud/ ▸*adj.* not having submitted to pressure or demands: *they are unbowed by centuries of colonial rule.*

un·brace /ˌənˈbrās/ ▸*v.* [*trans.*] remove a support from.

un·braid /ˌənˈbrād/ ▸*v.* untie (something braided): [*trans.*] *she may never unbraid her hair in the soft candlelight of a shared bedroom* | [*intrans.*] *removed the bobby pins from her left braid and began to unbraid.* ■ [*intrans.*] (of something braided) become untwisted: *he's aged gracefully, as an old rope will until it finally unbraids.*

un·bri·dle /ənˈbrīdl/ ▸*v.* [*trans.*] remove the bridle from (a horse or mule): *learn how to bridle and unbridle a horse.*■ release from restraint: [as *adj.*] *the forces of the world capitalist market were unbridled and spread quickly.*

un·bri·dled /ˌənˈbrīdld/ ▸*adj.* uncontrolled; unconstrained: *a moment of unbridled ambition* | *unbridled lust.*

un·bro·ken /ˌənˈbrōkən/ ▸*adj.* not broken, fractured, or damaged: *an unbroken glass.* ■ not interrupted or disturbed; continuous: *a night of sleep unbroken by nightmares.* ■ (of a record) not surpassed: *a 13-year unbroken record of increasing profits.* ■ (of a horse) not tamed or accustomed to being ridden. ■ (of land) not cultivated. —**un·bro·ken·ly** *adv.* —**un·bro·ken·ness** *n.*

un·buck·le /ˌənˈbəkəl/ ▸*v.* [*trans.*] unfasten the buckle of (something, esp. a belt).

un·build /ˌənˈbild/ ▸*v.* (*past* and *past part.* **-built**) [*trans.*] demolish or destroy (something, esp. a building or system). ■ [as *adj.*] (**unbuilt**) (of buildings or land) not yet built or built on: *a slope of unbuilt land.*

un·bun·dle /ˌənˈbəndl/ ▸*v.* [*trans.*] **1** market or charge for (items or services) separately rather than as part of a package. **2** split (a company or conglomerate) into its constituent businesses, esp. before selling them off. —**un·bun·dler** *n.* (in sense 2).

Pronunciation Key ə *ago*; ər *over*; ˈə or ˌə *up*; ˈər or ˌər *fur*; a *hat*; ā *rate*; ä *car*; CH *chew*; e *let*; ē *see*; e(ə)r *air*; i *fit*; ī *by*; i(ə)r *ear*; NG *sing*; ō *go*; ô *for*; oi *boy*; o͝o *good*; o͞o *goo*; ou *out*; SH *she*; TH *thin*; T͟H *then*; (h)w *why*; ZH *vision*

U

un·bur·den /ˌənˈbərdn/ ▸*v.* [*trans.*] relieve (someone) of something that is causing anxiety or distress: *the need to* **unburden yourself to** *someone who will listen.* ■ (usu. **be unburdened**) not cause (someone) hardship or distress: *they are unburdened by expectations of success.*

un·bur·y /ˌənˈberē/ ▸*v.* (**-bur·ies**, **-bur·ied**) [*trans.*] remove (something) from under the ground.

un·but·ton /ˌənˈbətn/ ▸*v.* [*trans.*] unfasten the buttons of (a garment). ■ [*intrans.*] *informal* relax and become less inhibited: *unbutton a little, Molly.*

un·called /ˌənˈkôld/ ▸*adj.* not summoned or invited. ■ (**uncalled for**) (esp. of a person's behavior) undesirable and unnecessary: *uncalled-for remarks.*

un·can·ny /ˌənˈkanē/ ▸*adj.* (**-ni·er**, **-ni·est**) strange or mysterious, esp. in an unsettling way: *an uncanny feeling that she was being watched.* ▷late 16th cent. (originally Scots in the sense 'relating to the occult, malicious'): from UN-[1] 'not' + CANNY. **—un·can·ni·ly** /-ˈkanəl-ē/ *adv.* **—un·can·ni·ness** *n.*

un·cap /ˌənˈkap/ ▸*v.* (**-capped**, **-cap·ping**) [*trans.*] remove the lid or cover from. ■ remove a limit or restriction on (a price, rate, or amount).

un·cared /ˌənˈke(ə)rd/ ▸*adj.* (**uncared for**) not looked after properly: *it was sad to see the old place uncared for and neglected | he grinned, showing surprisingly uncared-for teeth.*

un·car·ing /ˌənˈke(ə)riNG/ ▸*adj.* not displaying sympathy or concern for others: *an uncaring father.* ■ not feeling interest in or attaching importance to something: *she fled out into the weather,* **uncaring of** *the rain.* **—un·car·ing·ly** *adv.*

Un·cas /ˈəNGkəs/ (c.1588–1683) chief of the Mohegan Indians in what is now eastern Connecticut. He fought on the side of the British in the Pequot War 1637 and King Philip's War 1675–76.

un·case /ˌənˈkās/ ▸*v.* [*trans.*] remove from a cover or case.

un·ceas·ing /ˌənˈsēsiNG/ ▸*adj.* not coming to an end; continuous: *the unceasing efforts of the staff.* **—un·ceas·ing·ly** *adv.*

un·cel·e·brat·ed /ˌənˈseləˌbrātid/ ▸*adj.* not publicly acclaimed: *an uncelebrated but indispensable role.*

un·cer·e·mo·ni·ous /ˌənserəˈmōnēəs/ ▸*adj.* having or showing a lack of formality: *her entertaining was gracious but unceremonious.* ■ abrupt or discourteous: *he was known for his strong views and unceremonious manners | they make their unceremonious exit from the window.* **—un·cer·e·mo·ni·ous·ly** *adv.* **—un·cer·e·mo·ni·ous·ness** *n.*

un·cer·tain /ˌənˈsərtn/ ▸*adj.* not able to be relied on; not known or definite: *an uncertain future.* ■ (of a person) not completely confident or sure of something: *I was uncertain how to proceed.* **—un·cer·tain·ly** *adv.*

▸*PHRASE* □ **in no uncertain terms** clearly and forcefully: *she has already refused me, in no uncertain terms.*

un·cer·tain·ty /ˌənˈsərtntē/ ▸*n.* (*pl.* **-ties**) the state of being uncertain: *times of uncertainty and danger.* ■ (usu. **uncertainties**) something that is uncertain or that causes one to feel uncertain: *financial uncertainties.*

THE RIGHT WORD **doubt, dubiety, skepticism, uncertainty**

If you're not sure about something, you're probably experiencing a degree of **uncertainty**, which is a general term covering everything from a mere lack of absolute certainty (*uncertainty about the time of the dinner party*) to an almost complete lack of knowledge that makes it impossible to do more than guess at the result or outcome (*uncertainty about the country's future*).

Doubt implies both uncertainty and an inability to make a decision because the evidence is insufficient (*considerable doubt as to her innocence*).

Dubiety comes closer in meaning to *uncertainty* than to *doubt*, because it stresses a lack of sureness rather than an inability to reach a decision; but unlike *uncertainty*, it connotes wavering or fluctuating between one conclusion and another (*no one could fail to notice the dubiety in his voice*).

If you exhibit **skepticism**, you are not so much uncertain as unwilling to believe. It usually refers to a habitual state of mind or to a customary reaction (*she always listened to his excuses with skepticism*).

un·cer·tain·ty prin·ci·ple ▸*n.* *Physics* the principle that the momentum and position of a particle cannot both be precisely determined at the same time.

un·cer·ti·fied /ˌənˈsərtəˌfīd/ ▸*adj.* not officially recognized as having a certain status or meeting certain standards: *uncertified accountants.* ■ not attested or confirmed in a formal statement.

un·chain /ˌənˈCHān/ ▸*v.* [*trans.*] remove the chains fastening or securing (someone or something).

un·chal·lenge·a·ble /ˌənˈCHalənjəbəl/ ▸*adj.* not able to be disputed, opposed, or defeated: *the unchallengeable truth of these basic facts.* **—un·chal·lenge·a·bly** /-blē/ *adv.*

un·chal·lenged /ˌənˈCHalənjd/ ▸*adj.* not disputed or questioned: *the report's findings did not* **go unchallenged.** ■ (esp. of a person in power) not opposed or defeated: *a position of unchallenged supremacy.* ■ not called on to prove one's identity or allegiance: *they walked unchallenged into a hospital and stole a baby.*

un·chal·leng·ing /ˌənˈCHalənjiNG/ ▸*adj.* (of a task or situation) not testing one's abilities: *my job was unchallenging.* ■ not threatening someone's position: *his voice was gentle and unchallenging.*

un·chanc·y /ˌənˈCHansē/ ▸*adj.* (**-chanc·i·er**, **-chanc·i·est**) *chiefly Scottish* unlucky, inauspicious, or dangerous.

un·charged /ˌənˈCHärjd/ ▸*adj.* not charged, in particular: ■ not accused of an offense under the law: *she was released uncharged.* ■ not carrying an electric charge. ■ not charged to a particular account: *an uncharged fixed cost.*

un·char·i·ta·ble /ˌənˈCHaritəbəl/ ▸*adj.* (of a person's behavior or attitude toward others) unkind; unsympathetic: *this uncharitable remark possibly arose out of jealousy.* **—un·char·i·ta·ble·ness** *n.* **—un·char·i·ta·bly** /-blē/ *adv.*

un·chart·ed /ˌənˈCHärtid/ ▸*adj.* (of an area of land or sea) not mapped or surveyed.

un·chaste /ˌənˈCHāst/ ▸*adj.* relating to or engaging in sexual activity, esp. of an illicit or extramarital nature: *unchaste subjects in art.* **—un·chaste·ly** *adv.* **—un·chas·ti·ty** /-ˈCHastətē/ *n.*

un·chas·tened /ˌənˈCHāsənd/ ▸*adj.* (of a person) not restrained or subdued: *he was unchastened and ready for fresh mischief.*

un·checked /ˌənˈCHekt/ ▸*adj.* (esp. of something undesirable) not controlled or restrained: *unchecked population growth.* ■ not examined, esp. in order to determine the accuracy, quality, or condition of something.

un·chris·tian /ˌənˈkrisCHən/ ▸*adj.* not professing Christianity or its teachings. ■ (of a person or their behavior) unkind, unfair, or morally wrong. **—un·chris·tian·ly** *adv.*

un·church /ˌənˈCHərCH/ ▸*v.* [*trans.*] officially exclude (someone) from participation in the Christian sacraments; excommunicate. ■ deprive (a building) of its status as a church.

un·churched /ˌənˈCHərCHt/ ▸*adj.* [*attrib.*] not belonging to or connected with a church.

un·ci·al /ˈənSHəl; -sēəl/ ▸*adj.* **1** of or written in a majuscule script with rounded unjoined letters that is found in European manuscripts of the 4th–8th centuries and from which modern capital letters are derived. **2** *rare* of or relating to an inch or an ounce. ▸*n.* an uncial letter or script. ■ a manuscript in uncial script. ▷mid 17th cent.: from Latin *uncialis*, from *uncia* 'inch.' Sense 1 is in the late Latin sense of *unciales litterae* 'uncial letters,' the original application of which is unclear.

uncial

uncial 1

un·ci·form /ˈənsəˌfôrm/ ▸*adj.* another term for UNCINATE. ■ *dated* denoting the hamate bone of the wrist.

un·ci·na·ri·a·sis /ˌənsənəˈrīəsis/ ▸*n.* another term for ANCYLOSTOMIASIS. ▷early 20th cent.: from modern Latin *Uncinaria* (the name of a genus of hookworms) + -IASIS.

un·ci·nate /ˈənsənit; -ˌnāt/ ▸*adj.* *chiefly Anatomy* having a hooked shape. ▷mid 18th cent.: from Latin *uncinatus*, from *uncinus* 'hook.'

un·cir·cu·lat·ed /ˌənˈsərkyəˌlātid/ ▸*adj.* (esp. of paper money or coin) not having been in circulation.

un·cir·cum·cised /ˌənˈsərkəmˌsīzd/ ▸*adj.* (of a boy or man) not circumcised. ■ *archaic* irreligious or heathen. **—un·cir·cum·ci·sion** /-ˌsərkəmˈsiZHən/ *n.*

un·civ·il /ˌənˈsivəl/ ▸*adj.* discourteous; impolite. See note at RUDE. **—un·civ·il·ly** *adv.*

un·civ·i·lized /ˌənˈsivəˌlīzd/ ▸*adj.* (of a place or people) not considered to be socially, culturally, or morally advanced. ■ impolite; bad-mannered.

un·clad /ˌənˈklad/ ▸*adj.* **1** unclothed; naked. **2** not provided with cladding: *unclad girders.*

un·claimed /ˌənˈklāmd/ ▸*adj.* not demanded or requested as being something one has a right to: *unclaimed benefits.*

un·clamp /ˌənˈklamp/ ▸*v.* [*trans.*] remove from, or as if from, a clamp. ■ release or loosen the clamp of: *he unclamped its jaws and climbed out of its cage.*

un·clasp /ˌənˈklasp/ ▸*v.* [*trans.*] unfasten (a clasp or similar device): *they unclasped their seat belts.* ■ release the grip of: *I unclasped her fingers from my hair.*

un·clas·si·fied /ˌənˈklasəˌfīd/ ▸*adj.* not arranged in or assigned to classes or categories: *many texts remain unclassified or uncatalogued.* ■ (of information or documents) not designated as secret.

un·cle /ˈəNGkəl/ ▸*n.* the brother of one's father or mother or the husband of one's aunt. ■ *informal* an unrelated older male friend, esp. of a child. ■ *archaic informal* a pawnbroker. ▷Middle English: from Old French *oncle*, from late Latin *aunculus*, alteration of Latin *avunculus* 'maternal uncle' (see AVUNCULAR).

▸*PHRASE* □ **cry** (or **say**) **uncle** *informal* surrender or admit defeat.

-uncle ▸*suffix* forming chiefly diminutive nouns: *carbuncle | peduncle.* ▷from Old French *-oncle*, *-uncle*, or from Latin *-unculus*, a special form of *-ulus*.

un·clean /ˌənˈklēn/ ▸*adj.* dirty: *the company was fined for operating in unclean premises.* ■ morally wrong: *unclean thoughts.* ■ (of food) regarded in a particular religion as impure and unfit to be eaten: *pork is an unclean meat for Muslims.* ■ (in biblical use) ritually impure; (of a spirit) evil. ▷Old English *unclǣne* (see UN-[1], CLEAN). **—un·clean·ness** *n.*

un·clean·li·ness /ˌənˈklenlēnis/ ▸*n.* the state of being dirty: *head lice and general uncleanliness in schools.*

un·clean·ly /ˌənˈklenlē/ ▸*adj.* archaic term for UNCLEAN.

un·clear /ˌənˈkli(ə)r/ ▸*adj.* not easy to see, hear, or understand: *the motive for this killing is unclear.* ■ not obvious or definite; ambiguous: *their future remains unclear.* ■ having or feeling doubt or confusion: *users are still unclear about what middleware does.* **—un·clear·ly** *adv.* **—un·clear·ness** *n.*

un·cleared /ˌənˈkli(ə)rd/ ▸*adj.* not having been cleared or cleared up, in particular: ■ (of a check) not having passed through a clearinghouse and been paid into the payee's account. ■ (of land) not cleared of vegetation before cultivation.

Un·cle Joe see STILWELL.

un·clench /ˌənˈklenCH/ ▸*v.* [*trans.*] release (a clenched part of the body): *slowly she unclenched her fist.* ■ [*intrans.*] relax from a clenched state.

Un·cle Sam /sam/ a personification of the federal government or citizens of the U.S., typically portrayed as a tall, thin, bearded man wearing a suit of red, white, and blue. ▷early 19th cent.: said (from the time of the first recorded instances) to have arisen as a facetious expansion of the letters U.S.

Uncle Sam

Un·cle Tom /täm/ ▸*n.* *derogatory* a black man considered to be excessively obedient or servile. ▷1920s: from the name of the hero of H. B. Stowe's *Uncle Tom's Cabin* (1852). **—Un·cle Tom·ism** /ˈtämˌizəm/ *n.*

un·climbed /ˌənˈklīmd/ ▸*adj.* (of a mountain or rock face) not previously climbed: *the unclimbed south ridge.* **—un·climb·a·ble** /-ˈklīməbəl/ *adj.*

un·cloak /ˌənˈklōk/ ▸*v.* [*trans.*] *poetic/literary* uncover; reveal.

un·clog /ˌənˈklôg; -ˈkläg/ ▸*v.* (**-clogged**, **-clog·ging**) [*trans.*] remove accumulated matter from: *exfoliation unclogs pores and prevents blackheads.*

un·close /ˌənˈklōz/ ▸*v. rare* open.

un·clothe /ˌənˈklō<u>TH</u>/ ▸*v.* [*trans.*] remove the clothes from (oneself or someone).

un·cloud·ed /ˌənˈkloudid/ ▸*adj.* (of the sky) not dark or overcast: *you wake up to sunshine and unclouded skies.* ■ not troubled or spoiled by anything: *six months of unclouded happiness.*

un·co /ˈəNGkō; -kə/ *Scottish* ▸*adj.* unusual or remarkable.
▸*adv.* [*as submodifier*] remarkably; very: *it's got an unco fine taste.*
▸*n.* (*pl.* **-cos**) a stranger. ■ (**uncos**) news. ▷late Middle English (in the sense 'unknown, strange'): alteration of **UNCOUTH**.

un·coil /ˌənˈkoil/ ▸*v.* straighten or cause to straighten from a coiled or curled position: [*intrans.*] *the rope uncoiled like a snake* | [*trans.*] *she uncoiled her feather boa.*

un·col·lect·ed /ˌənkəˈlektid/ ▸*adj.* (esp. of money) not collected or claimed: *the reward remained uncollected.* ■ left awaiting collection: *bursting sacks of uncollected refuse.* ■ (of literary works) not previously published.

un·col·ored /ˌənˈkələrd/ (*Brit.* **un·col·oured**) ▸*adj.* having no color; neutral in color. ■ not influenced, esp. in a negative way: *explanations that are uncolored by the observer's feelings.*

un·com·fort·a·ble /ˌənˈkəmfərtəbəl; -ˈkəmftərbəl/ ▸*adj.* causing or feeling slight pain or physical discomfort: *athlete's foot is a painful and uncomfortable condition.* ■ causing or feeling unease or awkwardness: *he began to feel uncomfortable at the man's hard stare* | *an uncomfortable silence.* —**un·com·fort·a·ble·ness** *n.* —**un·com·fort·a·bly** /-blē/ *adv.* [*as submodifier*] *the house was dark and uncomfortably cold.*

un·com·ment /ˌənˈkämˌent/ ▸*v.* [*trans.*] *Computing* change (a piece of text within a program) from being a comment to being part of the program that is run by the computer by removing tagging that identifies the text as a comment.

un·com·mer·cial /ˌənkəˈmərSHəl/ ▸*adj.* not making, intended to make, or allowing a profit. ■ not having profit as a primary aim: *a seemingly uncommercial verse drama.*

un·com·mit·ted /ˌənkəˈmitid/ ▸*adj.* not committed to a particular course or policy: *uncommitted voters.* ■ (of resources) not pledged or set aside for future use: *there is very little uncommitted money to fund new policies.* ■ (of a person) not pledged to remain in a long-term emotional relationship with someone.

un·com·mon /ˌənˈkämən/ ▸*adj.* out of the ordinary; unusual: *prostate cancer is not uncommon in men over 60* | *an uncommon name.* ■ [*attrib.*] remarkably great (used for emphasis): *an uncommon amount of noise.*
▸*adv.* [*as submodifier*] *archaic* remarkably: *he was uncommon afraid.* —**un·com·mon·ly** *adv.* [*as submodifier*] *an uncommonly large crowd.* —**un·com·mon·ness** *n.*

un·com·mu·ni·ca·tive /ˌənkəˈmyo͞onəkətiv; -ˌkātiv/ ▸*adj.* (of a person) unwilling to talk or impart information. ■ (of something such as writing or art) not conveying much or any meaning or sense. —**un·com·mu·ni·ca·tive·ly** *adv.* —**un·com·mu·ni·ca·tive·ness** *n.*

un·com·pen·sat·ed /ˌənˈkämpənˌsātid/ ▸*adj.* (of a person or expense) not compensated or reimbursed: *the plaintiff remained uncompensated for his original injuries.* ■ (of an action) not compensated for: *uncompensated exploitation of the Third World.* ■ (of work) unpaid: *workers who performed uncompensated "off-the-clock" work for Ernst in violation of the law.*

un·com·pet·i·tive /ˌənkəmˈpetətiv/ ▸*adj.* (with reference to business or commerce) not competitive: *that would destroy jobs and make industry uncompetitive.* ■ characterized by a desire to avoid fair competition: *uncompetitive practices.* —**un·com·pet·i·tive·ly** *adv.* —**un·com·pet·i·tive·ness** *n.*

un·com·plain·ing /ˌənkəmˈplāniNG/ ▸*adj.* not complaining; resigned: *she was uncomplaining, accepting of her lot.* —**un·com·plain·ing·ly** *adv.*

un·com·pli·cat·ed /ˌənˈkämpləˌkātid/ ▸*adj.* simple or straightforward: *he was an extraordinarily uncomplicated man.*

un·com·pre·hend·ing /ˌənˌkämpriˈhendiNG/ ▸*adj.* showing or having an inability to comprehend something: *an uncomprehending silence.* —**un·com·pre·hend·ing·ly** *adv.*

un·com·pro·mis·ing /ˌənˈkämprəˌmīziNG/ ▸*adj.* showing an unwillingness to make concessions to others, esp. by changing one's ways or opinions. ■ harsh or relentless: *the uncompromising ugliness of her home.* —**un·com·pro·mis·ing·ly** *adv.* —**un·com·pro·mis·ing·ness** *n.*

un·con·cealed /ˌənkənˈsēld/ ▸*adj.* (esp. of an emotion) not concealed; obvious: *Sophie looked around her with unconcealed curiosity.*

un·con·cern /ˌənkənˈsərn/ ▸*n.* a lack of worry or interest, esp. when surprising or callous.

un·con·cerned /ˌənkənˈsərnd/ ▸*adj.* showing a lack of worry or interest, esp. when this is surprising or callous: *Scott seemed unconcerned by his companion's problem.* —**un·con·cern·ed·ly** /-ˈsərnədlē/ *adv.*

un·con·di·tion·al /ˌənkənˈdiSHənl; -ˈdiSHnəl/ ▸*adj.* not subject to any conditions: *unconditional surrender.* —**un·con·di·tion·al·i·ty** /-ˌdiSHəˈnalətē/ *n.* —**un·con·di·tion·al·ly** *adv.*

un·con·di·tioned /ˌənkənˈdiSHənd/ ▸*adj.* **1** not subject to conditions or to an antecedent condition; unconditional: *pure and unconditioned love.* **2** relating to or denoting instinctive reflexes or other behavior not formed or influenced by conditioning or learning: *an unconditioned response.* **3** not subjected to a conditioning process: *waste in its raw, unconditioned form.*

un·con·fessed /ˌənkənˈfest/ ▸*adj.* not acknowledged: *the hope that remains unconfessed.* ■ (of a sin) not confessed to a priest.

un·con·fined /ˌənkənˈfīnd/ ▸*adj.* not confined to a limited space: *sows should be unconfined at farrowing.* ■ (of joy or excitement) very great: *joy was unconfined.*

un·con·firmed /ˌənkənˈfərmd/ ▸*adj.* not confirmed as to truth or validity: *an unconfirmed report of shots being fired.*

un·con·form·a·ble /ˌənkənˈfôrməbəl/ ▸*adj. Geology* (of rock strata in contact) marking a discontinuity in the geological record, and typically not having the same direction of stratification. —**un·com·form·a·bly** /-blē/ *adv.*

un·con·form·i·ty /ˌənkənˈfôrmətē/ ▸*n. Geology* a surface of contact between two groups of unconformable strata. ■ the condition of being unconformable.

un·con·nect·ed /ˌənkəˈnektid/ ▸*adj.* not joined together or to something else: *the ground wire was left unconnected.* ■ not associated or linked in a sequence: *two unconnected events* | *the question was* ***unconnected to*** *anything they had been discussing.* ■ not having relatives in important or influential positions. —**un·con·nect·ed·ly** *adv.* —**un·con·nect·ed·ness** *n.*

un·con·quer·a·ble /ˌənˈkäNGk(ə)rəbəl/ ▸*adj.* (esp. of a place, people, or emotion) not conquerable: *an unconquerable pride.* —**un·con·quer·a·bly** /-blē/ *adv.*

un·con·scion·a·ble /ˌənˈkänSH(ə)nəbəl/ ▸*adj.* not right or reasonable: *the unconscionable conduct of his son.* ■ unreasonably excessive: *shareholders have had to wait an unconscionable time for the facts to be established.* ▷mid 16th cent.: from **UN-**[1] 'not' + obsolete *conscionable*, from **CONSCIENCE** (interpreted as a plural) + **-ABLE**. —**un·con·scion·a·bly** /-blē/ *adv.*

un·con·scious /ˌənˈkänSHəs/ ▸*adj.* not conscious: *the boy was beaten unconscious.* ■ done or existing without one realizing: *he would wipe back his hair in an unconscious gesture of annoyance.* ■ [*predic.*] (**unconscious of**) unaware of: *"What is it?" he said again, unconscious of the repetition.*
▸*n.* (**the unconscious**) the part of the mind that is inaccessible to the conscious mind but that affects behavior and emotions. —**un·con·scious·ly** *adv.* —**un·con·scious·ness** *n.*

un·con·sid·ered /ˌənkənˈsidərd/ ▸*adj.* disregarded and unappreciated: *a penchant for picking up unconsidered trifles.* ■ (of a statement or action) not thought about in advance, and therefore rash or harsh: *I realize that my unconsidered remarks were dangerously indiscreet.*

un·con·sol·a·ble /ˌənkənˈsōləbəl/ ▸*adj.* inconsolable. —**un·con·sol·a·bly** /-blē/ *adv.*

un·con·sti·tu·tion·al /ˌənˌkänstəˈt(y)o͞oSHənl/ ▸*adj.* not in accordance with a political constitution, esp. the U.S. Constitution, or with procedural rules. —**un·con·sti·tu·tion·al·i·ty** /-ˌt(y)o͞oSHəˈnalətē/ *n.* —**un·con·sti·tu·tion·al·ly** *adv.*

un·con·straint /ˌənkənˈstrānt/ ▸*n.* freedom from constraint.

un·con·struct·ed /ˌənkənˈstrəktid/ ▸*adj.* (of a garment) unstructured.

un·con·sumed /ˌənkənˈso͞omd/ ▸*adj.* (esp. of food or fuel) not consumed.

un·con·sum·mat·ed /ˌənˈkänsəˌmātid/ ▸*adj.* (of a marriage or other relationship) not having been consummated.

un·con·tain·a·ble /ˌənkənˈtānəbəl/ ▸*adj.* (esp. of an emotion) very strong: *his uncontainable enthusiasm.*

un·con·test·ed /ˌənkənˈtestid/ ▸*adj.* not contested: *these claims have not gone uncontested.* —**un·con·test·ed·ly** *adv.*

un·con·tro·vert·ed /ˌənˌkäntrəˈvərtid/ ▸*adj.* of which the truth or validity is not disputed or denied.

un·con·ven·tion·al /ˌənkənˈvenSHənl/ ▸*adj.* not based on or conforming to what is generally done or believed: *his unconventional approach to life.* —**un·con·ven·tion·al·i·ty** /-ˌvenSHəˈnalətē/ *n.* —**un·con·ven·tion·al·ly** *adv.*

un·con·vert·ed /ˌənkənˈvərtid/ ▸*adj.* not converted, in particular: ■ (of a building) not adapted to a different use. ■ not having adopted a different religion, belief, or practice: *unconverted pagans.*

un·con·vinced /ˌənkənˈvinst/ ▸*adj.* not certain that something is true or can be relied on or trusted: *Parisians remain* ***unconvinced that*** *the project will be approved.*

un·con·vinc·ing /ˌənkənˈvinsiNG/ ▸*adj.* failing to make someone believe that something is true or valid: *she felt the lie was unconvincing.* ■ failing to impress: *a slightly bizarre and unconvincing fusion of musical forces.* —**un·con·vinc·ing·ly** *adv.*

un·cool /ˌənˈko͞ol/ ▸*adj. informal* not fashionable or impressive: *an uncool haircut.*

un·co·op·er·a·tive /ˌənkōˈäp(ə)rətiv/ ▸*adj.* unwilling to help others or do what they ask. —**un·co·op·er·a·tive·ly** *adv.*

un·co·or·di·nat·ed /ˌənkōˈôrdnˌātid/ ▸*adj.* **1** badly organized: *expensive mistakes resulting from uncoordinated manufacturing strategies.* **2** (of a person or their movements) clumsy.

un·cork /ˌənˈkôrk/ ▸*v.* [*trans.*] pull the cork out of (a bottle or other container). ■ *figurative* allow (feelings) to be vented: *there are those who have tried to uncork some of the mounting frustrations and pressures of the job by turning to the bottle.* ■ *informal* (in a game or sport) deliver (a kick, throw, or punch): *he uncorked the best throw of his career.*

un·count·a·ble /ˌənˈkountəbəl/ ▸*adj.* too many to be counted (usually in hyperbolic use): *she'd spent uncountable nights in this very bed.* —**un·count·a·bil·i·ty** /-ˌkountəˈbilətē/ *n.* —**un·count·a·bly** /-blē/ *adv.*

un·count·ed /ˌənˈkountid/ ▸*adj.* not counted. ■ very numerous: *uncounted millions of dollars.*

un·cou·ple /ˌənˈkəpəl/ ▸*v.* [*trans.*] disconnect (something, esp. a railroad vehicle that has been coupled to another). ■ [*intrans.*] become disconnected: *the groups of cells commonly uncouple from surrounding tissue* | *figurative I have seen marriages uncouple under the strain.* ■ release (hunting dogs) from being fastened together in couples.

un·court·ly /ˌənˈkôrtlē/ ▸*adj.* not courteous or refined.

un·couth /ˌənˈko͞oTH/ ▸*adj.* (of a person or their appearance or behavior) lacking good manners, refinement, or grace: *he is unwashed, uncouth, and drunk most of the time.* See note at **RUDE**. ■ (esp. of art or language) lacking sophistication or delicacy: *uncouth sketches of peasants.* ■ *archaic* (of a place) uncomfortable, esp. because of remoteness or poor conditions. ▷Old English *uncūth* 'unknown,' from **UN-**[1] 'not' + *cūth* (past participle of *cunnan* 'know, be able'). —**un·couth·ly** *adv.* —**un·couth·ness** *n.*

un·cov·e·nant·ed /ˌənˈkəv(ə)nəntid/ ▸*adj.* not bound by or in accordance with a covenant or agreement. ■ not promised by or based on a covenant, esp. a covenant with God.

un·cov·er /ˌənˈkəvər/ ▸*v.* [*trans.*] remove a cover or covering from: *he uncovered the face of the dead man.* ■ discover (something previously secret or unknown): *further evidence has been uncovered.* ■ [*intrans.*] *archaic* remove one's hat, esp. as a mark of respect.

un·cov·ered /ˌənˈkəvərd/ ▸*adj.* **1** without a lid or cover: *bake uncovered until cheese begins to brown.* ■ having had the cover removed. ■ without a hat or other covering for the head: *no uncovered heads are seen on the street.* **2** not covered by insurance.■ (of loans) not secured by collateral: *the percentage of uncovered debt is only seven percent.* **3** not treated or dealt with along with other subjects: *he left the most important topic uncovered until the end of the class.*

un·crate /ˈənˌkrāt/ ▸*n.* [*trans.*] an item of merchandise removed from its shipping container.

un·cre·ate /ˌənkrēˈāt/ ▸*v.* [*trans.*] *poetic/literary* destroy.

U

un·cre·at·ed /ˌənkrēˈātid/ ▸*adj.* (esp. of a divine being) existing without having been created. ■ not yet created.

un·cred·it·ed /ˌənˈkreditid/ ▸*adj.* (of a person or their work) not publicly acknowledged as being part of something, esp. a publication or broadcast.

un·crit·i·cal /ˌənˈkritikəl/ ▸*adj.* not expressing criticism; complacently accepting: *the technique had received uncritical acclaim in the media.* ■ not using one's critical faculties: *uncritical apologists for the country.* ■ not in accordance with the principles of critical analysis: *uncritical reasoning.* —**un·crit·i·cal·ly** /-ik(ə)lē/ *adv.*

un·cross /ˌənˈkrôs; -ˈkräs/ ▸*v.* [*trans.*] move (something) back from a crossed position: *the reporter uncrossed his legs.*

un·crown /ˌənˈkroun/ ▸*v.* [*trans.*] deprive (a monarch) of their ruling position.

un·crowned /ˌənˈkround/ ▸*adj.* not formally crowned as a monarch.

UNCSTD ▸*abbr.* United Nations Conference on Science and Technology for Development.

UNCTAD /ˈəNGkˌtad/ ▸*abbr.* United Nations Conference on Trade and Development.

unc·tion /ˈəNG(k)SHən/ ▸*n.* **1** *formal* the action of anointing someone with oil or ointment as a religious rite or as a symbol of investiture as a monarch. ■ the oil or ointment so used. ■ short for EXTREME UNCTION. **2** *archaic* treatment with a medicinal oil or ointment. ■ an ointment: *mercury in the form of unctions.* **3** a manner of expression arising or apparently arising from deep emotion, esp. as intended to flatter: *he spoke the last two words with exaggerated unction.* ▷late Middle English: from Latin *unctio(n-)*, from *unguere* 'anoint.' Sense 3 arises from the link between religious fervor and "anointing" with the Holy Spirit.

unc·tu·ous /ˈəNG(k)CHo͞oəs/ ▸*adj.* **1** (of a person) excessively or ingratiatingly flattering; oily: *he seemed anxious to please but not in an unctuous way.* **2** (chiefly of minerals) having a greasy or soapy feel. ▷late Middle English (in the sense 'greasy'): from medieval Latin *unctuosus*, from Latin *unctus* 'anointing,' from *unguere* 'anoint.' —**unc·tu·ous·ly** *adv.* —**unc·tu·ous·ness** *n.*

un·cul·ti·vat·ed /ˌənˈkəltəˌvātid/ ▸*adj.* (of land) not used for growing crops. ■ (of a person) not highly educated or socially adept.

un·curl /ˌənˈkərl/ ▸*v.* straighten or cause to straighten from a curled position: [*intrans.*] *in spring the new leaves uncurl* | [*trans.*] *the doctor uncurled his fingers.*

un·cut /ˌənˈkət/ ▸*adj.* not cut: *her hair was left uncut.* ■ (of a text, movie, or performance) complete; unabridged. ■ (of a stone, esp. a diamond) not shaped by cutting. ■ (of alcohol or a drug) not diluted or adulterated: *large amounts of uncut heroin.* ■ *chiefly historical* (of a book) with the edges of its pages not slit open or trimmed off. ■ (of fabric) having its pile loops intact.

un·dat·ed /ˌənˈdātid/ ▸*adj.* not provided or marked with a date: *most of his letters are undated.*

un·daunt·ed /ˌənˈdôntid; -ˈdänt-/ ▸*adj.* not intimidated or discouraged by difficulty, danger, or disappointment: *they were undaunted by the huge amount of work needed.* —**un·daunt·ed·ly** *adv.* —**un·daunt·ed·ness** *n.*

un·dead /ˌənˈded/ ▸*adj.* (of a fictional being, esp. a vampire) technically dead but still animate.

un·dec·a·gon /ˌənˈdekəˌgän/ ▸*n.* another term for HENDECAGON. ▷early 18th cent.: formed irregularly from Latin *undecim* 'eleven,' on the pattern of *decagon.*

un·de·ceive /ˌəndiˈsēv/ ▸*v.* [*trans.*] tell (someone) that an idea or belief is mistaken: *they took her for a nun, and Mary said nothing to undeceive them.*

un·de·cid·a·ble /ˌəndiˈsīdəbəl/ ▸*adj.* not able to be firmly established or refuted. ■ *Logic* (of a proposition or theorem) not able to be proved or disproved. —**un·de·cid·a·bil·i·ty** /-ˌsīdəˈbilətē/ *n.*

un·de·cid·ed /ˌəndiˈsīdid/ ▸*adj.* (of a person) not having made a decision: *the jury remained undecided.* ■ not settled or resolved: *the match was still undecided.*
▸*n.* a person who has not decided how they are going to vote in an election. —**un·de·cid·ed·ly** *adv.*

un·de·ci·pher·a·ble /ˌəndiˈsīf(ə)rəbəl/ ▸*adj.* (of speech or writing) not able to be read or understood.

un·de·clared /ˌəndiˈkle(ə)rd/ ▸*adj.* not publicly announced, admitted, or acknowledged: *his undeclared candidacy, which surged in the polls last spring.* ■ (esp. of taxable income or dutiable goods) not declared.

un·de·filed /ˌəndiˈfīld/ ▸*adj.* not defiled; pure.

un·de·fined /ˌəndiˈfīnd/ ▸*adj.* not clear or defined: *undefined areas of jurisdiction* | *he felt an undefined longing.* —**un·de·fin·a·ble** /-ˈfīnəbəl/ *adj.* —**un·de·fin·a·bly** /-ˈfīnəblē/ *adv.*

un·de·lete /ˌəndiˈlēt/ ▸*v.* [*trans.*] *Computing* cancel the deletion of (text or a file).

un·de·mand·ing /ˌəndəˈmandiNG; ˌəndēˈmandiNG/ ▸*adj.* (esp. of a task or person) not demanding: *undemanding clerical jobs.*

un·de·mon·stra·tive /ˌəndiˈmänstrətiv/ ▸*adj.* (of a person) not tending to express feelings, esp. of affection, openly: *John is silent and undemonstrative, like Dad.* —**un·de·mon·stra·tive·ly** *adv.* —**un·de·mon·stra·tive·ness** *n.*

un·de·ni·a·ble /ˌəndiˈnīəbəl/ ▸*adj.* unable to be denied or disputed: *it is an undeniable fact that some dogs are easier to train than others* | *ornate fireplaces give the place undeniable class.* —**un·de·ni·a·bly** /-blē/ *adv.* [*sentence adverb*] *the topic is undeniably an important one.*

un·der /ˈəndər/ ▸*prep.* **1** extending or directly below: *vast stores of oil under Alaska* | *the streams that ran under the melting glaciers.* ■ below (something covering or protecting): *under several feet of water* | *a hot plate under an insulated lid.* **2** at a lower level or layer than: *the room under his study.* ■ behind (a physical surface): *it was written on the new canvas under a gluey coating.* ■ behind or hidden behind (an appearance or disguise): *he had a deep sense of fun under his quiet exterior.* ■ lower in grade or rank than: *under him in the hierarchy.* **3** used to express dominance or control: *I was under his spell.* ■ during (a specified time period, reign, or administration): *it occurred under the pontificate of Paul II.* ■ as a reaction to or undergoing the pressure of (something): *the sofa creaked under his weight* | *certain institutions may be under threat.* ■ as provided for by the rules of; in accordance with: *flowers supplied under contract by a local florist.* ■ used to express grouping or classification: *file it under "lost"* | *published under his own name.* ■ *Computing* within the environment of (a particular operating system): *the program runs under DOS.* **4** lower than (a specified amount, rate, or norm): *they averaged just under 2.8 percent.* **5** undergoing (a process): *under construction.* ■ in an existent state of: *children living under difficult circumstances.* ■ planted with: *fields under wheat.*
▸*adv.* **1** extending or directly below something: *weaving the body through the crossbars, over and under, over and under.* **2** under water: *he was floating for some time but suddenly went under.*
▸*adj.* **1** denoting the lowest part or surface of something; on the underside: *the under part of the shell is concave.* **2** unconscious, typically as a result of general anesthesia: *the operation was quick—she was only under for 15 minutes.* ▷Old English, of Germanic origin; related to Dutch *onder* and German *unter.* —**un·der·most** /-ˌmōst/ *adj.*
▸PHRASES □ **go under** see GO[1]. □ **under way** having started and making progress.■ (of a boat) moving through the water: *no time was lost in* **getting under way.** [mid 18th cent. (as a nautical term): from Dutch *onderweg.*]

under- ▸*prefix* **1** below; beneath: *underclothes* | *undercover.* ■ lower in status; subordinate: *undersecretary.* **2** insufficiently; incompletely: *undernourished.*

un·der·a·chieve /ˌəndərəˈCHēv/ ▸*v.* [*intrans.*] do less well than is expected, esp. in schoolwork. —**un·der·a·chieve·ment** *n.* —**un·der·a·chiev·er** *n.*

un·der·act /ˌəndərˈakt/ ▸*v.* [*intrans.*] act a part in a play or film in an overly restrained or unemotional way.

un·der·age /ˌəndərˈāj/ ▸*adj.* (of a person) too young to engage legally in a particular activity, esp. drinking alcohol or having sex. ■ [*attrib.*] (of an activity) engaged in by people who are underage: *underage drinking.*

un·der·arm /ˈəndərˌärm/ ▸*adj.* & *adv.* another term for UNDERHAND (sense 2).
▸*n.* a person's armpit: [as *adj.*] *use an underarm deodorant.*

un·der·banked /ˌəndərˈbaNGkt/ ▸*adj.* **1** (of an area) with insuffıcent banks to meet market demand. ■ (of consumers) lacking full use of banking facilities. **2** (of an investment issue) not adequately underwritten by financing institutions.

un·der·bel·ly /ˈəndərˌbelē/ ▸*n.* (*pl.* **-lies**) the soft underside or abdomen of an animal. ■ *figurative* an area vulnerable to attack: *these multinationals have a soft underbelly.* ■ *figurative* a hidden unpleasant or criminal part of society.

un·der·bid ▸*v.* /ˌəndərˈbid/ (**-bid·ding**; *past* and *past part.* **-bid**) [*trans.*] (in an auction or when seeking a contract) make a lower bid than (someone): *they were underbid by competitors who charged less.* ■ *Bridge* make a lower bid on (one's hand) than its strength warrants.
▸*n.* /ˈəndərˌbid/ a bid that is lower than another or than is justified. —**un·der·bid·der** /ˌəndərˈbidər/ *n.*

un·der·bite /ˈəndərˌbīt/ ▸*n.* (in nontechnical use) the projection of the lower teeth beyond the upper.

un·der·bod·y /ˈəndərˌbädē/ ▸*n.* (*pl.* **-bod·ies**) the underside of a road vehicle, ship, or animal's body.

un·der·boss /ˈəndərˌbôs; -ˌbäs/ ▸*n.* a boss's deputy, esp. in a criminal organization.

un·der·bred /ˌəndərˈbred/ ▸*adj. dated* ill-mannered; rude.

un·der·brush /ˈəndərˌbrəSH/ ▸*n.* shrubs and small trees forming the undergrowth in a forest.

un·der·cap·i·tal·ize /ˌəndərˈkapətlˌīz/ ▸*v.* [*trans.*] provide (a company) with insufficient capital to achieve desired results. —**un·der·cap·i·tal·i·za·tion** /-ˌkapətl-əˈzāSHən/ *n.*

un·der·card /ˈəndərˌkärd/ ▸*n.* the list of less important bouts on the same bill as a main boxing match.

un·der·car·riage /ˈəndərˌkarij/ ▸*n.* a wheeled structure beneath an aircraft, typically retracted when not in use, that receives the impact on landing and supports the aircraft on the ground. ■ the supporting frame under the body of a vehicle.

un·der·cast /ˌəndərˈkast/ ▸*v.* (*past* and *past part.* **-cast**) [*trans.*] (usu. **be undercast**) allocate the parts in (a play or movie) to insufficiently skilled actors.

un·der·charge ▸*v.* /ˌəndərˈCHärj/ [*trans.*] **1** charge (someone) a price or amount that is too low. **2** give less than the proper charge to (an electric battery).
▸*n.* /ˈəndərˌCHärj/ a charge that is insufficient.

un·der·class /ˈəndərˌklas/ ▸*n.* the lowest social stratum in a country or community, consisting of the poor and unemployed.

un·der·class·man /ˌəndərˈklasmən/ ▸*n.* (*plural* **underclassmen**) a student in high school or college who is not a senior: *one of the talented underclassmen leaving campus life early for the NFL.*

un·der·cling /ˈəndərˌkliNG/ *Climbing* ▸*n.* a handhold that faces down the rock face.
▸*v.* [*intrans.*] climb using such handholds.

un·der·clothes /ˈəndərˌklō(TH)z/ ▸*plural n.* clothes worn under others, typically next to the skin.

un·der·cloth·ing /ˈəndərˌklōTHiNG/ ▸*n.* underclothes.

un·der·coat /ˈəndərˌkōt/ ▸*n.* **1** a layer of paint applied after the primer and before the topcoat. **2** an animal's underfur or down.
▸*v.* [*trans.*] apply a coat of undercoat to (something).

un·der·con·sump·tion /ˌəndərkənˈsəm(p)SHən/ ▸*n.* *Economics* purchase of goods and services at a level lower than that of their supply.

un·der·cook /ˌəndərˈko͝ok; ˈəndərˌko͝ok/ ▸*v.* [*trans.*] [usu. as *adj.*] (**undercooked**) cook (something) insufficiently: *undercooked meats.*

un·der·cool /ˌəndərˈko͞ol/ ▸*v.* another term for SUPERCOOL.

un·der·count ▸*v.* /ˌəndərˈkount/ [*trans.*] enumerate (something, esp. a sector of a population in a census) at a lower figure than the actual figure.
▸*n.* /ˈəndərˌkount/ a count or figure that is inaccurately low. ■ the amount by which such a count or figure falls short of the actual figure.

un·der·cov·er /ˌəndərˈkəvər/ ▸*adj.* (of a person or their activities) involved in or involving secret work within a community or organization, esp. for the purposes of police investigation or espionage: *an undercover police operation.*
▸*adv.* as an undercover agent: *a special unit of the police that operates undercover.*

un·der·croft /ˈəndərˌkrôft; -ˌkräft/ ▸*n.* the crypt of a church. ▷late Middle English: from UNDER- + the rare term *croft* 'crypt,' from Middle Dutch *crofte* 'cave,' from Latin *crypta.*

un·der·cur·rent /ˈəndərˌkərənt/ ▸*n.* a current of water below the surface, moving in a different direction from any surface current. ■ *figurative* an underlying feeling or influence, esp. one that is contrary to the prevailing atmosphere and is not expressed openly: *an undercurrent of anger and discontent.*

un·der·cut ▸*v.* /ˌəndərˈkət/ (**-cut·ting**; *past* and *past part.* **-cut**) [*trans.*] **1** offer goods or services at a lower price than (a competitor): *these industries have been undercut by more efficient foreign producers.* **2** cut or wear away the part below or under (something, esp. a cliff). ■ *figurative* weaken; undermine: *the chairman denied his authority was being undercut.* ■ cut away material to leave (a carved design) in relief. **3** (in sports such as tennis or golf) strike (a ball) with a chopping motion so as to give it backspin.
▸*n.* /ˈəndərˌkət/ **1** a space formed by the removal or

absence of material from the lower part of something, such as a cliff, a coal seam, or part of a carving in relief. ■ a notch cut in a tree trunk to guide its fall when felled. **2** *Brit.* the underside of a sirloin of beef.

un·der·damp /ˌəndər'damp/ ▸*v.* [*trans.*] *Physics* damp (a system) incompletely, so as to allow a few oscillations after a single disturbance.

un·der·de·ter·mine /ˌəndərdi'tərmən/ ▸*v.* [*trans.*] (usu. **be underdetermined**) account for (a theory or phenomenon) with less than the amount of evidence needed for proof or certainty. **—un·der·de·ter·mi·na·tion** /-ˌtərmə'nāsHən/ *n.*

un·der·de·vel·oped /ˌəndərdi'veləpt/ ▸*adj.* not fully developed: *underdeveloped kidneys* | *the community services are underfunded and underdeveloped.* ■ (of a country or region) not advanced economically. ■ (of photographic film) not developed sufficiently to give a normal image. **—un·der·de·vel·op·ment** /-əpmənt/ *n.*

un·der·dog /'əndərˌdôg; -ˌdäg/ ▸*n.* a competitor thought to have little chance of winning a fight or contest. ■ a person who has little status in society. ▷late 19th cent.: with reference to the beaten dog in a dogfight.

un·der·done /ˌəndər'dən/ ▸*adj.* (of food) insufficiently cooked.

un·der·draw·ing /'əndərˌdrôiNG/ ▸*n.* sketched lines made by a painter as a preliminary guide, and subsequently covered with layers of paint.

un·der·dress /ˌəndər'dres/ ▸*v.* [*intrans.*] (also **be underdressed**) dress too plainly or too informally: *without a pinstripe you'd be underdressed.*

un·der·ed·u·cat·ed /ˌəndər'ejəˌkātid/ ▸*adj.* inadequately educated.

un·der·em·pha·size /ˌəndər'emfəˌsīz/ ▸*v.* [*trans.*] (usu. **be underemphasized**) place insufficient emphasis on: *history is underemphasized in the curriculum.* **—un·der·em·pha·sis** /-sis/ *n.*

un·der·em·ployed /ˌəndərim'ploid/ ▸*adj.* (of a person) not doing work that makes full use of their skills and abilities. ■ (of a person) not having enough paid work. **—un·der·em·ploy·ment** /-'ploimənt/ *n.*

un·der·es·ti·mate ▸*v.* /ˌəndər'estəˌmāt/ [*trans.*] estimate (something) to be smaller or less important than it actually is: *the administration has grossly underestimated the extent of the problem.* ■ regard (someone) as less capable than they really are: *he had underestimated the new president.*
▸*n.* /-mit/ [usu. in *sing.*] an estimate that is too low. **—un·der·es·ti·ma·tion** /-ˌestə'māsHən/ *n.*

un·der·ex·pose /ˌəndərik'spōz/ ▸*v.* [*trans.*] *Photography* expose (film or an image) for too short a time. **—un·der·ex·po·sure** /-'spōzHər/ *n.*

un·der·fed /ˌəndər'fed/ ▸*adj.* insufficiently fed or nourished.

un·der·floor /ˌəndər'flôr/ ▸*adj.* situated or operating beneath the floor.

un·der·flow /'əndərˌflō/ ▸*n.* **1** an undercurrent. ■ a horizontal flow of water through the ground, esp. one underneath a riverbed. **2** *Computing* the generation of a number that is too small to be represented in the device meant to store it.

un·der·foot /ˌəndər'fo͝ot/ ▸*adv.* under one's feet; on the ground: *it was very muddy underfoot* | *figurative genuine rights were being trodden underfoot.* ■ constantly present and in one's way: *the last thing my mother wanted was a child underfoot.*

un·der·fund /ˌəndər'fənd/ ▸*v.* [*trans.*] (usu. **be underfunded**) provide with insufficient funding. **—un·der·fund·ing** *n.*

un·der·fur /'əndərˌfər/ ▸*n.* an inner layer of short, fine fur or down underlying an animal's outer fur, providing warmth and waterproofing.

un·der·gar·ment /'əndərˌgärmənt/ ▸*n.* an article of underclothing.

un·der·gird /ˌəndər'gərd/ ▸*v.* [*trans.*] secure or fasten from the underside, esp. by a rope or chain passed underneath. ■ *formal* provide support or a firm basis for.

un·der·glaze /'əndərˌglāz/ ▸*adj.* (of decoration on pottery) done before the glaze is applied. ■ (of colors) used in such decoration.
▸*n.* a color or design applied in this way.

un·der·go /ˌəndər'gō/ ▸*v.* (**-goes**; *past* **-went**; *past part.* **-gone**) [*trans.*] experience or be subjected to (something, typically something unpleasant, painful, or arduous): *the baby underwent a life-saving brain operation.* ▷Old English *undergān* 'undermine' (see **UNDER-**, **GO**1).

un·der·grad /'əndərˌgrad/ ▸*n. informal* an undergraduate.

un·der·grad·u·ate /ˌəndər'grajəwit/ ▸*n.* a student at a college or university who has not yet earned a bachelor's or equivalent degree.
▸*adj.* designed for or typical of undergraduates: *I'm taking undergraduate classes.*

un·der·ground ▸*adv.* /ˌəndər'ground/ beneath the surface of the ground: *miners working underground.* ■ in or into secrecy or hiding, esp. as a result of carrying out subversive political activities: *many were forced to* **go underground** *by the government.*
▸*adj.* /'əndərˌground/ situated beneath the surface of the ground: *underground parking garages.* ■ of or relating to the secret activities of people working to subvert an established order: *Czech underground literature.* ■ of or denoting a group or movement seeking to explore alternative forms of lifestyle or artistic expression; radical and experimental: *the New York underground art scene.*
▸*n.* /'əndərˌground/ **1** a group or movement organized secretly to work against an existing regime: *I got involved with the French underground.* ■ a group or movement seeking to explore alternative forms of lifestyle or artistic expression: *the late sixties underground.* **2** (**the Underground**) *Brit.* a subway, esp. the one in London: *travel chaos on the Underground.*

un·der·ground e·con·o·my ▸*n.* the part of a country's economic activity that is unrecorded and untaxed by its government.

Un·der·ground Rail·road a secret network for helping slaves escape from the South to the North and to Canada in the years before the Civil War.

un·der·growth /'əndərˌgrōTH/ ▸*n.* a dense growth of shrubs and other plants, esp. under trees in woodland.

un·der·hand /'əndərˌhand/ ▸*adj.* **1** (of a throw or stroke in sports) made with the arm or hand below shoulder level: *he has a surprisingly good motion, more sidearm than underhand* | [as *adv.*] *I served underhand.* ■ with the palm of the hand upward or outward: *an underhand grip.* **2** another term for **UNDERHANDED**: *Laura would never agree to anything that smacked of underhand snooping.* ▷Old English in the sense 'in or into subjection, under control' (see **UNDER-**, **HAND**).

un·der·hand·ed /ˌəndər'handəd/ ▸*adj.* acting or done in a secret or dishonest way: *an underhanded method of snatching clients from rivals.* See note at **SECRET**. **—un·der·hand·ed·ly** *adv.*

un·der·hung /ˌəndər'həNG/ ▸*adj.* another term for **UNDERSHOT** (sense 2).

un·der·in·sured /ˌəndərin'sHo͝ord/ ▸*adj.* (of a person) having inadequate insurance coverage. **—un·der·in·sur·ance** /'əndərinˌsHo͝orəns/ *n.*

un·der·in·vest /ˌəndərin'vest/ ▸*v.* [*intrans.*] fail to invest sufficient money or resources in a project or enterprise: *we persistently underinvest in historic buildings.* **—un·der·in·vest·ment** *n.*

un·der·lay1 ▸*v.* /ˌəndər'lā/ (*past* and *past part.* **-laid**) [*trans.*] (usu. **be underlaid**) place something under (something else), esp. to support or raise it: *the green fields are underlaid with limestone* | *figurative a whine underlaid by an occasional choking sob.*
▸*n.* /'əndərˌlā/ something placed under or behind something else, esp. material laid under a carpet for protection or support. ■ *Music* the manner in which the words are fitted to the notes in a piece of vocal music. ▷Old English *underlecgan* (see **UNDER-**, **LAY**1).

un·der·lay2 ▸ past tense of **UNDERLIE**.

un·der·lay·ment /ˌəndər'lāmənt/ ▸*n.* a layer between a subfloor and a finished floor that facilitates leveling and adhesion: *the underlayment may be of hardboard or particle board of various thicknesses.*

un·der·let /ˌəndər'let/ ▸*v.* [*trans.*] (**-let·ting**; *past* and *past part.* **-let**) another term for **SUBLET**. ■ lease (land or property) at less than the true value.

un·der·lie /ˌəndər'lī/ ▸*v.* (**-ly·ing**; *past* **-lay**; *past part.* **-lain**) [*trans.*] (esp. of a layer of rock or soil) lie or be situated under (something). ■ be the cause or basis of (something): *the fundamental issue that underlies the conflict* | [as *adj.*] (**underlying**) *the underlying causes of poverty and drug addiction.* ▷Old English *underlicgan* 'be subject or subordinate to' (see **UNDER-**, **LIE**1).

un·der·life /'əndərˌlīf/ ▸*n.* a way of living that the general public does not normally encounter.

un·der·line /'əndərˌlīn/ ▸*v.* [*trans.*] draw a line under (a word or phrase) to give emphasis or indicate special type. ■ emphasize (something): *the improvement in retail sales was underlined by these figures.*
▸*n.* **1** a line drawn under a word or phrase, esp. for emphasis. **2** the line of the lower part of an animal's body.

un·der·lin·en /'əndərˌlinin/ ▸*n. archaic* underclothes, esp. those made of linen.

un·der·ling /'əndərliNG/ ▸*n.* (usu. **underlings**) *chiefly derogatory* a person lower in status or rank.

un·der·lip /'əndərˌlip/ ▸*n.* the lower lip of a person or animal.

un·der·ly·ing /ˌəndər'lī-iNG/ ▸ present participle of **UNDERLIE**.

un·der·man /ˌəndər'man/ ▸*v.* (**-manned**, **-man·ning**) [*trans.*] (usu. **be undermanned**) fail to provide with enough workers or crew: *the public prosecutor's offices are hopelessly undermanned.*

un·der·men·tioned /ˌəndər'mencHənd/ ▸*adj. Brit.* mentioned at a later place in a book or document.

un·der·mine /ˌəndər'mīn; 'əndərˌmīn/ ▸*v.* [*trans.*] erode the base or foundation of (a rock formation). ■ dig or excavate beneath (a building or fortification) so as to make it collapse. ■ *figurative* damage or weaken (someone or something), esp. gradually or insidiously: *this could undermine years of hard work.* ▷Middle English: from **UNDER-** + the verb **MINE**2, probably suggested by Middle Dutch *ondermineren.* **—un·der·min·er** *n.*

un·der·neath /ˌəndər'nēTH/ ▸*prep.* & *adv.* **1** situated directly below (something else): [as *prep.*] *our bedroom is right underneath theirs* | [as *adv.*] *his eyes were red-rimmed with black bags underneath* | [as *adj.*] *on longer hair, the underneath layers can be permed to give extra body.* ■ situated on a page directly below (a picture or another piece of writing): [as *prep.*] *four names written neatly underneath one another* | [as *adv.*] *there was writing underneath.* **2** so as to be concealed by (something else): [as *prep.*] *money changed hands underneath the table* | *figurative underneath his aloof air, Nicky was a warm and open young man* | [as *adv.*] *paint peeling off in flakes to reveal grayish plaster underneath.* ■ partly or wholly concealed by (a garment): [as *prep.*] *she could easily see the broadness of his shoulders underneath a tailored white shirt* | [as *adv.*] *I wear button-downs, and my T-shirts show underneath.*
▸*n.* [in *sing.*] the part or side of something facing toward the ground; the underside. ▷Old English *underneothan*; compare with **BENEATH**.

un·der·nour·ished /ˌəndər'nərisHt; -'nə-risht/ ▸*adj.* having insufficient food or other substances for good health and condition: *undernourished children.* **—un·der·nour·ish·ment** *n.*

un·der·paid /ˌəndər'pād/ ▸ past and past participle of **UNDERPAY**.

un·der·paint·ing /'əndərˌpāntiNG/ ▸*n.* paint subsequently overlaid with another layer or with a finishing coat.

un·der·pants /'əndərˌpan(t)s/ ▸*plural n.* an undergarment covering the lower part of the torso and having two holes for the legs.

un·der·part /'əndərˌpärt/ ▸*n.* a lower part or portion of something. ■ (**underparts**) the underside of an animal's body, esp. when of a specified color or pattern.

un·der·pass /'əndərˌpas/ ▸*n.* a road or pedestrian tunnel passing under another road or a railroad.

un·der·pay /ˌəndər'pā/ ▸*v.* (*past* and *past part.* **-paid**) [*trans.*] pay too little to (someone). ■ pay less than is due for (something): [as *adj.*] (**underpaid**) *late or underpaid tax.* **—un·der·pay·ment** /ˌəndər'pāmənt; 'əndərˌpā-/ *n.*

un·der·per·form /ˌəndərpər'fôrm/ ▸*v.* [*intrans.*] perform less well than expected. ■ [*trans.*] increase in value less than: *the shares have underperformed the market.* **—un·der·per·for·mance** /-'fôrməns/ *n.*

un·der·pin /ˌəndər'pin/ ▸*v.* (**-pinned**, **-pin·ning**) [*trans.*] support (a building or other structure) from below by laying a solid foundation below ground level or by substituting stronger for weaker materials. ■ support, justify, or form the basis for: *the theme of honor underpinning the two books.*

un·der·pin·ning /'əndərˌpiniNG/ ▸*n.* a solid foundation laid below ground level to support or strengthen a building. ■ a set of ideas, motives, or devices that justify or form the basis for something: *the theoretical underpinning for free-market economics.*

un·der·plant /ˌəndər'plant/ ▸*v.* [*trans.*] plant or cultivate the ground around (a tall plant) with smaller plants: *the roses* **are underplanted with** *pink and white bulbs.*

un·der·play /ˌəndər'plā; 'əndərˌplā/ ▸*v.* [*trans.*] perform (something) in a restrained way: *the violins un-*

derplayed the romantic element in the music. ■ represent (something) as being less important than it actually is: *I do not wish to underplay the tragedies that have occurred.*

un·der·plot /ˈəndərˌplät/ ▸*n.* a subordinate plot in a play, novel, or similar work.

un·der·pop·u·lat·ed /ˌəndərˈpäpyəˌlātid/ ▸*adj.* having an insufficient or very small population. —**un·der·pop·u·la·tion** /-ˌpäpyəˈlāsʜən/ *n.*

un·der·pow·ered /ˌəndərˈpou(-ə)rd/ ▸*adj.* lacking sufficient mechanical, electrical, or other power.

un·der·pre·pared /ˌəndərpriˈpərd/ ▸*adj.* not having prepared sufficiently to carry out a task.

un·der·price /ˌəndərˈprīs/ ▸*v.* [*trans.*] sell or offer something at a lower price than (the competition): *smaller banks may try to underprice the new giant in town.* ■ sell or offer (something) at too low a price: *we try not to underprice our books, while making sure they are still a good buy.*

un·der·priv·i·leged /ˌəndərˈpriv(ə)lijd/ ▸*adj.* (of a person) not enjoying the same standard of living or rights as the majority of people in a society.

un·der·pro·duce /ˌəndərprəˈd(y)o͞os/ ▸*v.* [*trans.*] **1** produce less of (a commodity) than is wanted or needed. **2** [often as *adj.*] (**underproduced**) record or produce (a song or movie) in such a basic way that it appears rough or unfinished: *many of the album's best tracks are relatively underproduced.* —**un·der·pro·duc·tion** /-prəˈdəksʜən/ *n.*

un·der·proof /ˌəndərˈpro͞of/ ▸*adj.* containing less alcohol than proof spirit does.

un·der·prop /ˌəndərˈpräp/ ▸*v.* (**-propped**, **-prop·ping**) [*trans.*] *archaic* support, esp. with a prop.

un·der·rate /ˌəndə(r)ˈrāt/ ▸*v.* [*trans.*] [often as *adj.*] (**underrated**) underestimate the extent, value, or importance of (someone or something): *a very underrated film.*

un·der·re·hearsed /ˌəndə(r)riˈhərst/ ▸*adj.* (of a performance or performer) having had insufficient rehearsals.

un·der·re·port /ˌəndə(r)riˈpôrt/ ▸*v.* [*trans.*] fail to report (something) fully: *athletes are inclined to underreport their use of drugs* | [as *adj.*] (**underreported**) *underreported domestic violence.*

un·der·rep·re·sent /ˌəndə(r)ˌrepriˈzent/ ▸*v.* [*trans.*] provide with insufficient or inadequate representation: *women are underrepresented at high levels.* —**un·der·rep·re·sen·ta·tion** /-ˌzenˈtāsʜən; -zən-/ *n.*

un·der·rep·re·sent·ed /ˌəndərˌrepriˈzentid/ ▸*adj.* not represented in adequate numbers or amounts: *women are underrepresented as senior scientists at the research center.*

un·der·re·sourced /ˌəndə(r)ˈrēˌsôrst; -riˈsôrst/ ▸*adj. chiefly Brit.* provided with insufficient resources: *an overstretched and under-resourced service.* —**un·der·re·sourc·ing** /-ˈrēˌsôrsiɴɢ; -riˈsôrs-/ *n.*

un·der·sat·u·rat·ed /ˌəndərˈsacʜəˌrātid/ ▸*adj. technical* falling short of being saturated with a particular constituent. —**un·der·sat·u·ra·tion** /-ˌsacʜəˈrāsʜən/ *n.*

un·der·score ▸*v.* /ˈəndərˌskôr; ˌəndərˈskôr/ another term for **UNDERLINE**.
▸*n.* /ˈəndərˌskôr/ another term for **UNDERLINE** (sense 1).

un·der·sea /ˌəndərˈsē/ ▸*adj.* below the sea or the surface of the sea: *undersea cables.*

un·der·sec·re·tar·y /ˌəndərˈsekriˌterē/ ▸*n.* (*pl.* **-tar·ies**) a subordinate official, in particular (in the U.S.) the principal assistant to a member of the cabinet, or (in the UK) a junior minister or senior civil servant.

un·der·sell /ˌəndərˈsel/ ▸*v.* (*past* and *past part.* **-sold**) [*trans.*] sell something at a lower price than (a competitor): *we can equal or undersell mail order.* ■ promote or rate (something) insufficiently; undervalue: *don't undersell yourself.*

un·der·set ▸*v.* /ˈəndərˌset/ (**-set·ting**; *past* and *past part.* **-set**) [*trans.*] *rare* place (something) under something else, esp. for support.
▸*n.* /ˈəndərset/ another term for **UNDERCURRENT**.

un·der·sexed /ˌəndərˈsekst/ ▸*adj.* having unusually weak sexual desires.

un·der·sher·iff /ˈəndərˌsherif/ ▸*n.* a deputy sheriff.

un·der·shirt /ˈəndərˌsʜərt/ ▸*n.* an undergarment worn under a shirt.

un·der·shoot ▸*v.* /ˌəndərˈsʜo͞ot/ (*past* and *past part.* **-shot**) [*trans.*] fall short of (a point or target): *the figure undershot the government's original estimate.* ■ (of an aircraft) land short of (the runway).
▸*n.* /ˈəndərsʜo͞ot/ an act of undershooting.

un·der·shorts /ˈəndərˌsʜôrts/ ▸*plural n.* underpants, esp. those worn by men or boys.

un·der·shot /ˈəndərˌsʜät/ ▸ past and past participle of **UNDERSHOOT**.
▸*adj.* **1** (of a waterwheel) turned by water flowing under it. **2** denoting or having a lower jaw that projects beyond the upper jaw.

un·der·side /ˈəndərˌsīd/ ▸*n.* the bottom or lower side or surface of something: *the butterfly's wings have a mottled brown pattern on the underside.* ■ *figurative* the less favorable aspect of something: *the sordid underside of the glamorous 1980s.*

un·der·signed /ˈəndərˌsīnd/ ▸*adj.* [usu. as *plural n.*] (**the undersigned**) *formal* whose signature is appended: *we, the undersigned, wish to protest at the current activities of the company.*

un·der·sized /ˌəndərˈsīzd/ (also **un·der·size**) ▸*adj.* of less than the usual size.

un·der·skirt /ˈəndərˌskərt/ ▸*n.* a skirt worn under another; a petticoat.

un·der·slung /ˌəndərˈsləɴɢ/ ▸*adj.* suspended from the underside of something: *helicopters hover to lift underslung loads.* ■ (of a vehicle chassis) hanging lower than the axles.

un·der·soil /ˈəndərˌsoil/ ▸*n.* subsoil.

un·der·sold /ˌəndərˈsōld/ ▸ past and past participle of **UNDERSELL**.

un·der·spend /ˌəndərˈspend/ ▸*v.* (*past* and *past part.* **-spent**) [*intrans.*] spend too little. ■ [*trans.*] spend less than (a specified or allocated amount): *schools have underspent their training budgets.*

un·der·staff /ˌəndərˈstaf/ ▸*v.* [*trans.*] provide (an organization) with too few staff members to operate effectively: [as *adj.*] (**understaffed**) *the department is understaffed and overworked.* —**un·der·staff·ing** *n.*

un·der·stand /ˌəndərˈstand/ ▸*v.* (*past* and *past part.* **-stood**) **1** [*trans.*] perceive the intended meaning of (words, a language, or speaker): *he didn't understand a word I said* | *he could usually* ***make himself understood*** | [with *clause*] *she understood what he was saying.* ■ perceive the significance, explanation, or cause of (something): *she didn't really understand the situation* | [with *clause*] *he couldn't understand why we burst out laughing* | [*intrans.*] *you don't understand—she has left me.* ■ be sympathetically or knowledgeably aware of the character or nature of: *Picasso understood color* | [with *clause*] *I understand how you feel.* ■ interpret or view (something) in a particular way: *as the term is usually understood, legislation refers to regulations and directives.* **2** [with *clause*] infer something from information received (often used as a polite formula in conversation): *I understand you're at art school* | [*trans.*] *as I understood it, she was flying back to New Zealand tomorrow.* ■ [*trans.*] (often **be understood**) regard (a missing word, phrase, or idea) as present; supply mentally: *"present company excepted" is always understood when sweeping generalizations are being made.* ■ [*trans.*] (often **be understood**) assume to be the case; take for granted: *he liked to play the field—that was understood.* ▷Old English *understandan* (see **UNDER-**, **STAND**). —**un·der·stand·er** *n.*

un·der·stand·a·ble /ˌəndərˈstandəbəl/ ▸*adj.* able to be understood: *though his accent was strange, the words were perfectly understandable.* ■ to be expected; natural, reasonable, or forgivable: *such fears are understandable.* —**un·der·stand·a·bil·i·ty** /-ˌstandəˈbilətē/ *n.* —**un·der·stand·a·bly** /-blē/ *adv.* [*sentence adverb*] *understandably, Richard did not believe me.*

un·der·stand·ing /ˌəndərˈstandiɴɢ/ ▸*n.* the ability to understand something; comprehension: *foreign visitors with little understanding of English.* ■ the power of abstract thought; intellect: *a child of sufficient intelligence and understanding.* ■ an individual's perception or judgment of a situation: *my understanding was that he would try to find a new supplier.* ■ sympathetic awareness or tolerance: *a problem that needs to be handled with understanding.* ■ an informal or unspoken agreement or arrangement: *he and I have an understanding* | *he had only been allowed to come* ***on the understanding that*** *he would be on his best behavior.*
▸*adj.* **1** sympathetically aware of other people's feelings; tolerant and forgiving: *people expect their doctor to be understanding.* **2** *archaic* having insight or good judgment. —**un·der·stand·ing·ly** *adv.*

un·der·state /ˌəndərˈstāt/ ▸*v.* [*trans.*] describe or represent (something) as being smaller, worse, or less important than it actually is: *the press has understated the extent of the problem.* —**un·der·stat·er** /ˈəndərˌstātər/ *n.*

un·der·stat·ed /ˌəndərˈstātid/ ▸*adj.* presented or expressed in a subtle and effective way: *understated elegance.* —**un·der·stat·ed·ly** *adv.*

un·der·state·ment /ˈəndərˌstātmənt/ ▸*n.* the presentation of something as being smaller, worse, or less important than it actually is: *a master of English understatement* | *to say I am delighted is an understatement.*

un·der·steer ▸*v.* /ˌəndərˈstir/ [*intrans.*] (of a motor vehicle) have a tendency to turn less sharply than is intended: *the car understeers on very fast bends.*
▸*n.* /ˈəndərˌstir/ the tendency of a vehicle to turn in such a way.

un·der·stood /ˌəndərˈsto͝od/ ▸ past and past participle of **UNDERSTAND**.

un·der·stored /ˈəndərˈstôrd/ ▸*adj.* supplied with fewer retail stores than the market demands: *specific market niches in which Chicago is understored compared to Los Angeles and New York.*

un·der·sto·ry /ˈəndərˌstôrē/ (*Brit.* **un·der·sto·rey**) ▸*n.* (*pl.* **-ries**) *Ecology* a layer of vegetation beneath the main canopy of a forest.

un·der·strap·per /ˈəndərˌstrapər/ ▸*n. informal, dated* an assistant or junior official.

un·der·stud·y /ˈəndərˌstədē/ ▸*n.* (*pl.* **-stud·ies**) (in the theater) a person who learns another's role in order to be able to act as a replacement at short notice.
▸*v.* (**-stud·ies**, **-stud·ied**) [*trans.*] learn (a role) or the role played by (an actor): *he had to understudy Prospero.*

un·der·sub·scribed /ˌəndərsəbˈskrībd/ ▸*adj.* (of a course or event) having more places available than applications.

un·der·sur·face /ˈəndərˌsərfəs/ ▸*n.* the lower or under surface of something.

un·der·take /ˌəndərˈtāk/ ▸*v.* (*past* **-took**; *past part.* **-tak·en**) [*trans.*] commit oneself to and begin (an enterprise or responsibility); take on: *a firm of builders undertook the construction work.* ■ [usu. with *infinitive*] promise to do a particular thing: *the firm undertook to keep price increases to a minimum.* ■ [with *clause*] guarantee or affirm something; give as a formal pledge: *a truck driver implicitly* ***undertakes that*** *he is reasonably skilled as a driver.*

un·der·tak·er /ˈəndərˌtākər/ ▸*n.* a person whose business is preparing dead bodies for burial or cremation and making arrangements for funerals.

un·der·tak·ing /ˈəndərˌtākiɴɢ; ˌəndərˈtā-/ ▸*n.* **1** a formal pledge or promise to do something: *I give* ***an undertaking that*** *we shall proceed with the legislation.* ■ a task that is taken on; an enterprise: *a mammoth undertaking that involved digging into the side of a cliff face.* ■ the action of undertaking to do something: *the knowing undertaking of an obligation.* **2** /ˈəndərˌtākiɴɢ/ the management of funerals as a profession.

un·der·things /ˈəndərˌᴛʜiɴɢz/ ▸*plural n.* underclothes, esp. those worn by a woman or girl.

un·der·thrust /ˌəndərˈᴛʜrəst/ *Geology* ▸*v.* (*past* and *past part.* **-thrust**) [*trans.*] force (a crustal plate or other body of rock) beneath another plate or block. ■ be forced underneath (another plate or block).
▸*n.* an instance of such forced movement.

un·der·tint /ˈəndərˌtint/ ▸*n.* a subdued or delicate tint.

un·der·tip /ˈəndərˈtip/ ▸*v.* (**-tipped**, **-tip·ping**) give (someone) an excessively small tip.

un·der·tone /ˈəndərˌtōn/ ▸*n.* a subdued or muted tone of sound or color: *they were talking in undertones* | *a pallid undertone to her tanned skin.* ■ an underlying quality or feeling: *the sexual undertones of most advertising.*

un·der·took /ˌəndərˈto͝ok/ ▸ past participle of **UNDERTAKE**.

un·der·tow /ˈəndərˌtō/ ▸*n.* a current below the surface of the sea moving in the opposite direction to the surface current, esp. away from the shore: *I was swept away by the undertow.* ■ *figurative* an implicit quality, emotion, or influence underlying the superficial aspects of something and leaving a particular impression: *there's a dark undertow of loss that links the novel with earlier works.*

un·der·trained /ˌəndərˈtrānd/ ▸*adj.* with insufficient training for a job, sport, etc.

un·der·trick /ˈəndərˌtrik/ ▸*n. Bridge* a trick by which the declarer falls short of their contract.

un·der·use ▸*v.* /ˌəndərˈyo͞oz/ [*trans.*] [usu. as *adj.*] (**underused**) use (something) below the optimum level: *the owner noted a lot of underused space in that garage.*
▸*n.* /ˌəndərˈyo͞os/ insufficient use: *underuse of existing services.*

un·der·u·ti·lize /ˌəndərˈyo͞otlˌīz/ ▸*v.* [*trans.*] underuse (something). —**un·der·u·ti·li·za·tion** /-ˌyo͞otl-əˈzāsʜən/ *n.*

un·der·val·ue /ˌəndərˈvalyo͞o/ ▸*v.* (**-val·ues**, **-val·ued**, **-val·u·ing**) [*trans.*] [often as *adj.*] (**undervalued**) rate (something) insufficiently highly; fail to appreciate: *the skills of the housewife remain undervalued in society.* ■ underestimate the financial value of (something):

the company's assets were undervalued in its balance sheet. —**un·der·val·u·a·tion** /-ˌvalyo͞oˈāsʜən/ *n.*

un·der·vest /ˈəndərˌvest/ ▸*n. chiefly Brit.* an undershirt.

un·der·vote /ˈəndərˌvōt/ ▸*n.* a ballot not counted because of unclear marking by the voter.

un·der·wa·ter /ˌəndərˈwôtər; -ˈwätər/ ▸*adj.* & *adv.* situated, occurring, or done beneath the surface of the water: [as *adj.*] *there are underwater volcanoes in the region* | [as *adv.*] *they learn to navigate underwater at night.*

un·der·wear /ˈəndərˌwer/ ▸*n.* clothing worn under other clothes, typically next to the skin.

un·der·weight /ˈəndərˌwāt; ˌəndərˈwāt/ ▸*adj.* below a weight considered normal or desirable: *he was thirty pounds underweight.* ■ *Finance* (also **un·der·weight·ed**) having less investment in a particular area than is considered desirable or appropriate: *the company is still underweight in Japan* | *underweighted in technology.* ▸*v.* [*trans.*] apply too little weight to (something): *we feared the hot-air balloon had been underweighted.* | *figurative clinicians tend to overweight parent and underweight child information when deriving diagnoses.* ▸*n.* insufficient weight.

un·der·went /ˌəndərˈwent/ ▸ past of **UNDERGO**.

un·der·whelm /ˌəndərˈ(h)welm/ ▸*v.* [*trans.*] (usu. **be underwhelmed**) *humorous* fail to impress or make a positive impact on (someone); disappoint: *American voters seem underwhelmed by the choices for president.* ▷1950s: suggested by **OVERWHELM**.

un·der·wing /ˈəndərˌwiɴɢ/ ▸*n.* **1** the hind wing of an insect, esp. when it is normally hidden by a forewing. **2** the underside of a bird's wing. **3** (also **un·der·wing moth**) [usu. with *adj.*] a moth with drab forewings and brightly colored hind wings, typically yellow or red with a black terminal band. • Several genera in the family Noctuidae.

un·der·wire /ˈəndərˌwīr/ ▸*n.* a semicircular wire support stitched under each cup of a bra. —**un·der·wired** *adj.*

un·der·wood /ˈəndərˌwo͝od/ ▸*n.* small trees and shrubs growing beneath taller timber trees.

un·der·work /ˌəndərˈwərk/ ▸*v.* [*trans.*] (usu. **be underworked**) impose too little work on (someone): *its members are viewed by the public as overpaid and underworked.*

un·der·world /ˈəndərˌwərld/ ▸*n.* **1** the world of criminals or of organized crime. **2** the mythical abode of the dead, imagined as being under the earth.

un·der·write /ˈəndə(r)ˌrīt; ˌəndə(r)ˈrīt/ ▸*v.* (*past* **-wrote**; *past part.* **-writ·ten**) [*trans.*] **1** sign and accept liability under (an insurance policy), thus guaranteeing payment in case loss or damage occurs. ■ accept (a liability or risk) in this way. **2** (of a bank or other financial institution) engage to buy all the unsold shares in (an issue of new securities). ■ undertake to finance or otherwise support or guarantee (something): *they were willing to underwrite the construction of a ship.* **3** *archaic* write (something) below something else, esp. other written matter. —**un·der·writ·er** /ˈəndə(r)ˌrītər/ *n.*

un·de·scend·ed /ˌəndiˈsendid/ ▸*adj. Medicine* (of a testicle) remaining in the abdomen instead of having descended normally into the scrotum.

un·de·served /ˌəndiˈzərvd/ ▸*adj.* not warranted, merited, or earned: *an undeserved term of imprisonment.* —**un·de·serv·ed·ly** /-ˈzərvədlē/ *adv.*

un·de·serv·ing /ˌəndiˈzərviɴɢ/ ▸*adj.* not deserving or worthy of something positive, esp. help or praise. —**un·de·serv·ing·ly** *adv.*

un·de·sir·a·ble /ˌəndiˈzīrəbəl/ ▸*adj.* not wanted or desirable because harmful, objectionable, or unpleasant: *the drug's undesirable side effects.* ▸*n.* a person considered to be objectionable in some way. —**un·de·sir·a·bil·i·ty** *n.* —**un·de·sir·a·ble·ness** *n.* —**un·de·sir·a·bly** /-blē/ *adv.*

un·de·sired /ˌəndiˈzīrd/ ▸*adj.* (esp. of an act or consequence) not wanted or desired.

un·de·ter·mined /ˌəndiˈtərmənd/ ▸*adj.* not authoritatively decided or settled: *the acquisition will result in an as yet undetermined number of lay-offs.* ■ not known: *the bus was traveling with an undetermined number of passengers when it crashed.*

un·de·vel·oped /ˌəndiˈveləpt/ ▸*adj.* not having been developed: *undeveloped coal reserves.* ■ not having developed: *undeveloped buds and shoots.*

un·did /ˌənˈdid/ ▸ past of **UNDO**.

un·dies /ˈəndēz/ ▸*plural n. informal* articles of underwear, esp. those of a woman or girl. ▷early 20th cent.: abbreviation.

un·dif·fer·enced /ˌənˈdif(ə)rənst/ ▸*adj. Heraldry* (of arms) not made distinct by a mark of difference.

un·dif·fer·en·ti·at·ed /ˌənˌdifəˈrenchēˌātid/ ▸*adj.* not different or differentiated: *ideologically undifferentiated candidates.*

un·dine /ˌənˈdēn; ˈənˌdēn/ ▸*n.* a female spirit or nymph inhabiting water. ▷early 19th cent.: from modern Latin *undina* (a word invented by Paracelsus), from Latin *unda* 'a wave.'

un·dip·lo·mat·ic /ˌənˌdipləˈmatik/ ▸*adj.* being or appearing insensitive and tactless. —**un·dip·lo·mat·i·cal·ly** /-ik(ə)lē/ *adv.*

un·di·rect·ed /ˌəndəˈrektəd; -ˌdī-/ ▸*adj.* lacking direction; without a particular aim, purpose, or target: *she was full of ineffectual undirected anger.*

un·dis·guised /ˌəndisˈgīzd/ ▸*adj.* (of a feeling) not disguised or concealed; open: *she looked at him with undisguised contempt.* —**un·dis·guis·ed·ly** /-ˈgīzidlē/ *adv.*

un·dis·mayed /ˌəndisˈmād/ ▸*adj.* not dismayed or discouraged by a setback.

un·dis·put·ed /ˌəndiˈspyo͞otid/ ▸*adj.* not disputed or called into question; accepted.

un·dis·so·ci·at·ed /ˌəndiˈsōsʜēˌātid; -ˈsōsē/ ▸*adj. Chemistry* (of a molecule) not dissociated into oppositely charged ions.

un·dis·tin·guish·a·ble /ˌəndiˈstiɴɢgwisʜəbəl/ ▸*adj.* indistinguishable.

un·dis·tin·guished /ˌəndiˈstiɴɢgwisʜt/ ▸*adj.* lacking distinction; unexceptional: *an undistinguished career.*

un·dis·trib·ut·ed mid·dle ▸*n. Logic* a fallacy arising from the failure of the middle term of a syllogism to refer to all the members of a class in at least one premise.

un·di·vid·ed /ˌəndəˈvīdid/ ▸*adj.* not divided, separated, or broken into parts. ■ concentrated on or devoted completely to one object: *I can now give you my undivided attention.*

un·do /ˌənˈdo͞o/ ▸*v.* (**-does** /-ˈdəz/; *past* **-did**; *past part.* **-done**) [*trans.*] **1** unfasten, untie, or loosen (something): *the knot was difficult to undo.* **2** cancel or reverse the effects or results of (a previous action or measure): *there wasn't any way Evelyn could undo the damage.* ■ cancel (the last one or more commands executed by a computer). **3** *formal* cause the downfall or ruin of: *Iago's hatred of women undoes him.* ▸*n. Computing* a feature of a computer program that allows a user to cancel or reverse the last one or more commands executed. ▷Old English *undōn* (see **UN-**[2], **DO**[1]).

un·dock /ˌənˈdäk/ ▸*v.* [*trans.*] **1** separate (a spacecraft) from another in space: *Conrad undocked Gemini and used his thruster to back slowly away* | [*intrans.*] *Atlantis is scheduled to undock from Mir today.* **2** take (a ship) out of or away from a dock.

un·do·cu·ment·ed /ˌənˈdäkyəˌmentid/ ▸*adj.* **1** not recorded in or proved by documents. **2** not having the appropriate legal document or license: *undocumented immigrants.*

un·do·ing /ˌənˈdo͞o-iɴɢ/ ▸*n.* [in *sing.*] a person's ruin or downfall: *he knew of his ex-partner's role in his undoing.* ■ the cause of such ruin or downfall: *that complacency was to be their undoing.*

un·done /ˌənˈdən/ ▸ past participle of **UNDO**. ▸*adj.* **1** not tied or fastened: *the top few buttons of his shirt were undone.* **2** not done or finished: *he had left his homework undone.* **3** *formal* or *humorous* (of a person) ruined by a disastrous or devastating setback or reverse: *I am undone!*

un·doubt·a·ble /ˌənˈdoutəbəl/ ▸*adj. rare* not able to be doubted; indubitable. —**un·doubt·a·bly** /-blē/ *adv.*

un·doubt·ed /ˌənˈdoutid/ ▸*adj.* not questioned or doubted by anyone: *her undoubted ability.* —**un·doubt·ed·ly** *adv.*

UNDP ▸*abbr.* United Nations Development Program.

un·draped /ˌənˈdrāpt/ ▸*adj.* not covered with cloth or drapery. ■ (esp. of a model or subject in art) naked.

un·dreamed /ˌənˈdrēmd/ (*Brit.* also **un·dreamt** /-ˈdremt/) ▸*adj.* (**undreamed of**) not thought to be possible (used to express pleasant surprise at the amount, extent, or level of something): *a level of comfort undreamed of in earlier times* | *she is now enjoying undreamed-of success.*

un·dress /ˌənˈdres/ ▸*v.* [*intrans.*] take off one's clothes: *she undressed and climbed into bed* | *I went into the bathroom to* **get undressed**. ■ [*trans.*] take the clothes off (someone else). ▸*n.* **1** the state of being naked or only partially clothed: *women in various states of undress.* **2** *Military* ordinary clothing or uniform, as opposed to that worn on ceremonial occasions. Compare with **FULL DRESS**.

un·dressed /ˌənˈdrest/ ▸*adj.* **1** wearing no clothes: *he was undressed and ready for bed.* **2** not treated, processed, or prepared for use: *undressed deerskin* | *a rough, undressed stone slab.* **3** (of food) not having a dressing: *an undressed salad.*

UNDRO ▸*abbr.* United Nations Disaster Relief Office.

un·due /ˌənˈd(y)o͞o/ ▸*adj.* unwarranted or inappropriate because excessive or disproportionate: *this figure did not give rise to undue concern.* —**un·du·ly** /-ˈd(y)o͞olē/ *adv.*

un·due in·flu·ence ▸*n. Law* influence by which a person is induced to act otherwise than by their own free will or without adequate attention to the consequences.

un·du·lant /ˈənjələnt; ˈəndyə-/ ▸*adj.* having a rising and falling motion or appearance like that of waves; undulating. ▷mid 19th cent.: from Latin *undulant-* 'moving like a wave,' from the verb *undulare.* —**un·du·lance** *n.*

un·du·lant fe·ver ▸*n.* brucellosis in humans. ▷late 19th cent.: so named because of the intermittent fever associated with the disease.

un·du·late ▸*v.* /ˈənjəˌlāt; ˈəndyə-/ [*intrans.*] move with a smooth wavelike motion: *her body undulated to the thumping rhythm of the music.* ■ [usu. *adj.*] (**undulating**) have a wavy form or outline: *delightful views over undulating countryside.* ▸*adj.* /-lit; -ˌlāt/ *Botany* & *Zoology* (esp. of a leaf) having a wavy surface or edge. ▷mid 17th cent.: from late Latin *undulatus*, from Latin *unda* 'a wave.' —**un·du·late·ly** /-litlē/ *adv.* —**un·du·la·tion** /ˌənjəˈlāsʜən; ˌəndyə-/ *n.* —**un·du·la·to·ry** /ˈənjələˌtôrē; ˈəndyə-/ *adj.*

un·dy /ˈəndē/ ▸*adj.* [usu. *postpositive*] *Heraldry* another term for **WAVY**.

un·dy·ing /ˌənˈdī-iɴɢ/ ▸*adj.* (esp. of an emotion) lasting forever: *promises of undying love.* —**un·dy·ing·ly** *adv.*

un·earned /ˌənˈərnd/ ▸*adj.* not earned or deserved: *unearned privileges.* ■ *Baseball* (of a run) scored as the result of or following an error made by the fielding side (specifically when the fielder has failed to make the third out of the inning), and not recorded in the pitcher's statistics.

un·earned in·come ▸*n.* income from investments rather than from work.

un·earned in·cre·ment ▸*n.* an increase in the value of land or property without labor or expenditure on the part of the owner.

un·earth /ˌənˈərʜ/ ▸*v.* [*trans.*] find (something) in the ground by digging. ■ discover (something hidden, lost, or kept secret) by investigation or searching: *they have done all they can to unearth the truth.*

un·earth·ly /ˌənˈərʜlē/ ▸*adj.* **1** unnatural or mysterious, esp. in a disturbing way: *unearthly quiet.* **2** *informal* unreasonably early or inconvenient: *a job that involves getting up at an unearthly hour.* —**un·earth·li·ness** *n.*

un·ease /ˌənˈēz/ ▸*n.* anxiety or discontent: *public unease about defense policy.*

un·eas·y /ˌənˈēzē/ ▸*adj.* (**-eas·i·er**, **-eas·i·est**) causing or feeling anxiety; troubled or uncomfortable: *she felt guilty now and a little uneasy* | *an uneasy silence.* —**un·eas·i·ly** /-zəlē/ *adv.* —**un·eas·i·ness** *n.*

un·ec·o·nom·ic /ˌənˌekəˈnämik; -ˌēkə-/ ▸*adj.* unprofitable: *costs for seven huge, uneconomic reactors.* ■ constituting an inefficient use of money or other resources: *it may be uneconomic to repair some goods.*

un·ec·o·nom·i·cal /ˌənˌekəˈnämikəl; -ˌēkə-/ ▸*adj.* wasteful of money or other resources; not economical: *the old buses eventually become uneconomical to run.* —**un·ec·o·nom·i·cal·ly** /-ik(ə)lē/ *adv.*

un·ed·i·fy·ing /ˌənˈedəˌfī-iɴɢ/ ▸*adj.* (esp. of an event taking place in public) distasteful; unpleasant: *the unedifying sight of the two leaders screeching conflicting proposals.* —**un·ed·i·fy·ing·ly** *adv.*

un·ed·u·cat·ed /ˌənˈejəˌkātid/ ▸*adj.* lacking an education; poorly educated. See note at **IGNORANT**. —**un·ed·u·ca·ble** /-kəbəl/ *adj.*

un·e·lect·a·ble /ˌəniˈlektəbəl/ ▸*adj.* (of a candidate or party) unable to be elected.

un·e·lect·ed /ˌəniˈlektid/ ▸*adj.* (of an official) not elected: *unelected bureaucrats.*

un·e·mo·tion·al /ˌəniˈmōsʜənl/ ▸*adj.* not having or showing strong feelings: *a flat, unemotional voice.* —**un·e·mo·tion·al·ly** /-sʜənl-ē/ *adv.*

Pronunciation Key ə *ago*; ər *over*; ˈə or ˌə *up*; ˈər or ˌər *fur*; a *hat*; ā *rate*; ä *car*; ᴄʜ *chew*; e *let*; ē *see*; e(ə)r *air*; i *fit*; ī *by*; i(ə)r *ear*; ɴɢ *sing*; ō *go*; ô *for*; oi *boy*; o͝o *good*; o͞o *goo*; ou *out*; sʜ *she*; ᴛʜ *thin*; ᴛʜ *then*; (h)w *why*; ᴢʜ *vision*

U

un·em·ploy·a·ble /ˌənim'ploiəbəl/ ▸*adj.* (of a person) not able or likely to get paid employment, esp. because of a lack of skills or qualifications.
▸*n.* an unemployable person. —**un·em·ploy·a·bil·i·ty** /-ˌploiə'bilətē/ *n.*

un·em·ployed /ˌənim'ploid/ ▸*adj.* (of a person) without a paid job but available to work: *I was unemployed for three years* | [as *plural n.*] (**the unemployed**) *a training program for the long-term unemployed.* ■ (of a thing) not in use.

un·em·ploy·ment /ˌənim'ploimənt/ ▸*n.* the state of being unemployed. ■ the number or proportion of unemployed people: *a time of high unemployment.* ■ short for UNEMPLOYMENT BENEFIT.

un·em·ploy·ment ben·e·fit (also **un·em·ploy·ment com·pen·sa·tion**) ▸*n.* a payment made by a government or a labor union to an unemployed person.

un·em·ploy·ment com·pen·sa·tion ▸*n.* money that substitutes for wages or salary, paid to recently unemployed workers under a program administered by a government or labor union.

un·end·ing /ˌən'endiNG/ ▸*adj.* having or seeming to have no end: *the charity rescues children from unending poverty.* See note at ETERNAL. ■ countless or continual: *unending demands.* —**un·end·ing·ly** *adv.* —**un·end·ing·ness** *n.*

un·en·dur·a·ble /ˌənin'd(y)o͝orəbəl/ ▸*adj.* not able to be tolerated or endured: *cries of unendurable suffering.* —**un·en·dur·a·bly** /-blē/ *adv.*

un-Eng·lish /ˌən'iNG(g)lisH/ ▸*adj.* not considered characteristic of English people or the English language.

un·en·riched /ˌənen'ricHt/ ▸*adj.* **1** (of foodstuffs or soil) without additional nutrients added: *unenriched white flour.* **2** (of uranium) in the natural state, containing less than one percent U-235 (an unstable, fissionable isotope of uranium ore).

un·en·tan·gle /ˌənin'taNGgəl/ ▸*v.* another term for DISENTANGLE.

un·en·vi·a·ble /ˌən'envēəbəl/ ▸*adj.* difficult, undesirable, or unpleasant: *he had the unenviable task of trying to reconcile their disparate interests* | *an unenviable reputation for drunkenness.* —**un·en·vi·a·bly** /-blē/ *adv.*

UNEP ▸*abbr.* United Nations Environment Programme.

un·e·qual /ˌən'ēkwəl/ ▸*adj.* **1** not equal in quantity, size, or value: *two rooms of unequal size* | *unequal odds.* ■ not fair, evenly balanced, or having equal advantage: *the ownership of capital is unequal in this country.* **2** [*predic.*] not having the ability or resources to meet a challenge: *she felt* **unequal to** *the task before her.*
▸*n.* a person or thing considered to be different from another in status or level. —**un·e·qual·ly** *adv.*

un·e·qualed /ˌən'ēkwəld/ (*Brit.* **un·e·qualled**) ▸*adj.* superior to all others in performance or extent: *a range of facilities unequaled in Chicago* | *trout of unequaled quality.*

un·e·quiv·o·cal /ˌəni'kwivəkəl/ ▸*adj.* leaving no doubt; unambiguous: *an unequivocal answer* | *he was unequivocal in condemning the violence.* —**un·e·quiv·o·cal·ly** /-ik(ə)lē/ *adv.* —**un·e·quiv·o·cal·ness** *n.*

un·err·ing /ˌən'əriNG; -'er-/ ▸*adj.* always right or accurate: *an unerring sense of direction.* —**un·err·ing·ly** *adv.* —**un·err·ing·ness** *n.*

un·es·cap·a·ble /ˌənə'skāpəbəl/ ▸*adj.* another term for INESCAPABLE.

UNESCO /yo͞o'neskō/ (also **Unesco**) an agency of the United Nations established in 1945 to promote the exchange of information, ideas, and culture. In 1984 the U.S. withdrew from the organization. ▷acronym from *United Nations Educational, Scientific, and Cultural Organization.*

un·es·cort·ed /ˌənə'skôrtid; -'esˌkôrtid/ ▸*adj.* not escorted, esp. for protection, security, or as a mark of rank: *their task was to prey on unescorted enemy merchant ships and sink them.* ■ unaccompanied by a social partner: *in some bars unescorted women were not served.*

un·es·sen·tial /ˌənə'sencHəl/ ▸*adj.* & *n.* another term for INESSENTIAL.

un·eth·i·cal /ˌən'eTHikəl/ ▸*adj.* not morally correct: *it is unethical to torment any creature for entertainment.* —**un·eth·i·cal·ly** /-ik(ə)lē/ *adv.*

un·e·ven /ˌən'ēvən/ ▸*adj.* not level or smooth: *the floors are cracked and uneven.* ■ not regular, consistent, or equal: *the uneven distribution of resources.* ■ (of a contest) not equally balanced: *Fran struggled briefly but soon gave up the uneven contest.* ▷Old English *unefen* 'not corresponding exactly' (see UN-[1], EVEN[1]). —**un·e·ven·ly** *adv.* —**un·e·ven·ness** *n.*

un·e·ven bars (also **un·e·ven par·al·lel bars**) ▸*plural n.* a pair of parallel bars set at different heights, used in women's gymnastics. ■ the set of exercises performed on such a piece of equipment.

un·ex·am·pled /ˌənig'zampəld/ ▸*adj. formal* having no precedent or parallel: *a regime that brought such unexampled disaster on its people.*

un·ex·cep·tion·a·ble /ˌənik'sepsH(ə)nəbəl/ ▸*adj.* not open to objection: *the unexceptionable belief that society should be governed by law.* —**un·ex·cep·tion·a·ble·ness** *n.* —**un·ex·cep·tion·a·bly** /-blē/ *adv.*

USAGE There is a clear distinction in meaning between **exceptionable** ('open to objection') and **exceptional** ('out of the ordinary, very good'). However, this distinction has become blurred in the negative forms **unexceptionable** and **unexceptional**. Strictly speaking, **unexceptionable** means 'not open to objection' (*this request is* ***unexceptionable*** *in itself*), while **unexceptional** means 'not out of the ordinary, usual' (*the hotel was adequate but* ***unexceptional***). But, although the distinction may be clear in these two examples, the meaning of **unexceptionable** is often indeterminate between 'not open to objection' and 'ordinary,' as in *the food was bland and* ***unexceptionable*** or *the candidates were pretty* ***unexceptionable***. See also **usage** at EXCEPTIONABLE.

un·ex·cep·tion·al /ˌənik'sepsHənl/ ▸*adj.* not out of the ordinary; usual: *an unexceptional movie.* —**un·ex·cep·tion·al·ly** *adv.*

USAGE See usage at UNEXCEPTIONABLE.

un·ex·cit·a·ble /ˌənik'sītəbəl/ ▸*adj.* (of a person) not easily excited. —**un·ex·cit·a·bil·i·ty** /-ˌsītə'bilətē/ *n.*

un·ex·pect·ed /ˌənik'spektid/ ▸*adj.* not expected or regarded as likely to happen: *his death was totally unexpected* | [as *n.*] (**the unexpected**) *he seemed to have a knack for saying the unexpected.* —**un·ex·pect·ed·ly** *adv.* [as *submodifier*] *an unexpectedly high price* —**un·ex·pect·ed·ness** *n.*

un·ex·pired /ˌənik'spīrd/ ▸*adj.* (of an agreement or period of time) not yet having come to an end: *the unexpired portion of the lease.*

un·ex·plain·a·ble /ˌənik'splānəbəl/ ▸*adj.* unable to be explained or accounted for: *unexplainable rages.* —**un·ex·plain·a·bly** /-blē/ *adv.*

un·ex·plained /ˌənik'splānd/ ▸*adj.* not described or made clear; unknown: *the reason for her summons was as yet unexplained.* ■ not accounted for or attributable to an identified cause: *SIDS is still an unexplained phenomenon.*

un·ex·ploit·ed /ˌənik'sploitid/ ▸*adj.* (of resources) not used to maximum benefit: *unexploited reserves of natural gas.*

un·ex·plored /ˌənik'splôrd/ ▸*adj.* (of a country or area) not investigated or mapped. ■ not evaluated or discussed in detail: *the research focuses on an unexplored theme in European history.*

un·ex·posed /ˌənik'spōzd/ ▸*adj.* covered or protected; not vulnerable. ■ [*predic.*] not introduced to or acquainted with something: *a person* ***unexposed to*** *spiritualist traditions.* ■ [*predic.*] not made public; concealed: *no secrets were left unexposed.* ■ (of photographic film) not subjected to light.

un·ex·pressed /ˌənik'sprest/ ▸*adj.* (of a thought or feeling) not communicated or made known: *he thought it best to leave his doubts unexpressed.* ■ *Genetics* (of a gene) not appearing in a phenotype.

un·face·a·ble /ˌən'fāsəbəl/ ▸*adj.* (of a situation or circumstance) not able to be confronted or dealt with.

un·fail·ing /ˌən'fāliNG/ ▸*adj.* without error or fault: *his unfailing memory for names.* ■ reliable or constant: *his mother had always been an unfailing source of reassurance.* —**un·fail·ing·ly** *adv.* —**un·fail·ing·ness** *n.*

un·fair /ˌən'fe(ə)r/ ▸*adj.* not based on or behaving according to the principles of equality and justice: *at times like these the legal system appears inhumane and unfair.* ■ unkind, inconsiderate, or unreasonable: *you're unfair to criticize like that when she's never done you any harm.* ■ not following the rules of a game or sport. ▷Old English *unfæger* 'not beautiful' (see UN-[1], FAIR[1]). —**un·fair·ly** *adv.* —**un·fair·ness** *n.*

un·faith·ful /ˌən'fāTHfəl/ ▸*adj.* not faithful, in particular: ■ engaging in sexual relations with a person other than one's regular partner in contravention of a previous promise or understanding: *you haven't* ***been unfaithful to*** *him, have you?* | *her unfaithful husband.* ■ disloyal, treacherous, or insincere: *she felt that to sell the house would be* ***unfaithful to*** *her parents' memory.* —**un·faith·ful·ly** *adv.* —**un·faith·ful·ness** *n.*

un·fa·mil·iar /ˌənfə'milyər/ ▸*adj.* not known or recognized: *his voice was* ***unfamiliar to*** *her.* ■ unusual or uncharacteristic: *the yellow taxicab was an unfamiliar sight on these roads.* ■ [*predic.*] (**unfamiliar with**) not having knowledge or experience of: *the organization was set up to advise people who might be unfamiliar with legal procedures.* —**un·fa·mil·i·ar·i·ty** /-ˌmilē'e(ə)ritē; -fəmil'yer-/ *n.*

un·fash·ioned /ˌən'fasHənd/ ▸*adj. chiefly poetic/literary* not made into a specific shape; formless.

un·fas·ten /ˌən'fasən/ ▸*v.* [*trans.*] open the fastening of; undo (something): *Allie stands before the mirror unfastening her earrings* | [as *adj.*] (**unfastened**) *he had left the door unfastened.* ■ [*intrans.*] become loose or undone.

un·fa·thered /ˌən'fāTHərd/ ▸*adj. dated* having no known or acknowledged father; illegitimate. ■ *chiefly poetic/literary* of unknown or obscure origin: *unfathered rumors.*

un·fa·vor·a·ble /ˌən'fāv(ə)rəbəl/ (*Brit.* **un·fa·vour·a·ble**) ▸*adj.* **1** expressing or showing a lack of approval or support: *single mothers are often the target of unfavorable press attention.* **2** adverse; inauspicious: *it would be unwise to sell the company while the economic circumstances are so unfavorable.* —**un·fa·vor·a·ble·ness** *n.* —**un·fa·vor·a·bly** /-blē/ *adv.*

un·feel·ing /ˌən'fēliNG/ ▸*adj.* unsympathetic, harsh, or callous. ■ lacking physical sensation or sensitivity. ▷late Old English *unfēlende* 'insensible' (see UN-[1], FEELING). —**un·feel·ing·ly** *adv.* —**un·feel·ing·ness** *n.*

un·feigned /ˌən'fānd/ ▸*adj.* genuine; sincere: *a broad smile of unfeigned delight.* —**un·feign·ed·ly** /-'fānidlē/ *adv.*

un·felt /ˌən'felt/ ▸*adj.* not felt or experienced: *he had no desire to trade unfelt greetings with his mother-in-law.*

un·fet·ter /ˌən'fetər/ ▸*v.* [*trans.*] [usu. as *adj.*] (**unfettered**) release from restraint or inhibition: *his imagination is unfettered by the laws of logic.*

un·fil·i·al /ˌən'filēəl; -'filyəl/ ▸*adj.* not having or showing the qualities associated with a son or daughter. —**un·fil·i·al·ly** *adv.*

un·fil·tered /ˌən'filtərd/ ▸*adj.* **1** not having been filtered: *unfiltered tap water.* **2** (of a cigarette) not provided with a filter.

un·fin·ished /ˌən'finisHt/ ▸*adj.* not finished or concluded; incomplete: *her last novel is unfinished.* ■ (of an object) not having been given an attractive surface appearance as the final stage of manufacture.

un·fit /ˌən'fit/ ▸*adj.* **1** [*predic.*] (of a thing) not of the necessary quality or standard to meet a particular purpose: *the land is* ***unfit for*** *food crops.* ■ (of a person) not having the requisite qualities or skills to undertake something competently: *she is unfit to have care and control of her children.* ■ *Biology* (of a species) not able to produce viable offspring or survive in a particular environment. **2** (of a person) not in good physical condition, typically as a result of failure to exercise regularly.
▸*v.* (**-fit·ted, -fit·ting**) [*trans.*] *archaic* make (something or someone) unsuitable; disqualify. —**un·fit·ly** *adv.* —**un·fit·ness** *n.*

un·fit·ted /ˌən'fitid/ ▸*adj.* **1** [*predic.*] (of a person) not fitted or suited for a particular task or vocation: *he seemed to know he was* ***unfitted for*** *such a role.* **2** (of furniture) not fitted.

un·fit·ting /ˌən'fitiNG/ ▸*adj.* not fitting or suitable; unbecoming. —**un·fit·ting·ly** *adv.*

un·fixed /ˌən'fikst/ ▸*adj.* not fixed, in particular: ■ not fixed in a definite place or position; unfastened; loose: *the green cloth cover had become unfixed in a dozen places.* ■ uncertain or variable: *a being of unfixed gender.* ■ *informal* (of a venture or situation) doubtful or unsuccessful; coming to nothing: *you don't have to do anything unless the deal* ***comes unfixed.*** —**un·fix** *v.*

un·flag·ging /ˌən'flagiNG/ ▸*adj.* tireless; persistent: *his apparently unflagging enthusiasm impressed her.* —**un·flag·ging·ly** *adv.*

un·flap·pa·ble /ˌən'flapəbəl/ ▸*adj. informal* having or showing calmness in a crisis. —**un·flap·pa·bil·i·ty** /-ˌflapə'bilətē/ *n.* —**un·flap·pa·bly** /-blē/ *adv.*

un·fla·vored /ˌən'flāvərd/ (*Brit.* **un·fla·voured**) ▸*adj.* (of food or drink) not containing additional flavorings.

un·fledged /ˌən'flejd/ ▸*adj.* (of a bird) not yet fledged. ■ *figurative* (of a person) inexperienced; youthful.

un·fleshed /ˌən'flesHt/ ▸*adj. chiefly poetic/literary* not covered with flesh.

un·flinch·ing /ˌən'flincHiNG/ ▸*adj.* not showing fear or hesitation in the face of danger or difficulty: *he has shown unflinching determination throughout the campaign.* —**un·flinch·ing·ly** *adv.*

un·fo·cused /ˌən'fōkəst/ (also **un·fo·cussed**) ▸*adj.* (of a person or their eyes) not seeing clearly; appearing glazed or expressionless. ■ (of an optical device) not adjusted to focus: *perpetually unfocused binoculars.* ■ (of a lens) not making incident light rays meet at a single point. ■ (of an object of vision) not in focus; indistinct. ■ (of feelings or plans) without a specific aim or direction: *my aspirations to write history were real but unfocused.*

un·fold /,ən'fōld/ ▶*v.* open or spread out from a folded position: [*trans.*] *he unfolded the map and laid it out on the table* | [*intrans.*] *a Chinese paper flower that unfolds in water.* ■ [*trans.*] reveal or disclose (thoughts or information): *Miss Eva* ***unfolded*** *her secret exploits* ***to*** *Mattie.* ■ [*intrans.*] (of information or a sequence of events) be revealed or disclosed: *there was a fascinating scene unfolding before me.* ▷Old English *unfealdan* (see UN-², FOLD¹). **—un·fold·ment** *n.*

un·forced /,ən'fôrst/ ▶*adj.* not produced by effort; natural: *an unforced cheerfulness.* ■ not compelled or constrained: *his retirement was an unforced departure.* **—un·forc·ed·ly** /-'fôrsədlē/ *adv.*

un·forced er·ror ▶*n.* *Sports* a mistake made on an easy shot by a competitor in a nonpressure situation.

un·fore·told /,ənfôr'tōld; -fər-/ ▶*adj. poetic/literary* not foretold; unpredicted.

un·for·get·ta·ble /,ənfər'getəbəl/ ▶*adj.* impossible to forget; very memorable: *that unforgettable first kiss.* **—un·for·get·ta·bly** /-blē/ *adv.*

un·for·giv·a·ble /,ənfər'givəbəl/ ▶*adj.* so bad as to be unable to be forgiven or excused: *losing your temper with him was unforgivable.* **—un·for·giv·a·bly** /-blē/ *adv.*

un·for·giv·ing /,ənfər'giviNG/ ▶*adj.* not willing to forgive or excuse people's faults or wrongdoings: *he was always a proud and unforgiving man.* ■ (of conditions) harsh; hostile: *the moor can be a wild and unforgiving place in bad weather.* **—un·for·giv·ing·ly** *adv.* **—un·for·giv·ing·ness** *n.*

un·formed /,ən'fôrmd/ ▶*adj.* without a definite form or shape: *she packed the unformed butter into the mold.* ■ not having developed or been developed fully: *he had an ambitious, albeit unformed, idea for a novel* | *unformed youths.*

un·forth·com·ing /,ənfôrTH'kəmiNG/ ▶*adj.* [*predic.*] **1** (of a person) not willing to divulge information: *the sergeant seemed unforthcoming, so he inquired at the gate.* **2** (of something required) not ready or made available when wanted or needed: *with money unforthcoming from the company, the project has had to be delayed.*

un·for·tu·nate /,ən'fôrCHənət/ ▶*adj.* having or marked by bad fortune; unlucky: *the unfortunate Cunningham was fired.* ■ (of a circumstance) unfavorable or inauspicious: *the delay at the airport was an unfortunate start to our vacation.* ■ regrettable or inappropriate: *his unfortunate remark silenced the gathering.*
▶*n.* (often **unfortunates**) a person who suffers bad fortune. ■ *archaic* a person who is considered immoral or lacking in religious faith or instruction, esp. a prostitute.

un·for·tu·nate·ly /,ən'fôrCHənətlē/ ▶*adv.* [*sentence adverb*] it is unfortunate that: *unfortunately, we do not have the time to interview every applicant.*

un·found·ed /,ən'foundid/ ▶*adj.* having no foundation or basis in fact: *her persistent fear that she had cancer was unfounded.* **—un·found·ed·ly** *adv.* **—un·found·ed·ness** *n.*

UNFPA ▶*abbr.* United Nations Fund for Population Activities.

un·free /,ən'frē/ ▶*adj.* deprived or devoid of liberty. **—un·free·dom** /-dəm/ *n.*

un·freeze /,ən'frēz/ ▶*v.* (*past* **-froze**; *past part.* **-fro·zen**) [*trans.*] cause (something) to thaw. ■ [*intrans.*] become thawed. ■ remove restrictions on the use or transfer of (an asset).

un·fre·quent·ed /,ən'frēkwəntid; -frē'kwen-/ ▶*adj.* (of a place) visited only rarely: *an unfrequented dirt path off the road to the beach.*

un·friend·ed /,ən'frendid/ ▶*adj. poetic/literary* without friends: *murder left innocent people bereft and unfriended.*

un·friend·ly /,ən'fren(d)lē/ ▶*adj.* (**-li·er**, **-li·est**) not friendly: *she shot him an unfriendly glance* | *Mildred felt unfriendly toward her* | *environmentally unfriendly activities.* **—un·friend·li·ness** *n.*

un·frock /,ən'fräk/ ▶*v.* another term for DEFROCK.

un·fro·zen /,ən'frōzən/ ▶ past participle of UNFREEZE.
▶*adj.* not or no longer frozen: *larvae remain unfrozen under the ice.*

un·fruit·ful /,ən'frootfəl/ ▶*adj.* **1** not producing good or helpful results; unproductive: *the meeting was unfruitful.* **2** not producing fruit or crops; unfertile. **—un·fruit·ful·ly** *adv.* **—un·fruit·ful·ness** *n.*

un·ful·filled /,ənfoo(l)'fild/ ▶*adj.* not carried out or brought to completion: *it was his unfulfilled ambition to write.* ■ not having fully utilized or exploited one's abilities or character. **—un·ful·fill·a·ble** /-'filəbəl/ *adj.* **—un·ful·fill·ing** /-'filiNG/ *adj.*

un·fun·ny /,ən'fənē/ ▶*adj.* (**-ni·er**, **-ni·est**) (typically of something intended to be funny) not amusing: *a hideously unfunny spoof film.* **—un·fun·ni·ly** /-'fənəlē/ *adv.* **—un·fun·ni·ness** *n.*

un·furl /,ən'fərl/ ▶*v.* make or become spread out from a rolled or folded state, esp. in order to be open to the wind: [*trans.*] *a man was unfurling a sail* | [*intrans.*] *the flags unfurl.*

un·fur·nished /,ən'fərnisHt/ ▶*adj.* **1** (of a house or apartment) without furniture, esp. available to be rented without furniture: *an unfurnished apartment.* **2** *archaic* not supplied: *he is* ***unfurnished with*** *the ideas of justice.*

un·fused /,ən'fyoozd/ ▶*adj.* **1** not fused or joined: *Darwin had predicted that a proto-bird would one day turn up with unfused wing fingers.* **2** not fitted or supplied with a fuse: *unfused electrical terminals.*

un·gain·ly /,ən'gānlē/ ▶*adj.* (of a person or movement) awkward; clumsy: *an ungainly walk.* ▷mid 17th cent.: from UN-¹ 'not' + obsolete *gainly* 'graceful,' based on Old Norse *gegn* 'straight.' **—un·gain·li·ness** *n.*

un·get·at·a·ble /,ən,get'atəbəl/ ▶*adj. informal* inaccessible.

un·gird /,ən'gərd/ ▶*v.* [*trans.*] *archaic* release or take off by undoing a belt or girth.

un·giv·ing /,ən'giviNG/ ▶*adj.* (of a person) cold or stubborn in relationships with other people. ■ (of a material) not bending or pliable; stiff.

un·glazed /,ən'glāzd/ ▶*adj.* not glazed: *unglazed porcelain.*

un·gloved /,ən'gləvd/ ▶*adj.* not wearing a glove or gloves.

un·glued /,ən'glood/ ▶*adj.* not or no longer stuck: *grease particles* ***come unglued*** *from the plate.* | *figurative it was only a matter of time before the whole operation came unglued.* ■ *informal* (of a person or state of mind) confused and emotionally strained: *it had been a long day, and tempers were* ***becoming unglued.***

un·god·ly /,ən'gädlē/ ▶*adj.* irreligious or immoral: *ungodly lives of self-obsession, lust, and pleasure.* ■ *informal* unreasonably early or inconvenient: *I've been troubled by telephone calls at ungodly hours.* **—un·god·li·ness** *n.*

un·gov·ern·a·ble /,ən'gəvərnəbəl/ ▶*adj.* impossible to control or govern. **—un·gov·ern·a·bil·i·ty** /-,gəvərnə'bilətē/ *n.* **—un·gov·ern·a·bly** /-blē/ *adv.*

un·gra·cious /,ən'grāsHəs/ ▶*adj.* **1** not polite or friendly: *after Anna's kindness I wouldn't want to seem ungracious.* **2** not graceful or elegant. **—un·gra·cious·ly** *adv.* **—un·gra·cious·ness** *n.*

un·grad·ed /,ən'grādid/ ▶*adj.* **1** not divided into grades or separate levels: *students are in ungraded classrooms.* **2** not required or subject to evaluation: *the ungraded part of the assignment.*

un·gram·mat·i·cal /,əngrə'matikəl/ ▶*adj.* not conforming to grammatical rules; not well formed: *ungrammatical sentences.* **—un·gram·mat·i·cal·i·ty** /-,mati'kalətē/ *n.* (*pl.* **-ties**). **—un·gram·mat·i·cal·ly** /-ik(ə)lē/ *adv.* **—un·gram·mat·i·cal·ness** *n.*

un·grasp·a·ble /,ən'graspəbəl/ ▶*adj.* impossible to comprehend or understand.

un·grate·ful /,ən'grātfəl/ ▶*adj.* not feeling or showing gratitude: *she's so ungrateful for everything we do.* ■ not pleasant or acceptable: *he turned to the ungrateful task of forming a police cordon.* **—un·grate·ful·ly** *adv.* **—un·grate·ful·ness** *n.*

un·green /,ən'grēn/ ▶*adj.* (of a product or practice) harmful to the environment; not ecologically acceptable: *an ungreen commercial development.* ■ (of a person or organization) not supporting protection of the environment. **—un·green·ly** *adv.*

un·ground /,ən'ground/ ▶*v.* [*trans.*] remove from a grounded state: *It's easy to jump in and ground airplanes. It's not so easy to unground them.*

un·ground·ed /,ən'groundid/ ▶*adj.* **1** having no basis or justification; unfounded: *ungrounded fears.* **2** not electrically grounded. **3** [*predic.*] (**ungrounded in**) not properly instructed or proficient in (a subject or activity).

un·group /,ən'groop/ ▶*v.* [*trans.*] *Computing* separate (items) from a group formed within a word-processing or graphics package.

un·gual /'əNGg(yə)wəl/ ▶*adj. Zoology & Medicine* of, relating to, or affecting a nail, hoof, or claw. ▷mid 19th cent.: from Latin *unguis* 'nail' + -AL.

un·guard·ed /,ən'gärdid/ ▶*adj.* without protection or a guard: *the museum was unguarded at night.* ■ not well considered; careless: *an unguarded remark.* **—un·guard·ed·ly** *adv.* **—un·guard·ed·ness** *n.*

un·guent /'əNGgwənt/ ▶*n.* a soft greasy or viscous substance used as an ointment or for lubrication. ▷late Middle English: from Latin *unguentum*, from *unguere* 'anoint.'

un·guic·u·late /,əNG'gwikyə,lāt; -lət/ ▶*adj. Zoology* having one or more nails or claws. ■ *Botany* (of a petal) having a narrow stalklike base. ▷early 19th cent.: from modern Latin *unguiculatus*, from Latin *unguiculus* 'fingernail, toenail,' diminutive of *unguis* 'nail.'

un·guid·ed /,ən'gīdid/ ▶*adj.* not guided in a particular path or direction; left to take its own course. ■ (of a missile) not directed by remote control or internal equipment. Compare with BALLISTIC MISSILE and GUIDED.

un·guis /'əNGgwis/ ▶*n.* (*pl.* **un·gues** /'əNGgwēz/) *Zoology* a nail, claw, or fang. ▷early 18th cent.: from Latin.

un·gu·late /'əNGgyələt; -,lāt/ ▶*n.* *Zoology* a hoofed mammal. See also EVEN-TOED UNGULATE, ODD-TOED UNGULATE. • Former order Ungulata, now divided into two unrelated orders (see ARTIODACTYLA and PERISSODACTYLA). ▷early 19th cent.: from late Latin *ungulatus*, from Latin *ungula* 'hoof.'

un·guled /'əNG,gyoold/ ▶*adj. Heraldry* (of an animal) having hoofs of a specified different tincture.

un·hal·lowed /,ən'halōd/ ▶*adj.* not formally consecrated: *unhallowed ground.* ■ unholy; wicked: *unhallowed retribution.*

un·hand /,ən'hand/ ▶*v.* [*trans.*] [usu. in *imperative*] *archaic* or *humorous* release (someone) from one's grasp: *"Unhand me, sir!" she cried.*

un·hand·some /,ən'han(d)səm/ ▶*adj.* [often with *negative*] not handsome: *Bobby was not unhandsome in his uniform.*

un·hand·y /,ən'handē/ ▶*adj.* **1** not easy to handle or manage; awkward. **2** not skillful in using the hands. **—un·hand·i·ly** /-dəlē/ *adv.* **—un·hand·i·ness** *n.*

un·hang /,ən'haNG/ ▶*v.* (*past* and *past part.* **-hung**) *rare* [*trans.*] take down from a hanging position.

un·hap·pen /,ən'hapən/ ▶*v.* [*intrans.*] (of an occurrence) become as though never having happened; be reversed: *things had happened that could never unhappen.* ■ [*trans.*] cause (something) not to have happened: *you can't unhappen it just by saying we won't speak of it again.*

un·hap·pi·ly /,ən'hapəlē/ ▶*adv.* in an unhappy manner. ■ [*sentence adverb*] unfortunately: *unhappily, such days do not come too often.*

un·hap·py /,ən'hapē/ ▶*adj.* (**-pi·er**, **-pi·est**) not happy: *an unhappy marriage* | *Aunt Millie looked unhappy.* ■ [*predic.*] (**unhappy at/about/with**) not satisfied or pleased with (a situation): *many were unhappy about the scale of the cuts.* ■ unfortunate: *an unhappy coincidence.* **—un·hap·pi·ness** *n.*

un·harmed /,ən'härmd/ ▶*adj.* [often as *complement*] not harmed; uninjured: *all the hostages were released unharmed.*

un·har·ness /,ən'härnəs/ ▶*v.* [*trans.*] remove a harness from (a horse or other animal).

un·hasp /,ən'hasp/ ▶*v.* [*trans.*] *archaic* unfasten.

UNHCR an agency of the United Nations set up in 1951 to aid, protect, and monitor refugees. ▷abbreviation of *United Nations High Commission for Refugees.*

un·health·ful /,ən'helTHfəl/ ▶*adj.* harmful to health: *radon can build up to unhealthful levels.* **—un·health·ful·ness** *n.*

un·health·y /,ən'helTHē/ ▶*adj.* (**-health·i·er**, **-health·i·est**) harmful to health: *an unhealthy diet.* ■ not having or showing good health: *his face looked pale and unhealthy.* ■ (of a person's attitude or behavior) not sensible or well balanced; abnormal and harmful: *an unhealthy obsession with fast cars.* **—un·health·i·ly** /-THəlē/ *adv.* **—un·health·i·ness** *n.*

un·heard /,ən'hərd/ ▶*adj.* not heard or listened to: *my protests went unheard.* ■ (**unheard of**) not previously known of or done: *sales tax was unheard of in Kansas up until 1937* | *wines from unheard-of villages.*

un·hedged /,ən'hejd/ ▶*adj.* **1** not bounded by a hedge: *an unhedged field.* **2** (of an investment or investor) not protected against loss by balancing or compensating contracts or transactions: *the bank collapsed due to unhedged trading.*

un·heed·ful /,ən'hēdfəl/ ▶*adj.* [*predic.*] not noticing or paying attention: *I charged down the stairs,* ***unheedful of*** *the missing bannister.*

Pronunciation Key ə *ago*; ər *over*; 'ə or ,ə *up*; 'ər or ,ər *fur*; a *hat*; ā *rate*; ä *car*; CH *chew*; e *let*; ē *see*; e(ə)r *air*; i *fit*; ī *by*; i(ə)r *ear*; NG *sing*; ō *go*; ô *for*; oi *boy*; oo *good*; oo *goo*; ou *out*; SH *she*; TH *thin*; TH *then*; (h)w *why*; ZH *vision*

un·heim·lich /ˌo͝onˈhīmlikн; ˌən-/ ▸*adj.* uncanny; weird. ▷German.

un·her·ald·ed /ˌənˈherəldid/ ▸*adj.* not previously announced, expected, or recognized.

un·hinge /ˌənˈhinj/ ▸*v.* [*trans.*] **1** [usu. as *adj.*] (**unhinged**) make (someone) mentally unbalanced: *I thought she must be unhinged by grief.* ■ deprive of stability or fixity; throw into disorder. **2** take (a door) off its hinges.

un·hip /ˌənˈhip/ ▸*adj.* (**-hip·per, -hip·pest**) *informal* unaware of or unaffected by current fashions or trends: *while it was remote and decidedly unhip, the town was otherwise right up-to-date.*

un·his·tor·ic /ˌənhiˈstôrik; -ˈstär-/ ▸*adj.* not historic or historical.

un·his·tor·i·cal /ˌənhiˈstôrikəl; -ˈstär-/ ▸*adj.* not in accordance with history or with historical analysis. —**un·his·tor·i·cal·ly** /-ik(ə)lē/ *adv.*

un·hitch /ˌənˈhicн/ ▸*v.* [*trans.*] unhook or unfasten (something tethered to or caught on something else).

un·hol·ster /ˌənˈhōlstər/ ▸*v.* [*trans.*] remove (a gun) from a holster.

un·ho·ly /ˌənˈhōlē/ ▸*adj.* (**-li·er, -li·est**) sinful; wicked. ■ not holy; unconsecrated: *an unholy marriage.* ■ denoting an alliance with potentially harmful implications between two or more parties that are not natural allies: *an unholy alliance between economic and political power.* ■ *informal* awful; dreadful (used for emphasis): *she was making an unholy racket.* ▷Old English *unhālig* (see UN-[1], HOLY). —**un·ho·li·ness** *n.*

un·hood /ˌənˈho͝od/ ▸*v.* [*trans.*] remove the hood from (something, esp. a falcon or horse).

un·hook /ˌənˈho͝ok/ ▸*v.* [*trans.*] unfasten or detach (something that is held or caught by a hook).

un·hoped /ˌənˈhōpt/ ▸*adj.* (**unhoped for**) exceeding hope or expectation: *an unhoped-for piece of good luck.*

un·horse /ˌənˈhôrs/ ▸*v.* [*trans.*] cause to fall from a horse: *having unhorsed each other, the two men finished the fight on foot | figurative her mission is to unhorse fashionable literary theories.*

un·hou·seled /ˌənˈhouzəld/ ▸*adj. archaic* (of a person) not having received the Eucharist. ▷mid 16th cent.: from UN-[1] 'not' + the past participle of obsolete *housel* 'offer the Eucharist to,' from *housel* 'Eucharist.'

un·hu·man /ˌənˈ(h)yo͞omən/ ▸*adj.* not resembling or having the qualities of a human being.

un·hung[1] /ˌənˈhəNG/ ▸*adj.* **1** (esp. of a picture) not hanging or hung. **2** [*predic.*] (of a wicked person) still living when expected to be executed by hanging.

un·hung[2] ▸ past and past participle of UNHANG.

un·hur·ried /ˌənˈhərēd; -ˈhə-rēd/ ▸*adj.* moving, acting, or taking place without haste or urgency. —**un·hur·ried·ly** *adv.*

un·husk /ˌənˈhəsk/ ▸*v.* [*trans.*] remove a husk or shell from (a seed or fruit): [as *adj.*] (**unhusked**) *unhusked rice.*

un·hy·gi·en·ic /ˌənhīˈjenik; ˌənhīˈjēnik/ ▸*adj.* not clean or sanitary: *damp, unhygienic accommodations.* —**un·hy·gi·en·i·cal·ly** /ˌənhīˈjenək(ə)lē; ˌənhīˈjēnək(ə)lē/ *adv.*

uni- ▸*comb. form* one; having or consisting of one: *unicellular | unicycle.* ▷from Latin *unus* ' one.'

U·ni·ate /ˈyo͞onēˌat; -it; -ˌāt/ (also **U·ni·at**) ▸*adj.* denoting or relating to any community of Christians in eastern Europe or the Near East that acknowledges papal supremacy but retains its own liturgy: *the Uniate churches.*
▸*n.* a member of such a community. ▷mid 19th cent.: from Russian *uniat*, from *uniya*, from Latin *unio* (see UNION).

u·ni·ax·i·al /ˌyo͞onēˈaksēəl/ ▸*adj.* having or relating to a single axis. ■ (of crystals) having one optic axis, as in the hexagonal, trigonal, and tetragonal systems.

u·ni·bod·y /ˈyo͞onəˌbädē/ ▸*n.* (*pl.* **-bod·ies**) a single molded unit forming both the bodywork and chassis of a vehicle.

u·ni·brow /ˈyo͞onəˌbrou/ ▸*n.* a pair of eyebrows that meet above the nose, giving the appearance of a single eyebrow. Also called MONOBROW. —**u·ni·browed** *adj.*

u·ni·cam·er·al /ˌyo͞onəˈkam(ə)rəl/ ▸*adj.* (of a legislative body) having a single legislative chamber. ▷mid 19th cent.: from UNI- 'one' + Latin *camera* 'chamber' + -AL.

u·ni·cast /ˈyo͞oniˌkast/ ▸*n.* transmission of a data package or an audiovisual signal to a single recipient: [as *adj.*] *the unicast method wastes a lot of bandwidth by sending duplicate information.* ▷1990s: on the pattern of *broadcast*.

UNICEF /ˈyo͞onəˌsef/ an agency of the United Nations established in 1946 to help governments (esp. in developing countries) improve the health and education of children and their mothers. ▷acronym from *United Nations Children's* (originally *International Children's Emergency*) *Fund*.

u·ni·cel·lu·lar /ˌyo͞onəˈselyələr/ ▸*adj. Biology* (of protozoans, certain algae and spores, etc.) consisting of a single cell. ■ (of an evolutionary or developmental stage) characterized by the formation or presence of a single cell or cells.

u·ni·cit·y /yo͞oˈnisətē/ ▸*n. rare* the fact of being or consisting of one, or of being united as a whole. ■ the fact or quality of being unique.

u·ni·col·or /ˈyo͞onəˌkələr/ (also **u·ni·col·ored**) (*Brit.* **-col·our** or **-col·oured**) ▸*adj.* of one color.

u·ni·com /ˈyo͞onəˌkäm/ ▸*n.* a radio communications system of a type used at small airports.

u·ni·corn /ˈyo͞onəˌkôrn/ ▸*n.* **1** a mythical animal typically represented as a horse with a single straight horn projecting from its forehead. ■ a heraldic representation of such an animal, with a twisted horn, a deer's feet, a goat's beard, and a lion's tail. **2** *historical* a carriage drawn by three horses, two abreast and one leader. ■ a team of three horses arranged in such a way. ▷Middle English: via Old French from Latin *unicornis*, from *uni-* 'single' + *cornu* 'horn,' translating Greek *monokerōs*.

unicorn 1

u·ni·corn root ▸*n.* any of a number of plants in the lily family, esp. those with roots having medicinal uses, in particular devil's bit and colicroot.

u·ni·cum /ˈyo͞onəkəm/ ▸*n.* (*pl.* **-ca** /-kə/) a unique example or specimen. ▷late 19th cent.: from Latin, neuter of *unicus* 'unique.'

u·ni·cur·sal /ˌyo͞onəˈkərsəl/ ▸*adj. Mathematics* relating to or denoting a curve or surface that is closed and can be drawn or swept out in a single movement. ▷mid 19th cent.: from UNI- 'one' + Latin *cursus* 'course' + -AL.

u·ni·cus·pid /ˌyo͞onəˈkəspid/ ▸*adj.* having one cusp or point.
▸*n.* a tooth with a single cusp, esp. a canine tooth.

u·ni·cy·cle /ˈyo͞onəˌsīkəl/ ▸*n.* a cycle with a single wheel, typically used by acrobats. —**u·ni·cy·clist** /-ˌsīklist/ *n.*

un·i·den·ti·fied fly·ing ob·ject ▸*n.* see UFO.

u·ni·di·men·sion·al /ˌyo͞onədəˈmensнənl; -sнənəl/ ▸*adj.* having one dimension: *a unidimensional model.*

u·ni·di·rec·tion·al /ˌyo͞onidiˈreksнənl/ ▸*adj.* moving or operating in a single direction. —**u·ni·di·rec·tion·al·i·ty** /-ˌreksнəˈnalitē/ *n.* —**u·ni·di·rec·tion·al·ly** *adv.*

UNIDO ▸*abbr.* United Nations Industrial Development Organization.

u·ni·fi·ca·tion /ˌyo͞onəfiˈkāsнən/ ▸*n.* the process of being united or made into a whole. —**u·ni·fi·ca·tor·y** /-ˈkātərē/ *adj.*

U·ni·fi·ca·tion Church an evangelistic religious and political organization founded in 1954 in Korea by Sun Myung Moon. Also called HOLY SPIRIT ASSOCIATION FOR THE UNIFICATION OF WORLD CHRISTIANITY.

u·ni·fied field the·o·ry ▸*n. Physics* a theory that describes two or more of the four interactions (electromagnetic, gravitational, weak, and strong) previously described by separate theories.

u·ni·form /ˈyo͞onəˌfôrm/ ▸*adj.* **1** not changing in form or character; remaining the same in all cases and at all times: *blocks of stone of uniform size | the decline in fertility was not uniform across social classes.* ■ of a similar form or character to another or others: *a uniform package of amenities at a choice of hotels.* **2** denoting a garment forming part of a person's uniform: *black uniform jackets.*
▸*n.* **1** the distinctive clothing worn by members of the same organization or body or by children attending certain schools: *airline pilots in dark blue uniforms | an officer in uniform.* ■ *informal* a police officer wearing a uniform: *uniforms were already on the scene.* **2** a code word representing the letter U, used in radio communication.
▸*v.* [*trans.*] **1** make uniform. **2** provide or dress (someone) in a uniform. ▷mid 16th cent. (as an adjective): from French *uniforme* or Latin *uniformis* (see UNI-, FORM). Sense 1 of the *noun* dates from the mid 18th cent. —**u·ni·form·ly** /ˈyo͞onəˌfôrmlē; ˌyo͞onəˈfôrm-/ *adv.*

U·ni·form Com·mer·ci·al Code (abbr.: **UCC**) ▸*n.* the body of laws governing commercial transactions in the U.S.

u·ni·formed /ˈyo͞onəˌfôrmd/ ▸*adj.* (of a person) wearing a uniform: *uniformed police officers.*

u·ni·form·i·tar·i·an·ism /ˌyo͞onəˌfôrməˈte(ə)rēəˌnizəm/ ▸*n. Geology* the theory that changes in the earth's crust during geological history have resulted from the action of continuous and uniform processes. Often contrasted with CATASTROPHISM. —**u·ni·form·i·tar·i·an** *adj.* & *n.*

u·ni·form·i·ty /ˌyo͞onəˈfôrmətē/ ▸*n.* (*pl.* **-ties**) the quality or state of being uniform: *an attempt to impose administrative and cultural uniformity.* ▷late Middle English: from Old French *uniformite* or late Latin *uniformitas*, from Latin *uniformis* (see UNIFORM).

u·ni·form re·source lo·ca·tor (abbr.: **URL**) ▸*n.* a location or address identifying where documents can be found on the Internet.

u·ni·fy /ˈyo͞onəˌfī/ ▸*v.* (**-fies, -fied**) make or become united, uniform, or whole: [*trans.*] *the government hoped to centralize and unify the nation* | [*intrans.*] *opposition groups struggling to unify around the goal of replacing the regime* | [as *adj.*] (**unified**) *a unified system of national education.* ▷early 16th cent.: from French *unifier* or late Latin *unificare* 'make into a whole.' —**u·ni·fi·er** *n.*

u·ni·lat·er·al /ˌyo͞onəˈlatərəl; -ˈlatrəl/ ▸*adj.* **1** (of an action or decision) performed by or affecting only one person, group, or country involved in a particular situation, without the agreement of another or the others: *unilateral nuclear disarmament.* **2** relating to, occurring on, or affecting only one side of an organ or structure, or of the body. —**u·ni·lat·er·al·ly** *adv.*

u·ni·lat·er·al·ism /ˌyo͞onəˈlatərəˌlizəm; -ˈlatrə-/ ▸*n.* the process of acting, reaching a decision, or espousing a principle unilaterally. —**u·ni·lat·er·al·ist** *n.* & *adj.*

u·ni·lin·e·ar /ˌyo͞onəˈlinēər/ ▸*adj.* developing or arranged serially and predictably, without deviation: *there is a unilinear path of language learning with a finite end.* ■ (of Web sites) allowing or designed for controlled navigation, following a single path. —**u·ni·lin·e·ar·ly** *adv.*

u·ni·lin·gual /ˌyo͞onəˈliNGg(yə)wəl/ ▸*adj.* conducted in, concerned with, or speaking only one language. —**u·ni·lin·gual·ly** *adv.*

u·ni·loc·u·lar /ˌyo͞onəˈläkyələr/ ▸*adj. Botany & Zoology* having, consisting of, or characterized by only one loculus or cavity; single-chambered.

un·im·ag·i·na·ble /ˌənəˈmaj(ə)nəbəl/ ▸*adj.* difficult or impossible to imagine or comprehend: *lives of almost unimaginable deprivation.* —**un·im·ag·i·na·bly** /-blē/ *adv.*

u·ni·mod·al /ˌyo͞onəˈmōdl/ ▸*adj.* having or involving one mode. ■ (of a statistical distribution) having one maximum.

u·ni·mo·lec·u·lar /ˌyo͞onəməˈlekyələr/ ▸*adj. Chemistry* consisting of or involving a single molecule.

un·im·paired /ˌənimˈpe(ə)rd/ ▸*adj.* not weakened or damaged: *unimpaired mobility.*

un·im·peach·a·ble /ˌənimˈpēcнəbəl/ ▸*adj.* not able to be doubted, questioned, or criticized; entirely trustworthy: *an unimpeachable witness.* —**un·im·peach·a·bly** /-blē/ *adv.*

un·im·por·tance /ˌənimˈpôrtns/ ▸*n.* the state or fact of lacking in importance or significance: *her tone conveyed the unimportance of anything that might have happened.*

un·im·pressed /ˌənimˈprest/ ▸*adj.* feeling no admiration, interest, or respect.

un·im·proved /ˌənimˈpro͞ovd/ ▸*adj.* not made better. ■ (of land) not cleared or cultivated.

un·in·cor·po·rat·ed /ˌəninˈkôrpəˌrātid; ˌəniNG-/ ▸*adj.* **1** (of a company or other organization) not formed into a legal corporation: *an unincorporated business.* **2** not included as part of a whole. ■ (of territory) not designated as belonging to a particular country, town, or area.

un·in·flect·ed /ˌənin'flektid/ ▸*adj.* **1** *Grammar* (of a word or a language) not undergoing changes to express grammatical functions or attributes: *English is largely uninflected.* **2** not varying in intonation or pitch: *her voice was flat and uninflected.*

un·in·hab·it·a·ble /ˌənin'habətəbəl/ ▸*adj.* (of a place) unsuitable for living in.

un·in·hib·it·ed /ˌənin'hibitid/ ▸*adj.* expressing one's feelings or thoughts unselfconsciously and without restraint: *fits of uninhibited laughter.* **—un·in·hib·it·ed·ly** *adv.* **—un·in·hib·it·ed·ness** *n.*

un·in·i·ti·at·ed /ˌənə'nishēˌātid/ ▸*adj.* without special knowledge or experience: *a bachelor neither prudish nor uninitiated* | [as *plural n.*] (**the uninitiated**) *the discussion wasn't easy to follow for the uninitiated.*

un·in·spired /ˌənin'spīrd/ ▸*adj.* **1** lacking in imagination or originality: *he writes repetitive and uninspired poetry.* **2** (of a person) not filled with excitement: *they were uninspired by the Nationalist Party.*

un·in·stall /ˌənin'stôl/ (*Brit.* also **un·in·stal**) ▸*v.* remove (an application or file) from a computer: [*trans.*] *if you wanted to uninstall them, you could never be certain which files could be safely deleted.*
▸*adj.* denoting a command, function, or capability to remove software: *complete uninstall capability.* **—un·in·stal·la·tion** /ˌən-instə'lāshən/ *n.* **—un·in·stall·er** *n.*

un·in·struct·ed /ˌənin'strəktid/ ▸*adj.* (of a person) not taught or having learned a subject or skill. ■ (of behavior) not acquired by teaching; natural or spontaneous: *her own instinctive, uninstructed response.*

un·in·sur·a·ble /ˌənin'shoŏrəbəl/ ▸*adj.* not eligible for insurance coverage: *some risky activities are uninsurable at any price.*

un·in·tel·li·gent /ˌənin'teləjənt/ ▸*adj.* having or showing a low level of intelligence: *a good-natured but unintelligent boy.* See note at STUPID. **—un·in·tel·li·gence** *n.* **—un·in·tel·li·gent·ly** *adv.*

un·in·tel·li·gi·ble /ˌənin'teləjəbəl/ ▸*adj.* impossible to understand: *dolphin sounds are* ***unintelligible to*** *humans.* **—un·in·tel·li·gi·bil·i·ty** /-ˌteləjə'bilətē/ *n.* **—un·in·tel·li·gi·bly** /-blē/ *adv.*

un·in·ter·est·ed /ˌən'intristid; -'intəˌrestid/ ▸*adj.* not interested in or concerned about something or someone: *I was totally* ***uninterested in*** *boys* | *an uninterested voice.* **—un·in·ter·est·ed·ly** *adv.* **—un·in·ter·est·ed·ness** *n.*

USAGE On the difference between **uninterested** and **disinterested**, see **usage** at DISINTERESTED.

un·in·ter·pret·a·ble /ˌənin'tərprətəbəl/ ▸*adj.* impossible to explain or understand in terms of meaning or significance.

un·in·ter·rupt·ed /ˌənˌintə'rəptid/ ▸*adj.* without a break in continuity: *an uninterrupted flow of traffic.* ■ (of a view) unobstructed. **—un·in·ter·rupt·ed·ly** *adv.*

un·in·ter·rupt·i·ble /ˌənˌintə'rəptəbəl/ ▸*adj.* not able to be broken in continuity: *an uninterruptible power supply.*

u·ni·nu·cle·ate /ˌyoōnə'n(y)oōklēit/ ▸*adj. Biology* having a single nucleus.

un·in·vit·ed /ˌənin'vītid/ ▸*adj.* (of a person) attending somewhere or doing something without having been asked: *their privacy was disrupted by a series of uninvited guests.* ■ (of a thought or act) involuntary, unwelcome, or unwarranted: *strange uninvited thoughts crossed her mind.* **—un·in·vit·ed·ly** *adv.*

un·in·voked /ˌənin'vōkt/ ▸*adj.* (of a god, spirit, or power) not invoked or called on in prayer.

Un·ion /'yoōnyən/ an industrial and residential township in northeastern New Jersey; pop. 50,024.

un·ion /'yoōnyən/ ▸*n.* **1** the action or fact of joining or being joined, esp. in a political context: *he was opposed to closer political or economic union with Europe* | *a currency union between the two countries.* ■ a state of harmony or agreement: *they live in perfect union.* ■ a marriage: *their union had not been blessed with children.* **2** an organized association of workers formed to protect and further their rights and interests; a labor union: *the National Farmers' Union.* ■ a club, society, or association formed by people with a common interest or purpose: *members of the Students' Union.* ■ short for RUGBY UNION. ■ *Brit., historical* a number of parishes consolidated for the purposes of administering the Poor Laws. ■ (also **un·ion work·house** or **un·ion house**) a workhouse set up by such a group of parishes. ■ *Brit.* an association of independent churches for purposes of cooperation. **3** (also **Un·ion**) a political unit consisting of a number of states or provinces with the same central government, in particular: ■ the U.S., esp. from its founding by the original thirteen states in 1787–90 to the secession of the Confederate states in 1860–61. ■ (also **the Fed·er·al Un·ion**) the northern states of the U.S. that opposed the seceding Confederate states in the Civil War. **4** a building at a college or university used by students for recreation and other nonacademic activities. **5** *Mathematics* the set that comprises all the elements (and no others) contained in any of two or more given sets. ■ the operation of forming such a set. **6** a pipe coupling. **7** a part of a flag with an emblem symbolizing national union, typically occupying the upper corner next to the staff. **8** a fabric made of two or more different yarns, typically cotton and linen or silk. ▷late Middle English: from Old French, or from ecclesiastical Latin *unio(n-)* 'unity,' from Latin *unus* 'one.'

un·ion-bash·ing ▸*n. informal* active or vocal opposition to labor unions and their rights.

un·ion cat·a·log ▸*n.* a list of the combined holdings of several libraries.

Un·ion Cit·y **1** a city in north central California, south of Oakland; pop. 53,762. **2** an industrial city in northeastern New Jersey, across the Hudson River from New York City; pop. 58,102.

Un·ion·dale /'yoōnyənˌdāl/ a residential and commercial village in southeastern New York, on Long Island; pop. 20,328.

un·ion·ist /'yoōnyənist/ ▸*n.* **1** a member of a labor union. ■ an advocate or supporter of labor unions. **2** (**Un·ion·ist**) a person who opposed secession during the Civil War. ■ a person in Northern Ireland, esp. a member of a political party, supporting or advocating union with Great Britain. **—un·ion·ism** /-ˌnizəm/ *n.* **—un·ion·is·tic** /ˌyoōnyə'nistik/ *adj.*

un·ion·ize /'yoōnyəˌnīz/ ▸*v.* become or cause to become members of a labor union. **—un·ion·i·za·tion** /ˌyoōnyəni'zāshən/ -ˌnī'zā-/ *n.*

un·ion·ized /'yoōnyəˌnīzd/ ▸*adj.* (of workers or their workplace) belonging to, or having workers belonging to, a labor union: *unionized factories.*

un·i·o·nized /ˌən'īəˌnīzd/ ▸*adj.* not ionized.

Un·ion Jack ▸*n.* **1** the national flag of the United Kingdom, consisting of red and white crosses on a blue background. [originally a small British union flag flown as the jack of a ship; compare with UNION *n.* 7.] **2** (**un·ion jack**) (in the U.S.) a small flag consisting of the union from the national flag, flown at the bows of vessels in harbor.

Un·ion of My·an·mar official name for MYANMAR.

Un·ion of So·vi·et So·cial·ist Re·pub·lics (abbr.: **USSR**) full name of SOVIET UNION.

un·ion shop ▸*n.* a place of work where employers may hire nonunion workers who must join a labor union within an agreed time. Compare with CLOSED SHOP, OPEN SHOP.

Un·ion Square a park in southern Manhattan in New York City, noted as a former theater and, later, labor union hub.

un·ion suit ▸*n. dated* a single undergarment combining shirt and pants.

Un·ion Ter·ri·to·ry any of several territories of India that are administered by the central government.

u·nip·ar·ous /yoō'nip(ə)rəs/ ▸*adj. chiefly Zoology* producing a single young at a birth. ▷mid 17th cent.: from modern Latin *uniparus* (from Latin *uni-* 'one' + *-parus* 'bearing') + -OUS.

u·ni·per·son·al /ˌyoōnə'pərsənəl/ ▸*adj. rare* comprising, or existing as, one person only.

u·ni·pla·nar /ˌyoōnə'plānər/ ▸*adj.* lying in one plane.

u·ni·po·lar /ˌyoōnə'pōlər/ ▸*adj.* having or relating to a single pole or kind of polarity: *a unipolar magnetic charge.* ■ (of psychiatric illness) characterized by either depressive or (more rarely) manic episodes but not both. Compare with BIPOLAR DISORDER. ■ (of a nerve cell) having only one axon or process. ■ *Electronics* (of a transistor or other device) using charge carriers of a single polarity. **—u·ni·po·lar·i·ty** /-pə'laritē; -pō-/ *n.*

u·nip·o·tent /yoō'nipətənt/ ▸*adj.* **1** *Mathematics* (of a subgroup) having only one idempotent element. **2** *Biology* (of an immature or stem cell) capable of giving rise to only one cell type.

u·nique /yoō'nēk/ ▸*adj.* being the only one of its kind; unlike anything else: *the situation was unique in modern politics* | *original and unique designs.* ■ particularly remarkable, special, or unusual: *a unique opportunity to see the spectacular Bolshoi Ballet.* ■ [*predic.*] (**unique to**) belonging or connected to (one particular person, group, or place): *a style of architecture that is unique to Portugal.*
▸*n. archaic* a unique person or thing. ▷early 17th cent.: from French, from Latin *unicus*, from *unus* 'one.' **—u·nique·ly** *adv.* **—u·nique·ness** *n.*

USAGE There is a set of adjectives—including **unique**, **complete**, **equal**, and **perfect**—whose core meaning embraces a mathematically absolute concept and which therefore, according to a traditional argument, cannot be modified by adverbs such as **really**, **quite**, or **very**. For example, since the core meaning of **unique** (from Latin 'one') is 'being only one of its kind,' it is logically impossible, the argument goes, to submodify it: it either is 'unique' or it is not, and there are no stages in between. In practice, the situation in the language is more complex than this. Words like **unique** have a core sense but they often also have a secondary, less precise (nonabsolute) sense of 'very remarkable or unusual,' as in *a really unique opportunity.* It is advisable, however, to use **unique** sparingly and not to modify it with *very, quite, really,* etc. Often, a writer can instead make accurate use of *rare, distinctive, unusual, remarkable,* or other nonabsolute adjectives.

u·ni·sex /'yoōnəˌseks/ ▸*adj.* (esp. of clothing or hairstyles) designed to be suitable for both sexes.
▸*n.* a style in which men and women look and dress in a similar way.

u·ni·sex·u·al /ˌyoōnə'sekshoōəl/ ▸*adj.* (of an organism) either male or female; not hermaphrodite. ■ *Botany* (of a flower) having either stamens or pistils but not both. **—u·ni·sex·u·al·i·ty** /-ˌsekshoō'alitē/ *n.* **—u·ni·sex·u·al·ly** *adv.*

u·ni·son /'yoōnəsən; -zən/ ▸*n.* **1** simultaneous performance of action or utterance of speech: *"Yes, sir," said the girls* ***in unison.*** **2** *Music* coincidence in pitch of sounds or notes: *the flutes play* ***in unison with*** *the violas.* ■ a combination of notes, voices, or instruments at the same pitch or (esp. when singing) in octaves: *good unisons are formed by flutes, oboes, and clarinets.*
▸*adj.* [*attrib.*] performed in unison. ▷late Middle English (sense 2): from Old French, or from late Latin *unisonus*, from Latin *uni-* 'one' + *sonus* 'sound.' **—u·nis·o·nous** /yoō'nisənəs/ *adj.*

un·is·sued /ˌən'ishoōd/ ▸*adj.* (esp. of shares of stock) not yet issued: *his rights to acquire any unissued shares were eliminated.* ■ (of a musical recording) recorded but not issued to the public: *the previously unissued song isn't any great shakes.*

u·nit /'yoōnit/ ▸*n.* **1** an individual thing or person regarded as single and complete, esp. for purposes of calculation: *the family unit.* ■ each of the individuals or collocations into which a complex whole may be divided: *large areas of land made up of smaller units* | *the sentence as a unit of grammar.* ■ a device that has a specified function, esp. one forming part of a complex mechanism: *the gearbox and transmission unit.* ■ a piece of furniture or equipment for fitting with others like it or made of complementary parts: *a sink unit.* ■ a self-contained section of accommodations in a larger building or group of buildings: *one- and two-bedroom units.* ■ a part of an institution such as a hospital having a special function: *the intensive care unit.* ■ a subdivision of a larger military grouping: *he returned to Germany with his unit.* ■ an amount of educational instruction, typically determined by the number of hours spent in class: *students take three compulsory core units.* ■ an item manufactured: [as *adj.*] *unit cost.* ■ a police car: *he eased into his unit and flicked the siren on.* **2** a quantity chosen as a standard in terms of which other quantities may be expressed: *a unit of measurement* | *fifty units of electricity.* **3** the number one. ■ (**units**) the digit before the decimal point in decimal notation, representing an integer less than ten. ▷late 16th cent. (as a mathematical term): from Latin *unus*, probably suggested by DIGIT.

UNITA /ˌyoō'nētə/ an Angolan nationalist movement founded in 1966 by Jonas Savimbi (b.1934) to fight Portuguese rule. After independence was achieved in 1975, UNITA continued to fight against the ruling Marxist MPLA, with help from South Africa. ▷acronym from Portuguese *UniÃ£o Nacional para a Independencia Total de Angola.*

u·ni·tard /'yoōnəˌtärd/ ▸*n.* a tight-fitting one-piece garment of stretchable fabric that covers the body from the neck to the knees or feet. ▷1960s: from UNI- 'single' + LEOTARD.

U

Pronunciation Key ə *ago;* ər *over;* 'ə or ˌə *up;* 'ər or ˌər *fur;* a *hat;* ā *rate;* ä *car;* CH *chew;* e *let;* ē *see;* e(ə)r *air;* i *fit;* ī *by;* i(ə)r *ear;* NG *sing;* ō *go;* ô *for;* oi *boy;* oŏ *good;* oō *goo;* ou *out;* SH *she;* TH *thin;* T͟H *then;* (h)w *why;* ZH *vision*

U·ni·tar·i·an /ˌyo͞oniˈte(ə)rēən/ ▸*n.* *Theology* a person, esp. a Christian, who asserts the unity of God and rejects the doctrine of the Trinity. ■ a member of a church or religious body maintaining this belief and typically rejecting formal dogma in favor of a rationalist and inclusivist approach to belief.
▸*adj.* of or relating to the Unitarians. ▷late 17th cent.: from modern Latin *unitarius* (from Latin *unitas* 'unity') + -AN. —**U·ni·tar·i·an·ism** /-ˌnizəm/ *n.*

U·ni·tar·i·an U·ni·ver·sal·ism /ˌyo͞onəˈvərsəˌlizəm/ ▸*n.* the religious denomination formed in 1961 by the merger of the Unitarians and the Universalists. —**U·ni·tar·i·an U·ni·ver·sal·ist** *adj. & n.*

u·ni·tar·y /ˈyo͞oniˌterē/ ▸*adj.* **1** single; uniform: *a sort of unitary wholeness.* ■ of or relating to a system of government or organization in which the powers of the separate constituent parts are vested in a central body: *a unitary rather than a federal state.* **2** unified; whole: *it was just this unitary beauty that the Ptolemaic cosmology lacked.* **3** of or relating to a unit or units. —**u·ni·tar·i·ly** /ˈyo͞onəˌterəlē; ˌyo͞onəˈte(ə)r-/ *adv.* —**u·ni·tar·i·ty** /ˌyo͞onəˈte(ə)ritē/ *n.*

U·ni·tas /yo͞oˈnītəs/, Johnny (1933–2002), U.S. football player; full name *John Constantine Unitas.* A quarterback with the Baltimore Colts 1956–72, he led them to three NFL titles in 1958, 1959, and 1968 and a Super Bowl win in 1971. He also played for the San Diego Chargers 1972–73. Football Hall of Fame (1979).

u·nit cell ▸*n.* *Crystallography* the smallest group of atoms of a substance that has the overall symmetry of a crystal of that substance, and from which the entire lattice can be built up by repetition in three dimensions.

u·nite /yo͞oˈnīt/ ▸*v.* come or bring together for a common purpose or action: [*intrans.*] *he called on the party to unite* | [*trans.*] *they are united by their love of cars.* ■ come or bring together to form a unit or whole, esp. in a political context: [*intrans.*] *the two Germanys officially united* | [*trans.*] *he aimed to unite Italy and Sicily under his imperial crown* | *his work unites theory and practice.* See note at JOIN.■ [*trans.*] *archaic* join in marriage. ▷late Middle English: from Latin *unit-* 'joined together,' from the verb *unire,* from *unus* 'one.' —**u·ni·tive** /ˈyo͞onətiv; yo͞oˈnī-/ *adj.*

u·nit·ed /yo͞oˈnītid/ ▸*adj.* joined together politically, for a common purpose, or by common feelings: *women acting together in a united way.* ■ *chiefly Brit.* used in names of soccer and other sports teams formed by amalgamation: *Oxford United.* —**u·nit·ed·ly** *adv.*

U·nit·ed Ar·ab E·mir·ates (abbr.: **UAE**) an independent state on the southern coast of the Persian Gulf, west of the Gulf of Oman; pop. 2,523,000; capital, Abu Dhabi; official language, Arabic.

The United Arab Emirates was formed in 1971 by the federation of the independent sheikhdoms formerly called the Trucial States: Abu Dhabi, Ajman, Dubai, Fujairah, Ras al Khaimah (joined early 1972), Sharjah, and Umm al Qaiwain.

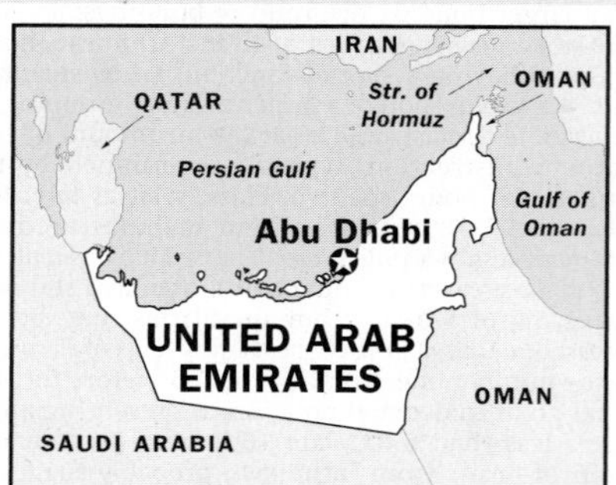

U·nit·ed Ar·ab Re·pub·lic (abbr.: **UAR**) a former political union established by Egypt and Syria in 1958. It was seen as the first step toward the creation of a pan-Arab union in the Middle East, but only Yemen entered into loose association with it 1958–66 and Syria withdrew in 1961. Egypt retained the name United Arab Republic until 1971.

U·nit·ed Art·ists a movie production company formed in 1919 by Charlie Chaplin, Douglas Fairbanks, Mary Pickford, and D. W. Griffith, to make movies without the artistic strictures of the larger companies. Its films have earned more than 100 Academy Awards. Since 1981, it has operated under the ownership of MGM.

U·nit·ed Breth·ren ▸*plural n.* a Protestant denomination founded in the U.S. in 1800.

U·nit·ed King·dom (abbr.: **UK**) a country in western Europe that consists of England, Wales, Scotland, and Northern Ireland; pop. 60,270,000; capital, London; language, English (official). Full name UNITED KINGDOM OF GREAT BRITAIN AND NORTHERN IRELAND.

England (which had incorporated Wales in the 16th century) and Scotland have had the same monarch since 1603, when James VI of Scotland succeeded to the English crown as James I; the kingdoms were formally united by the Act of Union in 1707. An Act of Parliament joined Great Britain and Ireland in 1801, but the Irish Free State (later the Republic of Ireland) broke away in 1921. The UK became a member of the EC (now the EU) in 1973.

U·nit·ed Na·tions (abbr.: **UN**) an international organization of countries set up in 1945, in succession to the League of Nations, to promote international peace, security, and cooperation.

Its members, originally the countries that fought against the Axis powers in World War II, now number more than 190 and include most sovereign states of the world. Administration is by a secretariat headed by a secretary-general. The chief deliberative body is the General Assembly, in which each member state has one vote; recommendations are passed but are not binding on members and generally have had little effect on world politics. The Security Council bears the primary responsibility for the maintenance of peace and security and may call on members to take action, chiefly peacekeeping action, to enforce its decisions. The UN's headquarters are in New York City.

U·nit·ed Prov·inc·es *historical* **1** the seven provinces united in 1579 that formed the basis of the republic of the Netherlands. **2** an Indian administrative division formed by the union of Agra and Oudh that has been called Uttar Pradesh since 1950.

U·nit·ed States (abbr.: **U.S.** or **US**) a country that occupies most of the southern half of North America as well as Alaska and the Hawaiian Islands; pop. 293,027,000; capital, Washington, D.C. Full name UNITED STATES OF AMERICA.

The U.S. is a federal republic comprising 50 states and the Federal District of Columbia. It originated in the American Revolution, the successful rebellion of the colonies on the eastern coast against British rule in 1775–83. The original 13 states that formed the Union drew up a federal constitution in 1787, and George Washington was elected the first president in 1789. In the 19th century the territory of the U.S. was extended across the continent through the westward spread of pioneers and settlers and acquisitions such as that of Texas and California from Mexico in the 1840s. After a long period of isolation in foreign affairs, the U.S. participated on the Allied side in both world wars and emerged from the Cold War as the world's leading military and economic power.

u·nit·ize /ˈyo͞onəˌtīz/ ▸*v.* [*trans.*] [usu. as *adj.*] (**unitized**) form into a single unit by combining parts into a whole: *a six-cylinder engine and a unitized body with thousands of welds.* ■ package (cargo) into unit loads: *a unitized load.*

u·nit mem·brane ▸*n.* *Biology* a lipoprotein membrane that encloses many cells and cell organelles and is composed of two electron-dense layers enclosing a less dense layer.

u·nit pric·ing ▸*n.* identification of and labeling of items for sale with the retail price per unit, permitting easier price comparisons among similar products in different sized containers.

u·nit train ▸*n.* a train transporting a single commodity.

u·nit trust ▸*n.* British term for MUTUAL FUND.

u·nit vec·tor ▸*n.* *Mathematics* a vector that has a magnitude of one.

u·ni·ty /ˈyo͞onətē/ ▸*n.* (*pl.* **-ties**) **1** the state of being united or joined as a whole, esp. in a political context: *European unity* | *economic unity.* ■ harmony or agreement between people or groups: *their leaders called for unity between opposing factions.* ■ the state of forming a complete and pleasing whole, esp. in an artistic context: *the repeated phrase gives the piece unity and cohesion.* ■ a thing forming a complex whole: *they speak of the three parts as a unity.* ■ in Aristotle's *Poetics,* each of the three dramatic principles requiring limitation of the supposed time of a drama to that occupied in acting it or to a single day (**unity of time**), use of one scene throughout (**unity of place**), and concentration on the development of a single plot (**unity of action**). **2** *Mathematics chiefly Brit.* the number one. ▷Middle English: from Old French *unite,* from Latin *unitas,* from *unus* 'one.'

Univ. ▸*abbr.* University.

univ. ▸*abbr.* ■ universal.

u·ni·va·lent ▸*adj.* /ˌyo͞onəˈvālənt; yo͞oˈnivələnt/ **1** *Biology* (of a chromosome) remaining unpaired during meiosis. **2** *Chemistry* another term for MONOVALENT.
▸*n.* /yo͞oˈnivələnt/ *Biology* a univalent chromosome.

u·ni·valve /ˈyo͞onəˌvalv/ *Zoology* ▸*adj.* having one valve or shell.
▸*n.* another term for GASTROPOD (see GASTROPODA).

U·ni·ver·sal /ˌyo͞onəˈvərsəl/ a movie production company formed by Carl Laemmle in 1912, one of the first studios to move from New York to the Los Angeles area. The company merged with MCA (Music Corporation of America) in 1962. The company produced movies starring Abbott and Costello, the series of Sherlock Holmes movies featuring Basil Rathbone and Nigel Bruce, and blockbusters such as *ET The Extra-Terrestrial* (1982).

u·ni·ver·sal /ˌyo͞onəˈvərsəl/ ▸*adj.* of, affecting, or done by all people or things in the world or in a particular group; applicable to all cases: *universal adult suffrage* | *the incidents caused universal concern.* ■ *Logic* denoting a proposition in which something is asserted of all of a class. Contrasted with PARTICULAR. ■ *Linguistics* denoting or relating to a grammatical rule, set of rules, or other linguistic feature that is found in all languages. ■ (of a tool or machine) adjustable to or appropriate for all requirements; not restricted to a single purpose or position.
▸*n.* a person or thing having universal effect, currency, or application, in particular: ■ *Logic* a universal proposition. ■ *Philosophy* a term or concept of general application. ■ *Philosophy* a nature or essence signified by a general term. ■ *Linguistics* a universal grammatical rule or linguistic feature. ▷late Middle English: from Old French, or from Latin *universalis,* from *universus* (see UNIVERSE). —**u·ni·ver·sal·i·ty** /-vərˈsalətē/ *n.*

THE RIGHT WORD **catholic, common, ecumenical, general, generic, universal**

Something that is **universal** applies to every case or individual in a class or category (*a universal practice among aboriginal tribesmen; a universal truth*).

General, on the other hand, is less precise; it implies applicability to all or most of a group or class,

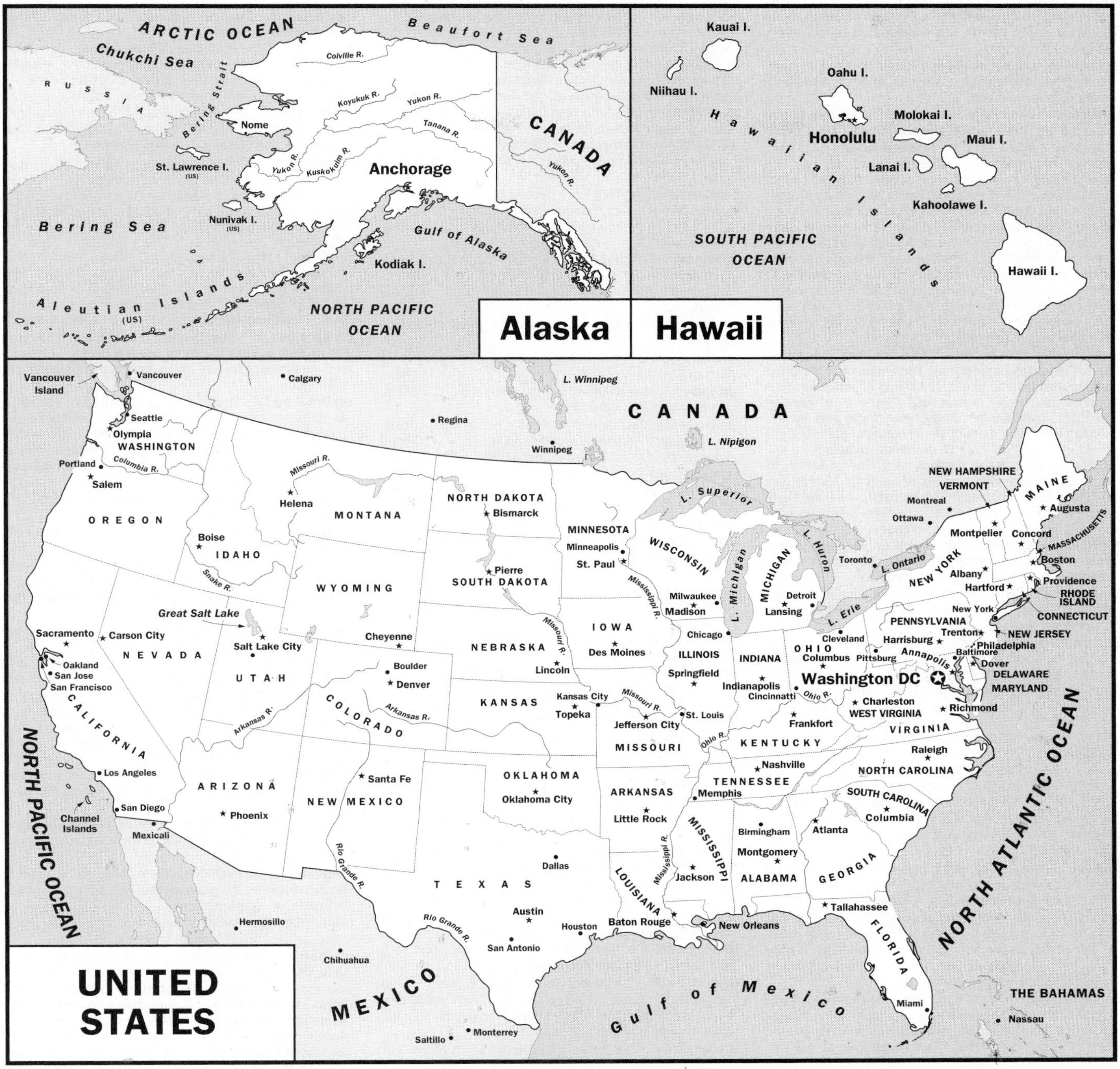

Alaska **Hawaii**

UNITED STATES

whether the members of that group are clearly defined or only casually associated (*a drug that has come into general use among women but has not yet won the universal acceptance of doctors*).

Generic is often used in place of *general* when referring to every member of a genus or clearly defined scientific category (*a generic characteristic of insects*); with reference to language, it means referring to both men and women (*a generic pronoun*).

Common implies participation or sharing by all members of a class (*a common interest in French culture*) or frequently occurring (*a common complaint*).

Catholic implies a wide-ranging or inclusive attitude (*known for his catholic tastes in music*), while **ecumenical** means pertaining to the whole Christian church or promoting unity among religious groups or divisions (*an ecumenical marriage ceremony*).

Uni·ver·sal Cit·y /ˈyo͞onəˌvərsəl/ a district in northwestern Los Angeles in California, in the San Fernando Valley, home to Universal Studios and other entertainment facilities.

u·ni·ver·sal do·nor ▶*n.* a person of blood group O, who can in theory donate blood to recipients of any ABO blood group.

u·ni·ver·sal·ist /ˌyo͞onəˈvərsəlist/ ▶*n.* **1** *Christian Theology* a person who believes that all humankind will eventually be saved. ■ (usu. **Universalist**) a member of an organized body of Christians who hold such beliefs. **2** a person advocating loyalty to and concern for others without regard to national or other allegiances.
▶*adj.* **1** *Christian Theology* of or relating to universalists. **2** universal in scope or character. —**u·ni·ver·sal·ism** /-ˌlizəm/ *n.* —**u·ni·ver·sal·is·tic** /-ˌvərsəˈlistik/ *adj.*

u·ni·ver·sal·ize /ˌyo͞onəˈvərsəˌlīz/ ▶*v.* [*trans.*] give a universal character or application to (something, esp. something abstract): *theories that universalize experience.* ■ bring into universal use; make available for all: *attempts to universalize basic education.* —**u·ni·ver·sal·iz·a·bil·i·ty** /-ˌvərsəˌlīzəˈbilətē/ *n.* —**u·ni·ver·sal·i·za·tion** /-ˌvərsəliˈzāSHən/ *n.*

u·ni·ver·sal joint (also **u·ni·ver·sal coup·ling**) ▶*n.* a coupling or joint that can transmit rotary power by a shaft over a range of angles.

u·ni·ver·sal·ly /ˌyo͞onəˈvərsəlē/ ▶*adv.* by everyone; in every case: *progress is not always universally welcomed.*

U·ni·ver·sal Prod·uct Code ▶*n.* more formal term for BAR CODE.

u·ni·ver·sal quan·ti·fi·er ▶*n.* *Logic* a formal expression used in asserting that a stated general proposition is true of all the members of the delineated universe or class.

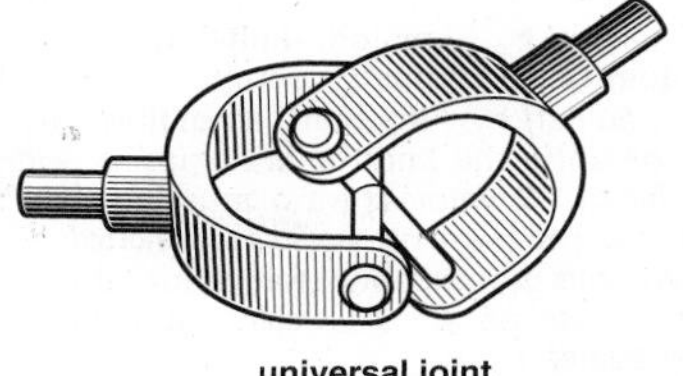

universal joint

Pronunciation Key ə *ago;* ər *over;* ˈə *or* ˌə *up;* ˈər *or* ˌər *fur;* a *hat;* ā *rate;* ä *car;* CH *chew;* e *let;* ē *see;* e(ə)r *air;* i *fit;* ī *by;* i(ə)r *ear;* NG *sing;* ō *go;* ô *for;* oi *boy;* o͝o *good;* o͞o *goo;* ou *out;* SH *she;* TH *thin;* TH *then;* (h)w *why;* ZH *vision*

u·ni·ver·sal re·cip·i·ent ▸*n.* a person of blood group AB, who can in theory receive donated blood of any ABO blood group.

u·ni·ver·sal set ▸*n. Mathematics & Logic* the set containing all objects or elements and of which all other sets are subsets.

U·ni·ver·sal Time (also **U·ni·ver·sal Time Co·or·di·nat·ed**) another term for GREENWICH MEAN TIME.

u·ni·verse /'yo͞onə,vərs/ ▸*n.* (**the universe**) all existing matter and space considered as a whole; the cosmos. The universe is believed to be at least 10 billion light years in diameter and contains a vast number of galaxies; it has been expanding since its creation in the big bang about 13 billion years ago. ■ a particular sphere of activity, interest, or experience: *the front parlor was the hub of her universe.* ■ (*Logic* also **u·ni·verse of dis·course**) another term for UNIVERSAL SET. ▷late Middle English: from Old French *univers* or Latin *universum*, neuter of *universus* 'combined into one, whole,' from *uni-* 'one' + *versus* 'turned' (past participle of *vertere*).

u·ni·ver·si·ty /,yo͞onə'vərsətē/ ▸*n.* (*pl.* **-ties**) an educational institution designed for instruction, examination, or both, of students in many branches of advanced learning, conferring degrees in various faculties, and often embodying colleges and similar institutions: [*in names*] *Oxford University | the University of California* | [*as adj.*] *the university buildings | a university professor.* ■ the members of this collectively. ■ the grounds and buildings of such an institution. ▷Middle English: from Old French *universite*, from Latin *universitas* 'the whole,' in late Latin 'society, guild,' from *universus* (see UNIVERSE).

▸*PHRASES* □ **at university** *chiefly Brit.* studying at a university. □ **the university of life** the experience of life regarded as a means of instruction.

U·ni·ver·si·ty Cit·y /,yo͞onə'vərsitē/ a city in eastern Missouri, west of St. Louis, home to Washington University; pop. 40,087.

U·ni·ver·si·ty Park a city in northeastern Texas, enclosed by northern Dallas, home to Southern Methodist University; pop. 22,259.

u·niv·o·cal /,yo͞onə'vōkəl; yo͞o'nivə-/ ▸*adj. Philosophy & Linguistics* (of a word or term) having only one possible meaning; unambiguous: *a univocal set of instructions.* —**u·niv·o·cal·i·ty** /,yo͞onə,vō'kalətē/ *n.* —**u·niv·o·cal·ly** *adv.*

U·nix /'yo͞oniks/ (also **UNIX**) ▸*n. trademark Computing* a widely used multiuser operating system. ▷1970s: from UNI- 'one' + a respelling of -ICS, on the pattern of an earlier less compact system called *Multics.*

un·joint /,ən'joint/ ▸*v.* [*trans.*] *rare* separate or dislocate the joints of.

un·just /,ən'jəst/ ▸*adj.* not based on or behaving according to what is morally right and fair: *resistance to unjust laws.* —**un·just·ly** *adv.* —**un·just·ness** *n.*

un·jus·ti·fi·a·ble /,ən'jəstə,fīəbəl; -,jəstə'fī-/ ▸*adj.* not able to be shown to be right or reasonable: *an unjustifiable restriction on their freedom.* —**un·jus·ti·fi·a·bly** /-blē/ *adv.* [*sentence adverb*] *they seemed, unjustifiably, to be taking things out on the students.*

un·kempt /,ən'kem(p)t/ ▸*adj.* (esp. of a person) having an untidy or disheveled appearance: *they were unwashed and unkempt.* ▷late Middle English: from UN-[1] 'not' + *kempt* 'combed' (past participle of archaic *kemb*, related to COMB). —**un·kempt·ly** *adv.* —**un·kempt·ness** *n.*

un·kept /,ən'kept/ ▸*adj.* **1** (of a commitment or undertaking) not honored or fulfilled: *unkept appointments and broken promises.* **2** not tidy or cared for.

un·kind /,ən'kīnd/ ▸*adj.* inconsiderate and harsh to others: *you were terribly* **unkind to** *her | he was the butt of some unkind jokes | it was* **unkind of** *her to criticize.* —**un·kind·ly** *adv.* —**un·kind·ness** *n.*

un·king /,ən'kiNG/ ▸*v.* [*trans.*] *archaic* remove (a monarch) from power.

un·kink /,ən'kiNGk/ ▸*v.* straighten or become straight.

un·knit /,ən'nit/ ▸*v.* (**-knit·ted**, **-knit·ting**) [*trans.*] separate (things that are joined, knotted, or interlocked).

un·knot /,ən'nät/ ▸*v.* (**-knot·ted**, **-knot·ting**) **1** [*trans.*] release or untie the knot or knots in: *he swiftly unknotted his tie.* **2** [*intrans.*] (of a muscle) relax after being tense and hard: *his shoulders unknotted.*

un·know·a·ble /,ən'nōəbəl/ ▸*adj.* not able to be known: *the total cost is unknowable.* —**un·know·a·bil·i·ty** /-,nōə'bilətē/ *n.*

un·know·ing /,ən'nō-iNG/ ▸*adj.* not knowing or aware: *the lions moved stealthily toward their unknowing victims.* ▸*n.* lack of awareness or knowledge. —**un·know·ing·ly** *adv.* —**un·know·ing·ness** *n.*

un·known /,ən'nōn/ ▸*adj.* not known or familiar: *exploration into unknown territory | his whereabouts are* **unknown to** *his family.* ■ (of a performer or artist) not well known or famous.
▸*n.* an unknown person or thing: *she is a relative unknown.* ■ *Mathematics* an unknown quantity or variable: *find the unknown in the following equations.* ■ (**the unknown**) that which is unknown: *our fear of the unknown.* —**un·known·ness** *n.*

▸*PHRASE* □ **unknown to** without the knowledge of: *unknown to Miller, the police had taped their telephone conversation.*

un·known quan·ti·ty ▸*n.* a person or thing whose nature, value, or significance cannot be determined or is not yet known: *the producers replaced her with an unknown quantity.*

Un·known Sol·dier ▸*n.* an unidentified representative member of a country's armed forces killed in war, given burial with special honors in a national memorial.

un·lace /,ən'lās/ ▸*v.* [*trans.*] undo the laces of (a shoe or garment).

un·lade /,ən'lād/ ▸*v.* [*trans.*] *archaic* unload (a ship or cargo).

un·lad·en /,ən'lādn/ ▸*adj.* not carrying a load: *unladen, the boat heeled to starboard.*

un·la·dy·like /,ən'lādē,līk/ ▸*adj.* not behaving or dressing in a way considered appropriate for a well-bred woman or girl: *Sharon gave an unladylike snort.* ■ (of an activity or occupation) not considered suitable for a woman or girl.

un·laid /,ən'lād/ ▸ past and past participle of UNLAY.
▸*adj.* not laid: *the table was still unlaid.*

un·la·ment·ed /,ənlə'mentid/ ▸*adj.* (of a person who has died or something that has gone or finished) not mourned or regretted.

un·lash /,ən'lasH/ ▸*v.* [*trans.*] unfasten (something securely tied with a cord or rope): *he unlashed the dinghy.*

un·latch /,ən'lacH/ ▸*v.* [*trans.*] unfasten the latch of (a door or gate).

un·law·ful /,ən'lôfəl/ ▸*adj.* not conforming to, permitted by, or recognized by law or rules: *the use of unlawful violence | they claimed the ban was unlawful.* —**un·law·ful·ly** /-f(ə)lē/ *adv.* —**un·law·ful·ness** *n.*

un·lay /,ən'lā/ ▸*v.* (*past* and *past part.* **-laid**) [*trans.*] *Nautical* untwist (a rope) into separate strands. ▷early 18th cent.: from UN-[2] (expressing reversal) + LAY[1].

un·lead·ed /,ən'ledid/ ▸*adj.* **1** (esp. of gasoline) without added tetraethyl lead. ■ *humorous* (of coffee) decaffeinated. **2** not covered, weighted, or framed with lead. **3** *Printing* (of type) with no space or leads added between lines.
▸*n.* gasoline without added lead.

un·learn /,ən'lərn/ ▸*v.* [*trans.*] discard (something learned, esp. a bad habit or false or outdated information) from one's memory: *teachers are being asked to unlearn rigid rules for labeling and placing children.*

un·learn·ed[1] /,ən'lərnid/ ▸*adj.* (of a person) not well educated. —**un·learn·ed·ly** *adv.*

un·learned[2] /,ən'lərnd/ ▸*adj.* not having been learned: *she found herself on the stage, lines unlearned.* ■ not needing to be learned because innate: *the unlearned responses of our inner world.*

un·leash /,ən'lēsH/ ▸*v.* [*trans.*] release from a leash or restraint: *we unleashed the dog and carried it down to our car | figurative the failure of the talks could unleash more fighting.*

un·leav·ened /,ən'levənd/ ▸*adj.* (of bread) made without yeast or other leavening agent.

un·less /ən'les; ,ən-/ ▸*conj.* except if (used to introduce a case in which a statement being made is not true or valid): *unless you have a photographic memory, repetition is vital | manuscripts cannot be returned unless accompanied by a self-addressed envelope.* ▷late Middle English: from ON or IN (assimilated through lack of stress to UN-[1]) + LESS.

un·let·tered /,ən'letərd/ ▸*adj.* (of a person) poorly educated or illiterate. See note at IGNORANT.

un·li·censed /,ən'līsənst/ (*Brit.* also **un·li·cenced**) ▸*adj.* not having an official license: *unlicensed weapons.* ■ *chiefly Brit.* (of a bar or restaurant) not having a license for the sale of liquor: *unlicensed clubs do not seek publicity.*

un·light·ed /,ən'lītid/ ▸*adj.* unlit.

un·lik·a·ble /,ən'līkəbəl/ (also **un·like·a·ble**) ▸*adj.* (esp. of a person) not likable: *a thoroughly unlikable bully.*

un·like /,ən'līk/ ▸*prep.* different from; not similar to: *they were unlike anything ever seen before | a large house not unlike Mr. Shaw's.* ■ in contrast to; differently from: *unlike Helen, he was not superstitious.* ■ uncharacteristic of (someone): *he sounded irritable, which was unlike him.*
▸*adj.* [*predic.*] dissimilar or different from each other: *they seemed utterly unlike, despite being twins.* ■ (**unlike to/from**) *archaic* not like; different from: *he was very unlike to any other man.* ▷Middle English: perhaps originally an alteration of Old Norse *Ú[ordm]líkr*; compare with Old English *ungelīc* 'not of the same kind, not comparable.' —**un·like·ness** *n.*

USAGE The use of **unlike** as a conjunction, as in *she was behaving* **unlike** *she'd* **ever** *behaved before*, is not considered standard English. It can be avoided by using **as** with a negative instead: *she was behaving* **as** *she'd* **never** *behaved before.*

un·like·ly /,ən'līklē/ ▸*adj.* (**-li·er**, **-li·est**) not likely to happen, be done, or be true; improbable: *an unlikely explanation |* **it is unlikely that** *they will ever be used |* [*with infinitive*] *the change is unlikely to affect many people.* —**un·like·li·hood** /-,ho͝od/ *n.* —**un·like·li·ness** *n.*

un·lim·ber /,ən'limbər/ ▸*v.* [*trans.*] detach (a gun) from its limber so that it can be used. ■ unpack or unfasten (something) ready for use: *we had to unlimber some of the gear.*

un·lim·it·ed /,ən'limitid/ ▸*adj.* not limited or restricted in terms of number, quantity, or extent: *the range of possible adaptations was unlimited.* ■ *Brit.* (of a company) not limited. ■ *Mathematics* (of a problem) having an infinite number of solutions. —**un·lim·it·ed·ly** *adv.* —**un·lim·it·ed·ness** *n.*

un·lined[1] /,ən'līnd/ ▸*adj.* not marked or covered with lines: *her face was still unlined | unlined paper.*

un·lined[2] ▸*adj.* (of a container or garment) without a lining: *unlined curtains.*

un·link /,ən'liNGk/ ▸*v.* [*trans.*] make no longer connected: *all three loops are linked, but cutting any one unlinks the other two.* ■ [*as adj.*] (**unlinked**) unconnected: *three previously unlinked murders.*

un·liq·ui·dat·ed /,ən'likwə,dātid/ ▸*adj.* (of a debt) not cleared or paid off.

un·list·ed /,ən'listid/ ▸*adj.* not included on a list. ■ (of a person or telephone number) not listed in a telephone directory or available through directory assistance, at the wish of the subscriber: *the nuisance calls stopped after he obtained an unlisted number.* ■ denoting or relating to a company whose shares are not listed on a stock exchange.

un·lis·ten·a·ble /,ən'lisənəbəl/ ▸*adj.* (esp. of music) impossible or unbearable to listen to: *today, his recordings seem unlistenable.*

un·lit /,ən'lit/ ▸*adj.* **1** not provided with lighting: *an unlit staircase.* **2** not having been set alight: *his unlit pipe.*

un·liv·a·ble /,ən'livəbəl/ ▸*adj.* not able to be lived in; uninhabitable: *the pollution that has made life virtually unlivable for our people there.*

un·lived-in /,ən'liv ,din/ ▸*adj.* not appearing to be used or inhabited; not homey or comfortable.

un·load /,ən'lōd/ ▸*v.* [*trans.*] **1** remove goods from (a vehicle, ship, container, etc.): *she hadn't finished unloading the car.* ■ remove (goods) from a vehicle, ship, container, etc.: *the men unloaded the wheat into the bays.* ■ [*intrans.*] (of a vehicle, ship, container, etc.) have goods removed: *the street was jammed with trucks unloading.* ■ *informal* get rid of (something unwanted): *he had* **unloaded** *his depreciating stock* **on** *his unsuspecting wife.* ■ *informal* give expression to (oppressive thoughts or feelings): *the meeting had been a chance for her to unload some of her feelings about her son.* **2** remove (ammunition) from a gun or (film) from a camera. —**un·load·er** *n.*

un·lock /,ən'läk/ ▸*v.* [*trans.*] undo the lock of (something) by using a key: *he unlocked the door to his room.* ■ make (something previously inaccessible or unexploited) available for use: *the campaign has helped us unlock rich reserves of talent among our employees.*

un·looked-for /,ən'lo͝okt ,fôr/ ▸*adj.* unexpected; unforeseen: *in his family he found unlooked-for happiness.*

un·loose /,ən'lo͞os/ (also **un·loos·en**) ▸*v.* [*trans.*] undo; let free: *his first action was to unloose that knotted necktie | figurative she unloosed a salvo of condescension.*

un·lov·a·ble /,ən'ləvəbəl/ (also **un·love·a·ble**) ▸*adj.* not lovable: *a very unlovable child.* —**un·lov·a·bil·i·ty** /-,ləvə'bilətē/ *n.*

un·love·ly /,ən'ləvlē/ ▸*adj.* not attractive; ugly. —**un·love·li·ness** *n.*

un·luck·y /,ən'ləkē/ ▸*adj.* (**-luck·i·er**, **-luck·i·est**) having, bringing, or resulting from bad luck: *an unlucky defeat* | [*with infinitive*] *the visitors were unlucky to have a goal disallowed.* —**un·luck·i·ly** /-'ləkəlē/ *adv.* —**un·luck·i·ness** *n.*

un·made /ˌən'mād/ ▸*adj.* **1** (of a bed) not having the bedclothes neatly arranged for sleeping in. **2** *Brit.* (of a road) without a hard, smooth surface.

un·maid·en·ly /ˌən'mādn-lē/ ▸*adj.* not befitting or characteristic of a young, sexually inexperienced woman. —**un·maid·en·li·ness** *n.*

un·make /ˌən'māk/ ▸*v.* (*past* and *past part.* **-made**) [*trans.*] reverse or undo the making of; annul: *Watergate made the independent prosecutor law necessary; Whitewater may unmake it.* ■ ruin; destroy: *human beings make cities and unmake them.*

un·man /ˌən'man/ ▸*v.* (**-manned, -man·ning**) [*trans.*] *poetic/literary* deprive of qualities traditionally associated with men, such as self-control or courage: *sitting in the dock awaiting a sentence will unman the stoutest heart.*

un·man·age·a·ble /ˌən'manijəbəl/ ▸*adj.* difficult or impossible to manage, manipulate, or control: *his behavior was becoming unmanageable at home.* —**un·man·age·a·ble·ness** *n.* —**un·man·age·a·bly** /-blē/ *adv.*

un·man·aged /ˌən'manijd/ ▸*adj.* **1** not controlled or regulated: *a critique of unmanaged capitalism.* **2** (of land) left wild; in a natural state.

un·man·ly /ˌən'manlē/ ▸*adj.* not manly; weak or cowardly: *unmanly behavior.* —**un·man·li·ness** *n.*

un·manned /ˌən'mand/ ▸*adj.* not having or needing a crew or staff: *an unmanned space flight.*

un·man·nered /ˌən'manərd/ ▸*adj.* not affected or artificial in style.

un·man·ner·ly /ˌən'manərlē/ ▸*adj.* not having or showing good manners: *uncouth, unmannerly fellows.* —**un·man·ner·li·ness** *n.*

un·mapped /ˌən'mapt/ ▸*adj.* (of an area or feature) not represented on a geographical map. ■ unexplored: *unmapped corners of Africa.* ■ *Biology* (of a gene or chromosome) not yet mapped.

un·marked /ˌən'märkt/ ▸*adj.* **1** not marked: *an unmarked police car | his skin was unmarked.* ■ *Linguistics* (of a word or other linguistic unit) having a more general meaning or use than a corresponding marked term: *"duck" is unmarked, whereas "drake" is marked.* **2** not noticed: *it's a pleasure to reward them for work which might otherwise go unmarked.*

un·mask /ˌən'mask/ ▸*v.* [*trans.*] expose the true character of or hidden truth about: *the trial unmasked him as a complete charlatan.* ■ [often as *adj.*] (**unmasked**) remove the mask from: *an unmasked gunman.* —**un·mask·er** *n.*

un·match·a·ble /ˌən'macHəbəl/ ▸*adj.* incapable of being matched, equaled, or rivaled. —**un·match·a·bly** /-blē/ *adv.*

un·matched /ˌən'macHt/ ▸*adj.* not matched or equaled: *he has a talent unmatched by any other politician.*

un·mean·ing /ˌən'mēniNG/ ▸*adj.* having no meaning or significance; meaningless: *a sweet, unmeaning smile.* —**un·mean·ing·ly** *adv.*

un·meas·ur·a·ble /ˌən'mezH(ə)rəbəl/ ▸*adj.* not able to be measured objectively: *the unmeasurable qualities of a scientist.* —**un·meas·ur·a·bly** /-blē/ *adv.*

un·meas·ured /ˌən'mezHərd/ ▸*adj.* **1** not having been measured: *unmeasured risk factors.* **2** *chiefly poetic/literary* immense; limitless: *he is regarded by his congregation with unmeasured adoration.*

un·me·di·at·ed /ˌən'mēdēˌātid/ ▸*adj.* without anyone or anything intervening or acting as an intermediate; direct.

un·melt·ed /ˌən'meltid/ ▸*adj.* not melted: *unmelted snow.*

un·men·tion·a·ble /ˌən'mencHənəbəl/ ▸*adj.* too embarrassing, offensive, or shocking to be spoken about: *the unmentionable subject of incontinence.*
▸*n.* (usu. **unmentionables**) *chiefly humorous* a person or thing that is too shocking or embarrassing to be mentioned by name: *wearing nothing but fig leaves over their unmentionables.* ■ (**unmentionables**) underwear. —**un·men·tion·a·bil·i·ty** /-ˌmencHənə'bilətē/ *n.* —**un·men·tion·a·ble·ness** *n.* —**un·men·tion·a·bly** /-blē/ *adv.*

un·men·tioned /ˌən'mencHənd/ ▸*adj.* not mentioned: *a monument unmentioned in all the architectural guides.*

un·mer·ci·ful /ˌən'mərsəfəl/ ▸*adj.* cruel or harsh; showing no mercy. —**un·mer·ci·ful·ly** /-f(ə)lē/ *adv.* —**un·mer·ci·ful·ness** *n.*

un·mer·it·ed /ˌən'meritid/ ▸*adj.* not deserved or merited: *an unmerited insult.*

un·met /ˌən'met/ ▸*adj.* (of a requirement) not achieved or fulfilled: *an unmet need.*

un·me·tered /ˌən'mētərd/ ▸*adj.* **1** not charged for according to amount or time used. **2** not supplied or fitted with a meter: *an unmetered taxi.* **3** not canceled or franked using a postage meter: *agents warned the public to be on the alert for unmetered packages.*

un·met·ri·cal /ˌən'metrikəl/ ▸*adj.* not composed in or using meter: *an unmetrical poet.*

un·mil·i·tar·y /ˌən'miliˌterē/ ▸*adj.* not typical of, suitable for, or connected with the military.

un·mind·ful /ˌən'mīn(d)fəl/ ▸*adj.* [*predic.*] not conscious or aware: *Danielle seemed* ***unmindful of*** *her parents' plight.* —**un·mind·ful·ly** *adv.* —**un·mind·ful·ness** *n.*

un·miss·a·ble /ˌən'misəbəl/ ▸*adj.* **1** so good that it should not be missed: *the special effects make this an unmissable treat.* **2** so clear or obvious that it cannot be missed.

un·mis·tak·a·ble /ˌənmə'stākəbəl/ (also **un·mis·take·a·ble**) ▸*adj.* not able to be mistaken for anything else; very distinctive: *the unmistakable sound of his laughter.* —**un·mis·tak·a·bil·i·ty** /-ˌstākə'bilətē/ *n.* —**un·mis·tak·a·bly** /-blē/ *adv.*

un·mis·tak·en /ˌənmə'stākən/ ▸*adj.* not mistaken; right, correct.

un·mit·i·gat·ed /ˌən'mitəˌgātid/ ▸*adj.* [*attrib.*] absolute; unqualified: *the tour had been* ***an unmitigated disaster.*** See note at **SEVERE**. —**un·mit·i·gat·ed·ly** *adv.*

un·mixed /ˌən'mikst/ ▸*adj.* not mixed: *bold unmixed colors.*

un·mixed bless·ing ▸*n.* [usu. with *negative*] a situation or thing having advantages and no disadvantages: *motherhood is not an unmixed blessing.*

un·mod·u·lat·ed /ˌən'mäjəˌlātid/ ▸*adj.* not modulated: *an unmodulated video signal.*

un·mo·lest·ed /ˌənmə'lestid/ ▸*adj.* not pestered or molested; left in peace: *they allowed him to pass unmolested.*

un·moor /ˌən'mo͝or/ ▸*v.* [*trans.*] release the moorings of (a vessel).

un·mor·al /ˌən'môrəl; -'mär-/ ▸*adj.* not influenced by or concerned with morality. Compare with **IMMORAL**. —**un·mo·ral·i·ty** /-mə'ralətē; -mô-/ *n.*

un·moth·er·ly /ˌən'məT͟Hərlē/ ▸*adj.* not having or showing the affectionate feelings associated with a mother.

un·mo·ti·vat·ed /ˌən'mōtəˌvātid/ ▸*adj.* **1** not having interest in or enthusiasm for something, esp. work or study. **2** without a reason or motive: *an unmotivated attack.*

un·mourned /ˌən'môrnd/ ▸*adj.* not mourned: *he would die alone and unmourned.*

un·moved /ˌən'mo͞ovd/ ▸*adj.* [*predic.*] not affected by emotion or excitement: *he was unmoved by her outburst.* ■ not changed in one's purpose or intention: *her opponents were unmoved and plan to return to court.* ■ not changed in position: *shares in some companies were initially unmoved.* —**un·mov·a·ble** /-vəbəl/ (also **un·move·a·ble**) *adj.*

un·mov·ing /ˌən'mo͞oviNG/ ▸*adj.* **1** not moving; still: *Claudia sat unmoving behind her desk.* **2** not stirring any emotion.

un·muf·fle /ˌən'məfəl/ ▸*v.* [*trans.*] free (something) from something that muffles or conceals.

un·muf·flered /ˌən'məflərd/ ▸*adj.* **1** (of an engine or vehicle) not fitted with a muffler: *the crescendo of unmufflered 400-horsepower engines.* **2** not restrained, muffled, or suppressed in any way: *unmufflered fun.*

un·mur·mur·ing /ˌən'mərməriNG/ ▸*adj. poetic/literary* not complaining. —**un·mur·mur·ing·ly** *adv.*

un·mu·si·cal /ˌən'myo͞ozikəl/ ▸*adj.* not pleasing to the ear. ■ unskilled in or indifferent to music. —**un·mu·si·cal·i·ty** /-ˌmyo͞ozi'kalətē/ *n.* —**un·mu·si·cal·ly** /-zik(ə)lē/ *adv.* —**un·mu·si·cal·ness** *n.*

un·muz·zle /ˌən'məzəl/ ▸*v.* [*trans.*] remove a muzzle from (an animal). ■ *figurative* allow (a person or the press) to express their views freely and without censorship.

un·muz·zled /ˌən'məzəld/ ▸*adj.* (of an animal) not wearing a muzzle.

un·name·a·ble /ˌən'nāməbəl/ (also **un·nam·a·ble**) ▸*adj.* not able to be named, esp. because too bad or horrific: *his mind was blank with an unnameable fear.*

un·named /ˌən'nāmd/ ▸*adj.* not having a name: *a new but yet unnamed African violet.* ■ not identified by name: *an old couple in an unnamed American city.*

un·nat·u·ral /ˌən'nacH(ə)rəl/ ▸*adj.* contrary to the ordinary course of nature; abnormal: *death by unnatural causes.* ■ not existing in nature; artificial: *the artificial turf looks an unnatural green.* ■ affected or stilted: *the formal tone of the programs caused them to sound stilted and unnatural.* ■ lacking feelings of kindness and sympathy that are considered to be natural: *they condemned her as an unnatural woman.* —**un·nat·u·ral·ly** *adv.* —**un·nat·u·ral·ness** *n.*

un·nav·i·ga·ble /ˌən'navəgəbəl/ ▸*adj.* (of a waterway or sea) not able to be sailed on by ships or boats. —**un·nav·i·ga·bil·i·ty** /-ˌnavəgə'bilətē/ *n.*

un·nec·es·sar·y /ˌən'nesəˌserē/ ▸*adj.* not needed: *a fourth Chicago airport is unnecessary.* ■ more than is needed; excessive: *the police used unnecessary force.* ■ (of a remark) not appropriate and likely to be offensive or impertinent.
▸*plural n.* (**unnecessaries**) unnecessary things. —**un·nec·es·sar·i·ly** /-ˌnesə'se(ə)rəlē/ *adv.* —**un·nec·es·sar·i·ness** *n.*

un·need·ed /ˌən'nēdid/ ▸*adj.* not needed: *the disposal of unneeded assets.*

un·nerve /ˌən'nərv/ ▸*v.* [*trans.*] make (someone) lose courage or confidence: *the bleakness of his gaze unnerved her |* [as *adj.*] (**unnerving**) *an unnerving experience.* —**un·nerv·ing·ly** *adv.*

un·no·tice·a·ble /ˌən'nōtisəbəl/ ▸*adj.* not easily observed or noticed: *the reverberation will be so slight as to be unnoticeable.* —**un·no·tice·a·bly** /-blē/ *adv.*

un·no·ticed /ˌən'nōtist/ ▸*adj.* [usu. as *complement*] not noticed: *a deliberate kick that went unnoticed by the referee.*

un·num·bered /ˌən'nəmbərd/ ▸*adj.* **1** not marked with or assigned a number. **2** not counted, typically because very great.

UNO /'yo͞onō/ ▸*abbr.* United Nations Organization.

un·ob·jec·tion·a·ble /ˌənəb'jeksHənəbəl/ ▸*adj.* not objectionable; acceptable: *he thought he would become a storyteller, an unobjectionable hobby.* —**un·ob·jec·tion·a·bly** /-blē/ *adv.*

un·o·blig·ing /ˌənə'blījiNG/ ▸*adj.* not helpful or cooperative.

un·ob·tain·i·um /ˌənəb'tānēəm/ (also **unobtanium**) ▸*n.* a fictional material with supernatural properties: *what type of cabling are we talking about, steel, composite, unobtainium?* ■ a material that it extremely rare and difficult to obtain.

un·ob·tru·sive /ˌənəb'tro͞osiv/ ▸*adj.* not conspicuous or attracting attention: *corrections should be neat and unobtrusive.* —**un·ob·tru·sive·ly** *adv.* —**un·ob·tru·sive·ness** *n.*

un·oc·cu·pied /ˌən'äkyəˌpīd/ ▸*adj.* **1** (of ground) not occupied by inhabitants. ■ (of premises) having fixtures and furniture but no inhabitants or occupants. Compare with **VACANT**. **2** not engaged in work or a pursuit; idle. **3** not occupied by enemy troops.

un·or·dained /ˌənôr'dānd/ ▸*adj.* not having been ordained as a priest or minister.

un·or·dered /ˌən'ôrdərd/ ▸*adj.* not put in order; unarranged or disorderly. ■ not ordered or asked for.

un·or·gan·ized /ˌən'ôrgəˌnīzd/ ▸*adj.* not organized: *a sea of unorganized data.* ■ not represented by or formed into a trade union: *unorganized white-collar workers.*

un·o·rig·i·nal /ˌənə'rijənl/ ▸*adj.* lacking originality; derivative: *an uninteresting and unoriginal essay.* —**un·o·rig·i·nal·i·ty** /-ˌrijə'nalətē/ *n.* —**un·o·rig·i·nal·ly** *adv.*

un·or·tho·dox /ˌən'ôrtHəˌdäks/ ▸*adj.* contrary to what is usual, traditional, or accepted; not orthodox: *he frequently upset other scholars with his unorthodox views.* —**un·or·tho·dox·ly** *adv.* —**un·or·tho·dox·y** /-ˌdäksē/ *n.*

un·owned /ˌən'ōnd/ ▸*adj.* **1** not having an owner. **2** not admitted to; unacknowledged: *the unowned anger of all the smiling females of unenlightened times.*

un·pack /ˌən'pak/ ▸*v.* [*trans.*] open and remove the contents of (a suitcase, bag, or package): *she unpacked her suitcase |* [*intrans.*] *he unpacked and put everything away.* ■ remove (something) from a suitcase, bag, or package: *we unpacked the sandwiches.* ■ *figurative* analyze (something) into its component elements: *let us unpack this question.* ■ *Computing* convert (data) from a compressed form to a usable form. —**un·pack·er** *n.*

un·pack·aged /ˌən'pakijd/ ▸*adj. chiefly Brit.* (of a vacation) not organized as an inclusive package.

un·paged /ˌən'pājd/ ▸*adj.* (of a book) not having the pages numbered: *a rare unpaged leaf.*

un·pag·i·nat·ed /ˌən'pajəˌnātid/ ▸*adj.* unpaged.

un·paid /ˌən'pād/ ▸*adj.* **1** (of a debt) not yet discharged by payment: *unpaid bills.* **2** (of work or a period of leave) undertaken without payment: *unpaid labor in the home.* ■ (of a person) not receiving payment for work done.

U

un·paired /ˌənˈpe(ə)rd/ ▸*adj.* **1** not arranged in pairs. **2** not forming one of a pair.

un·pal·at·a·ble /ˌənˈpalətəbəl/ ▸*adj.* not pleasant to taste. ■ difficult to tolerate or accept: *the unpalatable fact that many of the world's people are starving.* —**un·pal·at·a·bil·i·ty** /-ˌpalətəˈbilitē/ *n.* —**un·pal·at·a·bly** /-blē/ *adv.*

un·par·al·leled /ˌənˈparəˌleld/ ▸*adj.* having no parallel or equal; exceptional: *the sudden rise in unemployment is unparalleled in the postwar period.*

un·par·don·a·ble /ˌənˈpärdn-əbəl; -ˈpärdnə-/ ▸*adj.* (of a fault or offense) too severe to be pardoned; unforgivable: *an unpardonable sin.* —**un·par·don·a·ble·ness** *n.* —**un·par·don·a·bly** /-blē/ *adv.*

un·par·lia·men·ta·ry /ˌənˌpärləˈmentərē/ ▸*adj.* (esp. of language) contrary to the rules or procedures of a parliament: *an unparliamentary expression.*

un·peg /ˌənˈpeg/ ▸*v.* (**-pegged**, **-peg·ging**) [*trans.*] unfasten by the removal of pegs. ■ cease to maintain a fixed relationship between (a currency) and another currency.

un·peo·ple /ˌənˈpēpəl/ ▸*v.* [*trans.*] [usu. as *adj.*] (**unpeopled**) empty of people; depopulate.

un·per·ceived /ˌənpərˈsēvd/ ▸*adj.* [usu. as *complement*] not perceived; unobserved: *the full significance of this went unperceived.*

un·per·son /ˈənpərsən; -ˌpər-/ ▸*n.* (*pl.* **-per·sons**) a person whose name or existence is denied or ignored, esp. because of a political misdemeanor. ▷1949: coined by George Orwell in the novel *1984*.

un·per·turbed /ˌənpərˈtərbd/ ▸*adj.* not perturbed or concerned: *Kenneth seems unperturbed by the news.* —**un·per·turbed·ly** /-ˈtərbədlē/ *adv.*

un·phil·o·soph·i·cal /ˌənˌfiləˈsäfikəl/ ▸*adj.* not following philosophical principles or method. —**un·phil·o·soph·ic** *adj.* (*archaic*) —**un·phil·o·soph·i·cal·ly** /-ik(ə)lē/ *adv.*

un·phys·i·cal /ˌənˈfizikəl/ ▸*adj.* not in accordance with the laws or principles of physics; not corresponding to a physically possible situation.

un·phys·i·o·log·i·cal /ˌənˌfizēəˈläjikəl/ ▸*adj.* not in accordance with normal physiological conditions. —**un·phys·i·o·log·ic** *adj.* —**un·phys·i·o·log·i·cal·ly** /-ik(ə)lē/ *adv.*

un·pick /ˌənˈpik/ ▸*v.* [*trans.*] undo the sewing of (stitches or a garment): *I unpicked the seams of his trousers.* ■ *figurative* carefully analyze the different elements of, esp. in order to find faults.

un·picked /ˌənˈpikt/ ▸*adj.* **1** (of a flower, fruit, or vegetable) not picked: *unpicked tomatoes.* **2** not selected.

un·pin /ˌənˈpin/ ▸*v.* (**-pinned**, **-pin·ning**) [*trans.*] unfasten or detach by removing a pin or pins. ■ *Chess* release (a pinned piece or pawn), e.g., by moving away the piece it is shielding.

un·pit·y·ing /ˌənˈpitē-iNG/ ▸*adj.* not feeling or showing pity. —**un·pit·y·ing·ly** *adv.*

un·place·a·ble /ˌənˈplāsəbəl/ ▸*adj.* not able to be placed or classified: *an unplaceable accent.*

un·placed /ˌənˈplāst/ ▸*adj.* not having or assigned to a specific place. ■ *chiefly Horse Racing* not one of the first three to finish in a race or competition. ■ not appropriate or correct in the circumstances: *a feeling of unplaced alarm.*

un·planned /ˌənˈpland/ ▸*adj.* not planned: *an unplanned pregnancy.*

un·plant·ed /ˌənˈplantid/ ▸*adj.* (of land) uncultivated.

un·play·a·ble /ˌənˈplāəbəl/ ▸*adj.* not able to be played or played on: *hit a high-bouncing, unplayable chop over second | an unplayable golf course.* ■ (of music) too difficult or bad to perform. —**un·play·a·bly** /-blē/ *adv.*

un·pleas·ant /ˌənˈplezənt/ ▸*adj.* causing discomfort, unhappiness, or revulsion; disagreeable: *an unpleasant smell | the symptoms are extremely unpleasant.* ■ (of a person or their manner) unfriendly and inconsiderate; rude: *when drunk, he could become very unpleasant.* —**un·pleas·ant·ly** *adv.*

un·pleas·ant·ness /ˌənˈplezəntnəs/ ▸*n.* the state or quality of being unpleasant. ■ bad feeling or quarreling between people.

un·pleas·ant·ry /ˌənˈplezəntrē/ ▸*n.* (*pl.* **-ries**) **1** (**unpleasantries**) disagreeable matters or comments: *the day-to-day unpleasantries of dealing with an alien administration.* **2** *dated* quarreling or other disagreeable behavior: *a little unpleasantry with the authorities.*

un·pleas·ing /ˌənˈplēziNG/ ▸*adj.* not giving satisfaction, esp. of an aesthetic kind: *the sound was not unpleasing.* —**un·pleas·ing·ly** *adv.*

un·plea·sure /ˌənˈplezHər/ ▸*n.* *Psychoanalysis* the sense of inner pain, discomfort, or anxiety that results from the blocking of an instinctual impulse by the ego.

un·plowed /ˌənˈploud/ (*Brit.* **un·ploughed**) ▸*adj.* **1** (of an area of land) not having been plowed. **2** (of a road) not cleared of snow by a snowplow.

un·plug /ˌənˈpləg/ ▸*v.* (**-plugged**, **-plug·ging**) [*trans.*] **1** disconnect (an electrical device) by removing its plug from a socket: *she unplugged the fridge.* ■ sever the connection between a peripheral device and a computer: *the only thing you can do is to unplug the RJ45 | Why do I have to unplug the mouse to get the printer to work?* **2** remove an obstacle or blockage from: *a procedure to unplug blocked arteries.* **3** [intrans.] *informal* relax by disengaging from normal activities: *they've gone up to the cabin to unplug.*

un·plugged /ˌənˈpləgd/ ▸*adj.* *trademark* (of pop or rock music) performed or recorded with acoustic rather than electrically amplified instruments.

un·plumbed /ˌənˈpləmd/ ▸*adj.* **1** unsounded; unfathomed: *loomed to the surface like a stingray from unplumbed depths.* ■ not fully explored or understood: *one-dimensional performances that leave the play's psychological depths unplumbed.* **2** (of a building or room) not having water and drainage pipes installed and connected: *an indoor, unplumbed outhouse.* —**un·plumb·a·ble** /-ˈpləməbəl/ *adj.*

un·po·et·ic /ˌənpōˈetik/ ▸*adj.* not having a style of expression characteristic of poetry. —**un·po·et·i·cal** *adj.*

un·point·ed /ˌənˈpointid/ ▸*adj.* **1** not having a sharpened or tapered tip. **2** (of a Semitic language) written without dots or small strokes to indicate vowels or distinguish consonants. **3** (of brickwork, a brick structure, or tiling) having joints that are not filled in or repaired.

un·pol·ished /ˌənˈpälisHt/ ▸*adj.* not having a polished surface: *his shoes were unpolished.* ■ unrefined in style or behavior: *his work is unpolished and sometimes incoherent.*

un·pol·i·tic /ˌənˈpäliˌtik/ ▸*adj.* rare term for IMPOLITIC.

un·po·lit·i·cal /ˌənpəˈlitikəl/ ▸*adj.* not concerned with politics; apolitical: *large numbers of otherwise unpolitical people responded to the war.*

un·polled /ˌənˈpōld/ ▸*adj.* **1** (of a voter) not having voted, or registered to vote, at an election. ■ (of a vote) not cast at or registered for an election. **2** (of a person) not included in an opinion poll.

un·pop·u·lar /ˌənˈpäpyələr/ ▸*adj.* not liked or popular: *unpopular measures | Luke was* ***unpopular with*** *most of the teachers.* —**un·pop·u·lar·i·ty** /-ˌpäpyəˈlaritē/ *n.*

un·pop·u·lat·ed /ˌənˈpäpyəˌlātid/ ▸*adj.* (of a place) having no inhabitants: *three missiles landed in unpopulated areas.* ■ (of a printed circuit board) having no components fitted.

un·posed /ˌənˈpōzd/ ▸*adj.* (of a photograph) not having an artificially posed subject.

un·pos·sessed /ˌənpəˈzest/ ▸*adj.* not owned. ■ [*predic.*] (**unpossessed of**) not having (an ability, quality, or characteristic): *the money men are unpossessed of the social graces.*

un·pow·ered /ˌənˈpou(-ə)rd/ ▸*adj.* having no mechanical source of power for propulsion.

un·prac·ti·cal /ˌənˈpraktikəl/ ▸*adj.* another term for IMPRACTICAL (sense 1). —**un·prac·ti·cal·i·ty** /-ˌpraktiˈkalətē/ *n.*

un·prac·ticed /ˌənˈpraktist/ (*Brit.* **un·prac·tised**) ▸*adj.* (of a person or faculty) not trained or experienced: *to the unpracticed eye, the result might appear a hodgepodge.* ■ (of an action or performance) not often done before.

un·prec·e·dent·ed /ˌənˈpresəˌdəntid/ ▸*adj.* never done or known before: *the government took the unprecedented step of releasing confidential correspondence.* —**un·prec·e·dent·ed·ly** *adv.*

un·pre·dict·a·ble /ˌənpriˈdiktəbəl/ ▸*adj.* not able to be predicted: *the unpredictable weather of the Scottish islands.* ■ (of a person) behaving in a way that is not easily predicted: *he is emotional and unpredictable.* —**un·pre·dict·a·bil·i·ty** /-ˌdiktəˈbilətē/ *n.* —**un·pre·dict·a·bly** /-blē/ *adv.*

un·pre·dict·ed /ˌənpriˈdiktid/ ▸*adj.* (of an event or result) unforeseen: *the unpredicted change of weather.*

un·prej·u·diced /ˌənˈprejədist/ ▸*adj.* not having or showing a dislike or distrust based on fixed or preconceived ideas.

un·pre·med·i·tat·ed /ˌənpriˈmedəˌtātid; -prē-/ ▸*adj.* (of an act, remark, or state) not thought out or planned beforehand: *it was a totally unpremeditated attack.* See note at SPONTANEOUS. —**un·pre·med·i·tat·ed·ly** *adv.*

un·pre·pared /ˌənpriˈpe(ə)rd/ ▸*adj.* [*predic.*] not ready or able to deal with something: *she was totally* ***unprepared for*** *what happened next | the transformation caught them* ***unprepared.*** ■ [with *infinitive*] not willing to do something: *they were unprepared to accept what was proposed.* ■ (of a thing) not made ready for use: *paintings on unprepared canvas.* —**un·pre·par·ed·ness** /-ˈpe(ə)r(i)dnis/ *n.*

un·pre·pos·ses·sing /ˌənˌprēpəˈzesiNG/ ▸*adj.* not particularly attractive or appealing to the eye: *despite his unprepossessing appearance he had an animal magnetism.*

un·pre·sent·a·ble /ˌənpriˈzentəbəl/ ▸*adj.* not clean, well-dressed, or decent enough to be seen in public.

un·pressed /ˌənˈprest/ ▸*adj.* (of food or drink) not shaped, squeezed, or obtained by pressure. ■ (of clothing) unironed.

un·pres·sur·ized /ˌənˈpresHəˌrīzd/ ▸*adj.* (of a gas or its container) not having raised pressure that is produced or maintained artificially. ■ (of an aircraft cabin) not having normal atmospheric pressure maintained at a high altitude.

un·pre·tend·ing /ˌənpriˈtendiNG/ ▸*adj.* *archaic* not pretentious or false; genuine: *unpretending sympathy.*

un·pre·ten·tious /ˌənpriˈtenCHəs/ ▸*adj.* not attempting to impress others with an appearance of greater importance, talent, or culture than is actually possessed. ■ (of a place) pleasantly simple and functional; modest. —**un·pre·ten·tious·ly** *adv.* —**un·pre·ten·tious·ness** *n.*

un·primed /ˌənˈprīmd/ ▸*adj.* not made ready for use or action, in particular: ■ (of wood, canvas, or metal) not covered with primer or undercoat. ■ *Biology & Medicine* (of a cell) not having an induced susceptibility or proclivity.

un·prin·ci·pled /ˌənˈprinsəpəld/ ▸*adj.* (of a person or their behavior) not acting in accordance with moral principles: *the public's dislike of unprincipled press behavior.*

un·print·a·ble /ˌənˈprintəbəl/ ▸*adj.* (of words, comments, or thoughts) too offensive or shocking to be published: *Peter's first reply was unprintable.* —**un·print·a·bly** /-blē/ *adv.*

un·print·ed /ˌənˈprintid/ ▸*adj.* (of a book or piece of writing) not published: *unprinted law reports.*

un·priv·i·leged /ˌənˈpriv(ə)lijd/ ▸*adj.* not having special rights, advantages, or immunities.

un·prob·lem·at·ic /ˌənˌprābləˈmatik/ ▸*adj.* not constituting or presenting a problem or difficulty: *none of these approaches is unproblematic.* —**un·prob·lem·at·i·cal** *adj.* —**un·prob·lem·at·i·cal·ly** /-ik(ə)lē/ *adv.*

un·proc·essed /ˌənˈpräˌsest; -səst-; -ˈprō-/ ▸*adj.* unaltered from an original or natural state; not processed: *fresh, unprocessed food.*

un·pro·duc·tive /ˌənprəˈdəktiv/ ▸*adj.* not producing or able to produce large amounts of goods, crops, or other commodities: *unproductive land must be reforested.* ■ (of an activity or period) not achieving much; not very useful: *unproductive meetings.* —**un·pro·duc·tive·ly** *adv.* —**un·pro·duc·tive·ness** *n.*

un·pro·fes·sion·al /ˌənprəˈfesHənl/ ▸*adj.* below or contrary to the standards expected in a particular profession: *a report on unprofessional conduct.* —**un·pro·fes·sion·al·ism** /-ˌizəm/ *n.* —**un·pro·fes·sion·al·ly** *adv.*

un·prof·it·a·ble /ˌənˈpräfitəbəl/ ▸*adj.* (of a business or activity) not yielding profit or financial gain: *the mines became increasingly unprofitable.* ■ (of an activity) not beneficial or useful: *there has been much unprofitable speculation.* —**un·prof·it·a·bil·i·ty** /-ˌpräfitəˈbilitē/ *n.* —**un·prof·it·a·bly** /-blē/ *adv.*

un·pro·gres·sive /ˌənprəˈgresiv/ ▸*adj.* not favoring or implementing social reform or new, typically liberal, ideas.

un·prom·is·ing /ˌənˈpräməsiNG/ ▸*adj.* not giving hope of future success or good results: *the boy's natural intellect had survived in unpromising circumstances.* —**un·prom·is·ing·ly** *adv.*

un·prompt·ed /ˌənˈpräm(p)tid/ ▸*adv.* without being encouraged or assisted to say or do something: *unprompted, helpful conductors advised me to change at Thornaby | those are the notions they volunteered unprompted.*
▸*adj.* said, done, or acting without being encouraged or assisted: *unprompted remarks.*

un·pro·nounce·a·ble /ˌənprəˈnounsəbəl/ ▸*adj.* (of a word or name) too difficult to say. —**un·pro·nounce·a·bly** /-blē/ *adv.*

un·pro·pi·tious /ˌənprəˈpisHəs/ ▸*adj.* (of a circumstance) not giving or indicating a good chance of success; unfavorable: *his reports were submitted at a financially unpropitious time.* —**un·pro·pi·tious·ly** *adv.*

un·pros·per·ous /ˌənˈpräspərəs/ ▸*adj.* *rare* not enjoying or bringing financial success.

un·pro·tect·ed /ˌənprəˈtektid/ ▸*adj.* not protected or kept safe from harm or injury: *a high, unprotected* *plateau | health care workers remained* ***unprotected against*** *hepatitis B infection.* ■ (of a dangerous machine or mechanism) not fitted with safety guards. ■ (of sex) engaged in without a condom. ■ *Computing* (of data or a memory location) able to be accessed or used without restriction.

un·pro·test·ing /ˌənprəˈtesting; -prō-; -ˈprōˌtest-/ ▶*adj.* not objecting to what someone has said or done. —**un·pro·test·ing·ly** *adv.*

un·prov·a·ble /ˌənˈpro͞ovəbəl/ ▶*adj.* unable to be demonstrated by evidence or argument as true or existing: *the hypothesis is not merely unprovable, but false.* —**un·prov·a·bil·i·ty** /-ˌpro͞ovəˈbilətē/ *n.*

un·prov·en /ˌənˈpro͞ovən/ (also **un·proved** /-ˈpro͞ovd/) ▶*adj.* not demonstrated by evidence or argument as true or existing: *long-standing but unproven allegations | the risks are unproven.* ■ (of a new or alternative product, system, or treatment) not tried and tested.

un·pro·vid·ed /ˌənprəˈvīdid/ ▶*adj.* [*predic.*] not provided. ■ (**unprovided with**) not equipped with (something useful or necessary). ■ (**unprovided for**) (of a dependent) not supplied with sufficient money to cover the cost of living: *he left a widow and children totally unprovided for.*

un·pro·voked /ˌənprəˈvōkt/ ▶*adj.* (of an attack, or a display of aggression or emotion) not caused by anything done or said: *acts of unprovoked aggression.* ■ (of a person) not provoked to do something.

un·pruned /ˌənˈpro͞ond/ ▶*adj.* not subjected to any reducing, trimming, or refining process: *structured, unpruned data.*

un·pub·lished /ˌənˈpəblisht/ ▶*adj.* (of a piece of writing or music) not issued in print for public sale or consumption. ■ (of an author) having no writings issued in print. —**un·pub·lish·a·ble** /-lishəbəl/ *adj.*

un·punc·tu·al /ˌənˈpəngkcho͞oəl/ ▶*adj.* not happening or doing something at the agreed or proper time. —**un·punc·tu·al·i·ty** /-ˌpəng(k)cho͞oˈalitē/ *n.*

un·punc·tu·at·ed /ˌənˈpəngkcho͞oˌātid/ ▶*adj.* (of a continuing event) not interrupted or marked by something occurring at intervals: *we wished for sleep unpunctuated by the cry of gulls.* ■ (of text) not containing punctuation marks.

un·pun·ished /ˌənˈpənisht/ ▶*adj.* [*as complement*] (of an offense or offender) not receiving a penalty or sanction as retribution for transgression: *I can't allow such a mistake to* ***go unpunished.***

un·put·down·a·ble /ˌənˌpo͝otˈdounəbəl/ ▶*adj. informal* (of a book) so engrossing that one cannot stop reading it.

un·qual·i·fied /ˌənˈkwäləˌfīd/ ▶*adj.* **1** (of a person) not officially recognized as a practitioner of a particular profession or activity through having satisfied the relevant conditions or requirements. ■ [usu. with *infinitive*] not competent or sufficiently knowledgeable to do something: *I am singularly unqualified to write about football.* **2** without reservation or limitation; total: *the experiment was not an unqualified success.* —**un·qual·i·fied·ly** /-ˌfī(i)dlē/ *adv.*

un·quan·ti·fi·a·ble /ˌənˈkwäntəˌfīəbəl; -ˌkwäntəˈfī-/ ▶*adj.* impossible to express or measure in terms of quantity.

un·quan·ti·fied /ˌənˈkwäntəˌfīd/ ▶*adj.* not expressed or measured in terms of quantity: *we now have abundant, if unquantified, evidence.*

un·ques·tion·a·ble /ˌənˈkweschənəbəl/ ▶*adj.* not able to be disputed or doubted: *his musicianship is unquestionable.* —**un·ques·tion·a·bil·i·ty** /-ˈkweschənəˈbilətē/ *n.* —**un·ques·tion·a·bly** /-blē; -ˈkwesh-/ *adv.* [*sentence adverb*] *unquestionably, the loss of his father was a grievous blow.*

un·ques·tioned /ˌənˈkweschənd/ ▶*adj.* not disputed or doubted; certain: *his loyalty to John is unquestioned.* ■ not examined or inquired into: *an unquestioned assumption.* ■ not subjected to questioning.

un·ques·tion·ing /ˌənˈkweschəning/ ▶*adj.* accepting something without dissent or doubt: *an unquestioning acceptance of the traditional curriculum.* —**un·ques·tion·ing·ly** *adv.*

un·qui·et /ˌənˈkwīət/ ▶*adj.* not inclined to be quiet or inactive; restless: *she prowled at night like an unquiet spirit.* ■ uneasy; anxious: *her unquiet desperation.* —**un·qui·et·ly** *adv.* —**un·qui·et·ness** *n.*

un·quote /ˌənˈkwōt; ˈənˌkwōt/ ▶*v.* see QUOTE —— UNQUOTE at QUOTE.

un·quot·ed /ˌənˈkwōtid/ ▶*adj.* not quoted or listed on a stock exchange: *an unquoted company.*

un·rat·ed /ˌənˈrātid/ ▶*adj.* not having received a rating or assessment. ■ (of a film) not allocated an official classification, typically because regarded as unsuitable for general release. ■ *informal* not highly regarded.

un·rav·el /ˌənˈravəl/ ▶*v.* (**-raveled**, **-rav·el·ing**; *Brit.* **-rav·elled**, **-rav·el·ling**) [*trans.*] **1** undo (twisted, knitted, or woven threads). ■ [*intrans.*] (of twisted, knitted, or woven threads) become undone: *part of the crew neck had unraveled.* ■ unwind (something wrapped around another object): *he unraveled the cellophane from a small cigar.* **2** investigate and solve or explain (something complicated or puzzling): *they were attempting to unravel the cause of death.* ■ [*intrans.*] begin to fail or collapse: *his painstaking diplomacy of the last eight months could quickly unravel.*

un·read /ˌənˈred/ ▶*adj.* (of a book or document) not read. ■ *archaic* (of a person) not well read.

un·read·a·ble /ˌənˈrēdəbəl/ ▶*adj.* not clear enough to read; illegible. ■ too dull or difficult to be worth reading: *a heavy, unreadable novel.* ■ (of a facial expression) unable to be interpreted: *an unreadable expression in his eyes.* —**un·read·a·bil·i·ty** /-ˌrēdəˈbilətē/ *n.* —**un·read·a·bly** /-blē/ *adv.*

un·read·y /ˌənˈredē/ ▶*adj.* [*predic.*] not prepared for a situation or activity: *she was young and unready for motherhood.* ■ *archaic* slow to act; hesitant. —**un·read·i·ness** *n.*

un·re·al /ˌənˈrē(ə)l/ ▶*adj.* so strange as to appear imaginary; not seeming real: *in the half-light the tiny cottages seemed unreal.* ■ unrealistic: *unreal expectations.* ■ *informal* incredible; amazing. —**un·re·al·i·ty** /-rēˈalətē/ *n.* —**un·re·al·ly** *adv.*

un·re·al·iz·a·ble /ˌənˈrēəˌlīzəbəl; -ˌrēəˈlī-/ ▶*adj.* not able to be achieved or made to happen: *the summit might generate unrealizable public expectations.*

un·re·al·ized /ˌənˈrēəˌlīzd/ ▶*adj.* not achieved or created: *an unrealized plan for a full-length novel.* ■ not known: *a new, previously unrealized epidemic.* ■ not converted into money: *unrealized property assets.*

un·rea·son /ˌənˈrēzən/ ▶*n.* inability to act or think reasonably. ▷Middle English (in the senses 'unreasonable intention' and 'impropriety'): from UN-[1] 'lack of' + REASON.

un·rea·son·a·ble /ˌənˈrēz(ə)nəbəl/ ▶*adj.* not guided by or based on good sense: *your attitude is completely unreasonable.* See note at ABSURD. ■ beyond the limits of acceptability or fairness: *an unreasonable request.* —**un·rea·son·a·ble·ness** *n.* —**un·rea·son·a·bly** /-blē/ *adv.*

un·rea·soned /ˌənˈrēzənd/ ▶*adj.* not based on good sense or logic: *an unreasoned reaction to the idea.*

un·rea·son·ing /ˌənˈrēz(ə)ning/ ▶*adj.* not guided by or based on good sense; illogical: *unreasoning panic.* —**un·rea·son·ing·ly** *adv.*

un·re·cep·tive /ˌənriˈseptiv/ ▶*adj.* not receptive, esp. to new suggestions or ideas.

un·re·cip·ro·cat·ed /ˌənriˈsiprəˌkātid/ ▶*adj.* not reciprocated: *his feelings for her were unreciprocated.*

un·reck·oned /ˌənˈrekənd/ ▶*adj.* not calculated or taken into account.

un·re·claimed /ˌənriˈklāmd/ ▶*adj.* (esp. of land) not reclaimed.

un·rec·og·nized /ˌənˈrekəgˌnīzd/ ▶*adj.* not identified from previous encounters or knowledge. ■ not acknowledged as valuable or valid.

un·re·con·struct·ed /ˌənˌrēkənˈstrəktid/ ▶*adj.* not reconciled or converted to the current political theory or movement: *unreconstructed communists.*

un·re·cov·er·a·ble /ˌənriˈkəvərəbəl/ ▶*adj.* not able to be recovered or corrected.

un·reel /ˌənˈrēl/ ▶*v.* [*trans.*] unwind (something wrapped around another object): *she unreeled the plug from her headset.* ■ [*intrans.*] (of a film) wind from one reel to another during projection: *the film sequence unreeled meaninglessly in front of her.*

un·reeve /ˌənˈrēv/ ▶*v.* (*past* **-rove** /-ˈrōv/) [*trans.*] *Nautical* withdraw (a rope) from a pulley block or other object.

un·re·fined /ˌənriˈfīnd/ ▶*adj.* not processed to remove impurities or unwanted elements: *unrefined sugar.* ■ (of a person or their behavior) not elegant or cultured.

un·re·flect·ing /ˌənriˈflekting/ ▶*adj.* **1** not engaging in reflection or thought: *an unreflecting hedonist.* **2** not reflecting light. —**un·re·flect·ing·ly** *adv.* —**un·re·flect·ing·ness** *n.* —**un·re·flec·tive** /-tiv/ *adj.*

un·re·gard·ed /ˌənriˈgärdid/ ▶*adj.* not respected or considered; ignored: *her sarcasm went unregarded.*

un·re·gen·er·ate /ˌənriˈjenərət/ ▶*adj.* not reforming or showing repentance; obstinately wrong or bad. —**un·re·gen·er·a·cy** /-rəsē/ *n.* —**un·re·gen·er·ate·ly** *adv.*

un·reg·is·tered /ˌənˈrejəstərd/ ▶*adj.* not officially recognized and recorded: *unregistered births.*

un·reg·u·lat·ed /ˌənˈregyəˌlātid/ ▶*adj.* not controlled or supervised by regulations or laws.

un·re·hearsed /ˌənriˈhərst/ ▶*adj.* not practiced before a performance: *spontaneous and unrehearsed music.*

un·re·leased /ˌənriˈlēst/ ▶*adj.* (esp. of a film or recording) not released.

un·re·lent·ing /ˌənriˈlenting/ ▶*adj.* not yielding in strength, severity, or determination: *the heat was unrelenting.* ■ (of a person or their behavior) not giving way to kindness or compassion: *unrelenting opponents.* —**un·re·lent·ing·ly** *adv.* —**un·re·lent·ing·ness** *n.*

un·re·lieved /ˌənriˈlēvd/ ▶*adj.* lacking variation or change; monotonous: *flowing gowns of unrelieved black.* ■ not provided with relief; not aided or assisted. —**un·re·liev·ed·ly** /-ˈlēvidlē/ *adv.*

un·re·li·gious /ˌənriˈlijəs/ ▶*adj.* indifferent or hostile to religion. ■ not connected with religion.

un·re·mark·a·ble /ˌənriˈmärkəbəl/ ▶*adj.* not particularly interesting or surprising: *his early childhood was unremarkable | an unremarkable house.* —**un·re·mark·a·bly** /-blē/ *adv.*

un·re·marked /ˌənriˈmärkt/ ▶*adj.* not mentioned or remarked upon; unnoticed: *she let his bitterness* ***go unremarked.***

un·re·mit·ting /ˌənriˈmiting/ ▶*adj.* never relaxing or slackening; incessant: *unremitting drizzle.* —**un·re·mit·ting·ly** *adv.* —**un·re·mit·ting·ness** *n.*

un·re·mu·ner·a·tive /ˌənriˈmyo͞onərətiv; -ˌrātiv/ ▶*adj.* bringing little or no profit or income: *unremunerative research work.* —**un·re·mu·ner·a·tive·ly** *adv.*

un·re·peat·a·ble /ˌənriˈpētəbəl/ ▶*adj.* not able to be done or made again. ■ too offensive or shocking to be said again. —**un·re·peat·a·bil·i·ty** /-ˌpētəˈbilətē/ *n.*

un·re·pent·ant /ˌənriˈpentənt/ ▶*adj.* showing no regret for one's wrongdoings: *he was unrepentant and said that his comments were completely accurate.* —**un·re·pent·ant·ly** *adv.*

un·re·port·ed /ˌənriˈpôrtəd/ ▶*adj.* not reported: *many human rights abuses* ***went unreported.***

un·rep·re·sent·a·tive /ˌənˌrepriˈzentətiv/ ▶*adj.* not typical of a class, group, or body of opinion: *an unrepresentative survey.* —**un·rep·re·sen·ta·tive·ness** *n.*

un·re·quit·ed /ˌənriˈkwītid/ ▶*adj.* (of a feeling, esp. love) not returned or rewarded. —**un·re·quit·ed·ly** *adv.* —**un·re·quit·ed·ness** *n.*

un·re·serve /ˌənriˈzərv/ ▶*n. archaic* lack of reserve; frankness.

un·re·served /ˌənriˈzərvd/ ▶*adj.* **1** without reservations; complete: *he has had their unreserved support.* ■ frank and open: *a tall, unreserved young man.* **2** not set apart for a particular purpose or booked in advance: *unreserved grandstand seats.* —**un·re·serv·ed·ly** /-ˈzərvidlē/ *adv.* —**un·re·serv·ed·ness** /-ˈzərvədnəs/ *n.*

un·re·solved /ˌənriˈzälvd; -ˈzôlvd/ ▶*adj.* (of a problem, question, or dispute) not resolved: *a number of issues remain unresolved.* ■ *archaic* (of a person) uncertain of what to think or do. —**un·re·solv·ed·ly** /-ˈzälvidlē; -ˈzôl-/ *adv.* —**un·re·solv·ed·ness** /-ˈzälvidnəs; -ˈzôl-/ *n.*

un·rest /ˌənˈrest/ ▶*n.* a state of dissatisfaction, disturbance, and agitation in a group of people, typically involving public demonstrations or disorder: *the very worst years of industrial unrest.* ■ a feeling of disturbance and dissatisfaction in a person: *the frenzy and unrest of her own life.*

un·rest·ed /ˌənˈrestid/ ▶*adj.* (of a person) not refreshed by rest: *she woke feeling unrested.*

un·rest·ing /ˌənˈresting/ ▶*adj.* ceaselessly active. —**un·rest·ing·ly** *adv.*

un·re·stored /ˌənriˈstôrd/ ▶*adj.* not repaired or renovated: *an unrestored farmhouse.*

un·re·strained /ˌənriˈstrānd/ ▶*adj.* not restrained or restricted: *a display of unrestrained delight.* —**un·re·strain·ed·ly** /-ˈstrānidlē/ *adv.* —**un·re·strain·ed·ness** /-ˈstrānidnis/ *n.*

un·re·straint /ˌənriˈstrānt/ ▶*n.* lack of restraint, or freedom from it; wildness: *they enjoyed the unrestraint of drunkenness.*

un·re·strict·ed /ˌənriˈstriktid/ ▶*adj.* not limited or restricted: *unrestricted access to both military bases.* —**un·re·strict·ed·ly** *adv.*

un·re·turned /ˌənriˈtərnd/ ▶*adj.* not reciprocated or responded to: *phone calls go unreturned.*

Pronunciation Key ə *ago*; ər *over*; ˈə or ˌə *up*; ˈər or ˌər *fur*; a *hat*; ā *rate*; ä *car*; ch *chew*; e *let*; ē *see*; e(ə)r *air*; i *fit*; ī *by*; i(ə)r *ear*; ng *sing*; ō *go*; ô *for*; oi *boy*; o͝o *good*; o͞o *goo*; ou *out*; sh *she*; th *thin*; t͟h *then*; (h)w *why*; zh *vision*

U

un·re·versed /ˌənrəˈvərst/ ▸*adj.* (esp. of a decision, etc.) not reversed.

un·re·vised /ˌənriˈvīzd/ ▸*adj.* not revised; in an original form: *the manuscript was unrevised when he died.*

un·re·ward·ing /ˌənrəˈwôrdiNG/ ▸*adj.* not rewarding or satisfying: *it was dull, unrewarding work.*

un·rid·den /ˌənˈridn/ ▸*adj.* not ridden or never having been ridden or broken in.

un·rid·dle /ˌənˈridl/ ▸*v.* [*trans.*] *rare* solve; explain.

un·ride·a·ble /ˌənˈrīdəbəl/ (also **un·rid·a·ble**) ▸*adj.* not able to be ridden.

un·rig /ˌənˈrig/ ▸*v.* (**-rigged**, **-rig·ging**) [*trans.*] remove the rigging from (a ship).

un·right·eous /ˌənˈrīCHəs/ ▸*adj. formal* not righteous; wicked. ▹Old English *unrihtwīs* (see **UN-**[1], **RIGHTEOUS**). —**un·right·eous·ly** *adv.* —**un·right·eous·ness** *n.*

un·rip /ˌənˈrip/ ▸*v.* (**-ripped**, **-rip·ping**) [*trans.*] *rare* open by ripping: *he carefully unripped one of the seams.*

un·ri·valed /ˌənˈrīvəld/ (*Brit.* **un·ri·valled**) ▸*adj.* better than everyone or everything of the same type: *the paper's coverage of foreign news is unrivaled.*

un·riv·et /ˌənˈrivit/ ▸*v.* (**-riv·et·ed**, **-riv·et·ing**) [*trans.*] *rare* undo, unfasten, or detach by the removal of rivets.

un·road·wor·thy /ˌnˈrōdˌwərT͟Hē/ ▸*adj.* (of a vehicle) not roadworthy.

un·robe /ˌənˈrōb/ ▸*v.* less common term for **DISROBE**.

un·roll /ˌənˈrōl/ ▸*v.* open or cause to open out from a rolled-up state: [*intrans.*] *the blanket unrolled as he tugged it* | [*trans.*] *two carpets had been unrolled.*

un·roof /ˌənˈro͞of; -ˈro͝of/ ▸*v.* [*trans.*] *rare* remove the roof of.

un·roofed /ˌənˈro͞oft; -ˈro͝oft/ ▸*adj.* not provided with a roof.

un·root /ˌənˈro͞ot; -ˈro͝ot/ ▸*v.* [*trans.*] uproot (something).

un·rope /ˌənˈrōp/ ▸*v.* [*intrans.*] *Climbing* detach oneself from a rope.

un·round·ed /ˌənˈroundid/ ▸*adj.* not rounded. ■ *Phonetics* (of a vowel) pronounced with the lips not rounded.

un·rove /ˌənˈrōv/ ▸ past of **UNREEVE**.

un·ruf·fled /ˌənˈrəfəld/ ▸*adj.* not disordered or disarranged: *the unruffled waters of the lake.* ■ (of a person) not agitated or disturbed; calm.

un·ruled /ˌənˈro͞old/ ▸*adj.* **1** *poetic/literary* not ruled, governed, or under control: *men with passions unruled.* **2** (of paper) not having ruled lines.

un·ru·ly /ˌənˈro͞olē/ ▸*adj.* (**-li·er**, **-li·est**) disorderly and disruptive and not amenable to discipline or control: *complaints about unruly behavior.* ■ (of hair) difficult to keep neat and tidy. ▹late Middle English: from **UN-**[1] 'not' + archaic *ruly* 'amenable to discipline or order' (from **RULE**). —**un·ru·li·ness** *n.*

U

UNRWA /ˈənrə/ ▸*abbr.* United Nations Relief and Works Agency.

un·sad·dle /ˌənˈsadl/ ▸*v.* [*trans.*] remove the saddle from (a horse or other ridden animal). ■ dislodge from a saddle.

un·safe sex ▸*n.* sexual activity in which precautions are not taken to reduce the risk of spreading sexually transmitted diseases, esp. AIDS.

un·said /ˌənˈsed/ past and past participle of **UNSAY**. ▸*adj.* not said or uttered: *the rest of the remark he left unsaid.*

un·sal·a·ble /ˌənˈsāləbəl/ (also **un·sale·a·ble**) ▸*adj.* not able to be sold: *the house proved unsalable.* —**un·sal·a·bil·i·ty** /-ˌsāləˈbilətē/ *n.*

un·sal·a·ried /ˌənˈsalərēd/ ▸*adj.* not being paid or involving the payment of a salary: *an unsalaried post.*

un·sat·is·fac·to·ry /ˌənˌsatəsˈfakt(ə)rē/ ▸*adj.* unacceptable because poor or not good enough: *an unsatisfactory situation.* —**un·sat·is·fac·to·ri·ly** /-ˈfakt(ə)rəlē/ *adv.* —**un·sat·is·fac·to·ri·ness** *n.*

un·sat·u·rat·ed /ˌənˈsaCHəˌrātid/ ▸*adj. Chemistry* (of organic molecules) having carbon–carbon double or triple bonds and therefore not containing the greatest possible number of hydrogen atoms for the number of carbons. —**un·sat·u·ra·tion** /-ˌsaCHəˈrāSHən/ *n.*

un·saved /ˌənˈsāvd/ ▸*adj.* not saved, in particular (in Christian use) not having had one's soul saved from damnation.

un·sa·vor·y /ˌənˈsāv(ə)rē/ (*Brit.* **un·sa·vour·y**) ▸*adj.* disagreeable to taste, smell, or look at. ■ disagreeable and unpleasant because morally disreputable: *an unsavory reputation.* —**un·sa·vor·i·ly** /-rəlē/ *adv.* —**un·sa·vor·i·ness** *n.*

un·say /ˌənˈsā/ ▸*v.* (*past* and *past part.* **-said**) [*trans.*] withdraw or retract (a statement).

un·say·a·ble /ˌənˈsāəbəl/ ▸*adj.* not able to be said, esp. because considered too controversial or offensive to mention.

un·scal·a·ble /ˌənˈskāləbəl/ ▸*adj.* not able to be scaled or climbed: *a prison with unscalable walls.*

un·scaled /ˌənˈskāld/ ▸*adj.* (of a mountain) not yet climbed: *they had climbed a hitherto unscaled peak.*

un·scarred /ˌənˈskärd/ ▸*adj.* not scarred or damaged: *he did not escape unscarred.*

un·scathed /ˌənˈskāT͟Hd/ ▸*adj.* [*predic.*] without suffering any injury, damage, or harm: *I came through all those perils unscathed.*

un·schol·ar·ly /ˌənˈskälərlē/ ▸*adj.* not showing the learning, reasoning, and attention to detail characteristic of a scholar. —**un·schol·ar·li·ness** *n.* (*rare*).

un·schooled /ˌənˈsko͞old/ ▸*adj.* not educated at or made to attend school: *unschooled children.* ■ lacking knowledge or training in a particular field: *she was* **unschooled in** *the niceties of royal behavior.* ■ not affected or artificial; natural and spontaneous.

un·sci·en·tif·ic /ˌənˌsīənˈtifik/ ▸*adj.* **1** not in accordance with scientific principles or methodology: *our whole approach is hopelessly unscientific.* **2** lacking knowledge of or interest in science. —**un·sci·en·tif·i·cal·ly** /-ik(ə)lē/ *adv.*

un·scram·ble /ˌənˈskrambəl/ ▸*v.* [*trans.*] restore (something that has been scrambled) to an intelligible, readable, or viewable state. —**un·scram·bler** /-b(ə)lər/ *n.*

un·screened /ˌənˈskrēnd/ ▸*adj.* **1** not subjected to testing or investigation by screening: *a transfusion with unscreened blood.* ■ not filtered or sorted using a screen. **2** (of a movie or television program) not shown or broadcast: *copies of the unscreened episodes.* **3** not provided with or hidden by a screen.

un·screw /ˌənˈskro͞o/ ▸*v.* (with reference to a lid or other object held in place by a spiral thread) unfasten or be unfastened by twisting: [*trans.*] *Will unscrewed the cap from a metal flask* | [*intrans.*] *the spout usually unscrews or lifts off easily.* ■ [*trans.*] detach, open, or slacken (something) by removing or loosening the screws holding it in place.

un·script·ed /ˌənˈskriptid/ ▸*adj.* said or delivered without a prepared script; impromptu.

un·scrip·tur·al /ˌənˈskripCHərəl/ ▸*adj.* not in accordance with the Bible: *sacraments deemed unscriptural by Luther.*

un·scru·pu·lous /ˌənˈskro͞opyələs/ ▸*adj.* having or showing no moral principles; not honest or fair. —**un·scru·pu·lous·ly** *adv.* —**un·scru·pu·lous·ness** *n.*

un·seal /ˌənˈsēl/ ▸*v.* [*trans.*] remove or break the seal of: *she slowly unsealed the envelope.*

un·search·a·ble /ˌənˈsərCHəbəl/ ▸*adj. poetic/literary* unable to be clearly understood; inscrutable: *their motives in coming were complex and unsearchable.* —**un·search·a·ble·ness** *n.* —**un·search·a·bly** /-blē/ *adv.*

un·sea·son·a·ble /ˌənˈsēzənəbəl/ ▸*adj.* (of weather) unusual for the time of year: *an unseasonable warm spell.* ■ untimely; inopportune: *we visited the place at an unseasonable time.* —**un·sea·son·a·ble·ness** *n.* —**un·sea·son·a·bly** /-blē/ *adv.*

un·sea·son·al /ˌənˈsēzənəl/ ▸*adj.* (esp. of weather) unusual or inappropriate for the time of year: *unseasonal heavy rains have brought a great influx of snakes.*

un·sea·soned /ˌənˈsēzənd/ ▸*adj.* **1** (of food) not flavored with salt, pepper, or other spices or seasonings. **2** (of timber) not treated or matured. ■ (of a person) inexperienced.

un·seat /ˌənˈsēt/ ▸*v.* [*trans.*] cause (someone) to fall from a horse or bicycle. ■ remove from a position of power or authority.

un·sea·wor·thy /ˌənˈsēˌwərT͟Hē/ ▸*adj.* (of a boat or ship) not in a good enough condition to sail on the sea.

un·se·cured /ˌənsiˈkyo͝ord/ ▸*adj.* **1** (of a loan) made without an asset given as security. ■ (of a creditor) having made such a loan. **2** not made secure or safe.

un·see·a·ble /ˌənˈsēəbəl/ ▸*adj.* not able to be seen; invisible.

un·seed·ed /ˌənˈsēdid/ ▸*adj.* (chiefly of a competitor in a sports tournament) not seeded.

un·see·ing /ˌənˈsēiNG/ ▸*adj.* with one's eyes open but without noticing or seeing anything. —**un·see·ing·ly** *adv.*

un·seem·ly /ˌənˈsēmlē/ ▸*adj.* (of behavior or actions) not proper or appropriate: *an unseemly squabble.* —**un·seem·li·ness** *n.*

un·seen /ˌənˈsēn/ ▸*adj.* not seen or noticed: *it seemed she might escape unseen.* ■ not foreseen or predicted: *unseen problems.* ■ *chiefly Brit.* (of a passage for translation in a test or examination) not previously read or prepared.

un·self·con·scious /ˌənˌselfˈkänSHəs/ ▸*adj.* not suffering from or exhibiting self-consciousness; not shy or embarrassed. —**un·self·con·scious·ly** *adv.* —**un·self·con·scious·ness** *n.*

un·sel·fish /ˌənˈselfiSH/ ▸*adj.* willing to put the needs or wishes of others before one's own: *unselfish devotion.* —**un·self·ish·ly** *adv.* —**un·self·ish·ness** *n.*

un·sen·sa·tion·al /ˌənsenˈsāSHənl/ ▸*adj.* not sensational or seeking to provoke interest or excitement at the expense of accuracy. —**un·sen·sa·tion·al·ly** *adv.*

un·sen·ti·men·tal /ˌənˌsentəˈmen(t)l/ ▸*adj.* not displaying or influenced by sentimental feelings. —**un·sen·ti·men·tal·ly** *adv.*

Un·ser /ˈənsər/, Al(fred) (1939–) U.S. race car driver. He won four Indy 500 races 1970, 1971, 1978, 1987 before he retired in 1994.

un·se·ri·ous /ˌənˈsi(ə)rēəs/ ▸*adj.* not serious; lighthearted.

un·served /ˌənˈsərvd/ ▸*adj.* **1** (of a person or section of society) not attended to: *the needs of unserved and underserved audiences.* **2** *Law* (of a writ or summons) not officially delivered to a person: *there is no point in leaving a writ unserved.*

un·ser·vice·a·ble /ˌənˈsərvəsəbəl/ ▸*adj.* not in working order or fulfilling its function adequately; unfit for use. —**un·ser·vice·a·bil·i·ty** /-ˌsərvəsəˈbilətē/ *n.*

un·set /ˌənˈset/ ▸*adj.* **1** (of a jewel) not yet placed in a setting; unmounted: *ten unset sapphires.* **2** (of cement) not yet hardened.

un·set·tle /ˌənˈsetl/ ▸*v.* [*trans.*] cause to feel anxious or uneasy; disturb: *the crisis has unsettled financial markets* | [as *adj.*] (**unsettling**) *an unsettling conversation.* —**un·set·tle·ment** *n.* —**un·set·tling·ly** *adv.*

un·set·tled /ˌənˈsetld/ ▸*adj.* **1** lacking stability: *an unsettled childhood.* ■ worried and uneasy: *she felt edgy and unsettled.* ■ liable to change; unpredictable: *a spell of unsettled weather.* ■ not yet resolved: *one important question remains unsettled.* ■ (of a bill) not yet paid. **2** (of an area) having no settlers or inhabitants. —**un·set·tled·ness** *n.*

un·sex /ˌənˈseks/ ▸*v.* [*trans.*] deprive of gender, sexuality, or the characteristic attributes or qualities of one or other sex.

un·sexed /ˌənˈsekst/ ▸*adj.* having no sexual characteristics.

un·sex·y /ˌənˈseksē/ ▸*adj.* (**-sex·i·er**, **-sex·i·est**) not sexually attractive or exciting.

un·shack·le /ˌənˈSHakəl/ ▸*v.* [*trans.*] (usu. **be unshackled**) release from shackles, chains, or other physical restraints: *his feet were unshackled.* ■ *figurative* liberate; set free.

un·shad·ed /ˌənˈSHādid/ ▸*adj.* **1** (of a light bulb or lamp) not having a shade or cover. ■ not screened from direct light. **2** (of an area of a diagram) not shaded with pencil lines or a block of color.

un·shad·owed /ˌənˈSHadōd/ ▸*adj.* not covered or darkened by a shadow or shadows.

un·shak·a·ble /ˌənˈSHākəbəl/ (also **un·shake·a·ble**) ▸*adj.* (of a belief, feeling, or opinion) strongly felt and unable to be changed: *an unshakable faith in God.* ■ unable to be disputed or questioned: *an unshakable alibi.* —**un·shak·a·bil·i·ty** /-ˌSHākəˈbilətē/ *n.* —**un·shak·a·bly** /-blē/ *adv.*

un·shak·en /ˌənˈSHākən/ ▸*adj.* not disturbed from a firm position or state; steadfast and unwavering: *their trust in him remained unshaken.* —**un·sha·ken·ly** *adv.*

un·shaped /ˌənˈSHāpt/ ▸*adj.* having a vague, ill-formed, or unfinished shape.

un·shared /ˌənˈSHe(ə)rd/ ▸*adj.* not shared with or by another or others.

un·sharp /ˌənˈSHärp/ ▸*adj. Photography* (of a picture or image) not well defined. —**un·sharp·ness** *n.*

un·shaved /ˌənˈSHāvd/ ▸*adj.* unshaven.

un·shav·en /ˌənˈSHāvən/ ▸*adj.* not having recently shaved or been shaved.

un·sheathe /ˌənˈSHēT͟H/ ▸*v.* [*trans.*] draw or pull out (a knife, sword, or similar weapon) from its sheath or covering.

un·shed /ˌənˈSHed/ ▸*adj.* (of tears) welling in a person's eyes but not falling on their cheeks.

un·shelled /ˌənˈSHeld/ ▸*adj.* not extracted from its shell: *unshelled peanuts.*

un·ship /ˌənˈSHip/ ▸*v.* (**-shipped**, **-ship·ping**) [*trans.*] *chiefly Nautical* remove (an oar, mast, or other object) from its fixed or regular position: *they unshipped the oars.* ■ unload (a cargo) from a ship or boat.

un·shod /ˌənˈSHäd/ ▸*adj.* not wearing shoes.

un·shorn /ˌənˈSHôrn/ ▸*adj.* (of a person's hair) not cut.

un·shrink·a·ble /ˌənˈSHRINGkəbəl/ ▸*adj.* (of fabric, etc.) not liable to shrink. —**un·shrink·a·bil·i·ty** /-ˌSHRINGkəˈbilətē/ *n.*

un·shrink·ing /ˌənˈSHRINGkiNG/ ▸*adj.* unhesitating; fearless. —**un·shrink·ing·ly** *adv.*

un·sight·ed /ˌənˈsītid/ ▸*adj.* lacking the power of sight: *blind or unsighted people.* ■ not seen: *a distant unsighted object.* ■ (esp. in sports) prevented from having a clear view of something.

un·sight·ly /ˌənˈsītlē/ ▸*adj.* unpleasant to look at; ugly: *unsightly warts.* —**un·sight·li·ness** *n.*

un·signed /ˌənˈsīnd/ ▸*adj.* **1** not identified or authorized by a person's signature: *an unsigned check.* ■ (of a musician or sports player) not having signed a contract of employment. **2** *Mathematics & Computing* not having a plus or minus sign, or a bit representing this.

un·sink·a·ble /ˌənˈsiNGkəbəl/ ▸*adj.* (of a ship or boat) unable to be sunk: *the supposedly unsinkable ship hit an iceberg.* —**un·sink·a·bil·i·ty** /-ˌsiNGkəˈbilətē/ *n.*

un·sis·ter·ly /ˌənˈsistərlē/ ▸*adj.* not showing the support and affection that is thought to be characteristic of a sister.

un·sized /ˌənˈsīzd/ ▸*adj.* (of fabric, paper, or a wall) not treated with size. See SIZE[2].

un·skilled /ˌənˈskild/ ▸*adj.* not having or requiring special skill or training: *unskilled manual workers.*

un·skill·ful /ˌənˈskilfəl/ ▸*adj.* not having or showing skill. —**un·skill·ful·ly** *adv.* —**un·skill·ful·ness** *n.*

un·skimmed /ˌənˈskimd/ ▸*adj.* (of milk) not skimmed.

un·slak·a·ble /ˌənˈslākəbəl/ (also **un·slake·a·ble**) ▸*adj.* not able to be quenched or satisfied: *her unslakable desire.*

un·sleep·ing /ˌənˈslēpiNG/ ▸*adj.* not or never sleeping: *much of that night she lay unsleeping.* —**un·sleep·ing·ly** *adv.*

un·sliced /ˌənˈslīst/ *adj.* (esp. of a commercially produced loaf of bread) not having been cut into slices.

un·sling /ˌənˈsliNG/ ▸*v.* (*past* and *past part.* **-slung**) [*trans.*] remove (something) from the place where it has been slung or suspended.

un·smil·ing /ˌənˈsmīliNG/ ▸*adj.* (of a person or their manner or expression) serious or unfriendly; not smiling. —**un·smil·ing·ly** *adv.* —**un·smil·ing·ness** *n.*

un·smoked /ˌənˈsmōkt/ ▸*adj.* **1** (of meat or fish) not cured by exposure to smoke: *smoked and unsmoked bacon.* **2** (of tobacco or a cigarette) not having been smoked.

un·snap /ˌənˈsnap/ ▸*v.* (**-snapped**, **-snap·ping**) [*trans.*] unfasten or open with a brisk movement and a sharp sound: *he put the case on the table and unsnapped the clasps.*

un·snarl /ˌənˈsnärl/ ▸*v.* [*trans.*] disentangle; sort out.

un·so·cia·ble /ˌənˈsōSHəbəl/ ▸*adj.* not enjoying or making an effort to behave sociably in the company of others: *Terry was grumpy and unsociable.* ■ not conducive to friendly social relations: *watching TV is a fairly unsociable activity.* —**un·so·cia·bil·i·ty** /-ˌsōSHəˈbilətē/ *n.* —**un·so·cia·ble·ness** *n.* —**un·so·cia·bly** /-blē/ *adv.*

> ***USAGE*** There is some overlap in the use of the adjectives **unsociable**, **unsocial**, and **antisocial**, but they also have distinct core meanings. Generally speaking, **unsociable** means 'not enjoying, or avoiding, the company of others': *Terry was grumpy and* ***unsociable***. **Antisocial** can be used as a synonym for **unsociable**, but can further be used to mean 'contrary to the laws and customs of a society': *aggressive and* ***antisocial*** *behavior.* **Unsocial** can be used as a synonym for **unsociable** as well, but it may also denote a preference for solitude and not hostility toward company: *Ben's feeling a little tired and* ***unsocial*** *tonight.*

un·so·cial /ˌənˈsōSHəl/ ▸*adj.* not seeking the company of others: *woodchucks lead a relatively unsocial life.* ■ causing annoyance and disapproval in others; antisocial: *the unsocial behavior of young teenagers.* —**un·so·cial·ly** *adv.*

> ***USAGE*** See usage at UNSOCIABLE.

un·soiled /ˌənˈsoild/ ▸*adj.* not stained or dirty.

un·sold /ˌənˈsōld/ ▸*adj.* (of an item) not sold: *numerous copies of the book remained unsold | please return any unsold tickets by November 9.*

un·sol·der /ˌənˈsädər; -ˈsôdər/ ▸*v.* [*trans.*] undo the soldering of.

un·sol·dier·ly /ˌənˈsōljərlē/ ▸*adj.* inappropriate to or not befitting a soldier: *prisoners of war in their unsoldierly uniforms.*

un·so·lic·it·ed /ˌənsəˈlisitid/ ▸*adj.* not asked for; given or done voluntarily: *unsolicited junk mail.* —**un·so·lic·it·ed·ly** *adv.*

un·so·phis·ti·cat·ed /ˌənsəˈfistəˌkātid/ ▸*adj.* lacking refined worldly knowledge or tastes. See note at GULLIBLE. ■ not complicated or highly developed; basic: *unsophisticated computer software.* ■ not artificial: *the village has remained unspoiled and unsophisticated.* —**un·so·phis·ti·cat·ed·ly** *adv.* —**un·so·phis·ti·cat·ed·ness** *n.* —**un·so·phis·ti·ca·tion** /-ˌfistiˈkāSHən/ *n.*

un·sought /ˌənˈsôt/ ▸*adj.* not searched for, requested, or desired.

un·sound /ˌənˈsound/ ▸*adj.* not safe or robust; in poor condition: *the tower is structurally unsound.* ■ not based on sound evidence or reasoning and therefore unreliable or unacceptable: *unsafe and unsound banking practices.* ■ (of a person) not competent, reliable, or holding acceptable views. ■ injured, ill, or diseased, esp. (of a horse) lame. —**un·sound·ly** *adv.* —**un·sound·ness** *n.*

un·sound·ed[1] /ˌənˈsoundid/ ▸*adj.* not uttered, pronounced, or made to sound.

un·sound·ed[2] ▸*adj.* unfathomed.

un·sown /ˌənˈsōn/ ▸*adj.* not having been sown: *a strip of unsown soil.*

un·spar·ing /ˌənˈspe(ə)riNG/ ▸*adj.* **1** merciless; severe: *he is unsparing in his criticism of the arms trade.* **2** given freely and generously: *she had won her mother's unsparing approval.* —**un·spar·ing·ly** *adv.* —**un·spar·ing·ness** *n.*

un·speak·a·ble /ˌənˈspēkəbəl/ ▸*adj.* not able to be expressed in words: *I felt an unspeakable tenderness toward her.* ■ too bad or horrific to express in words. —**un·speak·a·ble·ness** *n.* —**un·speak·a·bly** /-blē/ *adv.*

un·speak·ing /ˌənˈspēkiNG/ ▸*adj.* not speaking; silent.

un·spe·cif·ic /ˌənspəˈsifik/ ▸*adj.* not specific; vague: *he was unspecific about his relationship with Marian.*

un·spec·i·fied /ˌənˈspesəˌfīd/ ▸*adj.* not stated clearly or exactly: *an unspecified number of people.*

un·spec·tac·u·lar /ˌənspekˈtakyələr; -spək-/ ▸*adj.* not spectacular; unremarkable: *she had been an unspectacular student.* —**un·spec·tac·u·lar·ly** *adv.*

un·spent /ˌənˈspent/ ▸*adj.* not spent. ■ not exhausted or used up: *he shook with unspent rage.*

un·spilled /ˌənˈspild/ (also **un·spilt** /-ˈspilt/) ▸*adj.* not spilled.

un·spir·i·tu·al /ˌənˈspiriCHo͞oəl/ ▸*adj.* not spiritual; worldly: *the clergymen were deplorably unspiritual.* —**un·spir·i·tu·al·i·ty** /-ˌspiriCHo͞oˈalitē/ *n.* —**un·spir·i·tu·al·ly** *adv.*

un·spoiled /ˌənˈspoild/ (*Brit.* also **un·spoilt** /ˌənˈspoilt/) ▸*adj.* not spoiled, in particular (of a place) not marred by development: *unspoiled countryside.*

un·spo·ken /ˌənˈspōkən/ ▸*adj.* not expressed in speech; tacit: *an unspoken assumption.*

un·spon·sored /ˌənˈspänsərd/ ▸*adj.* not supported or promoted by a sponsor.

un·spool /ˌənˈspo͞ol/ ▸*v.* [*intrans.*] unwind from or as if from a spool. ■ (of a film) be screened. ■ [*trans.*] show (a film).

un·sport·ing /ˌənˈspôrtiNG/ ▸*adj.* unsportsmanlike. —**un·sport·ing·ly** *adv.*

un·sports·man·like /ˌənˈspôrtsmənˌlīk/ ▸*adj.* not fair, generous, or sportsmanlike: *a penalty against us for unsportsmanlike conduct.*

un·sprayed /ˌənˈsprād/ ▸*adj.* not having been sprayed, esp. with pesticides or other chemicals.

un·sprung /ˌənˈsprəNG/ ▸*adj.* not provided with springs.

un·sta·ble /ˌənˈstābəl/ ▸*adj.* (**-bler**, **-blest**) prone to change, fail, or give way; not stable: *the unstable cliff tops | an unstable government.* ■ prone to psychiatric problems or sudden changes of mood: *he was mentally unstable.* —**un·sta·ble·ness** *n.* —**un·sta·bly** /-blē/ *adv.*

un·staffed /ˌənˈstaft/ ▸*adj.* not provided with a staff or official personnel: *the kitchen on the seventh floor is an unstaffed facility.*

un·stage·a·ble /ˌənˈstājəbəl/ ▸*adj.* (of a play) impossible or very difficult to present to an audience.

un·stamped /ˌənˈstam(p)t/ ▸*adj.* **1** not marked by stamping. **2** not having a postage stamp affixed.

un·starched /ˌənˈstärCHt/ ▸*adj.* (esp. of fabric or clothing) not starched.

un·stat·ed /ˌənˈstātid/ ▸*adj.* not stated or declared: *a series of unstated assumptions.*

un·states·man·like /ˌənˈstātsmənˌlīk/ ▸*adj.* not suitable for or befitting a statesman.

un·stayed /ˌənˈstād/ ▸*adj.* (especially of masts and rigging) not provided with stays; unsupported.

un·stead·y /ˌənˈstedē/ ▸*adj.* (**-stead·i·er**, **-stead·i·est**) **1** liable to fall or shake; not firm: *he was very unsteady on his feet.* **2** not uniform or regular: *a soft unsteady voice.* —**un·stead·i·ly** /-ˈstedl-ē/ *adv.* —**un·stead·i·ness** *n.*

un·step /ˌənˈstep/ ▸*v.* (**-stepped**, **-step·ping**) [*trans.*] remove (a vessel's mast) from its step.

un·ster·ile /ˌənˈsterəl/ ▸*adj. chiefly Medicine* not sterile; not sterilized: *unsterile needles.*

un·stick /ˌənˈstik/ ▸*v.* (*past* and *past part.* **-stuck**) [*trans.*] cause to become no longer stuck together.
▸*PHRASE* □ **come** (or **get**) **unstuck** become separated or unfastened.■ *informal* fail completely: *all their clever ideas came unstuck.*

un·stint·ed /ˌənˈstintid/ ▸*adj.* given without restraint; liberal: *we received unstinted support.* —**un·stint·ed·ly** *adv.*

un·stint·ing /ˌənˈstintiNG/ ▸*adj.* given or giving without restraint; unsparing: *he was unstinting in his praise.* —**un·stint·ing·ly** *adv.*

un·stirred /ˌənˈstərd/ ▸*adj.* not moved, agitated, or stirred.

un·stitch /ˌənˈstiCH/ ▸*v.* [*trans.*] undo the stitches of.

un·stop /ˌənˈstäp/ ▸*v.* (**-stopped**, **-stop·ping**) [*trans.*] free (something) from obstruction: *he must unstop the sink.* ■ remove the stopper from (a bottle or other container).

un·stop·pa·ble /ˌənˈstäpəbəl/ ▸*adj.* impossible to stop or prevent: *an unstoppable army.* —**un·stop·pa·bil·i·ty** /-ˌstäpəˈbilətē/ *n.* —**un·stop·pa·bly** /-blē/ *adv.*

un·stop·per /ˌənˈstäpər/ ▸*v.* [*trans.*] remove the stopper from (a bottle or other container): *he unstoppered the jar.*

un·strained /ˌənˈstrānd/ ▸*adj.* **1** not forced or produced by effort: *a lovely warm unstrained smile.* **2** not subjected or reacting to straining or stretching.

un·strap /ˌənˈstrap/ ▸*v.* (**-strapped**, **-strap·ping**) [*trans.*] undo the strap or straps of. ■ release (someone or something) by undoing straps: *they unstrapped themselves.*

un·stressed /ˌənˈstrest/ ▸*adj.* **1** *Phonetics* (of a syllable) not pronounced with stress: *an unstressed syllable.* **2** not subjected to stress: *a well-balanced, unstressed person.*

un·string /ˌənˈstriNG/ ▸*v.* (*past* and *past part.* **-strung**) [*trans.*] **1** [usu. as *adj.*] (**unstrung**) unnerve: *a mind unstrung by loneliness.* **2** remove or relax the string or strings of (a bow or musical instrument). **3** remove from a string: *unstringing the beads from the rosary.*

un·struc·tured /ˌənˈstrəkCHərd/ ▸*adj.* without formal organization or structure: *an unstructured interview.*

un·stuck /ˌənˈstək/ ▸ past and past participle of UNSTICK.

un·stud·ied /ˌənˈstədēd/ ▸*adj.* not labored or artificial; natural: *she had an unstudied grace in every step.* —**un·stud·ied·ly** *adv.*

un·stuffed /ˌənˈstəft/ *adj.* not containing stuffing.

un·stuff·y /ˌənˈstəfē/ ▸*adj.* **1** friendly, informal, and approachable: *colorful and unstuffy periodicals.* **2** having fresh air or ventilation.

un·styl·ish /ˌənˈstīliSH/ ▸*adj.* not elegant, fashionable, or stylish.

un·sub·scribe /ˌənsəbˈskrīb/ ▸*v.* [*intrans.*] cancel a subscription, esp. to an Internet newsletter, newsgroup, or electronic mailing list.

un·sub·stan·tial /ˌənsəbˈstanCHəl/ ▸*adj.* having little or no solidity, reality, or factual basis. —**un·sub·stan·ti·al·i·ty** /-ˌstanCHēˈalitē/ *n.* —**un·sub·stan·tial·ly** *adv.*

un·sub·stan·ti·at·ed /ˌənsəbˈstanCHēˌātid/ ▸*adj.* not supported or proven by evidence: *unsubstantiated claims.*

un·sub·tle /ˌənˈsətl/ ▸*adj.* not subtle; obvious; clumsy: *a grindingly unsubtle joke.* —**un·sub·tly** /-ˈsətl-ē/ *adv.*

un·sug·ared /ˌənˈSHo͝ogərd/ ▸*adj.* not sweetened or sprinkled with sugar.

un·suit·a·ble /ˌənˈso͞otəbəl/ ▸*adj.* not fitting or appropriate: *the display is unsuitable for young children.* —**un·suit·a·bil·i·ty** /-ˌso͞otəˈbilətē/ *n.* —**un·suit·a·ble·ness** *n.* —**un·suit·a·bly** /-blē/ *adv.*

un·suit·ed /ˌənˈso͞otid/ ▸*adj.* [*predic.*] not right or appropriate: *he was totally* ***unsuited for*** *the job.*

un·sul·lied /ˌənˈsəlēd/ ▸*adj.* not spoiled or made impure: *an unsullied reputation.*

Pronunciation Key ə *ago*; ər *over*; ˈə or ˌə *up*; ˈər or ˌər *fur*; a *hat*; ā *rate*; ä *car*; CH *chew*; e *let*; ē *see*; e(ə)r *air*; i *fit*; ī *by*; i(ə)r *ear*; NG *sing*; ō *go*; ô *for*; oi *boy*; o͝o *good*; o͞o *goo*; ou *out*; SH *she*; TH *thin*; T͟H *then*; (h)w *why*; ZH *vision*

un·sung /ˌən'səNG/ ▸*adj.* not celebrated or praised: *Harvey is one of the unsung heroes of the industrial revolution.*

un·su·per·vised /ˌən'so͞opərˌvīzd/ ▸*adj.* not done or acting under supervision: *unsupervised visits | a safe garden where children may play unsupervised.* ■ (of a person) not watched over in the interest of their or others' security: *roaming, unsupervised youths pose a threat.*

un·sup·port·a·ble /ˌənsə'pôrtəbəl/ ▸*adj.* another term for INSUPPORTABLE. —**un·sup·port·a·bly** /-blē/ *adv.*

un·sup·port·ed /ˌənsə'pôrtid/ ▸*adj.* (of a structure, object, or person) not supported physically: *a toddler who can stand unsupported.* ■ not borne out by evidence or facts: *the assumption was unsupported by evidence.* ■ (of a person or activity) not given financial or other assistance. ■ *Computing* (of a program, language, or device) not having assistance for the user available from a manufacturer or systems manager.

un·sup·port·ive /ˌənsə'pôrdiv/ ▸*adj.* not providing encouragement or emotional help: *the family environment is unsupportive.*

un·sure /ˌən'SHo͝or/ ▸*adj.* not feeling, showing, or done with confidence and certainty: *she was feeling nervous,* ***unsure of*** *herself* | [with *clause*] *she was unsure how to reply.* ■ (of a fact) not fixed or certain: *the date is unsure.* —**un·sure·ly** *adv.* —**un·sure·ness** *n.*

un·sur·faced /ˌən'sərfist/ ▸*adj.* (of a road or path) not provided with a durable finished upper layer.

un·sur·mount·a·ble /ˌənsər'moun(t)əbəl/ ▸*adj.* not able to be overcome; insurmountable: *unsurmountable problems.*

un·sur·pass·a·ble /ˌənsər'pasəbəl/ ▸*adj.* not able to be exceeded in quality or degree. —**un·sur·pass·a·bly** *adv.*

un·sur·passed /ˌənsər'past/ ▸*adj.* as good as or better than any other: *the quality of workmanship is unsurpassed.*

un·sur·prised /ˌənsə(r)'prīzd/ ▸*adj.* not feeling or showing surprise at something unexpected: *he replied in a flat and unsurprised voice.*

un·sur·pris·ing /ˌənsə(r)'prīziNG/ ▸*adj.* not unexpected and so not causing surprise: *the outcome of this somber film is unsurprising.* —**un·sur·pris·ing·ly** *adv.* [*sentence adverb*] *unsurprisingly, recession is the theme of most reports.*

un·sus·cep·ti·ble /ˌənsə'septəbəl/ ▸*adj.* **1** not likely or liable to be influenced or harmed by a particular thing: *infants are relatively* ***unsusceptible to*** *infections.* **2** [*predic.*] (**unsusceptible of**) not capable or admitting of: *their meaning is unsusceptible of analysis.* —**un·sus·cep·ti·bil·i·ty** /-ˌseptə'bilitē/ *n.*

un·sus·pect·ed /ˌənsə'spektid/ ▸*adj.* not known or thought to exist or be present; not imagined possible: *the actor displays an unsuspected talent for comedy.* ■ (of a person) not regarded with suspicion. —**un·sus·pect·ed·ly** *adv.*

un·sus·pect·ing /ˌənsə'spektiNG/ ▸*adj.* (of a person or animal) not aware of the presence of danger; feeling no suspicion: *antipersonnel mines lie in wait for their unsuspecting victims.* —**un·sus·pect·ing·ly** *adv.* —**un·sus·pect·ing·ness** *n.*

un·sus·pi·cious /ˌənsə'spiSHəs/ ▸*adj.* not having or showing suspicion. —**un·sus·pi·cious·ly** /ˌənsə'spiSHəslē/ *adv.* —**un·sus·pi·cious·ness** /ˌənsə'spiSHəsnəs/ *n.*

un·sus·tain·a·ble /ˌənsə'stānəbəl/ ▸*adj.* not able to be maintained at the current rate or level: *macroeconomic instability led to an unsustainable boom.* ■ *Ecology* upsetting the ecological balance by depleting natural resources: *unsustainable fishing practices.* ■ not able to be upheld or defended: *the old idea was unsustainable.* —**un·sus·tain·a·bly** /-blē/ *adv.*

un·sus·tained /ˌənsə'stānd/ ▸*adj.* not prolonged for an extended period or without interruption.

un·swayed /ˌən'swād/ ▸*adj.* [*predic.*] (of a person) not influenced or affected: *investors are unswayed by suggestions that the numbers are overblown.*

un·sweet·ened /ˌən'swētnd/ ▸*adj.* (of food or drink) without sugar or a similar substance having been added: *unsweetened grapefruit juice.*

un·swept /ˌən'swept/ *adj.* (of an area) not cleaned by having the dirt or litter on it swept up: *the walls were damp, the floor unswept.*

un·swerv·ing /ˌən'swərviNG/ ▸*adj.* not changing or becoming weaker; steady or constant: *unswerving loyalty.* —**un·swerv·ing·ly** *adv.*

un·sworn /ˌən'swôrn/ ▸*adj.* *Law* (of testimony or evidence) not given under oath.

un·sym·met·ri·cal /ˌənsə'metrikəl/ ▸*adj.* another term for ASYMMETRICAL. —**un·sym·met·ri·cal·ly** /-trik(ə)lē/ *adv.*

un·sym·pa·thet·ic /ˌənˌsimpə'THetik/ ▸*adj.* not feeling, showing, or expressing sympathy: *I'm not being unsympathetic, but I can't see why you put up with him.* ■ [*predic.*] not showing approval or favor toward an idea or action: *they were initially* ***unsympathetic toward*** *the cause of Irish freedom.* ■ (of a person) not friendly or cooperative; unlikeable: *a totally unsympathetic character.* —**un·sym·pa·thet·i·cal·ly** /-ik(ə)lē/ *adv.*

un·sys·tem·at·ic /ˌənˌsistə'matik/ ▸*adj.* not done or acting according to a fixed plan or system; unmethodical: *the burial mound was excavated in an unsystematic way | they were relatively unsystematic in their use of the data.* —**un·sys·tem·at·i·cal·ly** /-ik(ə)lē/ *adv.*

un·tack[1] /ˌən'tak/ ▸*v.* [*trans.*] detach (something) by the removal of tacks.

un·tack[2] ▸*v.* [*trans.*] remove the saddle and bridle from (a horse).

un·taint·ed /ˌən'tān(t)ᵊd/ ▸*adj.* not contaminated, polluted, or tainted: *the paper was untainted by age.*

un·tak·en /ˌən'tākən/ ▸*adj.* **1** (of a region or person) not taken by force; uncaptured. **2** (of an action) not put into effect: *hard decisions have been left untaken.*

un·tam·a·ble /ˌən'tāməbəl/ (also **un·tame·a·ble**) ▸*adj.* (of an animal) not capable of being domesticated. ■ not capable of being controlled: *her untamable mop of thick black hair.*

un·tamed /ˌən'tāmd/ ▸*adj.* not domesticated or otherwise controlled.

un·tan·gle /ˌən'taNGgəl/ ▸*v.* [*trans.*] free from a tangled or twisted state: *fishermen untangle their nets.* ■ make (something complicated or confusing) easier to understand or deal with.

un·tanned /ˌən'tand/ ▸*adj.* **1** (of a person or their skin) not tanned by exposure to the sun. **2** (of animal skin) not converted into leather by tanning: *untanned hides.*

un·tapped /ˌən'tapt/ ▸*adj.* **1** (of a resource) not yet exploited or used: *a huge, untapped market for bagels.* **2** (of a telephone, etc.) free from listening devices.

un·tar·nished /ˌən'tärniSHt/ ▸*adj.* (of metal or metalware) not having lost its luster, esp. as a result of exposure to air or moisture. ■ *figurative* not made less valuable or respected: *his ministers enjoyed an untarnished reputation.*

un·tast·ed /ˌən'tāstid/ ▸*adj.* (of food or drink) not sampled or tested for flavor: *Louis's untasted food was scraped into the dog's bowl.*

un·taught /ˌən'tôt/ ▸*adj.* (of a person) not trained by teaching: *she is totally untaught and will not listen.* ■ not acquired by teaching; natural or spontaneous: *by untaught instinct they know that scent means food.*

un·taxed /ˌən'takst/ ▸*adj.* **1** not subject to taxation. **2** (of an item, income, etc.) not having had the required tax paid on it.

un·teach /ˌən'tēCH/ ▸*v.* (*past* and *past part.* **-taught**) **1** cause (someone) to forget or discard previous knowledge. **2** remove from the mind (something known or taught) by different teaching.

un·teach·a·ble /ˌən'tēCHəbəl/ ▸*adj.* (of a student or skill) unable to be taught.

un·tech·ni·cal /ˌən'teknikəl/ ▸*adj.* not having or requiring technical knowledge.

un·tem·pered /ˌən'tempərd/ ▸*adj.* not moderated or lessened by anything: *the products of a technological mastery untempered by political imagination.* ■ (of a material) not brought to the proper hardness or consistency.

un·ten·a·ble /ˌən'tenəbəl/ ▸*adj.* (esp. of a position or view) not able to be maintained or defended against attack or objection: *this argument is clearly untenable.* —**un·ten·a·bil·i·ty** /-ˌtenə'bilitē/ *n.* —**un·ten·a·bly** /-blē/ *adv.*

un·tend·ed /ˌən'tendid/ ▸*adj.* not cared for or looked after; neglected: *untended gravestones.*

un·ten·ured /ˌən'tenyərd/ ▸*adj.* (of a teacher, lecturer, or other professional) not having a permanent post. ■ (of an academic or other post) not permanent.

Un·ter·mensch /'o͝ontərˌmenCH/ ▸*n.* (*pl.* **-mensch·en** /-ˌmenCHən/) a person considered racially or socially inferior. ▷German, literally 'underperson.'

Un·ter·mey·er /'əntərˌmīər/, Louis (1885–1977) U.S. writer and poet. He published critical anthologies, including *Modern American Poetry* (1919) and *The World's Great Stories* (1964), as well as his own poetry such as "Long Feud" (1962).

un·test·ed /ˌən'testid/ ▸*adj.* (of an idea, product, or person) not subjected to examination, experiment, or experience; unproven: *analyses based on dubious and untested assumptions.* —**un·test·a·ble** /-'testəbəl/ *adj.*

un·teth·er /ˌən'teT͟Hər/ ▸*v.* [*trans.*] release or free from a tether: *I reached the horses and untethered them.*

un·thanked /ˌən'THaNGkt/ ▸*adj.* without receiving thanks: *the women's kind gesture did not* ***go unthanked.***

un·thank·ful /ˌən'THaNGkfəl/ ▸*adj.* not feeling or showing pleasure, relief, or gratitude. —**un·thank·ful·ly** /ˌən'THaNGkfəlē/ *adv.* —**un·thank·ful·ness** /ˌən'THaNGkfəlnəs/ *n.*

un·thaw /ˌən'THô/ ▸*v.* **1** melt or thaw: [*trans.*] *the warm weather helped unthaw the rail lines.* **2** [as *adj.*] (**unthawed**) still frozen; unmelted: *it could not explain how future science might revive the unthawed dead.*

un·think·a·ble /ˌən'THiNGkəbəl/ ▸*adj.* (of a situation or event) too unlikely or undesirable to be considered a possibility: *it was unthinkable that John could be dead* | [as *n.*] (**the unthinkable**) *the unthinkable happened—I spoke up.* —**un·think·a·bil·i·ty** /-ˌTHiNGkə'bilitē/ *n.* —**un·think·a·bly** /-blē/ *adv.* [as *submodifier*] *a land of unthinkably vast spaces.*

un·think·ing /ˌən'THiNGkiNG/ ▸*adj.* expressed, done, or acting without proper consideration of the consequences: *she was at pains to correct unthinking prejudices.* —**un·think·ing·ly** *adv.* —**un·think·ing·ness** *n.*

un·thought /ˌən'THôt/ ▸*adj.* not formed by the process of thinking. ■ (**unthought of**) not imagined or dreamed of: *the old develop interests unthought of in earlier years.*

un·thread /ˌən'THred/ ▸*v.* [*trans.*] take (a thread) out of a needle. ■ remove (an object) from a thread.

un·threat·en·ing /ˌən'THretniNG/ ▸*adj.* not having a hostile or frightening quality or manner; not causing someone to feel vulnerable or at risk: *a quiet and unthreatening place.* —**un·threat·ened** /ˌən'THretnd/ *adj.*

un·thrift·y /ˌən'THriftē/ ▸*adj.* **1** not using money and other resources carefully; wasteful. **2** *chiefly archaic* or *dialect* (of livestock or plants) not strong and healthy. —**un·thrift·i·ly** /-təlē/ *adv.* —**un·thrift·i·ness** *n.*

un·throne /ˌən'THrōn/ ▸*v.* archaic term for DETHRONE.

un·ti·dy /ˌən'tīdē/ ▸*adj.* (**-ti·di·er**, **-ti·di·est**) not arranged neatly and in order: *the place was dreadfully untidy.* ■ (of a person) not inclined to keep one's possessions or appearance neat and in order. —**un·ti·di·ly** /-'tīdilē/ *adv.* —**un·ti·di·ness** *n.*

un·tie /ˌən'tī/ ▸*v.* (**-tied**, **-ty·ing**) [*trans.*] undo or unfasten (a cord or knot): *she knelt to untie her laces.* ■ undo a cord or similar fastening that binds (someone or something): *Morton untied the parcel.* ▷Old English *untīgan* (see UN-[2], TIE).

un·tied /ˌən'tīd/ ▸*adj.* not fastened or knotted.

un·til /ˌən'til; ən-/ ▸*prep.* & *conj.* up to (the point in time or the event mentioned): [as *prep.*] *the kidnappers have given us until October 11th to deliver the documents | he held the office until his death* | [as *conj.*] *you don't know what you can achieve until you try.* ▷Middle English: from Old Norse *und* 'as far as' + TILL[1] (the sense thus duplicated).

USAGE On the differences between **until** and **till**, see usage at TILL[1].

un·tilled /ˌən'tild/ ▸*adj.* (of land) not prepared and cultivated for crops.

un·time·ly /ˌən'tīmlē/ ▸*adj.* (of an event or act) happening or done at an unsuitable time: *Dave's untimely return.* ■ (of a death or end) happening too soon or sooner than normal: *his untimely death in military action.*
▸*adv. archaic* at a time that is unsuitable or premature: *the moment was very untimely chosen.* —**un·time·li·ness** *n.*

un·tinged /ˌən'tinjd/ ▸*adj.* [*predic.*] (**untinged by/with**) not in the slightest affected by: *a cold-blooded killing untinged by any remorse on your part.*

un·tir·ing /ˌən'tīriNG/ ▸*adj.* (of a person or their actions) continuing at the same rate without loss of vigor; indefatigable: *his untiring efforts on their behalf.* —**un·tir·ing·ly** *adv.*

un·ti·tled /ˌən'tītld/ ▸*adj.* **1** (of a book, composition, or other artistic work) having no name. **2** (of a person) not having a title indicating high social or official rank: *lesser untitled officials.*

un·to /'ənto͞o/ ▸*prep.* **1** archaic term for TO: *do unto others as you would have them do unto you | I say unto you, be gone.* **2** archaic term for UNTIL: *marriage was forever—unto death.* ▷Middle English: from UNTIL, with TO replacing TILL[1] (in its northern dialect meaning 'to').

un·told /ˌən'tōld/ ▸*adj.* **1** [*attrib.*] too much or too many to be counted or measured: *thieves caused un-*

told damage. **2** (of a story or event) not narrated or recounted: *no event, however boring, is left untold.* ▷Old English *untealđ* 'not counted' (see UN-[1], TOLD).

un·toned /ˌənˈtōnd/ ▸*adj.* **1** (of a person's body) lacking in tone or muscular definition. **2** (esp. of music) lacking in variation of tone or subtlety.

un·touch·a·ble /ˌənˈtəCHəbəl/ ▸*adj.* **1** not able or allowing to be touched or affected: *a receptionist looking gorgeous and untouchable.* ■ unable to be matched or rivaled: *we took the silver medal behind the untouchable U.S. team.* **2** of or belonging to the lowest-caste Hindu group or the people outside the caste system. ▸*n.* a member of the lowest-caste Hindu group or a person outside the caste system. Contact with untouchables is traditionally held to defile members of higher castes. —**un·touch·a·bil·i·ty** /-ˌtəCHəˈbilitē/ *n.*

USAGE In senses relating to the traditional Hindu caste system, the term **untouchable** and the social restrictions accompanying it were declared illegal in the constitution of India in 1949 and of Pakistan in 1953. The official term today is **scheduled caste.**

un·touched /ˌənˈtəCHt/ ▸*adj.* **1** not handled, used, or tasted: *Annabel pushed aside her untouched plate.* ■ (of a subject) not treated in writing or speech; not discussed: *no detail is left untouched.* **2** not affected, changed, or damaged in any way: *Prague was relatively untouched by the war.*

un·to·ward /ˌənˈtôrd; -t(ə)ˈwôrd/ ▸*adj.* unexpected and inappropriate or inconvenient: *both tried to behave as if nothing untoward had happened | untoward jokes and racial remarks.* —**un·to·ward·ly** *adv.* —**un·to·ward·ness** *n.*

un·trace·a·ble /ˌənˈtrāsəbəl/ ▸*adj.* unable to be found, discovered, or traced: *many use false addresses and are untraceable.* —**un·trace·a·bly** /-blē/ *adv.*

un·traced /ˌənˈtrāst/ ▸*adj.* not found or discovered by investigation: *patients with untraced records.*

un·tracked /ˌənˈtrakt/ ▸*adj.* (of land) not previously explored or traversed; without a path or tracks: *the Saxons usually hid in the untracked marshlands.* ■ (of snow or a snowy slope) not marked by skis, vehicles, people, or animals: *experts can go heli-skiing in untracked powder.*
▸not found after attempts at detection, esp. by means of radar or satellite: *the previously untracked object.*
▸*PHRASE* □ **get untracked** get into one's stride or find good form, esp. in sporting contexts.

un·tra·di·tion·al /ˌəntrəˈdiSHənl/ ▸*adj.* not existing in or as part of a tradition; not customary or long-established.

un·trained /ˌənˈtrānd/ ▸*adj.* not having been trained in a particular skill: *self-styled doctors* ***untrained in*** *diagnosis |* ***to the untrained eye,*** *the two products look remarkably similar.* —**un·train·a·ble** /-ˈtrānəbəl/ *adj.*

un·tram·meled /ˌənˈtraməld/ (*Brit.* also **un·tram·melled**) ▸*adj.* not deprived of freedom of action or expression; not restricted or hampered: *a mind untrammeled by convention.*

un·trans·fer·a·ble /ˌənˌtransˈfərəbəl; -ˈtransfərə-/ ▸*adj.* not able to be transferred to another place, occupation, or person.

un·trans·formed /ˌəntransˈfôrmd/ ▸*adj.* not having been transformed in form, appearance, or character.

un·trans·lat·a·ble /ˌənˌtransˈlātəbəl; -ˌtranz-/ ▸*adj.* (of a word, phrase, or text) not able to have its sense satisfactorily expressed in another language: *an untranslatable German pun.* —**un·trans·lat·a·bil·i·ty** /-transˌlātəˈbilitē; -tranz-/ *n.*

un·trans·lat·ed /ˌənˈtranzˌlātid; -ˈtrans-/ ▸*adj.* (of words or text) not having their sense expressed in another language: *a nine-volume work, as yet untranslated from the Icelandic.* ■ (of a sequence of nucleotides in messenger RNA) not converted to the amino acid sequence of a protein or polypeptide during synthesis.

un·trav·eled /ˌənˈtravəld/ (*Brit.* also **un·trav·elled**) ▸*adj.* (of a person) not having traveled much. ■ (of a road or region) not journeyed along or through: *an unknown and untraveled wilderness.*

un·treat·a·ble /ˌənˈtrētəbəl/ ▸*adj.* (of a patient, a disease or other condition) for whom or which no medical care is available or possible.

un·treat·ed /ˌənˈtrētid/ ▸*adj.* **1** (of a patient, disease, or other condition) not given medical care: *untreated cholera can kill up to half of those infected.* **2** not preserved, improved, or altered by the use of a chemical, physical, or biological agent: *untreated sewage is pumped directly into the sea.*

un·trend·y /ˌənˈtrendē/ ▸*adj. informal* not very fashionable or up to date: *his untrendy long hair.*

un·tried /ˌənˈtrīd/ ▸*adj.* **1** not yet tested to discover quality or reliability; inexperienced: *he chose two untried actors for leading roles.* **2** *Law* (of an accused person) not yet subjected to a trial in court.

un·trod·den /ˌənˈträdn/ ▸*adj.* (of a surface) not having been walked on: *untrodden snow.*

un·trou·bled /ˌənˈtrəbəld/ ▸*adj.* not feeling, showing, or affected by anxiety or problems: *a man untroubled by a guilty conscience | an untroubled gaze.*

un·true /ˌənˈtrōō/ ▸*adj.* **1** not in accordance with fact or reality; false or incorrect: *these suggestions are totally untrue | a malicious and untrue story.* **2** [*predic.*] not faithful or loyal. **3** incorrectly positioned or balanced; not upright or level. ▷Old English *untrēowe* 'unfaithful' (see UN-[1], TRUE). —**un·tru·ly** /-ˈtrōōlē/ *adv.*

un·truss /ˌənˈtrəs/ ▸*v.* [*trans.*] unfasten (esp. a trussed fowl).

un·trussed /ˌənˈtrəst/ ▸*adj.* (of a chicken or other bird prepared for eating) having had its wings and legs unfastened before cooking: *an untrussed chicken.*

un·trust·ing /ˌənˈtrəstiNG/ ▸*adj.* not tending to believe in other people's honesty or sincerity; suspicious.

un·trust·wor·thy /ˌənˈtrəstˌwərT͟Hē/ ▸*adj.* not able to be relied on as honest or truthful: *Thomas considered her to be devious and untrustworthy | these untrustworthy impressions were instinctive.* —**un·trust·wor·thi·ness** *n.*

un·truth /ˌənˈtrōōTH/ ▸*n.* (*pl.* **-truths** /-ˈtrōōT͟HZ; -ˈtrōōTHS/) a lie or false statement (often used euphemistically): *they go off and tell untruths about organizations for which they worked.* ■ the quality of being false. ▷Old English *untrēowth* 'unfaithfulness' (see UN-[1], TRUTH).

un·truth·ful /ˌənˈtrōōTHfəl/ ▸*adj.* saying or consisting of something that is false or incorrect: *companies issuing untruthful recruitment brochures.* —**un·truth·ful·ly** *adv.* —**un·truth·ful·ness** *n.*

un·tuck /ˌənˈtək/ ▸*v.* [*trans.*] free the edges or ends of (something) from being hidden or held in place.

un·tucked /ˌənˈtəkt/ ▸*adj.* with the edges or ends hanging loose; not tucked in: *an untucked shirt.*

un·tun·a·ble /ˌənˈt(y)ōōnəbəl/ ▸*adj.* (of a piano, etc.) that cannot be tuned.

un·tuned /ˌənˈt(y)ōōnd/ ▸*adj.* not tuned or properly adjusted.

un·tune·ful /ˌənˈt(y)ōōnfəl/ ▸*adj.* not having a pleasing melody; unmusical: *an untuneful hymn.* —**un·tune·ful·ly** *adv.*

un·turned /ˌənˈtərnd/ ▸*adj.* **1** not turned: *unturned soil.* **2** (of a wooden object) not shaped on a lathe.

un·tu·tored /ˌənˈt(y)ōōtərd/ ▸*adj.* not formally taught or trained: *the species are all much the same* ***to the untutored eye.*** See note at IGNORANT.

un·twine /ˌənˈtwīn/ ▸*v.* make or become unwound or untwisted: [*trans.*] *Robyn untwined her fingers.*

un·twist /ˌənˈtwist/ ▸*v.* open or cause to open from a twisted position: [*trans.*] *he untwisted the wire and straightened it out.*

un·ty·ing /ˌənˈtī-iNG/ ▸ present participle of UNTIE.

un·typ·i·cal /ˌənˈtipikəl/ ▸*adj.* not having the distinctive qualities of a particular type of person or thing; unusual or uncharacteristic: *the harsh dissonances give a sound that is quite* ***untypical of*** *that period.* —**un·typ·i·cal·ly** /-ik(ə)lē/ *adv.* [as *submodifier*] *I'll keep this review untypically short* | [*sentence adverb*] ***not untypically,*** *one large painting took her five months.*

un·us·a·ble /ˌənˈyōōzəbəl/ ▸*adj.* not fit to be used: *the steps were overgrown and unusable.*

un·used /ˌənˈyōōzd;/ ▸*adj.* **1** not being, or never having been, used: *any unused equipment will be welcomed back.* **2** /-ˈyōōst/ [*predic.*] (**unused to**) not familiar with or accustomed to something: *unused to spicy food, she took a long mouthful of water.*

un·u·su·al /ˌənˈyōōZHōōəl/ ▸*adj.* not habitually or commonly occurring or done: *the government has taken the unusual step of calling home its ambassador | it was unusual for Dennis to be late.* ■ remarkable or interesting because different from or better than others: *a man of unusual talent.* —**un·u·su·al·ly** *adv.* [*sentence adverb*] ***unusually for*** *a city hotel, it is set around a lovely garden* | [as *submodifier*] *he made an unusually large number of mistakes.* —**un·u·su·al·ness** *n.*

un·ut·ter·a·ble /ˌənˈətərəbəl/ ▸*adj.* too great, intense, or awful to describe: *those private moments of unutterable grief.* —**un·ut·ter·a·bly** /-blē/ *adv.* [as *submodifier*] *Juliet climbed the stairs, feeling unutterably weary.*

un·ut·tered /ˌənˈətərd/ ▸*adj.* (of words or thoughts) not spoken or expressed: *her lips mouthed unuttered thanks.*

un·vac·ci·nat·ed /ˌənˈvaksəˌnātid/ ▸*adj.* (of a person) not inoculated with a vaccine to provide immunity against a disease: *pockets of unvaccinated children.*

un·val·ued /ˌənˈvalyōōd/ ▸*adj.* **1** not considered to be important or beneficial: *he felt unvalued.* **2** *archaic* not valued or appraised with regard to monetary worth.

un·van·quished /ˌənˈvaNGkwiSHt/ ▸*adj.* (of an opponent or obstacle) not conquered or overcome: *the idea of humbling the hitherto unvanquished islanders.*

un·var·ied /ˌənˈve(ə)rēd/ ▸*adj.* not involving change; monotonous: *a plain, unvaried diet.*

un·var·nished /ˌənˈvärniSHt/ ▸*adj.* not covered with varnish. ■ (of a statement or manner) plain and straightforward: *please tell me the unvarnished truth.*

un·var·y·ing /ˌənˈve(ə)rē-iNG/ ▸*adj.* not changing; constant or uniform: *the unvarying routine of parsonage life.* —**un·var·y·ing·ly** *adv.* [as *submodifier*] *they found her to be unvaryingly polite* —**un·var·y·ing·ness** *n.*

un·veil /ˌənˈvāl/ ▸*v.* [*trans.*] remove a veil or covering from, esp. uncover (a new monument or work of art) as part of a public ceremony: *the mayor unveiled a plaque* | [as *n.*] (**unveiling**) *the unveiling of the memorial.* ■ show or announce publicly for the first time: *the manufacturer unveiled plans for expanding into aviation.*

un·vent·ed /ˌənˈventid/ ▸*adj.* **1** not provided with ventilation. **2** (of strong, usually negative feelings) not expressed: *unvented rage.*

un·ven·ti·lat·ed /ˌənˈventlˌātid/ ▸*adj.* (of a room or space) not provided with fresh air.

un·versed /ˌənˈvərst/ ▸*adj.* [*predic.*] (**unversed in**) not experienced or skilled in; not knowledgeable about: *he was unversed in Washington ways.*

un·vi·a·ble /ˌənˈvīəbəl/ ▸*adj.* not capable of working successfully; not feasible: *the commission found the plan to be financially unviable.* —**un·vi·a·bil·i·ty** /-ˌvīəˈbilitē/ *n.*

un·vi·o·lat·ed /ˌənˈvīəˌlātid/ ▸*adj.* not violated or desecrated: *the ground above the stone was undisturbed, the stone unviolated.* ■ (of a woman) virginal.

un·vis·it·ed /ˌənˈvizitid/ ▸*adj.* (of a place) having had no people visit it: *Antarctica remained unvisited until the late 18th century.*

un·vi·ti·at·ed /ˌənˈviSHēˌātid/ ▸*adj.* *archaic* pure and uncorrupted.

un·voiced /ˌənˈvoist/ ▸*adj.* **1** not expressed in words; unuttered: *a person's unvoiced thoughts.* **2** *Phonetics* (of a speech sound) uttered without vibration of the vocal cords.

un·walled /ˌənˈwôld/ ▸*adj.* (of a place) without enclosing or defensive walls.

un·want·ed /ˌənˈwäntid; -ˈwônt-/ ▸*adj.* not or no longer desired: *affairs can lead to unwanted pregnancies | she felt unwanted.*

un·warned /ˌənˈwôrnd/ ▸*adj.* (of a person) not warned in advance about something.

un·war·rant·a·ble /ˌənˈwôrəntəbəl; -ˈwär-/ ▸*adj.* not able to be authorized or sanctioned; unjustifiable: *an unwarrantable intrusion into personal matters.* —**un·war·rant·a·bly** /-blē/ *adv.*

un·war·rant·ed /ˌənˈwôrəntid; -ˈwär-/ ▸*adj.* not justified or authorized: *I am sure your fears are unwarranted.*

un·war·y /ˌənˈwe(ə)rē/ ▸*adj.* not cautious; not aware of possible dangers or problems: *accidents can happen to the unwary traveler* | [as *plural n.*] (**the unwary**) *hidden traps for the unwary.* —**un·war·i·ly** /-ˈwe(ə)rəlē/ *adv.* —**un·war·i·ness** *n.*

un·washed /ˌənˈwôSHt; -ˈwäSHt/ ▸*adj.* not having been washed.
▸*PHRASE* □ **the (great) unwashed** *derogatory* the mass or multitude of ordinary people.

un·watch·a·ble /ˌənˈwäCHəbəl/ ▸*adj.* (of a film or television program) too poor, tedious, or disturbing to be viewed.

un·wa·tered /ˌənˈwôtərd; -ˈwät-/ ▸*adj.* not supplied or sprinkled with water.

un·wa·ver·ing /ˌənˈwāvəriNG/ ▸*adj.* steady or resolute; not wavering: *she fixed him with an unwavering stare.* —**un·wa·ver·ing·ly** *adv.*

un·weaned /ˌənˈwēnd/ ▸*adj.* (of an infant or other young mammal) not accustomed to food other than its mother's milk.

un·wear·a·ble /ˌənˈwe(ə)rəbəl/ ▸*adj.* (of a garment) not fit to be worn.

un·wea·ried /ˌənˈwi(ə)rēd/ ▸*adj.* not tired or becoming tired. —**un·wea·ried·ly** *adv.*

un·wea·ry·ing /ˌənˈwi(ə)rē-iNG/ ▶*adj.* never tiring or slackening. —**un·wea·ry·ing·ly** *adv.*

un·wed /ˌənˈwed/ (also **un·wed·ded**) ▶*adj.* not married: *an unwed teenage mother.* —**un·wed·ded·ness** *n.*

un·weed·ed /ˌənˈwēdᵊd/ ▶*adj.* not cleared of weeds.

un·weighed /ˌənˈwād/ ▶*adj.* **1** not considered; hasty. **2** (of goods) not weighed.

un·weight /ˌənˈwāt/ ▶*v.* [*trans.*] momentarily stop pressing heavily on (a ski or skateboard) in order to make a turn more easily. ▷1930s: back-formation from UNWEIGHTED.

un·weight·ed /ˌənˈwātid/ ▶*adj.* **1** without a weight attached. **2** *Statistics* (of a figure or sample) not adjusted or biased to reflect importance or value.

un·wel·come /ˌənˈwelkəm/ ▶*adj.* (of a guest or new arrival) not gladly received: *guards kept out unwelcome visitors.* ■ not much needed or desired: *unwelcome attentions from men.* —**un·wel·come·ly** *adv.* —**un·wel·come·ness** *n.*

un·wel·com·ing /ˌənˈwelkəmiNG/ ▶*adj.* having an inhospitable or uninviting atmosphere or appearance: *Jean crept into her cold and unwelcoming bed.* ■ (of a person or their manner) not friendly toward someone arriving or approaching.

un·well /ˌənˈwel/ ▶*adj.* [*predic.*] sick: *consult a doctor if you feel unwell.*

un·wept /ˌənˈwept/ ▶*adj. chiefly poetic/literary* (of a person) not mourned or lamented.

un·whole·some /ˌənˈhōlsəm/ ▶*adj.* not characterized by or conducive to health or moral well-being: *the use of the living room as sleeping quarters led to unwholesome crowding.* —**un·whole·some·ly** *adv.* —**un·whole·some·ness** *n.*

un·wield·y /ˌənˈwēldē/ ▶*adj.* (**-wield·i·er**, **-wield·i·est**) difficult to carry or move because of its size, shape, or weight: *the first mechanical clocks were large and unwieldy.* ■ (of a system or bureaucracy) too big or badly organized to function efficiently. ▷late Middle English (in the sense 'lacking strength, infirm'): from UN-[1] 'not' + WIELDY (in the obsolete sense 'active'). —**un·wield·i·ly** *adv.* —**un·wield·i·ness** *n.*

un·will·ing /ˌənˈwiliNG/ ▶*adj.* [often with *infinitive*] not ready, eager, or prepared to do something: *he was unwilling to take on that responsibility | unwilling conscripts.* ▷Old English *unwillende* (see UN-[1], WILLING). —**un·will·ing·ly** *adv.* —**un·will·ing·ness** *n.*

un·wind /ˌənˈwīnd/ ▶*v.* (*past* and *past part.* **-wound** /-ˈwound/) undo or be undone after winding or being wound: [*trans.*] *Ella unwound the long woolen scarf from her neck* | [*intrans.*] *the net unwinds from the reel.* ■ [*intrans.*] relax after a period of work or tension: *the Grand Hotel is a superb place to unwind.*

un·wink·ing /ˌənˈwiNGkiNG/ ▶*adj.* (of a stare or a shining light) steady; unwavering: *the lights shone unwinking in the still air | unwinking blue eyes.* —**un·wink·ing·ly** *adv.*

un·wired /ˌənˈwī(ə)rd/ ▶*adj.* **1** wireless: *photo sharing between Macs on wired and unwired networks.* **2** disengaged or disconnected from electronic media: *the geographic terrain and the remoteness force you to be unwired.*

un·wis·dom /ˌənˈwizdəm/ ▶*n.* folly; lack of wisdom: *it stresses the unwisdom of fathers leaving their children.* ▷Old English *unwīsdōm* (see UN-[1], WISDOM).

un·wise /ˌənˈwīz/ ▶*adj.* (of a person or action) not wise or sensible; foolish: *it is unwise to rely on hearsay evidence | unwise policy decisions.* ▷Old English *unwīs* (see UN-[1], WISE[1]). —**un·wise·ly** *adv.* [*sentence adverb*] *unwisely, she repeated the remark to her mother.*

un·wished /ˌənˈwisHt/ ▶*adj.* (usu. **unwished-for**) not wanted or desired: *an unwished-for child.*

un·wit·nessed /ˌənˈwitnist/ ▶*adj.* (esp. of an event) not witnessed.

un·wit·ting /ˌənˈwitiNG/ ▶*adj.* (of a person) not aware of the full facts: *an unwitting accomplice.* ■ not done on purpose; unintentional: *we are anxious to rectify the unwitting mistakes made in the past.* ▷Old English *unwitende* 'not knowing or realizing' (see UN-[1], WIT[2]). —**un·wit·ting·ly** *adv.* [*sentence adverb*] *quite unwittingly, you played right into my hands that night.* —**un·wit·ting·ness** *n.*

un·wom·an·ly /ˌənˈwŏŏmənlē/ ▶*adj.* not having or showing qualities traditionally associated with women: *initiative of any overt sort was considered unwomanly.* —**un·wom·an·li·ness** *n.*

un·wont·ed /ˌənˈwôntid/ ▶*adj.* [*attrib.*] unaccustomed or unusual: *there was an unwonted gaiety in her manner.* —**un·wont·ed·ly** *adv.* [as *submodifier*] *she was unwontedly shy and subdued.* —**un·wont·ed·ness** *n.*

un·wood·ed /ˌənˈwŏŏdid/ ▶*adj.* **1** having few trees. **2** (of a wine) not having been stored in a wooden cask.

un·work·a·ble /ˌənˈwərkəbəl/ ▶*adj.* not able to function or be carried out successfully; impractical: *complex, unworkable theories.* ■ (of a material) not able to be worked: *the alloy becomes brittle and almost unworkable.* —**un·work·a·bil·i·ty** /-ˌwərkəˈbilitē/ *n.* —**un·work·a·bly** /-blē/ *adv.*

un·worked /ˌənˈwərkt/ ▶*adj.* not cultivated, mined, or carved: *unworked fields | an unworked vein of rich ore.*

un·work·man·like /ˌənˈwərkmənˌlīk/ ▶*adj.* badly done or made.

un·world·ly /ˌənˈwərldlē/ ▶*adj.* (of a person) not having much awareness of the realities of life, in particular, not motivated by material or practical considerations: *she was so shrewd in some ways, but hopelessly unworldly in others.* ■ not seeming to belong to this planet; strange: *the unworldly monolith loomed four stories high.* —**un·world·li·ness** *n.*

un·worn /ˌənˈwôrn/ ▶*adj.* not damaged or shabby-looking as a result of much use: *the tires appear unworn, even after many fast miles | unworn carpeting.* ■ (of a garment) never worn.

un·wor·ried /ˌənˈwərēd/ ▶*adj.* [*predic.*] not anxious or uneasy: *foreign investors are largely unworried by the government's fall.*

un·wor·thy /ˌənˈwərT͟Hē/ ▶*adj.* (**-thi·er**, **-thi·est**) not deserving effort, attention, or respect: *he was* ***unworthy of*** *trust and unfit to hold office.* ■ (of a person's action or behavior) not acceptable, esp. from someone with a good reputation or social position: *the expression of anger was frowned upon as being unworthy.* ■ having little value or merit: *many pieces are unworthy and ungrammatical.* —**un·wor·thi·ly** /-T͟Həlē/ *adv.* —**un·wor·thi·ness** *n.*

un·wound /ˌənˈwound/ ▶ past and past participle of UNWIND.
▶*adj.* (of a clock or watch) not wound or wound up.

un·wo·ven /ˌənˈwōvən/ ▶*adj.* (of fabric) not woven.

un·wrap /ˌənˈrap/ ▶*v.* (**-wrapped**, **-wrap·ping**) [*trans.*] remove the wrapping from a package: *children excitedly unwrapping and playing with their new presents.*

un·wrin·kled /ˌənˈriNGkəld/ ▶*adj.* (esp. of fabric or a person's skin) free from wrinkles.

un·writ·ten /ˌənˈritn/ ▶*adj.* not recorded in writing: *documenting unwritten languages.* ■ (esp. of a law) resting originally on custom or judicial decision rather than on statute: *an unwritten constitution.* ■ (of a convention) understood and accepted by everyone, although not formally established: *the unwritten rules of social life.*

un·wrought /ˌənˈrôt/ ▶*adj.* (of metals or other materials) not worked into a finished condition. ■ (of a mine or ore deposit) not worked or mined.

un·yield·ing /ˌənˈyēldiNG/ ▶*adj.* (of a mass or structure) not giving way to pressure; hard or solid: *the Atlantic hurled its waves at the unyielding rocks.* ■ (of a person or their behavior) unlikely to be swayed; resolute: *his unyielding faith.* —**un·yield·ing·ly** *adv.* —**un·yield·ing·ness** *n.*

un·yoke /ˌənˈyōk/ ▶*v.* [*trans.*] release (a pair of animals) from a yoke. ■ [*intrans.*] *archaic* cease work.

un·zip /ˌənˈzip/ ▶*v.* (**-zipped**, **-zip·ping**) [*trans.*] unfasten the zipper of (an item of clothing): *he unzipped his black jacket.* ■ *Computing* decompress (a file) that has previously been compressed.

up /əp/ ▶*adv.* **1** toward the sky or a higher position: *he jumped up | two of the men hoisted her up | the curtain went up.* ■ upstairs: *she made her way up to bed.* ■ out of bed: *Miranda hardly ever got up for breakfast | he had been up for hours.* ■ (of the sun) visible in the sky after daybreak: *the sun was already up when they set off.* ■ expressing movement toward or position in the north: *I drove up to Detroit.* ■ to or at a place perceived as higher: *going for a walk up to the stores.* ■ *Brit.* toward or in the capital or a major city: *give me a ring when you're up in London.* ■ *Brit.* at or to a university, esp. Oxford or Cambridge: *they were up at Cambridge about the same time.* ■ (of food that has been eaten) regurgitated from the stomach: *I was sick and vomited up everything.* ■ [as *exclam.*] used as a command to a soldier or an animal to stand up and be ready to move or attack: *up, boys, and at 'em.* **2** to the place where someone is: *Dot didn't hear Mrs. Parvis come creeping up behind her.* **3** at or to a higher level of intensity, volume, or activity: *she turned the volume up | liven up the graphics | U.S. environmental groups had been stepping up their attack on GATT.* ■ at or to a higher price, value, or rank: *sales are up 22.8 percent at $50.2 million | unemployment is up and rising.* ■ winning or at an advantage by a specified margin: *there they were in the fourth quarter, up by 11 points | we came away 300 bucks up on the evening.* **4** into the desired or a proper condition: *the mayor agreed to set up a committee.* ■ so as to be finished or closed: *I've got a bit of paperwork to finish up | I zipped up my sweater.* **5** into a happy mood: *I don't think anything's going to cheer me up.* **6** displayed on a bulletin board or other publicly visible site: *he put up posters around the city.* **7** (of sailing) against the current or the wind. ■ (of a ship's helm) moved so that the rudder is to leeward. **8** *Baseball* at bat: *every time up, he had a different stance.*
▶*prep.* from a lower to a higher point on (something); upward along: *she climbed up a flight of steps.* ■ from one end to another of (a street or other area), not necessarily on an upward slope: *bicycling up Pleasant Avenue toward Maywood Avenue | walking up the street.* ■ to a higher part of (a river or stream), away from the sea: *a cruise up the Rhine.*
▶*adj.* **1** [*attrib.*] directed or moving toward a higher place or position: *the up escalator.* ■ *Physics* denoting a flavor of quark having a charge of $+2/3$. Protons and neutrons are thought to be composed of combinations of up and down quarks. **2** [*predic.*] in a cheerful mood; ebullient: *the mood here is resolutely up.* **3** [*predic.*] (of a computer system or industrial process) functioning properly: *the system is now up.* **4** [*predic.*] at an end: *his contract was up in three weeks | time's up.* **5** (of a jockey) in the saddle.
▶*n. informal* a period of good fortune: *you can't have ups all the time in football.*
▶*v.* (**upped**, **up·ping**) **1** [*intrans.*] (**up and do something**) *informal* do something abruptly or boldly: *she upped and left him.* **2** [*trans.*] cause (a level or amount) to be increased: *capacity will be upped by 70 percent next year.* **3** [*trans.*] lift (something) up: *everybody was cheering and upping their glasses.* ■ [*intrans.*] (**up with**) *informal* raise or pick up (something): *this woman ups with a stone.* ▷Old English *up(p)*, *uppe*, of Germanic origin; related to Dutch *op* and German *auf*.
▶*PHRASES* □ **get it up** *vulgar slang* have a penile erection. □ **it is all up with** *informal* it is the end of or there is no hope for (someone or something). □ **on the up and up** *informal* **1** honest or sincere. **2** *Brit.* steadily improving or becoming more successful. □ **something is up** *informal* something unusual or undesirable is happening or afoot. □ **up against** close to or in contact with: *crowds pressed up against the police barricades.* ■ *informal* confronted with or opposed by: *I began to think of what teachers are up against today.* ■ (**up against it**) *informal* facing some serious but unspecified difficulty: *they play better when they're up against it.* □ **up and about** no longer in bed (after sleep or an illness). □ **up and down** **1** moving upward and downward: *bouncing up and down.* **2** to and fro: *pacing up and down in front of her desk.* ■ [as *prep.*] to and fro along: *strolling up and down the corridor.* **3** in various places throughout: *in clubs up and down the country.* **4** *informal* in varying states or moods; changeable: *my relationship with her was up and down.* □ **up and running** (esp. of a computer system) in operation; functioning: *the new computer is up and running.* □ **up the ante** see ANTE. □ **up before** appearing for a hearing in the presence of: *we'll have to come up before a magistrate.* □ **up for** **1** available for: *the house next door is up for sale.* **2** being considered for: *he had been up for promotion.* **3** due for: *his contract is up for renewal in June.* □ **up for it** *informal* ready to take part in a particular activity: *Nick wasn't really up for it.* □ **up hill and down dale** all over the place: *he led me up hill and down dale till my feet were dropping off.* □ **up on** well informed about: *he was up on the latest methods.* □ **up to** **1** as far as: *I could reach just up to his waist.* ■ (also **up until**) until: *up to now I hadn't had a relationship.* **2** indicating a maximum amount: *the process is expected to take up to two years.* **3** [with *negative* or in *questions*] as good as; good enough for: *I was not up to her standards.* ■ capable of or fit for: *he is simply not up to the job.* **4** the duty, responsibility, or choice of (someone): *it was up to them to gauge the problem.* **5** *informal* occupied or busy with: *what's he been up to?* □ **up top** *Brit., informal* in the brain (with reference to intelligence): *a man with nothing much up top.* □ **up with ——** an exclamation expressing support for a stated person or thing. □ **up yours** (also **up your ass**) *vulgar slang* an exclamation expressing contemptuous defiance or rejection of someone. □ **what's up?** *informal* **1** what is going on? **2** what is the matter?: ***what's up with*** *you?*

up- ▶*prefix* **1** (added to verbs and their derivatives) upward: *upturned | upthrow.* ■ to a more recent time; to a newer or better state: *upbeat | update | upgrade |*

upscale. **2** (added to nouns) denoting (direction of) motion up: *upriver* | *uphill* | *upwind.* **3** (added to nouns) higher: *upland* | *upstroke* ■ increased: *up-tempo.*

up·an·chor ▸*v.* [*intrans.*] (of a ship) weigh anchor.

up-and-com·ing ▸*adj.* (of a person beginning a particular activity or occupation) making good progress and likely to become successful: *up-and-coming young players.* —**up-and-com·er** *n.*

U·pan·i·shad /(y)o͞o'panə,shad; o͞o'pəni,shəd/ ▸*n.* each of a series of Hindu sacred treatises written in Sanskrit *c.*800–200 BC, expounding the Vedas in predominantly mystical and monistic terms. ▷from Sanskrit, literally 'sitting near (i.e., at the feet of a master),' from *upa* 'near' + *ni-ṣad* 'sit down.'

u·pas /'yo͞opəs/ (also **u·pas tree**) ▸*n.* a tropical Asian tree, the milky sap of which has been used as arrow poison and for ritual purposes. • *Antiaris toxicaria*, family Moraceae. ■ (in folklore) a Javanese tree alleged to poison its surroundings and said to be fatal to approach. ▷late 18th cent.: from Malay *(pohun) upas* 'poison (tree).'

up·beat /'əp,bēt/ ▸*n.* (in music) an unaccented beat preceding an accented beat.
▸*adj. informal* cheerful; optimistic.

up·bow /bō/ ▸*n.* (on a stringed instrument) a stroke begun with the tip of the bow and proceeding toward the base. Compare with DOWN-BOW.

up·braid /,əp'brād/ ▸*v.* [*trans.*] find fault with (someone); scold: *he was upbraided for his slovenly appearance.* See note at SCOLD. ▷late Old English *upbrēdan* 'allege (something) as a basis for censure,' based on BRAID in the obsolete sense 'brandish.' The current sense dates from Middle English.

up·bring·ing /'əp,bringing/ ▸*n.* the treatment and instruction received by a child from its parents throughout its childhood: *she had had a Christian upbringing.* ▷late 15th cent.: from obsolete *upbring* 'to rear' (see UP-, BRING).

up·build /,əp'bild/ ▸*v.* (*past* and *past part.* **-built**) [*trans.*] *chiefly poetic/literary* construct or develop (something).

UPC ▸*abbr.* ■ Universal Product Code.

up card ▸*n.* a playing card turned face up on the table, esp. the top card of the waste heap in rummy or a card turned face up in stud poker.

up·cast /'əp,kast/ ▸*n.* (also **up·cast shaft**) a shaft through which air leaves a mine.
▸*v.* (*past* and *past part.* **-cast**) [*trans.*] cast (something) upward: [as *adj.*] (**upcast**) *upcast light.*

up·chuck /'əp,chək/ *informal* ▸*v.* vomit: [*intrans.*] *don't let her upchuck on him* | [*trans.*] *I almost upchucked my toasted marshmallows.*
▸*n.* matter vomited from the stomach.

up·close /klōs/ ▸*adv.* at very close range: *he was able to experience glaciers calving up-close.*
▸*adj.* showing or allowing considerable detail: *an up-close look at a panorama of products and services.*

up·coast /,əp'kōst/ ▸*adv.* & *adj.* further up the coast.

up·code /,əp'kōd/ ▸*v.* [*trans.*] assign an inaccurate billing code to (a medical procedure or treatment) to increase reimbursement: *if you are asked to upcode drug charges to increase reimbursement, will you refuse to do so or go along with the flow?* | [*intrans.*] *auditors discovered that they had been upcoding for years.*

up·com·ing /'əp,kəming/ ▸*adj.* forthcoming; about to happen: *the upcoming election.*

up·coun·try /,əp'kəntrē; 'əp,kəntrē/ ▸*adv.* & *adj.* in or toward the interior of a country; inland: [as *adv.*] *she comes from somewhere upcountry* | [as *adj.*] *a little upcountry town.*

up·date ▸*v.* /,əp'dāt; 'əp,dāt/ [*trans.*] make (something) more modern or up to date: *security measures are continually updated and improved* | [as *adj.*] (**updated**) *an updated list of subscribers.* ■ give (someone) the latest information about something: *the reporter promised to keep the viewers updated.*
▸*n.* /'əp,dāt/ an act of bringing something or someone up to date, or an updated version of something: *an update on recently published crime figures.* —**up·dat·a·ble** *adj.* (*Computing*).

Up·dike /'əp,dīk/, John (Hoyer) (1932–), U.S. novelist, poet, and short-story writer. He is noted for his quartet of novels *Rabbit, Run* (1960), *Rabbit Redux* (1971), *Rabbit is Rich* (1981), and *Rabbit at Rest* (1990), the last two earning him Pulitzer Prizes. Other novels include *The Witches of Eastwick* (1984) and *S* (1998).

up·do /'əp,do͞o/ ▸*n. informal* a hairstyle in which the hair is swept up and fastened away from the face and neck.

up·dom·ing /'əp,dōming/ ▸*n. Geology* the upward deformation of a rock mass into a dome shape.

up·draft /'əp,draft/ (*Brit.* **up·draught**) ▸*n.* an upward current or draft of air.

up·end /,əp'end/ ▸*v.* [*trans.*] set or turn (something) on its end or upside down: *Kitty upended her purse, dumping out all her money* | [as *adj.*] (**upended**) *an upended box.* ■ [*intrans.*] (of a swimming duck or other waterbird) submerge the head and foreparts in order to feed, so that the tail is raised in the air.

up·field /,əp'fēld/ ▸*adv., adj. Football* another term for DOWNFIELD.

up·flung /'əp,fləng/ ▸*adj. chiefly poetic/literary* (esp. of limbs) flung upward, esp. in a gesture of helplessness or alarm.

up·front /,əp'frənt/ *informal* ▸*adv.* (usu. **up front**) **1** at the front; in front: *I was sitting up front.* **2** (of a payment) in advance: *the salesmen are paid commission up front.*
▸*adj.* **1** bold, honest, and frank: *he'd been upfront about his intentions.* **2** [*attrib.*] (of a payment) made in advance. **3** at the front or the most prominent position: *a literary weekly with an upfront section modeled on the New Yorker.*

up·grade ▸*v.* /'əp,grād; ,əp'grād/ [*trans.*] raise (something) to a higher standard, in particular improve (equipment or machinery) by adding or replacing components: *the cost of upgrading each workstation is around $300* | [as *adj.*] (**upgraded**) *upgraded computers.* ■ raise (an employee) to a higher grade or rank.
▸*n.* /'əp,grād/ an act of upgrading something. ■ an improved or more modern version of something, esp. a piece of computing equipment. —**up·grad·a·bil·i·ty** /,əp,grādə'bilitē/ (also **up·grade·a·bil·i·ty**) *n.* —**up·grad·a·ble** /,əp'grādəbəl/ (also **up·grade·a·ble**) *adj.*
▸PHRASE □ **on the upgrade** improving; progressing.

up·growth /'əp,grōth/ ▸*n.* the process or result of growing upward. ■ an upward growth.

up·heav·al /,əp'hēvəl/ ▸*n.* a violent or sudden change or disruption to something: *major upheavals in the financial markets* | *times of political upheaval.* ■ an upward displacement of part of the earth's crust.

up·heave /,əp'hēv/ ▸*v.* [*trans.*] *poetic/literary* heave or lift up (something, esp. part of the earth's surface): *the area was first upheaved from the primeval ocean.*

up·hill ▸*adv.* /,əp'hil/ in an ascending direction up a hill or slope: *follow the track uphill.*
▸*adj.* /'əp,hil/ sloping upward; ascending: *the journey is slightly uphill.* ■ *figurative* requiring great effort; difficult: *an uphill struggle to gain worldwide recognition.*
▸*n.* /'əp,hil/ an upward slope.

up·hold /,əp'hōld/ ▸*v.* (*past* and *past part.* **-held**) [*trans.*] confirm or support (something that has been questioned): *the court upheld his claim for damages.* ■ maintain (a custom or practice): *many furniture makers uphold the tradition of fine design.* —**up·hold·er** *n.*

up·hol·ster /əp'hōlstər; ə'pōl-/ ▸*v.* [*trans.*] provide (furniture) with a soft, padded covering: *the chairs were upholstered in red velvet* | [as *adj.*] (**upholstered**) *an upholstered stool.* ■ cover the walls or furniture in (a room) with textiles. ▷mid 19th cent.: back-formation from UPHOLSTERER.

up·hol·ster·er /əp'hōlstərər; ə'pōl-/ ▸*n.* a person who upholsters furniture, esp. professionally. ▷early 17th cent.: from the obsolete noun *upholster* (from UPHOLD in the obsolete sense 'keep in repair') + -STER.

up·hol·ster·y /əp'hōlst(ə)rē; ə'pōl-/ ▸*n.* soft, padded textile covering that is fixed to furniture such as armchairs and sofas. ■ the art or practice of fitting such a covering.

UPI ▸*abbr.* United Press International.

Up·john /'əp,jän/, Richard (1802–78), U.S. architect; born in England. He is best known for his buildings, such as Trinity Church 1839–46 in New York City, that are designed in Gothic Revival style.

up·keep /'əp,kēp/ ▸*n.* the process of keeping something in good condition: *we will be responsible for the upkeep of the access road.* ■ financial or material support of a person or animal: *payments for the children's upkeep.*

Up·land /'əplənd/ a city in southwestern California, east of Los Angeles and north of Ontario; pop. 63,374.

up·land /'əplənd; -,land/ ▸*n.* (also **uplands**) an area of high or hilly land: *conservation of areas of upland.*

up·land cot·ton ▸*n.* cotton of a type grown in the U.S. that typically yields medium- and short-staple forms of cotton. • *Gossypium hirsutum* var. *latifolium*, family Malvaceae.

up·land sand·pip·er ▸*n.* a North American sandpiper that breeds on upland fields. Also called UPLAND PLOVER. • *Bartramia longicauda.*

up·lift ▸*v.* /,əp'lift/ [*trans.*] **1** [usu. as *adj.*] (**uplifted**) lift (something) up; raise: *her uplifted face.* ■ (**be uplifted**) (of an island, mountain, etc.) be created by an upward movement of the earth's surface. **2** elevate or stimulate (someone) morally or spiritually: [as *adj.*] (**uplifting**) *an uplifting tune.*
▸*n.* /'əp,lift/ **1** an act of raising something. ■ *Geology* the upward movement of part of the earth's surface. ■ [often as *adj.*] support, esp. for a woman's bust, from a garment: *an uplift bra.* **2** a morally or spiritually elevating influence: *their love will prove an enormous uplift.* —**up·lift·er** /,əp'liftər/ *n.*

up·light /'əp,līt/ (also **up·light·er**) /-,lītər/ ▸*n.* a light placed or designed to throw illumination upward. —**up·light·ing** *n.*

up·link /'əp,lingk/ ▸*n.* a communications link to a satellite.
▸*v.* [*trans.*] provide (someone) with or send (something) by such a link: *I can uplink fax transmissions to a satellite.*

up·load *Computing* ▸*v.* /'əp,lōd; ,əp'lōd/ [*trans.*] transfer (data) to another computer system; transmit (data). Compare with DOWNLOAD.
▸*n.* /'əp,lōd/ the action or process of transferring data in such a way.

up·mar·ket /,əp'märkit; 'əp,mär-/ (also **up·mar·ket**) ▸*adj.* & *adv.* upscale.

up·most /'əp,mōst/ ▸*adj.* another term for UPPERMOST.

up·on /ə'pän; ə'pôn/ ▸*prep.* more formal term for ON, esp. in abstract senses: *it was based upon two principles* | *a school's dependence upon parental support.* ▷Middle English: from UP + ON, suggested by Old Norse *upp á.*

USAGE The preposition **upon** has the same core meaning as the preposition **on**. **Upon** is sometimes more formal than **on**, however, and is preferred in the phrases *once upon a time* and *upon my word*, and in uses such as *row upon row of seats* and *Christmas is almost upon us.*

up·per[1] /'əpər/ ▸*adj.* **1** situated above another part: *his upper arm* | *the upper atmosphere.* ■ higher in position or status: *the upper end of the social scale.* **2** situated on higher ground. ■ situated to the north: [in *place names*] *Upper California.* **3** *Geology* & *Archaeology* denoting a younger (and hence usually shallower) part of a stratigraphic division or archaeological deposit or the period in which it was formed or deposited: *the Upper Paleolithic age.*
▸*n.* **1** the part of a boot or shoe above the sole. **2** (**uppers**) upper dentures or teeth. ▷Middle English: from the adjective UP + -ER[2].
▸PHRASES □ **have** (or **gain**) **the upper hand** have or gain advantage or control over someone or something. □ **on one's uppers** *chiefly Brit., informal* extremely short of money.

up·per[2] ▸*n.* (usu. **uppers**) *informal* a stimulating drug, esp. amphetamine. ▷1960s: from the verb UP + -ER[1].

Up·per Can·a·da the mainly English-speaking region of Canada north of the Great Lakes and west of the Ottawa River, in what is now southern Ontario.

up·per·case /'əpər' kās/ (also **up·per case**) ▸*n.* capital letters as opposed to small letters (lowercase): *the keywords must be in uppercase* | [as *adj.*] *uppercase letters.* ▷referring originally to two type cases positioned on an angled stand, the case containing the capital letters being higher and further away from the compositor.

up·per cham·ber ▸*n.* another term for UPPER HOUSE.

up·per class ▸*n.* [treated as *sing.* or *pl.*] the social group that has the highest status in society, esp. the aristocracy.
▸*adj.* of, relating to, or characteristic of such a group: *upper-class accents.*

up·per·class·man /,əpər'klasmən/ ▸*n.* (*pl.* **-men**) a junior or senior in high school or college.

up·per crust ▸*n.* (**the upper crust**) *informal* the upper classes.

up·per·cut /'əpər,kət/ ▸*n.* a punch delivered with an upward motion and the arm bent. ■ *Baseball* an upward batting stroke, typically resulting in a fly ball.
▸*v.* [*trans.*] hit with an uppercut.

Up·per Dar·by /'därbē/ a township in southern Pennsylvania, southwest of Philadelphia; pop. 81,821.

U

Pronunciation Key ə *ago*; ər *over*; 'ə or ,ə *up*; 'ər or ,ər *fur*; a *hat*; ā *rate*; ä *car*; CH *chew*; e *let*; ē *see*; e(ə)r *air*; i *fit*; ī *by*; i(ə)r *ear*; NG *sing*; ō *go*; ô *for*; oi *boy*; o͝o *good*; o͞o *goo*; ou *out*; SH *she*; TH *thin*; TH *then*; (h)w *why*; ZH *vision*

up·per house ▸*n.* the smaller house in a bicameral legislature or parliament. ■ (**the Upper House**) (in the UK) the House of Lords.

up·per·most /ˈəpərˌmōst/ ▸*adj.* (also **up·most**) highest in place, rank, or importance: *the uppermost windows* | *her father was uppermost in her mind.*
▸*adv.* at or to the highest or most important position: *investors put environmental concerns uppermost on their list.*

Up·per Pe·nin·su·la (abbr.: **UP**) the northern section of Michigan that is separated from the southern part of the state by Lake Michigan, the Straits of Mackinac, and Lake Huron. Lake Superior is to the north.

up·per re·gions ▸*plural n. archaic* or *poetic/literary* the sky or heavens.

up·per school ▸*n.* a secondary school for children aged from about fourteen upward, generally following on from a middle school. ■ the section of a school that comprises or caters to the older students.

Up·per Vol·ta former name (until 1984) for **BURKINA FASO**.

up·pish /ˈəpisʜ/ ▸*adj. informal* arrogantly self-assertive. —**up·pish·ly** *adv.* —**up·pish·ness** *n.*

up·pi·ty /ˈəpətē/ ▸*adj. informal* self-important; arrogant: *an uppity sister-in-law.* ▷late 19th cent.: a fanciful formation from **UP**.

Upp·sa·la /ˈo͝opˌsälə/ a city in eastern Sweden; pop. 167,000.

up·raise /ˌəpˈrāz/ ▸*v.* [*trans.*] raise (something) to a higher level: *concentration upraises things* | [as *adj.*] (**upraised**) *an upraised arm.*

up·right /ˈəpˌrīt/ ▸*adj.* **1** vertical; erect: *the posts must be in an upright position.* ■ (of a piano) having vertical strings. ■ greater in height than breadth: *an upright freezer.* ■ denoting a device designed to be used in a vertical position: *an upright vacuum cleaner.* **2** (of a person or their behavior) strictly honorable or honest: *an upright member of the community.*
▸*adv.* in or into a vertical position: *she was sitting upright in bed.*
▸*n.* **1** a post or rod fixed vertically, esp. as a structural support: *the stone uprights of the parapet.* ■ (**uprights**) *Football* the vertical posts extending up from the goal post, between which a field goal must pass to score. **2** an upright piano. ▷Old English *upriht*, of Germanic origin; related to Dutch *oprecht* and German *aufrecht* (see **UP**, **RIGHT**). —**up·right·ly** *adv.* —**upright·ness** *n.*

up·rise /ˌəpˈrīz/ ▸*v.* (*past* **-rose**; *past part.* **-ris·en**) [*intrans.*] *archaic* or *poetic/literary* rise to a standing or elevated position: *bright and red uprose the morning sun.*

up·ris·ing /ˈəpˌrīzɪɴɢ/ ▸*n.* an act of resistance or rebellion; a revolt: *an armed uprising.*

> *THE RIGHT WORD* **insurgency, insurrection, mutiny, putsch, rebellion, revolution, uprising**
>
> There are a number of ways to defy the established order or overthrow a government.
>
> You can stage an **uprising**, which is a broad term referring to a small and usually unsuccessful act of popular resistance (*uprisings among angry workers all over the country*).
>
> An uprising is often the first sign of a general or widespread **rebellion**, which is an act of armed resistance against a government or authority; this term is usually applied after the fact to describe an act of resistance that has failed (*a rebellion against the landowners*).
>
> If it is successful, however, a rebellion may become a **revolution**, which often implies a war or an outbreak of violence (*the American Revolution*). Although a *revolution* usually involves the overthrow of a government or political system by the people, it can also be used to describe any drastic change in ideas, economic institutions, or moral values (*the sexual revolution*).
>
> An **insurrection** is an organized effort to seize power, especially political power, while an **insurgency** is usually aided by foreign powers.
>
> If you're on a ship, you can stage a **mutiny**, which is an insurrection against military or naval authority.
>
> But if you're relying on speed and surprise to catch the authorities off guard, you'll want to stage a **putsch**, which is a small, popular uprising or planned attempt to seize power.

up·riv·er /ˈəpˈrivər/ ▸*adv.* & *adj.* toward or situated at a point nearer the source of a river: [as *adv.*] *the salmon head upriver to spawn* | [as *adj.*] *they headed for the upriver side.*

up·roar /ˈəpˌrôr/ ▸*n.* a loud and impassioned noise or disturbance: *the room was in an uproar* | *the assembly dissolved in uproar.* ■ a public expression of protest or outrage: *it caused an uproar in the press.* ▷early 16th cent.: from Middle Dutch *uproer*, from *op* 'up' + *roer* 'confusion,' assimilated to **ROAR**.

up·roar·i·ous /ˌəpˈrôrēəs/ ▸*adj.* characterized by or provoking loud noise or uproar: *an uproarious party.* ■ provoking loud laughter; very funny. —**up·roar·i·ous·ly** *adv.* —**up·roar·i·ous·ness** *n.*

up·root /ˌəpˈro͞ot; -ˈro͝ot/ ▸*v.* [*trans.*] pull (something, esp. a tree or plant) out of the ground: *the elephant's trunk is powerful enough to uproot trees.* ■ move (someone) from their home or a familiar location: *my father traveled constantly and uprooted his family several times.* ■ *figurative* eradicate; destroy: *a revolution is necessary to uproot the social order.* —**up·root·er** *n.*

up·rose /ˌəpˈrōz/ ▸ past of **UPRISE**.

up·rush /ˈəpˌrəsʜ/ ▸*n.* a sudden upward surge or flow, esp. of a feeling: *an uprush of joy.*

UPS ▸*abbr.* uninterruptible power supply.

ups-a-dai·sy /ˈəpsəˈdāzē/ (also **up·sa-dai·sy**) ▸*exclam.* variant spelling of **UPSY-DAISY**.

ups and downs ▸*plural n.* a succession of both good and bad experiences: *I have my ups and downs.* ■ rises and falls, esp. in the value or success of something: *the ups and downs of the market.*

up·scale /ˌəpˈskāl; ˈəpˌskāl/ ▸*adj.* & *adv.* toward or relating to the more expensive or affluent sector of the market: [as *adj.*] *Hawaii's upscale boutique hotels* | [as *adv.*] *once known as the low-cost cousin of beef, fish has moved upscale.*

up·set /ˌəpˈset/ ▸*v.* (**-set·ting**; *past* and *past part.* **-set**) [*trans.*] **1** make (someone) unhappy, disappointed, or worried: *the accusation upset her* | [as *adj.*] (**upsetting**) *a painful and upsetting divorce.* **2** knock (something) over: *he upset a tureen of soup.* ■ cause disorder in (something); disrupt: *the dam will upset the ecological balance.* ■ disturb the digestion of (a person's stomach); cause (someone) to feel nauseous or unwell. **3** [often as *n.*] (**upsetting**) shorten and thicken the end or edge of (a metal bar, wheel rim, or other object), esp. by hammering or pressure when heated.
▸*n.* /ˈəpset/ **1** a state of being unhappy, disappointed, or worried: *domestic upsets* | *a legal dispute will cause worry and upset.* **2** an unexpected result or situation, esp. in a sports competition: *they caused one of last season's league upsets by winning 27–15.* **3** a disturbance of a person's digestive system: *a stomach upset.*
▸*adj.* /ˌəpˈset/ **1** [*predic.*] unhappy, disappointed, or worried: *she looked pale and upset.* **2** (of a person's stomach) having disturbed digestion, esp. because of something eaten. —**up·set·ter** /ˌəpˈsetər/ *n.* —**up·set·ting·ly** *adv.*

up·set price /ˈəpˌset/ ▸*n.* the lowest acceptable selling price for a property in an auction; a reserve price.

up·shift /ˈəpˌsʜift/ ▸*v.* [*intrans.*] change to a higher gear in a motor vehicle. ■ [*trans.*] increase: *stricter driving laws that upshifted the penalties for drunken driving.*
▸*n.* a change to a higher gear.

up·shot /ˈəpˌsʜät/ ▸*n.* [in *sing.*] the final or eventual outcome or conclusion of a discussion, action, or series of events: *the upshot of the meeting was that he was on the next plane to New York.*

up·side /ˈəpˌsīd/ ▸*n.* [in *sing.*] **1** the positive or favorable aspect of something. **2** an upward movement of stock prices.
▸*PHRASE* □ **upside the head** on the side of head: *she slapped him upside the head.*

up·side down ▸*adv.* & *adj.* with the upper part where the lower part should be; in an inverted position: [as *adv.*] *the bar staff put the chairs upside down on the tables* | [as *adj.*] *an upside-down canoe.* ■ in or into total disorder or confusion: [as *adv.*] *burglars have **turned** our house **upside down**.* ▷Middle English: originally *up so down*, perhaps in the sense 'up as if down.'

up·side-down cake ▸*n.* a cake that is baked over a layer of fruit in syrup and inverted for serving.

up·si·lon /ˈəpsəˌlän; ˈ(y)o͞op-/ ▸*n.* the twentieth letter of the Greek alphabet (**Υ, υ**), transliterated in the traditional Latin style as 'y' (as in *cycle*) or in the modern style as 'u' (as in the etymologies of this dictionary). ■ (**Upsilon**) [followed by Latin genitive] *Astronomy* the twentieth star in a constellation: *Upsilon Scorpii.* ■ (also **up·si·lon par·ti·cle**) *Physics* a meson thought to contain a *b* quark bound to its antiparticle, produced in particle accelerators. ▷mid 17th cent.: Greek, literally 'plain or simple U,' from *psilos* 'plain,' referring to the need to distinguish upsilon from the diphthong *oi*: in late Greek the two had (and in modern Greek still has) the same pronunciation.

up·size /ˈəpˌsīz/ ▸*v.* increase or cause to increase in size or complexity.

up·slope ▸*n.* /ˈəpˌslōp/ an upward slope.
▸*adv.* & *adj.* /ˌəpˈslōp/ at or toward a higher point on a slope.

up·stage /ˌəpˈstāj/ ▸*adv.* & *adj.* at or toward the back of a theater stage: [as *adv.*] *Hamlet turns to face upstage* | [as *adj.*] *an upstage exit.* ■ [as *adj.*] *informal, dated* superior; aloof.
▸*v.* [*trans.*] divert attention from (someone) toward oneself; outshine: *they were totally upstaged by their costar in the film.* ■ (of an actor) move toward the back of a stage to make (another actor) face away from the audience.

up·stairs ▸*adv.* /ˌəpˈste(ə)rz/ on or to an upper floor of a building: *I tiptoed upstairs.* ■ used to refer to someone's mental health: *is he, uh, all right upstairs?*
▸*adj.* /ˈəpˈsterz/ [*attrib.*] situated on an upper floor: *an upstairs bedroom.*
▸*n.* /ˌəpˈsterz; ˈəpˌsterz/ an upper floor: *she was cleaning the upstairs.*
▸*PHRASE* □ **the man upstairs** a humorous name for God.

up·stand·ing /ˌəpˈstandɪɴɢ; ˈəpˌstan-/ ▸*adj.* **1** honest; respectable: *an upstanding member of the community.* **2** standing up; erect: *upstanding feathered plumes.*

up·start /ˈəpˌstärt/ ▸*n. derogatory* a person who has risen suddenly to wealth or high position, esp. one who behaves arrogantly: *the upstarts who dare to challenge the legitimacy of his rule* | [as *adj.*] *an upstart leader.*

up·state /ˈəpˈstāt/ ▸*adj.* & *adv.* of, in, or to a part of a state remote from its large cities, esp. the northern part: [as *adj.*] *the Watermans bought 27 acres in upstate Vermont.*
▸*n.* such an area: *visiting farmers from upstate.* ■ (also **Upstate**) in New York, parts of the state north of New York City, thought of as distinct culturally and politically: *Concord table grapes from upstate* [as *adj.*] *the small community college in upstate New York.* —**up·stat·er** *n.*

up·stream /ˌəpˈstrēm/ ▸*adv.* & *adj.* moving or situated in the opposite direction from that in which a stream or river flows; nearer to the source: [as *adv.*] *a salmon swimming upstream* | [as *adj.*] *the upstream stretch of the Platte.* ■ *Biology* situated in or toward the part of a sequence of genetic material where transcription takes place earlier than at a given point. ■ at a stage in the process of gas or oil extraction and production before the raw material is ready for refining.

up·stroke /ˈəpˌstrōk/ ▸*n.* a stroke made upward: *the upstroke of the whale's tail.*

up·surge /ˈəpˌsərj/ ▸*n.* an upward surge in the strength or quantity of something; an increase: *an upsurge in separatist activity.*

up·sweep ▸*v.* /ˌəpˈswēp/ [*intrans.*] be arranged in an upswept fashion. ■ [*trans*] sweep upward.
▸*n.* /ˈəpˌswēp/ **1** an upward rise or sweep: *the gentle upsweep of the city wall.* ■ a marked rise in activity: *catching the market at the start of its upsweep.* **2** an upswept hairdo.

up·swell /ˈəpˌswel/ ▸*n. rare* an increase or upsurge.

up·swept /ˈəpˌswept/ ▸*adj.* curved, sloping, or directed upward: *an upswept mustache.* ■ (of the hair) brushed or held upward and off the face: *an elegant upswept style.*

up·swing /ˈəpˌswɪɴɢ/ ▸*n.* an increase in strength or quantity; an upward trend: *cigar smoking has been **on the upswing**.*

up·sy-dai·sy /ˈəpsē ˌdāzē/ (also **ups-a-dai·sy**, **up·sa-daisy** /ˈəpsə ˈdāzē/) ▸*exclam.* used to express encouragement to a child who has fallen or is being lifted. ▷mid 19th cent.: alteration of earlier *up-a-daisy*; compare with **LACKADAISICAL**.

up·take /ˈəpˌtāk/ ▸*n.* **1** the action of taking up or making use of something that is available: *a recent uptake in cigar smoking* | *the uptake and usage of microcomputers.* ■ the taking in or absorption of a substance by a living organism or bodily organ: *the uptake of glucose into the muscles.* **2** a pipe or flue leading air, smoke, or gases up to a chimney.
▸*PHRASE* □ **be quick** (or **slow**) **on the uptake** *informal* be quick (or slow) to understand something.

up·talk /ˈəpˌtôk/ ▸*n.* a manner of speaking in which declarative sentences are uttered with rising intonation at the end, as if they were questions.

up·tem·po /ˈəpˌtempō/ ▸*adj.* & *adv.* *Music* played with a fast or increased tempo: [as *adj.*] *uptempo guitar work.*

up·throw /ˈəpˌTHrō/ *Geology* ▸*v.* [*trans.*] [usu. as *adj.*] (**upthrown**) displace (a body of rock) upward on one side of a fault relative to the other..

▸*n.* an upward displacement of a body of rock on one side of a fault.

up·thrust /ˈəpˌTHrəst/ ▸*n.* *Physics* the upward force that a liquid or gas exerts on a body floating in it. ■ *Geology* another term for UPLIFT. ■ an upward thrust: *the upthrust of Manhattan skyscrapers.*

▸*v.* [*trans.*] [usu. as *adj.*] (**upthrust**) thrust (something) upward: *Turco's upthrust beard.*

up·tick /ˈəpˌtik/ ▸*n.* a small increase.

up·tight /ˌəpˈtīt/ ▸*adj.* *informal* anxious or angry in a tense and overly controlled way: *don't get so uptight about everything.*

up·time /ˈəpˌtīm/ ▸*n.* time during which a machine, esp. a computer, is in operation.

up to date ▸*adj.* incorporating the latest developments and trends: *a modern, up-to-date hospital.* ■ incorporating or aware of the latest information: *the book will keep you up to date.*

up-to-the-min·ute ▸*adj.* incorporating the very latest information or developments: *an up-to-the-minute news broadcast.*

up·town ▸*adj.* /ˌəpˈtoun/ of, in, or characteristic of the residential area of a city or town. ■ of or characteristic of an affluent area or people: *I don't pay uptown prices.*

▸*adv.* /ˌəpˈtoun/ in or into such an area.

▸*n.* /ˈəpˌtoun/ a residential area in a town or city. —**up·town·er** /ˌəpˈtounər/ *n.*

up·trend /ˈəpˌtrend/ ▸*n.* an upward tendency.

up·turn ▸*n.* /ˈəpˌtərn/ an improvement or upward trend, esp. in economic conditions or someone's fortunes: *an upturn in the economy.*

▸*v.* /ˈəpˌtərn; ˌəpˈtərn/ [*trans.*] [usu. as *adj.*] (**upturned**) turn (something) upward or upside down: *a sea of upturned faces.*

uPVC ▸*abbr.* unplasticized polyvinyl chloride, a rigid, chemically resistant form of PVC used for piping, window frames, and other structures.

up·ward /ˈəpwərd/ ▸*adv.* (also **up·wards**) toward a higher place, point, or level: *she peered upward at the sky.*

▸*adj.* moving, pointing, or leading to a higher place, point, or level: *an upward trend in sales.* ▷Old English *upweard(es)* (see UP, -WARD). —**up·ward·ly** *adv.*

▸*PHRASE* □ **upwards** (or **upward**) **of** more than: *upwards of 3,500 copies | Gooden can throw the ball at upward of 95 miles per hour.*

up·ward·ly mo·bile /ˈəpwərdlē/ ▸*adj.* moving to a higher social class; acquiring wealth and status. —**up·ward mo·bil·i·ty** *n.*

up·weight /ˈəpˌwāt/ ▸*v.* [*trans.*] **1** give increased importance, rank or weighting to: *some advertisers upweighted TV, while others upweighted press.* **2** *Finance* increase the proportion of (an asset or asset class) in a portfolio or fund: *an opportunity to upweight equities where feasible within your risk profile.*

up·well·ing /ˌəpˈweliNG/ ▸*n.* a rising of seawater, magma, or other liquid.

▸*adj.* (esp. of emotion) building up or gathering strength: *upwelling grief.*

up·wind /ˌəpˈwind/ ▸*adv.* & *adj.* against the direction of the wind: [as *adv.*] *you learn how to sail upwind* | [as *adj.*] *the upwind wing tip.*

Ur /ər; o͝or/ an ancient Sumerian city, formerly on the Euphrates River, in southern Iraq. One of the oldest cities in Mesopotamia, dating from the 4th millennium BC, it reached its zenith in the late 3rd millennium BC.

ur- ▸*comb. form* primitive; original; earliest: *urtext.* ▷from German.

u·ra·cil /ˈyo͝orəˌsil/ ▸*n.* *Biochemistry* a compound found in living tissue as a constituent base of RNA. In DNA its place is taken by thymine. • A pyrimidine derivative; chem. formula: $C_4H_4N_2O_2$. ▷late 19th cent.: from *ur(ea)* + *ac(etic)* + -IL.

u·rae·mi·a ▸*n.* British spelling of UREMIA.

u·rae·us /yo͝oˈrēəs/ ▸*n.* (*pl.* **u·rae·i** /yo͝oˈrēˌī; -ˈrēˌē/) a representation of a sacred serpent as an emblem of supreme power, worn on the headdresses of ancient Egyptian deities and sovereigns. ▷mid 19th cent.: modern Latin, from Greek *ouraios*, representing the Egyptian word for 'cobra.'

U·ral-Al·ta·ic /ˈyo͝orəl alˈtāik/ ▸*adj.* of, relating to, or denoting a hypothetical language group formerly proposed to include both the Uralic and the Altaic languages.

U·ral·ic /yo͝oˈralik/ ▸*adj.* **1** of, relating to, or denoting a family of languages spoken from northern Scandinavia to western Siberia, comprising the Finno-Ugric and Samoyedic groups. **2** of or relating to the Ural Mountains or the surrounding areas.

▸*n.* the Uralic languages collectively.

U·ral Moun·tains /ˈyo͝orəl/ (also **the U·rals**) a mountain range in northern Russia that extends 1,000 miles (1,600 km) south from the Arctic Ocean to the Aral Sea. It forms part of the conventional boundary between Europe and Asia.

U·ral Riv·er /ˈyo͝orəl/ a river, 1,575 miles (2,534 km) long, that rises at the southern end of the Ural Mountains in western Russia and flows through western Kazakhstan to the Caspian Sea at Atyraū.

U·ra·ni·a /yo͝oˈrānēə/ *Greek & Roman Mythology* the Muse of astronomy. ▷Greek, literally 'heavenly (female).'

U·ra·ni·an /yo͝oˈrānēən/ ▸*adj.* **1** of or relating to the planet Uranus. **2** *poetic/literary* homosexual. [late 19th cent.: with allusion to a reference to Aphrodite in Plato's *Symposium.*]

▸*n.* a homosexual.

u·ran·i·nite /yo͝oˈrānəˌnīt; -ˈranə-/ ▸*n.* a black, gray, or brown mineral that consists mainly of uranium dioxide and is the chief ore of uranium. PITCHBLENDE is a variety of uraninite. ▷late 19th cent.: from URANO-[2] + -ITE[1].

u·ra·ni·um /yo͝oˈrānēəm/ ▸*n.* the chemical element of atomic number 92, a gray, dense radioactive metal used as a fuel in nuclear reactors. (Symbol: **U**)

Uranium is a chemically reactive metal belonging to the actinide series. Becquerel discovered radioactivity in uranium in 1896, and its capacity to undergo fission led to its use as a source of energy, though the fissile isotope, uranium-235, has to be separated from the more common uranium-238 before it can be used in nuclear weapons. The atom bomb exploded over Hiroshima in 1945 contained uranium-235.

▷late 18th cent.: modern Latin, from URANUS + -IUM.

urano-[1] ▸*comb. form* relating to the heavens: *uranography.* ▷from Greek *ouranos* 'heavens, sky.'

urano-[2] ▸*comb. form* representing URANIUM.

u·ra·nog·ra·phy /ˌyo͝orəˈnägrəfē/ ▸*n.* *archaic* the branch of astronomy concerned with describing and mapping the heavens. —**u·ra·nog·ra·pher** *n.* —**u·ra·no·graph·ic** /-nəˈgrafik/ *adj.*

U·ran·us /ˈyo͝orənəs; yo͝oˈrā-/ **1** *Greek Mythology* a personification of heaven or the sky, the most ancient of the Greek gods and first ruler of the universe. He was overthrown and castrated by his son Cronus. **2** *Astronomy* a distant planet of the solar system, seventh in order from the sun, discovered by William Herschel in 1781.

Uranus orbits between Jupiter and Neptune at an average distance of 2,870 million km from the sun. It has an equatorial diameter of 50,800 km, and is one of the gas giants. The planet is bluish-green in color, having an upper atmosphere consisting almost entirely of hydrogen and helium. There are at least seventeen satellites, the largest of which are Oberon and Titania, and a faint ring system.

u·ra·nyl /ˈyo͝orəˌnil/ ▸*n.* [as *adj.*] *Chemistry* the cation UO_2^{2+}, present in some compounds of uranium: *uranyl acetate.* ▷mid 19th cent.: from URANIUM + -YL.

U·rar·ti·an /o͝oˈrärtēən/ ▸*adj.* of or relating to the ancient kingdom of Urartu in eastern Anatolia (*c.*1500–585 BC).

▸*n.* **1** a native or inhabitant of ancient Urartu. **2** the language of Urartu, related to Hurrian.

u·rate /ˈyo͝orˌāt/ ▸*n.* a salt or ester of uric acid.

ur·ban /ˈərbən/ ▸*adj.* in, relating to, or characteristic of a city or town: *the urban population.* ▷early 17th cent.: from Latin *urbanus*, from *urbs, urb-* 'city.'

Ur·ban·a /ərˈbanə/ an industrial and commercial city in east central Illinois; pop. 36,344.

Ur·ban·dale /ˈərbənˌdāl/ a city in south central Iowa, a northwestern suburb of Des Moines; pop. 29,072.

ur·bane /ˌərˈbān/ ▸*adj.* (of a person, esp. a man) suave, courteous, and refined in manner. ▷mid 16th cent. (in the sense 'urban'): from French *urbain* or Latin *urbanus* (see URBAN). —**ur·bane·ly** *adv.*

THE RIGHT WORD **cosmopolitan, genteel, sophisticated, suave, urbane**

In his long career as a film star, Cary Grant was known for playing **urbane, sophisticated** roles. *Urbane* in this context suggests the social poise and polished manner of someone who is well-traveled and well-bred, while *sophisticated* means worldly-wise as opposed to naive (*a sophisticated young girl who had spent her childhood in Paris and London*).

Cosmopolitan describes someone who is at home anywhere in the world and is free from provincial attitudes (*a cosmopolitan man who could charm women of all ages and nationalities*), while **suave** suggests the gracious social behavior of *urbane* combined with a certain glibness or superficial politeness (*she was taken in by his expensive clothes and suave manner*).

At one time **genteel** meant well-bred or refined, but nowadays it has connotations of self-consciousness or pretentiousness (*too genteel to drink wine from a juice glass*).

ur·ban for·est ▸*n.* a densely wooded area located in a city.

ur·ban·ism /ˈərbəˌnizəm/ ▸*n.* **1** the lifestyle of city dwellers. **2** urbanization.

ur·ban·ist /ˈərbənist/ ▸*n.* an advocate of or expert in city planning.

ur·ban·ite /ˈərbəˌnīt/ ▸*n.* *informal* a person who lives in a city or town.

ur·ban·i·ty /ˌərˈbanitē/ ▸*n.* **1** suavity, courteousness, and refinement of manner. **2** urban life. ▷mid 16th cent.: from French *urbanité* or Latin *urbanitas*, from *urbanus* 'belonging to the city' (see URBAN).

ur·ban·ize /ˈərbəˌnīz/ ▸*v.* make or become urban in character: [*trans.*] *once an agrarian society, the island has recently been urbanized* | [as *adj.*] (**urbanized**) *urbanized areas.* —**ur·ban·i·za·tion** /ˌərbənəˈzāSHən/ *n.*

ur·ban leg·end (also *chiefly Brit.* **ur·ban myth**) ▸*n.* a humorous or horrific story or piece of information circulated as though true, esp. one purporting to involve someone vaguely related or known to the teller; for example, a rumor that pet alligators flushed down toilets are alive in the sewers.

ur·ban re·new·al ▸*n.* the redevelopment of areas within a large city, typically involving the clearance of slums.

ur·ban sprawl ▸*n.* the uncontrolled expansion of urban areas.

urbs /ərbz/ ▸*n.* *chiefly poetic/literary* the city, esp. as a symbol of harsh or busy modern life. ▷Latin.

URC ▸*abbr.* United Reformed Church.

ur·chin /ˈərCHin/ ▸*n.* **1** a mischievous young child, esp. one who is poorly or raggedly dressed. ■ *archaic* a goblin. **2** short for SEA URCHIN. ■ *Brit., chiefly dialect* a hedgehog. ▷Middle English *hirchon, urchon* 'hedgehog,' from Old Northern French *herichon*, based on Latin *hericius* 'hedgehog.'

Ur·du /ˈo͝ordo͞o; ˈər-/ ▸*n.* a form of Hindustani written in Persian script, with many loanwords from Persian and Arabic. It is an official language of Pakistan and is widely used in India and elsewhere. ▷from Persian *(zabān-i-)urdū* '(language of the) camp' (because it developed after the Muslim invasions as a lingua franca between the occupying armies and the local people of the region around Delhi), *urdū* being from Turkic *ordu* (see HORDE).

-ure ▸*suffix* forming nouns: **1** denoting an action, process, or result: *censure* | *closure* | *scripture.* **2** denoting an office or function: *judicature.* **3** denoting a collective: *legislature.* ▷from Old French *-ure*, from Latin *-ura.*

u·re·a /yo͝oˈrēə/ ▸*n.* *Biochemistry* a colorless crystalline compound that is the main nitrogenous breakdown product of protein metabolism in mammals and is excreted in urine. • Chem. formula: $CO(NH_2)_2$. ▷early 19th cent.: modern Latin, from French *urée*, from Greek *ouron* 'urine.'

u·re·a·plas·ma /yo͝oˌrēəˈplazmə/ ▸*n.* a small bacterium related to the mycoplasmas, characterized by the ability to metabolize urea. • Genus *Ureaplasma*, order Mycoplasmatales.

u·re·ase /ˈyo͝orēˌās; -ˌāz/ ▸*n.* a naturally occurring enzyme that hydrolyzes urea into ammonium carbonate.

u·re·ide /ˈyo͝orēˌīd; -id/ ▸*n.* *Chemistry* any of a group of compounds that are acyl derivatives of urea.

u·re·mi·a /yo͝oˈrēmēə/ (*Brit.* **u·rae·mi·a**) ▸*n.* *Medicine* a raised level in the blood of urea and other nitrogenous waste compounds that are normally eliminated by the kidneys. ▷mid 19th cent.: modern Latin, from Greek *ouron* 'urine' + *haima* 'blood.' —**u·re·mic** /yo͞o'rēmik/ *adj.*

u·re·ter /'yo͞oritər; yo͞o'rētər/ ▶*n. Anatomy & Zoology* the duct by which urine passes from the kidney to the bladder or cloaca. ▷late 16th cent.: from French *uretÃ[die]re* or modern Latin *ureter*, from Greek *ourētēr*, from *ourein* 'urinate.' —**u·re·ter·al** /yo͞o'rētərəl/ *adj.* —**u·re·ter·ic** /ˌyo͞ori'terik/ *adj.*

u·re·thane /'yo͞orəˌTHān/ ▶*n. Chemistry* a synthetic crystalline compound used in making pesticides and fungicides, and formerly as an anesthetic. • Alternative name: **ethyl carbamate**; chem. formula: $CO(NH_2)OC_2H_5$. ■ short for POLYURETHANE. ▷mid 19th cent.: from French *uréthane* (see UREA, ETHANE).

u·re·thra /yo͞o'rēTHrə/ ▶*n. Anatomy & Zoology* the duct by which urine is conveyed out of the body from the bladder, and which in male vertebrates also conveys semen. ▷mid 17th cent.: from late Latin, from Greek *ourēthra*, from *ourein* 'urinate.' —**u·re·thral** *adj.*

u·re·thri·tis /ˌyo͞orə'THrītis/ ▶*n. Medicine* inflammation of the urethra.

U·rey /'yo͞orē/, Harold Clayton (1893–1981), U.S. chemist. He discovered deuterium in 1932, pioneered the use of isotope labeling, and served as director of the Manhattan Project at Columbia University. Nobel Prize for Chemistry (1934).

Ur·ga /'o͝orgə/ former name (until 1924) of **ULAANBAATAR**.

urge /ərj/ ▶*v.* [*trans.* usu. *infinitive*] try earnestly or persistently to persuade (someone) to do something: *he urged her to come and stay with us* | [with *direct speech*] *"Try to relax," she urged.* ■ recommend or advocate (something) strongly: *I urge caution in interpreting these results* | [with *clause*] *they are urging that more treatment facilities be provided.* ■ [*trans.*] encourage (a person or animal) to move more quickly or in a particular direction: *drawing up outside the house, he urged her inside.* ■ (**urge someone on**) encourage someone to continue or succeed in something: *he could hear her voice urging him on.*
▶*n.* a strong desire or impulse: *the urge for revenge.* ▷mid 16th cent.: from Latin *urgere* 'press, drive.'

ur·gent /'ərjənt/ ▶*adj.* (of a state or situation) requiring immediate action or attention: *the situation is far more urgent than politicians are admitting.* See note at CRUCIAL. ■ (of action or an event) done or arranged in response to such a situation: *she needs urgent treatment.* ■ (of a person or their manner) earnest and persistent in response to such a situation: *an urgent whisper.* ▷late 15th cent.: from Old French, from Latin *urgent-* 'pressing, driving,' from the verb *urgere* (see URGE). —**ur·gen·cy** *n.* —**ur·gent·ly** *adv.*

-uria ▶*comb. form* in nouns denoting that a substance is present in the urine, esp. in excess: *glycosuria.* ▷modern Latin, from Greek *-ouria*, from *ouron* 'urine.'

U·ri·ah /yo͞o'rīə/ (in the Bible) a Hittite officer in David's army, whom David, desiring his wife Bathsheba, caused to be killed in battle (2 Sam. 11).

ur·i·al /'o͝orēəl/ ▶*n.* (*pl.* same) a wild sheep with long legs and relatively small horns, native to central Asia. • *Ovis vignei*, family Bovidae. ▷mid 19th cent.: from Punjabi *ūrial.*

u·ric ac·id /'yo͞orik/ ▶*n. Biochemistry* an almost insoluble compound which is a breakdown product of nitrogenous metabolism. It is the main excretory product in birds, reptiles, and insects. • A bicyclic acid derived from purine; chem. formula: $C_5H_4N_4O_3$. ▷early 19th cent.: *uric* from French *urique*, from *urine* (see URINE). —**u·rate** /'yo͝orˌāt/ *n.*

u·ri·dine /'yo͞orəˌdēn; -dn/ ▶*n. Biochemistry* a compound formed by partial hydrolysis of RNA. It is a nucleoside containing uracil linked to ribose. ▷early 20th cent.: from *ur(acil)* + -IDE + -INE[4].

U·rim and Thum·mim /'(y)o͝orim; o͞o'rēm and 'THəmim; to͞o'mēm/ ▶*plural n. historical* two objects of a now unknown nature, possibly used for divination, worn on the breastplate of a Jewish high priest. ▷from Hebrew.

u·ri·nal /'yo͞orənl/ ▶*n.* a bowl or other receptacle, typically attached to a wall in a public toilet, into which men may urinate. ▷Middle English (denoting a glass container for the medical inspection of urine): via Old French from Latin *urinal*, from *urina* (see URINE).

u·ri·nal·y·sis /ˌyo͞orə'naləsis/ ▶*n.* (*pl.* **-ses** /-ˌsēz/) *Medicine* analysis of urine by physical, chemical, and microscopical means to test for the presence of disease, drugs, etc.

u·ri·nar·y /'yo͞orəˌnerē/ ▶*adj.* of or relating to urine. ■ of, relating to, or denoting the system of organs, structures, and ducts by which urine is produced and discharged, in mammals comprising the kidneys, ureters, bladder, and urethra.

u·ri·nate /'yo͞orəˌnāt/ ▶*v.* [*intrans.*] discharge urine; pass water. ▷late 16th cent.: from medieval Latin *urinat-* 'urinated,' from the verb *urinare.* —**u·ri·na·tion** /ˌyo͞orə'nāSHən/ *n.*

u·rine /'yo͞orən/ ▶*n.* a watery, typically yellowish fluid stored in the bladder and discharged through the urethra. It is one of the body's chief means of eliminating excess water and salt and also contains nitrogen compounds such as urea and other waste substances removed from the blood by the kidneys. ▷Middle English: via Old French from Latin *urina.*

u·ri·nif·er·ous tu·bule /ˌyo͞orə'nif(ə)rəs 't(y)o͞oˌbyo͞ol/ ▶*n.* another term for KIDNEY TUBULE.

Ur·is /'yo͞orəs/, Leon (Marcus) (1924–2003) U.S. writer. His works include *Battle Cry* (1953), *Exodus* (1958), *QB VII* (1970), *Trinity* (1976), *The Haj* (1984), and *Redemption* (1995).

URL ▶*abbr. Computing* uniform (or universal) resource locator, the address of a World Wide Web page.

urn /ərn/ ▶*n.* **1** a tall, rounded vase with a base, and often a stem, esp. one used for storing the ashes of a cremated person. **2** a large metal container with a tap, in which tea or coffee is made and kept hot, or water for making such drinks is boiled: *a tea urn.*
▶*v.* [*trans.*] *archaic* place (something) in an urn. ▷late Middle English: from Latin *urna*; related to *urceus* 'pitcher.'

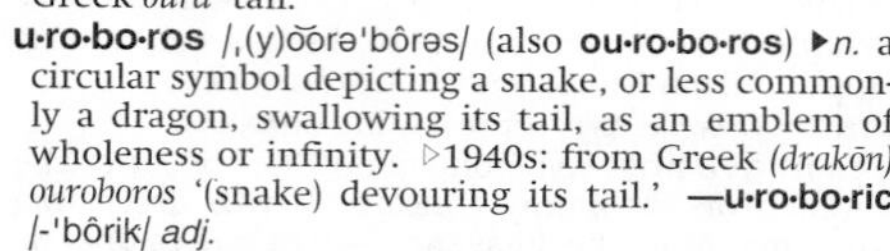

urn 1

uro-[1] ▶*comb. form* of or relating to urine or the urinary organs: *urogenital.* ▷from Greek *ouron* 'urine.'

uro-[2] ▶*comb. form Zoology* relating to a tail or the caudal region: *urodele.* ▷from Greek *oura* 'tail.'

u·ro·bo·ros /ˌ(y)o͞orə'bôrəs/ (also **ou·ro·bo·ros**) ▶*n.* a circular symbol depicting a snake, or less commonly a dragon, swallowing its tail, as an emblem of wholeness or infinity. ▷1940s: from Greek *(drakōn) ouroboros* '(snake) devouring its tail.' —**u·ro·bo·ric** /-'bôrik/ *adj.*

Ur·o·chor·da·ta /ˌyo͞orəkôr'dätə; -'dātə/ *Zoology* a group of chordate animals that comprises the tunicates. • Subphylum Urochordata, phylum Chordata. ▷modern Latin (plural), from URO-[2] 'tail' + CHORDATA. —**u·ro·chor·date** /-'kôrdət; -ˌdāt/ *n. & adj.*

Ur·o·de·la /ˌyo͞orə'dēlə/ *Zoology* an order of amphibians that comprises the newts and salamanders, which retain the tail as adults. Also called **CAUDATA**. ▷modern Latin (plural), from URO-[2] 'tail' + Greek *dēlos* 'evident.' —**u·ro·dele** /'yo͞orəˌdēl/ *n. & adj.*

ur·o·dy·nam·ics /ˌyo͞orədī'namiks/ ▶*plural n.* [treated as *sing.*] *Medicine* the diagnostic study of pressure in the bladder, in treating incontinence. —**u·ro·dy·nam·ic** *adj.*

u·ro·gen·i·tal /ˌyo͞orō'jenətl; ˌyo͞orə-/ ▶*adj.* of, relating to, or denoting both the urinary and genital organs.

u·rog·ra·phy /yo͞o'rägrəfē/ ▶*n.* another term for PYELOGRAPHY. —**u·ro·gram** /'yo͞orəˌgram/ *n.*

u·ro·ki·nase /ˌyo͞orō'kīˌnās; -ˌnāz/ ▶*n. Biochemistry* an enzyme produced in the kidneys that promotes the conversion of plasminogen to plasmin and can be used to dissolve blood clots.

u·ro·lag·nia /ˌyo͞orō'lagnēə/ ▶*n.* a tendency to derive sexual pleasure from the sight or thought of urination. Also called UROPHILIA. ▷early 20th cent.: from URO-[1] 'of urine' + Greek *lagneia* 'lust.'

u·ro·li·thi·a·sis /ˌyo͞orələ'THīəsis/ ▶*n. Medicine* the formation of stony concretions in the bladder or urinary tract.

u·rol·o·gy /yo͞o'räləjē/ ▶*n.* the branch of medicine and physiology concerned with the function and disorders of the urinary system. —**u·ro·log·ic** /ˌyo͞orə'läjik/ *adj.* —**u·ro·log·i·cal** *adj.* —**u·rol·o·gist** /-jist/ *n.*

u·ron·ic ac·id /yo͞o'ränik/ ▶*n. Biochemistry* any of a class of compounds that are derived from sugars by oxidizing a $-CH_2OH$ group to an acid group ($-COOH$). ▷1920s: *uronic* from URO-[1] 'urine' + -IC, with the insertion of *-n-*.

u·ro·phil·i·a /ˌyo͞orō'filēə/ ▶*n.* another term for UROLAGNIA.

u·ro·pod /'yo͞orəˌpäd/ ▶*n. Zoology* the sixth and last pair of abdominal appendages of lobsters and related crustaceans, forming part of the tail fan. ▷late 19th cent.: from URO-[2] 'tail' + Greek *pous, pod-* 'pod.'

u·ro·pyg·i·al gland /ˌyo͞orə'pijēəl/ ▶*n.* another term for PREEN GLAND.

u·ro·pyg·i·um /ˌyo͞orə'pijēəm/ ▶*n. Zoology* the rump of a bird, supporting the tail feathers. ▷late 18th cent.: via medieval Latin from Greek *ouropugion.* —**u·ro·pyg·i·al** *adj.*

u·ros·co·py /yo͞o'räskəpē/ ▶*n. historical Medicine* the diagnostic examination of urine by simple inspection.

u·ro·style /'yo͞orəˌstīl/ ▶*n. Zoology* a long bone formed from fused vertebrae at the base of the vertebral column in some lower vertebrates, esp. frogs and toads.

Ur·sa Ma·jor /'ərsə 'mājər/ *Astronomy* one of the largest and most prominent northern constellations (the Great Bear). The seven brightest stars form a familiar asterism known by various names (esp. the Big Dipper and the Plow) and include the Pointers. ■ [as *genitive*] (**Ur·sae Ma·jor·is** /'ərsē mə'jôris/) used with a preceding letter or numeral to designate a star in this constellation: *the star Delta Ursae Majoris.* ▷Latin, 'Big Bear,' from the story in Greek mythology that the nymph Callisto was turned into a bear and placed as a constellation in the heavens by Zeus.

Ur·sa Mi·nor /'ərsə 'mīnər/ *Astronomy* a northern constellation (the Little Bear) that contains the north celestial pole and the polar star Polaris. The brightest stars form a shape that is also known as the Little Dipper. ■ [as *genitive*] (**Ur·sae Mi·nor·is** /'ərsē mi'nôris/) used with a preceding letter or numeral to designate a star in this constellation: *the star Alpha Ursae Minoris.* ▷Latin 'Little Bear.'

ur·sine /'ərˌsin; -ˌsēn/ ▶*adj.* of, relating to, or resembling bears. ▷mid 16th cent.: from Latin *ursinus*, from *ursus* 'bear.'

Ur·su·la, St. /'ərs(y)ələ/ a legendary British saint and martyr, said to have been put to death with 11,000 virgins after being captured by Huns near Cologne while on a pilgrimage.

Ur·su·line /'ərs(y)əlin; -ˌlīn; -ˌlēn/ ▶*n.* a nun of an order founded by St. Angela Merici (1470–1540) at Brescia in 1535 for nursing the sick and teaching girls.
▶*adj.* of or relating to this order. ▷from St. *Ursula*, the founder's patron saint (see **URSULA, ST.**), + -INE[1].

ur·text /'o͝orˌtekst/ ▶*n.* (*pl.* **-tex·te** /-ˌtekstə/) an original or the earliest version of a text, to which later versions can be compared. ▷from German.

ur·ti·car·i·a /ˌərti'ke(ə)rēə/ ▶*n. Medicine* a rash of round, red welts on the skin that itch intensely, sometimes with dangerous swelling, caused by an allergic reaction, typically to specific foods. Also called NETTLERASH or HIVES. ▷late 18th cent.: modern Latin, from Latin *urtica* 'nettle,' from *urere* 'to burn.'

ur·ti·cate /'ərtiˌkāt/ ▶*v.* [*intrans.*] cause a stinging or prickling sensation like that given by a nettle: [as *adj.*] (**urticating**) *the urticating hairs.* ▷mid 19th cent.: from medieval Latin *urticat-* 'stung,' from the verb *urticare*, from Latin *urtica* (see URTICARIA). —**ur·ti·ca·tion** /ˌərti'kāSHən/ *n.*

U·ru·guay /'(y)o͝orəˌgwī; -ˌgwā/ a country on the Atlantic coast of South America south of Brazil; pop. 3,399,000 (est. 1991); official language, Spanish; capital, Montevideo. —**U·ru·guay·an** /ˌ(y)o͝orə'gwīən; -'gwā-/ *adj. & n.*

Uruguay was liberated from Spanish colonial rule in 1825, and in the early 20th century was molded into South America's first welfare state. Civil unrest beginning in the 1960s, and particularly fighting against the Marxist Tupamaro guerrillas, led to a period of military rule, but civilian government was restored in 1985.

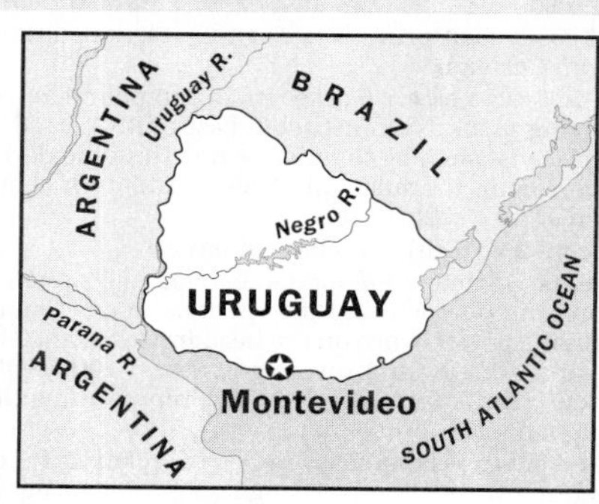

U

U·ruk /ˈoŏrŏŏk/ an ancient city in southern Mesopotamia, northwest of Ur, one of the greatest cities of Sumer. Built in the 5th millennium BC, it is associated with the hero Gilgamesh. Arabic name WARKA; biblical name ERECH.

U·rum·qi /ŏŏˈrŏŏmˈCHē/ (also **U·rum·chi**) the capital of Xinjiang autonomous region in northwestern China; pop. 1,110,000. Former name (until 1954) TIHWA.

u·rus /ˈyŏŏrəs/ ▸*n.* another term for AUROCHS. ▷early 17th cent.: from Latin, from Greek *ouros*.

u·ru·shi·ol /(y)ŏŏˈrŏŏshē,ôl; -,ōl; -,äl/ ▸*n. Biochemistry* an oily liquid that is the main constituent of Japanese lacquer and is responsible for the irritant properties of poison ivy and other plants. It consists of a mixture of catechol derivatives. ▷early 20th cent.: from Japanese *urushi* 'Japanese lacquer' + -OL.

US ▸*abbr.* ■ United States. ■ *Brit.* undersecretary. ■ *Brit., informal* unserviceable; useless.

us /əs/ ▸*pron.* [*first person plural*] **1** used by a speaker to refer to himself or herself and one or more other people as the object of a verb or preposition: *let us know | we asked him to come with us | both of* **us**. Compare with WE. ■ used after the verb "to be" and after "than" or "as": *it's us or them | they are richer than us.* ■ *informal* to or for ourselves: *we got us some good hunting.* **2** *informal* me: *give us a kiss.* ▷Old English *ūs*, accusative and dative of WE, of Germanic origin; related to Dutch *ons* and German *uns*.

▸*PHRASES* □ **one of us** a person recognized as an accepted member of a particular group, typically one that is exclusive in some way. □ **us and them** (or **them and us**) expressing a sense of division within a group of people: *negotiations were hampered by an "us and them" attitude between management and unions.*

> *USAGE* Is it correct to say *they are richer than* **us**, or is it better to say *they are richer than* **we (are)**? See usage at PERSONAL PRONOUN and THAN.

U.S. ▸*abbr.* United States.

USA ▸*abbr.* ■ United States of America. ■ United States Army.

U.S.A. ▸*abbr.* ■ United States of America. ■ United States Army.

us·a·ble /ˈyōōzəbəl/ (also **use·a·ble**) ▸*adj.* able or fit to be used: *usable information.* —**us·a·bil·i·ty** /,yōōzəˈbilətē/ *n.*

U.S.A.F. (also **USAF**) ▸*abbr.* United States Air Force.

us·age /ˈyōōsij; -zij/ ▸*n.* the action of using something or the fact of being used: *a survey of water usage | the usage of equipment.* ■ the way in which a word or phrase is normally and correctly used. ■ habitual or customary practice, esp. as creating a right, obligation, or standard. ▷Middle English (in the sense 'customary practice'): from Old French, from *us* 'a use' (see USE).

> *USAGE* **Usage** means 'manner of use, practice,' while **use** means 'the act of employing.' In discussions of writing, **usage** is the term for normal or prescribed practice: *standard usage calls for a plural.* In describing particular examples, however, employ **use**: *the use of the plural with this noun is incorrect.*

us·ance /ˈyōōzəns/ ▸*n. archaic* **1** another term for USAGE. **2** the time allowed for the payment of foreign bills of exchange, according to law or commercial practice. ▷late Middle English: from Old French, from the base of the verb *user* 'to use.'

USB ▸*abbr. Computing* universal serial bus, a connection technology for attaching peripheral devices to a computer, providing fast data exchange.

USB flash drive ▸*n. Computing* an external flash drive, small enough to carry on a key ring, that can be used with any computer with a USB port.

USC ▸*abbr. Law* United States Code.

U.S.C.G. (also **USCG**) ▸*abbr.* United States Coast Guard.

USD ▸*abbr.* United States dollar.

USDA (also **U.S.D.A.**) ▸*abbr.* United States Department of Agriculture.

use ▸*v.* **1** /yōōz/ [*trans.*] take, hold, or deploy (something) as a means of accomplishing a purpose or achieving a result; employ: *she used her key to open the front door | the poem uses simple language.* ■ take or consume (an amount) from a limited supply of something: *we have used all the available funds.* ■ exploit (a person or situation) for one's own advantage: *I couldn't help feeling that she was using me.* ■ [*trans.*] treat (someone) in a particular way: *use your troops well and they will not let you down.* ■ apply (a name or title) to oneself: *she still used her maiden name professionally.* ■ (**one could use**) *informal* one would like or benefit from: *I could use another cup of coffee.* ■ *informal* take (an illegal drug): *they were using heroin daily | [intrans.] had she been using again?* **2** /yōōst/ [in *past*] (**used to**) describing an action or state of affairs that was done repeatedly or existed for a period in the past: *this road used to be a dirt track | I used to give him lifts home.* **3** /yōōst/ (**be/get used to**) be or become familiar with someone or something through experience: *she was used to getting what she wanted | he's weird, but you just have to get used to him.*

▸*phrasal v.* □ **use something up** consume or expend the whole of something: *the money was soon used up.* ■ find a purpose for something that is left over: *I might use up all my odd scraps of wool to make a scarf.* ■ (**be used up**) *informal* (of a person) be worn out, esp. with overwork: *she was tired and used up.*

▸*n.* /yōōs/ the action of using something or the state of being used for some purpose: *a member of staff is present when the pool is* **in use** *| theater owners were charging too much for* **the use of** *their venues.* ■ the ability or power to exercise or manipulate something, esp. one's mind or body: *the horse lost* **the use of** *his hind legs.* ■ a purpose for or way in which something can be used: *the herb has various culinary uses.* ■ the value or advantage of something: *it was no use trying to persuade her | what's the use of crying?* ■ *historical Law* the benefit or profit of lands, esp. lands that are in the possession of another who holds them solely for the beneficiary. ■ the characteristic ritual and liturgy of a church or diocese. ■ the action of taking or habitual consumption of a drug. ▷Middle English: the noun from Old French *us*, from Latin *usus*, from *uti* 'to use'; the verb from Old French *user*, based on Latin *uti*.

▸*PHRASES* □ **have its** (or **one's**) **uses** *informal* be useful on certain occasions or in certain respects. □ **have no use for** be unable to find a purpose for; have no need for: *he had no use for a single glove.* ■ *informal* dislike or be impatient with. □ **make use of** use for a purpose.■ benefit from: *they were educated enough to make use of further training.* □ **use and wont** *formal* established custom. □ **use someone's name** quote someone as an authority or reference.

> *USAGE* 1 The construction **used to** is standard, but difficulties arise with the formation of negatives and questions. Traditionally, **used to** behaves as a modal verb, so that questions and negatives are formed without the auxiliary verb **do**, as in *it* **used not to** *be like that* and **used** *she* **to** *come here?* In modern English, this question form is now regarded as very formal or old-fashioned and the use with **do** is broadly accepted as standard, as in **did** *she* **use to** *come here?* Negative constructions with **do**, on the other hand (as in *it* **didn't use to** *be like that*), although common, are informal and are not generally accepted.
>
> 2 There is sometimes confusion over whether to use the form **used to** or **use to**, which has arisen largely because the pronunciation is the same in both cases. Except in negatives and questions, the correct form is **used to**: *we* **used to** *go to the movies all the time* (not *we* **use to** *go to the movies*). However, in negatives and questions using the auxiliary verb **do**, the correct form is **use to**, because the form of the verb required is the infinitive: *I* **didn't use to** *like mushrooms* (not *I* **didn't used to** *like mushrooms*). See also **usage** at USAGE and UTILIZE.

use·a·ble ▸*adj.* variant spelling of USABLE.

used /yōōzd/ ▸*adj.* **1** having already been used: *scrawling on the back of a used envelope.* **2** secondhand: *a used car.*

use·ful /ˈyōōsfəl/ ▸*adj.* able to be used for a practical purpose or in several ways: *aspirin is useful for headaches.* —**use·ful·ly** *adv.* —**use·ful·ness** *n.*

▸*PHRASE* □ **make oneself useful** do something that is of some value or benefit to someone: *make yourself useful—get Jenny a drink.*

use·ful load ▸*n.* the load able to be carried by an aircraft in addition to its own weight.

use·less /ˈyōōsləs/ ▸*adj.* not fulfilling or not expected to achieve the intended purpose or desired outcome: *a piece of useless knowledge | we tried to pacify him, but it was useless.* ■ *informal* having no ability or skill in a specified activity or area: *he was useless at football.* —**use·less·ly** *adv.* —**use·less·ness** *n.*

Use·net /ˈyōōz,net/ (also **USENET**) *Computing* an Internet service consisting of thousands of newsgroups.

us·er /ˈyōōzər/ ▸*n.* **1** a person who uses or operates something, esp. a computer or other machine. ■ a person who takes illegal drugs; a drug user: *the drug causes long-term brain damage in users | a heroin user.* ■ a person who manipulates others for their own gain: *he was a gifted user of other people.* **2** *Law* the continued use or enjoyment of a right.

us·er-de·fin·a·ble ▸*adj. Computing* having a function or meaning that can be specified and varied by a user.

us·er-friend·ly ▸*adj.* (of a machine or system) easy to use or understand: *the search software is user-friendly.* —**us·er-friend·li·ness** *n.*

us·er-hos·tile ▸*adj.* (of a machine or system) difficult to use or understand.

us·er in·ter·face ▸*n. Computing* the means by which the user and a computer system interact, in particular the use of input devices and software.

us·er·name /ˈyōōzər,nām/ ▸*n. Computing* an identification used by a person with access to a computer network.

us·er-o·ri·ent·ed ▸*adj.* (of a machine or system) designed primarily for the user's convenience.

ush·er /ˈəSHər/ ▸*n.* **1** a person who shows people to their seats, esp. in a theater or at a wedding. ■ an official in a court whose duties include swearing in jurors and witnesses and keeping order. ■ *Brit.* a person employed to walk before a person of high rank on special occasions. **2** *Brit., archaic* an assistant teacher.

▸*v.* [*trans.*] show or guide (someone) somewhere: *a waiter ushered me to a table.* ■ *figurative* cause or mark the start of (something new): *the railroads* **ushered in** *an era of cheap mass travel.* ▷late Middle English (denoting a doorkeeper): from Anglo-Norman French *usser*, from medieval Latin *ustiarius*, from Latin *ostiarius*, from *ostium* 'door.'

ush·er·ette /,əSHəˈret/ ▸*n.* a woman who shows people to their seats in a theater.

Us·hua·ia /ŏŏˈswīə/ a port in Argentina, in Tierra del Fuego; pop. 11,000. It is the southernmost town in the world.

USIA (also **U.S.I.A.**) ▸*abbr.* United States Information Agency.

Ãœs·kü·dar /,ŏŏskəˈdär/ a city in northwestern Turkey, across from Istanbul on the Bosporus where it joins the Sea of Marmara; pop. 396,000. Former name SCUTARI.

U.S.M.C. (also **USMC**) ▸*abbr.* ■ United States Marine Corps.

U.S.N. (also **USN**) ▸*abbr.* United States Navy.

us·nic ac·id /ˈəsnik/ ▸*n. Biochemistry* a yellow crystalline compound that is present in many lichens and is used as an antibiotic. • A tricyclic phenol; chem. formula: $C_{18}H_{16}O_7$. ▷mid 19th cent.: *usnic* from medieval Latin *usnea* (from Arabic *ushnah* 'moss') + -IC.

USO ▸*abbr.* ■ ultra stable oscillator. ■ United Service Organizations.

U·so·ni·an /yōōˈsōnēən/ ▸*adj.* of or relating to the United States: *the Usonian city.* ■ relating to or denoting the style of buildings designed in the 1930s by Frank Lloyd Wright, characterized by inexpensive construction and flat roofs.

▸*n.* a native or inhabitant of the United States. ■ a house built in the 1930s by Frank Lloyd Wright. ▷early 20th cent.: an acronym from *United States* + *-onian* after *Amazonian, Devonian*, etc.

Us·pa·lla·ta Pass /,ŏŏspäˈyätə; -ˈZHätə/ a pass over the Andes near Santiago in Chile, in southern South America. It links Argentina with Chile.

USPS (also **U.S.P.S.**) ▸*abbr.* ■ United States Postal Service.

us·que·baugh /ˈəskwə,bô; -,bä/ ▸*n. chiefly Irish Scottish* whiskey. ▷late 16th cent.: from Irish and Scottish Gaelic *uisge beatha* 'water of life'; compare with WHISKEY.

U.S.S. (also **USS**) ▸*abbr.* United States Ship, used in the names of ships in the U.S. Navy: *the U.S.S.* Maine *was launched in 1895.*

USSR (also **U.S.S.R.**) *historical* ▸*abbr.* Union of Soviet Socialist Republics.

Ust-A·ba·kan·sko·e /ˈŏŏst ,äbəˈkänskəyə/ former name (until 1931) of ABAKAN.

U·sta·she /ŏŏˈstäSHē/ (also **U·sta·shas** or **U·sta·shi**) ▸*plural n.* [treated as *sing.* or *pl.*] the members of a Croatian extreme nationalist movement that engaged in terrorist activity before World War II and ruled Croatia with Nazi support after Yugoslavia was invaded and divided by the Germans in 1941. ▷from Serbo-Croat *Ustaše* 'rebels.'

U·sti·nov[1] /ˈyoostəˌnôf; -ˌnôv; oōˈstēnəf/ former name (1984–87) of **IZHEVSK**.

U·sti·nov[2] /ˈyoostəˌnôf; -ˌnôv/, Sir Peter (Alexander) (1921–2004), British actor, director, and playwright. He wrote and acted in a number of plays, including *Romanoff and Juliet* (1956). Notable movies: *Spartacus* (1960), *Death on the Nile* (1978), and *Lorenzo's Oil* (1992).

usu. ▸*abbr.* ■ usual; usually.

u·su·al /ˈyoozhooəl/ ▸*adj.* habitually or typically occurring or done; customary: *he carried out his usual evening routine | their room was a shambles* **as usual**. See note at **NORMAL**.

▸*n.* **(the/one's usual)** *informal* the drink someone habitually orders or prefers. ■ the thing that is typically done or present: *it's a nice change from the usual.* ▷late Middle English: from Old French, or from late Latin *usualis*, from Latin *usus* 'a use' (see **USE**). **—u·su·al·ly** *adv. March usually has the heaviest rainfall.* **—u·su·al·ness** *n.*

u·su·fruct /ˈyoozəˌfrəkt; -sə-/ ▸*n. Roman Law* the right to enjoy the use and advantages of another's property short of the destruction or waste of its substance. ▷early 17th cent.: from medieval Latin *usufructus*, from Latin *usus (et) fructus* 'use (and) enjoyment,' from *usus* 'a use' + *fructus* 'fruit.' **—u·su·fruc·tu·ar·y** /ˌyoozəˈfrəkchooˌerē; -sə-/ *adj. & n.*

U·sum·bu·ra /ˌoosəmˈboorə/ former name (until 1962) of **BUJUMBURA**.

u·su·rer /ˈyoozhərər/ ▸*n.* a person who lends money at unreasonably high rates of interest. ▷Middle English: from Anglo-Norman French, from Old French *usure*, from Latin *usura* (see **USURY**).

u·su·ri·ous /yooˈzhoorēəs/ ▸*adj.* of or relating to the practice of usury: *they lend money at usurious rates.* **—u·su·ri·ous·ly** *adv.*

u·surp /yooˈsərp/ ▸*v.* [*trans.*] take (a position of power or importance) illegally or by force: *Richard usurped the throne.* ■ take the place of (someone in a position of power) illegally; supplant: *the Hanoverian dynasty had usurped the Stuarts.* ■ [*intrans.*] **(usurp on/upon)** *archaic* encroach or infringe upon (someone's rights): *the Church had usurped upon the domain of the state.* ▷Middle English (in the sense 'appropriate (a right) wrongfully'): from Old French *usurper*, from Latin *usurpare* 'seize for use.' **—u·sur·pa·tion** /ˌyoosərˈpāshən/ *n.* **—u·surp·er** *n.*

u·su·ry /ˈyoozh(ə)rē/ ▸*n.* the illegal action or practice of lending money at unreasonably high rates of interest. ■ *archaic* interest at such rates. ▷Middle English: from Anglo-Norman French *usurie*, or from medieval Latin *usuria*, from Latin *usura*, from *usus* 'a use' (see **USE**).

UT ▸*abbr.* ■ Universal Time. ■ Utah (in official postal use).

U·tah /ˈyooˌtô; -ˌtä/ a state in the western U.S.; pop. 2,233,169; capital, Salt Lake City; statehood, Jan. 4, 1896 (45). The region, a part of Mexico from 1821, was ceded to the U.S. in 1848. The first permanent settlers, who arrived in 1847, were Mormons fleeing persecution. Statehood was refused until the Mormons renounced polygamy—a dispute that led to the Utah War 1857–58. **—U·tah·an** /-tô(ə)n; -ˈtä(ə)n/ *adj. & n.*

U·tah Beach a name given to the westernmost of the beaches, north of Carentan in Normandy, where U.S. troops landed on D-day in June 1944.

u·tah·rap·tor /ˈyooˌtôˌraptər; -ˌtä-/ ▸*n.* a large dromaeosaurid dinosaur, the remains of which were discovered in Utah in 1992. It was twice the size of deinonychus. • Genus *Utahraptor*, family Dromaeosauridae, suborder Theropoda. ▷modern Latin, from **UTAH** + **RAPTOR**.

U·ta·ma·ro /ˌootəˈmärō/, Kitagawa (1753–1806), Japanese painter and printmaker; born *Kitagawa Netsuyoshi*. A leading exponent of the ukiyo-e school, he was noted for his sensual depictions of women.

UTC ▸*abbr.* Universal Time Coordinated. Also expanded as **COORDINATED UNIVERSAL TIME**.

Ute /yoot/ ▸*n.* (*pl.* same or **Utes**) **1** a member of an American Indian people living chiefly in Colorado and Utah. **2** the Uto-Aztecan language of this people.

▸*adj.* of or relating to this people or their language. ▷from earlier *Utah*, from Spanish *Yuta*; compare with **PAIUTE**.

ute /yoot/ ▸*n. informal* a utility vehicle: *ordinary families buy pickups and sport utes.* ▷1940s: abbreviation.

u·ten·sil /yooˈtensəl/ ▸*n.* an implement, container, or other article, esp. for household use. See note at **TOOL**. ▷late Middle English (denoting domestic implements or vessels collectively): from Old French *utensile*, from medieval Latin, neuter of Latin *utensilis* 'usable,' from *uti* 'to use' (see **USE**).

u·ter·i /ˈyootəˌrī; -ˌrē/ ▸ plural form of **UTERUS**.

u·ter·ine /ˈyootərin; -ˌrīn/ ▸*adj.* of or relating to the uterus or womb: *uterine contractions.* ■ [*attrib.*] born of the same mother but not having the same father: *a uterine sister.* ▷late Middle English: from **UTERUS** + **-INE**[1], or, in the sense 'born of the same mother,' from late Latin *uterinus*.

u·ter·us /ˈyootərəs/ ▸*n.* (*pl.* **u·ter·i** /ˈyootəˌrī; -ˌrē/) the organ in the lower body of a woman or female mammal where offspring are conceived and in which they gestate before birth; the womb. ▷Latin; related to Greek *hustera*. Compare with **HYSTERIC**.

U·ther Pen·drag·on /ˈ(y)oothər penˈdragən/ (in Arthurian legend) king of the Britons and father of Arthur.

U·ti·ca /ˈyootikə/ an industrial city in central New York, on the Mohawk River; pop. 60,651.

u·tile[1] /ˈyootl; ˈyooˌtīl/ ▸*adj. rare* advantageous. ▷late 15th cent.: via Old French from Latin *utilis*, from *uti* 'to use.'

u·ti·le[2] /ˈyootl-ē/ ▸*n.* a large tropical African hardwood tree with timber that is widely used as a substitute for mahogany. • *Entandrophragma utile*, family Meliaceae. ▷1950s: modern Latin, specific epithet; see **UTILE**[1].

u·til·i·tar·i·an /yooˌtiliˈte(ə)rēən/ ▸*adj.* **1** designed to be useful or practical rather than attractive. **2** *Philosophy* of, relating to, or adhering to the doctrine of utilitarianism: *a utilitarian theorist.*

▸*n. Philosophy* an adherent of utilitarianism.

u·til·i·tar·i·an·ism /yooˌtiləˈte(ə)rēəˌnizəm/ ▸*n.* the doctrine that actions are right if they are useful or for the benefit of a majority. ■ the doctrine that an action is right insofar as it promotes happiness, and that the greatest happiness of the greatest number should be the guiding principle of conduct.

u·til·i·ty /yooˈtilətē/ ▸*n.* (*pl.* **-ties**) **1** the state of being useful, profitable, or beneficial: *he had a poor opinion of the utility of book learning.* ■ (in game theory or economics) a measure of that which is sought to be maximized in any situation involving a choice. **2** a public utility. ■ stocks and bonds in public utilities. **3** *Computing* a utility program.

▸*adj.* [*attrib.*] **1** useful, esp. through being able to perform several functions: *a utility truck.* ■ denoting a player capable of playing in several different positions in a sport. **2** functional rather than attractive: *utility clothing.* **3** of or relating to the lowest U.S. government grade of beef. **4** (of domestic animals) raised for potential profit and not for show or as pets. ▷late Middle English: from Old French *utilite*, from Latin *utilitas*, from *utilis* 'useful.'

u·til·i·ty func·tion ▸*n. Economics* a mathematical function that ranks alternatives according to their utility to an individual.

u·til·i·ty knife ▸*n.* a knife with a small sharp blade, often retractable, designed to cut wood, cardboard, and other materials.

u·til·i·ty pole ▸*n.* another term for **TELEPHONE POLE**.

u·til·i·ty pro·gram ▸*n. Computing* a program for carrying out a routine function.

u·til·i·ty room ▸*n.* a room equipped with appliances for washing and other domestic work.

u·til·i·ty ve·hi·cle (also **u·til·i·ty truck**) ▸*n.* a truck with low sides designed for carrying small loads.

u·ti·lize /ˈyootlˌīz/ ▸*v.* [*trans.*] make practical and effective use of: *vitamin C helps your body utilize the iron present in your diet.* ▷early 19th cent.: from French *utiliser*, from Italian *utilizzare*, from *utile* (see **UTILE**[1]). **—u·ti·liz·a·ble** /ˌyootlˈīzəbəl; ˈyootlˌī-/ *adj.* **—u·ti·li·za·tion** /ˌyootl-əˈzāshən/ *n.* **—u·ti·liz·er** *n.*

USAGE **Utilize**, borrowed in the 19th century from the French *utiliser*, means 'make practical or effective use of.' Because it is a more formal word than **use** and is often used in contexts (as in business writing) where the ordinary verb **use** would be simpler and more direct, **utilize** may strike readers as pretentious jargon and should therefore be used sparingly. See also **usage** at **USAGE**.

-ution ▸*suffix* (forming nouns) equivalent to **-ATION** (as in *solution*). ▷via French from Latin *-utio(n-)*.

ut·most /ˈətˌmōst/ ▸*adj.* [*attrib.*] most extreme; greatest: *a matter of the utmost importance.*

▸*n.* **(the utmost)** the greatest or most extreme extent or amount: *a plot that stretches credulity to the utmost.* ▷Old English *ūt(e)mest* 'outermost' (see **OUT**, **-MOST**).

▸*PHRASE* □ **do one's utmost** do the most that one is able: *Dan was doing his utmost to be helpful.*

U·to-Az·tec·an /ˈyootōˈazˌtekən/ ▸*n.* a language family of Central America and western North America including Comanche, Hopi, Nahuatl (the language of the Aztecs), Paiute, Pima, and Shoshone.

▸*adj.* of, relating to, or denoting this language family.

U·to·pi·a /yooˈtōpēə/ (also **u·to·pi·a**) ▸*n.* an imagined place or state of things in which everything is perfect. The word was first used in the book *Utopia* (1516) by Sir Thomas More. The opposite of **DYSTOPIA**. ▷based on Greek *ou* 'not' + *topos* 'place.'

U·to·pi·an /yooˈtōpēən/ (also **u·to·pi·an**) ▸*adj.* modeled on or aiming for a state in which everything is perfect; idealistic.

▸*n.* an idealistic reformer. **—U·to·pi·an·ism** /-ˌnizəm/ *n.*

u·to·pi·an so·cial·ism ▸*n.* socialism achieved by the moral persuasion of capitalists to surrender the means of production peacefully to the people.

U·trecht /ˈyooˌtrekt; ˈYˌtrekHt/ a city in the central Netherlands, capital of a province of the same name; pop. 231,000.

U·trecht vel·vet ▸*n.* a strong, thick plush velvet, used in upholstery.

u·tri·cle /ˈyootrəkəl/ ▸*n.* a small cell, sac, or bladder-like protuberance in an animal or plant. ■ (also **u·tric·u·lus** /yooˈtrikyələs/) the larger of the two fluid-filled cavities forming part of the labyrinth of the inner ear (the other being the sacculus). It contains hair cells and otoliths which send signals to the brain concerning the orientation of the head. ▷mid 18th cent.: from French *utricule* or Latin *utriculus*, diminutive of *uter* 'leather bag.' **—u·tric·u·lar** /yooˈtrikyələr/ *adj.*

U·tril·lo /ooˈtrēō; yooˈtrilō/, Maurice (1883–1955), French painter, chiefly known for his depictions of Paris street scenes, esp. of the Montmartre district.

Ut·tar·an·chal /ˌootərˈənchəl/ a state in northern India, formed in 2000 from the northern part of Uttar Pradesh; capital, Dehra Dun.

Ut·tar Pra·desh /ˈootər prəˈdāsh; -ˈdesh/ a state in northern India that borders on Tibet and Nepal; capital, Lucknow. It was formed in 1950 from the United Provinces of Agra and Oudh.

ut·ter[1] /ˈətər/ ▸*adj.* [*attrib.*] complete; absolute: *Charles stared at her in utter amazement.* ▷Old English *ūtera*, *ūttra* 'outer,' comparative of *ūt* 'out'; compare with **OUTER**. **—ut·ter·ly** *adv.* [as *submodifier*] *he looked utterly ridiculous.*

ut·ter[2] ▸*v.* [*trans.*] **1** make (a sound) with one's voice: *he uttered an exasperated snort.* ■ say (something) aloud: *they are busily scribbling down every word she utters.* **2** *Law* put (forged money) into circulation. ■ publish, circulate, or deliver to another person (a document or other object). ▷late Middle English: from Middle Dutch *ūteren* 'speak, make known, give currency to (coins).' **—ut·ter·a·ble** *adj.* **—ut·ter·er** *n.*

ut·ter·ance /ˈətərəns/ ▸*n.* a spoken word, statement, or vocal sound. ■ the action of saying or expressing something aloud: *the simple utterance of a few platitudes.* ■ *Linguistics* an uninterrupted chain of spoken or written language.

ut·ter·most /ˈətərˌmōst/ ▸*adj. & n.* another term for **UTMOST**.

U-turn ▸*n.* the turning of a vehicle in a U-shaped course so as to face in the opposite direction. ■ *figurative* a change of plan, esp. a reversal of political policy: *another U-turn by the government.*

UV ▸*abbr.* ultraviolet.

UVA ▸*abbr.* ultraviolet radiation of relatively long wavelengths.

u·va·rov·ite /(y)ooˈväraˌvīt/ ▸*n.* an emerald green variety of garnet, containing chromium. ▷mid 19th cent.: from the name of Count Sergei S. *Uvarov* (1785–1855), Russian statesman, + **-ITE**[1].

UVB ▸*abbr.* ultraviolet radiation of relatively short wavelengths.

u·ve·a /ˈyoovēə/ ▸*n.* the pigmented layer of the eye, lying beneath the sclera and cornea, and comprising the iris, choroid, and ciliary body. ▷late Middle English (denoting the choroid layer of the eye): from medieval Latin, from Latin *uva* 'grape.' **—u·ve·al** *adj.*

u·ve·i·tis /ˌyoovēˈītis/ ▸*n. Medicine* inflammation of the uvea.

u·vu·la /ˈyoovyələ/ ▸*n.* (*pl.* **-lae** /-ˌlē; -ˌlī/) *Anatomy* (also **pal·a·tine u·vu·la**) a fleshy extension at the back of the soft palate that hangs above the throat. ■ a similar fleshy hanging structure in any organ of the body, particularly one at the opening of the bladder. ▷late Middle English: from late Latin, diminutive of Latin *uva* 'grape.'

u·vu·lar /ˈyo͞ovyələr/ ▶*adj.* **1** *Phonetics* (of a sound) articulated with the back of the tongue and the uvula, as *r* in French and *q* in Arabic. **2** *Anatomy* of or relating to the uvula.
▶*n. Phonetics* a uvular consonant.

UXO ▶*abbr.* unexploded ordnance.

ux·o·ri·al /ˌəkˈsôrēəl; əgˈzôr-/ ▶*adj.* of or relating to a wife. ▷early 19th cent.: from Latin *uxor* 'wife' + **-IAL**.

ux·o·ri·cide /ˌəkˈsôrəˌsīd; ˌəgˈzôr-/ ▶*n.* the killing of one's wife. ■ a man who kills his wife. ▷mid 19th cent.: from Latin *uxor* 'wife' + **-CIDE**. **—ux·o·ri·cid·al** /əkˌsôrəˈsīdl; əgˌzôr-/ *adj.*

ux·o·ri·ous /ˌəkˈsôrēəs; ˌəgˈzôr-/ ▶*adj.* having or showing an excessive or submissive fondness for one's wife. ▷late 16th cent.: from Latin *uxoriosus*, from *uxor* 'wife.' **—ux·o·ri·ous·ly** *adv.* **—ux·o·ri·ous·ness** *n.*

Uy·gur ▶*n.* & *adj.* variant spelling of **UIGHUR**.

Uz·bek /ˈo͝ozˌbek; ˈəz-; o͝ozˈbek/ ▶*n.* **1** a member of a Turkic people living mainly in the republic of Uzbekistan and elsewhere in southwestern Asia. ■ a native or national of Uzbekistan. **2** the Turkic language of Uzbekistan.
▶*adj.* of or relating to Uzbekistan, the Uzbeks, or their language. ▷the name in Uzbek.

Uz·bek·i·stan /o͝ozˈbekəˌstan; əz-; -ˌstän/ an independent republic in central Asia that lies south and southeast of the Aral Sea; pop. 26,410,000; capital, Tashkent; languages, Uzbek and Russian.

Uzbekistan was formerly a constituent republic of the Soviet Union. It became independent within the Commonwealth of Independent States when the Soviet Union broke up in 1991.

U·zi /ˈo͞ozē/ ▶*n.* a type of submachine gun of Israeli design. ▷1950s: from *Uziel* Gal, the Israeli army officer who designed it.

Vv

V

V[1] /vē/ (also **v**) ▸*n.* (*pl.* **Vs** or **V's**) **1** the twenty-second letter of the alphabet. ■ denoting the next after U in a set of items, categories, etc. **2** (also **vee**) a shape like that of a letter V: [in *combination*] *deep, V-shaped valleys.* ■ [as *adj.*] denoting an internal combustion engine with a number of cylinders arranged in two rows at an angle to each other in a V-shape: *a V-engine | a 32-valve V8 power plant.* **3** the Roman numeral for five.

V[2] ▸*abbr.* ■ volt(s).
▸*symbol* ■ the chemical element vanadium. ■ voltage or potential difference: $V = IR$. ■ (in mathematical formulae) volume: $pV = nRT$.

v. ▸*abbr.* ■ *Grammar* verb. ■ (in textual references) verse. ■ verso. ■ versus. ■ very. ■ (in textual references) vide.
▸*symbol* velocity.

V-1 ▸*n.* a small flying bomb powered by a simple jet engine, used by the Germans in World War II. Also called DOODLEBUG. ▷abbreviation of German *Vergeltungswaffe* 'reprisal weapon.'

V-2 ▸*n.* a rocket-powered flying bomb, which was the first ballistic missile, used by the Germans in World War II. ▷see **V-1**.

VA ▸*abbr.* ■ (in the UK) Order of Victoria and Albert. ■ Veterans Affairs (formerly Veterans Administration). ■ Vicar Apostolic. ■ Vice Admiral. ■ Virginia (in official postal use).

Va. ▸*abbr.* Virginia.

Vaal /väl/ a river in South Africa, the chief tributary of the Orange River, that rises in the Drakensberg Mountains and flows 750 miles (1,200 km) southwest to the Orange River near Douglas.

Vaa·sa /'väsə; -sä/ a port in western Finland, on the Gulf of Bothnia; pop. 53,000. Swedish name **VASA**.

vac /vak/ ▸*n.* **1** informal term for VACUUM CLEANER. **2** *Brit.* informal term for VACATION.

va·can·cy /'vākənsē/ ▸*n.* (*pl.* **-cies**) **1** an unoccupied position or job: *a vacancy for a shorthand typist.* ■ an available room in a hotel or other establishment providing accommodations. **2** empty space: *Cathy stared into vacancy, seeing nothing.* ■ emptiness of mind; lack of intelligence or understanding: *vacancy, vanity, and inane deception.* ■ *Crystallography* a defect in a crystal lattice, consisting of the absence of an atom or an ion from a position where there should be one.

va·cant /'vākənt/ ▸*adj.* (of premises) having no fixtures, furniture, or inhabitants; empty. Compare with UNOCCUPIED (sense 1). ■ (of a position or office) not filled: *the president resigned and the post was left vacant.* ■ (of a person or their expression) having or showing no intelligence or interest: *a vacant stare.* ▷Middle English: from Old French, or from Latin *vacant-* 'remaining empty,' from the verb *vacare*. **—va·cant·ly** *adv.*

va·cate /'vā,kāt/ ▸*v.* [*trans.*] **1** leave (a place that one previously occupied): *rooms must be vacated by noon on the last day of your vacation.* ■ give up (a position or office): *he will vacate a job in government sales.* **2** *Law* cancel or annul (a judgment, contract, or charge). ▷mid 17th cent. (as a legal term, also in the sense 'make ineffective'): from Latin *vacat-* 'left empty,' from the verb *vacare*.

va·ca·tion /vā'kāsʜən; və-/ ▸*n.* **1** an extended period of recreation, esp. one spent away from home or in traveling: *he took a vacation in the south of France | people come here* ***on vacation*** [as *adj.*] *a vacation home.* ■ a fixed holiday period between terms in schools and law courts. **2** the action of leaving something one previously occupied: *his marriage was the reason for the vacation of his fellowship.*
▸*v.* [*intrans.*] take a vacation: *I was vacationing in Europe with my family.* ▷late Middle English: from Old French, or from Latin *vacatio(n-)*, from *vacare* 'be unoccupied' (see VACATE). **—va·ca·tion·er** *n.* **—va·ca·tion·ist** /-ist/ *n.*

va·ca·tion·land /vā'kāsʜən,land; və-/ ▸*n.* an area providing attractions for people on vacation.

Vac·a·ville /'vakə,vil/ a city in west central California, southwest of Sacramento; pop. 71,479.

vac·ci·nate /'vaksə,nāt/ ▸*v.* [*trans.*] treat with a vaccine to produce immunity against a disease; inoculate: *all the children were* ***vaccinated against*** *diphtheria.* **—vac·ci·na·tion** /,vaksə'nāsʜən/ *n.* **—vac·ci·na·tor** /-,nātər/ *n.*

vac·cine /vak'sēn/ ▸*n.* *Medicine* a substance used to stimulate the production of antibodies and provide immunity against one or several diseases, prepared from the causative agent of a disease, its products, or a synthetic substitute, treated to act as an antigen without inducing the disease: *there is no* ***vaccine against*** *HIV infection.* ■ *Computing* a program designed to detect computer viruses, and inactivate them. ▷late 18th cent.: from Latin *vaccinus*, from *vacca* 'cow' (because of the early use of the cowpox virus against smallpox).

vac·cin·i·a /vak'sinēə/ ▸*n.* *Medicine* cowpox, or the virus that causes it. ▷early 19th cent.: modern Latin, from Latin *vaccinus* (see VACCINE).

Va·cher·in /,vasʜ(ə)'ran; ,väsʜ-/ ▸*n.* a type of soft French or Swiss cheese made from cow's milk. ▷French, from earlier *vachelin*, from *vache* 'cow.'

vac·il·late /'vasə,lāt/ ▸*v.* [*intrans.*] alternate or waver between different opinions or actions; be indecisive: *I had for a time vacillated between teaching and journalism.* ▷late 16th cent. (in the sense 'sway unsteadily'): from Latin *vacillat-* 'swayed,' from the verb *vacillare*. **—vac·il·la·tion** /,vasə'lāsʜən/ *n.* **—vac·il·la·tor** /-,lātər/ *n.*

vac·u·a /'vakyəwə/ ▸ plural form of VACUUM.

vac·u·ole /'vakyōō,ōl/ ▸*n.* *Biology* a space or vesicle within the cytoplasm of a cell, enclosed by a membrane and typically containing fluid. ■ a small cavity or space in tissue, esp. in nervous tissue as the result of disease. ▷mid 19th cent.: from French, diminutive of Latin *vacuus* 'empty.' **—vac·u·o·lar** /,vakyōō'ōlər; 'vakyōōələr/ *adj.* **—vac·u·o·la·tion** /,vakyōōə'lāsʜən/ *n.*

vac·u·ous /'vakyəwəs/ ▸*adj.* having or showing a lack of thought or intelligence; mindless: *a vacuous smile | vacuous slogans.* ■ *archaic* empty. ▷mid 17th cent. (in the sense 'empty of matter'): from Latin *vacuus* 'empty' + **-OUS**. **—va·cu·i·ty** /va'kyōōətē; və-/ *n.* **—vac·u·ous·ly** *adv.* **—vac·u·ous·ness** *n.*

vac·u·um /'vak,yōō(ə)m; -yəm/ ▸*n.* (*pl.* **-u·ums** or **-u·a** /-yōōə/) **1** a space entirely devoid of matter. ■ a space or container from which the air has been completely or partly removed. ■ [usu. in *sing.*] a gap left by the loss, death, or departure of someone or something formerly playing a significant part in a situation or activity: *the political vacuum left by the death of the Emperor.* **2** (*pl.* **-u·ums**) a vacuum cleaner.
▸*v.* [*trans.*] clean with a vacuum cleaner: *the room needs to be vacuumed.* ▷mid 16th cent.: modern Latin, neuter of Latin *vacuus* 'empty.'
▸*PHRASE* □ **in a vacuum** (of an activity or a problem to be considered) isolated from the context normal to it and in which it can best be understood or assessed.

vac·u·um bot·tle ▸*n.* another term for THERMOS.

vac·u·um brake ▸*n.* a railroad-vehicle brake operated by changes in pressure in a continuous pipe that is generally kept exhausted of air by a pump and controls similar brakes throughout the train.

vac·u·um clean·er ▸*n.* an electrical apparatus that by means of suction collects dust and small particles from floors and other surfaces. **—vac·uum-clean** *v.*

vac·u·um dis·til·la·tion ▸*n.* *Chemistry* distillation of a liquid under reduced pressure, enabling it to boil at a lower temperature than normal.

vac·u·um ex·trac·tion ▸*n.* the application of reduced pressure to extract something, particularly to assist childbirth or as a method of abortion, or as a technique for removing components of a chemical mixture.

vac·u·um ex·trac·tor ▸*n.* a cup-shaped appliance for performing vacuum extraction in childbirth. Also called VENTOUSE.

vac·u·um flask ▸*n.* another term for THERMOS.

vac·u·um gauge ▸*n.* a gauge for testing pressure after the production of a vacuum.

vac·u·um-pack ▸*v.* [*trans.*] seal (a product) in packaging after any air has been removed so that the packaging is tight and firm: *it is quickly vacuum-packed in foil pouches to ensure freshness |* [as *adj.*] (**vacuum-packed**) *vacuum-packed cheese.*

vac·u·um pump ▸*n.* a pump used for creating a vacuum.

vac·u·um tube ▸*n.* an electron tube containing a near-vacuum that allows the free passage of electric current.

va·de me·cum /,vädē 'mākəm; ,vādē 'mē-/ ▸*n.* a handbook or guide that is kept constantly at hand for consultation. ▷early 17th cent.: modern Latin, literally 'go with me,' from Latin *vadere* 'go,' from an Indo-European root shared by WADE.

Va·do·da·ra /və'dōdərə; -,rä/ a city in the state of Gujarat, western India; pop. 1,021,000.

va·dose /'vā,dōs/ ▸*adj.* relating to or denoting underground water above the water table. Compare with PHREATIC. ▷late 19th cent.: from Latin *vadosus*, from *vadum* 'shallow expanse of water.'

Va·duz /vä'dōōts; fä-/ the capital of Liechtenstein; pop. 5,000.

vag·a·bond /'vagə,bänd/ ▸*n.* a person who wanders from place to place without a home or job. ■ *informal, dated* a rascal; a rogue.
▸*adj.* [*attrib.*] having no settled home.
▸*v.* [*intrans.*] *archaic* wander about as or like a vagabond. ▷Middle English (originally denoting a criminal): from Old French, or from Latin *vagabundus*, from *vagari* 'wander.' **—vag·a·bond·age** /-dij/ *n.*

va·gal /'vāgəl/ ▸*adj.* of or relating to the vagus nerve.

va·gar·i·ous /və'ge(ə)rēəs; vā-/ ▸*adj.* *rare* erratic and unpredictable in behavior or direction. ▷late 18th cent. (in the sense 'changing, inconstant'): from VAGARY + -OUS.

va·gar·y /'vāgərē/ ▸*n.* (*pl.* **-gar·ies**) (usu. **vagaries**) an unexpected and inexplicable change in a situation or in someone's behavior: *the vagaries of the weather.* ▷late 16th cent. (also as a verb in the sense 'roam'): from Latin *vagari* 'wander.'

va·gi /'vā,gī; -,jī; -,gē; -,jē/ ▸ plural form of VAGUS.

va·gi·na /və'jīnə/ ▸*n.* (*pl.* **-nas** or **-nae** /-nē; -nī/) the muscular tube leading from the external genitals to the cervix of the uterus in women and most female mammals. ■ *Botany & Zoology* any sheathlike structure, esp. a sheath formed around a stem by the base of a leaf. ▷late 17th cent.: from Latin, literally 'sheath, scabbard,' which is also the source of the word VANILLA. **—vag·i·nal** /'vajənl/ *adj.*

va·gi·na den·ta·ta /den'tätə/ ▸*n.* the motif of a vagina with teeth, occurring in folklore and fantasy and said to symbolize male fears of the dangers of sexual intercourse, esp. of castration. ▷early 20th cent.: *dentata*, feminine of Latin *dentatus* 'having teeth.'

vag·i·nal plug ▸*n. Zoology* a secretion that blocks the vagina of some rodents and insectivores after mating.

vag·i·nis·mus /ˌvajəˈnizməs/ ▸*n.* painful spasmodic contraction of the vagina in response to physical contact or pressure (esp. in sexual intercourse). ▷mid 19th cent.: modern Latin, from Latin *vagina* (see VAGINA).

vag·i·ni·tis /ˌvajəˈnītis/ ▸*n.* inflammation of the vagina.

vag·i·no·plas·ty /ˈvajənōˌplastē/ ▸*n. Medicine* plastic surgery performed to create or repair a vagina. ▷late 19th cent.: from *vagina* + *-plasty.*

vag·i·no·sis /ˌvajəˈnōsəs/ ▸*n.* a bacterial infection of the vagina causing a malodorous white discharge.

va·got·o·my /vāˈgätəmē/ ▸*n.* (*pl.* **-mies**) a surgical operation in which one or more branches of the vagus nerve are cut, typically to reduce the rate of gastric secretion (e.g., in treating peptic ulcers). —**va·got·o·mized** /-ˌmīzd/ *adj.*

va·go·to·ni·a /ˌvagəˈtōnēə/ ▸*n.* the condition in which there is increased influence of the parasympathetic nervous system and increased excitability of the vagus nerve, producing bradycardia and faintness.

va·grant /ˈvāgrənt/ ▸*n.* a person without a settled home or regular work who wanders from place to place and lives by begging. ■ *archaic* a wanderer. ■ *Ornithology* a bird that has strayed or been blown from its usual range or migratory route. Also called ACCIDENTAL.
▸*adj.* [*attrib.*] characteristic of, relating to, or living the life of a vagrant: *vagrant beggars.* ■ moving from place to place; wandering: *vagrant whales.* ■ *poetic/literary* moving or occurring unpredictably; inconstant: *the vagrant heart of my mother.* ▷late Middle English: from Anglo-Norman French *vagarant* 'wandering around,' from the verb *vagrer.* —**va·gran·cy** /-grənsē/ *n.* —**va·grant·ly** *adv.*

vague /vāg/ ▸*adj.* of uncertain, indefinite, or unclear character or meaning: *many patients suffer vague symptoms.* ■ thinking or communicating in an unfocused or imprecise way: *he had been very vague about his activities.* ▷mid 16th cent.: from French, or from Latin *vagus* 'wandering, uncertain.' —**vague·ly** *adv.* —**vague·ness** *n.* —**vagu·ish** *adj.*

va·gus /ˈvāgəs/ ▸*n.* (*pl.* **va·gi** /-gī; -jī; -gē; -jē/) (also **vagus nerve**) *Anatomy* each of the tenth pair of cranial nerves, supplying the heart, lungs, upper digestive tract, and other organs of the chest and abdomen. ▷mid 19th cent.: from Latin (see VAGUE).

Vail /vāl/ a town in northern Colorado, a noted ski resort; pop. 3,659.

vail /vāl/ ▸*v.* [*trans.*] *archaic* take off or lower (one's hat or crown) as a token of respect or submission. ■ [*intrans.*] take off one's hat or otherwise show respect or submission to someone. ▷Middle English (originally in the sense 'lower (one's eyes, weapon, banner, etc.) as a sign of submission'): shortening of obsolete *avale,* from Old French *avaler* 'to lower,' from *a val* 'down' (literally 'in the valley').

vain /vān/ ▸*adj.* **1** having or showing an excessively high opinion of one's appearance, abilities, or worth: *their flattery made him vain.* **2** [*attrib.*] producing no result; useless: *a vain attempt to tidy up the room | the vain hope of finding work.* ■ having no meaning or likelihood of fulfillment: *a vain boast.* ▷Middle English (in the sense 'devoid of real worth'): via Old French from Latin *vanus* 'empty, without substance.' —**vain·ly** *adv.*
▸**PHRASES** □ **in vain** without success or a result: *they waited in vain for a response.* □ **take someone's name in vain** use someone's name in a way that shows a lack of respect.

vain·glo·ry /ˈvānˌglôrē; ˌvānˈglôrē/ ▸*n. poetic/literary* inordinate pride in oneself or one's achievements; excessive vanity. ▷Middle English: suggested by Old French *vaine gloire,* Latin *vana gloria.* —**vain·glo·ri·ous** /ˌvānˈglôrēəs/ *adj.* —**vain·glo·ri·ous·ly** /ˌvānˈglôrēəslē/ *adv.* —**vain·glo·ri·ous·ness** /ˌvānˈglôrēəsnəs/ *n.*

vair /ve(ə)r/ ▸*n.* **1** fur, typically bluish-gray, obtained from a variety of squirrel, used in the 13th and 14th centuries as a trimming or lining for garments. **2** *Heraldry* fur, represented by interlocking rows of shield-shaped or bell-shaped figures that are typically alternately blue and white, as a tincture. ▷Middle English: via Old French from Latin *varius* (see VARIOUS).

Vaish·na·va /ˈvīsHnəvə/ ▸*n.* a member of one of the main branches of modern Hinduism, devoted to the worship of the god Vishnu as the supreme being, esp. in his incarnation as Krishna. Compare with SHAIVA. ▷from Sanskrit *vaiṣṇava.*

Vaish·ya /ˈvīsHyə; ˈvīs-/ (also **Vais·ya**) ▸*n.* a member of the third of the four Hindu castes, comprising the merchants and farmers. ▷from Sanskrit *vaiśya* 'peasant, laborer.'

vaj·ra /ˈvəjrə/ ▸*n.* (in Buddhism and Hinduism) a thunderbolt or mystical weapon, esp. one wielded by the god Indra. ▷Sanskrit.

val·ance /ˈvaləns; ˈvāləns/ ▸*n.* a length of decorative drapery attached to the canopy or frame of a bed in order to screen the structure or the space beneath it. ■ a length of decorative drapery hung above a window to screen the curtain fittings. ■ an indirect-lighting fixture extending along the top of an interior wall. ■ a dust ruffle. ▷late Middle English: perhaps Anglo-Norman French, from a shortened form of Old French *avaler* 'descend' (see VAIL). —**val·anced** *adj.*

Val·dos·ta /valˈdästə/ a city in southern Georgia, southeast of Albany; pop. 43,724.

vale[1] /vāl/ ▸*n.* a valley (used in place names or as a poetic term): *the Vale of Glamorgan.* ▷Middle English: from Old French *val,* from Latin *vallis, valles.*
▸**PHRASE** □ **vale of tears** *poetic/literary* the world regarded as a scene of trouble or sorrow.

vale[2] /ˈvālā/ *archaic* ▸*exclam.* farewell.
▸*n.* a written or spoken farewell. ▷Latin, literally 'be well!, be strong!,' imperative of *valere.*

val·e·dic·tion /ˌvaləˈdiksHən/ ▸*n.* the action of saying farewell: *he spread his palm in valediction.* ■ a statement or address made at or as a farewell: *his official memorial valediction.* ▷mid 17th cent.: based on Latin *vale* 'goodbye' + *dicere* 'to say,' on the pattern of *benediction.*

val·e·dic·to·ri·an /ˌvaləˌdikˈtôrēən/ ▸*n.* a student, typically having the highest academic achievements of the class, who delivers the valedictory at a graduation ceremony. Compare with SALUTATORIAN.

val·e·dic·to·ry /ˌvaləˈdikt(ə)rē/ ▸*adj.* serving as a farewell: *a valedictory wave.*
▸*n.* (*pl.* **-ries**) a farewell address.

va·lence /ˈvāləns/ ▸*n. Chemistry* the combining power of an element, esp. as measured by the number of hydrogen atoms it can displace or combine with: *carbon always has a valence of 4.* ■ [as *adj.*] relating to or denoting electrons involved in or available for chemical bond formation: *molecules with unpaired valence electrons.* ■ *Linguistics* the number of grammatical elements with which a particular word, esp. a verb, combines in a sentence. ▷late Middle English: from late Latin *valentia* 'power, competence,' from *valere* 'be well or strong.'

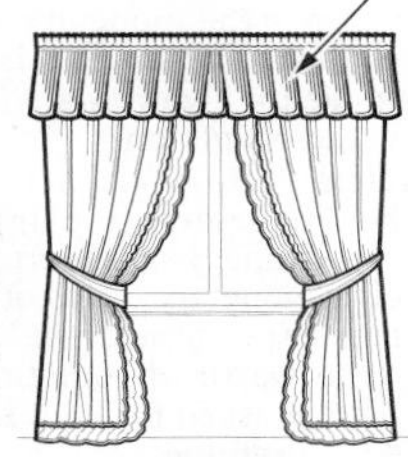
valance

Va·len·ci·a /vəˈlensēə; -ˈlencHēə/ **1** an autonomous region of eastern Spain, on the Mediterranean coast. It was formerly a Moorish kingdom (1021–1238). ■ its capital, a port on the Mediterranean coast; pop. 777,000. **2** a city in northern Venezuela; pop. 903,000.

Va·len·ci·ennes /vəˌlensēˈen; ˌvalən-/ ▸*n.* a type of bobbin lace. ▷named after a town in northeastern France, where it was made in the 17th and 18th centuries.

va·len·cy /ˈvālənsē/ ▸*n.* (*pl.* **-cies**) *Chemistry & Linguistics chiefly Brit.* another term for VALENCE. ▷early 17th cent.: from late Latin *valentia* 'power' (see VALENCE).

-va·lent ▸*comb. form* **1** having a valency of the specified number: *trivalent.* **2** *Genetics* (denoting a meiotic structure) composed of the specified number of chromosomes: *univalent.*

Val·en·tine, St. /ˈvalənˌtīn/ either of two early Italian saints (who may have been the same person) traditionally commemorated on February 14—a Roman priest martyred *c.*269 and a bishop of Terni martyred at Rome. St. Valentine was regarded as the patron of lovers.

val·en·tine /ˈvalənˌtīn/ ▸*n.* a card sent, often anonymously, on St. Valentine's Day (February 14) to a person one loves or is attracted to. ■ a person to whom one sends such a card or whom one asks to be one's sweetheart. ▷late Middle English (denoting a person chosen (sometimes by lot) as a sweetheart or special friend): from Old French *Valentin,* from Latin *Valentinus.*

Val·en·ti·no /ˌvalənˈtēnō/, Rudolph (1895–1926), U.S. actor, born in Italy; born *Rodolfo Guglielmi di Valentina d'Antonguolla.* He played the romantic hero in silent movies such as *The Sheikh* (1921) and *Blood and Sand* (1922).

Rudolph Valentino

Va·le·ra, Eamon de, see DE VALERA.

Va·le·ri·an /vəˈli(ə)rēən/ (died 260), Roman emperor 253–260; Latin name *Publius Licinius Valerianus.* He renewed the persecution of the Christians that was initiated by Decius.

va·le·ri·an /vəˈli(ə)rēən/ ▸*n.* a plant that typically bears clusters of small pink or white flowers. Native to Eurasia, several species have been introduced to North America. • Family Valerianaceae: several species, in particular **common valerian** (*Valeriana officinalis*), a valued medicinal herb, and the Mediterranean **red valerian** (*Centranthus ruber*), grown for its spurred flowers, which attract butterflies. ■ a drug obtained from the root of common valerian, used as a sedative and antispasmodic. ▷late Middle English: from Old French *valeriane,* from medieval Latin *valeriana (herba),* apparently the feminine of *Valerianus* 'of Valerius' (a personal name).

va·ler·ic ac·id /vəˈlerik; -ˈli(ə)r-/ ▸*n. Chemistry* another term for PENTANOIC ACID. ▷mid 19th cent.: *valeric* from VALERIAN + -IC. —**val·er·ate** /ˈvaləˌrāt/ *n.*

Va·lé·ry /ˌvälāˈrē/, (Ambroise) Paul (Toussaint Jules) (1871–1945), French poet, essayist, and critic. His poetry includes *La Jeune parque* (1917) and "Le Cimetière marin" (1922).

val·et /vaˈlā; ˈvalā; ˈvalit/ ▸*n.* **1** a man's personal male attendant, responsible for his clothes and appearance. ■ a hotel employee performing such duties for guests. ■ a rack or stand on which to hang clothing. **2** a person employed to park cars.
▸*v.* (**-eted, -et·ing**) [*trans.*] act as a valet to (a particular man). ■ [*intrans.*] work as a valet. ▷late 15th cent. (denoting a footman acting as an attendant to a horseman): from French; related to VASSAL.

val·et park·ing ▸*n.* a service provided at a restaurant, club, or airport whereby an attendant parks and retrieves patrons' vehicles.

val·e·tu·di·nar·i·an /ˌvaləˌt(y)o͞odnˈe(ə)rēən/ ▸*n.* a person who is unduly anxious about their health. ■ a person suffering from poor health.
▸*adj.* showing undue concern about one's health. ■ suffering from poor health. ▷early 18th cent.: from Latin *valetudinarius* 'in ill health' (from *valetudo* 'health,' from *valere* 'be well') + -AN. —**val·e·tu·di·nar·i·an·ism** /-ˌnizəm/ *n.*

val·e·tu·di·nar·y /ˌvaləˈt(y)o͞odnˌerē/ ▸*adj.* & *n.* (*pl.* **-naries**) another term for VALETUDINARIAN.

val·gus /ˈvalgəs/ ▸*n. Medicine* a deformity involving oblique displacement of part of a limb away from the midline. The opposite of VARUS. ▷early 19th cent.: from Latin, literally 'knock-kneed.'

Val·hal·la /valˈhalə; välˈhälə/ *Scandinavian Mythology* a hall in which heroes killed in battle were believed to feast with Odin for eternity. ▷modern Latin, from Old Norse *Valhǫll,* from *valr* 'the slain' + *hǫll* 'hall.'

val·iant /ˈvalyənt/ ▸*adj.* possessing or showing courage or determination: *she made a valiant effort to hold her anger in check | a valiant warrior.* ▷Middle English (also in the sense 'robust, well-built'): from Old French *vailant,* based on Latin *valere* 'be strong.' —**val·iant·ly** *adv.*

Pronunciation Key ə *ago;* ər *over;* ˈə *or* ˌə *up;* ˈər *or* ˌər *fur;* a *hat;* ā *rate;* ä *car;* CH *chew;* e *let;* ē *see;* e(ə)r *air;* i *fit;* ī *by;* i(ə)r *ear;* NG *sing;* ō *go;* ô *for;* oi *boy;* o͝o *good;* o͞o *goo;* ou *out;* SH *she;* TH *thin;* T͟H *then;* (h)w *why;* ZH *vision*

val·id /ˈvalid/ ▸*adj.* actually supporting the intended point or claim; acceptable as cogent: *a valid criticism.* See note at **BELIEVABLE.** ■ legally binding due to having been executed in compliance with the law: *a valid contract.* ■ legally acceptable: *the visas are valid for thirty days.* ▷late 16th cent.: from French *valide* or Latin *validus* 'strong,' from *valere* 'be strong.' —**va·lid·i·ty** /vəˈlidətē/ *n.* —**val·id·ly** *adv.*

val·i·date /ˈvaləˌdāt/ ▸*v.* [*trans.*] check or prove the validity or accuracy of (something): *these estimates have been validated by periodic surveys.* ■ demonstrate or support the truth or value of: *in a healthy family a child's feelings are validated.* ■ make or declare legally valid. ▷mid 17th cent. (in the sense 'make legally valid'): from medieval Latin *validat-* 'made legally valid,' from the verb *validare*, from Latin *validus* (see **VALID**). —**val·i·da·tion** /ˌvaləˈdāsHən/ *n.*

val·ine /ˈvalˌēn; ˈvāˌlēn/ ▸*n. Biochemistry* an amino acid that is a constituent of most proteins. It is an essential nutrient in the diet of vertebrates. • Chem. formula: $(CH_3)_2CHCH(NH_2)COOH$. ▷early 20th cent.: from *val(eric acid)* + **-INE**[4].

va·lise /vəˈlēs/ ▸*n.* a small traveling bag or suitcase. ▷early 17th cent.: from French, from Italian *valigia*; compare with medieval Latin *valesia*, of unknown origin.

Val·i·um /ˈvalēəm/ ▸*n.* trademark for **DIAZEPAM.** ▷1960s: of unknown origin.

Val·kyr·ie /valˈki(ə)rē; ˈvalkərē/ ▸*n. Scandinavian Mythology* each of Odin's twelve handmaidens who conducted the slain warriors of their choice from the battlefield to Valhalla. ▷from Old Norse *Valkyrja*, literally 'chooser of the slain,' from *valr* 'the slain' + *kyrja* 'chooser.'

Val·la·do·lid /ˌvalədəˈlid; ˌbäyədəˈlēd/ **1** a city in northern Spain, capital of Castilla-León region; pop. 345,000. It was the principal residence of the kings of Castile in the 15th century. **2** former name (until 1828) of **MORELIA.**

val·lec·u·la /vəˈlekyələ/ ▸*n.* (*pl.* **-lae** /-ˌlē; -ˌlī/) *Anatomy & Botany* a groove or furrow. ▷mid 19th cent.: from a late Latin variant of Latin *vallicula*, diminutive of Latin *vallis* 'valley.' —**val·lec·u·lar** /-lər/ *adj.*

Val·le·jo /vəˈlāō; -ˌhō/ an industrial port city in north central California, on San Pablo Bay, northeast of San Francisco; pop. 109,199.

Val·let·ta /vəˈletə/ the capital and chief port of Malta; pop. 9,000. ▷named after Jean de *La Valette*, grand master of the Knights of Malta, who built the town after 1565.

val·ley /ˈvalē/ ▸*n.* (*pl.* **-leys**) **1** a low area of land between hills or mountains, typically with a river or stream flowing through it. **2** *Architecture* an internal angle formed by the intersecting planes of a roof, or by the slope of a roof and a wall. ▷Middle English: from Old French *valee*, based on Latin *vallis, valles*; compare with **VALE**[1].

val·ley fe·ver (also **San Joa·quin Val·ley fe·ver**) ▸*n.* informal term for **COCCIDIOIDOMYCOSIS.**

Val·ley Forge the site on the Schuylkill River in Pennsylvania, about 20 miles (32 km) northwest of Philadelphia, where George Washington's Continental Army spent the winter of 1777–78 in conditions of extreme hardship during the American Revolution.

Val·ley Girl (also **Val·ley girl**) ▸*n. informal* a fashionable and affluent teenage girl from the San Fernando valley in southern California.

Val·ley of the Kings a valley near ancient Thebes in Egypt where the pharaohs of the New Kingdom (*c.*1550–1070 BC) were buried.

Val·ley Stream an industrial and commercial village in west central Long Island, southeast of New York; pop. 33,946.

Va·lois /valˈwä; ˈvalˌwä/ the French royal house from the accession of Philip VI, successor to the last Capetian king, in 1328 to the death of Henry III in 1589, when the throne passed to the Bourbons.

Va·lo·na /vəˈlōnə/ Italian name for **VLORË.**

va·lo·ni·a /vəˈlōnēə/ ▸*n.* (also **va·lo·ni·a oak**) an evergreen oak tree native to southern Europe and western Asia. See also **ALEPPO GALL.** • *Quercus macrolepis*, family Fagaceae. ■ the acorn cups of this tree, which yield a black dye and are used in tanning. ▷early 18th cent.: from Italian *vallonia*, based on Greek *balanos* 'acorn.'

val·or /ˈvalər/ (*Brit.* **val·our**) ▸*n.* great courage in the face of danger, esp. in battle: *the medals are awarded for acts of valor.* ▷Middle English (denoting worth derived from personal qualities or rank): via Old French from late Latin *valor*, from *valere* 'be strong.' —**val·or·ous** /-ərəs/ *adj.*

val·or·ize /ˈvaləˌrīz/ ▸*v.* [*trans.*] give or ascribe value or validity to (something): *the culture valorizes the individual.* ■ raise or fix the price or value of (a commodity or currency) by artificial means, esp. by government action. ▷1920s: back-formation from *valorization* (from French *valorisation*, from *valeur* 'value'). —**val·or·i·za·tion** /ˌvalərəˈzāsHən/ *n.*

Val·pa·raí·so /ˌvalpəˈrīzō; ˌbälpärəˈēsō/ the principal port of Chile, in the center of the country, near Santiago; pop. 277,000.

Val·po·li·cel·la /ˌvalˌpōləˈcHelə; ˌväl-/ ▸*n.* red Italian wine made in the Val Policella district.

val·pro·ic ac·id /valˈprō-ik/ ▸*n. Chemistry* a synthetic crystalline compound with anticonvulsant properties, used (generally as salts) in the treatment of epilepsy. • Alternative name: **2-propylpentanoic acid**; chem. formula: $C_7H_{15}COOH$. ▷1970s: *valproic* from *valeric* (see **VALERIC ACID**) + *pro(pyl)* + **-IC.** —**val·pro·ate** /-ˈprōˌāt; -ət/ *n.*

Val·sal·va ma·neu·ver /valˈsalvə/ ▸*n. Medicine* the action of attempting to exhale with the nostrils and mouth, or the glottis, closed. This increases pressure in the middle ear and the chest, as when bracing to lift heavy objects, and is used as a means of equalizing pressure in the ears. ▷late 19th cent.: named after Antonio M. *Valsalva* (1666–1723), Italian anatomist.

valse /väls/ ▸*n.* (*pl.* same) French term for **WALTZ** (esp. as used in the titles of pieces of music). ▷late 18th cent.: via French from German *Walzer.*

val·u·a·ble /ˈvalyə(wə)bəl/ ▸*adj.* worth a great deal of money: *a valuable antique.* ■ extremely useful or important: *my time is valuable.*
▸*n.* (usu. **valuables**) a thing that is of great worth, esp. a small item of personal property: *put all your valuables in the hotel safe.* —**val·u·a·bly** /-blē/ *adv.*

val·u·a·ble con·sid·er·a·tion ▸*n. Law* legal consideration having some economic value, which is necessary for a contract to be enforceable.

val·u·a·tion /ˌvalyo͞oˈāsHən/ ▸*n.* an estimation of something's worth, esp. one carried out by a professional appraiser: *it is wise to obtain an independent valuation.* ■ the monetary worth of something, esp. as estimated by an appraiser. —**val·u·ate** /ˈvalyo͞oˌāt/ *v.*

val·u·a·tor /ˈvalyəˌwātər/ ▸*n. archaic* a person who makes valuations.

val·ue /ˈvalyo͞o/ ▸*n.* **1** the regard that something is held to deserve; the importance or preciousness of something: *your support is of great value.* ■ the material or monetary worth of something: *prints seldom rise in value | equipment is included up to a total value of $500.* ■ the worth of something compared to the price paid or asked for it: *at $12.50 the book is a* ***good value.*** ■ the usefulness of something considered in respect of a particular purpose: *some new drugs are of great value in treating cancer.* ■ the relative rank, importance, or power of a playing card, chess piece, etc., according to the rules of the game. **2** (**values**) a person's principles or standards of behavior; one's judgment of what is important in life: *they internalize their parents' rules and values.* **3** the numerical amount denoted by an algebraic term; a magnitude, quantity, or number: *the mean value of x | an accurate value for the mass of Venus.* **4** *Music* the relative duration of the sound signified by a note. **5** *Linguistics* the meaning of a word or other linguistic unit. ■ the quality or tone of a spoken sound; the sound represented by a letter. **6** *Art* the relative degree of lightness or darkness of a particular color: *the artist has used adjacent color values as the landscape recedes.*
▸*v.* (**-ues, -ued, -u·ing**) [*trans.*] **1** (often **be valued**) estimate the monetary worth of (something): *his estate* ***was valued at*** *$45,000.* **2** consider (someone or something) to be important or beneficial; have a high opinion of: *she had come to value her privacy and independence |* [as *adj.*] (**valued**) *a valued friend.* ▷Middle English: from Old French, feminine past participle of *valoir* 'be worth,' from Latin *valere.*

val·ue add·ed ▸*n. Economics* the amount by which the value of an article is increased at each stage of its production, exclusive of initial costs.
▸*adj.* [*attrib.*] (**value-added**) (of goods) having features added to a basic line or model for which the buyer is prepared to pay extra. ■ (of a company) offering specialized or extended services in a commercial area.

val·ue-add·ed tax (abbr.: **VAT**) ▸*n.* a tax on the amount by which the value of an article has been increased at each stage of its production or distribution.

val·ue a·nal·y·sis ▸*n.* the systematic and critical assessment by an organization of every feature of a product to ensure that its cost is no greater than is necessary to carry out its functions.

val·ue-free ▸*adj.* free from criteria imposed by subjective values or standards; purely objective: *real science could and should be value-free.*

val·ue judg·ment /ˈvalyo͞o ˌjəjmənt/ ▸*n.* an assessment of something as good or bad in terms of one's standards or priorities.

val·ue-lad·en ▸*adj.* presupposing the acceptance of a particular set of values: *governments' judgments are value-laden.*

val·ue·less /ˈvalyo͞oləs/ ▸*adj.* having no value; worthless: *cherished but valueless heirlooms.* —**val·ue·less·ness** *n.*

val·ue-neu·tral ▸*adj.* not presupposing the acceptance of any particular values.

val·ue stock ▸*n. Finance* shares of a company with solid fundamentals that are priced below those of its peers, based on analysis of price/earnings ratio, yield, and other factors. Compare with **GROWTH STOCK.**

va·lu·ta /vəˈlo͞otə/ ▸*n.* the value of one currency with respect to its exchange rate with another. ■ foreign currency: *these internal flights supply valuta to the cash-starved confederation.* ▷late 19th cent.: from Italian, literally 'value.'

val·vate /ˈvalˌvāt/ ▸*adj. Botany* (of sepals or other parts) having adjacent edges abutting rather than overlapping. Compare with **IMBRICATE.** ▷early 19th cent.: from Latin *valvatus* 'having folding doors,' from *valva* 'valve.'

valve /valv/ ▸*n.* a device for controlling the passage of fluid through a pipe or duct, esp. an automatic device allowing movement in one direction only. ■ (in full **ther·mi·on·ic valve**) *Electronics* British term for **THERMIONIC TUBE.** ■ *Music* a cylindrical mechanism in a brass instrument that, when depressed or turned, admits air into different sections of tubing and so extends the range of available notes. ■ *Anatomy & Zoology* a membranous fold in a hollow organ or tubular structure, such as a blood vessel or the digestive tract, that maintains the flow of the contents in one direction by closing in response to any pressure from reverse flow. ■ *Zoology* each of the halves of the hinged shell of a bivalve mollusk or brachiopod, or of the parts of the compound shell of a barnacle. ■ *Botany* each of the halves or sections into which a dry fruit (esp. a pod or capsule) dehisces. ▷late Middle English (denoting a leaf of a folding or double door): from Latin *valva.* —**valved** *adj.* [in *combination*] *a branchiopod has a two-valved outer covering* —**valve·less** *adj.*

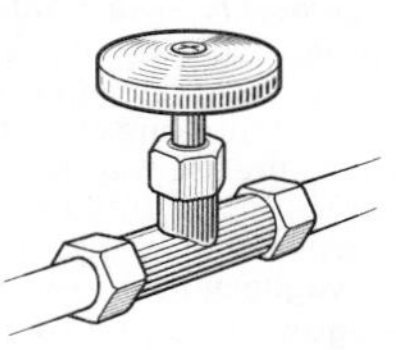

valve

valve head ▸*n.* the part of a vertically opening valve that is lifted off the valve aperture to open the valve.

val·vu·lar /ˈvalvyələr/ ▸*adj.* relating to, having, or acting as a valve or valves: *valvular heart disease | three pairs of valvular apertures.* ▷late 18th cent.: from modern Latin *valvula* (diminutive of Latin *valva* 'leaf of a door') + **-AR**[1].

val·vu·li·tis /ˌvalvyəˈlītis/ ▸*n. Medicine* inflammation of the valves of the heart.

vam·brace /ˈvamˌbrās/ ▸*n. historical* a piece of armor for the arm, esp. the forearm. ▷Middle English: from an Anglo-Norman French shortening of Old French *avantbras*, from *avant* 'before' + *bras* 'arm.' Compare with **VAMPLATE.**

va·moose /vaˈmo͞os; və-/ ▸*v.* [*intrans.*] *informal* depart hurriedly: *we'd better vamoose before we're caught.* ▷mid 19th cent.: from Spanish *vamos* 'let us go.'

vamp[1] /vamp/ ▸*n.* **1** the upper front part of a boot or shoe. **2** (in jazz and popular music) a short, simple introductory passage, usually repeated several times until otherwise instructed.
▸*v.* **1** [*trans.*] attach a new upper to (a boot or shoe). ■ (**vamp something up**) *informal* repair or improve something: *the production values have been vamped up.* **2** [*intrans.*] repeat a short, simple passage of music: *the band was vamping gently behind his busy lead guitar.* ▷Middle English (denoting the foot of a stocking): shortening of Old French *avantpie*, from *avant* 'before' + *pie* 'foot.' The musical sense of the verb developed from the general sense 'improvise.'

vamp[2] *informal* ▸*n.* a woman who uses sexual attraction to exploit men.

▸*v.* [*trans.*] **1** blatantly set out to attract: *she had not vamped him like some wicked Jezebel.* **2** (in fiction) turn (someone) into a vampire. ▹early 20th cent.: abbreviation of VAMPIRE. —**vamp·ish** *adj.* —**vamp·ish·ly** *adv.* —**vamp·y** *adj.*

vam·pire /ˈvamˌpī(ə)r/ ▸*n.* **1** a corpse supposed, in European folklore, to leave its grave at night to drink the blood of the living by biting their necks with long pointed canine teeth. ■ *figurative* a person who preys ruthlessly on others: *the protectionist vampires in the Congress.* **2** (also **vam·pire bat**) a small bat that feeds on the blood of mammals or birds using its two sharp incisor teeth and anticoagulant saliva, found mainly in tropical America. See also FALSE VAMPIRE. • Family Desmodontidae (or Phyllostomidae): three species, in particular the **common vampire** (*Desmodus rotundus*). ▹mid 18th cent.: from French, from Hungarian *vampir*, perhaps from Turkish *uber* 'witch.' —**vam·pir·ic** /vamˈpirik/ *adj.*

vam·pir·ism /ˈvampīˌrizəm/ ▸*n.* the action or practices of a vampire.

vam·plate /ˈvamˌplāt/ ▸*n. historical* a circular plate on a spear or lance designed to protect the hand. ▹Middle English: from Anglo-Norman French *vauntplate*, from *avant* 'before' + *plate* 'thin plate.' Compare with VAMBRACE.

Van, Lake /van; vän/ a large saltwater lake in the mountains of eastern Turkey.

van[1] /van/ ▸*n.* a covered boxlike motor vehicle, typically having a rear door and sliding doors on the side panels, used for transporting goods or people. ■ a covered truck used for moving goods, esp. furniture. ■ *Brit.* an enclosed railroad freight-car. ■ *Brit.* a caravan. ▹early 19th cent.: shortening of CARAVAN.

van[2] ▸*n.* (**the van**) the foremost part of a company of people moving or preparing to move forward, esp. the foremost division of an advancing military force: ***in the van** were the foremost chiefs and some of the warriors astride horses.* ■ *figurative* the forefront: *he was **in the van** of the movement to encourage the cultivation of wildflowers.* ▹early 17th cent.: abbreviation of VANGUARD.

van[3] ▸*n.* **1** *archaic* a winnowing fan. **2** *archaic* or *poetic/literary* a bird's wing. ▹late Middle English: dialect variant of FAN[1], probably reinforced by Old French *van* or Latin *vannus.*

van·a·date /ˈvanəˌdāt/ ▸*n. Chemistry* a salt in which the anion contains vanadium and oxygen, esp. one of the anion $VO_4{}^{3-}$. ▹mid 19th cent.: from VANADIUM + -ATE[1].

va·nad·i·nite /vəˈnādnˌīt; -ˈnadn-/ ▸*n.* a rare reddish-brown mineral consisting of a vanadate and chloride of lead, typically occurring as an oxidation product of lead ores. ▹mid 19th cent.: from VANADIUM + -ITE[1].

va·na·di·um /vəˈnādēəm/ ▸*n.* the chemical element of atomic number 23, a hard gray metal of the transition series, used to make alloy steels. (Symbol: **V**) ▹mid 19th cent.: modern Latin, from Old Norse *Vanadís* (a name of the Scandinavian goddess Freyja).

va·na·di·um steel ▸*n.* a strong alloy of steel containing vanadium.

Van Al·len /van ˈalən/, James Alfred (1914–), U.S. physicist. He used balloons and rockets to study cosmic radiation in the upper atmosphere and showed that specific zones of high radiation were the result of charged particles from the solar wind being trapped in two belts around the earth.

Van Al·len belt ▸*n.* each of two regions of intense radiation partly surrounding the earth at heights of several thousand kilometers.

Van·brugh /ˈvanbrə/, Sir John (1664–1726), British architect and playwright. His comedies include *The Relapse* (1696) and *The Provok'd Wife* (1697). His architectural works include Castle Howard (1702) and Blenheim Palace (1705), both produced in collaboration with Nicholas Hawksmoor (1661-1736).

Van Bur·en[1] /van ˈbyŏŏrən/, Abigail (1918–), U.S. journalist; born *Pauline Esther Friedman.* Author of the "Dear Abby" advice column from 1956, she competed with her twin sister, advice columnist Ann Landers. In 1987, Van Buren's column became coauthored with her daughter, Jeanne Phillips, who, by 2000, had assumed sole authorship.

Van Bu·ren[2], Martin (1782–1862), 8th president of the U.S. 1837–41. Before succeeding President Jackson, he served as vice president 1833–37. A Democrat, he is noted for his development of the two-party system. His measure of placing government funds, previously held in private banks, in an independent government treasury displeased many Democrats.

van·co·my·cin /ˌvaNGkəˈmīsin/ ▸*n. Medicine* a bacterial antibiotic used against resistant strains of streptococcus and staphylococcus. • This antibiotic is obtained from the bacterium *Streptomyces orientalis.* ▹1950s: from *vanco-* (of unknown origin) + -MYCIN.

Van·cou·ver[1] /vanˈkōōvər/ **1** a city and port in British Columbia, in southwestern Canada, on the mainland opposite Vancouver Island; pop. 471,844. It is the largest city and chief port in western Canada. **2** an industrial port city in southwestern Washington, on the Columbia River, north of Portland in Oregon; pop. 143,560.

Van·cou·ver[2], George (1757–98), English navigator. He led an exploration of the coasts of Australia, New Zealand, and Hawaii (1791–92) and later charted much of the west coast of North America between southern Alaska and California. Vancouver Island and the city of Vancouver, Canada, are named after him.

Van·cou·ver Is·land a large island off the Pacific coast of Canada, in southwestern British Columbia. Its capital, Victoria, is the capital of British Columbia.

Van·da /ˈvändə/ Swedish name for VANTAA.

van·dal /ˈvandl/ ▸*n.* **1** a person who deliberately destroys or damages public or private property: *the rear window of the car was smashed by vandals.* **2** (**Vandal**) a member of a Germanic people that ravaged Gaul, Spain, and North Africa in the 4th–5th centuries and sacked Rome in AD 455. ▹from Latin *Vandalus*, of Germanic origin. Sense 1 dates from the mid 17th cent.

van·dal·ism /ˈvandlˌizəm/ ▸*n.* action involving deliberate destruction of or damage to public or private property. —**van·dal·is·tic** /ˌvandlˈistik/ *adj.* —**van·dal·is·ti·cal·ly** /ˌvandlˈistik(ə)lē/ *adv.*

van·dal·ize /ˈvandlˌīz/ ▸*v.* [*trans.*] deliberately destroy or damage (public or private property): *stations have been wrecked and vandalized beyond recognition.*

Van de Graaff gen·er·a·tor /ˈvan də ˌgraf/ ▸*n. Physics* a machine devised to generate electrostatic charge by means of a vertical endless belt collecting charge from a voltage source and transferring it to a large insulated metal dome, where a high voltage is produced. ▹mid 20th cent.: named after Robert Jemison *Van de Graaff* (1901–67), American physicist.

Van·der·bijl·park /ˈvandərˌbīlˌpärk/ a steel-manufacturing city in South Africa, south of Johannesburg; pop. 540,000.

Van·der·bilt /ˈvandərˌbilt/, Cornelius (1794–1877), U.S. businessman and philanthropist. He amassed a fortune from shipping and railroads and made an endowment to found Vanderbilt University in Nashville, Tennessee (1873).

Van der Post /ˌvan dər ˈpōst/, Sir Laurens (Jan) (1906–96), South African explorer and writer.His books, including *Venture to the Interior* (1952) and *The Lost World of the Kalahari* (1958), combine travel writing and descriptions of fauna with philosophical speculation.

van der Waals forc·es /ˈvan dər ˌwôlz; -ˌvälz/ ▸*plural n. Chemistry* weak, short-range electrostatic attractive forces between uncharged molecules, arising from the interaction of permanent or transient electric dipole moments. ▹late 19th cent.: named after Johannes *van der Waals* (1837–1923), Dutch physicist.

Van De·van·ter /van dəˈvantər/, Willis (1859–1941), U.S. Supreme Court associate justice 1910–37. Appointed to the Court by President Taft, he was a conservative and stayed on the Court longer than he intended in hopes of blocking many of President Franklin D. Roosevelt's New Deal programs.

Martin Van Buren

van de Vel·de[1] /ˌvän də ˈveldə/ the name of a family of Dutch painters. ■ **Willem** (1611–93); known as **Willem van de Velde the Elder**. He painted marine subjects, was official artist to the Dutch fleet, and worked for Britain's Charles II. ■ **Willem** (1633–1707), son of Willem the Elder; known as **Willem van de Velde the Younger**. He was also a notable marine artist who painted for Charles II. ■ **Adriaen** (1636–72); son of Willem the Elder. He painted landscapes, portraits, and biblical and genre scenes.

van de Vel·de[2], Henri (Clemens) (1863–1957), Belgian architect, designer, and teacher. He pioneered the development of art nouveau design and architecture in Europe.

Van Die·men's Land /van ˈdēmənz/ former name (until 1855) of TASMANIA.

Van Dor·en /van ˈdôrən/ U.S. writers. **Carl (Clinton) Van Doren** (1885–1950), a historian and literary critic, was noted as the author of *Benjamin Franklin* (1938). His brother **Mark (Albert) Van Doren** (1894–1972) was a poet and educator whose work is collected in *Collected Poems* (1939). Mark's son, **Charles Lincoln Van Doren** (1926–), a writer and an educator, wrote *The Idea of Progress* (1967) and *A History of Knowledge* (1991). In 1959, he was involved in a quiz show scandal when it was revealed that he had been given the answers for his appearances on television's "Twenty One" in 1956 where he won $129,000.

Van Dyck /van ˈdīk/ (also **Van·dyke**), Sir Anthony (1599–1641), Flemish painter. He is noted for his portraits of members of the English court.

Van Dyke /van ˈdīk/, Dick (1925–), U.S. actor and comedian. He starred in the television series "The Dick Van Dyke Show" (1961–66) and "Diagnosis Murder" (1993–). His movies include *Bye Bye Birdie* (1963), which he also did on Broadway 1960–61, and *Mary Poppins* (1965).

Van·dyke (also **van·dyke**) ▸*n.* **1** a broad lace or linen collar with an edge deeply cut into large points (in imitation of a style frequently depicted in portraits by Sir Anthony Van Dyck), fashionable in the 18th century. ■ each of a number of large deep-cut points on the border or fringe of a garment or piece of material. **2** (also **Van·dyke beard**) a neat, pointed beard.
▸*adj.* [*attrib.*] denoting a style of garment or decorative design associated with the portraits of Van Dyck: *a Vandyke handkerchief.*

Vandyke beard

Van·dyke brown ▸*n.* a deep rich brown.

vane /vān/ ▸*n.* a broad blade attached to a rotating axis or wheel that pushes or is pushed by wind or water and forms part of a machine or device such as a windmill, propeller, or turbine. ■ short for WEATHERVANE. ■ the flat part on either side of the shaft of a feather. ■ a broad, flat projecting surface designed to guide the motion of a projectile, such as a feather on an arrow or a fin on a torpedo. ▹late Middle English: dialect variant of obsolete *fane* 'banner,' of Germanic origin. —**vaned** *adj.* [usu. in *combination*] *a three-vaned windmill.*

Vä·nern /ˈvenə(r)n/ a lake in southwestern Sweden, the largest lake in the country and the third largest in Europe.

Van Eyck /van ˈīk/, Jan (*c.*1370–1441), Flemish painter. Notable works: *The Adoration of the Lamb* (known as the Ghent Altarpiece, 1432) in the church of St. Bavon in Ghent and *The Arnolfini Marriage* (1434).

vang /vaNG/ ▸*n. Sailing* each of two guy ropes running from the end of a gaff to opposite sides of the deck. ▹mid 18th cent.: variant of obsolete *fang*, denoting a gripping device, from Old Norse *fang* 'grasp,' of Germanic origin.

Van Gogh /van ˈgō; ˈgäKH/, Vincent (Willem) (1853–90), Dutch painter. He is best known for his post-Impressionist work. His most famous pictures include several studies of sunflowers and *A Starry Night* (1889). Suffering from severe depression, he cut off part of his own ear and eventually committed suicide.

van·guard /ˈvanˌgärd/ ▸*n.* a group of people leading the way in new developments or ideas: *the experimental spirit of the modernist vanguard.* ■ a position at the forefront of new developments or ideas: *the prototype was* ***in the vanguard of*** *technical development.* ■ the foremost part of an advancing army or naval force. ▷late Middle English (denoting the foremost part of an army): shortening of Old French *avan(t)garde,* from *avant* 'before' + *garde* 'guard.' **—van·guard·ism** /-ˌizəm/ *n.* **—van·guard·ist** *n.*

va·nil·la /vəˈnilə/ ▸*n.* **1** a substance obtained from vanilla beans or produced artificially and used to flavor sweet foods or to impart a fragrant scent to cosmetic preparations: [as *adj.*] *vanilla ice cream.* ■ ice cream flavored with vanilla: *four scoops of vanilla with hot fudge sauce.* ■ [as *adj.*] of the yellowish-white color of vanilla ice cream: *a vanilla dress.* **2** a tropical climbing orchid that has fragrant flowers and long podlike fruit. • Genus *Vanilla,* family Orchidaceae: many species, in particular *V. planifolia,* the chief commercial source of vanilla beans. ■ (also **va·nil·la bean** or **va·nil·la pod**) the fruit of this plant, which is cured and then either used in cooking or processed to extract an essence that is used for flavor and fragrance.
▸*adj.* having no special or extra features; ordinary: *it will be able to do tricks that* ***plain vanilla*** *CD-ROMs can't.* ▷mid 17th cent.: from Spanish *vainilla* 'pod,' diminutive of *vaina* 'sheath, pod,' from Latin *vagina* 'sheath.' (See **VAGINA**.) The spelling change was due to association with French *vanille.*

va·nil·lin /vəˈnilin; ˈvanl-/ ▸*n. Chemistry* a fragrant compound that is the essential constituent of vanilla. • Alternative name: **3-methoxy-4-hydroxybenzaldehyde**; chem. formula: $CH_3OC_6H_3(OH)CHO$. ▷mid 19th cent.: from **VANILLA** + **-IN**[1].

Va·nir /ˈväni(ə)r/ ▸*n. Scandinavian Mythology* a race of Norse gods, allies of the Aesir, that function as fertility divinities.

van·ish /ˈvanish/ ▸*v.* [*intrans.*] **1** disappear suddenly and completely: *Mary vanished without trace.* ■ gradually cease to exist: *the days of the extended family are vanishing.* **2** *Mathematics* become zero. ▷Middle English: shortening of Old French *e(s)vaniss-,* lengthened stem of *e(s)vanir,* from Latin *evanescere* 'die away.'

van·ish·ing cream ▸*n. dated* a cream or ointment that leaves no visible trace when rubbed into the skin.

van·ish·ing·ly /ˈvanishinglē/ ▸*adv.* [as *submodifier*] in such a manner or to such a degree as almost to become invisible, nonexistent, or negligible: *an event of* ***vanishingly small*** *probability.*

van·ish·ing point ▸*n.* **1** the point at which receding parallel lines viewed in perspective appear to converge. **2** [in *sing.*] the point at which something that has been growing smaller or increasingly faint disappears altogether: *custody fees have dropped close to the vanishing point.*

van·i·tas /ˈvanəˌtäs/ ▸*n.* a still-life painting of a 17th-century Dutch genre containing symbols of death or change as a reminder of their inevitability. ▷Latin, literally 'vanity.'

van·i·ty /ˈvanətē/ ▸*n.* (*pl.* **-ties**) **1** excessive pride in or admiration of one's own appearance or achievements: *it flattered his vanity to think I was in love with him | the personal vanities and ambitions of politicians.* See notes at **EGOTISM, PRIDE**. ■ [as *adj.*] denoting a person or company that publishes works at the author's expense: *a vanity press.* **2** the quality of being worthless or futile: *the vanity of human wishes.* **3** a dressing table. ■ a bathroom unit consisting of a washbasin typically set into a counter with a cabinet beneath. ▷Middle English: from Old French *vanite,* from Latin *vanitas,* from *vanus* 'empty' (see **VAIN**).

van·i·ty case ▸*n.* a small case fitted with a mirror and compartments for makeup.

Van·i·ty Fair *n.* the world regarded as a place of frivolity and idle amusement (originally with reference to Bunyan's *Pilgrim's Progress*).

van·i·ty mir·ror ▸*n.* a small mirror used for applying makeup, esp. one fitted in a visor of a motor vehicle.

van·i·ty plate ▸*n.* a vehicle license plate bearing a distinctive or personalized combination of letters, numbers, or both.

van·i·ty ta·ble ▸*n.* a dressing table.

Van Nuys /van ˈnīz/ an industrial and residential section of northwestern Los Angeles in California, a center of aerospace manufacturing.

van·pool /ˈvanˌpo͞ol/ ▸*n.* an arrangement whereby commuters travel together in a van.

van·quish /ˈvangkwish/ ▸*v.* [*trans.*] defeat thoroughly: *Mexican forces vanquished the French army in a battle in Puebla.* ▷Middle English: from Old French *vencus, venquis* (past participle and past tense of *veintre*), *vainquiss-* (lengthened stem of *vainquir*), from Latin *vincere* 'conquer.' **—van·quish·a·ble** *adj.* **—van·quish·er** *n.*

Van Rens·se·laer /ˌvan ˌrensəˈli(ə)r; ˈrensələr/, Stephen (1764–1839), U.S. army officer and politician. He held various state positions in New York and participated in the War of 1812. A Federalist, he served in the U.S. House of Representatives 1822–29. He also founded the technical school (1824) that became Rensselaer Polytechnic Institute in Troy, New York.

Van·taa /ˈvänˌtä/ a city in southern Finland, a northern suburb of Helsinki; pop. 155,000. Swedish name **VANDA**.

van·tage /ˈvantij/ (usu. **van·tage point**) ▸*n.* a place or position affording a good view of something: *from my vantage point I could see into the front garden | figurative the past is continuously reinterpreted from the vantage point of the present.* ▷Middle English: from Anglo-Norman French, shortening of Old French *avantage* 'advantage.'

Va·nu·a·tu /ˌväno͞oˈäto͞o; ˌvano͞o-/ a country that consists of a group of islands in the southwestern Pacific Ocean; pop. 202,000; capital, Vila; languages, Bislama, English, and French (all official). **—Va·nu·a·tu·an** /-ˈäto͞oən/ *adj.* & *n.*

The islands were administered jointly by Britain and France as the New Hebrides. Vanuatu became an independent republic within the Commonwealth of Nations in 1980.

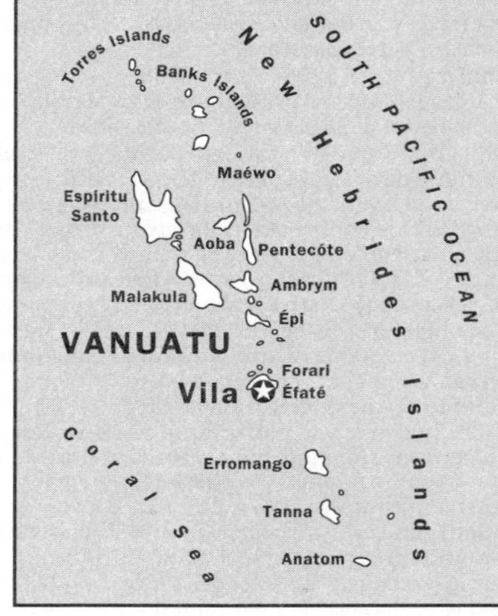

Van·zet·ti /vanˈzetē/, Bartolomeo (1888–1927), U.S. political radical; born in Italy. In 1921, along with Nicola Sacco, he was accused and convicted of murder in a sensational, controversial trial. In 1927, both men were executed in the electric chair; fifty years later, their names were cleared of any crimes.

vap·id /ˈvapid/ ▸*adj.* offering nothing that is stimulating or challenging: *tuneful but vapid musical comedies.* ▷mid 17th cent. (used originally in description of drinks as 'lacking in flavor'): from Latin *vapidus.* **—va·pid·i·ty** /vaˈpidətē/ *n.* **—vap·id·ly** *adv.*

va·por /ˈvāpər/ (*Brit.* **va·pour**) ▸*n.* a substance diffused or suspended in the air, esp. one normally liquid or solid: *dense clouds of smoke and toxic vapor | chemical vapors.* ■ *Physics* a gaseous substance that is below its critical temperature, and can therefore be liquefied by pressure alone. Compare with **GAS**. ■ (**the vapors**) *dated* a sudden feeling of faintness or nervousness or a state of depression.
▸*v.* [*intrans.*] talk in a vacuous, boasting, or pompous way: *he was vaporing on about the days of his youth.* ▷late Middle English: from Old French *vapour,* or from Latin *vapor* 'steam, heat.' The current verb sense dates from the early 17th cent. **—va·por·ish** *adj.* (*archaic*) **—va·por·ous** /ˈvāpərəs/ *adj.* **—va·por·ous·ness** /ˈvāpərəsnəs/ *n.* **—va·por·y** /ˈvāpərē/ *adj.*

va·por bar·ri·er ▸*n.* a thin layer of impermeable material, typically polyethylene sheeting, included in building construction to prevent moisture from damaging the fabric of the building.

va·por den·si·ty ▸*n. Chemistry* the density of a particular gas or vapor relative to that of hydrogen at the same pressure and temperature.

va·po·ret·to /ˌväpəˈretō; ˌvapə-/ ▸*n.* (*pl.* **-ret·ti** /-ˈretē/ or **-ret·tos**) (in Venice) a canal boat (originally a steamboat, now a motorboat) used for public transportation. ▷Italian, diminutive of *vapore* 'steam,' from Latin *vapor.*

va·por·ize /ˈvāpəˌrīz/ ▸*v.* convert or be converted into vapor: [*trans.*] *there is a large current which is sufficient to vaporize carbon* | [*intrans.*] *cold gasoline does not vaporize readily.* **—va·por·iz·a·ble** *adj.* **—va·por·i·za·tion** /ˌvāpərəˈzāshən; -ˌrīˈzā-/ *n.*

va·por·iz·er /ˈvāpəˌrīzər/ ▸*n.* a device that generates a particular substance in the form of vapor, esp. for medicinal inhalation.

va·por lock ▸*n.* an interruption in the flow of a liquid through a fuel line or other pipe as a result of vaporization of the liquid.

va·por pres·sure ▸*n. Chemistry* the pressure of a vapor in contact with its liquid or solid form.

va·por trail ▸*n.* another term for **CONTRAIL**.

va·por·ware /ˈvāpərˌwer/ (*Brit.* **va·pour·ware**) ▸*n. informal Computing* software or hardware that has been advertised but is not yet available to buy, either because it is only a concept or because it is still being written or designed.

va·pour ▸*n.* British spelling of **VAPOR**.

va·que·ro /väˈkerō/ ▸*n.* (*pl.* **-ros**) (in Spanish-speaking parts of the U.S.) a cowboy; a cattle driver. ▷Spanish, from *vaca* 'cow.'

VAR ▸*abbr.* value-added reseller, a company that adds extra features to products it has bought before selling them on. ■ value at risk, a method of quantifying the risk of holding a financial asset.

var. ▸*abbr.* variety.

va·ra /ˈvärə/ ▸*n.* **1** a unit of linear measure, formerly used in Latin America and Texas, equal to about 33 inches (84 cm). **2** a long spiked lance used by a picador.

va·rac·tor /ˈve(ə)rˌaktər; vəˈraktər/ ▸*n. Electronics* a semiconductor diode with a capacitance dependent on the applied voltage. ▷1950s: from elements of *variable reactor.*

Va·ra·na·si /vəˈränəsē/ a city on the Ganges River, in Uttar Pradesh, in northern India; pop. 926,000. It is a holy city and a place of pilgrimage for Hindus, who undergo ritual purification in the Ganges. Former name **BENARES**.

Va·rang·i·an /vəˈranjēən/ ▸*n.* any of the Scandinavian voyagers who traveled by land and up rivers into Russia in the 9th and 10th centuries AD, establishing the Rurik dynasty and gaining great influence in the Byzantine Empire. ▷from medieval Latin *Varangus* (a name ultimately from Old Norse, probably based on *vár* 'pledge') + **-IAN**.

Var·gas /ˈvärgəs/, Getúlio Dornelles (1883–1954), Brazilian statesman; president 1930–45 and 1951–54. After seizing power, he ruled as a virtual dictator until overthrown by a coup. Returned to power in 1951, he later committed suicide after widespread calls for his resignation.

Var·gas Llo·sa /ˈvärgəs ˈyōsə/, (Jorge) Mario (Pedro) (1936–), Peruvian novelist, playwright, and essayist. His novels include *Aunt Julia and the Scriptwriter* (1977) and *The War of the End of the World* (1982).

vari- ▸*comb. form* various: *variform.* ▷from Latin *varius.*

var·i·a·ble /ˈve(ə)rēəbəl/ ▸*adj.* **1** not consistent or having a fixed pattern; liable to change: *the quality of hospital food is highly variable | awards can be for variable amounts.* ■ (of a wind) tending to change direction. ■ *Mathematics* (of a quantity) able to assume different numerical values. ■ *Botany* & *Zoology* (of a species) liable to deviate from the typical color or form, or to occur in different colors or forms. **2** able to be changed or adapted: *the drill has variable speed.* ■ (of a gear) designed to give varying ratios or speeds.
▸*n.* an element, feature, or factor that is liable to vary or change: *there are too many variables involved to make any meaningful predictions.* ■ *Mathematics* a quantity that during a calculation is assumed to vary or be capable of varying in value. ■ *Computing* a data item that may take on more than one value during or between programs. ■ *Astronomy* short for **VARIABLE STAR**. ■ (**variables**) the region of light, variable winds to the north of the northeast trade winds or (in the southern hemisphere) between the southeast trade winds and the westerlies. ▷late Middle English: via Old French from Latin *variabilis,* from *variare* (see **VARY**). **—var·i·a·bil·i·ty** /ˌve(ə)rēəˈbilitē/ *n.* **—var·i·a·ble·ness** *n.* **—var·i·a·bly** /-blē/ *adv.*

var·i·a·ble cost ▸*n.* a cost that varies with the level of output.

var·i·a·ble-ge·om·e·try ▸*adj.* denoting a swing-wing aircraft.

var·i·a·ble-rate mort·gage ▸*n.* another term for ADJUSTABLE RATE MORTGAGE.

var·i·a·ble star ▸*n. Astronomy* a star whose brightness changes, either irregularly or regularly.

var·i·ance /ˈve(ə)rēəns/ ▸*n.* the fact or quality of being different, divergent, or inconsistent: *her light tone was **at variance with** her sudden trembling.* ■ the state or fact of disagreeing or quarreling: *they were **at variance with** all their previous allies.* ■ *chiefly Law* a discrepancy between two statements or documents. ■ *Law* an official dispensation from a rule or regulation, typically a building regulation. ■ *Statistics* a quantity equal to the square of the standard deviation. ■ (in accounting) the difference between expected and actual costs, profits, output, etc., in a statistical analysis. ▷Middle English: via Old French from Latin *variantia* 'difference,' from the verb *variare* (see VARY).

var·i·ant /ˈve(ə)rēənt/ ▸*n.* a form or version of something that differs in some respect from other forms of the same thing or from a standard: *clinically distinct variants of malaria* | [as *adj.*] *a variant spelling.* ▷late Middle English (as an adjective in the sense 'tending to vary'): from Old French, literally 'varying,' present participle of *varier* (see VARY). The noun dates from the mid 19th cent.

var·i·ate /ˈve(ə)rē-it; -ˌāt/ ▸*n.* another term for RANDOM VARIABLE.

var·i·a·tion /ˌve(ə)rēˈāsʜən/ ▸*n.* **1** a change or difference in condition, amount, or level, typically with certain limits: *regional variations in house prices* | *the figures showed marked variation from year to year.* ■ *Astronomy* a deviation of a celestial body from its mean orbit or motion. ■ *Mathematics* a change in the value of a function due to small changes in the values of its argument or arguments. ■ (also **mag·net·ic var·i·a·tion**) the angular difference between true north and magnetic north at a particular place. ■ *Biology* the occurrence of an organism in more than one distinct color or form. **2** a different or distinct form or version of something: *hurling is an Irish variation of field hockey.* ■ *Music* a version of a theme, modified in melody, rhythm, harmony, or ornamentation, so as to present it in a new but still recognizable form: *there is an eleven-bar theme followed by seven variations and a coda* | *figurative **variations on** the perennial theme of marital discord.* ■ *Ballet* a solo dance as part of a performance. ▷late Middle English (denoting variance or conflict): from Old French, or from Latin *variatio(n-)*, from the verb *variare* (see VARY). —**var·i·a·tion·al** /-sʜənl/ *adj.*

var·i·a·tion·ist /ˌve(ə)rēˈāsʜənist/ ▸*n.* a person who studies variations in usage among different speakers of the same language.

var·i·ce·al /ˌvarəˈsēəl/ ▸*adj. Zoology & Medicine* of, relating to, or involving a varix. ▷1960s: from Latin *varix, varic-*, on the pattern of words such as *corneal* and *laryngeal.*

var·i·cel·la /ˌvarəˈselə/ ▸*n. Medicine* technical term for CHICKEN POX. ■ (also **var·i·cel·la-zos·ter**) a herpesvirus that causes chicken pox and shingles; herpes zoster. ▷late 18th cent.: modern Latin, irregular diminutive of VARIOLA.

var·i·ces /ˈvarəˌsēz/ ▸ plural form of VARIX.

var·i·co·cele /ˈvarikōˌsēl/ ▸*n. Medicine* a mass of varicose veins in the spermatic cord. ▷mid 18th cent.: from Latin *varix, varic-* 'dilated vein' + -CELE.

var·i·col·ored /ˈve(ə)riˌkələrd/ (*Brit.* **var·i·col·oured**) ▸*adj.* consisting of several different colors. ▷mid 17th cent.: from Latin *varius* 'diverse' + COLORED.

var·i·cose /ˈvarəˌkōs/ ▸*adj.* [*attrib.*] affected by a condition causing the swelling and tortuous lengthening of veins, most often in the legs: *varicose veins.* ▷late Middle English: from Latin *varicosus*, from *varix* (see VARIX). —**var·i·cosed** *adj.* —**var·i·cos·i·ty** /ˌvariˈkäsitē/ *n.*

var·ied /ˈve(ə)rēd/ ▸*adj.* incorporating a number of different types or elements; showing variation or variety: *a little effort to make life pleasant and varied* | *a long and varied career.* —**var·ied·ly** *adv.*

var·i·e·gat·ed /ˈver(ē)əˌgātid/ ▸*adj.* exhibiting different colors, esp. as irregular patches or streaks: *variegated yellow bricks.* ■ *Botany* (of a plant or foliage) having or consisting of leaves that are edged or patterned in a second color, esp. white as well as green. ■ marked by variety: *his variegated and amusing observations.* ▷mid 17th cent.: from Latin *variegat-* 'made varied' (from the verb *variegare*, from *varius* 'diverse') + -ED[2]. —**var·i·e·gate** /ˈve(ə)r(ē)iˌgāt/ —**var·i·e·ga·tion** /ˌver(ē)iˈgāsʜən/ *n.*

va·ri·e·tal /vəˈrīətl/ ▸*adj.* **1** (of a wine or grape) made from or belonging to a single specified variety of grape. **2** *chiefly Botany Zoology* of, relating to, characteristic of, or forming a variety: *varietal names.*
▸*n.* a varietal wine. —**va·ri·e·tal·ly** *adv.*

va·ri·e·ty /vəˈrīətē/ ▸*n.* (*pl.* **-ties**) **1** the quality or state of being different or diverse; the absence of uniformity, sameness, or monotony: *it's the variety that makes my job so enjoyable.* ■ (**a variety of**) a number or range of things of the same general class that are different or distinct in character or quality: *the center offers a variety of leisure activities.* ■ a thing that differs in some way from others of the same general class or sort; a type: *fifty varieties of fresh and frozen pasta.* ■ a form of television or theater entertainment consisting of a series of different types of acts, such as singing, dancing, and comedy: *in 1937 she did another season of variety* | [as *adj.*] *a variety show.* **2** *Biology* a taxonomic category that ranks below subspecies (where present) or species, its members differing from others of the same subspecies or species in minor but permanent or heritable characteristics. Varieties are more often recognized in botany, in which they are designated in the style *Apium graveolens* var. *dulce*. Compare with FORM (sense 3) and SUBSPECIES. ■ a cultivated form of a plant. See CULTIVAR. ■ a plant or animal that varies in some trivial respect from its immediate parent or type. ▷late 15th cent.: from French *variété* or Latin *varietas*, from *varius* (see VARIOUS).
▸*PHRASE* □ **variety is the spice of life** *proverb* new and exciting experiences make life more interesting.

va·ri·e·ty meats ▸*plural n.* meat consisting of the entrails and internal organs of an animal.

va·ri·e·ty store ▸*n.* a small store selling a wide range of inexpensive items.

var·i·form /ˈve(ə)rəˌfôrm/ ▸*adj.* (of a group of things) differing from one another in form: *variform languages.* ■ (of a single thing or a mass) consisting of a variety of forms or things: *a variform education.* ▷mid 17th cent.: from Latin *varius* 'diverse' + -FORM.

va·ri·o·la /vəˈrīələ; ˌve(ə)rēˈōlə/ ▸*n. Medicine* technical term for SMALLPOX. ▷late 18th cent.: from medieval Latin, literally 'pustule, pock,' from Latin *varius* 'diverse.' —**va·ri·o·lar** /-lər/ *adj.* —**va·ri·o·lous** /-ləs/ *adj.* (*archaic*)

var·i·o·loid /ˈve(ə)rēəˌloid/ *Medicine* ▸*adj.* resembling smallpox.
▸*n.* a mild form of smallpox affecting people who have already had the disease or have been vaccinated against it.

var·i·om·e·ter /ˌve(ə)rēˈämitər/ ▸*n.* **1** a device for indicating an aircraft's rate of climb or descent. **2** an inductor whose total inductance can be varied by altering the relative position of two coaxial coils connected in series, or by permeability tuning, and so can be used to tune an electric circuit. **3** an instrument for measuring variations in the intensity of the earth's magnetic field.

var·i·o·rum /ˌve(ə)rēˈôrəm/ ▸*adj.* (of an edition of an author's works) having notes by various editors or commentators. ■ including variant readings from manuscripts or earlier editions.
▸*n.* a variorum edition. ▷early 18th cent.: genitive plural of *varius* 'diverse,' from Latin *editio cum notis variorum* 'edition with notes by various (commentators).'

var·i·ous /ˈve(ə)rēəs/ ▸*adj.* different from one another; of different kinds or sorts: *dresses of various colors* | *his grievances were many and various.* ■ having or showing different properties or qualities: *their environments are locally various.*
▸*adj. & pron.* more than one; individual and separate: [as *adj.*] *various people arrived late* | [as *pron.*] ***various of** her friends had called.* ▷late Middle English: from Latin *varius* 'changing, diverse' + -OUS. —**var·i·ous·ness** *n.*

USAGE In standard English, the word **various** is normally used as an adjective. It is best reserved for contexts indicating variety, and should not be used as a synonym for **several**. In colloquial American speech, **various** is sometimes also used (as though it were a pronoun) followed by *of*, as in ***various of** her friends had called*—another way of saying *some of* or *several of*. This use is discouraged by some traditionalists, however, because **various** is properly an adjective, not a pronoun, and **various of** erodes the sense of variety, diversity, and distinctness. This erosion or blurring of meaning is further evident in the use of **various different**, as in ***various different** kinds of oak*, a redundant wording that should be avoided.

var·i·ous·ly /ˈve(ə)rēəslē/ ▸*adv.* in several or different ways: *his early successes can be variously accounted for.*

Va·ris·can /vəˈriskən/ ▸*adj. Geology* another term for HERCYNIAN. ▷early 20th cent.: from Latin *Varisci* (the name of a Germanic tribe) + -AN.

var·is·tor /vəˈristər/ ▸*n.* a semiconductor diode with resistance dependent on the applied voltage. ▷1930s: contraction of *varying resistor.*

var·ix /ˈve(ə)riks/ ▸*n.* (*pl.* **var·i·ces** /ˈve(ə)riəˌsēz/) **1** *Medicine* a varicose vein. **2** *Zoology* each of the ridges on the shell of a gastropod mollusk, marking a former position of the aperture. ▷late Middle English: from Latin.

var·let /ˈvärlət/ ▸*n. historical* a man or boy acting as an attendant or servant. ■ a knight's page. ■ *archaic* an unprincipled rogue or rascal. ▷late Middle English: from Old French, variant of *valet* 'attendant' (see VALET). The sense 'rogue' dates from the mid 16th cent. —**var·let·ry** /-lətrē/ *n.*

var·mint /ˈvärmənt/ ▸*n. dialect, informal* a troublesome wild animal, esp. a fox. ■ a troublesome and mischievous person, esp. a child. ▷mid 16th cent.: alteration of VERMIN.

Var·na /ˈvärnə/ a port and resort in eastern Bulgaria, on the western shores of the Black Sea; pop. 321,000.

var·na /ˈvərnə; ˈvär-/ ▸*n.* each of the four Hindu castes, Brahman, Kshatriya, Vaishya, and Shudra. ▷Sanskrit, literally 'color, class.'

var·nish /ˈvärnisʜ/ ▸*n.* resin dissolved in a liquid for applying on wood, metal, or other materials to form a hard, clear, shiny surface when dry. ■ [in *sing.*] *archaic* an external or superficially attractive appearance of a specific quality: *an outward varnish of civilization.*
▸*v.* [*trans.*] apply varnish to: *we stripped the floor and varnished it.* ■ disguise or gloss over (a fact): *the White House is **varnishing over** the defeat of the president's proposal.* ▷Middle English: from Old French *vernis*, from medieval Latin *veronix* 'fragrant resin, sandarac' or medieval Greek *berenikē*, probably from *Berenice*, a town in Cyrenaica. —**var·nish·er** *n.*

var·nish tree ▸*n.* another term for LACQUER TREE.

Var·ro /ˈvarō/, Marcus Terentius (116–27 BC), Roman scholar and satirist. His works covered many subjects, including philosophy, agriculture, education, and the Latin language.

var·ro·a /ˈvarəwə/ (also **var·roa mite**) ▸*n.* a microscopic mite that is a debilitating parasite of the honeybee, causing loss of honey production. • *Varroa jacobsoni*, order (or subclass) Acari. ▷1970s: modern Latin, from VARRO (with reference to his work on beekeeping) + -A[1].

var·si·ty /ˈvärsətē/ ▸*n.* (*pl.* **-ties**) a sports team representing a school or college: *Miller promoted him to the varsity for his sophomore season* | [as *adj.*] *girls' varsity basketball.* ■ *Brit., dated* university: *he had his hair cut as soon as he got back from varsity.* ■ [as *adj.*] *Brit.* (esp. of a sporting event or team) of or relating to a university, esp. Oxford or Cambridge: *a varsity match.* ▷mid 17th cent.: shortening of UNIVERSITY, reflecting an archaic pronunciation.

Var·u·na /ˈvərŏŏnə; ˈvär-/ *Hinduism* one of the gods in the Rig Veda. Originally the sovereign lord of the universe and guardian of cosmic law, he is known in later Hinduism as god of the waters.

var·us /ˈve(ə)rəs/ ▸*n. Medicine* a deformity involving oblique displacement of part of a limb toward the midline. The opposite of VALGUS. ▷early 19th cent.: from Latin, literally 'bent, crooked.'

varve /ˈvärv/ ▸*n. Geology* a pair of thin layers of clay and silt of contrasting color and texture that represent the deposit of a single year (summer and winter) in a lake. Such layers can be used to determine the chronology of glacial sediments. ▷early 20th cent.: from Swedish *varv* 'layer.' —**varved** *adj.*

var·y /ˈve(ə)rē/ ▸*v.* (**var·ies, var·ied**) [*intrans.*] differ in size, amount, degree, or nature from something else of the same general class: *the properties **vary in** price* | [as *adj.*] (**varying**) *varying degrees of success.* ■ change from one condition, form, or state to another: *your skin's moisture content varies according to*

V

climatic conditions. ■ [*trans.*] introduce modifications or changes into (something) so as to make it different or less uniform: *he tried to vary his diet.* ▷Middle English: from Old French *varier* or Latin *variare*, from *varius* 'diverse' . **—var·y·ing·ly** *adv.*

vas /vas/ ▸*n.* (*pl.* **va·sa** /'vāsə; -zə/) *Anatomy* a vessel or duct. ▷late 16th cent.: from Latin, literally 'vessel.' **—va·sal** /'vāsəl; -zəl/ *adj.*

Va·sa /'väsə/ Swedish name for **VAASA**.

Va·sa·rely /ˌväsə'relē; ˌvas-/, Viktor (1908–97), French painter, born in Hungary. A pioneer of op art, he was best known for a style of geometric abstraction that used repeated geometric forms and interacting colors to create visual disorientation.

Va·sa·ri /və'särē/, Giorgio (1511–74), Italian painter, architect, and biographer. His *Lives of the Most Excellent Painters, Sculptors, and Architects* (1550, enlarged 1568) formed the basis for the later study of art history in the West.

Vas·co da Ga·ma /ˌväskō də 'gämə/ see **DA GAMA**.

vas·cu·lar /'vaskyələr/ ▸*adj. Anatomy, Zoology, & Medicine* of, relating to, affecting, or consisting of a vessel or vessels, esp. those that carry blood: *vascular disease | the vascular system.* ■ *Botany* relating to or denoting the plant tissues (xylem and phloem) that conduct water, sap, and nutrients in flowering plants, ferns, and their relatives. ▷late 17th cent.: from modern Latin *vascularis*, from Latin *vasculum* (see **VASCULUM**). **—vas·cu·lar·i·ty** /ˌvaskyə'laritē/ *n.*

vas·cu·lar bun·dle ▸*n. Botany* a strand of conducting vessels in the stem or leaves of a plant, typically with phloem on the outside and xylem on the inside.

vas·cu·lar cyl·in·der ▸*n.* another term for **STELE** (sense 1).

vas·cu·lar·ize /'vaskyələˌrīz/ ▸*v.* [*trans.*] *Biology & Anatomy* provide (a tissue or structure) with vessels, esp. blood vessels; make vascular: [as *adj.*] (**vascularized**) *the endocrine glands are highly vascularized tissues.* **—vas·cu·lar·i·za·tion** /ˌvaskyələrə'zāshən/ *n.*

vas·cu·lar plant ▸*n. Botany* a plant that is characterized by the presence of conducting tissue. • Subkingdom Tracheophyta: divisions Pteridophyta (ferns, horsetails, and club mosses) and Spermatophyta (cycads, conifers, and flowering plants).

vas·cu·lar tis·sue ▸*n.* the tissue in higher plants that constitutes the vascular system, consisting of phloem and xylem, by which water and nutrients are conducted throughout the plant.

vas·cu·la·ture /'vaskyələˌchoŏr; -chər/ ▸*n. Anatomy* the vascular system of a part of the body and its arrangement: *diseases affecting the pulmonary vasculature.*

vas·cu·li·tis /ˌvaskyə'lītis/ ▸*n.* (*pl.* **-lit·i·des** /-'litiˌdēz/) *Medicine* inflammation of a blood vessel or blood vessels. **—vas·cu·lit·ic** /-'litik/ *adj.*

vas·cu·lum /'vaskyələm/ ▸*n.* (*pl.* **-la** /-lə/) *Botany* a collecting box for plants, typically in the form of a flattened cylindrical metal case with a lengthwise opening, carried by a shoulder strap. ▷late 18th cent.: from Latin, diminutive of *vas* 'vessel.'

vas de·fe·rens /ˌvas 'defərənz; -ˌrenz/ ▸*n.* (*pl.* **va·sa de·fe·ren·ti·a** /ˌväsə ˌdefə'renshē)ə; ˌvāzə/) *Anatomy* the duct that conveys sperm from the testicle to the urethra. ▷late 16th cent.: from **VAS** + Latin *deferens* 'carrying away,' present participle of *deferre.*

vase /vās; vāz; väz/ ▸*n.* a decorative container, typically made of glass or china and used as an ornament or for displaying cut flowers. ▷late Middle English: from French, from Latin *vas* 'vessel.' **—vase·ful** /-ˌfoŏl/ *n.* (*pl.* **-fuls**).

vas·ec·to·my /və'sektəmē; va-/ ▸*n.* (*pl.* **-mies**) the surgical cutting and sealing of part of each vas deferens, typically as a means of sterilization. **—va·sec·to·mize** /-ˌmīz/ *v.*

Vas·e·line /ˌvasə'lēn; 'vasəˌlēn/ ▸*n. trademark* a type of petroleum jelly used as an ointment and lubricant. ▸*v.* [*trans.*] cover or smear with this. ▷late 19th cent.: formed irregularly from German *Wasser* 'water' + Greek *elaion* 'olive oil' + **-INE**[4].

vase shell ▸*n.* a predatory mollusk of warm seas, with a heavy ribbed shell that has blunt spines and is typically pale with chestnut markings. • Genus *Vasum*, family Vasidae, class Gastropoda.

vaso- ▸*comb. form* of or relating to a vessel or vessels, esp. blood vessels: *vasoconstriction.* ▷from Latin *vas* 'vessel.'

vas·o·ac·tive /ˌvāzō'aktiv; ˌvasō-/ ▸*adj. Physiology* affecting the diameter of blood vessels (and hence blood pressure).

vas·o·con·stric·tion /ˌvāzōkən'strikshən; ˌvasō-/ ▸*n.* the constriction of blood vessels, which increases blood pressure. **—vas·o·con·stric·tive** /-'striktiv/ *adj.* **—vas·o·con·stric·tor** /-'striktər/ *n.*

vas·o·di·la·tion /ˌvāzōdī'lāshən; ˌvasō-/ (also **vas·o·di·la·ta·tion** /-ˌdilə'tāshən/) ▸*n.* the dilatation of blood vessels, which decreases blood pressure. **—vas·o·di·la·tor** /-'dīˌlātər/ *n.* **—vas·o·dil·a·to·ry** /-'diləˌtôrē/ *adj.*

vas·o·mo·tor /ˌvāzō'mōtər; ˌvasō-/ ▸*adj.* [*attrib.*] causing or relating to the constriction or dilatation of blood vessels. ■ denoting a region in the medulla of the brain (the **vasomotor center**) that regulates blood pressure by controlling reflex alterations in the heart rate and the diameter of the blood vessels, in response to stimuli from receptors in the circulatory system or from other parts of the brain.

vas·o·pres·sin /ˌvāzō'presən; ˌvasō-/ ▸*n. Biochemistry* a pituitary hormone that acts to promote the retention of water by the kidneys and increase blood pressure. ▷1920s: from *vasopressor* 'causing constriction in blood vessels' + **-IN**[1].

va·so·pres·sor /'vasōˌpresər; 'vāzō-/ ▸*adj.* causing the constriction of blood vessels.
▸*n.* a drug with this effect.

va·so·spasm /'vasōˌspazəm; 'vāzō-/ ▸*n.* sudden constriction of a blood vessel, reducing its diameter and flow rate. **—va·so·spas·tic** /ˌvasō'spastik; ˌvāzō-/ *adj.*

va·so·va·gal /ˌvāzō'vāgəl; ˌvasō-/ ▸*adj.* [*attrib.*] *Medicine* relating to or denoting a temporary fall in blood pressure, with pallor, fainting, sweating, and nausea, caused by overactivity of the vagus nerve, esp. as a result of stress.

vas·sal /'vasəl/ ▸*n. historical* a holder of land by feudal tenure on conditions of homage and allegiance. ■ a person or country in a subordinate position to another: [as *adj.*] *a vassal state of the Chinese empire.* ▷late Middle English: via Old French from medieval Latin *vassallus* 'retainer,' of Celtic origin; compare with **VAVASOUR**. **—vas·sal·age** /-əlij/ *n.*

vast /vast/ ▸*adj.* of very great extent or quantity; immense: *a vast plain of buffalo grass.*
▸*n. archaic* an immense space. ▷late Middle English: from Latin *vastus* 'void, immense;' compare with **WASTE**. **—vast·ly** *adv.* **—vast·ness** *n.* **—vast·y** *adj.*

vas·ta·tion /va'stāshən/ ▸*n. poetic/literary* the action or process of emptying or purifying someone or something, typically violently or drastically. ▷mid 16th cent.: from Latin *vastatio(n-)*, from *vastare* 'lay waste.'

Väs·ter·ås /ˌvestə'rōs/ a port on Lake Mälaren in eastern Sweden; pop. 120,000.

vas·ti·tude /'vastiˌt(y)oōd/ ▸*n.* **1** the quality of being vast; immensity. **2** a vast extent or space.

VAT /vat/ ▸*abbr.* value added tax.

vat /vat/ ▸*n.* **1** a large tank or tub used to hold liquid, esp. in industry: *a vat of hot tar.* **2** (also **vat dye**) a water-insoluble dye, such as indigo, that is applied to a fabric in a reducing bath, which converts it to a soluble form, the color being obtained on subsequent oxidation in the fabric fibers.
▸*v.* (**vat·ted**, **vat·ting**) [*trans.*] (often **be vatted**) place or treat in a vat. ▷Middle English: southern and western English dialect variant of obsolete *fat* 'container,' of Germanic origin; related to Dutch *vat* and German *Fass.*

vat dye ▸*n.* a water-insoluble dye that is applied as an alkaline solution of a soluble leuco form, the color being obtained through oxidation. **—vat-dyed** *adj.*

vat·ic /'vatik/ ▸*adj. poetic/literary* describing or predicting what will happen in the future: *vatic utterances.* ▷early 17th cent.: from Latin *vates* 'prophet' + **-IC**.

Vat·i·can /'vatikən/ ▸*n.* (usu. **the Vatican**) the palace and official residence of the pope in Rome. ■ [treated as *sing.* or *pl.*] the administrative center of the Roman Catholic Church. ▷mid 16th cent.: from French, or from Latin *Vaticanus*, the name of a hill in Rome.

Vat·i·can Cit·y an independent papal state in the city of Rome, the seat of government of the Roman Catholic Church; pop. 1,000.

It covers an area of 109 acres (44 hectares) around St. Peter's Basilica and the palace of the Vatican. Having been suspended after the incorporation of the former Papal States into Italy in 1870, the temporal power of the pope was restored by the Lateran Treaty of 1929.

Vat·i·can Coun·cil ▸*n.* each of two general councils of the Roman Catholic Church, held in 1869–70 and 1962–65. The first (**Vatican I**) proclaimed the infallibility of the pope when speaking *ex cathedra*; the second (**Vatican II**) made numerous reforms, abandoning the universal Latin liturgy and acknowledging ecumenism.

va·tic·i·nate /və'tisəˌnāt/ ▸*v.* [*intrans.*] *rare* foretell the future. ▷early 17th cent.: from Latin *vaticinat-* 'prophesied,' from the verb *vaticinari*, from *vates* 'prophet.' **—va·tic·i·nal** /-ənl/ *adj.* **—va·tic·i·na·tion** /-ˌtisə'nāshən/ *n.* **—va·tic·i·na·tor** /-ˌnātər/ *n.* **—va·tic·i·na·to·ry** /-ənəˌtôrē/ *adj.*

Vät·tern /'vetə(r)n/ a lake in southern Sweden.

va·tu /'väˌtoō/ ▸*n.* (*pl.* same) the basic monetary unit of Vanuatu. ▷Bislama.

Vaud /vō/ a canton on the shores of Lake Geneva in western Switzerland; capital, Lausanne. German name **WAADT**.

vaude·ville /'vôd(ə)ˌvil; -vəl/ ▸*n.* a type of entertainment popular chiefly in the U.S. in the early 20th century, featuring a mixture of specialty acts such as burlesque comedy and song and dance. ■ a stage play on a trivial theme with interspersed songs. ■ *archaic* a satirical or topical song with a refrain. ▷mid 18th cent.: from French, earlier *vau de ville* (or *vire*), said to be a name given originally to songs composed by Olivier Basselin, a 15th-cent. fuller born in *Vau de Vire* in Normandy. **—vaude·vil·lian** /ˌvôd(ə)'vilyən; -'vilēən/ *adj. & n.*

Vau·dois /vō'dwä/ ▸*n.* (*pl.* same) *historical* a member of the Waldenses religious sect.
▸*adj.* of or relating to the Waldenses. ▷mid 16th cent.: French, representing medieval Latin *Valdensis* (see **WALDENSES**).

Vaughan[1] /vôn/, Henry (1621–95), Welsh religious writer and metaphysical poet.

Vaughan[2], Sarah (Lois) (1924–90), U.S. jazz singer and pianist. She was notable for her vocal range, her use of vibrato, and her improvisational skills.

Vaughan Wil·liams, Ralph (1872–1958), English composer. His strongly melodic music frequently reflects his interest in Tudor composers and English folk songs. Notable works: *Fantasia on a Theme by Thomas Tallis* (1910), *A London Symphony* (1914), and the *Mass in G minor* (1922).

vault[1] /vôlt/ ▸*n.* **1** a roof in the form of an arch or a series of arches, typical of churches and other large, formal buildings. ■ *poetic/literary* a thing resembling an arched roof, esp. the sky: *the vault of heaven.* ■ *Anatomy* the arched roof of a cavity, esp. that of the skull: *the cranial vault.* **2** a large room or chamber used for storage, esp. an underground one. ■ a secure room in a bank in which valuables are stored. ■ a chamber beneath a church or in a graveyard used for burials.
▸*v.* [*trans.*] [usu. as *adj.*] (**vaulted**) provide (a building or room) with an arched roof or roofs: *a vaulted arcade.* ■ make (a roof) in the form of a vault: *there was a high ceiling, vaulted with cut slate.* ▷Middle English: from Old French *voute*, based on Latin *volvere* 'to roll.'

vault[2] ▸*v.* [*intrans.*] leap or spring while supporting or propelling oneself with one or both hands or with the help of a pole: *he vaulted over the gate.* ■ [*trans.*] jump over (an obstacle) in such a way: *Ryker vaulted the barrier.*
▸*n.* an act of vaulting. ▷mid 16th cent.: from Old French *volter* 'to turn (a horse), gambol,' based on Latin *volvere* 'to roll.' **—vault·er** *n.*

vault·ing /'vôlting/ ▸*n.* **1** ornamental work in a vaulted roof or ceiling. **2** the action of vaulting over obstacles as a gymnastic or athletic exercise.

vault·ing horse ▸*n.* a padded wooden block used for vaulting over by gymnasts and athletes.

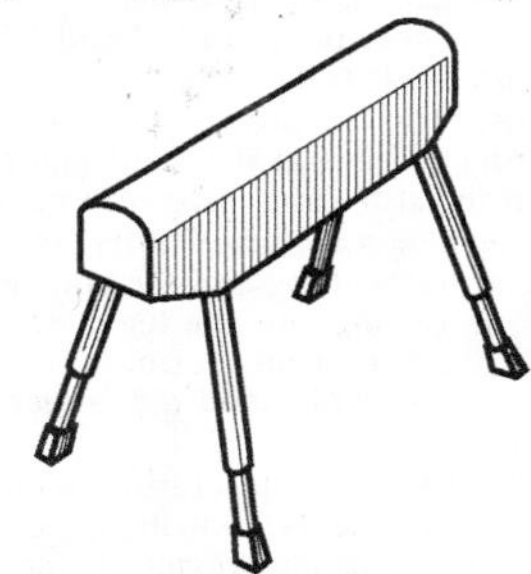

vaulting horse

vaunt /vônt; vänt/ ▸*v.* [*trans.*] [usu. as *adj.*] (**vaunted**) boast about or praise (something), esp. excessively: *the much vaunted information superhighway.*
▸*n. archaic* a boast. ▷late Middle English: the noun a shortening of obsolete *avaunt* 'boasting, a boast'; the verb (originally in the sense 'use boastful language')

from Old French *vanter*, from late Latin *vantare*, based on Latin *vanus* 'vain, empty.' —**vaunt·er** *n.* —**vaunt·ing·ly** *adv.*

vav /väv; vôv/ ▶*n.* the sixth letter of the Hebrew alphabet.

vav·a·so·ry /ˈvavəˌsôrē/ ▶*n.* (*pl.* **-ries**) *historical* the estate of a vavasour. ▷early 17th cent.: from Old French *vavasorie* or medieval Latin *vavasoria* (see VAVASOUR).

vav·a·sour /ˈvavəˌsôr/ ▶*n.* *historical* a vassal owing allegiance to a powerful lord and having other vassals under him. ▷Middle English: from Old French *vavas(s)our*, from medieval Latin *vavassor*, perhaps from *vassus vassorum* 'vassal of vassals.'

VC ▶*abbr.* ■ Vice-Chairman. ■ Vice-Chancellor. ■ Vice-Consul. ■ Victoria Cross. ■ Vietcong.

vCard ▶*n.* *trademark* virtual business card, an electronic representation of a business card, usually a file attached to an e-mail in place of a signature.

V-chip ▶*n.* a computer chip installed in a television receiver that can be programmed by the user to block or scramble material containing a special code in its signal indicating that it is deemed violent or sexually explicit.

vCJD ▶*abbr.* variant Creutzfeldt–Jakob disease, the human form of mad cow disease. Sometimes referred to as **nvCJD** (new variant Creutzfeldt–Jakob disease).

VCR ▶*abbr.* videocassette recorder.

VD ▶*abbr.* venereal disease.

V-day ▶*n.* Victory Day, esp. with reference to the Allied victories in World War II.

VDT ▶*abbr.* video display terminal.

've *informal* ▶*abbr.* have (usually after the pronouns *I*, *you*, *we*, and *they*): *we've tried our best.*

veal /vēl/ ▶*n.* the flesh of a calf, used as food. ▷Middle English: from Anglo-Norman French *ve(e)l*, from Latin *vitellus*, diminutive of *vitulus* 'calf.'

veal·er /ˈvēlər/ ▶*n.* a calf raised to become veal.

Veb·len /ˈveblən/, Thorstein (Bunde) (1857–1929), U.S. economist and social scientist. He coined the phrase "conspicuous consumption." His works include *The Theory of the Leisure Class* (1899), a critique of capitalism, and *The Theory of Business Enterprise* (1904).

vec·tor /ˈvektər/ ▶*n.* **1** *Mathematics & Physics* a quantity having direction as well as magnitude, esp. as determining the position of one point in space relative to another. Compare with SCALAR. ■ *Mathematics* a matrix with one row or one column. ■ a course to be taken by an aircraft. ■ [as *adj.*] *Computing* denoting a type of graphical representation using straight lines to construct the outlines of objects. **2** an organism, typically a biting insect or tick, that transmits a disease or parasite from one animal or plant to another. ■ *Genetics* a bacteriophage or plasmid that transfers genetic material into a cell, or from one bacterium to another.

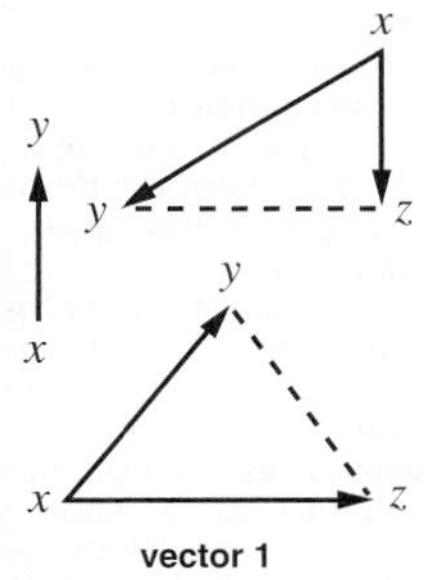

vector 1

▶*v.* [*trans.*] (often **be vectored**) direct (an aircraft in flight) to a desired point. ▷mid 19th cent.: from Latin, literally 'carrier,' from *vehere* 'convey.' —**vec·to·ri·al** /vekˈtôrēəl/ *adj.* (in sense 1 of the *noun*). —**vec·to·ri·al·ly** /vekˈtôrēəlē/ *adv.* (in sense 1 of the *noun*). —**vec·tor·i·za·tion** /ˌvektərəˈzāshən/ *n.* —**vec·tor·ize** /-ˌrīz/ *v.* (in sense 1 of the *noun*).

vec·tor field ▶*n.* *Mathematics* a function of a space whose value at each point is a vector quantity.

vec·tor proc·es·sor ▶*n.* *Computing* a processor that is able to process sequences of data with a single instruction.

vec·tor prod·uct ▶*n.* *Mathematics* the product of two real vectors in three dimensions that is itself a vector at right angles to both the original vectors. Its magnitude is the product of the magnitudes of the original vectors and the sine of the angle between their directions. Also called CROSS PRODUCT. Compare with INNER PRODUCT. • Written as **a** × **b**.

vec·tor space ▶*n.* *Mathematics* a space consisting of vectors, together with the associative and commutative operation of addition of vectors, and the associative and distributive operation of multiplication of vectors by scalars.

Ve·da /ˈvādə; ˈvēdə/ ▶*n.* [treated as *sing.* or *pl.*] the most ancient Hindu scriptures, written in early Sanskrit and containing hymns, philosophy, and guidance on ritual for the priests of Vedic religion. Believed to have been directly revealed to seers among the early Aryans in India, and preserved by oral tradition, the four chief collections are the Rig Veda, Sama Veda, Yajur Veda, and Atharva Veda. ▷Sanskrit, literally '(sacred) knowledge.'

Ve·dan·ta /vəˈdäntə; və-/ ▶*n.* a Hindu philosophy based on the doctrine of the Upanishads, esp. in its monistic form. ▷from Sanskrit *vedānta*, from *veda* (see VEDA) + *anta* 'end.' —**Ve·dan·tic** /-tik/ *adj.* —**Ve·dan·tist** /-tist/ *n.*

V-E Day ▶*n.* the day (May 8) marking the Allied victory in Europe in 1945. ▷*V-E*, abbreviation of *Victory in Europe*.

Ved·da /ˈvedə/ ▶*n.* a member of an aboriginal people inhabiting the forests of Sri Lanka. ▷from Sinhalese *vaddā* 'hunter.'

ve·dette /viˈdet/ (also **vi·dette**) ▶*n.* **1** *historical* a mounted sentry positioned beyond an army's outposts to observe the movements of the enemy. **2** a leading star of stage, screen, or television. ▷late 17th cent.: from French, literally 'scout,' from an alteration of southern Italian *veletta*, perhaps based on Spanish *velar* 'keep watch.'

Ve·dic /ˈvādik; ˈvēdik/ ▶*adj.* of or relating to the Veda or Vedas.
▶*n.* the language of the Vedas, an early form of Sanskrit. ▷from French *védique* or German *vedisch* (see VEDA).

Ve·dic re·li·gion ▶*n.* the ancient religion of the Aryan peoples who entered northwestern India from Persia *c.*2000–1200 BC. It was the precursor of Hinduism, and its beliefs and practices are contained in the Vedas.

Its characteristics included ritual sacrifice to many gods, especially Indra, Varuna, and Agni; social classes (varnas) that formed the basis of the caste system; and the emergence of the priesthood, which dominated orthodox Brahmanism from *c.*900 BC. Transition to classical Hinduism began in about the 5th century BC.

vee /vē/ ▶*n.* the letter V. ■ a thing shaped like a V: *a broken vee of birds points for the marshes.*

vee·jay /ˈvēˌjā/ ▶*n.* *informal* a person who introduces and plays popular music videos. ▷1980s: representing a pronunciation of *VJ*, short for *video jockey*, on the pattern of *deejay*.

vee·na /ˈvēnə/ (also **vi·na**) ▶*n.* an Indian stringed instrument, with four main and three auxiliary strings. The southern type has a lutelike body; the older northern type has a tubular body and a gourd fitted to each end as a resonator. ▷from Sanskrit *vīṇā*.

veep /vēp/ ▶*n.* *informal* a vice president. ▷1940s: from the initials *VP*.

veer[1] /vi(ə)r/ ▶*v.* [*intrans.*] change direction suddenly: *an oil tanker that had veered off course.* ■ *figurative* suddenly change an opinion, subject, type of behavior, etc.: *the conversation eventually veered away from theatrical things.* ■ (of the wind) change direction clockwise around the points of the compass: *the wind veered southwest.* The opposite of BACK.
▶*n.* a sudden change of direction. ▷late 16th cent.: from French *virer*, perhaps from an alteration of Latin *gyrare* (see GYRATE).

veer[2] ▶*v.* [*trans.*] *dated Nautical* slacken or let out (a rope or cable) in a controlled way. ▷late Middle English: from Middle Dutch *vieren*.

veer·y /ˈvi(ə)rē/ ▶*n.* a North American woodland thrush with a brown back and speckled breast. • *Catharus fuscescens*, subfamily Turdinae, family Muscicapidae. ▷mid 19th cent.: perhaps imitative.

veg[1] /vej/ ▶*v.* (**veg·ges**, **veg·ging**, **vegged**) [*intrans.*] *informal* relax to the point of complete inertia: *they were vegging out in front of the TV.* ▷1920s: abbreviation of VEGETATE.

veg[2] ▶*n.* (*pl.* same) *Brit.*, *informal* a vegetable or vegetables: *meat and two veg.* ▷late 19th cent.: abbreviation.

Ve·ga[1] /ˈvāgə/, Lope de (1562–1635), Spanish playwright and poet; full name *Lope Felix de Vega Carpio*. He is regarded as the founder of Spanish drama.

Ve·ga[2] *Astronomy* the fifth brightest star in the sky, and the brightest in the constellation Lyra, overhead in summer to observers in the northern hemisphere. ▷via Spanish or medieval Latin from Arabic, literally 'the falling eagle or vulture.'

ve·ga /ˈvāgə/ ▶*n.* (in Spain and Spanish America) a large plain or valley, typically a fertile and grassy one. ▷Spanish and Catalan.

veg·an /ˈvēgən; ˈvejən/ ▶*n.* a person who does not eat or use animal products: *I'm a strict vegan* | [as *adj.*] *a vegan diet.* ▷1940s: from VEGETARIAN + -AN.

Ve·gas /ˈˌvāgəs/ ▶*informal* Las Vegas.

veg·e·ta·ble /ˈvejtəbəl; ˈvəjətə-/ ▶*n.* **1** a plant or part of a plant used as food, typically as accompaniment to meat or fish, such as a cabbage, potato, carrot, or bean. **2** *informal, offensive* a person who is incapable of normal mental or physical activity, esp. through brain damage. ■ *informal* a person with a dull or inactive life: *I thought I'd sort of flop back and be a vegetable for a bit.*
▶*adj.* [*attrib.*] of or relating to vegetables as food: *a vegetable garden* | *vegetable soup.* ■ of or relating to plants or plant life, esp. as distinct from animal life or mineral substances: *vegetable matter.* ▷late Middle English (in the sense 'growing as a plant'): from Old French, or from late Latin *vegetabilis* 'animating,' from Latin *vegetare* (see VEGETATE). The noun dates from the late 16th cent.

veg·e·ta·ble but·ter ▶*n.* vegetable fat with the consistency of butter.

veg·e·ta·ble i·vo·ry ▶*n.* a hard white material obtained from the endosperm of the ivory nut.

veg·e·ta·ble mar·row ▶*n.* see MARROW (sense 1).

veg·e·ta·ble oil ▶*n.* an oil derived from plants, e.g., canola oil, olive oil, sunflower oil.

veg·e·ta·ble sheep ▶*n.* a New Zealand plant of the daisy family that has grayish hairy leaves and forms hummocks that from a distance look like sheep. • *Raoulia eximia*, family Compositae.

veg·e·ta·ble spa·ghet·ti ▶*n.* another term for SPAGHETTI SQUASH.

veg·e·ta·ble sponge ▶*n.* another term for LOOFAH.

veg·e·ta·ble tal·low ▶*n.* vegetable fat used as tallow.

veg·e·tal /ˈvejətl/ ▶*adj.* **1** *formal* of or relating to plants: *a vegetal aroma.* **2** [*attrib.*] *Embryology* of or relating to that pole of the ovum or embryo that contains the less active cytoplasm, and frequently most of the yolk, in the early stages of development: *vegetal cells* | *the vegetal region.* ▷late Middle English: from medieval Latin *vegetalis*, from Latin *vegetare* 'animate.' Sense 2 dates from the early 20th cent.

veg·e·tal pole /ˈvejitl/ ▶*n.* *Embryology* the portion of an ovum opposite the animal pole, containing most of the yolk and little cytoplasm.

veg·e·tar·i·an /ˌvejiˈte(ə)rēən/ ▶*n.* a person who does not eat meat, and sometimes other animal products, esp. for moral, religious, or health reasons.
▶*adj.* of or relating to the exclusion of meat or other animal products from the diet: *a vegetarian restaurant.* ▷mid 19th cent.: formed irregularly from VEGETABLE + -ARIAN. —**veg·e·tar·i·an·ism** /-ˌnizəm/ *n.*

veg·e·tate /ˈvejəˌtāt/ ▶*v.* [*intrans.*] **1** live or spend a period of time in a dull, inactive, unchallenging way: *if she left him there alone, he'd sit in front of the television set and vegetate.* **2** *dated* (of a plant or seed) grow; sprout. ■ [*trans.*] cause plants to grow in or cover (a place). **3** *Medicine* (of an abnormal growth) increase in size. ▷early 17th cent.: from Latin *vegetat-* 'enlivened,' from the verb *vegetare*, from *vegetus* 'active,' from *vegere* 'be active.'

veg·e·tat·ed /ˈvejəˌtātid/ ▶*adj.* covered with vegetation or plant life: *densely vegetated wetlands.*

veg·e·ta·tion /ˌvejəˈtāshən/ ▶*n.* **1** plants considered collectively, esp. those found in a particular area or habitat: *the chalk cliffs are mainly sheer with little vegetation.* **2** the action or process of vegetating. **3** *Medicine* an abnormal growth on or in the body. ▷mid 16th cent. (sense 2): from medieval Latin *vegetatio(n-)* 'power of growth,' from the verb *vegetare* (see VEGETATE). —**veg·e·ta·tion·al** /-shənl/ *adj.*

veg·e·ta·tive /ˈvejəˌtātiv/ ▶*adj.* **1** *Biology* of, relating to, or denoting reproduction or propagation achieved by asexual means, either naturally (budding, rhizomes, runners, bulbs, etc.) or artificially (grafting, layering, or taking cuttings): *vegetative spores* | *a vegetative replicating phase.* ■ of, relating to, or concerned with growth rather than sexual reproduction: *environmental factors trigger the switch from vegetative to floral development.* **2** of or relating to vegetation or plant life: *diverse vegetative types.* **3** *Medicine* (of a person) alive but comatose and without apparent brain activity or responsiveness.

See PERSISTENT VEGETATIVE STATE. ▷late Middle English (sense 2): from Old French *vegetatif, -ive* or medieval Latin *vegetativus* (see VEGETATE). —**veg·e·ta·tive·ly** *adv.* —**veg·e·ta·tive·ness** *n.*

veg·e·ta·tive cell ▸*n. Botany & Microbiology* a cell of a bacterium or unicellular alga that is actively growing rather than forming spores.

veg·gie /ˈvejē/ (also **veg·ie**) ▸*n.* & *adj. informal* **1** another term for VEGETABLE. **2** another term for VEGETARIAN. ▷1970s: abbreviation.

veg·gie burg·er ▸*n.* a patty resembling a hamburger but made with vegetable protein, soybeans, etc., instead of meat.

ve·he·ment /ˈvēəmənt/ ▸*adj.* showing strong feeling; forceful, passionate, or intense: *her voice was low but vehement* | *vehement criticism.* ▷late Middle English (describing pain or temperature, in the sense 'intense, high in degree'): from French *véhément* or Latin *vehement-* 'impetuous, violent,' perhaps from an unrecorded adjective meaning 'deprived of mind,' influenced by *vehere* 'carry.' —**ve·he·mence** *n.* —**ve·he·ment·ly** *adv.*

ve·hi·cle /ˈvēəkəl; ˈvēˌhikəl/ ▸*n.* **1** a thing used for transporting people or goods, esp. on land, such as a car, truck, or cart. **2** a thing used to express, embody, or fulfill something: *I use paint as a* ***vehicle*** *for my ideas.* ■ a substance that facilitates the use of a drug, pigment, or other material mixed with it. ■ the figurative language used in a metaphor, as distinct from the metaphor's subject. Often contrasted with TENOR[2] (sense 1). ■ a film, television program, song, etc., that is intended to display the leading performer to the best advantage. ▷early 17th cent.: from French *véhicule* or Latin *vehiculum*, from *vehere* 'carry.' —**ve·hic·u·lar** /vēˈhikyələr/ *adj.* (in sense 1).

veil /vāl/ ▸*n.* a piece of fine material worn by women to protect or conceal the face: *a white bridal veil.* ■ a piece of linen or other fabric forming part of a nun's headdress, resting on the head and shoulders. ■ a thing that conceals, disguises, or obscures something: *shrouded in an eerie veil of mist.* ■ *Botany* a membrane that is attached to the immature fruiting body of some toadstools and ruptures in the course of development, either (**universal veil**) enclosing the whole fruiting body or (**partial veil**) joining the edges of the cap to the stalk. ■ (in Jewish antiquity) the piece of precious cloth separating the sanctuary from the body of the Temple or the Tabernacle.

▸*v.* [*trans.*] cover with or as though with a veil: *she veiled her face.* ■ [usu. as *adj.*] (**veiled**) partially conceal, disguise, or obscure: *a thinly veiled threat.* ▷Middle English: from Anglo-Norman French *veil(e)*, from Latin *vela*, plural of *velum* (see VELUM). —**veil·less** *adj.*

▸*PHRASES* □ **beyond the veil** in a mysterious or hidden place or state, esp. the unknown state of life after death. □ **draw a veil over** avoid discussing or calling attention to (something), esp. because it is embarrassing or unpleasant. □ **take the veil** become a nun.

veil·ing /ˈvāliNG/ ▸*n.* **1** the action of wearing or covering someone or something with a veil: *the fundamentalist campaign for the veiling of women.* **2** a light gauzy fabric or fine lace used for veils.

vein /vān/ ▸*n.* **1** any of the tubes forming part of the blood circulation system of the body, carrying in most cases oxygen-depleted blood toward the heart. Compare with ARTERY. ■ (in general and figurative use) a blood vessel: *he felt the adrenaline course through his veins.* ■ (in plants) a slender rib running through a leaf or bract, typically dividing or branching, and containing a vascular bundle. ■ (in insects) a hardened branching rib that forms part of the supporting framework of a wing, consisting of an extension of the tracheal system; a nervure. ■ a streak or stripe of a different color in wood, marble, cheese, etc. ■ a fracture in rock containing a deposit of minerals or ore and typically having an extensive course underground. ■ subsurface water, esp. as considered a source or potential source of water for a well or wells and thought of as flowing in a channel. ■ *figurative* a source of a specified quality or other abstract resource: *he managed to tap into the thick vein of discontent to his own advantage.* **2** [in *sing.*] a distinctive quality, style, or tendency: *he closes his article in a somewhat humorous vein.* ▷Middle English: from Old French *veine*, from Latin *vena*. The earliest senses were 'blood vessel' and 'small natural underground channel of water.' —**vein·less** *adj.* —**vein·let** /-lit/ *n.* —**vein·like** /-ˌlīk/ *adj.* & *adv.* —**vein·y** *adj.* (**vein·i·er, vein·i·est**).

veined /vānd/ ▸*adj.* marked with or as if with veins: [in *combination*] *a blue-veined cheese.*

vein·ing /ˈvāniNG/ ▸*n.* a pattern of lines, streaks, or veins: *the marble's characteristic surface veining.*

vein·ous /ˈvānəs/ ▸*adj.* having prominent or noticeable veins. Compare with VENOUS.

vein·stone /ˈvānˌstōn/ ▸*n.* another term for GANGUE.

Ve·la /ˈvēlə; ˈvā-/ *Astronomy* a southern constellation (the Sails), lying partly in the Milky Way between Carina and Pyxis and originally considered part of Argo. ■ [as *genitive*] (**Velorum** /vēˈlôrəm/) used with a preceding letter or numeral to designate a star in this constellation: *the star Gamma Velorum.* ▷Latin, plural of *velum* 'sail.'

ve·la /ˈvēlə/ ▸ plural form of VELUM.

ve·la·men /vəˈlāmən/ ▸*n.* (*pl.* **-lam·i·na** /-ˈlamənə/) *Botany* an outer layer of empty cells in the aerial roots of epiphytic orchids and aroids. ▷late 19th cent.: from Latin, from *velare* 'to cover.'

ve·lar /ˈvēlər/ ▸*adj.* **1** of or relating to a veil or velum. **2** *Phonetics* (of a speech sound) pronounced with the back of the tongue near the soft palate, as in *k* and *g* in English.

▸*n.* a velar sound. ▷early 18th cent.: from Latin *velaris*, from *velum* (see VELUM).

ve·lar·i·um /viˈle(ə)rēəm/ ▸*n.* (*pl.* **-lar·i·a** /-ˈle(ə)rēə/) a large awning of a type used in ancient Rome to cover a theater or amphitheater as a protection against the weather, now more commonly used as an inner ceiling to improve acoustics. ▷Latin.

ve·lar·i·za·tion /ˌvēlərəˈzāSHən/ ▸*n. Phonetics* a secondary articulation involving movement of the back of the tongue toward the velum. —**ve·lar·ize** /ˈvēləˌrīz/ *v.*

ve·lar·ize /ˈvēləˌrīz/ ▸*v.* [*trans.*] make velar; articulate or supplement the articulation of (a sound, esp. a consonant) by raising the tongue to or toward the soft palate: *a velarized /l/.*

Ve·láz·quez /vəˈläsˌk(w)ez; -kəs/, Diego Rodríguez de Silva y (1599–1660), Spanish painter; court painter to Philip IV. His portraits humanized the formal Spanish tradition of idealized figures. Notable works: *Pope Innocent X* (1650), *The Toilet of Venus* (known as *The Rokeby Venus*, *c.*1651), and *Las Meninas* (*c.*1656).

Ve·láz·quez de Cué·llar /vəˈläsˌk(w)ez dā ˈkwāyär/, Diego (*c.*1465–1524), Spanish conquistador. After sailing with Columbus to the New World in 1493, he began the conquest of Cuba in 1511 and later initiated expeditions to conquer Mexico.

Vel·cro /ˈvelkrō/ ▸*n. trademark* a fastener for clothes or other items, consisting of two strips of thin plastic sheet, one covered with tiny loops and the other with tiny flexible hooks, which adhere when pressed together and can be separated when pulled apart deliberately.

▸*v.* [*trans.*] fasten, join, or fix with such a fastener. ▷1960s: from French *velours croché* 'hooked velvet.' —**Vel·croed** *adj.*

veld /velt/ (also **veldt**) ▸*n.* open, uncultivated country or grassland in southern Africa. It is conventionally classified by altitude into highveld, middleveld, and lowveld. ▷Afrikaans, from Dutch, literally 'field.'

Vel·de, van de[1], Henri, see VAN DE VELDE[2].

Vel·de, van de[2], Willem and sons, see VAN DE VELDE[1].

ve·li·ger /ˈveləjər; ˈvēlə-/ ▸*n. Zoology* the final larval stage of certain mollusks, having two ciliated flaps for swimming and feeding. ▷late 19th cent.: from VELUM + Latin *-ger* 'bearing.'

vel·le·i·ty /vəˈlēətē; ve-/ ▸*n.* (*pl.* **-ties**) *formal* a wish or inclination not strong enough to lead to action: *the notion intrigued me, but remained a velleity.* ▷early 17th cent.: from medieval Latin *velleitas*, from Latin *velle* 'to wish.'

vel·lum /ˈveləm/ ▸*n.* **1** fine parchment made originally from the skin of a calf. **2** smooth writing paper imitating vellum. ▷late Middle English: from Old French *velin*, from *veel* (see VEAL).

ve·lo·cim·e·ter /ˌveləˈsimitər; ˌvēlə-/ ▸*n.* an instrument for measuring velocity. ▷mid 19th cent.: from Latin *velox, veloc-* 'swift' + -METER. —**ve·lo·cim·e·try** /-itrē/ *n.*

ve·loc·i·pede /vəˈläsəˌpēd/ ▸*n. historical* an early form of bicycle propelled by working pedals on cranks fitted to the front axle. ■ a child's tricycle. ▷early 19th cent.: from French *vélocipède*, from Latin *velox, veloc-* 'swift' + *pes, ped-* 'foot.' —**ve·loc·i·ped·ist** /-dist/ *n.*

ve·loc·i·rap·tor /vəˈläsəˌraptər/ ▸*n.* a small dromaeosaurid dinosaur of the late Cretaceous period. • Genus *Velociraptor*, family Dromaeosauridae, suborder Theropoda. ▷modern Latin, from Latin *velox, veloc-* 'swift' + RAPTOR.

ve·loc·i·ty /vəˈläsətē/ ▸*n.* (*pl.* **-ties**) the speed of something in a given direction: *the velocities of the emitted particles.* ■ (in general use) speed: *the tank shot backward at an incredible velocity.* ■ (also **ve·loc·i·ty of cir·cu·la·tion**) *Economics* the rate at which money changes hands within an economy. ▷late Middle English: from French *vélocité* or Latin *velocitas*, from *velox, veloc-* 'swift.'

ve·lo·drome /ˈveləˌdrōm; ˈvēlə-/ ▸*n.* a cycle-racing track, typically with steeply banked curves. ■ a stadium containing such a track. ▷late 19th cent.: from French *vélodrome*, from *vélo* 'bicycle' + *-drome* (see -DROME).

ve·lour /vəˈlo͝or/ (also **ve·lours**) ▸*n.* a plush woven fabric resembling velvet, chiefly used for soft furnishings, clothing, and hats. ■ *dated* a hat made of such fabric. ▷early 18th cent.: from French *velours* 'velvet,' from Old French *velour*, from Latin *villosus* 'hairy,' from *villus* (see VELVET).

ve·lou·té /vəlo͞oˈtā/ ▸*n.* a rich white sauce made with chicken, veal, pork, or fish stock, thickened with cream and egg yolks. ▷French, literally 'velvety.'

ve·lum /ˈvēləm/ ▸*n.* (*pl.* **ve·la** /-lə/) a membrane or membranous structure, typically covering another structure or partly obscuring an opening, in particular: ■ *Anatomy* the soft palate. ■ *Zoology* a membrane, typically bordering a cavity, esp. in certain mollusks, medusae, and other invertebrates. ■ *Botany* the veil of a toadstool. ▷mid 18th cent.: from Latin, literally 'sail, curtain, covering, veil.'

ve·lure /vəˈlo͝or/ *archaic* ▸*n.* velvet.

▸*v.* [*trans.*] dress (a hat) by means of a velvet pad: *the hatter then velures the hats in a revolving device.*

vel·vet /ˈvelvət/ ▸*n.* a closely woven fabric of silk, cotton, or nylon, that has a thick short pile on one side. ■ soft downy skin that covers a deer's antler while it is growing. ▷Middle English: from Old French *veluotte*, from *velu* 'velvety,' from medieval Latin *villutus*, from Latin *villus* 'tuft, down.' —**vel·vet·ed** *adj.* —**vel·vet·y** *adj.*

▸*PHRASE* □ **on velvet** *informal, dated* in an advantageous or prosperous position.

vel·vet ant ▸*n.* an antlike velvety-bodied insect related to the wasps. The female is wingless, and the larvae parasitize the young of bees and wasps in the nest. • Family Mutillidae, superfamily Scolioidea: numerous species.

vel·vet·een /ˈvelvəˌtēn; ˌvelvəˈtēn/ ▸*n.* a cotton fabric with a pile resembling velvet. ■ (**velveteens**) *dated* trousers made of this fabric.

vel·vet grass ▸*n.* a common pasture grass with soft downy leaves, native to Eurasia and naturalized in North America. • *Holcus lanatus*, family Gramineae.

vel·vet·leaf /ˈvelvətˌlēf/ ▸*n.* (*pl.* same or **-leafs**) a Eurasian plant of the mallow family, with large heart-shaped velvety leaves and yellow flowers. It is naturalized in North America, where it has become a serious weed of farmland. • *Abutilon theophrasti*, family Malvaceae.

vel·vet rev·o·lu·tion ▸*n.* a nonviolent political revolution, esp. the relatively smooth change from communism to a Western-style democracy in Czechoslovakia at the end of 1989. ▷translating Czech *sametová revoluce.*

vel·vet worm ▸*n.* see ONYCHOPHORA.

Ven. ▸*abbr.* Venerable (as the title of an archdeacon): *the Ven. William Davies.*

ve·na /ˈvēnə/ ▸*n. Anatomy & Zoology* a vein.

ve·na ca·va /ˌvēnə ˈkävə; ˈkāvə/ ▸*n.* (*pl.* **ve·nae ca·vae** /ˈvēnē ˈkävē; ˈkāvē; ˈvēnī ˈkävī; ˈkāvī/) a large vein carrying deoxygenated blood into the heart. There are two in humans, the **inferior vena cava** (carrying blood from the lower body) and the **superior vena cava** (carrying blood from the head, arms, and upper body). ▷late 16th cent.: from Latin, literally 'hollow vein.'

ve·nal /ˈvēnl/ ▸*adj.* showing or motivated by susceptibility to bribery: *why should these venal politicians care how they are rated?* | *their generosity had been at least partly venal.* ▷mid 17th cent. (in the sense 'available for purchase,' referring to merchandise or a favor): from Latin *venalis*, from *venum* 'thing for sale.' —**ve·nal·i·ty** /vēˈnalətē; və-/ *n.* —**ve·nal·ly** *adv.*

USAGE **Venal** and **venial** are sometimes confused. **Venal** means 'corrupt, able to be bribed, or involving bribery': *local customs officials are notoriously* ***venal****, and smuggling thrives.* **Venial** is used to describe a sin or offense that is 'pardonable, excusable, not mortal': *in our high school, smoking cigarettes was a* ***venial*** *sin.*

ve·na·tion /vē'nāSHən/ ▸*n. Biology* the arrangement of veins in a leaf or in an insect's wing. ■ the system of venous blood vessels in an animal. ▷mid 17th cent.: from Latin *vena* 'vein' + -ATION. —**ve·na·tion·al** /-SHənl/ *adj.*

vend /vend/ ▸*v.* [*trans.*] offer (small items, esp. food) for sale, esp. either from a stall or from a slot machine: *there was a man vending sticky cakes and ices.* ■ *Law* or *formal* sell (something). ▷early 17th cent. (in the sense 'be sold'): from French *vendre* or Latin *vendere* 'sell,' from *venum* 'something for sale' + a variant of *dare* 'give.' —**vend·i·ble** (also **vend·a·ble**) *adj.*

Ven·da[1] /'vendə/ a former homeland established in South Africa for the Venda people, now part of Northern Province.

Ven·da[2] ▸*n.* (*pl.* same or **-das**) **1** a member of a people living in Northern Transvaal and southern Zimbabwe. **2** the Bantu language of this people.
▸*adj.* of or relating to this people or their language. ▷the stem of Venda *Muvenda* (in sense 1), *Tshivenda* (in sense 2).

ven·dange /vän'dänZH; vän-/ ▸*n.* (*pl.* same) (in France) the grape harvest. ▷French.

Ven·dé·mi·aire /,vändə'myer; ,vändā-; / ▸*n.* the first month of the French Republican calendar (1793–1805), originally running from September 22 to October 21. ▷French, from Latin *vindemia* 'vintage.'

vend·er /'vendər/ ▸*n.* variant spelling of VENDOR.

ven·det·ta /ven'detə/ ▸*n.* a blood feud in which the family of a murdered person seeks vengeance on the murderer or the murderer's family. ■ a prolonged bitter quarrel with or campaign against someone: *he has accused the British media of pursuing a vendetta against him.* ▷mid 19th cent.: from Italian, from Latin *vindicta* 'vengeance.'

vend·ing ma·chine ▸*n.* a machine that dispenses small articles such as food, drinks, or cigarettes when a coin, bill, or token is inserted.

ven·dor /'vendər; -,dôr/ (also **vend·er**) ▸*n.* a person or company offering something for sale, esp. a trader in the street: *an Italian ice cream vendor.* ■ a person or company whose principal product lines are office supplies and equipment. ■ *Law* the seller, esp. of property. ▷late 16th cent.: from Anglo-Norman French *vendour* (see VEND).

ven·dor plac·ing ▸*n. Finance* a type of placing used as a method of financing a takeover in which the purchasing company issues its own shares as payment to the company being bought, with the prearranged agreement that these shares are then placed with investors in exchange for cash.

ven·due /ven'd(y)o͞o; vän-/ ▸*n.* a public auction. ▷late 17th cent.: via Dutch from French dialect *vendue* 'sale,' from *vendre* 'sell.'

ve·neer /və'ni(ə)r/ ▸*n.* a thin decorative covering of fine wood applied to a coarser wood or other material. ■ a layer of wood used to make plywood. ■ [in *sing.*] an attractive appearance that covers or disguises someone or something's true nature or feelings: *her veneer of composure cracked a little.*
▸*v.* [*trans.*] [usu. as *adj.*] (**veneered**) cover (something) with a decorative layer of fine wood. ■ cover or disguise (someone or something's true nature) with an attractive appearance. ▷early 18th cent. (earlier as *fineer*): from German *furni(e)ren*, from Old French *fournir* 'furnish.'

ve·neer·ing /və'ni(ə)riNG/ ▸*n.* **1** material used as veneer. **2** the action of covering something with a veneer.

ven·e·punc·ture ▸*n. chiefly Brit.* variant spelling of VENIPUNCTURE.

ven·er·a·ble /'venərəbəl; 'venrə-/ ▸*adj.* accorded a great deal of respect, esp. because of age, wisdom, or character: *a venerable statesman.* ■ (in the Roman Catholic Church) a title given to a deceased person who has attained a certain degree of sanctity but has not been fully beatified or canonized. ■ (in the Anglican Church) a title given to an archdeacon. ▷late Middle English: from Old French, or from Latin *venerabilis*, from the verb *venerari* (see VENERATE). —**ven·er·a·bil·i·ty** /,venərə'bilətē/ *n.* —**ven·er·a·ble·ness** *n.* —**ven·er·a·bly** /-blē/ *adv.*

ven·er·ate /'venə,rāt/ ▸*v.* [*trans.*] (often **be venerated**) regard with great respect; revere: *Mother Teresa is venerated as a saint.* See note at REVERE. ▷early 17th cent.: from Latin *venerat-* 'adored, revered,' from the verb *venerari*. —**ven·er·a·tion** /,venə'rāSHən/ *n.* —**ven·er·a·tor** /-,rātər/ *n.*

ve·ne·re·al /və'ni(ə)rēəl/ ▸*adj.* of or relating to sexual desire or sexual intercourse. ■ of or relating to venereal disease. ▷late Middle English: from Latin *venereus* (from *venus, vener-* 'sexual love') + -AL. —**ve·ne·re·al·ly** *adv.*

ve·ne·re·al dis·ease ▸*n.* a disease typically contracted by sexual contact with a person already infected; a sexually transmitted disease.

ve·ne·re·ol·o·gy /və,ni(ə)rē'äləjē/ ▸*n.* the branch of medicine concerned with venereal diseases. —**ve·ne·re·o·log·i·cal** /-ə'läjikəl/ *adj.* —**ve·ne·re·ol·o·gist** /-jist/ *n.*

ven·er·y[1] /'venərē/ ▸*n. archaic* sexual indulgence. ▷late Middle English: from medieval Latin *veneria*, from *venus, vener-* 'sexual love.'

ven·er·y[2] ▸*n. archaic* hunting. ▷Middle English: from Old French *venerie*, from *vener* 'to hunt,' from Latin *venari*.

ven·e·sec·tion /'venə,sekSHən; 'venə-/ ▸*n.* another term for PHLEBOTOMY. ▷mid 17th cent.: from medieval Latin *venae sectio(n-)* 'cutting of a vein.'

Ve·ne·ti·a /və'nēSHə/ a region in northeastern Italy; capital, Venice. Italian name **VENETO** . ▷named after the *Veneti*, the pre-Roman inhabitants of the region.

Ve·ne·tian /və'nēSHən/ ▸*adj.* of or relating to Venice or its people.
▸*n.* a native or citizen of Venice. ■ the dialect of Italian spoken in Venice. ▷late Middle English: from Old French *Venicien*, assimilated to medieval Latin *Venetianus*, from Latin *Venetia* 'Venice.'

ve·ne·tian blind ▸*n.* a window blind consisting of horizontal slats that can be pivoted to control the amount of light that passes through it.

Ve·ne·tian glass ▸*n.* decorative glassware of a type associated with Venice, esp. the nearby island of Murano.

Ve·ne·tian red ▸*n.* a reddish-brown pigment consisting of ferric oxide. ■ a strong reddish-brown color.

Ve·ne·tian win·dow ▸*n.* a large window consisting of a central arched section flanked by two narrow rectangular sections.

Ve·ne·zia /və'netsēə/ Italian name for **VENICE**.

Ven·e·zue·la /,venəz(ə)'wālə/ a republic on the northern coast of South America, on the Caribbean Sea; pop. 25,017,000; capital, Caracas; language, Spanish (official). ▷Spanish, literally 'little Venice,' named by early explorers when they saw native houses built on stilts over water. —**Ven·e·zue·lan** *adj.* & *n.*

Colonized by the Spanish in the 16th century, Venezuela won its independence in 1821 after a ten-year struggle. It did not, however, emerge as a separate nation until its secession from federation with Colombia in 1830. It is a major oil-exporting country, with the industry based on the area around Lake Maracaibo in the northwest.

venge·ance /'venjəns/ ▸*n.* punishment inflicted or retribution exacted for an injury or wrong. ▷Middle English: from Old French, from *venger* 'avenge.'
▸*PHRASE* □ **with a vengeance** used to emphasize the degree to which something occurs or is true: *her headache was back with a vengeance.*

venge·ful /'venjfəl/ ▸*adj.* seeking to harm someone in return for a perceived injury: *a vengeful ex-con.* See note at VINDICTIVE. ▷late 16th cent.: from obsolete *venge* 'avenge' (see VENGEANCE), on the pattern of *revengeful*. —**venge·ful·ly** *adv.* —**venge·ful·ness** *n.*

ve·ni·al /'vēnēəl; 'vēnyəl/ ▸*adj. Christian Theology* denoting a sin that is not regarded as depriving the soul of divine grace. Often contrasted with **MORTAL**. ■ (of a fault or offense) slight and pardonable. ▷Middle English: via Old French from late Latin *venialis*, from *venia* 'forgiveness.' —**ve·ni·al·i·ty** /,vēnē'alətē/ *n.* —**ve·ni·al·ly** *adv.*

USAGE See usage at **VENAL**.

ve·ni·al sin ▸*n.* (in Roman Catholicism) a relatively slight sin that does not entail damnation of the soul: *she lost her patience, a venial sin she must report later to Father Damien.*

Ven·ice /'venəs/ **1** a city in northeastern Italy, on a lagoon of the Adriatic Sea, capital of Venetia region; pop. 318,000. It is built on numerous islands that are separated by canals and linked by bridges. Italian name **VENEZIA**. **2** /'venis/ a beachfront section of Los Angeles in California, west of downtown.

ven·i·punc·ture /'vēnə,pəNGkCHər; 'venə-/ (*chiefly Brit.* also **ven·e·punc·ture**) ▸*n.* the puncture of a vein as part of a medical procedure, typically to withdraw a blood sample or for an intravenous injection. ▷1920s: from Latin *vena* 'vein' + PUNCTURE.

ven·i·son /'venəsən; -zən/ ▸*n.* meat from a deer. ▷Middle English: from Old French *veneso(u)n*, from Latin *venatio(n-)* 'hunting,' from *venari* 'to hunt.'

Ve·ni·te /və'nitē; -'nētē; -'nē,tā/ ▸*n.* Psalm 95 used as a canticle in Christian liturgy, chiefly at matins. ▷Latin, literally 'come ye,' the first word of the psalm.

Venn di·a·gram /ven/ ▸*n.* a diagram representing mathematical or logical sets pictorially as circles or closed curves within an enclosing rectangle (the universal set), common elements of the sets being represented by the areas of overlap among the circles. ▷early 20th cent.: named after John *Venn* (1834–1923), English logician.

ve·no·gram /'vēnə,gram/ ▸*n. Medicine* an image produced by venography.

ve·nog·ra·phy /vi'nägrəfē/ ▸*n. Medicine* radiography of a vein after injection of a radiopaque fluid. ▷1930s: from Latin *vena* 'vein' + -GRAPHY. —**ve·no·graph·ic** /,vēnə'grafik/ *adj.* —**ve·no·graph·i·cal·ly** /,vēnə'grafik(ə)lē/ *adv.*

ven·om /'venəm/ ▸*n.* poisonous fluid secreted by animals such as snakes and scorpions and typically injected into prey or aggressors by biting or stinging. ■ *figurative* extreme malice and bitterness shown in someone's attitudes, speech, or actions: *his voice was full of venom.* ▷Middle English: from Old French *venim*, variant of *venin*, from an alteration of Latin *venenum* 'poison.'

ven·om·ous /'venəməs/ ▸*adj.* (of animals, esp. snakes, or their parts) secreting venom; capable of injecting venom by means of a bite or sting. ■ *figurative* (of a person or their behavior) full of malice or spite: *she replied with a venomous glance.* See note at VINDICTIVE. ▷Middle English: from Old French *venimeux*, from *venim* (see VENOM). —**ven·om·ous·ly** *adv.* —**ven·om·ous·ness** *n.*

ve·nous /'vēnəs/ ▸*adj.* of or relating to a vein or the veins.■ of or relating to the dark red, oxygen-poor blood in the veins and pulmonary artery. ▷early 17th cent.: from Latin *venosus* 'venous,' from *vena* 'vein.' —**ve·nos·i·ty** /vi'näsətē/ *n.* —**ve·nous·ly** *adv.*

ve·nous in·suf·fi·cien·cy ▸*n. Pathology* failure of the veins to adequately circulate the blood, esp. from the lower extremities.

vent[1] /vent/ ▸*n.* an opening that allows air, gas, or liquid to pass out of or into a confined space. ■ *figurative* release or expression of a strong emotion, energy, etc.: *children* **give vent to** *their anger in various ways.* ■ the opening of a volcano, through which lava and other materials are emitted. ■ *historical* the touch hole of a gun. ■ the anus, esp. one in a lower animal such as a fish that serves for both excretion and reproduction.
▸*v.* [*trans.*] **1** give free expression to (a strong emotion): *he had come to vent his rage and despair.* **2** provide with an outlet for air, gas, or liquid: *clothes dryers must be vented to the outside.* ■ discharge or expel (air, gas, or liquid) through an outlet: *the plant was isolated and the gas vented.* ■ permit air to enter (a beer cask). ▷late Middle English: partly from French *vent* 'wind,' from Latin *ventus*, reinforced by French *évent*, from *éventer* 'expose to air,' based on Latin *ventus* 'wind.' —**vent·less** *adj.*

vent[2] ▸*n.* a slit in a garment, esp. in the lower edge of the back of a coat through the seam. ▷late Middle English: alteration of dialect *fent*, from Old French *fente* 'slit,' based on Latin *findere* 'cleave.'

ven·tail /'ven,tāl/ ▸*n. historical* the lower movable front of a medieval helmet. ■ the whole movable front of such a helmet, including the visor.

V

ven·ter /ˈventər/ ▸*n. Zoology* the underside or abdomen of an animal. ▷early 18th cent.: from Latin, literally 'belly.'

ven·ti·fact /ˈventəˌfakt/ ▸*n. Geology* a stone shaped by the erosive action of windblown sand. ▷early 20th cent.: from Latin *ventus* 'wind' + *factum*, neuter past participle of *facere* 'make.'

ven·ti·late /ˈventəˌlāt/ ▸*v.* [*trans.*] **1** cause air to enter and circulate freely in (a room, building, etc.): *ventilate the greenhouse well* | [as *adj.*, in *combination*] (**-ventilated**) *gas heaters should only ever be used in well-ventilated rooms.* ■ (of air) purify or freshen (something) by blowing on or through it: *a colossus ventilated by the dawn breeze.* ■ *Medicine* subject to artificial respiration. ■ *archaic* oxygenate (the blood). **2** discuss or examine (an opinion, issue, complaint, etc.) in public: *he used the club to ventilate an ongoing complaint.* ▷late Middle English (in the sense 'winnow, scatter'): from Latin *ventilat-* 'blown, winnowed,' from the verb *ventilare*, from *ventus* 'wind.' The sense 'cause air to circulate in' dates from the mid 18th cent.

ven·ti·la·tion /ˌventəˈlāsʜən/ ▸*n.* **1** the provision of fresh air to a room, building, etc. ■ *Medicine* the supply of air to the lungs, esp. by artificial means. **2** public discussion or examination of an opinion, issue, complaint, etc. ▷late Middle English (in the sense 'current of air'): from Old French, or from Latin *ventilatio(n-)*, from the verb *ventilare* (see VENTILATE). Sense 1 dates from the mid 17th cent.

ven·ti·la·tor /ˈventəˌlātər/ ▸*n.* **1** an appliance or aperture for ventilating a room or other space. **2** *Medicine* an appliance for artificial respiration; a respirator.

ven·ti·la·to·ry /ˈventələˌtôrē/ ▸*adj. Physiology* of, relating to, or serving for the provision of air to the lungs or respiratory system.

Ven·tose /vänˈtōz/ (also **Ven·tôse**) ▸*n.* the sixth month of the French Republican calendar (1793–1805), originally running from February 19 to March 20. ▷French *Ventôse*, from Latin *ventosus* 'windy,' from *ventus* 'wind.'

ven·touse /ˈvenˌto͞os/ ▸*n. Medicine* a vacuum extractor for use in assisting childbirth. ▷1960s: from French, literally 'cupping glass,' based on Latin *ventus* 'wind.'

ven·tral /ˈventrəl/ ▸*adj. Anatomy, Zoology, & Botany* of, on, or relating to the underside of an animal or plant; abdominal: *a ventral nerve cord* | *the ventral part of the head.* Compare with DORSAL. ▷late Middle English: from Latin *venter, ventr-* 'belly' + -AL. —**ven·tral·ly** *adv.*

ven·tral fin ▸*n. Zoology* another term for PELVIC FIN. ■ an unpaired fin on the underside of certain fishes. ■ a single vertical fin under the fuselage or tail of an aircraft.

ven·tri·cle /ˈventrəkəl/ ▸*n. Anatomy* a hollow part or cavity in an organ, in particular: ■ each of the two main chambers of the heart, left and right. ■ each of the four connected fluid-filled cavities in the center of the brain. ▷late Middle English: from Latin *ventriculus*, diminutive of *venter* 'belly.' —**ven·tric·u·lar** /venˈtrikyələr/ *adj.*

ven·tri·cose /ˈventrəˌkōs/ ▸*adj.* **1** having a protruding belly. **2** *Botany* distended, inflated. ▷mid 18th cent.: formed irregularly from VENTRICLE + -OSE[1].

ven·tric·u·log·ra·phy /venˌtrikyəˈlägrəfē/ ▸*n. Medicine* radiography of the ventricles of the brain with the cerebral fluid replaced by air (pneumoencephalography) or radiopaque material or labeled with a radionuclide.

ven·tric·u·lus /venˈtrikyələs/ ▸*n.* technical term for GIZZARD.

ven·tril·o·quist /venˈtriləkwist/ ▸*n.* a person who can speak or utter sounds so that they seem to come from somewhere else, esp. an entertainer who makes their voice appear to come from a dummy of a person or animal. ▷mid 17th cent.: from modern Latin *ventriloquium* (from Latin *venter* 'belly' + *loqui* 'speak') + -IST. —**ven·tri·lo·qui·al** /ˌventrəˈlōkwēəl/ *adj.* —**ven·tril·o·quism** /-ˌkwizəm/ *n.* —**ven·tril·o·quize** /-ˌkwīz/ *v.* —**ven·tril·o·quy** /-kwē/ *n.*

ven·tro·lat·er·al /ˌventrōˈlatərəl; -ˈlatrəl/ ▸*adj. Biology* situated toward the junction of the ventral and lateral sides. —**ven·tro·lat·er·al·ly** *adv.*

ven·tro·me·di·al /ˌventrōˈmēdēəl/ ▸*adj. Biology* situated toward the middle of the ventral side. —**ven·tro·me·di·al·ly** *adv.*

Ven·tu·ra[1] /venˈcʜo͝orə/ (official name **San Buenaventura**) a city in southern California, on the Pacific Ocean; pop. 92,575.

Ven·tur·a[2], Jesse (1951–), U.S. politician; born *James George Janos*. A former professional wrestler 1975–86, who was called "The Body," he was governor of Minnesota 1999-2002.

ven·ture /ˈvencʜər/ ▸*n.* a risky or daring journey or undertaking: *pioneering ventures into little-known waters.* ■ a business enterprise involving considerable risk.

▸*v.* [*intrans.*] dare to do something or go somewhere that may be dangerous or unpleasant: *she* ***ventured out*** *into the blizzard.* ■ dare to do or say something that may be considered audacious (often used as a polite expression of hesitation or apology): *may I venture to add a few comments?* | *I ventured to write to her* | [*trans.*] *he ventured the opinion that Putt was now dangerously insane.* ■ [*trans.*] expose (something) to the risk of loss: *his fortune is ventured in an expedition over which he has no control.* ▷late Middle English (in the sense 'adventure,' also 'risk the loss of'): shortening of ADVENTURE.

▸*PHRASES* □ **at a venture** *archaic* trusting to chance rather than to previous consideration or preparation: *a man drew a bow at a venture.* □ **nothing ventured, nothing gained** *proverb* you can't expect to achieve anything if you never take any risks.

ven·ture cap·i·tal ▸*n.* capital invested in a project in which there is a substantial element of risk, typically a new or expanding business. —**ven·ture cap·i·tal·ist** *n.*

ven·tur·er /ˈvencʜərər/ ▸*n. archaic* a person who undertakes or shares in a trading venture.

ven·ture·some /ˈvencʜərsəm/ ▸*adj.* willing to take risks or embark on difficult or unusual courses of action. —**ven·ture·some·ly** *adv.* —**ven·ture·some·ness** *n.*

Ven·tu·ri /venˈto͝orē; -ˈcʜo͝orē/, Robert (Charles) (1925–), U.S. architect and writer; pioneer of post-modernist architecture. Among his buildings are the Humanities Classroom Building of the State University of New York at Purchase (1973) and the Sainsbury Wing of the National Gallery in London (1991).

ven·tu·ri /venˈto͝orē/ ▸*n.* (*pl.* **-ris**) a short piece of narrow tube between wider sections for measuring flow rate or exerting suction. ▷late 19th cent.: named after Giovanni B. *Venturi* (1746–1822), Italian physicist.

ven·ue /ˈvenˌyo͞o/ ▸*n.* the place where something happens, esp. an organized event such as a concert, conference, or sports event: *the river could soon be the venue for a powerboat world championship event.* ■ *Law* the county or district within which a criminal or civil case must be heard. ▷late 16th cent. (denoting a thrust or bout in fencing; also in the Law sense): from Old French, literally 'a coming,' feminine past participle of *venir* 'come,' from Latin *venire*.

ven·ule /ˈvenˌyo͞ol/ ▸*n. Anatomy* a very small vein, esp. one collecting blood from the capillaries. ▷mid 19th cent.: from Latin *venula*, diminutive of *vena* 'vein.'

Ve·nus /ˈvēnəs/ **1** *Roman Mythology* a goddess, worshiped as the goddess of love in classical Rome though apparently a spirit of kitchen gardens in earlier times. Greek equivalent APHRODITE. [Latin.] ■ [as *n.*] (**a Venus**) *chiefly poetic/literary* a beautiful woman. **2** *Astronomy* the second planet from the sun in the solar system, the brightest celestial object after the sun and moon and frequently appearing in the twilight sky as the evening or morning star.

> Venus orbits between Mercury and the earth at an average distance of 67.2 million miles (108 million km) from the sun. It is almost equal in size to the earth, with a diameter of 7,521 miles (12,104 km) and shows phases similar to the moon. The planet is completely covered by clouds consisting chiefly of sulfuric acid droplets, and no surface detail can be seen by telescope. There is a dense atmosphere of carbon dioxide, which traps the heat of the sun by the greenhouse effect to produce a surface temperature of 460°C. The planet has no natural satellite.

3 (also **ve·nus, Ve·nus shell**, or **Ve·nus clam**) a burrowing marine bivalve mollusk with clearly defined growth lines on the shell. • *Venus, Venerupis*, and other genera, family Veneridae. —**Ve·nu·si·an** /vəˈn(y)o͞osʜ(ē)ən; -zʜən; -sēən/ *adj.* & *n.*

Ve·nus·berg /ˈvēnəsˌbərg/ ▸*n.* (in German legend) the court of Venus.

Ve·nus de Mi·lo /də ˈmēlō; ˈmī-/ a classical sculpture of Aphrodite dated to *c.*100 BC. It was discovered on the Greek island of Melos in 1820 and is now in the Louvre in Paris. ▷French, 'Venus of Melos.'

Venus flytrap

Ve·nus fly·trap (also **Ve·nus's fly·trap**) ▸*n.* a small carnivorous bog plant with hinged leaves that spring shut on and digest insects that land on them. Native to the southeastern U.S., it is also kept as an indoor plant. • *Dionaea muscipula*, family Droseraceae.

Ve·nus's comb ▸*n.* another term for SHEPHERD'S NEEDLE.

Ve·nus's flow·er bas·ket ▸*n.* a slender upright sponge with a filmy, latticelike skeleton. • Genus *Euplectella*, class Hexactinellida.

Ve·nus's gir·dle ▸*n.* a large, almost transparent comb jelly with a flattened ribbonlike body, living chiefly in warmer seas. • Genus *Cestum*, phylum Ctenophora.

Ve·nus's hair ▸*n.* the maidenhair fern *Adiantum capillus-veneris.*

Ve·nus's look·ing glass ▸*n.* a blue-flowered plant of the bellflower family, whose shiny brown seeds inside their open capsule supposedly resemble mirrors. • Two species in the family Campanulaceae: *Legousia hybrida* of Europe, and *Triodanis perfoliata* of North America.

ve·ra·cious /vəˈrāsʜəs/ ▸*adj. formal* speaking or representing the truth. ▷late 17th cent.: from Latin *verax, verac-* (from *verus* 'true') + -IOUS. —**ve·ra·cious·ly** *adv.* —**ve·ra·cious·ness** *n.*

ve·rac·i·ty /vəˈrasətē/ ▸*n.* conformity to facts; accuracy: *officials expressed doubts concerning the veracity of the story.* ■ habitual truthfulness: *voters should be concerned about his veracity and character.* ▷early 17th cent.: from French *véracité* or medieval Latin *veracitas*, from *verax* 'speaking truly' (see VERACIOUS).

Ve·ra·cruz /ˌverəˈkro͞oz; -ˈkro͞os/ **1** a state in east central Mexico that has a long coastline on the Gulf of Mexico; capital, Jalapa Enriquez. **2** a city and port in Mexico, in Veracruz state, on the Gulf of Mexico; pop. 328,000.

ve·ran·da /vəˈrandə/ (also **ve·ran·dah**) ▸*n.* a roofed platform along the outside of a house, level with the ground floor. ▷early 18th cent.: from Hindi *varaṇḍā*, from Portuguese *varanda* 'railing, balustrade.' —**ve·ran·daed** *adj.*

ve·ra·pam·il /vəˈrapəməl/ ▸*n. Medicine* a synthetic compound that acts as a calcium antagonist and is used to treat angina pectoris and cardiac arrhythmias. ▷1960s: from *v(al)er(onitr)il(e)* (from VALERIC ACID + NITRILE), with the insertion of *-apam-* (of unknown origin).

ver·a·trine /ˈverəˌtrēn; -trin/ ▸*n. Chemistry* a poisonous substance consisting of a mixture of alkaloids that occurs in the seeds of sabadilla and related plants, used, esp. formerly, to relieve neuralgia and rheumatism. ▷early 19th cent.: from French *vératrine*, from Latin *veratrum* 'hellebore.'

ve·ra·trum /vəˈrātrəm/ ▸*n.* (*pl.* **-trums**) a plant of a genus that includes the false hellebores. • Genus *Veratrum*, family Liliaceae. ▷modern Latin, from Latin, literally 'hellebore.'

verb /vərb/ ▸*n. Grammar* a word used to describe an action, state, or occurrence, and forming the main part of the predicate of a sentence, such as *hear, become, happen.* ▷late Middle English: from Old French *verbe* or Latin *verbum* 'word, verb.' —**verb·less** *adj.*

ver·bal /ˈvərbəl/ ▸*adj.* **1** relating to or in the form of words: *the root of the problem is visual rather than verbal* | *verbal abuse.* ■ spoken rather than written; oral: *a verbal agreement.* ■ tending to talk a lot: *he's very verbal.* **2** *Grammar* of, relating to, or derived from a verb: *a verbal adjective.*

▸*n. Grammar* a word or words functioning as a verb. ■ a verbal noun. ▷late 15th cent. (describing a person who deals with words rather than things): from French, or from late Latin *verbalis*, from *verbum* 'word' (see VERB). —**ver·bal·ly** *adv.*

> *USAGE* It is sometimes said that the true sense of the adjective **verbal** is 'of or concerned with words,' whether spoken or written (as in *verbal abuse*), and that it should not be used to mean 'spoken rather than written' (as in *a verbal agreement*). For this strictly 'spoken' sense, it is said that the adjective **oral** should be used instead. In practice, however, **verbal** is well established in this sense

and, in certain idiomatic phrases (such as *a verbal agreement*), cannot be simply replaced by **oral**. Note that it is not incorrect to refer to a spoken agreement, order, etc., as **verbal**, but it is *more exact* to describe it as **oral**—a distinction lawyers are expected to observe.

ver·bal·ism /ˈvərbəˌlizəm/ ▶*n.* concentration on forms of expression rather than content. ■ a verbal expression. ■ excessive or empty use of language. —**ver·bal·ist** *n.* —**ver·bal·is·tic** /ˌvərbəˈlistik/ *adj.*

ver·bal·ize /ˈvərbəˌlīz/ ▶*v.* **1** [*trans.*] express (ideas or feelings) in words, esp. by speaking out loud: *they are unable to verbalize their real feelings.* **2** [*intrans.*] speak, esp. at excessive length and with little real content: *the dangers of verbalizing about art.* **3** [*trans.*] make (a word, esp. a noun) into a verb. —**ver·bal·iz·a·ble** *adj.* —**ver·bal·i·za·tion** /ˌvərbələˈzāsHən; -ˌlīˈzā-/ *n.* —**ver·bal·iz·er** *n.*

ver·bal noun ▶*n. Grammar* a noun formed by inflection of a verb and partly sharing its constructions, such as *smoking* in *smoking is forbidden.* See **-ING**1.

ver·bal o·ver·shad·ow·ing ▶*n. Psychology* the tendency of verbalization to impair the recall of visual memories, resulting in unreliable eyewitness accounts.

ver·bas·cum /vərˈbaskəm/ ▶*n.* a plant of a genus that comprises the mulleins. • Genus *Verbascum*, family Scrophulariaceae. ▷modern Latin, from Latin, literally 'mullein.'

ver·ba·tim /vərˈbātəm/ ▶*adv. & adj.* in exactly the same words as were used originally: [as *adv.*] *subjects were instructed to recall the passage verbatim* | [as *adj.*] *your quotations must be verbatim.* ▷late 15th cent.: from medieval Latin, from Latin *verbum* 'word.' Compare with **LITERATIM**.

ver·be·na /vərˈbēnə/ ▶*n.* a chiefly American herbaceous plant that bears heads of bright showy flowers, widely cultivated as a garden ornamental. • Genus *Verbena*, family Verbenaceae: many species, in particular a group of complex cultivars (*V.* × *hybrida*). ▷modern Latin, from Latin, literally 'sacred bough,' in medieval Latin 'vervain.'

ver·bi·age /ˈvərbē-ij/ ▶*n.* speech or writing that uses too many words or excessively technical expressions. ▷early 18th cent.: from French, from obsolete *verbeier* 'to chatter,' from *verbe* 'word' (see **VERB**).

ver·bose /vərˈbōs/ ▶*adj.* using or expressed in more words than are needed: *much academic language is obscure and verbose.* ▷late 17th cent.: from Latin *verbosus*, from *verbum* 'word.' —**ver·bose·ly** *adv.* —**ver·bos·i·ty** /-ˈbäsətē/ *n.*

ver·bo·ten /fərˈbōtn; vər-/ ▶*adj.* forbidden, esp. by an authority. ▷German.

verb phrase ▶*n. Grammar* the part of a sentence containing the verb and any direct or indirect object, but not the subject.

ver·dant /ˈvərdnt/ ▶*adj.* (of countryside) green with grass or other rich vegetation. ■ of the bright green color of lush grass: *a deep, verdant green.* ▷late 16th cent.: perhaps from Old French *verdeant*, present participle of *verdoier* 'be green,' based on Latin *viridis* 'green.' —**ver·dan·cy** /ˈvərdn-sē/ *n.* —**ver·dant·ly** *adv.*

verd an·tique /ˈvərd anˈtēk/ ▶*n.* a green ornamental marble consisting of serpentine with calcite and dolomite veins. ■ verdigris on ancient bronze or copper. ■ a green form of porphyry. ▷mid 18th cent.: from obsolete French, literally 'antique green.'

Ver·de·lho /vərˈdelyo͞o/ ▶*n.* (*pl.* **-lhos**) a white grape originally grown in Madeira, now also in Portugal, Sicily, Australia, and South Africa. ■ a medium Madeira made from this grape. ▷Portuguese, literally 'little green thing;' compare with **VERDICCHIO**.

ver·der·er /ˈvərdərər/ ▶*n. Brit.* a judicial officer of a royal forest. ▷mid 16th cent.: from Anglo-Norman French, based on Latin *viridis* 'green.'

Ver·di /ˈve(ə)rdē/, Giuseppe (Fortunino Francesco) (1813–1901), Italian composer. His many operas, such as *La Traviata* (1853), *Aida* (1871), and *Otello* (1887), emphasize the dramatic element and the treatment of personal stories on a heroic scale, often against backgrounds that reflect his political interests. He is also noted for *Requiem* (1874).

Ver·dic·chi·o /vərˈdēkēˌō/ ▶*n.* a variety of white wine grape grown in the Marche region of Italy. ■ a dry white wine made from this grape. ▷Italian, literally 'little green thing;' compare with **VERDELHO**.

ver·dict /ˈvərdikt/ ▶*n.* a decision on a disputed issue in a civil or criminal case or an inquest: *the jury returned a verdict of 'not guilty.'* ■ an opinion or judgment: *I'm anxious to know your verdict on me.* ▷Middle English: from Anglo-Norman French *verdit*, from Old French *veir* 'true' (from Latin *verus*) + *dit* (from Latin *dictum* 'saying').

ver·di·gris /ˈvərdəˌgrēs; -ˌgris; -ˌgrē/ ▶*n.* a bright bluish-green encrustation or patina formed on copper or brass by atmospheric oxidation, consisting of basic copper carbonate. ▷Middle English: from Old French *verte-gres*, earlier *vert de Grece* 'green of Greece.'

ver·din /ˈvərdn/ ▶*n.* a small songbird with a gray body and yellowish head, found in the semideserts of southwestern North America. • *Auriparus flaviceps*, family Remizidae. ▷late 19th cent.: from French, literally 'yellowhammer.'

ver·di·ter /ˈvərdətər/ ▶*n.* a light blue or bluish-green pigment, typically prepared by adding chalk or whiting to a solution of copper nitrate, used in making crayons and as a watercolor.
▶*adj.* of this color. ▷early 16th cent.: from Old French *verd de terre*, literally 'earth green.'

Ver·dun, Bat·tle of /vərˈdən/ a long and severe battle in 1916, during World War I, at the fortified town of Verdun in northeastern France.

ver·dure /ˈvərjər/ ▶*n.* lush green vegetation. ■ the fresh green color of such vegetation. ■ *poetic/literary* a condition of freshness. ▷late Middle English: via French from Old French *verd* 'green,' from Latin *viridis*. —**ver·dured** *adj.* —**ver·dur·ous** /-jərəs/ *adj.*

Ve·ree·ni·ging /vəˈrēnəgiNG; fə-/ a city in South Africa; pop. 774,000 (with Vanderbijlpark).

verge1 /vərj/ ▶*n.* an edge or border: *they came down to the verge of the lake.* See note at **BORDER**. ■ an extreme limit beyond which something specified will happen: *I was* ***on the verge of*** *tears.* ■ *Brit.* a grass edging such as that by the side of a road or path. ■ *Architecture* an edge of tiles projecting over a gable.
▶*v.* [*intrans.*] (**verge on**) approach (something) closely; be close or similar to (something): *despair verging on the suicidal.* ▷late Middle English: via Old French from Latin *virga* 'rod.' The current verb sense dates from the late 18th cent.

verge2 ▶*n.* a wand or rod carried before a bishop or dean as an emblem of office. ▷late Middle English: from Latin *virga* 'rod.'

verge3 ▶*v.* [*intrans.*] incline in a certain direction or toward a particular state: *his style verged into the art nouveau school.* ▷early 17th cent. (in the sense 'descend (to the horizon)'): from Latin *vergere* 'to bend, incline.'

ver·gence /ˈvərjəns/ ▶*n.* **1** *Physiology* the simultaneous movement of the pupils of the eyes toward or away from one another during focusing. **2** *Geology* the direction in which a fold is inclined or overturned: *a zone of opposing fold vergence.* ▷1980s: common element of **CONVERGENCE** and **DIVERGENCE**.

verg·er /ˈvərjər/ ▶*n.* **1** an official in a church who acts as a caretaker and attendant. **2** an officer who carries a rod before a bishop or dean as a symbol of office. ▷Middle English (sense 2): from Anglo-Norman French (see **VERGE**2). —**verg·er·ship** /-ˌSHip/ *n.*

Ver·gil variant spelling of **VIRGIL**.

ver·glas /verˈglä/ ▶*n.* a thin coating of ice or frozen rain on an exposed surface. ▷early 19th cent.: French, from *verre* 'glass' + *glas* (now *glace*) 'ice.'

ve·rid·i·cal /vəˈridikəl/ ▶*adj. formal* truthful. ■ coinciding with reality: *such memories are not necessarily veridical.* ▷mid 17th cent.: from Latin *veridicus* (from *verus* 'true' + *dicere* 'say') + **-AL**. —**ve·rid·i·cal·i·ty** /-ˌridəˈkalətē/ *n.* —**ve·rid·i·cal·ly** /-ik(ə)lē/ *adv.*

ver·i·est /ˈverēist/ ▶*adj.* [*attrib.*] (**the veriest**) *chiefly archaic* used to emphasize the degree to which a description applies to someone or something: *everyone but the veriest greenhorn knows by now.* ▷early 16th cent.: superlative of **VERY**.

ver·i·fi·ca·tion /ˌverəfiˈkāsHən/ ▶*n.* the process of establishing the truth, accuracy, or validity of something: *the verification of official documents.* ■ [often as *adj.*] *Philosophy* the establishment by empirical means of the validity of a proposition. ■ the process of ensuring that procedures laid down in weapons limitation agreements are followed. ▷early 16th cent.: from Old French or from medieval Latin *verificatio(n-)*, from the verb *verificare* (see **VERIFY**).

ver·i·fy /ˈverəˌfī/ ▶*v.* (**-fies, -fied**) [*trans.*] (often **be verified**) make sure or demonstrate that (something) is true, accurate, or justified: *his conclusions have been verified by later experiments* | [with *clause*] *"Can you verify that the guns are licensed?"* ■ *Law* swear to or support (a statement) by affidavit. ▷Middle English (as a legal term): from Old French *verifier*, from medieval Latin *verificare*, from *verus* 'true.' —**ver·i·fi·a·ble** /ˈverəˌfīəbəl; ˌverəˈfī-/ *adj.* —**ver·i·fi·a·bly** /ˈverəˌfīəblē; ˌverəˈfī-/ *adv.* —**ver·i·fi·er** *n.*

ver·i·ly /ˈverəlē/ ▶*adv. archaic* truly; certainly: *I verily believed myself to be a free woman.* ▷Middle English: from **VERY** + **-LY**2, suggested by Old French *verrai(e)ment*.

ver·i·si·mil·i·tude /ˌverəsəˈmiliˌt(y)o͞od/ ▶*n.* the appearance of being true or real: *the detail gives the novel some verisimilitude.* ▷early 17th cent.: from Latin *verisimilitudo*, from *verisimilis* 'probable,' from *veri* (genitive of *verus* 'true') + *similis* 'like.' —**ver·i·sim·i·lar** /-ˈsimələr/ *adj.*

ve·ris·mo /vəˈrizmō; ve-/ ▶*n.* realism in the arts, esp. late 19th-century Italian opera. ■ this genre of opera, as composed principally by Puccini, Mascagni, and Leoncavallo. ▷Italian.

ve·ris·tic /vəˈristik/ ▶*adj.* (of art or literature) extremely or strictly naturalistic. ▷late 19th cent.: from Latin *verum* (neuter) 'true' or Italian *vero* 'true' + **-IST** + **-IC**. —**ver·ism** /ˈverˌizəm/ *n.* —**ver·ist** /ˈverist/ *n. & adj.*

ver·i·ta·ble /ˈveritəbəl/ ▶*adj.* [*attrib.*] used as an intensifier, often to qualify a metaphor: *the early 1970s witnessed a veritable price explosion.* See note at **GENUINE**. ▷late Middle English: from Old French, from *verite* 'truth' (see **VERITY**). Early senses included 'true' and 'speaking the truth,' later 'genuine, actual.' —**ver·i·ta·bly** /-blē/ *adv.*

vé·ri·té /ˌveriˈtā/ ▶*n.* a genre of film, television, and radio programs emphasizing realism and naturalism. ▷French, literally 'truth.'

ver·i·ty /ˈveritē/ ▶*n.* (*pl.* **-ties**) a true principle or belief, esp. one of fundamental importance: *the* ***eternal verities.*** ■ truth: *irrefutable, objective verity.* ▷late Middle English: from Old French *verite*, from Latin *veritas*, from *verus* 'true.'

ver·juice /ˈvərˌjo͞os/ ▶*n.* a sour juice obtained from crab apples, unripe grapes, or other fruit, used in cooking and formerly in medicine. ▷Middle English: from Old French *vertjus*, from *vert* 'green' + *jus* 'juice.'

Ver·khne·u·dinsk /ˌverknəˈo͞odinsk/ former name (until 1934) of **ULAN-UDE**.

Ver·laine /vərˈlān; verˈlen/, Paul (1844–96), French symbolist poet. Notable collections of his poetry include *Poèmes saturniens* (1867), *Fêtes galantes* (1869), and *Romances sans paroles* (1874).

Ver·meer /vərˈmi(ə)r/, Jan (1632–75), Dutch painter. He generally painted domestic genre scenes, for example *The Kitchen Maid* (*c.*1658), *The Music Lesson* (*c.*1662–65), and *The Girl with a Pearl Earring* (*c.*1665–66). His work is distinguished by its clear design and simple form.

ver·meil /ˈvərməl; -ˌmāl; vərˈmā(l)/ ▶*n.* [often as *adj.*] **1** gilded silver or bronze. **2** *poetic/literary* vermilion. ▷late Middle English (sense 2): from Old French (see **VERMILION**).

vermi- ▶*comb. form* of or relating to a worm or worms, esp. parasitic ones: *vermiform.* ▷from Latin *vermis* 'worm.'

ver·mi·an /ˈvərmēən/ ▶*adj.* **1** *poetic/literary* relating to or resembling a worm; wormlike. **2** *Anatomy* of or relating to the vermis of the brain. ▷late 19th cent.: from Latin *vermis* 'worm' + **-IAN**.

ver·mi·cel·li /ˌvərməˈCHelē; -ˈselē/ ▶*n.* pasta made in long slender threads. ▷Italian, plural of *vermicello*, diminutive of *verme* 'worm,' from Latin *vermis*.

ver·mi·cide /ˈvərməˌsīd/ ▶*n.* a substance that is poisonous to worms.

ver·mic·u·lar /vərˈmikyələr/ ▶*adj.* **1** like a worm in form or movement; vermiform. **2** of, denoting, or caused by intestinal worms. **3** marked with close wavy lines. ▷late 17th cent.: from medieval Latin *vermicularis*, from Latin *vermiculus*, diminutive of *vermis* 'worm.'

ver·mic·u·late /vərˈmikyəˌlāt; -lət/ ▶*adj.* **1** another term for **VERMICULAR**. **2** another term for **VERMICULATED**. ▷early 17th cent.: from Latin *vermiculatus*, past participle of *vermiculari* 'be full of worms' (see **VERMICULAR**).

ver·mic·u·lat·ed /vərˈmikyəˌlātid/ ▶*adj.* **1** (esp. of the plumage of a bird) marked with sinuous or wavy lines. **2** *archaic* worm-eaten. **3** *Architecture* carved or molded with shallow wavy grooves resembling the tracks of worms. —**ver·mic·u·la·tion** /vərˌmikyəˈlāsHən/ *n.*

Pronunciation Key ə *ago*; ər *over*; ˈə or ˌə *up*; ˈər or ˌər *fur*; a *hat*; ā *rate*; ä *car*; CH *chew*; e *let*; ē *see*; e(ə)r *air*; i *fit*; ī *by*; i(ə)r *ear*; NG *sing*; ō *go*; ô *for*; oi *boy*; o͝o *good*; o͞o *goo*; ou *out*; SH *she*; TH *thin*; TH *then*; (h)w *why*; ZH *vision*

ver·mic·u·lite /vər'mikyə,līt/ ▸*n.* a yellow or brown mineral found as an alteration product of mica and other minerals, and used for insulation or as a moisture-retentive medium for growing plants. ▷early 19th cent.: from Latin *vermiculari* 'be full of worms' (because on expansion due to heat, it shoots out forms resembling small worms) + **-ITE**[1].

ver·mi·form /'vərmə,fôrm/ ▸*adj. chiefly Zoology* or *Anatomy* resembling or having the form of a worm.

ver·mi·form ap·pen·dix ▸*n.* technical term for **APPENDIX** (sense 1).

ver·mi·fuge /'vərmə,fyōōj/ ▸*n. Medicine* an anthelmintic medicine.

ver·mil·ion /vər'milyən/ (also **ver·mil·lion**) ▸*n.* a brilliant red pigment made from mercury sulfide (cinnabar). ■ a brilliant red color: *a lateral stripe of vermilion* | [as *adj.*] *vermilion streaks of sunset.* ▷Middle English: from Old French *vermeillon*, from *vermeil*, from Latin *vermiculus*, diminutive of *vermis* 'worm.'

ver·min /'vərmən/ ▸*n.* [treated as *pl.*] wild mammals and birds that are believed to be harmful to crops, farm animals, or game, or that carry disease, e.g., foxes, rodents, and insect pests. ■ parasitic worms or insects. ■ *figurative* people perceived as despicable and as causing problems for the rest of society: *the vermin who ransacked her house.* ▷Middle English (originally denoting animals such as reptiles and snakes): from Old French, based on Latin *vermis* 'worm.' **—ver·min·ous** /-mənəs/ *adj.*

ver·mis /'vərməs/ ▸*n. Anatomy* the rounded and elongated central part of the cerebellum, between the two hemispheres. ▷late 19th cent.: from Latin, literally 'worm.'

Ver·mont /vər'mänt/ a state in the northeastern U.S., on the border with Canada, one of the six New England States; pop. 608,827; capital, Montpelier; statehood, Mar. 4, 1791 (14). Explored and settled by the French during the 1600s and 1700s, it became an independent republic in 1777 until it was admitted as a U.S. state. **—Ver·mont·er** *n.*

ver·mouth /vər'mōōTH/ ▸*n.* a red or white wine flavored with aromatic herbs, chiefly made in France and Italy and drunk mixed with gin. ▷from French *vermout*, from German *Wermut* 'wormwood.'

ver·nac·cia /vər'nächə/ ▸*n.* a variety of wine grape grown in the San Gimignano area of Italy and in Sardinia. ■ a strong dry white wine made from this grape. ▷Italian.

ver·nac·u·lar /vər'nakyələr/ ▸*n.* **1** (usu. **the vernacular**) the language or dialect spoken by the ordinary people in a particular country or region: *he wrote in the vernacular to reach a larger audience.* See note at **DIALECT.** ■ [with *adj.*] the terminology used by people belonging to a specified group or engaging in a specialized activity: *gardening vernacular.* **2** architecture concerned with domestic and functional rather than monumental buildings: *buildings in which Gothic merged into farmhouse vernacular.*

▸*adj.* **1** (of language) spoken as one's mother tongue; not learned or imposed as a second language. ■ (of speech or written works) using such a language: *vernacular literature.* **2** (of architecture) concerned with domestic and functional rather than monumental buildings. ▷early 17th cent.: from Latin *vernaculus* 'domestic, native' (from *verna* 'home-born slave') + **-AR**[1]. **—ver·nac·u·lar·ism** /-,rizəm/ *n.* **—ver·nac·u·lar·i·ty** /-,nakyə'laritē/ *n.* **—ver·nac·u·lar·ize** /-,rīz/ *v.* **—ver·nac·u·lar·ly** *adv.*

ver·nal /'vərnl/ ▸*adj.* of, in, or appropriate to spring: *the vernal freshness of the land.* ▷mid 16th cent.: from Latin *vernalis*, from *vernus* 'of the spring,' from *ver* 'spring.' **—ver·nal·ly** *adv.*

ver·nal e·qui·nox ▸*n.* the equinox in spring, on about March 20 in the northern hemisphere and September 22 in the southern hemisphere.■ *Astronomy* the equinox in March. Also called **SPRING EQUINOX.** ■ *Astronomy* another term for **FIRST POINT OF ARIES** (see **ARIES**).

ver·nal grass ▸*n.* a sweet-scented Eurasian grass that is sometimes grown as a meadow or hay grass. Also called **sweet vernal grass.** • *Anthoxanthum odoratum*, family Gramineae.

ver·nal·i·za·tion /,vərnl-ə'zāSHən/ ▸*n.* the cooling of seed during germination in order to accelerate flowering when it is planted. ▷1930s: translation of Russian *yarovizatsiya.* **—ver·nal·ize** /'vərnl,īz/ *v.*

ver·na·tion /vər'nāSHən/ ▸*n. Botany* the arrangement of young leaves in a leaf bud before it opens. Compare with **ESTIVATION.** ▷late 18th cent.: from modern Latin *vernatio(n-)*, from Latin *vernare* 'to grow (as in the spring),' from *vernus* (see **VERNAL**).

Verne /vərn/, Jules (1828–1905), French novelist. One of the first writers of science fiction, he often anticipated later scientific and technological developments, such as in *Twenty Thousand Leagues under the Sea* (1870). Other novels include *Journey to the Center of the Earth* (1864) and *Around the World in Eighty Days* (1873).

Ver·ner's Law /'vernərz; 'vər-/ *Linguistics* the observation that voiceless fricatives in Germanic predicted by Grimm's Law became voiced if the preceding syllable in the corresponding Indo-European word was unstressed, as in the English words *death* and *dead.* ▷late 19th cent.: named after Karl A. *Verner* (1846–96), Danish philologist.

ver·ni·cle /'vərnəkəl/ ▸*n.* another term for **VERONICA** (sense 2). ▷Middle English: from Old French, alteration of *vernique*, from medieval Latin *veronica.*

ver·nier /'vərnēər/ ▸*n.* a small movable graduated scale for obtaining fractional parts of subdivisions on a fixed main scale of a barometer, sextant, or other measuring instrument. ▷mid 18th cent.: named after Pierre *Vernier* (1580–1637), French mathematician.

ver·ni·er cal·i·per ▸*n.* a linear measuring instrument consisting of a scaled rule with a projecting arm at one end, to which is attached a sliding vernier with a projecting arm that forms a jaw with the other projecting arm.

ver·nier en·gine ▸*n.* another term for **THRUSTER** (on a spacecraft). ▷mid 20th cent.: named after P. *Vernier* (see **VERNIER**).

ver·ni·er scale ▸*n.* see **VERNIER.**

ver·nis·sage /,vernə'säZH/ ▸*n.* (*pl.* same) a private viewing of paintings before public exhibition. ▷French, literally 'varnishing,' originally referring to the day prior to an exhibition when artists were allowed to retouch and varnish hung work.

ver·nix /'vərniks/ ▸*n.* (in full **ver·nix ca·se·o·sa**) /,kāsē'ōsə/ a greasy deposit covering the skin of a baby at birth. ▷late 16th cent.: from medieval Latin, variant of *veronix* 'fragrant resin' (see **VARNISH**).

Ver·ny /'vernē/ former name (until 1921) of **ALMATY.**

Ve·ro·na /və'rōnə/ a city on the Adige River, in northeastern Italy; pop. 259,000.

ve·ro·nal /'verə,nôl; -ənl/ ▸*n. trademark* another term for **BARBITAL.** ▷early 20th cent.: from German, from **VERONA** + **-AL.**

Ve·ro·ne·se /,vārə'nāzā/, Paolo (*c.*1528–88), Italian painter; born *Paolo Caliari.* He is particularly known for his richly colored feast scenes such as in *The Marriage at Cana* (1562).

ve·ron·i·ca /və'ränəkə/ ▸*n.* **1** a herbaceous plant of north temperate regions, typically with upright stems bearing narrow pointed leaves and spikes of blue or purple flowers. • Genus *Veronica*, family Scrophulariaceae: many species, including the speedwells. **2** a cloth supposedly impressed with an image of Jesus' face. [see **VERONICA, ST.**] ■ a picture of Jesus' face similar to this. **3** (in bullfighting) a slow movement of the cape away from a charging bull by the matador, who stands in place. [said to be by association of the attitude of the matador with the depiction of St. *Veronica* holding out a cloth to Jesus (see **VERONICA, ST.**).] ▷early 16th cent.: from medieval Latin, from the given name *Veronica.*

Ve·ron·i·ca, St. /və'ränəkə/ (in the Bible) a woman of Jerusalem who offered her veil, or handkerchief, to Jesus on the way to Calvary, to wipe the blood and sweat from his face. The cloth is said to have retained the image of his features.

ve·ron·ique /,verə'nēk; ,värô-/ ▸*adj.* [*postpositive*] denoting a dish, typically of fish or chicken, prepared or garnished with grapes. ▷from the French given name *Véronique.*

Ver·ra·za·no /,verät'sänō/, Giovanni da (c.1480–1527), Italian navigator in the service of France. He was the first European to enter New York Bay 1524.

Ver·ra·za·no-Nar·rows Bridge /,verə'zänō/ a suspension bridge across New York harbor between Brooklyn and Staten Island, the longest in the world when it was completed in 1964. ▷named after Giovanni da *Verrazano.*

ver·ru·ca /və'rōōkə/ ▸*n.* (*pl.* **-cae** /-kē; -kī/ or **-cas**) a contagious and usually painful wart on the sole of the foot; a plantar wart. ■ (in medical use) a wart of any kind. ▷late Middle English: from Latin. **—ver·ru·cose** /'verə,kōs; və'rōō-/ *adj.* **—ver·ru·cous** /və'rōōkəs/ *adj.*

Ver·sa·ce /vər'säCHē/, Gianni (1946–97), Italian fashion designer. He was killed outside his home in Miami.

Ver·sailles /vər'sī; ver-/ a palace built for Louis XIV near the town of Versailles, southwest of Paris. It was built around a chateau belonging to Louis XIII, which was transformed by additions in the grand French classical style.

Ver·sailles, Trea·ty of **1** a treaty that terminated the American Revolution in 1783. **2** a treaty signed in 1919 that brought a formal end to World War I.

The treaty redivided the territory of the defeated Central Powers, restricted Germany's armed forces, and established the League of Nations. It left Germany smarting under what it considered a vindictive settlement while not sufficiently restricting its ability eventually to rearm and seek forcible redress.

ver·sal /'vərsəl/ ▸*adj.* of or relating to a style of ornate capital letter used to start a verse, paragraph, etc., in a manuscript, typically built up by inking between pen strokes and with long, rather flat serifs.

▸*n.* a versal letter. ▷late 19th cent.: from Latin *vers-* 'turned' + **-AL**, influenced by **VERSE.**

ver·sant /'vərsənt/ ▸*n.* a region of land sloping in one general direction. ▷mid 19th cent.: from French, present participle (used as a noun) of *verser* 'tilt over,' from Latin *versare.*

ver·sa·tile /'vərsətl/ ▸*adj.* **1** able to adapt or be adapted to many different functions or activities: *a versatile sewing machine* | *he was versatile enough to play either position.* **2** *archaic* changeable; inconstant. ▷early 17th cent. (in the sense 'inconstant, fluctuating'): from French, or from Latin *versatilis*, from *versat-* 'turned around, revolved,' from the verb *versare*, frequentative of *vertere* 'to turn.' **—ver·sa·tile·ly** *adv.* **—ver·sa·til·i·ty** /,vərsə'tilətē/ *n.*

verse /vərs/ ▸*n.* writing arranged with a metrical rhythm, typically having a rhyme: *a lament in verse* | [as *adj.*] *verse drama.* ■ a group of lines that form a unit in a poem or song; a stanza: *the second verse.* ■ each of the short numbered divisions of a chapter in the Bible or other scripture. ■ a versicle. ■ *archaic* a line of poetry. ■ a passage in an anthem for a soloist or a small group of voices.

▸*v.* [*intrans.*] *archaic* speak in or compose verse; versify. ▷Old English *fers*, from Latin *versus* 'a turn of the plow, a furrow, a line of writing,' from *vertere* 'to turn'; reinforced in Middle English by Old French *vers*, from Latin *versus.* **—verse·let** /-lət/ *n.*

versed /vərst/ ▸*adj.* (**versed in**) experienced or skilled in; knowledgeable about: *a native Icelander* ***well versed in*** *her country's medieval literature.* ▷early 17th cent.: from French *versé* or Latin *versatus*, past participle of *versari* 'be engaged in.'

versed sine ▸*n. Mathematics* one minus cosine. ■ *Architecture* the rise of an arch of a bridge.

ver·si·cle /'vərsikəl/ ▸*n.* (usu. **versicles**) a short sentence said or sung by the minister in a church service, to which the congregation gives a response. ▷Middle English: from Old French *versicule* or Latin *versiculus*, diminutive of *versus* (see **VERSE**).

ver·si·col·ored /'vərsi,kələrd/ (*Brit.* **ver·si·col·oured**) ▸*adj. archaic* **1** changing from one color to another in different lights. **2** variegated. ▷early 18th cent.: from Latin *versicolor* (from *versus* 'turned' + *color* 'color') + **-ED**[2].

ver·si·fy /'vərsə,fī/ ▸*v.* (**-fies, -fied**) [*trans.*] turn into or express in verse: *he versifies others' ideas.* | [as *n.*] (**versifying**) *a talent for versifying.* ▷late Middle English: from Old French *versifier*, from Latin *versificare*, from *versus* (see **VERSE**). **—ver·si·fi·ca·tion** /,vərsəfi'kāSHən/ *n.* **—ver·si·fi·er** *n.*

ver·sine /'vər,sīn/ (also **ver·sin**) ▸*n. Mathematics* another term for **VERSED SINE.** ▷early 19th cent.: abbreviation.

ver·sion /'vərZHən/ ▸*n.* **1** a particular form of something differing in certain respects from an earlier form or other forms of the same type of thing: *a revised version of the paper was produced for a later meeting* | *they produce yachts in both standard and master versions.* ■ a particular edition or translation of a book or other work: *the English version will be published next year.* ■ [usu. with *adj.*] an adaptation of a novel, piece of music, etc., into another medium or style: *a film version of a wonderfully funny cult novel.* ■ a particular updated edition of a piece of computer software. ■ an account of a matter from a particular person's point of view: *he told her his version of events.* **2** *Medicine* the manual turning of a fetus in the uterus to make delivery easier. ■ an abnormal displacement of the uterus. ▷late Middle English (in the sense 'translation'): from French, or from medieval Latin *versio(n-)*, from Latin *vertere* 'to turn.' **—ver·sion·al** /-ZHənl/ *adj.*

ver·sion con·trol ▸*n. Computing* the task of keeping a software system consisting of many versions and configurations well organized.

vers li·bre /ˌver 'lēbrə/ ▸*n.* another term for **FREE VERSE.** ▷French, literally 'free verse.'

ver·so /'vərsō/ ▸*n.* (*pl.* **-sos**) **1** a left-hand page of an open book, or the back of a loose document. Contrasted with **RECTO. 2** the reverse of something such as a coin or painting. ▷mid 19th cent.: from Latin *verso (folio)* 'on the turned (leaf).'

verst /vərst/ ▸*n.* a Russian measure of length, about 0.66 mile (1.1 km). ▷from Russian *versta.*

Ver·ste·hen /fər'SHtāən/ ▸*n. Sociology* empathic understanding of human behavior. ▷German, literally 'understanding.'

ver·sus /'vərsəs; -səz/ (abbr.: **v.** or **vs.**) ▸*prep.* against (esp. in sports and legal use): *Penn versus Princeton.* ■ as opposed to; in contrast to: *weighing the pros and cons of organic versus inorganic produce.* ▷late Middle English: from a medieval Latin use of Latin *versus* 'toward.'

vert /vərt/ ▸*n.* green, as a heraldic tincture: [*postpositive*] *three piles vert.* ▷late Middle English (as an adjective): via Old French from Latin *viridis* 'green.'

ver·te·bra /'vərtəbrə/ ▸*n.* (*pl.* **-brae** /-ˌbrē; -ˌbrā/) each of the series of small bones forming the backbone, having several projections for articulation and muscle attachment, and a hole through which the spinal cord passes.

In the human spine (or vertebral column) there are seven cervical vertebrae (in the neck), twelve thoracic vertebrae (to which the ribs are attached), and five lumbar vertebrae (in the lower back). In addition, five fused vertebrae form the sacrum, and four the coccyx.

▷early 17th cent.: from Latin, from *vertere* 'to turn.' **—ver·te·bral** /-brəl; vər'tē-/ *adj.*

ver·te·bral col·umn ▸*n.* another term for **SPINAL COLUMN.**

ver·te·brate /'vərtəbrət; -ˌbrāt/ ▸*n.* an animal of a large group distinguished by the possession of a backbone or spinal column, including mammals, birds, reptiles, amphibians, and fishes. Compare with **INVERTEBRATE.** • Subphylum Vertebrata, phylum Chordata: seven classes.
▸*adj.* of or relating to the vertebrates. ▷early 19th cent.: from Latin *vertebratus* 'jointed,' from *vertebra* (see **VERTEBRA**).

ver·tex /'vərˌteks/ ▸*n.* (*pl.* **-ti·ces** /-təˌsēz/ or **-tex·es**) **1** the highest point; the top or apex. ■ *Anatomy* the crown of the head. **2** *Geometry* each angular point of a polygon, polyhedron, or other figure. ■ a meeting point of two lines that form an angle. ■ the point at which an axis meets a curve or surface. ▷late Middle English: from Latin, 'whirlpool, crown of a head, vertex,' from *vertere* 'to turn.'

ver·ti·cal /'vərtikəl/ ▸*adj.* **1** at right angles to a horizontal plane; in a direction, or having an alignment, such that the top is directly above the bottom: *the vertical axis | keep your back vertical.* **2** *archaic* denoting a point at the zenith or the highest point of something. **3** *Anatomy* of or relating to the crown of the head. **4** involving different levels of a hierarchy or progression, in particular: ■ involving all the stages from the production to the sale of a class of goods. ■ (esp. of the transmission of disease or genetic traits) passed from one generation to the next.
▸*n.* **1** (usu. **the vertical**) a vertical line or plane: *the columns incline several degrees away from the vertical.* **2** an upright structure: *we remodeled the opening with a simple lintel and unadorned verticals.* **3** short for **VERTICAL TASTING. 4** the distance between the highest and lowest points of a ski area: *the resort claims a vertical of 2100 meters.* ▷mid 16th cent. (in the sense 'directly overhead'): from French, or from late Latin *verticalis,* from *vertex* (see **VERTEX**). **—ver·ti·cal·i·ty** /ˌvərti'kalətē/ *n.* **—ver·ti·cal·ize** /-ˌlīz/ *v.* **—ver·ti·cal·ly** /-ik(ə)lē/ *adv.*

ver·ti·cal an·gles ▸*plural n. Mathematics* each of the pairs of opposite angles made by two intersecting lines.

ver·ti·cal cir·cle ▸*n.* a great circle of the celestial sphere whose diameter runs from zenith to nadir.

ver·ti·cal file ▸*n.* an alphabetized file for pamphlets and other small publications that do not merit a call number in a library system.

ver·ti·cal fin ▸*n. Zoology* any of the unpaired fins in the midline of a fish's body, i.e., a dorsal, anal, or caudal fin.

ver·ti·cal in·te·gra·tion ▸*n.* the combination in one company of two or more stages of production normally operated by separate companies.

ver·tic·al·ly chal·lenged /'vərtik(ə)lē/ ▸*adj. humorous* not tall in height; short.

ver·ti·cal sta·bi·liz·er ▸*n. Aeronautics* a small, flattened projecting surface or attachment on an aircraft or rocket for providing aerodynamic stability.

ver·ti·cal tast·ing ▸*n.* a tasting in order of year of several different vintages of a particular wine.

ver·ti·cal un·ion ▸*n.* a union whose members all work in various capacities in a single industry.

ver·ti·cil·li·um /ˌvərtə'silēəm/ ▸*n.* a fungus of a genus that includes a number of species that cause wilt in plants. • Genus *Verticillium,* subdivision Deuteromycotina, in particular *V. albo-atrum* and *V. dahliae.* ■ wilt caused by such fungi. ▷modern Latin, from Latin *verticillus* 'spindle whorl.'

ver·tig·i·nous /vər'tijənəs/ ▸*adj.* causing vertigo, esp. by being extremely high or steep: *vertiginous drops to the valleys below.* ■ relating to or affected by vertigo. ▷early 17th cent.: from Latin *vertiginosus,* from *vertigo* 'whirling around' (see **VERTIGO**). **—ver·tig·i·nous·ly** *adv.*

ver·ti·go /'vərtəgō/ ▸*n.* a sensation of whirling and loss of balance, associated particularly with looking down from a great height, or caused by disease affecting the inner ear or the vestibular nerve; giddiness. ▷late Middle English: from Latin, 'whirling,' from *vertere* 'to turn.'

ver·ti·sol /'vərtəˌsäl; -ˌsôl/ ▸*n. Soil Science* a clayey soil with little organic matter that occurs in regions having distinct wet and dry seasons. ▷1960s: from **VERTICAL** + Latin *solum* 'soil.'

ver·tu ▸*n.* variant spelling of **VIRTU.**

ver·vain /'vərˌvān/ ▸*n.* a widely distributed herbaceous plant with small blue, white, or purple flowers and a long history of use as a magical and medicinal herb. • *Verbena officinalis,* family Verbenaceae. ▷late Middle English: from Old French *verveine,* from Latin *verbena* (see **VERBENA**).

verve /vərv/ ▸*n.* vigor and spirit or enthusiasm: *Kollo sings with supreme verve and flexibility.* ▷late 17th cent. (denoting special talent in writing): from French, 'vigor,' earlier 'form of expression,' from Latin *verba* 'words.'

ver·vet /'vərvət/ (also **ver·vet mon·key**) ▸*n.* a common African guenon with greenish-brown upper parts and a black face. Compare with **GREEN MONKEY, GRIVET.** • *Cercopithecus aethiops,* family Cercopithecidae, in particular the race *C. a. pygerythrus* of southern and eastern Africa. ▷late 19th cent.: from French, of unknown origin.

Ver·viers /ver'vyā/ a manufacturing town in eastern Belgium; pop 53,000.

Ver·woerd /fər'vŏŏrt/, Hendrik (Frensch) (1901–66), South African statesman; prime minister 1958–66. As minister of Bantu affairs (1950–58), he developed the segregation policy of apartheid. As premier, he banned the ANC and the Pan-Africanist Congress in 1960 and declared South Africa a republic in 1961.

ver·y /'verē/ ▸*adv.* used for emphasis: ■ in a high degree: *very large | very quickly | very much so.* ■ [with *superlative* or **own**] used to emphasize that the following description applies without qualification: *the very best quality | his very own car.*
▸*adj.* actual; precise (used to emphasize the exact identity of a particular person or thing): *those were his very words | he might be phoning her at this very moment | transformed* **before our very eyes.** ■ emphasizing an extreme point in time or space: *from the very beginning of the book | at the very back of the skull.* ■ with no addition of or contribution from anything else; mere: *the very thought of drink made him feel sick.* ■ *archaic* real; genuine: *the very God of Heaven.* ▷Middle English (as an adjective in the sense 'real, genuine'): from Old French *verai,* based on Latin *verus* 'true.'
▸*PHRASES* □ **not very 1** in a low degree: *"Bad news?" "Not very."* **2** far from being: *I'm not very impressed.* □ **the very idea!** see **IDEA.** □ **the very same** see **SAME.** □ **very good** (or **well**) an expression of consent.

ver·y high fre·quen·cy ▸*n.* (abbr.: **VHF**) the band of frequencies between 30 and 300 megahertz, typically used for broadcasting television signals.

Ver·y Large Ar·ray (abbr.: **VLA**) ▸*n.* the world's largest radio telescope, consisting of 27 dish antennas in Socorro, New Mexico.

Ver·y light /'verē; 'vi(ə)rē/ ▸*n.* a flare fired into the air from a pistol for signaling or for temporary illumination. ▷early 20th cent.: named after Edward W. *Very* (1847–1910), American naval officer.

ver·y low fre·quen·cy ▸*n.* (abbr.: **VLF**) the band of frequencies between 3 and 30 kilohertz.

Ver·y pis·tol ▸*n.* a hand-held gun used for firing a Very light.

VESA ▸*abbr.* Video Electronics Standards Association, a U.S.-based organization that defines formats for displays and buses used in computers.

Ve·sak /'väˌsäk/ (also **We·sak** or **Vi·sā·kha** /vi'säkə/) ▸*n.* the most important Buddhist festival, commemorating the birth, enlightenment, and death of the Buddha, and celebrated at the full moon in the Indian month of Vaishaka (April–May). ▷Sinhalese *vesak,* via Pali from Sanskrit *vaiśākha,* denoting the month April–May.

Ve·sa·li·us /və'sālēəs/, Andreas (1514–64), Flemish anatomist; the founder of modern anatomy.

ve·si·cal /'vesəkəl/ ▸*adj. Anatomy & Medicine* of, relating to, or affecting the urinary bladder: *vesical function | the vesical artery.* ▷late 18th cent.: from Latin *vesica* 'bladder' + **-AL.**

ves·i·cant /'vesəkənt/ ▸*adj.* tending to cause blistering.
▸*n.* an agent that causes blistering. ▷late Middle English: from late Latin *vesicant-* 'forming pustules,' from the verb *vesicare,* from *vesica* 'bladder.'

ve·si·ca pis·cis /'vesikə 'pis(k)is; 'pīsis; və'sēkə; və'sīkə/ ▸*n.* (*pl.* **ve·si·cae pis·cis** /-ˌkī; -ˌkē/) another term for **MANDORLA.** ▷Latin, literally 'fish's bladder.'

ves·i·cate /'vesiˌkāt/ ▸*v.* [*trans.*] *chiefly Medicine* raise blisters on. ■ [*intrans.*] form blisters. ▷mid 17th cent.: from late Latin *vesicat-* 'having pustules,' from *vesica* 'bladder.' **—ves·i·ca·tion** /ˌvesi'kāSHən/ *n.* **—ves·i·ca·to·ry** /'vesəkəˌtôrē; və'sikə-/ *adj. & n.*

ve·si·cle /'vesikəl/ ▸*n.* a fluid- or air-filled cavity or sac, in particular: ■ *Anatomy & Zoology* a small fluid-filled bladder, sac, cyst, or vacuole within the body. ■ *Botany* an air-filled swelling in a plant, esp. a seaweed. ■ *Geology* a small cavity in volcanic rock, produced by gas bubbles in the molten lava. ■ *Medicine* a small blister full of clear fluid. ▷late 16th cent.: from French *vésicule* or Latin *vesicula,* diminutive of *vesica* 'bladder.' **—ve·sic·u·lar** /və'sikyələr/ *adj.* **—ve·sic·u·lat·ed** /və'sikyəˌlātid/ *adj.* **—ve·sic·u·la·tion** /vəˌsikyə'lāSHən/ *n.*

ves·i·co·u·re·ter·ic re·flux /ˌvesəkōˌyŏŏri'terik/ ▸*n. Medicine* flow of urine from the bladder back into the ureters, arising from defective valves and causing a high risk of kidney infection. ▷mid 20th cent.: *vesicoureteric* from Latin *vesica* 'bladder' + *ureteric* (see **URETER**).

ve·sic·u·late ▸*v.* /və'sikyəˌlāt/ make or become vesicular.
▸*adj.* /və'sikyəlit; -ˌlāt/ containing or covered with vesicles or small cavities.

Ves·pa·sian /ves'pāZHən/ (AD 9–79), Roman emperor 69–79 and founder of the Flavian dynasty; Latin name *Titus Flavius Vespasianus.* His reign saw the restoration of financial and military order and the initiation of a public building program.

ves·per /'vespər/ ▸*n.* evening prayer: [as *adj.*] *vesper service.* See also **VESPERS.** ■ *archaic* evening. ■ (**Vesper**) *poetic/literary* Venus as the evening star. ▷late Middle English: from Latin *vesper* 'evening (star),' which is related to Greek *hesperos* 'western; the evening star' (see **HESPERUS.**)

ves·per·al /'vespərəl/ ▸*adj.* **1** of or pertaining to evening. **2** of or pertaining to vespers.
▸*n.* a book containing the psalms, canticles, anthems and the like with their musical settings that are used at vespers.

ves·pers /'vespərz/ ▸*n.* a service of evening prayer in the Divine Office of the Western Christian Church (sometimes said earlier in the day). ■ a service of evening prayer in other churches. ▷late 15th cent.: from Old French *vespres* 'evensong,' from Latin *vesperas* (accusative plural), on the pattern of *matutinas* 'matins.'

ves·per spar·row ▸*n.* a small North American songbird related to the buntings, having streaked brown plumage and known for its evening song. • *Pooecetes gramineus,* family Emberizidae (subfamily Emberizidae).

ves·per·til·i·o·nid /ˌvespər'tilēəˌnid/ ▸*n. Zoology* a bat of a large family (Vespertilionidae) that includes most of the typical insectivorous bats of north temperate regions. ▷late 19th cent.: from modern Latin *Vespertilionidae* (plural), from Latin *vespertilio* 'bat.'

V

ves·per·tine /ˈvespər,tīn; -,tēn/ ▶*adj.* **1** *technical* or *poetic/literary* of, relating to, occurring, or active in the evening. **2** *Botany* (of a flower) opening in the evening. **3** *Zoology* active in the evening. ▷late Middle English: from Latin *vespertinus,* from *vesper* 'evening.'

ves·pi·ar·y /ˈvespē,erē/ ▶*n.* (*pl.* **-ar·ies**) a nest of wasps. ▷early 19th cent.: formed irregularly from Latin *vespa* 'wasp,' on the pattern of *apiary.*

ves·pid /ˈvespid/ ▶*n.* any wasp of the family Vespidae, including yellow jackets and hornets.

ves·pine /ˈves,pīn; -pin/ ▶*adj.* of or relating to wasps. ▷mid 19th cent.: from Latin *vespa* 'wasp' + **-INE**[1].

Ves·puc·ci /vesˈp(y)o͞ocнē/, Amerigo (1451–1512), Italian merchant and explorer. He reached the coast of Venezuela on his first voyage 1499–1500 and explored the Brazilian coastline 1501–02. The Latin form of his first name is believed to have given rise to the name of America.

ves·sel /ˈvesəl/ ▶*n.* **1** a ship or large boat. **2** a hollow container, esp. one used to hold liquid, such as a bowl or cask. ■ (chiefly in or alluding to biblical use) a person, esp. regarded as holding or embodying a particular quality: *giving honor unto the wife, as unto the weaker vessel.* **3** *Anatomy & Zoology* a duct or canal holding or conveying blood or other fluid. See also **BLOOD VESSEL.** ■ *Botany* any of the tubular structures in the vascular system of a plant, serving to conduct water and mineral nutrients from the root. ▷Middle English: from Anglo-Norman French *vessel(e),* from late Latin *vascellum,* diminutive of *vas* 'vessel.'

vest /vest/ ▶*n.* a close-fitting waist-length garment, typically having no sleeves or collar and buttoning down the front. ■ a similar garment worn on the upper part of the body for a particular purpose or activity: *a running vest | a bulletproof vest.* ■ a piece of material showing at the neck of a woman's dress. ■ *Brit.* an undershirt.

▶*v.* **1** [*trans.*] (usu. **be vested in**) confer or bestow (power, authority, property, etc.) on someone: *executive power is vested in the president.* ■ (usu. **be vested with**) give (someone) the legal right to power, property, etc.: *the socialists came to be vested with the power of legislation.* ■ [*intrans.*] (**vest in**) (of power, property, etc.) come into the possession of: *the bankrupt's property vests in his trustee.* **2** [*intrans.*] (of a chorister or member of the clergy) put on vestments. ■ [*trans.*] *poetic/literary* dress (someone): *the Speaker vested him with a rich purple robe.* ▷late Middle English (as a verb): from Old French *vestu* 'clothed,' past participle of *vestir,* from Latin *vestire;* the noun (early 17th cent., denoting a loose outer garment) from French *veste,* via Italian from Latin *vestis* 'garment.'

▶*PHRASE* □ **play** (or **keep**) **one's cards close to one's vest** see **CHEST.**

Ves·ta /ˈvestə/ *Roman Mythology* the goddess of the hearth and household. Her temple in Rome contained no image but a fire that was kept constantly burning and was tended by the Vestal Virgins.

ves·ta /ˈvestə/ ▶*n.* *chiefly historical* a short wooden or wax match. ▷mid 19th cent.: from the name of the goddess **VESTA.**

ves·tal /ˈvestl/ ▶*adj.* of or relating to the Roman goddess Vesta: *a vestal temple.* ■ *poetic/literary* chaste; pure.

▶*n.* a vestal virgin. ■ *poetic/literary* a chaste woman, esp. a nun.

Ves·tal Vir·gin (also **ves·tal vir·gin**) ▶*n.* (in ancient Rome) a virgin consecrated to Vesta and vowed to chastity, sharing the charge of maintaining the sacred fire burning on the goddess's altar.

vest·ed /ˈvestid/ ▶*adj.* **1** secured in the possession of or assigned to a person: *a state law vested the ownership of all wild birds to the individual counties.* ■ protected or established by law or contract: *parental rights are then vested by section 14 of the 1975 Act.* ■ (of a person) legally entitled to a future benefit, as from a pension: *he was completely vested after five years with the company.* **2** supplied or worn with a vest. **3** wearing vestments.

vest·ed in·ter·est ▶*n.* [usu. in *sing.*] a personal stake or involvement in an undertaking or state of affairs, esp. one with an expectation of financial gain: *banks have* ***a vested interest in*** *the growth of their customers.* ■ a person or group having such a personal stake or involvement: *the problem is that the authorities are a vested interest.* ■ *Law* an interest (usually in land or money held in trust) recognized as belonging to a particular person.

vest·ee /,veˈstē/ ▶*n.* a vestlike piece of material showing at the neck of a woman's dress.

Ves·ter·å·len /ˈvestə,rōlən/ a group of islands in Norway, in the Norwegian Sea, north of the Arctic Circle.

ves·ti·ar·y /ˈvestē,erē/ ▶*adj.* *poetic/literary* of or relating to clothes or dress.

▶*n.* (*pl.* **-ar·ies**) a room or building in a monastery or other large establishment in which clothes are kept. ▷Middle English (denoting a vestry): from Old French *vestiarie,* from Latin *vestiarium* (see **VESTRY**).

ves·tib·u·lar /veˈstibyələr; və-/ ▶*adj.* *chiefly Anatomy* of or relating to a vestibule, particularly that of the inner ear, or more generally to the sense of balance.

ves·ti·bule /ˈvestə,byo͞ol/ ▶*n.* **1** an antechamber, hall, or lobby next to the outer door of a building. ■ an enclosed entrance compartment in a railroad car. **2** *Anatomy* a chamber or channel communicating with or opening into another, in particular: ■ the central cavity of the labyrinth of the inner ear. ■ the part of the mouth outside the teeth. ■ the space in the vulva into which both the urethra and vagina open. ▷early 17th cent. (denoting the space in front of the main entrance of a Roman or Greek building): from French, or from Latin *vestibulum* 'entrance court.' **—ves·ti·buled** *adj.*

ves·ti·bu·lo·coch·le·ar nerve /ve,stibyəlōˈkāklēər/ ▶*n.* *Anatomy* each of the eighth pair of cranial nerves, conveying sensory impulses from the organs of hearing and balance in the inner ear to the brain. The vestibulocochlear nerve on each side branches into the **vestibular nerve** and the **cochlear nerve.**

ves·tige /ˈvestij/ ▶*n.* a trace of something that is disappearing or no longer exists: *the last* ***vestiges of*** *colonialism.* See note at **TRACE.** ■ [usu. with *negative*] the smallest amount (used to emphasize the absence of something): *he waited patiently, but without* ***a vestige of*** *sympathy.* ■ *Biology* a part or organ of an organism that has become reduced or functionless in the course of evolution. ▷late Middle English: from French, from Latin *vestigium* 'footprint.'

ves·tig·i·al /veˈstij(ē)əl/ ▶*adj.* forming a very small remnant of something that was once much larger or more noticeable: *he felt a vestigial flicker of anger from last night.* ■ *Biology* (of an organ or part of the body) degenerate, rudimentary, or atrophied, having become functionless in the course of evolution: *the vestigial wings of kiwis are entirely hidden.* **—ves·tig·i·al·ly** *adv.*

ves·ti·men·ta·ry /,vestəˈmentərē/ ▶*adj.* *formal* of or relating to clothing or dress: *lack of vestimentary rigor.* ▷early 19th cent.: from Latin *vestimentum* 'clothing' + **-ARY**[1].

ves·ti·men·tif·er·an /,vestə,menˈtifərən/ ▶*n.* *Zoology* a very large marine worm that lives in upright tubes near hydrothermal vents, subsisting on the products of chemoautotrophic bacteria. • Order Vestimentifera, phylum Pogonophora; sometimes regarded as a separate phylum. ▷late 20th cent.: from modern Latin *Vestimentifera* (from Latin *vestimentum* 'clothing' + *-fer* 'bearing') + **-AN.**

vest·ing /ˈvestiNG/ ▶*n.* **1** the conveying to an employee of unconditional entitlement to a share in a pension fund. **2** medium- to heavy-weight cloth with a decorated or raised pattern, used for vests and other garments.

ves·ti·ture /ˈvesticнər; -,cнo͝or/ ▶*n.* *archaic* clothing. ▷mid 19th cent.: based on Latin *vestire* 'clothe.'

Vest·man·na·ey·jar /ˈvest,mänəˈā,yär/ Icelandic name for **WESTMANN ISLANDS.**

vest·ment /ˈves(t)mənt/ ▶*n.* (usu. **vestments**) a chasuble or other robe worn by the clergy or choristers during services. ■ *archaic* a garment, esp. a ceremonial or official robe. ▷Middle English: from Old French *vestiment,* from Latin *vestimentum,* from *vestire* 'clothe' (see **VEST**).

vest-pock·et ▶*adj.* [*attrib.*] (esp. of a reference book) small enough to fit into a pocket: *a series of popular vest-pocket dictionaries.* ■ very small in size or scale: *a vest-pocket park.*

ves·try /ˈvestrē/ ▶*n.* (*pl.* **-tries**) a room or building attached to a church, used as an office and for changing into vestments. ■ a meeting of parishioners, originally in a vestry, for the conduct of parochial business. ■ a body of parishioners meeting in such a way. ▷late Middle English: probably from an Anglo-Norman French alteration of Old French *vestiarie,* from Latin *vestiarium.*

ves·try·man /ˈvestrēmən/ ▶*n.* (*pl.* **-men**) a member of a parochial vestry.

ves·ture /ˈvescнər/ ▶*n.* *poetic/literary* clothing; dress: *a man garbed in ancient vesture.* ▷Middle English: from Old French, based on Latin *vestire* 'clothe.'

ve·su·vi·an·ite /vəˈso͞ovēə,nīt/ ▶*n.* another term for **IDOCRASE.** ▷late 19th cent.: from **VESUVIUS** + **-AN** + **-ITE**[1].

Ve·su·vi·us /vəˈso͞ovēəs/ an active volcano near Naples, in southern Italy, 4,190 feet (1,277 m) high. A violent eruption in AD 79 buried the towns of Pompeii and Herculaneum.

vet[1] /vet/ ▶*n.* *informal* a veterinary surgeon.

▶*v.* (**vet·ted, vet·ting**) [*trans.*] make a careful and critical examination of (something): *proposals for vetting large takeover bids.* ■ (often **be vetted**) *Brit.* investigate (someone) thoroughly, esp. in order to ensure that they are suitable for a job requiring secrecy, loyalty, or trustworthiness: *each applicant will be vetted by police.* ▷mid 19th cent: abbreviation of **VETERINARY** or **VETERINARIAN.**

vet[2] ▶*n.* *informal* a veteran. ▷mid 19th cent.: abbreviation.

vetch /vecн/ ▶*n.* a widely distributed scrambling herbaceous plant of the pea family that is cultivated as a silage or fodder crop. See also **TARE**[1]. • Genus *Vicia,* family Leguminosae: several species, in particular the **common** or (**spring**) **vetch** (*V. sativa*) and **purple vetch** (*V. americana*). ▷Middle English: from Anglo-Norman French *veche,* from Latin *vicia.*

vetch·ling /ˈvecнliNG/ ▶*n.* a widely distributed scrambling plant related to the vetches, typically having fewer leaflets. • Genus *Lathyrus,* family Leguminosae: several species, including *L. palustris.*

vet·er·an /ˈvetərən; ˈvetrən/ ▶*n.* a person who has had long experience in a particular field: ■ a person who has served in the military: *a veteran of two world wars.* ▷early 16th cent.: from French *vétéran* or Latin *veteranus,* from *vetus* 'old.'

Vet·er·ans Day ▶*n.* a public holiday held on the anniversary of the end of World War I (November 11) to honor U.S. veterans and victims of all wars. It replaced Armistice Day in 1954.

vet·er·i·nar·i·an /,vet(ə)rəˈne(ə)rēən/ ▶*n.* a person qualified to treat diseased or injured animals.

vet·er·i·nar·y /ˈvet(ə)rə,nerē/ ▶*adj.* of or relating to the diseases, injuries, and treatment of animals: *veterinary medicine | a veterinary nurse.*

▶*n.* (*pl.* **-nar·ies**) *dated* a veterinarian. ▷late 18th cent.: from Latin *veterinarius,* from *veterinae* 'cattle.'

vet·er·i·nar·y sur·geon ▶*n.* British term for **VETERINARIAN.**

vet·i·ver /ˈvetəvər/ (also **vet·i·vert** /-vərt/) ▶*n.* a fragrant extract or essential oil obtained from the root of an Indian grass, used in perfumery and aromatherapy. • The grass is *Vetiveria zizanioides,* family Gramineae. ▷mid 19th cent.: from French *vétiver,* from Tamil *vettivēr,* from *vēr* 'root.'

ve·to /ˈvētō/ ▶*n.* (*pl.* **-toes**) a constitutional right to reject a decision or proposal made by a law-making body: *the legislature would have a veto over appointments to key posts.* ■ such a rejection. ■ a prohibition: *his veto on our drinking after the meal was annoying.*

▶*v.* (**-toes, -toed**) [*trans.*] exercise a veto against (a decision or proposal made by a law-making body): *the president vetoed the bill.* ■ refuse to accept or allow: *the film star often has a right to veto the pictures used for publicity.* ▷early 17th cent.: from Latin, literally 'I forbid,' used by Roman tribunes of the people when opposing measures of the Senate. **—ve·to·er** *n.*

vex /veks/ ▶*v.* [*trans.*] make (someone) feel annoyed, frustrated, or worried, esp. with trivial matters: *the memory of the conversation still vexed him |* [as *adj.*] (**vexing**) *the most vexing questions for policymakers.* ■ *archaic* cause distress to: *thou shalt not vex a stranger.* ▷late Middle English: from Old French *vexer,* from Latin *vexare* 'shake, disturb.' **—vex·er** *n.* **—vex·ing·ly** *adv.*

vex·a·tion /vekˈsāsнən/ ▶*n.* the state of being annoyed, frustrated, or worried: *Jenny bit her lip in vexation.* ■ something that causes annoyance, frustration, or worry: *the cares and vexations of life.* ▷late Middle English: from Old French, or from Latin *vexatio(n-),* from *vexare* (see **VEX**).

vex·a·tious /vekˈsāsнəs/ ▶*adj.* causing or tending to cause annoyance, frustration, or worry: *the vexatious questions posed by software copyrights.* ■ *Law* denoting an action or the bringer of an action that is brought without sufficient grounds for winning, purely to cause annoyance to the defendant. **—vex·a·tious·ly** *adv.* **—vex·a·tious·ness** *n.*

vexed /vekst/ ▶*adj.* **1** [*attrib.*] (of a problem or issue) difficult and much debated; problematic: ***the vexed question*** *of exactly how much money the government is going to spend.* **2** annoyed, frustrated, or worried: *I'm very vexed with you!* **—vex·ed·ly** /ˈveksədlē/ *adv.*

vex·il·lol·o·gy /ˌveksə'läləjē/ ▸*n.* the study of flags. ▷1950s: from Latin *vexillum* 'flag' + **-LOGY**. —**vex·il·lo·log·i·cal** /-lə'läjikəl/ *adj.* —**vex·il·lol·o·gist** /-jist/ *n.*

vex·il·lum /vek'siləm/ ▸*n.* (*pl.* **vex·il·la** /vek'silə/) **1** a Roman military standard or banner, esp. one of a maniple. [Latin, from *vehere* 'carry.'] ■ a body of troops under such a standard. **2** *Botany* the standard of a papilionaceous flower. **3** *Ornithology* the vane of a feather.

VF ▸*abbr.* ■ video frequency. ■ visual field.

VFR ▸*abbr.* visual flight rules, used to regulate the flying and navigating of an aircraft under conditions of good visibility.

VG ▸*abbr.* ■ very good. ■ vicar-general.

VGA ▸*abbr.* video graphics array, a standard for defining color display screens for computers.

vgc ▸*abbr.* very good condition (used in advertisements).

VHF ▸*abbr.* very high frequency, denoting radio waves of a frequency of about 30–300 MHz and a wavelength of about 1–10 meters.

VHS *trademark* ▸*abbr.* video home system, denoting the video system and tape used by domestic video recorders and some camcorders.

VHS-C *trademark* ▸*abbr.* VHS compact, denoting a video system used by some camcorders, which records signals in VHS format on smaller videocassettes.

VI ▸*abbr.* Virgin Islands.

vi·a /'vīə; 'vēə/ ▸*prep.* traveling through (a place) en route to a destination: *they came to Europe via Turkey.* ■ by way of; through: *they can see the artists' works via a camera hookup.* ■ by means of: *a file sent via electronic mail.* ▷late 18th cent.: from Latin, ablative of *via* 'way, road.'

Vi·a Ap·pi·a /'vēə 'apēə; 'vīə/ Latin name for **APPIAN WAY**.

vi·a·ble /'vīəbəl/ ▸*adj.* capable of working successfully; feasible: *the proposed investment was economically viable.* ■ *Botany* (of a seed or spore) able to germinate. ■ *Biology* (of a plant, animal, or cell) capable of surviving or living successfully, esp. under particular environmental conditions. ■ *Medicine* (of a fetus or unborn child) able to live after birth. ▷early 19th cent.: from French, from *vie* 'life,' from Latin *vita*. —**vi·a·bil·i·ty** /ˌvīə'bilətē/ *n.* —**vi·a·bly** /-blē/ *adv.*

Vi·a Cru·cis /'vēə 'kro͞ocHis/ ▸*n.* another term for **THE WAY OF THE CROSS** (see **WAY**). ■ *figurative* a lengthy and distressing or painful procedure: *we embarked on a Via Crucis of tired comic formulae.* ▷Latin.

vi·a dol·o·ro·sa /'vēə ˌdälə'rōsə; ˌdōlə-/ ▸*n.* (**the Via Dolorosa**) the route believed to have been taken by Jesus through Jerusalem to Calvary. ■ *figurative* a distressing or painful journey or process: *he commenced a via dolorosa to the coast.* ▷Latin, literally 'painful path.'

vi·a·duct /'vīəˌdəkt/ ▸*n.* a long bridgelike structure, typically a series of arches, carrying a road or railroad across a valley or other low ground. ▷early 19th cent.: from Latin *via* 'way,' on the pattern of *aqueduct*.

Vi·ag·ra vī'agrə ▸*n.* trademark for **SILDENAFIL CITRATE**. ▷1990s: apparently a blend of **VIRILITY** and **NIAGARA**.

vi·al /'vī(ə)l/ ▸*n.* a small container, typically cylindrical and made of glass, used esp. for holding liquid medicines. ▷Middle English: alteration of **PHIAL**.

vi·a me·di·a /'vēə 'mādēə; 'vīə 'mēdēə/ ▸*n.* *formal* a middle way or compromise between extremes: *the settlement is a via media between Catholicism and Protestantism.* ▷Latin.

vi·and /'vīənd/ ▸*n.* (usu. **viands**) *poetic/literary* an item of food: *an unlimited assortment of viands.* ▷late Middle English: from Old French *viande* 'food,' from an alteration of Latin *vivenda*, neuter plural gerundive of *vivere* 'to live.'

vi·a ne·ga·ti·va /'vēə ˌnegə'tēvə; 'vīə/ ▸*n.* *Theology* a way of describing something by saying what it is not, esp. denying that any finite concept of attribute can be identified with or used of God or ultimate reality. ▷Latin, literally 'negative path.'

vi·at·i·cal set·tle·ment /vī'atikəl; vē-/ ▸*n.* an arrangement whereby a person with a terminal illness sells their life insurance policy to a third party for less than its mature value, in order to benefit from the proceeds while alive. ▷1990s: *viatical* from Latin *viaticus* 'relating to a journey or departing' + **-AL**.

vi·at·i·cum /vī'atikəm; vē-/ ▸*n.* (*pl.* **-ca** /-kə/) **1** the Eucharist as given to a person near or in danger of death. **2** *archaic* a supply of provisions or an official allowance of money for a journey. ▷mid 16th cent.: from Latin, neuter of *viaticus*, from *via* 'road.'

vibe /vīb/ ▸*n.* *informal* **1** (usu. **vibes**) a person's emotional state or the atmosphere of a place as communicated to and felt by others: *a lot of moody people giving off* **bad vibes**. [abbreviation of *vibrations*.] **2** (**vibes**) another term for **VIBRAPHONE**.

vib·ist /'vībist/ ▸*n.* a musician who plays the vibraphone.

vi·brac·u·lum /vī'brakyələm/ ▸*n.* (*pl.* **-la** /-lə/) *Zoology* (in some bryozoans) any of a number of modified zooids that bear a long whiplike seta, serving to prevent other organisms from settling on the colony. Compare with **AVICULARIUM**. ▷mid 19th cent.: modern Latin, from Latin *vibrare* (see **VIBRATE**). —**vi·brac·u·lar** /-lər/ *adj.*

vi·bra·harp /'vībrəˌhärp/ ▸*n.* another term for **VIBRAPHONE**.

vi·brant /'vībrənt/ ▸*adj.* full of energy and enthusiasm: *a vibrant cosmopolitan city.* ■ quivering; pulsating: *Rose was* **vibrant with** *anger.* ■ (of color) bright and striking. ■ (of sound) strong or resonating: *a vibrant male voice.* ▷early 17th cent. (in the sense 'moving rapidly, vibrating'): from Latin *vibrant-* 'shaking to and fro,' from the verb *vibrare* (see **VIBRATE**). —**vi·bran·cy** /-brənsē/ *n.* —**vi·brant·ly** *adv.*

vi·bra·phone /'vībrəˌfōn/ ▸*n.* a musical percussion instrument with a double row of tuned metal bars, each above a tubular resonator containing a motor-driven rotating vane, giving a vibrato effect. ▷1920s: from **VIBRATO** + **-PHONE**. —**vi·bra·phon·ist** /-ˌfōnist/ *n.*

vibraphone

vi·brate /'vīˌbrāt/ ▸*v.* move or cause to move continuously and rapidly to and fro: [*intrans.*] *the cabin started to vibrate* | [*trans.*] *the bumblebee vibrated its wings for a few seconds.* ■ [*intrans.*] (**vibrate with**) quiver with (a quality or emotion): *his voice vibrated with terror.* ■ [*intrans.*] (of a sound) resonate; continue to be heard: *a low rumbling sound that began to vibrate through the car.* ■ [*intrans.*] (of a pendulum) swing to and fro. ▷late Middle English (in the sense 'give out (light or sound) as if by vibration'): from Latin *vibrat-* 'moved to and fro,' from the verb *vibrare*.

vi·bra·tile /'vībrətl; -ˌtīl/ ▸*adj.* *Biology* (of cilia, flagella, or other small appendages) capable of or characterized by oscillatory motion. ▷early 19th cent.: alteration of **VIBRATORY**, on the pattern of words such as *pulsatile*.

vi·bra·tion /vī'brāsHən/ ▸*n.* an instance of vibrating: *powerful vibrations from an earthquake* | *the big-capacity engine generated less vibration.* ■ *Physics* an oscillation of the parts of a fluid or an elastic solid whose equilibrium has been disturbed, or of an electromagnetic wave. ■ (**vibrations**) *informal* a person's emotional state, the atmosphere of a place, or the associations of an object, as communicated to and felt by others. ▷mid 17th cent.: from Latin *vibratio(n-)*, from the verb *vibrare* (see **VIBRATE**). —**vi·bra·tion·al** /-sHənl/ *adj.*

vi·bra·tion white fin·ger ▸*n.* Raynaud's disease, when caused by exposure to chronic vibration.

vi·bra·to /və'brätō; vī-/ ▸*n.* *Music* a rapid, slight variation in pitch in singing or playing some musical instruments, producing a stronger or richer tone. Compare with **TREMOLO**. ▷mid 19th cent.: Italian, past participle of *vibrare* 'vibrate.'

vi·bra·tor /'vīˌbrātər/ ▸*n.* a device that vibrates or causes vibration, in particular: ■ a device used for massage or sexual stimulation. ■ *Music* a reed in a reed organ.

vi·bra·to·ry /'vībrəˌtôrē/ ▸*adj.* of, relating to, or causing vibration.

vib·ri·o /'vibrēˌō/ ▸*n.* (*pl.* **-os**) *Medicine* a waterborne bacterium of a group that includes some pathogenic kinds that cause cholera, gastroenteritis, and septicemia. • *Vibrio* and related genera; motile Gram-negative bacteria occurring as curved flagellated rods. ▷modern Latin, from Latin *vibrare* 'vibrate.'

vi·bris·sa /vī'brisə/ ▸*n.* (*pl.* **-bris·sae** /-brisē; -'brisˌī/) *Zoology* any of the long stiff hairs growing around the mouth or elsewhere on the face of many mammals, used as organs of touch; whiskers. ■ *Ornithology* each of the coarse bristlelike feathers growing around the gape of certain insectivorous birds that catch insects in flight. ▷late 17th cent.: from Latin, literally 'nostril hair.'

vi·bro·tac·tile /ˌvībrə'taktl; -ˌtīl/ ▸*adj.* relating to or involving the perception of vibration through touch.

vi·bur·num /vī'bərnəm/ ▸*n.* a shrub or small tree of temperate and warm regions, typically bearing flat or rounded clusters of small white flowers. • Genus *Viburnum*, family Caprifoliaceae: many species and ornamental hybrids, including the guelder rose and wayfaring tree. ▷modern Latin, from Latin, 'wayfaring tree.'

Vic. ▸*abbr.* Victoria.

vic·ar /'vikər/ ▸*n.* (in the Roman Catholic Church) a representative or deputy of a bishop. ■ (in the Episcopal Church) a member of the clergy in charge of a chapel. ■ (in the Church of England) an incumbent of a parish where tithes formerly passed to a chapter or religious house or layman. ■ (in other Anglican Churches) a member of the clergy deputizing for another. ■ a cleric or choir member appointed to sing certain parts of a cathedral service. ▷Middle English: via Anglo-Norman French from Old French *vicaire*, from Latin *vicarius* 'substitute,' from *vic-* 'change, turn, place' (compare with **VICE**[3]). —**vic·ar·ship** /-ˌsHip/ *n.*

vic·ar·age /'vikərij/ ▸*n.* the residence of a vicar. ■ *historical* the benefice or living of a vicar.

vic·ar ap·os·tol·ic ▸*n.* a Roman Catholic missionary. ■ a titular bishop.

vic·ar·gen·er·al ▸*n.* (*pl.* **vic·ars-gen·er·al**) an Anglican official serving as a deputy or assistant to a bishop or archbishop. ■ (in the Roman Catholic Church) a bishop's representative in matters of jurisdiction or administration.

vi·car·i·al /vī'ke(ə)rēəl; vi-/ ▸*adj.* *archaic* of, relating to, or serving as a vicar.

vi·car·i·ance /vī'ke(ə)rēəns; vi-/ ▸*n.* *Biology* the geographical separation of a population, typically by a physical barrier such as a mountain range or river, resulting in a pair of closely related species. ▷1950s: from Latin *vicarius* 'substitute' + **-ANCE**.

vic·ar·i·ate /vi'ke(ə)rēit; vī-; -ˌāt/ ▸*n.* the office or authority of a vicar. ■ a church or parish ministered to by a vicar.

vi·car·i·ous /vī'kerēəs; vi-/ ▸*adj.* experienced in the imagination through the feelings or actions of another person: *I could glean vicarious pleasure from the struggles of my imaginary film friends.* ■ acting or done for another: *a vicarious atonement.* ■ *Physiology* of or pertaining to the performance by one organ of the functions normally discharged by another. ▷mid 17th cent.: from Latin *vicarius* 'substitute' (see **VICAR**) + **-OUS**. —**vi·car·i·ous·ly** *adv.* —**vi·car·i·ous·ness** *n.*

Vic·ar of Christ ▸*n.* (in the Roman Catholic Church) a title of the pope.

vice[1] /vīs/ ▸*n.* immoral or wicked behavior. See note at **SIN**. ■ criminal activities involving prostitution, pornography, or drugs. ■ an immoral or wicked personal characteristic. ■ a weakness of character or behavior; a bad habit: *cigars happen to be my father's vice.* ▷Middle English: via Old French from Latin *vitium*. —**vice·less** *adj.*

vice[2] ▸*n.* British spelling of **VISE**.

vice[3] /vīs; 'vīsē; 'vīsə/ ▸*prep.* as a substitute for: *the letter was drafted by David Hunt, vice Bevin who was ill.* ▷Latin, ablative of *vic-* 'change.'

vice[4] (also **vice-**) ▸*comb. form* acting as deputy or substitute for; next in rank: *vice regent* | *vice-consul.* ▷from Latin *vice* 'in place of' (compare with **VICE**[3]).

vice ad·mi·ral /vīs/ ▸*n.* a naval officer of very high rank, in particular an officer in the U.S. Navy or Coast Guard ranking above rear admiral and below admiral.

vice chan·cel·lor /vīs/ ▸*n.* **1** a deputy chancellor, esp. one of a British university who discharges most of its administrative duties. **2** *Law* a judge appointed to assist a chancellor, esp. in chancery court or court of equity.

vice·ge·rent /ˌvīs'ji(ə)rənt/ ▸*n.* *formal* a person exercising delegated power on behalf of a sovereign or ruler. ■ a person regarded as an earthly

Pronunciation Key ə ago; ər over; 'ə or ˌə up; 'ər or ˌər fur; a hat; ā rate; ä car; cH chew; e let; ē see; e(ə)r air; i fit; ī by; i(ə)r ear; NG sing; ō go; ô for; oi boy; o͝o good; o͞o goo; ou out; SH she; TH thin; T͟H then; (h)w why; ZH vision

representative of God or a god, esp. the pope. ▷mid 16th cent.: from medieval Latin *vicegerent-* '(person) holding office,' from Latin *vic-* 'office, place, turn' + *gerere* 'carry on, hold.' —**vice·ge·ren·cy** *n.* (*pl.* **-cies**).

Vi·cen·te /vē'sentä/, Gil (*c.*1465–*c.*1536), Portuguese playwright and poet.

Vi·cen·za /vē'cHentsə/ a city in northeastern Italy; pop. 109,000.

vice pres·i·dent /vīs/ ▸*n.* an official or executive ranking below and deputizing for a president. —**vice pres·i·den·cy** *n.* (*pl.* **-cies**) —**vice pres·i·den·tial** /ˌprezi'dencHəl/ *adj.*

vice·re·gal /ˌvīs'rēgəl/ ▸*adj.* of or relating to a viceroy.

vice·reine /'vīsˌrān/ ▸*n.* the wife of a viceroy. ■ a female viceroy. ▷early 19th cent.: from French, from *vice-* 'in place of' + *reine* 'queen.'

vice·roy /'vīsˌroi/ ▸*n.* **1** a ruler exercising authority in a colony on behalf of a sovereign. **2** a migratory orange and black butterfly that closely resembles the monarch but is typically somewhat smaller. The caterpillar feeds on willow leaves, and the adult mimics the unpalatable monarch. • *Limenitis archippus*, subfamily Limenitidinae, family Nymphalidae. ▷early 16th cent.: from archaic French, from *vice-* 'in place of' + *roi* 'king.' —**vice·roy·al** /ˌvīs'roi-əl/ *adj.* —**vice·roy·ship** /-ˌsHip/ *n.*

vice·roy·al·ty /ˌvīs'roi-əltē; 'vīsˌroi-/ (also **Vice·roy·al·ty**) ▸*n.* (*pl.* **-ties**) the office, position, or authority of a viceroy. ■ a territory governed by a viceroy.

vice squad /vīs/ ▸*n.* a department or division of a police force that enforces laws against prostitution, drug abuse, illegal gambling, etc.

vice ver·sa /'vīs 'vərsə; 'vīsə/ ▸*adv.* with the main items in the preceding statement the other way around: *science must be at the service of man, and not vice versa.* ▷early 17th cent.: from Latin, literally 'in-turned position.'

Vi·chy /'vēsHē; 'visHē/ a town in south central France; pop. 28,000. A noted spa town, it is the source of an effervescent mineral water. During World War II, it was the headquarters of the regime set up after the German occupation of northern France to administer unoccupied France and the colonies. Never recognized by the Allies, the regime functioned as a puppet government for the Nazis.

vi·chys·soise /ˌvēsHē'swäz; ˌvisHē-; 'vēsHēˌswäz; 'visHē-/ ▸*n.* a soup made with potatoes, leeks, and cream and typically served chilled. ▷French (feminine), 'of Vichy' (see **VICHY**).

vic·i·nage /'visənij/ ▸*n.* another term for **VICINITY**. ▷Middle English: from Old French *vis(e)nage*, from an alteration of Latin *vicinus* 'neighbor.'

vic·i·nal /'visənl/ ▸*adj.* *rare* neighboring; adjacent. ■ *Chemistry* relating to or denoting substituents attached to adjacent atoms in a ring or chain. ▷early 17th cent.: from French, or from Latin *vicinalis*, from *vicinus* 'neighbor.'

vi·cin·i·ty /və'sinətē/ ▸*n.* (*pl.* **-ties**) the area near or surrounding a particular place: *the number of people living in the immediate vicinity was small.* ■ *archaic* proximity in space or relationship: *the abundance and vicinity of country seats.* ▷mid 16th cent. (in the sense 'proximity'): from Latin *vicinitas*, from *vicinus* 'neighbor.'

vi·cious /'visHəs/ ▸*adj.* **1** deliberately cruel or violent: *a vicious assault.* ■ (of an animal) wild and dangerous to people. ■ *figurative* serious or dangerous: *a vicious flu bug.* ■ *poetic/literary* immoral: *every soul on earth, virtuous or vicious, shall perish.* **2** *archaic* (of language or a line of reasoning) imperfect; defective. ▷Middle English (in the sense 'characterized by immorality'): from Old French *vicious* or Latin *vitiosus*, from *vitium* 'vice.' —**vi·cious·ly** *adv.* —**vi·cious·ness** *n.*

vi·cious cir·cle (also **vi·cious cy·cle**) ▸*n.* **1** a sequence of reciprocal cause and effect in which two or more elements intensify and aggravate each other, leading inexorably to a worsening of the situation. **2** *Logic* a definition or statement that begs the question.

vi·cis·si·tude /və'sisəˌt(y)o͞od/ ▸*n.* (usu. **vicissitudes**) a change of circumstances or fortune, typically one that is unwelcome or unpleasant: *her husband's sharp vicissitudes of fortune.* ■ *poetic/literary* alternation between opposite or contrasting things: *the vicissitude of the seasons.* ▷early 17th cent. (in the sense 'alternation'): from French, or from Latin *vicissitudo*, from *vicissim* 'by turns,' from *vic-* 'turn, change.' —**vi·cis·si·tu·di·nous** /-ˌsisə't(y)o͞odn-əs; -'t(y)o͞odnəs/ *adj.*

Vicks·burg /'viksˌbərg/ a city on the Mississippi River, in western Mississippi; pop. 26,407. In 1863, during the Civil War, it was successfully besieged by Union forces. The last Confederate outpost on the river, its loss effectively split the secessionist states in half.

vi·comte /vē'kônt/ ▸*n.* (*pl.* same) a French nobleman corresponding in rank to a viscount. ▷French.

vi·com·tesse /ˌvēkôn'tes/ ▸*n.* (*pl.* same) a French noblewoman corresponding in rank to a viscountess. ▷French.

vic·tim /'viktəm/ ▸*n.* a person harmed, injured, or killed as a result of a crime, accident, or other event or action. ■ a person who is tricked or duped: *the victim of a hoax.* ■ a living creature killed as a religious sacrifice. ▷late 15th cent. (denoting a creature killed as a religious sacrifice): from Latin *victima*.

▸**PHRASE** □ **fall victim to** be hurt, killed, damaged, or destroyed by: *many streams have fallen victim to the recent drought.*

vic·tim·ize /'viktəˌmīz/ ▸*v.* [*trans.*] single (someone) out for cruel or unjust treatment: *scam artists who victimize senior citizens.* —**vic·tim·i·za·tion** /ˌviktəmə'zāsHən/ *n.* —**vic·tim·iz·er** *n.*

vic·tim·less /'viktəmləs/ ▸*adj.* denoting a crime in which there is no injured party.

vic·tim·less crime ▸*n.* a legal offense to which all parties consent and no party is injured: *software piracy is far from a victimless crime.*

vic·tim·ol·o·gy /ˌviktə'mäləjē/ ▸*n.* (*pl.* **-gies**) the study of the victims of crime and the psychological effects on them of their experience. ■ the possession of an outlook, arising from real or imagined victimization, that seems to glorify and indulge the state of being a victim.

vic·tor /'viktər/ ▸*n.* **1** a person who defeats an enemy or opponent in a battle, game, or other competition. **2** a code word representing the letter V, used in radio communication. ▷Middle English: from Anglo-Norman French *victo(u)r* or Latin *victor*, from *vincere* 'conquer.'

Victor Em·man·u·el II /'viktər i'manyəwəl/ (1820–78), ruler of the kingdom of Sardinia 1849–61 and first king of united Italy 1861–78. He hastened the drive toward Italian unification by appointing Cavour as premier of Piedmont in 1852. He added Venetia to the kingdom in 1866 and Rome in 1870.

Victor Em·man·u·el III (1869–1947), last king of Italy 1900–46. He invited Mussolini to form a government in 1922 and lost all political power. After the loss of Sicily to the Allies in 1943, he acted to dismiss Mussolini and conclude an armistice.

Vic·to·ri·a[1] /vik'tôrēə/ **1** a state in southeastern Australia; pop. 4,394,000; capital, Melbourne. **2** a port at the southern tip of Vancouver Island, capital of British Columbia; pop. 71,228. **3** the capital of the Seychelles, a port on the island of Mahé; pop. 24,000. **4** the capital of Hong Kong; pop. 591,000. **5** a city in southern Texas; pop. 55,076.

Vic·to·ri·a[2] (1819–1901), queen of Great Britain and Ireland 1837–1901 and empress of India 1876–1901. She took an active interest in the policies of her ministers, but largely retired from public life after Prince Albert's death in 1861. Her reign was the longest in British history.

Vic·to·ri·a[3] (also **vic·to·ri·a**) ▸*n.* *historical* a light four-wheeled horse-drawn carriage with a collapsible hood, seats for two passengers, and an elevated driver's seat in front. ▷late 19th cent.: named after Queen *Victoria* (see **VICTORIA**[2]).

Vic·to·ri·a, Lake the largest lake in Africa, in Uganda and Tanzania and bordering on Kenya, drained by the Nile River. Also called **VICTORIA NYANZA**.

Vic·to·ri·a Cross (abbr.: **VC**) ▸*n.* a decoration awarded for conspicuous bravery in the British Commonwealth armed services, instituted by Queen Victoria in 1856.

Vic·to·ri·a Day ▸*n.* (in Canada) the Monday preceding May 24, observed as a national holiday to commemorate the birthday of Queen Victoria.

Vic·to·ri·a de Du·ran·go /vik'tôrēə dā do͞o'ränggō; d(y)o͞o'rang-/ full name for **DURANGO**.

Vic·to·ri·a Falls a waterfall 355 feet (109 m) high, on the Zambezi River, on the Zimbabwe–Zambia border. Its native (Kalolo-Lozi) name is *Mosi-oa-tunya* ("the smoke that thunders").

Vic·to·ri·a Is·land an island in Canada, in the Arctic archipelago, in the Northwest Territories.

Vic·to·ri·a lil·y ▸*n.* a tropical South American water lily that has gigantic floating leaves with raised sides. • Genus *Victoria*, family Nymphaeaceae: two species.

Vic·to·ri·an /vik'tôrēən/ ▸*adj.* of or relating to the reign of Queen Victoria: *a Victorian house.* ■ of or relating to the attitudes and values of this period, regarded as characterized esp. by a stifling and prudish moral earnestness.

▸*n.* a person who lived during the Victorian period. —**Vic·to·ri·an·ism** /-ˌnizəm/ *n.*

Vic·to·ri·an·a /vikˌtôrē'anə; -'änə/ ▸*plural n.* articles, esp. collectors' items, from the Victorian period. ■ matters or attitudes relating to or characteristic of this period.

Vic·to·ri·a Nile the upper part of the White Nile River, between lakes Victoria and Albert.

Vic·to·ri·a Ny·an·za /nē'anzə; nī-; 'nyänzə/ another name for Lake Victoria (see **VICTORIA, LAKE**).

Vic·to·ri·a Peak a mountain on Hong Kong Island that rises to 1,818 ft. (554 m.).

vic·to·ri·ous /vik'tôrēəs/ ▸*adj.* having won a victory; triumphant: *a victorious army | the team defied the odds and emerged victorious.* ■ of or characterized by victory: *he'd participated in the victorious campaigns of the Franco-Prussian War.* ▷late Middle English: from Anglo-Norman French *victorious*, from Latin *victoriosus*, from *victoria* (see **VICTORY**). —**vic·to·ri·ous·ly** *adv.* —**vic·to·ri·ous·ness** *n.*

Vic·tor·ville /'viktərˌvil/ an industrial and residential city in southern California, northeast of Los Angeles; pop. 40,674.

vic·to·ry /'vikt(ə)rē/ ▸*n.* (*pl.* **-ries**) an act of defeating an enemy or opponent in a battle, game, or other competition: *an election victory | they won their heat and went on to victory in the final.* ▷Middle English: from Anglo-Norman French *victorie*, from Latin *victoria*.

vic·to·ry bond ▸*n.* a bond issued by a government during or immediately after a major war.

vic·to·ry gar·den ▸*n.* a vegetable garden, esp. a home garden, planted to increase food production during a war.

vic·to·ry lap ▸*n.* a celebratory circuit of a sports field, track, or court by the person or team that has won a contest.

vic·to·ry roll ▸*n.* a roll performed by an aircraft as a sign of triumph, typically after a successful mission.

vic·to·ry sign ▸*n.* a signal of triumph or celebration made by holding up the hand with the palm outward and the first two fingers spread apart to represent the letter V.

vict·ual /'vitl/ *dated* ▸*n.* (**victuals**) food or provisions, typically as prepared for consumption.

▸*v.* (**-ualed, -ual·ing**; *Brit.* **-ualled, -ual·ling**) [*trans.*] provide with food or other stores: *the ship wasn't even properly victualed.* ■ [*intrans.*] *archaic* obtain or lay in food or other stores: *a voyage of such length, that no ship could victual for.* ■ [*intrans.*] *archaic* eat: *victual with me next Saturday.* ▷Middle English: from Old French *vitaille*, from late Latin *victualia*, neuter plural of Latin *victualis*, from *victus* 'food'; related to *vivere* 'to live.' The pronunciation still represents the early spelling *vittel*; later spelling has been influenced by the Latin form.

vict·ual·er /'vitl-ər/ (*Brit.* **vic·tu·al·ler**) ▸*n.* **1** *dated* a person providing or selling food or other provisions. ■ a ship providing supplies for troops or other ships. **2** (also **li·censed vic·tu·al·er**) *Brit.* a person who is licensed to sell alcoholic liquor. ▷late Middle English: from Old French *vitaill(i)er*, from *vitaille* (see **VICTUAL**).

vi·cu·ña /vī'k(y)o͞onə və-; 'ko͞onyə/ ▸*n.* a wild relative of the llama, inhabiting mountainous regions of South America and valued for its fine silky wool. • *Vicugna vicugna*, family Camelidae. ■ cloth made from this wool or an imitation of it. ▷early 17th cent.: from Spanish, from Quechua.

vid /vid/ ▸*n.* *informal* short for **VIDEO**.

Vi·dal /vi'däl/, Gore (1925–), U.S. novelist, playwright, and essayist; born *Eugene Luther Vidal*. His novels, many of them satirical comedies, include *Williwaw* (1946), *Myra Breckenridge* (1968), and *Lincoln* (1984). His essays are a satirical commentary on U.S. political and cultural life.

vi·de /'vēdē; 'vēˌdā; 'vīdē/ ▸*v.* [*trans.*] see; consult (used as an instruction in a text to refer the reader to a specified passage, book, author, etc., for fuller or further information): *vide the comments cited in Schlosser.* ▷Latin, 'see!,' imperative of *videre*.

vi·de·li·cet /və'deləˌset; -sət; -'dāləˌket/ ▸*adv.* more formal term for **VIZ.** ▷Latin, from *videre* 'to see' + *licet* 'it is permissible.'

vid·e·o /'vidēˌō/ ▸*n.* (*pl.* **-os**) the system of recording, reproducing, or broadcasting moving visual images on or from videotape. ■ a movie or other piece of material recorded on videotape. ■ a videocassette: *a blank video | the film will soon be released* ***on video.*** ■ a short movie made by a pop or rock group to accompany a song when broadcast on television. ■ *Brit.* a videocassette recorder. ▷1930s: from Latin *videre* 'to see,' on the pattern of *audio*.

vid·e·o ar·cade ▶*n.* an indoor area containing coin-operated video games.

vid·e·o cam·er·a ▶*n.* a camera for recording images on videotape or for transmitting them to a monitor screen.

vid·e·o card ▶*n. Computing* a printed circuit board controlling output to a display screen.

vid·e·o·cas·sette /ˌvidēōkəˈset/ ▶*n.* a cassette of videotape.

vid·e·o·cas·sette re·cord·er (abbr.: **VCR**) ▶*n.* a device that, when linked to a television set, can be used for recording on and playing videotapes.

vid·e·o·con·fer·ence /ˈvidēōˌkänf(ə)rəns; -ˌkänf(ə)rns/ ▶*n.* an arrangement in which television sets, videophones, or computers are used to enable a group of people in several different locations to communicate with each other in sound and vision. **—vid·e·o·con·fer·enc·ing** *n.*

vid·e·o di·a·ry ▶*n.* a record on videotape of a notable period of someone's life, or of a particular event, made using a camcorder.

vid·e·o·disc /ˈvidēōˌdisk/ (also **vid·e·o·disk**) ▶*n.* a CD-ROM or other disk used to store visual images and sound.

vid·e·o dis·play ter·min·al (abbr.: **VDT**) ▶*n. Computing* a device for displaying input signals as characters on a screen, typically a monitor.

vid·e·o dra·ma ▶*n.* another term for **TELEPLAY**.

vid·e·o game ▶*n.* a game played by electronically manipulating images produced by a computer program on a television screen or other display screen.

vid·e·o·graph·ics /ˌvidēōˈgrafiks/ ▶*plural n.* visual images produced using computer technology. ■ [treated as *sing.*] the manipulation of video images using a computer.

vid·e·og·ra·phy /ˌvidēˈägrəfē/ ▶*n.* the process or art of making video films. **—vid·e·og·ra·pher** /-fər/ *n.*

vid·e·o jock·ey ▶*n.* a person who introduces and plays music videos for a broadcast, party, or other entertainment.

vid·e·o mail ▶*n.* an e-mail message with a video clip attached.

vid·e·o-on-de·mand ▶*n.* a system in which viewers choose their own filmed entertainment, by means of a PC or interactive TV system, from a wide selection.

vid·e·o·phile /ˈvidēəˌfīl/ ▶*n.* an enthusiast for or devotee of video recordings or video technology.

vid·e·o·phone /ˈvidēōˌfōn/ ▶*n.* a telephone device transmitting and receiving a visual image as well as sound.

vid·e·o pill ▶*n.* a capsule containing a tiny camera that, when swallowed, transmits photographs of the stomach and intestines to a recording device: *video pills can be used to diagnose ulcers.* Also called **CAPSULE ENDOSCOPE**.

vid·e·o·play /ˈvidēōˌplā/ ▶*n.* another term for **TELEPLAY**.

vid·e·o re·cord·er ▶*n.* another term for **VIDEOCASSETTE RECORDER**. **—vid·e·o re·cord·ing** *n.*

vid·e·o·scope /ˈvidēəˌskōp/ ▶*n.* a fiber-optic rod attached to a camera that transmits images from within the body to a television monitor, used in diagnosis and surgery.

vid·e·o·sur·ger·y /ˈvidēōˌsərjərē/ ▶*n.* a minimally invasive approach to surgery using from one to five small incisions, each between ¼ inch and 1 inch in length, through which specially designed instruments are inserted into the body. One of these is a tiny fiber-optic rod attached to a camera, enabling the surgeon to see what is happening inside the body on a television monitor.

vid·e·o·tape /ˈvidēōˌtāp/ ▶*n.* magnetic tape for recording and reproducing visual images and sound. ■ a videocassette. ■ a film or other piece of material recorded on videotape.

▶*v.* [*trans.*] make a video recording of (an event or broadcast): *his arrest was videotaped.*

vid·e·o·tex /ˈvidēōˌteks/ (also **vid·e·o·text** /-ˌtekst/) ▶*n.* an electronic information system such as teletext or viewdata. ▷1970s: from **VIDEO** + **TEXT**.

vi·dette ▶*n.* variant spelling of **VEDETTE**.

vid·i·con /ˈvidiˌkän/ ▶*n. Electronics* a small television camera tube in which the image is formed on a transparent electrode coated with photoconductive material, the current from which varies as it is scanned by a beam of low-speed electrons. ▷1950s: from the initial elements of **VIDEO** and *iconoscope* (an early television camera tube).

vid·i·ot /ˈvidēət/ ▶*n. informal* a habitual, undiscriminating watcher of television or videotapes. ▷1960s: blend of **VIDEO** and **IDIOT**.

vie /vī/ ▶*v.* (**vy·ing**) [*intrans.*] compete eagerly with someone in order to do or achieve something: *rival mobs vying for control of the liquor business.* ▷mid 16th cent.: probably a shortening of obsolete *envy*, via Old French from Latin *invitare* 'challenge.'

vie de Bo·hème /ˈvē də bōˈem/ ▶*n.* (usu. **la vie de Bohème**) an unconventional or informal way of life, esp. as practiced by an artist or writer. ▷French, literally 'bohemian's life.'

Vi·en·na /vēˈenə/ the capital of Austria, in the northeastern part of the country on the Danube River; pop. 1,533,000. From 1278 to 1918 it was the seat of the Habsburgs and has long been a center of the arts, esp. music. Mozart, Beethoven, and the Strauss family were among the composers who lived and worked there. German name **WIEN**. **—Vi·en·nese** /ˌvēəˈnēz; -ˈnēs/ *adj.* & *n.*

Vi·en·na, Con·gress of an international conference held 1814–15 to agree upon the settlement of Europe after the Napoleonic Wars. The guiding principle of the settlement was the restoration and strengthening of hereditary and sometimes despotic rulers; the result was a political stability that lasted for three or four decades.

Vi·en·na Cir·cle a group of empiricist philosophers, scientists, and mathematicians active in Vienna from the 1920s until 1938, including Rudolf Carnap and Kurt Gödel. Their work laid the foundations of logical positivism.

Vi·en·na sau·sage ▶*n.* a small frankfurter made of pork, beef, or veal.

Vi·en·na Se·ces·sion ▶*n.* see **SEZESSION**.

Vi·en·nese waltz ▶*n.* a waltz characterized by a slight anticipation of the second beat of the bar and having a romantic quality. ■ a piece of music written in this style.

Vien·tiane /ˌvyenˈtyän; vēˌentēˈän/ the capital and chief port of Laos, on the Mekong River; pop. 377,000.

Vier·wald·stät·ter·see /firˈvältˌshtetərˌzā/ German name for Lake Lucerne (see **LUCERNE, LAKE**).

Vi·et·cong /vēˌetˈkông; ˌvyet-; ˌvēət-; -ˈkäng/ (also **Viet Cong**) ▶*n.* (*pl.* same) a member of the communist guerrilla movement in Vietnam that fought the South Vietnamese government forces 1954–75 with the support of the North Vietnamese army and opposed the South Vietnamese and U.S. forces in the Vietnam War. ▷Vietnamese, literally 'Vietnamese Communist.'

Vi·et·minh /vēˌetˈmin; ˌvyet-; ˌvēət-/ ▶*n.* (*pl.* same) a member of a communist-dominated nationalist movement, formed in 1941, that fought for Vietnamese independence from French rule. Members of the Vietminh later joined with the Vietcong. ▷from Vietnamese *Viet*-Nam Dôc-Lâp Dông-*Minh* 'Vietnamese Independence League.'

Vi·et·nam /vēˌetˈnäm; ˌvyet-; ˌvēət-; -ˈnam/ a country in Southeast Asia, on the South China Sea; pop. 82,689,000; capital, Hanoi; language, Vietnamese (official). ▷from Vietnamese *Viet*, the name of the inhabitants, + *nam* 'south.'

Traditionally dominated by China, Vietnam came under French influence between 1862 and 1954. After World War II, the Vietminh defeated the French, who then withdrew. Vietnam was partitioned along the 17th parallel between communist North Vietnam (capital, Hanoi) and noncommunist South Vietnam (capital, Saigon). The Vietnam War between the North and the U.S.-backed South ended in victory for the North in 1975 and the reunification of the country under a communist regime the following year.

Vi·et·nam·ese /vēˌetnəˈmēz; ˌvyet-; ˌvēət-; -ˈmēs/ ▶*adj.* of or relating to Vietnam, its people, or their language.

▶*n.* (*pl.* same) **1** a native or national of Vietnam, or a person of Vietnamese descent. **2** the language of Vietnam, which is probably a Mon-Khmer language although much of its vocabulary is derived from Chinese.

Viet·nam·ese pot·bel·lied pig ▶*n.* see **POTBELLIED PIG**.

Vi·et·nam·i·za·tion /vēˌetnəməˈzāshən; ˌvyet-; ˌvēət-/ ▶*n.* (in the Vietnam War) the U.S. policy of withdrawing its troops and transferring the responsibility and direction of the war effort to the government of South Vietnam.

Vi·et·nam War a war between communist North Vietnam and U.S.-backed South Vietnam.

After the partition of Vietnam in 1954, the communist North attempted to unite the country as a communist state, fueling U.S. concern over the possible spread of communism in Southeast Asia. After two U.S. destroyers were reportedly fired on in the Gulf of Tonkin in 1964, U.S. Army forces were sent to Vietnam, supported by contingents from South Korea, Australia, New Zealand, and Thailand, while U.S. aircraft bombed North Vietnamese forces and areas of Cambodia. The Tet Offensive of 1968 damaged U.S. confidence and U.S. forces began to be withdrawn, finally leaving in 1973. The North Vietnamese captured the southern capital Saigon to end the war in 1975.

view /vyo͞o/ ▶*n.* **1** the ability to see something or to be seen from a particular place: *the end of the tunnel came into view | they stood on the bar to get a better view.* ■ a sight or prospect, typically of attractive natural scenery, that can be taken in by the eye from a particular place: *a fine view of the castle.* ■ a work of art depicting such a sight. ■ the visual appearance or an image of something when looked at in a particular way: *an aerial view of the military earthworks.* ■ an inspection of things for sale by prospective purchasers, esp. of works of art at an exhibition. ■ *Law* (in court proceedings) a formal inspection by the judge and jury of the scene of a crime or property mentioned in evidence. **2** a particular way of considering or regarding something; an attitude or opinion: *strong political views.* See note at **OPINION**.

▶*v.* **1** [*trans.*] look at or inspect (something): *the public can view the famous hall with its unique staircase.* ■ watch (something) on television. ■ *Hunting* see (a fox) break cover. **2** [*trans.*] regard in a particular light or with a particular attitude: *farmers are viewing the rise in rabbit numbers with concern.* ▷Middle English: from Anglo-Norman French *vieue*, feminine past participle of *veoir* 'see,' from Latin *videre*. The verb dates from the early 16th cent. **—view·a·ble** *adj.*

▶*PHRASES* □ **in full view** clearly visible. □ **in view** visible to someone: *the youth was keeping him in view.* ■ as one's aim or objective: *his arrest is the principal object I **have in view**.* ■ in one's mind when forming a judgment: *it is important to **have in view** the position reached at the beginning of the 1970s.* □ **in view of** because or as a result of. □ **on view** (esp. of a work of

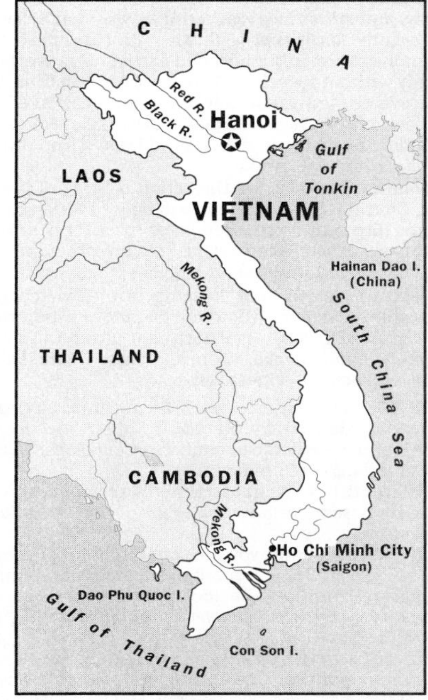

V

Pronunciation Key ə *ago*; ər *over*; ˈə *or* ˌə *up*; ˈər *or* ˌər *fur*; a *hat*; ā *rate*; ä *car*; ch *chew*; e *let*; ē *see*; e(ə)r *air*; i *fit*; ī *by*; i(ə)r *ear*; ng *sing*; ō *go*; ô *for*; oi *boy*; o͝o *good*; o͞o *goo*; ou *out*; sh *she*; th *thin*; t͟h *then*; (h)w *why*; zh *vision*

art) being shown or exhibited to the public. □ **with a view to** with the hope, aim, or intention of.

view·da·ta /ˈvyo͞oˌdatə; -ˌdātə/ ▸*n.* a news and information service in which computer data is sent by a telephone link and displayed on a television screen.

view·er /ˈvyo͞oər/ ▸*n.* **1** a person who looks at or inspects something. ■ a person watching television or a movie. **2** a device for looking at slides or similar photographic images.

view·er·ship /ˈvyo͞oərˌsʜip/ ▸*n.* [treated as *sing.* or *pl.*] the audience for a particular television program or channel.

view·find·er /ˈvyo͞oˌfīndər/ ▸*n.* a device on a camera showing the field of view of the lens, used in framing and focusing the picture.

view·graph /ˈvyo͞oˌgraf/ ▸*n.* a graph or other data produced as a transparency for projection onto a screen or for transmission during a teleconference.

view hal·loo ▸*n.* a shout given by a hunter on seeing a fox break cover.

view·ing /ˈvyo͞oiɴɢ/ ▸*n.* the action of inspecting or looking at something: *the owner may allow viewing by appointment.* ■ the action of watching something on television: *it is quite unsuitable for family viewing.* ■ an opportunity to see something, esp. a work of art.

view·less /ˈvyo͞oləs/ ▸*adj.* **1** not having or affording a pleasant sight or prospect. **2** *poetic/literary* unable to be seen; invisible: *the enormous viewless mantle of the night.*

view·point /ˈvyo͞oˌpoint/ ▸*n.* another term for POINT OF VIEW.

view·port /ˈvyo͞oˌpôrt/ ▸*n.* a window in a spacecraft or in the conning tower of an oil rig. ■ *Computing* a framed area on a display screen for viewing information.

viff /vif/ (also **VIFF**) *informal Aeronautics* ▸*n.* a technique used by a vertical takeoff aircraft to change direction abruptly by altering the direction of thrust of the aircraft's jet engines.
▸*v.* [*intrans.*] (of a vertical takeoff aircraft) change direction in such a way. ▷1970s: acronym from *vectoring in forward flight.*

vig /vig/ ▸*n.* short for VIGORISH.

vi·ga /ˈvēgə/ ▸*n.* a rough-hewn roof timber or rafter, esp. in an adobe building. ▷Spanish.

Vi·gée-Le·brun /vēˈzʜā ləˈbrœn/, (Marie Louise) Élisabeth (1755–1842), French painter. She is known for her portraits of women and children, esp. of Marie Antoinette and of Lady Hamilton.

vi·ges·i·mal /viˈjesəməl/ ▸*adj. rare* relating to or based on the number twenty. ▷mid 17th cent.: from Latin *vigesimus* (from *viginti* 'twenty') + -AL.

vig·il /ˈvijəl/ ▸*n.* **1** a period of keeping awake during the time usually spent asleep, esp. to keep watch or pray: *my birdwatching vigils lasted for hours | as he lay in a coma the family* ***kept vigil.*** ■ a stationary, peaceful demonstration in support of a particular cause, typically without speeches. **2** (in the Christian Church) the eve of a festival or holy day as an occasion of religious observance. ■ (**vigils**) nocturnal devotions. ▷Middle English (sense 2): via Old French from Latin *vigilia*, from *vigil* 'awake.'

vig·i·lance /ˈvijələns/ ▸*n.* the action or state of keeping careful watch for possible danger or difficulties. ▷late 16th cent.: from French, or from Latin *vigilantia*, from *vigilare* 'keep awake,' from *vigil* (see VIGIL).

vig·i·lance com·mit·tee ▸*n.* a body of vigilantes.

vig·i·lant /ˈvijələnt/ ▸*adj.* keeping careful watch for possible danger or difficulties: *the burglar was spotted by vigilant neighbors.* ▷late 15th cent.: from Latin *vigilant-* 'keeping awake,' from the verb *vigilare*, from *vigil* (see VIGIL). —**vig·i·lant·ly** *adv.*

THE RIGHT WORD **alert, careful, cautious, circumspect, vigilant, wary, watchful**

All of these adjectives connote being on the lookout for danger or opportunity.

Watchful is the most general term, meaning closely observant (*a watchful young man who noticed everything*).

If you're **vigilant**, you are watchful for a purpose (*to be vigilant in the presence of one's enemies*), and **wary** suggests being on the lookout for treachery or trickery (*wary of his neighbor's motives in offering to move the fence*).

If you're **alert**, you are quick to apprehend a danger, an opportunity, or an emergency (*she was much more alert after a good night's sleep*), and if you're **careful**, you may be able to avoid danger or error altogether.

Cautious and **circumspect** also emphasize the avoidance of danger or unpleasant situations. To be *circumspect* is to be watchful in all directions and with regard to all possible consequences (*these journalists have to be circumspect, not criticizing anyone too harshly*); to be *cautious* is to guard against contingencies (*a cautious approach to treating illness*).

vig·i·lan·te /ˌvijəˈlantē/ ▸*n.* a member of a self-appointed group of citizens who undertake law enforcement in their community without legal authority, typically because the legal agencies are thought to be inadequate. ▷mid 19th cent.: from Spanish, literally 'vigilant.' —**vig·i·lan·tism** /-ˌtizəm/ *n.*

vig·il light ▸*n.* a candle lighted and placed on a shrine as an act of devotion.

vig·ne·ron /ˌvēnyəˈrôn; -ˈrōn/ ▸*n.* a person who cultivates grapes for winemaking. ▷French, from *vigne* 'vine.'

vi·gnette /vinˈyet/ ▸*n.* **1** a brief evocative description, account, or episode. **2** a small illustration or portrait photograph that fades into its background without a definite border. ■ a small ornamental design filling a space in a book or carving, typically based on foliage.
▸*v.* [*trans.*] portray (someone) in the style of a vignette. ■ produce (a photograph) in the style of a vignette by softening or shading away the edges of the subject. ▷late Middle English (sense 2; also as an architectural term denoting a carved representation of a vine): from French, diminutive of *vigne* 'vine.' —**vi·gnet·tist** /-ˈyetist/ *n.*

Vi·gny /vēnˈyē/, Alfred Victor, Comte de (1797–1863), French poet, novelist, and playwright. His poetry reveals his faith in "man's unconquerable mind."

Vi·go /ˈvēgō/ a port on the Atlantic Ocean in Galicia, in northwestern Spain; pop. 277,000.

vig·or /ˈvigər/ (*Brit.* **vig·our**) ▸*n.* **1** physical strength and good health. ■ effort, energy, and enthusiasm: *they set about the new task with vigor.* ■ strong, healthy growth of a plant. **2** *Law* legal or binding force; validity. ▷Middle English: from Old French *vigour*, from Latin *vigor*, from *vigere* 'be lively.' —**vig·or·less** /ˈvigərləs/ *adj.*

vig·or·ish /ˈvigərisʜ/ ▸*n. informal* **1** [in *sing.*] an excessive rate of interest on a loan, typically one from an illegal moneylender. **2** the percentage deducted from a gambler's winnings by the organizers of a game. ▷early 20th cent.: probably from Yiddish, from Russian *vyigrysh* 'gain, winnings.'

vig·or·ous /ˈvig(ə)rəs/ ▸*adj.* (of a person) strong, healthy, and full of energy. ■ characterized by or involving physical strength, effort, or energy: *vigorous aerobic exercise.* ■ (of language) forceful: *a vigorous denial.* ■ (of a plant) growing strongly. ▷Middle English: via Old French from medieval Latin *vigorosus*, from Latin *vigor* (see VIGOR). —**vig·or·ous·ly** *adv.* —**vig·or·ous·ness** *n.*

vi·ha·ra /viˈhärə/ ▸*n.* a Buddhist monastery. ▷Sanskrit.

vi·hue·la /vēˈ(h)wālə/ ▸*n.* a type of early Spanish stringed musical instrument, in particular: ■ (**vi·hue·la de ma·no** /de ˈmānō/) a type of guitar. ■ (**vi·hue·la de ar·co** /ˈärkō/) a type of viol. ▷mid 19th cent.: Spanish.

Vi·ja·ya·wa·da /ˌvijəyəˈwädə/ a city on the Krishna River in Andhra Pradesh, in southeastern India; pop. 701,000.

Vi·king[1] /ˈvīkiɴɢ/ ▸*n.* any of the Scandinavian seafaring pirates and traders who raided and settled in many parts of northwestern Europe in the 8th–11th centuries.
▸*adj.* of or relating to the Vikings or the period in which they lived. ▷from Old Norse *víkingr*, from *vík* 'creek' or Old English *wīc* 'camp, dwelling place.'

Vi·king[2] either of two American space probes sent to Mars in 1975, each of which consisted of a lander that conducted experiments on the surface and an orbiter.

Vi·la /ˈvēlə/ (also **Port Vi·la**) the capital of Vanuatu, on the southwestern coast of the island of Efate; pop. 20,000.

vi·la·yet /ˌvēləˈyet/ ▸*n.* (in Turkey, and formerly in the Ottoman Empire) a major administrative district or province with its own governor. ▷Turkish, from Arabic *wilāya(t)* 'government, administrative district.'

vile /vīl/ ▸*adj.* extremely unpleasant: *he has a vile temper | vile smells.* ■ morally bad; wicked: *as vile a rogue as ever lived.* See note at DEPRAVED.■ *archaic* of little worth or value. ▷Middle English: via Old French from Latin *vilis* 'cheap, base.' —**vile·ly** *adv.* —**vile·ness** *n.*

vil·i·fy /ˈviləˌfī/ ▸*v.* (**-fies, -fied**) [*trans.*] speak or write about in an abusively disparaging manner: *he has been vilified in the press.* See note at MALIGN. ▷late Middle English (in the sense 'lower in value'): from late Latin *vilificare*, from Latin *vilis* 'of low value' (see VILE). —**vil·i·fi·ca·tion** /ˌviləfiˈkāsʜən/ *n.* —**vil·i·fi·er** *n.*

vil·i·pend /ˈviləˌpend/ ▸*v.* [*trans.*] *archaic* **1** regard as worthless or of little value; despise. **2** speak slightingly or abusively of; vilify. —**vil·i·pend·er** *n.* —**vil·i·pens·ive** *adj.*

Vil·la /ˈvēyə/, Pancho (1878–1923), Mexican revolutionary; born *Doroteo Arango.* He helped Venustiano Carranza to overthrow the dictatorial regime of General Victoriano Huerta in 1914, but then helped Emiliano Zapata to rebel against Carranza's regime.

vil·la /ˈvilə/ ▸*n.* (esp. in continental Europe) a large and luxurious country residence. ■ a large country house of Roman times, having an estate and consisting of farm and residential buildings arranged around a courtyard. ■ *Brit.* a detached or semidetached house in a residential district, typically one that is Victorian or Edwardian in style. ▷early 17th cent.: from Italian, from Latin.

Vil·la·fran·chi·an /ˌviləˈfraɴɢkēən/ ▸*adj.* of, relating to, or denoting an age (or stage) in Europe crossing the boundary of the Upper Pliocene and Lower Pleistocene, lasting from about 3 to 1 million years ago. ■ [as *n.*] (**the Villafranchian**) the Villafranchian age or stage, or the system of deposits laid down during it. ▷late 19th cent.: from French *villafranchien*, from *Villafranca* d'Asti, the village in northern Italy near which exposures of this period occur.

vil·lage /ˈvilij/ ▸*n.* a group of houses and associated buildings, larger than a hamlet and smaller than a town, situated in a rural area. ■ a self-contained district or community within a town or city, regarded as having features characteristic of village life: *the Olympic village.* ■ (in the U.S.) a small municipality with limited corporate powers. ▷late Middle English: from Old French, from Latin *villa* 'country house.' —**vil·lag·er** *n.*

vil·lage id·i·ot ▸*n. chiefly archaic* a person of very low intelligence resident and well known in a village.

vil·lag·i·za·tion /ˌvilijəˈzāsʜən/ ▸*n.* (in Africa and Asia) the concentration of the population in villages as opposed to scattered settlements, typically to ensure more efficient control and distribution of services such as health care and education. ■ the transfer of land to the communal control of villagers.

vil·lain /ˈvilən/ ▸*n.* **1** a person guilty or capable of a crime or wickedness. ■ the person or thing responsible for specified trouble, harm, or damage: *the industrialized nations are the real environmental villains.* ■ (in a play or novel) a character whose evil actions or motives are important to the plot. **2** *archaic* variant spelling of VILLEIN. ▷Middle English (in the sense 'a rustic, boor'): from Old French *vilein*, based on Latin *villa* (see VILLA). —**vil·lain·ess** /ˈvilənəs/ *n.*

vil·lain·ous /ˈvilənəs/ ▸*adj.* relating to, constituting, or guilty of wicked or criminal behavior: *the villainous crimes of the terrorists.* ■ *informal* extremely bad or unpleasant: *a villainous smell.* —**vil·lain·ous·ly** *adv.* —**vil·lain·ous·ness** *n.*

vil·lain·y /ˈvilənē/ ▸*n.* (*pl.* **-lain·ies**) wicked or criminal behavior: *the villainy of professional racketeers | minor villainies.* ▷Middle English: from Old French *vilenie*, from *vilein* (see VILLAIN).

vil·la·nel·la /ˌviləˈnelə/ ▸*n.* (*pl.* **-nel·le** /-ˈnelē/ or **-nel·las**) a form of Italian part-song originating in Naples in the 16th century, in rustic style with a vigorous rhythm. ▷Italian, feminine of *villanello* 'rural,' diminutive of *villano* 'peasant.'

vil·la·nelle /ˌviləˈnel/ ▸*n.* a nineteen-line poem with two rhymes throughout, consisting of five tercets and a quatrain, with the first and third lines of the opening tercet recurring alternately at the end of the other tercets and with both repeated at the close of the concluding quatrain. ▷late 19th cent.: from French, from Italian *villanella* (see VILLANELLA).

-ville ▸*comb. form informal* used in fictitious place names with reference to a particular quality: *dullsville.* ▷from French *ville* 'town,' used in many U.S. town names.

vil·lein /ˈvilən; -ˌān/ ▸*n.* (in medieval England) a feudal tenant entirely subject to a lord or manor to whom he paid dues and services in return for land. ▷Middle English: variant of VILLAIN.

vil·lein·age /ˈvilənij; -ˌānij/ ▸*n. historical* the tenure or status of a villein.

vil·lous /ˈviləs/ ▸*adj. Anatomy* (of a structure, esp. the epithelium) covered with villi. ■ *Medicine* (of a condition) affecting the villi: *villous atrophy.* ■ *Botany* shaggy.

vil·lus /ˈviləs/ (*pl.* **vil·li** /ˈvilī; ˈvilē/) ▸*n.* **1** *Anatomy* any of numerous minute elongated projections set closely together on a surface, typically increasing its surface area for the absorption of substances, in particular: ■ a fingerlike projection of the lining of the small intestine. ■ a fold of the chorion. **2** [(usu. in *pl.*)] *Botany* a long slender hair. ▷early 18th cent.: from Latin, literally 'shaggy hair.'

Vil·ni·us /ˈvilnēəs/ the capital of Lithuania, in the southeastern part of the country; pop. 593,000.

vim /vim/ ▸*n. informal* energy; enthusiasm: *in his youth he was full of vim and vigor.* ▷mid 19th cent. (originally U.S.): perhaps from Latin, accusative of *vis* 'energy.'

Vi·my Ridge, Bat·tle of /ˈvēme; ˈvimē; vēˈmē/ an Allied attack on the German position of Vimy Ridge, near the town of Arras, France, during World War I. One of the key points on the Western Front, it had long resisted assaults, but on April 9, 1917, it was taken by Canadian troops in fifteen minutes, at the cost of heavy casualties.

VIN /vin/ ▸*abbr.* vehicle identification number.

vin /van; van/ ▸*n.* [usu. with *adj.*] French wine: *vin blanc.* ▷French, literally 'wine.'

vi·na ▸*n.* variant spelling of **VEENA**.

vi·na·ceous /vīˈnāsHəs; və-/ ▸*adj.* of the color of red wine. ▷late 17th cent.: from Latin *vinaceus* (from *vinum* 'wine') + **-OUS**.

vin·ai·grette /ˌvinəˈgret/ ▸*n.* **1** (also **vin·ai·grette dress·ing**) salad dressing of oil, wine vinegar, and seasoning. **2** *historical* a small ornamental bottle for holding smelling salts. ▷French, diminutive of *vinaigre* 'vinegar.'

vin·blas·tine /vinˈblasˌtēn/ ▸*n. Medicine* a cytotoxic compound of the alkaloid class obtained from the Madagascar periwinkle and used to treat Hodgkin's disease and other cancers of the lymphatic system. ▷1960s: from modern Latin *Vinca* (see **VINCA**) + *(leuco)blast* (a cell from which a leucocyte develops) + **-INE**[4].

vin·ca /ˈviNGkə/ ▸*n.* another term for **PERIWINKLE**[1]. ▷1930s: from modern Latin *Vinca* (genus name), from late Latin *pervinca* (see **PERIWINKLE**[1]).

Vin·cennes /vinˈsenz/ **1** **2** a historic commercial and industrial city in southwestern Indiana, on the Wabash River; pop. 19,859.

Vin·cent de Paul, St. /ˈvinsənt də ˈpôl/ (1581–1660), French priest. He devoted his life to work among the poor and the sick and established institutions for his work, including the Daughters of Charity (Sisters of Charity of St. Vincent de Paul) 1633. Feast day, July 19.

Vin·cen·tian /vinˈsensHən/ ▸*n.* a member of the Congregation of the Mission, a Catholic organization founded at the priory of St. Lazare in Paris by St. Vincent de Paul to preach to the rural poor and train candidates for the priesthood. Also called **LAZARIST**.

Vin·cent's an·gi·na ▸*n.* a painful ulcerative condition of the inside of the mouth or of the gums, associated with trench mouth.

Vin·ci, Leonardo da, see **LEONARDO DA VINCI**.

vin·ci·ble /ˈvinsəbəl/ ▸*adj. poetic/literary* (of an opponent or obstacle) able to be overcome or conquered. ▷mid 16th cent.: from Latin *vincibilis*, from *vincere* 'to overcome.' —**vin·ci·bil·i·ty** /ˌvinsəˈbilətē/ *n.*

vin·cris·tine /vinˈkrisˌtēn/ ▸*n. Medicine* a cytotoxic compound of the alkaloid class obtained from the Madagascar periwinkle and used to treat acute leukemia and other cancers. ▷1960s: from modern Latin *Vinca* (see **VINCA**) + a second element perhaps based on **CRISTA** + **-INE**[4].

vin·cu·lum /ˈviNGkyələm/ ▸*n.* (*pl.* **-la** /-lə/) **1** *Anatomy* a connecting band of tissue, such as that attaching a flexor tendon to the bone of a finger or toe. **2** *Mathematics* a horizontal line drawn over a group of terms in a mathematical expression to indicate that they are to be operated on as a single entity by the preceding or following operator. ▷mid 17th cent. (in the sense 'bond, tie'): from Latin, literally 'bond,' from *vincire* 'bind.' The term has been used in anatomy since the mid 19th cent. —**vin·cu·lar** /-lər/ *adj.*

vin·da·loo /ˈvindəˌlo͞o; ˌvindəˈlo͞o/ ▸*n.* a highly spiced hot Indian curry made with meat or fish. ▷probably from Portuguese *vin d'alho* 'wine and garlic (sauce),' from *vinho* 'wine' + *alho* 'garlic.'

vin de pays /ˌvan dʏ pāˈē; ˌvan do͞o/ (also **vin du pays**) ▸*n.* (*pl.* **vins de pays** *pronunc.* same) the third-highest French classification of wine, indicating that the wine meets certain standards including area of production, strength, and quality. ■ French wine produced locally. ▷French, literally 'wine of the region.'

vin de ta·ble /ˌvan də ˈtäbl(ə); ˌvan/ ▸*n.* (*pl.* **vins de ta·ble** *pronunc.* same) French table wine of reasonable quality, suitable for accompanying a meal. ▷French, literally 'table wine.'

vin·di·cate /ˈvindəˌkāt/ ▸*v.* [*trans.*] clear (someone) of blame or suspicion: *hospital staff were vindicated by the inquest verdict.* See note at **ABSOLVE**. ■ show or prove to be right, reasonable, or justified: *more sober views were vindicated by events.* ▷mid 16th cent. (in the sense 'deliver, rescue'): from Latin *vindicat-* 'claimed, avenged,' from the verb *vindicare*, from *vindex*, *vindic-* 'claimant, avenger.' —**vin·di·ca·ble** /-kəbəl/ *adj.* —**vin·di·ca·tion** /ˌvindəˈkāsHən/ *n.* —**vin·di·ca·tor** /-ˌkātər/ *n.* —**vin·di·ca·to·ry** /-kəˌtôrē/ *adj.*

vin·dic·tive /vinˈdiktiv/ ▸*adj.* having or showing a strong or unreasoning desire for revenge: *the criticism was both vindictive and personalized.* ▷early 17th cent.: from Latin *vindicta* 'vengeance' + **-IVE**. —**vin·dic·tive·ly** *adv.* —**vin·dic·tive·ness** *n.*

THE RIGHT WORD **rancorous, spiteful, vengeful, venomous, vindictive**

Someone who is motivated by a desire to get even might be described as **vindictive**, a word that suggests harboring grudges for perceived wrongs (*a vindictive person who had alienated friends and neighbors alike*).

Spiteful is a stronger term, implying a bitter or vicious vindictiveness (*a spiteful child who broke the toy she had been forced to share*).

Vengeful implies a strong urge to actually seek vengeance (*vengeful after losing her husband in a hit-and-run accident*).

Someone who is **rancorous** suffers from a deep-seated and lasting bitterness, although it does not imply a desire to hurt or to be vindictive (*his rancorous nature made him difficult to befriend*).

Venomous takes its meaning from "venom," referring to someone or something of a spiteful, malignant nature and suggesting a poisonous sting (*a critic's venomous attack on the author's first novel*).

Vine /vīn/, Frederick John (1939–), English geologist. He and his colleague **Drummond H. Matthews** (1931–97) showed that magnetic data from the earth's crust under the Atlantic Ocean provided evidence for seafloor spreading.

vine /vīn/ ▸*n.* a climbing or trailing woody-stemmed plant of the grape family. • *Vitis* and other genera, family Vitaceae. ■ used in names of climbing or trailing plants of other families, e.g., **potato vine**. ■ the slender stem of a trailing or climbing plant. ▷Middle English: from Old French, from Latin *vinea* 'vineyard, vine,' from *vinum* 'wine.' —**vin·y** *adj.*

vine dress·er ▸*n.* a person who prunes, trains, and cultivates vines.

vin·e·gar /ˈvinəgər/ ▸*n.* a sour-tasting liquid containing acetic acid, obtained by fermenting dilute alcoholic liquids, typically wine, cider, or beer, and used as a condiment or for pickling. ■ *figurative* sourness or peevishness of behavior, character, or speech: *her aggrieved tone held a touch of vinegar.* ▷Middle English: from Old French *vyn egre*, based on Latin *vinum* 'wine' + *acer* 'sour.' —**vin·e·gar·ish** *adj.* —**vin·e·gar·y** *adj.*

Vin·e·gar Joe see **STILWELL**.

Vine·land /ˈvīnlənd/ a commercial and industrial city in southern New Jersey; pop. 54,780.

vin·er·y /ˈvīn(ə)rē/ ▸*n.* (*pl.* **-er·ies**) a greenhouse for grapevines. ■ a vineyard.

vine·yard /ˈvinyərd/ ▸*n.* a plantation of grapevines, typically producing grapes used in winemaking. ■ *figurative* a sphere of action or labor (in allusion to Matt. 20:1): *women professors laboring in feminist vineyards.*

vingt-et-un /ˌvant ā ˈən; ˌvan tā ˈœn/ ▸*n.* the card game blackjack. ▷French, literally 'twenty-one.'

vi·nho ver·de /ˈvinyō ˈverdē; ˈvēnyo͞o ˈverdə/ ▸*n.* a young Portuguese wine, not allowed to mature. ▷Portuguese, literally 'green wine.'

vini- ▸*comb. form* of or relating to wine: *viniculture.* ▷from Latin *vinum* 'wine.'

vin·i·cul·ture /ˈvinəˌkəlCHər/ ▸*n.* the cultivation of grapevines for winemaking. ▷late 19th cent.: from Latin *vinum* 'wine' + **CULTURE**, on the pattern of words such as *agriculture.* —**vin·i·cul·tur·al** /ˌvinəˈkəlCHərəl/ *adj.* —**vin·i·cul·tur·ist** /ˌvinəˈkəlCHərist/ *n.*

vin·i·fi·ca·tion /ˌvinəfiˈkāsHən/ ▸*n.* the conversion of grape juice or other vegetable extract into wine by fermentation. —**vin·i·fy** /ˈvinəˌfī/ *v.* (**-fies**, **-fied**).

vin·ing /ˈvīniNG/ ▸*adj.* [*attrib.*] (of a plant) growing as a vine with climbing or trailing woody stems.

Vin·land /ˈvinlənd/ the region of the northeastern coast of North America that was visited in the 11th century by Norsemen led by Leif Ericsson. It was so named from the report that grapevines were found growing there. The exact location is uncertain.

Vin·ny·tsya /ˈvēnitsyə/ a city in central Ukraine; pop. 379,000. Russian name **VINNITSA** .

vi·no /ˈvēnō/ ▸*n.* (*pl.* **-nos**) Spanish or Italian wine. ▷Spanish and Italian, 'wine.'

vi·no da ta·vo·la /ˈvēno dä ˈtävōlə/ ▸*n.* Italian wine of reasonable quality, suitable for drinking with a meal. ▷Italian, literally 'table wine.'

vin or·di·naire /ˌvann ˌôrdēˈne(ə)r; ˈvan/ ▸*n.* (*pl.* **vins or·di·naires** /ˌvanz ˌôrdēˈne(ə)r; ˈvanz/) cheap table wine for everyday use. ▷French, literally 'ordinary wine.'

vi·nous /ˈvīnəs/ ▸*adj.* of, resembling, or associated with wine: *a vinous smell.* ■ fond of or influenced by drinking wine: *his vinous companion.* ■ of the reddish color of wine. ▷late Middle English: from Latin *vinum* 'wine' + **-OUS**. —**vi·nos·i·ty** /vīˈnäsətē/ *n.* —**vi·nous·ly** *adv.*

Vin·son /ˈvinsən/, Frederick Moore (1890–1953), U.S. chief justice 1946–53. Before being appointed to the chief justiceship by President Truman, he had been a member of the U.S. House of Representatives 1924–29 and 1931–38, had held several federal positions during World War II, and had served in the president's cabinet as secretary of the Treasury 1945–46.

Vin·son Mas·sif /ˈvinsən maˈsēf/ the highest mountain in Antarctica, in Ellsworth Land. It rises to 16,863 feet (5,140 m).

vin·tage /ˈvintij/ ▸*n.* the year or place in which wine, esp. wine of high quality, was produced. ■ a wine of high quality made from the crop of a single identified district in a good year. ■ *poetic/literary* wine. ■ the harvesting of grapes for winemaking. ■ the grapes or wine produced in a particular season. ■ the time that something of quality was produced: *rifles of various sizes and vintages.*
▸*adj.* of, relating to, or denoting wine of high quality: *vintage claret.* ■ denoting something of high quality, esp. something from the past or characteristic of the best period of a person's work: *a vintage Sherlock Holmes adventure.* ▷late Middle English: alteration (influenced by **VINTNER**) of earlier *vendage*, from Old French *vendange*, from Latin *vindemia* (from *vinum* 'wine' + *demere* 'remove').

vin·tage port ▸*n.* port wine of special quality, all of one year, bottled early and aged in the bottle.

vin·tag·er /ˈvintijər/ ▸*n.* a person who harvests grapes.

vin·tage year ▸*n.* the year that a particular wine was produced. ■ a particularly successful year for some pursuit or product: *it was a vintage year for home-run hitters.*

vint·ner /ˈvintnər/ ▸*n.* **1** a wine merchant. **2** a wine maker. ▷late Middle English: via Anglo-Latin from Old French *vinetier*, from medieval Latin *vinetarius*, from Latin *vinetum* 'vineyard,' from *vinum* 'wine.'

vi·nyl /ˈvīnl/ ▸*n.* **1** synthetic resin or plastic consisting of polyvinyl chloride or a related polymer, used esp. for wallpapers and other covering materials and for phonograph records: *light-reflecting vinyls can be hung in the usual way.* ■ vinyl used as the standard material for phonograph records: *fans had to wait almost a year before the song eventually appeared on vinyl.* **2** [as *adj.*] *Chemistry* of or denoting the unsaturated hydrocarbon radical $-CH{=}CH_2$, derived from ethylene by removal of a hydrogen atom: *a vinyl group.* ▷mid 19th cent.: from Latin *vinum* 'wine' + **-YL**.

vi·nyl ac·e·tate ▸*n. Chemistry* a colorless liquid ester used in the production of polyvinyl acetate and other commercially important polymers. • Chem. formula: $CH_2CHOCOCH_3$.

vi·nyl chlo·ride ▸*n. Chemistry* a colorless toxic gas used in the production of polyvinyl chloride and other commercially important polymers. • Chem. formula: CH_2CHCl.

vi·ol /ˈvīəl/ ▸*n.* a musical instrument of the Renaissance and baroque periods, typically six-stringed, held vertically and played with a bow. ▷late 15th cent. (originally denoting a violinlike instrument): from Old French *viele*, from Provençal *viola*; probably related to FIDDLE.

vi·o·la[1] /vī'ōlə; vē-; 'vīələ/ ▸*n.* an instrument of the violin family, larger than the violin and tuned a fifth lower. ▷early 18th cent.: from Italian and Spanish; compare with VIOL.

vi·o·la[2] /vē'ōlə/ ▸*n.* a plant of a genus that includes the pansies and violets. • Genus *Viola*, family Violaceae: many species. ▷modern Latin, from Latin, literally 'violet.'

vi·o·la·ceous /,vīə'lāsHəs/ ▸*adj.* **1** of a violet color. **2** *Botany* of, relating to, or denoting plants of the violet family (Violaceae). ▷mid 17th cent.: from Latin *violaceus* (from *viola* 'violet') + -OUS.

vi·o·la da brac·cio /vē'ōlə də 'brächō/ ▸*n.* an early musical instrument of the violin family (as distinct from a viol), specifically one corresponding to the modern viola. ▷Italian, literally 'viol for the arm.'

vi·o·la da gam·ba /vē'ōlə də 'gämbə; 'gam-/ (also **vi·ol da gam·ba**) ▸*n.* a viol, specifically a bass viol (corresponding to the modern cello). ▷Italian, literally 'viol for the leg.'

vi·o·la d'a·mo·re /vē'ōlə dä'môrā; də-; -'môrē/ ▸*n.* a sweet-toned 18th-century musical instrument similar to a viola, but with six or seven strings, and additional sympathetic strings below the fingerboard. ▷Italian, literally 'viol of love.'

vi·o·late /'vīə,lāt/ ▸*v.* [*trans.*] break or fail to comply with (a rule or formal agreement): *they violated the terms of a cease-fire.* ■ fail to respect (someone's peace, privacy, or rights): *they denied that human rights were being violated.* ■ treat (something sacred) with irreverence or disrespect: *he was accused of violating a tomb.* ■ rape or sexually assault (someone). ▷late Middle English: from Latin *violat-* 'treated violently,' from the verb *violare*. —**vi·o·la·tor** /-,lātər/ *n.* —**vi·o·la·ble** /-ləbəl/ *adj.* (*rare*). —**vi·o·la·tive** *adj.*

vi·o·la·tion /,vīə'lāsHən/ ▸*n.* the action of violating someone or something: *the aircraft were* ***in violation of*** *UN resolutions.*

vi·o·lence /'vī(ə)ləns/ ▸*n.* behavior involving physical force intended to hurt, damage, or kill someone or something. ■ strength of emotion or an unpleasant or destructive natural force: *the violence of her own feelings.* ■ *Law* the unlawful exercise of physical force or intimidation by the exhibition of such force. ▷Middle English: via Old French from Latin *violentia*, from *violent-* 'vehement, violent' (see VIOLENT).

▸*PHRASE* □ **do violence to** damage or adversely affect.

vi·o·lent /'vī(ə)lənt/ ▸*adj.* using or involving physical force intended to hurt, damage, or kill someone or something: *a violent confrontation with riot police.* ■ (esp. of an emotion or unpleasant or destructive natural force) very strong or powerful: *violent dislike | the violent eruption killed 1,700 people.* ■ (of a color) vivid. ■ *Law* involving an unlawful exercise or exhibition of force. ▷Middle English (in the sense 'having a marked or powerful effect'): via Old French from Latin *violent-* 'vehement, violent.' —**vi·o·lent·ly** *adv.*

vi·o·lent storm ▸*n.* a wind of force 11 on the Beaufort scale (56–63 knots or 64-72 mph).

vi·o·let /'vī(ə)lət/ ▸*n.* **1** a herbaceous plant of temperate regions, typically having purple, blue, or white five-petaled flowers, one of which forms a landing pad for pollinating insects. • Genus *Viola*, family Violaceae (the **violet family**): many species, including the **dog violet** and **sweet violet**. See also VIOLA[2]. ■ used in names of similar-flowered plants of other families, e.g., **African violet**. **2** a bluish-purple color seen at the end of the spectrum opposite red.

▸*adj.* of a purplish-blue color. ▷Middle English: from Old French *violette*, diminutive of *viole*, from Latin *viola* 'violet.'

vi·o·lin /,vīə'lin/ ▸*n.* a stringed musical instrument of treble pitch, played with a horsehair bow. The classical European violin was developed in the 16th century. It has four strings and a body of characteristic rounded shape, narrowed at the middle and with two f-shaped sound holes. ▷late 16th cent.: from Italian *violino*, diminutive of *viola* (see VIOLA[1]). —**vi·o·lin·ist** /-ist/ *n.* —**vi·o·lin·is·tic** /-lin'istik/ *adj.*

violin

vi·o·lin spi·der ▸*n.* another term for BROWN RECLUSE.

vi·o·list ▸*n.* **1** /vē'ōlist/ a viola player. **2** /'vīəlist/ a viol player.

vi·o·lon·cel·lo /,vīələn'cHelō; ,vē-/ ▸*n.* formal term for CELLO. ▷early 18th cent.: Italian, diminutive of *violone* (see VIOLONE). —**vi·o·lon·cel·list** /-'cHelist/ *n.*

vi·o·lo·ne /,vēə'lōnā/ ▸*n.* an early form of double bass, esp. a large bass viol. ▷Italian, augmentative of *viola* (see VIOLA[1]).

VIP ▸*abbr.* ■ very important person. ■ *Biochemistry* vasoactive intestinal polypeptide (or peptide), a substance which acts as a neurotransmitter, esp. in the brain and gastrointestinal tract.

vi·pas·sa·na /vi'päsənə/ (also **Vi·pas·sa·na**) ▸*n.* (in Theravada Buddhism) meditation involving concentration on the body or its sensations, or the insight that this provides. ▷Pali, literally 'inward vision.'

vi·per /'vīpər/ ▸*n.* a venomous snake with large hinged fangs, typically having a broad head and stout body, with dark patterns on a lighter background. • Family Viperidae: numerous genera and species. See also PIT VIPER, ADDER[1]. ■ a spiteful or treacherous person. ▷early 16th cent.: from French *vipère* or Latin *vipera*, from *vivus* 'alive' + *parere* 'bring forth.' —**vi·per·ine** /'vīpə,rīn; -rin/ *adj.* —**vi·per·ish** *adj.* —**vi·per·ous** /'vīp(ə)rəs/ *adj.*

▸*PHRASE* □ **viper in one's bosom** a person who betrays those who have helped them.

vi·per·fish /'vīpər,fisH/ ▸*n.* (*pl.* same or **-fish·es**) a small, elongated deep-sea fish that has large jaws with long protruding fangs. • Family Chauliodontidae: several genera and species.

vi·per's bu·gloss ▸*n.* a bristly plant of the borage family, with pink buds that open to blue flowers. It was formerly used in the treatment of snake bites. Native to Eurasia, it is now widespread throughout North America. • *Echium vulgare*, family Boraginaceae.

vi·rae·mia ▸*n.* British spelling of VIREMIA.

vi·ra·go /və'rägō; -'rā-/ ▸*n.* (*pl.* **-gos** or **-goes**) a domineering, violent, or bad-tempered woman. ■ *archaic* a woman of masculine strength or spirit; a female warrior. ▷Old English (used only as the name given by Adam to Eve, following the Vulgate), from Latin, 'heroic woman, female warrior,' from *vir* 'man.' The current sense dates from late Middle English.

vi·ral /'vīrəl/ ▸*adj.* of the nature of, caused by, or relating to a virus or viruses. —**vi·ral·ly** *adv.*

vi·ral load ▸*n.* a measurement of the amount of a virus in an organism, typically in the bloodstream, usu. stated in virus particles per milliliter.

vi·ral mar·ket·ing ▸*n.* a method of product promotion that relies on getting customers to market an idea, product, or service on their own by telling their friends about it, usually by e-mail: [as *adj.*] *a carefully designed viral marketing strategy ripples outward extremely rapidly.*

Vir·chow /'firkHō/, Rudolf Karl (1821–1902), German physician and pathologist. He founded cellular pathology.

vir·e·lay /'virə,lā/ (also **vir·e·lai**) ▸*n.* a medieval French lyric poem of indefinite length composed of stanzas of long lines rhyming with each other and short lines rhyming with each other, the short lines of each stanza furnishing the rhyme for the long lines of the next, with the short lines of the last stanza taking their rhyme from the short lines of the first. ▷late Middle English: from Old French *virelai*.

vi·re·mi·a /vī'rēmēə/ (*Brit.* also **vi·rae·mi·a**) ▸*n.* *Medicine* the presence of viruses in the blood. ▷1940s: from VIRUS + -EMIA. —**vi·re·mic** /-mik/ *adj.*

vir·e·o /'virē,ō/ ▸*n.* (*pl.* **-os**) a small American songbird, typically having a green or gray back and yellow or white underparts. • Family Vireonidae (the **vireo family**): two genera, esp. *Vireo*, and several species. The vireo family also includes the greenlets and peppershrikes. ▷mid 19th cent.: from Latin, perhaps denoting a greenfinch.

vi·res·cent /və'resənt; vī-/ ▸*adj.* *poetic/literary* greenish. ▷early 19th cent.: from Latin *virescent-* 'turning green,' inceptive of *virere* 'be green.' —**vi·res·cence** *n.* —**vi·res·cent·ly** *adv.*

vir·ga /'vərgə/ ▸*n.* (*pl.* **-gae** /-gē; -gī/) *Meteorology* a mass of streaks of rain appearing to hang under a cloud and evaporating before reaching the ground. ▷1940s: from Latin, literally 'rod, stripe.'

vir·gate /'vərgət; -,gāt/ ▸*n.* *Brit., historical* a varying measure of land, typically 30 acres. ▷mid 17th cent.: from Latin *virgatus*, from *virga* 'rod.'

Vir·gil /'vərjəl/ (also **Ver·gil**) (70–19 BC), Roman poet; Latin name *Publius Vergilius Maro*. He wrote three major works: the *Eclogues*, ten pastoral poems that blend traditional themes of Greek bucolic poetry with contemporary political and literary themes; the *Georgics*, a didactic poem on farming; and the *Aeneid*, an epic poem about Aeneas, a Trojan (see AENEID). —**Vir·gil·i·an** /vər'jilēən/ *adj.*

vir·gin /'vərjən/ ▸*n.* a person, typically a woman, who has never had sexual intercourse. ■ a naive, innocent, or inexperienced person, esp. in a particular context: *a political virgin.* ■ (**the Virgin**) the mother of Jesus; the Virgin Mary. ■ a woman who has taken a vow to remain a virgin. ■ (**the Virgin**) the zodiacal sign or constellation Virgo. ■ *Entomology* a female insect that produces eggs without being fertilized.

▸*adj.* **1** [*attrib.*] being, relating to, or appropriate for a virgin: *his virgin bride.* **2** not yet touched, used, or exploited: *acres of virgin forests | virgin snow.* ■ (of clay) not yet fired. ■ (of wool) not yet, or only once, spun or woven. ■ (of olive oil) obtained from the first pressing of olives. ■ (of metal) made from ore by smelting. ▷Middle English: from Old French *virgine*, from Latin *virgo*, *virgin-*.

vir·gin·al /'vərjənl/ ▸*adj.* being, relating to, or appropriate for a virgin: *virginal shyness.*

▸*n.* (usu. **virginals**) an early spinet with the strings parallel to the keyboard, typically rectangular, and popular in 16th and 17th century houses. [perhaps because usually played by young women (see origin below).] ▷late Middle English: from Old French, or from Latin *virginalis*, from *virgo* 'young woman.' —**vir·gin·al·ist** /-jənl-ist/ *n.* —**vir·gin·al·ly** *adv.*

vir·gin birth ▸*n.* **1** (**the Virgin Birth**) the doctrine of Christ's birth from a mother, Mary, who was a virgin. **2** *Zoology* parthenogenesis.

Vir·gin·ia[1] /vər'jinyə/ a state in the eastern U.S., on the Atlantic coast; pop. 7,078,515; capital, Richmond; statehood, June 25, 1788 (10). It was the site of the first permanent European settlement in North America at Jamestown in 1607. One of the original thirteen states, it saw the British surrender at Yorktown in 1781 to end the American Revolution, as well as many Civil War battles. —**Vir·gin·ian** *n.* & *adj.*

Vir·gin·ia[2] ▸*n.* a type of tobacco grown and manufactured in Virginia. ■ a cigarette made of such tobacco. —**Vir·gin·ian** *n.* & *adj.*

Vir·gin·ia Beach a city and resort on the Atlantic coast of southeastern Virginia; pop. 425,257.

Vir·gin·ia blue·bell ▸*n.* a North American woodland plant of the borage family, bearing nodding, trumpet-shaped blue flowers. Also called VIRGINIA COWSLIP. • *Mertensia virginica*, family Boraginaceae.

Vir·gin·ia Cit·y a historic settlement in western Nevada, south of Reno, site of the Comstock Lode gold and silver boom in the 1850s–60s.

Vir·gin·ia cow·slip ▸*n.* another term for VIRGINIA BLUEBELL.

Vir·gin·ia creep·er ▸*n.* a North American vine of the grape family, chiefly cultivated for its red autumn foliage. • Genus *Parthenocissus*, family Vitaceae: several species, in particular *P. quinquefolia*.

Vir·gin·ia ham ▸*n.* a smoke-cured ham from a hog fed on peanuts and corn.

Vir·gin·ia o·pos·sum ▸*n.* see OPOSSUM.

Vir·gin·ia reel ▸*n.* a lively American country dance performed by a number of couples facing each other in parallel lines.

Vir·gin·ia snake·root ▸*n.* see SNAKEROOT.

Vir·gin·ia stock ▸*n.* a low-growing, sweetly scented plant with white, pink, or lilac flowers, native to the Mediterranean and cultivated elsewhere. • *Malcolmia maritima*, family Brassicaceae.

Vir·gin Is·lands /'vərjən/ a group of Caribbean islands at the eastern end of the Greater Antilles,

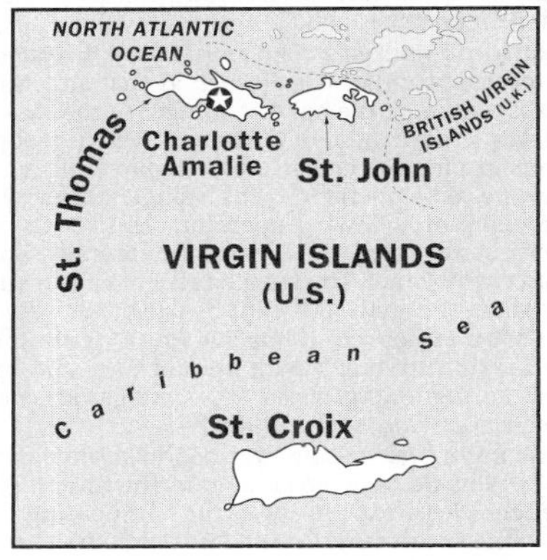

divided between U.S. and British administration. The islands were settled, mainly in the 17th century, by British and Danish sugar planters. The U.S. islands include about 50 islands; pop. 108,000; capital, Charlotte Amalie (on St. Thomas). They were purchased from Denmark in 1917 because of their strategic position. The British islands consist of about 40 islands in the northeastern part of the group; pop. 17,000; capital, Road Town (on Tortola).

vir·gin·i·ty /vərˈjinətē/ ▸*n.* the state of never having had sexual intercourse: *he* **lost his virginity** *in college.* ■ the state of being naive, innocent, or inexperienced in a particular context: *his political virginity.* ▷Middle English: from Old French *virginite*, from Latin *virginitas*, from *virgo* (see VIRGIN).

Vir·gin Mar·y the mother of Jesus (see MARY[1]).

vir·gin queen ▸*n.* **1** an unfertilized queen bee. **2** (**the Virgin Queen**) Queen Elizabeth I of England, who died unmarried.

vir·gin's bow·er ▸*n.* a North American clematis with white flowers. Also called OLD MAN'S BEARD, because of the fluffy gray plumes that stick to the seeds in autumn. • *Clematis virginiana*, family Ranunculaceae.

Vir·go /ˈvərgō/ **1** *Astronomy* a large constellation (the Virgin), said to represent a maiden or goddess associated with the harvest. It contains several bright stars, the brightest of which is Spica, and a dense cluster of galaxies. ■ [as *genitive*] (**Virginis**) used with a preceding letter or numeral to designate a star in this constellation: *the star Gamma Virginis.* **2** *Astrology* the sixth sign of the zodiac, which the sun enters about August 23. ■ (**a Virgo**) (*pl.* **-gos**) a person born when the sun is in this sign. ▷Latin. **—Vir·go·an** /-gōən/ *n.* & *adj.* (in sense 2).

vir·go in·tac·ta /ˈvərgō inˈtaktə/ ▸*n. chiefly Law* a girl or woman who has never had sexual intercourse, originally a virgin whose hymen is intact. ▷Latin, literally 'untouched virgin.'

vir·gule /ˈvər,gyo͞ol/ ▸*n.* another term for SLASH[1] (sense 2). ▷mid 19th cent.: from French, literally 'comma,' from Latin *virgula*, diminutive of *virga* 'rod.'

vir·i·des·cent /,virəˈdesənt/ ▸*adj.* greenish or becoming green. ▷mid 19th cent.: from late Latin *viridescent-* 'becoming green,' from the verb *viridescere*, from Latin *viridis* 'green.' **—vir·i·des·cence** *n.*

vi·rid·i·an /vəˈridēən/ ▸*n.* a bluish-green pigment consisting of hydrated chromium hydroxide. ■ the bluish-green color of this. ▷late 19th cent.: from Latin *viridis* 'green' (from *virere* 'be green') + -IAN.

vir·ile /ˈvirəl/ ▸*adj.* (of a man) having strength, energy, and a strong sex drive. See note at MALE. ■ having or characterized by strength and energy: *a strong, virile performance of the Mass.* ▷late 15th cent. (in the sense 'characteristic of a man'): from French *viril* or Latin *virilis*, from *vir* 'man.' **—vi·ril·i·ty** /vəˈrilitē/ *n.*

vir·il·ism /ˈvirə,lizəm/ ▸*n. Medicine* the condition that results from virilization.

vir·il·i·za·tion /,virələˈzāsʜən/ ▸*n. Medicine* the development of male physical characteristics (such as muscle bulk, body hair, and deep voice) in a female or precociously in a boy, typically as a result of excess androgen production.

vi·ri·no /viˈrēnō; və-/ ▸*n.* (*pl.* **-nos**) *Microbiology* a hypothetical infectious particle postulated as the cause of scrapie, BSE, and Creutzfeldt–Jakob disease, consisting of noncoding nucleic acid in a protective coat made from host cell proteins. Compare with PRION[2]. ▷1970s: from VIRUS + the diminutive suffix *-ino*.

vi·ri·on /ˈvirē,än; ˈvī-/ ▸*n. Microbiology* the complete, infective form of a virus outside a host cell, with a core of RNA or DNA and a capsid. ▷1950s: from VIRUS + -ON.

vi·roid /ˈvī,roid/ ▸*n. Microbiology* an infectious entity affecting plants, smaller than a virus and consisting only of nucleic acid without a protein coat.

vi·rol·o·gy /vīˈräləjē/ ▸*n.* the branch of science that deals with the study of viruses. **—vi·ro·log·i·cal** /,vīrəˈläjikəl/ *adj.* **—vi·ro·log·i·cal·ly** *adv.* **—vi·rol·o·gist** /-jist/ *n.*

vir·tu /,vərˈto͞o/ (also **ver·tu**) ▸*n.* **1** knowledge of or expertise in the fine arts. ■ curios or objets d'art collectively. **2** *poetic/literary* the good qualities inherent in a person or thing. ▷early 18th cent.: from Italian *virtù* 'virtue'; the variant *vertu* is an alteration, as if from French.

▸*PHRASE* □ **article** (or **object**) **of virtu** an article that is interesting because of its antiquity, beauty, quality of workmanship, etc.

vir·tu·al /ˈvərcʜo͞oəl/ ▸*adj.* almost or nearly as described, but not completely or according to strict definition: *the virtual absence of border controls.* ■ *Computing* not physically existing as such but made by software to appear to do so: *a virtual computer.* See also VIRTUAL REALITY. ■ *Optics* relating to the points at which rays would meet if produced backward. ■ *Physics* denoting particles or interactions with extremely short lifetimes and (owing to the uncertainty principle) indefinitely great energies, postulated as intermediates in some processes. ▷late Middle English (also in the sense 'possessing certain virtues'): from medieval Latin *virtualis*, from Latin *virtus* 'virtue,' suggested by late Latin *virtuosus*. **—vir·tu·al·i·ty** /,vərcʜo͞oˈalitē/ *n.*

vir·tu·al com·mun·i·ty ▸*n.* a community of people sharing common interests, ideas, and feelings over the Internet.

vir·tu·al im·age ▸*n. Optics* an optical image formed from the apparent divergence of light rays from a point, as opposed to an image formed from their actual divergence.

vir·tu·al·ize /ˈvərcʜo͞oə,līz/ ▸*v.* convert (something) to a computer-generated simulation of reality: [*trans.*] *traditional universities have begun to virtualize parts of their curricula* | [*intrans.*] *our method makes it easy to virtualize.* **—vir·tu·al·i·za·tion** *n.* **—vir·tu·a·li·zer** *n.*

vir·tu·al·ly /ˈvərcʜə(wə)lē/ ▸*adv.* nearly; almost: *virtually all those arrested were accused* | *the college became virtually bankrupt.* ■ *Computing* by means of virtual reality techniques.

vir·tu·al mem·o·ry (also **vir·tu·al stor·age**) ▸*n. Computing* memory that appears to exist as main storage although most of it is supported by data held in secondary storage, transfer between the two being made automatically as required.

vir·tu·al of·fice ▸*n.* the operational domain of any business or organization whose work force includes a significant proportion of workers using technology to perform their work at home.

vir·tu·al pet ▸*n.* another term for CYBERPET.

vir·tu·al pri·vate net·work (abbr.: **VPN**) ▸*n. Computing* a method employing encryption to provide secure access to a remote computer over the Internet.

vir·tu·al re·al·i·ty ▸*n. Computing* the computer-generated simulation of a three-dimensional image or environment that can be interacted with in a seemingly real or physical way by a person using special electronic equipment, such as a helmet with a screen inside or gloves fitted with sensors.

vir·tue /ˈvərcʜo͞o/ ▸*n.* **1** behavior showing high moral standards: *paragons of virtue.* See note at GOODNESS. ■ a quality considered morally good or desirable in a person: *patience is a virtue.* ■ a good or useful quality of a thing: *Mike was extolling the virtues of the car* | *there's* **no virtue in** *suffering in silence.* ■ *archaic* virginity or chastity, esp. of a woman. **2** (**virtues**) (in traditional Christian angelology) the seventh highest order of the ninefold celestial hierarchy. ▷Middle English: from Old French *vertu*, from Latin *virtus* 'valor, merit, moral perfection,' from *vir* 'man.' **—vir·tue·less** *adj.*

▸*PHRASES* □ **by** (or **in**) **virtue of** because or as a result of. □ **make a virtue of** derive benefit or advantage from submitting to (an unwelcome obligation or unavoidable circumstance).

vir·tu·o·so /,vərcʜo͞oˈōsō/ ▸*n.* (*pl.* **-si** /-sē/ or **-sos**) a person highly skilled in music or another artistic pursuit: *a celebrated clarinet virtuoso* | [as *adj.*] *virtuoso guitar playing.* ■ a person with a special knowledge of or interest in works of art or curios. ▷early 17th cent.: from Italian, literally 'learned, skillful,' from late Latin *virtuosus* (see VIRTUOUS). **—vir·tu·os·ic** /-ˈäsik; -ˈōsik/ *adj.* **—vir·tu·os·i·ty** /-ˈäsitē/ *n.*

vir·tu·ous /ˈvərcʜəwəs/ ▸*adj.* having or showing high moral standards: *she considered herself very virtuous because she neither drank nor smoked.* See note at MORAL. ■ *archaic* (esp. of a woman) chaste. ▷Middle English: from Old French *vertuous*, from late Latin *virtuosus*, from *virtus* 'virtue.' **—vir·tu·ous·ly** *adv.* **—vir·tu·ous·ness** *n.*

vir·u·lence gene ▸*n.* a gene whose presence or activity in an organism's genome is responsible for the pathogenicity of an infective agent.

vir·u·lent /ˈvir(y)ələnt/ ▸*adj.* **1** (of a disease or poison) extremely severe or harmful in its effects. ■ (of a pathogen, esp. a virus) highly infective. **2** bitterly hostile: *a virulent attack on liberalism.* ▷late Middle English (originally describing a poisoned wound): from Latin *virulentus*, from *virus* 'poison' (see VIRUS). **—vir·u·lence** *n.* **—vir·u·lent·ly** *adv.*

vi·rus /ˈvīrəs/ ▸*n.* an infective agent that typically consists of a nucleic acid molecule in a protein coat, is too small to be seen by light microscopy, and is able to multiply only within the living cells of a host: [as *adj.*] *a virus infection.* ■ *informal* an infection or disease caused by such an agent. ■ *figurative* a harmful or corrupting influence: *the virus of cruelty that is latent in all human beings.* ■ (also **com·pu·ter vi·rus**) a piece of code that is capable of copying itself and typically has a detrimental effect, such as corrupting the system or destroying data. ▷late Middle English (denoting the venom of a snake): from Latin, literally 'slimy liquid, poison.' The earlier medical sense, superseded by the current use as a result of improved scientific understanding, was 'a substance produced in the body as the result of disease, esp. one that is capable of infecting others with the same disease.'

Vis. ▸*abbr.* Viscount.

vi·sa /ˈvēzə/ ▸*n.* an endorsement on a passport indicating that the holder is allowed to enter, leave, or stay for a specified period of time in a country. ▷mid 19th cent.: via French from Latin *visa*, past participle (neuter plural) of *videre* 'to see.'

vis·age /ˈvizij/ ▸*n.* [usu. in *sing.*] *poetic/literary* a person's face, with reference to the form or proportions of the features: *an elegant, angular visage.* ■ a person's facial expression: *there was something hidden behind his visage of cheerfulness.* ■ *figurative* the surface of an object presented to view: *the moonlit visage of the port's whitewashed buildings.* ▷Middle English: via Old French from Latin *visus* 'sight,' from *videre* 'to see.' **—vis·aged** *adj.* [in *combination*] *a stern-visaged old man.*

Vi·sā·kha /viˈsäkə/ ▸*n.* variant spelling of VESAK.

Vi·sa·kha·pat·nam /vi,sʜäkəˈpətnəm/ a port on the coast of Andhra Pradesh, in southeastern India; pop. 750,000.

Vi·sa·lia /viˈsālyə; vī-/ a city in south central California, in the San Joaquin Valley; pop. 75,636.

vis-à-vis /ˈvēz ə ˈvē/ ▸*prep.* in relation to; with regard to: *many agencies now have a unit to deal with women's needs vis-à-vis employment.* ■ as compared with; as opposed to: *the advantage for U.S. exports is the value of the dollar vis-à-vis other currencies.*

▸*adv. archaic* in a position facing a specified or implied subject: *he was there* **vis-à-vis with** *Miss Arundel.*

▸*n.* (*pl.* same) **1** a person or group occupying a corresponding position to that of another person or group in a different area or domain; a counterpart: *his admiration for the U.S. armed services extends to their vis-à-vis, the Russian military.* **2** a face-to-face meeting: *the dreaded vis-à-vis with his boss.* ▷mid 18th cent.: French, literally 'face to face,' from Old French *vis* 'face.'

USAGE The expression **vis-à-vis** literally means 'face to face.' Avoid using it to mean 'about, concerning,' as in *he wanted to talk to me vis-à-vis next weekend.* In the sense 'in contrast, comparison, or relation to,' however, **vis-à-vis** is generally acceptable: *let us consider government regulations vis-à-vis employment rates.*

Visc. ▸*abbr.* Viscount.

vis·ca·cha /viˈskäcʜə/ ▸*n.* a large South American burrowing rodent of the chinchilla family, sometimes hunted for its fur and flesh. • Genera *Lagidium* and *Lagostomus*, family Chinchillidae: four species. ▷early 17th cent.: via Spanish from Quechua *(h)uiscacha*.

vis·cer·a /ˈvisərə/ ▸*plural n.* (*sing.* **vis·cus** /ˈviskəs/) the internal organs in the main cavities of the body, esp. those in the abdomen, e.g., the intestines. ▷mid 17th cent.: from Latin, plural of *viscus* (see VISCUS).

vis·cer·al /ˈvis(ə)rəl/ ▸*adj.* of or relating to the viscera: *the visceral nervous system.* ■ relating to deep inward feelings rather than to the intellect: *the voters' visceral fear of change.* **—vis·cer·al·ly** *adv.*

vis·cer·o·trop·ic /,visərəˈtrōpik; -ˈträpik/ ▸*adj.* (of a microorganism) tending to attack or affect the viscera.

vis·cid /ˈvisid/ ▸*adj.* glutinous; sticky: *the viscid mucus lining of the intestine.* ▷mid 17th cent.: from late Latin *viscidus*, from Latin *viscum* 'birdlime.' **—vis·cid·i·ty** /vəˈsidətē/ *n.*

vis·co·e·las·tic·i·ty /,viskō-i,lasˈtisitē; -,ēla-/ ▸*n. Physics* the property of a substance of exhibiting both elastic and viscous behavior, the application of stress causing temporary deformation if the stress is quickly removed but permanent deformation if it is maintained. **—vis·co·e·las·tic** /,-iˈlastik/ *adj.*

vis·com·e·ter /vi'skämətər/ ▸*n.* an instrument for measuring the viscosity of liquids. ▷late 19th cent.: from late Latin *viscosus* 'viscous' + **-METER**. —**vis·co·met·ric** /ˌviskə'metrik/ *adj.* —**vis·co·met·ri·cal·ly** /ˌviskə'metrik(ə)lē/ *adv.* —**vis·com·e·try** /-ətrē/ *n.*

Vis·con·ti /və'skäntē/, Luchino (1906–76), Italian movie and theater director; full name *Don Luchino Visconti, Conte di Modrone*. His movies include *Obsession* (1942), *The Leopard* (1963), and *Death in Venice* (1971).

vis·cose /'visˌkōs; -ˌkōz/ ▸*n.* a viscous orange-brown solution obtained by treating cellulose with sodium hydroxide and carbon disulfide, used as the basis of manufacturing rayon fiber and transparent cellulose film. ■ rayon fabric or fiber made from this. ▷late 19th cent.: from late Latin *viscosus*, from Latin *viscus* 'birdlime.'

vis·co·sim·e·ter /ˌviskə'simitər/ ▸*n.* another term for **VISCOMETER**.

vis·cos·i·ty /ˌvi'skäsitē/ ▸*n.* (*pl.* **-ties**) the state of being thick, sticky, and semifluid in consistency, due to internal friction. ■ a quantity expressing the magnitude of such friction, as measured by the force per unit area resisting a flow in which parallel layers unit distance apart have unit speed relative to one another. ▷late Middle English: from Old French *viscosite* or medieval Latin *viscositas*, from late Latin *viscosus* (see **VISCOUS**).

vis·count /'vīˌkount/ ▸*n.* a British nobleman ranking above a baron and below an earl. ▷late Middle English: from Old French *visconte*, from medieval Latin *vicecomes, vicecomit-* (see **VICE-**, **COUNT**[2]). —**vis·count·cy** /-ˌkountsē/ *n.*

vis·count·ess /'vīˌkountəs/ ▸*n.* the wife or widow of a viscount. ■ a woman holding the rank of viscount in her own right.

vis·count·y /'vīˌkountē/ ▸*n.* the land under the authority of a viscount.

vis·cous /'viskəs/ ▸*adj.* having a thick, sticky consistency between solid and liquid; having a high viscosity: *viscous lava.* ▷late Middle English: from Anglo-Norman French *viscous* or late Latin *viscosus*, from Latin *viscum* 'birdlime.' —**vis·cous·ly** *adv.* —**vis·cous·ness** *n.*

vis·cus /'viskəs/ ▸ singular form of **VISCERA**. ▷Latin.

vise /vīs/ (*Brit.* **vice**) ▸*n.* a metal tool with movable jaws that are used to hold an object firmly in place while work is done on it, typically attached to a workbench. ▷Middle English (denoting a screw or winch): from Old French *vis*, from Latin *vitis* 'vine.' —**vise·like** *adj.*

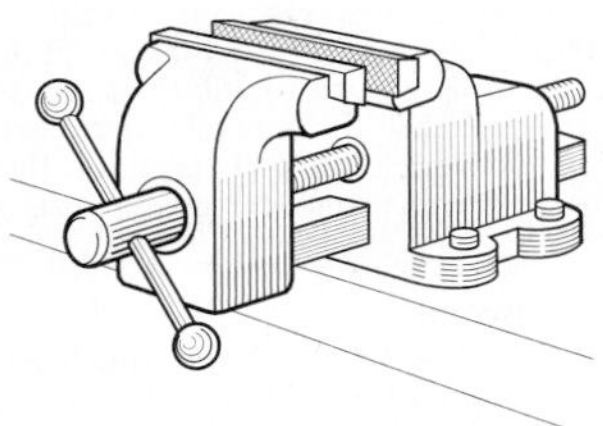

vise

Vish·nu /'vishno͞o/ *Hinduism* a god, originally a minor Vedic god, now regarded by his worshipers as the supreme deity and savior, by others as the preserver of the cosmos in a triad with Brahma and Shiva. Vishnu is considered by Hindus to have had nine earthly incarnations or avatars, including Rama, Krishna, and the historical Buddha; the tenth avatar will herald the end of the world. ▷from Sanskrit *Viṣṇu*. —**Vish·nu·ism** /-ˌizəm/ *n.* —**Vish·nu·ite** /-ˌīt/ *n.* & *adj.*

vis·i·bil·i·ty /ˌvizə'bilitē/ ▸*n.* the state of being able to see or be seen: *a reduction in police presence and visibility on the streets.* ■ the distance one can see as determined by light and weather conditions: *visibility was down to 15 yards.* ■ the degree to which something has attracted general attention; prominence: *the issue began to lose its visibility.* ▷late Middle English: from French *visibilite* or late Latin *visibilitas*, from Latin *visibilis* (see **VISIBLE**).

vis·i·ble /'vizəbəl/ ▸*adj.* **1** able to be seen: *the church spire is visible from miles away.* ■ *Physics* (of light) within the range of wavelengths to which the eye is sensitive. ■ able to be perceived or noticed easily: *a visible improvement.* ■ in a position of public prominence: *a highly visible member of the royal entourage.* **2** of or relating to imports or exports of tangible commodities: *the visible trade gap.* ▷Middle English: from Old French, or from Latin *visibilis*, from *videre* 'to see.' —**vis·i·ble·ness** *n.* —**vis·i·bly** /-blē/ *adv. he was visibly uncomfortable.*

Vis·i·goth /'vizəˌgäth/ ▸*n.* a member of the branch of the Goths who invaded the Roman Empire between the 3rd and 5th centuries AD and ruled much of Spain until overthrown by the Moors in 711. ▷from late Latin *Visigothus*, the first element possibly meaning 'west' (compare with **OSTROGOTH**). —**Vis·i·goth·ic** /ˌvizə'gäthik/ *adj.*

vi·sion /'vizhən/ ▸*n.* **1** the faculty or state of being able to see: *she had defective vision.* ■ the ability to think about or plan the future with imagination or wisdom: *the organization had lost its vision and direction.* ■ a mental image of what the future will or could be like: *a socialist vision of society.* ■ the images seen on a television screen. **2** an experience of seeing someone or something in a dream or trance, or as a supernatural apparition: *the idea came to him in a vision.* ■ (often **visions**) a vivid mental image, esp. a fanciful one of the future: *he **had visions of** becoming the Elton John of his time.* ■ a person or sight of unusual beauty.
▸*v.* [*trans.*] *rare* imagine. ▷Middle English (denoting a supernatural apparition): via Old French from Latin *visio(n-)*, from *videre* 'to see.' —**vi·sion·al** /-zhənl/ *adj.* —**vi·sion·less** *adj.*

vi·sion·ar·y /'vizhəˌnerē/ ▸*adj.* **1** (esp. of a person) thinking about or planning the future with imagination or wisdom: *a visionary leader.* ■ *archaic* (of a scheme or idea) not practical. **2** of, relating to, or able to see visions in a dream or trance, or as a supernatural apparition: *a visionary experience.* ■ *archaic* existing only in a vision or in the imagination.
▸*n.* (*pl.* **-ar·ies**) a person with original ideas about what the future will or could be like. —**vi·sion·ar·i·ness** *n.*

vi·sion quest ▸*n.* an attempt to achieve a vision of a future guardian spirit, traditionally undertaken at puberty by boys of the Plains Indian peoples, typically through fasting or self-torture.

vis·it /'vizit/ ▸*v.* (**-it·ed**, **-it·ing**) [*trans.*] **1** go to see and spend time with (someone) socially: *I came to visit my grandmother.* ■ go to see and spend time in (a place) as a tourist. ■ stay temporarily with (someone) or at (a place) as a guest: *we hope you enjoy your stay and will visit us again* | [*intrans.*] *I don't live here—I'm only visiting.* ■ go to see (someone or something) for a specific purpose, such as to make an inspection or to receive or give professional advice or help: *inspectors visit all the hotels.* ■ [*intrans.*] (**visit with**) go to see (someone) socially: *he went out to visit with his pals.* ■ [*intrans.*] *informal* chat: *there was nothing to do but visit with one another.* ■ go to (a Web site or Web page): *visit us at www.flycreekcidermill.com.* ■ (chiefly in biblical use) (of God) come to (a person or place) in order to bring comfort or salvation. **2** (often **be visited**) inflict (something harmful or unpleasant) on someone: *the mockery **visited upon** him by his schoolmates.* ■ (of something harmful or unpleasant) afflict (someone): *they were **visited with** epidemics of a strange disease.* ■ *archaic* punish (a person or a wrongful act): *offenses were visited with the loss of eyes or ears.*
▸*n.* an act of going or coming to see a person or place socially, as a tourist, or for some other purpose: *a visit to the doctor.* ■ a temporary stay with a person or at a place. ■ an informal conversation. ▷Middle English: from Old French *visiter* or Latin *visitare* 'go to see,' frequentative of *visare* 'to view,' from *videre* 'to see.' —**vis·it·a·ble** *adj.*

vis·it·a·bil·i·ty /ˌvizitə'bilitē/ ▸*n.* a measure of a place's ease of access for people with disabilities: *we endeavor to create a community that is not only accessible to disabled persons, but is also a model of visitability.* —**vis·it·a·ble** *adj.*

vis·it·ant /'vizətənt/ ▸*n.* *chiefly poetic/literary* a supernatural being or agency; an apparition. ■ *archaic* a visitor or guest. ■ *Ornithology* a visitor.
▸*adj.* *archaic* or *poetic/literary* paying a visit: *the housekeeper was abrupt with the poor visitant niece.* ▷late 16th cent.: from French, or from Latin *visitant-* 'going to see,' from the verb *visitare* (see **VISIT**).

vis·it·a·tion /ˌvizə'tāshən/ ▸*n.* **1** an official or formal visit, in particular: ■ (in church use) an official visit of inspection, esp. one by a bishop to a church in the bishop's diocese. ■ the appearance of a divine or supernatural being. ■ a gathering with the family of a deceased person before the funeral. ■ *Law* a divorced person's right to spend time with their children in the custody of a former spouse. **2** a disaster or difficulty regarded as a divine punishment: *a visitation of the plague.* **3** (**the Visitation**) the visit of the Virgin Mary to Elizabeth related in Luke 1:39–56. ■ the festival commemorating this on May 31 (formerly July 2). ▷Middle English: from Old French, or from late Latin *visitatio(n-)*, from the verb *visitare* (see **VISIT**).

vis·it·a·to·ri·al /ˌvizətə'tôrēəl/ ▸*adj.* another term for **VISITORIAL**.

vis·it·ing /'viziting/ ▸*adj.* [*attrib.*] (of a person) on a visit to a person or place: *a visiting speaker.* ■ (of an academic) working for a fixed period of time at another institution: *a visiting professor.*

vis·it·ing card ▸*n.* British term for **CALLING CARD**.

vis·it·ing fire·man ▸*n.* *informal* an important visitor to a city or organization who is given an official welcome and especially cordial treatment. ■ a visitor or tourist who is accorded special attention because they are expected to spend extravagantly.

vis·it·ing nurse ▸*n.* a nurse who visits and treats patients in their homes, operating as part of a social service agency.

vis·it·ing pro·fes·sor ▸*n.* a professor on a short-term contract to teach at a college or university other than the one that mainly employs them.

vis·i·tor /'vizitər/ ▸*n.* a person visiting a person or place, esp. socially or as a tourist. ■ (usu. **visitors**) a member of a sports team on tour or playing away from home. ■ *chiefly Brit.* a person with the right or duty of occasionally inspecting and reporting on a college or other academic institution. ■ *Ornithology* a migratory bird present in a locality for only part of the year. ▷late Middle English: from Anglo-Norman French *visitour*, from Old French *visiter* (see **VISIT**).

vis·i·to·ri·al /ˌvizə'tôrēəl/ ▸*adj.* of or relating to an official visitor or visitation: *visitorial jurisdiction.*

Vis·king /'visking/ (also **Vis·king tub·ing**) ▸*n.* *trademark* a type of seamless cellulose tubing used as a membrane in dialysis and as an edible casing for sausages. ▷1930s: named after the *Visking* Corporation of Chicago, Illinois.

vis me·di·ca·trix na·tu·rae /'vis ˌmedi'kātriks nə'to͝orē; 'wēs ˌmedi'kātriks nä'to͝orˌī/ ▸*n.* the body's natural ability to heal itself. ▷Latin, 'the healing power of nature.'

vis·na /'visnə/ ▸*n.* *Veterinary Medicine* a fatal disease of sheep in which there is progressive demyelination of neurons in the brain and spinal cord, caused by a virus. ▷1950s: from Old Norse, 'to wither.'

vi·sor /'vīzər/ (also **vi·zor**) ▸*n.* a stiff brim at the front of a cap. ■ a movable part of a helmet that can be pulled down to cover the face. ■ a screen for protecting the eyes from unwanted light, esp. one at the top of a vehicle windshield. ■ *historical* a mask. ▷Middle English: from Anglo-Norman French *viser*, from Old French *vis* 'face,' from Latin *visus* (see **VISAGE**). —**vi·sored** *adj.*

Vis·queen /'visˌkwēn/ ▸*n.* *trademark* a durable polyethylene sheeting, used in various building applications and in the manufacture of waterproof household articles. ▷1940s: from **VISKING**, with humorous alteration of *-king* to *-queen*.

VISTA /'vistə/ ▸*abbr.* Volunteers in Service to America.

Vis·ta /'vistə/ a city in southwestern California, north of San Diego; pop. 71,872.

vis·ta /'vistə/ ▸*n.* a pleasing view, esp. one seen through a long, narrow opening: *a vista of church spires.* ■ a mental view of a succession of remembered or anticipated events: *vistas of freedom seemed to open ahead of him.* ▷mid 17th cent.: from Italian, literally 'view,' from *visto* 'seen,' past participle of *vedere* 'see,' from Latin *videre*.

Vis·ta·vi·sion /'vistəˌvizhən/ ▸*n.* *trademark* a form of wide-screen cinematography employing standard 35 mm film in such a way as to give a larger projected image using ordinary methods of projection.

Vis·tu·la /'vischələ/ a river in Poland that rises in the Carpathian Mountains and flows north for 592 miles (940 km) through Cracow and Warsaw, to the Baltic Sea near Gdańsk. Polish name **WISŁA**.

vis·u·al /'vizho͞oəl/ ▸*adj.* of or relating to seeing or sight: *visual perception.*
▸*n.* (usu. **visuals**) a picture, piece of film, or display used to illustrate or accompany something. ▷late Middle English (originally describing a beam imagined to proceed from the eye and make vision possible): from late Latin *visualis*, from Latin *visus* 'sight,' from *videre* 'to see.' The current noun sense dates from the 1950s. —**vis·u·al·i·ty** /ˌvizho͞o'alitē/ *n.* —**vis·u·al·ly** *adv.*

vis·u·al a·cu·i·ty ▸*n.* sharpness of vision, measured by the ability to discern letters or numbers at a given distance according to a fixed standard.

vis·u·al ag·no·sia ▸*n. Medicine* a condition in which a person can see but cannot recognize or interpret visual information, due to a disorder in the parietal lobes.

vis·u·al aid ▸*n.* (usu. **visual aids**) an item of illustrative matter, such as a film, slide, or model, designed to supplement written or spoken information so that it can be understood more easily.

vis·u·al an·gle ▸*n. Optics* the angle formed at the eye by rays from the extremities of an object viewed.

vis·u·al bi·na·ry ▸*n. Astronomy* a binary star of which the components are sufficiently far apart to be resolved by an optical telescope.

vis·u·al cor·tex ▸*n. Anatomy* the part of the cerebral cortex that receives and processes sensory nerve impulses from the eyes.

vis·u·al field ▸*n.* another term for FIELD OF VISION.

vis·u·al·ize /ˈvizʜ(ə)wə,līz/ ▸*v.* [*trans.*] **1** form a mental image of; imagine: *it is not easy to visualize the future.* **2** make (something) visible to the eye: *the cells were better visualized by staining.* —**vis·u·al·iz·a·ble** *adj.* —**vis·u·al·i·za·tion** /,vizʜ(ə)wələˈzāsʜən/ *n.*

vis·u·al pur·ple ▸*n.* another term for RHODOPSIN.

vis·u·al ray ▸*n. Optics* an imaginary line representing the path of light from an object to the eye.

vi·su·o·mo·tor /,vizʜəwōˈmōtər/ ▸*adj.* [*attrib.*] relating to or denoting the coordination of movement and visual perception by the brain.

vis·u·o·spa·tial /,vizʜəwōˈspāsʜəl/ ▸*adj.* [*attrib.*] *Psychology* relating to or denoting the visual perception of the spatial relationships of objects.

vi·ta /ˈvītə; ˈvē-/ ▸*n.* **1** a fresh start or new direction in life, esp. following a powerful emotional experience. **2** a biography or biographical sketch.

vi·tal /ˈvītl/ ▸*adj.* **1** absolutely necessary or important; essential: *secrecy is of vital importance | it is vital that the system is regularly maintained.* ■ indispensable to the continuance of life: *the vital organs.* **2** full of energy; lively: *a beautiful, vital girl.* See note at ALIVE. **3** *archaic* fatal: *the wound is vital.*
▸*n.* (**vitals**) the body's important internal organs, esp. the gut or the genitalia. ■ short for VITAL SIGNS. ▷late Middle English (describing the animating principle of living beings, also in sense 2): via Old French from Latin *vitalis*, from *vita* 'life.' The sense 'essential' dates from the early 17th cent. —**vi·tal·ly** *adv.*

vi·tal ca·pac·i·ty ▸*n.* the greatest volume of air that can be expelled from the lungs after taking the deepest possible breath.

vi·tal force ▸*n.* the energy or spirit that animates living creatures; the soul. ■ *Philosophy* (in some theories, particularly that of Bergson) a hypothetical force, independent of physical and chemical forces, regarded as being the causative factor in the evolution and development of living organisms. [translating French *élan vital*.] ■ a person or thing that gives something vitality and strength: *he was a vital force in British music.*

vi·tal·ism /ˈvītl,izəm/ ▸*n.* the theory that the origin and phenomena of life are dependent on a force or principle distinct from purely chemical or physical forces. ▷early 19th cent.: from French *vitalisme*, or from VITAL + -ISM. —**vi·tal·ist** *n.* & *adj.* —**vi·tal·is·tic** /,vītlˈistik/ *adj.*

vi·tal·i·ty /vīˈtalitē/ ▸*n.* the state of being strong and active; energy: *changes that will give renewed vitality to our democracy.* ■ the power giving continuance of life, present in all living things: *the vitality of seeds.* ▷late 16th cent.: from Latin *vitalitas*, from *vitalis* (see VITAL).

vi·tal·ize /ˈvītl,īz/ ▸*v.* [*trans.*] give strength and energy to: *yoga calms and vitalizes body and mind.* See note at QUICKEN. —**vi·tal·i·za·tion** /,vītl-əˈzāsʜən/ *n.*

vi·tal signs /ˈvīdl sīnz/ ▸*plural n.* clinical measurements, specifically pulse rate, temperature, respiration rate, and blood pressure, that indicate the state of a patient's essential body functions.

vi·tal sta·tis·tics /ˈvīdl stəˈtistiks/ ▸*plural n.* **1** quantitative data concerning a population, such as the number of births, marriages, and deaths. **2** *informal* the measurements of a woman's bust, waist, and hips.

vi·ta·min /ˈvītəmən/ ▸*n.* any of a group of organic compounds that are essential for normal growth and nutrition and are required in small quantities in the diet because they cannot be synthesized by the body. ▷early 20th cent.: from Latin *vita* 'life' + AMINE, because vitamins were originally thought to contain an amino acid.

vi·ta·min A ▸*n.* another term for RETINOL.

vi·ta·min B ▸*n.* any of a group of substances (the **vitamin B complex**) that are essential for the working of certain enzymes in the body and, although not chemically related, are generally found together in the same foods. They include thiamine (**vitamin B_1**), riboflavin (**vitamin B_2**), pyridoxine (**vitamin B_6**), and cyanocobalamin (**vitamin B_{12}**).

vi·ta·min C ▸*n.* another term for ASCORBIC ACID.

vi·ta·min D ▸*n.* any of a group of vitamins found in liver and fish oils, essential for the absorption of calcium and the prevention of rickets in children and osteomalacia in adults. They include calciferol (**vitamin D_2**) and cholecalciferol (**vitamin D_3**).

vi·ta·min E ▸*n.* another term for TOCOPHEROL.

vi·ta·min H ▸*n.* another term for BIOTIN.

vi·ta·min K ▸*n.* any of a group of vitamins found mainly in green leaves and essential for the blood-clotting process. They include phylloquinone (**vitamin K_1**) and menaquinone (**vitamin K_2**).

vi·ta·min M ▸*n.* another term for FOLIC ACID.

vi·ta·min P ▸*n.* the bioflavonoids, regarded collectively as a vitamin.

Vi·tebsk /ˈvētipsk/ Russian name for VITSEBSK.

vi·tel·li /vəˈtel,ī; vī-; -ˈtelē/ ▸ plural form of VITELLUS.

vi·tel·lin /vəˈtelən; vī-/ ▸*n. Biochemistry* the chief protein constituent of egg yolk. ▷mid 19th cent.: from VITELLUS + -IN[1].

vi·tel·line /vəˈtelən; vī-; -,ēn; -,īn/ ▸*adj. Zoology* or *Embryology* of or relating to the yolk (or yolk sac) of an egg or embryo, or to yolk-producing organs. ▷late Middle English (in the sense 'colored like egg yolk'): from medieval Latin *vitellinus*, from *vitellus* (see VITELLUS).

vi·tel·line mem·brane ▸*n. Embryology* a transparent membrane surrounding and secreted by the fertilized ovum, preventing the entry of further spermatozoa.

Vi·tel·li·us /vəˈtelēəs/, Aulus (15–69), Roman emperor. He was acclaimed emperor in January 69 by the legions in Germany during the civil wars that followed the death of Nero. He defeated Otho but was killed by the supporters of Vespasian.

vi·tel·lo·gen·in /vīˈtelə,jenən; və-/ ▸*n. Biochemistry* a protein present in the blood, from which the substance of egg yolk is derived. ▷1960s: from VITELLUS + -GEN + -IN[1].

vi·tel·lus /vəˈteləs; vī-/ ▸*n. Embryology* the yolk of an egg or ovum. ▷early 18th cent.: from Latin, literally 'yolk.'

vi·tex /ˈvīteks/ ▸*n.* **1** another term for CHASTE TREE. **2** a medicinal preparation extracted from the berries of the chaste tree, used to treat gynecological conditions.

vi·ti·ate /ˈvisʜē,āt/ ▸*v.* [*trans.*] *formal* spoil or impair the quality or efficiency of: *development programs have been vitiated by the rise in population.* ■ destroy or impair the legal validity of. ▷mid 16th cent.: from Latin *vitiat-* 'impaired,' from the verb *vitiare*, from *vitium* (see VICE[1]). —**vi·ti·a·tion** /,visʜēˈāsʜən/ *n.* —**vi·ti·a·tor** /-,ātər/ *n.*

vit·i·cul·ture /ˈviti,kəlcʜər/ ▸*n.* the cultivation of grapevines. ■ the study of grape cultivation. ▷late 19th cent.: from Latin *vitis* 'vine' + CULTURE, on the pattern of words such as *agriculture*. —**vit·i·cul·tur·al** /,vitiˈkəlcʜərəl/ *adj.* —**vit·i·cul·tur·ist** /-rist/ *n.*

Vi·ti Le·vu /ˈvētē ˈlā,vōō; ˈlev,ōō/ the largest of the Fiji islands. Its chief settlement is Suva.

vit·i·li·go /,vitlˈīgō; -ˈēgō/ ▸*n. Medicine* a condition in which the pigment is lost from areas of the skin, causing whitish patches, often with no clear cause. Also called LEUCODERMA. ▷late 16th cent.: from Latin, literally 'tetter.'

Vi·to·ria /viˈtôrēə/ a city in northeastern Spain, capital of the Basque Provinces; pop. 209,000.

Vi·tó·ri·a /viˈtôrēə/ a port in eastern Brazil, capital of the state of Espírito Santo; pop. 276,000.

vit·rec·to·my /vəˈtrektəmē/ ▸*n.* the surgical operation of removing the vitreous humor from the eyeball.

vit·re·ous /ˈvitrēəs/ ▸*adj.* like glass in appearance or physical properties. ■ (of a substance) derived from or containing glass: *the toilet and bidet are made of vitreous china.* ▷late Middle English: from Latin *vitreus* (from *vitrum* 'glass') + -OUS. —**vit·re·ous·ness** *n.*

vit·re·ous hu·mor ▸*n.* the transparent jellylike tissue filling the eyeball behind the lens. Compare with AQUEOUS HUMOR.

vi·tres·cent /vəˈtresənt/ ▸*adj. rare* capable of or susceptible to being turned into glass. ▷mid 18th cent.: from Latin *vitrum* 'glass' + -ESCENT. —**vi·tres·cence** *n.*

vit·ri·form /ˈvitrə,fôrm/ ▸*adj.* having the form or appearance of glass.

vit·ri·fy /ˈvitrə,fī/ ▸*v.* (**-fies**, **-fied**) [*trans.*] (often **be vitrified**) convert (something) into glass or a glasslike substance, typically by exposure to heat. ▷late Middle English: from French *vitrifier* or based on Latin *vitrum* 'glass.' —**vit·ri·fac·tion** /,vitrəˈfaksʜən/ *n.* —**vit·ri·fi·a·ble** /ˈvitrə,fīəbəl; ,vitrəˈfī-/ *adj.* —**vit·ri·fi·ca·tion** /,vitrəfiˈkāsʜən/ *n.*

vi·trine /vəˈtrēn/ ▸*n.* a glass display case. ▷French, from *vitre* 'glass pane.'

vit·ri·ol /ˈvitrēəl; -,ôl/ ▸*n. archaic* or *poetic/literary* sulfuric acid. ■ *figurative* cruel and bitter criticism: *her mother's sudden gush of fury and vitriol.* ▷late Middle English (denoting the sulfate of various metals): from Old French, or from medieval Latin *vitriolum*, from Latin *vitrum* 'glass.' —**vit·ri·ol·ic** /,vitrēˈälik/ *adj.*

Vi·tru·vi·us /vəˈtrōōvēəs/ (*fl.* 1st century BC), Roman architect and military engineer; full name *Marcus Vitruvius Pollio*. He wrote a comprehensive 10-volume treatise on architecture.

Vi·tsebsk /ˈvēt,sepsk/ a city in northeastern Belarus; pop. 356,000. Russian name VITEBSK.

vit·ta /ˈvitə/ ▸*n.* (*pl.* **vit·tae** /ˈvitē; ˈvitī/) **1** *Botany* an oil tube in the fruit of some plants. **2** *Zoology* a band or stripe of color. ▷early 19th cent.: from Latin, literally 'band, chaplet.'

vit·tle ▸*n. archaic* variant spelling of VICTUAL.

vi·tu·per·ate /vəˈt(y)ōōpə,rāt; vī-/ ▸*v.* [*trans.*] *archaic* blame or insult (someone) in strong or violent language. See note at SCOLD. ▷mid 16th cent.: from Latin *vituperat-* 'censured, disparaged,' from the verb *vituperare*, from *vitium* 'fault' + *parare* 'prepare.' —**vi·tu·per·a·tor** /-,rātər/ *n.*

vi·tu·per·a·tion /və,t(y)ōōpəˈrāsʜən; vī-/ ▸*n.* bitter and abusive language: *no one else attracted such vituperation from him.*

vi·tu·per·a·tive /vəˈt(y)ōōpə,rātiv; vī-; -p(ə)rətiv/ ▸*adj.* bitter and abusive: *the criticism soon turned into a vituperative attack.*

Vi·tus, St. /ˈvītəs/ (died *c.*300), Christian martyr. He is the patron of those who suffer from epilepsy and certain nervous disorders, including St. Vitus's dance (Sydenham's chorea). Feast day, June 15.

vi·va /ˈvēvə/ ▸*exclam.* long live! (used to express acclaim or support for a specified person or thing): *"Viva Mexico!"*
▸*n.* a cry of this as a salute or cheer. ▷Italian and Spanish.

vi·va·ce /vēˈvä,cʜā; -cʜē/ *Music* ▸*adv.* & *adj.* (esp. as a direction) in a lively and brisk manner.
▸*n.* a passage or movement marked to be performed in this manner. ▷Italian, 'brisk, lively,' from Latin *vivax*, *vivac-*.

vi·va·cious /vəˈvāsʜəs; vī-/ ▸*adj.* (esp. of a woman) attractively lively and animated. ▷mid 17th cent.: from Latin *vivax*, *vivac-* 'lively, vigorous' (from *vivere* 'to live') + -IOUS. —**vi·va·cious·ly** *adv.* —**vi·va·cious·ness** *n.* —**vi·vac·i·ty** /vəˈvasitē; vī-/ *n.*

Vi·val·di /viˈväldē; -ˈvôldē/, Antonio (Lucio) (1678–1741), Italian composer and violinist; known as **the Red Priest.** His feeling for texture and melody is evident in his numerous compositions such as *The Four Seasons* (concerto, 1725).

vi·var·i·um /vīˈve(ə)rēəm/ ▸*n.* (*pl.* **-var·i·a** /-ˈve(ə)rēə/) an enclosure, container, or structure adapted or prepared for keeping animals under seminatural conditions for observation or study or as pets; an aquarium or terrarium. ▷early 17th cent.: from Latin, literally 'game enclosure, fishpond,' from *vivus* 'living,' from *vivere* 'to live.'

vi·vat /ˈvē,vat; -,vät; ˈvī,vat/ ▸*exclam.* & *n.* Latin term for VIVA.

vi·va vo·ce /,vēvə ˈvōcʜā; ,vīvə ˈvōsē/ ▸*adj.* (esp. of an examination) oral rather than written.
▸*adv.* orally rather than in writing.
▸*n.* (also **vi·va**) *Brit.* an oral examination, typically for an academic qualification. ▷mid 16th cent.: from medieval Latin, literally 'with the living voice.'

vive la dif·fé·rence /ˈvēv(ə) lä ,difəˈräns/ ▸*exclam. chiefly humorous* an expression of approval of difference, esp. that between the sexes. ▷from French, literally 'long live the difference.'

vi·ver·id /vīˈverid; vi-/ ▸*n. Zoology* a mammal of the

V

civet family (Viverridae). ▷early 20th cent.: from modern Latin *Viverridae*, from Latin *viverra* 'ferret.'

viv·i·an·ite /ˈvivēəˌnīt/ ▸n. a mineral consisting of a phosphate of iron that occurs as a secondary mineral in ore deposits. It is colorless when fresh but becomes blue or green with oxidization. ▷early 19th cent.: named after John H. *Vivian* (1785–1855), British mineralogist, + -ITE[1].

viv·id /ˈvivid/ ▸adj. **1** producing powerful feelings or strong, clear images in the mind: *memories of that evening were still vivid* | *a vivid description.* See note at GRAPHIC. ■ (of a color) intensely deep or bright. **2** *archaic* (of a person or animal) lively and vigorous. ▷mid 17th cent.: from Latin *vividus*, from *vivere* 'to live.' —**viv·id·ly** *adv.* —**viv·id·ness** *n.*

viv·i·fy /ˈvivəˌfī/ ▸v. (**-fies, -fied**) [*trans.*] enliven or animate: *outings vivify learning for children.* ▷late Middle English: from French *vivifier*, from late Latin *vivificare*, from Latin *vivus* 'living,' from *vivere* 'to live.' —**viv·i·fi·ca·tion** /ˌvivəfiˈkāSHən/ *n.*

vi·vip·a·rous /vīˈvip(ə)rəs; vi-/ ▸adj. *Zoology* (of an animal) bringing forth live young that have developed inside the body of the parent. Compare with OVIPAROUS and OVOVIVIPAROUS. ■ *Botany* (of a plant) reproducing from buds that form plantlets while still attached to the parent plant, or from seeds that germinate within the fruit. ▷mid 17th cent.: from Latin *viviparus* (from *vivus* 'alive' + *-parus* 'bearing') + -OUS. —**viv·i·par·i·ty** /ˌvivəˈparitē; ˌvīvə-/ *n.* —**vi·vip·a·rous·ly** *adv.*

viv·i·sect /ˈvivəˌsekt; ˌvivəˈsekt/ ▸v. [*trans.*] perform vivisection on (an animal) (used only by people who are opposed to the practice). ▷mid 19th cent.: back-formation from VIVISECTION. —**viv·i·sec·tor** /-tər/ *n.*

viv·i·sec·tion /ˌvivəˈsekSHən/ ▸n. the practice of performing operations on live animals for the purpose of experimentation or scientific research (used only by people who are opposed to such work). ■ *figurative* ruthlessly sharp and detailed criticism or analysis: *the vivisection of America's seamy underbelly.* ▷early 18th cent.: from Latin *vivus* 'living,' on the pattern of *dissection.* —**viv·i·sec·tion·ist** /-ist/ *n.* & *adj.*

vix·en /ˈviksən/ ▸n. a female fox. ■ a spiteful or quarrelsome woman. ▷late Middle English *fixen*, perhaps from the Old English adjective *fyxen* 'of a fox.' The *v-* is from the form of the word in southern English dialect. —**vix·en·ish** *adj.*

Vi·yel·la /vīˈelə/ ▸n. *trademark* a fabric made from a twilled mixture of cotton and wool. ▷late 19th cent.: from *Via Gellia*, a valley in Derbyshire, north central England, where it was first made.

viz. /viz/ or said as /ˈnāmlē/ ▸adv. namely; in other words (used esp. to introduce a gloss or explanation): *the first music reproducing media, viz., the music box and the player piano.* ▷abbreviation of VIDELICET, *z* being a medieval Latin symbol for *-et.*

viz·ard /ˈvizərd/ ▸n. *archaic* a mask or disguise. ▷mid 16th cent.: alteration of VISOR.

vi·zier /vəˈzi(ə)r/ ▸n. *historical* a high official in some Muslim countries, esp. in Turkey under Ottoman rule. ▷mid 16th cent.: via Turkish from Arabic *wazīr* 'caliph's chief counselor.' —**vi·zier·ate** /-ˈzi(ə)rit; -ˈzi(ə)rˌāt/ *n.* —**vi·zier·i·al** /-ˈzi(ə)rēəl/ *adj.* —**vi·zier·ship** /-ˌSHip/ *n.*

vi·zor ▸n. variant spelling of VISOR.

vizs·la /ˈvizHlə; ˈvēzlə/ ▸n. a dog of a breed of golden-brown pointer with large drooping ears. ▷1940s: from the name of a town in Hungary.

VJ ▸abbr. video jockey.

V-J Day ▸n. the day (August 15) in 1945 on which Japan ceased fighting in World War II, or the day (September 2) when Japan formally surrendered. ▷*V-J*, abbreviation of *Victory over Japan.*

VLA ▸abbr. Very Large Array (telescope).

Vlach /vläk; vlak/ ▸n. a member of the indigenous population of Romania and Moldova, claiming descent from the inhabitants of the Roman province of Dacia.
▸adj. of or relating to this people. ▷from a Slavic word meaning 'foreigner,' from a Germanic word related to Old English *Wælisc* (see WELSH). Compare with WALLACHIA.

Vla·di·kav·kaz /ˌvladəˌkäfˈkäz; -ˈkäs/ a city in southwestern Russia, capital of the autonomous republic of North Ossetia; pop. 306,000. Former names ORDZHONIKIDZE (1931–44 and 1954–93) and DZAUDZHIKAU (1944–54).

Vlad·i·mir /ˈvladəˌmi(ə)r; vləˈd(y)ēmir/ a city in western Russia, east of Moscow; pop. 353,000.

Vlad·i·mir I (956–1015), grand prince of Kiev 980–1015; known as **Vladimir the Great**; canonized as **St. Vladimir**. His marriage to a sister of the Byzantine emperor Basil II resulted in his conversion to Christianity. Feast day, July 15.

Vla·di·vos·tok /ˌvladəˈväsˌtäk; -vəˈstäk/ a city in southeastern Russia, on the coast of the Sea of Japan, capital of Primorsky; pop. 643,000.

Vla·minck /vləˈmaNGk; -ˈmaNk/, Maurice de (1876–1958), French painter and writer. With Derain and Matisse he became a leading exponent of fauvism.

vlast /vläst/ ▸n. (*pl.* **vla·sti** /-tē/) (in countries of the former USSR) political power or authority. ■ (**the vlasti**) members of the government; people holding political power. ▷Russian.

VLF ▸abbr. very low frequency (denoting radio waves of frequency 3–30 kHz and wavelength 10–100 km).

Vlo·rë /ˈvlôrə/ a port in southwestern Albania, on the Adriatic coast; pop. 56,000. Also called VLONA, Italian name VALONA.

VLSI *Electronics* ▸abbr. very large-scale integration, the process of integrating hundreds of thousands of components on a single silicon chip.

Vl·ta·va /ˈvəltəvə/ a river in the Czech Republic that rises in the Bohemian Forest on the German–Czech border and flows north for 270 miles (435 km), passing through Prague before joining the Elbe River north of the city. German name MOLDAU.

V-mail ▸n. **1** a method of microfilming U.S. soldiers' mail to and from home to cut down on shipping costs during World War II, with "V" standing for "victory." **2** short for VOICEMAIL. **3** short for VIDEOMAIL.

VMD ▸abbr. ■ Doctor of Veterinary Medicine. ▷from Latin, *Veterinariae Medicinae Doctor.*

V-neck ▸n. a neckline of a garment, having straight sides meeting at a point to form a V-shape. ■ a garment with a neckline of this type. —**V-necked** *adj.*

voc. ▸abbr. ■ vocational. ■ *Grammar* vocative.

vocab. ▸abbr. ■ vocabulary.

vo·ca·ble /ˈvōkəbəl/ ▸n. a word, esp. with reference to form rather than meaning. ▷late Middle English (denoting a name): from French, or from Latin *vocabulum*, from *vocare* 'call.'

vo·cab·u·lar·y /vōˈkabyəˌlerē; vi-/ ▸n. (*pl.* **-lar·ies**) the body of words used in a particular language. ■ a part of such a body of words used on a particular occasion or in a particular sphere: *the vocabulary of law* | *the term became part of business vocabulary.* ■ the body of words known to an individual person: *he had a wide vocabulary.* ■ a list of difficult or unfamiliar words with an explanation of their meanings, accompanying a piece of specialist or foreign-language text. ■ a range of artistic or stylistic forms, techniques, or movements: *dance companies have their own vocabularies of movement.* ▷mid 16th cent. (denoting a list of words with definitions or translations): from medieval Latin *vocabularius*, from Latin *vocabulum* (see VOCABLE).

vo·cal /ˈvōkəl/ ▸adj. **1** of or relating to the human voice: *nonlinguistic vocal effects like laughs and sobs.* ■ *Anatomy* used in the production of speech sounds: *the vocal apparatus.* ■ *Phonetics* (of a sound in speech) made with the voice rather than the breath alone; voiced. **2** expressing opinions or feelings freely or loudly: *he was vocal in condemning the action.* **3** (of music) consisting of or incorporating singing.
▸n. (often **vocals**) a part of a piece of music that is sung. ■ a musical performance involving singing. ▷late Middle English: from Latin *vocalis*, from *vox, voc-* (see VOICE). Current senses of the noun date from the 1920s. —**vo·cal·i·ty** /vōˈkalətē/ *n.* —**vo·cal·ly** *adv.*

vo·cal cords (also **vo·cal folds**) ▸*plural n.* folds of membranous tissue that project inward from the sides of the larynx to form a slit across the glottis in the throat, and whose edges vibrate in the airstream to produce the voice.

vo·cal·ese /ˌvōkəˈlēz/ ▸n. a style of singing in which singers put words to jazz tunes, esp. to previously improvised instrumental solos. See SCAT[2].

vo·cal·ic /vōˈkalik; və-/ ▸adj. *Phonetics* of, relating to, or consisting of a vowel or vowels.

vo·ca·lise /ˈvōkəˌlēz; ˌvōkəˈlēz/ ▸n. *Music* a singing exercise using individual syllables or vowel sounds to develop flexibility and control of pitch and tone. ■ a vocal passage consisting of a melody without words: *the second movement is in the spirit of a vocalise.*

vo·cal·ism /ˈvōkəˌlizəm/ ▸n. **1** the use of the voice or vocal organs in speech. ■ the skill or art of exercising the voice in singing. **2** *Phonetics* a vowel sound or articulation. ■ a system of vowels used in a given language.

vo·cal·ist /ˈvōkəlist/ ▸n. a singer, typically one who regularly performs with a jazz or pop group.

vo·cal·ize /ˈvōkəˌlīz/ ▸v. [*trans.*] **1** utter (a sound or word): *the child vocalizes a number of distinct sounds* | [*intrans.*] *a warbler vocalized from a reed bed.* ■ express (something) with words: *Gillie could scarcely vocalize her responses.* ■ [*intrans.*] *Music* sing with several notes to one vowel. **2** *Phonetics* change (a consonant) to a semivowel or vowel. **3** write (a language such as Hebrew) with vowel points. —**vo·cal·i·za·tion** /ˌvōkələˈzāSHən/ *n.* —**vo·cal·iz·er** *n.*

vo·cal sac ▸n. *Zoology* (in many male frogs) a loose fold of skin on each side of the mouth, which can be inflated to produce sound.

vo·cal score ▸n. a musical score showing the voice parts in full, but with the accompaniment reduced or omitted.

vo·ca·tion /vōˈkāSHən/ ▸n. a strong feeling of suitability for a particular career or occupation: *not all of us have a vocation to be nurses or doctors.* ■ a person's employment or main occupation, esp. regarded as particularly worthy and requiring great dedication: *her vocation as a poet.* ■ a trade or profession. ▷late Middle English: from Old French, or from Latin *vocatio(n-)*, from *vocare* 'to call.'

vo·ca·tion·al /vōˈkāSHənl/ ▸adj. of or relating to an occupation or employment: *they supervised prisoners in vocational activities.* ■ (of education or training) directed at a particular occupation and its skills: *vocational school* | *specialized vocational courses.* —**vo·ca·tion·al·ism** /-ˌizəm/ *n.* —**vo·ca·tion·al·ize** /-ˌīz/ *v.* —**vo·ca·tion·al·ly** *adv.*

voc·a·tive /ˈväkətiv/ *Grammar* ▸adj. relating to or denoting a case of nouns, pronouns, and adjectives in Latin and other languages, used in addressing or invoking a person or thing.
▸n. a word in the vocative case. ■ (**the vocative**) the vocative case. ▷late Middle English: from Old French *vocatif, -ive* or Latin *vocativus*, from *vocare* 'to call.'

vo·cif·er·ate /vəˈsifəˌrāt; vō-/ ▸v. [*intrans.*] shout, complain, or argue loudly or vehemently: *he then began to vociferate pretty loudly* | [*trans.*] *he entered, vociferating curses.* ▷late 16th cent.: from Latin *vociferat-* 'exclaimed,' from the verb *vociferari*, from *vox* 'voice' + *ferre* 'carry.' —**vo·cif·er·ant** /-rənt/ *adj.* —**vo·cif·er·a·tion** /-ˌsifəˈrāSHən/ *n.*

vo·cif·er·ous /vəˈsifərəs; vō-/ ▸adj. (esp. of a person or speech) vehement or clamorous: *he was a vociferous opponent of the takeover.* —**vo·cif·er·ous·ly** *adv.* —**vo·cif·er·ous·ness** *n.*

THE RIGHT WORD **boisterous, clamorous, obstreperous, strident, vociferous**

An angry crowd might be **vociferous**, which implies loud and unrestrained shouting or crying out (*a vociferous argument*).

A happy crowd might be **boisterous**, which implies noisy exuberance or high-spirited rowdiness (*a boisterous celebration of spring*).

A crowd that wants something is likely to be **clamorous**, which suggests an urgent or insistent vociferousness in demanding or protesting something.

If people's demands are not met, they might become **obstreperous**, which means noisy in an unruly and aggressive way, usually in defiance of authority (*an obstreperous child*).

Strident suggests a harsh, grating loudness that is particularly distressing to the ear (*her strident voice could be heard throughout the building*).

vo·cod·er /ˈvōˌkōdər/ ▸n. a synthesizer that produces sounds from an analysis of speech input. ▷1930s: from VOICE + CODE + -ER[1].

VOD ▸abbr. video-on-demand.

vod·ka /ˈvädkə/ ▸n. an alcoholic spirit of Russian origin made by distillation of rye, wheat, or potatoes. ▷Russian, diminutive of *voda* 'water.'

vo·dun /vōˈdo͞on/ ▸n. another term for VOODOO. ▷Fon, 'fetish.'

vogue /vōg/ ▸n. [usu. in *sing.*] the prevailing fashion or style at a particular time: *the vogue is to make realistic films.* ■ general acceptance or favor; popularity: *the 1920s and 30s, when art deco was much* ***in vogue.***
▸adj. [*attrib.*] popular; fashionable: *"citizenship" was to be the government's vogue word.*
▸v. (**vogued, vogue·ing** or **vogu·ing**) [*intrans.*] dance to music in such a way as to imitate the characteristic poses struck by a model on a catwalk. [1980s: from the name of the fashion magazine *Vogue.*] ▷late

V

16th cent. (in *the vogue*, denoting the foremost place in popular estimation): from French, from Italian *voga* 'rowing, fashion,' from *vogare* 'row, go well.' **—vogu·ish** *adj.*

voice /vois/ ▶*n.* **1** the sound produced in a person's larynx and uttered through the mouth, as speech or song: *Meg raised her voice | a worried tone of voice.* ■ an agency by which a particular point of view is expressed or represented: *once the proud voice of middle-class conservatism, the paper had fallen on hard times.* ■ [in *sing.*] the right to express an opinion: *the new electoral system gives minority parties a voice.* ■ a particular opinion or attitude expressed: *a dissenting voice.* ■ the ability to speak or sing: *she'd* **lost her voice**. ■ (usu. **voices**) the supposed utterance of a guiding spirit, typically giving instructions or advice. ■ the distinctive tone or style of a literary work or author: *she had strained and falsified her literary voice.* **2** *Music* the range of pitch or type of tone with which a person sings, such as soprano or tenor. ■ a vocal part in a composition. ■ a constituent part in a fugue. ■ each of the notes or sounds able to be produced simultaneously by a musical instrument (esp. an electronic one) or a computer. ■ (in an electronic musical instrument) each of a number of preset or programmable tones. **3** *Phonetics* sound uttered with resonance of the vocal cords (used in the pronunciation of vowels and certain consonants). **4** *Grammar* a form or set of forms of a verb showing the relation of the subject to the action: *the passive voice.*
▶*v.* [*trans.*] **1** express (something) in words: *get teachers to voice their opinions on important subjects.* **2** [usu. as *adj.*] (**voiced**) *Phonetics* utter (a speech sound) with resonance of the vocal cords (e.g., *b, d, g, v, z*). **3** *Music* regulate the tone quality of (organ pipes). ▷Middle English: from Old French *vois*, from Latin *vox, voc-*. **—voiced** *adj.* [in *combination*] *deep-voiced.* **—voic·er** *n.* (in sense 3 of the *verb*).
▶*PHRASES* □ **give voice to** allow (a particular emotion, opinion, or point of view) to be expressed. ■ allow (a person or group) to express their emotions, opinion, or point of view. □ **in voice** in proper vocal condition for singing or speaking: *the soprano is in marvelous voice.* □ **with one voice** in complete agreement; unanimously.

voice box ▶*n.* the larynx.

voice chan·nel ▶*n.* *Telecommunications* a channel with a bandwidth sufficiently great to accommodate speech.

voice coil ▶*n.* *Telecommunications* a coil that drives the cone of a loudspeaker according to the signal current flowing in it. ■ a similar coil with the converse function in a moving-coil microphone.

voice·ful /'voisfəl/ ▶*adj.* *poetic/literary* possessing a voice: *the swelling of the voiceful sea.*

voice·less /'voislis/ ▶*adj.* mute; speechless: *how could he have remained voiceless in the face of her cruelty?* ■ not expressed: *the air was charged with voiceless currents of thought.* ■ (of a person or group) lacking the power or right to express an opinion or exert control over affairs. ■ *Phonetics* (of a speech sound) uttered without resonance of the vocal cords, e.g., *f* as opposed to *v*, *p* as opposed to *b*, and *s* as opposed to *z*. **—voice·less·ly** *adv.* **—voice·less·ness** *n.*

voice mail (also **voice·mail**) ▶*n.* a centralized electronic system that can store messages from telephone callers.

Voice of A·mer·i·ca an official U.S. radio station that broadcasts around the world in English and other languages. It was founded in 1942 and is operated by the Board for International Broadcasting.

voice-o·ver ▶*n.* a piece of narration in a movie or broadcast, not accompanied by an image of the speaker.

voice·print /'vois,print/ ▶*n.* a visual record of speech, analyzed with respect to frequency, duration, and amplitude. ▷1960s: from the noun **VOICE**, on the pattern of *fingerprint*.

voice rec·og·ni·tion tech·nol·o·gy ▶*n.* the technology that enables a machine or computer program to receive and interpret dictation or to understand and carry out spoken commands.

voice vote ▶*n.* a vote taken by noting the relative strength and volume of calls of *aye* and *no*.

void /void/ ▶*adj.* **1** not valid or legally binding: *the contract was void.* ■ (of speech or action) ineffectual; useless: *all the stratagems you've worked out are rendered void.* **2** completely empty: *void spaces surround the tanks.* ■ [*predic.*] (**void of**) free from; lacking: *what were once the masterpieces of literature are now void of meaning.* ■ *formal* (of an office or position) vacant. **3** [*predic.*] (in bridge and whist) having been dealt no cards in a particular suit.
▶*n.* **1** a completely empty space: *the black void of space.* ■ an emptiness caused by the loss of something: *the void left by the collapse of communism.* ■ an unfilled space in a wall, building, or structure. **2** (in bridge and whist) a suit in which a player is dealt no cards.
▶*v.* [*trans.*] **1** declare that (something) is not valid or legally binding: *the Supreme Court voided the statute.* **2** discharge or drain away (water, gases, etc.). ■ *chiefly Medicine* excrete (waste matter). ■ [usu. as *adj.*] (**voided**) empty or evacuate (a container or space). ▷Middle English (in the sense 'unoccupied'): from a dialect variant of Old French *vuide*; related to Latin *vacare* 'vacate'; the verb partly a shortening of **AVOID**, reinforced by Old French *voider*. **—void·a·ble** *adj.* **—void·ness** *n.*

THE RIGHT WORD **abrogate, annul, invalidate, negate, nullify, void**

To **void** a check, to **invalidate** a claim, to **abrogate** a law, and to **annul** a marriage all refer to the same basic activity, which is putting an end to something or depriving it of validity, force, or authority. But these verbs are not always interchangeable.

Annul is the most general term, meaning to end something that exists or to declare that it never really existed (*the charter was annulled before it could be challenged*).

Abrogate implies the exercise of legal authority (*Congress abrogated the treaty between the two warring factions*), while **nullify** means to deprive something of its value or effectiveness (*nullify the enemy's attempt to establish communications*).

Void and *invalidate* are often used interchangeably as they both mean to make null or worthless (*void a legal document by tearing it up; invalidate a check by putting the wrong date on it*).

Negate means to prove an assertion false (*her version of the story negated everything her brother had said*) or to nullify or make something ineffective (*the study's findings were negated by its author's arrest for fraud*).

void·ance /'voidns/ ▶*n.* the action of voiding something or the state of being voided: *the voidance of exhaust gases.* ■ *chiefly Law* an annulment of a contract. ■ *Christian Church* a vacancy in a benefice. ▷late Middle English: from Old French, from the verb *voider* (see **VOID**).

void·ed /'voidid/ ▶*adj.* *Heraldry* (of a bearing) having the central area cut away so as to show the field.

voi·là /vwä'lä/ (also **voi·la**) ▶*exclam.* there it is; there you are: *"Voilà!" she said, producing a pair of strappy white sandals.* ▷French.

voile /voil/ ▶*n.* a thin, plain-weave, semitransparent fabric of cotton, wool, or silk. ▷late 19th cent.: French, literally 'veil.'

VoIP (also **VOIP**) ▶*abbr.* voice over Internet protocol, a communications protocol that allows for telephonic communication via the Internet.

voir dire /'vwär 'di(ə)r/ ▶*n.* *Law* a preliminary examination of a witness or a juror by a judge or counsel. ■ an oath taken by such a witness. ▷Law French, from Old French *voir* 'true' + *dire* 'say.'

voix ce·leste /'vwä sə'lest/ ▶*n.* French term for **VOX ANGELICA**. ▷late 19th cent.: French, literally 'heavenly voice.'

Voj·vo·di·na /'voivə,dēnə/ a mainly Hungarian-speaking province in northern Serbia in Yugoslavia, on the Hungarian border; capital, Novi Sad.

vol. ▶*abbr.* volume.

Vo·lans /'vōlənz/ *Astronomy* an inconspicuous southern constellation (the Flying Fish), between Carina and the south celestial pole. ■ [as *genitive*] (**Volantis**) used with a preceding letter or numeral to designate a star in this constellation: *the star Beta Volantis.* ▷Latin, from the former name *Piscis Volans* 'the flying fish'.

vo·lant /'vōlənt/ ▶*adj.* *Zoology* (of an animal) able to fly or glide: *newly volant young.* ■ of, relating to, or characterized by flight: *volant ways of life.* ■ [usu. *postpositive*] *Heraldry* represented as flying: *a falcon volant.* ■ *poetic/literary* moving rapidly or lightly: *her sails caught a volant wind.* ▷mid 16th cent. (as a military term in the sense 'capable of rapid movement'): from French, literally 'flying,' present participle of *voler*, from Latin *volare* 'to fly.'

Vo·la·pük /'vōlə,po͝ok; 'vôlə-; 'välə-/ ▶*n.* an artificial language devised in 1879 and proposed for international use by a German cleric, Johann M. Schleyer, and based on extremely modified forms of words from English and Romance languages. ▷from *vol* representing English *world* + *-a-* (as a connective) + *pük* representing English *speak* or *speech*.

vo·lar /'vōlər/ ▶*adj.* *Anatomy* relating to the palm of the hand or the sole of the foot. ▷early 19th cent.: from Latin *vola* 'hollow of hand or foot' + **-AR**[1].

vol·a·tile /'välətl/ ▶*adj.* **1** (of a substance) easily evaporated at normal temperatures. **2** liable to change rapidly and unpredictably, esp. for the worse: *the political situation was becoming more volatile.* ■ (of a person) liable to display rapid changes of emotion. ■ (of a computer's memory) retaining data only as long as there is a power supply connected.
▶*n.* (usu. **volatiles**) a volatile substance. ▷Middle English (in the sense 'creature that flies,' also, as a collective, 'birds'): from Old French *volatil* or Latin *volatilis*, from *volare* 'to fly.' **—vol·a·til·i·ty** /,välə'tilitē/ *n.*

vol·a·tile oil ▶*n.* another term for **ESSENTIAL OIL**.

vol·a·til·ize /'välətl,īz/ ▶*v.* [*trans.*] cause (a substance) to evaporate or disperse in vapor. ■ [*intrans.*] become volatile; evaporate. **—vol·a·til·iz·a·ble** *adj.* **—vol·a·til·i·za·tion** /,välətl-ə'zāsнən/ *n.*

vol-au-vent /,vôl ō 'vän/ ▶*n.* a small round case of puff pastry filled with a savory mixture, typically of meat or fish in a richly flavored sauce. ▷French, literally 'flight in the wind.'

vol·can·ic /väl'kanik; vôl-/ ▶*adj.* of, relating to, or produced by a volcano or volcanoes. ■ *figurative* (esp. of a feeling or emotion) bursting out or liable to burst out violently: *the kind of volcanic passion she'd felt last night.* ▷late 18th cent.: from French *volcanique*, from *volcan* (see **VOLCANO**). **—vol·can·i·cal·ly** /-ik(ə)lē/ *adv.*

vol·can·ic bomb ▶*n.* see **BOMB** (sense 2).

vol·can·ic glass ▶*n.* another term for **OBSIDIAN**.

vol·can·ic·i·ty /,välkə'nisitē; ,vôl-/ ▶*n.* another term for **VOLCANISM**.

vol·can·i·clas·tic /väl,kanə'klastik; vôl-/ ▶*adj.* *Geology* relating to or denoting a clastic rock that contains volcanic material.

vol·can·ic neck ▶*n.* see **NECK** (sense 2).

vol·can·ism /'välkə,nizəm; 'vôl-/ (also **vul·can·ism**) ▶*n.* *Geology* volcanic activity or phenomena.

vol·ca·no /väl'kānō; vôl-/ ▶*n.* (*pl.* **-noes** or **-nos**) a mountain or hill, typically conical, having a crater or vent through which lava, rock fragments, hot vapor, and gas are or have been erupted from the earth's crust. ■ *figurative* an intense suppressed emotion or situation liable to burst out suddenly: *what volcano of emotion must have been boiling inside that youngster.* ▷early 17th cent.: from Italian, from Latin *Volcanus* 'Vulcan.' *See page 1882*

vol·can·ol·o·gy /,välkə'näləjē; ,vôl-/ (also **vul·can·ol·o·gy**) ▶*n.* the scientific study of volcanoes. **—vol·can·o·log·i·cal** /,välkanl'äjikəl; ,vôl-/ *adj.* **—vol·can·ol·o·gist** /-jist/ *n.*

vole /vōl/ ▶*n.* a small, typically burrowing, mouselike rodent with a rounded muzzle, found in both Eurasia and North America. • Subfamily Microtinae (or Arvicolinae), family Muridae: several genera, in particular *Microtus*, and numerous species. ▷early 19th cent. (originally *vole-mouse*): from Norwegian *voll(mus)* 'field (mouse).'

Vol·ga /'vōlgə; 'väl-; 'vôl-/ the longest river in Europe, rising in northwestern Russia and flowing east for 2,292 miles (3,688 km) to Kazan, where it turns southeast to the Caspian Sea. It has been dammed at several points to provide hydroelectric power and is navigable for most of its length.

Vol·go·grad /'vōlgə,grad; 'väl-; 'vôl-/ an industrial city in southwestern Russia, at the junction of the Don and Volga rivers; pop. 1,005,000. Former names **TSARITSYN** (until 1925) and **STALINGRAD** (1925–61).

vo·li·tion /və'lisнən; vō-/ ▶*n.* the faculty or power of using one's will: *without conscious volition she backed into her office.* ▷early 17th cent. (denoting a decision or choice made after deliberation): from French, or from medieval Latin *volitio(n-)*, from *volo* 'I wish.' **—vo·li·tion·al** /-sнənl/ *adj.* **—vo·li·tion·al·ly** /-sнənl-ē/ *adv.* **—vol·i·tive** /'välətiv/ *adj.* (*formal* or *technical*).
▶*PHRASE* □ **of** (or **by** or **on**) **one's own volition** voluntarily: *they choose to leave early of their own volition.*

Völ·ker·wan·de·rung /'fœlkər,vändə,ro͝oNG; 'fœl-/ ▶*n.* a migration of peoples, esp. that of Germanic and Slavic peoples into Europe from the 2nd to the 11th

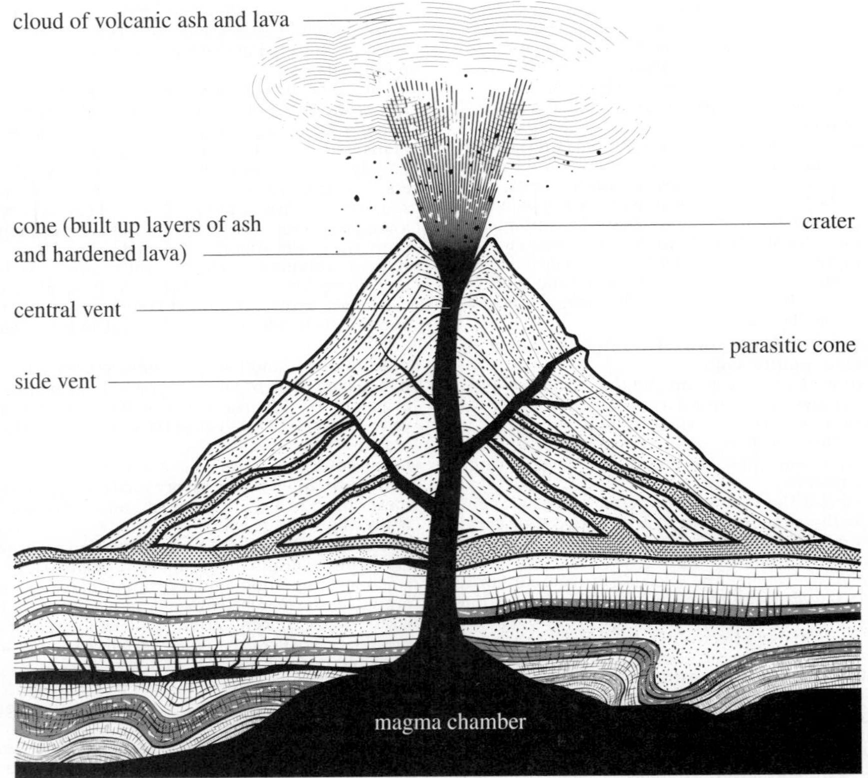

volcano

centuries. ▷German, from *Völker* 'nations' + *Wanderung* 'migration.'

völ·kisch /ˈfəlkisн; ˈfœl-/ (also **vol·kisch** /ˈfōkisн; ˈfōlk-/) ▶*adj.* (of a person or ideology) populist or nationalist, and typically racist: *völkisch ideas and traditions.* ▷German.

volks·lied /ˈfōks,lēt; ˈfôlks-/ ▶*n.* a German folk song, or a song in the style of one. ■ a national anthem, esp. that of the 19th-century Transvaal Republic.

vol·ley /ˈvälē/ ▶*n.* (*pl.* **-leys**) **1** a number of bullets, arrows, or other projectiles discharged at one time: *the infantry let off a couple of volleys.* ■ a series of utterances directed at someone in quick succession: *he unleashed a volley of angry questions.* ■ *Tennis* an exchange of shots. **2** (in sports, esp. tennis or soccer) a strike or kick of the ball made before it touches the ground.
▶*v.* (**-leys, -leyed**) [*trans.*] (in sports, esp. tennis or soccer) strike or kick (the ball) before it touches the ground: *he volleyed home the ball.* ■ score (a goal) with such a shot. ■ [*intrans.*] (in tennis and similar games) play a pregame point, sometimes in order to determine who will serve first. ■ utter or discharge in quick succession: *the dog was volleying joyful barks.* ▷late 16th cent.: from French *volée*, based on Latin *volare* 'to fly.' —**vol·ley·er** *n.*

vol·ley·ball /ˈvälē,bôl/ ▶*n.* a game for two teams, usually of six players, in which a large ball is hit by hand over a high net, the aim being to score points by making the ball reach the ground on the opponent's side of the court. ■ the inflated ball used in this game.

Vo·log·da /ˈvôləgdə/ a city in northern Russia; pop. 286,000.

Vo·los /ˈvō,läs; -,lôs/ a port on an inlet of the Aegean Sea, in Thessaly, in eastern Greece; pop. 77,000. Greek name **Vólos** .

vol·plane /ˈväl,plān; ˈvôl-/ *Aeronautics* ▶*n.* a controlled dive or downward flight at a steep angle, esp. by an airplane with the engine shut off.
▶*v.* [*intrans.*] (of an airplane) make such a dive or downward flight. ▷early 20th cent.: from French *vol plané*, literally 'glided flight.'

vols ▶*abbr.* volumes.

Vol·scian /ˈvälsнən; ˈvôlskēən/ ▶*n.* **1** a member of an ancient Italic people who fought the Romans in Latium in the 5th and 4th centuries BC until absorbed into Rome after their final defeat in 304 BC. **2** the Italic language of the Volscians.
▶*adj.* of or relating to the Volscians. ▷from Latin *Volsci* (the name of the people) + **-AN**.

Vol·stead Act /ˈväl,sted; ˈvôl-; ˈvōl-/ a law that enforced alcohol prohibition in the U.S. from 1920–33. ▷named after Andrew J. *Volstead* (1860–1947), American legislator.

volt[1] /vōlt/ (abbr.: **V**) ▶*n.* the SI unit of electromotive force, the difference of potential that would drive one ampere of current against one ohm resistance. ▷late 19th cent.: named after A. *Volta* (see **VOLTA**[2]).

volt[2] /vōlt; vôlt; vält/ (also **volte**) ▶*n.* *Fencing* a sudden quick jump or other movement to escape a thrust.
▶*v.* [*intrans.*] *Fencing* make a quick movement to avoid a thrust. ▷late 17th cent.: from French *volter* (see **VOLTE**).

Vol·ta[1] /ˈvōltə; ˈväl-; ˈvôl-/ a river in West Africa that is formed in central Ghana by the junction of its headwaters, the Black Volta, the White Volta, and the Red Volta rivers, all of which rise in Burkina Faso. It flows south to the Bight of Benin. At Akosombo in southeastern Ghana the river has been dammed to create Lake Volta, one of the world's largest man-made lakes.

Vol·ta[2] /ˈvōltə/, Alessandro Giuseppe Antonio Anastasio, Count (1745–1827), Italian physicist. He is best known for the voltaic pile or electrochemical battery in 1800, which was the first device to produce a continuous electric current.

volt·age /ˈvōltij/ ▶*n.* *Physics* an electromotive force or potential difference expressed in volts.

volt·age clamp *Physiology* ▶*n.* a constant electrical potential applied to a cell membrane, typically in order to measure ionic currents.
▶*v.* (**volt·age-clamp**) [*trans.*] apply a voltage clamp to (a membrane, cell, etc.).

volt·age di·vid·er ▶*n.* a series of resistors or capacitors that can be tapped at any intermediate point to produce a specific fraction of the voltage applied between its ends.

Vol·ta·ic /välˈtā-ik; vōl-; vôl-/ ▶*adj.* & *n.* another term for **GUR**.

vol·ta·ic /välˈtā-ik; vōl-; vôl-/ ▶*adj.* of or relating to electricity produced by chemical action in a primary battery; galvanic. ▷early 19th cent.: from the name of A. *Volta* (see **VOLTA**[2]) + **-IC**.

Vol·taire /vōlˈte(ə)r; vôl-/ (1694–1778), French writer, playwright, and poet; pseudonym of *François-Marie Arouet*. A leading figure of the Enlightenment, he frequently came into conflict with the establishment as a result of his radical views and satirical writings. Notable works: *Lettres philosophiques* (1734) and *Candide* (1759).

volt-am·pere ▶*n.* a unit of electrical power equal to the product of one volt and one ampere and equivalent to one watt of direct current.

volte ▶*n.* **1** variant spelling of **VOLT**[2]. **2** a movement performed in dressage and classical riding, in which a horse describes a circle of 6 yards diameter. ▷late 17th cent. (as a fencing term): from French, from Italian *volta* 'a turn,' from *volgere* 'to turn.' Sense 2 dates from the early 18th cent.

volte-face /,vält(ə) ˈfäs; ,vōlt(ə); ,vôlt(ə)/ ▶*n.* (*pl.* same) an act of turning around so as to face in the opposite direction. ■ an abrupt and complete reversal of attitude, opinion, or position: *a remarkable volte-face on taxes.* ▷early 19th cent.: from French, from Italian *voltafaccia*, based on Latin *volvere* 'to roll' + *facies* 'appearance, face.'

volt·me·ter /ˈvōlt,mētər/ ▶*n.* an instrument for measuring electric potential in volts.

vol·u·ble /ˈvälyəbəl/ ▶*adj.* speaking or spoken incessantly and fluently: *she was as voluble as her husband was silent.* See note at **TALKATIVE**. ▷late 16th cent.: from French, or from Latin *volubilis*, from *volvere* 'to roll.' Earlier use in late Middle English included the senses 'rotating around an axis' and 'having a tendency to change,' also meanings of the Latin word. —**vol·u·bil·i·ty** /,välyəˈbilətē/ *n.* —**vol·u·ble·ness** *n.* —**vol·u·bly** /-blē/ *adv.*

vol·ume /ˈvälyəm; -,yōōm/ ▶*n.* **1** a book forming part of a work or series. ■ a single book or a bound collection of printed sheets. ■ a consecutive sequence of issues of a periodical. ■ *historical* a scroll of parchment or papyrus containing written matter. **2** the amount of space that a substance or object occupies, or that is enclosed within a container, esp. when great: *the sewer could not cope with the volume of rainwater | a volume of air.* ■ the amount or quantity of something, esp. when great: *changes in the volume of consumer spending.* ■ (**a volume of/volumes of**) a certain, typically large amount of something: *the volumes of data handled are vast.* ■ fullness or expansive thickness of something, esp. of a person's hair. **3** quantity or power of sound; degree of loudness: *he turned the volume up on the radio.* ▷late Middle English (originally denoting a roll of parchment containing written matter): from Old French *volum(e)*, from Latin *volumen* 'a roll,' from *volvere* 'to roll.' An obsolete meaning 'size or extent (of a book)' gave rise to sense 2.

vol·u·met·ric /,välyəˈmetrik/ ▶*adj.* of or relating to the measurement of volume. ■ (of chemical analysis) based on measuring the volumes of reagents, esp. by titration. ▷mid 19th cent.: from **VOLUME** + **METRIC**[1]. —**vol·u·met·ri·cal·ly** /-trik(ə)lē/ *adv.*

vol·u·met·ric ef·fi·cien·cy ▶*n.* the ratio of the volume of fluid actually displaced by a piston or plunger to its swept volume.

vol·u·met·ric sen·sor ▶*n.* a security device that detects the movement of people or objects by sensing their shapes.

vo·lu·mi·nous /vəˈlōōmənəs/ ▶*adj.* occupying or containing much space; large in volume, in particular: ■ (of clothing or drapery) loose and ample. ■ (of writing) very lengthy and full. ■ (of a writer) producing many books. ▷early 17th cent.: partly from late Latin *voluminosus* 'having many coils,' partly from Latin *volumen, volumin-* (see **VOLUME**). —**vo·lu·mi·nous·ly** *adv.* —**vo·lu·mi·nous·ness** *n.*

vol·u·mize /ˈvälyə,mīz; -yōō-/ ▶*v.* [*trans.*] (of a product or styling technique) give body to (hair). —**vol·um·iz·er** *n.*

vol·un·ta·rism /ˈväləntə,rizəm/ ▶*n.* **1** the principle of relying on voluntary action (used esp. with reference to the involvement of voluntary organizations in social welfare). ■ *historical* (esp. in the 19th century) the principle that churches or schools should be independent of the state and supported by voluntary contributions. **2** *Philosophy* the doctrine that the will is a fundamental or dominant factor in the individual or the universe. ▷mid 19th cent.: formed irregularly from **VOLUNTARY**. —**vol·un·ta·rist** *n.* & *adj.* —**vol·un·ta·ris·tic** /,väləntəˈristik/ *adj.*

vol·un·tar·y /ˈvälən,terē/ ▶*adj.* done, given, or acting of one's own free will: *we are funded by voluntary contributions.* ■ working, done, or maintained without payment: *a voluntary helper.* ■ supported by contributions rather than taxes or fees: *voluntary hospitals.*

■ *Physiology* under the conscious control of the brain. ■ *Law* (of a conveyance or disposition) made without return in money or other consideration.
▸*n.* (*pl.* **-tar·ies**) an organ solo played before, during, or after a church service. ■ *historical* a piece of music performed extempore, esp. as a prelude to other music, or composed in a free style. ▷late Middle English: from Old French *volontaire* or Latin *voluntarius*, from *voluntas* 'will.' **—vol·un·tar·i·ly** /ˌvälən'te(ə)rəlē; 'välənˌter-/ *adv.* **—vol·un·tar·i·ness** *n.*

vol·un·tar·y·ism /'välənˌterēˌizəm/ ▸*n.* less common term for VOLUNTARISM (sense 1). **—vol·un·tar·y·ist** *n.*

vol·un·teer /ˌvälən'tir/ ▸*n.* a person who freely offers to take part in an enterprise or undertake a task. ■ a person who works for an organization without being paid. ■ a person who freely enrolls for military service rather than being conscripted, esp. a member of a force formed by voluntary enrollment and distinct from the regular army. ■ a plant that has not been deliberately planted. ■ *Law* a person to whom a voluntary conveyance or deposition is made.
▸*v.* [*intrans.*] freely offer to do something: *he volunteered for the job* | [with *infinitive*] *I rashly volunteered to be a contestant.* ■ [*trans.*] offer (help) in such a way: *he volunteered his services as a driver for the convoy.* ■ [*reporting verb*] say or suggest something without being asked: [*trans.*] *it never paid to volunteer information* | [with *direct speech*] *"Her name's Louise," Christina volunteered.* ■ work for an organization without being paid. ■ [*trans.*] commit (someone) to a particular undertaking, typically without consulting them: *he was volunteered for parachute training by friends.* ▷late 16th cent. (as a noun, with military reference): from French *volontaire* 'voluntary.' The change in the ending was due to association with **-EER**.

vol·un·teer·ism /ˌvälən'ti(ə)rˌizəm/ ▸*n.* the use or involvement of volunteer labor, esp. in community services.

Vol·un·teer State a nickname for the state of TENNESSEE.

vo·lup·tu·ar·y /və'ləpCHo͞oˌerē/ ▸*n.* (*pl.* **-ar·ies**) a person devoted to luxury and sensual pleasure.
▸*adj.* concerned with luxury and sensual pleasure: *a voluptuary decade when high living was in style.* ▷early 17th cent.: from Latin *volupt(u)arius*, from *voluptas* 'pleasure.'

vo·lup·tu·ous /və'ləpCHəwəs/ ▸*adj.* of, relating to, or characterized by luxury or sensual pleasure: *long curtains in voluptuous crimson velvet.* See note at SENSUOUS. ■ (of a woman) curvaceous and sexually attractive. ▷late Middle English: from Old French *voluptueux* or Latin *voluptuosus*, from *voluptas* 'pleasure.' **—vo·lup·tu·ous·ly** *adv.* **—vo·lup·tu·ous·ness** *n.*

vo·lute /və'lo͞ot/ ▸*n.* **1** *Architecture* a spiral scroll characteristic of Ionic capitals and also used in Corinthian and composite capitals. **2** a deep-water marine mollusk with a thick spiral shell that is colorful and prized by collectors. • Family Volutidae, class Gastropoda: *Voluta* and other genera.

volute 1

▸*adj.* forming a spiral curve or curves: *spoked wheels with outside volute springs.* ▷mid 16th cent.: from French, or from Latin *voluta*, feminine past participle of *volvere* 'to roll.' **—vo·lut·ed** *adj.*

vo·lu·tion /və'lo͞oSHən/ ▸*n.* **1** *poetic/literary* a rolling or revolving motion. **2** a single turn of a spiral or coil. ▷late 15th cent.: from late Latin *volutio(n-)*, from Latin *volut-* 'rolled,' from the verb *volvere*.

vol·va /'välvə; 'vôl-/ ▸*n. Botany* (in certain fungi) a veil that encloses the fruiting body, often persisting after rupture as a sheath at the base of the stalk. ▷mid 18th cent.: modern Latin, from Latin *volvere* 'to roll, wrap around.'

vol·vox /'välˌväks; 'vôl-/ ▸*n. Biology* a green, single-celled aquatic organism that forms minute, free-swimming spherical colonies. • Genus *Volvox*, division Chlorophyta (or phylum Chlorophyta, kingdom Protista). ▷modern Latin, from Latin *volvere* 'to roll.'

vol·vu·lus /'välvyələs; 'vôl-/ ▸*n.* (*pl.* **-li** /-ˌlī; -ˌlē/ or **-lus·es**) *Medicine* an obstruction caused by twisting of the stomach or intestine. ▷late 17th cent.: modern or medieval Latin, from Latin *volvere* 'to roll.'

Volzh·sky /'vôlSH(s)kē/ an industrial city in southwestern Russia, on the Volga River; pop. 275,000.

vo·mer /'vōmər/ ▸*n. Anatomy* the small thin bone separating the left and right nasal cavities in humans and most other vertebrates. ▷early 18th cent.: from Latin, literally 'plowshare' (because of the shape).

vom·it /'vämət/ ▸*v.* (**-it·ed**, **-it·ing**) [*intrans.*] eject matter from the stomach through the mouth: *the sickly stench made him want to vomit* | [*trans.*] *she used to* **vomit up** *her food.* ■ [*trans.*] emit (something) in an uncontrolled stream or flow: *the machine vomited fold after fold of paper.*
▸*n.* **1** matter vomited from the stomach. **2** *archaic* an emetic. ▷late Middle English: from Old French *vomite* (noun) or Latin *vomitus*, from *vomere* 'to vomit.' **—vom·it·er** *n.*

vom·i·to·ri·um /ˌvämə'tôrēəm/ ▸*n.* (*pl.* **-tor·i·a** /-'tôrēə/) **1** each of a series of entrance or exit passages in an ancient Roman amphitheater or theater. **2** a place in which, according to popular misconception, the ancient Romans are supposed to have vomited during feasts to make room for more food. ▷Latin.

vom·i·to·ry /'väməˌtôrē/ ▸*adj.* **1** denoting the entrance or exit passages in a theater or amphitheater. **2** *rare* relating to or inducing vomiting.
▸*n.* (*pl.* **-ries**) another term for VOMITORIUM (sense 1). ▷early 17th cent.: from Latin *vomitorius*, based on *vomere* 'to vomit,' partly as an Anglicization of Latin *vomitorium* (see VOMITORIUM).

vom·i·tous /'vämətəs/ ▸*adj.* nauseating.

vom·i·tus /'vämətəs/ ▸*n. chiefly Medicine* matter that has been vomited. ▷early 20th cent.: from Latin.

von Braun /vän 'brôn; fôn 'broun/ see BRAUN[3].

Von·ne·gut /'vänigət/, Kurt, Jr. (1922–), U.S. novelist and short-story writer. His works blend elements of realism, science fiction, fantasy, and satire and include *Cat's Cradle* (1963); *Slaughterhouse-Five* (1969), based on the fire-bombing of Dresden in 1945, which Vonnegut himself experienced as a prisoner of war; and *Hocus Pocus* (1991).

von Neu·mann /vän 'noiˌmän; -mən/ see NEUMANN.

von Reck·ling·hau·sen's dis·ease /ˌvän 'rekliNGˌhouzənz/ ▸*n.* **1** a hereditary disease in which numerous benign tumors develop in various parts of the body, esp. the skin and the fibrous sheaths of the nerves. It is a form of neurofibromatosis. **2** a disease in which the bones are weakened as a result of excessive secretion of the parathyroid hormone, leading to bowing and fracture of long bones and sometimes deformities of the chest and spine. Also called OSTEITIS FIBROSA CYSTICA (see OSTEITIS). ▷early 20th cent.: named after Friedrich *von Recklinghausen* (1833–1910), German pathologist.

von Stern·berg /vän 'stərnˌbərg/, Josef (1894–1969), U.S. movie director, born in Austria. His best-known movie *Der Blaue Engel* (1930; *The Blue Angel*) made Marlene Dietrich an international star. He also worked with her on a series of Hollywood movies that included *Dishonored* (1931) and *Shanghai Express* (1932).

von Wil·le·brand's dis·ease /ˌvän 'viləˌbränts/ ▸*n. Medicine* an inherited disorder characterized by a tendency to bleed, caused by deficiency or abnormality of a plasma coagulation factor (**von Willebrand factor**). ▷1940s: named after Erik A. *von Willebrand* (1870–1949), Finnish physician.

voo·doo /'vo͞oˌdo͞o/ ▸*n.* a black religious cult practiced in the Caribbean and the southern U.S., combining elements of Roman Catholic ritual with traditional African magical and religious rites, and characterized by sorcery and spirit possession. ■ a person skilled in such practice.
▸*v.* (**-doos**, **-dooed**) [*trans.*] affect (someone) by the practice of such witchcraft. ▷early 19th cent.: from Louisiana French, from Kwa *vodũ*. **—voo·doo·ism** /-ˌizəm/ *n.* **—voo·doo·ist** /-ist/ *n.*

Voor·trek·ker /'fo͞orˌtrekər; 'fôr-/ ▸*n. S. African historical* a member of one of the groups of Dutch-speaking people who migrated by wagon from the Cape Colony into the interior from 1836 onwards, in order to live beyond the borders of British rule. ▷Afrikaans, from Dutch *voor* 'fore' + *trekken* 'to travel.'

VOR ▸*abbr.* visual omnirange, denoting a type of navigation system using a series of radio beacons.

-vora ▸*comb. form* in names of groups corresponding to adjectives ending in *-vorous* (such as *Insectivora* corresponding to *insectivorous*).

vo·ra·cious /və'rāSHəs/ ▸*adj.* wanting or devouring great quantities of food: *he had a voracious appetite.* ■ having a very eager approach to an activity: *his voracious reading of literature.* ▷mid 17th cent.: from Latin *vorax, vorac-* (from *vorare* 'devour') + **-IOUS**. **—vo·ra·cious·ly** *adv.* **—vo·ra·cious·ness** *n.* **—vo·rac·i·ty** /-'rasitē/ *n.*

-vore ▸*comb. form* in names of members of groups corresponding to adjectives ending in *-vorous* (such as *detritivore* corresponding to *detritivorous*).

Vo·ro·nezh /və'rôniSH; -'rō-/ a city in Russia, south of Moscow; pop. 895,000.

Vo·ro·shi·lov·grad /vərə'shēləvˌgräd; ˌvôrə-/ former name (1935–58; and 1970–91) for LUHANSK. ▷named in honor of Marshal Kliment *Voroshilov* (1881–1969), Soviet military and political leader.

-vorous ▸*comb. form* feeding on a specified food: *carnivorous* | *herbivorous.* ▷from Latin *-vorus* (from *vorare* 'devour') + **-OUS**.

Vor·stel·lung /'fôrˌSHteloo͝NG/ ▸*n.* (*pl.* **-stel·lung·en** /-ˌSHteloo͝NGən/) *Philosophy* a mental image or idea produced by prior perception of an object, as in memory or imagination, rather than by actual perception. ▷German.

vor·tal /'vôrtl/ ▸*n.* an Internet site that provides a directory of links to information related to a particular industry. ▷1990s: blend of *v(ertical)* (as in *vertical industry*, an industry specializing in a narrow range of goods and services), and *(p)ortal*.

vor·tex /'vôrˌteks/ ▸*n.* (*pl.* **-tex·es** or **-ti·ces** /-təˌsēz/) a mass of whirling fluid or air, esp. a whirlpool or whirlwind. ■ *figurative* something regarded as a whirling mass: *the vortex of existence.* ▷mid 17th cent.: from Latin *vortex, vortic-*, literally 'eddy,' variant of VERTEX. **—vor·ti·cal** /'vôrtikəl/ *adj.* **—vor·ti·cal·ly** /'vôrtik(ə)lē/ *adv.* **—vor·tic·i·ty** /vôr'tisitē/ *n.* **—vor·ti·cose** /'vôrtəˌkōs/ *adj.* **—vor·tic·u·lar** /vôr'tikyələr/ *adj.*

vor·ti·cel·la /ˌvôrtə'selə/ ▸*n. Zoology* a sedentary, single-celled aquatic animal with a contractile stalk and a bell-shaped body bearing a ring of cilia. • Genus *Vorticella*, phylum Ciliophora, kingdom Protista. ▷late 18th cent.: modern Latin, diminutive of Latin *vortex, vortic-* 'eddy.'

Vor·ti·cist /'vôrtəsist/ ▸*n. historical* a member of a British artistic movement of 1914–15 influenced by cubism and futurism and favoring machinelike forms. ▷from Latin *vortex, vortic-* 'eddy' + **-IST**. **—Vor·ti·cism** /-ˌsizəm/ *n.*

Vosges /vōZH/ a mountain system in eastern France, in Alsace near the border with Germany.

Vos·tok /'väsˌtäk; ˌvə'stôk/ a series of six manned Soviet orbiting spacecraft, the first of which, launched in April 1961, carried the first man in space (Yuri Gagarin).

vo·ta·ry /'vōtərē/ ▸*n.* (*pl.* **-ries**) a person, such as a monk or nun, who has made vows of dedication to religious service. ■ a devoted follower, adherent, or advocate of someone or something: *he was a votary of John Keats.* ▷mid 16th cent.: from Latin *vot-* 'vowed' (from the verb *vovere*) + **-ARY**[1]. **—vo·ta·rist** /-rist/ *n.*

vote /vōt/ ▸*n.* a formal indication of a choice between two or more candidates or courses of action, expressed typically through a ballot or a show of hands or by voice. ■ an act of expressing such an indication of choice: *they are ready to* **put it to a vote**. ■ (**the vote**) the choice expressed collectively by a body of electors or by a specified group: *the Republican vote in Florida.* ■ (**the vote**) the right to indicate a choice in an election.
▸*v.* [*intrans.*] give or register a vote: *they voted against the resolution* | [with *complement*] *I voted Republican.* ■ [*trans.* or *complement*] cause (someone) to gain or lose a particular post or honor by means of a vote: *incompetent judges are voted out of office.* ■ [with *clause*] *informal* used to express a wish to follow a particular course of action: *I vote we have one more game.* ■ [*trans.*] (of a legislature) grant or confer by vote. ■ [*trans.*] (**vote something down**) reject (something) by means of a vote. ▷late Middle English: from Latin *votum* 'a vow, wish,' from *vovere* 'to vow.' The verb dates from the mid 16th cent. **—vote·less** *adj.*
▸*PHRASES* □ **vote of confidence** a vote showing that a majority continues to support the policy of a leader or governing body. □ **vote of no confidence** (or **vote of censure**) a vote showing that a majority does not support the policy of a leader or governing body. □ **vote with one's feet** *informal* indicate an opinion by being present or absent or by some other course of action.

V

vot·er /ˈvōtər/ ▸*n.* a person who votes or has the right to vote at an election.

vot·ing booth ▸*n.* a compartment with one open side in which one voter at a time stands to mark their ballot.

vot·ing ma·chine ▸*n.* a machine for the automatic registering of votes.

vo·tive /ˈvōtiv/ ▸*adj.* offered or consecrated in fulfillment of a vow: *votive offerings.*
▸*n.* an object offered in this way, such as a candle used as a vigil light. ▷late 16th cent.: from Latin *votivus*, from *votum* (see **VOTE**). The original sense was 'expressing a desire,' preserved in **VOTIVE MASS**.

vo·tive Mass ▸*n.* (in the Roman Catholic Church) a Mass celebrated for a special purpose or occasion.

vouch /vouCH/ ▸*v.* [*intrans.*] (**vouch for**) assert or confirm as a result of one's own experience that something is true or accurately so described: *they say New York is the city that never sleeps, and I can certainly* **vouch for** *that.* ■ confirm that someone is who they say they are or that they are of good character: *he was refused entrance until someone could vouch for him.* ▷Middle English (as a legal term in the sense 'summon (a person) to court to prove title to property'): from Old French *voucher* 'summon,' based on Latin *vocare* 'to call.'

vouch·er /ˈvouCHər/ ▸*n.* a small printed piece of paper that entitles the holder to a discount or that may be exchanged for goods or services. ■ a receipt. ▷early 17th cent.: from **VOUCH**.

vouch·safe /vouCHˈsāf; ˈvouCH,sāf/ ▸*v.* [with *two objs.*] (often **be vouchsafed**) give or grant (something) to (someone) in a gracious or condescending manner: *it is a blessing vouchsafed him by heaven.* ■ [*trans.*] reveal or disclose (information): *you'd never vouchsafed that interesting tidbit before.* ▷Middle English: originally as the phrase *vouch* something *safe* on someone, i.e., 'warrant the secure conferment of (something on someone).'

vous·soir /vo͞oˈswär/ ▸*n. Architecture* a wedge-shaped or tapered stone used to construct an arch. ▷early 18th cent: via French from popular Latin *volsorium*, based on Latin *volvere* 'to roll.' The word, borrowed from Old French, was also used for a time in late Middle English.

Vou·vray /vo͞oˈvrā/ ▸*n.* dry white wine, either still or sparkling, produced in the Vouvray district of the Loire valley. ▷French.

vow /vou/ ▸*n.* a solemn promise. ■ (**vows**) a set of such promises committing one to a prescribed role, calling, or course of action, typically to marriage or a monastic career.
▸*v.* **1** [*reporting verb*] solemnly promise to do a specified thing: [with *clause*] *he vowed that his government would not tolerate a repeat of the disorder* | [with *direct speech*] *one fan vowed, "I'll picket every home game."* **2** [*trans.*] *archaic* dedicate to someone or something, esp. a deity: *I* **vowed** *myself* **to** *this enterprise.* ▷Middle English: from Old French *vou*, from Latin *votum* (see **VOTE**); the verb from Old French *vouer*.

vow·el /ˈvouəl/ ▸*n.* a speech sound that is produced by comparatively open configuration of the vocal tract, with vibration of the vocal cords but without audible friction and is a unit of the sound system of a language that forms the nucleus of a syllable. Contrasted with **CONSONANT**. ■ a letter representing such a sound, such as *a, e, i, o, u.* ▷Middle English: from Old French *vouel*, from Latin *vocalis (littera)* 'vocal (letter).' **—vow·eled** /ˈvou(ə)ld/ (*Brit.* **vow·elled**) *adj.* [usu. in *combination*] **—vow·el·less** *adj.*

vow·el gra·da·tion ▸*n.* another term for **ABLAUT**.

vow·el har·mo·ny ▸*n.* the phenomenon in some languages, e.g., Turkish, in which all the vowels in a word are members of the same subclass, for example all front vowels or all back vowels.

vow·el height ▸*n. Phonetics* the degree to which the tongue is raised or lowered in the articulation of a particular vowel.

vow·el·ize /ˈvouə,līz/ ▸*v.* [*trans.*] supply (something such as a Hebrew or shorthand text) with vowel points or signs representing vowels.

vow·el point ▸*n.* each of a set of marks indicating vowels in writing phonetically explicit text in Semitic languages such as Hebrew and Arabic.

vow·el shift ▸*n. Phonetics* a phonetic change in a vowel or vowels. ■ (**the Great Vowel Shift**) a series of changes between medieval and modern English affecting the long vowels of the standard language.

vox an·gel·i·ca /ˈväks anˈjelikə/ ▸*n.* a soft stop on an organ or harmonium that is tuned slightly sharp to produce a tremolo effect. ▷mid 19th cent.: from late Latin, literally 'angelic voice.'

vox·el /ˈväksəl/ ▸*n.* (in computer-based modeling or graphic simulation) each of an array of elements of volume that constitute a notional three-dimensional space, esp. each of an array of discrete elements into which a representation of a three-dimensional object is divided. ▷1970s: from the initial letters of **VOLUME** and **ELEMENT**, with the insertion of *-x-* for ease of pronunciation.

vox hu·ma·na /ˈväks (h)yo͞oˈmänə; -ˈmanə; -ˈmānə/ ▸*n.* an organ stop with a tone supposedly resembling the human voice. ▷early 18th cent.: from Latin, literally 'human voice.'

vox po·pu·li /ˈväks ˈpäpyə,lī; -,lē/ ▸*n.* [in *sing.*] the opinions or beliefs of the majority. ▷mid 16th cent.: from Latin, literally 'the people's voice.'

voy·age /ˈvoi-ij/ ▸*n.* a long journey involving travel by sea or in space: *a six-year voyage to Jupiter* | *figurative writing a biography is a* **voyage of discovery**. See note at **JOURNEY**.
▸*v.* [*intrans.*] go on a long journey, typically by sea or in space: *he has voyaged through places like Venezuela and Peru.* ■ [*trans.*] *archaic* sail over or along (a sea or river). ▷Middle English (as a noun denoting a journey): from Old French *voiage*, from Latin *viaticum* 'provisions for a journey' (in late Latin 'journey'). **—voy·age·a·ble** *adj.* (*archaic*) **—voy·ag·er** *n.*

Voy·ag·er /ˈvoi-ijər/ either of two American space probes launched in 1977 to investigate the outer planets. Voyager 1 encountered Jupiter and Saturn, while Voyager 2 reached Jupiter, Saturn, Uranus, and finally Neptune (1989).

vo·ya·geur /,vwäyəˈZHər; ,voi-ə-/ ▸*n. historical* (esp. in Canada) a boatman employed by the fur companies in transporting goods and passengers to and from trading posts. ▷French, literally 'voyager,' from *voyager* 'to travel.'

Vo·ya·geurs National Park /,vwäyəˈZHərz; ,voi-ə-/ a preserve in northern Minnesota, along the Canadian border, whose name recalls the French fur traders of the 18th century.

vo·yeur /voiˈyər; vwä-/ ▸*n.* a person who gains sexual pleasure from watching others when they are naked or engaged in sexual activity. ■ a person who enjoys seeing the pain or distress of others. ▷early 20th cent.: from French, from *voir* 'see.' **—vo·yeur·ism** /ˈvoiyə,rizəm; voiˈyər,izəm; vwäˈyər-/ *n.* **—voy·eur·is·tic** /,voiyəˈristik; ,vwäyə-/ *adj.* **—voy·eur·is·ti·cal·ly** *adv.*

VP ▸*abbr.* Vice President.

VPL ▸*abbr.* ■ visible programming language. ■ *informal* visible panty line.

VPN ▸*abbr.* virtual private network.

VR ▸*abbr.* ■ Queen Victoria. [abbreviation of Latin *Victoria Regina*.] ■ variant reading. ■ virtual reality.

VRAM /ˈvē,ram/ ▸*n. Electronics* a type of RAM used in computer display cards. ▷1990s: abbreviation of *video RAM*.

VRML *Computing* ▸*abbr.* virtual reality modeling language.

vroom /vro͞om; vro͝om/ *informal* ▸*v.* [*intrans.*] (of an engine in a vehicle) make a roaring sound by being run at very high speed. ■ [*trans.*] cause (an engine in a vehicle) to make such a sound in this way. ■ [*intrans.*] (of a vehicle or its driver) travel at great speed: *she still had the car and she would vroom up at midnight.*
▸*n.* the roaring sound of an engine or motor vehicle.
▸*exclam.* used to express or imitate such a sound to suggest speed or acceleration: *press the ignition button and vroom!* ▷1960s: imitative.

VS ▸*abbr.* Veterinary Surgeon.

vs. ▸*abbr.* versus.

V-sign ▸*n.* **1** a sign resembling the letter V made with the palm of the hand facing outward, used as a symbol or gesture of victory. **2** *Brit.* a similar sign made with the first two fingers pointing up and the back of the hand facing outward, used as a gesture of abuse or contempt.

VSO ▸*abbr.* Voluntary Service Overseas.

VSOP ▸*abbr.* Very Special Old Pale, a kind of brandy.

VT ▸*abbr.* Vermont (in official postal use).

Vt. ▸*abbr.* Vermont.

VTO ▸*abbr.* vertical takeoff.

VTOL /ˈvē,täl; -,tôl/ ▸*abbr.* vertical takeoff and landing.

VTR ▸*abbr.* videotape recorder.

vug /vəg/ ▸*n. Geology* a cavity in rock, lined with mineral crystals. ▷early 19th cent.: from Cornish *vooga*. **—vug·gy** /ˈvəgē/ *adj.* **—vug·u·lar** /ˈvəgyələr/ *adj.*

Vuil·lard /vwēˈyär/, (Jean) Édouard (1868–1940), French painter and graphic artist. A member of the Nabi Group, he produced decorative panels, murals, paintings, and lithographs, particularly of domestic interiors and portraits.

Vul·can /ˈvəlkən/ *Roman Mythology* the god of fire. Greek equivalent **HEPHAESTUS**.

Vul·ca·ni·an /,vəlˈkānēən/ ▸*adj.* **1** associated with the god Vulcan. ■ (also **vulcanian**) associated with metalworking or metallurgy. **2** (also **vulcanian**) *Geology* relating to or denoting a type of volcanic eruption marked by periodic explosive events. [early 20th cent.: from *Vulcano*, the name of a volcano in the Lipari Islands, Italy, + **-IAN**.]

vul·can·ism /ˈvəlkə,nizəm/ ▸*n.* variant spelling of **VOLCANISM**.

vul·can·ite /ˈvəlkə,nīt/ ▸*n.* hard black vulcanized rubber. ▷mid 19th cent.: from **VULCAN** + **-ITE**[1].

vul·can·ize /ˈvəlkə,nīz/ ▸*v.* [*trans.*] harden (rubber or rubberlike material) by treating it with sulfur at a high temperature. ▷early 19th cent. (in the sense 'throw into a fire'): from **VULCAN** + **-IZE**. **—vul·can·iz·a·ble** *adj.* **—vul·can·i·za·tion** /,vəlkənəˈzāSHən/ *n.* **—vul·can·iz·er** *n.*

vul·can·ol·o·gy /,vəlkəˈnäləjē/ ▸*n.* variant spelling of **VOLCANOLOGY**.

Vulg. ▸*abbr.* ■ Vulgate.

vul·gar /ˈvəlgər/ ▸*adj.* lacking sophistication or good taste; unrefined: *the vulgar trappings of wealth.* ■ making explicit and offensive reference to sex or bodily functions; coarse and rude: *a vulgar joke.* ■ *dated* characteristic of or belonging to the masses. ▷late Middle English: from Latin *vulgaris*, from *vulgus* 'common people.' The original sense was 'used in ordinary calculations' (surviving in **VULGAR FRACTION**) and 'in ordinary use, used by the people' (surviving in **VULGAR LATIN** and **VULGAR TONGUE**). **—vul·gar·i·ty** /,vəlˈgaritē/ *n.* (*pl.* **-ties**) **—vul·gar·ly** *adv.*

vul·gar frac·tion ▸*n.* British term for **COMMON FRACTION**.

vul·gar·i·an /,vəlˈge(ə)rēən/ ▸*n.* an unrefined person, esp. one with newly acquired power or wealth.

vul·gar·ism /ˈvəlgə,rizəm/ ▸*n.* a word or expression that is considered inelegant, esp. one that makes explicit and offensive reference to sex or bodily functions. ■ *archaic* an instance of rude or offensive behavior.

vul·gar·ize /ˈvəlgə,rīz/ ▸*v.* [*trans.*] make less refined: *her voice, vulgarized by its accent, was full of caressing tones.* ■ make commonplace or less subtle or complex: [as *adj.*] (**vulgarized**) *a vulgarized version of the argument.* **—vul·gar·i·za·tion** /,vəlgərəˈzāSHən/ *n.*

vul·gar Lat·in ▸*n.* informal Latin of classical times.

vul·gar tongue ▸*n.* (**the vulgar tongue**) *dated* the national or vernacular language of a people (used typically to contrast such a language with Latin).

Vul·gate /ˈvəl,gāt; -gət/ ▸*n.* **1** the principal Latin version of the Bible, prepared mainly by St. Jerome in the late 4th century, and (as revised in 1592) adopted as the official text for the Roman Catholic Church. **2** (**vul·gate**) [in *sing.*] *formal* common or colloquial speech: *I required a new, formal language in which to address him, not the vulgate.* **3** (**vul·gate**) the traditionally accepted text of any author. ▷from Latin *vulgata (editio)* '(edition) prepared for the public,' feminine past participle of *vulgare*, from *vulgus* 'common people.'

vuln[1] /vəln/ ▸*v.* [*trans.*] *Heraldry* wound. ▷late 16th cent.: formed irregularly from Latin *vulnerare* 'to wound.'

vuln[2] ▸*n.* a vulnerability, esp. one associated with computer security: *the total of 10 vulns discovered are described as highly critical.*

vul·ner·a·ble /ˈvəln(ə)rəbəl/ ▸*adj.* susceptible to physical or emotional attack or harm: *we were in a vulnerable position* | *small fish are* **vulnerable to** *predators.* ■ *Bridge* (of a partnership) liable to higher penalties, either by convention or through having won one game toward a rubber. ▷early 17th cent.: from late Latin *vulnerabilis*, from Latin *vulnerare* 'to wound,' from *vulnus* 'wound.' **—vul·ner·a·bil·i·ty** /,vəln(ə)rəˈbilitē/ *n.* (*pl.* **-ties**) **—vul·ner·a·ble·ness** *n.* **—vul·ner·a·bly** /-blē/ *adv.*

vul·ner·ar·y /ˈvəlnə,rerē/ *archaic* ▸*adj.* (of a drug, plant, etc.) of use in the healing of wounds.
▸*n.* (*pl.* **-ar·ies**) a medicine of this kind. ▷late 16th cent.: from Latin *vulnerarius*, from *vulnus* 'wound.'

Vul·pec·u·la /,vəlˈpekyələ/ *Astronomy* an inconspicuous northern constellation (the Fox), lying in the Milky Way between Cygnus and Aquila. ■ [as *genitive*] (**Vulpeculae** /-yəlē/) used with a preceding letter or numeral to designate a star in this constellation:

the star Alpha Vulpeculae. ▷Latin, diminutive of *vulpes* 'fox.'

vul·pine /'vəl,pīn/ ▸*adj.* of or relating to a fox or foxes. ■ crafty; cunning: *Karl gave a vulpine smile.* ▷early 17th cent.: from Latin *vulpinus*, from *vulpes* 'fox.'

vul·ture /'vəlCHər/ ▸*n.* **1** a large bird of prey with the head and neck more or less bare of feathers, feeding chiefly on carrion and reputed to gather with others in anticipation of the death of a sick or injured animal or person. • Order Accipitriformes: the **Old World vultures** (family Accipitridae, esp. *Gyps* and *Aegypius*) and the **New World vultures** (with the condors in the family Cathartidae). **2** a contemptible person who preys on or exploits others. ▷late Middle English: from Anglo-Norman French *vultur*, from Latin *vulturius*. **—vul·tur·ine** /-,rīn/ *adj.* **—vul·tur·ish** *adj.* **—vul·tur·ous** /-CHərəs/ *adj.*

vul·va /'vəlvə/ ▸*n. Anatomy* the female external genitals. ■ *Zoology* the external opening of the vagina or reproductive tract in a female mammal or nematode. ▷late Middle English: from Latin, literally 'womb.' **—vul·val** *adj.* **—vul·var** *adj.*

vul·vi·tis /,vəl'vītis/ ▸*n. Medicine* inflammation of the vulva.

vul·vo·vag·in·i·tis /,vəlvō,vajə'nītis/ ▸*n.* inflammation of the vulva and vagina.

vv. ▸*abbr.* ■ verses. ■ volumes.

Vyat·ka /'vyätkə; vē'ät-/ an industrial town in western Russia, in the central part of European Russia, on the Vyatka River; pop. 487,000. Former name (1934–92) **Kirov**.

vy·ing /'vī-iNG/ ▸ present participle of **vie**.

Ww

W[1] /ˈdəbəl,yo͞o/ (also **w**) ▸*n.* (*pl.* **Ws** or **W's**) **1** the twenty-third letter of the alphabet. ■ denoting the next after V in a set of items, categories, etc. **2** a shape like that of a letter W: [in *combination*] *the* **W-shaped** *northern constellation of Cassiopeia.*

W[2] ▸*abbr.* ■ Wales. ■ *Baseball* WALK (sense 3 of the *noun*). ■ warden. ■ (in tables of sports results) games won. ■ watt(s). ■ Wednesday. ■ week. ■ (**w**) weight. ■ Welsh. ■ West or Western: *104° W | W Europe.* ■ (in personal ads) White. ■ *Cricket* (on scorecards) wicket(s). ■ width: *23 in. H x 20.5 in. W x 16 in. D.* ■ (in personal ads) widowed. ■ (in genealogies) wife. ■ (in shortwave transmissions) with. ■ women's (clothes size). ■ *Physics* work.
▸*symbol* ■ the chemical element tungsten. [from modern Latin *wolframium.*]

WA ▸*abbr.* ■ Washington (State) (in official postal use). ■ Western Australia.

Wa /wä/ ▸*n.* (*pl.* same or **Was**) **1** a member of a hill people living on the border between China and Myanmar (Burma). **2** the Mon-Khmer language of this people.
▸*adj.* of, relating to, or denoting this people or their language.

Waac /wak/ ▸*n.* a member of the Women's Army Auxiliary Corps (later the WAC) formed in 1942, now no longer a separate branch. ▷acronym.

Waadt /vät/ German name for **VAUD**.

Waal /väl/ a river in south central Netherlands. The most southern of two major distributaries of the Rhine River, it flows for 52 miles (84 km) from the point where the Rhine forks, just west of the border with Germany, to the estuary of the Meuse (Maas) River on the North Sea.

Wa·bash Riv·er /ˈwô,basʜ/ a river that flows for 475 miles (765 km) from western Ohio across Indiana and then along the Indiana-Illinois border to the Ohio River.

wa·bi /ˈwäbē/ ▸*n.* (in Japanese art) a quality of austere and serene beauty expressing a mood of spiritual solitude recognized in Zen Buddhist philosophy. ▷Japanese, literally 'solitude.'

WAC /wak/ ▸*abbr.* Women's Army Corps. See **WAAC**. ■ (also **Wac**) a member of the Women's Army Corps.

wack /wak/ *informal* ▸*adj.* bad; inferior: *a wack radio station.*
▸*n.* **1** a crazy or eccentric person. **2** worthless or stupid ideas, work, or talk; rubbish: *this track is a load of wack.* ▷1930s: probably a back-formation from **WACKY**.

wack·e /ˈwakə/ ▸*n. Geology* a sandstone of which the mud matrix in which the grains are embedded amounts to between 15 and 75 percent of the mass. ▷early 19th cent.: from German, from Middle High German *wacke* 'large stone,' Old High German *wacko* 'pebble.'

wacked ▸*adj.* variant spelling of **WHACKED**.

wack·o /ˈwakō/ (also **whack·o**) *informal* ▸*adj.* mad; insane: *wacko fundamentalists.*
▸*n.* (*pl.* **-os**) a crazy person. ▷1970s: from **WACKY** + **-O**.

wack·y /ˈwakē/ (also **whack·y**) ▸*adj.* (**wack·i·er, wack·i·est**) *informal* funny or amusing in a slightly odd or peculiar way: *a wacky chase movie.* ▷mid 19th cent. (originally dialect): from the noun **WHACK** + **-Y**[1]. **—wack·i·ly** /ˈwakəlē/ *adv.* **—wack·i·ness** *n.*

Wa·co /ˈwākō/ a commercial and industrial city in east central Texas; pop. 103,590.

wad /wäd/ ▸*n.* **1** a lump or bundle of a soft material, used for padding, stuffing, or wiping: *a* **wad of** *cotton.* ■ *chiefly historical* a disk of felt or another material used to keep powder or shot in place in a gun barrel. ■ a portion of chewing gum, or of tobacco or another narcotic when used for chewing. **2** a bundle of paper, banknotes, or documents: *a thick* **wad of** *index cards.* ■ *informal* a large amount of something, esp. money: *she was working on TV and had* **wads of** *money.*
▸*v.* (**wad·ded, wad·ding**) [*trans.*] [usu. as *adj.*] (**wadded**) **1** compress (a soft material) into a lump or bundle: *a wadded handkerchief.* **2** stop up (an aperture or a gun barrel) with a bundle or lump of soft material: *he had something wadded behind his teeth.* ■ line or stuff (a garment or piece of furniture) with wadding: *a wadded sheepskin coat.* ▷mid 16th cent. (denoting wadding): perhaps related to Dutch *watten*, French *ouate* 'padding, absorbent cotton.'
▸*PHRASE* □ **shoot one's wad** spend all one's money. [originally, to fire one's gun with only the wad for a projectile when one's ammunition is exhausted.]

wad·cut·ter /ˈwäd,kətər/ ▸*n.* a bullet designed to cut a neat hole in a paper range target.

wad·ding /ˈwädiɴɢ/ ▸*n.* soft, thick material used to line garments or pack fragile items, esp. absorbent cotton. ■ a material from which wads for guns are made.

wad·dle /ˈwädl/ ▸*v.* [*intrans.*] walk with short steps and a clumsy swaying motion: *three geese waddled across the road.*
▸*n.* [in *sing.*] a waddling gait: *I walk with a waddle.* ▷late 16th cent.: perhaps a frequentative of **WADE**. **—wad·dler** /ˈwädlər; ˈwädl-ər/ *n.*

wad·dy /ˈwädē/ ▸*n.* (*pl.* **-dies**) an Australian Aboriginal's war club. ■ *Austral./NZ* a club or stick, esp. a walking stick. ▷from Dharuk *wadi* 'tree, stick, club.'

Wade /wād/, (Sarah) Virginia (1945–), English tennis player. She won singles titles at the U.S. Open in 1968, at the Australian Open in 1972, and at Wimbledon in 1977.

wade /wād/ ▸*v.* [*intrans.*] walk through water or another liquid or soft substance: *we waded ashore.* ■ [*trans.*] walk through (something filled with water): *firefighters waded the waist-deep flood water.* ■ (**wade through**) read laboriously through (a long piece of writing). ■ (**wade into**) *informal* get involved in (something) vigorously or forcefully: *he waded into the yelling, fighting crowd.* ■ (**wade in**) *informal* make a vigorous attack or intervention: *Nicola waded in and grabbed the baby.*
▸*n.* [in *sing.*] an act of wading. ▷Old English *wadan* 'move onward,' also 'penetrate,' from a Germanic word meaning 'go (through),' from an Indo-European root shared by Latin *vadere* 'go,' as in **VADE MECUM**. **—wad·a·ble** (also **wade·a·ble**) *adj.*

Wade–Giles /ˈwād ˈjīlz/ ▸*n.* a system of romanized spelling for transliterating Chinese, devised by Sir Thomas Francis Wade (1818–95) and Herbert Allen Giles (1845–1935). It has been largely superseded by Pinyin.

wad·er /ˈwādər/ ▸*n.* **1** a person or animal, esp. a bird, that wades, in particular: ■ a wading bird of the order Ciconiiformes, which comprises the herons, storks, and ibises. ■ *chiefly Brit.* a wading bird of the order Charadriiformes, which comprises the sandpipers, plovers, and related birds. Also called **SHOREBIRD**, esp. in North America. **2** (**waders**) high waterproof boots, or a waterproof garment for the legs and body, used esp. by anglers when fishing.

wa·di /ˈwädē/ ▸*n.* (*pl.* **-dis** /-ēz/ or **-dies** /-ēz/) (in certain Arabic-speaking countries) a valley, ravine, or channel that is dry except in the rainy season. ▷early 17th cent.: from Arabic *wādī*.

wad·ing pool ▸*n.* a shallow artificial pool for children to paddle in.

WAF /waf/ ▸*abbr.* Women in the Air Force.
▸*n.* a member of the WAF.

wa·fer /ˈwāfər/ ▸*n.* a very thin, light, crisp, sweet cookie or cracker, esp. one of a kind eaten with ice cream. ■ a thin disk of unleavened bread used in the Eucharist. ■ *Electronics* a very thin slice of a semiconductor crystal used as the substrate for solid-state circuitry. ■ *historical* a small disk of dried paste formerly used for fastening letters or holding papers together. ■ a round, thin piece of something: *a wafer of ice.*
▸*v.* [*trans.*] *rare* fasten or seal (a letter, document, etc.) with a wafer. ▷late Middle English: from an Anglo-Norman French variant of Old French *gaufre* (see **GOFFER**), from Middle Low German *wāfel* 'waffle'; compare with **WAFFLE**[2]. **—wa·fer·y** *adj.*

wa·fer-thin ▸*adj.* & *adv.* very thin or thinly: [as *adj.*] *plates of wafer-thin metal* | [as *adv.*] *slicing meats wafer-thin.*

Waf·fen SS /ˈväfən/ ▸*n.* (**the Waffen SS**) the combat units of the SS in Nazi Germany during World War II. ▷German *Waffen* 'arms, weapons.'

waf·fle[1] /ˈwäfəl; ˈwô-/ *informal* ▸*v.* [*intrans.*] **1** fail to make up one's mind: *Joseph had been waffling over where to go.* **2** *chiefly Brit.* speak or write, esp. at great length, without saying anything important or useful: *he* **waffled on** *about everything that didn't matter.*
▸*n.* **1** a failure to make up one's mind: *his waffle on abortion.* **2** *chiefly Brit.* lengthy but trivial or useless talk or writing. ▷late 17th cent. (originally in the sense 'yap, yelp'): frequentative of dialect *waff* 'yelp,' of imitative origin. **—waf·fler** /ˈwäf(ə)lər; ˈwô-/ *n.* **—waf·fly** /ˈwäf(ə)lē; ˈwô-/ *adj.*

waf·fle[2] ▸*n.* a small crisp batter cake, baked in a waffle iron and eaten hot with butter or syrup.
▸*adj.* denoting a style of fine honeycomb weaving or a fabric woven to give a honeycomb effect. ▷mid 18th cent.: from Dutch *wafel*; compare with **WAFER** and **GOFFER**.

waf·fle i·ron ▸*n.* a utensil, typically consisting of two shallow metal pans hinged together, used for baking waffles.

waft /wäft; waft/ ▸*v.* pass or cause to pass easily or gently through or as if through the air: [*intrans.*] *the smell of stale fat wafted out from the café* | [*trans.*] *each breeze would waft pollen around the house.*
▸*n.* a gentle movement of air. ■ a scent or odor carried on such a movement of air. ▷early 16th cent. (in the sense 'escort (a ship)'): back-formation from obsolete *wafter* 'armed convoy vessel,' from Low German, Dutch *wachter*, from *wachten* 'to guard.' A sense 'convey by water' gave rise to the current use of the verb.

wag[1] /wag/ ▸*v.* (**wagged, wag·ging**) (with reference to an animal's tail) move or cause to move rapidly to and fro: [*intrans.*] *his tail began to wag* | [*trans.*] *the dog went out, wagging its tail.* ■ [*trans.*] move (an upward-pointing finger) from side to side to signify a warning or reprimand: *she wagged a finger at Elinor.* ■ [*intrans.*] (used of a tongue, jaw, or chin, as representing a person) talk, esp. in order to gossip or spread rumors: *this is a small island, and tongues are beginning to wag.*
▸*n.* a single rapid movement from side to side: *a chirpy wag of the head.* ▷Middle English (as a verb): from the Germanic base of Old English *wagian* 'to sway.'
▸*PHRASES* □ **how the world wags** *dated* how affairs are going or being conducted. □ **the tail wags the dog** see **TAIL**[1].

wag[2] ▸*n. dated* a person who makes facetious jokes. ▷mid 16th cent. (denoting a young man or mischievous boy, also used as a term of endearment to an infant): probably from obsolete *waghalter* 'person likely to be hanged' (see **WAG**[1], **HALTER**).

wage /wāj/ ▸*n.* (usu. **wages**) a fixed regular payment,

W

typically paid on a daily or weekly basis, made by an employer to an employee, esp. to a manual or unskilled worker: *we were struggling to get better wages.* Compare with SALARY. ■ (**wages**) *Economics* the part of total production that is the return to labor as earned income as distinct from the remuneration received by capital as unearned income. ■ *figurative* the result or effect of doing something considered wrong or unwise: *the wages of sin is death.*

▸*v.* [*trans.*] carry on (a war or campaign): *it is necessary to destroy their capacity to wage war.* ▷Middle English: from Anglo-Norman French and Old Northern French, of Germanic origin; related to GAGE[1] and WED.

wage drift ▸*n. Finance* the tendency for the average level of wages actually paid to rise above wage rates through increases in overtime and other factors.

wa·ger /ˈwājər/ ▸*n.* & *v.* more formal term for BET. ▷Middle English (also in the sense 'solemn pledge'): from Anglo-Norman French *wageure,* from *wager* 'to wage.'

wage slave ▸*n. informal* a person wholly dependent on income from employment, typically employment of an arduous or menial nature. —**wage slav·er·y** *n.*

wag·ger·y /ˈwagərē/ ▸*n.* (*pl.* **-ger·ies**) *dated* waggish behavior or remarks; jocularity. ■ *archaic* a waggish action or remark.

wag·gish /ˈwagisн/ ▸*adj. dated* humorous in a playful, mischievous, or facetious manner: *a waggish riposte.* —**wag·gish·ly** *adv.* —**wag·gish·ness** *n.*

wag·gle /ˈwagəl/ ▸*v. informal* move or cause to move with short quick movements from side to side or up and down: [*intrans.*] *his arm waggled* | [*trans.*] *Mary waggled a glass at them.* ■ [*trans.*] swing (a golf club) loosely to and fro over the ball before playing a shot.

▸*n.* an act of waggling. ▷late 16th cent.: frequentative of WAG[1].

wag·gle dance ▸*n.* a waggling movement performed by a honeybee at the hive or nest, to indicate to other bees the direction and distance of a source of food.

wag·gly /ˈwag(ə)lē/ ▸*adj.* moving with quick short movements from side to side or up and down: *a waggly tail.*

Wag·ner[1] /ˈwagnər/, Honus (1874–1955), U.S. baseball player and coach; full name *John Peter Wagner;* known as the **Flying Dutchman**. Joining the National League in 1897 and playing shortstop for the Pittsburgh Pirates 1900–1917, he was noted for hitting, stealing bases, and speed. Baseball Hall of Fame (1936).

Wag·ner[2] /ˈvägnər/, (Wilhelm) Richard (1813–83), German composer. He developed an operatic genre that he called music drama, synthesizing music, drama, verse, legend, and spectacle. Notable works: *The Flying Dutchman* (1841), *Der Ring des Nibelungen* (1847–74), *Tristan and Isolde* (1859), and the *Siegfried Idyll* (1870).

Wag·ne·ri·an /vägˈne(ə)rēən/ ▸*adj.* of, relating to, or characteristic of the operas of Richard Wagner. ■ *figurative* having the enormous dramatic scale and intensity of a Wagner opera: *a strategic predicament of positively Wagnerian proportions.*

▸*n.* an admirer of Wagner or his music.

Wag·ner tu·ba ▸*n.* a brass instrument of baritone pitch with an oval shape and upward-pointing bell, combining features of the tuba and the French horn and first used in Wagner's *Der Ring des Nibelungen.*

wag·on /ˈwagən/ (*Brit.* also **wag·gon**) ▸*n.* a vehicle used for transporting goods or another specified purpose: *a coal wagon* | *an ammunition wagon.* ■ a four-wheeled trailer for agricultural use, or a small version of this for use as a child's toy. ■ a horse-drawn vehicle, esp. a covered wagon used by early settlers in North America and elsewhere. ■ a wheeled cart or hut used as a food stall. ■ a small cart or wheeled table used for serving drinks or food. ■ a vehicle like a camper used by gypsies or circus performers. ■ *informal* short for STATION WAGON. ■ *Brit.* a railroad freight car. ▷late 15th cent.: from Dutch *wagen;* related to WAIN.

▸**PHRASES** □ **fix someone's wagon** bring about a person's downfall or spoil their chances of success. □ **hitch one's wagon to a star** see HITCH. □ **off the wagon** (of an alcoholic) drinking after a period of abstinence: *she* **fell off the wagon** *two days after making a resolution to quit.* □ **on the wagon** *informal* (of an alcoholic) abstaining from drinking: *Agnes was thinking of* **going on the wagon** *again.*

wag·on·er /ˈwagənər/ (*Brit.* also **wag·goner**) ▸*n.* the driver of a horse-drawn wagon. ▷mid 16th cent.: from Dutch *wagenaar,* from *wagen* (see WAGON).

wag·on·ette /ˌwagəˈnet/ (*Brit.* also **wag·gon·ette**) ▸*n.* a four-wheeled horse-drawn pleasure vehicle, typically open, with facing side seats and one or two seats arranged crosswise in front.

wag·on-lit /ˈvägôɴ ˈlē/ ▸*n.* (*pl.* **wag·ons-lits** *pronunc.* same) a sleeping car on a Continental railroad. ▷from French *wagon* 'railroad car' + *lit* 'bed'.

wag·on·load /ˈwagənˌlōd/ ▸*n.* an amount of something that can be carried in one wagon: *a* **wagonload** *of food.*

wag·on train ▸*n. historical* a convoy or train of covered horse-drawn wagons, as used by pioneers or settlers in North America.

wag·tail /ˈwagˌtāl/ ▸*n.* a slender Eurasian and African songbird with a long tail that is frequently wagged up and down, typically living by water. • Family Motacillidae: two genera, in particular *Motacilla,* and several species.

Wah·ha·bi /wəˈhäbē; wä-/ (also **Wa·ha·bi**) ▸*n.* (*pl.* **-bis** /-bēz/) a member of a strictly orthodox Sunni Muslim sect founded by Muhammad ibn Abd al-Wahhab (1703–92). It advocates a return to the early Islam of the Koran and Sunna, rejecting later innovations; the sect is still the predominant religious force in Saudi Arabia. —**Wah·ha·bism** /-bizəm/ *n.* —**Wah·ha·bite** *n.* & *adj.*

wa·hi·ne /wäˈhēnē/ ▸*n.* **1** a Polynesian woman or wife, esp. in Hawaii or New Zealand. **2** a young woman surfer. ▷Hawaiian or Maori.

wa·hoo[1] /ˈwäˌho͞o; ˌwäˈho͞o/ ▸*n.* **1** (also **wa·hoo elm**) another term for WINGED ELM. ▷perhaps from Creek *ahá-hwa* 'walnut.'

wa·hoo[2] ▸ a North American burning bush. • *Euonymus atropurpurea,* family Celastraceae. ▷from Dakota.

wa·hoo[3] ▸ a large predatory tropical marine fish of the mackerel family, prized as a game fish. • *Acanthocybium solanderi,* family Scombridae. ▷early 20th cent.: of unknown origin.

wa·hoo[4] ▸*exclam.* another term for YAHOO[2]. ▷1940s: probably a natural exclamation.

wah-wah /ˈwä ˈwä/ (also **wa-wa**) ▸*n.* a musical effect achieved on brass instruments by alternately applying and removing a mute and on an electric guitar by controlling the output from the amplifier with a pedal. ■ a pedal for producing such an effect on an electric guitar. ▷1920s: imitative.

waif /wāf/ ▸*n.* **1** a homeless and helpless person, esp. a neglected or abandoned child: *she is foster-mother to various* **waifs and strays.** ■ an abandoned pet animal. **2** *Law* a piece of property thrown away by a fleeing thief and held by the state in trust for the owner to claim. ▷late Middle English: from an Anglo-Norman French variant of Old Northern French *gaif,* probably of Scandinavian origin. Early use was often in *waif and stray,* as a legal term denoting a piece of property found and, if unclaimed, falling to the lord of the manor. —**waif·ish** *adj.*

Wai·ka·to /wīˈkätō; -ˈkatō/ a river in New Zealand that flows northwest for 270 miles (434 km) from the center of North Island to the Tasman Sea, the country's longest river.

Wai·ki·ki /ˌwīkiˈkē/ a beach resort in Hawaii, a suburb of Honolulu, on the island of Oahu.

wail /wāl/ ▸*n.* a prolonged high-pitched cry of pain, grief, or anger: *Christopher let out a wail.* ■ a sound resembling this: *the wail of an air-raid siren.*

▸*v.* [*intrans.*] give such a cry of pain, grief, or anger: *Tina ran off wailing* | [with *direct speech*] *"But why?" she wailed.* ■ make a sound resembling such a cry: *the wind wailed and buffeted the timber structure.* ■ [*trans.*] *poetic/literary* manifest or feel deep sorrow for; lament: *she wailed her wretched life.* ▷Middle English: from Old Norse; related to WOE. —**wail·er** *n.* —**wail·ful** /-fəl/ *adj.* (*poetic/literary*) —**wail·ing·ly** *adv.*

Wail·ing Wall /ˈwāliɴɢ/ another name for WESTERN WALL.

Wai·mea Can·yon /wīˈmāə/ (also **the Grand Canyon of the Pacific**) a deep canyon in western Kauai Island in Hawaii.

Wain /wān/, John (Barrington) (1925–94), English writer and critic. One of the Angry Young Men of the early 1950s, he was later professor of poetry at Oxford 1973–78.

wain /wān/ ▸*n. archaic* a wagon or cart. ■ (**the Wain**) short for CHARLES'S WAIN. ▷Old English *wæg(e)n,* of Germanic origin; related to Dutch *wagen* and German *Wagen,* also to WAY and WEIGH[1].

wain·scot /ˈwānˌskōt; -skət; -ˌskät/ ▸*n.* [in *sing.*] an area of wooden paneling on the lower part of the walls of a room. ■ *Brit., historical* imported oak of fine quality, used mainly to make paneling.

▸*v.* (**-scot·ed**, **-scot·ing** or **-scot·ted**, **-scot·ting**) [*trans.*] line (a room or wall) with wooden paneling. ▷Middle English: from Middle Low German *wagenschot,* apparently from *wagen* 'wagon' + *schot,* probably meaning 'partition.'

wain·scot·ing /ˈwānˌskōtiɴɢ; -ˌskä-/ (also **wain·scot·ting**) ▸*n.* wooden paneling that lines the lower part of the walls of a room. ■ material for such paneling.

Wain·wright /ˈwānˌrīt/, Jonathan Mayhew (1883–1953), U.S. army officer. The general in charge of all U.S. troops on the Philippine Islands from 1942, he was forced to surrender at Corregidor 1942 and was held as a prisoner of war by the Japanese until 1945.

wain·wright /ˈwānˌrīt/ ▸*n. historical* a wagon-builder.

Wai·pa·hu /wīˈpäho͞o/ a city in Hawaii, on southern Oahu Island, west of Pearl City; pop. 33,108.

WAIS /wās/ ▸*abbr. Computing* wide area information service, designed to provide access to information across a computer network.

waist /wāst/ ▸*n.* the part of the human body below the ribs and above the hips. ■ the circumference of this: *her waist is 28 inches.* ■ a narrowing of the trunk of the body at this point: *the last time you had a waist was around 1978.* ■ the part of a garment encircling or covering the waist. ■ the point at which a garment is shaped so as to narrow between the rib cage and the hips: *a jacket with a high waist.* ■ a blouse or bodice. ■ a narrow part in the middle of anything, such as a violin, an hourglass, the body of wasp, etc. ■ the middle part of a ship, between the forecastle and the quarterdeck. ▷late Middle English: apparently representing an Old English word from the Germanic root of WAX[2]. —**waist·ed** *adj.* [in *combination*] *high-waisted.* —**waist·less** *adj.*

waist·band /ˈwās(t)ˌband/ ▸*n.* a strip of cloth forming the waist of a garment such as a skirt or a pair of trousers.

waist cloth ▸*n.* a loincloth.

waist·coat /ˈwās(t)ˌkōt; ˈweskət/ ▸*n. Brit.* a vest, esp. one worn by men over a shirt and under a jacket. ■ *historical* a man's quilted long-sleeved garment worn under a doublet in the 16th and 17th centuries.

waist-deep (also **waist-high**) ▸*adj.* & *adv.* of or at a depth to reach the waist: [as *adj.*] *the waist-deep water* | [as *adv.*] *Ellwood stood waist-high in the water.* ■ of or at a height to reach the waist: [as *adj.*] *a ruin surrounded by waist-high grass and nettles.*

waist·line /ˈwās(t)ˌlīn/ ▸*n.* an imaginary line around a person's body at the waist, esp. with respect to its size: *eliminating inches from the waistline.* ■ the shaping and position of the waist of a garment.

wait /wāt/ ▸*v.* [*intrans.*] **1** stay where one is or delay action until a particular time or until something else happens: *he did not* **wait for** *a reply* | *they will* **wait on** *a Supreme Court ruling* | [with *infinitive*] *Ben stood on the street corner waiting to cross* | [*trans.*] *I had to wait my turn to play.* ■ remain in readiness for some purpose: *he found the car waiting on the platform.* ■ be left until a later time before being dealt with: *we shall need a statement later, but that will have to wait.* ■ [*trans.*] *informal* defer (a meal) until a person's arrival: *he will wait supper for me.* ■ (**wait on/upon**) *chiefly Brit.* await the convenience of: *we can't wait on the government; we have to do it ourselves.* **2** (**cannot wait**) used to indicate that one is eagerly impatient to do something or for something to happen: *I can't wait for tomorrow* | [with *infinitive*] *I can't wait to get started again.* **3** act as a waiter or waitress, serving food and drink: *a local man was employed to* **wait on** *them at table* | [*trans.*] *we had to wait tables in the mess hall.*

▸*phrasal v.* □ **wait on** (or **upon**) act as an attendant to (someone): *a maid was appointed to wait on her.* ■ serve (a customer) in a store. ■ *archaic* pay a respectful visit to. □ **wait up** **1** not go to bed until someone arrives or something happens. **2** go more slowly or stop until someone catches up.

▸*n.* **1** [in *sing.*] a period of waiting: *we had a long wait.* **2** (**waits**) *Brit., archaic* street singers of Christmas carols. ■ *historical* official bands of musicians maintained by a city or town. ▷Middle English: from Old Northern French *waitier,* of Germanic origin; related to WAKE[1]. Early senses included 'lie in wait (for),' 'observe carefully,' and 'be watchful.'

▸**PHRASES** □ **wait and see** wait to find out what will

Pronunciation Key ə *ago*; ər *over*; ˈə or ˌə *up*; ˈər or ˌər *fur*; a *hat*; ā *rate*; ä *car*; CH *chew*; e *let*; ē *see*; e(ə)r *air*; i *fit*; ī *by*; i(ə)r *ear*; NG *sing*; ō *go*; ô *for*; oi *boy*; o͝o *good*; o͞o *goo*; ou *out*; SH *she*; TH *thin*; T͟H *then*; (h)w *why*; ZH *vision*

happen before doing or deciding something. □ **you wait** used to convey a threat, warning, or promise: *just you wait till your father comes home!*

wait-a-bit (also **wait-a-bit thorn**) ▸*n. chiefly S. African* an African bush with hooked thorns that catch the clothing, in particular an acacia. ▷translating Afrikaans *wag-'n-bietjie*, literally 'wait a bit.'

Waite /wāt/, Morrison Remick (1816–88), U.S. chief justice 1874–88. Appointed to the chief justiceship by President Grant, he wrote over 100 opinions, many of which upheld the power of state governments.

wait·er /ˈwātər/ ▸*n.* **1** a man whose job is to serve customers at their tables in a restaurant. **2** a person who waits for a time, event, or opportunity. **3** a small tray; a salver.

wait·ing /ˈwātiNG/ ▸*n.* **1** the action of staying where one is or delaying action until a particular time or until something else happens. **2** official attendance at court. See also LADY-IN-WAITING.

wait·ing game ▸*n.* a tactic in which one refrains from action for a time in order to act more effectively at a later date or stage: *policemen were playing a waiting game outside a country cottage.*

wait·ing list ▸*n.* a list of people waiting for something, esp. housing or admission to a school.

wait·ing room ▸*n.* a room provided for the use of people who are waiting to be seen by a doctor or dentist or who are waiting in a station for a bus or train.

wait list ▸*n.* another term for WAITING LIST.
▸*v.* (**wait-list**) [*trans.*] put (someone) on a waiting list.

wait·per·son /ˈwātˌpərsən/ ▸*n.* a waiter or waitress (used as a neutral alternative).

wait·ress /ˈwātris/ ▸*n.* a woman whose job is to serve customers at their tables in a restaurant.

wait·ress·ing /ˈwātrisiNG/ ▸*n.* the action or occupation of working as a waitress.

wait·ron /ˈwāträn; -trən/ ▸*n.* a waiter or waitress (used as a neutral alternative).

wait·staff /ˈwātstaf/ ▸*n.* [treated as *sing.* or *pl.*] waiters and waitresses collectively.

wait state ▸*n.* the condition of computer software or hardware being unable to process further instructions while waiting for some event such as the completion of a data transfer.

waive /wāv/ ▸*v.* [*trans.*] refrain from insisting on or using (a right or claim): *he will waive all rights to the money.* See note at RELINQUISH. ■ refrain from applying or enforcing (a rule, restriction, or fee): *her tuition fees would be waived.* ▷Middle English (originally as a legal term relating to removal of the protection of the law): from an Anglo-Norman French variant of Old French *gaiver* 'allow to become a waif, abandon.'

USAGE **Waive** and **waiver** should not be confused with **wave** and **waver**. **Waive** is a transitive verb that means 'surrender (a right or claim),' and **waiver** is its related noun, meaning 'an instance of waiving' or 'a document recording such waiving': *he **waived** potential rights in the case by signing the **waiver**.* **Wave**, as a transitive verb, means 'move (one's hand, or something in one's hand) to and fro': *she **waved** the paper to get their attention.* **Waver** is an intransitive verb that means 'shake with a quivering motion' or 'be undecided about two courses of action': *the tall grass **wavered** silently; at the last minute, he **wavered** and said he wasn't sure whether he should go.*

W

waiv·er /ˈwāvər/ ▸*n.* an act or instance of waiving a right or claim. ■ a document recording such waiving of a right or claim.

Wa·kam·ba /wäˈkämbə/ ▸ plural form of KAMBA.

wa·ka·me /ˈwäkəˌmā; wäˈkämā/ ▸*n.* an edible brown seaweed used, typically in dried form, in Chinese and Japanese cooking. • *Undaria pinnatifida*, class Phaeophyceae. ▷Japanese.

Wa·kash·an /wäˈkaSHən/ ▸*adj.* of, relating to, or denoting a small family of almost extinct American Indian languages of the northern Pacific coast, including Kwakiutl and Nootka.
▸*n.* this family of languages. ▷formed by Captain Cook from Nootka *wakash* 'bravo!' + -AN.

wake[1] /wāk/ ▸*v.* (*past* **woke** /wōk/ or **waked**; *past part.* **wok·en** /ˈwōkən/ or **waked**) **1** emerge or cause to emerge from a state of sleep; stop sleeping: [*intrans.*] *she **woke up** feeling better* | [*trans.*] *I wake him gently.* ■ [*intrans.*] (**wake up to**) become alert to or aware of: *he needs to wake up to reality.* ■ [*trans.*] *figurative* cause (something) to stir or come to life: *it wakes desire in others.* **2** [*trans.*] *dialect* hold a vigil beside (someone who has died): *we waked Jim last night.*
▸*n.* **1** a watch or vigil held beside the body of someone who has died, sometimes accompanied by ritual observances including eating and drinking. **2** (**wakes**) [treated as *sing.*] *chiefly historical* (in some parts of the UK) a festival and holiday held annually in a rural parish, originally on the feast day of the patron saint of the church. [probably from Old Norse *vaka*.] ▷Old English (recorded only in the past tense *wōc*), also partly from the weak verb *wacian* 'remain awake, hold a vigil,' of Germanic origin; related to Dutch *waken* and German *wachen*; compare with WATCH. **—wak·er** *n.*
▸*PHRASE* □ **wake up and smell the coffee** [usu. in *imperative*] *informal* become aware of the realities of a situation, however unpleasant.

wake[2] ▸*n.* a trail of disturbed water or air left by the passage of a ship or aircraft. ■ *figurative* used to refer to the aftermath or consequences of something: *the committee was set up **in the wake of** the inquiry.* ▷late 15th cent. (denoting a track made by a person or thing): probably via Middle Low German from Old Norse *vǫk, vaka* 'hole or opening in ice.'

wake·board /ˈwākˌbôrd/ ▸*n.* a board shaped like a broad waterski that is towed behind a motorboat and ridden like a surfboard.
▸*v.* [*intrans.*] ride a wakeboard: *I have wakeboarded for three years* | [as *n.*] (**wakeboarding**) *wakeboarding went from an unknown to a craze practically overnight.* ▷1990s: from WAKE[2], on the pattern of *surfboard.* **—wake·board·er** *n.*

Wake·field /ˈwākˌfēld/ an industrial town in eastern Massachusetts, north of Boston; pop. 24,825.

wake·ful /ˈwākfəl/ ▸*adj.* (of a person) unable or not needing to sleep: *he had been wakeful all night.* ■ alert and vigilant. ■ (of a period of time) passed with little or no sleep: *wakeful nights.* **—wake·ful·ly** *adv.* **—wake·ful·ness** *n.*

Wake Is·land /wāk/ a coral atoll in the Pacific Ocean, north of the Marshall Islands. Controlled by the U.S. since 1898, it was the scene of World War II fighting after the Japanese occupied it in December 1941.

wak·en /ˈwākən/ ▸*v.* poetic/literary term for WAKE[1] (sense 1). ▷Old English *wæcnan* 'be aroused,' of Germanic origin; related to WAKE[1].

wake-rob·in ▸*n.* **1** another term for TRILLIUM. **2** *Brit.* another term for CUCKOOPINT.

wake-up ▸*n.* [in *sing.*] an instance of a person waking up or being woken up.

wake-up call ▸*n.* a telephone call made according to a prior arrangement to wake the person called. ■ *figurative* a person or thing that causes people to become fully alert to an unsatisfactory situation and to take action to remedy it: *today's statistics will be a wake-up call for the administration.*

wak·ing /ˈwākiNG/ ▸*n.* the state of being awake: *he hangs between sleeping and waking.*

wa·ki·za·shi /ˌwäkēˈzäSHē/ ▸*n.* (*pl.* same) a Japanese sword shorter than a katana. ▷Japanese, from *waki* 'side' + *sasu* 'wear at one's side.'

Waks·man /ˈwäksmən; ˈwak-/, Selman Abraham (1888–1973), U.S. microbiologist, born in Russia. He discovered the antibiotic streptomycin for use esp. against tuberculosis. Nobel Prize for Physiology or Medicine (1952).

Wa·la·chi·a variant spelling of WALLACHIA.

Wal·cott /ˈwôlkət/ , Louis Eugene, see FARRAKHAN.

Wal·den Pond /ˈwôldən/ a pond in Concord in Massachusetts, associated with the writer Henry David Thoreau, now within a state park.

Wal·den·ses /wôlˈdensēz; wä-/ ▸*plural n.* a Christian sect that was founded in southern France *c.*1170 by Peter Valdes (d.1205), a merchant of Lyons, and adopted Calvinist doctrines during the Reformation, now existing chiefly in Italy and America. **—Wal·den·si·an** /-sēən/ *adj.* & *n.*

Wald·heim /ˈvôldˌhīm; ˈwôld-; ˈvält-/, Kurt (1918–), Austrian diplomat and statesman; president 1986–92. He was secretary-general of the UN 1972–81. His later career was blemished by revelations about his service as a German officer in World War II.

Wal·dorf sal·ad /ˈwôlˌdôrf/ ▸*n.* a salad made from apples, walnuts, celery, and mayonnaise. ▷named after the *Waldorf*-Astoria Hotel in New York, where it was first served.

wale /wāl/ ▸*n.* **1** a ridge on a textured woven fabric such as corduroy. **2** *Nautical* a plank running along the side of a wooden ship, thicker than the usual planking, and strengthening and protecting the hull. **3** a horizontal band around a woven basket. ▷late Old English *walu* 'stripe, weal.'

wale knot ▸*n.* another term for WALL KNOT.

Wal·er /ˈwālər/ ▸*n.* **1** a horse of a typically light breed from Australia, esp. from New South Wales. **2** *informal* a native or inhabitant of Australia, esp. New South Wales.

Wales /wālz/ a principality of Great Britain and the United Kingdom, west of central England; pop. 2,798,000; capital, Cardiff. The Celtic inhabitants of Wales successfully maintained independence from the Anglo-Saxons who settled in England following the withdrawal of the Romans. Norman colonization from England began in the 12th century, and English control over the country was assured by Edward I's conquest 1277–84. Edward began the custom of making the English sovereign's eldest son Prince of Wales. Wales was formally brought into the English legal and parliamentary system by Henry VIII in 1536 but has retained a distinct cultural identity. In 1997, a referendum narrowly approved proposals for a Welsh assembly. Welsh name CYMRU.

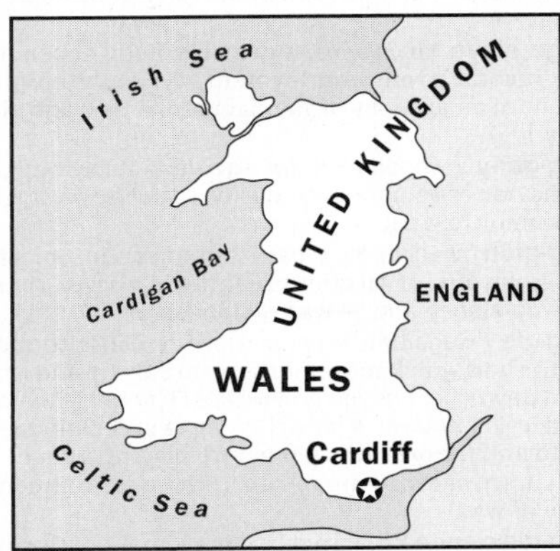

Wales, Prince of see PRINCE OF WALES; CHARLES, PRINCE.

Wa·łę·sa /vəˈlensə; vəˈwensə/, Lech (1943–), Polish labor leader and statesman; president 1990–95.The founder of the labor union called Solidarity (1980), he was imprisoned 1981–82 after the movement was banned. After Solidarity's landslide victory in the 1989 elections, he became president. Nobel Peace Prize (1983).

wa·li /ˈwälē/ ▸*n.* the governor of a province in an Arab country. ▷from Arabic *wālī*.

walk /wôk/ ▸*v.* **1** [*intrans.*] move at a regular and fairly slow pace by lifting and setting down each foot in turn, never having both feet off the ground at once: *I walked across the lawn* | *she turned and walked a few paces.* ■ use similar movements but of a different part of one's body or a support: *he could walk on his hands, carrying a plate on one foot.* ■ go on foot for recreation and exercise: *you can walk in 21,000 acres of mountain and moorland.* ■ [*trans.*] travel along or over (a route or area) on foot: *the police department has encouraged officers to walk the beat.* ■ (of a quadruped) proceed with the slowest gait, always having at least two feet on the ground at once. ■ [*trans.*] ride (a horse) at this pace: *he walked his horse toward her.* ■ *informal* abandon or suddenly withdraw from a job, commitment, or situation: *they can **walk away** from the deal* | *we were expecting the merger with Bell to go through—we didn't expect Bell to walk on the deal.* ■ *informal* be released from suspicion or from a charge: *had any of the others come clean during the trial, he might have walked.* ■ used to suggest that someone has achieved a state or position easily or undeservedly: *no one has the right to **walk straight into** a well-paid job for life.* ■ (of a ghost) be present and visible: *the ghosts of Bannockburn walked abroad.* ■ *archaic* used to describe the way in which someone lives or behaves: *walk humbly with your God.* ■ *Baseball* be awarded first base after not swinging at four balls pitched outside the strike zone. ■ [*trans.*] *Baseball* allow or enable (a batter) to do this. ■ *Baseball* (of a pitcher) give a walk with the bases loaded so as to force in (a run). ■ *Basketball* another term for TRAVEL (sense 2). **2** [*trans.*] cause or enable (someone or something) to walk or move as though walking: *she walked her fingers over the dresses.* ■ guide, accompany, or escort (someone) on foot: *he walked her home to her door.* ■ [*trans.*] take (a domestic animal, typically a dog) out for exercise: *a man walking his retriever.* ■ push (a bicycle or motorcycle) while walking alongside it.
▸*phrasal v.* □ **walk away** easily, casually, or irresponsibly abandon a situation in which one is involved or

for which one is responsible. □ **walk away with** *informal* another way of saying WALK OFF WITH. □ **walk in on** enter suddenly or unexpectedly. ■ intrude on: *he was clearly not expecting her to walk in on him just then.* □ **walk into** *informal* encounter or become involved in through ignorance or carelessness: *I had walked into a situation from which there was no escape.* □ **walk off with** *informal* **1** steal. **2** win: *the team walked off with a silver medal.* □ **walk something off** exercise on foot in order to undo the effects of a heavy meal. □ **walk out 1** depart suddenly or angrily. ■ leave one's job suddenly. ■ go on strike. ■ abandon someone or something toward which one has responsibilities: *he* ***walked out on*** *his wife.* **2** *Brit., informal, dated* go for walks in courtship: *you were* ***walking out with*** *Tom.* □ **walk over** *informal* another way of saying WALK ALL OVER. □ **walk through** rehearse (a play or other piece), reading the lines aloud from a script and performing the actions of the characters. ■ act or perform in a perfunctory or lackluster manner. □ **walk someone through** guide (someone) carefully through a process: *a meeting to walk parents through the complaint process.*

▸*n.* **1** an act of traveling or an excursion on foot: *he was too restless to sleep, so he went out for a walk.* ■ [in *sing.*] used to indicate the time that it will take someone to reach a place on foot or the distance that they must travel: *the library is within five minutes' walk.* ■ a route recommended or marked out for recreational walking. ■ a sidewalk or path. ■ a part of a forest under one keeper. ■ *chiefly Brit.* the round followed by a mail carrier. **2** [in *sing.*] an unhurried rate of movement on foot: *they crossed the field at a leisurely walk.* ■ the slowest gait of an animal. ■ a person's manner of walking: *the spring was back in his walk.* **3** *Baseball* an instance of being awarded (or allowing a batter to reach) first base after not swinging at four balls pitched outside the strike zone. ▷Old English *wealcan* 'roll, toss,' also 'wander,' of Germanic origin. The sense 'move around,' and specifically 'go around on foot,' arose in Middle English. **—walk·a·ble** /ˈwôkəbəl/ *adj.*

▸*PHRASES* □ **walk all over** *informal* treat in a thoughtless, disrespectful, and exploitative manner: *they thought they could come in and walk all over us.* ■ defeat easily. □ **walking encyclopedia** (also **walking dictionary**) *informal* a person who has an impressive knowledge of facts or words. □ **walk someone off their feet** walk with someone until they are exhausted. □ **walk of life** the position within society that someone holds or the part of society to which they belong as a result of their job or social status: *the courses attracted people from all walks of life.* □ **walk on air** see AIR. □ **walk on eggshells** be extremely cautious about one's words or actions. □ **walk one's talk** (also **walk the walk**) suit one's actions to one's words. □ **walk the plank** see PLANK. □ **walk the streets 1** walk freely in a town or city. **2** work as a prostitute. □ **walk the wards** *dated* gain experience as a clinical medical student. □ **win in a walk** win without effort or competition.

walk·a·bout /ˈwôkə,bout/ ▸*n. Austral.* a journey on foot undertaken by an Australian Aboriginal in order to live in the traditional manner. ■ *chiefly Brit.* an informal stroll among a crowd conducted by an important visitor. ■ a walking tour.

▸*PHRASE* □ **go walkabout** (of an Australian Aboriginal) wander into the bush away from white society in order to live in the traditional manner. ■ wander around from place to place in a protracted or leisurely way.

walk·a·thon /ˈwôkə,THän/ ▸*n. informal* a long-distance walk organized as a fund-raising event. ▷1930s: from WALK, on the pattern of *marathon.*

Walk·er[1] /ˈwôkər/, Alice (Malsenior) (1944–), U.S. writer and critic. She wrote the award-winning *The Color Purple* (1982), a story about a black woman rebuilding her life after being raped by her supposed father, which was made into a movie in 1985. She also wrote *Possessing the Secret of Joy* (1992) and *By the Light of My Father's Smile* (1998).

Walk·er[2], Jimmy (1881–1946), U.S. politician; full name *James John Walker.* He was mayor of New York City 1926–32 but resigned when his involvement in fraud was exposed.

Walk·er[3], Sarah Breedlove (1867–1919), U.S. entrepreneur and philanthropist; known as **Madame C. J. Walker**. She invented and marketed a preparation to straighten kinky hair 1905 and built her business into the largest African-American–owned firm in the U.S., the Madame C. J. Walker Manufacturing Co. She generously gave of her wealth, mainly to African-American educational institutions and charities.

walk·er /ˈwôkər/ ▸*n.* a person who walks, esp. for exercise or enjoyment. ■ a device for helping a baby learn to walk, consisting of a harness set into a frame on wheels. ■ a frame used by disabled or infirm people for support while walking, typically made of metal tubing with small wheels or rubber-tipped feet.

Walk·er Cup a golf tournament held every two years and played between teams of male amateurs from the U.S. and from Great Britain and Ireland, first held in 1922. The tournament was instituted by George Herbert Walker, a former president of the U.S. Golf Association.

walk·ie-talk·ie /ˈwôkē ˈtôkē/ ▸*n.* a portable two-way radio.

walk-in ▸*adj.* **1** (esp. of a storage area) large enough to walk into: *a walk-in closet.* **2** (of a service) available for customers or clients without the need for an appointment: *a walk-in clinic.*

▸*n.* a walk-in customer or a walk-in storage-area.

walk·ing bass /bās/ ▸*n. Music* a bass part in 4/4 time in which a note is played on each beat of the bar and which typically moves up and down the scale in small steps.

walk·ing fern ▸*n.* a North American fern with long slender tapering fronds that form new plantlets where the tips touch the ground, typically growing on limestone. • *Asplenium* (or **Camptosorus**) *rhizophyllus*, family Aspleniaceae.

walk·ing frame ▸*n. Brit.* full form of WALKER.

walk·ing leaf ▸*n.* **1** another term for LEAF INSECT. **2** another term for WALKING FERN.

walk·ing leg ▸*n. Zoology* (in certain arthropods, esp. crustaceans) a limb used for walking.

walk·ing pa·pers ▸*plural n. informal* notice of dismissal from a job: *the reporter has been given his walking papers.*

walk·ing pneu·mo·ni·a ▸*n.* a type of pneumonia caused by mycoplasmas, with symptoms similar to but milder than those of bacterial or viral pneumonia. It spreads easily and typically affects school-age children and adults under 40.

walk·ing shoe ▸*n.* a sturdy, practical shoe with good treads, suitable for regular or extensive walking.

walk·ing stick ▸*n.* **1** a stick, typically with a curved handle, used for support when walking. **2** (also **walk·ing·stick**) a long, slender, slow-moving insect that resembles a twig. In many species, its appears that there are no males and that the females lay fertile eggs without mating. • Family Phasmatidae, order Phasmida: many genera.

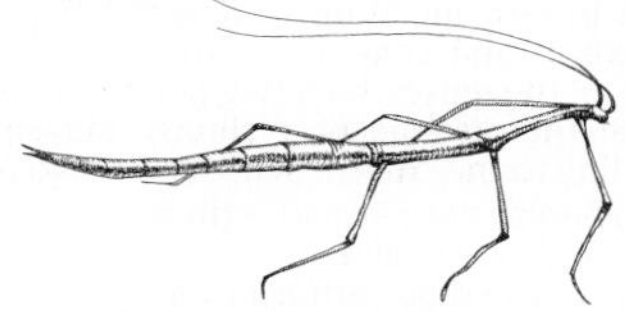

walking stick 2

walk·ing tour ▸*n.* a sightseeing tour made on foot.

walk·ing wound·ed /ˈwo͝ondid/ ▸*plural n.* (usu. **the walking wounded**) people who have been injured in a battle or major accident but who are still able to walk. ■ people who have suffered emotional wounds.

Walk·man /ˈwôkmən; -,man/ ▸*n.* (*pl.* **-mans** or **-men**) *trademark* a type of personal stereo.

walk-on ▸*adj.* [*attrib.*] denoting a small nonspeaking part in a play or film.

▸*n.* a person who plays such a part, or the part itself. ■ a sports player with no regular status in a team.

walk·out /ˈwôk,out/ ▸*n.* a sudden angry departure, esp. as a protest or strike.

walk·o·ver /ˈwôk,ōvər/ ▸*n.* **1** an easy victory: *they won in a 12–2 walkover.* ■ a win by forfeit. **2** a somersault in which a gymnast performs a handstand and then slowly moves the feet backward and down to the floor, or first arches back into a handstand and then slowly moves the feet forward and down to the floor.

walk-through ▸*n.* **1** a careful demonstration or explanation of the details of a process or procedure. ■ a rough rehearsal of a play, film, or other performance, without an audience or cameras. ■ *Computing* a product review of software carried out before release. **2** an undemanding task. ■ an unchallenging role in a play or other performance. ■ a perfunctory or lackluster performance. **3** *Computing* a software model of a building or other object in which the user can simulate walking around or through.

▸*adj.* [*attrib.*] designed to be walked through: *a walk-through gallery | walk-through registration.*

walk-up ▸*adj.* (of a building) allowing access to the upper floors by stairs only; having no elevator: *a walk-up hotel.* ■ (of a room or apartment) accessed in this way. ■ (of a building or service) easily accessible to pedestrians: *a walk-up food stand.* ■ (of a travel fare) at the price charged for immediate use rather than at the lower level provided when a customer makes a reservation in advance: *the one-way walk-up fare from Baltimore to San Francisco.*

▸*n.* a building allowing access to the upper floors by stairs only.

walk·way /ˈwôk,wā/ ▸*n.* a passage or path for walking along, esp. a raised passageway connecting different sections of a building or a wide path in a park or garden.

wall /wôl/ ▸*n.* a continuous vertical brick or stone structure that encloses or divides an area of land: *a garden wall | farmland traversed by drystone walls.* ■ a side of a building or room, typically forming part of the building's structure. ■ any high vertical surface or facade, esp. one that is imposing in scale: *the eastern wall of the valley | figurative a wall of sound.* ■ a thing perceived as a protective or restrictive barrier: *a wall of silence.* ■ *Soccer* a line of defenders forming a barrier against a free kick taken near the penalty area. ■ short for CLIMBING WALL. ■ *Mining* the rock enclosing a lode or seam or forming the side of a mine-working. ■ *Anatomy & Zoology* the membranous outer layer or lining of an organ or cavity: *the wall of the stomach.* ■ *Biology* see CELL WALL.

▸*v.* [*trans.*] enclose (an area) within walls, esp. to protect it or lend it some privacy: *housing areas that are* ***walled off*** *from the indigenous population.* ■ (**wall something up**) block or seal a place by building a wall around or across it: *one doorway has been walled up.* ■ (**wall someone/something in/up**) confine or imprison someone or something in a restricted or sealed place: *the gray tenements walled in the space completely.* ▷Old English, from Latin *vallum* 'rampart,' from *vallus* 'stake.' **—wall-less** *adj.*

▸*PHRASES* □ **between you and me and the wall** see BEDPOST. □ **drive someone up the wall** *informal* make someone very irritated or angry. □ **go to the wall** *informal* **1** (of a business) fail; go out of business. **2** support someone or something, no matter what the cost to oneself: *the tendency for poets to* ***go to the wall for*** *their beliefs.* □ **hit the wall** (of an athlete) experience a sudden loss of energy in a long race. □ **off the wall** *informal* **1** eccentric or unconventional. **2** (of a person) angry: *the president was off the wall about the article.* **3** (of an accusation) without basis or foundation. □ **walls have ears** *proverb* be careful what you say as people may be eavesdropping. □ **wall-to-wall** (of a carpet or other floor covering) fitted to cover an entire floor. ■ *informal* denoting great extent or number: *wall-to-wall customers.*

Wall·a·bout Bay /ˈwôlə,bout/ a former inlet of the East River in Brooklyn in New York City, the site of the imprisonment of thousands of American prisoners during the American Revolution, many of whom died here.

wal·la·by /ˈwäləbē/ ▸*n.* (*pl.* **-bies**) an Australasian marsupial that is similar to, but smaller than, a kangaroo. • Family Macropodidae: several genera and numerous species, including the **agile wallaby** (*Macropus agilis*). ▷early 19th cent.: from Dharuk *walabi* or *waliba.*

agile wallaby

Wal·lace[1] /ˈwôləs; ˈwäl-/, Alfred Russel (1823–1913), English naturalist; a founder of zoogeography.

Pronunciation Key ə *ago;* ər *over;* ˈə *or* ,ə *up;* ˈər *or* ,ər *fur;* a *hat;* ā *rate;* ä *car;* CH *chew;* e *let;* ē *see;* e(ə)r *air;* i *fit;* ī *by;* i(ə)r *ear;* NG *sing;* ō *go;* ô *for;* oi *boy;* o͝o *good;* o͞o *goo;* ou *out;* SH *she;* TH *thin;* T͟H *then;* (h)w *why;* ZH *vision*

W

Wal·lace[2], (Richard Horatio) Edgar (1875–1932), English novelist, screenwriter, and playwright. He wrote the screenplay for the movie *King Kong*, which was made shortly after his death.

Wal·lace[3], Henry Agard (1888–1965), U.S. politician, agriculturist, and editor. He was editor of *Wallaces' Farmer* and its successor 1910–33. He was U.S. secretary of agriculture 1933–40, U.S. vice president 1941–45, and U.S. secretary of commerce 1945–46. He was the presidential candidate for the new Progressive Party in 1948.

Wal·lace[4], George Corley (1919–98), U.S. politician. A four-term governor of Alabama 1963–67, 1971–79, 1983–87, he gained national attention in the early 1960s when he defied the civil rights legislation that outlawed segregation in public schools. While campaigning for the 1972 Democratic presidential nomination, he was shot and paralyzed by would-be assassin Arthur Bremer.

Wal·lace[5], Mike (1918–), U.S. journalist; born *Myron Leon Wallace*. A news correspondent with CBS from 1963, he appeared on the television news program "60 Minutes" from 1968.

Wal·lace[6], Sir William (*c.*1270–1305), Scottish national hero. A leader of Scottish resistance to Edward I, he defeated the English army at Stirling in 1297. After Edward's second invasion of Scotland in 1298, he was defeated and subsequently executed.

Wal·lace's line *Zoology* a hypothetical line, proposed by Alfred Russel Wallace, marking the boundary between the Oriental and Australian zoogeographical regions. Wallace's line is now placed along the continental shelf of Southeast Asia, east of the islands of Borneo, Bali, and the Philippines. To the west of the line, Asian animals such as monkeys predominate, while to the east of it, the fauna is dominated by marsupials.

Wal·la·chi·a /wä'lākēə; wə-/ (also **Wa·la·chi·a**) a former principality in southeastern Europe, between the Danube River and the Transylvanian Alps. In 1861, it was united with Moldavia to form Romania. ▷based on a variant of **VLACH**. **—Wal·la·chi·an** *adj.* & *n.*

wal·lah /'wälə/ ▶*n.* [in *combination* or with *adj.*] *Indian* or *informal* a person concerned or involved with a specified thing or business: *ice cream wallahs.* ■ a native or inhabitant of a specified place: *Bombay wallahs.* ▷from the Hindi suffix *-vālā* 'doer' (commonly interpreted in the sense 'fellow'), from Sanskrit *pālaka* 'keeper.'

wal·la·roo /,wôlə'roo/ ▶*n.* a large Australian kangaroo, the female of which is paler than the male. • Genus *Macropus*, family Macropodidae: two species, in particular the **common wallaroo** (*M. robustus*). ▷early 19th cent.: from Dharuk *walaru*.

Wal·la Wal·la /,wälə 'wälə/ a historic commercial and industrial city in southeastern Washington; pop. 26,478.

wall·board /'wôl,bôrd/ ▶*n.* a type of board made from wood pulp, plaster, or other material, used for covering walls and ceilings. ■ a piece of such board.

wall chart ▶*n.* a chart or poster designed for display on a wall as a teaching aid or source of information.

wall cov·er·ing ▶*n.* material such as wallpaper or textured fabric used as a decorative covering for interior walls.

W

wall·creep·er /'wôl,krēpər/ ▶*n.* a Eurasian songbird related to the nuthatches, having mainly gray plumage with broad bright red wings, and living among rocks in mountainous country. • *Tichodroma muraria*, family Sittidae (or Tichodromadidae).

wall cress ▶*n.* another term for **ARABIS**.

Wal·len·berg /'wôlən,bərg; 'välən,ber(yə)/, Raoul (1912–?), Swedish diplomat in Budapest. In 1944, he helped many thousands of Jews escape death by issuing them Swedish passports. Arrested by the Soviets in 1945, he was imprisoned in Moscow. Although Soviet authorities stated that he died in prison in 1947, his fate remains uncertain.

Wal·ler /'wälər/, Fats (1904–43), U.S. jazz pianist, songwriter, bandleader, and singer; born *Thomas Wright Waller*. The composer of the songs "Ain't Misbehavin'" (1928) and "Honeysuckle Rose" (1929), he was the foremost exponent of the New York "stride school" of piano playing.

wal·let /'wälit; 'wô-/ ▶*n.* a pocket-sized, flat, folding holder for money and plastic cards. ■ *archaic* a bag for holding provisions, esp. when traveling, typically used by peddlers and pilgrims. ▷late Middle English (denoting a bag for provisions): probably via Anglo-Norman French from a Germanic word related to **WELL**[2]. The current sense (originally U.S.) dates from the mid 19th cent.

wall·eye /'wôl,ī/ ▶*n.* **1** an eye with a streaked or opaque white iris. ■ an eye directed abnormally outward. **2** a North American pikeperch with large, opaque silvery eyes. It is a commercially valuable food fish and a popular sporting fish. • *Stizostedion vitreum*, family Percidae. ▷early 16th cent.: back-formation from earlier *wall-eyed*, from Old Norse *vagleygr*; related to Icelandic *vagl* 'film over the eye.' **—wall-eyed** *adj.*

wall·flow·er /'wôl,flou(-ə)r/ ▶*n.* **1** a southern European plant of the cabbage family, with fragrant yellow, orange-red, dark red, or brown flowers, cultivated for its early spring blooming. • *Cheiranthus cheiri*, family Brassicaceae. **2** *informal* a person who has no one to dance with or who feels shy, awkward, or excluded at a party.

wall hang·ing ▶*n.* a large decorative piece of fabric or other material to be hung on the wall of a room.

wall-hung ▶*adj.* another term for **WALL-MOUNTED**.

Wal·ling·ford /'wäliNGfərd/ an industrial town in south central Connecticut; pop. 40,822.

Wal·lis and Fu·tu·na Is·lands /'wäləs and foo'toonə; 'wôləs/ an overseas territory of France that consists of two groups of islands to the west of Samoa in the central Pacific Ocean; pop. 15,000; capital, Mata-Utu.

wall knot (also **wale knot**) ▶*n.* a knot made at the end of a rope by intertwining strands to prevent unraveling or act as a stopper.

wall-mount·ed ▶*adj.* fixed to a wall.

wall of hon·or ▶*n.* a wall on which are inscribed the names of individuals whose acts or achievements are deemed praiseworthy.

Wal·loon /wä'loon/ ▶*n.* **1** a member of a people who speak a French dialect and live in southern and eastern Belgium and neighboring parts of France. Compare with **FLEMING**[3]. **2** the French dialect spoken by this people.
▶*adj.* of or concerning the Walloons or their language. ▷from French *Wallon*, from medieval Latin *Wallon-*, from the same Germanic origin as **WELSH**.

wal·lop /'wäləp/ *informal* ▶*v.* (**-loped**, **-lop·ing**) [*trans.*] strike or hit (someone or something) very hard: *they walloped the back of his head with a stick | figurative they were tired of getting walloped with income taxes.* ■ heavily defeat (an opponent).
▶*n.* **1** a heavy blow or punch. ■ [in *sing.*] *figurative* a potent effect: *the script* **packs a wallop**. **2** *Brit.* alcoholic drink, esp. beer. ▷Middle English (as a noun denoting a horse's gallop): from Old Northern French *walop* (noun), *waloper* (verb), perhaps from a Germanic phrase meaning 'run well,' from the bases of **WELL**[1] and **LEAP**. Compare with **GALLOP**. From 'gallop' the senses 'bubbling noise of a boiling liquid' and then 'sound of a clumsy movement' arose, leading to the current senses. **—wal·lop·er** *n.*

wal·lop·ing /'wäləpiNG/ *informal* ▶*n.* [in *sing.*] a beating: *she gave him a good walloping.*
▶*adj.* [*attrib.*] large and powerful: *a walloping shock.*

Wal·lops Is·land /'wäləps/ an island in eastern Virginia, on the Delmarva Peninsula, the site of a U.S. rocket and high-altitude balloon facility.

wal·low /'wälō/ ▶*v.* [*intrans.*] **1** (chiefly of large mammals) roll about or lie relaxed in mud or water, esp. to keep cool, avoid biting insects, or spread scent: *watering places where buffalo liked to wallow.* ■ (of a boat or aircraft) roll from side to side: *the small jet wallowed in the sky.* **2** (**wallow in**) (of a person) indulge in an unrestrained way in (something that creates a pleasurable sensation): *I was wallowing in the luxury of the hotel | he had been wallowing in self-pity.*
▶*n.* **1** an act of wallowing: *a* **wallow in** *nostalgia.* **2** an area of mud or shallow water where mammals go to wallow, typically developing into a depression in the ground over long use. ▷Old English *walwian* 'to roll around,' of Germanic origin, from an Indo-European root shared by Latin *volvere* 'to roll.' **—wal·low·er** *n.*

Wal·low·a Moun·tains /wä'lôə/ a range in northeastern Oregon. The Wallowa River valley, on its east, is home to the Nez Perce Indians.

wall paint·ing ▶*n.* a painting made directly on a wall, such as a fresco or mural.

wall·pa·per /'wôl,pāpər/ ▶*n.* paper that is pasted in vertical strips over the walls of a room to provide a decorative or textured surface. ■ *Computing* an optional background pattern or picture on a computer screen.
▶*v.* [*trans.*] apply wallpaper to (a wall or room).

wall pass ▶*n.* *Soccer* a short pass to a teammate who immediately returns it.

wall·pep·per (also **wall pep·per**) ▶*n.* another term for **MOSSY STONECROP** (see **STONECROP**).

wall plate ▶*n.* **1** a piece of lumber laid horizontally in or on a wall as a support for a girder, rafter, or joist. **2** a metal plate fixed to a wall, for attaching a bracket or other device.

wall rock ▶*n.* *Geology* the rock adjacent to or enclosing a vein, hydrothermal ore deposit, fault, or other geological feature.

wall rock·et ▶*n.* a yellow-flowered European plant that resembles mustard and emits a foul smell when crushed. • *Diplotaxis muralis*, family Brassicaceae.

wall rue ▶*n.* a small delicate spleenwort (fern) that resembles rue, growing on walls and rocks in both Europe and North America and sensitive to atmospheric pollution. • *Asplenium ruta-muraria*, family Aspleniaceae.

Wall Street a street at the south end of Manhattan in New York City, where the New York Stock Exchange and other leading U.S. financial institutions are located. ■ used allusively to refer to the U.S. money market or financial interests. ▷named after a wooden stockade that was built in 1653 around the original Dutch settlement of New Amsterdam.

wall tent ▶*n.* a tent with nearly perpendicular sides.

wall u·nit ▶*n.* a piece of furniture having various sections, typically shelves and cabinets, designed to stand against a wall.

wal·ly·ball /'wôlē'bôl; 'wä-/ ▶*n.* a game played on a four-walled court with rules similar to volleyball, and with a ball the same size as but harder than a volleyball. The ball is allowed to bounce once against the ceiling or one of the walls before being returned over the net.

wal·nut /'wôl,nət/ ▶*n.* **1** the large wrinkled edible seed of a deciduous tree, consisting of two halves contained within a hard shell that is enclosed in a green fruit. **2** (also **wal·nut tree**) the tall tree that produces this nut, with compound leaves and valuable ornamental timber that is used chiefly in cabinetmaking and gunstocks. • Genus *Juglans*, family Juglandaceae: several species, including the **common** (or **English**) **walnut** (*J. regia*) and the **black walnut** (*J. nigra*). ▷late Old English *walh-hnutu*, from a Germanic compound meaning 'foreign nut.' See also **WELSH**.

Wal·nut Creek a residential and industrial city in north central California, northeast of Oakland; pop. 60,569.

Wal·pole[1] /'wôl,pōl/, Horace, 4th Earl of Orford (1717–97), English writer and politician; son of Sir Robert Walpole. He wrote *The Castle of Otranto* (1764), one of the first Gothic novels.

Wal·pole[2], Sir Hugh (Seymour) (1884–1941), British novelist, born in New Zealand. He is noted for *The Herries Chronicle* (1930–33), a historical sequence.

Wal·pole[3], Sir Robert, 1st Earl of Orford (1676–1745), British statesman; first lord of the treasury and chancellor of the exchequer 1715–17 and 1721–42; father of Horace Walpole. He is generally thought of as the first British prime minister, since he presided over the cabinet for George I and George II.

Wal·pur·gis·nacht /väl'poogis,näKHt; -,näkt/ ▶*n.* German for **WALPURGIS NIGHT**.

Wal·pur·gis night /väl'poorgis/ ▶*n.* (in German folklore) the night of April 30 (May Day's eve), when witches meet on the Brocken mountain and hold revels with the Devil. ▷named after St. *Walburga*, an English nun who in the 8th cent. helped to convert the Germans to Christianity; her feast day coincided with an ancient pagan festival whose rites were intended to give protection from witchcraft.

Wal·ras' law /'valrəs/ *Economics* a law stating that the total value of goods and money supplied equals that of goods and money demanded. ▷1940s: named after M. E. Léon *Walras* (1834–1910), French economist. **—Wal·ra·si·an** *adj.*

wal·rus /'wôlrəs; 'wä-/ ▶*n.* a large gregarious marine mammal related to the eared seals, having two large downward-pointing tusks and found in the Arctic Ocean. • *Odobenus rosmarus*, the only member of the family Odobenidae. ▷early 18th cent.: probably from Dutch *walrus*, perhaps by an inversion of elements (influenced by *walvis* 'whale-fish') of Old Norse *hrosshvalr* 'horse-whale.'

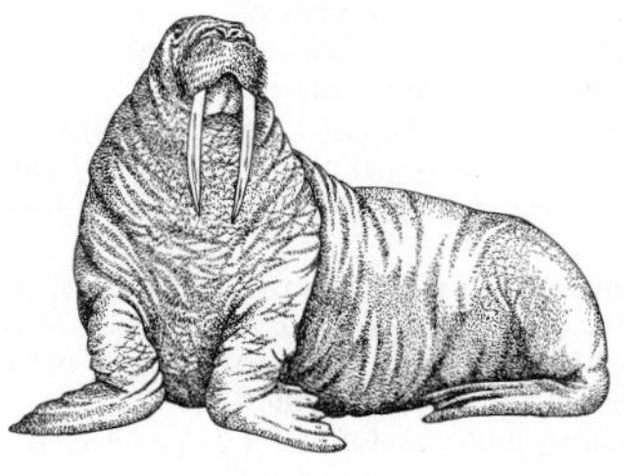
walrus

wal·rus mus·tache ▸*n.* a long, thick, drooping mustache.

Wal·sall /ˈwôlˌsôl; ˈwälˌsäl/ an industrial town western central England; pop. 256,000.

Wal·ter Mit·ty /ˈwôltər ˈmitē/ the hero of a story (by James Thurber) who indulged in extravagant daydreams of his own triumphs. ■ [as *n.*] [often as *adj.*] used to refer to a person who fantasizes about a life much more exciting and glamorous than their own life: *his ultimate Walter Mitty fantasy is to be secretary of state.*

Wal·ters /ˈwôltərz/, Barbara (1931–), U.S. television journalist. Noted for her interviews of celebrities, she has appeared on the television programs "20/20" (1979–2004) and "The View" (1997–). She is also noted for her once-in-a-while "Barbara Walters Specials" that involve timely celebrity interviews.

Wal·tham /ˈwôlˌTHam; -ˌTHam/ a historic industrial and academic city in eastern Massachusetts, on the Charles River, west of Boston; pop. 59,226.

Wal·ton[1] /ˈwôltn/, Ernest Thomas Sinton (1903–95), Irish physicist. In 1932 he succeeded, with Sir John Cockcroft, in splitting the atom. Nobel Prize for Physics (1951, shared with Cockcroft).

Wal·ton[2], Izaak (1593–1683), English writer. He is chiefly known for *The Compleat Angler* (1653; rewritten, 1655), which combines practical information on fishing with folklore and is interspersed with pastoral songs and ballads.

Wal·ton[3], Sam (1918–92), U.S. businessman. He founded Wal-Mart discount stores in 1962 and by 1966, with 20 stores, had begun to computerize inventory. By 1991, Wal-Mart was the largest retailer in the U.S.

waltz /wôlts/ ▸*n.* a dance in triple time performed by a couple who as a pair turn rhythmically around and around as they progress around the dance floor. ■ a piece of music written for or in the style of this dance.
▸*v.* [*intrans.*] dance a waltz: *I waltzed across the floor with the lieutenant.* ■ [*trans.*] guide (someone) in or as if in a waltz: *he waltzed her around the table.* ■ [*intrans.*] move or act lightly, casually, or inconsiderately: *you can't just* **waltz in** *and expect to make a mark | it is the third time that he has* **waltzed off with** *the coveted award.* ▷late 18th cent.: from German *Walzer*, from *walzen* 'revolve.' **—waltz·er** *n.*
▸*PHRASE* □ **waltz Matilda** see MATILDA[2].

Wal·vis Bay /ˈwôlvəs; ˈwäl-/ a port in Namibia; pop. 25,000. Administratively, it was an exclave of the former Cape Province in South Africa until it was transferred to Namibia in 1994.

Wam·pa·no·ag /ˌwämpəˈnō-ag/ ▸*n.* (*pl.* same or **-ags**) a member of a confederacy of native peoples of southeastern Massachusetts who spoke the extinct Algonquian language Massachusett.
▸*adj.* of, relating to, or denoting these people. ▷from an Algonquian name, literally 'easterners.'

wam·pum /ˈwämpəm/ ▸*n. historical* a quantity of small cylindrical beads made by North American Indians from quahog shells, strung together and worn as a decorative belt or other decoration or used as money. ▷from Massachusett *wampumpeag*, literally 'white strings'.

WAN /wan/ ▸*abbr.* ■ *Computing* wide area network. [1980s: acronym.]

wan /wän/ ▸*adj.* (of a person's complexion or appearance) pale and giving the impression of illness or exhaustion: *she was looking wan and bleary-eyed.* See note at PALE. ■ (of light) pale; weak: *the wan dawn light.* ■ (of a smile) weak; strained. ■ *poetic/literary* (of the sea) without luster; dark and gloomy. ▷Old English *wann* 'dark, black,' of unknown origin. **—wan·ly** *adv.* **—wan·ness** *n.*

Wan·a·mak·er /ˈwänəˌmākər/, John (1838–1922) U.S. businessman. A pioneering department store merchant, he cofounded a men's clothing store in Philadelphia in 1861. After his partner's death, he made it into a department store 1877 and opened another in New York City 1896. The success of his stores was based on advertising. He also served as U.S. postmaster general 1889–93.

wand /wänd/ ▸*n.* a long, thin stick or rod, in particular: ■ a stick or rod thought to have magic properties, held by a magician, fairy, or conjuror and used in casting spells or performing tricks: *the fairy godmother waves her magic wand and grants the heroine's wishes.* ■ a staff or rod held as a symbol of office. ■ *informal* a conductor's baton. ■ a hand-held electronic device that can be passed over a bar code to read the encoded data. ■ a device emitting a laser beam, used esp. to create a pointer on a projected image or text. ■ a small stick with a brush at one end used for the application of mascara. ■ *Archery* a target 6 feet (1.83 meters) high and 2 inches (5.8 cm) wide, set at 100 yards (91.44 meters) for men and 60 yards (54.86 meters) for women. ■ (**wands**) one of the suits in some tarot packs, corresponding to batons in others. ▷Middle English: from Old Norse *vǫndr*, probably of Germanic origin and related to WEND and WIND[2].

wan·der /ˈwändər/ ▸*v.* [*intrans.*] walk or move in a leisurely, casual, or aimless way: *he wandered aimlessly through the narrow streets.* ■ move slowly away from a fixed point or place: *please don't* **wander off** *again | figurative his attention had wandered.* ■ (of a road or river) wind with gentle twists and turns in a particular direction; meander. ■ [*trans.*] move or travel slowly through or over (a place or area): *she found her wandering the streets.* ■ be unfaithful to one's spouse or regular sexual partner.
▸*n.* an act or instance of wandering: *she'd go on wanders like that in her nightgown.* ▷Old English *wandrian*; related to WEND and WIND[2]. **—wan·der·er** *n.*

wan·der·ing al·ba·tross ▸*n.* a very large albatross of southern oceans, having white plumage with black wings and a wingspan of up to 11 feet (3.3 m). • *Diomedea exulans*, family Diomedeidae.

Wan·der·ing Jew (also **wan·der·ing Jew**) ▸*n.* **1** a legendary person said to have been condemned by Jesus Christ to wander the earth until the second coming. ■ a person who never settles down. **2** a tender trailing tradescantia, typically having striped leaves that are suffused with purple. • Genus *Tradescantia*, family Commelinaceae: *T. albiflora* and *T. pendula* (formerly *Zebrina pendula*).

Wan·der·jahr /ˈvändərˌyär/ ▸*n.* (*pl.* **-jahre**) /-ˌyärə/ a year spent traveling abroad, typically immediately before or after a university or college course. ▷late 19th cent.: German, literally 'wander year.'

wan·der·lust /ˈwändərˌləst/ ▸*n.* a strong desire to travel: *a man consumed by wanderlust.* ▷early 20th cent.: from German *Wanderlust*.

wan·der·oo /ˌwändəˈrōō/ ▸*n.* (in Sri Lanka) a leaf monkey or langur. • Genus *Presbytis*, family Cercopithecidae: the purple-faced leaf monkey (*P. vetulus*), or the hanuman (*P. entellus*). ▷late 17th cent.: from Sinhalese *wanderu* 'monkey.'

Wan·der·vo·gel /ˈvändərˌfōgəl/ ▸*n.* (*pl.* **-vö·gel** /-ˌfəgəl/) a member of a German youth organization founded at the end of the 19th century for the promotion of outdoor activities and folk culture. ■ a wanderer, esp. someone who travels the world on foot. ▷German, literally 'bird of passage.'

wane[1] /wān/ ▸*v.* [*intrans.*] (of the moon) have a progressively smaller part of its visible surface illuminated, so that it appears to decrease in size. ■ (esp. of a condition or feeling) decrease in vigor, power, or extent; become weaker: *confidence in the dollar waned.* ▷Old English *wanian* 'lessen,' of Germanic origin; related to Latin *vanus* 'vain.'
▸*PHRASE* □ **on the wane** becoming weaker, less vigorous, or less extensive: *the epidemic was on the wane.*

wane[2] ▸*n.* the amount by which a plank or log is beveled or falls short of a squared shape. ▷mid 17th cent.: from WANE[1]. **—wane·y** *adj.*

Wang /wäNG/, An (1920–90), U.S. computer engineer; born in China. In 1948, he invented a magnetic core memory for computers. The founder of Wang Laboratories in 1951, he held 40 patents.

wan·gle /ˈwaNGgəl/ *informal* ▸*v.* [*trans.*] obtain (something that is desired) by persuading others to comply or by manipulating events: *I wangled an invitation to her party | I think we should be able to* **wangle it** *so that you can start tomorrow.*
▸*n.* an act or an instance of obtaining something in such a way: *they regarded the coalition as a wangle.* ▷late 19th cent. (first recorded as printers' slang): of unknown origin; perhaps based on the verb WAGGLE. **—wan·gler** /ˈwaNG(ə)lər/ *n.*

wank /waNGk/ *Brit., vulgar slang* ▸*v.* [*intrans.*] (typically of a man) masturbate.
▸*phrasal v.* □ **wank oneself/someone off** (or **wank off**) masturbate.
▸*n.* an act of masturbating. ▷1940s: of unknown origin.

Wan·kel en·gine /ˈwäNGkəl; ˈwaNG-/ ▸*n.* a rotary internal combustion engine in which a curvilinear, triangular, eccentrically pivoted piston rotates in an elliptical chamber, forming three combustion spaces that vary in volume as the piston turns. ▷1960s: named after Felix *Wankel* (1902–88), German engineer.

wank·er /ˈwaNGkər/ ▸*n. Brit., vulgar slang* a person who masturbates (used as a term of abuse).

wan·ky /ˈwäNGkē; ˈwaNG-/ ▸*adj.* (**-ki·er**, **-ki·est**) *vulgar slang, chiefly Brit.* contemptible, worthless, or stupid: *I was determined not to end up as some Nigel doing wanky beer ads.* ▷late 20th cent.: from *wank* 'masturbate' (of unknown origin) + *-y*.

wan·na /ˈwônə; ˈwä-/ *informal* ▸*contraction of* want to; want a.

wan·na·be /ˈwänəbē; ˈwô-/ ▸*n. informal, derogatory* a person who tries to be like someone else or to fit in with a particular group of people: *a star-struck wannabe.* ▷1980s: representing a pronunciation of *want to be*.

want /wänt; wônt/ ▸*v.* **1** [*trans.*] have a desire to possess or do (something); wish for: *I want an apple |* [with *infinitive*] *we want to go to the beach |* [*trans.*] *she wanted me to go to her room |* [*intrans.*] *I'll give you a lift into town if you want.* ■ wish to consult or speak to (someone): *Tony wants me in the studio.* ■ (usu. **be wanted**) (of the police) desire to question or apprehend (a suspected criminal): *he is wanted by the police in connection with an arms theft.* ■ desire (someone) sexually: *I've wanted you since the first moment I saw you.* ■ [with *present participle*] *informal, chiefly Brit.* (of a thing) require to be attended to in a specified way: *the wheel wants greasing.* ■ [with *infinitive*] *informal* ought, should, or need to do something: *you don't want to believe everything you hear.* ■ [*intrans.*] (**want in/into/out/away**) *informal* desire to be in or out of a particular place or situation: *if anyone wants out, there's the door.* **2** [*intrans.*] *chiefly archaic* lack or be short of something desirable or essential: *you shall* **want for nothing** *while you are with me.* See note at LACK. ■ [*trans.*] (chiefly used in expressions of time) be short of or lack (a specified amount or thing): *it* **wanted** *twenty minutes* **to** *midnight | it* **wants** *a few minutes* **of** *five o'clock.*
▸*n.* **1** *chiefly archaic* a lack or deficiency of something: *Victorian houses which are* **in want of** *repair | it won't be through want of trying.* ■ the state of being poor and in need of essentials; poverty: *freedom from want.* **2** a desire for something: *the expression of our wants and desires.* ▷Middle English: the noun from Old Norse *vant*, neuter of *vanr* 'lacking'; the verb from Old Norse *vanta* 'be lacking.' The original notion of "lack" was early extended to "need," and from this developed the sense 'desire.'
▸*PHRASE* □ **for want of** because of a lack of (something): *for want of a better location we ate our picnic lunch in the cemetery.*

want ad ▸*n. informal* a classified advertisement in a newspaper or magazine; a small ad.

want·ing /ˈwäntiNG; wônt-/ ▸*adj.* [*predic.*] lacking in a certain required or necessary quality: *they weren't* **wanting in** *confidence | their products would be* **found wanting** *in a direct comparison.* ■ not existing or supplied; absent: *the knee-cap is wanting in amphibians and reptiles.*

want list ▸*n.* a list of stamps, books, recordings, or similar items required by a collector.

wan·ton /ˈwäntn/ ▸*adj.* **1** (of a cruel or violent action) deliberate and unprovoked: *sheer wanton vandalism.* **2** (esp. of a woman) sexually immodest or promiscuous. ■ *poetic/literary* growing profusely; luxuriant: *where wanton ivy twines.* ■ *poetic/literary* lively; playful: *a wanton fawn.*
▸*n. archaic* a sexually immodest or promiscuous woman.
▸*v.* [*intrans.*] *archaic* or *poetic/literary* **1** play; frolic. **2** behave in a sexually immodest or promiscuous way. ▷Middle English *wantowen* 'rebellious, lacking

Pronunciation Key ə ago; ər over; ˈə or ˌə up; ˈər or ˌər fur; a hat; ā rate; ä car; CH chew; e let; ē see; e(ə)r air; i fit; ī by; i(ə)r ear; NG sing; ō go; ô for; oi boy; ŏŏ good; ōō goo; ou out; SH she; TH thin; TH then; (h)w why; ZH vision

discipline,' from *wan-* 'badly' + Old English *togen* 'trained' (related to TEAM and TOW[1]). **—wan·ton·ly** *adv.* **—wan·ton·ness** *n.*

WAP /wap/ ▸*abbr.* Wireless Application Protocol, a set of protocols for connecting cellular phones and other radio devices to the Internet.

wap·en·take /'wäpən,tāk; 'wa-/ ▸*n. historical* (in the UK) a subdivision of certain northern and midland English counties, corresponding to a hundred in other counties. ▷late Old English *wǣpen(ge)tæc*, from Old Norse *vápnatak*, from *vápn* 'weapon' + *taka* 'take,' perhaps with reference to voting in an assembly by a show of weapons.

wap·i·ti /'wäpitē/ ▸*n.* (*pl.* **-tis**) another term for ELK. ▷early 19th cent.: from Shawnee, literally 'white rump.'

Wap·si·pin·i·con Riv·er /,wäpsə'pinikən/ a river that flows for 225 miles (360 km) across eastern Iowa to the Mississippi River. Its valley is associated with the regional painting of Grant Wood and others.

waqf /wəkf; vəkf/ ▸*n.* (*pl.* same) an endowment made by a Muslim to a religious, educational, or charitable cause. ▷from Arabic, literally 'stoppage, immobilization (of ownership of property),' from *waqafa* 'come to a standstill.'

war /wôr/ ▸*n.* a state of armed conflict between different nations or states or different groups within a nation or state: *Japan* **declared war** *on Germany | Iran and Iraq had been* **at war** *for six years.* ■ a particular armed conflict: *after the war, they emigrated to America.* ■ a state of competition, conflict, or hostility between different people or groups: *she was* **at war with** *her parents | a price war among discount retailers.* ■ a sustained effort to deal with or end a particular unpleasant or undesirable situation or condition: *the authorities are* **waging war against** *all forms of smuggling |* **a war on** *drugs.*
▸*v.* (**warred, war·ring**) [*intrans.*] engage in a war: *small states warred against each another | figurative conflicting emotions warred within her.* ▷late Old English *werre*, from an Anglo-Norman French variant of Old French *guerre*, from a Germanic base shared by WORSE.
▸*PHRASES* □ **go to war** declare, begin, or see active service in a war. □ **go to the wars** *archaic* serve as a soldier. □ **war clouds** /'wôr ,kloudz/ a threatening situation of instability in international relations: *the war clouds were looming.* □ **war of attrition** a prolonged war or period of conflict during which each side seeks to gradually wear out the other by a series of small-scale actions. □ **war of nerves** see NERVE. □ **war of words** a prolonged debate conducted by means of the spoken or printed word. □ **war to end all wars** a war, esp. World War I, regarded as making subsequent wars unnecessary.

war ba·by ▸*n.* **1** a child born in wartime, esp. World War II. **2** a child born in wartime, esp. one fathered illegitimately by a serviceman.

war·bird /'wôr,bərd/ ▸*n.* a vintage military aircraft.

war·ble[1] /'wôrbəl/ ▸*v.* [*intrans.*] (of a bird) sing softly and with a succession of constantly changing notes: *larks were warbling in the trees.* ■ (of a person) sing in a trilling or quavering voice: *he warbled in an implausible soprano.*
▸*n.* a warbling sound or utterance. ▷late Middle English (as a noun in the sense 'melody'): from Old Northern French *werble* (noun), *werbler* (verb), of Germanic origin; related to WHIRL.

war·ble[2] ▸*n.* a swelling or abscess beneath the skin on the back of cattle, horses, and other mammals, caused by the presence of the larva of a warble fly. ■ the larva causing this. ▷late Middle English: of uncertain origin.

war·ble fly ▸*n.* a large fly that lays its eggs on the legs of mammals such as cattle and horses. The larvae migrate internally to the host's back, where they form a small lump with a breathing hole, dropping to the ground later when fully grown. • Genus *Hypoderma*, family Oestridae: several species, including the widespread *H. bovis*.

war·bler /'wôrb(ə)lər/ ▸*n.* **1** any of a number of small insectivorous songbirds that typically have a warbling song: • (also **wood war·bler**) a New World bird of the subfamily Parulinae, family Emberizidae. • an Old World bird of the family Sylviidae, which includes the blackcap, whitethroat, and chiffchaff. **2** *informal* a person who sings in a trilling or quavering voice.

war·blog ▸*n.* a weblog dealing with a war, or written by an active participant in or witness to warfare.

war bon·net ▸*n.* see BONNET (sense 1).

war bride ▸*n.* a woman who marries a man whom she met while he was on active service.

War·burg /'wôr,bərg/, Otto Heinrich (1883–1970), German biochemist. He pioneered the use of the techniques of chemistry for biochemical investigations, esp. for his work with the respiratory enzyme. Nobel Prize for Physiology or Medicine (1931); the Nazis prohibited him from accepting a second one in 1944 because of his Jewish ancestry.

war·chalk·ing /'wôr,CHôkiNG/ (also **war chalk·ing**) ▸*n. Computing* the practice of marking chalk symbols on sidewalks and other outdoor surfaces to indicate the location of unsecured wireless network connections: *savvy IT managers check their buildings' facades for signs of warchalking.* **—war·chalk** *v.*

war chest ▸*n.* a reserve of funds used for fighting a war. ■ a sum of money used for conducting a campaign or business.

war col·lege ▸*n.* a college providing advanced instruction for senior officers of the armed services.

war cor·re·spond·ent ▸*n.* a journalist reporting from a scene of war.

war crime ▸*n.* an action carried out during the conduct of a war that violates accepted international rules of war. **—war crim·i·nal** *n.*

war cry ▸*n.* a call made to rally soldiers for battle or to gather together participants in a campaign.

Ward[1] /wôrd/, Artemas (1727–1800), American politician and soldier. He served as a general during the American Revolution, second in command to George Washington. Later he was a member of the Continental Congress 1780–82 and of the U.S. House of Representatives 1791–95.

Ward[2], (Aaron) Montgomery (1843–1913), U.S. businessman. In 1872, he founded a dry-goods business, which became Montgomery Ward & Co., the first mail-order firm in the U.S.

ward /wôrd/ ▸*n.* **1** a separate room in a hospital, typically one allocated to a particular type of patient: *a children's ward* | [as *adj.*] *a ward nurse.* ■ one of the divisions of a prison. **2** an administrative division of a city or borough that typically elects and is represented by a councilor or councilors. ■ a territorial division of the Mormon Church presided over by a bishop. **3** a person, usually a minor, under the care and control of a guardian appointed by their parents or a court. ■ *archaic* guardianship or the state of being subject to a guardian: *the ward and care of the Crown.* **4** (usu. **wards**) any of the internal ridges or bars in a lock that prevent the turning of any key that does not have grooves of corresponding form or size. ■ the corresponding grooves in the bit of a key. **5** *archaic* the action of keeping a lookout for danger: *I saw them keeping ward at one of those huge gates.* **6** *historical* an area of ground enclosed by the encircling walls of a fortress or castle. **7** *Fencing* a defensive position or motion.
▸*v.* [*trans.*] **1** *archaic* guard; protect: *it was his duty to ward the king.* **2** admit (a patient) to a hospital ward.
▸*phrasal v.* □ **ward someone/something off** prevent from harming or affecting one: *she put up a hand as if to ward him off.* ▷Old English *weard* (in sense 5, also 'body of guards'), *weardian* 'keep safe, guard,' of Germanic origin; reinforced in Middle English by Old Northern French *warde* (noun), *warder* (verb) 'guard,' variants of Old French *garde, garder*; compare with GUARD. **—ward·ship** /-,SHip/ *n.*
▸*PHRASE* □ **ward of the court** a person, usually a minor or of unsound mind, for whom a guardian has been appointed by a court or who has become directly subject to the authority of that court.

-ward (also **-wards**) ▸*suffix* added to nouns of place or destination and to adverbs of direction: **1** (usu. **-wards**) (forming adverbs) toward the specified place or direction: *eastward | homewards.* **2** (usu. **-ward**) (forming adjectives) turned or tending toward: *onward | upward.* ▷Old English *-weard*, from a Germanic base meaning 'turn.' The forms in *-s* are all remnants of the old genitive singular inflection.

war dance ▸*n.* a ceremonial dance performed before a battle or to celebrate victory.

war·den /'wôrdn/ ▸*n.* a person responsible for the supervision of a particular place or thing or for ensuring that regulations associated with it are obeyed: *the warden of a local nature reserve | an air-raid warden.* ■ the head official in charge of a prison. ■ a churchwarden. ■ *Brit.* the head of certain schools, colleges, or other institutions. ▷Middle English (originally denoting a guardian or protector): from Anglo-Norman French and Old Northern French *wardein*, variant of Old French *guarden* 'guardian.' **—war·den·ship** /-,SHip/ *n.*

ward·er /'wôrdər/ ▸*n. chiefly Brit.* a prison guard. ▷late Middle English (denoting a watchman or sentinel): from Anglo-Norman French *wardere*, from Old Northern French *warder* 'to guard.' The current sense dates from the mid 19th cent.

ward heel·er ▸*n. informal, chiefly derogatory* a person who assists in a political campaign by canvassing votes for a party and performing menial tasks for its leaders.

war di·al·er ▸*n.* a program used to find phone numbers that connect to a modem, often used by someone seeking to access the computers of others without permission. **—war di·al·ing** *n.*

war·driv·ing /'wôr,drīviNG/ ▸*n.* the practice of seeking out and taking advantage of free connection to unsecured wireless networks. ▷2003: allegedly coined by Pete Shipley, a San Francisco Bay-area IT consultant, from *war* + *driving*, described by him as "driving around looking for unsecured wireless networks."

ward·robe /'wôr,drōb/ ▸*n.* a large, tall cabinet in which clothes may be hung or stored. ■ a person's entire collection of clothes: *her wardrobe is extensive.* ■ the costume department or costumes of a theater or movie company: [as *adj.*] *a wardrobe assistant.* ■ a department of a royal or noble household in charge of clothing. ▷Middle English (in the sense 'private chamber'): from Old Northern French *warderobe*, variant of Old French *garderobe* (see GARDEROBE).

ward·robe mis·tress ▸*n.* a woman in charge of the construction and organization of the costumes in a theatrical company.

ward·robe trunk ▸*n.* a trunk fitted with rails and shelves for use as a traveling wardrobe.

ward·room /'wôrd,ro͞om; -,ro͝om/ ▸*n.* a commissioned officers' mess on board a warship.

war drum ▸*n.* a drum beaten as a summons or an accompaniment to battle.

-wards ▸*suffix* variant spelling of -WARD.

ware[1] /we(ə)r/ ▸*n.* [usu. with *adj.*] pottery, typically that of a specified type: *blue-and-white majolica ware* | (**wares**) *Minoan potters produced an astonishing variety of wares.* ■ manufactured articles of a specified type: *crystal ware | aluminum ware.* ■ (**wares**) articles offered for sale: *traders in the street markets displayed their wares.* ▷Old English *waru* 'commodities,' of Germanic origin, perhaps the same word as Scots *ware* 'cautiousness,' and having the primary sense 'object of care'; related to WARE[2].

ware[2] ▸*adj.* [*predic.*] *archaic* aware: *thou speak'st wiser than thou art ware of.* ▷Old English *wær*, from the Germanic base of WARE[1].

ware[3] (also **'ware**) ▸*v.* [in *imperative*] beware (used as a warning cry, typically in a hunting context). ▷Old English *warian* 'be on one's guard,' from a Germanic base meaning 'observe, take care.'

ware·house ▸*n.* /'we(ə)r,hous/ a large building where raw materials or manufactured goods may be stored before their export or distribution for sale. ■ a large wholesale or retail store: *a discount warehouse.*
▸*v.* /-,hous; -,houz/ [*trans.*] store (goods) in a warehouse. ■ place (imported goods) in a bonded warehouse pending the payment of import duty. ■ *informal* place (someone, typically a prisoner or a psychiatric patient) in a large, impersonal institution in which their problems are not satisfactorily addressed.

ware·house club ▸*n.* an organization that operates from a large out-of-town store and sells goods in bulk at discounted prices to business and private customers who must first become club members.

ware·house·man /'we(ə)r,housmən/ ▸*n.* (*pl.* **-men**) a person who is employed in, manages, or owns a warehouse.

ware·hous·ing /'we(ə)r,houziNG/ ▸*n.* the practice or process of storing goods in a warehouse. ■ warehouses considered collectively. ■ *informal* the practice of placing people, typically prisoners or psychiatric patients, in large, impersonal institutions.

war·fare /'wôr,fe(ə)r/ ▸*n.* engagement in or the activities involved in war or conflict: *guerrilla warfare.*

war·fa·rin /'wôrfərin/ ▸*n.* a water-soluble compound with anticoagulant properties, used as a rat poison and in the treatment of thrombosis. • A coumarin derivative; chem. formula: $C_{19}H_{16}O_4$. ▷1950s: from the initial letters of *Wisconsin Alumni Research Foundation* + *-arin* on the pattern of *coumarin.*

war·fight·er /'wôr,fītər/ ▸*n.* a soldier in combat: *the lease proposal balances the urgent needs of the warfighter with the demands of our other vital programs.*

W

USAGE The burgeoning usage of this term with reference to ground troops in Iraq, mostly in sympathetic contexts, suggests that the old-fashioned *soldier* no longer captures the imagination of listeners and readers.

war game ▸*n.* a military exercise carried out to test or improve tactical expertise. ■ a simulated military conflict carried out as a game, leisure activity, or exercise in personal development.
▸*v.* [*trans.*] (**war-game**) engage in (a campaign or course of action) using the strategies of such a military exercise: *there seemed to be no point war-gaming an election 15 months away.* —**war-gam·er** *n.*

war-gam·ing /'wôr,gāmiNG/ (also **war gam·ing**) ▸*n.* the action of playing a war game as a leisure activity or exercise in personal development. ■ the action of engaging in a campaign or course of action using the strategies of a military exercise.

war·head /'wôr,hed/ ▸*n.* the explosive head of a missile, torpedo, or similar weapon.

War·hol /'wôr,hôl; -,hōl/, Andy (*c.*1928–87), U.S. painter, graphic artist, and moviemaker; born *Andrew Warhola.* A major exponent of pop art, he achieved fame for a series of silkscreen prints and acrylic paintings of familiar objects (such as Campbell's soup cans) and famous people (such as Marilyn Monroe), that are treated with objectivity and precision.

war·horse /'wôr,hôrs/ ▸*n.* (in historical contexts) a large, powerful horse ridden in battle. ■ *informal* an elderly person such as a soldier, politician, or sports player who has fought many campaigns or contests. ■ a musical, theatrical, or literary work that has been heard or performed repeatedly: *that old warhorse Liszt's "Hungarian Rhapsody No. 2."*

War·ka /wər'kä/ Arabic name for **URUK**.

war·like /'wôr,līk/ ▸*adj.* disposed toward or threatening war; hostile: *a warlike clan.* ■ (of plans, preparations, or munitions) directed toward or prepared for war.

war·lock /'wôr,läk/ ▸*n.* a man who practices witchcraft; a sorcerer. ▷Old English *wǣrloga* 'traitor, scoundrel, monster,' also 'the Devil,' from *wǣr* 'covenant' + an element related to *lēogan* 'belie, deny.' From its application to the Devil, the word was transferred in Middle English to a person in league with the devil, and hence a sorcerer. It was chiefly Scots until given wider currency by Sir Walter Scott.

war·lord /'wôr,lôrd/ ▸*n.* a military commander, esp. an aggressive regional commander with individual autonomy.

warm /wôrm/ ▸*adj.* **1** of or at a fairly or comfortably high temperature: *a warm September evening* | [as *complement*] *I walked quickly to keep warm.* ■ (of clothes or coverings) made of a material that helps the body to retain heat; suitable for cold weather: *a warm winter coat.* ■ (of a color) containing red, yellow, or orange tones: *her fair coloring suited soft, warm shades.* ■ *Hunting* (of a scent or trail) fresh; strong. ■ (of a soil) quick to absorb heat or retaining heat. **2** having, showing, or expressive of enthusiasm, affection, or kindness: *they exchanged warm, friendly smiles* | *a warm welcome.* ■ *archaic* characterized by lively or heated disagreement: *a warm debate arose.* ■ *archaic* sexually explicit or titillating. **3** [*predic.*] *informal* (esp. in children's games) close to discovering something or guessing the correct answer: *you're getting warmer.*
▸*v.* make or become warm: [*trans.*] *I stamped my feet to* ***warm them up*** | *figurative the film warmed our hearts* | [*intrans.*] *it's a bit chilly in here, but it'll soon* ***warm up.***
▸*phrasal v.* □ **warm down** recover from strenuous physical exertion by doing gentle stretches and exercises. □ **warm to/toward** (or **warm up to/toward**) begin to like (someone): *she and Will had really warmed up to each other.* ■ become more interested in or enthusiastic about (something): *I never really warmed to the idea of moving.* □ **warm up** prepare for physical exertion or a performance by exercising or practicing gently beforehand: *the band was warming up.* ■ (of an engine or electrical appliance) reach a temperature high enough to allow it to operate efficiently. ■ become livelier or more animated: *after several more rounds, things began to warm up in the bar.* □ **warm something up** (or **over**) reheat previously cooked food. ■ amuse or entertain an audience or crowd so as to make them more receptive to the main act. ▷Old English *wearm* (adjective), *werman, wearmian* (verb), of Germanic origin; related to Dutch and German *warm*, from an Indo-European root shared by Latin *formus* 'warm' and Greek *thermos* 'hot.' —**warm·er** *n.* [usu. in *combination*] *a towel-warmer.* —**warm·ish** *adj.* —**warm·ly** *adv.* —**warm·ness** *n.*
▸*PHRASE* □ **keep something warm for someone** hold or occupy a place or post until another person is ready to do so.

war ma·chine ▸*n.* **1** the military resources of a country organized for waging war. **2** an instrument or weapon of war.

warm·blood /'wôrm,bləd/ ▸*n.* a horse of a breed that is a cross between an Arab or similar breed and another breed of the draft or pony type.

warm-blood·ed ▸*adj.* **1** relating to or denoting animals (chiefly mammals and birds) that maintain a constant body temperature, typically above that of the surroundings, by metabolic means; homeothermic. **2** ardent; passionate. —**warm-blood·ed·ness** *n.*

warm-down ▸*n.* a series of gentle exercises designed to relax the body after strenuous physical exertion.

warmed-o·ver ▸*adj.* **1** (also **warmed-up**) (of food or drink) reheated: *warmed-over chicken and pasta.* **2** (of an idea or product) secondhand; stale: *warmed-over communism.*

war me·mo·ri·al ▸*n.* a monument commemorating those killed in a war.

warm front ▸*n. Meteorology* the boundary of an advancing mass of warm air, in particular the leading edge of the warm sector of a low-pressure system.

warm fuz·zy ▸*n.* see **FUZZY**.

warm·heart·ed /'wôrm 'härtəd/ ▸*adj.* (of a person or their actions) sympathetic and kind. —**warm·heart·ed·ly** *adv.* —**warm·heart·ed·ness** *n.*

warm·ing pan ▸*n. historical* a wide, flat brass pan on a long handle, filled with hot coals and used for warming a bed.

war·mon·ger /'wôr,məNGgər; -,mäNG-/ ▸*n.* a sovereign or political leader or activist who encourages or advocates aggression or warfare toward other nations or groups. —**war·mon·ger·ing** *n. & adj.*

Warm Springs a resort in northwestern Georgia, associated with Franklin D. Roosevelt and his "Little White House," where he died; pop. 407.

warmth /wôrmTH/ ▸*n.* the quality, state, or sensation of being warm; moderate and comfortable heat: *the warmth of the sun on her skin.* ■ enthusiasm, affection, or kindness: *she smiled with real warmth.* ■ vehemence or intensity of emotion: *"Of course not," he snapped, with a warmth that he regretted.*

warm-up (also **warm·up**) ▸*n.* a period or act of preparation for a game, performance, or exercise session, involving gentle exercise or practice. ■ (**warm-ups**) a garment worn during light exercise or training; a sweatsuit. ■ a period before a stage performance in which the audience is amused or entertained in order to make it more receptive to the main act.

warn /wôrn/ ▸*v.* [*reporting verb*] inform someone in advance of an impending or possible danger, problem, or other unpleasant situation: [*trans.*] *his father had* ***warned*** *him* ***of*** *what might happen* | [with *direct speech*] *"He's going to humiliate you," John warned* | [with *clause*] *the union warned that its members were close to going on strike.* ■ give someone forceful or cautionary advice about their actions or conduct: [*trans.*] *friends* ***warned*** *her* ***against*** *the marriage* | [*trans.*] *they warned people not to keep large amounts of cash in their homes* | [*intrans.*] *they* ***warned against*** *false optimism.*
▸*phrasal v.* □ **warn someone off** tell someone forcefully or threateningly to go away or stay. ■ advise someone forcefully against (a particular thing or course of action): *he has been warned off booze.* ▷Old English *war(e)nian, wearnian*, from a West Germanic base meaning 'be cautious'; compare with **WARE**[2]. —**warn·er** *n.*

War·ner /'wôrnər/, Pop (1871–1954), U.S. football coach; full name *Glenn Scobey Warner.* While a coach at Carlisle Indian Industrial School 1907–14, Jim Thorpe was one of his players. He also coached football teams at Cornell University 1897–98, and 1904–06, The University of Pittsburgh 1915–23, and Stanford University 1924–32. A football league for youths is named for him.

War·ner Broth·ers /'wôrnər/ a movie production company founded in 1923 by the brothers Harry, Jack, Sam, and Albert Warner. The company produced the first full-length sound movie, *The Jazz Singer*, in 1927 and went on to release successful gangster films with Humphrey Bogart, Busby Berkeley musicals in the 1930s and 1940s, and the Looney Tunes cartoons.

War·ner Rob·ins /,wôrnər 'räbinz/ an industrial city in central Georgia, site of a U.S. Air Force base; pop. 48,804.

warn·ing /'wôrniNG/ ▸*n.* a statement or event that indicates a possible or impending danger, problem, or other unpleasant situation: *a warning about heavy thunderstorms* | *suddenly and without any warning, the army opened fire* | [as *adj.*] *a red warning light.* ■ cautionary advice: *a word of warning—don't park illegally.* ■ advance notice of something: *she had only had four days' warning before leaving Berlin.* ■ an experience or sight that serves as a cautionary example to others: *his death should be a warning to everyone.* ▷Old English *war(e)nung* (see **WARN**, **-ING**[1]). —**warn·ing·ly** *adv.*

warn·ing col·or·a·tion ▸*n. Zoology* conspicuous coloring that warns a predator that an animal is unpalatable or poisonous.

warn·ing track ▸*n. Baseball* a grassless strip around the outside of the outfield grass that warns fielders that they are approaching the outfield wall.

War of 1812 a conflict between the U.S. and the UK (1812–14), prompted by restrictions on U.S. trade resulting from the British blockade of French and allied ports during the Napoleonic Wars, and by British and Canadian support for American Indians trying to resist westward expansion. It was ended by a treaty that restored all conquered territories to their owners before outbreak of war.

War of A·mer·i·can In·de·pend·ence see **AMERICAN REVOLUTION**.

War of Jen·kins's Ear see **JENKINS'S EAR, WAR OF**.

warp /wôrp/ ▸*v.* **1** become or cause to become bent or twisted out of shape, typically as a result of the effects of heat or dampness: [*intrans.*] *wood has a tendency to warp* | [*trans.*] *moisture had warped the box.* ■ [*trans.*] cause to become abnormal or strange; have a distorting effect on: *your judgment has been warped by your obvious dislike of him* | [as *adj.*] (**warped**) *a warped sense of humor.* **2** [*trans.*] move (a ship) along by hauling on a rope attached to a stationary object on shore. ■ [*intrans.*] (of a ship) move in such a way. **3** [*trans.*] (in weaving) arrange (yarn) so as to form the warp of a piece of cloth. **4** [*trans.*] cover (land) with a deposit of alluvial soil by natural or artificial flooding.
▸*n.* **1** a twist or distortion in the shape or form of something: *the head of the racket had a curious warp.* ■ *figurative* an abnormality or perversion in a person's character. ■ [as *adj.*] relating to or denoting (fictional or hypothetical) space travel by means of distorting space-time: *the craft possessed warp drive* | *warp speed.* **2** [in *sing.*] (in weaving) the threads on a loom over and under which other threads (the weft) are passed to make cloth: *the warp and weft are the basic constituents of all textiles* | *figurative rugby is woven into the warp and weft of South African society.* **3** a rope attached at one end to a fixed point and used for moving or mooring a ship. **4** *archaic* alluvial sediment; silt. ▷Old English *weorpan* (verb), *wearp* (noun), of Germanic origin; related to Dutch *werpen* and German *werfen* 'to throw.' Early verb senses included 'throw,' 'fling open,' and 'hit (with a missile)'; the sense 'bend' dates from late Middle English. The noun was originally a term in weaving (see sense 2). —**warp·age** /'wôrpij/ *n.* (in sense 1 of the *verb*). —**warp·er** *n.* (in sense 3 of the *verb*).

war·paint /'wôr,pānt/ ▸*n.* a pigment or paint traditionally used in some societies, esp. those of North American Indians, to decorate the face and body before battle. ■ *informal* elaborate or excessively applied makeup.

war·path /'wôr,paTH/ ▸*n.* (in phrase **on the warpath**) in an angry and aggressive state about a conflict of dispute: *he intends to go on the warpath with a national campaign to reverse the decision.* ▷with reference to American Indians heading toward a battle with an enemy.

war·plane /'wôr,plān/ ▸*n.* an airplane designed and equipped to engage in air combat or to drop bombs.

war po·et ▸*n.* a poet writing at the time of and on the subject of war, esp. one on military service during World War I.

war·rant /'wôrənt; 'wä-/ ▸*n.* **1** a document issued by a legal or government official authorizing the police or some other body to make an arrest, search premises, or carry out some other action relating to the administration of justice: *magistrates issued a* *warrant for his arrest | an extradition warrant.* ■ a document that entitles the holder to receive goods, money, or services: *we'll issue you with a travel warrant.* ■ *Finance* a negotiable security allowing the holder to buy shares at a specified price at or before some future date. ■ [usu. with *negative*] justification or authority for an action, belief, or feeling: *there is* ***no warrant for*** *this assumption.* **2** an official certificate of appointment issued to an officer of lower rank than a commissioned officer.

▸*v.* [*trans.*] justify or necessitate (a certain course of action): *that offense is serious enough to warrant a court marshal.* ■ officially affirm or guarantee: *the vendor warrants the accuracy of the report.* ▷Middle English (in the senses 'protector' and 'safeguard,' also, as a verb, 'keep safe from danger'): from variants of Old French *guarant* (noun), *guarantir* (verb), of Germanic origin; compare with **GUARANTEE**. **—war·rant·er** *n.*

▸*PHRASE* □ **I** (or **I'll**) **warrant (you)** *dated* used to express the speaker's certainty about a fact or situation: *I'll warrant you'll thank me for it in years to come.*

war·rant·a·ble /'wôrəntəbəl; 'wä-/ ▸*adj.* (of an action or statement) able to be authorized or sanctioned; justifiable: *a warrantable assertion.* **—war·rant·a·ble·ness** *n.* **—war·rant·a·bly** /-blē/ *adv.*

war·ran·tee /ˌwôrən'tē; ˌwä-/ ▸*n. Law* a person to whom a warranty is given.

> ***USAGE*** Warrantee means 'person to whom a warranty is made'; it is not a spelling variant of **warranty**.

war·rant of·fi·cer ▸*n.* an officer in the U.S. armed forces ranking below the commissioned officers and above the noncommissioned officers.

war·ran·tor /'wôrəntər; 'wä-/ ▸*n.* a person or company that provides a warranty.

war·ran·ty /'wôrəntē; 'wä-/ ▸*n.* (*pl.* **-ties**) a written guarantee, issued to the purchaser of an article by its manufacturer, promising to repair or replace it if necessary within a specified period of time: *the car comes with a three-year warranty | as your machine is under warranty, I suggest getting it checked.* ■ (in contract law) a promise that something in furtherance of the contract is guaranteed by one of the contractors, esp. the seller's promise that the thing being sold is as promised or represented. ■ (in an insurance contract) an engagement by the insured party that certain statements are true or that certain conditions shall be fulfilled, the breach of it invalidating the policy. ■ (in property law) a covenant by which the seller binds themselves and their heirs to secure to the buyer the estate conveyed in the deed. ■ (in contract law) a term or promise in a contract, breach of which entitles the innocent party to damages but not to treat the contract as discharged by breach. ■ [usu. with *negative*] *archaic* justification or grounds for an action or belief: *you have no warranty for such an audacious doctrine.* ▷Middle English: from Anglo-Norman French *warantie*, variant of *garantie* (see **GUARANTY**). Early use was as a legal term denoting a covenant annexed to a conveyance of property, in which the vendor affirmed the security of the title.

> ***USAGE*** See usage at **WARRANTEE**.

war·ran·ty deed ▸*n. Law* a deed that guarantees a clear title to the buyer of real property.

War·ren[1] /'wôrən; 'wär-/ **1** an industrial city in southeastern Michigan, north of Detroit; pop. 138,247. **2** an industrial city in northeastern Ohio, on the Mahoning River; pop. 50,793.

War·ren[2], American family of physicians. **Joseph Warren** (1741–75), a patriot active in the events leading up to the American Revolution, was killed at the Battle of Bunker Hill. His brother, **John Warren** (1753–1815), was a leading medical practitioner in New England, a surgeon in the American Revolution, and the founder of Harvard Medical School in 1783. **John Collins Warren** (1778–1856), the son of John Warren, helped to found Massachusetts General Hospital in 1811.

War·ren[3], Earl (1891–1974), U.S. chief justice 1953–69. He did much to extend civil liberties, including the prohibition of segregation in schools. He is also remembered for heading the Warren Commission 1964 that investigated into the assassination of President Kennedy and concluded that Lee Harvey Oswald was the sole gunman.

War·ren[4], Mercy Otis (1728–1814), American writer and political satirist; the sister of James Otis. She wrote *The Adulateur* (1773) and *The Group* (1775), as well as the play *History of the Rise, Progress, and Termination of the American Revolution* (1805).

War·ren[5], Robert Penn (1905–89), U.S. poet, novelist, and critic. The first person to win Pulitzer Prizes in both fiction and poetry categories, he was made the U.S.'s first poet laureate in 1986. Notable works: *All the King's Men* (1946), *A Place To Come To* (1977), *Promises* (1957), *Now and Then* (1978).

war·ren /'wôrən; 'wä-/ ▸*n.* (also **rabbit warren**) a network of interconnecting rabbit burrows. ■ a densely populated or labyrinthine building or district: *a warren of narrow gas-lit streets.* ■ *Brit., historical* an enclosed piece of land set aside for breeding game, esp. rabbits. ▷late Middle English: from an Anglo-Norman French and Old Northern French variant of Old French *garenne* 'game park,' of Gaulish origin.

war·ren·er /'wôrənər; 'wä-/ ▸*n. historical* a gamekeeper. ■ a person in charge of a rabbit warren, either as owner or on behalf of its owner. ▷late Middle English: from Anglo-Norman French *warener*, from *warenne* 'game park.'

war·ring /'wôriNG/ ▸*adj.* [*attrib.*] (of two or more people or groups) in conflict with each other: *warring factions | a warring couple.*

war·ri·or /'wôrēər/ ▸*n.* (esp. in former times) a brave or experienced soldier or fighter. ▷Middle English: from Old Northern French *werreior*, variant of Old French *guerreior*, from *guerreier* 'make war,' from *guerre* 'war.'

war room ▸*n.* a room from which a war is directed. ■ a room from which business or political strategy is planned.

War·saw /'wôrˌsô/ the capital of Poland, in the eastern central part of the country, on the Vistula River; pop. 1,656,000. The city suffered severe damage and the loss of 700,000 lives during World War II and was almost completely rebuilt. Polish name **WARSZAWA**.

War·saw Pact a treaty of mutual defense and military aid signed at Warsaw on May 14, 1955, by communist states of Europe under Soviet influence, in response to the admission of West Germany to NATO. The pact was dissolved in 1991.

war·ship /'wôrˌSHip/ ▸*n.* a ship equipped with weapons and designed to take part in warfare at sea.

Wars of Re·li·gion another term for **FRENCH WARS OF RELIGION**.

Wars of the Ros·es the 15th-century English civil wars between the Houses of York and Lancaster, represented by white and red roses respectively, during the reigns of Henry VI, Edward IV, and Richard III. The struggle was largely ended in 1485 by the defeat and death of the Yorkist king Richard III at the Battle of Bosworth and the accession of the Lancastrian Henry Tudor (Henry VII), who united the two houses by marrying Elizabeth, daughter of Edward IV.

wart /wôrt/ ▸*n.* a small, hard, benign growth on the skin, caused by a virus. ■ any rounded excrescence on the skin of an animal or the surface of a plant. ■ *informal* an obnoxious or objectionable person. ■ an undesirable or disfiguring feature: *few products are without their warts.* ▷Old English *wearte*, of Germanic origin; related to Dutch *wrat* and German *Warze*. **—wart·y** /'wôrtē/ *adj.*

▸*PHRASE* □ **warts and all** *informal* including features or qualities that are not appealing or attractive: *Philip must learn to accept me, warts and all.*

wart·hog /'wôrtˌhäg/ ▸*n.* an African wild pig with bristly gray skin, a large head, warty lumps on the face, and curved tusks. • *Phacochoerus aethiopicus*, family Suidae.

war·time /'wôrˌtīm/ ▸*n.* a period during which a war is taking place.

Earl Warren

war-torn ▸*adj.* (of a place) racked or devastated by war: *a war-torn republic.*

War·wick[1] /'wôrik; 'wär-; -wik/ a city in east central Rhode Island, south of Providence; pop. 85,808.

War·wick[2] /'wôrwik/, Dionne (1941–), U.S. singer. Her many hit songs are collected in albums such as *Here I Am* (1966), *The Windows of the World* (1968), *I'll Never Fall in Love Again* (1970), and *I Say a Little Prayer for You* (2000).

War·wick[3] /'wôr(w)ik/, Richard Neville, Earl of (1428–71), English statesman; known as **Warwick the Kingmaker**. During the Wars of the Roses he fought first on the Yorkist side, helping Edward IV to gain the throne in 1461, and then on the Lancastrian side, briefly restoring Henry VI to the throne in 1470. He was killed at the battle of Barnet.

war·y /'we(ə)rē/ ▸*adj.* (**war·i·er**, **war·i·est**) feeling or showing caution about possible dangers or problems: *dogs that have been mistreated often remain very* ***wary of*** *strangers | a wary look.* See note at **VIGILANT**. ▷late 15th cent.: from **WARE**[2] + **-Y**[1]. **—war·i·ly** /-rəlē/ *adv.* **—war·i·ness** *n.*

was /wəz/ ▸ first and third person singular past of **BE**.

wa·sa·bi /wə'säbē/ ▸*n.* a Japanese plant with a thick green root that tastes like strong horseradish and is used in cooking, esp. in powder or paste form as an accompaniment to raw fish. • *Eutrema wasabi*, family Brassicaceae. ▷early 20th cent.: from Japanese.

Wa·satch Range /'wôˌsaCH/ a range of the Rocky Mountains that extends south from Idaho into central Utah, where Salt Lake City and its suburbs lie on its west.

wash /wäSH; wôSH/ ▸*v.* **1** [*trans.*] clean with water and, typically, soap or detergent: *I stripped and washed myself all over.* ■ [*intrans.*] clean oneself, esp. one's hands and face with soap and water. ■ (of an animal) clean (itself or another) by licking. ■ [*trans.*] remove (a stain or dirt) from something by cleaning with water and detergent: *they have to keep washing the mold off the walls | figurative all that hate can't wash away the guilt.* ■ [*intrans.*] (of dirt or a stain) be removed in such a way: *the dirt on his clothes would easily wash out.* ■ [*intrans.*] (of fabric, a garment, or dye) withstand cleaning to a specified degree without shrinking or fading: *a linen-mix yarn that washes well.* ■ [*intrans.*] do one's laundry: *I need someone to cook and wash for me.* ■ (usu. **be washed**) *poetic/literary* wet or moisten (something) thoroughly: *you are beautiful with your face washed with rain.* **2** [*trans.*] (of flowing water) carry (someone or something) in a particular direction: *floods washed away the bridges.* ■ [*intrans.*] be carried by flowing water: *an oil slick washed up on the beaches.* ■ [*intrans.*] (esp. of waves) sweep, move, or splash in a particular direction: *the sea began to wash along the decks.* ■ [*trans.*] (usu. **be washed**) (of a river, sea, or lake) flow through or lap against (a country, coast, etc.): *offshore islands washed by warm blue seas.* ■ [*intrans.*] (**wash over**) (of a feeling) affect (someone) suddenly: *a deep feeling of sadness washed over her.* ■ [*intrans.*] (**wash over**) occur all around without greatly affecting (someone): *she allowed the babble of conversation to wash over her.* ■ [*trans.*] sift metallic particles from (earth or gravel) by running water through it. **3** [*trans.*] (usu. **be washed**) brush with a thin coat of diluted paint or ink: *the walls were washed with shades of umber.* ■ (**wash something with**) coat inferior metal with (a film of gold or silver from a solution). **4** [*intrans.*] *informal* seem convincing or genuine: *charm won't wash with this crew.*

▸*phrasal v.* □ **wash something down 1** wash or clean something thoroughly: *she washed down the walls.* **2** accompany or follow food with a drink: *bacon and eggs* ***washed down with*** *a cup of tea.* □ **wash out** (or **wash someone out**) be excluded (or exclude someone) from a course or position after a failure to meet the required standards: *a lot of them had washed out of pilot training.* □ **wash something out 1** clean the inside of something with water. **2** wash something, esp. a garment, quickly or briefly: *I don't have time to wash a blouse out every night.* **3** (usu. **be washed out**) cause an event to be postponed or canceled because of rain: *the game was washed out.* **4** (of a flood or downpour) make a breach in a road.

▸*n.* **1** [usu. in *sing.*] an act of washing something or an instance of being washed. ■ a quantity of clothes needing to be or just having been washed: *she hung out her Tuesday wash.* ■ a medicinal or cleansing solution: *mouth wash.* **2** [in *sing.*] the disturbed water or air behind a moving boat or aircraft or the sound made by this: *the wash of a motorboat.* ■ the surging of water or breaking of waves or the sound made by this: *the wash of waves on the pebbled beach.* **3** a layer of paint or metal spread thinly on a surface: *the walls were covered with a pale lemon wash.* **4** silt or gravel carried by a stream or river and deposited as sediment. ■ a sandbank exposed only at low tide. ■ (in the western U.S.) a dry bed of a stream, typically in a ravine, that flows only seasonally. **5** kitchen slops and other food waste fed to pigs. **6** malt fermenting in preparation for distillation. **7** [in *sing.*] *informal* a situation or result that is of no benefit to either of two opposing sides: *the plan's impact on jobs would be a wash, creating as many as it costs.* ▷Old English *wæscan* (verb), of Germanic origin; related to Dutch *wassen*, German *waschen*, also to **WATER**.

▸*PHRASES* □ **come out in the wash** *informal* be resolved eventually with no lasting harm: *he's not happy, but he assures me* ***it'll all come out in the wash.*** □ **in the wash** (of clothes, bed linen, or similar) put aside for washing or in the process of being washed. □ **one hand washes the other** mutual favors are exchanged: *you can be on the list if you also link to our page. One hand washes the other.* □ **wash one's dirty linen** (or **laundry**) **in public** *informal* (of an individual or a member of an organization) discuss or argue about one's private affairs in public. □ **wash one's hands** go to the toilet (used euphemistically). □ **wash one's hands of** disclaim responsibility for: *the social services washed their hands of his daughter.* [originally with biblical allusion to Matt. 27:24.]

Wash. ▸*abbr.* Washington.

wash·a·ble /ˈwäsHəbəl; ˈwôsH-/ ▸*adj.* (esp. of fabric or clothes) able to be washed without shrinkage or other damage: *washable curtains* | [as *n.*] *fine washables.* **—wash·a·bil·i·ty** /ˌwäsHəˈbilitē; ˌwôsH-/ *n.*

wash-and-wear ▸*adj.* (of a garment or fabric) easily washed, drying quickly, and not needing to be ironed.

wash·a·ter·i·a ▸*n.* variant form of **WASHETERIA**.

wash·ba·sin /ˈwäsHˌbāsən; ˈwôsH-/ ▸*n.* a basin, typically fixed to a wall or on a pedestal, used for washing one's hands and face.

wash·board /ˈwäsHˌbôrd; ˈwôsH-/ ▸*n.* **1** a board made of ridged wood or a sheet of corrugated zinc, used when washing clothes as a surface against which to scrub them. ■ a similar board played as a percussion instrument by scraping. ■ the surface of a worn, uneven road. ■ [as *adj.*] denoting a man's stomach that is lean and has well-defined muscles. **2** a board fixed along the side of a boat to prevent water from spilling in over the edge.
▸*v.* [*trans.*] [usu. as *adj.*] (**washboarded**) cause ridges to develop in (a road or road surface): *a road left washboarded by winter frost.*

wash·cloth /ˈwäsHˌklôTH; ˈwôsH-/ ▸*n.* a cloth for washing one's face and body, typically made of terrycloth or other absorbent material.

wash·day /ˈwäsHˌdā; ˈwôsH-/ ▸*n.* a day on which a household's clothes, bed linens, etc., are washed, esp. when the same day each week.

wash draw·ing ▸*n.* a picture or sketch made by laying on washes of watercolor, typically in monochrome, over a pen or pencil drawing.

washed-out ▸*adj.* faded by or as if by sunlight or repeated washing: *washed-out jeans.* ■ (of a person) pale and tired.

washed-up ▸*adj.* deposited by the tide on a shore: *washed-up jellyfish.* ■ *informal* no longer effective or successful: *a washed-up actress.*

wash·er /ˈwäsHər; ˈwôsH-/ ▸*n.* **1** [usu. with *adj.*] a person or device that washes something: *a glass washer.* ■ a washing machine. **2** a small flat ring made of metal, rubber, or plastic fixed under a nut or the head of a bolt to spread the pressure when tightened or between two joining surfaces as a spacer or seal.

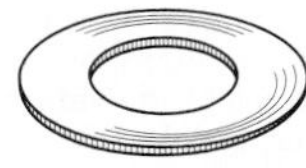

washer 2

wash·er-dry·er ▸*n.* a washing machine with a built-in tumble-dryer.

wash·er·wom·an /ˈwäsHərˌwo͝omən; ˈwôsH-/ ▸*n.* (*pl.* **-wom·en**) a woman whose occupation is washing clothes.

wash·e·te·ri·a /ˌwäsHəˈti(ə)rēə; ˌwôsH-/ (also **wash·a·te·ri·a**) ▸*n.* another term for **LAUNDROMAT**. ▷1950s: from **WASH**, on the pattern of *cafeteria.*

wash·ing /ˈwäsHiNG; ˈwôsH-/ ▸*n.* the action of washing oneself or laundering clothes, bed linen, etc. ■ a quantity of clothes, bed linen, etc., that is to be washed or has just been washed: *she took her washing around to the launderette.*

wash·ing ma·chine ▸*n.* a machine for washing clothes, bed linens, etc.

wash·ing so·da ▸*n.* sodium carbonate, used dissolved in water for washing and cleaning.

Wash·ing·ton[1] /ˈwôsHiNGtən; ˈwäsH-/ **1** a state in the northwestern U.S., on the Pacific coast, bordered by Canada; pop. 5,894,121; capital, Olympia; statehood, Nov. 11, 1889 (42). By agreement with Britain, Washington's northern border was set at the 49th parallel in 1846. **2** the capital of the U.S.; pop. 572,059. It is coextensive with the District of Columbia, a federal district on the Potomac River bordering on the states of Virginia and Maryland. Founded in 1790, during the presidency of George Washington, the city was planned by engineer Pierre-Charles L'Enfant (1754–1825) and built as the capital. Full name **WASHINGTON, D.C.**. **—Wash·ing·to·ni·an** /ˌwôsHiNGˈtōnēən; ˌwäsH-/ *n.* & *adj.*

Wash·ing·ton[2], Booker T. (1856–1915), U.S. educator; full name *Booker Taliaferro Washington.* A leading commentator for black Americans, he established the Tuskegee Institute in Alabama (1881). His support for segregation and his emphasis on vocational skills for blacks were criticized by other black leaders.

Booker T. Washington

Wash·ing·ton[3], Bushrod (1762–1829), U.S. Supreme Court associate justice 1798–1829; a nephew of George Washington. Appointed to the Court by President John Adams, he helped to establish the supremacy of the Court over states' rights.

Wash·ing·ton[4], Denzel (1954–), U.S. actor. His many movies include *Glory* (Academy Award, 1989), *Malcolm X* (1992), *Philadelphia* (1993), *The Preacher's Wife* (1996), *The Hurricane* (1999), and *The Manchurian Candidate* (2004).

Wash·ing·ton[5], George (1732–99), 1st president of the U.S. 1789–97. Commander in chief of the Continental Army, he helped to win the American Revolution by keeping his army together through the winter of 1777–78 at Valley Forge and by winning a decisive battle at Yorktown in 1781. In 1787, he chaired the convention at Philadelphia that drew up the U.S. Constitution. In his two terms as president, he followed a policy of neutrality in international affairs and of expansion on the domestic front.

George Washington

Wash·ing·ton, Mount a peak in north central New Hampshire, the highest in the Presidential Range of the White Mountains and in the northeastern U.S. at 6,288 feet (1,918 m)

Wash·ing·ton Mon·u·ment a colossal obelisk erected in honor of George Washington as a national memorial in Washington, D.C. The square base of the obelisk measures 55 feet (17 m) on a side, and the tapering hollow shaft, containing a stairway and elevator to the top, is 555 feet (169 m) high. The cornerstone to the monument was laid on July 4, 1848; the monument was finished in 1884 and opened to the public in 1886.

Washington Monument

Wash·ing·ton Square a park in lower Manhattan in New York City, a focal point of Greenwich Village.

Wash·i·ta Riv·er /ˈwôsHiˌtô; ˈwäsH-/ a river that flows for 500 miles (800 km) from the Texas Panhandle across southern Oklahoma to the Red River at Lake Texoma.

wash·out /ˈwäsHˌout; ˈwôsH-/ ▸*n.* **1** [usu. in *sing.*] *informal* an event that is spoiled by constant or heavy rain. ■ a disappointing failure: *the film was a washout.* **2** a breach in a road or railroad track caused by flooding. ■ *Geology* a channel cut into a sedimentary deposit by rushing water and filled with younger material. **3** *Medicine* the removal of material or a substance from the body or a part of it, either by washing with a fluid, or by allowing it to be eliminated over a period.

wash·rag /ˈwäsHˌrag; ˈwôsH-/ ▸*n.* another term for **WASHCLOTH**.

wash·room /ˈwäsHˌro͞om; ˈwôsH-; -ˌro͝om/ ▸*n.* a room with washing and toilet facilities.

wash·stand /ˈwäsHˌstand; ˈwôsH-/ ▸*n. chiefly historical* a piece of furniture designed to hold a jug, bowl, or basin for the purpose of washing one's hands and face.

wash·tub /ˈwäsHˌtəb; ˈwôsH-/ ▸*n.* a large metal tub used for washing clothes and linen.

wash-up ▸*n.* an act of washing, esp. washing oneself or dishes.

wash·y /ˈwäsHē; ˈwôsHē/ ▸*adj.* (**wash·i·er**, **wash·i·est**) **1** *archaic* (of food or drink) too watery: *washy potatoes.* ■ lacking in strength or vigor; insipid: *a weak and washy production.* **2** (of a color) having a faded look. **—wash·i·ness** *n.*

was·n't /ˈwəzənt/ ▸*contraction of* was not.

Wasp /wäsp/ (also **WASP**) ▸*n.* an upper- or middle-class American white Protestant, considered to be a member of the most powerful group in society. ▷1950s: acronym from *white Anglo-Saxon Protestant.* **—Wasp·ish** *adj.* **—Wasp·y** *adj.*

wasp /wäsp/ ▸*n.* **1** a social winged insect that has a narrow waist and a sting. It constructs a paper nest from wood pulp and raises the larvae on a diet of insects. • Family Vespidae, superfamily Vespoidea, order Hymenoptera: several genera, in particular *Vespula* and *Polistes.* **2** a solitary winged insect with a narrow waist, mostly distantly related to the social wasps and including many parasitic kinds. • Several superfamilies in the sections Aculeata (digger, mason, and potter wasps) and Parasitica (parasitic wasps and gall wasps), order Hymenoptera. ▷Old English *wæfs, wæps, wæsp,* from an Indo-European

Pronunciation Key ə *ago;* ər *over;* ˈə or ˌə *up;* ˈər or ˌər *fur;* a *hat;* ā *rate;* ä *car;* CH *chew;* e *let;* ē *see;* e(ə)r *air;* i *fit;* ī *by;* i(ə)r *ear;* NG *sing;* ō *go;* ô *for;* oi *boy;* o͝o *good;* o͞o *goo;* ou *out;* SH *she;* TH *thin;* T̲H̲ *then;* (h)w *why;* ZH *vision*

W

root shared by Latin *vespa*; perhaps related to WEAVE[1] (from the weblike form of its nest). —**wasp·like** /-ˌlīk/ *adj.*

wasp·ish /ˈwäspiSH/ ▸*adj.* readily expressing anger or irritation: *he had a waspish tongue.* —**wasp·ish·ly** *adv.* —**wasp·ish·ness** *n.*

wasp waist ▸*n.* a very narrow or tightly corseted waist. —**wasp-waist·ed** *adj.*

was·sail /ˈwäsəl; -ˌsāl/ *archaic* ▸*n.* spiced ale or mulled wine drunk during celebrations for Twelfth Night and Christmas Eve. ■ lively and noisy festivities involving the drinking of plentiful amounts of alcohol; revelry.
▸*v.* **1** [*intrans.*] drink plentiful amounts of alcohol and enjoy oneself with others in a noisy, lively way. **2** go from house to house at Christmas singing carols: *here we go a-wassailing.* ▷Middle English *wæs hæil* 'be in (good) health!': from Old Norse *ves heill* (compare with HAIL[2]). The drinking formula *wassail* (and the reply *drinkhail* 'drink good health') were probably introduced by Danish-speaking inhabitants of England, and then spread, so that by the 12th cent. the usage was considered by the Normans to be characteristic of Englishmen. —**was·sail·er** *n.*

was·sail bowl (also **was·sail cup**) ▸*n.* a large bowl in which wassail was made and from which it was dispensed for the drinking of toasts.

Was·ser·mann test /ˈwäsərmən; ˈvä-/ ▸*n.* *Medicine* a diagnostic test for syphilis using a specific antibody reaction (the **Wassermann reaction**) of the patient's blood serum. ▷early 20th cent.: named after August P. *Wassermann* (1866–1925), German pathologist.

Was·ser·stein /ˈwäsərˌstīn; -ˌstēn/, Wendy (1950–), U.S. playwright. She is most noted for her award-winning play *The Heidi Chronicles* (1988). She also wrote *The Sisters Rosensweig* (1992) and *An American Daughter* (1997).

wast /wəst; wäst/ ▸ *archaic* or *dialect* second person singular past of BE.

wast·age /ˈwāstij/ ▸*n.* **1** the action or process of losing or destroying something by using it carelessly or extravagantly: *the wastage of natural resources.* ■ the amount of something lost or destroyed in such a way: *wastage was cut by 50 percent.* **2** the weakening or deterioration of a part of the body, typically as a result of illness or lack of use: *the wastage of muscle tissue.*

waste /wāst/ ▸*v.* **1** [*trans.*] use or expend carelessly, extravagantly, or to no purpose: *we can't afford to waste electricity* | *I don't use the car, so why should I* ***waste*** *precious money* ***on*** *it?* ■ (usu. **be wasted on**) bestow or expend on an unappreciative recipient: *her small talk was wasted on this guest.* ■ (usu. **be wasted**) fail to make full or good use of: *we're wasted in this job.* **2** [*intrans.*] (of a person or a part of the body) become progressively weaker and more emaciated: *she was dying of AIDS, visibly* ***wasting away*** [as *adj.*] (**wasting**) *a wasting disease.* ■ [*trans.*] *archaic* cause to do this: *these symptoms wasted the patients very much.* **3** [*trans.*] *poetic/literary* devastate or ruin (a place): *he seized their cattle and wasted their country.* See note at RAVAGE. ■ *informal* kill or severely injure (someone): *I saw them waste the guy I worked for.* **4** [*intrans.*] *poetic/literary* (of time) pass away; be spent: *the years were wasting.*
▸*adj.* [*attrib.*] **1** (of a material, substance, or byproduct) eliminated or discarded as no longer useful or required after the completion of a process: *ensure that waste materials are disposed of responsibly* | *plants produce oxygen as a waste product.* **2** (of an area of land, typically in a city or town) not used, cultivated, or built on: *a patch of waste ground.*
▸*n.* **1** an act or instance of using or expending something carelessly, extravagantly, or to no purpose: *it's a waste of time trying to argue with him* | *they had learned to avoid waste.* ■ *archaic* the gradual loss or diminution of something: *he was pale and weak from waste of blood.* **2** material that is not wanted; the unusable remains or byproducts of something: *bodily waste* | (**wastes**) *hazardous industrial wastes.* **3** (usu. **wastes**) a large area of barren, typically uninhabited land: *the icy wastes of the Antarctic.* **4** *Law* damage to an estate caused by an act or by neglect, esp. by a life-tenant. ▷Middle English: from Old Northern French *wast(e)* (noun), *waster* (verb), based on Latin *vastus* 'unoccupied, uncultivated;' compare with VAST.
▸*PHRASES* □ **go to waste** be unused or expended to no purpose. □ **lay waste to** (or **lay something (to) waste**) completely destroy: *a land laid waste by war.* □ **waste one's breath** see BREATH. □ **waste not, want not** *proverb* if you use a commodity or resource carefully and without extravagance, you will never be in need. □ **waste words** see WORD.

waste·bas·ket /ˈwāstˌbaskit/ ▸*n.* a receptacle for small quantities of rubbish.

wast·ed /ˈwāstid/ ▸*adj.* **1** used or expended carelessly, extravagantly, or to no purpose: *wasted fuel* | *a wasted opportunity.* ■ (of an action) not producing the desired result: *I'm sorry you've had a wasted journey.* **2** (of a person or a part of the body) weak and emaciated: *her wasted arm.* ■ *informal* under the influence of alcohol or illegal drugs: *he looked kind of wasted.*

waste·ful /ˈwāstfəl/ ▸*adj.* (of a person, action, or process) using or expending something of value carelessly, extravagantly, or to no purpose: *wasteful energy consumption.* —**waste·ful·ly** *adv.* —**waste·ful·ness** *n.*

waste·gate /ˈwāstˌgāt/ ▸*n.* a device in a turbocharger that regulates the pressure at which exhaust gases pass to the turbine by opening or closing a vent to the exterior.

waste·land /ˈwāstˌland/ ▸*n.* an unused area of land that has become barren or overgrown. ■ a bleak, unattractive, and unused or neglected urban or industrial area: *the restoration of industrial wasteland* | *figurative the mid 70s are now seen as something of a cultural wasteland.*

waste·pa·per bas·ket ▸*n.* a wastebasket.

waste pipe ▸*n.* a pipe carrying waste water, such as that from a sink, bathtub, or shower, to a drain.

wast·er /ˈwāstər/ ▸*n.* a wasteful person or thing: *you are a great waster of time.* ■ *informal* a person who does little or nothing of value. ■ a discarded piece of defective pottery.

wast·rel /ˈwāstrəl/ ▸*n.* **1** *poetic/literary* a wasteful or good-for-nothing person. **2** *archaic* a waif; a neglected child. ▷late 16th cent. (denoting a strip of wasteland): from the verb WASTE + -REL.

wat /wät/ ▸*n.* (in Thailand, Cambodia, and Laos) a Buddhist monastery or temple. ▷Thai, from Sanskrit, *vāṭa* 'enclosure.'

watch /wäCH/ ▸*v.* **1** [*trans.*] look at or observe attentively, typically over a period of time: *Lucy watched him go* | [*intrans.*] *as she watched, two women came into the garden* [with *clause*] *everyone stopped to watch what was going on.* ■ keep under careful or protective observation: *a large set of steel doors,* ***watched over*** *by a single guard.* ■ secretly follow or spy on: *he told me my telephones were tapped and I was being watched.* ■ follow closely or maintain an interest in: *the girls watched the development of this relationship with incredulity.* ■ exercise care, caution, or restraint about: *most women watch their diet during pregnancy* | [with *clause*] *you should watch what you say!* ■ [*intrans.*] (**watch for**) look out or be on the alert for: *in spring and summer, watch for kingfishers* | ***watch out for*** *broken glass.* ■ [*intrans.*] [usu. in *imperative*] (**watch out**) be careful: *credit-card fraud is on the increase, so watch out.* ■ (**watch it/yourself**) [usu. in *imperative*] *informal* be careful (used as a warning or threat): *if anyone finds out, you're dead meat; so watch it.* **2** [*intrans.*] *archaic* remain awake for the purpose of religious observance: *she watched whole nights in the church.*
▸*n.* **1** a small timepiece worn typically on a strap on one's wrist. **2** [usu. in *sing.*] an act or instance of carefully observing someone or something over a period of time: *the security forces have been* ***keeping a close watch on*** *our activities.* ■ a period of vigil during which a person is stationed to look out for danger or trouble, typically during the night: *Murray took the last watch before dawn.* ■ a fixed period of duty on a ship, usually lasting four hours. ■ (also **star·board** or **port watch**) the officers and crew on duty during one such period. ■ *figurative* the period someone spends in a particular role or job. ■ (usu. **the watch**) *historical* a watchman or group of watchmen who patrolled and guarded the streets of a town before the introduction of the police force. ■ a body of soldiers making up a guard. ▷Old English *wæcce* 'watchfulness,' *wæccende* 'remaining awake'; related to WAKE[1]. The sense 'small timepiece' probably developed by way of a sense 'alarm device attached to a clock.' —**watch·er** *n.* [often in *combination*] *a bird-watcher.*
▸*PHRASES* □ **be on the watch** be carefully looking out for something, esp. a possible danger. □ **keep watch** stay on the lookout for danger or trouble. □ **watch one's mouth** see MOUTH. □ **the watches of the night** *poetic/literary* the hours of night, portrayed as a time when one cannot sleep. □ **watch (one's) pennies** see PENNY. □ **watch one's step** used as a warning to someone to walk or act carefully. □ **watch this space** see SPACE. □ **watch the time** ensure that one is aware of the time in order to avoid being late.

wat·cha /ˈwəCHə; ˈwä-/ ▸*pron.* variant spelling of WHATCHA.

watch·a·ble /ˈwäCHəbəl/ ▸*adj.* (of a film or television program) moderately enjoyable to watch. —**watch·a·bil·i·ty** /ˌwäCHəˈbilitē/ *n.*

watch cap ▸*n.* a close-fitting knitted cap of a kind worn by members of the U.S. Navy in cold weather.

watch·case /ˈwäCHˌkās/ ▸*n.* a metal case enclosing the works of a watch.

watch chain ▸*n.* a metal chain securing a pocket watch.

watch·dog /ˈwäCHˌdôg/ ▸*n.* a dog kept to guard private property. ■ a person or group whose function is to monitor the practices of companies providing a particular service or utility: *a watchdog for the global banking industry.*
▸*v.* (**-dogged, -dog·ging**) [*trans.*] maintain surveillance over (a person, activity, or situation): *how can we watchdog our investments?*

watch·fire /ˈwäCHˌfīr/ ▸*n.* a fire maintained during the night as a signal or for the use of someone who is on watch.

watch·ful /ˈwäCHfəl/ ▸*adj.* watching or observing someone or something closely; alert and vigilant: *they attended dances under the* ***watchful eye*** *of their father.* See note at VIGILANT. ■ *archaic* wakeful; sleepless. —**watch·ful·ly** *adv.* —**watch·ful·ness** *n.*

watch list ▸*n.* a list of individuals, groups, or items that require close surveillance, typically for legal or political reasons.

watch·mak·er /ˈwäCHˌmākər/ ▸*n.* a person who makes and repairs watches and clocks. —**watch·mak·ing** /-kiNG/ *n.*

watch·man /ˈwäCHmən/ ▸*n.* (*pl.* **-men**) a man employed to look after an empty building, esp. at night. ■ *historical* a member of a body of people employed to keep watch in a town at night.

watch night ▸*n.* a religious service held on New Year's Eve or Christmas Eve.

watch spring ▸*n.* a mainspring in a watch.

watch·tow·er /ˈwäCHˌtou(-ə)r/ ▸*n.* a tower built to create an elevated observation point.

watch·word /ˈwäCHˌwərd/ ▸*n.* a word or phrase expressing a person's or group's core aim or belief: *the watchword for the market is be prepared for anything.* ■ *archaic* a military password.

wa·ter /ˈwôtər; ˈwä-/ ▸*n.* **1** a colorless, transparent, odorless, tasteless liquid that forms the seas, lakes, rivers, and rain and is the basis of the fluids of living organisms. ■ this as supplied to houses or commercial establishments through pipes and taps: *each bedroom has a washbasin with hot and cold water* | [as *adj.*] *water pipes.* ■ one of the four elements in ancient and medieval philosophy and in astrology (considered essential to the nature of the signs Cancer, Scorpio, and Pisces): [as *adj.*] *a water sign.* ■ (usu. **the waters**) the water of a mineral spring, typically as used medicinally for bathing in or drinking: *resorts where southerners came to* ***take the waters.*** ■ [with *adj.*] a solution of a specified substance in water: *ammonia water.* ■ urine: *drinking alcohol will make you need to* ***pass water*** *more often.* ■ (**waters**) the amniotic fluid surrounding a fetus in the womb, esp. as discharged in a flow shortly before birth: *I think my waters have broken.*

> Water is a compound of oxygen and hydrogen (chem. formula: H_2O) with highly distinctive physical and chemical properties: it is able to dissolve many other substances; its solid form (ice) is *less* dense than the liquid form; its boiling point, viscosity, and surface tension are unusually high for its molecular weight, and it is partially dissociated into hydrogen and hydroxyl ions.

2 (**the water**) a stretch or area of water, such as a river, sea, or lake: *the lawns ran down to the water's edge.* ■ the surface of such an area of water: *she ducked under the water.* ■ [as *adj.*] found in, on, or near such areas of water: *a water plant.* ■ (**waters**) the water of a particular sea, river, or lake: *the waters of Hudson Bay* | *figurative the government is taking us into unknown waters with these changes in the legislation.* ■ (**waters**) an area of sea regarded as under the jurisdiction of a particular country: *Japanese coastal waters.* **3** the quality of transparency and brilliance shown by a diamond or other gem. **4** *Finance* capital stock that represents a book value greater than the true assets of a company.
▸*v.* **1** [*trans.*] pour or sprinkle water over (a plant or an area of ground), typically in order to encourage plant growth: *I went out to water the geraniums.* ■ give a drink of water to (an animal): *they stopped to water the horses and to refresh themselves.* ■ [*intrans.*] (of an animal) drink water. ■ (usu. **be watered**) (of a river)

flow through (an area of land): *the valley is watered by the Pines River.* ■ take a fresh supply of water on board (a ship or steam train): *the ship was watered and fresh livestock taken aboard.* ■ *Finance* increase (a company's debt, or nominal capital) by the issue of new shares without a corresponding addition to assets. **2** [*intrans.*] (of the eyes) become full of moisture or tears: *Rory blinked, his eyes watering.* ■ (of the mouth) produce saliva, typically in response to the sight or smell of appetizing food: *the smell of frying bacon made Hilary's mouth water.* **3** [*trans.*] dilute or adulterate (a drink, typically an alcoholic one) with water: *staff at the club had been* **watering down** *the drinks.* ■ (**water something down**) make a statement or proposal less forceful or controversial by changing or leaving out certain details: *the army's report of its investigation was considerably watered down.* ▷Old English *wæter* (noun), *wæterian* (verb), of Germanic origin; related to Dutch *water*, German *Wasser*, from an Indo-European root shared by Russian *voda* (compare with VODKA), also by Latin *unda* 'wave' and Greek *hudōr* 'water.' **—wa·ter·er** *n.* **—wa·ter·less** *adj.*

▸*PHRASES* □ **by water** using a ship or boat for travel or transport: *at the end of the lake was a small gazebo, accessible only by water.* □ **cast one's bread upon the waters** see BREAD. □ **like water** in great quantities: *George was spending money like water.* □ **make water 1** urinate. **2** (of a ship or boat) take in water through a leak. □ **of the first water** (of a diamond or pearl) of the greatest brilliance and transparency. ■ (typically of someone or something perceived as undesirable or annoying) extreme or unsurpassed of their kind: *she was a bore of the first water.* □ **under water** submerged; flooded. □ **the water of life** whiskey. □ **water off a duck's back** see DUCK[1]. □ **water on the brain** *informal* hydrocephalus. □ **water under the bridge** (or **water over the dam**) used to refer to events or situations that are in the past and consequently no longer to be regarded as important or as a source of concern.

wa·ter ar·um ▸*n.* a plant of the arum family, with heart-shaped leaves, a white spathe, and a green spadix. It grows in swamps and boggy ground in north temperate regions. Also called WILD CALLA. • *Calla palustris*, family Araceae.

water arum

wa·ter bag /bäg; bôg/ ▸*n.* a bag made of leather, canvas, or other material, used for carrying water.

wa·ter-based ▸*adj.* (of a substance or solution) using or having water as a medium or main ingredient: *a water-based paint.*

wa·ter bath ▸*n. Chemistry* a container of water heated to a given temperature, used for heating substances placed in smaller containers.

wa·ter bear ▸*n.* a minute invertebrate with a short plump body and four pairs of stubby legs, living in water or in the film of water on plants such as mosses. • Phylum Tardigrada.

Wa·ter Bear·er (**the Water Bearer**) the zodiacal sign or constellation Aquarius.

wa·ter·bed /ˈwôtərˌbed; ˈwä-/ ▸*n.* a bed with a water-filled rubber or plastic mattress.

wa·ter bee·tle ▸*n.* any of a large number of beetles that live in fresh water. • Several families, in particular Dytiscidae (the predatory diving beetles) and Hydrophilidae (scavenging beetles).

wa·ter·bird /ˈwôtərˌbərd; ˈwä-/ ▸*n.* a bird that frequents water, esp. one that habitually wades or swims in fresh water.

wa·ter birth ▸*n.* a birth in which the mother spends the final stages of labor in a birthing pool, with delivery taking place either in or out of the water.

wa·ter bis·cuit ▸*n.* a thin, crisp unsweetened cracker made from flour and water.

wa·ter bloom ▸*n.* another term for ALGAL BLOOM (see BLOOM).

wa·ter boat·man ▸*n.* an aquatic bug that spends much of its time on the bottom, using its front legs to sieve food from the water and its hair-fringed rear legs for swimming. • Family Corixidae, suborder Heteroptera: *Corixa*, *Sigara*, and other genera. ■ another term for BACKSWIMMER.

wa·ter·bod·y /ˈwôtərˌbädē; ˈwä-/ ▸*n.* (*pl.* **-bod·ies**) a body of water forming a physiographical feature, for example a sea or a reservoir.

wa·ter-bomb·er ▸*n.* an aircraft used for extinguishing forest fires by dropping water.

wa·ter·borne ▸*adj.* (of a vehicle or goods) conveyed by, traveling on, or involving travel or transportation on water. ■ (of a disease) communicated or propagated by contaminated water.

wa·ter·buck /ˈwôtərˌbək; ˈwä-/ ▸*n.* a large African antelope occurring near rivers and lakes in the savanna. • *Kobus ellipsiprymnus*, family Bovidae.

wa·ter buf·fa·lo ▸*n.* a large black domesticated buffalo with heavy swept-back horns, used as a beast of burden throughout the tropics. • Genus *Bubalus*, family Bovidae: the domesticated *B. bubalis*, descended from the wild *B. arnee*, which is confined to remote parts of India and Southeast Asia.

Wa·ter·bury /ˈwôtərˌberē; ˈwätər-/ an industrial city in western Connecticut, on the Naugatuck River, a historic brass-manufacturing center; pop. 107,271.

wa·ter can·non ▸*n.* a device that ejects a powerful jet of water, typically used to disperse a crowd.

wa·ter chest·nut ▸*n.* **1** (also **Chi·nese wa·ter chest·nut**) the tuber of a tropical sedge that is widely used in Asian cooking, its white flesh remaining crisp after cooking. **2** the sedge that yields this tuber, which is cultivated in flooded fields in Southeast Asia. • *Eleocharis tuberosa*, family Cyperaceae. **3** (also **wa·ter cal·trop**) an aquatic plant with small white flowers, producing an edible rounded seed with two large projecting horns. • *Trapa natans*, family Trapaceae.

wa·ter clock ▸*n. historical* a clock that used the flow of water to measure time.

wa·ter clos·et ▸*n. dated* a flush toilet. ■ a room containing such a toilet.

wa·ter·cock /ˈwôtərˌkäk; ˈwä-/ ▸*n.* a brown and gray aquatic Asian rail, the male of which develops black plumage and a red frontal shield in the breeding season. • *Gallicrex cinerea*, family Rallidae.

wa·ter·col·or /ˈwôtərˌkələr; ˈwä-/ (*Brit.* **wa·ter·col·our**) ▸*n.* (also **watercolors**) artists' paint made with a water-soluble binder such as gum arabic, and thinned with water rather than oil, giving a transparent color. ■ a picture painted with watercolors. ■ the art of painting with watercolors, esp. using a technique of producing paler colors by diluting rather than by adding white. **—wa·ter·col·or·ist** *n.*

wa·ter cool·er ▸*n.* a dispenser of cooled drinking water, typically used in office workplaces. ■ [as *adj.*] *informal* denoting the type of informal conversation or socializing among office workers that takes place in the communal area in which such a dispenser is located: *a water-cooler chat about the president.*

wa·ter·course /ˈwôtərˌkôrs; ˈwä-/ ▸*n.* a brook, stream, or artificially constructed water channel. ■ the bed along which this flows.

wa·ter·craft /ˈwôtərˌkraft; ˈwä-/ ▸*n.* (*pl.* same) **1** a boat or other vessel that travels on water. **2** skill in sailing and other activities that take place on water.

wa·ter·cress /ˈwôtərˌkres; ˈwä-/ ▸*n.* a cress that grows in running water and whose pungent leaves are used in salad. • *Nasturtium officinale*, family Brassicaceae.

wa·ter crow·foot ▸*n.* see CROWFOOT.

wa·ter cure ▸*n. chiefly historical* a session of treatment by hydropathy.

wa·ter cy·cle ▸*n.* the cycle of processes by which water circulates between the earth's oceans, atmosphere, and land, involving precipitation as rain and snow, drainage in streams and rivers, and return to the atmosphere by evaporation and transpiration.

wa·ter·dog /ˈwôtərˌdôg; ˈwä-/ ▸*n.* an aquatic North American salamander that is a smaller relative of the mudpuppy, typically living in flowing water. • Genus *Necturus*, family Proteidae: several species.

wa·tered silk ▸*n.* silk that has been treated in such a way as to give it a wavy lustrous finish.

wa·ter·fall /ˈwôtərˌfôl; ˈwä-/ ▸*n.* a cascade of water falling from a height, formed when a river or stream flows over a precipice or steep incline.

wa·ter fern ▸*n.* **1** a small aquatic or semiaquatic fern that is either free-floating or anchored by the roots, found chiefly in tropical and warm countries. • Families Azollaceae, Marsileaceae and Salviniaceae: many species, in particular the minute floating *Azolla filiculoides* of tropical America, which has been naturalized elsewhere. **2** an Australian fern with large coarse fronds, typically growing in marshy areas and rain forests. • Genus *Blechnum*, family Blechnaceae: several species.

wa·ter flea ▸*n.* another term for DAPHNIA.

Wa·ter·ford /ˈwôtərfərd; ˈwätər-/ **1** a county in southeastern Republic of Ireland, in the province of Munster; main administrative center, Dungarvan. ■ its county town, a port on an inlet of St. George's Channel; pop. 40,000. It is noted for its clear, colorless flint glass, known as Waterford crystal. **2** a town in southeastern Connecticut, east of New London; pop. 17,930. **3** a city in southeastern Michigan, northwest of Pontiac; pop. 66,692.

Wa·ter·ford glass ▸*n.* fine clear, colorless flint glassware first manufactured in Waterford, Ireland in the 18th and 19th centuries.

wa·ter·fowl /ˈwôtərˌfoul; ˈwä-/ ▸*plural n.* ducks, geese, or other large aquatic birds, esp. when regarded as game.

wa·ter·front /ˈwôtərˌfrənt; ˈwä-/ ▸*n.* a part of a town that borders a body of water.

wa·ter gap ▸*n.* a transverse gap in a mountain ridge through which a stream or river flows.

wa·ter gar·den ▸*n.* a garden with pools or a stream, for growing aquatic plants.

wa·ter gas ▸*n.* a fuel gas consisting mainly of carbon monoxide and hydrogen, made by passing steam over incandescent coke.

Wa·ter·gate /ˈwôtərˌgāt; ˈwä-/ a political scandal in which an attempt to bug the national headquarters of the Democratic Party (in the Watergate building in Washington, D.C.) led to the resignation of President Nixon (1974).

wa·ter·gate /ˈwôtərˌgāt; ˈwä-/ ▸*n.* a gate of a town or castle opening on to a lake, river, or sea. ■ *archaic* a sluice; a floodgate.

wa·ter glass ▸*n.* **1** a solution of sodium or potassium silicate. It solidifies on exposure to air and is used to make silica gel and for preserving eggs and hardening artificial stone. **2** an instrument for making observations beneath the surface of water, consisting of a bucket with a glass bottom. **3** a glass for holding drinking water.

wa·ter gun ▸*n.* a water pistol.

wa·ter ham·mer ▸*n.* a knocking noise in a water pipe that occurs when a tap is turned off briskly.

wa·ter hem·lock ▸*n.* a highly poisonous plant of the parsley family that grows in ditches and marshy ground. • Genus *Cicuta*, family Umbelliferae: several species, in particular the North American *C. maculata* (also called **spotted cowbane**).

wa·ter·hen /ˈwôtərˌhen; ˈwä-/ ▸*n.* an aquatic rail, esp. a moorhen or related bird. • Genera *Gallinula* and *Amaurornis*, family Rallidae.

wa·ter·hole /ˈwôtərˌhōl; ˈwä-/ ▸*n.* a depression in which water collects, esp. one from which animals regularly drink.

wa·ter hy·a·cinth ▸*n.* a free-floating tropical American water plant that has been introduced elsewhere as an ornamental and in some warmer regions has become a serious weed of waterways. • *Eichhornia crassipes*, family Pontederiaceae.

wa·ter ice ▸*n.* sorbet.

waterfall

Pronunciation Key ə *ago*; ər *over*; ˈə or ˌə *up*; ˈər or ˌər *fur*; a *hat*; ā *rate*; ä *car*; CH *chew*; e *let*; ē *see*; e(ə)r *air*; i *fit*; ī *by*; i(ə)r *ear*; NG *sing*; ō *go*; ô *for*; oi *boy*; o͝o *good*; o͞o *goo*; ou *out*; SH *she*; TH *thin*; T͟H *then*; (h)w *why*; ZH *vision*

W

wa·ter·ing can ▸*n.* a portable water container with a long spout and a detachable perforated cap, used for watering plants.

wa·ter·ing hole ▸*n.* a waterhole from which animals regularly drink. ■ *informal* a tavern or bar.

wa·ter·ing place ▸*n.* a watering hole. ■ a spa or seaside resort.

wa·ter jack·et ▸*n.* a casing containing water surrounding and protecting something from extremes of temperature. —**wa·ter-jack·et·ed** *adj.*

wa·ter jump ▸*n.* an obstacle in a jumping competition or steeplechase, where a horse must jump over or into water.

wa·ter·leaf /ˈwôtər,lēf; ˈwä-/ ▸*n.* a North American woodland plant with bell-shaped flowers and leaves that appear to be stained with water. • Genus *Hydrophyllum*, family Hydrophyllaceae.

wa·ter let·tuce ▸*n.* a tropical aquatic plant of the arum family that forms a floating rosette of leaves. • *Pistia stratiotes*, family Araceae.

wa·ter lev·el ▸*n.* **1** the height reached by the water in a reservoir, river, storage tank, etc. ■ another term for WATER TABLE. **2** an instrument that uses water to indicate the horizontal.

wa·ter li·ly ▸*n.* an ornamental aquatic plant with large round floating leaves and large, typically cup-shaped, floating flowers. • Family Nymphaeaceae: several genera and many species, including the white-flowered **fragrant water lily** (*Nymphaea odorata*) of eastern North America, and the yellow-flowered **Indian pond lily** of California (*Nuphar polysepalum*).

fragrant water lily

wa·ter·line /ˈwôtər,līn; ˈwä-/ ▸*n.* **1** the line to which a vessel's hull is immersed when loaded in a specified way. ■ the level reached by the sea or a river visible as a line on a rock face, beach, or riverbank. ■ any of a set of structural lines of a ship, parallel with the surface of the water, representing the contour of the hull at various heights above the keel and drawn on shipbuilding plans. **2** a vertical watermark made in laid paper.

wa·ter·logged /ˈwôtər,lôgd; ˈwä-/ ▸*adj.* saturated with or full of water: *the race was called off after parts of the course were found to be waterlogged.* ▷mid 18th cent.: past participle of the verb *waterlog* 'make (a ship) unmanageable by flooding,' from WATER + the verb LOG[1].

Wa·ter·loo /,wôtərˈlo͞o; ,wä-; ˈwôtər,lo͞o; ˈwä-/ **1** an industrial and commercial city in northeastern Iowa; pop. 68,747. **2** see AUSTIN[1] sense 2.

Wa·ter·loo, Battle of /ˈwôtər,lo͞o; ˈwä-/ a battle fought on June 18, 1815, near the village of Waterloo (in what is now Belgium), in which Napoleon's army was defeated by the British (under the Duke of Wellington) and Prussians. The allied pursuit caused Napoleon's army to disintegrate entirely, ending his bid to return to power. ■ [as *n.*] (**a Waterloo**) a decisive defeat or failure: *the coach rued the absence of his top player as his team* ***met their Waterloo***.

wa·ter main ▸*n.* a main line in a water supply system.

wa·ter·man /ˈwôtərmən; ˈwä-/ ▸*n.* (*pl.* **-men**) a boatman. ■ an oarsman who has attained a particular level of knowledge or skill.

wa·ter·mark /ˈwôtər,märk; ˈwä-/ ▸*n.* a faint design made in some paper during manufacture, that is visible when held against the light and typically identifies the maker.
▸*v.* [*trans.*] mark with such a design.

wa·ter mass ▸*n.* a large body of seawater that is distinguishable esp. by its characteristic temperature and salinity range.

wa·ter meas·ur·er ▸*n.* a long, thin aquatic bug that walks slowly on the surface film of water and spears small prey with its beak. • Genus *Hydrometra*, family Hydrometridae, suborder Heteroptera: several species.

wa·ter·mel·on /ˈwôtər,melən; ˈwä-/ ▸*n.* **1** the large melonlike fruit of a plant of the gourd family, with smooth green skin, red pulp, and watery juice. **2** the widely cultivated African plant that yields this fruit. • *Citrullus lanatus*, family Cucurbitaceae.

wa·ter mil·foil ▸*n.* see MILFOIL (sense 2).

wa·ter mill /ˈwôtər,mil; ˈwä-/ ▸*n.* a mill worked by a waterwheel.

wa·ter moc·ca·sin ▸*n.* another term for COTTONMOUTH.

wa·ter mold ▸*n.* any of a group of fungi-like organisms that live in water or soil, many of which are parasitic on plants. • Phlya Chytridiomycota and Oomycota, kingdom Protista.

wa·ter nymph ▸*n.* (in folklore and classical mythology) a nymph inhabiting or presiding over water, esp. a Naiad or Nereid.

wa·ter of crys·tal·li·za·tion ▸*n.* *Chemistry* water molecules forming an essential part of the crystal structure of some compounds.

wa·ter o·pos·sum (also **wa·ter pos·sum**) ▸*n.* another term for YAPOK.

wa·ter ou·zel ▸*n.* another term for DIPPER (sense 1).

wa·ter pars·nip ▸*n.* a tall plant of the parsley family that lives in or near water. • *Sium latifolium* and *Berula erecta*, family Umbelliferae.

wa·ter pep·per ▸*n.* a widely distributed plant of the dock family that grows in wet ground, with peppery-tasting leaves and sap that is a skin irritant. • Genus *Polygonum*, family Polygonaceae: several species, in particular *P. hydropiper*.

wa·ter pipe ▸*n.* **1** a pipe for conveying water. **2** a pipe for smoking tobacco, cannabis, etc., that draws the smoke through water to cool it.

wa·ter pis·tol ▸*n.* a toy pistol that shoots a jet of water.

wa·ter plan·tain ▸*n.* an aquatic or marshland plant of north temperate regions, with leaves that resemble those of plantains and a tall stem bearing numerous white or pink flowers. • Genus *Alisma*, family Alismataceae: several species, including *A. trivale*.

wa·ter po·lo ▸*n.* a seven-a-side game played by swimmers in a pool, with a ball like a volleyball that is thrown into the opponent's net.

wa·ter pow·er ▸*n.* power that is derived from the weight or motion of water, used as a force to drive machinery. —**wa·ter-pow·ered** *adj.*

wa·ter·proof /ˈwôtər,pro͞of; ˈwä-/ ▸*adj.* impervious to water: *a waterproof hat.* ■ not liable to be washed away by water: *waterproof ink.*
▸*n.* *Brit.* a garment, esp. a coat, that keeps out water.
▸*v.* [*trans.*] make impervious to water. —**wa·ter·proof·er** *n.* —**wa·ter·proof·ness** *n.*

wa·ter rat ▸*n.* a large, semiaquatic, ratlike rodent.

wa·ter-re·pel·lent ▸*adj.* not easily penetrated by water, esp. as a result of being treated for such a purpose with a surface coating.

wa·ter-re·sis·tant ▸*adj.* able to resist the penetration of water to some degree but not entirely. —**wa·ter-re·sis·tance** *n.*

wa·ter right ▸*n.* **1** [usu. *pl.*] the right to make use of the water from a stream, lake, or irrigation canal. **2** *Nautical* the right to navigate on particular waters.

Wa·ters[1] /ˈwôtərz; ˈwä-/, Ethel (1896–1977), U.S. singer and actress. A blues and jazz singer, she made songs such as "Dinah" (1925) and "Stormy Weather" (1933) popular. She acted on Broadway in *Cabin in the Sky* (1940) and *The Member of the Wedding* (1950) and in movies such as *Pinky* (1949).

Wa·ters[2], Muddy (1915–83), U.S. blues singer and guitarist; born *McKinley Morganfield.* He became well known for his song "Rollin' Stone" (1950). In the same year, he formed a blues band, with which he recorded such hits as "Got My Mojo Working" (1957). The Rolling Stones took their name from his 1950 song.

wa·ter·scape /ˈwôtər,skāp; ˈwä-/ ▸*n.* a landscape in which an expanse of water is a dominant feature.

wa·ter scor·pi·on ▸*n.* a mainly tropical predatory water bug with grasping forelegs, breathing from the surface via a bristlelike "tail." • Family Nepidae, suborder Heteroptera: several genera including the *Nepa* and *Ranatra*.

wa·ter·shed /ˈwôtər,SHed; ˈwä-/ ▸*n.* an area or ridge of land that separates waters flowing to different rivers, basins, or seas. ■ an area or region drained by a river, river system, or other body of water. ■ an event or period marking a turning point in a course of action or state of affairs: *these works mark a watershed in the history of music.* ▷early 19th cent.: from WATER + *shed* in the sense 'ridge of high ground' (related to SHED[2]), suggested by German *Wasserscheide*, literally 'water-divide'.

wa·ter shrew ▸*n.* a large semiaquatic shrew that preys on aquatic invertebrates. • Four genera, family Soricidae: several species, in particular the **American water shrew** (*Sorex palustris* and the **Eurasian water shrew** (*Neomys fodiens*).

wa·ter·side /ˈwôtər,sīd; ˈwä-/ ▸*n.* the edge of or area adjoining a sea, lake, or river.

wa·ter·ski /ˈwôtər,skē; ˈwä-/ ▸*n.* (*pl.* **-skis**) each of a pair of skis enabling the wearer to skim the surface of the water when towed by a motorboat.
▸*v.* [*intrans.*] skim the surface of water on waterskis. —**wa·ter·ski·er** *n.*

wa·ter slide ▸*n.* a slide into a swimming pool, typically flowing with water and incorporating a number of twists and turns.

wa·ter snake ▸*n.* a harmless snake that is a powerful swimmer and spends part of its time in fresh water hunting for prey. Water snakes are found in Africa, Asia, and America. • *Natrix* and other genera, family Colubridae: several species.

wa·ter sof·ten·er ▸*n.* a device or substance that softens hard water by removing certain minerals.

wa·ter sol·dier ▸*n.* an aquatic European plant with slender, spiny-toothed leaves in submerged rosettes that rise to the surface at flowering time. • *Stratiotes aloides*, family Hydrocharitaceae.

wa·ter spi·der ▸*n.* a semiaquatic spider. • Several species, including the European *Argyroneta aquatica* (family Argyronetidae), which lives in an underwater dome of silk filled with air.

wa·ter sports ▸*plural n.* sports that are carried out on water, such as waterskiing and windsurfing. ■ *informal* sexual activity involving urination.

wa·ter·spout /ˈwôtər,spout; ˈwä-/ ▸*n.* a rotating column of water and spray formed by a whirlwind occurring over the sea or other body of water.

wa·ter stone ▸*n.* a whetstone used with water rather than oil.

wa·ter strid·er ▸*n.* a slender predatory bug that moves quickly across the surface film of water, using its front legs for catching prey. • Family Gerridae, suborder Heteroptera: *Gerris* and other genera.

wa·ter ta·ble ▸*n.* the level below which the ground is saturated with water. Compare with PHREATIC, VADOSE.

wa·ter·thrush /ˈwôtər,THrəSH; ˈwä-/ ▸*n.* a thrushlike North American warbler related to the ovenbird, found near woodland streams and swamps. • Genus *Seiurus*, subfamily Parulinae, family Emberizidae: two species.

wa·ter·tight /ˈwôtər,tīt; ˈwä-/ ▸*adj.* closely sealed, fastened, or fitted so that no water enters or passes through: *a watertight seal.* ■ (of an argument or account) unable to be disputed or questioned: *their alibis are watertight.*

wa·ter·tight com·part·ment ▸*n.* any of the sections with intervening watertight partitions into which the interior of a large ship is now usually divided for safety.

wa·ter tor·ture ▸*n.* a form of torture in which the victim is exposed to the incessant dripping of water on the head or to the sound of dripping.

wa·ter tow·er ▸*n.* a tower supporting an elevated water tank, whose height creates the pressure required to distribute the water through a piped system. ■ a firefighting apparatus for lifting hoses to great heights.

Wa·ter·town /ˈwôtər,toun; ˈwä-/ **1** an industrial town in eastern Massachusetts, on the Charles River, west of Boston; pop. 33,284. **2** an industrial and commercial city in north central New York, near Lake Ontario and the Thousand Islands; pop. 29,429. **3** a city in northeastern South Dakota; pop. 20,237. **4** an industrial city in south central Wisconsin; pop. 19,142.

wa·ter-vas·cu·lar sys·tem ▸*n.* *Zoology* (in an echinoderm) a network of water vessels in the body, the tube feet being operated by hydraulic pressure within the vessels.

Wa·ter·ville /ˈwôtərvil; ˈwä-/ a commercial city in south central Maine, on the Kennebec River; pop. 17,173.

wa·ter·way /ˈwôtər,wā; ˈwä-/ ▸*n.* **1** a river, canal, or other route for travel by water. **2** a thick plank or angle iron at the outer edge of the deck of a vessel, which joins the vessel's side to its deck and directs water overboard via the scuppers.

wa·ter·weed /ˈwôtər,wēd; ˈwä-/ ▸*n.* **1** any aquatic plant with inconspicuous flowers, esp. a pondweed. **2** a submerged aquatic American plant that is grown in aquariums and ornamental ponds. • Genus *Elodea*, family Hydrocharitaceae: several species, in particular *E. canadensis*.

wa·ter·wheel /ˈwôtər,(h)wēl; ˈwä-/ ▸*n.* a large wheel

driven by flowing water, used to work machinery or to raise water to a higher level.

water wheel

wa·ter wings ▸*plural n.* inflated floats that may be fixed to the arms of someone learning to swim to give increased buoyancy.

wa·ter witch (also **wa·ter witch·er**) ▸*n.* a person who searches for underground water by using a dowsing rod. —**wa·ter witch·ing** *n.*

Wa·ter Won·der·land a nickname for the state of MICHIGAN.

wa·ter·works /ˈwôtər,wərks; ˈwä-/ ▸*plural n.* **1** [treated as *sing.*] an establishment for managing a water supply. **2** *informal* used to refer to the shedding of tears: *"Don't* **turn on the waterworks,***" he advised.*

wa·ter·y /ˈwôtərē; ˈwä-/ ▸*adj.* consisting of, containing, or resembling water: *a watery fluid.* ■ thin or tasteless as a result of containing too much water: *watery coffee.* ■ weak; pale: *watery sunshine.* ■ (of a person's eyes) full of or running with tears. ▷Old English *wæterig* (see WATER, -Y[1]). —**wa·ter·i·ness** *n.*

WATS /wäts/ ▸*abbr.* ■ Wide Area Telecommunications Service.

Wat·son[1] /ˈwätsən/, James Dewey (1928–), U.S. biologist. Together with Francis Crick, he proposed the double-helix model for the structure of the DNA molecule. Nobel Prize for Physiology or Medicine (1962, shared with Crick and Wilkins).

James Watson

Wat·son[2], John Broadus (1878–1958), U.S. psychologist; founder of the school of behaviorism. He held that the role of the psychologist was to discern, through observation and experimentation, the innate behavior and acquired behavior in an individual.

Wat·son·ville /ˈwätsən,vil/ a city in west central California, south of San Jose; pop. 31,099.

Wat·son-Watt /ˈwätsən ˈwät/, Sir Robert Alexander (1892–1973), Scottish physicist. He led a team that developed radar into a practical system for locating aircraft; this played a vital role in World War II.

Wat·su /ˈwätsoo/ ▸*n.* a form of shiatsu massage that takes place in water. ▷1980s: blend of *water* and *shiatsu.*

Watt /wät/, James (1736–1819), Scottish engineer. Among his many innovations, he greatly improved the efficiency of the Newcomen steam engine, which was then adopted for a variety of purposes. He also introduced the term *horsepower.*

watt /wät/ (abbr.: **W**) ▸*n.* the SI unit of power, equivalent to one joule per second, corresponding to the power in an electric circuit in which the potential difference is one volt and the current one ampere. ▷late 19th cent.: named after J. WATT.

watt·age /ˈwätij/ ▸*n.* a measure of electrical power expressed in watts. ■ the operating power of a lamp or other electrical appliance expressed in watts.

Wat·teau /wäˈtō/, Jean Antoine (1684–1721), French painter. An initiator of the rococo style, he is also known for his invention of the *fête galante.*

watt-hour ▸*n.* a measure of electrical energy equivalent to a power consumption of one watt for one hour.

wat·tle[1] /ˈwätl/ ▸*n.* **1** a material for making fences, walls, etc., consisting of rods or stakes interlaced with twigs or branches. **2** *chiefly Austral.* an acacia. • Genus *Acacia*, family Leguminosae: many species, including the **golden wattle**.
▸*v.* [*trans.*] make, enclose, or fill up with wattle. ▷Old English *watul*, of unknown origin.

wat·tle[2] ▸*n.* a colored fleshy lobe hanging from the head or neck of domestic chickens, turkeys, and some other birds. ▷early 16th cent.: of unknown origin. —**wat·tled** *adj.*

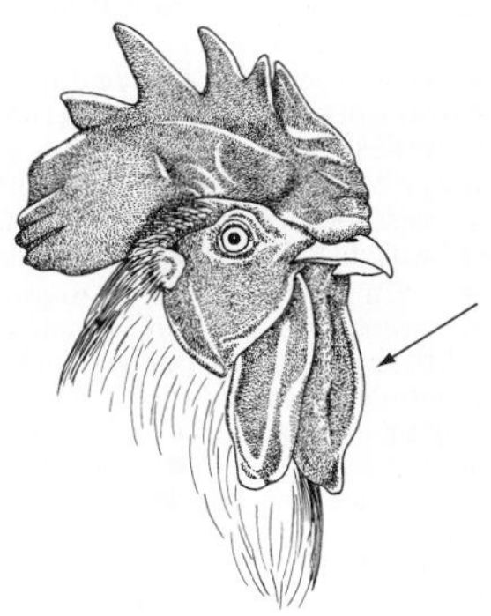

wattle[2]

wat·tle and daub ▸*n.* a material formerly or traditionally used in building walls, consisting of a network of interwoven sticks and twigs covered with mud or clay.

wat·tle·bird /ˈwätl,bərd/ ▸*n.* the largest of the honeyeaters found in Australia, with a wattle hanging from each cheek. • Genus *Anthochaera* (and *Melidectes*), family Meliphagidae: four species.

watt·me·ter /ˈwät,mētər/ ▸*n.* a meter for measuring electric power in watts.

Watts /wäts/ a district in southern Los Angeles in California, home to much of the black population of the city.

Wa·tu·si /wäˈtoosē/ ▸*n.* **1** (also **Wa·tut·si** /-ˈtootsē/) *dated* [treated as *pl.*] the Tutsi people collectively. **2** an energetic dance popular in the 1960s.
▸*v.* [*intrans.*] dance the Watusi. ▷from the Kinyarwanda language of the Bantu family, from the plural prefix *wa-* + TUTSI.

Waugh /wô/, Evelyn (Arthur St. John) (1903–66), English novelist. His work was profoundly influenced by his conversion to Roman Catholicism in 1930. Notable works: *Decline and Fall* (1928) and *Brideshead Revisited* (1945).

Wau·ke·gan /wôˈkēgən/ an industrial port city in northeastern Illinois, on Lake Michigan; pop. 87,901.

Wau·ke·sha /ˈwôki,shô/ an industrial city in southeastern Wisconsin, west of Milwaukee; pop. 64,825.

waul /wôl/ ▸*v.* [*intrans.*] give a loud plaintive cry like that of a cat. ▷early 16th cent.: imitative.

Wau·sau /ˈwô,sô/ an industrial and commercial city in central Wisconsin; pop. 37,060.

Wau·wa·to·sa /,wô-wəˈtōsə/ a city in southeastern Wisconsin, west of Milwaukee; pop. 47,271.

wave /wāv/ ▸*v.* **1** [*intrans.*] move one's hand to and fro in greeting or as a signal: *he waved to me from the train.* ■ [*trans.*] move (one's hand or arm, or something held in one's hand) to and fro: *he waved a sheaf of papers in the air.* ■ move to and fro with a swaying or undulating motion while remaining fixed to one point: *the flag waved in the wind.* ■ [*trans.*] convey (a greeting or other message) by moving one's hand or something held in it to and fro: *we waved our farewells* | [with *two objs.*] *she waved him goodbye.* ■ [*trans.*] instruct (someone) to move in a particular direction by moving one's hand: *he waved her back.* **2** [*trans.*] style (hair) so that it curls slightly: *her hair had been carefully waved for the evening.* ■ [*intrans.*] (of hair) grow with a slight curl: [as *adj.*] (**waving**) *thick, waving gray hair sprouted back from his forehead.*
▸*phrasal v.* □ **wave something aside** dismiss something as unnecessary or irrelevant: *he waved the objection aside and carried on.* □ **wave someone/something down** use one's hand to give a signal to stop to a driver or vehicle.
▸*n.* **1** a long body of water curling into an arched form and breaking on the shore. ■ a ridge of water between two depressions in open water: *gulls and cormorants bobbed on the waves.* ■ a shape seen as comparable to a breaking wave: *a wave of treetops stretched to the horizon.* ■ (usu. **the wave**) an effect resembling a moving wave produced by successive sections of the crowd in a stadium standing up, raising their arms, lowering them, and sitting down again. ■ (**the waves**) *poetic/literary* the sea. ■ an intense burst of a particular feeling or emotion: *horror came over me in waves* | *a new wave of apprehension assailed her.* ■ a sudden occurrence of or increase in a specified phenomenon: *a wave of strikes had effectively paralyzed the government.* **2** a gesture or signal made by moving one's hand to and fro: *he gave a little wave and walked off.* **3** a slightly curling lock of hair: *his hair was drying in unruly waves.* ■ a tendency to curl in a person's hair: *her hair has a slight natural wave.* **4** *Physics* a periodic disturbance of the particles of a substance that may be propagated without net movement of the particles, such as in the passage of undulating motion, heat, or sound. See also STANDING WAVE and TRAVELING WAVE. ■ a single curve in the course of this motion. ■ a similar variation of an electromagnetic field in the propagation of light or other radiation through a medium or vacuum. ▷Old English *wafian* (verb), from the Germanic base of WAVER; the noun by alteration (influenced by the verb) of Middle English *wawe* '(sea) wave.' —**wave·less** *adj.* —**wave·like** *adj.* & *adv.*
▸*PHRASE* □ **make waves** *informal* create a significant impression: *he has already made waves as a sculptor.* ■ cause trouble: *I don't want to risk her welfare by making waves.*

USAGE See usage at WAIVE.

wave·band /ˈwāv,band/ ▸*n.* a range of wavelengths falling between two given limits, used in radio transmission.

wave e·qua·tion ▸*n.* *Mathematics* a differential equation expressing the properties of motion in waves.

wave·form /ˈwāv,fôrm/ ▸*n.* *Physics* a curve showing the shape of a wave at a given time.

wave·front /ˈwāv,frənt/ ▸*n.* *Physics* a surface containing points affected in the same way by a wave at a given time.

wave func·tion ▸*n.* *Physics* a function that satisfies a wave equation and describes the properties of a wave.

wave·guide /ˈwāv,gīd/ ▸*n.* a metal tube or other device confining and conveying microwaves.

wave·length /ˈwāv,length/ ▸*n.* *Physics* the distance between successive crests of a wave, esp. points in a sound wave or electromagnetic wave. (Symbol: λ) ■ this distance as a distinctive feature of radio waves from a transmitter. ■ *figurative* a person's ideas and way of thinking, esp. as it affects their ability to communicate with others: *when we met we hit it off immediately—we're* **on the same wavelength.**

wave·let /ˈwāvlit/ ▸*n.* a small wave of water; a ripple.

wave me·chan·ics ▸*plural n.* [treated as *sing.*] *Physics* a method of analysis of the behavior of atomic phenomena with particles represented by wave equations.

wave num·ber ▸*n.* *Physics* the number of waves in a unit distance.

wave pack·et ▸*n.* *Physics* a group of superposed waves that together form a traveling localized disturbance, esp. one described by Schrödinger's equation and regarded as representing a particle.

wa·ver /ˈwāvər/ ▸*v.* [*intrans.*] shake with a quivering motion: *the flame wavered in the draft.* ■ become unsteady or unreliable: *his love for her had never wavered.* ■ be undecided between two opinions or courses of action; be irresolute: *she never* **wavered from** *her intention.* ▷Middle English: from Old Norse *vafra* 'flicker,' of Germanic origin. Compare with WAVE. —**wa·ver·er** *n.* —**wa·ver·ing·ly** *adv.* —**wa·ver·y** *adj.*

USAGE See usage at WAIVE.

WAVES /wāvz/ ▶*plural n.* the women's section of the U.S. Naval Reserve, established in 1942, or, since 1948, of the U.S. Navy. ▷acronym from *Women Appointed* (later *Accepted*) *for Volunteer Emergency Service*.

wave·ta·ble /ˈwāvˌtābəl/ ▶*n. Computing* a file or memory device containing data that represents a sound such as a piece of music.

wave the·o·ry ▶*n. historical Physics* the theory that light is propagated through the ether by a wave motion imparted to the ether by the molecular vibrations of the radiant body.

wave train ▶*n.* a group of waves of equal or similar wavelengths traveling in the same direction.

wav file /wāv/ (also **wave file**) ▶*n. Computing* a format for storing audio files that produces CD-quality audio: *save the recording as a wav file on your hard drive.*

wav·i·cle /ˈwāvikəl/ ▶*n. Physics* an entity having characteristic properties of both waves and particles. ▷1920s: blend of WAVE and PARTICLE.

wav·y /ˈwāvē/ ▶*adj.* (**wav·i·er**, **wav·i·est**) (of a line or surface) having or consisting of a series of undulating and wavelike curves: *she had long, wavy hair.* ■ [usu. *postpositive*] *Heraldry* divided or edged with a line formed of alternating shallow curves. —**wav·i·ly** /ˈwāvəlē/ *adv.* —**wav·i·ness** *n.*

wa-wa ▶*n.* variant spelling of WAH-WAH.

wax[1] /waks/ ▶*n.* a sticky yellowish moldable substance secreted by honeybees as the material of honeycomb; beeswax. ■ a white translucent material obtained by bleaching and purifying this substance and used for such purposes as making candles, modeling, and as a basis of polishes. ■ a similar viscous substance, typically a lipid or hydrocarbon. ■ earwax. ■ *informal* used in reference to phonograph records: *he didn't get* **on wax** *until 1959.*
▶*v.* [*trans.*] **1** cover or treat (something) with wax or a similar substance, typically to polish or protect it: *I washed and waxed the floor.* ■ remove unwanted hair from (a part of the body) by applying wax and then peeling off the wax and hairs together. **2** *informal* make a recording of: *he waxed a series of tracks that emphasized his lead guitar work.* ▷Old English *wæx*, *weax*, of Germanic origin; related to Dutch *was* and German *Wachs*. The verb dates from late Middle English. —**wax·er** *n.*

wax[2] ▶*v.* [*intrans.*] (of the moon between new and full) have a progressively larger part of its visible surface illuminated, increasing its apparent size. ■ *poetic/literary* become larger or stronger: *his anger waxed.* ■ [with *complement*] begin to speak or write about something in the specified manner: *they* **waxed lyrical** *about the old days.* ▷Old English *weaxan*, of Germanic origin; related to Dutch *wassen* and German *wachsen*, from an Indo-European root shared by Greek *auxanein* and Latin *augere* 'to increase.'
▶*PHRASE* □ **wax and wane** undergo alternate increases and decreases: *companies whose fortunes wax and wane with the economic cycle.*

wax[3] ▶*n.* [usu. in *sing.*] *Brit., informal, dated* a fit of anger: *she is* **in a wax** *about the delay to the wedding.* ▷mid 19th cent.: origin uncertain; perhaps from phrases such as *wax angry*.

wax bean ▶*n.* a dwarf bean of a variety with yellow, stringless pods.

wax·ber·ry /ˈwaksˌberē/ ▶*n.* a shrub with berries that have a waxy coating, in particular a bayberry or wax myrtle.

wax·bill /ˈwaksˌbil/ ▶*n.* a small, finchlike Old World songbird, typically brightly colored and with a red bill that resembles sealing wax in color. • Family Estrildidae (the **waxbill family**): several genera, esp. *Estrilda*, and several species. The waxbill family also includes the avadavats, mannikins, cordon-bleu, Java sparrow, zebra finch, etc., many popular as cage birds.

waxed pa·per (also **wax pa·per**) ▶*n.* paper that has been impregnated with wax to make it waterproof or greaseproof, used esp. in cooking and the wrapping of foodstuffs.

wax·en /ˈwaksən/ ▶*adj.* having a smooth, pale, translucent surface or appearance like that of wax: *a canopy of waxen, creamy blooms.* ■ *archaic* or *poetic/literary* made of wax: *a waxen effigy.*

wax light ▶*n. historical* a taper or candle made from wax.

wax moth ▶*n.* a brownish moth that lays its eggs in beehives. The caterpillars cover the combs with silken tunnels and feed on beeswax. • Genera *Galleria* and *Achroea*, family Pyralidae: several species, in particular *G. mellonella*.

wax mu·se·um ▶*n.* an exhibition of wax dummies, typically representing famous people and fictional characters: *no wax museum is complete without its chamber of horrors.*

wax myr·tle ▶*n.* an evergreen bayberry, esp. the common *Myrica cerifera* of the southern U.S. The wax covering its nutlets is used for making scented candles.

wax palm ▶*n.* either of two South American palm trees from which wax is obtained: • an Andean palm with a stem coated in a mixture of resin and wax (*Ceroxylon alpinum*, family Palmae). • a carnauba.

wax re·sist ▶*n.* a process similar to batik used in pottery and printing.

wax tree (also **Jap·a·nese wax tree**) ▶*n.* an eastern Asian tree with white berries that produce a wax that is used as a substitute for beeswax. • *Rhus succedanea*, family Anacardiaceae.

wax·wing /ˈwaksˌwiNG/ ▶*n.* a crested Eurasian and American songbird with mainly pinkish-brown plumage, having small tips like red sealing wax on some wing feathers. • Genus *Bombycilla*, family Bombycillidae: three species.

wax·work /ˈwaksˌwərk/ ▶*n.* a lifelike dummy modeled in wax. ■ (**waxworks**) [treated as *sing.*] an exhibition of wax dummies.

wax·y /ˈwaksē/ ▶*adj.* (**wax·i·er**, **wax·i·est**) resembling wax in consistency or appearance: *waxy potatoes.* —**wax·i·ly** /ˈwaksəlē/ *adv.* —**wax·i·ness** *n.*

way /wā/ ▶*n.* **1** a method, style, or manner of doing something: *worry was their way of showing how much they cared* | *there are two ways of approaching this problem.* ■ a person's characteristic or habitual manner of behavior or expression: *it was not his way to wait passively for things to happen.* ■ (**ways**) the customary modes of behavior or practices of a group: *foreigners who adopt French ways.* ■ [in *sing.*] the typical manner in which something happens or in which someone or something behaves: *he was showing off, as is the way with adolescent boys.* **2** a road, track, path, or street for traveling along: [in *place names*] *No. 3, Church Way.* ■ [usu. in *sing.*] a course of travel or route taken in order to reach a place: *can you tell me the way to Duffy Square?* ■ a means of entry or exit from somewhere, such as a door or gate: *we're going in the back way.* ■ [in *sing.*] (also *informal* **ways**) a distance traveled or to be traveled; the distance from one place to another: *they still had a long way ahead of them* | *figurative the area's wine industry still has some way to go to full maturity.* ■ [in *sing.*] a period between one point in time and another: *September was a long way off.* ■ [in *sing.*] travel or motion along a particular route; the route along which someone or something would travel if unobstructed: *Christine tried to follow but Martin blocked her way.* ■ [in *sing.*] a specified direction: *we just missed another car coming the other way.* ■ (often **ways**) parts into which something divides or is divided: *the national vote split three ways* | [in *combination*] *a five-way bidding war.* ■ (**one's way**) used with a verb and adverbial phrase to intensify the force of an action or to denote movement or progress: *I shouldered my way to the bar.* ■ forward or backward motion of a ship or boat through water: *the dinghy lost way and drifted toward the shore.* **3** [in *sing.*] [with *adj.* or *possessive*] *informal* a particular area or locality: *I've got a sick cousin over Fayetteville way.* **4** a particular aspect of something; a respect: *I have changed in every way.* **5** [in *sing.*] [with *adj.*] a specified condition or state: *the family was in a poor way.* **6** (**ways**) a sloping structure down which a new ship is launched.
▶*adv. informal* at or to a considerable distance or extent; far (used before an adverb or preposition for emphasis): *his understanding of what constitutes good writing is way off target* | *my grandchildren are way ahead of others their age.* ■ [as *submodifier*] much: *I was cycling way too fast.* ■ [usu. as *submodifier*] extremely; really (used for emphasis): *the guys behind the bar were way cool.* [shortening of AWAY.] ▷Old English *weg*, of Germanic origin; related to Dutch *weg* and German *Weg*, from a base meaning 'move, carry.'
▶*PHRASES* □ **across the way** nearby, esp. on the opposite side of the street. □ **all the way** see ALL. □ **be on one's way** have started one's journey. ■ [in *imperative*] (**(be) on your way**) *informal* go away: *on your way, and stop wasting my time!* □ **by a long way** by a great amount; by far. □ **by the way 1** incidentally (used to introduce a minor topic not connected with what was being spoken about previously): *by the way, pay in advance if you can.* **2** during the course of a journey: *you will have a fine view of Moray Firth by the way.* □ **by way of 1** so as to pass through or across; via: *we approached the Berlin Wall by way of Checkpoint Charlie.* **2** constituting; as a form of: *"I can't help it," shouted Tom by way of apology.* **3** by means of: *noncompliance with the regulations is punishable by way of a fine.* □ **come one's way** happen or become available to one: *he did whatever jobs came his way.* □ **find a way** discover a means of obtaining one's object. □ **get** (or **have**) **one's** (**own**) **way** get or do what one wants in spite of opposition. □ **give way 1** yield to someone or something: *he was not a man to* **give way to** *this kind of pressure.* ■ (of a support or structure) be unable to carry a load or withstand a force; collapse or break. ■ (**give way to**) allow oneself to be overcome by or to succumb to (an emotion or impulse): *she gave way to a burst of weeping.* **2** allow someone or something to be or go first: **give way to** *traffic coming from the right.* ■ (**give way to**) be replaced or superseded by: *Alan's discomfort gave way to anger.* □ **go all the** (or **go the whole**) **way** continue a course of action to its conclusion. ■ *informal* have sexual intercourse with someone. □ **go out of one's way** [usu. with *infinitive*] make a special effort to do something: *Mrs. Mott went out of her way to be courteous to Sara.* □ **go one's own way** act independently or as one wishes, esp. against contrary advice. □ **go one's way 1** (of events, circumstances, etc.) be favorable to one: *I was just hoping things went my way.* **2** leave: *each went his way singing hallelujahs.* □ **go someone's way** travel in the same direction as someone: *wait for Owen, he's going your way.* □ **have it your** (**own**) **way** [in *imperative*] *informal* used to indicate angrily that although one disagrees with something someone has said or proposed, one is not going to argue further: *have it your way–we'll go to Princetown.* □ **have it both ways** see BOTH. □ **have a way with** have a particular talent for dealing with or ability in: *she's got a way with animals.* □ **have one's way with** *humorous* have sexual intercourse with (someone) (typically implying that it is against their wishes or better judgment). □ **in more ways than one** used to indicate that a statement has more than one meaning: *Shelley let her hair down in more ways than one.* □ **in a way** (or **in some ways** or **in one way**) to a certain extent, but not altogether or completely (used to reduce the effect of a statement): *in some ways television is more challenging than theater.* □ **in the family way** see FAMILY. □ **in the** (or **one's**) **way** forming an obstacle or hindrance to movement or action: *his head was in the way of my view.* □ **in the way of** another way of saying BY WAY OF (sense 2) above. □ **in someone/something's** (**own**) **way** if regarded from a particular standpoint appropriate to that person or thing: *it's a good enough book in its way.* □ **in no way** not at all: *quasars in no way resemble normal galaxies.* □ **keep** (or **stay**) **out of someone's way** avoid someone. □ **know one's way around** be familiar with (an area, procedure, or subject). □ **lead the way** go first along a route to show someone the way. ■ be a pioneer in a particular activity. □ **look the other way** deliberately avoid seeing or noticing someone or something. □ **no two ways about it** see NO. □ **one way and another** taking most aspects or considerations into account: *it's been quite a day one way and another.* □ **one way or another** (or **one way or the other**) used to indicate that something is the case for any of various unspecified reasons: *one way or another she brought it on herself.* ■ by some means: *he wants to get rid of me one way or another.* ■ whichever of two given alternatives is the case: *the question is not yet decided, one way or the other.* □ **on the** (or **one's**) **way** in the course of a journey: *I'll tell you on the way home.* □ **on the** (or **its**) **way** about to arrive or happen: *there's more snow on the way.* ■ *informal* (of a child) conceived but not yet born. □ **on the** (or **one's**) **way out** in the process of leaving. ■ *informal* going out of fashion or favor. □ **the other way around** in the opposite position or direction. ■ the opposite of what is expected or supposed: *it was you who sought me out, not the other way around.* □ **out of one's way** not on one's intended route. □ **put someone in the way of** *dated* give someone the opportunity of. □ **that way** *dated* used euphemistically to indicate that someone is homosexual: *he was a bit that way.* □ **to someone's** (or **one's**) **way of thinking** in someone's (or one's) opinion. □ **way back** (also **way back when**) *informal* long ago. □ **the way of the Cross 1** the journey of Jesus to the place of his crucifixion. **2** a set of images representing the Stations of the Cross. **3** *figurative* the suffering and self-sacrifice of a Christian. □ **way of life** the typical pattern of behavior of a person or group: *the rural way of life.* □ **the way of the world** the manner in which people typically behave or things typically happen (used to express one's resignation to it): *all those millions are not going to create many jobs, but that's the way of the world.* □ **ways and means** the methods and

resources at someone's disposal for achieving something: *the company is seeking ways and means of safeguarding jobs.* □ **way to go** *informal* used to express pleasure, approval, or excitement.

-way ▸*suffix* equivalent to **-WAYS**.

wa·yang /ˈwäyäNG/ ▸*n.* (in Indonesia and Malaysia) a theatrical performance employing puppets or human dancers. ■ (also **wa·yang ku·lit**) a Javanese and Balinese shadow puppet play. ▷Javanese.

way·bill /ˈwā,bil/ ▸*n.* a list of passengers or goods being carried on a vehicle.

way·far·er /ˈwā,fe(ə)rər/ ▸*n. poetic/literary* a person who travels on foot. **—way·far·ing** *n.*

way·far·ing tree /ˈwā,fe(ə)riNG/ ▸*n.* a white-flowered Eurasian shrub that has berries at different stages of ripening (green, red, and black) occurring together, growing chiefly on calcareous soils. • *Viburnum lantana*, family Caprifoliaceae.

way·lay /ˈwā,lā/ ▸*v.* (*past* and *past part.* **-laid**) [*trans.*] stop or interrupt (someone) and detain them in conversation or trouble them in some other way: *he waylaid me on the stairs.* **—way·lay·er** *n.*

Wayne[1] /wān/ **1** an industrial city in southeastern Michigan, southwest of Detroit; pop. 19,899. **2** a residential and commercial township in northeastern New Jersey, northwest of Paterson; pop. 47,025.

Wayne[2], Anthony (1745–96), American soldier; known as **Mad Anthony**. A general noted for his courage and military brilliance, he is credited with saving West Point from British occupation following Benedict Arnold's betrayal. He retired in 1783, but returned to active duty in the 1790s, defeating the Indians at the Battle of Fallen Timbers in Ohio in 1794.

Wayne[3], James Moore (c.1790–1867), U.S. Supreme Court associate justice 1835–67. Before being appointed to the Court by President Jackson, he served in the U.S. House of Representatives 1829–35 as a member from Georgia. On the Court, he worked to achieve a compromise between slavery and preservation of the Union.

Wayne[4], John (1907–79), U.S. actor; born *Marion Michael Morrison*; known as **the Duke**. Associated with movie director John Ford from 1930, Wayne became a Hollywood star with *Stagecoach* (1939) and appeared in classic westerns such as *Red River* (1948), *The Searchers* (1956), and *True Grit* (1969), for which he won an Academy Award.

John Wayne

Wayne Coun·ty a county in southeastern Michigan that includes the city of Detroit; pop. 2,061,162.

way-out ▸*adj. informal* regarded as extremely unconventional, unusual, or avant-garde.

way·point /ˈwā,point/ ▸*n.* a stopping place on a journey. ■ an endpoint of the leg of a course, esp. one whose coordinates have been generated by a computer.

-ways ▸*suffix* forming adjectives and adverbs of direction or manner: *edgeways* | *lengthways.* Compare with **-WISE**.

way·side /ˈwā,sīd/ ▸*n.* the edge of a road.

▸*PHRASE* □ **fall by the wayside** fail to persist in an endeavor or undertaking: *many readers will fall by the wayside as the terminology becomes more complicated.* [with biblical allusion to Luke 8:5.]

way sta·tion ▸*n.* a stopping point on a journey. ■ a minor station on a railroad.

way·ward /ˈwāwərd/ ▸*adj.* difficult to control or predict because of unusual or perverse behavior: *her wayward, difficult sister* | *figurative his wayward emotions.* ▷late Middle English: shortening of obsolete *awayward* 'turned away'; compare with **FROWARD**. **—way·ward·ly** *adv.* **—way·ward·ness** *n.*

way·worn /ˈwā,wôrn/ (also **way-worn**) ▸*adj. archaic* weary with traveling.

wa·zir /wäˈzi(ə)r/ ▸*n.* another term for **VIZIER**.

wa·zoo /wäˈzo͞o/ ▸*n. informal* the anus.

▸*PHRASE* □ **up** (or **out**) **the wazoo** very much; in great quantity; to a great degree: *he's insured out the wazoo* | *Jack and I have got work up the wazoo already.*

Wb ▸*abbr.* weber(s).

WBA ▸*abbr.* World Boxing Association.

WBC ▸*abbr.* World Boxing Council.

W bo·son /ˈbō,sän/ ▸*n.* another term for **W PARTICLE**.

WC ▸*abbr.* ■ *Brit.* water closet. ■ (of a region) west central.

WCC ▸*abbr.* World Council of Churches.

we /wē/ ▸*pron.* [*first person plural*] **1** used by a speaker to refer to himself or herself and one or more other people considered together: *shall we have a drink?* ■ used to refer to the speaker together with other people regarded in the same category: *nobody knows kids better than we teachers do.* ■ people in general: *we should eat as varied and well-balanced a diet as possible.* **2** used in formal contexts for or by a royal person, or by a writer or editor, to refer to himself or herself: *in this section we discuss the reasons.* **3** used condescendingly to refer to the person being addressed: *how are we today?* ▷Old English, of Germanic origin; related to Dutch *wij* and German *wir*.

weak /wēk/ ▸*adj.* **1** lacking the power to perform physically demanding tasks; lacking physical strength and energy: *she was recovering from the flu and was very weak.* ■ lacking political or social power or influence: *the central government had grown too weak to impose order* | [as *plural n.*] (**the weak**) *the new king used his powers to protect the weak.* ■ (of a crew, team, or army) containing too few members or members of insufficient quality. ■ (of a faculty or part of the body) not able to fulfill its functions properly: *he had a weak stomach.* ■ of a low standard; performing or performed badly: *the choruses on this recording are weak.* ■ not convincing or logically forceful: *the argument is an extremely weak one* | *a weak plot.* ■ exerting only a small force: *a weak magnetic field.* **2** liable to break or give way under pressure; easily damaged: *the salamander's tail may be broken off at a weak spot near the base.* ■ lacking the force of character to hold to one's own decisions, beliefs, or principles; irresolute. ■ (of a belief, emotion, or attitude) not held or felt with such conviction or intensity as to prevent its being abandoned or dispelled: *their commitment to the project is weak.* ■ not in a secure financial position: *people have no faith in weak banks.* ■ (of prices or a market) having a downward tendency. **3** lacking intensity or brightness: *a weak light from a single street lamp.* ■ (of a liquid or solution) lacking flavor or effectiveness because of being heavily diluted: *a cup of weak coffee.* ■ displaying or characterized by a lack of enthusiasm or energy: *she managed a weak, nervous smile.* ■ (of features) not striking or strongly marked: *his beard covered a weak chin.* ■ (of a syllable) unstressed. **4** *Grammar* denoting a class of verbs in Germanic languages that form the past tense and past participle by addition of a suffix (in English, typically *-ed*); contrasted with **STRONG**. **5** *Physics* of, relating to, or denoting the weakest of the known kinds of force between particles, which acts only at distances less than about 10^{-15} cm, is very much weaker than the electromagnetic and the strong interactions, and conserves neither strangeness, parity, nor isospin. ▷Old English *wāc* 'pliant,' 'of little worth,' 'not steadfast,' reinforced in Middle English by Old Norse *veikr*, from a Germanic base meaning 'yield, give way.' **—weak·ish** *adj.*

▸*PHRASES* □ **the weaker sex** [treated as *sing.* or *pl.*] *dated, derogatory* women regarded collectively. □ **weak in the knees** helpless with emotion. □ **the weak link** the point at which a system, sequence, or organization is most vulnerable; the least dependable element or member.

THE RIGHT WORD **debilitated, decrepit, feeble, frail, infirm, weak**

Someone who is **weak** lacks physical, mental, or moral strength (*a weak heart; a weak excuse; too weak to resist temptation*). But there's nothing to suggest what the cause of this lack of strength might be.

Someone who is **frail**, on the other hand, is weak because he or she has a slight build or delicate constitution (*a small, frail man*).

Calling someone **feeble** implies that his or her weakness is pitiable (*too feeble to get out of bed*); when applied to things, *feeble* means faint or inadequate (*a feeble light*).

Infirm suggests a loss of soundness, as from aging or illness (*poverty and illness had made him infirm*).

Debilitated and **decrepit** also suggest that strength once present has been lost. But while someone who is young may be *debilitated* by disease, *decrepit* specifically refers to a loss of strength due to advanced age or long use (*a decrepit old woman who seldom left her house; a decrepit building that would soon be torn down*).

weak·en /ˈwēkən/ ▸*v.* make or become weaker in power, resolve, or physical strength: [*trans.*] *fault lines had weakened and shattered the rocks* | [*intrans.*] *his resistance had weakened.* **—weak·en·er** *n.*

weak end·ing ▸*n. Prosody* an unstressed syllable in a place at the end of a line of verse that normally receives a stress.

weak·fish /ˈwēk,fiSH/ ▸*n.* (*pl.* same or **-fish·es**) a large, slender-bodied marine fish living along the east coast of North America, popular as a food fish and for sport. Also called **SEA TROUT**. • *Cynoscion regalis*, family Sciaenidae. ▷late 18th cent.: from obsolete Dutch *weekvisch*, from *week* 'soft' + *visch* 'fish.'

weak in·ter·ac·tion ▸*n. Physics* interaction at short distances between subatomic particles mediated by the weak force.

weak-kneed ▸*adj.* weak and shaky as a result of fear or excitement. ■ lacking in resolve or courage; cowardly.

weak·ling /ˈwēkliNG/ ▸*n.* a person or animal that is physically weak and frail. ■ an ineffectual or cowardly person.

weak·ly /ˈwēklē/ ▸*adv.* in a way that lacks strength or force: *she leaned weakly against the wall.*

▸*adj.* (**-li·er**, **-li·est**) sickly; not robust. **—weak·li·ness** *n.*

weak-mind·ed ▸*adj.* lacking determination, emotional strength, or intellectual capacity. **—weak-mind·ed·ness** *n.*

weak·ness /ˈwēknis/ ▸*n.* the state or condition of lacking strength: *the country's weakness in international dealings.* ■ a quality or feature regarded as a disadvantage or fault: *you must recognize your product's strengths and weaknesses.* ■ a person or thing that one is unable to resist or likes excessively: *you're his one weakness—he should never have met you.* ■ [in *sing.*] (**weakness for**) a self-indulgent liking for: *he had a great weakness for Scotch whisky.*

weak side ▸*n. Sports* (on teams with an odd number of players) the half of an offensive or defensive alignment that has one player fewer.

weak sis·ter ▸*n. informal* a weak, ineffectual, or unreliable member of a group.

weal[1] /wēl/ (also *chiefly Medicine* **wheal**) ▸*n.* a red, swollen mark left on flesh by a blow or pressure. ■ *Medicine* an area of the skin that is temporarily raised, typically reddened, and usually accompanied by itching. ▷early 19th cent.: variant of **WALE**, influenced by obsolete *wheal* 'suppurate.'

weal[2] ▸*n. formal* that which is best for someone or something: *I am holding this trial behind closed doors in the public weal.* ▷Old English *wela* 'wealth, well-being'; related to **WELL**[1].

Weald /wēld/ a formerly wooded district of southeastern England that included parts of Kent, Surrey, and East Sussex. ▷Old English, variant of *wald* (see **WOLD**).

wealth /welTH/ ▸*n.* an abundance of valuable possessions or money: *he used his wealth to bribe officials.* ■ the state of being rich; material prosperity: *some people buy boats and cars to display their wealth.* ■ plentiful supplies of a particular resource: *the country's mineral wealth.* ■ [in *sing.*] a plentiful supply of a particular desirable thing: *the tables and maps contain a wealth of information.* ■ *archaic* well-being; prosperity. ▷Middle English *welthe*, from **WELL**[1] or **WEAL**[2], on the pattern of *health*.

wealth·y /ˈwelTHē/ ▸*adj.* (**wealth·i·er**, **wealth·i·est**) having a great deal of money, resources, or assets; rich: *the wealthy nations of the world* | [as *plural n.*] (**the wealthy**) *the burden of taxation on the wealthy.* **—wealth·i·ly** /-THəlē/ *adv.*

Pronunciation Key ə *ago*; ər *over*; ˈə or ˌə *up*; ˈər or ˌər *fur*; a *hat*; ā *rate*; ä *car*; CH *chew*; e *let*; ē *see*; e(ə)r *air*; i *fit*; ī *by*; i(ə)r *ear*; NG *sing*; ō *go*; ô *for*; oi *boy*; o͝o *good*; o͞o *goo*; ou *out*; SH *she*; TH *thin*; T͟H *then*; (h)w *why*; ZH *vision*

THE RIGHT WORD affluent, flush, opulent, prosperous, rich, wealthy, well-to-do

If you have an abundance of money, you are **rich**. Another term for *rich* is **wealthy**, which may further imply that you are an established and prominent member of the community whose lifestyle is in keeping with your income (*a wealthy family whose influence on public opinion could not be ignored*).

Affluent comes from a Latin word meaning to flow, and it connotes a generous income (*an affluent neighborhood*), while **opulent** suggests lavish spending or an ostentatious display of wealth (*an opulent mansion with every imaginable luxury*). One may come from an *affluent* family, in other words, and not have a particularly *opulent* lifestyle.

If you're **prosperous**, you are thriving or flourishing (*a prosperous merchant; a prosperous business*).

While *prosperous* suggests an economic situation that is on the rise, **flush** means having plenty of money on hand at a particular time (*she was feeling flush after receiving her first paycheck*).

Well-to-do implies prosperity, enough to support more-than-comfortable living but not necessarily enough to be considered among the world's richest (*they were known as a well-to-do family with a strong commitment to educating their children*).

wean[1] /wēn/ ▸*v.* [*trans.*] accustom (an infant or other young mammal) to food other than its mother's milk. ■ accustom (someone) to managing without something on which they have become dependent or of which they have become excessively fond: *the doctor tried to* **wean** *her* **off** *the sleeping pills.* ■ (**be weaned on**) be strongly influenced by (something), esp. from an early age: *I was weaned on a regular diet of Hollywood fantasy.* ▷Old English *wenian*, of Germanic origin; related to Dutch *wennen* and German *entwöhnen*.

wean[2] ▸*n. Scottish & N. English* a young child. ▷late 17th cent.: contraction of *wee ane* 'little one.'

wean·ling /ˈwēnliNG/ ▸*n.* a newly weaned animal.

weap·on /ˈwepən/ ▸*n.* a thing designed or used for inflicting bodily harm or physical damage: *nuclear weapons.* ■ *figurative* a means of gaining an advantage or defending oneself in a conflict or contest: *resignation threats had long been a weapon in his armory.* ▷Old English *wǣp(e)n*, of Germanic origin; related to Dutch *wapen* and German *Waffe*. **—weap·oned** *adj.* **—weap·on·less** *adj.*

weap·on·ize ▸*v.* [*trans.*] **1** convert to use as a weapon: *a list of pathogens that terrorists might weaponize.* **2** supply or equip with weapons: *a plan to weaponize space.* **—weap·on·i·za·tion** *n.*

weap·on of mass de·struc·tion ▸*n.* [usu. plural] (**weapons of mass destruction**) a chemical, biological or radioactive weapon capable of causing widespread death and destruction.

weap·on·ry /ˈwepənrē/ ▸*n.* [treated as *sing.* or *pl.*] weapons regarded collectively.

wear[1] /we(ə)r/ ▸*v.* (*past* **wore** /wôr/; *past part.* **worn** /wôrn/) **1** [*trans.*] have on one's body or a part of one's body as clothing, decoration, protection, or for some other purpose: *he was wearing a dark suit | both ladies wore a bunch of violets.* ■ habitually have on one's body or be dressed in: *although she was a widow, she didn't wear black.* ■ exhibit or present (a particular facial expression or appearance): *they wear a frozen smile on their faces.* ■ [*trans.* or *adverbial*] have (one's hair or beard) at a specified length or arranged in a specified style: *the students wore their hair long.* ■ (of a ship) fly (a flag). **2** [*trans.* or *complement*] damage, erode, or destroy by friction or use: *the track has been worn down in part to bare rock.* ■ [*intrans.* or *complement*] undergo such damage, erosion, or destruction: *mountains are wearing down with each passing second.* ■ [*trans.*] form (a hole, path, etc.) by constant friction or use: *the water was forced up through holes it had worn.* ■ [*intrans.*] (**wear on**) cause weariness or fatigue to: *some losses can wear on you.* **3** [*intrans.*] withstand continued use or life in a specified way: *a carpet-type finish seems to* **wear well**. ■ [*trans.*] [usu. with *negative*] *Brit., informal* tolerate; accept: *the environmental health people wouldn't wear it.* **4** [*intrans.*] (**wear on**) (of a period of time) pass, esp. slowly or tediously: *as the afternoon wore on, he began to look unhappy.* ■ [*trans.*] *poetic/literary* pass (a period of time) in some activity: *spinning long stories, wearing half the day.*

▸*phrasal v.* □ **wear someone/something down** overcome or exhaust someone or something by persistence. □ **wear off** lose effectiveness or intensity. □ **wear something out** (or **wear out**) **1** use or be used until no longer in good condition or working order: *wearing out the stair carpet | the type was used again and again until it wore out.* **2** (**wear someone/something out**) exhaust or tire someone or something: *an hour of this wandering wore out Lampard's patience.*

▸*n.* **1** the wearing of something or the state of being worn as clothing: *some new tops for wear in the evening.* **2** [with *adj.*] clothing suitable for a particular purpose or of a particular type: *evening wear.* **3** damage or deterioration sustained from continuous use: *you need to make a deduction for* **wear and tear** *on all your belongings.* ■ the capacity for withstanding continuous use without such damage: *old things were relegated to the bedrooms because there was plenty of wear left in them.* ▷Old English *werian*, of Germanic origin, from an Indo-European root shared by Latin *vestis* 'clothing.' **—wear·er** *n.*

▸*PHRASES* □ **wear one's heart on one's sleeve** see **HEART**. □ **wear thin** be gradually used up or become less convincing or acceptable: *his patience was wearing thin | the joke had started to wear thin.* □ **wear the pants** see **PANTS**.

wear[2] ▸*v.* (*past* and *past part.* **wore**) [*trans.*] *Sailing* bring (a ship) about by turning its head away from the wind: *Shannon gives the order to* **wear ship**. ▷early 17th cent.: of unknown origin.

wear·a·ble /ˈwe(ə)rəbəl/ ▸*adj.* capable of being worn on the body.

▸*n.* (also **wear·a·ble com·put·er**) a computer that is small or portable enough to be worn or carried on one's body. **—wear·a·bil·i·ty** /ˌwe(ə)rəˈbilitē/ *n.*

wear·ing /ˈwe(ə)riNG/ ▸*adj.* mentally or physically tiring. **—wear·ing·ly** *adv.*

wear·i·some /ˈwi(ə)rēsəm/ ▸*adj.* causing one to feel tired or bored. **—wea·ri·some·ly** *adv.* **—wea·ri·some·ness** *n.*

wear·y /ˈwi(ə)rē/ ▸*adj.* (**wear·i·er, wear·i·est**) feeling or showing tiredness, esp. as a result of excessive exertion or lack of sleep: *he gave a long, weary sigh.* See note at **TIRED**. ■ reluctant to see or experience any more of; tired of: *she was* **weary of** *their constant arguments |* [in *combination*] *war-weary Americans.* ■ calling for a great amount of energy or endurance; tiring and tedious: *the weary journey began again.*

▸*v.* (**wear·i·es, wear·i·ed**) [*trans.*] cause to become tired: *she was wearied by her persistent cough.* ■ [*intrans.*] (**weary of**) grow tired of or bored with: *she wearied of the sameness of her life.* ▷Old English *wērig, wǣrig*. **—wea·ri·less** *adj.* **—wea·ri·ly** /ˈwirəlē/ *adv.* **—wea·ri·ness** *n.* **—wea·ry·ing·ly** *adv.*

▸*PHRASE* □ **no rest** (or **peace**) **for the weary** *humorous* one's heavy workload or lack of tranquility is due to one's own choices, or to one's sinful life. [with biblical allusion to Isa. 48:22, 57:21.]

wea·sel /ˈwēzəl/ ▸*n.* a small, slender, carnivorous mammal related to, but generally smaller than, the stoat. • Genus *Mustela*, family Mustelidae (the **weasel family**): several species, in particular *M. nivalis* of northern Eurasia and northern North America. The weasel family also includes the polecats, minks, martens, skunks, wolverine, otters, and badgers. ■ *figurative, informal* a deceitful or treacherous person.

▸*v.* (**-seled, -sel·ing**; *Brit.* **-selled, -sel·ling**) [*intrans.*] achieve something by use of cunning or deceit: *she suspects me of trying to* **weasel my way into** *his affections.* ■ behave or talk evasively. ▷Old English *wesle, wesule*; related to Dutch *wezel* and German *Wiesel*. **—wea·sel·ly** *adj.*

wea·sel-faced ▸*adj.* (of a person) having a face with unattractively thin, sharp, or pointed features.

wea·sel words ▸*plural n.* words or statements that are intentionally ambiguous or misleading.

weath·er /ˈweT͟Hər/ ▸*n.* the state of the atmosphere at a place and time as regards heat, cloudiness, dryness, sunshine, wind, rain, etc.: *if the weather's good, we can go for a walk.* ■ a report on such conditions as broadcast on radio or television. ■ cold, wet, and unpleasant or unpredictable atmospheric conditions; the elements: *stone walls provide shelter from wind and weather.* ■ [as *adj.*] denoting the side from which the wind is blowing, esp. on board a ship; windward: *the weather side of the yacht.* Contrasted with **LEE**.

▸*v.* [*trans.*] **1** wear away or change the appearance or texture of (something) by long exposure to the atmosphere: [*trans.*] *his skin was weathered almost black by his long outdoor life |* [as *adj.*] (**weathered**) *chemically weathered rock.* ■ [*intrans.*] (of rock or other material) be worn away or altered by such processes: *the ice sheet preserves specimens that would* **weather away** *more quickly in other regions.* ■ [usu. as *n.*] (**weathering**) *Falconry* allow (a hawk) to spend a period perched on a block in the open air. **2** come safely through (a storm). ■ withstand (a difficulty or danger): *this year has tested industry's ability to weather recession.* ■ *Sailing* (of a ship) get to the windward of (a cape or other obstacle). **3** make (boards or tiles) overlap downward to keep out rain. ■ (in building) slope or bevel (a surface) to throw off rain. ▷Old English *weder*, of Germanic origin; related to Dutch *weer* and German *Wetter*, probably also to the noun **WIND**[1].

▸*PHRASES* □ **in all weathers** in every kind of weather, both good and bad. □ **keep a weather eye on** observe very carefully, esp. for changes or developments. □ **under the weather** *informal* slightly unwell or in low spirits.

weath·er bal·loon ▸*n.* a balloon equipped with meteorological apparatus that is sent into the atmosphere to provide information about the weather.

weath·er-beat·en ▸*adj.* damaged or worn by exposure to the weather: *a tiny weather-beaten church.* ■ (of a person or a person's face) having skin that is lined and tanned or reddened through prolonged time spent outdoors.

weath·er·board /ˈweT͟Hərˌbôrd/ ▸*n.* each of a series of horizontal boards nailed to outside walls with edges overlapping to keep out the rain; clapboard.

▸*v.* [*trans.*] fit or supply with weatherboards.

weath·er·board·ing /ˈweT͟HərˌbôrdiNG/ ▸*n.* weatherboards collectively.

weath·er·cock /ˈweT͟Hərˌkäk/ ▸*n.* a weathervane in the form of a rooster.

▸*v.* [*intrans.*] (of a boat or aircraft) tend to turn its head into the wind; gripe.

weath·er helm ▸*n. Nautical* a tendency in a sailing ship to head into the wind if the tiller is released.

weath·er·ize /ˈweT͟Həˌrīz/ ▸*v.* [*trans.*] to make (a house or other building) resistant to cold weather by adding insulation, siding, storm windows, etc.

weath·er·ly /ˈweT͟Hərlē/ ▸*adj. Sailing* (of a boat) able to sail close to the wind without drifting much to leeward. **—weath·er·li·ness** *n.*

weath·er·man /ˈweT͟Hərˌman/ ▸*n.* (*pl.* **-men**) a man who broadcasts a description and forecast of weather conditions.

weath·er map ▸*n.* a map showing the state of the weather over a large area.

weath·er·proof /ˈweT͟Hərˌpro͞of/ ▸*adj.* resistant to the effects of bad weather, esp. rain: *the building is structurally sound and weatherproof.*

▸*v.* [*trans.*] make (something) resistant to the effects of bad weather, esp. rain.

weath·er sta·tion ▸*n.* an observation post where weather conditions and meteorological data are observed and recorded.

weath·er·strip /ˈweT͟Hərˌstrip/ ▸*n.* a strip of rubber, metal, or other material used to seal the edges of a door or window against rain and wind.

▸*v.* (**-stripped, -strip·ping**) [*trans.*] apply such a strip to (a door or window). **—weath·er·strip·ping** *n.*

weath·er·tight /ˈweT͟Hərˌtīt/ ▸*adj.* (of a building) sealed against rain and wind.

weath·er·vane /ˈweT͟HərˌvānI ▸*n.* a revolving pointer to show the direction of the wind, typically mounted on top of a building.

weathervane

weath·er·worn /ˈweT͟Hərˌwôrn/ ▸*adj.* eroded or altered by being exposed to the weather: *a weather-worn gravestone.*

weave[1] /wēv/ ▸*v.* (*past* **wove** /wōv/; *past part.* **woven** /ˈwōvən/ or **wove**) [*trans.*] form (fabric or a fabric item) by interlacing long threads passing in one direction with others at a right angle to them: *linen was woven in the district.* ■ form (thread) into fabric in this way: *some thick mohairs can be difficult to weave.* ■ [*intrans.*] [usu. as *n.*] (**weaving**) make fabric in this way typically by working at a loom: *cotton spinning and weaving was done in mills.* ■ (**weave something into**) include something as an integral part or element of (a woven fabric): *a gold pattern was woven into the material.* ■ make (basketwork or a wreath) by interlacing rods or flowers. ■ make (a complex story or pattern) from a number of interconnected elements: *he weaves colorful, cinematic plots.* ■ (**weave something into**) include an element in (such a story or pattern): *interpretative comments are woven into the narrative.*

▸*n.* [usu. with *adj.*] a particular style or manner in

which something is woven: *scarlet cloth of a very fine weave.* ▷Old English *wefan*, of Germanic origin, from an Indo-European root shared by Greek *huphē* 'web' and Sanskrit *ūrṇavābhi* 'spider,' literally 'wool-weaver.' The current noun sense dates from the late 19th cent.

weave[2] ▶*v.* [*intrans.*] twist and turn from side to side while moving somewhere in order to avoid obstructions: *he had to **weave his way** through the crowds.* ■ take evasive action in an aircraft, typically by moving it from side to side. ■ (of a horse) repeatedly swing the head and forepart of the body from side to side (considered to be a vice). ▷late 16th cent.: probably from Old Norse *veifa* 'to wave, brandish.'

weav·er /ˈwēvər/ ▶*n.* **1** a person who weaves fabric. **2** (also **weav·er·bird**) a finchlike songbird of tropical Africa and Asia, related to the sparrows and building elaborately woven nests. • Family Ploceidae: several genera, in particular *Ploceus*, and numerous species.

weav·er's knot (also **weav·er's hitch**) ▶*n.* a sheet bend used for joining threads in weaving.

web /web/ ▶*n.* **1** a network of fine threads constructed by a spider from fluid secreted by its spinnerets, used to catch its prey. ■ a similar filmy network spun by some insect larvae, esp. communal caterpillars. ■ *figurative* a complex system of interconnected elements, esp. one perceived as a trap or danger: *he found himself caught up in **a web of** bureaucracy.* ■ (**the Web**) short for WORLD WIDE WEB. **2** a membrane between the toes of a swimming bird or other aquatic animal. ■ a thin flat part connecting thicker or more solid parts in machinery. **3** a roll of paper used in a continuous printing process. ■ the endless wire mesh in a papermaking machine on which such paper is made. **4** a piece of woven fabric.
▶*v.* (**webbed**, **web·bing**) [*intrans.*] move or hang so as to form a weblike shape: *an intricate transportation network webs from coast to coast.* ■ [*trans.*] (usu. **be webbed**) cover with or as though with a web: *she noticed his tanned skin, webbed with fine creases.* ▷Old English *web(b)* 'woven fabric,' of Germanic origin; related to Dutch *web*, also to WEAVE[1]. Early use of the verb was in the sense 'weave (fabric) on a loom.' **—web·like** /-ˌlīk/ *adj.*

Webb /web/ , Loretta, see LYNN.

webbed /webd/ ▶*adj.* **1** (of the feet of a swimming bird or other aquatic animal) having the toes connected by a membrane. ■ *Medicine* (of fingers or toes) abnormally united for all or part of their length by a fold of skin. **2** (of a band or strip of tough material) made from webbing or similar fabric: *a heavy webbed strap.*

web·bing /ˈwebiNG/ ▶*n.* **1** strong, closely woven fabric used for making items such as straps and belts, and for supporting the seats of upholstered chairs. **2** the part of a baseball glove between the thumb and forefinger.

web·cam /ˈwebˌkam/ ▶*n.* a video camera that inputs to a computer connected to the Internet, so that its images can be viewed by Internet users. ▷1990s: blend of *web* in the sense 'World Wide Web' and *cam(era)*.

web·cast /ˈwebˌkast/ (also **Web·cast**) ▶*n.* a live video broadcast of an event transmitted across the Internet: *an estimated 1.5 million to 2 million surfers clicked on to the live Webcast of the Victoria's Secret annual fashion show.* **—web·cast·ing** *n.*

web-en·able ▶*v.* [trans.] make accessible via or compatible with the World Wide Web: *a project to web-enable legacy accounting systems | web-enable your small business.*

We·ber[1] /ˈvābər/, Carl Maria (Friedrich Ernst) von (1786–1826), German composer. He is regarded as the founder of the German romantic school of opera. Notable works: *Der Freischütz* (1817–21) and *Euryanthe* (1822–23).

We·ber[2], Max (1864–1920), German economist and sociologist; regarded as one of the founders of modern sociology. In *The Protestant Ethic and the Spirit of Capitalism* (1904), he argued that there was a direct relationship between the Protestant work ethic and the rise of capitalism.

We·ber[3], Wilhelm Eduard (1804–91), German physicist. He proposed a unified system for electrical units and determined the ratio between the units of electrostatic and electromagnetic charge.

we·ber /ˈwebər/ (abbr.: **Wb**) ▶*n.* the SI unit of magnetic flux, causing the electromotive force of one volt in a circuit of one turn when generated or removed in one second. ▷late 19th cent.: named after W. E. *Weber* (see WEBER[3]).

We·bern /ˈvābərn/, Anton (Friedrich Ernst) von (1883–1945), Austrian composer. A leading exponent of serialism, his music is marked by its brevity. The atonal *Five Pieces for Orchestra* (1911–13) lasts under a minute.

web-foot·ed ▶*adj.* (of a swimming bird or other aquatic animal) having webbed feet.

Web host·ing ▶*n.* *Computing* the activity or business of providing storage space and access for Web sites.

web·log /ˈwebˌlôg; -ˌläg/ ▶*n.* a Web site on which an individual or group of users produces an ongoing narrative. ▷1990s: from *web* in the sense 'World Wide Web' and *log* in the sense 'regular record of incidents.' **—web·log·ger** *n.*

Web·mail /ˈwebˌmāl/ (also **web·mail**) ▶*n.* e-mail available for use online and stored in the Internet server mailbox, and that is not downloaded to an e-mail program or used offline.

Web·mas·ter /ˈwebˌmastər/ (also **web·mas·ter**) ▶*n.* *Computing* a person who designs and develops Web sites.

web off·set ▶*n.* offset printing on continuous paper fed from a reel.

Web page (also **web page**) ▶*n.* *Computing* a document connected to the World Wide Web and viewable by anyone with an Internet connection and a browser.

Web site (also **web site** or **web·site**) ▶*n.* *Computing* a location connected to the Internet that maintains one or more pages on the World Wide Web.

web-spin·ner ▶*n.* a slender mainly tropical insect with a soft brownish body, living under stones or logs in a tunnel of silk produced by glands on the front legs. • Order Embioptera: several families.

Web·ster[1] /ˈwebstər/, Daniel (1782–1852), U.S. statesman and lawyer. A noted orator, he represented New Hampshire 1813–17 and then Massachusetts 1823–27 in the U.S. House of Representatives, as well as Massachusetts in the U.S. Senate 1827–41 and 1845–50. As secretary of state 1841–43 under President W. H. Harrison, he negotiated the Webster-Ashburton Treaty, which settled boundary disputes with Canada.

Daniel Webster

Web·ster[2], John (*c.*1580–*c.*1625), English playwright. Notable works: *The White Devil* (1612) and *The Duchess of Malfi* (1623), both revenge tragedies.

Web·ster[3], Noah (1758–1843), U.S. lexicographer. His *American Dictionary of the English Language* (1828) in two volumes and containing 70,000 words was the first dictionary to give comprehensive coverage of usage in the U.S.

Web·ster Groves /ˌwebstər ˈgrōvz/ a city in eastern Missouri, southwest of St. Louis; pop. 22,987.

web·work /ˈwebˌwərk/ ▶*n.* a mesh or network of links or connecting pieces: *a webwork of beams and girders.*

web·worm /ˈwebˌwərm/ ▶*n.* a caterpillar that spins a web in which to rest or feed. When present in large numbers, it can become a serious pest. • *Loxostega* and other genera, family Pyralidae.

web·zine /ˈwebˌzēn/ ▶*n.* a magazine published on the Internet: *a webzine seeking to become essential reading rather than just another online pastime.*

wed /wed/ ▶*v.* (**wed·ding**; *past* and *past part.* **wed·ded** or **wed**) [*trans.*] *chiefly formal* or *archaic* get married to: *he was to wed the king's daughter.* ■ [*intrans.*] get married: *they wed a week after meeting* | (**be wed**) *after a three-month engagement, they were wed in London.* ■ give or join in marriage: *will you wed your daughter to him?* ■ [as *adj.*] (**wedded**) of or concerning marriage: *a celebration of 25 years' **wedded bliss**.* ■ combine (two factors or qualities, esp. desirable ones): *in this recording he weds an excellent program with a distinctive vocal style.* ■ (**be wedded to**) be obstinately attached or devoted to (an activity, belief, or system): *foreign policy has remained wedded to outdated assumptions.* ▷Old English *weddian*, from the Germanic base of Scots *wed* 'a pledge'; related to Latin *vas* 'surety,' also to GAGE[1].

we'd /wēd/ ▶*contraction of* we had: *we'd already been on board.* ■ we should or we would: *we'd like to make you an offer.*

Wed. ▶*abbr.* Wednesday.

Wed·dell Sea /ˈwedl; wəˈdel/ an arm of the Atlantic Ocean, off the coast of Antarctica. ▷named after the British explorer James Weddell (1787–1834), who visited it in 1823.

Wed·dell seal ▶*n.* a large mottled gray seal with a small head, ranging farther south than any other seal and breeding on the fast ice of Antarctica. • *Leptonychotes weddelli*, family Phocidae. ▷early 20th cent.: named after James *Weddell* (see WEDDELL SEA).

wed·ding /ˈwediNG/ ▶*n.* a marriage ceremony, esp. considered as including the associated celebrations. ▷Old English *weddung* (see WED, -ING[1]).

wed·ding band ▶*n.* a wedding ring.

wed·ding bells ▶*plural n.* bells rung to celebrate a wedding (used to allude to the likelihood of marriage between two people): *the two were seen going everywhere together, and all her friends could hear wedding bells.*

wed·ding cake ▶*n.* a rich iced cake, typically in two or more tiers, served at a wedding reception. ■ [as *adj.*] denoting a building or architectural style that is very decorative or ornate: *a wedding-cake mansion.*

wed·ding day ▶*n.* the day or anniversary of a wedding.

wed·ding march ▶*n.* a piece of march music played at the entrance of the bride or the exit of the couple at a wedding.

wed·ding night ▶*n.* the night after a wedding (esp. with reference to its consummation).

wed·ding plan·ner ▶*n.* someone who plans and organizes weddings as a profession.

wed·ding ring ▶*n.* a ring worn by a married person, given by the spouse at their wedding.

wedge /wej/ ▶*n.* a piece of wood, metal, or some other material having one thick end and tapering to a thin edge, that is driven between two objects or parts of an object to secure or separate them. ■ an object or piece of something having such a shape: ***a wedge of** cheese.* ■ a formation of people or animals with such a shape. ■ a golf club with a low, angled face for maximum loft. ■ a shot made with such a club. ■ a shoe, typically having a fairly high heel, of which the heel and sole form a solid block, with no gap under the instep. ■ a heel of this kind. ■ *Music* another term for DASH.
▶*v.* **1** [*trans.*] fix in position using a wedge: [*trans.*] *the door was wedged open.* **2** [*trans.*] force into a narrow space: *I wedged the bags into the back seat.* ▷Old English *wecg* (noun), of Germanic origin; related to Dutch *wig*.
▶*PHRASES* □ **drive a wedge between** separate: *the general aimed to drive a wedge between the city and its northern defenses.* ■ cause disagreement or hostility between: *I'm not trying to drive a wedge between you and your father.* □ **thin end of the wedge** *informal* an action or procedure of little importance in itself, but likely to lead to more serious developments.

wedge is·sue ▶*n.* a divisive political issue, esp. one that is raised by a candidate for public office in hopes of attracting or alienating an opponent's supporters.

wedg·ie /ˈwejē/ ▶*n.* *informal* **1** a shoe with a wedged heel. **2** an uncomfortable tightening of the underpants between the buttocks, typically produced when someone pulls the underpants up from the back as a practical joke.

Wedg·wood /ˈwejˌwo͝od/ ▶*n.* *trademark* ceramic ware made by the English potter Josiah Wedgwood (1730–95) and his successors. Wedgwood is most associated with the powder-blue stoneware pieces with white embossed cameos that first appeared in 1775. ■ a powder-blue color characteristic of this stoneware.

wed·lock /ˈwedˌläk/ ▶*n.* the state of being married. ▷late Old English *wedlāc* 'marriage vow,' from *wed* 'pledge' (related to WED) + the suffix *-lāc* (denoting action).

Pronunciation Key ə *ago*; ər *over*; ˈə *or* ˌə *up*; ˈər *or* ˌər *fur*; a *hat*; ā *rate*; ä *car*; CH *chew*; e *let*; ē *see*; e(ə)r *air*; i *fit*; ī *by*; i(ə)r *ear*; NG *sing*; ō *go*; ô *for*; oi *boy*; o͝o *good*; o͞o *goo*; ou *out*; SH *she*; TH *thin*; T͟H *then*; (h)w *why*; ZH *vision*

▸*PHRASE* □ **born in** (or **out of**) **wedlock** born of married (or unmarried) parents.

Wednes·day /ˈwenz,dā; -,dē/ ▸*n.* the day of the week before Thursday and following Tuesday: *a report goes before the councilors* **on Wednesday** | *they finish early on Wednesdays* | [as *adj.*] *on a Wednesday morning.*

▸*adv.* on Wednesday: *see you Wednesday.* ■ (**Wednesdays**) on Wednesdays; each Wednesday: *Wednesdays, the jazz DJ hosts a jam session.* ▷Old English *Wōdnesdæg*, named after the Germanic god **ODIN**; translation of late Latin *Mercurii dies*; compare with Dutch *woensdag*.

Weds. ▸*abbr.* Wednesday.

wee /wē/ ▸*adj.* (**we·er**, **we·est**) *chiefly Scottish* little: *when I was just a wee bairn.* ▷Middle English (originally a noun use in Scots, usually as *a little wee* 'a little bit'): from Old English *wēg(e)*.

▸*PHRASE* □ **the wee hours** the early hours of the morning after midnight: *nights of dining and dancing until the wee hours.*

weed /wēd/ ▸*n.* a wild plant growing where it is not wanted and in competition with cultivated plants. ■ any wild plant growing in salt or fresh water. ■ *informal* marijuana. ■ (**the weed**) *informal* tobacco. ■ *informal* a leggy, loosely built horse.

▸*v.* [*trans.*] remove unwanted plants from (an area of ground or the plants cultivated in it): *I was weeding a flower bed.* ■ (**weed something out**) remove something, esp. inferior or unwanted items or members from a group or collection: *we must raise the level of research and weed out the poorest work.* ▷Old English *wēod* (noun), *wēodian* (verb), of unknown origin; related to Dutch *wieden* (verb). —**weed·er** *n.* —**weed·less** *adj.*

weed kill·er ▸*n.* a substance used to destroy weeds.

weeds /wēdz/ ▸*plural n.* short for **WIDOW'S WEEDS**.

weed whack·er ▸*n.* an electrically powered grass trimmer with a nylon cutting cord that rotates rapidly on a spindle.

weed·y /ˈwēdē/ ▸*adj.* (**weed·i·er**, **weed·i·est**) **1** containing or covered with many weeds: *a weedy path led to the gate.* ■ of the nature of or resembling a weed: *a weedy species of plant.* **2** *informal* (of a person) thin and physically weak in appearance. —**weed·i·ness** *n.*

wee·juns /ˈwējənz/ (also **Wee·juns**) *trademark* ▸*plural n.* moccasin-style shoes for casual wear. ▷1950s: a fanciful formation.

week /wēk/ ▸*n.* a period of seven days: *the course lasts sixteen weeks* | *he'd cut the grass a week ago.* ■ the period of seven days generally reckoned from and to midnight on Saturday night: *she has an art class twice a week.* ■ workdays as opposed to the weekend; the five days from Monday to Friday: *I work during the week, so I can only get to this shop on Saturdays.* ■ the time spent working in this period of five to seven days: *she works a 48-hour week.* ■ a period of five or seven days devoted to a specified purpose or beginning on a specified day: *Super Bowl week* | *the week of June 23.* ■ *informal, chiefly Brit.* used after the name of a day to indicate that something will happen seven days after that day: *the program will be broadcast on Sunday week.* ▷Old English *wice*, of Germanic origin; related to Dutch *week* and German *Woche*, from a base probably meaning 'sequence, series.'

▸*PHRASES* □ **week after week** during each successive week, esp. over a long period: *week after week of overcast skies.* □ **week by week** gradually and steadily over the weeks: *Monday evening demonstrations grew week by week.* □ **a week from ——** used to state that something is due to happen seven days after the specified day or date: *we'll be back a week from Friday.* □ **week in, week out** every week without exception.

week·day /ˈwēk,dā/ ▸*n.* a day of the week other than Saturday or Sunday.

week·end /ˈwēk,end/ ▸*n.* the period from Friday evening through Sunday evening, esp. regarded as a time for leisure: *she spent the weekend camping* | [as *adj.*] *a weekend break.* ■ (also **long week·end**) this period plus one or two days immediately before or after: *the long holiday weekend.*

▸*v.* [*intrans.*] *informal* spend a weekend somewhere: *he was weekending in the country.*

week·end·er /ˈwēk,endər/ ▸*n.* a person who spends time in a particular place only on weekends. ■ a bag or suitcase suitable for weekend travel. ■ a small pleasure boat.

week-long (also **weeklong**) ▸*adj.* [*attrib.*] lasting for a week: *a week-long visit to New Zealand.*

week·ly /ˈwēklē/ ▸*adj.* [*attrib.*] done, produced, or occurring once a week: *there was a weekly dance on Wednesdays.* ■ relating to or calculated in terms of a week: *the difference in weekly income is $290.*

▸*adv.* once a week: *interviews were given weekly.*

▸*n.* (*pl.* **-lies**) a newspaper or periodical issued every week.

week·night /ˈwēk,nīt/ ▸*n.* a night of the week other than Saturday or Sunday.

ween /wēn/ ▸*v.* [*intrans.*] *archaic* be of the opinion; think or suppose: *he, I ween, is no sacred personage.* ▷Old English *wēnan*, of Germanic origin; related to Dutch *wanen* 'imagine,' German *wähnen* 'suppose wrongly,' also to **WISH**.

wee·nie /ˈwēnē/ ▸*n.* **1** another term for **WIENER** (sense 1). **2** *vulgar slang* a man's penis. ■ (also **wie·ner**) *informal* a weak, socially inept, or boringly studious person: *newer programming languages are a favorite of the tech weenies.*

wee·ny /ˈwēnē/ ▸*adj.* (**-ni·er**, **-ni·est**) *informal* tiny. ▷late 18th cent.: from **WEE**, on the pattern of *tiny*; compare with **TEENY**.

weep /wēp/ ▸*v.* (*past* and *past part.* **wept** /wept/) [*intrans.*] **1** shed tears: *a grieving mother wept over the body of her daughter* | [*trans.*] *he wept bitter tears at her cruelty.* ■ utter or express with tears: [with *direct speech*] *"No!" she wept.* ■ [*trans.*] *archaic* mourn for; shed tears over: *a young widow weeping her lost lord.* **2** exude liquid: *she rubbed one of the sores, making it weep.*

▸*n.* [in *sing.*] a fit or spell of shedding tears. ▷Old English *wēpan* (verb), of Germanic origin, probably imitative.

weep·er /ˈwēpər/ ▸*n.* **1** a person who weeps. ■ *historical* a hired mourner at a funeral. ■ a small image of a mourner on a monument. ■ another term for **WEEPIE**. **2** (**weepers**) *historical* funeral garments, in particular: ■ a man's crepe hatband worn at funerals. ■ a widow's black crepe veil and white cuffs.

weep·ie /ˈwēpē/ ▸*n.* (*pl.* **-ies**) *informal* a sentimental or emotional film, novel, or song.

weep·ing /ˈwēpiNG/ ▸*adj.* [*attrib.*] **1** shedding tears. ■ exuding liquid. **2** used in names of tree and shrub varieties with drooping branches, e.g., **weeping cherry**. —**weep·ing·ly** *adv.*

weep·ing wid·ow ▸*n.* a mushroom that has a buff cap with purplish-black gills that appear to secrete drops of fluid when damp, found commonly in both Eurasia and North America. • *Lacrymaria velutina*, family Coprinaceae, class Hymenomycetes.

weep·ing wil·low ▸*n.* a Eurasian willow with trailing branches and foliage reaching down to the ground, widely grown as an ornamental in waterside settings. • Genus *Salix*, family Salicaceae: several species and hybrids, in particular *S. babylonica*.

weep·y /ˈwēpē/ ▸*adj.* (**weep·i·er**, **weep·i·est**) *informal* tearful; inclined to weep: *a weepy clingy child.* ■ sentimental: *a weepy made-for-TV movie.* —**weep·i·ly** /-əlē/ *adv.* —**weep·i·ness** *n.*

wee·ver /ˈwēvər/ (also **wee·ver fish**) ▸*n.* a small, long-bodied fish with eyes at the top of the head and venomous dorsal spines. It occurs along eastern Atlantic coasts, typically buried in the sand with just the eyes and spines protruding. • Family Trachinidae: several genera and species. ▷early 17th cent.: perhaps a transferred use of Old French *wivre* 'serpent, dragon,' from Latin *vipera* 'viper.'

wee·vil /ˈwēvəl/ ▸*n.* a small beetle with an elongated snout, the larvae of which typically develop inside seeds, stems, or other plant parts. Many are pests of crops or stored foodstuffs. Also called **SNOUT BEETLE**. • Curculionidae and other families in the superfamily Curculionoidea: numerous genera. ■ *informal* any small insect that damages stored grain. ▷Old English *wifel* 'beetle,' from a Germanic base meaning 'move briskly.' —**wee·vil·y** *adj.*

wee-wee *informal* ▸*n.* a child's word for urine.

▸*v.* [*intrans.*] urinate. ▷1930s: imitative.

w.e.f. *Brit.* ▸*abbr.* with effect from: *a budget to allocate w.e.f. April 1st.*

weft /weft/ ▸*n.* [in *sing.*] (in weaving) the crosswise threads on a loom over and under which other threads (the warp) are passed to make cloth. ▷Old English *weft(a)*, of Germanic origin; related to **WEAVE**[1].

Wehr·macht /ˈver,mäkt; -,mäKHt/ the German armed forces, esp. the army, from 1921 to 1945. ▷German, literally 'defensive force.'

Wei /wā/ the name of several dynasties that ruled in China, esp. that of AD 386–535.

Weich·sel /ˈvīksəl/ ▸*n.* [usu. as *adj.*] *Geology* the final Pleistocene glaciation in northern Europe. ■ the system of deposits laid down at this time. ▷1930s: from the German name of the Vistula River in Poland. —**Weich·sel·i·an** /vīkˈsilēən/ *adj.* & *n.*

Wei·fang /ˈwāˈfäNG/ a city in Shandong province, in eastern China; pop. 565,000. Former name **WEIHSIEN**.

wei·ge·la /wīˈjēlə/ ▸*n.* an Asian flowering shrub of the honeysuckle family, that has pink, red, or yellow flowers and is a popular ornamental. • Genus *Weigela*, family Caprifoliaceae: several species, in particular *W. florida*. ▷modern Latin, named after Christian E. *Weigel* (1748–1831), German physician.

weigh[1] /wā/ ▸*v.* **1** [*trans.*] find out how heavy (someone or something) is, typically using scales: *weigh yourself on the day you begin the diet* | *the vendor weighed the vegetables.* ■ have a specified weight: *when the twins were born, they weighed ten pounds.* ■ balance in the hands to guess or as if to guess the weight of: *she picked up the brick and weighed it in her right hand.* ■ (**weigh something out**) measure and take from a larger quantity of a substance a portion of a particular weight: *she weighed out two ounces of loose tobacco.* ■ [*intrans.*] (**weigh on**) be depressing or burdensome to: *his unhappiness would weigh on my mind so much.* **2** assess the nature or importance of, esp. with a view to a decision or action: *the consequences of the move would need to be very carefully weighed.* ■ (**weigh something against**) compare the importance of one factor with that of (another): *they need to weigh benefit against risk.* ■ [*intrans.*] influence a decision or action; be considered important: *the evidence weighed heavily against him.*

▸*phrasal v.* □ **weigh someone down** be heavy and cumbersome to someone: *my waders and fishing gear weighed me down.* ■ be oppressive or burdensome to someone: *she was weighed down by the responsibility of looking after her sisters.* □ **weigh in** (chiefly of a boxer or jockey) be officially weighed before or after a contest: *Mason* **weighed in at** *203 lb.* □ **weigh in at** *informal* be of (a specified weight). ■ *informal* cost (a specified amount). □ **weigh in with** *informal* make a forceful contribution to a competition or argument by means of: *Baker weighed in with a three-pointer.* □ **weigh into** *informal* join in forcefully or enthusiastically: *they weighed into the election campaign.* ■ attack physically or verbally: *he weighed into the companies for their high costs.* □ **weigh out** (of a jockey) be weighed before a race. □ **weigh someone/something up** *Brit.* carefully assess someone or something: *investors weighed up their next move.* ▷Old English *wegan*, of Germanic origin; related to **WAGON** and **WAIN**, and to Dutch *wegen* 'weigh,' German *bewegen* 'move,' from an Indo-European root shared by Latin *vehere* 'convey.' Early senses included 'transport from one place to another' and 'raise up.' —**weigh·a·ble** *adj.* —**weigh·er** *n.*

▸*PHRASES* □ **weigh anchor** see **ANCHOR**. □ **weigh one's words** carefully choose the way one expresses something.

weigh[2] ▸*n.* (in phrase **under weigh**) *Nautical* another way of saying **UNDER WAY** (see **UNDER**). ▷late 18th cent.: from an erroneous association with *weigh anchor* (see **WEIGH**[1]).

weigh-in ▸*n.* an official or regular weighing of something or someone, e.g., of boxers before a fight.

weigh sta·tion ▸*n.* a roadside station where commercial vehicles are required to stop and be inspected, thus protecting the road from travel by overweight or unsafe vehicles.

weight /wāt/ ▸*n.* **1** a body's relative mass or the quantity of matter contained by it, giving rise to a downward force; the heaviness of a person or thing: *he was at least 175 pounds in weight.* ■ *Physics* the force exerted on the mass of a body by a gravitational field. Compare with **MASS**. ■ the quality of being heavy: *as he came upstairs the boards creaked under his weight.* ■ a unit or system of units used for expressing how much an object or quantity of matter weighs. ■ a piece of metal known to weigh a definite amount and used on scales to determine how heavy an object or quantity of a substance is. ■ the amount that a jockey is expected or required to weigh, or the amount that a horse can easily carry. ■ any of several divisions based on relative lightness and heaviness into which boxers and wrestlers are classified for competition. ■ the surface density of cloth, used as a measure of its quality. ■ *Printing* the degree of blackness of a type font. **2** a heavy object, esp. one being lifted or carried. ■ a heavy object used to give an impulse or act as a counterweight in a mechanism. ■ a heavy object thrown by a shotputter. ■ (**weights**) blocks or discs of metal or other heavy material used in weightlifting or weight training. ■ a burden or responsibility. **3** the ability of someone or something to influence decisions or actions: *a recommendation by the committee will carry great weight.* ■ the importance attached to something: *individuals differ in the weight they attach to various aspects of a job.* ■ *Statistics* a factor associated with one of a set of numerical quantities, used to represent its importance relative to the other members of the set.

▸*v.* [*trans.*] **1** hold (something) down by placing a heavy object on top of it: *a mug half filled with coffee* ***weighted down*** *a stack of papers.* ■ make (something) heavier by attaching a heavy object to it, esp. so as to make it stay in place: *the jugs were covered with muslin veils weighted with colored beads.* **2** attach importance or value to: *speaking, reading, and writing should be weighted equally in the assessment.* ■ (**be weighted**) be planned or arranged so as to put a specified person, group, or factor in a position of advantage or disadvantage: *the balance of power is weighted in favor of the government.* ■ *Statistics* multiply the components of (an average) by factors to take account of their importance. **3** assign a handicap weight to (a horse). **4** treat (a fabric) with a substance to make it seem thicker and heavier. ▷Old English *(ge)wiht*, of Germanic origin; related to Dutch *wicht* and German *Gewicht*. The form of the word has been influenced by **WEIGH**[1].

▸*PHRASES* □ **put on** (or **lose**) **weight** become fatter (or thinner). □ **throw one's weight around** *informal* be unpleasantly self-assertive. □ **throw one's weight behind** *informal* use one's influence to help support. □ **the weight of the world** used in reference to a very heavy burden of worry or responsibility: *he continues to carry the weight of the world on his shoulders.* □ **be a weight off one's mind** come as a great relief after one has been worried. □ **worth one's weight in gold** (of a person) exceedingly useful or helpful.

weight belt ▸*n.* a belt to which weights are attached, designed to help divers stay submerged.

weight·ed av·er·age ▸*n. Statistics* an average resulting from the multiplication of each component by a factor reflecting its importance.

weight·ing /ˈwātiNG/ ▸*n.* allowance or adjustment made in order to take account of special circumstances or compensate for a distorting factor. ■ an allocated proportion of something, esp. an investment: *the company continues to recommend a 35% weighting in bonds.* ■ emphasis or priority: *they will give due weighting to quality as well as price.*

weight·less /ˈwātlis/ ▸*adj.* (of a body, esp. in an orbiting spacecraft) not apparently acted on by gravity. **—weight·less·ly** *adv.* **—weight·less·ness** *n.*

weight·lift·ing /ˈwātˌliftiNG/ ▸*n.* the sport or activity of lifting barbells or other heavy weights. There are two standard lifts in modern weightlifting: the single-movement lift from floor to extended position (the **snatch**), and the two-movement lift from floor to shoulder position, and from shoulders to extended position (the **clean and jerk**). **—weight·lift·er** *n.*

weight train·ing ▸*n.* physical training that involves lifting weights.

weight-watch·er ▸*n.* a person who is concerned about their weight, esp. one who diets. ▷from the proprietary name *Weight Watchers*, an organization promoting dietary control as a means of losing weight. **—weight-watch·ing** *n.* & *adj.*

weight·y /ˈwātē/ ▸*adj.* (**weight·i·er, weight·i·est**) weighing a great deal; heavy: *a weighty candelabra.* See note at **HEAVY**. ■ of great seriousness and importance: *he threw off all weighty considerations of state.* ■ having a great deal of influence on events or decisions. **—weight·i·ly** /-təlē/ *adv.* **—weight·i·ness** *n.*

Wei·hsien /ˈwā-ăēˈen/ former name for **WEIFANG**.

Weil /vīl; vā/, Simone (1909–43), French essayist, philosopher, and mystic. She joined the resistance movement in England during World War II and later died of tuberculosis while weakened by voluntary starvation to call attention to the plight of her French compatriots.

Weill /vīl/, Kurt (1900–50), German composer, resident in the U.S. from 1935. He is best known for the operas he wrote with Bertolt Brecht, political satires that include *The Threepenny Opera* (1928).

Weil's dis·ease /vīlz/ ▸*n.* a severe, sometimes fatal, form of leptospirosis transmitted by rats via contaminated water. ▷late 19th cent.: named after H. Adolf *Weil* (1848–1916), German physician.

Wei·mar /ˈvīˌmär/ a city in Thuringia, in central Germany; pop. 59,000.

Wei·mar·an·er /ˈwīməˌränər; ˈvī-/ ▸*n.* a dog of a thin-coated, typically gray breed of pointer used as a gun dog. ▷1940s: from German, from **WEIMAR** in Germany, where the breed was developed.

Wei·mar Re·pub·lic the German republic of 1919–33, so called because its constitution was drawn up at Weimar. The republic was faced with huge reparation costs deriving from the Treaty of Versailles as well as soaring inflation and high unemployment. The 1920s saw a growth in support for right-wing groups, and the Republic was eventually overthrown by the Nazi Party of Adolf Hitler.

Wein·berg /ˈwīnˌbərg/, Steven (1933–), U.S. theoretical physicist. He devised a theory to unify electromagnetic interactions and the weak forces within the nucleus of an atom. Nobel Prize for Physics (1979, shared with Sheldon Glashow 1932– and Abdus Salam).

Wein·stein /ˈwīnˌstīn/, Nathan Wallenstein, see **WEST**[5].

wei qi /wā CHē/ (also **wei ch'i**) ▸*n.* a traditional Chinese board game of territorial possession and capture. ▷Chinese, from *wéi* 'surround' + *qí* 'chess.'

weir /wi(ə)r/ ▸*n.* a low dam built across a river to raise the level of water upstream or regulate its flow. ■ an enclosure of stakes set in a stream as a trap for fish. ▷Old English *wer*, from *werian* 'dam up.'

weird /wi(ə)rd/ ▸*adj.* suggesting something supernatural; uncanny: *the weird crying of a seal.* ■ *informal* very strange; bizarre: *a weird coincidence | all sorts of* ***weird and wonderful*** *characters.* ■ *archaic* connected with fate.

▸*n. archaic, chiefly Scottish* a person's destiny.

▸*v.* [*trans.*] (**weird someone out**) *informal* induce a sense of disbelief or alienation in someone. ▷Old English *wyrd* 'destiny,' of Germanic origin. The adjective (late Middle English) originally meant 'having the power to control destiny,' and was used esp. in *the Weird Sisters*, originally referring to the Fates, later the witches in Shakespeare's *Macbeth*; the latter use gave rise to the sense 'unearthly' (early 19th cent.). **—weird·ly** *adv.* **—weird·ness** *n.*

weird·o /ˈwi(ə)rdō/ ▸*n.* (*pl.* **-dos**) *informal* a person whose dress or behavior seems strange or eccentric.

weird sis·ters ▸*plural n.* (usu. **the weird sisters**) the Fates. ■ witches, esp. those in Shakespeare's *Macbeth*.

Weir·ton /ˈwi(ə)rtn/ an industrial city in northern West Virginia, on the Ohio River; pop. 20,411.

Weis·mann /ˈvīsmən/, August Friedrich Leopold (1834–1914), German biologist, one of the founders of modern genetics. He expounded the theory of germ plasm and suggested that variability in individuals came from the recombination of chromosomes during reproduction. **—Weis·mann·ism** /-ˌnizəm/ *n.* **—Weis·mann·ist** /ˈvīsmənist/ *n.* & *adj.*

Weiss·mul·ler /ˈwīˌsmələr/, Johnny (1904–84), U.S. swimmer and actor; full name *John Peter Weissmuller*. He won three Olympic gold medals in 1924 and two in 1928. He starred in the Tarzan movies in the 1930s and 1940s.

weiss·wurst /ˈvīsˌwərst; -ˌwo͝orst/ ▸*n.* whitish German sausage made chiefly of veal. ▷German, literally 'white sausage.'

Weiz·mann /ˈvītsmən/, Chaim (Azriel) (1874–1952), Israeli statesman, born in Russia; president 1949–52. He played an important role in persuading the U.S. government to recognize the new state of Israel in 1948.

we·ka /ˈwekə/ ▸*n.* a large flightless New Zealand rail with heavily built legs and feet. • *Gallirallus australis*, family Rallidae. ▷mid 19th cent.: from Maori, imitative of its cry.

welch /welCH/ ▸*v.* variant spelling of **WELSH**.

wel·come /ˈwelkəm/ ▸*n.* an instance or manner of greeting someone: *you will receive a warm welcome | he went to meet them with his hand stretched out in welcome.*

▸*exclam.* used to greet someone in a glad or friendly way: ***welcome to*** *the Wildlife Park.*

▸*v.* [*trans.*] greet (someone arriving) in a glad, polite, or friendly way: *hotels should welcome guests in their own language* | [as *adj.*] (**welcoming**) *a welcoming smile.* ■ be glad to entertain (someone) or receive (something): *we welcome any comments.* ■ react with pleasure or approval to (an event or development): *the bank's decision to cut its rates was widely welcomed.*

▸*adj.* (of a guest or new arrival) gladly received: *visitors with disabilities are always welcome.* ■ very pleasing because much needed or desired: *after your walk, the café serves a welcome pot of coffee | deregulation is* ***welcome to*** *consumers.* ■ [*predic.*, with *infinitive*] allowed or invited to do a specified thing: *anyone is welcome to join them at their midday meal.* ■ [*predic.*] (**welcome to**) used to indicate that one is relieved to be relinquishing the control or possession of something to another: *the job is all yours and you're welcome to it!* ▷Old English *wilcuma* 'a person whose coming is pleasing,' *wilcumian* (verb), from *wil-* 'desire, pleasure' + *cuman* 'come.' The first element was later changed to *wel-* 'well,' influenced by Old French *bien venu* or Old Norse *velkominn*. **—wel·come·ly** *adv.* **—wel·come·ness** *n.* **—wel·com·er** *n.* **—wel·com·ing·ly** *adv.*

▸*PHRASES* □ **make someone welcome** receive and treat someone hospitably. □ **wear out** (or **overstay** or **outstay**) **one's welcome** stay as a visitor longer than one is wanted. □ **you're welcome** used as a polite response to thanks.

Wel·come Wag·on ▸*n. trademark* a vehicle bringing gifts and samples from local merchants to newcomers in a community.

weld[1] /weld/ ▸*v.* [*trans.*] join together (metal pieces or parts) by heating the surfaces to the point of melting with a blowpipe, electric arc, or other means, and uniting them by pressing, hammering, etc.: *the truck had spikes welded to the back.* ■ forge (an article) by such means. ■ unite (pieces of plastic or other material) by melting or softening of surfaces in contact. ■ *figurative* cause to combine and form a harmonious or effective whole: *his efforts to* ***weld together*** *the religious parties ran into trouble.*

▸*n.* a welded joint. ▷late 16th cent. (in the sense 'become united'): alteration (probably influenced by the past participle) of **WELL**[2] in the obsolete sense 'melt or weld (heated metal).' **—weld·a·bil·i·ty** /ˌweldəˈbilitē/ *n.* **—weld·a·ble** *adj.* **—weld·er** *n.*

weld[2] ▸*n.* a widely distributed plant related to mignonette, yielding a yellow dye. • *Reseda luteola*, family Resedaceae. ■ the yellow dye made from this plant, which has been used since Neolithic times and was a popular color for Roman wedding garments. ▷late Middle English: related to Dutch *wouw*, perhaps also to **WOLD**.

wel·fare /ˈwelˌfe(ə)r/ ▸*n.* the health, happiness, and fortunes of a person or group: *they don't give a damn about the welfare of their families.* ■ statutory procedure or social effort designed to promote the basic physical and material well-being of people in need: *the protection of rights to education, housing, and welfare.* ■ financial support given for this purpose. ▷Middle English: from the adverb **WELL**[1] + the verb **FARE**.

▸*PHRASE* □ **on welfare** receiving government financial assistance for basic material needs.

wel·fare re·form ▸*n.* a movement to change the federal government's social welfare policy by shifting some of the responsibility to the states and cutting benefits.

wel·fare state ▸*n.* a system whereby the government undertakes to protect the health and well-being of its citizens, esp. those in financial or social need, by means of grants, pensions, and other benefits. The foundations for the modern welfare state in the U.S. were laid by the New Deal programs of President Franklin D. Roosevelt. ■ a country practicing such a system.

wel·fare-to-work ▸*adj.* denoting government policies that encourage those receiving welfare benefits to find a job, for example by providing job training: *Wisconsin's hard-nosed welfare-to-work program.*

wel·fare work ▸*n.* organized effort to promote the basic physical and material well-being of people in need. **—wel·fare work·er** *n.*

wel·far·ism /ˈwelfe(ə)ˌrizəm/ ▸*n.* the principles or policies associated with a welfare state. **—wel·far·ist** *n.* & *adj.*

wel·kin /ˈwelkin/ ▸*n. poetic/literary* the sky. ■ heaven. ▷Old English *wolcen* 'cloud, sky'; related to Dutch *wolk* and German *Wolke*.

▸*PHRASE* □ **make the welkin ring** make a very loud sound: *the crew made the welkin ring with its hurrahs.*

Wel·kom /ˈvelkəm/ a town in central South Africa; pop. 185,000.

well[1] /wel/ ▸*adv.* (**bet·ter, best**) **1** in a good or satisfactory way: *the whole team played well.* ■ in a way that is appropriate to the facts or circumstances: *you did well to come and tell me* | [as *submodifier*, in *combination*] *a well-timed exit.* ■ so as to have a fortunate outcome: *his campaign did not go well.* ■ in a kind way: *the animals will remain loyal to humans if treated well.* ■ with praise or approval: *people spoke well of him | the film was quite well reviewed at the time.* ■ with equanimity: *she*

Pronunciation Key ə *ago*; ər *over*; ˈə or ˌə *up*; ˈər or ˌər *fur*; a *hat*; ā *rate*; ä *car*; CH *chew*; e *let*; ē *see*; e(ə)r *air*; i *fit*; ī *by*; i(ə)r *ear*; NG *sing*; ō *go*; ô *for*; oi *boy*; o͝o *good*; o͞o *goo*; ou *out*; SH *she*; TH *thin*; T͟H *then*; (h)w *why*; ZH *vision*

took it very well, all things considered. ■ profitably; advantageously: *she would marry well or not at all.* ■ in a condition of prosperity or comfort: *they lived well and were generous with their money.* ■ *archaic* luckily; opportunely: *hail fellow, well met.* **2** in a thorough manner: *add the mustard and lemon juice and mix well.* ■ to a great extent or degree (often used for emphasis): *the visit had been planned well in advance* | [as *submodifier*, in *combination*] *a well-loved mother.* ■ intimately; closely: *he knew my father very well.* ■ [as *submodifier*] *Brit., informal* very; extremely: *he was well out of order.* ■ [with *submodifier*] used as an intensifier: *I should bloody well hope so.* **3** [with *modal*] very probably; in all likelihood: *being short of breath may well be the first sign of asthma.* ■ without difficulty: *she could well afford to pay for the reception herself.* ■ with good reason: *"What are we doing here?" "You may well ask."*

▸*adj.* (**bet·ter**, **best**) [*predic.*] **1** in good health; free or recovered from illness: *I don't feel very well* | *it would be some time before Sarah was completely well* | [*attrib.*] *informal he was not a well man.* ■ in a satisfactory state or position: *all is not well in post-Soviet Russia.* **2** sensible; advisable: *it would be well to know just what this suggestion entails.*

▸*exclam.* used to express a range of emotions including surprise, anger, resignation, or relief: *Well, really! The manners of some people!* ■ used when pausing to consider one's next words: *well, I suppose I could fit you in at 3:45.* ■ used to express agreement or acceptance, often in a qualified or slightly reluctant way: *well, all right, but be quick.* ■ used to introduce the resumption of a narrative or a change of subject. ■ used to mark the end of a conversation or activity: *well, cheers, Tom—I must run.* ■ used to indicate that one is waiting for an answer or explanation from someone: *Well? You promised to tell me all about it.* ▷Old English *wel(l)*, of Germanic origin; related to Dutch *wel* and German *wohl*; probably also to the verb **WILL**[1].

▸*PHRASES* □ **all's well that ends well** see **ALL**. □ **all very well** see **ALL**. □ **as well 1** in addition; too: *the museum provides hours of fun and a few surprises as well* | *a shop that sold books* **as well as** *newspapers.* **2** (**as well** or **just as well**) with equal reason or an equally good result: *I* **may as well** *have a look.* ■ sensible, appropriate, or desirable: *it would be as well to let him go.* □ **as well he** (or **she**, etc.) **might** (or **may**) used to convey the speaker's opinion that a reaction is appropriate or unsurprising: *she sounded rather chipper, as well she might, given her bright prospects.* □ **be well out of** *Brit., informal* be fortunate to be no longer involved in (a situation). □ **be well in with** *informal* have a good relationship with (someone in a position of influence or authority): *you're well in with O'Brien, aren't you?* □ **be well up on** (or **in**) know a great deal about (a particular thing). □ **do well for oneself** be successful, typically in material or financial terms. □ **leave** (or **let**) **well enough alone** refrain from interfering with or trying to improve something that is satisfactory or adequate as it is. □ **very well** used to express agreement or understanding, sometimes grudging: *oh very well then, come in.* □ (**all**) **well and good** used to express acceptance of a first statement before introducing a contradictory or confirming second statement: *well, that's all well and good, but why didn't he phone her to say so?* □ **well and truly** completely: *Leith was well and truly rattled.* □ **well enough** to a reasonable degree: *he liked Isobel well enough, but wouldn't want to make a close friend of her.* □ **well worth** certainly worth: *Salzburg is well worth a visit.*

USAGE 1 The adverb **well** is often used in combination with past participles to form compound adjectives: **well-adjusted, well-intentioned, well-known**, and so on. As far as hyphenation is concerned, there are three general rules: (1) if the compound adjective is placed before the noun (i.e., in the attributive position), it should be hyphenated (*a **well-intentioned** remark*); (2) if the compound adjective is preceded by an adverb (*much, very, surprisingly,* etc.), the compound adjective is open (*a thoroughly **well prepared** student*); (3) if the compound adjective is placed after the noun or verb (i.e., in the predicate position), it may, but need not, be hyphenated (*her remark was **well-intentioned*** or *her remark was **well intentioned***). Likewise, other, similar compounds with *better, best, ill, little, lesser, least,* etc., are hyphenated before the noun (*a **little-known** author*), often open after a noun or verb (*the author was **little known***), and open if modified by an adverb (*a very **little known** author*).
2 On uses of **well** and **good**, see **usage** at **GOOD**.

well[2] ▸*n.* **1** a shaft sunk into the ground to obtain water, oil, or gas. ■ a plentiful source or supply: *she could feel a deep well of sympathy and compassion.* ■ *archaic* a water spring or fountain. ■ short for **INKWELL**. ■ a depression made to hold liquid: *put the flour on a flat surface and make a well to hold the eggs.* ■ (**Wells**) [in *place names*] *chiefly Brit.* a place where there are mineral springs: *Tunbridge Wells.* **2** an enclosed space in the middle of a building, giving room for stairs or an elevator, or to allow light or ventilation. ■ *Brit.* the place in a court of law where the clerks and ushers sit. **3** *Physics* a region of minimum potential: *a gravity well.*

▸*v.* [*intrans.*] (of a liquid) rise to the surface and spill or be about to spill: *tears were beginning to well in her eyes.* ■ (of an emotion) arise and become more intense: *all the old bitterness began to* **well up** *inside her again.* ▷Old English *wella*, of Germanic origin; related to Dutch *wel* and German *Welle* 'a wave.'

we'll /wēl/ ▸*contraction of* we shall; we will.

well-ad·just·ed ▸*adj.* successfully altered or moved so as to achieve a desired fit, appearance, or result: *her eyes were well adjusted to the darkness.* ■ (of a person) mentally and emotionally stable: *a well-adjusted, happy child is less likely to be physically ill.*

well-ad·vised ▸*adj.* [with *infinitive*] sensible; wise: *you would be well advised to obtain legal advice.*

Wel·land Ca·nal /ˈwelənd/ (also **Wel·land Ship Ca·nal**) a canal in southern Canada, 26 mi. (42 km.) long, that links Lake Erie with Lake Ontario. It bypasses Niagara Falls and forms part of the St. Lawrence Seaway.

well-ap·point·ed ▸*adj.* (of a building or room) having a high standard of equipment or furnishing.

well-a·ware ▸*adj.* having full knowledge of a situation or fact: *we are well aware of the dangerous side effects that some herbs can have.*

well-be·haved ▸*adj.* conducting oneself in an appropriate manner: *the crowd was very well behaved.* ■ (of a computer program) communicating with hardware via standard operating system calls rather than directly and therefore able to be used on different machines.

well-be·ing ▸*n.* the state of being comfortable, healthy, or happy: *an improvement in the patient's well-being.*

well-born ▸*adj.* from a noble or wealthy family.

well-bred ▸*adj.* having or showing good breeding or manners.

well-built ▸*adj.* (of a person) large and strong. ■ of strong, solid construction: *the well-built and massively thick walls.*

well-con·duct·ed ▸*adj.* properly organized or carried out: *responsible, well-conducted businesses.* ■ *archaic* well behaved.

well-con·nect·ed ▸*adj.* acquainted with or related to people with prestige or influence.

well deck ▸*n.* an open space on the main deck of a ship, lying at a lower level between the forecastle and poop.

well-dis·posed ▸*adj.* having a positive, sympathetic, or friendly attitude toward someone or something: *the company is* **well-disposed to** *the idea of partnership.*

well-done ▸*adj.* **1** (of a task or undertaking) carried out successfully or satisfactorily: *the decoration is very well done* | [*postpositive*] *the satisfaction of* **a job well done**. **2** (of meat) thoroughly cooked: *well-done roast beef.*

▸*exclam.* used to express congratulation or approval: *Well done—you've worked very hard!*

well-dressed ▸*adj.* wearing smart or fashionable clothes.

well-earned ▸*adj.* fully merited or deserved: *a well-earned rest.*

well-en·dowed ▸*adj.* having plentiful supplies of a resource: *the country is* **well endowed with** *mineral resources.* ■ well provided with money; wealthy. ■ *informal, humorous* (of a man) having large genitals. ■ *informal, humorous* (of a woman) large-breasted.

Welles /welz/, (George) Orson (1915–85), U.S. movie director and actor. His realistic radio dramatization in 1938 of H. G. Wells's *The War of the Worlds* persuaded many listeners that a Martian invasion was really happening. Notable movies: *Citizen Kane* (Academy Award for best screenplay, 1941), *The Lady from Shanghai* (1948), and *The Third Man* (1949).

Welles·ley /ˈwelzlē/ a town in eastern Massachusetts, west of Boston, home to Wellesley College; pop. 26,615.

well-fa·vored ▸*adj.* having special advantages, esp. good looks.

well-fed ▸*adj.* having good meals regularly.

well-formed ▸*adj.* correctly or attractively proportioned or shaped. ■ (esp. of a sentence or phrase) constructed according to grammatical rules. ■ conforming to the formation rules of a logical system.

well-found ▸*adj.* (chiefly of a boat) well equipped and maintained.

well-found·ed ▸*adj.* (esp. of a suspicion or belief) based on good evidence or reasons: *their apprehensions were well founded.*

well-groomed ▸*adj.* (esp. of a person) clean, tidy, and well dressed.

well-ground·ed ▸*adj.* based on good evidence or reasons. ■ having a good training in or knowledge of a subject: *boys who are* **well grounded in** *traditional academic subjects.*

well·head /ˈwel,hed/ ▸*n.* **1** the place where a spring comes out of the ground. **2** the structure over a well, typically an oil or gas well.

well-heeled ▸*adj. informal* wealthy.

well house ▸*n.* a small building or room enclosing a well and its apparatus.

well-hung ▸*adj.* **1** *informal, humorous* (of a man) having large genitals. **2** (of meat or game) hung until sufficiently dry, tender, or high before cooking.

wel·lie ▸*n.* variant spelling of **WELLY**.

well-in·formed ▸*adj.* having or showing much knowledge about a wide range of subjects, or about one particular subject.

Wel·ling·ton[1] /ˈweliNGtən/ the capital of New Zealand, at the southern tip of North Island; pop. 150,000. It became the capital in 1865, when the seat of government was moved from Auckland.

Wel·ling·ton[2], Arthur Wellesley, 1st Duke of (1769–1852), British soldier and statesman; prime minister 1828–30 and 1834; known as **the Iron Duke**. He served as commander of the British forces against Napoleon 1808–14 and defeated him at the Battle of Waterloo 1815, which ended the Napoleonic Wars.

wel·ling·ton /ˈweliNGtən/ (also **wel·ling·ton boot**) ▸*n. chiefly Brit.* a knee-length waterproof rubber or plastic boot. ▷early 19th cent.: named after the 1st Duke of *Wellington* (see **WELLINGTON**[2]).

wel·ling·to·nia /,weliNGˈtōnēə/ ▸*n. Brit.* another term for **giant redwood** (see **REDWOOD**). ▷mid 19th cent.: modern Latin, from the former binomial *Wellingtonia gigantea* (from **WELLINGTON**[2]).

well-in·ten·tioned ▸*adj.* having or showing good intentions despite a lack of success or fortunate results: *well-intentioned advice.*

well-kept ▸*adj.* (esp. of property) kept clean, tidy, and in good condition. ■ (of a secret) not told to anyone or made widely known.

well-knit ▸*adj.* (of a person or animal) strongly and compactly built.

well-known ▸*adj.* known widely or thoroughly: *a well-known television personality.*

well-made ▸*adj.* strongly or skillfully constructed: *a well-made film.*

well-man·nered ▸*adj.* having or showing good manners; polite: *they were well mannered and eager to please.*

well-matched ▸*adj.* (of two or more people or items) appropriate for or very similar to each other: *a fiercely contested quarterfinal between two well-matched sides.*

well-mean·ing (also **well-meant**) ▸*adj.* well intentioned: *well-meaning friends.*

well·ness /ˈwelnis/ ▸*n.* the state or condition of being in good physical and mental health: *when you come right down to it, stress affects every aspect of wellness.*

well-nigh ▸*adv. chiefly poetic/literary* almost: *a task that is well-nigh impossible.*

well-off ▸*adj.* wealthy: *her family is quite well off.* ■ in a favorable situation or circumstances: *they were well off without her.*

well-oiled ▸*adj.* **1** [*predic.*] *informal* drunk. **2** (esp. of an organization) operating smoothly: *the ruling party's well-oiled political machine.*

well-pleased ▸*adj.* [*predic.*] highly gratified or satisfied: *Moore paused, well pleased with the effect.*

well-pre·served ▸*adj.* (of something old) having remained in good condition. ■ (of an old person) showing little sign of aging.

well-round·ed ▸*adj.* having a smooth, curved shape: *well-rounded quartz pebbles.* ■ (of a person) plump. ■ pleasingly varied or balanced: *a dry, robust, well-rounded wine.* ■ (of a person) having a personality that is fully developed in all aspects. ■ (of a phrase or sentence) carefully composed and balanced. ■ (of an education) covering well the necessary areas of instruction.

Wells[1] /welz/, H. G. (1866–1946), English novelist; full name *Herbert George Wells.* He wrote some of the earliest science-fiction novels, such as *The War of the Worlds* (1898), which combined political satire with warnings about the powers of science.

Wells[2], Henry, see **WELLS, FARGO & CO.**.

well-set ▸*adj.* (of a construction) firmly established; solidly fixed or arranged. ■ (also **well-set-up**) (of a person) strongly built.

Wells, Far·go & Co. /ˌwelz ˈfärgō/ a U.S. transportation company founded in 1852 by the businessmen Henry Wells (1805–78) and William Fargo (1818–81) and others. It carried mail to and from the newly developed West, founded a San Francisco bank, and later ran a stagecoach service.

well-spent ▸*adj.* (of money or time) usefully or profitably expended: *time spent in taking stock is time well spent.*

well-spo·ken ▸*adj.* (of a person) speaking in an educated and refined manner.

well·spring /ˈwelˌspriNG/ ▸*n. poetic/literary* an original and bountiful source of something: *sadness is the wellspring of creativity.*

well-tak·en ▸*adj.* (of a comment, argument, etc.) shrewd and accurate: *though she often makes her case too earnestly, her points are well-taken.*

well-tem·pered ▸*adj.* (of a person or animal) having a cheerful or emotionally stable disposition. ■ (of a process or activity) properly regulated, controlled, or moderated.

well-thumbed ▸*adj.* (of a book, magazine, etc.) having been read often and bearing marks of frequent handling.

well-to-do ▸*adj.* wealthy; prosperous: *a well-to-do family.*

well-trav·eled ▸*adj.* **1** (of a person) having traveled widely. **2** (of a route) much frequented by travelers.

well-trod·den ▸*adj.* much frequented by travelers: *a well-trodden path.*

well-turned ▸*adj.* **1** (of a compliment, phrase, or verse) elegantly expressed. **2** (esp. of an ankle or leg) having an elegant and attractive shape. ▷originally with reference to the turning of a piece of work on a lathe.

well-up·hol·stered ▸*adj.* (of a chair or sofa) having plenty of padding. ■ *humorous* (of a person) fat.

well-used ▸*adj.* much used: *a well-used route.* ■ worn or shabby through much use, handling, or wear: *a well-used manual typewriter.*

well-wish·er ▸*n.* a person who desires happiness or success for another, or who expresses such a desire.

well-worn ▸*adj.* showing the signs of extensive use or wear: *a well-worn leather armchair.* ■ (of a phrase, idea, or joke) used or repeated so often that it no longer has interest or significance.

well-wrought ▸*adj.* skillfully constructed or put together: *a well-wrought argument.*

wel·ly /ˈwelē/ (also **wel·lie**) ▸*n.* (*pl.* **-lies**) *Brit., informal* **1** short for **WELLINGTON**. **2** power or vigor: *I like big, fat voices with plenty of welly.*

Welsh /welsH/ ▸*adj.* of or relating to Wales, its people, or their Celtic language.
▸*n.* **1** the Celtic language of Wales, spoken by about 500,000 people (mainly bilingual in English). Descended from the Brythonic language spoken in most of Roman Britain, it has been strongly revived after a long decline. **2** [as *plural n.*] (**the Welsh**) the people of Wales collectively. ▷Old English *Welisc, Wælisc*, from a Germanic word meaning 'foreigner;' compare with Latin *Volcae*, the name of a Celtic people in southern Gaul. —**Welsh·ness** *n.*

welsh /welsH/ (also **welch**) ▸*v.* [*intrans.*] (**welsh on**) fail to honor (a debt or obligation incurred through a promise or agreement): *banks began welshing on their agreement not to convert dollar reserves into gold.* ▷mid 19th cent.: of unknown origin. —**welsh·er** *n.*

Welsh cor·gi ▸*n.* (*pl.* **Welsh cor·gis**) a dog of a short-legged breed with a foxlike head. ▷1920s: from Welsh, from *cor* 'dwarf' + *ci* 'dog.'

Welsh corgi

Welsh·man /ˈwelsHmən/ ▸*n.* (*pl.* **-men**) a male native or national of Wales, or a man of Welsh descent.

Welsh pop·py ▸*n.* a yellow- or orange-flowered European poppy of shady rocky places. • *Meconopsis cambrica*, family Papaveraceae.

Welsh rare·bit (also **Welsh rab·bit**) ▸*n.* another term for **RAREBIT**.

Welsh spring·er ▸*n.* (usu. **Welsh spring·er span·iel**) see **SPRINGER** (sense 1).

Welsh ter·ri·er ▸*n.* a stocky, rough-coated, typically black-and-tan terrier of a breed with a square muzzle and drop ears.

Welsh·wom·an /ˈwelsHˌwo͝omən/ ▸*n.* (*pl.* **-wom·en**) a female native or national of Wales, or a woman of Welsh descent.

welt /welt/ ▸*n.* **1** a leather rim sewn around the edge of a shoe upper to which the sole is attached. ■ a ribbed, reinforced, or decorative border of a garment or pocket. **2** a red, swollen mark left on flesh by a blow or pressure. ■ a heavy blow.
▸*v.* [*trans.*] **1** provide with a welt. **2** strike (someone or something) hard and heavily: *I could have welted her.* ■ [*intrans.*] develop a raised scar: *his lip was beginning to thicken and welt from the blow.* ▷late Middle English: of unknown origin.

Welt·an·schau·ung /ˈveltˌänˌsHouəNG/ ▸*n.* (*pl.* **-schau·ung·en** /-sHouəNGən/) a particular philosophy or view of life; the worldview of an individual or group. ▷German, from *Welt* 'world' + *Anschauung* 'perception.'

wel·ter[1] /ˈweltər/ ▸*v.* [*intrans.*] *poetic/literary* move in a turbulent fashion: *the streams foam and welter.* ■ lie steeped in blood with no help or care.
▸*n.* a large number of items in no order; a confused mass: *there's such a welter of conflicting rules.* ■ a state of general disorder: *the attack petered out in a welter of bloody, confused fighting.* ▷Middle English (in the sense 'writhe, wallow'): from Middle Dutch, Middle Low German *welteren.*

wel·ter[2] ▸*n.* short for **WELTERWEIGHT**.

wel·ter·weight /ˈweltərˌwāt/ ▸*n.* a weight in boxing and other sports intermediate between lightweight and middleweight. In the amateur boxing scale it ranges from 140 to 147 pounds (63.5–67 kg). ■ a boxer or other competitor of this weight. ▷early 19th cent.: *welter* of unknown origin.

Welt·schmerz /ˈveltˌsHmerts/ ▸*n.* a feeling of melancholy and world-weariness. ▷German, from *Welt* 'world' + *Schmerz* 'pain.'

Wel·ty /ˈweltē/, Eudora (1909–2001), U.S. novelist, short-story writer, and critic. Her novels chiefly focus on life in the South and contain Gothic elements; they include *Delta Wedding* (1946) and *The Optimist's Daughter* (1972), which won a Pulitzer Prize.

wel·wit·schi·a /welˈwicHēə/ ▸*n.* a gymnospermous plant of desert regions in southwestern Africa that has a dwarf, massive trunk, two long strap-shaped leaves, and male and female flowers in the scales of scarlet cones. It is remarkable for its ability to extract moisture from fog. • Genus *Welwitschia*, family Welwitschiaceae: one species, *W. mirabilis.* ▷mid 19th cent.: modern Latin, named after Friedrich *Welwitsch* (1806–72), Austrian botanist.

wen[1] /wen/ ▸*n.* a boil or other swelling or growth on the skin, esp. a sebaceous cyst. ■ *archaic* an outstandingly large or overcrowded city: *the great wen of London.* ▷Old English *wen(n)*, of unknown origin; compare with Low German *wehne* 'tumor, wart.'

wen[2] (also **wyn** /win/) ▸*n.* a runic letter, used in Old and Middle English, later replaced by *w.* ▷Old English, literally 'joy'; so named because it is the first letter of this word. Compare with sense 3 of **THORN** and sense 2 of **ASH**[2].

We·natch·ee /wəˈnacHē/ a city in central Washington, on the Columbia River, near the Wenatchee Mountains; pop. 21,756.

Wen·ces·las /ˈwensəsˌläs; -ˌlôs/ (also **Wen·ces·laus**) (1361–1419), king of Bohemia (as Wenceslas IV) 1378–1419. He became king of Germany, Holy Roman Emperor, and king of Bohemia in the same year, but was deposed by the German electors in 1400.

Wen·ce·slas, St. (also **Wen·ces·laus**) (*c.*907–29), duke of Bohemia and patron saint of the Czech Republic; also known as **Good King Wenceslas**. He worked to Christianize the people of Bohemia but was murdered by his brother; he later became venerated as a martyr. Feast day, September 28.

wench /wencH/ ▸*n. archaic* or *humorous* a girl or young woman. ■ *archaic* a prostitute.
▸*v.* [*intrans.*] *archaic* (of a man) consort with prostitutes. ▷Middle English: abbreviation of obsolete *wenchel* 'child, servant, prostitute'; perhaps related to Old English *wancol* 'unsteady, inconstant.' —**wench·er** *n.*

Wen-Chou /ˈwen ˈcHō/ variant of **WENZHOU**.

Wend /wend/ ▸*n.* another term for **SORB**. ▷from German *Wende*, of unknown origin.

wend /wend/ ▸*v.* [*intrans.*] (**wend one's way**) go in a specified direction, typically slowly or by an indirect route: *they wended their way across the city.* ▷Old English *wendan* 'to turn, depart,' of Germanic origin; related to Dutch and German *wenden*, also to **WIND**[2].

wen·di·go ▸*n.* variant spelling of **WINDIGO**.

Wend·ish /ˈwendisH/ ▸*adj.* & *n.* another term for **SORBIAN**.

Wens·ley·dale /ˈwenzlēˌdāl/ ▸*n.* a light-yellow, firm-textured cow's milk cheese made in England.

went /went/ ▸ past of **GO**[1].

wen·tle·trap /ˈwentlˌtrap/ ▸*n.* a marine mollusk that has a tall spiral shell with many whorls that are ringed with oblique ridges. • Family Epitoniidae, class Gastropoda: numerous species. ▷mid 18th cent.: from Dutch *wenteltrap*, literally 'winding stair.'

Wen·zhou /ˈwənˈjō; ˈwen-/ (also **Wen-Chou** /ˈwen ˈcHō/) an industrial city in Zhejiang province, in eastern China; pop. 1,650,400.

wept /wept/ ▸ past and past participle of **WEEP**.

were /wər/ ▸ second person singular past, plural past, and past subjunctive of **BE**.

we're /wi(ə)r/ ▸*contraction of* we are.

weren't /wər(ə)nt/ ▸*contraction of* were not.

were·wolf /ˈwe(ə)rˌwo͝olf/ ▸*n.* (*pl.* **-wolves**) (in myth or fiction) a person who changes for periods of time into a wolf, typically when there is a full moon. ▷late Old English *werewulf*; the first element has usually been identified with Old English *wer* 'man.' In modern use the word has been revived through folklore studies.

Wer·ner /ˈvernər/, Alfred (1866–1919), Swiss chemist, born in France. He showed that stereochemistry was general to the whole of chemistry and was a pioneer in the study of coordination compounds. Nobel Prize for Chemistry (1913).

Wer·ner's syn·drome /ˈwərnərz/ ▸*n. Medicine* a rare hereditary syndrome causing rapid premature aging, susceptibility to cancer, and other disorders. ▷1930s: named after Carl O. *Werner* (1879–1936), German physician.

Wer·nick·e's ar·e·a /ˈve(ə)rnikēz; -kəz/ ▸*n. Anatomy* a region of the brain concerned with the comprehension of language, located in the cortex of the dominant temporal lobe. Damage in this area causes **Wernicke's aphasia**, characterized by superficially fluent, grammatical speech but an inability to use or understand more than the most basic nouns and verbs. ▷late 19th cent.: named after Karl *Wernicke* (1848–1905), German neuropsychiatrist.

Wer·nick·e's en·ceph·a·lop·a·thy (also **Wer·nick·e's syn·drome**) ▸*n. Medicine* a neurological disorder caused by thiamine deficiency, typically from chronic alcoholism or persistent vomiting, and marked by mental confusion, abnormal eye movements, and unsteady gait. ▷late 19th cent.: named after K. *Wernicke* (see **WERNICKE'S AREA**).

wert /wərt/ ▸ archaic second person singular past of **BE**.

We·sak ▸*n.* variant spelling of **VESAK**.

We·ser /ˈvāzər/ a river in northwestern Germany that forms at the junction of the Werra and Fulda rivers in Lower Saxony and flows north for 182 miles (292 km) to the North Sea near Bremerhaven.

Wes·ley /ˈwezlē; ˈweslē/, John (1703–91), English preacher and cofounder of Methodism. Wesley won many working-class converts, but the opposition encountered from the establishment of the Church of England led to the Methodists forming a separate denomination in 1791. His brother **Charles** (1707–88) was also a founding Methodist.

Wes·ley·an /ˈweslēən/ ▸*adj.* of, relating to, or denoting the teachings of John Wesley or the main branch of the Methodist Church that he founded.
▸*n.* a follower of Wesley or adherent of the main Methodist tradition. —**Wes·ley·an·ism** /-ˌnizəm/ *n.*

Wes·sex /ˈwesiks/ the kingdom of the West Saxons, established in Hampshire in the early 6th century

W

and gradually extended by conquest to include much of southern England.

Wes·si /ˈwesē; ˈvesē/ *informal* ▸*n.* a citizen of West Germany. Compare with **Ossi.** ▷probably from German *Westdeutsche* 'West German.'

West[1] /west/, Benjamin (1738–1820), U.S. painter, resident in Britain from 1763. He became historical painter to George III in 1769 and the second president of the Royal Academy in 1792.

West[2], Dorothy (1907–98), U.S. writer. She wrote about racism and class and was a spokesman for the Harlem Renaissance during the 1920s. Her novels included *The Living Is Easy* (1948) and *The Wedding* (1995). *The Richer, the Poorer* (1995) is a collection of autobiographical pieces.

West[3], Jerry (Alan) (1938–), U.S. basketball player and coach. A guard, he played for the Los Angeles Lakers 1960–74. After retiring as a player, he coached the Lakers 1976–79 and then became their general manager in 1982. Basketball Hall of Fame (1979).

West[4], Mae (1892–1980), U.S. actress and playwright. She established her reputation on Broadway in her own comedies, *Sex* (1926) and *Diamond Lil* (1928), which are memorable for their spirited approach to sexual matters, before she embarked on her successful Hollywood career in the 1930s.

West[5], Nathanael (1903–40), U.S. writer; born *Nathan Wallenstein Weinstein*. He wrote mainly during the Great Depression years of the 1930s. His works included novels such as *Miss Lonelyhearts* (1933), *A Cool Million* (1934), and *The Day of the Locust* (1939).

West[6], Dame Rebecca (1892–1983), British writer and feminist, born in Ireland; born *Cicily Isabel Fairfield*. She is best remembered for *The Meaning of Treason* (1949), a study of the Nuremberg trials. Other notable works: *Black Lamb and Grey Falcon* (1942) and *The Fountain Overflows* (1957).

west /west/ ▸*n.* (usu. **the west**) **1** the direction toward the point of the horizon where the sun sets at the equinoxes, on the left-hand side of a person facing north, or the part of the horizon lying in this direction: *the evening sun glowed from the west* | *a patrol aimed to create a diversion* **to the west of** *the city.* ■ the compass point corresponding to this. **2** the western part of the world or of a specified country, region, or town: *it will become windy in the west.* ■ (usu. **the West**) Europe and its culture seen in contrast to other civilizations. ■ (usu. **the West**) *historical* the noncommunist states of Europe and North America, contrasted with the former communist states of eastern Europe. ■ (usu. **the West**) the western part of the U.S., esp. the states west of the Mississippi. **3** [as *name*] (**West**) *Bridge* the player sitting to the right of North and partnering East.
▸*adj.* **1** [*attrib.*] lying toward, near, or facing the west: *the west coast.* ■ (of a wind) blowing from the west. **2** of or denoting the western part of a specified area, city, or country or its inhabitants: *West Africa.*
▸*adv.* to or toward the west: *he faced west and watched the sunset* | *the accident happened a mile* **west of** *Bowes.* ▷Old English, of Germanic origin; related to Dutch and German *west*, from an Indo-European root shared by Greek *hesperos*, Latin *vesper* 'evening.'

West Af·ri·ca the western part of the African continent, esp. the countries bounded by and including Mauritania, Mali, and Niger in the north and Gabon in the south.

West Al·lis /ˈalis/ an industrial city in southeastern Wisconsin, southwest of Milwaukee; pop. 61,254.

West Bank a region west of the Jordan River and northwest of the Dead Sea. It includes Jericho, Hebron, Nablus, Bethlehem, and other settlements. It became part of Jordan in 1948 and was occupied by Israel following the Six Day War of 1967. An agreement was signed in 1993 that granted limited autonomy to the Palestinians, who comprise 97 percent of its inhabitants; withdrawal of Israeli troops began in 1994.

West Bend an industrial city in southeastern Wisconsin, on the Milwaukee River; pop. 23,916.

West Ben·gal a state in eastern India; capital, Calcutta.

West Ber·lin See **Berlin.**

west·bound /ˈwestˌbound/ ▸*adj.* leading or traveling toward the west: *I need a westbound train.*

West Brom·wich /ˈbrämiCH/ an industrial town in western central England; pop. 155,000.

West·brook /ˈwestˌbro͝ok/ a city in southern Maine; a western suburb of Portland; pop. 16,142.

West·ches·ter Coun·ty /ˈwesˌCHestər/ a suburban county in southeastern New York, northeast of New York City; pop. 923,459.

West Coast ▸*n.* the western seaboard of the U.S. from Washington to California.

West Coun·try the southwestern counties of England.

West Co·vi·na /kōˈvēnə/ a city in southwestern California, east of Los Angeles; pop. 96,086.

West Des Moines a city in south central Iowa, a western suburb of Des Moines; pop. 46,403.

West End the entertainment and shopping area of London to the west of the City.

west·er·ing /ˈwestəriNG/ ▸*adj. poetic/literary* (esp. of the sun) nearing the west. ▷mid 17th cent.: from the literary verb *wester*, from **west.**

Wes·ter·ly /ˈwestərlē/ an industrial and resort town in southwestern Rhode Island, on the Connecticut border; pop. 22,966.

west·er·ly /ˈwestərlē/ ▸*adj.* & *adv.* in a westward position or direction: [as *adj.*] *the westerly end of Sunset Boulevard* | [as *adv.*] *our plan was to keep westerly.* ■ (of a wind) blowing from the west: [as *adj.*] *a stiff westerly breeze.*
▸*n.* (often **westerlies**) a wind blowing from the west. ■ (**westerlies**) the belt of prevailing westerly winds in the mid-latitudes of the northern and southern hemispheres. ▷late 15th cent.: from obsolete *wester* 'western' + **-ly**[1].

west·ern /ˈwestərn/ ▸*adj.* **1** [*attrib.*] situated in the west, or directed toward or facing the west: *there will be showers in some western areas.* ■ (of a wind) blowing from the west. **2** (usu. **West·ern**) living in or originating from the west, in particular Europe or the U.S.: *Western society.* ■ of, relating to, or characteristic of the west or its inhabitants: *the history of western art.* ■ *historical* of or originating from the noncommunist states of Europe and North America in contrast to the Eastern bloc.
▸*n.* (also **West·ern**) a film, television drama, or novel about cowboys in western North America, esp. in the late 19th and early 20th centuries. ▷Old English *westerne* (see **west, -ern**). **—west·ern·most** /-ˌmōst/ *adj.*

West·ern Aus·tra·lia a state in western Australia; pop. 1,643,000; capital, Perth. It was colonized by the British in 1826 and was federated with the other states of Australia in 1901.

West·ern blot ▸*n. Biochemistry* an adaptation of the Southern blot procedure, used to identify specific amino-acid sequences in proteins. ▷suggested by **Southern blot.**

West·ern Cape a province in southwestern South Africa, formerly part of Cape Province; capital, Cape Town.

West·ern Church the part of the Christian Church historically originating in the Latin Church of the Western Roman Empire, including the Roman Catholic Church and the Anglican, Lutheran, and Reformed Churches, esp. as distinct from the Eastern Orthodox Church.

West·ern Em·pire the western part of the Roman Empire, after its division in AD 395.

West·ern·er /ˈwestərnər/ (also **west·ern·er**) ▸*n.* a native or inhabitant of the west, esp. of western Europe or North America.

West·ern Front the zone of fighting in western Europe in World War I, in which the German army engaged the armies to its west, i.e., France, the UK (and its dominions), and, from 1917, the U.S. For most of the war the front line stretched from the Vosges mountains in eastern France through Amiens to Ostend in Belgium.

west·ern hem·i·sphere the half of the earth that contains the Americas.

west·ern hem·lock ▸*n.* a large coniferous tree with flattened needles of two different sizes, grown for pulp and as an ornamental. It occurs chiefly along the Pacific coast from northern California to Alaska and in the northern Rocky Mountains. • *Tsuga heterophylla*, family Pinaceae.

West·ern Isles another name for **Hebrides.**

west·ern·ize /ˈwestərˌnīz/ ▸*v.* [*trans.*] (usu. **be westernized**) cause (a country, person, or system) to adopt or be influenced by the cultural, economic, or political systems of Europe and North America: *the agreement provided for the legal system to be westernized* | [as *adj.*] (**westernized**) *the more westernized parts of the city.* ■ [*intrans.*] be in the process of adopting or being influenced by the systems of the West: [as *adj.*] (**westernizing**) *a westernizing tribe.* **—west·ern·i·za·tion** /ˌwestərniˈzāSHən/ *n.* **—west·ern·iz·er** *n.*

west·ern om·e·let ▸*n.* an omelet containing a filling of onion, green pepper, and ham.

West·ern Ro·man Em·pire see **Roman Empire.**

West·ern sad·dle ▸*n.* a saddle with a deep seat, high pommel and cantle, and broad stirrups.

West·ern Sa·har·a a region in northwestern Africa, on the Atlantic coast between Morocco and Mauritania; pop. 187,000; capital, La'youn. Formerly an overseas Spanish province called Spanish Sahara, it was renamed and annexed by Morocco and Mauritania in 1976. Mauritania withdrew in 1979 and Morocco extended its control over the entire region. A liberation movement, the Polisario Front, which had launched a guerrilla war against the Spanish in 1973, continued its struggle against Morocco in an attempt to establish an independent Saharawi Arab Democratic Republic; a cease-fire came into effect in 1991.

West·ern Sa·mo·a see **Samoa.**

west·ern sand·wich ▸*n.* a sandwich having a western omelet as a filling.

West·ern swing ▸*n.* a style of country music influenced by jazz, popular in the 1930s.

West·ern Wall a high wall in Jerusalem said to stand on the site of Herod's temple, where Jews traditionally pray and lament on Fridays. Also called **Wailing Wall.**

Western Wall

West·ern Zhou see **Zhou.**

Wes·ter·ville /ˈwestərˌvil/ a city in central Ohio, northeast of Columbus; pop. 30,193.

West·fa·len /vestˈfälən/ German name for **Westphalia.**

West Far·go a city in southwestern North Dakota, a western suburb of Fargo; pop. 14,940.

West·field /ˈwestˌfēld/ **1** an industrial city in western Massachusetts; pop. 38,372. **2** a historic town in northeastern New Jersey, west of Elizabeth; pop. 28,870.

West Flan·ders a province of northwestern Belgium; capital, Bruges.

West Fri·sian Is·lands see **Frisian Islands.**

West Ger·man·ic ▸*n.* the western group of Germanic languages, comprising High and Low German, Dutch, Frisian, and English.
▸*adj.* of or relating to West Germanic.

West Ger·ma·ny see **Germany.**

West Hart·ford a town in central Connecticut, west of Hartford; pop. 63,589.

West Ha·ven a town in southwestern Connecticut, west of New Haven; pop. 54,021.

West High·land ter·ri·er (also **West High·land white ter·ri·er**) ▸*n.* a dog of a small, short-legged breed of terrier with a white coat and erect ears and tail, developed in the West Highlands.

West Hol·ly·wood a city in southwestern California, northeast of Beverly Hills; pop. 36,118.

West In·di·an ▸*n.* a native or national of any of the islands of the West Indies. ■ a person of West Indian descent.
▸*adj.* of or relating to the West Indies or its people.

West In·di·an sat·in·wood ▸*n.* see **satinwood.**

West In·dies a chain of islands that extends from the Florida peninsula to the coast of Venezuela and lies between the Caribbean Sea and the Atlantic Ocean. They consist of three main island groups: the Greater and Lesser Antilles and the Bahamas, with Bermuda lying further to the north. Originally inhabited by Arawak and Carib Indians, the islands were visited by Columbus in 1492 and named by him in the belief that he had reached the coast of India. The islands now consist of a number of independent states and British, French, Dutch, and U.S. dependencies.

west·ing /ˈwestiNG/ ▸*n.* distance traveled or measured westward, esp. at sea. ■ a figure or line representing westward distance on a map.

West·ing·house /ˈwestiNG,hous/, George (1846–1914), U.S. engineer. He is best known for developing vacuum-operated safety brakes and electrically controlled signals for railroads. He held over 400 patents and built up a huge company to manufacture his products.

West I·ri·an another name for IRIAN JAYA.

West Jor·dan a city in north central Utah, south of Salt Lake City; pop. 68,336.

West La·fay·ette a city in west central Indiana, across the Wabash River from Lafayette, home to Purdue University; pop. 25,907.

West·land /ˈwestlənd/ a city in southeastern Michigan, a western suburb of Detroit; pop. 86,602.

West·mann Is·lands /ˈwes(t)mən; ˈves(t)-/ a group of fifteen volcanic islands off the southern coast of Iceland. Icelandic name VESTMANNAEYJAR.

West·meath /,wes(t)ˈmēTH; -ˈmēTH/ a county of the Republic of Ireland, in the province of Leinster; county town, Mullingar.

West Mem·phis an industrial and commercial city in northeastern Arkansas, across the Mississippi River from Memphis in Tennessee; pop. 27,666.

West Mif·flin /ˈmiflən/ an industrial borough in southwestern Pennsylvania, southeast of Pittsburgh; pop. 23,644.

West·min·ster /ˈwes(t),minstər; ,wes(t)ˈmin-/ **1** an industrial and commercial city in southwestern California, southeast of Los Angeles; pop. 78,118. **2** a city in north central Colorado, northwest of Denver; pop. 100,940. **3** an inner London borough that contains the Houses of Parliament and many government offices. Full name CITY OF WESTMINSTER. ■ used in reference to the British Parliament: *Westminster enforced successive cuts in pay.*

West·min·ster Ab·bey the collegiate church of St. Peter in Westminster, London, originally the abbey church of a Benedictine monastery. Nearly all the kings and queens of England have been crowned in Westminster Abbey; it is also the burial place of many of England's monarchs and other leading figures.

West New York an industrial and residential town in northeastern New Jersey, on the Hudson River, across from New York City; pop. 38,125.

West Nile vi·rus ▸*n.* a flavivirus of African origin that can be spread to humans and other mammals via mosquitoes, causing encephalitis and flulike symptoms, with some fatalities.

west-north·west ▸*n.* the direction or compass point midway between west and northwest.

West Or·ange a suburban township in northeastern New Jersey, northwest of Newark; pop. 39,013.

West Palm Beach a resort city in southeastern Florida; pop. 67,643.

West·pha·lia /wes(t)ˈfālyə; -ˈfālēə/ a former province of northwestern Germany. German name WESTFALEN. **—West·pha·lian** *adj.* & *n.*

West·pha·li·a, Trea·ty of the peace accord (1648) that ended the Thirty Years War, signed simultaneously in Osnabrück and Münster.

West Point the U.S. Military Academy, founded in 1802, located on the site of a former strategic fort on the west bank of the Hudson River in New York.

West·port /ˈwest,pôrt/ **1** a town in southwestern Connecticut, an affluent suburb southwest of Bridgeport; pop. 24,410. **2** a former town, now part of Kansas City in Missouri, that was a 19th-century gateway to the westbound Santa Fe Trail.

West Quod·dy Head /ˈkwädē/ the easternmost (66° 57′ W) point in the U.S., in Lubec in Maine, south of Passamaquoddy Bay.

West Rox·bury a southwestern district of Boston, Massachusetts. It was a separate town until 1874 and was the site of the experimental Brook Farm.

West Sax·on ▸*n.* **1** a native or inhabitant of the Anglo-Saxon kingdom of Wessex. **2** the dialect of Old English used by the West Saxons, the chief literary dialect of Old English.
▸*adj.* of or relating to the West Saxons or their dialect.

West Sen·e·ca a town in western New York, southeast of Buffalo; pop. 47,830.

West Side the residential and commercial districts west of Fifth Avenue in Manhattan in New York City.

west-south·west ▸*n.* the direction or compass point midway between west and southwest.

West Val·ley Cit·y a city in north central Utah, south of Salt Lake City; pop. 108,896.

West Vir·gin·ia a state in the eastern U.S.; pop. 1,808,344; capital, Charleston; statehood, June 20, 1863 (35). It separated from Virginia in 1861, at the beginning of the Civil War, because the two areas were at odds over the questions of secession and of slavery. **—West Vir·gin·ian** *n.* & *adj.*

west·ward /ˈwestwərd/ ▸*adj.* toward the west: *the journey covers eight time zones in a westward direction.*
▸*adv.* (also **west·wards**) in a westerly direction: *the vast prairie lands extending from northern Ohio westward.*
▸*n.* (**the westward**) a direction or region toward the west: *he sees a light* **to the westward.** **—west·ward·ly** *adv.*

West War·wick /ˈwôrwik/ a town in central Rhode Island, southwest of Providence; pop. 29,581.

West·wood /ˈwest,wo͝od/ a section in western Los Angeles in California, home to the University of California at Los Angeles (UCLA).

wet /wet/ ▸*adj.* (**wet·ter, wet·test**) **1** covered or saturated with water or another liquid: *she followed, slipping on the wet rock.* ■ (of the weather) rainy: *a wet, windy evening.* ■ (of paint, ink, plaster, or a similar substance) not yet having dried or hardened. ■ (of a baby or young child) having urinated in its diaper or underwear. ■ involving the use of water or liquid: *wet methods of photography.* **2** *informal* (of a country or region or of its legislation) allowing the sale of alcoholic beverages. ■ (of a person) addicted to alcohol. **3** *Brit., informal* showing a lack of forcefulness or strength of character; feeble: *they thought the cadets were a bit wet.*
▸*v.* (**wet·ting**; *past* and *past part.* **wet** or **wet·ted**) [*trans.*] cover or touch with liquid; moisten: *he wet a finger and flicked through the pages* | [as *n.*] (**wetting**) *the wetting caused an aggravation of his gout.* ■ (esp. of a baby or young child) urinate in or on: *the child wet the bed.* ■ (**wet oneself**) urinate involuntarily.
▸*n.* **1** liquid that makes something damp: *I could feel the wet of his tears.* ■ (**the wet**) rainy weather: *the race was held in the wet.* ■ a person opposed to the prohibition of alcoholic beverages. **2** *Brit., informal* a person lacking forcefulness or strength of character. ▷Old English *wǣt* (adjective and noun), *wǣtan* (verb); related to WATER. **—wet·ly** *adv.* **—wet·ness** *n.* **—wet·ta·ble** *adj.* **—wet·tish** *adj.*
▸*PHRASES* □ **all wet** completely wrong. □ **wet behind the ears** *informal* lacking experience; immature. □ **wet through** (or **to the skin**) with one's clothes soaked; completely drenched. □ **wet one's whistle** *informal* have a drink.

we·ta /ˈwetə/ ▸*n.* a large brown wingless insect related to the grasshoppers, with long spiny legs and wood-boring larvae, found only in New Zealand. • Family Stenopelmatidae: several genera, including *Deinacrida* (the **giant wetas**). ▷mid 19th cent.: from Maori.

wet·back /ˈwet,bak/ ▸*n. informal, derogatory* a Mexican living in the U.S., esp. one who is an illegal immigrant. ▷1920s: so named from the practice of swimming the Rio Grande to reach the U.S.

wet bar ▸*n.* a bar or counter equipped with running water and a sink, for serving alcoholic drinks at home.

wet blan·ket ▸*n. informal* a person who spoils other people's fun by failing to join in with or by disapproving of their activities.

wet bulb ▸*n.* one of the two thermometers of a psychrometer, the bulb of which is enclosed in wetted material so that water is constantly evaporating from it and cooling the bulb.

wet cell ▸*n.* a primary electric cell in which the electrolyte is a liquid. Compare with DRY CELL.

wet dock ▸*n.* a dock in which water is maintained at a level that keeps a vessel afloat.

wet dream ▸*n.* an erotic dream associated with involuntary ejaculation of semen.

wet fly ▸*n.* an artificial fishing fly designed to sink below the surface of the water.

weth·er /ˈweTHər/ ▸*n.* a castrated ram. ▷Old English, of Germanic origin; related to Dutch *weer* and German *Widder.*

Weth·ers·field /ˈweTHərz,fēld/ a historic town in central Connecticut, south of Hartford on the Connecticut River; pop. 25,651.

wet·land /ˈwet,land; -lənd/ ▸*n.* (also **wetlands**) land consisting of marshes or swamps; saturated land.

wet look ▸*n.* [in *sing.*] an artificially wet or shiny appearance, in particular one possessed by a clothing fabric or achieved by applying a type of gel to the hair.

wet nurse ▸*n. chiefly historical* a woman employed to suckle another woman's child.
▸*v.* (**wet-nurse**) [*trans.*] act as a wet nurse to. ■ *informal* look after (someone) as though they were a helpless infant.

wet pack ▸*n.* a session of hydrotherapy in which the body is wrapped in wet cloth.

wet plate ▸*n. Photography* a sensitized collodion plate exposed in the camera while the collodion is moist.

wet·suit /ˈwet,so͞ot/ ▸*n.* a close-fitting garment of neoprene or similar material typically covering most of the body but not designed to exclude water, worn for warmth in water sports or diving. Compare with DRY SUIT.

wet·ting a·gent ▸*n.* a chemical that can be added to a liquid to reduce its surface tension and make it more effective in spreading over and penetrating surfaces.

wet·ware /ˈwet,we(ə)r/ ▸*n. humorous* human brain cells or thought processes regarded as analogous to, or in contrast with, computer systems. ■ (chiefly in science fiction) computer technology in which the brain is linked to artificial systems, or used as a model for artificial systems based on biochemical processes.

we've /wēv/ ▸*contraction of* we have.

Wex·ford /ˈweksfərd/ a county in southeastern Republic of Ireland, in the province of Leinster. ■ its county town, a port on the Irish Sea; pop. 10,000 (1991).

Wey·mouth /ˈwāməTH/ a town in eastern Massachusetts, southeast of Boston; pop. 54,063.

w.f. *Printing* ▸*abbr.* wrong font (used as a proofreading mark).

whack /(h)wak/ *informal* ▸*v.* [*trans.*] strike forcefully with a sharp blow: *his attacker whacked him on the head* | [*intrans.*] *she found a stick to* **whack at** *the branches.* ■ murder: *he was whacked while sitting in his car.*
▸*phrasal v.* □ **whack off** *vulgar slang* masturbate.
▸*n.* **1** a sharp or resounding blow. **2** a try or attempt: *we decided to* **take a whack at** *spotting the decade's trends.* **3** *Brit.* a specified share of or contribution to something: *motorists* **pay** *a fair* **whack** *for the use of the roads through taxes.* ▷early 18th cent.: imitative, or perhaps an alteration of THWACK. **—whack·er** *n.*
▸*PHRASES* □ **at a** (or **one**) **whack** at one time: *he built twenty houses at one whack.* □ **out of whack** out of order; not working: *all their calculations were out of whack.*

whacked /(h)wakt/ (also **whacked out**) ▸*adj. informal* completely exhausted: *I'm not staying long—I'm whacked.* ■ under the influence of drugs: *a whacked-out, drug-addicted child.*

whack·ing /ˈ(h)wakiNG/ ▸*adj.* [*attrib.*] *Brit., informal* very large: *she poured us two whacking drinks* | [as *submodifier*] *he dug a whacking great hole.*

whack·o ▸*adj.* & *n.* (*pl.* **-os**) variant spelling of WACKO.

whack·y ▸*adj.* variant spelling of WACKY.

whale[1] /(h)wāl/ ▸*n.* (*pl.* same or **whales**) a very large marine mammal with a streamlined hairless body, a horizontal tail fin, and a blowhole on top of the head for breathing. • Order Cetacea. See BALEEN WHALE and TOOTHED WHALE. ▷Old English *hwæl,* of Germanic origin. *See page 1910*
▸*PHRASES* □ **a whale of a ——** *informal* an exceedingly good example of a particular thing: *you've been doing a whale of a job.* □ **have a whale of a time** enjoy oneself very much.

whale[2] ▸*v.* [*trans.*] *informal* beat; hit: *Dad came upstairs and whaled me* | [*intrans.*] *they* **whaled at** *the water with their paddles.* ▷late 18th cent.: variant of WALE.

whale·back /ˈ(h)wāl,bak/ ▸*n.* a thing that is shaped like a whale's back, esp. an arched structure over the bow or stern part of the deck of a steamer, or a large elongated hill: [as *adj.*] *a whaleback ridge.*

whale·boat /ˈ(h)wāl,bōt/ ▸*n.* a long rowboat with a bow at either end for easy maneuverability, formerly used in whaling. ■ a similar boat used as a ship's lifeboat and utility boat.

sperm whale
Physeter catodon
up to 60 feet
orca
Orcinus orca
up to 30 feet
humpback whale
Megaptera novaeangliae
30 to 60 feet
narwhal
Monodon monoceros
up to 14 feet
bottlenose dolphin
Tursiops truncatus
8 to 12 feet
harbor porpoise
Phocoena phocoena
4 to 6 feet

whales

whale·bone /ˈ(h)wāl,bōn/ ▸*n.* an elastic horny substance that grows in a series of thin parallel plates in the upper jaw of some whales and is used by them to strain plankton from the seawater. Also called BALEEN. ■ strips of this substance, much used formerly as stays in corsets and dresses: [as *adj.*] *a whalebone bodice.* ■ bone or ivory from a whale or walrus.

whale·bone whale ▸*n.* another term for BALEEN WHALE.

whale oil ▸*n.* oil obtained from the blubber of a whale, formerly used in oil lamps and for making soap.

whal·er /ˈ(h)wālər/ ▸*n.* a whaling ship. ■ a seaman engaged in whaling.

whale shark ▸*n.* a very large tropical shark that typically swims close to the surface, where it feeds chiefly on plankton. It is the largest known fish. • *Rhincodon typus,* the sole member of the family Rhincodontidae.

whal·ing /ˈ(h)wāliNG/ ▸*n.* the practice or industry of hunting and killing whales for their oil, meat, or whalebone.

wham /(h)wam/ *informal* ▸*exclam.* used to express the sound of a forcible impact: *the bombs landed—wham!—right on target.* ■ used to express the idea of a sudden, dramatic, and decisive occurrence: *he asked me out for a drink, and—wham!—that was it.*
▸*v.* (**whammed**, **wham·ming**) [*intrans.*] strike something forcefully: *trucks whammed into each other.* ■ make a loud sound as of a forceful impact: *my heart was whamming away like a drum.* ▷1920s: imitative.

wham bam *informal* ▸*exclam.* used to express the idea of a sudden or dramatic occurrence or change of events: *Wham bam!—we were sitting in a wreck at the foot of the cliff.* ▷1950s (as *wham-bang*): from WHAM + BAM or the verb BANG[1].
▸*PHRASE* □ **wham-bam-thank-you-ma'am** used in reference to sexual activity conducted roughly and quickly, without tenderness.

wham·mo /ˈ(h)wamō/ ▸*exclam.* another term for WHAM.

wham·my /ˈ(h)wamē/ ▸*n.* (*pl.* **-mies**) *informal* an event with a powerful and unpleasant effect; a blow: *the third whammy was the degradation of the financial system.* See also DOUBLE WHAMMY. ■ an evil or unlucky influence: *I've come to **put the whammy on** them.* ▷1940s: from the noun WHAM + -Y[1]; associated from the 1950s with the comic strip *Li'l Abner*, in which the hillbilly Evil-Eye Fleagle could "shoot a whammy" (put a curse on somebody) by pointing a finger with one eye open, and a 'double whammy' with both eyes open.

whang /(h)waNG/ *informal* ▸*v.* [*intrans.*] make or produce a resonant noise: *the cheerleader whanged on a tambourine.* ■ [*trans.*] strike or throw heavily and loudly: *he whanged down the receiver.*
▸*n.* a noisy blow: *he gave a whang with his hammer.* ▷late 17th cent. (in the sense 'strike as if with a thong'): variant of THONG; senses describing noise are imitative.

whap /(h)wap/ ▸*v.* (**whapped**, **whap·ping**) & *n.* variant spelling of WHOP.

wharf /(h)wôrf/ ▸*n.* (*pl.* **wharves** /(h)wôrvz/ or **wharfs**) a level quayside area to which a ship may be moored to load and unload. ▷late Old English *hwearf*, of Germanic origin.

wharf·age /ˈ(h)wôrfij/ ▸*n.* accommodations provided at a wharf for the loading, unloading, or storage of goods. ■ payment made for such accommodations.

wharf·in·ger /ˈ(h)wôrfinjər/ ▸*n.* an owner or keeper of a wharf. ▷Middle English: from WHARFAGE + -ER[1].

Whar·ton /ˈ(h)wôrtn/, Edith (Newbold) (1862–1937), U.S. novelist and short-story writer, resident in France from 1907. Her novels are concerned with the conflict between social and individual fulfillment. They include *Ethan Frome* (1911) and *The Age of Innocence* (1920), which won a Pulitzer Prize.

wharves /(h)wôrvz/ ▸ plural form of WHARF.

what /(h)wət; (h)wät/ ▸*pron.* **1** [*interrog. pron.*] asking for information specifying something: *what is your name?* | *I'm not sure what you mean.* ■ asking for repetition of something not heard or confirmation of something not understood: *what? I can't hear you* | *you did what?* **2** [*relative pron.*] the thing or things that (used in specifying something): *what we need is a commitment.* ■ (referring to the whole of an amount) whatever: *I want to do what I can to make a difference.* ■ *dialect* who or that: *the one what got to my house.* **3** (in exclamations) emphasizing something surprising or remarkable: *what some people do for attention!*
▸*adj.* **1** [*interrog. adj.*] asking for information specifying something: *what time is it?* | *do you know what excuse he gave me?* **2** [*relative adj.*] (referring to the whole of an amount) whatever: *he had been robbed of what little money he had.* **3** (in exclamations) how great or remarkable: [as *adj.*] *what luck!* | [as *predeterminer*] *what a fool she was.*
▸*interrog. adv.* **1** to what extent?: *what does it matter?* **2** used to indicate an estimate or approximation: *see you, what, about four?* **3** *informal, dated* used for emphasis or to invite agreement: *pretty poor show, what?* ▷Old English *hwæt*, of Germanic origin; related to Dutch *wat* and German *was*, from an Indo-European root shared by Latin *quod*.
▸*PHRASES* □ **and** (or **or**) **what have you** *informal* and/or anything else similar: *for a binder try soup, gravy, cream, or what have you.* □ **and what not** *informal* and other similar things. □ **give someone what for** see GIVE. □ **what about ——? 1** used when asking for information or an opinion on something: *what about the practical angle?* **2** used to make a suggestion: *what about a walk?* □ **what-d'you-call-it** (or **what's-its name**) *informal* another term for WHATCHAMACALLIT. □ **what ever** used for emphasis in questions, typically expressing surprise or confusion: *what ever did I do to deserve him?* See **usage** below. □ **what for?** *informal* for what reason? □ **what if ——? 1** what would result if ——?: *what if nobody shows up?* **2** what does it matter if ——?: *what if our house is a mess? I'm clean.* □ **what is more** and as an additional point; moreover. □ **what next** see NEXT. □ **what of ——?** what is the news concerning ——? □ **what of it?** why should that be considered significant? □ **what's-his** (or **-its**) **-name** another term for WHATSHISNAME. □ **what say —— ?** used to make a suggestion: *what say we take a break?* □ **what's what** *informal* what is useful or important: *I'll teach her what's what.* □ **what with** because of (used usually to introduce several causes of something): *what with the drought and the neglect, the garden is in a sad condition.*

USAGE On the distinction between **what ever** and **whatever**, see usage at WHATEVER.

what·cha /ˈ(h)wəCHə; ˈ(h)wä-/ (also **wat·cha** /ˈwəCHə; ˈwä-/) ▸*pron.* nonstandard contraction of: ■ what are you: *hey, whatcha gonna do?* ■ what have you: *whatcha got this hammer for?* ■ what do you: *whatcha want to make a mess like that for?*

what·cha·ma·call·it /ˈ(h)wəCHəmə,kôlit; ˈ(h)wä-/ ▸*n.* *informal* used to refer to a person or thing whose name one cannot recall, does not know, or does not wish to specify: *she wanted me to get the whatchamacallit from her bureau.*

what·e'er /,(h)wətˈe(ə)r; ,(h)wät-/ *poetic/literary* ▸*contraction of* whatever.

what·ev·er /(h)wətˈevər; ,(h)wät-/ ▸*relative pron.* & *adj.* used to emphasize a lack of restriction in referring to any thing or amount, no matter what: [as *pron.*] *do whatever you like* | [as *adj.*] *take whatever action is needed.* ■ regardless of what: [as *pron.*] *you have our support, whatever you decide* | [as *adj.*] *whatever decision he made I would support it.*
▸*interrog. pron.* used for emphasis instead of "what" in questions, typically expressing surprise or confusion: *whatever is the matter?* See **usage** below.
▸*adv.* **1** [with *negative*] at all; of any kind (used for emphasis): *they received no help whatever.* **2** *informal* no matter what happens: *we told him we'd back him whatever.*
▸*exclam.* used to express skepticism or exasperation: *Joseph's commentary amounted to "Yeah, well. Whatever."*
▸*PHRASES* □ **or whatever** *informal* or anything similar: *use chopped herbs, nuts, garlic, or whatever.* □ **whatever next** see NEXT.

USAGE In the sentence *I will do **whatever** you ask of me* (in which **whatever** = *anything*), **whatever** is correctly spelled as one word. But in the interrogative sense (***what ever** was Mary thinking?*), the emphasis is on *ever*, and it should be spelled as the two words **what ever** because *ever* is serving as an intensifier to the pronoun *what*.
See also **usage** at HOWEVER and WHEREVER.

what·not /ˈ(h)wət,nät; ˈ(h)wät-/ ▸*n.* **1** *informal* used to refer to an item or items that are not identified but are felt to have something in common with items already named: *little flashing digital displays, electric zooms and whatnots* | *pictures and books and manuscripts and whatnot.* **2** a stand with shelves for small objects.

whats·his·name /ˈ(h)wətsiz,nām; ˈ(h)wät-/ (also **whats·his·name**, **whats·his·face** /-,fās/, or **whats·her·name** /-sər,nām/) ▸*n.* *informal* used to refer to a person whose name one cannot recall, does not know, or does not wish to specify: *poor Mr. Whatsisname just blew a fuse.*

whats·is /ˈ(h)wətsəs; ˈ(h)wät-/ ▸*n.* *informal* used to refer to a thing whose name one cannot recall, does not know, or does not wish to specify: *I am up to my whatsis in snow and slush.*

whats·it /ˈ(h)wətsit; ˈ(h)wät-/ ▸*n.* another term for WHATCHAMACALLIT.

what·so /ˈ(h)wət,sō; ˈ(h)wät-/ ▸*pron.* & *adj. archaic* whatever: [as *pron.*] *whatso goes into their brain comes out as prose.* ▷Middle English: reduced form of Old English *swā hwæt swā* 'so what so.'

what·so·e'er /,(h)wətsōˈe(ə)r; ,(h)wät-/ *poetic/literary* ▸*contraction of* whatsoever.

what·so·ev·er /,(h)wətsōˈevər; ,(h)wät-/ ▸*adv.* [with *negative*] at all (used for emphasis): *I have no doubt whatsoever.*
▸*adj.* & *pron. archaic* whatever.

what-you-see-is-what-you-get ▸*adj.* see **WYSIWYG**.

wheal /(h)wēl/ ▸*n.* variant spelling of WEAL[1].

wheat /(h)wēt/ ▸*n.* a cereal plant that is the most important kind grown in temperate countries, the grain of which is ground to make flour for bread, pasta, pastry, etc. • Genus *Triticum*, family Gramineae: several species, including **bread wheat** (*T. aestivum*) and **durum wheat**, and many distinctive cultivars. ■ the grain of this plant. ▷Old English *hwǣte*, of Germanic origin; related to Dutch *weit*, German *Weizen*, also to WHITE.
▸*PHRASE* □ **separate the wheat from the chaff** see CHAFF[1].

wheat belt ▸*n.* (**the wheat belt**) a region where wheat is the chief agricultural product.

wheat·ear /ˈ(h)wēt,ir/ ▸*n.* a mainly Eurasian and African songbird related to the chats, with black and buff or black and white plumage and a white rump. • Genus *Oenanthe*, subfamily Turdinae, family Muscicapidae: several species, in particular the gray-backed **northern wheatear** (*O. oenanthe*), found in the arctic barrens of Eurasia and northeastern Canada. ▷late 16th cent.: apparently from WHITE (assimilated to WHEAT) + ARSE (assimilated to EAR[2]).

wheat·en /ˈ(h)wētn/ ▸*adj.* (esp. of bread) made of wheat. ■ of a color resembling that of wheat; a pale yellow-beige.

wheat·en ter·ri·er ▸*n.* a terrier of a breed with a pale golden soft wavy coat.

wheat germ ▸*n.* a nutritious foodstuff of a dry floury consistency consisting of the extracted embryos of grains of wheat.

wheat·grass /ˈ(h)wēt,gras/ ▸*n.* another term for COUCH GRASS.

Wheat·ley /ˈ(h)wētlē/, Phillis (c.1752–84), American poet; born in Africa. She was sold as a slave at age eight to the John Wheatley family of Boston. She was educated by them and then accompanied a member of the family to London, where her first volume of poetry, *Poems on Various Subjects, Religious and Moral* (1773), was published.

wheat·meal /ˈ(h)wēt,mēl/ ▸*n.* flour made from wheat from which some of the bran and germ has been removed.

Whea·ton /ˈ(h)wētn/ a city in northeastern Illinois, west of Chicago; pop. 51,464.

Wheat State a nickname for the state of **KANSAS**.

Wheat·stone /ˈ(h)wēt,stōn/, Sir Charles (1802–75), English physicist and inventor. He is best known for his electrical inventions.

Wheat·stone bridge ▸*n.* a simple circuit for measuring an unknown resistance by connecting it so as to form a quadrilateral with three known resistances and applying a voltage between a pair of opposite corners.

whee /(h)wē/ ▸*exclam.* used to express delight, excitement, or exhilaration: *as the car began to bump down the track he felt a lightening of his spirits—whee!* ▷natural exclamation: first recorded in English in the 1920s.

whee·dle /ˈ(h)wēdl/ ▸*v.* [*intrans.*] employ endearments or flattery to persuade someone to do something or give one something: *you can contrive to **wheedle your way** onto a court* | [with *direct speech*] *"Please, for my* *sake," he wheedled.* ■ [*trans.*] (**wheedle someone into doing something**) coax or persuade someone to do something. ■ [*trans.*] (**wheedle something out of**) coax or persuade (someone) to say or give something. ▷mid 17th cent.: perhaps from German *wedeln* 'cringe, fawn,' from *Wedel* 'tail, fan.' —**whee·dler** *n.* —**whee·dling·ly** *adv.*

wheel /(h)wēl/ ▶*n.* **1** a circular object that revolves on an axle and is fixed below a vehicle or other object to enable it to move easily over the ground. ■ a circular object that revolves on an axle and forms part of a machine. ■ (**the wheel**) used in reference to the cycle of a specified condition or set of events: *the final release from the wheel of life.* ■ (**the wheel**) *historical* a large wheel used as an instrument of punishment or torture, esp. by binding someone to it and breaking their limbs: *a man sentenced to be* ***broken on the wheel.*** **2** a machine or structure having a wheel as its essential part. ■ (**the wheel**) a steering wheel (used in reference to driving or steering a vehicle or vessel): *his crew knows when he wants to* ***take the wheel.*** ■ a vessel's propeller or paddle-wheel. ■ a device with a revolving disk or drum used in various games of chance. ■ a system, or a part of a system, regarded as a relentlessly moving machine: *the wheels of justice.* **3** (**wheels**) *informal* a car: *she's got wheels now.* ■ a bicycle. **4** a thing resembling a wheel in form or function, in particular a cheese made in the form of a disk. **5** an instance of wheeling; a turn or rotation. **6** *informal* short for BIG WHEEL.
▶*v.* **1** [*trans.*] push or pull (a vehicle with wheels): *the sea sled was* ***wheeled out*** *to the flight deck.* ■ [*trans.*] carry (someone or something) in or on a vehicle with wheels: *a young woman is wheeled into the operating room.* ■ (**wheel something in/on/out**) *informal* produce something that is unimpressive because it has been frequently seen or heard before: *the old journalistic arguments have to be wheeled out.* **2** [*intrans.*] (of a bird or aircraft) fly in a wide circle or curve: *the birds wheeled and dived.* ■ turn around quickly so as to face another way: *Robert* ***wheeled around*** *to see the face of Mr. Mafouz.* ■ turn or seem to turn on an axis or pivot: *the stars wheeled through the sky.* ▷Old English *hwēol* (noun), of Germanic origin, from an Indo-European root shared by Sanskrit *cakra* 'wheel, circle' and Greek *kuklos* 'circle.' —**wheeled** *adj.* [in *combination*] *a four-wheeled cart.* —**wheel·less** *adj.*
▶*PHRASES* □ **on wheels 1** by, or traveling by, car or bicycle: *a journey on wheels.* ■ (of a service) brought to one's home or district; mobile. **2** *informal* used to emphasize one's distaste or dislike of the person or thing mentioned: *she was a bitch on wheels.* □ **wheel and deal** engage in commercial or political scheming, esp. unscrupulously: [as *n.*] (**wheeling and dealing**) *the wheeling and dealing of the Wall Street boom years.* □ **the wheel of Fortune** the wheel that the deity Fortune is fabled to turn as a symbol of random luck or change. □ **wheels within wheels** used to indicate that a situation is complicated and affected by secret or indirect influences.

wheel and ax·le ▶*n.* a simple lifting machine consisting of a rope that unwinds from a wheel onto a cylindrical drum or shaft joined to the wheel to provide mechanical advantage.

wheel arch ▶*n.* an arch-shaped cavity in the body of a vehicle, which houses a wheel.

wheel·bar·row /'(h)wēl,barō/ ▶*n.* a small cart with a single wheel at the front and two supporting legs and two handles at the rear, used typically for carrying loads in building-work or gardening.
▶*v.* [*trans.*] carry (a load) in a wheelbarrow.

wheelbarrow

wheel·base /'(h)wēl,bās/ ▶*n.* the distance between the front and rear axles of a vehicle: [in *combination*] *a short-wheelbase model.*

wheel·chair /'(h)wēl,CHe(ə)r/ ▶*n.* a chair built on wheels for an invalid or disabled person, pushed by another person or propelled by the occupant, or motorized.

wheel dog ▶*n.* the dog harnessed nearest to the sleigh in a dog team.

Whee·ler /'(h)wēlər/, John Archibald (1911–), U.S. theoretical physicist. Wheeler worked with Niels Bohr on nuclear fission and collaborated with Richard Feynman on problems concerning the retarded effects of action at a distance. He coined the term **black hole** in 1968.

wheel·er /'(h)wēlər/ ▶*n.* **1** [in *combination*] a vehicle having a specified number of wheels: *a huge eighteen-wheeler truck.* **2** a wheelwright. **3** a horse harnessed next to the wheels of a cart and behind a leading horse.

wheel·er-deal·er (also **wheel·er and deal·er**) ▶*n.* a person who engages in commercial or political scheming. —**wheel·er-deal·ing** *n.*

Whee·ler Peak /'(h)wēlər/ a peak in the Sangre de Cristo Mountains, northeast of Taos, the highest peak in New Mexico at 13,161 feet (4,011 m)

wheel horse ▶*n.* a horse harnessed nearest the wheels of a vehicle. ■ *figurative* a responsible and hardworking person, esp. an experienced and conscientious member of a political party.

wheel·house /'(h)wēl,hous/ ▶*n.* a part of a boat or ship serving as a shelter for the person at the wheel.

wheel·ie /'(h)wēlē/ ▶*n. informal* a trick or maneuver whereby a bicycle or motorcycle is ridden for a short distance with the front wheel raised off the ground.

Whee·ling /'(h)wēliNG/ a historic industrial city in northern West Virginia, on the Ohio River; pop. 31,419.

wheel lock ▶*n. historical* a kind of gunlock having a steel wheel that rubbed against a flint. ■ a gun having such a gunlock.

wheel·man /'(h)wēl,mən/ ▶*n.* (*pl.* **-men**) a person who drives a car or takes the wheel of a boat. ■ a cyclist.

wheels·man /'(h)wēlzmən/ ▶*n.* (*pl.* **-men**) a person who steers a ship or boat.

wheel·spin /'(h)wēl,spin/ ▶*n.* rotation of a vehicle's wheels without traction.

wheel well ▶*n.* a recess in a vehicle in which a wheel is located.

wheel·wright /'(h)wēl,rīt/ ▶*n. chiefly historical* a person who makes or repairs wooden wheels.

wheeze /(h)wēz/ ▶*v.* [*intrans.*] (of a person) breathe with a whistling or rattling sound in the chest, as a result of obstruction in the air passages: *the illness often leaves her wheezing.* ■ [*trans.*] utter with such a sound: *he could barely wheeze out his pleas for a handout* | [with *direct speech*] *"Don't worry son," he wheezed.* ■ [*intrans.*] walk or move slowly with such a sound: *she wheezed up the hill toward them.* ■ (of a device) make an irregular rattling or spluttering sound: *the engine coughed, wheezed, and shrieked into life.*
▶*n.* [usu. in *sing.*] **1** a sound of or as of a person wheezing: *I talk with a wheeze.* **2** an old joke, story, aphorism, act, or routine: *the old wheeze about the diner complaining about the fly in his soup.* ■ *Brit., informal* a clever or amusing scheme, idea, or trick: *a new wheeze to help farmers.* ▷late Middle English: probably from Old Norse *hvæsa* 'to hiss.' —**wheez·er** *n.* —**wheez·ing·ly** *adv.*

wheez·y /'(h)wēzē/ ▶*adj.* making the sound of a person wheezing: *a wheezy laugh.* —**wheez·i·ly** /-əlē/ *adv.* —**wheez·i·ness** *n.*

whelk[1] /(h)welk/ ▶*n.* a predatory marine mollusk with a heavy, pointed spiral shell, some kinds of which are edible. • Family Buccinidae, class Gastropoda: *Buccinum* and other genera. ▷Old English *wioloc, weoloc,* of unknown origin; the spelling with *wh-* was perhaps influenced by WHELK[2].

whelk[1]

whelk[2] ▶*n. archaic* a pimple. ▷Old English *hwylca,* related to *hwelian* 'suppurate.'

whelm /(h)welm/ ▶*v.* [*trans.*] *archaic* or *poetic/literary* engulf, submerge, or bury (someone or something): *a swimmer whelmed in a raging storm.* ■ [*intrans.*] flow or heap up abundantly: *the brook whelmed up from its source.*
▶*n. archaic* or *poetic/literary* an act or instance of flowing or heaping up abundantly; a surge: *the whelm of the tide.* ▷Middle English: representing an Old English form parallel to *hwelfan* 'overturn (a vessel).'

whelp /(h)welp/ ▶*n.* a puppy. ■ a cub. ■ a boy or young man (often as a disparaging form of address). ■ (**whelps**) a set of projections on the barrel of a capstan or windlass, designed to reduce the slippage of a rope.
▶*v.* [*trans.*] (of a female dog) give birth to (a puppy): *Copper whelped seven puppies* | [*intrans.*] *a bitch due to whelp.* ▷Old English *hwelp* (noun), of Germanic origin; related to Dutch *welp* and German *Welf.*
▶*PHRASE* □ **in whelp** (of a female dog) pregnant.

when /(h)wen/ ▶*interrog. adv.* at what time: *when did you last see him?* | [with *prep.*] *since when have you been interested?* ■ how soon: *when can I see you?* ■ in what circumstances: *when would such a rule be justifiable?*
▶*relative adv.* at or on which (referring to a time or circumstance): *Saturday is the day when I get my hair done.*
▶*conj.* **1** at or during the time that: *I loved math when I was in school.* ■ after: *call me when you're finished.* ■ at any time that; whenever: *can you spare five minutes when it's convenient?* **2** after which; and just then (implying suddenness): *he had just drifted off to sleep when the phone rang.* **3** in view of the fact that; considering that: *why bother to paint it when you can photograph it with the same effect?* **4** although; whereas: *I'm saying it now when I should have told you long ago.* ▷Old English *hwanne, hwenne,* of Germanic origin; related to German *wenn* 'if,' *wann* 'when.'

whence /(h)wens/ (also **from whence**) ▶*interrog. adv. formal* or *archaic* from what place or source: *whence does Congress derive this power?*
▶*relative adv. formal* or *archaic* from which; from where: *the Ural mountains, whence the ore is procured.* ■ to the place from which: *he will be sent back whence he came.* ■ as a consequence of which: *whence it followed that the strategies were obsolete.* ▷Middle English *whennes,* from earlier *whenne* (from Old English *hwanon,* of Germanic origin) + **-s**[3] (later respelled *-ce* to denote the unvoiced sound).

USAGE Strictly speaking, **whence** means 'from what place,' as in ***whence** did you come?* Thus, the preposition **from** in *from whence did you come?* is redundant and its use is considered incorrect by some. The use with **from** is very common, though, and has been used by reputable writers since the 14th century. It is now broadly accepted in standard English.

whence·so·ev·er /,(h)wensō'evər/ ▶*relative adv. formal* or *archaic* from whatever place or source.

when·e'er /(h)wən'e(ə)r; (h)wen-/ *poetic/literary* ▶*contraction of* whenever.

when·ev·er /(h)wən'evər/ ▶*conj.* at whatever time; on whatever occasion (emphasizing a lack of restriction): *you can ask for help whenever you need it.* ■ every time that: *the springs in the armchair creak whenever I change position.*
▶*interrog. adv.* used for emphasis instead of "when" in questions, typically expressing surprise or confusion: *whenever shall we get there?*
▶*PHRASE* □ **or whenever** *informal* or at any time: *if you lay eyes on him, either tonight or tomorrow or whenever, call me right away.*

USAGE See usage at WHATEVER.

when-is·sued ▶*adj. Finance* of or relating to trading in securities that have not yet been issued.

when·so·e'er /,(h)wensō'e(ə)r/ *poetic/literary* ▶*contraction of* whensoever.

when·so·ev·er /,(h)wensō'evər/ ▶*conj.* & *adv.* formal term for WHENEVER.

where /(h)we(ə)r/ ▶*interrog. adv.* in or to what place or position: *where do you live?* | *where is she going?* | [with *prep.*] *where do you come from?* ■ in what direction or respect: *where does the argument lead?* ■ in or from what source: *where did you read that?* ■ in or to what situation or condition: *just where is all this leading us?*
▶*relative adv.* **1** at, in, or to which (used after reference to a place or situation): *I first saw him in Paris, where I lived in the early sixties.* **2** the place or situation in which: *this is where I live.* ■ in or to a place or situation in which: *sit where I can see you* | *where people were concerned, his threshold of boredom was low.* ■ in or to any place in which; wherever: *he was free to go where he liked.*
▶*conj. informal* **1** that: *do you see where the men in your life are emotionally unavailable to you?* | *I see where the hotel has changed hands again.* **2** whereas: *where some care-givers burn out, others become too involved.*
▶*n.* [(prec. by the)] the place; the scene of something (see WHEN *n.*). ▷Old English *hwǣr,* of Germanic origin; related to Dutch *waar* and German *wo.*

where·a·bouts /'(h)we(ə)rə,bouts/ ▶*interrog. adv.* where or approximately where: *whereabouts do you come from?*
▶*n.* [treated as *sing.* or *pl.*] the place where someone or something is: *his whereabouts remain secret.*

where·af·ter /(h)we(ə)r'aftər/ ▶*relative adv. formal* after which: *dinner was taken at a long wooden table, whereafter we sipped liqueurs in front of a roaring fire.*

where·as /(h)we(ə)r'az/ ▶*conj.* in contrast or comparison with the fact that: *you treat the matter lightly,*

W

whereas I myself was never more serious. ■ (esp. in legal preambles) taking into consideration the fact that.

USAGE See **usage** at **WHILE**.

where·at /(h)we(ə)r'at/ ▸*relative adv. & conj. archaic* or *formal* at which: *they demanded an equal share in the high command, whereat negotiations broke down.*

where·by /(h)we(ə)r'bī/ ▸*relative adv.* by which: *a system whereby people could vote by telephone.*

wher·e'er /(h)we(ə)r'e(ə)r/ *poetic/literary* ▸*contraction of* wherever.

where·fore /'(h)we(ə)r,fôr/ *archaic* ▸*interrog. adv.* for what reason: *she took an ill turn, but wherefore I cannot say.*
▸*relative adv. & conj.* as a result of which: [as *conj.*] *truly he cared for me, wherefore I title him with all respect.*
▸PHRASE □ **whys and wherefores** see **WHY**.

where·from /,(h)we(ə)r'frəm/ ▸*relative adv. archaic* from which or from where: *one day you may lose this pride of place wherefrom you now dominate.*

where·in /(h)we(ə)r'in/ *formal* ▸*adv.* **1** [*relative adv.*] in which: *the situation wherein the information will eventually be used.* **2** [*interrog. adv.*] in what place or respect?: *so wherein lies the difference?*

where·of /(h)we'räv; -'əv/ ▸*relative adv. formal* of what or which: *I know whereof I speak.*

where·on /(h)we(ə)r'än; -'ôn/ ▸*relative adv. archaic* on which: *the cliff side whereon I walked.*

where·so·e'er /,(h)we(ə)rsō'e(ə)r/ *poetic/literary* ▸*contraction of* wheresoever.

where·so·ev·er /,(h)we(ə)rsō'evər/ ▸*adv. & conj. formal* word for **WHEREVER**.

where·to /(h)we(ə)r'to͞o/ ▸*relative adv. archaic* or *formal* to which: *young ambition's ladder, whereto the climber-upward turns his face.*

where·up·on /,(h)we(ə)rə'pän/ ▸*conj.* immediately after which: *he qualified in February, whereupon he was promoted to sergeant.*

wher·ev·er /(h)we(ə)r'evər/ ▸*relative adv.* in or to whatever place (emphasizing a lack of restriction): *meet me wherever you like.* ■ in all places; regardless of where: *it should be available wherever you go to shop.*
▸*interrog. adv.* used for emphasis instead of "where" in questions, typically expressing surprise or confusion: *wherever can he have gone to?* See **usage** below.
▸*conj.* in every case when: *use whole grain breakfast cereals wherever possible.*
▸PHRASE □ **or wherever** *informal* or any similar place: *it is bound to have originated in Taiwan or wherever.*

USAGE In formal writing, **where ever**, in which *ever* is an intensifier of the question *where* (as distinct from **wherever** in the sense of 'anywhere') is written as two words: ***where ever** can he have gone?* See explanation in **usage** at **HOWEVER** and **WHATEVER**.

where·with /(h)we(ə)r'wiTH; -'wiT͟H/ ▸*relative adv. archaic* or *formal* with or by which: *the instrumental means wherewith the action is performed.*

where·with·al /'(h)we(ə)rwiT͟H,ôl; -wiTH-/ ▸*n.* [usu. with *infinitive*] (**the wherewithal**) the money or other means needed for a particular purpose: *they lacked the wherewithal to pay.*

wher·ry /'(h)werē/ ▸*n.* (*pl.* **-ries**) a light rowboat used chiefly for carrying passengers. ■ *Brit.* a large light barge. ▷late Middle English: of unknown origin. **—wher·ry·man** /'(h)werēmən/ *n.* (*pl.* **-men**).

whet /(h)wet/ ▸*v.* (**whet·ted, whet·ting**) [*trans.*] sharpen the blade of (a tool or weapon): *her husband is whetting his knife.* ■ excite or stimulate (someone's desire, interest, or appetite): *here's an extract to whet your appetite.*
▸*n. archaic* a thing that stimulates appetite or desire: *he swallowed his two dozen oysters as a whet.* ▷Old English *hwettan*, of Germanic origin; related to German *wetzen*, based on an adjective meaning 'sharp.' **—whet·ter** *n.* (*rare*).

wheth·er /'(h)weT͟Hər/ ▸*conj.* expressing a doubt or choice between alternatives: *he seemed undecided **whether** to go **or** stay* | *it is still not clear **whether or not** he realizes.* ■ expressing an inquiry or investigation (often used in indirect questions): *I'll see whether she's at home.* ■ indicating that a statement applies whichever of the alternatives mentioned is the case: *I'm going **whether** you like it **or not**.* ▷Old English *hwæther, hwether*, of Germanic origin; related to German *weder* 'neither.'
▸PHRASE □ **whether or no 1** whether or not: *the only issue arising would be whether or no the publication was defamatory.* **2** *archaic* in any case: *God help us, whether or no!*

USAGE On the difference between **whether** and **if**, see **usage** at **IF**.

whet·stone /'(h)wet,stōn/ ▸*n.* a fine-grained stone used for sharpening cutting tools.

whew /hyo͞o; hwyo͞o/ ▸*exclam.* used to express surprise, relief, or a feeling of being very hot or tired: *Whew—and I thought it was serious!* ▷late Middle English: imitative; compare with **PHEW**.

whey /(h)wā/ ▸*n.* the watery part of milk that remains after the formation of curds. ▷Old English *hwæg, hweg*, of Germanic origin; related to Dutch *wei*.

whey-faced ▸*adj.* (of a person) pale, esp. as a result of ill health, shock, or fear.

which /(h)wiCH/ ▸*interrog. pron. & adj.* asking for information specifying one or more people or things from a definite set: [as *pron.*] *which are the best varieties of grapes for long keeping?* | *which of the suspects murdered him?* | [as *adj.*] *which way is the wind blowing?*
▸*relative pron. & adj.* used referring to something previously mentioned when introducing a clause giving further information: [as *pron.*] *a conference in Vienna, which ended on Friday* | [after *prep.*] *it was a crisis for which he was totally unprepared* | [as *adj.*, after *prep.*] *your claim ought to succeed, **in which case** the damages will be substantial.* ▷Old English *hwilc*, from the Germanic bases of **WHO** and **ALIKE**.
▸PHRASE □ **which is which** used when two or more people or things are difficult to distinguish from each other: *there is no confusion as to which is which.*

USAGE In U.S. English, it is usually recommended that **which** be employed only for nonrestrictive (or nonessential) clauses: *the horse, which is in the paddock, is six years old* (the *which* clause contains a nonessential fact, noted in passing; the horse would be six years old wherever it was). A *that* clause is restrictive (or essential), as it identifies a particular thing: *the horse that is in the paddock is six years old* (not any horse, but the one in the paddock). See also **usage** at **RESTRICTIVE** and **THAT**.

which·a·way /'(h)wiCHə,wā/ ▸*interrog. adv. informal* or *dialect* **1** in which direction? **2** how? in which way?
▸*relative adv.* however; in whatever way.
▸PHRASE □ **every whichaway** in a disorderly fashion: *books are skewed and lounge against one another every whichaway.*

which·ev·er /,(h)wiCH'evər/ ▸*relative adj. & pron.* used to emphasize a lack of restriction in selecting one of a definite set of alternatives: [as *adj.*] *choose whichever brand you prefer* | [as *pron.*] *their pension should be increased annually in line with earnings or prices, whichever is the higher.* ■ regardless of which: [as *adj.*] *they were in a position to intercept him whichever way he ran* | [as *pron.*] *whichever they choose, we must accept it.*

which·so·ev·er /,(h)wiCHsō'evər/ ▸*adj. & pron. archaic* whichever: [as *pron.*] *on any occasion whichsoever it be.*

whick·er /'(h)wikər/ ▸*v.* [*intrans.*] **1** utter a half-suppressed laugh; snigger; titter: *a half-loony whicker of nerves.* ■ (of a horse) give a soft breathy whinny: *the palomino whickered when she saw him and stamped her foreleg.* **2** move with a sound as of something hurtling through or beating the air: *the soft whicker of the wind flowing through the July corn.*
▸*n.* **1** a snigger; a soft, breathy whinny. **2** the sound of something beating the air. ▷mid 17th cent. (in the sense 'to snigger, titter'): imitative.

whid·ah ▸*n.* archaic spelling of **WHYDAH**.

Whid·bey Is·land /'(h)widbē/ an island in northwestern Washington, north of Puget Sound.

whiff /(h)wif/ ▸*n.* **1** a smell that is only smelled briefly or faintly: *I **caught a whiff** of peachy perfume.* ■ [in *sing.*] an act of sniffing or inhaling, typically so as to determine or savor a scent: *one whiff of clothing and Fido was off.* ■ [in *sing.*] a trace or hint of something bad, menacing, or exciting: *here was a man with a whiff of danger about him.* **2** a puff or breath of air or smoke. **3** *informal* (chiefly in baseball or golf) an unsuccessful attempt to hit the ball.
▸*v.* **1** [*trans.*] get a brief or faint smell of: *he screwed up his nose as if he'd whiffed Limburger.* **2** [*intrans.*] *informal* (chiefly in baseball or golf) try unsuccessfully to hit the ball. ▷late 16th cent. (originally in the senses 'gust of wind' and 'inhalation of tobacco smoke,' also, as a verb, 'blow with a slight gust'): imitative.

whif·fle /'(h)wifəl/ ▸*v.* [*intrans.*] (of the wind) blow lightly in a specified direction: *as we walked, air began whiffling down off Bald Peak.* ■ move lightly as if blown by a puff of air: *the geese came whiffling down onto the grass.* ■ [*trans.*] blow or move (something) with or as if with a puff of air: *the mouse whiffled its whiskers.*
▸*n.* **1** a slight movement of air or the sound of such a movement. **2** (also **whif·fle cut**) *informal* a very short haircut worn by U.S. soldiers in World War II. ▷mid 16th cent.: frequentative (verb), diminutive (noun) of **WHIFF**.

whif·fle·tree /'(h)wifəl,trē/ ▸*n.* a singletree. ▷mid 19th cent.: variant of **WHIPPLETREE**.

Whig /(h)wig/ *historical* ▸*n.* **1** a member of the British reforming and constitutional party that sought the supremacy of Parliament and was eventually succeeded in the 19th century by the Liberal Party. **2** an American colonist who supported the American Revolution. ■ a member of an American political party in the 19th century, succeeded by the Republicans. **3** a 17th-century Scottish Presbyterian. **4** [as *adj.*] denoting a historian who interprets history as the continuing and inevitable victory of progress over reaction. ▷probably a shortening of Scots *whiggamore*, the nickname of 17th-cent. Scottish rebels, from *whig* 'to drive' + **MARE**[1]. **—Whig·ger·y** /-ərē/ *n.* **—Whig·gish** *adj.* **—Whig·gism** /-,izəm/ *n.*

while /(h)wīl/ ▸*n.* **1** a period of time: *we chatted **for a while*** | *she retired **a little while** ago.* ■ (**a while**) for some time: *can I keep it a while?* **2** (**the while**) at the same time; meanwhile: *he starts to draw, talking the while.* ■ *poetic/literary* during the time that: *beseeching him, the while his hand she wrung.*
▸*conj.* **1** during the time that; at the same time as: *nothing much changed while he was away.* **2** whereas (indicating a contrast): *one person wants out, while the other wants the relationship to continue.* ■ in spite of the fact that; although: *while I wouldn't recommend a night-time visit, by day the area is full of interest.*
▸*relative adv.* during which: *the period while the animal remains alive.*
▸*v.* [*trans.*] (often **while away the time**) pass time in a leisurely manner: *a diversion to while away the long afternoons.* ▷Old English *hwīl* 'period of time,' of Germanic origin; related to Dutch *wijl*, German *Weile*; the conjunction is an abbreviation of Old English *thā hwīle the* 'the while that.'
▸PHRASES □ **between whiles** *archaic* at intervals: *add potassium carbonate, shaking vigorously between whiles.* □ **worth one's while** worth the time or effort spent.

USAGE 1 **While** is sometimes used, without causing any misunderstandings, in the sense of **whereas** ('although,' 'by contrast,' 'in comparison with the fact that'). This usage is frowned on by some traditionalists, but **while** is sometimes preferable, as in contexts in which **whereas** might sound inappropriately formal: ***while** you say you like her, you've never stood up for her*). **Whereas** is preferable, however, for preventing ambiguity in contexts in which **while** might be read as referring to time, or might falsely suggest simultaneity: ***whereas** Burton promised to begin at once, he was delayed nine months for lack of funding*; ***whereas** Jonas was an excellent planter and cultivator, Julius was a master harvester.*
2 On the distinction between **awhile** and **a while**, see **usage** at **AWHILE**.
3 On the distinction between **worth while** and **worthwhile**, see **usage** at **WORTHWHILE**.

whiles /(h)wīlz/ ▸*conj.* archaic form of **WHILE**. ▷Middle English: originally in adverbs such as *somewhiles* 'formerly,' *otherwhiles* 'at times.'

while-you-wait ▸*adj.* [*attrib.*] (of a service) performed immediately: *a while-you-wait oil change.*

whi·lom /'(h)wīləm/ *archaic* ▸*adv.* formerly; in the past: *the wistful eyes which whilom glanced down upon the fields.*
▸*adj.* former; erstwhile: *a whilom circus acrobat.* ▷Old English *hwīlum* 'at times,' dative plural of *hwīl* (see **WHILE**).

whilst /(h)wīlst/ ▸*conj. & relative adv. chiefly Brit.* while. ▷late Middle English: from **WHILES** + *-t* as in **AGAINST**.

whim /(h)wim/ ▸*n.* **1** a sudden desire or change of mind, esp. one that is unusual or unexplained: *she bought it **on a whim*** | *he appeared and disappeared **at whim**.* **2** *archaic* a windlass for raising ore or water from a mine. ▷late 17th cent.: of unknown origin. Sense 2 (mid 18th cent.) is a transferred use.

whim·brel /'(h)wimbrəl/ ▸*n.* a small migratory curlew of northern Eurasia and northern Canada, with a striped crown and a trilling call. • *Numenius phaeopus*, family Scolopacidae. ▷mid 16th cent.: from

Pronunciation Key ə *ago*; ər *over*; 'ə *or* ,ə *up*; 'ər *or* ,ər *fur*; a *hat*; ā *rate*; ä *car*; CH *chew*; e *let*; ē *see*; e(ə)r *air*; i *fit*; ī *by*; i(ə)r *ear*; NG *sing*; ō *go*; ô *for*; oi *boy*; o͝o *good*; o͞o *goo*; ou *out*; SH *she*; TH *thin*; T͟H *then*; (h)w *why*; ZH *vision*

WHIMPER or synonymous dialect *whimp* (imitative of the bird's call) + -REL.

whim·per /ˈ(h)wimpər/ ▸v. [*intrans.*] (of a person or animal) make a series of low, feeble sounds expressive of fear, pain, or discontent: *a child in a bed nearby began to whimper.* ■ [with *direct speech*] say something in a low, feeble voice expressive of such emotions: *"He's not dead, is he?" she whimpered.*
▸n. a low, feeble sound expressive of such emotions: *she gave a little whimper of protest.* ■ (**a whimper**) a feeble or anticlimactic tone or ending: *their first appearance in the top flight ended with a whimper rather than a bang.* [with allusion to T. S. Eliot's "This is the way the world ends Not with a bang but a whimper" (*Hollow Men*, 1925).] ▹early 16th cent.: from dialect *whimp* 'to whimper,' of imitative origin. —**whim·per·er** *n.* —**whim·per·ing·ly** *adv.*

whim·si·cal /ˈ(h)wimzikəl/ ▸*adj.* **1** playfully quaint or fanciful, esp. in an appealing and amusing way: *a whimsical sense of humor.* **2** acting or behaving in a capricious manner: *the whimsical arbitrariness of autocracy.* —**whim·si·cal·i·ty** /ˌ(h)wimziˈkalitē/ *n.* —**whim·si·cal·ly** /-ik(ə)lē/ *adv.*

whim·sy /ˈ(h)wimzē/ (also **whim·sey**) ▸n. (*pl.* **-sies** or **-seys**) playfully quaint or fanciful behavior or humor: *the film is an awkward blend of whimsy and moralizing.* ■ a whim. ■ a thing that is fanciful or odd: *the stone carvings and whimsies.* ▹early 17th cent. (in the sense 'caprice'): probably based on WHIM-WHAM.

whim-wham ▸n. *archaic* a quaint and decorative object; a trinket. ■ a whim: *the follies and whim-whams of the metropolis.* ▹early 16th cent.: fanciful reduplication.

whin[1] /(h)win/ ▸n. *chiefly N. English* furze; gorse. ▹late Middle English: probably of Scandinavian origin; compare with Swedish *ven* 'bent grass.'

whin[2] (also **whin·stone**) ▸n. *Brit.* hard, dark basaltic rock such as that of the Whin Sill in Northern England. ▹Middle English: of unknown origin.

whin·chat /ˈwinˌCHat/ ▸n. a small Eurasian and North African songbird related to the stonechat, with a brown back and orange-buff underparts. • *Saxicola rubetra*, subfamily Turdinae, family Muscicapidae. ▹late 17th cent.: from WHIN[1] + CHAT[2].

whine /(h)wīn/ ▸n. a long, high-pitched complaining cry: *the dog gave a small whine.* ■ a long, high-pitched unpleasant sound: *the whine of the engine.* ■ a complaining tone of voice. ■ a feeble or petulant complaint: *a constant whine about the quality of public services.*
▸v. [*intrans.*] give or make a long, high-pitched complaining cry or sound: *the dog whined and scratched at the back door.* ■ [*reporting verb*] complain in a feeble or petulant way: [*intrans.*] *the waitress whined about the increased work* | [with *direct speech*] *"What about him?" he whined.* ▹Old English *hwīnan* 'whistle through the air,' related to WHINGE. The noun dates from the mid 17th cent. —**whin·er** *n.* —**whin·ing·ly** *adv.* —**whin·y** *adj.*

whinge /(h)winj/ *Brit., informal* ▸v. (**whinge·ing**) [*intrans.*] complain persistently and in a peevish or irritating way: *stop whingeing and get on with it!*
▸n. an act of complaining in such a way. ▹late Old English *hwinsian*, of Germanic origin; related to German *winseln*; compare with WHINE. —**whinge·ing·ly** *adv.* —**whing·er** *n.* —**whing·y** /-jē/ *adj.*

whin·ny /ˈ(h)winē/ ▸n. (*pl.* **-nies**) a gentle, high-pitched neigh.
▸v. (**-nies, -nied**) [*intrans.*] (of a horse) make such a sound: *the pony whinnied and tossed his head happily.* ▹late Middle English (as a verb): imitative. The noun dates from the early 19th cent.

whin·stone /ˈ(h)winˌstōn/ ▸n. another term for WHIN[2].

whip /(h)wip/ ▸n. **1** a strip of leather or length of cord fastened to a handle, used for flogging or beating a person or for urging on an animal. ■ *figurative* a thing causing mental or physical pain or acting as a stimulus to action: *councils are attempting to find new sites* ***under the whip*** *of a powerful agency.* **2** a thing or person resembling a whip in form or function: *a licorice whip.* ■ a utensil such as a whisk or an eggbeater for beating cream, eggs, or other food. ■ a slender, unbranched shoot or plant. ■ short for WHIPPER-IN. ■ short for WHIP ANTENNA. ■ [with *adj.*] a scythe for cutting specified crops: *a grass whip.* ■ a rope-and-pulley hoisting apparatus. **3** an official of a political party appointed to maintain discipline among its members in Congress or Parliament, esp. so as to ensure attendance and voting in debates. ■ *Brit.* a written notice from such an official requesting attendance for voting. ■ (**the whip**) *Brit.* party membership of a Member of Parliament or other elected body: *he asked for the whip to be withdrawn from them.* **4** a dessert consisting of cream or eggs beaten into a light fluffy mass with fruit, chocolate, or other ingredients. **5** [in *sing.*] a violent striking or beating movement. ■ [in *sing.*] in metaphorical use referring to something that acts as a stimulus to work or action: *the governor* ***cracked the whip*** *in the city.*
▸v. (**whipped, whip·ping**) [*trans.*] **1** beat (a person or animal) with a whip or similar instrument, esp. as a punishment or to urge them on. ■ (of a flexible object or rain or wind) strike or beat violently: *the wind whipped their faces* | [*intrans.*] *ferns and brambles* ***whipped at*** *him.* ■ beat (cream, eggs, or other food) into a froth. ■ (**whip someone into**) urge or rouse someone into (a specified state or position): *the radio host whipped his listeners into a frenzy* | *the city had been* ***whipped into shape.*** ■ *informal* (of a player or team) defeat (a person or team) heavily in a sporting contest. **2** [*intrans.*] move fast or suddenly in a specified direction: *I whipped around the corner.* ■ [*trans.*] take out or move (something) fast or suddenly: *he whipped out his revolver and shot him.* **3** bind (something) with spirally wound twine. ■ sew or gather (something) with overcast stitches.
▸*phrasal v.* □ **whip in** act as whipper-in. □ **whip something out** (or **off**) write something hurriedly: *you'll find the software ideal for whipping out memos and proposals.* □ **whip someone up** deliberately excite someone into having a strong feeling or reaction: *Dad had managed to* ***whip himself up into*** *a fantastic rage.* □ **whip something up 1** cause water, sand, etc., to rise up and be flung about in a violent manner: *the sea was whipped up by a force-nine gale.* ■ stimulate a particular feeling in someone: *we tried hard to whip up interest in the products.* **2** make or prepare something, typically something to eat, very quickly. ▹Middle English: probably from Middle Low German and Middle Dutch *wippen* 'swing, leap, dance,' from a Germanic base meaning 'move quickly.' The noun is partly from the verb, reinforced by Middle Low German *wippe* 'quick movement.' —**whip·like** /-ˌlīk/ *adj.* —**whip·per** *n.*
▸*PHRASES* □ **the whip hand** a position of power or control over someone. □ **whip someone's ass** see ASS[2].

whip an·ten·na ▸n. an antenna in the form of a long flexible wire or rod with a connection at one end.

whip·cord /ˈ(h)wipˌkôrd/ ▸n. **1** thin, tough, tightly twisted cord used for making the flexible end part of whips. **2** a closely woven ribbed worsted fabric, used for making garments such as jodhpurs.

whip·lash /ˈ(h)wipˌlaSH/ ▸n. **1** [usu. in *sing.*] the lashing action of a whip: *figurative he cringed before the icy whiplash of Curtis's tongue.* ■ the flexible part of a whip or something resembling it. **2** injury caused by a severe jerk to the head, typically in a motor-vehicle accident.
▸v. [*trans.*] jerk or jolt (someone or something) suddenly, typically so as to cause injury: *the force of impact had whiplashed the man's head.* ■ [*intrans.*] move suddenly and forcefully, like a whip being cracked: *he rammed the yacht, sending its necklace of lights whiplashing from the bridge.*

whip pan ▸n. a camera panning movement fast enough to give a blurred picture.
▸v. (**whip-pan**) [*intrans.*] pan quickly to give a blurred picture.

whipped /(h)wipt/ ▸*adj.* **1** [*attrib.*] having been flogged or beaten with a whip: *a whipped dog.* ■ [*predic.*] *informal* worn out; exhausted. **2** (of cream, eggs, or other food) beaten into a froth.

whip·per-in ▸n. (*pl.* **whip·pers-in**) a huntsman's assistant who brings straying hounds back into the pack.

whip·per·snap·per /ˈ(h)wipərˌsnapər/ ▸n. *informal* a young and inexperienced person considered to be presumptuous or overconfident. ▹late 17th cent.: perhaps representing *whipsnapper*, expressing noise and unimportance.

whip·pet /ˈ(h)wipit/ ▸n. a dog of a small slender breed originally produced as a cross between the greyhound and the terrier or spaniel, bred for racing. ▹early 17th cent.: partly from obsolete *whippet* 'move briskly.'

whip·ping /ˈ(h)wipiNG/ ▸n. **1** a thrashing or beating with a whip or similar implement: *she saw scars on his back from the whippings* | *whipping was to be abolished as a punishment* **2** cord or twine used to bind or cover a rope.

whip·ping boy ▸n. a person who is blamed or punished for the faults or incompetence of others. ▹extended use of the original term (mid 17th cent.) denoting a boy educated with a young prince or other royal person and punished instead of him.

whip·ping cream ▸n. fairly thick cream containing enough butterfat to make it suitable for whipping.

whip·ping post ▸n. *historical* a post to which offenders were tied in order to be whipped as a public punishment.

whip·pit /ˈ(h)wipit/ ▸n. a small container of nitrous oxide intended for home use in whipped cream charging bottles but often used as an inhalant.

whip·ple·tree /ˈ(h)wipəlˌtrē/ ▸n. archaic term for SINGLETREE. ▹mid 18th cent.: apparently from WHIP + TREE.

whip·poor·will /ˈ(h)wipərˌwil/ (also **whip-poor-will**) ▸n. a North and Central American nightjar with a distinctive call. • *Caprimulgus vociferus*, family Caprimulgidae. ▹early 18th cent.: imitative of its call.

whip·py /ˈ(h)wipē/ ▸*adj.* flexible; springy: *new growths of whippy sapling twigs.* —**whip·pi·ness** *n.*

whip·saw /ˈ(h)wipˌsô/ ▸n. a saw with a narrow blade and a handle at both ends, used typically by two people.
▸v. (*past part.* **-sawn** or **-sawed**) [*trans.*] cut with a whipsaw: *he was whipsawing lumber.* ■ *informal* subject to two difficult situations or opposing pressures at the same time: *the army has been whipsawed by a shrinking budget and a growing pool of recruits.* ■ *informal* compel to do something. ■ (usu. **be whipsawed**) *informal Stock Market* subject to a double loss, as when buying a security before the price falls and selling before the price rises. ■ cheat or beat (someone) in two ways at once or by the collusion of two others.

whip scor·pi·on ▸n. an arachnid that resembles a scorpion, with stout pincerlike mouthparts and a long, slender taillike appendage, living in leaf litter and under stones in tropical and semitropical regions. • Order Uropygi.

whip snake ▸n. any of a number of slender, fast-moving snakes that often feed on lizards and catch their prey by pursuing it, in particular: • a harmless snake found in Eurasia, America, and Africa (*Coluber* and other genera, family Colubridae, including the Eurasian *C. viridiflavus*). • a venomous Australian snake (*Desmansia* and other genera, family Elapidae, including the widespread *D. psammophis*).

whip·stitch /ˈ(h)wipˌstiCH/ ▸n. an overcast stitch.
▸v. [*trans.*] sew (something) with such stitches.

whip·stock /ˈ(h)wipˌstäk/ ▸n. the handle of a whip.

whip·tail /ˈ(h)wipˌtāl/ (also **whip·tail liz·ard**) ▸n. a slender long-tailed American lizard with an alert manner and a jerky gait. • Genus *Cnemidophorus*, family Teiidae: several species.

whip·worm /ˈ(h)wipˌwərm/ ▸n. a parasitic nematode worm with a stout posterior and slender anterior part, esp. one that infests the intestines of domestic animals. • Genus *Trichuris*, class Aphasmida (or Adenophorea).

whir /(h)wər/ (also **whirr**) ▸v. (**whirred, whir·ring**) [*intrans.*] (esp. of a machine or a bird's wings) make a low, continuous, regular sound: *the ceiling fans whirred in the smoky air.*
▸n. a sound of such a type: *the whir of the projector.* ▹late Middle English (in the sense 'move with a whirring sound'): probably of Scandinavian origin; compare with WHIRL.

whirl /(h)wərl/ ▸v. move or cause to move rapidly around and around: [*intrans.*] *leaves whirled in eddies of wind* | [*trans.*] *I* ***whirled*** *her* ***around*** *the dance floor.* ■ move or cause to move rapidly: [*intrans.*] *Sybil stood waving as they whirled past* | [*trans.*] *he was whirled into the bushes.* ■ [*intrans.*] (of the head, mind, or senses) seem to spin around: *Kate made her way back to the office, her mind whirling.* ■ [*intrans.*] (of thoughts or mental images) follow each other in bewildering succession: *a kaleidoscope of images whirled through her brain.*
▸n. [in *sing.*] a rapid movement around and around. ■ frantic activity of a specified kind: *the event was all part of the mad social whirl.* ■ [with *adj.*] a specified kind of candy or cookie with a spiral shape: *a hazelnut whirl.* ▹Middle English: the verb probably from Old Norse *hvirfla* 'turn around'; the noun partly from Middle Low German, Middle Dutch *wervel* 'spindle,' or from Old Norse *hvirfill* 'circle,' from a Germanic base meaning 'rotate.' —**whirl·er** *n.* —**whirl·ing·ly** *adv.*
▸*PHRASES* □ **give something a whirl** *informal* give something a try. □ **in a whirl** in a state of confusion.

whirl·i·gig /ˈ(h)wərlēˌgig/ ▸n. **1** a toy that spins around, for example, a top or a pinwheel. ■ another term for MERRY-GO-ROUND. **2** [in *sing.*] a thing regarded as hectic or constantly changing: *the whirligig of time.* **3** (also **whirl·i·gig bee·tle**) a small black predatory beetle that swims rapidly in circles on the surface of still or slow-moving water and dives when alarmed. • Family Gyrinidae: *Gyrinus* and other genera. ▷late Middle English: from WHIRL + obsolete *gig* 'a top.'

whirl·ing der·vish ▸*n.* see DERVISH.

whirl·ing dis·ease ▸*n.* a disease of juvenile trout and salmon caused by a parasitic protozoan, affecting the balance of the fish and causing it to swim with a whirling motion. • The protozoan is *Myxobolus cerebralis*, phylum Sporozoa.

whirl·pool /ˈ(h)wərl,po͞ol/ ▸*n.* a rapidly rotating mass of water in a river or sea into which objects may be drawn, typically caused by the meeting of conflicting currents. ■ *figurative* a turbulent situation from which it is hard to escape: *he was drawing her down into an emotional whirlpool.* ■ (also **whirl·pool bath**) a heated pool in which hot, typically aerated water is continuously circulated.

whirl·wind /ˈ(h)wərl,wind/ ▸*n.* a column of air moving rapidly around and around in a cylindrical or funnel shape. ■ used in similes and metaphors to describe a very energetic or tumultuous person or process: *a whirlwind of activity* [as *adj.*] *a whirlwind romance.*

▸*PHRASE* □ (**sow the wind and**) **reap the whirlwind** suffer serious consequences as a result of one's actions. [with biblical allusion to Hos. 8:7.]

whirl·y·bird /ˈ(h)wərlē,bərd/ ▸*n. informal* a helicopter.

whirr ▸*n.* & *v.* variant spelling of WHIR.

whisht /(h)wisHt/ (also **whist**) ▸*exclam. chiefly Scottish Irish* hush (used to demand silence): *"Whisht, child. Away and do what you're told."* ▷natural exclamation: first recorded in English in the mid 16th cent.

▸*PHRASE* □ **hold one's whisht** keep silent.

whisk /(h)wisk/ ▸*v.* **1** [*trans.*] take or move (someone or something) in a particular direction suddenly and quickly: *his jacket was whisked away for dry cleaning.* ■ move (something) through the air with a light, sweeping movement: *hippopotamuses spread their scents by whisking their tails.* **2** [*trans.*] beat or stir (a substance, esp. cream or eggs) with a light, rapid movement. **3** brush with a whisk broom.

▸*n.* **1** a utensil for whipping eggs or cream. **2** short for WHISK BROOM. **3** (also **fly whisk**) a bunch of grass, twigs, or bristles for removing dust or flies. **4** [in *sing.*] a brief, rapid action or movement: *a whisk around St. Basil's cathedral.* ▷late Middle English: of Scandinavian origin.

whisk n. 1

whisk broom ▸*n.* a small, stiff, short-handled broom used esp. to brush clothing.

whisk·er /ˈ(h)wiskər/ ▸*n.* **1** a long projecting hair or bristle growing from the face or snout of many mammals. ■ (**whiskers**) the hair growing on a man's face, esp. on his cheeks. ■ a single crystal of a material in the form of a filament with no dislocations. **2** (a **whisker**) *informal* a very small amount: *they won the election by a whisker.* **3** a spar for extending the clews of a sail so that it can catch more wind. ▷late Middle English (originally denoting a bundle of feathers, twigs, etc., used for whisking): from the verb WHISK + -ER[1]. —**whiskered** *adj.* —**whiskery** *adj.*

▸*PHRASE* □ **within a whisker of** *informal* extremely close or near to doing, achieving, or suffering something.

whis·key /ˈ(h)wiskē/ ▸*n.* (*pl.* **-keys**) **1** (also **whis·ky** (*pl.* **-kies**)) a spirit distilled from malted grain, esp. barley or rye. **2** a code word representing the letter W, used in radio communication. ▷early 18th cent.: abbreviation of obsolete *whiskybae*, variant of USQUEBAUGH.

USAGE Is it **whiskey** or **whisky**? Note that the British and Canadian spelling is without the *e*, so that properly one would write of ***Scotch whisky*** or ***Canadian whisky***, but ***Kentucky bourbon whiskey*** or ***Irish whiskey***.

whis·key jack ▸*n. informal* another term for GRAY JAY.

whis·key sour ▸*n.* a drink consisting of whiskey mixed with sugar and lemon or lime juice.

whis·per /ˈ(h)wispər/ ▸*v.* [*intrans.*] speak very softly using one's breath without one's vocal cords, esp. for the sake of privacy: *Alison was whispering in his ear* | [*trans.*] *he managed to whisper a faint goodbye* | [with *direct speech*] *"Are you all right?" he whispered.* ■ *poetic/literary* (of leaves, wind, or water) rustle or murmur softly. ■ (**be whispered**) be rumored: *it was whispered that he would soon die.*

▸*n.* a soft or confidential tone of voice; a whispered word or phrase: *she spoke in a whisper.* ■ *poetic/literary* a soft rustling or murmuring sound: *the thunder of the surf became a muted whisper.* ■ a rumor or piece of gossip: *whispers of a blossoming romance.* ■ [usu. in *sing.*] a slight trace; a hint: *he didn't show even a whisper of interest.* ▷Old English *hwisprian*, of Germanic origin; related to German *wispeln*, from the imitative base of WHISTLE. —**whis·per·er** *n.* —**whis·per·y** *adj.*

whis·per·ing cam·paign ▸*n.* a systematic circulation of a rumor, typically in order to damage someone's reputation.

whis·per·ing gal·ler·y ▸*n.* a gallery or dome with acoustic properties such that a faint sound may be heard around its entire circumference.

whist[1] /(h)wist/ ▸*n.* a card game, usually for two pairs of players, in which points are scored according to the number of tricks won. ▷mid 17th cent. (earlier as *whisk*): perhaps from WHISK (with reference to whisking away the tricks); perhaps associated with WHIST[2].

whist[2] ▸*exclam.* variant spelling of WHISHT.

whis·tle /ˈ(h)wisəl/ ▸*n.* a clear, high-pitched sound made by forcing breath through a small hole between partly closed lips, or between one's teeth. ■ a similar sound, esp. one made by a bird, machine, or the wind. ■ an instrument used to produce such a sound, esp. for giving a signal.

▸*v.* **1** [*intrans.*] emit a clear, high-pitched sound by forcing breath through a small hole between one's lips or teeth: *the audience cheered and whistled* | [as *n.*] (**whistling**) *I awoke to their cheerful whistling* | [as *adj.*] (**whistling**) *a whistling noise.* ■ express surprise, admiration, or derision by making such a sound: *Bob whistled. "You look beautiful!" he said.* ■ [*trans.*] produce (a tune) in such a way. ■ (esp. of a bird or machine) produce a similar sound: *the kettle began to whistle.* ■ [*intrans.*] produce such a sound by moving rapidly through the air or a narrow opening: *the wind was whistling down the chimney.* ■ blow an instrument that makes such a sound, esp. as a signal: *the referee did not whistle for a foul.* ■ [*trans.*] (**whistle someone/something up**) summon something or someone by making such a sound. **2** (**whistle for**) wish for or expect (something) in vain: *you can go home and whistle for your wages.* ▷Old English *(h)wistlian* (verb), *(h)wistle* (noun), of Germanic origin; imitative and related to Swedish *vissla* 'to whistle.'

▸*PHRASES* □ **blow the whistle on** *informal* bring an illicit activity to an end by informing on the person responsible. □ (**as**) **clean as a whistle** extremely clean or clear. ■ *informal* free of incriminating evidence: *the cops raided the warehouse but the place was clean as a whistle.* □ **whistle something down the wind** let something go; abandon something. ■ turn a trained hawk loose by casting it off with the wind. □ **whistle in the dark** pretend to be unafraid. □ **whistle in the wind** try unsuccessfully to influence something that cannot be changed.

whis·tle-blow·er (also **whis·tle·blow·er**) ▸*n.* a person who informs on someone engaged in an illicit activity. —**whis·tle-blow·ing** *n.*

Whis·tler /ˈ(h)wislər/, James (Abbott) McNeill (1834–1903), U.S. painter and etcher. He mainly painted in one or two colors and sought to achieve harmony of color and tone. Notable works: *Arrangement in Gray and Black: The Artist's Mother* (portrait known as *Whistler's Mother*, 1872) and *Old Battersea Bridge: Nocturne—Blue and Gold* (*c.*1872–75).

whis·tler /ˈ(h)wis(ə)lər/ ▸*n.* **1** a person who whistles. ■ an atmospheric radio disturbance heard as a whistle that falls in pitch, caused by lightning. **2** a robust Australasian and Indonesian songbird with a strong and typically hooked bill and a loud melodious call. Also called THICKHEAD. • Family Pachycephalidae: four genera, in particular *Pachycephala*, and many species. **3** another term for HOARY MARMOT.

whis·tle-stop ▸*adj.* [*attrib.*] very fast and with only brief pauses: *a whistle-stop tour of Britain.*

▸*n.* a small unimportant town on a railroad. ■ a brief pause in a tour by a politician for an electioneering speech.

whis·tling duck ▸*n.* a long-legged duck with an upright stance and a whistling call, often perching on branches. Also called TREE DUCK. • Genus *Dendrocygna*, family Anatidae: several species.

whis·tling swan ▸*n.* a bird of the North American race of the tundra swan, breeding in northern Canada and overwintering on the coasts of the U.S. • *Cygnus columbianus columbianus*, family Anatidae.

whit /(h)wit/ ▸*n.* [in *sing.*] a very small part or amount: *the last whit of warmth was drawn off by the setting sun.* ▷late Middle English: apparently an alteration of obsolete *wight* 'small amount.'

▸*PHRASES* □ **every whit** wholly: *my mother was fond of her and I shall be every whit as fond.* □ **not** (or **never**) **a whit** not at all: *Sara had not changed a whit.*

White[1] /(h)wīt/, Byron Raymond (1917–2002), U.S. Supreme Court associate justice 1962–93. Appointed to the Court by President Kennedy, he was considered a moderate, or centrist, and was often the swing vote when the Court was evenly divided. Before becoming a lawyer in 1946, he played professional football and studied at Oxford University as a Rhodes scholar.

White[2], E(lwyn) B(rooks) (1899–1985), U.S. writer. He was a chief contributor to the *New Yorker* magazine from 1926 and *Harper's* magazine 1938–43 and the author of the children's classics *Stuart Little* (1945), *Charlotte's Web* (1952), and *The Trumpet of the Swan* (1970).

White[3], Edward Douglass, Jr. (1845–1921), U.S. chief justice 1910–21. Before being appointed to the Court as an associate justice 1894–1910 by President Cleveland, he served as a U.S. senator from Louisiana 1891–94. Appointed chief justice by President Taft, he was the first associate justice to go on to that higher post. He was noted for his work on antitrust legislation.

White[4], Edward H., see GRISSOM.

White[5], Patrick (Victor Martindale) (1912–90), Australian novelist, born in Britain. He is especially noted for the novels *The Tree of Man* (1955) and *Voss* (1957). Nobel Prize for Literature (1973).

White[6], T. H. (1906–64), British novelist, born in India; full name *Terence Hanbury White.* He is best known for the tetralogy *The Once and Future King*, his reworking of the Arthurian legend, that began with *The Sword in the Stone* (1938).

White[7], Theodore H. (1915–86), U.S. journalist and historian. He is best known for *The Making of the President 1960* (Pulitzer Prize, 1962). Other works include *In Search of History* (1978) and *America in Search of Itself* (1982).

white /(h)wīt/ ▸*adj.* **1** of the color of milk or fresh snow, due to the reflection of most wavelengths of visible light; the opposite of black: *a sheet of white paper.* ■ approaching such a color; very pale: *her face was white with fear.* ■ *figurative* morally or spiritually

W

James MacNeil Whistler
portrait by Walter Greaves, 1877

Pronunciation Key ə ago; ər over; ˈə or ˌə up; ˈər or ˌər fur; a hat; ā rate; ä car; CH chew; e let; ē see; e(ə)r air; i fit; ī by; i(ə)r ear; NG sing; ō go; ô for; oi boy; o͝o good; o͞o goo; ou out; SH she; TH thin; T̲H̲ then; (h)w why; ZH vision

pure; innocent and untainted: *he is as pure and white as the driven snow.* ■ (of a plant) having white flowers or pale-colored fruit. ■ (of a tree) having light-colored bark. ■ (of wine) made from white grapes, or dark grapes with the skins removed, and having a yellowish color. ■ *Brit.* (of coffee or tea) served with milk or cream. ■ (of glass) transparent; colorless. ■ (of bread) made from a light-colored, sifted, or bleached flour. **2** (also **White**) belonging to or denoting a human group having light-colored skin (chiefly used of peoples of European extraction): *a white farming community.* ■ of or relating to such people: *white Australian culture.* **3** *historical* counter-revolutionary or reactionary. Contrasted with RED (sense 2).

▸*n.* **1** white color or pigment: *garnet-red flowers flecked with white | the woodwork was an immaculate white.* ■ white clothes or material: *he was dressed from head to foot in white.* ■ (**whites**) white clothes, esp. as worn for playing tennis, or as naval uniform, or in the context of washing: *wash whites separately.* ■ white wine. ■ (**White**) the player of the white pieces in chess or checkers. ■ the white pieces in chess. ■ a white thing, in particular the white ball (the cue ball) in billiards. ■ the outer part (white when cooked) that surrounds the yolk of an egg; the albumen. ■ white bread: *tuna on white.* **2** the visible pale part of the eyeball around the iris. **3** (also **White**) a member of a light-skinned people, esp. one of European extraction. **4** [with *adj.*] a white or cream butterfly that has dark veins or spots on the wings. It can be a serious crop pest. • *Pieris* and other genera, family Pieridae. See also CABBAGE WHITE.

▸*v.* [*trans.*] *archaic* paint or turn (something) white: *your passion hath whited your face.*

▸*phrasal v.* □ **white out** (of vision) become impaired by exposure to sudden bright light. ■ (of a person) lose color vision as a prelude to losing consciousness. □ **white something out 1** obliterate a mistake with white correction fluid. ■ cover one's face or facial blemishes completely with makeup. **2** impair someone's vision with a sudden bright light. ▷late Old English *hwīt*, of Germanic origin; related to Dutch *wit* and German *weiss*, also to WHEAT. **—white·ly** *adv.* **—white·ness** *n.* **—whit·ish** *adj.*

▸*PHRASES* □ **bleed someone/something white** drain someone or something of wealth or resources. □ **whited sepulcher** *poetic/literary* a hypocrite. [with biblical allusion to Matt. 23:27.] □ **white man's burden** the task that white colonizers believed they had to impose their civilization on the black inhabitants of their colonies. [from Rudyard Kipling's *The White Man's Burden* (1899).] □ **whiter than white** extremely white. ■ morally beyond reproach.

white ad·mi·ral ▸*n.* a North American butterfly that has black wings bearing a broad white band and a marginal row of blue dashes. • *Limenitis arthemis*, subfamily Limenitinae, family Nymphalidae. See RED-SPOTTED PURPLE.

white ant ▸*n.* another term for TERMITE.

White Ar·my ▸*n.* any of the armies that opposed the Bolsheviks during the Russian Civil War of 1918–21.

white ar·se·nic ▸*n.* an extremely toxic soluble white solid made by burning arsenic. • Alternative name: **arsenic trioxide**; chem. formula: As_2O_3.

white·bait /ˈ(h)wīt,bāt/ ▸*n.* the small silvery-white young of herrings, sprats, and similar marine fish, eaten in numbers as food.

white bal·ance ▸*n.* the color balance on a video camera. ■ a control or system for adjusting this.

white bass /bās/ ▸*n.* a North American freshwater bass with dark horizontal stripes. • *Morone chrysops*, family Percichthyidae.

White Bear Lake a city in southeastern Minnesota, northeast of St. Paul; pop. 24,704.

white belt ▸*n.* a white belt worn by a beginner in judo or karate. ■ a person wearing such a belt.

white birch ▸*n.* a birch tree with white bark, esp. the paper birch or the European silver birch.

white blood cell ▸*n.* less technical term for LEUKOCYTE.

white·board /ˈ(h)wīt,bôrd/ ▸*n.* a wipeable board with a white surface used for teaching or presentations. ■ *Computing* an area on a display screen common to several users, on which they can write and draw. As a teleconferencing tool, it enables visual communication.

white book ▸*n.* a book of rules, standards, or records, esp. an official government report, bound in white.

white-bread ▸*adj. informal* of, belonging to, or representative of the white middle classes; not progressive, radical, or innovative: *inoffensive white-bread comedies.*

white bry·o·ny ▸*n.* see BRYONY (sense 1).

white·cap /ˈ(h)wīt,kap/ ▸*n.* a small wave with a foamy crest.

white ce·dar ▸*n.* a North American tree of the cypress family. • *Thuja* and other genera, family Cupressaceae: several species, in particular the **northern white cedar** (*T. occidentalis*), which yields timber and medicinal oil.

white cell ▸*n.* less technical term for LEUKOCYTE.

white choc·o·late ▸*n.* a white candy flavored with cocoa.

white Christ·mas ▸*n.* a Christmas during which there is snow on the ground.

white clo·ver ▸*n.* see CLOVER.

white-col·lar ▸*adj.* of or relating to the work done or those who work in an office or other professional environment. ■ denoting nonviolent crime committed by white-collar workers, esp. fraud.

white cur·rant ▸*n.* a cultivated variety of red currant with pale edible berries. The berries are insipid and generally used for jams and jellies, in combination with other fruits.

white dwarf ▸*n. Astronomy* a small very dense star that is typically the size of a planet. A white dwarf is formed when a low-mass star has exhausted all its central nuclear fuel and lost its outer layers as a planetary nebula.

white el·e·phant ▸*n.* a possession that is useless or troublesome, esp. one that is expensive to maintain or difficult to dispose of. ▷from the story that the kings of Siam gave such animals as a gift to courtiers considered obnoxious, in order to ruin the recipient by the great expense incurred in maintaining the animal.

white-eye ▸*n.* a small Old World songbird with a ring of white feathers around the eye. • Family Zosteropidae: several genera, in particular *Zosterops*, and numerous species.

white·face /ˈ(h)wīt,fās/ ▸*n.* **1** white stage makeup. **2** a Hereford cow or bull.

White Fa·ther ▸*n.* **1** a white man regarded by people of a nonwhite race as having authority over them. **2** a member of the Society of Missionaries of Africa, a Roman Catholic order founded in Algiers in 1868. ▷translating French *Père Blanc*.

white feath·er ▸*n.* a white feather given to someone as a sign that the giver considers them a coward. ▷late 18th cent.: with reference to a white feather in the tail of a game bird, being a mark of bad breeding.

▸*PHRASE* □ **show the white feather** *Brit., dated* behave in a cowardly fashion.

white fir ▸*n.* a North American fir that has a whitish coloration on both sides of its flat needles. White firs are common in the mountainous coastal areas of California, the Sierra Nevada, and the southern Rockies. • *Abies concolor*, family Pinaceae.

white·fish /ˈ(h)wīt,fisн/ ▸*n.* (*pl.* same or **-fish·es**) a mainly freshwater fish of the salmon family, widely used as food. • *Coregonus* and other genera, family Salmonidae: several species.

white fish ▸*n.* fish with pale flesh, such as plaice, halibut, cod, and haddock.

white flag ▸*n.* a white flag or cloth used as a symbol of surrender, truce, or a desire to parley.

white flight ▸*n.* the move of native-born white city-dwellers to the suburbs to escape the influx of immigrants or migrants.

white flour ▸*n.* fine wheat flour, typically bleached, from which most of the bran and germ have been removed.

white·fly /ˈ(h)wīt,flī/ ▸*n.* (*pl.* same or **-flies**) a minute winged bug covered with powdery white wax, damaging plants by feeding on the sap and coating them with honeydew. • Family Aleyrodidae, suborder Homoptera: numerous genera and species.

white-foot·ed mouse ▸*n.* a common deer mouse with white feet, found in the U.S. and Mexico. • *Peromyscus leucopus*, family Muridae.

White Fri·ar ▸*n.* a Carmelite monk. ▷late Middle English: so named because of the white habits worn by the monks.

white·front /ˈ(h)wīt,frənt/ (also **white-front·ed goose**) ▸*n.* a migratory goose with mainly gray plumage and a white forehead, breeding in northern Eurasia and North America. • Genus *Anser*, family Anatidae: two species.

white gold ▸*n.* a silver-colored alloy of gold with nickel, platinum, or another metal.

white goods ▸*plural n.* **1** large electrical goods used domestically such as refrigerators and washing machines, typically white in color. Compare with BROWN GOODS. **2** *archaic* domestic linen.

White·hall /ˈ(h)wīt,hôl/ a street in Westminster, London, on which many government offices are located. ■ used as an allusive reference to the British Civil Service. ■ used as an allusive reference to the British government, its offices, or its policy: *a pledge was given by Whitehall to protect British troops in Bosnia.*

white-hand·ed gib·bon ▸*n.* the common gibbon, which has white hands and feet and is found in Thailand and Malaysia. Also called LAR GIBBON. • *Hylobates lar*, family Hylobatidae.

White·head /ˈ(h)wīt,(h)ed/, Alfred North (1861–1947), English philosopher and mathematician. He is remembered chiefly for *Principia Mathematica* (1910–13), on which he collaborated with his student Bertrand Russell.

white·head /ˈ(h)wīt,hed/ ▸*n. informal* a pale or white-topped pustule on the skin.

white heat ▸*n.* the temperature or state of something that is so hot that it emits white light. ■ [in *sing.*] *figurative* a state of intense passion or activity.

white hole ▸*n. Astronomy* a hypothetical celestial object that expands outward from a space-time singularity and emits energy, in the manner of a time-reversed black hole.

white hope ▸*n.* a person expected to bring much success to a group or organization: *he was the* ***great white hope*** *for many kids trapped in bad lives.* ■ formerly, a white boxer believed by fans to be able to beat a black champion.

White·horse /ˈ(h)wīt,hôrs/ the capital of Yukon Territory in northwestern Canada; pop. 17,925. Situated on the Alaska Highway, it is the center of a copper-mining and fur-trapping region.

white hors·es ▸*plural n.* white-crested sea waves.

white-hot ▸*adj.* at white heat: *a shower of white-hot embers.*

White House 1 the official residence of the U.S. president in Washington, D.C. ■ the U.S. president, presidency, or government: *the White House denounced the charge.* **2** the Russian parliament building.

White House 1

white i·bis ▸*n.* a white ibis with a red face and a long decurved red bill, found chiefly from the southern U.S. to northern South America. • *Eudocimus albus*, family Threskiornithidae.

white ibis

white knight ▸*n.* a person or thing that comes to someone's aid. ■ a person or company making an acceptable counteroffer for a company facing a hostile takeover bid.

white-knuck·le ▸*adj.* [*attrib.*] (esp. of a vehicle, boat, or airplane ride) causing excitement or tension. ▷1970s: with reference to the effect caused by gripping tightly to steady oneself.

white-knuck·led ▸*adj. informal* (of a person) showing signs of extreme tension due to fear or anger.

white-la·bel ▸*adj.* denoting a musical recording for which the fully printed commercial label is not yet available, and which has been supplied with a plain white label before general release for promotional purposes.

▸*n.* (**white label**) a recording released in such a way.

White La·dy ▸*n.* a cocktail made with gin, orange liqueur, and lemon juice.

white lead /led/ ▸*n.* a white pigment consisting of a mixture of lead carbonate and lead hydroxide.

white lie ▸*n.* a harmless or trivial lie, esp. one told to avoid hurting someone's feelings.

white light ▸*n.* apparently colorless light, for example ordinary daylight. It contains all the wavelengths of the visible spectrum at equal intensity.

white light·ning ▸*n.* illicit homemade whiskey, typically colorless and distilled from corn.

white list ▸*n. informal* a list of people or products viewed with approval. Compare with BLACK LIST.

white·list·ing /ˈ(h)wītˌlistiNG/ ▸*n. Computing* the use of antispam filtering software to allow only specified e-mail addresses to get through. ▷on the pattern of *blacklisting*.

white mag·ic ▸*n.* magic used only for good purposes. **—white ma·gi·cian** *n.*

white mat·ter ▸*n.* the paler tissue of the brain and spinal cord, consisting mainly of nerve fibers with their myelin sheaths. Compare with GRAY MATTER.

white meat ▸*n.* pale meat such as poultry, veal, and rabbit. Often contrasted with RED MEAT.

white met·al ▸*n.* a white or silvery alloy, esp. a tin-based alloy used for the surfaces of bearings.

White Moun·tains a range that rises to 6,288 feet (1,918 m) at Mount Washington, situated in northern New Hampshire, part of the Presidential range in the Appalachian system.

white mouse ▸*n.* an albino form of the house mouse, widely bred as a pet and laboratory animal.

whit·en /ˈ(h)wītn/ ▸*v.* make or become white: [*trans.*] *snow whitened the mountain tops* | [*intrans.*] *she gripped the handle until her knuckles whitened.* **—whit·en·er** *n.*

white night ▸*n.* **1** a sleepless night. [translating French *nuit blanche*.] **2** a night when it is never properly dark, as in high latitudes in summer.

White Nile the name for the main, western branch of the Nile River that flows between the Uganda–Sudan border and its confluence with the Blue Nile at Khartoum.

white noise ▸*n. Physics* noise containing many frequencies with equal intensities.

white·out /ˈ(h)wītˌout/ ▸*n.* **1** a blizzard, esp. in polar regions, that reduces visibilities to near zero. ■ a weather condition in which the features and horizon of snow-covered country are indistinguishable due to uniform light diffusion. **2** white correction fluid for covering typing or writing mistakes. **3** a loss of color vision due to rapid acceleration, often before a loss of consciousness.

white pa·ges ▸*n.* the part of the telephone book that lists residential and business telephone numbers in alphabetical order by name, usually without any advertising copy.

white pa·per ▸*n.* a government or other authoritative report giving information or proposals on an issue.

White Pass a pass from Skagway in Alaska into British Columbia that provided a route for gold seekers in the 1890s Klondike rush. A railroad here, opened in 1900, draws tourists.

white pep·per ▸*n.* the husked ripe or unripe berries of the pepper (see PEPPER sense 2), typically ground and used as a condiment.

white phos·pho·rus ▸*n.* see PHOSPHORUS.

white pine ▸*n.* any of a number of coniferous trees with whitish timber, in particular: • a North American tree that yields high-quality timber that is valued for intricate work (*Pinus strobus*, family Pinaceae). • the kahikatea.

White Plains a commercial city in southeastern New York, the seat of Westchester County; pop. 53,077.

white point·er ▸*n.* another term for GREAT WHITE SHARK.

white pop·lar ▸*n.* a Eurasian poplar with lobed leaves that are white underneath and gray-green above. Also called ABELE. • *Populus alba*, family Salicaceae.

white rhi·noc·er·os ▸*n.* a very large two-horned African rhinoceros with broad lips. • *Ceratotherium simum*, family Rhinocerotidae.

White Riv·er **1** a river that flows for 720 miles (1,160 m) from northwestern Arkansas across the Ozark Plateau to the Mississippi River. **2** a river that flows in two main branches through Indiana, past Indianapolis, to the Wabash River. **3** a river that flows for 500 miles (800 km) from northwestern Nebraska into South Dakota to the Missouri River.

White Rus·sia another name for BELARUS.

White Rus·sian ▸*n.* **1** a Belorussian. ■ an opponent of the Bolsheviks during the Russian Civil War. **2** a cocktail made of vodka, coffee liqueur, and milk served on ice.
▸*adj.* Belorussian. ■ of or relating to the opponents of the Bolsheviks.

white sage ▸*n.* see SAGE[1] (sense 2).

white sale ▸*n.* a store's sale of household linens.

white san·dal·wood ▸*n.* see SANDALWOOD.

White Sands an area of white gypsum salt flats in central New Mexico, designated a national monument in 1933. It is surrounded by a large missile-testing range, which, in 1945, was the site of the detonation of the first nuclear weapon.

white sauce ▸*n.* a sauce of flour, melted butter, and milk or cream.

White Sea an inlet of the Barents Sea off the coast of northwestern Russia.

white sea bass /bas/ ▸*n.* see SEA BASS.

white shark ▸*n.* see GREAT WHITE SHARK.

white-shoe ▸*adj. informal* denoting a company, esp. a law firm, owned and run by members of the WASP elite, generally regarded as cautious and conservative. ▷with reference to the white shoes fashionable among Ivy League college students in the 1950s.

white slave ▸*n.* a woman tricked or forced into prostitution, typically one taken to a foreign country for this purpose. **—white slav·er** *n.* **—white slav·er·y** *n.*

white·smith /ˈ(h)wītˌsmiTH/ ▸*n.* a person who makes articles out of metal, esp. tin. ■ a polisher or finisher of metal goods. ▷Middle English: from WHITE (denoting 'white iron,' i.e., tin) + SMITH.

white snake·root ▸*n.* see SNAKEROOT.

white spruce ▸*n.* a North American spruce with yellow-green or blue-green needles and cylindrical cones, found principally in Canada. • *Picea glauca*, family Pinaceae.

White·stone /ˈ(h)wītˌstōn/ a largely residential section of northern Queens in New York City, on the East River, across from the Bronx, to which it is joined by the Bronx-Whitestone Bridge.

white sug·ar ▸*n.* purified sugar.

White Sul·phur Springs a historic resort city in southeastern West Virginia, in the Allegheny Mountains; pop. 2,779.

white su·prem·a·cy ▸*n.* the belief that white people are superior to those of all other races, esp. the black race, and should therefore dominate society.

white·tail deer /(h)wīt ˌtāl/ (also **white-tailed deer** or **white·tail**) ▸*n.* a reddish to grayish American deer with white on the belly and the underside of the tail. • *Odocoileus virginianus*, family Cervidae.

whitetail deer

white·thorn /ˈ(h)wītˌTHôrn/ ▸*n.* the hawthorn.

white·throat /ˈ(h)wītˌTHrōt/ ▸*n.* a migratory Eurasian and North African warbler with a gray head and white throat. • Genus *Sylvia*, family Sylviidae: three species, in particular the common *S. communis*.

white-throat·ed spar·row ▸*n.* a sparrow that winters in southern and eastern North America. It has prominent yellow eyebrows and a white patch at the throat. • *Zonotrichia albicollis*, family Emberizidae.

white tie ▸*n.* a white bow tie worn by men as part of full evening dress. ■ full evening dress with a white bow tie: *he was wearing immaculate white tie and tails.*
▸*adj.* (of an event) requiring full evening dress to be worn, including a white bow tie.

white trash ▸*n. informal, offensive* poor white people, esp. those living in the southern U.S.

white truf·fle ▸*n.* an underground fungus eaten in Europe as a delicacy. Also called TARTUFO. • *Tuber magnatum*, family Tuberaceae, subdivision Ascomycotina. Alternative name: **Piedmont truffle**.

white vit·ri·ol /ˈvitrēəl/ ▸*n. archaic* crystalline zinc sulfate.

white·wall /ˈ(h)wītˌwôl/ ▸*n.* **1** (also **white·wall tire**) a tire with a white stripe around the outside, or a white sidewall. **2** [as *adj.*] denoting a haircut in which the sides of the head are shaved and the top and back are left longer.

white wal·nut ▸*n.* another term for BUTTERNUT (sense 1).

white·wash /ˈ(h)wītˌwäSH; -ˌwôSH/ ▸*n.* **1** a solution of lime and water or of whiting, size, and water, used for painting walls white. ■ (also **white·wash·ing**) a deliberate concealment of someone's mistakes or faults in order to clear their name. **2** a victory in a game in which the loser scores no points.
▸*v.* [*trans.*] **1** [usu. as *adj.*] (**whitewashed**) paint (a wall, building, or room) with whitewash. ■ try to clear (someone or their name) by deliberately concealing their mistakes or faults: *his wife must have wanted to whitewash his reputation.* ■ deliberately conceal (someone's mistakes or faults): *this is not to whitewash the actual political practice of the government.* **2** defeat (an opponent), keeping them from scoring. **—white·wash·er** *n.*

white·wa·ter /(h)wītˈwôtər; ˈwä-/ (also **white wa·ter**) ▸*n.* [often as *adj.*] (also **white-wa·ter**) fast shallow stretches of water in a river: *whitewater rafting.*

white whale ▸*n.* another term for BELUGA (sense 1).

white wil·low ▸*n.* a Eurasian streamside willow that has narrow leaves with silky white hairs on both sides, and the bark of which contains salicin. • *Salix alba*, family Salicaceae.

white witch ▸*n.* a person, typically a woman, who practices magic for altruistic purposes.

white·wood /ˈ(h)wītˌwo͝od/ ▸*n.* **1** light-colored wood, esp. when made up into furniture and ready for staining, varnishing, or painting. **2** any of a number of trees that yield pale timber, in particular: • a silver fir. • a basswood. • the tulip tree.

white·work /ˈ(h)wītˌwərk/ ▸*n.* embroidery worked in white thread on a white ground.

whit·ey /ˈ(h)wītē/ ▸*n.* (*pl.* **-eys**) *informal, offensive* a contemptuous term used by black people to refer to a white person. ■ [in *sing.*] white people collectively: *her ambitions in publishing have been thwarted by whitey.*

whith·er /ˈ(h)wiT͟Hər/ ▸*interrog. adv. archaic* or *poetic/literary* to what place or state: *whither are we bound?* | *they asked people whither they would emigrate.* ■ what is the likely future of: *whither modern architecture?*
▸*relative adv. archaic* or *poetic/literary* to which (with reference to a place): *the barbecue had been set up by the lake, whither Matthew and Sara were conducted.* ■ to whatever place; wherever: *we could drive whither we pleased.* ▷Old English *hwider*, from the Germanic base of WHICH; compare with HITHER and THITHER.

whith·er·so·ev·er /ˌ(h)wiT͟Hərsōˈevər/ ▸*relative adv. archaic* wherever: *she was free to drift whithersoever she chose.*

whit·ing[1] /ˈ(h)wītiNG/ ▸*n.* (*pl.* same) **1** a slender-bodied marine fish of the cod family, which lives in shallow European waters and is a commercially important food fish. • *Merlangius merlangus*, family Gadidae. **2** [usu. with *adj.*] any of a number of similar marine fishes, in particular: • the northern kingfish of eastern North America. ▷Middle English: from Middle Dutch *wijting*, from *wijt* 'white.'

whit·ing[2] ▸*n.* ground chalk used for purposes such as whitewashing and cleaning metal plate.

whit·leath·er /ˈ(h)witˌleT͟Hər/ ▸*n.* leather that has been prepared by dressing with alum and salt so as to retain its natural color. ▷late Middle English: from WHITE + LEATHER.

whit·low /ˈ(h)witˌlō/ ▸*n.* an abscess in the soft tissue near a fingernail or toenail. ▷late Middle English (also as *whitflaw, -flow*), apparently from WHITE + FLAW[1] in the sense 'crack,' but perhaps related to Dutch *fijt* 'whitlow.'

whit·low grass ▸*n.* a dwarf European plant with a rosette of leaves at the base of a low flowering stem, growing widely on rocks and walls. It was formerly believed to cure whitlows. • Genus *Erophila*, family Brassicaceae: several species, in particular *E. verna*.

Whit·man[1] /ˈ(h)witmən/, Christine Todd (1946–) U.S. politician. She served as the governor of New Jersey 1995–2001 and administrator of the U.S. Environmental Protection Agency 2001–2003.

Whit·man[2], Walt (1819–92), U.S. poet. In 1855, he published a free verse collection, *Leaves of Grass*, that includes "I Sing the Body Electric" and "Song

W

of Myself"; eight further editions followed during Whitman's lifetime. Other notable works: *Drum-Taps* (1865) and *Sequel to Drum-Taps* (1865).

Whit·ney[1] /ˈ(h)witnē/, Eli (1765–1825), U.S. inventor. He is best known for his invention of the cotton gin (patented 1794) to automate the removal of seeds from raw cotton. He also is known to have developed the idea of mass-producing interchangeable parts in order to fulfill a contract in 1797 to supply muskets for the government.

Whit·ney[2], Gertrude Vanderbilt (1876–1942) U.S. sculptor and philanthropist; the daughter of Cornelius Vanderbilt. She sculpted the *Titanic* Women's Memorial in 1931 in Washington, DC, and that same year founded the Whitney Museum of American Art in New York City, the first museum in the U.S. devoted exclusively to native art.

Whit·ney, Mount a mountain in the Sierra Nevada in California. Rising to 14,495 feet (4,418 m), it is the highest peak in the continental U.S. outside of Alaska.

Whit·sun /ˈ(h)witsən/ ▸*n.* Whitsuntide. ▷Middle English: from **WHITSUNDAY**, reduced as if from *Whitsun Day*.

Whit·sun·day /ˈ(h)witˈsənˌdā/ ▸*n.* another term for **PENTECOST** (sense 1). ▷late Old English *Hwīta Sunnandæg*, literally 'white Sunday,' probably with reference to the white robes of those newly baptized at Pentecost.

Whit·sun·tide /ˈ(h)witsənˌtīd/ ▸*n.* the weekend or week including Whitsunday.

Whit·ta·ker /ˈ(h)witikər/, Charles Evans (1901–73), U.S. Supreme Court associate justice 1957–62. Appointed to the Court by President Eisenhower, he was considered a conservative, esp. regarding civil rights.

Whit·ti·er[1] /ˈ(h)witēər/ an industrial city in southwestern California, southeast of Los Angeles; pop. 77,671.

Whit·ti·er[2], John Greenleaf (1807–92), U.S. poet and abolitionist. From the early 1840s, he edited various periodicals and wrote poetry for the abolitionist cause. He is best known for his poems on rural themes, esp. "Snow-Bound" (1866).

Whit·ting·ton /ˈ(h)witiNGtən/, Dick (died 1423), English merchant and lord mayor of London 1397–98, 1406–07, and 1419–20; full name *Sir Richard Whittington*. The legend of his early life as a poor orphan was first recorded in 1605.

Whit·tle /ˈ(h)witl/, Sir Frank (1907–96), English aeronautical engineer, test pilot, and inventor of the jet aircraft engine. He took out the first patent for a turbojet engine in 1930. The first flight using Whittle's jet engine was made in 1941.

whit·tle /ˈ(h)witl/ ▸*v.* [*trans.*] carve (wood) into an object by repeatedly cutting small slices from it. ■ carve (an object) from wood in this way. ■ (**whittle something away/down**) reduce something in size, amount, or extent by a gradual series of steps: *the short list of fifteen was whittled down to five* | [*intrans.*] *the censors had* **whittled away at** *the racy dialogue.* ▷mid 16th cent.: from dialect *whittle* 'knife.' —**whit·tler** *n.*

whiz /(h)wiz/ (also **whizz**) ▸*v.* (**whizzed, whiz·zing**) **1** [*intrans.*] move quickly through the air with a whistling or whooshing sound: *the Iraqi missiles whizzed past* | *figurative the weeks whizzed by.* ■ (**whiz through**) do or deal with quickly: *Audrey would whiz through a few chores in the shop.* ■ [*intrans.*] cause to rotate in a machine, esp. a food processor: *add remaining sauce and whiz until smooth.* **2** [*intrans.*] *informal* urinate.

▸*n.* **1** a whistling or whooshing sound made by something moving fast through the air. **2** (also **wiz**) *informal* a person who is extremely clever at something: *a computer whiz.* [early 20th cent.: influenced by **WIZARD**.] **3** *informal* an act of urinating. ▷mid 16th cent.: imitative.

whiz-bang (also **whizz-bang**) *informal* ▸*n.* (esp. during World War I) a low-velocity shell. ■ a resounding success: *Dan was a whiz-bang at mechanical things.*

▸*adj.* lively or sensational; fast-paced: *a whiz-bang publicity campaign.*

whiz kid ▸*n.* *informal* a young person who is outstandingly skillful or successful at something: *a computer whiz-kid.*

whiz·zy /ˈ(h)wizē/ ▸*adj.* technologically innovative or advanced: *a whizzy new technology.*

WHO ▸*abbr.* World Health Organization.

who /ho͞o/ ▸*pron.* **1** [*interrog. pron.*] what or which person or people: *who is that woman?* | *I wonder who that letter was from.* **2** [*relative pron.*] used to introduce a clause giving further information about a person or people previously mentioned: *Joan Fontaine plays the mouse who married the playboy.* ■ *archaic* the person that; whoever: *who holds the sea, perforce doth hold the land.* ▷Old English *hwā*, of Germanic origin; related to Dutch *wie* and German *wer*.

▸*PHRASES* □ **as who should say** *archaic* as if to say: *he meekly bowed to him, as who should say "Proceed."* □ **who am I** (or **are you, is he,** etc.) **to do something** what right or authority do I (or you, he, etc.) have to do something: *who am I to object?* □ **who goes there?** see **GO**[1].

USAGE **1** A continuing debate in English usage is the question of when to use **who** and when to use **whom**. According to formal grammar, **who** forms the subjective case and so should be used in subject position in a sentence, as in *who decided this?* The form **whom**, on the other hand, forms the objective case and so should be used in object position in a sentence, as in *whom do you think we should support?* or *to* **whom** *do you wish to speak?* Although there are some speakers who still use **who** and **whom** according to the rules of formal grammar as stated here, there are many more who rarely use **whom** at all; its use has retreated steadily and is now largely restricted to formal contexts. The normal practice in modern English is to use **who** instead of **whom** (**who** *do you think we should support?*) and, where applicable, to put the preposition at the end of the sentence (**who** *do you wish to speak to?*). Such uses are today broadly accepted in standard English, but in formal writing it is best to maintain the distinction.
2 On the use of **who** and **that** in relative clauses see **usage** at **THAT**.

whoa /wō/ ▸*exclam.* used as a command to a horse to make it stop or slow down. ■ *informal* used as a greeting, to express surprise or interest, or to command attention: *whoa, that's huge!* ▷late Middle English: variant of **HO**[2].

who'd /ho͞od/ ▸*contraction of* ■ who had: *some Americans who'd arrived after lunch.* ■ who would: *he knew many of the people who'd be there.*

who·dun·it /ho͞oˈdənit/ (*Brit.* **who·dun·nit**) ▸*n.* *informal* a story or play about a murder in which the identity of the murderer is not revealed until the end. ▷1930s: from *who done it?*, nonstandard form of *who did it?*

who·e'er /ho͞oˈe(ə)r/ *poetic/literary* ▸*contraction of* whoever.

who·ev·er /ho͞oˈevər/ ▸*relative pron.* the person or people who; any person who: *whoever did it hated him.* ■ regardless of who: *come out, whoever you are.*

▸*interrog. pron.* used for emphasis instead of "who" in questions, typically expressing surprise or confusion: *whoever would want to make up something like that?* See **usage** below.

USAGE In the emphatic use (**who ever** *does he think he is?*) **who ever** should be written as two words in formal writing.
See also **usage** at **HOWEVER** and **WHATEVER**.

whole /hōl/ ▸*adj.* **1** [*attrib.*] all of; entire: *he spent the whole day walking* | *she wasn't telling the whole truth.* ■ used to emphasize a large extent or number: *whole shelves in libraries are devoted to the subject* | **a whole lot** *of money.* **2** in an unbroken or undamaged state; in one piece: *owls usually swallow their prey whole.* ■ [*attrib.*] (of milk, blood, or other substances) with no part removed. ■ [*predic.*] healthy: *all people should be whole in body, mind, and spirit.*

▸*n.* **1** a thing that is complete in itself: *the subjects of the curriculum form a coherent whole.* **2** (**the whole**) all of something: *the effects will last for the whole of his life.*

▸*adv.* [*as submodifier*] *informal* used to emphasize the novelty or distinctness of something: *the man who's given a whole new meaning to the term "cowboy."* ▷Old English *hāl*, of Germanic origin; related to Dutch *heel* and German *heil*, also to **HAIL**[2]. The spelling with *wh-* (reflecting a dialect pronunciation with *w-*) first appeared in the 15th cent. —**whole·ness** *n.*

▸*PHRASES* □ **as a whole** as a single unit and not as separate parts; in general: *a healthy economy is in the best interests of society as a whole.* □ **in whole** entirely or fully: *a number of stone churches survive in whole or in part.* □ **in the whole** (**wide**) **world** anywhere; of all: *he was the nicest person in the whole world.* □ **on the whole** taking everything into account; in general. □ **the whole nine yards** *informal* everything possible or available: *send in the troops, aircraft, nuclear submarine experts, the whole nine yards.*

whole blood ▸*n.* blood drawn directly from the body from which none of the components, such as plasma or platelets, has been removed.

whole bod·y scan ▸*n.* a CT scan of the torso, especially one obtained for health screening purposes. —**whole bod·y scan·ning** *n.*

whole cloth ▸*n.* cloth of the full size as manufactured, as distinguished from a piece cut off for a garment or other item.

▸*PHRASE* □ **out of** (**the**) **whole cloth** *informal* totally false: *the allegations had been created out of whole cloth.*

whole food ▸*n.* (also **whole foods**) food that has been processed or refined as little as possible and is free from additives or other artificial substances.

whole-grain ▸*adj.* made with or containing whole unprocessed grain: *whole-grain cereals.*

whole·heart·ed /ˈhōlˈhärtid/ ▸*adj.* showing or characterized by complete sincerity and commitment: *you have my wholehearted support.* —**whole·heart·ed·ly** *adv.* —**whole·heart·ed·ness** *n.*

whole lan·guage ▸*n.* a method of teaching children to read at an early age that allows students to select their own reading matter and that emphasizes the use and recognition of words in everyday contexts.

whole-life ▸*adj.* relating to or denoting a life insurance policy that pays a specified amount only on the death of the person insured.

whole life in·sur·ance ▸*n.* life insurance that pays a benefit on the death of the insured and also accumulates a cash value. Compare with **TERM LIFE INSURANCE**.

whole note ▸*n.* *Music* a note having the time value of two half notes or four quarter notes, represented by a ring with no stem. It is the longest note now in common use. Also called **SEMIBREVE**.

whole num·ber ▸*n.* a number without fractions; an integer.

whole·sale /ˈhōlˌsāl/ ▸*n.* the selling of goods in large quantities to be retailed by others.

▸*adv.* being sold in such a way: *bottles from this region sell wholesale at about $72 a case.* ■ on a large scale: *the safety clauses seem to have been taken wholesale from union documents.*

▸*adj.* done on a large scale; extensive: *the wholesale destruction of Iraqi communications.*

▸*v.* [*trans.*] sell (goods) in large quantities at low prices to be retailed by others. ▷late Middle English: originally as *by whole sale* 'in large quantities.' —**whole·sal·er** *n.*

whole·some /ˈhōlsəm/ ▸*adj.* conducive to or suggestive of good health and physical well-being: *the food is plentiful and very wholesome.* ■ conducive to or promoting moral well-being: *good wholesome fun.* ▷Middle English: probably already in Old English (see **WHOLE, -SOME**[1]). —**whole·some·ly** *adv.* —**whole·some·ness** *n.*

whole step ▸*n.* *Music* an interval of a (whole) tone.

whole-tone scale ▸*n.* *Music* a scale consisting entirely of intervals of a tone, with no semitones.

whole-wheat ▸*adj.* denoting flour or bread made from whole grains of wheat, including the husk or outer layer.

▸*n.* whole-wheat bread or flour.

who·lism /ˈhōlizəm/ ▸*n.* variant spelling of **HOLISM**. —**who·lis·tic** *adj.* —**who·lis·ti·cal·ly** *adv.*

whol·ly /ˈhōl(l)ē/ ▸*adv.* entirely; fully: *she found herself given over wholly to sensation* | [*as submodifier*] *the distinction is not wholly clear.* ▷Middle English: probably already in Old English (see **WHOLE, -LY**[2]).

whol·ly-owned ▸*adj.* denoting a company all of whose shares are owned by another company.

whom /ho͞om/ ▸*pron.* used instead of "who" as the object of a verb or preposition: [*interrog. pron.*] *whom did he marry?* | [*relative pron.*] *her mother, in whom she confided, said it wasn't easy for her.*

USAGE On the use of **who** and **whom**, see **usage** at **WHO**.

whom·ev·er /ho͞omˈevər/ ▸*pron.* *chiefly formal* or *poetic/literary* used instead of "whoever" as the object of a verb or preposition: *I'll sing whatever I like to whomever I like.*

whomp /(h)wämp; (h)wômp/ *informal* ▸*v.* [*trans.*] strike heavily; thump: *whomp the club head on the ground* | [*intrans.*] *giant comet chunks whomped into Jupiter.* ■ defeat decisively: *that was our last fight and I whomped him good.*

▸*phrasal v.* □ **whomp something up** produce something quickly: *I might whomp up a couple of gallons of spaghetti sauce.*

▸*n.* a dull heavy sound. ▷1920s: imitative.

W

whom·so /ˈho͞omsō/ ▸*pron. archaic* used instead of "whoso" as the object of a verb or preposition: *whomso thou meetest, say thou this to each.*

whom·so·ev·er /ˌho͞omsōˈevər/ ▸*relative pron. formal* used instead of "whosoever" as the object of a verb or preposition: *they supported his right to marry whomsoever he chose.*

whoomp /(h)wo͝omp/ (also **whoomph** /(h)wo͝omf/) ▸*n.* a sudden sound, such as that made by a muffled or distant explosion: *the distant whoomp of antiaircraft shells bursting.* ▷1950s: imitative.

whoop /(h)wo͞op; ho͞op/ ▸*n.* a loud cry of joy or excitement. ■ a hooting cry or sound: *the whoop of fast-approaching sirens.* ■ a long rasping indrawn breath, typically of someone with whooping cough.
▸*v.* [*intrans.*] give or make a whoop: *all at once they were* ***whooping with*** *laughter.* ▷Middle English: probably imitative.
▸*PHRASES* □ **not give** (or **care**) **a whoop** *informal, dated* be totally indifferent. □ **whoop it up** *informal* enjoy oneself or celebrate in a noisy way. ■ create or stir up excitement or enthusiasm.

whoop·ee /ˈ(h)wo͝opē; ˈ(h)wo͞oˈpē/ *informal* ▸*exclam.* expressing wild excitement or joy.
▸*n.* wild revelry: *hours of parades and whoopee.* ■ *dated* a wild party.
▸*PHRASE* □ **make whoopee** **1** celebrate wildly. **2** have sexual intercourse.

whoop·ee cush·ion /ˈwo͝opē/ (also **whoop·ie cush·ion**) ▸*n.* a rubber cushion that makes a sound like a fart when someone sits on it.

whoop·er /ˈ(h)wo͞opər; ˈho͞opər/ ▸*n.* (also **whoop·er swan**) **1** a large migratory swan with a black and yellow bill and a loud trumpeting call, breeding in northern Eurasia and Greenland. • *Cygnus cygnus*, family Anatidae. **2** short for WHOOPING CRANE.

whoop·ing cough ▸*n.* a contagious bacterial disease chiefly affecting children, characterized by convulsive coughs followed by a whoop. Also called PERTUSSIS. • The organism responsible is *Bordetella pertussis*, a Gram-negative bacterium intermediate between a coccus and a bacillus.

whoop·ing crane ▸*n.* a large mainly white crane with a trumpeting call, breeding in central Canada and now endangered. • *Grus americana*, family Gruidae.

whoops /wo͝ops; wo͞ops/ ▸*exclam. informal* another term for OOPS. ▷1920s: probably an alteration of UPSY-DAISY; compare with OOPS.

whoosh /(h)wo͞osH; (h)wo͝osH/ (also **woosh**) ▸*v.* [*intrans.*] move quickly or suddenly with a rushing sound: *a train whooshed by* | [as *adj.*] (**whooshing**) *there was a loud whooshing noise.* ■ [*trans.* or *complement*] move (something) in such a way: *he whooshed the curtains open.*
▸*n.* a sudden movement accompanied by a rushing sound: *there was a big whoosh of air.*
▸*exclam.* used to imitate such a movement and sound. ▷mid 19th cent.: imitative.

whop /(h)wäp/ (also **whap**) *informal* ▸*v.* (**whopped**, **whop·ping**) [*trans.*] hit hard: *Smith whopped him on the nose.* ■ defeat; overcome.
▸*n.* a heavy blow or the sound of such a blow. ■ the regular pulsing sound of a helicopter rotor. ▷late Middle English (in the sense 'take or put sharply'): variant of dialect *wap* 'strike,' of unknown origin.

whop·per /ˈ(h)wäpər/ ▸*n. informal* a thing that is extremely or unusually large: *the novel is a 1,079 page whopper.* ■ a gross or blatant lie.

whop·ping /ˈ(h)wäpiNG/ ▸*adj. informal* very large: *a whopping $74 million loss* | [as *submodifier*] *a whopping big party.*

whore /hôr/ ▸*n. derogatory* a prostitute. ■ a promiscuous woman.
▸*v.* [*intrans.*] (of a woman) work as a prostitute: *she spent her life whoring for dangerous men.* ■ [often as *n.*] (**whoring**) (of a man) use the services of prostitutes: *he lived by night, indulging in his two hobbies, whoring and eating.* ■ debase oneself by doing something for unworthy motives, typically to make money: *he had never whored after money.* ▷late Old English *hōre*, of Germanic origin; related to Dutch *hoer* and German *Hure*, from an Indo-European root shared by Latin *carus* 'dear.'
▸*PHRASE* □ **the Whore of Babylon** *derogatory* the Roman Catholic Church. [with biblical allusion to Rev. 17:1, 5, etc.).]

whore·dom /ˈhôrdəm/ ▸*n. dated* prostitution or other promiscuous sexual activity.

whore·house /ˈhôrˌhous/ ▸*n. informal* a brothel.

whore·mas·ter /ˈhôrˌmastər/ ▸*n. archaic* **1** a whoremonger. **2** a procurer or pimp.

whore·mon·ger /ˈhôrˌmäNGgər; -ˌməNG-/ ▸*n. archaic* a person who has dealings with prostitutes, esp. a sexually promiscuous man.

whore·son /ˈhôrsən/ ▸*n. archaic* an unpleasant or greatly disliked person. ▷Middle English: from WHORE + SON, suggested by Anglo-Norman French *fiz a putain.*

Whorf /(h)wôrf/, Benjamin Lee (1897–1941), U.S. linguist and insurance worker, known for his contribution to the Sapir-Whorf hypothesis. A student of linguistics in his spare time, Whorf studied Hopi and other American Indian languages and attended Edward Sapir's courses at Yale.

whor·ish /ˈhôrisH/ ▸*adj.* belonging to or characteristic of a prostitute. —**whor·ish·ly** *adv.* —**whor·ish·ness** *n.*

whorl /(h)wôrl/ ▸*n.* a coil or ring, in particular: ■ *Zoology* each of the turns or convolutions in the shell of a gastropod or ammonoid mollusk. ■ *Botany* a set of leaves, flowers, or branches springing from the stem at the same level and encircling it. ■ *Botany* (in a flower) each of the sets of organs, esp. the petals and sepals, arranged concentrically around the receptacle. ■ a complete circle in a fingerprint. ■ *chiefly historical* a small wheel or pulley in a spinning wheel, spinning machine, or spindle.
▸*v.* [*intrans.*] *poetic/literary* spiral or move in a twisted and convoluted fashion: *the dances are kinetic kaleidoscopes where steps whorl into wildness.* ▷late Middle English (denoting a small flywheel): apparently a variant of WHIRL, influenced by Old English *wharve* 'whorl of a spindle.' —**whorled** *adj.*

whor·tle·ber·ry /ˈ(h)wərtlˌberē/ ▸*n.* a bilberry. ▷late 16th cent.: dialect variant of Middle English *hurtleberry*, of unknown origin.

who's /ho͞oz/ ▸*contraction of* ■ who is: *who's that?* ■ who has: *who's done the reading?*

USAGE A common written mistake is to confuse **who's** with **whose**. The form **who's** represents a contraction of 'who is' or 'who has': ***who's*** *going to feed the dog?; I wonder* ***who's*** *left the light on again?* The word **whose** is a possessive pronoun or adjective: ***whose*** *is this?;* ***whose*** *turn is it?*

whose /ho͞oz/ ▸*interrogative possessive adj.* & *pron.* belonging to or associated with which person: [as *adj.*] *whose round is it?* | [as *pron.*] *a minivan was parked at the curb and Juliet wondered whose it was.*
▸*relative possessive adj.* of whom or which (used to indicate that the following noun belongs to or is associated with the person or thing mentioned in the previous clause): *he's a man whose opinion I respect.* ▷Old English *hwæs*, genitive of *hwā* 'who' and *hwæt* 'what.'

USAGE On the differences in use between **whose** and **who's**, see **usage** at WHO'S.

whose·so·ev·er /ˌho͞ozsōˈevər/ ▸*relative pron.* & *adj. formal* whoever's: [as *adj.*] *the story will have been told you by your fathers, whosesoever sons you are.*

whos·ev·er /ˌho͞ozˈevər/ ▸*relative pron.* & *adj. rare* belonging to or associated with whichever person; whoever's: [as *pron.*] *the choice, whosever it was, is interesting* | [as *adj.*] *she dialed whosever number she could still remember.*

who·sis /ˈho͞ozis/ (also **who·sit** /-zit/) ▸*n. informal* (often in titles) a person whose name one cannot recall, does not know, or does not wish to specify: *lunch with Senator Whosis who was so fond of bourbon.* ▷1920s: contraction of *who is this?*

who·so /ˈho͞osō/ ▸*pron.* archaic term for WHOEVER: *whoso took such things into account was a fool.* ▷Middle English: shortening of Old English *swā hwā swā* 'so who so.'

who·so·ev·er /ˌho͞osōˈevər/ ▸*pron.* formal term for WHOEVER: *a belief that whosoever steals will be blinded.*

who's who ▸*n.* a list or directory of facts about notable people.

wh-ques·tion ▸*n.* a question in English introduced by a wh-word and requiring more information in reply than simply *yes* or *no.*

whump /(h)wəmp/ ▸*n.* [usu. in *sing.*] a dull thudding sound: *the horse fell with a great whump.*
▸*v.* [*intrans.*] make such a sound: *he pitched a snowball that whumped into the car.* ■ [*trans.*] strike (something) heavily with such a sound: *she began whumping him on his lower back.* ▷late 19th cent.: imitative.

whup /(h)wo͝op/ ▸*v.* (**whupped**, **whup·ping**) [*trans.*] *informal* beat; thrash: *they would whup him and send him home.* ■ defeat convincingly: *if you lined up our guys against the 49ers, they'd get whupped.* ▷late 19th cent.: variant of WHIP.

wh-word ▸*n. Grammar* any of a class of English words used to introduce questions and relative clauses. The main wh-words are *why, who, which, what, where, when*, and *how.*

why /(h)wī/ ▸*interrog. adv.* for what reason or purpose: *why did he do it?* ■ [with *negative*] used to make or agree to a suggestion: *why don't I give you a lift?*
▸*relative adv.* (with reference to a reason) on account of which; for which: ***the reason why*** *flu shots need repeating every year is that the virus changes.* ■ the reason for which: *each has faced similar hardships, and perhaps that is why they are friends.*
▸*exclam.* **1** expressing surprise or indignation: *Why, that's absurd!* **2** used to add emphasis to a response: *"You think so?" "Why, yes."*
▸*n.* (*pl.* **whys**) a reason or explanation: *the* ***whys and wherefores*** *of these procedures need to be explained to students.* ▷Old English *hwī, hwȳ* 'by what cause,' instrumental case of *hwæt* 'what,' of Germanic origin.
▸*PHRASE* □ **why so?** for what reason or purpose?

whyd·ah /ˈ(h)widə/ (also **why·da**) ▸*n.* an African weaverbird, the male of which has a black back and a very long black tail used in display flight. • Genus *Vidua*, family Ploceidae: several species. ▷late 18th cent. (originally *widow-bird*): alteration by association with *Whidah* (now Ouidah), a town in Benin.

WI ▸*abbr.* ■ West Indies. ■ Wisconsin (in official postal use). ■ *Brit.* Women's Institute.

WIC /wik/ ▸*abbr.* Women, Infants, and Children (a federal or state program to ensure proper nutrition for poor mothers and their children).

Wic·ca /ˈwikə/ ▸*n.* the religious cult of modern witchcraft, esp. an initiatory tradition founded in England in the mid 20th century and claiming its origins in pre-Christian pagan religions. ▷representing Old English *wicca* 'witch.' —**Wic·can** *adj.* & *n.*

Wich·i·ta /ˈwicHəˌtô; -ˌtä/ a city in southern Kansas, on the Arkansas River, the largest city in the state; pop. 344,284.

Wich·i·ta Falls an industrial and commercial city in north central Texas; pop. 96,259.

wick[1] /wik/ ▸*n.* a strip of porous material up which liquid fuel is drawn by capillary action to the flame in a candle, lamp, or lighter. ■ *Medicine* a gauze strip inserted in a wound to drain it.
▸*v.* [*trans.*] absorb or draw off (liquid) by capillary action: *these excellent socks will* ***wick away*** *the sweat* | [*intrans.*] *synthetics with hollow fibers that wick well.* ▷Old English *wēoce*; related to Dutch *wiek* and German *Wieche* 'wick yarn.'
▸*PHRASE* □ **dip one's wick** *vulgar slang* (of a man) have sexual intercourse.

wick[2] ▸*n.* **1** [in *place names*] a town, hamlet, or district: *Hampton Wick* | *Warwick.* **2** *Brit., dialect* a dairy farm. ▷Old English *wīc* 'dwelling place,' probably based on Latin *vicus* 'street, village.'

wick·ed /ˈwikid/ ▸*adj.* (**-ed·er**, **-ed·est**) evil or morally wrong: *a wicked and unscrupulous politician.* ■ intended to or capable of harming someone or something: *he should be punished for his wicked driving.* ■ *informal* extremely unpleasant: *despite the sun, the wind outside was wicked.* ■ playfully mischievous: *Ben has a wicked sense of humor.* ■ *informal* excellent; wonderful: *Sophie makes wicked cakes.* ■ *informal* [as *submodifier*] very; extremely: *he runs wicked fast.* ▷Middle English: probably from Old English *wicca* 'witch' + -ED[1]. —**wick·ed·ly** *adv.* —**wick·ed·ness** *n.*

wick·er /ˈwikər/ ▸*n.* pliable twigs, typically of willow, plaited or woven to make items such as furniture and baskets: [as *adj.*] *a wicker chair.* ▷Middle English: of Scandinavian origin; compare with Swedish *viker* 'willow'; related to *vika* 'to bend.'

wick·er·work /ˈwikərˌwərk/ ▸*n.* wicker. ■ furniture or other items made of wicker.

wick·et /ˈwikit/ ▸*n.* **1** (also **wick·et door** or **wick·et gate**) a small door or gate, esp. one beside or in a larger one. ■ an opening in a door or wall, often fitted with glass or a grille and used for selling tickets or a similar purpose. ■ one of the wire hoops on a croquet course. **2** *Cricket* each of the sets of three stumps with two bails across the top at either end of the pitch, defended by a batsman. ■ the prepared strip of ground between these two sets of stumps. ■ the dismissal of a batsman; each of ten dismissals regarded as marking a division of a side's innings: *Darlington won by four wickets.* ▷Middle English (in the sense 'small door or grille'): from Anglo-Norman French and Old Northern French *wiket*; origin uncertain, usually referred to the Germanic root of Old Norse *víkja* 'to turn, move.' Cricket senses date from the late 17th cent.

▸*PHRASES* □ **a sticky wicket** *Cricket* a pitch that has been drying after rain and is difficult to bat on. ■ [in *sing.*] *informal* a tricky or awkward situation: *the problem of who sits where can create a sticky wicket.* □ **take a wicket** *Cricket* (of a bowler or a fielding side) dismiss a batsman.

wick·et·keep·er /ˈwikit,kēpər/ ▸*n. Cricket* a fielder stationed close behind a batsman's wicket and typically equipped with gloves and pads. **—wick·et·keep·ing** *n.*

wick·i·up /ˈwikē,əp/ ▸*n.* an American Indian hut consisting of an oval frame covered with brushwood or grass. ▷Fox 'house;' compare with **WIGWAM**.

Wick·low /ˈwiklō/ a county in eastern Republic of Ireland, in the province of Leinster. ■ its county town, on the Irish Sea; pop. 6,000.

wid·der·shins /ˈwidər,SHinz/ (also **with·er·shins**) ▸*adv. chiefly Scottish* in a direction contrary to the sun's course, considered as unlucky; counterclockwise. ▷early 16th cent.: from Middle Low German *weddersins*, from Middle High German *widersinnes*, from *wider* 'against' + *sin* 'direction'; the second element was associated with Scots *sin* 'sun.'

wide /wīd/ ▸*adj.* (**wid·er, wid·est**) **1** of great or more than average width: *a wide road.* ■ (after a measurement and in questions) from side to side: *it measures 15 cm long by 12 cm wide | how wide do you think this house is?* ■ open to the full extent: *wide eyes.* ■ considerable: *tax revenues have undershot Treasury projections by a wide margin.* **2** including a great variety of people or things: *a wide range of opinion.* ■ spread among a large number of people or over a large area: *the business is slowly gaining wider acceptance.* ■ [in *combination*] extending over the whole of: *an industry-wide trend.* **3** at a considerable or specified distance from a point or mark: *Bodie's shot was inches wide.* ■ *Baseball* (of a pitch) outside: *the ball was* **wide of** *the plate.* ■ *Baseball* (of a throw) to either side of a base: *forced a wide throw to first.* ■ (in field sports) at or near the side of the field: *he played in a wide left position.* **4** *Phonetics* another term for **LAX**.

▸*adv.* **1** to the full extent: *his eyes opened wide.* **2** far from a particular point or mark: *a shot that went wide to the right.* ■ at or near the side of the field; toward the sideline: *he will play wide on the right.*

▸*n. Cricket* a ball that is judged to be too wide of the stumps for the batsman to play, for which an extra is awarded to the batting side. ■ a run scored because of a delivery of this kind. ▷Old English *wīd* 'spacious, extensive,' *wīde* 'over a large area,' of Germanic origin. **—wide·ness** *n.* **—wid·ish** *adj.*

▸*PHRASES* □ **give someone/something a wide berth** see **BERTH**. □ **wide awake** fully awake. □ **wide of the mark** a long way away from an intended target. ■ inaccurate: *the accusation was a little wide of the mark.* □ **wide open 1** stretching over an outdoor expanse: *the wide open spaces of Montana.* **2** offering a great variety of opportunities: *suddenly the whole world was* **wide open to** *her.* **3** (of a contest) of which the outcome is not predictable. **4** vulnerable, esp. to attack.

wide-an·gle ▸*adj.* (of a lens) having a short focal length and hence a field covering a wide angle.

wide ar·e·a net·work (abbr.: **WAN**) ▸*n.* a computer network in which the computers connected may be far apart, generally having a radius of half a mile or more. Compare with **LOCAL AREA NETWORK**.

wide-a·wake ▸*n.* a soft felt hat with a low crown and wide brim. ▷mid 19th cent.: punningly so named, because the hat does not have a nap.

wide-band ▸*adj.* (of a radio, or other device or activity involving broadcasting) having or using a wide band of frequencies or wavelengths.

wide-bod·y /ˈwīd,bädē/ ▸*adj.* [*attrib.*] (also **wide-bod·ied**) having a wide body, in particular: ■ (of a large jet airplane) having a wide fuselage. ■ (of a tennis racket) having a wide head.

▸*n.* (*pl.* **-bod·ies**) (also **wide·bod·y**) **1** a large jet airplane with a wide fuselage. **2** a tennis racket with a wide head. **3** *informal* a large, heavily built person, esp. one who plays a team sport.

wide-eyed ▸*adj.* having one's eyes wide open in amazement. ■ *figurative* innocent: *people think of Pinocchio as the wide-eyed, sweet-voiced puppet.*

▸*adv.* with one's eyes wide open in amazement: *we looked at each other wide-eyed.*

wide·ly /ˈwīdlē/ ▸*adv.* **1** over a wide area or at a wide interval: *he smiled widely and held out a hand | a tall man with widely spaced eyes.* ■ to a large degree in nature or character (used to describe considerable variation or difference): *lending policies vary widely between different banks |* [as *submodifier*] *people in widely different circumstances.* **2** over a large area or range; extensively: *Deborah has traveled widely |* [as *submodifier*] *she was widely read.* ■ by many people or in many places: *credit cards are widely accepted.*

wid·en /ˈwīdn/ ▸*v.* make or become wider: [*trans.*] *the incentive to dredge and widen the river |* [*intrans.*] *his grin widened | the lane* **widened out** *into a small clearing.* **—wid·en·er** *n.*

wide·out /ˈwīd,out/ ▸*n.* a wide receiver.

wide-rang·ing ▸*adj.* covering an extensive range: *a wide-ranging discussion.*

wide re·ceiv·er ▸*n. Football* an offensive player who is positioned at a distance from the end and is used primarily as a pass receiver.

wide-screen (also **wide·screen**) ▸*adj.* [*attrib.*] designed with or for a screen presenting a wide field of vision in relation to its height: *a wide-screen TV.*

▸*n.* (**widescreen**) a movie or television screen presenting a wide field of vision in relation to its height. ■ a film format presenting a wide field of vision in relation to height.

wide·spread /ˈwīdˈspred/ ▸*adj.* found or distributed over a large area or number of people: *there was widespread support for the war.*

widg·eon ▸*n.* variant spelling of **WIGEON**.

widg·et /ˈwijit/ ▸*n. informal* a small gadget or mechanical device, esp. one whose name is unknown or unspecified. ■ *Computing* a component of a user interface that operates in a particular way. ▷1930s : perhaps an alteration of **GADGET**.

wid·ow /ˈwidō/ ▸*n.* **1** a woman who has lost her husband by death and has not remarried. ■ [with *adj.*] *humorous* a woman whose husband is often away participating in a specified sport or activity: *a golf widow.* **2** *Printing* a last word or short last line of a paragraph falling at the top of a page or column and considered undesirable.

▸*v.* [*trans.*] [usu. as *adj.*] (**widowed**) make into a widow or widower: *she had to care for her widowed mother.* ▷Old English *widewe*, from an Indo-European root meaning 'be empty'; compare with Sanskrit *vidh* 'be destitute,' Latin *viduus* 'bereft, widowed,' and Greek *ēitheos* 'unmarried man.'

wid·ow·er /ˈwidō-ər/ ▸*n.* a man who has lost his wife by death and has not remarried.

wid·ow·hood /ˈwidō,ho͝od/ ▸*n.* the state or period of being a widow or widower.

wid·ow-mak·er ▸*n. informal* a thing with the potential to kill men. ■ a dead branch caught precariously high in a tree which may fall on a person below.

wid·ow's mite ▸*n.* a small monetary contribution from someone who is poor. ▷with biblical allusion to Mark 12:43.

wid·ow's peak ▸*n.* a V-shaped growth of hair toward the center of the forehead, esp. one left by a receding hairline in a man. ▷mid 19th cent.: so called because it was formerly believed to be a predictor of widowhood for a woman.

wid·ow's walk ▸*n.* a railed or balustraded platform built on a roof, originally in early New England houses, typically for providing an unimpeded view of the sea. ▷1930s: with reference to its use as a viewpoint for the hoped-for return of a seafaring husband.

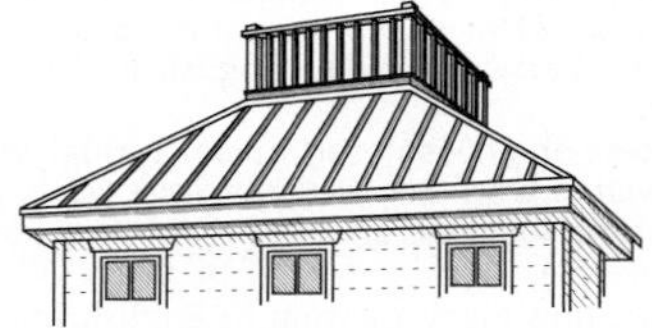

widow's walk

wid·ow's weeds ▸*plural n.* black clothes worn by a widow in mourning. ▷early 18th cent. (earlier as *mourning weeds*): *weeds* (obsolete in the general sense 'garments') is from Old English *wǣd(e)*, of Germanic origin.

width /widTH; witTH/ ▸*n.* the measurement or extent of something from side to side: *the yard was about seven feet* **in width** *| the shoe comes in a variety of widths.* ■ a piece of something at its full extent from side to side: *a single* **width of** *hardboard.* ■ the sideways extent of a swimming pool as a measure of the distance swum. ■ the quality of covering or accepting a broad range of things; scope: *the width of experience required for these positions.* ▷early 17th cent.: from **WIDE** + **-TH**[2], on the pattern of *breadth* (replacing *wideness*).

width·wise /ˈwidTH,wīz; ˈwitTH-/ (also **width·ways** /-,wāz/) ▸*adv.* in a direction parallel with a thing's width: *fold the pastry in half widthwise.*

wield /wēld/ ▸*v.* [*trans.*] hold and use (a weapon or tool): *a masked raider wielding a handgun.* ■ have and be able to use (power or influence): *faction leaders wielded enormous influence within the party.* ▷Old English *wealdan, wieldan* 'govern, subdue, direct,' of Germanic origin; related to German *walten*. **—wield·er** *n.*

wield·y /ˈwēldē/ ▸*adj.* (**wield·i·er, wield·i·est**) easily controlled or handled: *the beefy Bentley is far from wieldy.* ▷late 16th cent.: back-formation from **UNWIELDY**.

Wien /vēn/ German name for **VIENNA**.

Wie·ner /ˈwēnər/, Norbert (1894–1964), U.S. mathematician. He established the science of cybernetics in the late 1940s and made major contributions to the study of stochastic processes, integral equations, harmonic analysis, and related fields.

wie·ner /ˈwēnər/ (also *informal* **wee·nie, wie·nie** /-nē/) ▸*n.* **1** a frankfurter or similar sausage. **2** another term for **WEENIE**. ▷early 20th cent.: abbreviation of German *Wienerwurst* 'Vienna sausage.'

Wie·ner schnit·zel /ˈvēnər ,SHnitsəl/ ▸*n.* a dish consisting of a thin slice of veal that is breaded, fried, and garnished. ▷from German, literally 'Vienna cutlet.'

Wies·ba·den /ˈvēs,bädn/ a city in western Germany, the capital of the state of Hesse, on the Rhine River, opposite Mainz; pop. 264,000.

Wie·sel /vēˈzəl; ˈvēzəl; wiˈzel/, Elie (1928–), U.S. human rights campaigner, novelist, and academic, born in Romania; full name *Eliezer Wiesel*. A survivor of the Auschwitz and Buchenwald concentration camps, he became an authority on the Holocaust, documenting and publicizing Nazi war crimes. Nobel Peace Prize (1986).

Wie·sen·thal /ˈvēzən,täl; -,THäl/, Simon (1908–), Austrian Jewish investigator of Nazi war crimes. After spending three years in concentration camps, he began a campaign to bring Nazi war criminals to justice, tracing some 1,000 unprosecuted criminals including Adolf Eichmann.

wife /wīf/ ▸*n.* (*pl.* **wives** /wīvz/) a married woman considered in relation to her husband. ■ [with *adj.*] the wife of a man with a specified occupation: *a faculty wife.* ■ *archaic* or *dialect* a woman, esp. an old or uneducated one. ▷Old English *wīf* 'woman,' of Germanic origin; related to Dutch *wijf* and German *Weib*. **—wife·hood** /-,ho͝od/ *n.* **—wife·less** *adj.* **—wife·like** /-,līk/ *adj.* **—wife·li·ness** /ˈwīflēnis/ *n.* **—wife·ly** *adj.*

▸*PHRASE* □ **take a woman to wife** *archaic* marry a woman.

wife-swap·ping ▸*n. informal* the practice within a group of married couples of exchanging sexual partners on a casual basis.

wif·ey /ˈwifē/ ▸*n.* (*pl.* **-eys**) *informal* a condescending way of referring to a man's wife.

Wif·fle ball /ˈwifəl/ ▸*n. trademark* a light perforated ball used in a type of baseball. ■ a game played with such a ball. ▷1950s: *Wiffle*, variant of **WHIFFLE**.

Wi-Fi /ˈwīˈfī/ ▸*abbr.* Wireless Fidelity, a group of technical standards enabling the transmission of data over wireless networks.

▸*v.* (**-Fies, -Fied, -Fy·ing**) [*trans.*] convert or adapt for Wireless Fidelity compatibility: *what type of electronics will be immune from being Wi-Fied?*

wig[1] /wig/ ▸*n.* a covering for the head made of real or artificial hair, typically worn by people for adornment or by people trying to conceal their baldness or in England by judges and barristers in courts of law. ▷late 17th cent.: shortening of **PERIWIG**. **—wigged** *adj.* **—wig·less** *adj.*

wig[2] ▸*v.* (**wigged, wig·ging**) [*trans.*] *Brit., informal, dated* rebuke (someone) severely: *I had often occasion to wig him for getting drunk.*

▸*phrasal v.* □ **wig out** *informal* become deliriously excited; go completely wild. ▷early 19th cent.: apparently from **WIG**[1], perhaps from **BIGWIG** and associated with a rebuke given by a person in authority.

wig·eon /ˈwijən/ (also **widg·eon**) ▸*n.* a dabbling duck with mainly reddish-brown and gray plumage, the male having a whistling call. • Genus *Anas*, family

Anatidae: several species, in particular the **American wigeon** (*A. americana*)and the **Eurasian wigeon** (*A. penelope*). ▷early 16th cent.: perhaps of imitative origin and suggested by PIGEON[1].

wig·ger *informal* ▸*n.* **1** a white person who tries to emulate or acquire African-American cultural behavior and tastes: *Whites who pal around with Blacks are called "wannabes" or "wiggers".* **2** an unreliable or flaky person: *the '80s wigger is the same as the '50s greaser, the '60s hippie,or the '70s burnout.*

wig·gle /ˈwigəl/ ▸*v.* move or cause to move up and down or from side to side with small rapid movements: [*trans.*] *Stasia wiggled her toes* | [*intrans.*] *my tooth was wiggling around.* ■ (**wiggle out of**) avoid (something), esp. by devious means: *they're trying to wiggle out of their agreement.*

▸*n.* a wiggling movement: *a slight wiggle of the hips.* ■ a deviation in a line: *a wiggle on a chart.* ▷Middle English: from Middle Low German and Middle Dutch *wiggelen* (frequentative). **—wig·gly** /ˈwig(ə)lē/ *adj.* (**-gli·er**, **-gli·est**).

▸*PHRASE* □ **get a wiggle on** *informal* get moving; hurry.

wig·gler /ˈwig(ə)lər/ ▸*n.* a person or thing that wiggles or causes something to wiggle. ■ *Physics* a magnet designed to make a beam of particles in an accelerator follow a sinusoidal path, in order to increase the amount of radiation they produce. ■ *dialect* an earthworm. ■ *informal* a mosquito larva.

wig·gle room ▸*n.* *informal* room to maneuver; flexibility, esp. in one's options or interpretation: *he had precious little wiggle room because of the budget deficit.*

wig·gy /ˈwigē/ ▸*adj.* (**-gi·er**, **-gi·est**) *informal* emotionally uncontrolled or weird: *Jerry and Susan were gloriously wiggy.* ▷1960s: from *wig out* (see WIG[2]).

Wight, Isle of see ISLE OF WIGHT.

wight /wīt/ ▸*n.* [usu. with *adj.*] *archaic* or *dialect* a person of a specified kind, esp. one regarded as unfortunate: *he always was an unlucky wight.* ■ *poetic/literary* a spirit, ghost, or other supernatural being. ▷Old English *wiht* 'thing, creature,' of Germanic origin; related to Dutch *wicht* 'little child' and German *Wicht* 'creature.'

wig·wag /ˈwig,wag/ ▸*v.* (**-wagged**, **-wag·ging**) [*intrans.*] *informal* move to and fro: *the dog wigwagged his way up the porch steps.* ■ signal by waving an arm, flag, light, or other object: *Ned furiously wigwagged at her.* ▷late 16th cent.: reduplication of WAG[1].

wig·wam /ˈwig,wäm/ ▸*n.* a dome-shaped hut or tent made by fastening mats, skins, or bark over a framework of poles, used by some North American Indian peoples. ▷early 17th cent.: from Abnaki, 'their house,' from an Algonquian base meaning 'dwell,' shared with WICKIUP.

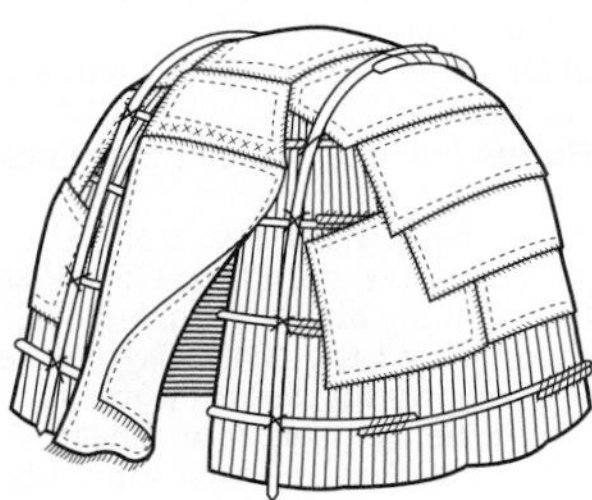

wigwam

wi·ki /ˈwikē/ ▸*n.* a Web site that allows collaborative editing of its content and structure by its users. ▷coined by programmer Ward Cunningham (1949-), from Hawaiian *wiki-wiki* 'quick-quick.'

wil·co /ˈwilkō/ ▸*exclam.* expressing compliance or agreement, esp. acceptance of instructions received by radio: *roger, wilco.* ▷1940s (originally in military use): abbreviation of *will comply.*

wild /wīld/ ▸*adj.* **1** (of an animal or plant) living or growing in the natural environment; not domesticated or cultivated. ■ (of people) not civilized; barbarous: *the wild tribes from the north.* ■ (of scenery or a region) desolate-looking: *the wild coastline of Cape Wrath.* **2** uncontrolled or unrestrained, esp. in pursuit of pleasure: *she went through a wild phase of drunken parties and desperate affairs.* ■ haphazard, esp. rashly so: *a wild guess.* ■ extravagant or unreasonable; fanciful: *who, even* **in their wildest dreams**, *could have anticipated such a victory?* ■ stormy: *the wild sea.* ■ *informal* very enthusiastic or excited: *I'm not wild about the music.* ■ *informal* very angry. ■ (of looks, appearance, etc.) indicating distraction: *her wild eyes were darting back and forth.* ■ (of a playing card) deemed to have any value, suit, color, or other property in a game at the discretion of the player holding it. See also WILD CARD.

▸*adv.* in an uncontrolled manner: *the bad guys shoot wild.* ■ in a very excited or angry state: *the crowd went wild with enthusiasm.*

▸*n.* (**the wild**) a natural state or uncultivated or uninhabited region: *kiwis are virtually extinct* **in the wild**. ■ (**the wilds**) a remote uninhabited or sparsely inhabited area: *he spent a year in* **the wilds of** *Canada.* ▷Old English *wilde*, of Germanic origin; related to Dutch and German *wild.* **—wild·ish** *adj.* **—wild·ly** *adv.* **—wild·ness** *n.*

▸*PHRASES* □ **run wild** (of an animal, plant, or person) grow or develop without restraint or discipline: *these horses have been running wild since they were born* | *figurative her imagination had run wild.* □ **wild and woolly** uncouth in appearance or behavior.

wild ar·um ▸*n.* another term for CUCKOOPINT.

wild boar ▸*n.* see BOAR (sense 1).

wild cal·la /ˈkalə/ ▸*n.* another term for WATER ARUM.

wild cane ▸*n.* another name for GIANT REED.

wild card ▸*n.* a playing card that can have any value, suit, color, or other property in a game at the discretion of the player holding it. ■ a person or thing whose influence is unpredictable or whose qualities are uncertain. ■ *Computing* a character that will match any character or sequence of characters in a search. ■ an opportunity to enter a sports competition without having to take part in qualifying matches or be ranked at a particular level. ■ a player or team given such an opportunity.

wild car·rot ▸*n.* another term for QUEEN ANNE'S LACE.

wild·cat /ˈwīld,kat/ ▸*n.* **1** a small native Eurasian and African cat that is typically gray with black markings and a bushy tail, noted for its ferocity. • *Felis silvestris*, family Felidae, the African race of which is believed to be the ancestor of the domestic cat. ■ any of the smaller members of the cat family, esp. the bobcat. ■ a hot-tempered or ferocious person, typically a woman. **2** an exploratory oil well.

▸*adj.* [*attrib.*] (of a strike) sudden and unofficial: *legislation to curb wildcat strikes.* ■ commercially unsound or risky.

▸*v.* [*intrans.*] prospect for oil.

wild·cat·ter /ˈwīld,katər/ ▸*n.* a prospector who sinks exploratory oil wells. ■ a risky investor.

wild-caught ▸*adj.* (of an animal) taken from the wild rather than bred from captive stock.

wild·craft /ˈwīld,kraft/ ▸*v.* [*intrans.*] gather herbs, plants, and fungi from the wild.

▸*n.* the action or practice of wildcrafting.

wild dog ▸*n.* a wild member of the dog family, esp. the hunting dog of Africa, the dhole of India, or the dingo of Australia.

Wilde /wīld/, Oscar (Fingal O'Flahertie Wills) (1854–1900), Irish playwright, novelist, poet, and wit. His advocacy of "art for art's sake" is evident in his only novel, *The Picture of Dorian Gray* (1890). As a playwright, he achieved success with the comedies *Lady Windermere's Fan* (1892) and *The Importance of Being Earnest* (1895).

Oscar Wilde

wil·de·beest /ˈwildə,bēst/ ▸*n.* (*pl.* same or **-beests**) another term for GNU. ▷early 19th cent.: from Afrikaans, literally 'wild beast.'

Wil·der[1] /ˈwīldər/, Billy (1906–2002), U.S. movie director and screenwriter, born in Austria; born *Samuel Wilder*. His numerous film successes include *Double Indemnity* (1944), *The Lost Weekend* (1945), *Sunset Boulevard* (1950), *Sabrina* (1954), *Some Like It Hot* (1959), and *The Apartment* (1960). He won six Academy Awards.

Wil·der[2], Gene (1935–), U.S. actor; born *Jerome Silberman*; husband of Gilda Radner. He cowrote, directed, and starred in *The Woman in Red* (1984). He cowrote and starred in *Young Frankenstein* (1974) and also starred in *Willy Wonka and the Chocolate Factory* (1971) and *Blazing Saddles* (1973).

Wil·der[3], Laura Ingalls (1867–1957), U.S. writer. She wrote a series of children's books about her experiences growing up on the U.S. frontier during the late 1800s. Her most well known is *Little House on the Prairie* (1935), which was the basis for a television series 1974–83. Other books include *Little House in the Big Woods* (1932) and *These Happy Golden Years* (1943).

Wil·der[4], Thornton (Niven) (1897–1975), U.S. novelist and playwright. His work is particularly concerned with the universality of human experience, irrespective of time or place. He wrote the novel *The Bridge of San Luis Rey* (1927) and the plays *Our Town* (1938) and *The Skin of Our Teeth* (1942).

wild·er /ˈwildər/ ▸*v.* [*trans.*] *archaic* cause to lose one's way; lead or drive astray: *unknowne Lands, where we have wildered ourselves.* ■ perplex; bewilder: *the sad Queen, wildered of thought.* ▷early 17th cent.: origin uncertain; perhaps based on WILDERNESS.

wil·der·ness /ˈwildərnis/ ▸*n.* [usu. in *sing.*] an uncultivated, uninhabited, and inhospitable region. ■ a neglected or abandoned area of a garden or town. ■ *figurative* a position of disfavor, esp. in a political context: *the man who led the Green Party out of the wilderness* | [as *adj.*] *his wilderness years.* ▷Old English *wildēornes* 'land inhabited only by wild animals,' from *wild dēor* 'wild deer' + -NESS.

▸*PHRASE* □ **a voice in the wilderness** an unheeded advocate of reform (see Matt. 3:3, etc.)

Wil·der·ness Road a historic route, opened by Daniel Boone in the 1770s and used until the 1840s, that allowed western migration through the Allegheny Mountains by way of the Cumberland Gap between Tennessee and Kentucky.

Wil·der·ness, the a wooded region of Spotsylvania County in northeastern Virginia, site of an inconclusive Civil War battle in 1864.

wild-eyed ▸*adj.* (of a person or animal) with an expression of panic or desperation in their eyes. ■ *figurative* emotionally volatile, typically fearful or desperate: *wild-eyed zealots.* ■ senseless or impractical: *a wild-eyed fantasy.*

wild·fire /ˈwīld,fīr/ ▸*n.* **1** a large, destructive forest- or brush-fire that spreads quickly. **2** *historical* a combustible liquid such as Greek fire that was readily ignited and difficult to extinguish, used esp. in warfare. **3** less common term for WILL-O'-THE-WISP.

▸*PHRASE* □ **spread like wildfire** spread with great speed: *the news had spread like wildfire.*

wild·flow·er /ˈwīld,flou(-ə)r/ (also **wild flow·er**) ▸*n.* a flower of an uncultivated variety or a flower growing freely without human intervention.

wild·fowl /ˈwīld,foul/ ▸*plural n.* game birds, esp. aquatic ones; waterfowl.

wild gin·ger ▸*n.* a North American plant with large heart-shaped leaves and hairy leafstalks. Its aromatic root is used as a ginger substitute. • *Asarum canadense*, family Aristolochiaceae.

wild-goose chase ▸*n.* a foolish and hopeless pursuit of something unattainable.

wild horse ▸*n.* a domestic horse that has returned to the wild, or that is allowed to live under natural conditions; a feral horse. ■ a horse that has not been broken in. ■ a wild animal of the horse family.

▸*PHRASE* □ **wild horses wouldn't ——** used to convey that nothing could persuade or force someone to do something: *wild horses wouldn't have kept me away.*

wild·ing[1] /ˈwīldiNG/ ▸*n.* *informal* the activity by a gang of youths of going on a protracted and violent rampage in a public place, attacking people at random. ▷1980s: from the adjective WILD + -ING[1].

wild·ing[2] (also **wild·ling** /-liNG/) ▸*n.* a wild plant, esp. an apple tree descended from cultivated varieties, or its fruit. ▷early 16th cent.: from the adjective WILD + -ING[3].

wild·life /ˈwīld,līf/ ▸*n.* wild animals collectively; the native fauna (and sometimes flora) of a region.

wild·life park ▸*n.* see PARK (sense 1).

wild man ▸*n.* a man with a fierce or wildly unruly nature. ■ the image of a primitive or uncivilized man as a symbol of the wild side of human nature or of

W

seasonal fertility. ▪ a supposed manlike animal such as a yeti.

wild mus·tard ▸*n.* charlock.

wild oat ▸*n.* an Old World grass that is related to the cultivated oat and is commonly found as a weed of other cereal plants. • *Avena fatua,* family Gramineae.
▸*PHRASE* □ **sow one's wild oats** see **OAT**.

wild pitch *Baseball* ▸*n.* an errant pitch that is not hit by the batter and cannot be stopped by the catcher, enabling a base runner to advance.
▸*v.* (**wild-pitch**) [*trans.*] enable (a base runner) to advance by making such a pitch: *Reed was wild-pitched to second.*

wild rice ▸*n.* a tall aquatic North American grass related to rice, with edible grains. • *Zizania aquatica,* family Gramineae. ▪ the grain of this plant used as food.

wild serv·ice tree ▸*n.* see **SERVICE TREE**.

wild silk ▸*n.* coarse silk produced by wild silkworms, esp. tussore.

wild type ▸*n. Genetics* a strain, gene, or characteristic that prevails among individuals in natural conditions, as distinct from an atypical mutant type.

Wild West the western U.S. in a time of lawlessness in its early history. The Wild West was the last of a succession of frontiers formed as settlers moved gradually further west. The frontier was officially declared closed in 1890.

wild·wood /ˈwīldˌwo͝od/ ▸*n. chiefly poetic/literary* an uncultivated wood or forest that has been allowed to grow naturally.

wile /wīl/ ▸*n.* (**wiles**) devious or cunning stratagems employed in manipulating or persuading someone to do what one wants.
▸*v.* [*trans.*] **1** *archaic* lure; entice: *she could be neither driven nor wiled into the parish kirk.* **2** (**wile away the time**) another way of saying **WHILE AWAY THE TIME**. See **WHILE**. ▷Middle English: perhaps from an Old Norse word related to *vél* 'craft.'

wil·ful ▸*adj.* variant spelling of **WILLFUL**.

wil·ga /ˈwilgə/ ▸*n.* a small white-flowering Australian tree that is resistant to drought and a valuable source of fodder. In North America, it is also planted as an ornamental. • *Geijera parviflora,* family Rutaceae. ▷late 19th cent.: from Wiradhuri *wilgar.*

Wil·helm I /ˈvilˌhelm/ (1797–1888), king of Prussia 1861–88 and emperor of Germany 1871–88. He became the first emperor of Germany after Prussia's victory against France in 1871. The latter part of his reign was marked by the rise of German socialism, to which he responded with harsh, repressive measures.

Wil·helm II (1859–1941), emperor of Germany 1888–1918; grandson of Wilhelm I and of Queen Victoria; known as **Kaiser Wilhelm**. After forcing Bismarck to resign in 1890, he proved unable to exercise a strong or consistent influence over German policies. Vilified by Allied propaganda as the instigator of World War I, he abdicated and went into exile in 1918.

Wil·hel·mi·na /ˌvilhelˈmēnə/, (1880–1962), queen of the Netherlands 1890–1948. During World War II, she maintained a government in exile in London and through frequent radio broadcasts became a symbol of resistance to the Dutch people. She returned to the Netherlands in 1945.

W

Wilkes /wilks/, Charles (1798–1877), U.S. naval officer and explorer. He determined that Antarctica is a continent during an 1838–42 expedition. Antarctica's Wilkes Land was named in his honor. In 1861, he was involved in the Trent Affair, an incident on the high seas in which Confederate commissioners to England and France were forcibly detained by the U.S. navy.

Wilkes-Barre /ˈwilks ˌbarə; ˌbarē/ an industrial city in northeastern Pennsylvania, on the Susquehanna River, in the Wyoming Valley; pop. 47,523.

Wilkes Land /wilks/ a region of Antarctica that has a coast on the Indian Ocean. It is claimed by Australia. ▷named after the U.S. naval officer Charles *Wilkes*, who sighted and surveyed it between 1838 and 1842.

Wil·kie /ˈwilkē/, Sir David (1785–1841), Scottish painter. He established his reputation with the painting *Village Politicians* (1806). His style contributed to the growing prestige of genre painting.

Wil·kins1 /ˈwilkinz/, Maurice Hugh Frederick (1916–2004), British biochemist and molecular biologist, born in New Zealand. From X-ray diffraction analysis of DNA, he and his colleague Rosalind Franklin confirmed the double helix structure proposed by Francis Crick and James Watson in 1953. Nobel Prize for Physiology or Medicine (1962, shared with Crick and Watson).

Wil·kins2, Roy (1901–81), U.S. civil rights leader. He edited the NAACP's magazine, *The Crisis*, from 1934 until 1949 and then served as executive secretary of the NAACP 1955–77.

Will /wil/, George F. (1941–), U.S. journalist. A columnist and television commentator, his syndicated newspaper column first appeared in *The Washington Post*. He also wrote a column for *Newsweek* magazine from 1976, and appeared on television's "This Week." His books include *Men at Work: The Craft of Baseball* (1989) and *The Woven Figure: Conservatism and America's Fabric 1994–1997* (1997).

will1 /wil/ ▸*modal verb* (*3rd sing. present* **will**; *past* **would** /wo͝od; wəd/) **1** expressing the future tense: *you will regret it when you are older.* ▪ expressing a strong intention or assertion about the future: *come what may, I will succeed.* **2** expressing inevitable events: *accidents will happen.* **3** expressing a request: *will you stop here, please.* ▪ expressing desire, consent, or willingness: *will you have a cognac?* **4** expressing facts about ability or capacity: *a rock so light that it will float on water | your tank will hold about 26 gallons.* **5** expressing habitual behavior: *she will dance for hours.* ▪ (pronounced stressing "will") indicating annoyance about the habitual behavior described: *he will keep intruding.* **6** expressing probability or expectation about something in the present: *they will be miles away by now.* ▷Old English *wyllan*, of Germanic origin; related to Dutch *willen*, German *wollen*, from an Indo-European root shared by Latin *velle* 'will, wish.'
▸*PHRASE* □ **will do** *informal* expressing willingness to carry out a request or suggestion: *"Might be best to check." "Righty-oh, will do."*

USAGE On the differences in use between **will** and **shall**, see usage at **SHALL**.

will2 ▸*n.* **1** [usu. in *sing.*] the faculty by which a person decides on and initiates action: *she has an iron will | a battle of wills between children and their parents | an act of will.* ▪ (also **will·pow·er**) control deliberately exerted to do something or to restrain one's own impulses: *a stupendous effort of will.* ▪ a deliberate or fixed desire or intention: *Jane had not wanted them to stay* ***against their will*** | [with *infinitive*] *the will to live.* ▪ the thing that one desires or ordains: *the disaster was God's will.* **2** a legal document containing instructions as to what should be done with one's money and property after one's death.
▸*v.* [*trans.*] **1** *chiefly formal poetic/literary* intend, desire, or wish (something) to happen: *he was doing what the saint willed* | [with *clause*] *marijuana, dope, grass—call it what you will.* ▪ [*trans.*] make or try to make (someone) do something or (something) happen by the exercise of mental powers: *reluctantly he willed himself to turn and go back | she stared into the fog, willing it to clear.* **2** (**will something to**) bequeath something to (someone) by the terms of one's will. ▪ [with *clause*] leave specified instructions in one's will: *he willed that his body be given to the hospital.* ▷Old English *willa* (noun), *willian* (verb), of Germanic origin; related to Dutch *wil*, German *Wille* (nouns), also to **WILL**1 and the adverb **WELL**1. **—willed** *adj.* [in *combination*] *I'm strong-willed.* **—will-less·ness** *n.* **—will·er** *n.*
▸*PHRASES* □ **at will** at whatever time or in whatever way one pleases: *it can be molded and shaped at will | he was shoved around at will.* □ **have a will of one's own** have a willful character. □ **have one's will** *archaic* obtain what one wants. □ **if you will** said when politely inviting a listener or reader to do something or when using an unusual or fanciful term: *imagine, if you will, a typical silversmith's shop.* □ **where there's a will there's a way** *proverb* determination will overcome any obstacle. □ **with the best will in the world** however good one's intentions (used to imply that success in a particular undertaking is unlikely although desired). □ **with a will** energetically and resolutely.

Wil·lam·ette Riv·er /wəˈlamit/ a river that flows for 300 miles (480 km) through western Oregon to the Columbia River.

Wil·lard1 /ˈwilərd/, Emma (1787–1870), U.S. educator. She founded a boarding school in Vermont in 1814 to teach subjects, such as mathematics and philosophy, not then available to women.

Wil·lard2, Frances Elizabeth Caroline (1839–98), U.S. women's rights and temperance activist. She was president of the Women's Christian Temperance Union 1879, an organizer of the Prohibition Party in 1882, and president of the National Council of Women 1890. She wrote *Woman and Temperance* (1883).

will-call ▸adj. relating to a place (usu. a ticket window or office) where items previously purchased can be picked up: *Those picking up tickets at the will-call window must use the Trumbull entrance.*

wil·lem·ite /ˈwiləˌmīt/ ▸*n.* a mineral, typically greenish-yellow and fluorescent, consisting of a silicate of zinc. ▷mid 19th cent.: from the name of *Willem* I (1772–1843), king of the Netherlands, + **-ITE**1.

Wil·lem·stad /ˈviləmˌstät; ˈwil-/ the capital of the Netherlands Antilles, on the southwestern coast of the island of CuraÃ‡ao; pop. 50,000.

wil·let /ˈwilit/ ▸*n.* (*pl.* same or **-lets**) a large North American sandpiper. • *Catoptrophorus semipalmatus,* family Scolopacidae. ▷mid 19th cent.: imitative of its call, *pill-will-willet.*

will·ful /ˈwilfəl/ (also **wil·ful**) ▸*adj.* (of an immoral or illegal act or omission) intentional; deliberate: *willful acts of damage.* ▪ having or showing a stubborn and determined intention to do as one wants, regardless of the consequences or effects: *the pettish, willful side of him.* ▷Middle English: from the noun **WILL**2 + **-FUL**. **—will·ful·ly** /ˈwilfəlē/ *adv.* **—will·ful·ness** /ˈwilfəlnəs/ *n.*

Wil·liam /ˈwilyəm/ the name of two kings of England and two of Great Britain and Ireland: ▪ **William I** (*c.*1027–87), reigned 1066–87; the first Norman king of England; known as **William the Conqueror**. He invaded England and defeated Harold II at the Battle of Hastings (1066). He introduced Norman institutions and customs (including feudalism) and instigated the Domesday Book. ▪ **William II** (*c.*1060–1100), son of William I; reigned 1087–1100; known as **William Rufus**. He crushed rebellions in 1088 and 1095 and also campaigned against his brother Robert, Duke of Normandy (1089–96), ultimately acquiring the duchy. ▪ **William III** (1650–1702), grandson of Charles I, husband of Mary II; reigned 1689–1702; known as **William of Orange**. In 1688, he deposed James II at the invitation of disaffected politicians and was crowned along with his wife Mary. ▪ **William IV** (1765–1837), son of George III; reigned 1830–7; known as **the Sailor King**. Having served in the Royal Navy, he came to the throne after the death of his brother George IV.

Will·iam I1 (1143–1214), grandson of David I; king of Scotland 1165–1214; known as **William the Lion**.

Will·iam I2 (1533–84), prince of the House of Orange; first stadtholder (chief magistrate) of the United Provinces of the Netherlands 1572–84; known as **William the Silent**.

Will·iam of Oc·cam /ˈäkəm/ (also **Ock·ham**) (*c.*1285–1349), English philosopher and Franciscan friar. A defender of nominalism, he is known for the maxim called "Occam's razor."

Will·iam of Or·ange, William III of Great Britain and Ireland (see **WILLIAM**).

Will·iam Ru·fus /ˈro͞ofəs/, William II of England (see **WILLIAM**).

Will·iams1 /ˈwilyəmz/, Hank (1923–53), U.S. country singer and songwriter; born *Hiram King Williams*. He had the first of many hits, "Lovesick Blues," in 1949 and that year joined the *Grand Ole Opry* television program. Many of his songs were successfully recorded by other artists."Your Cheatin' Heart," recorded in 1952, was released after his sudden death.

Wil·liams2, Myrna see **LOY**.

Wil·liams3, Roger (*c.*1603–83), American clergyman; born in England. Banished from Massachusetts, he founded the colony of Rhode Island and, within it, the settlement of Providence in 1636 as a refuge from political and religious persecution. He served as Rhode Island's president 1654–57.

Wil·liams4 ▸, Rowan Douglas (1950–), Welsh Anglican clergyman; archbishop of Canterbury from 2002. His many books include: *Writing in the Dust: Reflections on 11th September and Its Aftermath* (2002) and *Anglican Identities* (2004).

Wil·liams5 ▸, Serena (1981–), U.S. tennis player. She won the singles titles at the U.S. Open 1999 and 2002, Wimbledon 2002 and 2003, French Open 2002, Australian Open 2003. She is the sister of Venus Williams.

Wil·liams6, Ted (1918–2002), U.S. baseball player; full name *Theodore Samuel Williams*; nickname the **Splendid Splinter**. An outfielder for the Boston Red Sox 1939–1960, except for two stints in military service, he managed the Washington Senators (later the Texas Rangers) 1968–72. Baseball Hall of Fame (1966).

Wil·liams[7], Tennessee (1911–83), U.S. playwright; born *Thomas Lanier Williams.* His success began with *The Glass Menagerie* (1944) and *A Streetcar Named Desire* (1947), which deal with vulnerable heroines living in fragile fantasy worlds that are shattered by brutal reality. Other notable works: *Cat on a Hot Tin Roof* (1955) and *The Night of the Iguana* (1962).

Wil·liams[8] ▶, Venus (1980–), U.S. tennis player. She won the singles titles at the U.S. Open 2000 and 2001 and Wimbledon 2000 and 2001. She is the sister of Serena Williams.

Wil·liams[9], William Carlos (1883–1963), U.S. poet, essayist, novelist, and short-story writer. His poetry illuminates the ordinary by vivid, direct observation; it is characterized by avoidance of emotional content and the use of U.S. vernacular. Collections include *Spring and All* (1923) and *Pictures from Brueghel* (1963).

Wil·liams·burg /ˈwilyəmz,bərg/ **1** a city in southeastern Virginia, between the James and York rivers; pop. 11,530. It was the state capital of Virginia from 1699, when it was renamed in honor of William III, until 1799, when Richmond became the capital. A large part of the town has been restored and reconstructed so that it appears as it was during the colonial era. **2** a residential and industrial section of northern Brooklyn in New York City, noted for its Hasidic Jewish community and arts colony.

Wil·liams·port /ˈwilyəmz,pôrt/ an industrial city in north central Pennsylvania, on the Susquehanna River; the birthplace of Little League baseball; pop. 31,933.

Will·iam the Con·quer·or, William I of England (see WILLIAM).

wil·lies /ˈwilēz/ ▶*plural n.* (**the willies**) *informal* a strong feeling of nervous apprehension and discomfort: *that room **gave him the willies**.* ▷late 19th cent. (originally U.S.): of unknown origin.

will·ing /ˈwiliNG/ ▶*adj.* [often with *infinitive*] ready, eager, or prepared to do something: *he was quite willing to compromise.* ■ given or done readily: *willing and prompt obedience.* **—will·ing·ly** *adv.* **—will·ing·ness** *n.*

Will·ing·bo·ro /ˈwiliNG,bərə/ a residential township in west central New Jersey, near the Delaware River; pop. 36,291. It was founded as Levittown in 1959.

Will·is·ton /ˈwiləstən/ a city in northwestern North Dakota, on the northern banks of the Missouri River; pop. 12,512.

wil·li·waw /ˈwilē,wô/ ▶*n.* a sudden violent squall blowing offshore from a mountainous coast. ▷mid 19th cent.: of unknown origin.

Will·kie, Wendell Lewis (1882–1944) U.S. politician and lawyer. The Republican presidential candidate in 1940, he unsuccessfully ran against incumbent Franklin D. Roosevelt who was running for his third term. He later supported Roosevelt's war effort programs and policies.

will-o'-the-wisp /ˈwil ə T͟Hə ˈwisp/ ▶*n.* an ignis fatuus. ■ *figurative* a person or thing that is difficult or impossible to find, reach, or catch. ▷early 17th cent.: originally as *Will with the wisp*, the sense of *wisp* being 'handful of (lighted) hay.'

wil·low /ˈwilō/ ▶*n.* **1** (also **wil·low tree**) a tree or shrub of temperate climates that typically has narrow leaves, bears catkins, and grows near water. Its pliant branches yield osiers for basketry, and its wood has various uses. • Genus *Salix*, family Salicaceae: many species. **2** a machine with revolving spikes used for cleaning cotton, wool, or other fibers. ▷Old English *welig*, of Germanic origin; related to Dutch *wilg*.

wil·low grouse ▶*n.* another term for WILLOW PTARMIGAN.

wil·low herb (also **wil·low-herb**) ▶*n.* a plant of temperate regions that typically has willowlike leaves and pink or pale purple flowers. • *Epilobium* and related genera, family Onagraceae: many species, including the common **hairy willow herb** (*E. hirsutum*) and the common fireweed (*E. angustifolium*).

wil·low pat·tern ▶*n.* a conventional design representing a Chinese scene in blue on white pottery, typically showing three figures on a bridge, with a willow tree and two birds above: [as *adj.*] *a willow-pattern plate.*

wil·low ptar·mi·gan ▶*n.* a common Eurasian and North American grouse with reddish-brown and white plumage, turning mainly white in winter. • *Lagopus lagopus*, family Tetraonidae (or Phasianidae). See also RED GROUSE.

wil·low·ware /ˈwilō,we(ə)r/ ▶*n.* pottery with a willow-pattern design.

wil·low·y /ˈwilōē/ ▶*adj.* **1** bordered, shaded, or covered by willows: *willowy meadow land.* **2** (of a person) tall, slim, and lithe.

will·pow·er /ˈwil,pou(ə)r/ ▶*n.* see WILL[2] (sense 1).

Wills Mood·y /wilz/, Helen (1905–98), U.S. tennis player; born *Helen Newington Wills.* She won the Wimbledon women's singles championship eight times 1927–30, 1932–33, 1935, 1938; the U.S. Open seven times 1923–25, 1927–29, 1931; and the French Open four times 1932–34, 1936.

wil·ly /ˈwilē/ (also **wil·lie**) ▶*n.* (*pl.* **-lies**) *informal* a penis. ▷early 20th cent.: nickname for the given name *William.*

wil·ly-nil·ly /ˈwilē ˈnilē/ ▶*adv.* **1** whether one likes it or not: *he would be forced to collaborate willy-nilly.* **2** without direction or planning; haphazardly: *politicians expanded spending programs willy-nilly.* ▷early 17th cent.: later spelling of *will I, nill I* 'I am willing, I am unwilling.'

Wil·ming·ton /ˈwilmiNGtən/ **1** the largest city in Delaware, on the Delaware River, in the northeastern part of the state; pop. 72,664. **2** an industrial port city in southeastern North Carolina, on the Cape Fear River and the Atlantic Ocean; pop. 75,838.

Wilms' tu·mor /wilmz/ ▶*n.* a malignant tumor of the kidney, of a type that occurs in young children. ▷early 20th cent.: named after Max *Wilms* (1867–1918), German surgeon.

Wil·son[1] /ˈwilsən/ an industrial city in east central North Carolina; pop. 36,930.

Wil·son[2] /ˈwilsən/, Charles Thomson Rees (1869–1959), Scottish physicist. He invented the cloud chamber, building his first one in 1895. He later improved the design and by 1911 had a chamber in which the track of an ion could be made visible. This became a major tool of particle physicists. Nobel Prize for Physics (1927, shared with Arthur Compton).

Wil·son[3], Edmund (1895–1972), U.S. critic, essayist, and short-story writer. He is remembered chiefly for works of literary and social criticism. He was a friend of F. Scott Fitzgerald and edited the latter's unfinished novel *The Last Tycoon* (1941).

Wil·son[4], Edward Osborne (1929–), U.S. social biologist. He worked principally on social insects, notably ants and termites, extrapolating his findings to the social behavior of other animals, including humans.

Wil·son[5], (James) Harold, Baron Wilson of Rievaulx (1916–95), British statesman; prime minister 1964–70 and 1974–76. Although faced with severe economic problems, his government introduced a number of social reforms, such as comprehensive schooling, and renegotiated Britain's terms of entry into the European Economic Community.

Wil·son[6], James (1742–98), U.S. Supreme Court associate justice 1789–98; born in Scotland. A signer of the Declaration of Independence 1776 and a member of the Continental Congress 1775–77; 1782–83; 1785–87, he was appointed to the Court by President Washington.

Wil·son[7], John Tuzo (1908–93), Canadian geophysicist. He was a pioneer in the study of plate tectonics, introducing the term *plate* in this context in the early 1960s.

Wil·son[8], Teddy (1912–86), U.S. jazz pianist; full name *Theodore Shaw Wilson.* He was a member of Benny Goodman's band and trio 1935–39 and then went on to play with various small groups and to perform by himself.

Wil·son[9], (Thomas) Woodrow (1856–1924), 28th president of the U.S. 1913–21. A Democrat, he eventually took the U.S. into World War I in 1917 and later played a leading role in the peace negotiations and the formation of the League of Nations. The Senate, however, failed to ratify the peace treaty. Semi-incapacitated by a stroke in 1919, he did not seek reelection. Nobel Peace Prize (1920).

Woodrow Wilson

Wil·son, Mount a peak in the San Gabriel Mountains of southwestern California, near Pasadena, site of a major astronomical observatory.

wilt[1] /wilt/ ▶*v.* [*intrans.*] (of a plant, leaf, or flower) become limp through heat, loss of water, or disease; droop. ■ (of a person) lose one's energy or vigor.
▶*n.* [usu. with *adj.*] any of a number of fungal or bacterial diseases of plants characterized by wilting of the foliage. ▷late 17th cent. (originally dialect): perhaps an alteration of dialect *welk* 'lose freshness,' of Low German origin.

wilt[2] ▶ archaic second person singular of WILL[1].

Wil·ton /ˈwiltn/ ▶*n.* a woven carpet resembling a Brussels carpet but with a velvet pile. ▷late 18th cent.: from *Wilton*, the name of a town in southern England, noted for the manufacture of carpets.

Wilts. ▶*abbr.* Wiltshire.

Wilt·shire /ˈwilt,SHi(ə)r; -SHər/ a county of southern England; county town, Trowbridge.

wil·y /ˈwīlē/ ▶*adj.* (**wil·i·er**, **wil·i·est**) skilled at gaining an advantage, esp. deceitfully: *his wily opponents.* **—wil·i·ly** /ˈwīləlē/ *adv.* **—wil·i·ness** *n.*

Wim·ble·don /ˈwimbəldən/ an annual international tennis championship played on grass for individual players and pairs, held at the headquarters of the All England Lawn Tennis and Croquet Club in the London suburb of Wimbledon. Now one of the world's major tennis championships, it has been played since 1877.

wim·min /ˈwimin/ ▶*plural n.* nonstandard spelling of "women" adopted by some feminists to avoid the word ending *-men.*

WIMP[1] /wimp/ ▶*n.* [often as *adj.*] *Computing* a graphical user interface designed to simplify or demystify computing operations. ▷1980s: acronym from *windows, icons, menus, and pointing (device).*

WIMP[2] ▶*n.* *Physics* a hypothetical subatomic particle of large mass that interacts only weakly with ordinary matter, postulated as a constituent of the dark matter of the universe. ▷1980s: acronym from *weakly interacting massive particle.*

wimp /wimp/ *informal* ▶*n.* a weak and cowardly or unadventurous person.
▶*v.* [*intrans.*] (**wimp out**) withdraw from a course of action or a stated position in a way that is seen as feeble or cowardly. ▷1920s: origin uncertain, perhaps from WHIMPER. **—wimp·ish** *adj.* **—wimp·ish·ly** *adv.* **—wimp·ish·ness** *n.* **—wimp·y** *adj.*

wim·ple /ˈwimpəl/ ▶*n.* a cloth headdress covering the head, the neck, and the sides of the face, formerly worn by women and still worn by some nuns. ▷late Old English *wimpel*, of Germanic origin; related to German *Wimpel* 'pennon, streamer.' **—wim·pled** *adj.*

wimple

win /win/ ▶*v.* (**win·ning**; *past* and *past part.* **won** /wən; wän/) [*trans.*] **1** be successful or victorious in (a contest or conflict): *the Mets have won four games in a row* | [*intrans.*] *a determination to win* | [with *complement*] *the Pirates won 2–1.* **2** acquire or secure as a result of a contest, conflict, bet, or other endeavor: *there are hundreds of prizes to be won* | [with *two objs.*] *the sort of play that won them the World Cup.* ■ gain (a person's attention, support, or love), typically gradually or by effort: *you will find it difficult to win back their attention.* ■ (**win someone over**) gain the support or favor of someone by action or persuasion: *her sense of humor had won him over at once.* ■ [*intrans.*] (**win out**) manage to succeed or achieve something by effort: *talent won out over bureaucracy.* ■ *archaic* manage to reach (a place) by effort: *many lived to win the great cave.* ■ obtain (ore) from a mine.

▸*n.* a successful result in a contest, conflict, bet, or other endeavor; a victory: *a win against Norway.* ▷Old English *winnan* 'strive, contend,' also 'subdue and take possession of, acquire,' of Germanic origin. **—win·less** *n.* **—win·na·ble** *adj.*

▸*PHRASES* □ **one can't win** *informal* said when someone feels that no course of action open to them will bring success or please people. □ **win the day** be victorious in battle, sport, or argument. □ **win or lose** whether one succeeds or fails: *win or lose, the important thing for him is to set a good example.* □ **win** (or **earn**) **one's spurs** *historical* gain a knighthood by an act of bravery. ■ *informal* gain one's first distinction or honors. □ **you can't win them all** (or **win some, lose some**) *informal* said to express consolation or resignation after failure in a contest.

wince[1] /wins/ ▸*v.* [*intrans.*] give a slight involuntary grimace or shrinking movement of the body out of or in anticipation of pain or distress: *he winced at the disgust in her voice.*

▸*n.* [in *sing.*] a slight grimace or shrinking movement caused by pain or distress. ▷Middle English (originally in the sense 'kick restlessly from pain or impatience'): from an Anglo-Norman French variant of Old French *guenchir* 'turn aside.' **—winc·er** *n.* **—winc·ing·ly** *adv.*

THE RIGHT WORD **cower, cringe, flinch, recoil, wince**

The same person might **wince** when receiving a flu shot, **flinch** from a difficult task, and **cower** in fear at the approach of a tornado. All of these verbs mean to draw back in alarm, disgust, faintheartedness, or servility, but there are subtle differences among them.

To *wince* is to make a slight recoiling movement, often an involuntary contraction of the facial features, in response to pain or discomfort (*to wince when a singer misses a high note*), while *flinch* may imply a similar drawing-back motion or, more abstractly, a reluctance or avoidance (*to tackle the job without flinching*).

Cower and **cringe** both refer to stooped postures, although *cower* is usually associated with fearful trembling (*he cowered in the doorway*) while *cringe* is usually linked to servile, cowardly, or fawning behavior (*she cringed before her father's authority*).

More than any of the other verbs here, **recoil** suggests a physical movement away from something (*recoil at the sight of a poisonous snake*), although that movement may also be psychological (*recoil at the very thought of a family reunion*).

wince[2] ▸*n.* *Brit.* a roller for moving textile fabric through a dyeing vat. ▷late 17th cent. (in the sense 'winch'): variant of **WINCH**.

winch /winCH/ ▸*n.* **1** a hauling or lifting device consisting of a rope, cable, or chain winding around a horizontal rotating drum, turned by a crank or by motor or other power source; a windlass. **2** the crank of a wheel or axle.

▸*v.* [*trans.*] hoist or haul with a winch. ▷late Old English *wince* 'reel, pulley,' of Germanic origin; related to the verb **WINK**. The verb dates from the early 16th cent. **—winch·er** *n.*

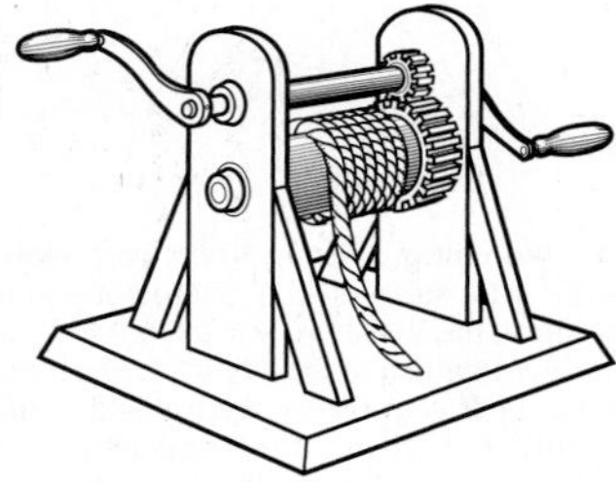

winch 1

Win·ches·ter[1] /ˈwin,CHestər; -CHəstər/ a historic city in northwestern Virginia, in the Shenandoah Valley; pop. 21,947.

Win·ches·ter[2] ▸*n.* **1** (also **Win·ches·ter ri·fle**) *trademark* a breech-loading side-action repeating rifle. [named after Oliver F. *Winchester* (1810–80), the U.S. manufacturer of the rifle.] **2** (in full **Win·ches·ter disk** or **drive**) *Computing* a disk drive in a sealed unit containing a high-capacity hard disk and the read-write heads. [so named because its original numerical designation (30-30) corresponded to the caliber (.30") and the load (30 grains of powder) of the rifle (see sense 1).]

wind[1] ▸*n.* /wind/ **1** the perceptible natural movement of the air, esp. in the form of a current of air blowing from a particular direction: *the wind howled about the building | an easterly wind | gusts of wind.* ■ [as *adj.*] relating to or denoting energy obtained from harnessing the wind with windmills or wind turbines. ■ used to suggest something very fast, unrestrained, or changeable: *run like the wind | she could be as free and easy as the wind.* ■ used in reference to an influence or tendency that cannot be resisted: *a wind of change.* ■ used in reference to an impending situation: *he had seen which way the wind was blowing.* ■ the rush of air caused by a fast-moving body. ■ a scent carried by the wind, indicating the presence or proximity of an animal or person. **2** breath as needed in physical exertion or in speech. ■ the power of breathing without difficulty while running or making a similar continuous effort: *he waited while Jerry got his wind back.* See also **SECOND WIND**. **3** empty, pompous, or boastful talk; meaningless rhetoric. ■ air swallowed while eating or gas generated in the stomach and intestines by digestion. **4** air or breath used for sounding an organ or a wind instrument. ■ (also **winds**) [treated as *sing.* or *pl.*] wind instruments, or specifically woodwind instruments, forming a band or a section of an orchestra: *concerto for piano, violin, and thirteen winds |* [as *adj.*] *wind players.*

▸*v.* /wind/ [*trans.*] **1** (often **be winded**) cause (someone) to have difficulty breathing because of exertion or a blow to the stomach: *the fall nearly winded him.* **2** detect the presence of (a person or animal) by scent: *the birds could not have seen us or winded us.* **3** /wīnd/ (*past* and *past part.* **wind·ed** /ˈwīndid/ or **wound** /wound/) *poetic/literary* sound (a bugle or call) by blowing: *but scarce again his horn he wound.* ▷Old English, of Germanic origin; related to Dutch *wind* and German *Wind*, from an Indo-European root shared by Latin *ventus*. **—wind·less** *adj.*

▸*PHRASES* □ **before the wind** *Sailing* with the wind blowing more or less from astern. □ **get wind of** *informal* begin to suspect that (something) is happening; hear a rumor of: *Marty got wind of a plot being hatched.* [referring originally to the scent of game in hunting.] □ **it's an ill wind that blows no good** *proverb* few things are so bad that no one profits from them. □ **off the wind** *Sailing* with the wind on either quarter. □ **on a wind** *Sailing* against a wind on either bow. □ **put** (or **have**) **the wind up** *Brit., informal* alarm or frighten (or be alarmed or frightened): *he was trying to put the wind up him with stories of how hard teaching was.* □ **sail close to** (or **near**) **the wind** **1** *Sailing* sail as nearly against the wind as possible while still making headway. **2** *informal* verge on indecency, dishonesty, or disaster. □ **take the wind out of someone's sails** frustrate someone by unexpectedly anticipating an action or remark. □ **to the wind** (**s**) (or **the four winds**) in all directions: *my little flock scatters to the four winds.* ■ so as to be abandoned or neglected: *I threw my friends' advice to the winds.* [from 'And fear of death deliver to the winds' (Milton's *Paradise Lost*).]

wind[2] /wīnd/ ▸*v.* (*past* **wound** /wound/) **1** [*intrans.*] move in or take a twisting or spiral course: *the path wound among olive trees.* **2** [*trans.*] pass (something) around a thing or person so as to encircle or enfold: *he wound a towel around his midriff.* ■ repeatedly twist or coil (a length of something) around itself or a core: *Anne wound the wool into a ball.* ■ [*intrans.*] be twisted or coiled in such a way: *large vines wound around every tree.* ■ wrap or surround (a core) with a coiled length of something: *devices wound with copper wire.* **3** [*trans.*] make (a clock or other device, typically one operated by clockwork) operate by turning a key or handle: *he* **wound up** *the clock every Saturday night | she was winding the gramophone.* ■ turn (a key or handle) repeatedly around and around: *I wound the handle as fast as I could.* ■ [*trans.*] cause (an audio or videotape or a film) to move back or forward to a desired point: *wind your tape back and listen to make sure everything is okay.* ■ [*trans.*] hoist or draw (something) with a windlass, winch, or similar device.

▸*phrasal v.* □ **wind down** (of a mechanism, esp. one operated by clockwork) gradually lose power. ■ *informal* (of a person) relax after stress or excitement. ■ (also **wind something down**) draw or bring gradually to a close: *business began to wind down as people awaited the new regime.* □ **wind up** *informal* **1** arrive or end up in a specified state, situation, or place: *Kevin winds up in New York.* **2** another way of saying **WIND SOMETHING UP** (sense 2): *he wound up by attacking Nonconformists.* **3** *Baseball* (of a pitcher) use the windup delivery. □ **wind someone up 1** (usu. **be wound up**) make tense or angry: *he was clearly wound up and frantic about his daughter.* **2** *Brit., informal* tease or irritate someone: *she's only winding me up.* □ **wind something up 1** arrange the affairs of and dissolve a company: *the company has since been wound up.* **2** gradually or finally bring an activity to a conclusion: *the experiments had to be wound up because the funding stopped.* **3** *informal* increase the tension, intensity, or power of something: *he wound up the engine.*

▸*n.* **1** a twist or turn in a course. **2** a single turn made when winding. ▷Old English *windan* 'go rapidly,' 'twine,' of Germanic origin; related to **WANDER** and **WEND**.

wind·age /ˈwindij/ ▸*n.* the air resistance of a moving object, such as a vessel or a rotating machine part, or the force of the wind on a stationary object. ■ the effect of the wind in deflecting a missile such as a bullet.

Win·daus /ˈvin,dous/, Adolf (1876–1959), German organic chemist. He did pioneering work on the chemistry and structure of steroids and their derivatives, notably cholesterol. He also investigated the D vitamins and vitamin B_1 and discovered histamine. Nobel Prize for Chemistry (1928).

wind·bag /ˈwind,bag/ ▸*n.* *informal, derogatory* a person who talks at length but says little of value. **—wind·bag·ger·y** /-ərē/ *n.*

wind band /wind/ ▸*n.* a group of musicians playing mainly woodwind instruments.

wind-borne ▸*adj.* carried by the wind: *wind-borne paper bags and candy wrappers caught on a fence.*

wind·bound /ˈwind,bound/ ▸*adj.* (of a sailing ship) unable to sail because of extreme or contrary winds.

wind·break /ˈwind,brāk/ ▸*n.* a thing, such as a row of trees or a fence, wall, or screen, that provides shelter or protection from the wind.

wind·break·er /ˈwind,brākər/ ▸*n.* *trademark* a wind-resistant jacket with a close-fitting neck, waistband, and cuffs.

wind·burn /ˈwind,bərn/ ▸*n.* reddening and soreness of the skin caused by prolonged exposure to the wind. **—wind·burned** (also *chiefly Brit.* **wind·burnt**) *adj.*

Wind Cave Na·tion·al Park /wind/ a preserve in the Black Hills of South Dakota, noted for its caves and wildlife.

wind·chill /ˈwin(d),CHil/ (also **wind·chill fac·tor** or **chill fac·tor**) ▸*n.* a quantity expressing the effective lowering of the air temperature caused by the wind, esp. as affecting the rate of heat loss from an object or human body or as perceived by an exposed person.

wind chimes /wind/ ▸*plural n.* a decorative arrangement of small pieces of glass, metal, or shell suspended from a frame, typically hung near a door or window so as make a tinkling sound in the breeze.

wind·er /ˈwīndər/ ▸*n.* a device or mechanism used to wind something, esp. something such as a watch or clock or the film in a camera.

Win·der·mere /ˈwində(r),mi(ə)r/ a lake in northwestern England, in the southeastern part of the Lake District. About 10 miles (17 km) in length, it is the largest lake in England.

wind·fall /ˈwind,fôl/ ▸*n.* an apple or other fruit blown down from a tree or bush by the wind. ■ a piece of unexpected good fortune, typically one that involves receiving a large amount of money: [as *adj.*] *windfall profits.*

wind·fall prof·its tax (also **wind·fall tax**) ▸*n.* a tax levied on an unforeseen or unexpectedly large profit, esp. one regarded to be excessive or unfairly obtained.

wind farm /wind/ ▸*n.* an area of land with a group of energy-producing windmills or wind turbines.

wind·flow·er /ˈwind,flou(-ə)r/ ▸*n.* an anemone.

wind·gall /ˈwind,gôl/ ▸*n.* a small painless swelling just above the fetlock of a horse, caused by inflammation of the tendon sheath.

wind gap /wind/ ▸*n.* a valley cut through a ridge by erosion by a river that no longer follows a course through the valley.

wind gauge /wind/ ▸*n.* an anemometer. ■ an apparatus attached to the sights of a gun enabling allowance to be made for the wind in shooting.

wind harp /wind/ ▸*n.* another term for **AEOLIAN HARP**.

Wind·hoek /ˈvint,ho͝ok; ˈwind-/ the capital of Namibia, in the center of the country; pop. 59,000.

wind·hov·er /ˈwind,həvər/ ▸*n. Brit., dialect* a kestrel.

win·di·go /ˈwindi,gō/ (also **wen·di·go**) ▸*n.* (*pl.* **-gos** or **-goes**) (in the folklore of some northern Algonquian peoples) a cannibalistic giant; a person who has been transformed into a monster by the consumption of human flesh. ▷from Ojibwa.

wind·ing /ˈwīndiNG/ ▸*n.* **1** the action of winding something or of moving in a twisting or spiral course. ■ (**windings**) twisting movements: *the windings of the stream.* ■ an electrical conductor that is wound around a magnetic material, esp. one encircling part of the stator or rotor of an electric motor or generator or forming part of a transformer. ■ (**windings**) things that wind or are wound around something. **2** [in *sing.*] (**winding up**) the process of arranging and closing someone's business affairs: *the winding up of a deceased person's affairs.* ■ the process of closing down a company or a financial institution: *the return of capital on a winding up* [as *adj.*] *a winding-up order was issued against BCCI.* **3** [in *sing.*] (**winding down**) the action of gradually drawing or being drawn to a close: *the winding down of the investigation.*
▸*adj.* following a twisting or spiral course: *our bedroom was at the top of a winding staircase.*

wind·ing sheet /ˈwīndiNG/ ▸*n.* a sheet in which a corpse is wrapped for burial; a shroud.

wind in·stru·ment /wind/ ▸*n.* a musical instrument in which sound is produced by the vibration of air, typically by the player blowing into the instrument. ■ a woodwind instrument as distinct from a brass instrument.

wind·jam·mer /ˈwind,jamər/ ▸*n. historical* a merchant sailing ship.

wind·lass /ˈwindləs/ ▸*n.* a type of winch used esp. on ships to hoist anchors and haul on mooring lines and, esp. formerly, to lower buckets into and hoist them up from wells.
▸*v.* [*trans.*] haul or lift (something) with a windlass. ▷late Middle English: probably an alteration of obsolete *windas*, via Anglo-Norman French from Old Norse *vindáss*, literally 'winding pole.'

windlass

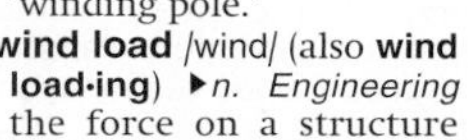
wind load /wind/ (also **wind load·ing**) ▸*n. Engineering* the force on a structure arising from the impact of wind on it.

wind ma·chine /wind/ ▸*n.* a machine used in the theater or in filmmaking for producing a blast of air or imitating the sound of wind. ■ a wind-driven turbine for producing electricity.

wind·mill /ˈwind,mil/ ▸*n.* a building with sails or vanes that turn in the wind and generate power to grind grain into flour. ■ a similar structure used to generate electricity or draw water. ■ *Brit.* a pinwheel. ■ a propeller, esp. one used formerly on an autogiro.
▸*v.* [*trans.*] move (one's arms) around in a circle in a manner suggestive of the rotating sails or vanes of a windmill. ■ [*intrans.*] (of one's arms) move in such a way. ■ [*intrans.*] (of the propeller or rotor of an aircraft, or the aircraft itself) spin unpowered.
▸PHRASE □ **tilt at windmills** see TILT.

windmill

win·dow /ˈwindō/ ▸*n.* **1** an opening in the wall or roof of a building or vehicle that is fitted with glass or other transparent material in a frame to admit light or air and allow people to see out. ■ a pane of glass filling such an opening: *thieves smashed a window and took $600.* ■ an opening in a wall or screen through which customers are served in a bank, ticket office, or similar building. ■ a space on the inside of a store's window where goods are displayed for sale: *I prefer the red dress that's in the window* | [as *adj.*] *beautiful window displays.* **2** a thing resembling such an opening in form or function, in particular: ■ a transparent panel on an envelope to show an address. ■ *Computing* a framed area on a display screen for viewing information. ■ (**window on/into/to**) a means of observing and learning about: *television is a window on the world.* ■ *Physics* a range of electromagnetic wavelengths for which a medium (esp. the atmosphere) is transparent. **3** an interval or opportunity for action: *February 15 to March 15 should be the final window for new offers.* ■ an interval during which atmospheric and astronomical circumstances are suitable for the launch of a spacecraft. **4** strips of metal foil or metal filings dispersed in the air to obstruct radar detection. [military code word.] ▷Middle English: from Old Norse *vindauga*, from *vindr* 'wind' + *auga* 'eye.' —**win·dow·less** *adj.* (in sense 1).
▸PHRASES □ **go out the window** *informal* (of a plan or pattern or behavior) no longer exist; disappear. □ **window of opportunity** a favorable opportunity for doing something that must be seized immediately if it is not to be missed. □ **window of vulnerability** an opportunity to attack something that is at risk (esp. as a cold war claim that America's land-based missiles were easy targets for a Soviet first strike). □ **windows of the soul** organs of sense, esp. the eyes.

win·dow box ▸*n.* a long narrow box in which flowers and other plants are grown, placed on an outside windowsill.

win·dow clean·er ▸*n.* a person employed to clean windows. ■ a substance used for cleaning windows.

win·dow dress·ing ▸*n.* the arrangement of an attractive display in a shop window. ■ an adroit but superficial or actually misleading presentation of something, designed to create a favorable impression: *the government's effort has amounted to little more than window dressing.*

win·dowed /ˈwindōd/ ▸*adj.* **1** having a window or windows for admitting light or air: [in *combination*] *a row of bay-windowed houses.* **2** *Computing* having or using framed areas on a display screen for viewing information.

win·dow frame ▸*n.* a supporting frame for the glass of a window.

win·dow·ing /ˈwindō-iNG/ ▸*n. Computing* the use of windows for the simultaneous display of more than one item on a screen.

win·dow ledge ▸*n.* another term for WINDOWSILL.

win·dow·pane /ˈwindō,pān/ ▸*n.* **1** a pane of glass in a window. **2** a broad flatfish with numerous dark spots, found in the western Atlantic. Also called SAND DAB. • *Scophthalmus aquosus*, family Scophthalmidae (or Bothidae). **3** (in full **win·dow·pane ac·id**) *informal* a gelatin chip containing LSD.

Win·dow Rock a community in northeastern Arizona, capital of the Navajo reservation, named for a limestone formation; pop. 3,306.

Win·dows /ˈwindōz/ ▸*plural n.* [treated as *sing.*] *trademark* a computer operating system with a graphical user interface.

win·dow seat ▸*n.* a seat below a window, esp. one in a bay or alcove. ■ a seat next to a window in an aircraft, train, or other vehicle.

win·dow-shop ▸*v.* [*intrans.*] look at the goods displayed in shop windows, esp. without intending to buy anything: [as *n.*] (**window-shopping**) *window-shopping is the favorite pastime of all New Yorkers.* —**win·dow-shop·per** *n.*

win·dow·sill /ˈwindō,sil/ (also **win·dow sill**) ▸*n.* a ledge or sill forming the bottom part of a window.

win·dow treat·ment ▸*n.* interior decoration for a window or window frame.

wind·pack /ˈwind,pak/ ▸*n.* snow that has been compacted by the wind.

wind·pipe /ˈwind,pīp/ ▸*n.* the air passage from the throat to the lungs; the trachea.

Wind Riv·er Range /wind/ a range of the Rocky Mountains in western Wyoming that rises to 13,804 feet (4,207 m) at Gannett Peak, the highest in the state.

wind rose /wind/ ▸*n.* a diagram showing the relative frequency of wind directions at a place.

wind·row /ˈwind,rō/ ▸*n.* a long line of raked hay or sheaves of grain laid out to dry in the wind. ■ a long line of material heaped up by the wind.

wind·sail /ˈwind,sāl/ ▸*n. historical* a long wide tube or funnel of sailcloth used to convey air to the lower parts of a ship.

wind scor·pi·on /wind/ ▸*n.* another term for SUN SPIDER.

wind·screen /ˈwind,skrēn/ ▸*n.* British term for WINDSHIELD.

wind shear /wind/ ▸*n.* variation in wind velocity occurring along a direction at right angles to the wind's direction and tending to exert a turning force.

wind·shield /ˈwind,SHēld/ ▸*n.* a window at the front of the passenger compartment of a motor vehicle.

wind·shield wip·er (*Brit.* **wind·screen wip·er**) ▸*n.* a power-operated device for keeping a windshield clear of rain, typically one with a rubber blade on an arm that moves in an arc.

wind·slab /ˈwind,slab/ ▸*n.* a thick crust formed on the surface of soft snow by the wind, of a kind liable to slip and create an avalanche.

wind·sock /ˈwind,säk/ ▸*n.* a light, flexible cylinder or cone mounted on a mast to show the direction and strength of the wind, esp. at an airfield.

Wind·sor[1] /ˈwinzər/ **1** a town in southern England, on the Thames River, opposite Eton; pop. 32,000. **2** an industrial city and port in Ontario, southern Canada, on Lake Ontario, opposite the U.S. city of Detroit; pop. 191,435. **3** /ˈwin(d)zər/ a commercial and residential town in north central Connecticut, north of Hartford; pop. 27,817.

Wind·sor[2] the name of the British royal family since 1917. Previously Saxe-Coburg-Gotha, it was changed in response to anti-German feeling in World War I.

Wind·sor, Duke of the title conferred on Britain's Edward VIII upon his abdication in 1936.

Wind·sor Cas·tle a royal residence at Windsor, founded by William the Conqueror on the site of an earlier fortress and extended by his successors, particularly Edward III. The castle was severely damaged by fire in 1992.

Wind·sor chair ▸*n.* a wooden dining chair with a semicircular back supported by upright rods.

Wind·sor knot ▸*n.* a large, loose triangular knot in a necktie, produced by making extra turns when tying.

Wind·sor tie ▸*n. dated* a wide silk bias-cut necktie, tied in a loose double knot.

Windsor chair

wind sprint /wind/ ▸*n. Track & Field* a form of exercise consisting of repeated alternation between a walk or slow run and a faster run.

wind·storm /ˈwind,stôrm/ ▸*n.* a storm with very strong wind but little or no rain or snow; a gale.

wind-suck·ing /wind/ ▸*n.* (in a horse) habitual behavior involving repeated arching of the neck and sucking in and swallowing air, often accompanied by a grunting sound. —**wind-suck·er** *n.*

wind·surf·er /ˈwind,sərfər/ ▸*n.* a person who takes part in windsurfing. ■ *trademark* a sailboard.

wind·surf·ing /ˈwind,sərfiNG/ ▸*n.* the sport or pastime of riding on water on a sailboard. —**wind·surf** *v.*

wind·swept /ˈwind,swept/ ▸*adj.* **1** (of a place) exposed to strong winds: *the windswept moors.* **2** (of a person or their appearance) affected, shaped, or mussed by exposure to the wind: *his windswept hair.*

wind tun·nel /wind/ ▸*n.* a tunnel-like apparatus for producing an airstream of known velocity past models of aircraft, buildings, etc., in order to investigate flow or the effect of wind on the full-size object. ■ an open space through which strong winds are channeled by surrounding tall buildings.

wind tur·bine /wind/ ▸*n.* a turbine having a large vaned wheel rotated by the wind to generate electricity.

wind·up /ˈwīnd,əp/ ▸*n.* **1** an act of concluding or finishing something: *the windup of the convention.* **2** *Baseball* the motions of a pitcher immediately before delivering the ball, in which they take a step back, lift the hands over the head, and step forward. **3** *Brit., informal* an attempt to tease or irritate someone.
▸*adj.* (of a toy or other device) functioning by means of winding a key or handle: *a windup clock.*

wind·ward /ˈwindwərd/ ▸*adj.* & *adv.* facing the wind or on the side facing the wind: [as *adj.*] *the windward side of the boat.* Contrasted with LEEWARD.
▸*n.* the side or direction from which the wind is

blowing: *the ships drifted west, leaving the island quite a distance **to windward**.*

▸PHRASE □ **to windward of** *dated* in an advantageous position in relation to: *I happen to have **got to windward of** the young woman.*

Wind·ward Is·lands **1** a group of islands in the eastern Caribbean Sea that constitute the southern part of the Lesser Antilles. They include Martinique, Dominica, St. Lucia, Barbados, St. Vincent and the Grenadines, and Grenada. Their name refers to their position further upwind, in terms of the prevailing southeastern winds, than the Leeward Islands. **2** an island group in the eastern Society Islands in French Polynesia that include Moorea and Tahiti. French name **ILES DU VENT**.

Wind·ward Pas·sage an ocean channel between Cuba on the west and Haiti on the east that connects the Caribbean Sea with the Atlantic Ocean.

wind·y[1] /ˈwindē/ ▸*adj.* (**wind·i·er**, **wind·i·est**) **1** (of weather, a period of time, or a place) marked by or exposed to strong winds: *a very windy day.* ■ resembling the wind in sound or force: *Pratt's sigh was windy.* **2** *Brit.* suffering from, marked by, or causing an accumulation of gas in the alimentary canal. ■ *informal* using or expressed in many words that sound impressive but mean little: *windy speeches.* ▷Old English *windig* (see **WIND**[1], **-Y**[1]). **—wind·i·ly** /-əlē/ *adv.* **—wind·i·ness** *n.*

wind·y[2] /ˈwīndē/ ▸*adj.* (of a road or river) following a curving or twisting course.

wine /wīn/ ▸*n.* an alcoholic drink made from fermented grape juice. ■ [with *adj.*] an alcoholic drink made from the fermented juice of specified other fruits or plants: *a glass of dandelion wine.* ■ short for **WINE RED**.

▸*v.* [*trans.*] (**wine and dine someone**) entertain someone by offering them drinks or a meal: *members of Congress have been lavishly wined and dined by lobbyists for years.* ■ [*intrans.*] (of a person) take part in such entertainment: *we wined and dined with Eddie's and Bernie's friends.* ▷Old English *wīn*, of Germanic origin; related to Dutch *wijn*, German *Wein*, based on Latin *vinum*. **—wine·y** (also **win·y**) *adj.*

▸PHRASE □ **good wine needs no bush** *proverb* there's no need to advertise or boast about something of good quality as people will always discover its merits. [a *bush* was an innkeeper's sign, originally depicting a bunch of ivy used (in place of grape leaves) to show that the establishment sold wine.]

wine bar ▸*n.* a bar or small restaurant where wine is the main drink available.

wine·ber·ry /ˈwīn,berē/ ▸*n.* a bristly deciduous shrub native to China and Japan, producing scarlet berries used in cooking. • *Rubus phoenicolasius*, family Rosaceae. ■ the fruit of this bush.

wine·bib·ber /ˈwīn,bibər/ ▸*n.* *archaic* or *poetic/literary* a habitual drinker of alcohol. **—wine·bib·bing** /-,bibiNG/ *n.* & *adj.*

wine bot·tle ▸*n.* a glass bottle for wine, the standard size holding 75 cl or 26 2/3 fl. oz.

wine cel·lar ▸*n.* a cellar in which wine is stored. ■ a stock of wine.

wine cool·er ▸*n.* a container for chilling a bottle of wine. ■ a bottled drink made from wine, fruit juice, and carbonated water.

wine·glass /ˈwīn,glas/ ▸*n.* a glass with a stem and foot, used for drinking wine. **—wine·glass·ful** /ˈwīnglas,fo͝ol/ *n.* (*pl.* **-fuls**).

wine·grow·er /ˈwīn,grōər/ ▸*n.* a cultivator of grapes for wine.

wine list ▸*n.* a list of the wines available in a restaurant: ■ a restaurant's selection or stock or wines.

wine·mak·er /ˈwīn,mākər/ ▸*n.* a producer of wine; a winegrower.

wine·mak·ing /ˈwīn,mākiNG/ ▸*n.* the production of wine.

wine·press /ˈwīn,pres/ ▸*n.* a press in which grapes are squeezed in making wine.

wine red ▸*n.* a dark red color like that of red wine.

win·er·y /ˈwīnərē/ ▸*n.* (*pl.* **-er·ies**) an establishment where wine is made.

Wine·sap /ˈwīn,sap/ ▸*n.* a large red apple, used for cooking and as a dessert apple.

wine·skin /ˈwīn,skin/ ▸*n.* an animal skin sewn up and used to hold wine.

wine stew·ard ▸*n.* a waiter responsible for serving wine.

wine tast·ing ▸*n.* an event at which people taste and compare a number of wines. ■ the action of judging the quality of wine by tasting it. **—wine tast·er** *n.*

wine vin·e·gar ▸*n.* vinegar made from wine rather than malt.

Win·frey /ˈwinfrē/, Oprah (1954–), U.S. television talk-show host, actress, and publisher. In 1984, she started as a talk-show host on "A.M. Chicago," which evolved into the nationally televised "Oprah Winfrey Show" in 1986. She also played Sofia in the movie *The Color Purple* (1985) and began publishing *O* magazine in 2000.

Oprah Winfrey

wing /wiNG/ ▸*n.* **1** any of a number of specialized paired appendages that enable some animals to fly, in particular: ■ (in a bird) a modified forelimb that bears large feathers. ■ (in a bat or pterosaur) a modified forelimb with skin stretched between or behind the fingers. ■ (in most insects) each of two or four flat extensions of the thoracic cuticle, either transparent or covered in scales. ■ the meat on the wing bone of a bird used as food. ■ (usu. **wings**) *figurative* power or means of flight or rapid motion: *time flies by **on wings**.* **2** a rigid horizontal structure that projects from both sides of an aircraft and supports it in the air. ■ (**wings**) a pilot's certificate of ability to fly a plane, indicated by a badge representing a pair of wings: *Michael earned his wings as a commercial pilot.* **3** a part that projects, in particular: ■ *Brit.* a raised part of the body of a car or other vehicle above the wheel. ■ [usu. with *adj.*] a part of a large building, esp. one that projects from the main part: *the maternity wing at South Cleveland Hospital.* ■ either end (port or starboard) of a ship's navigational bridge. ■ *Anatomy* a lateral part or projection of an organ or structure. ■ *Botany* a thin membranous appendage of a fruit or seed that is dispersed by the wind. **4** a group within a political party or other organization that holds particular views or has a particular function: *Sinn Fein, the political wing of the IRA.* **5** a side area, or a person or activity associated with that area, in particular: ■ (**the wings**) the sides of a theater stage out of view of the audience. ■ (in soccer, rugby, and other games) the part of the field close to the sidelines. ■ (in soccer, ice hockey, and other games) an attacking player who plays mostly forward close to one side of the field or rink. ■ a flank of a battle array. **6** an air force unit of several squadrons or groups.

▸*v.* **1** [*intrans.*] travel on wings or by aircraft; fly: *a bird came winging around the corner.* ■ move, travel, or be sent quickly, as if flying: *the prize will be **winging its way** to you soon.* ■ [*trans.*] throw with the arm: *he scooped up the ball and winged it toward Freddie.* ■ [*trans.*] send or convey (something) quickly, as if by air: *just jot down the title on a postcard and wing it to us.* ■ [*trans.*] *archaic* enable (someone or something) to fly or move rapidly: *the convent was at some distance, but fear would wing her steps.* **2** [*trans.*] shoot (a bird) in the wing, so as to prevent flight without causing death: *one bird was winged for every bird killed.* ■ wound (someone) superficially, esp. in the arm or shoulder. **3** (**wing it**) *informal* speak or act without preparation; improvise: *a little boning up puts you ahead of the job seekers who try to wing it.* [from theatrical slang, originally meaning 'to play a role without properly knowing the text' (either by relying on a prompter in the wings or by studying the part in the wings between scenes).] ▷Middle English (originally in the plural): from Old Norse *vængir*, plural of *vængr*. **—wing·less** *adj.* **—wing·like** /-,līk/ *adj.*

▸PHRASES □ **in the wings** ready to do something or to be used at the appropriate time: *there are no obvious successors **waiting in the wings**.* □ **on the wing** (of a bird) in flight. □ **on a wing and a prayer** with only the slightest chance of success. □ **spread** (or **stretch** or **try**) **one's wings** extend one's activities and interests or start new ones. □ **take wing** (of a bird, insect, or other winged creature) fly away. □ **under one's wing** in or into one's protective care.

wing·back ▸*n.* **1** *Football* an offensive back who lines up outside an end. **2** *Soccer* a player who plays in a wide position on the field, taking part both in attack and defense.

wing·beat /ˈwiNG,bēt/ ▸*n.* one complete set of motions of a wing in flying.

wing case ▸*n.* each of a pair of modified toughened forewings that cover the functional wings in certain insects, esp. an elytron of a beetle.

wing chair ▸*n.* a high-backed armchair with side pieces projecting from the back, originally in order to protect the sitter from drafts.

wing chair

wing col·lar ▸*n.* a high stiff shirt collar with turned-down corners.

wing cov·ert ▸*n.* (in a bird's wing) each of the smaller feathers covering the bases of the flight feathers.

wing dam ▸*n.* a dam or barrier built into a stream to deflect the current.

wing·ding /ˈwiNG,diNG/ ▸*n.* *informal* a lively event or party. ▷1920s (in the sense 'spasm, seizure,' esp. one associated with drug-taking): of unknown origin.

winged /wiNGd/ ▸*adj.* **1** having wings for flight: *the earliest winged insects.* ■ /ˈwiNGid/ *figurative, poetic/literary* gracefully swift; able to move as if with wings: *the entire evening had gone by on winged feet.* **2** having one or more lateral parts, appendages, or projections: *those eyeglasses with the winged frames were very popular.*

winged bean ▸*n.* a tropical Asian pea plant that has four-sided pods with longitudinal flanges. The entire pod and the roots are edible and are noted for their high protein content. • *Psophocarpus tetragonolobus*, family Leguminosae.

winged elm ▸*n.* a North American elm that has extremely short leafstalks and flat corky projections on its branchlets. • *Ulmus alata*, family Ulmaceae.

Winged Vic·to·ry ▸*n.* a winged statue of Nike, the Greek goddess of victory, esp. the Nike of Samothrace (*c.*200 BC) preserved in the Louvre in Paris.

winged words ▸*plural n.* *poetic/literary* highly apposite or significant words.

wing·er /ˈwiNGər/ ▸*n.* **1** an attacking player on the wing in soccer, hockey, and other sports. **2** [in *combination*] a member of a specified political wing: *a left-winger.*

wing for·ward ▸*n.* *Soccer* see **WING** (sense 5 of the *noun*).

wing·let /ˈwiNGlit/ ▸*n.* a little wing. ■ a vertical projection on the tip of an aircraft wing for reducing drag.

wing·man /ˈwiNG,mən/ ▸*n.* (*pl.* **-men**) **1** a pilot whose aircraft is positioned behind and outside the leading aircraft in a formation. **2** another term for **WINGER** (sense 1).

wing nut ▸*n.* **1** (also **wing·nut**) a nut with a pair of projections for the fingers to screw it on. **2** an Asian tree of the walnut family, with a deeply fissured trunk, compound leaves, and characteristic broad-winged nutlets. • Genus *Pterocarya*, family Juglandaceae.

wing·o·ver /ˈwiNG,ōvər/ ▸*n.* a maneuver in which an aircraft turns at the top of a steep climb and flies back along its original path.

wing oys·ter ▸*n.* an edible marine bivalve mollusk with a fragile flattened shell, the hinge of which bears winglike projections. • Family Pteridae: *Pteria* and other genera.

wing sail ▸*n.* a rigid or semirigid structure similar to an aircraft wing fixed vertically on a boat to provide thrust from the action of the wind.

wing shoot·ing ▸*n.* the shooting of birds in flight.

wing·span /ˈwiNG,span/ (also **wing·spread** /-,spred/) ▸*n.* the maximum extent across the wings of an aircraft, bird, or other flying animal, measured from tip to tip. ■ the distance between opposite fingertips of the outstretched arms of an athlete, especially a basketball player: *Warrick's massive wingspan got in the way of Kansas's national championship hopes.*

wing·stroke /ˈwiNG,strōk/ ▸*n.* another term for **WINGBEAT**.

wing tip (also **wing·tip**) ▸*n.* **1** the tip of the wing of an aircraft, bird, or other animal. **2** a shoe with a toe cap having a backward extending point and curving sides, resembling the shape of a wing.

wing tip 2

wing walk·ing ▸*n.* acrobatic stunts performed on the wings of an airborne aircraft as a public entertainment.

wink /wiNGk/ ▸*v.* [*intrans.*] close and open one eye quickly, typically to indicate that something is a joke or a secret or as a signal of affection or greeting: *he winked at Nicole as he passed.* ■ (**wink at**) pretend not to notice (something bad or illegal): *the authorities winked at their illegal trade.* ■ (of a bright object or a light) shine or flash intermittently.
▸*n.* an act of closing and opening one eye quickly, typically as a signal: *Barney gave him a knowing wink.* ▷Old English *wincian* 'close the eyes,' of Germanic origin; related to German *winken* 'to wave,' also to WINCE[1].
▸*PHRASES* □ **as easy as winking** *informal* very easy or easily. □ **in the wink of an eye** (or **in a wink**) very quickly. □ **not sleep** (or **get**) **a wink** (or **not get a wink of sleep**) not sleep at all.

win·kle /'wiNGkəl/ ▸*n.* a small herbivorous shore-dwelling mollusk with a spiral shell. Also called PERIWINKLE[2]. • Family Littorinidae, class Gastropoda: many genera and species, including the common and edible *Littorina littorea*.
▸*v.* [*trans.*] (**winkle something out**) *chiefly Brit.* extract or obtain something with difficulty: *I swore I wasn't going to tell her, but she* **winkled** *it all* **out of** *me.* ▷late 16th cent.: shortening of PERIWINKLE[2]. —**win·kler** /'wiNGk(ə)lər/ *n.*

win·kle-pick·er ▸*n. Brit., informal* a shoe with a long pointed toe, popular in the 1950s.

Win·ne·ba·go /,winə'bāgō/ ▸*n.* (*pl.* same or **-gos**) **1** a member of an American Indian people formerly living in eastern Wisconsin and now mainly in southern Wisconsin and Nebraska. **2** the Siouan language of this people. **3** (*pl.* **-gos**) *trademark* a motor vehicle with living accommodations used when traveling long distances or camping.
▸*adj.* of or relating to the Winnebago people or their language. ▷Algonquian, literally 'person of the dirty water,' referring to the muddy Fox River.

Win·ne·ba·go, Lake /,winə'bāgō/ the largest lake in Wisconsin, in the east central part of the state.

win·ner /'winər/ ▸*n.* a person or thing that wins something: *a Nobel Prize winner.* ■ a goal or shot that wins a winner or point. ■ *Bridge* a card that can be relied on to win a trick. ■ *informal* a thing that is a success or is likely to be successful: *the changes failed to make the soap opera a winner.*

win·ner's cir·cle ▸*n.* a small circular area or enclosure at a racetrack where the winning horse and jockey are brought to receive their awards and have photographs taken.

win·ning /'winiNG/ ▸*adj.* **1** [*attrib.*] gaining, resulting in, or relating to victory in a contest or competition: *a winning streak.* **2** attractive; endearing: *a winning smile.*
▸*n.* **1** (**winnings**) money won, esp. by gambling: *he went to collect his winnings.* **2** *Mining* a shaft or pit together with the apparatus for extracting coal or other minerals. —**win·ning·ly** *adv.* (in sense 2 of the *adjective*).

win·ning·est /'winiNGist/ ▸*adj. informal* having achieved the most success in competition: *the winningest coach in pro-football history.*

win·ning post ▸*n.* a post marking the end of a race.

Win·ni·peg /'winə,peg/ a city in southern central Canada, the capital of the province of Manitoba, at the confluence of the Assiniboine and Red rivers, south of Lake Winnipeg; pop. 616,790.

Win·ni·peg, Lake a large lake in central Canada, in southern central Manitoba, north of the city of Winnipeg. Fed by the Saskatchewan, Winnipeg, and Red rivers from the east and south, the lake is drained by the Nelson River, which flows northeast to Hudson Bay.

Win·ni·pe·sau·kee, Lake /,winəpə'sôkē; -'säkē/ the largest lake in New Hampshire, a resort center in the east central part of the state.

win·now /'winō/ ▸*v.* **1** [*trans.*] blow a current of air through (grain) in order to remove the chaff. ■ remove (chaff) from grain: *women* **winnow** *the chaff from piles of unhusked rice.* ■ reduce the number in a set of (people or things) gradually until only the best ones are left: *the contenders had been winnowed to five.* ■ find or identify (a valuable or useful part of something): *amidst this welter of confusing signals, it's difficult to* **winnow out** *the truth.* ■ identify and remove (the least valuable or useful people or things): *guidelines that would help* **winnow out** *those not fit to be soldiers.* **2** [*intrans.*] *poetic/literary* (of the wind) blow: *the autumn wind winnowing its way through the grass.* ■ [*trans.*] (of a bird) fan (the air) with wings. ▷Old English *windwian*, from *wind* (see WIND[1]). —**win·now·er** *n.*

win·o /'wīnō/ ▸*n.* (*pl.* **-os**) *informal* a person who drinks excessive amounts of cheap wine or other alcohol, esp. one who is homeless.

Wi·no·na /wə'nōnə/ an industrial city in southeastern Minnesota, on the Mississippi River; pop. 25,399.

win·some /'winsəm/ ▸*adj.* attractive or appealing in appearance or character: *a winsome smile.* ▷Old English *wynsum*, from *wyn* 'joy' + -SOME[1]. —**win·some·ly** *adv.* —**win·some·ness** *n.*

Win·ston-Sa·lem /,winstən 'sāləm/ an industrial and commercial city in north central North Carolina, a tobacco-processing center; pop. 185,776.

win·ter /'wintər/ ▸*n.* the coldest season of the year, in the northern hemisphere from December to February and in the southern hemisphere from June to August: *the tree has a good crop of berries in winter* | [as *adj.*] *the winter months.* ■ *Astronomy* the period from the winter solstice to the vernal equinox. ■ (**winters**) *poetic/literary* years: *he seemed a hundred winters old.*
▸*adj.* [*attrib.*] (of fruit and vegetables) ripening late in the growing season and suitable for storage over the winter: *a winter apple.* ■ (of wheat or other crops) sown in autumn for harvesting the following year.
▸*v.* [*intrans.*] (esp. of a bird) spend the winter in a particular place: *birds wintering in the Channel.* ■ [*trans.*] keep or feed (plants or cattle) during winter. ▷Old English, of Germanic origin; related to Dutch *winter* and German *Winter*, probably also to WET. —**win·ter·er** *n.* —**win·ter·less** *adj.* —**win·ter·ly** *adj.*

win·ter ac·o·nite ▸*n.* see ACONITE.

win·ter·ber·ry /'wintər,berē/ (also **win·ter·ber·ry hol·ly**) ▸*n.* (*pl.* **-ries**) a North American holly with toothed, nonprickly leaves and berries that persist through the winter. • Genus *Ilex*, family Aquifoliaceae: several species, in particular the **common winterberry** (*I. verticillata*) and the **smooth winterberry** (*I. laevigata*).

win·ter·bourne /'wintər,bôrn/ ▸*n. Brit.* a stream, typically on chalk or limestone, that flows only after wet weather. ▷Old English *winterburna* (see WINTER, BURN[2]).

win·ter cher·ry ▸*n.* a plant of the nightshade family, with cherrylike fruit that ripens in winter. • Several species in the family Solanaceae, in particular *Physalis alkekengi*, the Chinese lantern plant.

win·ter creep·er ▸*n.* an evergreen clinging vine that is native to China and cultivated elsewhere as an ornamental ground cover. It has escaped cultivation and is regarded as an ecological threat in some eastern U.S. states. • *Euonymus fortunei*, family Celastraceae.

win·ter cress ▸*n.* a bitter-tasting cress of north temperate regions. • Genus *Barbarea*, family Brassicaceae: several species, in particular *B. vulgaris*.

win·ter cur·rant ▸*n.* another term for RED-FLOWERING CURRANT (see FLOWERING CURRANT).

win·ter floun·der ▸*n.* a common flatfish of the western Atlantic, having cryptic gray-brown coloration and popular as food in winter in North America. • *Pseudopleuronectes americanus*, family Pleuronectidae.

win·ter gar·den ▸*n.* a garden of plants, such as evergreens, that flourish in winter. ■ a conservatory in which flowers and other plants are grown in winter.

win·ter·green /'wintər,grēn/ ▸*n.* **1** a North American plant from which a pungent oil is obtained, in particular the checkerberry or related shrubs. ■ (also **oil of win·ter·green**) a pungent oil containing methyl salicylate, now obtained chiefly from the sweet birch or made synthetically, used medicinally and as a flavoring. **2** a low-growing plant of acid soils in north temperate regions, with spikes of white bell-shaped flowers. • *Chimaphila*, *Pyrola* and other genera, family Pyrolaceae (the wintergreen family): several species, including the **spotted wintergreen** (*C. maculata*). ▷mid 16th cent.: the plants so named because of remaining green in winter, suggested by Dutch *wintergroen*, German *Wintergrün*.

Win·ter Ha·ven a resort and industrial city in central Florida; pop. 24,725.

win·ter·ize /'wintə,rīz/ ▸*v.* [*trans.*] (usu. **be winterized**) adapt or prepare (something, esp. a house or an automobile) for use in cold weather: *a waterfront cottage that Dixon had winterized.* —**win·ter·i·za·tion** /,wintəri'zāSHən/ *n.*

win·ter jas·mine ▸*n.* a yellow-flowered Chinese jasmine that blooms during the winter. • *Jasminum nudiflorum*, family Oleaceae.

win·ter mel·on ▸*n.* a variety of muskmelon with a sweet, edible flesh that requires a long growing season and ripens in late autumn, making it available in many supermarkets during the winter.

win·ter moth ▸*n.* a moth that emerges in the winter, the female of which has only vestigial wings. It was formerly a major pest of fruit trees. • Several species in the family Geometridae.

Win·ter O·lym·pics an international contest of winter sports held every four years at a two-year interval from the summer games. They have been held separately from the main games since 1924.

Win·ter Pal·ace the former Russian imperial residence in St. Petersburg, stormed in the Revolution of 1917 and later used as a museum and art gallery.

Win·ter Park a resort and citrus-growing city in east central Florida, northeast of Orlando; pop. 22,242.

win·ter quar·ters ▸*plural n.* accommodations for the winter, esp. for soldiers.

win·ter sleep ▸*n.* hibernation.

win·ter sol·stice ▸*n.* the solstice that marks the onset of winter, at the time of the shortest day, about December 22 in the northern hemisphere and June 21 in the southern hemisphere. ■ *Astronomy* the solstice in December.

win·ter sports ▸*plural n.* sports performed on snow or ice, such as skiing and ice skating.

win·ter squash ▸*n.* a squash that has a hard rind and may be stored. • Cultivars of *Cucurbita moschata* and *C. maxima*, family Cucurbitaceae.

win·ter·sweet /'wintər,swēt/ ▸*n.* a deciduous Chinese shrub that produces heavily scented yellow flowers in winter before the leaves appear, grown in North America as an ornamental. • *Chimonanthus praecox*, family Calycanthaceae.

win·ter·tide /'wintər,tīd/ ▸*n.* poetic/literary term for WINTERTIME.

win·ter·time /'wintər,tīm/ ▸*n.* the season or period of winter.

Win·throp[1] /'winTHrəp/, John (1588–1649), American colonial leader; born in England. He was the first governor 1630–49 of the Massachusetts Bay Colony. His son **John Winthrop, Jr.**, served as the governor of Connecticut 1657, 1659–76.

Win·throp[2], John (1714–79), American astronomer and physicist. He was the first American to practice rigorous experimental science, giving laboratory demonstrations of electricity in 1746 and predicting the return of Halley's Comet in 1759.

win·try /'wintrē/ (also **win·ter·y** /'wint(ə)rē/) ▸*adj.* (**-tri·er**, **-tri·est**) characteristic of winter, esp. in feeling or looking very cold and bleak: *a wintry landscape* | *figurative his eyes were decidedly wintry.* ▷Old English *wintrig* (see WINTER, -Y[1]). —**win·tri·ly** /-trəlē/ *adv.* —**win·tri·ness** *n.*

win·try mix ▸*n.* variable precipitation consisting of rain, freezing rain, sleet, or snow: *the wintry mix slowed down drivers crossing the Blue Ridge Mountains.*

win-win ▸*adj.* [*attrib.*] of or denoting a situation in which each party benefits in some way: *we are aiming for a win-win situation.*

WIP ▸*abbr.* work in progress (chiefly in business and financial contexts).

wipe /wīp/ ▸*v.* [*trans.*] clean or dry (something) by rubbing its surface with a cloth, a piece of paper, or one's hand: *Paul wiped his face with a handkerchief* | *he* **wiped down** *the kitchen wall.* ■ [*trans.*] remove (dirt or moisture) from something by rubbing its surface with a cloth, a piece of paper, or one's hand: *she wiped away a tear.* ■ clean (something) by rubbing it against a surface: *the man wiped his hands on his hips.* ■ [*trans.*] spread (a liquid) over a surface by rubbing:

gently wipe the lotion over the eyelids. ■ [*trans.*] *figurative* remove or eliminate (something) completely: *things have happened to wipe the smile off Kate's face.* ■ erase (data) from a magnetic medium.

▶*phrasal v.* □ **wipe something off** subtract an amount from a value or debt: *the crash wiped 24 percent off stock prices.* □ **wipe out** *informal* fall over or off a vehicle. ■ be capsized by a wave while surfing. □ **wipe someone out 1** kill a large number of people: *the plague had wiped out whole villages.* **2** (usu. **be wiped out**) ruin someone financially. **3** *informal* exhaust or intoxicate someone. □ **wipe something out** eliminate something completely: *their life savings were wiped out.*

▶*n.* **1** an act of wiping. **2** a piece of disposable absorbent cloth or paper, esp. one treated with a cleansing agent, for wiping something clean. **3** a cinematographic effect in which an existing picture seems to be wiped out by a new one as the boundary between them moves across the screen. ▷Old English *wīpian*, of Germanic origin; related to WHIP. **—wipe·a·ble** *adj.*

▶*PHRASES* □ **wipe the floor with** *informal* inflict a humiliating defeat on: *they wiped the floor with us in a 36-6 win.* □ **wipe the slate clean** forgive or forget past faults or offenses; make a fresh start.

wipe·out /ˈwīpˌout/ ▶*n. informal* an instance of complete destruction: *a nuclear wipeout.* ■ a complete failure. ■ the obliteration of one radio signal by another. ■ a fall from a surfboard.

wip·er /ˈwīpər/ ▶*n.* **1** a windshield wiper. **2** an electrical contact that moves across a surface.

WIPO ▶*abbr.* World Intellectual Property Organization.

Wi·ra·dhur·i /ˌwērəˈjŏŏrē/ ▶*n.* an Aboriginal language of southeastern Australia, now extinct.

wire /wīr/ ▶*n.* **1** metal drawn out into the form of a thin flexible thread or rod. ■ a piece of such metal. ■ a length or quantity of wire used, for example, for fencing or to carry an electric current. ■ *Horse Racing* a wire stretched across and above the track at the finish line of a racetrack. ■ an electronic listening device that can be concealed on a person. **2** *informal* a telegram or cablegram.

▶*v.* [*trans.*] **1** install electric circuits or wires in: *wiring a plug* | *they wired the place themselves.* ■ connect (someone or something) to a piece of electronic equipment: *a microphone wired to a loudspeaker.* **2** provide, fasten, or reinforce with wires: *they wired his jaw.* **3** *informal* send a telegram or cablegram to: *she wired her friend for advice.* ■ [with *two objs.*] send (money) to (someone) by means of a telegram or cablegram: *he was expecting a friend in Australia to wire him $1,500.* **4** snare (an animal) with wire. **5** (usu. **be wired**) *Croquet* obstruct (a ball, shot, or player) by a wicket. ▷Old English *wīr*, of Germanic origin, probably from the base of Latin *viere* 'plait, weave.' **—wir·er** *n.*

▶*PHRASES* □ **by wire** by telegraph. □ **down to the wire** *informal* used to denote a situation whose outcome is not decided until the very last minute: *it was probable that the test of nerves would go down to the wire.* □ **get one's wires crossed** see CROSS. □ **under the wire** *informal* at the last possible opportunity; just in time.

wire cloth ▶*n.* fabric woven from wire.

wire cut·ter ▶*n.* (usu. **wire cutters**) a tool for cutting wire.

wired /wīrd/ ▶*adj. informal* **1** making use of computers and information technology to transfer or receive information, esp. by means of the Internet: *the economic arguments for getting your business wired.* **2** [*predic.*] in a nervous, tense, or edgy state: *not much sleep lately—I'm a little wired.* ■ under the influence of drugs or alcohol.

wire-draw ▶*v.* (*past* **-drew**; *past part.* **-drawn**) [*trans.*] [often as *n.*] (**wire-drawing**) draw out (metal) into wire by passing it through a series of holes of diminishing diameter in a steel plate. ■ *figurative, archaic* refine (an argument or idea) excessively, in such a way that it becomes strained or forced. **—wire-draw·er** *n.*

wire·frame /ˈwīrˌfrām/ ▶*n. Computing* a skeletal three dimensional model in which only lines and vertices are represented.

wire fraud ▶*n.* financial fraud involving the use of telecommunications or information technology.

wire gauge ▶*n.* a gauge for measuring the diameter of wire. ■ the diameter of wire; any of a series of standard sizes in which wire is made.

wire gauze ▶*n.* see GAUZE.

wire grass ▶*n.* a grass with tough wiry stems. • Genera *Aristida* and *Poa*, family Gramineae: several species, including the European *P. compressa*, which has become naturalized in North America.

wire-guid·ed ▶*adj.* (of a missile) directed by means of electrical signals transmitted along fine connecting wires that uncoil during the missile's flight.

wire-haired ▶*adj.* (esp. of a dog breed) having stiff or wiry hair: *a wire-haired terrier.*

wire·less /ˈwīrlis/ ▶*n. dated, chiefly Brit.* **1** (also **wireless set**) a radio receiving set. **2** computer networking, broadcasting, telephony, or telegraphy using radio signals.

▶*adj.* lacking or not requiring wires.

wire·less hot spot (also **wireless hotspot**) ▶*n.* an area with a usable signal to allow wireless connection to the Internet or some other computer network.

wire·less·ly /ˈwī(ə)rlislē/ ▶*adv.* without a wire connection; using a wireless technology: *a patented FM technology that broadcasts music wirelessly.*

wire·line /ˈwīrˌlīn/ ▶*n.* **1** a telegraph or telephone wire. **2** (in the oil industry) a cable for lowering and raising tools and other equipment in a well shaft. ■ an electric cable used to connect measuring devices in an oil well with indicating or recording instruments at the surface. **3** a horizontal watermark in laid paper.

wire·man /ˈwīrmən/ ▶*n.* (*pl.* **-men**) **1** an electrician. **2** a journalist working for a news agency. **3** *Informal* a professional wiretapper.

wire·pull·er /ˈwīrˌpŏŏlər/ ▶*n. informal* a person, esp. a politician, who exerts control or influence from behind the scenes. **—wire·pull·ing** /-ˌpŏŏliNG/ *n.*

wire rope ▶*n.* a length of rope made from wires twisted together as strands; cable.

wire serv·ice ▶*n.* a news agency that supplies syndicated news by wire to newspapers, radio, and television stations.

wire·tap·ping /ˈwīrˌtapiNG/ ▶*n.* the practice of connecting a listening device to a telephone line to secretly monitor a conversation. **—wire·tap** *n.* & *v.* **—wire·tap·per** /-ˌtapər/ *n.*

wire wheel ▶*n.* a wheel on a car, esp. a sports car, having narrow metal spokes.

wire·worm /ˈwīrˌwərm/ ▶*n.* a wormlike hard-skinned larva, esp. of a click beetle. Many wireworms feed on the underground parts of plants and can cause damage to arable and other crops. ■ a myriapod, esp. of the millipede genus *Iulus*, which damages plant roots.

wir·ing /ˈwīriNG/ ▶*n.* a system of wires providing electric circuits for a device or building. ■ the installation of this. ■ *informal* the structure of the nervous system or brain perceived as determining a basic or innate pattern of behavior.

Wir·ral /ˈwi(ə)rəl/ a peninsula on the coast of northwestern England, between the estuaries of the rivers Dee and Mersey. Full name THE WIRRAL PENINSULA.

Wirt·schafts·wun·der /ˈvirtsHäftsˌvŏŏndər/ ▶*n.* an economic miracle, esp. the economic recovery of the Federal Republic of West Germany after World War II. ▷German.

wir·y /ˈwī(ə)rē/ ▶*adj.* (**wir·i·er**, **wir·i·est**) resembling wire in form and texture: *his wiry black hair.* ■ (of a person) lean, tough, and sinewy: *Bernadette was a small, wiry woman.* **—wir·i·ly** /ˈwīrəlē/ *adv.* **—wir·i·ness** *n.*

Wis. ▶*abbr.* Wisconsin.

Wis·con·sin[1] /wisˈkänsən/ a state in the northern U.S. that borders on lakes Superior (in the northwest) and Michigan (in the east); pop. 5,363,675; capital, Madison; statehood, May 29, 1848 (30). Ceded to Britain by the French in 1763 and acquired by the U.S. in 1783 as part of the former Northwest Territory, it was the site of the Black Hawk War, the last armed Indian resistance to white settlement in the area, in 1832. **—Wis·con·sin·ite** /-səˌnīt/ *n.*

Wis·con·sin[2] ▶*n.* [usu. as *adj.*] *Geology* the last (or last two) of the Pleistocene glaciations of North America, approximating to the Weichsel of northern Europe. ■ the system of deposits laid down at this time.

Wis·con·sin Riv·er a river that flows for 430 miles (690 km) through central Wisconsin to the Mississippi River at Prairie du Chien. The **Dells of the Wisconsin** are a popular scenic area.

Wisd. ▶*abbr.* (in biblical references) Wisdom of Solomon (Apocrypha).

wis·dom /ˈwizdəm/ ▶*n.* the quality of having experience, knowledge, and good judgment; the quality of being wise. ■ the soundness of an action or decision with regard to the application of such experience, knowledge, and good judgment: *some questioned the wisdom of building the dam so close to an active volcano.* ■ the body of knowledge and principles that develops within a specified society or period: *oriental wisdom.* See note at KNOWLEDGE. ▷Old English *wīsdōm* (see WISE[1], -DOM).

▶*PHRASE* □ **in someone's wisdom** used ironically to suggest that an action is not well judged: *in their wisdom they decided to dispense with him.*

wis·dom lit·er·a·ture ▶*n.* the biblical books of Job, Proverbs, Ecclesiastes, Song of Songs, Wisdom of Solomon, and Ecclesiasticus collectively. ■ similar works, esp. from the ancient Near East, containing proverbial sayings and practical maxims.

Wis·dom of Sol·o·mon a book of the Apocrypha ascribed to Solomon and containing a meditation on wisdom. The book is thought actually to date from about the 1st century BC to the 1st century AD.

wis·dom tooth ▶*n.* each of the four hindmost molars in humans, which usually appear at about the age of twenty.

wise[1] /wīz/ ▶*adj.* having or showing experience, knowledge, and good judgment: *she seems kind and wise* | *a wise precaution.* ■ responding sensibly or shrewdly to a particular situation: *it would be wise to discuss the matter with the chairman of the committee.* ■ [*predic.*] having knowledge in a specified subject: *families wise in the way of hurricane survival.* ■ [*predic.*] (**wise to**) *informal* alert to or aware of: *at seven she was already wise to the police.*

▶*phrasal v.* □ **wise off** *Informal* make wisecracks: *Jake and I would wise off to him.* □ **wise up** [often in *imperative*] *informal* become alert to or aware of something: *wise up and sort yourselves out before it's too late.* ▷Old English *wīs*, of Germanic origin; related to Dutch *wijs* and German *weise*, also to WIT[2]. **—wise·ly** *adv.*

▶*PHRASES* □ **get wise** become alert or aware: *the birds get wise and figure out it's just noise.* □ **be wise after the event** understand and assess an event or situation only after its implications have become obvious. □ **be none** (or **not any**) **the wiser** know no more than before.

wise[2] ▶*n. archaic* the manner or extent of something: *he did it this wise.* ▷Old English *wīse*, of Germanic origin; related to WIT[2].

▶*PHRASE* □ **in no wise** not at all.

-wise ▶*suffix* forming adjectives and adverbs of manner or respect such as *clockwise, otherwise.* Compare with **-WAYS**. ■ *informal* with respect to; concerning: *security-wise, there are few problems.* ▷from WISE[2].

USAGE In modern English, the suffix **-wise** is attached to nouns to form a sentence adverb meaning 'concerning or with respect to,' as in *tax-wise, money-wise, time-wise*, etc. The suffix is widely used, but most of the words so formed are considered inelegant or in poor English style.

wise·a·cre /ˈwīzˌākər/ ▶*n.* a person with an affectation of wisdom or knowledge, regarded with scorn or irritation by others; a know-it-all. ▷late 16th cent.: from Middle Dutch *wijsseggher* 'soothsayer,' probably from the Germanic bases of WIT[2] and SAY. The assimilation to ACRE remains unexplained.

wise·ass /ˈwīzˌas/ ▶*n. & adj. Informal* another term for SMART ALECK.

wise·crack /ˈwīzˌkrak/ *informal* ▶*n.* a clever and pithy spoken witticism.

▶*v.* [*intrans.*] make a wisecrack: [as *n.*] (**wisecracking**) *his warmth, boisterousness, and constant wisecracking.* **—wise·crack·er** *n.*

wise guy *informal* ▶*n.* **1** a person who speaks and behaves as if they know more than others. **2** a member of the Mafia.

wise man ▶*n.* a man versed in magic, witchcraft, or astrology. See also THREE WISE MEN.

wis·en·heim·er /ˈwīzənˌhīmər/ ▶*n. informal* a person who behaves in an irritatingly smug or arrogant fashion, typically by making clever remarks and displaying their knowledge. ▷early 20th cent.: from WISE[1] + the suffix *-(n)heimer* found in surnames such as *Oppenheimer.*

wi·sent /ˈvēzent/ ▶*n.* the European bison. See BISON. ▷mid 19th cent.: from German; related to BISON.

wise saw ▶*n.* a proverbial saying.

wise wom·an ▶*n. chiefly historical* a woman considered to be knowledgeable in matters such as herbal healing, magic charms, or other traditional lore.

wish /wiSH/ ▶*v.* [*intrans.*] feel or express a strong desire or hope for something that is not easily attainable; want something that cannot or probably will not happen: *we* **wished for** *peace* | [with *clause*] *he wished* *that he had practiced the routines.* ■ silently invoke such a hope or desire, esp. in a ritualized way: *I closed my eyes and wished.* ■ [with *infinitive*] feel or express a desire to do something: *they wish to become involved.* ■ [*trans.*] ask (someone) to do something or that (something) be done: *I wish it to be clearly understood.* ■ [with *two objs.*] express a desire for (the success or good fortune) of (someone): *they wish her every success.* ■ [*trans.*] (**wish something on**) hope that something unpleasant will happen to: *I would not* **wish it on** *the vilest soul.*

▸*n.* a desire or hope for something to happen: *the union has reiterated its wish for an agreement* | [with *infinitive*] *it is their wish to continue organizing similar exhibitions.* ■ (usu. **wishes**) an expression of such a desire, typically in the form of a request or instruction: *she must carry out her late father's wishes.* ■ an invocation or recitation of a hope or desire: *he* **makes a wish.** ■ (usu. **wishes**) an expression of a desire for someone's success or good fortune: *they had received kindness and* **good wishes** *from total strangers.* ■ a thing or event that is or has been desired; an object of desire: *the petitioners eventually got their wish.* ▷Old English *wȳscan*, of Germanic origin; related to German *wünschen*, also to **WEEN** and **WONT**. —**wish·er** *n.* [in *combination*] *an ill-wisher.*

▸*PHRASES* □ **if wishes were horses, beggars would ride** *proverb* if you could achieve your aims simply by wishing for them, life would be very easy. □ **wish someone well** feel or express a desire for someone's well-being. □ **the wish is father to the thought** *proverb* we believe a thing because we wish it to be true.

USAGE Is it more correct to say *I wish I* **were** *rich* or *I wish I* **was** *rich*? On the question of the use of the subjunctive mood, see **usage** at **SUBJUNCTIVE**.

wish·bone /ˈwisʜˌbōn/ ▸*n.* **1** a forked bone (the furcula) between the neck and breast of a bird. According to a popular custom, this bone from a cooked bird is broken by two people, with the holder of the longer portion being entitled to make a wish. **2** an object of similar shape, in particular: ■ *Football* an offensive formation in which the fullback lines up immediately behind the quarterback with the two halfbacks behind and on either side of the fullback. ■ a forked element in the suspension of a motor vehicle or aircraft, typically attached to a wheel at one end with the two arms hinged to the chassis. ■ *Sailing* a boom in two halves that curve outward around a sail and meet aft of it.

wish book ▸*n. informal* a mail-order catalog.

wish·ful /ˈwisʜfəl/ ▸*adj.* having or expressing a desire or hope for something to happen. ■ expressing or containing a desire or hope for something impractical or unfeasible: *without resources the proposed measures were merely* **wishful thinking.** —**wish·ful·ly** *adv.* —**wish·ful·ness** *n.*

wish ful·fil·ment ▸*n.* the satisfying of unconscious desires in dreams or fantasies.

wish·ing well ▸*n.* a well into which one drops a coin and makes a wish.

wish list ▸*n.* a list of desired things or occurrences.

wish-wash ▸*n. informal* a weak or watery drink: *one pot of wish-wash called "tea."* ■ insipid or excessively sentimental talk or writing: *this isn't just emotional wish-wash.* ▷late 18th cent.: reduplication of **WASH**.

wish·y-wash·y /ˈwisʜē ˈwäsʜē; -ˈwôsʜē/ ▸*adj.* (of drink or liquid food such as soup) weak; watery. ■ feeble or insipid in quality or character; lacking strength or boldness: *wishy-washy liberalism.* ▷early 18th cent.: reduplication of **WASHY**.

Wis·ła /ˈvēswä/ Polish name for **VISTULA**.

wisp /wisp/ ▸*n.* a small thin or twisted bunch, piece, or amount of something: **wisps of** *smoke rose into the air.* ■ a small bunch of hay or straw used for drying or grooming a horse. ■ a small thin person, typically a child: *a fourteen-year-old wisp of a girl.* ▷Middle English: origin uncertain; perhaps related to **WHISK**. —**wisp·i·ly** /ˈwispilē/ *adv.* —**wisp·i·ness** /ˈwispēnis/ *n.* —**wisp·y** *adj.* (**wisp·i·er, wisp·i·est**).

Wis·sen·schaft /ˈvisənˌsʜäft/ ▸*n.* the systematic pursuit of knowledge, learning, and scholarship (esp. as contrasted with its application). ▷German, literally 'knowledge, science.'

wist /wist/ ▸ past and past participle of **WIT**².

Wis·tar rat /ˈwistər/ ▸*n. Biology & Medicine* a rat of a strain developed for laboratory purposes. ▷1930s: named after the *Wistar* Institute of Anatomy and Biology, Philadelphia, Pennsylvania.

wis·te·ri·a /wiˈsti(ə)rēə/ (also **wis·ta·ri·a** /-ˈste(ə)r-/) ▸*n.* a climbing shrub of the pea family, with hanging clusters of pale bluish-lilac flowers. Native to North America and eastern Asia, ornamental varieties are widely grown on walls and pergolas. • Genus *Wisteria*, family Leguminosae: several species. ▷modern Latin, named after Caspar *Wistar* (or *Wister*) (1761–1818), American anatomist.

wist·ful /ˈwistfəl/ ▸*adj.* having or showing a feeling of vague or regretful longing: *a wistful smile.* ▷early 17th cent.: apparently from obsolete *wistly* 'intently,' influenced by **WISHFUL**. —**wist·ful·ly** *adv.* —**wist·ful·ness** *n.*

wit¹ /wit/ ▸*n.* **1** mental sharpness and inventiveness; keen intelligence: *he does not lack perception or native wit.* ■ (**wits**) the intelligence required for normal activity; basic human intelligence: *he needed all his wits to figure out the way back.* **2** a natural aptitude for using words and ideas in a quick and inventive way to create humor: *a player with a sharp tongue and a quick wit.* ■ a person who has such an aptitude: *she is such a wit.* ▷Old English *wit(t)*, *gewit(t)*, denoting the mind as the seat of consciousness, of Germanic origin; related to Dutch *weet* and German *Witz*, also to **WIT**². —**wit·ted** *adj.* [in *combination*] *slow-witted.*

▸*PHRASES* □ **be at one's wits' end** be overwhelmed with difficulties and at a loss as to what to do next. □ **be frightened** (or **scared**) **out of one's wits** be extremely frightened; be immobilized by fear. □ **gather** (or **collect**) **one's wits** allow oneself to think calmly and clearly in a demanding situation. □ **have** (or **keep**) **one's wits about one** be constantly alert and vigilant. □ **live by one's wits** earn money by clever and sometimes dishonest means, having no regular employment. □ **pit one's wits against** compete with (someone or something).

THE RIGHT WORD **humor, irony, repartee, sarcasm, satire, wit**

If you're good at perceiving analogies between dissimilar things and expressing them in quick, sharp, spontaneous observations or remarks, you have **wit**.

Humor, on the other hand, is the ability to perceive what is comical, ridiculous, or ludicrous in a situation or character, and to express it in a way that makes others see or feel the same thing. It suggests more sympathy, tolerance, and kindliness than *wit* (*she maintained a sense of humor in the midst of trying circumstances*).

Irony is the implicit humor in the contradiction between what is meant and what is expressed, or in the discrepancy between appearance and reality. An example would be to shout, in the midst of a hurricane, "What a perfect day for a wedding!"

Although **sarcasm** may take the form of irony, it is less subtle and is often used harshly or bitterly to wound or ridicule someone. Unlike irony, however, *sarcasm* depends on tone of voice for its effect (*"a fine friend you turned out to be!" he said, with obvious sarcasm*).

Satire usually implies the use of sarcasm or irony for the purpose of ridicule or criticism, often directed at institutions or political figures (*she wrote political satire for the comedy team*).

If you are good at making quick, witty replies, you will be known for your **repartee**, which is the art of responding pointedly and skillfully with wit or humor in a conversational exchange (*no one could compete with her witty repartee*).

wit² ▸*v.* (**wot** /wät/, **wit·ting**; *past* and *past part.* **wist** /wist/) [*intrans.*] **1** *archaic* have knowledge: *I addressed a few words to the lady you* **wot of** | [*trans.*] *I wot that but too well.* **2** (**to wit**) that is to say (used to make clearer or more specific something already said or referred to): *the textbooks show an irritating parochialism, to wit an almost total exclusion of papers not in English.* ▷Old English *witan*, of Germanic origin; related to Dutch *weten* and German *wissen*, from an Indo-European root shared by Sanskrit *veda* 'knowledge' and Latin *videre* 'see.'

wit·an /ˈwitn/ ▸*n.* another term for **WITENAGEMOT**. ▷representing the Old English plural of *wita* 'wise man.'

witch /wicʜ/ ▸*n.* **1** a woman thought to have evil magic powers. Witches are popularly depicted as wearing a black cloak and pointed hat, and flying on a broomstick. ■ a follower or practitioner of modern witchcraft; a Wiccan priest or priestess. ■ *informal* an ugly or unpleasant old woman; a hag. ■ a girl or woman capable of enchanting or bewitching a man. **2** an edible North Atlantic flatfish that is of some commercial value. • *Glyptocephalus cynoglossus*, family Pleuronectidae.

▸*v.* [*trans.*] (of a witch) cast an evil spell on: *Mrs. Mucharski had somehow witched the house.* ■ (of a girl or woman) enchant (a man): *she witched Jake.* ▷Old English *wicca* (masculine), *wicce* (feminine), *wiccian* (verb); current senses of the verb are probably a shortening of **BEWITCH**. —**witch·like** /-ˌlīk/ *adj.* —**witch·y** *adj.*

▸*PHRASE* □ **as cold as** (or **colder than**) **a witch's tit** *vulgar slang* very cold.

witch·craft /ˈwicʜˌkraft/ ▸*n.* the practice of magic, esp. black magic; the use of spells and the invocation of spirits. See also **WICCA**.

witch doc·tor ▸*n.* (among tribal peoples) a magician credited with powers of healing, divination, and protection against the magic of others.

witch elm ▸*n.* variant spelling of **WYCH ELM**.

witch·er·y /ˈwicʜərē/ ▸*n.* the practice of magic: *warding off evil spirits and acts of witchery.* ■ compelling power exercised by beauty, eloquence, or other attractive or fascinating qualities.

witch·es' broom ▸*n.* dense twiggy growth in a tree caused by infection with fungus (esp. rusts), mites, or viruses.

witch·es' sab·bath ▸*n.* see **SABBATH** (sense 2).

witch·grass /ˈwicʜˌgras/ (also **witch grass**) ▸*n.* a tough creeping grass that can become an invasive weed: • couch grass. • a North American grass (*Panicum capillare*, family Gramineae).

witch ha·zel ▸*n.* a shrub with fragrant yellow flowers that is widely grown as an ornamental. American species flower in autumn, and Asian species in winter. • Genus *Hamamelis*, family Hamamelidaceae: several species, esp. *H. virginiana*, which is the source of the lotion. ■ an astringent lotion made from the bark and leaves of this plant. ▷mid 16th cent.: *witch*, variant of *wych* (see **WYCH ELM**).

witch-hunt ▸*n. historical* a search for and subsequent persecution of a supposed witch. ■ *informal* a campaign directed against a person or group holding unorthodox or unpopular views. —**witch-hunt·ing** *n.*

witch·ing /ˈwicʜiNG/ ▸*n.* the practice of witchcraft.

▸*PHRASE* □ **the witching hour** midnight (with reference to the belief that witches are active and magic takes place at that time). [with allusion to *the witching time of night* from Shakespeare's *Hamlet* (III. ii. 377).]

witch·weed /ˈwicʜˌwēd/ ▸*n.* a small parasitic plant that attaches itself to the roots of other plants. Native to the Old World tropics and southern Africa, it has been introduced into North America and can cause serious damage to crops such as corn and sugar. • Genus *Striga*, family Scrophulariaceae.

wit·e·na·ge·mot /ˈwitn-əgəˌmōt/ ▸*n. historical* an Anglo-Saxon national council or parliament. Also called **WITAN**. ▷Old English, from *witena*, genitive plural of *wita* 'wise man' + *gemōt* 'meeting' (compare with **MOOT**).

with /wiᴛʜ; wiᴛʜ/ ▸*prep.* **1** accompanied by (another person or thing): *a nice steak with a bottle of red wine.* ■ in the same direction as: *marine mammals generally swim with the current.* ■ along with (with reference to time): *wisdom comes with age.* ■ in proportion to: *the form of the light curve changes with period in a systematic way.* **2** possessing (something) as a feature or accompaniment: *a flower-sprigged blouse with a white collar.* ■ marked by or wearing: *a tall dark man with a scar on one cheek* | *a small man with thick glasses.* **3** indicating the instrument used to perform an action: *cut it with a knife* | *treatment with acid before analysis.* ■ indicating the material used for some purpose: *fill the bowl with water.* **4** in opposition to: *we started fighting with each other.* **5** indicating the manner or attitude of the person doing something: *with great reluctance.* **6** indicating responsibility: *leave it with me.* **7** in relation to: *my father will be angry with me.* **8** employed by: *she's with IBM now.* ■ as a member or employee of: *he plays with the Cincinnati Cyclones.* ■ using the services of: *I bank with the TSB.* **9** affected by (a particular fact or condition): *with no hope* | *in bed with lumbago.* ■ indicating the cause of an action or condition: *trembling with fear* | *the paper was yellow with age.* **10** indicating separation or removal from something: *to part with one's dearest possessions* | *their jobs could be dispensed with.* ▷Old English, probably a shortening of a Germanic preposition related to obsolete English *wither* 'adverse, opposite.'

Pronunciation Key ə *ago*; ər *over*; ˈə or ˌə *up*; ˈər or ˌər *fur*; a *hat*; ā *rate*; ä *car*; cʜ *chew*; e *let*; ē *see*; e(ə)r *air*; i *fit*; ī *by*; i(ə)r *ear*; NG *sing*; ō *go*; ô *for*; oi *boy*; o͝o *good*; o͞o *goo*; ou *out*; sʜ *she*; ᴛʜ *thin*; ᴛʜ *then*; (h)w *why*; zʜ *vision*

▸*PHRASES* □ **away** (or **off** or **out**, etc.) **with** used in exhortations to take or send someone or something away, in, out, etc.: *off with his head.* □ **be with someone** **1** agree with or support someone: *we're all with you on this one.* **2** *informal* follow someone's meaning: *I'm not with you.* □ **with it** **1** knowledgeable about and following modern ideas and fashions: *a young, with-it film buyer.* **2** [usu. with *negative*] alert and comprehending: *I'm not really with it this morning.* □ **with that** at that point; immediately after saying or doing something dramatic: *with that, she flounced out of the room.*

with·al /wiTH'ôl; wiTH-/ *archaic* ▸*adv.* in addition; as a further factor or consideration: *the whole is light and portable, and ornamental withal.* ■ all the same; nevertheless (used when adding something that contrasts with a previous comment): *she gave him a grateful smile, but rueful withal.*
▸*prep.* with (used at the end of a clause): *we sat with little to nourish ourselves withal but vile water.* ▷Middle English: originally as *with all.*

with·draw /wiTH'drô; wiTH-/ ▸*v.* (*past* **-drew**; *past part.* **-drawn**) **1** [*trans.*] remove or take away (something) from a particular place or position: *slowly Ruth withdrew her hand from his.* ■ take (money) out of an account: *normally you can withdraw up to $50 in cash.* ■ take back or away (something bestowed, proposed, or used): *the party threatened to withdraw its support for the government.* ■ (in parliamentary procedure) remove or recall a motion, amendment, etc., from consideration. ■ say that (a statement one has made) is untrue or unjustified: *he failed to withdraw his remarks and apologize.* ■ [*intrans.*] (of a man) practice coitus interruptus. **2** [*intrans.*] leave or come back from a place, esp. a war zone: *Iraqi forces* ***withdrew from*** *Kuwait.* ■ [*trans.*] cause (someone) to leave or come back from a place, esp. a war zone: *both countries agreed to withdraw their troops.* ■ no longer participate in an activity or be a member of a team or organization: *his rival withdrew from the race on the second lap.* ■ depart to another room or place, esp. in search of quiet or privacy. ■ retreat from contact or communication with other people: *he went silent and* ***withdrew into himself.*** **3** [*intrans.*] cease to take an addictive drug: *for the cocaine user, it is possible to withdraw without medication.* ▷Middle English: from the prefix *with-* 'away' + the verb DRAW.

with·draw·al /wiTH'drôl; wiTH-/ ▸*n.* the action of withdrawing something: *the withdrawal of legal aid.* ■ an act of taking money out of an account. ■ a sum of money withdrawn from an account: *a $30,000 cash withdrawal.* ■ the action of ceasing to participate in an activity: *the Soviet withdrawal from Afghanistan.* ■ the process of ceasing to take an addictive drug. ■ coitus interruptus.
▸*PHRASE* □ **withdrawal symptoms** the unpleasant physical reaction that accompanies the process of ceasing to take an addictive drug.

with·drawn /wiTH'drôn; wiTH-/ ▸ past participle of WITHDRAW.
▸*adj.* not wanting to communicate with other people: *a disorder characterized by withdrawn and fearful behavior.*

withe /wiTH; wiTH/ ▸*n.* variant spelling of WITHY.

with·er /'wiTHər/ ▸*v.* **1** [*intrans.*] (of a plant) become dry and shriveled: *the grass had withered to an unappealing brown* | [as *adj.*] (**withered**) *withered leaves.* ■ (of a person, limb, or the skin) become shrunken or wrinkled from age or disease: [as *adj.*] (**withered**) *a girl with a withered arm.* ■ cease to flourish; fall into decay or decline: *programs would* ***wither away*** *if they did not command local support.* **2** [*trans.*] cause harm or damage to: *a business that can wither the hardiest ego.* ■ mortify (someone) with a scornful look or manner: *she withered me with a look.* ▷late Middle English: apparently a variant of WEATHER, ultimately differentiated for certain senses.
▸*PHRASE* □ **wither on the vine** fail to be implemented or dealt with because of neglect or inaction.

with·er·ing /'wiTHəriNG/ ▸*adj.* **1** intended to make someone feel mortified or humiliated: *a withering look.* **2** (of heat) intense; scorching.
▸*n.* the action of becoming dry and shriveled. ■ the action of declining or decaying: *the withering of the PLO's revolutionary threat.* —**with·er·ing·ly** *adv.* (in sense 1 of the *adjective*).

with·er·ite /'wiTHə,rīt/ ▸*n.* a rare white mineral consisting of barium carbonate, occurring esp. in veins with galena. ▷late 18th cent.: from the name of William *Withering* (1741–99), the English physician and scientist who first described it, + -ITE[1].

with·ers /'wiTHərz/ ▸*plural n.* the highest part of a horse's back, lying at the base of the neck above the shoulders. The height of a horse is measured to the withers. ▷early 16th cent.: apparently a reduced form of *widersome*, from obsolete *wither-* 'against, contrary' (as the part that resists the strain of the collar) + a second element of obscure origin.

with·er·shins /'wiTHər,SHinz/ ▸*adv.* variant spelling of WIDDERSHINS.

with·hold /wiTH'hōld; wiTH-/ ▸*v.* (*past* and *past part.* **-held**) [*trans.*] refuse to give (something that is due to or is desired by another): *the name of the dead man is being withheld* | [as *n.*] (**withholding**) *the withholding of consent to treatment.* ■ suppress or hold back (an emotion or reaction). ■ (of an employer) deduct (tax) from an employee's paycheck and send it directly to the government. ▷Middle English: from the prefix *with-* 'away' + the verb HOLD[1]. —**with·hold·er** *n.*

with·hold·ing tax ▸*n.* the amount of an employee's pay withheld by the employer and sent directly to the government as partial payment of income tax.

with·in /wiTH'in; wi'TH-/ ▸*prep.* inside (something): *the spread of fire within the building.* ■ inside the range of (an area or boundary): *a field located within the city.* ■ inside the range of (a specified action or perception): *within reach.* ■ not further off than (used with distances): *Bob lives* ***within*** *a few miles* ***of*** *Honesdale.* ■ occurring inside (a particular period of time): *sold out within two hours* | *33% were rearrested* ***within*** *two years* ***of*** *their release.* ■ inside the bounds set by (a concept, argument, etc.): *full cooperation within the terms of the treaty.*
▸*adv.* inside; indoors: *inquire within.* ■ internally or inwardly: *beauty coming from within.* ▷late Old English *withinnan* 'on the inside.'
▸*PHRASE* □ **within doors** indoors.

with·out /wiTH'out; wiTH-/ ▸*prep.* **1** in the absence of: *he went to Sweden without her.* ■ not having the use or benefit of: *the first person to make the ascent without oxygen.* ■ [often with *verbal n.*] in circumstances in which the action mentioned does not happen: *they sat looking at each other without speaking.* **2** *archaic* or *poetic/literary* outside: *the barbarians without the gates.*
▸*adv. archaic* or *poetic/literary* outside: *the enemy without.*
▸*conj. archaic* or *dialect* without it being the case that: *he won't be able to go without we know it.* ■ unless: *I'd never have known you without you spoke to me.* ▷Old English *withūtan* 'on the outside.'
▸*PHRASES* □ **do without** see DO[1]. □ **go without** see GO[1].

with·stand /wiTH'stand; wiTH-/ ▸*v.* (*past* and *past part.* **-stood**) [*trans.*] remain undamaged or unaffected by; resist: *the structure had been designed to withstand winds of more than 100 mph.* ■ offer strong resistance or opposition to (someone or something). ▷Old English *withstandan*, from the prefix *with-* 'against' + the verb STAND. —**with·stand·er** *n.*

with·y /'wiTHē; 'wiTHē/ (also **withe** /wiTH; wiTH; wiTH/) ▸*n.* (*pl.* **with·ies** or **withes** /wiTHs; wiTHz/) a tough flexible branch of an osier or other willow, used for tying, binding, or basketry. ■ another term for OSIER. ▷Old English *withig*, of Germanic origin; related to German *Weide.*

wit·less /'witlis/ ▸*adj.* foolish; stupid: *a witless retort.* ■ [as *complement*] to such an extent that one cannot think clearly or rationally: *I was scared witless.* ▷Old English *witlēas* 'crazy, dazed' (see WIT[1], -LESS). —**wit·less·ly** *adv.* —**wit·less·ness** *n.*

wit·ling /'witliNG/ ▸*n. archaic, chiefly derogatory* a person who considers themselves to be witty.

wit·loof /'wit,lōf/ ▸*n.* chicory of a broad-leaved variety grown for blanching. ▷late 19th cent.: from Dutch, literally 'white leaf.'

wit·ness /'witnis/ ▸*n.* **1** a person who sees an event, typically a crime or accident, take place: *police are appealing for* ***witnesses to*** *the accident* | *I was witness to one of the most amazing comebacks in sprinting history.* ■ a person giving sworn testimony to a court of law or the police. ■ a person who is present at the signing of a document and signs it themselves to confirm this. **2** evidence; proof: *the memorial service was* ***witness to*** *the wide circle of his interest.* ■ used to refer to confirmation or evidence given by signature, under oath, or otherwise: ***in witness thereof,*** *the parties sign this document.* ■ open profession of one's religious faith through words or actions: *he told us of faithful Christian witness by many in his country.* **3** a member of the Jehovah's Witnesses.
▸*v.* **1** [*trans.*] see (an event, typically a crime or accident) take place: *a bartender who witnessed the murder.* ■ have knowledge of (an event or change) from personal observation or experience: *what we are witnessing is the birth of a dangerously liberal orthodoxy.* ■ (of a time, place, or other context) be the setting in which (a particular event) takes place: *the 1980s witnessed an unprecedented increase in the scope of the electronic media.* ■ be present as someone signs (a document) or gives (their signature) to a document and sign it oneself to confirm this: *the clerk witnessed her signature.* ■ [in *imperative*] look at (used to introduce a fact illustrating a preceding statement): *the nuclear family is a vulnerable institution—witness the rates of marital breakdown.* **2** [*intrans.*] (**witness to**) give or serve as evidence of; testify to: *his writings witness to an inner toughness.* ■ (of a person) openly profess one's religious faith in: *one of the purposes of his coming was to nerve the disciples to witness to Jesus.* ▷Old English *witnes* (see WIT[1], -NESS).
▸*PHRASES* □ **as God is my witness** (or **God be my witness**) an invocation of God as confirmation of the truth of a statement: *God be my witness, sir, I didn't!* □ **call someone or something to witness** *archaic* appeal or refer to someone or something for confirmation or evidence of something: *his hands extended upward as if to call the heavens to witness this injustice.*

wit·ness stand (*Brit.* **wit·ness box**) ▸*n. Law* the place in a court where a witness stands to give evidence.

Witt /vit/, Katarina (1965–), German figure skater. A four-time world champion 1984, 1985, 1987, 1988, she won Olympic gold medals for East Germany in 1984 and 1988.

Wit·ten·berg /'witn,bərg; 'vitn,berk/ a town in eastern Germany, on the Elbe River northeast of Leipzig; pop. 87,000. It was the scene in 1517 of Martin Luther's campaign against the Roman Catholic Church that was a major factor in the rise of the Reformation.

Witt·gen·stein /'vitgən,stīn; -,SHtīn/, Ludwig (Josef Johann) (1889–1951), British philosopher, born in Austria. His two major works, *Tractatus Logico-Philosophicus* (1921) and *Philosophical Investigations* (1953), examine language and its relationship to the world.

wit·ti·cism /'witi,sizəm/ ▸*n.* a witty remark. ▷1677: coined by Dryden from WITTY, on the pattern of *criticism.*

wit·ting /'witiNG/ ▸*adj.* done in full awareness or consciousness; deliberate: *the witting and unwitting complicity of the institutions.* ■ (of a person) conscious or aware of the full facts of a situation: *there is no proof that the Chinese were witting accomplices.* ▷late Middle English: from WIT[2] + -ING[2]. —**wit·ting·ly** *adv.*

wit·tol /'witl/ ▸*n. archaic* a man who is aware and tolerant of his wife's infidelity; an acquiescent cuckold. ▷late Middle English: apparently from WIT[2] + the last syllable (with the loss of *-d*) of CUCKOLD.

wit·ty /'witē/ ▸*adj.* (**-ti·er**, **-ti·est**) showing or characterized by quick and inventive verbal humor: *a witty remark* | *Marlowe was charming and witty.* ▷Old English *wit(t)ig* 'having wisdom' (see WIT[1], -Y[1]). —**wit·ti·ly** /'witəlē/ *adv.* —**wit·ti·ness** *n.*

Wit·wa·ters·rand /'wit,wôtərz,rand; -,wätərz-; -,ränd/ (**the Witwatersrand**) a region in South Africa, around the city of Johannesburg. A series of parallel rocky ridges, it forms a watershed between the Vaal and Olifant rivers. The region contains rich gold deposits that were first discovered in 1886. Also called THE RAND (see RAND[1]). ▷Afrikaans, literally 'ridge of white waters.'

wi·vern ▸*n.* archaic spelling of WYVERN.

wives /wīvz/ ▸ plural form of WIFE.

wiz /wiz/ ▸*n.* variant spelling of WHIZ (sense 2).

wiz·ard /'wizərd/ ▸*n.* **1** a man who has magical powers, esp. in legends and fairy tales. ■ a person who is very skilled in a particular field or activity: *a financial wizard.* **2** *Computing* a help feature of a software package that automates complex tasks by asking the user a series of easy-to-answer questions.
▸*adj. informal, dated, chiefly Brit.* wonderful; excellent. ▷late Middle English (in the sense 'philosopher, sage'): from WISE[1] + -ARD. —**wiz·ard·ly** *adj.* (in sense 1 of the *noun*).

wiz·ard·ry /'wizərdrē/ ▸*n.* the art or practice of magic: *Merlin used his powers of wizardry for good.* ■ great skill in a particular area of activity: *his wizardry with leftovers.* ■ the product of such skill: *the car is full of hi-tech wizardry.*

wiz·en /'wizən; 'wē-/ ▸*adj.* archaic variant of WIZENED.

wiz·ened /'wizənd; 'wē-/ ▸*adj.* shriveled or wrinkled with age: *a wizened, weather-beaten old man.* ▷early 16th cent.: past participle of archaic *wizen* 'shrivel,' of Germanic origin.

W

wk. ▸*abbr.* week: *75 mg per day for 3 wks.*

Wła·dys·ław II /vlä'dis,läf; -,wäf/ see **Ladislaus II.**

WLAN /'dəbəlyōō ,lan/ ▸*abbr. Computing* wireless local area network.

WLTM ▸*abbr.* would like to meet (used in lonely hearts advertisements).

Wm ▸*abbr.* William.

WMD ▸*abbr.* weapon(s) of mass destruction.

WMO ▸*abbr.* World Meteorological Organization.

WNW ▸*abbr.* west-northwest.

WO ▸*abbr.* Warrant Officer.

w/o ▸*abbr.* ■ without.

woad /wōd/ ▸*n.* a yellow-flowered European plant of the cabbage family. It was formerly grown as a source of blue dye, which was extracted from the leaves after they had been dried, powdered, and fermented. • *Isatis tinctoria*, family Brassicaceae. ■ the dye obtained from this plant, now superseded by synthetic products. ▹Old English *wād*, of Germanic origin; related to Dutch *wede* and German *Waid*.

wob·ble /'wäbəl/ ▸*v.* [*intrans.*] move unsteadily from side to side: *the table wobbles where the leg is too short.* ■ [*trans.*] cause to move in such a way. ■ [with *adverbial of direction*] move in such a way in a particular direction: *they wobble around on their bikes.* ■ (of the voice) tremble; quaver: *her voice wobbled dangerously, but she brought it under control.* ■ *figurative* hesitate or waver between different courses of action; vacillate: *the president wobbled on Bosnia.*

▸*n.* an unsteady movement from side to side. ■ a tremble or quaver in the voice. ■ a moment of hesitation or vacillation. ▹mid 17th cent. (earlier as *wabble*): of Germanic origin; compare with Old Norse *vafla* 'waver'; related to the verb **wave.**

wob·bler /'wäb(ə)lər/ ▸*n.* a person or thing that wobbles. ■ (in angling) a lure that wobbles and does not spin.

Wob·blies /'wäblēz/ ▸*plural n.* popular name for members of **Industrial Workers of the World.** ▹early 20th cent.: of unknown origin.

wob·bly /'wäb(ə)lē/ ▸*adj.* (**-bli·er, -bli·est**) tending to move unsteadily from side to side: *the car had a wobbly wheel.* ■ (of a person or their legs) weak and unsteady from illness, tiredness, or anxiety. ■ (of a person, action, or state) uncertain, wavering, or insecure: *the evening gets off to a wobbly start.* ■ (of a speaker, singer, or voice) having a tendency to move out of tone or slightly vary in pitch. ■ (of a line or handwriting) not straight or regular; shaky. **—wob·bli·ness** *n.*

Wo·burn /'wōōbərn; 'wō-/ an industrial city in northeastern Massachusetts, northwest of Boston; pop. 35,943.

Wode·house /'wōōd,hous/, Sir P. G. (1881–1975), English writer; full name *Pelham Grenville Wodehouse*. His best-known works are humorous stories of the upper-class world of Bertie Wooster and his valet Jeeves, the first of which appeared in 1917.

Wo·den /'wōdn/ another name for **Odin.**

woe /wō/ ▸*n. often humorous* great sorrow or distress: *they had a complicated tale of woe.* ■ (**woes**) things that cause sorrow or distress; troubles: *to add to his woes, customers have been spending less.* ▹natural exclamation of lament: recorded as *wā* in Old English and found in several Germanic languages.

▸*PHRASES* □ **woe betide someone** (or **woe to someone**) used humorously to warn someone that they will be in trouble if they do a specified thing: *woe betide anyone wearing the wrong color!* □ **woe is me!** an ironical or humorous exclamation of sorrow or distress.

woe·be·gone /'wōbi,gôn; -,gän/ ▸*adj.* sad or miserable in appearance: *don't look so woebegone, Joanna.* ▹Middle English (in the sense 'afflicted with grief'): from **woe** + *begone* 'surrounded' (past participle of obsolete *bego* 'go around, beset').

woe·ful /'wōfəl/ ▸*adj.* characterized by, expressive of, or causing sorrow or misery: *her face was woeful.* ■ very bad; deplorable: *the remark was enough to establish his woeful ignorance about the theater.* **—woe·ful·ly** *adv.* [as *submodifier*] *the police response was woefully inadequate.* **—woe·ful·ness** *n.*

wog /wäg/ ▸*n. Brit., offensive* a person who is not white. ▹1920s: of unknown origin.

Wöh·ler /'vœlər/, Friedrich (1800–82), German chemist. His synthesis of urea from ammonium cyanate in 1828 demonstrated that organic compounds could be made from inorganic compounds. He was also the first to isolate the elements aluminum and beryllium.

wok /wäk/ ▸*n.* a bowl-shaped frying pan used typically in Chinese cooking. ▹Chinese (Cantonese dialect).

wok

woke /wōk/ ▸ past of **wake**[1].

wok·en /'wōkən/ ▸ past participle of **wake**[1].

wold /wōld/ ▸*n.* [often in *place names*] (usu. **wolds**) (in Britain) a piece of high, open, uncultivated land or moor: *the Lincolnshire Wolds.* ▹Old English *wald* 'wooded upland,' of Germanic origin; perhaps related to **wild.** Compare with **Weald.**

wolf /wōōlf/ ▸*n.* (*pl.* **wolves** /wōōlvz/) **1** a wild carnivorous mammal that is the largest member of the dog family, living and hunting in packs. It is native to both Eurasia and North America, but has been widely exterminated. • *Canis lupus*, family Canidae; it is the chief ancestor of the domestic dog. ■ used in names of similar or related mammals, e.g., **maned wolf, Tasmanian wolf. 2** used in similes and metaphors to refer to a rapacious, ferocious, or voracious person or thing. ■ *informal* a man who habitually seduces women. **3** a harsh or out-of-tune effect produced when playing particular notes or intervals on a musical instrument, caused either by the instrument's construction or by divergence from equal temperament.

▸*v.* [*trans.*] devour (food) greedily: *he wolfed down his breakfast.* ▹Old English *wulf*, of Germanic origin; related to Dutch *wolf* and German *Wolf*, from an Indo-European root shared by Latin *lupus* and Greek *lukos*. The verb dates from the mid 19th cent. **—wolf·ish** *adj.* **—wolf·ish·ly** *adv.* **—wolf·like** /-,līk/ *adj.*

▸*PHRASES* □ **cry wolf** call for help when it is not needed, with the effect that one is not believed when one really does need help. [with allusion to Aesop's fable of the shepherd boy who deluded people with false cries of "Wolf!"] □ **hold** (or **have**) **a wolf by the ears** be in a precarious position. □ **keep the wolf from the door** have enough money to avert hunger or starvation (used hyperbolically): *I work part-time to pay the mortgage and keep the wolf from the door.* □ **throw someone to the wolves** leave someone to be roughly treated or criticized without trying to help or defend them. □ **a wolf in sheep's clothing** a person or thing that appears friendly or harmless but is really hostile. [with biblical allusion to Matt. 7:15.]

Wolfe[1] /wōōlf/, James (1727–59), British general. One of the leaders of the expedition sent to seize French Canada, he commanded the attack on Quebec, the French capital, in 1759. He was fatally wounded while leading his troops to victory on the Plains of Abraham.

Wolfe[2], Thomas (Clayton) (1900–38), U.S. novelist. His intense, romantic works, including his first autobiographical novel *Look Homeward Angel* (1929), dwell idealistically on the U.S. Other notable works: *Of Time and the River* (1935), *The Web and the Rock* (1938), and *You Can't Go Home Again* (1940).

Wolfe[3], Tom (1931–), U.S. writer; born *Thomas Kennerley Wolfe, Jr.* Having been a news reporter for the *Washington Post* 1959–62 and the *Herald Tribune* 1962–66, he examined contemporary culture in the U.S. in *The Electric Kool-Aid Acid Test* (1968), *The Bonfire of the Vanities* (1988), and *A Man in Full* (1998).

wolf·fish /'wōōlf,fish/ ▸*n.* a large long-bodied marine fish with a long-based dorsal fin and sharp doglike teeth, inhabiting the deep waters of the northern hemisphere. Also called **catfish, sea wolf.** • Family Anarhichadidae: several genera and species, including the edible *Anarhichas lupus*.

wolf·hound /'wōōlf,hound/ ▸*n.* a dog of a large breed originally used to hunt wolves.

wolf pack ▸*n.* a group of people or things that operate as a hunting and attacking pack, in particular a group of attacking submarines or aircraft.

wolf·ram /'wōōlfrəm/ ▸*n.* tungsten or its ore, esp. as a commercial commodity. ▹mid 18th cent.: from German, assumed to be a miners' term, perhaps from *Wolf* 'wolf' + Middle High German *rām* 'soot,' probably originally a pejorative term referring to the ore's inferiority to tin, with which it occurred.

wolf·ram·ite /'wōōlfrə,mīt/ ▸*n.* a black or brown mineral that is the chief ore of tungsten. It consists of a tungstate of iron and manganese.

Wolf Riv·er a river that flows for 210 miles (340 km) through central Wisconsin.

wolfs·bane /'wōōlfs,bān/ ▸*n.* a northern European aconite. • Genus *Aconitum*, family Ranunculaceae: several species, in particular the purple-flowered *A. lycoctonum*.

Wolfs·burg /'wōōlfs,bərg; 'vôlfs,bōōrk/ an industrial city on the Mittelland Canal in Lower Saxony, in northwestern Germany; pop. 129,000.

wolf·skin /'wōōlf,skin/ ▸*n.* the skin or pelt of a wolf.

wolf spi·der ▸*n.* a fast-moving ground spider that runs after and springs on its prey. • Family Lycosidae, order Araneae.

wolf whis·tle ▸*n.* a whistle with a rising and falling pitch, directed toward someone to express sexual attraction or admiration.

▸*v.* (**wolf-whis·tle**) [*trans.*] whistle in such a way at: *fans wolf-whistled her as she took off her jacket* | [*intrans.*] *they wolf-whistled at me.*

Wol·las·ton /'wōōləstən/, William Hyde (1766–1828), English chemist and physicist. He discovered palladium and rhodium and pioneered techniques in powder metallurgy.

wol·las·ton·ite /'wōōləstə,nīt/ ▸*n.* a white or grayish mineral typically occurring in tabular masses in metamorphosed limestone. It is a silicate of calcium and is used as a source of rock wool. ▹early 19th cent.: from the name of W. H. *Wollaston* (see **Wollaston**) + **-ite**[1].

Wol·lon·gong /'wōōlən,gông; -,gäng/ a city on the coast of New South Wales, in southeastern Australia; pop. 211,000.

Woll·stone·craft /'wōōlstən,kraft/, Mary (1759–97), English writer and feminist. Her *A Vindication of the Rights of Woman* (1792) defied assumptions about male supremacy and championed educational equality for women. In 1797 she married William Godwin and died shortly after giving birth to their daughter Mary Shelley.

Wo·lof /'wō,läf/ ▸*n.* (*pl.* same or **-lofs**) **1** a member of a people living in Senegal and Gambia. **2** the Niger–Congo language of this people.

▸*adj.* of or relating to the Wolof or their language. ▹the name in Wolof.

Wol·sey /'wōōlzē/, Thomas (*c.*1474–1530), English prelate and statesman; known as **Cardinal Wolsey.** He incurred royal displeasure through his failure to secure the papal dispensation necessary for Henry VIII's divorce from Catherine of Aragon. He was arrested on a charge of treason and died on his way to trial.

Wol·ston·i·an /wôl'stōnēən/ ▸*adj. Geology* of, relating to, or denoting the penultimate Pleistocene glaciation in Britain, identified with the Saale of northern Europe (and perhaps the Riss of the Alps). ■ [as *n.*] (**the Wolstonian**) the Wolstonian glaciation or the system of deposits laid down during it. ▹1960s: from *Wolston*, the name of a village in central England, + **-ian.**

Wol·ver·hamp·ton /'wōōlvər,ham(p)tən; ,wōōlvər'ham(p)-/ an industrial city in western central England, northwest of Birmingham; pop. 240,000.

wol·ver·ine /,wōōlvə'rēn/ ▸*n.* **1** a heavily built short-legged carnivorous mammal with a shaggy dark coat and a bushy tail, native to the tundra and forests of arctic and subarctic regions. • *Gulo luscus* of North America and *G. gulo* of Europe, family Mustelidae. **2** (**Wolverine**) *Informal* a native or inhabitant of Michigan. ▹late 16th cent. (earlier as *wolvering*): formed obscurely from *wolv-*, plural stem of **wolf.**

European wolverine

Wol·ver·ine State a nickname for the state of **Michigan.**

W

Pronunciation Key ə *ago*; ər *over*; 'ə or ,ə *up*; 'ər or ,ər *fur*; a *hat*; ā *rate*; ä *car*; ch *chew*; e *let*; ē *see*; e(ə)r *air*; i *fit*; ī *by*; i(ə)r *ear*; ng *sing*; ō *go*; ô *for*; oi *boy*; ōō *good*; ōō *goo*; ou *out*; sh *she*; th *thin*; th *then*; (h)w *why*; zh *vision*

wolves /wo͝olvz/ ▸ plural form of WOLF.

wom·an /ˈwo͝omən/ ▸*n.* (*pl.* **wom·en** /ˈwimin/) an adult human female. ■ a female worker or employee. ■ a wife, girlfriend, or lover: *he wondered whether Billy had his woman with him.* ■ [with *adj.*] a female person associated with a particular place, activity, or occupation: *a young American woman.* ■ [in *sing.*] female adults in general: *woman is intuitive.* ■ a female paid to clean someone's house and carry out general domestic duties. ■ a peremptory form of address to a woman: *don't be daft, woman.* ▷Old English *wīfmon, -man* (see WIFE, MAN), a formation peculiar to English, the ancient word being WIFE. **—wom·an·less** *adj.* **—wom·an·like** /-ˌlīk/ *adj.*

▸*PHRASES* □ **be one's own woman** see OWN. □ **the little woman** a condescending way of referring to a man's wife. □ **my good woman** *Brit., dated* a patronizing form of address to a woman: *you're mistaken, my good woman.* □ **woman of letters** a female scholar or author. □ **woman of the streets** *dated* used euphemistically to refer to a prostitute. □ **woman of the world** see WORLD. □ **woman to woman** in a direct and frank way between two women.

-woman ▸*comb. form* in nouns denoting: ■ a female of a specified nationality: *Frenchwoman.* ■ a woman of specified origin or place of abode: *Yorkshirewoman.* ■ a woman belonging to a distinct specified group: *laywoman.* ■ a woman having a specified occupation or professional status: *chairwoman | saleswoman.* ■ a woman skilled in or associated with a specified activity, esp. a craft or sport: *needlewoman | oarswoman.*

wom·an·hood /ˈwo͝omənˌho͝od/ ▸*n.* the state or condition of being a woman: *she was on the very brink of womanhood.* ■ the qualities considered to be natural to or characteristic of a woman: *Mary was cultivated as an ideal of womanhood.* ■ women considered collectively: *images of African-American womanhood.*

wom·an·ish /ˈwo͝oməniSH/ ▸*adj. derogatory* suitable to or characteristic of a woman: *he confused introspection with womanish indecision.* ■ (of a man) effeminate; unmanly: *Burden thought him a weak womanish fool.* **—wom·an·ish·ly** *adv.* **—wom·an·ish·ness** *n.*

wom·an·ism /ˈwo͝oməˌnizəm/ ▸*n.* a form of feminism that emphasizes women's natural contribution to society (used by some in distinction to the term *feminism* and its association with white women). **—wom·an·ist** *n.*

wom·an·ize /ˈwo͝oməˌnīz/ ▸*v.* [*intrans.*] (of a man) engage in numerous casual sexual affairs with women: [as *n.*] (**womanizing**) *there were rumors that his womanizing had now become intolerable.* **—wom·an·iz·er** *n.*

wom·an·kind /ˈwo͝omənˌkīnd/ ▸*n.* women considered collectively: *a giant step forward for womankind.*

wom·an·ly /ˈwo͝omənlē/ ▸*adj.* relating to or having the characteristics of a woman or women: *her smooth, womanly skin.* ■ (of a girl's or woman's body) fully developed and curvaceous: *I've got a womanly figure.* **—wom·an·li·ness** *n.*

womb /wo͞om/ ▸*n.* the uterus. ■ a place of origination and development: *the womb of evil.* ▷Old English *wamb, womb*, of Germanic origin. **—womb·like** /-ˌlīk/ *adj.*

wom·bat /ˈwämˌbat/ ▸*n.* a burrowing plant-eating Australian marsupial that resembles a small bear with short legs. • Family Vombatidae: two genera and three species, in particular the **common wombat** (*Vombatus ursinus*). ▷late 18th cent.: from Dharuk.

common wombat

wom·en /ˈwimin/ ▸ plural form of WOMAN.

wom·en·folk /ˈwiminˌfōk/ ▸*plural n.* the women of a particular family or community considered collectively.

wom·en's lib ▸*n. informal* short for WOMEN'S LIBERATION. **—wom·en's lib·ber** *n.*

wom·en's lib·er·a·tion ▸*n.* the advocacy of the liberation of women from inequalities and subservient status in relation to men, and from attitudes causing these (now generally replaced by the term *feminism*).

wom·en's move·ment ▸*n.* a broad movement campaigning for women's liberation and rights.

wom·en's rights ▸*plural n.* rights that promote a position of legal and social equality of women with men.

wom·en's room ▸*n.* another term for LADIES' ROOM.

wom·en's stud·ies ▸*plural n.* [usu. treated as *sing.*] academic courses in sociology, history, literature, and psychology that focus on the roles, experiences, and achievements of women in society.

wom·en's suf·frage ▸*n.* the right of women to vote.

wom·ens·wear /ˈwiminzˌwe(ə)r/ (also **wom·en's wear**) ▸*n.* clothing for women.

wom·en's work ▸*n.* work traditionally and historically undertaken by women, esp. tasks of a domestic nature such as cooking, needlework, and child rearing.

wom·yn /ˈwimin/ ▸*plural n.* nonstandard spelling of "women" adopted by some feminists in order to avoid the word ending *-men.*

won[1] /wən/ ▸ past and past participle of WIN.

won[2] /wän/ ▸*n.* (*pl.* same) the basic monetary unit of North and South Korea, equal to 100 jun in North Korea and 100 jeon in South Korea. ▷from Korean *wŏn.*

Won·der /ˈwəndər/, Stevie (1950–), U.S. singer, songwriter, and musician; born *Steveland Judkins Morris.* His repertoire includes soul, rock, funk, and romantic ballads, as heard on albums such as *Innervisions* (1973) and *Songs in the Key of Life* (1976). Blind since birth, he has had many hit songs, including "I Just Called to Say I Love You" and "Ebony and Ivory."

won·der /ˈwəndər/ ▸*n.* a feeling of surprise mingled with admiration, caused by something beautiful, unexpected, unfamiliar, or inexplicable: *he had stood in front of it, observing the intricacy of the ironwork with the wonder of a child.* ■ the quality of a person or thing that causes such a feeling: *Athens was a place of wonder and beauty.* ■ a strange or remarkable person, thing, or event: *the electric trolley car was looked upon as the wonder of the age.* ■ [as *adj.*] having remarkable properties or abilities: *a wonder drug.* ■ [in *sing.*] a surprising event or situation: *it is a wonder that losses are not much greater.*

▸*v.* [*intrans.*] **1** desire or be curious to know something: *how many times have I written that, I wonder?* | [with *clause*] *I can't help wondering how Stasia and Katie are feeling.* ■ [with *clause*] used to express a polite question or request: *I wonder whether you have thought more about it?* ■ feel doubt: *I* **wonder about** *such a marriage.* **2** feel admiration and amazement; marvel: *people stood by and* **wondered at** *such bravery* | [as *adj.*] (**wondering**) *a wondering look on her face.* ■ be surprised: *if I feel compassion for her, it is not to be wondered at.* ▷Old English *wundor* (noun), *wundrian* (verb), of Germanic origin; related to Dutch *wonder* and German *Wunder*, of unknown ultimate origin. **—won·der·er** *n.* **—won·der·ing·ly** *adv.*

▸*PHRASES* □ **I shouldn't wonder** *informal, chiefly Brit.* I think it likely. □ **no** (or **little** or **small**) **wonder** it is not surprising: ***it is little wonder that*** *the fax machine is so popular.* □ **ninety-day** (or **thirty-day** or **one-day**) **wonder** something that attracts enthusiastic interest for a short while but is then ignored or forgotten. ■ (usu. **ninety-day** (or **thirty-day**) **wonder**) a person who has had intensive military training for the specified time. □ **wonders will never cease** an exclamation of great surprise at something pleasing. □ **work** (or **do**) **wonders** have a very beneficial effect on someone or something: *a good night's sleep can work wonders for mind and body.*

won·der·ful /ˈwəndərfəl/ ▸*adj.* inspiring delight, pleasure, or admiration; extremely good; marvelous: *they all think she's wonderful | the climate was wonderful all the year round.* ▷late Old English *wunderfull* (see WONDER, -FUL). **—won·der·ful·ly** /-f(ə)lē/ *adv.* [as *submodifier*] *the bed was wonderfully comfortable.* **—won·der·ful·ness** *n.*

won·der·land /ˈwəndərˌland/ ▸*n.* a land or place full of wonderful things: *London was a wonderland of historical sites, museums, theaters, shops, and entertainment.*

won·der·ment /ˈwəndərmənt/ ▸*n.* a state of awed admiration or respect: *Corbett shook his head in silent wonderment.*

won·der·struck /ˈwəndərˌstrək/ ▸*adj.* (of a person) experiencing a sudden feeling of awed delight or wonder.

won·der·work·er /ˈwəndərˌwərkər/ ▸*n.* a person who performs miracles or wonders. **—won·der·work·ing** *adj.*

won·drous /ˈwəndrəs/ ▸*adj. poetic/literary* inspiring a feeling of wonder or delight; marvelous: *this wondrous city.*

▸*adv.* [as *submodifier*] *archaic* marvelously; wonderfully: *she is grown wondrous pretty.* ▷late 15th cent.: alteration of obsolete *wonders* (adjective and adverb), genitive of WONDER, on the pattern of *marvelous.* **—won·drous·ly** *adv.* **—won·drous·ness** *n.*

wonk /wäNGk/ ▸*n. informal, derogatory* a studious or hardworking person: *any kid with an interest in science was a wonk.* ■ a person who takes an excessive interest in minor details of political policy: *he is a* ***policy wonk*** *in tune with a younger generation of voters.* ▷1920s: of unknown origin.

won·ky /ˈwäNGkē/ ▸*adj.* (**-ki·er**, **-ki·est**) *informal* crooked; off-center; askew: *you have a wonky nose and a crooked mouth.* ■ (of a thing) unsteady; shaky: *they sat drinking, perched on the wonky stools.* ■ faulty: *your sense of judgment is a bit wonky at the moment.* ▷early 20th cent.: fanciful formation. **—won·ki·ly** /ˈwäNGkəlē/ *adv.* **—won·ki·ness** *n.*

wont /wônt; wōnt/ ▸*adj.* [*predic.*] *poetic/literary* (of a person) in the habit of doing something; accustomed: *he was wont to arise at 5:30 every morning.*

▸*n.* (**one's wont**) *formal* or *humorous* one's customary behavior in a particular situation: *Constance, as was her wont, had paid her little attention.*

▸*v.* (*3rd sing. present* **wonts** or **wont**; *past* **wont** or **wonted**) *archaic* make or be or become accustomed: [*trans.*] *wont thy heart to thoughts hereof* | [*intrans.*] *sons wont to nurse their parents in old age.* ▷Old English *gewunod*, past participle of *wunian*, 'dwell, be accustomed' of Germanic origin.

won't /wōnt/ ▸*contraction of* will not.

wont·ed /ˈwôntid; ˈwōn-/ ▸*adj. poetic/literary* habitual; usual: *the place had sunk back into its wonted quiet.* ▷late Middle English: from WONT.

won·ton /ˈwänˌtän/ (also **won ton**) ▸*n.* (in Chinese cooking) a small dumpling or roll with a savory filling, often of minced pork, usually eaten boiled in soup. ▷from Chinese (Cantonese dialect) *wān t'ān.*

woo /wo͞o/ ▸*v.* (**woos, wooed**) [*trans.*] try to gain the love of (someone, typically a woman), esp. with a view to marriage: *he wooed her with quotes from Shakespeare.* ■ seek the favor, support, or custom of: *pop stars are being wooed by film companies eager to sign them up.* ▷late Old English *wōgian* (intransitive), *āwōgian* (transitive), of unknown origin. **—woo·a·ble** *adj.* **—woo·er** *n.*

Wood[1] /wo͝od/, Grant (De Volsen) (1892–1942), U.S. artist. He is most noted for his scenes of his native Iowa in paintings such as *Woman with Plant(s)* (1929), *American Gothic* (1930), and *Spring in Town* (1941).

Wood[2], Natalie (1938–81), U.S. actress. She played the vulnerable adolescent heroine in *Rebel Without A Cause* (1955) and similar roles in *Cry in the Night* (1956), *West Side Story* (1961), and *Inside Daisy Clover* (1966).

wood /wo͝od/ ▸*n.* **1** the hard fibrous material that forms the main substance of the trunk or branches of a tree or shrub. ■ such material when cut and used as timber or fuel: *a large table made of dark, polished wood | best quality woods were used for joinery* | [as *adj.*] *a wood cross.* ■ a golf club with a wooden or other head that is relatively broad from face to back (often with a numeral indicating the degree to which the face is angled to loft the ball). ■ a shot made with such a club. **2** (also **woods**) an area of land, smaller than a forest, that is covered with growing trees: *a thick hedge divided the wood from the field | a long walk in the woods.* ▷Old English *wudu*, from a Germanic word related to Welsh *gwŷdd* 'trees.' **—wood·less** *adj.*

▸*PHRASES* □ **out of the wood** (or **woods**) out of danger or difficulty. □ **get wood** *vulgar slang* have an erection. □ **knock on wood** said in order to prevent a confident statement from bringing bad luck: *I haven't been banned yet, knock on wood.* [with reference to the custom of touching something wooden to ward off bad luck.]

wood al·co·hol ▸*n.* crude methanol made by distillation from wood.

wood a·nem·o·ne ▸*n.* see ANEMONE.

wood ant ▸*n.* a large reddish-brown ant found chiefly in woodlands, living in nest mounds, which it defends by spraying formic acid at the attacker. • *Formica rufa*, family Formicidae.

wood bet·o·ny ▸*n.* see LOUSEWORT.

wood·bine /ˈwo͝odˌbīn/ ▸*n.* either of two climbing plants: • Virginia creeper. • *Brit.* the common honeysuckle.

wood·block /ˈwo͝odˌbläk/ ▸*n.* a block of wood, esp.

one from which woodcut prints are made. ■ a print made in such a way. ■ a hollow wooden block used as a percussion instrument.

Wood·bridge /ˈwo͝odˌbrij/ an industrial, commercial, and residential township in northeastern New Jersey; pop. 97,203.

Wood·bur·y /ˈwo͝odˌberē; -bərē/, Levi (1789–1851), U.S. Supreme Court associate justice 1846–51. Before being appointed to the Court by President Polk, he served as the governor of New Hampshire 1823–24 and as a U.S. senator 1825–31, 1841–45.

wood·carv·ing /ˈwo͝odˌkärviNG/ ▶*n.* the action or skill of carving wood to make functional or ornamental objects. ■ an object made in this way. —**wood·carv·er** *n.*

wood·chat /ˈwo͝odˌCHat/ (also **wood·chat shrike**) ▶*n.* a shrike of southern Europe, North Africa, and the Middle East, having black and white plumage with a chestnut head. • *Lanius senator*, family Laniidae.

wood·chuck /ˈwo͝odˌCHək/ ▶*n.* a North American marmot with a heavy body and short legs. • *Marmota monax*, family Sciuridae. ▷late 17th cent.: alteration (by association with **wood**) of an American Indian name.

wood·cock /ˈwo͝odˌkäk/ ▶*n.* (*pl.* same) a woodland bird of the sandpiper family, with a long bill, brown camouflaged plumage, and a distinctive display flight. • Genus *Scolopax*, family Scolopacidae: several species, in particular the **Eurasian woodcock** (*S. rusticola*), which is sometimes regarded as a game bird.

wood·craft /ˈwo͝odˌkraft/ ▶*n.* **1** skill in woodwork. **2** knowledge of the woods, esp. with reference to camping and other outdoor pursuits.

wood·cut /ˈwo͝odˌkət/ ▶*n.* a print of a type made from a design cut in a block of wood, formerly widely used for illustrations in books. Compare with **wood engraving**. ■ the technique of making such prints.

wood·cut·ter /ˈwo͝odˌkətər/ ▶*n.* **1** a person who cuts down trees or branches, esp. for fuel. **2** a person who makes woodcuts. —**wood·cut·ting** *n.*

wood duck ▶*n.* a tree-nesting North American duck, the male of which has brightly colored plumage. Also called **Carolina duck**. • *Aix sponsa*, family Anatidae.

wood ear ▶*n.* an edible fungus, black or brown in color, that grows on trees and is sold in dry wrinkled shapes somewhat resembling ears. • *Auricularia auricula*, family Auriculariaceae.

wood·ed /ˈwo͝odid/ ▶*adj.* (of an area of land) covered with woods or many trees: *a wooded valley.*

wood·en /ˈwo͝odn/ ▶*adj.* **1** made of wood: *a wooden spoon | she closed the heavy wooden door.* **2** like or characteristic of wood: *a kind of dull wooden sound.* ■ stiff and awkward in movement or manner: *she is one of the most wooden actresses of all time.* —**wood·en·ly** *adv.* (in sense 2) —**wood·en·ness** *n.* (in sense 2).

wood en·grav·ing ▶*n.* a print made from a finely detailed design cut into the end grain of a block of wood. Compare with **woodcut**. ■ the technique of making such prints. —**wood en·grav·er** *n.*

wood·en·head ▶*n. informal* a stupid person. —**wood·en·head·ed** *adj.* —**wood·en·head·ed·ness** *n.*

wood·fern /ˈwo͝odˌfərn/ ▶*n.* an evergreen fern with leathery dark-green fronds. • Genus *Dryopteris*, family Polypodiaceae, numerous species, including the common **evergreen** (or **marginal**) **woodfern** (*D. marginalis*).

wood fi·ber /ˈwo͝od ˌfībər/ ▶*n.* fiber obtained from wood and used esp. in the manufacture of paper.

wood·grain /ˈwo͝odˌgrān/ ▶*n.* a texture seen in a cut surface of wood. ■ [as *adj.*] denoting a surface or finish imitating such a pattern: *the doors are available in woodgrain finish.*

evergreen woodfern

wood·grouse /ˈwo͝odˌgrous/ ▶*n.* a grouse that frequents woodlands, esp. a capercaillie, spruce grouse, or willow grouse.

wood-hoo·poe /ˈho͞oˌpō; -po͞o/ ▶*n.* a long-tailed African bird with a long, slender, down-curved bill and blackish plumage with a blue or green gloss. • Genus *Phoeniculus*, family Phoeniculidae: several species.

wood i·bis ▶ **1** *n.* a stork with a slightly down-curved bill and a bare face or head, found in America and Africa. Also called **wood stork**. • Genus *Mycteria*, family Ciconiidae: the black-faced *M. americana* of America, and the red-faced *M. ibis* of Africa. **2** (**crest·ed wood i·bis**) a mainly brown ibis with a greenish crest, found only in Madagascar. • *Lophotibis cristata*, family Threskiornithidae.

wood·ie /ˈwo͝odē/ ▶*n.* **1** *vulgar slang* (also **wood·y**) (of a man) a penile erection. **2** a station wagon with wood exterior paneling.

Wood·land /ˈwo͝odlənd/ a city in north central California, northwest of Sacramento; pop. 39,802.

wood·land /ˈwo͝odlənd; -ˌland/ ▶*n.* (also **woodlands**) land covered with trees: *large areas of ancient woodland | [as adj.] woodland birds are often drably colored.*

wood·land·er /ˈwo͝odləndər; -ˌlandər/ ▶*n.* an inhabitant of woodland.

wood·lark /ˈwo͝odˌlärk/ ▶*n.* a small European and North African lark with a short tail and melodious song, frequenting open ground with scattered trees. • *Lullula arborea*, family Alaudidae.

Wood·lawn /ˈwo͝odˌlôn/ a residential section of the northern Bronx in New York City, site of the noted Woodlawn Cemetery.

wood louse ▶*n.* (*pl.* **wood lice**) a small terrestrial crustacean with a grayish segmented body and seven pairs of legs, living in damp habitats. • *Oniscus* and other genera, order Isopoda.

wood·man /ˈwo͝odmən/ ▶*n.* (*pl.* **-men**) *chiefly historical* a person working in woodland, esp. a forester or woodcutter.

wood mouse ▶*n.* a dark brown Eurasian mouse with a long tail and large eyes. Also called **field mouse**. • Genus *Apodemus*, family Muridae: several species, in particular the widespread *A. sylvaticus.*

wood mush·room ▶*n.* an edible mushroom with a white cap and brown gills, smelling strongly of aniseed and found in woodland in both Eurasia and North America. • *Agaricus silvicola*, family Agaricaceae, class Hymenomycetes.

wood·note /ˈwo͝odˌnōt/ ▶*n. poetic/literary* a natural and untrained musical note resembling the song of a bird.

wood nymph ▶*n.* **1** (in folklore and classical mythology) a nymph inhabiting woodland, esp. a Dryad or Hamadryad. **2** a brown American butterfly of grassy habitats and light woodlands, with large eyespots on the forewings and smaller ones on the hind wings. • Genus *Cercyonis*, subfamily Satyrinae, family Nymphalidae: several species, in particular the widespread *C. pegala*. **3** (also **wood·nymph**) a dark-colored, green-throated hummingbird, found from Mexico to Argentina. • Genus *Thalurania*, family Trochilidae: several species, including the **common wood nymph** (*T. furcata*) and the **Mexican wood nymph** (*T. ridgwayi*).

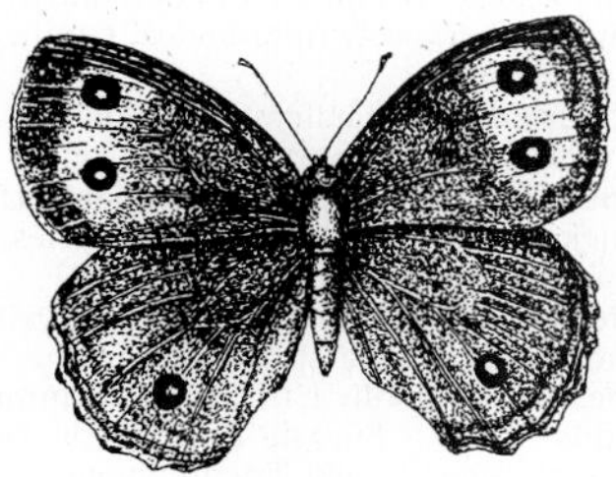

wood nymph 2

wood·peck·er /ˈwo͝odˌpekər/ ▶*n.* a bird with a strong bill and a stiff tail, that climbs tree trunks to find insects and drums on dead wood to mark territory. • Family Picidae (the **woodpecker family**): many genera and numerous species. The woodpecker family also includes the wrynecks, piculets, flickers, and sapsuckers.

wood pi·geon ▶*n.* a large Eurasian and African pigeon with mainly gray plumage, using wing claps in display flight. • Genus *Columba*, family Columbidae: several species, in particular the widespread *C. palumbus* (also called **ringdove**).

wood·pile /ˈwo͝odˌpīl/ ▶*n.* a stack of wood stored for fuel.

wood pulp ▶*n.* wood fiber reduced chemically or mechanically to pulp and used in the manufacture of paper.

wood rat ▶*n.* another term for **pack rat**.

wood·ruff /ˈwo͝odˌrəf/ ▶*n.* a white-flowered plant of the bedstraw family with whorled leaves, smelling of new-mown hay when dried or crushed. • Genera *Galium* and *Asperula*, family Rubiaceae: several species, esp. **sweet woodruff** (*G. odoratum*). ▷Old English *wudurofe*, from *wudu* 'wood' + an element of unknown meaning.

Wood·ruff key /ˈwo͝odrəf/ ▶*n.* a key whose cross section is part circular, to fit into a curved keyway in a shaft, and part rectangular, used chiefly in machinery. ▷late 19th cent.: named after the *Woodruff* Manufacturing Company, Hartford, Connecticut.

wood·rush /ˈwo͝odˌrəSH/ ▶*n.* a grasslike plant that typically has long flat leaves fringed with long hairs. • Genus *Luzula*, family Juncaceae: many species.

Woods[1] /wo͝odz/, Tiger (1975–), U.S. golfer; full name *Eldrick Woods*. Since turning professional in 1996, he has won several championships, including the Masters (1997, 2001, 2002), the PGA (1999, 2000), the U.S. Open (2000, 2002), and the British Open (2000).

Tiger Woods

Woods[2], William Burnham (1824–87), U.S. Supreme Court associate justice 1880–87. A judge on the circuit court, he was appointed to the Supreme Court by President Hayes.

wood sage ▶*n.* another term for **American germander** (see **germander**).

wood screw ▶*n.* a tapering metal screw with a sharp point.

wood·shed /ˈwo͝odˌSHed/ ▶*n.* a shed where wood for fuel is stored.
▶*v.* [*intrans.*] practice a musical instrument: *he's off woodshedding again.*
▶*PHRASE* □ **take someone to the woodshed** *informal* reprove or punish someone, esp. discreetly.

Woods Hole a village in Falmouth in southeastern Massachusetts, at the southwest corner of Cape Cod, a resort and noted ocean research center.

wood·si·a /ˈwo͝odzēə/ ▶*n.* a small tufted fern that grows among rocks in mountains in temperate and cool regions. • Genus *Woodsia*, family Woodsiaceae. ▷modern Latin, named after Joseph Woods (1776–1864), English architect and botanist.

woods·man /ˈwo͝odzmən/ ▶*n.* (*pl.* **-men**) a person living or working in the woods, esp. a forester, hunter, or woodcutter.

wood·smoke /ˈwo͝odˌsmōk/ ▶*n.* the smoke from a wood fire.

wood sor·rel ▶*n.* a small woodland plant with cloverlike leaves and five-petaled flowers. • Genus *Oxalis*, family Oxalidaceae: several species, including the yellow-flowered creeping **yellow wood sorrel** (*O. stricta*) and the purple-flowered **violet wood sorrel** (*O. violacea*).

wood spir·it ▶*n.* another term for **wood alcohol**.

Wood·stock /ˈwo͝odˌstäk/ a small town in southwestern New York, near Albany. It gave its name in the summer of 1969 to a huge rock music festival held about 60 miles (96 km) to the southwest.

wood stork ▶*n.* another term for **wood ibis**.

woods·y /ˈwo͝odzē/ ▶*adj.* of, relating to, or characteristic of wood or woodlands: *trails through woodsy countryside | the woodsy smells of cedar and pine.* ▷mid 19th cent.: formed irregularly from **wood** (differentiated from *woody*).

wood thrush ▶*n.* a thrush of eastern North America, with a brown back, rufous head, and dark-spotted white breast, and a loud liquid song. • *Hylocichla mustelina*, subfamily Turdinae, family Muscicapidae.

wood tick ▸*n.* a North American tick that infests wild and domestic animals, often found clinging to plants and responsible for transmitting spotted fever. • Genus *Dermacentor*, family Ixodidae, in particular *D. andersoni.*

wood tick

wood·turn·ing /ˈwo͝od-ˌtərniNG/ ▸*n.* the action of shaping wood with a lathe. —**wood·turn·er** /-ˌtərnər/ *n.*

wood war·bler ▸*n.* a migratory European leaf warbler found in woodlands, with plaintive calls and a trilling song. • *Phylloscopus sibilatrix*, family Sylviidae. ■ any New World warbler of the subfamily Parulinae, family Emberizidae.

Wood·ward[1] /ˈwo͝odwərd/, Joanne (1930–), U.S. actress. She starred in *The Three Faces of Eve* (Academy Award, 1957); *The Long Hot Summer* (1958); *Rachel, Rachel* (1968), which was directed by her husband, Paul Newman; *The Glass Menagerie* (1987), and *Mr. & Mrs. Bridge* (1990).

Wood·ward[2], Robert Burns (1917–79), U.S. organic chemist. He was the first to synthesize quinine, cholesterol, chlorophyll, and vitamin B_{12}, and with **Roald Hoffmann** (1937–), a U.S. chemist, born in Poland, discovered symmetry-based rules governing the course of rearrangement reactions involving cyclic intermediates. Nobel Prize for Chemistry (1965).

Wood·ward[3] **1** , Robert (Upshur) (1943–), **2** U.S. journalist. He was the *Washington Post* reporter who, with Carl Bernstein, broke the story of the Watergate burglary and traced the financial payoffs to President Nixon. With Bernstein, he wrote *All the President's Men* (1974) and *The Final Days* (1976). He is also the author of *The Choice* (1996), *Shadow: Five Presidents and the Legacy of Watergate* (1999), and *Plan of Attack* (2004).

wood·wasp /ˈwo͝odˌwäsp/ ▸*n.* another term for HORNTAIL.

wood·wind /ˈwo͝odˌwind/ ▸*n.* [treated as *sing.* or *pl.*] wind instruments other than brass instruments forming a section of an orchestra, including flutes, oboes, clarinets, and bassoons: *striking passages for woodwind and brass.*

wood wool·ly foot ▸*n.* see WOOLLY FOOT.

wood·work /ˈwo͝odˌwərk/ ▸*n.* the wooden parts of a room or building, such as window frames or doors: *the woodwork was painted blue.* —**wood·work·er** *n.*

▸*PHRASE* □ **come out of the woodwork** (of an unpleasant person or thing) emerge from obscurity; be revealed.

wood·work·ing /ˈwo͝odˌwərkiNG/ ▸*n.* the activity or skill of making things from wood.

wood·worm /ˈwo͝odˌwərm/ ▸*n.* the worm or larva of a beetle that bores into wood. ■ the damaged condition of wood resulting from infestation with this larva.

wood·y /ˈwo͝odē/ ▸*adj.* (**wood·i·er**, **wood·i·est**) (of an area of land) covered with trees: *a woody dale.* ■ made of, resembling, or suggestive of wood: *cut out the woody central core before boiling.* ■ *Botany* (of a plant or its stem) of the nature of or consisting of wood; lignified. —**wood·i·ness** *n.*

wood·yard /ˈwo͝odˌyärd/ ▸*n.* a yard where wood is chopped or stored.

wood·y night·shade ▸*n.* see NIGHTSHADE.

woof[1] /wo͝of/ ▸*n.* the barking sound made by a dog.
▸*v.* [*intrans.*] (of a dog) bark: *the dog started to woof.* ■ *black slang* say something in an ostentatious or aggressive manner but with no intention to act: *King start woofing to keep folks off our case. Just woofing. Just talk.* ▷early 19th cent.: imitative.

woof[2] ▸*n.* another term for WEFT. ▷Old English *ōwef*, a compound from the base of WEAVE[1]; Middle English *oof* later became *woof* by association with WARP in the phrase *warp and woof.*

woof·er /ˈwo͝ofər/ ▸*n.* a loudspeaker designed to reproduce low frequencies. ▷1930s: from the verb WOOF[1] + -ER[1].

wool /wo͝ol/ ▸*n.* **1** the fine soft curly or wavy hair forming the coat of a sheep, goat, or similar animal, esp. when shorn and prepared for use in making cloth or yarn. ■ yarn or textile fiber made from such hair: *carpets made of 80 percent wool and 20 percent nylon | a sampler in colored wools* | [as *adj.*] *her blue wool suit.* **2** a thing resembling such hair in form or texture, in particular: ■ [with *adj.*] the soft underfur or down of some other mammals: *beaver wool.* ■ [with *adj.*] a metal or mineral made into a mass of fine fibers: *lead wool.* ▷Old English *wull*, of Germanic origin; related to Dutch *wol* and German *Wolle*, from an Indo-European root shared by Latin *lana* 'wool,' *vellus* 'fleece.' —**wool·like** /-ˌlīk/ *adj.*

▸*PHRASE* □ **pull the wool over someone's eyes** deceive someone by telling untruths.

wool clip ▸*n.* the total quantity of wool shorn from a particular flock or in a particular area in the course of a year.

wool·en /ˈwo͝olən/ (*Brit.* **wool·len**) ▸*adj.* [*attrib.*] of or relating to the production of wool: *the woolen industry | a woolen mill.* ■ made wholly or partly of wool: *thick woolen blankets.*
▸*n.* (usu. **woolens**) an article of clothing made of wool. ▷late Old English *wullen* (see WOOL, -EN[2]).

Woolf /wo͝olf/, Virginia (1882–1941), English novelist, essayist, and critic; born *Adeline Virginia Stephen.* A member of the Bloomsbury Group, she gained recognition with *Jacob's Room* (1922). Subsequent novels, such as *Mrs. Dalloway* (1925) and *To the Lighthouse* (1927), established her as an exponent of modernism.

wool·gath·er·ing /ˈwo͝olˌgaT͟H(ə)riNG/ ▸*n.* indulgence in aimless thought or dreamy imagining; absentmindedness: *he wanted to be free to indulge his woolgathering.* —**wool·gath·er** /-ˌgaT͟Hərər/ *v.*

wool·grow·er /ˈwo͝olˌgrō(ə)r/ ▸*n.* a breeder of sheep for wool.

Wooll·cott /ˈwo͝olkət/, Alexander (Humpreys) (1887–1943), U.S. critic. He was the drama critic for *The New York Times* (1914–22) and the *New York World* (1925–28) and also had a radio show called "Town Crier" (1929–42). The lead character in *The Man Who Came to Dinner* (1939), a play by Moss Hart and George S. Kaufman, was based on Woollcott.

Wool·ley /ˈwo͝olē/, Sir (Charles) Leonard (1880–1960), English archaeologist. He directed a British-U.S. excavation of the Sumerian city of Ur 1922–34 that uncovered rich royal tombs and thousands of clay tablets.

wool·ly /ˈwo͝olē/ (also **wool·y**) ▸*adj.* (**-li·er**, **-li·est**) **1** made of wool: *a red woolly hat.* ■ (of an animal, plant, or part) bearing or naturally covered with wool or hair resembling wool. ■ resembling wool in texture or appearance: *woolly wisps of cloud.* **2** vague or confused in expression or character: *woolly thinking.* ■ (of a sound) indistinct or distorted: *an opaque and woolly recording.*
▸*n.* (*pl.* **-lies**) **1** (usu. **woollies**) *informal, chiefly Brit.* a garment made of wool, esp. a pullover. **2** a sheep. —**wool·li·ness** *n.* (in sense 2 of the *adjective*).

wool·ly a·del·gid /əˈdeljid/ ▸*n.* any of several small aphidlike insects that feed on conifers, esp. hemlocks, spruces, and firs. By sucking the sap from young twigs, the insect retards or prevents tree growth and causes needles to discolor and drop prematurely. • Superfamily Aphidoidea, family Adelgidae.

wool·ly bear ▸*n.* a large hairy caterpillar, esp. that of a tiger moth.

wool·ly·butt /ˈwo͝olēˌbət/ ▸*n.* an Australian eucalyptus with thick fibrous bark. • Several species in the genus *Eucalyptus*, family Myrtaceae.

wool·ly foot (also **wood wool·ly foot**) ▸*n.* a yellowish-brown toadstool with a slender stem, the base of which bears long woolly hairs, found commonly in woodlands in both Eurasia and North America. • *Collybia peronata*, family Tricholomataceae, class Hymenomycetes.

wool·ly mam·moth ▸*n.* a mammoth that was adapted to the cold periods of the Pleistocene, with a long shaggy coat, small ears, and a thick layer of fat. Individuals are sometimes found frozen in the permafrost of Siberia. • *Mammuthus primigenius*, family Elephantidae.

woolly mammoth

wool·ly rhi·noc·er·os ▸*n.* an extinct two-horned Eurasian rhinoceros that was adapted to the cold periods of the Pleistocene, with a long woolly coat. • Genus *Coelodonta*, family Rhinocerotidae.

wool·ly spi·der mon·key ▸*n.* a large spider monkey with long thin limbs and tail, dense woolly fur, and a large protruding belly, native to the rain forests of southeastern Brazil. • *Brachyteles arachnoides*, family Cebidae.

Wool·mark /ˈwo͝olˌmärk/ ▸*n.* an international quality symbol for wool instituted by the International Wool Secretariat.

Wool·sack /ˈwo͝olˌsak/ ▸*n.* (in the UK) the Lord Chancellor's wool-stuffed seat in the House of Lords. It is said to have been adopted in Edward III's reign as a reminder to the Lords of the importance to England of the wool trade. ■ (**the woolsack**) the position of Lord Chancellor.

wool·sort·er's dis·ease ▸*n.* see ANTHRAX.

wool·sta·pler ▸*n.* *archaic* a person who buys wool from a producer, grades it, and sells it to a manufacturer.

wool work ▸*n.* needlework executed in wool on a canvas foundation.

Wool·worth /ˈwo͝olwərTH/, Frank Winfield (1852–1919), U.S. businessman. He pioneered the concept of low-priced retailing in 1878 and from this built a large international chain of stores.

wool·y ▸*adj.* variant spelling of WOOLLY.

Woo·me·ra /ˈwo͝omərə; ˈwo͝omə-/ a town in central South Australia, the site of a vast military testing ground used in the 1950s for nuclear tests and since the 1960s for tracking space satellites.

woo·mer·a /ˈwo͝omərə/ ▸*n.* *Austral.* an Aboriginal stick used to throw a dart or spear more forcibly. ▷from Dharuk *wamara.*

woo·nerf /ˈvo͞onərf/ ▸*n.* a road in which devices for reducing or slowing the flow of traffic have been installed. ▷1970s: from Dutch, from *wonen* 'reside' + *erf* 'premises, ground.'

Woon·sock·et /wo͞onˈsäkit/ an industrial city in northern Rhode Island, on the Blackstone River; pop. 43,224.

woop·ie /ˈwo͞opē/ (also **woop·y**) ▸*n.* (*pl.* **-ies**) *informal* an affluent retired person able to pursue an active lifestyle. ▷1980s: elaboration of the acronym from *well-off older person.*

woosh ▸*v., n., exclam.,* & *adv.* variant spelling of WHOOSH.

Woos·ter /ˈwo͝ostər/ an industrial and academic city in north central Ohio; pop. 22,191.

wooz·y /ˈwo͞ozē/ ▸*adj.* (**wooz·i·er**, **wooz·i·est**) *informal* unsteady, dizzy, or dazed: *I still felt woozy from all the pills.* ▷late 19th cent.: of unknown origin. —**wooz·i·ly** /-zəlē/ *adv.* —**wooz·i·ness** *n.*

wop /wäp/ ▸*n.* *informal, offensive* a contemptuous term for an Italian or other southern European. ▷early 20th cent. (originally U.S.): origin uncertain, perhaps from Italian *guappo* 'bold, showy,' from Spanish *guapo* 'dandy.'

Worces·ter[1] /ˈwo͝ostər/ an industrial and college city in central Massachusetts, on the Blackstone River; pop. 172,648.

Worces·ter[2] /ˈwo͝ostər/ (also **Roy·al Worces·ter**) ▸*n.* *trademark* porcelain made at Worcester, England, in a factory founded in 1751. The porcelain (largely tableware) at first showed strong influence from Chinese and Dresden designs before being produced in a wider variety of designs.

Worces·ter·shire sauce /ˈwo͝ostərˌSHi(ə)r; -SHər/ ▸*n.* a pungent sauce containing soy sauce and vinegar, first made in Worcester, England.

Worcs. ▸*abbr.* Worcestershire.

word /wərd/ ▸*n.* a single distinct meaningful element of speech or writing, used with others (or sometimes alone) to form a sentence and typically shown with a space on either side when written or printed. ■ a single distinct conceptual unit of language, comprising inflected and variant forms. ■ (usu. **words**) something that someone says or writes; a remark or piece of information: *his grandfather's words had been meant kindly | a word of warning.* ■ speech as distinct from action: *he conforms in word and deed to the values of a society that he rejects.* ■ [with *negative*] (**a word**) even the smallest amount of something spoken or written: *don't believe a word of it.* ■ (**one's word**) a person's account of the truth, esp. when it differs from that of another person: *in court it would have been his word against mine.* ■ (**one's word**) a promise or assurance: *everything will be taken care of—you have my word.* ■ (**words**) the text or spoken part of a play, opera, or other performed piece; a script: *he had to learn his words.* ■ (**words**) angry talk: *her father would have* **had words with** *her about that.* ■ a message; news: *I was afraid to leave Washington in case there was word from the office.* ■ a command, password, or motto: *someone* **gave me the word** *to start playing.* ■ a basic unit of data in a computer, typically 16 or 32 bits long.
▸*v.* [*trans.*] choose and use particular words in order to say or write (something): *he words his request in a*

particularly ironic way | [as *adj.*, with *submodifier*] (**worded**) *a strongly worded letter of protest.*
▸*phrasal v.* ▫ **word up** [as *imperative*] *informal* listen: *word up, my brother, you got me high as a kite.*
▸*exclam. informal* used to express agreement: *"That Jay is one dangerous character." "Word."* ▷Old English, of Germanic origin; related to Dutch *woord* and German *Wort*, from an Indo-European root shared by Latin *verbum* 'word.' —**word·age** /ˈwərdij/ *n.* —**word·less** *adj.* —**word·less·ly** *adv.* —**word·less·ness** *n.*
▸*PHRASES* ▫ **at a word** as soon as requested: *ready to leave again at a word.* ▫ **be as good as one's word** do what one has promised to do. ▫ **break one's word** fail to do what one has promised. ▫ **have a word** speak briefly to someone: *I'll just* **have a word with** *him.* ▫ **in other words** expressed in a different way; that is to say. ▫ **in so many words** [often with *negative*] in the way mentioned: *I haven't told him in so many words, but he'd understand.* ▫ **in a word** briefly. ▫ **keep one's word** do what one has promised. ▫ **a man/woman of his/her word** a person who keeps their promises. ▫ **(on/upon) my word** an exclamation of surprise or emphasis: *my word, you were here quickly!* ▫ **of few words** taciturn: *he's a man of few words.* ▫ **put something into words** express something in speech or writing: *he felt a vague disappointment which he couldn't put into words.* ▫ **put words into someone's mouth** falsely or inaccurately report what someone has said. ■ prompt or encourage someone to say something that they may not otherwise have said. ▫ **take someone at their word** interpret a person's words literally or exactly, esp. by believing them or doing as they suggest. ▫ **take the words out of someone's mouth** say what someone else was about to say. ▫ **take someone's word (for it)** believe what someone says or writes without checking for oneself. ▫ **too —— for words** *informal* extremely ——: *going around by the road was too tedious for words.* ▫ **waste words 1** talk in vain. **2** talk at length. ▫ **the Word (of God) 1** the Bible, or a part of it. **2** Jesus Christ (see **LOGOS**). ▫ **word for word** in exactly the same or, when translated, exactly equivalent words. ▫ **word of honor** a solemn promise: *I'll be good to you always, I give you my word of honor.* ▫ **word of mouth** spoken language; informal or unofficial discourse. ▫ **the word on the street** *informal* a rumor or piece of information currently being circulated. ▫ **words fail me** used to express one's disbelief or dismay. ▫ **a word to the wise** a hint or brief explanation given, that being all that is required.

-word ▸*comb. form* denoting a word that may be offensive or have a negative connotation, specified by the word's first letter: *the F-word.*

word as·so·ci·a·tion ▸*n.* the spontaneous and unreflective production of other words in response to a given word, as a game, a prompt to creative thought or memory, or a technique in psychiatric evaluation.

word blind·ness ▸*n.* less technical term for **ALEXIA**, or (less accurately) for **DYSLEXIA**.

word·book /ˈwərd,bo͝ok/ ▸*n.* a reference book containing lists of words and meanings or other related information.

word break (also **word di·vi·sion**) ▸*n. Printing* a point at which a word is split between two lines of text by means of a hyphen.

word class ▸*n.* a category of words of similar form or function; a part of speech.

word deaf·ness ▸*n.* an inability to identify spoken words, resulting from a brain defect such as Wernicke's aphasia.

word game ▸*n.* a game involving the making, guessing, or selection of words.

word·ing /ˈwərdiNG/ ▸*n.* the words used to express something; the way in which something is expressed: *the standard form of wording for a consent letter.*

word length ▸*n. Computing* the number of bits in a word.

word or·der ▸*n.* the sequence of words in a sentence, esp. as governed by grammatical rules and as affecting meaning.

word-per·fect /ˈpərfəkt/ ▸*adj.* another term for **LETTER-PERFECT**.

word pic·ture ▸*n.* a vivid description in writing.

word·play /ˈwərd,plā/ ▸*n.* the witty exploitation of the meanings and ambiguities of words, esp. in puns.

word prob·lem ▸*n.* a mathematics exercise presented in the form of a hypothetical situation that requires an equation to be solved; for example, "if George earns a salary of $18,500 and 28% of it is deducted in taxes, how much take-home pay remains?"

word proc·ess·ing ▸*n.* the production, storage, and manipulation of text on a word processor or personal computer. —**word-proc·ess** *v.*

word proc·es·sor ▸*n.* a dedicated computer or program for storing, manipulating, and formatting text entered from a keyboard and providing a printout. ■ a person who uses such a program.

word sal·ad ▸*n.* a confused or unintelligible mixture of seemingly random words and phrases, specifically ■ (in psychiatry) as a form of speech indicative of advanced schizophrenia. ■ as a means of bypassing a spam filter for e-mail.

word search ▸*n.* a puzzle consisting of letters arranged in a grid, containing several hidden words written in any direction.

word·smith /ˈwərd,smiTH/ ▸*n.* a skilled user of words.

word square ▸*n.* a puzzle requiring the discovery of a set of words of equal length written one under another to read the same down as across, e.g., *too old ode.*

Words·worth[1] /ˈwərdz,wərTH/, Dorothy (1771–1855), English diarist, sister of William Wordsworth. Her *Grasmere Journal* (1800–03) documents her intense response to nature.

Words·worth[2], William (1770–1850), English poet. Much of his work was inspired by the Lake District. "Lyrical Ballads" (1798), which was composed with Coleridge and included "Tintern Abbey," was a landmark in romanticism. He was appointed poet laureate in 1843. Other notable poems:"I Wandered Lonely as a Cloud" (1815) and "The Prelude" (1850).

word wrap ▸*n.* a feature on a word processor that automatically moves a word that is too long to fit on a line to the beginning of the next line.

word·y /ˈwərdē/ ▸*adj.* (**word·i·er**, **word·i·est**) using or expressed in too many words: *a wordy and repetitive account.* ■ *archaic* consisting of words: *on the publication of Worcester's dictionary, a wordy war arose.* ▷Old English *wordig* (see **WORD**, **-Y**[1]). —**word·i·ly** /-dəlē/ *adv.* —**word·i·ness** *n.*

wore[1] /wôr/ ▸ past of **WEAR**[1].

wore[2] ▸ past and past participle of **WEAR**[2].

work /wərk/ ▸*n.* **1** activity involving mental or physical effort done in order to achieve a purpose or result: *he was tired after a day's work in the fields.* See note at **LABOR**. ■ (**works**) [in *combination*] a place or premises for industrial activity, typically manufacturing: *he found a job in the ironworks.* **2** such activity as a means of earning income; employment: *I'm still looking for work.* ■ the place where one engages in such activity: *I was returning home from work on a packed subway.* ■ the period of time spent during the day engaged in such activity: *he was going to the theater after work.* **3** a task or tasks to be undertaken; something a person or thing has to do: *they made sure the work was progressing smoothly.* ■ the materials for this: *she frequently took work home with her.* ■ (**works**) *Theology* good or moral deeds: *the Clapham sect was concerned with works rather than with faith.* **4** something done or made: *her work hangs in all the main American collections.* ■ the result of the action of a specified person or thing: *the bombing had been* **the work of** *a German-based cell.* ■ a literary or musical composition or other piece of fine art: *a work of fiction.* ■ (**works**) all such pieces by a particular author, composer, or artist, regarded collectively: *the works of Schubert fill several feet of shelf space.* ■ a piece of embroidery, sewing, or knitting, typically made using a specified stitch or method. ■ (usu. **works**) *Military* a defensive structure. ■ (**works**) an architectural or engineering structure such as a bridge or dam. ■ the record of the successive calculations made in solving a mathematical problem: *show your work on a separate sheet of paper.* **5** (**works**) the operative part of a clock or other machine: *she could almost hear the tick of its works.* **6** *Physics* the exertion of force overcoming resistance or producing molecular change. **7** (**the works**) *informal* everything needed, desired, or expected: *the heavens put on a show: sheet lightning, hailstones—the works.*
▸*v.* (*past* **worked** or *archaic* **wrought** /rôt/) [*intrans.*] **1** be engaged in physical or mental activity in order to achieve a purpose or result, esp. in one's job; do work: *an engineer who had been* **working on** *a design for a more efficient wing* | *new contracts forcing employees to work longer hours.* ■ be employed, typically in a specified occupation or field: *Taylor has* **worked in** *education for 17 years.* ■ (**work in**) (of an artist) produce articles or pictures using (a particular material or medium): *he works in clay over a very strong frame.* ■ [*trans.*] produce (an article or design) using a specified material or sewing stitch: *the castle itself is* **worked in** *tent stitch.* ■ [*trans.*] set to or keep at work: *Jane is working you too hard.* ■ [*trans.*] cultivate (land) or extract materials from (a mine or quarry): *contracts and leases to work the mines.* ■ [*trans.*] solve (a puzzle or mathematical problem): *she spent her days working crosswords.* ■ [*trans.*] practice one's occupation or operate in or at (a particular place): *I worked a few clubs and so forth.* ■ make efforts to achieve something; campaign: *we spend a great deal of our time* **working for** *the lacto-vegetarian cause.* **2** (of a machine or system) operate or function, esp. properly or effectively: *his cell phone doesn't work unless he goes to a high point.* ■ (of a machine or a part of it) run; go through regular motions: *it's designed to go into a special "rest" state when it's not working.* ■ (esp. of a person's features) move violently or convulsively: *hair wild, mouth working furiously.* ■ [*trans.*] cause (a device or machine) to operate: *teaching customers how to work a VCR.* ■ (of a plan or method) have the desired result or effect: *the desperate ploy had worked.* ■ [*trans.*] bring about; produce as a result: *with a dash of blusher here and there, you can work miracles.* ■ [*trans.*] *informal* arrange or contrive: *the chairman was prepared to work it for Phillip if he was interested.* ■ (**work on/upon**) exert influence or use one's persuasive power on (someone or their feelings): *she worked upon the sympathy of her associates.* ■ [*trans.*] use one's persuasive power to stir the emotions of (a person or group of people): *the born politician's art of working a crowd.* **3** [*trans.* or *complement*] bring (a material or mixture) to a desired shape or consistency by hammering, kneading, or some other method: *work the mixture into a paste with your hands.* ■ bring into a specified state, esp. an emotional state: *Harold had worked himself into a minor rage.* **4** move or cause to move gradually or with difficulty into another position, typically by means of constant movement or pressure: [*trans.* or *complement*] *comb from tip to root, working out the knots at the end* | [*intrans.* or *complement*] *its stanchion bases were already working loose.* ■ (of joints, such as those in a wooden ship) loosen and flex under repeated stress. ■ [with *adverbial*] *Sailing* make progress to windward, with repeated tacking: *trying to work to windward in light airs.*
▸*phrasal v.* ▫ **work something in** include or incorporate something, typically in something spoken or written. ▫ **work something off 1** discharge a debt by working. **2** reduce or get rid of something by work or activity: *one of those gimmicks for working off aggression.* ▫ **work out 1** (of an equation) be capable of being solved. ■ (**work out at**) be calculated at: *the losses work out at $2.94 a share.* **2** have a good or specified result: *things don't always work out that way.* **3** engage in vigorous physical exercise or training, typically at a gym. ▫ **work someone out** understand someone's character. ▫ **work something out 1** solve a sum or determine an amount by calculation. ■ solve or find the answer to something: *I couldn't work out whether it was a band playing or a record.* **2** plan or devise something in detail: *work out a seating plan.* **3** *poetic/literary* accomplish or attain something with difficulty: *malicious fates are bent on working out an ill intent.* **4** (usu. **be worked out**) work a mine until it is exhausted of minerals. **5** another way of saying **WORK SOMETHING OFF** above. ▫ **work someone over** *informal* treat someone with violence; beat someone severely: *the cops had worked him over a little just for the fun of it.* ▫ **work through** go through a process of understanding and accepting (a painful or difficult situation): *they should be allowed to feel the pain and work through their emotions.* ▫ **work to** follow or operate within the constraints of (a plan or system): *working to tight deadlines.* ▫ **work up to** proceed gradually toward (something more advanced or intense): *the course starts with landing technique, working up to jumps from an enclosed platform.* ▫ **work someone up** (often **get worked up**) gradually bring someone, esp. oneself, to a state of intense excitement, anger, or anxiety: *he got all worked up and started shouting and swearing.* ▫ **work something up 1** bring something gradually to a more complete or satisfactory state: *painters were accustomed to working up compositions from drawings.* **2** develop or produce by activity or effort: *despite the cold, George had already worked up a fair sweat.* ▷Old English *weorc* (noun), *wyrcan* (verb), of Germanic origin; related to Dutch *werk* and German

Pronunciation Key ə *ago*; ər *over*; ˈə or ˌə **up**; ˈər or ˌər *fur*; a *hat*; ā *rate*; ä *car*; CH *chew*; e *let*; ē *see*; e(ə)r *air*; i *fit*; ī *by*; i(ə)r *ear*; NG *sing*; ō *go*; ô *for*; oi *boy*; o͝o *good*; o͞o *goo*; ou *out*; SH *she*; TH *thin*; TH *then*; (h)w *why*; ZH *vision*

Werk, from an Indo-European root shared by Greek *ergon*. —**work·less** *adj.*

▸*PHRASES* □ **at work** engaged in work. ■ in action: *researchers were convinced that one infectious agent was at work.* □ **give someone the works** *informal* treat someone harshly. ■ kill someone. □ **have one's work cut out** be faced with a hard or lengthy task. □ **in the works** being planned, worked on, or produced. □ **out of work** unemployed. □ **set to work** (or **set someone to work**) begin or cause to begin work. □ **the work of ——** a task occupying a specified amount of time: *it was the work of a moment to discover the tiny stab wound.* □ **work one's ass** (**butt**, etc.) **off** *vulgar slang* work extremely hard. □ **work one's fingers to the bone** see BONE. □ **work one's passage** pay for one's journey on a ship with work instead of money. □ **work one's way through college** (or **school**, etc.) obtain the money for educational fees or one's maintenance as a student by working. □ **work one's will on/upon** accomplish one's purpose on: *she set a coiffeur to work his will on her hair.* □ **work wonders** see WONDER.

-work ▸*comb. form* denoting things or parts made of a specified material or with specified tools: *silverwork | fretwork.* ■ denoting a mechanism or structure of a specified kind: *bridgework | clockwork.* ■ denoting ornamentation of a specified kind, or articles having such ornamentation: *knotwork.*

work·a·ble /ˈwərkəbəl/ ▸*adj.* **1** able to be worked, fashioned, or manipulated: *more flour and salt can be added until they make a workable dough.* **2** capable of producing the desired effect or result; practicable; feasible: *a workable peace settlement.* —**work·a·bil·i·ty** /ˌwərkəˈbilitē/ *n.* —**work·a·bly** /-blē/ *adv.*

work·a·day /ˈwərkəˌdā/ ▸*adj.* of or relating to work or one's job: *the workaday world of timecards and performance reviews.* ■ not special, unusual, or interesting in any way; ordinary: *your humble workaday PC.*

work·a·hol·ic /ˌwərkəˈhôlik; -ˈhälik/ ▸*n.* *informal* a person who compulsively works hard and long hours. —**work·a·hol·ism** /ˈwərkəˌhôlizəm; -ˌhäl-/ *n.*

work·a·like /ˈwərkəˌlīk/ ▸*n.* *Computing* a computer that is able to use the software of another specified machine without special modification. ■ a piece of software identical in function to another software package.

work·a·round /ˈwərkəˌround/ ▸*n.* *Computing* a method for overcoming a problem or limitation in a program or system.

work·bas·ket /ˈwərkˌbaskət/ (also **work·bag**) ▸*n.* a basket (or bag) used for storing sewing materials.

work·bench /ˈwərkˌbench/ ▸*n.* a bench at which carpentry or other mechanical or practical work is done.

work·boat /ˈwərkˌbōt/ ▸*n.* a boat used for work such as commercial fishing or transporting freight, rather than leisure or naval service.

work·book /ˈwərkˌbo͝ok/ ▸*n.* a student's book containing instruction and exercises relating to a particular subject. ■ *Computing* a single file containing several different types of related information as separate worksheets.

work·box /ˈwərkˌbäks/ ▸*n.* a portable box used for storing or holding tools and materials for activities such as sewing.

work camp ▸*n.* a camp at which community work is done, esp. by young volunteers. ■ another term for LABOR CAMP.

work·day /ˈwərkˌdā/ ▸*n.* a day on which one works: *Saturdays were workdays for him.* ■ the part of the day devoted or allotted to work: *18-hour workdays.*

work·er /ˈwərkər/ ▸*n.* **1** a person or animal that works, in particular: ■ [with *adj.*] a person who does a specified type of work: *a farm worker.* ■ an employee, esp. one who does manual or nonexecutive work. ■ (**workers**) used in Marxist or leftist contexts to refer to the working class. ■ [with *adj.*] a person who works in a specified way: *she's a good worker.* ■ *informal* a person who works hard: *I got a reputation for being a worker.* ■ (in social insects such as bees, wasps, ants, and termites) a neuter or undeveloped female that is a member of what is usually the most numerous caste and does the basic work of the colony. **2** a creator or producer of a specified thing: *a worker of precious metals.*

work·er priest ▸*n.* a Roman Catholic priest, esp. in postwar France, or an Anglican priest who engages part-time in ordinary secular work.

work eth·ic ▸*n.* [in *sing.*] the principle that hard work is intrinsically virtuous or worthy of reward. See also PROTESTANT ETHIC.

work·fare /ˈwərkˌfe(ə)r/ ▸*n.* a welfare system that requires those receiving benefits to perform some work or to participate in job training. ▷1960s: from WORK + a shortened form of WELFARE.

work·flow /ˈwərkˌflō/ ▸*n.* the sequence of industrial, administrative, or other processes through which a piece of work passes from initiation to completion.

work force (also **work·force**) ▸*n.* [treated as *sing.* or *pl.*] the people engaged in or available for work, either in a country or area or in a particular company or industry.

work func·tion ▸*n.* *Physics* the minimum quantity of energy that is required to remove an electron to infinity from the surface of a given solid, usually a metal. (Symbol: ϕ.)

work·group /ˈwərkˌgro͞op/ ▸*n.* a group within a workforce that normally works together. ■ *Computing* a group that shares data via a local network.

work-hard·en ▸*v.* [*trans.*] [often as *n.*] (**work-hardening**) *Metallurgy* toughen (a metal) by cold-working.

work·horse /ˈwərkˌhôrs/ ▸*n.* a horse used for work on a farm. ■ a person or machine that dependably performs hard work over a long period of time: *the aircraft was the standard workhorse of Soviet medium-haul routes.*

work·house /ˈwərkˌhous/ ▸*n.* **1** *historical* (in the UK) a public institution in which the destitute of a parish received board and lodging in return for work. **2** a prison in which petty offenders are expected to work.

work·ing /ˈwərking/ ▸*adj.* [*attrib.*] **1** having paid employment: *the size of the working population.* ■ engaged in manual labor: *the vote is no longer sufficient protection for the working man.* ■ relating to, suitable for, or for the purpose of work: *improvements in living and working conditions.* ■ (of a meal) during which business is discussed: *Meredith was at a working lunch in Rose's office.* ■ (of an animal) used in farming, hunting, or for guard duties; not kept as a pet or for show. ■ (of something possessed) sufficient to work with: *they **have a working knowledge of** contract law.* ■ (of a theory, definition, or title) used as the basis for work or argument and likely to be developed, adapted, or improved later: *the working hypothesis is tested and refined through discussion.* **2** functioning or able to function: *the mill still has a working waterwheel.* ■ (of parts of a machine) moving and causing a machine to operate: *the working parts of a digital watch.* ■ (of the face or features) moving convulsively: *she mumbled, blood spilling from her working lips.*

▸*n.* **1** the action of doing work. ■ the action of extracting minerals from a mine. ■ (usu. **workings**) a mine or a part of a mine from which minerals are being extracted. **2** (**workings**) the way in which a machine, organization, or system operates: *we will be less secretive about the workings of government.*

work·ing cap·i·tal ▸*n.* *Finance* the capital of a business that is used in its day-to-day trading operations, calculated as the current assets minus the current liabilities.

work·ing class ▸*n.* [treated as *sing.* or *pl.*] the social group consisting of people who are employed for wages, esp. in manual or industrial work: *the housing needs of the working classes.*

▸*adj.* (**working-class**) of, relating to, or characteristic of people belonging to such a group: *a working-class community.*

work·ing day ▸*n.* another term for WORKDAY.

work·ing draw·ing ▸*n.* a scale drawing that serves as a guide for the construction or manufacture of something such as a building or machine.

work·ing girl ▸*n.* *informal, chiefly dated* a woman who goes out to work rather than remaining at home. ■ a prostitute.

work·ing group ▸*n.* a committee or group appointed to study and report on a particular question and make recommendations based on its findings.

work·ing load ▸*n.* the maximum load that a machine or other structure is designed to bear during normal operation.

work·ing mem·o·ry ▸*n.* *Psychology* the part of short-term memory that is concerned with immediate conscious perceptual and linguistic processing. ■ *Computing* an area of high-speed memory used to store programs or data currently in use.

work·ing stor·age ▸*n.* *Computing* a part of a computer's memory that is used by a program for the storage of intermediate results or other temporary items.

work·load /ˈwərkˌlōd/ ▸*n.* the amount of work to be done by someone or something: *he had been given three deputies to ease his workload.*

work·man /ˈwərkmən/ ▸*n.* (*pl.* **-men**) a man employed to do manual labor. ■ [with *adj.*] a person with specified skill in a job or craft: *you check it through, like all good workmen do.*

work·man·like /ˈwərkmənˌlīk/ ▸*adj.* showing efficient competence: *a steady, workmanlike approach.*

work·man·ship /ˈwərkmənˌship/ ▸*n.* the degree of skill with which a product is made or a job done: *cracks on the bridge girders were caused by poor workmanship.*

work·mate /ˈwərkˌmāt/ ▸*n.* *chiefly Brit.* a person with whom one works.

work of art ▸*n.* a creative product with strong imaginative or aesthetic appeal.

work·out /ˈwərkˌout/ ▸*n.* a session of vigorous physical exercise or training.

work per·mit ▸*n.* an official document giving a foreigner permission to take a job in a country.

work·piece /ˈwərkˌpēs/ ▸*n.* an object being worked on with a tool or machine.

work·place /ˈwərkˌplās/ ▸*n.* a place where people work, such as an office or factory.

work re·lease ▸*n.* leave of absence from prison by day enabling a prisoner to continue in normal employment.

work·room /ˈwərkˌro͞om; -ˌro͝om/ ▸*n.* a room for working in, esp. one equipped for a particular kind of work.

works coun·cil ▸*n.* *chiefly Brit.* a group of employees representing a workforce in discussions with their employers.

work·sheet /ˈwərkˌshēt/ ▸*n.* **1** a paper listing questions or tasks for students. **2** a paper for recording work done or in progress. ■ *Computing* a data file created and used by a spreadsheet program, which takes the form of a matrix of cells when displayed.

work·shop /ˈwərkˌshäp/ ▸*n.* **1** a room or building in which goods are manufactured or repaired. **2** a meeting at which a group of people engage in intensive discussion and activity on a particular subject or project.

▸*v.* [*trans.*] present a performance of (a dramatic work), using intensive group discussion and improvisation in order to explore aspects of the production before formal staging: *the play was workshopped briefly at the Shaw Festival.*

work-shy ▸*adj.* (of a person) lazy and disinclined to work.

work·site /ˈwərkˌsīt/ ▸*n.* an area where an industry is located or where work takes place.

work·space /ˈwərkˌspās/ ▸*n.* space in which to work: *the kitchen is all white, with maximum workspace.* ■ an area rented or sold for commercial purposes. ■ *Computing* a memory storage facility for temporary use.

work·sta·tion /ˈwərkˌstāshən/ ▸*n.* **1** a general-purpose computer with a higher performance level than a personal computer. **2** an area where work of a particular nature is carried out, such as a specific location on a manufacturing assembly line. **3** a desk with a computer or a computer terminal and keyboard.

work-stud·y ▸*adj.* [*attrib.*] of or relating to a college program that enables students to work part-time while attending school.

work sur·face ▸*n.* another term for COUNTERTOP.

work·wear /ˈwərkˌwe(ə)r/ ▸*n.* heavy-duty clothes for physical or manual work.

work·week /ˈwərkˌwēk/ ▸*n.* the total number of hours or days worked in a week: *a six-day workweek.*

world /wərld/ ▸*n.* **1** (usu. **the world**) the earth, together with all of its countries, peoples, and natural features: *he was doing his bit to save the world.* ■ (**the world**) all of the people, societies, and institutions on the earth: [as *adj.*] *world affairs.* ■ [as *adj.*] denoting one of the most important or influential people or things of its class: *they had been brought up to regard France as a world power.* ■ another planet like the earth: *the possibility of life on other worlds.* ■ the material universe or all that exists; everything. **2** a part or aspect of human life or of the natural features of the earth, in particular: ■ a region or group of countries: *the English-speaking world.* ■ a period of history: *the ancient world.* ■ a group of living things: *the animal world.* ■ the people, places, and activities to do with a particular thing: *they were a legend in the world of British theater.* ■ human and social interaction: *he has almost completely withdrawn from the world | how inexperienced she is in the ways of the world.* ■ average, respectable, or fashionable people or their customs or

W

opinions. ■ (**one's world**) a person's life and activities: *he felt his whole world had collapsed.* ■ everything that exists outside oneself. ■ [in *sing.*] a stage of human life, either mortal or after death: *in this world and the next.* ■ secular interests and affairs: *parents are not viewed as the primary educators of their own children, either in the world or in the church.* ▷Old English *w(e)oruld*, from a Germanic compound meaning 'age of man'; related to Dutch *wereld* and German *Welt*.

▸*PHRASES* □ **be not long for this world** have only a short time to live. □ **the best of both** (or **all possible**) **worlds** the benefits of widely differing situations, enjoyed at the same time. □ **bring someone into the world** give birth to or assist at the birth of someone. □ **come into the world** be born. □ **come up** (or **go down**) **in the world** rise (or drop) in status, esp. by becoming richer (or poorer). □ **in the world** used for emphasis in questions, esp. to express astonishment or disbelief: *why in the world did you not reveal yourself sooner?* □ **look for all the world like** look precisely like (used for emphasis): *fossil imprints that look for all the world like motorcycle tracks.* □ **man** (or **woman**) **of the world** a person who is experienced in the ways of sophisticated society. □ **not do something for the world** not do something whatever the inducement: *I wouldn't miss it for the world.* □ **out of this world** *informal* extremely enjoyable or impressive: *an herb and lemon dressing that's out of this world.* □ **see the world** travel widely and gain wide experience. □ **think the world of** have a very high regard for (someone): *I thought the world of my father.* □ **the world, the flesh, and the devil** all forms of temptation to sin. □ **a** (or **the**) **world of** a very great deal of: *there's a world of difference between being alone and being lonely.* □ (**all**) **the world over** everywhere on the earth. □ **worlds apart** very different or distant.

World Bank an international banking organization established to control the distribution of economic aid among member nations, and to make loans to them in times of financial crisis. See also **INTERNATIONAL BANK FOR RECONSTRUCTION AND DEVELOPMENT.**

world beat ▸*n.* Western music incorporating elements of traditional music from any part of the world, esp. from developing nations: *the booming sounds of world beat in the background.*

world-beat·er ▸*n.* a person or thing that is better than all others in its field. —**world-beat·ing** *adj.*

world ci·ty ▸*n.* a cosmopolitan city, with resident and visiting foreigners.

world-class ▸*adj.* (of a person, thing, or activity) of or among the best in the world.

World Coun·cil of Church·es (abbr.: **WCC**) an association established in 1948 to promote unity among the many different Christian Churches. Its member Churches number over 300, and include virtually all Christian traditions except Roman Catholicism and Unitarianism. Its headquarters are in Geneva.

World Cup ▸*n.* a sports competition between teams from several countries, in particular an international soccer tournament held every four years. ■ a trophy awarded for such a competition.

world fair ▸*n.* see **WORLD'S FAIR.**

world-fa·mous ▸*adj.* known throughout the world: *the world-famous tenor José Carreras.*

World Health Or·gan·i·za·tion (abbr.: **WHO**) an agency of the United Nations, established in 1948 to promote health and control communicable diseases.

World Her·it·age Site ▸*n.* a natural or man-made site, area, or structure recognized as being of outstanding international importance and therefore as deserving special protection. Sites are nominated to and designated by the World Heritage Convtention (an organization of UNESCO).

World In·tel·lec·tu·al Pro·per·ty Or·gan·i·za·tion (abbr.: **WIPO**) an organization, established in 1967 and an agency of the United Nations from 1974, for cooperation between governments in matters concerning patents, trademarks, and copyright, and the transfer of technology between countries. Its headquarters are in Geneva.

world lan·guage ▸*n.* a language known or spoken in many countries: *English is now the world language.* ■ an artificial language for international use: *there have been attempts to introduce a standard world language.*

world line ▸*n. Physics* a curve in space-time joining the positions of a particle throughout its existence.

world·ling /ˈwərldliNG/ ▸*n.* a cosmopolitan and sophisticated person.

world·ly /ˈwərldlē/ ▸*adj.* (**-li·er, -li·est**) of or concerned with material values or ordinary life rather than a spiritual existence: *his ambitions for worldly success.* ■ (of a person) experienced and sophisticated. ▷Old English *woruldlic* (see **WORLD, -LY**[1]). —**world·li·ness** *n.*

▸*PHRASE* □ **worldly goods** (or **possessions** or **wealth**) everything that someone owns.

world·ly-mind·ed ▸*adj.* intent on worldly things.

world·ly-wise ▸*adj.* prepared by experience for life's difficulties; not easily shocked or deceived: *Lisa was sufficiently worldly-wise to understand the situation.* —**world·ly wis·dom** *n.*

World Me·te·or·o·log·i·cal Or·gan·i·za·tion (abbr.: **WMO**) an agency of the United Nations, established in 1950 with the aim of facilitating worldwide cooperation in meteorological observations, research, and services. Its headquarters are in Geneva.

world mu·sic ▸*n.* traditional music from the developing world. ■ Western popular music incorporating elements of such music.

world or·der ▸*n.* a system controlling events in the world, esp. a set of arrangements established internationally for preserving global political stability.

world pow·er ▸*n.* a country that has significant influence in international affairs.

World Se·ries the professional championship for North American major league baseball, played at the end of the season between the champions of the American League and the National League. It was first played in 1903.

World Serv·ice a service of the British Broadcasting Corporation that transmits radio programs in English and over thirty other languages around the world twenty-four hours a day. A worldwide television station was established in 1991 on a similar basis.

world's fair (also **world fair**) ▸*n.* an international exhibition of the industrial, scientific, technological, and artistic achievements of the participating nations.

world-shak·ing ▸*adj.* (in hyperbolic use) of supreme importance or having a momentous effect: *a world-shaking announcement.*

world soul ▸*n. Philosophy* the immanent cause or principle of life, order, consciousness, and self-awareness in the physical world. ▷mid 19th cent.: translating German *Weltgeist.*

World Trade Cen·ter a complex of buildings in New York featuring twin skyscrapers 110 stories high, designed by Minoru Yamasaki and completed in 1972. The twin towers were destroyed in a terrorist attack on September 11, 2001, with the loss of about 2,700 lives.

World Trade Or·gan·i·za·tion (abbr.: **WTO**) an international body founded in 1995 to promote international trade and economic development by reducing tariffs and other restrictions.

world-view /ˈwərld,vyo͞o/ (also **world view**) ▸*n.* a particular philosophy of life or conception of the world: *a Christian worldview revolves around the battle of good and evil.*

world war ▸*n.* a war involving many large nations in all different parts of the world. The name is commonly given to the wars of 1914–18 and 1939–45, although only the second of these was truly global. See **WORLD WAR I, WORLD WAR II.**

World War I a war (1914–18) in which the Central Powers (Germany and Austria–Hungary, joined later by Turkey and Bulgaria) were defeated by an alliance of Britain and its dominions, France, Russia, and others, joined later by Italy and the U.S.

Political tensions over the rise of the German Empire were the war's principal cause, although it was set off by the assassination of Archduke Franz Ferdinand of Austria by a Bosnian Serb nationalist in Sarajevo, an event used as a pretext by Austria for declaring war on Serbia. Most of the fighting took place on land in Europe and was generally characterized by long periods of bloody stalemate; the balance eventually shifted in the Allies' favor in 1917 when the U.S. joined the war. Total casualties of the war are estimated at 10 million killed. One of the consequences of the war was the collapse of the German, Austro-Hungarian, Russian, and Ottoman empires.

World War II a war (1939–45) in which the Axis Powers (Germany, Italy, and Japan) were defeated by an alliance eventually including the United Kingdom and its dominions, the Soviet Union, and the U.S.

Hitler's invasion of Poland in September 1939 led Great Britain and France to declare war on Germany. Germany defeated and occupied France the following year and soon overran much of Europe. Italy joined the war in 1940, and the U.S. and Japan entered after the Japanese attack on the U.S. fleet at Pearl Harbor. Italy surrendered in 1943, and the Allies launched a full-scale invasion in Normandy in June 1944. The war in Europe ended when Germany surrendered in May 1945; Japan surrendered after the U.S. dropped atom bombs on Hiroshima and Nagasaki in August 1945. An estimated 55 million people were killed during the war, including a much higher proportion of civilians than in World War I.

world-wea·ry ▸*adj.* feeling or indicating feelings of weariness, boredom, or cynicism as a result of long experience of life: *their world-weary, cynical talk.* —**world-wea·ri·ness** *n.*

world·wide /ˈwərldˈwīd/ ▸*adj.* extending or reaching throughout the world: *worldwide sales of television rights.*

▸*adv.* throughout the world: *she travels worldwide as a consultant.*

World Wide Web *Computing* a widely used information system on the Internet that provides facilities for documents to be connected to other documents by hypertext links, enabling the user to search for information by moving from one document to another.

WORM /wərm/ ▸*abbr.* write-once read-many, denoting a type of computer memory device.

worm /wərm/ ▸*n.* **1** any of a number of creeping or burrowing invertebrate animals with long, slender, soft bodies and no limbs. • Phyla Annelida (segmented worms), Nematoda (roundworms), and Platyhelminthes (flatworms), and up to twelve minor phyla. ■ short for **EARTHWORM.** ■ (**worms**) intestinal or other internal parasites. ■ used in names of long, slender insect larvae, esp. those in fruit or wood, e.g., **army worm, woodworm.** ■ used in names of other animals that resemble worms in some way, e.g., **slow-worm, shipworm.** ■ a maggot supposed to eat buried corpses: *food for worms.* ■ *Computing* a self-replicating program able to propagate itself across a network, typically having a detrimental effect. **2** *informal* a weak or despicable person (used as a general term of contempt). **3** a helical device or component, in particular: ■ the threaded cylinder in a worm gear. ■ the coiled pipe of a still in which the vapor is cooled and condensed.

▸*v.* **1** [*intrans.*] move with difficulty by crawling or wriggling: *I **wormed my way** along the roadside ditch.* ■ (**worm one's way into**) insinuate one's way into: *the educated dealers may later worm their way into stockbroking.* ■ [*trans.*] move (something) into a confined space by wriggling it: *I wormed my right hand between my body and the earth.* ■ (**worm something out of**) obtain information from (someone) by cunning persistence: *I did manage to worm a few details out of him.* **2** [*trans.*] treat (an animal) with a preparation designed to expel parasitic worms. **3** [*trans.*] *archaic Nautical* make (a rope) smooth by winding small cordage between the strands. ▷Old English *wyrm* (noun), of Germanic origin; related to Latin *vermis* 'worm' and Greek *rhomox* 'woodworm.' —**worm·like** /-,līk/ *adj.*

▸*PHRASE* □ (**even**) **a worm will turn** *proverb* (even) a meek person will resist or retaliate if pushed too far.

worm cast (also **worm cast·ing**) ▸*n.* a convoluted mass of soil, mud, or sand thrown up by an earthworm or lugworm on the surface after passing through the worm's body.

worm-eat·en ▸*adj.* (of organic tissue) eaten into by worms: *a worm-eaten corpse.* ■ (of wood or a wooden object) full of holes made by woodworm.

worm·er /ˈwərmər/ ▸*n.* a substance administered to animals or birds to expel parasitic worms.

worm-fish·ing ▸*n.* the activity or practice of angling with worms for bait.

worm gear ▸*n.* a mechanical arrangement consisting of a toothed wheel worked by a

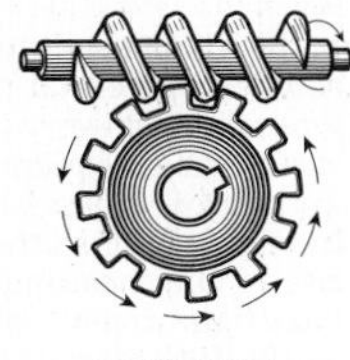

worm gear

Pronunciation Key ə *ago;* ər *over;* ˈə *or* ˌə *up;* ˈər *or* ˌər *fur;* a *hat;* ā *rate;* ä *car;* CH *chew;* e *let;* ē *see;* e(ə)r *air;* i *fit;* ī *by;* i(ə)r *ear;* NG *sing;* ō *go;* ô *for;* oi *boy;* o͝o *good;* o͞o *goo;* ou *out;* SH *she;* TH *thin;* T͟H *then;* (h)w *why;* ZH *vision*

short revolving cylinder (worm) bearing a screw thread.

worm·hole /ˈwərm,hōl/ ▸*n.* a hole made by a burrowing insect larva or worm in wood, fruit, books, or other materials. ■ *Physics* a hypothetical connection between widely separated regions of space-time.

worm liz·ard ▸*n.* **1** a subterranean burrowing reptile that resembles an earthworm, being blind, apparently segmented, and typically without limbs. • Suborder Amphisbaenia, order Squamata: four families and numerous species. **2** a legless lizard.

Worms /wərmz; vôrms/ an industrial town in western Germany, on the Rhine River, northwest of Mannheim; pop. 77,000. The Diet of Worms 1521 condemned Martin Luther's teaching.

Worms, Di·et of see **DIET OF WORMS.**

worm·seed /ˈwərm,sēd/ ▸*n.* a plant whose seeds have anthelmintic properties: • (also **Levant wormseed**) santonica. • (also **American wormseed**) an American plant of the goosefoot family (*Chenopodium ambrosioides*, family Chenopodiaceae).

worm's-eye view ▸*n.* a view as seen from below or from a humble position: *being assigned to the secretariat provided a worm's-eye view of international diplomacy.*

worm snake ▸*n.* **1** a small harmless North American snake that resembles an earthworm. • *Carphophis amoena*, family Colubridae. **2** another term for **BLIND SNAKE.**

worm wheel ▸*n.* the wheel of a worm gear.

worm·wood /ˈwərm,wo͝od/ ▸*n.* **1** a woody shrub with a bitter aromatic taste, used, esp. formerly, as an ingredient of vermouth and absinthe and in medicine. • Genus *Artemisia*, family Compositae: several species, in particular the Eurasian *A. absinthium*. **2** *figurative* a state or source of bitterness or grief. ▷Old English *wermōd*. The change in spelling in late Middle English was due to association with **WORM** and **WOOD**. Compare with **VERMOUTH.**

worm·y /ˈwərmē/ ▸*adj.* (**worm·i·er, worm·i·est**) **1** (of organic tissue) infested with or eaten into by worms: *the prisoners received wormy vegetables.* ■ (of wood or a wooden object) full of holes made by woodworm. **2** *informal* (of a person) weak, abject, or revolting. —**worm·i·ness** *n.*

worn /wôrn/ ▸ past participle of **WEAR**[1].

▸*adj.* damaged and shabby as a result of much use: *a worn, frayed denim jacket.* ■ very tired: *his face looked worn and old.*

worn out ▸*adj.* **1** (of a person or animal) extremely tired; exhausted: *you look worn out.* **2** damaged or shabby to the point of being no longer usable: *worn-out shoes.* ■ (of an idea, method, or system) used so often or existing for so long as to be considered valueless: *he portrayed the Democrats as the party of worn-out ideas.*

wor·ri·ment /ˈwərēmənt/ ▸*n.* archaic or humorous term for **WORRY.**

wor·ri·some /ˈwərē,səm/ ▸*adj.* causing anxiety or concern: *a worrisome problem.* —**wor·ri·some·ly** *adv.*

wor·ry /ˈwərē/ ▸*v.* (**-ries, -ried**) **1** [*intrans.*] give way to anxiety or unease; allow one's mind to dwell on difficulty or troubles: *he* ***worried about*** *his soldier sons in the war* | [with *clause*] *I began to worry whether I had done the right thing.* ■ [*trans.*] cause to feel anxiety or concern: *there was no need to worry her* | *I've been* ***worrying myself sick*** *over my mother* | [*trans.*] *he is worried that we are not sustaining high employment* | [as *adj.*] (**worrying**) *the level of inflation has improved but remains worrying.* ■ [as *adj.*] (**worried**) expressing anxiety: *there was a worried frown on his face.* ■ [*trans.*] cause annoyance to: *the noise never really stops, but it doesn't worry me.* **2** [*trans.*] (of a dog or other carnivorous animal) tear at, gnaw on, or drag around with the teeth: *I found my dog contentedly worrying a bone.* ■ (of a dog) chase and attack (livestock, esp. sheep). ■ [*intrans.*] (**worry at**) pull at or fiddle with repeatedly: *he began to worry at the knot in the cord.*

▸*n.* (*pl.* **-ries**) a state of anxiety and uncertainty over actual or potential problems: *her son had been a constant source of worry to her.* ■ a source of anxiety: *the idea is to secure peace of mind for people whose greatest worry is fear of attack.* ▷Old English *wyrgan* 'strangle.' In Middle English the original sense of the verb gave rise to the meaning 'seize by the throat and tear,' later figuratively 'harass,' whence 'cause anxiety to' (early 19th century, the date also of the noun). —**wor·ried·ly** *adv.* —**wor·ri·er** *n.* —**wor·ry·ing·ly** *adv.* [as *submodifier*] *trade deficits are worryingly large.*

▸*PHRASE* □ **not to worry** *informal* used to reassure someone by telling them that a situation is not serious: *not to worry—no harm done.*

wor·ry beads ▸*plural n.* a string of beads that one fingers and moves in order to calm oneself.

wor·ry·wart /ˈwərē,wôrt/ ▸*n. informal* a person who tends to dwell unduly on difficulty or troubles.

worse /wərs/ ▸*adj.* **1** comparative of **BAD, ILL. 2** of poorer quality or a lower standard; less good or desirable: *the accommodations were awful, and the food was worse.* ■ more serious or severe: *the movement made the pain worse.* ■ more reprehensible or evil: *it is worse to intend harm than to be indifferent.* ■ [*predic.* or as *complement*] in a less satisfactory or pleasant condition; more ill or unhappy: *he felt worse, and groped his way back to bed.*

▸*adv.* **1** comparative of **BADLY, ILL. 2** less well or skillfully: *the more famous I became the worse I painted.* ■ more seriously or severely: *the others had been drunk too, worse than herself.* ■ [*sentence adverb*] used to introduce a statement of circumstances felt by the speaker to be more serious or undesirable than others already mentioned: *The system will find it hard to sort out property disputes. Even worse, the law will discourage foreign investment.*

▸*n.* a more serious or unpleasant event or circumstance: *the small department was already stretched to the limit, but worse was to follow.* ■ (**the worse**) a less good, favorable, or pleasant condition: *the weather changed for the worse.* ▷Old English *wyrsa, wiersa* (adjective), *wiers* (adverb), of Germanic origin; related to **WAR.**

▸*PHRASES* □ **none the worse for** not adversely affected by: *we were none the worse for our terrible experience.* □ **or worse** used to suggest a possibility that is still more serious or unpleasant than one already considered, but that the speaker does not wish or need to specify: *the child might be born blind or worse.* □ **so much the worse for ——** used to suggest that a problem, failure, or other unfortunate event or situation is the fault of the person specified and that the speaker does not feel any great concern about it: *if his subjects were unwilling to accept the progress her offered, so much the worse for them.* □ **the worse for wear** *informal* **1** damaged by use or weather over time; battered and shabby. **2** (of a person) feeling rather unwell, esp. as a result of drinking too much alcohol. □ **worse luck** see **LUCK.** □ **worse off** in a less advantageous position; less fortunate or prosperous.

wors·en /ˈwərsən/ ▸*v.* make or become worse: [*intrans.*] *her condition worsened on the flight* | [*trans.*] *arguing actually worsens the problem* | [as *adj.*] (**worsening**) *Romania's rapidly worsening economic situation.*

wor·ship /ˈwərsʜəp/ ▸*n.* the feeling or expression of reverence and adoration for a deity: *the worship of God* | *ancestor worship.* ■ the acts or rites that make up a formal expression of reverence for a deity; a religious ceremony or ceremonies: *the church was opened for public worship.* ■ adoration or devotion comparable to religious homage, shown toward a person or principle: *Krushchev threw the worship of Stalin overboard.* ■ *archaic* honor given to someone in recognition of their merit. ■ [as *title*] (**His/Your Worship**) *chiefly Brit.* used in addressing or referring to an important or high-ranking person, esp. a magistrate or mayor: *we were soon joined by His Worship the Mayor.*

▸*v.* (**-shiped, -ship·ing**; also **-shipped, -ship·ping**) [*trans.*] show reverence and adoration for (a deity); honor with religious rites: *the Maya built jungle pyramids to worship their gods.* ■ treat (someone or something) with the reverence and adoration appropriate to a deity: *she adores her sons and they worship her.* See note at **REVERE.** ■ [*intrans.*] take part in a religious ceremony: *he went to the cathedral because he chose to worship in a spiritually inspiring building.* ▷Old English *weorthscipe* 'worthiness, acknowledgment of worth' (see **WORTH, -SHIP**). —**wor·ship·er** (also **wor·ship·per**) *n.*

wor·ship·ful /ˈwərsʜəpfəl/ ▸*adj.* feeling or showing reverence and adoration: *her voice was full of worshipful admiration.* ■ *archaic* entitled to honor or respect. ■ (**Worshipful**) *Brit.* used in titles given to justices of the peace and to certain old corporations or their officers: *the Worshipful Company of Goldsmiths.* —**wor·ship·ful·ly** *adv.* —**wor·ship·ful·ness** *n.*

worst /wərst/ ▸*adj.* superlative of **BAD, ILL.** ■ of the poorest quality or the lowest standard: *the speech was the worst he had ever made.* ■ least pleasant, desirable, or tolerable: *they were to stay in the worst conditions imaginable.* ■ most severe, serious, or dangerous: *at least 32 people died in Australia's worst bus accident.* ■ least suitable or advantageous: *the worst time to take out a bond is when rates are low but rise suddenly.*

▸*adv.* **1** superlative of **BADLY, ILL. 2** most severely or seriously: *manufacturing and mining are the industries worst affected by falling employment.* ■ least well, skillfully, or pleasingly: *he was voted the worst dressed celebrity.* ■ [*sentence adverb*] used to introduce the fact or circumstance that the speaker considers most serious or unpleasant: *her mother had rejected her, and worst of all, her adoptive father turned out to be a cheat and a deceiver.*

▸*n.* the most serious or unpleasant thing that could happen: *when I saw the ambulance outside her front door, I began to* ***fear the worst.*** ■ the most serious, dangerous, or unpleasant part or stage of something: *there are signs that the recession is past its worst.*

▸*v.* [*trans.*] (usu. **be worsted**) get the better of; defeat: *this was not the time for a deep discussion—she was tired and she would be worsted.* ▷Old English *wierresta, wyrresta* (adjective), *wierst, wyrst* (adverb), of Germanic origin; related to **WORSE.**

▸*PHRASES* □ **at its** (or **someone's**) **worst** in the most unpleasant, unimpressive, or unattractive state of which someone or something is capable: *nothing's working at the moment, so I suppose you've seen us at our worst.* ■ at the most severe or serious point or level: *harsh lines appeared in his face when his rheumatism was at its worst.* □ **at worst** (or **the worst**) in the most serious case: *at worst the injury could mean months in the hospital.* ■ under the most unfavorable interpretation: *the cabinet's reaction to the crisis was at best ineffective and at worst irresponsible.* □ **be one's own worst enemy** see **ENEMY.** □ **do one's worst** (in the view of one's opponent) do as much damage as one can (often used to express defiance in the face of threats): *let them do their worst—he would never surrender.* □ **get** (or **have**) **the worst of it** be in the least advantageous or successful position; suffer the most. □ **if worst comes to worst** if the most serious or difficult circumstances arise. □ **in the worst way** *informal* very much: *he wants to win in the worst way.*

worst-case ▸*adj.* (of a projected development) characterized by the worst of the possible foreseeable circumstances: *in* ***the worst-case scenario****, coastal resorts and communities face disaster.*

wor·sted /ˈwo͝ostid; ˈwərstid/ ▸*n.* a fine smooth yarn spun from combed long-staple wool. ■ fabric made from such yarn, having a close-textured surface with no nap: [as *adj.*] *a worsted suit.* ▷Middle English: from *Worstead*, the name of a parish in Norfolk, England.

wort /wərt; wôrt/ ▸*n.* **1** [in *combination*] used in names of plants and herbs, esp. those used, esp. formerly, as food or medicinally, e.g., **butterwort, woundwort.** ■ *archaic* such a plant or herb. **2** the sweet infusion of ground malt or other grain before fermentation, used to produce beer and distilled malt liquors. ▷Old English *wyrt*, of Germanic origin; related to **ROOT**[1].

Worth /wərʜ/, Charles Frederick (1825–95), English couturier, resident in France from 1845. Regarded as the founder of Parisian *haute couture*, he is noted for designing gowns with crinolines and for introducing the bustle.

worth /wərʜ/ ▸*adj.* [*predic.*] equivalent in value to the sum or item specified: *jewelry worth $450 was taken.* ■ sufficiently good, important, or interesting to justify a specified action; deserving to be treated or regarded in the way specified: *the museums in the district are well worth a visit.* ■ used to suggest that the specified course of action may be advisable: *a meat and potato dish that's worth checking out.* ■ having income or property amounting to a specified sum: *she is worth $10 million.*

▸*n.* the value equivalent to that of someone or something under consideration; the level at which someone or something deserves to be valued or rated: *they had to listen to every piece of gossip and judge its worth.* ■ an amount of a commodity equivalent to a specified sum of money: *he admitted stealing 10,000 dollars' worth of computer systems.* ■ the amount that could be achieved or produced in a specified time: *the companies have debts greater than two years' worth of their sales.* ■ high value or merit: *he is noble and gains his position by showing his inner worth.* ▷Old English *w(e)orth* (adjective and noun), of Germanic origin; related to Dutch *waard* and German *wert*.

▸*PHRASES* □ **for all someone is worth** *informal* **1** as energetically or enthusiastically as someone can: *he thumps the drums for all he's worth.* **2** so as to obtain everything one can from someone: *the youths milked him for all he was worth and then disappeared.* □ **for what it is worth** used to present a comment, suggestion, or opinion without making a claim as to its importance or validity: *for what it's worth, she's very highly thought of abroad.* □ **worth it** *informal* sufficiently good, enjoyable, or successful to repay any effort,

W

trouble, or expense: *it requires a bit of patience to learn, but it's well worth it.* □ **worth one's salt** see SALT. □ **worth one's while** (or **worth while**) see WHILE.

worth·less /ˈwərTHlis/ ▶*adj.* having no real value or use: *that promise is worthless.* ■ (of a person) having no good qualities; deserving contempt: *Joan had been deserted by a worthless husband.* —**worth·less·ly** *adv.* —**worth·less·ness** *n.*

worth·while /ˈwərTHˈ(h)wīl/ ▶*adj.* worth the time, money, or effort spent; of value or importance: *extra lighting would make a worthwhile contribution to road safety.* —**worth·while·ness** *n.*

USAGE The adjective **worthwhile** is used both attributively (that is, before the noun) and predicatively (that is, when it stands alone and comes after the verb). In both positions, it is almost always written as one word: *a* **worthwhile** *book, the book was* **worthwhile**. But it is occasionally hyphenated (*a* **worth-while** *book*) or written as two words (*the book was* **worth while**).

wor·thy /ˈwərT͟Hē/ ▶*adj.* (**-thi·er**, **-thi·est**) deserving effort, attention, or respect: *generous donations to worthy causes.* ■ having or showing the qualities or abilities that merit recognition in a specified way: *issues* **worthy of** *further consideration.* ■ good enough; suitable: *no composer was considered* **worthy of** *the name until he had written an opera.*

▶*n.* (*pl.* **-thies**) *often derogatory* or *humorous* a person notable or important in a particular sphere: *schools governed by local worthies.* ▷Middle English: from WORTH + -Y¹. —**wor·thi·ly** /-T͟Həlē/ *adv.* —**wor·thi·ness** *n.*

-worthy ▶*comb. form* deserving of a specified thing: *newsworthy.* ■ suitable or fit for a specified thing: *roadworthy.* ▷from WORTHY.

wot¹ /wät/ ▶*pron., adj., & interrog. adv. Brit.* nonstandard spelling of WHAT, chiefly representing informal, dialectical, or humorous use.

wot² ▶ singular present of WIT².

Wo·tan /ˈvōˌtän/ another name for **ODIN**.

Wouk /wōk; wo͝ok/, Herman (1915–), U.S. writer. His novels include *The Caine Mutiny* (1951), *Marjorie Morningstar* (1955), *The Winds of War* (1971), *War and Remembrance* (1978), and *The Glory* (1994).

would /wo͝od/ ▶*modal verb* (*3rd sing. present* **would**) **1** past of WILL¹, in various senses: *he said he would be away for a couple of days | he wanted out, but she wouldn't leave | the windows would not close.* **2** (expressing the conditional mood) indicating the consequence of an imagined event or situation: *he would lose his job if he were identified.* ■ (**I would**) used to give advice: *I wouldn't drink that if I were you.* **3** expressing a desire or inclination: *I would love to work in Prague | would you like some water?* **4** expressing a polite request: *would you pour the wine, please?* ■ expressing willingness or consent: *who would live here?* **5** expressing a conjecture, opinion, or hope: *I would imagine that they'll want to keep it | I guess some people would consider it brutal | I would have to agree.* **6** used to make a comment about behavior that is typical: *every night we would hear the boy crying | derogatory they would say that, wouldn't they?* **7** [with *clause*] *poetic/literary* expressing a wish or regret: *would that he had lived to finish it.* ▷Old English *wolde*, past of *wyllan* (see WILL¹).

USAGE On the differences in use between **would** and **should**, see **usage** at SHOULD.

would-be ▶*adj. often derogatory* [*attrib.*] desiring or aspiring to be a specified type of person: *a would-be actress who dresses up as Marilyn Monroe.*

would·n't /ˈwo͝odnt/ ▶*contraction of* would not.

▶*PHRASE* □ **I wouldn't know** *informal* used to indicate that one can't be expected to know the answer to someone's question or to comment on a matter: *"It was a lot better than last year's dance." "I wouldn't know about that."*

wouldst /wo͝odst/ (also **would·est** /ˈwo͝odist/) ▶ archaic second person singular of WOULD.

wound¹ /wo͞ond/ ▶*n.* an injury to living tissue caused by a cut, blow, or other impact, typically one in which the skin is cut or broken. ■ an injury to a person's feelings or reputation: *the new crisis has opened old wounds.*

▶*v.* [*trans.*] (often **be wounded**) inflict an injury on (someone): *the sergeant was seriously wounded | [as adj.]* (**wounded**) *a wounded soldier.* ■ injure (a person's feelings): *you really wounded his pride when you turned him down | [as adj.]* (**wounded**) *her wounded feelings.* ▷Old English *wund* (noun), *wundian* (verb), of Germanic origin; related to Dutch *wond* and German *Wunde*, of unknown ultimate origin. —**wound·ing·ly** *adv.* —**wound·less** *adj.*

wound² /wound/ ▶ alternate past and past participle of WIND¹.

wound³ /wound/ ▶ past and past participle of WIND².

Wound·ed Knee /ˈwo͞ondid/ a village in southwestern South Dakota, in the Pine Ridge Indian reservation, the site of an 1890 massacre and 1973 demonstrations.

Wound·ed Knee, Bat·tle of /ˈwo͞ondid ˈnē/ the last major confrontation (1890) between the U.S. Army and American Indians, at the village of Wounded Knee on a reservation in South Dakota. More than 150 largely unarmed Sioux men, women, and children were massacred. A civil rights protest at the site in 1973 led to clashes with the authorities.

wound·wort /ˈwo͞ondˌwərt; -ˌwôrt/ ▶*n.* a hairy Eurasian plant resembling a dead-nettle, formerly used in the treatment of wounds. • Genus *Stachys*, family Labiatae: several species.

wove /wōv/ ▶ past of WEAVE¹.

wo·ven /ˈwōvən/ ▶ past participle of WEAVE¹.

▶*adj.* (of fabric) formed by interlacing long threads passing in one direction with others at a right angle to them: *women in striped, woven shawls.* ■ (of basketwork or a wreath) made by interlacing items such as cane, stems, flowers, or leaves. ■ [with *submodifier*] (of a complex story or pattern) made in a specified way from a number of interconnected elements: *a neatly woven tale of intrigue in academia.*

wove pa·per ▶*n.* paper made on a wire-gauze mesh so as to have a uniform unlined surface. Compare with LAID PAPER. ▷early 19th cent.: *wove*, variant of WOVEN.

wow¹ /wou/ *informal* ▶*exclam.* (also **wow·ee** /ˈwouē; ˈwouˈ(w)ē/) expressing astonishment or admiration: *"Wow!" he cried enthusiastically.*

▶*n.* a sensational success: *your play's a wow.*

▶*v.* [*trans.*] impress and excite (someone) greatly: *they wowed audiences on their recent British tour.* ▷natural exclamation: first recorded in Scots in the early 16th cent.

wow² ▶*n.* slow pitch fluctuation in sound reproduction, perceptible in long notes. Compare with FLUTTER (sense 1). ▷mid 20th cent.: imitative.

wow·ser /ˈwouzər/ ▶*n. Austral./NZ informal* a person who is publicly critical of others and the pleasures they seek; a killjoy. ▷late 19th cent.: of obscure origin.

Woz·ni·ak /ˈwäznēˌak/, Steve (1950–), U.S. computer entrepreneur. He cofounded the Apple computer company in 1976 with Steve Jobs and helped to lead it until 1981 and again from 1983 until 1985, leaving to devote his time to other projects.

WP ▶*abbr.* word processing or word processor.

w.p. ▶*abbr.* weather permitting: *I hope to arrive in London that evening (w.p.).*

W par·ti·cle ▶*n. Physics* a heavy charged elementary particle considered to transmit the weak interaction between other elementary particles. ▷*W*, the initial letter of *weak.*

wpb ▶*abbr.* wastepaper basket.

wpm ▶*abbr.* words per minute (used after a number to indicate typing speed).

WRAC /rak/ ▶*abbr.* Women's Royal Army Corps (in the UK, until 1993).

wrack¹ ▶*v.* variant spelling of RACK¹ (sense 1).

USAGE On the complicated relationship between **wrack** and **rack**, see **usage** at RACK¹.

wrack² /rak/ ▶*n.* any of a number of coarse brown seaweeds that grow on the shoreline, frequently each kind forming a distinct band in relation to high- and low-water marks. Many have air bladders for buoyancy. • Genera *Fucus*, *Ascophyllum*, and *Pelvetia*, class Phaeophyceae. ▷early 16th cent.: apparently from WRACK⁴.

wrack³ ▶*n.* variant spelling of RACK⁵. ▷late Middle English: variant of RACK⁵.

wrack⁴ ▶*n. archaic, dialect* a wrecked ship; a shipwreck. ■ wreckage. ▷late Middle English: from Middle Dutch *wrak*; related to WREAK and WRECK.

WRAF /raf/ ▶*abbr.* Women's Royal Air Force (in the UK, until 1994).

wraith /rāTH/ ▶*n.* a ghost or ghostlike image of someone, esp. one seen shortly before or after their death. ■ used in similes and metaphors to describe a pale, thin, or insubstantial person or thing: *heart attacks had reduced his mother to a wraith.* ■ *poetic/literary* a wisp or faint trace of something: *a sea breeze was sending a gray* **wraith of** *smoke up the slopes.* ▷early 16th cent. (originally Scots): of unknown origin. —**wraith·like** /-ˌlīk/ *adj.*

Wran·gel Is·land /ˈraNGgəl/ an island in the East Siberian Sea, off the coast of northeastern Russia. It was named after Russian admiral and explorer Baron Ferdinand Wrangel (1794–1870).

Wran·gell Moun·tains /ˈraNGgəl/ a range in southeastern Alaska, within Wrangell–St. Elias National Park, along the Pacific coast and the border of the Yukon Territory.

wran·gle /ˈraNGgəl/ ▶*n.* a dispute or argument, typically one that is long and complicated: *an insurance wrangle is holding up compensation payments.*

▶*v.* **1** [*intrans.*] have such a dispute or argument: [as *n.*] (**wrangling**) *weeks of political wrangling.* See note at QUARREL. **2** [*trans.*] round up, herd, or take charge of (livestock): *the horses were wrangled early.* **3** another term for WANGLE. ▷late Middle English: compare with Low German *wrangeln*, frequentative of *wrangen* 'to struggle'; related to WRING.

wran·gler /ˈraNGglər/ ▶*n.* **1** a person in charge of horses or other livestock on a ranch. ■ a person who trains and takes care of the animals used in a movie. **2** a person engaging in a lengthy and complicated quarrel or dispute.

wrap /rap/ ▶*v.* (**wrapped**, **wrap·ping**) **1** [*trans.*] cover or enclose (someone or something) in paper or soft material: *he wrapped the Christmas presents | Leonora wrapped herself in a large white bath towel.* ■ clasp; embrace: *she wrapped him in her arms.* ■ cover (the body) with a body wrap. ■ cover (the fingernails) with a nail wrap. **2** [*trans.*] (**wrap something around**) arrange paper or soft material around (someone or something), typically as a covering or for warmth or protection: *wrap the bandage around the injured limb.* ■ place an arm, finger, or leg around (someone or something): *he wrapped an arm around her waist.* ■ *informal* crash a vehicle into (a stationary object): *Richard wrapped his car around a telephone pole.* **3** [*trans.*] *Computing* cause (a word or unit of text) to be carried over to a new line automatically as the margin is reached, or to fit around embedded features such as pictures. ■ [*intrans.*] (of a word or unit or text) be carried over in such a way. **4** [*intrans.*] *informal* finish filming or recording: *we wrapped on schedule three days later.*

▶*phrasal v.* □ **wrap up** (also **wrap someone up**) put on (or dress someone in) warm clothes: *wrap up warm | Tim was well wrapped up against the weather.* □ **wrap something up** complete or conclude a discussion or agreement: *they hope to wrap up negotiations within sixty days.* ■ win a game or competition: *Australia wrapped up the series 4–0.*

▶*n.* **1** a loose outer garment or piece of material. ■ [as *adj.*] denoting a garment having one part overlapping another; wraparound: *a wrap skirt.* ■ paper or soft material used for wrapping: *plastic food wrap.* ■ (usu. **wraps**) *figurative* a veil of secrecy maintained about something, esp. a new project: *details of the police operation are being kept* **under wraps**. **2** [usu. in *sing.*] *informal* the end of a session of filming or recording: *right, it's a wrap.* **3** a sandwich in which the filling is rolled in a soft tortilla. **4** short for BODY WRAP. ■ short for NAIL WRAP. ▷Middle English: of unknown origin.

▶*PHRASE* □ **be wrapped up in** be so engrossed or absorbed in (something) that one does not notice other people or things.

wrap·a·round /ˈrapəˌround/ ▶*adj.* [*attrib.*] curving or extending around at the edges or sides: *wraparound sunglasses.* ■ (of a garment) having one part overlapping another and fastened loosely: *a wraparound skirt.*

▶*n.* **1** a wraparound garment. **2** *Computing* a facility by which a linear sequence of memory locations or screen positions is treated as a continuous circular series.

wrap·a·round mort·gage ▶*n.* a second mortgage held by a lender who collects payments on it and the first mortgage from the borrower. The lender makes the payments to the original mortgage holder.

wrap·a·round porch ▶*n.* a shallow veranda enclosing two or more sides of a house: *three-story million-dollar houses with wraparound porches perched on pilings.*

wrap·per /ˈrapər/ ▶*n.* **1** a piece of paper, plastic, or foil covering and protecting something sold. ■ a cover enclosing a newspaper or magazine for mailing. ■ the dust jacket of a book. ■ a tobacco leaf of superior quality enclosing a cigar. **2** a loose robe or gown.

wrap·per ap·pli·ca·tion ▸*n.* a computer program that works only with another fully developed program, which it enhances in some way: *we have created a viewer that is a simple wrapper application for the underlying multimedia system.*

wrap·ping /ˈrapiNG/ ▸*n.* paper or soft material used to cover or enclose someone or something: *she took the cellophane wrapping off the box.*

wrap·ping pa·per ▸*n.* strong or decorative paper for wrapping parcels or presents.

wrapt /rapt/ ▸*adj.* archaic or poetic form of WRAPPED: *wrapt in her music no birdsong shall ever equal.*

wrap-up ▸*n.* a summary or résumé, in particular: ■ a review of a sporting event. ■ an overview of the products of one company or in one field.
▸*adj.* serving to summarize, complete, or conclude something: *200 campaign volunteers celebrated during wrap-up festivities.*

wrasse /ras/ ▸*n.* (*pl.* same or **wrass·es**) a marine fish with thick lips and strong teeth, typically brightly colored with marked differences between the male and female. • Family Labridae: numerous genera and species. ▷late 17th cent.: from Cornish *wrah*; related to Welsh *gwrach*, literally 'old woman.'

wrath /raTH/ ▸*n.* extreme anger (chiefly used for humorous or rhetorical effect): *he hid his pipe for fear of incurring his father's wrath.* ▷Old English *wrǣththu*, from *wrāth* (see WROTH).

wrathful /ˈraTHfəl/ ▸*adj. poetic/literary* full of or characterized by intense anger: *natural calamities seemed to be the work of a wrathful deity.* **—wrath·ful·ly** *adv.* **—wrath·ful·ness** *n.*

wrath·y /ˈraTHē/ ▸*adj. informal, dated* another term for WRATHFUL.

wreak /rēk/ ▸*v.* [*trans.*] cause (a large amount of damage or harm): *torrential rainstorms* ***wreaked havoc*** *yesterday | the environmental damage wreaked by ninety years of phosphate mining.* ■ inflict (vengeance): *he was determined to* ***wreak*** *his revenge* ***on*** *the girl who had rejected him.* ■ *archaic* avenge (someone who has been wronged): *grant me some knight to wreak me for my son.* ▷Old English *wrecan* 'drive (out), avenge,' of Germanic origin; related to Dutch *wreken* and German *rächen*; compare with WRACK[4], WRECK, and WRETCH. **—wreak·er** *n.*

> *USAGE* The phrase **wrought havoc**, as in *they* ***wrought havoc*** *on the countryside*, is an acceptable variant of **wreaked havoc**. Here, **wrought** is an archaic past tense of **work**. It is not, as is sometimes assumed, a past tense of **wreak**.

wreath /rēTH/ ▸*n.* (*pl.* **wreaths** /rē<u>TH</u>z; rēTHs/) **1** an arrangement of flowers, leaves, or stems fastened in a ring and used for decoration or for laying on a grave. ■ a carved representation of such a wreath. ■ a similar ring made of or resembling soft, twisted material: *a gold wreath.* ■ *Heraldry* a representation of such a ring below a crest (esp. where it joins a helmet). ■ a curl or ring of smoke or cloud: *wreaths of mist swirled up into the cold air.* **2** *archaic, chiefly Scottish* a snowdrift. ▷Old English *writha*, related to WRITHE.

wreathe /rē<u>TH</u>/ ▸*v.* [*trans.*] (usu. **be wreathed**) cover, surround, or encircle (something): *he sits wreathed in smoke | his face was wreathed in smiles.* ■ [*trans.*] *poetic/literary* twist or entwine (something flexible) around or over something: *shall I once more wreathe my arms about Antonio's neck?* ■ form (flowers, leaves, or stems) into a wreath. ■ [*intrans.*] (esp. of smoke) move with a curling motion: *he watched the smoke wreathe into the night air.* ▷mid 16th cent.: partly a back-formation from archaic *wrethen*, past participle of WRITHE, reinforced by WREATH.

wreck /rek/ ▸*n.* the destruction of a ship at sea; a shipwreck: *the survivors of the wreck.* ■ a ship destroyed in such a way: *the salvaging of treasure from wrecks.* ■ *Law* goods brought ashore by the sea from a wreck and not claimed by the owner within a specified period (usually a year): *the profits of wreck.* ■ something, esp. a vehicle or building, that has been badly damaged or destroyed: *the plane was reduced to a smoldering wreck | figurative the wreck of their marriage.* ■ the disorganized remains of something that has suffered damage or destruction. ■ a road or rail crash: *a train wreck.* ■ a person whose physical or mental health or strength has failed: *the scandal left the family emotional wrecks.*
▸*v.* [*trans.*] (usu. **be wrecked**) cause the destruction of (a ship) by sinking or breaking up: *he was drowned when his ship was wrecked.* ■ involve (someone) in such a wreck: *sailors who had the misfortune to be wrecked on these coasts.* ■ [*intrans.*] [usu. as *n.*] (**wrecking**) *chiefly historical* cause the destruction of a ship in order to steal the cargo: *the locals reverted to the age-old practice of wrecking.* ■ [*intrans.*] *archaic* suffer or undergo shipwreck. ■ destroy or severely damage (a structure or vehicle): *the blast wrecked more than 100 houses.* ■ spoil completely: *an eye injury wrecked his chances of a professional career.* ■ [*intrans.*] [usu. as *n.*] (**wrecking**) engage in breaking up badly damaged vehicles, demolishing old buildings, or similar activities to obtain usable spares or scrap. ▷Middle English (as a legal term denoting wreckage washed ashore): from Anglo-Norman French *wrec*, from the base of Old Norse *reka* 'to drive'; related to WREAK.

wreck·age /ˈrekij/ ▸*n.* the remains of something that has been badly damaged or destroyed: *firemen had to cut him free from the wreckage of the car.*

wrecked /rekt/ ▸*adj.* **1** having been wrecked: *an old wrecked barge lay upside down | a wrecked marriage.* **2** *informal* under the influence of or suffering the effects of drugs or alcohol: *they got wrecked on tequila.*

wreck·er /ˈrekər/ ▸*n.* **1** a person or thing that wrecks, damages, or destroys something: [in *combination*] *she was cast as a home-wrecker.* ■ a person who breaks up damaged vehicles, demolishes old buildings, salvages wrecked ships, etc., to obtain usable spares or scrap. ■ *chiefly historical* a person on the shore who tries to bring about a shipwreck in order to profit from the wreckage. **2** a tow truck.

wreck·ing ball (also **wreck·er's ball**) ▸*n.* a heavy metal ball swung from a crane into a building to demolish it.

Wren[1] /ren/, Sir Christopher (1632–1723), English architect. Following the Fire of London in 1666, he was responsible for the design of the new St. Paul's Cathedral 1675–1711 and many of the city's churches.

Wren[3] ▸*n.* (in the UK) a member of the former Women's Royal Naval Service. ▷early 20th cent.: originally in the plural, from the abbreviation **WRNS**.

wren /ren/ ▸*n.* **1** a small short-winged songbird found chiefly in the New World. • Family Troglodytidae: many genera and numerous species, in particular the very small *Troglodytes troglodytes* (**winter wren**), which has a short cocked tail and is the only wren that occurs the Old World. **2** [usu. with *adj.*] any of a number of small songbirds that resemble the true wrens in size or appearance. ▷Old English *wrenna*, of Germanic origin.

wrench /renCH/ ▸*n.* **1** [usu. in *sing.*] a sudden violent twist or pull: *with a wrench Tony wriggled free.* ■ *figurative* an act of leaving someone or something that causes sadness or distress: *it will be a real wrench to leave after eight years.* **2** a tool used for gripping and turning nuts, bolts, pipes, etc. **3** *Mechanics* a combination of a couple with a force along its axis.
▸*v.* [*trans.*] pull or twist (someone or something) suddenly and violently: *Casey grabbed the gun and wrenched it upward from my hand | [trans.] she wrenched herself free of his grip | [intrans.] figurative the betrayal wrenched at her heart.* ■ injure (a part of the body) as a result of a sudden twisting movement: *she slipped and wrenched her ankle.* ■ turn (something, esp. a nut or bolt) with a wrench. ■ *archaic* distort to fit a particular theory or interpretation: *to wrench our Bible to make it fit a misconception of facts.* ▷late Old English *wrencan* 'twist,' of unknown origin.
▸*PHRASE* □ **a wrench in the works** another way of saying A MONKEY WRENCH IN THE WORKS (see MONKEY WRENCH).

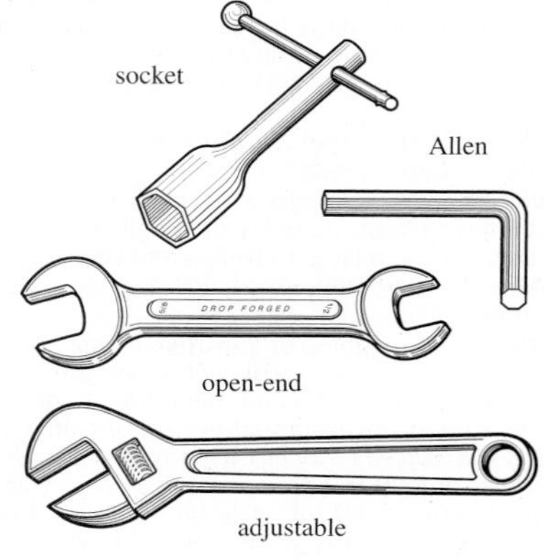

wrench 2

wrench fault ▸*n.* another term for STRIKE-SLIP FAULT.

wren·tit /ˈrenˌtit/ ▸*n.* a long-tailed North American songbird that is the only American member of the babbler family, with dark plumage. • *Chamaea fasciata*, family Timaliidae.

wrest /rest/ ▸*v.* [*trans.*] forcibly pull (something) from a person's grasp: *Leila tried to wrest her arm from his hold.* ■ take (something, esp. power or control) from someone or something else after considerable effort or difficulty: *they wanted to allow people to wrest control of their lives from impersonal bureaucracies.* ■ *archaic* distort the meaning or interpretation of (something) to suit one's own interests or views: *you appear convinced of my guilt, and wrest every reply I have made.*
▸*n. archaic* a key for tuning a harp or piano. ▷Old English *wrǣstan* 'twist, tighten,' of Germanic origin; related to Danish *vriste*, also to WRIST.

wres·tle /ˈresəl/ ▸*v.* [*intrans.*] take part in a fight, either as a sport or in earnest, that involves grappling with one's opponent and trying to throw or force them to the ground: *as the policeman* ***wrestled with*** *the gunman a shot rang out.* ■ [*trans.*] force (someone) into a particular position or place by fighting in such a way: *the security guards wrestled them to the ground.* ■ *figurative* struggle with a difficulty or problem: *for over a year David* ***wrestled with*** *a guilty conscience.* ■ [*trans.*] move or manipulate (something) in a specified way with difficulty and some physical effort: *she wrestled the keys out of the ignition.*
▸*n.* [in *sing.*] a wrestling bout or contest: *a wrestle to the death.* ■ a hard struggle: *a lifelong wrestle with depression.* ▷Old English, frequentative of *wrǣstan* 'wrest.' **—wres·tler** /ˈres(ə)lər/ *n.*

wres·tling /ˈres(ə)liNG/ ▸*n.* the sport or activity of grappling with an opponent and trying to throw or hold them down on the ground, typically according to a code of rules.

> Popular in ancient Egypt, China, and Greece, wrestling was introduced to the Olympic Games in 704 BC; many of the holds and throws used now are the same as those of antiquity. The two main competition styles are Greco-Roman (in which holds below the waist are prohibited) and freestyle, which has become a popular televised sport.
> See also SUMO.

wretch /reCH/ ▸*n.* an unfortunate or unhappy person: *can the poor wretch's corpse tell us anything?* ■ *informal* a despicable or contemptible person: *ungrateful wretches.* ▷Old English *wrecca* (also in the sense 'banished person'); related to German *Recke* 'warrior, hero,' also to the verb WREAK.

wretch·ed /ˈreCHid/ ▸*adj.* (**-ed·er, -ed·est**) (of a person) in a very unhappy or unfortunate state: *I felt so wretched because I thought I might never see you again.* ■ of poor quality; very bad: *the wretched conditions of the slums.* ■ used to express anger or annoyance: *she disliked the wretched man intensely.* ▷Middle English: formed irregularly from WRETCH + -ED[1]. **—wretch·ed·ly** *adv.* [as *submodifier*] *a wretchedly poor country.* **—wretch·ed·ness** *n.*

wrig·gle /ˈrigəl/ ▸*v.* [*intrans.*] twist and turn with quick writhing movements: *he kicked and wriggled but she held him firmly.* ■ [*trans.*] cause to move in such a way: *she wriggled her bare, brown toes.* ■ [*intrans.*] move in a particular direction with wriggling movements: *Susie wriggled out of her clothes.* ■ (**wriggle out of**) avoid (something), esp. by devious means: *don't try and wriggle out of your contract.*
▸*n.* [in *sing.*] a wriggling movement: *she gave an impatient little wriggle.* ▷late 15th cent.: from Middle Low German *wriggelen*, frequentative of *wriggen* 'twist, turn.' **—wrig·gly** /ˈrig(ə)lē/ *adj.*

wrig·gler /ˈrig(ə)lər/ ▸*n.* a person or thing that wriggles. ■ a wriggling animalcule or the larva of a mosquito. Also called WIGGLER.

Wright[1] /rīt/, Frank Lloyd (1869–1959), U.S. architect. His "prairie-style" houses, characterized by a close relationship among building, landscape, and materials used, revolutionized domestic architecture in the U.S. Notable buildings include the Kaufmann House, which incorporated a waterfall, in Pennsylvania 1935–39 and the Guggenheim Museum of Art in New York 1956–59.

Wright[2], Orville (1871–1948) and Wilbur (1867–1912), U.S. aviation pioneers. In 1903, the Wright brothers were the first to make brief sustained and controlled powered flights in an airplane, which was designed and built by them. They were also the first to make and fly a practical powered airplane 1905 and a passenger-carrying airplane 1908.

wright /rīt/ ▸*n. archaic* a maker or builder. ▷Old English *wryhta, wyrhta;* related to **WORK**.

wring /riNG/ ▸*v.* (*past* **wrung** /rəNG/) [*trans.*] squeeze and twist (something) to force liquid from it: *she* **wrung** *the cloth* **out** *in the sink.* ■ [*trans.*] extract (liquid) by squeezing and twisting something: *I wrung out the excess water.* ■ break (an animal's neck) by twisting it forcibly. ■ squeeze (someone's hand) tightly, esp. with sincere emotion. ■ [*trans.*] obtain (something) with difficulty or effort: *few concessions were wrung from the government.* ■ cause pain or distress to: *the letter must have wrung her heart.*
▸*n.* [in *sing.*] an act of squeezing or twisting something. ▷Old English *wringan* (verb); related to Dutch *wringen*, also to **WRONG**.
▸*PHRASE* □ **wring one's hands** clasp and twist one's hands together as a gesture of great distress, esp. when one is powerless to change the situation.

wring·er /ˈriNGər/ ▸*n.* a device for wringing water from wet clothes, mops, or other objects.
▸*PHRASE* □ **put someone through the wringer** *informal* subject someone to a very stressful experience, esp. a severe interrogation.

wrin·kle /ˈriNGkəl/ ▸*n.* **1** a slight line or fold in something, esp. fabric or the skin of the face. ■ *informal* a minor difficulty; a snag: *the organizers have the wrinkles pretty well ironed out.* **2** *informal* a clever innovation, or useful piece of information or advice: *learning the wrinkles from someone more experienced saves time.*
▸*v.* [*trans.*] [often as *adj.*] (**wrinkled**) make or cause lines or folds in (something, esp. fabric or the skin): *Dotty's wrinkled stockings.* ■ grimace and cause wrinkles on (a part of the face): *he sniffed and wrinkled his nose.* ■ [*intrans.*] form or become marked with lines or folds: *her brow wrinkled.* ▷late Middle English: origin obscure, possibly a back-formation from the Old English past participle *gewrinclod* 'sinuous' (of which no infinitive is recorded).

wrin·kly /ˈriNGk(ə)lē/ ▸*adj.* (**-kli·er, -kli·est**) having many lines or folds: *he's old and wrinkly.*

wrist /rist/ ▸*n.* **1** the joint connecting the hand with the forearm. See also **CARPUS**. ■ the equivalent joint (the carpal joint) in the foreleg of a quadruped or the wing of a bird. ■ the part of a garment covering the wrist; a cuff. **2** (also **wrist pin**) (in a machine) a stud projecting from a crank as an attachment for a connecting rod. ▷Old English, of Germanic origin, probably from the base of **WRITHE**.

wrist·band /ˈristˌband/ ▸*n.* a strip of material worn around the wrist, in particular: ■ a small strap or bracelet, esp. one used for identification or as a fashion item. ■ a strip of absorbent material worn during sports or strenuous exercise to soak up sweat. ■ the cuff of a shirt or blouse.

wrist·drop ▸*n.* paralysis of the muscles that normally raise the hand at the wrist and extend the fingers, typically caused by nerve damage.

wrist·guard /ˈristˌgärd/ ▸*n.* a band of leather or leatherlike material worn around the wrist for support and protection, esp. for athletic activities such as archery and fencing.

wrist·let /ˈristlit/ ▸*n.* a band or bracelet worn on the wrist, typically as an ornament.

wrist pin ▸*n.* another term for **WRIST** (sense 2).

wrist·watch /ˈristˌwäCH/ ▸*n.* a watch worn on a strap around the wrist.

wrist·work /ˈristˌwərk/ ▸*n.* the action of working the hand without moving the arm, esp. in fencing and ball games.

wrist·y /ˈristē/ ▸*adj. Tennis* (of a stroke) performed using a pronounced movement of the wrist: *he uses a fast, wristy swing to hit his forehand.*

writ[1] /rit/ ▸*n.* a form of written command in the name of a court or other legal authority to act, or abstain from acting, in some way. ■ (**one's writ**) one's power to enforce compliance or submission; one's authority: *you have business here which is out of my writ and competence.* ▷Old English, as a general term denoting written matter, from the Germanic base of **WRITE**.

writ[2] ▸*v.* archaic past participle of **WRITE**.
▸*PHRASE* □ **writ large** clear and obvious: *the unspoken question writ large upon Rose's face.* ■ in a stark or exaggerated form: *bribing people by way of tax allowances is the paternalistic state writ large.*

write /rīt/ ▸*v.* (*past* **wrote** /rōt/; *past part.* **writ·ten** /ˈritn/) [*trans.*] **1** mark (letters, words, or other symbols) on a surface, typically paper, with a pen, pencil, or similar implement: *he wrote his name on the paper | Alice* **wrote down** *the address* | [*intrans.*] *he wrote very neatly in blue ink.* ■ [*intrans.*] have the ability to mark coherent letters or words in this way: *he couldn't read or write.* ■ fill out or complete (a sheet, check, or similar) in this way: *he had to write a check for $800.* ■ [*intrans.*] write in a cursive hand, as opposed to printing individual letters. **2** compose, write, and send (a letter) to someone: *I* **wrote** *a letter* **to** *Alison* | [with *two objs.*] *I wrote him a short letter* | [*intrans.*] *he wrote almost every day.* ■ write and send a letter to (someone): *Mother wrote me and told me about poor Simon's death.* ■ [*trans.*] (**write in**) write to an organization, esp. a broadcasting station, with a question, suggestion, or opinion: *write in with your query.* **3** compose (a text or work) for written or printed reproduction or publication; put into literary form and set down in writing: *I didn't know you wrote poetry* | [*intrans.*] *he wrote under a pseudonym | he had written about the beauty of Andalucia.* ■ compose (a musical work): *he has written a song specifically for her.* ■ (**write someone into/out of**) add or remove a character to or from (a long-running story or series). ■ *archaic* describe in writing: *if I could write the beauty of your eyes.* **4** [*trans.*] *Computing* enter (data) into a specified storage medium or location in store. **5** underwrite (an insurance policy).
▸*phrasal v.* □ **write something down 1** reduce the nominal value of stock or goods. **2** write as if for those considered inferior. □ **write someone in** (when voting) add the name of someone not on the original list of candidates and vote for them. □ **write something off 1** (**write someone/something off**) dismiss someone or something as insignificant: *the boy had been written off as a nonachiever.* **2** cancel the record of a bad debt; acknowledge the loss of or failure to recover an asset: *he urged the banks to write off debt owed by poorer countries.* □ **write something up 1** write a full or formal account of something: *I was too tired to write up my notes.* ■ make entries to bring a diary or similar record up to date: *he wrote up a work journal which has never been published.* **2** increase the nominal value of stock or goods. ▷Old English *wrītan* 'score, form (letters) by carving, write,' of Germanic origin; related to German *reissen* 'sketch, drag.' —**writ·a·ble** *adj.*
▸*PHRASES* □ **be nothing to write home about** *informal* be very mediocre or unexceptional. □ **be** (or **have something**) **written all over one** (or **one's face**) *informal* used to convey that the presence of a particular quality or feeling is clearly revealed by a person's expression: *guilt was written all over his face.* □ **be written in stone** see **STONE**. □ (**and**) **that's all she wrote** *informal* used to convey that there is or was nothing more to be said about a matter: *we were arguing about who should pay the bill, but he pulled out a couple of hundreds and that's all she wrote.*

write-back ▸*n. Finance* the process of restoring to profit a provision for bad or doubtful debts previously made against profits and no longer required.

write-down ▸*n. Finance* a reduction in the estimated or nominal value of an asset.

write-in ▸*n.* a vote cast for an unlisted candidate by writing their name on a ballot paper: *the results showed 70 blank ballots and 770 write-ins.* ■ a candidate for whom votes are cast in such a way.

write-off ▸*n.* **1** *Finance* a cancellation from an account of a bad debt or worthless asset. **2** a worthless or ineffectual person or thing: *she burns the toast and decides the weekend is a write-off.*

write-once ▸*adj. Computing* denoting a memory or storage device, typically an optical one, on which data, once written, cannot be modified.

write-pro·tect ▸*v.* [*trans.*] *Computing* protect (a disk) from accidental writing or erasure, as by removing the cover from a notch in the plastic casing of a floppy disk.
▸*adj.* denoting a notch or other device that fulfills this function.

writ·er /ˈrītər/ ▸*n.* a person who has written a particular text: *the writer of the letter.* ■ a person who writes books, stories, or articles as a job or regular occupation: *the distinguished travel writer Freya Stark.* ■ [with *adj.*] a person who writes in a specified way: *Dickens was a prolific writer.* ■ a composer of musical works: *a writer of military music.* ■ *Computing* a device that writes data to a storage medium. ■ *Stock Market* a broker who makes an option available for purchase or sells options. ■ [with *adj.*] a person who has a specified kind of handwriting: *neat writers.* ■ *Brit., historical* a scribe. ■ *Brit., archaic* a clerk, esp. in the navy or other government offices. ▷Old English *wrītere* (see **WRITE**).
▸*PHRASES* □ **writer's block** the condition of being unable to think of what to write or how to proceed with writing. □ **writer's cramp** pain or stiffness in the hand caused by excessive writing.

writ·er-in-res·i·dence ▸*n.* (*pl.* **writ·ers-in-res·i·dence**) a writer holding a temporary residential post in an academic establishment, in order to share their professional insights.

writ·er·ly /ˈrītərlē/ ▸*adj.* of or characteristic of a professional author: *the mixture of writerly craft and stamina that Greene had.* ■ consciously literary: *novels as tricksy and writerly as those of Robbe-Grillet.*

write-up ▸*n.* **1** a full written account. ■ a newspaper or magazine article giving the author's opinion of a recent event, performance, or product. **2** *Finance* an increase in the estimated or nominal value of an asset.

writhe /rīTH/ ▸*v.* [*intrans.*] make continual twisting, squirming movements or contortions of the body: *he writhed in agony on the ground.* ■ [*trans.*] cause to move in such a way: *a snake writhing its body in a sinuous movement.* ■ (**writhe in/with/at**) respond with great emotional or physical discomfort to (a violent or unpleasant feeling or thought): *she bit her lip, writhing in suppressed fury.*
▸*n. rare* a twisting, squirming movement. ▷Old English *wrīthan* 'make into coils, plait, fasten with a cord,' of Germanic origin; related to **WREATHE**.

writh·en /ˈriTHən/ ▸*adj.* **1** *poetic/literary* twisted or contorted out of normal shape or form. **2** (of antique glass or silver) having spirally twisted ornamentation. ▷Old English in the sense 'plaited, entwined,' archaic past participle of **WRITHE**.

writ·ing /ˈrītiNG/ ▸*n.* **1** the activity or skill of marking coherent words on paper and composing text: *parents want schools to concentrate on reading, writing, and arithmetic.* ■ the activity or occupation of composing text for publication: *she made a decent living from writing.* **2** written work, esp. with regard to its style or quality: *the writing is straightforward and accessible.* ■ (**writings**) books, stories, articles, or other written works: *he was introduced to the writings of Gertrude Stein.* ■ (**the Writings**) the Hagiographa. **3** a sequence of letters, words, or symbols marked on paper or some other surface: *a leather product with gold writing on it.* ■ handwriting: *his writing looked crabbed.*
▸*PHRASES* □ **in writing** in written form, esp. as proof of an agreement or grievance: *he asked them to* **put** *their complaints* **in writing**. □ **the writing** (or **handwriting**) **is on the wall** there are clear signs that something unpleasant or unwelcome is going to happen: *the writing was on the wall for the old system.* [with biblical allusion to Dan. 5:5, 25–8.]

writ·ing desk ▸*n.* a piece of furniture with a surface for writing on and with drawers and other compartments for pens and paper.

writ·ing pad ▸*n.* a pad of paper for writing on.

writ·ing pa·per ▸*n.* paper of good quality used for writing, esp. letter-writing.

writ of ex·e·cu·tion ▸*n. Law* a judicial order that a judgment be enforced.

writ·ten /ˈritn/ ▸ past participle of **WRITE**.

WRNS *historical* ▸*abbr.* (in the UK) Women's Royal Naval Service.

Wro·cław /ˈvrôtˌswäf; -ˌsläf/ an industrial city on the Oder River, in western Poland; pop. 643,000. German name **BRESLAU**.

wrong /rôNG/ ▸*adj.* **1** not correct or true: *that is the wrong answer.* ■ [*predic.*] mistaken: *I was* **wrong about** *him being on the yacht that evening.* ■ unsuitable or undesirable: *they asked all the wrong questions.* ■ [*predic.*] in a bad or abnormal condition; amiss: *something was* **wrong with** *the pump.* **2** unjust, dishonest, or immoral: *they were* **wrong to** *take the law into their own hands | it was* **wrong of** *me to write you such an angry note.*
▸*adv.* in an unsuitable or undesirable manner or direction: *what am I doing wrong?* ■ with an incorrect result: *she guessed wrong.*
▸*n.* an unjust, dishonest, or immoral action: *I have done you a great wrong.* ■ *Law* a breach, by commission or omission, of one's legal duty. ■ *Law* an invasion of right to the damage or prejudice of another.
▸*v.* [*trans.*] act unjustly or dishonestly toward (someone): *please forgive me these things and the people I have wronged.* ■ mistakenly attribute bad motives to; misrepresent: *perhaps I wrong him.* ▷late Old English *wrang*, from Old Norse *rangr* 'awry, unjust'; related

to WRONG. **—wrong·er** *n.* **—wrong·ly** *adv.* **—wrong·ness** *n.*

▶*PHRASES* □ **get someone wrong** misunderstand someone, esp. by falsely imputing malice. □ **go down the wrong way** (of food) enter the windpipe instead of the gullet. □ **go wrong** develop in an undesirable way. □ **in the wrong** responsible for a quarrel, mistake, or offense. □ **two wrongs don't make a right** *proverb* the fact that someone has done something unjust or dishonest is no justification for acting in a similar way.

wrong·do·ing /ˈrôNG,do͞oiNG/ ▶*n.* illegal or dishonest behavior: *the head of the bank has denied any wrongdoing.* **—wrong·do·er** *n.*

wrong-foot ▶*v.* [*trans.*] (in a game) play so as to catch (an opponent) off balance: *Cook wrong-footed the defense with a low free kick.* ■ *Brit.* put (someone) in a difficult or embarrassing situation by saying or doing something that they do not expect: *an announcement regarded as an attempt to wrong-foot the opposition.*

wrong·ful /ˈrôNGfəl/ ▶*adj.* (of an act) not fair, just, or legal: *he is suing the police for wrongful arrest.* **—wrong·ful·ly** *adv.* **—wrong·ful·ness** *n.*

wrong·ful death ▶*adj.* denoting a civil action in which damages are sought against a party for causing a death, typically when criminal action has failed or is not attempted: *a wrongful death lawsuit.*

wrong·head·ed /ˈrôNG,hedid/ ▶*adj.* having or showing bad judgment; misguided: *this approach is both wrong-headed and naive.* **—wrong·head·ed·ly** *adv.* **—wrong·head·ed·ness** *n.*

wrong side ▶*n.* the reverse side of a fabric.

▶*PHRASES* □ **born on the wrong side of the blanket** see BLANKET. □ **get out of bed on the wrong side** see BED. □ **on the wrong side of 1** out of favor with: *she knew not to get on the wrong side of him.* **2** somewhat more than (a specified age): *he cheerfully admits he is the wrong side of fifty.* □ **on the wrong side of the tracks** see TRACK[1]. □ **wrong side out** inside out.

wrote /rōt/ ▶ past tense of WRITE.

wroth /rôTH/ ▶*adj. archaic* angry: *Sir Leicester is majestically wroth.* ▷Old English *wrāth*, of Germanic origin; related to Dutch *wreed* 'cruel,' also to WRITHE.

wrought /rôt/ archaic past and past participle of WORK. ▶*adj.* (of metals) beaten out or shaped by hammering.

USAGE See usage at WREAK.

wrought i·ron ▶*n.* a tough, malleable form of iron suitable for forging or rolling rather than casting, obtained by puddling pig iron while molten. It is nearly pure but contains some slag in the form of filaments.

wrought up ▶*adj.* [*predic.*] upset and anxious: *she didn't get too wrought up about things.*

wrung /rəNG/ ▶ past and past participle of WRING.

WRVS ▶*abbr.* (in the UK) Women's Royal Voluntary Service.

wry /rī/ ▶*adj.* (**wry·er**, **wry·est** or **wri·er**, **wri·est**) **1** using or expressing dry, esp. mocking, humor: *a wry smile* | *wry comments.* **2** (of a person's face or features) twisted into an expression of disgust, disappointment, or annoyance. ■ *archaic* (of the neck or features) distorted or turned to one side: *a remedy for wry necks.* ▷early 16th cent. (in the sense 'contorted'): from Old English *wrigian* 'tend, incline,' in Middle English 'deviate, swerve, contort.' **—wry·ly** *adv.* **—wry·ness** *n.*

wry·neck /ˈrī,nek/ ▶*n.* **1** an Old World bird of the woodpecker family, with brown camouflaged plumage and a habit of twisting and writhing the neck when disturbed. • Genus *Jynx*, family Picidae: two species, in particular the **northern wryneck** (*J. torquilla*) of Eurasia. **2** another term for TORTICOLLIS.

WSW ▶*abbr.* west-southwest.

wt ▶*abbr.* weight.

WTF ▶*abbr. offensive* what the fuck.

WTO ▶*abbr.* World Trade Organization.

Wu /wo͞o/ ▶*n.* a dialect of Chinese spoken in Jiangsu and Zhejiang provinces and the city of Shanghai. ▷the name in Chinese.

Wu·han /ˈwo͞oˈhän/ a port in eastern China, the capital of Hubei province; pop. 3,710,000. Situated at the confluence of the Han and the Yangtze rivers, it is a conurbation of three adjacent towns (Hankow, Hanyang, and Wuchang) that have been administered jointly since 1950.

wul·fen·ite /ˈwo͝olfə,nīt/ ▶*n.* an orange-yellow mineral consisting of a molybdate of lead, typically occurring as tabular crystals. ▷mid 19th cent.: from the name of F. X. von *Wulfen* (1728–1805), Austrian scientist, + -ITE[1].

Wun·der·kam·mer /ˈvo͝ondər,kämər/ ▶*n.* (*pl.* **-kam·mern**) a place where a collection of curiosities and rarities is exhibited. ▷German, literally 'wonder chamber.'

wun·der·kind /ˈwo͝ondər,kind/ ▶*n.* (*pl.* **-kinds** or **-kind·er** /-,kindər/) a person who achieves great success when relatively young. ▷late 19th cent.: from German, from *Wunder* 'wonder' + *Kind* 'child.'

Wundt /vo͝ont/, Wilhelm (1832–1920), German psychologist. He founded psychology as a separate discipline and established a laboratory devoted to its study.

wun·ner·ful /ˈwənərfəl/ ▶*adj.* nonstandard spelling of WONDERFUL, representing dialect pronunciation.

Wup·per·tal /ˈvo͞opər,täl; ˈwo͞op-/ an industrial city in western Germany, in North Rhine-Westphalia northeast of Düsseldorf; pop. 385,000.

Wur·litz·er /ˈwərlitsər/ ▶*n. trademark* a large pipe organ or electric organ, esp. one used in the movie theaters of the 1930s. ▷named after Rudolf *Wurlitzer* (1831–1914), the German-born American instrument-maker who founded the manufacturing company.

Würm /vo͝orm/ ▶*n.* [usu. as *adj.*] *Geology* the final Pleistocene glaciation in the Alps, possibly corresponding to the Weichsel of northern Europe. ■ the system of deposits laid down at this time. ▷early 20th cent.: the former name of the Starnberger See, a lake in Bavaria.

wurst /wərst; wo͝orst/ ▶*n.* German or Austrian sausage. ▷from German *Wurst.*

wurtz·ite /ˈwərt,sīt/ ▶*n.* a mineral consisting of zinc sulfide, typically occurring as brownish-black pyramidal crystals. ▷mid 19th cent.: from the name of Charles A. Wurtz (1817–84), French chemist, + -ITE[1].

Würz·burg /ˈvərts,bərg; ˈwərts-; ˈvʏrts,bo͝ork/ an industrial city on the Main River in Bavaria, in southern Germany; pop. 128,000.

wu·shu /ˈwo͞oSHo͞o/ ▶*n.* the Chinese martial arts. ▷from Chinese *wǔshù*, from *wǔ* 'military' + *shù* 'art.'

wuss /wo͝os/ ▶*n. informal* a weak or ineffectual person (often used as a general term of abuse). ▷late 20th cent.: of unknown origin. **—wuss·y** *adj.*

Wu·xi /ˈwo͞oˈSHē/ (also **Wu-hsi**) a city on the Grand Canal in Jiangsu province, in eastern China; pop. 930,000 .

Wu·xia /ˈwo͞oˈSHyä/ ▶*n.* a genre of Chinese fiction or film dealing with martial arts, sorcery, and chivalry. ▷from Chinese *wuxia*, from *wu* 'martial art' + *xia* 'warrior'.

wuz /wəz/ ▶*v.* nonstandard spelling of WAS, representing dialect or informal pronunciation.

WV ▶*abbr.* West Virginia (in official postal use).

W.Va ▶*abbr.* West Virginia.

WWF ▶*abbr.* ■ World Wrestling Federation.

WWI ▶*abbr.* World War I.

WWII ▶*abbr.* World War II.

WWW ▶*abbr.* World Wide Web.

WY ▶*abbr.* Wyoming (in official postal use).

Wy·an·dot /ˈwīən,dät/ (also **Wy·an·dotte**) ▶*n.* **1** a member of an American Indian community formed by Huron-speaking peoples, originally in Ontario, now living mainly in Oklahoma and Quebec. **2** the Iroquoian language of this people. **3** (usu. **Wyandotte**) a domestic chicken of a medium-sized breed. ▶*adj.* of or relating to the Wyandot people or their language. ▷mid 18th cent.: from French *Ouendat*, from Huron *Wendat*.

Wy·an·dotte /ˈwīən,dät/ an industrial city in southeastern Michigan, south of Detroit; pop. 30,938.

wych elm /wiCH/ (also **witch elm**) ▶*n.* a European elm with large rough leaves, chiefly growing in woodland or near flowing water. • *Ulmus glabra*, family Ulmaceae. ▷early 17th cent.: *wych*, used in names of trees with pliant branches, from Old English *wic(e)*, apparently from a Germanic root meaning 'bend'; related to WEAK.

Wych·er·ley /ˈwiCHərlē/, William (*c.*1640–1716), English playwright. His Restoration comedies are characterized by their acute examination of sexual morality and marriage conventions.

Wyc·lif /ˈwiklif/ (also **Wyc·liffe**), John (*c.*1330–84), English religious reformer. He criticized the wealth and power of the Church and upheld the Bible as the sole guide for doctrine; Wyclif instituted the first English translation of the complete Bible. His followers were known as Lollards.

Wye /wī/ a river that rises in the mountains of western Wales and flows southeast for about 132 miles (208 km) before entering the Severn estuary at Chepstow. In its lower reaches it forms part of the border between Wales and England.

wye /wī/ ▶*n.* a support or other structure shaped like a Y, in particular: ■ a triangle of railroad track, used for turning locomotives or trains. ■ (in plumbing) a short pipe with a branch joining it at an acute angle. ▷mid 19th cent.: the letter *Y* represented as a word.

Wy·eth /ˈwīəTH/, a U.S. family of artists, notably **N. C.** (1882–1944); full name *Newell Convers Wyeth*, whose many illustrations appeared in publications; his son **Andrew Newell** (1917–), whose paintings include *Christina's World* (1948) and the Helga series (1971–85); and his son **Jamie** (1946–), full name *James Browning Wyeth*, whose notable paintings include *Portrait of J.F.K.* (1965), *Wolfbane* (1984), and his series of portraits of Orca Bates.

Wy·ler /ˈwīlər/, William (1902–81), U.S. director; born in Germany. He is noted for his award-winning movies such as *Jezebel* (1938), *Mrs. Miniver* (Academy Award, 1941), *The Best Years of Our Lives* (1946), *Ben-Hur* (1959), and *Funny Girl* (1968).

wyn /win/ ▶*n.* variant spelling of WEN[2].

Wynd·ham /ˈwindəm/, John (1903–69), English writer of science fiction; pseudonym of *John Wyndham Parkes Lucas Beynon Harris.* Notable novels: *The Day of the Triffids* (1951), *The Chrysalids* (1955), and *The Midwich Cuckoos* (1957).

Wy·nette /wīˈnet/, Tammy (1942–98), U.S. country singer; born *Virginia Wynette Pugh.* Her unique lamenting voice brought her success with songs such as "Apartment No. 9" (1966) and "Stand by Your Man" (1968).

Wyo. ▶*abbr.* Wyoming.

Wy·o·ming /wīˈōmiNG/ **1** a state in the western central U.S.; pop. 493,782; capital, Cheyenne; statehood, July 10, 1890 (44). Acquired, in part, by the Louisiana Purchase in 1803, it gave the vote to women in 1869, the first state to do so. **2** a city in southwestern Michigan, southwest of Grand Rapids; pop. 69,368. **—Wy·o·ming·ite** /-miNG,īt/ *n.*

Wy·o·ming Val·ley a valley in northeastern Pennsylvania, along the Susquehanna River.

Wy·o·tan·a /,wīōˈtanə/ ▶*n. informal* a region consisting largely of mountain wilderness lying partly in southern Montana and partly in northern Wyoming. ▷blend of *Wyoming* and *Montana.*

WYSIWYG /ˈwizē,wig/ (also **wysiwyg**) ▶*adj. Computing* denoting the representation of text on screen in a form exactly corresponding to its appearance on a printout. ▷1980s: acronym from *what you see is what you get.*

wy·vern /ˈwīvərn/ ▶*n. Heraldry* a winged two-legged dragon with a barbed tail. ▷late Middle English (denoting a viper): from Old French *wivre*, from Latin *vipera.*

wyvern

X[1] /eks/ (also **x**) ▶*n.* (*pl.* **Xs** or **X's**) **1** the twenty-fourth letter of the alphabet. ■ denoting the next after W in a set of items, categories, etc. ■ denoting an unknown or unspecified person or thing: *there is nothing in the data to tell us whether X causes Y or Y causes X.* ■ (**x**) (used in describing play in bridge) denoting an unspecified card other than an honor. ■ (usu. ***x***) the first unknown quantity in an algebraic expression, usually the independent variable. [the introduction of *x*, *y*, and *z* as symbols of unknown quantities is due to Descartes (*Géométrie*, 1637), who took *z* as the first unknown and then proceeded backward in the alphabet.] ■ (usu. ***x***) denoting the principal or horizontal axis in a system of coordinates: [in *combination*] *the* ***x-axis***. **2** a cross-shaped written symbol, in particular: ■ used to indicate a position on a map or diagram. ■ used to indicate a mistake or incorrect answer. ■ used in a letter or message to symbolize a kiss. ■ used to indicate one's vote on a paper ballot. ■ used in place of the signature of a person who cannot write. **3** a shape like that of a letter X: *two wires in the form of an X* | [in *combination*] *an* ***X-shaped*** *cross.* **4** the Roman numeral for ten.
▶*v.* (**X's, X'd, X'ing**) [*trans.*] mark or make a sign with an X. ■ overwrite or obliterate with an X or series of X's. ■ make void or annul; invalidate: *we're all* ***X-ing*** *things* ***out*** *of our curricula.*

X[2] ▶*symbol* **1** a rating assigned to movies classified as suitable for adults only. Replaced in 1990 by **NC-17**. **2** (in systematic names of organisms) hybrid. [from **CROSS** *n.* 3.]

-x ▶*suffix* forming the plural of many nouns ending in *-u* taken from French: *tableaux.* ▷from French.

X-act·o knife /ig'zaktō/ ▶*n. trademark* a utility knife with a very sharp replaceable blade. ▷1940s: respelling of the adjective **EXACT** + **-O**.

Xan·a·du /'zanə,do͞o/ ▶*n.* (*pl.* **-dus**) used to convey an impression of a place as almost unattainably luxurious or beautiful: *three architects and a planner combine to create a Xanadu.* ▷alteration of *Shang-tu*, the name of an ancient city in southeastern Mongolia, as portrayed in Coleridge's poem *Kubla Khan* (1816).

Xan·ax /'zan,aks/ ▶*n.* trademark for **ALPRAZOLAM**.

Xan·kän·di /,ḵhänkan'dē/ the capital of Nagorno-Karabakh in southern Azerbaijan; pop. 58,000. Russian name **STEPANAKERT**.

xan·than gum /'zanTHən; -,THan/ ▶*n. Chemistry* a substance produced by bacterial fermentation or synthetically and used in foods as a gelling agent and thickener. It is a polysaccharide composed of glucose, mannose, and glucuronic acid. ▷1960s: from the modern Latin name of the bacterium *Xanthomonas campestris* + **-AN**.

xan·thene /'zan,THēn/ ▶*n. Chemistry* a yellowish crystalline compound whose molecule contains two benzene rings joined by a methylene group and an oxygen atom, and whose derivatives include brilliant, often fluorescent dyes such as fluorescein and rhodamines. • Chem. formula: $C_{13}H_{10}O$. ▷late 19th cent.: from Greek *xanthos* 'yellow' + **-ENE**.

xan·thic ac·id /'zanTHik/ ▶*n. Chemistry* an organic acid containing the group $-OCS_2H$, examples of which are typically reactive solids. ▷early 19th cent.: *xanthic* from Greek *xanthos* 'yellow' + **-IC**. —**xan·thate** /'zan,THāt/ *n.*

xan·thine /'zan,THēn; -THin/ ▶*n. Biochemistry* a crystalline compound that is found in blood and urine and is an intermediate in the metabolic breakdown of nucleic acids to uric acid. • A purine derivative; chem. formula: $C_5H_4N_4O_2$. ■ any of the derivatives of this, including caffeine and related alkaloids. ▷mid 19th cent.: from *xanthic* (from Greek *xanthos* 'yellow' + **-IC**) + **-INE**[4].

Xan·thip·pe /zan'tipē; -'THipē/ (also **Xan·tip·pe** /-'tipē/) (5th century BC), wife of Socrates. Her allegedly bad-tempered behavior toward her husband made her proverbial as a shrew.

xan·tho·ma /zan'THōmə/ ▶*n.* (*pl.* **-mas** or **-ma·ta** /-mətə/) *Medicine* an irregular yellow patch or nodule on the skin, caused by deposition of lipids. ▷mid 19th cent.: from Greek *xanthos* 'yellow' + **-OMA**.

xan·tho·phyll /'zanTHə,fil/ ▶*n. Biochemistry* a yellow or brown carotenoid plant pigment that causes the autumn colors of leaves. ▷mid 19th cent.: from Greek *xanthos* 'yellow' + *phullon* 'leaf.'

Xa·vi·er, St. Fran·cis /(ig)'zāvēər/ (1506–52), Spanish Catholic missionary; known as **the Apostle of the Indies**. One of the original seven Jesuits, from 1540 he traveled to southern India, Sri Lanka, Malacca, the Moluccas, and Japan where, he made thousands of converts. Feast day, December 3.

X chro·mo·some ▶*n. Genetics* (in humans and other mammals) a sex chromosome, two of which are normally present in female cells (designated XX) and only one in male cells (designated XY). Compare with **Y CHROMOSOME**.

xd ▶*abbr.* ex dividend.

Xe ▶*symbol* the chemical element xenon.

xe·bec /'zē,bek/ (also **ze·bec**) ▶*n. historical* a small three-masted Mediterranean sailing ship with lateen and sometimes square sails. ▷mid 18th cent.: alteration (influenced by Spanish *xabeque*) of French *chebec*, via Italian from Arabic *šabbāk*.

Xe·lo·da /zə'lōdə/ ▶*n.* trademark for **CAPECITABINE**.

Xe·na·kis /ze'näkēs/, Iannis (1922–), French composer and architect, of Greek descent. He is noted for his use of electronic and aleatory techniques in music.

Xe·nar·thra /zə'närTHrə/ *Zoology* an order of mammals that comprises the edentates. Also called **EDENTATA**. ▷modern Latin (plural), from **XENO-** 'strange' + Greek *arthron* 'joint' (because of the peculiar accessory articulations in the vertebrae). —**xe·nar·thran** *n.* & *adj.*

Xe·nia /'zēnyə/ a commercial and industrial city in southwestern Ohio; pop. 24,664.

xe·ni·a /'zēnēə; -nyə/ ▶*n. Botany* the influence or effect of pollen on the endosperm or embryo, resulting in hybrid characteristics in form, color, etc., of the derived seed.

Xen·i·cal /'zenikal/ ▶*n. trademark* a synthetic drug that blocks pancreatic enzymes used in the digestion of fats, used to treat obesity.

xeno- ▶*comb. form* relating to a foreigner or foreigners: *xenophobia.* ■ other; different in origin: *xenograft.* ▷from Greek *xenos* 'stranger, foreigner,' (adjective) 'strange.'

xen·o·bi·ot·ic /,zenəbī'ätik; ,zēnə-/ ▶*adj.* relating to or denoting a substance, typically a synthetic chemical, that is foreign to the body or to an ecological system.
▶*n.* (usu. **xenobiotics**) a substance of this kind.

xen·o·cryst /'zenə,krist; 'zēnə-/ ▶*n. Geology* a crystal in an igneous rock that is not derived from the original magma. ▷late 19th cent.: from **XENO-** 'foreign' + **CRYSTAL**.

xe·nog·a·my /zə'nägəmē/ ▶*n. Botany* fertilization of a flower by pollen from a flower on a genetically different plant. Compare with **GEITONOGAMY**. —**xe·nog·a·mous** /-məs/ *adj.*

xen·o·ge·ne·ic /,zenōjə'nē-ik; ,zēnō-/ ▶*adj. Immunology* denoting, relating to, or involving tissues or cells belonging to individuals of different species. Compare with **ALLOGENEIC**.

xen·o·graft /'zenə,graft; 'zēnə-/ ▶*n.* a tissue graft or organ transplant from a donor of a different species from the recipient.

xen·o·lith /'zenə,liTH; 'zēnə-/ ▶*n. Geology* a piece of rock within an igneous rock that is not derived from the original magma but has been introduced from elsewhere, esp. the surrounding country rock.

xen·ol·o·gy /zə'näləjē/ ▶*n.* (chiefly in science fiction) the scientific study of alien biology, cultures, etc. ▷1950s: from Greek *xenos* 'stranger, foreigner', (adjective) 'strange.' —**xen·ol·o·gist** *n.*

xe·non /'zē,nän; 'zen,än/ ▶*n.* the chemical element of atomic number 54, a member of the noble gas series. It is obtained by distillation of liquid air and is used in some specialized electric lamps. (Symbol: **Xe**) ▷late 19th cent.: from Greek, neuter of *xenos* 'strange.'

Xe·noph·a·nes /zə'näfə,nēz/ (*c.*570–*c.*480 BC), Greek philosopher. A member of the Eleatic school, he argued for a form of pantheism and criticized belief in anthropomorphic gods.

xen·o·phile /'zenə,fil; 'zē-/ ▶*n.* an individual who is attracted to foreign peoples, manners, or cultures.

xen·o·pho·bi·a /,zēnə'fōbēə; ,zenə-/ ▶*n.* intense or irrational dislike or fear of people from other countries: *racism and xenophobia are steadily growing in Europe.* —**xen·o·phobe** /'zēnə,fōb; 'zenə-/ *n.* —**xen·o·pho·bic** /-'fōbik/ *adj.*

Xen·o·phon /'zenə,fän/ (*c.*435–*c.*354 BC), Greek historian, writer, and military leader. From 401, he fought with Cyrus the Younger against Artaxerxes II. The campaign and retreat are recorded in the *Anabasis*. Other notable writings include the *Hellenica*, a history of Greece.

Xe·no·pus /'zenəpəs/ ▶*n.* the African clawed toad, much used in embryological research and formerly in pregnancy testing, as it produces eggs in response to substances in the urine of a pregnant woman. • *Xenopus laevis*, family Pipidae. ▷late 19th cent.: modern Latin, from **XENO-** 'strange' + Greek *pous* 'foot.'

xen·o·time /'zenə,tīm; 'zēnə-/ ▶*n.* a yellowish-brown mineral that occurs in some igneous rocks and consists of a phosphate of yttrium and other rare-earth elements. ▷mid 19th cent.: from **XENO-**, apparently erroneously for Greek *kenos* 'vain, empty,' + *timē* 'honor' (because it was wrongly supposed to contain a new metal).

xen·o·trans·plan·ta·tion /,zenə,transplan'tāSHən; ,zēnə-/ ▶*n.* the process of grafting or transplanting organs or tissues between members of different species. —**xen·o·trans·plant** /-'trans,plant/ *n.*

X·er /'eksər/ ▶*n.* another term for **GEN-XER**. ▷shortening.

xe·ric /'zi(ə)rik; 'zer-/ ▶*adj. Ecology* (of an environment or habitat) containing little moisture; very dry. Compare with **HYDRIC** and **MESIC**[1]. ▷1920s: from **XERO-** 'dry' + **-IC**.

xe·ri·scape /'zi(ə)rə,skāp; 'zerə-/ ▶*n.* a style of landscape design requiring little or no irrigation or other maintenance, used in arid regions. ■ a garden or landscape created in such a style.
▶*v.* [*trans.*] landscape (an area) in such a style. ▷1980s: from **XERIC** + **-SCAPE**.

xero- ▶*comb. form* dry: *xeroderma* | *xerophyte.* ▷from Greek *xēros* 'dry.'

xe·ro·der·ma /,zi(ə)rə'dərmə/ ▶*n.* any of various diseases characterized by extreme dryness of the skin,

Pronunciation Key ə *ago*; ər *over*; 'ə *or* ,ə *up*; 'ər *or* ,ər *fur*; a *hat*; ā *rate*; ä *car*; CH *chew*; e *let*; ē *see*; e(ə)r *air*; i *fit*; ī *by*; i(ə)r *ear*; NG *sing*; ō *go*; ô *for*; oi *boy*; o͝o *good*; o͞o *goo*; ou *out*; SH *she*; TH *thin*; TH *then*; (h)w *why*; ZH *vision*

esp. a mild form of ichthyosis. ▷mid 19th cent.: modern Latin, from **XERO-** 'dry' + Greek *derma* 'skin.'

xe·ro·der·ma pig·men·to·sum /ˌpigmənˈtōsəm; -men-/ ▸*n.* a rare hereditary defect of the enzyme system that repairs DNA after damage from ultraviolet rays, resulting in extreme sensitivity to sunlight and a tendency to develop skin cancer. ▷late 19th cent.: *pigmentosum*, neuter of Latin *pigmentosus* 'pigmented.'

xe·rog·ra·phy /ziˈrägrəfē/ ▸*n.* a dry copying process in which black or colored powder adheres to parts of a surface remaining electrically charged after being exposed to light from an image of the document to be copied. **—xe·ro·graph·ic** /ˌzi(ə)rəˈgrafik/ *adj.* **—xe·ro·graph·i·cal·ly** *adv.*

xe·roph·i·lous /ziˈräfələs/ ▸*adj. Botany & Zoology* (of a plant or animal) adapted to a very dry climate or habitat, or to conditions where moisture is scarce. **—xer·o·phile** /ˈzi(ə)rəˌfīl/ *n.*

xe·roph·thal·mi·a /ˌzi(ə)räfˈTHalmēə; ˌzi(ə)räp-/ ▸*n. Medicine* abnormal dryness of the conjunctiva and cornea of the eye, with inflammation and ridge formation, typically associated with vitamin A deficiency.

xe·ro·phyte /ˈzi(ə)rəˌfīt/ ▸*n. Botany* a plant that needs very little water. **—xe·ro·phyt·ic** /ˌzi(ə)rəfitik/ *adj.*

Xerox /ˈzi(ə)rˌäks/ ▸*n. trademark* a xerographic copying process. ■ a copy made using such a process. ■ a machine for copying by xerography.
▸*v.* (**xerox**) [*trans.*] copy (a document) by such a process. ▷1950s: an invented name, based on **XEROGRAPHY**.

Xerx·es I /ˈzərkˌsēz/ (*c.*519–465 BC), son of Darius I; king of Persia 486–465. He continued his father's attack on the Greeks but was forced to withdraw after defeats at Salamis in 480 and Plataea in 479.

x-height ▸*n.* the height of a lower-case x, considered characteristic of a given typeface or script.

Xho·sa /ˈkōsə; ˈkô-; ˈKHō-; ˈKHô-/ ▸*n.* (*pl.* same or **-sas**) **1** a member of a South African people traditionally living in the Eastern Cape Province. They form the second largest ethnic group in South Africa after the Zulus. **2** the Nguni language of this people.
▸*adj.* of or relating to this people or their language. ▷from the stem of Xhosa *umXhosa* (plural *amaXhosa*).

XHTML ▸*abbr. Computing* Extensible Hypertext Markup Language, an HTML system for tagging text files to achieve font, color, graphic, and hyperlink effects on World Wide Web pages, incorporating user-defined elements.

xi /zī; ksī/ ▸*n.* the fourteenth letter of the Greek alphabet (Ξ, ξ), transliterated as 'x.' ■ (**Xi**) [followed by Latin genitive] *Astronomy* the fourteenth star in a specified constellation: *Xi Cygni.*

Xia·men /ˈSH(y)äˈmən/ (also **Hsia-men**) a port in Fujian province, in southeastern China; pop. 639,000. Also called **AMOY**.

Xi·an /ˈSHēˈän/ (also **Hsi·an**) an industrial city in central China, capital of Shaanxi province; pop. 2,710,000. The city has been inhabited since the 11th century BC, having previously been the capital of the Han, Sui, and Tang dynasties. Former names **CHANGAN, SIKING**.

Xi·ang /SHēˈäNG/ (also **Hsi·ang**) ▸*n.* a dialect of Chinese spoken by about 36 million people, mainly in Hunan province.

Xing·tai /ˈSHiNGˈtī/ a city in northeastern China, south of Shijiazhuang, in the province of Hebei; pop. 1,167,000.

Xin·gú /SHiNGˈgōō/ a South American river that rises in the Mato Grosso of western Brazil and flows north for about 1,230 miles (1,979 km) to join the Amazon delta.

Xi·ning /ˈSHēˈniNG/ (also **Hsi·ning**) a city in northern central China, capital of Qinghai province; pop. 698,000.

Xin·jiang /ˈSHinjēˈäNG/ an autonomous region in northwestern China, on the border with Mongolia and Kazakhstan; pop. 15,170,000; capital, Urumqi. A remote mountainous region, it includes the Tien Shan and Kunlun Shan mountains, the Taklimakan Desert, and the arid Tarim Basin.

-xion ▸*suffix* forming nouns such as *fluxion*. ▷from Latin participial stems (see also **-ION**).

xiph·i·ster·num /ˌzifəˈstərnəm/ ▸*n. Anatomy* the lowest part of the sternum; the xiphoid process. ▷mid 19th cent.: from Greek *xiphos* 'sword' + **STERNUM**.

xiph·oid proc·ess (also **xiph·oid car·ti·lage**) ▸*n. Anatomy* the cartilaginous section at the lower end of the sternum, which is not attached to any ribs and gradually ossifies during adult life. ▷mid 18th cent. (as *xiphoid cartilage*): *xiphoid* from Greek *xiphoeidēs*, from *xiphos* 'sword.'

X-ir·ra·di·a·tion ▸*n.* irradiation with X-rays.

Xi·zang /ˈSHēˈdzäNG/ Chinese name for **TIBET**.

XL ▸*abbr.* extra large (as a clothes size).

Xmas /ˈkrisməs; ˈeksməs/ ▸*n.* informal term for **CHRISTMAS**. ▷X representing the initial chi of Greek *Khristos* 'Christ.'

XML ▸*abbr.* Extensible Markup Language, a metalanguage that allows users to define their own customized markup languages, especially in order to display documents on the World Wide Web.

XMS ▸*abbr.* extended memory system, a system for increasing the amount of memory available to a personal computer.

XO ▸*abbr. Military* executive officer.

XOR ▸*n.* another term for **EXCLUSIVE OR**.

x-ra·di·a·tion ▸*n.* treatment with or exposure to X-rays. ■ radiation in the form of X-rays.

X-rat·ed /ˈeks ˌrātid/ ▸*adj.* pornographic or indecent: *there was some X-rated humor.* ■ (of a movie) given an X classification (see **X**[2]).

X-ray /ˈeks ˌrā/ (also **x-ray** or **X ray**) ▸*n.* **1** electromagnetic radiation of high energy and very short wavelength (between ultraviolet light and gamma rays) that is able to pass through many materials opaque to light. ■ [as *adj.*] *informal* denoting an apparent or supposed faculty for seeing beyond an outward form: *you didn't need X-ray eyes to know what was going on.* **2** a photographic or digital image of the internal composition of something, esp. a part of the body, produced by X-rays being passed through it and being absorbed to different degrees by different materials. ■ an act of photographing someone or something in this way: *he will have an X-ray today | would you send her for X-ray?* **3** a code word representing the letter X, used in radio communication.
▸*v.* [*trans.*] photograph or examine with X-rays: *luggage bound for the hold is X-rayed.* ▷translation of German *X-Strahlen* (plural), from *X-* (because, when discovered in 1895, the nature of the rays was unknown) + *Strahl* 'ray.'

X-ray as·tron·o·my ▸*n.* the branch of astronomy concerned with the detection and measurement of high-energy electromagnetic radiation emitted by celestial objects.

X-ray crys·tal·log·ra·phy ▸*n.* the study of crystals and their structure by means of X-ray diffraction.

X-ray dif·frac·tion ▸*n.* the scattering of X-rays by the regularly spaced atoms of a crystal, useful in obtaining information about the structure of the crystal.

X-ray fish ▸*n.* a small almost transparent freshwater fish with an opaque body cavity. Native to South America, it is popular in aquariums. • *Pristella riddlei*, family Characidae.

X-ray mi·cro·scope ▸*n.* an instrument that uses X-rays to produce a magnified image.

X-ray tel·e·scope ▸*n.* a telescope designed to detect sources of X-rays.

X-ray ther·a·py ▸*n.* medical treatment of a disease using controlled doses of X-rays.

X-ray tube ▸*n. Physics* a device for generating X-rays by accelerating electrons to high energies and causing them to strike a metal target from which the X-rays are emitted.

xu /sōō/ ▸*n.* (*pl.* same) a monetary unit of Vietnam, equal to one hundredth of a dong. ▷Vietnamese, from French *sou*.

Xu·zhou /ˈSHōōˈjō/ (also **Hsu-chou** /ˈSHōōˈjō/) a city in Jiangsu province, in eastern China; pop. 910,000. Former name (1912–45) **TONGSHAN**.

XXL ▸*abbr.* extra extra large (as a clothes size).

xy·lan /ˈzīlan; -lən/ ▸*n.* a polysaccharide found in plant cell walls that hydrolyzes to xylose.

xy·lem /ˈzīləm/ ▸*n. Botany* the vascular tissue in plants that conducts water and dissolved nutrients upward from the root and also helps to form the woody element in the stem. Compare with **PHLOEM**. ▷late 19th cent.: from Greek *xulon* 'wood' + the passive suffix *-ēma*.

xy·lene /ˈzīˌlēn/ ▸*n. Chemistry* a volatile liquid hydrocarbon obtained by distilling wood, coal tar, or petroleum, and used in fuels and solvents, and in chemical synthesis. • Alternative name: **dimethylbenzene**; chem. formula: $C_6H_4(CH_3)_2$; three isomers. ▷mid 19th cent.: from **XYLO-** 'of wood' + **-ENE**.

xy·li·dine /ˈzīliˌdēn; -din; ˈzili-/ ▸*n.* any one of six isomeric compounds that are derived from xylene and used in the manufacture of dyes. • Chem. formula: $(CH_3)_2C_6H_3NH_2$ ■ a mixture of xylidine isomers in the form of an oily liquid.

xy·li·tol /ˈzīləˌtôl; -ˌtäl/ ▸*n. Chemistry* a sweet-tasting crystalline alcohol derived from xylose, present in some plant tissues and used as an artificial sweetener in foods. • Chem. formula: $CH_2OH(CHOH)_3CH_2OH$. ▷late 19th cent.: from **XYLOSE** + **-ITE**[1] + **-OL**.

xylo- ▸*comb. form* of or relating to wood: *xylophagous | xylophone.* ▷from Greek *xulon* 'wood.'

xy·log·ra·phy /zīˈlägrəfē/ ▸*n. rare* the art of making woodcuts or wood engravings, esp. by a relatively primitive technique. **—xy·lo·graph·ic** /ˌzīləˈgrafik/ *adj.*

xy·loph·a·gous /zīˈläfəgəs/ ▸*adj. Zoology* (esp. of an insect larva or mollusk) feeding on or boring into wood.

xy·lo·phone /ˈzīləˌfōn/ ▸*n.* a musical instrument played by striking a row of wooden bars of graduated length with one or more small wooden or plastic mallets. ▷mid 19th cent.: from **XYLO-** 'of wood' + **-PHONE**. **—xy·lo·phon·ic** /ˌzīləˈfänik/ *adj.* **—xy·lo·phon·ist** /ˈzīləˌfōnist/ *n.*

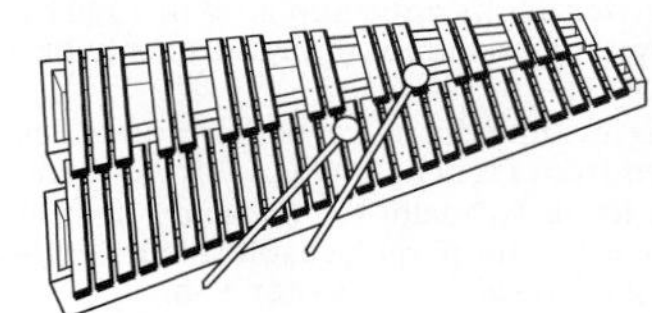

xylophone

xy·lose /ˈzīˌlōs; -ˌlōz/ ▸*n. Chemistry* a sugar of the pentose class that occurs widely in plants, esp. as a component of hemicelluloses.

XYZ Af·fair an incident in Franco-American relations in which a bribery attempt perpetrated by French agents in 1797 led the U.S. to the brink of formal war with France.

In 1797, President John Adams sent delegates Elbridge Gerry, John Marshall, and Charles Cotesworth Pinckney to France in order to negotiate a peaceful resolution of problems that existed between the two nations. The U.S. delegates were informed by three French agents that negotiations could not begin until the U.S. granted a $10 million loan to the French government and paid $250,000 to French foreign minister Talleyrand. The U.S. delegation refused the French demands and negotiations were suspended. In 1798, the delegation's dispatches regarding the incident were made public. These documents, in which the French agents were identified only as X, Y, and Z, incited American outrage and precipitated an undeclared naval war (1798–1800) between the U.S. and France. A treaty in 1800 finally averted a major war.

Yy

Y1 /wī/ (also **y**) ▸*n.* (*pl.* **Ys** or **Y's**) **1** the twenty-fifth letter of the alphabet. ■ denoting the next after X in a set of items, categories, etc. ■ denoting a second unknown or unspecified person or thing: *the claim that chemical X causes birth defect Y.* ■ (usu. ***y***) the second unknown quantity in an algebraic expression, usually the dependent variable. [the introduction of *x*, *y*, and *z* as symbols of unknown quantities is due to Descartes (see **X**1).] ■ (usu. ***y***) denoting the secondary or vertical axis in a system of coordinates: [in *combination*] *the* y*-axis.* **2** (**Y**) a shape like that of a capital Y: [in *combination*] *rows of tiny* ***Y-shaped*** *motifs.*

Y2 ▸*abbr.* ■ yen: *Y140.* ■ *informal* a YMCA, YWCA, YMHA, or YWHA facility: *Scott was living at the Y.*
▸*symbol* the chemical element yttrium.

y ▸*abbr.* year(s): *orbital period (Pluto): 248.5y.*

-y1 /ē/ ▸*suffix* forming adjectives: **1** (from nouns and adjectives) full of; having the quality of: *messy* | *milky* | *mousy.* ■ with depreciatory reference: *boozy* | *tinny.* **2** (from verbs) inclined to; apt to: *sticky.* ▷Old English *-ig*, of Germanic origin.

-y2 (also **-ey** or **-ie**) ▸*suffix* forming diminutive nouns and adjectives, nicknames, hypocoristics, etc.: *aunty* | *Tommy* | *nightie.* ■ forming verbs: *shinny.* ▷Middle English: originally Scots.

-y3 ▸*suffix* forming nouns: **1** denoting a state, condition, or quality: *glory* | *jealousy* | *orthodoxy.* **2** denoting an action or its result: *blasphemy* | *victory.* ▷from French *-ie*, from Latin *-ia*, *-ium*, or Greek *-eia*, *-ia*.

Y2K ▸ *abbr.* the year 2000.

ya /yə/ ▸*pron. & possessive adj.* nonstandard spelling of **YOU** or **YOUR**, used to represent informal pronunciation: *see ya later.*

yab·ber /ˈyabər/ ▸*v.* [*intrans.*] *informal* chatter. ▷probably from Wuywurung (an Aboriginal language).

YAC ▸*abbr. Biology* yeast artificial chromosome.

yacht /yät/ ▸*n.* a medium-sized sailboat equipped for cruising or racing. ■ [with *adj.*] a powered boat or small ship equipped for cruising, typically for private or official use: *a steam yacht.*
▸*v.* [*intrans.*] race or cruise in a yacht. ▷mid 16th cent.: from early modern Dutch *jaghte*, from *jaghtschip* 'fast pirate ship,' from *jag(h)t* 'hunting' + *schip* 'ship.'

yacht·ing /ˈyätiNG/ ▸*n.* the sport or pastime of racing or sailing in yachts.

yachts·man /ˈyätsmən/ ▸*n.* (*pl.* **-men**) a man who sails yachts.

yachts·wom·an /ˈyätsˌwo͝omən/ ▸*n.* (*pl.* **-wom·en**) a woman who sails yachts.

yack /yak/ ▸*n.* & *v.* variant spelling of **YAK**2.

yack·e·ty-yak /ˈyakətē ˈyak/ (also **yack·et·y-yack**) ▸*n.* & *v.* another term for **YAK**2. ▷1950s: imitative.

yad·da yad·da yad·da /ˈyädə ˈyädə ˈyädə/ *informal* ▸used as a substitute in written and spoken contexts for actual words where they are too lengthy or tedious to recite in full: *boy meets girl, boy loses girl, yadda yadda yadda.*

Yad·kin Riv·er /ˈyadkin/ a river that flows for 200 miles (320 km) through western North Carolina to join the Uwharrie River to form the Pee Dee River.

Ya·fo /ˈyäfō/ Hebrew name for **JAFFA**.

YAG /yag/ ▸*n.* a synthetic crystal of yttrium aluminum garnet, used in certain lasers and as an imitation diamond in jewelry. ▷1960s: acronym from *yttrium aluminum garnet.*

ya·gé /ˈyäˌZHā ˈyäˌhā/ ▸*n.* another term for **AYAHUASCA**. ▷1920s: from American Spanish.

Ya·gi an·ten·na /ˈyägē; ˈyagē/ ▸*n.* a highly directional radio antenna made of several short rods mounted across an insulating support and transmitting or receiving a narrow band of frequencies. ▷1940s: named after Hidetsugu *Yagi* (1886–1976), Japanese engineer.

yag·na ▸*n.* variant spelling of **YAJNA**.

yah /yä/ ▸*n. Brit. informal* an upper-class person: *the cafe is full of yahs whose daddies own chateaux in France.*

yah /yä; ya/ ▸*exclam.* expressing derision: *yah, you missed!* ▷natural exclamation: first recorded in English in the early 17th cent.

ya·hoo1 /ˈyäˌho͞o; yäˈho͞o/ ▸*n. informal* a rude, noisy, or violent person. ▷mid 18th cent.: from the name of an imaginary race of brutish creatures in Swift's *Gulliver's Travels* (1726).

ya·hoo2 /yäˈho͞o/ ▸*exclam.* expressing great joy or excitement: *yahoo—my plan worked!* ▷natural exclamation: first recorded in English in the 1970s.

yahr·zeit /ˈyärˌtsīt; ˈyôr-/ ▸*n.* (among Jews) the anniversary of someone's death, esp. a parent's. ▷mid 19th cent.: Yiddish, literally 'anniversary time.'

Yah·weh /ˈyäˌwā; -ˌwe; -ˌvā/ (also **Yah·veh** /-ˌvā; -ˌve/) ▸*n.* a form of the Hebrew name of God used in the Bible. The name came to be regarded by Jews (*c.*300 BC) as too sacred to be spoken, and the vowel sounds are uncertain. ▷from Hebrew *YHWH* with added vowels; compare with **JEHOVAH**, **YHVH**.

Yah·wist /ˈyäwist; -vist/ (also **Yah·vist** /-vist/) ▸*n.* the postulated author or authors of parts of the first six books of the Bible, in which God is regularly named *Yahweh.* Compare with **ELOHIST**.

yaj·na /ˈyəgnə; -nyə/ (also **yag·na**) ▸*n. Hinduism* a ritual sacrifice with a specific objective. ▷from Sanskrit *yajña* 'worship, sacrifice.'

Yaj·ur Ve·da /ˈyəjo͝or ˈvādə; ˈvēdə/ *Hinduism* one of the four Vedas, based on a collection of sacrificial formulae in early Sanskrit used in the Vedic religion by the priest in charge of sacrificial ritual. ▷from Sanskrit *yajus* 'sacrificial formula' and **VEDA**.

yak1 /yak/ ▸*n.* a large domesticated wild ox with shaggy hair, humped shoulders, and large horns, used in Tibet as a pack animal and for its milk, meat, and hide. • Genus *Bos*, family Bovidae; the domesticated *B. grunniens*, descended from the wild *B. mutus*, which rarely is still found at high altitude. ▷late 18th cent.: from Tibetan *gyag.*

yak1

yak2 (also **yack** or **yack·et·y-yak**) *informal* ▸*n.* [in *sing.*] a trivial or unduly persistent conversation.
▸*v.* (**yakked**, **yak·king**) [*intrans.*] talk at length about trivial or boring subjects. ▷1950s: imitative.

Yak·i·ma1 /ˈyakəmə; -ˌmô/ a commercial and industrial city in south central Washington; pop. 71,845.

Yak·i·ma2 ▸*n.* (*pl.* same or **-mas**) **1** a member of a North American Indian people of south central Washington. **2** the Sahaptin dialect of this people.
▸*adj.* of or relating to this people or their language. ▷unknown, but possibly from a Salish language.

ya·ki·to·ri /ˌyäkiˈtôrē/ ▸*n.* a Japanese dish of chicken pieces grilled on a skewer. ▷Japanese, from *yaki* 'grilling, toasting' + *tori* 'bird.'

Ya·kut /yəˈko͞ot/ ▸*n.* (*pl.* same or **-kuts**) **1** a member of an indigenous people living in scattered settlements in northern Siberia. **2** the Turkic language of this people.
▸*adj.* of or relating to this people or their language. ▷via Russian from Yakut.

Ya·ku·tia /yəˈko͞oSH(ē)ə/ an autonomous republic in eastern Russia; pop. 1,081,000; capital, Yakutsk. It is the coldest inhabited region in the world, with 40 percent of its territory lying north of the Arctic Circle. Official name **SAKHA, REPUBLIC OF**.

Ya·kutsk /yəˈko͞otsk/ a city in eastern Russia, on the Lena River, capital of the republic of Yakutia; pop. 187,000.

ya·ku·za /yäˈko͞ozə; ˈyäko͞oˌzä/ ▸*n.* (*pl.* same) a Japanese gangster or racketeer. ■ a Japanese organized crime syndicate similar to the Mafia. ▷Japanese, from *ya* 'eight' + *ku* 'nine' + *za* 'three,' referring to the worst hand in a gambling game.

Yale1 /yāl/, Elihu (1649–1721), English colonial administrator. He was a large benefactor of the Collegiate School in Saybrook, Connecticut, which was named Yale College in his honor in 1718, after its move to New Haven.

Yale2, Linus, Jr. (1821–68), U.S. inventor and manufacturer. He invented the pin tumbler cylinder lock and the combination lock. In 1868, he cofounded the Yale Lock Manufacturing Company.

Yale3 (also **Yale lock**) ▸*n.* [often as *adj.*] *trademark* a type of lock with a latch bolt and a flat key with a serrated edge. ▷mid 19th cent.: named after Linus *Yale*, Jr., who invented the mechanism it uses.

Yale U·ni·ver·si·ty an Ivy League university in New Haven, Connecticut, founded in 1701.

Yal·ie /ˈyālē/ ▸*n.* (*pl.* **-ies**) *informal* a student or graduate of Yale University.

y'all /yôl/ ▸*contraction of* you-all.

Yal·ta Con·fer·ence /ˈyôltə; ˈyäl-/ a meeting between the Allied leaders Churchill, Roosevelt, and Stalin in February 1945 at Yalta, a Crimean port on the Black Sea. The leaders planned the final stages of World War II and agreed on the subsequent territorial division of Europe.

Ya·lu /ˈyäˌlo͞o/ a river in eastern Asia that rises in the mountains of Jilin province in northeastern China and flows southwest for about 500 miles (800 km) to the Yellow Sea. It forms most of the border between China and North Korea. In November 1950, the advance of UN troops toward the Yalu River precipitated the Chinese invasion of North Korea.

yam /yam/ ▸*n.* **1** the edible starchy tuber of a climbing plant, widely distributed in tropical and subtropical countries. **2** the plant that yields this tuber. • Genus *Dioscorea*, family Dioscoreaceae: many species. **3** a sweet potato. ▷late 16th cent.: from Portuguese *inhame* or obsolete Spanish *iñame*, probably of West African origin.

Ya·ma /ˈyəmə; ˈyämə/ (in Hindu legend) the first man to die. He became the guardian, judge, and ruler of the dead, and is represented as carrying a noose and riding a buffalo. ▷from Sanskrit *yama* 'restraint' (from *yam* 'restrain').

Ya·ma·mo·to /ˌyäməˈmōtō/, Isoroku (1884–1943), Japanese admiral. As commander in chief of the combined fleet (air and naval forces) from 1939, he was responsible for planning the Japanese attack on Pearl Harbor in 1941.

Ya·ma·sa·ki /ˌyäməˈsäkē/, Minoru (1912–86), U.S. architect. He designed the barrel-vaulted St. Louis

Pronunciation Key ə *ago*; ər *over*; ˈə *or* ˌə *up*; ˈər *or* ˌər *fur*; a *hat*; ā *rate*; ä *car*; CH *chew*; e *let*; ē *see*; e(ə)r *air*; i *fit*; ī *by*; i(ə)r *ear*; NG *sing*; ō *go*; ô *for*; oi *boy*; o͝o *good*; o͞o *goo*; ou *out*; SH *she*; TH *thin*; TH *then*; (h)w *why*; ZH *vision*

Municipal Airport terminal in 1956 and the World Trade Center in New York in 1972.

Ya·ma·to-e /yä'mätō ˌā/ ▶*n.* a style of decorative painting in Japan during the 12th and early 13th centuries, characterized by strong color and flowing lines. ▷Japanese, from *Yamato* 'Japan' + *e* 'picture.'

ya·men /'yämən/ ▶*n. informal* the office or residence of a public official in the Chinese Empire.

yam·mer /'yamər/ ▶*n. informal* or *dialect* loud and sustained or repetitive noise: *the yammer of their animated conversation* | *the yammer of enemy fire.*
▶*v.* [*intrans.*] *informal* or *dialect* make a loud repetitive noise. ■ talk volubly. ▷late Middle English (as a verb meaning 'lament, cry out'): alteration of earlier *yomer* (from Old English *geōmrian* 'to lament') suggested by Middle Dutch *jammeren.* **—yam·mer·er** *n.*

Ya·mous·sou·kro /ˌyäməˈsōōkrō/ the capital of the Ivory Coast; pop. 120,000. It replaced Abidjan as the capital in 1983.

yam·pa /'yampə/ ▶*n.* a wild plant of the parsley family, native to central and western North America, that has an edible root. It has clusters of small white flowers somewhat resembling Queen Anne's lace. • *Perideridia gairdneri*, family Umbelliferae.

Yam·pa Riv·er /'yampə/ a river that flows for 250 miles (400 km) across northwestern Colorado to join the Green River.

yam·pee /'yampē/ ▶*n.* another term for **CUSH-CUSH**.

Ya·mu·na /'yəmōōnə/ Hindi name for **JUMNA**.

Yan·cheng /'yan'CHəNG/ (also **Yen-cheng** /'yen-/) a city in Jiangsu province, in eastern China; pop. 380,000.

yang /yaNG; yäNG/ ▶*n.* (in Chinese philosophy) the active male principle of the universe, characterized as male and creative and associated with heaven, heat, and light. Contrasted with **YIN**. ▷from Chinese *yáng* 'male genitals,' 'sun,' 'positive.'

Yan·gon /ˌyäNG'gōn/ Burmese name for **RANGOON**.

Yang·tze /'yaNG'(t)sē/ the principal river in China. It rises as the Jinsha in the Tibetan highlands and flows south and then east for 3,964 miles (6,380 km) through central China before it enters the East China Sea at Shanghai. Also called **CHANG JIANG**.

Yank /yaNGk/ ▶*n.* another term for **YANKEE** (senses 1 and 2).

yank /yaNGk/ *informal* ▶*v.* [*trans.*] pull with a jerk: *her hair was yanked, and she screamed* | [*trans.*] *he yanked her to her feet* | [*intrans.*] *Liz* **yanked at** *her arm.*
▶*n.* [in *sing.*] a sudden hard pull: *one of the other girls gave her ponytail a yank.* ▷late 18th cent. (as a Scots word in the sense 'sudden sharp blow'): of unknown origin.

Yan·kee /'yaNGkē/ ▶*n. informal* **1** *often derogatory* a person who lives in, or is from, the U.S. **2** an inhabitant of New England or one of the northern states. ■ *historical* a Union soldier in the Civil War. **3** a code word representing the letter Y, used in radio communication. **4** (also **Yan·kee jib**) *Sailing* a large jib set forward of a staysail in light winds. **5** a bet on four or more horses to win (or be placed) in different races. ▷mid 18th cent.: origin uncertain; recorded in the late 17th cent. as a nickname; perhaps from Dutch *Janke*, diminutive of *Jan* 'John.'

Yan·kee Doo·dle /'dōōdl/ ▶*n.* **1** (also **Yan·kee Doo·dle Dan·dy**) a song popular during the American Revolution. Informally regarded as a national song, it is the official state song of Connecticut. **2** *Brit.* another term for **YANKEE** (senses 1 and 2).

Yank·ton /'yaNGktən/ ▶*n.* (*pl.* same or **-tons**) **1** a member of an American Indian people of the Great Plains of North and South Dakota. **2** the Siouan language of this people.
▶*adj.* of or relating to this people or their language. ▷from Sioux *ihą̃kthų̃wą̃*, literally 'those dwelling at the end.'

Yank·to·nai /ˌyaNGktə'nī/ ▶*n.* a Sioux people now living in the Dakotas and eastern Montana, formerly living in northern Minnesota. ■ a member of this people.

Y

Ya·no·ma·mi /ˌyänə'mämē/ (also **Ya·no·ma·mö** /-'mämō/) ▶*n.* (*pl.* same) **1** a member of a native people living mainly in the forests of southern Venezuela and northern Brazil. **2** either of the two related languages of this people.
▶*adj.* of or relating to this people or their language. ▷the name in Yanomami, literally 'people.'

Yan·qui ▶*n.* variant spelling of **YANKEE**, typically used in Latin American contexts.

Yan·tai /'yan'tī/ (also **Yen-tai** /'yen-/) a port in eastern China, on the Yellow Sea, in Shandong province; pop. 3,204,600. Former name (3rd century BC–15th century) **CHEFOO**.

yan·tra /'yəntrə; 'yan-; 'yän-/ ▶*n.* a geometric diagram, or any object, used as an aid to meditation in tantric worship. ▷Sanskrit, literally 'device for holding or fastening.'

Yao /you/ ▶*n.* (*pl.* same) **1** a member of a mountain-dwelling people of southern China. **2** the language of this people.
▶*adj.* of or relating to this people or their language. ▷from Chinese *Yáo*, literally 'precious jade.'

Ya·oun·dé /ˌyoun'dā/ the capital of Cameroon; pop. 800,000.

yap /yap/ ▶*v.* (**yapped**, **yap·ping**) [*intrans.*] give a sharp, shrill bark: *the dachshunds yapped at his heels.* ■ *informal* talk at length in an irritating manner.
▶*n.* **1** a sharp, shrill bark. **2** *informal* a person's mouth (used in expressions to do with speaking): *shut your yap.* ■ loud, irritating talk: *she'll give you a lot of yap.* ▷early 17th cent. (denoting a dog that yaps): imitative. **—yap·per** *n.*

ya·pok /yə'päk/ (also **ya·pock**) ▶*n.* a semiaquatic carnivorous opossum with dark-banded gray fur and webbed hind feet, native to tropical America. Also called **WATER OPOSSUM**. • *Chironectes minimus*, family Didelphidae. ▷early 19th cent.: from *Oyapock*, the name of a northern Brazilian river.

yapp /yap/ ▶*n. Brit.* a form of bookbinding with a limp leather cover projecting to fold over the edges of the leaves, typically used for bibles. ▷late 19th cent.: named after William *Yapp*, a London bookseller, for whom this style of binding was first made (*c.*1860).

yap·py /'yapē/ ▶*adj.* (**-pi·er**, **-pi·est**) *informal* (of a dog) inclined to bark in a sharp, shrill way. ■ inclined to talk foolishly or at length.

Ya·qui /'yäkē/ ▶*n.* (*pl.* same or **-quis**) **1** a member of an American Indian people of northwestern Mexico and Arizona. **2** the Uto-Aztecan language of this people.
▶*adj.* of or relating to this people or their language. ▷Spanish, from earlier *Hiaquis*, from Yaqui *Hiaki.*

yar·ak /'yarˌak/ ▶*n.* (in phrase **in yarak**) (of a trained hawk) fit and in a proper condition for hunting. ▷mid 19th cent.: perhaps from Persian *yārakī* 'strength, ability' or from Turkish *yarağ* 'readiness.'

yar·bor·ough /'yärˌb(ə)rə; -ˌbərō/ ▶*n.* (in bridge or whist) a hand with no card above a nine. ▷early 20th cent.: named after the Earl of *Yarborough* (died 1897), said to have bet 1000 to 1 against its occurrence.

yard[1] /yärd/ ▶*n.* **1** (abbr.: **yd.**) a unit of linear measure equal to 3 feet (0.9144 meter). ■ (**yards of**) *informal* a great length: *yards and yards of fine lace.* ■ a square or cubic yard, esp. of sand or other building materials. ■ a cloth measure, of three feet in length and varying widths. **2** a cylindrical spar, tapering to each end, slung across a ship's mast for a sail to hang from. **3** *informal* one hundred dollars; a one hundred dollar bill. ▷Old English *gerd* (in sense 2); related to Dutch *gard* 'twig, rod' and German *Gerte.*
▶*PHRASE* □ **by the yard** in large numbers or quantities: *golf continues to inspire books by the yard.*

yard[2] ▶*n.* a piece of ground adjoining a building or house. ■ an area of ground surrounded by walls or buildings. ■ an area of land used for a particular purpose or business: *a storage yard.* ■ an area where deer or moose gather as a herd for the winter.
▶*v.* **1** [*trans.*] store or transport (timber) in or to a log yard. **2** [*intrans.*] (of deer or moose) gather as a herd for the winter. ▷Old English *geard* 'building, home, region,' from a Germanic base related to Russian *gorod* 'town.' Compare with **GARDEN** and **ORCHARD**.
▶*PHRASE* □ **the Yard** *Brit.* informal term for **SCOTLAND YARD**.

yard·age /'yärdij/ ▶*n.* **1** a distance or length measured in yards: *the caddie was working out yardages from tee to green.* ■ *Football* the distance covered in advancing the ball. **2** *archaic* the use of a yard for storage or the keeping of animals or payment for such use.

yar·dang /'yärˌdäNG; -ˌdaNG/ ▶*n.* a sharp irregular ridge of compact sand lying in the direction of the prevailing wind in exposed desert regions, formed by the wind erosion of adjacent material that is less resistant. ▷early 20th cent.: Turkic; compare with Turkish *yar* 'steep bank.'.

yard·arm /'yärdˌärm/ ▶*n.* the outer extremity of a ship's yard.
▶*PHRASE* □ **the sun is over the yardarm** *dated* used to refer to the time of day when it is permissible to begin drinking.

yard·bird /'yärdˌbərd/ ▶*n. informal* **1** a new military recruit, esp. one assigned to menial tasks. **2** a convict. ▷1940s: perhaps suggested by **JAILBIRD**.

yard·man /'yärdˌman/ ▶*n.* (*pl.* **-men**) **1** a person working in a railroad or lumberyard. **2** a person who does various outdoor jobs.

yard·mas·ter /'yärdˌmastər/ ▶*n.* a person who is in charge of a railroad yard.

yard of ale ▶*n. chiefly Brit.* the amount of beer (typically two to three pints) held by a narrow glass about a yard high. ■ a glass of this kind.

yard sale ▶*n.* a garage sale.

yard·stick /'yärdˌstik/ ▶*n.* a measuring rod a yard long, typically divided into inches. ■ a standard used for comparison: *the consumer price index, the government's yardstick for the cost of living.*

yare /yär; ye(ə)r/ ▶*adj.* (of a ship) responding promptly to the helm; easily manageable. ▷Old English *gearu* 'prepared, ready,' of Germanic origin; related to Dutch *gaar* 'done, dressed' and German *gar* 'ready.'

Yar·mouth /'yärməTH/ a resort town in southeastern Massachusetts, on southern Cape Cod; pop. 21,174.

yar·mul·ke /'yämə(l)kə/ (also **yar·mul·ka**) ▶*n.* a skullcap worn in public by Orthodox Jewish men or during prayer by other Jewish men. ▷early 20th cent.: from Yiddish *yarmolke.*

yarmulke

yarn /yärn/ ▶*n.* **1** spun thread used for knitting, weaving, or sewing. **2** *informal* a long or rambling story, esp. one that is implausible.
▶*v.* [*intrans.*] *informal* tell a long or implausible story: *they were yarning about local legends and superstitions.* ▷Old English *gearn*, of Germanic origin; related to Dutch *garen.*
▶*PHRASE* □ **spin a yarn** see **SPIN**.

yarn-dyed ▶*adj.* (of fabric) dyed as yarn, before being woven.

Ya·ro·slavl /ˌyärə'slävəl/ a port in western Russia, on the Volga River, northeast of Nizhni Novgorod; pop. 636,000.

yar·row /'yarō/ ▶*n.* a Eurasian plant of the daisy family, with feathery leaves and heads of small white, yellow, or pink aromatic flowers. Also called **MILFOIL**. • *Achillea millefolium*, family Compositae. ▷Old English *gearwe*; related to Dutch *gerwe.*

yarrow

yash·mak /yäsH'mäk; 'yasHˌmak/ ▶*n.* a veil concealing all of the face except the eyes, worn by some Muslim women in public. ▷mid 19th cent.: via Arabic from Turkish.

Yas·trzem·ski /yə'stremskē/, Carl (Michael) (1939–) U.S. baseball player; known as **Yaz**. An outfielder for the Boston Red Sox from 1961 until 1983, he had 452 career home runs and 3,419 career hits. Baseball Hall of Fame (1989).

yat·a·ghan /'yatəgən; -ˌgan/ ▶*n. chiefly historical* a sword without a guard and typically with a double-curved blade, used in Muslim countries. ▷from Turkish *yatağan.*

ya·tra /'yätrə/ ▶*n. Indian* a procession or pilgrimage, esp. one with a religious purpose. ▷from Sanskrit *yātrā* 'journey,' from *yā* 'go.'

yat·ter /'yatər/ *informal* ▶*v.* [*intrans.*] talk incessantly; chatter.
▶*n.* incessant talk. ▷early 19th cent.: imitative, perhaps suggested by **YAMMER** and **CHATTER**.

yau·pon /'yôˌpän; 'yōō-/ (also **yau·pon hol·ly**) ▶*n.* a holly of the southern U.S. Sometimes dried and brewed as a tea, its bitter leaves contain caffeine and have emetic properties. • *Ilex vomitoria*, family Aquifoliaceae. ▷early 18th cent.: from Catawba (a Siouan language spoken in South Carolina) *yopún*, diminutive of *yop* 'tree, shrub.'

yau·ti·a /you'tēə/ ▶*n.* a tropical American plant of the arum family that is cultivated for its edible tubers and sometimes its leaves. • Genus *Xanthosoma*, family Araceae: several species, in particular the fleshy-leaved **malanga** (*X. atrovirens*) of Latin America. ▷late 19th cent.: American Spanish, from Maya *yaaj* 'wound, poison' + *té* 'mouth' with reference to its caustic properties.

yaw /yô/ ▸*v.* [*intrans.*] (of a moving ship or aircraft) twist or oscillate about a vertical axis: [with *adverbial of direction*] *the jet yawed sharply to the right.*
▸*n.* a twisting or oscillation of a moving ship or aircraft around a vertical axis. ▷mid 16th cent.: of unknown origin.

yawl /yôl/ ▸*n.* a two-masted fore-and-aft-rigged sailboat with the mizzenmast stepped far aft so that the mizzen boom overhangs the stern. ■ *historical* a ship's jolly boat with four or six oars. ▷late 16th cent.: from Middle Low German *jolle* or Dutch *jol*, of unknown origin; compare with JOLLY[2].

yawn /yôn/ ▸*v.* [*intrans.*] involuntarily open one's mouth wide and inhale deeply due to tiredness or boredom: *he began yawning and looking at his watch.* ■ [usu. as *adj.*] (**yawning**) be wide open: *a yawning chasm.*
▸*n.* a reflex act of opening one's mouth wide and inhaling deeply due to tiredness or boredom. ■ *informal* a thing that is considered boring or tedious: *the awards show was a four-hour yawn.* ▷Old English *geonian*, of Germanic origin, from an Indo-European root shared by Latin *hiare* and Greek *khainein*. Current noun senses date from the early 18th cent. **—yawn·ing·ly** *adv.*

yawn·er /ˈyônər/ ▸*n. informal* a thing that is considered extremely boring: *the game was a real yawner.*

yawp /yôp/ ▸*n.* a harsh or hoarse cry or yelp. ■ foolish or noisy talk.
▸*v.* [*intrans.*] shout or exclaim hoarsely. ■ talk foolishly or noisily. ▷Middle English (as a verb): imitative. The noun dates from the early 19th cent. **—yawp·er** *n.*

yaws /yôz/ ▸*plural n.* [treated as *sing.*] a contagious disease of tropical countries, caused by a bacterium that enters skin abrasions and gives rise to small crusted lesions that may develop into deep ulcers. Also called FRAMBESIA. • The bacterium is the spirochete *Treponema pallidum* subsp. *pertenue.* ▷late 17th cent.: probably from Carib *yaya.*

yay[1] /yā/ ▸*exclam. informal* expressing triumph, approval, or encouragement: *Yay! Great, Julie!* ▷1960s: perhaps an alteration of YEAH.

yay[2] (also **yea**) ▸*adv. informal* (with adjectives of measure) so; to this extent: *I knew him when he was yay big.* ▷1960s: probably a variant of the adverb YEA[1].

Yaz·oo Riv·er /yaˈzo͞o/ a river that flows for 190 miles (305 km) from northern Mississippi to join the Mississippi River at Vicksburg. The fertile land between the rivers is the Mississippi **Delta,** or **Yazoo Delta.**

Yb ▸*symbol* the chemical element ytterbium.

Y·bor Cit·y /ˈēˌbôr/ an industrial and commercial section of Tampa in Florida, noted for its Cuban culture and cigar industry.

Y chro·mo·some ▸*n. Genetics* (in humans and other mammals) a sex chromosome that is normally present only in male cells, which are designated XY. Compare with **X** CHROMOSOME.

y·clept /iˈklept/ ▸*adj.* [*predic.*] *archaic* or *humorous* by the name of: *a lady yclept Eleanora.* ▷Old English *gecleopod*, past participle of *cleopian* 'call,' of Germanic origin.

yd. ▸*abbr.* yard (measure).

ye[1] /yē/ ▸*pron.* [*second person plural*] *archaic* or *dialect* plural form of THOU[1]: *gather ye rosebuds, while ye may.* ▷Old English *gē*, of Germanic origin; related to Dutch *gij* and German *ihr.*
▸*PHRASE* □ **ye gods!** an exclamation of astonishment.

ye[2] /yē; T͟Hē/ ▸*adj.* pseudo-archaic term for THE: *Ye Olde Bookshoppe.* ▷graphic variant; in late Middle English þ (see THORN) came to be written identically with y, so that *the* could be written *ye.* This spelling (usually y[e]) was kept as a convenient abbreviation in handwriting until the 19th cent., and in printers' types during the 15th and 16th cent., but it was never pronounced as "ye."

yea[1] /yā/ ▸*adv. archaic* or *formal* yes: *she has the right to say yea or nay.* ■ used for emphasis, esp. to introduce a stronger or more accurate word than one just used: *he was full, yea, crammed with anxieties.*
▸*n. archaic* or *formal* an affirmative answer: *the assembly would give the final yea or nay.* ■ (in the U.S. Congress) an affirmative vote. ▷Old English *gēa, gē*, of Germanic origin; related to Dutch and German *ja.*

yea[2] ▸*adv.* variant spelling of YAY[2].

Yea·ger /ˈyāgər/, Chuck (1923–), U.S. pilot; full name *Charles Elwood Yeager.* He became the first person to break the sound barrier when he piloted the Bell X-1 rocket research aircraft at high altitude to a level-flight speed of 670 mph in 1947.

Chuck Yeager

yeah /ˈye(ə); ˈya(ə)/ (also **yeh**) ▸*exclam.* & *n.* nonstandard spelling of YES, representing informal pronunciation.

yean /yēn/ ▸*v.* [*trans.*] *archaic* (of a sheep or goat) give birth to (a lamb or kid). ▷late Middle English: perhaps representing an Old English verb related to *ēanian* 'to lamb.'

year /yi(ə)r/ ▸*n.* **1** the time taken by a planet to make one revolution around the sun.

The length of the earth's year depends on the manner of calculation. For ordinary purposes the important period is the **solar year** (also called **astronomical year, equinoctial year,** or **tropical year**), which is the time between successive spring or autumnal equinoxes, or winter or summer solstices, roughly 365 days, 5 hours, 48 minutes, and 46 seconds in length. This period thus marks the regular cycle of the seasons.
See also SIDEREAL YEAR, ANOMALISTIC YEAR.

2 (also **cal·en·dar year** or **civ·il year**) the period of 365 days (or 366 days in leap years) starting from the first of January, used for reckoning time in ordinary affairs. ■ a period of the same length as this starting at any point: *the year starting July 1.* ■ [with *adj.*] such a period regarded in terms of the quality of produce, typically wine: *single-vineyard wine of a good year.* ■ a similar period used for reckoning time according to other calendars: *the Muslim year.* **3** (**one's years**) one's age or time of life: *she had a composure well beyond her years.* **4** (**years**) *informal* a very long time; ages: *it's going to take years to put that right.* **5** a set of students grouped together as being of roughly similar ages, mostly entering a school or college in the same academic year: *most of the girls in my year were leaving school at the end of the term.* ▷Old English *gē(a)r*, of Germanic origin; related to Dutch *jaar* and German *Jahr*, from an Indo-European root shared by Greek *hōra* 'season.'
▸*PHRASES* □ **in the year of our Lord** (or *dated* **in the year of grace**) —— in the year AD—— : *I was born in the year of our Lord 1786.* [*year of grace*, suggested by medieval Latin *anno gratiae*, used by chroniclers.] □ —— **of the year** a person or thing chosen as outstanding in a specified field or of a specified kind in a particular year: *the sports personality of the year.* □ **put years on** (or **take years off**) **someone** make someone feel or look older (or younger). □ **a year and a day** the period specified in some legal matters to ensure the completion of a full year. □ **year in and year out** continuously or repeatedly over a period of years: *they rented the same bungalow year in and year out.*

year·book /ˈyi(ə)rˌbo͝ok/ ▸*n.* an annual publication giving current information and listing events or aspects of the previous year, esp. in a particular field: *Yearbook of Physical Anthropology.* ■ a book containing photographs of the senior class in a school or college and details of school activities in the previous year.

year end (also **year's end**) ▸*n.* the end of the fiscal year: *we will discuss additional changes* **at year end** | [as *adj.*] *the year-end figures were impressive.*

year·ling /ˈyi(ə)rliNG/ ▸*n.* an animal (esp. a sheep, calf, or foal) a year old, or in its second year. ■ a racehorse in the calendar year after its year of foaling.
▸*adj.* [*attrib.*] having lived or existed for a year; a year old: *a yearling calf.* ■ of or relating to an something that is a year old: *the yearling market.*

year·long (also **year-long**) ▸*adj.* [*attrib.*] lasting for or throughout a year: *his yearlong battle with lung cancer.*

year·ly /ˈyi(ə)rlē/ ▸*adj.* & *adv.* happening or produced once a year or every year: [as *adj.*] *yearly visits to Africa* | [as *adv.*] *rent was paid yearly.* ▷Old English *gēarlic* (see YEAR, -LY[1]).

yearn /yərn/ ▸*v.* [*intrans.*] have an intense feeling of loss or lack and longing for something: [with *infinitive*] *they yearned to go home* | [as *n.*] (**yearning**) *he felt a* **yearning for** *the mountains.* ■ *archaic* be filled with compassion or warm feeling: *no fellow spirit yearned toward her.* ▷Old English *giernan*, from a Germanic base meaning 'eager.' **—yearn·er** *n.* **—yearn·ing·ly** *adv.*

year-round ▸*adj.* & *adv.* happening or continuing throughout the year: [as *adj.*] *an indoor pool for year-round use* | [as *adv.*] (also **year round**) *the center is open year round.*

yea·say·er /ˈyāˌsāər/ ▸*n.* **1** a person with a positive, confident outlook. **2** a person who always agrees with or is submissive to others.

yeast /yēst/ ▸*n.* a microscopic fungus consisting of single oval cells that reproduce by budding, and are capable of converting sugar into alcohol and carbon dioxide. • Genus *Saccharomyces*, subdivision Ascomycotina. ■ a grayish-yellow preparation of this obtained chiefly from fermented beer, used as a fermenting agent, to raise bread dough, and as a food supplement. ■ *Biology* any unicellular fungus that reproduces vegetatively by budding or fission, including forms such as candida that can cause disease. ▷Old English, of Germanic origin; related to Dutch *gist* and German *Gischt* 'froth, yeast,' from an Indo-European root shared by Greek *zein* 'to boil.' **—yeast·like** /-ˌlīk/ *adj.*

yeast·y /ˈyēstē/ ▸*adj.* (**yeast·i·er, yeast·i·est**) of, resembling, or containing yeast: *the yeasty smell of rising dough.* ■ *figurative* characterized by or producing upheaval or agitation; in a state of turbulence, typically a creative or productive one: *the yeasty days of yesterday's revolution.* **—yeast·i·ly** /ˈyēstəlē/ *adv.* **—yeast·i·ness** *n.*

Yeats /yāts/, W. B. (1865–1939), Irish poet and playwright; full name *William Butler Yeats.* His play *The Countess Cathleen* (1892) and his collection of stories *The Celtic Twilight* (1893) stimulated Ireland's theatrical, cultural, and literary revival. Notable poetry: "Sailing to Byzantium" and "Leda and the Swan." Nobel Prize for Literature (1923).

Willam Butler Yeats

yech /yəKH; yək; yeKH; yek/ (also **yecch**) ▸*exclam. informal* expressing aversion or disgust. ▷1960s: imitative; compare with YUCK. **—yech·y** *adj.*

yee-haw /ˈyēˌhô/ (also **yee-hah** /ˈyēˌhä/) ▸*exclam.* an expression of enthusiasm or exuberance, typically associated with cowboys or rural inhabitants of the southern U.S. ▷natural exclamation: first recorded in American English in the 1970s.

yegg /yeg/ ▸*n. informal* a burglar or safecracker. ▷early 20th cent.: of unknown origin.

yeh /ye/ ▸*exclam.* variant spelling of YEAH.
▸*pron.* /yə/ nonstandard spelling of YOU, used to represent various accents or dialects: *are yeh all right, lads?*

Ye·ka·te·rin·burg /yiˈkatərinˌbərg; yiˌkətyərinˈbo͝ork/ another name for **EKATERINBURG.**

Ye·ka·te·ri·no·dar /yəˌkätəˈrēnəˌdär/ (also **E·ka·te·ri·no·dar**) former name (until 1922) for **KRASNODAR.**

Pronunciation Key ə *ago;* ər *over;* ˈə or ˌə *up;* ˈər or ˌər *fur;* a *hat;* ā *rate;* ä *car;* CH *chew;* e *let;* ē *see;* e(ə)r *air;* i *fit;* ī *by;* i(ə)r *ear;* NG *sing;* ō *go;* ô *for;* oi *boy;* o͝o *good;* o͞o *goo;* ou *out;* SH *she;* TH *thin;* T͟H *then;* (h)w *why;* ZH *vision*

Ye·ka·te·ri·no·slav /yəˌkätəˈrēnəˌsläf; -ˌsläv/ (also **E·ka·te·ri·no·slav**) former name (1787–1926) for DNIPROPETROVSK.

yell /yel/ ▸*n.* a loud, sharp cry, esp. of pain, surprise, or delight; a shout. ■ an organized cheer, esp. one used to support a sports team.
▸*v.* [*intrans.*] give a loud, sharp cry: *you heard me* ***yelling at*** *her.* | [with *direct speech*] *"Happy New Year!" Ashley yelled.* ▷Old English *g(i)ellan* (verb), of Germanic origin; related to Dutch *gillen* and German *gellen.*

yel·low /ˈyelō/ ▸*adj.* **1** of the color between green and orange in the spectrum, a primary subtractive color complementary to blue; colored like ripe lemons or egg yolks: *curly yellow hair.* ■ *offensive* having a naturally yellowish or olive skin (as used to describe Chinese or Japanese people). ■ denoting a warning of danger that is thought to be near but not actually imminent: *he put Camp Visoko* ***on yellow alert.*** **2** *informal* cowardly: *he'd better get back there quick and prove he's not yellow.* ■ *archaic* showing jealousy or suspicion. **3** (of a book or newspaper) unscrupulously sensational.
▸*n.* **1** yellow color or pigment: *the craft detonated in a blaze of red and yellow* | *painted in vivid blues and yellows.* ■ yellow clothes or material: *everyone dresses in yellow.* **2** the yolk of an egg. **3** (**yellows**) any of a number of plant diseases in which the leaves turn yellow, typically caused by viruses and transmitted by insects.
▸*v.* [*intrans.*] become a yellow color, esp. with age: *the cream paint was beginning to yellow* | [as *adj.*] (**yellowing**) *yellowing lace curtains* | [as *adj.*] (**yellowed**) *a yellowed newspaper cutting.* ▷Old English *geolu, geolo;* related to Dutch *geel* and German *gelb,* also to GOLD. —**yel·low·ish** *adj.* —**yel·low·ly** *adv.* —**yel·low·ness** *n.* —**yel·low·y** *adj.*
▸PHRASE □ **the yellow peril** *offensive* the political or military threat regarded as being posed by the Chinese or by the peoples of Southeast Asia.

yel·low·back /ˈyelōˌbak/ ▸*n. historical* a cheap and typically sensational novel, with a yellow board or cloth binding.

yel·low-bel·lied sap·suck·er ▸*n.* a woodpecker of eastern North America with black-and-white plumage, a pale yellow belly, and, in the male, a scarlet crown and throat. • *Sphyrapicus varius,* family Picidae.

yel·low-bel·ly ▸*n. informal* **1** a coward. **2** any of various animals with yellow underparts. —**yel·low-bel·lied** *adj.*

yel·low bile ▸*n. historical* another term for CHOLER.

yel·low-billed /ˈyelōˌbild/ ▸*adj.* (of a bird) having a yellow bill. Used in the name of numerous such birds, including: • the North American **yellow-billed cuckoo** (*Coccyzus americanus,* family Cuculidae) • the African **yellow-billed duck** (*Anas undulata,* family Anatidae).

yel·low birch ▸*n.* see BIRCH (sense 1).

yel·low bunt·ing ▸*n.* another term for YELLOWHAMMER (sense 2).

yel·low·cake /ˈyelōˌkāk/ ▸*n.* impure uranium oxide obtained during processing of uranium ore. ▷1950s: so named because it is obtained as a yellow precipitate.

yel·low card ▸*n.* (in soccer and some other games) a yellow card shown by the referee to a player being cautioned. Compare with RED CARD.

yel·low dog *informal* ▸*n.* a contemptible or cowardly person or thing.
▸*adj.* (of a party-line voter, esp. a Democrat) inclined to support any candidate affiliated with one's chosen party, regardless of the candidate's personal qualities or political qualifications: *he is a self-proclaimed yellow dog Democrat.*

yel·low dog con·tract ▸*n.* a contract between a worker and an employer in which the worker agrees not to remain in or join a union.

yel·low dog Dem·o·crat (also **Yellow Dog Democrat**) ▸*n. informal* see YELLOW DOG. Compare with BLUE DOG DEMOCRAT.

yel·low earth ▸*n.* a yellowish loess occurring in northern China.

yel·low fe·ver ▸*n.* a tropical viral disease affecting the liver and kidneys, causing fever and jaundice and often fatal. It is transmitted by mosquitoes.

yel·low·fin /ˈyelōˌfin/ (also **yel·low·fin tu·na**) ▸*n.* a widely distributed, commercially important tuna that has yellow anal and dorsal fins. • *Thunnus albacares,* family Scombridae.

yel·low flag ▸*n.* **1** a ship's yellow flag, denoting the letter Q for 'quarantine.' When flown with another flag, it indicates disease on board; when flown alone, it indicates the absence of disease and signifies a request for customs clearance. Also called QUARANTINE FLAG. ■ *Auto Racing* a yellow flag used to signal to drivers that there is a hazard such as oil or a crashed car on the track. **2** a yellow-flowered iris that grows by water and in marshy places, native to Europe and naturalized in North America. • *Iris pseudacorus,* family Iridaceae.

yel·low·ham·mer /ˈyelōˌhamər/ ▸*n.* **1** another term for YELLOW-SHAFTED FLICKER (see FLICKER[2]). **2** a common Eurasian bunting, the male of which has a yellow head, neck, and breast. • *Emberiza citrinella,* family Emberizidae (subfamily Emberizinae). ▷mid 16th cent.: *-hammer* is perhaps from Old English *amore* (a kind of bird), possibly conflated with *hama* 'feathers.'

Yel·low·ham·mer State a nickname for the state of ALABAMA.

yel·low jack ▸*n.* **1** another term for YELLOW FLAG (sense 1). **2** archaic term for YELLOW FEVER. **3** an edible marine fish with yellowish underparts, found primarily in the Gulf of Mexico and the Caribbean Sea. • *Caranx bartholomaei,* family Carangidae.

yel·low jack·et ▸*n. informal* a wasp or hornet with bright yellow markings.

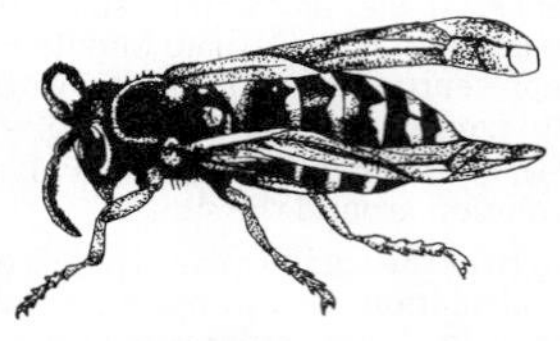

yellow jacket

yel·low jas·mine (also **yel·low jes·sa·mine**) ▸*n.* an ornamental climbing shrub with fragrant yellow flowers, native to the southeastern U.S. Its rhizome yields gelsemium. • *Gelsemium sempervirens,* family Loganiaceae.

yel·low jer·sey ▸*n.* (in a cycling race involving stages) a yellow jersey worn by the overall leader in a cycle race, at the end of any one day, and ultimately presented to the winner.

yel·low jour·nal·ism ▸*n.* journalism that is based upon sensationalism and crude exaggeration: *equating murder and dismemberment with smoking pot is the worst yellow journalism.* ▷1895: from the appearance in an issue of the *New York World* of a cartoon in which a child in a yellow dress ('The Yellow Kid') was the central figure. The color printing was an experiment designed to attract customers. —**yel·low jour·nal·ist** *n.*

Yel·low·knife /ˈyelōˌnīf/ the capital, since 1967, of the Northwest Territories in Canada, on the northern shore of Great Slave Lake; pop. 15,179.

yel·low·legs /ˈyelōˌlegz/ ▸*n.* a migratory sandpiper with bright yellow legs, breeding in Alaska and Canada. • Genus *Tringa,* family Scolopacidae: two species, the **greater yellowlegs** (*T. melanoleuca*) and the **lesser yellowlegs** (*T. flavipes*).

yel·low mom·bin /mōmˈbēn/ ▸*n.* see HOG PLUM.

yel·low o·cher ▸*n.* a yellow pigment that usually contains limonite, a yellowish-brown oxide of iron. ■ a moderate orange color with yellow overtones.

Yel·low Pag·es (also **yel·low pag·es**) ▸*plural n.* a telephone directory, or a section of one, printed on yellow paper and listing businesses and other organizations according to the goods or services they offer. ■ a similar directory available online through the Internet.

yel·low pine ▸*n.* any of several North American pines having a strong yellowish wood. ■ the wood of such a tree.

yel·low pop·lar ▸*n.* another term for TULIP TREE.

yel·low rain ▸*n.* a toxic yellow substance reported as falling in Southeast Asia, alleged to be a chemical warfare agent but now believed to consist of contaminated bee droppings.

Yel·low Riv·er the second largest river in China. It rises in the mountains of western central China and flows for more than 3,000 miles (4,830 km) in a huge semicircle before it enters Bo Hai, an inlet of the Yellow Sea. Chinese name HUANG HO.

Yel·low Sea an arm of the East China Sea that separates the Korean peninsula from the eastern coast of China. Chinese name HUANG HAI.

yel·low spot ▸*n.* the region of greatest visual acuity around the fovea of the eye; the macula lutea (see MACULA).

Yel·low·stone Na·tion·al Park /ˈyelōˌstōn/ a national park in northwestern Wyoming and Montana, known for Old Faithful geyser.

yel·low·tail /ˈyelōˌtāl/ ▸*n.* (*pl.* same or **-tails**) a marine fish that has yellow coloration on the fins, esp. a number of species prized as food fish. • Several genera and species, including the large sport fish **yellowtail** (*Seriola lalandi,* family Carangidae) of southern California, the **yellowtail flounder** (*Limanda ferruginea,* family Pleuronectidae) of the Atlantic coast from Labrador to Virginia, and the **yellowtail snapper** (*Ocyurus chrysurus,* family Lutjanidae) of Bermuda and the West Indies.

yel·low·throat /ˈyelōˌTHrōt/ ▸*n.* a small American warbler with a bright yellow throat. • Genus *Geothlypis,* subfamily Parulinae, family Emberizidae: several species.

yel·low un·der·wing ▸*n.* an underwing moth that has yellow hind wings with a black terminal band. • *Noctua* and other genera, family Noctuidae: several species, including the **large yellow underwing** (*N. pronuba*), the larva of which is a destructive cutworm.

yel·low·wood /ˈyelōˌwo͝od/ ▸*n.* any of a number of trees that have yellowish timber or yield a yellow dye, in particular: • a North American tree of the pea family (*Cladrastis lutea,* family Leguminosae). • a podocarp.

yelp /yelp/ ▸*n.* a short sharp cry, esp. of pain or alarm: *she uttered a yelp as she bumped into a table.*
▸*v.* [*intrans.*] utter such a cry: *my dogs were yelping at Linus.* ▷Old English *g(i)elpan* (verb) 'to boast,' from a Germanic imitative base. From late Middle English 'cry or sing with a loud voice' the current sense arose in the 16th cent. —**yelp·er** *n.*

Yel·tsin /ˈyeltsən/, Boris (Nikolaevich) (1931–), Russian statesman; president of the Russian Federation 1991–99. Impatient with the slow pace of Gorbachev's reforms, Yeltsin resigned from the Communist Party after becoming president of the Russian Soviet Federative Socialist Republic in 1990. As president of the independent Russian Federation, he faced opposition to his reforms.

Yem·en /ˈyemən/ a country in southwestern part of the Arabian peninsula; pop. 20,024,000; capital, Sana'a; official language, Arabic. —**Yem·e·ni** /ˈyemənē/ *adj.* & *n.*

An Islamic country since the mid 7th century, Yemen was part of the Ottoman Empire from the 16th century. During the 19th century, the port of Aden was developed as a British military base. After World War II, civil war between royalist and republican forces ended with British withdrawal and the partition of the country in 1967. South Yemen declared itself independent as the People's Democratic Republic of Yemen, and the North became the Yemen Arab Republic. In 1990, the countries reunited to form the Republic of Yemen; the South briefly seceded in 1994 but was defeated in a short civil war.

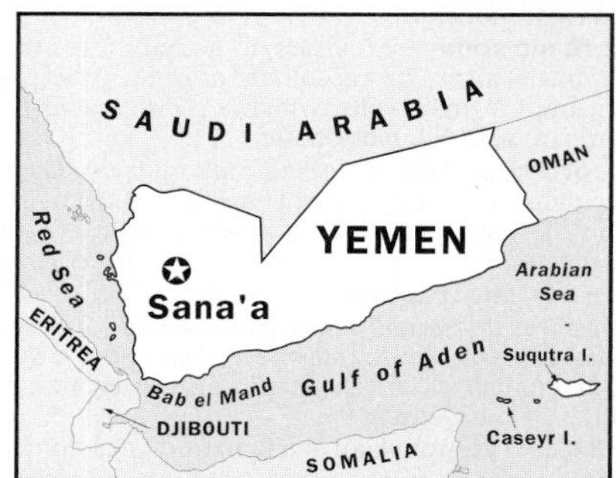

Yem·en·ite /ˈyeməˌnīt/ ▸*n.* **1** another term for YEMENI (see YEMEN). **2** ■ a Jew who was, or whose ancestors were, formerly resident in Yemen.
▸*adj.* of or relating to Yemeni Arabs or Jews. ▷from Arabic *yamanī* 'Yemeni' + -ITE[1].

yen[1] /yen/ ▸*n.* (*pl.* same) the basic monetary unit of Japan. ▷from Japanese *en* 'round.'

yen[2] *informal* ▸*n.* [in *sing.*] a longing or yearning: [with *infinitive*] *she always had a yen to be a writer.*
▸*v.* (**yenned, yen·ning**) [*intrans.*] feel a longing or yearning: *it's no use* ***yenning for*** *the old simplicities.* ▷late 19th cent. (in the sense 'craving (of a drug addict) for a drug'): from Chinese *yăn.*

Yen·i·sei /ˌyenəˈsā/ a river in Siberia, in Russia, that rises in the mountains on the Mongolian border and flows north for 2,566 miles (4,106 km) to the Arctic coast, where it empties into the Kara Sea.

yen·ta /ˈyentə/ ▸*n.* a woman who is a gossip or busybody. ▷1920s: Yiddish, originally a given name.

yeo·man /ˈyōmən/ ▸*n.* (*pl.* **-men**) **1** *historical* a man holding and cultivating a small landed estate; a freeholder. ■ a person qualified for certain duties and rights, such as to serve on juries and vote for the knight of the shire, by virtue of possessing free land of an annual value of 40 shillings. **2** *historical* a servant in a royal or noble household, ranking between a sergeant and a groom or a squire and a page. **3** *Brit.* a member of the yeomanry force. **4** a petty officer in the U.S. Navy or Coast Guard performing clerical duties on board ship. ■ (also **yeo·man of sig·nals**) (in the British Royal Navy and other Commonwealth navies) a petty officer concerned with signaling. ▷Middle English: probably from YOUNG + MAN. —**yeo·man·ly** *adj.*

▸*PHRASE* □ **yeoman service** efficient or useful help in need.

Yeo·man of the Guard ▸*n.* a member of the British sovereign's bodyguard, first established by Henry VII, now having only ceremonial duties and wearing Tudor dress as uniform. Also called BEEFEATER. ■ used erroneously to refer to a Yeoman Warder.

yeo·man·ry /ˈyōmənrē/ ▸*n.* [treated as *sing.* or *pl.*] *historical* a group of men who held and cultivated small landed estates. ■ (in Britain) a volunteer cavalry force raised from such a group (1794–1908).

Yeo·man Ward·er ▸*n.* a warder at the Tower of London. Also called BEEFEATER.

yeow /you; yēˈou/ ▸*exclam.* another word for YOW. ▷natural exclamation: first recorded in American English in the 1920s.

yep /yep/ (also **yup**) ▸*exclam.* & *n.* nonstandard spelling of YES, representing informal pronunciation.

yer /yər/ ▸*possessive adj.* nonstandard spelling of YOUR, used in representing dialectal speech: *eat yer dinner.*

▸*contraction of* you are, used in representing dialectal speech: *yer a dang fool.*

▸*pron.* nonstandard spelling of YOU, used in representing dialectal speech: *well, are yer comin'?*

▸*adv.* nonstandard spelling of HERE, used in representing dialectal speech: *I hate mighty bad to bus' up dis yer ax-helve.*

-yer ▸*suffix* variant spelling of -IER esp. after *w* (as in *lawyer, sawyer*).

yer·ba /ˈyerbə; ˈyər-/ (also **yer·ba ma·té** /ˈmätā; mäˈtā/) ▸*n.* another term for MATÉ. ▷early 19th cent.: from Spanish, literally 'herb.'

Yer·ba Bue·na /ˈyərbə ˈbwānə/ an island in San Francisco Bay in California; also, the name of the 1820s mainland settlement that became the city of San Francisco.

yer·ba bue·na /ˈbwānə/ ▸*n.* a trailing aromatic herb with whitish or lilac flowers, related to savory. Native to the western U.S., it has been used medicinally and as a local tea. • *Satureja douglasii*, family Labiatae. ▷mid 19th cent.: from Spanish, literally 'good herb.'

yer·ba ma·té /ˈye(ə)rbə mäˈtā/ ▸*n.* see MATÉ.

Yer·by /ˈyərbē/, Frank (Garvin) (1916–91), U.S. writer. He wrote action-packed novels such as *The Foxes of Harrow* (1946), *Judas, My Brother* (1968), and *The Dahomean* (1971). Discrimination against blacks in the U.S. caused him to live in Spain from 1955.

Ye·re·van /ˌyeriˈvän/ (also **E·re·van**) the capital of Armenia; pop. 1,202,000.

yes /yes/ ▸*exclam.* **1** used to give an affirmative response: *"Do you understand?" "Yes."* ■ expressing agreement with a positive statement just made: *"That was a grand evening." "Yes, it was."* ■ expressing contradiction of a negative statement: *"You don't want to go." "Yes, I do."* **2** used as a response to someone addressing one or otherwise trying to attract one's attention: *"Oh, Mr. Lawrence." "Yes?"* **3** used to question a remark or ask for more detail about it: *"It should be easy to check." "Oh yes? How?"* ■ asked at the end of a statement to indicate the expectation of agreement: *you think I perhaps killed Westbourne, yes?* **4** encouraging someone to continue speaking: *"When you bought those photographs . . ." "Yes?"* **5** expressing delight: *plenty to eat, including hot roast beef sandwiches (yes!).*

▸*n.* (*pl.* **yes·es** or **yes·ses**) an affirmative answer or decision, esp. in voting: *answering with assured and ardent yeses.* ▷Old English *gēse, gīse*, probably from an unrecorded phrase meaning 'may it be so.'

▸*PHRASE* □ **yes and no** partly and partly not: *"Did it come as a surprise to you?" "Yes and no."*

ye·shi·va /yəˈsʜēvə/ ▸*n.* an Orthodox Jewish college or seminary. ■ an Orthodox Jewish elementary or secondary school. ▷from Hebrew *yĕšīḇāh*.

yes-man ▸*n.* (*pl.* **-men**) *informal* a weak person who always agrees with their political leader or their superior at work.

yes·sir /ˈyesər; ˈyesˈsər/ (also **yes·sir·ee** /-səˈrē/) *informal* ▸*exclam.* used to express assent: *"Do you understand me?" "Yessir!"* ■ used to express emphatic affirmation: *yessir the food was cheap.* ▷early 20th cent.: alteration of *yes sir.*

yes·sum /ˈyesəm/ ▸*exclam. dated, chiefly black English* used as a polite form of assent addressed to a woman: *"You feel all right?" she asked. "Yessum."* ▷early 20th cent.: alteration of *yes ma'am.*

yester- ▸*comb. form poetic/literary* or *archaic* of yesterday: *yestereve* | *yesteryear.* ▷Old English *geostran*, of Germanic origin; related to Dutch *gisteren* and German *gestern* 'yesterday,' from an Indo-European root shared by Latin *heri* and Greek *khthes*.

yes·ter·day /ˈyestərˌdā; -dē/ ▸*adv.* on the day before today: *he returned to a hero's welcome yesterday.* ■ in the recent past: *everything seems to have been built yesterday.*

▸*n.* the day before today: *yesterday was Tuesday.* ■ the recent past: *yesterday's best sellers.* ▷Old English *giestran dæg* (see YESTER-, DAY).

▸*PHRASES* □ **yesterday morning** (or **afternoon**, etc.) in the morning (or afternoon, etc.) of yesterday. □ **yesterday's man** a man, esp. a politician, whose career is finished or past its peak. □ **yesterday's news** a person or thing that is no longer of interest.

yes·ter·night /ˈyestərˌnīt/ ▸*n. archaic* last night.

▸*adv.* during last night.

yes·ter·year /ˈyestərˌyir/ ▸*n. poetic/literary* last year or the recent past, esp. as nostalgically recalled: *return with us now to those thrilling days of yesteryear.*

yet /yet/ ▸*adv.* **1** up until the present or an unspecified or implied time; by now or then: *I haven't told anyone else yet* | *aren't you ready to go yet?* | *I* **have yet to** *be convinced* | [with *superlative*] *the congress was widely acclaimed as the best yet.* ■ [with *negative*] as soon as the present or a specified or implied time: *wait, don't go yet.* ■ from now into the future for a specified length of time: *I hope to continue for some time yet.* ■ referring to something that will or may happen in the future: *further research may yet explain the enigma* | *I know she's alive and I'll find her yet.* ■ up to and including the present or time mentioned; still: *is it raining yet?* **2** still; even (used to emphasize increase or repetition): *snow, snow, and yet more snow* | *yet another diet book* | *the rations were reduced* **yet again**. **3** nevertheless; in spite of that: *every week she gets worse, and yet it could go on for years.*

▸*conj.* but at the same time; but nevertheless: *the path was dark, yet I slowly found my way.* ▷Old English *giet(a)*, of unknown origin.

▸*PHRASES* □ **as yet** see AS[1]. □ **nor yet** and also not.

yet·i /ˈyetē; ˈyātē/ ▸*n.* a large hairy creature resembling a human or bear, said to live in the highest part of the Himalayas. ▷1930s: from Tibetan *yeh-teh* 'little manlike animal.'

Yev·tu·shen·ko /ˌyevtəˈsʜeNGkō/, Yevgeni (Aleksandrovich) (1933–), Russian poet. *Third Snow* (1955) and *Zima Junction* (1956) were regarded as encapsulating the feelings and aspirations of the post-Stalin generation. He incurred official hostility because of the outspoken nature of some of his poetry, notably *Babi Yar* (1961).

yew /yo͞o/ ▸*n.* (also **yew tree**) a coniferous tree that has red berrylike fruits, and most parts of which are highly poisonous. Yews are linked with folklore and superstition and can live to a great age; the timber is used in cabinetmaking and (formerly) to make longbows. • Genus *Taxus*, family Taxaceae: several species, in particular the **American yew** (*T. canadensis*) and the **English** (or **European**) **yew** (*T. baccata*). ▷Old English *īw, ēow*, of Germanic origin.

yez /yəz/ ▸*pron.* nonstandard spelling of YOUSE, used in representing dialectal speech.

Ygg·dra·sil /ˈigdrəsəl; -ˌsil/ *Scandinavian Mythology* a huge ash tree located at the center of the earth, with three roots, one extending to Niflheim (the underworld), one to Jotunheim (land of the giants), and one to Asgard (land of the gods). ▷from Old Norse *yg(g)drasill*, apparently from *Yggr* 'Odin' + *drasill* 'horse.'

YHVH (also **YHWH**) ▸*abbr.* the Hebrew Tetragrammaton representing the name of God. See also TETRAGRAMMATON, YAHWEH.

yi /yi/ ▸*pron.* nonstandard spelling of YOU, used in representing Scottish speech.

Yi·chun /ˈēˈcʜo͝on/ (also **I-chun**) a city in northeastern China, in Heilongjiang province; pop. 882,000.

Yid /yid/ ▸*n. informal, offensive* a Jew. ▷late 19th cent.: back-formation from YIDDISH.

Yid·dish /ˈyidisʜ/ ▸*n.* a language used by Jews in central and eastern Europe before the Holocaust. It was originally a German dialect with words from Hebrew and several modern languages and is today spoken mainly in the U.S., Israel, and Russia.

▸*adj.* of or relating to this language. ▷late 19th cent.: from Yiddish *yidish (daytsh)* 'Jewish German.'

Yid·dish·er /ˈyidisʜər/ ▸*n.* a person speaking Yiddish.

Yid·dish·ism /ˈyidəˌsʜizəm/ ▸*n.* **1** a Yiddish word or idiom, esp. one adopted into another language. **2** advocacy of Yiddish culture. —**Yid·dish·ist** *n.* (in sense 2).

Yid·dish·keit /ˈyidisʜˌkīt/ ▸*n.* the quality of being Jewish; the Jewish way of life or its customs and practices. ▷late 19th cent.: from Yiddish *yidishkeyt*.

yield /yēld/ ▸*v.* **1** [*trans.*] produce or provide (a natural, agricultural, or industrial product): *the land yields grapes and tobacco.* ■ (of an action or process) produce or deliver (a result or gain): *this method yields the same results.* ■ (of a financial or commercial process or transaction) generate (a specified financial return): *such investments yield direct cash returns.* **2** [*intrans.*] give way to arguments, demands, or pressure: *the Western powers now yielded when they should have resisted* | *he* **yielded to** *the demands of his partners.* ■ [*trans.*] relinquish possession of (something); give (something) up: *they might* **yield up** *their secrets* | *they are forced to yield ground.* See note at RELINQUISH.■ [*trans.*] cease to argue about: *I yielded the point.* ■ (esp. in a legislature) allow another the right to speak in a debate: *I yield to the gentleman from Kentucky.* ■ give right of way to other traffic. ■ (of a mass or structure) give way under force or pressure: *he reeled into the house as the door yielded.*

▸*n.* the full amount of an agricultural or industrial product: *the milk yield was poor.* ■ *Finance* the amount of money brought in, e.g., interest from an investment or revenue from a tax; return: *an annual dividend yield of 20 percent.* ■ *Chemistry* the amount obtained from a process or reaction relative to the theoretical maximum amount obtainable. ■ (of a nuclear weapon) the force in tons or kilotons of TNT required to produce an equivalent explosion: *yields ranging from five kilotons to 100 tons.* ▷Old English *g(i)eldan* 'pay, repay,' of Germanic origin. The senses 'produce, bear' and 'surrender' arose in Middle English. —**yield·er** *n.* (usu. in sense 1).

yield curve ▸*n. Finance* a curve on a graph in which the yield of fixed-interest securities is plotted against the length of time they have to run to maturity.

yield gap ▸*n. Finance* the difference between the return on government-issued securities and that on common stock.

yield·ing /ˈyēldiNG/ ▸*adj.* **1** (of a substance or object) giving way under pressure; not hard or rigid: *she dropped on to the yielding cushions.* ■ (of a person) complying with the requests or desires of others: *a gentle, yielding person.* **2** [in *combination*] giving a product or generating a financial return of a specified amount: *higher-yielding wheat.* —**yield·ing·ly** *adv.*

yield man·age·ment ▸*n.* the process of making frequent adjustments in the price of a product in response to certain market factors, such as demand or competition.

yield point ▸*n. Physics* the stress beyond which a material becomes plastic.

yield strength ▸*n. Physics* (in materials that do not exhibit a well-defined yield point) the stress at which a specific amount of plastic deformation is produced, usually taken as 0.2 percent of the unstressed length.

yield stress ▸*n. Physics* the value of stress at a yield point or at the yield strength.

yikes /yīks/ ▸*exclam. informal* expressing shock and alarm, often for humorous effect: *I had a dip in the 40-degree pool (yikes!).* ▷1970s: of unknown origin; compare with YOICKS.

Pronunciation Key ə *ago*; ər *over*; ˈə *or* ˌə *up*; ˈər *or* ˌər *fur*; a *hat*; ā *rate*; ä *car*; cʜ *chew*; e *let*; ē *see*; e(ə)r *air*; i *fit*; ī *by*; i(ə)r *ear*; NG *sing*; ō *go*; ô *for*; oi *boy*; o͝o *good*; o͞o *goo*; ou *out*; sʜ *she*; тʜ *thin*; T̲H̲ *then*; (h)w *why*; zʜ *vision*

symbol for yin and yang

yin /yin/ ▸*n.* (in Chinese philosophy) the passive female principle of the universe, characterized as female and sustaining and associated with earth, dark, and cold. Contrasted with YANG. ▷from Chinese *yīn* 'feminine,' 'moon,' 'shade.'

Yin·chuan /ˈyinˈCHwän/ a city in northern central China, on the Yellow River, capital of autonomous region Ningxia; pop. 658,000.

yip /yip/ ▸*n.* a short, sharp cry or yelp, esp. of excitement or delight.
▸*v.* (**yipped, yip·ping**) [*intrans.*] give such a cry or yelp. ▷early 20th cent. (originally U.S.): imitative.

yipe /yīp/ ▸*exclam.* an expression of surprise, fear, pain, etc.

yip·pee /ˈyipē; ˌyipˈē/ ▸*exclam.* expressing wild excitement or delight. ▷natural exclamation: first recorded in American English in the 1920s.

yip·pie /ˈyipē/ ▸*n.* (*pl.* **-pies**) a member of a group of politically active hippies, originally in the U.S. ▷1960s: acronym from *Youth International Party* + the suffix *-ie*, on the pattern of *hippie*.

yips /yips/ ▸*plural n.* (**the yips**) *informal* extreme nervousness causing a golfer to miss easy putts. ▷mid 20th cent.: of unknown origin.

Yi·shuv /yiˈSHo͞ov/ the Jewish community or settlement in Palestine during the 19th century and until the formation of the state of Israel in 1948. ▷from Hebrew *yiššūḇ* 'settlement.'

Yiz·kor /ˈyiskər; ˈyiz-; yēzˈkôr/ ▸*n.* (*pl.* same or **-kors**) a memorial service held by Jews on certain holy days for deceased relatives or martyrs. ▷from Hebrew *yizkōr*, literally 'may (God) remember.'

-yl ▸*suffix Chemistry* forming names of radicals: *hydroxyl* | *phenyl*. ▷from Greek *hulē* 'wood, material.'

y·lang-y·lang /ˈēˌläNG ˈēˌläNG/ (also **i·lang-i·lang**) ▸*n.* **1** a sweet-scented essential oil obtained from the flowers of a tropical tree, used in perfumery and aromatherapy. **2** the yellow-flowered tree, native to the Malay peninsula and the Philippines, from which this oil is obtained. • *Cananga odorata*, family Annonaceae. ▷late 19th cent.: from Tagalog *ilang-ilang*.

y·lem /ˈīləm/ ▸*n. Astronomy* (in the big bang theory) the primordial matter of the universe, originally conceived as composed of neutrons at high temperature and density. ▷1940s: from late Latin *hylem* (accusative) 'matter,' from Greek *hūlē*.

yl·id /ˈilid/ (also **yl·ide** /ˈilīd/) ▸*n. Chemistry* a compound that has an uncharged molecule containing a negatively charged carbon atom directly bonded to a positively charged atom of sulfur, phosphorus, nitrogen, or another element. ▷1950s: from -YL + -IDE.

YMCA ▸*n.* a welfare movement that began in London in 1844 and now has branches all over the world. ■ a hostel or recreational facility run by this association. ▷abbreviation of *Young Men's Christian Association*.

YMHA ▸*abbr.* Young Men's Hebrew Association.

Y·mir /ˈēˌmi(ə)r/ *Scandinavian Mythology* the primeval giant from whose body the gods created the world.

-yne ▸*suffix Chemistry* forming names of unsaturated organic compounds containing a triple bond: *ethyne*. ▷alteration of -INE[4].

yo[1] /yō/ ▸*exclam. informal* used to greet someone, attract their attention, or express excitement. ▷natural exclamation: first recorded in late Middle English.

yo[2] ▸*pron.* nonstandard spelling of YOU, used to represent black English.
▸*possessive adj.* nonstandard spelling of YOUR, used to represent black English.

yob /yäb/ ▸*n. Brit., informal* a rude, noisy, and aggressive young man. ▷mid 19th cent.: backward spelling of BOY. —**yob·bish** *adj.* —**yob·bish·ly** *adv.* —**yob·bish·ness** *n.* —**yob·by** *adj.*

yob·bo /ˈyäbō/ ▸*n.* (*pl.* **-bos** or **-boes**) *Brit., informal* another term for YOB.

yock /yäk/ ▸*n.* variant form of YUK.

yocto- ▸*comb. form* (used in units of measurement) denoting a factor of 10^{-24}: *yoctojoule*. ▷adapted from OCTO-, on the pattern of combining forms such as *peta-* and *exa-*.

yod /yôd; yo͝od; yäd/ ▸*n.* **1** the tenth and smallest letter of the Hebrew alphabet. **2** *Phonetics* the semivowel or glide *y*. **3** *Astrology* another term for FINGER OF GOD. ▷from Hebrew *yōḏ*; related to *yaḏ* 'hand.'

yo·del /ˈyōdl/ ▸*v.* (**-deled, -del·ing**; *Brit.* **-delled, -del·ling**) [*intrans.*] practice a form of singing or calling marked by rapid alternation between the normal voice and falsetto.
▸*n.* a song, melody, or call delivered in such a way. ▷early 19th cent.: from German *jodeln*. —**yo·del·er** *n.*

yo·ga /ˈyōgə/ ▸*n.* a Hindu spiritual and ascetic discipline, a part of which, including breath control, simple meditation, and the adoption of specific bodily postures, is widely practiced for health and relaxation.

> The yoga widely known in the West is based on **hatha yoga**, which forms one aspect of the ancient Hindu system of religious and ascetic observance and meditation, the highest form of which is **raja yoga** and the ultimate aim of which is spiritual purification and self-understanding leading to *samadhi* or union with the divine.

▷Sanskrit, literally 'union.' —**yo·gic** /-gik/ *adj.*

yogh /yōg; yōKH/ ▸*n.* a Middle English letter (ȝ) used mainly where modern English has *gh* or *y*. ▷Middle English: of unknown origin.

yo·gi /ˈyōgē/ ▸*n.* (*pl.* **-gis**) a person who is proficient in yoga. ▷from Sanskrit *yogī*, from *yoga* (see YOGA).

yo·gic fly·ing ▸*n.* a technique used chiefly by Transcendental Meditation practitioners that involves thrusting oneself off the ground while in the lotus position.

yo·gurt /ˈyōgərt/ (also **yo·ghurt** or **yo·ghourt**) ▸*n.* a semisolid sourish food prepared from milk fermented by added bacteria, often sweetened and flavored. ▷early 17th cent.: from Turkish *yoğurt*.

Yog·ya·kar·ta /ˌyägyəˈkärtə/ (also **Jog·ja·kar·ta** /ˌjägyə-; ˌjägjə-/) a city in Indonesia, on the southern coast of the island of Java; pop. 412,000. It was formerly the capital of Indonesia 1945–49.

yo-heave-ho /ˈyō ˌhēv ˈhō/ ▸*exclam.* & *n.* another term for HEAVE-HO.

yo·him·be /yōˈhimbā; -bē/ ▸*n.* a tropical West African tree of the bedstraw family, from which the drug yohimbine is obtained. • *Pausinystalia johimbe*, family Rubiaceae. ▷late 19th cent.: a local word.

yo·him·bine /yōˈhimˌbēn/ ▸*n. Chemistry* a toxic crystalline compound obtained from the bark of the yohimbe tree, used as an adrenergic blocking agent and also in the treatment of impotence. • An alkaloid; chem. formula: $C_{21}H_{26}O_3N_2$. ▷late 19th cent.: from YOHIMBE + -INE[4].

yo-ho-ho /ˈyō ˌhō ˈhō/ (also **yo-ho**) ▸*exclam.* **1** *dated* used to attract attention. **2** *archaic Nautical* a seaman's chant used while hauling ropes or performing other strenuous work.

yoicks /yoiks/ ▸*exclam.* used by fox hunters to urge on the hounds. ▷mid 18th cent.: of unknown origin.

yoke /yōk/ ▸*n.* **1** a wooden crosspiece that is fastened over the necks of two animals and attached to the plow or cart that they are to pull. ■ (*pl.* same or **yokes**) a pair of animals coupled together in such a way: *a yoke of oxen*. ■ *archaic* the amount of land that one pair of oxen could plow in a day. ■ a frame fitting over the neck and shoulders of a person, used for carrying pails or baskets. ■ used of something that is regarded as oppressive or burdensome: *the yoke of imperialism*. ■ used of something that represents a bond between two parties: *the yoke of marriage*. **2** something resembling or likened to such a crosspiece, in particular: ■ a part of a garment that fits over the shoulders and to which the main part of the garment is attached, typically in gathers or pleats. ■ the crossbar at the head of a rudder, to whose ends ropes are fastened. ■ a bar of soft iron between the poles of an electromagnet. ■ (in ancient Rome) an arch of three spears under which a defeated army was made to march. ■ a control lever in an aircraft.
▸*v.* [*trans.*] **1** put a yoke on (a pair of animals); couple or attach with or to a yoke: *a plow drawn by a camel and donkey yoked together* | *figurative Hong Kong's dollar has been* **yoked to** *America's*. **2** *informal* rob; mug: *two crackheads yoked this girl*. ▷Old English *geoc* (noun), *geocian* (verb), of Germanic origin; related to Dutch *juk*, German *Joch*, from an Indo-European root shared by Latin *jugum* and Greek *zugon*, also by Latin *jungere* 'to join.'

yoke 1

yo·kel /ˈyōkəl/ ▸*n. informal, often derogatory* an uneducated and unsophisticated person from the countryside. ▷early 19th cent.: perhaps figuratively from dialect *yokel* 'green woodpecker.'

Yok·na·pa·taw·pha Coun·ty /ˌyäknəpəˈtôfə/ a fictional county in northern Mississippi, the setting for most of the work of William Faulkner.

Yo·ko·ha·ma /ˌyōkəˈhämə/ a seaport in central Japan, on the southern side of the island of Honshu; pop. 3,220,000. It is a major port and the second largest city in Japan.

yo·ko·zu·na /ˌyōkəˈzo͞onə/ ▸*n.* (*pl.* same) a grand champion sumo wrestler. ▷Japanese, from *yoko* 'crosswise' + *tsuna* 'rope' (originally denoting a kind of belt presented to the champion).

yolk /yōk/ ▸*n.* the yellow internal part of a bird's egg, which is surrounded by the white, is rich in protein and fat, and nourishes the developing embryo. ■ *Zoology* the corresponding part in the ovum or larva of all egg-laying vertebrates and many invertebrates. ▷Old English *geol(o)ca*, from *geolu* 'yellow.' —**yolked** *adj.* [also in *combination*] —**yolk·less** *adj.* —**yolk·y** *adj.*

yolk sac ▸*n. Zoology* a membranous sac containing yolk attached to the embryos of reptiles and birds and the larvae of some fishes. ■ a sac lacking yolk in the early embryo of a mammal.

yolk stalk ▸*n.* a tubular connection between the yolk sac and the digestive tract of a developing embryo.

Yol·la Bol·ly Moun·tains /ˈyälə ˌbälē/ a range of the Klamath Mountains, in northwestern California, noted for its wilderness and wildlife.

Yom Kip·pur /ˈyôm kiˈpo͝or; ˈyōm; ˈyäm; ˈkipər/ ▸*n.* the most solemn religious fast of the Jewish year, the last of the ten days of penitence that begin with Rosh Hashanah (the Jewish New Year). Also called DAY OF ATONEMENT. ▷Hebrew.

Yom Kip·pur War the Israeli name for the Arab–Israeli conflict in 1973. Arab name OCTOBER WAR.

> The war lasted for less than three weeks; it started on the festival of Yom Kippur (in that year, October 6) when Egypt and Syria simultaneously attacked Israeli forces from the south and north, respectively. The Syrians were repulsed, and the Egyptians were surrounded. A cease-fire followed, and disengagement agreements over the Suez area were signed in 1974 and 1975.

yon /yän/ ▸*adj.* & *adv. poetic/literary* or *dialect* yonder; that: [as *adj.*] *you'll find some big ranches yon side of the Sierra*.
▸*pron. poetic/literary* or *dialect* yonder person or thing: *what do you make of yon?* ▷Old English *geon*, of Germanic origin; related to German *jener* 'that one.'
▸*PHRASE* □ **hither and yon** another term for HITHER AND THITHER.

yond /yänd/ ▸*adv.* & *adj. archaic* yonder.

yon·der /ˈyändər/ ▸*adv. archaic* or *dialect* at some distance in the direction indicated; over there: *there's a ford south of here, about nine miles yonder*.
▸*adj. archaic* or *dialect* that or those (used to refer to something situated at a distance): *what light through yonder window breaks?*
▸*n.* (**the yonder**) the far distance: *attempting to fly off into* **the wild blue yonder**. ▷Middle English: of Germanic origin; related to Dutch *ginder* 'over there,' also to YON.

yo·ni /ˈyōnē/ ▸*n.* (*pl.* **-nis**) *Hinduism* the vulva, esp. as a symbol of divine procreative energy conventionally represented by a circular stone. Compare with LINGAM. ▷Sanskrit, literally 'source, womb, female genitals.'

Yon·kers /ˈyäNGkərz/ an industrial city in southeastern New York, on the Hudson River, north of the Bronx in New York City; pop. 196,086.

yonks /yäNGks/ ▸*plural n. Brit., informal* a very long time: *I haven't seen him* **for yonks**. ▷1960s: origin unknown; perhaps related to *donkey's years* (see DONKEY).

yoo-hoo /ˈyo͞o ˌho͞o/ ▸*exclam.* a call used to attract attention to one's arrival or presence: *Yoo-hoo!—Is anyone there?*
▸*v.* [*intrans.*] (of a person) make such a call. ▷natural exclamation: first recorded in English in the 1920s.

Yor·ba Lin·da /ˌyôrbə ˈlində/ a city in southwestern California, southeast of Los Angeles; pop. 52,422.

yore /yôr/ ▸*n.* (in phrase of **yore**) *poetic/literary* of long ago or former times (used in nostalgic or mock-nostalgic recollection): *a great empire in days of yore.* ▷Old English *geāra, geāre*, of unknown origin.

York /yôrk/ **1** a city in northern England, on the Ouse River; pop. 101,000. **2** a commercial and industrial city in southeastern Pennsylvania; pop. 42,192. **3** the southwestern tip of Hayes Peninsula, on Baffin Bay in Greenland. It served as a base for U.S. explorer Robert E. Peary's polar expedition. A 100-ton meteorite found here was brought to the U.S. by Peary. ▷(as the name of the English city) from Danish *Jorvik.*

York, Cape a cape that extends into Torres Strait at the northeast tip of Australia, in Queensland.

York, House of the English royal house that ruled England from 1461 (Edward IV) until the defeat and death of Richard III in 1485, with a short break in 1470–01 (the restoration of Henry VI).

York·ie /ˈyôrkē/ ▸*n.* (*pl.* **-ies**) *informal* YORKSHIRE TERRIER.

York·ist /ˈyôrkist/ *historical* ▸*n.* an adherent or a supporter of the House of York, esp. in the Wars of the Roses.

▸*adj.* of or relating to the House of York: *the town rallied itself to the Yorkist cause.*

Yorks. ▸*abbr.* Yorkshire.

York·shire /ˈyôrk,SHi(ə)r; -SHər/ a former county in northern England, traditionally divided into East, West, and North Ridings. **—York·shire·man** /-mən/ *n.* (*pl.* **-men**) **—York·shire·wom·an** /-ˌwo͝omən/ *n.* (*pl.* **-wom·en**).

York·shire pud·ding ▸*n.* a popover made of baked unsweetened egg batter, typically eaten with roast beef.

York·shire ter·ri·er ▸*n.* a dog of a small, long-haired blue-gray and tan breed of terrier.

Yorkshire terrier

York·town /ˈyôrk,toun/ a historic site in southeastern Virginia, on the York River, north of Newport News, site of both the last (October 1781) battle of the American Revolution and a Civil War battle (1862).

Yo·ru·ba /ˈyôrəbə/ ▸*n.* (*pl.* same or **-bas**) **1** a member of a people of southwestern Nigeria and Benin. **2** the Kwa language of this people and an official language of Nigeria.

▸*adj.* of or relating to the Yoruba or their language. ▷the name in Yoruba.

Yor·vik /ˈyôrvik/ (also **Jor·vik**) Viking name for YORK sense 1.

Yo·sem·i·te Na·tion·al Park /yōˈsemətē/ a national park in the Sierra Nevada, in central California. It includes Yosemite Valley, with its sheer granite cliffs, and Yosemite Falls, the highest waterfall in the U.S.

Yo·shkar-O·la /yəSHˈkär əˈlä/ a city in western Russia, southeast of Nizhni Novgorod, capital of the republic of Mari El; pop. 246,000.

yotta- ▸*comb. form* (used in units of measurement) denoting a factor of 10^{24}: *yottameter.* ▷apparently adapted from Italian *otto* 'eight' (see also YOCTO-).

you /yo͞o/ ▸*pron.* [*second person singular* or *plural*] **1** used to refer to the person or people that the speaker is addressing: *are you listening?* | *I love you.* ■ used to refer to the person being addressed together with other people regarded in the same class: *you Australians.* ■ used in exclamations to address one or more people: *you fools* | *hey, you!* **2** used to refer to any person in general: *after a while, you get used to it.* ▷Old English *ēow*, accusative and dative of *gē* (see YE[1]); related to Dutch *u* and German *euch.* During the 14th cent. *you* began to replace YE[1], THOU[1], and THEE; by the 17th cent. it had become the ordinary second person pronoun for any number and case.

▸*PHRASES* □ **you and yours** you together with your family and close friends. □ **you-know-who** (or **you-know-what**) used to refer to someone (or something) known to the hearer without specifying their identity: *the minister was later to be sacked by you-know-who.*

you-all /ˈyo͞o ,ôl; yôl/ (also **y'all**) ▸*pron. dialect* (in the southern U.S.) you (used to refer to more than one person): *how are you-all?*

you'd /yo͞od/ ▸*contraction of* ■ you had: *you'd better remember it.* ■ you would: *I was afraid you'd ask me that.*

Yough·io·ghe·ny Riv·er /ˌyäkəˈgānē/ a river that flows for 135 miles (220 km) from West Virginia into Pennsylvania where it joins the Monongahela River at McKeesport.

you'll /yo͞ol/ ▸*contraction of* you will; you shall: *you'll find many exciting features.*

Young[1] /yəNG/, Andrew (Jackson, Jr.) (1932–), U.S. politician, civil rights leader, and clergyman. He served in various capacities with the Southern Christian Leadership Conference 1964–70 before becoming a Democratic representative from Georgia in the U.S. Congress 1973–79. He was the U.S. ambassador to the UN 1977–79 and mayor of Atlanta 1982–90.

Young[2], Brigham (1801–77), U.S. Mormon leader. He succeeded Joseph Smith as leader of the Mormons in 1844, led them westward, and established their headquarters at Salt Lake City, Utah. He served as governor of the territory of Utah from 1850 until 1857.

Young[3], Cy (1867–1955), U.S. baseball player; born *Denton True Young*; also know as the **Cyclone**. The all-time pitching leader in wins (511), he pitched for the Cleveland Spiders 1890–98, the St. Louis Cardinals 1899–1900, the Boston Red Sox 1901–08, and, briefly, the Cleveland Indians and the Boston Braves before retiring in 1911. Baseball's Cy Young Award for outstanding pitchers is named for him. Baseball Hall of Fame (1937).

Cy Young

Young[4], Steve (1961–) U.S. football player; full name *Jon Steven Young.* He began his professional career with the Tampa Bay Bucaneers 1985–87 and continued as a quarterback with the San Francisco 49ers 1987–2000. Named the NFL's most valuable player in 1992 and 1994, he led his team to victory in the Super Bowl in 1995.

Young[5], Thomas (1773–1829), English physicist, physician, and Egyptologist. His major work in physics concerned the wave theory of light. He also played a major part in the deciphering of the Rosetta Stone.

young /yəNG/ ▸*adj.* (**young·er** /ˈyəNGgər/, **young·est** /ˈyəNGgəst/) having lived or existed for only a short time: *a young girl* | [as *plural n.*] (**the young**) *the young are amazingly resilient.* ■ not as old as the norm or as would be expected: *more people were dying young.* ■ [*attrib.*] relating to, characteristic of, or consisting of young people: *young love* | *the Young Communist League.* ■ immature or inexperienced: *she's very* **young for her age.** ■ having the qualities popularly associated with young people, such as enthusiasm and optimism: *all those who are* **young at heart.** ■ (**the Younger**) used to denote the younger of two people of the same name: *Pitt the Younger.* ■ (**younger**) [*postpositive*] *Scottish* denoting the heir of a landed commoner: *Hugh Magnus Macleod, younger of Macleod.*

▸*n.* [treated as *pl.*] offspring, esp. of an animal before or soon after birth: *this species carries its young.* ▷Old English *g(e)ong*, of Germanic origin; related to Dutch *jong* and German *jung*, also to YOUTH; from an Indo-European root shared by Latin *juvenis.* **—young·ish** /ˈyəNGiSH/ *adj.*

▸*PHRASE* □ **with young** (of an animal) pregnant.

young·ber·ry /ˈyəNG,berē/ ▸*n.* (*pl.* **-ries**) a bramble of a variety that bears large, edible reddish-black fruit, believed to be a hybrid of a dewberry. ▷1920s: named after B. M. *Young* (*fl.* 1905), the American horticulturalist who first raised it.

young fus·tic ▸*n.* the smoke tree.

young gun ▸*n. informal* a young man perceived as assertive and aggressively self-confident.

young la·dy ▸*n.* a woman who is not far advanced in life; a girl. ■ a form of address used by an adult to a girl, often in anger: *I don't know what's got into you, young lady.* ■ *dated* a girlfriend.

young·ling /ˈyəNGliNG/ ▸*n. poetic/literary* a young person or animal.

young man ▸*n.* a man who is not far advanced in life; a boy. ■ a form of address used by an adult to a boy, often in anger: *don't waste my time, young man.* ■ *dated* a boyfriend.

Young Pre·tend·er see STUART[1].

Young's mod·u·lus /ˈyəNGz/ ▸*n. Physics* a measure of elasticity, equal to the ratio of the stress acting on a substance to the strain produced. ▷mid 19th cent.: named after T. *Young* (see YOUNG[5]).

young·ster /ˈyəNGstər/ ▸*n.* a child, young person, or young animal.

Youngs·town /ˈyəNGz,toun/ an industrial city in northeastern Ohio, in the Mahoning River valley; pop. 82,026.

Young Turk ▸*n.* a member of a revolutionary party in the Ottoman Empire who carried out the revolution of 1908 and deposed the sultan Abdul Hamid II. ■ a young person eager for radical change to the established order.

young 'un ▸*n. informal* a youngster.

youn·ker /ˈyəNGkər/ ▸*n. dated* a youngster. ▷early 16th cent. (denoting a young nobleman): from Middle Dutch *jonckher*, from *jonc* 'young' + *hēre* 'lord.' Compare with JUNKER.

your /yôr; yo͝or/ ▸*possessive adj.* **1** belonging to or associated with the person or people that the speaker is addressing: *what is your name?* **2** belonging to or associated with any person in general: *the sight is enough to break your heart.* ■ *informal* used to denote someone or something that is familiar or typical of its kind: *I'm just* **your average** *Joe* | *she is one of your chatty types.* **3** (**Your**) used when addressing the holder of certain titles: *Your Majesty* | *Your Eminence.* ▷Old English *ēower*, genitive of *gē* (see YE[1]), of Germanic origin; related to German *euer.*

you're /yo͝or; yôr/ ▸*contraction of* you are: *you're an angel, Deb!*

yourn /yôrn; yo͝orn/ ▸*possessive pron.* regional or archaic form of YOURS.

yours /yôrz; yo͝orz/ ▸*possessive pron.* **1** used to refer to a thing or things belonging to or associated with the person or people that the speaker is addressing: *the choice is yours* | *it's no business* **of yours.** ■ *dated* (chiefly in commercial use) your letter: *Mr. Smythe has sent me yours of the 15th inst. regarding the vacancy.* **2** used in formulas ending a letter: *Yours sincerely, John Watson* | *Yours, Jim Lindsay.*

▸*PHRASES* □ **up yours** see UP. □ **you and yours** see YOU. □ **yours truly** see TRULY.

your·self /yərˈself; yôr-; yo͝or-/ ▸*pron.* [*second person singular*] (*pl.* **-selves** /-ˈselvz/) **1** [*reflexive*] used to refer to the person being addressed as the object of a verb or preposition when they are also the subject of the clause: *help yourselves, boys* | *see for yourself.* **2** [*emphatic*] you personally (used to emphasize the person being addressed): *you're going to have to do it yourself.*

▸*PHRASES* □ (**not**) **be yourself** see BE ONESELF, NOT BE ONESELF at BE. □ **by yourself** see BY ONESELF at BY. □ **how's yourself?** *informal* how are you? (used esp. after answering a similar inquiry).

youse /yo͞oz/ ▸*pron. dialect* you (usually more than one person).

youth /yo͞oTH/ ▸*n.* (*pl.* **youths** /yo͞oTHs; yo͞o<u>TH</u>z/) **1** [in *sing.*] the period between childhood and adult age: *he had been a keen sportsman in his youth.* ■ the state or quality of being young, esp. as associated with vigor, freshness, or immaturity: *she imagined her youth and beauty fading.* ■ an early stage in the development of something: *this publishing sector is no longer in its youth.* **2** [treated as *sing.* or *pl.*] young people considered as a group: *middle-class youth have romanticized poverty* | [as *adj.*] *youth culture.* ■ a young man: *he was attacked by a gang of youths.* ▷Old English *geoguth*, of Germanic origin; related to Dutch *jeugd*, German *Jugend*, also to **YOUNG**.

youth cen·ter (also **youth club**) ▸*n.* a place or organization providing leisure activities for young people.

youth·ful /ˈyo͞oᴛʜfəl/ ▸*adj.* young or seeming young: *people aspiring to remain youthful.* ■ typical or characteristic of young people: *youthful enthusiasm.* **—youth·ful·ly** *adv.* **—youth·ful·ness** *n.*

THE RIGHT WORD **adolescent, callow, immature, juvenile, puerile, youthful**

Everyone wants to look **youthful**, an adjective that means possessing, or appearing to possess, the qualities associated with youth (*she is remarkably more youthful than her twin*).

But no one wants to be called **immature**, which means childish or emotionally underdeveloped and usually pertains to behavior and attitudes rather than to physical appearance (*still immature despite the fact that he was almost thirty*).

Juvenile suggests immaturity of mind or body and is applied especially to things that are designed for boys and girls in their early teens (*juvenile books*), while **adolescent** applies to the period between puberty and maturity and suggests the physical awkwardness and emotional instability associated with the teenage years (*an adolescent response to criticism*).

Young men in particular are often described as **callow**, which means immature in terms of experience (*a callow youth who had never lived away from his family*).

Of all these words, **puerile** is probably the most insulting, because it is so often used to describe adults who display the immature behavior of a child (*a puerile piece of writing; a puerile revolt against his aging parents*).

youth hos·tel ▸*n.* a place providing cheap accommodations aimed mainly at young people on hiking or cycling tours.

you've /yo͞ov/ ▸*contraction of* you have: *you've changed.*

yow /you/ (also **yeow**) ▸*exclam.* used to express pain or shock. ▷late Middle English: imitative. The word was not recorded again until the mid 19th cent., when it was used to express the cry of a dog or cat.

yowl /youl/ ▸*n.* a loud wailing cry, esp. one of pain or distress.

▸*v.* [*intrans.*] make such a cry: *he yowled as he touched one of the hot plates.* ▷Middle English: imitative.

yo-yo /ˈyō ˌyō/ ▸*n.* (*pl.* **-yos**) a toy consisting of a pair of joined discs with a deep groove between them in which string is attached and wound, which can be spun alternately downward and upward by its weight and momentum as the string unwinds and rewinds. ■ [often as *adj.*] a thing that repeatedly falls and rises again: *the yo-yo syndrome of repeatedly losing weight and gaining it again.* ■ *informal* a stupid, insane, or unpredictable person.

▸*v.* (**-yoes, -yoed**) [*intrans.*] move up and down; fluctuate: *popularity polls yo-yo up and down with the flow of events.* ■ [*trans.*] manipulate or maneuver (someone or something): *I don't want the job if it means he gets to yo-yo me around.* ▷early 20th cent.: of unknown origin.

Y·pres /ˈēpr(ə)/ a town in northwestern Belgium, near the border with France, in the province of West Flanders; pop. 35,000. It was the scene of some of the bitterest fighting during World War I (see **YPRES, BATTLE OF**). Flemish name **IEPER**.

Y·pres, Bat·tle of each of three battles on the Western Front near Ypres during World War I in 1914, 1915, and 1917. See also **PASSCHENDAELE, BATTLE OF**.

Yp·si·lan·ti /ˌipsəˈlantē/ an industrial city in southeastern Michigan, near Ann Arbor; pop. 24,846.

Y·quem /ēˈkem/ ▸*n.* a sweet white wine from the estate of Château d'Yquem in the Sauternes region of France.

yr. ▸*abbr.* ■ year or years. ■ younger. ■ your.

yrs. ▸*abbr.* ■ years. ■ yours (as a formula ending a letter).

YT ▸*abbr.* Yukon Territory (in official postal use).

YTD ▸*abbr.* year-to-date.

yt·ter·bi·um /iˈtərbēəm/ ▸*n.* the chemical element of atomic number 70, a silvery-white metal of the lanthanide series. (Symbol: **Yb**) ▷late 19th cent.: modern Latin, from *Ytterby*, the name of a Swedish town where it was first found in a quarry.

yt·tri·um /ˈitrēəm/ ▸*n.* the chemical element of atomic number 39, a grayish-white metal generally included among the rare-earth elements. (Symbol: **Y**) ▷early 19th cent.: modern Latin, from *Ytterby* (see **YTTERBIUM**).

Yu·an /yo͞oˈän/ a dynasty that ruled China AD 1259–1368, established by the Mongols under Kublai Khan. It preceded the Ming dynasty.

yu·an /yo͞oˈän/ ▸*n.* (*pl.* same) the basic monetary unit of China, equal to 10 jiao or 100 fen. ▷Chinese, literally 'round'; compare with **YEN**[1].

Yuan Jiang /yo͞oˈän jēˈäɴɢ/ Chinese name for **RED RIVER** (sense 1).

Yu·ba Cit·y /ˈyo͞obə/ a commercial city in north central California, northwest of Sacramento; pop. 27,437.

yuc·a /ˈyo͞okə/ ▸*n.* another term for **CASSAVA**. ▷Carib.

Yu·cai·pa /yo͞oˈkīpə/ a city in southern California, southeast of San Bernardino; pop. 32,824.

Yu·ca·tán /ˌyo͞okəˈtan; -ˈtän; ˈyo͞okəˌtan; -ˌtän/ a state in southeastern Mexico, at the northern tip of the Yucatán Peninsula; capital, Mérida. ▷adapted from a Mayan name for the language of the Mayan Indians in Oaxaca, Mexico.

Yu·ca·tán Pen·in·su·la a peninsula in southern Mexico that lies between the Gulf of Mexico and the Caribbean Sea.

Yu·ca·tec /ˈyo͞okəˌtek/ ▸*n.* (*pl.* same or **-tecs**) **1** a member of a native people of the Yucatán peninsula. ■ *informal* a native or inhabitant of the peninsula or the state of Yucatán. **2** the Mayan language of the Yucatec people.

▸*adj.* of or relating to the Yucatec or their language. ▷from Spanish *yucateco*. **—Yu·ca·tec·an** /ˌyo͞okəˈtekən/ *adj.*

yuc·ca /ˈyəkə/ ▸*n.* a plant of the agave family with stiff swordlike leaves and spikes of white bell-shaped flowers that are dependent upon the yucca moth for fertilization, found esp. in warm regions of North America and Mexico. • Genus *Yucca*, family Agavaceae: many species, including Spanish bayonet and Adam's-needle. See illustration at **ADAM'S-NEEDLE**. ▷mid 16th cent. (denoting cassava): from Carib.

yuc·ca moth ▸*n.* a small white American moth that lays its eggs in the ovary of a yucca plant. While doing so it deposits a ball of pollen on the stigma, thereby fertilizing the seeds on which the larvae feed. • Genus *Tegeticula*, family Incurvariidae: several species, in particular *T. yuccasella*.

Yu·chi /ˈyo͞oᴄʜē/ ▸*n.* (*pl.* same or **-chis**) **1** a member of an American Indian people now incorporated into the Creek Confederacy in Oklahoma. **2** the language of this people. ▷Creek, of uncertain origin.

yuck /yək/ *informal* ▸*exclam.* (also **yuk**) used to express strong distaste or disgust: *"Raw herrings! Yuck!"*

▸*n.* something messy or disgusting: *I can't bear the sight of blood and yuck.* ▷1960s (originally U.S.): imitative.

yuck·y /ˈyəkē/ (also **yuk·ky**) ▸*adj.* (**yuck·i·er, yuck·i·est**) *informal* messy or disgusting: *yucky green-gray slushy cabbage.*

Yue /yo͞oˈā/ ▸*n.* another term for **CANTONESE** (the language).

yu·ga /ˈyo͞ogə/ ▸*n.* *Hinduism* any of the four ages of the life of the world. ▷Sanskrit.

Yu·go·slav /ˈyo͞ogōˌsläv; ˌyo͞ogōˈsläv; -gə-/ ▸*n.* a native or national of Yugoslavia or its former constituent republics, or a person of Yugoslav descent.

▸*adj.* of or relating to Yugoslavia, its former constituent republics, or its people. ▷from Austrian German *Jugoslav*, from Serbo-Croat *jug* 'south' + **SLAV**.

Yu·go·sla·vi·a /ˌyo͞ogōˈslävēə; ˌyo͞ogə-/ a former federation of states in southeastern Europe, in the Balkans. **—Yu·go·sla·vi·an** *adj.* & *n.*

The country was formed as the Kingdom of Serbs, Croats, and Slovenes in the peace settlements at the end of World War I. It included Serbia, Montenegro, and the former South Slavic provinces of the Austro-Hungarian empire and assumed the name of Yugoslavia in 1929; its capital was Belgrade. After World War II, during which time Yugoslavia was invaded by Germany, the country emerged as a nonaligned communist federal republic under Marshal Tito. In 1990, communist rule was formally ended. Four of the six constituent republics (Slovenia, Croatia, Bosnia–Herzegovina, and Macedonia) then seceded amid serious civil and ethnic conflict. The two remaining republics, Serbia and Montenegro, declared a new Federal Republic of Yugoslavia in 1992 and formed a loose federation called Serbia and Montenegro in 2003.

yuh /yə/ ▸*pron.* nonstandard spelling of **YOU**, used in representing black English speech.

▸*possessive adj.* nonstandard spelling of **YOUR**, used in representing black English speech.

Yu·it /ˈyo͞oət/ ▸*n.* (*pl.* same or **Yu·its**) & *adj.* another term for **YUPIK**. ▷Siberian Yupik, literally 'people.'

yuk ▸*exclam.* variant spelling of **YUCK**.

▸*n.* *informal* a laugh, esp. a loud hearty one. [1930s: (theatrical slang): probably imitative.]

▸***PHRASE*** □ **yuk it up** (**yukked, yuk·king**) laugh, esp. in a loud hearty way.

Yu·ka·ghir /ˌyo͞okəˈgir/ ▸*n.* (*pl.* same or **-ghirs**) **1** a member of a people of Arctic Siberia. **2** the language of this people, of uncertain affinity but possibly Uralic.

▸*adj.* of or relating to this people or their language. ▷Yakut.

yu·ka·ta /yo͞oˈkätə/ ▸*n.* (*pl.* same or **-tas**) a light cotton kimono. ▷Japanese, from *yu* 'hot water' (because originally worn indoors after a bath) + *kata(bira)* 'light kimono.'

yuk·ky ▸*adj.* variant spelling of **YUCKY**.

Yu·kon /ˈyo͞oˌkän/ a river in northwestern North America that rises in Yukon Territory in northwestern Canada and flows west for 1,870 miles (3,020 km) through central Alaska to the Bering Sea.

Yu·kon stove ▸*n.* a lightweight portable stove consisting of a small metal box divided into firebox and oven.

Yu·kon Ter·ri·to·ry a territory in northwestern Canada, on the border with Alaska; pop. 27,797; capital, Whitehorse. The population increased briefly during the Klondike gold rush 1897–99.

yu·lan /ˈyo͞oˌlan; -lən/ ▸*n.* a Chinese magnolia with showy white flowers. • *Magnolia heptapeta*, family Magnoliaceae. ▷early 19th cent.: from Chinese *yùlán*, from *yù* 'gem' + *lán* 'plant.'

Yule /yo͞ol/ ▸*n.* archaic term for **CHRISTMAS**. ▷Old English *gēol(a)* 'Christmas Day'; compare with Old Norse *jól*, originally applied to a heathen festival lasting twelve days, later to Christmas.

yule log ▸*n.* a large log traditionally burned in the fireplace on Christmas Eve. ■ a log-shaped chocolate cake eaten at Christmas.

Yule·tide /ˈyo͞olˌtīd/ ▸*n.* archaic term for **CHRISTMAS**.

yum /yəm/ (also **yum-yum**) *informal* ▸*exclam.* used to express pleasure at eating, or at the prospect of eating, a particular food.

▸*adj.* (of food) delicious. ▷late 19th cent.: imitative.

Yu·ma[1] /ˈyo͞omə/ a city in southwestern Arizona, near the Colorado River and the Mexican border; pop. 77,515.

Yu·ma[2] ▸*n.* **1** (*pl.* same or **-mas**) a member of an American Indian people living mainly in southwestern Arizona. **2** the Yuman language of this people.

▸*adj.* of or relating to this people. ▷from Pima *yumĭ*.

Yu·man /ˈyo͞omən/ ▸*n.* a family of American Indian languages including Yuma.

▸*adj.* of or relating to the Yuman languages or their speakers. ▷from **YUMA** + **-AN**.

yum·my /ˈyəmē/ ▸*adj.* (**-mi·er, -mi·est**) *informal* (of food) delicious: *yummy pumpkin cakes.* ■ highly attractive and desirable: *I scooped up this yummy young man.* ▷late 19th cent.: from **YUM** + **-Y**[1].

Yun·nan /yo͞oˈnän/ a province in southwestern China, on the border with Vietnam, Laos, and Myanmar (Burma); capital, Kunming.

yup[1] /yəp/ ▸*exclam.* & *n.* variant spelling of **YEP**.

yup[2] ▸*n.* short for **YUPPIE**.

Yu·pik /ˈyo͞opik/ ▸*n.* (*pl.* same or **-piks**) **1** a member of an Eskimo people of Siberia, the Aleutian Islands, and southwestern Alaska. **2** any of the Eskimo languages of this people.

▸*adj.* of or relating to this people or their languages. ▷from Alaskan Yupik *Yup'ik* 'real person.'

USAGE See usage at **INUIT**.

yup·pie /ˈyəpē/ (also **yup·py**) ▸*n.* (*pl.* **-pies**) *informal, derogatory* a well-paid young middle-class professional who works in a city job and has a luxurious lifestyle. ▷1980s: elaboration of the acronym from *young urban professional*. **—yup·pie·dom** /-dəm/ *n.*

yup·pie flu (also **yup·pie dis·ease**) ▶*n.* informal derogatory term for **CHRONIC FATIGUE SYNDROME**.

yup·pi·fy /ˈyəpəˌfī/ ▶*v.* (**-fies**, **-fied**) [*trans.*] *informal, derogatory* make more affluent and upmarket in keeping with the taste and lifestyle of yuppies: *Kreuzberg is slowly being yuppified with smart little eating places.* **—yup·pi·fi·ca·tion** /ˌyəpəfiˈkāsHən/ *n.*

Yu·rok /ˈyo͝orˌäk; -ək/ ▶*n.* (*pl.* same or **-roks**) **1** a member of an American Indian people of northern California. **2** the language of this people, distantly related to Algonquian.
▶*adj.* of or relating to this people or their language. ▷from Karok *yúruk*, literally 'downstream.'

yurt /yo͝ort; yərt/ ▶*n.* a circular tent of felt or skins on a collapsible framework, used by nomads in Mongolia, Siberia, and Turkey. ▷from Russian *yurta*, via French or German from Turkic *jurt*.

Yu·zov·ka /ˈyo͞ozəfkə/ former name (1872–1924) for **DONETSK**. ▷named in honor of John Hughes (1814–89), a Welshman who established its first ironworks.

YWCA ▶*n.* a welfare movement with branches in many countries that began in Britain in 1855. ■ a hostel or recreational facility run by this association. ▷abbreviation of *Young Women's Christian Association*.

YWHA ▶*abbr.* Young Women's Hebrew Association.

Zz

Z[1] /zē/ (also **z**) ▸*n.* (*pl.* **Zs** or **Z's**) **1** the twenty-sixth letter of the alphabet. ▪ denoting the next after Y in a set of items, categories, etc. ▪ denoting a third unknown or unspecified person or thing: *X sold a car to Y (a car dealer) who in turn sold it to Z (a finance company).* ▪ (usu. ***z***) the third unknown quantity in an algebraic expression. [the introduction of *x, y,* and *z* as symbols of unknown quantities is due to Descartes (see **X**[1]).] ▪ (usu. ***z***) denoting the third axis in a three-dimensional system of coordinates: [in *combination*] *the z-axis.* **2** a shape like that of a capital Z: [in *combination*] *the same old **Z-shaped** crack in the paving stone.* **3** used in repeated form to represent the sound of buzzing or snoring.

▸*PHRASE* □ **catch some** (or **a few**) **Zs** *informal* get some sleep: *I'll go back to the hotel and catch some Zs.*

Z[2] ▸*symbol Chemistry* atomic number.

za·ba·glio·ne /ˌzäbəlˈyōnē/ ▸*n.* an Italian dessert made of whipped and heated egg yolks, sugar, and Marsala wine, served hot or cold. ▷Italian.

Zab·rze /ˈzäbzHə/ an industrial and mining city in southern Poland, in Upper Silesia; pop. 205,000. From 1915 to 1945, it was a German city called Hindenburg.

Za·ca·te·cas /ˌzäkəˈtākəs; ˌsäkə-/ a state in northern central Mexico. ▪ its capital, a silver-mining city located at an altitude of 8,200 feet (2,500 m); pop. 165,000.

zaf·fer /ˈzafər/ (also **zaf·fre**) ▸*n.* impure cobalt oxide, formerly used to make smalt and blue enamels. ▷mid 17th cent.: from Italian *zaffera* or French *safre.*

zaf·tig /ˈzäftig; -tik/ (also **zof·tig**) ▸*adj. informal* (of a woman) having a full, rounded figure; plump. ▷1930s: Yiddish, from German *saftig* 'juicy.'

zag /zag/ ▸*n.* a sharp change of direction in a zigzag course: *we traveled in a series of zigs and zags.*

▸*v.* (**zagged**, **zag·ging**) [*intrans.*] make a sharp change of direction: *a long path zigged and **zagged through** the woods.* ▷late 18th cent.: shortening of **ZIGZAG**.

Za·ga·zig /ˌzägəˈzēg; zäˈgäzig/ (also **Za·qa·ziq** /ˌzäkäˈzēk/) a city in northern Egypt, located on the Nile delta; pop. 279,000.

Za·greb /ˈzäˌgreb/ a city in northern central Croatia, the country's capital; pop. 707,000.

Zag·ros Moun·tains /ˈzagrəs; -ˌrōs/ a mountain range in western Iran that rises to 14,921 feet (4,548 m) at Zard Kuh. Most of Iran's oil fields lie along the western foothills.

Za·har·i·as /zəˈharēəs/, Babe (1914–56), U.S. track and field athlete and golfer; full name *Mildred Ella Didrikson Zaharias.* After winning gold medals in the javelin throw and 80-millimeter hurdle events at the 1932 Olympic games, she turned to golf and won many major professional titles between 1936 and 1954.

zai·ba·tsu /zīˈbätˌsoō; -ˈbat-/ ▸*n.* (*pl.* same) a large Japanese business conglomerate. ▷Japanese, from *zai* 'wealth' + *batsu* 'clique.'

Za·ire /zäˈi(ə)r/ Former name (until 1997) of **CONGO, DEMOCRATIC REPUBLIC OF THE.** —**Za·ir·e·an** /-ˈi(ə)rēən/ (also **Za·ir·i·an**) *adj.* & *n.*

za·ire /zäˈi(ə)r/ ▸*n.* (*pl.* same) the basic monetary unit of Zaire (now the Democratic Republic of the Congo), equal to 100 makuta. ▷from *Zaire,* a local name for the Congo River in central Africa.

Za·ire Riv·er see **CONGO**.

za·kat /zəˈkät; -ˈkat/ ▸*n.* obligatory payment made annually under Islamic law on certain kinds of property and used for charitable and religious purposes. ▷via Persian and Urdu from Arabic *zakā(t)* 'almsgiving.'

Za·kin·thos /ˈzäkinˌTHôs; zəˈkinTHəs/ (also **Za·kyn·thos**) a Greek island off the southwestern coast of mainland Greece, in the Ionian Sea, one of the Ionian Islands; pop. 33,000. Also called **ZANTE**.

za·kus·ka /zəˈkoōskə/ (also **za·kous·ka**) ▸*n.* (*pl.* **-ski** /-skē/ or **-skas**) a substantial Russian hors d'oeuvre item such as caviar sandwiches or vegetables with sour cream dip, all served with vodka. ▷Russian.

zal·cit·a·bine /zalˈsitəˌbēn/ ▸*n.* another term for **DIDEOXYCYTIDINE**. ▷1990s: from *zal-* (of unknown origin) + *-citabine* apparently formed by arbitrary alteration of **CYTIDINE**.

Zam·be·zi /zamˈbēzē/ a river in East Africa that rises in northwestern Zambia and flows for 1,600 miles (2,560 km), first south and then east, through Angola and the Democratic Republic of the Congo (formerly Zaire) to Victoria Falls where it turns to form the border between Zambia and Zimbabwe before crossing Mozambique and entering the Indian Ocean.

Zam·bi·a /ˈzambēə/ a landlocked country in central Africa, separated from Zimbabwe by the Zambezi River; pop. 10,462,000; capital, Lusaka; languages, English (official) and various Bantu languages. —**Zam·bi·an** *adj.* & *n.*

Formerly a British protectorate called Northern Rhodesia, Zambia became an independent republic within the Commonwealth of Nations in 1964, under Kenneth Kaunda (president 1964–91). Zambia's economy was adversely affected by its involvement in the Zimbabwe independence struggle 1965–79.

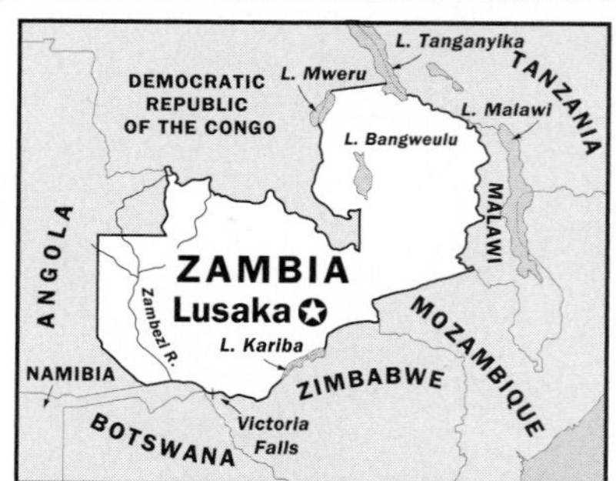

Zam·bo·an·ga /ˌzambōˈäNGgə/ a port in southern Philippines, on the western coast of the island of Mindanao; pop. 442,000.

Zam·bo·ni /zamˈbōnē/ ▸*n. trademark* a machine used to resurface ice for skating.

za·mi·a /ˈzāmēə/ (*Austral.* also **za·mi·a palm**) ▸*n.* an American or Australian cycad, some kinds of which produce roots or seeds that are edible after careful preparation. • Genera *Zamia* (of America) and *Macrozamia* (of Australia), family Zamiaceae. ▷early 19th cent.: modern Latin, from *zamiae,* misreading (in Pliny) of *azaniae* 'pine cones.'

za·min·dar /ˈzamənˌdär; zəˌmēnˈdär/ (also **ze·min·dar**) ▸*n. Indian* a landowner, esp. one who leases his land to tenant farmers. ▷via Urdu from Persian *zamīndār,* from *zamīn* 'land' + *-dār* 'holder.'

zam·in·dar·i /ˌzamənˈdärē; zəˌmēn-/ ▸*n. Indian historical* the system under which zamindars held land. ▪ the office or territory of a zamindar. ▷Urdu.

Zan·de /ˈzandē/ (also **A·zan·de** /əˈzandē/) ▸*n.* (*pl.* same or **A·zan·de**) **1** a member of a central African people of mixed ethnic origin. **2** the Niger-Congo language of this people, spoken mainly in northern Democratic Republic of the Congo (formerly Zaire) and Sudan.

▸*adj.* of or relating to this people or their language. ▷the name in Zande.

Zan·tac /ˈzanˌtak/ ▸*n.* trademark for **RANITIDINE**. ▷late 20th cent.: probably from *Z-* + **ANTACID**.

Zan·te /ˈzantē/ another name for **ZAKINTHOS**.

ZANU /ˈzanˌoō/ ▸*abbr.* Zimbabwe African National Union.

Zan·uck /ˈzanək/, Darryl F. (1902–79), U.S. movie producer; full name *Darryl Francis Zanuck.* He was the controlling executive of Twentieth Century Fox and its president from 1965 until his retirement in 1971.

ZANU–PF ▸*abbr.* Zimbabwe African National Union (Patriotic Front).

za·ny /ˈzānē/ ▸*adj.* (**-ni·er**, **-ni·est**) amusingly unconventional and idiosyncratic: *zany humor.*

▸*n.* an erratic or eccentric person. ▪ *historical* a comic performer partnering a clown, whom he imitated in an amusing way. ▷late 16th cent.: from French *zani* or Italian *zan(n)i,* Venetian form of *Gianni, Giovanni* 'John,' stock name of the servants acting as clowns in the *commedia dell'arte.* —**za·ni·ly** /-nəlē/ *adv.* —**za·ni·ness** *n.*

Zan·zi·bar /ˈzanzəˌbär/ an island off the coast of East Africa, part of Tanzania; pop. 641,000. In 1964, it became a republic and united with Tanganyika to form Tanzania. —**Zan·zi·ba·ri** /ˌzanzəˈbärē/ *adj.* & *n.*

Zao·zhuang /ˈdzouˈjwäNG; -jəˈwäNG/ (also **Tsao-chuang**) a city in eastern China, in Shandong province; pop. 3,192,000.

zap /zap/ *informal* ▸*v.* (**zapped**, **zap·ping**) **1** [*trans.*] destroy or obliterate: *zap the enemy's artillery before it can damage your core units | it's vital to zap stress fast.* **2** [*trans.*] cause to move suddenly and rapidly in a specified direction: *the boat zapped us up river.* ▪ [*intrans.*] move suddenly and rapidly, esp. between television channels or sections of videotape by use of a remote control: *video recorders mean the audience will zap through the ads.* **3** [*trans.*] cook or warm (food or a hot drink) in a microwave oven.

▸*n.* a sudden effect or event that makes a dramatic impact, esp. a sudden burst of energy or sound: *the eggs get an extra zap of UV light.* ▷1920s (originally U.S.): imitative.

Za·pa·ta /zəˈpätə/, Emiliano (1879–1919), Mexican revolutionary. He attempted to implement his program of agrarian reform by means of guerrilla warfare. From 1914, he and Pancho Villa fought against the regimes of General Huerta and Venustiano Carranza.

za·pa·te·a·do /ˌzäpətēˈädō; -tā-/ ▸*n.* (*pl.* **-dos**) a flamenco dance with rhythmic stamping of the feet. ▷mid 19th cent.: Spanish, from *zapato* 'shoe.'

Za·pa·tis·ta /ˌzäpəˈtēstə/ ▸*n.* a member or supporter of a revolutionary force working for social and agrarian reform ideals similar to those of Emilio Zapata (1879-1919), and which launched a popular uprising in the southern Mexican state of Chiapas in January 1994: [as [adj.]] *the Zapatista Army said thousands of armed men and women seized San Cristobal de las Casas.* ▷Spanish.

Za·po·rizhzh·ya /ˌzäpəˈrēzH(y)ə/ an industrial city in Ukraine, on the Dnieper River; pop. 891,000. Russian name **ZAPOROZHYE**; former name (until 1921) **ALEKSANDROVSK**.

Za·po·tec /ˈzäpəˌtek/ ▸*n.* (*pl.* same or **-tecs**) **1** a member of a native people living in and around Oaxaca in southern Mexico. **2** the Otomanguean language of this people.

▸*adj.* of or relating to the Zapotec or their language. ▷from Spanish *zapoteco,* from Nahuatl *tzapoteca,* plural of *tzapotecatl,* literally 'person of the place of the sapodilla.'

Zap·pa /ˈzapə/, Frank (1940–93), U.S. rock singer, musician, and songwriter. In 1965, he formed the Mothers of Invention, a group that combined psychedelic rock with elements of jazz and satire. In his later career he often mixed flowing guitar improvisations with scatological humor.

zap·per /ˈzapər/ ▶*n. informal* **1** a remote control for a television, video, or other piece of electronic equipment. **2** an electronic device used for killing insects: *a bug zapper.*

zap·py /ˈzapē/ ▶*adj.* (**-pi·er, -pi·est**) *informal* lively; energetic: *a zappy musical tapestry.*

ZAPU /ˈzap,o͞o/ ▶*abbr.* Zimbabwe African People's Union.

Za·qa·ziq /ˈzäkə,zik/ variant spelling of **ZAGAZIG**.

Za·ra·go·za /,särəˈgōsə; ,THärəˈgōTHə/ Spanish name for **SARAGOSSA**.

Zar·a·thus·tra /,zarəˈTHo͞ostrə/ the Avestan name for the Persian prophet Zoroaster. **—Zar·a·thus·tri·an** /-ˈTHo͞ostrēən/ *adj. & n.*

za·ri /ˈzärē/ ▶*n.* [usu. as *adj.*] a type of gold thread used decoratively on Indian clothing. ▷from Urdu *zarī*, from Persian *zar* 'gold.'

Za·ri·a /ˈzärēə/ a city in northern Nigeria; pop. 345,000.

za·ri·ba /zəˈrēbə/ (also **za·re·ba**) ▶*n.* (also **za·re·ba, za·ree·ba**) a protective enclosure of thorn bushes or stakes surrounding a campsite or village in northeastern Africa. ■ a cattle corral. ▷from Arabic *zarība* 'cattle pen; stockade.'

Zar·qa /ˈzärkə/ (also **Az Zar·qa** /az/) a city in northwestern Jordan; pop. 359,000.

zar·zue·la /zärˈzwālə/ ▶*n.* **1** a Spanish traditional form of musical comedy. **2** a Spanish dish of various kinds of seafood cooked in a rich sauce. ▷Spanish, apparently from a place name.

za·yin /ˈzäyin/ ▶*n.* the seventh letter of the Hebrew alphabet.

za·zen /,zäˈzen/ ▶*n.* Zen meditation, usually performed in the lotus position. ▷Japanese, from *za* 'sitting' + *zen* (see **ZEN**).

Z bo·son ▶*n.* another term for **Z PARTICLE**.

Z-DNA ▶*n. Biochemistry* DNA in which the double helix has a left-handed rather than the usual right-handed twist and the sugar phosphate backbone follows a zigzag course.

zeal /zēl/ ▶*n.* great energy or enthusiasm in pursuit of a cause or an objective: *his zeal for privatization | Laura brought a missionary zeal to her work.* ▷late Middle English: via ecclesiastical Latin from Greek *zēlos*.

Zea·land /ˈzēlənd/ the principal island of Denmark, located between the Jutland peninsula and the southern tip of Sweden. Its chief city is Copenhagen. Danish name **SJÆLLAND**.

zeal·ot /ˈzelət/ ▶*n.* a person who is fanatical and uncompromising in pursuit of their religious, political, or other ideals. ■ (**Zeal·ot**) *historical* a member of an ancient Jewish sect aiming at a world Jewish theocracy and resisting the Romans until AD 70. ▷mid 16th cent. (in the sense 'member of an ancient Jewish sect'): via ecclesiastical Latin from Greek *zēlōtēs*, from *zēloun* 'be jealous,' from *zēlos* (see **ZEAL**). **—zeal·ot·ry** /-ətrē/ *n.*

THE RIGHT WORD **bigot, enthusiast, extremist, fanatic, zealot**

An **enthusiast** displays an intense and eager interest in something (*a sky-diving enthusiast*).

A **fanatic** is not only intense and eager but possibly irrational in his or her enthusiasm; *fanatic* suggests extreme devotion and a willingness to go to any length to maintain or carry out one's beliefs (*a fly-fishing fanatic who hired a helicopter to reach his favorite stream*).

A **zealot** exhibits not only extreme devotion but vehement activity in support of a cause or goal (*a feminist zealot who spent most of her time campaigning for women's rights*).

An **extremist** is a supporter of extreme doctrines or practices, particularly in a political context (*a paramilitary extremist who anticipated the overthrow of the government*).

But it is the **bigot** who causes the most trouble, exhibiting obstinate and often blind devotion to his or her beliefs and opinions. In contrast to *fanatic* and *zealot*, the term *bigot* implies intolerance and contempt for those who do not agree (*a bigot who could not accept his daughter's decision to marry outside her religion*).

zeal·ous /ˈzeləs/ ▶*adj.* having or showing zeal: *the council was extremely zealous in the application of the regulations.* See note at **EAGER**. ▷early 16th cent.: from a medieval Latin derivative of Latin *zelus* 'zeal, jealousy.' **—zeal·ous·ly** *adv.* **—zeal·ous·ness** *n.*

ze·bec ▶*n.* variant spelling of **XEBEC**.

ze·bra /ˈzēbrə/ ▶*n.* **1** an African wild horse with black-and-white stripes and an erect mane. • Genus *Equus*, family Equidae: three species, the **common zebra** (*E. burchellii*), **Grevy's zebra** (*E. grevyi*), and the **mountain zebra** (*E. zebra*). See also **QUAGGA**. **2** a large butterfly with pale bold stripes on a dark background, in particular: • a yellow and black American butterfly (*Heliconius charitonius*, subfamily Heliconiinae, family Nymphalidae). **3** (also **ze·bra fish**) *S. African* a silvery-gold sea bream with vertical black stripes. • *Diplodus cervinus*, family Sparidae. **4** *informal* a person whose characteristic garb is a black-and-white striped uniform, esp. a football official or a convict. ▷early 17th cent.: from Italian, Spanish, or Portuguese, originally in the sense 'wild ass,' perhaps ultimately from Latin *equiferus*, from *equus* 'horse' + *ferus* 'wild.'

Grevy's zebra

ze·bra cross·ing ▶*n. Brit.* an area of road painted with broad white stripes, where vehicles must stop if pedestrians wish to cross.

ze·bra finch ▶*n.* a small Australian waxbill with black and white stripes on the face, popular as a pet bird. • *Poephila guttata*, family Estrildidae.

ze·bra mule /ˈzēbrə myo͞ol/ ▶*n.* another term for **ZORSE**.

ze·bra mus·sel ▶*n.* a small freshwater bivalve mollusk with zigzag markings on the shell, sometimes becoming a pest because it blocks water pipes. • *Dreissena polymorpha*, family Dreissenidae.

ze·bra·wood /ˈzēbrə,wo͝od/ ▶*n.* any of a number of tropical trees that produce ornamental striped timber that is used chiefly in cabinetmaking. • Species in several families, such as *Connarus guianensis* (family Connaraceae) of Guyana, and *Diospyros marmorata* (family Ebenaceae) of the Andaman Islands.

ze·bu /ˈzē,b(y)o͞o/ ▶*n.* another term for **BRAHMAN** (sense 3). ▷late 18th cent.: from French *zébu*, of unknown origin.

Zeb·u·lun /ˈzebyələn/ (also **Zeb·u·lon**) (in the Bible) a Hebrew patriarch, son of Jacob and Leah (Gen. 30:20). ■ the tribe of Israel traditionally descended from him.

Zech. ▶*abbr. Bible* Zechariah.

Zech·a·ri·ah /,zekəˈrīə/ a Hebrew minor prophet of the 6th century BC. ■ a book of the Bible including his prophecies.

zed /zed/ ▶*n. Brit.* the letter Z. ▷late Middle English: from French *zède*, via late Latin from Greek *zēta* (see **ZETA**).

Zed·e·ki·ah /,zedəˈkīə/ (in the Bible) the last king of Judea, who rebelled against Nebuchadnezzar and was carried off to Babylon into captivity (2 Kings 24–25, 2 Chron. 36).

zed·o·a·ry /ˈzedō,erē/ ▶*n.* an Indian plant related to turmeric, with an aromatic rhizome. • *Curcuma zedoaria*, family Zingiberaceae. ■ a gingerlike substance made from this rhizome, used in medicine, perfumery, and dyeing. ▷late Middle English: from medieval Latin *zedoarium*, from Persian *zadwār*.

zee /zē/ ▶*n.* the letter Z. ▷late 17th cent.: variant of **ZED**.

Zee·man ef·fect /ˈzēmən; ˈzā-/ ▶*n. Physics* the splitting of the spectrum line into several components by the application of a magnetic field. ▷late 19th cent.: named after Pieter *Zeeman* (1865–1943), Dutch physicist.

Zef·fi·rel·li /,zefəˈrelē/, Franco (1923–), Italian movie and theater director; born *Gianfranco Corsi*. His operatic productions are noted for the opulence of their sets and costumes. Notable movies: *Romeo and Juliet* (1968), *Hamlet* (1990), and *Tea with Mussolini* (1999).

ze·in /ˈzē-in/ ▶*n. Biochemistry* the principal protein of corn. ▷early 19th cent.: from modern Latin *Zea* (genus name of corn) + **-IN**[1].

zeit·ge·ber /ˈtsīt,gābər; ˈzīt-/ ▶*n. Physiology* a cue given by the environment, such as a change in light or temperature, to reset the internal body clock. ▷mid 20th cent.: from German *Zeitgeber*, from *Zeit* 'time' + *Geber* 'giver.'

zeit·geist /ˈtsīt,gīst; ˈzīt-/ ▶*n.* [in *sing.*] the defining spirit or mood of a particular period of history as shown by the ideas and beliefs of the time: *the story captured the zeitgeist of the late 1960s.* ▷mid 19th cent.: from German *Zeitgeist*, from *Zeit* 'time' + *Geist* 'spirit.'

Zel·ig /ˈzelig/ ▶*n.* a person who is able to change their appearance, behavior, or attitudes, so as to be comfortable in any situation: *a financial Zelig, he was the only man to advise all four of the major networks on deals in one year.* ▷1980s: from the name of Leonard *Zelig*, the chameleonic subject of Woody Allen's film *Zelig* (1983).

zel·ko·va /zelˈkōvə/ ▶*n.* an Asian tree of the elm family, often cultivated as an ornamental, for its timber, or as a bonsai tree. • Genus *Zelkova*, family Ulmaceae: several species, in particular **Japanese zelkova** (*Z. serrata*).

ze·min·dar /zəˈmēn,där/ ▶ variant spelling of **ZAMINDAR**.

zem·stvo /ˈzemst-vō/ ▶*n.* one of a system of elected councils established in czarist Russia to administer local affairs after the abolition of serfdom.

Zen /zen/ (also **Zen Bud·dhism**) ▶*n.* a Japanese school of Mahayana Buddhism emphasizing the value of meditation and intuition.

Zen Buddhism was introduced to Japan from China in the 12th century and has had a profound cultural influence. The aim of Zen is to achieve sudden enlightenment (satori) through meditation in a seated posture (zazen), usually under the guidance of a teacher and often using paradoxical statements (koans) to transcend rational thought.

▷Japanese, literally 'meditation,' from Chinese *chán* 'quietude,' from Sanskrit *dhyāna* 'meditation.' **—Zen Bud·dhist** *n.*

ze·na·na /zəˈnänə/ ▶*n.* (in India and Iran) the part of a house for the seclusion of women. ▷from Persian and Urdu *zanānah*, from *zan* 'woman.'

Zend /zend/ ▶*n.* an interpretation of the Avesta, each Zend being part of the Zend-Avesta. ▷from Persian *zand* 'interpretation.'

Zend-A·ves·ta ▶*n.* the Zoroastrian sacred writings, comprising the Avesta (the text) and Zend (the commentary).

Ze·ner /ˈzēnər/ (in full **Ze·ner di·ode**) ▶*n. Electronics* a form of semiconductor diode in which at a critical reverse voltage a large reverse current can flow. ▷1950s: named after Clarence M. *Zener* (1905–93), American physicist.

Ze·ner cards ▶*plural n.* a set of 25 cards each with one of five different symbols, used in ESP research. ▷1930s: named after Karl E. *Zener* (1903–61), American psychologist.

ze·nith /ˈzēniTH/ ▶*n.* [in *sing.*] the highest point reached by a celestial or other object: *the sun was well past the zenith | the missile reached its zenith and fell.* ■ the point in the sky or celestial sphere directly above an observer. The opposite of **NADIR**. ■ the time at which something is most powerful or successful: *under Justinian, the Byzantine Empire reached its zenith of influence.* ▷late Middle English: from Old French or medieval Latin *cenit*, based on Arabic *samt (ar-ra's)* 'path (over the head).' **—ze·nith·al** /-nəTHəl/ *adj.*

Ze·no[1] /ˈzēnō/ (*fl.* 5th century BC), Greek philosopher. A member of the Eleatic school, he defended Parmenides' theories by formulating paradoxes that appeared to demonstrate the impossibility of motion.

Ze·no[2] (*c.*335–*c.*263 BC), Greek philosopher; founder of Stoicism; known as **Zeno of Citium**. He founded the school of Stoic philosophy *c.*300 (see **STOICISM**).

Ze·no·bi·a /zəˈnōbēə/ (3rd century AD), queen of Palmyra *c.*267–272. She conquered Egypt and much of Asia Minor. When she proclaimed her son emperor, the Roman emperor Aurelian attacked, defeated, and captured her.

ze·o·lite /ˈzēə,līt/ ▶*n.* any of a large group of minerals consisting of hydrated aluminosilicates of sodium,

Pronunciation Key ə *ago*; ər *over*; ˈə or ,ə *up*; ˈər or ,ər *fur*; a *hat*; ā *rate*; ä *car*; CH *chew*; e *let*; ē *see*; e(ə)r *air*; i *fit*; ī *by*; i(ə)r *ear*; NG *sing*; ō *go*; ô *for*; oi *boy*; o͝o *good*; o͞o *goo*; ou *out*; SH *she*; TH *thin*; T͟H *then*; (h)w *why*; ZH *vision*

potassium, calcium, and barium. They can be readily dehydrated and rehydrated, and are used as cation exchangers and molecular sieves. ▷late 18th cent.: from Swedish and German *zeolit*, from Greek *zein* 'to boil' + **-LITE** (from their characteristic swelling when heated in the laboratory). **—ze·o·lit·ic** /ˌzēəˈlitik/ *adj.*

Zeph. ▸*abbr. Bible* Zephaniah.

Zeph·a·ni·ah /ˌzefəˈnīə/ a Hebrew minor prophet of the 7th century BC. ■ a book of the Bible containing his prophecies.

zeph·yr /ˈzefər/ ▸*n.* **1** *poetic/literary* a soft gentle breeze. **2** *historical* a fine cotton gingham. ■ a very light article of clothing. ▷late Old English *zefferus*, denoting a personification of the west wind, via Latin from Greek *zephuros* '(god of) the west wind.' Sense 1 dates from the late 17th cent.

Zep·pe·lin[1] /ˈzep(ə)lən/, Ferdinand (Adolf August Heinrich), Count von (1838–1917), German aviation pioneer. An army officer until his retirement in 1890, he devoted the rest of his life to the development of the dirigible airship named after him.

Zep·pe·lin[2] ▸*n. historical* a large German dirigible airship of the early 20th century, long and cylindrical in shape and with a rigid framework. Zeppelins were used during World War I for reconnaissance and bombing, and after the war as passenger transports until the 1930s.

zepto- ▸*comb. form* (used in units of measurement) denoting a factor of 10^{-21}: *zeptosecond.* ▷adapted from **SEPTI-**, on the pattern of combining forms such as *peta-* and *exa-*.

Zer·matt /ˈzərˌmät; (t)serˈmät/ an Alpine ski resort and mountaineering center near the Matterhorn, in southern Switzerland.

ze·ro /ˈzi(ə)rō; ˈzēˌrō/ ▸*cardinal number* (*pl.* **-ros**) no quantity or number; naught; the figure 0: *figures from zero to nine | you've left off a zero—it should be five hundred million.* ■ a point on a scale or instrument from which a positive or negative quantity is reckoned: *the gauge dropped to zero* | [as *adj.*] *a zero rate of interest.* ■ the temperature corresponding to 0° on the Celsius scale (32° Fahrenheit), marking the freezing point of water: *the temperature was below zero.* ■ the temperature corresponding to 0° on the Fahrenheit scale (approximately minus 18° Celsius), considered a very cold temperature, esp. for outdoor activities: *thirty below zero!* See also **SUB-ZERO.** ■ [usu. as *adj.*] *Linguistics* the absence of an actual word or morpheme to realize a syntactic or morphological phenomenon: *the zero plural in "three sheep."* ■ the lowest possible amount or level; nothing at all: *I rated my chances as zero.* ■ short for **ZERO HOUR.** ■ *informal* a worthless or contemptibly undistinguished person: *her husband is an absolute zero.*
▸*v.* (**-roes, -roed**) [*trans.*] **1** adjust (an instrument) to zero: *zero the counter when the tape has rewound.* **2** set the sights of (a gun) for firing.
▸*phrasal v.* □ **zero in** take aim with a gun or missile: *jet fighters* ***zeroed in on*** *the rebel positions.* ■ focus one's attention: *they* ***zeroed in on*** *the clues he gave away about.* □ **zero out** phase out or reduce to zero: *the bill would zero out capital gains taxes.* ▷early 17th cent.: from French *zéro* or Italian *zero*, via Old Spanish from Arabic *ṣifr* 'cipher.'

ze·ro-based ▸*adj. Finance* (of a budget or budgeting) having each item costed anew, rather than in relation to its size or status in the previous budget.

ze·ro-cou·pon ▸*adj.* of or relating to a debt obligation that pays no interest to the holder until it reaches maturity or is sold: *volatile zero-coupon bonds pay no interest but are issued of a discount to face value.*

ze·ro-cou·pon bond ▸*n.* a bond that is issued at a deep discount to its face value but pays no interest.

ze·ro-de·fect ▸*adj.* having no errors or flaws: *the shop provides zero-defect and on-time delivery services.*

ze·ro-e·mis·sion ▸*adj.* denoting a road vehicle that emits no pollutants from its exhaust.

ze·ro G ▸*abbr.* zero gravity.

ze·ro grav·i·ty ▸*n. Physics* the state or condition in which there is no apparent force of gravity acting on a body, either because the force is locally weak, or because both the body and its surroundings are freely and equally accelerating under the force.

ze·ro hour ▸*n.* the time at which a planned operation, typically a military one, is set to begin.

ze·ro op·tion ▸*n.* a disarmament proposal for the total removal of certain types of weapons on both sides.

ze·ro-point ▸*adj. Physics* relating to or denoting properties and phenomena in quantized systems at absolute zero.

ze·ro pop·u·la·tion growth ▸*n.* maintaining a population at a constant level by limiting the number of live births to only what is needed to replace the existing population.

ze·ro-sum ▸*adj.* [*attrib.*] (of a game or situation) in which whatever is gained by one side is lost by the other: *altruism is not a zero-sum game.*

ze·roth /ˈzi(ə)rōTH; ˈzēˌrōTH/ ▸*adj.* [*attrib.*] immediately preceding what is regarded as first in a series. ▷late 19th cent.: from **ZERO** + **-TH**[1].

ze·ro tol·er·ance ▸*n.* refusal to accept antisocial behavior, typically by strict and uncompromising application of the law.

zest /zest/ ▸*n.* **1** great enthusiasm and energy: *they campaigned with zest and intelligence* | [in *sing.*] *she had a great* ***zest for*** *life.* ■ a quality of excitement and piquancy: *I used to try to beat past records to add zest to my monotonous job.* **2** the outer colored part of the peel of citrus fruit, used as flavoring. ▷late 15th cent.: from French *zeste* 'orange or lemon peel,' of unknown origin. **—zest·ful** /-fəl/ *adj.* **—zest·ful·ly** /-fəlē/ *adv.* **—zest·ful·ness** /-fəlnəs/ *n.* **—zest·y** *adj.*

zest·er /ˈzestər/ ▸*n.* a kitchen utensil for removing fine shreds of zest from citrus fruit.

ze·ta /ˈzātə/ ▸*n.* the sixth letter of the Greek alphabet (Ζ, ζ), transliterated as 'z.' ■ (**Ze·ta**) [followed by Latin genitive] *Astronomy* the sixth star in a constellation: *Zeta Ursae Majoris.*

ze·ta po·ten·tial ▸*n. Chemistry* the potential difference existing between the surface of a solid particle immersed in a conducting liquid (e.g., water) and the bulk of the liquid.

ze·tet·ic /zəˈtetik/ ▸*adj. rare* proceeding by inquiry. ▷mid 17th cent.: from Greek *zētētikos*, from *zētein* 'seek.'

ze·tet·ics ▸*n.* [treated as *sing.*] a historical branch of algebra concerned with the direct search for unknown quantities.

zetta- ▸*comb. form* (used in units of measurement) denoting a factor of 10^{21}: *zettahertz.* ▷apparently adapted from Italian *sette* 'seven' (see also **ZEPTO-**).

zeug·ma /ˈzo͞ogmə/ ▸*n.* a figure of speech in which a word applies to two others in different senses (e.g., *John and his license expired last week*) or to two others of which it semantically suits only one (e.g., *with weeping eyes and hearts*). Compare with **SYLLEPSIS.** ▷late Middle English: via Latin from Greek, from *zeugnunai* 'to yoke'; related to *zugon* 'yoke.' **—zeug·mat·ic** /zo͞ogˈmatik/ *adj.*

Zeus /zo͞os/ *Greek Mythology* the supreme god, the son of Cronus (whom he dethroned) and Rhea, and brother and husband of Hera. Zeus was the protector and ruler of humankind, the dispenser of good and evil, and the god of weather and atmospheric phenomena (such as rain and thunder). Roman equivalent **JUPITER.** ▷Greek: related to the first syllable in Latin *Jupiter* and Sanskrit *dyauḥ* 'sky.'

ZEV ▸*abbr.* zero-emission vehicle.

Ze·ya Riv·er /ˈzāyə/ a river in eastern Russia that rises in the Stanovoy Range and flows south for 800 miles (1,290 km) into the Amur River at Blagoveshchensk.

Zhang·jia·kou /ˈjäNGjēˈäˈkō/ (also **Chang-chia-kow**) a city in northeastern China, in Hebei province, near the Great Wall; pop. 720,000. Mongolian name **KALGAN.**

Zhan·jiang /ˈjänjēˈäNG/ (also **Chan-chiang**) a port in southern China, in Guangdong province; pop. 1,049,000.

Zhda·nov /ˈZHdänəf/ former name (1948–89) of **MARIUPOL.** ▷named after the Soviet Politburo official Andrei *Zhdanov* (1896–1948), the defender of Leningrad during the siege of 1941–44.

Zhe·jiang /ˈjəjēˈäNG/ (also **Che-kiang**) a province in eastern China; capital, Hangzhou.

Zheng·zhou /ˈjəNGˈjō/ (also **Cheng-chow**) a city in northeastern central China, the capital of Henan province; pop. 1,660,000.

Zhen·jiang /ˈjənjēˈäNG/ (also **Chen-chiang, Chinkiang**) a port in eastern China, in Jiangsu province, on the Yangtze River; pop. 1,280,000.

Zhi·to·mir /ZHēˈtōmir/ Russian name for **ZHYTOMYR.**

Zhong·shan /jo͞oNGˈSHän/ (also **Chung-shan**) a city in southeastern China, in Guangdong province; pop. 1,073,000.

Zhou /jō/ (also **Chou**) a dynasty that ruled in China from the 11th century BC to 256 BC.

The dynasty's rule is commonly divided into **Western Zhou** (which ruled from a capital in the west of the region near Xian until 771 BC) and **Eastern Zhou** (which ruled after 771 BC from a capital based in the east). The rule of the Eastern Zhou, although weak and characterized by strife, saw the Chinese classical age of Confucius and Lao-tzu.

Zhou En·lai /ˈjō ˈenˈlī/ (also **Chou En-lai**) (1898–1976), Chinese communist statesman; prime minister of China 1949–76. A founder of the Chinese Communist Party, he organized a communist workers' revolt in 1927 in Shanghai in support of the Kuomintang forces surrounding the city. As premier, he was a moderating influence during the Cultural Revolution and presided over the moves toward détente with the U.S. in 1972–73.

Zhu·kov /ˈZHo͞oˌkôf; -ˌkôv; -kəf/, Georgi (Konstantinovich) (1896–1974), Soviet military leader, born in Russia. During World War II, he defeated the Germans at Stalingrad in 1943, lifted the siege of Leningrad in 1944, and led the final assault on Germany and the capture of Berlin in 1945.

Zhy·to·myr /ZHiˈtōmir/ an industrial city in central Ukraine; pop. 296,000. Russian name **ZHITOMIR.**

Z·ia ul-Haq /ˈzēə o͝ol ˈhäk/, Muhammad (1924–88), Pakistani general and statesman; president 1978–88. As chief of staff, he led the coup that deposed President Zulfikar Bhutto in 1977. He banned all political parties and introduced strict Islamic laws.

zib·e·line /ˈzibəˌlīn; -ˌlēn; -lin/ ▸*n.* **1** a thick soft fabric made of wool and other animal hair, such as mohair, with a flattened silky nap. **2** the fur of the sable.
▸*adj.* of or relating to the sable. ▷French 'sable', from Italian *zibellino*, probably from a Slavic word; compare with **SABLE**[1].

Zi·bo /ˈ(d)zəˈbō/ (also **Tzu-po**) a city in eastern China, in Shandong province; pop. 2,484,000.

zi·do·vu·dine /zīˈdävyəˌdēn; zə-; -ˈdō-/ ▸*n. Medicine* an antiviral drug used in the treatment of AIDS. It slows the growth of HIV infection in the body, but is not curative. • A thymidine derivative; chem. formula: $C_{10}H_{13}N_5O_4$. ▷1980s: arbitrary alteration of **AZIDOTHYMIDINE.**

Zieg·feld /ˈzēgˌfeld; -ˌfēld/, Florenz (1869–1932), U.S. theater manager. In 1907, he produced the first of the *Ziegfeld Follies*, a series of revues in New York City that were based on those of the Folies-Bergère in Paris.

ZIF sock·et /zif/ ▸*n.* a type of socket for mounting electronic devices that is designed not to stress or damage them during insertion. ▷late 20th cent.: *ZIF*, acronym from *zero insertion force.*

zig /zig/ ▸*n.* a sharp change of direction in a zigzag course: *he went round and round in zigs and zags.*
▸*v.* (**zigged, zig·ging**) [*intrans.*] make a sharp change of direction: *we zigged to the right.* ▷1960s: shortening of **ZIGZAG.**

zig·gu·rat /ˈzigəˌrat/ ▸*n.* (in ancient Mesopotamia) a rectangular stepped tower, sometimes surmounted by a temple. Ziggurats are first attested in the late 3rd millennium BC and probably inspired the biblical story of the Tower of Babel (Gen. 11:1–9). ▷from Akkadian *ziqqurratu.*

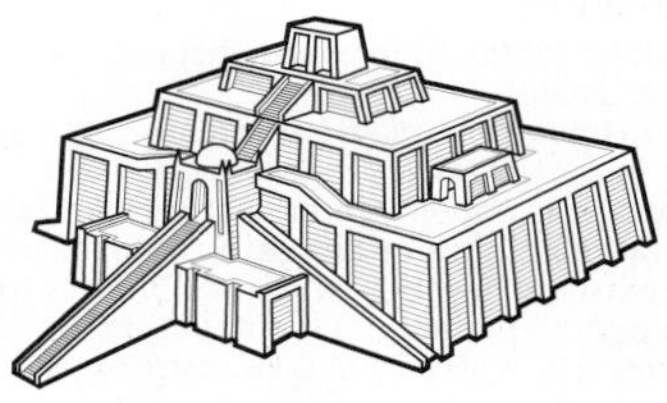

ziggurat

zig·zag /ˈzigˌzag/ ▸*n.* a line or course having abrupt alternate right and left turns: *she traced a zigzag on the metal with her finger.* ■ a turn on such a course: *the road descends in a series of sharp zigzags.*
▸*adj.* having the form of a zigzag; veering to right and left alternately: *when chased by a predator, some animals take a zigzag course.*
▸*adv.* so as to move right and left alternately: *she drives zigzag across the city.*
▸*v.* (**-zagged, -zag·ging**) [*intrans.*] have or move along in a zigzag course: *the path zigzagged between dry rises in the land.* ▷early 18th cent.: from French, from German *Zickzack*, symbolic of alternation of direction, first applied to fortifications. **—zig·zag·ged·ly** /-ˌzagədlē/ *adv.*

zi·kr /ˈzēkər/ ▸ variant spelling of **DHIKR.**

zilch /zilCH/ *informal* ▸*pron.* nothing: *I did absolutely zilch.*
▸*adj.* not any; no: *the character has zilch class.* ▷1960s: of unknown origin.

zil·lion /'zilyən/ ▸*cardinal number informal* an extremely large number of people or things: *we had **zillions** of customers.* ▷1940s: from Z (perhaps as a symbol of an unknown quantity) + MILLION. **—zil·lionth** /-yənTH/ *adj.*

zil·lion·aire /ˌzilyə'ne(ə)r/ ▸*n. informal* an extremely rich person.

Zim·bab·we /zim'bäbwā; -wē/ a landlocked country in southeastern Africa, separated from Zambia by the Zambezi River; pop. 12,671,000; capital, Harare; languages, English (official), Shona, Ndebele, and others. ▷from Shona *dzimbabwe* 'walled grave,' originally referring to *Great Zimbabwe*, a complex of stone ruins in one of the country's fertile valleys, the remains of a city at the center of a flourishing civilization in the 14th and 15th centuries. **—Zim·bab·we·an** /-wāən; -wēən/ *adj.* & *n.*

Formerly known as Southern Rhodesia, Zimbabwe was a self-governing British colony from 1923. In 1965, the white minority government of the colony (then called Rhodesia) issued a unilateral declaration of independence (UDI) under its prime minister, Ian Smith. Despite UN sanctions, illegal independence lasted until 1979, when the Lancaster House Agreement led to all-party elections in 1980 and black majority rule under Robert Mugabe. The country then became an independent republic and a member of the Commonwealth of Nations.

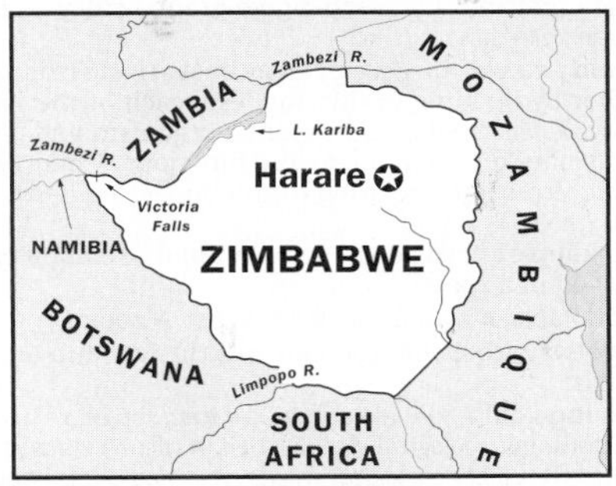

Zim·bab·we Af·ri·can Na·tion·al Un·ion (abbr.: **ZANU** or **ZANU–PF**) a Zimbabwean political party formed in 1963 as a guerrilla organization and led from 1975 by Robert Mugabe.

Having formed an alliance (called the Patriotic Front) with ZAPU in 1976 to coordinate opposition to white rule, ZANU won a large majority in the first post-independence elections (1980). ZANU and ZAPU ruled Zimbabwe as a coalition until a rift developed between them in 1982; in 1987, however, the parties agreed formally to merge, adopting the name ZANU–PF in 1989.

Zim·bab·we Af·ri·can Peo·ple's Un·ion (abbr.: **ZAPU**) a Zimbabwean political party formed in 1961 as a guerrilla organization and led by Joshua Nkomo. It merged with ZANU in 1989.

Zim·mer·man /'zimərmən/, Ethel, see MERMAN.

zinc /ziNGk/ ▸*n.* the chemical element of atomic number 30, a silvery-white metal that is a constituent of brass and is used for coating (galvanizing) iron and steel to protect against corrosion. (Symbol: **Zn**) ■ [usu. as *adj.*] galvanized iron or steel, esp. as the material of domestic utensils or corrugated roofs: *a zinc roof.*
▸*v.* [*trans.*] [usu. as *adj.*] (**zinced**) coat (iron) with zinc or a zinc compound to prevent rust. ▷mid 17th cent.: from German *Zink*, of unknown origin.

zinc blende ▸*n.* another term for SPHALERITE.

zinc fin·ger ▸*n. Biochemistry* a fingerlike loop of peptides enclosing a bound zinc ion at one end, typically part of a larger protein molecule (in particular one regulating transcription).

zinc·ite /'ziNGˌkīt/ ▸*n.* a rare deep red or orange-yellow mineral consisting chiefly of zinc oxide, occurring typically as granular or foliated masses. ▷mid 19th cent.: from ZINC + -ITE[1].

zin·co /'ziNGkō/ ▸*n.* (*pl.* **-cos**) an etched letterpress printing plate made of zinc.

zinc oint·ment (in full **zinc ox·ide oint·ment**) ▸*n.* ointment containing zinc oxide, used for various skin conditions.

zinc ox·ide ▸*n.* an insoluble white solid used as a pigment and in medicinal ointments. • Chem. formula: ZnO.

zinc white ▸*n.* a white pigment consisting of zinc oxide.

zine /zēn/ (also **'zine**) ▸*n. informal* a magazine, esp. a fanzine. ■ a webzine.

zin·eb /'zinˌeb/ ▸*n.* a white compound used as a fungicidal powder on vegetables and fruit. • Alternative name: **zinc ethylene bisdithiocarbamate**; chem. formula: $C_4H_6N_2S_4Zn$. ▷1950s: from *zin(c)* + *e(thylene)* + *b(is-)* from the systematic name.

Zin·fan·del /'zinfənˌdel/ ▸*n.* a variety of wine grape grown in California. ■ a red or blush dry wine made from this grape. ▷of unknown origin.

zing /ziNG/ *informal* ▸*n.* energy, enthusiasm, or liveliness: *he was expected to add some zing to the lackluster team.* ■ strong or piquant flavor: *sprinkle the seasoning on fish to give it zing.*
▸*v.* [*intrans.*] move swiftly: *he could send an arrow zinging through the air.* ■ [*trans.*] attack or criticize sharply: *he zinged the budget deal in interviews with journalists.* ▷early 20th cent.: imitative. **—zing·y** *adj.*

zing·er /'ziNGər/ ▸*n. informal* a striking or amusing remark: *open a speech with a zinger.* ■ an outstanding person or thing: *a zinger of a shot.*

Zin·jan·thro·pus /ˌzin'janTHrəpəs; ˌzinjan'THrō-/ ▸*n.* a genus name sometimes applied to AUSTRALOPITHECUS. ▷1950s: modern Latin, from Arabic *Zinj*, the early medieval name for East Africa, + Greek *anthrōpos* 'man.'

Zinne·mann /'zinəmən/, Fred (1907–97), U.S. movie director, born in Austria. He won Academy Awards for the short *That Mothers Might Live* (1938) and for the movies *From Here to Eternity* (1953) and *A Man For All Seasons* (1966).

zin·ni·a /'zinēə/ ▸*n.* an American plant of the daisy family that is widely cultivated for its bright showy flowers. • Numerous species and cultivars of the genus *Zinnia*, family Compositae. ▷modern Latin, named after Johann G. Zinn (1727–59), German physician and botanist.

Zi·on /'zīən/ (also **Si·on**) ▸*n.* **1** the hill of Jerusalem on which the city of David was built. ■ the citadel of ancient Jerusalem. ■ Jerusalem. ■ (in Christian thought) the heavenly city or kingdom of heaven. ■ the Jewish people or religion. ■ the Christian Church. **2** (among Rastafarians) Africa. ▷Old English, from ecclesiastical Latin *Sion*, from Hebrew *ṣiyōn*.

Zi·on·ism /'zīəˌnizəm/ ▸*n.* a movement for (originally) the reestablishment and (now) the development and protection of a Jewish nation in what is now Israel. It was established as a political organization in 1897 under Theodor Herzl, and was later led by Chaim Weizmann. **—Zi·on·ist** *n.* & *adj.*

zip /zip/ ▸*v.* (**zipped, zip·ping**) **1** [*trans.*] fasten with a zipper: *I **zipped up** my sweater.* ■ (**zip someone up**) fasten the zipper of a garment that someone is wearing: *he zipped himself up.* ■ *Computing* compress (a file) so that it takes less space in storage. **2** [*intrans.*] *informal* move at high speed: *swallows zipped back and forth across the lake.* ■ [*trans.*] cause to move or be delivered or dealt with rapidly: *he zipped a pass out to his receiver.*
▸*n.* **1** (also **zip fas·ten·er**) *chiefly Brit.* a zipper. ■ [as *adj.*] denoting something fastened by a zipper: *a zip pocket.* **2** *informal* energy; vigor: *he's full of zip.* **3** short for ZIP CODE.
▸*pron.* (also **zip·po**) *informal* nothing at all: *you got zip to do with me and my kind, buddy.* ▷mid 19th cent.: imitative.

zip code (also **ZIP code**) ▸*n.* a group of five or nine numbers that are added to a postal address to assist the sorting of mail. ▷1960s: *zip*, acronym from *zone improvement plan.*

zip·cuff /'zipˌkəf/ ▸*n.* a plastic strip with a loop on one end that is secured with notches on the other end, used as a temporary handcuff.
▸*v.* [trans.] to restrain with zipcuffs: *One cop called someone on the phone while the other one zipcuffed me* [as adj.] *zipcuffed protesters.*

Zip drive ▸*n. trademark Computing* a disk drive that stores data on high-capacity removable magnetic disks, often used for data backup.

zip file (also **ZIP file, zipped file**) ▸*n.* a computer file whose contents of one or more files are compressed for storage or transmission, often carrying the extension .ZIP: *a self-extracting zip file.* ▷from the shareware program *WinZip*, a popular file compression utility.

zip gun ▸*n. informal* a cheap homemade or makeshift gun: *I made the zip gun in class out of a toy airplane launcher.*

zip·less /'ziplis/ ▸*adj. informal* (of a sexual encounter) brief, uncomplicated, and passionate. ▷1970s: from the phrase *Zipless Fuck*, in Erica Jong's *Fear of Flying.*

zip·lock /'zipˌläk/ (also *trademark* **Zip·loc**) ▸*adj.* denoting a sealable plastic bag with a two-part strip along the opening that can be pressed together and readily reopened.

zip·per /'zipər/ ▸*n.* **1** a device consisting of two flexible strips of metal or plastic with interlocking projections closed or opened by pulling a slide along them, used to fasten garments, bags, and other items. **2** a display of news or advertisements that scrolls across an illuminated screen fixed to the upper part of a building.
▸*v.* [*trans.*] fasten or provide (something) with a zipper: *he wore a running suit **zippered up** tight.*

zip·per·head /'zipərˌhed/ ▸*n. offensive* an Asian person.

Zip·po /'zipō/ ▸*n.* (*pl.* **-pos**) *trademark* a type of cigarette lighter with a hinged lid, using lighter fluid as fuel. ▷1930s: of unknown origin.

zip·po /'zipō/ ▸*pron.* another term for ZIP.

zip·py /'zipē/ ▸*adj.* (**-pi·er, -pi·est**) *informal* bright, fresh, or lively: *a zippy, zingy, almost citrusy tang.* ■ fast or speedy: *zippy new sedans.* **—zip·pi·ly** /'zipəlē/ *adv.* **—zip·pi·ness** *n.*

zip-up ▸*adj.* [*attrib.*] *chiefly Brit.* (of a garment, pocket, bag, etc.) able to be fastened with a zipper: *a white zip-up jacket.*

zir·ca·loy /'zərkəˌloi/ ▸*n.* an alloy of zirconium, tin, and other metals, used chiefly as cladding for nuclear reactor fuel. ▷1950s: from ZIRCONIUM + ALLOY.

zir·con /'zərˌkän/ ▸*n.* a mineral occurring as prismatic crystals, typically brown but sometimes in translucent varieties of gem quality. It consists of zirconium silicate and is the chief ore of zirconium. ▷late 18th cent.: from German *Zirkon*; compare with JARGON[2].

zir·co·ni·a /ˌzər'kōnēə/ ▸*n.* zirconium dioxide, a white solid used in ceramic glazes and refractory coatings and as a synthetic substitute for diamonds in jewelry. See also CUBIC ZIRCONIA. • Chem. formula: ZrO_2. ▷late 18th cent.: from ZIRCON + -IA[1].

zir·co·ni·um /ˌzər'kōnēəm/ ▸*n.* the chemical element of atomic number 40, a hard silver-gray metal of the transition series. (Symbol: **Zr**) ▷early 19th cent.: modern Latin, from ZIRCON.

zit /zit/ ▸*n. informal* a pimple on the skin. ▷1960s: of unknown origin; apparently originally American teenagers' slang.

zith·er /'ziTHər; 'ziTH-/ ▸*n.* a musical instrument consisting of a flat wooden sound box with numerous strings stretched across it, placed horizontally and played with the fingers and a plectrum. It is used esp. in central European folk music. ▷mid 19th cent.: from German, from Latin *cithara* (see CITTERN). **—zith·er·ist** /-ərist/ *n.*

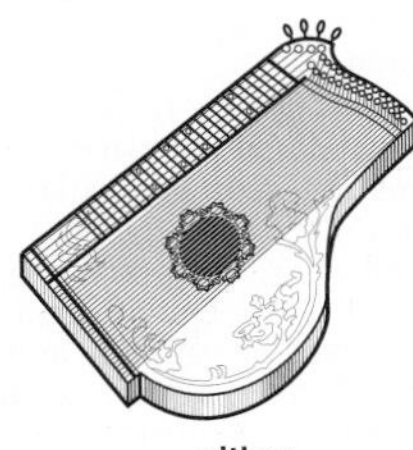
zither

zi·ti /'zētē/ ▸*n.* pasta in the form of tubes resembling large macaroni. ▷Italian.

zi·zith /tsē'tsēt/ ▸*plural n. Judaism* the 613 fringes of thread, symbolizing the 613 commandments in the Hebrew Scriptures, formerly worn at the corners of the shawl-like garment known as a tallith.

zizz /ziz/ *informal* ▸*n.* [in *sing.*] **1** a whizzing or buzzing sound: *there's a nasty zizz from the engine.* **2** *chiefly Brit.* a short sleep: *Philip's having a zizz.*
▸*v.* [*intrans.*] **1** make a whizzing or buzzing sound: *the crane whirred and zizzed.* **2** *chiefly Brit.* doze; sleep: *when everyone inside the building had **zizzed off** he sneaked inside.* ▷early 19th cent.: imitative.

zlo·ty /ˈzlôtē; ˈzlä-/ ▸*n.* (*pl.* same, **-tys**) the basic monetary unit of Poland, equal to 100 groszy. ▷Polish, literally 'golden.'

Zn ▸*symbol* the chemical element zinc.

zo- ▸*comb.form* variant spelling of **ZOO-**, shortened before a vowel (as in *Zoantharia*)

Zo·an·thar·ia /ˌzōənˈTHe(ə)rēə/ *Zoology* a group of coelenterates with polyps that bear more than eight tentacles, including the sea anemones and stony corals. • Subclass Zoantharia, class Anthozoa. ▷modern Latin (plural), from Greek *zōion* 'animal' + *anthos* 'flower.' **—zo·an·thar·i·an** *n.* & *adj.*

zo·ca·lo /ˈsōkəˌlō; sôˈkäˌlō/ ▸*n.* (in Mexico) a public square or plaza.

zo·di·ac /ˈzōdēˌak/ ▸*n.* *Astrology* a belt of the heavens within about 8° either side of the ecliptic, including all apparent positions of the sun, moon, and most familiar planets. It is divided into twelve equal divisions or signs (Aries, Taurus, Gemini, Cancer, Leo, Virgo, Libra, Scorpio, Sagittarius, Capricorn, Aquarius, Pisces). ■ a representation of the signs of the zodiac or of a similar astrological system.

The supposed significance of the movements of the sun, moon, and planets within the zodiacal band forms the basis of astrology. However, the modern constellations do not represent equal divisions of the zodiac, and the ecliptic now passes through a thirteenth (Ophiuchus). Also, owing to precession, the signs of the zodiac now roughly correspond to the constellations that bear the names of the *preceding* signs.

▷late Middle English: from Old French *zodiaque*, via Latin from Greek *zōidiakos*, from *zōidion* 'sculptured animal figure,' diminutive of *zōion* 'animal.' **—zo·di·a·cal** /zōˈdīəkəl/ *adj.*

zo·di·a·cal light ▸*n.* *Astronomy* a faint elongated cone of light sometimes seen in the night sky, extending from the horizon along the ecliptic. It is thought to be due to the reflection of sunlight from particles of ice and dust within the plane of the solar system.

zo·di·a·cal sign ▸*n.* see **SIGN** (sense 3).

zo·e·a /zōˈēə/ ▸*n.* (*pl.* **zo·e·ae** /zōˈēˌē/ or **zo·e·as**) a larval form of certain crustaceans, such as the crab, having a spiny carapace and rudimentary limbs on the abdomen and thorax.

zo·e·trope /ˈzō-ēˌtrōp/ ▸*n.* a 19th-century optical toy consisting of a cylinder with a series of pictures on the inner surface that, when viewed through slits with the cylinder rotating, give an impression of continuous motion. ▷mid 19th cent.: formed irregularly from Greek *zōē* 'life' + *-tropos* 'turning.'

zof·tig ▸*adj.* variant spelling of **ZAFTIG**.

Zog I /zôg/ (1895–1961), Albanian statesman and ruler; prime minister 1922–24; president 1925–28; king 1928–39; full name *Ahmed Bey Zogu*. His autocratic rule resulted in relative political stability; he went into exile when the country was invaded by Italy in 1939.

Zo·har /ˈzōˌhär/ ▸*n.* the chief text of the Jewish Kabbalah, presented as an allegorical or mystical interpretation of the Pentateuch. ▷from Hebrew *zōhar*, literally 'light, splendor.'

-zo·ic ▸*suffix* **1** forming adjectives relating to a particular manner of animal existence (such as *cryptozoic*). **2** of or relating to a particular geologic era (such as *Paleozoic*).

zois·ite /ˈzoiˌsīt/ ▸*n.* a grayish-white or grayish-green crystalline mineral of the epidote group consisting of a hydroxyl silicate of calcium and aluminum. ▷early 19th cent.: from the name of Baron S. von Edelstein *Zois* (1747–1819), Austrian scholar, + **-ITE**[1].

Zo·la /ˌzōˈlä; ˈzōˌlä/, Émile (Édouard Charles Antoine) (1840–1902), French novelist and critic. His series of 20 novels collectively entitled *Les Rougon-Macquart* (1871–93), including *Nana* (1880), *Germinal* (1885), and *La Terre* (1887), shows how human behavior is determined by environment and heredity.

Zol·ling·er–El·li·son syn·drome /ˈzäliNGər ˈeləsən; ˈzälənjər/ ▸*n.* *Medicine* a condition in which a gastrin-secreting tumor or hyperplasia of the islet cells in the pancreas causes overproduction of gastric acid, resulting in recurrent peptic ulcers. ▷1950s: named after Robert M. Zollinger (1903–92) and Edwin H. *Ellison* (1918–70), American physicians.

Zöll·ner il·lu·sion /ˈtsəlnər; ˈzôl-/ ▸*n.* an optical illusion in which long parallel lines appear to diverge or converge when crossed by rows of short oblique lines. ▷late 19th cent.: named after Johann K. F. *Zöllner* (1834–82), German physicist.

Zoll·ver·ein /ˈtsôlfəˌrīn; ˈzôl-/ ▸*n.* *historical* the customs union of German states in the 19th century. ▷from German *Zoll* 'customs' + *Verein* 'union.'

zom·bie /ˈzämbē/ ▸*n.* **1** originally, a snake-deity of or deriving from West Africa and Haiti. **2** a soulless corpse said to be revived by witchcraft, esp. in certain African and Caribbean religions. ■ *informal* a person who is or appears lifeless, apathetic, or completely unresponsive to their surroundings. **3** a tall mixed drink consisting of several kinds of rum, liqueur, and fruit juice. ▷early 19th cent.: of West African origin; compare with Kikongo *zumbi* 'fetish.' **—zom·bie·like** /-ˌlīk/ *adj.*

zom·bi·fy /ˈzämbəˌfī/ ▸*v.* [*trans.*] [usu. as *adj.*] (**zombified**) *informal* deprive of energy or vitality: *exhausted, screaming kids and their zombified parents.*

zo·na pel·lu·ci·da /ˈzōnə pəˈlo͞osədə/ ▸*n.* (*pl.* **zo·nae pel·lu·ci·dae** /ˈzōˌnē pəˈlo͞osəˌdē; ˈzōˌnī pəˈlo͞osəˌdī/) *Anatomy* & *Zoology* the thick transparent membrane surrounding a mammalian ovum before implantation. ▷mid 19th cent.: from Latin, literally 'pellucid girdle.'

zo·na·tion /zōˈnāSHən/ ▸*n.* distribution in zones or regions of definite character: *quartz grains can exhibit zonation and rounding.* ■ *Ecology* the distribution of plants or animals into specific zones according to such parameters as altitude or depth, each characterized by its dominant species.

zone /zōn/ ▸*n.* **1** [usu. with *adj.*] an area or stretch of land having a particular characteristic, purpose, or use, or subject to particular restrictions: *a pedestrian zone* | *the government has declared the city a disaster zone* | *a no-smoking zone.* ■ *Geography* a well-defined region extending around the earth between definite limits, esp. between two parallels of latitude: *a zone of easterly winds.* See also **FRIGID ZONE**, **TEMPERATE ZONE**, **TORRID ZONE**. ■ (also **time zone**) a range of longitudes where a common standard time is used. ■ *Sports* in basketball, football, and hockey, a specific area of the court, field, or rink, esp. one to be defended by a particular player, or the mode of defensive play using this system. See **ZONE DEFENSE** below. ■ a specific region or area within which uniform rates are charged for transportation, parcel post delivery, or other service. ■ (in full **post·al zone**) formerly, any of the numbered areas into which a large city or metropolitan area was divided for facilitating mail delivery. ■ *chiefly Botany* & *Zoology* an encircling band or stripe of distinctive color, texture, or character. **2** *archaic* a belt or girdle worn around a person's body. **3** *Mathematics* an area between two exact or approximate concentric circles. ■ a part of the surface of a sphere enclosed between two parallel planes, or of a cone or cylinder, etc., between such planes cutting it perpendicularly to the axis. **4** *Geology Paleontology* a range between specified limits of depth, height, etc., esp. a section of strata distinguished by characteristic fossils.

▸*v.* [*trans.*] **1** divide into or assign to zones, in particular: ■ [often as *n.*] (**zoning**) divide (a town or stretch of land) into areas subject to particular planning restrictions: *an experimental system of zoning.* ■ designate (a specific area) for use or development in such a manner: *the land is zoned for housing.* **2** *archaic* encircle as or with a band or stripe.

▸*phrasal v.* □ **zone out** *informal* fall asleep or lose concentration or consciousness: *I just zoned out for a moment.* [compare with sense 3 of **ZONED**.] ▷late Middle English: from French, or from Latin *zona* 'girdle,' from Greek *zōnē*. **—zon·al** /ˈzōnl/ *adj.* **—zon·al·ly** /ˈzōnl-ē/ *adv.*

▸*PHRASE* □ **zone defense** *Sports* in basketball, football, and hockey, a system of defensive play in which each player guards an allotted area of the field of play and guards an opponent only when the opponent is in his area.

zoned /zōnd/ ▸*adj.* **1** divided into zones, in particular (of land) designated for a particular type of use or development: *zoned industrial land.* **2** *chiefly Botany Zoology* marked with circles or bands of color: *strongly zoned leaves.* **3** *informal* under the influence of drugs or alcohol: *she's zoned on downers* | *a zoned-out hippie.* [1970s: blend of **ZONKED** and **STONED**.]

zone plate ▸*n.* a plate of glass marked out into concentric zones or rings alternately transparent and opaque, used like a lens to bring light to a focus.

zone re·fin·ing ▸*n.* a method of purifying a crystalline solid, typically a semiconductor or metal, by causing a narrow molten zone to travel slowly along an otherwise solid rod or bar to one end, at which impurities become concentrated.

zonk /zäNGk; zôNGk/ *informal* ▸*v.* **1** [*trans.*] hit or strike: *Charley really zonked me.* **2** fall or cause to fall suddenly and heavily asleep or lose consciousness: [*intrans.*] *I always just **zonk out** and sleep straight through* | [*trans.*] *I go rowing because it **zonks** me **out**.* ▷1940s: imitative.

zonked /zäNGkt; zôNGkt/ ▸*adj.* *informal* under the influence of drugs or alcohol: *the others got zonked on acid* | *a **zonked-out** beach bum.* ■ exhausted; tired out: *we hit the sack, **zonked out**.*

zon·ule /ˈzōnˌyo͞ol/ ▸*n.* *technical, chiefly Anatomy* a small zone, band, or belt.

zoo /zo͞o/ ▸*n.* an establishment that maintains a collection of wild animals, typically in a park or gardens, for study, conservation, or display to the public. ■ *Informal* a situation characterized by confusion and disorder: *it's a zoo in the lobby.* ▷mid 19th cent.: abbreviation of **ZOOLOGICAL GARDEN**, originally applied specifically to that of Regent's Park, London. **—zoo·ey** *adj. informal* .

zoo- ▸*comb. form* of animals; relating to animal life: *zoogeography.* ▷from Greek *zōion* 'animal.'

zo·o·gen·ic /ˌzōəˈjenik/ ▸*adj.* **1** produced by or originating in animals. **2** related or relating to animal development or evolution.

zoo·ge·o·graph·i·cal re·gion /ˌzōəˌjēəˈgrafikəl/ ▸*n.* *Zoology* each of a number of major areas of the earth having characteristic fauna (esp. mammals). They include the Palearctic, Ethiopian, Oriental, Australian, Nearctic, and Neotropical regions. Also called **FAUNAL REGION**.

zoo·ge·og·ra·phy /ˌzōəjēˈägrəfē/ ▸*n.* the branch of zoology that deals with the geographical distribution of animals. **—zo·o·ge·og·ra·pher** /-fər/ *n.* **—zo·o·ge·o·graph·ic** /-ˌjēəˈgrafik/ *adj.* **—zo·o·ge·o·graph·i·cal** /-ˌjēəˈgrafikəl/ *adj.* **—zo·o·ge·o·graph·i·cal·ly** /-ˌjēəˈgrafik(ə)lē/ *adv.*

zo·oid /ˈzōˌoid/ ▸*n.* *Zoology* an animal arising from another by budding or division, esp. each of the individuals that make up a colonial organism and typically have different forms and functions. ▷mid 19th cent.: from **ZOO-** 'relating to animals' + **-OID**. **—zo·oi·dal** /ˌzōˈoidl/ *adj.*

zoo·keep·er /ˈzo͞oˌkēpər/ ▸*n.* an animal attendant employed in a zoo.

zool. ▸*abbr.* ■ zoological. ■ zoologist. ■ zoology.

zo·ol·a·try /zōˈälətrē; zo͞o-/ ▸*n.* *rare* the worship of animals.

zo·o·log·i·cal /ˌzōəˈläjikəl; ˌzo͞oə-/ ▸*adj.* of or relating to zoology: *zoological classification.* ■ of or relating to animals: *eighty zoological woodcuts.* **—zo·o·log·i·cal·ly** /-ik(ə)lē/ *adv.*

zo·o·log·i·cal gar·den ▸*n.* *dated* a zoo.

zo·ol·o·gy /zōˈäləjē; zo͞o-/ ▸*n.* the scientific study of the behavior, structure, physiology, classification, and distribution of animals. ■ the animal life of a particular area or time: *the zoology of Russia's vast interior.* ▷mid 17th cent.: from modern Latin *zoologia* (see **ZOO-**, **-LOGY**). **—zo·ol·o·gist** /-jist/ *n.*

zoom /zo͞om/ ▸*v.* [*intrans.*] **1** (esp. of a car or aircraft) move or travel very quickly: *we watched the fly zooming about* | *he jumped into his car and zoomed off.* ■ [*intrans.*] (of prices) rise sharply: *the share index zoomed by about 136 points.* **2** (of a camera) change smoothly from a long shot to a close-up or vice versa: *the camera **zoomed in** for a close-up of his face* | *zoom out for a wide view of the garden again.* ■ [*trans.*] cause (a lens or camera) to do this.

▸*n.* a camera shot that changes smoothly from a long shot to a close-up or vice versa: [as *adj.*] *the zoom button.* ■ short for **ZOOM LENS**.

▸*exclam.* used to express sudden fast movement: *then suddenly, zoom!, he's off.* ▷late 19th cent.: imitative.

zoom lens ▸*n.* a lens allowing a camera to change smoothly from a long shot to a close-up or vice versa by varying the focal length.

zo·o·mor·phic /ˌzōəˈmôrfik/ ▸*adj.* having or representing animal forms or gods of animal form: *pottery decorated with anthropomorphic and zoomorphic designs.* ▷late 19th cent.: from **ZOO-** 'of animals' + Greek *morphē* 'form' + **-IC**. **—zo·o·mor·phism** /-ˈmôrˌfizəm/ *n.*

zo·on·o·sis /zōəˈnōsəs; zōˈänə-/ ▸*n.* (*pl.* **-ses** /-ˌsēz/) a disease that can be transmitted to humans from animals. ▷late 19th cent.: from **ZOO-** 'of animals' + Greek *nosos* 'disease.' **—zo·o·not·ic** /ˌzōəˈnätik/ *adj.*

zo·o·phile /ˈzōəˌfīl/ ▸*n.* **1** a person who loves animals; an opponent of cruelty to animals. **2** a person who is sexually attracted to animals. ▷late 19th cent. (originally in the botanical sense 'a plant pollinated by animals'): from *zoo* + *-phile*. The current senses date from the early 20th cent. **—zo·o·phil·i·a** /ˌzōəˈfilēə/ *n.* **—zo·o·phil·ic** *adj.*

Z

zo·o·phyte /ˈzōəˌfit/ ▸*n. dated Zoology* a plantlike animal, esp. a coral, sea anemone, sponge, or sea lily. ▹early 17th cent.: from Greek *zōiophuton* (see **ZOO-**, **-PHYTE**).

zo·o·plank·ton /ˈzōəˌplaNGktən/ ▸*n. Biology* plankton consisting of small animals and the immature stages of larger animals.

zo·o·spo·ran·gi·um /ˌzōəspəˈranjēəm/ ▸*n. Botany* (*pl.* **-gi·a** /-jēə/) a sporangium or spore case in which zoospores develop.

zo·o·spore /ˈzōəˌspôr/ ▸*n. Biology* a spore of certain algae, fungi, and protozoans, capable of swimming by means of a flagellum. Also called **SWARMER**.

zoot suit /zo͞ot/ ▸*n.* a man's suit of an exaggerated style, characterized by a long loose jacket with padded shoulders and high-waisted tapering trousers, popular in the 1940s. ▹1940s: rhyming formation on **SUIT**.

zo·o·xan·thel·la /ˌzōəzanˈTHelə/ ▸*n.* (*pl.* **-thel·lae** /-ˈTHelē/) *Biology* a yellowish-brown symbiotic dinoflagellate present in large numbers in the cytoplasm of many marine invertebrates. ▹late 19th cent.: modern Latin, from **zoo-** 'of animals' + Greek *xanthos* 'yellow' + the diminutive suffix *-ella*. **—zo·o·xan·thel·late** /-ˈTHelˌāt/ *adj.*

zorb·ing /ˈzôrbiNG/ ▸*n.* a sport in which a participant is secured inside an inner capsule in a large, transparent ball that is then rolled along the ground or down hills. ▹1990s: from *zorb*, the invented name for the ball, + *-ing*.

zo·ri /ˈzôrē/ ▸*n.* (*pl.* **zo·ris**) a traditional Japanese style of sandal, much like a flip-flop, originally made with a straw sole. ▹Japanese.

zo·ril·la /zəˈrilə/ (also **zo·ril** or **zo·rille** /ˈzôril; ˈzär-/) ▸*n.* a black and white carnivorous mammal that resembles a skunk, inhabiting arid regions of southern Africa. Also called **STRIPED POLECAT**. • *Ictonyx striatus*, family Mustelidae. ▹late 18th cent.: via French from Spanish *zorrilla*, diminutive of *zorro* 'fox.'

Zo·ro·as·ter /ˈzôrōˌastər/ (*c.*628–*c.*551 BC), Persian prophet and founder of Zoroastrianism; Avestan name *Zarathustra*. Traditionally, he was born in Persia and began to preach the tenets of what was later called Zoroastrianism after receiving a vision from Ahura Mazda.

Zo·ro·as·tri·an·ism /ˌzôrōˈastrēəˌnizəm/ ▸*n.* a monotheistic pre-Islamic religion of ancient Persia founded by Zoroaster in the 6th century BC.

According to the teachings of Zoroaster, the supreme god, named Ahura Mazda, created twin spirits, one of which chose truth and light, the other untruth and darkness. Later writings present a more dualistic cosmology in which the struggle is between Ahura Mazda (Ormazd) and the evil spirit Ahriman. The scriptures of Zoroastrianism are the Zend-Avesta. The language survives in isolated areas of Iran and in India, where its followers are known as Parsees.

—Zo·ro·as·tri·an *adj.* & *n.*

zorse /zôrs/ (also **ze·bra mule**) ▸*n.* the offspring of a zebra and a horse (strictly, a male zebra and a female horse), typically sterile. Zorses resemble horses or mules with dark zebra stripes.

zos·ter /ˈzästər/ ▸*n.* **1** short for **HERPES ZOSTER**. **2** (in ancient Greece) a belt or girdle.

Zou·ave /zo͞oˈäv; zwäv/ ▸*n.* **1** a member of a light-infantry corps in the French army, originally formed of Algerians and long retaining their oriental uniform. ■ a member of such an infantry unit patterned on the French Zouaves, esp. in the Union Army in the Civil War. **2** (**zouaves**) *dated* women's trousers with wide tops, tapering to a narrow ankle. ▹mid 19th cent.: from French, from Kabyle *Zouaoua*, the name of a tribe.

Zoug /zo͞og/ French name for **ZUG**.

zouk /zo͞ok/ ▸*n.* an exuberant style of popular music combining Caribbean and Western elements and having a fast heavy beat. ▹1970s: Guadeloupian Creole, literally 'to party.'

zounds /zoundz/ ▸*exclam. archaic* or *humorous* expressing surprise or indignation. ▹late 16th cent.: contraction from *(God)'s wounds* (i.e., those of Jesus Christ on the Cross).

Zo·vi·rax /zōˈvīˌraks/ ▸*n.* trademark for **ACYCLOVIR**.

zow·ie /ˈzou-ē; zouˈē/ ▸*exclam. informal* expressing astonishment or admiration. ▹natural exclamation: first recorded in American English in the early 20th cent.

zoy·si·a /ˈzoisēə; -zēə; -SHə; -ZHə/ ▸*n.* a low-growing grass of the genus *Zoysia*, native to tropical Asia and New Zealand and widely used for lawns. • Family Gramineae: several species and cultivars, including *Z. matrella* and *Z. japonica*.

Z par·ti·cle ▸*n. Physics* a heavy, uncharged elementary particle considered to transmit the weak interaction between other elementary particles.

ZPG ▸*abbr.* zero population growth.

Z-plas·ty /ˈzēˌplastē/ ▸*n.* a technique in orthopedic and cosmetic surgery in which one or more Z-shaped incisions are made, the diagonals forming one straight line, and the two triangular sections so formed are drawn across the diagonal before being stitched.

Zr ▸*symbol* the chemical element zirconium.

Zsig·mon·dy /ˈZHigˌmôndē/, Richard Adolph (1865–1929), German chemist, born in Austria. He investigated the properties of various colloidal solutions and invented the ultramicroscope for counting colloidal particles. Nobel Prize for Chemistry (1925).

zuc·chet·to /(t)so͞oˈketō; zo͞o-/ ▸*n.* (*pl.* **-tos**) a Roman Catholic cleric's skullcap: black for a priest, purple for a bishop, red for a cardinal, and white for the pope. ▹mid 19th cent.: from Italian *zucchetta*, diminutive of *zucca* 'gourd, head.'

zuc·chi·ni /zo͞oˈkēnē/ ▸*n.* (*pl.* same or **-nis**) a green variety of smooth-skinned summer squash. ▹Italian, plural of *zucchino*, diminutive of *zucca* 'gourd.'

Zug /tso͝ok; zo͞og/ a mainly German-speaking canton in central Switzerland. The smallest canton, it joined the confederation in 1352. ■ its capital; pop. 21,000. French name **ZOUG**.

zug·zwang /ˈzəgˌzwaNG; ˈtso͞ogˌtsvaNG/ ▸*n. Chess* a situation in which the obligation to make a move in one's turn is a serious, often decisive, disadvantage: *black is in zugzwang*. ▹early 20th cent.: from German *Zug* 'move' + *Zwang* 'compulsion.'

Zui·der Zee /ˌzīdər ˈzē; ˈzā/ a former shallow inlet of the North Sea, in the Netherlands. A dam across its entrance was completed in 1932, and since then large parts have been drained and reclaimed as polders. The remainder forms the IJsselmeer. ▹Dutch, literally 'southern sea.'

Zu·kor /ˈzo͞okər/, Adolph (1873–1973), U.S. movie producer and executive; born in Hungary. He created the Famous Players Co. in 1912. Through mergers and name changes it evolved as Paramount Pictures with Zukor at the head.

Zu·lu /ˈzo͞olo͞o/ ▸*n.* **1** a member of a South African people living mainly in KwaZulu-Natal province. ■ the Nguni language of this people. **2** a code word representing the letter Z, used in radio communication.

▸*adj.* of or relating to the Zulu people or language.

The Zulus formed a powerful military empire in southern Africa during the 19th century before being defeated in a series of engagements with white Afrikaner and British settlers. Some Zulus still live under the traditional clan system in the province of KwaZulu-Natal, but many now work in the cities.

▹from the stem of Zulu *umZulu* (plural *amaZulu*).

Zu·ni /ˈzo͞onē/ (also **Zu·ñi** /ˈzo͞onyē/) ▸*n.* (*pl.* same or **Zu·nis**) **1** a member of a Pueblo Indian people of western New Mexico. **2** the language of this people.

▸*adj.* of or relating to this people or their language. ▹from Spanish *Zuñi*, probably from Keresan.

zup·pa in·gle·se /ˈtso͞opə iNGˈglāzā; ˈzo͞opə; -zē/ ▸*n.* a rich Italian dessert resembling trifle. ▹Italian, literally 'English soup.'

Zu·rich /ˈzo͝orik/ a city in northern central Switzerland, on Lake Zurich; pop. 343,000. The largest city in Switzerland, it is a major international financial center.

Zwick·au /ˈtsvikˌou/ a mining and industrial city in southeastern Germany, in Saxony; pop. 113,000.

zwie·back /ˈswēˌbak; ˈzwē-; ˈswī-; ˈzwī-/ ▸*n.* a rusk or cracker made by baking a small loaf and then toasting slices until they are dry and crisp. ▹German, literally 'twice-bake.'

Zwing·li /ˈzwiNG(g)lē; ˈswiNG-; ˈtsfiNG-/, Ulrich (1484–1531), Swiss religious reformer, the principal figure of the Swiss Reformation. He rejected papal authority and many orthodox doctrines and, although he had strong local support in Zurich, his ideas met with fierce resistance in some regions. Zwingli was killed in the civil war that resulted from his reforms. **—Zwing·li·an** /-lēən/ *adj.* & *n.*

zwit·ter·i·on /ˈ(t)switərˌīən/ ▸*n. Chemistry* a molecule or ion having separate positively and negatively charged groups. ▹early 20th cent.: from German, from *Zwitter* 'a hybrid' + *Ion* 'ion.' **—zwit·ter·i·on·ic** /ˌ(t)switərīˈänik/ *adj.*

Zwor·y·kin /ˈzwôrikən; ˈzvôr-/, Vladimir (Kuzmich) (1889–1982), U.S. physicist and television pioneer, born in Russia. He invented a precursor to the television camera, the first to scan an image electronically. This had been developed into the first practical television camera by about 1929.

Zy·ban /ˈzīˌban/ ▸*n.* trademark for **BUPROPION**. ▹1990s: an invented name, probably from *ban* or *banish*.

zy·de·co /ˈzīdəˌkō/ ▸*n.* a kind of black American dance music originally from southern Louisiana, typically featuring accordion and guitar. ▹1960s: Louisiana Creole, possibly from a pronunciation of French *les haricots* in a dance-tune title.

zyg·a·poph·y·sis /ˌzigəˈpäfəsis; ˌzīgə-/ ▸*n.* one of the two paired processes of a vertebra that interlock it with the adjacent vertebrae.

zygo- ▸*comb. form* relating to joining or pairing: *zygodactyl*. ▹from Greek *zugon* 'yoke.'

zy·go·dac·tyl /ˌzīgōˈdaktl/ ▸*adj.* (of a bird's feet) having two toes pointing forward and two backward.

▸*n.* a bird with zygodactyl feet. **—zy·go·dac·ty·lous** /-ˈdaktələs/ *adj.*

zy·go·ma /zīˈgōmə/ ▸*n.* (*pl.* **-ma·(ə)ta** /-mətə/) *Anatomy* the bony arch of the cheek formed by connection of the zygomatic and temporal bones. ▹late 17th cent.: from Greek *zugōma*, from *zugon* 'yoke.' **—zy·go·mat·ic** /ˌzīgəˈmatik/ *adj.*

zy·go·mat·ic arch ▸*n. Anatomy* the zygoma.

zy·go·mat·ic bone ▸*n. Anatomy* the bone that forms the prominent part of the cheek and the outer side of the eye socket.

zy·go·mat·ic proc·ess ▸*n. Anatomy* a projection of the temporal bone that forms part of the zygoma.

zy·go·mor·phic /ˌzīgəˈmôrfik/ ▸*adj. Botany* (of a flower) having only one plane of symmetry, as in a pea or snapdragon; bilaterally symmetrical. Compare with **ACTINOMORPHIC**. **—zy·go·mor·phy** /ˈzīgəˌmôrfē/ *n.*

zy·go·spore /ˈzīgəˌspôr/ ▸*n. Biology* the thick-walled resting cell of certain fungi and algae, arising from the fusion of two similar gametes. Compare with **OOSPORE**.

zy·gote /ˈzīˌgōt/ ▸*n. Biology* a diploid cell resulting from the fusion of two haploid gametes; a fertilized ovum. ▹late 19th cent.: from Greek *zugōtos* 'yoked,' from *zugoun* 'to yoke.' **—zy·got·ic** /zīˈgätik/ *adj.*

zy·go·tene /ˈzīgəˌtēn/ ▸*n. Biology* the second stage of the prophase of meiosis, following leptotene, during which homologous chromosomes begin to pair.

Zy·klon B /ˈzīˌklän/ ▸*n.* hydrogen cyanide adsorbed on or released from a carrier in the form of small tablets, used as an insecticidal fumigant and by the Nazis for killing concentration-camp prisoners. ▹1930s: from German, of unknown origin.

zy·mase /ˈzīˌmās; -ˌmāz/ ▸*n. Biochemistry* a mixture of enzymes obtained from yeast that catalyze the breakdown of sugars in alcoholic fermentation. ▹late 19th cent.: from French, from Greek *zumē* 'leaven.'

zymo- (also **zym-** before a vowel) ▸*comb. form* relating to enzymes or fermentation: *zymogen* | *zymase*. ▹from Greek *zumē* 'leaven.'

zy·mo·gen /ˈzīməjən/ ▸*n. Biochemistry* an inactive substance that is converted into an enzyme when activated by another enzyme.

zy·mur·gy /ˈzīˌmərjē/ ▸*n.* the study or practice of fermentation in brewing, winemaking, or distilling. ▹mid 19th cent.: from Greek *zumē* 'leaven,' on the pattern of *metallurgy*.

Ready Reference

Rules of English: Understanding Grammar

Grammar is the system and structure of a language. It embodies all the principles by which the language works. All good writing begins with an understanding of the fundamentals of grammar:

- parts of speech
- parts of sentences
- sentence structures
- sentence functions

PARTS OF SPEECH

Noun

A **noun** is a word that identifies or names a person, place, thing, action, or quality. There are two types of nouns: proper and common.

Proper nouns

A noun that names a particular person, place, or thing is a **proper noun**. It always begins with a capital letter:

Benito Mussolini
Cairo
the Chrysler Building
Jell-O
Mount Everest

Common nouns

A noun that names a type of person, place, or thing is a **common noun**. There are three kinds of common nouns: concrete, abstract, and collective.

A **concrete noun** names someone or something that you can see or touch:

arm
giraffe
hamburger
lake
stapler

An **abstract noun** names something intangible (that is, something that can neither be seen nor touched):

assistance
bravery
disappointment
flavor
wit

A **collective noun** names a group of persons or things:

audience
colony
herd
platoon
set

SINGULAR AND PLURAL NOUNS

A noun that names one person, place, or thing is **singular**. A noun that names more than one person, place, or thing is **plural**. The spelling of a singular noun almost always changes when it becomes a plural. Most plurals can be formed by adding *s* or *es*, but many nouns do not follow this format.

beach/beaches
bean/beans
hairbrush/hairbrushes
leaf/leaves
mouse/mice
party/parties
school/schools
woman/women

If the spelling of a plural noun is in doubt, it is always advisable to consult a dictionary.

APPOSITIVES

An **appositive** is a noun (or a unit of words that acts as a noun) whose meaning is a direct copy or extension of the meaning of the preceding noun in the sentence. In other words, the appositive and the preceding noun refer to the same person, place, or thing. The appositive helps to characterize or elaborate on the preceding noun in a specific way.

The wedding cake, a chocolate masterpiece, was the hit of the reception.
[The noun *cake* and the appositive *masterpiece* are the same thing.]

His primary objective, to write the great American novel, was never realized.
[The noun *objective* and the appositive *to write the great American novel* are the same thing.]

Eleanor's math teacher, Mrs. Kennedy, is retiring next year.
[The noun *teacher* and the appositive *Mrs. Kennedy* are the same person.]

POSSESSIVES

A **possessive** is a noun whose form has changed in order to show possession. Certain rules can be followed to determine how the form should change for any given noun.

In the case of a singular noun, add an apostrophe and an *s*:

Lincoln's inaugural address
the baby's favorite blanket

Exception: Most singular nouns that end in *s* follow the preceding rule with no difficulty (e.g., *Chris's*, *Dickens's*), but some singular nouns that end in *s* may be exempted from the rule because the pronunciation of the plural is less awkward with just an apostrophe and no final *s*:

Ramses' dynasty
Aristophanes' great comedic works

In the case of a plural noun that ends in *s*, add just an apostrophe:

the Lincolns' summer home
our babies' double stroller

In the case of a plural noun that does not end in *s*, add an apostrophe and an *s*:

men's footwear
the fungi's rapid reproduction

In the case of a compound noun (a noun made of more than one word), only the last word takes the possessive form:

my sister-in-law's house
the commander in chief's personal staff

In the case of joint possession (that is, two or more nouns possess the same thing together), only the last of the possessing nouns takes the possessive form:

Ryan and Saul's nickel collection
[There is only one nickel collection, and *both* Ryan and Saul own it *together*.]

Gramma and Grampa's photo albums
[However many photo albums there may be, they all belong to *both* Gramma and Grampa *together*.]

In the case of individual possession by two or more nouns (that is, two or more nouns possess the same type of thing, but separately and distinctly), each of the possessing nouns takes the possessive form:

Lenny's and Suzanne's footprints on the beach
[Lenny and Suzanne *each* left *their own distinct* footprints on the beach.]

Strauss's and Khachaturian's waltzes
[Strauss and Khachaturian *each* composed *their own distinct* waltzes.]

Pronoun

A **pronoun** is a word that represents a person or thing without giving the specific name of the person or thing. There are five classes of pronouns: personal, relative, demonstrative, indefinite, and interrogative.

A **personal pronoun** is used to refer to the person speaking (first person), the person spoken to (second person), or the person or thing spoken about (third person). A pronoun formed from certain personal pronouns by adding the suffix *-self* (singular) or *-selves* (plural) is called "reflexive."

PERSON	SINGULAR	PLURAL	REFLEXIVE SINGULAR	REFLEXIVE PLURAL
first person	*I*	*we*	—	—
	my	*our*	*myself*	*ourselves*
	mine	*ours*	—	—
	me	*us*	—	—
second person	*you*	*you*	—	—
	your	*your*	*yourself*	*yourselves*
	yours	*yours*	—	—
	you	*you*	—	—
third person masculine	*he*	*they*	—	—
	his	*their*	—	—
	his	*theirs*	—	—
	him	*them*	*himself*	*themselves*
third person feminine	*she*	*they*	—	—
	her	*their*	—	—
	hers	*theirs*	—	—
	her	*them*	*herself*	*themselves*
third person neuter	*it*	*they*	—	—
	its	*their*	—	—
	its	*theirs*	—	—
	it	*them*	*itself*	*themselves*

Note that the gender designations of masculine, feminine, and neuter apply only to the third person singular.

Reflexive personal pronouns are so called because they reflect the action of the verb back to the subject. It is incorrect to use a reflexive pronoun by itself; there must be a subject to which it refers.

incorrect: Denise and myself will fix the car.
[The reflexive pronoun *myself* has no subject to refer to; the wording should be "Denise and I."]

correct: I will fix the car myself.
[The reflexive pronoun *myself* refers to the subject *I*.]

A reflexive pronoun that adds force or emphasis to a noun or another pronoun is called "intensive":

You yourself must return the ladder.
Terri and Phil want to wallpaper the kitchen themselves.

A **relative pronoun** introduces a descriptive clause. The relative pronouns are *which*, *that*, *who*, *whoever*, *whose*, *whom*, and *whomever*.

Wendy was the pianist who won the scholarship.
Is Mr. Leonard the teacher whose book was just published?
Whoever wrote the speech is a genius.
I attended the morning meeting, which lasted for three hours.

A **demonstrative pronoun** is specific. It is used to point out particular persons, places, or things. The demonstrative pronouns are *this*, *that*, *these*, and *those*.

These are the finest fabrics available.
I'll look at those first.
What is this?

An **indefinite pronoun** is nonspecific. It is used to refer to persons, places, or things without particular identification. There are numerous indefinite pronouns, including the following:

all	everyone	none
any	everything	no one
anybody	few	other
anyone	little	others
anything	many	several
both	most	some
each	much	somebody
either	neither	someone
everybody	nobody	something

George brought two desserts, but I didn't try either.
Many are called, but few are chosen.
Can somebody please answer the phone?

An **interrogative pronoun** is used to ask a question. The interrogative pronouns are *who*, *which*, and *what*.

Who wants to buy a raffle ticket?
Which of the two applicants has more practical experience?
What is the purpose of another debate?

PRONOUN CASES

The case of a pronoun is what determines its relation to the other words in the sentence. There are three pronoun cases: nominative, objective, and possessive.

Nominative case
The nominative pronouns are *I*, *we*, *you*, *he*, *she*, *it*, *they*, *who*, and *whoever*.

A pronoun that is the subject (or part of the subject) of a sentence is in the nominative case:

They loved the movie.
Mark and I are going to the Bahamas.

A pronoun that is a predicate is in the nominative case:

It was she who wrote the poem.
The winner will probably be you.

Objective case
The objective pronouns are *me*, *us*, *you*, *him*, *her*, *it*, *them*, *whom*, and *whomever*.

A pronoun that is the direct object of a verb is in the objective case:

Stephen already invited them.
Should we keep it?

A pronoun that is the indirect object of a verb is in the objective case:

Captain Mackenzie told us many seafaring tales.
I'll give you the recipe tomorrow.

A pronoun that is the object of a preposition is in the objective case:

Does she think this job is beneath her?
To whom was it addressed?

Possessive case
A possessive pronoun shows ownership.

The possessive pronouns used as predicate nominatives are *mine*, *ours*, *yours*, *his*, *hers*, *its*, *theirs*, and *whose*.

The blue station wagon is mine.
None of the cash was theirs.

The possessive pronouns used as adjectives are *my*, *our*, *your*, *his*, *her*, *its*, *their*, and *whose*.

Whose test scores were the highest?
I believe this is your package.

TIP

A possessive pronoun never has an apostrophe. Remember, the word *it's* is the contraction of *it is* or *it has*—not the possessive form of *it*.

- possessive: Life has its ups and downs.
- contraction: It's good to see you.

SINGULAR AND PLURAL AGREEMENT

It is important to identify a pronoun as singular or plural and to make certain that the associated verb form is in agreement. The pronouns that tend to cause the most problems for writers and speakers are the indefinite pronouns.

Some indefinite pronouns are always singular and therefore always require a singular verb. These include *everybody*, *everyone*, *somebody*, *someone*, *nobody*, *one*, *either*, and *neither*.

Nobody wants to leave.
Don't get up unless someone knocks on the door.
Either of these two colors is fine.

Other indefinite pronouns may be singular or plural, depending on the particular reference. These include *any*, *all*, *some*, *most*, and *none*.

> If any of these marbles are yours, let me know.
> [The noun *marbles* is plural.]
>
> If any of this cake is yours, let me know.
> [The noun *cake* is singular.]
>
> Most of the potatoes are already gone.
> [The noun *potatoes* is plural.]
>
> Most of the evening is already gone.
> [The noun *evening* is singular.]

Verb

A **verb** is a word that expresses an action or a state of being.

An **action verb** expresses a physical or mental action:

> break
> eat
> intercept
> operate
> unveil
> wish

A **state of being verb** expresses a condition or state of being:

> be
> become
> is
> lack
> seem
> smell

TRANSITIVE VERBS

A **transitive verb** expresses an action that is performed on someone or something. The someone or something is the **direct object.** Notice in each of the following examples that the direct object receives the action of the verb.

> Ingrid restores antique furniture.
> [transitive verb: *restores*; direct object: *furniture*]
>
> Hernandez pitched the ball.
> [transitive verb: *pitched*; direct object: *ball*]
>
> Did you feed the animals?
> [transitive verb: *feed*; direct object: *animals*]

Sometimes a transitive verb has both a direct object and an indirect object. An **indirect object** is the person or thing to whom or for whom the verb's action is being performed. Notice in each of the following examples that the direct object receives the action of the verb, while the indirect object identifies who or what the action affected.

> The captain handed us our orders.
> [transitive verb: *handed*; direct object: *orders*; indirect object: *us*]
>
> Did you give the plants some water?
> [transitive verb: *give*; direct object: *water*; indirect object: *plants*]

I tossed a pen to Herman.
[transitive verb: *tossed*; direct object: *pen*; indirect object: *Herman*]

TIP

Remember: A direct object answers *what?* An indirect object answers *to whom?* (or *to what?*) or *for whom?* (or *for what?*).

direct objects:	*What* does Ingrid restore?	furniture
	What did Hernandez pitch?	ball
	Did you feed *what*?	animals
	What did the captain hand?	orders
	Did you give *what*?	water
	What did I toss?	pen
indirect objects:	*To whom* did the captain hand orders?	us
	Did you give water *to what*?	plants
	To whom did I toss a pen?	Herman

INTRANSITIVE VERBS

An **intransitive verb** does not have an object. Notice in each of the following examples that the verb expresses an action that occurs without needing to be received.

We marched in the parade.
The tea kettle whistled.
Heidi sleeps on the third floor.

TIP

Remember: Because an intransitive verb does not have an object, the question *what?* will be unanswerable.

What did we march?
What did the kettle whistle?
What does Heidi sleep?

These questions simply cannot be answered; therefore the verbs are intransitive.

LINKING VERBS

A **linking verb** joins a word (or unit of words) that names a person or thing to another word (or unit of words) that renames or describes the person or thing. It is always intransitive and always expresses a state of being. The most common linking verbs are *to be* and all the forms of *to be*, which include *am*, *are*, *is*, *was*, and *were*. Other common linking verbs include the following:

act	feel	remain	sound
appear	grow	seem	taste
become	look	smell	turn

The air seemed humid yesterday.
What smells so good?
The days grow shorter.

I am a registered voter.
Kim remains a devout Catholic.
Butch and Sundance were the title characters.

Predicate adjectives and nominatives

The word (or unit of words) that a linking verb joins to the subject can be either an adjective or a noun, but its function is always the same: to tell something about the subject. An adjective that follows a linking verb is a **predicate adjective**. A noun that follows a linking verb is a **predicate nominative**.

predicate adjective: The air seemed humid yesterday.
What smells so good?
The days grow shorter.

predicate nominative: I am a registered voter.
Kim remains a devout Catholic.
Butch and Sundance were the title characters.

VOICE

The subject of a transitive verb either performs or receives the action. A verb whose subject performs is said to be in the **active voice**. A verb whose subject receives is said to be in the **passive voice**.

active voice: Brainerd & Sons built the storage shed.
[The subject *Brainerd & Sons* performed the action of building.]

Lydia will curry the horses.
[The subject *Lydia* will perform the action of currying.]

passive voice: The storage shed was built by Brainerd & Sons.
[The subject *shed* received the action of building.]

The horses will be curried by Lydia.
[The subject *horses* will receive the action of currying.]

MOOD

Verbs have a quality that shows the attitude or purpose of the speaker. This quality is called the **mood**. There are three verb moods: indicative, imperative, and subjunctive.

The **indicative mood** shows a statement or question of fact:

Does Paula know the combination to the safe?
Dr. Sliva is my dentist.

The **imperative mood** shows a command or request:

Make the most of your situation.
Proceed to the third traffic light.

The **subjunctive mood** shows a condition of doubtfulness, possibility, desirability, improbability, or unreality:

Should you decide to return the blouse, you will need the receipt.
If I were rich, I'd quit my job.

PERSON AND NUMBER

The **person** (first, second, or third) of a verb depends on to whom or to what the verb refers: the person speaking (first person), the person spoken to (second person), or the person or thing spoken about (third person).

The **number** (singular or plural) of a verb depends on whether the verb refers to a singular subject or a plural subject.

For nearly all verbs, the form of the verb changes only in the third person singular.

PERSON	SINGULAR	PLURAL
first person	I *know*	we *know*
second person	you *know*	you *know*
third person	he *knows* she *knows* it *knows*	they *know* they *know* they *know*
	Chris *knows* Mrs. Hansen *knows* God *knows* the teacher *knows* the heart *knows*	Chris and Pat *know* the Hansens *know* the gods *know* the teachers *know* our hearts *know*

TENSE

The **tense** of a verb shows the time of the verb's action. There are six verb tenses: present, present perfect, past, past perfect, future, and future perfect.

The **present tense** shows action occurring in the present:

I smell fresh coffee.

The present tense can also show the following:

action that is typical or habitual:	I design greenhouses. Stuart daydreams during math class.
action that will occur:	Lynne retires in six months. Our plane lands at midnight.
facts and beliefs:	March follows February. Greed destroys the spirit.

TIP

Yet another function of the present tense is what is called the **historical present**. This usage allows the writer or speaker to relate past actions in a present tone, which may enhance the descriptive flow of the text.

> The United States acquires the Oklahoma Territory from France in 1803 as part of the Louisiana Purchase. Following the War of 1812, the U.S. government begins a relocation program, forcing Indian tribes from the eastern United States to move into certain unsettled western areas, including Oklahoma. Because of their opposition to the U.S. government, most of these native people lend their support to the Confederate South during the American Civil War. In 1865, the war ends in utter defeat for the Confederacy, and all of the Oklahoma Territory soon falls under U.S. military rule.

When using the historical present, writers and speakers must be careful not to lapse into the past tense. For example, it would be an incorrect mix of tenses to say, "In 1865, the war ended in utter defeat for the Confederacy, and all of the Oklahoma Territory soon falls under U.S. military rule."

The **present perfect tense** is formed with the word *has* or *have*. It shows action begun in the past and completed by the time of the present:

James has checked the air in the tires at least three times.
I have read the book you're talking about.

The **past tense** shows action that occurred in the past:

> Greg memorized his speech.
> The mouse scurried across the room.

The **past perfect tense** is formed with the word *had*. It shows action that occurred in the past, prior to another past action:

> Eugene had finished his story by the time we got to the airport.
> The parrot had flown into another room long before we noticed an empty cage.

The **future tense** is formed with the word *will*. It shows action that is expected to occur in the future:

> The president will address the nation this evening.
> Tempers will flare when the truth comes out.

The **future perfect tense** is formed with the words *will have*. It shows action that is expected to occur in the future, prior to another future or expected action:

> Noreen will have finished painting by the time we're ready to lay the carpet.
> The candidates will have traveled thousands of miles before this campaign is over.

VERBALS

A verb form that acts as a part of speech other than a verb is a **verbal**. There are three types of verbals: infinitives, participles, and gerunds.

An **infinitive** is a verb form that can act as a noun, an adjective, or an adverb. It is preceded by the preposition *to*.

noun: To steal is a crime.
[The infinitive *to steal* is the subject.]

Our original plan, to elope, was never discovered.
[The infinitive *to elope* is an appositive.]

adjective: Those are words to remember.
[The infinitive *to remember* modifies the noun *words*.]

adverb: The hill was too icy to climb.
[The infinitive *to climb* modifies the predicate adjective *icy*.]

He lived to golf.
[The infinitive *to golf* modifies the verb *lived*.]

A **participle** is a verb form that has one of two uses: to make a verb phrase ("they were trying"; "the car has died") or to act as an adjective. A participle is a verbal only when it acts as an adjective.

> A **present participle** always ends in *-ing*:
>
> catching
> laughing
> winding
>
> A **past participle** usually ends in *-ed*, *-en*, or *-t*:
>
> given
> lost
> toasted

In the following examples, each participle acts as an adjective and is therefore a verbal:

> Does the zoo have a laughing hyena?
> We live on a winding road.

It was a lost opportunity.
Add a cup of toasted coconut.

A **gerund** is a verb form that acts as a noun. It always ends in *–ing*:

Reading is my favorite pastime.
The next step, varnishing, should be done in a well-ventilated area.
The doctor suggested guidelines for sensible dieting.

TIP

Remember: Both gerunds and present participles always end in *–ing*, but their functions are quite distinct. Also remember that a present participle is only a verbal when it acts as an adjective, *not* when it acts as a verb phrase.

verbal: Her singing has improved this year.
[Used as a noun, *singing* is a gerund, which is always a verbal.]

Peterson hired the singing cowboys.
[Used as an adjective, *singing* is a present participle that is also a verbal.]

not a verbal: The birds are singing.
[Used to form a verb phrase, *singing* is a present participle, but not a verbal]

Adjective

An **adjective** is a word that modifies a noun. There are two basic types of adjectives: descriptive and limiting.

Descriptive adjectives

A **descriptive adjective** describes a noun. That is, it shows a quality or condition of a noun:

She is an upstanding citizen.
Josh has invited his zany friends.
That was a mighty clap of thunder.
I prefer the white shirt with the long sleeves.

Limiting adjectives

A **limiting adjective** shows the limits of a noun. That is, it indicates the number or quantity of a noun, or it points out a certain specificity of a noun. There are three types of limiting adjectives: numerical adjectives, pronominal adjectives, and articles.

A **numerical adjective** is a number. It may be cardinal ("how many") or ordinal ("in what order"):

cardinal: We have served one million customers.
There are three prizes.
After Arizona was admitted, there were forty-eight states.

ordinal: You are the one millionth customer.
We won third prize.
Arizona was the forty-eighth state to be admitted.

A **pronominal adjective** is a pronoun that acts as an adjective. A pronominal adjective may be personal (*my, our, your, his, her, their, its*), demonstrative (*this, that, these, those*), indefinite (*all, any, few, other, several, some*), or interrogative (*which, what*).

personal: We loved her goulash.
The squirrel returned to its nest.

demonstrative: Those directions are too complicated.
This window is broken.

indefinite: Pick any card from the deck.
All luggage will be inspected.

interrogative: Which radios are on sale?
What color is the upholstery?

There are three **articles** in English: *a*, *an*, and *the*. Articles are classified as either indefinite (*a, an*) or definite (*the*).

indefinite: At dawn, a helicopter broke the silence.
An usher seated us.

definite: The paintings lacked imagination.

Comparison of adjectives

Descriptive adjectives are able to indicate qualities and conditions by three degrees of comparison: positive, comparative, and superlative. Adjectives may be compared in downward or upward order.

For **downward comparisons**, all adjectives use the words *less* (comparative) and *least* (superlative).

Downward Comparisons

positive (the quality or condition)	**comparative** (a degree lower than the positive)	**superlative** (the lowest degree of the positive)
intelligent	less intelligent	least intelligent
kind	less kind	least kind
salty	less salty	least salty

For **upward comparisons**, there are three different formats:

Upward Comparisons

positive (the quality or condition)	**comparative** (a degree higher than the positive)	**superlative** (the highest degree of the positive)

1. Almost all one-syllable adjectives use the endings *–er* (comparative) and *–est* (superlative). Some adjectives with two or more syllables follow this format as well.

kind	kinder	kindest
straight	straighter	straightest
salty	saltier	saltiest

2. Most adjectives with two or more syllables use the words *more* (comparative) and *most* (superlative). Most one-syllable adjectives may use this format as an optional alternative to using *–er* and *–est*.

harmonious	more harmonious	most harmonious
impatient	more impatient	most impatient
talkative	more talkative	most talkative
kind	more kind	most kind

3. Some adjectives have irregular forms.

bad/ill	worse	worst
good/well	better	best
far	farther/further	farthest/furthest
little	less	least
many	more	most

TIP

Never "double compare" an adjective. Remember:

- Sometimes a descriptive adjective may use either *–er* or *more*, but it never uses both.

  correct: The red grapes are sweeter than the green ones.
  The red grapes are more sweet than the green ones.

  incorrect: The red grapes are more sweeter than the green ones.

- Sometimes a descriptive adjective may use either *–est* or *most*, but it never uses both.

  correct: Samson is the friendliest dog in the building.
  Samson is the most friendly dog in the building.

  incorrect: Samson is the most friendliest dog in the building.

Adverb

An **adverb** is a word that modifies a verb, an adjective, or another adverb.

Adverb meanings

An adverb usually describes how, where, when, or to what extent something happens.

An **adverb of manner** describes *how*:

They argued loudly.

An **adverb of place** describes *where*:

Please sit near me.

An **adverb of time** describes *when*:

I'll call you later.

An **adverb of degree** describes *to what extent*:

The laundry is somewhat damp.

Adverb functions

A **relative adverb** introduces a subordinate clause:

I'll be out on the veranda when the clock strikes twelve.

A **conjunctive adverb** (also called a **transitional adverb**) joins two independent clauses:

Dinner is ready; however, you may have to heat it up.

An **interrogative adverb** introduces a question:

Where did Lisa go?

TIP

A great number of adverbs are created by adding the suffix *–ly* to an adjective:

hesitant + *-ly* = hesitantly
strong + *-ly* = strongly

This does not mean, however, that all adverbs end in *–ly*.

adverbs: fast, seldom, now

Nor does it mean that all words ending in *–ly* are adverbs.

adjectives: friendly, homely, dastardly

The way to determine if a word is an adverb or an adjective is to see how it is used in the sentence:

- If it modifies a noun, it is an adjective.
- If it modifies a verb, an adjective, or another adverb, it is an adverb.

An **independent adverb** functions independently from the rest of the sentence. That is, the meaning and grammatical correctness of the sentence would not change if the independent adverb were removed:

Besides, I never liked living in the city.

COMPARISON OF ADVERBS

Like adjectives, adverbs of manner may be compared in three degrees: positive, comparative, and superlative.

Most adverbs, especially those that end in *–ly*, take on the upward comparing words *more* and *most*.

positive	**comparative**	**superlative**
nicely	more nicely	most nicely
diligently	more diligently	most diligently

Some adverbs take on the upward comparing suffixes *–er* and *–est*:

positive	**comparative**	**superlative**
early	earlier	earliest
soon	sooner	soonest
close	closer	closest

Some adverbs have irregular upward comparisons.

positive	**comparative**	**superlative**
much	more	most
little	less	least
badly	worse	worst
well	better	best
far	farther	farthest
far	further	furthest

Almost all adverbs take on the downward comparing words *less* and *least*:

positive	**comparative**	**superlative**
nicely	less nicely	least nicely
diligently	less diligently	least diligently
early	less early	least early
soon	less soon	least soon
close	less close	least close

Preposition

A **preposition** is a word or group of words that governs a noun or pronoun by expressing its relationship to another word in the clause.

> The suspects landed in jail.
> [The relationship between the noun *jail* and the verb *landed* is shown by the preposition *in*.]
>
> Please hide the packages under the bed.
> [The relationship between the noun *bed* and the noun *packages* is shown by the preposition *under*.]
>
> The guitarist playing with our band is Samantha's uncle.
> [The relationship between the noun *band* and the participle *playing* is shown by the preposition *with*.]
>
> I already knew about it.
> [The relationship between the pronoun *it* and the verb *knew* is shown by the preposition *about*.]

TIP

Many words used as prepositions may be used as other parts of speech as well.

The closest village is over that hill.	[preposition]
He leaned over and whispered in my ear.	[adverb]
I told no one but Corinne.	[preposition]
We played our best, but the other team won.	[conjunction]
She is but a shadow of her former self.	[adverb]

Common prepositions

aboard
about
above
according to
across
after
against
ahead
along
along with
amid
around
as
as far as
as for
as to
aside from
at
because of
before
behind
below
beneath
beside
besides
between
beyond
but
but for
by
by means of
by way of
concerning
contrary to
despite
down
during
except
for
from
in
in addition to
in back of
in case of
in front of
in lieu of
in place of
in regard to
in spite of
inside
instead of
into
like
near
next to
of
off
on
on account of
on behalf of
onto
opposite
out
out of
outside
over
past
per
prior to
regarding
round
since
thanks to
through
throughout
till
to
toward
under
underneath
unlike
until
up
upon
up to
with
within
without

Conjunction

A **conjunction** is a word (or unit of words) that connects words, phrases, clauses, or sentences. There are three kinds of conjunctions: coordinating, subordinating, and correlative.

Coordinating conjunctions

A **coordinating conjunction** connects elements that have the same grammatical rank—that is, it connects words to words (nouns to nouns, verbs to verbs, etc.), phrases to phrases, clauses to clauses, sentences to sentences. A coordinating conjunction is almost always one of these seven words: *and, but, for, nor, or, so, yet.*

Would you prefer rice <u>or</u> potatoes?
[The coordinating conjunction *or* connects the two nouns *rice* and *potatoes.*]

I have seen <u>and</u> heard enough.
[The coordinating conjunction *and* connects the two verbs *seen* and *heard.*]

Vinnie's cat lay on the chair purring softly <u>yet</u> twitching its tail.
[The coordinating conjunction *yet* connects the two participial phrases *purring softly* and *twitching its tail.*]

O'Donnell is the reporter whose name is on the story <u>but</u> who denies having written it.
[The coordinating conjunction *but* connects the two subordinate clauses *whose name is on the story* and *who denies having written it.*]

We wanted to see batting practice, <u>so</u> we got to the stadium early.
[The coordinating conjunction *so* connects the two sentences *We wanted to see batting practice* and *We got to the stadium early*, creating one sentence. Notice that a comma precedes the conjunction when two sentences are joined.]

Subordinating conjunctions

A **subordinating conjunction** belongs to a subordinate clause. It connects the subordinate clause to a main clause.

I could get there on time <u>if only</u> the ferry were still running.
[The subordinating conjunction *if only* connects the subordinate clause *if only the ferry were still running* to the main clause *I could get there on time.*]

> **TIP**
>
> A noun clause or an adjective clause may or may not be introduced by a subordinating conjunction, but an adverb clause is always introduced by a subordinating conjunction.
>
> - noun clause introduced by subordinating conjunction:
>   Jack asked the question <u>even though he knew the answer</u>.
> - noun clause with no subordinating conjunction:
>   We gave <u>every single detail</u> our fullest attention.
> - adjective clause introduced by subordinating conjunction:
>   This is the farm <u>where we boarded our horses</u>.
> - adjective clause with no subordinating conjunction:
>   The people <u>we met last night</u> are Hungarian.
> - adverb clause with subordinating conjunction (as is always the case):
>   I will speak <u>as soon as the crowd quiets down</u>.

Common subordinating conjunctions

after	but	since	until
although	even if	so	when
as	even though	so that	whenever
as if	how	than	where
as long as	if	that	whereas
as though	if only	though	wherever
because	in order that	till	while
before	rather than	unless	why

CORRELATIVE CONJUNCTIONS

Two coordinating conjunctions that function together are called a pair of **correlative conjunctions**. These are the most common pairs of correlative conjunctions:

both . . . and
either . . . or
neither . . . nor
not only . . . but
not only . . . but also
whether . . . or

The site in Denver offers the potential for <u>both</u> security <u>and</u> expansion.
[The pair of correlative conjunctions *both . . . and* connects the two nouns *security* and *expansion*.]

I'm running in tomorrow's race <u>whether</u> it is sunny <u>or</u> rainy.
[The pair of correlative conjunctions *whether . . . or* connects the two adjectives *sunny* and *rainy*.]

TIP

It would be incorrect to say:

Their dog is <u>neither</u> quiet <u>nor</u> obeys simple commands.

Why? Because the pair of correlative conjunctions *neither . . . nor* is being used to connect the adjective *quiet* to the verb phrase *obeys simple commands*. This is not a grammatically valid connection.

Remember: A pair of correlative conjunctions is comprised of two coordinating conjunctions, and a coordinating conjunction must connect elements that have the same grammatical rank—that is, it must connect words to words (nouns to nouns, verbs to verbs, etc.), phrases to phrases, clauses to clauses, sentences to sentences.

Therefore, the sentence must be reworded to make the grammatical ranks match. Here are two such corrected versions:

Their dog is <u>neither</u> quiet <u>nor</u> obedient.
[The adjective *quiet* is connected to the adjective *obedient*.]

Their dog <u>neither</u> stays quiet <u>nor</u> obeys simple commands.
[The verb phrase *stays quiet* is connected to the verb phrase *obeys simple commands*.]

Interjection

An interjection is a word or phrase that expresses emotion, typically in an abrupt or emphatic way. It is not connected grammatically to the rest of the sentence. When the emotion expressed is very strong, the interjection is followed by an exclamation point. Otherwise it is followed by a comma:

Stop! I can't let you in here.
Yeah! Dempsey has won another fight.

Ah, that was a wonderful meal.
Oh no, I left my sweater on the train.

> **TIP**
>
> Interjections occur more often in speech than in writing. It is not wrong to use interjections in writing, but writers should do so sparingly. Remember, an interjection is essentially an interruption, and too many may disrupt the flow of the text.

PHRASES, CLAUSES, SENTENCES, AND PARAGRAPHS

Phrases

A **phrase** is a unit of words that acts as a single part of speech.

NOUN PHRASES

A phrase made up of a noun and its modifiers is a **noun phrase**:

The biggest pumpkin won a blue ribbon.
A magnificent whooping crane flew overhead.

Most noun phrases can be replaced with a pronoun:

Give the tickets to the tall, dark-haired gentleman.
Give the tickets to him.

VERB PHRASES

A phrase made up of a main verb and its auxiliaries is a **verb phrase** (also called a **complete verb**):

We have been waiting for three hours.
What type of music do you prefer?

ADJECTIVE PHRASES

A phrase made up of a participle and its related words is an **adjective phrase** (also called an **adjectival phrase** or a **participial phrase**). Acting as a single adjective, it modifies a noun or pronoun:

Awakened by the siren, we escaped to safety.
[The adjective phrase *Awakened by the siren* modifies the pronoun *we*.]

Following his grandmother's directions, Harry baked a beautiful apple pie.
[The adjective phrase *Following his grandmother's directions* modifies the noun *Harry*.]

PREPOSITIONAL PHRASES

A phrase that begins with a preposition is a **prepositional phrase**. It can act as an adjective or an adverb:

adjective: The car with the sunroof is mine.
[The noun *car* is modified by the prepositional phrase *with the sunroof*.]

adverb: After the storm, we gathered the fallen branches.
[The verb *gathered* is modified by the prepositional phrase *After the storm*.]

Clauses

A clause is a unit of words that contains a subject and a predicate.

INDEPENDENT CLAUSES

A clause that can stand by itself as a complete thought is an **independent clause**. Any independent clause can stand alone as a complete sentence:

The Milwaukee Brewers joined the National League in November 1997.
It is snowing.
Vitus is the patron saint of actors.
Bob called.
The Celts were highly ritualistic.
Read what child development experts have to say.

SUBORDINATE CLAUSES

A clause that cannot stand by itself as a complete thought is a **subordinate clause** (also called a **dependent clause**). It cannot be a part of a sentence unless it is related by meaning to the independent clause. Essentially, it exists to build upon the information conveyed by the independent clause. A subordinate clause can relate to the independent clause as an adjective, an adverb, or a noun:

adjective:	The Milwaukee Brewers, who play at Miller Park, joined the National League in November 1997.
adverb:	Bob called when you were at the store.
noun:	Read what child development experts have to say about the virtues and drawbacks of homeschooling.

ELLIPTICAL CLAUSES

An **elliptical clause** deviates from the rule that states "a clause contains a subject and a predicate." What an elliptical clause does is *imply* both a subject and a predicate, even though both elements do not in fact appear in the clause:

While vacationing in Spain, Jo received word of her promotion.
[The elliptical clause implies the subject "she" and the predicate "was vacationing"—that is, it implies "While she was vacationing in Spain."]

Myers arrived on Saturday the 12th; Anderson, the following Monday.
[The elliptical clause implies the predicate "arrived the following Monday"—that is it implies "Anderson arrived the following Monday."]

Elliptical clauses are valuable devices, as they allow the writer to avoid excessive wordiness, preserve a sense of variety, and enhance the rhythm of the text.

RESTRICTIVE CLAUSES

A clause that is essential to the meaning of the sentence—that is, it *restricts* the meaning of the sentence—is a **restrictive clause**. The content of a restrictive clause identifies a particular person, place, or thing. If the restrictive clause were to be removed, the meaning of the sentence would change. A restrictive clause begins with the relative pronoun *that*, *who*, or *whom*. It should never be set off with commas.

I'm returning the coat that I bought last week.
[The identification of the coat is important. It's not just any coat. It's specifically the one and only coat "that I bought last week." Without the restrictive clause, the identification would be lost.]

The president who authorized the Louisiana Purchase was Thomas Jefferson.
[The point of this sentence is to identify specifically the one and only president responsible for the Louisiana Purchase. Without the restrictive clause, the point of the sentence would be lost.]

NONRESTRICTIVE CLAUSES

A clause that is not essential to the meaning of the sentence—that is, it does *not restrict* the meaning of the sentence—is a **nonrestrictive clause**. The content of a nonrestrictive clause adds information to what has already been identified. If the nonrestrictive clause were to be removed, the meaning of the sentence would not change. A nonrestrictive clause begins with the relative pronoun *which*, *who*, or *whom*. It should always be set off with commas.

I'm returning my new coat, which doesn't fit.

President Jefferson, who authorized the Louisiana Purchase, was the third U.S. president.

[The clauses *which doesn't fit* and *who authorized the Louisiana Purchase* are informative but not necessary. Without them, the meaning of each sentence is still clear.]

Sentences

Properly constructed sentences are integral to good communication. By definition, a sentence is "a set of words that is complete in itself, typically containing a subject and predicate, conveying a statement, question, exclamation, or command, and consisting of a main clause and sometimes one or more subordinate clauses." Simply put, a sentence is a group of words that expresses a complete thought.

SUBJECT AND PREDICATE

The primary building blocks of a sentence are the subject and the predicate.

The **subject** (usually a noun or pronoun) is the part that the sentence is telling about. A **simple subject** is simply the person, place, or thing being discussed. A **complete subject** is the simple subject along with all the words directly associated with it:

The large tropical plant in my office has bloomed every summer.
[Here, the simple subject is *plant*. The complete subject is *The large tropical plant in my office*.]

Two or more subjects that belong to the same verb comprise what is called a **compound subject**:

Stan Garrison and the rest of the department are relocating next week.
[Here, the compound subject consists of *Stan Garrison* and *the rest of the department*. They share the verb phrase *are relocating*.]

The **predicate** (a verb) is the "action" or "being" part of the sentence—the part that tells something about the subject. A **simple predicate** is simply the main verb and its auxiliaries. A **complete predicate** is the simple predicate along with all the words directly associated with it:

The setting sun has cast a scarlet glow across the skyline.
[Here, the simple predicate is *has cast*. The complete predicate is *has cast a scarlet glow across the skyline*.]

Two or more predicates that have the same subject comprise what is called a **compound predicate**:

I wanted to buy some art but left empty-handed.
[Here, the compound predicate consists of *wanted to buy some art* and *left empty-handed*. They share the subject *I*.]

FOUR SENTENCE STRUCTURES

A **simple sentence** contains one independent clause. Its subject and/or predicate may or may not be compound, but its one and only clause is always independent:

Paula rode her bicycle. [subject + predicate]
Honus Wagner and Nap Lajoie are enshrined in the Baseball Hall of Fame. [compound subject + predicate]
The correspondents traveled across the desert and slept in makeshift shelters. [subject + compound predicate]

Lunch and dinner are discounted on Sunday but are full price on Monday. [compound subject + compound predicate]

A **compound sentence** contains two or more independent clauses. The following examples show the various ways that coordinating conjunctions (e.g., *and*, *but*, *yet*), conjunctive adverbs (e.g., *however*, *therefore*), and punctuation may be used to join the clauses in a compound sentence:

Ken made the phone calls and Maria addressed the envelopes.
The war lasted for two years, but the effects of its devastation will last for decades.
Judges and other officials should sign in by noon; exhibitors will start arriving at 2:00.
I have decided to remain on the East Coast; however, I am willing to attend the monthly meetings in Dallas.
FDR initiated the New Deal, JFK embraced the New Frontier, and LBJ envisioned the Great Society.

A **complex sentence** contains one independent clause and one or more subordinate clauses:

Even though I majored in English, I was hired to teach applied physics.
We can have the party indoors if it gets too windy.
Before I agree, I have to read the final report that you drafted.
[The independent clauses are *I was hired to teach applied physics; We can have the party indoors; I have to read the final report*. The subordinate clauses are *Even though I majored in English; if it gets too windy; Before I agree; that you drafted.*]

A **compound-complex sentence** contains two or more independent clauses and one or more subordinate clauses:

Because the candidates have been so argumentative, some voters are confused and many have become disinterested.
We will begin painting tomorrow if the weather's nice; if it rains,we will start on Thursday.
[The independent clauses are *some voters are confused; many have become disinterested; We will begin painting tomorrow, we will start on Thursday.* The subordinate clauses are *Because the candidates have been so argumentative; if the weather's nice; if it rains.*]

FOUR SENTENCE FUNCTIONS

A **declarative sentence** states a fact, an assertion, an impression, or a feeling. It ends with a period:

Florence is a beautiful city.
Lewis Carroll died in 1898.
I'm sorry I missed the end of your speech.

An **interrogative sentence** asks a question. It ends with a question mark:

Did you read the article about migrating geese patterns?
How do spell your last name?
Mr. Young owns a kennel?

An **imperative sentence** makes a request or gives an order. It typically ends with a period but occasionally may end with an exclamation point:

Please lock the doors.
Do not throw trash in the recycling bins.
Think before you speak!

An **exclamatory sentence** expresses surprise, shock, or strong feeling. It ends with an exclamation point:

Look at this mess!
I can't believe how great this is!
I lost my purse!

Paragraphs

A paragraph is a series of sentences that conveys a single theme. Paragraphs help writers organize thoughts, actions, and descriptions into readable units of information. The paragraph, as a unit of text, may have one of several functions. It may be descriptive, giving certain details or impressions about a person, thing, or event. It may be instructive, explaining a method or procedure. It may be conceptual, stating thoughts, feelings, or opinions.

Every paragraph should contain a sentence that states the main idea of the paragraph. This is called the **topic sentence**. The other sentences in the paragraph are the **supporting sentences**, and their function is just that—to support or elaborate on the idea set forth in the topic sentence. Most paragraphs begin with the topic sentence, as in the following example:

> Each Thanksgiving we make place cards decorated with pressed autumn leaves. After gathering the smallest and most colorful leaves from the maples and oaks in our backyard, we place the leaves between sheets of blotter paper, which we then cover with a large, heavy book. In just a day or two, the leaves are ready to be mounted on cards. We use plain index cards, folded in half. Using clear adhesive paper, we put one leaf on each card, leaving room for the guest's name.

Try reading the preceding paragraph without the topic sentence (the first sentence). The supporting information becomes less unified because it has no main idea to support. Now imagine adding to the paragraph the following sentence:

> Last year, three of our guests were snowed in at the airport.

This would be a misplaced addition to the paragraph, as it is unrelated to the topic sentence (that is, it has nothing to do with making Thanksgiving place cards). Because it introduces a new and distinct idea, it should become the topic sentence for a new and distinct paragraph.

SENTENCE DEVELOPMENT: AVOIDING PROBLEMS

Sentence style

Getting one's ideas across in words is the core of communication. Sentences provide the means to arrange ideas in a coherent way. Certainly, the rules of grammar should be observed when constructing a sentence, but the general rhythm of the sentence is also important. Sentences may be categorized into three general types: loose, periodic, and balanced. Good writers typically use a combination of these styles in order to create a flow of ideas that will hold the reader's interest.

A **loose sentence** gets to the main point quickly. It begins with a basic and complete statement, which is followed by additional information:

> The power went out, plunging us into darkness, silencing the drone of the television, leaving our dinner half-cooked.
> [The basic statement is *The power went out*. Everything that follows is additional information.]

A **periodic sentence** ends with the main point. It begins with additional information, thus imposing a delay before the basic statement is given:

> With no warning, like a herd of stampeding bison, a mob of fans crashed through the gate.
> The basic statement is *a mob of fans crashed through the gate*. Everything that precedes is additional information.

A **balanced sentence** is comprised of grammatically equal or similar structures. The ideas in the sentence are linked by comparison or contrast:

> To visit their island villa is to sample nirvana.

As writers become more comfortable with the basic rules of grammar and the general patterns of sentence structure, they are able to remain compliant with the rules while getting more creative with the patterns. Many well-constructed sentences will not agree precisely with any of the three preceding examples, but they should always evoke an answer of "yes" to two fundamental questions:

- Is the sentence grammatically correct?
- Will the meaning of the sentence be clear to the reader?

Flawed sentences

Three types of "flawed sentences" are sentence fragments, run-on sentences, and sentences with improperly positioned modifiers.

SENTENCE FRAGMENTS

A **sentence fragment** is simply an incomplete sentence. Fundamental to every sentence is a complete thought that is able to stand on its own. Because a phrase or subordinate clause is not an independent thought, it cannot stand on its own as a sentence. To be a part of a sentence, it must either be connected to an independent clause or be reworded to become an independent clause. Consider this sentence fragment:

My English guest who stayed on for Christmas.

Here are three possible ways to create a proper sentence from that fragment:

Everyone left on Tuesday except Dan, my English guest who stayed on for Christmas.
[The fragment is added to the independent clause *Everyone left on Tuesday except Dan.*]

My English guest stayed on for Christmas.
[The fragment becomes an independent clause by removing the word *who*.]

Dan was my English guest who stayed on for Christmas.
[The fragment becomes an independent clause by adding the words *Dan was*.]

RUN-ON SENTENCES

A **run-on sentence** results when two or more sentences are improperly united into one sentence. Characteristic of a run-on sentence is the absence of punctuation between the independent clauses or the use of incorrect punctuation (typically a comma) between the independent clauses:

Our flight was canceled we had to spend the night in Boston.
Our flight was canceled, we had to spend the night in Boston.

Here are three possible ways to correct the preceding run-on sentences:

Our flight was canceled; we had to spend the night in Boston.
[A semicolon provides a properly punctuated separation of the two independent clauses.]

Our flight was canceled, so we had to spend the night in Boston.
[A comma followed by a conjunction (*so*) provides a properly worded and punctuated separation of the two independent clauses.]

Our flight was canceled. We had to spend the night in Boston.
[The creation of two distinct sentences provides an absolute separation of the two independent clauses.]

MODIFIER PROBLEMS

The improper placement of modifying words, phrases, and clauses is a common mistake. The result is a sentence in which the modifier unintentionally refers to the wrong person or thing. The three principal culprits are dangling modifiers, misplaced modifiers, and squinting modifiers. Writers must be careful to avoid these troublesome errors in sentence construction. Review the following examples to see how an improperly placed modifier can be confusing to the reader. It is important to recognize the subtle differences between the incorrect sentences and their corrected versions.

A **dangling modifier** is an adjectival phrase or clause that lacks a proper connection because the word it is supposed to modify is missing.

dangling: While waiting for my son, a cat jumped onto the hood of my car.
[This wrongly implies that "a cat was waiting for my son."]

correct: While I was waiting for my son, a cat jumped onto the hood of my car.
While waiting for my son, I saw a cat jump onto the hood of my car.
A cat jumped onto the hood of my car while I was waiting for my son.
[The word that was missing is "I."]

dangling: At age seven, her grandfather died of diphtheria.
[This wrongly implies that "her grandfather died when he was seven."]

correct: When she was seven, her grandfather died of diphtheria.
Her grandfather died of diphtheria when she was seven.
At age seven, she lost her grandfather when he died of diphtheria.
[The word that was missing is "she."]

A **misplaced modifier** is a phrase or clause that is not positioned close enough to the word it is supposed to modify. It will seem to the reader that a different word is being modified.

misplaced: There was an outbreak in our school of chicken pox.
[This wrongly implies that there is "a school of chicken pox."]

correct: There was an outbreak of chicken pox in our school.
In our school there was an outbreak of chicken pox.
Our school experienced an outbreak of chicken pox.

misplaced: I was stopped by a policeman without a driver's license.
[This wrongly implies that there was "a policeman without a driver's license."]

correct: Driving without a license, I was stopped by a policeman.
I was stopped by a policeman, and I did not have a driver's license.

A **squinting modifier** is an adverb placed between two verbs. For the reader, it is often difficult to determine which verb the adverb is supposed to modify.

squinting: The stack of chairs she had arranged carefully collapsed in the wind.
[Was the stack of chairs "arranged carefully" or did it "carefully collapse"?]

correct: The stack of chairs she had carefully arranged collapsed in the wind.
[Of the two possible meanings, this is only one that makes sense.]

squinting: The stack of chairs she had arranged quickly collapsed in the wind.
[Was the stack of chairs "arranged quickly" or did it "quickly collapse"?]

correct: The stack of chairs she had quickly arranged collapsed in the wind.
The stack of chairs she had arranged collapsed quickly in the wind.
[Either meaning could make sense, so only the writer would know which version is correct.]

Guide to Spelling

Any reader or writer knows that spelling is an important component of writing. Some individuals seem to have little or no trouble spelling words correctly, while others seem to struggle with spelling, often misspelling the same words over and over.

For those who have experienced the struggle, it is important to remember that spelling is a skill that improves with practice. Regular reading and writing, accompanied by a dictionary for consultation, are the best methods for improving one's spelling. Anyone who has encountered trouble with spelling knows that the English language contains numerous irregularities. Even so, there are basic spelling rules that can be followed in most cases.

[For spelling guidelines for plural nouns and possessive nouns, refer to the "Noun" section under "Parts of Speech."]

> **TIP**
>
> Keep a list of words that you find difficult to spell. Use a dictionary to confirm the correct spellings. Add to your list whenever you encounter a troublesome word. Refer to your list often, and quiz yourself. Make up sentences that include words from the list, writing them without going back and forth to double-check the spelling. Compare the words in your sentences to the words on your list. Make a note of the words that continue to give you trouble, and write these words in sentences every day until you have learned to spell them.

COMPOUND ADJECTIVES AND NOUNS

A compound adjective or noun is a single term formed from two or more distinct words. There are three spelling formats for compounds: open, hyphenated, and closed.

In an **open compound**, the component words are separate, with no hyphen (*well fed; wagon train*).
In a **hyphenated compound**, the component words are joined by a hyphen (*half-baked; city-state*).
In a **closed compound**, the component words are joined into a single word (*hardheaded; campfire*).

Compound Adjectives

For most cases of open compound adjectives, there is a general rule of thumb: the compound is left open when it is not followed by the modified noun; the compound is hyphenated when it is followed by the modified noun:

She was well known in the South for her poetry.
[The compound *well known* is open because it is not followed by the modified noun *She.*]

In the South, she was a well-known poet.
[The compound *well-known* is hyphenated because it is followed by the modified noun *poet.*]

A notable exception occurs when the first part of the compound adjective is an adverb that ends in *–ly*. In this case, the compound remains open, even when it is followed by the noun:

The woman who met us in the lobby was beautifully dressed.
A beautifully dressed woman met us in the lobby.

Compound Nouns

For spellers, the least troublesome compound nouns are familiar closed compounds:

briefcase
cupcake
downstairs
fireplace

Other compound nouns can be troublesome. Although certain ones, such as *mother-in-law*, are always hyphenated, many compound nouns commonly occur in more than one acceptable format, such as *ice cap* or *icecap* and *vice president* or *vice-president*. For most spelling questions, the best resource is a dictionary; for questions pertaining specifically to compounds, an unabridged edition is recommended.

> **TIP**
>
> Different dictionaries often disagree on the preferred spelling formats for a number of compounds, so writers are well advised to consult just one dictionary when establishing a spelling style.

PREFIXES

A prefix is a group of letters added to the beginning of a word to adjust its meaning.

In most cases, prefixes are affixed to the root word without hyphenation:

antibacterial
postwar
semicircle

Often, however, a hyphen is customary, necessary, or preferable.

Certain prefixes almost always take a hyphen: *all-*, *ex-*, *full-*, *quasi-*, *self-*:

all-encompassing
ex-partner
full-bodied
quasi-liberal
self-confidence

When the root word begins with a capital letter, the prefix takes a hyphen:

anti-American
pre-Conquest

Sometimes, without a hyphen, a word could be easily confused with another:

We <u>recovered</u> our furniture.

Does this mean we *found* our *missing* furniture? Or did we *put new coverings on* our furniture? If the latter is meant, a hyphen would have avoided confusion:

We <u>re-covered</u> our furniture.

Sometimes, a hyphen is not necessary but preferable. Without it, the word may look awkward. One such circumstance is when the last letter of the prefix and the first letter of the root word are both vowels, or when an awkward double consonant is created. For each of the following pairs of words, either spelling is acceptable:

antiknock / anti-knock
preadapt / pre-adapt
semiindependent / semi-independent
nonnegative / non-negative

TIP

Regarding the use of optional hyphens, the writer should establish a preferred style. Keeping a running list of hyphenated terms can help writers keep track of which spellings they have already used in their text, thus making the style consistent.

SUFFIXES

A suffix is a group of letters added to the end of a word to create a derivative of the word. There are exceptions to the following guidelines on how to spell with suffixes, but in most cases these rules apply:

A root word that ends in *e* drops the *e* when the suffix begins with a vowel:

rehearse / rehearsing

However, most words that end in *ce* or *ge* keep the *e* when the suffix begins with *a* or *o*:

service / serviceable
advantage / advantageous

A root word that ends in *e* keeps the *e* when the suffix begins with a consonant:

wise / wisely

A root word that ends in a *y* preceded by a consonant changes the *y* to *i* when the suffix begins with any letter other than *i*:

satisfy / satisfies / satisfying

A root word that ends in *ie* changes the *ie* to *y* when the suffix is *–ing*:

lie / lying

A root word that ends in *oe* keeps the *e* when the suffix begins with a vowel, unless the vowel is *e*:

toe / toeing / toed

A one-syllable root word that ends in a single consonant preceded by a single vowel doubles the consonant when the suffix is *–ed, –er,* or *–ing*. This rule also applies to root words with two or more syllables if the accent is on the last syllable.

stir / stirred
refer / referring

WORD DIVISION

Sometimes it is necessary to "break" a word when the line on the page has run out of space. Dividing a word at the end of a line is perfectly acceptable, as long as two conditions are met: the word must be divisible, and the division must be made in the right place.

When a word is properly divided, a hyphen is attached to its first part, so that the hyphen is at the end of the line:

At the conclusion of the interview, I had two minutes to sum-
marize my management experiences.

What words are never divisible?	*for example:*
• one-syllable words	catch; flutes; strange; through
• contractions	didn't; doesn't; wouldn't; you're
• abbreviations	Calif.; NASCAR; RSVP; YMCA
• numbers written as numerals	1776; $2,800; 9:45; 0.137

Where is a correct place to divide a word?	*good break:*	*bad break:*
• after a prefix	inter-national	interna-tional
• before a suffix that has more than two letters	govern-ment	gov-ernment
• between the main parts of a closed compound	nut-cracker	nutcrack-er
• at the hyphen of a hyphenated compound	gender-neutral	gen-der-neutral
• after double consonants if the root word ends in the double consonants	address-ing	addres-sing
• otherwise, between double consonants	rib-bon	ribb-on
• in general (for words that don't fall into the previous categories), between syllables	whis-per	whi-sper

Where is an incorrect place to divide a word?	*good break:*	*bad break:*
• before a two-letter suffix	——	odd-ly
• after the first syllable if it has only one letter	Ameri-can	A-merican
• before the last syllable if it has only one letter	nu-tria	nutri-a
• before the ending *–ed* if the *–ed* is not pronounced	——	abash-ed

TIP

When dividing a word at the end of a line, it is always a good idea to use a dictionary to verify the word's proper syllabification.

NUMBERS

Numbers are an important part of everyday communication, yet they often cause a writer to stumble, particularly over questions of spelling and style. The guidelines on *how* to spell out a number are fairly straightforward. The guidelines on *when* to spell out a number are not so precise.

How to Spell Out Numbers

CARDINAL NUMBERS

The most common problem associated with the spelling of whole cardinal numbers is punctuation. The rules are actually quite simple: Numeric amounts that fall between twenty and one hundred are always hyphenated. No other punctuation should appear in a spelled-out whole number, regardless of its size.

26	twenty-six
411	four hundred eleven
758	seven hundred fifty-eight
6,500	six thousand five hundred
33,003	thirty-three thousand three
972,923	nine hundred seventy-two thousand nine hundred twenty-three

Note: The word *and* does not belong in the spelling of a number. For example, "758" should not be spelled "seven hundred and fifty-eight."

ORDINAL NUMBERS

The punctuation of spelled-out ordinal numbers typically follows the rules for cardinal numbers.

> What should we do for their fifty-fifth anniversary?
> He graduated two hundred twenty-ninth out of a class of two hundred thirty.

When ordinal numbers appear as numerals, they are affixed with *–th*, with the exception of those ending with the ordinal *first*, *second*, or *third*.

1st	581st
2nd	32nd
3rd	73rd
4th	907th

Note: Sometimes 2nd is written as 2d, and 3rd as 3d.

FRACTIONS

A fraction can appear in a number of formats, as shown here:

$\frac{3}{8}$	case fraction (or split fraction)
3/8	fraction with solidus
0.375	decimal fraction
three-eighths	spelled-out fraction

When acting as an adjective, a spelled-out fraction should always be hyphenated.

> The Serbian democrats have won a two-thirds majority.

When acting as a noun, a spelled-out fraction may or may not be hyphenated, according to the writer's or publisher's preferred style.

> At least four-fifths of the supply has been depleted.
> *or*
> At least four fifths of the supply has been depleted.

When to Spell Out Numbers

When to spell out a number, whole or fractional, is as much a matter of sense as of style. Text that is heavy with numbers, such as scientific or statistical material, could become virtually unreadable if the numbers were all spelled out. Conversely, conventional prose that occasionally makes mention of a quantity may look unbalanced with an occasional numeral here and there.

Often, the decision to spell or not to spell comes down to simple clarity:

> Our standard paper size is 8½ by 11.
> Our standard paper size is 8 1/2 by 11.
> Our standard paper size is eight and a half by eleven.
> Our standard paper size is eight and one-half by eleven.

The preceding four sentences say exactly the same thing, but the best choice for readability is the first.

TIP

Numerals and other symbols should never begin a sentence. If the symbol should not or cannot be spelled out, the sentence needs to be reworded.

> 19 students have become mentors.
> *should be:*
> Nineteen students have become mentors.
>
> 2006 is the year we plan to get married.
> *should be:*
> We plan to get married in 2006.
>
> $10 was found on the stairs.
> *should be:*
> Ten dollars was found on the stairs.
>
> 6:00 is the earliest I can leave.
> *should be:*
> Six o'clock is the earliest I can leave.
> *or:*
> The earliest I can leave is 6:00.
>
> $y = 2x + 1$ is a line with a slope of 2.
> *should be:*
> The line $y = 2x + 1$ has a slope of 2.

Even the most comprehensive books of style and usage do not dictate absolute rules regarding the style of numbers in text. When writing, it is most important to be as consistent as possible with a style once one has been established. For example, some writers or publishers may adopt a policy of spelling out the numbers zero through ten. Others may prefer to spell out the numbers zero through ninety-nine. Either style is perfectly acceptable, as long as the style is followed throughout the written work.

Sometimes, even after adopting a basic number style, the writer may wish to incorporate certain style allowances and exceptions. Perhaps the decision has been made by the writer to spell out only the numbers zero though ninety-nine. But in one paragraph, a sentence reads, "There must have been more than 1,000,000 people there." In this case, it may be better to write, "There must have been more than a million people there."

SYMBOLS

In most contexts of formal writing, the use of symbols should be strictly limited, but there are occasions when a symbol may be a better choice than a word. Text that deals largely with commerce, for instance, may rely on the use of various monetary symbols to keep the text organized and readable. In any text, mathematical equations and scientific formulas are much easier to read if written with symbols rather than words. Also, it is usually appropriate to use symbols within tables and charts; as symbols conserve space, they prevent a "cluttered look."

Here are some of the most common symbols found in print:

@	at	/	per *or* solidus
c/o	care of	%	percent
$	dollar	°	degree
¢	cent	+	plus
Can$	Canadian dollar	–	minus
£	pound sterling	÷	divided by
¥	yen	×	times
#	number *or* pound	±	plus or minus

Symbol	Meaning	Symbol	Meaning
$=$	equals	©	copyright
$\approx$	is approximately equal to	®	registered
$\neq$	is not equal to	™	trademark
$<$	is less than	¶	paragraph
$>$	is greater than	§	section
$\leqslant$	is less than or equal to	*	asterisk
$\geqslant$	is greater than or equal to	†	dagger
$\sqrt{}$	square root	‡	double dagger
∞	infinity	‖	parallels *or* pipes

Symbols are sometimes used to point out note references to the reader. In a table or chart, for instance, the writer may wish to indicate that an item is further explained or identified elsewhere on the page. A symbol placed with the item signals the reader to look for an identical symbol, which precedes the additional information. Sometimes, numerals are the symbols of choice, but if the material within the table or chart consists of numerals, it is probably better to use non-numeric symbols for the note references. The conventional set of symbols used for this purpose, in the conventional sequence in which to use them, is *, †, ‡, §, ‖, #.

COMMONLY MISSPELLED WORDS

abbreviated
absence
absolutely
acceptance
accessible
accidentally
accommodate
accompany
accuracy
ache
achieve
achievement
acquaintance
acquire
acre
across
actually
administration
admittance
adolescent
advantageous
advertisement
advisable
affectionate
affidavit
aficionado
afraid
again
aggravate
aghast
aisle
allege
allotment
ally
amateur
analysis
analyze
anesthetic
angel
angle
annihilation
annually
answer
anticipate
anxiety
apartheid
aperitif
apology
apparatus
apparent
appearance
appetite
appreciate
approach
appropriate
approximately
argue
argument
arithmetic
arrangement
ascend
ascertain
assistant
athletic
attendance
authority
auxiliary
available
awkward
bachelor
because
beggar
beginning
behavior
believe
benefit
benefited
bicycle
bouillon
boundary
bulletin
bureau
buried
business
cafeteria
calendar
campaign
cancellation
captain
carburetor
career
ceiling
cemetery
census
certificate
chamois

changeable
character
characteristic
chauffeur
chic
chief
chocolate
choice
choose
chose
Christian
clothes
collateral
colonel
color
column
commercial
commission
committee
community
compel
competitor
completely
conceivable
concentrate
condemn
confidence
confidential
confusion
connoisseur
conscience
conscious
continuous
controlled
controversial
conversant
convertible
cooperate
copyright
corps
correspondence
counterfeit
courageous
courteous
criticism
criticize
cruelly
curiosity
curious
cylinder
dealt
debtor
deceive
decision
definite
dependent
describe
despair
desperate
despise
develop
difference
dilemma
diphthong
disappearance
disappoint
disastrous
discipline
discrepancy
disease
diuretic
doctor
duplicate
easily
ecclesiastical
ecstasy
effect
efficient
eighth
elementary
eligible
embarrass
eminent
emphasize
encouragement
encumbrances
enforceable
entirely
entourage
envelope
environment
equipped
escape
especially
essential
et cetera (*abbreviated* etc.)
exaggerate
excellent
exciting
exercise
exhilarating
exhort
existence
expense
experience
experiment
extraordinary
extremely
facsimile
familiar
fantasy
fascinate
fashionable
fasten
fatal
favorite
February
field
fiery
finally
financial
fluorescent
forehead
foreign
forfeit
fortunately
forty
forward
fourth
freight
friend
fulfill
further
gauge
genius
gourmet
government
governor
gracious
grammar
guarantee
guerrilla
guess
guidance
gymnasium
gypsy
handsome
hangar
hanger
happened
happiness
harass
Hawaii

Commonly Misspelled Words (*cont.*)

heavily
height
heinous
heroine
hors d'oeuvre
hospital
humor
humorous
hungrily
hygiene
hypocrisy
hypocrite
hysterical
ignorance
illiterate
imagine
immediately
impossible
incidentally
increase
indefinite
independent
indictment
indispensable
individually
inevitable
influence
ingredient
innocence
inoculate
insurance
intelligence
intelligent
interference
interrupt
iridescent
irrelevant
itinerary
jealous
jewelry
knowledge
laboratory
laborer
laid
legitimate
leisure
liaison
library
license
lieutenant

lightning
likely
liquefy
liquidate
listener
literature
livelihood
lively
loneliness
luxury
magazine
magnificent
maintenance
maneuver
manufacturer
marriage
marvelous
mathematics
meant
mechanic
medical
medicine
melancholy
merchandise
millionaire
miniature
minimum
minuscule
minute
miscellaneous
mischief
mischievous
Massachusetts
misspell
mortgage
muscle
mysterious
narrative
naturally
necessary
nickel
niece
ninety
noisily
non sequitur
noticeable
obstacle
occasionally
occurrence
offensive

official
often
omission
omit
omitted
once
operate
opponent
opportunity
optimistic
orchestra
ordinarily
organization
originally
outrageous
pageant
paid
parallel
paralleled
paralyze
parliament
particular
pastime
peaceful
peculiar
performance
permanent
perseverance
personality
personnel
perspiration
persuade
pessimistic
phenomenal
Philippines
philosophy
physical
picnicking
pleasant
politician
Portuguese
possession
possibility
practically
practice
prairie
preferred
prejudice
preparation
presence

pressure
pretension
privilege
probably
procedure
proceed
procure
professor
proffered
promissory
pronunciation
propaganda
psychic
psychology
pumpkin
punctual
punctuation
pursuit
questionnaire
quiet
quite
quotient
raspberry
realize
really
realtor
realty
receipt
recipe
recognize
recommend
referred
reign
relevant
relieve
religious
removal
rendezvous
repertoire
repetition
rescind
reservoir
resistance
resource
responsibility
restaurant
rheumatism
rhythm
ridiculous
roommate
sachet
sacrifice
sacrilegious
safety
satisfied
scarcely
scarcity
scene
schedule
scholar
scissors
scurrilous
seance
secretary
seize
semester
separate
sergeant
shepherd
siege
similar
sincerely
skein
skiing
skillful
sophomore
soufflé
source
souvenir
specialty
specifically
specimen
sponsor
statistics
straight
strength
stretch
strictly
stubborn
substitute
subtle
succeed
successful
suede
sufficient
summary
superintendent
supersede
surgeon
surprise
susceptible
suspense
swimming
sympathetic
synonym
temperamental
temperature
tendency
therefore
thorough
though
thoughtful
tomorrow
tragedy
transferred
traveled
tremendous
truly
twelfth
typical
unanimous
unnecessary
useful
useless
usually
vacillate
vacuum
vague
valuable
variety
various
vegetable
vengeance
vilify
villain
warrant
weather
Wednesday
weird
whether
whole
yacht
yield

FOREIGN TERMS

Foreign words and phrases that are likely to be unfamiliar to the reader should be set in italics. When such terms are to be included in writing or speech, a dictionary should be consulted by the writer to insure proper placement of accents and other diacritical marks and by the speaker to insure correct pronunciations. Each of the following sample terms gives the literal translation, the English-usage definition, and an example sentence.

annus mirabilis: [Latin, 'wonderful year'] a remarkable or auspicious year.
This has been our team's *annus mirabilis.*

cause célèbre: [French, 'famous case'] a controversial issue that attracts a great deal of public attention.
The trial of Lizzie Borden became a *cause célèbre* throughout New England.

Weltschmerz: [German, 'world pain'] a feeling of melancholy and world-weariness.
A sense of *Weltschmerz* permeated his later works of art.
[Note that it is correct to capitalize a German noun.]

Familiar Foreign Terms

Many foreign terms have become so familiar and well-established in standard English usage that it is not necessary to put them in italic type. For most of these words, it is also not necessary to use accents and other diacritical marks, but in certain cases the inclusion of diacritics remains customary. There are, however, no absolute rules regarding when to italicize and when not to italicize, when to use diacritics and when not to use diacritics. Some foreign words may be more familiar to one group of readers than to another; therefore, targeted readership should be considered. Often, the style adopted is a matter of preference. As always, it is important for the writer to be consistent once this preference has been introduced.

Some familiar foreign terms:

ad absurdum
ad hoc
ad infinitum
ad interim
ad lib
ad nauseam
aficionado
à la carte (*or* a la carte)
à la king (*or* a la king)
à la mode (*or* a la mode)
al fresco
alter ego
annus mirabilis
Anno Domini
apartheid
aperitif
a priori
apropos
au contraire
au courant
au fait
au fond
au gratin
au jus
au naturel
au pair
avant-garde
ballet
basmati
bas-relief
baton
beau
beau monde
belle
bête noire
billet doux
bona fide
bonbon
bon mot
bon vivant
bouclé
boudoir
bouffant
bouillabaisse
bouillon
bouquet
bouquet garni
bourgeois
bric-a-brac
burka (*or* burkha)
burrito
cabaret
café (*or* cafe)
camisole
canapé
capo
carafe
carpe diem
carte blanche
cause célèbre
chaise longue
chalet
chamois
chapeau
chateau (*or* château)
chauffeur
chic
ciao
cognac
coiffeur
connoisseur
consommé

contretemps
corps
crepe (*or* crêpe)
croquette
cul-de-sac
de facto
déjà vu
de jure
de rigeur
dolce vita
doppelgänger
élan
elite
enchilada
enfant terrible
en masse
en route
entourage
entrée (*or* entree)
entre nous
eureka
ex cathedra
ex post facto
fait accompli
fajita
faux
faux pas
fiancé (*or* fiance)
fiancée (*or* fiancee)
fiesta
flagrante delicto
glasnost
gourmand
gourmet
hacienda
haute cuisine
hoi polloi
hors d'oeuvre
incognito
ingénue
in loco parentis
in re
in situ
in toto
in vitro
in vivo
jabot
judo
julienne
karma
karate
kasha
kibitz
kitsch
laissez-faire
lanai
lèse-majesté
loco
lorgnette
madame
mademoiselle
maître d' (*or* maitre d')
mañana
masseur
masseuse
materiel (*or* matériel)
mea culpa
modus operandi
monsieur
mot juste
née
ne plus ultra
nom de guerre
nom de plume
non sequitur
nota bene
nouveau riche
objet d'art
objet trouvé
pace
par excellence
pasha
pâté de foie gras
patio
per capita
persona non grata
pièce de résistance
pied-à-terre
piccolo
poncho
portière (*or* portiere)
post mortem
prima donna
prima facie
pro bono
pro forma
pronto
protégé (*or* protege)
purée (*or* puree)
quid pro quo
qui vive
raison d'être
re
rendezvous
repertoire
résumé (*or* resume)
revue
roué
roulette
sachet
salsa
samovar
samurai
sangfroid
sans souci
savoir faire
seance
serape
siesta
sine die
sine qua non
sombrero
soufflé
status quo
sub judice
suede
tableau
table d'hôte
tabula rasa
taco
tango
terra incognita
tête-à-tête
tour de force
tout le monde
trompe l'oeil
trousseau
verboten
vice versa
villa
viva voce
viz.
vox populi
Wanderjahr
Weltanschauung
Weltschmerz
yin/yang
yoga
Zeitgeist

Guide to Capitalization and Punctuation

CAPITALIZATION

Beginnings

The first word in a sentence is capitalized:

Dozens of spectators lined the street.

The first word in a direct quotation is capitalized:

Andy stood by the window and remarked, "The view from here is spectacular."

If a colon introduces more than one sentence, the first word after the colon is capitalized:

We went over our findings, one piece of evidence at a time: The custodian had discovered the body just before midnight. The keys to the victim's office were found in the stairwell. In the adjoining office, three file cabinets had been overturned.

If a colon introduces a formal and distinct statement, the first word after the colon is capitalized:

All my years on the basketball court have taught me one thing: Winning is more of a process than an outcome.

If a colon introduces a complete statement that is merely an extension of the statement preceding the colon, the first word after the colon is usually lowercased:

Everything in the house was a shade of pink: the sofa was carnation blush, the tiles were misty mauve, and the carpet was dusty rose.

If a colon introduces an incomplete statement, the first word after the colon is lowercased:

The caterer provided three choices: chicken, beef, and shrimp.

Proper Names

Proper names are capitalized. This is true of all proper names, including those of persons, places, structures, organizations, vessels, vehicles, brands, etc. Notice from the following examples that when a properly named entity is referred to in a "non-named" general sense, the general sense is almost always lowercased:

Eleanor Roosevelt
J. D. Salinger
Carson City / a city in Nevada
Ural Mountains / a view of the mountains
New York Public Library / borrowing books from the public library
Washington Monument / our photos of the monument
Calvin Leete Elementary School / the rear entrance of the school
Amherst Historical Society / when the society last met
Boeing 747
USS *Missouri* [note that the names of specific ships, aircraft, spacecraft, etc., are italicized]
Chevy Malibu
Slinky

Titles

The titles of works are capitalized. Titled works include:

- written material (books, periodicals, screenplays, etc.)
- components of written material (chapters, sections, etc.)
- filmed and/or broadcast works (movies, television shows, radio programs, etc.)
- works of art (paintings, sculptures, etc.)
- musical compositions (songs, operas, oratorios, etc.)

There are certain rules of convention regarding which words in the titles are capitalized.

Capitalize:

- first word in the title
- last word in the title
- nouns and pronouns
- adjectives
- verbs
- adverbs
- subordinating conjunctions (*although*, *as*, *because*, *if*, *since*, *that*, *whenever*, etc.)

Do not capitalize (unless they are first or last words in the title):

- articles (*a, an, the*)
- coordinating conjunctions (*and, but, for, nor, or, so, yet*)
- prepositions (although some guides suggest capitalizing prepositions of more than four letters)
- the word *to* in infinitives

The King, the Sword, and the Golden Lantern
A Room within a Room (*or* A Room Within a Room)
Seventy Ways to Make Easy Money from Your Home
The Stars Will Shine Because You Are Mine

If a subtitle is included, it typically follows a colon. It follows the capitalization rules of the main title, thus its first word is always capitalized:

Aftermath Explored: The Confessions of a Nuclear Physicist

The first element in a hyphenated compound is always capitalized. The subsequent elements are capitalized unless they are articles, prepositions, or coordinating conjunctions. But if the compound is the last word in the title, its final element is always capitalized, regardless of its part of speech:

Nineteenth-Century Poets
Over-the-Top Desserts
The Love-in of a Lifetime
The Year of the Love-In

An element that follows a hyphenated prefix is capitalized only if it is a proper noun or adjective:

Pre-Columbian Artifacts
Memoirs of a Semi-independent Child

Education

An academic title is capitalized (whether it is spelled out or abbreviated) when it directly accompanies a personal name. Otherwise, it is lowercased:

Professor Sarah McDonald
Assoc. Prof. Brown
my chemistry professor

An academic degree or honor is capitalized (whether it is spelled out or abbreviated) when it directly accompanies a personal name. Otherwise, it is lowercased:

Harold L. Fox, Ph.D.
Charles Gustafson, Fellow of the Geological Society
working toward her master's degree

Academic years are lowercased:

the senior prom
he's a sophomore
the fourth grade

The course name of a particular school subject is capitalized. A general field of study is lowercased (unless the word is normally capitalized, such as "English"):

Astronomy 101
Algebra II
taking classes in psychology, French literature, and chemistry

Calendar Terms and Time

The names of the days of the week and months of the year are capitalized:

Sunday	September
Monday	October
Tuesday	November

The names of the four seasons are lowercased:

winter	summer
spring	fall *or* autumn

TIP

Which titles should be set in italics, and which should be set off by quotation marks? In printed material, the distinction can be significant. Here's a handy list of the most common categories of titles and their standard treatments in type:

italics:

- books
  Crossroads of Freedom: Antietam, by James M. McPherson
- pamphlets
  Thomas Paine's *Common Sense*
- magazines
  Popular Mechanics
- newspapers
  USA Today
- movies
  One Flew Over the Cuckoo's Nest
- television or radio series
  This Week in Baseball
- plays
  Neil Simon's *Lost in Yonkers*
- long poems
  Beowulf

The names of holidays (religious and secular) and periods of religious observance are capitalized:

Arbor Day
Easter
Halloween
Lent
Memorial Day
Ramadan

The names of time zones and the time systems they designate are lowercased (except for any words that are proper names). Their abbreviations are capitalized:

eastern daylight time (EDT)
Greenwich mean time (GMT)
Pacific standard time (PST)

Legislation, Treaties, etc.

The formal name of a policy, treaty, piece of legislation, or similar agreement is capitalized. A general reference to such is lowercased:

Volstead Act
the act sponsored by Congressman Volstead
Treaty of Versailles
the treaty at Versailles
Bottle Bill
Articles of Confederation
Connecticut Constitution
Connecticut's constitution
North American Free Trade Agreement

- collections of poems and other anthologies
  The Collected Poems of Emily Dickinson
- operas, oratorios, and other long musical compositions
  Madame Butterfly
- painting, sculptures, and other works of art
  Thomas Cole's *Mount Etna from Taormina*

quotation marks:

- articles
  "How to Remove Wallpaper"
- chapters
  "Betsy Saves the Day"
- short stories
  "The Pit and the Pendulum," by Edgar Allan Poe
- short poems
  "Tree at My Window," by Robert Frost
- essays
  Emerson's "Spiritual Laws"
- television or radio episodes
  "Lucy Does a TV Commercial"
- songs and other short musical compositions
  "Are You Lonesome Tonight?"

Military Service

A military title or rank is capitalized (whether it is spelled out or abbreviated) when it directly accompanies a personal name. Otherwise, it is lowercased:

Gen. George Patton
Ensign Irene Mahoney
promoted to admiral
James Kirk, captain of the USS *Enterprise*

There are two significant exceptions to the preceding rule: the U.S. military titles "Fleet Admiral" and "General of the Army" should always be capitalized, even when not directly accompanying a personal name:

became General of the Army in 1950
a visit from the Fleet Admiral

The full official name of a military group or force is capitalized. A general reference to a military group or force is lowercased:

the Royal Air Force
the British air force
the Army Corps of Engineers
the Third Battalion
our battalion
the U.S. Navy
joined the navy

The full name of a battle or war is capitalized. A general reference to a battle or war is lowercased:

the Russian Revolution
fought in the revolution
the Spanish-American War
the war in Vietnam
the Battle of the Bulge
the first battle of the campaign
the Norman Conquest

The official name of a military award or medal is capitalized:

the Purple Heart
the Silver Star
the Victoria Cross
the Congressional Medal of Honor

Science

The capitalization rules governing scientific terminology cover a wide range of categories and applications. Some of the basic rules are discussed here.

Taxonomic nomenclature—that is, the scientific classification of plants and animals—follows specific rules for both capitalization and italics.

The names of the phylum, class, order, and family of a plant or animal are capitalized and set in roman type. This format also applies to the intermediate groupings (suborder, subfamily, etc.) within these divisions:

The North American river otter belongs to the phylum Chordata, the subphylum Vertebrata, the class Mammalia, the order Carnivora, and the family Mustelidae.

The divisions lower than family—that is, genus, species, and subspecies—are set in italic type. Of these, only the genus is capitalized. When a plant or animal is identified by its "scientific name" or "Latin name," the name given is the genus and species (and, when applicable, the subspecies):

The scientific name of the river otter is *Lutra canadensis*.
The Manitoban elk (*Cervus elaphus manitobensis*) is a subspecies of the North American elk.

The common names of plants and animals, as well as their hybrids, varieties, and breeds, are lowercased and set in roman type. A part of the name may be capitalized if that part is a term normally capitalized (that is, a proper name). If there is doubt, a dictionary should be consulted.

Alaskan malamute
Christmas cactus
Johnny-jump-up
maidenhair fern
rainbow trout
rose-breasted grosbeak
Swainson's hawk
Vietnamese potbellied pig

The names of astronomical entities, such as planets, stars, constellations, and galaxies, are capitalized:

Alpha Centauri
Canis Major
Crab Nebula
Ganymede
Mercury
Milky Way
Orion
Sirius

TIP

The names *sun*, *moon*, and *earth* are frequently lowercased. It is customary to capitalize them only when they are being referred to as components of the solar system. Also noteworthy is the fact that, in any context, the words *sun* and *moon* typically are preceded by the definite article, *the*. In non-astronomical contexts, the word *earth* often is preceded by *the*, but it is never preceded by *the* when used specifically as the name of a planet. Hence, *the Earth* would not be an appropriate use of capitalization.

We enjoyed the warmth of the sun.
The glow of the moon has inspired poets for centuries.
Countless species inhabit the earth.
What on earth are you doing?
In size, Venus is comparable to Earth.
The eclipse of the Moon will be visible from the night side of Earth.
They made observations of Neptune's orbit around the Sun.

The names of geological eras, periods, epochs, etc., are capitalized. When included with the name, the words *era*, *period*, *epoch*, etc., are lowercased.

Mesozoic era
Quaternary period
Oligocene epoch
Upper Jurassic

Abbreviations

Although the use of abbreviations in formal writing should be limited, abbreviations are legitimate components of the language and deserve the same attention to spelling as do other words. Certain capitalization

TIP

If the name of an entity such as an organization, institution, or movement is to be abbreviated, its full name should be identified. Upon first mention, both abbreviation and full name should appear together, with either one being set within parentheses. (Usually the lesser known format goes in the parentheses.) Thereafter in the text, only the abbreviation need appear:

> In February 1909, a group of activists founded what would become the NAACP (National Association for the Advancement of Colored People). For more than ninety years, the NAACP has persevered to honor its founders' vision of racial equality and social justice.
>
> Plans to rebuild at the site of the World Trade Center (WTC) are being discussed today. Various designs for new office space are expected to be considered. Thousands of suggestions for a WTC memorial have already been submitted.

guidelines for a few types of abbreviations are given below. Because the possible variations are numerous, a standard dictionary should be consulted for more thorough guidance on the spelling, capitalization, and punctuation of a specific abbreviation.

When a capitalized term is abbreviated, the abbreviation is capitalized. If the abbreviation is comprised of initials, all the initials are capitalized:

> Professor J. Leggett / Prof. J. Leggett
> Sergeant David Potter / Sgt. David Potter
> Master of Business Administration / MBA
> United States Marine Corps / USMC

When a lowercased term is abbreviated as a simple shortening, the abbreviation is usually lowercased. But if the abbreviation is comprised of initials, all the initials are usually capitalized. When there is a compound word in the term, the initials may include the first letter of the root word:

> especially / esp.
> teaspoon / tsp.
> deoxyribonucleic acid / DNA
> monosodium glutamate / MSG
> most favored nation / MFN

Usually, an abbreviation that ends in a capital letter is not followed by a period. An abbreviation that ends in a lowercase letter usually is followed by a period, although the period may be optional, depending on the prevailing style of the particular piece of writing.

One group of abbreviations that never ends with a period is the set of chemical symbols. Also, these abbreviations are always initially capitalized even though the terms they represent are lowercased:

Ar	argon	Na	sodium
Dy	dysprosium	Sb	antimony
H	hydrogen	Sn	tin
Kr	krypton	U	uranium
Lr	lawrencium	Xe	xenon

Note that some chemical symbols appear to be straightforward abbreviations (*Ca* for *calcium*) while others seem unrelated to their corresponding terms (*Au* for *gold*). In fact, these symbols are abbreviations of the official scientific, or Latin, names (*Au* for *aurum*, which is Latin for *gold*).

PUNCTUATION

Punctuation is an essential element of good writing because it makes the author's meaning clear to the reader. Although precise punctuation styles may vary somewhat among published sources, there are a number of fundamental principles worthy of consideration. Discussed below are these punctuation marks used in English:

comma	apostrophe
semicolon	quotation marks
colon	parentheses
period	dash
question mark	hyphen
exclamation point	

Comma

The **comma** is the most used mark of punctuation in the English language. It signals to the reader a pause, which generally clarifies the author's meaning and establishes a sensible order to the elements of written language. Among the most typical functions of the comma are the following:

1. It can separate the clauses of a compound sentence when there are two independent clauses joined by a conjunction, especially when the clauses are not very short:

   It never occurred to me to look in the attic, and I'm sure it didn't occur to Rachel either.

   The Nelsons wanted to see the Grand Canyon at sunrise, but they overslept that morning.

2. It can separate the clauses of a compound sentence when there is a series of independent clauses, the last two of which are joined by a conjunction:

   The bus ride to the campsite was very uncomfortable, the cabins were not ready for us when we got there, the cook had forgotten to start dinner, and the rain was torrential.

3. It is used to precede or set off, and therefore indicate, a nonrestrictive dependent clause (a clause that could be omitted without changing the meaning of the main clause):

   I read her autobiography, which was published last July.

   They showed up at midnight, after most of the guests had gone home.

   The coffee, which is freshly brewed, is in the kitchen.

4. It can follow an introductory phrase:

   Having enjoyed the movie so much, he agreed to see it again.

   Born and raised in Paris, she had never lost her French accent.

   In the beginning, they had very little money to invest.

5. It can set off words used in direct address:

   Listen, people, you have no choice in the matter.

   Yes, Mrs. Greene, I will be happy to feed your cat.

6. It can separate two or more coordinate adjectives (adjectives that could otherwise be joined with *and*) that modify one noun:

   The cruise turned out to be the most entertaining, fun, and relaxing vacation I've ever had.

   The horse was tall, lean, and sleek.

   Note that cumulative adjectives (those not able to be joined with *and*) are not separated by a comma:

   She wore bright yellow rubber boots.

7. It is used to separate three or more items in a series or list:

   Charlie, Melissa, Stan, and Mark will be this year's soloists in the spring concert.

We need furniture, toys, clothes, books, tools, housewares, and other useful merchandise for the benefit auction.

Note that the comma between the last two items in a series is sometimes omitted in less precise style:

The most popular foods served in the cafeteria are pizza, hamburgers and nachos.

8. It is used to separate and set off the elements in an address or other geographical designation:

   My new house is at 1657 Nighthawk Circle, South Kingsbury, Michigan.

   We arrived in Pamplona, Spain, on Thursday.

9. It is used to set off direct quotations (note the placement or absence of commas with other punctuation):

   "Kim forgot her gloves," he said, "but we have a pair she can borrow."

   There was a long silence before Jack blurted out, "This must be the world's ugliest painting."

   "What are you talking about?" she asked in a puzzled manner.

   "Happy New Year!" everyone shouted.

10. It is used to set off titles after a person's name:

    Katherine Bentley, M.D.

    Martin Luther King, Jr., delivered the sermon.

Semicolon

The **semicolon** has two basic functions:

1. It can separate two main clauses, particularly when these clauses are of equal importance:

   The crowds gathered outside the museum hours before the doors were opened; this was one exhibit no one wanted to miss.

   She always complained when her relatives stayed for the weekend; even so, she usually was a little sad when they left.

2. It can be used as a comma is used to separate such elements as clauses or items in a series or list, particularly when one or more of the elements already includes a comma:

   The path took us through the deep, dark woods; across a small meadow into a cold, wet cave; and up a hillside overlooking the lake.

   Listed for sale in the ad were two bicycles; a battery-powered, leaf-mulching lawn mower; and a maple bookcase.

Colon

The **colon** has five basic functions:

1. It can introduce something, especially a list of items:

   In the basket were three pieces of mail: a postcard, a catalog, and a wedding invitation.

   Students should have the following items: backpack, loose-leaf notebook, pens and pencils, pencil sharpener, and ruler.

2. It can separate two clauses in a sentence when the second clause is being used to explain or illustrate the first clause:

   We finally understood why she would never go sailing with us: she had a deep fear of the water.

   Most of the dogs in our neighborhood are quite large: two of them are St. Bernards.

3. It can introduce a statement or a quotation:

   His parents say the most important rule is this: Always tell the truth.

   We repeated the final words of his poem: "And such is the plight of fools like me."

4. It can be used to follow the greeting in a formal or business letter:

   Dear Ms. Daniels:

   Dear Sir or Madam:

5. It is used in the United States to separate minutes from hours, and seconds from minutes, in showing time of day and measured length of time:

   Please be at the restaurant before 6:45.

   Her best running time so far has been 00:12:35.

Period

The **period** has two basic functions:

1. It is used to mark the end of a sentence:

   It was reported that there is a shortage of nurses at the hospital. Several of the patients have expressed concern about this problem.

2. It is often used at the end of an abbreviation:

   On Fri., Sept. 12, Dr. Brophy noted that the patient's weight was 168 lb. and that his height was 6 ft. 2 in.

   (Note that another period is not added to the end of the sentence when the last word is an abbreviation.)

Question Mark and Exclamation Point

The only sentences that do not end in a period are those that end in either a question mark or an exclamation point.

Question marks are used to mark the end of a sentence that asks a direct question (generally, a question that expects an answer):

Is there any reason for us to bring more than a few dollars?

Who is your science teacher?

Exclamation points are used to mark the end of a sentence that expresses a strong feeling, typically surprise, joy, or anger:

I want you to leave and never come back!

What a beautiful view this is!

Apostrophe

The **apostrophe** has two basic functions:

1. It is used to show where a letter or letters are missing in a contraction.

   The directions are cont'd [continued] *on the next page.*
   We've [we have] *decided that if she can't* [cannot] *go, then we aren't* [are not] *going either.*

2. It can be used to show possession:

   The possessive of a singular noun or an irregular plural noun is created by adding an apostrophe and an *s*:

the pilot's uniform
Mrs. Mendoza's house
a tomato's bright red color
the oxen's yoke

The possessive of a regular plural noun is created by adding just an apostrophe:

the pilots' uniforms [referring to more than one pilot]
the Mendozas' house [referring to the Mendoza family]
the tomatoes' bright red color [referring to more than one tomato]

Quotation Marks

Quotation marks have two basic functions:

1. They are used to set off direct quotations (an exact rendering of someone's spoken or written words):

   "I think the new library is wonderful," she remarked to David.

   We were somewhat lost, so we asked, "Are we anywhere near the gallery?"

   In his letter he had written, "The nights here are quiet and starry. It seems like a hundred years since I've been wakened by the noise of city traffic and squabbling neighbors."

   Note that indirect quotes (which often are preceded by *that*, *if*, or *whether*) are not set off by quotation marks:

   He told me that he went to school in Boston.

   We asked if we could still get tickets to the game.

2. They can be used to set off words or phrases that have specific technical usage, or to set off meanings of words, or to indicate words that are being used in a special way in a sentence:

   The part of the flower that bears the pollen is the "stamen."

   When I said "plain," I meant "flat land," not "ordinary."

   Oddly enough, in the theater, the statement "break a leg" is meant as an expression of good luck.

   What you call "hoagies," we call "grinders" or "submarine sandwiches."

   He will never be a responsible adult until he outgrows his "Peter Pan" behavior.

   Note that sometimes single quotation marks, rather than double quotation marks, may be used to set off words or phrases:

   The part of the flower that bears the pollen is the 'stamen.'

   What is most important is to be consistent in such usage. Single quotation marks are also used to set off words or phrases within material already in double quotation marks, as:

   "I want the sign to say 'Ellen's Bed and Breakfast' in large gold letters," she explained.

Parentheses

Parentheses are used, in pairs, to enclose information that gives extra detail or explanation to the regular text. Parentheses are used in two basic ways:

1. They can separate a word or words in a sentence from the rest of the sentence:

   On our way to school, we walk past the Turner Farm (the oldest dairy farm in town) and watch the cows being fed.

   The stores were filled with holiday shoppers (even more so than last year).

Note that the period goes outside the parentheses, because the words in the parentheses are only part of the sentence.

2. They can form a separate complete sentence:

   Please bring a dessert to the dinner party. (It can be something very simple.) I look forward to seeing you there.

   Note that the period goes inside the parentheses, because the words in the parentheses are a complete and independent sentence.

Dash

A **dash** is used most commonly to replace the usage of parentheses within sentences. If the information being set off is in the middle of the sentence, a pair of long (or "em") dashes is used; if it is at the end of the sentence, just one long dash is used:

On our way to school, we walk past the Turner Farm—the oldest dairy farm in town—and watch the cows being fed.

The stores were filled with holiday shoppers—even more so than last year.

Hyphen

A **hyphen** has three basic functions:

1. It can join two or more words to make a compound, especially when doing so makes the meaning more clear to the reader:

   We met to discuss long-range planning.

   There were six four-month-old piglets at the fair.

   That old stove was quite a coal-burner.

2. It can replace the word "to" when a span or range of data is given. This kind of hyphen is sometimes keyed as a short (or "en") dash:

   John Adams was president of the United States 1797–1801.

   Today we will look for proper nouns in the L–N section of the dictionary.

   The ideal weight for that breed of dog would be 75–85 pounds.

3. It can indicate a word break at the end of a line. The break must always be between syllables:

It is important for any writer to know that there are numerous punctuation principles that are consid-ered standard and proper, but there is also flexibility regarding acceptable punctuation. Having learned the basic "rules" of good punctuation, the writer will be able to adopt a specific and consistent style of punc-tuation that best suits the material he or she is writing.

WORDS: MAKING THE RIGHT CHOICES

The building blocks of written or spoken communication are, of course, words. When we speak informally to one another throughout the day, we use our familiar vocabulary and patterns of expression without giving the individual words much thought. When our communication is more formal—as in a letter, an article, or a speech—our choice of words becomes more important.

Synonyms

Knowing which words to choose depends largely on knowing how to use synonyms. A **synonym** is a term that means exactly or nearly the same as another term in the same language. For example, *glad* is a synonym of *pleased*. By exploring synonym choices, writers are likely to keep their writing fresh and interesting.

Thoughtfully selected words not only convey the writer's message, they can enhance readability and demonstrate the writer's competency. It is usually well worth the writer's time to be guided by such resources as thesauruses and synonym studies.

Using thesauruses

A thesaurus, essentially a book of synonyms, can be an indispensable tool for the writer. There are two conventional types of thesauruses: one arranges the material by theme; the other arranges the headwords in an A-to-Z format, much like a dictionary. Most modern thesauruses are compiled in the latter format.

There are several reasons that one might consult a thesaurus. Perhaps "the right word" is somewhere in the writer's mind, but it just isn't coming to the writer at that moment. The writer thinks, "The word means something like *to pause*." When the writer looks up *pause* in the thesaurus, there in a list of synonyms is the very word! The writer is relieved and thinks, "Yes, that's what I was thinking of—the word *hesitate*."

Another valuable function of a thesaurus is to help the writer avoid repetition. Using the same word over and over again can be monotonous to the reader and may suggest weak vocabulary skills on the part of the writer. Consider the following paragraph:

> The movie we saw last night was very exciting. It started with an exciting car chase, and it just got more and more exciting as the plot developed. There were many moments that had me on the edge of my seat, but the scene in the train station was definitely the most exciting part of the story.

The writer risks losing the reader's attention because the reader may be thinking, "Doesn't this person know any word other than *exciting*?" If the writer were to consult a thesaurus, the paragraph could be greatly improved. One such revision might read as follows:

> The movie we saw last night was very <u>exciting</u>. It started with a <u>sensational</u> car chase, and it just got more and more <u>thrilling</u> as the plot developed. There were many moments that had me on the edge of my seat, but the scene in the train station was definitely the most <u>electrifying</u> part of the story.

A thesaurus can expand a writer's use of vocabulary and perk up a piece of writing, but it is the writer's responsibility to make certain that the words chosen are appropriate for the intended context. If a writer is not certain of the precise meaning or correct usage of a term listed in a thesaurus, a dictionary should be consulted as well.

Using synonym studies

Many dictionaries feature synonym studies, which expound on the usage of synonyms for selected terms. They offer an analytical treatment of the nuances of meaning that distinguish a set of closely related synonyms. If a synonym study were to appear at the dictionary entry for *distinguish*, for example, it might look like this:

> SYNONYM STUDY: **distinguish**
>
> DESCRY, DIFFERENTIATE, DISCERN, DISCRIMINATE. What we **discern**, we see apart from all other objects (*to discern the lighthouse beaming on the far shore*). **Descry** puts even more emphasis on the distant or unclear nature of what we're seeing (*the lookout was barely able to descry a man approaching*). To **discriminate** is to perceive the differences between or among things that are very similar; it may suggest that some aesthetic evaluation is involved (*to discriminate between two singers' styles*). **Distinguish** requires making even finer distinctions among things that resemble each other even more closely (*unable to distinguish the shadowy figures moving through the forest*). *Distinguish* can also mean recognizing by some special mark or outward sign (*the sheriff could be distinguished by his badge*). **Differentiate**, on the other hand, suggests the ability to perceive differences between things that are easily confused. In contrast to *distinguish*, *differentiate* suggests subtle differences that must be compared in some detail (*the color of the first paint sample was difficult to differentiate from the third sample*).

Clichés

A **cliché** is a worn-out expression. It was once fresh and meaningful, but it has lost its original impact through overuse. Numerous clichés have become so familiar that it would be virtually impossible to eradicate them from one's vocabulary. However, writers and speakers should make the effort to avoid using them, especially in formal material.

Common clichés to avoid

above and beyond the call of duty
accident waiting to happen
acid test
add insult to injury
after all is said and done
all hands on deck
all in all
all wet
all's well that ends well
almighty dollar
along the same lines
A-OK
as luck would have it
at a loss for words
at arm's length
avoid like the plague
back in the saddle
back on track
backseat driver
ball is in your court
barking up the wrong tree
be your own worst enemy
beat a dead horse
beat around the bush
been there, done that
beggars can't be choosers
be an open book
believe me
better late than never
between a rock and a hard place
between you, me, and the lamppost
big picture
big spender
bigger fish to fry
bird's-eye view
bitter end
bone of contention
born and bred
both sides of the coin
brain trust
bring home the bacon
broad spectrum
broaden one's horizons
bundle of nerves
bury the hatchet
busy as a bee
buy into
by leaps and bounds
by the skin of one's teeth
call her bluff
can't judge a book by its cover
can't take a joke
cast the net
catbird seat
catch as catch can
center of attention
cheat death
chew the fat
clear as a bell
clear as mud
cloak and dagger
coast is clear
cold as ice
cold shoulder
come full circle
come to no good
come up for air
conspicuous by their absence
cool it
cop out
could eat a horse
counting on you
count your blessings
cover all the bases
crazy like a fox
cream of the crop
creature of habit
crossing the line
cut me some slack
cut to the chase
dead in the water
dead wrong
dog-eat-dog
done deal
done to death
don't know him from Adam
down and dirty
down and out
down in the dumps
down in the mouth
dressed to the nines
due in large measure to

duly noted
dumb luck
easier said than done
easy come, easy go
easy mark
easy target
eat crow
end of discussion
every fiber of my being
face the music
fair and square
fall from grace
fall through the cracks
far and away
feast or famine
few and far between
fighting the tide
fill the bill
find it in your heart
fit as a fiddle
fit to be tied
fits like an old shoe
flat as a pancake
fly in the ointment
fly off the handle
for all intents and purposes
for love or money
for your information
fork it over
free as a bird
from the frying pan into the fire
from time immemorial
game plan
get behind the eight ball
get down to brass tacks
get off scot-free
get our ducks in a row
get the lead out
get the show on the road
get to the bottom of it
give a damn
give rise to
go for the kill
go it alone
go the distance
go the extra mile
go to pieces
go with the flow
goes without saying
good for nothing
goodly number
grass is always greener
green with envy
grist for the mill
hammer out the details
handwriting on the wall
hang in there
has a screw loose
have your heart in your mouth
head over heels
heated argument
his bark is worse than his bite
hit or miss
hit the ceiling
hit the ground running
hit the nail on the head
hold that thought
holding back the tide
hook, line, and sinker
hour of need
I wasn't born yesterday
icing on the cake
if looks could kill
if the price is right
I'm all over it
I'm speechless
in a nutshell
in due course
in hot water
in layman's terms
in one fell swoop
in over their heads
in seventh heaven
in the bag
in the ballpark
in the driver's seat
in the event that
in the final analysis
in the groove
in the near future
in the neighborhood of
in the nick of time
in the same boat
in the zone
in this day and age
irons in the fire
it could be worse
it stands to reason
it takes all kinds
it takes guts
it's your baby
join the club
keep your fingers crossed
keep the home fires burning
keeping score
kill the fatted calf

kiss of death
knock on wood
knock the socks off of
know the ropes
last but not least
last straw
lay an egg
learning curve
leave no stone unturned
left to his own devices
lend me an ear
let the cat out of the bag
let your hair down
letter perfect
lie low
light of day
like a bull in a china shop
like a bump on a log
like greased lightning
like rolling off a log
little does he know
live it up
lock, stock, and barrel
look like a million bucks
low man on the totem pole
make ends meet
make tracks
makes her blood boil
method in (*or* to) my madness
millstone around your neck
mince words
misery loves company
moment of truth
Monday-morning quarterback
monkey on your back
more money than God
more than meets the eye
more than you could shake a stick at
nail to the wall
naked truth
nearing the finish line
needle in a haystack
needs no introduction
never a dull moment
nip and tuck
nip in the bud
no harm, no foul
no skin off my nose
no strings attached
no-brainer
none the worse for wear
nose to the grindstone
not one red cent
nothing new, under the sun
off the cuff
old as the hills
old hat
old soldiers never die
older than dirt
on cloud nine
on the one hand/on the other hand
on the road
on the same page
on the same track
on the wagon
on top of the world
out of my league
out of the woods
over a barrel
pan out
par for the course
pass the buck
pay the piper
perish the thought
piece of cake
playing for keeps
powers that be
practice makes perfect
proud as a peacock
pulling my leg
pulling no punches
put faces to names
put on hold
put the bite on
put words in one's mouth
put your money where your mouth is
quick and dirty
rags to riches
rant and rave
reading me like a book
real McCoy
red as a beet
regret to inform you
reign supreme
rings a bell
ripe old age
rise and shine
rolling over in his grave
rub elbows
rule the roost
run circles around
run it up the flagpole
run off at the mouth
sadder but wiser
safe to say
salt of the earth

scarce as hen's teeth
sea of faces
see the forest for the trees
sell like hotcakes
set in stone
shake a leg
sharp as a tack
ships that pass in the night
shoot the breeze
shooting himself in the foot
shot in the arm
shot to hell
sight for sore eyes
sitting duck
skeleton in the closet
skin alive
sleep on it
smells fishy
smooth sailing
snake in the grass
spill the beans
stay in the loop
steal the limelight
stem the tide
stick to your guns
stick your neck out
straight from the horse's mouth
strange bedfellows
strike a balance
strong as an ox
stubborn as a mule
sturdy as an oak
suffice it to say
sweating bullets
take a breather
take into consideration
take on board
take one's word for
take pleasure in
take the bitter with the sweet
take the easy way out
take the liberty of
talk shop
talk the talk
talk through your hat
talk your ear off
that's all she wrote
the die is cast
they'll be sorry
thick as thieves
thin as a rail
think outside the box
think tank
those are the breaks
through thick and thin
throw caution to the wind
thrown to the wolves
tighten our belts
time is money
time marches on
time waits for no man
to each his own
to your heart's content
too funny for words
took the words right out of my mouth
touch base
turn the other cheek
turn up your nose
two peas in a pod
ugly as sin
under the wire
up a creek
upset the applecart
venture a guess
vicious circle
waiting for the other shoe to drop
walk the walk
walking encyclopedia
walking on air
welcome with open arms
when the cows come home
where angels fear to tread
where there's smoke, there's fire
whole nine yards
wild-goose chase
wipe the slate clean
wishful thinking
with bated breath
without further ado
without further delay
wonders never cease
words fail me
wreak havoc
yadda, yadda, yadda
you said a mouthful
you'll never know if you don't try

Redundant Expressions

A redundant expression is a group of words (usually a pair) in which at least one word is superfluous—that is, unnecessary. The superfluous element can be removed without affecting the meaning of the expression. In formal speech or writing, redundant expressions should be strictly avoided.

In the following list of common redundant expressions, the superfluous elements have been crossed out.

~~absolute~~ guarantee
~~absolutely~~ certain
~~absolutely~~ essential
~~absolutely~~ necessary
AC ~~current~~
~~actual~~ fact
~~actual~~ truth
add ~~an additional~~
adding ~~together~~
~~advance~~ reservations
~~advance~~ warning
after ~~the end of~~
all meet ~~together~~
alongside ~~of~~
~~already~~ existing
~~and~~ moreover
~~annoying~~ pest
ATM ~~machine~~
~~awkward~~ predicament
bald-~~headed~~
~~basic~~ essentials
~~basic~~ fundamentals
blend ~~together~~
~~brief~~ moment
~~but~~ however
~~but~~ nevertheless
came ~~at a time~~ when
cancel ~~out~~
~~chief~~ protagonist
~~clearly~~ obvious
climb ~~up~~
~~close~~ proximity
~~close~~ scrutiny
collaborate ~~together~~
combine ~~into one~~
commute ~~back and forth~~
~~complete~~ monopoly
~~completely~~ destroyed
~~completely~~ eliminated
~~completely~~ empty
~~completely~~ filled
~~completely~~ random
consensus ~~of opinion~~
continue ~~on~~
~~continue to~~ remain
cooperate ~~together~~
currently ~~today~~
DC ~~current~~
~~decorative~~ garnish
~~deep~~ chasm
~~definitely~~ decided
descend ~~down~~
~~different~~ varieties
~~difficult~~ dilemma
~~direct~~ confrontation
drop ~~down~~
during ~~the course of~~
dwindled ~~down~~
each ~~and every~~
earlier ~~in time~~
~~empty~~ space
~~end~~ result
enter ~~in~~
equal ~~to one another~~
~~established~~ fact
estimated at ~~about~~
estimated ~~roughly~~ at
~~every~~ now and then
~~evil~~ fiend
~~exact~~ duplicate
~~exact~~ opposites
~~fake~~ copy
~~false~~ pretenses
~~fellow~~ classmates
~~fellow~~ teammates
few ~~in number~~
filled ~~to capacity~~
~~final~~ conclusion
~~final~~ outcome
first ~~and foremost~~
~~first~~ began
~~first~~ introduction
first ~~of all~~
~~first~~ started
follow ~~after~~
for ~~a period of~~ six months
for ~~the purpose of~~
~~foreign~~ exports
~~foreign~~ imports
forever ~~and ever~~
foundered ~~and sank~~
~~free~~ gift
~~free~~ pass
~~future~~ prospects

gather ~~together~~
gave birth to a ~~baby~~ girl/boy
~~glowing~~ ember
~~good~~ bargain
~~good~~ benefits
had done ~~previously~~
~~harmful~~ injury
HIV ~~virus~~
~~honest~~ truth
~~hopeful~~ optimism
~~hot~~ water heater
I ~~myself personally~~
if ~~and when~~
~~important~~ breakthrough
in ~~close~~ proximity
~~intense~~ fury
introduced ~~for the first time~~
~~invited~~ guests
ISBN ~~number~~
joined ~~together~~
~~just~~ recently
kneel ~~down~~
last ~~of all~~
lift ~~up~~
look back ~~in retrospect~~
~~major~~ breakthrough
may ~~possibly~~
~~mental~~ telepathy
merged ~~together~~
meshed ~~together~~
~~midway~~ between
might ~~possibly~~
mix ~~together~~
~~mutual~~ cooperation
~~natural~~ instinct
never ~~at any time~~
~~new~~ beginning
~~new~~ bride
~~new~~ innovation
~~new~~ recruit
nine A.M. ~~in the morning~~
no trespassing ~~allowed~~
none ~~at all~~
~~now~~ pending
null ~~and void~~
~~old~~ cliché
~~old~~ proverb
~~opening~~ introduction
~~originally~~ created
over ~~and done with~~
~~over~~exaggerate
~~pair of~~ twins
parched ~~dry~~
~~passing~~ fad
~~past~~ experiences
~~past~~ history
~~past~~ memories
~~past~~ records
penetrate ~~into~~
~~perfect~~ ideal
permeate ~~throughout~~
~~personal~~ friend
~~personal~~ opinion
~~personally~~ believes
PIN ~~number~~
plan ~~in advance~~
~~poisonous~~ venom
~~positively~~ true
~~possibly~~ might
postponed ~~until a later time~~
~~pre~~recorded
~~present~~ incumbent
probed ~~into~~
proceed ~~ahead~~
protest ~~against~~
protrude ~~out~~
~~proven~~ facts
raise ~~up~~
reason ~~why~~
refer ~~back~~
reflect ~~back~~
repeat ~~again~~
reply ~~back~~
revert ~~back~~
Rio Grande ~~River~~
~~sad~~ tragedy
same ~~identical~~
seemed ~~to be~~
share ~~together~~
short ~~in length~~
since ~~the time when~~
~~sincerely~~ mean it
skipped ~~over~~
~~solemn~~ vow
spelled out ~~in detail~~
stacked ~~on top of each other~~
~~still~~ continues
~~still~~ persists
~~still~~ remains
strangled ~~to death~~
~~stupid~~ fool
~~suddenly~~ exploded
sufficient ~~enough~~
~~sum~~ total
summer ~~season~~
~~sworn~~ affidavit

~~temporary~~ recess
~~temporary~~ reprieve
~~terrible~~ tragedy
~~thoughtful~~ contemplation
~~thoughtful~~ deliberation
~~totally~~ eliminated
~~true~~ fact
~~twelve~~ midnight
~~twelve~~ noon
~~two~~ twins
~~ultimate~~ conclusion
~~unexpected~~ surprise
~~unintentional~~ mistake
~~uninvited~~ party crashers
UPC ~~code~~
~~usual~~ custom
~~utter~~ annihilation
~~very~~ unique
ways ~~and means~~
~~well-known old~~ adage
when ~~and if~~
whether ~~or not~~
widow ~~woman~~
written ~~down~~

Proofreader's Marks

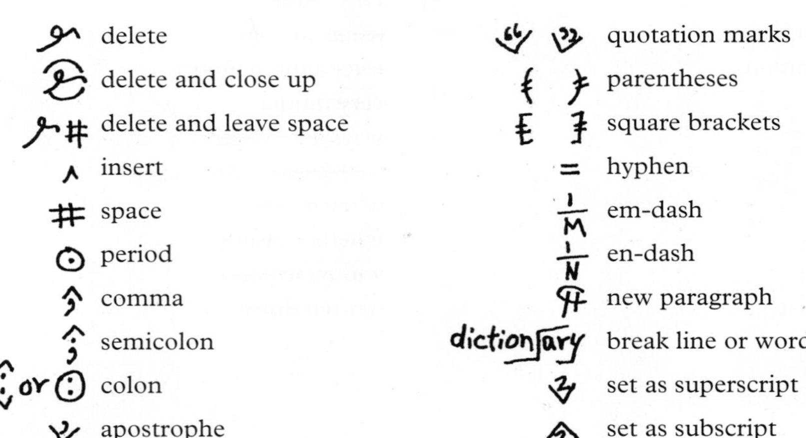

dictionray transpose
(tr) transpose (note in margin)
(3) spell out
(sp) spell out (note in margin)
dictionary capitalize
(cap) set as capitals (note in margin)
Dictionary make lower case
(lc) set in lower case (note in margin)
dictionary make boldface
(bf) set in boldface (note in margin)
dictionary make italic
(ital) set in italic (note in margin)
dictionary small caps
(sc) set in small caps (note in margin)
(lf) lightface (note in margin)
(rom) set in roman (note in margin)

The History of English

1. Fifteen centuries of English cannot easily be summarized, so this account is intended to pick out features on the landscape of language rather than to describe the scene in detail. This may afford some perspective on the information given in the dictionary, and help to make more sense of the strange and often unpredictable ways in which words seem to behave.

Origins

2.1 English belongs to the Indo-European family of languages, a vast group with many branches, thought to be derived from a common ancestor-language called Proto-Indo-European. The words we use in English are derived from a wide range of sources, mostly within this family. The earliest sources are Germanic, Norse, and Romanic; later, they are the languages of Europe more generally; and most recently, with developments in such areas as medicine, electronics, computers, and communications, they have been worldwide.

2.2 It is difficult to be sure exactly what we mean by an "English" word. Most obviously, words are English if they can be traced back to the Anglo-Saxons, Germanic peoples who settled in Britain from the fifth century and eventually established several kingdoms together corresponding roughly to present-day England. From this time are derived many common words such as *eat, drink, speak, work, house, door, man, woman, husband, wife*. The Anglo-Saxons displaced the Celtic peoples, whose speech survives in Scottish and Irish Gaelic, in Welsh, and in the local languages of two extremities of the British Isles, Manx (in the Isle of Man) and Cornish (in Cornwall, a county in southwestern England). Little Celtic influence remains in English, except in names of places such as *Brecon, Carlisle*, and *London*, and in many river names, such as *Avon, Thames*, and *Trent*. This fact may be attributed to a lack of cultural interaction, the Celts being forced back into the fringes of the British Isles by the Anglo-Saxon invaders.

3. Anglo-Saxon Britain continued to have contact with the Roman Empire, of which Britain had formerly been a part, and with Latin, which was the official language throughout the Empire and survived as a language of ritual (and for a time also of learning and communication) in the Western Christian Church. Christianity was brought to England with the mission of St. Augustine in AD 597. The Christianized Anglo-Saxons built churches and monasteries, and there were considerable advances in art and learning. At this time English was enriched by words from Latin, many of which are still in use, such as *angel, disciple, martyr*, and *shrine*. Other words came from Latin via the Germanic languages, for example *copper, mint* (in the sense of coinage), *pound, sack*, and *title*, and others were ultimately of more remote origin, for example *camel* (Semitic) and *shampoo* (Hindi).

4.1 The next important influence on the vocabulary of English came from the Danish and other Scandinavian invaders of the ninth and tenth centuries, collectively called Vikings. They occupied much of the eastern portion of England, and under Cnut (Canute) ruled the whole country for a time. The Danes had much more contact with the Anglo-Saxons than did the Celts, and their period of occupation has left its mark in the number of Scandinavian (Old Norse) words taken into English. Because Old Norse was also a Germanic language (of a different branch from English) many words were similar to the Anglo-Saxon ones, and it is difficult to establish the extent of the Old Norse influence. However, a number of Norse words are identifiable and are still in use, such as *call, take*, and *law*, names of parts of the body such as *leg*, and other basic words such as *egg, root*, and *window*. Many more Norse words are preserved in some dialects of eastern England, in English place names ending in *-thwaite* and *-thorpe* (both meaning 'settlement') and in *-by (Grimsby, Rugby*, and so on), and in English street names ending in *-gate* (from the Old Norse *gata* meaning 'street') such as *Coppergate* in New York.

4.2 In the Saxon kingdom of Wessex, King Alfred (reigned 871–899) and his successors did much to keep English alive by using it (rather than Latin) as the language of education and learning; by the tenth century there was a considerable amount of English prose and verse literature. Saxon and Danish kingdoms existed side by side for several generations, and there was much linguistic interaction. One very important effect on English was the gradual disappearance of many word endings, or inflections, leading to a simpler grammar. This was partly because the stems of English and Norse words were often very close in form (for example, *stān* and *steinn*, meaning 'stone'), and only the inflections differed as an impediment to mutual understanding. So other forms such as *stāne, stānes*, etc., began to be simplified and, eventually, eliminated. The process continued for hundreds of years into Middle English (see below).

The Norman Conquest

5. In 1066 William of Normandy defeated the English king, Harold, at the Battle of Hastings; he was crowned King of England on Christmas Day. The arrival of the French-speaking Normans as a ruling nobility brought a transforming Romance influence on the language. The Romance languages (chiefly French, Italian, Spanish, Portuguese, and Romanian) have their roots in the spoken or "vulgar" Latin *(vulgar* here meaning 'of the (common) people') that continued in use until about AD 600. For two hundred years after the Norman Conquest, French (in its regional Norman form) was the language of the aristocracy, the law courts, and the Church hierarchy in England. Gradually the Normans were integrated into English society, and by the reign of Henry II (1154–89) many of the aristocracy spoke English. During these years many French words were adopted into English. Some were connected with law and government, such as *justice, council*, and *tax*, and some were abstract terms such as *liberty, charity*, and *conflict*. The Normans also had an important effect on the spelling of English words. The combination of letters *cw-*, for example, was standardized in the Norman manner to *qu-*, so that *cwēn* became *queen* and *cwic* became *quik* (later *quick*).

6. This mixture of conquering peoples and their languages—Germanic, Scandinavian, and Romance—had a decisive effect on the forms of words in modern English. The three elements make up the basic stock of English vocabulary, and different practices of putting sounds into writing are reflected in each. The different grammatical characteristics of each element can be seen in the structure and endings of many words. Many of the variable endings such as *-ant* and *-ent*, *-er* and *-or*, *-able* and *-ible* exist because the Latin words on which they are based belonged to different classes of verbs and nouns, each of which had a different ending. For example, *important* comes from the Latin verb *portare*, meaning 'to carry' (which belongs to one verb class or conjugation) while *repellent* comes from the Latin verb *pellere*, meaning 'to drive' (which belongs to another). *Capable* comes from a Latin word ending in *-abilis*, while *sensible* comes from one ending in *-ibilis*, and so on.

Middle English

7. Middle English, as the English of *c.*1100–1500 is called, emerged as the spoken and written form of the language under these influences. The use of French diminished, especially after King John (reigned 1199–1216) lost possession of Normandy in 1204, severing an important Anglo-French link. Many Anglo-Saxon words continued in use, while others disappeared altogether: for example, *niman* was replaced by the Old Norse (Scandinavian) *taka* (meaning 'take'), and the Old English *sige* was replaced by a word derived from Old French, *victory*. Other Old English words that disappeared are *Mdl* (disease), *lof* (praise), and *lyft* (air: compare German *Luft*). Sometimes new and old words continued in use side by side, in some cases on a roughly equal footing, and in others with a distinction in meaning (as with *doom* and *judgment*, and *stench* and *smell*). This has produced pairs of words which are both in use today, such as *shut* and *close*, and *buy* and *purchase*, in which the second word of each pair is Romance in origin. Sometimes an even larger overlap was produced, as when *commence* (from the French) was added to the existing Old English *begin* and *start*. (The original meaning of *start* was 'leap,' 'move suddenly,' which is still current though no longer the main sense.)

8. Hundreds of the Romance words were short, simple words that would now be distinguished with difficulty from Old English words if their origin were not known: for example, *bar*, *cry*, *fool*, *mean*, *pity*, *stuff*, *touch*, and *tender*. Others, such as *commence* and *purchase*, have more formal connotations. The result was a mixture of types of words, a feature of modern English. For many meanings we now have a choice of less and more formal words, the more formal ones used only in very specific circumstances. For example, the word *vendor* is used instead of *seller* only in commercial contexts. Many technical words derived from or ultimately from Latin, such as *estop* and *usucaption*, survive only in legal contexts, to the great confusion of the layperson. These levels of formality are reflected in the dictionary's identification of usage level in particular cases as colloquial, formal, and so on.

Printing

9. There was much regional variation in the spelling and pronunciation of Middle English, although a good measure of uniformity was imposed by the development of printing from the fifteenth century. This uniformity was based as much on practical considerations of the printing process as on what seemed most "correct" or suitable. It became common practice, for example, to add a final *e* to words to fill a line of print. The printers—many of them foreign— used rules from their own languages, especially Dutch and Flemish, when setting English into type. William Caxton, the first English printer (1422–91), exercised an important but not always beneficial influence. The unnecessary insertion of *h* in *ghost*, for example, is due to Caxton (who learned the business of printing on the Continent), and the change had its effect on other words such as *ghastly* and (perhaps) *ghetto*. In general, Caxton used the form of English prevalent in the southeast of England, although the East Midland dialect was the more extensive. This choice, together with the importance of London as the English capital, gave the dialect of southeastern England a significance and influence that survives to the present day.

Pronunciation

10. At roughly the same time as the early development of printing, the pronunciation of English was also undergoing major changes. The main change, which began in the fourteenth century during the lifetime of the poet Chaucer (*c.*1342–1400), was in the pronunciation of vowel sounds. The so-called great vowel shift resulted in the reduction of the number of words that are pronounced with the vowel sound in long vowels *(deed* as distinct from *dead*). It also affected the pronunciation of other vowels: the word *life*, for example, was once pronounced as we now pronounce *leaf*, and *name* was pronounced as two syllables to rhyme with *comma*. In many cases, as with *name*, the form of the word did not change; this accounts for many of the "silent" vowels at the ends of words. The result of these developments was a growing difference between what was spoken and what was written.

The Renaissance

11. The rediscovery in Europe of the culture and history of the ancient Greek and Roman worlds exercised a further Romanizing influence on English. This began at the end of the Middle Ages and blossomed in the European Renaissance of the fifteenth to seven-teenth centuries. Scholarship flourished, and the language used by scholars and writers was Latin. During the Renaissance words such as *arena*, *dexterity*, *excision*, *genius*, *habitual*, *malignant*, *specimen*, and *stimulus* came into use in English. They are familiar and useful words but their origins sometimes make them awkward to handle, as, for example, when we use *arena*, *genius*, and *stimulus* in the plural. There was also a tendency in the Renaissance to try to emphasize the Greek or Latin origins of words when writing them. This accounts for the *b* in *debt* (the earlier English word was *det*; in Latin it is *debitum*), the *l* in *fault* (earlier *faut*; the Latin source is *fallere*), the *s* in *isle* (earlier *ile*; *insula* in Latin), and the *p* in *receipt* (earlier *receit*; *recepta* in Latin). Some words that had gone out of use were reintroduced, usually with changed meanings, for example *artificial*, *disk* (originally the same as *dish*), and *fastidious*.

Later Influences

12. The development of machines and technology from the eighteenth century onward, followed by the electronic revolution of our own times, has also played a part in continuing the influence of Latin. New technical terms have come into use, and they have often been formed on Latin or Greek source words because these can convey precise ideas in easily combinable forms, for example *bacteriology*, *microscope*, *radioactive*, and *semiconductor*. Combinations of Germanic elements are also used, as in *software*, *splashdown*, and *takeoff*. This process has sometimes produced etymologically odd mixtures, such as *television*, which is half Greek and half Latin, and *microchip*, which is half Greek and half Germanic.

13.1 In recent times English speakers have come into contact with people from other parts of the world, through trade, international relations, and improved communications generally. This contact has produced a rich supply of new words. India, where the British first had major dealings in the seventeenth century, is the source of words such as *bungalow*, *jodhpurs*, and *khaki*. Examples from other parts of the world are *harem* and *mufti* (from Arabic), *bazaar* (from Persian), *kiosk* (from Turkish), *ukulele* (from Hawaiian), *futon* (from Japanese), and *anorak* (from Eskimo). From European countries we have acquired *balcony* (from Italian), *envelope* (from French), and *yacht* (from Dutch).

13.2 Thousands of such words, though not English in the Germanic sense, are regarded as fully absorbed into English. In addition, there are many unnaturalized words and phrases that are used in English contexts but are generally regarded as "foreign," and are conventionally printed in italics to distinguish them when used in an English context. Very many of these are French, for example *accouchement* (childbirth), *bagarre* (a scuffle), *bonhomie* (geniality), *flânerie* (idleness), and *rangé* (domesticated), but other languages are represented, as with *echt* (genuine) and *Machtpolitik* (power politics) from German, and *mañana* (tomorrow) from Spanish.

14.1 Usage often recognizes the difficulties of absorbing words from various sources by assimilating them into familiar forms. The word *picturesque*, which came into use in the eighteenth century, is a compromise between its French source *pittoresque* and the existing Middle English word *picture*, to which it is obviously related. The English word *cockroach* is a conversion of its Spanish source word *cucaracha* into a pair of familiar words, *cock* (a bird) and *roach* (a fish). Cockroaches have nothing to do with cocks or roaches, and the association is simply a matter of linguistic convenience.

14.2 Problems of inflection arise with words taken from other languages. The ending *-i* in particular is very unnatural in English, and usage varies between *-is* and *-ies* for the plural. A similar difficulty occurs with the many adopted nouns ending in *-o*, some of which come from the Italian *(solo)*, some from Spanish *(armadillo)*, and some from Latin *(hero)*; here usage varies between *-os* and *-oes*. Verbs often need special treatment, as *bivouac* (from French, and before that probably from Swiss German), which needs a *k* in the past tense *(bivouacked*, not *bivouaced*, which might be mispronounced), and *ski* (from Norwegian, where usage allows both *ski'd* and *skied* as past forms).

Dictionaries

15.1 One obvious consequence of the development of printing in the fifteenth century was that it allowed the language to be recorded in glossaries and dictionaries, and this might be expected to have had a considerable effect on the way words were used and spelled. However, listing all the words in the language systematically in alphabetical order with their spellings and meanings is a relatively recent idea. There was nothing of the sort in Shakespeare's time, for example. In 1580, when Shakespeare was sixteen, a schoolmaster named William Bullokar published a manual for the "ease, speed, and perfect reading and writing of English," and he called for the writing of an English dictionary. Such a dictionary, the work of Robert Cawdrey (another schoolmaster), was not published until 1604. Like the dictionaries that followed in quick succession (including John (son of William) Bullokar's *An English Expositor*), its purpose was described as being for the understanding of "hard words." It was not until the eighteenth century that dictionaries systematically listed all the words in general use at the time regardless of how "easy" or "hard" they were; the most notable of these were compiled by Nathaniel Bailey (1721) and, especially, Samuel Johnson (1755). They were partly a response to a call, expressed by Swift, Pope, Addison, and other writers, for the language to be fixed and stabilized, and for the establishment of an English Academy to monitor it. None of these hopes as such were realized, but the dictionaries played an important role in setting the form and senses of English words. Noah Webster's American dictionaries set new standards for spelling and concision, starting with his edition in 1828.

15.2 The systematic investigation and recording of words in all their aspects and on a historical basis is represented in the *Oxford English Dictionary*, begun by the Scottish schoolmaster James A. H. Murray in 1879 as the *New English Dictionary on Historical Principles*. This work describes historically the spelling, inflection, origin, and meaning of words, and is supported by citations from printed literature and other sources of evidence from Old English to the present day. A new edition integrating the original dictionary and its *Supplement* (1972–1986) appeared in 1989. Because of its depth of scholarship, the *Oxford English Dictionary* forms a major basis of all English dictionaries produced since it was first published. Smaller desktop, college, and other abridged dictionaries that aim at recording the main vocabulary in current use began to appear early in the twentieth century, and in recent years the number has grown remarkably.

15.3 Dictionaries of current English, as distinct from historical dictionaries, generally record the language as it is being used at the time, and with usage constantly changing the distinction between "right" and "wrong" is sometimes difficult to establish. Unlike French, which is guided by the rulings of the *Académie Française*, English is not monitored by any single authority; established usage is the principal criterion. One result of this is that English tolerates many more alternative spellings than other languages. The alternatives are based on patterns of word formation and variation in the different languages through which they have passed before reaching ours.

15.4 It should also be remembered that general dictionaries provide a selection, based on currency, from a recorded stock of well over half a million words; that is to say, they represent a small percentage of what is attested to exist by printed sources and other materials. Dictionaries therefore differ in the selection they make, beyond the core of vocabulary and idiom that can be expected to be found in any dictionary.

English Worldwide

16.1 Modern usage is greatly influenced by rapid worldwide communications, by newspapers, and, in particular, by television and radio. The influence of American English, often regarded by the British as unsettling or harmful, has had a considerable effect on the vocabulary, idiom, and spelling of British English, and continues to do so. Among the many words and idioms in general use in British English, usually without any awareness of or concern about their American origin, are *OK*, *to fall for*, *to fly off the handle*, *round trip*, and *to snoop*. American English often has more regular spellings, for example the use of *-er* for *-re* in words such as theater (Brit. *theatre*), the standardization of *-or* and *-our* to *-or* in words such as *harbor* (Brit. *harbour*), and the use of *-se* in forms such as *defense* and *license*, where British English either has *-ce* only or both forms (for example, *a practice* but *to practise*).

16.2 English is now used all over the world; as a result, there are many varieties of English, with varying accents, vocabulary, and usage, as in South Africa, India, Australia, New Zealand, Canada, and elsewhere. These varieties have an equal claim to be regarded as "English" and, although learners of English may look to British and American English as the two poles of an English-speaking world, it is very important that dictionaries should take account of other varieties of English, especially as it affects that in use elsewhere. The process is a strengthening and enriching one, and is the mark of a living and flourishing language.

Further Reading

17. Those who are interested in exploring further will find a host of books on the history and development of English. Good general accounts are A. C. Baugh and T. Cable, *A History of the English Language* (4th ed., New Jersey, 1993) and B. M. H. Strang, *A History of English* (London, 1970). At a more popular level, and more up to date on recent trends, are R. W. Burchfield, *The English Language* (Oxford, 1985) and R. McCrum *et al.*, *The Story of English* (New York, 1993). *The Oxford Companion to the English Language* (ed. T. McArthur, New York and Oxford, 1996) contains much that will interest those who want to know more about the English of today and its place among the languages of the world.

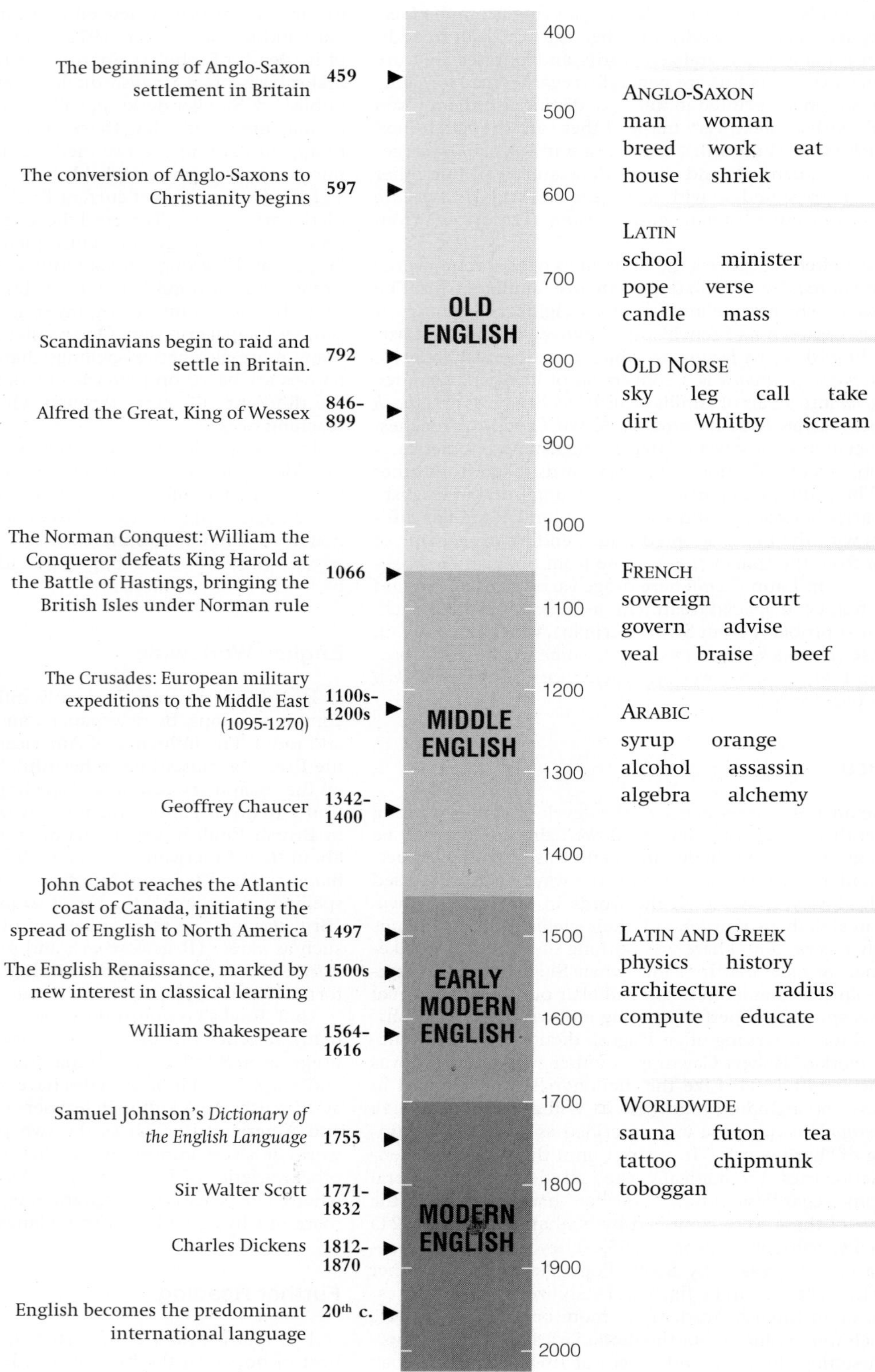
400
The beginning of Anglo-Saxon settlement in Britain 459
500
ANGLO-SAXON
man woman
breed work eat
house shriek
The conversion of Anglo-Saxons to Christianity begins 597
600
LATIN
school minister
pope verse
candle mass
700
OLD ENGLISH
Scandinavians begin to raid and settle in Britain. 792
800
OLD NORSE
sky leg call take
dirt Whitby scream
Alfred the Great, King of Wessex 846–899
900
1000
The Norman Conquest: William the Conqueror defeats King Harold at the Battle of Hastings, bringing the British Isles under Norman rule 1066
FRENCH
sovereign court
govern advise
veal braise beef
1100
The Crusades: European military expeditions to the Middle East (1095-1270) 1100s–1200s
1200
MIDDLE ENGLISH
ARABIC
syrup orange
alcohol assassin
algebra alchemy
1300
Geoffrey Chaucer 1342–1400
1400
John Cabot reaches the Atlantic coast of Canada, initiating the spread of English to North America 1497
1500
LATIN AND GREEK
physics history
architecture radius
compute educate
The English Renaissance, marked by new interest in classical learning 1500s
EARLY MODERN ENGLISH
William Shakespeare 1564–1616
1600
1700
WORLDWIDE
sauna futon tea
tattoo chipmunk
toboggan
Samuel Johnson's Dictionary of the English Language 1755
Sir Walter Scott 1771–1832
1800
MODERN ENGLISH
Charles Dickens 1812–1870
1900
English becomes the predominant international language 20th c.
2000

History of the English Language

Anglo-Saxon English developed from Anglo-Saxon (also known as Old English), the language brought to Britain by Germanic tribes (the Angles, Saxons, and Jutes), in the fifth century AD. These invaders gave England its name, "the land of the Angles", and provided the language with many common basic terms.

Latin At the end of the sixth century, a group of monks came as missionaries from Rome to strengthen Christianity in Britain. The words that came into English from Latin at this time are mainly connected with religion and learning.

Old Norse In the ninth and tenth centuries, invaders came from Scandinavia and occupied a large part of eastern England and northern Britain. Many everyday words in modern English come from their language, Old Norse, which is related to Anglo-Saxon, and many place names end in *-by* from their word for village.

French When Britain was conquered by the Normans in 1066, French became the language of the ruling classes. Many words in modern English that describe government and the legal system, as well as terms connected with cooking, came from French at this time.

Arabic During the Christian military expeditions to the Middle East in the twelfth and thirteenth centuries, English Crusaders came into contact with the Arab world and brought many of their words back to Britain. These words tended to relate to Islam, to Arab society and culture, and to learning, particularly in the fields of mathematics and astronomy.

Latin and Greek Many words of Latin origin came into English through French, but the Renaissance of the fifteenth and sixteenth centuries brought new interest in classical learning and an influx of words from Latin and Greek. Latin and Greek continue to be used in the invention of new words, particularly in the fields of science and technology.

Worldwide Beginning with English colonization of North America in the sixteenth century, English spread to many parts of the world where it was influenced by the native languages of these lands. English speakers today take words from a wide variety of other languages for phenomena that have no existing English name.

English Today As a result of absorbing words from all of these sources, English often has many synonyms from different languages to express the same idea, such as *fear* (from Old English), *terror* (from French), *alarm* (from Italian), *trepidation* (from Latin), and *angst* (from German).

States of the United States of America

State	Traditional & Postal Abbreviations	Capital
Alabama	Ala.; AL	Montgomery
Alaska	Alas.; AK	Juneau
Arizona	Ariz.; AZ	Phoenix
Arkansas	Ark.; AR	Little Rock
California	Calif.; CA	Sacramento
Colorado	Col.; CO	Denver
Connecticut	Conn.; CT	Hartford
Delaware	Del.; DE	Dover
Florida	Fla.; FL	Tallahassee
Georgia	Ga.; GA	Atlanta
Hawaii	Haw.; HI	Honolulu
Idaho	Ida,; ID	Boise
Illinois	Ill.; IL	Springfield
Indiana	Ind.; IN	Indianapolis
Iowa	Ia.; IA	Des Moines
Kansas	Kan.; KS	Topeka
Kentucky	Ky.; KY	Frankfort
Louisiana	La.; LA	Baton Rouge
Maine	Me.; ME	Augusta
Maryland	Md.; MD	Annapolis
Massachusetts	Mass.; MA	Boston
Michigan	Mich.; MI	Lansing
Minnesota	Minn.; MN	St. Paul
Mississippi	Miss.; MS	Jackson
Missouri	Mo.; MO	Jefferson City
Montana	Mont.; MT	Helena
Nebraska	Nebr.; NE	Lincoln
Nevada	Nev.; NV	Carson City
New Hampshire	N.H.; NH	Concord
New Jersey	N.J.; NJ	Trenton
New Mexico	N. Mex.; NM	Santa Fe
New York	N.Y.; NY	Albany
North Carolina	N.C.; NC	Raleigh
North Dakota	N. Dak.; ND	Bismarck
Ohio	O.; OH	Columbus
Oklahoma	Okla.; OK	Oklahoma City
Oregon	Ore.; OR	Salem
Pennsylvania	Pa.; PA	Harrisburg
Rhode Island	R.I.; RI	Providence
South Carolina	S.C.; SC	Columbia
South Dakota	S. Dak.; SD	Pierre
Tennessee	Tenn.; TN	Nashville
Texas	Tex.; TX	Austin
Utah	Ut.; UT	Salt Lake City
Vermont	Vt.; VT	Montpelier
Virginia	Va.; VA	Richmond
Washington	Wash.; WA	Olympia
West Virginia	W. Va.; WV	Charleston
Wisconsin	Wis.; WI	Madison
Wyoming	Wyo.; WY	Cheyenne

Presidents of the United States of America

Name and life dates	Party (term in office)
1. George Washington 1732–99	Federalist (1789–97)
2. John Adams 1735–1826	Federalist (1797–1801)
3. Thomas Jefferson 1743–1826	Democratic-Republican (1801–09)
4. James Madison 1751–1836	Democratic-Republican (1809–17)
5. James Monroe 1758–1831	Democratic-Republican (1817–25)
6. John Quincy Adams 1767–1848	Democratic-Republican (1825–29)
7. Andrew Jackson 1767–1845	Democrat (1829–37)
8. Martin Van Buren 1782–1862	Democrat (1837–41)
9. William Henry Harrison 1773–1841	Whig (1841)
10. John Tyler 1790–1862	Whig (1841–45)
11. James Knox Polk 1795–1849	Democrat (1845–49)
12. Zachary Taylor 1784–1850	Whig (1849–50)
13. Millard Fillmore 1800–74	Whig (1850–53)
14. Franklin Pierce 1804–69	Democrat (1853–57)
15. James Buchanan 1791–1868	Democrat (1857–61)
16. Abraham Lincoln 1809–65	Republican (1861–65)
17. Andrew Johnson 1808–75	Democrat (1865–69)
18. Ulysses Simpson Grant 1822–85	Republican (1869–77)
19. Rutherford Birchard Hayes 1822–93	Republican (1877–81)
20. James Abram Garfield 1831–81	Republican (1881)
21. Chester Alan Arthur 1830–86	Republican (1881–85)
22. (Stephen) Grover Cleveland 1837–1908	Democrat (1885–89)
23. Benjamin Harrison 1833–1901	Republican (1889–93)
24. (Stephen) Grover Cleveland 1837–1908	Democrat (1893–97)
25. William McKinley 1843–1901	Republican (1897–1901)
26. Theodore Roosevelt 1858–1919	Republican (1901–09)
27. William Howard Taft 1857–1930	Republican (1909–13)
28. (Thomas) Woodrow Wilson 1856–1924	Democrat (1913–21)
29. Warren Gamaliel Harding 1865–1923	Republican (1921–23)
30. Calvin Coolidge 1872–1933	Republican (1923–29)
31. Herbert Clark Hoover 1874–1964	Republican (1929–33)
32. Franklin Delano Roosevelt 1882–1945	Democrat (1933–45)
33. Harry S Truman 1884–1972	Democrat (1945–53)
34. Dwight David Eisenhower 1890–1969	Republican (1953–61)
35. John Fitzgerald Kennedy 1917–63	Democrat (1961–63)
36. Lyndon Baines Johnson 1908–73	Democrat (1963–69)
37. Richard Milhous Nixon 1913–94	Republican (1969–74)
38. Gerald Rudolph Ford 1913–	Republican (1974–77)
39. James Earl Carter, Jr. 1924–	Democrat (1977–81)
40. Ronald Wilson Reagan 1911– 2004	Republican (1981–89)
41. George Herbert Walker Bush 1924–	Republican (1989–93)
42. William Jefferson Clinton 1946–	Democrat (1993–2001)
43. George Walker Bush 1946–	Republican (2001–)

The Declaration of Independence

Action of Second Continental Congress, July 4, 1776
The unanimous Declaration of the thirteen United States of America

WHEN in the Course of human Events,

it becomes necessary for one People to dissolve the Political Bands which have connected them with another, and to assume among the Powers of the Earth, the separate and equal Station to which the Laws of Nature and of Nature's God entitle them, a decent Respect to the Opinions of Mankind requires that they should declare the causes which impel them to the Separation.

WE hold these Truths to be self-evident, that all Men are created equal, that they are endowed by their Creator with certain unalienable Rights, that among these are Life, Liberty and the Pursuit of Happiness — That to secure these Rights, Governments are instituted among Men, deriving their just Powers from the Consent of the Governed, that whenever any Form of Government becomes destructive of these Ends, it is the Right of the People to alter or to abolish it, and to institute new Government, laying its Foundation on such Principles, and organizing its Powers in such Form, as to them shall seem most likely to effect their Safety and Happiness. Prudence, indeed, will dictate that Governments long established should not be changed for light and transient Causes; and accordingly all Experience hath shewn, that Mankind are more disposed to suffer, while Evils are sufferable, than to right themselves by abolishing the Forms to which they are accustomed. But when a long Train of Abuses and Usurpations, pursuing invariably the same Object, evinces a Design to reduce them under absolute Despotism, it is their Right, it is their Duty, to throw off such Government, and to provide new Guards for their future Security. Such has been the patient Sufferance of these Colonies; and such is now the Necessity which constrains them to alter their former Systems of Government. The History of the present King of Great- Britain is a History of repeated Injuries and Usurpations, all having in direct Object the Establishment of an absolute Tyranny over these States. To prove this, let Facts be submitted to a candid World.

HE has refused his Assent to Laws, the most wholesome and necessary for the public Good.

HE has forbidden his Governors to pass Laws of immediate and pressing Importance, unless suspended in their Operation till his Assent should be obtained; and when so suspended, he has utterly neglected to attend to them.

HE has refused to pass other Laws for the Accommodation of large Districts of People, unless those People would relinquish the Right of Representation in the Legislature, a Right inestimable to them, and formidable to Tyrants only.

HE has called together Legislative Bodies at Places unusual, uncomfortable, and distant from the Depository of their public Records, for the sole Purpose of fatiguing them into Compliance with his Measures.

HE has dissolved Representative Houses repeatedly, for opposing with manly Firmness his Invasions on the Rights of the People.

HE has refused for a long Time, after such Dissolutions, to cause others to be elected; whereby the Legislative Powers, incapable of the Annihilation, have returned to the People at large for their exercise; the State remaining in the mean time exposed to all the Dangers of Invasion from without, and Convulsions within.

HE has endeavoured to prevent the Population of these States; for that Purpose obstructing the Laws for Naturalization of Foreigners; refusing to pass others to encourage their Migrations hither, and raising the Conditions of new Appropriations of Lands.

HE has obstructed the Administration of Justice, by refusing his Assent to Laws for establishing Judiciary Powers.

HE has made Judges dependent on his Will alone, for the Tenure of their Offices, and the Amount and Payment of their Salaries.

HE has erected a Multitude of new Offices, and sent hither Swarms of Officers to harrass our People, and eat out their Substance.

HE has kept among us, in Times of Peace, Standing Armies, without the consent of our Legislatures.

HE has affected to render the Military independent of and superior to the Civil Power.

HE has combined with others to subject us to a Jurisdiction foreign to our Constitution, and unacknowledged by our Laws; giving his Assent to their Acts of pretended Legislation:

FOR quartering large Bodies of Armed Troops among us;

FOR protecting them, by a mock Trial, from Punishment for any Murders which they should commit on the Inhabitants of these States:

FOR cutting off our Trade with all Parts of the World:

FOR imposing Taxes on us without our Consent:

FOR depriving us, in many Cases, of the Benefits of Trial by Jury:

FOR transporting us beyond Seas to be tried for pretended Offences:

FOR abolishing the free System of English Laws in a neighbouring Province, establishing therein an arbitrary Government, and enlarging its Boundaries, so as to render it at once an Example and fit Instrument for introducing the same absolute Rules into these Colonies:

FOR taking away our Charters, abolishing our most valuable Laws, and altering fundamentally the Forms of our Governments:

FOR suspending our own Legislatures, and declaring themselves invested with Power to legislate for us in all Cases whatsoever.

HE has abdicated Government here, by declaring us out of his Protection and waging War against us.

HE has plundered our Seas, ravaged our Coasts, burnt our Towns, and destroyed the Lives of our People.

HE is, at this Time, transporting large Armies of foreign Mercenaries to compleat the Works of Death, Desolation, and Tyranny, already begun with circumstances of Cruelty and Perfidy, scarcely paralleled in the most barbarous Ages, and totally unworthy the Head of a civilized Nation.

HE has constrained our fellow Citizens taken Captive on the high Seas to bear Arms against their Country, to become the Executioners of their Friends and Brethren, or to fall themselves by their Hands.

HE has excited domestic Insurrections amongst us, and has endeavoured to bring on the Inhabitants of our Frontiers, the merciless Indian Savages, whose known Rule of Warfare, is an undistinguished Destruction, of all Ages, Sexes and Conditions.

IN every stage of these Oppressions we have Petitioned for Redress in the most humble Terms: Our repeated Petitions have been answered only by repeated Injury. A Prince, whose Character is thus marked by every act which may define a Tyrant, is unfit to be the Ruler of a free People.

NOR have we been wanting in Attentions to our British Brethren. We have warned them from Time to Time of Attempts by their Legislature to extend an unwarrantable Jurisdiction over us. We have reminded them of the Circumstances of our Emigration and Settlement here. We have appealed to their native Justice and Magnanimity, and we have conjured them by the Ties of our common Kindred to disavow these Usurpations, which, would inevitably interrupt our Connections and Correspondence. They too have been deaf to the Voice of Justice and of Consanguinity. We must, therefore, acquiesce in the Necessity, which denounces our Separation, and hold them, as we hold the rest of Mankind, Enemies in War, in Peace, Friends.

WE, therefore, the Representatives of the UNITED STATES OF AMERICA, in GENERAL CONGRESS, Assembled, appealing to the Supreme Judge of the World for the Rectitude of our Intentions, do, in the Name, and by Authority of the good People of these Colonies, solemnly Publish and Declare, That these United Colonies are, and of Right ought to be, FREE AND INDEPENDENT STATES; that they are absolved from all Allegiance to the British Crown, and that all political Connection between them and the State of Great-Britain, is and ought to be totally dissolved; and that as FREE AND INDEPENDENT STATES, they have full Power to levy War, conclude Peace, contract Alliances, establish Commerce, and to do all other Acts and Things which INDEPENDENT STATES may of right do. And for the support of this Declaration, with a firm Reliance on the Protection of divine Providence, we mutually pledge to each other our Lives, our Fortunes, and our sacred Honor.

Signed by ORDER AND IN BEHALF of
the CONGRESS,
JOHN HANCOCK, President.
Attest:
CHARLES THOMSON, Secretary.

SIGNERS:

JOHN HANCOCK

New-Hampshire:
Josiah Bartlett
Wm. Whipple
Matthew Thornton

Massachusetts-Bay:
Saml. Adams
John Adams
Robt. Treat Paine
Elbridge Gerry

Rhode-Island and Providence, &c.:
Step. Hopkins
William Ellery

Connecticut:
Roger Sherman
Saml. Huntington
Wm. Williams
Oliver Wolcott

New-York:
Wm. Floyd
Phil. Livingston
Frans. Lewis
Lewis Morris

New-Jersey:
Richd. Stockton
Jno. Witherspoon
Fras. Hopkinson
John Hart
Abra. Clark

Pennsylvania:
Robt. Morris
Benjamin Rush
Benja. Franklin
John Morton
Geo. Clymer
Jas. Smith
Geo. Taylor
James Wilson
Geo. Ross

Delaware:
Caesar Rodney
Geo. Read
Tho. McKean

Maryland:
Samuel Chase
Wm. Paca
Thos. Stone
Charles Carroll, of Carrollton

Virginia:
George Wythe
Richard Henry Lee
Ths. Jefferson
Benja. Harrison
Thos. Nelson, Jr.
Francis Lightfoot Lee
Carter Braxton

North-Carolina:
Wm. Hooper
Joseph Hewes
John Penn

South-Carolina:
Edward Rutledge
Thos. Heyward, Jr.
Thomas Lynch, Jr.
Arthur Middleton

Georgia:
Button Gwinnett
Lyman Hall
Geo. Walton

Constitution of the United States

PREAMBLE.

We the People of the United States, in Order to form a more perfect Union, establish Justice, insure domestic Tranquility, provide for the common defense, promote the general Welfare, and secure the Blessings of Liberty to ourselves and our Posterity, do ordain and establish this Constitution for the United States of America.

Article I.

Section 1.

All legislative Powers herein granted shall be vested in a Congress of the United States, which shall consist of a Senate and House of Representatives.

Section. 2.

Clause 1:
The House of Representatives shall be composed of Members chosen every second Year by the People of the several States, and the Electors in each State shall have the Qualifications requisite for Electors of the most numerous Branch of the State Legislature.

Clause 2:
No Person shall be a Representative who shall not have attained to the Age of twenty five Years, and been seven Years a Citizen of the United States, and who shall not, when elected, be an Inhabitant of that State in which he shall be chosen.

Clause 3:
[Representatives and direct Taxes shall be apportioned among the several States which may be included within this Union, according to their respective Numbers, which shall be determined by adding to the whole Number of free Persons, including those bound to Service for a Term of Years, and excluding Indians not taxed, *three fifths of all other Persons.*][1] The actual Enumeration shall be made within three Years after the first Meeting of the Congress of the United States, and within every subsequent Term of ten Years, in such Manner as they shall by Law direct. The Number of Representatives shall not exceed one for every thirty Thousand, but each State shall have at Least one Representative; and until such enumeration shall be made, the State of New Hampshire shall be entitled to chuse three, Massachusetts eight, Rhode-Island and Providence Plantations one, Connecticut five, New-York six, New Jersey four, Pennsylvania eight, Delaware one, Maryland six, Virginia ten, North Carolina five, South Carolina five, and Georgia three.

Clause 4:
When vacancies happen in the Representation from any State, the Executive Authority thereof shall issue Writs of Election to fill such Vacancies.

Clause 5:
The House of Representatives shall chuse their Speaker and other Officers; and shall have the sole Power of Impeachment.

Section. 3.

Clause 1:
The Senate of the United States shall be composed of two Senators from each State, [*chosen by the Legislature thereof,*][2] for six Years; and each Senator shall have one Vote.

Clause 2:
Immediately after they shall be assembled in Consequence of the first Election, they shall be divided as equally as may be into three Classes. The Seats of the Senators of the first Class shall be vacated at the Expiration of the second Year, of the second Class at the Expiration of the fourth Year, and of the third Class at the Expiration of the sixth Year, so that one third may be chosen every second Year; [*and if Vacancies happen by Resignation, or otherwise, during the Recess of the Legislature of any State, the Executive thereof may make temporary Appointments until the next Meeting of the Legislature, which shall then fill such Vacancies.*][3]

Clause 3:
No Person shall be a Senator who shall not have attained to the Age of thirty Years, and been nine Years a Citizen of the United States, and who shall not, when elected, be an Inhabitant of that State for which he shall be chosen.

Clause 4:
The Vice President of the United States shall be President of the Senate, but shall have no Vote, unless they be equally divided.

Clause 5:
The Senate shall chuse their other Officers, and also a President pro tempore, in the Absence of the Vice President, or when he shall exercise the Office of President of the United States.

Clause 6:
The Senate shall have the sole Power to try all Impeachments. When sitting for that Purpose, they shall be on Oath or Affirmation. When the President of the United States is tried, the Chief Justice shall preside: And no Person shall be convicted without the Concurrence of two thirds of the Members present.

Clause 7:
Judgment in Cases of Impeachment shall not extend further than to removal from Office, and disqualification to hold and enjoy

[1] Changed in Section 2, Amendment XIV.
[2] Changed in Section 1, Amendment XVII.
[3] Changed in Section 2, Amendment XVII.

any Office of honor, Trust or Profit under the United States: but the Party convicted shall nevertheless be liable and subject to Indictment, Trial, Judgment and Punishment, according to Law.

Section. 4.

Clause 1:
The Times, Places and Manner of holding Elections for Senators and Representatives, shall be prescribed in each State by the Legislature thereof; but the Congress may at any time by Law make or alter such Regulations, except as to the Places of chusing Senators.

Clause 2:
The Congress shall assemble at least once in every Year, and such Meeting [shall be on the first Monday in December][4], unless they shall by Law appoint a different Day.

Section. 5.

Clause 1:
Each House shall be the Judge of the Elections, Returns and Qualifications of its own Members, and a Majority of each shall constitute a Quorum to do Business; but a smaller Number may adjourn from day to day, and may be authorized to compel the Attendance of absent Members, in such Manner, and under such Penalties as each House may provide.

Clause 2:
Each House may determine the Rules of its Proceedings, punish its Members for disorderly Behaviour, and, with the Concurrence of two thirds, expel a Member.

Clause 3:
Each House shall keep a Journal of its Proceedings, and from time to time publish the same, excepting such Parts as may in their Judgment require Secrecy; and the Yeas and Nays of the Members of either House on any question shall, at the Desire of one fifth of those Present, be entered on the Journal.

Clause 4:
Neither House, during the Session of Congress, shall, without the Consent of the other, adjourn for more than three days, nor to any other Place than that in which the two Houses shall be sitting.

Section. 6.

Clause 1:
The Senators and Representatives shall receive a Compensation for their Services, to be ascertained by Law, and paid out of the Treasury of the United States. They shall in all Cases, except Treason, Felony and Breach of the Peace, be privileged from Arrest during their Attendance at the Session of their respective Houses, and in going to and returning from the same; and for any Speech or Debate in either House, they shall not be questioned in any other Place.

Clause 2:
No Senator or Representative shall, during the Time for which he was elected, be appointed to any civil Office under the Authority of the United States, which shall have been created, or the Emoluments whereof shall have been increased during such time; and no Person holding any Office under the United States, shall be a Member of either House during his Continuance in Office.

Section. 7.

Clause 1:
All Bills for raising Revenue shall originate in the House of Representatives; but the Senate may propose or concur with Amendments as on other Bills.

Clause 2:
Every Bill which shall have passed the House of Representatives and the Senate, shall, before it become a Law, be presented to the President of the United States; If he approve he shall sign it, but if not he shall return it, with his Objections to that House in which it shall have originated, who shall enter the Objections at large on their Journal, and proceed to reconsider it. If after such Reconsideration two thirds of that House shall agree to pass the Bill, it shall be sent, together with the Objections, to the other House, by which it shall likewise be reconsidered, and if approved by two thirds of that House, it shall become a Law. But in all such Cases the Votes of both Houses shall be determined by yeas and Nays, and the Names of the Persons voting for and against the Bill shall be entered on the Journal of each House respectively. If any Bill shall not be returned by the President within ten Days (Sundays excepted) after it shall have been presented to him, the Same shall be a Law, in like Manner as if he had signed it, unless the Congress by their Adjournment prevent its Return, in which Case it shall not be a Law.

Clause 3:
Every Order, Resolution, or Vote to which the Concurrence of the Senate and House of Representatives may be necessary (except on a question of Adjournment) shall be presented to the President of the United States; and before the Same shall take Effect, shall be approved by him, or being disapproved by him, shall be repassed by two thirds of the Senate and House of Representatives, according to the Rules and Limitations prescribed in the Case of a Bill.

Section. 8.

Clause 1:
The Congress shall have Power To lay and collect Taxes, Duties, Imposts and Excises, to pay the Debts and provide for the common Defence and general Welfare of the United States; but all Duties, Imposts and Excises shall be uniform throughout the United States;

Clause 2:
To borrow Money on the credit of the United States;

Clause 3:
To regulate Commerce with foreign Nations, and among the several States, and with the Indian Tribes;

Clause 4:
To establish a uniform Rule of Naturalization, and uniform Laws on the subject of Bankruptcies throughout the United States;

Clause 5:
To coin Money, regulate the Value thereof, and of foreign Coin, and fix the Standard of Weights and Measures;

Clause 6:
To provide for the Punishment of counterfeiting the Securities and current Coin of the United States;

Clause 7:
To establish Post Offices and post Roads;

Clause 8:
To promote the Progress of Science and useful Arts, by securing for limited Times to Authors and Inventors the exclusive Right to their respective Writings and Discoveries;

Clause 9:
To constitute Tribunals inferior to the supreme Court;

Clause 10:
To define and punish Piracies and Felonies committed on the high Seas, and Offences against the Law of Nations;

Clause 11:
To declare War, grant Letters of Marque and Reprisal, and make Rules concerning Captures on Land and Water;

[4] Changed in Section 2, Amendment XX.

Clause 12:
To raise and support Armies, but no Appropriation of Money to that Use shall be for a longer Term than two Years;

Clause 13:
To provide and maintain a Navy;

Clause 14:
To make Rules for the Government and Regulation of the land and naval Forces;

Clause 15:
To provide for calling forth the Militia to execute the Laws of the Union, suppress Insurrections and repel Invasions;

Clause 16:
To provide for organizing, arming, and disciplining, the Militia, and for governing such Part of them as may be employed in the Service of the United States, reserving to the States respectively, the Appointment of the Officers, and the Authority of training the Militia according to the discipline prescribed by Congress;

Clause 17:
To exercise exclusive Legislation in all Cases whatsoever, over such District (not exceeding ten Miles square) as may, by Cession of particular States, and the Acceptance of Congress, become the Seat of the Government of the United States, and to exercise like Authority over all Places purchased by the Consent of the Legislature of the State in which the Same shall be, for the Erection of Forts, Magazines, Arsenals, dock-Yards, and other needful Buildings;—And

Clause 18:
To make all Laws which shall be necessary and proper for carrying into Execution the foregoing Powers, and all other Powers vested by this Constitution in the Government of the United States, or in any Department or Officer thereof.

Section. 9.

Clause 1:
The Migration or Importation of such Persons as any of the States now existing shall think proper to admit, shall not be prohibited by the Congress prior to the Year one thousand eight hundred and eight, but a Tax or duty may be imposed on such Importation, not exceeding ten dollars for each Person.

Clause 2:
The Privilege of the Writ of Habeas Corpus shall not be suspended, unless when in Cases of Rebellion or Invasion the public Safety may require it.

Clause 3:
No Bill of Attainder or ex post facto Law shall be passed.

Clause 4:
No Capitation, or other direct, Tax shall be laid, unless in Proportion to the Census or Enumeration herein before directed to be taken.

Clause 5:
No Tax or Duty shall be laid on Articles exported from any State.

Clause 6:
No Preference shall be given by any Regulation of Commerce or Revenue to the Ports of one State over those of another: nor shall Vessels bound to, or from, one State, be obliged to enter, clear, or pay Duties in another.

Clause 7:
No Money shall be drawn from the Treasury, but in Consequence of Appropriations made by Law; and a regular Statement and Account of the Receipts and Expenditures of all public Money shall be published from time to time.

Clause 8:
No Title of Nobility shall be granted by the United States: And no Person holding any Office of Profit or Trust under them, shall, without the Consent of the Congress, accept of any present, Emolument, Office, or Title, of any kind whatever, from any King, Prince, or foreign State.

Section. 10.

Clause 1:
No State shall enter into any Treaty, Alliance, or Confederation; grant Letters of Marque and Reprisal; coin Money; emit Bills of Credit; make any Thing but gold and silver Coin a Tender in Payment of Debts; pass any Bill of Attainder, ex post facto Law, or Law impairing the Obligation of Contracts, or grant any Title of Nobility.

Clause 2:
No State shall, without the Consent of the Congress, lay any Imposts or Duties on Imports or Exports, except what may be absolutely necessary for executing its inspection Laws: and the net Produce of all Duties and Imposts, laid by any State on Imports or Exports, shall be for the Use of the Treasury of the United States; and all such Laws shall be subject to the Revision and Controul of the Congress.

Clause 3:
No State shall, without the Consent of Congress, lay any Duty of Tonnage, keep Troops, or Ships of War in time of Peace, enter into any Agreement or Compact with another State, or with a foreign Power, or engage in War, unless actually invaded, or in such imminent Danger as will not admit of delay.

Article II.

Section. 1.

Clause 1:
The executive Power shall be vested in a President of the United States of America. *He shall hold his Office during the Term of four Years,* and, together with the Vice President, chosen for the same Term, be elected, as follows:

Clause 2:
Each State shall appoint, in such Manner as the Legislature thereof may direct, a Number of Electors, equal to the whole Number of Senators and Representatives to which the State may be entitled in the Congress: but no Senator or Representative, or Person holding an Office of Trust or Profit under the United States, shall be appointed an Elector.

Clause 3:
[*The Electors shall meet in their respective States, and vote by Ballot for two Persons, of whom one at least shall not be an Inhabitant of the same State with themselves. And they shall make a List of all the Persons voted for, and of the Number of Votes for each; which List they shall sign and certify, and transmit sealed to the Seat of the Government of the United States, directed to the President of the Senate. The President of the Senate shall, in the Presence of the Senate and House of Representatives, open all the Certificates, and the Votes shall then be counted. The Person having the greatest Number of Votes shall be the President, if such Number be a Majority of the whole Number of Electors appointed; and if there be more than one who have such Majority, and have an equal Number of Votes, then the House of Representatives shall immediately chuse by Ballot one of them for President; and if no Person have a Majority, then from the five highest on the List the said House shall in like Manner chuse the President. But in chusing the President, the Votes shall be taken by States, the Representation from each State having one Vote; A quorum for this Purpose shall consist of a Member or Members from two thirds of the States, and a Majority of all the States shall be necessary to a Choice. In every Case, after the Choice of the President, the Person having the greatest Number of Votes of the Electors shall be the Vice President. But if there should remain two or more who have equal Votes, the Senate shall chuse from them by Ballot the Vice President.*][1]

[1] Superseded by Amendment XII.

Clause 4:
The Congress may determine the Time of choosing the Electors, and the Day on which they shall give their Votes; which Day shall be the same throughout the United States.

Clause 5:
No Person except a natural born Citizen, or a Citizen of the United States, at the time of the Adoption of this Constitution, shall be eligible to the Office of President; neither shall any Person be eligible to that Office who shall not have attained to the Age of thirty five Years, and been fourteen Years a Resident within the United States.

Clause 6:
In Case of the Removal of the President from Office, or of his Death, Resignation, or Inability to discharge the Powers and Duties of the said Office, the Same shall devolve on the VicePresident, and the Congress may by Law provide for the Case of Removal, Death, Resignation or Inability, both of the President and Vice President, declaring what Officer shall then act as President, and such Officer shall act accordingly, until the Disability be removed, or a President shall be elected.

Clause 7:
The President shall, at stated Times, receive for his Services, a Compensation, which shall neither be encreased nor diminished during the Period for which he shall have been elected, and he shall not receive within that Period any other Emolument from the United States, or any of them.

Clause 8:
Before he enter on the Execution of his Office, he shall take the following Oath or Affirmation:—"I do solemnly swear (or affirm) that I will faithfully execute the Office of President of the United States, and will to the best of my Ability, preserve, protect and defend the Constitution of the United States."

Section. 2.

Clause 1:
The President shall be Commander in Chief of the Army and Navy of the United States, and of the Militia of the several States, when called into the actual Service of the United States; he may require the Opinion, in writing, of the principal Officer in each of the executive Departments, upon any Subject relating to the Duties of their respective Offices, and he shall have Power to grant Reprieves and Pardons for Offences against the United States, except in Cases of Impeachment.

Clause 2:
He shall have Power, by and with the Advice and Consent of the Senate, to make Treaties, provided two thirds of the Senators present concur; and he shall nominate, and by and with the Advice and Consent of the Senate, shall appoint Ambassadors, other public Ministers and Consuls, Judges of the supreme Court, and all other Officers of the United States, whose Appointments are not herein otherwise provided for, and which shall be established by Law: but the Congress may by Law vest the Appointment of such inferior Officers, as they think proper, in the President alone, in the Courts of Law, or in the Heads of Departments.

Clause 3:
The President shall have Power to fill up all Vacancies that may happen during the Recess of the Senate, by granting Commissions which shall expire at the End of their next Session.

Section. 3.

He shall from time to time give to the Congress Information of the State of the Union, and recommend to their Consideration such Measures as he shall judge necessary and expedient; he may, on extraordinary Occasions, convene both Houses, or either of them, and in Case of Disagreement between them, with Respect to the Time of Adjournment, he may adjourn them to such Time as he shall think proper; he shall receive Ambassadors and other public Ministers; he shall take Care that the Laws be faithfully executed, and shall Commission all the Officers of the United States.

Section. 4.

The President, Vice President and all civil Officers of the United States, shall be removed from Office on Impeachment for, and Conviction of, Treason, Bribery, or other high Crimes and Misdemeanors.

Article III.

Section. 1.

The judicial Power of the United States, shall be vested in one supreme Court, and in such inferior Courts as the Congress may from time to time ordain and establish. The Judges, both of the supreme and inferior Courts, shall hold their Offices during good Behaviour, and shall, at stated Times, receive for their Services, a Compensation, which shall not be diminished during their Continuance in Office.

Section. 2.

Clause 1:
The judicial Power shall extend to all Cases, in Law and Equity, arising under this Constitution, the Laws of the United States, and Treaties made, or which shall be made, under their Authority;—to all Cases affecting Ambassadors, other public Ministers and Consuls;—to all Cases of admiralty and maritime Jurisdiction;—to Controversies to which the United States shall be a Party;—to Controversies between two or more States;[*—between a State and Citizens of another State;—*][1] between Citizens of different States,—between Citizens of the same State claiming Lands under Grants of different States, and *between a State, or the Citizens thereof, and foreign States, Citizens or Subjects.*

Clause 2:
In all Cases affecting Ambassadors, other public Ministers and Consuls, and those in which a State shall be Party, the supreme Court shall have original Jurisdiction. In all the other Cases before mentioned, the supreme Court shall have appellate Jurisdiction, both as to Law and Fact, with such Exceptions, and under such Regulations as the Congress shall make.

Clause 3:
The Trial of all Crimes, except in Cases of Impeachment, shall be by Jury; and such Trial shall be held in the State where the said Crimes shall have been committed; but when not committed within any State, the Trial shall be at such Place or Places as the Congress may by Law have directed.

Section. 3.

Clause 1:
Treason against the United States, shall consist only in levying War against them, or in adhering to their Enemies, giving them Aid and Comfort. No Person shall be convicted of Treason unless on the Testimony of two Witnesses to the same overt Act, or on Confession in open Court.

Clause 2:
The Congress shall have Power to declare the Punishment of Treason, but no Attainder of Treason shall work Corruption of Blood, or Forfeiture except during the Life of the Person attainted.

[1] Clause affected by Amendment XI.

Article IV.

Section. 1.

Full Faith and Credit shall be given in each State to the public Acts, Records, and judicial Proceedings of every other State. And the Congress may by general Laws prescribe the Manner in which such Acts, Records and Proceedings shall be proved, and the Effect thereof.

Section. 2.

Clause 1:
The Citizens of each State shall be entitled to all Privileges and Immunities of Citizens in the several States.

Clause 2:
A Person charged in any State with Treason, Felony, or other Crime, who shall flee from Justice, and be found in another State, shall on Demand of the executive Authority of the State from which he fled, be delivered up, to be removed to the State having Jurisdiction of the Crime.

Clause 3:
[*No Person held to Service or Labour in one State, under the Laws thereof, escaping into another, shall, in Consequence of any Law or Regulation therein, be discharged from such Service or Labour, but shall be delivered up on Claim of the Party to whom such Service or Labour may be due.*][1]

Section. 3.

Clause 1:
New States may be admitted by the Congress into this Union; but no new State shall be formed or erected within the Jurisdiction of any other State; nor any State be formed by the Junction of two or more States, or Parts of States, without the Consent of the Legislatures of the States concerned as well as of the Congress.

Clause 2:
The Congress shall have Power to dispose of and make all needful Rules and Regulations respecting the Territory or other Property belonging to the United States; and nothing in this Constitution shall be so construed as to Prejudice any Claims of the United States, or of any particular State.

Section. 4.

The United States shall guarantee to every State in this Union a Republican Form of Government, and shall protect each of them against Invasion; and on Application of the Legislature, or of the Executive (when the Legislature cannot be convened) against domestic Violence.

Article V.

The Congress, whenever two thirds of both Houses shall deem it necessary, shall propose Amendments to this Constitution, or, on the Application of the Legislatures of two thirds of the several States, shall call a Convention for proposing Amendments, which, in either Case, shall be valid to all Intents and Purposes, as Part of this Constitution, when ratified by the Legislatures of three fourths of the several States, or by Conventions in three fourths thereof, as the one or the other Mode of Ratification may be proposed by the Congress; Provided that no Amendment which may be made prior to the Year One thousand eight hundred and eight shall in any Manner affect the first and fourth Clauses in the Ninth Section of the first Article; and that no State, without its Consent, shall be deprived of its equal Suffrage in the Senate.

Article VI.

Clause 1:
All Debts contracted and Engagements entered into, before the Adoption of this Constitution, shall be as valid against the United States under this Constitution, as under the Confederation.

Clause 2:
This Constitution, and the Laws of the United States which shall be made in Pursuance thereof; and all Treaties made, or which shall be made, under the Authority of the United States, shall be the supreme Law of the Land; and the Judges in every State shall be bound thereby, any Thing in the Constitution or Laws of any State to the Contrary notwithstanding.

Clause 3:
The Senators and Representatives before mentioned, and the Members of the several State Legislatures, and all executive and judicial Officers, both of the United States and of the several States, shall be bound by Oath or Affirmation, to support this Constitution; but no religious Test shall ever be required as a Qualification to any Office or public Trust under the United States.

Article VII.

The Ratification of the Conventions of nine States, shall be sufficient for the Establishment of this Constitution between the States so ratifying the Same.

Done in Convention by the Unanimous Consent of the States present the Seventeenth Day of September in the Year of our Lord one thousand seven hundred and Eighty seven and of the Independence of the United States of America the Twelfth In witness whereof We have hereunto subscribed our Names,

GEORGE WASHINGTON—
Presidt. and deputy from Virginia

New Hampshire
John Langdon
Nicholas Gilman

Delaware
Geo: Read
Gunning Bedford, Junior
John Dickinson
Richard Bassett
Jaco: Broom

Massachusetts
Nathaniel Gorham
Rufus King

Maryland
James McHenry
Dan: of St. Thos. Jenifer
Danl Carroll

Connecticut
Wm. Saml. Johnson
Roger Sherman

Virginia
John Blair—
James Madison, Junior

New York
Alexander Hamilton

New Jersey
Wil: Livingston
David Brearley.Wm. Paterson.
Jona: Dayton

North Carolina
Wm. Blount
Richd. Dobbs Spaight
Hugh Williamson

Pennsylvania
Benjamin Franklin
Thomas Mifflin
Robt. Morris
Geo. Clymer
Thos. FitzSimons
Jared Ingersoll
James Wilson
Gouverneur Morris

South Carolina
J. Rutledge
Charles Cotesworth Pinckney
Charles Pinckney
Pierce Butler

Georgia
William Few
Abr Baldwin

Attest:
William Jackson, *Secretary*

[1] Superseded by Amendment XIII.

Amendments to the Constitution

CONSTITUTION OF THE UNITED STATES ARTICLES IN ADDITION TO, AND AMENDMENT OF, THE CONSTITUTION OF THE UNITED STATES OF AMERICA, PROPOSED BY CONGRESS, AND RATIFIED BY THE LEGISLATURES OF THE SEVERAL STATES, PURSUANT TO THE FIFTH ARTICLE OF THE ORIGINAL CONSTITUTION

Article I.

Congress shall make no law respecting an establishment of religion, or prohibiting the free exercise thereof; or abridging the freedom of speech, or of the press; or the right of the people peaceably to assemble, and to petition the Government for a redress of grievances.

Article II.

A well regulated Militia, being necessary to the security of a free State, the right of the people to keep and bear Arms, shall not be infringed.

Article III.

No Soldier shall, in time of peace be quartered in any house, without the consent of the Owner, nor in time of war, but in a manner to be prescribed by law.

Article IV.

The right of the people to be secure in their persons, houses, papers, and effects, against unreasonable searches and seizures, shall not be violated, and no Warrants shall issue, but upon probable cause, supported by Oath or affirmation, and particularly describing the place to be searched, and the persons or things to be seized.

Article V.

No person shall be held to answer for a capital, or otherwise infamous crime, unless on a presentment or indictment of a Grand Jury, except in cases arising in the land or naval forces, or in the Militia, when in actual service in time of War or public danger; nor shall any person be subject for the same offence to be twice put in jeopardy of life or limb; nor shall be compelled in any criminal case to be a witness against himself, nor be deprived of life, liberty, or property, without due process of law; nor shall private property be taken for public use, without just compensation.

Article VI.

In all criminal prosecutions, the accused shall enjoy the right to a speedy and public trial, by an impartial jury of the State and district wherein the crime shall have been committed, which district shall have been previously ascertained by law, and to be informed of the nature and cause of the accusation; to be confronted with the witnesses against him; to have compulsory process for obtaining witnesses in his favor, and to have the Assistance of Counsel for his defence.

Article VII.

In Suits at common law, where the value in controversy shall exceed twenty dollars, the right of trial by jury shall be preserved, and no fact tried by a jury, shall be otherwise re-examined in any Court of the United States, than according to the rules of the common law.

Article VIII.

Excessive bail shall not be required, nor excessive fines imposed, nor cruel and unusual punishments inflicted.

Article IX.

The enumeration in the Constitution, of certain rights, shall not be construed to deny or disparage others retained by the people.

Article X.

The powers not delegated to the United States by the Constitution, nor prohibited by it to the States, are reserved to the States respectively, or to the people.

Article XI.

The Judicial power of the United States shall not be construed to extend to any suit in law or equity, commenced or prosecuted against one of the United States by Citizens of another State, or by Citizens or Subjects of any Foreign State.

Proposal and Ratification

The eleventh amendment to the Constitution of the United States was proposed to the legislatures of the several States by the Third Congress, on the 4th of March 1794; and was declared in a message from the President to Congress, dated the 8th of January, 1798, to have been ratified by the legislatures of three-fourths of the States. The dates of ratification were: New York, March 27, 1794; Rhode Island, March 31, 1794; Connecticut, May 8, 1794; New Hampshire, June 16, 1794; Massachusetts, June 26, 1794; Vermont, between October 9, 1794 and November 9, 1794; Virginia, November 18, 1794; Georgia, November 29, 1794; Kentucky, December 7, 1794; Maryland, December 26, 1794; Delaware, January 23, 1795; North Carolina, February 7, 1795.

Ratification was completed on February 7, 1795.

The amendment was subsequently ratified by South Carolina on December 4, 1797. New Jersey and Pennsylvania did not take action on the amendment.

Article XII.

The Electors shall meet in their respective states, and vote by ballot for President and Vice-President, one of whom, at least, shall not be an inhabitant of the same state with themselves; they shall name in their ballots the person voted for as President, and in distinct ballots the person voted for as Vice-President, and they shall make distinct lists of all persons voted for as President, and of all persons voted for as Vice-President, and of the number of votes for each, which lists they shall sign and certify, and transmit sealed to the seat of the government of the United States, directed to the President of the Senate;—The President of the Senate shall, in the presence of the Senate and House of Representatives, open all the certificates and the votes shall then be counted;—The person having the greatest number of votes for President, shall be the President, if such number be a majority of the whole number of Electors appointed; and if no person have such majority, then from the persons having the highest numbers not exceeding three on the list of those voted for as President, the House of Representatives shall choose immediately, by ballot, the President. But in choosing the President, the votes shall be taken by states, the representation from each state having one vote; a quorum for this purpose shall consist of a member or members from two-thirds of the states, and a majority of all the states shall be necessary to a choice. And if the House of Representatives shall not choose a President whenever the right of choice shall devolve upon them, before *the fourth day of March next following, then the Vice-President shall act as President, as in the case of the death or other constitutional disability of the President.*—The person having the greatest number of votes as Vice-President, shall be the Vice-President, if such number be a majority of the whole number of Electors appointed, and if no person have a majority, then from the two highest numbers on the list, the Senate shall choose the Vice-President; a quorum for the purpose shall consist of two-thirds of the whole number of Senators, and a majority of the whole number shall be necessary to a choice. But no person constitutionally ineligible to the office of President shall be eligible to that of Vice-President of the United States.

Proposal and Ratification

The twelfth amendment to the Constitution of the United States was proposed to the legislatures of the several States by the Eighth Congress, on the 9th of December, 1803, in lieu of the original third paragraph of the first section of the second article; and was declared in a proclamation of the Secretary of State, dated the 25th of September, 1804, to have been ratified by the legislatures of 13 of the 17 States. The dates of ratification were: North Carolina, December 21, 1803; Maryland, December 24, 1803; Kentucky, December 27, 1803; Ohio, December 30, 1803; Pennsylvania, January 5, 1804; Vermont, January 30, 1804; Virginia, February 3, 1804; New York, February 10, 1804; New Jersey, February 22, 1804; Rhode Island, March 12, 1804; South Carolina, May 15, 1804; Georgia, May 19, 1804; New Hampshire, June 15, 1804.

Ratification was completed on June 15, 1804.

The amendment was subsequently ratified by Tennessee, July 27, 1804. The amendment was rejected by Delaware, January 18, 1804; Massachusetts, February 3, 1804; Connecticut, at its session begun May 10, 1804.

Article XIII.

Section 1.

Neither slavery nor involuntary servitude, except as a punishment for crime whereof the party shall have been duly convicted, shall exist within the United States, or any place subject to their jurisdiction.

Section 2.

Congress shall have power to enforce this article by appropriate legislation.

Proposal and Ratification

The thirteenth amendment to the Constitution of the United States was proposed to the legislatures of the several States by the Thirty-eighth Congress, on the 31st day of January, 1865, and was declared, in a proclamation of the Secretary of State, dated the 18th of December, 1865, to have been ratified by the legislatures of twenty-seven of the thirty-six States. The dates of ratification were: Illinois, February 1, 1865; Rhode Island, February 2, 1865; Michigan, February 2, 1865; Maryland, February 3, 1865; New York, February 3, 1865; Pennsylvania, February 3, 1865; West Virginia, February 3, 1865; Missouri, February 6, 1865; Maine, February 7, 1865; Kansas, February 7, 1865; Massachusetts, February 7, 1865; Virginia, February 9, 1865; Ohio, February 10, 1865; Indiana, February 13, 1865; Nevada, February 16, 1865; Louisiana, February 17, 1865; Minnesota, February 23, 1865; Wisconsin, February 24, 1865; Vermont, March 9, 1865; Tennessee, April 7, 1865; Arkansas, April 14, 1865; Connecticut, May 4, 1865; New Hampshire, July 1, 1865; South Carolina, November 13, 1865; Alabama, December 2, 1865; North Carolina, December 4, 1865; Georgia, December 6, 1865.

Ratification was completed on December 6, 1865.

The amendment was subsequently ratified by Oregon, December 8, 1865; California, December 19, 1865; Florida, December 28, 1865 (Florida again ratified on June 9, 1868, upon its adoption of a new constitution); Iowa, January 15, 1866; New Jersey, January 23, 1866 (after having rejected the amendment on March 16, 1865); Texas, February 18, 1870; Delaware, February 12, 1901 (after having rejected the amendment on February 8, 1865); Kentucky, March 18, 1976 (after having rejected it on February 24, 1865). The amendment was rejected (and not subsequently ratified) by Mississippi, December 4, 1865.

Article XIV.

Section 1.

All persons born or naturalized in the United States, and subject to the jurisdiction thereof, are citizens of the United States and of the State wherein they reside. No State shall make or enforce any law which shall abridge the privileges or immunities of citizens of the United States; nor shall any State deprive any person of life, liberty, or property, without due process of law; nor deny to any person within its jurisdiction the equal protection of the laws.

Section 2.

Representatives shall be apportioned among the several States according to their respective numbers, counting the whole number of persons in each State, excluding Indians not taxed. But when the right to vote at any election for the choice of electors for President and Vice President of the United States, Representatives in Congress, the Executive and Judicial officers of a State, or the members of the Legislature thereof, is denied to any of the male inhabitants of such State, being twenty-one years of age, and citizens of the United States, or in any way abridged, except for participation in rebellion, or other crime, the basis of representation therein shall be reduced in the proportion which the number of such male citizens shall bear to the whole number of male citizens twenty-one years of age in such State.

Section 3.

No person shall be a Senator or Representative in Congress, or elector of President and Vice President, or hold any office, civil or military, under the United States, or under any State, who, having previously taken an oath, as a member of Congress, or as an officer of the United States, or as a member of any State legislature, or as an executive or judicial officer of any State, to support the Constitution of the United States, shall have engaged in insurrection or rebellion against the same, or given aid or comfort to the enemies thereof. But Congress may by a vote of two-thirds of each House, remove such disability.

Section 4.

The validity of the public debt of the United States, authorized by law, including debts incurred for payment of pensions and bounties for services in suppressing insurrection or rebellion, shall not be questioned. But neither the United States nor any State shall assume or pay any debt or obligation incurred in aid of insurrection or rebellion against the United States, or any claim for the loss or emancipation of any slave; but all such debts, obligations and claims shall be held illegal and void.

Section 5.

The Congress shall have power to enforce, by appropriate legislation, the provisions of this article.

Proposal and Ratification

The fourteenth amendment to the Constitution of the United States was proposed to the legislatures of the several States by the Thirty-ninth Congress, on the 13th of June, 1866. It was declared, in a certificate of the Secretary of State dated July 28, 1868 to have been ratified by the legislatures of 28 of the 37 States. The dates of ratification were: Connecticut, June 25, 1866; New Hampshire, July 6, 1866; Tennessee, July 19, 1866; New Jersey, September 11, 1866 (subsequently the legislature rescinded its ratification, and on March 24, 1868, readopted its resolution of rescission over the Governor's veto, and on Nov. 12, 1980, expressed support for the amendment); Oregon, September 19, 1866 (and rescinded its ratification on October 15, 1868); Vermont, October 30, 1866; Ohio, January 4, 1867 (and rescinded its ratification on January 15, 1868); New York, January 10, 1867; Kansas, January 11, 1867; Illinois, January 15, 1867; West Virginia, January 16, 1867; Michigan, January 16, 1867; Minnesota, January 16, 1867; Maine, January 19, 1867; Nevada, January 22, 1867; Indiana, January 23, 1867; Missouri, January 25, 1867; Rhode Island, February 7, 1867; Wisconsin, February 7, 1867; Pennsylvania, February 12, 1867; Massachusetts, March 20, 1867; Nebraska, June 15, 1867; Iowa, March 16, 1868; Arkansas, April 6, 1868; Florida, June 9, 1868; North Carolina, July 4, 1868 (after having rejected it on December 14, 1866); Louisiana, July 9, 1868 (after having rejected it on February 6, 1867); South Carolina, July 9, 1868 (after having rejected it on December 20, 1866).

Ratification was completed on July 9, 1868.

The amendment was subsequently ratified by Alabama, July 13, 1868; Georgia, July 21, 1868 (after having rejected it on November 9, 1866); Virginia, October 8, 1869 (after having rejected it on January 9, 1867); Mississippi, January 17, 1870; Texas, February 18, 1870 (after having rejected it on October 27, 1866); Delaware, February 12, 1901 (after having rejected it on February 8, 1867); Maryland, April 4, 1959 (after having rejected it on March 23, 1867); California, May 6, 1959; Kentucky, March 18, 1976 (after having rejected it on January 8, 1867).

Article XV.

Section 1.

The right of citizens of the United States to vote shall not be denied or abridged by the United States or by any State on account of race, color, or previous condition of servitude.

Section 2.

The Congress shall have power to enforce this article by appropriate legislation.

Proposal and Ratification

The fifteenth amendment to the Constitution of the United States was proposed to the legislatures of the several States by the Fortieth Congress, on the 26th of February, 1869, and was declared, in a proclamation of the Secretary of State, dated March 30, 1870, to have been ratified by the legislatures of twenty-nine of the thirty-seven States. The dates of ratification were: Nevada, March 1, 1869; West Virginia, March 3, 1869; Illinois, March 5, 1869; Louisiana, March 5, 1869; North Carolina, March 5, 1869; Michigan, March 8, 1869; Wisconsin, March 9, 1869; Maine, March 11, 1869; Massachusetts, March 12, 1869; Arkansas, March 15, 1869; South Carolina, March 15, 1869; Pennsylvania, March 25, 1869; New York, April 14, 1869 (and the legislature of the same State passed a resolution January 5, 1870, to withdraw its consent to it, which action it rescinded on March 30, 1970); Indiana, May 14, 1869; Connecticut, May 19, 1869; Florida, June 14, 1869; New Hampshire, July 1, 1869; Virginia, October 8, 1869; Vermont, October 20, 1869; Missouri, January 7, 1870; Minnesota, January 13, 1870; Mississippi, January 17, 1870; Rhode Island, January 18, 1870; Kansas, January 19, 1870; Ohio, January 27, 1870 (after having rejected it on April 30, 1869); Georgia, February 2, 1870; Iowa, February 3, 1870.

Ratification was completed on February 3, 1870, unless the withdrawal of ratification by New York was effective; in which event ratification was completed on February 17, 1870, when Nebraska ratified.

The amendment was subsequently ratified by Texas, February 18, 1870; New Jersey, February 15, 1871 (after having rejected it on February 7, 1870); Delaware, February 12, 1901 (after having rejected it on March 18, 1869); Oregon, February 24, 1959; California, April 3, 1962 (after having rejected it on January 28, 1870); Kentucky, March 18, 1976 (after having rejected it on March 12, 1869). The amendment was approved by the Governor of Maryland, May 7, 1973; Maryland having previously rejected it on February 26, 1870. The amendment was rejected (and not subsequently ratified) by Tennessee, November 16, 1869.

Article XVI.

The Congress shall have power to lay and collect taxes on incomes, from whatever source derived, without apportionment among the several States, and without regard to any census or enumeration.

Proposal and Ratification

The sixteenth amendment to the Constitution of the United States was proposed to the legislatures of the several States by the Sixty-first Congress on the 12th of July, 1909, and was declared, in a proclamation of the Secretary of State, dated the 25th of February, 1913, to have been ratified by 36 of the 48 States. The dates of ratification were: Alabama, August 10, 1909; Kentucky, February 8, 1910; South Carolina, February 19, 1910; Illinois, March 1, 1910; Mississippi, March 7, 1910; Oklahoma, March 10, 1910; Maryland, April 8, 1910; Georgia, August 3, 1910; Texas, August 16, 1910; Ohio, January 19, 1911; Idaho, January 20, 1911; Oregon, January 23, 1911; Washington, January 26, 1911; Montana, January 30, 1911; Indiana, January 30, 1911; California, January 31, 1911; Nevada, January 31, 1911; South Dakota, February 3, 1911; Nebraska, February 9, 1911; North Carolina, February 11, 1911; Colorado,

February 15, 1911; North Dakota, February 17, 1911; Kansas, February 18, 1911; Michigan, February 23, 1911; Iowa, February 24, 1911; Missouri, March 16, 1911; Maine, March 31, 1911; Tennessee, April 7, 1911; Arkansas, April 22, 1911 (after having rejected it earlier); Wisconsin, May 26, 1911; New York, July 12, 1911; Arizona, April 6, 1912; Minnesota, June 11, 1912; Louisiana, June 28, 1912; West Virginia, January 31, 1913; New Mexico, February 3, 1913.

Ratification was completed on February 3, 1913.

The amendment was subsequently ratified by Massachusetts, March 4, 1913; New Hampshire, March 7, 1913 (after having rejected it on March 2, 1911).

The amendment was rejected (and not subsequently ratified) by Connecticut, Rhode Island, and Utah.

Article XVII.

The Senate of the United States shall be composed of two Senators from each State, elected by the people thereof, for six years; and each Senator shall have one vote. The electors in each State shall have the qualifications requisite for electors of the most numerous branch of the State legislatures.

When vacancies happen in the representation of any State in the Senate, the executive authority of such State shall issue writs of election to fill such vacancies: *Provided,* That the legislature of any State may empower the executive thereof to make temporary appointments until the people fill the vacancies by election as the legislature may direct.

This amendment shall not be so construed as to affect the election or term of any Senator chosen before it becomes valid as part of the Constitution.

Proposal and Ratification

The seventeenth amendment to the Constitution of the United States was proposed to the legislatures of the several States by the Sixty-second Congress on the 13th of May, 1912, and was declared, in a proclamation of the Secretary of State, dated the 31st of May, 1913, to have been ratified by the legislatures of 36 of the 48 States. The dates of ratification were: Massachusetts, May 22, 1912; Arizona, June 3, 1912; Minnesota, June 10, 1912; New York, January 15, 1913; Kansas, January 17, 1913; Oregon, January 23, 1913; North Carolina, January 25, 1913; California, January 28, 1913; Michigan, January 28, 1913; Iowa, January 30, 1913; Montana, January 30, 1913; Idaho, January 31, 1913; West Virginia, February 4, 1913; Colorado, February 5, 1913; Nevada, February 6, 1913; Texas, February 7, 1913; Washington, February 7, 1913; Wyoming, February 8, 1913; Arkansas, February 11, 1913; Maine, February 11, 1913; Illinois, February 13, 1913; North Dakota, February 14, 1913; Wisconsin, February 18, 1913; Indiana, February 19, 1913; New Hampshire, February 19, 1913; Vermont, February 19, 1913; South Dakota, February 19, 1913; Oklahoma, February 24, 1913; Ohio, February 25, 1913; Missouri, March 7, 1913; New Mexico, March 13, 1913; Nebraska, March 14, 1913; New Jersey, March 17, 1913; Tennessee, April 1, 1913; Pennsylvania, April 2, 1913; Connecticut, April 8, 1913.

Ratification was completed on April 8, 1913.

The amendment was subsequently ratified by Louisiana, June 11, 1914. The amendment was rejected by Utah (and not subsequently ratified) on February 26, 1913.

Article XVIII.

Section 1.

After one year from the ratification of this article the manufacture, sale, or transportation of intoxicating liquors within, the importation thereof into, or the exportation thereof from the United States and all territory subject to the jurisdiction thereof for beverage purposes is hereby prohibited.

Section 2.

The Congress and the several States shall have concurrent power to enforce this article by appropriate legislation.

Section 3.

This article shall be inoperative unless it shall have been ratified as an amendment to the Constitution by the legislatures of the several States, as provided in the Constitution, within seven years from the date of the submission hereof to the States by the Congress.

Proposal and Ratification

The eighteenth amendment to the Constitution of the United States was proposed to the legislatures of the several States by the Sixty-fifth Congress, on the 18th of December, 1917, and was declared, in a proclamation of the Secretary of State, dated the 29th of January, 1919, to have been ratified by the legislatures of 36 of the 48 States. The dates of ratification were: Mississippi, January 8, 1918; Virginia, January 11, 1918; Kentucky, January 14, 1918; North Dakota, January 25, 1918; South Carolina, January 29, 1918; Maryland, February 13, 1918; Montana, February 19, 1918; Texas, March 4, 1918; Delaware, March 18, 1918; South Dakota, March 20, 1918; Massachusetts, April 2, 1918; Arizona, May 24, 1918; Georgia, June 26, 1918; Louisiana, August 3, 1918; Florida, December 3, 1918; Michigan, January 2, 1919; Ohio, January 7, 1919; Oklahoma, January 7, 1919; Idaho, January 8, 1919; Maine, January 8, 1919; West Virginia, January 9, 1919; California, January 13, 1919; Tennessee, January 13, 1919; Washington, January 13, 1919; Arkansas, January 14, 1919; Kansas, January 14, 1919; Alabama, January 15, 1919; Colorado, January 15, 1919; Iowa, January 15, 1919; New Hampshire, January 15, 1919; Oregon, January 15, 1919; Nebraska, January 16, 1919; North Carolina, January 16, 1919; Utah, January 16, 1919; Missouri, January 16, 1919; Wyoming, January 16, 1919.

Ratification was completed on January 16, 1919. See ***Dillon v. Gloss,*** *256 U.S. 368, 376 (1921).*

The amendment was subsequently ratified by Minnesota on January 17, 1919; Wisconsin, January 17, 1919; New Mexico, January 20, 1919; Nevada, January 21, 1919; New York, January 29, 1919; Vermont, January 29, 1919; Pennsylvania, February 25, 1919; Connecticut, May 6, 1919; and New Jersey, March 9, 1922. The amendment was rejected (and not subsequently ratified) by Rhode Island.

Article XIX.

The right of citizens of the United States to vote shall not be denied or abridged by the United States or by any State on account of sex.

Congress shall have power to enforce this article by appropriate legislation.

Proposal and Ratification

The nineteenth amendment to the Constitution of the United States was proposed to the legislatures of the several States by the Sixty-sixth Congress, on the 4th of June, 1919, and was declared, in a proclamation of the Secretary of State, dated the 26th of August, 1920, to have been ratified by the legislatures of 36 of the 48 States. The dates of ratification were: Illinois, June 10, 1919 (and that State readopted its resolution of ratification June 17, 1919); Michigan, June 10, 1919; Wisconsin, June 10, 1919; Kansas, June 16, 1919; New York, June 16, 1919; Ohio, June 16, 1919; Pennsylvania, June 24, 1919; Massachusetts, June 25, 1919; Texas, June 28, 1919; Iowa, July 2, 1919; Missouri, July 3, 1919; Arkansas, July 28, 1919; Montana, August 2, 1919; Nebraska, August 2, 1919; Minnesota, September 8, 1919; New Hampshire, September 10, 1919; Utah, October 2, 1919; California, November 1, 1919; Maine, November 5, 1919; North Dakota, December 1, 1919; South Dakota, December 4, 1919; Colorado, December 15, 1919; Kentucky, January 6, 1920; Rhode

Island, January 6, 1920; Oregon, January 13, 1920; Indiana, January 16, 1920; Wyoming, January 27, 1920; Nevada, February 7, 1920; New Jersey, February 9, 1920; Idaho, February 11, 1920; Arizona, February 12, 1920; New Mexico, February 21, 1920; Oklahoma, February 28, 1920; West Virginia, March 10, 1920; Washington, March 22, 1920; Tennessee, August 18, 1920.

Ratification was completed on August 18, 1920.

The amendment was subsequently ratified by Connecticut on September 14, 1920 (and that State reaffirmed on September 21, 1920); Vermont, February 8, 1921; Delaware, March 6, 1923 (after having rejected it on June 2, 1920); Maryland, March 29, 1941 (after having rejected it on February 24, 1920, ratification certified on February 25, 1958); Virginia, February 21, 1952 (after having rejected it on February 12, 1920); Alabama, September 8, 1953 (after having rejected it on September 22, 1919); Florida, May 13, 1969; South Carolina, July 1, 1969 (after having rejected it on January 28, 1920, ratification certified on August 22, 1973); Georgia, February 20, 1970 (after having rejected it on July 24, 1919); Louisiana, June 11, 1970 (after having rejected it on July 1, 1920); North Carolina, May 6, 1971; Mississippi, March 22, 1984 (after having rejected it on March 29, 1920).

Article XX.

Section 1.

The terms of the President and Vice President shall end at noon on the 20th day of January, and the terms of Senators and Representatives at noon on the 3d day of January, of the years in which such terms would have ended if this article had not been ratified; and the terms of their successors shall then begin.

Section 2.

The Congress shall assemble at least once in every year, and such meeting shall begin at noon on the 3d day of January, unless they shall by law appoint a different day.

Section 3.

If, at the time fixed for the beginning of the term of the President, the President elect shall have died, the Vice President elect shall become President. If a President shall not have been chosen before the time fixed for the beginning of his term, or if the President elect shall have failed to qualify, then the Vice President elect shall act as President until a President shall have qualified; and the Congress may by law provide for the case wherein neither a President elect nor a Vice President elect shall have qualified, declaring who shall then act as President, or the manner in which one who is to act shall be selected, and such person shall act accordingly until a President or Vice President shall have qualified.

Section 4.

The Congress may by law provide for the case of the death of any of the persons from whom the House of Representatives may choose a President whenever the right of choice shall have devolved upon them, and for the case of the death of any of the persons from whom the Senate may choose a Vice President whenever the right of choice shall have devolved upon them.

Section 5.

Sections 1 and 2 shall take effect on the 15th day of October following the ratification of this article.

Section 6.

This article shall be inoperative unless it shall have been ratified as an amendment to the Constitution by the legislatures of three-fourths of the several States within seven years from the date of its submission.

Proposal and Ratification

The twentieth amendment to the Constitution was proposed to the legislatures of the several states by the Seventy-Second Congress, on the 2d day of March, 1932, and was declared, in a proclamation by the Secretary of State, dated on the 6th day of February, 1933, to have been ratified by the legislatures of 36 of the 48 States. The dates of ratification were: Virginia, March 4, 1932; New York, March 11, 1932; Mississippi, March 16, 1932; Arkansas, March 17, 1932; Kentucky, March 17, 1932; New Jersey, March 21, 1932; South Carolina, March 25, 1932; Michigan, March 31, 1932; Maine, April 1, 1932; Rhode Island, April 14, 1932; Illinois, April 21, 1932; Louisiana, June 22, 1932; West Virginia, July 30, 1932; Pennsylvania, August 11, 1932; Indiana, August 15, 1932; Texas, September 7, 1932; Alabama, September 13, 1932; California, January 4, 1933; North Carolina, January 5, 1933; North Dakota, January 9, 1933; Minnesota, January 12, 1933; Arizona, January 13, 1933; Montana, January 13, 1933; Nebraska, January 13, 1933; Oklahoma, January 13, 1933; Kansas, January 16, 1933; Oregon, January 16, 1933; Delaware, January 19, 1933; Washington, January 19, 1933; Wyoming, January 19, 1933; Iowa, January 20, 1933; South Dakota, January 20, 1933; Tennessee, January 20, 1933; Idaho, January 21, 1933; New Mexico, January 21, 1933; Georgia, January 23, 1933; Missouri, January 23, 1933; Ohio, January 23, 1933; Utah, January 23, 1933.

Ratification was completed on January 23, 1933.

The amendment was subsequently ratified by Massachusetts on January 24, 1933; Wisconsin, January 24, 1933; Colorado, January 24, 1933; Nevada, January 26, 1933; Connecticut, January 27, 1933; New Hampshire, January 31, 1933; Vermont, February 2, 1933; Maryland, March 24, 1933; Florida, April 26, 1933.

Article XXI.

Section 1.

The eighteenth article of amendment to the Constitution of the United States is hereby repealed.

Section 2.

The transportation or importation into any State, Territory, or possession of the United States for delivery or use therein of intoxicating liquors, in violation of the laws thereof, is hereby prohibited.

Section 3.

This article shall be inoperative unless it shall have been ratified as an amendment to the Constitution by conventions in the several States, as provided in the Constitution, within seven years from the date of the submission hereof to the States by the Congress.

Proposal and Ratification

The twenty-first amendment to the Constitution was proposed to the several states by the Seventy-Second Congress, on the 20th day of February, 1933, and was declared, in a proclamation by the Secretary of State, dated on the 5th day of December, 1933, to have been ratified by 36 of the 48 States. The dates of ratification were: Michigan, April 10, 1933; Wisconsin, April 25, 1933; Rhode Island, May 8, 1933; Wyoming, May 25, 1933; New Jersey, June 1, 1933; Delaware, June 24, 1933; Indiana, June 26, 1933; Massachusetts, June 26, 1933; New York, June 27, 1933; Illinois, July 10, 1933; Iowa, July 10, 1933; Connecticut, July 11, 1933; New Hampshire, July 11, 1933; California, July 24, 1933; West Virginia, July 25, 1933; Arkansas, August 1, 1933; Oregon, August 7, 1933; Alabama, August 8, 1933; Tennessee, August 11, 1933; Missouri, August 29, 1933; Arizona, September 5, 1933; Nevada, September 5, 1933; Vermont, Septem-

ber 23, 1933; Colorado, September 26, 1933; Washington, October 3, 1933; Minnesota, October 10, 1933; Idaho, October 17, 1933; Maryland, October 18, 1933; Virginia, October 25, 1933; New Mexico, November 2, 1933; Florida, November 14, 1933; Texas, November 24, 1933; Kentucky, November 27, 1933; Ohio, December 5, 1933; Pennsylvania, December 5, 1933; Utah, December 5, 1933.

Ratification was completed on December 5, 1933.

The amendment was subsequently ratified by Maine, on December 6, 1933, and by Montana, on August 6, 1934. The amendment was rejected (and not subsequently ratified) by South Carolina, on December 4, 1933.

Article XXII.

Section 1.

No person shall be elected to the office of the President more than twice, and no person who has held the office of President, or acted as President, for more than two years of a term to which some other person was elected President shall be elected to the office of the President more than once. But this Article shall not apply to any person holding the office of President when this Article was proposed by the Congress, and shall not prevent any person who may be holding the office of President, or acting as President, during the term within which this Article becomes operative from holding the office of President or acting as President during the remainder of such term.

Section 2.

This article shall be inoperative unless it shall have been ratified as an amendment to the Constitution by the legislatures of three-fourths of the several States within seven years from the date of its submission to the States by the Congress.

Proposal and Ratification

This amendment was proposed to the legislatures of the several States by the Eightieth Congress on Mar. 21, 1947 by House Joint Res. No. 27, and was declared by the Administrator of General Services, on Mar. 1, 1951, to have been ratified by the legislatures of 36 of the 48 States. The dates of ratification were: Maine, March 31, 1947; Michigan, March 31, 1947; Iowa, April 1, 1947; Kansas, April 1, 1947; New Hampshire, April 1, 1947; Delaware, April 2, 1947; Illinois, April 3, 1947; Oregon, April 3, 1947; Colorado, April 12, 1947; California, April 15, 1947; New Jersey, April 15, 1947; Vermont, April 15, 1947; Ohio, April 16, 1947; Wisconsin, April 16, 1947; Pennsylvania, April 29, 1947; Connecticut, May 21, 1947; Missouri, May 22, 1947; Nebraska, May 23, 1947; Virginia, January 28, 1948; Mississippi, February 12, 1948; New York, March 9, 1948; South Dakota, January 21, 1949; North Dakota, February 25, 1949; Louisiana, May 17, 1950; Montana, January 25, 1951; Indiana, January 29, 1951; Idaho, January 30, 1951; New Mexico, February 12, 1951; Wyoming, February 12, 1951; Arkansas, February 15, 1951; Georgia, February 17, 1951; Tennessee, February 20, 1951; Texas, February 22, 1951; Nevada, February 26, 1951; Utah, February 26, 1951; Minnesota, February 27, 1951.

Ratification was completed on February 27, 1951.

The amendment was subsequently ratified by North Carolina on February 28, 1951; South Carolina, March 13, 1951; Maryland, March 14, 1951; Florida, April 16, 1951; Alabama, May 4, 1951. The amendment was rejected (and not subsequently ratified) by Oklahoma in June 1947, and Massachusetts on June 9, 1949.

Certification of Validity

Publication of the certifying statement of the Administrator of General Services that the amendment had become valid was made on Mar. 1, 1951, F.R. Doc. 51 092940, 16 F.R. 2019.

Article XXIII.

Section 1.

The District constituting the seat of Government of the United States shall appoint in such manner as the Congress may direct:

> A number of electors of President and Vice President equal to the whole number of Senators and Representatives in Congress to which the District would be entitled if it were a State, but in no event more than the least populous State; they shall be in addition to those appointed by the States, but they shall be considered, for the purposes of the election of President and Vice President, to be electors appointed by a State; and they shall meet in the District and perform such duties as provided by the twelfth article of amendment.

Section 2.

The Congress shall have power to enforce this article by appropriate legislation.

Proposal and Ratification

This amendment was proposed by the Eighty-sixth Congress on June 17, 1960 and was declared by the Administrator of General Services on Apr. 3, 1961, to have been ratified by 38 of the 50 States. The dates of ratification were: Hawaii, June 23, 1960 (and that State made a technical correction to its resolution on June 30, 1960); Massachusetts, August 22, 1960; New Jersey, December 19, 1960; New York, January 17, 1961; California, January 19, 1961; Oregon, January 27, 1961; Maryland, January 30, 1961; Idaho, January 31, 1961; Maine, January 31, 1961; Minnesota, January 31, 1961; New Mexico, February 1, 1961; Nevada, February 2, 1961; Montana, February 6, 1961; South Dakota, February 6, 1961; Colorado, February 8, 1961; Washington, February 9, 1961; West Virginia, February 9, 1961; Alaska, February 10, 1961; Wyoming, February 13, 1961; Delaware, February 20, 1961; Utah, February 21, 1961; Wisconsin, February 21, 1961; Pennsylvania, February 28, 1961; Indiana, March 3, 1961; North Dakota, March 3, 1961; Tennessee, March 6, 1961; Michigan, March 8, 1961; Connecticut, March 9, 1961; Arizona, March 10, 1961; Illinois, March 14, 1961; Nebraska, March 15, 1961; Vermont, March 15, 1961; Iowa, March 16, 1961; Missouri, March 20, 1961; Oklahoma, March 21, 1961; Rhode Island, March 22, 1961; Kansas, March 29, 1961; Ohio, March 29, 1961.

Ratification was completed on March 29, 1961.

The amendment was subsequently ratified by New Hampshire on March 30, 1961 (when that State annulled and then repeated its ratification of March 29, 1961). The amendment was rejected (and not subsequently ratified) by Arkansas on January 24, 1961.

Certification of Validity

Publication of the certifying statement of the Administrator of General Services that the amendment had become valid was made on Apr. 3, 1961, F.R. Doc. 61 093017, 26 F.R. 2808.

Article XXIV.

Section 1.

The right of citizens of the United States to vote in any primary or other election for President or Vice President, for electors for President or Vice President, or for Senator or Representative in Congress, shall not be denied or abridged by the United States or any State by reason of failure to pay any poll tax or other tax.

Section 2.

The Congress shall have power to enforce this article by appropriate legislation.

Proposal and Ratification

This amendment was proposed by the Eighty-seventh Congress by Senate Joint Resolution No. 29, which was approved by the Senate on Mar. 27, 1962, and by the House of Representatives on Aug. 27, 1962. It was declared by the Administrator of General Services on Feb. 4, 1964, to have been ratified by the legislatures of 38 of the 50 States. This amendment was ratified by the following States: Illinois, November 14, 1962; New Jersey, December 3, 1962; Oregon, January 25, 1963; Montana, January 28, 1963; West Virginia, February 1, 1963; New York, February 4, 1963; Maryland, February 6, 1963; California, February 7, 1963; Alaska, February 11, 1963; Rhode Island, February 14, 1963; Indiana, February 19, 1963; Utah, February 20, 1963; Michigan, February 20, 1963; Colorado, February 21, 1963; Ohio, February 27, 1963; Minnesota, February 27, 1963; New Mexico, March 5, 1963; Hawaii, March 6, 1963; North Dakota, March 7, 1963; Idaho, March 8, 1963; Washington, March 14, 1963; Vermont, March 15, 1963; Nevada, March 19, 1963; Connecticut, March 20, 1963; Tennessee, March 21, 1963; Pennsylvania, March 25, 1963; Wisconsin, March 26, 1963; Kansas, March 28, 1963; Massachusetts, March 28, 1963; Nebraska, April 4, 1963; Florida, April 18, 1963; Iowa, April 24, 1963; Delaware, May 1, 1963; Missouri, May 13, 1963; New Hampshire, June 12, 1963; Kentucky, June 27, 1963; Maine, January 16, 1964; South Dakota, January 23, 1964; Virginia, February 25, 1977.

Ratification was completed on January 23, 1964.

The amendment was subsequently ratified by North Carolina on May 3, 1989. The amendment was rejected by Mississippi (and not subsequently ratified) on December 20, 1962. Certification of Validity Publication of the certifying statement of the Administrator of General Services that the amendment had become valid was made on Feb. 5, 1964, F.R. Doc. 64 091229, 29 F.R. 1715.

Article XXV.

Section 1.

In case of the removal of the President from office or of his death or resignation, the Vice President shall become President.

Section 2.

Whenever there is a vacancy in the office of the Vice President, the President shall nominate a Vice President who shall take office upon confirmation by a majority vote of both Houses of Congress.

Section 3.

Whenever the President transmits to the President pro tempore of the Senate and the Speaker of the House of Representatives his written declaration that he is unable to discharge the powers and duties of his office, and until he transmits to them a written declaration to the contrary, such powers and duties shall be discharged by the Vice President as Acting President.

Section 4.

Whenever the Vice President and a majority of either the principal officers of the executive departments or of such other body as Congress may by law provide, transmit to the President pro tempore of the Senate and the Speaker of the House of Representatives their written declaration that the President is unable to discharge the powers and duties of his office, the Vice President shall immediately assume the powers and duties of the office as Acting President.

Thereafter, when the President transmits to the President pro tempore of the Senate and the Speaker of the House of Representatives his written declaration that no inability exists, he shall resume the powers and duties of his office unless the Vice President and a majority of either the principal officers of the executive department or of such other body as Congress may by law provide, transmit within four days to the President pro tempore of the Senate and the Speaker of the House of Representatives their written declaration that the President is unable to discharge the powers and duties of his office. Thereupon Congress shall decide the issue, assembling within forty-eight hours for that purpose if not in session. If the Congress, within twenty-one days after receipt of the latter written declaration, or, if Congress is not in session, within twenty-one days after Congress is required to assemble, determines by two-thirds vote of both Houses that the President is unable to discharge the powers and duties of his office, the Vice President shall continue to discharge the same as Acting President; otherwise, the President shall resume the powers and duties of his office.

Proposal and Ratification

This amendment was proposed by the Eighty-ninth Congress by Senate Joint Resolution No. 1, which was approved by the Senate on Feb. 19, 1965, and by the House of Representatives, in amended form, on Apr. 13, 1965. The House of Representatives agreed to a Conference Report on June 30, 1965, and the Senate agreed to the Conference Report on July 6, 1965. It was declared by the Administrator of General Services, on Feb. 23, 1967, to have been ratified by the legislatures of 39 of the 50 States. This amendment was ratified by the following States: Nebraska, July 12, 1965; Wisconsin, July 13, 1965; Oklahoma, July 16, 1965; Massachusetts, August 9, 1965; Pennsylvania, August 18, 1965; Kentucky, September 15, 1965; Arizona, September 22, 1965; Michigan, October 5, 1965; Indiana, October 20, 1965; California, October 21, 1965; Arkansas, November 4, 1965; New Jersey, November 29, 1965; Delaware, December 7, 1965; Utah, January 17, 1966; West Virginia, January 20, 1966; Maine, January 24, 1966; Rhode Island, January 28, 1966; Colorado, February 3, 1966; New Mexico, February 3, 1966; Kansas, February 8, 1966; Vermont, February 10, 1966; Alaska, February 18, 1966; Idaho, March 2, 1966; Hawaii, March 3, 1966; Virginia, March 8, 1966; Mississippi, March 10, 1966; New York, March 14, 1966; Maryland, March 23, 1966; Missouri, March 30, 1966; New Hampshire, June 13, 1966; Louisiana, July 5, 1966; Tennessee, January 12, 1967; Wyoming, January 25, 1967; Washington, January 26, 1967; Iowa, January 26, 1967; Oregon, February 2, 1967; Minnesota, February 10, 1967; Nevada, February 10, 1967.

Ratification was completed on February 10, 1967.

The amendment was subsequently ratified by Connecticut, February 14, 1967; Montana, February 15, 1967; South Dakota, March 6, 1967; Ohio, March 7, 1967; Alabama, March 14, 1967; North Carolina, March 22, 1967; Illinois, March 22, 1967; Texas, April 25, 1967; Florida, May 25, 1967.

Certification of Validity

Publication of the certifying statement of the Administrator of General Services that the amendment had become valid was made on Feb. 25, 1967, F.R. Doc. 67 092208, 32 F.R. 3287.

Article XXVI.

Section 1.

The right of citizens of the United States, who are eighteen years of age or older, to vote shall not be denied or abridged by the United States or by any State on account of age.

Section 2.

The Congress shall have power to enforce this article by appropriate legislation.

Proposal and Ratification

This amendment was proposed by the Ninety-second Congress by Senate Joint Resolution No. 7, which was approved by the Senate on Mar.

10, 1971, and by the House of Representatives on Mar. 23, 1971. It was declared by the Administrator of General Services on July 5, 1971, to have been ratified by the legislatures of 39 of the 50 States. This amendment was ratified by the following States: Connecticut, March 23, 1971; Delaware, March 23, 1971; Minnesota, March 23, 1971; Tennessee, March 23, 1971; Washington, March 23, 1971; Hawaii, March 24, 1971; Massachusetts, March 24, 1971; Montana, March 29, 1971; Arkansas, March 30, 1971; Idaho, March 30, 1971; Iowa, March 30, 1971; Nebraska, April 2, 1971; New Jersey, April 3, 1971; Kansas, April 7, 1971; Michigan, April 7, 1971; Alaska, April 8, 1971; Maryland, April 8, 1971; Indiana, April 8, 1971; Maine, April 9, 1971; Vermont, April 16, 1971; Louisiana, April 17, 1971; California, April 19, 1971; Colorado, April 27, 1971; Pennsylvania, April 27, 1971; Texas, April 27, 1971; South Carolina, April 28, 1971; West Virginia, April 28, 1971; New Hampshire, May 13, 1971; Arizona, May 14, 1971; Rhode Island, May 27, 1971; New York, June 2, 1971; Oregon, June 4, 1971; Missouri, June 14, 1971; Wisconsin, June 22, 1971; Illinois, June 29, 1971; Alabama, June 30, 1971; Ohio, June 30, 1971; North Carolina, July 1, 1971; Oklahoma, July 1, 1971.

Ratification was completed on July 1, 1971.

The amendment was subsequently ratified by Virginia, July 8, 1971; Wyoming, July 8, 1971; Georgia, October 4, 1971.

Certification of Validity

Publication of the certifying statement of the Administrator of General Services that the amendment had become valid was made on July 7, 1971, F.R. Doc. 71 099691, 36 F.R. 12725.

Article XXVII.

No law, varying the compensation for the services of the Senators and Representatives, shall take effect, until an election of Representatives shall have intervened.

Proposal and Ratification

This amendment, being the second of twelve articles proposed by the First Congress on Sept. 25, 1789, was declared by the Archivist of the United States on May 18, 1992, to have been ratified by the legislatures of 40 of the 50 States. This amendment was ratified by the following States: Maryland, December 19, 1789; North Carolina, December 22, 1789; South Carolina, January 19, 1790; Delaware, January 28, 1790; Vermont, November 3, 1791; Virginia, December 15, 1791; Ohio, May 6, 1873; Wyoming, March 6, 1978; Maine, April 27, 1983; Colorado, April 22, 1984; South Dakota, February 21, 1985; New Hampshire, March 7, 1985; Arizona, April 3, 1985; Tennessee, May 23, 1985; Oklahoma, July 10, 1985; New Mexico, February 14, 1986; Indiana, February 24, 1986; Utah, February 25, 1986; Arkansas, March 6, 1987; Montana, March 17, 1987; Connecticut, May 13, 1987; Wisconsin, July 15, 1987; Georgia, February 2, 1988; West Virginia, March 10, 1988; Louisiana, July 7, 1988; Iowa, February 9, 1989; Idaho, March 23, 1989; Nevada, April 26, 1989; Alaska, May 6, 1989; Oregon, May 19, 1989; Minnesota, May 22, 1989; Texas, May 25, 1989; Kansas, April 5, 1990; Florida, May 31, 1990; North Dakota, March 25, 1991; Alabama, May 5, 1992; Missouri, May 5, 1992; Michigan, May 7, 1992; New Jersey, May 7, 1992.

Ratification was completed on May 7, 1992.

The amendment was subsequently ratified by Illinois on May 12, 1992.

Certification of Validity

Publication of the certifying statement of the Archivist of the United States that the amendment had become valid was made on May 18, 1992, F.R. Doc. 92 0911951, 57 F.R. 21187.

[***Editorial note:*** *There is some conflict as to the exact dates of ratification of the amendments by the several States. In some cases, the resolutions of ratification were signed by the officers of the legislatures on dates subsequent to that on which the second house had acted. In other cases, the Governors of several of the States "approved" the resolutions (on a subsequent date), although action by the Governor is not contemplated by article V, which required ratification by the legislatures (or conventions) only. In a number of cases, the journals of the State legislatures are not available. The dates set out in this document are based upon the best information available.*]

Countries of the World

Country	Capital	Continent/Area	Nationality
Afghanistan	Kabul	Asia	Afghan
Albania	Tirana (Tiranë)	Europe	Albanian
Algeria	Algiers	Africa	Algerian
Andorra	Andorra la Vella	Europe	Andorran
Angola	Luanda	Africa	Angolan
Antigua and Barbuda	Saint John's	North America	Antiguan, Barbudan
Argentina	Buenos Aires	South America	Argentinian
Armenia	Yerevan	Europe	Armenian
Australia	Canberra	Australia	Australian
Austria	Vienna	Europe	Austrian
Azerbaijan	Baku	Europe	Azerbaijani
Bahamas, The	Nassau	North America	Bahamian
Bahrain	Manama	Asia	Bahraini
Bangladesh	Dhaka	Asia	Bangladeshi
Barbados	Bridgetown	North America	Barbadian
Belarus	Minsk	Europe	Belorussian, Belarussian, *or* Belarusian
Belgium	Brussels	Europe	Belgian
Belize	Belmopan	North America	Belizean
Benin	Porto Novo	Africa	Beninese
Bhutan	Thimphu	Asia	Bhutanese
Bolivia	La Paz; Sucre	South America	Bolivian
Bosnia and Herzegovina	Sarajevo	Europe	Bosnian, Herzegovinian
Botswana	Gaborone	Africa	Motswana, *sing.*, Batswana, *pl.*
Brazil	Brasilia	South America	Brazilian
Brunei	Bandar Seri Begawan	Asia	Bruneian
Bulgaria	Sofia	Europe	Bulgarian
Burkina Faso	Ouagadougou	Africa	Burkinese
Burma *(see* Myanmar)			
Burundi	Bujumbura	Africa	Burundian, *n.*; Burundi, *adj.*
Cambodia	Phnom Penh	Asia	Cambodian
Cameroon	Yaoundé	Africa	Cameroonian
Canada	Ottawa	North America	Canadian
Cape Verde	Praia	Africa	Cape Verdean
Central African Republic	Bangui	Africa	Central African
Chad	N'Djamena	Africa	Chadian
Chile	Santiago	South America	Chilean
China	Beijing	Asia	Chinese
Colombia	Bogotá	South America	Colombian
Comoros	Moroni	Africa	Comoran
Congo, Democratic Republic of the (*formerly* Zaire)	Kinshasa	Africa	Congolese
Congo, Republic of the	Brazzaville	Africa	Congolese, *n.*; Congolese *or* Congo, *adj.*
Costa Rica	San José	North America	Costa Rican
Côte d'Ivoire	Yamoussoukro	Africa	Ivorian
Croatia	Zagreb	Europe	Croat, *n.*; Croatian, *adj.*
Cuba	Havana	North America	Cuban
Cyprus	Nicosia	Europe	Cypriot

Country	Capital	Continent/Area	Nationality
Czech Republic	Prague	Europe	Czech
Denmark	Copenhagen	Europe	Dane, *n.*; Danish, *adj.*
Djibouti	Djibouti	Africa	Djiboutian
Dominica	Roseau	North America	Dominican
Dominican Republic	Santo Domingo	North America	Dominican
East Timor	Dili	Asia	East Timoran
Ecuador	Quito	South America	Ecuadorean
Egypt	Cairo	Africa	Egyptian
El Salvador	San Salvador	North America	Salvadoran
Equatorial Guinea	Malabo	Africa	Equatorial Guinean *or* Equatoguinean
Eritrea	Asmara	Africa	Eritrean
Estonia	Tallinn	Europe	Estonian
Ethiopia	Addis Ababa	Africa	Ethiopian
Fiji	Suva	Oceania	Fijian
Finland	Helsinki	Europe	Finn, *n.*; Finnish, *adj.*
France	Paris	Europe	French
Gabon	Libreville	Africa	Gabonese
Gambia, The	Banjul	Africa	`Gambian
Georgia	Tbilisi	Europe	Georgian
Germany	Berlin	Europe	German
Ghana	Accra	Africa	Ghanaian
Greece	Athens	Europe	Greek
Grenada	Saint George's	North America	Grenadian
Guatemala	Guatemala City	North America	Guatemalan
Guinea	Conakry	Africa	Guinean
Guinea-Bissau	Bissau	Africa	Guinea-Bissauan
Guyana	Georgetown	South America	Guyanese
Haiti	Port-au-Prince	North America	Haitian
Holy See	Vatican City	Europe	
Honduras	Tegucigalpa	North America	Honduran
Hungary	Budapest	Europe	Hungarian
Iceland	Reykjavik	Europe	Icelander, *n.*; Icelandic, *adj.*
India	New Delhi	Asia	Indian
Indonesia	Djakarta	Asia	Indonesian
Iran	Tehran	Asia	Iranian
Iraq	Baghdad	Asia	Iraqi
Ireland, Republic of	Dublin	Europe	Irish
Israel	Jerusalem	Asia	Israeli
Italy	Rome	Europe	Italian
Jamaica	Kingston	North America	Jamaican
Japan	Tokyo	Asia	Japanese
Jordan	Amman	Asia	Jordanian
Kazakhstan	Astana	Asia	Kazakhstani
Kenya	Nairobi	Africa	Kenyan
Kiribati	Bairiki (on Tarawa)	Oceania	I-Kiribati
Korea, North (*see* North Korea)			
Korea, South (*see* South Korea)			
Kuwait	Kuwait City	Asia	Kuwaiti
Kyrgyzstan	Bishkek	Asia	Kyrgyz
Laos	Vientiane	Asia	Lao *or* Laotian
Latvia	Riga	Europe	Latvian
Lebanon	Beirut	Asia	Lebanese
Lesotho	Maseru	Africa	Mosotho, *sing.*; Basotho, *pl.*; Basotho, *adj.*
Liberia	Monrovia	Africa	Liberian
Libya	Tripoli	Africa	Libyan
Liechtenstein	Vaduz	Europe	Liechtensteiner, *n.*; Liechtenstein, *adj.*
Lithuania	Vilnius	Europe	Lithuanian
Luxembourg	Luxembourg	Europe	Luxembourger, *n.*; Luxembourg, *adj.*
Macedonia	Skopje	Europe	Macedonian
Madagascar	Antananarivo	Africa	Malagasy
Malawi	Lilongwe	Africa	Malawian
Malaysia	Kuala Lumpur	Asia	Malaysian
Maldives	Male	Asia	Maldivian

Country	Capital	Continent/Area	Nationality
Mali	Bamako	Africa	Malian
Malta	Valletta	Europe	Maltese
Marshall Islands	Majuro	Oceania	Marshallese
Mauritania	Nouakchott	Africa	Mauritanian
Mauritius	Port Louis	Africa	Mauritian
Mexico	Mexico City	North America	Mexican
Micronesia	Kolonia	Oceania	Micronesian
Moldova	Chişinău	Europe	Moldovan
Monaco	Monaco	Europe	Monacan *or* Monegasque
Mongolia	Ulaanbaatar	Asia	Mongolian
Morocco	Rabat	Africa	Moroccan
Mozambique	Maputo	Africa	Mozambican
Myanmar (Burma)	Yangoon	Asia	Burmese
Namibia	Windhoek	Africa	Namibian
Nauru	Yaren District	Oceania	Nauruan
Nepal	Kathmandu	Asia	Nepalese
Netherlands	Amsterdam; The Hague	Europe	Dutchman *or* Dutchwoman, *n.*; Dutch, *adj.*
New Zealand	Wellington	Oceania	New Zealander, *n.*; New Zealand, *adj.*
Nicaragua	Managua	North America	Nicaraguan
Niger	Niamey	Africa	Nigerien
Nigeria	Abuja	Africa	Nigerian
North Korea	P'yongyang	Asia	North Korean
Norway	Oslo	Europe	Norwegian
Oman	Muscat	Asia	Omani
Pakistan	Islamabad	Asia	Pakistani
Palau	Koror	Oceania	Palauan
Panama	Panama City	North America	Panamanian
Papua New Guinea	Port Moresby	Oceania	Papua New Guinean
Paraguay	Asunción	South America	Paraguayan
Peru	Lima	South America	Peruvian
Philippines	Manila	Asia	Filipino, *n.*; Philippine, *adj.*
Poland	Warsaw	Europe	Pole, *n.*; Polish, *adj.*
Portugal	Lisbon	Europe	Portuguese
Qatar	Doha	Asia	Quatari
Romania	Bucharest	Europe	Romanian
Russia	Moscow	Europe & Asia	Russian
Rwanda	Kigali	Africa	Rwandan, Rwandese
Saint Kitts and Nevis	Basseterre	North America	Kittsian; Nevisian
Saint Lucia	Castries	North America	St. Lucian
Saint Vincent and the Grenadines	Kingstown	North America	St. Vincentian *or* Vincentian
Samoa (*formerly* Western Samoa)	Apia	Oceania	Samoan
San Marino	San Marino	Europe	Sammarinese
São Tomé and Príncipe	São Tomé	Africa	Sao Tomean
Saudi Arabia	Riyadh	Asia	Saudi *or* Saudi Arabian
Scotland	Edinburgh	Europe	Scot, *n.*; Scots *or* Scottish, *adj.*
Senegal	Dakar	Africa	Senegalese
Serbia and Montenegro	Belgrade	Europe	Serbian; Montenegram
Seychelles	Victoria	Indian Ocean	Seychellois, *n.*; Seychelles, *adj.*
Sierra Leone	Freetown	Africa	Sierra Leonean
Singapore	Singapore	Asia	Singaporean, *n.*; Singapore, *adj.*
Slovakia	Bratislava	Europe	Slovak
Slovenia	Ljubljana	Europe	Slovene, *n.*; Slovenian, *adj.*
Solomon Islands	Honiara	Oceania	Solomon Islander
Somalia	Mogadishu	Africa	Somali
South Africa	Pretoria; Cape Town; Bloemfontein	Africa	South African
South Korea	Seoul	Asia	South Korean
Spain	Madrid	Europe	Spanish
Sri Lanka	Colombo	Asia	Sri Lankan
Sudan	Khartoum	Africa	Sudanese
Suriname	Paramaribo	South America	Surinamer, *n.*; Surinamese, *adj.*
Swaziland	Mbabane	Africa	Swazi

Country	Capital	Continent/Area	Nationality
Sweden	Stockholm	Europe	Swede, *n.*; Swedish, *adj.*
Switzerland	Bern	Europe	Swiss
Syria	Damascus	Asia	Syrian
Taiwan	Taipei	Asia	Taiwanese
Tajikistan	Dushanbe	Asia	Tajik
Tanzania	Dar es Salaam	Africa	Tanzanian
Thailand	Bangkok	Asia	Thai
Togo	Lomé	Africa	Togolese
Tonga	Nuku'alofa	Oceania	Tongan
Trinidad and Tobago	Port-of-Spain	South America	Trinidadian; Tobagonian
Tunisia	Tunis	Africa	Tunisian
Turkey	Ankara	Asia & Europe	Turk, *n.*; Turkish, *adj.*
Turkmenistan	Ashgabat	Asia	Turkmen
Tuvalu	Funafuti	Oceania	Tuvaluan
Uganda	Kampala	Africa	Ugandan
Ukraine	Kiev	Europe	Ukrainian
United Arab Emirates	Abu Dhabi	Africa	Emirian
United Kingdom	London	Europe	Briton, n.; British, *collective pl. & adj.*
United States of America	Washington, DC	North America	American
Uruguay	Montevideo	South America	Uruguayan
Uzbekistan	Tashkent	Asia	Uzbek
Vanuatu	Vila	Oceania	Ni-Vanuatu
Venezuela	Caracas	South America	Venezuelan
Vietnam	Hanoi	Asia	Vietnamese
Western Samoa (*see* Samoa)			
Yemen	Sana'a	Asia	Yemeni
Yugoslavia (*see* Serbia and Montenegro)			
Zaire (*see* Congo)			
Zambia	Lusaka	Africa	Zambian
Zimbabwe	Harare	Africa	Zimbabwean

Chemical Elements

Element	Symbol	Atomic Number
actinium	Ac	89
aluminum	Al	13
americium	Am	95
antimony	Sb	51
argon	Ar	18
arsenic	As	33
astatine	At	85
barium	Ba	56
berkelium	Bk	97
beryllium	Be	4
bismuth	Bi	83
bohrium*	Ns	107
boron	B	5
bromine	Br	35
cadmium	Cd	48
calcium	Ca	20
californium	Cf	98
carbon	C	6
cerium	Ce	58
cesium	Cs	55
chlorine	Cl	17
chromium	Cr	24
cobalt	Co	27
copper	Cu	29
curium	Cm	96
dubnium*	Db	105
dysprosium	Dy	66
einsteinium	Es	99
erbium	Er	68
europium	Eu	63
fermium	Fm	100
fluorine	F	9
francium	Fr	87
gadolinium	Gd	64
gallium	Ga	31
germanium	Ge	32
gold	Au	79
hafnium	Hf	72
hassium*	Hs	108
helium	He	2
holmium	Ho	67
hydrogen	H	1
indium	In	49
iodine	I	53
iridium	Ir	77
iron	Fe	26
krypton	Kr	36
lanthanum	La	57
lawrencium	Lr	103
lead	Pb	82
lithium	Li	3
lutetium	Lu	71
magnesium	Mg	12
manganese	Mn	25
meitnerium*	Mt	109
mendelevium	Md	101
mercury	Hg	80
molybdenum	Mo	42
neodymium	Nd	60
neon	Ne	10
neptunium	Np	93
nickel	Ni	28
niobium	Nb	41
nitrogen	N	7
nobelium	No	102
osmium	Os	76
oxygen	O	8
palladium	Pd	46
phosphorus	P	15
platinum	Pt	78
plutonium	Pu	94
polonium	Po	84
potassium	K	19
praseodymium	Pr	59
promethium	Pm	61
protactinium	Pa	91
radium	Ra	88
radon	Rn	86
rhenium	Re	75
rhodium	Rh	45
rubidium	Rb	37
ruthenium	Ru	44
rutherfordium*	Rf	104
samarium	Sm	62
scandium	Sc	21
seaborgium*	Sg	106
selenium	Se	34
silicon	Si	14
silver	Ag	47
sodium	Na	11
strontium	Sr	38
sulfur	S	16
tantalum	Ta	73
technetium	Tc	43
tellurium	Te	52
terbium	Tb	65
thallium	Tl	81
thorium	Th	90
thulium	Tm	69
tin	Sn	50
titanium	Ti	22
tungsten (wolfram)	W	74
uranium	U	92
vanadium	V	23
xenon	Xe	54
ytterbium	Yb	70
yttrium	Y	39
zinc	Zn	30
zirconium	Zr	40

* Names formed systematically based on atomic numbers are preferred by the International Union of Pure and Applied Chemistry (IUPAC) for numbers from 104 onward. These names are formed on the numerical roots *nil* (= 0), *un* (= 1), *bi* (= 2), etc. (e.g., *unnilquadium* = 104, *unnilpentium* = 105, *unnilhexium* = 106, *unnilseptium* = 107, *unniloctium* = 108, *unnilnovium* = 109, etc.).

Standard Weights and Measures with Metric Equivalents and Conversions

Equivalents

1 inch	= 2.54 centimeters
1 foot = 12 inches	= 0.3048 meter
1 yard = 3 feet	= 0.9144 meter
= 36 inches	
1 (statute) mile = 1,760 yards	= 1.609 kilometers
= 5,280 feet	

Square Measure

1 sq. inch	= 6.45 sq. centimeters
1 sq. foot = 144 sq. inches	= 9.29 sq. decimeters
1 sq. yard = 9 sq. feet	= 0.836 sq. meter
1 acre = 4,840 sq. yards	= 0.405 hectare
1 sq. mile = 640 acres	= 259 hectares

Cubic Measure

1 cu. inch	= 16.4 cu. centimeters
1 cu. foot = 1,728 cu. inches	= 0.0283 cu. meter
1 cu. yard = 27 cu. feet	= 0.765 cu. meter

Capacity Measure

DRY MEASURE

1 pint = 33.60 cu. inches	= 0.550 liter
1 quart = 2 pints	= 1.101 liters
1 peck = 8 quarts	= 8.81 liters
1 bushel = 4 pecks	= 35.3 liters

LIQUID MEASURE

1 fluid ounce	= 29.573 milliliters
1 gill = 4 fluid ounces	= 118.294 milliliters
1 pint = 16 fluid ounces	= 0.473 liter
= 28.88 cu. inches	
1 quart = 2 pints	= 0.946 liter
1 gallon = 4 quarts	= 3.785 liters

Avoirdupois Weight

1 grain	= 0.065 gram
1 dram	= 1.772 grams
1 ounce = 16 drams	= 28.35 grams
1 pound = 16 ounces	= 0.4536 kilograms
= 7,000 grains	
1 stone (British) = 14 pounds	= 6.35 kilograms
1 ton = 2,000 pounds	
1 hundredweight (U.S.) = 100 pounds	
20 hundredweight (U.S.) = 2,000 pounds	

Conversions

Standard	Multiply By	To Get Metric
Length		
inches	2.5	centimeters
feet	30	centimeters
yards	0.9	meters
miles	1.6	kilometers
Area		
square inches	6.5	square centimeters
square feet	0.09	square meters
square yards	0.8	square meters
square miles	2.6	square kilometers
acres	0.4	hectares
Weight		
ounces	28	grams
pounds	0.45	kilograms
short tons	0.9	metric tons
Volume		
teaspoons	5	milliliters
tablespoons	15	milliliters
cubic inches	16	milliliters
fluid ounces	30	milliliters
cups	0.24	liters
pints	0.47	liters
quarts	0.95	liters
gallons	3.8	liters
cubic feet	0.03	cubic meters
cubic yards	0.76	cubic meters
Temperature		
degrees Fahrenheit	subtract 32, then multiply by 5/9	degrees Celsius

Metric Weights and Measures with Standard Equivalents and Conversions

Equivalents

Linear Measure

1 millimeter (mm)	= 0.039 inch
1 centimeter (cm) = 10 millimeters	= 0.394 inch
1 decimeter (dm) = 10 centimeters	= 3.94 inches
1 meter (m) = 10 decimeters	= 1.094 yards
1 decameter = 10 meters	= 10.94 yards
1 hectometer = 100 meters	= 109.4 yards
1 kilometer (km) = 1,000 meters	= 0.6214 mile

Square Measure

1 sq. centimeter	= 0.155 sq. inch
1 sq. meter = 10,000 sq. centimeters	= 1.196 sq. yards
1 are = 100 sq. meters	= 119.6 sq. yards
1 hectare = 100 ares	= 2.471 acres
1 sq. kilometer = 100 hectares	= 0.386 sq. mile

Cubic Measure

1 cu. centimeter	= 0.061 cu. inch
1 cu. meter = 1,000,000 cu. centimeters	= 1.308 cu. yards

Capacity Measure

1 milliliter (ml)	= 0.034 fluid ounce
1 centiliter (cl) = 10 milliliters	= 0.34 fluid ounce
1 deciliter (dl) = 10 centiliters	= 3.38 fluid ounces
1 liter (l) = 10 deciliters	= 1.06 quarts
1 decaliter = 10 liters	= 2.64 gallons
1 hectoliter = 100 liters	= 2.75 bushels

Weight

1 milligram (mg)	= 0.015 grain
1 centigram = 10 milligrams	= 0.154 grain
1 decigram (dg) = 10 centigrams	= 1.543 grains
1 gram (g) = 10 decigrams	= 15.43 grains
1 decagram = 10 grams	= 5.64 drams
1 hectogram = 100 grams	= 3.527 ounces
1 kilogram (kg) = 1,000 grams	= 2.205 pounds
1 ton (metric ton) = 1,000 kilograms	= 0.984 (long) ton

Conversions

Metric	Multiply By	To Get Standard
Length:		
millimeters	0.04	inches
centimeters	0.4	inches
meters	3.3	feet
meters	1.1	yards
kilometers	0.6	miles
Area:		
square centimeters	0.16	square inches
square meters	1.2	square yards
square kilometers	0.4	square miles
hectares	2.5	acres
Weight:		
grams	0.035	ounces
kilograms	2.2	pounds
metric tons	1.1	short tons
Volume:		
milliliters	0.03	fluid ounces
milliliters	0.06	cubic inches
liters	2.1	pints
liters	1.06	quarts
liters	0.26	gallons
cubic meters	35	cubic feet
cubic meters	1.3	cubic yards
Temperatures:		
degrees Celsius	9/5, then add 32	degress Fahrenheit

Arabic

Alone	Final	Medial	Initial		
ا	ـا			'alif	'
ب	ـب	ـبـ	بـ	bā'	b
ت	ـت	ـتـ	تـ	tā'	t
ث	ـث	ـثـ	ثـ	thā'	th
ج	ـج	ـجـ	جـ	jīm	j
ح	ـح	ـحـ	حـ	ḥā'	ḥ
خ	ـخ	ـخـ	خـ	khā'	kh
د	ـد			dāl	d
ذ	ـذ			dhāl	dh
ر	ـر			rā'	r
ز	ـز			zay	z
س	ـس	ـسـ	سـ	sīn	s
ش	ـش	ـشـ	شـ	shīn	sh
ص	ـص	ـصـ	صـ	ṣād	ṣ
ض	ـض	ـضـ	ضـ	ḍād	ḍ
ط	ـط	ـطـ	طـ	ṭā'	ṭ
ظ	ـظ	ـظـ	ظـ	ẓā'	ẓ
ع	ـع	ـعـ	عـ	'ayn	'
غ	ـغ	ـغـ	غـ	ghayn	gh
ف	ـف	ـفـ	فـ	fā'	f
ق	ـق	ـقـ	قـ	qāf	q
ك	ـك	ـكـ	كـ	kāf	k
ل	ـل	ـلـ	لـ	lām	l
م	ـم	ـمـ	مـ	mīm	m
ن	ـن	ـنـ	نـ	nūn	n
ه	ـه	ـهـ	هـ	hā'	h
و	ـو			wāw	w
ى	ـى	ـيـ	يـ	yā'	y

Hebrew

א	aleph	'
ב	beth	b, bh
ג	gimel	g, gh
ד	daleth	d, dh
ה	he	h
ו	waw	w
ז	zayin	z
ח	ḥeth	ḥ
ט	ṭeth	ṭ
י	yodh	y
כ ך	kaph	k, kh
ל	lamedh	l
מ ם	mem	m
נ ן	nun	n
ס	samekh	s
ע	'ayin	'
פ ף	pe	p, ph
צ ץ	ṣadhe	ṣ
ק	qoph	q
ר	resh	r
שׂ	śin	ś
שׁ	shin	sh
ת	taw	t, th

Greek

Α α	alpha	a
Β β	beta	b
Γ γ	gamma	g
Δ δ	delta	d
Ε ϵ	epsilon	e
Ζ ζ	zeta	z
Η η	eta	ē
Θ θ	theta	th
Ι ι	iota	i
Κ κ	kappa	k
Λ λ	lambda	l
Μ μ	mu	m
Ν ν	nu	n
Ξ ξ	xi	x
Ο ο	omicron	o
Π π	pi	p
Ρ ρ	rho	r, th
Σ σ ς	sigma	s
Τ τ	tau	t
Υ υ	upsilon	u
Φ φ	phi	ph
Χ χ	chi	kh
Ψ ψ	psi	ps
Ω ω	omega	ō

Russian

А а	a
Б б	b
В в	v
Г г	g
Д д	d
Е е	e, ye
Ё ё	yo
Ж ж	zh
З з	z
И и	i
Й й	i
К к	k
Л л	l
М м	m
Н н	n
О о	o
П п	p
Р р	r
С с	s
Т т	t
У у	u
Ф ф	f
Ь х	kh
Ц ц	ts
Ч ч	ch
Ш ш	sh
Щ щ	shch
Ъ ъ ('hard sign')	”
Ы ы	y
Ь ь ('soft sign')	'
Э э	e
ю	yu
Я я	ya

Illustration Credits

Illustration	Source
Abdullah, King	NATO Photos
Adams, John	Library of Congress
Adams, John Quincy	Library of Congress
Adams, Abigail	Library of Congress
Addams, Jane	The Schlesinger Library, Radcliffe institute, Harvard University
Alamo, The	Brice Hammack
Albright, Madeleine	Courtesy of the United Nations
Alhambra, The	Brice Hammack
amphitheater	Brice Hammack
Angkor Wat	Library of Congress
Annan, Kofi	Courtesy of the United Nations
Anthony, Susan B.	Library of Congress
aqueduct, Roman	Library of Congress
Arc de Triomphe	Library of Congress
Arlington National Cemetery	Brice Hammack
Armstrong, Neil	Library of Congress
Arthur, Chester Alan	Library of Congress
Aung San Suu Kyi	The Nobel Foundation
Ball, Lucille	Library of Congress
Barton, Clara	American Red Cross
Baryshnikov, Mikhail	Walter Chin @December 2003
Beatles, The	Getty Images
Benny, Jack	Library of Congress
Bernstein, Leonard	Library of Congress
Berry, Chuck	Library of Congress
Bradley, Omar	Library of Congress
Brandenburg Gate	Library of Congress
Brooklyn Bridge	Library of Congress
Buchanan, James	Library of Congress
Buffalo Bill	Library of Congress
Burns, George	The Museum of Modern Art
Bush, George H. W.	Library of Congress
Bush, George W.	Office of George W. Bush
Calamity Jane	Library of Congress
Capitol, U.S.	Brice Hammack
Capote, Truman	Library of Congress
Carter, Jimmy	Library of Congress
Carver, George Washington	Library of Congress
Castro, Fidel	Library of Congress
Chaplin, Charlie	Library of Congress
Chartres Cathedral	Library of Congress
Chiang Kai-shek	Library of Congress
Churchill, Winston	The Nobel Foundation
Cleveland, Grover	Library of Congress
Clinton, Hillary Rodham	Office of Hillary Rodham Clinton
Clinton, William Jefferson	The White House
Cole, Nat King	Photofest
Colosseum	Library of Congress
Coolidge, Calvin	Library of Congress
Crawford, Joan	The Museum of Modern Art
Crick, Francis	The Nobel Foundation
Cronkite, Walter	Library of Congress
Crosby, Bing	Library of Congress
Curie, Marie	Library of Congress
Curie, Pierre	The Nobel Foundation
Dali, Salvador	Library of Congress
Davis, Bette	The Museum of Modern Art
Davis, Jefferson	Library of Congress
Dean, James	The Museum of Modern Art
De Niro, Robert	The Museum of Modern Art
Dickinson, Emily	Amherst College Archives and Special Collections, by permission of the Trustees of Amherst College
Dietrich, Marlene	The Museum of Modern Art
DiMaggio, Joe	National Baseball Hall of Fame Library, Cooperstown, NY
Dome of the Rock	Library of Congress
Douglas, Stephen A.	Library of Congress
Douglass, Frederick	National Archives
Earhart, Amelia	National Archives
Easter Island Statues	Brice Hammack
Eiffel Tower	Library of Congress
Einstein, Albert	National Archives
Eisenhower, Dwight D.	Library of Congress
Elizabeth I	Library of Congress
Elizabeth II	Library of Congress
Empire State Building	Library of Congress
Farragut, David	Library of Congress
Fillmore, Millard	Library of Congress
Fitzgerald, Ella	Library of Congress
Fonda, Henry	The Museum of Modern Art
Forbidden City	Brice Hammack
Ford, Gerald	Library of Congress
Ford, Harrison	The Museum of Modern Art
Fox Quesada, Vicente	Courtesy of the United Nations
Franco, Francisco	Library of Congress
Franklin, Benjamin	Harvard University Art Museums
Friedan, Betty	College Archives, Smith College
Gable, Clark	Library of Congress
Garbo, Greta	Library of Congress
Garfield, James A.	Library of Congress
Gates, Bill	Microsoft Corporation
Gateway Arch	Library of Congress
Gehrig, Lou	National Baseball Hall of Fame Library, Cooperstown, NY
Geronimo	Library of Congress
Gish, Lillian	Library of Congress

Illustration	Source
Golden Gate Bridge	(c) 2001 PhotoDisc, Inc.
Gordimer, Nadine	The Nobel Foundation
Gore, Al	The White House
Grand Canyon	Library of Congress
Grant, Ulysses S.	Library of Congress
Great Wall of China	Brice Hammack
Hamilton, Alexander	Library of Congress
Hammarskjold, Dag	Courtesy of the United Nations
Harding, Warren G.	U.S. Senate Historical Office
Harlow, Jean	The Museum of Modern Art
Harrison, Benjamin	Library of Congress
Harrison, William Henry	U.S. Senate Historical Office
Hayes, Rutherford B.	Library of Congress
Hemingway, Ernest	John Fitzgerald Kennedy Library
Henry VIII	Library of Congress
Henry, Patrick	Colonial Williamsburg Foundation
Hepburn, Katharine	The Museum of Modern Art
Hirohito	Library of Congress
Hitchcock, Alfred	Library of Congress
Ho Chi Minh	Library of Congress
Hoover, Herbert Clark	Library of Congress
Hoover Dam	Brice Hammack
Houdini, Harry	Library of Congress
Houses of Parliament	Library of Congress
Houston, Samuel	Library of Congress
Humphrey, Hubert H.	Library of Congress
Jackson, Andrew	Library of Congress
Jackson, Jesse	Library of Congress
Jackson, Thomas "Stonewall"	Library of Congress
Jay, John	Library of Congress
Jefferson, Thomas	Library of Congress
Johnson, Andrew	US Senate Historical Office
Johnson, Lyndon Baines	Library of Congress
Jordan, Michael	Chicago Bulls
Joseph, Chief	Library of Congress
Kennedy, John F.	Courtesy of the Smithsonian
King, Jr., Martin Luther	Library of Congress
Laurel and Hardy	The Museum of Modern Art
Lee, Robert E.	Library of Congress
Lenin, Vladimir	Library of Congress
Liberty Bell	Library of Congress
Lincoln, Abraham	Library of Congress
Lincoln Memorial	Brice Hammack
Luther, Martin	Library of Congress
Madison, James	Library of Congress
Machu Picchu	Brice Hammack
Malcolm X	Library of Congress
Mandela, Nelson	Courtesy of the United Nations
Marshall, Thurgood	Collection of the Supreme Court of the United States
Matterhorn	Library of Congress
Mays, Willie	National Baseball Hall of Fame Library, Cooperstown, NY
McClintock, Barbara	The Nobel Foundation
McKinley, William	Library of Congress
Meir, Golda	Israeli Government Press Office
Michelangelo	Library of Congress
Monroe, James	Library of Congress
Monroe, Marilyn	Library of Congress
Monticello	(c) 2001 PhotoDisc, Inc.
Morrison, Toni	The Nobel Foundation
Moses, Grandma	Library of Congress
Murrow, Edward R.	Martin Luther King Library
Mussolini, Benito	National Archives
Nader, Ralph	David Alfaya
Nefertiti	Library of Congress
Nehru, Jawaharlal	Library of Congress
Newman, Paul	The Museum of Modern Art
Niagara Falls	(c) 2001 PhotoDisc, Inc.
Nicholson, Jack	The Museum of Modern Art
Nixon, Richard M.	Library of Congress
Notre Dame	Library of Congress
Oakley, Annie	Library of Congress
O'Keeffe, Georgia	Library of Congress
Old North Church	Library of Congress
Onassis, Jacqueline Kennedy	John F. Kennedy Library
Oxford	Brice Hammack
Pantheon	Library of Congress
Parks, Rosa	Schomburg Center for Research in Black Culture
Parthenon	Brice Hammack
Pentagon	Library of Congress
Petronas Towers	Tourism Malaysia
Picasso, Pablo	Library of Congress
Pierce, Franklin	Library of Congress
Pisa, Leaning Tower of	Brice Hammack
Plath, Sylvia	College Archives, Smith College
Poitier, Sidney	The Museum of Modern Art
Polk, James K.	Library of Congress
pyramid of Giza	Library of Congress
Reagan, Ronald W.	Ronald Reagan Library
redwood tree	Brice Hammack
Rehnquist, William H.	Collection of the Supreme Court of the United States
Renoir, Auguste	Library of Congress
Rhodes, Cecil	Library of Congress
Ride, Sally	National Archives
Rivera, Diego (painting of Zapata 1932)	Library of Congress
Robinson, Jackie	Library of Congress
Robinson, Mary	Courtesy of the United Nations
Rodin, Auguste	Library of Congress
Roosevelt, Eleanor	FDR Library
Roosevelt, Franklin D.	FDR Library
Roosevelt, Theodore	Library of Congress
Rushmore, Mount	(c) 2001 PhotoDisc, Inc.
Ruth, Babe	National Archives
Rutherford, Ernest	The Nobel Foundation
Sacajawea	State Historical Society of North Dakota
Sagrada Familia	Brice Hammack
Sanger, Margaret	Library of Congress
Shakespeare, William	Folger Shakespeare Library
Sherman, William Tecumseh	National Archives
Sinatra, Frank	Photofest
Sitting Bull	Library of Congress
Sphinx, The	Library of Congress
Spock, Benjamin	Library of Congress
St. Basil's Cathedral	Library of Congress
St. Paul's Cathedral	Library of Congress
Stalin, Joseph	Library of Congress
Stanton, Elizabeth Cady	Library of Congress
Statue of Liberty	Library of Congress
Steinem, Gloria	Library of Congress
Stengel, Casey	National Baseball Hall of Fame Library, Cooperstown, NY
Stewart, James	Library of Congress
Stonehenge	VisitBritain
Sun Yat-sen	Library of Congress
Supreme Court Building	Brice Hammack
Taft, William Howard	Library of Congress
Taj Mahal	Library of Congress
Taylor, Elizabeth	The Museum of Modern Art
Taylor, Zachary	Library of Congress
Tecumseh	Cincinnati Museum Center
Temple, Shirley	The Museum of Modern Art
Teresa, Mother	Martin Luther King Library
Thant, U	Courtesy of the United Nations
Tiananmen Square	Brice Hammack
Times Square	(c) NYC & Company

Illustration	Source
Tolstoy, Leo	Library of Congress
Tower of London	VisitBritain
Trevi Fountain	Courtesy of the Italian Government Tourist Board
Truman, Harry S	National Archives
Tubman, Harriet	Courtesy of the Smithsonian
Tutankhamen	Library of Congress
Twain, Mark	Library of Congress
Tyler, John	Library of Congress
Uncle Sam	Library of Congress
Valentino, Rudolph	Library of Congress
Van Buren, Martin	Library of Congress
Wailing Wall	Library of Congress
Warren, Earl	Collection of the Supreme Court of the United States
Washington, Booker T.	Library of Congress
Washington, George	Library of Congress
Washington Monument	Library of Congress
waterfall	Brice Hammack
Watson, James	The Nobel Foundation
Wayne, John	The Museum of Modern Art
Webster, Daniel	Library of Congress
Whistler, James MacNeil	Library of Congress
White House	Library of Congress
Wilde, Oscar	William Andrews Clark Memorial Library, UCLA
Wilson, Woodrow	Library of Congress
Woods, Tiger	(c) 2001 PGA Tour
Yeager, Chuck	Courtesy of the U.S. Air Force
Yeats, William Butler	The Nobel Foundation
Young, Cy	National Baseball Hall of Fame Library, Cooperstown, NY